Dictionary of American Regional English

Dictionary of American Regional English

Volume IV   P-Sk

Joan Houston Hall
Chief Editor

The Belknap Press of Harvard University Press
Cambridge, Massachusetts, and London, England
2002

P-Sk

Design by Marianne Perlak

Library of Congress Cataloging in Publication Data

Dictionary of American regional English.

1. English language—Dialects—United States—Dictionaries.
2. English language—United States—Dictionaries.
3. Americanisms—Dictionaries.
I. Cassidy, Frederic Gomes, 1907–
II. Hall, Joan Houston.
PE2843.D52   1985   427′.973   84-29025
ISBN 0-674-20511-1 (v. 1 : alk. paper)
ISBN 0-674-20512-X (v. 2)
ISBN 0-674-20519-7 (v. 3)
ISBN 0-674-00884-7 (v. 4)

Contents

DARE Staff, Volume IV

CHIEF EDITOR
Joan Houston Hall

SENIOR EDITOR, PRODUCTION
Luanne von Schneidemesser

SENIOR SCIENCE EDITOR
Sheila Y. Kolstad

REVIEW EDITOR
George H. Goebel

GENERAL EDITOR, BIBLIOGRAPHER
Leonard Zwilling

SCIENCE EDITOR
Roland L. Berns

SENIOR EDITOR, EDITORIAL COMPUTING
Craig M. Carver

ADJUNCT EDITOR
Audrey R. Duckert

CONTRIBUTING EDITORS
Matt Hogan (1978–97)
Jean Howell Patau (1986–97)
Beth Lee Simon (1986–95)

PRODUCTION ASSISTANT,
TECHNICAL TYPIST
Catherine R. Attig

SENIOR PROOFREADER
Elizabeth R. Gardner

PROOFREADERS
Elizabeth Blake
Margaret E. Kailhofer (2001–02)
Stephen M. Kratky (1987–97)

OFFICE MANAGER
Karen J. Krause

RESEARCH ASSISTANTS
Mary Jo Heck (1992–98)
Rebecca V. Roeder (1998–99; 2001)
Jason Sweet (2002)
Conrad Treff (1998–2001)

DIRECTOR OF DEVELOPMENT
David H. Simon

IN MEMORIAM

Frederic G. Cassidy

1907–2000

Creator, heart, and soul of the *Dictionary of American Regional English*
Chief Editor, 1962–2000

*"And thou in this shalt find thy monument,
When tyrants' crests and tombs of brass are spent."*
William Shakespeare, Sonnet 107

Preface

Readers of this volume are reminded that a full explanation of the background of the *DARE* project and the method of presentation of the entries can be found in the front matter to Volume I, with additional comments in the prefaces to Volumes II and III. It may be useful here to point to particular parts of the introductory materials in Volume I that elucidate the entries in each volume: a thorough discussion of pronunciation variation in American English is provided on pp. xli–lxi; the full text of each question asked in the *DARE* fieldwork is found on pp. lxii–lxxxv; and the specifics of each Informant's age, sex, race, education level, and community type are listed on pp. lxxxvi–cli. Because readers have suggested it would be useful to them, we reprint in this volume two explanatory items from earlier ones: from Volume I we include the figure contrasting the *DARE* map with the conventional map of the United States to make it easier for readers to "translate" the *DARE* map; from Volume III we reprint the explanatory page called "The Anatomy of an Entry." New to Volume IV is a brief Pronunciation Guide listing the phonetic symbols that appear in the head sections and the quotations in *DARE* entries.

The illustrative quotations in the *Dictionary* cover a span of nearly four hundred years and come from myriad sources. They are identified by date, author, and an abbreviated title, information that is intended to allow a reader to find the precise source from which the quote was taken. (Details of bibliographic and short-title procedures are explained on p. xxi of Volume I; the full bibliography of all sources will appear in the final volume of *DARE*.) An innovation in Volume IV, which reflects the staggering increase in the number of electronic sources available to lexicographers in the last few years, is the inclusion of quotations from digital libraries and from the World Wide Web.

Several archives have been particularly useful in documenting or antedating *DARE* headwords: *The Making of America (MOA)*, a collaborative effort of the University of Michigan and Cornell University (<http://moa.umdl.umich.edu> and <http://library5.library.cornell.edu/moa>), is a digital library of nineteenth-century primary sources in American social history, with emphases on education, psychology, American history, sociology, religion, and science and technology; *American Memory: Historical Collections for the National Digital Library* (<http://memory.loc.gov/ammem/amhome.html>), assembled by the Library of Congress, contains a wide array of sources, including historical documents, manuscripts, memoirs, letters, interviews, periodicals, pamphlets, maps, photographs, films, and music; and *Documenting the American South* (<http://docsouth.unc.edu/

dasmain.html>), developed by the Academic Affairs Library at the University of North Carolina at Chapel Hill, includes first-person narratives, Civil War documents, church histories, and literary works that document the Southern experience. Many other valuable collections, including databases of scientific names for plants and animals, are also used by *DARE* Editors, and still others will be used as they become available.

Developing a clear and systematic way of citing the wide range of materials available on the Internet has proved to be a considerable challenge. The policies we have developed represent a compromise—tailored to our particular situation—between the competing goals of precision and concision. For citation purposes we have divided Internet materials into four main groups, as follows:

1. Previously published works reproduced in the form of digital *images* in an on-line library (such as *MOA*) are cited exactly as if we had seen the original hard copy.

   1859 Storke *Family Farm* 2.172
   1880 *Harper's New Mth. Mag.* 61.865

(The case of a previously published work that has been converted into digital *text*—as by keyboarding or the use of Optical Character Recognition software—is quite different. It is effectively a new edition and falls into the following category of material.)

2. Works that have been formally published on the Internet are given individual short-titles analogous to those for print publications, with the addition of a parenthetical "Internet" at the end. By "formally published" we mean that the item forms a substantial, self-contained unit, that it has a definite date of publication, and that it appears under the auspices of an institutional or commercial body that appears to assure its authenticity, stability, and continued availability. (In individual cases, of course, it may be hard to determine whether an item meets these requirements; a deciding factor may be whether a bibliographic record is found on OCLC.) Sources treated in this way include electronic periodicals, electronic editions of print periodicals, and electronic "reprints" of previously published material. In the last case, following our pattern for reprint editions, the boldface date will be the date of original publication, with the date of the Internet publication following in parentheses.

   1999 *Cattle Today* Mar (Internet)
   2001 *Denver Post* (CO) 9 Sept sec K 1 (Internet)
   1845 (1997) Horton *Poet. Works* xiii (Internet)

3. For other material appearing on major governmental and institutional Internet sites we have created a short-title for the site as a whole, and, since such a site is rarely fixed and often

contains undated material, we always—with one exception noted below—give the date (year) of access, followed by the parenthetical abbreviation "acc." If the particular item within the site is dated, that date may precede the access date.

> **1999** (acc) U.S. Dept. Ag. *Integrated Taxonomic Info. System* (Internet)
>
> **1948** in 2001 (acc) Lexis–Nexis. Legal Research *State Case Law: CT* (Internet)

The single exception to this policy occurs when we quote from a digital *image* of a document appearing on such a site; in that case we give only the date of the original document, as in

> **1938** in Lib. of Congress *Amer. Memory: WPA Life Hist.* (Internet)

4. All other Internet material is cited under the general short-title "**date** *DARE* File—Internet," analogous to the "**date** *DARE* File" short-title we use for ephemeral printed matter (as well as all sorts of unpublished material). (We routinely print out hard copy of Internet pages or parts of pages that we cite, which become a permanent part of our files.) Since the date immediately preceding "*DARE* File" will always be the year of access, it is not specifically labeled as such. If the material we are quoting is dated, that date may precede the access date. When it appears useful to provide some idea of the nature of the item being quoted, a bracketed note may give its title or a description.

> **1999** *DARE* File—Internet
>
> **1809** in 2001 *DARE* File—Internet
>
> **1998** *DARE* File—Internet [Language of the Hayna Valley]
>
> **1998** *DARE* File—Internet [Weeds—Botanical Names]

Acknowledgments

Funding for Volume IV has come from a wide variety of sources, including several major long-term supporters as well as many new foundations and individual contributors. We are deeply indebted to the National Endowment for the Humanities (an independent federal agency), the Andrew W. Mellon Foundation, and the National Science Foundation, whose continuing support—both financial and moral—for the *DARE* project has allowed us to continue through economically uncertain times. In particular, we thank Helen Agüera and George Farr at NEH and Paul Chapin and Cecile McKee at NSF for their unflagging enthusiasm, encouragement, and advice; we are grateful to President William G. Bowen, former Secretary Richard Ekman, and Program Officer Joseph Meisel of the Mellon Foundation for their appreciation of the humanities and their understanding of the special needs of projects such as *DARE*.

Other foundations that have very generously contributed to the ongoing work at *DARE* are the Brittingham Fund, Inc., the Connemara Fund, the Charles A. Dana Foundation, the Gladys Krieble Delmas Foundation, the Franklin Philanthropic Foundation, Furthermore (a program of the J. M. Kaplan Fund), the Horace W. Goldsmith Foundation, the Hillsdale Fund, Inc., the Grace Jones Richardson Trust, the John C. Sime Trust, and the H. W. Wilson Foundation. We also gratefully acknowledge gifts from the Andrews McMeel Universal Foundation, the Anonymous Fund, the Butterfly Foundation, the Dawson Family Fund, the BFGoodrich Company, the David Greenewalt Charitable Trust, the Hidden Pond Foundation, Houghton Mifflin Company, the Margaret Banta Humleker Foundation, the Louise H. and David S. Ingalls Foundation, the New York Times Company Foundation, the PPC Foundation, the Hamilton Roddis Foundation, Inc., the Wilbert and Genevieve Schauer Foundation, Inc., the William E. Simon Foundation, the Sidney Stern Memorial Trust, and the Arthur W. Strelow Charitable Trust.

Several individuals have been extremely generous in their support for *DARE,* and we extend our sincere gratitude to them along with our thanks to the hundreds of other word lovers who have cast their votes for *DARE* by making contributions to the project. In the last few years, a group of particularly supportive individuals has joined together to form a Board of Visitors for *DARE,* providing assistance of many kinds in the effort to ensure completion of the project. We owe special thanks to Greg Alfus, John Bordie, Richard Ekman, Harlan Ellison, Jane Appleby Flint, Morris F. Goodman, James J. Kilpatrick, Robert D. King, Marianne Means, Jacquelyn Mitchard, Mary Lu Mitchell, Cynthia L. Moore, Robert H. Moore, Donald Oresman, William Safire, John A. Shea, Bruce Walker, and Simon Winchester.

Many of the gifts mentioned above would not have been received had it not been for the willingness of Phillip R. Certain, Dean of the College of Letters and Science at the University of Wisconsin–Madison, to take a chance on *DARE*. His offer to provide the funding for a development specialist for a three-year period was bold and unprecedented; it proved to be prescient and well justified. We are grateful that his confidence in the worth of the project, combined with the talents of Development Director David Simon and the generosity of *DARE*'s many supporters, has increased the momentum that will take us to the letter Z.

Assistance of many other kinds has also been invaluable to the project: Professor Emerita Audrey R. Duckert, of the University of Massachusetts at Amherst, has, since the project's inception, provided both insightful comments on entries and general advice and support; lexicographers Jesse Sheidlower (*Oxford English Dictionary*), E. Ward Gilman, Joanne Despres, and Jim Rader (Merriam-Webster, Inc.), Michael Agnes (Webster's New World Dictionaries), and David Jost (Houghton Mifflin Company) have all been extremely helpful colleagues, providing suggestions, citations, and feedback; Barry Popik has done prodigious research into etymologies and antedatings, yielding many useful citations; Lee Pederson and Michael M. Montgomery have allowed us generous access to the resources of the *Linguistic Atlas of the Gulf States* and the forthcoming *Dictionary of Smoky Mountain English,* respectively; C. Richard Beam has made suggestions regarding the treatment of Pennsylvania German words; several watchful contributors send lexical material on a continuing basis; and a dedicated group of volunteers from the Madison community has provided steady, cheerful assistance with a myriad of tasks, thereby lightening our daily load. Judith A. Taylor and Marjory McMickle deserve particular thanks, having helped us steadily for fifteen and fourteen years, respectively.

On the campus of the University of Wisconsin–Madison, librarians deserve special notice for their consistent helpfulness. We extend general thanks to administrators Kenneth L. Frazier, Louis Pitschmann, and Robin Rider, for understanding the needs of a project such as *DARE;* to Elsa Althen, Ed Duesterhoeft, Dineen Grow, Geraldine Laudati, Deb Shafer, Judith Tuohy, Ed Van Gemert, Heather Weltin, and Tanner Wray, for their persistence in solving problems and their resourcefulness in tracking down elusive sources; to Kathleen Horning and Megan Schliesman, for assistance with the resources of the Cooperative Children's Book Center; and to John Toussaint, of the Friends of the Library, for keeping *DARE* in mind as the book sales are organized.

Others in the UW–Madison community to whom we owe gratitude include former Chancellor David Ward and current Chancellor John Wiley, who understand both the challenges of supporting a project like *DARE* and the inherent value in doing so; Associate Deans Judith Kornblatt and Jane Tylus, of the Graduate School and the College of Letters and Science, respectively, who have provided both advice and financial support for graduate assistants; and W. Charles Read, Jo-seph Wiesenfarth, and the late Fannie LeMoine, who, with external reviewers John Algeo and Sidney I. Landau, made a convincing case for *DARE*'s continuation. We are also grateful to the University of Wisconsin Foundation, where President Andrew A. ("Sandy") Wilcox has been extremely supportive of the effort to fund *DARE* to its conclusion, and where Vice-Presidents Walter Keough and Mollie Buckley, as well as many other staff members, have graciously assisted David Simon and enthusiastically embraced the *DARE* project.

The Anatomy of a *DARE* Entry

headword.

part-of-speech abbreviation.

variant form. All variants are cross-referenced; a reader who looks up *drop egg* will find a reference to **dropped egg.**

etymology. *DARE* doesn't try to trace every word back to its ultimate origin, but only to explain how it got into American English. This etymology suggests that *dropped egg* is from Scots dialect, and refers the reader to the relevant entry in the *Scottish National Dictionary,* where the earliest citation is from 1824.

regional label. This generalization is based on all the available evidence, but especially, when possible, on evidence from the *DARE* survey.

social label. Like the regional label, this is based on all available evidence, but especially on evidence from the *DARE* survey.

definition.

dropped egg n Also *drop egg* [Prob from Scots dial; cf *SND drap* v. 5. (2) (b) 1824 →] **chiefly NEng** See Map *somewhat old-fash*
A poached egg.

map. The computer-generated map is deliberately distorted so that the area of each state is roughly proportional to its population. If every informant who was asked question H35 had answered *dropped egg,* the map would show 1,002 evenly spaced dots, each representing one of the communities selected for the *DARE* survey. This uniform spacing makes it much easier to interpret the map, since any "bunching" of dots is potentially significant, though it does take a little practice to recognize the states in their distorted forms.

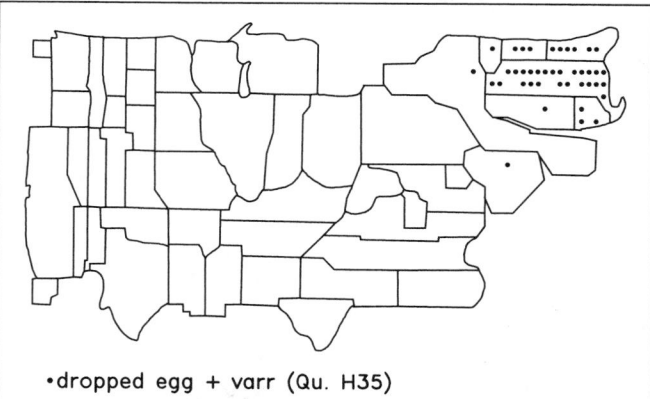
•dropped egg + varr (Qu. H35)

quotation block. The quotations provide examples of the headword, beginning with the earliest known U.S. example. All quotations, unless explicitly attributed to a secondary source, have been verified in the original.

short-title. The bibliography, to be published in the last volume, will give precise bibliographic details on every source cited in *DARE* (there are currently over 9,500), but the abbreviated titles allow the interested reader to identify the source.

1884 *Harper's New Mth. Mag.* 69.306/1 **MA,** Martha was . . eating her toast and a dropped egg. **1896** (c1973) Farmer *Orig. Cook Book* 93, *Dropped Eggs* (Poached). **1933** *Hanley Disks* **neMA,** Dropped egg—take and put a pan of milk on the stove and boil and drop the egg in and let it cook. **1941** *LANE* Map 295 (Poached Eggs), **through-out NEng,** *Dropped eggs.* . . 1 inf, **ceVT,** Drop eggs. **1948** Peattie *Berkshires* 323 **wMA,** In Berkshire . . you could not get a poached egg, but you could get a "dropped" egg, which was the same thing. **1965** *PADS* 43.24 **seMA,** 6 [infs] poached eggs, 4 [infs] dropped eggs, 1 [inf] dropped egg on toast. **1965–70** *DARE* (Qu. H35, *When eggs are taken out of the shell and cooked in boiling water, you call them _____ eggs*) 40 Infs, **chiefly NEng,** Dropped; **NH15,** Dropped egg on toast. [33 of 41 Infs old] **1975** Gould *ME Lingo* 82, *Dropped egg*—Maine for poached egg, usually on toast. **1977** *Yankee* Jan 73 **Isleboro ME,** The people on Isleboro eat dropped eggs instead of poached.

regional label. Whenever possible, regional information is given for individual quotations. In this example, the reader finds that the story quoted was set in Massachusetts.

***DARE* question.** This is the question to which *dropped egg* was a reply. The full questionnaire is printed in Volume I.

summary statement. This summarizes the regional distribution of the informants who gave this response.

informant code. Rarer responses are attributed to individual informants; a list in Volume I gives basic data on each one.

social statistics. In this entry, this is the main evidence for the social label *"somewhat old-fash."* When there are more informants, more elaborate statistics may be justified.

The *DARE* Map of the United States with a Conventional Map for Comparison

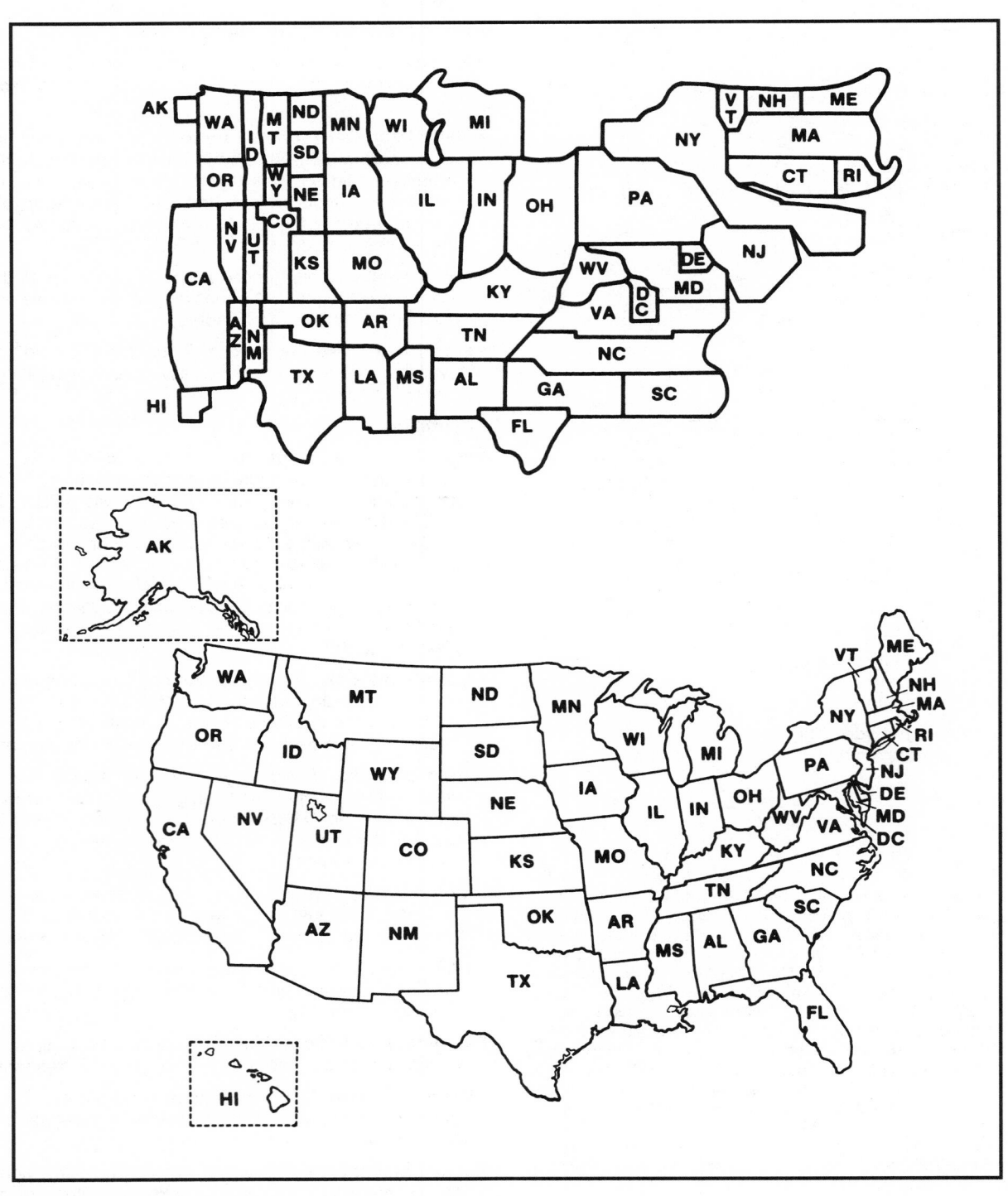

Pronunciation Guide

The following list of phonetic symbols and sample words is intended to provide a ready-reference guide to the system of transcription used in *DARE* entries. For an explanation of the criteria for inclusion of pronunciations and a more detailed discussion of the sounds and their regional distributions, readers are referred to the "Guide to Pronunciation" found on pp. xli–lxi of Volume I.

Pronunciations in the head sections of *DARE* entries are in "broadly phonetic" transcriptions using International Phonetic Alphabet (IPA) characters* enclosed in vertical lines. Those in quotations from *DARE* fieldwork are usually much more narrowly phonetic and are enclosed in square brackets. When quotations from sources other than *DARE* include pronunciations, the transcriptions are reproduced faithfully, with two exceptions: archaic or idiosyncratic systems are silently translated to *DARE*'s transcriptional system, and some of the minute details in sources such as the *Linguistic Atlas of the Gulf States* have not been preserved. Characters that are raised above the line of text are to be interpreted as weakly articulated; those enclosed in parentheses are variably present. Sequences of symbols not listed here should be interpreted as the sum of their parts. When two vowels in a transcription are contiguous but do not constitute a diphthong, they are separated by a hyphen.

In the list below, each symbol on the left is followed by a sample word containing the sound it represents. It must be remembered, however, that regional variation is complex, and one person's pronunciation of *father,* for instance, will not necessarily match another's. (In a few cases where readers are likely to recognize sounds characteristic of a particular region, notes regarding geographic distribution have been included.) Indented under the sample words are symbols for similar sounds that occur in the same phonetic environments. These include both those variants that occur frequently in *DARE* transcriptions and (in an effort to include symbols found in sources other than *DARE* materials) those that are less common. No attempt is made to determine an overall phonemic system.

*A few exceptions to the use of IPA characters are *DARE*'s use of |ɚ|, |š|, |ž|, |č|, and |ǰ|, which are traditional Linguistic Atlas symbols.

The Vowels

|i| *beat;* a higher-high-front unrounded vowel
     [ɪi] upgliding variant
     [iə] ingliding variant
     [ɨ] centralized variant
     [y] rounded variant

|ɪ| *bit;* a lower-high-front unrounded vowel
     [ɪə] ingliding variant
     [ɨ] centralized variant; usu unstressed
     [ʏ] rounded variant

|e| *bait;* a higher-mid-front unrounded vowel
     [eɪ] upgliding variant
     [eə] ingliding variant

|ɛ| *bet;* a lower-mid-front unrounded vowel
     [ɛɪ] upgliding variant
     [ɛə] ingliding variant
     [ɵ] rounded variant

|æ| *bat;* a higher-low-front unrounded vowel
     [æɪ] upgliding variant
     [æə] ingliding variant
     [a] lowered variant; used esp in parts of New England in such words as *ask, dance, path,* etc

|u| *boot;* a higher-high-back rounded vowel
[ʊu], [ʌu] upgliding variants
     [uə] ingliding variant
     [ʉ] centralized variant
     [ɯ] unrounded variant; see also |l|

|ʊ| *book;* a lower-high-back rounded vowel
     [ʊə] ingliding variant
     [ʊɪ] front-gliding variant
     [ʉ] centralized variant
     [ɤ] unrounded variant

|o| *boat;* a higher-mid-back rounded vowel
[ou], [ɤu] upgliding variants
     [oə] ingliding variant
     [ɵ] slightly fronted variant (the "New England short *o*")

|ʌ| *cut;* a fronted, lower-mid-back unrounded vowel occurring in stressed syllables
     [ʌɪ] upgliding variant
     [ʌə] ingliding variant

|ɔ| *bought;* a higher-low-back rounded vowel; see also |ɔɪ| and Pronc Intro 3.II.9
     [ɔu] upgliding variant
     [ɔə] ingliding variant
     [ɒ] lowered variant

|ɑ| *cot;* a lower-low-central unrounded vowel; see also Pronc Intro 3.II.9, 10
     [a] fronted variant
     [ɑ̠] retracted variant

|ə| *sofa;* also *mother* (for speakers without postvocalic *r*); a mid-central unrounded, unconstricted vowel occur-

ring in unstressed syllables (except when the first element of a diphthong; see |aɪ|, |aʊ|)
   [ɐ] lowered variant

|ɚ| *mother* (for speakers with postvocalic *r*); a mid-central unrounded, constricted vowel occurring in unstressed syllables

|ɜ| *bird* (for speakers without postvocalic *r*); a mid-central slightly rounded, unconstricted vowel occurring in stressed syllables
   [ɜɪ] upgliding variant
   [ɵ] fully rounded variant

|ɝ| *bird* (for speakers with postvocalic *r*); a mid-central slightly rounded, constricted vowel occurring in stressed syllables

|aɪ| *bite;* a front-upgliding diphthong
   [ɑɪ], [ɒɪ] retracted variants
   [əɪ], [ʌɪ] centralized variants (esp in Mid Atl and Canadian border regions)
   [aə], [ɑə] ingliding variants
   [a:] monophthongized variant (esp in parts of Sth and S Midl)

|aʊ| *about;* a back-upgliding diphthong
   [ɑʊ] retracted variant
   [əʊ], [ʌʊ] centralized variants (esp in Mid Atl and Canadian border regions)
   [a:] monophthongized variant (esp in parts of Midl)

|ɔɪ| *boy;* a front-upgliding diphthong
   [oɪ] raised variant
   [ɒɪ] lowered variant
   [ɔə] ingliding variant
   [ɔ:] monophthongized variant (esp in parts of Sth and Midl)

The Consonants

|p| *pat;* a voiceless bilabial stop

|b| *bat;* a voiced bilabial stop
   [ƀ] fricativized variant

|t| *tap;* a voiceless alveolar stop

|d| *dog;* a voiced alveolar stop

|k| *keep;* a voiceless velar stop
   [x] fricativized variant

|g| *get;* a voiced velar stop

|ʔ| *bottle;* a glottal stop

|f| *fist;* a voiceless labiodental fricative

|v| *vice;* a voiced labiodental fricative

|θ| *thing;* a voiceless interdental fricative

|ð| *this;* a voiced interdental fricative

|s| *see;* a voiceless alveolar fricative

|z| *zoo;* a voiced alveolar fricative

|š| *shoe;* a voiceless palatal fricative (also represented as [ʃ])

|ž| *vision;* a voiced palatal fricative (also represented as [ʒ])

|č| *chin;* a voiceless palatal affricate (also represented as [tʃ])

|ĵ| *jump;* a voiced palatal affricate (also represented as [dʒ])

|m| *mad;* a voiced bilabial nasal
   [ɱ] labiodental variant

|n| *new;* a voiced alveolar nasal
   [ɲ] palatalized variant

|ŋ| *spring;* a voiced velar nasal

|h| *high;* a voiceless glottal fricative

|w| *witch;* a voiced velar frictionless continuant

|hw| *which;* a voiceless continuant, for those who distinguish it from *witch;* (also represented as [ʍ])

|j| *you;* a voiced palatal frictionless continuant

|r| *run;* a voiced alveolar frictionless continuant
   [ɾ] flapped variant
   [ɹ] fricativized variant

|l| *light;* a voiced alveolar lateral
   [l̡] palatalized or "clear" variant
   [ł] velarized or "dark" variant
   [ɯ] fully vocalized variant; see also |u|

Diacritical Marks

' (raised, preceding a syllable) = having primary stress

ˌ (lowered, preceding a syllable) = having secondary stress

˜ (over a symbol) = nasalized

– (through the middle of a symbol) = articulated toward the center of the mouth

· (following a symbol) = slightly lengthened

: (following a symbol) = significantly lengthened

< or ⊢ (following a symbol) = forward in the mouth

> or ⊣ (following a symbol) = retracted in the mouth

^ or ⊤ (following a symbol) = higher in the mouth

ˇ or ⊥ (following a symbol) = lower in the mouth

' (following a symbol) = aspirated

¯ (following a symbol) = unreleased

₀ (beneath a symbol) = voiceless

ˬ (beneath a symbol) = voiced

‿ (beneath a symbol) = labialized

ˌ (beneath a consonant) = dentalized

‿ (beneath |ə|) = unsyllabic

. (beneath a consonant) = syllabic

. (beneath a vowel) = constricted

List of Abbreviations

Note: Periods are used for abbreviations in short-titles, but are generally omitted elsewhere.

a	ante (before); auxiliary informant	BBC	British Broadcasting Corporation
abbr(s)	abbreviated, abbreviation(s)	bd	board
absol	absolute(ly)	betw	between
abstr	abstract	bib	bibliographical, bibliography
acad	academy	biog	biographical, biography
acc	[date of] access; accusative	biol	biological, biology
accd	according to	bot	botanical
acct(s)	account(s)	Brit	Britain, Britannica, British
ADD	*American Dialect Dictionary*	bur	bureau
addit	addition(al)		
adj(s)	adjectival, adjective(s)	c	central; circa (about); copyright
admin	administration	Can	Canadian
adv(s)	adverb(s), adverbial	CanEngl	Canadian English (language)
advent	adventure(s)	CanFr	Canadian French (language)
advt	advertisement(s), advertiser	cap	capital
Afr	African	capt	captain
Afro-Amer	Afro-American	CB	citizens band
ag	agricultural, agriculture	cent(s)	central; century (-ies)
agric	agriculturalist	*Cent D*	*Century Dictionary*
AHD	*American Heritage Dictionary*	cf	confer (compare)
alt(s)	alternation(s), alternative	ch	chapter; church
alter(s)	alteration(s)	chem	chemical, chemistry
Amer	America(n), Americana	Chr	Christian
AmFr	American French	chron	chronicle(s)
AmInd	American Indian (language)	co	company; county
AmPort	American Portuguese (language)	cogn	cognate
AmSp	*American Speech*	col	colonel
AmSpan	American Spanish (language)	coll	collected, collection(s), collective; college
AND	*Australian National Dictionary*	colloq	colloquial
anon	anonymous	comb(s)	combination(s), combine(s)
AN&Q	*American Notes & Queries*	comm(s)	commission(ers); committee(s); community (-ies)
anthol	anthology	comp	compiler, compiled, composition
anthro	anthropological, anthropology	compar	comparative
antiq	antiquarian, antiquity	concr	concrete(ly)
aphet	aphetic	Cong	Congress
apoc	apocopated, apocopation	conj	conjunction
app	appendix	conjug	conjugation
appar	apparent(ly)	cons	consonant
approx	approximate(ly)	conserv	conservancy, conservation
Apr	April	constr(s)	construct(ed), construction(s); construed
arch	archaic	contemp	contemporary
archeol	archeological, archeology	contr	contracted, contraction
art	article	contrib	contribution(s)
assim	assimilated, assimilation	conv	conversation(al)
assoc	associate(d), association	coop	cooperative
asst	assistant	Corn	Cornish, Cornwall
astron	astronomical, astronomy	corr(s)	correct, corrected, correction(s)
Atl	Atlantic	correl	correlated, correlation, correlative
attrib	attribution, attributive(ly)	corresp	correspondence
Aug	August	cpd	compound, compounded, compounding
Austr	Australia(n)	crit	critical
autobiog	autobiographical, autobiography	cv	cultivar
aux	auxiliary	cyclop	cyclopedia

d	died
DA	*Dictionary of Americanisms*
DAE	*Dictionary of American English*
Dan	Danish
DARE	*Dictionary of American Regional English*
DAS	*Dictionary of American Slang*
dat	dative
DBE	*Dictionary of Bahamian English*
DCan	*Dictionary of Canadianisms*
Dec	December
def art	definite article
defin	defining, definition(s), definitive
Delmarva	DE, eMD, eVA
dem	demonstrative
dept	department
deriv	derivation, derived, derivative
derog	derogatory
descr	description, descriptive
dial(s)	dialect(s), dialectal
dicc	diccionario
dict	dictionary
dimin(s)	diminutive(s)
diss	dissertation(s)
dissim	dissimilated, dissimilation
distrib	distribute(d), distribution, distributive
div	division
DJE	*Dictionary of Jamaican English*
DN	*Dialect Notes*
DNE	*Dictionary of Newfoundland English*
DNZE	*Dictionary of New Zealand English*
doc	document(ary)
DOST	*Dictionary of the Older Scottish Tongue*
Dr	Doctor
DS	Data Summary
DSL	*Dictionary of the Scottish Language*
DSNA	Dictionary Society of North America
Du	Dutch
e	east(ern)
ed	edition, editor, editorial
EDD	*English Dialect Dictionary*
EDG	*English Dialect Grammar*
educ	educated, education(al)
ellip	ellipsis, elliptical(ly)
EModE	Early Modern English
encycl	encyclopedia, encyclopedic
engin	engineering
Engl	England, English
entomol	entomologica, entomological, entomology (-ist)
epenth	epenthesis, epenthetic
Episc	Episcopal
equiv	equivalence, equivalent
erron	erroneous(ly)
esp	especially
est	established
et al	et alii (and others)
etc	et cetera (and so forth)
etym(s)	etymological, etymology (-ies)
euphem(s)	euphemism(s), euphemistic(ally)
eve	evening
evid	evident(ly)
ex(x)	example(s)
exag	exaggerated
exc	except
exclam	exclamation, exclamatory
excr	excrescent
exped	expedition(s)
exper	experiment(al)
expl(s)	explain(ed), explanation(s)

explor	exploration(s), exploring
expr(s)	expression(s)
ext	extended, extension
eye-dial	eye-dialect
f, ff	and following
famil	familiar(izing)
Feb	February
fem	feminine
fig	figurative(ly), figure
Fin	Finnish
folk-etym	folk-etymological, folk-etymology
folkl	folklore
foll	follow(s), followed, following
Fr	French
Franco-Amer	Franco-American
FrCan	French Canadian (people)
freq	frequent(ly)
Fri	Friday
Fris	Frisian
ft	foot (measures); fort
funct	function(al)
fut	future
F&W	*Funk and Wagnalls Standard Dictionary*
FW(s)	fieldworker(s)
Gael	Gaelic
gaz	gazette(er)
gen	general(ly); genitive
geneal	genealogical, genealogy
genl	general
geog	geography
geogr(s)	geographer(s), geographic(al)
geol	geological, geology
Ger	German
Gk	Greek
gloss	glossary
Gmc	Germanic
gov	governor
govt	government
gram	grammar, grammatical
gs	grade school
gt	great
Haw	Hawaiian
hdbk	handbook
Heb	Hebrew
herb	herbaceous
hist	historic, historical(ly), history
horticult	horticultural(ist), horticulture
hon	honorable
hs	high school
Hung	Hungarian
hydrog	hydrographical, hydrography
ibid	ibidem (in the same place)
ie	id est (that is)
illit	illiterate
illustr	illustrate(d), illustration
imit	imitation, imitative
imper	imperative(ly)
imperf	imperfect(ly)
impers	impersonal(ly)
in	inch
inc	incorporated
incl	include(d), including, inclusive
Ind	Indian
indef	indefinite(ly)
indic	indicative(ly)

inf(s)	informant(s)		mod	modern
infin	infinitive(ly)		ModE	Modern English
infl	influence(d)		Mon	Monday
info	information		monogr	monograph(s)
infreq	infrequent(ly)		ms(s)	manuscript(s)
init	initial(ly)		mt(s)	mount, mountain(s)
inst	institute, institution		mth(s)	monthly, month(s)
internatl	international		MW	midwest
interp	interpretation, interpreter			
interrog	interrogative(ly)		n	noun; north(ern)
intj	interjection		*NADS*	*Newsletter of the American Dialect Society*
intr	intransitive(ly)		N Amer	North America(n)
intro	introduced, introducing, introduction		narr(s)	narrative(s)
Ir	Irish		nat	natural
irreg	irregular(ly)		natl	national
is	island(s)		naut	nautical
Ital	Italian		NB	New Brunswick
iter	iteration, iterative		nd	no date
			ne	northeast
Jan	January		NEast	northeast
jct	junction		neg	negative
joc	jocular(ly)		NEng	New England
jrl(s)	journal(s)		neut	neuter
			newsl	newsletter
l, ll	lake; line(s)		newsp	newspaper(s)
lab	laboratory		Nfld	Newfoundland
LaFr	Louisiana French		no(s)	number(s)
LAGS	*Linguistic Atlas of the Gulf States*		nom	nominative
LAMSAS	*Linguistic Atlas of the Middle and South Atlantic States*		non-std	nonstandard
			Norw	Norwegian
LANCS	*Linguistic Atlas of the North Central States*		Nov	November
LANE	*Linguistic Atlas of New England*		np	no page
lang(s)	language(s)		*N&Q*	*Notes & Queries*
Lat	Latin		ns	new series
LAUM	*Linguistic Atlas of the Upper Midwest*		nth(n)	north(ern)
lect	lecture(s)		nw	northwest
LGer	Low German		NYC	New York City
lib	library		*NYT*	*New York Times*
ling	linguistic(s)		NZ	New Zealand
lit	literature, literary			
Luth(s)	Lutheran(s)		obj	objective
			obs	obsolete
m	meter(s); monsieur		occas	occasional(ly)
mag	magazine		Oct	October
malaprop	malapropism		OE	Old English
Mar	March		*OED2*	*Oxford English Dictionary,* 2nd ed
masc	masculine		*OED(S)*	*Oxford English Dictionary (Supplement)*
math	mathematical, mathematics		OF	Old French
ME	Middle English (in etymologies; elsewhere = Maine)		old-fash	old-fashioned
med	medic(in)al, medicine		ON	Old Norse
MED	*Middle English Dictionary*		orig	origin, original(ly)
mem(s)	memorial(s)		ornith	ornithological, ornithologist (-gists('')), ornithology
metall	metallurgical, metallurgy		Oxfd	Oxford
metaph	metaphor, metaphorical(ly)			
metath	metathesis, metathetic(ally)		p, pp	post (after); page(s)
Mex	Mexican, Mexico		*PADS*	*Publication of the American Dialect Society*
MexSpan	Mexican Spanish		PaGer	Pennsylvania German
mfg(r)(s)	manufacture, manufacturer(s), manufacturing		pejor	pejorative
mid	middle		perf	perfect
mid-aged	middle-aged (of Infs: 40–59)		perh	perhaps
midl	midland		pers	person
midwest	midwestern		pert	pertaining
misc	miscellaneous, miscellany (-ies)		petrol	petroleum
mispronc	mispronunciation		philol	philological, philology
Missip	Mississippi		philos	philosopher, philosophical, philosophy
MJLF	*Midwestern Journal of Language and Folklore*		phon	phonetic
MLG	Middle Low German		phr(r)	phrase(s)
MLJ	*Modern Language Journal*		phys	physical
MLN	*Modern Language Notes*		pl	plate; plural

PMLA	*Publications of the Modern Language Association of America*	sig	signature
		SND	*Scottish National Dictionary*
poet	poetical	soc	society (-ies)
Pol	Polish	sociol	sociological, sociology
pop	popular(ly)	sp(p)	spelling(s), spelled; species
Port	Portuguese	Span	Spanish
poss	possessive; possible	SpanAm	Spanish American (people)
ppl	participial	spec	specific(ally)
pple(s)	participle(s)	sp-pronc(s)	spelling-pronunciation(s)
prec	preceded, preceding	st	saint; street
pred	predicate, predication, predicative(ly)	sta	station
pref	prefix(ation)	statist	statistical(ly)
prehist	prehistoric, prehistory	std	standard, standardized
prelim	preliminary	StdE	Standard English
prep(s)	preposition(s)	sth(n)	south(ern)
pres	present	subj	subject
pret	preterite	subjunc	subjunctive
prob	probable, probably	subseq	subsequent(ly)
proc	proceedings	subsp(p)	subspecies
progr	progressive	suff	suffix(ation)
pron	pronoun	sugg	suggest(ed), suggestion
pronc(s)	pronounced, pronouncing, pronunciation(s)	Sun	Sunday
pronc-sp(p)	pronunciation-spelling(s)	superl	superlative
Prot	Protestant	suppl	supplement(ary)
prov	proverb(ial); provincial	surv	survey(s)
psych	psychological, psychology	sw	southwest
pt	part; port	Sw	Swedish
pub	public; publication(s), published, publisher, publishing	syll	syllable
punct	punctuation	syn	synonym(ous)
QR	questionnaire	tech	technical, technological, technology
qrly	quarterly	terr	territory (-ies)
qu, qq	question(s)	Thu	Thursday
quot(s)	quotation(s)	topog	topographic(al), topography
		tr	transitive
r	recto; river	trans	transaction(s)
rec	record(s)	transcr	transcribe, transcription
recoll	recollections	transf	transfer(red)
redund	redundant	transl	translate(d), translation, translator, translating
redup	reduplicated, reduplication, reduplicative	treas	treasury
ref(s)	refer, reference(s)	Tue	Tuesday
refl	reflexive		
reg	register; regular(ly)	ult	ultimate(ly)
rel	related, relation, relative	uncert	uncertain
relig	religion, religious	uncom	uncommon
repet	repetition, repetitive	uncult	uncultivated
repr	representative(s); represented, represent(s), representing; reprint(ed)	univ	university
		unpub	unpublished
rept	report(s)	unstr	unstressed
resp(s)	response(s)	US(A)	United States (of America)
rev	review	usu	usual(ly)
revol	revolution(ary)		
rr	railroad(s)	v	verb; verso
Russ	Russian	var(r)	variant(s), various, varying; variety (-ies)
		vbl	verbal
s	south(ern)	vd	various dates
Sat	Saturday	vet	veterinarian, veterinary
Scan	Scandinavian	viz	videlicet (namely)
sci	science(s)	vocab(s)	vocabulary (-ies)
Scotl	Scotland	vol(s)	volume(s)
Scots	Scottish	vs	versus
se	southeast		
sec(s)	section(s)	w	west(ern); weekly
secy	secretary	*W2*	*Webster's New International Dictionary,* 2nd ed
Sept	September	*W3*	*Webster's Third New International Dictionary*
ser	series	wd	word
serv	service	Wed	Wednesday
sess	session	*WELS*	*Wisconsin English Language Survey*
sg	singular	wildfl	wildflower

wks	works		MT	Montana
WNID	*Webster's New International Dictionary*		NC	North Carolina
wrn	western		ND	North Dakota
WWI, WWII	World War I, World War II		NE	Nebraska
			NH	New Hampshire
yd	yard		NJ	New Jersey
yr(s)	year(s)		NM	New Mexico
			NV	Nevada
zool	zoological, zoology		NY	New York
			OH	Ohio
			OK	Oklahoma
			OR	Oregon

State Abbreviations

AK	Alaska		PA	Pennsylvania
AL	Alabama		RI	Rhode Island
AR	Arkansas		SC	South Carolina
AZ	Arizona		SD	South Dakota
CA	California		TN	Tennessee
CO	Colorado		TX	Texas
CT	Connecticut		UT	Utah
DC	Washington DC		VA	Virginia
DE	Delaware		VT	Vermont
FL	Florida		WA	Washington
GA	Georgia		WI	Wisconsin
HI	Hawaii		WV	West Virginia
IA	Iowa		WY	Wyoming
ID	Idaho			
IL	Illinois			
IN	Indiana			
KS	Kansas			
KY	Kentucky			
LA	Louisiana			
MA	Massachusetts			
MD	Maryland			
ME	Maine			
MI	Michigan			
MN	Minnesota			
MO	Missouri			
MS	Mississippi			

Signs and Symbols

~   is used to avoid repetition of a previously spelled-out word or phrase

‡   is used to indicate a word or sense of questionable genuineness

*   is used to indicate unattested or hypothetical forms

+   is used for "and"

→   is used with dates to indicate first or last attestation

<   is used for "derived from"

>   is used for "from which is derived"

=   is used for "equals"

p'- See **pre-** pref[1]

pa n [*OED2* 1811→]

A Forms. Cf ma A

1 |pɑ, pа|. Note: The "std" sp *pa* is also included here; in cases where the pronc is neither given nor implied by contrast with the sp *paw,* it is possible that some other pronc was intended. **widespread, but esp NEast, N Cent, Upper MW** See Map

1840 *U.S. Democratic Rev.* 7.79 **NEng,** It will do, Caleb, for *sartin,* . . for your Pa would never think of *licking* you after you are free. **1858** in 1983 *PADS* 70.45 **ce,sePA,** Saw 2 girls out on horseback while i was waiting for Pa. **1899** (1912) Green *VA Folk-Speech* 309, *Pa.* . . A childish form of *papa.* **1906** *DN* 3.122 **sIN,** *Pa* . . *paw.* . . The only words used for *father;* the latter not heard at all. **1910–20** in 1944 *ADD* **cNY,** *Pa* [pɑ]. **1948** Davis *Word Atlas Gt. Lakes* 63, [The chart shows that in the Gt. Lakes Atlas oral interviews *pa* was common in the northern section but rare or not found in the central and southern sections, while *paw* was rare or not found in the northern section but common in the central and southern sections.] **c1955** Reed–Person *Ling. Atlas Pacific NW,* 4 infs, Pa. **1961** Kurath–McDavid *Pronc. Engl.* 164, *Grandma.* . . The /ɑ ~ ɑ ~ a/ of *father* is used (1) throughout the North, including Metropolitan New York, and (2) in large parts of the South. The /ɔ ~ ɒ/ of *law* (1) predominates in the Midland. . . It is universal in West Virginia; in western Pennsylvania, /æ/ occurs alongside of it, in the Carolinas and Georgia /ɑ ~ ɑ/. (2) /ɔ/ occurs also, besides /ɑ/, from Albemarle Sound northward to lower Chesapeake Bay. The /æ/ of *bad* predominates (1) in the Low Country of South Carolina, (2) on the Eastern Shore of Maryland and in southern New Jersey, and occurs (3) as a minority variant in western Pennsylvania. . . In *grandpa, pa,* and *ma,* the regional dissemination of the variants is nearly the same as in *grandma.* **1965–70** *DARE* (Qu. Z1, . . *'Father')* 98 Infs, **widespread, but esp NEast, N Cent, Upper MW,** Pa [no transcriptions recorded, but FWs were expected to distinguish between spp *pa* and *paw*]; **MA1, ND2,** [pɑ]; **NY52, 69,** [pɑ(:)]—old-fashioned; **MI75,** [pɑ]—country people; **NY75,** [pɑ]—occasional; **SC3,** [pɑ]—her parents used this; **SC34,** [pɑˤ]; **MI5, SC26, 40,** [pɑ]; (Qu. M21b) Inf **MI36,** Ma and Pa; (Qu. N37) Inf **MD31,** [mɔ] and [pɑ]; (Qu. Z3) Infs **DC13, FL26, NJ19, NY96, OR3, PA225, TN30,** Pa; (Qu. AA23) Infs **MN35, WI31,** Pa; (Qu. NN12a) Inf **CA8,** Ask your pa. **1966** Dakin *Dial. Vocab. Ohio R. Valley* 2.419, In addition to *father* . . speakers commonly use these names: . . *pa* ([pa] or [pɑ]) . . ; *paw* ([pɔ] or [pɒ]). *Ibid* 422, *Paw* appears, chiefly in the speech of the oldest generation, everywhere in the Valley. *Pa* is less common, but this variant is used in the Ohio Company area and the upper Muskingum Valley, the Bluegrass and Pennyroyal, and in southeastern Illinois. . . [T]hese terms are unquestionably disappearing and may be characterized as "old-fashioned." **1970** *DARE* Tape **CA186,** Sunday morning . . Pa [pɑ] would hitch up the surrey and we'd get all cleaned up and we'd come clopping down Sunset Boulevard. **1973** Allen *LAUM* 1.338 **Upper MW** (as of c1950), *Pa* and *paw,* both informal, exhibit some distributional contrast. *Pa* dominates Minnesota and is favored in the Dakotas. *Paw* /pɔ/, on the contrary, is clearly Midland. Kurath found only one instance, as [pɒ], in southeastern New England. In the U[pper] M[idwest] its range is chiefly Iowa and Nebraska, where its greater frequency among Type I [=old, with little educ] speakers suggests that it is being considered as old-fashioned. **1973** Gawthrop *Dial. Calumet* 46 **nwIN,** This vowel [=ɑ] occurs in the speech of all informants in all representative locations. A low central lax vowel. . before a final juncture: ma, pa.

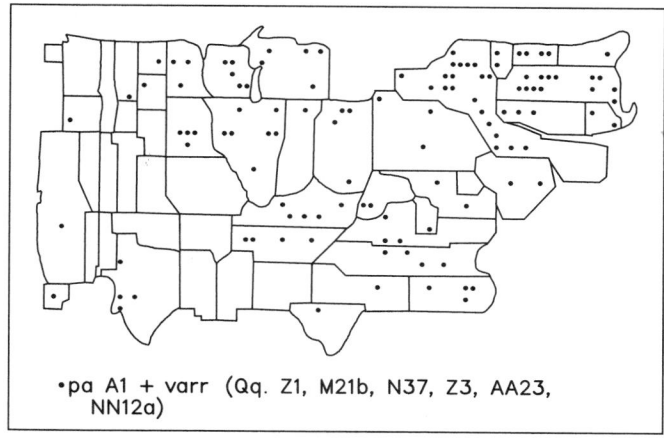

•pa A1 + varr (Qq. Z1, M21b, N37, Z3, AA23, NN12a)

2 |pɔ, pɑ|; for addit varr see quots; pronc-sp *paw.* **widespread exc NEast** See Map *somewhat old-fash*

1873 *Appletons' Jrl.* 10.487, There comes her paw and maw. **1890** *DN* 1.68 **KY,** *Pa* [pɑ] or [pɔ]. **1891** (1900) French *Otto* 162 **AR,** Paw made out to eat it, but I knowed 't was n't right. **1892** *DN* 1.240 **MO,** The native pronunciation in Kansas City for *ma* . . is [mɔ]. The same is true of *pa.* **1902** *DN* 2.240 **sIL,** *Pa* [pɔ]. **1903** *DN* 2.324 **seMO,** *Paw.* . . (In the North *pa* . .). **1903** Murrie *White Castle LA* 165 (as of c1865), Sancho. . . was a saucy fellow. If you gave him an inch he took an ell, but he never spoke of his "maw" and "paw" like so many of the other negroes. **1906** [see **A1** above]. **1907** *DN* 3.224 **nwAR,** *'Pa* [pɔ]. **1909** *DN* 3.356 **eAL, wGA,** *Paw.* **1936** *AmSp* 11.24 **eTX,** The context may similarly determine the variation in the pronunciation in monosyllables. 'I wonder if pa knows' [a 'wᴧndɚ ɛf pɔ noʊz]; 'Ask pa.[']' . . [æˢs 'pɔ:ə]. **1942** Faulkner *Go Down* 120 **MS,** I'm the man here. I'm the one to say in my house, like you and your paw and his paw were the ones to say in his. **1942** Hall *Smoky Mt. Speech* 29 **wNC, eTN,** *Father* . . is frequently replaced by ['dædɪ], used by young and old alike, less often by [pɔ:] and ['pæp(ɪ)]. **1942** Warnick *Garrett Co. MD* 1 **nwMD** (as of 1900–18), *Paw* (pɑ). **1942** McAtee *Dial. Grant Co. IN* 48 (as of 1890s), *Paw.* **1948** [see **A1** above]. **1961** [see **A1** above]. **1965–70** *DARE* (Qu. Z1, . . *'Father')* 90 Infs, **widespread exc NEast,** Paw [no transcriptions recorded, but FWs were expected to distinguish

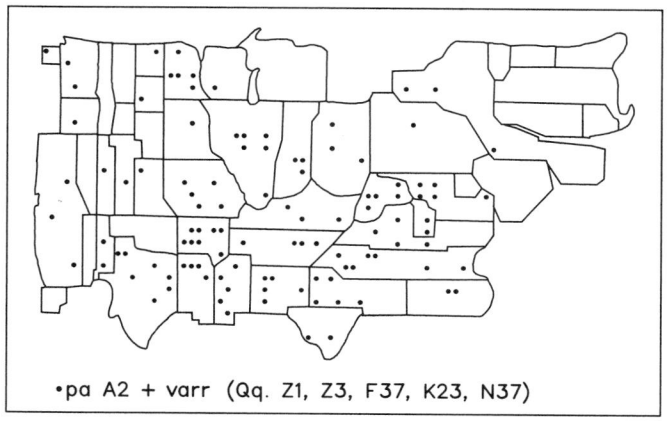

•pa A2 + varr (Qq. Z1, Z3, F37, K23, N37)

between spp *pa* and *paw*]; **AL**22, **MS**23, 30, 36, [pɔ]; **LA**12, [pɔ]—old-fashioned; **NY**52, [pɔ]—occasional; more a humorous way of putting it; **SC**29, [pɔ]—old; **GA**72, [pɑʊ]; **MO**13, My [pɒ] made me [FW: heard in conv] [Of all Infs responding to the question, 65% were old, 43% male, 65% comm type 5, 33% coll educ; of those giving these responses, 76% were old, 51% male, 48% comm type 5, 23% coll educ.]; (Qu. Z3) 10 Infs, **Sth, S Midl**, Paw; (Qu. F37) Inf **AR**47, Paw's room; (Qu. K23) Inf **IL**65, The [pɒ]; (Qu. N37) Inf **TX**51, Paw and Maw. **1966** [see **A1** above]. **1967** *DARE* Tape **TX**36, We had a party once in a while and if Ma and Pa ['mɔ n̩ 'pɒ] could go along and carry us, well, we went. **1973** [see **A1** above].

3 |pæ|. **chiefly Mid Atl, esp SC**   See Map

1888 *Amer. Jrl. Philol.* 9.205 **Charleston SC**, *Pa, ma,* are pronounced [pæ, mæ]. **1890** *DN* 1.8 **MD**, Baltimore peculiarities . . [pæ], [mæ] for *pa, ma.* **1905** *DN* 3.103 **nwAR**, [pæ, mæ, pɔ, mɔ]. **1930** *DN* 6.82 **cSC**, *Ma* and *pa* [mæ, pæ]. . . Fairly common; once universal. **1955** *PADS* 23.46 **e,cSC, eNC, seGA**, /æ/ in *pa, ma.* **1961** [see **A1** above]. **1966–67** *DARE* (Qu. Z1, . . 'Father') Infs **SC**2, 4, 46, [pæ]; **SC**7, [pæ]—her parents used this; **SC**10, His mother used [pæ]; **SC**11, [pæɨ]—others her age used; **SC**19, [pæ] [FW sugg]; his mother used this too; **SC**24, [pæ]—you never hear that word now; **SC**29, [pæ]—old; **SC**32, [pæ]—niggers; **SC**40, [pa, pæ] [FW sugg]; **SC**44, [pæ]—old-fashioned; **MD**13, [pæːə]—used in Inf's childhood.

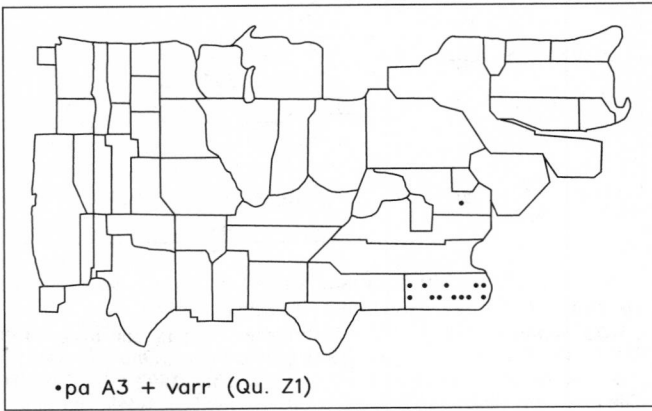

•pa A3 + varr (Qu. Z1)

B Senses.

1 A grandfather—also used as a quasi-personal name. **chiefly Sth, S Midl**   See Map   Cf **ma** n **B1**

1956 Ker *Vocab. W. TX* 307, *Grandfather* (usual terms and terms of affection). . . *pa*—colloq. for papa [2 of 67 infs]. **1961** Folk *Word Atlas N. LA* map 1206 *(Grandfather)*, [*Pa* is the least frequent of eight terms grouped together as "others."] **1965–70** *DARE* (Qu. Z3, . . 'Grandfather') 10 Infs, **Sth, S Midl**, Paw; **DC**13, **FL**26, **NJ**19, **OR**3, **PA**225, **TN**30, Pa; **NY**96, Pa—our grandchildren say this. **1986** Pederson *LAGS Concordance* **Gulf Region** *(Grandfather)* 8 infs, Pa; 1 inf, Pa—called grandfather; Pa Price—called the other one; 1 inf, Pa—grandchildren call him; 1 inf, Pa—by his own; 1 inf, Pa—some used this; 1 inf, Pa—one grandfather was called; 1 inf, Pa—his term; 1 inf, Pa—used by country people and negroes; 1 inf, Pa—paternal grandfather; 1 inf, Pa and Ma.

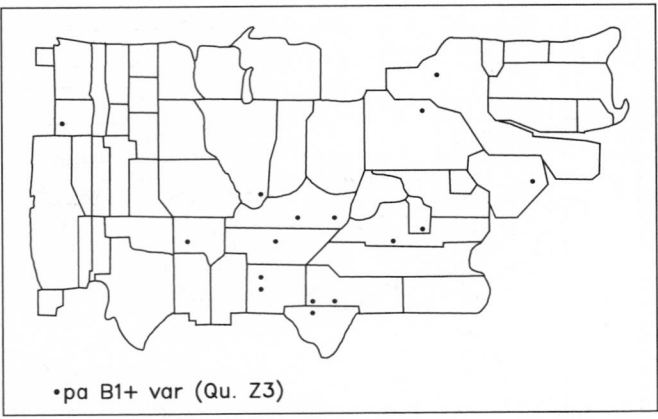

•pa B1+ var (Qu. Z3)

2 A husband—also used as a quasi-personal name.

1941 *LANE* Map 374 *(My husband)* 1 inf, **ceMA**, [pɑˋ], sometimes used [*LANE* Ed: uttered with signs of amusement]; 1 inf, **neMA**, [paˀ.ə], sometimes used; 1 inf, **swVT**, [pɑː], also used. **1968** *DARE* (Qu. AA23, *Joking names that a woman may use to refer to her husband: "It's time to go and get supper for my _____."*) Inf **MN**35, Pa; **WI**31, For pa [FW: Inf used in conv]. **1976** Garber *Mountain-ese* 66 **sAppalachians**, *Pa* . . father, husband. **1986** Pederson *LAGS Concordance* **Gulf Region** *(Husband)* 3 infs, Pa; 1 inf, Pa—old woman calls husband—in joke he tells; 1 inf, Pa—she calls her husband.

3 with *the:* A male animal kept for breeding purposes. *euphem*   Cf **daddy** n **5**, **father** n **B2**

1969 *DARE* (Qu. K23, *Words used by women or in mixed company for a bull*) Inf **IL**65, The paw [pɒ].

paa'dnuh   See **partner**

paa'lance   See **parlance**

paas blumes   See **pass blummies**

pac n Also *pac boot, pack*   [Perh < Delaware *pacu, paku* shoe, but perh abbr for **shoepack**]   Cf **bootpack, larrigan**
Orig a waterproof moccasin; later a moccasin-type waterproof or rubber-soled shoe or boot, esp one with a leather upper; a felt shoe worn inside an overshoe.

1872 (1876) Knight *Amer. Mech. Dict.* 2.1590, *Pac; Pack.* A moccasin having a sole turned up and sewed to the upper. Though now made of leather of various kinds, the *pac,* as used by the Indians of the Six Nations, for instance, was made of hide boiled in tallow and wax; or of *tawed* hide subsequently stuffed with tallow or wax. **1902** (1969) Sears *Catalogue* 1048, *Lumbermen's Pacs,* $1.98. . . *our best hand sewed Pac* with 10-inch leg of oil grain leather and oil tan pac leather uppers. *Ibid,* *Men's Pacs,* $0.98. **1911** *Century Dict. Suppl., Pack.* . . Also *pac.* . . 1. A moccasin made of hide prepared with tallow and wax, used by various North American Indian tribes.—2. A heavy felt or waterproof half-boot worn by loggers in the lumber-camps in winter. **1916** Kephart *Camping & Woodcraft* 1.157, *Pacs.*—A "shoe-pac" or "larrigan" is a beefhide moccasin with eight to ten-inch top, and with or without a light, flexible sole. It is practically waterproof so long as the seams (which are on top where they get less strain than those of a shoe) remain sound, and they are kept well greased. They are lighter and more pliable than shoes, and are first-rate "extras" to take along for wet days. **1922** *Outing* 80.68, Footwear, pac boots 16 inches; rubber boots. **1927** (1970) Sears *Catalogue* 341, An excellent combination consisting of a heavy rolled edge rubber over, with leather and light blanket lined stormproof arctic cloth top, together with a warm natural sheepskin wool Pac. **1944** *Sears Cat.* (ed. 189) 345 *(DA),* Leather top work Pac. . . Not rationed. **1950** *WELS* (*Canvas-top shoes with rubber soles)* 1 Inf, **seWI**, Pacs. **1950** *WELS Suppl.* **nwWI**, Packs—1. Boots with rubber shoes and leather tops. 2. Felt-boots made especially for wear inside galoshes or rubbers. **1956** Sorden-Ebert *Logger's Words* 25 **Gt Lakes**, *Packs,* Winter footwear worn by lumber-jacks. Made of rubber bottoms with leather tops. They were worn with several pairs of wool socks. **1968** *DARE* (Qu. W21, *Soft shoes that people wear only inside the house)* Inf **VA**28, Pacs [FW: Inf's spelling]—like a moccasin. **1991** Tabbert *Dict. Alaskan Engl.* 281, *Shoepac / shoepack—pac / pack*—These terms, which now usually refer to laceup boots with rubber bottoms and leather uppers, are from a word borrowed from the seventeenth-century Delaware Indian trade language (ultimately from Delaware) listed variously as *shipak, sippack, seppock,* etc. meaning 'shoes'. English speakers early misidentified the first part with English *shoe.* However, the second portion has been maintained in the un-English-looking form *pac,* though a more familiar *pack* rendering also has become established.

paccan   See **pecan**

pachuco n, also attrib Also sp *pachuko;* fem *pachuca*   [*OED2 pachuco* "a[dopted from] Mexican Sp. *pachuco* flashily dressed, vulgar"]   **SW, esp sCA, TX** *derog*   Cf **cholo, chuco**
A young Mexican-American, esp a gang member, often identifiable by distinctive clothing, hairstyle, and dialect; the dialect of such a person.

1943 *Crisis* (NY NY) July 200/1, *Pachuo* [sic] is a Mexican expression which originally meant "bandit" but has degenerated by usage into a description of a juvenile delinquent. . . In Mexican districts in the county of Los Angeles, small bands of pachucos have organized into gangs to fight each other. **1946** McWilliams *S. CA Country* 320, Since the Sleepy Lagoon case . . , open warfare has existed between the police and the Mexican boy and girl *pachucos* in Los Angeles. . . The continuance of these absurd police tactics has . . crystallized the hostility of the *pachucos* and solidified their "gang" organizations. **1947** *Common Ground* Summer 79/1 *(OED2)*, The Pachuco dialect is a mélange composed of *Caló*, Hispanicized English, Anglicized Spanish, and words of pure invention. **1956** Algren *Walk on the Wild Side* 50 **TX**, Two jungle bums diverted her. One was a kind of Mexican bear, a regular little Pachuco, sideburns and all. **1957** Laxalt *Sweet Promised Land* 69 **nNV**, After we came to like them [=young Mexicans on a sheep-shearing crew], it came as a shock one night to learn that they both carried knives, that at home in southern California they wore pegged pants and got into knife fights, that they were of the "Pachucos" we had been hearing so much about. **1966** T. Pynchon *Crying of Lot 49* i.II *(OED2)* **Los Angeles CA**, Hostile Pachuco dialect full of chingas and maricones. **1967** *DARE* (QR, near Qu. W42a) Inf **TX**27, Mexican teenage boys, *juvenil delincuentes,* are called pachucos or chucos; (Qu. HH26, *A person who is always ready to stir up trouble*) Inf **TX**4, Pachuco [pɑ'čuː.ko]—if he's young and Mexican; (Qu. HH28, *Names and nicknames . . for people of foreign background*) Inf **CA**15, Pachuco [pə'čukoʊ]—Mexican teenager. **1968** Fulbright *Cow-Country Counselor* 74 **AZ**, During the same period we were also troubled in Pinal County, as were the state of Arizona generally and other states, with *pachukos.* These were Mexican boys who wore long hair, . . wide-bottom trousers and usually had a knife concealed somewhere on their person. **1972** Wambaugh *Blue Knight* 71 **Los Angeles CA**, "Órale, panzón," he said like a pachuco, which he put on for me. He spoke beautiful Spanish. . . but the barrios of El Paso Texas died hard. **1976** *Word 1971* XXVII.294 [sic *OED2*—quot not found], *Pachuco* . . is used not only by felons, delinquents . . and others outside respectable society, but also by younger males throughout the Southwest as a street variety and for its slangy effect. **1986** Pederson *LAGS Concordance* **csTX**, 1 inf, Pachuco—Mexican, hoodlum, hippie; 1 inf, Pachuco—young Mexican-American; obsolete word; chuco—reduced form; 1 inf, Pachuco—"a little no-good Mexican boy"; pachucos—teenagers, long-haired, violent; 1 inf, Pachuco—old, full form of Chink, Chinko; Spanish; 1 inf, Pachucos—lower-class Mexicans with switchblades; 1 inf, Pachucos—long-haired Mexicans, wear tight pants; 1 inf, Pachucos—black fancy dressers; no longer used; 1 inf, Pachuco—Mexican teenage boy, rough, obscene; 1 inf, Pachucos—Mexican males, "white trash" equivalent; 1 inf, Pachucos—zoot-suits, hippie-acting. **1993** *DARE* File **TX**, *Pachuco/a* is the familiar term for homeboy/girl, fellow gangster, no? *Ibid,* My friend Debra down in San Antonio received a "pachuca vest" (presumably a vest worn by a pachuca) from one of her new friends when she was dating a Chicano (*his* designation, by the way).

Pacific cat n
=ring-tailed cat.
    1937 Grinnell et al. *Fur-Bearing Mammals CA* 1.166, *Ring-tailed Cats. . . Other Names. . .* Pacific Cat. *Ibid* 173, In the early days, [the late W.H.] Parkinson's father mined in the vicinity of the Tuolumne River and, when he returned home, he told of seeing one of these animals [=*Bassariscus astutus*], which he called "Pacific cat." . . Other people in the neighborhood called this species "miner's cat."

Pacific deer n Also *Pacific buck, ~-coast deer* **CA**
=mule deer.
    1967–70 *DARE* (Qu. P32, *. . Other kinds of wild animals*) Infs **CA**31, 36, 52, 87, Pacific deer; **CA**101, Pacific buck—used to be, no longer in this area; **CA**120, Pacific buck; **CA**181, Pacific-coast deer.

Pacific kingfish See **kingfish 4**

Pacific mackerel n
Std: **=chub mackerel.** Note: Formerly regarded as a distinct species from **chub mackerel.** Also called **Easter mackerel, greenback ~, little ~, night ~**

pacifity See **precipitate**

pack v
1 To carry, lug, tote (esp a heavy object). **chiefly West, Missip Valley, sAppalachians** See Map
    1805 (1905) Clark *Orig. Jrls. Lewis & Clark Exped.* 3.280, Proced up the 1st. right hand fork 4 miles & pack the meat from the woods to the

canoes from 4 miles to 3 miles distance all hands pack not one man exempted from this labour. **1849** in 1955 Lee *Mormon Chron.* 1.112, Some 20 or 30 person would suround the waggon . . , some of them with consternation depicted on their countenances, their Teams worn out, wumen & children on foot & som packing their provision[s], trying to reach Some point of Refuge. **1890** *DN* 1.79 **ID, KY, LA, MT, WA**, *Pack*. . . general word for *carry*. **1895** *DN* 1.373 **seKY, eTN, wNC**, *Pack:* to carry. **1902** *DN* 2.240 **sIL**, *Pack*. . . To carry, a word which is not used. *Pack* is used exclusively in sense of carry. **1903** *DN* 2.323 **seMO**, *Pack*. . . Carry. **1905** *DN* 3.63 **eNE**, *Pack*. . . Carry. **1906** *DN* 3.122 **sIN**, *Pack*. . . To carry, even a small thing. "I don't pack a watch." *Ibid* 149 **nwAR**, What'll you give me for packing this coal up to your office? **1911** *DN* 3.539 **eKY**. **1916** *DN* 4.347 **TX** (as of 1896), We'll have to pack a bushel of water from the well to the house. **1918** *DN* 5.19 **KS, NC, TN**. **1920** *DN* 5.83 **NW**. **1927** *AmSp* 2.361 **cwWV**. **1933** *AmSp* 8.1.23 **Appalachians**, *Pack* for *carry* is used in southwestern Virginia, southern West Virginia and in Kentucky, but it is not often heard in northern West Virginia or the adjoining part of Virginia. **1937** *Hall Coll.* **wNC**, When [Joe] Gunter moved, a wagon could not go above the hill at my father's place. . . [M]y oldest brother helped pack Gunter's things up to his new home. *Ibid,* If any goods were to be carried they would have to be unloaded and "packed" part of the way. **1950** *WELS* **WI** (To move something with you from one place to another: "He was _____ the box on his shoulder.") 1 Inf, Packing; ("Do you think you can _____ these cans to the shed?") 1 Inf, Pack; 1 Inf [who answered "carry" said], My Mother always "packs" things, she never carries them. **1965–70** *DARE* (Qu. Y30b, *To take something heavy up and move it from one place to another—for example, a bushel of apples*) 63 Infs, **chiefly West, Missip Valley, sAppalachians**, Pack; (Qu. Y30a, *To take something up and move it from one place to another—for example, a paper sack of groceries*) 56 Infs, **chiefly West, Missip Valley, sAppalachians**, Pack [Of all Infs responding to these questions, 28% were comm type 4 or 5, 64% old; of those giving this response, 89% were comm type 4 or 5, 72% old.]; (Qu. Y31, *If a child asked his father to carry him on his back . . "Give me a _____."*) Infs **IL**116, **KY**42, Pack me on your back; (Qu. JJ15a, *Sayings about a person who seems to you very stupid: "He hasn't sense enough to _____."*) Inf **CA**161, Pack guts to a hog. **1967–69** *DARE* Tape **AZ**2, They [=pack rats] will take something out of the nest and pack it elsewhere; **CA**145, I cut off all the good meat that I could pack . . and started back to climb over this ridge that I had run down; **CA**162, Every day we'd pack water for drinking water; **CA**163, Pack rat. . . They pack off everything. **1968** *DARE* FW Addits **KY**34, 44, Pack [FW: Infs used in conv] **LA**18A, *Pack*—carry, said of garbage which had to be carried some distance. Competes with "carry" and old-fashioned "tote." **1971** Wood *Vocab. Change* 41 **Sth**, When someone picks up and transports a heavy object such as a suitcase, he *carries* it in half of the [approx 1000] responses. . . *Hike* and *pack* also occur. *Ibid* 334, [The map shows 88 responses for *pack.* Of these, 60 are from **nAL, TN**, 10 from **swMS** and **seLA**; the others are scattered.] **1973** Allen *LAUM* 1.394 (as of c1950), For nearly two-thirds of the U[pper] M[idwest] infs, *lug* is the customary term for carrying an object heavy enough to require extra effort. . . Two minor equivalents are found in all the five states except South Dakota—*pack* and *tote*. *Ibid,* The written [checklist] replies are proportionately much greater for *pack,* which they conspicuously demonstrate to be dominantly Midland. **1991** Tabbert *Dict. Alaskan Engl.* 228, In rural Alaska the verb *pack* is used with high frequency in the sense 'to transport something carrying it by hand or on one's back'. It is especially common in the combination "to pack water."

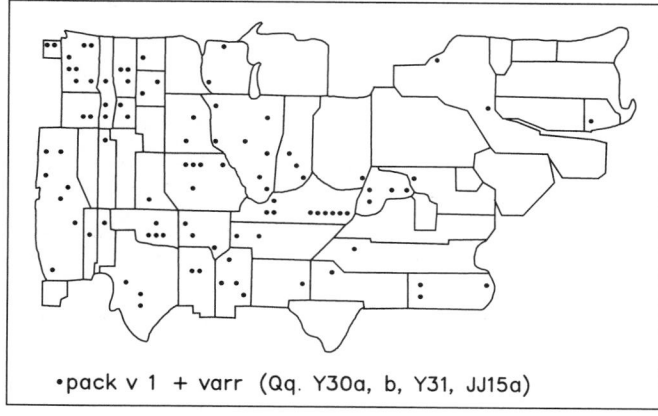

•pack v 1 + varr (Qq. Y30a, b, Y31, JJ15a)

a *pack news* (or *tales*): To gossip; to tattle, tell tales; hence nouns *news packer, tale* ~ a tattletale, a gossip. **esp S Midl**

   1903 *DN* 2.323 seMO, *Pack news.* . . Tattle. 'She's the worst woman in our settlement about packing news.' **1907** *DN* 3.234 nwAR, *Pack news.* . . To tattle. **1939** *AmSp* 14.92 eTN, *Tale packer.* Gossiper. 'That old woman's a tale packer.' **1942** Berrey–Van den Bark *Amer. Slang* 199.5, *Pack news, to communicate news. Ibid* 200.3, *Gossip.* . . pack news. **1950** Stuart *Hie Hunters* 113 eKY, "Ye'd better clear out, Brier-patch," Sparkie said. "Ye've packed enough tales fer one day!" **1983** *MJLF* 9.1.49 ceKY, *Newspacker* . . a tattletale.

b *pack guts to a bear* and varr: =carry guts to a bear.

   1903 *DN* 2.323 seMO, *Pack guts to a bear.* . . Signifying a low occupation. . . 'He isn't fitten to pack guts to a bear.' An expression of extreme contempt. **1922** *DN* 5.172 ME, NH, *Pack guts to a bear* or *carry guts to a bear.* . . "He ain't got sense enough to carry guts to a bear." "He isn't fitten to pack guts to a bear." **1927** *AmSp* 2.361 cwWV, *Pack guts to a goose* . . to work at dishonorable employment. "If he does that, he will be packing guts for the geese." **1969** *DARE* (Qu. JJ15a, *Sayings about a person who seems to you very stupid: "He hasn't sense enough to* _____.") Inf CA161, Pack guts to a hog.

c *pack (something) on* (or *onto, off on*): To blame (something) on; to lay responsibility for (something) on. [Cf *EDD* to pack *it upon a person* (at *pack* v. 11) "to foist an offence upon another"] **sAppalachians**

   1911 *DN* 3.539 eKY, *Pack-off on.* To blame; e.g., "He packed it off on me." = "He held me to account for it." **1915** *DN* 4.242 eTN, *Pack onto.* . . To lay the blame of (something) upon (one). "He packed my getting sick onto my getting dinner." **1952** Brown *NC Folkl.* 1.573, *Pack off on.* . . To blame another for something one is guilty of himself. "He tried to pack that stealing off on Ed."—General. **1966–69** *DARE* (Qu. II32, *To manage some way to shift the responsibility: "He said it wasn't his fault and tried to* _____.") Inf GA72, Saddle it off on me; lay it off on me; pack it off on me; NC33, Pack it on somebody else; TN13, Pack it on the other fellow. **1974** Fink *Mountain Speech* 19 wNC, eTN, *Pack* . . blame. "Hit was all packed on him."

d *pack the mail:* To ride or move quickly.

   1942 Berrey–Van den Bark *Amer. Slang* 921.5, *Ride a horse.* . . *Spec.* carry *or* pack the mail, *to ride fast. Ibid* 925.3, *Go fast; run.* . . pack *or* tote the mail. **1944** *AmSp* 19.156 sIN, *Pack (carry) the mail, to* (to run rapidly). **1976** Sublette Co. Artist Guild *More Tales* 57 WY (as of c1900), One of the first sayings I heard being used when I came to this country was when one was going fast, working hard, or doing something with extreme energy, they'd say, "He's really packin' the mail!"

pack n[1] See **pac**

pack n[2] See **packenham**

package n **HI**
A paper bag.

   1967 *DARE* (Qu. F22a, *A smaller paper container for bringing groceries home from the store*) Inf HI9A, Package—even though not closed or tied. **1972** McCormick *Vocab. HI* 70, *Package*—Paper container for groceries, bag, sack. **1972** Carr *Da Kine Talk* 143 HI, *Package* vs. *paper sack*—"Gimme one package. I like buy five poun' orange." The usual meaning of *package* 'a bundle of something', 'a parcel' has been widened in Hawaii to include the flat, unopened paper sack seen in markets. Many speakers continue to call the sack a *package,* however, even after it has been filled with groceries. This semantic shift can be heard in the conversation of speakers of [all levels of pidgin].

pack and back v phr
   1975 Gould *ME Lingo* 201, *Pack and back*—One of several woods terms to describe the carrying of two packsacks at once, which is done by alternating them on the trail. Carrying one ahead and then returning for the other, a man would tote the second one ahead of the first, and so repeat until he arrived in camp with both. Experienced woodsmen long ago proved it is faster and easier than making two trips, because you rest while you're back-tracking. In prohibition days, this was the customary way to bring booze down from Canada for guests at sporting camps. . . *Pack and back* is often called "walk and hide."

pack and boodle n [*pack* a group of people + **boodle 1**] Cf **kit n 2a**
A crowd, group.

   1950 *WELS* ("*They made a lot of noise and so he sent the whole* _____ *home.*") 1 Inf, WI, Pack and boodle, kit and caboodle.

packback n [Perh by metath from *backpack,* infl by **pack v 1**] Cf **packhorse ride**
A piggyback ride.

   1969–70 *DARE* (Qu. Y31, *If a child asked his father to carry him on his back . . "Give me a* _____.") Inf IL116, Packback; [IL116, KY42, Pack me on your back; PA67, Piggy-back; it's really peck-a-back].

pack barn See **packhouse**

packenham n Also sp *packingham;* abbr *pack* **FL**
Cheap or illegally made liquor; moonshine.

   1929 *AmSp* 4.386 KS, *Black-strap alky* or *pack* is made from New Orleans molasses; the term *pack* is used in many parts of the South also, and a gentleman at Palm Beach once told me that it refers to the English General Packenham, who was killed at the battle of New Orleans, and whose body was shipped home in a cask of liquor. **1966** *DARE* (Qu. DD21c, *Nicknames for whiskey, especially illegally made whiskey*) Inf FL32, Packenham; FL35, Packenham ['pækɪnhæm]—old-fashioned. [Both Infs old] **1966** *DARE* FW Addit FL35, The old folks all used to call "shine" packenham. **1986** Pederson *LAGS Concordance* (*Cheap whiskey* . . *home brewed beer or whiskey*) 1 inf, ceFL, Packing ham. [*LAGS* Ed: He didn't know the source of this.] [Inf old]

packer n
1 One who loads and manages pack-animals. **chiefly West**

   1788 (1888) Cutler *Life* 1.402, Here we met a Packer with ten pack-horses. **1825** (1933) Sibley *Santa Fe Diary* 140, I wrote to Mr. Baillio . . desiring him to send me over 10 Packing Mules, saddles & a sufficient number of Packers. **1871** *Scribner's Mth.* 2.4 MT, The dexterity with which a skillful packer will load and unload his horses is remarkable. **1888** *Century Illustr. Mag.* 36.202 MT, The Missourian was an expert packer, versed in the mysteries of the "diamond hitch," the only arrangement of the ropes that will insure a load staying in its place. **1900** Garland *Eagle's Heart* 291 West, "I'm no packer," growled Dan. [*Ibid* 292, Six piles of "truck," . . lay in a row. Each consisted of a sack of flour, a bundle of bacon, a bag of beans, a box, a camp stove, a pick, a shovel, and a tent. These were to be packed, covered with a mantle, and caught by "the diamond hitch."] **1923** Sinclair *Parowan Bonanza* 111 SW, There are some strangers camped right beside me. Government men—but I didn't like the look of their packer. **1930** Shoemaker *1300 Words* 48 cPA Mts (as of c1900), *Packer*—One who made a business of transporting goods on horses along the Jersey Shore—Coudersport Pike. **1969** *DARE* Tape CA161, Red Bluff got to be the head of navigation and the big distributing point with hundreds of teamsters and packers in here and out all the time.

2 in combs *news packer, tale* ~: See **pack v 2a**.

pack guts to a bear See **pack v 2b**

packhorse ride n Also *packsaddle ride* Cf **packback**
A piggyback ride.

   1965–70 *DARE* (Qu. Y31, *If a child asked his father to carry him on his back . . "Give me a* _____.") Infs NC40, OK12, Packhorse ride; IL114, Packhorse ride [FW sugg]; IL131, Packsaddle ride; TX86, [pɛk] horse ride. [4 of 5 Infs old]

packhouse n Also *pack barn,* ~ *shed* **esp GA, NC, eSC, VA**
See Map
A building used for storing cured tobacco or for preparing it for market or processing.

   c1937 in 1970 Yetman *Voices* 31 NC, Dey can have de meetin'. You tell 'em, Dave, dat I said dat dey can meet on Tuesday in de pack house. **1940** *AmSp* 15.134 KY [Language of the tobacco market], *Pack house.* Packing houses or barns in which tobacco is packed in hogsheads. **1944** *PADS* 2.68 sVA, *Pack-house.* . . A house in which tobacco is stored after it is cured. **1965–70** *DARE* (Qu. M1, . . *Kinds of barns* . . *according to their use or the way they are built*) Infs GA17, NC15, 24, Packhouse; GA19, Packhouse—tobacco house; SC1, Packhouse—for storing and working tobacco; SC7, Packhouse—for working up and storage of tobacco; SC24, Packhouse—for grading and working up tobacco; NC6, VA40, Pack barn—for tobacco after it is cured; VA43, Pack barn—storage barn; storing cured tobacco; (Qu. M22, . . *Kinds of* *buildings . . on farms*) Infs **NC**8, 49, Packhouse; **SC**12, Packhouse—large barn for working up tobacco and making it ready for market; **VA**38, Packhouses—for packing or storing cured tobacco; **NC**68, Pack shed. **1966** *PADS* 45.18 **cnKY**, *Pack house*. . . The place where cured tobacco is prized into hogsheads after its purchase by a tobacco processing company. . . "At the pack house, they use a press to prize the tobacco down in hogsheads." **1966–70** *DARE* Tape **NC**3, Then they put these sticks in the packhouse which has rooms in it, and they start off with a low heat to yellow the tobacco; **NC**8, They cure it, and then it's removed from the barn and put in the packhouse. Every farm must have some type of a packhouse. . . It must be dry and free of leaks; **NC**15, They put it [=tobacco] in the green state or ripen state, you know, and they pack it down in the packhouses. . . and then they will work it up and get it ready for market; **SC**12, We was grading and tying tobacco in the packhouse; **SC**17, You take it to the packhouse, and you bulk it down and then fix it up for the market. . . You . . want a good packhouse. . . Your floor ought to be four foot high from the ground. . . just . . to keep the water off of it and the dampness out of it; **VA**38, You let your fires go out then and you move that barn [=barnful of tobacco] out to your pack barn. **1969** *NC Folkl.* 17.34 **wNC**, In an effort not to be so dependent on the vagaries of weather, [tobacco] farmers often dug *casing houses,* also called *pack houses* or simply basements. These were work rooms dug into a bank or the side of a hill. Earthen rooms and walls afforded an atmosphere constantly damp and moist. **1986** Pederson *LAGS Concordance* **csGA**, 1 inf, Packhouse—where cured tobacco stored; 1 inf, Packhouses = packinghouses for meat or tobacco. [*DARE* Ed: 4 other Infs who offered *packhouse* did not specify its purpose.]

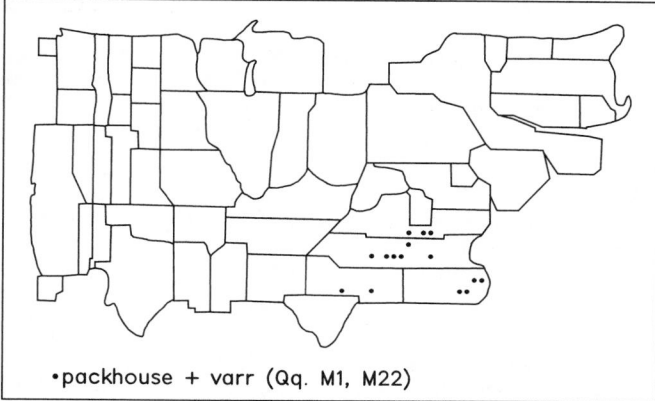

•packhouse + varr (Qq. M1, M22)

packie n Also sp *packy* **NEng** [Abbr for *package store*]
A liquor store.

    1982 Chaika *Speaking RI* [7], *Packie* = affectionate name faw *package staw.* **1996** *DARE* File **CT**, Her colleagues, from Enfield and Windsor, . . can't imagine calling a liquor store anything other than "packy." **1997** *Ibid* **seMA, eCT**, We always talked about going to a packy—a package store where you could buy alcohol but not open it on the premises. *Ibid* **neMA**, In New England, at least in northeastern Massachusetts a packie is a liquor store. **1999** *Ibid* **NH** (as of c1975), A common term in New Hampshire . . is "the packie", meaning the liquor store. **1999** *DARE* File—Internet **eMA** [Boston Online *The Wicked Good Guide to Boston English*], *Packie* run—What you make when you go downna Mahty's or some otha packie.

packingham See **packenham**

pack news See **pack** v **2a**

packout n
Food prepared and packaged by a restaurant to be consumed off the premises; take-out food.

    1955 *DARE* File **WA**, Food put up by a restaurant 'to go'—"Lunches, Hamburgers, Packouts." **1967** *DARE* FW Addit **NV**, Pak-out [sic] menu. **1998** *Ibid, Packout.* . . About two years ago I heard a woman use that expression. . . The woman was from Seattle, but I have no idea if that is where she was from originally.

pack peddler n Also *pack pedlar* **old-fash**
An itinerant peddler who sells goods from a pack.

    1859 *Ladies' Repository* 19.721, Even the appearance of two pack peddlers trudging up the front walk did not disturb my equanimity. **1880** *Ibid* 61.892, There was a pack peddler with smuggled shawls and laces at the door. **1917** Sinclair *King Coal* 250 **CO**, Betty . . [was] working at the . . task of making the children of a pack-pedlar into leaders in the "younger set." **1939** (1962) Thompson *Body & Britches* 165 **NY**, Shortly after a pack-peddler had got the better of "Wit" in what was thought an unethical manner, Cook's cat died. He skinned her and waited until the peddler called again one evening. . . Next day the itinerant drove into the yard. **1945** Wilson *Passing Institutions* 70 **KY**, We . . married and died in a small area, learning of the big outside world only through books and an occasional pack peddler or clock tinker who came in. **1968–69** *DARE* (Qu. U5, *Someone who sells small articles on a street corner*) Inf **MA**15, Used to have a pack peddler in neighborhood; (Qu. U7, *A man who goes from town to town selling things*) Inf **CT**20, Pack peddler; **IN**19, Pack peddler—clothing, jewelry, table linens, all imported things; **IN**60, Pack peddler—one who travels on foot with a canvas full of lace, notions, etc; **KY**28, Pack peddlers—old-fashioned, before the use of trucks; **KY**42, Pack peddler—house to house; **NY**75, Pack peddlers—years ago they carried wares on their back. [All Infs comm type 4 or 5; 5 of 7 Infs old] **1975** McDonough *Garden Sass* 131 **AR**, From the earliest days, when there were only trails to the homes, the "pack peddler" or "foot peddler" came with all his goods in a pack on his back. As roads were cleared, a new kind of salesman, called the "chicken peddler," made the rounds. **1977** Norman *Kinfolks* 89 **eKY**, We lived right in the very head of the holler, you see, and we never saw anybody up there much except a few old pack peddlers from time to time, and now and then some kind of candidate out lectioneering from house to house. **1986** Pederson *LAGS Concordance*, 1 inf, **swLA**, Pack peddlers—came to island to peddle wares.

pack rat n [See quot 1885] **West**
=**wood rat** (here: *Neotoma* spp).

    1885 (1891) Roosevelt *Hunting* 13, These rats were christened pack rats, on account of their curious and inveterate habit of dragging off to their holes every object they can possibly move. **1912** Wason *Friar Tuck* 238 **West**, We had the blamedest time with a pack-rat I ever did have. **1923** Cook *50 Yrs.* 163 **NM**, Metal buttons and buckles, and even parts of clothing, stored near by by the pack-rats, often added their mute testimony. **1929** *Ruppenthal Coll.* **KS**, Pack rat—wood rat; a large brown rat on the plains eastward from the Rocky Mountains. **1941** Jaeger *Wildflowers* 155 **Desert SW**, Curiously, pack rats *(Neotoma)* transport the prickly joints [of *Opuntia bigelovii*] and use them to protect their runways and nests. **1958** McCulloch *Woods Words* 131 **Pacific NW**, *Pack rat.* . . Also known as bush tail rat or trader rat. A woods rat with the habit of packing off anything loose at night—watch, keys, false teeth, etc. Generally trades a pine cone, stick, etc., for articles removed from camp. Makes a mess of unused cabins, building up a big ant's nest of sticks and trash. **1966–68** *DARE* (Qu. P29) Inf **TX**43, Pack rat; (Qu. P32, *. . Other kinds of wild animals*) Infs **AZ**2, **CA**2, 65, **NM**3, **WY**1, Pack rat. **1967–69** *DARE* Tape **AZ**2, Pack rats that we have out in the West. . . so called because they carry something in their mouth most everywhere they go. . . [T]he pack rat home gets to be several feet tall; **CA**163, [FW:] What's the difference between a wood rat and. . . [Inf:] Pack rat. They're the same. Pack rat, they pack off everything.

pack room n Cf **junk room**
A storage room.

    1956 Ker *Vocab. W. TX* 107, Room for storing disused articles. . . pack room. [1 of 67 infs] **1972** *PADS* 58.13 **cwAL**, Storage room. . . Some of the terms obtained are *storage room . . utility room . . pack room, cubby hole, glory hole,* and *junk room.* **1986** Pederson *LAGS Concordance (Loft)* 1 inf, **swGA**, Pack room—used for storing saddles, hay; *(Junk room)* 1 inf, **cwAL**, Pack room.

packsaddle(r) See **packsaddle worm**

packsaddle ride See **packhorse ride**

packsaddle worm n Also *packsaddle(r)* [See quot c1960] **esp sAppalachians** See Map
=**saddleback caterpillar.**

    1884 Smith *Bill Arp's Scrap Book* 72 **GA**, I wonder if Harris ever saw a pack saddle. Well, its as putty as a rainbow, just like most all of the devil's contrivances, and when you crowd one of em on a fodderblade you'd think that forty yaller jackets had stung you all in a bunch. **1925** Dargan *Highland Annals* 208 **cwNC**, You said I must git another big mess 'fore the frost struck 'em heavy, an' that field was plum full o' pack-saddlers. One stung me ever' time I laid my hand on a roas'in' year. Hit hurts worse'n a hornet fer a minute, an' it's harder on a body's temper than a hornet is. **1953** *PADS* 19.12 **sAppalachians,** *Pack saddler.* . . A beautiful green worm with markings like a saddle on its back. The worm stings. It is found on fodder. **c1960** *Wilson Coll.* **csKY,** *Pack-saddle worm*—The larva of an insect often found on corn blades with a very violent sting; the worm itself is quite pretty, actually suggesting the form of an old-fashioned pack-saddle. **1965–70** *DARE* (Qu. R21, . . *Other kinds of stinging insects*) Inf **NC35,** Packsaddle—fuzzy, looks like woolly worm with horns; **NC54,** Packsaddle—looks like a saddle and stays on corn; light green; **TN22,** Packsaddle—lives on corn; (Qu. R27, . . *Kinds of caterpillars or similar worms*) Infs **AL32, KY28,** Packsaddle—stinging worm; **GA77,** Packsaddle—brown, short, has black square on back; **KY40,** Packsaddle—found on corn blades, has poisonous spines [FW: Inf used in conv]; **TN6,** Packsaddle—has a stinger; **VA2,** Packsaddle; **VA7,** Packsaddle—long, green, with stingers in their backs, corn pests; (Qu. R30) Inf **VA3,** Packsaddle—wormlike; fuzzy, stings, eats corn [FW: It stings if you brush against its spines when picking corn.] **1982** Slone *How We Talked* 44 **eKY** (as of c1950), *"Pack saddler"*—a worm that was found on the blades of corn. We were always afraid of them when we were pulling the fodder. It stung by projecting spines from its back. It had a ring of these hair-like spines along its back that resembled a saddle.

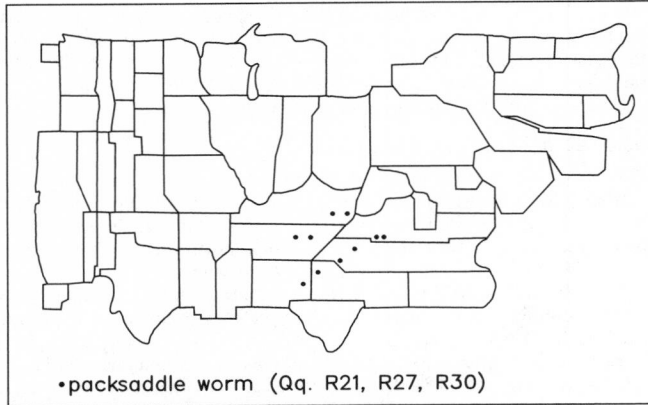

•packsaddle worm (Qq. R21, R27, R30)

pack shed See **packhouse**

pack (something) on (or onto, off on) See **pack** v 2c

pack tales See **pack** v 2a

pack the mail See **pack** v 2d

packwack n Also *paddywack, patti-whack* [Varr of *paxwax* nuchal ligament of an animal; gristle; varr recorded in *EDD* include *pack-wack* and *packywhack*]
See quots.
   1944 *PADS* 2.47 **NC, VA,** *Patti-whack* ['pætɪ,hwæk]. . . Cartilage, the wide white band found in beef; something regarded as tough. **1966** *DARE* FW Addit **MA6,** *Packwack*—meat that is neither bone nor meat. Inf says it's "sort of givey. Not really gristle." Father's term. **2000** *NADS Letters* **cPA,** I have heard the variant of pax-wax you list as patti-whack or paddywack (as we spelled it), used for that chewy gristle piece. The old folks would actually chew on it, for the beef juices. Two generations ago beef was not affordable to most families in my area, and on those rare occasions when they had some, they used everything.

pack-water n [**pack** v 1]
   1902 *DN* 2.240 **sIL,** *Pack-water.* . . One who is at another's beck and call; a drudge. One who will do drudgery for small favors, or favorable opinion. 'I ain't your pack-water.'

paczki n, sometimes pl Also sp *paczski* Pronc-spp *po(o)nchka, poonchkey, punchkey;* for addit varr see quots [Polish *pączek* ['pɔnček], pl *pączki* ['pɔnčki]] **in Polish settlement areas, esp MI, WI** Cf **fastnacht 1, kolacky, pascha**
A type of yeast-leavened, usu filled, doughnut traditionally associated with Shrove Tuesday.
   c1965 *DARE* FW Addit **seWI,** *Ponchka* ['pɔnčkə]. . . A Polish word used in Polish areas for a jelly-filled doughnut [Inf of Polish descent]. **1968** *DARE* (Qu. H28, *Different shapes or types of doughnuts*) Inf **WI47,** Poonchka [punškə]; (Qu. H29, *A round cake, cooked in deep fat,*

with jelly inside) Inf **WI47,** Poonchka—a Polish word for this. We use it for any solid doughnut. **1970** *DARE* Tape **MI**120A, Before Lent, all these Polish people would. . . have what was called a ['po^nski] party. . . Ponskies is something like a doughnut. **1981** Hachten *Flavor* **WI** 167, *Paczki* (Polish). . . Hedwig A. (Mrs. Victor) Semram, Milwaukee, submitted this recipe that has been handed down in her family which came from Poland in 1919. "These doughnuts are made on Shrove Tuesday which is the day before Ash Wednesday," she wrote. "So this is the last big feed before the long six-week fast." **1989** *WI Trails* Dec 26 **cWI,** Point Bakery was there first. . . and it's Polish through and through. . . Ponczaks [sic] (pronounced poonchkas), delightful crosses between a jelly donut and a Danish pastry, are still made from the handed-down, inherited recipes. **1996** *WI State Jrl.* (Madison) 18 Feb [Advt circular, in "The Corner Bakery" section:] *Special* of the week! Mix & Match, Filled with Prune, Jelly or Vanilla Buttercreme *Lenten Paczki Sale* 2 for 99¢. **1997** *NY Times* (NY) 10 Feb sec A 8/1 **Detroit MI,** For a growing number of southeastern Michigan residents, the day before Lent means a trip to this Polish–American enclave within the city of Detroit and the purchase of paczki: Polish jelly doughnuts. **1998** *Daily Hampshire Gaz.* (Northampton MA) sec W 1/2, Paczki, pronounced "pooch-key" or "punch-key" or even "poonch-key", is a Polish pastry, which looks like an extra large fried doughnut. **1998** *DARE* File **cMA,** Paczki ['pački]. **1999** *DARE* File **seMI,** Shrove Tuesday. . . Packzi Day!! (pronounce it poonch-kee). . . Here in Detroit, . . we have a surprisingly large Polish population and this particular bit of tradition has spread itself pretty much over all of Southeast Michigan.

pad n[1] [*OED2* pad sb.[2] 1 1567 →; "Orig *slang,* now also *dial.*"]
A road, path—usu in phr *on the pad* on the go, away from home.
   1899 (1912) Green *VA Folk-Speech* 309, *Pad.* . . A path; a footpath; a road. . . To be *on the pad,* to be on the go all the time. **1954** *Harder Coll.* **cwTN,** *On the pad*—not staying home much. **1956** McAtee *Some Dialect NC* 32, *Pad, on the.* . . On the go. "They kept me on the pad."

pad n[2]
1 See **lily pad 1.**
2 The flattened stem joint of a **prickly pear 1**; see quots. Cf **nopal, pear pad, tuna**
   1942 Hylander *Plant Life* 318, The genus *Opuntia* is recognized by its fleshy jointed stems, which are made up of either cylindrical or flattened joints known as "pads"; these succulent stems are green and take the place of leaves. . . One group of *Opuntia* species has distinctly flattened joints or "pads"; this includes the common Atlantic Prickly Pear. . . far up on the Atlantic coast. **1967** Dodge *Roadside Wildflowers* 49 **SW,** The name pricklypear is applied to the many cactuses with flat-jointed stems, called pads. The fruits are somewhat pear-shaped and are eaten, when mature, by birds and other small animals. **1979** Spellenberg *Audubon Guide N. Amer. Wildflowers W. Region* 440, *Opuntia polyacantha.* . . This Cactus is a nuisance on rangeland. . . The spiny pads often break off and stick in the noses and throats of livestock.
3 often in combs: A set of sheets of paper fastened at one edge so that single sheets can be torn off; see quots. [*OED2* pad sb.[3] 4 1865→] **widespread, but esp NEast** See Map Cf **block** n 3, **tablet**
   1860 *Harper's New Mth. Mag.* 21.601, Joseph and the Colonel had returned to camp, leaving me with my sketch-book. . . A huge drop on the paper-pad was the first warning that the storm threatened all day had really come. **1890** *Century Dict.* 4227, *Pad.* . . A number of sheets of

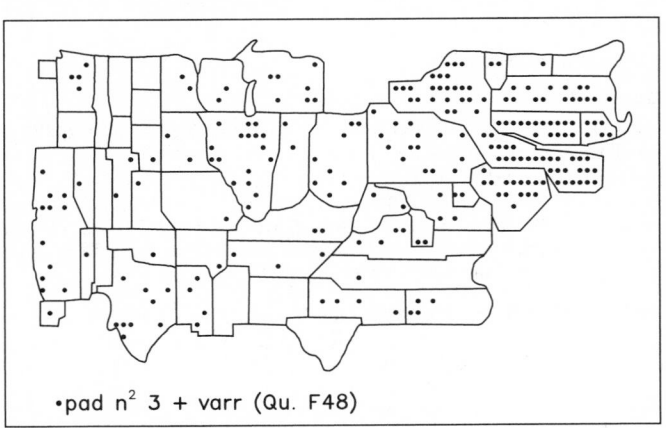

•pad n[2] 3 + varr (Qu. F48)

writing-, drawing-, or blotting-paper held together by glue at one or more edges, forming a tablet from which the sheets can be removed singly as used: as a writing-*pad;* a blotting-*pad.* **1912** Green *VA Folk-Speech* 309, *Pad.* . . Sheets of blank paper glued together at the edges, and used to write on. Writing-*pad.* **1930** Winkler *Morgan* 170 (as of 1863), The pad shover was a messenger clerk whose duty it was, in those days before the ticker or quotation boards, to display pads of paper containing latest stock prices. **1965–70** DARE (Qu. F48, . . *Pages of writing paper glued together at the top with a cardboard back;* not asked in early QRs) 209 Infs, **widespread, but esp NEast,** Pad; 16 Infs, **scattered,** Writing pad; 10 Infs, **scattered,** Scratch pad; **IN**64, **OH**84, Note pad; **CA**64, Composition pad; **OK**56, Pencil pad; **IL**84, **MI**68, Pad of paper.

Pad n³ See **paddy** n¹ 1

pad v See **pat** v 3

paddle n
1 A hand.
  1942 Berrey–Van den Bark *Amer. Slang* 121.54, *Hands.* . . paddles. **1968** DARE (Qu. X32, *Joking or uncomplimentary words for the hands* . . *"Those are mine. You keep your _____ [out of them]."*) Inf **MN**12, Paddles.
2 also *boat paddle, paddlefoot, paddlewheel:* A foot, esp a large one.
  1966–69 DARE (Qu. X38, *Joking names for unusually big or clumsy feet*) Infs **IN**13, 30, Paddlefoot; **GA**7, **TX**106, Boat paddles; **MN**12, Big paddles; **FL**33, Paddles; **PA**184, Paddlewheels.
3 in comb *fly paddle:* A flyswatter.
  1967 DARE (Qu. F47, . . *Wire or rubber device with a handle, that is used to kill flies;* not asked in early QRs) Inf **LA**14, Fly paddle. **1986** Pederson *LAGS Concordance,* 1 inf, **cLA,** Fly paddle; i.e. flyswatter.

paddlebill See **paddlefish**

paddle boat n Also *paddling boat*
A small, often flat-bottomed, boat propelled by a paddle.
  1874 Long *Amer. Wild-Fowl* 78, The size and shape of a paddle-boat . . must depend . . upon the locality intended for its use. **1905** in 1961 Pringle *Woman Rice Planter* 144 **GA,** She jumped into her paddling boat . . and . . paddled herself across. **1953** (1977) Hubbard *Shantyboat* 47 **Missip-Ohio Valleys,** As we drifted from one section [of river] to another our johnboat was called flatboat, joeboat, footboat, dinkyboat, paddleboat, and on the Lower Mississippi, bateau. **1965–70** DARE (Qu. O1, . . *A small rowboat, not big enough to hold more than two people*) Infs **AR**5, **DC**5, **GA**72, 82, Paddle boat; **SC**40, Paddle boat—same as bateau or fishing boat; **SC**9, Paddling boat; [(Qu. O2, *Nicknames . . for an old, clumsy boat*) Inf **IL**17, Paddle boat; (Qu. O10, . . *Kinds of boats . . used around here*) Infs **AR**40, **IL**16, 17, **IN**35, **KY**49, **NC**72, **PA**83, Paddle boats; **VA**28, Paddle boats—on artificial lakes near here]. [DARE Ed: Because of the absence of descriptions it is not possible to determine to what many of the Infs were referring.] **1975** Gould *ME Lingo* 202, *Paddle-boat*—A small version of the Rangeley boat made for small ponds in the Franklin County region. It could hold two, had no oarlocks, and was handled by a single paddle. A few survive in the area. **1986** Pederson *LAGS Concordance* **scattered Gulf Region, but esp freq eTN, nGA** (Rowboat) 39 infs, Paddle boat(s); 3 infs, Paddling boat. [Recorded comments show wide divergence on details: 5 infs specify that it is flat-bottomed, but 2 equate it with a canoe, and one says the shape of the bottom is irrelevant. It may be pointed at one, both, or neither end, and hold from two to four people.]

paddle cat n Cf **patter cat**
Prob =**cat** n 3c.
  1968 DARE (Qu. EE11, *Bat-and-ball games for just a few players [when there aren't enough for a regular game]*) Inf **SC**58, Paddle cat. **1968** DARE Tape **SC**58, [Inf:] Paddle cat. [FW:] How do you play that? [Inf:] It would have two batters, an' you had a batter here and one over here, and then each batter had a pitcher behind him and a catcher, and then we'd have fielders, and these pitchers they'd throw to that batter over here, and then he hit that ball and hit it out in the field, one of these fielders caught it, why he got [to go to] bat. **1986** Pederson *LAGS Concordance,* 1 inf, **ceAL,** Paddle cat—game played with ball.

paddlefish n Also *paddlebill* [See quots 1807, 1933]
A fish (*Polyodon spathula*) with a broad, flat snout, found chiefly in the Mississippi River drainage area.   Also called

channel digger, duckbill cat, flatbill, shovel cat, shovelfish 2, spadefish, spoonbill cat, ~ sturgeon
  1807 (1935) Janson *Stranger in Amer.* 197 **OH,** The paddle fish . . is four feet and four inches in length. The snout resembles in shape the paddle used by Indians in crossing rivers. **1820** Rafinesque *Ohio R. Fishes* 83, Paddlefish. Planirostra. . . Toothless Paddlefish. *Planinostra* [sic] *edentula.* . . Head as long as the body, snout longer than the head, somewhat cuneiform, obtuse. **1879** U.S. Natl. Museum *Bulletin* 14.64, *Polyodon folium* . . Paddle-fish.—Fresh waters of Mississippi Valley. **1908** *Century Illustr. Mag.* 76.457, In Louisiana it is known as billfish, billdom, and paddle-fish; in Mississippi, spoon-billed-cat or spooney; and in Arkansas as the spoonbill or spoon-billed-sturgeon. . . "Polyodon spatula" is the . . title by which the spoonbill is known to naturalists. **1933** LA Dept. of Conserv. *Fishes* 374, Spoonbill, Duckbill Cat, Shovelfish and Spadefish, all these popular names refer to the Paddlefish's most striking characteristic, the long, thin, expanded, blade-like snout which, extending far beyond its mouth, appears to be a sensitive organ of touch. **1948** *Sat. Review* 15 May 26, My ears . . were assailed by questions about the Paddlefish, the Brindled Stonecat, or the Tessellated Darter. **1981** Pederson *LAGS Basic Materials,* 1 inf, **ceTN,** Paddle bill (he had a bill).

paddle-foot n
1 A cottontail rabbit (*Sylvilagus* spp).
  1969 DARE (Qu. P30, . . *Wild rabbits*) Inf **KY**53, Paddle-foot—light-colored, white and gray.
2 See **paddle 2.**

paddlewheel See **paddle 2**

paddling boat See **paddle boat**

paddock n Also *pudick* [OED2 "Also *Sc.* . . *puddock*" c1350 →; "Now *Sc.* and *north. dial.*"] **esp NEng** Cf **bull paddock, Paddy-got-drunk**
A frog.
  1939 *LANE* Map 231 *(Frog)* 5 infs, **nNEng,** Paddock(s); 1 inf, **ceVT,** ['pʌdək], Scotch term. **1941** *Nature Mag.* 34.138, Bullfrog. . . In the Northeast, most of the names applied to this species contained in part or in entirety the term paddock, a Scottish and Old English word for frog. **1967** DARE (Qu. P21, *Small frogs that sing or chirp loudly in spring*) Inf **OH**3, Pudicks is what my husband called them. I think that's Scottish.

paddy n¹ [Common nickname among the Irish for *Patrick*]
1 cap; also rarely *Pad, Paddyman, Pat(sy), Patty:* An Irish person; someone of Irish descent. **chiefly Nth, N Midl, West, esp NEast** See Map Cf **Mick** n 1, **paddywhack** n¹ 1
  1784 in 1877 Belknap *Papers* 2.168, By yours of the 10th I find you have some knowledge of *Paddy* the Socinian, though he has none of you. **1838** Kettell *Yankee Notions* 154, Sometimes I hearde the truckmen sweare,/ And Broade-Streete Paddies fille the aire / With their sweete jargoning. **1914** DN 4.146, One may . . hear in current speech instead of the usual appellative "Irish" such substitutes as: "Paddy", "Mick", . . "Turk". . . [F]requent use has worn some of the edge from these cutting epithets and today they are often used . . with no shade of malice. **1941** *LANE* Map 454 *(Nicknames for an Irishman)* **throughout NEng,** Paddy; **scattered, but esp nNEng,** Pat; 1 inf, **csMA,** Pad; 1 inf, **cnMA,** Paddyman; 1 inf, **swCT,** Paddy from Cork; 1 inf, **ceCT,** A regular Paddy, as a child; 1 inf, **cCT,** Paddy, 'This younger generation never heard that word'; 1 inf, **neCT,** Paddy—an insult; Irish Paddies, used of Irish girls at school 'when I was a girl'; 1 inf, **neRI,** Paddy, 'a slum Irishman'; 1 inf, **ceMA,** Paddy, 'an old dirty Irishman'; 1 inf, **swMA,** Paddy, 'an Irishman when he's drunk'; 1 inf, **seNH,** I shouldn't think of calling them Paddies; 1 inf, **seRI,** It's not right to call them Paddy or Mick; 1 inf, **swMA,** Patsy. **1950** WELS (*Entirely, all the way:* "*He's Irish _____.*") 5 Infs, **WI,** As Paddy's pig. **1956** Ker *Vocab. W. TX* 367, For an Irishman's nickname, *Paddy* and its variants *Pat* and *Patty* have the greatest currency. Twenty-five such responses are offered by all types of informants, scattered throughout the central and eastern part of the designated counties. **1961** Folk *Word Atlas N. LA* map 1411, *Irishman* (nicknames) . . paddy [11% of 137 infs]. **1962** Atwood *Vocab. TX* 73, *Irishman.* An older nickname for an Irishman is *Paddy* or *Patty* . . which is infrequent among the younger informants. **1965–70** DARE (Qu. HH28, *Names and nicknames . . for people of foreign background: Irish*) 54 Infs, **scattered, but esp NEast,** Paddy; **PA**66, Patty; **NY**80, Pat, Patty's pig; **WI**44, Pat; **MA**68, He's as Irish as Paddy Murphy's pig; **NY**93, Irish as Paddy's pig; **CA**76, Irish as Pat's pig;

MI51, Patsies; NY88, Patsy; (Qu. LL26b, . . 'Entirely'—for example, "He's Irish _____.") 17 Infs, **Nth, N Midl, West,** (As) Paddy's pig; IL26, MA5, PA175, TN1, (As) Pat's pig; CT22, MA71, RI15, VT12, As Pat Murphy's pig; CA105, NJ9, As Patty's pig; (Qu. HH30, *Things that are nicknamed for different nationalities*) Inf MA58, Paddy barrow—small wheelbarrow; NY43, Paddy squabble—March 17th, Irish brawl; WI65, Irish as Paddy's pig; (Qu. U41b, . . "He's poor as _____.") Infs NJ1, PA107, Paddy's pig; CA112, Patty's flea; [(Qu. CC4, . . *for various religions or religious groups*) Inf MD23, Patsy—Catholic]. **1985** DARE File cwIN, Irish as "Paddy Boddy's pig." **1986** Pederson *LAGS Concordance* (*Irishman;* this question was asked chiefly in urban areas) 3 infs, **GA, TN, AR,** Paddy. [All infs 47 years old or younger]

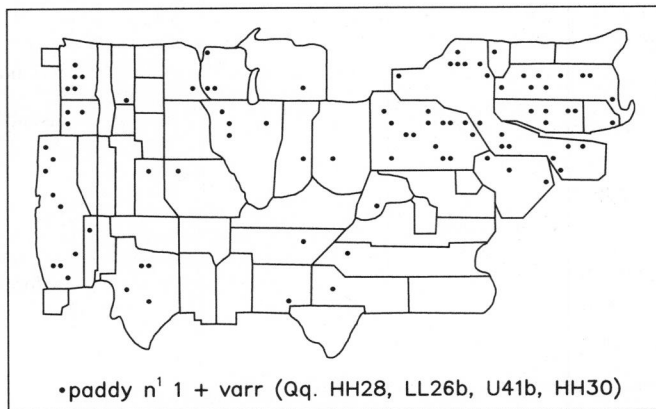

•paddy n¹ 1 + varr (Qq. HH28, LL26b, U41b, HH30)

2a By ext: a menial or manual laborer; hence rarely v *paddy* to perform menial labor.

1856 Emerson *English Traits* 282, The men were common masons, with paddies to help. **1863** in 1983 *PADS* 70.45 ce,sePA, Ben is ward master [in a military hospital] and Sam and I and two other paddies and another nice man assist. **1876** in 1969 *PADS* 52.54 seIL, Brother Frank is still Paddying on the G. and M. R.R. **1930** Shoemaker *1300 Words* 45 cPA Mts (as of c1900), *Paddy*—An Irish laborer on the old Pennsylvania canal. **1989** (1990) Baden *Maryland's E. Shore* 103, Crews who live in the area now and work willingly [on oyster-dredging boats] are called "paddies."

b A tramp. [Prob by ext from **2a** above, but perh infl by *on the pad* (at **pad** n¹)]

1967–70 DARE (Qu. HH19, *Other words or nicknames for a tramp*) Infs IL73, MO10, TX37, 104, Paddy.

3 in combs *paddy barrow, Paddy's car, ~ coach, paddy wagon:* A wheelbarrow. Cf **Irish buggy**

1911 *Century Dict. Suppl., Paddy-barrow.* . . A wheel-barrow having a curved bottom and no removable sides. [*Century* Ed: Colloq., U.S.] **1939** LANE Map 163 *(Wheelbarrow)* 1 inf, seNH, Paddy's coach [laughter]. **1949** McDavid Coll. cwNY, Paddy barrow—wheelbarrow. **1968–69** DARE (Qu. L41, *A device for moving dirt and other loads, with one wheel in front and handles to lift and push it behind*) Inf NY105, Paddy wagon; (Qu. HH30) Inf MA58, Paddy barrow—small wheelbarrow. **1973** Allen *LAUM* 1.225 (as of c1950), *Wheelbarrow.* . . paddy's car [1 inf, csMN] [laughter].

4 sometimes cap; also *paddywood, patty:* A White person; see quot 1980. [By ext from **1** above] *chiefly among Black speakers* Cf **Charlie 2**

1946 in 1973 Himes *Black on Black* 256, "Hey, don't spit in the sink where you wash the glasses," some paddy down the bar said. **1964** *PADS* 42.31 **Chicago IL,** The most characteristic feature of Negro terms for Caucasian is the tendency to expand particularized designations for Caucasians to include all members of the race, e.g. . . terms for nationality groups: *hunky, Paddy,* and *spick.* **1966** *Sat. Rev.* (U.S.) 15 Oct. 74/2 [sic *OED2*—quot not found], Man, how I hate Paddies (white people)! **1968** DARE (Qu. HH28, *Names and nicknames*) Inf CA81, Whites are called, by Negroes: Paddy—most common; PA66, Caucasian—Patty. [Both Infs Black] **1970** Abrahams *Positively Black* 8, The black became beautiful and the white became nothing but a honky and a paddy. **1972** Wambaugh *Blue Knight* 254 **LA,** I spotted a paddy hustler taking a guy up the back stairs. *Ibid,* Paddy hustling was always a Negro flimflam and that's where the name came from, but lately I've seen

white hustlers using this scam on other paddies. **1979** *New Yorker* 5 Feb 101, There were a few years, beginning in the late sixties, when almost any Mexican *barrio* in Southern California was dangerous territory for Anglo police. For those years . . gang members were transformed into Brown Berets, street toughs began thinking of themselves as Chicano militants, juvenile offenders learned to refer to the rest of the world as "the Anglo-dominant society" instead of "paddies." **1980** Folb *Runnin' Down* 54 cwCA [Black], Many made no distinction between Chicanos and whites and often characterized them in terms usually identified with white people—*grey, honky, white, peckerwood, paddywood.* *Ibid* 60, Some of the potentially neutral vernacular terms for whites such as *paddy, paddywood, the Man,* or *Charlie* carry little in the way of stereotyped qualities. **1986** Pederson *LAGS Concordance* ceTX *(Caucasian)* 1 inf, Paddies—insulting, old word; *(A rustic)* 1 inf, Country Paddy—white. [Same Black inf]

5 See quot.

1966–69 DARE (Qu. CC4, . . *Nicknames . . for various religions or religious groups*) Inf KY51, Paddies—Roman Catholics; makes no difference if they're Irish or not, as long as they're Catholics; MA11, Paddy church.

6 also *paddywhack:* =**ruddy duck.**

1888 Trumbull *Names of Birds* 112 NC, *Ruddy Duck.* . . At Newberne, N.C., *Paddy* and *Noddy.* *Ibid* 113, In the neighborhood of Morehead, N.C., *Paddy-whack.* **1895** Ridgway *Ornith.* IL 2.1.185, Ruddy Duck. . . [is called] Hickory-head, Greaser, Paddy, Noddy, Paddy-whack [etc.]. **1917** (1923) *Birds Amer.* 1.152, *Ruddy Duck. . . Other Names. . .* Paddywhack; . . Paddy. **1944** Hausman *Amer. Birds* 521, Paddy. . . Paddywhack—see Duck, Ruddy. **1960** *AmSp* 35.299, The *paddywhack* is the ruddy duck, common to Illinois.

paddy n² Also *paddy cow*
A bull.

1939 *LANE* Map 190 *(Bull)* 1 inf, swME, [pæᵊdɹ], so called from the enclosed [pædɐˇk] where he is kept. **1968** DARE FW Addit NY73, *Paddy cow, gentleman cow*—terms for bull in polite conversation. Old-fashioned.

paddy n³
See quot.

1908 *German Amer. Annals* 10.37 sePA, *Paddy.* . . Molasses candy. "Fine paddy, 20 cents a pound."

paddy v See **paddy** n¹ **2a**

paddy barrow See **paddy** n¹ **3**

paddybass v [Cf *SND* paddy bass n. "Sc. form of Fr. *pas de bas(que),* a basic step in Scottish country dancing"]

1993 *Coast Watch* Sept/Oct 13 **Outer Banks NC,** [Caption:] Paddybass—to walk back and forth.

paddy-cake See **pat-a-cake**

paddy cow See **paddy** n²

paddy frog n [Scots var of **paddock**] Cf *bull Paddy* (at **bull paddock**), **Paddy-got-drunk**

1986 Pederson *LAGS Concordance* (*Bullfrog*) 1 inf, cnAL, Paddy frog.

Paddy-got-drunk phr Also *Paddy-get-home* Cf **jugarum**
Used to represent the call of a **bullfrog 1** (here: *Rana catesbiana*). Cf **patty-go-round**

1939 *LANE* Map 231 *(Frog)* 1 inf, ceMA, The bullfrog says [dʒʌgə ˈrʌm, ~rʌᵊm] or [ˈpæˇdɹ ˌgɛt ˈhoum]. **1941** *Nature Mag.* 34.139, The "song" of the bull-frog . . has been worded in a variety of ways, the most familiar of which is "jug-o'-rum." Others are be-drowned . . and Paddy-got-drunk.

Paddyman See **paddy** n¹ **1**

Paddy's car (or coach) See **paddy** n¹ **3**

Paddy's hurricane n [**paddy** n¹ **1**]
=**Irishman's hurricane.**

[**1821** Welby *Visit N. Amer.* 6, We are now first experiencing a calm attended by a heavy swell of the sea;—the sailors call this "Paddy's Hurricane."] **1891** *AN&Q* 7.204, "Paddy's hurricane . ." is explained in books of sea phrases as meaning "not wind enough to stir a pennant".

1897 'F.B. Williams' *On Many Seas* 43 (*OED2*) **NEng,** We came on deck to find a 'Paddy's Hurricane'—a calm. **1903** A. Sonnichsen *Deep Sea Vagabonds* 114 (*OED2*), The winds here never blew at all, or, often in the manner of Paddy's hurricane up and down. **1945** Colcord *Sea Language* 47 **ME, Cape Cod, Long Island,** Other names for a calm are Irish hurricane or Paddy's hurricane.

paddywack n[1] See **paddywhack** n[1] 1

paddywack n[2] See **packwack**

paddy wagon See **paddy** n[1] 3

paddywhack n[1]

1 also *paddywack, paddywhacker:* =**paddy** n[1] 1.
1871 *Galaxy* 11.65, "Git in, you paddywhack," said Glover [=a Yankee] to Sweeney. **1900** Day *Up in ME* 198, Mother says it's something fearful—way this pesky young one acts,/ And she's called the Johnson children by the name of "Paddywhacks." **1909** *DN* 3.421 **Cape Cod MA** (as of a1857), *Paddywhacker.* . . An Irish ragamuffin. **1912** Green *VA Folk-Speech* 310, *Paddy Whack.* . . An Irishman. **1941** *LANE* Map 454 *(Nicknames for an Irishman)* 1 inf, **ceMA,** Paddywhacker; 1 inf, **nME,** Paddywhack; 1 inf, **seRI,** Cf. the rime sung by children to annoy an Irishman: [pædəwækə], *chew tobacco, if you die it'll be no great matter.* **1942** Berrey-Van den Bark *Amer. Slang* 385.11, *Irishman.* . . Paddy, Paddywack, Paddywhack.

2 See **paddy** n[1] 6.

paddywhack n[2]
1916 *DN* 4.327 **NY,** The hand, esp. of a baby: used by little children. . . *paddywhack.*

paddywhacker See **paddywhack** n[1] 1

paddywood See **paddy** n[1] 4

padiddle n Also *bediddle, padoodle, padungle, perdiddle, perdiddo* Cf **cockeye piddle**
=**cockeye.**
1959 in 1980 Koch *Folkl. KS* 6, If a fellow sees a car coming with only one light and says "padiddle," he may kiss his girl. If she sees it first and says "padiddle," she may slap the boy. [Offered by 5 female infs] **1968** *DARE* FW Addit **cwIN,** In high school—[pɚ'dɪdl]—to be spoken on seeing a car with only one headlight burning, especially on dates. Whoever says it first gets to kiss who she/he wants; "a game." **1980** *Hand Coll.* **WA,** *Padungle* [if you see the] backlight. **CA,** *Padoodle* [if you see the] headlight. **1985** *DARE* File **WI** (as of 1960s), In Madison, Wisconsin, when young people in cars saw a car with only one headlight approaching, the one who said "padiddle" first won a kiss from his "date." The one-headlight car thus became a "padiddle." *Ibid* **cwCA** (as of c1960), A boy who moved to California from Illinois told us about perdiddles—cars with one headlight out. **1985** *WI Alumnus Letters* **seWI,** A new word "Per diddle" (sp) for a car with only one light. **1994** *DARE* File **seWI,** A car with only one headlight is a perdiddo [pɚ'dɪdoʊ]; **sIL,** I've heard both padiddle and perdiddle. **1997** *Ibid* **csWI,** When a car with one working headlight and one non-working headlight passes by you say bediddle and hit the ceiling of the car you are in. **1998** *Ibid,* My mother, who was born and raised in Kalispell, Montana (b. 1940) taught me the word "padiddle". . . When she was in high school, if the boy saw the padiddle he could kiss the girl, but if the girl saw it she could either slap or kiss the boy. . . By the time I was in high school [in Seattle] in the 1970s . . not as many kids used the word. . . Now, if I use it, I usually get . . she-must-be-mad puzzled expressions. *Ibid* **neIL, NJ, Long Is. NY** (as of 1950s–60s). **2000** *NADS Letters,* Can't help being reminded of "padoodle," a car with one headlight (upper midwest [Minn./N.D./MT], commonly in use 1960s-and-probably-before/70s, not heard since nor in Calif.) If you see one coming, you're supposed to kiss any handy members of the opposite sex and pinch any of the same sex.

padogie See **pierogi**

padoodle, padungle See **padiddle**

pad walker See **bonnet walker**

pafisticated adj Cf **pifflicated**
Tipsy.
1966 *DARE* (Qu. DD13, *When a drinker is just beginning to show the effects of the liquor . . he's _____*) Inf **NC1,** Pafisticated.

pagoda bells n
A **twisted-stalk** (here: *Streptopus amplexifolius*).
1949 Moldenke *Amer. Wild Flowers* 336, The *pagodabells* . . has greenish white flowers and its leaves are green on both surfaces.

pagoda dogwood n Also *pagoda cornel*
A **dogwood** 1 (here: *Cornus alternifolia*).
1924 Deam *Shrubs IN* 235, *Cornus alternifolia* . . Pagoda Dogwood. **1942** Tehon *Fieldbook IL Shrubs* 219, Alternate-leaved Dogwood—Pagoda Dogwood. **1966** Grimm *Recognizing Native Shrubs* 208, Alternate-leaf Dogwood. . . Also called Blue or Pagoda Dogwood. **1979** Little *Checklist U.S. Trees* 97, Pagoda dogwood, blue dogwood, greenosier, pagoda-cornel.

pagoda oak n
=**cherrybark oak.**
1960 Vines *Trees SW* 188, A second variety [of *Quercus falcata*], now known as Swamp Red Oak . . is described by some botanists as a separate species (Pagoda Oak, *Q. pagoda* Raf.) . . The leaves are distinctly pagoda-shaped, with 5–13 lobes.

pagoda plant n
A **horsemint** 1 (here: *Monarda pectinata*).
1967 Dodge *Roadside Wildflowers* 61 **West,** Plains beebalm—white horsemint. . . The arrangement of blossoms and leaves as clusters, with bare stem between, has given it the name of pagoda plant in some localities.

pahmetto See **palmetto**

pahn See **pound** n[1]

pahoehoe n Also sp *pahoihoi* [Haw] **HI** Cf **aa**
Hardened basaltic lava with a smooth, shiny surface.
1859 *Amer. Jrl. Science* 2d ser 28.70 **HI,** We . . saw '*pahoihoi*' or solid lava forming, and also '*aa*' or clinkers. **1873** in 1966 Bishop *Sandwich Is.* 52 **HI,** We travelled as before in single file over an immense expanse of lava of the kind called *pahoehoe*, or satin rock, to distinguish it from the *a-a,* or jagged, rugged, impassable rock. Savants all use these terms in the absence of any equally expressive in English. **1938** Reinecke *Hawaiian Loanwords* 27, Pahoehoe. . . Lava that is laid down with a relatively smooth, billowy surface, in places ropy. . . F[requent]. **1955** (1959) Longwell-Flint *Phys. Geol.* 73 **HI,** Smooth, ropy lava called pahoehoe (pah-hō'-ā-hō'-ā). **1978** Chesterman *Audubon Field Guide Rocks* 689, Recent lava flows (e.g. in Hawaii) also illustrate the contrasting shapes in which basalt may solidify. They are either "molded" into twisted coils of rope or form cindery, jagged blocks, which are referred to by their Hawaiian names, "pahoehoe" and "aa" respectively. **1994** Stone-Pratt *Hawai'i's Plants* 85, The Mauna Ulu series of flows (1969–1974). . . are primarily smooth pāhoehoe; most still glisten with a glassy sheen and support little vegetation. Even more recent are the flows, both rough 'a'ā and smoother pahoehoe, that continue (as of 1994) to emerge . . from vents at the base of the Pu'u 'Ō'ō cone.

pahute weed n [Perh var of *Paiute*]
A **sea blite** (here: *Suaeda depressa*).
1923 in 1925 Jepson *Manual Plants CA* 333, *S[uaeda] depressa* . . var. *erecta* . . Pahute Weed. . . Coastal S. Cal.; Modoc Co.; e. to Rocky Mts. **1961** Peck *Manual OR* 292, *S. depressa.* . . Pahute Weed. . . Alkaline areas. **1973** Hitchcock-Cronquist *Flora Pacific NW* 101, Pahute weed . . *S. depressa.*

paid out See **pay out**

pail n Cf **bucket, slop pail**

1 A usu cylindrical vessel of wood, metal, or plastic having a handle, used esp for carrying liquids. **formerly chiefly Nth, now more widespread** Note: Although *bucket* and *pail* are basically synonymous, many speakers who are familiar with both terms distinguish between them in various, often idiosyncratic, ways. For a discussion of this phenomenon, see 1973 *AmSp* 48.62–3.
1622 Mourt's Relation *Iournall Plimoth* 12 **MA,** We found . . also an English Paile or Bucket. **1874** (1895) Eggleston *Circuit Rider* 214 **sOH** (as of early 19th cent), This vile vender of Yankee tins, who called a bucket a "pail," and said "noo" for new, and talked nasally. **1892** Eggleston *Hoosier Schoolmaster* 180, The total absence of the word *pail*

not only from the dialect, but even from cultivated speech in the Southern and Border States until very recently, is a fact I leave to be explained
on further investigation. **1899** (1912) Green *VA Folk-Speech* 310,
Pail. . . A vessel of wooden staves, nearly or quite cylindrical, with a
looped handle, used for carrying water, milk or other liquid. **1910** *DN*
3.446 **cwNY**, *Pail.* . . Bucket. So "water-pail"; "milk-pail"; "dinner-
pail." The term *bucket* . . is never used in this ordinary sense. **1912** *DN*
3.568 **cNY**, *Pail.* . . Wood, pulp, or tin vessel used for carrying milk, water, etc. *Bucket* is used in phrase *sap buckets*, as it is also in Vermont. In
the Southern states *bucket* is always used, and also in western Pennsylvania and Philadelphia, except in *milk pail* and *lard kettle* (any vessel
used for lard). **1949** Kurath *Word Geog.* 12, *Pail* . . is the regular name
throughout the North for the well-known container with flaring sides and
a bail. The compounds *water pail, milk pail, swill pail* likewise are current in this entire area. *Ibid* 13, All of the Midland and the South use
bucket in this sense, but *pail* is not unknown in the cities of Philadelphia
and Washington. . . Most New Englanders use *pail* indiscriminately for
the metal and the wooden varieties, as such expressions as *cedar pail*
and *wooden pail* show; but along the coast, from Narragansett Bay to
New Brunswick, many apply *pail* only to the modern metal container
and call the older wooden one a *bucket*. *Ibid*, It is fairly clear that early
New England had both *pail* and *bucket* and that *pail* had largely replaced
bucket at least in Western New England . . by the time of the Revolution.
The development in the Midland and the South is the precise opposite.
Here *bucket* came to be the general term, and *pail* survives only in North
Carolina and Tidewater Virginia as the name for an old-fashioned
wooden water or milk pail with one long stave for a handle. **1962**
Atwood *Vocab. TX* 102, Quite a number of informants state that a metal
container is a *bucket* if for water, a *pail* if for milk; moreover, there are
eighteen occurrences of *milk pail*, only three of *water pail*. (This does
not represent majority usage, in which *bucket* is used for both.) **1966**
DARE Tape **MI**9, He made me put a water pail over my head so I
wouldn't inhale any smoke. **1972** *PADS* 57.35 **Marietta OH** [Older
native speakers], *Pail*, which has more currency in the New England settlement area, occurs as a primary response only in . . [1 of 6 infs]. Midland and Southern *bucket* occurs among the other informants. But *pail*
occurs in combinations in all informants. The Northern *swill pail* occurs
in . . [1 inf]. *Garbage pail* occurs in . . [2 infs]. *Dinner pail* occurs in . .
[3 infs]. **1972** *PADS* 58.14 **cwAL**, *Pail*. *Bucket* (26 [of 27 infs]) predominates as the term for the wooden vessel; only one informant (Negro) used the older Southern term *pail*. *Pail* (6) is somewhat more common as the term for a metal container, but this Northern term is
generally restricted to younger, cultured usage. **1973** Allen *LAUM*
1.195 **Upper MW** (as of c1950), *Bucket* (wooden vessel). . . *Bucket* is
slightly favored in the U[pper] M[idwest], with some evidence of Midland orientation. *Ibid* 196, Some Northern speakers identify the term
[bucket] only with the object celebrated in Samuel Wordworth's poem;
for them a bucket is always "oaken." These speakers and others in Minnesota distinguish the vessel with the flaring sides as a *wooden pail*.
Ibid, The 1,008 respondents checking this item are divided almost precisely like the field infs., 62% with *bucket* and 44% with *pail*, the Iowa
pattern strongly indicating a Midland orientation; northern Iowa 46% for
bucket and 57% for *pail*; southern Iowa 84% for *bucket* and only 20%
for *pail*. *Ibid* 197, *Pail* (the metal vessel). . . The two terms, *pail* and
bucket, for a metal vessel for water or milk exhibit a rather sharp North-
ern-Midland contrast. The frequency for *pail* is Mn. 98%, Ia. 79%, N.D.
96%, S.D. 96%, Nb. 76%; for *bucket*: Mn. 8%, Ia. 54%, N.D. 12%, S.D.
26%, Nb. 59%. The *bucket* responses in Iowa, furthermore, occur in the
southern two-thirds of the state. *Ibid*, Responses from 1,055 persons
conform to the field data, with an 85% dominance of *pail* and only 26%
for *bucket*, the latter reported chiefly in southern Iowa and Nebraska.
1992 in 1993 *DARE* File **cwWA**, In Seattle. . . The container used with a
mop is called a "pail."

2 A spec type of such a vessel according to its construction or
use, as:

a *cedar pail*: One made of cedar and used esp to hold water.
   1772 in 1914 *MA Hist. Soc. Coll.* 7th ser 9.420 **RI**, Here is also a parcel of Cedar pails. **1852** *Harper's New Mth. Mag.* 5.854, We settled
down upon a cedar-pail or bucket for the elder of two boys. **1949**
Kurath *Word Geog.* 13 **NEng**, Most New Englanders use *pail* indiscriminately for the metal and the wooden varieties, as such expressions as *cedar pail* and *wooden pail* show. **1965-68** *DARE* (Qu. F30, *What is a
pail made of? What is it used for?*) Inf **LA**40, Cedar pail—mostly for
water; **MS**27, Cedar pail. **1967** LeCompte *Word Atlas* 138 **seLA**,
Wooden vessel for water. . . cedar pail [1 of 21 infs]. **1986** Pederson
LAGS Concordance (*What would you use to carry water in?*) 4 infs,

AL, TN, **cGA**, Cedar pail; 1 inf, **cMS**, Cedar pail—some call larger
bucket this; 1 inf, **cLA**, Cedar pail = cedar bucket, water pail; (*Large,
open tin vessel for water or milk*), 1 inf, **cwMS**, Cedar pail.

b usu in comb *coal pail*; also *hod-pail*: One used to carry
coal. **scattered, but esp Nth, N Midl** See Map
   1965-70 *DARE* (Qu. F44, . . *A container for coal to use in a stove*) 32
Infs, **scattered, but esp Nth, N Midl**, Coal pail; **KS**19, Hod-pail; **MA**8,
Pail. **1973** Allen *LAUM* 1.224 **Upper MW** (as of c1950), *Coal hod*. . .
(*Coal*) *pail*, a minority form correlating with Northern *pail* (for milk or
water), apparently was tending to replace the older special terms at the
time when coal stoves became obsolete, as its incidence is higher in the
western, more recently settled, states. . . The mail survey does not
closely correspond with the field data. Of the 1,060 respondents only
14% reported older *hod* and 19% *scuttle*, while the two newer generic
terms *pail* and *bucket*, were checked by 45% and 41% respectively.
1986 Pederson *LAGS Concordance* (*Coal scuttle*) 5 infs, **Gulf Region,**
Coal pail.

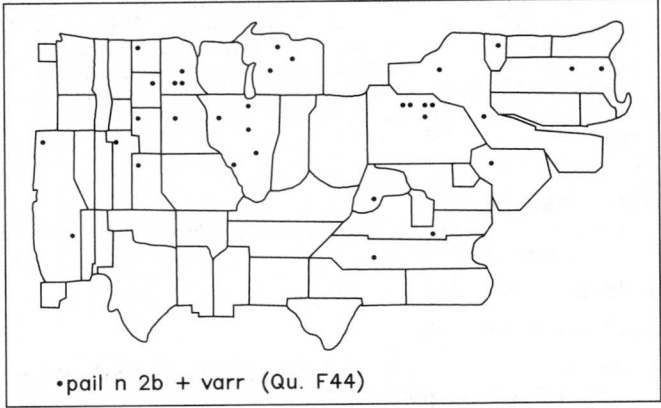

•pail n 2b + varr (Qu. F44)

c also in combs *lunch* (or *dinner*) *pail*: A container for carrying one's lunch; also fig.
   1855 (1888) Holmes *Homestead Hillside* 274, The little "tin
bucket,'[1] . . serves the . . purpose of dinner-pail. **1891** (1967) Freeman
New Engl. Nun 44, Matilda came in . . with her tin lunch-pail on her
arm. **1910** *DN* 3.446 **cwNY**, *Pail*. . . Bucket. . . "dinner-pail." **1917**
Sinclair *King Coal* 365, Union literature . . would be slipped . . into their
dinner pails. **1926** (1939) Hemingway *Torrents* 71, He set down his
lunch-pail. **1965-70** *DARE* (Qu. F22b, *A smaller paper container for
carrying a lunch:* "*He had his lunch in a _____.*") Infs **AR**14, **CA**4,
91, **IL**36, **IN**60, **OH**46, 65, **PA**248, Lunch pail; **MI**66, **MA**14, **MN**13,
NY128, 226, **WI**5, Dinner pail; **CA**9, 144, **NC**30, **PA**245, **TX**27, Pail;
[**CA**4, Lard pail]; (Qu. U39, *Somebody
who has lost all his money*) Inf **OR**1, Turned in his lunch pail; (Qu.
X31, . . *A woman's breasts*) Inf **OK**7, Lunch pails. **1981** Bly *Letters* 9
swMN, For city people who don't know it: *lunch* isn't a noon meal; it is
what you eat out of a black lunch pail at 9 A.M. and 3 P.M.

d *candy pail*: One used for bulk shipment of candy. Cf **pail
candy**
   1973 Allen *LAUM* 1.196 (as of c1950), 3 infs, **MN, NE, SD**, Candy
pail; 1 inf, **ND**, Wooden candy pail.

e *mop* (or *scrub*) *pail*: One used in household cleaning.
   1868 Chase *Manual School-Houses* 63, A broom, dust-brush, and
dust-pan, mop and mop-pail. **1967-68** *DARE* (Qu. F30) Infs **IA**38,
IL5, **MI**68, **NY**41, Scrub pail; **MA**6, Mop pail; (Qu. F31) Inf **OH**18,
Mop pail or scrub bucket. **1973** Allen *LAUM* 1.196 (as of c1950), 1 inf,
SD, Scrub pail. *Ibid* 197, 1 inf, **SD**, Scrub pail. **1986** Pederson *LAGS
Concordance* (*Plastic pail*) 5 infs, **TN, AL, AR**, Mop pail.

3 in redund comb *pail bucket*: See quots.
   1948 Davis *Word Atlas Gt. Lakes* 127, Large open tin vessel for water,
milk etc.—1 inf, **csIN**, Pail-bucket. **1966** Dakin *Dial. Vocab. Ohio R.
Valley* 2.110, *Bucket* (Wooden Vessel) . . Pail bucket. [*DARE* Ed: The re-
production of the map (Figure 50) does not allow a count of informants
to be made.] *Ibid* 116, [One informant] says that a *pail bucket* "is to
milk a cow in." One can only speculate about the precise meaning intended by *pail bucket*, but it seems that in the mind of this speaker . . his
pail bucket probably means *milk(ing) bucket*. **1986** Pederson *LAGS
Concordance* (*Large open tin vessel for water or milk*) 1 inf, **cnGA**, Pail

bucket; 1 inf, **swGA,** Pail bucket (as a unit); 1 inf, **swAL,** Pail bucket—metal; *(Wooden vessel)* 1 inf, **seGA,** Pail bucket (apparently usual term, repeats this).

pail v

1 To milk (a cow). **chiefly Inland Nth, N Midl, West** See Map

1892 *KS Univ. Qrly.* 1.98 **PA,** *Pail:* to milk, as, to pail the cow. **1897** *KS Univ. Qrly.* (ser B) 6.90 **neKS,** *Pail:* to milk. "Pail the cow." **1912** in 1983 Truman *Dear Bess* 87 **MO,** I had to pail the cow when I got in, which is a job I hate. **1913** *DN* 4.5 **ME,** *Pail.* . . To milk (a cow). **1915** *DN* 4.227 **wTX,** *Pail.* . . To milk. "Have you pailed the cow?" Universal. *Ibid* 245 **MT,** Takes Row half an hour to pail old Red. **1916** *DN* 4.278 **NE, KS,** *Pail.* . . It's time to go pail the cow. **1939** FWP *Guide NE* 111, Peculiarly expressive are the terms describing the sandhill region. . . and eloquent of the life of the sandhiller are: . . to juice or pail a cow. **1965–70** *DARE* (Qu. K8, *Joking terms for milking a cow: A farmer might say, "Well, it's time to go out and _____."*) 61 Infs, **chiefly Inland Nth, N Midl, West,** Pail (the cow *or* the cows, etc).

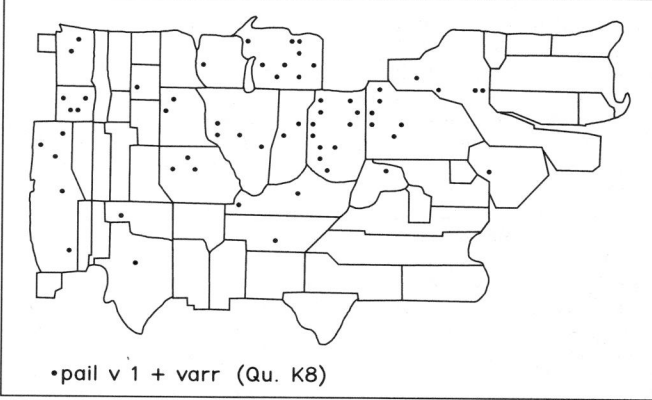

•pail v 1 + varr (Qu. K8)

2 See quot.

1911 *DN* 3.550 **WY,** *Pail the cow,* water the cow.

3 See quot.

1916 *DN* 4.291 **sAppalachians,** Sal, go *pail (draw and put into a pail)* some water.

pail bucket See **pail** n **3**

pail candy n

=**bucket candy.**

1967 *DARE* (Qu. H82b, *Kinds of cheap candy that used to be sold years ago*) Inf **SC32,** Pail candy—mixed hard candy in a bucket.

pailer See **peeler crab**

pail feed v phr, hence ppl adj *pail-fed*

To feed skim milk to (a calf) from a bucket or pail.

1944 Adams *Western Words* 111, *Pail fed*—Said of a calf raised on skimmed milk. **1966** *DARE* Tape **ND3,** We had about twenty-five cows which required the milking and the skimming of the milk. Then we'd have the young stock in the . . feeding stalls, that had 'em bring the milk down to them and pour it in their troughs, or they were pail-fed or whatever way. We had some of 'em, you know—it took time—some were stall-fed, some were pail-fed.

pail feed n [**pail feed** v phr] Cf **churn dash calf, skimmy**

A **bucket-fed** calf.

1911 *DN* 3.550 **WY,** *Pail feeds,* calves raised on skim milk. **1916** *DN* 4.280 **NE,** *Skimmies.* . . Calves raised on skim milk. Also *pail-feeds.*

paille-en-queue n Also *pian queue* [LaFr *paille-en-queue* literally "straw-in-[its-]tail," (in std Fr applied to the tropic bird)] **LA**

=**pintail 1.**

1898 Elliot *Wild Fowl* 125 **LA,** This Duck [=pintail] is known . . as Pian Queue in Louisiana. **1899** in 1900 LA Soc. Naturalists *Proc.* 89 **LA,** *Dafila acuta.* . . Pin-tail; Paille en queue. Very common in winter. **1916** *Times–Picayune* (New Orleans LA) 26 Mar 2, Pintail. . . Paille-en-

Queue; Pian Queue.—The long, pointed tail feathers of this abundant winter visitor gives [sic] this duck its very expressive and suitable common name. **1923** U.S. Dept. Ag. *Misc. Circular* 13.15 **LA,** Pintail. . . *Vernacular Names.* . . *In local use.* . . Paille-en-queue (straw-tail) (Que., La.)

paille fine n [LaFr *paille fine,* literally "fine straw"]

1 also *paille fin(ne), pifine:* =**maiden cane. LA**

1925 *Book of Rural Life* 4127, *Paille finne,* . . *grass,* or *pifine,* as it is popularly called, is a grass growing abundantly on the low, open prairies of Louisiana which are not overflowed by high tides. . . For years, people living along the Gulf coast of Louisiana had used the grass as a hay crop and found it highly satisfactory. The state then investigated its value and reported it excellent forage if cut at the proper stage of growth. **1926** *Torreya* 26.4 **LA,** *Panicum hemitomum* . . Paille fine (pyfeen), Vermillion Parish, La. **1947** *Jrl. Wildlife Management* 2.55 **seLA,** Maidencane (*Panicum hemitomon;* "paille-fine" or "canouche") . . is the dominant plant.

2 A **cordgrass** (here: *Spartina patens*).

1928 Ashbrook *Fur-Farming* 215, The favorite food of the muskrat is the tender bases, roots, and tubers of the three-square rushes (mainly *Scirpus americanus, S. olneyi* and *S. robustus*). The animals are also very fond of a grass known as Paille-fin (*Spartina patens juncea*), and cat-tails (*Typha angustifolia* and *T. latifolia*).

paille finne See **paille fine 1**

pail of steam See **steam**

pain See **pen A**

painful adj [*OED2* 1549 →]

Diligent, careful.

1931 Goodrich *Mt. Homespun* 49 **sAppalachians,** As the days went on many comments on the school were reported to her, not all favorable. . . "You're the most *painful* teacher . . we've ever had in this country; but they's some 'lows you'll never make an out of it lessn you use the hickory on some of them rough boys."

pain perdu n Also *pan-pan-do(ux)* [LaFr < Fr dial *pain perdu* lost bread] **chiefly LA** Cf **lost bread**

French toast.

1896 *Daily News Cook Book* 597 [Index], Pain perdu (see French toast). **1940** Brown *Amer. Cooks* 292 **LA,** Pain Perdu ("Lost Bread" in the sense that it's stale.) . . In other states this is popular under the alias "French Toast." **1941** Percy *Lanterns* 11 **nwMS,** Oh, the poor little boys who never . . lolled their tongues over pain-perdu. **1941** Writers' Program *Guide LA* 690, Pain perdu—Fr. lost bread. Stale bread dipped in egg and fried. **1968** *DARE* FW Addit **LA23,** Pan-pan-doux [ˌpænˌpænˈdu]—bread coated with egg and fried; stale bread is usually used. Also called lost bread. [FW: This is listed in recipe books as *pain perdu,* but the spelling is the one given by the Inf.] **1983** Reinecke *Coll.* 7 **LA,** Lost Bread. . . French Toast, also in English "pain perdu" [ˈpɜ̃ pədu][·] Translation or adaptation from French. **1992** Scott *Cajun Vernacular Engl.* 48, Pain perdu is but one example of a number of foods C[ajun] V[ernacular] E[nglish] speakers know or recognize only by the Cajun French term. **2000** *NADS Letters* **csLA,** I've only heard of French toast being called "lost bread" or "pan pan do" here in New Iberia.

paint adj, also used absol [Calque from AmSpan *pinto* spotted < *pintar* to paint] **widespread, but chiefly SW, esp TX** See Map Cf **pinto** adj

Of a horse: marked by irregular areas of white and black or some other color.

1845 *Amer. Whig Rev.* 2.511 **TX,** Most of them rode what are called "paint horses"; that is, the mustang, spotted with all the deeper colors on a milk-white ground. **1848** Bartlett *Americanisms* 243, In some of the Southern States, a horse or other animal which is spotted, is called a *paint.* **1856** *Harper's New Mth. Mag.* 13.756, The color of the American wild horse is generally chestnut; but hundreds are often seen which are known as "calico" or "paint horses" from their many colors. **1892** Duval *Young Explorers* 71 **TX,** A Mexican lad mounted on a milk-white (piebald) pony . . cantered off. **1920** Hunter *Trail Drivers TX* 165, I remember a squabble I had with two other buyers over a big white and black paint stud that happened to be in the bunch. **1929** Dobie *Vaquero* 252 **West,** Amos was riding his pet horse, a beautiful paint, which he thought more of than of his sweetheart. *Ibid* 253, It took him several hours to tell me . . what his paint horse had done. **c1960** *Wilson Coll.* **csKY,** *Paint horse* is a very modern term; older people said calico horse. **1962** Atwood *Vocab. TX* 55, *Little horse with big spots.* The familiar western pony is usually referred to as a *paint* . . although *pinto* . . is also in fairly frequent use. *Paint* is general throughout the state, whereas *pinto* is more concentrated in the Southwest and West. . . Neither word is at all usual in Louisiana. **1965–70** *DARE* (Qu. K37, . . *A horse of mixed colors*) 100 Infs, **chiefly SW, esp TX,** Paint; **NM**3, Pinto, paint—same, white and another color; red paints, black paints; **PA**163, Paint horse; (Qu. K39, . . *Names . . for horses according to their colors*) Infs **AL**26, **IN**80, Paint; **TX**10, Paint—spotted horse; **PA**72, Spotted paint; [**MI**27, **VA**68, ['pento]]. **1975** Hansen *Troublemaker* 2, She led out a little paint mare. **1976** *Billings* (Montana) *Gaz.* 2 July 11–C/6 (Advt.) *(OED2),* 8 yr old paint gelding. Child broke. Possible show horse.

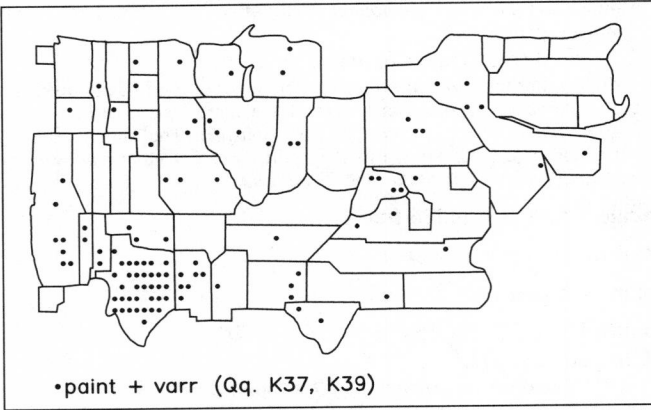

•paint + varr (Qq. K37, K39)

paint box n

A running game; see quot.

1967 *DARE* Tape **CA**68, Paint box . . there's a whole bunch of people on one side and whole bunch of people on one [=the other] side. The person in the middle calls any color, and . . if you've got the color [i.e. if you're thinking of that color], you run over to the other side, and if the people . . on the other side have that color, you run over to this side. [FW:] And he tries to touch as many that go through as he can. [Inf:] Uhm, then they're it, too, with him.

paintbrush n [From the supposed resemblance of the flower(s) or flowering stalk to a paintbrush] Cf **devil's paintbrush, Indian ~, white ~**

1 also *painter's brush:* =**Indian paintbrush 1. widespread, but esp West**

1869 Bowles *New West* 104 **CO,** The painter's brush, as familiarly called here, is . . something like the soldier's pompon in form, . . in every shade of red from deepest crimson to pale pink, and again in straw colors from almost white to deep lemon. **1888** Lindley–Widney *CA of South* 329, Here, too, is *Castilleia,* the painter's brush or Indian plume, identical with that of the East. **1892** *Jrl. Amer. Folkl.* 5.101 **nwIL, NH,** *Castilleja coccinea,* paint-brush. **1899** in 1919 Hale *Letters* 345 **wCA,** Mariposa lilies, painter's-brush, poppies, and dozens of others. **1915** (1926) Armstrong–Thornber *Western Wild Flowers* 472, Paint Brush—*Castilleja miniata.* . . This is a magnificent plant. . . the handsomest and commonest sort around Yosemite. *Ibid,* Paint Brush—*Castilleja angustifolia.* . . The whole plant is most beautiful and harmonious in color . . the upper part is clothed with innumerable delicate yet vivid tints of salmon, rose, and deep pink, shading to scarlet and crimson, forming a charming contrast to the quiet tones of the lower foliage. **1936** McDougall–Baggley *Plants of Yellowstone* 112, Paintbrush (*Castilleja*).—The State flower of Wyoming. . . The flowers are subtended by leafy bracts, which are usually much larger and more conspicuous than the flowers themselves. **1967–70** *DARE* (Qu. S26a, . . *Wildflowers. . . Roadside flowers*) Infs **CA**22, 24, 31, 79, 80, **TX**33, Paintbrush; **NV**5, Paintbrush or Indian flower; (Qu. S21) Inf **NY**233, Paintbrush—tall, red and yellow flower. [*DARE* Ed: Some of these Infs may refer instead to other senses below.] **1967** *DARE* Wildfl QR (Craighead) Pl.18.3 Infs **CA**24, **CO**29, Paintbrush; Pl.18.4 Inf **CA**24, Early paintbrush; **CO**15, Paintbrush; (Wills–Irwin) Pl.45A Inf **TX**44, Western paintbrush. **1968** in 1970 Johnson *White House Diary* 9 Apr 656, Great splashes of wildflowers began to appear along the road and in the pastures . . pale

pink buttercups, wild verbena, coral paint brush, Indian blanket. **1979** Spellenberg *Audubon Guide N. Amer. Wildflowers W. Region* 750, *Castilleja chromosa.* . . is one of the West's most common dry-land Paint-brushes.

2 A **St. John's wort** (here: *Hypericum prolificum*).

1896 *Jrl. Amer. Folkl.* 9.183, *Hypericum prolificum,* L., paint-brush, near Oakdam, Ind. [Footnote:] From resemblance of flowers to a small paint-brush. **1960** Vines *Trees SW* 756, It [=*Hypericum prolificum*] is known also as Broom-brush, Paint-brush, and Rock-rose.

3 =**owl's clover. West**

1897 Parsons *Wild Flowers CA* 228, The bright-magenta tufts of the pink paint-brush are often so abundant that they give the country a purplish hue for miles at a stretch. **1902** U.S. Natl. Museum *Contrib. Herbarium* 387, *Orthocarpus lithospermoides.* . . A herbaceous yellow or pink flowered plant about a foot high, the upper flowering half of which is a simple, dense, cylindrical spike, like a painter's brush. The name "paint brush" has been given to the plant on this account. **1959** Anderson *Flora AK* 421, *O[rthocarpus] hispidus* . . Lesser Paintbrush. . . Skagway. **1967** *DARE* Wildfl QR (Craighead) Pl.18.1 Inf **CO**15, Paintbrush.

4 A **hawkweed,** esp *Hieracium aurantiacum.* Cf **Flora's paintbrush 1, old-maid's-~, orange ~**

1900 *Plant World* 3.132 **nePA,** Italian Daisy—Paint Brush, for *Hieracium aurantiacum.* **1925** *Book of Rural Life* 7.4128, *Paintbrush,* a species of hawkweed found on poor soils in southeastern Canada and northeastern United States (see *Hawkweed*). **1935** (1943) Muenscher *Weeds* 501, *Hieracium pratense.* . . Yellow paintbrush. . . Very abundant from Quebec and Ontario to New York and Pennsylvania; infrequent westward to Michigan. **1967** *DARE* Wildfl QR Pl.223B Inf **NY**16, Paintbrush. **1967–69** *DARE* (Qu. S21, . . *Weeds . . that are a trouble in gardens and fields*) Infs **NY**30, **PA**192, Paintbrush; **NY**134, Paintbrush—rusty color; (Qu. S26a, . . *Wildflowers. . . Roadside flowers*) Infs **IN**32, **NY**20, Paintbrush; **NY**6, (Devil's) paintbrush; **WI**58, Paintbrush—right name is orange hawkweed; (Qu. S26c, *Wildflowers that grow in woods*) Inf **NY**28, Paintbrushes; (Qu. S26d, *Wildflowers that grow in meadows;* not asked in early QRs) Inf **NY**148, Paintbrush. [*DARE* Ed: Some of these Infs may refer instead to **1** above.]

painted box turtle n Also *painted box tortoise* Cf **painted turtle**

A **box turtle** (here: *Terrapene ornata*).

1908 Biol. Soc. DC *Proc.* 21.79 **TX,** *Terrapene ornata.* . . *Painted Box Tortoise.* Very common on the flats west of the city of Waco. **1928** Pope–Dickinson *Amphibians* 78, *Painted Box Turtle.* . . This species is dark-brown with numerous radiating, yellow lines. . . The plastron is distinctly marked with yellow and brown. The head is spotted with red or yellow and the neck banded with the same color. The scales on the forelimbs are bright orange or red. **1937** Cahn *Turtles IL* 96, *Terrapene ornata* . . Painted box turtle; sand turtle.

painted buckeye n

A **buckeye** n 1 (here: *Aesculus sylvatica*).

1952 Blackburn *Trees* 85, Small tree or tree-like shrub . . flowers red or red and yellow. . . Painted Buckeye. **1962** Harrar–Harrar *Guide S. Trees* 482, The painted buckeye is a small southern tree rarely exceeding 30′ in height and 10″ in diameter. It is most common from North Carolina to Georgia and Alabama but is also found in Florida near Pensacola.

painted bunting n

1 A small finch (*Passerina ciris*), the male of which is colored blue, green, and red. Also called **butterfly bird 1, English robin 2, green pop, Mexican canary 1, nonpareil, painted finch 1, pape, paradise finch, pope n[1] 1, red pop, sweet pop, Texas canary**

1811 Wilson *Amer. Ornith.* 3.68, Painted Bunting. . . This is one of the most numerous of the little summer birds of Lower Louisiana, where it is universally known among the French inhabitants, and called by them "Le Pape," and by the Americans the *Nonpareil.* **1832** Nuttall *Manual Ornith.* 1.477, Painted Bunting or Finch. . . known to the Americans as the *Nonpareil,* and to the French Louisianians as the *Pape.* **1839** Audubon *Synopsis Birds* 108, Spiza Ciris . . Blue-headed Painted-Bunting.—Painted-Bunting. **1858** Baird *Birds* 503, *Cyanospiza ciris* . . Nonpareil—Painted Bunting. . . South Atlantic and Gulf States to the Pecos river, Texas. **1898** (1900) Davie *Nests N. Amer. Birds* 405, *Painted Bunting.* . . The male is a bird of handsome variegated plumage—blue,

green, vermilion-red, yellowish-green, etc., and the female plain olive-green. **1946** Goodrich *Birds in KS* 298, *Painted Bunting* . . *Male,* gaudily colored in blue on head, red on rump and under parts, and green across shoulders. **1966** *DARE* (Qu. Q21, . . *Kinds of sparrows*) Inf **FL39,** Painted buntings. **1977** Bull–Farrand *Audubon Field Guide Birds* 586, *Painted Bunting.* . . Perhaps our most brilliant bird.
2 also *painted lark-bunting:* A **longspur** (here: *Calcarius pictus*).

1834 Nuttall *Manual Ornith.* 2.584, Painted Bunting . . *Emberiza (Plectrophanes) picta.* . . This beautifully marked species was observed associating with the Lapland Buntings or Long-Spurs, on the banks of the Saskatchewan. **1839** Audubon *Synopsis Birds* 99, Painted Lark-Bunting. **1890** *Century Dict.* 4234, *Painted bunting, Plectrophanes pictus,* a very common longspur of western and northwestern America, of many variegated colors. **1936** [see **painted longspur**]. **1955** [see **painted longspur**].
3 =**indigo bunting.**

1946 Goodrich *Birds in KS* 313, Bunting, painted—bunting, indigo.

painted cup n Cf Indian paintcup
=**Indian paintbrush 1.**
1819 (1821) Nuttall *Jrl.* 143, I was pleased to see the Painted Cup of the eastern states. **1837** Darlington *Flora Cestrica* 375 **sePA,** *Crimson Euchroma* . . Painted cup. Red Robin. **1882** *Harper's New Mth. Mag.* 65.853 **NEng,** What elf took pity on the painted-cup, and decked its leaves with the brilliant scarlet denied its hidden flower. **1917** Eaton *Green Trails* 88, If it [=*Castilleja miniata*] thrives as well . . as its eastern cousin, the brilliant painted cup, our farmers may not thank me! **1937** U.S. Forest Serv. *Range Plant Hdbk.* W49, The paintbrushes and painted-cups, although common, are never particularly abundant, always grow in association with other species and compose but a small part of the plant cover. **1963** Craighead *Rocky Mt. Wildflowers* 168, Yellow paintbrush—*Castilleja sulphurea.* . . Painted-cup, Squaw-feather.

painted daisy n Cf brown-eyed Susan 2
Prob a **gaillardia B.**
1967–70 *DARE* (Qu. S7, *A kind of daisy, bright yellow with a dark center, that grows along roadsides in late summer*) Inf **CO15,** Painted daisy; (Qu. S26a, . . *Wildflowers.* . . *Roadside flowers*) Inf **TX85,** Painted daisies; (Qu. S26d, *Wildflowers that grow in meadows;* not asked in early QRs) Inf **NC52,** Painted daisy.

painted duck n
=**harlequin duck.**
[**1831** Richardson *Fauna Boreali-Amer.* 459, *Clangula histrionica.* . . Painted Duck, also Mountain Duck—*Hudson's Bay Residents.*] **1917** (1923) *Birds Amer.* 1.142, Harlequin Duck. . . Painted Duck. **1949** Kitchin *Birds Olympic Peninsula* 52 **wWA,** *Western Harlequin Duck.* . . Other common names . . Painted Duck. . . The male birds first appear on the rivers in early April. . . in . . brilliant spring nuptial plumage, gorgeous in colors and markings. **1953** Jewett *Birds WA* 144, *Western Harlequin Duck* . . Other names: Painted Duck [etc.]. **1982** Elman *Hunter's Field Guide* 223, Harlequin Duck (*Histrionicus histrionicus*)—Common & regional names: painted duck [etc.].

painted finch n
1 =**painted bunting 1.**
1730 Royal Soc. London *Philos. Trans.* 36.431, *Fringilla tricolor,* the painted Finch. This is a most beautiful Bird; its Head and Neck are blue; its Back green, and the Belly red: The Hen is plain brown like a Sparrow, and so are the Cocks too, when hatched. **1831** Audubon *Ornith. Biog.* 1.279, Few vessels leave the port of New Orleans during the summer months, without taking some Painted Finches. **1832** [see **painted bunting 1**]. **1872** Coues *Key to N. Amer. Birds* 149, Painted Finch. Nonpareil. . . South Atlantic and Gulf States, common; an exquisite little creature of matchless hues. **1916** *Times–Picayune* (New Orleans LA) 23 Apr mag sec 21/5 **LA,** *Painted bunting* (Passerina ciris). Nonpareil; Painted Finch. **1946** Hausman *Eastern Birds* 575, *Painted Bunting.* . . Other Names—Nonpareil, Painted Finch, Mexican Canary.
2 =**indigo bunting.**
1946 Goodrich *Birds in KS* 315, Finch, painted—bunting, indigo.

painted goose n [See quot 1944]
The emperor goose *(Philacte canagica).*
1872 Coues *Key to N. Amer. Birds* 283, *Painted Goose. Emperor Goose.* . . N. W. coast; abundant at mouth of Yukon. **1903** Studer *Birds*

N. Amer. 162, Painted Goose; Emperor Goose. *(Philacte canagica.)* . . A species that is quite common . . on the Northwest coast of the United States. **1944** Hausman *Amer. Birds* 111, [*Philacte canagica.* . . Plumage, bluish-gray, each feather bearing a small black bar and a white tip. Head and hind neck, white or whitish soiled with rusty-orange; chin and throat, a dusky brownish or blackish. Tail, white. Bill, small and bluish or pinkish-white; feet, orange. . . Said to be the . . most beautiful of all the North American geese.] *Ibid* 514, Goose, Painted—see Goose, Emperor. **1982** Elman *Hunter's Field Guide* 280, *Emperor Goose* . . *Common & Regional Names* . . painted goose. . . Out beyond a wide, northwestern beach, almost skimming the breakers, an emperor goose looks ash-gray, barred with black and white.

painted lady n
1 An **Indian paintbrush 1** (here: *Castilleja coccinea*).
1899 *Plant World* 2.199, Painted Lady for *Castilleja coccinea* . . The adjective is obviously suggested by the brilliantly colored bracts, but why the lady is implicated is not so clear.
2 A brush-footed butterfly: usu the widely distributed *Vanessa cardui,* but also the related *V. annabella* and *V. virginiensis.* [*OED2* 1829 →]
1871 MO State Entomol. *Annual Rept.* 151, The Painted Lady (*Cynthia cardui*) . . has been known also to swarm in Canada. **1938** Brimley *Insects NC* 256, *V[anessa] cardui.* . . Painted Lady. Mountain region. . . Very irregular in its occurrence. **1972** Harris *Butterflies GA* 247, American Painted Lady. . . *Vanessa virginiensis.* . . Common throughout the state in open areas. *Ibid* 248, Painted Lady. . . *Vanessa cardui.* . . Occurs widely over the state. It is usually local and rare except from late August through October. **1986** Scott *Butterflies N. Amer.* 283, *Vanessa virginiensis*—American Painted Lady. . . Many flights all year in s Fla., s Tex., and s Calif.; only two flights in the north, the second flight apparently overwintering. *Ibid, Vanessa caryae*—Western Painted Lady. . . In open areas and suburbs [in the wUS]. **1995** *Smithsonian* Aug 16, At a June party in the garden, dozens of youngsters gently coaxed painted lady butterflies . . into taking flight.
3 A **trillium** (here: *Trillium undulatum*).
1933 Small *Manual SE Flora* 308, *T[rillium] undulatum.* . . Painted-lady. Painted-trillium. **1949** Moldenke *Amer. Wild Flowers* 339 **VT,** Of far more delicate and untarnished beauty is the *painted wakerobin* or *paintedlady* . . whose narrow white petals are daintily penciled with pink or purple veins or stripes. . . I have never seen it elsewhere in such splendid profusion as in the Green Mountains of Vermont, where many roadsides in the deep woods are veritably lined with this magnificent plant.

painted lark-bunting See painted bunting 2

painted leaf n Also paintleaf
A **spurge:** either *Euphorbia heterophylla* or **fire-on-the-mountain.**
1914 Georgia *Manual Weeds* 270, Painted Leaf—*Euphorbia heterophylla.* . . Sometimes the upper leaves are fiddle-shaped, and to add to their oddity are blotched with deep red. **1930** OK Univ. Biol. Surv. *Pub.* 2.1.70, *Euphorbia heterophylla* . . Painted-leaf. **1949** Moldenke *Amer. Wild Flowers* 118, In the paintedleaf, *P[oinsettia] heterophylla* . . the bracts are blotched with red, scarlet, or purple at the base. . . The fiddle paintedleaf, *P. cyathophora,* has some of its leaves fiddle-shaped, others variously lobed or toothed. **1968** Barkley *Plants KS* 222, Euphorbia cyathophora. Painted Leaf. Fire-on-the-mountain. **1976** Bailey–Bailey *Hortus Third* 463, *[Euphorbia] heterophylla* . . Paintleaf, Painted Leaf.

painted longspur n
A **longspur** (here: *Calcarius pictus*).
1884 Coues *Key to N. Amer. Birds* 358, *C[entrophanes] pictus.* . . Painted Longspur. . . is common on the prairies of Dakota, Montana, and Southward. **1898** (1900) Davie *Nests N. Amer. Birds* 367, The Painted Longspur inhabits Arctic America. . . It is a common bird on the prairies of Minnesota, Dakota, Montana, etc. **1911** *Century Dict. Suppl., Longspur* . . *Painted longspur, Smith's longspur* . . so named from its black, white, and yellowish markings. **1917** (1923) *Birds Amer.* 3.21, Smith's Longspur, or the Painted Longspur (*Calcarius pictus*), found on the interior plains of North America east of the Rocky Mountains from the Arctic coast in summer south to Texas in winter. **1936** Roberts *MN Birds* 2.448, Smith's Longspur. . . Painted Longspur, Painted Bunting. **1955** Forbush–May *Birds* 536, Smith's Longspur. . . Painted Longspur, Painted Bunting.

painted mackerel n

A **Spanish mackerel** (here: *Scomberomorus regalis*).

1946 LaMonte *N. Amer. Game Fishes* 28, Painted Mackerel. . . This fish is easily, and very generally, confused with the Spanish Mackerel. **1955** Zim–Shoemaker *Fishes* 84, Spanish, Painted, and Sierra Mackerels are spotted. **1973** Knight *Cook's Fish Guide* 384.

painted pod n Also *painted milkvetch* [From the mottled pod]

A **milk vetch** (here: *Astragalus ceramicus*).

1936 Winter *Plants NE* 102, Long-leaved Painted Pod. Bird-egg Pea. In sandy soil in western Nebr. **1973** Hitchcock–Cronquist *Flora Pacific NW* 233, Pod membranous, inflated, purplish-mottled; . . c Ida to e Mont and e and s; painted m[ilkvetch] . . A[stragalus] ceramicus.

painted quail n

Either the **harlequin quail** or the **mountain quail 1.**

1911 *Century Dict. Suppl.*, Quail. . . Painted quail. . . The mountain quail, *Oreortyx pictus,* of the western United States; so named from its bright marking of white and chestnut. **1982** Elman *Hunter's Field Guide* 92, Mountain quail—plumed quail, painted quail, San Pedro quail, mountain partridge. *Ibid* 102, In southeastern Arizona the desert blends into high, grassy country where yet a third quail species may go into a mixed bag. It is the harlequin, or Mearns, quail *(Cyrtonyx montezumae),* also called Montezuma quail, Massena quail, crazy quail, black quail, or painted quail. It has a small range, chiefly in Mexico.

painted robin n

=**varied thrush.**

1923 Dawson *Birds CA* 2.768, Varied Thrush. . . Synonyms. . . Painted Robin. [*Ibid* 771, The Varied Thrush is. . . a Robin in size, prevailing color, and general make-up.] **1953** Jewett *Birds WA* 511, Pacific Varied Thrush . . Other names . . Painted Robin. . . *Adult male: Under parts bright rusty brown, throat crossed by blackish necklace;* belly mixed white and gray; upper parts dark bluish slate, feathers edged with lighter; wings banded and edged with brown; side of head black, bordered above by brown streak.

painted tail n

A **black bass 1** such as the **largemouth bass.**

1820 Rafinesque *Ohio R. Fishes* 26, Genus. Calliurus. Painted Tail. *Ibid,* Dotted Painted Tail. *Calliurus Punctulatuse* [sic]. . . Vulgar names, Painted-tail or Bride-perch. **1933** LA Dept. of Conserv. *Fishes* 313, Large-mouthed Black Bass; . . Dotted Paintedtail; . . Paintedtail [etc]. [**1955** Zim–Shoemaker *Fishes* 98, Spotted Bass. . . Fingerlings are easily distinguished by their bright orange tail.]

painted terrapin (or tortoise) See **painted turtle**

painted trillium n Also *painted wake-robin* [See quot 1964] **chiefly NEast, esp NEng**

A **trillium** (here: *Trillium undulatum*).

1824 Bigelow *Florula Bostoniensis* 142 **VT,** Painted Trillium. . . Petals white, striped at base with purple, undulate at the edge. A very handsome species.—On the Ascutney mountain, Vermont. **1855** *Harvard Mag.* I.236 *(DA),* The Painted Trillium *(pictum)* is by far the most delicate of the species. **a1862** (1864) Thoreau *ME Woods* 320, *Trillium erythrocarpum* (painted trillium), common West Branch and Moosehead carry. **1891** Jesup *Plants Hanover NH* 45, T[rillium] erythrocarpum . . (Painted Trillium.) Moist woods; common. **1931** Harned *Wild Flowers Alleghanies* 126, *Painted Trillium. . .* is certainly one of the most beautiful of the genus; besides it is very common. **1949** [see **painted lady 3**]. **1964** Campbell et al. *Gt. Smoky Wildflowers* 24, One of the 10 trilliums . . of the Great Smokies, the painted trillium. . . blooms in April and May. The "painted" part of the name refers to the pink "V" at the base of the white petals. **1966–69** DARE (Qu. S2, . . *The flower that comes up in the woods early in spring, with three white petals that turn pink as the flower grows older*) Infs NY134, VT13, Painted trillium(s); MA6, White trillium, painted trillium, red trillium; NY97, Stink-pot— the red ones, painted trilliums—the others; (Qu. S21, . . *Weeds . . that are a trouble in gardens and fields*) Inf PA99, Painted trillium; (Qu. S26c, *Wildflowers that grow in woods*) Inf PA99, Painted trillium. **1979** Niering–Olmstead *Audubon Guide N. Amer. Wildflowers E. Region* 612, *Painted Trillium. . .* Easily recognized by the splash of pink in the center of the white flower.

painted turtle n Also *painted terrapin,* ~ *tortoise, paint turtle* Cf **painted box turtle**

A **red-bellied turtle,** usu *Chrysemys picta.*

1837 (1962) Williams *Territory FL* 63, The Painted Tortoise, testudo picta, is found in our rivers where they become brackish with the tide. **1842** DeKay *Zool. NY* 3.12, The Painted Tortoise. *Emys picta.* [*Ibid* 13, For the variety and the beauty of its markings, this is unquestionably the handsomest of our fresh-water species.] **1883** WI Chief Geologist *Geol. WI* 1.422 **WI,** Chrysemys marginata. . . Western Painted Turtle. Abundant everywhere. Probably this is a western form of *C. picta* of the eastern states. **1907** NJ State Museum *Annual Rept. for 1906* 201, *Chrysemys picta. . .* Painted Terrapin. . . Several found in a pond near Grenloch. **1917** Eaton *Green Trails* 242 **MA,** Of . . inhabitants of the land below the river bank, the painted turtle is most common. **1937** Cahn *Turtles IL* 129, *Chrysemys picta marginata* . . Painted turtle; red-legged turtle; mud turtle; pond turtle. *Ibid* 160, *Pseudemys troostii* (Holbrook) . . Red-head; painted turtle; pond terrapin. . . *Chrysemys scripta elegans* Boulenger 1889. **1950** WELS **WI** (*Kinds of turtles found in your neighborhood*) 4 Infs, Painted turtle(s); 1 Inf, Painted tortoise. **1958** Conant *Reptiles & Amphibians* 54, Painted Turtles: Genus *Chrysemys*—These are readily identified by their *smooth, unkeeled shells* and attractive patterns of *red, yellow,* and *black* (or olive). **1965–70** DARE (Qu. P24, . . *Kinds of turtles*) 19 Infs, **esp NY, PA,** Painted turtle(s); **NJ**10, **NY**156, **OH**16, **RI**6, Painted; **CT**31, **MI**123, Paint turtle; **ME**8, Eastern painted turtle. **1986** Pederson *LAGS Concordance (Turtle)* 1 inf, **New Orleans LA,** Painted turtle. **1996** *Audubon Mag.* Nov–Dec 44 **MA,** The river is high, and we . . sneak up on painted turtles basking on the branches of deadfalls. . . They crane their black-and-yellow-striped necks and study us with narrow eyes.

painted wake-robin See **painted trillium**

painter See **panther A1**

painter's brush See **paintbrush 1**

paint horse See **paint**

painting plant See **paint plant**

painting the double shovel n Also *painting the flat iron*
Either of two kissing games; see quot.

1964 Wallace *Frontier Life* 120 **swOK** (as of 1893–1906), The most exciting and daring of the new games the family from Iowa introduced were the various "kissing" games, such as "Painting the Double Shovel," where the boy knelt, first on one knee and then the other, while the girl he had chosen to "paint the shovel" sat on the proffered knee and kissed both cheeks. *Ibid* 121, In another kissing game, "Painting the Flat Iron," a couple tried to kiss by reaching under their arms with the palms of both their hands flat against the wall, an almost impossible feat which afforded the onlookers much entertainment.

paintleaf See **painted leaf**

paint plant n Also *painting plant* [See quots] Cf **Indian paint 3**

A **gromwell** (here: either *Lithospermum canescens* or *L. arvense*).

1900 Lyons *Plant Names* 227, L[ithospermum] arvense. . . Painting-plant. . . *Root* of this and the following species [=*L. canescens*] yields a red dye. **1914** Georgia *Manual Weeds* 341, Hoary Puccoon. . Paint Plant, Gray Gromwell. . . The thick, deep-boring, red root of this plant yields a red stain or dye; the Indians used it for decorating their naked bodies, before battle or on ceremonial occasions.

paint pony See **paint**

paint pot n **West**

A hot spring of usu boiling mud colored by various minerals; also used as the name of such a spring.

1876 Ludlow *Rept. Reconnaisance MT* 25 **WY,** Passing over a low ridge . . , we came upon the "Paint Pots." This singular phenomenon consists of a "pool" some 60 by 40 feet . . within which numerous mud puffs slowly rose and fell, some through the partially liquid mass, which again closed over them, others possessing a small crater of their own. . . The pool displayed various colors, white, yellow, and red predominating. **1885** *Overland Mth.* 5.13 **WY,** One peculiar class of geysers are known as "paint-pots," because, instead of discharging boiling water, they spit out lumps of scalding mud of all these vivid hues. **1939** FWP *Guide MT* 279, West Yellowstone. . . Long ago the Sheepeaters, a peaceful people, lived in the lofty cliffs near the steaming hot springs, bubbling "paint pots," and spouting geysers that other tribes dared not approach. **1946** Waters *Colorado* 146 **seCA,** These were probably the mud volcanoes, geysers and [*"*]paintpots" of Mullet Island in the Salton Sink. **1969** *Natl. Observer* 10 Feb 15/2 **sCA,** Mrs. Burns ticked off some of the curiosities of the Salton Sea. . . She talked of the "paint pots" at the south end of the sea; these are hot springs that now and then perform like geysers. **1972** Macdonald *Volcanoes* 331, These "paint pots" commonly are boiling . . , and . . their surfaces may be constantly disturbed by bursting bubbles of gas. Such boiling mud pools are well seen . . in Yellowstone and Lassen National Parks. **1987** Bates–Jackson *Gloss. Geol.* 475, *Paint pot*—A type of *mud pot* containing multicolored mud.

paint-root n Cf Indian paint 1, yellow ~ =redroot c.

1927 Boston Soc. Nat. Hist. *Proc.* 38.7.247 **Okefenokee GA,** *Gyrotheca tinctoria* 'Paintroot'. **1951** Teale *North with Spring* 41, The Kissimmee cranes are specialists at finding the underground tubers of *Gyrotheca tinctoria,* the pinkroot, bloodroot, Indian root, or painroot [sic] of the prairie. **1995** Brako et al. *Scientific & Common Names Plants* 197, Paint-root—*Lachnanthes caroliniana* [formerly *L. tinctoria*].

paint turtle See painted turtle

paint worm n
Perh a **redworm 1.**

1969 *DARE* (Qu. P6, . . *Kinds of worms . . used for bait*) Inf **GA**77, Paint worm—red, 5 inches long.

painy See -y

pair n [*OED2 pair* sb.[1] 6.a 13 . . →] See also **pair of bars**
A set or succession of more than two things—used esp in combs *pair of beads,* ~ *stairs.*

1765 in 1959 Franklin *Papers* 294, Salley has the Southroom two pairs of stairs. **1770** in 1891 Chase *Hist. Dartmouth College* 1.133, It is in . . a very narrow place in the great river for a bridge; and it is by a long pair of falls. **1833** Neal *Down-Easters* 1.108 **NEng,** And then ye koted some varses, pair o' varses we call 'em—about fools an adminstrations. **1840** *S. Lit. Messenger* 6.158, The girl, however, was determined to take me, and jumped into my arms one night, from a three-pair-of-stairs window. **1847** [see **pair of bars**]. **1874** *Catholic World* 19.849, Her attention was at once arrested by a tiny pair of beads [=a rosary] which she perceived dangling from Kathleen's wrist. **1894** [see **pair of bars**]. **1926** *AmSp* 1.442, A number of Iowa students tell me that the phrase *a pair of beads* is in common usage in Iowa to denote a string of beads. One girl from Oregon and another from Michigan are familiar with the expression at home. **1944** *PADS* 2.59 **MO,** Pair of beads. **1952** Brown *NC Folkl.* 1.573, *Pair*. . . A set of things—not necessarily two—closely related or connected: *a pair of balances* (or *scales*), *a pair of beads, a pair of stairs* (or *steps*), etc. *Ibid,* Pair of minutes (seconds). . . "I'll be with you in a pair of minutes." **1953** Randolph–Wilson *Down in Holler* 269 **Ozarks,** *Pair*. . . A considerable number, a set of things. A necklace is "a pair of beads." A stairway is "a pair of steps." Five or six treble hooks, fastened together for use in snagging or grabbing fish, are called "a pair of grabs." A denture, whether in two plates or one, is often "a pair of teeth." At the Veterans Hospital in Fayetteville, Ark., I heard "pair of cards" instead of pack or deck. **1955** *AmSp* 30.50, *Pair of beads* . . is frequently heard in all areas of the Eastern seaboard, in most of the speech areas east of the Mississippi, and to some extent west of the Mississippi. **1957** *Sat. Eve. Post Letters* **ceMO,** I found a pair of beads lying [on] the sidewalk. **c1960** *Wilson Coll.* **csKY,** *Pair of beads*—A string. Widely used. . . Much more used than string. *Ibid, Pair of stairs*—A flight of stairs, a stairway. **1965** *PADS* 43.21 **seMA,** Jewelry: She wore a _____ of beads . . pair; old term [1 of 9 infs]. **1965–70** *DARE* (Qu. LL20, *Beads to wear around the throat: "She wore a _____ of green beads."*) Infs **AL**24, **PA**16, **SC**26, 45, **TN**61, **TX**32, **VT**16, **VA**15, **WV**16, Pair; **IN**38, Pair—I've heard people say it but I never understood it; **MD**2, Pair—some people use this; **MA**5, Pair—heard; **MA**6, Pair [FW: Inf objects to this, but has heard it]; **MA**54, People ask for a string but not a pair; I've heard pair of beads—that's way back; **NJ**40, Pair—said around here too; **OH**61, Pair—old-fashioned; **SC**3, Pair—said it when a child; **SC**8, Pair—has heard; **SC**9, 19, 32, 39, Pair [FW sugg]; **VA**11, Pair—heard, very old term; **WI**21, Pair—heard somewhere, I see no sense in it; **WI**71, Pair [corr to] string; (Qu. A14, . . *A very short period of time: "I'll be ready in _____."* or *"It won't take any longer than _____."*) Inf **LA**24, Pair of minutes; (Qu. D6, *To get to the second floor, you walk up the _____*) Inf **NJ**2, Stairs, pair of stairs; **NY**75, Pair of stairs—I don't know why they put

the "pair" on. **c1970** Pederson *Dial. Surv. Rural GA* **seGA** (*If a woman is wearing beads around her neck, you might say, "That's certainly a pretty _____ of beads."*) 12 [of 64] infs, Pair.

pairie See purie

pair of bars n [*pair*; cf *EDD*] *old-fash*
See quot 1910.

1798 MA Hist. Soc. *Coll.* (1st ser) 5.108, They had taken down a pair of bars on the north side of the road. **1847** Hurd *Grammatical Corrector* 49, *Pair of stairs,* for *flight,* or *set of stairs;* as, "There were two pair of stairs." "We ascended the first pair of stairs." . . So, the expression, *a pair of bars,* where there are more than *two bars,* for a *set of bars* . . , is equally erroneous. **1872** U.S. Dept. Ag. *Rept. of Secy. for 1871* 498 **OH,** Nearly all inclosures are now provided with gates. There are scarcely more than one pair bars to fifteen gates. **1894** *DN* 1.342 **wCT,** *Pair of bars:* set of bars, five or six generally. Pair (=flight) of stairs is the only word in use. **1899** (1912) Green *VA Folk-Speech* 310, *Pair-of-bars*. . . Poles made to draw out of posts with large holes morticed in them, and placed on each side of the road to let a cart pass through. **1907** *DN* 3.195 **seNH,** *Pair of bars*. . . A fenced entrance to an inclosure, consisting of fence-rails that are pushed through holes in two upright posts. "You can drive in through that pair of bars." **1910** *DN* 3.446 **cwNY,** *Pair of bars*. . . A "gate stoppage" made of light fence-rails or narrow boards inserted in holes in two upright posts. "You can get into the lot thru that pair of bars." Becoming less common, with the scarcity of fence-rails and the inexpensiveness of gates. **1912** *DN* 3.568 **cNY,** *Pair of bars*. . . Five or six detached rails or pieces of board; when all are fastened together so that the whole can be moved at once, called a *gate.* **1935** Lincoln *Cape Cod Yesterdays* 117, There was a "pair of bars" where the path ended and it was my privilege to take down the upper bar so that the "women folks" might get over easily. **1942** McAtee *Dial. Grant Co. IN* 47 (as of 1890s), *Pair of bars* . . a gate of movable poles almost always more than two in number.

pairsawl, pairsol See parasol

paisano n [Span]

1a also sp *pisano;* abbr *pie;* similarly fem *paisana:* A Spanish-speaking peasant, farmer, or cowhand; a native person of Spanish and Indian descent, esp in California. **SW**

1824 in 1924 Austin *Papers* 1.723, Private citizens paisanos Military or Eclesiastics, shall be punished severely. **1856** *Spirit of Age* (Sacramento CA) 26 Mar 4/1, He . . wished good luck to his *pisanos,* and bid good bye to all. **1893** Lummis *Land of Poco Tiempo* 86 **NM,** [It is perhaps the most unreclaimed Mexican village in New Mexico. Not half a dozen of its people speak the language of the United States.] *Ibid* 88, Every one was out, but they were no longer the friendly *paisanos* we had known. **1910** Hart *Vigilante Girl* 196 **nCA,** She was a feminine replica of the native *caballero* of the time—very fair to look upon, seemingly not displeasing to the *vaqueros,* but with equal seeming eyed with horror by their womankind, the *paisanos.* **1935** (1937) Steinbeck *Tortilla Flat* 11 **cwCA,** What is a paisano? . . His ancestors have lived in California for a hundred or two years. **1939** Coolidge *Old CA Cowboys* 79, In a country where a white man would burn black in a month they were always drawing the color line and speaking of the Mexicans as "pies." That is all that is left of the word *paisano* after a Texan has chewed it up and spit it out; but it really means a countryman, a fellow citizen, and in Mexico is a term of respect. *Ibid* 108, The round-up dragged along as always, with such a circle of "pies" around the herd that they could hardly cut out the cows. . . At the same time the Mexicans were politer than ever. **1940** Fergusson *Our Southwest* 247 **NM,** They came from semi-arid Mexico and Spain. . . Unlike the Nordic pioneer who settled on isolated farms, the Spanish clustered in towns. They fought Indians only when they had to, to assure safety and security. Security was what the *paisano* wanted.

b By ext: see quot. *derog*

1950 *Western Folkl.* 9.158 **nCA** [Mountaineering vocab], *Paisano.* See *cotton picker. Ibid, Cotton picker.* An ignorant, foolish, or uninitiated person. A "rube."

2 also *Mexican paisano:* =**roadrunner 1.** [MexSpan; prob folk-etym for *faisán* pheasant]

[**1844** (1954) Gregg *Commerce* 138, There is to be found in Chihuahua and other southern districts a very beautiful bird called *paisano* (literally 'countryman'), which when domesticated, performs all the offices of a cat in ridding the dwelling-houses of mice and other vermin.] **1858** Baird *Birds* 73, This remarkable genus [=*Geococcyx*] is represented in the United States by a single species known as the Paisano, Chapparal Cock, or sometimes Road Runner. **1897** *Oölogist* 14.79 **TX,** In Texas this bird [=roadrunner] is almost universally known as the Chaparal Bird or Mexican Peafowl; sometimes it is called the Ground Cuckoo, Snake Killer and Paisano. **1926** TX Folkl. Soc. *Pub.* 5.88, As crazy as a *paisano* (road-runner or chaparral bird). **1940** Writers' Program *Guide TX* 28, The road runner or ground cuckoo, also locally called the chaparral bird, "Texas bird of paradise," and *paisano,* found over the entire middle and western parts of the State, is the clown of the highways. **1957** *AmSp* 32.185 **TX,** Mexican paisano—Roadrunner. **1958** *AZ Highways* May 2, Born and reared in Southwest Texas, I was grown before I knew that the bird [=the roadrunner] had any other name than paisano . . , by which Mexicans of Texas and northern Mexico know it. **1961** Ligon *NM Birds* 139, So much a part of the Southwest is the Roadrunner that in Texas, southern New Mexico, and particularly in Mexico, where it is regarded with affection and even reverence, it is commonly referred to as "Paisano," meaning "fellow countryman." **1966–67** *DARE* (Qu. Q7, *Names and nicknames for . . game birds*) Inf **TX**1, Roadrunner, chaparral, paisanos; (Qu. Q23) Inf **NM**13, Roadrunner = chaparral = paisano [paɪˈsɑno]. **1994** *DARE* File **San Antonio TX,** The University of Texas at San Antonio (mascot, the roadrunner) publishes its student newspaper named *The Paisano,* on a bi-weekly basis. Beside the word is a sketch of a running roadrunner.

pait n [Echoic]
=**ivory-billed woodpecker.**
    [**1831** Audubon *Ornith. Biog.* 1.343, No sooner has this bird [=the ivory-billed woodpecker] alighted than its remarkable voice is heard. . . Its notes are clear, loud, and yet rather plaintive. . . They are usually repeated three times in succession, and may be represented by the monosyllable *pait, pait, pait.*] **1954** Sprunt *FL Bird Life* 282, Ivory-billed Woodpecker. . . Local Names: Pait.

Paiute cabbage n
Either a **wild cabbage** (here: usu *Caulanthus inflatus*) or a **prince's-plume 2** (here: *Stanleya elata* and *S. pinnata*).
    [**1878** *Amer. Naturalist* 12.604, *Caulanthus crassicaulis* and *Stanleya pinnatifida* are eaten raw in the spring by the Pah-Ute Indians, the young plants being tender, and when cooked taste like cabbage.] **1941** Jaeger *Wildflowers* 74 **CA,** In Death Valley both species [=*Stanleya elata* and *S. pinnata*] of *Stanleya* are called "Paiute cabbage"; but that English name properly belongs to *Caulanthus inflatus,* which is not found in Death Valley. Mr. French Gilman informs me that the Indians use the young leaves of *Stanleya* for greens. [**1970** Kirk *Wild Edible Plants W. U.S.* 35, *Stanleya* spp. . . The tender stems and leaves have a cabbage-like taste and may be prepared in the same way as cabbage.]

pake n, adj |pɑˈke, ˈpɑˌke| [Prob < Cantonese dial; see quots 1938, 1971] **HI** *sometimes derog*
A Chinese person; Chinese.
    1938 Reinecke *Hawaiian Loanwords* 27, *Pake* . . n., adj, [Cantonese *pak ye* . . uncle or father.] 1. A Chinese. 2. Pertaining to the Chinese . . V[ery] F[requent]. *Ibid* 11, *Hapa pake*. . . A person of mixed Hawaiian and Chinese blood. **1954–60** Hance et al. *Hawaiian Sugar* 5, *Pake* [ˈpɑke]—Chinese. (slang—derogatory). **1967** *DARE* (Qu. U12, *If you were buying something and you argued with the person selling it till you made him lower the price . . "I _____."*) Inf **HI**6, Jew the [ˈpɑˈke] (= Chinese) down; (Qu. W22, . . *A loose, full housedress that ties at the waist*) Inf **HI**4, [ˌpɑˈke] muu muu—with tight neck and form-fit bodice; (Qu. HH28, *Names and nicknames . . for people of foreign background: Chinese*) Inf **HI**4, [ˌpɑˈke]; **HI**13, [ˈpɑˌke]; (Qu. HH29a, . . *People of mixed blood*) Inf **HI**4, [ˌhɑpa ˈpake] = Half Chinese, the other half is Hawaiian; (Qu. II23) Inf **HI**13, Rich pakes [ˌpɑˈkez]. [**1971** Pukui–Elbert *Hawaiian Dict.* 281, *Pākē*. . . China; Chinese. One theory is that this word derives from a fast, colloquial, and rather substandard Cantonese-dialect *pai kei* replacing standard Cantonese *pai ya* meaning "father," said in a friendly and joking way in answer to the question "Who are you?"] **1972** Carr *Da Kine Talk* 41 **HI,** My grandfather is pure *Pākē*. *Ibid* 99, Most of the Chinese laborers who came to Hawaii between 1876 and 1897 were from the vicinity of Canton in South China. They were given a nickname by people of other ethnic groups in Hawaii—the term *Pākē*. **1981** *Pidgin To Da Max* np **HI,** *Pake* . . Chinese. Nevah like spend money. *Ibid,* [Cartoon:] Bruce so *Pake*! Hees toilet peppah dispensah only geev one square at a time!

palamity See **palmity**

paláo See **pelado**

pale v
1 also with *in, up:* To enclose with (*or* as with) a **paling fence;** hence ppl adj phr *paled-in.* [*OED2* 1330 →] **esp Sth, S Midl** See also *paled fence* (at **pale fence**), *paled garden* (at **pale garden**)
    1808 (1892) Summer *Tour OH* 1.78 **VA,** Passed the remains of an old block-house, near which a number of graves . . the graves neatly paled in. **1847** in 1927 Jones *FL Plantation Recs.* 239 **nwFL,** 2 [hands] pailing [sic] in my yard, 14 [hands] plowing corn in woods paster. **1850** *De Bow's Rev.* 9.202 **Sth,** Each tenement has its separate door and window . . , and nearly all have a garden paled in. **1935** Sheppard *Cabins* 180 **wNC,** Then she will sweep the yard, put out a garden and "pale" a few flowers in "brash" [=brush] against the ravages of the dogs and chickens. **1937** *Hall Coll.* **eTN,** They paled in the garden. **1969** Gt. Smoky Mt. Natl. Park *Recordings* 25:2:17 (*Montgomery Coll.*) **wNC, eTN,** They [had] a little paled-in garden there. **1986** Pederson *LAGS Concordance (Picket fence)* 1 inf, **cwTN,** To pale a garden with—to keep rabbits out; 1 inf, **cwGA,** Paled up; 1 inf, **cwGA,** Paled in—of yard fenced in with paling fence; 1 inf, **neAR,** Pale the garden and the yard; 1 inf, **cnAL,** I'd pale my garden with palings.
2 To make a pale; to cut wood to form a picket or pale.
    1986 Pederson *LAGS Concordance,* 1 inf, **neAR,** Paled—make paling, of the verb "to pale"; 1 inf, **cnGA,** Pale them—sharpen so rain runs off top.

pale-belly n Also *pale-breast* **esp MA**
The young of either the **golden plover** or the **black-bellied plover.**
    1888 Trumbull *Names of Birds* 195, American Golden Plover. . . In Massachusetts . . at Ipswich and North Scituate, *Pale-Breast;* at Provincetown, New Bedford, and Chatham, *Pale-Belly;* these last two names being applied only to the young birds, which are regarded by many as a distinct species or variety. **1892** *Auk* 9.144 **MA,** I have at times shot large specimens of young American Golden Plover *(C. dominicus)*—Pale-bellies as they are called. **1917** (1923) *Birds Amer.* 1.256, *Black-bellied Plover*. . . Other Names. . . Pale-belly (young). *Ibid* 257, These "pale-bellies" are readily distinguished. They arrive on the New England coast early in September, whereas the adults begin to appear about July 25. *Ibid, Golden Plover*. . . Other Names. . . Pale-belly (young). **1918** Grinnell *Game Birds CA* 454, The young [of the black-bellied plover] in the fall are often called Pale-bellies because of the lighter coloration of the under parts. **1955** MA Audubon Soc. *Bulletin* 39.445, *American Golden Plover*. . . Pale-breast (Mass. The young, yellowish or brownish mottled below, in contrast to the black of adults, are sometimes considered a distinct variety.) *Ibid, Black-bellied Plover*. . . Pale-belly (Mass. The immature.)

pale crappie n
The white **crappie** (*Pomoxis annularis*).
    1908 Forbes–Richardson *Fishes of IL* 239, When separately mentioned the present species [=*Pomoxis annularis*] is often called the pale crappie, or the white crappie, or the ringed crappie. **1933** LA Dept. of Conserv. *Fishes* 333. **1939** Natl. Geogr. Soc. *Fishes* 110, White Crappie. . . A fish of so wide range naturally has many local names. Around the Great Lakes it is called ringed crappie, pale crappie, and strawberry bass.

paled fence See **pale fence**

paled garden See **pale garden**

paled-in See **pale 1**

paled road See **pale road**

paleface n
1 also *paleface rose-mallow:* A **hibiscus** (here: *Hibiscus denudatus*).
    1925 Jepson *Manual Plants CA* 626, H[ibiscus] denudatus . . Pale Face. . . petals white or pale lavender, often deep purple at center. **1942** Hylander *Plant Life* 378, In the west there are California Rose Mallow . . and the Pale Face, a species with lavender to white blossoms, marked with purple in the center, growing on the southwestern deserts and west to Texas. **1960** Vines *Trees SW* 739, Paleface Rose-mallow.
2 See quot.
    1970 *DARE* (Qu. B18, . . *Special kinds of wind*) Inf **VA**47, Paleface; whiteface; whiteface northeast—northeast wind with no rain.

paleface rose-mallow See **paleface 1**

pale fence n Also *paled fence* **chiefly Atlantic, esp PA** See Map Cf **pale 1, pale garden**
=**paling fence.**

1664 in 1897 *CT Hist. Soc. Coll.* 6.143, Ther shall be a suffishant palle fens set up Round about the sd bering yard. **1834** (1898) Kemper *Jrl.* 423 **WI,** In walking over the meadow from the mill to the landing passed an indian burial place, 2 poles with white flags flying a pale fence partly surrounding the place. **1839** *S. Lit. Messenger* 5.67, A handsome pale-fence skirted the lawn on the road-side. **1850** (1869) Watson *Camp-Fires* 28, Their ranks looked like a broken pale-fence. **1886** Stockton *Casting Away* 73 **PA,** Of all the foolish things that ever came under my eye, the buildin' a wall around a garden, when a pale fence would do just as well, is the foolishest. **1889** *Century Illustr. Mag.* 39.300, A high pale fence surrounded the house yard. **1939** *LANE* Map 115 (*Picket fence*) 1 inf, **seNH,** Pale fence; cf. *pales, palings*. **1949** [see **paling fence**]. **1956** [see **paling fence**]. **1965–70** *DARE* (Qu. L64, *The kind of wooden fence that's built around a garden or near a house*) 12 Infs, **esp PA,** Pale fence; **DC5,** Pale fence; **MD48,** Pale fence—vertical boards, spaces between; **MA5,** Pale fence—perh flat pieces; **PA6,** Pale fence—locust trees for posts. **1967** [see **paling fence**]. **1981** in 1982 *Barrick Coll.* **csPA,** Pale fence—picket fence [< paling fence]. **1986** Pederson *LAGS Concordance* **Gulf Region** (*Picket fence*) 7 infs, Pale fence; 1 inf, Pale fence—straight up and down; 1 inf, Pale fences—vertical strips; 1 inf, Pale fence—pointed at top, not sure; [1 inf, Pales—the pickets; 1 inf, Pale—used in making picket fence].

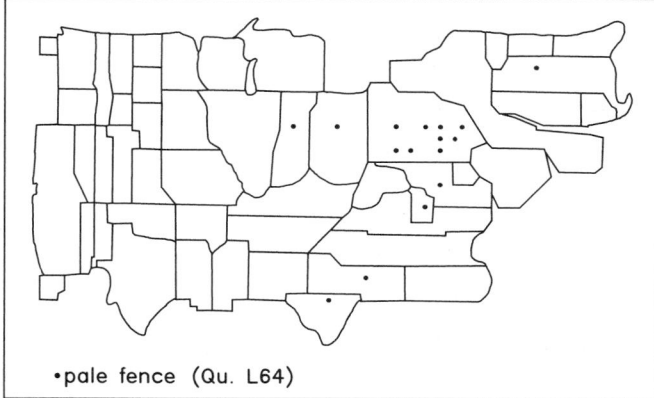

•pale fence (Qu. L64)

pale garden n Also *paled garden, pale yard, paling garden* [Cf *OED2 paled garden* (at *paled* ppl. a.[1] 2) 1531 →] **esp S Midl** Cf **pale 1, pale fence**
A garden or yard surrounded by a **paling fence.**

1835 *S. Lit. Messenger* 1.357 **WV,** The grand assault was from the east side, under cover of a paled garden, and a few half faced cabins within 40 or 50 yards of the fort. **1896** *Harper's New Mth. Mag.* 93.774 **TN,** Within the paled garden June-roses grow. **1949** Kurath *Word Geog.* Map 63, [There are four instances of *pale yard* in **NC** and **VA.**] **1966** Dakin *Dial. Vocab. Ohio R. Valley* 2.97, Eastern Kentucky also has a few instances of *pale yard* . . and *pale garden*. **1971** Wood *Vocab. Change* 300, 9 infs, **AR, GA, TN,** Pale garden. **1986** Pederson *LAGS Concordance,* 1 inf, **cnMS,** Paling garden.

pale in See **pale 1**

palement n Also *paling* [Prob varr of *pavement, paving;* cf **pale road**] **GA, SC** *among Black speakers* Cf **pavement**
A paved road; a sidewalk.

1892 (1969) Christensen *Afro-Amer. Folk Lore* 20 **seSC,** Br'er Rabbit say, "Br'er Elephan,' bein' you so heaby, you mus' run on the palement an' I run in de street." **c1970** [see **pale road**]. **1986** Pederson *LAGS Concordance* (*Sidewalk*) 1 inf, **swGA,** Palement = pavement, sidewalk; paling = pavement. [Inf Black]

‡**palement fence** n Cf **pale fence, palement**
1986 Pederson *LAGS Concordance* (*Picket fence*) 1 inf, **cTN,** Palement fence—boards are horizontal. [Inf Black]

pale road n Also *paled road* [Prob varr of *paved road:* cf **palement**] **GA** *among Black speakers*

c1970 Pederson *Dial. Surv. Rural GA* **seGA** (*Kinds of roads depending on what they are made out of*) 1 inf, Pale; 1 inf, Pale road, palement; 1 inf, [p'ɛˆɪə] road. [All infs Black] **1986** Pederson *LAGS Concordance* (*Cement road*) 1 inf, **cGA,** Pale road = paved road? made of tar; 1 inf, **swGA,** Pale roads = paved roads; 1 inf, **swGA,** Paled road—must be the same as "paved road." [All infs Black]

palette n [LaFr]
A spatula.

1968 *DARE* (Qu. F3, *When you're frying things—for example, eggs— you turn them over with a _____*) Inf **LA24,** Palette ['pælɪt].

pale up See **pale 1**

pale yard See **pale garden**

pali n, also attrib [Haw] **HI** Note: Haw has only one liquid consonant, which early writers often represented with *r* rather than *l*.
A steep slope, precipice.

1833 in 1934 Frear *Lowell & Abigail* 65 **HI,** Mr. Smith . . [invited] the mission families to ride up the valley of Nuuanu to see the parry [Frear: *pali* (precipice)] which is seven miles distant. **1838** *Ibid* 129, Abba was carried in a chair by natives, excepting a few rods on the steep part of the pari [Frear: pali]. **1951** *AmSp* 26.23 **HI,** Other common Hawaiian words are . . *pali* (cliff, precipice). **1965** Krauss-Alexander *Grove Farm* xvi **HI,** Pali—cliff. **1967** Reinecke-Tsuzaki *Hawaiian Loanwords* 107, *Pali;* /pali/. . . A precipice. On the island of Oahu, the *Pali* is Nuuanu Pali, not far from the city of Honolulu; or, sometimes, the whole precipitous windward side of the Koolau Mountain Range. V[ery] F[requent]. **1994** Stone-Pratt *Hawai'i's Plants* 68 **HI,** *Black Noddy or Noio.* . . Rocky coastal areas, especially pali (cliffs). *Ibid* 86, Trees are restricted to steep pali slopes and rough 'a'ā. *Ibid* 103, In only a few localities on steep slopes and pali faces are sizable thickets of lantana encountered.

palila n [Haw] **HI**
A honeycreeper (*Loxioides bailleui*) native to Hawaii.

1892 in 1903 Bernice P. Bishop Museum *Special Pub.* 6.436 **HI,** The food of the Palila is to a very large extent derived from the Mamani trees, on the seeds of which it chiefly feeds. **1944** Munro *Birds HI* 125, *Palila.* . . The name refers perhaps to the gray color of the bird. . . Neck, throat and breast yellow, rest of under surface mostly ashy gray. . . Rather a nice looking bird. **1972** Berger *Hawaiian Birdlife* 163, On a few occasions I have tramped through the open parkland forest for several hours without seeing or hearing a Palila. At other times of the year, they are very common. **1994** Stone-Pratt *Hawai'i's Plants* 329, On Mauna Kea . . palila populations seem to be rebuilding with drastic reduction of sheep and goats from the mountain. **1995** *Defenders* Fall 21, Hawaii has lost many . . habitats. . . A palila, an endangered woodland songbird, [is] deprived of habitat by cattle grazing.

paling n[1] **chiefly Sth, Midl**
1 =**paling fence.** [*OED2 paling* vbl. sb. 3.b 1558 →]

1806 *Balance* (Hudson NY) 22 July 231 **MS,** 1,200 feet of new cypress paling from around captain Randolph's lots blown down. **1839** *S. Lit. Messenger* 5.751, Before the door was a . . row of trees . . fenced in by a white paling, along the top of which ran a cornice. **1890** Howells *Shadow* 47, Some former proprietor had built a paling of slender strips of wood ten or twelve feet high. **1902** *DN* 2.240 **sIL,** Palin [peĺɪn]. . . A stave or picket; a picket fence. **1906** *DN* 3.122 **sIN,** *Palin.* . . Stave, picket; a picket fence. **1966** [see **paling fence**]. **1966–69** *DARE* (Qu. L64, *The kind of wooden fence that's built around a garden or near a house*) Infs **AL53, FL20, GA68, IN32, MO39, WV5,** Paling; **FL9,** Picket or paling. [*DARE* Ed: Perh *fence* is to be understood.]
2 A vertical bar or slat forming part of a fence; hence *palings* a set of bars or slats composing a **paling fence.** [*OED2 paling* vbl. sb. 3.c 1834 →]

1845 Thompson *Pineville* 167 **GA,** And you've [=a mule] broke the major's palins down, you unnatural cus. **1867** Harris *Sut Lovingood Yarns* 143 **TN,** I jis' tore off a palin frum the fence, an' tuck hit in bof hans. **1871** Eggleston *Hoosier Schoolmaster* 92 **sIN,** Palings—pickets she called them—of the garden fence. . . Miss Hawkins was recently from Massachusetts. **1902** [see **1** above]. **1903** *DN* 2.323 **seMO,** They're pullin' palins offen your fence. **1904** *DN* 2.419 **nwAR,** *Paling:* [peĺɪn]. . . Picket. 'The old hound had his head fast between two palins.' **1906** [see **1** above]. **1909** *DN* 3.355 **eAL, wGA,** *Palin(g).* . . A picket, a fence stave; *paling* is practically the only term in use in the South. **1913** Wharton *Custom of Country* 52 **NY**, The earliest had been spent in the yellow "frame" cottage where she had hung on the fence, kicking her toes against the broken palings. **1941** Stuart *Men of Mts.* 98 **KY**, The palins were tall and the tops sharpened so a body couldn't climb over the fence. **1956** [see **paling fence**]. **1965–70** *DARE* (Qu. L64, *The kind of wooden fence that's built around a garden or near a house*) Infs **FL**7, 26, **GA**3, 9, 14, **MD**18, **TN**1, **VA**14, Palings; (Qu. L65, . . *Kinds of fences*) Inf **GA**22, Palings. **1967** [see **paling fence**]. **1967** Fetterman *Stinking Creek* 38 **seKY**, The yard is surrounded by its "palings," a fence of slender slats that encircles and protects the yard. **1967** *PADS* 47.20, [Footnote 16:] The *Third* [=Webster's *Third New International Dictionary*] does not clearly distinguish between *palings* and *pickets.* For many Southerners the former are riven out with a froe and wattled (woven) around the stringers of a fence; the latter are sawed out and nailed on. **1970** [see **paling fence**]. **1972** *PADS* 58.14 **cwAL**, *Picket fence.* South and Midland *palings* (11 [of 27 infs]) and *paling fence* (2) are more frequent than Northern *picket fence* (10, without social distinction). Of those using *picket fence,* three gave *paling fence* as an alternate. **1989** [see **paling fence**].

paling n[2] See **palement**

paling fence n [*OED2* (at *paling* vbl. sb. 4) 1805 →; cf **paling** n[1] **2**] **chiefly Sth, S Midl** See Map Cf **pale fence**
A fence made of vertical bars or slats; a picket fence.

    1843 *Amer. Pioneer* 2.308 **WV**, A strong body [of enemy fighters] occupied the yard of Ebenezer Zane . . using a paling fence as a cover. **1873** Twain–Warner *Gilded Age* 60, Hawkins put up the first "paling" fence that had ever adorned the village. **1901** Merwin–Webster *Calumet "K"* 68 **Chicago IL**, They were standing . . near the paling fence which bounded the C. & S.C. right of way. **1939** *LANE* Map 115 *(Picket fence)* 2 infs, **sRI, sNH**, Paling fence = picket fence; 2 infs, **ceMA, seNH**, Paling fence. **1942** Faulkner *Go Down* 49 **MS**, He entered the gate in the paling fence. **1946** *PADS* 5.30 **VA**, *Paling fence.* . . A fence made of pales, pointed slats; common everywhere. **1949** Kurath *Word Geog.* 55, Fences with pointed or blunt upright slats which commonly surround the dwelling and the garden are known as . . *paling fences, paled fences,* or simply as *palings* in the Midland and the Southern area. The variant *paled fence* is characteristic of the Philadelphia area. **1950** *PADS* 13.18 **cTX**, *Paling fence.* . . A fence made of pales (pointed slats) joined by wire. A picket fence is made by nailing pickets to cross-members. **1956** Ker *Vocab. W. TX* 156, For the modern trade term . . *picket fence,* there are thirty-five responses [from 67 infs], eleven more than for the Midland and Southern *paling fence.* For *palings* there are seven entries and for *paled fence* one. The fact that *picket fence* is now used as a trade name, may explain why it is winning the preference. **c1960** *Wilson Coll.* **csKY**, *Paling fence*—A fence made with home-made palings or pickets, which had been rived out of timber with a froe; just after rail-timber became scarce, paling fences were common until wire fences arrived. **1965–70** *DARE* (Qu. L64, *The kind of wooden fence that's built around a garden or near a house*) 147 Infs, **chiefly Sth, Midl,** Paling fence; (Qu. L62, *A fence made of split logs*) Inf **IN**13, Paling fence ['pelɪn fens]; (Qu. L65, . . *Kinds of fences*) Infs **AL**11, **VA**10, Paling fence; **AR**55, Paling fence—made of strips rived out of logs; **GA**72, Palin' fence—old-fashioned, out of oak 4 to 5 feet high. **1966** Dakin *Dial. Vocab. Ohio R. Valley* 2.92, In general, *picket fence* predominates north of the Ohio River, in the Bluegrass, and in the eastern Pennyroyal Corridor. *Paling fence* is still fairly common in parts of this area, however, and predominates to the virtual exclusion of *picket fence* in the Kentucky Mountains. Elsewhere in Kentucky it is the more common term. In the mountains and among older people the most common form is *palings.* In the Bluegrass and north of the Ohio (except in the Hanging Rock region) *paling fence* is usual. *Ibid* 95, The somewhat more frequent use of *paling fence*—also *palings, paled fence* (rare), *pale fence* (rare), and *a paling* (rare)—among the oldest generation of informants north of the river suggests that this was the more common older usage. **1967** Faries *Word Geog. MO* 77, The primary expression used by the Missouri informants for a fence with pointed wooden slats is the general term *picket fence* (80 percent [of 700 infs]). There are four South and South Midland expressions current in much lesser degree: *paling fence* (145 occurrences), which does not appear in a twenty-one county area north of the Missouri River and west of the Chariton River; *palings* (20 occurrences), which appears only once north of the Missouri River; *paled fence* (8 occurrences); and *pale fence* (7 occurrences). **1970** Tarpley *Blinky* 125 **neTX**, The most common term . . is *picket fence.* . .

Paling fence is practically unknown among informants under 30 in Northeast Texas. Several informants define *pickets* as narrow, pointed slats joined together with wire and *palings* as broader slats . . which are nailed individually to the framework of the fence. Another common distinction is that a *paling fence* is the homemade variety and that a *picket fence* is purchased or constructed by skilled carpenters. **1972** [see **paling** n[1] 2]. **1989** Pederson *LAGS Tech. Index* 62 **Gulf Region**, 497 infs, Picket fence; 121 infs, Paling fence; 113 infs, Paling(s). [*DARE* Ed: Resps recorded as *paling* appear for the most part either to represent *paling fence* or to refer to an individual fence-picket.]

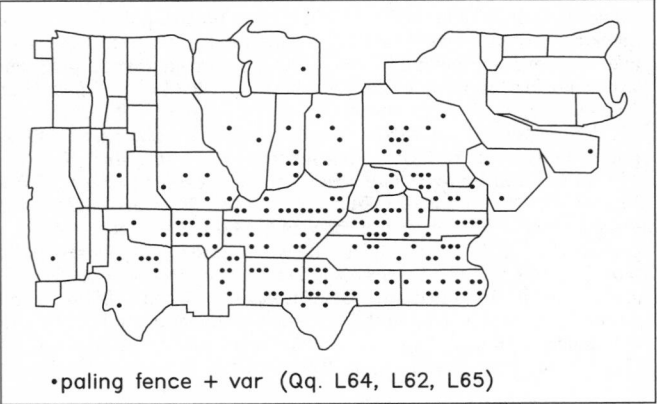

•paling fence + var (Qq. L64, L62, L65)

paling garden See **pale garden**

palings See **paling** n[1] **2**

pallance See **parlance**

pallet n Also sp *pallit* [*OED2 pallet* sb.[2] 1 c1374 →; "A straw bed; a mattress; a small, poor, or mean bed or couch."] **chiefly Sth, W Midl, SW** See Map See also **Baptist pallet, Methodist ~**
A makeshift bed on the floor or ground.

    1840 *S. Lit. Messenger* 6.263, A pallet was spread out for the pedler in the room where we supped. **1885** Twain *Huck. Finn* 220 **MO**, Up garret was a little cubby, with a pallet in it. **1894** in 1941 Warfel–Orians *Local-Color Stories* 741 **sAR**, With elaborate apologies for the state of her cabin, which was indeed strewn with trash, improvised rag babies, and pallets, she proceeded to wipe off a chair. **1899** (1912) Green *VA Folk-Speech* 311, *Pallet.* . . A bed on the floor made up with quilts, or blankets, sheets and a pillow, on which children of a house were put to sleep while visitors occupied their beds. **1902** *DN* 2.240 **sIL**, *Pallit.* . . Bed on the floor. **1903** *DN* 2.323 **seMO**, *Pallet.* . . A bed made on the floor. 'I haven't got a spare bed, but I can make down a pallet for you.' **1904** *DN* 2.420 **nwAR**, *Pallet.* . . A bed on the floor improvised from a folded blanket or quilt. **1906** *DN* 3.122 **sIN**, *Pallet.* **1909** *DN* 3.355 **eAL, wGA**, *Pallet.* . . A bed of quilts made on the floor. If a mattress is used, it is called a "bed on the floor." **1915** *DN* 4.187 **swVA**, *Pallet.* **1923** *DN* 5.216 **swMO**, *Pallet.* **1930** Faulkner *As I Lay Dying* 7 **MS**, I used to lie on the pallet in the hall, waiting. **1944** *PADS* 2.59 **cnMO**, *Pallet.* **1965–70** *DARE* (Qu. E18, *A temporary or emergency bed made*

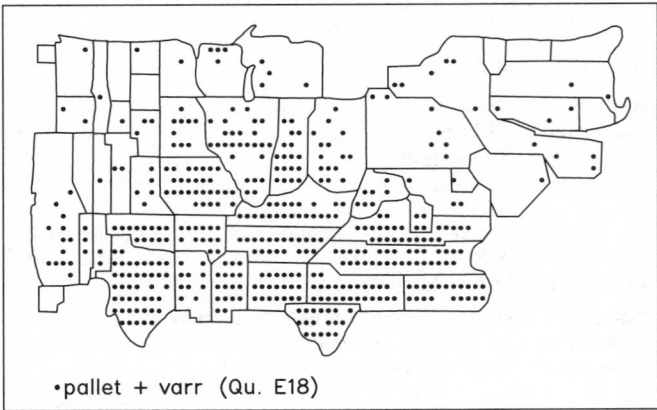

•pallet + varr (Qu. E18)

up on the floor) 453 Infs, **chiefly Sth, W Midl, SW,** Pallet; **AL**11, **MS**1, Baptist pallet; **AR**47, Free-will Baptist pallet; **AR**47, **TX**40, Methodist pallet. **1973** Allen *LAUM* 1.230 (as of c1950), *Pallet* (bed on the floor). . . Although most infs. have no name for a temporary bed on the floor, the 35 infs. using *pallet* exhibit a clear South Midland distribution that at one time was strong enough to spread slightly into western Nebraska. Competing *shakedown,* though with only 20 occurrences, has a suggestively Northern distribution. Both terms are usually considered old-fashioned if known at all. **1989** Pederson *LAGS Tech. Index* 105 **Gulf Region,** 700 infs, Pallet; 8 infs, Pallet on the floor; 6 infs, Baptist pallet; 3 infs, Methodist pallet; 2 infs, Floor pallet; 1 inf, Down pallet; 1 inf, Hard-shell pallet. **1998** *DARE* File **OK, TX,** The Dallas informant born in 1954 uses the word *pig blanket* for what he also calls *pallet*—a blanket spread on the floor for small children. *Pallet* is universal in Oklahoma. I was put on a *pallet* when I was small.

pallet baby n
See quot.
    1958 Randolph *Sticks* 111 **Ozarks,** There was one creeper, one walker, two pallet babies, one suckling, and an apron child. The census taker says, "Do all these children belong to you and Jim?"

pallit See **pallet**

palm n, v Usu |pɑm, pɒm|; also **chiefly Sth, S Midl, occas NEng** |pæm|; sp-proncs |palm, pɑlm|; for addit varr see quots at **A** below   Pronc-spp *pam, parm*   Similarly adj *pammy* Cf **balm, calm, pan** n[1]**, panel**
A Forms.
    1893 Shands *MS Speech* 6, Among the educated classes *palm, calm* . . are correctly pronounced, but the illiterate of both colors pronounce ɑ as [æ]. **1909** *DN* 3.355 **eAL, wGA,** Pam [pæm]. . . Palm. *Pammy.* . . Palmy. **1915** *DN* 4.187 **swVA,** Palm [pæm]. **1923** *DN* 5.216 **swMO,** *Pa'm.* . . Palm. **1931** (1991) Hughes–Hurston *Mule Bone* 143 **cFL** [Black], Take yo' rusty pams offen me. **1933** *AmSp* 8.2.29 **KY,** Bless me, the elder (the Vicar) cyarved me a fleek (slice) of ham-meat the size of my pam (palm) spread plum wide (indicating with wide spread hand). **c1938** in 1970 Hyatt *Hoodoo* 2.1480 **seGA,** Jest tack one in de pam . . of each hand [in a drawing of the person]. **c1940** Eliason *Word Lists FL* 14 **wFL,** Palm [pæm]: Used by old persons. **1941** *LANE* Map 490, (*Palm* (of the hand)), [Proncs of the type [pɑ·m] occur **throughout NEng;** those of the types [pa·m, pæ⁽ᵊ⁾m] are **scattered;** 1 inf, swCT, [pɑ˃lm]; 1 inf, swCT, [pælm]; 1 inf, cCT, [pɒˡm].] [*LANE* Ed: Pronunciations with final [lm] . . are presumably overcareful forms not in habitual use.] **1955** *PADS* 23.46 **e,cSC, eNC, seGA,** /æ/ in *palm, calm,* etc., even in cultured speech (old-fashioned elsewhere). **1961** Kurath–McDavid *Pronc. Engl.* 142, *Palm* (of the hand) exhibits a regional and social dissemination of variants similar to that observed in *calm,* but in the Midland and the South the vowel of *barn* is decidedly more common in *palm* than in *calm.* In Pennsylvania, /ɔ ~ ɒ/ occurs as in *calm,* but rather more frequently. **1964** O'Hare *Ling. Geog. E. MT* 194, [The map shows] [t]he vowel nucleus of 'palm' [6 infs, /ɑ/; 3 infs, /ɑ/; 3 infs /ɒ/]. **c1970** Pederson *Dial. Surv. Rural GA* **seGA** (*Palm*) [28 infs, [pɑ(ə)m]; 19 infs, [pɑ(ə)m]; 5 infs, [pɑlm]; 4 infs [pæm]; 1 inf, [pɑᵁm].] **1975** Gould *ME Lingo* 202, Palm is pronounced "parm" in Maine. **1976** Allen *LAUM* 3.21 (as of c1950), In *palm* . . /ɑ/ is usual in the U[pper] M[idwest]. *Ibid* 279, In the UM two Type I rural infs. in Iowa, with Midland and South Midland ancestry, reflect the minority eastern /pæm/ . . . Although most other UM speakers have /ɑ/ or its backed equivalent /ɑ/, a scattering of infs. have the rounded /ɒ/ or /ɔ/. Some of these latter instances in Iowa are clearly due to a South Midland background. **1989** Pederson *LAGS Tech. Index* 264 **Gulf Region** (*Palm*) [The main pronc types, excluding the variants in which the final *m* has been changed to *n,* are: [pɑʊm, pɒʊm] 321 infs; [pɑm] 215; [pɒm, pɔm] 71; [pɑlm, pɒlm] 66; [pæm] 19; [pæʊm] 5; and [pælm] 1.] **1991** *Macoupin Co. Enquirer* (Carlinville IL) 6 **cwIL,** [From a 1961 issue quoting "oldsters":] Some sly persons pammed off things they wished to be shet of.
B As noun.
The sole of the foot. **chiefly Sth** [*OED2 palm* sb.[2] 2.c 1460 →]
    1845 Thompson *Pineville* 62 **cGA,** Caused him to stand rather in a jumping attitude, upon the palms of his feet. **1890** (1895) Riley *Rhymes of Childhood* 88 **IN,** Turn to the lane where we used to "teeter-totter,"/ Printing little foot-palms in the mellow mould. **1927** Kennedy *Gritny* 29 **sLA** [Black], Cut de palms his feets in de bargain, so he can't run no

mo'. **1929** Wolfe *Look Homeward* 227 **NC,** [Eugene's] feet were numb and dead, sore on the palms. **c1938** in 1970 Hyatt *Hoodoo* 1.555 **seNC,** Git de dirt out of nine of his tracks right in *de palm of his foot*—yo' know, where he step on, de palm.

palma Christi n Also rarely, *esp among Black speakers, palm Crystal, palm of Christa, palm of Christian, pammy Christy, pomer Christer, prong of Christian, pumma Crissul* [*OED2* 1548 →] **chiefly Sth**
The castor bean *(Ricinus communis).*
    1737 (1911) Brickell *Nat. Hist. NC* 21, *Palma-Christi,* several sorts of *Mint, Red-Dock, Jamestown-Weed.* **1831** Peck *Guide for Emigrants* 158 **swIL,** The *Palma christi,* or castor oil bean, is produced in considerable quantities in Madison, Randolph, and other counties. **1836** *Farmers' Reg.* Sept [298], There is yet another growth that bids fair to become of great value to the agricultural interest of the Eastern Shore of Maryland, namely, the *palma christi,* or castor bean plant, sometimes known by the name of *mole plant.* **1869** Porcher *Resources* 134 **Sth,** *Palma Christi.* . . This valuable plant thrives so well in the Southern States that it might be made a source of profit. On some of the plantations the seeds are boiled, and the supernatant oil given as a cathartic. **1903** Small *Flora SE U.S.* 705, *Ricinus communis.* . . Escaped from cultivation, New Jersey to Florida to Texas. Widely naturalized in warm and tropical regions. *Palma Christi.* **1927** Kennedy *Gritny* 148 **sLA** [Black], Y'oughta eat you a few dese pumma-crissuls you got hyuh in yo' yard. **c1937** in 1977 *Amer. Slave Suppl. 1* 1.280 **AL,** If us niggers got sick dey would give us pomer-christer, mashed up fer castor oil. **c1938** in 1970 Hyatt *Hoodoo* 1.626 **TN** [Black], Yo' git chew nine grains of red peppah outa de pods, nine grains. Git two teaspoon fulla sugah an' yo' git chew *one palm of Christian* seed. *Ibid* 2.982 **seGA,** Well, dey call it de stingin' nettle. It got a little ball on it like a prong of Christian seed, like mah fingernail. Yo' have seen a prong of Christian seed, ain't chew? **1945** FWP *Lay My Burden Down* 29 **Sth** (as of c1865) [Black], Two, three Pammy Christy beans,/ Little piece o' rusty iron. **1967** *DARE* FW Addit **LA**2, Palm Crystals [pam krısčəlz]—alternate name for castor beans, probably more common than 'castor beans.' **1972** GA Dept. Ag. *Farmers Market Bulletin* 5 Jan 8/2 **swGA,** [Letter:] The Palma Christi, Castor Bean, or mole bean, are these same and will they get rid of ground moles? . . [Response:] These are all the same and do, for some reason, cause Mr. Mole to find a new home. **1972** *Names SC* 29.28, *Palm of Christa* (Dorchester County), another version of Red Leaf Palmachristi, identified as *Ricinus communis.* **1986** Pederson *LAGS Concordance,* 1 inf, swGA, Palma Christi—children lie on leaves—for fever; 1 inf, swGA, Palma Christi leaves—used for breaking a fever; 1 inf, seFL, (Palma) Christi leaves—tear up; 1 inf, seFL, Palma Christi trees. [All infs Black]

palmalla See **palmilla 1**

palm cabbage See **palmetto cabbage**

palm Crystal See **palma Christi**

palmeeter See **palmetto**

palmella See **palmilla 1**

palmetto n Also sp *palmeto*   Pronc-spp *pahmetto, palmeeter, palmeta, (pa')meeter, pa'metter, permeeter*
A Forms.
    1743 [see **B** below]. **1747** in 1895 *Documents Colonial & Post-Revol. Hist. NJ* 12.364, The woman . . [wore] blue worsted stockings, palmeta hat, scarlet cloth cloak [etc]. **1927** Kennedy *Gritny* 35 **sLA** [Black], You ain' laid aside dis ole palmeeter hat. **1927** Boston Soc. Nat. Hist. *Proc.* 38.7.213 **Okefenokee GA,** *Serenoa serrulata*—Saw-palmetto; 'pa'metter'; 'pa'meeter'. *Ibid* 220, *Sabal glabra*—'Blue pa'metter'. *Ibid* 312, You find 'em [=skunks] around big high pa'meeters an' clayroots in piney woods. **1933** Rawlings *South Moon* 14 **FL,** Nothin' won't make excusin' palmeeters and that sorry pine. **c1940** Eliason *Word Lists FL* 3, Meeter buds . . Palmetto scrub thicket. **1946** *PADS* 6.23 **eNC,** Permeeter [pə'mitɚ, -ə]. . . Palmetto. Pamlico. Common till 1880; rare now. **1965–70** *DARE* (Qu. S17, . . *Kinds of plants . . that . . cause itching and swelling*) Inf **LA**43, Palmetto ['pæl'meto]; (Qu. S26b, *Wildflowers that grow in water or wet places*) Inf **FL**35, Palmetto blooms, [pæl'metɚz]; (Qu. T16, . . *Kinds of trees . . 'special'*) Inf **FL**17, Palmettos ['pælmetouz]; **FL**20, Palmettos [pæl'metəz]; **SC**10, Palmetto ['pæl'metə]; **SC**69, Palmetto [pæl'medə]—state tree. **1969** *DARE* FW

Addit **seGA,** [pæl'mɛtæ-z]. **1984** *WI State Jrl.* (Madison) 20 Dec sec 4 1, People around me say "pahmetto," as if the first syllable rhymed with "palm" as in palm tree or palm of the hand. People looked at me funny when I said my kids went to Pal-metto High School, instead of Pahm-etto. I stubbornly stick with "pal." It's not only a Southern word, it's the right way to say it. You could look it up.

B Sense.

Usu a palm of the genus *Sabal,* but also a palm such as the **saw palmetto 1.** For other names of var spp of *Sabal* see **cabbage palm, dwarf palmetto 1, scrub cabbage, ~ palmetto;** for terms relating to the leaf or leaf-stalk of these palms see **boot v² 2, bootjack 2, fan** n, **latanier** Cf **blue palmetto 1, silver-top ~**

1606 in 1624 Smith *Genl. Hist. VA* 26, Plums there are of three sorts. The red and white are like our hedge plums, but the other which they call *Putchamins,* grow as high as a *Palmeta.* **1743** Catesby *Nat. Hist. Carolina* 2 [app] iii **SC,** At *Sullivans* Island . . the Sea on the West Side has so encroached. . . that, it has gained in three Years Time, a Quarter of a Mile laying prostrate, and swallowing up vast Pine, and Palmeto-Trees. **1765** (1942) Bartram *Diary of a Journey* 37, The hammocks of . . palmettos are generally surrounded . . with swamp. **1784** (1968) Hutchins *Hist. Narr. LA & W. FL* 34, The whole is . . covered with thick wood, Palmetto bushes, &c. **1814** Brackenridge *Views of LA* 172, The wind here became too strong, and we were compelled to put to shore on a little point of land overgrown with palmettoes. **1853** Hammett *Stray Yankee in TX* 55, A wolf skin, or the nearest palmetto brake, furnishes him with a hat. **1879** Bishop *4 Months* 298 **FL,** With their venison these men served a very palatable dish made from the terminal bud of the palmetto known as the "cabbage." **1898** Sudworth *Forest Trees* 37, *Sabal palmetto. . . Range.*—Coast region from North Carolina . . to Florida . . , and on the Gulf coast. . . *Names in use. . .* Palmetto (N.C., S.C.) **1927** Boston Soc. Nat. Hist. *Proc.* 38.7.377 **Okefenokee GA,** They [=deer] eat huckleberries, . . palmetto [*Serenoa*] berries, . . possum haws [*Viburnum nudum*]—nearly all the berries they can reach. **1942** (1960) Robertson *Red Hills* 163 **SC,** Women in their best taffeta dresses fanned themselves with palmettos. **1965–70** *DARE* T16, . . *Kinds of trees . . 'special'*) Infs **FL**17, 20, **GA**91, **SC**4, 10, 21, 63, **TX**9, 22, Palmetto; **FL**16, Palmetto palm—good for docks; **LA**10, Palmetto—just a low bunch of fan-shaped leaves; **SC**67, Palmetto—Palmetto State, in fact; **SC**69, Palmetto—state tree; (Qu. I44, *What kinds of berries grow wild around here?*) Inf **GA**23, Palmettos; (Qu. S17, . . *Kinds of plants . . that . . cause itching and swelling*) Inf **LA**43, Palmetto; (Qu. S26b, *Wildflowers that grow in water or wet places*) Inf **FL**35, Palmetto blooms; **LA**43, Palmettos; (Qu. T1, . . *A bunch of trees growing together in open country, especially on a hill*) Inf **SC**10, Palmetto hatchet [hæɪč̣ɪt]—like a grape arbor; (Qu. T5, . . *Kinds of evergreens, other than pine*) Inf **GA**3, Palmetto palms; **SC**63, Palmetto. **1966–68** *DARE* Tape **AL**20, And she told about the palmetto hats. We have a palm, I guess belongs to the palm family. Did you ever see a palmetto thing made out of the thorn of these things and dried? . . They would gather these and strip them off . . and plait them and sew them together and make a hat; **FL**45, They had built a pathway between a narrow row of palmetto trees all the way from the railroad track down to the hotel; **GA**25, And for salt, they had to dig up these palmettos, like you see growing here, you know them palmettos with the fans on them. **1980** Little *Audubon Guide N. Amer. Trees E. Region* 314, "Carolina Palmetto". . . Medium-sized, spineless, evergreen palm with . . *very large, fan-shaped leaves* spreading around top. [*Ibid* 315, The names are from the Spanish *palmito,* meaning "small palm."]

palmetto bug n esp FL

Any of several cockroaches, but usu those of the genus *Periplaneta.*

1985 Shore *Sachertorte Algorithm* 73, As a marketing achievement, this terminology [="user-friendly"] ranks with "Palmetto bugs," which is a term used in Florida—at the instigation of some genius in the real estate industry, I'm told—for large, flying cockroaches. **1991** Leonard *Maximum Bob* 110 **FL,** A dump full of palmetto bugs, called roaches other places. **1992** Hoffman *Turtle Moon* 42 **ceFL,** The lights are on beneath the water, so the pool seems to float in space, a black hole surrounded by white moths and palmetto bugs. **1994** FL Coop. Extension Serv. *Fact Sheet ENY* 258.110, The remaining 5 species are. . . the American, *Periplaneta americana,* Australian, *P. australasiae,* Brown, *P. brunnea,* Smokybrown, *P. fuliginosa,* and the Florida Woods cockroaches, *Eurycotis floridana.* Collectively, this group of cockroaches is

what the homeowner commonly refers to as "palmettobugs." **1995** *DARE* File **Sth,** Terms like *water bug, croton bug, steam fly,* and *palmetto bug* are easier to talk about than admitting you have "roaches."

palmetto cabbage n Also *palm cabbage* Cf **swamp cabbage**

The edible bud of **cabbage palm.**

1847 (1979) Rutledge *Carolina Housewife* 99, To dress palmetto cabbage. Trim off carefully the hard folds of the palmetto cabbage; then boil the inner part for two hours. . . When the cabbage is quite soft, pour off the water, and mash the vegetable up with a wooden or silver spoon. **1875** (1876) Hallock *Camp Life* 75 **FL,** When the popularly known "staff" is gone, he can repair to the nearest hammock and cut a "palmeer cabbage." **1946** FL Dept. Ag. *Qrly. Bulletin* 77.31, *Sabal palmetto—Cabbage Palmetto.* Our fine native palm, yielding palm-cabbage and medicinal berries. *Ibid* 41, *Palmetto Cabbage* or the terminal bud of our cabbage palmetto was also used for food and is still used, but no tree should ever be sacrificed for a pot of cabbage.

palmetto pounder n Cf **goose-drownder,** *DS* B24–25

A heavy rain.

1980 *DARE* File **Miami FL** (as of c1960), We had a real palmetto pounder last night.

palmilla n [MexSpan, literally "little palm"] **Desert SW**

1 also *palmalla, palmella, palmillo, pamilla:* Usu a **soapweed** (here: *Yucca elata*), but also other **yuccas.**

1844 (1954) Gregg *Commerce* 113, Among the wild productions of New Mexico is the *palmilla*—a species of palmetto, which might be termed the *soap-plant*—whose roots, as well as those of another species known as *palma* (or palm), when bruised, form a saponaceous pulp called *amole,* much used by the natives for washing clothes. **1901** [see **2** below]. **1937** U.S. Forest Serv. *Range Plant Hdbk.* B157, Soaptree yucca, more often known simply as soapweed or palmilla (Mexican for little palm), is a somewhat palmlike plant, crowned with a dense tuft of swordlike leaves. **1949** Moldenke *Amer. Wild Flowers* 369, The official state flower of New Mexico is the "yucca". . . the palmilla, *Y. elata,* is a very likely contender for this honor. **1960** Vines *Trees SW* 68, *Yucca. . . glauca. . .* Also known under the vernacular names of Adam's-needle and Palmillo. The short crowns were sometimes used as a soap substitute by Indians. **1970** Correll *Plants TX* 400, *Yucca elata* . . Palmella, soap-tree, soap-weed. **1985** Dodge *Flowers SW Deserts* 28, Narrowleaf Yuccas . . Soaptree Yucca, Whipple Yucca, Palmalla, [etc]. **1987** Kindscher *Edible Wild Plants* 225, *Yucca glauca—Common names . .* New Mexican Spanish pamilla.

2 An **agave** (here: *Manfreda virginica*).

1901 Lounsberry *S. Wild Flowers* 66, False Aloe.—*Agave Virginica. . .* Although the custom is very prevalent, it is quite improperly that the agaves are called aloes and century plants. The narrow-leaved species, such as the present one, a fact also true of yuccas with this characteristic, are again known to the natives of the south and southwest under the name of "palmilla."

palmillo See **palmilla 1**

palmity n Also *palamity, palmity talk* [Perh < *palmateer* var of *parliamenteer* to electioneer; see quots 1855, 1859; cf *OED2 parliament* v. 4 "*fig. (humorous)* To vociferate, gabble."]

Ridiculous or excessive speech.

[**1855** Haliburton *Nature* 2.16, Our people talk a great deal of nonsense about emancipation, but they know it's all bunkum, and it serves to palmeteer on, and makes a pretty party catch-word.] [**1859** (1968) Bartlett *Americanisms* 309, *To parmateer,* or *palmateer.* To electioneer; evidently a corruption of *parliamenteer,* to electioneer for a seat in parliament. This term is very common in the State of Rhode Island, beyond which I think it does not extend.] **1928** Chapman *Happy Mt.* 17 **seTN,** When you've had time to take your share of that, you'll not talk such high palamity this way. **1936** *AmSp* 11.276 **cTN,** Palamity. Affectation or much talk. 'Listen to her palamity.' **1938** Matschat *Suwannee R.* 122 **neFL, seGA,** Freeman's makin' palmity talk as how she be too young. *Ibid* 289 [Glossary], *Palmity:* much ado about nothing.

palm-leaf oriole n Also *palm oriole* [Because it sometimes makes or suspends its nest from palm leaves]

=**hooded oriole.**

1923 Dawson *Birds CA* 89, Arizona Hooded Oriole . . *Icterus cucullatus nelsoni* . . Palm Oriole. [*Ibid* 92, The birds idled away the month of July making trial, or decoy, nests. These were invariably of palm fiber. *Ibid,* He constructed a nest on the under side of a palm leaf.] **1928** Bailey *Birds NM* 653, In the towns of southern California the Arizona Hooded Oriole merits its name of Palm-leaf Oriole, as it hangs its shallow basket nest, woven of palm-leaf fibers, from the underside of the outstretched, protecting fan palms.

palm of Christa, palm of Christian See **palma Christi**

palm of gilyum n
=**balm of Gilead 2a.**
    1968 *DARE* (Qu. T12, *The kind of poplar tree that has sticky, sweet-smelling buds*) Inf **MD22,** Palm of gilyum ['pæm ə 'gɪljəm]—buds heated in mutton tallow, strained, used to make salve for sores and painful joints.

palm oriole See **palm-leaf oriole**

palm-polly n
An epiphytic orchid *(Polyrrhiza lindenii)* native to southern Florida. Also called **white butterfly orchid**
    1933 Small *Manual SE Flora* 398, *Palm-polly.* . . Restricted mostly to Big Cypress Swamp. . . The elongate worm-like roots are supplied with chlorophyll and function as leaves. **1950** Correll *Native Orchids* 375 **FL,** In Collier County, the palm-polly is frequently found in dense shade. . . When one . . sees the extraordinary flowers of this little orchid for the first time, one is instantly impressed with its likeness to a thin flat snow-white frog suspended in mid-air—caught, as it were, in the middle of a leap from one branch to another. **1953** Greene–Blomquist *Flowers South* 23, In Fla. is the small, white, spectral palm-polly *(Polyrrhiza Lindenii).*

palo amarillo n [MexSpan, literally "yellow wood"]   **Desert SW** Cf **yellowwood**
1 Any of several **barberries.**
    [1848 (1962) U.S. Army Corps. Topog. Engineers *Abert's NM Rept.* 117, We saw . . also, a "mahonia," the leaves of which are very much like the holly; this the Mexicans call "palomereo."] **1931** U.S. Dept. Ag. *Misc. Pub.* 101.36, Hollygrape is commonly known by a number of other names, such as Oregon grape, hollyleaf barberry, mahonia, and palo amarillo. **1960** Vines *Trees SW* 273, Laredo Mahonia—*Mahonia trifoliata.* . . Vernacular names are Wild Currant . . and Palo Amarillo. **1976** Elmore *Shrubs & Trees SW* 69, Frémont Barberry . . Frémont holly-grape, bérbero, agracejo [small grape], palo amarillo [yellow wood].
2 =**bee brush.**
    1970 Correll *Plants TX* 1335, *Aloysia gratissima* . . Common bee-brush, white bush, white brush, palo amarillo [etc].

palo blanco n [MexSpan, literally "white wood"]
1 =**hackberry. esp TX**
    1838 in 1952 Green *Samuel Maverick* 83, Griffin & Granville can cut posts or pickets, and haul them to the (palo-blanco) hackberry tree. **1884** Sargent *Forests of N. Amer.* 126, Hackberry. Palo Blanco. Western Texas . . to the mountains of southern Arizona, and through the Rocky mountains to eastern Oregon. **1897** Sudworth *Arborescent Flora* 185 **TX,** *Celtis occidentalis reticulata.* . . Palo Blanco. **1908** Britton *N. Amer. Trees* 358, Thick-leaved Hackberry—*Celtis reticulata.* . . It is also called Palo Blanco and simply Hackberry, in Texas. **1938** Van Dersal *Native Woody Plants* 92, *Celtis lindheimeri* . . Paloblanco. **1965** Teale *Wandering Through Winter* 132 **TX,** It was the native hackberry. Because of the whiteness of its trunk it is known locally as "palo blanco." **1967** *DARE* (Qu. T13, . . *Hackberry*) Infs **TX**1, 22, 28, Palo blanco. **1970** Correll *Plants TX* 493, *Celtis laevigata* . . Texas sugarberry, palo blanco. *Ibid, Celtis reticulata* . . Netleaf hackberry, palo blanco. **1981** Benson–Darrow *Trees SW Deserts* 154, Celtis [spp]—Hackberry, Palo Blanco.
2 A **forestiera** (here: *Forestiera neomexicana*). **Desert SW**
    1913 Wooton *Trees NM* 128, Palo blanco . . is a good sized shrub 10–15 feet high with smooth greenish or pale bark, pale green leaves and dark blue to almost black berries the size of currants. **1938** Van Dersal *Native Woody Plants* 128, *Forestiera neomexicana* . . Paloblanco . . A small or commonly large, spiny, much-branched, spreading shrub. **1960** Vines *Trees SW* 851, New Mexico Forestiera. . . is also known as Desert Olive and Palo Blanco.
3 A **lotebush** (here: *Ziziphus obtusifolia*).

1931 U.S. Dept. Ag. *Misc. Pub.* 101.113, *Southwestern jujube* . . known locally as whitethorn and by a variety of Mexican names including . . paloblanco, is the most widely distributed and best known of these native species.
4 A **soapberry** (here: *Sapindus drummondii*).
    1960 Vines *Trees SW* 683, Vernacular names [for *Sapindus drummondii*] are Amole de Bolita, Tehuistle, Palo Blanco [etc]. **1975** Lamb *Woody Plants SW* 141, Western soapberry—*Sapindus drummondii* . . Jaboncillo, Palo blanco.

palo Cristo n
A **paloverde 1** (here: *Parkinsonia microphylla*).
    1931 U.S. Dept. Ag. *Misc. Pub.* 101.80, *Littleleaf paloverde* . . locally known as palo Christo [sic] . . is found in southern California, Lower California, southern Arizona, and Sonora.

palo de hierro n Also *arbol de hierro, palo fier(r)o* [Mex-Span, literally "iron wood (or tree)"]
=**desert ironwood.**
    1884 Sargent *Forests of N. Amer.* 56, *Olneya Tesota.* . . *Iron wood. Arbol de hierro.* California, . . southwestern Arizona. . . A small tree in the United States. **1894** *Amer. Anthropologist* 7.293 **AZ,** During the rest of the year the Indians devote themselves to . . the gathering of the fruit of the cactus, mesquite beans, and the bean of the *palo fiero* or iron-wood. **1897** Sudworth *Arborescent Flora* 263, *Olneya tesota.* . . *Common Names.* . . Arbol De Hierro (Cal.). Palo de Hierro (Ariz., etc.) **1910** Jepson *Silva CA* 261, The Desert Ironwood, or Arbol de Hierro of the Spanish Californians. . . Its wood is remarkably hard and heavy. **1945** Benson–Darrow *Manual SW Trees* 195, *Palo fierro.* . . Gravelly or sandy mesas or rocky foothills of the desert. **1975** Lamb *Woody Plants SW* 80, "Palo de Hierro". . . Seeds edible when roasted. Plant valuable for food, cover, erosion control. **1980** Little *Audubon Guide N. Amer. Trees W. Region* 498, It is known locally as "Ironwood" and . . as *palo de hierro.* The hard, dark brown wood . . is easily polished but dulls tools used to work it.

palo dulce n [MexSpan, literally "sweet wood"]
A **kidneywood** (here: *Eysenhardtia polystachya*).
    1975 Lamb *Woody Plants SW* 80, *Kidneywood* ("Palo dulce"). . . Supposed to have medicinal value for kidney, bladder infections.

paloduro n [MexSpan, literally "hard wood"]
1 A **hackberry.**
    1907 Cook *Border & Buffalo* 62 **SW,** There was a thicket of stunted hackberry and paloduro [sic], hard poles of chinawood, close to where the old camp-fire had been. **[1942** Santamaría *Dicc. Americanismos* 2.387, *Palo duro* . . En Nuevo Méjico . . se llama así una ulmácea *(Celtis caudata),* denominada en Méjico . . palo blanco. [=*Palo duro* . . an ulmaceous plant *(Celtis caudata)* so called in New Mexico . . in Mexico called . . palo blanco.]]
2 A **mountain mahogany 2** (here: *Cercocarpus montanus*).
    1976 Elmore *Shrubs & Trees SW* 62, *Alderleaf Mountain-mahogany.* . . The Spanish name palo duro means hard wood. The Navajo name signifies a plant "whose wood is as heavy as stone." They use its wood because of its hardness, as staffs to hold wool while spinning it.

palo fier(r)o See **palo de hierro**

palometa n [AmSpan]
Any of var **pompanos 1;** see quots.
    1896 U.S. Natl. Museum *Bulletin* 47.940, *Trachinotus glaucus.* . . Gaff-topsail Pámpano; Old Wife; Palometa. *Ibid* 941, *Trachinotus falcatus.* . . round Pámpano; Palometa. *Ibid* 942, *Trachinotus kennedyi.* . . Palometa. *Ibid* 943, *Trachinotus goodei.* . . Permit; Palometa. **1946** LaMonte *N. Amer. Game Fishes* 38, *Round Pompano.* . . Names: Indian River Permit, Palometa [etc]. *Ibid, Permit.* . . Names: Great Pompano . . Palometa. **1972** Sparano *Outdoors Encycl.* 378, *Permit*—Common Names: Permit, great pompano, round pompano, palometa.

palo santo n [MexSpan, literally "holy wood"]
A **yerba buena** (here: *Eriodictyon californicum*).
    1894 *Jrl. Amer. Folkl.* 7.94 **CA,** *Eriodictyon glutinosum,* . . palo santo, yerba santa.

palouse See **palouser 2**

palouse lightning n Cf *DS* BB19

1966 *DARE* FW Addit **neWA**, Palouse lightning—intestinal flu; Palouse hills are the hills of Whitman County, Washington.

palouser n [*Palouse* a farming region in eastern Washington] **chiefly NW**

1 A novice or greenhorn; a country bumpkin. Cf *DS* HH1, 15

1903 *Outing* 42.144, No, all were not British "remittance men," Arizona "palousers," and bank clerks on the trail. **1918** *DN* 5.27 **NW,** *Palouser. . .* A greenhorn; a country fellow. From the fact that the Palouse is a farming country.

2 also *palouse:* A makeshift lantern; see quots.

1918 *DN* 5.27 **NW,** *Palouser. . .* A lantern made by attaching a bale, horizontally, to an empty can and by inserting a candle through a hole in the side. **1923** *Outing* 81.257 **MT,** I found a bright new lard pail left by some former camper, and made a palouse (pronounced paloose), an Indian invention of inestimable value in camp. **1939** FWP *ID Lore* 243, Mining jargon in the Pierce City area: . . *Palouser*—a lard pail and candle converted into a lantern. **1958** McCulloch *Woods Words* 131 **Pacific NW,** *Palouser*—A lantern made by sticking a candle through a hole in a tin can. **1997** *DARE* File, [Reader letter to Random House Dictionaries:] A palouser was a primative latern made by turning a lard can, (or any other large can with a shiney inside), on its side, reconnect the bail from top to bottom, cut a star shaped hole in the "bottom" (side opposite the bail), and insert a candle up thru the hole. My Grandfather, of French/Canadian heritage, used to make "palousers" for light when we spent time in our primative hunting cabin in western Montana in the mid-30's and early 40's.

3 See quot. [Perh infl by **lalapalooza 1**]

1918 *DN* 5.27 **NW,** *Palouser. . .* A gorgeous sunset. From the circumstance that the sunsets in the Palouse are very magnificent.

paloverde n [MexSpan, literally "green wood"]

1 A tree or shrub of the genus *Parkinsonia.* For other names of var spp see **horse bean 2, Jerusalem thorn, male paloverde, palo Cristo**

1852 (1854) Bartlett *Personal Narr.* 2.188 **SW,** The vegetation consisted of mezquit and palo verde. **1884** Sargent *Forests of N. Amer.* 60, *Parkinsonia Torreyana. . .* Green-bark acacia. Palo verde. **1910** Jepson *Silva CA* 259, *Cercidium Torreyanum . .* Palo Verde. . . The leaves fall soon after they appear in March but the trees still present a cheerful appearance on account of the bright green bark (whence the Spanish name), which is all the more pleasing on account of the contrast with the parched desert scenery. **1931** U.S. Dept. Ag. *Misc. Pub.* 101.79, *Jerusalem-thorn . .* known also as girasol-thorn, horse-bean . . , paloverde [etc]. *Ibid* 80, *Border paloverde . .* known also as Texas paloverde . . ranges from southwestern Texas to southern California. . . *Littleleaf paloverde . .* is found in southern California, Lower California, southern Arizona, and Sonora. *Texas paloverde,* or dwarf paloverde . . often forms dense thickets in the Rio Grande region of southwestern Texas. **1936** Whitehouse *TX Flowers* 50, Horse Bean (*Parkinsonia aculeata*) is also known as Jerusalem-thorn, shower-of-gold, and palo verde, the latter meaning "green timber" from the green trunk and branches. **1944** (1967) McNichols *Crazy Weather* 24 **AZ,** Up ahead Havek trudged on past a paloverde tree, green of trunk, branch, and stem, and very beautiful against the white sand of the wash. **1945** Benson–Darrow *Manual SW Trees* 174, *Parkinsonia.* Palo Verde. This genus of palo verdes is well known in cultivation in southwestern cities and towns. *Ibid* 176, *Cercidium.* Palo Verde. The common native palo verdes belong to *Cercidium.* . . The genus is differentiated readily from *Parkinsonia* by the absence of long, narrow streamers. [*DARE* Ed: *Cercidium* spp are now included in *Parkinsonia.*] **1967** *DARE* Wildfl QR (Wills-Irwin) Pl.16D Inf **TX44,** Paloverde. **1969–70** *DARE* (Qu. T5, . . *Kinds of evergreens, other than pine*) Inf **AZ13,** Paloverde; **AZ16,** [pælo'vɝdi]; (Qu. T16, . . *Kinds of trees . . 'special'*) Inf **AZ16,** Paloverde—green stick. **1971** Dodge *100 Desert Wildflowers* 31, Blue palo-verde trees cover themselves with masses of yellow blossoms in April and May. . . During much of the year the trees are relatively leafless, the green bark of the trunk and branches taking over the function of leaves. The word palo-verde . . means "green stick" in Spanish, referring to the color of the bark. **1993** Kingsolver *Pigs in Heaven* 176 **AZ,** His eyes follow the golden, drawn-out shape of . . a coyote circling the trunk of a palo verde tree.

2 =**crucifixion thorn 3.**

1931 U.S. Dept. Ag. *Misc. Pub.* 101.116, Canotia (*Canotia hola-*

cantha), also called crucifixion thorn, Mohave-thorn, paloverde, and tree of Christ.

palsy-walsy adj, n |'pælzi 'wælzi| Also sp *palsey-walsey* [Redup of *palsy*] **esp Nth, N Midl, West**

Friendly, or giving the appearance of friendliness; a friend.

[**1930** *AmSp* 6.82, Call me Palsy.] [**1937** J. Curtis *There ain't no Justice* xxvi.287 (*OED2*), What are you having, palsy-walsy?] **1941** Smith *Gang's All Here* 266, There was nothing to do but I must go along with them. I even went into SRO [=Standing Room Only] with them. Talk about palsywalsies! **1947** *Philadelphia Bull.* 17 Feb. 8/3 (*OED2*), Army planes will drop on them pictures of General MacArthur and Hirohito in palsey-walsey attitudes, to convince them that hostilities have ceased. **1951** Johnson *Resp. to PADS 20* **DE** (*People who are very friendly toward each other:* "*They're _____.*") Palsy-walsy. **1965–70** *DARE* (Qu. II3, *Expressions to say that people are very friendly toward each other:* "*They're _____.*") 42 Infs, **esp Nth, C Atl, sCA,** (All) palsy-walsy; [**NJ2, PA29,** Palsy;] (Qu. II2a, *When two people begin to be friendly:* "*He has just recently _____ with John.*") Inf **CA119,** Become palsy-walsy; **NJ1,** Getting to be palsy-walsy; [**PA74,** Gotten palsy;] (Qu. II2b, *When two people have become friendly . .* "*It's been quite a while that Mary and Jane have been _____.*") 9 Infs, **esp Nth,** Palsy-walsy; [**CT5, MT2, PA29,** Palsy;] (Qu. AA8, *When people make too much of a show of affection in a public place . .* "*There they were at the church supper _____ [with each other].*") Inf **CO27,** Palsy-walsy. **1995** *DARE* File **cwCA** (as of 1950s), I wouldn't want to get too palsy-walsy ['pælzi 'wælzi] with them.

pam See **palm**

pa'meeter, pa'metter See **palmetto**

pamilla See **palmilla 1**

pammy See **palm**

pammy Christy See **palma Christi**

pampano See **pompano 1**

pan n[1] [Var, prob by folk-etym, of **palm** (pronounced [pæm])] The palm of the hand.

1961 Kurath–McDavid *Pronc. Engl.* 142, In the folk speech of the South and the South Midland *palm* has been largely replaced by *pan.* **c1970** Pederson *Dial. Surv. Rural GA* seGA (*Palm*) 6 infs, [pæn]; 1 inf, [pɑən]. [4 of 7 infs Black] **1986** Pederson *LAGS Concordance* (*Palm*) 51 infs, **Gulf Region,** Pan. [21 of 51 infs Black]

pan n[2] See **panguingue**

panacake See **pannicake**

panada n Pronc-spp *panady, penaidie, pernady* [*OED2 panada* 1625 →, *panade* 1598 →] *old-fash*

A soft dish consisting primarily of sweetened bread or crackers soaked in boiling water, served esp to invalids.

1847 (1852) Crowen *Amer. Cookery* 410, *Panada.*—Break stale bread or soda crackers small, . . and pour boiling water over . . ; add sugar and nutmeg. . . Raisins . . may be put in with the bread, when there is no objection to the effect produced by them—they being laxative. **1867** Harris *Sut Lovingood Yarns* 250 **TN,** Oh yu dam puney, panady eatin siterzens. **1871** (1975) Levy *Jewish Cookery* 122, Diet for Invalids. . . *Panada, made in five minutes.*—Set a little water on the fire, add a glass of white wine, some sugar, a scrape of nutmeg and lemon peel, and some grated bread crumbs. . . When of a proper thickness to drink, take it off. **1879** (1965) Tyree *Housekeeping in Old VA* 482, *Diet and remedies for the sick. . . Panada.* Lay six nice crackers in a bowl. Sprinkle over them powdered sugar and a pinch of salt. . . Pour boiling water over the crackers, and let them remain near the fire half an hour. Then add a teaspoonful of good French brandy. **1890** James *Mother James' Cooking* 466, *Food for the sick. . .* Cracker Panada. **1923** *DN* 5.237 **swWI,** *Penaidie. . .* Bread crumbs served with butter, sugar, and hot water. (Fr. *pain?*) "He's feelin' kind o' bad; had some penaidie for breakfast." **1944** *PADS* 2.20 **sAppalachians,** *Pernady* [pɚ'nedɪ]. . . A dish prepared with bread crumbs and sorghum, and placed in the oven to heat or brown.

panas See **panhas**

pan bread n Also *pan biscuit, pan corn bread* Cf **skillet bread, spider bread**
Any of var quick breads cooked in a frying pan; see quots.
1918 *DN* 5.27 NW, *Panbread*. . . Baking-powder bread, usually cooked by the open fire. General. **1958** McCulloch *Woods Words* 131 **Pacific NW,** *Pan bread*—Usually a pretty tough looking kind of biscuit or bread made in a frying pan set on the coals of a camp fire. **1966** Dakin *Dial. Vocab. Ohio R. Valley* 2.315 **IN, KY,** *Corn bread*. . . [2 of c200 infs] *pan bread.* **1966–70** *DARE* (Qu. H14, *Bread that's made with cornmeal*) Inf **FL49,** Pan bread—corn bread cooked in the stove; **KY57,** Pan corn bread—made in a skillet; **MS2,** Corn bread—different kinds: muffins, pan bread, pone bread; (Qu. H18, . . *Special kinds of bread*) Inf **CO27,** Pan bread is spider bread; **LA33,** Pan bread—not as crispy as the French bread; **OK53,** Pan bread; (Qu. H19, *What do you mean by a biscuit? How are they made?*) Inf **CA77,** Pan biscuit—called if men are camping, or pan bread; **CA170,** Pan biscuits; **WI20,** Pan biscuits. **c1970** Pederson *Dial. Surv. Rural GA* (*What other things are made from corn meal?*) 1 inf, **seGA,** Pan bread. [Inf Black] **1986** Pederson *LAGS Concordance,* 1 inf, **ceGA,** Pan bread—cooked in iron frying pan; 1 inf, **swGA,** Pan bread; 1 inf, **seLA,** Pan bread—wheat flour. **1993** *DARE* File, Among other things, my family says . . "loaf bread" (as opposed to pan bread or pan biscuits) because Mom grew up in Silsbee Texas.

pancake n
1 A **heelsplitter:** either *Lasmigona complanata* or *Potamilus alata.*
1908 Kunz–Stevenson *Book of the Pearl* 73 **Missip Valley,** Other well-known species are the pancake (*Lampsilis alatus*), the maple-leaf (*Quadrula wardi*), and the hackle-back (*Symphynota complanata*). **1941** *AmSp* 16.156 **Missip Valley,** There are many varieties of fresh-water mussels, but the button cutter is ignorant of any technical terminology for them. His names are mostly descriptive and frequently picturesque. The following list gives the common names as applied by the cutter and fisher of shells. . . Arkansas[,] . . Pancake [etc]. **1982** U.S. Fish & Wildlife Serv. *Fresh-Water Mussels* 2.38, White Heelsplitter. Pancake. Historically widespread, common; now sporadic, increasingly rare. **1992** Cummings–Mayer *Field Guide Freshwater Mussels Midwest* 92, *Lasmigona complanata*. . . Pancake. . . Shell large, rounded, and compressed, very thin in young individuals, becoming thicker in adults. *Ibid* 124, *Potamilus alatus* [sic]. . . Pancake. . . Shell large, elongate, laterally compressed and somewhat rectangular, thin in young shells to moderately thick in older individuals.
2 =**belly-flop 2.**
1965–70 *DARE* (Qu. EE29, *When swimmers are diving and one comes down flat onto the water, that's a* _____) Infs **NJ30,** 46, **NY211,** 220, **OH42, PA94, VA93, WA3,** Pancake.
3 A children's game; see quot.
1970 *DARE* (Qu. EE33, . . *Outdoor games . . that children play*) Inf **KY85,** Pancake—a version of leapfrog where you slap the other player on the rump as you jump over him in the opposite direction as leapfrog.

pancake cactus See **pancake pear**

pancake flipper (or lifter) See **pancake turner**

pancake pear n Also *pancake cactus* [Prob from the fancied resemblance of the flat yellowish joints to pancakes]
A **prickly pear 1** (here: *Opuntia chlorotica*).
1940 Benson *Cacti AZ* 4.62, *Opuntia chlorotica*. . . Pancake pear. Arborescent prickly pear . . 3 to 6 feet high and several feet in diameter. **1957** Jaeger *N. Amer. Deserts* 141, On the mountain sides and in rocky canyons grow the pancake cactus (*Opuntia chlorotica* . .), and a number of low-growing nipple cacti. *Ibid* 250, *Pancake cactus*. . . A cactus . . of tree-like form . . and formed of large disk-like joints 3 to 8 inches in diameter. The spines are close-set and yellow. **1974** Munz *Flora S. CA* 316, *Pancake-Pear.* . . Joints circular to broadly obovate, yellow-green, . . flat. . . Usually on dry rocky walls, 3000–5500 ft.

pancake plant n [See quot 1924]
A **mallow B:** usu *Malva rotundifolia,* but also *M. sylvestris.*
1900 Lyons *Plant Names* 238, *M[alva] sylvestris.* . . Cheese-flower, Cheese-cake plant . . Pancake plant. **1924** *Amer. Botanist* 30.105, The best known and most abundant species is *Malva rotundifolia* an insignificant weed but known to children as "cheeses," and "pancake-plant" because of the round flat groups of ovaries which are edible when

young. **1959** Carleton *Index Herb. Plants* 89, *Pancake-plant:* Malva rotundifolia.

pancake squash n
A **pattypan squash.**
1968 *DARE* (Qu. I23, . . *Kinds of squash*) Inf **VA28,** Pancake squash—[same as] pattypan.

pancake turner n Also *pancake flipper, ~ lifter;* for addit varr see quots **widespread, but somewhat less freq Sth, S Midl, PA** See Map Cf **cake turner, egg ~**
A spatula.
1847 (1852) Crowen *Amer. Cookery* 34 NY, Fish should be turned with a broad blade knife, or a pancake turner. **1946** *AmSp* 21.55, *American*. . . Pancake-turner (never heard in English). **1954** *Harder Coll.* **cwTN,** *Pancake turner*. . . Instrument used to turn over frying food. **c1960** *Wilson Coll.* **csKY,** *Pancake turner*. . . A kitchen utensil used to turn frying eggs, pancakes, etc. **1965–70** *DARE* (Qu. F3, *When you're frying things—for example, eggs—you turn them over with a* _____) 207 Infs, **widespread, but somewhat less freq Sth, S Midl, PA,** Pancake turner; **IL98,** Pancake turner-over; **CA2,** Pancake flapper; **CA162,** Pancake flipper; **IL63, VA42,** Pancake lifter; **NC84,** Pancake spatula. **1968** *DARE* FW Addit NV, Pancake turner—what you use when you turn things you are frying.

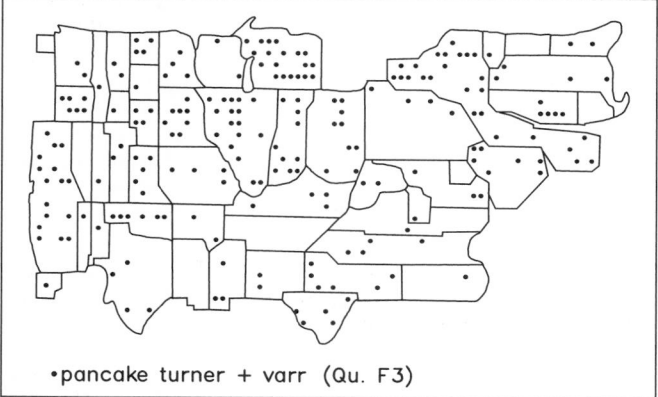

•pancake turner + varr (Qu. F3)

pan corn bread See **pan bread**

pan cream n
1952 Tracy *Coast Cookery* 295, *Pan cream.* Thick cream skimmed from the top of fresh milk. Much thicker than city "heavy cream."

pandowdy n chiefly NEng Cf **apple pandowdy, pan pie 1**
A **deep-dish pie** or cobbler, usu made with apples.
1830 in 1834 Smith *Life Jack Downing* 107 ME, You dont know how queer it looks to see . . politics and pan-dowdy . . jumbled up together. **1838** Kettell *Yankee Notions* 221, I doubt what learned Thebans call / The same, but Yankee natives all / Have *christened* it Pan-Dowdy. [Footnote:] This rustical and true Yankee dish . . is a prodigious apple-pie, with a brown crust, baked in a deep pan, *unde nomen* [=whence the name]. Crust and contents are crushed into a chaos; and when served up cold, as the Doctor says, *credite Pisones* [=believe [me], Pisos], it is fit for an Archduke. **1847** *Knickerbocker* 29.498 eMA, Oh! those were joyous olden times,/ The times of which we've read,/ Of good old-fashioned pandowdy,/ Of rye-and-Indian bread. **1852** Hawthorne *Blithedale* 241 NEng, Hollingsworth [would] fill my plate from the great dish of pandowdy. **1873** *Harper's New Mth. Mag.* 46.593, He should relish an old-fashioned pandowdy, such as his mother used to make forty years ago. **1913** *DN* 4.55 ME, *Apple-dowdy*. . . A kind of pudding made of apples with bread or batter, baked in a deep dish for a long time, and cut so that the crust comes in the middle. It is eaten with sugar and cream. Also *pan-dowdy.* **1949** Kurath *Word Geog.* 21 eNEng, *Dowdy, pan dowdy* . . is the name of a desert [sic] made of fruit and sweetened dough—a sort of cobbler—that has currency on Massachusetts Bay and in New Hampshire and Maine, and is not unknown on Cape Cod and Narragansett Bay. **1979** Flagg *Cape Cod Cooking* 121 eMA, *Rhubarb Pan Dowdy.* . . Butter a baking dish. Into it put the rhubarb. . . Pour the batter over the rhubarb and bake in a 350° oven until crusty and brown on top.

pan dulce n [AmSpan] **SW** Cf **pão doce**
Any of var sweet breads or pastries.

    1922 Bogan *Ceremonial Dances Yaqui* 27 **csAZ,** Booths for the sale of soda waters, *pan dulce,* pies and coffee appear as if by magic. **1932** Bentley *Spanish Terms* 176, *Pan dulce.* . . Sweet bread; sweet meats. The phrase is only occasionally used by English-speaking people when referring to the particular Mexican confections to be found in border towns. **1967** *DARE* (Qu. H18, . . *Special kinds of bread*) Inf **TX**3, Pan dulces [ˌpan ˈdulses]; (Qu. H32, . . *Fancy rolls and pastries*) Inf **TX**28, Pan dulce. **1996** *NADS Letters* **TX** (as of c1960s), What I remember most about pan dulce [pan dulse] is that it did not seem sweet. . . I was impressed with the colors and the variety of shapes and textures. . . Some varieties look like kaiser rolls; others look more like something made with strudel dough. **1997** *Ibid* **cwCA,** "Pan dulce," the sweet breads you can buy at Mexican grocery stores in (at least) Northern California. I've seen pan dulce in small markets since I moved to San Francisco Bay Area and environs, 12 years ago. *Ibid* **sCA,** Pan dulce is sweet bread in *any* Mexican bakery in Southern California. *Ibid* **TX,** I am a native of El Paso, TX, which is the only place I have ever seen "pan dulce" or "Mexican sweetbread." It is an airy, yellowish, mildly sweet circular thin flat bread. . . What makes it really sweet is the "icing" on the top.

panel n [Folk-etym for **pan** n[1]] *chiefly among Black speakers*
The palm of the hand.

    c1970 Pederson *Dial. Surv. Rural GA* (*Palm*) 1 inf, [pæ·nə]. [Inf Black] **1986** Pederson *LAGS Concordance,* 15 infs, **Gulf Region,** Panel = palm. [12 of 15 infs Black]

panel entry n
In coal mining: =**entry** 2.

    [**1947** Natl. Coal Assoc. *Gloss.* 16, *Panel*—A group of rooms; also any large rectangular block of coal.] **1973** *PADS* 59.35 **eKY, sWV,** An *entry cut* at a right angle to the *main entry* from which *rooms* are *neck*ed *off* and [which] serves as a *haulage road* to the main haulage system. . . [P]anel entry.

panel fence n Also *paneling fence* **chiefly Sth** See Map
Any of var types of fences made in sections (as a rail fence); now esp a picket fence or board fence.

    1800 in 1969 Herndon *Wm. Tatham Tobacco* 10 **VA,** The *worm* or *pannel fence, originally of Virginia,* consists of logs or malled rails from about four to six or eight inches thick, and eleven feet in length. A good fence consists of ten rails and a rider, or perhaps nine rails and two riders. **1858** Warder *Hedges* 113, A half-acre lot, with a seven-foot panel-fence on one side, and a hedge on the other. **1931** Webb *Gt. Plains* 281, The fence might be made straight, thus avoiding many of the defects of the worm fence, by setting posts upright and in pairs, tying each pair together at the top, and placing the rails end to end. This was called a panel fence. **1940** U.S. Dept. Ag. *Farmers' Bulletin* 1832.30, [Caption:] A panel fence suitable for stony land. [*DARE* Ed: Photo shows fence of rails or poles fastened to posts which are supported by a slanted brace.] **1949** Faulkner *Knight's Gambit* 134 **MS,** They would ride past mile after mile of white-painted panel fence. **1965–70** *DARE* (Qu. L61, *Fences made of solid logs, now or in the past*) Inf **NC**49, Panel [pænl] fence; (Qu. L64, *The kind of wooden fence that's built around a garden or near a house*) Infs **NC**68, **PA**71, **SC**3, **VA**49, Panel fence; **DC**8, Panel [pænl] fence; **MD**40, Panel [pænl] fence [FW: that which others call picket or paling]; **GA**80, Wood panel fence—slats horizontal or vertical; (Qu. L65, . . *Kinds of fences*) Inf **LA**15, Panel fence—made with one-by-sixes about six or eight inches apart; **MD**3, Panel fences—posts with milled lumber boards running between horizontally, usually three with spaces between; **OR**7, Panel fence—loose panels—often one-by-sixes—set to posts, nailed to posts; [**UT**7, Panel fencing]. **c1970** Pederson *Dial. Surv. Rural GA* (*Different kinds of wood fences*) 2 infs, **seGA,** Panel. **1970** Tarpley *Blinky* 124 **neTX,** *Fence made of slats standing upright.* . . pale fence, panel fence, plank fence, railing fence [5 of 200 infs]. **1976** Brown *Gloss. Faulkner* 144, *Panel fence* . . a fence made of posts set in the ground with planks between them. A favorite design uses horizontal top and bottom planks, with two planks crossing each other to form an X between them. Panel fences are usually painted white and are characteristic of horse farms, pretentious estates, etc. **1986** Pederson *LAGS Concordance* **Gulf Region** (*What kinds of fences do you have around the yards and gardens?*) 3 infs, Panel fence; 1 inf, Panel fence—wood boards, vertical; 1 inf, Panel fence—planks come to a point; 1 inf, Panel fence—four inch wide boards, palings; 1 inf, Panel fence—a board fence, substantial; 1 inf, Panel fence—two types: per-

pendicular or longways; 1 inf, Picket panel fence; 1 inf, Panel fence—pointed at top; [1 inf, Panel fencing;] 1 inf, Panel—of fence; 1 inf, Panel—fence; 1 inf, Panel—fence, picket fence; 1 inf, A bunch of pickets together makes the panel; 4 infs, Paneling fence.

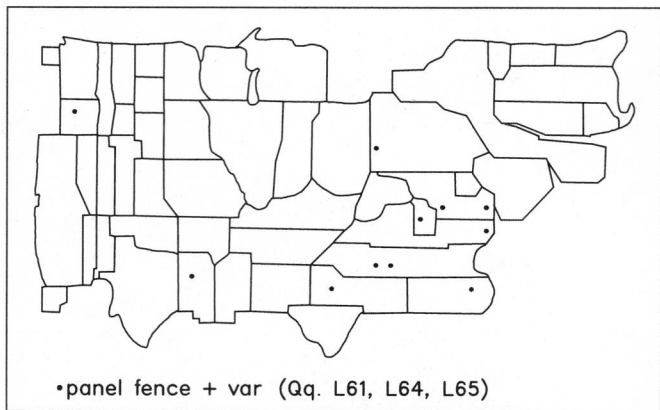

•panel fence + var (Qq. L61, L64, L65)

pan-fried potatoes n pl Also *pan-fried raw potatoes, pan fries* **chiefly NEast, Midl** See Map Cf **American fried potatoes, cottage fried ~, fresh fried ~, home fried ~**
Potatoes that have been sliced and fried in a small amount of fat.

    1940 Brown *Amer. Cooks* 919 **WI,** *Pan-Fried Raw Potatoes*—1 Quart Raw Sliced Potatoes . . salt . . fat . . pepper. Peel potatoes and slice very thin. Cover with cold water. . . Heat fat in spider, add potatoes, seasoning, cover tightly, and let steam slowly. . . When browned at bottom, turn and brown on other side. Chopped onions may be added. **1945** in 1953 Botkin–Harlow *Treas. Railroad Folkl.* 348, The baked beans and bread puddings, the pork chops and pan-fried potatoes . . sustained many and many a famished brakeman and conductor. **1950** *WELS* **WI** (*Kinds of fried potatoes*) 1 Inf, Pan-fried—cooked potatoes, fried; 1 Inf, Pan-fried; 1 Inf, Pan-fried—in a small amount of fat. **1965–70** *DARE* (Qu. H47) 40 Infs, **chiefly NEast, Midl,** Pan-fried (potatoes); **NC**30, **WV**11, Pan fries.

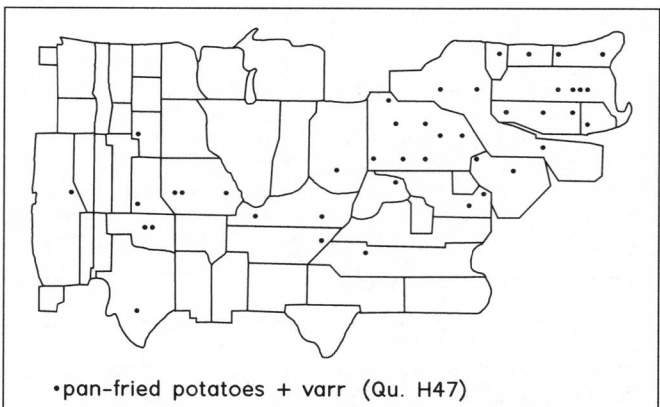

•pan-fried potatoes + varr (Qu. H47)

panga See **peng**

panguingue n Also *pangingi, pang(u)ingui;* pronc-spp *panginky, panginny, panguinea;* abbr *pan* [Tagalog *pangguinggui*] **AK, NW, CA** Cf **cooncan**
A card game similar to rummy; see quot 1991.

    1905 (1906) Beach *Spoilers* 70 **AK,** Outside in the main gambling-room there were but few women. Men crowded in dense masses about the faro lay-out, the wheel, craps, the Klondike game, pangingi, and the card-tables. **1913** *Official Rules of Card Games* 10, *Pangingui. The Pack.*—Eight decks, with the eights, nines and tens of each suit omitted, as in Conquian. (In some localities as few as five decks are used.) *Number of Players.*—Any number may play. **1953** *AmSp* 28.117 **Pacific coast** (as of late 1940s) [Carnie talk], *Panguinea.* . . A card game employing several decks, usually the cheapest game in a gambling place. **1966–69** *DARE* (Qu. DD35, . . *Card games*) Inf **CA**7, Panginny; **CA**168, [ˌpænˈgini]; **CA**147, Pan—for panginky; **MT**1, **WA**22, Pan.

1967 *AK Sportsman* June 27 (1991 Tabbert *Dict. Alaskan Engl.*), For recreation there is a choice between pool and pan nightly at Jim Huntington's, the Thursday night movie, and Bingo on Saturday night. **1973** *All-Alaska Weekly* (Fairbanks) Dec 7 (Tabbert *Dict. Alaskan Engl.*), In fact in 1901, when the first gambling raid took place in Fairbanks, there were no moves by law enforcement officers to move against pinochle and panguingui. . . Panguingui, or "pan" as it is commonly called, requires seven decks of cards and seven players. **1976** Maclean *River Runs Through* 186 wMT (as of 1919), The ones I watched were playing "pan" and pinochle, and they were playing for "chits," not chips. **1991** Tabbert *Dict. Alaskan Engl.* 236, Panguingue[,] pan—A card game which developed in the Philippines as a multiple-player variation of con-quian (also called *coon-can*), the source of all rummy-type games. It is played with from five to eight combined Spanish decks (i.e., without the eights, nines, and tens) by six to fifteen players. The object is to meld groupings of cards, with certain melds being more valuable. It became popular in the U.S. West in the late nineteenth century and was transplanted to Alaska during the gold rush.

panhagen n Also *panhaden* [See quot 1842] **NEast** Cf **pauhagen**
=**menhaden 1.**

   1842 DeKay *Zool. NY* 4.260, This fish is known under the various names of *Bony-fish*, . . *Panhagen* and *Menhaden;* the last being the name given by the Manhattans, and *Panhagen* (pronounced *panhangen*) the Narraganset epithet. **1873** in 1878 Smithsonian Inst. *Misc. Coll.* 14.2.33 NEng, *Brevoortia menhaden* . . panhaden, panhagen. **1889** (1971) Farmer *Americanisms* 75, *Bony Fish (Alosa menhaden)*. . . It has many names, amongst which are . . *panhagen, menhaden* (Massachusetts and Rhode Island).

panhandle grape n [See quot 1970]
A **grape** (here: *Vitis acerifolia*).

   1938 Van Dersal *Native Woody Plants* 337, Panhandle [grape] (*Vitis doaniana*). **1970** Correll *Plants TX* 1017, *Vitis acerifolia* . . Panhandle grape, bush grape. . . In low open woods in stream bottoms, and on dunes and rocky slopes in Tex. Panhandle, s.e., to n.w. part of n.-cen. Tex. **1976** Bailey–Bailey *Hortus Third* 1162, *[Vitis] acerifolia* . . Bush g[rape], panhandle g[rape].

panhas n Usu |ˈpɑnˌhɔs, ˈpɑnˌhɑs, ˈpɔnˌhɔs, ˈpʌnˌhɔs|; also |ˈpɑnˌhɔrs| Pronc-spp *panas, panhoss, pawnhaus, ponhaws, ponhorse, ponhoss, pony-horse;* for addit pronc and sp varr see quots [PaGer *pannhas*, literally "pan-rabbit"; in some areas perh directly from Ger dial *panhaas*] **scattered, but chiefly N Midl, esp PA** See Map Cf **headcheese 1, pan-rabbit**
=**scrapple.**

   1869 *Atlantic Mth.* 24.483 sePA, Some make *pawn-haus* from the liquor in which the pudding meat was boiled, adding thereto corn-meal. **1896** *DN* 1.422, *Pon-hoss.* . . Place, Myersville, Md., and Gettysburg, Pa.; means *scrapple* (see dictionary). . . Used to hear college students jocosely call it "pan rabbit." . . Strange to say that in this community (Tannersville, Pa.) where Pa. Dutch abounds, "scrapple" is the word used; while in the two places above, where Pa. Dutch is unknown, "ponhoss" is the word used. **1908** *German Amer. Annals* 10.39 sePA, *Ponhaws.* . . A dish like fried mush, made by boiling buckwheat flour and corn meal with the juice of fried meat, and sometimes scraps of pork. When cold this is cut into slices and fried. "We had ponhaws for breakfast." **c1910** in 1953 *PA Dutchman* 15 Feb 9, We made "ponhaus." **1923** *DN* 5.236 swWI, *Ponhaws.* . . Scrapple. **1942** Warnick *Garrett Co. MD* 12 nwMD (as of 1900–18), *Ponhoss* . . scrapple. **1942** McAtee *Dial. Grant Co. IN* 50 (as of 1890s), *Ponhoss* (phonetic spelling, both o's the same) . . scrapple. **1944** *PADS* 2.47 NC, *Pan has* [pɑn hɑs]. . . Liver-pudding. Caldwell and Catawba cos., N.C. Rare. **1946** *PADS* 6.24 swVA, *Pon hosh* [ˈpɑn ˈhɑʃ, -ˈhɔʃ]. . . Grease from hog-killing mixed with corn meal, fried, and sliced. "Scrapple." "Solidified liquid leavings from liver pudding, etc., cooked (fried) with corn meal." Rural region of Salem, 1940, 1946. **1949** *AmSp* 24.112 cnGA, nwSC, *Ponhoss.* . . A kind of scrapple. **1949** Kurath *Word Geog.* 32, *Ponhaws*, a synonym of *(Philadelphia) scrapple*, is in use from the Pennsylvania German section westward to Ohio and has survived also on the upper reaches of the Potomac in Maryland and West Virginia. **1952** Brown *NC Folkl.* 1.578 c,eNC, *Pon horse.* . . Corn meal cooked in stock from liver pudding. **1953** *PA Dutchman* Apr 4 (as of 1932), Would I supervise the preparing and cooking the panhaws? **c1955** Reed–Person *Ling. Atlas Pacific NW*, 1 inf, Panhoss. **1962** Atwood *Vocab. TX* 83, *Ponhaws* (a pork mixture) occurs only among in-

formants of German background in Kerr, Kendall, and Bexar Counties, in the recorded form *panas*. **1965–70** *DARE* (Qu. H43, *Foods made from parts of the head and inner organs of an animal*) Inf CO27, [ˈpɒhɑs]—scrapple seasoned with coriander; MO34, [ˈpɑn,uᵛuˑs]—made with cornmeal, some might call it scrapple; PA110, [pʌnhɔs]—with cornmeal, scrapple same thing; PA176, [panhɑs]—with cornmeal, scrapple same thing; PA210, [ˈpʌnhɔs]—buckwheat flour, wheat flour, and cornmeal; PA213, [ˈpʌnhɔs]—with cornmeal; WV8, [panhɒːz] is made like scrapple but without meat; scrapple is made with cornmeal, broth, and meat; WV11, [panhɑəs]—with cornmeal; MO12, [ˈpan,hɑst]; MD30, [ˈpɑnhɔs]—broth and some of the meat mixed with cornmeal; MD17, [ˈpɔn,hɔz]—old-time word for scrapple; OH90, Panhas; MD19, 24, Pondhorse; IN23, [ˈpɔnhɔs]—broth from pigs' feet cooked with cornmeal; PA136, Scrapple—called [ˈpʌn,hɑus]; (Qu. H24, . . *Names or nicknames . . for boiled cornmeal*) Inf IL134, [panhɔs]; PA9, [panhɔs]—mush with pork and the broth of pork; (Qu. H25, . . *Names or nicknames . . for fried cornmeal*) Inf MO12, [ˈpan,hɑˑs]; PA206, [pɔnhɔs]; VA30, [ˈpænhɔs]—they use the broth from the liver pudding fried with cornmeal; IL29, [ˈpɔnhɔs]—made with meat broth; IL5, [panhaus]—German dish with fried cornmeal, also has meat; CA64, Panhas—fried cornmeal seasoned with pork, served with honey, a German dish; (Qu. H45, *Dishes made with meat, fish, or poultry that everybody around here would know, but that people in other places might not*) Inf IL5, [panˈhaus]—German; PA143, 210, Panhas; PA242, [ˈpanhɔs]—similar to scrabble; (Qu. H65, *Foreign foods favored by people around here*) Inf IL5, Panhas—like polenta, German. **1967–68** *DARE* Tape IL5, The German dish is panhas [ˈpɑᶜn,hɑᶜˑs]. . . We make it of pork. We mix lean pork in mush, cooked mush, in mush, and then fry it; MD24, We would add cornmeal and flour . . and make a, like a mush, only it was flavored with the broth from the hog head. And then it was called panhas [ˈpɑˑən,hɔs]. . . It was more of a breakfast food. It would be fried crisp in a skillet; MD26, When we butcher, why, we just take the broth off the cooking—the head meat—and put salt and pepper in it and we put so much flour and so much cornmeal in it and we call it panhas [ˈpɑˑn,hɔɚs]. **1968** *DARE* FW Addit csNY, Pannhorse [ˈpan,hɔrs]—food made by a German family near here with all sorts of pork innards in it. Like headcheese. Inf is uncertain he is pronouncing this word right. **1971** Wood *Vocab. Change* 44 Sth, *Ponhaws* and a phonological variant *ponhoss* occur irregularly in the region; its reasonably frequent occurrence in Louisiana may indicate German influences there. **1973** Allen *LAUM* 1.288 (as of c1950), *Head cheese.* . . *Ponhaws* lives in the speech of a Nebraska housewife whose father came from Maryland. . . Nineteen respondents check *ponhoss* (spelled *panihoss* on the checklist and respelled by two respondents . . as *poonhuss*). **1973** Flach *Yankee German–America* 17 csTX, There would be three kinds of sausage—meat, liver and blood. The first was smoked, the other two cooked in that great copper kettle. During this process the water would boil down and to this juice cornmeal would be added to make pannas. **1982** *Barrick Coll.* csPA, *Panhoss*—[pron. [ˈpanhɑs]] scrapple[,] common. **1990** *Inside UVA* (Charlottesville VA) 15 Dec 2/1 wVA (as of c1940), Pony-horse was another product made from hogs. **1993** Thomas Co. Hist. Soc. (KS) *Prairie Winds* Mar 7 (as of c1890), 'Pon Hos' . . was made from the bits and pieces left over after a butchering.

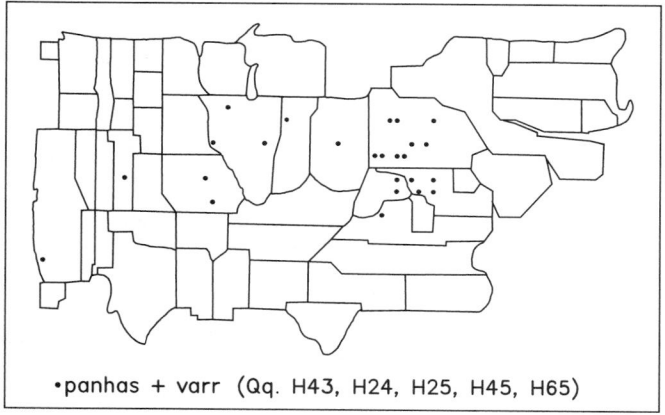

•panhas + varr (Qq. H43, H24, H25, H45, H65)

panicake See **pannicake**

panic grass n
Std: a grass of the genus *Panicum*, or of one of the genera such as *Dichanthelium* that were formerly included in this genus.

Also called **witchgrass**. For other names of var spp see **corn grass 2, deer-tongue ~, dogtooth ~, fool hay 1, guinea corn 2, ~ grass 1, hurrah grass b, Johnson ~ 2, maiden cane, millet, mutton cane 2, old-witch grass, quack ~ 3, redtop 1d, sour grass, switch ~, tickle ~, torpedo ~, tumbleweed, vine mesquite, witch's hair**

panini n [See quots 1929, 1948] **HI**

A **prickly pear 1** (here: *Opuntia ficus-indica*).

1928 Pan-Pacific Research Inst. *Jrl.* 3.2.8 **HI**, Opuntia, prickly pear, panini. 1929 Pope *Plants HI* 153, The Hawaiian name "Panini" [for *Opuntia ficus-indica*] has been explained to the writer as a corruption of Manini, the Hawaiian name for Don Marin, a resident [formerly of Mexico], who introduced plants in Hawaii between 1791 and 1837. 1948 Neal *In Gardens HI* 532, Panini. Opuntia megacantha [=*O. ficus-indica*]. . . Spiny, having one to five white, inch-long spines, as well as brown wool and a few yellow bristles, borne on each cushion. *Ibid* 533, The Hawaiian name, panini, means "very unfriendly" *(nini)* "wall" *(pa)*. 1951 *AmSp* 26.23 **HI**, Other common Hawaiian words are . . *panini* (cactus). 1965 Neal *Gardens HI* 607, Pa-nini. . . About 15 feet high. [*Ibid* 608, This is the common wild cactus of Hawaii, where it was introduced possibly about 1800.]

paniolo n Also *paniola*; rarely *paniolo pipi* [Haw pronc-sp for Span *español* Spanish, Spaniard] **HI**

A cowboy.

1892 Hawaiian Hist. Soc. *Papers* 2.26, At Waimea, the Mexican Hispano-Indian found his home and occupation. . . He was called generically "Paniolo" or "Espagnol," the word that now-a-days means "cowboy." 1932 Hawaiian Hist. Soc. *Annual Rept. for 1931* 17, These men were of Spanish, Mexican or Indian origin. The Hawaiians called them *paniolo* from the word *espagnol*. Indeed, today the Hawaiian word for cowboy is *paniolo*. 1938 Reinecke *Hawaiian Loanwords* 27, Paniola. . . Cowboy. S[eldom]. [*Ibid* 29, Pipi. . . [Eng. *beef*.] A head of neat cattle. . . F[requently].] 1951 *AmSp* 26.22 **HI**, Names of nationalities are generally transliterations, such as . . *paniolo* for Spaniard (*español;* the first cowboys in the islands were Mexicans, and a *paniolo* came to mean a cowpuncher). 1967 *DARE* (Qu. HH28, *Names and nicknames . . for people of foreign background*) Inf **HI**4, Paniolo = Spanish; Hawaiian cowboy = paniolo pipi. [*DARE* Ed: literally "Spanish beef" or "Spanish head of cattle"] 1980 Bushnell *Water of Kane* 246 **HI** (as of 1876-77), The paniolos, cracking whips, whooping, whistling, chased the animals up the slope toward a corral under the trees near the kitchen tent. 1984 Sunset *HI Guide* 85, Paniolo—cowboy.

pank v [Perh blend of *pack* + *spank,* but cf Norw, Dan *banke,* Sw *banka* knock, tap, beat] **chiefly nMI; also PA, Upstate NY**

To pack or tamp down; to crush.

1937 in 1975 W3 File **nwMI**, Our snow is often too deep to dig a path, so we don snowshoes and stamp along snow, and finally it becomes hard and crusted enough to walk in without snowshoes. The process we call 'panking' a path. . . It is especially prevalent among Cornish people. . . It is especially used in the northern part of the Upper Peninsula of Michigan. 1957 *Sat. Eve. Post Letters* **nwMI**, Another word we have is pank. It means to pat down something, as, "He panked down the sand around his sand castle." 1966 *DARE* (Qu. KK21, *When something hollow is crushed by a heavy weight, or by a fall: "They ran the wagon over the coffee pot and _____."*) Inf **MI**33, Panked [pæŋkt] it—also for like crushing a milk carton. 1966 *DARE* File **nwMI**, Pank = tamp. To pank snow in the hands to form a snowball; to pank the earth with a tamper. Used in the Upper Peninsula of Michigan and in coal mining in . . Penna. 1967 *DARE* FW Addit **nwMI**, Pank [pæŋk]—Pank the snow down. Pank the earth over the potatoes. Pank the pillow. 1972 *DARE* File **nwMI**, Pank [pæŋk] = to pack down (snow) with a shovel. Current. 1975 *Ibid* **nwMI**, Pank [pæŋk]—To tamp, pack; said of sand, snow, hair, etc. Gogebic, Ontonagon, Iron, Houghton Counties, Upper Peninsula, Mich. 1980 *NYT Article Letters* **nePA**, When I was a little girl growing up in Nanticoke, Pa., in the early '40's, it was a must to (s)pank the snow with the back of the shovel when building a solid fort for a snowball fight. *Ibid* **nePA** (as of 1920s), When I was a child in Scranton Pennsylvania in the early 1920's, we *panked* down the snow for sledding. *Ibid* **NY**, I told my grandson last month that his sand castle would be improved if he 'panked' the sand down harder. In upstate New York, where I lived for many years, it was used in connection with snow but additionally with sand or dirt for planting. 1993 *Detroit Free Press* (MI) 30 July sec F 3/3 **Upper Peninsula MI,** *Pank:* compound word formed from "pack" and "spank." Describes what you do with the sole of a boot or flat of a shovel to get snow to stay

where you want. "Pank it down." 1997 *NADS Letters* **nePA**, Pank. . . We used it to mean "to flatten" or "to smoosh" and we use it in association with snow, clay (like Play-Doh), bread dough, etc. *Ibid* **neMN**, "Pank" is used in the Iron Range of Northern Minnesota . . [to mean] to pat down the snow.

pan mush n
=**fried mush.**

1967 *DARE* (Qu. H25, . . *Names or nicknames . . for fried cornmeal*) Inf **PA**40, Fried mush or pan mush.

pannicake n Also sp *panicake, pan(n)acake, panniecake, pannycake* [Varr of *pancake,* perh infl by cognate forms in other langs; cf Du *pannekoek,* Norw *pannekake*] **chiefly Nth, esp NY, WI**

1941 *Language* 17.335 **WI** [LANCS fieldwork], A three-syllable form was used by three [of 50] informants, with middle syllable unstressed and varying from [ɪ] to [ə]: [the first inf] (Dutch deriv.) *pannacake,* [the second] . . (Belgian deriv.) *pannycake,* [the third] . . (Vermont deriv.) *pancakes,* 'but *pannycakes* is the real name.' . . Most current is *pancake.* 1949 *WELS Suppl.* **WI**, Pannacakes—country version of pancakes. 1950 *WELS* **WI** (*What other names do you have for pancakes*) 3 Infs, Pannicakes; 1 Inf, Panacakes—fairly common, pannicakes also heard. 1952 Henderson *Home Is Upriver* 97 **sLA**, Welcome to panny-cake alley. 1953 Van Wagenen *Golden Age* 71 **ceNY** (as of late 19th cent), There are plenty of oldsters who would deny that the phrase "in excess" had any meaning when applied to the laudable habit of riotous consumption of buckwheat "pannie-cakes." 1966–69 *DARE* (Qu. H20b) Infs **NH**11, **NY**1, [pænɪkeks], **NY**126, ['pænɪ,keks]—old people; **NY**220, ['pæni,keks]; **MN**30, **SC**9, Pannicake(s). 1968 *Chatham Courier–Rough Notes* (NY) 20 June sec B 7/4, He [="Grandpa"] thought of next November and buckwheat panny cakes, or hot saleratus biscuits drenched in honey from a wild bee tree. 1973 Allen *LAUM* 1.283 (as of c1950), *Griddle cakes* (of wheat). . . The older variant *pani-cake* or *pannicake,* recorded 3 times in Wisconsin fieldwork, has echoes in Minnesota and was overheard locally by an inf. in a Dutch community in North Dakota. This variant may be derived from Dutch *pannekack.*

pannikin n
1 A small pan or cup. [OED2 1823 →] Cf **cannikin 1**

1867 *Galaxy* 3.731, The salt pork or beef is placed in a small tub on the floor . . , and each man . . rapidly eats it, using his left hand as a fork to steady the meat in his private pannikin. 1869 *Scientific Amer.* 20.37, Those anxious to propagate the fish artificially throw a net over the female when she comes to deposit the egg, and by bending her back slightly over a pannikin, the eggs are expressed. 1889 in 1899 Warman *Story RR* 243 **West,** They swarmed into the old freight cars which had been fitted up with long planks for benches and tables. On the latter were tin pannikins, iron knives and forks, and pewter spoons. 1930 Shoemaker *1300 Words* 45 **cPA Mts** (as of c1900), *Pannikin*—A small pan. 1969 Sorden *Lumberjack Lingo* 84 **NEng, Gt Lakes,** *Pannikin*—A small pan or cup for tea or coffee.

‡**2** Transf: food cooked in such a cup. [Perh infl by *ramekin*]

1896 *Daily News Cook Book* 284, Pannikins—Chop fine enough cold meat to make a pint. . . Put the meat on to heat with two tablespoonfuls water and a cup of rich sweet milk. Thicken [and season] . . ; pour this creamed hash into the center of a hot platter; bake as many eggs as are required in hot, buttered cups; turn them out and arrange them around the creamed meat.

pannycake See **pannicake**

panocha, panoche See **penoche**

pan-pan-doux See **pain perdu**

pan pie n
1 =**pandowdy.** Cf **potpie 2**

1862 Dodge *Country Living* 70 **MA**, No pan-pie with hot brown bread on Sunday morning. 1883 ME Bd. Ag. *Ag. ME for 1882* 403, You have all heard of the pan-dowdy, or pan-pie, the pride of our grandmothers. 1940 Brown *Amer. Cooks* 386 **MA**, Pan pie—A pie crust made with buttermilk having large globules of butter swimming in it is the first requisite. . . Line a bread tin with this, cut small pieces of fat salt pork as thin as possible, and place them around the sides and on the bottom; then fill the tin with slices of fine tart apples and place a few more pieces of pork over the top. Pour over ⅔ cup molasses, sprinkle with ½ teaspoon each of cinnamon, allspice, and nutmeg. Cover with crust and bake 1½ hours.

This classic dish was also called pork apple pie. **1969** *DARE* (Qu. H63, *Kinds of desserts*) Inf **KY**37, Fruit cobblers or pan pies—gooseberry, blackberry, peach. **1986** Pederson *LAGS Concordance* **Gulf Region, esp GA, TN** (*Apple . . cobbler*) 3 infs, Pan pie(s); 1 inf, Pan pie—apple pie, not in a deep dish; 1 inf, Pan pies—layers of fruit and pastry; 1 inf, Pan pies—small; 1 inf, Pan pie—shallow; 1 inf, Pan pie = deep dish pie, no bottom crust; 1 inf, Pan pies—flat, one crust; 1 inf, Pan pies— [*LAGS* Ed: as opposed to cobblers?]

2 =**potpie 1.**
   1968 *DARE* (Qu. H45, *Dishes made with meat, fish, or poultry that everybody around here would know, but that people in other places might not*) Inf **GA**24, Chicken pan pie.

pan plow n [Prob < hard*pan*]
   1968 *DARE* (Qu. L18, *Kinds of plows*) Inf **LA**15, Turning plow—threw dirt to one side, used to be called "pan plow."

pan-rabbit n [Calque from **panhas**]
=**scrapple.**
   1896 *DN* 1.422 **sePA, neMD,** *Pon-hoss. . .* Used to hear college students jocosely call it "pan rabbit." **1940–41** Cassidy *WI Atlas,* 1 inf [of 50], ['pɒnhɒɒs] or ['pæn,ræbət]—cook the meat off a pig's head, stir in buckwheat flour, press in mold.

pan squash See **pattypan squash**

pansy n [*OED2* a1500 →] Cf **field pansy, pansy violet, wild pansy**
   Any of several usu wild **violets,** but esp a **johnny-jump-up 1.**
   1822 Eaton *Botany* 514, *[Viola] tricolor* (garden violet, hearts-ease, pansy). **1876** Hobbs *Bot. Hdbk.* 86, Pansy, Heartsease, Viola tricolor. **1891** Coulter *Botany W. TX* 25, *V. tricolor . . var. arvensis. . . Pansy. . .* Dry or sandy soil, and apparently indigenous, at least in Texas. It is the wild representative of the common garden pansy. **1893** *Jrl. Amer. Folkl.* 6.138 **nwIL,** *Viola pedata,* pansy, Peoria, Il. **1909** *DN* 3.413 **nME,** *Johnny jump up. . .* The pansy. **1920** Rice–Rice *Pop. Studies CA Wild Flowers* 57, *Viola pedunculata . . .* is found throughout the Coast Range and its valleys. . . They are . . called Violets, Pansies, Johnny-Jump-Up, or . . "Gallitos." **1965–70** *DARE* (Qu. S3, *A flower like a large violet with a yellow center and small ragged leaves—it comes up early in spring on open, stony hilltops*) 10 Infs, **scattered,** Pansy; **CA**53, 117, Baby pansy; (Qu. S11, *. . Blue violet, . . dog-tooth violet*) Infs **CA**165, **GA**28, **IL**30, 138, **OR**4, **WA**8, 15, Pansy.

pansy bird n
=**horned lark.**
   1955 *AmSp* 30.184, *Pansy bird* (horned lark, Colo.) from the resemblance of its head and throat markings to a pansy flower.

pansy violet n Cf **pansy**
   Any of several **violets,** but esp the **bird's-foot violet 1.**
   1933 Small *Manual SE Flora* 886, *V[iola] pedata. . .* Crowfoot-violet. Pansy-violet [etc.]. **1940** Gates *Flora KS* 154, Viola arvensis . . Pansy Violet. **1961** Smith *MI Wildflowers* 237, Bird-foot or Crow-foot Violet, Pansy Violet. **1968** *DARE* FW Addit **LA**21, A violet with pale top petals and dark at the inside of lower petals is a *pansy violet.* It is treasured; girls always let everyone know about it when they find one of those for their bouquet. **1970** Kirk *Wild Edible Plants W. U.S.* 223, *Viola pedunculata. . .* Pansy Violet, Violet, Johnny-Jump-Up. **1976** Bruce *How to Grow Wildflowers* 89, The Birdsfoot Violet, *Viola pedata.* With finely cut leaves like buttercup or anemone and showy, flat pansy-form flower (one of its common names is "Pansy Violet"), it is the glory of the roadsides.

pant v Also *pants*
   To provide (one) with trousers or pants; to allow (one) to wear long trousers.
   1934 *W2,* Pant. . . To clothe in "pants." *Southern U.S.* **1944** Howard *Walkin' Preacher* 219 **Ozarks,** Hogs shore hain't afetchin' nothin'. . . Takes a hull hog to pants me, pants goin' up in price like they air. **1952** Brown *NC Folkl.* 1.573 **nwNC,** Pant. . . To put pants (trousers) on for the first time. "I knowed him before he was panted."

pantaloon flower n
=**Dutchman's breeches 1.**
   1959 Carleton *Index Herb. Plants* 89, *Pantaloon-flower:* Dicentra cucullaria.

pant-ass n [See quot]
   Either the **willet** or the **spotted sandpiper.**
   1954 McAtee *Suppl. to Nomina Abitera* [8], Willett (*Catoptrophorus semipalmatus*)—Big pant-ass, coastal North Carolina, C. Cottam. The much smaller spotted sandpiper is commonly called "pant-ass"; pant has the meaning of "to throb", in reference to the constant tail-bobbing of the bird.

pant cat See **panther A2**

panter See **panther A1, 2**

panter cat See **panther A2**

panther n Usu |'pænθə(r)|; for varr see **A** below
   A Pronc varr. [The sp *panter* was common through the 16th cent; presumably the corresponding pronc survived esp in folk speech long after the sp with *h* became std (cf the name *Thomas*). For the vowel change in *painter* cf **can** v[1] **1b, hain't.**]
   1 |'pentə(r)| and varr; pronc-spp *pa(i)nter.* **scattered, but more freq Appalachians, Inland Sth** See Map
   1738 in 1974 Franklin *Sayings Poor Richard* 97 **PA,** *Mercury* will have his share in these affairs, and so confound the speech of the people, that when a *Pennsylvanian* would say *panther* he shall say *painter.* **1818** in 1824 Knight *Letters* 107 **KY,** Some words are used . . by the lower classes in society, pronounced very uncouthly, as . . painter for panther. **1823** [see **C1** below]. **1848** (1855) Ruxton *Life Far West* 109 **Rocky Mts,** "Painter meat can't 'shine' with this," says a hunter. **1853** Simms *Sword & Distaff* 88 **SC,** The only chance is in jest playing the scout, as ef you had a wolf on one quarter, and a yellow painter (panther) on t'other. **1859** Taliaferro *Fisher's R.* 76 **nwNC** (as of 1820s), There sot the biggest painter that ever walked the Blue Ridge. **1903** *DN* 2.323 **seMO,** *Painter.* **1907** *DN* 3.234 **nwAR,** *Painter.* **1913** London *Valley of Moon* 320 **CA,** An' panthers!—all the old folks called 'em painters an' catamounts an' varmints. **1917** *DN* 4.431 **LA, IL, NY,** *Painter.* **1923** *DN* 5.216 **swMO,** *Painter. Ibid* 236 **swWI,** He screamed like a painter. **1926** [see **C1** below]. **1927** *AmSp* 2.361 **cwWV,** *Painter.* **1930** Shoemaker *1300 Words* 47 **cPA Mts** (as of c1900), *Painter.* **1939** Writers' Program *Guide KY* 12, Hair-raising stories are still told about the panther or puma (locally called "painter"), once fairly common but now extinct in the State. **1939** [see **A2** below]. **1950** [see **C1** below]. **1952** Brown *NC Folkl.* 1.573, *Panter* ['pentə, -ɚ]. . . Panther. **c1960** [see **A2** below]. **1965–70** *DARE* (Qu. P31) 28 Infs, **esp sAppalachians,** Painter [5 Infs indicated that this was old-fashioned.]; **LA**14, Painter ['peintə]—among very ignorant Negroes; **WY**1, Painter—mountain men used to say this; **MS**53, ['peinθɚ]. **1983** *MJLF* 9.1.49 **ceKY** (as of 1956), *Painter.*

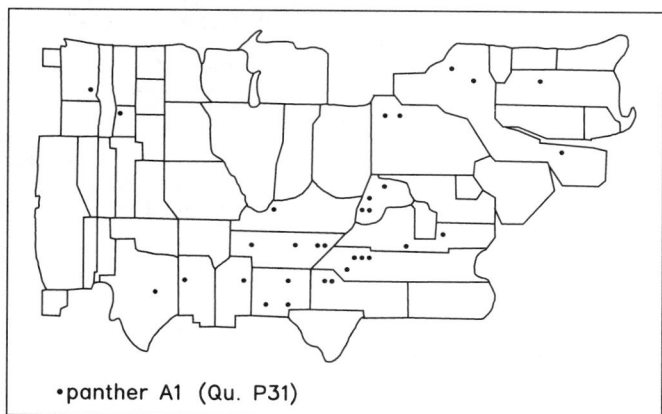

•panther A1 (Qu. P31)

   2 |'pæntə(r)| and varr; pronc-sp *panter;* also *pant(er) cat.* **chiefly Sth, S Midl**
   1840 *S. Lit. Messenger* 6.264 **TN,** I would'nt [sic] think it any more sin to put a ball through such fellows, than through a panter or a wolf. **1845** Hooper *Advent. Simon Suggs* 47 **AL,** We did'nt [sic] make quite as much noise as a panter and a pack of hounds. **1848** Thompson *Major Jones's Travel* 114 **GA,** It kicked and squalled like a young panter. **1872** Schele de Vere *Americanisms* 368, The *painter* or *panter,* the familiar corruption of panther, [is] found in the everglades of Florida. **1909** *DN* 3.355 **eAL, wGA,** *Panter. . .* Panther. **1915** *DN* 4.187 **swVA,** *Panter. . .* Variant of *panther.* Pron. [pɛantɚ]. **1934** Hurston *Jonah's*

Gourd Vine 107 **AL** [Black], Pant'er got 'im, maybe. **1939** McGuire *FL Cracker Dial.* 152, [One informant] reported she had often heard [pentɚ] and [pæntɚ]. **c1960** *Wilson Coll.* **csKY,** *Panther*—used to be /'pæntə/ or /'pentə/. **1966–69** *DARE* (Qu. P31) Infs **AL**17, **GA**84, **NC**36, Panter(s); **KY**24, ['pæntɚz]; **FL**7, ['pæntɚz], ['pæntə] cat; **NC**8, Panter cat; **LA**12, Panters—that's what they said long time ago; that's what niggers called 'em; **NC**49, Pant cat. **1966** *DARE* Tape **FL**47, There was panthers ['pæntəz], there was wildcats, there was bear, and there was all kinds of small animals. **1984** Hancock *Choestoe* 13 **neGA,** One of Jep's tales concerned a panther, they called it "a panter."

B Gram form.

Sg used as pl. Cf Intro "Language Changes" II.7

1927 *AmSp* 3.10 **Ozarks,** Singular forms like *coon, skunk, mink, . . bar* and *panter* are regularly used as plurals. **1967–69** *DARE* Tape **TX**24, There was lots of panther here when, up till, oh, I'll say till about nineteen and three or four; **TX**70, There was a few panther in the country when I was a kid. **1986** [see **C1** below].

C Sense.

1 also *panther cat:* **=mountain lion. widespread, but chiefly NEast, Sth, S Midl** See Map and Map Section

1683 (1771) Penn *Select Wks.* 408 [sic for 608] **PA,** The creatures . . that are natural to these parts, are the Wild Cat, Panther, Otter, Wolf [etc]. **1743** Catesby *Nat. Hist. Carolina* 2 [app] xxv, The Panther at its full Growth is three Feet high, of a redish Colour, like that of a Lyon, without the Spots of a Leopard, or the Stripes of a Tyger, the Tail is very long. **1775** (1962) Romans *Nat. Hist. FL* 190, But should you wound a bear, or the *American* panther, so as to disable him from flight, he will prove dangerous. **1823** Cooper *Pioneers* 2.174 **cNY,** We'd like to have had a bad job of that panther, or painter's work—some calls it one, and some calls it t'other—but I know little of the beast. **1831** (1973) Pattie *Personal Narr.* 54 **NM,** I was aroused from slumber by a noise in the leaves, and raising my head saw a panther streched [sic] on the log by which I was lying, within six feet of me. **1842** DeKay *Zool. NY* 1.48, The *Cougar* or *Painter* (a corruption of the word *Panther*,) is now rarely seen in the southern parts of the State; though the writer remembers, when a boy, the consternation occasioned by the appearance of one of these animals in Westchester county, not more than twenty-five miles from New-York. **1917** Anthony *Mammals Amer.* 146, In the Northwest they call it the "Mountain Lion," in the Southwest the "Cougar;" . . in the Gulf States it answers to the chill-producing name of "Panther," while the early settlers in the East called it the "Catamount," and the "Painter." **1926** (1949) McQueen–Mizell *Hist. Okefenokee* 104 **seGA,** Our panther, which is called by some the "painter," is a member of the puma family. **1938** Rawlings *Yearling* 48 **FL,** They had Injuns to fight and bears and panther-cats. **1945** FWP *Lay My Burden Down* 78 **TX** (as of c1861) [Black], I seed wildcats and coons and bunches of wolves and heared the panthers scream like the woman. **1950** *WELS,* 1 Inf, **cwWI,** Have not had a panther here in 40 years; 1 Inf, **cWI,** Painter. **1965–70** *DARE* (Qu. P31, . . *Names or nicknames . . for the . . panther, . . wildcat*) 106 Infs, **chiefly Atlantic, Sth, S Midl, TX,** Panther; **MS**32, **NY**68, Black panther; **FL**16, Florida panther; **NH**14, Indian panther; **PA**121, Panther—most common name; mountain lion—once in a great while; **VA**8, Panther—similar to western cougar or mountain lion, but not called that here, just panther; 30 Infs, **esp sAppalachians,** Painter; **AL**17, **FL**7, **GA**84, **KY**24, **LA**12, **NC**8, 36, Panter (cat); **NC**49, Pant cat; **MS**53, ['peɪnθɚ]; (Qu. CC17) 22 Infs, **scattered,** (Black) panthers; (Qu. P32, . .

Other kinds of wild animals) Infs **MO**9, **NY**23, Panther. **1967–69** *DARE* Tape **GA**48, Now this old panther ['pænθɚ]—I've seen those but didn't ever see any tigers; **GA**51, Tiger, now, and panther ['pænθɚ] I think is what in our way of speaking is the same thing; **NC**53, A panther or a cougar, they've got a real long tail like a puma or a mountain lion; **PA**141, Right close by . . is where the last panther in this area was killed. . . That was, I'd say, in the seventies [=1870s]; **PA**142, It was the last panther that was killed in the lower valley; **TX**19, She looked back and there was a panther. **1986** Pederson *LAGS Concordance,* 7 infs, **Gulf Region,** Panther(s); 1 inf, **cFL,** Used to be some panther; 1 inf, **cnAL,** Panther—not many of these left—screams like a woman in distress.

2 usu in combs *panther piss, ~ poison, ~ sweat;* for addit varr, see quots: Strong or inferior liquor; moonshine.

1929 *AmSp* 4.386 **KS** [Wet words], *Panther-sweat, monkey-swill* and *rat-track whiskey* are less easily classified, to say nothing of a number of more or less vulgar terms which are best omitted here. **1930** *AmSp* 5.239 [University slang], The author has collected the following expressions around the campus of Colgate University. . . *Panther-sweat:* a term for intoxicating liquor. "The boys became unmanageable from drinking panther-sweat." **1932** *AmSp* 7.436 [Stanford Univ expressions], "Panther" is the common name for gin. **1940** (1941) Bell *Swamp Water* 75 **Okefenokee GA,** What you trembling about, Cousin Jesse? Give Ben Ragan a drink of that panther water. **1942** Berrey–Van den Bark *Amer. Slang* 99.3, *Inferior liquor.* . . Panther piss *or* sweat. *Ibid* 99.8, *Strong liquor.* . . Panther piss, -pizen *or* sweat. *Ibid* 100.9, *Gin.* . . Panther. **1946** *AmSp* 21.194 [Stillers' argot], A young, wild, bitey whiskey may be called 'panther sweat,' but the term has an indelicate variation which is more frequently used. **1946** Heggen *Mr. Roberts* 134, 'That whiskey they make,' said Dowdy, 'is really panther-piss. Two drinks of that will knock you on your ass like nothing you ever saw!' **1958** McCulloch *Woods Words* 132 **Pacific NW,** *Panther juice*—A stout drink. **1965–70** *DARE* (Qu. DD21c, *Nicknames for whiskey, especially illegally made whiskey*) Infs **CT**13, **IL**14, **NY**105, **PA**76, **TN**44, **WI**48, Panther piss; **IL**128, **NY**163, Panther piss [FW sugg]; **NY**219, Ol' panther piss; **AZ**2, **TX**11, Panther juice; **TX**26, Panther piss—this is illegal, not bad store-bought; (Qu. DD21a, *General words . . for any kind of liquor*) Inf **IA**8, Panther piss; (Qu. DD21b, *General words . . for bad liquor*) Inf **TX**26, Panther piss [laughter]; (Qu. DD25, . . *Nicknames . . for beer*) Inf **LA**14, Panther piss; (Qu. DD28b, . . *Fermented drinks . . made at home*) Inf **NC**37, Pink panther—various juices and whiskey; (Qu. DD31, *Joking names for homemade hard liquor;* total Infs questioned, 75) Inf **MS**1, Panther piss. **1985** Wilkinson *Moonshine* 28 **neNC,** "After that they'd serve you North Carolina Corn." It is called . . panther's breath. **1986** Pederson *LAGS Concordance,* 1 inf, **swAL,** Panther piss—poor moonshine.

panther cat See **panther C1**

panther lily n [*OED2* 1884 →]

A **leopard lily 1** (here: *Lilium pardalinum*).

1889 *Century Dict.* 3454, Among the eight species of the Pacific slope are the Washington lily . . the panther-lily, *L. pardalinum* [etc]. **1938** MacFarland et al. *Garden Bulbs* 136, Lilium pardalinum. Sometimes called the Western Tiger Lily, this highly esteemed California native also has the common names of Leopard Lily and Panther Lily. **1961** Thomas *Flora Santa Cruz* 118 **cwCA,** *L[ilium] pardalinum* . . Panther, Leopard, or Tiger Lily, California Tiger Lily. Wet meadows, along springs, and near streams, mainly on the western slopes of the Santa Cruz Mountains. **1979** Spellenberg *Audubon Guide N. Amer. Wildflowers W. Region* 585, The similar Leopard Lily or Panther Lily (*L. pardalinum*), which grows along forest streams or near springs over most of California, has bright orange-red flowers.

panther owl n

=great horned owl.

1955 *AmSp* 30.178 **MS,** For its strikingly predatory nature, the great horned owl has the folk title *panther owl* (Miss.) and in writing has been called *tiger among birds.*

panther piss (or poison, sweat) See **panther C2**

panther tongue n

A noisemaker supposed to imitate the cry of the **panther C1.**

1968 *DARE* (Qu. CC17) Inf **VA**26, Children made noise with panther tongues. **1968** *DARE* Tape **VA**26, [FW:] I was just wondering if you could tell me how you make those panther tongues [mentioned by Inf at Qu. CC17]. . . [Inf:] You just take a little block of cedar . . about an inch

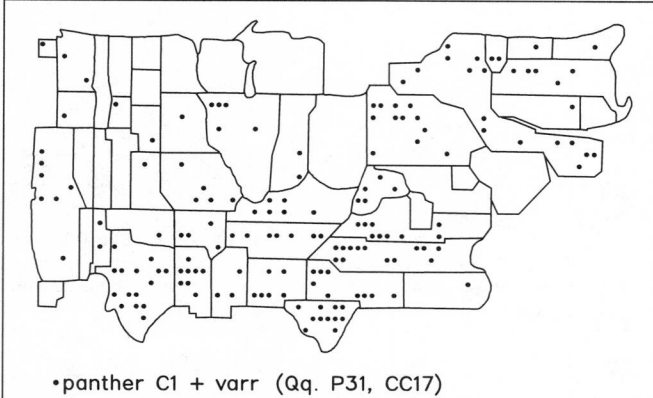

•panther C1 + varr (Qq. P31, CC17)

wide and about four inches long, and you just hollow it down through the middle . . kind of like a ship's hull . . . And you take another little flat piece of cedar and get it real thin, lay it right on top of that. Then it's just about big enough to go in your mouth where that thin piece strikes that hull, and you blow in there and just push that thing up and down a little bit and it'll just make an awful panthery racket. . . It'd make an awful weird sound, sound like a panther. **1998** *NADS Letters* **seKY,** Panther tongue—This sounded more like "painter tongue." . . What I recall was a pair of resonators (resembling woodwind reeds, but hand carved out of local materials) attached to some ring-shaped holder. Blowing into the ring made the resonators rasp against each other, producing a sound not unlike a bilabial trill. (I hesitate to call it a "Bronx cheer" because I remember a painter tongue only from my time in another AFSC work camp, this one in Leslie Co., Ky, in the summer of 1946.) **2000** *Ibid* **VA,** Panther tongue . . a blade of grass held between the thumbs. When you cup your hands and blow over it, an awful sound results. **2001** *Ibid,* Panther tongue was made from a broken balloon or old piece of inner-tube. 63 yr old female, white, New York City.

pantod n [Prob var of **fantod**] **NEast**
A vague or undefined illness; an imaginary illness; a fit.

1901 *DN* 2.144 **NY,** Pantod. . . The colic or a similar disorder. **1903** *DN* 2.352 **CT, MA,** Pant-od. . . Reported in such a sentence as 'What's the matter? You act as though you had the pantod.' **1904** *DN* 2.399 **NY,** Pantod. . . 1. A violent pain. 2. A mild discomfort corresponding to a "conniption fit." **1955** Taber *Stillmeadow Daybook* 47 **swCT,** I never go into a pantod wondering if I were on a desert island and had to choose would I choose a cat or dog? Why worry? **1969** *DARE* (Qu. BB28, *Joking names . . for imaginary diseases:* "He must have the _____.") Inf **MA14,** Pantod [ˌpænˈtɑd]; **NY186,** Pantod on the rummit.

pantry shower n Also *pantry party* Cf **pound party**
1965–70 *DARE* (Qu. FF3, . . *'Showers' or 'gift parties'*) Inf **CA8,** Pantry shower—type of bridal; **CO17,** Pantry shower—for lunchroom and for brides; **GA13,** Pantry shower—give food; **GA81,** Pantry shower—for a new minister, or for the needy; **GA86,** Pantry shower—people bring something, one person gets it; **NE11,** Pantry shower—for new preacher to stock his cupboard; **GA32, IL5, NY166,** Pantry shower(s); **IA3,** Pantry parties—usually for a minister, everybody brought a pound of something, especially for a new minister; **OH95,** Pantry party—a pound of food or supplies taken to minister (also for newlyweds).

pants See **pant**

pants hangers n pl Also *pants garters, ~ supporters*
Suspenders.

1950 *WELS* (What does a man wear over his shoulders to hold up his trousers?) 1 Inf, **ceWI,** Pants supporters; 1 Inf, **swWI,** Pants hangers. **1970** *DARE* (Qu. W7) Inf **PA244,** Pants garters.

pants rabbit n Also *pants rat; rarely pant rabbit*
A **louse B1** or other body vermin.

1918 *Natl. Geogr. Mag.* June 499, They [=soldiers] . . call the things "pants rabbits" and "seam squirrels." **1937** Sandoz *Slogum* 115 **NE,** The place was getting to be just like any other damned dirty hog ranch, with the bunks full o' pants rabbits. **1937** Steinbeck *Of Mice* 36 **CA,** What the hell kind of bed you giving us, anyways. We don't want no pants rabbits. **1940** *AmSp* 15.451 [Argot of the sea], *Pant rabbits.* Any form of body vermin. **1950** *WELS* (Other names [include joking and nicknames] for body and head lice) 3 Infs, **ce,csWI,** Pants rabbit. **1956** Sorden–Ebert *Logger's Words* 25 **Gt Lakes,** *Pants-rabbits,* Body vermin. Lice. **1958** McCulloch *Woods Words* 132 **Pacific NW,** *Pants rabbits*—Parasites. **1968** Adams *Western Words* 219, *Pants rats*—What the cowboy calls body lice.

pants supporters See **pants hangers**

pants, the n
c1960 *Wilson Coll.* **csKY,** Pants. . . A fit of panting. "I run so fast I've got the pants."

pantywaist n **chiefly Nth, N Midl** See Map Cf **milquetoast**
A timid or effeminate man or boy; a sissy; hence adj *pantywaist* sissified.

1936 *AmSp* 11.280 **SD** [College slang], *Panty-waist.* A sissy. **1937** *Sun* (Baltimore MD) 28 Apr. 6 *(OED2),* [Advt:] Now Mike don't be calling *me* a panty waist. **1941** *Sun* (Baltimore MD) 21 Mar 14/7 *(Hench Coll.),* Three of them [=synonyms for *conscript*] . . are "draftee," "trainee," and "selectee." All of them are panty-waist words, inevitably suggestive of an itty, bitty, piggy-wiggy, worse even than the "Sammy" that soft-headed persons tried in vain to hang on the doughboys in 1917. **1942** *AmSp* 17.170 **sIL** [Campus slang], The most vivid are given here: . . *fancy-pants* or *panty-waist* (a 'sissy'). **1951** *Harper's Mag.* 203.5.96, The hurt . . pantywaist ran off a number of copies of his letter. **1958** Babcock *I Don't Want* 11 **eSC,** Now skedaddle and show those pantywaist aristocrats what a real dog is like! **1965–70** *DARE* (Qu. Y5, . . *To urge somebody to do something he shouldn't:* "Johnny wouldn't have tried that if the other boys hadn't _____.") Inf **UT7,** Called him pantywaist; (Qu. AA21, . . *Joking expressions . . about a wife who gives the orders and a husband who takes them from her*) Infs **MI78, MN15, OH56, 57, PA163,** (He's a) pantywaist; (Qu. HH10, *A very timid or cowardly person:* "He's _____.") Infs **CT3, HI1, MI78, WA1,** Pantywaist; (Qu. HH11a, *Someone who is too particular or fussy—if it's a man*) Infs **MA6, OH57, PA223, 230,** Pantywaist; (Qu. HH38, *A womanish man*) Infs **HI1, IN5, 68, MI116, NY187, PA227, TX19, WI57,** Pantywaist; (Qu. HH39, *A homosexual man*) Inf **IL50,** Pantywaist; (Qu. JJ3b, *When a school child makes a special effort to 'get in good' with the teacher in hopes of getting a better grade:* "She's an awful _____.") Inf **WA1,** Pantywaist.

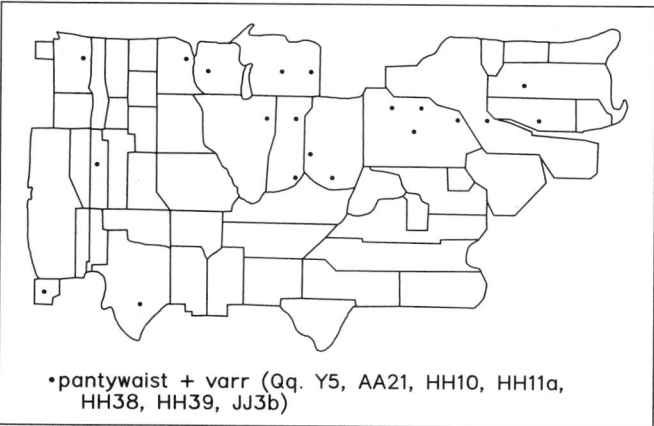

•pantywaist + varr (Qq. Y5, AA21, HH10, HH11a, HH38, HH39, JJ3b)

pan weed n
See quot.

1967 *DARE* FW Addit **seOR,** Pan weed—a wild weed that grows among [sic] alfalfa, gets in milk of cows.

pão doce n [Port] **HI** Cf **malassada, pan dulce**
A kind of sweet bread.

1967 *DARE* (Qu. H18, . . *Special kinds of bread*) Inf **HI1,** Portuguese bread—still available; also called sweet bread: [ˌpɔnˈdus] in Portuguese; made with yolks of eggs, therefore yellow; sweet; **HI6,** Portuguese sweet bread—pão doce [ˈpanˈdus]—"now commercial" (was primarily homemade); **HI9A,** [pɔndus]—sweet bread, 1½', yellow inside, brown outside, and sweet. **1972** Carr *Da Kine Talk* 96 **HI,** Hawaii's Portuguese heritage, gastronomically speaking, comes to mind in connection with the popular *pão doce,* the sweet-bread known to all. **1981** Pap *Port.-Americans* 216, In Hawaii, . . Portuguese sweetbreads *(pão doce)* and doughnuts *(malassadas),* too, are quite popular. **1991** Kirlin–Kirlin *Smithsonian Folklife Cookbook* 275 **HI,** Pao Doce (Portuguese Sweet Bread). **1996** *DARE* File **HI,** Pao doce . . is most commonly known as Portuguese sweet bread or sweet bread; it's a soft yellow bread with a brown crust usually baked in a round loaf. Well-loved! **1996** *NADS Letters* **ceMA,** Pao Doce (sweet bread) is well and very much alive. Every Portuguese bakery *anywhere* bakes these—usually reserving them for the weekends. My mother [from Fall River] brings loaves . . every time she visits. . . We can get pao doce at the local Stop and Shop [in Lexington].

paopao n [Haw] **HI** Cf **papio**
An **ulua** (here: *Caranx speciosus*).

1926 Pan-Pacific Research Inst. *Jrl.* 1.1.9 **HI,** Gnathanodon speciosus. . . Pao-pao. . . Pel[agic]. C[ommon].

paounding berrel See **pounding barrel**

pap n |pæp| Rarely *paps*

1 A father—usu used as a quasi-personal name. **chiefly Midl, S Atl** See Map *old-fash*

1844 *Knickerbocker* 23.15, They said, pap wasn't at home. **1858** in 1983 *PADS* 70.45 **ce,sePA,** Met Pap coming down in a one horse vehicle. **1871** Eggleston *Hoosier Schoolmaster* 81 **IN,** Pap wants to know ef you would spend tomorry and Sunday at our house? **1890** *DN* 1.68 **KY,** *Pap* [pæp]. **1891** Garland *Main-Travelled Roads* 211 **WI,** He knows his poor old pap when he comes home from the war. **1901** *DN* 2.182 **neKY,** *Father*. . . Pap. **1902** *DN* 2.240 **sIL,** *Pap*. . . Father; the latter is not often used, but almost always pa [pɔ] or pap. **1903** *DN* 2.323 **seMO,** *Pap*. . . Father. It is not uncommon to hear a grown man or woman speak of 'pap.' This, however, is only among quite old-fashioned people. **1906** *DN* 3.122 **sIN,** *Pap* . . father. **1907** *DN* 3.234 **nwAR,** *Pap*. . . Father. **1909** *DN* 3.355 **eAL, wGA,** *Pap(py)*. . . Father. **1923** *DN* 5.216 **swMO,** *Pap*. . . Father. **1930** Shoemaker *1300 Words* 46 **cPA Mts** (as of c1900), *Pap*—father. **1934** Carmer *Stars Fell on AL* 39, Mattie Sue's pap and mammy. **1940** Faulkner *Hamlet* 50 **MS,** So me and Pap went on. **1941** *LANE* Map 371 *(Dad, Pa)* 1 inf, **cnNH,** Pap [*DARE* Ed: used only as a child]; 1 inf, **swCT,** *Pap, daddy,* both common, the latter more frequent; 1 inf, **swMA,** *Pap,* 'That's what I and my two own brothers, older than me, called our stepfather—a real old-fashioned word.'; 3 infs, **ce,seNH, ceME,** Pap [*DARE* Ed: regarded as older or old-fashioned though still in use]. **1942** Hall *Smoky Mt. Speech* 77 **wNC, eTN,** ['pæpɪ] . . is often shortened to [pæp]. **1965–70** *DARE* (Qu. Z1, . . *'Father'*) 21 Infs, **chiefly Midl, S Atl,** Pap; **KY10, MD21,** Pap—old-fashioned; **GA33,** Pap—Inf's father called father this; **MD24,** Pap—heard occasionally; **MD31,** Pap [FW: used in conversation]; **NC40,** Pap—her parents said this. [23 of 27 Infs old, 17 comm type 5] **1966** Dakin *Dial. Vocab. Ohio R. Valley* 2.423, *Pap* and *pappy* are clearly "more Mountain," but are by no means limited to this section. Older and middle-aged speakers throughout Kentucky use these affectionate terms and they are also used north of the Ohio. Above the river only *pap* is common, however, and is rarely used except by the oldest speakers. **1986** Pederson *LAGS Concordance (Father)* 1 inf, **cnTN,** Pap—local term; 4 infs, **ne,ceTN,** Pap; 1 inf, **neTN,** She called her own father pap; 1 inf, **neTN,** Pap—called his father when a child; 1 inf, **neTN,** When younger called father pap; 1 inf, **ceTN,** Everyone called his father and grandfather pap; 1 inf, **neGA,** Pap—others' term; 1 inf, **ceGA,** Grandfather called great-grandfather pap; 1 inf, **cnTN,** She called him pap; 1 inf, **cTN,** Called his father pap; 1 inf, **cTN,** Pap—other people's term; 1 inf, **cGA,** Paps—she has heard the term.

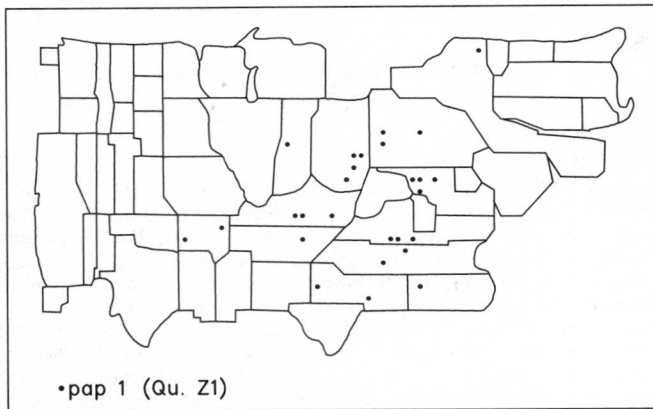

•pap 1 (Qu. Z1)

2 A grandfather; an old man. Cf **pap-pap**

1955 *PADS* 24.105 [Argot of pickpockets], A *pappy* (or *pap*) is an elderly man. **1965–70** *DARE* (Qu. Z3, . . *'Grandfather'*) Infs **AL46, NC40, TN13,** (Old) Pap. **1986** Pederson *LAGS Concordance,* 1 inf, **ceTN,** Everyone called his father and grandfather pap; (Grandfather) 1 inf, **cGA,** Paps—she has heard the term. **1998** *DARE* File **cwPA,** I now live in Indiana, PA, . . where some native speakers . . call their grandfather "Pap." **2000** *Ibid* Pittsburgh PA, "Pap" . . = "grandfather" (and absolutely not "father").

papa n[1] See **pawpaw**

papa n[2] Usu |'pɑpə, 'pɔpə|; also |pə'pɑ|; **chiefly Nth, esp NEng** |'pʌpə|; **esp SC** |'pæpə, pə'pæ|; for addit proncs see quots Also sp *papah, poppa, popper, poppo, puppa(h)* Cf **mamma**

1 A father—often used as a quasi-personal name, esp by a man's children or wife. [*OED2* 1681 →]

1806 (1970) Webster *Compendious Dict.* 215, *Papa, . . a name for father.* [*DARE* Ed: This entry was carried over from Webster's English model.] **1818** *N. Amer. Rev.* 7.77 **MA,** What is meant, Papa, by a boy's being bound to his master? **a1876** in 1983 *PADS* 70.45 **ce,sePA,** Papa went down to _____ [sic] in the morning in a sleigh. **1907** *DN* 3.197 **seNH,** *Puppa*. . . Papa. The latter is a book word. **1909** *DN* 3.355 **eAL, wGA,** *Pap(py)*. . . Perhaps not so common as *paw,* or *papa.* **1910–20** in 1944 *ADD* **cNY,** [pɑ], [pɑpə], not [pɔ], [pæp(ɪ)]. **1913** Wharton *Custom of Country* 314 **NY,** He was subjected by Mrs. Spragg to searching enquiries as to how his food set, and whether he didn't think his Popper was too strict with him. **1925** *DN* 5.349 **SC,** Charleston, (S.C.) has kept the æ in *palm* and *calm,* and (with stress on the ultima) *a* final, in papa and mamma. [pə'pæ, mə'mæ]. **1936** *AmSp* 11.21 **eTX,** *Papa, drop,* . . *crop* are pronounced both [ɑ] and [æ]. *Ibid* 159, The vowel in the final syllable of all the words listed below is usually [ə]. . . papa. **1938** Daniels *Southerner* 327 **SC,** Miss Amelia sadly . . parted with ancestral spoons in order that papá (behind each "p" the "a" is short) . . might have the best imported sherry. **1941** in 1944 *ADD* 438 **wWV,** [pʌpə] always in 1 family. **1941** *LANE* Map 371, [Proncs of the type ['pɑpə, 'pɒ-, 'pɔ-] are common **throughout NEng;** also **esp eNEng** freq ['pʌpə]; occas ['pɑpə, 'pæ-].] **1948** *WELS Suppl.* **ceWI,** The Roberts children called our parents mummah and papah, and over the hill the Steuersons said puppah and mamma. **1965–70** *DARE* (Qu. Z1, . . *'Father'*) 305 Infs, **widespread, but somewhat more freq Sth, S Midl,** Papa (or poppa); **CT23, MI9, NY83, SC40, 42,** ['pɑpə]; **SC44, 58,** ['pɔpə]; **CA21, FL26, NC55, SC19,** ['pɔpə]; **ME9, MA44, 69, MI17,** ['pʌpə]; **MA73,** ['pʌpə] not heard much now; **MA73, MO5,** ['pɑpə]; **CA59, MA5, 40,** [,pə'pɑ]; **LA6,** ['pɒpə]; **SC10,** [pæpə]; **SC11,** [pə'pæ]; **SC46,** Papa [papə, pæpæ, pə'pɑ]; **MN34,** Poppo. [*DARE* Ed: In comments recorded by FWs, 47 Infs indicated that *papa* (*poppa*) was old-fashioned (though 2 said it was less old-fashioned than *pa* or *paw*), 9 that they used or heard it when they were children, 3 that it was used by children, and 6 simply that it was rare or uncommon. Other comments recorded were: "By people of Jewish extraction"; "Girls use that more"; "In Scandinavian families"; "If you were trying to wheedle something out of your dad"; "Lower class"; "Some of her children"; "Most common."] **1965–70** *DARE* Tape **CA110,** Now I told this to mamma, papa ['pɑpə]; **IN12,** When we were little . . papa ['pɑpə] and mamma always took us to church; **MI17,** The mamma and papa ['pɑ^pə] had the middle room; **TX24,** When papa ['pɔpə] first came here; **TX40,** Papa ['pɑpə] put it down in salt; **TX46,** Before papa ['pɑpə] was born. **1966** Dakin *Dial. Vocab. Ohio R. Valley* 2.419, *Father* . . *papa*—[papə], [pɑpə], or (occasionally) [pɑpə]—sometimes with primary stress on the initial syllable, usually with even stress, and never with stress on the second syllable. **1992** Hunter-Gault *In My Place* 58 **GA** [Black], Once Poppa was on a roll, he could go for hours, and no one would think about leaving.

2 A grandfather—often used as a quasi-personal name. **chiefly Sth, S Midl, SW** See Map Cf **pa-paw** n[2]

1965–70 *DARE* (Qu. Z3, . . *'Grandfather'*) 16 Infs, **esp Sth, S Midl, SW,** Papa (or poppa); **LA6,** Poppa ['pɒpə]; **LA18,** Papa—newfangled; pappy—old-fashioned; **LA20,** Papa—occasional; papaw [pə'pɔ]; **CA166,** Papa—[FW: Papa Charlie is what Inf called her grandfather.]; **CA194,** Papa Frank; **TN65,** Papa plus given name, as Papa Joe. **1970** Tarpley *Blinky* 210 **neTX,** *Usual term of affection for grandfather* . . papa [9 of 200 infs].

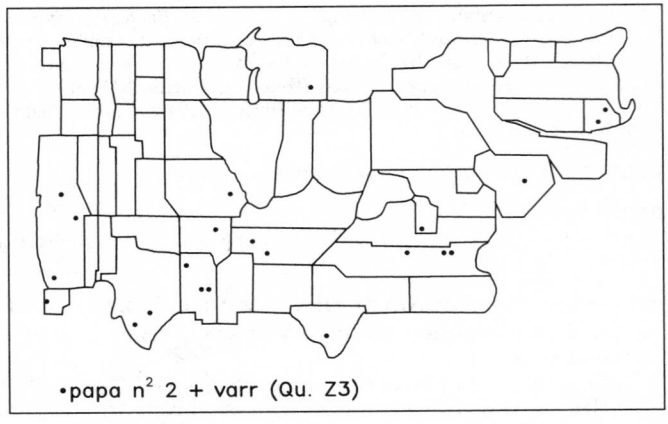

•papa n[2] 2 + varr (Qu. Z3)

3 usu attrib: A male animal, esp one used for breeding purposes. *euphem* Cf **daddy** n 5, **father** n B2

1950 *WELS* **WI** (*Words used for a bull*) 3 Infs, Papa cow; (*Words used by women or in mixed company for a bull*) 4 Infs, Papa cow; (*Words used by women or in mixed company for a male breeding pig*) 5 Infs, Papa pig. **1951** Johnson *Resp. to PADS 20* **DE** (*Words used by women or in mixed company for a male sheep*) Papa sheep; (*Words . . for a male breeding pig*) Papa pig. **c1955** Reed–Person *Ling. Atlas Pacific NW*, 2 [of 52] infs, Poppa cow. **c1960** *Wilson Coll.* **csKY**, Papa cow. . . A very mild substitute for bull. *Papa pig*. . . Euphemism for boar. **1960** Criswell *Resp. to PADS 20* **Ozarks** (*Words used by women or in mixed company for a male sheep*) Papa sheep. **1965–70** *DARE* (Qu. K23, *Words used by women or in mixed company for a bull*) 23 Infs, **scattered,** Papa cow; FL12, Papa bull; FL7, Papa; (Qu. K22, *Words used for a bull*) Infs ID3, IA41, Papa cow; FL12, Papa bull; (Qu. K52, *A male pig kept for breeding*) Infs CO11, LA33, MA58, Papa pig; VA10, Papa hog; VA46, Poppa hog; (Qu. K53, *Words used by women or in mixed company for a male breeding-pig; total Infs questioned, 75*) Inf OK33, Papa hog. **1973** Allen *LAUM* 1.244 **Upper MW** (as of c1950), *Bull*. . . papa cow [1 inf, **IA**]. *Ibid* 250, *Boar*. . . papa hog [1 inf, **NE**]. **1986** Pederson *LAGS Concordance* (*Bull*) 1 inf, **swMS**, Others say papa cow—old, usual term in past; 1 inf, **swMS**, Papa cow; (*Boar*) 2 infs, **ce,cwMS**, Papa hog; 1 inf, **cnGA**, Papa pigs; (*Stallion*) 1 inf, **swAL**, Papa horse—euphemism, joking; 1 inf, **cwMS**, Papa horse—polite term; 1 inf, **cMS**, Papa horse—I've heard; 1 inf, **ceTX**, Papa horse—mother told them to say.

4 in phr *your papa likes you best:* =**father** n B5.

1968 *DARE* (Qu. W24a, . . *Expressions . . to warn a woman slyly that her slip is showing*) Inf **IN19**, Your papa likes you best.

papabotte n Also *papabot(e)*   Pronc-sp *poppa body*   [Prob echoic]   **LA**

An **upland plover** (here: *Bartramia longicauda*).

1838 Audubon *Ornith. Biog.* IV.34 (*DA*), In the neighbourhood of New Orleans, where it [the Bartram sandpiper] is called the 'Papabote,' it usually arrives in great bands in the spring. **1881** *Chicago Field* 11 June 281 **LA**, That species of plover, designated with us by the peculiarly local name of papabotte, but, ornithologically *Totanus bartramius*. . . In season . . they are found . . feeding largely upon Spanish-flies and insects of the beetle order, which excites fat, and whose peculiar influences impregnate their flesh and produce a most delicate *morceau* for the epicure. **1888** Trumbull *Names of Birds* 173, At New Orleans, La. it is the *Papabote;* this is Audubon's spelling of the name; it is also written "Papabot" and "Papabotte." **1899** in 1900 *LA Soc. Naturalists Proc.* 96, *Bartramia longicauda*. . . Papabotte. . . Eagerly hunted and highly prized in lower Louisiana as a game bird. **1949** *N.O. Times-Picayune Mag.* 27 Nov 16 (*DA*), Some call this 'upland' variety the Papabotte, from the sound of his call. **1951** Teale *North with Spring* 100 **LA**, Across the field, where the rain had left shallow puddles here and there, plover were feeding. Maurice told me they were called locally "poppabodies"—apparently a corruption of the French word for upland plover, "pappabotte." **1962** Imhof *AL Birds* 237, *Upland Plover*. . . Papabotte. **1983** Reinecke *Coll.* 8 **LA**, Papabotte. . . [papəbɑt] the upland plover or sandpiper, once much sought after as a supposed aphrodisiac, said to have consumed Spanish fly in migration. Served in plusher Basin Street houses. Known among hunters from La. Fr., prob. onomatap [sic].

Papago bluebells n

A **blue dicks** (here: *Dichelostemma capitatum*).

1942 Castetter–Bell *Pima & Papago Ag.* 60, Bulbs of *covenas* or Papago blue bells (*Brodiaea capitata* var. *pauciflora*) were . . usually eaten raw in early spring before other foods were available.

papah See **papa**

pa-pap See **pap-pap**

papau, papaw n[1] See **pawpaw**

pa-paw n[2] Usu |'pæˌpɔ, 'pɑˌpɔ, 'pɔˌpɔ| Also sp *pappaw, pawpaw, pop-paw;* for addit pronc and sp varr see quots   **scattered, but chiefly Sth, S Midl**   See Map   Cf **mam-maw, pap-pap**

A grandfather; rarely a father or stepfather—also used as a quasi-personal name.

1942 Hall *Smoky Mt. Speech* 77 **wNC, eTN**, ['pæˌpɔ:] for *grandfather* is also said to be current. **1956** Ker *Vocab. W. TX* 308, *Pa-paw* and/or *paw-paw* [for grandfather] is offered by [3 of 67] informants. **c1960**

Wilson Coll. **csKY**, *Papaw* is becoming common for grandpa. **1962** Atwood *Vocab. TX* 66, Miscellaneous nicknames recorded for this item [=*grandfather*] include: . . Papaw, Poppaw. **1965–70** *DARE* (Qu. Z3, . . 'Grandfather') 17 Infs, **chiefly Sth, S Midl**, Pa-paw [no transcription recorded]; 19 Infs, **chiefly Sth, S Midl**, Pa-paw ['pæˌpɔ]; AL30, LA11, 40, MS47, 51, Pa-paw ['pɑˌpɔ]; KY44, Pa-paw [papɔ]; 14 Infs, **scattered, but esp Sth, S Midl**, Paw-paw; LA2, 28, NC55, OK42, Paw-paw ['pɔˌpɔ]; CA132, GA6, 7, 11, NC31, PA1, 241, VA93, Pa-pa; IL51, SC34, Pa-pa [papɑ]; SC40, MA125, Pa-pa ['papa]; SC44, Pa-pa [pæpæ]; PA241, Paw-pa; IL25, Pa-po ['pɑːpo]; NC31, Po-po ['pouˌpou]; AR51, Peepaw ['piˌpɔ]. **1970** Tarpley *Blinky* 210 **neTX**, *Usual term of affection for grandfather* . . pappy, pop, pop-paw [rare]. **1975** *Appalachian Jrl.* 2.154 **wNC**, Grandparents were usually designated by the terms *mammaw* and *pappaw*. **1992** *NADS Letters* **AL**, The Alabama term for "grandfather" is . . *papaw*. Perhaps I should spell it *pappaw* to reflect the first vowel [æ]. I'm afraid I can't give any accurate dialect boundaries. *Ibid* **cIN**, *Mamaw & papaw*. . . Our local Monroe County people use these two words, often in death and thank-you notes in paper: our beloved grandpa, dad, brother, and papaw, and many seem to use it as an affectionate term for a grandparent or even parent. *But my local life-long resident cleaning lady insists that its real true and correct meaning is: Step-father and Step-mother. **1993** *Ibid* **TX**, The word for grandfather was paw-paw with equal accent on both syllables. **1996** *DARE File* **sOH**, The area using "mammaw/mamaw" and "pappaw/papaw" extends at least as far west as Portsmouth, OH . . , and as far north of the river as Hillsboro and Chillicothe. *Ibid*, My "spousal equivalent" . . called her maternal grandparents mammaw [=['mæˌmɔ]] and papaw [=['pæˌpɔ]] and her paternal grandmother mami with stress on the last syllable. . . In south Louisiana mami and mimi (so accented) are common. I never heard this or mammaw growing up in Tenn. but I did hear papaw and pawpaw.

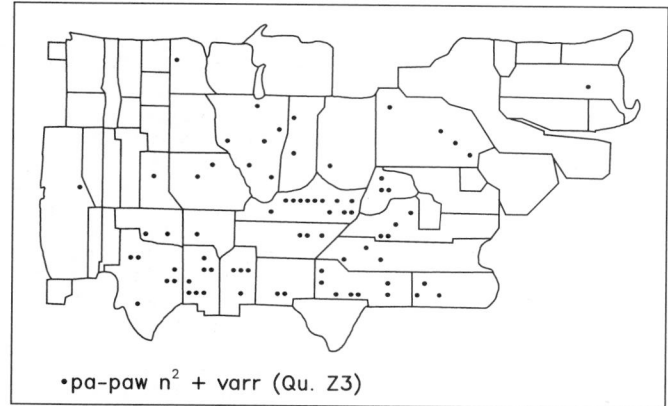
•pa-paw n[2] + varr (Qu. Z3)

pape n |pap| Pronc-sp *pop*   [LaFr *pape,* literally "pope"; cf **cardinal 1, king eveque**]   **LA**   Cf **blue pop, green ~, pope** n[1] 1, **poplaree, red pop, sweet ~**

Any of var small, brightly colored birds, but esp the **painted bunting 1**; hence v *pop* to hunt this bird.

[**1758** Le Page du Pratz *Histoire Louisiane* 2.139, Le Pape est un oiseau dont le pluma[ge] est rouge & noir. [=The pape is a bird whose plumage is red and black.]] [**1811** Wilson *Amer. Ornith.* 3.68, Painted Bunting. . . This is one of the most numerous of the little summer birds of Lower Louisiana, where it is universally known among the French inhabitants, and called by them *"Le Pape,"* and by the Americans the *Nonpareil*.] **1831** Audubon *Ornith. Biog.* 1.281 **LA**, Some persons give the name of *Nonpareil* to this species [=painted bunting], but it is more commonly known by the name of *Pape*, which, in fact, is a general appellation given by the inhabitants of Louisiana to all the smaller species of thick-billed birds. **1882** Nuttall *Ornith. Club Bulletin* 7.163 **LA**, I saw several males [of *Passerina ciris*] in confinement in New Orleans. . . They are called "Pops" here, the derivation of which name I could not make out. **1945** *AmSp* 20.49 **New Orleans LA**, The English-speaking people of New Orleans call the bird [=the painted bunting] 'pop.' As a boy I went 'popping' (trapping 'pops') in the 'sticks' (reeds, canes, weeds ten feet high) within the city limits of New Orleans. **1968** *DARE* (Qu. Q14, . . *Goldfinch*) Inf LA33, Pops. **1983** Reinecke *Coll.* 8 **LA**, *Pape, Pop* . . [pɑp]—a small very colorful song-bird, esp. painted bunting. . . Also "red-pop" La. Fr. "pape," pope, by entertaining analogy with "cardinal" and "évèque" or bishop = indigo bunting.

paperback See **papershell 1**

paper-bag bush n
=**bladder sage.**

    1941 Jaeger *Wildflowers* 226, Paper-bag bush. . . A very handsome rounded shrub, presenting a singular appearance because of its numerous inflated, papery pods, which in age are often tinged with rose. . . more or less common over the northern Colorado and Mohave deserts; to Utah and Mex. **1960** Vines *Trees SW* 906, Bladder-sage. . . A vernacular name for the species is Paperbag-bush, because of the inflated calyx. **1981** Benson–Darrow *Trees SW Deserts* 204, *Salazaria mexicana* . . Bladder Sage, Paper-Bag Bush.

paper-bark tree n
A **madrone** (here: *Arbutus texana*).

    1951 *PADS* 15.37 **TX,** *Arbutus texana*. . . Paper-bark tree. Strips of pinkish, orange-red, or red-brown bark, thin and curly like birch, floating down clear little streams in mountain canons [sic] are one means of detecting the presence of this beautiful Texas tree.

paperbelly n
1 =**lake trout 1.** [See quot 1983]

    1965 McClane *McClane's Std. Fishing Encycl.* 461, Presently identified as a race resembling the siscowet in its external appearance is the humper lake trout, which is known to the commercial fishermen as the "paperbelly" or "bank trout." **1983** Becker *Fishes WI* 331, The humper's thin ventral body wall ("paper-belly") and the limited amount of fat on its viscera would distinguish it from the siscowet.

2 A **kiyi** (here: *Coregonus kiyi*).

    1983 Becker *Fishes WI* 361, *Coregonus kiyi*. . . Other common names: bigeye, paperbelly [etc].

paper birch n [See quot 1900]
A birch: usu *Betula papyrifera,* but also **gray birch a** and **western birch.** For other names of *B. papyrifera* see **canoe birch, gray ~ d, red ~ 4, silver ~, spoolwood, white birch**

    1785 Marshall *Arbustrum* 19, *Betula papyrifera*. White Paper Birch. This is a variety of the last [=the Red Birch], growing to a middling size and pretty much resembling it except in having a very white smooth bark. **1810** Michaux *Histoire des Arbres* 1.25, Betula papyracea . . Canoe birch (Bouleau à canot), Paper birch (Bouleau à papier), Dénominations également usitées dans les Etats de New-Hampshire, Vermont, le District de Maine, la Nouvelle-Écosse, et plus au nord. [= . . Both names used in the States of New-Hampshire, Vermont, the District of Maine, Nova Scotia, and further north.] **1861** Wood *Class-Book* 649, *B[etula] papyracea* . . Paper Birch. **1900** (1927) Keeler *Our Native Trees* 304, The Paper Birch possesses the most wonderful bark of any of our native trees. . . Beneath the smooth white skin are the paper-like layers which readily separate into thin sheets and vary in color from cream to light tan. . . The thin papery layers into which the bark separates are of so firm a texture that it is possible both to write and paint upon them. **1938** Van Dersal *Native Woody Plants* 325, Paper [birch] *(Betula papyrifera, Betula populifolia).* Ibid, Western paper [birch] *(Betula papyrifera).* **1961** Douglas *My Wilderness* 110 **neMN,** Behind it were a few paper (canoe) birch and a thick stand of black spruce towering eighty or a hundred feet. **1967** Gilkey–Dennis *Hdbk. NW Plants* 85, *Betula occidentalis* . . the *Western paper birch.* . . a large tree reaching a trunk diam. of 9–12 dm., and closely related to the *Eastern paper birch, B. papyrifera,* and sometimes treated as a variety of this species. **1969** *DARE* (Qu. T16, . . *Kinds of trees* . . *'special'*) Inf **RI5,** Paper birch.

paper chase n Also *paper trail* [*OED2* (at *paper* sb. 12) 1856 →]
See quot 1899.

    [**1891** *Harper's New Mth. Mag.* 82.658, The instruction of the French army has been developed, and even its amusements have become more serious, and those which necessitate exercises useful in warfare, such as drag hunts, raids, and "rally-papier," or paper chases, are very popular.] **1895** Ibid 90.506, Nevertheless, the sporting fever was rampant in the land, and a paper-chase club led in 1876 to the organization of a hunt. **1899** Champlin–Bostwick *Young Folks' Games* 404, *Hare and hounds,* or *paper chase,* a running game played by any number of persons. One or two of the players are chosen as hares, and each is provided with a bag filled with small clippings of paper, called the "scent." The hares start off together. . . After from five to fifteen minutes . . the hounds set off in pursuit. **1906** *DN* 3.149 **nwAR,** *Paper trail.* . . Hare and hounds. **1957** *Sat. Eve. Post Letters* **neKS,** Paper chase—torn newspapers spread in a trail for those who were chasing to follow. Used by kids in Clay Center, Kansas around 1909. **1967–68** *DARE* (Qu. EE33, . . *Outdoor*

games . . *that children play*) Inf **AK9,** Paper chase—fox and hounds; **CT8, OR15, PA35, 104,** Paper chase.

paper daisy n
1 =**paperflower.** [See quot 1945]

    1945 Benson–Darrow *Manual SW Trees* 337, *Psilostrophe Cooperi.* . . Yellow Paper Daisy. . . Ray flowers . . becoming papery at fruiting time. **1967** Dodge *Roadside Wildflowers* 87, *Paper Daisy.* . . With age, the bright yellow flowers . . become papery in texture, and may remain on the plant for weeks. . . Stockmen report the plants poisonous to sheep. *Psilostrophe tagetina.* **1968** Schmutz et al. *Livestock-Poisoning Plants AZ* 50, Paperdaisy *(Psilostrophe sparsiflora. . . P. tagetina). Ibid* 146, Yellow paperdaisy—*Psilostrophe cooperi.* . . It may cause some poisoning similar to the other paperflowers.

2 A **desert marigold** (here: *Baileya multiradiata*). [See quot 1957]

    1957 Jaeger *N. Amer. Deserts* 274, *Gold Dollars, Paper Daisy,* or *Desert Marigold. Baileya multiradiata.* . . The floral rays are papery and turn down with age. A common and very showy roadside plant. **1961** Wills–Irwin *Flowers TX* 242, A common and attractive plant of hills and flats in the Trans-Pecos, Paper Daisy, or Desert Baileya, flowers intermittently throughout most of the year. **1985** Dodge *Flowers SW Deserts* 90, Blossom petals (rays) become bleached and papery as the blossoms age, thus giving the plant in some localities the name "paper-daisy."

paperflower n [See quot 1915]
A plant of the genus *Psilostrophe,* native chiefly to the southwestern US. Also called **paper daisy 1**

    1915 (1926) Armstrong–Thornber *Western Wild Flowers* 542, *Psilostrophe . . sparsiflora.* . . *Paper Flowers—Psilostrophe Cooperi.* . . the pretty flowers . . [have] yellow rays, . . turning back and becoming papery as they fade. **1936** Whitehouse *TX Flowers* 180, *Plains Paper-Flower (Psilotrophe villosa)* . . has foliage covered with a dense white wooly coat of hairs. . . Near El Paso is found the lovely western paper-flower . . *(Psilostrophe cooperi). . . Psilostrophe tagetinae* [sic] . . is probably the most abundant paper-flower in the state. **1948** Stevens *KS Wild Flowers* 389, *Psilostrophe villosa—Paperflower.* . . Ray flowers . . with age becoming whitened and papery. **1968** Schmutz et al. *Livestock-Poisoning Plants AZ* 50, *Psilostrophe sparsiflora. . . P. tagetina.* . . These paperflowers are erect, perennial herbs. . . most abundant on overgrazed ranges. **1985** Dodge *Flowers SW Deserts* 92, Although the paperflower does not form great masses of color, the blossom covered clumps are conspicuous among the cactus, mesquite and creosotebush of the desert.

paper-flowered onion n
A **wild onion** (here: *Allium hyalinum*).

    1923 Abrams *Flora Pacific States* 1.396 **CA,** *Allium hyalinum.* . . Paper-flowered Onion. . . Foothills of the Sierra Nevada. **1961** Thomas *Flora Santa Cruz* 124 **cwCA,** Paper-flowered Onion. Known locally only from the vicinity of Uvas Creek and Almaden. April–May.

paper hearts n
A **ground-cherry** (here: *Physalis viscosa* subsp *mollis*).

    1951 *PADS* 15.38 **TX,** *Physalis mollis.* . . Cowslip vines; paper hearts.

paper hornet See **paper wasp**

paperleaf alder n [See quot 1908]
An alder (here: *Alnus tenuifolia*).

    1908 Rogers *Tree Book* 179, The *Paperleaf Alder.* . . A small tree with thin, firm-textured leaves, . . one of the prettiest of the alders. **1938** Van Dersal *Native Woody Plants* 322, Alder, Paperleaf *(Alnus tenuifolia).*

papermaker, paper-making wasp See **paper wasp**

papermouth n Also *papermouth bass, ~ perch* [See quot 1956]
=**crappie.**

    1902 Jordan–Evermann *Amer. Fishes* 334 **IN, IL,** The crappie. . . is a fish of wide distribution and has, in consequence, received many vernacular names. It is called . . tin-mouth or papermouth in northern Indiana and Illinois. **1946** LaMonte *N. Amer. Game Fishes* 143, White Crappie. . . Papermouth [etc]. *Ibid,* Black Crappie. . . Papermouth, Tin-mouth. **1947** Dalrymple *Panfish* 85, Here, my friend, are the various names by which you would address that little gamester, the Crappie, depending on where you happened to be at the moment: Bachelor . .

Papermouth[,] Papermouth Bass [etc]. **1956** Harlan–Speaker *IA Fish* 221, Care must be used in landing a crappie once he is hooked. In some regions they are known as "paper-mouths", which is a very descriptive term. Keep a tight line, or he will be off your hook right now, but don't "horse" them too much either, or the hook will tear out. **1972** Sparano *Outdoors Encycl.* 361, *White Crappie* . . Common Names: White crappie, papermouth, . . papermouth perch [etc]. *Ibid* 362, *Black Crappie* . . Common Names . . papermouth, grass bass.

paper-shade Irish n Cf **lace-curtain 2**
 1967 *DARE* File **csMA** (as of c1950), Paper-shade Irish—Lower class Irish. This is [also] common in Boston and perhaps wherever there is an Irish population. I have heard variations on it, too.

papershell n
 1 also *paperback:* A molted crab whose shell is just beginning to harden. **esp MD, DE** Cf **buckram, leatherback 8**
 1884 Goode *Fisheries U.S.* 776, On different parts of the coast, Crabs in the soft state are known respectively as "Soft Crabs," "Shedders," or "Peelers." The terms "Soft Crab," "Paper-shell," and "Buckler" denote the different stages of consistency of the shell, from the time of shedding until it has become nearly hard again. **1905** U.S. Bur. Fisheries *Rept. for 1904* 419, There are six stages of a crab's life, commonly classified as follows: First, the "hard crab," . . second, a "snot," . . third, a "peeler," . . fourth, a "buster," . . fifth, the "soft crab;" sixth, a "papershell," when the new shell is beginning to harden. **1934** *Sun* (Baltimore MD) 2 Apr 6/2–3 *(Hench Coll.)* **seMD**, Floats . . have to be fished several times during each twenty-four hours, in order that the soft crab may be taken out at once and placed in grass, otherwise they would become papershell or buckram crabs, which are illegal to market. **1953** MD Dept. Educ. *Our Underwater Farm* 25, A crab molts 25 or 26 times during its life, each time increasing in size. The molting process goes on step by step from hard crab to peeler, to buster, to soft shell, to paper shell, and back to hard crab again. **1968** *DARE* Tape **DE**2, Paperbacks are just a stage in between a soft-shell and a hard-shell. . . We like to throw them back if we realize it's a papershell. **1976** Warner *Beautiful Swimmers* 22 **eMD**, In the case of the blue crab . . what is remarkable is the extreme softness of the new skin after moulting. . . Left in the water, the blue crab's new exo-skeleton hardens rapidly. It becomes "paper shell" or slightly stiff in twelve hours. **1984** *DARE* File **Chesapeake Bay** [Watermen's vocab], Papershell.
 2 Any of several **freshwater clams** of the genera *Anodonta, Leptodea* or *Potamilus,* or *Anodontoides ferussacianus.* [From the thinness of the shell]
 1941 *AmSp* 16.156, There are many varieties of fresh-water mussels. . . The following list gives the common names as applied by the cutter and fisher of shells. . . Paper-shell [etc]. **1982** U.S. Fish & Wildlife Serv. *Fresh-Water Mussels* 1.18, Pink Papershell . . *Proptera* [= *Potamilus*] *laevissima. Ibid* 21, Fragile papershell . . *Leptodea fragilis. Ibid* 22, Narrow Papershell . . *Leptodea leptodon.* **1982** *WI State Jrl.* (Madison) 22 Aug sec 7 3, [Caption:] Several of the clams that may be found in Wisconsin rivers include . . fragile paper shell [etc]. **1991** IL Nat. Hist. Surv. *Biol. Notes* 137.11 **IL**, *Anodontoides ferussacianus* . . cylindrical papershell. . . 50 individuals of this headwater species were collected at ten stations and constituted more than 2% of the total sample. *Ibid* 12, *Leptodea fragilis.* . . Widespread and common in both small streams and rivers . . , the fragile papershell was the third most commonly collected species in the current survey. *Ibid* 14, *Potamilus ohiensis* . . pink papershell. **1992** Cummings–Mayer *Field Guide Freshwater Mussels MW* 74, *Utterbackia* (=*Anodonta*) *imbecillis.* . . Papershell. . . Shell extremely thin, transparent in young individuals. *Ibid* 78, *Pyganodon* (=*Anodonta*) *grandis.* . . Papershell. . . Shell extremely thin in young mussels. *Ibid* 80, *Cylindrical papershell*—*Anodontoides ferussacianus. Ibid* 118, *Leptodea leptodon.* . . Narrow papershell. *Ibid* 120, *Leptodea fragilis.* . . Papershell. . . *Ibid* 122, *Potamilus ohiensis.* . . Papershell.
 3 See **papershell pecan.**

papershell cockle n Cf **hard-shell clam 2**
 A **littleneck 2** (here: *Protothaca tenerrima*).
 1920 CA Fish & Game Comm. *Fish Bulletin* 4.38, In the Los Angeles markets. . . the more brittle *Paphia* [=*Prototheca tenerrima*] . . is called a soft-shell or paper-shell cockle.

papershell pecan n Also *papershell*
 The thin-shelled nut of any of var **pecan B1** cultivars.
 1912 *Outing* 61.377, The only difference between the so-called "paper-shell" pecan and the fruit from the wild tree of the forest is that the

former has been grown on a budded or grafted tree. **1945** *N. Eng. Homestead* 27 Oct. 20/2 *(DA)*, Paper shell pecan in Shell 50¢ per pound. **1967** *DARE* (Qu. I53, . . *Fruits grown around here . . special varieties*) Inf **SC**29, Papershell pecans. **1969** *DARE* Tape **IL**83, I have two big papershell pecan trees—they's big huge'uns in the front. **1976** Bailey–Bailey *Hortus Third* 830, Thin-shelled nuts are often advertised and sold as "paper shell" pecans. This is not a pecan cultivar but a characteristic of many cultivars. **1986** Pederson *LAGS Concordance,* 10 infs, **Gulf Region,** Papershell (pecans). **1989** Whealy *Fruit Inventory* 312, *Papershell*—Thin shelled nut, not quite as large as Mahan and Stuart. Good quality. Fine shaped, fast growing tree. Excellent pollinator.

paper trail See **paper chase**

paper wasp n Also *paper hornet, papermaker, paper-making wasp* **chiefly NEast, N Cent** See Map
 A wasp of the family Vespidae, usu of the genus *Polistes.* For other names of *Dolichovespula maculata* see **bald-faced hornet**
 1854 Riley *Puddleford People* 216, The 'paper-wasp' was gathering wild cotton and flax. **1867** *Amer. Naturalist* 1.140, The odor that arises from the Tarantula Killer when she uses her sting . . resembles the odor of the paper-making wasp (Vespa), only much stronger. **1869** (1870) *Ibid* 3.52 **OH**, The Paper Hornet (*Vespa maculata*) often enters my nucleus hives, when I am rearing Italian queen bees. **1939** *LANE* Map 239 *(Wasp)* Small yellowish wasps that build comb-shaped paper nests. These are commonly known simply as *wasps.* . . 3 infs, **swCT, cwCT, ceMA,** Paper wasp. **1940** Teale *Insects* 121, One summer, I spent hours watching the building of a nest by paper-making wasps. . . All the workers made trips afield to find wood out of which they bit chunks and chewed them into pulp for making paper. **1949** Swain *Insect Guide* 176, The paper wasps construct sometimes massive nests, which may be suspended from the branches of trees, eaves, and barn roofs, or placed in cavities in trees or in the ground. *Ibid* 177, Paper Wasp—*Polistes fuscatus.* **1965–70** *DARE* (Qu. R21, . . *Stinging insects*) 17 Infs, **chiefly NEast, N Cent,** Paper wasp; OK52, Black wasp, red wasp—also called papermakers; (Qu. R20, *Wasps that build their nests of mud*) Infs **NY**60, 171, **PA**126, 163, 168, **RI**15, Paper wasp; **CT**29, Paper wasp—looks like mud wasp but makes nest of paper-like substance; **NJ**16, Paper wasp—tubes of paper, yellow head, 1½ inches; **NY**183, Paper wasp—about one inch long, build nests of paper and mud, about the size and shape of a man's clenched hand. **1972** Swan–Papp *Insects* 545, *P[olistes] f[uscatus] pallipes*—sometimes referred to as the "dark paper wasp". . . *P. annularis*—the "large paper wasp". . . *P. exclamans*—known as the "zebra paper wasp." **1980** Milne–Milne *Audubon Field Guide Insects* 834, Paper Wasps (*Polistes* spp.) *Ibid* 835, Paper Wasps are much more tolerant of people and minor disturbances than are hornets and yellow jackets. The Northern Paper Wasp (*P. fuscatus*) . . is dark reddish brown and yellow. . . The Southwestern Texas Paper Wasp (*P. apachus*) . . is reddish brown with yellow markings. It occurs in Texas, New Mexico, southern California, and Mexico.

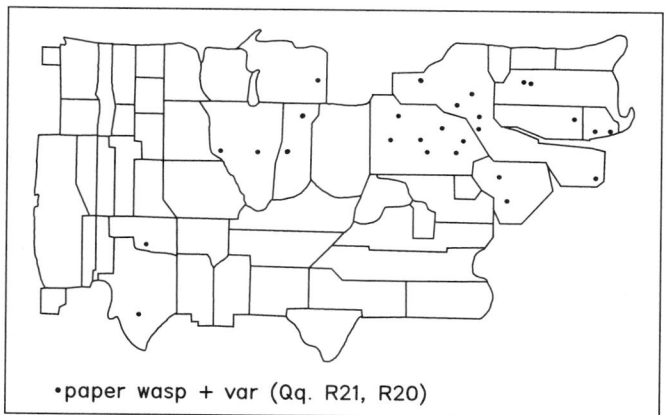
•paper wasp + var (Qq. R21, R20)

paperwood pine n
 =**jack pine 1.**
 1969 *DARE* (Qu. T16, . . *Kinds of trees . . 'special'*) Inf **PA**214, Paperwood pine—same as jack pine.

papio n [Haw] **HI**
 The young of any of several **ulua;** see quots.
 1960 Gosline–Brock *Hawaiian Fishes* 176, *Caranx helvous* . . *Papio*

[young]. . . *Caranx ignobilis* . . *Papio* [young]. . . One of the commonest of the uluas found in Hawaiian waters. *Ibid* 178, *Caranx lugubris* . . *Papio* [young]. *Ibid* 179, *Caranx sexfasciatus* . . *Papio* [young]. . . The papio (juvenile fish) range from tide pools and brackish-water areas to deeper coastal waters. **1967** *Honolulu Star–Bulletin* (HI) 31 May sec F 1/4, Baby ulua called papio. **1967** *DARE* Tape **HI**9, They catch that kind of papio [pɑˈpio]. Papio is a small size of ulua. **1979** Bushnell *Stone of Kannon* 394 **HI** (as of 1876–77), Koi pulled in a fine papio. Five minutes later, when he hooked a weke, the native fishermen gathered around Koi and Aiko. **1994** Stone–Pratt *Hawaiʻi's Plants* 81, Fishes such as . . papio (young ulua . . *Caranx* sp.) were probably introduced into the pools from the ocean by humans, for use as food.

papoose root n

1 also *pappoose root, poppoos ~, poppose ~:* =**blue cohosh 1.** [See quot 1951]
1815 Drake *Natural View Cincinnati* 85, Leontice thalictoides [sic]—poppoos root. **1822** Eaton *Botany* 227, *Caulophyllum* . . *thalictroides* (poppose root, false cohosh). **1828** Rafinesque *Med. Flora* 97, *Caulophyllum thalictroides*. . . Vulgar Names—Cohosh, Cohush, Blueberry, Papoose root [etc]. **1859** (1968) Bartlett *Americanisms* 309, *Pappoose-Root (Caulophyllum thalictroides.)* A plant called also Blue Cohosh. **1901** Lounsberry *S. Wild Flowers* 188, *Blue Cohosh. Pappoose Root.*. . All about, it is known by the native people whose belief it is, that it does good to all young creatures, the faith, no doubt, transmitted to them by the Indians who dosed with it their pappooses. **1943** Peattie *Great Smokies* 190, The old wives of the mountains today are not averse to . . giving their teething children a little papooseroot. **1951** Voss–Eifert *IL Wild Flowers* 67, The medicinal root was used by the Indians as an antispasmodic in infant convulsions—papoose root—and as an aid in quick childbirth—squawroot.
2 A **bugbane 1** (here: *Cimicifuga racemosa*).
1971 Krochmal *Appalachia Med. Plants* 96, *Cimicifuga racemosa*. . . Common Names: Cohosh bugbane . . papoose root [etc]. **1974** (1977) Coon *Useful Plants* 219, *Cimicifuga racemosa* . . papoose root, bugbane, etc. . . As a medicine it is said . . to be of value for snakebites, while the extractions from the roots and rhizomes are listed as valuable as a sedative, and antispasmodic.

pa-pop See **pop-pop**

pap-pap n |ˈpæ(p) ˈpæp| Also sp *pa-pap, pu-pap* [Hypocoristic] **PA, MD** Cf **pop-pop**
A grandfather—also used as a quasi-personal name.
1967–69 *DARE* (Qu. Z3, . . *'Grandfather'*) Infs **MD**24, 27, Pap-pap [pæp pæp]—only small children say; **PA**76, Pap-pap [pæp pæp]; **PA**134, 213, Pap-pap; **PA**164, Pa-pap [pæ pæp]; **PA**14, Pu-pap.

pappaw See **papaw**

pappie See **pappy** v

pappoose adv
1912 *DN* 3.359 **cNY**, *Pappoose*. . . Same as pig-a-back. "Carry me pappoose."

pappoose root See **papoose root**

pappy n

1 A father—also used as a quasi-personal name. [*OED2* 1763 →] **chiefly S Midl** See Map Cf **poppy** n² **1**
1854 *Ladies' Repository* 14.51, Pappy's face is as cold as ice, and I don't feel him stir any more. **1887** (1967) Harris *Free Joe* 129 **nGA**, Nobody never ketched me whinin' 'roun' atter your pappy 'fore we wuz married. **1890** *DN* 1.68 **KY**, *Pa*. . . Note also . . [pæp] and . . [pæpi]. **1893** Shands *MS Speech* 49, *Pappy* [pæpi]. A term used by negro children for *father*. **1899** (1912) Green *VA Folk-Speech* 311, *Pappy*. . . Papa; father. A childish word. **1903** Murrie *White Castle LA* 165 (as of c1865), Sancho. . . was a saucy fellow. If you gave him an inch he took an ell, but he never spoke of his "maw" and "paw" like so many of the other negroes; it was "mammy" and "pappy." **1909** *DN* 3.355 **eAL, wGA**, *Pap(py)*. . . Father. Perhaps not so common as *paw*, or *papa*. **1914** *DN* 4.60 **cVA**, *Pappy*. . . Father. Wheah's yo' pappy? **1915** *DN* 4.187 **swVA**, *Pappy*. . . Diminutive of *pap*, father. **1919** *DN* 5.39 **eTN**, *Pappy*. . . Father. **1923** *DN* 5.216 **swMO**, *Pap*. . . Father. Also, *Pappy* and *Poppy*. **1928** in 1952 Mathes *Tall Tales* 43 **sAppalachians**, Pappy's dead an' gone, an' John Cutshaw's been in the pen fer five years now. **1936** *AmSp* 11.160 **eTX**, Among older or less well educated people in rural districts, *algebra, Arnica,* [etc]. . . are pronounced with [ɪ] in the

final syllable. . . [ˈmæmɪ], [ˈpæpɪ] for *mama, papa,* are also often heard among such speakers. **1942** Hall *Smoky Mt. Speech* 77 **wNC, eTN**, *Mama* and *papa*, now usually [ˈmɑmə] and [ˈpɑpə], may still occasionally be heard as [ˈmæmɪ] and [ˈpæpɪ]; the latter is often shortened to [pæp]. **1942** Faulkner *Go Down* 47 **MS**, The same thing made my pappy that made your grandmaw. **1953** [see **2** below]. **c1960** [see **2** below]. **1962** Dykeman *Tall Woman* 255 **NC** (as of c1860), But everyone knows there's only one person would have put him up to such mischief: the man he was tenant and pappy-in-law to. **1965–70** *DARE* (Qu. Z1, . . *'Father'*) 22 Infs, **chiefly S Midl**, Pappy; **KY**5, 25, 59, 70, Pappy—old-fashioned; **KY**60, Some say pappy; **TN**1, Pappy—mostly by children; **TN**27, Pappy—older than papa; **TX**35, Pappy—long time ago; (Qu. P37b, *Nicknames for a shotgun*) Inf **MO**36, Pappy's standby; (Qu. U38a, . . *A great deal of money: "He's got _____ [of money]."*) Inf **NY**249, Got money, his mammy and pappy; (Qu. Z11b, . . *[A child whose parents were not married]*) Inf **MD**36, Don't know his pappy. [15 of 32 total Infs comm type 5, 14 gs educ or less] **1986** Pederson *LAGS Concordance (Father)* 20 infs, **chiefly TN, nAL, nAR**, Pappy; 1 inf, **cAL**, Is exactly like his pappy in looks; 1 inf, **ceAR**, Sure looks like his pappy; 1 inf, **cwFL**, Ol' Pappy Parker.

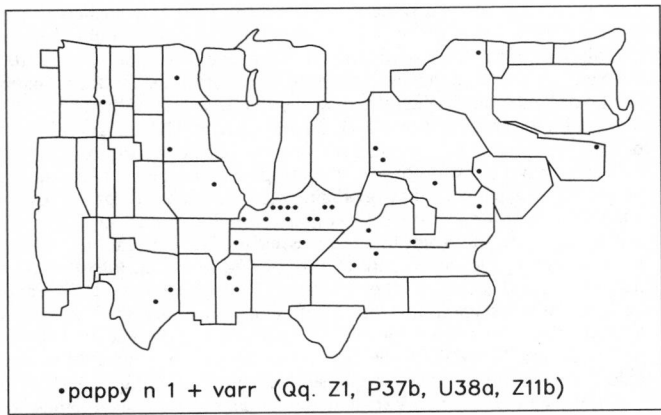
•pappy n 1 + varr (Qq. Z1, P37b, U38a, Z11b)

2 also *great pappy, old ~:* A grandfather; occas a great-uncle—also used as a quasi-personal name.
1953 Randolph–Wilson *Down in Holler* 270 **Ozarks**, *Pappy*. . . Father. *Pap, paw,* and *poppy* are also common. In some families the father is called *paw*, while *pappy* designates a grandfather or even a great-uncle. **c1960** *Wilson Coll.* **csKY**, *Pappy*. . . Father, formerly common; still used by middle-aged people and, because of this, by some grandchildren, to mean grandfather. **1965–70** *DARE* (Qu. Z3, . . *'Grandfather'*) 15 Infs, **scattered, but esp Midl**, Pappy; **NY**209, Great pappy; **GA**28, Granddaddy, old pappy; **1986** Pederson *LAGS Concordance (Grandfather)* 11 infs, **Gulf Region**, Pappy; 1 inf, **neTN**, Her grandchildren called her husband pappy. **2000** *DARE* File **seKY** (as of c1950), We called our Grandmother and Grandfather Mammy and Pappy.

pappy v Also sp *pappie*
1 To father (a child). Cf **daddy** v **1**
1940 Stuart *Trees of Heaven* 169 **eKY**, Funny how a man that ugly could pappie a gal purty as Subrinea. **1941** *Sat. Eve. Post* 10 May 113 **KY**, Once I knew a man had a passel o' children. . . Married two times and pappied twenty-three.
2 See quot. Cf **daddy** v **3**
1953 Randolph–Wilson *Down in Holler* 263 **Ozarks**, *Mammy*. . . to transmit the mother's likeness to offspring. . . The word *pappy* is used in the same way, meaning that the progeny *take after* the father rather than the mother.

pappyfish n
A **harvestfish** (here: *Peprilus alepidotus*).
1896 U.S. Bur. Fisheries *Rept. for 1895* 351, *Rhombus paru*. . . *Pappyfish*. South Atlantic Coast of United States. **1897** NY Forest Fish & Game Comm. *Annual Rept. for 1896* 239, *Rhombus paru* . . Harvestfish; Pappy-fish.—A summer visitor in Gravesend Bay and sometimes rare, but formerly abundant. **1903** NY State Museum & Sci. Serv. *Bulletin* 60.456, *Pappyfish*. . . Profile of head very obtuse. . . The species reaches a length of 8 inches.

pappy sack n Also sp *pa sack*
1994 NC Lang. & Life Project *Dial. Dict. Lumbee Engl.* 9 **seNC**,

Pappy sack. . . Also *pa sack.* Term of endearment for a male child. *Come here, my little pappy sack!*

paps See **pap**

par n Cf **head and footer**

A children's game; see quot 1891; also a measure of distance in the game.

1891 *Jrl. Amer. Folkl.* 4.228 **Brooklyn NY,** *Par.* This game is identical with "Head and Footer" up to the point where all have leaped over the back of the one who is "it." The latter then moves forward a certain distance, which he measures by placing one foot lengthwise beside the base line and the other foot in the hollow of the ankle at right angles to the first. This distance, amounting to the length of the boy's foot plus the width at the instep, is called a "par." The boys then leap over as before, and this is continued until the distance is so great that some one fails to make the leap, or the one who is "it" is "spurred." The game is then started again from the original line, the one failing to go over, or "spurring," becomes "it." **1901** *DN* 2.144 **cwNY,** *Par.* . . Distance of length and width of foot in the game of the same name. Ithaca.

parable n

In phr *speak a parable:* To make a wise or pithy statement.

1950 *PADS* 14.50 **SC,** *Parable:* . . A wise statement. Mostly in the phrase: "You have spoken, or you spoke a parable." **1952** Brown *NC Folkl.* 1.573, *Parable, to speak a:* To say something to the point, something wise.—Central and east.

paraboo n [Cf **parachute**]

1967 *DARE* (Qu. W1c, . . *Joking names . . for an umbrella*) Inf **NY10,** Paraboo ['pɛrəbu]—my paraboo blew outside [sic] out.

parachute n Also sp *parashoot* *joc* Cf **bumbershoot**

An umbrella or parasol.

1870 *Punchinello* 1.379, Foldin' my Filacteries, an' pickin' up my bloo cotton parashoot, I fled the seen. **1901** *DN* 2.144 **PA, NY,** *Parachute.* . . A variant of *parasol.* Crawford Co., Pa., Ithaca [NY]. **1965–70** *DARE* (Qu. W1c, . . *Joking names . . for an umbrella*) 55 Infs, **widespread,** Parachute; **GA77,** Handmade parachute [Of all Infs responding to this question, 72% were old, 22% were gs educ or less, 38% were male; of those giving this response, 89% were old, 41% were gs educ or less, 54% were male.]; (Qu. W1a, *What do you open up and hold over your head when it rains?*) Inf **NY49,** Parachute; (Qu. W1b, *If you use an umbrella . . when the sun is too hot, you call it a* _____) Infs **CT20, FL17, MO16, WA24, WV8,** Parachute. **1986** Pederson *LAGS Concordance* (Umbrella) 1 inf, **csAL,** Parachute; 1 inf, **neAR,** Children called it a parachute.

parachute plant n [See quot 1941]

A **tobaccoweed** (here: *Atrichoseris platyphylla*).

1941 Jaeger *Wildflowers* 306 **Desert SW,** *Atrichoseris platyphylla.* . . The name parachute plant was given because in large plants the inflorescence, with its canopy of white flowers and converging pedicels, appears like a parachute floating in mid-air, the lower stem being quite inconspicuous against its background of dark-surfaced soil. **1960** Abrams *Flora Pacific States* 4.584, Parachute Plant. . . Sandy desert washes, . . California, and adjacent Nevada, east to southwestern Utah and western Arizona.

parada n Also *paratha, peratha, prada* [Appar < Span *parada,* perh in sense "relay of horses"] **CA, OR, NV**

A herd of cattle or horses.

1924 James *Cowboys N. & S.* 25, A "main herd" in Montana, Wyoming, Arizona, and Texas, goes under the name of "parada" in California, Oregon, and Nevada. *Ibid* 38, As a rule, when a bunch of broncs was wanted out of the "stock"—there'd be a "parada" (herd of about 100 broke horses) held together by a few riders—the wild ones would be hazed . . toward the "parada." **1940** Writers' Program *Guide NV* 76, The *cavvy* or *caviatha* is the band of saddle horses, while the *peratha* is any large band. **1964** Jackman–Long *OR Desert* 392, *Parada*—Group of horses or cattle. **c1983** in Lib. of Congress *Amer. Memory: Buckaroos in Paradise* (Internet) **nNV,** Usage of prada, parada, or paratha varies. Here Les uses the term to name the group of animals, often dry cows, cut from the rodera. . . Les said that parada can also name a group of horses, a meaning reported by folklorist Gary Stanton after interviewing other cowboys from the region. One former mustanger told Gary that he had used tame horses to lure wild horses into a trap, and called the bunch of tame animals a parada. (Personal communication from Gary Stanton, August 14, 1984.)

parade key See **key** n 1

paradise apple n [Cf Ger *Paradiesapfel* tomato]

=tomato.

1952 Brown *NC Folkl.* 1.573, *Paradise apple.* . . The tomato.

paradise finch n

=painted bunting 1.

1932 Bennitt *Check-list* 60 **MO,** Painted bunting. *Passerina ciris* . . Nonpareil . . paradise finch. **1969** Longstreet *Birds FL* 147, *Painted Bunting*—Other names: Nonpareil; Mariposa; Paradise Finch [etc].

paradise flower n

A **cat's-claw** (here: *Acacia greggii*).

1897 Sudworth *Arborescent Flora* 250 **NM,** *Acacia greggii.* . . Paradise Flower. **1931** U.S. Dept. Ag. *Misc. Pub.* 101.71, *Catclaw,* also called . . paradise flower, varies in size and form from a very prickly bush to a tall shrub or small tree. **1937** U.S. Forest Serv. *Range Plant Hdbk.* B2, Catclaw, known also as . . paradise-flower, . . is a southwestern species ranging from western Texas to southern Nevada, northern Lower California, and northern Chihuahua, Mexico. **1960** Vines *Trees SW* 499, Paradise Flower. . . The fragrant yellow flowers furnish an excellent bee food, and honey from it is of light yellow and of good flavor.

paradise seed n Also *seed of paradise* Cf **guinea seed**

A grain of paradise (*Aframomum melegueta*).

1931 *Jrl. Amer. Folkl.* 44.412 **Sth** [Black], Take a picture of St. Peter and put it at the front door and a picture of St. Michael at the back door. Put the Paradise seeds in little bags and put one behind each saint. It is known as "feeding the saint." **c1938** in 1970 Hyatt *Hoodoo* 1.709 **LA** [Black], You put the seed of paradise and the codfish together and that *fast luck* together, cinnamon and sugar. *Ibid* 2.1146, Yo' shove dis name down in dere wit red peppah, salt, *gumbo filet,* an' nine *paradise seeds,* an' bury it right at de fo'k of a road.

paradise tree n

A tree (*Simarouba glauca*) native to southern Florida.

1884 Sargent *Forests of N. Amer.* 32, *Paradise Tree.* Semi-tropical Florida. . . A tree sometimes 15 meters in height. **1901** Lounsberry *S. Wild Flowers* 293, That its beauty is appreciated by the people seems to be voiced by its common name of Paradise Tree. **1908** Rogers *Tree Book* 351, *Paradise Tree.* . . grows in lower Florida and the West Indies. . . For weeks in spring the immense loose clusters of tiny yellow flowers spread like a delicate veil over the treetop. . . This is one of the most beautiful trees in tropical gardens, as its name implies. **1939** FWP *Guide FL* 346 **ceFL,** In this jungle . . are found trees growing more than 200 miles north of their native habitat on the Florida Keys. . . [A]mong others, ironwood, gumbo limbo, soapberry, torchwood, strangling fig, paradise tree, pond apple, and necklace bean. **1961** Douglas *My Wilderness* 148 **sFL,** The satinleaf, paradise tree, fiddlewood, Cherokee bean, . . and wax myrtle were strange. **1979** Little *Checklist U.S. Trees* 275, *Paradise-tree.* . . N. on e. coast [of FL] to Cape Canaveral and w. coast to Collier Co. **1992** Hoffman *Turtle Moon* 12 **ceFL,** Every night he drank a bitter tea made from the bark of the paradise tree to ensure his good health.

parakeet n Also sp *paroquet*

1 Std: the Carolina parakeet (*Conuropsis carolinensis*). Also called **gabby bird, parrot**

2 =puffin.

1917 *Wilson Bulletin* 29.2.75 **ME,** *Fratercula arctica.*—Parakeet, Matinicus I[slan]d, Me. **1925** (1928) Forbush *Birds MA* 1.31, *Fratercula arctica arctica.* . . Other names: sea-parrot; paroquet. **1946** Hausman *Eastern Birds* 339, Atlantic Puffin . . Sea Parrot, Common Puffin, Paroquet [etc]. **1956** MA Audubon Soc. *Bulletin* 40.80, Common Puffin . . Parakeet (Maine, Mass. From its high, arched back.)

3 =cedar waxwing.

1917 *Wilson Bulletin* 29.2.84 **KY,** *Bombycilla cedrorum.*—Rice-bird, paroquet, Hickman, Ky.

paralyzed adj Also *poralized*

Used as an intensive in phr *take a paralyzed oath.*

1924 (1946) Greer-Petrie *Angeline Gits an Eyeful* 12 **csKY,** I'll take a poralized oath ev'ry word I'm a-tellin' you is the Gospel truth. **1940** *AmSp* 15.220 **cwTX,** If there is any question as to the veracity of the speaker, . . the narrator gives strongest assurance by repeating: 'I'll take a paralyzed oath.' **1957** *Sat. Eve. Post* 22 June 85 **neTX,** One man said, "I'll take a paralyzed oath that this little old hound won't hunt anything but coons. He won't even notice a rabbit." **1997** *DARE* File—Internet **TX**, Texas Tech head football coach Spike Dykes announced the signing of 25 players to national letters of intent. . . "I really am excited. I will take a paralyzed oath about that."

pararie See **prairie**

parashoot See **parachute**

parasitic jaeger n

Std: a **jaeger 1** (here: *Stercorarius parasiticus*) noted for stealing prey from other birds.   Also called **gull hunter, jiddy hawk, man-o'-war, marlinspike 1, pigeon-tailed gull, puke hawk, robber gull, sea hawk 1, ~ hen 1, teaser**

parasol n Pronc-spp *pairsawl, pairsol, parasole, parasolt, parrysawl;* for addit varr see quots

A Forms.

   1883 (1971) Harris *Nights with Remus* 111 **GA** [Black], Ef I gits win' er any 'spicious racket maybe I mought take down my pairsol en foller long atter you.   **1890** *DN* 1.40 **csME,** *Parasol:* [pærə'sɔl] *and* ['pærəsɔl].   **1922** Gonzales *Black Border* 318 **sSC, GA coasts** [Gullah glossary], *Parrysawl*—parasol, parasols.   **1938** Faulkner *Unvanquished* 90 **MS,** Take that pairsawl and wear hit out on him!   **1968–69** *DARE* (Qu. W1b, *If you use an umbrella . . when the sun is too hot, you call it a _____*) 638 Infs, **widespread,** Parasol; 111 Infs, **widespread,** Parasole; **CA107, IN13,** Parasolt; **NY24, WI56,** Sun parasol(e); **LA6,** Parasoil ['pæˌsɔil]; (Qu. W1c) Inf **TN13,** Parashol ['pærəʃɔl].

B Senses.

1 A rain umbrella (as opposed to a light umbrella used as a sunshade).   **scattered, but chiefly Sth, S Midl, Cent, TX** See Map

   1828 Webster *Amer. Dict., Parasol.* . . A small umbrella used by ladies to defend themselves from rain, or their faces from the sun's rays.   **c1960** *Wilson Coll.* **csKY,** *Parasol.* . . Strictly speaking, a sunshade; used often for umbrella, too.   **1965–70** *DARE* (Qu. W1a, *What do you open up and hold over your head when it rains?*) 82 Infs, **chiefly Sth, S Midl, Cent, TX,** Parasol; **AL17, FL28, SC10, 29,** Parasole; (Qu. W1c, . . *Joking names . . for an umbrella*) 14 Infs, **chiefly Sth, S Midl,** Parasol.   **1971** Bright *Word Geog. CA & NV* 161, *Umbrella . . parasol* 18% [of 300 infs] P[attern] XI [=rural]. Twenty-three said it was used only as a sunshade, 9 that it was old-fashioned.   **1973** Allen *LAUM* 1.227 **Upper MW** (as of c1950), *Umbrella.* . . Use of *parasol* . . to designate the device for protection against rain . . seems Midland-oriented.   **1989** Pederson *LAGS Tech. Index* 103 **Gulf Region** (*What do you hold over your head when it rains*) 271 infs, Parasol; [41 infs, Parasol (for sun)].

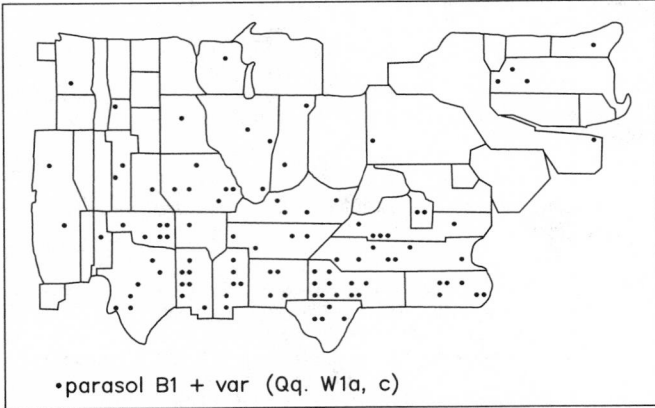

•parasol B1 + var (Qq. W1a, c)

2 A **marsh pennywort** (here: *Hydrocotyle ranunculoides*).
   1942 *Torreya* 42.163 **LA,** *Hydrocotyle ranunculoides.* . . Water parsley, parasol.

3 See **parasol mushroom.**

4 pl: **=mayapple 1.   Cf umbrella leaf, ~ plant**
   1898 *Jrl. Amer. Folk.* 11.222 **OH,** *Podophyllum peltatum,* L., "parasols," Mansfield, Ohio.

parasol mushroom n Also *parasol*

A **mushroom B1** of the genus *Lepiota,* esp *L. procera.*

1890 *Century Dict.* 4284, *Parasol mushroom,* an edible mushroom, *Agaricus procerus,* having a red-brown obtusely obconic, or at length campanulate, fleshy pileus, from three to seven inches broad.   **1908** Hard *Mushroom Edible* 46, *Lepiota procera.* . . The Parasol Mushroom. . . The stem is very long. . . The ring is rather thick and firm, though in mature plants it becomes loosened and movable on the stem. This and the form of the plant suggest the name, parasol.   **1964** Kingsbury *Poisonous Plants U.S.* 98, The genus *Lepiota* contains several species—for example *L. procera,* the parasol mushroom—that are among the prized edible mushrooms.   **1967** *PA Game News* Aug 6, Soft cream-colored cap with brown scales; loose, cottony ring; woody stem roughened with minute scales; base enlarged, no sheath or scales—parasol mushroom. . . I spotted a lineup of stately parasol mushrooms along the road. . . Sauteed in butter (not too much) with a dash of salt and a turn of the pepper mill, they were terrific when eaten on toast.   **1968** *DARE* (Qu. I37, *Small plants shaped like an umbrella that grow in woods and fields—which are safe to eat*) Inf **NC55,** Parasol—have purple gills; (Qu. S18) Inf **NC55,** ['peəˌsɔl].   **1980** Marteka *Mushrooms* 36, My wife and I have long rated the parasol mushroom as one of the outstanding edible species. The cap is the best part, and we have found specimens fruiting in New Hampshire with caps so large that the fruiting bodies had toppled over.   **1987** McKnight–McKnight *Mushrooms* 241, Parasol Mushroom . . Genus *Lepiota.   Ibid* 242, Shield Parasol—*Lepiota clypeolaria.   Ibid* 243, Smoothcap Parasol—*Leucoagaricus naucina.   Ibid* 244, American Parasol—*Leucoprinus americana.*

parasolt See **parasol**

paratha See **parada**

paratoed See **parrot-toed**

parboil v Usu |'pɑ(r)bɔɪl|; also |'pɛ(ə)r-, 'pær-, -baɪl| Pronc-spp *parebile, pareboil;* by folk-etym, *power boil* [Cf *OED2 parboil,* with varr *perbuille* (15th cent) and *perboyl(e), perboile* (16th–17th cent)] Cf **boil** n[1], v

Std senses, var forms.

   1909 *DN* 3.355 **eAL, wGA,** *Pare-boil* [pær]. . . To parboil.   **1915** *DN* 4.187 **swVA,** *Parboil* [pɛərbaɪl].   **1963** Watkins–Watkins *Yesterday Hills* 54 **cnGA,** Rabbit parebiled and then fried.   **1968** *DARE* FW Addit **LA21,** *Parboil*—common pronunciation is [pɑ:bɔɪəl], but old-fashioned is [pærbɔɪəl].   **1970** *DARE* Tape **TX104,** That's the kind [of greens] you have to parboil ['pɛrˌbɔɪl].   **1975** in 1981 *NC Folkl. Jrl.* 29.32, If you have any kind of wild meats, just break up some of the spice wood and wash clean, power boil [parboil] with your wild meat.   **1976** Garber *Mountain-ese* 66 **sAppalachians,** You allers pare-boil possum afore you start to roast it.

parbuckle n Cf **crosshaul** n **3**

A contrivance for moving any heavy cylindrical object, consisting of one or more (usu two) ropes or chains anchored at the point to or from which it is to be raised or lowered and passed under and around it; hence v *parbuckle* to move by this contrivance; vbl n *parbuckling.*

   1859 *Scientific Amer.* 1.226, Capt. G.B. Cornish . . has patented an improvement in the Cunningham rig, consisting principally in the employment for the purpose of reefing square sails, by rolling them upon their yards, of a single reef pennant applied in the form of a parbuckle, around the middle of a yard.   **1861** Scott *Military Dict.* 452, To parbuckle a gun, is to roll it in either direction from the spot in which it rests. To do this, place the gun on skids, and if it is to be moved up or down a slope, two 4½-inch ropes are made fast to some place on the upper part of the slope, the ends are carried under the chase and breech of the gun respectively round it, and up the slope. If the running ends of these ropes are hauled upon, the gun ascends; if eased off, it descends.   **1872** (1876) Knight *Amer. Mech. Dict.* 2.1632, *Parbuckle.* . . A means for raising or lowering. . . The bight of the rope is placed round a post; the cask, spar, or gun lies in the double loop.   **1945** Colcord *Sea Language* 139 **ME, Cape Cod, Long Island,** *Parbuckle.* To roll a cask or similar object by means of slings. The word was originated by sailors, but it and the process are familiar to brewery workers and others who handle barrels ashore.   **1950** *Western Folkl.* 9.119 **nwOR** [Logger speech], *Parbuckle.* See *Gilhooly.* [*Ibid* 117, *Gilhooly.* Term applied to a method of extracting logs from behind stumps and other obstructions.]   **1958** McCulloch *Woods Words* 132 **Pacific NW,** *Parbuckle*—a. A crosshaul; a cable passed under and back over a log causing it to roll when the cable is pulled. This was the usual method of loading cars in the early days of railroad logging before steam loading rigs were common. . . Parbuckling is still used in small shows to put logs onto flat bed trucks where a big loading rig is not required. . . **b.** A method of freeing a log hung up behind a stump. A swamp hook is stuck on the power side of the stump and a line run from it down under the log and around over the top of log and stump and back to the source of power. A stout pull will parbuckle the log over the stump. **1969** Sorden *Lumberjack Lingo* 85 **NEng, Gt Lakes,** *Parbuckle*—Line or chain is passed under and back over a log causing the log to roll when the chain or line is pulled. This became a loading method at landings when railroads began to haul logs to the mills.

parcel n, v Usu |ˈpɑ(r)səl|; also |ˈpæsəl|, rarely |ˈpɑ́ršəl| Pronc-sp *passel* [Spp of the type *passel* are attested from the 15th century onward and appear widely in Engl dial; *parshel, parshal* are occas attested in Scots, nEngl dial.] Cf **parsnip, partridge** Note: At **A** below, the var *passel* and its corresponding proncs are included when they illustrate std senses of *parcel;* exx of *passel* (and varr) in the sense "a group, bunch, batch; an indefinite, usu large, number or quantity" are treated at **passel 2.**
A Forms.
  1874 (1895) Eggleston *Circuit Rider* 80 **sOH** (as of early 19th cent), Hello, boys! Howdy? Got a nice passel of furs, eh? **1911** *DN* 3.539 **eKY,** *Parcel.* Pronounced [pæsl]. **1915** *DN* 4.187 **swVA,** *Parcel* [pæsl]. **1923** [see **passel 2**]. **1924** Raine *Land of Saddle-Bags* 10 **sAppalachians,** "I'd love to git to a place once whar I could see a big passel o' land that hadn't been stood up on edge like," said one woman out of her experience of precipitous and imprisoning horizons. **1959** *VT Hist.* 27.151, *Parcel* [ˈpɑrsl]. . pronc. A parcel of land or ground. Common. **1984** Hancock *Choestoe* 11 **neGA,** Jep said he rode a stallion horse, brought a "passel" of tobacco and two jeans suits from Virginia. **1996** *DARE* File **csWI** (as of 1950s), In the phr *parcel post, parcel* was pronounced [ˈpɑ́ršl] by a woman at the information and mailing desk [at the University of Wisconsin]. I heard this more than once. She was a Wisconsin native.
B As noun.
=passel 2. Note: This sense is now usu associated with the pronc |ˈpæsəl| and the sp *passel;* exx of the sp *parcel* are included here, but it is of course usu impossible to know what pronc the writer had in mind. [*OED2 parcel* sb. 6 1588 →]
  1690 (1892) Hammond *Diary* 153 **MA,** They [=Indians] were set upon by a parcel of English. **1808** (1898) Hunt *Diary* 16 **PA,** Saw a parcel of hounds in pursuit of a Fox, hard upon him. **1814** in 1915 *PA Mag. Hist. & Biog.* 39.326 **PA,** Isaac and a parcel of negroes were to have gone a Maying. **1849** in 1956 Eliason *Tarheel Talk* 287 **cn,cNC,** A parcel of noisy students . . are giving us what is called a serinade. **1885** Twain *Huck. Finn* 48 **MO,** And after that he polished off with a kind of a general cuss all round, including a considerable parcel of people which he didn't know the names of. **1912** [see **passel 2**]. **1966–69** *DARE* (Qu. LL8b, . . *A large number . . "She has a whole _____ of cousins."*) Infs **AR**39, **GA**11, [ˈpɑrsl]; **NY**92, [ˈpɑrsəl]; **NY**155, [ˈpɑrsəl]; (Qu. LL10, *A whole group of people: "They made too much noise, so he sent the whole _____ home."*) Inf **ME**16, Parcel and kaboodle; **MS**15, Kit and parcel. **1986** Pederson *LAGS Concordance* (*Passel*) 1 inf, **cwGA,** Parcel of food—more than she would eat; 1 inf, **seFL,** Parcel—not of children.
C As verb.
With *out:* **=deacon** v **1.** Cf **line out 1**
  1984 Wilder *You All Spoken Here* 180 **Sth,** Line the song; line out; passel out: The song leader reads aloud the first two lines of the song to be sung, and the congregation sings them. The next two lines are read, then sung, and in this piecemeal fashion the whole song is sung.

parcel shower n Cf **pantry shower**
  1906 *DN* 3.149 **nwAR,** *Parcel shower.* . . A party given in honor of a prospective bride at which she receives presents in parcels. "The parcel shower tendered Miss Sykes Monday afternoon was a social success."

parch v, hence ppl adj *parched* [*OED2* 1398 →] **chiefly Sth, S Midl**
To toast, roast (foodstuffs, esp nuts, grains, and the like); to pop (corn).
  1622 Mourt's *Relation Iournall Plimoth* 46, At this towne of *Massasoyts . .* wee . . bought about a handfull of Meale of their parched Corne. **1674** in 1897 *SC Hist. Soc. Coll.* 5.458, Two fatt Turkeys to helpe out

wth our parcht corne flower broth. **1797** Imlay *Western Terr.* 237, Parched meal. . is a very nourishing food, and is an excellent provision for travellers. **1817** (1965) *N. Amer. Rev.* 4.177 **NEng,** Drank coffee made of parched beans, and black pepper. **1849** in 1850 Cooper *Rural Hours* 388 **NY,** Besides these different ways of cooking the maize, we should not forget parched or "popped" corn, in which the children delight so much. **1866** Devens *Pictorial Book* 484, Putting his hand into his pocket and hauling out a handful of parched coffee. **1906** *DN* 3.149 **nwAR, MS,** *Parched pindar.* . . Roasted peanut. **1909** *DN* 3.355 **eAL, wGA,** *Parched pindar.* . . Roasted peanut. *Ibid* 401 **nwAR,** *Parch.* To roast. "Parch the coffee." **1935** Hurston *Mules & Men* 87 **FL,** The refreshments are parched peanuts, fried rabbit, fish, chicken and chitterlings. **1945** FWP *Lay My Burden Down* 196 **LA** (as of c1865) [Black], I dunno if you ever parch popcorn. That the way the little guns sound. **1956** McAtee *Some Dialect NC* 32, *Parched peanuts.* . . A more general term is roasted peanuts. **1965–70** *DARE* (Qu. H50, *Dishes made with beans, peas, or corn that everybody around here knows, but people in other places might not*) Inf **WA**6, Parched corn; (Qu. BB50a, . . *Favorite remedies . . for a cough*) Inf **MS**63, Parch hog feet and hoofs and make syrup of this; [(Qu. DD24, . . *Diseases that come from continual drinking*) Inf **FL**52, Parched liver]. **1965** *DARE* FW Addit **FL**18, Parch—to roast peanuts. "You just parch them in the oven til the skins come loose." **1966–68** *DARE* Tape **FL**41, You have to parch your peanuts. . . Just put them in the stove, parch them like you would bake bread; **IN**30, They didn't have very many treats then because it would have to be taffy, or maple molasses, or parched corn, or popcorn balls; **NC**10, I've parched many a pound of coffee. . . You take the green coffee and parch it and grind it in a mill; **NC**41, You had to parch your own coffee, come in the beans, you know. . . Put that skillet on an' put this here green coffee . . an' put that in, like parchin' peanuts. **1971** *Foxfire* 5.89 **nGA,** Popcorn was popped ("parched") by putting the shelled kernels in a covered metal box. **1982** Slone *How We Talked* 90 **eKY** (as of c1950), *Parch corn*—the regular white corn used for feed or bread. Brown in a hot skillet, to which has been added a little salt and grease. Stir until it becomes brown and "crunchie" or "bricklie." Eat as popcorn. **1986** Pederson *LAGS Concordance* **Gulf Region,** 1 inf, Parch corn; 1 inf, Parch peanuts—cook on low heat for a long time; 1 inf, Parching corn—heating corn in oven; 1 inf, Peanut parching—sometimes after wedding; 2 infs, Parching peanuts; 1 inf, Parching some peanuts; 1 inf, Some people parches corn; 1 inf, Of green coffee, parch it brown; 1 inf, Of coffee, parch it your own self; 1 inf, Parch the coffee—roasting the beans; 1 inf, **cnTN,** Parching coffee—baking beans to dry and brown; (*How is coffee prepared?*) 8 infs, Parch it; 1 inf, Parch it—of beans before grinding; 1 inf, Parch it—using green coffee; 2 infs, Parch the coffee; 1 inf, People parched the green coffee in a skillet; 1 inf, Parched green coffee; 2 infs, Parched (it); 1 inf, Parched it, then ground it, then boiled it; 1 inf, When green you parched it until it was brown; 1 inf, A-parching coffee; *(In bulk)* 1 inf, Parched or unparched, loose coffee = bulk coffee; 1 inf, Of coffee preparation, like parching peanuts; *(Peanuts)* 2 infs, Parch them; 1 inf, Parched—roasted in oven, skin slides off easily; 1 inf, Parched or boiled—only kinds of peanuts; 1 inf, Parched, peanut bean; 1 inf, Parched peanuts. **1998** *DARE* File **neIA** (as of c1980), One of my college roommates used her popcorn popper to make parched corn. She heated the kernels (which were larger than unpopped popcorn kernels) in oil; rather than popping, they browned and became hard and crunchy.

‡parcheese n Cf **cheese B1**
The fruit of a **mallow B** (here: *Malva rotundifolia*).
  1901 Lounsberry *S. Wild Flowers* 337, We find growing by fences and along waysides . . Malva rotundifolia with graceful rounded leaves and small, bluish purple flowers which later produce the parcheeses eaten and beloved by children.

pard See **partner**

pardelle n Cf **leopard flower**
=blackberry lily.
  1933 Small *Manual SE Flora* 327, B[elamcanda] chinensis. . . Blackberry-lily, Pardelle . . Dry hills, roadsides, and fence-rows. **1949** Moldenke *Amer. Wild Flowers* 363, The remarkable *blackberrylily* or *pardelle, Belamcanda chinensis,* . . though a native of China, is now found on dry hills and along roadsides and fencerows from Connecticut to Georgia and westward to Indiana.

pard(e)ner See **partner**

parebile, pareboil See **parboil**

parfect(ly) See **perfect**

pargo n [Appar < Span *pagro, pargo* for *Pagrus pagrus;* cf
porgy n[1]]
=**muttonfish 1.**
   1898 U.S. Natl. Museum *Bulletin* 47.1265, *Neomaenis analis* . . Mut-
ton-fish; Pargo.   **1902** Jordan–Evermann *Amer. Fishes* 412, *Muttonfish.* . . This snapper, which is also called pargo or pargo criollo, reaches
2 feet or more in length.   **1933** John G. Shedd Aquarium *Guide* 105,
Lutianus analis—Muttonfish; Pargo.   **1946** LaMonte *N. Amer. Game
Fishes* 60, Muttonfish. . . Pargo, Sama, Red Snapper, Green Snapper,
Pargo Criolla.

paring bee n Also *paring* **chiefly NEast** *old-fash* Cf *DCan*
=**apple bee.**
   [**1826** (1832) Pickering *Inquiries* 109 **Canada,** A *"paring bee,"* or
"be;" . . an assemblage of neighbours invited to one house, to prepare
apples for drying.]   **1845** *Lowell Offering* 5.269 **NH,** When we were
about to have a paring bee, we sent out our invitations a day or two previous.   **1857** *Quinland* 1.191 **NY,** Went . . with the young people to a
paring-bee. . . some pared, some quartered, some cored, some strung.
1887 *Century Illustr. Mag.* 35.331 **Nth,** There was nothin' wuth de-
clarin',/ 'Cept I'd kissed her onct or twice,/ At a huskin' or a parin'.
1896 VT State Bd. Ag. *Report* 16.97, The old fashioned husking and
paring bees have been done away with.   **1963** Early Amer. Industries
Assoc. *Chronicle* 16.35 **VT** (as of 1850s), Describing the typical activity
after harvesting the fall's apple crop, a Vermont woman wrote: "All the
neighbors would meet at one house for a paring bee."   **1968** *DARE* Tape
NY105, There was an apple paring bee up south of town in a log
cabin. . . When they went to these paring bees, as a rule they wound up
in a good donnybrook. They had a good fight.

parish See **perish**

park n
1 A high-elevation valley surrounded by mountains.   **chiefly
West, esp Rocky Mts**
   1806 in 1810 Pike *Expeditions* 123 **West,** Passed the *Park,* which is
ten miles round, and not more than three quarters of a mile across.
1839 in 1913 OR Hist. Soc. *Hist. Qrly.* 14.263 **Rocky Mts,** At noon we
entered a very large valley, called *the Park,* at the entrance of which we
crossed the North Fork of the River Platte.   **1843** (1973) Farnham
Travels Prairies 1.264 **CO** (as of 1839), The valleys that lie upon this
stream and some of its tributaries, are called by the hunters "The Old
Park." If the qualifying term were omitted, they would be well described
by their name. Extensive meadows running up the valleys of the streams,
woodlands skirting the mountain bases and dividing the plains, over
which the antelope, black and white tailed deer, . . and the buffalo and
elk range—a splendid park indeed.   **1878** Beadle *Western Wilds* 487,
Colorado is divided nearly down the center by the main chain of the
Rocky Mountains. . . As depressions in the Summit appear the great
parks, a curious and attractive feature of Colorado. As summer retreats
and grazing grounds, they will ultimately be of great value.   **1888**
(1958) Wister *Out West* 71 **WY,** I steered as well as I could for the dip in
the woods below the range, and we came out on a big sage park.   **1907**
White *AZ Nights* 137 **CO,** We kept them over the hills in some "parks,"
as these sots call meadows in that country.   **1910** Johnson *Highways
Rocky Mts.* 140, Some of the valleys are fully fifty miles long and nearly
as wide, and are open grazing and farm land. Whether large or small, a
mountain valley of this type is called "a park."   **1917** Eaton *Green
Trails* 85 **nwMT,** It [=squaw grass] climbs to the high "parks" just below the passes and flourishes close to the snowfields.   **1918** Visher
Geog. SD 44, The [Black] Hills as a whole are a mountainous region
which has an average elevation of more than 5000 feet, . . extensive exposures of firm rock, and heavy forests. . . The more open "park area," . .
has many broad valleys lower than the limestone plateau, but includes
the higher peaks such as Harney, Terry, and Custer.   **1952** Peattie *Black
Hills* 25, The little mountain meadows ("parks" in the Western vernacular) are untouched by the mowing machine.   **1960** *PADS* 34.34 **CO,**
Two of the terms . . are surely limited by the nature of the environment.
Park in the sense 'mountain meadow' is limited to the mountain area and
the nearby foothills communities.   *Ibid* 64, [In a list of words more
common among speakers under 60 yrs old:] Park 'clearing'.   **1961**
Douglas *My Wilderness* 42 **WY,** The meadows like the ones we saw at
Elkhart are called parks by our local people. They are grazed by
permittees.   **1966–68** *DARE* (Qu. C29, *A good-sized stretch of level
land with practically no trees*) Inf **CO41,** Park—in the mountains;
NM11, In timber country it might be a meadow or a park; **UT14,** A
park; meadow.   **1967** *DARE* Tape **WY1,** I've seen bulls that had a little
herd of cows off in a little park. . . We rode out in a little park and there

stood a big bull elk on the other side of the park looking at us. . . I said,
"Well, Doc, step down and kill that bull across the meadow there."
1973 Allen *LAUM* 1.234 (as of c1950), *Meadow* (low-lying grassland). . . Park [1 inf, **cwSD**].   **2000** Launspach *ID Dial. Project* 3 **seID,**
(Level open space among mountains) 1 inf, Park.

2 also *park line* (or *strip*): =**parking 2a.**
   1966–70 *DARE* (Qu. N44, *In a town, the strip of grass and trees between the sidewalk and the curb*) Infs **GA30, MA122, NM5, OH20,
TX26,** 102, Park; **NC38,** Park strip.   **1973** Allen *LAUM* 1.381 (as of
c1950), The strip of grass between a sidewalk and the street. . . Minor
variants . . *park* [3 infs, **IA, SD;** 2 infs query the resp].   *Ibid,* The
checklists report sparse appearance of the following terms volunteered
as write-ins: . . park line [1 inf, **SD**].   **1984** *DARE* File **UT,** *(In a town,
the strip of grass and trees between the sidewalk and the curb)* Park
strip.   **2000** Launspach *ID Dial. Project* 3 **seID,** *(Grassy strip between a
sidewalk and the street)* 1 inf, Park.

3 also *center park:* =**median (strip) 1.**
   1968–70 *DARE* (Qu. N17, . . *The separating area in the middle [of a
four-lane road]*) Inf **GA17,** Center park; **NY231,** Park—if green.

park v *obs* Cf **parking** n
To provide with park-like areas; esp, to provide a street with
strips of lawn, often planted with trees or shrubs, on each side
or down the middle; hence vbl n *parking* the act or practice of
doing this.
   1855 Roberts *Sketches Detroit* 65 **MI,** Washington avenue . . is 200
feet in width, which is wide enough to admit of being parked 100 feet in
the centre, and still leave ample carriage way on either side.   **1873**
Howard *Monumental City* 365 **DC,** Large spaces of ground between
curb and dwelling, allowed in some avenues the monotony of system to
be broken and relieved by *double rows* of trees; so that this plan of *parking* the capital has, to some extent, indemnified property owners.   **1875**
Appletons' Jrl. 14.412 **DC,** Six or seven years ago Congress authorized
the parking of the *centre* of the streets. . . One or two such "parks" were
made—that is to say, stones were put down on each side of the street,
and for a breadth of twenty feet in the middle turf. It was soon a question which was the barer and more disagreeable, the pavement or the
parking.   **1884** *Century Illustr. Mag.* 27.649 **DC,** The great boule-
vards . . were three times as wide as was necessary . . ; it was determined to use a portion of them only for a roadway, another portion for
foot-walks, and to devote fully half of the street to lawns in front of the
houses. . . In Washington . . the streets were wide enough to permit this
without sacrificing any private property, and the system of 'parking' thus
became the rule, and not the exception.   **1897** *Atlantic Mth.* 79.220
cwNY, By the influence of a Village Improvement Society the streets
were parked.

parka n Usu |ˈpɑrkə|; also **chiefly AK** |ˈpɑrki| Pronc-spp
parkee, parki(e), parky [See quot 1958]
Std sense, var forms.
   1865 (1982) Adams *Life on Yukon* 121 **AK,** Tonight I got a Reindeer
Skin coat Russian name of which is Parkie.   **1866** in 1942 James *First
Scientific Explor.* 266 **AK,** The parky is a skin coat with a hood to go
over the head trimmed with fox or wolf skins.   **1893** Barnum *Life AK
Mission* 13 **AK,** The parki is a long loose garment made of skins.   **1915**
Stuck *10000 Miles* 35 **AK,** The parkee . . is primarily a windbreak.
1933 Marshall *Arctic Village* 144 **AK,** The parky is a loose-fitting garment which is slipped over the head and comes down about to the knees.
1939 FWP *Guide AK* xli, *Parka.* . . (E[skimauan]) (pronounced "parky")
overgarment of skin, fur, or wool.   **1958** Carrighar *Moonlight* 43 **AK,**
Parki, incidentally, is the way the word is pronounced in the North. It is
of Russian-Siberian origin, and was introduced as the name of the shirts
of bird skins worn in the Aleutian Islands.   **1965** Bowen *Alaskan Dict.*
25, *Parka* (Pronounced *parkee* by *old time Alaskans* and many *natives*).
The hooded coat worn as an outer garment by *natives* and whites alike
in the *Arctic*.

parkage n
=**parking 2a.**
   1967 *DARE* (Qu. N44, *In a town, the strip of grass and trees between
the sidewalk and the curb*) Inf **OH18,** Tree lawn, parkage.   **1997** *DARE*
File **OH,** It may be called the devil's strip in Akron, but 30 miles from
Akron it is the parkage.

parka squirrel n Also *parkee squirrel, parkie ~, parky ~* [See
quot 1948]   **AK**
A **ground squirrel b** (here: *Spermophilus parryi*).

1933 *Anchorage Daily Times* (AK) 25 Aug *(Tabbert Coll.),* Many grouse and thousands of Parka squirrel also were seen. **1948** *AK Sportsman* Mar 18, [Caption:] Alaska's little parka squirrel . . is considered an asset to Territorial economy. His soft grayish fur, light and warm, is in demand for the finest of dress parkas. **1961** *Ibid* Sept 11, The flurry of eagle wings lifting off with a parkie squirrel. **1965** Bowen *Alaskan Dict.* 26, *Parka squirrel* or *Parkee squirrel.* A small ground squirrel, the pelt of which makes a delicate, lasting, and warm parka. Eskimos prize the parka squirrel parka over others although various skins are used according to the use of the parkas as for hunting, extreme cold weather, or beauty. **1968** *DARE* (Qu. P27, . . *Kinds of squirrels)* Inf **AK9,** Parka squirrel—good eating—also make parkas from hides; (Qu. P29, . . *'Gophers' . . other name . . or what other animal are they most like)* Inf **AK1,** Ground squirrel—further north, parka squirrel—fur used to line parkas. **1991** Tabbert *Dict. Alaskan Engl.* 122, Another common Alaskan English name for the arctic ground squirrel is *parka* or *parky squirrel,* so called from the fact that the skins are used in many traditional Eskimo and Indian parkas, especially the elaborate women's parkas.

parkee See **parka**

parkee squirrel See **parka squirrel**

parkerberry n Also *parkleberry*
=**farkleberry.**

1926 *Torreya* 26.6 **GA,** *Batodendron arboreum.* . . Parker berry, "only the negroes call it sparkle berry," said my informant, Sapelo I[slan]d, Ga. **1968** *DARE* FW Addit **swLA,** Parkleberries—a dark purple berry good to eat after frost comes. The bushes grow on sandy land.

parki(e) See **parka**

parkie squirrel See **parka squirrel**

parking vbl n See **park** v

parking n [**park** v]
1 Land beside or in the middle of a street or intersection, or around a building, that is covered with lawn and often planted with trees or shrubs. *?obs*

1873 Howard *Monumental City* 365 **DC,** The extent of this embellishment may be judged from the fact that . . the parking then completed amounted to nearly six hundred thousand yards. **1885** Ingle *Local Institutions VA* 109, Spaces were left [in Williamsburg] for a market-place, court-house green and parking for the palace. **1888** *Encycl. Brit.* (9th ed) 24.382 **DC,** As the width of the streets is in most cases in excess of the demands of travel, a portion of this width has, in the residence streets, been left between the side walks and the houses, and has been improved as a public parking. In some cases, similar parking has been left in the middle of the streets. **1893** *Congressional Record* 20 Feb. 24.3.1856/2 **DC,** It is not an usual thing to find parking around manufacturing establishments in the heart of cities.

2a also in combs *parking area,* ~ *lot,* ~ *place,* ~ *space:* An area of such land; spec, a strip of lawn, often planted with trees, between a street and sidewalk. **chiefly NW, Plains States, IA; also N Cent, sCA** See Map Cf **parkway 3**

1900 *Congressional Record* 17 Feb. 33.2.1895/2 **DC,** The little plats of ground at the intersection of streets which are generally denominated "parkings." **1918** ID Ag. Exper. Sta. *Bulletin* 105.46, If necessary to place the poles [=utility poles] in the parking they should be set next the walks and painted green. **a1944** in 1946 White *Autobiog.* 98 **KS,** Elm trees and cottonwoods were on the parking. **1945** *AmSp* 20.154 **ceMN,** *Parking.* The grassed area between curbing and sidewalk. The term is used by some Minnesotans instead of *Boulevard,* by others as an alternate. **1950** *Aurora* (Ill.) *Beacon News* 8 Sept. 3/1 *(Mathews Coll.),* Residents . . are asked to set their waste paper on the parkings in front of their homes in time for collection. **c1955** Reed–Person *Ling. Atlas Pacific NW* (Grass between sidewalk and street) 10 infs, Parking; 1 inf, Parking area. **1962** Bailey *Jayhawker* 83 **KS,** They give me Hail Columbia for letting my horse get on their parkings and eat their grass. **1965–70** *DARE* (Qu. N44, *In a town, the strip of grass and trees between the sidewalk and the curb)* 55 Infs, **chiefly NW, Plains States, IA; also N Cent, sCA,** Parking; **CO20, IA22, KS6, MN10, WA3,** Parking area; **NE7,** Parking lot; (Qu. N17, . . *The separating area in the middle [of a four-lane road])* Inf **MO6,** Not parking, is it? The strip between sidewalk and street is called parking. **1966** *Milwaukee Jrl.* (WI) 19 Jan 22 **CO,** I learned that a parking is the grassy area between the

sidewalk and the street. **1971** Wood *Vocab. Change* 53 **Sth,** *Parking* is first [choice] in Oklahoma . . [but is] unreported in Alabama, Mississippi, Florida, and Louisiana. *Ibid* 303, Parking [offered by 47 of approx 1000 infs]. **1973** Gawthrop *Dial. Calumet* 71 **nwIN,** *Grass strip between sidewalk and street:* . . parking 4 [of 125 checklist infs]. **1973** Allen *LAUM* 1.381 (as of c1950), The strip of grass between a sidewalk and the street. . . *Parking,* the most common, dominates with its use in the Midland area of Iowa and South Dakota and in extreme eastern and extreme western Nebraska. . . Minor variants . . *parking space* [1 inf, **NE**]. *Ibid,* The checklists report sparse appearance of the following terms volunteered as write-ins: . . *parking place* [1 inf, **NE**]. **1984** *DARE* File **ID, UT,** *(In a town, the strip of grass and trees between the sidewalk and the curb)* Parking. **2000** Launspach *ID Dial. Project* 3 **seID,** *(Grassy strip between a sidewalk and the street)* 8 infs, *Parking.*

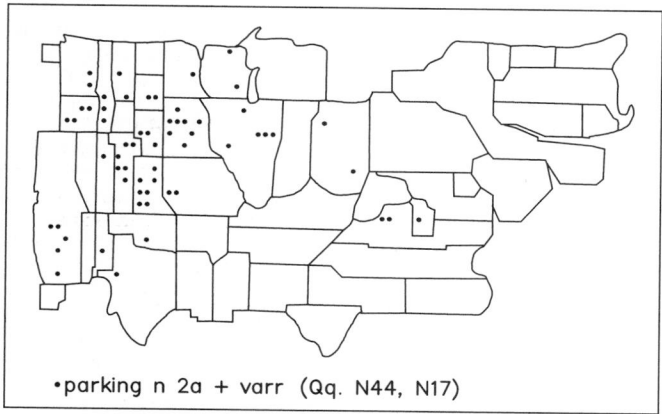
•parking n 2a + varr (Qq. N44, N17)

b in comb *parking strip.* **chiefly NW, esp WA** See Map

c1955 Reed–Person *Ling. Atlas Pacific NW* (Grass between sidewalk and street) 23 infs, 20 **WA,** Parking strip. **1962** *Sat. Eve. Post* 10 Mar 60 **NW,** She felt herself fly over the handlebars and land on the grass of the parking strip. **1965–70** *DARE* (Qu. N44, *In a town, the strip of grass and trees between the sidewalk and the curb)* 17 Infs, 11 **WA,** Parking strip. **1971** Wood *Vocab. Change* 53 **Sth,** The choice of *boulevard* occurs everywhere in a second or lesser preference as does *boulevard strip,* and *parking strip.* *Ibid* 304, Parking strip 67 [of approx 1000 infs]. **1973** Gawthrop *Dial. Calumet* 71 **nwIN,** *Grass strip between sidewalk and street:* . . parking strip 3 [of 125 checklist infs]. **1973** Allen *LAUM* 1.381 (as of c1950), The strip of grass between a sidewalk and the street. . . Minor variants . . *parking strip* [1 inf, **SD**]. **1979** Stegner *Recapitulation* 153 **UT,** His feet are light on the sidewalk, lighter yet on the parking-strip grass where he prefers to walk. **1984** *DARE* File **UT,** *(In a town, the strip of grass and trees between the sidewalk and the curb)* Parking strip. **1995** *DARE* File **WA,** I call those grassy strips between the sidewalk and the street "parking strips." *Ibid* **swID** (as of 1950s), When I visited relatives in Idaho, I learned about parking strips; we didn't have them at home in California.

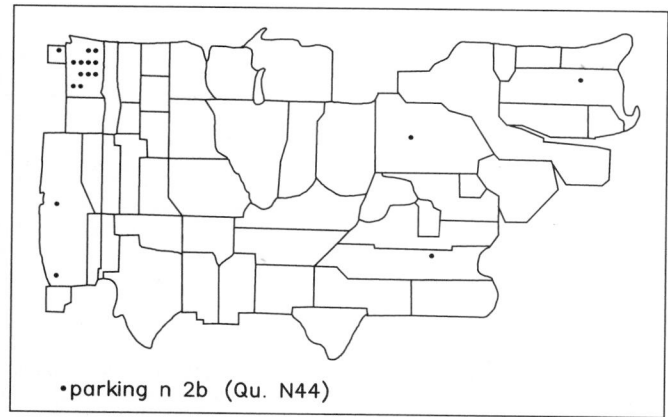
•parking n 2b (Qu. N44)

parking terrace See **terrace**

parkleberry See **parkerberry**

park line (or strip) See **park 2**

parkrow n
=parking 2a.

2000 *Tower Times* (Stoughton WI) Summer 4 **csWI,** Before you decide to plant a tree in the city parkrow, you need to request a pre-approved parkrow tree listing and planting permit. *Ibid* 5, Garage sale signs may be placed in the parkrow, in front of the residence where the sale is being held. **2001** *Ashland City Source* (OR) Apr (Internet), Spring Cleaning for Parkrows and Vacant Lots. . . A parkrow is the strip of land between the curb of a street and the sidewalk, usually with a width of four to eight feet.

parkway n

1 A broad street or highway laid out with strips of lawn, often planted with trees or shrubs. **chiefly NEast, esp NY, CT, NJ** See Map

1878 *Scribner's Mth.* 16.302 **Brooklyn NYC,** As the lots are 30.5 meters deep, one block of tenements and one block of dwellings, with a park-way or narrow street between them, or two blocks of dwellings with broad park-way or short street between them, can be placed on the lots as now divided. **1893** *New Engl. Mag.* 14.790 **eMA,** Beacon Street was widened into a park way from 160 to 180 feet in width, with a reservation for street-car service near the centre. **1897** *Atlantic Mth.* 79.95, The Chicago park system contains nearly nineteen hundred acres of land, most of which is in six parks . . , three in one chain, and all, with one exception, connected by park-ways. **1956** *Chicago Daily News* (IL) 1 Dec. 8/3 *(Mathews Coll.),* The 450-mile Natchez parkway, which memorializes the wilderness path that once linked Nashville, Tenn., with Natchez, Miss., is almost half finished. **1965–70** *DARE* (Qu. N16a, *Names for a highway with two lanes on each side and a separation down the middle*) 39 Infs, **chiefly NEast, esp NY, CT, NJ,** Parkway; **GA**23, Sunshine State Parkway; (Qu. N16b, *Names for a highway with two lanes on each side and a separation down the middle—if you have to pay to drive on it*) Infs **KY**72, **NY**206, Parkway; **NY**63, Toll parkway. **1967** *State* (Raleigh NC) 15 Aug. 20/2 *(Mathews Coll.),* Another early term was "The Scenic Highway," and we still are directed to the Parkway with this term. **1986** Pederson *LAGS Concordance* **Gulf Region,** 1 inf, Parkway—an open highway; not a grass strip; 1 inf, Parkway—with trees, landscaping; 3 infs, Parkway; 11 infs, Parkway [in var proper names]. **1995** [see **3** below].

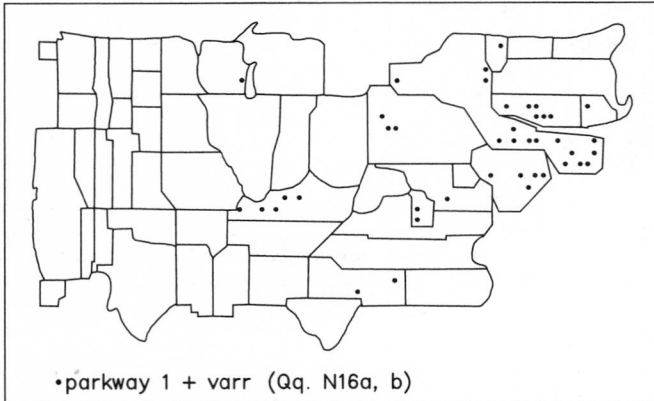

•parkway 1 + varr (Qq. N16a, b)

2 **=median (strip) 1.**

1903 *NY Times* (NY) 16 Aug 29/5, The contractors have laid out with mathematical exactness a so-called "park strip," to replace the beautiful, tree-covered parkway they demolished. **1938** *Sun* (Baltimore MD) 30 Nov 5/7 *(Hench Coll.),* It may be possible, they say, to install . . guard rails on such heavily traveled thoroughfares . . where inability to obtain a sufficiently wide right-of-way precludes use of a "parkway" to separate traffic lanes. **1939** *Ibid* 30 May 6/7 *(Hench Coll.),* That road is a triumph for Maryland at least. . . The raw edges have been softened by intelligent roadside planting and . . the parkway in between is being landscaped. **1965–70** *DARE* (Qu. N17, . . *The separating area in the middle [of a four-lane road]*) 14 Infs, **scattered,** Parkway. **1966** *DARE* FW Addit **sFL,** Parkway—median or divider in a four-lane highway. "Don't Drive on Parkway." Road sign. **1986** Pederson *LAGS Concordance,* 1 inf, **seGA,** Parkway—on divided street; 1 inf, **csGA,** Parkway—in center of street; 1 inf, **cAL,** Parkway—in middle of street; [1 inf, **csTX,** Parkways—wider than medians; 10 ft. across; grass].

3 **=parking 2a. scattered, but esp Missip-Ohio Valleys, West** See Map

1948 *Dly. Ardmoreite* (Ardmore, Okla.) 2 May 13/1 *(DA),* He is also putting in the sprinkler system on the parkway. **1950** *WELS Suppl.* *(Strip of grass between sidewalk and street)* 4 infs, **sWI, nIL,** Parkway. **c1955** Reed–Person *Ling. Atlas Pacific NW (Grass between sidewalk and street)* 3 infs, **WA, ID,** Parkway. **1965–70** *DARE* (Qu. N44, *In a town, the strip of grass and trees between the sidewalk and the curb*) 55 Infs, **scattered, but esp Missip-Ohio Valleys, West,** Parkway. **1971** Wood *Vocab. Change* 53 **Sth,** *Parkway* is the first choice in Arkansas . . [but is] unreported in Louisiana. *Ibid* 306, Parkway [offered by 152 of approx 1000 infs]. **1973** Gawthrop *Dial. Calumet* 71 **nwIN,** *Grass strip between sidewalk and street:* parkway 73 [of 125 checklist infs]. **1973** Allen *LAUM* 1.381 (as of c1950), The strip of grass between a sidewalk and the street. . . Minor variants . . *parkway* [5 infs, **IA, SD, NE**]. **1986** Pederson *LAGS Concordance* **Gulf Region,** 6 infs, Parkway; 6 infs, Parkway—grass strip; 1 inf, Parkway—is a boulevard; 1 inf, Parkway—official municipal designation; 1 inf, Parkway—grass strip; city property; 1 inf, Parkway—with trees; 1 inf, Parkway—grass strip between sidewalk and street. **1995** *DARE* File **CO,** Within the last 20 years after moving to Colorado Springs, I picked up an extra definition for *parkway,* which previously connoted for me wide, green-scaped, paved roads. In Colorado Springs, a lot of neighborhoods have 2-foot to 10-foot strips of grass running parallel to, and between the sidewalk and the street. These are called parkways as well.

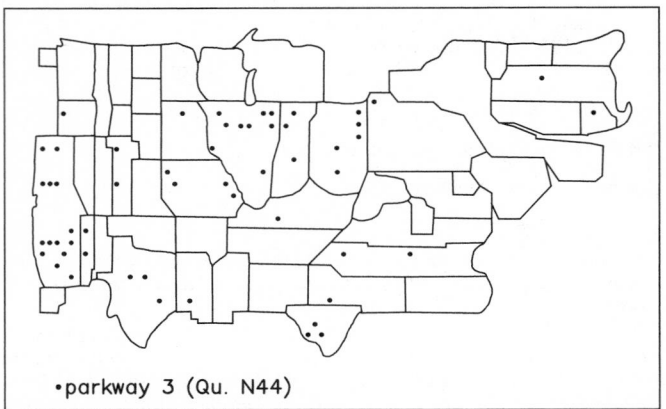

•parkway 3 (Qu. N44)

parky n[1] See **parka**

parky n[2] **NYC, IL, WI**
A playground attendant or other park employee.

1941 *AmSp* 16.188 **NYC,** *Parky.* . . A park attendant. **1997** *NADS Letters* **ceWI,** "Parky". . . This term was used in Green Bay, WI in the 1970's to refer to playground supervisors in the city park system. *Ibid* **ceWI,** My son David was employed by the Green Bay Park District as a parky in 1993 or so. He supervised play, organized games and skits, and taught fundamentals of some team sports. *Ibid* **seWI,** *Parky* is a word that I've always heard to refer to State Park police. **1997** *DARE* File **Bronx NYC,** In the early to mid 1950s *Parky* was the customary designation for the city employee who was in charge of the neighborhood playground. The commonest interaction we kids would have with the *parky* was when we wanted to check out game equipment, such as shuffleboard sets, basketballs, chinese checker sets, and the like, and someone was deputed to ask the *parky* who was in charge of distributing same. *Ibid* **NYC,** When I used to work in Rockaway, we called the guys from the Parks Department who picked up trash on the beach "parkies." **1998** *NADS Letters* **cnIL,** "Parky" as a playground attendant. . . It was a common usage among my playmates in northern Illinois (Rockford) in the mid 1930s. **2001** *DARE* File **NYC,** I had the chance to speak to a park attendant recently . . and he said, "Yeah, technically we're 'park attendants,' but we get called 'parkies' too. And a lot of other things I can't say with kids around."

parky squirrel See **parka squirrel**

parlance n, v Pronc-spp *paa'lance, pallance* [*OED2 parlance* sb. 1 1579–80 →]
Speech, discussion; to speak, have conversation.
1953 Brewer *Word Brazos* 23 **eTX** [Black], Ah calls to min' a ole man

what use to come ovuh here constant to paa'lance wid me 'fo' his daughtuh move offen de plannuhtation dat's way yonnuh pas' de li'l' rivuh. **1969** Emmons *Deep Rivers* 90 **eTX** [Black], "Come on now, let's talk about the Lord, and we'll have pallance together." We did have parlance, Susan and I. We often had long talks about the Lord and His dealings with us.

parley exclam Also with *out*
=barley.

[**1895** *DN* 1.397 **NYC**, *I tebár* . . in children's games when one wishes to withdraw temporarily, in order to avoid being caught, he says, "I tebar."] **1901** *DN* 2.144 **PA**, *Parley* . . . The same as *I tebar*. **1968** *DARE* (Qu. EE17, *In a game of tag, if a player wants to rest, what does he call out so that he can't be tagged?*) Inf **PA**130, Parley out ['pɑrli ˌaʊt].

parliament house n Also *parliament building* [Cf *EDD* *parliament* 5 "A necessary house"]

1966–67 *DARE* (Qu. M21a, *An outside toilet building*) Inf **WA**1, Parliament building [laughter]; (Qu. M21b, *Joking names for an outside toilet building*) Inf **NY**20, Parliament house.

parlor n

A Form.

Pronc-sp *porler*.   Cf Pronc Intro 3.I.1.c

1987 Childress *Out of the Ozarks* 15 **eTX** (as of c1945), First off, the rich farmer talked the way we did. He pronounced parlor "porler." "Less go own in th' porler," he announced in his East Texas accent.

B Senses.

1 usu in combs *dairy* (or *milk(ing)*) *parlor*: A special room or building where cows are milked. **scattered, but esp C Atl, N Cent, NW**   See Map

1965–70 *DARE* (Qu. M10, *The part of the barn where cows are kept*) Infs **IN**63, **OH**61, 95, **VA**10, Milking parlor; **IL**125, Milk parlor; **OH**10, Milking parlor, milking area—two different places; **OH**44, Milking parlor—now; **MI**64, Milking parlor—nowadays; **MI**49, Milking parlors—now the more up-to-date barns have loafing parlors and milking parlors; **MO**18, Parlor—in a modern dairy; (Qu. M1, . . *Kinds of barns . . according to their use or the way they are built*) Infs **IL**108, **MO**5, **VA**26, **WA**25, Milking parlor; **NJ**6, Dairy parlor ['pɑlə]; **DE**1, Milking parlor [pɑlɚ]—where a cow is in the barn where she's being milked; **MD**34, Milking parlor—big enough to milk 6–8 cows at a time; they go through by turns; now replacing larger barns; **TX**33, Milking parlor—air-conditioned for dairy cattle, with Muzak; **MN**34, Loafing barn—a barn with a large open area inside and a milking parlor; (Qu. M18, *The separate building where milk is kept cool*) Infs **FL**29, **IN**35, **MD**29, **MI**94, 95, **NE**3, **TN**1, **VA**14, **WA**20, Milk(ing) parlor; **IN**35, Dairy parlor; **MI**97, Milk parlor—modern; **OH**88, Milk parlor—everything is in one place; (Qu. M22, . . *Kinds of buildings . . on farms*) Infs **MT**4, **OR**1, **VA**14, **WA**23, Milk(ing) parlor; **MO**11, Milking parlor—where they drive the cows through. **1967–68** *DARE* Tape **MA**32, [Inf:] We don't have a milk parlor. . . [Aux Inf:] That's the most modern; **NJ**10, They have a milk parlor—they are all modern. **1968** *Post–Reg.* (Idaho Falls ID) 25 Jan 32/3, 126 Acres, 4 bedroom home, 3 stall elevated milking parlor. **1985** McPhee *Table of Contents* 158 **ME**, She began her day washing down the "parlor" in the family barn and doing what she calls calf chores. **1986** Pederson *LAGS Concordance* (*Where cows are staked or penned for milking*) 4 infs, **swAL, cwLA, seTN,**

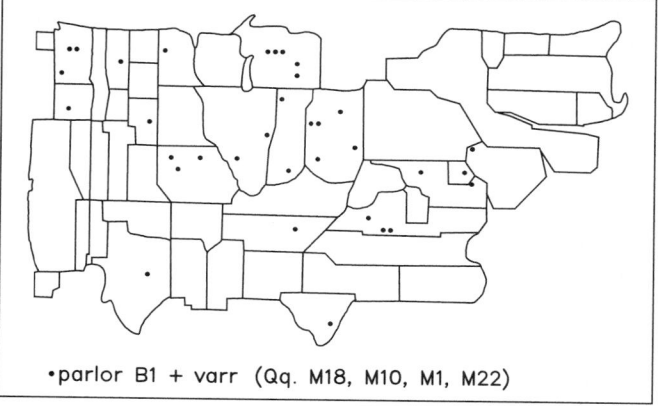

•parlor B1 + varr (Qq. M18, M10, M1, M22)

neGA, Milking parlor(s); 1 inf, **ceTN**, Milk parlor—in dairies; 1 inf, **neMS**, Milk parlor; 1 inf, **ceTN**, Milking parlor—modern indoor structure; 1 inf, **cnGA**, Milking parlor—concrete floor; 1 inf, **cwGA**, Milking parlor—dairies have this; 1 inf, **cAL**, Milking parlor—modern term; 1 inf, **seLA**, Milking parlor—heard, not locally; 1 inf, **cLA**, Milking parlor—inside the barn.

2 usu in combs *hog* (or *pig*) *parlor*: A room or building, or infreq a fenced area outside, where animals are kept. **chiefly Sth, S Midl**   See Map   Cf *loafing parlor* (at **loafing barn**)

1958 *Sat. Eve. Post* 24 May 92 **TN**, Using carefully engineered plans . . , the Gills built a "pig parlor"—a fancy name for a new-style pork factory. . . It was designed to keep the pigs healthy and well fed with a minimum of labor. **1965–70** *DARE* (Qu. M1, . . *Kinds of barns . . according to their use or the way they are built*) Infs **GA**60, **KY**72, 93, Hog parlor; **KY**72, Pig parlor; **MO**11, Pig parlors [pɪg pɑrlɚz]; **IL**63, Cow parlor—3 sides, cows are loose inside, not in stanchions; (Qu. M15, *The place outdoors where pigs are kept*) Infs **AL**15, **MS**81, **MO**11, **NC**87, Pig parlor; **NC**49, Pig parlor [pɪg pɑɚlə]—for raising pigs; **TX**63, Pig parlor—where mama pigs are kept; **GA**68, Hog parlor; (Qu. M17, *A building where chickens or hens are kept*) Inf **SC**43, Chicken parlor; (Qu. M22, . . *Kinds of buildings . . on farms*) Inf **KY**84, Hog parlor—heat, water, feeders; **VA**46, Pig parlor. **1966** Dakin *Dial. Vocab. Ohio R. Valley* 2.84, The term *hog parlor,* used in advertising and on farm programs . . in the corn belt to refer to the more elaborate modern enclosures with concrete floors, running water, etc., has apparently not caught on . . at least . . at the time the survey was made [=1933–58]. . . but another generation may be using *parlor* in a new sense. **1969** *Daily Progress* (Charlottesville VA) 31 July sec A 3/7 (*Hench Coll.*) **cVA**, In a pig pen, the farmers explained, hogs live like pigs. But in a hog parlor, the hog is raised on concrete and never allowed to wallow. Moreover, a properly maintained hog parlor is flushed daily with a high pressure hose. **1971** O'Connor *Complete Stories* 493 **cGA**, "Their feet never touch the ground. We have a pig-parlor—that's where you raise them on concrete," she explained to the pleasant lady, "and Claud scoots them down with the hose every afternoon and washes off the floor." **1986** Pederson *LAGS Concordance* **Gulf Region** (*Shelter and enclosure for hogs and pigs*) 12 infs, Pig parlor(s); 11 infs, Hog parlor(s); 1 inf, Hog parlor—floored, modern; 1 inf, Hog parlor—with shelter; 1 inf, Hog parlor—concrete floor, running water, etc.; 1 inf, Hog parlor—called now; 1 inf, Hog parlor—they're kept inside, would be cleaner; 1 inf, Hog parlor—dressed up place for a hog; 1 inf, Hog parlor—of concrete; 1 inf, Hog parlor—with concrete floor; 1 inf, Hog parlor or pig parlor—more recently.

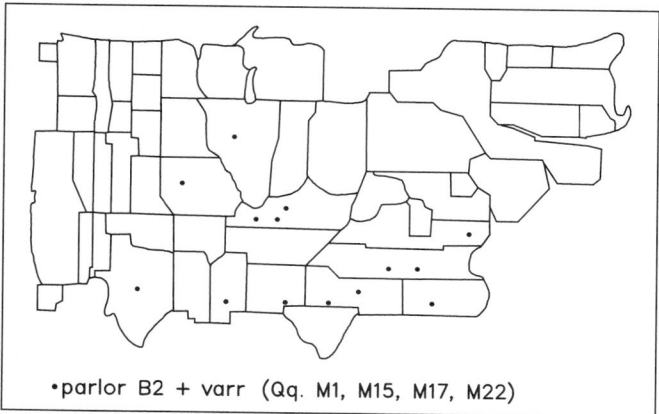

•parlor B2 + varr (Qq. M1, M15, M17, M22)

3 In railroading: a caboose.

1931 *Writer's Digest* 11.42 [Railroad terms], *Parlor*—Caboose. **1938** Beebe *High Iron* 223 [Railroad terms], *Parlor*: Caboose.

4 One of the chambers in a lobster trap with two chambers; see quots. Cf **kitchen** n[1] **2**

1957 Beck *Folkl. ME* 126, Some [=lobster traps] had two openings or "heads" at opposite ends, others one "head" leading into a "parlor" and thence into the "kitchen" where the lobster was finally caught. **1978** Merriam *Illustr. Lobstering* 64, *Parlor Trap*. . . The lobsters get to the parlor by going through the kitchen . . and then through the large head. The head into the parlor is larger than the head which the lobsters entered through.

parlor broom n
=**hearth broom.**
   1908 *DN* 3.319 **eAL, eGA,** *Hearth-broom.* . . A small broom used only about the open fireplace. Sometimes called *parlor-broom.* **1950** *WELS (Different kinds of brooms used around the house)* 2 Infs, **ceWI,** Parlor broom.

parlor match n *old-fash* Cf **brimstone match**
A match that contains no sulfur.
   1864 *Scientific Amer.* 11.350, *Diamond Parlor Matches.* These Matches are the *best in the world, sure fire, without sulphur,* no disagreeable smell, and a luxury and comfort to smokers and people with weak lungs. **1873** Howard *Monumental City* 124 **MD,** Both Sulphur and Parlor matches are made [in Baltimore] which compare favorably in quality, with those manufactured elsewhere in the country. **1927** *Scribner's Mag.* 81.326 **NEng,** There is only one good match—that is the big, soft-nosed parlor-match that will light on anything. **1927** (1970) Sears *Catalogue* 929, *Ever-Brite Gasoline Table Lamp.* . . It lights almost instantly with an ordinary parlor match. **1947** *McDavid Coll.* **FL,** Parlor matches = kitchen matches (big). **1965–70** *DARE* (Qu. F46, . . *Matches you can strike anywhere;* not asked in early QRs) 11 Infs, **scattered,** Parlor matches [all Infs old]. **1973** Allen *LAUM* 1.160 **Upper MW** (as of c1950), *Kitchen matches* (that will strike anywhere). . . parlor matches [16 infs] [all infs born before 1890].

parlor rugby n
A children's kissing game.
   1968 *DARE* (Qu. EE33, . . *Outdoor games . . that children play*) Inf **CT**11, Parlor rugby—person who is "it" sits in middle, calls two numbers, boy and girl; the girl must kiss the boy who is "it" before the other boy kisses her.

parm See **palm**

paroquet See **parakeet**

parrain n [Fr] **sLA** Cf **nenaine**
A godfather.
   1923 *DN* 5.244 **sLA,** *Parin* [sic] [pɑræ]. . . Godfather. **1961** *PADS* 36.11 **sLA,** The special Louisiana additions to the questionnaire produced a considerably longer list of terms which are almost surely confined to the area. . . That they could be generally current in other areas is extremely doubtful. . . *Parrain* (Godfather)—84.2 [percent of 70 informants]. **1967** LeCompte *Word Atlas* 268 **seLA,** *Godfather.* . . *parrain* [19 of 21 infs]. **1968** *DARE* FW Addit **LA**39, Parrain ['pɑ,ræ] = godfather. Common New Orleans and southwards, no matter whether speaker is of French descent or not. **1983** *Reinecke Coll.* 8 **LA,** *Parrain* [pəræ] . . godfather. Less common than Nainaine, Nanny. Known to people not of Fr. descent. **1986** Pederson *LAGS Concordance,* 1 inf, **seLA,** Parrain—godfather.

parrot n
=**parakeet 1.**
   1588 (1903) Hariot *Briefe Rept.* **VA** sig D3ʳ, There are also *Parats, Faulcons, & Marlin haukes,* which although with vs they bee not vsed for meate, yet for other causes I thought good to mention. **1612** Smith *Map VA* 1.15, In winter thare are great plenty of Swans, . . Oxeies, Parrats and Pigeons. **1731** Catesby *Nat. Hist. Carolina* 1.11, *The Parrot of Carolina.* This Bird is of the bigness, or rather less than a Black-bird, weighing three ounces and an half. . . This is the only one of the Parrot kind in Carolina. **1779** in 1916 Mereness *Travels* 621 **KY,** Here was several flocks of Parrots flying about. **1858** in 1859 Gosse *Letters from AL* 298, I had the pleasure of seeing a flock of parrots (*Psittacus Carolinensis*). . . There were eighty or a hundred in one compact flock, and as they swept past me, screaming as they went, I fancied that they looked like an immense shawl of green satin, on which an irregular pattern was worked in scarlet and gold and azure. **1874** Coues *Birds NW* 296 **IA,** A resident of Decatur County told me that he had several times seen a flock of Parrots . . on a tall, dead cottonwood-tree, known to the neighboring people as the 'parrot-tree,' from its having been frequented at intervals by the same flock for several years. **1903** Dawson *Birds OH* 2.369, There are gray-haired men still among us who remember the shrieking companies of "parrots" which used to haunt the bottom lands and go charging about the sycamores like gusts of mad leaves; but to-day only the cunning plume-hunter or thrice-lucky ornithologist may penetrate to the remaining fastnesses of the species in the everglades of

Florida. **1962** Imhof *AL Birds* 298, Carolina Parakeet . . other names: Carolina Paroquet, Carolina Parrot, Parrot.

parrotbill n
=**razor-billed auk.**
   1956 MA Audubon Soc. *Bulletin* 40.79 **RI,** Razor-billed Auk. . . Noddy, Parrot-bill.

parrot blackbird n
The smooth-billed ani (*Crotophaga ani*).
   1954 Sprunt *FL Bird Life* 245, Smooth-billed Ani. . . *Local Names:* Parrot Blackbird. . . Entirely black, plumage with purple and greenish reflections; . . upper mandible forming a high, thin crest.

parrot feather See **parrot's feather 1**

parrot feathers See **parrot's feather 3**

parrot's beak See **parrot's head**

parrot's feather n
1 also *parrot feather:* =**water milfoil,** esp *Myriophyllum brasiliense.* Cf **green parrot('s) feather**
   1923 *Amer. Botanist* 29.140 **seGA,** In the wettest places in the bayhead are purple and yellow *Iris versicolor* . . and in the open water great masses of the dainty parrot's feather (*Myriophyllum*). **1936** McDougall–Baggley *Plants of Yellowstone* 94, *Myriophyllum.* . . The genus is commonly known as *parrotfeather.* **1950** Gray–Fernald *Manual of Botany* 1074, *Parrot's-feather.* . . Tends to persist southw. (n. to Mo. and casually to s.N.Y.) **1956** St. John *Flora SE WA* 269 **ID,** *Myriophyllum brasiliense.* . . *Parrot's Feather.* . . Established in slough, mouth of Potlatch River, Ida. **1970** Correll *Plants TX* 1138, *Myriophyllum brasiliense.* . . *Parrot's-feather.* . . Widely scattered in ponds, ditches, streams and on seepage slopes.
2 A **mermaid weed 1** (here: *Proserpinaca palustris*).
   1940 Clute *Amer. Plant Names* 268, *Proserpinacea* [sic] *palustris.* Parrot's feather.
3 as *parrot feathers:* A bladderwort (*Utricularia* spp).
   1951 *PADS* 15.40 **TX,** *Utricularia* spp.—Parrot feathers.

parrot's head n Also *parrot's beak*
A **lousewort 1** (here: *Pedicularis racemosa*).
   1920 Rice–Rice *Pop. Studies CA Wild Flowers* 112, *P[edicularis] ornithorhyncha,* the quaint little Duck's Bill, grows in Washington and Oregon. . . Then there are the "Parrot's Head" and the "Walrus Head." **1963** Craighead *Rocky Mt. Wildflowers* 175, Parrots-beak . . *P[edicularis] racemosa* . . has upper lip of corolla prolonged into a distinct beak.

parrot-toed adj Pronc-spp *paratoed,* *parry-toed,* *pear-toed* **chiefly Mid and S Atl** See Map
Having feet that turn inward; pigeon-toed; hence n pl *parrot toes* inward-turning feet.
   1824 *N. Amer. Rev.* 19.223, Who ever before thought of General Washington . . marching with the true aboriginal parrot toed gait in an elegant costume of party colored feathers, and porcupine's quills! **1845** (1969) Willis *Dashes* 4.215 **NEast,** To aid the likeness, he is slightly parry-toed. **1849** Lynch *Exped. Jordan* 91 **VA,** Most of the Turks walk what

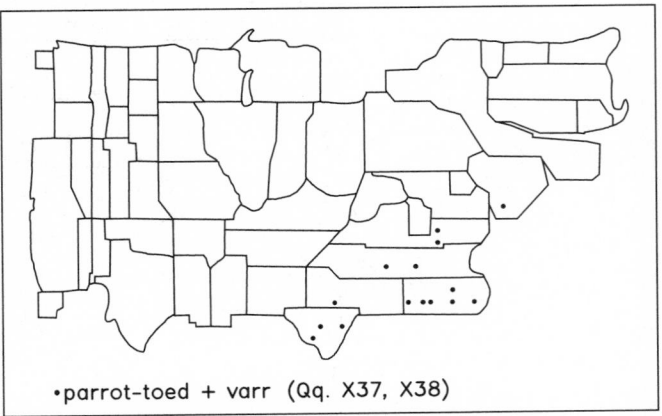

•parrot-toed + varr (Qq. X37, X38)

is termed "parrot-toed,"—very much like our Indians. **1899** (1912) Green *VA Folk-Speech* 312, *Parrot-toed. . . Parry-toed,* with the toes turned in in walking. **1930** *DN* 6.82 cSC, *Paratoed. . .* Pigeon-toed. Probably the expression was originally parrot-toed, although no one associates it with a parrot now. Universal. **1947** *McDavid Coll.* **GA,** Parrot toed = pigeon toed. **1950** *PADS* 14.50 **SC,** *Paratoed. . . Parrot-toed,* a milder degree of pigeon-toed. **1965–70** *DARE* (Qu. X37, . . *Words . . to describe people's legs if they're noticeably bent, or uneven, or not right*) 10 Infs, **chiefly S Atl,** Parrot-toed; VA69, 73, Parrot toes; FL33, Pear-toed [pɛɪɚˈtoʊd]—they point their toes in when they walk; GA43, Pear-toed—same as slew-footed; (Qu. X38, *Joking names for unusually big or clumsy feet*) Inf NC49, Pear [pɛɚ]-toed. [10 of 15 Infs Black or Amer Ind] **1986** Pederson *LAGS Concordance,* 1 inf, **csAL,** Pear-toed = pigeon-toed? [Inf Black]

parrysawl See **parasol**

parry-toed See **parrot-toed**

parsley n Usu |ˈpɑ(r)sli|; also |ˈpæsli| Pronc-spp *pas(s)ley* Cf **passel**
A Forms.
1891 *DN* 1.119 cNY, [ˈpɑrslɪ] (also [ˈpæslɪ] with loss of *r*). **1899** (1912) Green *VA Folk-Speech* 312, *Pasley. . .* Parsley. **1967** *DARE* FW Addit **NH**11, [We] also eat passley greens. **1969** *DARE* (Qu. I28a) Inf MO37, [ˈkʰɑuˌpˈæsliⁱi].
B Senses. Cf **cow parsley, desert ~, hog ~, Jerusalem ~, sea ~, water ~, whiskbroom ~, wild ~**
1 usu with adj: Any of var **biscuit roots 1,** but often *Lomatium foeniculaceum.*
1936 Winter *Plants NE* 85, *C[ogswellia] orientale. . .* White-flowered Parsley. . . *C. daucifolia. . .* Carrot-leaved Parsley. . . *C. foeniculacea. . .* Hairy Parsley. **1937** Stemen–Myers *OK Flora* 364, *Carrot-leaved Parsley.* Foliage tomentose, becoming less dense in age. *Ibid* 365, *Hairy Parsley.* Perennial with a fusiform root. **1940** Steyermark *Flora MO* 397, Hairy Parsley (*Lomatium daucifolium*). **1967** Gilkey–Dennis *Hdbk. NW Plants* 291, *Lomatium dissectum. . . Purple parsley. . .* Leaves with . . blades many times divided into narrow ultimate segments. . . Common along the roadsides. **1967** *DARE* Wildfl QR (Craighead) Pl.13.5 Inf **CO**29, Parsley. **1987** Kindscher *Edible Wild Plants* 147, Prairie parsley [=*Lomatium foeniculaceum*] is one of the first prairie plants to bloom in the spring. Its edible leaves have a strong parsley taste and are good in salads.
2 with adj: Any of several related umbelliferous plants that somewhat resemble parsley (*Petroselinum crispum*); see quots.
1941 Jaeger *Wildflowers* 177 **Desert SW,** *Gilman Parsley. Cymopterus Gilmani. . .* In the mountains of the Death Valley Nat[ional] Mon[ument]. **1953** Nelson *Plants Rocky Mt. Park* 112, *Mountain parsley, Harbouria trachypleura. . .* A plant with umbels of small yellow flowers. . . *Alpine parsley . . , Oreoxis alpina. . .* A dwarf . . plant with . . pinnate leaves with narrow segments and very short stem. . . *wild yellow-parsley . . , Pseudocymopterus montanus.* **1970** Correll *Plants TX* 1160, *Pseudocymopterus montanus. . . Mountain parsley. . .* Usually in rocky places.

parsley hawthorn n Also *parsley(-leaved) haw, parsley-leaf (or -leaved) hawthorn, parsley-leaved thorn*
A hawthorn (here: *Crataegus marshallii*) noted for its finely cut leaves. Also called **red haw 1**
1813 Muhlenberg *Catalogus Plantarum* 49, [*Crataegus*] *apiifolia*—parsley-leaved [hawthorn]. **1860** Curtis *Cat. Plants NC* 83, Parsley-leaved Haw. . . The leaves are about 1 inch long, and much cut up into small divisions, from which this handsome shrub or small tree derives its name, and by which it is easily distinguished from all the other species. **1868** (1870) Gray *Field Botany* 128, Parsley-leaved T[horn]. **1908** Rogers *Tree Book* 316, Parsley Haw. . . Its graceful, parsley-like leaves at once distinguish it from other species. **1967** *DARE* (Qu. I46, . . *Kinds of fruits that grow wild around here*) Inf LA2, Parsley haw—red haw. **1976** Elmore *Shrubs & Trees SW* 146, Acerola, the tiny applelike fruit of parsely-leaved [sic] hawthorn is richer in natural Vitamin C than any other fruit. **1979** Little *Checklist U.S. Trees* 114, Parsley-leaf hawthorn. **1995** Brako et al. *Scientific & Common Names Plants* 199, Parsley hawthorn—*Crataegus marshallii.*

parsley worm n
The larva of the black swallowtail (*Papilio polyxenes asterias*).

1842 Harris *Treatise Insects* 211, In the month of June, there may be found, on the leaves of the parsley and carrot, certain caterpillars, more commonly called parsley-worms. **1882** (1903) Treat *Injurious Insects* 55, In July, in the New England and Middle States, and earlier further South, there will be found upon Parsley especially, and sometimes upon other cultivated umbelliferous plants, . . a showy caterpillar, known as the "Parsley-worm." . . If disturbed it at once . . gives off, what has been called a "scent," but is better described as a stench which pervades the air for some distance. **1966** *DARE* (Qu. R27, . . *Kinds of caterpillars or similar worms*) Inf **PA**1, Parsley worm. **1972** Swan–Papp *Insects* 204, *Black Swallowtail (Parsleyworm). . .* Also variously called . . celery-worm, carrotworm. . . Sometimes a pest of garden and field crops. **1989** Entomol. Soc. Amer. *Common Names Insects* 44, Parsleyworm. . . Adult called black swallowtail.

parsnip n Usu |ˈpɑ(r)snɪp, -snəp|; also |ˈpæsnɪp| Pronc-spp *pasnep, pasnet, pasnip, pasnup* Arch sp *parsnep* Cf **parsley, passel**
A Forms.
1790 in 1793 Amer. Philos. Soc. *Trans.* 3.234 **VA,** I have heard this poisonous herb, called by the names of Wild-Carrot, Wild-Parsnep [etc]. **1843** Torrey *Flora NY* 1.271, *Zizia aurea. . .* Golden Meadow Parsnep. **1894** *Century Illustr. Mag.* 48.869 **swIN,** No types can express . . the long-drawn flatness of the accented vowel in apast, yander, and paster, or for that matter, in "pasnips" for parsnips. **1899** (1912) Green *VA Folk-Speech* 312, *Pasnip. . .* Pasnep, for parsnip. **1903** *DN* 2.291 **Cape Cod MA** (as of a1857), Pasnup. **1911** *DN* 3.539 **eKY,** *Parsnip.* Pronounced [pæsnɪp]. **1917** in 1944 *ADD* **sWV,** Pa'snip. **1952** Brown *NC Folkl.* 1.573, *Pasnip* [ˈpæsnɪp]. **1964** *PADS* 42.21 **cwKY,** *Parsnip.* Older people said [ˈpæsnɪp]. **1982** Slone *How We Talked* 26 **eKY** (as of c1950), *Pasnet*—parsnip.
B freq with adj: Any of several related umbelliferous plants that somewhat resemble parsnip (*Pastinaca sativa*); see quots. Cf **bladder parsnip, cowbane ~, cow ~, golden ~, Hercules ~, Indian ~, lace ~, meadow ~, pestle ~, poison ~, sheep ~, wafer ~, water ~, wild ~**
1892 *Jrl. Amer. Folkl.* 5.97 **ME,** *Daucus carota,* parsnip. Harmony, Me. **1911** Jepson *Flora CA* 303, *P[eucedanum] caruifolium. . . Alkali Parsnip. . .* peduncles 3 or 4 from a common stout taproot. **1937** U.S. Forest Serv. *Range Plant Hdbk.* W52, Such related plants as angelicas . . and woollyhead-parsnip (*Sphenosciadium capitellatum*) are harmless and good forage. **1967** *DARE* Wildfl QR Pl.12, Parsnip—cow parsnip has bigger leaves. *Ibid* (Craighead; *Lomatium dissectum*) Pl.13.5 Inf **CA**24, Desert parsnip. **1976** Bailey–Bailey *Hortus Third* 679, [*Lomatium*] *triternatum. . . Buck parsnip. . .* Al[ber]ta s. to Wyo. and n. Calif.

parson See **person**

parson-in-a-pillory n Also *parson-in-the-pillory* Cf **parson-in-the-pulpit**
=skunk cabbage 1a.
1933 Small *Manual SE Flora* 245, Sepals and filaments fitting tightly around the style: fruit-head persistent. . . *Parson-in-the-Pillory.* Skunk-cabbage. **1949** Moldenke *Amer. Wild Flowers* 347, *Symplocarpus foetidus. . .* This plant, also called . . *parson-in-a-pillory,* . . is found in swamps and low meadows from Georgia (and possibly Florida) to Missouri, northward to Minnesota and Nova Scotia. **1970** *Living Museum* 31.180 **IL,** Known by such descriptive epithets as swamp cabbage, parson-in-a-pillory, polecatweed, and devil's tobacco, the skunk cabbage, a relative of jack-in-the-pulpit, ushers in the growing season.

parson-in-the-pulpit n Cf **parson plant, preacher-in-the-pulpit 2**
A jack-in-the-pulpit 1 (here: *Arisaema triphyllum pusillum*).
1933 Small *Manual SE Flora* 247, *A[risaema] acuminatum. . .* Parson-in-the-Pulpit. **1976** Fleming *Wild Flowers FL* 39, Parson-in-the-Pulpit grows in the deep shade of hammocks in rich mucky soil and may be seen along old woods' roads; it blooms in early spring in central and south Florida.

parson plant n Cf **parson-in-the-pulpit**
A jack-in-the-pulpit 1.
1968 *DARE* (Qu. S1, . . *Jack-in-the-pulpit*) Inf **NY**123, Parson plant.

parson's face See **minister's face 1**

parson's nose n Also *parson's snout* [Engl dial] **chiefly S Atl** See Map
=**pope's nose 1.**
1839 Longfellow *Hyperion* 1.142, An epicurean morsel,—a parson's nose. **c1960** *Wilson Coll.* **csKY**, *Parson's nose*. . . The tail or rump of a chicken; called elsewhere the "pope's nose" or the "pope's toe." **1965–70** *DARE* (Qu. K73, . . *Names . . for the rump of a cooked chicken*) 13 Infs, **chiefly S Atl**, Parson's nose; **FL6**, Parson's snout.

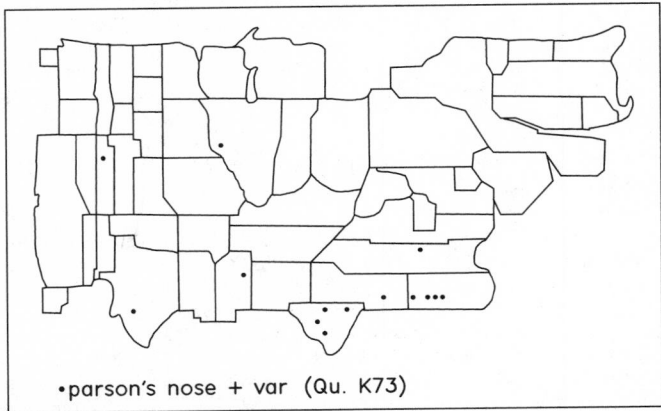

•parson's nose + var (Qu. K73)

parster, parstur See **pasture** n¹, v¹

particular adj, n, adv   Usu |pə(r)ˈtɪkjələ(r)|; also |pɑr-, -ˈtɪk(ə)lə(r)| Similarly adv *particularly;* see quot 1936   Pronc-spp *partikeler, pertick(e)ler, pertic'lar, peticular, petickler, pretick(e)lar, p'tickler, puhtickluh*
A Forms.
1853 [see **B1** below]. **1858** [see **B2** below]. **1871** Eggleston *Hoosier Schoolmaster* 101 **sIN**, I rather guess as how the ole man Bosaw will give perticeler fits to our folks to-day. **1871** [see **D** below]. **1890** *DN* 1.68 **KY**, *Particular.* Pronounced [pətɪklə]. **1892** *DN* 1.217, [Re quot 1890:] The accent of [pətɪklə] is on the [ɪ]. **1904** Day *Kin o' Ktaadn* 118 **ME**, The gen'ral public don't see that p'tickler side of a woodsman. **1910** Hart *Vigilante Girl* 17 **nCA**, Oh, I don't know what pettickler thing they done right now. **1916** *DN* 4.278 **NE**, *Peticular.* . . Particular. . . [Also N.Y.] **1917** [see **C** below]. **1922** Gonzales *Black Border* 320 **sSC, GA coasts** [Gullah glossary], Puhtickluh—particular, particularly. **1936** *AmSp* 11.245 **eTX**, Particular—*[Plantation-Type:]* [pəˈtɪk(jə)lə]—*[Hill-Type:]* [pəˈtɪklə]—*[Negro:]* [pəˈtɪklə]. *Ibid* 310 **Upstate NY**, *Particular* occurs 49 times with [j], and 4 times without it; *particularly,* 7 times with [j], and once without it. *Ibid* 313, Particular—[[r] *in-cluded:*] 89 [times; [r] *omitted:*] 75. . . In *particularly,* both [r] and [l] may be dissimilated; [pəˈtɪkjrlɪ], one of several variations, illustrates both types. **1937** Crane *Let Me Show You VT* 30 **VT**, There are words which some persons perpetuate in mispronunciation. . . F'r instance . . *partikeler* for particular. **1942** *AmSp* 17.153 **seNY**, Particular—*[Both r's pronounced:]* 25—*[First r omitted:]* 24—*[Second r omitted:]* 1—*[Both r's omitted:]* 31. **1942** Hall *Smoky Mt. Speech* 68 **wNC, eTN**, The vowel [represented by *u*] is frequently omitted [in] *particular* [pəˈtɪklə]. **1959** *VT Hist.* 27.151, *Particular* [pɑrˈtɪklə]. . . Common. **1970** *DARE* (Qu. HH11a, *Someone who is too particular or fussy—if it's a man*) Inf **IL126**, Pertic'lar.
B As adj.
1 Cautious, chary, careful.   **chiefly Sth, S Midl**
1853 Simms *Sword & Distaff* 376 **SC** [Black], Be berry preticklar, jis' when you gitting off de hoss; and when you's a-walking up de steps. **1952** Brown *NC Folkl.* 1.573, *Particular.* . . Careful, cautious. "Be particular when you cross the street." **c1960** *Wilson Coll.* **csKY**, *Particular.* . . Cautious, careful. **1965–70** *DARE* (Qu. BB2, *If a person is careful not to put much weight on his injured leg, you might say he was _____ that leg*) Infs **GA8, KY77, MS63, SC34, 40, TN30, 65, VA71**, Particular with. **1966** *DARE* Tape **GA7**, It's in a fine mist when it goes on that tree, and if you're not particular, the wind can be blowin' back from the tree towards you, and it'll just blow it all over you. . . If you're not particular, it'll come back on you. **1986** Pederson *LAGS Concordance (He should be careful)* 1 inf, **cGA**, Be particular; 1 inf, **ceAL**, Better be particular—better be careful.

2 Used as a general expression of intensification—usu in phrr *to give (someone) particular hell* (or *jesse, lightning,* etc).
1846 *Spirit of Times* 6 June 176/2 *(DA)*, Our boys did give them 'most particular Jesse,' and that is all I have time to tell you about the battle. **1847** (1962) Robb *Squatter Life* 31, Don't forgit to gin the town below particular saltpetre. **1854** in 1956 Eliason *Tarheel Talk* 147 **NC**, I chained him hand & foot & took a cowhide 4 feet long and gave him particular Jessey. **1858** Hammett *Piney Woods Tavern* 68, They . . made pretickelar Judies [=fools] of theyselves ginerally. **1871** *Harper's New Mth. Mag.* 43.690, Ef *Pat* Role, or any other consarned Irishman, kicks up a muss 'bout these yer diggins, he'll kotch *par*tic'lar lightnin'. **1966** Barnes–Jensen *Dict. UT Slang* 18, *Give particular hell, to:* . . used as an intensive.
C As noun.
1 pl: See quot 1917.
1917 *DN* 4.415 **wNC**, *Particulars* [pɪtklæz]. . . Perishable foodstuffs. **1996** in 2001 *Montgomery Coll.* **eTN**, When you're going to dinner on the ground, you better be careful about your particulars.
2 in phr *that's a particular:* That's a fact. [Appar by ext from *particular* an item of information]
1943 Weslager *DE Forgotten Folk* 153, Everybody knows that I got my faults, but I ain't never told a lie in my life and that's a particular. *Ibid* 169, It didn't taste good, but it was a sure cure, that's a particular.
D As adv.   Cf Intro "Language Changes" II.8
Especially, in particular, particularly.   **esp Sth, S Midl**
1871 Eggleston *Hoosier Schoolmaster* 41 **sIN**, He didn't think she had no great sight to be pertickler thankful fer. **1922** [see **A** above]. **1938** Rawlings *Yearling* 76 **nFL**, Never perticklar mean. **1939** in 1944 *ADD* 442 **nwAR**, I ain't worried pertic'lar. **1965** *DARE* (Qu. KK51, *Very plainly or abruptly:* "I asked him _____ what he meant by that.") Inf **MS61**, Particular. **1986** Pederson *LAGS Concordance,* 1 inf, **neTN**, He particular used shoulders.

partida n [Span]   **West**   Cf **parada**
See quot 1932.
1892 *DN* 1.192 **TX**, *Partída:* a drove of cattle. This word answers to the common American words 'a lot,' 'a heap,' etc., speaking of an indefinite quantity. **1929** Dobie *Vaquero* 66 **West**, Mustang Gray . . rounded up a *partida* of Cortina bandits. **1932** Bentley *Spanish Terms* 176, *Partida.* . . From *partir,* to divide. A party, a band, squad; an outlaw band.

partidge See **partridge** A4

partikeler See **particular**

partment n [Aphet form of *apartment,* perh by metanalysis; cf Intro "Language Changes" I.2]   **esp Sth, S Midl**
1965–70 *DARE* (Qu. D23, *A house that is divided in two through the middle so that two families can live in it*) Infs **AL55, KY40, NY70, TX35, VA38, 47**, Partment; (Qu. D24, *Living quarters in a building where several other families live*) Infs **FL21, KY40, 68, MO4, 5, 19, 20, VA38, 75**, Partment; (Qu. D26, . . *Different kinds of apartments*) Inf **AL11**, Partment. **1986** Pederson *LAGS Concordance,* 24 infs, **Gulf Region**, (A)partment(s) [=partment(s), in var combs]; 1 inf, **seLA**, It's a partment hotel.

partner n
A Forms.   Pronc-spp *paa'dnuh, pard(e)ner, podna, podner;* abbr *pard*   **scattered, but chiefly Sth, S Midl, SW**   See Map
1795 Dearborn *Columbian Grammar* 137, *List of Improprieties.* . . Pardener for Partner. **1837** Sherwood *Gaz. GA* 71, *Pardner,* for partner. **1843** in 1940 Chabot *TX Letters* 46, I am chained now to Milvern Harold who makes a first rate pard. **1849** in 1956 Eliason *Tarheel Talk* 315 **nw,cnNC**, Pardner. **1883** Twain *Life on Missip.* (Boston) 50, I was on watch and boss of the stabboard oar forrard, and one of my pards was a man named Dick Allbright. **1899** (1912) Green *VA Folk-Speech* 312, *Pardner.* **1905** *DN* 3.63 **NE**, *Pard.* . . Short for *pardner.* **1906** *DN* 3.150 **nwAR**, "Who's your pardner this dance?" "Come on. You're my pardner. Help me." Common. **1909** *DN* 3.355 **eAL, wGA**, *Pard.* . . Short for *pardner.* **1922** Gonzales *Black Border* 317 **sSC, GA coasts** [Gullah glossary], *Paa'dnuh*—partner, partners. **1925** *AmSp* 1.152 **West**, Western Speech is full of differences from Eastern Speech. . . "Pardner" is so firmly established that many think it a typographical error when they see the word spelled with a "t." **1928** *AmSp* 3.405

Ozarks (as of 1916–27), *Partner* is turned into *pardner.* **1942** Warnick *Garrett Co. MD* 1 **nwMD** (as of 1900–18), *Pardner* (partner). **1945** [see **B1** below]. **1965–70** *DARE* (Qu. II1) 19 Infs, **esp Sth, S Midl, SW,** Pardner; (Qu. II10b) 9 Infs, **scattered,** Pardner; (Qu. AA15b) Inf **MI49,** Got himself a pardner; **OR13,** Took him a pardner; (Qu. II2b) Inf **MS88,** Running pardners; (Qu. II8) Inf **MD36,** Go in pardners; (Qu. II10a) Infs **ND5, TX1,** Pardner; **DE1,** Pard; (Qu. NN10a) Inf **OK27,** Howdy, pardner. **1976** Garber *Mountain-ese* 66 **sAppalachians,** *Pardner . . * partner, cohort. **1990** Burke *Morning for Flamingos* 127 **seLA,** "I respect your feelings, Tony." "You don't rattle, do you?" "Morning and night, podna. I've got a problem here. Ray doesn't want my friend along on the tarpon trip."

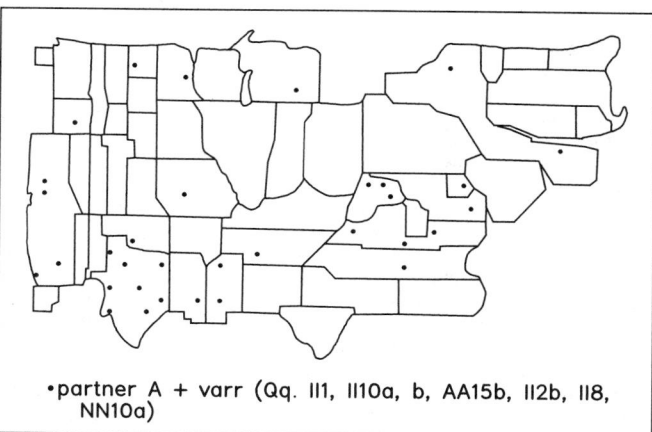

•partner A + varr (Qq. II1, II10a, b, AA15b, II2b, II8, NN10a)

B Senses.

1 A very close friend.   Cf **compañero**
    1894 Riley *Armazindy* 73 **IN,** We're old pards.—But Frank he jest / Can't stay still! **1942** McAtee *Dial. Grant Co. IN* 48 (as of 1890s), *Pard, pardner . . * partner, or more often crony or friend. Slang, chiefly U.S. **1945** Street *Gauntlet* 103 **MO** (as of 1920s), "You know Ben Thigpen. He's my podner. Me and Ben are just like this." He held up two fingers and they were close together. **1965–70** *DARE* (Qu. II1, . . *A close friend . . "He's my _____."*) 19 Infs, **esp Sth, S Midl, SW,** Pardner; **IL98, IN75,** Partner.

2 Used as a term of address; see quots.   Cf **buddy** n **1**
    1887 *Amer. Field* 27.61 **West,** A "cow puncher" rode up and pointing at the umbrella asked: "What is she pard?" **1904** *DN* 2.420 **nwAR,** *Pardner. . * Sir. Common in addressing a stranger. "Won't you come in, pardner?" **1927** *AmSp* 3.169 **SW** [Cowboy speech], If cowboys agree with you upon a subject, it is "y'u said it," "y'u hit 'er, pard," or "that's its shape." **1962** Atwood *Vocab. TX* 70, Familiar greeting. . . one [inf, of approx 270] gave *hi, pardner!* **1965–70** *DARE* (Qu. II10b, *Asking directions of somebody on the street when you don't know his name— what you'd say to a man: "Say, _____, how far is it to the next town?"*) 9 Infs, **scattered,** Pardner; **MS56,** Partner; (Qu. II10a, *Asking directions of somebody on the street when you don't know his name— what you'd say to a boy: "Say, _____, where's the post office?"*) Infs **ND5, TX1,** Pardner; **DE1,** Pard; (Qu. NN10a, *Expressions [such as 'hello'] used when you meet somebody you know quite well)* Inf **CA160,** Hi there, partner; **OK27,** Howdy, partner. **1971** Bright *Word Geog. CA & NV* 192, Partner 67% [of 300 infs] . . *pardner* 45%. . . Of those using *partner,* 35 would use it in the vocative, 75 would not. Of those who gave *pardner,* 33 would use it in the vocative, 56 would not. Many of those who said that they would use the word in the vocative qualified it as a jocular term. **1983** Beyle *How Talk Cape Cod* 27, The Portuguese here sometimes refer to folks as "pard" (short for pardner).

partridge n Usu |'pɑrtrɪǰ, pɑr-, -trɨǰ|; for varr see **A** below   Cf **cartridge**

A Forms.

1 |'pɑtrɪǰ| and varr; pronc-sp *podridge.*   **chiefly NEng, Sth, S Midl**   See Map   Note: While this type represents the expected pronc in r-less areas, it also appears to be common beyond the normal boundaries of this area.   Cf Pronc Intro 3.III.1
    1965–70 *DARE* (Qu. Q7) 67 Infs, **chiefly NEng, Sth, S Midl,** [Proncs of the type ['pɑtrɪǰ, 'pɑ-, -trɨǰ, -drɪǰ]]; **FL27, GA76, SC19, VA21,**

['pɒtrɪǰ(ɪz)]; **DC2, IN14,** ['pɒtrɪǰ]; **NC49,** ['pɒdrɪǰ]; **MS11,** ['pɑdwɪǰ]; **MS53,** ['pɑtwɪǰ]. **1967** *DARE* Wildfl QR Pl.80 Inf **TX34,** Podridge pea. **1975** Gould *ME Lingo* 203, *Pa'tridge*—There are no native partridges in Maine, but the two grouses are called *pa'tridges:* the ruffed grouse and the spruce grouse. Up to late hour, no Mainer has ever called a grouse a grouse. **1981** Pederson *LAGS Basic Materials,* 1 inf, **cwGA,** [p'aˑˑətrɪdʒ].

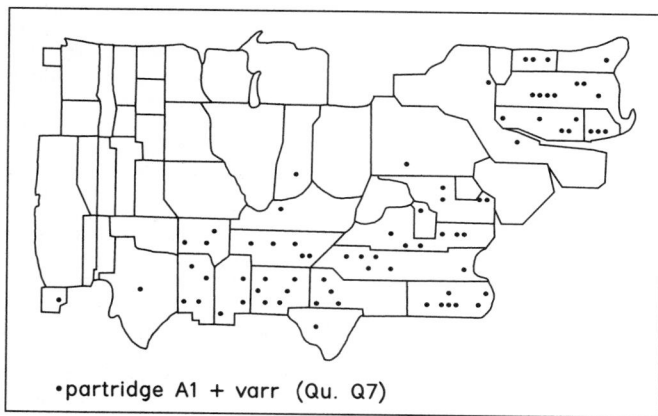

•partridge A1 + varr (Qu. Q7)

2 |'pætrɪǰ| and varr; pronc-spp *patri(d)ge, pattridge.*   **chiefly Nth, Midl, now esp NEng, NY**   See Map   Cf **pat** n³   Note: The related type ['pætɚ(ɪ)ǰ], which is **chiefly S Midl,** is included at **A3** below.
    1818 (1937) Guild *Jrl.* 3.251 **VT,** I spied a patrige. . . and with a stone brought the partridge to the ground. **1841** in 1934 *AmSp* 9.263 **eTN,** *Patridge.* **1843** in 1956 Eliason *Tarheel Talk* 315 **c,cnNC,** Patriges. **1847** Hurd *Grammatical Corrector* 87, *Partridge* ["incorrect" pronc = ['pætrɪǰ]; "correct" pronc = ['pɑrtrɪǰ]]. **1853** Simms *Sword & Distaff* 116 **SC,** I cook myse'f 'fore I guine let Mass Cappin want for dinner. So long as . . dere's pattridge and dub (dove) . . Tom will always hab 'nough somet'ing to cook! **1887** (1895) Robinson *Uncle Lisha* 62 **wVT,** Naow an' ag'in he'd be gone for days an' days, . . sneakin' ontu squirrels an' pa'tridges an' ducks sly as foxes. **1888** Jones *Negro Myths* 19 **GA coast,** Buh Pattridge and Buh Rabbit jine compny fuh kill cow. **1891** *DN* 1.163 **cNY,** ['pætrɪǰ] < *partridge.* **1892** *DN* 1.240 **cwMO,** ['pætrɪǰ]. **1893** Shands *MS Speech* 49, *Patridge* ['pætrɪǰ]. A pronunciation of *partridge* common among negroes and illiterate whites. **1903** *DN* 2.290 **Cape Cod MA** (as of a1857), Other peculiarities of *r* are seen in pattridge . . for partridge [etc]. *Ibid* 325 **seMO,** *Patridge.* **1907** *DN* 3.234 **nwAR,** ['pætrɪǰ]. **1915** *DN* 4.187 **swVA,** ['pætrɪǰ]. **1917** *DN* 4.397 **neOH,** ['pætrɪǰ]. **1950** *WELS (Other names for . . quail)* 1 inf, **ceWI,** Partridge—most people call them patridge. **1959** *VT Hist.* 27.151, *Partridge* ['pætrɪǰ]. . . Common. **1965–70** *DARE* (Qu. Q7) 32 Infs, **scattered Nth, Midl, but esp NEng, NY,** [Proncs of the type ['pætrɪǰ, -drɪǰ]]; **MI17,** ['pætrɪǰ]—when we were kids, we used to call them ['pætrɪǰ]; **CT23, VT13,** ['pærtrɪǰ]. [18 of 35 Infs gs educ or less] **1978** *DARE* File **cnMA,** Partridge—I heard this pronounced ['pæt͡rɪǰ] by a man between 65 and 70, high school education. **1992** Phelps *Famous Last Words* 14 **NEng,** We also had lots of Patridge and deer.

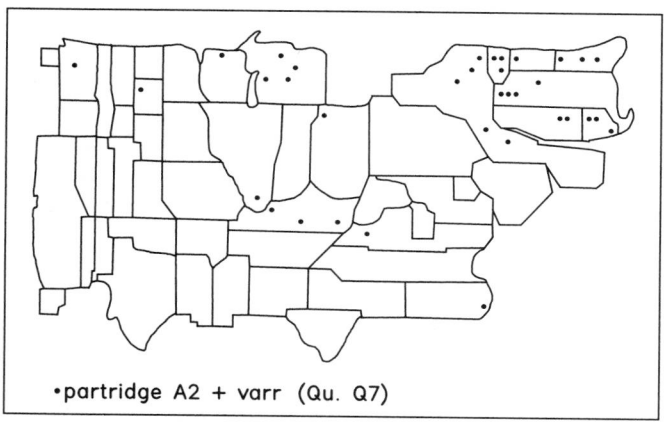

•partridge A2 + varr (Qu. Q7)

3 |ˈpatɚ(ɪ)ǰ, ˈpæ-, ˈpɔ-| and varr; pronc-spp *paterage, patterge, patteridge, pot(t)eridge.* **chiefly Sth, S Midl** See Map

1771 in 1915 *New Engl. Hist. & Geneal. Reg.* 69.15 **MA,** Capt Ivory & Capt Sawtell & fourteen more of us killed in all about 75 Squarreels & Potteridges. **1853** in 1956 Eliason *Tarheel Talk* 315 **cnNC,** Paterage. **c1862** in 1943 Wiley *Life Johnny Reb* 163 **TX,** One little fellow develed me so much about Fly home to thy native home gentle dove he sayed that I looked more like a paterage. **1891** *PMLA* 6.175 **TN,** Metathesis of *r* in such words as *purty . .* , and *pătŭrge* for *partridge,* is common. **c1940** Eliason *Word Lists FL* 11 **wFL,** Poteridge [potrɪdʒ]. **1942** Hall *Smoky Mt. Speech* 30 **wNC, eTN,** Partridge [ˈpætrɪdʒ] (beside [ˈpatɚdʒ]). **1955** Ritchie *Singing Family* 188 **seKY,** And a patterge in a pear-bush! **1961** *Mt. Life* Spring 7 **sAppalachians,** R has succeeded in crossing the vowel in some instances: . . *apern, gorm* (grime . .), and. . . *patteridge* (partridge). **1965–70** *DARE* (Qu. Q7), Infs **AL53, DE4, MA40, NC41, SC2, 3, 11, 24, 32, 34, 43, TX51,** [Proncs of the type [ˈpatɚɪǰ]]; **NC24,** [ˈpatɚrɪǰ]; [Proncs of the type [ˈpatɚ·ɪǰ, pa-, -dɚ·ǰ]]; **FL22, KY28, TX35, VA57,** [Proncs of the type [ˈpatɚ·ɪǰ, pɒ-, -dɚ·ɪǰ]]; **DC8, GA77, NC3, 37, TX99,** [Proncs of the type [ˈpɔtɚ·ɪǰ, pɒ-, -dɚ·ɪǰ]]; **NC54,** [ˈpɒdɚ·ǰɪz]; **KY21, 31, 56, 86, 88, TX32, VA15,** [ˈpætɚ·ǰ, ˈpædɚ·ǰ]; **IN17, KY24, 47, 84, NC44, TN26,** [ˈpætɚ·ɪǰ, ˈpædɚ·ɪǰ]. [36 of 37 Infs White; cf **A4** below] **1966** [see **partridge pea**]. **1966–67** [see **partridge pea**]. **1975** Gainer *Witches* 14 **sAppalachians,** He shot a patteridge with his new gun. **1981** Pederson *LAGS Basic Materials,* 1 inf, **cwTN,** [ˈpa·tɚ·dʒ]; 1 inf, **cwTN,** [ˈpˈæᶜ·rɚ·dʒ]; 1 inf, **csMS,** [ˈpaᶜtɚ·dʒ]; 1 inf, **ceTX,** [ˈpaˀtɚrɪˀdʒ]; 1 inf, **ceTX,** [ˈpaᶜdɚ·dʒɪz].

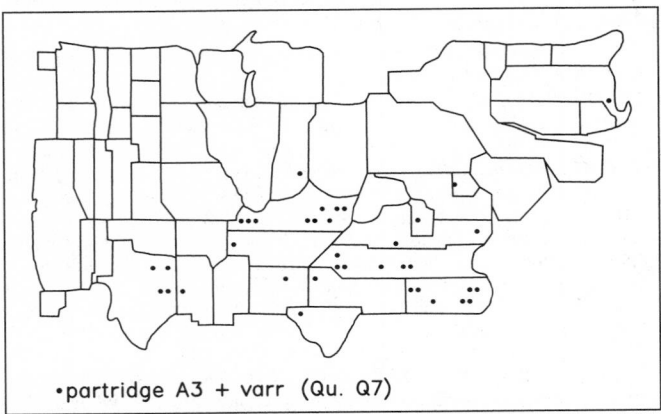

•partridge A3 + varr (Qu. Q7)

4 |ˈpɑ(r)trɪǰ, -dɪǰ, ˈpætɪǰ, -dɪǰ| and varr; pronc-spp *partidge, pattige, potti(d)ge.* **chiefly Lower Missip Valley, Mid Atl** See Map *esp freq among Black speakers*

1909 *DN* 3.356 **eAL, wGA,** Pattige, pottige. . . Partridge. **1955** [see **B2** below]. **1958** [see **B1** below]. **1965–70** *DARE* (Qu. Q7) 18 Infs, **chiefly Lower Missip Valley, Mid Atl,** [Proncs of the type [ˈpɑtɪǰ, -tɪǰ, -dɪǰ]]; **SC57,** [ˈpɑɚtɪǰ]; **VA43,** [ˈpatɪǰɪz]; **GA20, KY82, MD15, 20, MS81, NJ69, VA26, 40,** [Proncs of the type [ˈpɑrtɪǰ, -tɪǰ, -dɪǰ]]; **AR51, GA35, IL32, MI96, SC26,** [Proncs of the type [ˈpætɪǰ, -tɪǰ, -dɪǰ]]. [14 of 31 total Infs Black; cf **A3** above] **1967** *DARE* FW Addit **TN17,** [ˈpadɪǰɪz]—used by country people. **1981** Pederson *LAGS Basic Materials,* 1 inf, **ceAL,** [ˈpaˀtɪˀdʒɪz]; 1 inf, **swGA,** [ˈpˈɑˀ·ᵊtɪtʃ]; 1 inf, **cAL,**

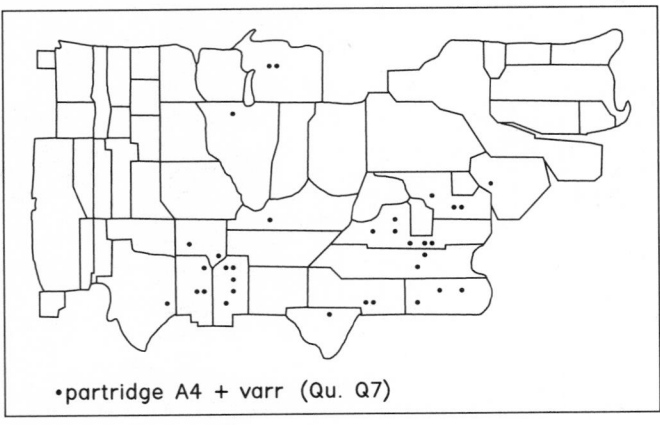

•partridge A4 + varr (Qu. Q7)

[ˈpaᶜtɪʌdʒɪz]; 1 inf, **seAL,** [ˈpˈaˀtɪdʒɪz]; 1 inf, **seAL,** [ˈpaˀ·tɚˀdʒ]; 1 inf, **nwFL,** [ˈpaᶜɚtɪˀdʒɪz].

5 other varr: See quots.

1966–67 [see **partridge pea**]. **1967–70** *DARE* (Qu. Q7) Inf **IN35,** [ˈpɔrtrɪtʃɪs]; **PA128,** [ˈpɔrtˌrɪǰ]; **PA132,** [ˈpɒɚtrɪǰ]—obsolete; **TX40,** [ˈpɔrtrɪǰ]; **TN6,** [ˈparrɪǰ]—common pronunciation; **VA61,** [ˈpɑrčɪǰ]; **VA105,** [ˈpačɪǰ]. **1981** Pederson *LAGS Basic Materials,* 1 inf, **cwTN,** [ˈpaˀrɪdʒɪz].

B Senses. Cf **quail**

1 =**bob-white.** **chiefly Sth, S Midl**

[**1587** (1964) Laudonnière *Notable Hist.* (transl. Hakluyt) 6ʳ, As we passed throw these woods we saw . . Partridges gray and redde, little different from ours, but chiefly in bignesse.] **1612** Smith *Map VA* 1.15, Patridges there are little bigger then our Quailes, wilde Turkies are as bigge as our tame. **1676** Royal Soc. London *Philos. Trans.* 11.631, The Fowls that keep the Woods are, wild *Turkies, Turkie Buzzards, Turtle-Doves, Partridges, Hawks* of several sorts. **1743** Catesby *Nat. Hist. Carolina* 2 app 12, The American Partridge.—This is about half the size of the *Perdix Cinerea,* or common Partridge, which it somewhat resembles in colour, though differently marked; particularly the head has three black lines, one above and two below the eyes, with two intermediate yellowish white lines. **1792** Belknap *Hist. NH* 3.171, Partridge,— *Tetrao marilandicus.* . . In the southern and middle States, the quail is called a partridge, and the partridge a pheasant. **1812** Wilson *Amer. Ornith.* 6.25, The food of the Partridge consists of grain, seeds, insects, and berries. *Ibid* 26, The *Quail,* as it is called in New England, or the *Partridge,* as in Pennsylvania, is nine inches long. **1872** Coues *Key to N. Amer. Birds* 236, *Virginia Partridge,* or *Quail. Bob-white. Quail;* New England and Middle States, wherever the ruffed grouse is called "partridge." *Partridge;* Southern States, wherever the ruffed grouse is called "pheasant." **1907** *DN* 3.234 **nwAR,** Partridge. . . Quail. **1913** *Auk* 30.494 Okefenokee **GA,** *Colinus virginianus virginianus.* Bob-white; 'Partridge.' **1938** Matschat *Suwannee R.* 208 **neFL, seGA,** Quail, commonly called partridges throughout the South, are very shy and timid. **1950** *WELS (Names and nicknames for other kinds of game birds in your section)* 8 Infs, **WI,** Partridge; *(Other names for . . quail)* 1 Inf, **cWI,** Partridge. [*DARE* Ed: Some of these Infs may refer instead to other senses below.] **1955** MA Audubon Soc. *Bulletin* 39.443 **NH,** Bob-white. . . Brown Partridge. . . The general tone of the plumage of both sexes is reddish brown. **1958** Babcock *I Don't Want* 175 **eSC,** But you'd better say "pottidges" rather than "quail" [in speaking to "plantation Negroes"]. **1965–70** *DARE* (Qu. Q7, *Names and nicknames for . . game birds*) 175 Infs, **chiefly Sth, S Midl,** Partridge; **NY71,** Partridge— weigh about a pound—half as big as a grouse. [*DARE* Ed: Some of these Infs may refer instead to other senses below.] **1982** Elman *Hunter's Field Guide* 84, *Colinus virginianus . . Common & regional names . .* Virginia partridge.

2 =**ruffed grouse.** **chiefly NEast, Gt Lakes** Cf **pat** n³

1630 Higginson *Nevv Englands Plantation* sig C2ʳ, And my selfe . . sprung a Partridge so bigge that through the heauinesse of his Body could fly but a little way. **1670** (1937) Denton *Brief Descr.* 5 **Long Is. NY,** Wild fowl there is great store of, as Turkies, Heath-Hens, Quailes, Partridges, Pidgeons, . . and divers others. **1844** Giraud *Birds Long Is.* 192 **NY,** This species of Grouse is well known in the State of New York by the name of Partridge; in the Western States it has received the appellation of Pheasant. **1874** Coues *Birds NW* 421, It would simplify matters much to discard altogether the terms "Pheasant" and "Partridge," by which this species is known in, respectively, the Northern and Southern States, and call it by its proper name of "Ruffed Grouse." **1890** Warren *Birds PA* 107, The Ruffed Grouse is known generally throughout Pennsylvania as the Pheasant, but in some parts of the northeastern counties it is usually called "Partridge," a name by which the quail is commonly designated in most parts of this state. **1917** Eaton *Green Trails* 102 **MA,** When the blue cedar berries are ripe . . , ruffed grouse (partridge) find them a ready food. **1950** *WELS* **WI** *(Names and nicknames for other kinds of game birds in your section)* 16 Infs, Partridge; 1 Inf, Ruffed grouse (also called partridge); 1 Inf, Ruffed grouse—partridge; 1 Inf, Partridge—larger than prairie chicken, longer neck with ruff; 1 Inf, Partridge—grouse [FW: Inf thinks they're same bird.]; 1 Inf, Partridge—like a small hen; *(Other names . .)* 1 Inf, **ceWI,** Partridge— most people call them patridge, also wood hen. [*DARE* Ed: Some of these Infs may refer to other senses.] **1955** MA Audubon Soc. *Bulletin* 39.443 **NEng,** Partidge (Sometimes Patridge or Pat). **1965–70** *DARE* (Qu. Q7, *Names and nicknames for . . game birds*) 183 Infs, **chiefly NEast, Gt Lakes,** Partridge. [*DARE* Ed: Some of these Infs may refer instead to other senses.] **1966** *DARE* Tape **MI**2, We have the partridge or ruff grouse, the real name of them. **1996** *Capital Times* (Madison WI) 29 Nov sec B, Although it [=the spruce grouse] resembles a ruffed grouse, which many old timers simply refer to as a partridge, it is larger.

3 Any of var game birds native to the western US such as the **California quail 1** or **harlequin ~,** or the introduced **Hungarian partridge 1** or the chukar *(Alectoris chukar).* Cf **Gambel's quail, mountain partridge 2**

1851 *Acad. Nat. Sci. Philadelphia Proc. for 1851* 221 **TX,** Gambel's Quail, or Partridge, . . is much disposed to seek the farms, if any be within reach, and to cultivate the acquaintance of man. **1898** (1900) Davie *Nests N. Amer. Birds* 166, The shape of the eggs is characteristic of all eggs of the Partridge [=*Callipepla squamata*]. *Ibid* 168, Mr. Otho C. Poling found this Partridge [=*Cyrtonyx montezumae*] to be fairly common in parts of . . Southern Arizona. **1904** Wheelock *Birds CA* 120, So closely allied are the California partridge and the Valley Partridge that only by direct comparison of the two species may the lighter coloring of the latter be distinguished. **1929** in 1936 Roberts *MN Birds* 1.405, The Partridges have done well since released in late March, 1926. **1950** *WELS* **WI** *(Names and nicknames for other kinds of game birds in your section)* 4 Infs, Partridges; 1 Inf, Huns (partridges). **1953** Jewett *Birds WA* 220, A covey of partridges [=*Perdix perdix*] "gets up in a bunch and goes in a hurry." *Ibid* 228, These partridges [=*Alectoris chukar*] are doing well in extremely dry areas. **1966–69** *DARE* (Qu. Q7, *Names and nicknames for . . game birds)* Infs **CA**105, 155, **ID**4, **OR**1, 14, **SD**2, **WA**24, Partridge; **HI**14, Partridge—chukar; **MN**38, Partridge—chukars and Huns; **ND**1, Partridge—Hungarian; **OH**23, Hunkies or pats—those are partridges; **SD**8, Partridge (Hungarian). **1969** *DARE* Tape **CA**170, [Inf:] Oh, they're gonna have some kind of partridge. . . [FW:] Pheasant? [Inf:] Pheasant? No. Something in the chicken family.

4 Either the white-tailed **ptarmigan** *(Lagopus leucurus)* or the **willow ptarmigan.** Cf **snow partridge, white ~, willow ~**

1967 *DARE* (Qu. Q7, *Names and nicknames for . . game birds)* Inf **CO**7, Ptarmigan—a partridge. **1982** Elman *Hunter's Field Guide* 79, *Common & Regional names:* For willow ptarmigan—*snow grouse, . . Alaska partridge.*

partridgeberry n [Because the fruits are eaten by birds in winter]

1 also *partridge plum:* A creeping evergreen plant of the genus *Mitchella,* esp *M. repens,* or its fruit. For other names of *M. repens* see **boxberry 2, checkerberry 3, chickberry, chickenberry 2, cowberry 2, creep chequerberry, deerberry c, foxberry 3, groundberry 2, heath-hen plum, hive vine 1, moonshine** n **4, one-berry 1, partridge vine, pheasant berry, pigeonberry 4, pigeon plum 2, running box, snakeberry, squawberry, squaw plum, ~ vine, teaberry, turkeyberry, twinberry, two-eyed berry, winter clover**

1717 Royal Soc. London *Philos. Trans. for 1714, 1715, 1716* 29.63 **MA,** Another Plant, . . Partridge-berries, excellent in curing the *Dropsy.* **1784** in 1785 Amer. Acad. Arts & Sci. *Memoirs* 1.410, *Mitchella. . . Partridgeberry.* The stems trailing. . . Blossoms white. In thick woods and swamps. **1811** Wilson *Amer. Ornith.* 3.109, A favourite article of their [=pinnated grouses'] diet, is the *heath-hen plum,* or partridgeberry. **1875** (1876) Stowe *Betty's Bright Idea* 121 **NEng,** Little Love gathered stores of bright checker-berries and partridge plums. **1949** Moldenke *Amer. Wild Flowers* 172, Our *American partridgeberry* is a creeping herb. . . The red (rarely white) fruits are double. . . Being edible and persistent through the winter, they are great favorites of partridges, foxes, deer, and other animals that can get at them during the winter months. **1966–70** *DARE* (Qu. I44, *What kinds of berries grow wild around here?)* Infs **NY**52, 97, Partridgeberries; (Qu. S26b, *Wildflowers that grow in water or wet places)* Inf **MA**6, Partridgeberries; (Qu. S26c, *Wildflowers that grow in woods)* Infs **RI**15, **VA**52, Partridgeberry. [*DARE* Ed: Some of these Infs may refer instead to other senses below.] **1966–67** *DARE* Wildfl QR Pl.211B Infs **NC**36, **OH**14, 37, **MI**7, 57, **SC**41, **WI**80, Partridgeberry. **1979** *DARE* File **cnMA** (as of c1915), People used to pick "patridge berries" when I was a child and make "patridge-berry" bowls.

2 A plant of the genus *Vaccinium,* usu **mountain cranberry 1** (here: *Vaccinium vitis-idaea*).

[**1748** Ellis *Voyage* 169 **Canada,** Shrubs bearing red and black Berries,

which the Partridges feed on, therefore called Partridge Berries.] [**1790** in 1792 Cartwright *Jrl. Labrador* 2.168, After breakfast I sent the Indian women to Signal Hill to pick partridge-berries and watch for deer.] **1943** Fernald–Kinsey *Edible Wild Plants E. N. Amer.* 317, Export of the Partridge-berries from Newfoundland alone to Minneapolis and the neighboring markets has sometimes reached the annual total of more than 8600 barrels. **1955** U.S. Arctic Info. Center *Gloss.* 53, Mountain cranberry. . . Also called . . 'partridge berry' [etc]. **1972** Viereck–Little *AK Trees* 233, *Mountain-cranberry . .* Other names: lingenberry [sic], . . partridgeberry [etc].

3 also *partridge bush, ~ plant:* A **wintergreen 2** (here: *Gaultheria procumbens*).

1814 Bigelow *Florula Bostoniensis* 101, *Gaultheria procumbens. . . Partridge berry. . .* A plant universally known for its pleasant, aromatic flavour. **1843** *Amer. Pioneer* 2.125 **PA, NY,** The vivid green leaves and bright scarlet berries of the "Partridge bush," or "Checkerberry." **1848** Gray *Manual of Botany* 264, Creeping Wintergreen. . . In the interior of the country it is everywhere called *Wintergreen,* or sometimes *Tea-berry.* Eastward it is called *Checquer-berry* or *Partridge-berry* (names also applied to Mitchella, the latter especially so). **1894** *Jrl. Amer. Folkl.* 7.93, *Gaultheria procumbens . .* partridge-berry, N.H.[,] partridge-plant, N.Y. **1931** Bell *Cape Cod Color* 101 **seMA,** The wintergreen berry grows under many an alias; checker-berry, box-berry, tea-berry, spice-berry, ground-holly, and partridge-berry. **1969** *DARE* (Qu. T5, . . *Kinds of evergreens, other than pine)* Inf **NY**165, Partridgeberry—like wintergreen. **1974** (1977) Coon *Useful Plants* 135, Teaberry, boxberry, partridgeberry, wintergreen [etc].

4 A **snowberry** (here: *Symphoricarpos* spp).

1924 *Amer. Botanist* 32 **West,** *Symphoricarpos occidentalis* is known variously, and often incorrectly, of course, as . . "June-berry" and "partridge-berry." **1939** Tharp *Vegetation TX* 70, Partridge berry *(Symphoricarpus).*

partridgeberry vine See **partridge vine**

partridge bush See **partridgeberry 3**

partridge duck n
=**green-winged teal.**

1923 U.S. Dept. Ag. *Misc. Circular* 13.13 **MD,** *Green-winged Teal. . .* partridge-duck. **1982** Elman *Hunter's Field Guide* 178, When flushed, a greenwing explodes into the air—hence the name partridge duck or water-partridge.

partridge foot n [See quot 1954]
A mat-forming plant *(Luetkea pectinata)* native to the Pacific Northwest.

1934 Haskin *Wild Flowers Pacific Coast* 169, *Partridge Foot. . .* This little spiraea-like plant forms dense mats close to the ground in high mountain meadows. **1954** Sharpe *101 Wildflowers* 17 **nwWA,** The name "partridge foot" appears to have been derived from the shape of the leaves. **1973** Hitchcock–Cronquist *Flora Pacific NW* 214, Partridgefoot. . . Moist or shaded areas, mostly where snow lies late in spring.

partridge hawk n [See quot 1893] Cf **grouse hawk**
Usu the **goshawk 1,** but also the **sharp-shinned hawk.**

[**1781** Latham *Genl. Synopsis Birds* 1.1.78, This bird . . was sent from *Severn River, Hudson's Bay,* where it is called *Speckled Partridge Hawk.*] **1890** Warren *Birds PA* 120, *Accipiter velox. . .* Sharp-shinned Hawk; Partridge Hawk. **1893** Fisher *Hawks & Owls U.S.* 45, In some parts of the country the Goshawk hunts the ruffed grouse so persistently that it is known by the name of 'Partridge Hawk.' **1895** U.S. Dept. Ag. *Yearbook for 1894* 231, From the persistency with which this species [=*Accipiter gentilis*] hunts the ruffed grouse in many of the Northern States, it has received the name "partridge hawk." **1895** Minot *Land-Birds New Engl.* 374, American Goshawk. "Partridge Hawk." **1927** Forbush *Birds MA* 2.116, Goshawk. *Other names:* Blue hawk; partridge hawk. **1955** MA Audubon Soc. *Bulletin* 39.441, Goshawk. . . Partridge Hawk (Mass., Conn. As preying upon Ruffed Grouse, or Partridge.)

partridge pea n
A plant of the genus *Chamaecrista,* esp *C. fasciculata.* Also called **bee-blossom 3, honeycup 1, sensitive pea;** for other names of var spp see **gold coins, negro coffee, pepperbox, prairie senna, rattlebox 1f, sensitive plant 2, sleeping plant**

1787 *Amer. Museum* 2.451 **VA,** The eastern shore bean. . . has been mistaken, by some, for the common tare or partridge-pea. **1837** Darlington *Flora Cestrica* 433 se**PA**, *C[assia] Chamaecrista. . . Vulgò—* Sensitive Pea. Partridge Pea. Magothy-bay Bean. **1912** Blatchley *IN Weed Book* 89, The partridge pea (*C. chamaecrista* L.) is another senna. **1933** Small *Manual SE Flora* 662, *Chamaecrista. . .* Honey-cups. Bee-blossoms. Partridge-peas. **1953** Greene–Blomquist *Flowers South* 54, The partridge-pea or golden-cassia *(C. fasciculata)* is the most frequent and widely distributed species in e. U.S. and is especially abundant in some of the open, sandy areas in the outer Coastal Plain. **1961** Wills–Irwin *Flowers TX* 130, Partridge-peas in general often colonize poor soils and should be encouraged in fallow fields. **1966** *DARE* Tape **NC24**, We have a wild—what we call partridge pea ['pɑtɚɪ̆ ˌpi]. **1966–67** *DARE* Wildfl QR (Wills–Irwin) Pl.16C Inf **TX44**, Partridge pea; Pl.105A Inf **NC28**, ['pɔtɚɪ̆ pi]; Pl.105B Infs **NC28**, **OH14**, Partridge pea; **SC41**, Partridge pea, [corr to] porridge pea. **1970** *DARE* (Qu. S26a, *. . Wildflowers. . . Roadside flowers)* Inf **VA77**, Partridge pea; (Qu. S26d, *Wildflowers that grow in meadows;* not asked in early QRs) Inf **KY89**, ['pædɚj̆] pea.

partridge plant See **partridgeberry 3**

partridge plum See **partridgeberry 1**

partridge vine n Also *partridgeberry vine*
A **partridgeberry 1** (here: *Mitchella repens*).
1860 *Ladies' Repository* 20.137, Setting my feet on the mosses / And the tangled partridge-vine. **1876** Hobbs *Bot. Hdbk.* 87, Partridge berry vine . . *Mitchella repens.* **1880** *Harper's New Mth. Mag.* 61.864 **NEast**, Here are soft beds of rich green moss studded with scarlet berries of wintergreen and partridge vine. **1901** Lounsberry *S. Wild Flowers* 476, Partridge vine. Checker-berry. Squaw-vine. *Mitchella repens. . .* Well into the winter the berries last. **1911** Henkel *Amer. Med. Leaves* 34, *Mitchella repens. . .* boxberry, foxberry, partridge vine. **1940** *Sun* (Baltimore MD) 9 Dec 8/4 *(OED2),* In Christmas seasons when holly berries are comparatively scarce, the berries of the smoke bush come as a substitute, and often of the dogwood and of the partridge vines in the woodlands. **1962** Dykeman *Tall Woman* 293 **NC**, And yet here she was, . . with the first rays of the sun burning away the moist fog, revealing familiar trails bordered by thick clumps of shining green galax leaves, tall Solomon's-seal, running partridge vines.

partridge woodpecker n esp **NEast**
=**flicker** n[2] **1.**
1896 Robinson *In New Engl. Fields* 59, Thoreau often termed him [= *Colaptes auratus*] partridge-woodpecker. **1920** Packard *Old Plymouth* 193 se**MA**, Partridge woodpeckers flocked in, drolly jollying each other and making much talk, sotto voce. . . More than one cried, "flicker, flicker, flicker." **1955** *AmSp* 30.180, *Partridge woodpecker* (yellow-shafted flicker, Maine, Vt., Mass., N.Y., Wis.) [seems to refer to] speckled plumage, with perhaps some harking back to the use of this species as game.

part that went over the fence last n For varr, see quots Cf **north end of a chicken flying south**
=**pope's nose 1.**
1871 *Scribner's Mth.* 3.160, Miss Marigold got up courage to say that she *had* rather a weakness for the part that went over the fence last, although she always had some scruples about mentioning it. **1911** Shute *Plupy* 298, se**NH**, Jest think of the stuffin' and gravy. . . And the drumsticks. . . And the gizzard and the part that goes over the fence last. **1942** McAtee *Dial. Grant Co. IN* 48 (as of 1890s), *Part that goes over the fence last. . .* Pope's nose, or uropygium of a fowl; usually heard at table. **1954** *Harder Coll.* cw**TN**, The rump of a cooked chicken. . . "Heerd [sic] called *last part through the fence."* **1956** McAtee *Some Dialect NC* 32, *Part that goes over the fence last. . .* euphemism for rump of a fowl. c**1960** *Wilson Coll.* cs**KY**, *Part of the chicken that goes over the fence last. . .* A humorous reference to the piece of chicken that includes the tail. **1965–70** *DARE* (Qu. K73, *. . Names . . for the rump of a cooked chicken)* 321 Infs, **widespread**, Part that went over the fence last [and varr]; 46 Infs, Piece that went over the fence last [and varr]; 44 Infs, Last piece (*or* part) over the fence [and varr]; 7 Infs, End that went over the fence last; 4 Infs, Last thing that went over the fence [and varr]; 3 Infs, Last end (that gets) over the fence; 1 Inf, Jump over the fence; 1 Inf, Last over the fence; 1 Inf, Last that went over the fence; 1 Inf, One dat cross de fence last; 1 Inf, One that went over the fence last; 1 Inf, Over the fence last; 1 Inf, Thing that goes over the fence last; 1 Inf, What went over the fence last.

pa sack See **pappy sack**

pascha n Also sp *paska* [Appar transf from Russ *paskha* Easter; a mixture of sweetened cheese curd, butter, and fruit traditionally eaten at Easter; see quot 1972] Cf **paczki**
A kind of sweet bread associated with Easter.
1957 Showalter *Mennonite Cookbook* 9 **MN**, *Russian Easter Bread—Paska. . .* 2 cups flour . . cream . . sugar . . 10 eggs . . butter . . lemon extract . . yeast cakes. *Ibid* 10, *Cheese Spread for Paska. . .* Press [cottage] cheese and egg yolks through a sieve. Bring cream to a boil and then cool. Cream together the butter and sugar and add the other ingredients. Mix thoroughly. This is now ready to use as a spread when serving Paska. **1968** *DARE* (Qu. H18, *. . Special kinds of bread)* Inf **PA110**, Holy bread, Pascha—Easter bread, plait bread in ring for crown of thorns—birds in the thorns; a non-raised bread; it's a secret recipe. [**1972** *Complete World Cookery* 225, Pascha, a traditional Easter dish [in Russia], is usually eaten with slices of rich yeast cake called koolich.]

pasear n [Span *pasear* to take a walk] **SW**
An excursion, tour.
[**1840** (1841) Dana *2 Yrs.* 313, We found him at the landing-place . . saying he was going to pasear with our captain a little.] **1868** *Overland Mth.* 1.26, The mode of life [in Mexico City] differs little, if at all, from that of most large Spanish-American cities: the early rising to enjoy the fresh balcony air; the morning coffee, ride, bath and pasear; [etc.] **1887** Harte *Crusade Excelsior* 158 **SW**, I don't know but I'd take a little *pasear* into the town if I had my horse ready. **1907** White *AZ Nights* 144, It will be appreciated when the crowd comes back from that little *pasear* into Buck Cañon. *Ibid* 330, "What's up, Buck?" he inquired. "Just going out for a pasear with the little horse, Jed." **1929** Dobie *Vaquero* 129 **West**, Now . . I made . . a considerable *pasear* into the Devil's River country to the south and west. A part of the time on this *pasear* I had with me a Seminole Indian. **1946** Mora *Trail Dust* 209 **West**, The few coastal roads were miserable, and the stages operating over them were no inducement for the invalid who sought a restful pasear. **1958** *Julian Apple Day* [7] cs**CA**, Many years ago a prospector arrived at Yaqui Well late one gloomy afternoon after a pasear into the Santa Rosa area. **1969** O'Connor *Horse & Buggy West* 62 **AZ**, Americans took a *welta* instead of a turn and a *pasear* instead of a walk.

pa'sel See **passel 2**

paska See **pascha**

pasley See **parsley**

pasnep, pasnet, pasnip, pasnup See **parsnip**

pasqueflower n Cf **honey-in-the-dale**
Std: a plant of the genus *Pulsatilla,* esp *P. patens* (formerly *Anemone patens*). For other names of this sp see **April fools, badger 5, blue angel, ~ tulip, crocus** n[1] **2a, crow** n[3]**, crowfoot 1b, Easter flower 1, gosling 2, grandfather's whiskers, hartshorn plant, headache ~, lion's beard 1, mayflower 3b, prairie smoke 2, rock lily 2, stone ~, wild crocus, windflower;** for other names of *P. occidentalis* see **old-man-of-the-mountain 2.** For other names of the fruit or seed head see **lion's beard 1, old-man-of-the-mountain 2, little dish mops**

pass v
1 also with var advs (see below): To die; hence vbl n *passing.* *euphem* Cf **cross 5** Note: The comb *pass away* is widespread and std and is not illustrated here.
a without adv. Note: The vbl n *passing* "death" is std and is not illustrated here. [*OED2* 1340 →; "Now *arch.* or *dial.*"] **chiefly Sth, S Midl** *esp freq among Black speakers*
1959 Lomax *Rainbow Sign* 160 **LA** [Black], My first wife didn't live more than a year and six months. Then she passed. **1965–70** *DARE* (Qu. BB42, *If a person is very sick . . he's _____*) Inf **VA69**, About to pass; (Qu. BB54, *When a sick person is past hope of recovery . . he's [a] _____*) Inf **TX86**, Passing; (Qu. BB55, *. . To say that a person died. . . Serious expressions;* total Infs questioned, 75) Inf **MS60**, Passed; (Qu. BB56, *Joking expressions for dying: "He _____."*) Infs **LA18, MA6, NJ21, 67, OK55, SC27, TX3, VA41**, Passed. [6 of 11 Infs Black] **1966–69** *DARE* Tape **AL14**, And he just passed back here about . . four years ago, he just passed; **GA79**, My brother passed, my

sister passed, and now there's just the two of us left. [Both Infs Black] **1967** *Mebane Enterprise & Hillsborough Jrl.* (NC) 13 Apr sec B 8/1, [Headline:] Davis passes at age of 80. **1967** *Raymond Herald & Advt.* (WA) 9 Mar 7/1, [Headline:] William Merchant Passes Suddenly. **1967** *DARE* FW Addit AR55, Passed—died. Used by Blacks. **1969** Emmons *Deep Rivers* 42 eTX [Black], And the night he passed, I was with him by myself. . . I just called the doctor, and then the next day I called the minister, and I went to the funeral home. **c1970** *DARE* File csWI (as of 1930s), Leonard has passed. **1971** Roberts *Third Ear* np [Black], Passed . . died; expired. **1984** Burns *Cold Sassy* 304 nGA (as of 1906), She said, 'If'n I pass, I hope. . . Well, find you another wife and I'll take it as a compli-ment.' **1991** Pederson *LAGS Social Matrix* 200 **Gulf Region**, [Of the 116 infs who said *pass(ed)*, 86 (or 74%) were Black, as against 22% in the total sample of 914 primary infs.] [*DARE* Ed: Cf quot 1991 at **1b** below.] **1994** *DARE* File **PA**, My grandmother, who "passed" last month, used the verb in that way. She grew up in Pennsylvania and taught English in New York. *Ibid* LA, I have used all [= *passed, passed away, passed on*]. *Ibid* cwCA (as of 1965–70), When I was a teenager . . I . . first heard the word "passed" for "died"—without the word "on" or "away"—from African Americans I worked with, ages ranging from 15 to 60. **1997** Frazier *Cold Mountain* 147 **NC** (as of c1866), They guessed he haid died. Birch offered to go spit juice in his eye to see would he blink, but Teague said, We don't need to test him. He's passed.

b with *on.*   [*OED2* 1804–20 →]

1860 *Ladies' Repository* 20.277, Do they wait us there with changeless lore,/ The dear ones who passed on before? **1884** Barber *Diary* np **MA**, Atwood passed on this morn. aged 74 years. **1884** *150th Anniv. Settlement of Boscawen & Webster, New Hampsh.* 44 *(OED2)*, They have all passed on to become soldiers of the unseen army. **1923** *Amer. Mag.* June 15, The murderer took poison and so the two passed on. **1925** *AmSp* 1.155 **West**, There is an attitude toward death which is reflected in the expressions "passed away" and "passed on." **1926** *AmSp* 1.350, My observation is that of one who was born in New York State sixty-odd years ago, and who has lived nearly all his life in that state and the District of Columbia. I give some of the terms erroneously listed as peculiarly Western, with my comments. . . "[P]assed away" and "passed on" for "died;" *passed away* was the usual polite expression of my childhood, and *passed on* has in a considerable degree superseded it among my Eastern acquaintance. **1936** *AmSp* 11.197 [Euphemisms for dying], Passed on/away/out/over. **1965–70** *DARE* (Qu. BB56, *Joking expressions for dying: "He _____."*) 57 Infs, **scattered**, Passed on; **AL20**, Pass on; **PA35**, Passed on to glory [Of all Infs responding to the question, 93% were White; of those giving these resps, 100% were White.]; (Qu. BB55, *. . To say that a person died. . Serious expressions;* total Infs questioned, 75) 17 Infs, Passed on; (Qu. BB54, *When a sick person is past hope of recovery . . he's [a] _____*) Inf **OH2**, Going to pass on. **1967–69** *DARE* Tape CA172A, He had passed on before any of these big companies came in here; MI66, And in my life I have seen several of those mammoth old big oaks become targets of wind and storm and they have passed on too; WI72, His father had had the business before him. And then, when my father passed on, it was handin [sic] down to my brother. **1991** Pederson *LAGS Social Matrix* 200 **Gulf Region**, [Of the 108 infs who said *passed on*, 93 (or 86%) were White, as against 78% in the total sample of 914 primary infs.]

c with *out.*   [*OED2* 1899 →]   *somewhat old-fash*

c1867 in 1986 *DARE* File seMI, [Inscription on a tombstone in a Flushing MI cemetery:] Caroline / wife of E.J. Langston / born on / March 23, 1833 / Passed out / Dec. 18, 1867. **1911** (1916) Porter *Harvester* 394 **IN**, The Harvester made passing out so natural, so easy, so a part of elemental forces, that I almost have forgotten her tortured body. **1924** Marks *Plastic Age* 12, He left us a whale of a lot of jack when he passed out. **1925** *AmSp* 1.24, The slang terms associated with medical functions are innumerable and represent ignorance, a form of prudery, or attempts to evade the unpleasant. A conspicuous example is the number of slang terms and phrases used to describe death. Among these I list readily from memory: "Give up the ghost"; "pass out"; "kick the bucket"; "croak." **1936** [see **1b** above]. **1939** *Hall Coll.* wNC, I stayed with him [=Horace Kephart] until he passed out. **1954** *Harder Coll.* cwTN, Pass out. . . To die. **1965–70** *DARE* (Qu. BB56, *Joking expressions for dying: "He _____."*) 59 Infs, **scattered**, Passed out; **MO7**, Pass out; MO3, Passed out on me; NC41, NY220, VA11, Passing out [55 of 64 Infs old, none young]; [NV2, Passed out of the picture;] (Qu. BB55, *. . To say that a person died. . Serious expressions;* total Infs questioned, 75) Infs **DC3**, **FL30**, **MS63**, Passed out; DC3, Pass out; (Qu. BB54, *When a sick person is past hope of recovery . . he's [a] _____*) Inf **MA24**, About to pass out; (Qu. GG31, *To laugh very*

hard: *"I thought I'd _____."*) Infs **MS71**, **SC45**, **TN12**, Die, pass out; IL64, Die laughing, pass out laughing. **1966** *PADS* 46.28 **cnAR** (as of 1952), *Pass out. . . Die.*—"When he passed out, he was buried with his dogs." **1969** *DARE* FW Addit MA30, Passed out = died; MA48, *Pass out*—to die. A serious, not a joking, expression. **1969** *DARE* Tape CT20, When my father was passing out, he felt so sorry he didn't have money to leave us. **1991** Pederson *LAGS Social Matrix* 200 **Gulf Region**, [Of the 24 infs who used *passed out*, 20 were more than 65 years old; none was under 45.]

d with *over.*   [*OED2* 1909 →]

1911 (1916) Porter *Harvester* 344 **IN**, Said he loved red roses livin', so he was goin' to have them when he passed over. **1936** [see **1b** above]. **1967–68** *DARE* (Qu. BB56, *Joking expressions for dying: "He _____."*) Infs **MI96**, **OH41**, **TX33**, Passed over; [VA5, Passed over the river]. **1986** Pederson *LAGS Concordance (To die)* 1 inf, **ceTX**, Passed over—has heard; doesn't usually use; 1 inf, **ceTX**, He passed over; [1 inf, **csAL**, He passed over the hill—joking].

e with *off.*

1969 *DARE* (Qu. BB56, *Joking expressions for dying: "He _____."*) Inf MI108, Passed off. **1986** Pederson *LAGS Concordance (To die)* 1 inf, **cGA**, Passed off.

2 freq with *by:* To come or go to a place; to visit or stop by (a place). [In LA, infl by Cajun Fr; see quot 1992] **chiefly Sth, S Midl, esp LA**   Cf **by prep 1**

1941 O'Donnell *Great Big Doorstep* 6 sLA, Oh, Tope, let's pass and ask Father Pennygrass to bless her [=a statue]! *Ibid* 23, 'Well, send Evvie for two cigarettes. Here's two coppers.' 'Evvie's restin. Pass on your way.' 'I wunna smoke now. Can't she run to Zhule's?' 'Pass the store on your way.' **1942** *AmSp* 17.172 **sIL**, Several verbs in daily use in this community are of interest: . . *to stop by for* or *to pass for* (for 'to call for'). **1951** *PADS* 15.70 nLA, Pass by for. . . To call for someone. "Just pass by for me and I'll be ready to go." **1954** *Harder Coll.* cwTN, Pass by for. . . To call for someone. **1967–69** *DARE* (Qu. II14, *To pay a short visit: "Last night our new neighbors _____."*) Infs AL33, MI75, Passed by; GA77, Passed by and said howdy. **1968** *DARE* FW Addit LA33, Pass = go. "She said you can pass out there tomorrow sometime." **1972** *Thompson Coll.* **New Orleans LA**, *Pass* = to come to a place. . . [A] man asked a woman who had come for the ironing 'How come you passin so soon this moynin?' . . The milkman passes on Tuesdays and Fridays. **1992** Scott *Cajun Vernacular Engl.* 41 sLA, When a speaker says "I'm going to pass by your house," he means that he will stop and enter that house, usually to visit. This usage is a literal translation from the Cajun French verb *passer,* which can mean "to go to," as in *passer pa ta maison.*

3 in var senses infl by Fr idiom: See quots. [Calque of Fr *passer*]   **chiefly sLA**   Cf **make v¹ C18, pass n 3**

1968 *DARE* FW Addit LA28, The French people say pass him to the church; we say bring him to the church. Said of a man who had died and was being taken to his funeral. *Ibid* LA32, We passed a good time—used frequently in place of "had a good time." *Ibid* LA33, To pass = to wipe, to rub. "And then we passed furniture polish on the shelves." **1984** *Yeah You Rite* (Video recording) **New Orleans LA**, We forget that some of the words we use every day might not make sense to somebody from out of town: Words like . . *I pass the mop and pass the vacuum.* **1992** Scott *Cajun Vernacular Engl.* 41 sLA, *Before you go, you need to pass the broom. (Before you go, you need to sweep.)* In another sense, C[ajun] V[ernacular] E[nglish] uses *pass* to mean "to spend [time]," (in Cajun French, *passer du temps*), as in "to pass a good time". Mais, *let's get a six-pack, and we'll pass a good time, yeah? Eh! You passed a good time last night at the fais-do-do?* Yet another CVE idiom involving *pass* is "to pass someone a slap," from *passer une tape,* meaning "to slap." In CVE, this can also be used synonymously with "spank." *You stop that right now, or I'm gonna pass you a slap. You got my permission to pass him a slap if he don't behave in class.*

4 To deliver (newspapers).

1943 in 1944 *ADD* wWV, When I was in Junior High School I passed papers. **1998** *DARE* File cOH (as of c1950), A gentleman in his late 50s, early 60s was telling about his childhood in this region of Ohio, a little southwest of Columbus. . . He was referring to the newspaper route he had as a teen. . . He said he *passed papers.* **2001** *NADS Letters,* "Pass papers" was a common expression in my boyhood in southern Indiana in the 1940's–50's. It was also common in Kentucky, Illinois, and maybe Ohio. *Ibid,* My husband, age 52, born & raised in New Castle, Indiana. . . says when he was in junior high, he was a paperboy and "passed papers."

pass n

1 with *the:* =**passing** n **1.**

1916 Macy–Hussey *Nantucket Scrap Basket* 141, *"Pass, the"*—People on the street. All Nantucketers enjoy "watching the pass." **1986** *DARE* File (as of 1907–20), On Nantucket Island, "pass" refers to pedestrian traffic. Old houses in Nantucket Town are sited right next to the side-walks. It was common for residents to sit at their windows in summer and observe . . this pedestrian traffic. This was called "watching the pass."

2 also *passing:* A place in a road where animals cross regu-larly. **scattered, but chiefly Inland Nth, N Midl, esp Up-state NY** See Map

1965–70 *DARE* (Qu. N31, *A place in a road where animals regularly go across*) 34 Infs, **scattered**, Cattle pass; 19 Infs, **chiefly NEast,** Cow pass; **CA**75, **IA**41, **LA**40, **NY**23, 100, **OH**29, 50, **VA**13, Pass; **CA**63, **IL**48, **ME**19, **NY**117, 226, **OH**58, Animal pass; **NM**5, **NY**75, 123, 214, **WI**18, Deer pass; **MS**60, Pig passes; **MN**12, Cattle passing; **PA**247, Horse passing; **NY**210, Pig passing. **1970** *DARE* File, *Cattle pass:* Vermont has numerous road signs with this wording, and few with *cattle crossing;* Massachusetts has only one *cattle pass* sign that I have seen and a thousand *cattle crossing.*

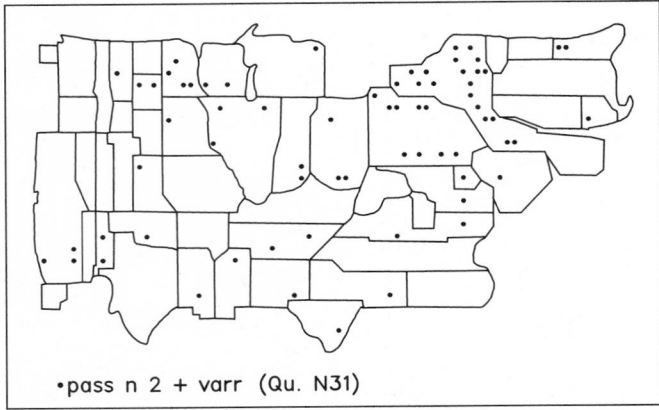

•pass n 2 + varr (Qu. N31)

3 in phr *make a pass* (or *passé*): See quots. [Cf **pass** v **3**] **LA**

1967 LeCompte *Word Atlas* 281 **seLA,** *To pass by one's house.* . . to make a pass [3 of 21 infs]. **1968** *DARE* FW Addit **LA**33, "I want to make a little pass upstairs." She meant to walk through and expect [sic for *inspect*] the upstairs rooms. **1983** *Reinecke Coll.* 8 **LA,** *Passé* ['pɑse]. . . in phrase "make a passé" a short trip to a given place and back or to second destination, or to run an errand, etc. "I'm uh make a passe [sic] by de liquor sto." Chiefly Cajun or humorous.

passage n Also *passageway* **Sth, S Midl, esp SC**

A hallway; a breezeway.

1835 in 1868 McCall *Letters Frontiers* 280 **AR,** The house . . was one of those structures called in the West *"two pens and a passage."* **1843** (1969) Lewis *Odd Leaves* 147 **LA,** The house consisted of a double log cabin, of small dimensions, a passage, the full depth of the house, run-ning between the "pens." **1886** *S. Bivouac* 4.343 **sAppalachians,** Pass-age (hall). **1899** (1912) Green *VA Folk-Speech* 312, *Passage.* . . An av-enue or alley leading to the various divisions or apartments in a building. *Hall* not generally used. **1910** Porter *Strictly Business* 219, There was a long hallway (or "passageway," as they call it in the land of the Colo-nels) with one side latticed, running along the rear of the house. **1966** Dakin *Dial. Vocab. Ohio R. Valley* 56, Several field records from Ken-tucky . . have entries which would seem to refer to the open hall be-tween two parts of a house. *Dog walk,* . . *passage, breezeway* each ap-pear one time. **1966–67** *DARE* (Qu. D11, *When you go into a house, the part just beyond the front door is the _____*) Inf **SC**19, Passage—same as hallway; **SC**22, Passageway antedates hall; runs front-to-back; **SC**29, Hall, passageway; **SC**43, Passageway; same as hallway; (Qu. D16, . . *Parts added on to the main part of a house*) Inf **SC**4, Used to have the kitchen as a separate building and a passageway connecting it to house; **SC**19, Breezeway connected kitchen and house; passage same as breezeway. **1976** Ryland *Richmond Co. VA* 374, *Passage*—hall. **1986** Pederson *LAGS Concordance,* 1 inf, **cwGA,** Passageway—to separate kitchen; 1 inf, **swAL,** Passageway; 1 inf, **seLA,** Passageway between buildings; 1 inf, **seLA,** Covered passageway.

pass and repass v phr **chiefly Sth, S Midl**

To meet casually and then part, after little or no conversation; to meet (someone) in such a way.

1937 *Hall Coll.* **wNC,** I pass and repass him without speakin'. **1950** *PADS* 14.51 **SC,** *Pass and repass.* . . "We pass and repass," i.e., we are on fairly friendly terms. **1966–68** *DARE* (Qu. II5a, *When you don't want to have anything to do with a certain person because you don't like him* . . *"I'd certainly like to get _____ of him."*) Inf **MS**56, Pass and repass; (Qu. II12, *Talking about meeting somebody on the street and speaking only a few words with him: "We just _____."*) Infs **FL**31, **IN**30, **NC**82, **SC**34, Passed and repassed; [**MO**15, Repassed]. **1984** Wilder *You All Spoken Here* 103 **Sth,** *Pass and repass:* Speak when they meet but not on good terms.

pass blummies n Also *paas blumes* [Du *Paas-* Easter- + *bloem* flower] Cf **Easter flower 3**

A **hepatica** (here: *Hepatica nobilis*).

1896 *Jrl. Amer. Folkl.* 9.180 **NY,** *Hepatica acutiloba* . . pass blummies, Alcove, N.Y. [Footnote:] Probably corrupted from *Pasque Blumen.* **1940** Clute *Amer. Plant Names* 3, *H[epatica] triloba* . . paas blumes.

pass by See **pass** v **2**

pass-down See **pass-me-down**

passé n

1 in phr *make a passé:* See **pass** n **3.**

2 =**keep-away.** [See quot 1983] **LA**

1981 Pederson *LAGS Basic Materials,* 1 inf, **seLA,** [ˌpˈɑˑˑsˈseˇɨ]; keep away; gets "rowdy"—one runs with ball until tackled—can pass it to an-other; if you are tackled, throw it up in the air. **1983** *Reinecke Coll.* 8 **LA,** *Passé* ['pɑse] . . a simple game of pitch and catch, often with an ob-ject, not a ball, owned or valued by the third person, from whom the other two try to withhold it. Sometimes among Creole Blacks, ['fase]. In playing, the pitchers alternately, are told "passé, passé" by the would-be receiver. "Let's play passé with little Charlie's new pencil-box." From Fr. "passez," plural imperative [of *passer*] to pass, convey.

passel n

1 See **parcel.**

2 also sp *pa'sel, passell, passle, passul:* A group, bunch, batch (of people, animals, or things); an indefinite, usu large, number or quantity. [Orig pronc-spp for *parcel,* but now usu felt as a separate word, to which one of the senses of *parcel* has be-come attached. The semantic split is not yet complete; see **parcel A** for exx of forms of the *passel* type associated with other senses of *parcel,* and **parcel B** for *parcel* in the sense il-lustrated here.] **formerly chiefly Sth, S Midl, now wide-spread** Cf **ornery**

1835 Longstreet *GA Scenes* 213, "How did you come on raisin' chick-ens this year, Mis' Shad?" . . "La messy, honey! I have had mighty bad luck. I had the prettiest pa'sel you most ever seed till the varment took to killin' 'em." **1859** Taliaferro *Fisher's R.* 126 **nwNC** (as of 1820s), I seen a passel ov men com trucklin' to me, rockin' along. **1884** *Anglia* 7.276 **Sth, S Midl** [Black], *Er passle er fokes* = a 'parcel' of people. **1890** *DN* 1.68 **KY,** *Passel* [pæsl]: for *parcel.* "She bought a whole pas-sel o' things," "There was a whole passel o' folks there." Becoming rare. **1893** Shands *MS Speech* 49, *Passle.* . . Used to some extent by all classes, but principally by the uneducated to mean a *parcel,* not in the sense of a small bundle or a small quantity, but in that of a considerable number. **1894** *Century Illustr. Mag.* 48.869 **swIN,** "Passell" I give as equivalent to parcel, but it has in the dialect the sense of a portion or quantity, as "he spilt a whole passell of eggs in the road." It is also ap-plied to people in contempt, as "a passell of nateral born fools," and es-pecially "a passell of thieves." **1902** *DN* 2.240 **sIL,** *Parcel.* . . Com-monly pronounced [pæsl] and applied only to a small assemblage of persons. **1906** Casey *Parson's Boys* 136 **sIL** (as of c1860), I . . didn't see another blessed thing but a passel of juggen hens. **1909** *DN* 3.356 **eAL, wGA,** *Passel.* . . Parcel, batch, lot, etc. **1912** *DN* 3.584 **wIN,** *Par-cel.* . . A batch; a lot; a crowd. In this sense often pronounced *passel,* but never in the sense of *package.* **1920** (1921) Sandburg *Smoke & Steel* 147 **nwIL,** Long ago I learned how to sleep,/. . . / In a passel of trees where the branches trapped the wind. **1923** *DN* 5.216 **swMO,** *Pas-sel.* . . Parcel. Also, a large number, as a 'passel o' people.' **1927** Ken-nedy *Gritny* 104 **sLA** [Black], My name bin walked on by a passul o' mean-minded Gritny niggers. **1933** Thurber *My Life* 2 **cOH,** On these occasions he was usually gone six or eight days and returned growling and out of temper, with the news that the federal Union was run by a passel of blockheads. **1940** Faulkner *Hamlet* 36 **MS,** Setting there bragging and lying to a passel of shiftless men. **1946** *PADS* 6.22 **eNC** (as of 1900–10), *Passel.* . . A group of nondescript boys and girls. Used derogatorily. . . Common. **1947** *PADS* 8.15 **sIN** (as of 1900–10), *Passel. Ibid* 22 **KY,** *Passel:* Used only by older people. **1965–70** *DARE* (Qu. LL8b, . . *A large number* . . *"She has a whole _____ of cousins."*) 64 Infs, **widespread,** Passel [Of all Infs responding to the question, 63% were old; of those giving this resp, 36% were old.]; (Qu. U38b, . . *A great deal of money: "He made a _____ [of money]."*) Inf **WI**68, Passel; (Qu. LL9a, *As much as you need or more* . . *"We've got _____ of apples."*) Inf **IA**5, Passel; (Qu. LL10, *A whole group of people: "They made too much noise, so he sent the whole _____ home."*) Infs **MD**32, **MS**73, **MO**11, **NC**61, **NY**105, Passel; **FL**38, **VA**31, Passel of them. **1967** *DARE* FW Addit **AR**52, They's a passel ['pæsəl] of things to be done. **1972** *Time* 27 Mar 25, There are nine varieties of bumper stickers, George Wallace watches selling for $16.50, a passel of buttons (10 cents each). **1993** *Time* 3 May 21, Los Angeles voters pared a passel of 24 politicians vying to replace Mayor Tom Bradley and picked two polar opposites.

passez exclam [Cajun Fr; 1984 Daigle *Dict. Cajun Lang.* 2.114, "*Passez,* interj. Word used to chase away dogs."] **sLA**
    1968 *DARE* (Qu. NN22c, *Expressions used to drive away a dog*) Infs **LA**35, 37, Passez; (Qu. NN22d, . . *Expressions used to drive away people or animals*) Inf **LA**25, Passez.

passing n
1 The people or vehicles going past. Cf **pass** n **1**
    1871 *Scribner's Mth.* 3.161, Miss Pinkham proposed that they should take their nuts and raisins over to the window, and hold their plates in their laps. . . "It places one so entirely at leisure, and at the same time allows one to see all the passing." **1929** *AmSp* 5.128 **ME,** The old folks watched "the passing" and knew everyone's horse.
2 See **pass** n **2.**

passing the scissors See **scissors**

passion bite (or blister, bump) See **passion mark**

passion flower n Also *passion vine* [*OED2* 1633 →; see quot 1938] **esp Sth**   Cf **Holy Trinity flower**
=maypop 1.
    1802 (1803) Ellicott *Jrl.* 287, The China root . . and passion flower . . are abundant in the rich grounds. **1808** (1910) Ayer *Diary* 53 **MA,** In the forenoon Mr. Mosely called to see our passion vine. **1851** *De Bow's Rev.* 9.49 **LA,** May Pop, Passion Flower, is also abundant here. **1887** (1967) Harris *Free Joe* 182 **GA,** Wild passion-flowers clambering along the broken-down fence of pine-poles. **1897** IN Dept. Geol. & Nat. Resources *Rept. for 1896* 658, P[assiflora] lutea . . Northern Passion Flower. **1929** Neal *Honolulu Gardens* 216, A passion vine that climbs vigorously on arbors and trellises in a few places in Honolulu bears one of the most edible kinds of passion fruit. **1938** FWP *U.S. One* 256 **neFL,** On high ground beside the road grows the vine of the passionflower, so called by Spanish missionaries because to them the bloom symbolized the passion of Christ. In the center of the blossom is a cross; the stigmas, they said, represented the nails, the anthers the wounds and the rays of the corona the crown of thorns. **1965–70** *DARE* (Qu. S4, . . *Mayapple: [Woodside plant, not a tree, with two large spreading leaves; they grow in patches and have a small yellow fruit late in summer]*) Infs **FL**16, **GA**38, **NC**10, 16, 21, 24, Maypop or passion flower; **AR**35, Maypop, passion flower—same; **MS**1, Passion flower; (Qu. S26a, . . *Wildflowers* . . *Roadside flowers*) Inf **AR**52, Passion flower or maypop; (Qu. S26e, *Other wildflowers not yet mentioned;* not asked in early QRs) Inf **KY**82, Maypop (passion flower)—a vine with big purple flowers and small fruits later on; (Qu. T16) Inf **GA**84, Maypop is called passion flower. **1967** *DARE* FW Addit **SC**41, Passion flower = maypop = *Passiflora incarnata.* **1967** *DARE* Wildfl QR (Wills–Irwin) Pl.27A Inf **TX**34, Passion flower if you buy it—if it's wild, wild maypop. **1981** Pederson *LAGS Basic Materials,* 1 inf, **nwMS,** Maypops = passion flowers.

passion mark n Also *passion bite, ~ blister, ~ bump, ~ kiss, ~ pimple, ~ spot* **scattered, but less freq NEng, Upper Missip Valley, West** See Map Cf **hickey** n[2] **c**
A mark on the skin caused by sucking or biting.
    1965–70 *DARE* (Qu. X39, *A mark on the skin where somebody has*

sucked it hard and brought the blood to the surface) 38 Infs, **scattered, but less freq NEng, Upper Missip Valley, West,** Passion mark; **NY**210, Passion bite; **PA**69, Passion blister; **NY**224, Passion bump; **MO**26, Passion kiss; **NY**224, Passion pimple; **OK**57, Passion spot. [19 of 42 Infs coll educ, 17 young] **1981** Pederson *LAGS Basic Materials,* 1 inf, **New Orleans LA,** Lump on the head [is] called a hickey (an egg-like swelling, not a passion mark).

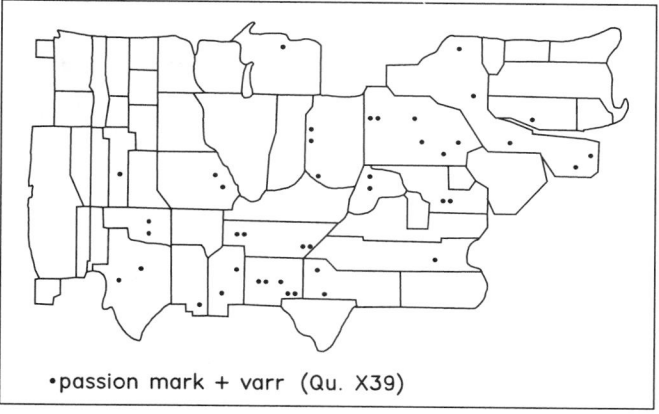

•passion mark + varr (Qu. X39)

passion pimple n
1 also *passion rash:* **=jack bump.** Cf **fuck bump, jerk ~, love ~ 1**
    1967 *DARE* (Qu. X59, . . *The small infected pimples that form usually on the face*) Inf **MN**10, Passion pimples, passion rash.
2 See **passion mark.**

passion rash See **passion pimple 1**

passion spot See **passion mark**

passion vine See **passion flower**

pass kittens See **kittens, have**

passle See **passel 2**

passley See **parsley**

pass-me-down n Also *pass-down, pass-(me-)on*
A piece of secondhand clothing.
    1965–70 *DARE* (Qu. U3, *A coat, dress, or other garment that is passed on from one person to another [or an older child to a younger one]*) Infs **MD**19, 26, **NY**156, Pass-down; **CA**9, **IN**26, **NJ**3, Pass-me-down; **NY**40, **PA**126, Pass-me-on; **CA**177, Pass-on; [**MA**5, Passed-down; **CA**83, Passed-on-down].

pass off See **pass** v **1e**

pass on v See **pass** v **1b**

pass-on n See **pass-me-down**

passonne See **possum** n **1**

pass out See **pass** v **1c**

pass over v phr See **pass** v **1d**

passover n
An impending storm that fails to bring rain.
    1975 *Appalachian Jrl.* 2.158 **wNC,** A heavy rainfall is a *gully-washer,* and rain clouds that seem to be bringing rain may, after all, be only a *passover.*

pass through the rubbers See **rubbers**

passul See **passel 2**

password n [**pass words**]
    1914 *DN* 4.111 **cKS,** Password. . . A greeting.

pass words v phr For varr see quots
1 To converse briefly. **esp Sth, S Midl** See Map
    1906 *DN* 3.150 **nwAR,** Pass words. . . To converse. "We passed a few

words." **1923** *DN* 5.216 **swMO,** *Pass a word or two. . .* To hold a short conversation.   **1965–70** *DARE* (Qu. II12, *Talking about meeting somebody on the street and speaking only a few words with him: "We just _____."*) 22 Infs, **esp Sth, S Midl,** Passed a few words; **NE3,** Passed a few remarks; **MS6,** Passed words. [7 of 24 Infs Black]

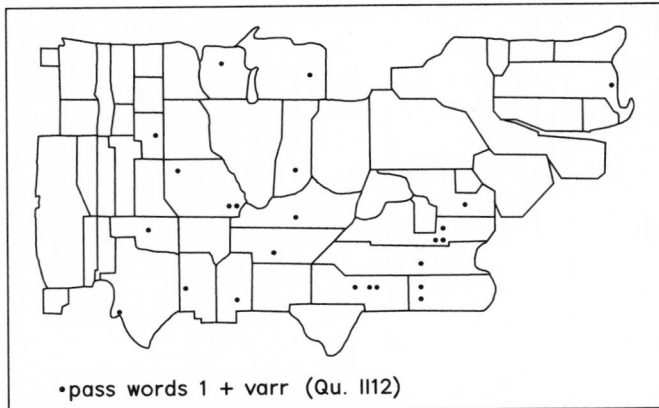

•pass words 1 + varr (Qu. II12)

2 To exchange hostile words; to quarrel.

1909 *DN* 3.401 **nwAR,** *Pass words. . .* To exchange words, usually leading up to a quarrel.   **1952** Brown *NC Folkl.* 1.574 **c,eNC,** *Pass words. . .* To quarrel. "They passed some words before John hit him."   **1984** Wilder *You All Spoken Here* 47 **Sth,** *Pass some words:* Quarrel, as "They commenced to pass some words an' then they fell in an' fit."

past prep

Std sense, var syntax.

Postposed in expressions referring to age.   [*OED2 past* prep. 1.b 1676–1720]   Cf **long** adj **B4, rising** adj **2**

1774 in 1877 Smith *Genl. Hist. Duchess Co.* 300 **NY,** Came into the pasture of James Young . . a sorrel mare, two years old past, marked with the letter B on the near hind thigh.   **1835** (1940) Arnold *Diaries* 120 **VT,** This morning my white mare died, being 8 years old past.   **1943** in 1944 *ADD* **seWV,** Grandson B_____ . . , 7 years past, of Hillsboro, came up Washington's Birthday.   **1967–69** *DARE* FW Addit **cnNY,** Eighty past—past eighty (in years). Occasional; **ceKY,** "He's ninety year past"—he's over ninety years old. [Used in conversation by two Infs.]

pasta fazool n Also *pasta fasuli,* ~ *fazoole,* ~ *fazul* [From a dialect var of Ital *pasta e fagioli* pasta and beans; cf Sicilian *fasula,* Neapolitan *fasulo* bean]

A dish of pasta and beans or other legumes.

1940 *New York Daily Mirror* 23 Jan 26/1 (*Popik Coll.*), He is slipping like . . the sale of pasta fazoole in Naples.   **1952** *NY Herald Tribune* (NY) 21 May 16/6 (*Popik Coll.*), [Headline:] *Pasta Fazool Makes Its Debut At a Colony Restaurant Lunch.*   **1968** *DARE* (Qu. H36, *Kinds of soup*) Inf **MA7,** Pasta fasuli—chopped-up spaghetti with white beans, oil.   **1975** Pepitone-Stainback *Joe* 158 **NYC,** He told him to fix us a huge pile of pastafazool, which is peas and macaroni.   **1993** *Amer. Spectator* May 72, Sometime, it must have been around 1940, I heard the term *pastafazool.* It may have been a spoken interjection during a jazz vocal by one of the Italian-American musicians of the era.   **1998** *DARE* File—Internet **sePA** [Language of the Hayna Valley], Pasta Fazul—*Pasta e Fagioli,* a pasta and bean dish.

paste n

Also in var combs: Thick gravy.

1905 *DN* 3.89 **nwAR,** *Paste. . .* Gravy. 'The boys at the dorm say "Pass the paste," when they want the gravy.'   **1942** Berrey–Van den Bark *Amer. Slang* 91.46, *Gravy. . . Spec.* paste, *thick gravy.*   **1950** *WELS* (*What words do you have for gravy? [Include joking ones]*) 1 Inf, **cnWI,** Paste; 1 Inf, **ceWI,** Kite paste.   **1966–70** *DARE* (Qu. H37, . . *Words . . for gravy. Any joking ones?*) Inf **CA212,** Paperhanger's paste; **FL15,** Paste [laughter]; **OR1,** Wallpaper paste.

paster See **pasture** n[1], v

pastern n Pronc-spp *paster, pasture*

Std sense, var forms.

1915 *DN* 4.187 **swVA,** *Paster. . .* Variant of both *pastern* and *pasture.*   **1940** Yoder *Rosanna* 175 **PA,** Well, he has a slight limp when he trots and he has a slight enlargement above the pasture joint.

pastor n[1] Also *pastore* [Span *pastor*]   **SW**

A sheepherder.

1849 U.S. Congress *Serial Set* 64 Doc 132, The flock [of sheep] was under Mexican and not Navajo control, and, from my conversation with the *pastor,* became assured that our apprehensions were groundless.   **1906** Adams *Cattle Brands* 20 (*DA*), Here I found a flock of sheep and a pastore.   **1940** Fergusson *Our Southwest* 177, The *pastor,* shepherd, was at everybody's beck and call. But he had the constant companionship of his dog, and no finer beast was ever known than a well-trained sheep dog.   **1986** Pederson *LAGS Concordance,* 1 inf, **csTX,** Pastor = shepherd; took care of goats and sheep.

pastor v, hence vbl n *pastoring*   **esp Sth, S Midl**

To serve (a church or congregation) as a pastor; to hold the position of pastor; to employ as a pastor.

1894 *Kingdom* (Minneapolis) 20 Apr. (*OED2*), Having given half his life to pastoring and preaching.   **1931** (1991) Hughes–Hurston *Mule Bone* 76 **cFL** [Black], I ain't never pastored no town so way-back as this one here.   **1936** in 1970 Hyatt *Hoodoo* 1.51 (as of c1904), This story happened . . at a church near Greenville, South Carolina, where we pastored [Hyatt: the informant's husband was pastor of the church].   **1939** in Lib. of Congress *Amer. Memory: WPA Life Hist.* (Internet) **FL** [Black], I belong to the Freewill Baptist Church, pastored by Rev. Williams, over on Fourth Street.   *Ibid* **NC** [Black], The next eight years of my life I pastored in little country churches in my home conference.   *Ibid* **SC,** I worked in the store and pastored this church for four years.   *Ibid* **NC,** I worked at my trade in the factory while pastoring this church.   **1967** *DARE* FW Addit **GA19,** "Where does he pastor?" Woman in office: "He pastors in Jacksonville." (Conversation was about a revival evangelist.)   **c1974** Jones *Ozark Hill Boy* 27 **AR** (as of c1933), Bill was an Assembly of God preacher and pastored a country church.   **1986** Pederson *LAGS Concordance,* 1 inf, **seGA,** He's a preacher but not a pastor because he don't pastor a church; 1 inf, **swAL,** He don't pastor no church; 1 inf, **nwMS,** Preacher who is not pastored; 1 inf, **neAR,** He pastored the church; 1 inf, **cwAR,** The largest church he'd ever pastored; 1 inf, **nwAL,** I quit pastoring—i.e., retired from the ministry; 1 inf, **seAL,** Pastors two or three churches.

pastor n[2] See **pasture** n[1], v

pastore See **pastor** n[1]

pasture n[1], v Usu |ˈpæsčə(r)|; also **esp NEng** |ˈpɑsčə, pɑstə|; **chiefly Sth, S Midl** |ˈpæstə(r)|; for addit varr see quots   Pronc-spp *pa(r)ster, pa(r)stur, pastor, pastuh, postur(e)*

Std sense, var forms.

1859 in 1956 Eliason *Tarheel Talk* 315 **c,csNC,** Paster.   **1871** Eggleston *Hoosier Schoolmaster* 99 **sIN,** I see Pete Jones, and them others . . a crossin' the blue-grass paster.   **a1883** (1911) Bagby *VA Gentleman* 56, The native Virginian. . . says . . "down in the parster."   **1893** Shands *MS Speech* 49, Pastur [ˈpæstə]. Illiterate white for *pasture.*   **1898** Lloyd *Country Life* 19 **AL,** Drive the geese down to the paster.   **1899** (1912) Green *VA Folk-Speech* 312, Parster. . . For pasture. "The horses are all in the parster."   **1909** *DN* 3.356 **eAL, wGA,** Paster, *n.* and *v.* Pasture.   **1910** *DN* 3.454 **seVT,** Parstur, corrupt form of *pasture.* Rare.   **1915** *DN* 4.187 **swVA,** Paster. . . Variant of both *pastern* and *pasture.*   **1921** Haswell *Daughter Ozarks* 20 (as of 1880s), His hosses is out to his Paw's paster.   **1922** Gonzales *Black Border* 318 **sSC, GA coasts** [Gullah glossary], Pastuh . . pasture, pastures.   **1929** *AmSp* 5.131 **ME,** Parster.   **1939** *LANE* Map 114 (*Pasture*), [Most common proncs are of the types [pæstʃə] and, **esp eNEng,** [pastʃə, pɑ(ə)stʃə]; less frequent are [pæstə, pa·stə]; 1 inf, **swNEng,** also [pæstʃr;] 1 inf, **swCT,** [pɑrstr], still commonly heard; 1 inf, **sRI,** [pæstjuə, -tʃuə], spelling-pron. (The informant has taught school.); 1 inf, **seMA,** [pastʃuə], spelling-pron. (The informant has taught school.); 1 inf, **ceMA,** [paˑ·stə, pa·s-], still commonly heard, especially from old people; 1 inf, **neVT,** [pæsʃə]; 1 inf, **seNH,** [pæᵻstʃə], modern pron.]   **1941** Writers' Program *SC Folk Tales* 101, But when she make staat tuh trabble dat paat tru duh pastor leadin tuh she son boat, . . sumptin grab her holt!   **1956** Ker *Vocab. W. TX* 158, *Place where cows are enclosed. .* pasture [13 of 67 infs], postur [1 inf].   **1958** Francis *Structure of Amer. Engl.* 523 **eVA,** /a/ in *pasture* and a few other words. I [=old-fashioned, rustic, poorly educated speakers].   **1961** Kurath–McDavid *Pronc. Engl.* 137, *Pasture. . .* In this word /a/ is common only (1) in Massachusetts Bay area and (2) in Maine from Casco Bay . . eastward. . . In Virginia . . *pasture* is pronounced as /ˈpɑstə/ from Chesapeake Bay to the Blue Ridge and southward into the northern counties of North Carolina; it predominates, moreover, in highly conservative northeastern North Carolina. **1974** Gilbreth *Dictionary* 13 seSC, *Pastor:* Field where cows graze. *Ibid* 14, *Posture.* **1989** Pederson *LAGS Tech. Index* 59, [The prevailing proncs of *pasture* are of the types [ˈpæsča(r)] (483 infs), [ˈpɑstə(r)] (219), and [ˈpæstjə(r)] (90). Substitution of [š] for [s] is fairly common (50); significant variation in the first vowel is almost nonexistent.]

pasture n[2] See **pastern**

pasture baby n Cf **pasture-bred, pasture colt**
A child born out of wedlock.
   1967 *DARE* (Qu. Z11b, . . *[A child whose parents were not married]*) Inf **SC**32, Pasture baby.

pasture bird n
1 =**golden plover.** Cf **pasture plover**
   1888 Trumbull *Names of Birds* 195 **swMA,** To the old people at West Barnstable, [the golden plover is known as] *pasture-bird* (a name now seldom heard, but used there by every one until fifteen or twenty years ago). **1917** (1923) *Birds Amer.* 1.257, Golden Plover, *Charadrius dominicus dominicus.* . . Other Names . . Pasture-bird. **1955** MA Audubon Soc. *Bulletin* 39.444, [American Golden Plover. . . Field Bird (Maine, Mass. It resorts to grasslands more than do its relatives, except the Killdeer.)] *Ibid,* Pasture Bird (Mass. See note on Field Bird.)
2 =**vesper sparrow.**
   1944 Hausman *Amer. Birds* 506, Bird, pasture—see Sparrow, vesper.
3 =**cowbird 1.**
   1969 *DARE* (Qu. Q14, . . *Names . . for . . cowbird*) Inf **IN**80, Pasture bird.

pasture brake n
A **brake** n[1] (here: *Pteridium aquilinum*).
   1891 *Jrl. Amer. Folkl.* 4.149 **NH,** All ferns we knew as *Brakes,* and the common pasture brake we called Polypod, probably an Asplenium. **1974** (1977) Coon *Useful Plants* 199, *Pteridium aquilinum*—Bracken fern, brake fern, pasture brake, fiddleheads (or necks). **1976** Bailey-Bailey *Hortus Third* 924, *[Pteridium] aquilinum* . . Brake, pasture b[rake], hog-pasture b[rake], bracken.

pasture-bred adj chiefly N Midl See Map Cf **field-bred**
Of a domestic animal: conceived or impregnated by accident; also transf.
   1950 *WELS (A horse that was not intentionally bred)* 3 Infs, **WI,** Pasture-bred. **1965–70** *DARE* (Qu. K43, *A horse that was not intentionally bred, or bred by accident*) 36 Infs, **chiefly N Midl,** Pasture-bred; **MD**22, Pasture-bred—used for calf bred by accident [FW: Inf assumes the same applies to horse]; **MI**101, Pasture-bred—associated more often with cattle; **NC**36, Pasture-bred—for horses or cattle; **OK**33, Pasture-bred—said for cows, used to say it for horses [37 of 40 Infs male]; [**IL**84, **PA**174, Bred in the pasture]; (Qu. Z11b, . . *[A child whose parents were not married]*) Inf **IA**11, She was pasture-bred—meaning the pregnant woman was laid in the field before being married—this would be a very degrading thing to say of a woman.

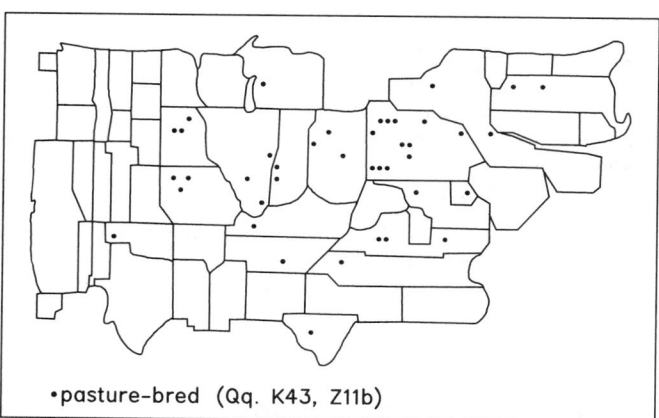

•pasture-bred (Qq. K43, Z11b)

pasture colt n
A foal that is **pasture-bred;** by ext, a **pasture baby.**

1967 Faries *Word Geog.* MO 116, A child born out of wedlock. . . Write-ins (one occurrence for each) are: *love child, pasture colt, shame baby.* **1968–69** *DARE* (Qu. K43, *A horse that was not intentionally bred, or bred by accident*) Infs **MN**40, **TN**31, Pasture colt.

pasture gooseberry n
A **gooseberry 1** (here: *Ribes cynosbati*).
   1924 Deam *Shrubs IN* 87, *Pasture Gooseberry.* . . of no economic importance, although its fruit was used by the pioneers for jelly. **1938** Van Dersal *Native Woody Plants* 234, *Ribes cynosbati.* . . *Pasture gooseberry.* . . A small spiny shrub; flowers April–June. **1942** Tehon *Fieldbook IL Shrubs* 94, The Pasture Gooseberry . . is . . seldom more than 2 feet high . . [and] generally covered more or less densely with long, reddish prickles. **1966** Grimm *Recognizing Native Shrubs* 116, *Ribes cynosbati.* . . New Brunswick to Manitoba; south to Georgia, Alabama, and Missouri. Also called Pasture Gooseberry.

pasture mushroom n
1 A **field mushroom** (here: either *Agaricus arvensis* or *A. campestris*).
   1943 Fernald-Kinsey *Edible Wild Plants E. N. Amer.* 381, *Meadow or Pasture Mushroom, Agaricus arvensis* and *campestris.* [*Ibid* 382, *A. campestris,* although technically different in many details, is the commoner of the two in old pastures and manured areas.] **1980** Marteka *Mushrooms* 113, *Agaricus campestris.* . . pasture mushroom. . . This short, stocky, white mushroom . . grows in grassy areas.
2 also *pasture puffball:* A **puffball 1** such as *Lycoperdon cyathiforme.*
   1969 *DARE* (Qu. S18, *A kind of mushroom that grows like a globe . . sometimes gets as big as a man's head*) Inf **NY**183, Pasture mushrooms. **1980** Marteka *Mushrooms* 131, *Calvatia cyathiformis* . . pasture puffball. . . There are other large puffballs that have a similar size and shape, . . but all are edible when the interior is white. . . Fruits on lawns, meadows, pastures, and other open grassy areas.

pasture petunia n
=**wild petunia.**
   1951 *PADS* 15.40 **TX,** *Ruellia* spp.—Wild, wild prairie, or pasture, petunias.

pasture plover n Cf **pasture bird 1**
An **upland plover** (here: *Bartramia longicauda*).
   1917 (1923) *Birds Amer.* 1.247, Upland Plover. . . Other Names. . . Pasture Plover. **1925** (1928) Forbush *Birds MA* 1.447, *Bartramia longicauda.* . . Pasture Plover. . . Seen in meadows, fields and hill pastures. **1956** MA Audubon Soc. *Bulletin* 40.17 **NH, MA,** Pasture Plover.

pasture puffball See **pasture mushroom 2**

pasture pup n
A **marmot a** (here: *Marmota monax*).
   1982 Elman *Hunter's Field Guide* 408, Marmot . . Common & regional names . . eastern or flatland species—*woodchuck, groundhog, monax, pasture pup.*

pasture rose n Cf **meadow rose**
A **wild rose:** usu *Rosa carolina,* but also *R. virginiana.*
   1899 MacMillan *MN Plant Life* 291, The swamp rose and the pasture rose may be known by the presence of a pair of extra large prickles just below the stipules at the base of each leaf. **1900** Lyons *Plant Names* 324, *R[osa] humilis* [=*R. carolina*]. . . Pasture Rose, . . the common Wild Rose of eastern U.S. **1919** (1923) House *Wild Flowers NY* 1.139, *Low or Pasture Rose—Rosa virginiana.* . . In dry or rocky soil. **1924** Deam *Shrubs IN* 131, *Rosa carolina.* . . Pasture Rose. **1929** Stemen-Myers *Spring Flora OK* 62, *Rosa virginiana.* . . Pasture Rose. **1953** Greene-Blomquist *Flowers South* 50, *Pasture-, Low-,* or *Carolina-Rose (Rosa carolina).* . . differs from the Virginia-rose (*Rosa virginiana*) in having more coarsely serrate leaves and more slender infrastipular prickles. **1967** *DARE* (Qu. S26e, *Other wildflowers not yet mentioned;* not asked in early QRs) Inf **MN**6, Pasture rose. **1967** *DARE* Wildfl QR Pl.102 *(Rosa virginiana)* Inf **AR**44, Pasture rose. **1973** Wharton-Barbour *Trees KY* 533, *Rosa carolina.* . . Pasture Rose. This pretty little rose, pink and delightfully fragrant, grows . . in old fields throughout the state.

pasture salvia See **salvia**

pasture thistle n
A **thistle:** usu *Cirsium pumilum,* occas also *C. altissimum.*

1824 Bigelow *Florula Bostoniensis* 292 **MA**, *Cnicus pumilus. . . Pasture Thistle. . .* Very common in dry pastures and by road sides. **1847** Wood *Class-Book* 356, *C[irsium] pumilum. . . Pasture Thistle. . .* Very large heads of fragrant, purple flowers. **1891** Jesup *Plants Hanover NH* 24, C[nicus] pumilus. . . (Pasture Thistle.) Fields; common. **1912** Mathews *Amer. Wild Flowers* 522, *Pasture Thistle—Cirsium pumilum. . .* The largest-flowered thistle of all. . . In dry pastures and fields, Me. to Del. and Pa., near the coast. **1940** Gates *Flora KS* 251, Cirsium altissimum. . . Pasture Thistle. . . Thickets, open rocky slopes, low alluvial woods and waste ground. **1946** Tatnall *Flora DE* 278, *C. pumilum. . . Pasture Thistle. . .* In pastures of the Piedmont province. **1968** Barkley *Plants KS* 376, Cirsium altissimum. . . Pasture Thistle. Tall Thistle. . . East two-thirds [of KS] or more.

pasture weed n

A **star thistle** (here: *Centaurea melitensis*).

1896 *Jrl. Amer. Folkl.* 9.191 **CA**, *Centaurea Melitensis*, pasture weed, tocolote [sic].

pasty n |ˈpæsti|

1 A pie or turnover filled with meat and vegetables, usu baked without a pan. [*OED2* a1300 →] **scattered, but chiefly Gt Lakes, esp MI** See Map

1763 in 1939 Wolcott *Yankee Cook Book* 277 ceMA, *Marrow pasties*—Cut half a pound of marrow in little Lumps . . ; skin shred six apples small and mix therewith; to which, add a quarter of a pound of Sugar. Season with beaten Mace, Cinnamon, and Nutmeg; mix half a pound of currants . . , well with all the other Ingredients, . . to make them into turn-over Pasties with Puff Paste. **1940** Brown *Amer. Cooks* 411 **MI**, A Pasty may be eaten hot or cold, and if it is of generous size is a meal in itself. It is a perfect picnic dish, as it keeps hot for hours, wrapped in napkins, and will not get soggy. **1944** Nute *Lake Superior* 251 **MI, WI, MN,** They gave the Copper Country their delicious pasties or meat turnovers. **1950** *WELS (Dishes made with beef)* 1 Inf, **cWI**, Pasties; 1 Inf, **swWI**, Pasty (Cornish); *(Dishes made with meat and vegetables mixed)* 3 Infs, **WI**, Pasties; 1 Inf, **cWI**, English pasties. **1959** Tallman *Dict. Amer. Folkl.* 217, *Pasty. . .* This term was used by the Cornishmen for their popular meat pie. They brought the custom with them from Wales to the mines in Michigan, where the dish is still a great favorite. **1961** *Daily Mining Gaz.* (Houghton MI) 1 Aug sec 4 11/8, He has given the cook his recipe for fish pasties and every Friday, fish pasties are on the day's menu. **1965–70** *DARE* (Qu. H45, *Dishes made with meat, fish, or poultry that everybody around here would know, but that people in other places might not)* Inf **CA126**, Cornish pasty—old-fashioned [FW sugg]; **CA132, DC4,** Cornish pasty—meat pie; **MI22, 34, MN1, NV1,** Cornish pasty; **CO40, 47,** Cousin Jack pasty; **CA146,** Pasties—eaten by Cornish miners, a turnover, men would put them in their buckets; **IA30,** Pasty—a turnover or a meat pie—taters, meat, onions; **IL3,** Pasty [ˈpæstɪ]—a Cornish dish made of meat and potato in a baked crust; **MI9,** Pasties [ˈpæstɪz]; **MI13,** Pasty—more so in the Ishpeming and Negaunee area; the Cornish pasty has a suet crust rather than just a regular crust; **MI52,** Pasty [ˈpæstɪ]; **NJ2,** Pasty—meat pie not in dish, not really native; **NJ4,** Pasties [ˈpæstɪz]—came with English miners—meat, onions, and potatoes in crust, meat pie with no gravy; **PA105,** Pasties; **WI47,** Pasties [ˈpæstɪz]—hand-held meat pie; **MI18, MN14, WI52,** Pasty; (Qu. H65, *Foreign foods favored by people around here)* Infs **CA132, PA110,** Pasties; **MI1,** Pasties [pæstɪz]—Cornish or Welsh: meat, carrots, onions, turnips (or beggies—ruta-

bagas)—thicker than a crust, not as thick as a biscuit or a meat pie—filling lies between; **MI9,** Pasties—Cornish; **MI46, 52,** Pasties [ˈpæstɪz]; **MI94, NV1,** Pasty; (Qu. HH30, *Things that are nicknamed for different nationalities—for example, a 'Dutch treat')* Inf **MN2,** Cousin Jack pasty. [23 of 28 total Infs female] **1966–67** *DARE* Tape **MI22,** Make a crust like you would for a pie, but not quite so rich. . . Peel potatoes and dice them up, and a little turnip. Then . . cut up meat and onions . . and put this in the crust. . . Turn it over and crimp the edges. And you put it on a pan and . . bake it for one hour. But make sure you put a hole in the top of the pasty [ˈpæstɪ]; **MI40,** Batching . . was a group of three of us boys getting together, renting an apartment, . . and quite often bringing the material goods from home, such as pasties [ˈpæ·stɪz], pies, and sometimes carrying a bushel of potatoes along; **MI43,** Things were getting . . bad up there for funds, so a bunch of us . . women got together and we organized a pasty [ˈpæˆɛstɪ] group. . . [But] the winters were getting too hard for me . . to deliver pasties [ˈpæstɪz] in Houghton. **1996** *DARE* File **csWI,** When I first came to Madison in 1975 I discovered that pasties [ˈpæstɪz] make a great take-out food.

2 Transf: see quot.

1972 *DARE* File **nwMI,** Pasty [pæstɪ]—a "cow's pie," dropping of cow dung.

pat n¹ Cf **pat** v 3

A small, flat cake or patty made of breaded oysters.

1968 [see **pat** v 3].

pat v

1a also in phr *pat it down:* To clap, slap one's body, or strike the ground with one's foot rhythmically as an accompaniment to dancing; hence vbl n *patting;* n *patter* one who excels at this. **chiefly Sth, S Midl**

1850 in 1910 *Annals IA* (3d ser) 9.467, I heard some good fiddling and thought . . of sweet home and the merry ones that, no doubt, at that time were "patting it down" to some old favorite air. **1853** (1855) Northup *12 Yrs. Slave* 219 **LA** [Black], The patting is performed by striking the hands on the knees, then striking the hands together, then striking the right shoulder with one hand, the left with the other—all the while keeping time with the feet, and singing. **1860** Hundley *Social Relations S. States* 357, The distant "thrum, tumpe tum" of the merry banjo, may be accompanied by a flute or violin, or "patting." **1869** *Atlantic Mth.* 24.74 **OH,** I [=a minstrel] was made to dance "Juba" to the time which the comedian himself gave me by means of his two hands and one foot, and which is technically called "patting." **1883** (1971) Harris *Nights with Remus* 50 **GA** [Black], De gals done make 'rangerments wid Brer Rabbit fer ter pat fer um, en in dem days Brer Rabbit wuz a patter, mon. He mos' sho'ly wuz. **1894** Riley *Armazindy* 136 **IN,** Ponchus *pats* fer me an' sings. **1908** (1966) Thorp *Songs Cowboys* 41 **TX,** When they go to their dances some dance while others pat / They ride their bucking broncos and wear their broad brimmed hats. **1922** Talley *Negro Folk Rhymes* 259, Now when I first witnessed this dance, there were no words said at all. There was simply patting with the hands and dancing. **1945** FWP *Lay My Burden Down* 114 **LA** (as of c1865) [Black], Some of us young bucks just step up and say we was good dancers, and we start shuffling while the rest of the niggers pat. **1959** Lomax *Rainbow Sign* 25 **AL** [Black], Francie never sings so you can hear her, and Sukie, well, she could *pat* the best I ever heard. **1967** *DARE* Tape **TX49,** If you'd get together, lots of times some fellers'd pat, you know. One would jump out in front and commence dancing. We'd get together a crowd of us. . . Someone'd pat for you like [Inf demonstrates clapping and stamping]. That's way you'd dance. **1972** in 1982 Powers *Cataloochee* 171 **cwNC** (as of a1940), They'us playin' the ole Virginia Reel, and she was a-pattin'. . . A-pattin' for that dance!

b tr: To do this as accompaniment to (a verse). See also *pat juba* (at **juba** 1)

1922 Talley *Negro Folk Rhymes* 297, "Juba Circle, raise de latch,/ Juba dance dat Long Dog Scratch, Juba! Juba!" While this was being patted and repeated, the dancers within the circle described a circle with raised foot and ended doing a dance step called "Dog Scratch."

2 To tap or stamp (one's foot), clap (one's hands) in time to music or dancing; to beat (time). **chiefly Sth** *esp freq among Black speakers*

1848 *Ladies' Repository* 8.292, The moving agent of the whole operation was a son of Ham, patting his foot, and drawing a horse-hair across a piece of cat-gut. **1849** Foster *NY in Slices* 31, A splendidly-attired woman in the prime of life and loveliness . . sits at one of the little marble tables, resting her bonnet . . on her hand and patting her foot rapidly

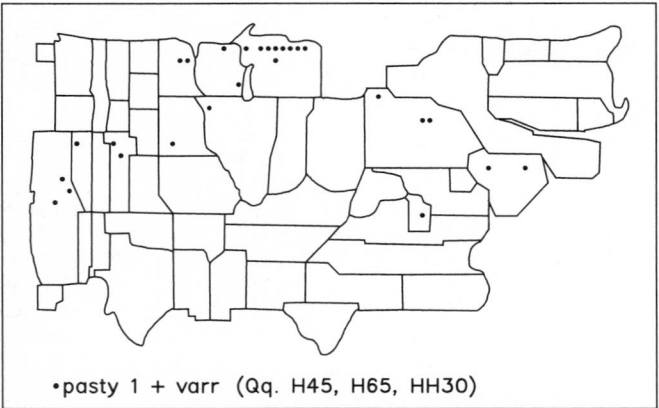

•pasty 1 + varr (Qq. H45, H65, HH30)

on the floor. **1873** *Ladies' Repository* 11.353 **PA,** Here stands an old woman in the corner singing "diddle, diddle, diddle," without beginning or end, time or tune, sense or rhyme, patting her foot for accompaniment to the cracked voice. **1883** (1971) Harris *Nights with Remus* 45 **GA** [Black], He 'uz . . one er dem ar kinder fiddlers w'at can't git de chune down fine 'less dey pats der foot. **1888** Jones *Negro Myths* 121 **GA coast,** Buh Wolf . . duh play eh fiddle. . . Buh Wolf yeye shet tight, an eh dis bin er rock from side ter side, an draw eh bow . . en der pat de time wid eh foot. **1922** Talley *Negro Folk Rhymes* 232, But those forming the circle, for most of the time, repeated the Rhyme, clapping their hands together, and patting their feet in rhythmic time with the words of the Rhyme being repeated. *Ibid* 233, Every one who has listened to a well sung Negro Jubilee Song knows that it is almost impossible to hear one sung and not pat the foot. **1930** Stoney-Shelby *Black Genesis* 182 **seSC,** Br' Rabbit seddown on a stump, an' start for play on he fiddle, an' sing, an' pat he foot. **1966** *DARE* Tape **MS76** [Black], The others'd be pattin' their hand while we skippin'. **1974** Dance *World of Swing* 13, I just think swing is a matter of some good things put together that you can really pat your foot by. **1986** Pederson *LAGS Concordance (Stamp the floor)* 1 inf, **nwGA,** Pat your foot.

3 also *pad:* To coat with bread crumbs or batter before frying. esp **MD** Cf **pat** n[1]
1968 *DARE* Tape **MD3,** The old old-time suppers, we used to get a colored woman in the neighborhood and she would put three or four oysters in one pat. . . And they'd stay together, and nobody now knows how to pat oysters. . . At the last one that I attended. . . Somebody . . ordered 300 more oysters patted. **1968–69** *DARE* FW Addit **MD37,** *Pad* fish or oysters—dip them in bread crumbs or batter before frying; **sePA,** *Padded oysters*—sign in front of a tray of *breaded* oysters being sold at the Carlisle Farmers Market.

Pat n[2] See **paddy** n[1] **1**

pat n[3] [Abbr for *partridge*, based on the pronc ['pætrɪǰ] or a similar form; cf **partridge A2, 3, 4, B2**] **Nth, esp MI** See Map =ruffed grouse.
1933 White *Dog Days* 29 **CA,** When the "pat," as he was always known in affectionate diminution of the local "partridge," flushed, he did so under full pressure from the very start. **1955** [see **partridge B2**]. **1965–70** *DARE* (Qu. Q7, *Names and nicknames for . . game birds*) Inf **MI10,** Rough grouse—call those pats, from "partridge"; **MI27,** ['pɑrtrɪǰ]—they call them pats [pæts]; **MI53,** Ruffed grouse—synonymous with partridge, pats; **MI104,** ['pɑrtrɪǰ] [FW: Inf uses the nickname "pat"]; **MI116,** ['pætrɪǰ]—also called pats; **MI120,** ['pætrɪ]—pats; **MI123,** ['pɑrtrɪ] or pat; **NY52,** Partridge or pat; **OH23,** Hunkies or pats—those are partridge. **1966** *Newberry News* (MI) 29 Sept 1/1, Failing to measure up to last fall are ruffed grouse populations in the upper peninsula which appear to have slipped the most in the west end of the region. In 1965, an estimated 210,000 pats were taken above the Straits. **1966** *DARE* Tape **MI14,** [FW:] Do you know another name for ruffed grouse? Are they called anything else? [Inf:] Well, they're called partridge or in lower Michigan they call them pats. **1966** *DARE* File **nMI,** [Real estate advt:] *Sportsmen*—If you are looking for an ideal hunting and fishing club—try this. 560 acres—deer, bear, "pats", trout stream. **1982** Elman *Hunter's Field Guide* 15, *Ruffed Grouse.* . . Common & Regional Names: partridge, pa'tridge, pat [etc].

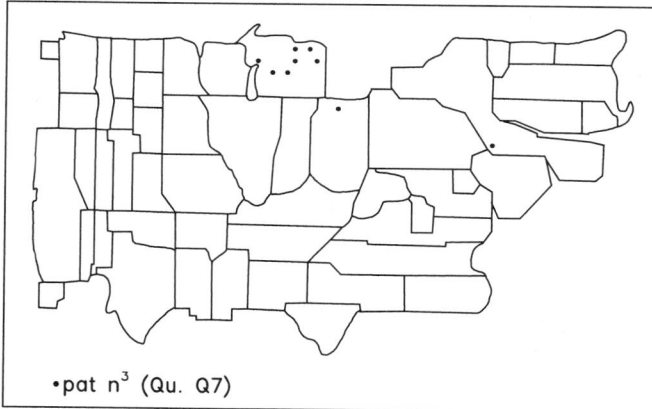

•pat n[3] (Qu. Q7)

pat-a-cake n Also *patty-cake, paddy-cake* esp **Sth, S Midl** A pancake or similar quick bread.

1966–70 *DARE* (Qu. H20b, . . *Names . . for pancakes*) Infs **CA105, FL51, GA4,** Patty-cakes; **NJ8,** Paddy-cakes; (Qu. F3, *When you're frying things—for example, eggs—you turn them over with a _____*) Inf **GA4,** Patty-cake turner. **1986** Pederson *LAGS Concordance (Pancakes)* 3 infs, **TN, LA,** Pat-a-cakes; 1 inf, **swGA,** Pat-a-cakes—old-fashioned term; 1 inf, **neFL,** Pat-a-cakes—made like pancakes but smaller; *(Other kinds of bread and cakes made of cornmeal)* 2 infs, **AR, GA,** Pat-a-cake.

pat-a-cat See **patter cat**

patager n Also *patowga, patawka* [Varr of **catalpa** or **catawba**]
1966–68 *DARE* (Qu. P6, . . *Kinds of worms . . used for bait*) Inf **SC32,** Patager [pə'tagɚ] worm—on trees; **SC7,** Patowga [pə'taʊgə] worm; (Qu. T9) Inf **DE5,** Patawka [pə'tɔkə].

patalca n Also *patalky* [Varr of **catalpa**]
1968–70 *DARE* (Qu. P6, . . *Kinds of worms . . used for bait*) Inf **MO24,** Patalky [pə'tælki]; (Qu. T9, *The common shade tree with large heart-shaped leaves, clusters of white blossoms, and long thin seed pods or 'beans'*) Inf **IA22,** Patalca [pə'tælkə]; **MO15,** [pə'tælkə] tree.

patalfy See **patalpha**

patalky See **patalca**

patalpa n [Var of **catalpa**]
1903 *DN* 2.324 seMO, *Patalpa.* . . Catalpa. A curious but common mispronunciation. **1969** *DARE* (Qu. P6) Inf **KY43,** [pə'tælpə] worm—found on ['tælpə].

patalpha n Also *patalfy* [Varr of **catalpa**]
1882 U.S. Natl. Museum *Proc.* 5.70 **IN,** *Catalpa speciosa.* Catalpa; "Patalpha"; "Wahoo." **1968** *DARE* (Qu. T9) Inf **TN26,** Patalfy [pə'tælfi].

Pat and Charlie n
One's own legs; hence v phr *Pat and Jerry* to go on **shank's mare.**
1966–67 *DARE* (Qu. Y24, . . *To walk, to go on foot: "I can't get a ride, so I'll just have to _____.")* Inf **SC24,** Walk, hoof it, Pat and Jerry; **SC26,** Take Pat and Charlie; **SC44,** Go on Pat and Charlie.

patapan squash See **pattypan squash**

patata n[1] [Cf Span *patata* potato]
A **povertyweed h** (here: *Monolepis nuttalliana*).
1923 in 1925 Jepson *Manual Plants CA* 323, *M[onolepis] nuttalliana.* . . *Patata.* . . Infrequent, but widely distributed. **1941** Jaeger *Wildflowers* 49 **Desert SW,** *Patata.* . . Cismontane and desert valleys, and barren clay hills at low elevations. **1967** Harrington *Edible Plants Rocky Mts.* 80, *Poverty Weed, Patata.* . . This plant makes a very good potherb. Select young and tender plants; we advise removing the roots, especially if they appear to be tough and fibrous. [*Ibid* 81, The Indians were reported to have used the roots for food. We tried them, boiling them for 30 minutes and frying them in butter. They were acceptable but some of the older ones were a bit tough.] **1974** (1977) Coon *Useful Plants* 96, Poverty weed, patata. . . It is rated as a "very good pot-herb, to be cooked and boiled 20 to 30 minutes with one change of water."

patata n[2] See **potato A1**

patawber n [Var of **catawba**]
1968 *DARE* (Qu. P6, . . *Kinds of worms . . used for bait*) Inf **GA25,** [pə'tɔrbɚ] worm; (Qu. T9, *The common shade tree with large heart-shaped leaves, clusters of white blossoms, and long thin seed pods or 'beans'*) Inf **GA25,** Patawber [pətɔbɚ].

patawka See **patager**

patch n

1 in phrr *isn't a patch on* (rarely *to*): Is in no way comparable to. [*OED2 patch* sb.[1] 1.e 1860 →, but probably much older; cf *EDD patch* sb. 1] Cf **hold** v **C2c, patching**
1860 *Vanity Fair* 20.245, We trust the reader is convinced now that *Haynau* is not a patch to *Miramon*. **1892** *Overland Mth.* 20.408 **CA,** Talk about San Francisco fogs. They ain't a patch on the one we are in here. **1965–70** *DARE* (Qu. LL32, *Expressions meaning that one man's ability is not nearly as great as another man's: "John can't [or doesn't, or isn't] _____ Bill."*) Infs **IL53, 97, LA23, MD30, NY107, OH56,**

TN39, **TX**13, (Isn't) a patch on; **LA**45, Isn't a patch on Bill's ass; [**TX**104, Can't put a patch on].

2 A small town or neighborhood of ramshackle houses, esp one associated with a mine; a shantytown—often used with *the* or in var combs as a nickname for such a settlement; hence n *patcher* an inhabitant of such a settlement. **chiefly Nth, N Midl** See Map

1877 (1971) McCabe *Hist. Gt. Riots* 460 **PA,** The whole population of the coal regions living in cities, towns and small settlements, often called 'patches.' **1901** *DN* 2.145 **PA,** *Patch.* . . In the mining villages of Pa., the part of the village occupied by the miners, distinct from that occupied by the superintendent and manager. **1902** Rice *Mrs. Wiggs* 4 **KY,** The Wiggses lived in the Cabbage Patch. It was not a real cabbage patch, but a queer neighborhood, where ramshackle cottages played hopscotch over the railroad tracks. **1938** (1964) Korson *Minstrels Mine Patch* 316 **nePA,** *Patcher:* An inhabitant of a mine patch. **1953** *Reading Times* (PA) 15 July 7/1, Getting into their [=miners'] ramshackle "patches" was almost like entering an enemy fortress. **1965–70** *DARE* (Qu. C33, . . *Joking names . . for an out-of-the-way place, or a very small or unimportant place*) Inf **IA**22, Patch—if small; **KY**68, Cabbage patch, rabbit patch; **OH**91, Cow patch; **TX**71, Dogpatch [FW sugg; Inf doubtful]; (Qu. C34, *Nicknames for nearby settlements, villages, or districts*) Inf **IN**69, Howe Patch—the old name of Wollcott; **MO**16, We got a dogpatch back here; **MA**30, The patch—the south end of Turners [= Turners Falls]; **NY**43, Pumpkin patch; **NY**198, Dogpatch = Dolgeville; **PA**74, Patches—name for mining towns; **PA**131, Linesville—the onion patch; (Qu. C35, *Nicknames for the different parts of your town or city*) Inf **CT**36, Gadpatch; **IL**32, Irish patch—Catholic church, Catholic school, and a devil of a lot of Irish; **KS**5, Dogpatch—for the northwest part of town; **MI**27, Dogpatch—trash live there; **MA**62, The patch; **NJ**2, The patch—Irish district, now gone; **NY**223, The patch—area where they were not very particular who their neighbors were; (Qu. II25, *Names or nicknames for the part of a town where the poorer people, special groups, or foreign groups live*) Infs **IL**30, **MA**30, The patch; **MA**61, The patch—where Irish live; **NY**224, The patch—here in Bath, old-fashioned; **MI**28, Dogpatch; **IL**36, Kerry patch—where the poor Irish lived. [20 of 23 total Infs old] **1969** *Chicago Daily News* (IL) 27–8 Sept 5/1 *(Mathews Coll.),* It is seedy, dreary, congested, despairing—a multi-racial poor people's patch, Appalachia in Chicago. **1998** *DARE* File **swPA,** Both of my grandfathers were coal miners, and my parents were raised in various patches, depending upon where the mines were working. **1998** Millersville Univ. Center for PA Ger. Studies *Jrl.* Autumn 11, Imagine rustic mining houses and fences. . . Could there be such a place? Well there was, the tiny mining patch of Rausch Creek in western Schuylkill County. The term patch is used to describe the mining shacks which made up a village around the local colliery.

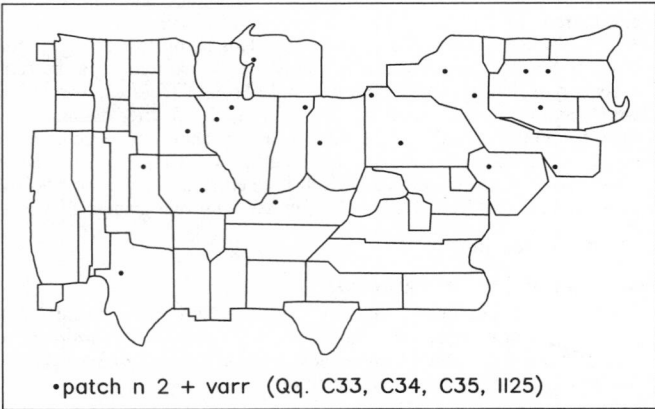

•patch n 2 + varr (Qq. C33, C34, C35, II25)

patch v Cf **patch farm**
To grow (a crop) on a small area of land.

1940 (1978) Still *River of Earth* 101 **KY,** Though Grandma was seventy-eight, she had patched two acres of corn. Even with the crows, the crab grass, and the dwarf stalks she had made enough bread to feed us through the winter.

patchbill coot n Also *patchbill* Cf **patchhead**
=surf scoter.

1899 Howe–Sturtevant *Birds RI* 40, *Oidemia perspicillata.* . . Patch-

bill Coot. . . A common winter resident along the coast and in Narragansett Bay. **1955** MA Audubon Soc. *Bulletin* 39.377 **RI,** *Surf Scoter.* . . Patch-bill Coot (R.I. The male has a round black spot "like a piece of court-plaster" on each side of the bill.) **1982** Elman *Hunter's Field Guide* 240, *Melanitta perspicillata.* . . Patch-bill.

patches n Cf **poor man's patches**
=tick trefoil.

1916 *Torreya* 16.238 **VA,** *Meibonia* spp.—Patches, Revels I[slan]d, Va. **1941** *Nature Mag.* 34.136 **VA,** For these flat fuzzy seeds that stick so closely to our clothes, what more neatly appropriate name than "patches," a term I heard on Revels Island, Virginia.

patch farm n Cf **pea patch**
A piece of land planted only in sections; hence v phr *patch farm* to work such a piece of land; vbl n *patch farming*.

1939 FWP *Guide TN* 22, Thousands of tiny "patch-farms" are scattered through the uplands. **1952** *Sun* (Baltimore MD) 12 Dec sec B 16/2 **cMD,** Mr. Smith estimates that it [=the 93-acre farm] had lain idle for fifteen years, having been only "patch farmed" during that period. . . [N]ow the principal product is unrestrained brush. **1954** *Britannica Book of Yr.* 752, *Patch-farm, v.t.* To farm (a piece of land) in patches. (1952). **1970** *DARE* Tape TX100, I'm gon' keep a little of my land. . . and do a little patch farming, and I expect to consider myself a farmer. **1986** Pederson *LAGS Concordance,* 1 inf, **swMS,** Patch farming.

patchhead n Also *patchhead coot, patch-poll(ed)* ~ [See quot 1917]
=surf scoter.

1888 Trumbull *Names of Birds* 103, *Surf Scoter.* . . at Ash Point (near Rockland), Bath, Portland, Pine Point, and Kennebunk [ME], *Patchhead;* in Massachusetts about Fairhaven and New Bedford, to many upon Martha's Vineyard, and at Stonington, Conn., *Patch-polled Coot.* **1899** Howe–Sturtevant *Birds RI* 40, *Patch-poll Coot.* . . September 1 to May 14. July and August. **1917** (1923) *Birds Amer.* 1.151, *Surf Scoter.* . . *Other Names.* . . Patch-head; Patch-head Coot; Patch-polled Coot. . . *Adult Male:* . . a triangular white patch on forehead pointing forward; another one on nape pointing downward. **1946** Hausman *Eastern Birds* 166, Patchhead. . . The white head patches are: one on the forehead and one farther back on the crown toward the nape. **1955** MA Audubon Soc. *Bulletin* 39.377, Patch-head (Maine, Mass., R.I.); Patch-head Coot (Maine); Patch-poll Coot (Mass., Conn.) **1982** Elman *Hunter's Field Guide* 240, *Melanitta perspicillata.* . . Patch-head.

patching n
In phr *isn't a patching to:* Is in no way comparable to. Cf **patch** n 1

[**1836** in 1965 *AmSp* 40.131, [Song lyrics:] There's been a nigger here singing about a long tail blue, But he ain't a Patching and that's very true. If you want the cut of a coat or anything so Just look at the rigging of Billy Barlow.] **1851** Burke *Polly Peablossom* 52 **GA,** All the sailors an' French parrots in Orleans ain't a patchin' to him. **1871** Eggleston *Hoosier Schoolmaster* 105 **sIN,** Them crack oxen over at Clifty-ah ha'n't a patchin' to mine-ah. **1878** Hart *Sazerac Lying Club* 54 **NV,** It gits pretty cold in this country sometimes, but it aint a patchin' to what it is back in the State of Wisconsin, whar I come from. **1903** *DN* 2.324 **seMO,** *Patching.* . . In expression 'not a patching,' not comparable. 'Smith's speech wasn't a patching to the one Jones made.' **1906** Casey *Parson's Boys* 91 **sIL** (as of c1860), Well, this ain't a patchin' to what I'll give ye if ye ever call me names ag'in. **1907** *DN* 3.234 **nwAR,** *Patching.* . . In the expression, "not a patching," not comparable. "A rack-rabbit [sic] ain't a patching to an antelope when it comes to speed." **1915** *DN* 4.187 **swVA,** *Patchin'.* . . In *not a patchin',* by no means equal or comparable (to). "Slick Jim's coon dog's not a patchin' to mine." **1921** *DN* 5.116 **KY,** *Patchin'.* . . Usually used in unfavorable comparison, e.g.: "Nance ain't a patchin' to that Barnes gal." **1921** (1923) Greer-Petrie *Angeline Seelbach* 2 **eKY,** The Phoenix Hotel. . . aint a-patchin' to Miss Seelback's place. **1944** *PADS* 2.25 **cwNC,** *Patchin',* not a patchin' to: . . No comparison with. "Your dog ain't a patchin' ter mine." **1967–69** *DARE* (Qu. LL32, *Expressions meaning that one man's ability is not nearly as great as another man's: "John can't [or doesn't, or isn't]* _____ *Bill.")* Inf **TX**19, Isn't a patchin' to—old times; **TX**72, He isn't a patchin' to.

patch-nosed snake n Also *patch-nose (snake)* [See quot 1974]

A snake of the genus *Salvadora,* native to the southwestern US. For other names of *S. grahamiae* see **striped mouse snake**

1915 *Copeia* 15.4 **CA,** The following snakes were observed within one-half day's walk of the city of Los Angeles during the years 1913 and 1914: . . Patch-nosed Snake, *Salvadora grahamiae* [etc]. **1928** Baylor Univ. Museum *Contrib.* 16.15, Patch-nose Snake—*Salvadora grahamiae.* **1947** Pickwell *Amphibians* 44 **Pacific,** The Patch-nosed Snake [is] so named for the blunt nose formed by the rostral scale, which is free on all margins. **1974** Shaw–Campbell *Snakes West* 95, The patch-nosed snakes . . have an enlarged rostral scale, sometimes as extreme as the "leaf" of the leaf-nosed snake, that gives them their common name. *Ibid* 97, Where the western patch-nose is a snake of sage, creosote, and Joshua tree, the mountain patch-nose is found on rocky slopes or in grassy glades among stands of cedar and pine. **1979** Behler–King *Audubon Field Guide Reptiles* 650, Like the Western Patch-nosed Snake, this species [=*Salvadora deserticola*] can tolerate higher temperatures than most other snakes.

patch-poll(ed) coot See **patchhead**

patent-leather beetle n
=**betsy bug.**
   1954 Borror–DeLong *Intro. Insects* 382, Passalid Beetles. These beetles are called by a variety of names—bessbugs, betsy-beetles, patent-leather beetles [etc]. . . The Eastern species . . is a shining black beetle. **1980** Milne–Milne *Audubon Field Guide Insects* 555, Patent-leather Beetle . . (*Odontotaenius disjunctus*) . . Shiny black.

patent note n
=**shape note.**
   1822 Ely *Sacred Music, Containing a Great Variety of Psalm and Hymn Tunes; . . The Greater Part of Which Were Never Published in the Patent Notes* [title]. **1848** *Ladies' Repository* 8.286, The old patent notes, as they were called, are discarded in this book, much to the joy, we should think, of all lovers of good music. **1860** *Ibid* 20.215, Another work, called the "Minstrel of Zion" . . was stereotyped and published at Philadelphia. The music was compiled and arranged by Dr. S. Wakefield . . and was in patent notes. The system of patent notes being a mere sectionalism, and never becoming very popular, operated somewhat against the acceptability of the "Minstrel." **1895** Howells *Recollections* 143 **ceOH** (as of 1825), As it was very difficult to fix these syllables to the right notes, the books were printed in what they called patent notes. **1953** *PA Dutchman* 1 Mar 3/2 *(Mathews Coll.),* Here were the singers duly instructed in all the mysteries of 'the heavenly maid' as far as the 'patent notes' were concerned.

paterage See **partridge A3**

paternoster tree n Cf **bead tree**
=**Chinaberry 1.**
   1920 *Torreya* 20.22 **VA,** *Melia azedarach* . . Paternoster tree.

patet(t)a See **potato A1**

path n
1 Used allusively in var combs and phrr to refer to an outside toilet building.
   1967–70 *DARE* (Qu. M21b, *Joking names for an outside toilet building*) Infs **IN30, VA59,** (The) path; **MO20,** The bath with a path; **KY68,** Path house—always a path a-going to it; **WY5,** A path rather than a bath. **1986** Pederson *LAGS Concordance,* 1 inf, **ceLA,** So many rooms and a path—joking for outhouse. **1998** *DARE* File **seIA** (as of 1930s), The neighbors on the next farm had more money than we did. They had an indoor bath; we had an outdoor path.
2 See quot.
   1973 *DARE* File **ceMA,** Just recently at work, two of the guys (natives of Newton and Dedham) have used *path* meaning a part in the hair. 'I used to make my path on this side.' At first I thought they were kidding, but they weren't. That's what they call it.

pathmaster n Also *path man* [*DCan* 1799 →] **chiefly Nth** Cf **maintainer, overseer 2, patrolman**
One whose job it is to maintain public paths and roads.
   1842 Kirkland *Forest Life* 1.230 **MI,** So it is with regard to roads. The consultation about them, the choice of commissioner and of path-

masters, . . certainly tend to improve the faculties of those concerned. **1851** Turner *Hist. Pioneer Settlement* 126 **NY,** At the third town meeting, in 1791, Trueworthy Cook, of Pompey, and Jeremiah Gould of Salina . . , and James Wadworth of Geneseo, were chosen path masters. **1869** U.S. Dept. Ag. *Rept. of Secy. for 1868* 348, The immediate supervision of construction and repairs is generally under the direction of local "road supervisors," or "path masters," as they are termed in some districts. **1892** *New Engl. Mag.* 13.47, The average path-master has never given one hour's study to engineering, but is all the more self-confident that he comprehends all that needs to be known. **1950** *WELS* (A man whose job it is to take care of roads in a certain locality) **WI,** Pathmaster. **1965–70** *DARE* (Qu. N33) Inf **AL59,** Path man; **MI64,** Pathmaster—used to be called "pastmaster"; **MI71,** Pathmaster—years ago we used to call them; **MA58,** Pathmaster—Maine term; **PA104,** Pathmaster—old term; **NY32, WI31,** Pathmaster; **WI51,** Pathmaster—in charge of a mile of road, haven't heard for a long time; super pathmaster—head of a gang of pathmasters.

pathweed n
=**dog fennel 1.**
   1940 Clute *Amer. Plant Names* 74, A[*nthemis*] *cotula.* . . path-weed.

patica See **hepatica**

patience n
   1909 *DN* 3.356 **eAL, wGA,** Patience. . . A candy made of burnt sugar and pecans.

patience along v phr [Cf *OED2* patience v. 2 "*rare*"]
To endure patiently.
   1942 (1960) Robertson *Red Hills* 253 **SC,** I been here God knows how long—just patiencing along.

Patience Mary n
=**jewelweed 1.**
   1976 Ryland *Richmond Co. VA* 374, *Patience Mary*—impatiens (plant).

patient v [*OED2* 1551 →; "*Obs.*"]
To make patient; to content.
   1895 *DN* 1.373 **seKY, eTN, wNC,** *Patien'* (v.): content. "I never could patien' myself to keep pets."

pat it down See **pat** v 1a

pat jawbone See **jawbone** n 2

pat juba See **juba 1**

patootie n Usu |ˌpəˈtuti|; for varr see quot 1965–70   Also *patoot(y)* [Perh varr of *potato*]
1 usu in comb *sweet patootie:* A sweetheart or wife.
   1921 *DN* 5.110 **CA,** *Patootie.* . . [pəˈtuti] Sweetheart. Reported from four different localities. **1924** *DN* 5.274 [Exclams], Sweet patooty. **1935** *Nation* 15 May 562, He calls the object of his affection a "hot patootie." **1965–70** *DARE* (Qu. AA3, *Nicknames or affectionate names for a sweetheart*) 10 Infs, **scattered,** Sweet [pəˈtuti, -ɪ]; **FL19, NM5,** Sweet patootie; [**IL26,** Sweet [pəˈtuni];] **KY74,** Sweet [pətudijə]; **MS1,** Sweet [pəˈtudɪ]; **OK1,** Sweet [pɚˈtuti]; **PA148,** Sweet [pɪˈtuti]; **PA175,** Sweet [pəˈtut]; **AL10,** [pɑtu·ti·]. **1977** *New Yorker* 26 Sept 32, She was, successively, . . the wife and/or sweet patootie of the quartet. **1986** Pederson *LAGS Concordance (Girl friend)* 1 inf, **cnMS,** Patootie; 1 inf, **seLA,** Sweet patootie.
2 See quots. Cf **boody 2, doody** n[1]
   1967–68 *DARE* (Qu. X35, *Joking words for the part of the body that you sit on . . "He slipped and came down hard on his _____."*) Inf **MN28,** Patoot; **SC55,** Patootie—grandson's word. **1996** Evanovich *Two Dough* 224 **NJ,** Well, I thought, it could be worse. I could still be married to Dickie Orr, the horse's patoot.

patowga See **patager**

patri(d)ge See **partridge A2**

Patriots' Day n
The anniversary of the Battle of Lexington (April 19, 1775), observed as a legal holiday in Maine and Massachusetts.
   1894 *Boston Eve. Transcript* (MA) 18 Apr 8/4 **MA,** Lowell mill

agents, having heard the indignant protest against the running of machinery in the mills Patriots' Day, have decided to reconsider their action. **1925** *Ibid* 21 Apr 10/1 **MA,** [Headline:] Sesquicentennial of Patriots' Day passes into history. **1944** Holton *Yankees Were Like This* 243 **Cape Cod MA,** I don't remember just when it was that the Massachusetts legislature made up its mind it was silly to have a legal holiday called Fast Day on which nobody did any fasting. So they gave us April 19 instead and called it Patriots' Day. **1969** *Yankee* Feb 42, Observed only in New England are. . . Patriots' Day, Maine and Massachusetts, April 19. **1988** Nickerson *Days to Remember* 272 **Cape Cod MA,** Another change has been the lengthening of Cape Cod's season. . . Columbus Day weekend, Veterans Day, Washington's Birthday and Patriot's Day often see our streets crowded with cars "from away".

patrolman n Also *road patrolman, highway ~*
=**pathmaster.**

1965–70 *DARE* (Qu. N33, *A man whose job is to take care of roads in a certain locality*) 18 Infs, **scattered, but esp Upper Missip Valley, nNEng, Upstate NY,** Patrolman; **GA9, IA11, IL85, ME19, 22, OH103, TN11,** Road patrolman; **WI12,** Road patrolman—in county; **CO46,** Patrolman—it makes it confusing with "officer patrolman"; **VT4,** Patrolman—take care of large highway; **IL78, 87,** Highway patrolman.

patron See **pattern**

patruskie See **petrushki**

Patsy n[1] See **paddy** n[1] 1

patsy n[2] See **potsy** 1

patte jaune See **pied jaune**

patter See **pat** v 1a

patter cat n Also *pat-a-cat* Cf **paddle cat**
A children's ball game; see quots.

1969 *DARE* (Qu. EE11, *Bat-and-ball games for just a few players [when there aren't enough for a regular game]*) Inf **GA89,** Patter cat or town ball—played with a rubber ball. **1986** Pederson *LAGS Concordance,* 1 inf, **cwGA,** Pat-a-cat—ball game similar to dodge ball.

patterge, patteridge See **partridge A3**

pattern n Pronc-spp *patron, pattren;* for addit varr see below [Scots, Engl dial]
Std sense, var forms.

1771 in 1956 Eliason *Tarheel Talk* 315 **NC,** Pattren. **1799** *Ibid,* Partron. **1841** *Ibid,* Patron. **1852** *Ibid,* Pattron. **1899** (1912) Green *VA Folk-Speech* 314, *Patron.* . . For *pattern.* A model or plan. **1968** Kellner *Aunt Serena* 64 **IN,** A child could study lessons or a new crochet pattern (called "pattren") or read a few pages of *Pilgrim's Progress.*

pattige See **partridge A4**

patting See **pat** v 1a

pattipan squash See **pattypan squash**

patti-whack See **packwack**

pattren See **pattern**

pattridge See **partridge A2**

Patty n See **paddy** n[1] 1, 4

pattyauguh See **periagua**

patty-cake See **pat-a-cake**

patty-go-round n Cf **brother rounds, paddock, Paddy-got-drunk**
A **bullfrog** 1.

1963 *PADS* 39.14 **MA,** For the bullfrog, . . *patty-go-round* appeared in Seekonk.

pattypan squash n Also *pan squash, patapan ~, pattipan squash, pattypan (scallop)* **scattered, but esp C Atl** See Map Cf **bunch squash, cymling, dish squash**

A cultivated **summer squash** with a scalloped edge (here: *Cucurbita pepo* var). Also called **pancake squash, pie-crust ~, pie ~, round ~, saucer ~, scallop ~, ten-toed ~**

1863 Burr *Field & Garden* 208, Early White Bush Scolloped [Squash].—White Pattypan. Cymbling [etc]. *Ibid* 209, Early Yellow Bush Scolloped [Squash].—Cymbling. Pattypan. Yellow Summer Scollop. **1907** *Suburban Life* April 237 *(DA),* We put in four egg-plants, two hills of crookneck squash and two hills of pattypan squash. **1925** *Book of Rural Life* 9.5252, [Caption:] The large Hubbard squash for winter use is shown above, while below are the crookneck and "pattypan" types of summer squashes. **1950** *PADS* 14.50 **SC,** *Pan squash.* . . The cymling. So named from its shape. **1965–70** *DARE* (Qu. 123, . . *Kinds of squash*) 26 Infs, **scattered, but esp C Atl,** Pattypan squash; **KS20,** Pattypan squash—white, flat scallop squash; **NJ46,** Pattypans; **NJ56,** Pattypan—flat, white, knobs all around; **OH15,** Pattypan squash—looks like a yellow, round pie; **PA9,** Pattypan—white ones with scalloped edges; **TN4,** Patapan ['pætə,pæn] squash. **1968** *DARE* FW Addit **cnNY,** Pattypan squash—may be yellow or light green, round with fluted edges. Vegetable entry, Booneville Fair. **1984** Klein *Ceremonies* 387, Bert's married daughter, Irma, had just had an entire plot of pattypan squash wiped out, almost overnight, by a particularly voracious breed of corpulent grey slug that had never been seen in the area before. **1988** Whealy *Garden Seed Inventory* (2d ed) 344, *Scallop, Patty Pan* (Patty Pan White Bush Scallop). **1995** *DARE* File **csWI,** "Patti-pan squash"—sign at Madison, Wisconsin, Farmers' Market.

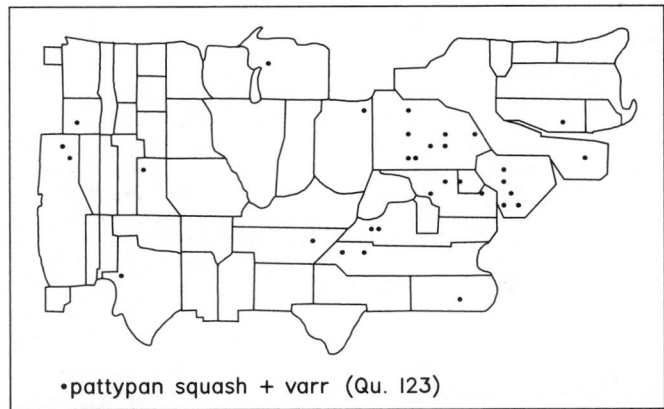

•pattypan squash + varr (Qu. 123)

patty pug See **pug**

pau adj |pau| [Haw] **HI**
Finished, done, consumed; hence phr *pau hana* work is finished; the time when or after one quits work; the afternoon or weekend.

1938 Reinecke *Hawaiian Loanwords* 28, *Pau.* . . Through; done; finished; used up. . . *Pauhana.* . . 1. Through work. 2. That part of the afternoon after quitting time. 3. The afternoon generally. **1942** *AmSp* 17.21 **HI** [English of Hawaiian children], *Through*[b] *finish* . . two words which have been almost replaced by a Hawaiian word, *pau.* **1967** Clark *All the Best* **HI** 55, *Pau*—finished; all done. No Hawaiian word is more thoroughly absorbed into haole speech than is pau. **1967** *DARE* (Qu. LL17, . . *There's no more of something: "The potatoes are _____."*) Inf **HI1,** Pau; all pau [pau]; **HI6,** All pau. **1967** *DARE* Tape **HI4,** During the night only. . . Twelve to four. When the chicken crow, four o'clock, pau . . no more work. **1969** *DARE* FW Addit **HI,** Pau [pau]—through, finished; e.g., Are you pau? *Pau hana* [pau 'hana]—after work, quitting time; e.g., a weekend store sale might be called a pau-hana sale. **1972** Carr *Da Kine Talk* 116 **HI,** *No pau yet!* . . 'It's not finished!' 'I'm not finished yet!' . . *pau-hana time.* . . 'Quitting time'. **1976** *Parade* 29 Aug 2, What's happened to the Dean Martin–Cathy Hawn marriage? I hear it's gone pau. . . L.G.L., Honolulu, Hawaii. **1986** *Amer. Tongues* (Video recording) **HI,** "If I'm in Honolulu and then it's quitting time, what do you say?" "Well . . you would use the Hawaiian term that everybody knows, which is *pau hana* ['pau 'hana] 'work is finished,' and everybody knows that." **1997** *NY Times* (NY) 2 Mar sec F 14/4 **HI,** "All pau, sir?" the Hawaiian flight attendant asks. The island businessman smiles, handing her his empty tray. "I certainly hope not," he says, "fo' real!" They share a laugh lost on the tourists across the aisle. . . "[A]way from Waikiki, dese haoles dey all pau, brudda," a friend used to say, cranking up his pidgin. . . In other words, when you travel outside the tourist spots, you're finished (pau).

pa'u n |'pɑ'ʔu| [Haw] **HI**
A woman's skirt; see quots.

1873 in 1966 Bishop *Sandwich Is.* 47 **HI,** Females wore the *pau,* a short petticoat made of *tapa,* which reached from the waist to the knees. **1938** Reinecke *Hawaiian Loanwords* 28, *Pa-u* [pɑ'ʔu]. . . A woman's skirt, especially a very full type of riding skirt in vogue half a century ago, and still seen in costume parades. **1951** *AmSp* 26.23 **HI,** *Pa-u* (a voluminous riding skirt). **1955** Day *HI People* 300, The women wore a short kapa skirt called a *pa-u.* **1984** Sunset *HI Guide* 85, *Pa'u*—wrap-around skirt.

paughaden See **pauhagen**

paugie See **pogy 2**

paugy See **pogy 1, 2**

pauhagen n Also *paughaden, pauhaugen, poghaden, pohagen, pohegan* [Of Algonquian origin] Cf **panhagen, pogy**
A **menhaden 1** (here: *Brevoortia tyrannus*).

1833 Smith *Nat. Hist. Fishes MA* 160 **NH, ME,** The menhaden, amongst the older class of fishermen, towards New Hampshire and Maine, bears the Indian name of Pauhagen. **1838** *MA Zool. & Bot. Surv. Repts. Zool.* 48, I have made an estimate of the fish caught by the fishermen of this place (Lynn). . . There are nearly three hundred and twelve thousand *pohegans* used for bait—and nearly as many thrown away, and strewed on the land for manure. **1843** (1844) Johnson *Farmer's Encycl.* 769, *Manhaden.* . . A species of herring frequenting the waters of the New England States and Long Island, where it goes under the various names of *Bony Fish, Moss* or *Marsbanker, Hardhead,* and *Pauhaugen.* **1859** (1968) Bartlett *Americanisms* 267, *Menhaden. (Alosa menhaden.)* . . It is also known by the names of . . *Mossbonker,* and *Pauhagen. Ibid* 313, *Pauhagen,* or *Pohagen.* See *Menhaden.* **1878** *Amer. Naturalist* 12.737, The Abnaki (*i.e.,* coast of Maine) name was *Pookagan* as Rasles wrote it. . . The older fishermen of Northern Massachusetts, New Hampshire and Maine called the fish by the Indian name "pauhagen," and I myself have heard it called "poghaden" by old fishermen about Cape Cod. **1910** Hodge *Hdbk. Amer. Indians* 2.212, *Pauhagen.* One of the New England names of the menhaden, or mossbunker. . . Other spellings are paughaden, poghaden, pauhagen.

pau hana See **pau** adj

pauhaugen See **pauhagen**

Paula Pry See **Paul Pry**

Paul Bunyan mosquito n
A **mosquito** n[1] **B1.**

1969 *DARE* (Qu. R15b, . . *An extra-big mosquito*) Inf **MI**108, Paul Bunyan mosquito.

Paul Henry See **Paul Jones 2**

Paul Jones n

1 also *John Paul Jones:* A circle dance that involves frequent changing of partners; a method of choosing or changing partners in a dance.

1920 *Atlantic Mth.* 126.89 **WA,** The whole sprightly, smiling, hand-clasping population seems engaged in one vast 'Paul Jones' . . with no one . . refusing to join the dance. **1948** Shaw *Round Dance Book* 398, *Circle Two-Step (or Paul Jones)* This favorite of all the circle mixers tends to be called, forthrightly, the "circle two-step" in many parts of the West. In other parts of the country it is called "Paul Jones." **1952** *American Girl* Apr 12 (*W3* File), I drew him in a Paul Jones and we bandied a few jaunty words. **1954** Basso *View from Pompey's Head* 210 **Sth,** The story is that he went to a party in Savannah, where one of his friends has a daughter who's coming out, and worked up enough ambition to try to dance the Paul Jones. **1965–70** *DARE* (Qu. FF5a, . . *Different steps and figures in dancing—in past years*) Infs **CA**136, **DC**8, **GA**11, **MA**48, **NY**87, **PA**205, 223, **VA**92, Paul Jones; **CA**113, Paul Jones—mixer, changing partners; **CA**209, Paul Jones—a two-step; **MD**26, Paul Jones—two circles, one within the other, music plays, when it stops, you dance with the person opposite you in the other circle—a mixer-type

dance; **CA**53, Paul Jones's—not as much changing of partners as a square dance; (Qu. EE2, *Games that have one extra player—when a signal is given, the players change places, and the extra one tries to get a place*) Inf **LA**2, Tag dance or Paul Jones—a dance in which one without a partner tags someone who has one. **1973** *NYT Mag.* 2 Dec 124, How graceful my grandmother looked, in spite of her bulk, doing the waltz and the John Paul Jones. **1986** Pederson *LAGS Concordance (A dance)* 1 inf, neFL, Paul Jones—new name for square dance. **1997** *NADS Letters* wMD, [I knew] "Paul Jones," aka "John Paul Jones" in Western Maryland, ca. 1950, when I was painfully, imperfectly learning the graces of ballroom dancing. *Ibid* csTX (as of 1950s), The specific version of the Paul Jones that was employed in the folk group that I belonged to was to form two concentric circles, males on the outside and females on the inside. While music played, the circles would rotate in opposite directions. When the music stopped, the circles were to stop, and each male was then supposed to dance with the closest female. *Ibid* ceTX (as of 1950s), When she did the Paul Jones, men would form one line and women would form another. The music would begin, and at the sound of a whistle the men and women would run toward one another and pick partners. These partners would dance with each other until the whistle was blown again. *Ibid* cTX, The arrangement . . is called the Paul Jones. I suggested that the motion by men and women in opposite directions continued while music played but stopped when the music stopped. He corrected me, saying that the signal to stop circling was the blowing of a whistle. *Ibid* seTX (as of 1930s), The Paul Jones was a good mixer. Often, during one dance the whistle was blown several times. Thus, one could dance with several people, meeting new friends (or not getting stuck with a jerk). *Ibid* **CT,** Paul Jones.

2 also *Paul Henry:* One's signature. Cf **John Hancock, ~ Henry**

1965–66 *DARE* (Qu. JJ13, . . *Joking words . . for a name signed to a paper:* "I'll put my _____ on that.") Inf **OK**9, Paul Henry; **ND**3, Paul Jones.

Paul Pry n Also *Paula Pry* [Popularized by the meddlesome character of that name in the comedy *Paul Pry* (1825) by John Poole, but see quot 1820; *OED2* (at *Paul* sb. 3.a) 1829 →] Cf **meddlesome Mattie**
A meddlesome or interfering person.

[**1820** in 1965 *AmSp* 40.131, [Song lyrics:] I've just dropp'd in to make a Call, I hope I don't intrude now, 'Tis but Paul Pry how are you all, Pray do not think me rude now.] **1840** *S. Lit. Messenger* 6.580, Here is . . no officious Paul Pry, to intrude on your retirement. **1875** in 1987 Alcott *Selected Letters* 193 **NEng,** I wish you'd write an article on the rights of authors, & try to make the public see that the books belong to them but not the peace, time, comfort and lives of the writers. It is a new kind of slavery & these horrid Paul Prys *must* be put down. **1892** *Harper's New Mth. Mag.* 84.549, He [=the gray squirrel] is the Paul Pry, the news-gatherer, of the woods. **1934** *Sun* (Baltimore MD) 27 Apr. 12/2 (*OED2*), The Senate's theory that the way to enforce the tax laws is to give the Paul Prys of every community access to the private details of every man's gross and net income. **1944** Adams *Western Words* 113, *Paul Pry*—A meddler. **1950** *WELS* (Names for the kind of person who is always prying into somebody else's affairs: "She's a _____." "She's the _____ person I know!") 1 Inf, **cwWI,** Paul Pry; 1 Inf, seWI, Paula Pry; (Somebody who is always meddling) 1 Inf, **cwWI,** Paul Pry. **1968** *DARE* (Qu. GG36a, *The kind of person who is always poking into other people's affairs:* "She's an awful _____.") Inf **CT**4, Paul Pry. **1985** Rattray *Advent. Dimon* 230 **Long Is.** NY (as of c1890), He seems to have taken a particular dislike to the two of you. I didn't know as he'd even noticed you, but he says he's sneaks and Paul-prys. **1998** Tyler *Patchwork Planet* 149 eMD, "Barnaby here is the Paul Pry Burglar," Len told Kirsten. . . "That's the name the newspaper gave him," Len said. "People would come home and find their silver still in place, stereo still in place; but all their mail had been opened and their photo albums rifled."

paunch n Usu |pɔnč, panč|; also **Sth, S Midl** |pʌnč| Pronc-spp *ponch, punch* Similarly adj *punchy*
A Forms.

1963 [see B below]. **1968** *DARE* (Qu. X50, *Names or nicknames for a person who is very fat*) Inf **GA**59, Punchy-fat. **1972** [see B below]. **1981** Pederson *LAGS Basic Materials* **Gulf Region,** [Of 31 exx of *paunch,* 13 had proncs of the types [pʌ(ə)nč], 9 of the types [pɔɔnč, pɒˑnč], and 9 of the types [pɑ(ə)nč].] **1982** [see B below]. **1985**

Wilkinson *Moonshine* 60 **neNC,** I didn't recognize you just now. Since I last saw you, you got a little punch on you. **2000** [see **B** below].

B Sense.

The stomach of an animal, esp as used for food. [*OED2 paunch* sb.2 c1420 →] **Sth, S Midl**

1850 Lanman *Haw-ho-noo* 134 **MI,** The largest perch I ever saw . . was taken from the paunch of a Maskinonge. **1859** Storke *Family Farm* 3.205 **NY,** The capacious paunch of the pig, and its great powers of digestion, are what render it so beneficial to us. **1899** (1912) Green *VA Folk-Speech* 314, *Paunch* . . the stomach of an animal. **1963** Watkins-Watkins *Yesterday Hills* 92 **cnGA,** A mad stone taken from the stomach or "punch" of a deer was supposed to prevent and cure rabies. **1966** Dakin *Dial. Vocab. Ohio R. Valley* 2.262, *Chittlins*—Many records do not include an entry for this item and others have various terms—*entrails, intestines, guts, insides, innards, paunch, bowels, casings . .* —which would seem to be simply general terms for intestines. . . *Tripe* appears infrequently in the field records for this item. **1968** DARE (Qu. H43, *Foods made from parts of the head and inner organs of an animal*) Inf **IN48,** Paunch. **1972** *Foxfire Book* 206 **nGA,** *Stomach* [of a hog] (*also called the "paunch" or "punch"*)—Cut the stomach free of intestines, split, and wash out well. Scrape it down and soak in salt water for three days. Then rinse, cut up, and cook like chitlins. **1982** Slone *How We Talked* 37 **eKY** (as of c1950), *Ponch*—hog's stomach. **1986** Pederson *LAGS Concordance* (Haslet) 5 infs, **Gulf Region,** Paunch; 3 infs, **nwGA, ceLA,** Paunch—stomach; 1 inf, **cnGA,** The paunch of a cow = beef tripe, stomach, edible; 1 inf, **cGA,** Paunch on a hog—same as "tripe" on cow; 1 inf, **nwFL,** Paunch has the goody in it, haslet; 1 inf, **cwFL,** Paunch of calf, hog, organs inside; 1 inf, **cAL,** Paunch of cow; 1 inf, **ceTX,** Tripe is the paunch—the stomach; 1 inf, **ceAR,** Paunch part—stomach; 1 inf, **csMS,** Paunch = tripe; 1 inf, **seMS,** Paunch—maw, in a hog, like the tripe; 1 inf, **cnAR,** Paunch—fed to chickens; 1 inf, **ceTX,** Paunch—of hog; 1 inf, **ceTX,** Paunch—generic term for cow's entrails; 1 inf, **nwLA,** Cow paunch—tripe; *(Chitterlings, intestines)* 1 inf, **cnGA,** Paunch—stomach, edible; 1 inf, **cwTN,** Paunch used to make chitterlings; 1 inf, **seMS,** Paunch—stomach, boiled or baked; 1 inf, **seMS,** Paunch—hog; 1 inf, **nwAR,** Paunch—intestines, before "guts"; 1 inf, **cwLA,** Paunch and guts—chitterlings; 1 inf, **cLA,** Paunch—something from butchered hog; 1 inf, **cAL,** The paunch—the tripe or stomach of a cow. **2000** *NADS Letters* **PA,** One friend's mother was from Easton, PA. . . Her grandmother made that Pa Dutch dish and her mother called it "Pig Punch." This friend is in her mid-to-late 60s.

paupaw See **pawpaw**

pauson n
=**bloodroot 1.**

1830 Rafinesque *Med. Flora* 2.78, Sanguinaria canadensis. . . Red Puccoon, Bloodwort, Redroot, Pauson, Turmeric. **1892** (1974) Mills-paugh *Amer. Med. Plants* 22-1, Bloodroot, red puccoon, puccoon, tetterwort, redroot, pauson [etc]. **1930** Sievers *Amer. Med. Plants* 14, Redroot. . . pauson. **1979** Erichsen-Brown *Med. N. Amer. Plants* 318, Puccoon root, red-puccoon, red Indian paint, redroot, pauson, snake-bite.

pave n
1 A pavement; a city street or pavement.

1835 *S. Lit. Messenger* 1.357, I met a friend on the *pave* last week. **1843** (1916) Hall *New Purchase* 65 **IN,** The *pave* [of a courtroom] was, of course, dust sometimes, sometimes mortar. **1851** Hall *Manhattaner* 39, Would that . . time-honored ex-street commissioner Ewen, were in New Orleans to behold *its paves and trottoirs.* **1882** McCabe *NY by Sunlight* 144 **NYC,** The silence and emptiness will be alone relieved by the . . rattling of a casual carriage over the stony pave. **1911** (1916) Porter *Harvester* 31 **IN,** Down the street went the Harvester, passing over city pave with his free, swinging stride.

2 =**pave road.** **chiefly Gulf States, GA**

1958 McDavid in Francis *Structure of Amer. Engl.* 532, In southwest Louisiana, chiefly but not exclusively among bilinguals, a concrete highway is the *pave.* **1961** *PADS* 36.11 **sLA,** We might begin with a small group of words that are positively confined to the informants of southern Louisiana. . . *pave* (paved highway)—12.9 [percent of 70 informants]. [*Ibid* 15, In only one interview, in which French responses were sought, . . a rather large number of such loan-words [from English] were elicited: pave [pe:v] (highway) [etc].] **1967** LeCompte *Word Atlas* 245 **seLA,** Hard-surfaced road made of concrete. . . *(le)* pave [9 of 21 infs]. . . paved [2 infs]. . . pave road [1 inf]. . . The response "pave" is used both in French and English. **c1970** Pederson *Dial. Surv. Rural GA* **seGA** *(Kinds of roads)* 4 infs, Pave; *(A paved road with a light-colored*

surface [or] *paved with concrete)* 1 inf, Pave. **1971** Wood *Vocab. Change* 149 **GA, LA, OK, TN,** *A road paved with concrete. . .* Pave [9 of c1000 infs]. **1986** Pederson *LAGS Concordance* (Cement road) 6 infs, **cn,swGA, neFL, csLA,** Pave; 1 inf, **cLA,** Concrete pave; asphalt pave; 1 inf, **ceTX,** Asphalt pave; *(Sidewalk)* 1 inf, **neTN,** Pave. [DARE Ed: Some of these infs may have been using *pave* as an adjective. All proncs are of the type [peɪv].]

pave highway See **pave road**

pavement n Pronc-sp *payment* **scattered, but chiefly C Atl, esp sePA; also Gulf States** Cf **palement**
A sidewalk.

1816 *N. Amer. Rev.* 2.247 **Boston MA,** How few of our young men are in the habit of riding on horse-back, and as to walking! a walk of three or four miles is apt to excite their surprise, and a feeling of something like degradation at being seen on foot off the pavement. **1872** Schele de Vere *Americanisms* 516, *Pavement* denotes in the United States more frequently the sidewalk than the paved street. This arises from the fact that, in the countless new towns springing up every year in all the new States, the sidewalks are generally first made, long before the roads are macadamised or the streets paved, and hence they are first spoken of as the *pavement.* **1907** *St. Nicholas* Oct 1111 **NYC,** The streets and not even the pavements can be blocked even for a few hours. **1937** AmSp 12.203 [Engl of PaGer area], The doctor, lawyer, or professor in a Pennsylvania German community. . . will, however, use words like . . 'pavement' (sidewalk), and many another word which might startle his colleagues from other parts of the nation. *Ibid* 205, [']Pavement,' and 'spritz,' for example, merit regular newspaper use, as also does, 'he left me do it.' **1949** Kurath *Word Geog.* 62, *Sidewalk.* . . Throughout the Eastern States *sidewalk* is in general use, excepting only the Philadelphia trade area, which extends westward to the Alleghenies, northward to the fork of the Susquehanna, and southward on Delaware Bay and Chesapeake Bay. Here the Philadelphia term *pavement* is current. **1954** DE Folkl. Bulletin 1.16, Pavement (sidewalk). **1956** Ker *Vocab. W. TX* 92, *Place to walk at side of street. . .* Pavement [1 of 67 infs]. **1968** DARE FW Addit **cnMD,** *Pavement* is used for what most people call a *sidewalk*—a strip of cement for pedestrians. **1972** *NYT Article Letters* **sePA,** In Philadelphia (25 years ago, at any rate) "square" was used in reference to a city block, and "pavement" for "sidewalk." **1972** *PADS* 58.17 **cwAL,** Sidewalk. Sidewalk (22 [of 27 infs]) is the usual term, but Eastern Pennsylvania *pavement* (4) also occurs. **1977–78** Foster *Lexical Variation* 32 **NJ,** *Pavement* 'sidewalk' proved difficult to elicit, although the word is used in this sense at least in the Philadelphia Suburbs and Central Jersey. **1986** Pederson *LAGS Concordance* **Gulf Region** *(Sidewalk)* 21 infs, Pavement(s); 4 infs, Pavement(s)—(same as) sidewalk(s); 1 inf, Pavement—old term for sidewalk; 1 inf, Pavement—in town; sidewalk; 1 inf, Pavement—in Philadelphia; 1 inf, The grass between the pavement and the street; 1 inf, Cement pavement—to walk on. **1996** Salvucci *Philadelphia Dial. Dict.* 51, *Pavement. . . Southern Phila., North Phila., Kensington.* sidewalk. Also *payment.* **1997** DARE File **Philadelphia PA,** Since my childhood (1950s) in Philly, I have heard and used the terms *pavement* and *sidewalk* synonymously. My family, natives of Philadelphia, still unconsciously alternate between these two terms. **1997** DARE File—Internet **cePA** [CoalSpeak], *Payment:* What you walk on when you're outside.

pave road n Also *pave highway,* ~ *street* [Perh **pave** n **2,** used attrib, but perh assim pronc of *paved road*] **chiefly Gulf States, GA**
A hard-surfaced road; see quots; rarely n *pave walk* a sidewalk.

1967 LeCompte *Word Atlas* 245 **seLA,** *Hard-surfaced road made of concrete. . .* pave road [1 of 21 infs]. **c1970** Pederson *Dial. Surv. Rural GA* **seGA** *(Kinds of roads)* 13 infs, Pave road(s); *(A paved road with a light-colored surface* [or] *paved with concrete)* 2 infs, Pave road; *(A paved road with a black surface)* 3 infs, Pave road. **1986** Pederson *LAGS Concordance* **Gulf Region** *(Cement road)* 48 infs, Pave road(s); 3 infs, Pave street(s); 1 inf, Pave highway—light-colored; *(Byway)* 7 infs, Pave road(s); *(Sidewalk)* 1 inf, Pave walk = sidewalk.

paw See **pa** A2

pawdogger See **pod auger** v

pawn n [EDD *pawn* sb.2 "In games: an article deposited by an individual player . . , and redeemable by some sportive fine or penalty imposed by the judge."]

=**forfeit.**

1771 in 1893 *Atlantic Mth.* 72.222 **Boston MA,** For variety we woo'd a widow, hunted the whistle, threaded the needle, and while the company was collecting, we diverted ourselves with playing of pawns. **1831** (1858) Smith *Festivals* 330 **NEng,** The village and country lasses enjoy their *spinning* and *quilting* bevies, singing-schools, and *pawn* parties, with at least an equal zest. **1897** (1952) McGill *Narrative* 137 **SC,** Some of the boys were skilled in the dispensation of suitable redemption of these pawns, and when exhibited to them they inquire: "Fine or superfine?" **1938** in Lib. of Congress *Amer. Memory: WPA Life Hist.* (Internet) **SC,** Then there was the game that everybody knows I guess. One person went around and took something from all the children who were going to play the game. . . One child sat in the center and the one who collected the pawns stood over the one in the center. He held one of the pawns in his closed hand over the one sitting down and said . . "Heavy, heavy hangs over your head." Child sitting: "Fine or superfine?" Child standing: "Fine (or super-fine, depending on what the object was). What shall the owner of this pawn do?" **1959** Lomax *Rainbow Sign* 36 **AL** [Black], We'd play a kissing game, like Fine and Superfine. . . [W]e all say to the one in the chair, say, "Heavy, heavy hang over your head." Chair say, "Fine, superfine." They all say, "What shall Nora do to redeem this pawn?" **1972** Jones–Hawes *Step it Down* 166 **eGA** [Black], When the players tire of the first game, the earning back of the "pawns" (the articles given up) forms a kind of coda. . . (The Islanders used the term "pawn" for both the forfeited article and the task assigned to redeem it.)

Pawnee lettuce n Cf **Shawnee**

=**lamb's lettuce.**

1847 Wood *Class-Book* 309, F[edia] olitoria . . *Pawnee Lettuce.* **1939** Medsger *Edible Wild Plants* 157, The Corn Salad is a native of Europe, where it is much cultivated as a potherb and salad plant. . . It is commonly sold in the markets about New York, where it usually goes by the name of Field Salad. The names Fetticus and Pawnee Lettuce are also used for this plant.

pawnhaus See **panhas**

pawpaw n[1] Usu |'pɑˌpɔ, 'pɔˌpɔ| Also *pawpaw apple* Also sp *papa(u), papaw, paupaw, pop-paw;* for addit pronc and sp varr see quots [Varr or doublets of *papaya*, orig applied to the tropical tree *Carica papaya* and its fruit] **chiefly Midl** See Map A tree or shrub of the genus *Asimina*, esp *A. triloba;* also the fruit of such a plant. Also called **banana B1, custard apple 2, dog ~ 1.** For other names of *A. triloba* see **fetid shrub;** for other names of var spp see **flag pawpaw**

1709 (1967) Lawson *New Voyage* 111, The *Papau* is not a large Tree. I think, I never saw one a Foot through; but has the broadest Leaf of any Tree in the Woods, and bears an Apple about the Bigness of a Hen's Egg, yellow, soft, and as sweet as any thing can well be. **1733** (1876) Byrd *Journey to Eden* 27, We also saw in this Place abundance of papa Trees. **1739** (1946) Gronovius *Flora Virginica* 61, *Anona* foliis ovalilanceolatis glabris nitidis planis. . . *Papaw-tree.* **1773** in 1845 Cist *Cincinnati Misc.* 1.265, Spent some time in fitting poles of pawpawwood. **1773** (1865) Jones *Jrl.* 47 **OH,** The wood . . is called paupaw, it is very light, and bears a kind of fruit in shape resembling a cucumber. **1822** Woods *2 Yrs. Residence* 227 **seIL,** Papaws, or pawpaws, grow in clusters of three or four on a shrub 20 feet high. **1830** Rafinesque *Med. Flora* 2.197, *Papaw, Custard Apple.* . . The *A[simina] triloba,* found from Ohio to Mexico. Fruit with a bad smell, but when ripe after frost, the pulp is sweet, laxative and healthy. **1849** Howitt *Our Cousins in OH* 77, Here . . the paw-paw, or custard-apple, was in bloom. **1894** Riley *Armazindy* 48 **IN,** And sich pop-paws! Lumps o' raw / Gold and green, jes oozy th'ough / With ripe yaller. **1897** Barton *Hero in Homespun* 335 **sAppalachians,** Elizabeth returned soon afterward from the woods, bringing with her the first ripe papaws, which were to serve as a relish for the frugal dinner. **1912** Green *VA Folk-Speech* 314, *Pawpaw.* . A fruit in shape and size like a banana. **1923** *DN* 5.217 **swMO,** *Pop-paw.* . . Papaw. **1942** Faulkner *Go Down* 178 **MS,** Laying right there by the road in that pawpaw thicket! **1965–70** *DARE* (Qu. I46, . . *Kinds of fruits that grow wild around here*) 89 Infs, **chiefly Midl,** Pawpaw(s) [DARE Ed: In the 22 cases where FWs recorded proncs, they were mostly of the type ['pɑˌpɔ, 'pɑˌpɔ]; single instances were recorded of [pəˈpɔ], ['papa], and ['ɔˌpɔ]. Proncs were prob recorded only when they seemed inconsistent with the sp *paw-paw* printed in the QR.]; **VA56,** ['pʌpɔ] apples; **VA78,** Pawpaw apples; **MS16,** Pop-alls; **VA24,** Pop-haws; (Qu. S4) Inf **FL6,** [pɔˑpɔˑ]; **MD13,** ['pɔpɔ] apple—develops a

cylindrical fruit, yellow, not edible—grows in bushes in swamps; (Qu. S17, . . *Kinds of plants . . that . . cause itching and swelling*) Inf **OK47,** Pawpaw—causes swelling of my face, but not everybody's; (Qu. T15, . . *Kinds of swamp trees*) Inf **IL96,** Pawpaw; (Qu. T16, . . *Kinds of trees . . 'special'*) Inf **AR48,** Cow cucumber has that great big white flower on it—another tree like the pawpaw; **IL55,** [pɔpɔ]—fruit tree, tastes like banana, green skin with soft inside, big brown trees. **1970** Green *Ely* 99 **TN** [Black], I was keeping customers supplyed with chalybeate water, flowers, berrys, pawpaw apples. **1982** Slone *How We Talked* 48 **eKY** (as of c1950), Pop paws—eaten for the fruit. **1998** *DARE* File **seOH,** Intrusive /l/ can also be linking . . , and it is common in southeastern Ohio and much of South Midland as well. . . Thus, I hear both "paw(l)paw" for the fruit (intrusive) and "draw(l)ing" (linking).

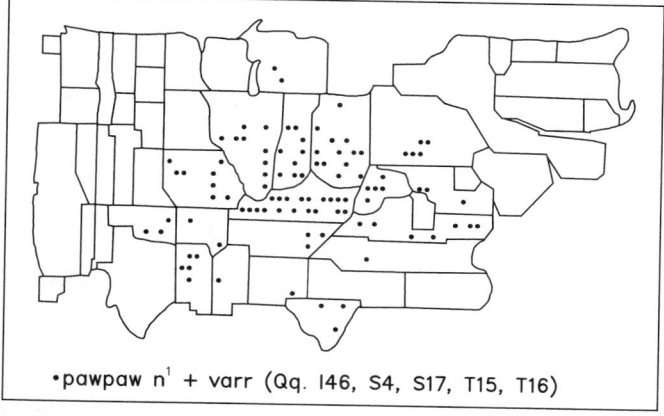

•pawpaw n[1] + varr (Qq. I46, S4, S17, T15, T16)

paw-paw n[2] See **pa-paw**

pawpaw apple See **pawpaw** n[1]

pawpaw gum n

A **tupelo gum** (here: *Nyssa aquatica*).

1924 (1925) Stansbury *Lake of Gt. Dismal* 101 **VA,** In many parts of the swamp cotton gum, known locally as papaw gum, is plentiful. It bears large leaves and fruit.

payment See **pavement**

payoff n esp **NEast** See Map The last straw; the limit of one's patience.

1965–70 *DARE* (Qu. GG22a, *When you have come to the end of your patience . . "Well that's the _____."*) Infs **IN32, MA71, NY10,** 32, 54, 59, 78, 113, **PA82,** Payoff; (Qu. GG22b, *When you have come to the end of your patience . . "Well, that certainly _____."*) Inf **WA3,** The payoff. [9 of 10 Infs old]

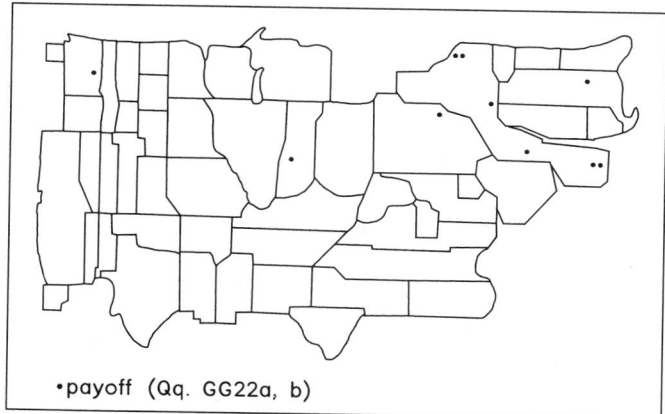

•payoff (Qq. GG22a, b)

pay of the fiddler See **fiddler, pay the**

payote See **peyote**

pay out v phr esp **S Midl**

To pay off a debt; hence ppl adj phr *paid out* out of debt.

1903 *DN* 2.324 **seMO,** *Pay out.* . . To settle in full; to get out of debt. **1906** *DN* 3.150 **nwAR,** "He's about paid out," i.e., "He has almost paid off his debt." **1942** Thomas *Blue Ridge Country* 280 **sAppalachians,** Clate was company-owned! If he lived to be a hundred he'd never be paid out. **1967** *DARE* FW Addit **AR**47, Pay out—pay up. **1984** Wilder *You All Spoken Here* 106 **Sth,** *Pay out:* Settle a debt with a farm owner if you are a tenant, or with a time-store merchant if you are a farm owner, when crops are sold.

pay the fiddler See **fiddler, pay the**

pay-toll (road) n

1968 *DARE* (Qu. N16b, *Names for a highway with two lanes on each side and a separation down the middle—if you have to pay to drive on it*) Inf **MN**19, Pay-toll road; **GA**40, Pay-toll ['pe,tɔl].

p.b. See **place back(s)**

pea n¹ Cf **peavine, wild pea**

1 Std: =**garden pea.** Note: The term *pea* is occas used for other legumes such as those of the genera *Phaseolus* and *Vicia,* but such usage is not regional.

2 =**black-eyed pea;** hence n *pea hay* the cut plant dried for fodder. **chiefly Sth, S Midl**

1787 in 1891 Washington *Writings* 11.179, Wheat . . will average about 4s. sterling per bushel. . . Beans, pease, &co., have not been sold in any quantities.—Barley is not made here. **1881** Phares *Farmer's Book of Grasses* 17 **Sth,** The Red Ripper, Black, Cow Pea and others yield a heavy crop of seed and hay. . . Peas sown in June rarely yield half so much vine and leaf as those planted in May. . . A hand will pick as many pounds of peas as of cotton in a given time. **1890** McAllister *Society* 97 **GA,** "What is pea pie?" I asked. "Cow peas and bacon," was the answer. **1932** Kelley *Inchin' Along* 55 **AL,** Everybody knows there is nothing a mule likes better than pea-vine hay with the peas left on. **c1960** *Wilson Coll.* **csKY,** Peas (that is, cowpeas or stock peas) grown on most farms of other times. Some used for hay. **1965–70** *DARE* (Qu. L9b, *Hay from other kinds of plants [not grass]; not asked in early QRs*) Infs **KY**84, **LA**2, 3, **MD**15, **MS**87, **MO**10, **NC**30, **VA**77, Pea hay; **GA**33, **NC**73, 81, Peas; (Qu. L9a, *. . Kinds of grass . . grown for hay*) Infs **FL**26, **GA**33, Peas; **MD**15, **NC**85, Pea hay; (Qu. I19, *Small white beans with a black spot where they were joined to the pod*) Inf **LA**28, Just peas, [corr to] black-eyed peas. **1967–70** *DARE* FW Addit **AL,** Order *peas* and you will get either *field peas* (black-eyed peas) or *lady peas* (small white peas); in order to get green peas, one must order *English peas.* I can't tell how many times I have gotten into trouble on this one; **KY**85, *Crowder peas:* white—a variety of field peas not usually grown in the garden; used for pea hay, though also used for human consumption; old-fashioned. **1972** Hilliard *Hog Meat* 275, There were several varieties of peas grown in the southeastern states. Known locally by such names as "crowders," or "blackeyes," they were much more commonly grown than green peas [=*Pisum sativum*] or any of the beans. The species was *Vigna sinensis* [=*V. unguiculata*]. **1981** Pederson *LAGS Basic Materials,* 1 inf, **GA,** Peavine hay—a kind of hay with which you pick all the peas off of it before cutting. **1984** *NADS Letters* **ceGA,** One student did report, however, that he had seen a movie in which poor people who couldn't pay fines were sent to work on public pea farms. **1994** (1995) Snead *Hollow Boy* 32 **nVA** (as of c1930), Uncle John complained that he couldn't get his pea hay made because it wouldn't stop raining.

3 =**vetchling. CA**

1911 Jepson *Flora CA* 238, *Lathyrus.* Pea. **1923** Davidson–Moxley *Flora S. CA* 192, *Lathyrus.* Pea. Much resembling *Vicia,* but the flowers larger. **1961** Thomas *Flora Santa Cruz* 220 **cwCA,** *Lathyrus. . .* Pea. Leaflets 2, tendrils well developed. **1974** Munz *Flora S. CA* 443, *Lathyrus. . .* Pea. Annual or mostly perennial herbs with rootstocks or sometimes taproots.

4 =**peanut 1.** Cf **field pea, goober ~**

1954 *Harder Coll.* **cwTN,** Peas. . . Peanuts; see *goobers.* **1970** *DARE* Tape **VA**70, We have peanut combine that will pick the peas all green and carry 'em to a dryer and dry 'em with gas heat and air, and a fan. And now one man can go out and do the whole job right by hisself.

5 in phrr *come nigh as a p(ea), come in a pea* and varr: To come very close to (doing something). **esp S Midl**

1901 Harben *Westerfelt* 131 **nGA,** Ward Billingsley wus thar at the house tryin' to get 'er to run off with him, an' . . Marthy come as nigh as pease a-doin' of it. **1909** *DN* 3.351 **eAL, wGA,** *Near as peas. . .* Very near. "I come near as peas killin' myself." Often *nigh as peas.* **1931**

PMLA 46.1304 **sAppalachians,** He come as nigh as a p gittin' thar. **1936** *Esquire* Nov 223 **KY,** If ever I meet the fellow that hit me with that rock we are going to tangle. . . W'y it come as nigh as a pea keeping me out of the war. **1959** Roberts *Up Cutshin* 14 **seKY,** You talk about white-eyeing on the job—I come in a pea a-doing it on my first job in the mines. [**1968** *Foxfire* Fall–Winter 24 **neGA, cwNC,** "Nigh as a pea" (meaning very close to).]

6 in combs *Pea Ridge, ~ Hill, ~ Sticks:* Used as a name or nickname for a small, poor, or out-of-the-way place. **chiefly S Midl** *derog*

1851 U.S. Post Office Dept. *Table Post Offices* 209, Pea Ridge—Union [Co.]—South Carolina. . . Pea Ridge—Montgomery—Tennessee. . . Pea Ridge—Benton—Arkansas. **1876** VA Bd. Immigration *VA Geogr. Political Summary* 257, *Seaboard and Roanoke Railroad.* Stations.—Portsmouth . . Pea Ridge . . Bower's Hill . . [etc]. **1949** Barringer *Nat. Bent* 23 **NC,** Although the farm lands in this valley were exceptionally rich, there was a god-forsaken pea-ridge between the two creeks so poor that it was practically untenanted. **1963** Berry *Almost White* 19 **KY,** In Cumberland and Monroe counties there are a similar people known as the Coe Clan, or the Pea Ridge Group. **1966–70** *DARE* (Qu. C34, *Nicknames for nearby settlements, villages, or districts*) Inf **NC**15, Pea Hill; **GA**9, Pea Ridge—county-line settlement; **KY**56, Pea Sticks—small community across Slate Creek; (Qu. II25, *Names or nicknames for the part of a town where the poorer people, special groups, or foreign groups live*) Inf **GA**23, Pea Ridge—colored section, Homerville; **TX**104, Pea Ridge—colored section. **1986** Pederson *LAGS Concordance,* 1 inf, **nwAL,** Pea Ridge—MS; 1 inf, **nwTN,** Pea Ridge—TN; 1 inf, **cnAR,** Battle of Pea Ridge—in Civil War.

7 in var combs: A thing of very little value. [By analogy with *hill of beans, row of pins,* etc]

1965–68 *DARE* (Qu. HH20b, *Of an idle, worthless person . . "He doesn't amount to _____."*) Infs **MS**30, **NC**33, **IN**19, Hill (*or* pot, row) of peas.

8 in phr *not to know peas:* To be very stupid. Cf **beans, not to know**

1965 *DARE* (Qu. LL16, *The most basic thing, the simplest thing: "He doesn't know _____ thing about plumbing.";* total Infs questioned, 75) Inf **MS**30, Peas.

pea n² Also sp *pee* [Prob back-formation from obs or dial *peise* understood as pl] **esp Sth, S Midl**
See quot 1946.

1761 in 1898 *Documents Colonial & Post-Revol. Hist. NJ* 20.529, To be sold. . . a large Quantity of old refuse cast Iron, . . Sash-weights, Stove-plates, Steelyard-peas [etc]. **1899** Green *VA Folk-Speech* 314, *Pea. . .* A pear-shaped mass of iron hung on the arm of steelyards and slid along, when ballancing [sic] the thing weighed the weight is read off. The weight used in weighing anything with the steelyards. **1903** *DN* 2.325 **seMO,** *Pea. . .* The balance weight of a steelyards or scales. **1909** *DN* 3.356 **eAL, wGA.** **1943** Writers' Program NC *Bundle of Troubles* 39, Uncle George set the pea at fifteen pound, and the beam jerked up. . . When he put the pea at thirty-five pound, the beam leveled off. **1946** *PADS* 6.23 **ceNC,** *Pea. . .* A sliding weight (counterpoise) used on scales and steelyard(s). Pamlico, 1900–. Common. **1954** *Harder Coll.* **cwTN,** *Pea. . .* A weight for scales. **1982** *Barrick Coll.* **csPA,** *Pee*—counterpoise of a steelyard of balance scale. **1986** Pederson *LAGS Concordance,* 1 inf, **swGA,** The pea—weight on cotton scale.

pea bag See **pea sack**

pea bean n **chiefly NEast, Gt Lakes** See Map
A **navy bean** or similar smaller, usu white, dry bean (*Phaseolus vulgaris* cv).

1863 Burr *Field & Garden* 467, *Pea-Bean. . .* As a garden variety, it is of little value, though the young pods are crisp and tender. It is cultivated almost exclusively as a field-bean. . . The Pea-bean, the White Marrow, and the Blue Pod are the principal if not the only kinds of much commercial importance. *Ibid* 468, By many, and perhaps by a majority, the Pea-bean is esteemed the best of all baking varieties. **1896** (c1973) Farmer *Orig. Cook Book* 211, *Boston Baked Beans.* Pick over one quart pea beans, cover with cold water, and soak over night. **1939** Wolcott *Yankee Cook Book* 101, *Baked Beans with Maple Syrup—[A Vermont recipe]*—1 quart pea beans [etc]. **1947** Bowles–Towle *New Engl.*

Cooking 66, You may own a traditional Boston bean pot, you may choose pea beans, . . but if you do not give beans a long baking, you will not serve the dish that New Englanders relish for Saturday supper and Sunday breakfast. **1965–70** *DARE* (Qu. I18, *The smaller beans that are white when they are dry*) 143 Infs, **chiefly NEast, Gt Lakes,** Pea beans; **MA**8, 34, 98, **NH**3, California pea bean(s); **MA**27, California pea beans—small; New York pea beans—large; **MA**40, York State or California pea beans; **MA**125, Pea beans or California pea beans; **RI**3, Pea beans—two kinds—New York State [and] California—smaller; **RI**9, California pea beans; **RI**15, California or New York pea [beans]; **MA**122, **TX**38, Pea [beans]; **MD**37, Soup beans, navy beans, pea beans—same thing; **MA**6, many kinds. Baked beans use pea beans; **NJ**8, Pea beans—look like pod of peas, only are a bean—mainly a Southern dish; **NJ**9, Soup beans—other people call them pea beans; **NY**48, Pea beans—used for baked beans; **ME**12, Maine pea beans; **MI**108, Michigan pea beans; **VA**7, Navy pea beans; (Qu. I19, *Small white beans with a black spot where they were joined to the pod*) Infs **IA**30, **IN**30, 76, 79, **MD**17, **NJ**5, **NY**1, 109, 230, **OH**65, **PA**128, Pea beans; (Qu. I14) Inf **NJ**8, Pea beans; (Qu. I15) Inf **KY**12, Pea beans; (Qu. I17, *Beans . . that are dark red when they are dry*) Infs **ME**5, **NC**50, Pea bean(s); **MA**15, Pea beans—dark red and white—came from Texas; (Qu. I20, . . *Kinds of beans*) Infs **NY**84, **PA**166, **SC**29, **VA**2, Pea beans; **NY**224, White bean, medium [bean], pea bean—all three [are the same as] the marrow bean; **CT**29, California pea beans. **1967** *DARE* Tape **MA**6, When they got thoroughly brown, she turned the beans into a bowl, . . poured boiling water over it, and told Dad he must drink the infusion. . . You have to have white beans, that's pea beans. **1972** *Yesterday* 1.2.30, By itself, the navy, or, its slightly smaller cousin, the pea bean doesn't taste like much. **1979** *Today Show Letters* ce**MA** (as of c1927), I discovered that what were listed in the Harvard Sq. cafeterias as "pea beans" were what in Kansas I had known as navy beans or, sometimes, white beans. **1981** Pederson *LAGS Basic Materials,* 1 inf, sw**GA,** Pea beans = navy beans. **1988** Whealy *Garden Seed Inventory* (2d ed) 33, *Navy* (Boston Pea . . Bean) . . pods with small white beans, . . excel[lent] for baked beans or soup. **1997** *DARE* File nw**MA** (as of c1920), My father always grew yelloweyes, yelloweye beans, so we always used these for baked beans. They're big beans. Some of my cousins used pea beans. They're little beans. My father used to call them buckshot. *Ibid* ne**MA,** My grandmother illustrated and contributed recipes to a cookbook published by her church in 1951. The only beans listed for Boston baked bean recipes are pea beans. Navy beans were used for ham and bean soup. Navy beans are big white beans.

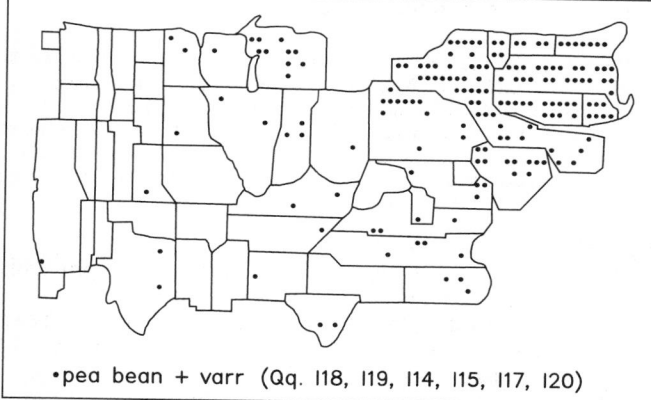

•pea bean + varr (Qq. I18, I19, I14, I15, I17, I20)

peaberry n Cf **coffeeweed 1a, pea tree**
Perh a **coffeeberry 2.**

1929 Dobie *Vaquero* 232 **West,** We "borrowed" some peaberry out of the mesquite, took water from our canteens, and boiled coffee.

peabird n [From its fondness for the **garden pea**]
1 Either the black-headed grosbeak (*Pheucticus melanocephalus*) or the **rose-breasted grosbeak.**

1872 *Amer. Naturalist* 6.397 **UT,** The black-headed grosbeak is. . . well known as the "Pea-bird," from its fondness for green peas. **1936** Roberts *MN Birds* 2.337, *Rose-breasted Grosbeak. . .* "Pea Bird." [*Ibid* 2.340, The most serious complaint against it [=the rose-breasted grosbeak] is its fondness for garden peas. In small patches where the birds are numerous it and the Baltimore Oriole may take the entire crop if it is left unprotected.]

2 =**Baltimore oriole.**

1917 (1923) *Birds Amer.* 2.258, Baltimore Oriole. Icterus galbula. . . Fire-bird; Pea-bird. [*Ibid* 261, The Baltimore Oriole. . . often gives cause for complaint by his bad habit of eating green peas; he sometimes strips the pods to such an extent that crops are severely damaged.] **1946** Hausman *Eastern Birds* 556, Baltimore Oriole. . . Baltimore Bird, Peabird, etc.

peabody bird n Also *peabody (sparrow), peverly bird, Sam Peabody* [Echoic] esp **NEng** =**white-throated sparrow.**

1856 Lanman *Advent. Wilds U.S.* 2.80, And here, by a strain now ringing in our ears, we are reminded of the fact that the quaint sweet whistling of the *Peabody-bird,* has accompanied us on our journey, all the way from the far off Potomac. **1865** U.S. Dept. Ag. *Rept. of Secy. for 1864* 422, White-throated Sparrow—Peabody Bird—Wheat Bird. . . This beautiful sparrow arrives in Massachusetts by the first week in April. **1885** Torrey *Birds* 83 **White Mts NH,** A farmer named Peverly was walking about his fields one spring morning, trying to make up his mind whether the time had come to put in his wheat. The question was important, and he was still in a deep quandary, when a bird spoke up out of the wood and said, "Sow wheat, Peverly, Peverly, Peverly!—Sow wheat, Peverly, Peverly, Peverly!" That settled the matter. The wheat was sown, and in the fall a most abundant harvest was gathered; and ever since then this little feathered oracle has been known as the Peverly bird. **1897** Chapman *Bird-Life* 188, Later, you will hear the sweet, plaintive notes that give to this bird the name Peabody-bird. **1902** *New Engl. Mag.* 26.218, The spring whistle of the Peabody sparrow, the cat-bird, practising broken bars of her medley song. **1909** *DN* 3.415 n**ME,** *Sam Peabody. . .* The white-throated sparrow, which seems to say *poor old Sam Peabody, Peabody, Peabody.* **1917** Eaton *Green Trails* 140 **MA,** When we reach this hedgerow, where the Peabodies are always fluting in early summer, the dog abandons us. **1940** (1948) Seton *Trail of Artist* 224, My sweet singer of the tamaracks, . . the night-singer of the Assiniboine, was neither more nor less than the white-throated sparrow, the Peabody bird of New England, the nightingale of the farther north. **1956** MA Audubon Soc. *Bulletin* 40.255, White-throated sparrow. . . Peabody Bird (All. One rendering of the song is "Sow wheat. Peabody. Peabody. Peabody."); Peverly Bird (N.H. On the same principle as the preceding.); Sam Peabody [sic] (Maine. Another syllabilization of the song is "Old Sam Peabody, Peabody, Peabody.") **1987** Stegner *Crossing* 5 **VT,** Off in the woods I hear a Peabody bird tentatively try out a song he seems to have half forgotten.

peabush n Cf **feather peabush**
An **indigo bush 2:** usu *Dalea* spp.

1931 U.S. Dept. Ag. *Misc. Pub.* 101.84, In general, livestock seem seldom to exhibit any fondness for the herbage of the shrubby peabushes of the Western States unless other palatable vegetation is absent or scarce. **1970** Kirk *Wild Edible Plants W. U.S.* 256, *Dalea terminalis* . . Pea Bush, Smokethorn. . . Pea Bush is found in sandy soil from western Texas to southern Utah, Arizona and Chihuahua. **1971** Dodge *100 Desert Wildflowers* 36, In common with other daleas . . it [=*Dalea fremontii*] is usually called "indigobush" or "peabush." **1985** Dodge *Flowers SW Deserts* 101, *Dalea* [spp] . . Smokethorn, Indigobush, Peabush.

peace n [*OED2 peace* sb. 13 a1310 →; *"arch"*] **widespread in literary use, but chiefly Sth, S Midl in oral use** See Map
In phrr *hold* (or *keep*) *one's peace:* To remain silent, not to speak—freq used in imper.

1745 (1888) Washington *Rules* 12 **VA,** Speak not when you should hold your peace. **1860** Emerson *Conduct* 171 **MA,** If you have headache, or sciatica, or leprosy, . . I beseech you, by all angels, to hold your peace. **1875** *Ladies' Repository* 1.399, She must learn when to speak, and when to hold her peace. **1954** *New Republic* 22 Nov 63, Believing that in time the solid human virtue of consideration for the rights of others would prevail, I should have held my peace. **1965–70** *DARE* (Qu. GG23b, *If you speak sharply to somebody to make him be patient . . "Hold _____!"*) 14 Infs, **chiefly Sth, S Midl,** Your peace; (Qu. GG23a, *If you speak sharply to somebody to make him be patient . . "Now just keep your _____."*) Infs **AL**28, **LA**8, Peace; (Qu. GG23c, . . *Expressions [to tell someone to be patient]*) Inf **VA**1, Hold your peace; (Qu. GG27a, *To get somebody out of an unhappy mood . . "Everything's going to be all right, so _____."*) Inf **NJ**64, Keep your peace. **1986** Pederson *LAGS Concordance* (Keep calm!) 2 infs, ne**FL,** ce**AR,** Hold your peace; 1 inf, se**MS,** Keep your peace a little.

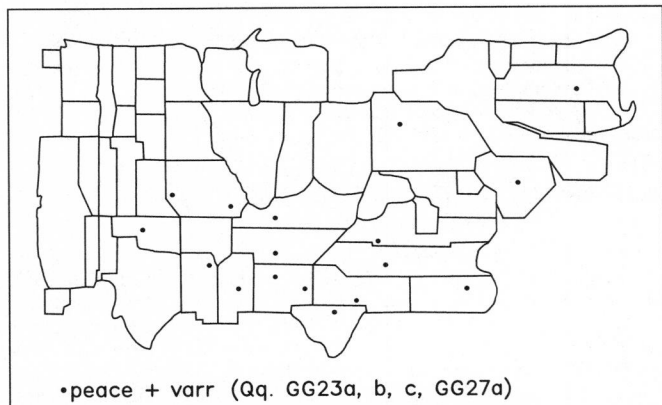

• peace + varr (Qq. GG23a, b, c, GG27a)

peacebreaker n Also *peace disturber* [*OED2* 1552 →]
chiefly Sth, S Midl See Map *esp freq among Black speakers*
A disruptive person, troublemaker.
1873 *Appletons' Jrl.* 10.431, Like the Quaker who, being sued for
debt, was horrified at being styled in the writ as "detaining money by
force and arms," complaint is made of injustice. "It is only the *stylus
curiæ*," explained the magistrate. "I don't know *curiæ*," said the Quaker,
"but he should not call us peace-breakers." **1965–70** *DARE* (Qu. HH26,
A person who is always ready to stir up trouble) Infs **CA**81, **GA**77, 83,
LA8, **NC**84, 87, **TN**48, **VA**69, Peacebreaker; **MO**23, Peace disturber. [8
of 9 Infs Black] **1986** Pederson *LAGS Concordance* (*Nicknames for
one who tattles*) 1 inf, **nwFL**, A peacebreaker; 1 inf, **nwLA**, Peacebreaker—adult who makes trouble, tattler.

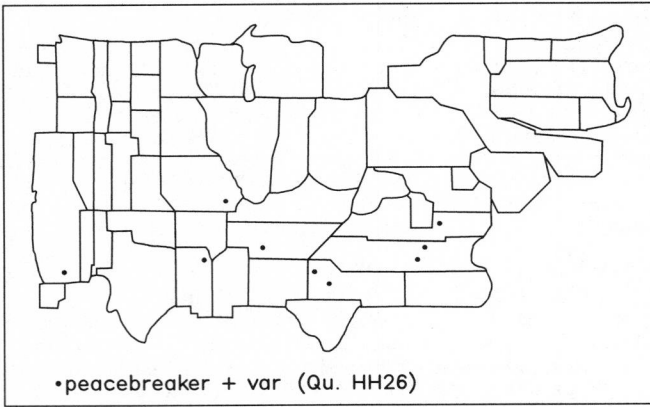

• peacebreaker + var (Qu. HH26)

pea chaparral See **chaparral pea**

peach b(r)ush See **wild peach**

peachleaf oak See **peach oak 1**

peachleaf willow n Also *peach(-leaved) willow*
A **willow** (*Salix amygdaloides*) native chiefly from the Great
Lakes region through much of the western US. Also called
black willow 1
1908 Rogers *Tree Book* 158, *Peach-leaf Willow.* . . Erect, straight-
branched tree. [*Ibid* 159, The resemblance of the foliage of this tree to
that of peach is striking. . . Rare in the East, it is common in the valley
of the Ohio, and along streams that flow down the eastern slopes of the
Rocky Mountains.] **1908** Sudworth *Forest Trees Pacific* 216, *Salix
amygdaloides.* . . This willow, also called "peach willow" (from a resemblance of its leaves to those of the peach), produces one straight, or
sometimes leaning, trunk. **1923** Abrams *Flora Pacific States* 1.490,
Peach-leaved Willow. . . A tree . . yellowish-green in mass-color, youngest twigs yellow, slender, somewhat drooping. **1950** Peattie *Nat. Hist.
Trees* 107, The Peach Willow, named for the shape of its handsome
blades, so like the foliage of the Peach, grows 60 or 70 feet tall. **1980**
Little *Audubon Guide N. Amer. Trees W. Region* 348, *Peachleaf Willow*—"Peach Willow." [*Ibid* 349, This [=*Salix amygdaloides*] is the
common willow across the northern plains.]

peach-leaved oak See **peach oak 1, 3**

peach-leaved willow See **peachleaf willow**

peach limb tea See **peach tree tea**

peach melon n Cf **vegetable peach**
=**mango 3.**
1956 Ker *Vocab. W. TX* 295, Peach melon—used instead of fruit for
pies in early days, longer than cantaloupe.

peach oak n
1 also *peachleaf oak, peach-leaved* ~: A **willow oak** (here:
Quercus phellos). [See quots c1830, 1947]
c1830 Martin *VA & DC* 209, Peach oak (so called from the resemblance of its leaves to that of the peach tree). **1884** Sargent *Forests of
N. Amer.* 154, Willow Oak. Peach Oak. . . A tree 18 to 24 meters in
height . . bottom lands or rich sandy uplands. **1890** Newhall *Trees NE
Amer.* 126, *Willow Oak, Peach-leaved Oak. Q*[*uercus*] *phellos.* . . Found,
from Staten Island and New Jersey southward along the coast to Northeastern Florida and the Gulf States, and from Kentucky southwestward.
1947 Collingwood–Brush *Knowing Trees* 199, The long, narrow entire
leaf, which is common to only a few other oaks, leads occasionally to
the common name—peach-leaf oak. **1980** Little *Audubon Guide N.
Amer. Trees E. Region* 404, Willow Oak . . "Peach Oak." [*Ibid* 405,
While superficially the foliage resembles that of willows, it is recognized
as an oak by the acorns and the tiny bristle-tip [of the leaf].]
2 A **tanbark oak** (here: *Lithocarpus densiflorus*). **West**
1884 Sargent *Forests of N. Amer.* 155, Tanbark Oak. Chestnut Oak.
Peach Oak. Valley of the Umpqua river, Oregon, south through the
Coast ranges to the Santa Lucia mountains, California. **1897** Sudworth
Arborescent Flora 179 **OR**, *Quercus densiflora* . . Common Names. . .
Peach Oak. **1967** *DARE* (Qu. T5, . . *Kinds of evergreens, other than
pine*) Inf **CA**31, Peach oak—a tan oak laurel; (Qu. T10, . . *Kinds of oak
trees*) Inf **CA**31, Peach oak.
3 also *peach-leaved oak*: =**shingle oak.** [See quot 1897]
1897 IN Dept. Geol. & Nat. Resources *Rept. for 1896* 616, *Q*[*uercus*]
imbricaria . . Shingle Oak. Laurel Oak. Peach-leaved Oak. . . Distinguished by its shining, lanceolate entire leaves, resembling in general appearance those of the peach. **1921** Deam *Trees IN* 119, *Quercus
imbricaria* . . Shingle Oak. . . It is also called black oak, peach oak, jack
oak and water oak. **1968** *DARE* (Qu. T10, . . *Kinds of oak trees*) Inf
IN35, Peach oak.

peach-orchard beau n [Folk-etym or perh deliberately punning var of **peach-orchard boar**]
A clandestine lover.
1949 *AmSp* 24.111 **ceSC**, *Peach-orchard beau.* . . Clandestine sweetheart. **1997** *DARE* File **MO**, My dad was from Peach Orchard, Missouri and my grandma used to talk about a *peach orchard beau.* It was
usually a "forbidden" romance by local standards, such as interracial, in-
cestuous, feuding families, adulterous, etc., hence the term *peach-orchard crazy* because of the extreme passion involved when you're doing
something you're not supposed to be doing.

peach-orchard boar n
1 also *peach-orchard pig,* ~ *borer:* Used in var proverbial
comparisons, usu referring to wild or unrestrained behavior;
see quots. [In ref to the practice of pasturing hogs in peach
orchards to eat the windfalls] **scattered, but esp Sth, S Midl**
Cf **peach-orchard crazy**
[**1885** *Century Illustr. Mag.* 29.681 **cTN**, An' don't stan' ther' a-
gawpin' like er runt pig in er peach orchard.] [**1953** Randolph–Wilson
Down in Holler 108 **Ozarks**, A candidate for Congress once said that
his opponent, a handsome fellow and popular with the ladies, was "wild
as a boar in a peach orchard."] **1967** *DARE* Tape **WA**30, [FW:] Can
you tell me how hungry you were before you started eating? [Inf:] You
mean tonight? Hungrier than a peach orchard boar. **1986** *DARE* File,
Crazier than a peach orchard boar. **1992** *Houston Chron.* (TX) 5 Apr
sec G 1, *Crazy:* . . Nuttier than a peach orchard pig. **1995** Brophy Coll.
54 **swMO** (as of c1960), Peach-orchard borer, crazy as a. **1997** *NADS
Letters* **nFL**, I have heard this from my native North Floridian in-laws as
"peach orchard boar." The idea is that wild hogs ate the peaches whole,
and became agitated when they passed the pits. Thus one can be "wilder
than a peach orchard boar." **1998** *Ibid* **TX**, I have . . heard the phrase
"peach orchard boar" all my life from mostly rural folks in West Texas,
East Texas, New Mexico, Oklahoma, Arkansas, Missouri and Florida. It
is a widespread and commonly used phrase always used as "drunk as a

peach orchard boar" or "crazy as a. . . " or "wild as a. . . ". This phrase comes from the fact that if hogs eat the rotting, fermenting fruit that has fallen to the ground . . they actually get drunk, stagger around, fall down, and run into things. *Ibid*, I . . often heard from my mother-in-law "crazy (or wild) as a peach-orchard boar." She explained that it was from the fact that pigs foraged among the fermented fallen fruit in peach orchards and got drunk and disorderly.

2 See quot. Cf **peach-orchard beau**

1953 Randolph–Wilson *Down in Holler* 108 **Ozarks,** The term peach orchard carries some obscure reference to sexual excess. General Daniel E. Sickles, of Civil War fame, used to be described as "the hero of the Peach Orchard," a phrase which sent any Ozark audience into gales of laughter. . . The phrase "peach orchard boars" is applied to men who appear sexually passionate and unrestrained. . . [I]n some sections of Missouri and Arkansas . . it is a serious breach of the proprieties to say peach orchard in polite conversation with respectable women.

peach-orchard crazy adj phr

1953 Randolph–Wilson *Down in Holler* 108 **Ozarks,** A very passionate, licentious woman is said to be "peach orchard crazy." **1997** [see **peach-orchard beau**].

peach pickle n **chiefly Sth, S Midl, TX**   See Map
A peach preserved in vinegar, sugar, and usu spices.

1827 Mrs. Hall *Letters* 165 *(DA),* One of the best pickles I ever ate is peach pickle. **1847** (1852) Crowen *Amer. Cookery* 397, *Mrs. Cowing's Peach Pickles.*—Take ripe sound cling-stone peaches . . ; make a gallon of good vinegar hot, add to it four pounds of brown sugar . . ; stick five or six cloves into each of the peaches, then pour the vinegar hot over them. **1864** *Hist. NW Soldiers' Fair* 139, [Donations include] 1 keg peach pickles. **1891** *Harper's New Mth. Mag.* 82.222 **eTN,** Jack, hev ye ever tasted my sweet-spiced peach pickles? **1957** Showalter *Mennonite Cookbook* 404, *Sweet Peach Pickle.* . . Sugar . . vinegar . . cinnamon . . cloves. **1965** *Colonial Kitchens* 146 **neGA,** Peach Pickle, No. 1. **1965–70** DARE (Qu. H56, *Names for . . pickles*) 40 Infs, **chiefly Sth, S Midl, TX,** (Sweet) peach pickle(s); (Qu. H57, *Tasty or spicy side-dishes served with meats*) Infs TN52, VA13, 18, 35, 42, 45, Peach pickle(s). **1986** Pederson *LAGS Concordance,* 2 infs, **cTN, ceAR,** Peach pickle—made of (the) Indian peach(es); 1 inf, **ceAL,** Make peach pickle of plum peach; 1 inf, **nwTN,** Cling peach used for making peach pickle; 1 inf, **cMS,** Peach pickle. **1993** Thomas Co. Hist. Soc. (KS) *Prairie Winds* Mar 6 (as of c1890), There were pickles as well, peach pickles, long yellow beans were pickled, chopped vegetable pickles, spiced gooseberry, . . one friend made brandied pears.

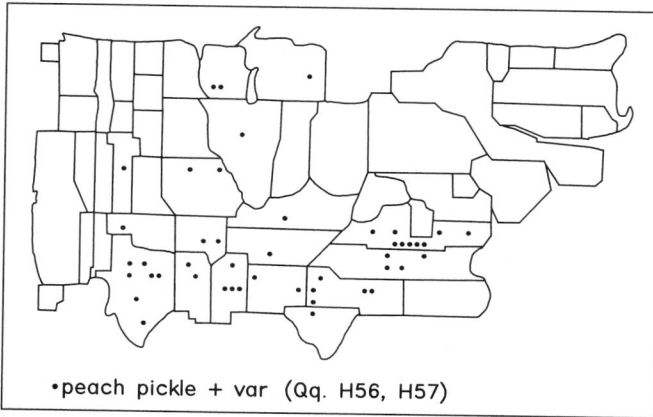

•peach pickle + var (Qq. H56, H57)

peach pit n
A type of hard candy.

1968 DARE (Qu. H82a, *Cheap candies sold especially for schoolchildren*) Inf **NY37,** Peach pits—hard candy; (Qu. H82b, *Kinds of cheap candy that used to be sold years ago*) Inf **NY99,** Peach pits.

peach thorn n **Desert SW**
A **wolfberry** (here: *Lycium cooperi*).

1925 Jepson *Manual Plants CA* 891, *L[ycium] cooperi.* . . Peach Thorn. . . Thorny compact densely leafy shrub, . . fruit . . subglobose, . . hard or bony at maturity. **1941** Jaeger *Wildflowers* 229 **Desert SW,** *Peach-thorn.* . . The several-seeded, greenish fruits, peculiarly constricted just above the middle, distinguish this thornbush from all others of its range. **1951** Abrams *Flora Pacific States* 3.667, *Lycium*

Cooperi. . . Peach Thorn. . . Fruit ovoid, greenish yellow. . . Desert mesa, arroyos, and slopes, . . California, to southwestern Utah, and western Arizona.

peach tree oil See **peach tree tea**

peach-tree rose n
The flowering almond (*Prunus triloba*).

1944 *PADS* 2.35 **nwNC,** Peach-tree rose. . . Flowering almond. The leaves are like those of a peach tree, and the flowers are like tiny roses.

peach-tree tea n Also *peach-limb tea, peach-tree oil*   **Sth, Midl**   Cf **hickory** n B3, **oil of hazel, strap oil**
A whipping.

1912 *DN* 3.584 **wIN,** Peach tree tea. . . Punishment with a peach tree switch. **1915** *DN* 4.187 **swVA,** Peach tree tea. . . Punishment with a peach tree switch. **1940** *AmSp* 15.215 **FL,** My mother never gave me any *hickory tea,* 'whipping'. . . but she talked a lot about giving me *hickory oil.* Peachtree-oil, though, was what she enjoyed giving me most. **1941** Writers' Program *Guide AR* 87, Students . . were grouped according to their ability in reading or arithmetic, and the wayward were urged on with liberal doses of "peach limb tea." c**1960** *Wilson Coll.* **csKY,** Peach tree tea. . . A switching. The peach tree holds the same place in MC [=Mammoth Cave] area that the birch does in more northern sections; this is shared, on a rougher scale, with the hickory, which seems useful in many areas. **1972** *Press* (Pittsburgh PA) 10/2, A whipping is "peach tree tea" in Georgia, but in Arkansas it is "peach limb tea." **1972** DARE File **IN** (as of c1920), Peach tree tea. . . A whipping. **1984** Gilmore *Ozark Baptizings* 178 **MO,** Veiled or overt threats of arrest were frequent, though one editor recommended the more direct approach of administering a little "'peach tree tea,' which would do the kids more good in less time than all the courts in America."

peach willow See **peachleaf willow**

peachwort n [*OED2* 1597]
A **lady's thumb** (here: *Polygonum persicaria*).

1876 Hobbs *Bot. Hdbk.* 87, Peach wort, Heartsease, Polygonum persicaria. **1900** Lyons *Plant Names* 300, P[olygonum] Persicaria. . . Lover's-pride, Peachwort [etc]. **1940** Clute *Amer. Plant Names* 139, *P[olygonum] persicaria.* . . heart's-ease, peach-wort [etc].

peacify v
To pacify, quiet, bring peace to; hence adj *peacified* pacified, peaceable.

1887 *Scribner's Mag.* 1.590 **wMD** [Black], Marse Archie tell her not to worry, dat he gwine 'member he's his pa . . , an' he peacify her, an' dey talk long time. **1902** *DN* 2.241 **sIL,** Peacify. . . To soothe, to quiet, or subdue. **1903** *DN* 2.323 **seMO,** Pacify. . . Pronounced peacify ['pisɪfaɪ]. **1930s** in 1944 *ADD* 446 **eWV,** Peacify. . . To pacify. . . Usual. **1942** Berrey–Van den Bark *Amer. Slang* 269.1, Peacify, *to pacify.* **1952** Brown *NC Folkl.* 1.574, Peacified. . . Peaceable.

pea clam n
A **freshwater clam** of the family Sphaeriidae.   Also called **pill clam**

1992 Cummings–Mayer *Field Guide Freshwater Mussels MW* 172, *Fingernailclams and Peaclams* (Family Sphaeriidae) *Musculium, Piscidium,* and *Sphaerium.* . . Shell rounded to slightly oval and inflated. . . Peaclams. . . have disappeared from many streams where they were formerly abundant (such as the Illinois River).

peacock sunfish n
1 =**flier 2.** [See quot 1933]
1933 John G. Shedd Aquarium *Guide* 92, *Centrarchus macropterus*—Round Sunfish; Peacock Sunfish; Flier. . . The young have an ocellated black spot on the soft part of the dorsal fin similar to the spots on the peacock's tail. **1991** Amer. Fisheries Soc. *Common Names Fishes* 177, Sunfish, . . peacock—see flier.
2 Any of several **sunfish** of the genus *Lepomis;* see quot.
1949 Caine *N. Amer. Sport Fish* 43, This plethora of nicknames [listed below] covers the pumpkinseed and its six closely related cousins. . . Big-ear Bream . . Peacock Sunfish [etc].

peadabber n Cf **jackleg** adj 1
1930 *Herald–Advt.* (Huntington WV) 30 Nov sec 3 6/8 **KY, WV,** Describing lawyers, two words are often used—"jack-leg" and "pea-

dabber." The former relates to one who has but recently hung out his shingle; the latter, to one who is venerable.

peadoodle See **peedoodle** n

pea-eater n Cf **pea soup 2**
    1966 *DARE* (Qu. HH28, *Names and nicknames . . for people of foreign background: French*) Inf **SD5**, Pea-eaters.

pea eye n[1]
A small, round eye; hence adj *pea-eyed.*
    1966–70 *DARE* (Qu. X21b, *If the eyes are very sharp or piercing*) Infs **FL33, MO23, NJ33**, Pea-eyed; **OH65**, Pea eye; (Qu. X21c, *If the eyes are very round*) Inf **FL33**, Pea-eyed—small, round, beady eyes; **MS16**, Pea eyes—very small eyes.

pea eye n[2] See **P.I.**

pea-eyed See **pea eye** n[1]

pea ham See **ham** n[2]

pea hay See **pea** n[1] **2**

pea hill See **pea** n[1] **6**

pea hulling n Also *pea shelling, ~ whipping* [**hull** v **1**] **sAppalachians** Cf **bean hulling**
A social gathering or *bee* at which peas are shelled.
    1919 *Jrl. Amer. Folkl.* 32.388 **NC**, Formerly, a decade or so ago, people would have large quilting-parties, likewise "a corn-huskin'" and a "pea-whippin'," when corn was to be husked or peas shelled. On these occasions a "big dinner" was supplied. **1967** *Hall Coll.* **wNC, eTN,** *Pea-shellin'. . .* A get-together or party at someone's home to shell peas. "They had corn-shuckin's and pea-shellin's. They used to have molassy-pullin's." **1969** *DARE* (Qu. FF2, . . *Kinds of parties*) Inf **KY5**, Pea hullings. **1978** in **1996** *Montgomery Coll.* **eTN,** We didn't have anything like children do nowadays to entertain ourselves, just being at home and going to a corn shucking or a pea hulling or something like that. *Ibid,* They'd gather together, a bunch of girls and boys, and have what they call pea hulling. *Ibid,* They had corn shuckin's and pea shellin's. **1986** Pederson *LAGS Concordance,* 1 inf, **ceTN,** Pea-hulling—parties.

peak and pine v phr [*OED2* (at *peak* v.[1] 4) 1605 →]
To go about dispiritedly or listlessly; hence adj phr *peaked and pined* (or *piney*) listless, sickly.
    1851 *N. Amer. Rev.* 72.141, He is left to "peak and pine"—to wander "a man forbid." **1872** *Appletons' Jrl.* 7.287 **GA,** The latter, a little round, dumpy body, with a face that naturally ought to have been fat, glistening, and cheerful, but was in reality "peaked and pined," rocked backward and forward. **1898** Westcott *Harum* 149 **NY,** She peaked an' pined, an' died when Billy P. was about fifteen or so. **1902** (1904) Rowe *Maid of Bar Harbor* 5 **ME,** That any woman . . should peak and pine into such a faded middle age. **1957** *DE Folkl. Bulletin* 1.28, Peaked and piney (not feeling up to par).

peaked adj Usu |'pikɪd|; also esp **nNEng** |'pɪkɪd|; occas |pikt|; rarely |pɪkt|; for other varr see quots 1965–70, 1981 Pronc-spp *peekid, picked, pickid*
Std senses, var forms.
    1864 in **1986** Messer *Civil War Letters* 26 **VT,** I have seen Nathaniel he thinks you look rather picked but Simon is fat as a pig. **1914** *DN* 4.78 **ME, nNH,** Pickid. . . feeble, in poor health. "Sarah's mighty pickid this winter." **1941** *LANE* Map 459 (*Emaciated, peaked*), [In **CT, RI, MA,** and much of **VT,** proncs of the type ['pikɪd] are the most common; in **NH** and **ME,** those of the type ['pɪkɪd] occur almost exclusively; [pikt] and [pɪkt] occur rarely.] **1965–70** *DARE* (Qu. X52, . . *A person . . who had been sick was looking _____*) 255 Infs, **widespread,** Peaked [proncs of the type ['pikəd, -ɪd, -ɪd]]; **TX39, 51,** [pikɪd]—old-fashioned; **MI33,** ['pikəd]—older people; **NY69,** ['pikɪd]—you never hear that any more; 10 Infs, **scattered,** [pikt]; **NJ67,** ['pikɪd], [pikt]; **CA93, ME5, MA4,** [Proncs of the type ['pɪkɪd, -əd, -ɛd]]; **ME15,** ['pikɛd]—some say ['pɪkɛd]; **GA7,** ['pikɪt]; **LA3,** ['pikɪt]; **UT12,** ['pikɪd]; **VA65, 90, 93,** ['pikɪt]; 6 Infs, Peaked [no transcription]; (Qu. BB38, *When a person doesn't look healthy, or looks as if he hadn't been well for some time . . "He looks _____."*) 260 Infs, **widespread,** Peaked [proncs of the type ['pikəd, -ɪd, -ɪd]]; **NY69, 211, TX40,** ['pikɪd, -ɪd]—old-fashioned; 13 Infs, **esp NEast, N Cent,** [pikt]; **GA84,**

['pikɪd]; [pikt]—common; **MI13,** ['pikəd]; might also hear [pikt]; **TN3,** ['pɪkɪd] or [pikt]—old-fashioned; **SC44,** ['pikɪd]; **IL25, WA6,** ['piəkəd, -ɪd]; **IL36,** ['pɪʌkɪd] [FW: pronc of first vowel about halfway between [i] and [ɪ]]; **LA3, NY27,** ['pikɪt]; 23 Infs, **scattered,** Peaked [no transcription]. **1975** Gould *ME Lingo* 204, You look a little pee-kid. **1981** Pederson *LAGS Basic Materials,* 1 inf, **csGA,** [p'iˇikɪd]—older term; 2 infs, **ceAL, seLA,** [p'iˇkt]; 1 inf, **nwMS,** [p'iˇkt], [p'iˇd] [sic]; 1 inf, **swMS,** [p'ɪ̆iˇkɪs] [sic]; 1 inf, **swMS,** She says [p'ɪ̆iˇkt]; some say ['p'ɪ̆ikt]; 1 inf, **csLA,** [p'iˇkɪt]; 1 inf, **csLA,** [p'ɪ̆ŋkɪ^] [sic]. [*DARE* Ed: The *LAGS Technical Index* lists 342 exx of *peaked,* but gives no indication of pronc.]

peaked and piney See **peak and pine**

peaked-bill n
=**hooded merganser.**
    1923 U.S. Dept. Ag. *Misc. Circular* 13.7 **SC,** Hooded Merganser. . . Vernacular names. . . *In local use.* . . peaked-bill.

peakedy adj Cf Intro "Language Changes" III.1, **fadedy**
Peaked.
    1956 Algren *Walk on the Wild Side* 65 **wTX,** Folks looken a little peakedy. **1981** Pederson *LAGS Basic Materials,* 1 inf, **neGA,** Looks ['p'iˇkɪdiˇ]; 1 inf, **swGA,** You look ['p'ɪ̆gɪdi].

peaking adj
Sickly, peaked.
    1902 (1904) Rowe *Maid of Bar Harbor* 5 **ME,** Four strong, stout, healthy boys! And every one after the same pattern,—no pindlin', peakin', half-breeds, but Hadlocks to the backbone. **1941** *LANE* Map 459 (*Emaciated, peaked*) 1 inf, **swCT,** [pikɪn].

peaky adj Also *peakish* [Varr of *peaked*]
Sickly, peaked.
    1877 Bartlett *Americanisms* 455, Peaky or peeky. Sickly-looking; peakish. **1888** *Scribner's Mag.* 3.69 **NYC,** Her mother said she was a "peaky, Miss Nancy sort of a fussy child." **1932** Stribling *Store* 123 **AL,** I feel sorter peaky. **1941** *LANE* Map 459 (*Emaciated, peaked*) 1 inf, **Block Is. RI,** ['pikɪʃ]. **1958** *DE Folkl. Bulletin* 1.32, Peaky (sickly looking). **1965–70** *DARE* (Qu. BB38, *When a person doesn't look healthy, or looks as if he hadn't been well for some time . . "He looks _____."*) Infs **IL138, KY94, MI13, NY40, 80, OR3, SC4, 32, WV20,** Peaky; **NC72, NY226, SC19,** Peakish; (Qu. X52, . . *A person . . who had been sick was looking _____*) Infs **CA184, 202, FL25, NY20, SC66,** Peaky; **MD9,** Peakish. **1979** *Verbatim* 6.3.14 **MO,** Peaky meant 'poorly' and 'not up to snuff.' **1986** Pederson *LAGS Concordance* (*Someone's been sick a while; he's up and about now, but still looks a bit _____*) 6 infs, **FL, MS, LA,** Peakish; 1 inf, **nwFL,** Peaky.

peal v[1] See **peel** v[2]

peal n, v[2] See **pial**

pea lark n [Var of **field lark**] Cf **fee lark**
=**meadowlark 1.**
    1966 *DARE* (Qu. Q15, . . *Kinds of larks*) Inf **GA7,** Pea lark ['pilɑˇk]—same as field lark. **1986** Pederson *LAGS Concordance,* 1 inf, **swLA,** Pea larks.

pealay See **piler**

pealer See **peeler** n[2]

pea-lip sucker n
=**harelip sucker.**
    1889 U.S. Natl. Museum *Proc. for 1888* 11.45 **IN,** *Lagochila lacera.* . . It is known here as the Pea-lip Sucker. **1897** U.S. Natl. Museum *Bulletin* 47.199, *Lagochila lacera.* . . Rabbit-mouth Sucker; Pea-lip Sucker. **1902** Jordan–Evermann *Amer. Fishes* 66, Genus *Lagochila.* . . This is the most peculiar genus of suckers and may be known readily by the nonprotractile upper lip and the split lower lip. The single species is the hare-lip sucker, cutlips, split-mouth sucker, rabbit-mouth sucker, pea-lip sucker, or May sucker, *L. lacera.* . . It is most common in the Ozark region.

peamouth n
A **minnow B1** (here: *Mylocheilus caurinus*) native to rivers of the northwestern US. Also called **freshwater herring 2, trout, whitefish**

1957 Blair et al. *Vertebrates U.S.* 104, *Mylocheilus caurinum.* . . Peamouth. Columbia River system and north to the Fraser River. Recorded from Montana, Idaho, Oregon, Washington [etc]. **1966** *DARE* (Qu. P3, *Freshwater fish that are not good to eat*) Inf **MT**4, Peamouths. **1971** Brown *Fishes MT* 95, In early times the peamouth was called "whitefish" around Flathead Lake and was served in the hotels and restaurants there. **1983** *Audubon Field Guide N. Amer. Fishes* 427, *Peamouth.* . . Mouth small; *barbel present* at each corner of jaw. *Ibid* 428, The Peamouth. . . lives about 13 years, unusually long for a minnow. **1991** *Amer. Fisheries Soc. Common Names Fishes* 124, Chub . . peamouth—see peamouth.

peanukle See **pinochle**

peanut n

1 Std: a legume *(Arachis hypogaea)* cultivated esp in the southern US for its edible seed, for the oil produced from the seed, and as a forage crop. Also called **field pea, goober** n[1] **1, ~ pea, googleberry, grass nut 4, groundnut B2, ground pea 1, grundniss, hognut 3, hog peanut 2, monkey food 2, ~ nut 1, pea** n[1] **4, pignut 5, pinder, spudnut, underground pea**

2 Used in the names of var social gatherings at which peanuts are shelled or eaten.

1933 Rawlings *South Moon* 235 **FL**, In September he had let a setting of mash go flat because he had promised to go with her to a peanut-boiling. **1941** Writers' Program *Guide WV* 347 **ceWV**, Whole families walk five or six miles to enjoy a few hours of entertainment at pie suppers, peanut socials, square dances, and bingo parties. **1966–68** *DARE* (Qu. FF2, . . *Kinds of parties*) Infs **GA**8, **SC**11, Peanut boilings; **SC**58, Peanut picking—old-fashioned; **GA**28, Peanut shelling—old-fashioned. **1986** Pederson *LAGS Concordance*, 1 inf, **swGA**, Peanut boiling—party, when young; 1 inf, **cnFL**, A peanut boiling—at the church; 1 inf, **swAL**, Peanut parching—sometimes after weddings; 1 inf, **neMS**, Peanut parching; 1 inf, **csGA**, Peanut shellings—held in winter; 2 infs, **swGA, cnFL**, Peanut shellings.

3 A small or insignificant person—sometimes used as an affectionate term for a small child.

1915 *DN* 4.203, *Peanut*, an insignificant person. "You peanut!" **1919** *DN* 5.69 **NM** [Among hs students], *Peanut*, a term of disparagement. "He is a peanut, but he is clever." **1934** (1940) Weseen *Dict. Amer. Slang* 377, *Peanut*—An insignificant person; a pugnosed person. **1967–70** *DARE* (Qu. Z12, *Nicknames and joking words meaning 'a small child'*: "He's a healthy little _____.") Infs **CT**5, **NJ**35, **VA**93, Peanut; (Qu. NN12a, *Things that people say to put a child off when he asks too many questions:* "What's that for?") Inf **NY**30, That's enough from peanuts. **1981** *Children's Folkl. Newsl.* Spring 3 **ceMN**, Peanut. . . Small boy. **1996** *DARE* File **csWI**, The nurses at the Children's Hospital frequently refer affectionately to an infant, and occasionally to a toddler, as "peanut" or as "a peanut."

4 A small or insignificant enterprise; esp used in nicknames for a local train.

1938 Hertzler *Horse & Buggy Dr.* 86 **KS** (as of early 20th cent), The trains were made up of "shoebox" coaches. One of these, the "peanut special" which many Missourians will recognize, was a fair example. **1950** *WELS (Names for a train that stops at every station along the way)* 1 Inf, **cwWI**, Peanut Limited; (*Joking names for a branch railroad that is not very important or that does not give the best of service*) 1 Inf, **cwWI**, Peanut train; 1 Inf, **cwWI**, Peanut Special or Peanut Limited. **1961** Hall *String Too Short* 136 **NH**, The old Boston and Maine train which I always took from North Station [Boston] was called the Peanut in New Hampshire. (Once it had been the *Pénult* and went to Montreal.) It stopped every two miles. **1967** Fetterman *Stinking Creek* 40 **seKY**, I just shop around these little places—I call them peanut stores. **1967–69** *DARE* (Qu. N37, *Joking names for a branch railroad that is not very important or gives poor service*) Infs **IL**81, **TN**6, Peanut; **NY**226, Peanut—one near Akron, taken out; **NY**176, Peanut Line; **CA**23, The Peanut Special.

5 Used in nicknames for small or out-of-the-way places; see quot. *derog* Cf **pea** n[1] **6**

1968–70 *DARE* (Qu. C33, . . *Joking names . . for an out-of-the-way place, or a very small or unimportant place*) Inf **PA**131, Hick village, Peanutsville; (Qu. C35, *Nicknames for the different parts of your town or city*) Inf **MI**115, Peanut Row.

6 A **freshwater clam** (here: *Tritogonia verrucosa*).

1992 Cummings–Mayer *Field Guide Freshwater Mussels MW* 26,

Pistolgrip—Tritogonia verrucosa. . . *Other common names* . . peanut. . . Widespread but relatively uncommon.

peanut bum n Also *peanut scramble*
See quot 1899.

1871 Bagg *4 Yrs. at Yale* 70, After that, only a few upper-class men will be found there, except there be some special attraction, as a contested election of officers, or a play, or a "peanut bum." **1899** Champlin–Bostwick *Young Folks' Games* 519, *Peanut bum*, a scramble for peanuts, in which any number of persons may take part. A bag of peanuts, containing at least a bushel, is emptied in the middle of a large room. . . The object of each is to get the most peanuts. . . The Peanut Bum was once a common sport at Yale College, but is now discontinued. **1945** *Sun* (Baltimore MD) 23 July 10/4 *(Hench Coll.)*, Rosen directed the novelty games, including a husband-calling contest, a dizzy-izzy race, and a peanut scramble.

peanut clover n
A clover (here: *Trifolium amphianthum*).

1970 Correll *Plants TX* 809 **TX, LA**, *Trifolium amphianthum.* . . *Peanut clover.* Perennial. . . Some fruit borne underground. Frequent in wooded sandy areas.

peanut-eater n [Prob in ref to the vegetarianism encouraged by the church] Cf **chicken-eater 3, fish-eater, mackerel-snapper**
A member of the Seventh-Day Adventist church.

1967 *DARE* (Qu. CC4, . . *Nicknames . . for various religions or religious groups*) Inf **OR**15, Peanut-eaters—Seven-Day A's.

peanut float n
A nonexistent object used as the basis of a practical joke.

1968 *DARE* (Qu. HH14, *Ways of teasing a beginner or inexperienced person—for example, by sending him for a 'left-handed monkey wrench':* "Go get me _____.") Inf **PA**71, Peanut float.

peanut gallery n scattered, but chiefly east of Missip R See Map Cf **peanut heaven, ~ roost,** *DS* D40
The top balcony of a theater.

1876 Knight *Amer. Mech. Dict.* 3.2476, The occupants of our peanut galleries, however, use it [=the whistle] indiscriminately for praise or blame. **1888** *Lippincott's* 42.734, Go to the lowest theatre in any of our large cities, or . . mark what is called the "Family Circle" by theatre-proprietors and to the general world is more felicitously known as the "Peanut Gallery." **1893** (1896) Post *Harvard Stories* 108, On the strength of my promise he bought a seat in the peanut gallery. **1945** *New Yorker* 5 May 15, We were sitting in the peanut gallery of the Opera House. **1950** *WELS (Names and nicknames for the upper balcony of a theater)* 3 Infs, **WI**, Peanut gallery. **1965–70** *DARE* (Qu. D40) 120 Infs, **scattered, but chiefly east of Missip R**, Peanut gallery.

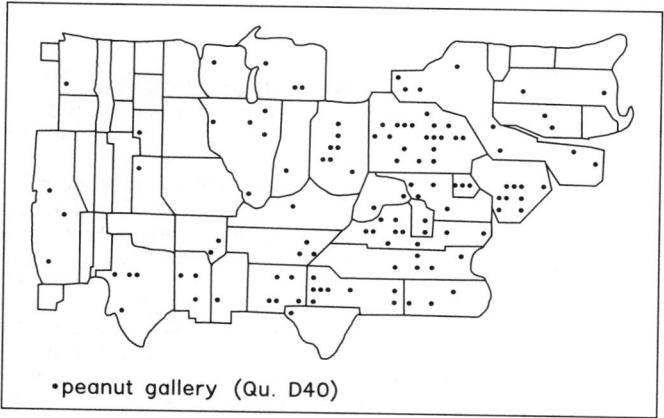

•peanut gallery (Qu. D40)

peanut heaven n chiefly OH, PA, C Atl See Map on p. 68
Cf **nigger heaven 1**
=peanut gallery.

1897 *KS Univ. Qrly.* (ser B) 6.90, *Peanut heaven:* the highest gallery in a theatre.—General. **1965–70** *DARE* (Qu. D40, *Names and nicknames . . for the upper balcony in a theater*) 37 Infs, **chiefly OH, PA, C Atl**, Peanut heaven.

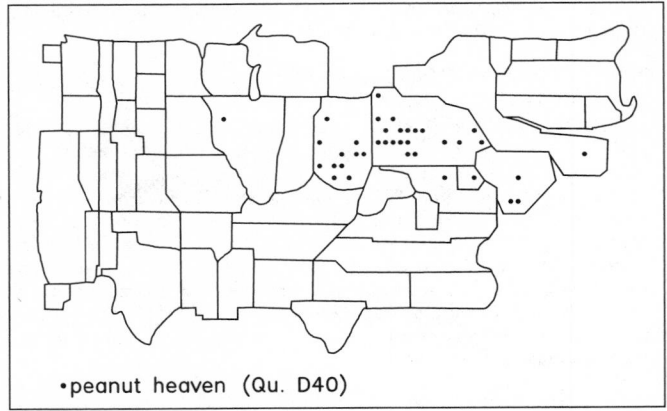

• peanut heaven (Qu. D40)

peanut roaster n Cf **coffeepot 1**

Among railroaders and loggers: a small steam engine.

 1945 Hubbard *Railroad Ave.* 354, *Peanut roaster*—Any small steam engine. **1958** McCulloch *Woods Words* 133 **Pacific NW,** *Peanut roaster*—A small steam locie or donkey.

peanut roost n Cf **buzzard roost 2, chicken ~ 1, crow's nest 4,** *DS* **D40**

=**peanut gallery.**

 1966–70 *DARE* (Qu. D40, *Names and nicknames . . for the upper balcony in a theater*) Infs **FL**15, **TX**5, 28, 31, **VA**44, Peanut roost.

peanut scramble See **peanut bum**

peanut squash n

Perh a **winter squash;** see quot.

 1969 *DARE* (Qu. I23, . . *Kinds of squash*) Inf **MI**108, Peanut squash—green-colored with yellow specks.

pea patch n esp Gulf States Cf **patch farm**

A small field of tillable land; hence v (phr) *pea-patch(-farm)* to work a small farm; n *pea-patcher* one who works a small farm or other small enterprise.

 c1940 Eliason *Word Lists FL* 10, *Pea-patcher:* A small country farmer, one that does not tend much land. It is a general term on the bay section for any one who comes to the bay or gulf and takes up fishing, oystering, or any of the work that pertains to the water. **1986** Pederson *LAGS Concordance* **Gulf Region** (*Field*) 45 infs, (The) pea patch [17 infs indicated that it is small, or smaller than a field.]; 4 infs, (The) pea patches; 1 inf, You done planted your pea patch out there; 1 inf, He pea-patch-farmed = he operated a very small farm; 1 inf, Pea-patching—"to run a small operation."

pea picker n

1 One's hand. Cf **cotton picker 1, pea-picking**

 1967 *DARE* (Qu. X32, *Joking or uncomplimentary words for the hands . . "Those are mine. You keep your _____ [out of them]."*) Inf **SC**40, Pea pickers.

2 A rube, hick; an unskilled laborer. Cf **cotton picker 3**

 1927 *AmSp* 3.24 **eTX** [Sawmill talk], Farmers who come to work in the mill after their crops are "laid by" are called "pea pickers." **1942** Berrey–Van den Bark *Amer. Slang* 391.3, *Rustic; bumpkin. . .* Pea picker. **1948** *PADS* 9.43 **OK** [Oil refinery terms], *Pea picker. . .* A common laborer that has neither the intelligence nor the training to become skilled in the petroleum distillation processes. The term arose in East Texas during the oil boom there when farm labor was employed in large numbers because of the lack of oil distillers. **1963** Owens *Look to River* 86 **TX,** All you other peapickers. You know what jobs you got. Make haste. Cut the wood. Haul the water. Clean up what's got to be cleaned up. **1966** *DARE* (Qu. HH1, *Names and nicknames for a rustic or countrified person*) Inf **GA**11, Pea picker.

pea-picking adj Cf **cotton-picking**

Used as a term of disparagement; see quot.

 1966–69 *DARE* (Qu. X32, *Joking or uncomplimentary words for the hands . . "Those are mine. You keep your _____ [out of them]."*) Infs **AR**51, **GA**72, **MS**16, Pea-picking fingers (*or* hands); (Qu. KK55b, *To* deny something very firmly: "Would you work for him?" "Not on your _____.") Inf **IL**45, Pea-pickin' life.

peapod n Also *peapod dory* [From the shape] **chiefly ME**

An open double-ended boat with rounded stem and stern used esp in lobster fishing.

 1884 U.S. Natl. Museum *Bulletin* 27.696 **ME,** *Double-ender or peapod. . .* Open; lapstreak; sharp forward and aft; rounding stem and sternpost; both ends alike; rounding bilge; keel; rudder; two thwarts; two oars; one sail. This model (built at Jonesport, Me.) represents a class of boats used in the general fisheries of the coast of Maine, but chiefly employed in the lobster-fisheries in certain localities. **1895** *Searcher* 1.79 **ME,** A pea-pod is a small open rowboat, much in demand among the Maine lobster fishermen. It is about fourteen feet long on top, built of cedar, with oak timbers, alike at both ends, and of such general appearance as to suggest the familiar pea-pod. **1915** *Rudder* 89 (*Mathews Coll.*), In her youth she had been a Maine 'pea pod', a double ended keel rowboat, with a slack bilge and no stability. **1932** Wasson *Sailing Days* 108 **cME coast,** Peculiar to the lower Penobscot region were double-ended, lap-streaked boats universally known as "pea-pods" and famed for being especially able in rough water. **1957** Beck *Folkl. ME* 128, On Matinicus Island the peapod dory served the purpose admirably. **1965** *PADS* 43.19 **seMA,** Small rowboat large enough for two . . peapod [1 of 9 infs]. **1966** *DARE* (Qu. O1, *What do you call a small rowboat?*) Inf **ME**6, Peapod—especially used for a saltwater boat pickèd [=peaked] at both ends. **1975** Gould *ME Lingo* 204, *Peapod*—A double-ended rowing and less often a sailing boat that originated in the Jonesport area. Still used and still being built. **1978** Merriam *Illustr. Lobstering* 65 **ME,** *Pea Pod*—A small, sixteen foot or so, double-ended rowing boat. Its name derives from the shape. Used in early lobstering.

pear n Also *pear cactus* Cf **Indian pear 2, pancake pear**

=**prickly pear 1** or its fruit; hence n *pear apple* the fruit of the **prickly pear 1.**

 1889 Vasey *Ag. Grasses* 100 **TX,** John C. Chesley, . . central Texas [writes]: The prickly pear is used here to a great extent. We have a ranch in Stephens County where we are now feeding the pear to over a hundred of our poorest cattle, and they are doing well on it. . . The pear should be cut and hauled to the feed-lots while the sap is in the roots. **1898** Canfield *Maid of Frontier* 205 **TX,** He knew . . which of the "pear apples" were good to eat. **1905** U.S. Bur. Plant Industry *Bulletin* 74.20, It is universally recognized throughout the pear region of southwestern Texas that the plant has a decided tendency to increase the flow of milk. **1929** Ellis *Ordinary Woman* 10 **CO** (as of early 20th cent), My mother would gather, very carefully, pear cactus and split it more carefully, throwing it into the water. **1949** *Sun. World-Herald Mag.* (Omaha) 1 May 10/4 (*DA*), By 1925 the pear covered something like 60 million acres, including some of the best land. **1956** Gipson *Old Yeller* 99 **TX,** The sight made me wonder again how a hog could be tough enough to eat prickly-pear apples with their millions of little hairlike spines. I ate them, myself, sometimes; for pear apples are good eating. **1966** *DARE* (Qu. S15, . . *Weed seeds that cling to clothing*) Inf **GA**11, Pear cactus [same as] prickly pear. **1976** Bailey–Bailey *Hortus Third* 793, *[Opuntia] microdasys. . .* Var. *rufida. . . Blind pear.*

pear v Also sp *peer* [ME *peren,* aphet form of *aperen* to appear; *OED2* c1375 →; "Obs. exc. *dial.*"] **chiefly S Midl**

1 To appear; to seem.

 1851 (1852) Stowe *Uncle Tom's Cabin* 2.175 **Sth** [Black], 'Pears like he jus grew crosser, every day. **1885** Murfree *Prophet of Smoky Mts.* 177 **TN,** It always 'peared ter me ez he war a mighty cur'ous man. **1890** *DN* 1.65 **KY,** *'Pears:* for *appears.* [DN Ed: Common in Elizabethan English.] **1891** *DN* 1.158 **cNY,** Aphæresis is very common in Ith[aca] D[ialect]. It occurs in . . [piɚd] < *appeared.* **1899** Chesnutt *Conjure Woman* 25 **csNC** [Black], De med'cine did n' 'pear ter do no good. **1899** (1912) Green *VA Folk-Speech* 315, In pears to . . **1903** *DN* 2.300 **Cape Cod MA** (as of a1857), *Pear to. . .* To haunt. 'If you marry again I'll pear to you.' For appear. *Ibid* 324 **seMO,** It pears like you don't know me. **1907** *DN* 3.234 **nwAR,** *'Pears like. . .* Appears as if. **1909** *DN* 3.356 **eAL, wGA,** *Pears like. . .* Appears as if. The subject is usually omitted. *Ibid* 401 **nwAR,** *Pears. . .* Appears. **1912** *DN* 3.584 **wIN,** *'Pears like. . .* It appears as if. " 'Pears like he don't want to do it." *'Pears to me. . .* It appears (or seems) to me. **1916** *DN* 4.341 **seOH,** *Peers.* Aphetic form of *appears.* **1927** *AmSp* 2.361 **WV,** It 'pears to me that I have seen you before. **1942** Warnick *Garrett Co. MD* 1 **nwMD** (as of 1900–18). **1946** *AmSp* 21.98 **sIL.** **1949** Turner *Africanisms* 272 **seSC** [Gullah], [ɑn dɛn ɪt pye lɛɪk ʋɪ rɛɪz] [=And then it appear like I rise.] **c1960** *Wilson Coll.* **csKY,** *Appears* is sometimes ['pjɪrz]. **1979** *AmSp* 54.94 sME (as of 1899–1910), *Loss of syllables*—This feature is very common in the notes, as it is in Wasson's fiction. Examples [include] . . *'pear* 'appear.'

2 in phr *pear out:* See quot.

1909 *DN* 3.414 nME, *Pear out.* . . To appear at church after marriage; to appear in new garments.

pear apple (or cactus) See **pear** n

pearch See **perch** n²

'pearently See **appearently**

pear hawthorn n Also *pear haw, ~ thorn, pearleaf thorn, pear-leaved (haw)thorn*

A **hawthorn** (here: *Crataegus calpodendron*) native to much of the eastern half of the US. Also called **red haw 1, sugar ~, thorn, ~ apple, ~ plum, whitethorn**

1813 Muhlenberg *Catalogus Plantarum* 48, *Cratægus* . . *pyrifolia* [= *C. calpodendron*]—Hawthorn . . pear-leaved. **1822** Eaton *Botany* 254, [*Crataegus*] *pyrifolia* . . pear-leaf thorn. **1848** Gray *Manual of Botany* 128, *C[rataegus] tomentosa* [=*C. calpodendron*] . . (Black or Pear Thorn). . . A tall shrub rather than a tree, with fragrant flowers and large leaves. **1850** Emerson *Rept. Trees & Shrubs* 435, The Pear-leaved Thorn. *C. tomentosa.* **1884** Sargent *Forests of N. Amer.* 79, Black thorn. Pear haw. . . the most widely-distributed of the North American *Crataegi,* varying greatly in the size, shape, and color of the fruit, form of the leaves [etc]. **1921** Deam *Trees IN* 191, *Crataegus Calpodendron.* . . Pear-thorn. Pear or Red Haw. **1950** Peattie *Nat. Hist. Trees* 365, *Pear Hawthorn.* . . New York State and Ontario to Minnesota and Arkansas, and south to the mountains of Georgia. **1979** Little *Checklist U.S. Trees* 109, *Crataegus calpodendron* . . *pear hawthorn.* . . Other common names—pear haw, pear thorn.

pea-ridge See **pea** n¹ **6**

pea ripper n Cf **piss-ripper**

A very hot day; hence adj *pea-ripping* hot.

1984 Wilder *You All Spoken Here* 143 Sth, *Pea ripper:* Hot enough to bust open peas on the vine. **1984** *Commercial Appeal* (Memphis TN) 20 May mag sec 10/1, The older people [in the South] are more tied to a rural environment, and so many similes are straight out of rural life, comparing things to animals (*"scarce as hen's teeth"*), natural events (*"went like forty"*), the weather (*"like a pea-ripping day"*) and so on.

pearl n Cf **jewelhead**

The otolith of the catfish; see quot.

1973 Knight *Cook's Fish Guide* 25, Jewelry hobbyists and youngsters appreciate some catfish heads. Boil them in plenty of water long enough for the flesh to fall off . . and pick out the catfish "pearls"—the earbones—and the cross-shaped bone in which they are set. Both are used by hobby jewelers.

pearleaf thorn, pear-leaved (haw)thorn See **pear hawthorn**

pearl everlasting See **pearly everlasting 1**

pearl-finder n Also *pearl snake*

A **water snake** (here: *Nerodia* spp).

1938 Burman *Blow for a Landing* 110 **Lower Missip Valley,** Wonder if we can git a pearl-finder, Captain Joe. . . It's a snake with markings on him like a pearl. *Ibid,* When you git the pearl snake you tie a string to him so he can't git away. And first place he goes into the water, you put in your rakes and dig. . . If you do it right, you git a pearl every time. *Ibid* 111, As he was striding down a muddy trail, a long yellow body flashed beneath his feet and glided off toward the brush. . . 'He's a pearl-finder sure. . . Look at them pearls!' With his stick he pointed to the odd beadlike markings which formed the pattern of the reptile's vivid skin.

pearl grass n [*OED2* 1633 → for *Briza maxima*]

=**rattlesnake grass 1.**

1894 *Jrl. Amer. Folkl.* 7.104 **MA,** *Glyceria Canadensis,* . . pearl-grass, Waverley, Mass. . . Name given by a few children, some years ago. **1910** Graves *Flowering Plants* 74 **CT,** *Glyceria canadensis.* . . Pearl Grass. . . Frequent. Bogs, open swamps and ditches.

pearl harlequin n Cf **cliff harlequin**

=**Dutchman's breeches 1.**

1933 Small *Manual SE Flora* 550, *B[icuculla] Cucullaria.* . . Butterfly-banner. Pearl-harlequin [etc].

pearlie n Also sp *pearly* Cf **purie**

In marble play: see quot.

c1970 Wiersma *Marbles Terms* swMI (as of c1960), *Pearlies* ['pɪɚ·liz]—a pearly in Muskegon meant a clear glass marble of tinted color. They were highly prized in Muskegon; *Pearlie* ['pɪɚ·li] . . light-colored, solid-colored marble. (Mich. 1945; Pacific N.W. 1931; Utah 1965); *Pearlie*—a clear marble, perhaps similar to a "moonie." . . He got 3 pearlies.

pearl millet n

1 An introduced cereal grass (*Pennisetum glaucum*) grown esp for forage in the southern US. Also called **cattail 2f, foxtail 1**

1884 Vasey *Ag. Grasses* 43, *Penicillaria spicata.* . . Pearl Millet. . . cultivated, especially in the Southern States. **1887** Beal *Grasses N. Amer.* 1.187, *P[ennisetum] spicatum.* Pearl . . Millet.—This grass has been spoken of very highly as a meadow grass for the South, where it has been grown for many years. . . It may be cut two or three times a year, and yield an abundant crop of rather coarse hay. **1948** Wolfe *Farm Gloss.* 213, Pearl Millet. . . Small seed in a "head" or bushy top. **1976** Bailey–Bailey *Hortus Third* 837, *Pearl Millet.* . . Cult[ivated] for forage in the s[outhern] states.

2 A **sorghum** (here: *Sorghum bicolor*).

1895 Gray–Bailey *Field Botany* 468, *Sorghum vulgare* [=*S. bicolor*]. . . *Pearl* . . *Millet.* . . A tall, maize-like plant. **1901** Mohr *Plant Life AL* 135, Various kinds of sorghum, known as durrha or kafir corn, millo maize, and pearl millet[,] . . and the so-called Johnson grass (*Sorghum halepense*) furnish green forage and hay crops throughout the summer.

pearlo See **pilau** n¹

pearl plant n

A **false gromwell** (here: *Onosmodium virginianum*).

1900 Lyons *Plant Names* 266, *O[nosmodium] Virginianum.* . . Eastern U.S. . . Necklace-weed, Pearl-plant [etc]. **1910** Graves *Flowering Plants* 330 **CT,** Gravel-weed. Pearl-plant [etc].

pearls n pl [*OED2* 1586 →]

Teeth, false teeth.

1950 *WELS* (Joking names for teeth) 3 Infs, **WI,** Pearls; (For false teeth) 1 Inf, **csWI,** Plaster pearls. **1965–70** *DARE* (Qu. X13a) Infs **CA36, 128, IL78, 84, IN60, NY224, PA216, TN35, WI50,** Pearls; **PA74,** Matched set of pearls; (Qu. X13b) Inf **CA79,** New pearls; **NJ33,** Plaster pearls.

pearl snake See **pearl-finder**

pearl-twist n [See quot 1963]

=**ladies' tresses.**

1933 Small *Manual SE Flora* 380, *Ibidium* [=*Spiranthes*]. . . About 80 species, natives of temperate and tropical America.—*Ladies'-tresses. Pearl-twists.* **1963** Craighead *Rocky Mt. Wildflowers* 39, Ladies-Tresses—*Spiranthes romanzoffiana.* . . Other names: Pearltwist. . . The small white flowers appear in a dense terminal spike . . [and] partially spiral about the stem. **1976** Bailey–Bailey *Hortus Third* 1066, *Spiranthes* [spp]. . . Ladies'-tresses, pearl-twist.

pearly See **pearlie**

pearly bill n

=**ivory-billed woodpecker.**

1925 Bailey *Birds FL* 81, Ivory-billed woodpecker. . . *Campephilus principalis* (Pearly Bill) . . this large, handsome bird is still far from being extinct in Florida.

pearly everlasting n

1 also *pearl everlasting:* A woolly composite plant (*Anaphalis margaritacea*) with a flat cluster of white flower heads often used in dried flower arrangements. Also called **cat's-paw 5, cottonweed 1a, everlasting n 1, Indian posy 3, ~ tobacco 6, ladies'-tobacco b, lady-in-white, life-everlasting 2, moonshine 1, none-so-pretty 1, povertyweed b, rabbit tobac-**

co 1e, silver button, silverleaf 2, strawflower   See also **life-of-man 2**

1848 Gray *Manual of Botany* 238, A[ntennaria] margaritacea. . . Pearly Everlasting. . . scales of the pearly white involucre obtuse or rounded.   **1897** Parsons *Wild Flowers CA* 102, Pearly everlasting flower. . . The flowers of the pearly everlasting have a peculiarly pure pearly look before they are entirely open, and their sharp-pointed little scales give them a prim, set look, like very regular, tiny white roses. **1937** U.S. Forest Serv. *Range Plant Hdbk.* W13, Pearl everlasting, a bunched or loosely tufted perennial herb of the aster family, also called pearly everlasting, cudweed, Indian-tobacco, and life everlasting, is often confused with the related pussytoes (*Antennaria* spp.), plants which also produce everlasting flowers.   **1949** Moldenke *Amer. Wild Flowers* 208, The common pearleverlasting, *Anaphalis margaritacea* . . occurs usually in large patches in dry sterile or often somewhat acid soil of woods, hillsides, and clearings from Newfoundland to Alaska and south to North Carolina, Kansas, and Oregon.   **1967** *DARE* FW Addit **AR**44, Pearly everlasting—some say "moonshine"—Anaphalis margaritacea.   **1975** Hamel–Chiltoskey *Cherokee Plants* 48, Pearly everlasting. . . make cold tea, pour over hot rock and breathe fumes.

2 A **pussytoes** (here: *Antennaria plantaginifolia*).

1896 *Jrl. Amer. Folkl.* 9.191 **MA**, Antennaria plantaginifolia. . . four toes, mouse-ear, pearly everlasting, Salem, Mass.

pear out See pear v 2

pear pad n   Cf pad n² 2, pear n

A **prickly pear 1** (here: esp *Opuntia humifusa*); hence n *pear pad apple* the fruit of this plant.

1946 *PADS* 6.23 **NC**, Pear pad. . . A variety of cactus which grows in sandy soil on the N.C. coast. Pamlico. Common. *Pear pad apple*. . . A sort of seed or fruit produced by the pear pad. Carteret Co., N.C. Heard a few times, 1941.   **1966–69** *DARE* (Qu. S15, . . *Weed seeds that cling to clothing*) Inf **NC**76, Pear pads [FW: These are little cactus, prickly pears, which grow wild here.]; (Qu. S17, . . *Kinds of plants . . that . . cause itching and swelling*) Inf **MS**16, Pear pads.

pear pickle n chiefly Sth   See Map   Cf peach pickle

1965–70 *DARE* (Qu. H56, *Names for . . pickles*) 15 Infs, **chiefly Sth**, Pear pickle(s); **GA**1, **NC**23, **SC**11, Pear; (Qu. H57, *Tasty or spicy side-dishes served with meats*) Infs **VA**35, 42, 45, Pear pickle. [17 of 21 Infs old, 4 mid-aged]

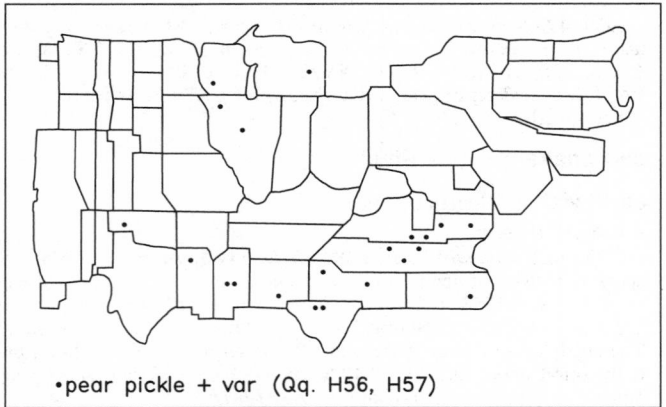

•pear pickle + var (Qq. H56, H57)

peart adj |pɪrt, pirt, pjɚt|; for addit varr see quots   Also *peartish* Also sp *peert, piert, pyert*   [Varr of *pert;* cf *OED2* pert adj. 6.β "*dial.* and *U.S.* (*[peart]* often viewed as a distinct word).")] **chiefly Sth, S Midl**   See Map

Lively; chipper; in good health; clever; hence n *peartness*.

1828 Hall *Letters West* 304, These little fixens . . make a man feel right peart.   **1871** Eggleston *Hoosier Schoolmaster* 39 **sIN**, They mos' always do, you see, kase he's the peartest *ole* man in this deestrick.   **1872** (1973) Thompson *Major Jones's Courtship* 175 **GA**, Mary's right piert, and little Henry Clay is makin a monstrous good beginning in the world. **a1883** (1911) Bagby *VA Gentleman* 261, "Ah!" said I, turning around, "how do you do, sir?" "Right peart; how d' y' come on yourself?" The speaker was a fine specimen of a Virginia countryman.   **1884** *Anglia* 7.269 **Sth, S Midl** [Black], *To look peart* = to be well.   **1887** Kirkland *Zury* 538 **IL**, Peart. . . Bright, smart, pert, in good condition.   **1899**

(1912) Green *VA Folk-Speech* 315, Peart. . . Lively; smart; feeling well; in good spirits; brisk; clever.   **1902** *DN* 2.241 **sIL**, [pirt]. . . Sprightly; lively; intelligent. Always used of persons in sickness, as 'Jim aint as peert,' or 'is a heap peerter than he was yestdy.'   **1903** *DN* 2.324 **seMO**, 'Hit's a mighty peart baby.' This is the usual compliment passed on a young infant.   **1906** *DN* 3.122 **sIN**, [pɪɚt]. . . Strong; healthy. "He's a peart child."   **1907** *DN* 3.224 **nwAR**, [pirt]. . . Sprightly, lively, intelligent. *Ibid* 235 **nwAR**, [pirt]. . . Lively, bright. "Yes, I'm like the nigger's rabbit, poor but peart."   **1911** *DN* 3.539 **eKY**, P͞eart. . . 1. sound in health; 2. mentally keen, alert.   **1912** *DN* 3.585 **wIN**, Peart. . . Lively.   **1921** Haswell *Daughter Ozarks* 57 (as of 1880s), At eighteen she had the reputation of being the "prettiest and peartest girl on Turtle Creek."   **1938** Rawlings *Yearling* 89 **nFL**, Well, son . . you look right peart.   **1952** Brown *NC Folkl.* 1.574, Peartish ['pjɚtɪʃ]. . . Somewhat well, somewhat lively; showing improvement. *Ibid* 575, Peartness ['pjɚtnɪs]. . . Liveliness.   **1962** Atwood *Vocab. TX* 72, An unusually active old person is usually said to be *spry* (70 [infs]), but *peart* (18 [infs]) is still fairly current in the older groups.   **1965–70** *DARE* (Qu. KK27, *A very lively, active old person: "For his age, he's _____."*) Infs **KY**47, **SC**31, **TX**1, **VA**15, **WV**16, (Awful, plumb, *or* right) peart [piɚt]; **AR**52, **GA**36, **SC**39, 45, **WV**4, 5, 8, (Real *or* right) peart [piɚt]; **GA**31, Peart—[pjɚt] or [piɚt]; **MS**69, Peart [pjʌɚt]; **MO**9, [piˇiɚt]; **SC**34, Peart [piɛɚt]; I reckon; **TX**32, Peart [pjɚt] as a cricket; **VA**11, Peart [piɚt] as a cricket; **TN**44, Real peart [piiɚt]; (Qu. Y22, *To move around in a way to make people take notice of you: "Look at him _____."*) Inf **MO**10, Peart [piɚt]; (Qu. BB47, *Feeling in the best of health and spirits: "I'm feeling _____!"*) Inf **KY**46A, Peart [pjɛɚt]; (Qu. GG29, *To be in a good or pleasant mood: "This morning he seems to be feeling _____."*) Inf **IL**143, Peart [piɚt]; **VA**15, Peart [pjɛɚt]; (Qu. KK28, *Feeling ambitious and eager to work*) Inf **MS**73, Mighty peart [pjʌɚt]; (Qu. KK29, *To start working very hard: "He was slow at first but now he's really _____."*) Inf **KY**85, Getting peart [piɚt]; **VA**38, Peart [pjɚt].   **1966** Dakin *Dial. Vocab. Ohio R. Valley* 463, Peart . . is clearly old and seems to be primarily a South Midland term which was brought into the Ohio Valley through the Cumberland Gap.   **1978** *DARE* File **cnMA** (as of c1915), One old man that I knew used to answer the usual "How are you this morning?" with "Peart, right peart." Other old people used the word, pronounced ['piɚt] or [piɚt]—sometimes with no *r*—as in "Well, you're lookin' peart today."   **1984** *Annals Internal Med.* 100.6.900 **cwAL**, *Peart and pyert* are variations of pert, lively, in good health.   **1989** Pederson *LAGS Tech. Index* 273 **Gulf Region**, *(Lively [of older people])* [20 infs offered proncs of the type [pɪrt], 11 of the type [pʌrt], 8 of the type [pjɪrt], 2 of the type [pʌɜt], and 1 each of the types [pɛrt, pɪɜt, pjɪɜt].]   **1994** NC Lang. & Life Project *Dial. Dict. Lumbee Engl.* 9 **seNC**, Pyert. . . Lively, good. *I feel pyert today.*

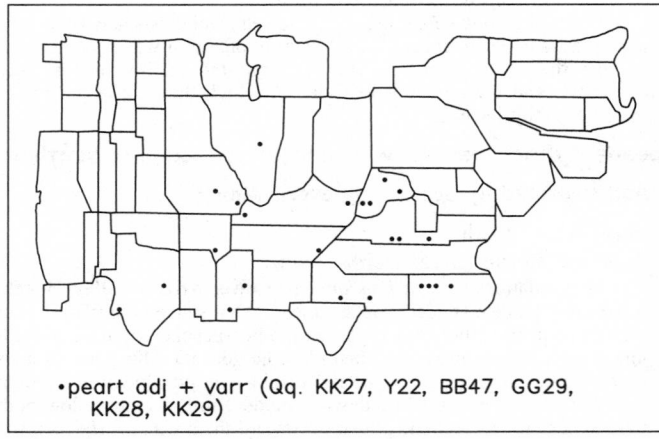

•peart adj + varr (Qq. KK27, Y22, BB47, GG29, KK28, KK29)

peart adv   Also *peartly;* also sp *peert*   **chiefly Sth, S Midl**

Briskly, quickly; in a lively or agreeable way.

1832 (1919) Irving *Jrls.* 3.171 **NY**, My horse goes quite peart.   **1856** Brewerton *War in KS* 383, To "get along" in a happy-go-lucky sort of way, which he [=a pro-slavery man] calls "a-doin'-right-peartly."   **1867** Harris *Sut Lovingood Yarns* 87 **TN**, I passed 'em [=his legs] a-pas' each uther tuther day, right peart.   **1899** (1912) Green *VA Folk-Speech* 315, Peartly. . . In a peart manner. Readily [sic]; briskly; promptly.   **1901** Harben *Westerfelt* 40 **nGA**, I reckon you must 'a' rid purty peert.   **1909** *DN* 3.356 **eAL, wGA**, Peart. . . Lively. . . "The old mare went along right peart."   **1924** Raine *Land of Saddle-Bags* 100 **sAppalachians**, We rode considerable *peart* and shunned the worst places. **1928** Peterkin *Scarlet Sister Mary* 274 **SC**, Beat de mule, Andrew, make em step more pearter. **1937** (1977) Hurston *Their Eyes* 225 **FL** [Black], Then she found out that one of her hands was all stepped on and her fingers were bleeding pretty peart. **1940** (1978) Still *River of Earth* 16 **KY**, We heered you was living in the smokehouse and getting along peart. **1942** Perry *Texas* 54, If the March wind's been blowing peart, you may have to take time off to throw a little dirt against your corn stalks to keep 'em from getting blown loose in the ground. **1952** Brown *NC Folkl.* 1.575, *Peartly* ['pjɝtlɪ]. . . Lively, quickly. **1968** *DARE* FW Addit **LA30**, Peart—adv. Briskly, actively. "It's rainin' pretty peart out there!"

pearten v Usu with *up* Also *perten* Pronc-spp *peerten*, *pyeerten* **chiefly Sth, S Midl**

1 also *pert*: To make lively or cheerful; to enliven, hasten; hence vbl n *peart(en)ing* enlivening, in combs *peartening juice, peart(en)ing powder*.

1827 (1939) Sherwood *Gaz. GA* 139, *Provincialisms. . . Pertend up*, for better, more cheerful. **1876** in 1884 Lanier *Poems* 168 **GA**, Lord, peerten de hoein' fas'. **1907** Wright *Shepherd* 225 **Ozarks**, You think I'm drunk. But I ain't, not so mighty much. Jest enough t' perten me up a pepper grain. **1914** Furman *Sight* 32 **KY**, I allow it'll pyeerten Aunt Dalmanuthy up to hear some new thing. **1929** Sale *Tree Named John* 19 **MS**, Hit goes into de baby en peartens up dem teethes en gives de baby strengt' to stan' it. **1952** Brown *NC Folkl.* 1.574, *Pearten (up)* ['pjɝtn]. . . To enliven, to cheer up; to become lively, cheerful. "That fellow certainly peartens a body up with his lively jokes." "I hear that Mary's baby is peartening up some." **1962** Dykeman *Tall Woman* 74 **NC** (as of c1860), "You're looking peart," Paul said. "Peartens a feller up best to see homefolks." **1974** Fink *Mountain Speech* 19 **wNC, eTN**, *Peartnin' powders* . . tonic, vitamins. "Doc, John wants some more of those peartnin' powders that done him so good." **1976** Garber *Mountain-ese* 67 **sAppalachians**, *Peartin'-powders* . . tonic—All I need is some peartin'-powders to liven me up fer the winter. **1984** Wilder *You All Spoken Here* 201, *Pearted up*: If you weren't peart earlier, you improved with treatment. Maybe you got a sympathetic listener, or a bowl of hot pot likker with cornbread crumbled in it, or a dollop of peartenin' juice high in alcoholic content. **1985** *NC Folkl. Jrl.* 33.35 **wNC** (as of c1920), [At a corn shucking] there were a few jugs of peartenin' juice circulating around among the boys in the dark corners or outside the building, especially if the night was frosty.

2 To become lively, active, or cheerful; to hasten.

1851 Hooper *Widow Rugby's Husband* 78 **AL**, I peartened up then, and gin [=gave] him as good as he sent. **1894** *Scribner's Mag.* 15.59 **Sth**, "I hope yo' mendin'." "Thank you, Brother March, I'm peart'nin', as they say." **1899** (1912) Green *VA Folk-Speech* 315, *Pearten up*. . . To become more lively and active: as, a horse *peartens up* when he goes along better and makes better time on the road. **1909** *DN* 3.356 **eAL, wGA**, *Pearten*. . . To hasten, go faster: often with *up*. "We will have to pearten up if we expect to get there on time." **1915** *DN* 4.187 **swVA**, *Pearten*. . . Used with *up*. 1. To seem more lively. "The old man peartened up about ten o'clock for a few minutes." 2. To go more briskly. "We'll have to pearten up, or night will get us." **1917** *DN* 4.415 **wNC, KY**, *Pearten up*. . . To become lively or cheerful. **1923** (1946) Greer-Petrie *Angeline Doin' Society* 22 **csKY**, So fur, they hadn't pearten'd up a bit. **1952** [see **1** above]. **1962** Dykeman *Tall Woman* 262 **NC** (as of c1860), "Pearten up, boy," Mark said to him, "your mama will think of something to help." **1967–70** *DARE* (Qu. JJ26, *If somebody has been doing poor work or not enough, the boss might say, "If he wants to keep his job he'd better _____."*) Inf **KY85**, Pearten [piɑˑtn] up; **OH49**, Pearten up ['pɪɑɚtən ˌəp]—that means get on the ball; **TX37**, Pearten up ['pɛɾtɛn [sic] ʌp] a little; (Qu. KK29, *To start working very hard*) Inf **KY85**, Pearten [piɑˑtn] up. **1967** Green *Horse Tradin'* 290 **TX**, Ol' Nothin' had savvied what was going to happen and had pertened-up some, too. . . Wat dropped his hat and hollered: "Go!" **1986** Pederson *LAGS Concordance*, 1 inf, **neTN**, [Toad] pertens up when the sun shines.

pear thorn See **pear hawthorn**

pearting (powder) See **pearten 2**

peartish See **peart** adj

peartly See **peart** adv

peartness See **peart** adj

pear-toed See **parrot-toed**

pea sack n Also *pea bag*
See quot 1968.

1968 *DARE* (Qu. F19, *A cloth container for grain*) Inf **MD14**, Pea bag—finer, cotton fiber. **1986** Pederson *LAGS Concordance*, 1 inf, **cwTN**, Pea sack—for feed, in "old days," like tow sack.

pea shelling See **pea hulling**

peasly adj Cf **peezaltree**
1969 *DARE* (Qu. BB38, *When a person doesn't look healthy, or looks as if he hadn't been well for some time . . "He looks _____."*) Inf **NY196**, Peasly ['pizlɪ].

pea snipe n
Either the **least sandpiper** or the **semipalmated sandpiper**.
1923 U.S. Dept. Ag. *Misc. Circular* 13.55 **IN**, Least Sandpiper. . . Vernacular Names. . . In local use. . . pea-snipe [etc]. *Ibid* 57, Semipalmated Sandpiper. . . Vernacular Names. . . In local use. . . pea-snipe.

pea soup n
1 A thick soup made from dried peas. [*OED2* 1711 →] **chiefly NEast, nGt Lakes** See Map Cf **split pea soup**
1845 Frémont *Rept. Rocky Mts.* 234, We had to-night an extraordinary dinner—pea soup, mule, and dog. **1879** (1965) Tyree *Housekeeping in Old VA* 83, Pea soup. Soak one pint of split peas in water for twelve hours. **1948** *WELS Suppl.* **ME** [In lumber camps], And "Pea soup and Johnnycake make a Frenchman's belly ache," I've often heard, but I've seen enough Frenchmen, with their Sunday plaid wool shirts and their hair slicked back and faces scrubbed, dive into that combination to know that it's the quantity consumed that makes the dire result. **1950** *WELS* (*Kinds of soup favored in your neighborhood*) 24 Infs, **WI**, Pea soup. **1965–70** *DARE* (Qu. H36, *Kinds of soup*) 60 Infs, **chiefly NEast, nGt Lakes**, Pea soup; **NJ2**, Bean and pea soup; **MN11**, Pea soup and ham; **MA122**, Pea soup with ham hocks; (Qu. H50, *Dishes made with beans, peas, or corn that everybody around here knows, but people in other places might not*) 9 Infs, **esp NEast**, Pea soup.

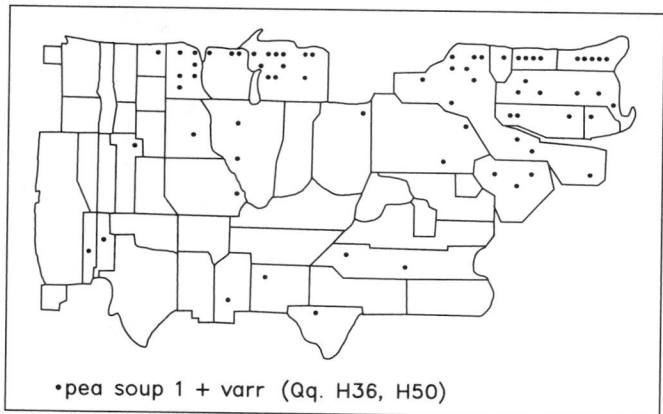

•pea soup 1 + varr (Qq. H36, H50)

2 also attrib; also *pea souper*: A person of French background or heritage, esp a French Canadian. [*DCan peasoup* a French Canadian; 1896 →; "through long association with pea soup"] **chiefly Nth**
[**1897** Rogers *Folk-Stories N. Border* 25 **nwNY**, [FrCan speaker:] Me no 'fraid watter, Ahm cum off Montrahall, me. Ahm no peesoup Frencher.] **1930** Williams *Logger-Talk* 16 **Pacific NW**, Pea-souper: A French Canadian. **1931** 'D. Stiff' *Milk & Honey Route* 38 (*OED2*), A Canadian Frenchman is a 'Canuck' or sometimes a 'pea soup'. **1942** Berrey–Van den Bark *Amer. Slang* 385.5, Pea-souper, *a French-Canadian*. [**1948** see **1** above.] **1956** Sorden–Ebert *Logger's Words* 25 **Gt Lakes**, *Pea-soup*, A French Canadian lumber-jack. **1958** McCulloch *Woods Words* 133 **Pacific NW**, Peasouper—A Frenchman or Quebecker working in the woods; from their fondness for pea soup. Ted Flynn tells of one peasouper cook who prepared a huge pot of the soup and let it stand outside so it would freeze in order to keep. Ted's father, the camp boss, cut a square chunk out of the frozen pot, poked a hole in it, threaded it on an ax handle, and said "come on, boy, we're off for work. This is lunch." **1959** *VT Hist.* 27.152, Pea-soupers. . . French Canadians. Rare. **1965–70** *DARE* (Qu. HH28, *Names and nicknames . . for people of foreign background: French*) Infs **CT23, MN10, NY12**, Pea soup(s); **CT37**, Pea souper; (Qu. HH28, . . *French-Canadian*) Infs **ND3,**

OR3, WI52, Pea soup(s); **MA**40, Canuck, pea souper ['pi supə]; **NY**1, Pea-soup Frenchman, Canuck.   **1973** Allen *LAUM* 1.408 (as of c1950) 1 inf, **ND**, Pea soup. A French-Canadian.

pea sticks See **pea** n[1] **6**

pea-tad n

Something small and insignificant.

1968 *DARE* (Qu. LL2, . . *Too small to be worth much: "I don't want that little _____ potato."*) Inf **VA**15, Pea-tad ['pitæd] [FW: 2 words, "tad" is the noun].

pea thrasher n Cf **peabird**

=**brown thrasher.**

1969 *DARE* (Qu. Q14, . . *Names . . for . . brown thrasher*) Inf **GA**77, Pea thrasher.

peat pink n Cf **wild pink**

A **catchfly 1** (here: *Silene caroliniana*).

1959 Carleton *Index Herb. Plants* 90, *Peat-pink: Silene caroliniana.*

pea tree n Cf **bean tree**

=**catalpa B1**; hence n *pea-tree worm* =**catalpa B2.**

1968 *DARE* (Qu. P6, . . *Kinds of worms . . used for bait*) Inf **VA**14, Pea-tree worm [FW:=catalpa worm]; (Qu. T9, *The common shade tree with large heart-shaped leaves, clusters of white blossoms, and long thin seed pods or 'beans'*) Inf **VA**15, Pea tree.

pea-turkey n

1 in phrr *not to say* (or *hear*) *pea-turkey* and varr: Not to say (or hear) a single word.   **chiefly Sth, S Midl**

1909 *DN* 3.356 **eAL, wGA,** *Pea-turkey.* . . A single word, anything. "She never said pea-turkey to me about it."   **1967** *DARE* FW Addit **eTN,** "I didn't say 'pea-turkey'" meaning "I didn't say a word," "I didn't say goodbye."   **1984** Burns *Cold Sassy* 16 **nGA** (as of 1906), If she don't write them and don't hear from them and don't ever say pea-turkey about them to anybody, something's wrong. *Ibid* 58, Ain't nobody in Cold Sassy ever heard pea-turkey from him since.   **1984** Wilder *You All Spoken Here* 152 **Sth,** *Never said pea turkey:* Failed to give information, or to invite one to some function, as "She lef' heah, I tell you, an' nevah said pea turkey.["]   **1992** *DARE* File, The expression "He didn't say pea-turkey," meaning "He didn't say anything at all," is one my mother heard growing up in Southern Alabama and has heard recently from friends in Georgia and Mississippi, who say they have known it all their lives.

2 in phr *not to know pea-turkey:* Not to know the simplest thing.   Cf **pea** n[1] **4**

1984 Burns *Cold Sassy* 112 **nGA** (as of 1906), He'd just showed he didn't know pea-turkey about how grown daughters feel when a young stepmother is brought into the family.   **1992** *Sacramento Bee* (CA) 19 Nov sec A 2/4 **AR,** *He don't know pea turkey*—absolutely ignorant.

peatweed n [Appar from its habitat]

A **swamp loosestrife** (here: *Decodon verticillatus*).

1900 Lyons *Plant Names* 133, *D[ecodon] verticillatus.* . . Swamp Loose-strife. . . **1919** (1923) House *Wild Flowers NY* 1.183, [*Swamp Loosestrife.* . . An herblike perennial growing usually in swamps or shallow water.] *Ibid* 184, [Swamp loosestrife is] also known as peatweed.   **1933** Small *Manual SE Flora* 929, *Peat-weed.* . . Swamps and ponds, var. provinces, Fla. to La., Minn., and Me.   **1959** Carleton *Index Herb. Plants* 90, *Peat-weed: Decodon verticillatus.*

peavine n

1a Any of var usu twining plants of the family Fabaceae.   Cf **pea** n[1] Note: These quots may refer spec to other senses below.

1675 in 1882 *PA Mag. Hist & Biog.* 6.89, You have Grass as high as a Man's Knees . . interlac'd with Pea-Vines, and other Weeds that Cattel much delight in.   **1797** Imlay *Western Terr.* 518 **TN,** In the state of Tenasee cattle at present support themselves among the reeds, pea-vines, rye-grass, and clover.   **1806** in 1852 U.S. Congress *Debates & Proc.* 9th Cong 2nd Sess 1107 **cLA,** The banks of the river are covered with pea vine and several sorts of grass, bearing seed.   **1850** Gallaher *W. Sketch-book* 371, The plains and hills were covered with the rank, luxuriant pea-vine.   **1880** Tourgée *Bricks* 61 **NC,** Richards. . . came from up North somewhere about 1790, when everybody thought this pea-vine

country was a sort of new Garden of Eden.   **1892** (1972) Allen *Blue-Grass Region KY* 14, [The] forest . . together with cane-brakes and pea-vines, covered the face of the country when it was first beheld by pioneers.

b Spec:

(1) Std: =**garden pea.**

(2) A **black-eyed pea** or related species of *Vigna,* the cut plant of which is often used as fodder or silage.   **Sth**

1804 in 1930 Dunbar *Life* 217 **MS,** The banks of the [Red] river are luxuriantly clothed with pea-vine and several kinds of grasses yielding seed.   **1846** (1878) Aime *Plantation Diary* 111, Pea vine hay is excellent this year, the vine being still green and juicy.   **1858** *S. Cultivator* 16.58 **Sth,** Now, as 1000 pounds of dry clover, or pea-vine hay, consumed by domestic animals, is reduced to 450 pounds in their dry excrements, it is clear that if such clover or pea-vines be plowed in on the fields where they are grown, the soil will receive 550 pounds more of the organized constituents of these plants in every 1000 pounds, than it would if the latter were fed to live stock and their dung and urine returned to the land.   **1881** Phares *Farmer's Book of Grasses* 16 **MS,** [*Southern Field Pea.*] *Ibid* 18, Now a word as to pea vine hay. . . It is highly relished by all live stock and is worth much more than all the labor and expense of saving. . . The analysis of the pea and vine confirms the . . value of both as food for animals and land.   **1883** GA Dept. Ag. *Pub. Circular No. 26* 8.21, There is too little attention paid to the cow pea, for it is certainly the clover of the South. . . Peavine hay cannot be excelled as a stock feed when properly saved.   [**1925** *Book of Rural Life* 3190, Cowpea hay is the most important legume hay in the Cotton Belt.] **1932** Kelley *Inchin' Along* 55 **AL,** Everybody knows there is nothing a mule likes better than pea-vine hay with the peas left on.   **1965–70** *DARE* (Qu. L9a, . . *Kinds of grass . . grown for hay*) Infs **GA**3, **FL**7, **NC**18, Peavine(s); **GA**7, 17, 60, **NC**49, Peavine hay; (Qu. L9b, *Hay from other kinds of plants [not grass];* not asked in early QRs) Infs **GA**19, **SC**1, 3, 23, **GA**45, Peavine; **AR**52, **GA**60, 87, **SC**19, 26, 39, 40, 43, Peavine hay.   **1969** *DARE* Tape **GA**77, [FW:] What would you plant for hay? [Inf:] Well, . . for sorghum seed hay we'd mostly require a low, kind of a low land for sorghum hay. And, you know, peavine hay, that'll produce mostly where nothing else won't.   **1981** Pederson *LAGS Basic Materials,* 6 infs, **GA, LA, MS,** Peavine hay; 1 inf, **GA,** Peavine hay—a kind of hay with which you pick all the peas off of it before cutting.

(3) =**hog peanut 1.**

1814 Bigelow *Florula Bostoniensis* 173, Glycine monoica [=*Amphicarpaea bracteata*]. . . *Pea vine.* . . A very delicate wood vine, twining upon the bushes, and flowering in July and August.   **1830** Rafinesque *Med. Flora* 2.190, *Amphicarpa monoica.* . . *Pea Vine.* Cattle are greedy of this plant, and destroy it almost every where, ought to be cultivated for fodder. The seeds are like peas, and as good to eat. In Carolina they begin to cultivate it for the table.   **1840** MA Zool. & Bot. Surv. *Herb. Plants & Quadrupeds* 61, *A[mphicarpa] monoica.* . . *Pea Vine.* Has a hairy, twining, slender stem, and purple flowers.   **1861** Wood *Class-Book* 322, *Amphicarpaea.* . . *Pea Vine.*   **1958** Jacobs–Burlage *Index Plants NC* 121, *Amphicarpa monoica.* . . *Pea vine.* . . Common in rich damp woodland sections of North Carolina and South Carolina. . . The subterranean pod is cultivated for use as a vegetable.

(4) =**lupine.**   **West**

1870 *Amer. Naturalist* 4.30 **NV,** The meadows are bounded . . by the Pea-vine mountains (so-called from the frequency with which the lupines or wild peas are met with on its sides).   **1901** U.S. Dept. Ag. Div. Entomol. *Bulletin* 26.100 **MT,** *Lupinus* spp. . . Other names: Blue pea, . . Pea vine. . . A number of stockmen call these plants lupines, but perhaps the names wild bean, blue bean, and blue pea are more generally applied to them in Montana.   **1913** (1979) Barnes *Western Grazing* 265, *Lupines.* . . Eaten at certain times and under certain conditions it is extremely injurious to horses, cattle and sheep. The common name among stockmen is wild pea, blue pea, blue bean and peavine. . . It is often mistaken for a variety of loco.

(5) A **vetch** (here: *Vicia* spp), esp *Vicia americana.*   Cf **Canada pea 1, deer pea 1**

1900 Lyons *Plant Names* 393, *V[icia] Americana.* . . American or Purple Vetch, Pea-vine.   **1903** Small *Flora SE U.S.* 655, *Vicia.* . . Trailing or climbing herbs. . . Pod short or elongated, flattened. . . *Vetch. Pea Vine.*   **1953** Greene–Blomquist *Flowers South* 61, *Vetches, Tares,* or *Pea-Vines* (*Vicia*). . . Some of these are used for winter cover-crops and some for ornamental purposes. . . Various localities, Ga. to Kans. and n. to w. N.Y.

(6) A **tick trefoil**; see quots.

1901 Mohr *Plant Life* AL 571, Naked-stemmed Peavine. . . *Desmodium nudiflorum*. . . Large-flowered Peavine. . . *Hedysarum grandiflorum* [=*Desmodium g.*]. . . Few-flowered Peavine. . . *Desmodium pauciflorum*. [c1967 GA Univ. *Weeds S. U.S.* 30, *Desmodium tortuosum*. . . Flower clusters of pea-like blooms producing jointed pods which break into pieces with one seed.]

(7) =**vetchling**. **chiefly West** Cf **marsh pea, pea** n¹ 3

1937 U.S. Forest Serv. *Range Plant Hdbk.* W102, Peavines (Lathyrus spp.). . . The best known member of the genus is undoubtedly the cultivated sweetpea. . . Peavines occur from near sea level on the Pacific coast to above timber line in the Rocky Mountains. **1954** Harrington *Manual Plants CO* 327, *Lathyrus* [spp]. . . Peavine. **1963** Murie *Birds Mt. McKinley* Pl. 3 **AK**, [Caption:] The foreground is torn up by grizzlies seeking peavine roots. **1967** Dodge *Roadside Wildflowers* 37 **SW**, Peavine is . . often found at 5,000 to 7,000 feet in dry, open, pinyon woodlands blooming May to August. The sweetpea-like flowers are large and showy. . . *Lathyrus eucosmus*. **1973** Hitchcock–Cronquist *Flora Pacific NW* 261, *Lathyrus* [spp]. . . Peavine; Sweet-pea; Vetchling. **1986** Scott *Butterflies N. Amer.* 536, Hostplant Catalogue. . . Pea Vine: *Lathyrus*.

2 Either of two plants of the family Convolvulaceae: **hedge bindweed 1** or **man-of-the-earth 1.** **esp OH** See Map

1897 *Jrl. Amer. Folkl.* 10.51 **OH**, *Convolvulus sepium* . . pea vine, Sulphur Grove, Ohio. *Ibid, Ipomoea pandurata* . . wild sweet potato, pea vine, Sulphur Grove, Ohio. **1965–70** DARE (Qu. S5, . . *Wild morning glory*) Infs IL4, 25, **OH**25, 78, 90, 95, Peavine; **OH**98, Wild peavine; **DC**2, Peavine—grows up fences, etc; (Qu. S9, . . *Kinds of grass that are hard to get rid of*) Infs **OH**48, 88, Peavines; (Qu. S21, . . *Weeds . . that are a trouble in gardens and fields*) Inf **OH**25, Peavine; **OH**56, Peavines; **MD**20, Peavine—something like morning glory—white flower.

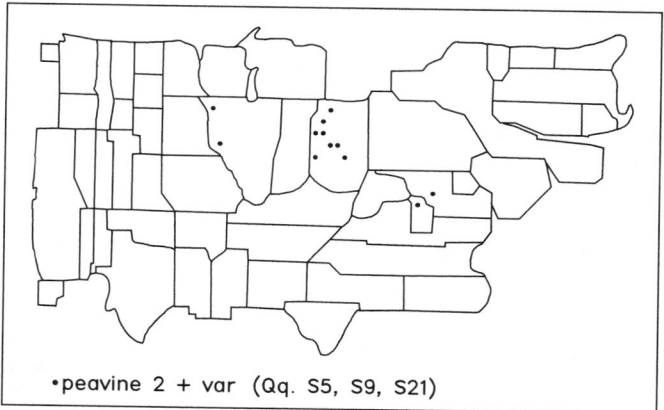

•peavine 2 + var (Qq. S5, S9, S21)

3 also *peavine railroad,* ~ *train*: A small, local railroad line or train.

1950 *Western Folkl.* 9.119 **nwOR** [Logger speech], Peavine, The. A logging railroad. **1956–59** *Hall Coll.*, Pea vine railroad (or *train*). The railroad that went under bushes and trees from Newport, Tenn., to Mt. Sterling, N.C.; **wNC**, The pea-vine railroad was called that because of the wild pea vines growing along the [Pigeon] River; **eTN**, They had a party up at Mount Starlin'. The pea vine train run an' they was loaded that day—a whole batch of deputies on it; **eTN**, "I came up on the pea vine" (i.e., on the logging railroad). **1966–69** DARE (Qu. N37, *Joking names for a branch railroad that is not very important or gives poor service*) Infs **KS**1, **MO**17, **TN**11, **WV**2, Peavine; **FL**1, Peavine—between here and Rochelle; **OH**53, Peavine—it was so crooked; **VT**12, The peavine—a particular train. **1984** Wilder *You All Spoken Here* 187 **Sth**, *Peavine railroad*: One with a rambling route—no beeline here—as in a mountain lumbering operation. **1986** Pederson *LAGS Concordance*, 1 inf, **cFL**, The Peavine—small railroad, served phosphate area.

4 See quot.

1968–70 DARE (Qu. B10, . . *Long trailing clouds high in the sky*) Infs **GA**92, **NY**116, Peavines.

peavine clover n

Either **zigzag clover** or **red clover.**

1900 Lyons *Plant Names* 377, *T[rifolium] medium* . . , Zigzag Clover, . . Pea-vine Clover. **1910** Graves *Flowering Plants* 248 **CT**,

Trifolium pratense. . . Red . . or Pea-vine Clover. . . Extensively cultivated for fodder and for fertilizer. **1911** CA Ag. Exper. Sta. Berkeley *Bulletin* 217.1001, *Trifolium pratense*. . . Pea Vine Clover. . . Beekeepers in the vicinity of Sacramento report bees to work on it. **1922** *Amer. Botanist* 28.34, *Trifolium medium*, a species greatly resembling the red clover, is known as "zig-zag clover" probably from its flexuous stems. . . In addition it is sometimes called "pea-vine clover."

peavine railroad (or train) See **peavine 3**

peaweed n

Prob =**red-stemmed peavine.**

1949 PADS 11.9 **cwTX** (as of 1911–29), Pea weed. . . A type of loco weed; apparently so named because of its pea-green color.

pea whipping See **pea hulling**

peawood n Also *peewood, pisswood* Cf **tisswood wNC, eTN**

A **silver bell 1** (here: *Halesia carolina*).

1908 Britton *N. Amer. Trees* 793, Silverbell tree—*Halesia carolina.* . . This very beautiful small tree or shrub is also known as the Snowdrop tree, Wild olive tree, Bell tree, Opossomwood, Calicowood, Tisswood, Peawood, and Rattle box. **1937** Thornburgh *Gt. Smoky Mts.* 28, The chittim tree or silver bell he [=a mountain guide] calls "peawood." **1954** McAtee *Suppl. to Nomina Abitera* [4] **NC**, Silverbell (*Halesia monticola*)—Pee-wood, rarely piss-wood, Great Smoky Mountains, North Carolina. The name tiss-wood of books, thus is probably an enphemism [sic]. **1961** Douglas *My Wilderness* 160 **wNC**, The silverbells had reclaimed it. This tree, which the mountain people call "pea-wood," often sends a shaft seventy-five feet into the sky. **1967** DARE (Qu. T16, . . *Kinds of trees . . 'special'*) Inf **TN**14, Peawood—same as bluebell—blue, looks like a peablossom, gets plumb full of little bells, real pretty. **1970** Campbell et al. *Gt. Smoky Wildflowers* 48, Silverbell. . . abundant in rich, loamy, shaded soils from 900 to 5,000 foot elevation in the Smokies. . . Peawood is another common name.

peazzer See **piazza**

pebbings-in n Cf **peg C2**

In marble play: see quot.

1969 DARE (Qu. EE7, . . *Kinds of marble games*) Inf **RI**12, Pebbings-in—put allie between legs, if other guy hits it, he gets it, if not, you get all marbles he throws.

pebble n [See quot]

A **striped bass** (here: *Morone saxatilis*).

1959 *Washington Post & Times Herald* (DC) 26 June sec C 9/2 **cMD**, Deale has a good school of pan-size to 2-pound rockfish on Holland Point bar, but among them are the ubiquitous "pebbles"—rockfish considerably less than the minimum legal length.

pecan n Usu |pɪˈkɑn, pə-, -ˈkæn| Pronc-spp *paccan, pecon*; for addit pronc and sp varr see quots and *DA(E)*, *OED2* [Algonquian]

A Forms.

[**1712** in 1846 Kip *Early Jesuit Missions* 198, Pacanes. [DARE Ed: Fr author gives this as the term used by the Illinois.]] [**1772** Ulloa *Noticias* 116, La una de estas llaman *Pacanos*, que es un genero de *Nogál* de mas corpulencia que ellos, pero en madera y hoja muy semejante. [=One of these they call *Pacanos*, which is a kind of walnut, only fatter, but in wood and leaf very similar.]] **1773** in 1778 Hutchins *Topog. Descr.* 52, The timber. . . or Paccan, Maple, Ash, Button Wood. **1786** in 1903 Jefferson *Writings* 2.74 **VA**, The paccan-nut is, as you conjecture, the Illinois nut. The former is the vulgar name south of the Potomac. **1792** Imlay *Western Terr.* 212, The Carolina ground-nut grows low down on the Mississippi, and the peccane in the Illinois. **1793** (1948) Toulmin *Western Country* 67 **KY**, Hickory nuts, walnuts, puccoon nuts (a very fine fruit). **1797** in 1908 Mathews *A. Ellicott* 152, I have a large Keg of Pecon Nuts put up for you. **1804** in 1930 Dunbar *Life* 217 **MS**, Black oak, packawn, hickory, elm &c. **1836** (1935) Field *3 Yrs. TX* 40, The timber with few exceptions is percon, which bears a fruit not unlike the shagbark walnut. **1854** Wailes *Rept. on Ag. & Geol.* MS 343, Pacon, Carya olivaefermis [sic]. Pacon, bitter, Hicorea texana. **1897** *KS Univ. Qrly.* (ser B) 6.91 **LA**, Puccon: pecan. **1903** DN 2.324 **seMO**, [pɛˈkɑn]. This pronunciation is universal. **1907** DN 3.234 **nwAR**, Pecan. . . Universally pronounced [pɪˈkɔn]. **1909** DN 3.356 **eAL, wGA**,

Pecan. . . Pronounced [pɪˈkɔn]. **1919** *DN* 5.37 **OK,** *Puccoon.* . . Negro pronunciation of *pecan.* [*DARE* Ed: This may be erroneous; cf **puccoon.**] **1929** Sale *Tree Named John* 70 **MS,** How you spec' me t' swallow 'at ole nasty, bloody thing an' it's big ez a puck-cawn, too? **1941** *LANE* Map 278 **NEng,** [Of 24 infs who said *pecan,* 9 said [ˈpikæn] or [pɪˈkæn], 5 [pɪˈkæn], 7 [pikən], and one each [pikaˆn] and [pɪkaˆn]. One inf said that [pikaˆn] was proper, but [pikæn] was usual.] **1942** *Collier's* 12 Sept 36 **Sth** [Black], Yonder her house, Boss, settin' in de edge er de puck-kon grove. **1944** *AmSp* 19.148 **LA,** The writer has collected nine other specimens [=pronunciations of *pecan,* in addition to [pɪˈkɑn] and [pəˈkɑn]] to date. . . 1. [ˈpiˌkæn] 2. [pɪˈkæn] 3. [ˈpiːkɑn] 4. [ˈpikən] 5. [pɪˈkɑn] 6. [pəˈkɑn] 7. [pʌˈkɑn] 8. [ˈpʌˈkɔn] 9. [ˈpəˈkɔ] 10. [pəˈkɔ] 11. [pəˈkɔrn]. **c1960** *Wilson Coll.* **csKY,** Pecan [pɪˈkɑn], [ˈpiˌkɑn]. **1965–70** *DARE* (Qq. L34, I43, 53, T15, 16) 288 Infs, **chiefly Sth, S Midl, OK, TX,** (Bitter, Burkett, McCulley, Schley, sweet, wild, etc) pecans [Proncs of the type [pɪˈkɑn, pəˈkɑn, -ˈkɔn] are most common; those of the type [pɪˈkɑn, pɪ-, pi-] are also frequent, as are [ˈpiˌkæn, -ˌkɑn, -ˌkɔn]; less freq are the types [ˈpʌˌkɑn, pɪˈkʌn, pəˈkʌn]; others, such as [pɑˈkɑn, pəˈkæn, ˈpikn̩], also occur.]; (Qu. H32) Infs **CO47, DE2, IN3, IA36, MN14, NE7, WV8, WI70,** [ˈpiˌkɑn, ˈpi-]; **MA2, PA119,** [ˈpiˌkæn]; **NM5, KS4,** [pɪˈkɑn]; **NY169,** [pɪˈkæn]; **OH98,** [piˈkɑn]; **MI111,** [pəˈkɑn]; **PA136,** [ˈpiˈkn̩]; (Qu. H63) Infs **AL33, LA14, CA178, IL122, KY74,** 85, **TX94,** [pəˈkɑn]; **VA4,** 35, 45, [ˈpiˌkɑn]; **KY25, VA18,** [piˈkɑn]; **GA36,** [pɪˈkæn]; **KY85,** [piˈkɔn]; **LA6,** [ˈpʌˌkɑn]; **TX36,** [pɪˈkɑn]; (Qu. H80) Inf **LA9,** [pəˈkɔn]; **MS34,** [ˈpʌkɑn]; **SC34,** [ˈpikæn]; **TX26,** [pˈɪˈkɑn]; **TX37,** [pikɑn]; **TX85,** [pikɑn]; **TX91,** [pəkɑn]; **WY3,** [ˈpiˌkɑn]. [*DARE* Ed: Because of the way in which *pecan* was elicited, esp in Qq. I43 and T16, the bulk of this information is from areas in which pecans are grown.] **1967** *DARE* Tape **LA7,** They were eating up those people's [ˈpʌkɔˑnz]. **1989** Pederson *LAGS Tech. Index* 182 **Gulf Region,** [Pronunciations of the type [pɪˈkɑn, pəˈkɑn, -ˈkɔn] are most common; those of the type [ˈpiˌkɑn, -ˌkɔn, -ˌkæn, ˌpiˈkɑn] are also common; less freq are [ˌpiˈkæn, ˈpʌˌkɑn, ˌbɪˈkɑn, ˌbə-]; others, such as [ˈpikn̩, ˈpiˌkɛn, -ˌkjæn, ˈpɑˌkɔn, ˈpʊˌkɑn, ˈpʌˌkæn] also occur.]

B Senses.

1 Std: a **hickory** n **B1** (here: *Carya illinoiensis*); also the fruit of this tree. Also called **bitter pecan, Illinois nut, nogal, papershell pecan, soft-shelled hickory, sweet pecan** Cf **wild pecan**

2 A nose.

1968 *DARE* (Qu. X14, *Joking words for the nose*) Inf **LA37,** Schnozzola, potato, pecan, ski jump.

3 See quot.

1968 *DARE* (Qu. HH28, *Names and nicknames . . for people of foreign background: Negro*) Inf **LA20,** Pecan.

pêche prêtre n Also *pesce prétre* [Fr *pêche prêtre,* literally "priest-fish"; see quot 1887] Cf **priestfish**
=**black rockfish 1.**

1882 U.S. Natl. Museum *Bulletin* 16.659, *S[ebastichthys] mystinus.* . . Pêche Prêtre; Black Rock-fish. . . Puget Sound to San Diego. **1887** Goode *Amer. Fishes* 268 **CA,** *Sebastichthys mystinus,* is most generally called the "Black Rockfish" . . . The Portuguese at Monterey call it "Pesce Prêtre," or Priest-fish, in allusion to its dark colors, so different from those of most of the other members of the family. **1898** U.S. Natl. Museum *Bulletin* 47.1784, *Sebastodes mystinus.* . . Pêche Prêtre.

peck n¹ [Engl dial var of *pick; OED2* 1514 →] *old-fash*
A tool for dressing millstones—often in comb *mill-peck;* hence v *peck* to dress a millstone with this tool.

1899 (1912) Green *VA Folk-Speech* 282, *Mill-peck.* . . A hammer wlth [sic] two chisel-heads, used for deepening the grooves of millstones. *Ibid* 316, *Peck.* . . Peckaxe. A pickaxe. A mill-*peck.* **1952** Brown *NC Folkl.* 1.575, *Peck.* . . To dress a millstone. **1982** Ginns *Snowbird Gravy* 85 **nwNC,** When I'd sharpen it, I'd take a mill peck. That's a rock, and you just peck furrows in it, in the millstone. The stone was about forty inches across. I had to peck those furrows in it so it would grind.

peck n² [Cf *OED2 peck* sb.³ 3 "Food, meat, 'grub'"; 1567 →; "slang," orig. *Thieves' Cant"*]
Chiefly among railroad workers: a short lunch break.

1932 *RR Mag.* Oct 369, *Peck*—20 minutes allowed for lunch. **1938** Beebe *High Iron* 223 [Railroad terms], *Peck:* Twenty-minute stop allowed for a meal in a railroad restaurant.

peck v¹

1 To knock or tap on something, as a door. **chiefly Sth, S Midl**

1902 *DN* 2.241 **sIL,** *Peckin.* . . Frequently used for 'pounding.' **1903** *DN* 2.324 **seMO,** *Peck.* . . To tap; to rap. 'He was pecking at the door.' **1907** *DN* 3.234 **nwAR,** *Peck.* . . To rap, to tap. **1968** *DARE* FW Addit **MD18,** *Peck*—meaning "knock" in connection with door. "Somebody pecked at the door." **1982** Ginns *Snowbird Gravy* 176 **nwNC,** Got tired, wanted some water, and stopped at a house and pecked at the door. **1986** Pederson *LAGS Concordance,* 1 inf, **cMS,** I can peck on wood (= knock on wood for luck). **2000** *DARE* File **WV,** I heard an interesting expression from an older lady from West Virginia I thought I'd share. "Peck on wood" for "knock on wood."

2 with *at* or *on:* =**pick** v **2.** **scattered, but more freq Sth, S Midl**

1870 *Galaxy* 9.218 **NEng,** Whatever person liked Susie, . . that person he pecked at. The pecking was good-natured in appearance; . . but it was just as serious in purpose as open anger. **1899** (1912) Green *VA Folk-Speech* 316, *Peck.* . . To *peck* at, to attack repeatedly with petty criticism; to carp at. "Peck on." **1906** *DN* 3.150 **nwAR,** *Peck on.* . . To bully. "What you want to peck on him for?" **1909** *DN* 3.356 **eAL, wGA,** *Peck on.* . . To take advantage of, bully, impose on. **1952** Brown *NC Folkl.* 1.575, *Peck at (on).* . . To nag at, to find fault with. **c1960** *Wilson Coll.* **csKY,** *Peck at.* . . To nag, pick at. **1965–69** *DARE* (Qu. Y7, *When one person never misses a chance to be mean to another . . : "I don't know why she keeps _____ me all the time!"*) Infs **AL51, NY37, OH72, PA104, TX65,** Pecking at; **OK42,** Pecking on; (Qu. Y8, *To keep after a person so as to get him to do things: "He never gets a minute's peace—she's always _____";* total Infs questioned, 75) Infs **NM12, OK1,** Pecking at him. **1982** *DARE* File **swNH,** Pecking at someone (being a verbal nuisance).

3 See **peck** n¹.

peck n³ Also *pecker* [Abbrs for **peckerwood 2**] **chiefly Sth, S Midl** *chiefly among Black speakers*
A White person, esp a **poor White 1.**

1932 *Evening Sun* (Baltimore) 9 Dec 31/5 (*OED2*), *Peck,* a white person. **1934** *AmSp* 9.288 **sePA** [Negro slang in Lincoln Univ], *Pale* (also *peck; pink*). A white person. Sometimes used in lieu of the more general Negro term for whites, *o'fay* or *fay.* **1965–70** *DARE* (Qu. HH1, *Names and nicknames for a rustic or countrified person*) Inf **KY85,** Country peck; **SC69,** Pecks—Whites; (Qu. HH28, *Names and nicknames . . for people of foreign background*) Inf **LA6,** For White folks: cracker—for poor ones, poorer than we are; peck—for poor ones; **VA41,** Cracker, old peck—nicknames used by Negroes for Whites; **VA71,** Call Whites of whatever origin "pecks" or "crackers." [4 of 5 Infs Black] **1969** in 1972 Chapman *New Black Voices* 183, A poor white peck will cuss. A poor white peck will cuss worse'n a nigger. I am talking about white men who ain't poor like them pecks. **1970** Major *Dict. Afro-Amer. Slang* 90, *Peck* . . a white person. **1986** Pederson *LAGS Concordance,* 1 inf, **swAL,** Peck—seems to mean "poor white" here; 1 inf, **ceTX,** Country peck—white; 1 inf, **swGA,** Peck—Negro pejorative for a white person; *(The poor whites—black man's terms)* 5 infs, **GA, cLA, seAR,** (Poor) peck; 1 inf, **nwMS,** Peck—"niggers say"; 1 inf, **swGA,** A nasty peck; 1 inf, **swGA,** A peck—worse than cracker, a lazy person; 1 inf, **ceAL,** Peck—a southern white, not used now; 1 inf, **cwMS,** Poor peck—ain't got nothing, don't know nothing; 1 inf, **ceTX,** That's a poor peck; 1 inf, **swMS,** White peck; 2 infs **ceLA, cnGA,** (Poor) pecker(s); 1 inf, **ceTN,** A pecker, old white peckers—could apply to any whites; *(Caucasian)* 2 infs, **swTN, cnAL,** Peck—derogatory; 1 inf, **cwTN,** A peck; 1 inf, **nwLA,** Pecker—derogatory. [18 of 22 infs Black, 1 of Fr background]

peck n⁴ [*peck* to nag, scold] Cf *have a mad on* (at **mad** n); **peck, on the**
An angry mood, bad temper—in phr *to have a peck on.*

1968 *DARE* FW Addit **nwKS,** "She has a peck on"—something upset her and as a result she's annoyed and irritable.

peck v² [Var of **peg C2;** cf *OED2 peck* v.² 1 "To pitch, cast, fling. . . *Obs. exc. dial.*"]
To throw, make a throw (at something); hence n *peck* a toss, throw (at something).

1967 *DARE* (Qu. Y10, *To throw something . . "The dog came at him, so he picked up a stone and _____ it at him."*) Inf **NY10A,** Pecked. **c1970** Wiersma *Marbles Terms* **swMI** (as of c1905), It's your turn to peck at the glassy. *Ibid,* Peck . . a peg. [Peg . . an overhand shot at a large marble with a smaller one.] **1998** *NADS Letters* **eMA** (as of c1950), I clearly remember "peck" in the sense of "To throw something or make a throw at" in the context of informal baseball games. . . "Peck it home," or "Peck it here." *Ibid* **ceWI,** A friend of mine in Appleton, WI (in the mid-1960s) was nicknamed "Pecker." The nickname had no sexual connotation whatever. It was a reference to basketball. My friend was notorious for shooting (or "pecking") the ball from just about anywhere on the court, rather than passing it to a teammate. *Ibid* **MD,** In the mid- to late 1960s, when I was playing . . baseball in Hagerstown, Maryland, "Peck it in here" was often used for a hard throw. . . from the outfield to the infield. . . It was rarely used regarding the pitcher throwing to the hitter, except in the case of a knock-down pitch: "He pecked it right at him." **1999** *Ibid* **nwOH** (as of c1960), In Toledo, Ohio in little league baseball we used the term peck to mean a throw. Peck it home; he really pecked that one in there or he pecked it away (missed who he was throwing to).

peck n[5] See **peck** v[2]

peck at See **peck** v[1] 2

peck eggs See **pick eggs**

pecker n
1 also *peckerbird:* A **woodpecker.** [*OED2* 1697 →]
1906 *DN* 3.150 **nwAR,** *Pecker.* . . Woodpecker. **1956** Ker *Vocab. W. TX* 229, Bird that pecks holes in trees. . . pecker [1 of 67 infs]. **1965–70** *DARE* (Qu. Q18, *Joking names and nicknames for woodpeckers*) Infs **CT5, IA22, IL77, MN33, MS81, OH97, SC69, SD5, TN65, WI54,** Pecker; **CO20, IL4, MI108,** Peckerbird; **AZ2,** Pesty pecker. **1986** Pederson *LAGS Concordance (Woodpecker)* 1 inf, **cnFL,** Red pecker; 2 infs, **ceAL, nwFL,** Pecker woodpecker(s); 1 inf, **nwMS,** Redheaded wooden peckers = woodpeckers.
2 The penis.
[**1902** Farmer–Henley *Slang* 156, *Pecker.* . . The *penis.*] **1936** (1938) Miller *Black Spring* 142 **Brooklyn NYC,** Ought to stand on Times Square with my pecker in my hand and piss in the gutter. **1942** McAtee *Dial. Grant Co. IN Suppl. 1* 7 (as of 1890s), *Pecker* . . the most common word for penis. **1954** *Harder Coll.* **cwTN,** *Pecker:* The penis. This taboo term has by analogy caused the word *woodpecker* to be changed to *woodchuck.* **1968** *DARE* (Qu. II20b, *A person who tries too hard to gain somebody else's favor*) Inf **CA105,** Pecker-sucker—woods term. **1985** Irving *Cider House* 41 **eME,** By mistake, trying to get out of her lap, he'd put his hand on her breast and she'd sharply pinched what the private school boy in Waterville had called his pecker. **1985** Keillor *Lake Wobegon* 170 **MN,** It was an honor to have Sylvester's desk, a boy who probably sat and whiled away the hours with similar thoughts about Washington and Lincoln, cars, peckers, foreign lands, lunch. **1986** Pederson *LAGS Concordance,* 1 inf, **csTN,** Pecker = dick—penis—as abusives, not equivalents; 1 inf, **cLA,** Pecker = penis—in anecdote; 1 inf, **cAL,** His pecker = his penis.
3 See **peck** n[3].

peckerbird See **pecker** 1

peckerhead n
1 A **woodpecker.**
1967–70 *DARE* (Qu. Q18, *Joking names and nicknames for woodpeckers*) Infs **CT26, MD9, MI112, MO18,** Peckerhead; **NH14,** Peckerhead—wouldn't use it before women. **1986** Pederson *LAGS Concordance,* 1 inf, **csTN,** A pecker head—most of them say—not woodpecker.
2 A disparaging term for a person; see quots.
1955 *Time* 14 Nov 116, When the girl's husband . . , a got-rich peckerhead, finds out about that hotel visit, he ravishes his wife, just to even the score. **1969** *DARE* (Qu. N12, . . *Somebody who drives carelessly or not well*) Inf **IL81,** Jackass; half-wit; peckerheads—now, you[=FW]'re of age, and you're married, and that's what I'd call him. **1977** Leonard *Unknown* 239 **LA,** Them peckerheads'd never make it. **1986** Pederson *LAGS Concordance,* 1 inf, **cnAL,** Pecker head—peckerwood—thickheaded person—stupid; 1 inf, **ceTX,** Pecker-head—people—he hasn't heard much; 1 inf, **cnGA,** Pecker heads = peckerwoods + redheads—term for boys. **1995** Lesley *Sky Fisherman* 284 **OR,** Think of these poor Indian people. Lost about everything they have, then lose even more while I diddle around rescuing peckerheads like you.

pecker pole n
See quots.
1956 *AmSp* 31.151 **nwCA,** *Pecker pole.* . . A long, thin log. **1958** McCulloch *Woods Words* 133 **Pacific NW,** *Pecker pole*—A small tree or sapling. **1977** Jones *OR Folkl.* 101, *Peckerpole:* a small tree.

peckerwood n Pronc-sp *peckawood* [Metath for *woodpecker;* cf Intro "Language Changes" I.1]
1 also *peckerwooder, peckwood:* A **woodpecker. chiefly Sth, S Midl** See Map Cf **French peckerwood**
1835 in 1910 *Talladega Daily Home* (AL) 28 Feb 2/3, The following "old timers" lived on the highway . . From the mouth of Peckerwood creek to the Sulphur Springs . . Henry G. Woodward [etc]. **1859** (1968) Bartlett *Americanisms* 314, *Peckerwood.* . . Western for Woodpecker. **1885** Thompson *By-Ways* 24, Allus thut 'at a Peckwood wer' a leetle, tinty, stripedy feller; never hyeard er them air big ole woodcocks a bein' called Peckwoods. **1893** Shands *MS Speech* 49, *Peckerwood. Woodpecker.* Bartlett says that this word is Western. It is also heard very frequently in Mississippi, as in Tennessee. **1893** Owen *Voodoo Tales* 53 **MO** [Black], "Granny, that wasn't a woodpecker. . ." "Hit b'long in fam'bly o' de peckerwoods des de same." **1903** *DN* 2.324 **seMO,** *Peckerwood.* . . Woodpecker. **1906** *DN* 3.150 **nwAR,** *Peckerwood.* **1906** Johnson *Highways Missip. Valley* 87 **TN,** Off among the trees I could hear . . the drum-beat of the "peckerwoods." **1909** *DN* 3.356 **eAL, wGA,** *Peckerwood.* **1915** *DN* 4.187 **swVA,** *Peckerwood. Ibid* 227 **wTX,** *Peckerwood.* **1916** *DN* 4.345 **FL,** *Peckerwood.* **1927** *DN* 5.476 **Ozarks,** *Peckerwood.* **1929** Sale *Tree Named John* 127 **MS** [Black], Yistiddy e'nin', a peckerwood lit on my house en pecked, he did, twel Ah th'owed fus' a knife en den a fock at 'im. **1946** *AmSp* 21.98 **sIL,** *Peckerwood,* woodpecker. **1949** Kurath *Word Geog.* 74, *Woodpecker.* . . The variant *peckerwood* is common in the folk speech of the Virginia Piedmont and can be heard also in the mountains of North Carolina. **1950** *PADS* 14.51 **SC,** *Peckerwood.* **1955** *Oriole* 20.1.9, Yellow-shafted flicker. . . Peckerwood, Peckwood [etc]. **1965–70** *DARE* (Qu. Q18, *Joking names and nicknames for woodpeckers*) 171 Infs, **chiefly Sth, S Midl,** Peckerwood; **KY21,** Peckerwood—regular, not joking, name; **KY76,** Peckerwood [FW: used in conv; not joking]; **KY82,** Peckerwood—serious word; **TN24,** Peckerwood—this seems to be the most common word; **GA54, 76,** Peckerwooder. **1989** Pederson *LAGS Tech. Index* 203 **Gulf Region,** 358 infs, Peckerwood; 3 infs, Peckerwood bird.

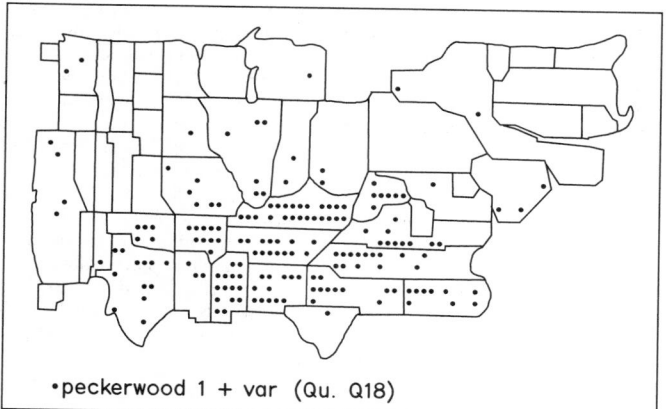

•peckerwood 1 + var (Qu. Q18)

2 A poor, backward, rural White person—often used as a vague term of abuse for a White person, esp by Black speakers. **chiefly Sth, S Midl** *derog* Cf **poor White 1**
1928 McKay *Home to Harlem* 46 **NYC** [Black], What's the matter, buddy, the peckawoods them was doing you in? **1929** Gordon *Born to Be* 126 **cwFL** [Black], All these peckerwoods runs around with these black gals when they can git 'em. **1934** Stribling *Unfinished Cathedral* 189 **AL,** Hello, old peckerwood, what's up? **1942** *Amer. Mercury* 55.223.96 **Harlem NYC** [Black], Peckerwood—poor and unloved class of Southern whites. **1942** Faulkner *Go Down* 360 **MS,** You sound almost like a Northerner even, not like the draggle-tailed women of these Delta peckerwoods. **1952** Brown *NC Folkl.* 1.575, *Peckerwood.* . . A poor, low-class white person. **1953** Randolph–Wilson *Down in Holler* 270 **Ozarks,** *Peckerwood.* . . In some parts of Arkansas it refers to rural whites of low origin, comparable to the *white trash* of the Deep South.

1964 *Chicago Daily News* (IL) 23 Sept 36/8 **MS** [Black], 40 percent of my business was whites, and not just peckerwoods . . , but good whites. 1964 *PADS* 42.31 **Chicago IL,** The most characteristic feature of Negro terms for Caucasians is the tendency to expand particularized designations for Caucasians to include all members of the race, e.g., terms for poor Southerners: *peckerwood, white trash* [etc]. 1967–70 *DARE* (Qu. HH1, *Names and nicknames for a rustic or countrified person*) Infs **MS**88, **TN**53, (Poor) peckerwood; **NC**87, Peckerwood—Whites; (Qu. HH5, *Someone who is queer but harmless*) Inf **TX**27, Peckerwood; (Qu. HH28, *Names and nicknames . . for people of foreign background*) Inf **CA**81, Whites are called by Negroes: peckerwoods; (Qu. HH40, *Uncomplimentary words for an old man*) Inf **AR**55, Peckerwood. [4 of 6 Infs Black] 1980 *AR Gaz.* (Little Rock) 23 Nov sec B 4, "Peckerwoods," in South Arkansas deer-hunting parlance, are outsiders coming into an area to hunt. 1989 Pederson *LAGS Tech. Index* 253 **Gulf Region** *(Poor whites [white usage])* 19 infs, Peckerwoods; 3 infs, No-worm *(or regular, sorry)* peckerwood; 1 inf, Peckerwood farmer; *(Poor whites [black usage])* 41 infs, Peckerwood; 4 infs, Lazy *(or old, mean, poor)* peckerwood. 1994 *DARE* File **NM, OK,** In at least western Oklahoma and eastern New Mexico, in at least the more rural areas (I taught in a very small, very rural, very typical school) *peckerwood* was often used by the staff there, even to a student's face, to refer to a student who was a little dickens, a skeezix, a loveable rascal, someone who even was a pleasant diversion. . . With adults it had a different connotation: someone (always a male; it was never used to refer to females) who was shiftless, engaged in borderline legal activities, if indeed any activities at all. . . There I knew of no racial distributions, but that was 20 years ago. 1996 McDowell *Leaving Pipe Shop* 18 **AL** [Black], You are the oldest and you know how to stand up to these plant folks. You got to have enough gumption to deal with these peckerwoods.

3 In logging: used attrib in ref to a small-scale transient logging and milling operation, as:

a *peckerwood (saw)mill.* **chiefly Sth, S Midl**

1937 Morley *Characteristics Labor Market AL* 40, There are also a great number of small so-called "peckerwood" mills which operate in small tracts. 1938 *FWP Guide CT* 483, The highway . . swings around the hill . . entering an area where a 'peckerwood' (transient) sawmill has worked in native softwoods and left the usual 'slash.' 1943 *Clarke Co. Democrat* (Grove Hill AL) 1 July 2/2 *(DA),* The peckerwood mills are almost as rare in Clarke as the ivory-billed woodpecker. 1945 *News-Age Herald* (Birmingham) 23 Sep. two-B/6 *(DA)* **AL,** It jumped from Walter's first little 'peckerwood' sawmill to a substantial wholesale lumber business. 1946 *Newsweek* 15 Apr 68 **sAppalachians,** Operators of fly-by-night "peckerwood" sawmills are busy in the backwoods supplying the black market in lumber. *Ibid,* Conditions encourage . . the peckerwood . . operators who cut undergrown trees ruthlessly. 1949 Webber *Backwoods Teacher* 14 **Ozarks,** The gables . . were of lumber which still showed the ancient curving marks of the circular saw which had sliced it from the logs at some little "peckerwood" mill. 1955 *Seattle Daily Times* (WA) 11 Dec 8/4, [Letter:] A small portable mill of the type commonly called "haywire" or "pecker-wood" saws from five to ten thousand board-feet per day. 1978 *Natl. Geogr. Mag.* Mar 415 **AR,** Delmar operates a small mill, a 440 Corley, on a few acres in the Ozarks. . . Peckerwood mills—as those like Delmar's are called in this region—are remnants of the past, when timbering was done mostly by small entrepreneurs scattered about in the woods. 1989 Flynt *Poor But Proud* 149 **ceAL,** Portable operations, often called "peckerwood sawmills," actually went on the trains with crews.

b *peckerwood operator.*

1946 [see **3a** above].

c *peckerwood outfit.* Cf **gyppo** n **b**

1958 McCulloch *Woods Words* 133 **Pacific NW,** *Peckerwood outfit*—a. A small gypo outfit. b. A small portable sawmill in the woods.

peckerwooder See **peckerwood 1**

peckerwood mill See **peckerwood 3a**

peckerwood operator See **peckerwood 3b**

peckerwood outfit See **peckerwood 3c**

peckerwood sawmill See **peckerwood 3a**

peck horn n
An althorn, esp the mellophone.

1926 Ferber *Show Boat* 96, Up the levee they scrambled—two cornets, a clarinet, a tuba, an alto (called a peck horn. Magnolia loved its ump-a ump-a ta-ta-ta, ump-a ump-a ta-ta-ta). 1936 *Amer. Mercury* 38.1.x, *Peck Horn*—mellophone. 1966 *New Yorker* 25 June 46 **New Orleans LA,** From the age of eight I played the upright alto—the peck horn—in my father's band. 1971 *Today Show Letters* **AR,** Peck Horn—French Horn or Alto Horn. . . Plays after beats [in] music. 1991 Ruff *Call to Assembly* 122, The men all played mellophones, which are also called "peck horns." (The peck horns, a poor substitute for the French horn in bands, is [sic] an alto horn that typically plays simple repeated notes that sound like "peck, pecka, peck, peck, peck, peck.")

peckie n
=**least sandpiper.**

1887 *Forest & Stream* 28.84 **seMA,** Shore Bird Nomenclature. . . In Nantucket. . . the semi-palmated and other small sandpipers are called peckies.

peckinall See **pegging awl**

peckish adj
1 Hungry.

1838 (1843) Haliburton *Clockmaker* (2d ser) 12, I don't care if I stop and breakfast with you, for I feel considerable peckish this mornin'. 1899 (1912) Green *VA Folk-Speech* 316, *Peckish*. . . Inclined to eat; somewhat hungry. 1903 *DN* 2.353, *Peckish*. . . Slightly hungry; ready for a lunch. 1946 *PADS* 6.23 **eNC** (as of 1925), *Peckish*. . . Somewhat hungry. 1952 Brown *NC Folkl.* 1.575, *Peckish*. . . Hungry. 1969 *DARE* FW Addit **ceNC,** *Peckish,* meaning hungry. "I'm feeling a little peckish." 1978 Gould *Greenleaf* 125 **ME,** Why, Alcott, you sure look peckish today. Merry Christmas to you. 1998 *DARE* File **cwCA** (as of 1960s), My parents, both from the Northwest, used to say "I'm feeling a little peckish this evening." I could hear the quote marks around *peckish,* though, so I knew they were using it as if it were someone else's word, not theirs.

2 also *pecky:* Short-tempered; nagging, hypercritical. Cf **peck** n[4]; **peck, on the**

1895 *DN* 1.392 **swVA,** *Peckish* . . easily offended. 1949 Guthrie *Way West* 271, The Indians would get over being meddlesome and pecky. 1952 Brown *NC Folkl.* 1.575, *Peckish* . . inclined to nag. 1969 *DARE* (Qu. HH12, *A person who is always finding fault about unimportant things*) Inf **IL**71, Pecky.

peck on See **peck** v[1] **2**

peck, on the adj phr [Prob < *peck* to carp, nag, scold] **chiefly West** Cf **peck** n[4], **peckish 2, prod, on the**
Irritable, angry, ready to fight.

1907 White *AZ Nights* 118, You can chase a cow safely only until she gets hot and winded. Then she stands her ground and gets emphatically "on the peck." 1914 *DN* 4.165 **AZ,** *Get on the peck* (or *prod*). . . To assume the defensive. 1923 *DN* 5.216 **swMO,** *On the peck*. . . Pugnaciously inclined. 1958 McCulloch *Woods Words* 126 **Pacific NW,** *On the peck*—Mad; short-tempered. 1966–69 *DARE* (Qu. K16, *A cow with a bad temper*) Inf **NM**3, On the peck; (Qu. GG8, *When a person is very easily offended: "Be careful what you say to him, he's _____."*) Inf **OR**6, Always on the peck; (Qu. GG39, *Somebody who seems to be looking for reasons to be angry: "He's a _____."*) Inf **TX**43, On the peck.

peck-sap n
1965 *McDavid Coll.* **GA,** Peck-sap = sapsucker. [From] middle-aged Black woman.

peckwood See **peckerwood 1**

pecky adj
1 See **peckish 2.**
2 See quot.

1967 *DARE* FW Addit **AR**52, Making the ears and feet [of stuffed animals] is pecky work. [FW: Pecky = tedious, intricate, requiring patience and attention to detail.]

pecon See **pecan**

pecos v [*Pecos* River]
See quot 1929.

1929 Dobie *Vaquero* 292 **West,** If in the old days a man said of another, "He is a cowboy of the Pecos," that might mean many things. . . It might mean that he was a rustler. It might mean that he ran the risk of being "pecosed" either for his integrity or the lack of it; on the other hand, it might mean that he had helped to "pecos" some other rider of the range. *Ibid* 293, To "pecos" a man one shot him and rolled his body into the river—the one river that drained an empire. **1940** Writers' Program *Guide TX* 561 **cwTX,** Not only was homicide frequent but the tough *hombres* of the town added a distinctive touch in their manner of disposing of the body and were responsible for the creation of a new verb, to "Pecos." "Pecosin' a feller," meant killing him, filling the body with rocks and dropping it into the waters of the river.

Pecos strawberry See **strawberry**

pectoral sandpiper n

Std: a sandpiper *(Calidris melanotos)* noted for the male's developing a pouch at the breast in breeding season.   Also called **brownback 2, cherook, cow snipe, dowitch 1, fatbird, grass-bird 2a, grass plover 2, ~ snipe, haybird, hay plover, jack** n[1] **23b, jacksnipe 1, krieker, marsh plover, May ~, meadow snipe 2, oxeye 1a, prairie pigeon d, shortneck, sand snipe, squat ~, squatter, triddler**

peculiar n Cf **gem**

A type of muffin; see quot.

1896 *Daily News Cook Book* 344, Peculiars—Two cups of flour, one teaspoonful baking powder, one-half teaspoonful salt, one egg, one pint sweet milk. . . Bake in gem pans in a quick oven.

pecune See **picayune**

pedab See **pee-dab**

peddle v

Used in var phrr meaning to mind one's own business, as:
a *peddle* (or *sell*) *one's papers* and varr.   **chiefly Nth, West, Mid Atl**   See Map

1938 FWP NYC *NY Panorama* 156, *Go peddle your papers* . . may mean *go away; be a good fellow and leave; go away before you get hurt; mind your own business, you lug . . ; or leave us alone, can't you see we're busy?*   **1947** in 1960 Wentworth–Flexner *Slang* 380, I told him to go peddle his papers.   **1949** *Ibid,* He had been told to peddle his papers elsewhere.   **1950** WELS (*Expressions used to tell somebody to keep to himself and mind his own business*) 4 Infs, **WI,** Go (*or just, run along and*) peddle your papers.   **c1950** Halpert Coll. 47 **wKY, nwTN,** Aw, go peddle your papers = said to get rid of someone who is bothering you. (College).   **1965–70** DARE (Qu. II22, *Expressions to tell somebody to keep to himself and mind his own business*) 42 Infs, **chiefly Nth, West, Mid Atl,** Go peddle your (own) papers; **CA1,** 169, **CT35, IA30,** Peddle your (own) papers; **WA1,** Run along and peddle your own papers; **MD24,** You peddle your papers; **DC3, KY94, MA71,** 77, Go sell (your) papers; (Qu. JJ24, *To refuse firmly: "He wanted to get some more money, but this time I _____."*) Inf **WI34,** Told him to go peddle his papers elsewhere; (Qu. NN12a, *Things that people say to put a child off when he asks too many questions: "What's that for?"*) Inf **OK31,** Go peddle your papers; (Qu. NN12b, *Things that people say to put off a child when he asks, "What are you making?"*) Inf **MD22,** Go peddle

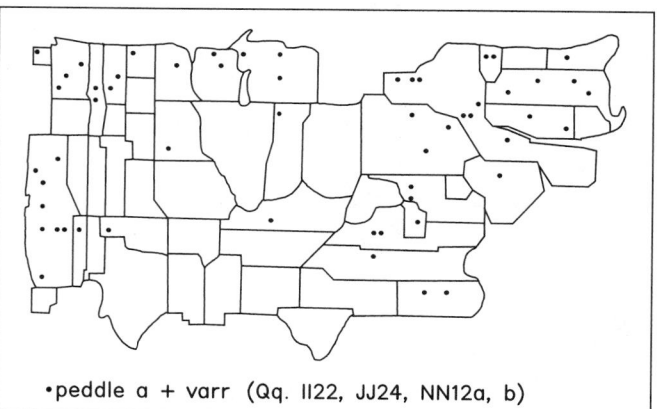

•peddle a + varr (Qq. II22, JJ24, NN12a, b)

your papers; **ME16,** Go sell your papers someplace else; [(Qu. Y19, *To begin to go away from a place: "It's about time for me to _____."*) Inf **MN24,** Peddle my papers].

b *peddle one's fish* (or *cucumbers,* etc) and varr.

1932 *AmSp* 7.335 [Johns Hopkins jargon], *Peddle your fish*—mind your own business.   **1950** WELS (*Expressions used to tell somebody to keep to himself and mind his own business*) 1 Inf, **seWI,** Peddle your fish.   **1965–70** DARE (Qu. II22, *Expressions to tell somebody to keep to himself and mind his own business*) 15 Infs, **scattered,** Go peddle your cucumbers (*or* apples, bananas, blarney, fish, peaches, peanuts); **TX9,** 29, Go peddle your own apples; **MD34,** Go peddle your fish in your own backyard; **MA56, 61,** Go peddle your wares elsewhere (*or* somewhere else); **MI4,** Peddle your own fish; [**FL35,** Pedal your own wagon;] (Qu. NN12a, *Things that people say to put a child off when he asks too many questions: "What's that for?"*) Inf **MS1,** Peddle your ducks somewhere else; (Qu. NN22b, *Expressions used to drive away children*) Inf **NY30,** Peddle your business; (Qu. NN22c, *Expressions used to drive away a dog*) Inf **NY1,** Go peddle fish.

peddler n Cf DS N36–37

In railroading: see quots.

1926 *AmSp* 1.652 [Hobo lingo], *Peddler*—local or slow freight train.   **1932** *RR Mag.* Oct 369, *Peddler*—Local way freight.   **1976** Gould *Blackie's RR Hdbk.* 6, *Train (doing switching and merchandise work):* Peddler—Local.

pede See **pedro**

pedestrian n joc

Prob a Presbyterian.

1967–69 DARE (Qu. CC4, *. . Nicknames . . for various religions or religious groups*) Infs **CA10, CT35, OH40,** Pedestrians.

pedigree n

One's personal history, esp an account of one's misdeeds; a police record; hence phr *to read* (or *tell*) *one's pedigree* and varr, to reveal frankly someone's faults.   Cf **read one's title clear**

1902 *DN* 2.241 **sIL,** Pedigree. . . One's antecedents or personal history.   **1903** *DN* 2.324 **seMO,** Pedigree. . . History. 'If he doesn't go straight I'll tell his pedigree.' Not applying to family descent, but to personal history.   **1907** *DN* 3.234 **nwAR,** Pedigree. . . Personal history; biography.   **1915** *DN* 4.187 **swVA,** Pedigree. . . Biography. "He's give us his whole pedigree from childhood on."   **1917** (1968) Phillips *Susan Lenox* 2.397 **NYC,** "Oh, she's got a record. . . Why the hell didn't you say so?" "I thought you remembered. You took her pedigree."   **1927** Ruppenthal Coll. **KS,** To read one's pedigree—to scold one esp. by stating in detail the shortcomings for which he is scolded.   **1942** Berrey–Van den Bark *Amer. Slang* 477.5, Pedigree, a prisoner's police record.   **1965–70** DARE (Qu. JJ35b, *. . Expressions [. . when you have just about reached the point of telling somebody what you think of him]*) Infs **CA101, IL5, 17, 115, KS13, OH22, 31, OK9, PA142,** I'm going to read his pedigree; **KS8,** I'd like to read his pedigree.

pedro n |'pidro, pid| Also *pede* **chiefly Inland Nth (exc Upper MW, NW), CA** See Map Cf **cinch** n[1] **3, double pedro, setback 2**

A card game, derived from **pitch** n[2] **1,** in which a special value is put on the five of trump—also used in var combs referring to varr of this game; in this or related games: the five of trump and sometimes also the five of the other suit of the same color.

1874 *Reno* (Nev.) *Crescent* 8 May 2/3 *(DA),* The five of trumps is 'pedro.'   **1899** Champlin-Bostwick *Young Folks' Games* 7, *Pedro Sancho,* or *Sancho Pedro.* A kind of Auction Pitch in which the dealer sells the privilege of making or pitching the trump. . . The five of trumps (called Pedro) counts five points, and the nine of trumps (called Sancho) nine points, each in favor of the player who wins the trick containing it. . . When a Joker . . is used in this game, it is called Dom, and the game Dom Pedro. . . Sancho may be omitted from the game, which is then called Pedro.   **1908** Day *King Spruce* 239 **ME,** I reckon some of us better spend our winter evenin's readin' instead of playin' pitch pede.   **1913** U.S. Playing Card Co. *Official Rules* 154, *Pedro* (or *pedro sancho*). A variety of Pitch in which the 9 (sancho) and 5 (pedro) of trumps count 9 and 5 points respectively for players winning tricks on which they are played.   **1929** Lynd–Lynd *Middletown* 281 **IN,** The growing rigidity of the social system today is centering parties more and more upon cards, pedro among the workers and bridge among the others.   **1947** *Sat. Eve. Post* 17 May 102 **LA,** He operates a pedro game for the Sabine and Chinese shrimpers.   **1950** *New Haven* (Mich.) *Herald* 19 Oct 1/5 *(Mathews Coll.),* Mrs. Fred Spens of Richmond entertained the North End pedro club Tuesday afternoon.   **1965–70** *DARE* (Qu. DD35, . . *Card games*) 21 Infs, **chiefly Inland Nth (exc Upper MW, NW), CA,** Pedro ['pidro]; **CA**97, Pedro ['pidro]—high-low-jack in the game; **MA**6, Pedro ['pidro]—a pitch game, deuces count and black fives high; **NV**9, Pedro ['pidro]—a simple game, nine cards, partners, four people; **NY**232, Pedro ['pidro]—fives are pedro, they count ten; **OH**4, Used to be pedro that the men played; **PA**104, Pedro ['pidro]—called [pid]; **NY**9, Pedro ['pidro] or [pid]; **WI**77, Right and left pedro; **NV**9, Single (*or* double) pedro; **IN**13, King pedro; **NY**68, Double-king pede [pid]—aces high, left and right king, jack, queen; some played 100 points, some 99; **VT**7, King pede [pid]; **VT**16, Pede [pid] used to be all they played around here for a while—eighty-eight pede, one hundred pede, pede, sixty-three pede; (Qu. DD37, . . *Table games played a lot by adults*) Inf **CA**158, Pedro ['pidro]. [34 of 35 Infs comm type 4 or 5, 30 old]   **1968** *Courier-Freeman* (Potsdam NY) 21 Mar 19, A pedro party for the benefit of Winthrop Grange was held Saturday evening.   **1974** Gibson *Hoyle* 66, [In the rules of *cinch:*] Bids can run as high as fourteen, which is the greatest number of points that a team can take during play, according to the following schedule, which pertains strictly to trump cards: . . right pedro, the five, 5; left pedro, the five of the same color, 5.   *Ibid* 172, *Pedro:* This covers developments of *Auction Pitch . . ,* which include two interrelated features: Simplification of play, and additional points for various trump cards taken in play.

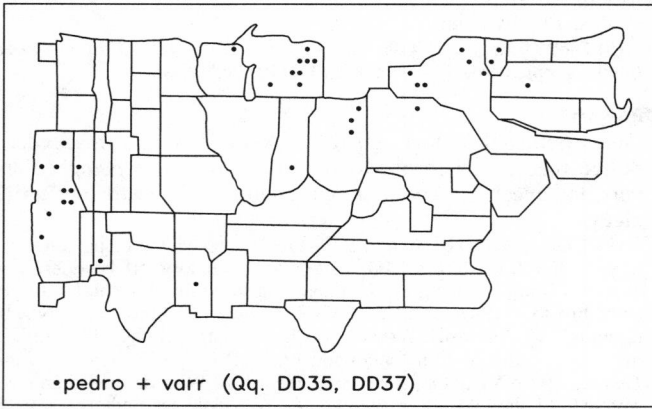

•pedro + varr (Qq. DD35, DD37)

pee n See **pea** n[2]

pee exclam See **pee-pee** exclam

pee-anna See **piano**

pee ant n [Euphem]   **chiefly S Midl**   See Map
=**piss ant** n 1.
   1954 *Harder Coll.* **cwTN,** Little ants are pee-ants or piss ants. We don't say them words.   **1965–70** *DARE* (Qu. R17, . . *Names . . for the big black ants that sting*) Infs **GA**6, **KY**11, 16, **NC**30, Pee ants; **VA**34, Piss ant; pee ants; (Qu. R18, . . *Kinds of ants*) Inf **CA**99, Pee ant; **KY**34,

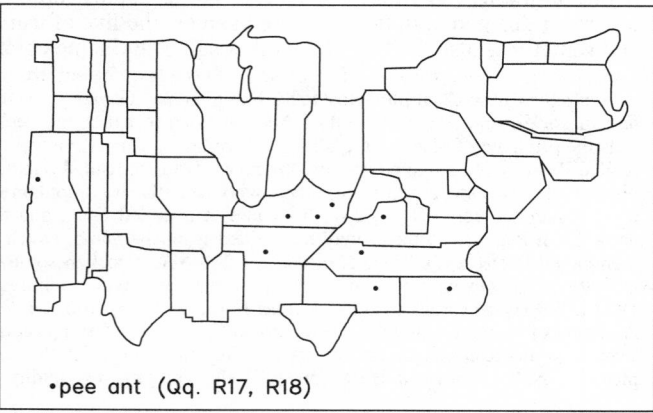

•pee ant (Qq. R17, R18)

Pee ants—small; **SC**53, Pee ants—sting; **TN**52, Pee ants—have a smell. [6 of 9 Infs female]   **1982** *Barrick Coll.* **csPA,** Peeants—euphemism for pissants.

pee-bed See **piss-a-bed** 2

pee-dab n Also *pee-dad, pee-dookie* Also sp *pedab* [Varr of **peewee** n[1] **2;** cf **dab** n[2], **doogie**]
=**pee-jib.**
   1957 *Sat. Eve. Post Letters* **sIN** (as of c1905), We had at least four grades of marbles, "aggies," "glassies," "crockies" and "peedads."   **1965–70** *DARE* (Qu. EE6b, *Small marbles or marbles in general*) Inf **TN**44, Pee-dabs; **IN**56, Pee-dads; **GA**77, Pee-dookies; [**IN**14, Pea marbles;] (Qu. EE6c, *Cheap marbles*) Inf **IN**56, Pee-dads—small brown ones made of clay.   **1973** Ferretti *Marble Book* 49, *Pedab.* Another name for Doughie.   **1975** in 1981 *NC Folkl. Jrl.* 29.33 **nwNC,** Benny Yates, a Boone native, recalls that in his youth every boy in his school had a small poke in which he carried a wide assortment of marbles suitable for any contest. "Pedabs, of course, were the most common. They were small, clay marbles that weren't worth much."   **1992** *DARE* File **eTN,** [From catalog for Smoky Mountain Knife Works:] Playing Marbles is our "National Sport" up here in the Smoky Mountains! . . "*Big Poke*" Contains approx. 300 marbles: 100 Tall Boys & 200 Pee-Dabs.

peedee n [Echoic]
1 A **pipit** (here: *Anthus spinoletta*).
   1951 *PADS* 15.58 **neIN** (as of 1890s), Peedee . . Pipit (*Anthus spinoletta rubescens*). My boyhood name for them imitated the notes of the birds flying overhead.
2 as *peedee frog, peeteet:* A **tree frog.**
   1968 *DARE* (Qu. P21, *Small frogs that sing or chirp loudly in spring*) Inf **IN**3, Peeteets; **PA**136, Peedee frogs.

peedoodle n Also *peadoodle, peadoddle* [Cf *EDD* peadoddle "To dawdle"]   **chiefly Sth, S Midl**
1 pl; with *the:* The jitters, nervousness.
   1835 Longstreet *GA Scenes* 231, "The stranger's got the *peedoddles,*" said a fourth, with humorous gravity.   **1992** *Houston Chron.* (TX) 5 Apr sec G 1/4, *Nervous:* . . Bad case of the peadoodles.   **1995** *Brophy Coll.* 54 **swMO** (as of c1960), Peedoodles. [A] certain nervous disorder of women.   **1997** *NADS Letters* **cAR,** The peadoodles is a nervousness that makes you feel like you don't know what to do with yourself.   *Ibid* **sTX,** I encountered the term [=*peadoodles*] during the early 50s in South Texas near Corpus Christi.
2 also pl; also *peadoodle crap;* in phr *knock* (or *scare*) *the peadoodles out of one* and varr: To give one a severe blow (or fright).
   2000 *NADS Letters* **eTX, swLA,** A sentence that I heard growing up was: "You scared the peadoodle crap out of me." or "You scared the peadoodles out of me." The first example was by far the most commonly used one. . . This comes from the East Texas, Southeast Texas and Southwest Louisiana areas. The age group using this term were all in their 80's though some of their children in their 50's also used the term. I have only heard this in rural areas and not in urban areas like Houston.   *Ibid* **TX,** His mother (b. Waxahachi TX 1923) used to say to her kids (in the loving way that mothers have) "Quit that, or I'll knock the peedoodle out of you." He doesn't know exactly what she meant, but he thought it sounded too serious to chance it.   *Ibid,* My grandmother (1880–1948) used the word *peadoodle* in this sense: If you don't quit that, I'm gonna knock the peadoodle out of you. I always took it to mean I would be rendered senseless. That usage still occurs in my family in Texas, Pennsylvania, North Carolina and South Carolina.   *Ibid* **IN,** I'm 53 and this expression was used a lot by Indiana farmers, especially kids. I always thought you got the peadoodles scared out of you, meaning you pooped and peed at the same time.
3 in phr *not to know peadoodle:* Not to know anything.
   2000 *NADS Letters* **SC,** I have always heard it used as "He doesn't know peadoodle." That is used in S.C.

pee-doodle v
See quot.
   2000 *NADS Letters* **WI,** I would spell this "peedoodle." This is an expression I occasionally heard my mother use. It means to briefly lose control of one's bladder. . . Can be caused by nerves, or a strong cough, a sneeze or even a laugh. . . My mother grew up here in Wisc., near Clinton and Mount Horeb. She was born in 1934.   *Ibid,* My grand-

mother 1887–1973, who was born near Mobile and lived in East Texas from 1890 until her death, retained many language characteristics. When she said "peedoodle," she meant to lose control of one's bladder momentarily. For example, "Quit tickling your sister—you're going to make her peedoodle."

pee-dookie See **pee-dab**

peeg See **pig** n[1] **A**

pee-gee See **pee-jib**

pee-in-the-bed See **piss-a-bed 3, 6**

pee-jib n Also *pee-gee, pee-jink(er)* [Var of **peewee** n[1] **2**; cf **jib** n[2]] esp **S Atl, Inland Sth** See Map
A small, usu cheap, playing marble.

1958 *Resp. to PADS 29* **cnOK**, Pee Jinker . . a pottie smaller than ⅜ [inch] in diameter. **1965–70** *DARE* (Qu. EE6a, . . *Different kinds of marbles—the big one that's used to knock others out of the ring*) Inf **VA**1, Pee-gee; (Qu. EE6b, *Small marbles or marbles in general*) Infs **KY**40, 41, **VA**1A, Pee-jibs; **GA**3, Pee-gees; **AL**3, Pee-jinks; **AL**32, Pee-jinks ['pijɪŋks]; **GA**23, Pee-jinkers; (Qu. EE6c, *Cheap marbles*) Inf **KY**40, Pee-jibs; **KY**41, Pee-jibs ['pijɪbz]; **AL**3, Pee-jinks.

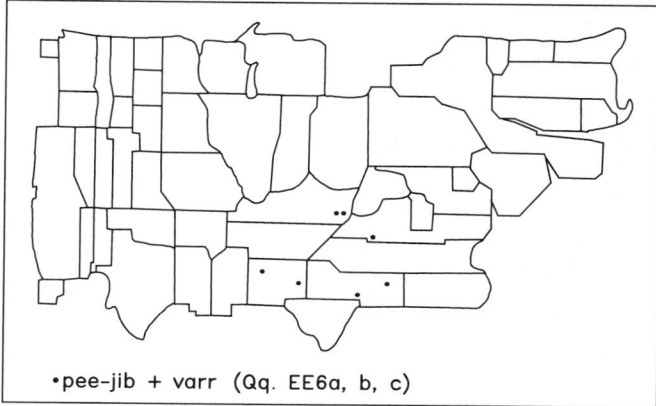

•pee-jib + varr (Qq. EE6a, b, c)

peekid See **peaked**

peel v[1], hence vbl n *peeling*, n *peeler*

1 To shell, hull, or husk (beans, peas, nuts, or ears of corn); hence ppl adj *peeled.* **scattered, but esp LA, TX** Cf **peeling** n
1938 *AmSp* 13.19 **MO** [Cornhusking terms], Pulling the ripe ear from its covering of dried shucks on the stalk, in western Nebraska and South Dakota is sometimes called *snapping* or *picking* as well as husking. Boys from Missouri farms have told me that they also call it *peeling* and *shucking.* **1965–70** *DARE* (Qu. I11, *When somebody takes peas out of the covering . . "She's _____ peas."*) Infs **LA**24, 37, **MA**7, Peeling; (Qu. I13, *When you take dry beans out of the cover you are _____ them*) Infs **GA**23, **LA**37, **MA**7, **NY**83, **TX**26, Peeling. **1972** *Thompson Coll.* **New Orleans LA**, Peelin(g) peas = peas from which the pods/shells/shucks/hulls are removed (and that takes in almost all kinds). They're peeled rather than shelled/hulled/shucked in New Orleans. **1975** *Times-Picayune* (New Orleans LA) 5 June 3/1, And how about a two-pound container of peeled pecans going at $3.00? **1986** Pederson *LAGS Concordance* **Gulf Region** (*To shell beans*) 12 infs, 7 **LA, TX**, Peel (them); 1 inf, **neFL**, Peeling the peas; 1 inf, **csLA**, Pea peeler—peels peas. **1997** *DARE* File **csTX**, I remember John Broughton of San Antonio saying that he "peeled" the pecans which fell from the tree in his yard.

2 To remove the skin from (an animal).
1929 *AmSp* 5.73 **NE** [Cattle country talk], "To peel" a "critter" is to pull the skin from it, often by means of a "double tree" and a horse. "To peel" is also "to skin" a rabbit or other small animal. **1968** Adams *Western Words* 223, *Peeler*—A cowboy's term for a man who skins the hides off cattle; also called *stripper. Ibid, Peeling*—A cowboy's term for skinning the hide off cattle.

peel v[2] Also sp *peal* [Prob *EDD* pail v. (also *peal, peel, pele*) "2. To strike continuously; to beat, thrash. . . 6. To hurry; to run at full speed." (Cf also *OED2* peal v.[1])]

1 To strike, beat; hence n *peeling* a beating.
1931–33 *LANE Worksheets* **csCT**, *Peeling*. . . Spanking. "I'll give you a good peeling." **1935** Davis *Honey* 104 **OR**, I picked up a club and peeled him one over the head. **1953** Randolph–Wilson *Down in Holler* 270 **Ozarks**, *Peel*. . . To slap or spank, as in punishing a child. "Quit that foolishness, Johnny, or I'll peel ye good!" **1954** *Harder Coll.* **cwTN**, *Peel*. . . Slap or spank, as in punishing a child.

2 with *out*: To scold, chide; hence n *peeling* a scolding; n *peeler* a rebuke.
1899 (1912) Green *VA Folk-Speech* 316, *Peeler*. . . A speech or letter scoring a person. **1968–70** *DARE* (Qu. II27, *If somebody gives you a very sharp scolding . . "I certainly got a _____ for that."*) Inf **PA**68, Peeled out; **NY**234, Peeling.

3 usu with *it*: To go or leave rapidly, run fast. Note: Colloq or slang *peel (out)* "to accelerate fast enough to burn rubber" is not included here.
1858 Hammett *Piney Woods Tavern* 178, Whang went an old musket slap at us, and we peeled it for hum as if the old sarpent was behind. **1859** (1968) Bartlett *Americanisms* 314, *To peel it.* To run at full speed. "Come, boys; peel it now, or you'll be late." **1942** Berrey–Van den Bark *Amer. Slang* 58.6, *Depart hurriedly;* "cut and run." . . Peel it. **1997** *DARE* File **Baltimore MD**, A person could peel down the street, if walking sufficiently fast.

4 To ride and break (a horse); hence vbl n *peeling*. [Cf **peeler** n[2] **2**]
1909 in 1947 Lomax *Advent. Ballad Hunter* 52 **Plains States, SW**, He knew some songs but me and another fellow were pealing some bronks for hat collections and I did not have time to copy them. **1929** *AmSp* 5.63 **NE**, An intelligent "bronco buster" will "break" a good horse to saddle without "spoiling" him. . . Sometimes, "breaking" is called "peeling" and "twisting." Many ranchers employ "peelers" by occasionally [sic], only because such men often are experts and are little interested in other kinds of work. **1939** (1973) FWP *Guide MT* 415, *Peel broncs*—To ride, drive, or break horses, especially with free use of the whip. **1940** White *Wild Geese* 5 **NW** (as of 1890s), He punched cattle as a cowboy; he peeled cayuses as a bronco buster.

5 To throw (a rock, ball, or other object).
1969 *DARE* (Qu. Y10, *To throw something . . "The dog came at him, so he picked up a stone and _____ it at him."*) Inf **PA**179, Threw, peeled. **1997** *DARE* File, "Peel," meaning "throw," is a childhood usage of mine. I was born in Northern Montana to rural Idaho/Utah parents; moved to Burley, Idaho at age 11. [A colleague] from rural Utah . . volunteered it in a sentence: "Hey, peel it to me," or "He peeled me a good one." *Ibid* **nAL**, "Peel" = "to throw." Yes, it was common in this usage in North Alabama, where I was born in 1935. *Ibid* **PA** (as of 1960s-70s), I used this word [=peal/peel] as a youth . . , but seldom do now. *Ibid* **Chicago IL** (as of 1930s). [*Ibid* **Canada**, "I was down on the beach peeling rocks at the gulls." I learned this from my father, who . . grew up . . just across the lake from Bay City, Michigan.] **1998** *Ibid* **nGA**, I use *peel* to mean . . to throw a ball (or some other object) at someone. *Ibid* **cKY** (as of 1960s); **swMI** (as of 1970s); **neOH** (as of 1950s); **cwPA** (as of 1970s).

peeled See **peel** v[1] **1**

peeler n[1]
1 See **peeler crab**.
2 See **peel** v[1].

peeler n[2] Also sp *pealer* [Perh from *EDD* pail v. (also *peal, peel, pele*) "5. To set about anything with energy." Cf **peel** v[2]]
1 Something remarkable of its kind; esp a hard-working, energetic person. **chiefly NEast**
1823 Cooper *Pioneers* 1.212 **NY**, It's a peeler without, I can tell you, good woman; but what cares I, blow high or blow low, d'ye see, it's all the same thing to Ben. **1830** in 1834 Smith *Life Jack Downing* 46 **ME**, My patience, he's a real peeler for speaking. **1845** Kirkland *Western Clearings* 74 **MI**, We's goin' straight to a bee-tree that I lit upon two or three days ago. . . It's a reel peeler, I tell ye! There's a hundred and fifty weight of honey in it, if there's a pound. **1859** (1968) Bartlett *Americanisms* 314, *Pealer.* A dashing, go ahead person or thing; a rouser. **1869** Stowe *Oldtown Folks* 117 **NEng**, She was spoken of with applause under such titles as "a staver," "a pealer," "a roarer to work." **1902** Day *Pine Tree Ballads* 90 **ME**, The storm came down upon us from the nor'-nor'east by east,/ —'Twas an equinoctial pealer,/ A reg'lar ring-tail

squealer. **1954** Forbes *Rainbow* 166 **NEng,** Half the time she was just one more farmer's wife—a real peeler for work. Some said she worked so beyond the usual limits of female endurance to smother up disappointment at having reached a considerable age childless. **1959** *VT Hist.* 27.152 **cn,neVT,** *Peeler.* . . A good worker. She's a *peeler.* Common. **1967** *DARE* FW Addit **MI66,** Peeler—synonym for *brat,* defined for me as "a boy that is not to be disciplined." **1969** *DARE* (Qu. X20, . . *A black eye*) Inf **IL60,** Peeler ['pilɚ].

2 A ranch hand or cowboy; spec one who tames wild horses, a bronco-buster. [The more spec sense appears to be derived from **peel** v[2] **4,** but if, as the quots suggest, the more general sense is the older, then the verb is a back-formation.] **West**
   1894 in 1958 Wister *Out West* 198, *Peeler*—cowpuncher. **1903** (1965) Adams *Log Cowboy* 85 **West,** My peelers and I are riding Circle Dot horses, as well as reaching the wagon in time for breakfast and lining our flues with Lovell's good chuck. **1916** *DN* 4.347 **nwTX** (as of 1896), *Peeler.* . . A ranch hand: among cattlemen in N.W. Texas. **1929** *AmSp* 5.57 **NE** [Cattle country talk], A cowboy is a "puncher," "cow puncher," "cow hand," "cow poke," "waddie," or "ranchman." The rodeo has made common the terms "bronc peeler," "bronco twister," "bronco buster," "buster," and "rider." **1929** Dobie *Vaquero* 127, Joe always carried two six-shooters, a rifle in a scabbard, a dirk, and wore, of course, the usual leggins, boots, and spurs that went to make up a peeler's rig. **1937** *DN* 6.618 **swTX,** Many . . Western terms are associated with the cowboy's taming of wild horses. . . Used in its strictest sense, the *peeler* refers to the cowpuncher who rides into the herd and "cuts" out the horse desired. **1940** (1966) Writers' Program *Guide AZ* 63, Two bronc-fighters, or peelers. **1940** Writers' Program *Guide NV* 76, A *broncho* or *bronch* is an unbroken horse, and the rider who breaks him is the *peeler.* **1941** Cleaveland *No Life* 128, Our cowhands who had been over to the Staked Plains came back with tales of how their hair had turned white at the way Texas 'peelers' ran over prairie-dog towns where there seemed to be no solid ground beneath their feet . . of a walnut that you have to break) Inf **LA37,** Shell, to become "a peeler." **1945** Thorp *Pardner* 139 **SW,** One day, along with a bunch of Block peelers, he visited the saloon in the little settlement of Seven Rivers.

3 See **peel** v[2] **2.**

peeler crab n Also *peeler* Pronc-sp *pailer* [*OED2* 1866 →] **chiefly Delmarva** Cf **buster 5, rank** adj **4, red sign (crab)**
A crab (or rarely other crustacean) nearly ready to shed its shell; see quots.
   1877 Bartlett *Americanisms* 456, *Peeler.* . . A crab just before shedding and becoming *soft,* when his shell is loose, so that it can be *peeled* off with the fingers, is called a *peeler.* It is the favorite bait for salt-water fishing, in Maryland and Virginia. **1883** *Century Illustr. Mag.* 26.378 **KY,** Large craw-fish, which were about to shed their outer cases, or shells, and which for this reason are called "shedders," or "Peelers". **1905** U.S. Bur. Fisheries *Rept. for 1904* 419, There are six stages of a crab's life, commonly classified as follows: First, the "hard crab," . . second, a "snot," . . third, a "peeler," when the old shell has begun to break. . . During hot weather it takes from two to three days for a "snot" to become a "peeler." **1942** Chesapeake Biol. Lab. *Pub.* 52.8 **Chesapeake Bay,** When the female [blue crab] becomes a peeler about to shed for the last time she is sought out by a male, who carries and protects her until she sheds. **1968–70** *DARE* (Qu. P18, . . *Kinds of shellfish*) Inf **MD15,** Peeler crab—crab exactly ready to shed shell; **VA55,** Peeler—about to become a sook. **1968–69** *DARE* FW Addit **eMD,** Peeler—a crab due to shed his shell soon; heard all over Eastern Shore of Maryland and Smith Island; **neNC,** Peeler—a crab about to shed; makes good bait. **1970** *DARE* Tape **VA47,** When they're catching peeler crabs, they . . put jimmy crabs, which is the . . male crab, in the pots and close it so he can't get out, and the little peelers, which are going to be soft, will go get in the pot with him. Sometimes you can catch as many as two hundred in a pot; **VA112,** They . . have a crab trap . . that catches these little peelers that sheds out to become soft-shell crabs. **1976** Warner *Beautiful Swimmers* 248 **eMD,** On the way back a little boy greets you. "Do you love this island?" he says. "I can show you some pailers." In Tangier vocabulary love equals favor or like and pailers are peeler crabs. **1982** Heat Moon *Blue Highways* 390 **Chesapeake Bay,** "Some people prefer a baked pailer to a fresh oyster." "What's a pailer?" "Peeler. Here, they say 'pailer,' and 'dredging' is 'drudgin'.'" **1984** *DARE* File **Chesapeake Bay** [Watermen's vocab], Red peeler. Ripe peeler. **1994** *DARE* File **DE,** A peeler is a crab that's about to molt. Crabs molt about once a month—that's where soft crabs come from. **1996** Horton *Island Out of Time* 62 **Chesapeake Bay MD,** Into one tub will go "green peelers." Placed in holding tanks back at Ed's shedding

shanty, these will emerge soft in several days. "Rank" peelers, which will shed sooner, go to another tub.

peeling n[1] [**peel** v[1] **1**]
The shell or hull of a nut; the pod of a legume.
   1966 Dakin *Dial. Vocab. Ohio R. Valley* 2.364, *Walnut hull.* . . Two Kentuckians say *rind;* one says *husk;* and one says *peeling.* **1968–70** *DARE* (Qu. I10, *The outside covering of green peas that you break open to get the peas out*) Infs **GA79, PA239,** Peeling; (Qu. I12, *The outside covering of dry beans*) Inf **GA79,** Peeling; (Qu. I40, *The hard part inside the husk . . of a walnut that you have to break*) Inf **LA37,** Shell, peelings. **1973** Allen *LAUM* 1.307 (as of c1950), *Shell* (hard case of a walnut or hickory nut). . . peeling [1 inf, **NE;** inf doubtful]. **1986** Pederson *LAGS Concordance* (*Walnut shell*) 8 infs, **Gulf Region,** Peeling(s) [*DARE* Ed: These infs specify the soft or outer cover of the nut.]; 1 inf, **cTN,** Peeling—hard outer cover; 1 inf, **ceLA,** Thick peeling—outer cover; 1 inf, **nwLA,** Top peeling—or green hull.

peeling n[2] See **peel** v[2] **1, 2**

peeling vbl n[1] See **peel** v[1]

peeling vbl n[2] See **peel** v[2] **4**

peel it See **peel** v[2] **3**

peel out See **peel** v[2] **2**

pee-low See **pelado**

peeny n[1] See **peony** n[1] **3**

peeny n[2] Also *peenuckle, peeny stick, peonie, peony* Cf **pee-wee** n[1] **3**
=cat n **3a.**
   1949 *WELS Suppl.* **csWI,** I have played game called peony (pē'ōnee) using 2 sticks mentioned on your program this morning. *Ibid* **cWI,** My husband, whose home is Stevens Point, says that the game played with sticks was called peonie (?spelling) by him & his playmates. **1950** *WELS* **WI** (*Game in which you flip a short stick into the air and try to hit it with a longer stick*) 2 Infs, Peeny; 1 inf, Peeny stick. **1967–68** *DARE* (Qu. EE10) Infs **IA3, WI72,** Peeny; **WI40,** Peenuckle—never see it played anymore.

peeny in the pot n
   1950 *WELS* (*Different kinds of marble games*) 1 Inf, **cWI,** Peeny in the pot.

peeny stick See **peeny**

peep n
1 **=sora.**
   1792 Belknap *Hist. NH* 3.169, Peep, *Rallus carolinus.* **1955** MA Audubon Soc. *Bulletin* 39.443 **ME, NH,** Sora . . Peep . . sonic.

2 also *peep-squeak:* Any of var sandpipers, esp the **least sandpiper.** Cf **bull peep, little ~, marsh ~**
   1794 in 1810 MA Hist. Soc. *Coll.* 1st ser 3.199, Sea fowl are plenty on the shores and in the bay; particularly the gannet, . . widgeon, and peep. **1834** Nuttall *Manual Ornith.* 2.122, The Peeps, as they are here called, are seen in the salt marshes around Boston, as early as the 8th of July. **1844** DeKay *Zool. NY* 2.244, *Wilson's Sandpiper.* . . This little sandpiper, commonly known as the *Peep,* from its usual note, and as the *Oxeye,* from the size and brilliancy of its eye, is one of our most abundant species. **1880** *Forest & Stream* 15.4, Long-legged sandpiper (*Micropalama himantopus*); stilt; bastard dowitch . . peep [etc]. **1940** Todd *Birds W. PA* 237, This species [=the semipalmated sandpiper] and the Least Sandpiper resemble each other closely in size, coloration, and general habits; both have been given the name of "Peep." **1954** Sprunt *FL Bird Life* 183, *White-rumped Sandpiper.* . . This little "Peep" is one of the sandpipers. *Ibid* 185, *Red-backed Sandpiper.* . . Local Names: Sand-snipe; Peep. **1955** Lowery *LA Birds* 259, The Baird Sandpiper. . . is a rather nondescript "peep." **1968–70** *DARE* (Qu. Q10, . . *Water birds and marsh birds*) Inf **IA20,** Peep-squeak—a nickname for a sand bird—a least sandpiper; **MA98,** Peeps, sandpeeps, sandpipes—make good stew. **1995** *DARE* File **eMA,** Peep stew was a great favorite in Plymouth, Mass, early in the twentieth century. The boys went to the beach and shot the peep (plural) there.

3 also *pee-pee, peeper, peepie, peepy:* A small chick or turkey poult. **chiefly PA, MD** Cf **pee-pee** exclam

1890 *DN* 1.74 **ePA**, *Pee-pee* . . a very small chicken. **1908** *German Amer. Annals* 10.37 **sePA**, *Peepy.* Young chicken. "There's the hen with her peepies." . . Probably onamatopoetic [sic]. **1913** Johnson *Highways St. Lawrence to VA* 272 **MD**, "Scat cat!" she cried. "If I ketch you ketchin' the peepies 'twill be the worst for you." **1916** *DN* 4.338 **PA**, *Peepy.* . . A chicken, especially a chick. *Ibid* 343 **nwMD**, *Peep.* . . A small chick. Also in *pl.*, *peepies.* **1930** Shoemaker *1300 Words* 45 **cPA Mts** (as of c1900), *Peeps*—Baby chickens. **1931** *AmSp* 7.20 **swPA**, *Peeps.* Little chickens. **1935** *AmSp* 10.171 **PA** [Engl of PA Germans], *Peep.* A chick just hatched, or a small chicken. **1942** Warnick *Garrett Co. MD* 11 **nwMD** (as of 1900–18), *Peepies* . . chicks. **1946** *PADS* 6.23 **swVA**, *Peepies.* . . Chickens. **1950** Klees *PA Dutch* 281, *Klook* and *peep* are universally used in the Dutch country for a broody hen and a baby chicken. **1952** Brown *NC Folkl.* 1.575, *Peepy.* . . A small chicken or turkey; perhaps onomatopoeic.—General. **1953** *AmSp* 28.252 **csPA**, *Pee-pee.* . . A newborn or very young chick. Most commonly pronounced as though it were *peepy.* Presumably an onomatopoeic reduplication (normally used by children, sometimes by adults), from the young chick's shrill, weak cry, 'peep. . . peep. . . peep.' **1968** *DARE* FW Addit **nwMD**, *Peepie* . . baby chicken . . no aspiration on second [p]—this word is not identical with the common euphemism for urine. **1969** *DARE* (Qu. M16, *The small shelter for a hen that can be moved about from place to place*) Inf **PA**207, *Pee-pee house.* **1982** *Barrick Coll.* **csPA**, *Peepy*—small chicken. **1994** (1995) Snead *Hollow Boy* 43 **nVA** (as of c1930), She might say, "kill me five frying-size chickens." These were chickens that probably came in the mail as little peepers around Easter time. **2000** Millersville Univ. Center for PA Ger. Studies *Jrl.* Spring 6, Susie took special interest in a black peep named Chooky. When all the chicks were taken to market to be sold, Susie hid Chooky under a strawberry basket.

4 also *peepie;* Transf: a young woman. [By analogy with *chick*]

1968 *DARE* (Qu. HH34, *General words . . for a woman, not necessarily uncomplimentary*) Inf **PA**94, Broad, chick, peep. **1996** Huth *Famil. Words* 105 **csPA**, *Peepie.* . . any young girl.

peep exclam See **pee-pee** exclam

pee-paw n Cf **mee-maw, pa-paw** n[2]

A grandfather.

1967 *DARE* (Qu. Z3, . . *'Grandfather'*) Inf **AR**51, Pee-paw ['pi,pɔ]— little ones uses [sic] this. **1992** *NADS Letters* **cNC**, Our granddaughter refers to me as Meemaw and has from the first. Originally she referred to my husband as Peepaw, but within the past year she has begun to call him Grandpa. (She has just turned five.) *Ibid* **neSC**, I have a late 30s-aged friend . . who always talks of *meemaw* and *peepaw* when referring to little old people who look like grandparents.

peep-by-night n

A **four-o'clock 1.**

1944 *PADS* 2.47 **NC**, *Peep-by-night.* . . A flower that opens at night, the four-o'clock. Swain Co., N.C. **1984** Wilder *You All Spoken Here* 176 **Sth**, *Pretty-by-nights; peep-by-nights:* Four o'clocks, flowers that bloom in late afternoon.

pee-pee n See **peep** n 3

pee-pee exclam Also *pee(p), peepie(-peepie), peep-peep* **esp PA, Mid Atl;** also **LA, TX** Cf **bee** v, **peep** n 3

Used as a call to chickens or turkeys.

1899 (1912) Green *VA Folk-Speech* 316, *Pee-pee.* Call for turkeys. **1950** *PADS* 14.51 **SC**, *Pee-pee.* . . A call to turkeys. Imitative of the cry of the poults. **1956** Ker *Vocab. W. TX* 209, Call to turkeys. . . Pee, pee! Pee, pee! . . peep [2 of 67 infs]. **1961** *PADS* 36.11 **sLA**, Various calls to animals in this area . . appear to be unique. . . [C]hickens [are called] by *kee!, keetie!* or *pee(p)!* **1962** Atwood *Vocab. TX* 55, Of those who know how to call turkeys, most use *turk(ee).* . . Some others use *pee(p)* (9) [of approx 270 infs]. **1967–70** *DARE* (Qu. K79, *How do you call the chickens to you at feeding time?*) Infs **MD**20, **PA**137, 147, 211, Pee-pee; pee-pee(-pee); **SC**69, **PA**37, 153, Peep-peep(-peep); **MD**26, Peepie-peepie-peepie. **1970** Greatman *Dial. Atlas MD* 76, Peepie—"chicken call" 2 [of 50 infs]. **1970** Tarpley *Blinky* 156 **neTX**, Call to turkeys to come get the feed . . pee-pee-pee [7 of 200 infs] . . peep-peep-peep [rare]. **1986** Pederson *LAGS Concordance* (Calls to chickens) 1 inf, **seLA**, Pee (x 3)—falsetto; 1 inf, **csLA**, Pee (x 7)—first syllable high pitched; [1 inf, **neMS**, Pitta-pee (x 2)—call to turkeys—falsetto].

peeper n[1]

1 also *peep(er) frog, ~ toad, peeping frog:* A **tree frog.** **chiefly NEast, N Cent** See Map Cf **cricket frog, hyla, March peeper, marsh ~, night ~, spring ~**

1842 DeKay *Zool. NY* 3.70, The Cricket Hylodes . . *Hylodes gryllus.* . . This species is known under the names of *Peeper* and *Cricket Frog*, in New-York. **1857** Hammond *Wild N. Scenes* 30 **NY**, All is still now, save the piping notes of the little peeper along the shore. **1891** in 1898 IL State Lab. Nat. Hist. Urbana *Bulletin* 3.340, *Acris gryllus* . . Cricket-frog, Peeper [etc.]. **1906** (1907) Dickerson *Frog Book* 139, Peeping Frogs are tiny things an inch or less long. *Ibid* 140, There is a Peeper! The thin, sweet "pe-ep, pe-ep, pe-ep, pe-ep," sounding much like a bird's call-note, comes from the moss and leaves at the water's edge. **1930** Shoemaker *1300 Words* 48 **cPA Mts** (as of c1900), *Peeper*—Pickering's frog, called by some "swamp lizard", the much loved musical harbinger of spring in Pennsylvania bogs and ponds. **1939** *LANE* Map 231 (*Frog*), The *peeper* (*peeping frog, peep* [*frog*] . .) is described by ten informants as a small frog or as smaller than a bullfrog. . . Seven informants mention that peepers appear in early spring . ., three specify the time of their appearance as March. **1949–50** *WELS Suppl.,* 1 Inf, **csWI**, Peepers—little frogs with big throats; 1 Inf, **neWI**, Never heard little frogs called "peepers" until 1942 in Door County, but must have been deaf, because it seems the only common name. **1950** *WELS* **WI** (*Small frogs that sing or chirp loudly in spring*) 7 Infs, Peepers; 1 Inf, Green peepers; (*Names for the tree-frog*) 1 Inf, Peeper; 1 Inf, Tree toad; my folks out East called him a "peeper." **1965–70** *DARE* (Qu. P21, *Small frogs that sing or chirp loudly in spring*) 129 Infs, **chiefly NEast, N Cent,** Peepers; **CT**4, 22, 23, 26, 36, 39, **MA**68, 74, **NC**30, 31, 35, 53, **PA**182, 198, Peep frogs; **CT**36, 39, Peepers, peep frogs; **RI**4, 6, Peep toads; **IN**27, **PA**155, Peeper frogs; **NY**223, Peepers have to freeze up three times before spring; **NY**231, Peepers—they got to be froze up three times before you get good weather; [**NY**2, Not peepers; they're bug or animal that peep [sic] in spring;] (Qu. P20, *Very young frogs—when they still have tails but no legs*) Inf **NY**36, Peepers; [(Qu. R7, *Insects that sit in trees or bushes in hot weather and make a sharp, buzzing sound*) Inf **NC**48, Peepers; **PA**9, Tree frogs, peepers;] (Qu. R8, . . *Kinds of creatures that make a clicking or shrilling or chirping kind of sound*) Inf **NJ**8, Peepers—come out in spring [FW: He's never seen them, just heard them.]; **NY**156, Peepers. **1966** Dakin *Dial. Vocab. Ohio R. Valley* 388, Kentucky has *sprat frog, swamp ~, pond ~, little ~, kitin' ~, squeaking ~, skracking ~, mud quackers,* and *peeper toad.* **1968** *PA Game News* Dec 20 **PA**, Peeping frogs are eaten by almost every kind of predator, from birds in the treetops to fish under water. **1973** Allen *LAUM* 1.325 **SD** (as of c1950), One South Dakotan offers both *peeping frog* and *peep toad.* **1989** Mosher *Stranger* 58 **nVT** (as of 1952), Although the quality of the maple syrup wouldn't be as high as earlier in the spring, we wouldn't have missed this final "frog run"—so-called because the peeper frogs had already started to sing—for the world.

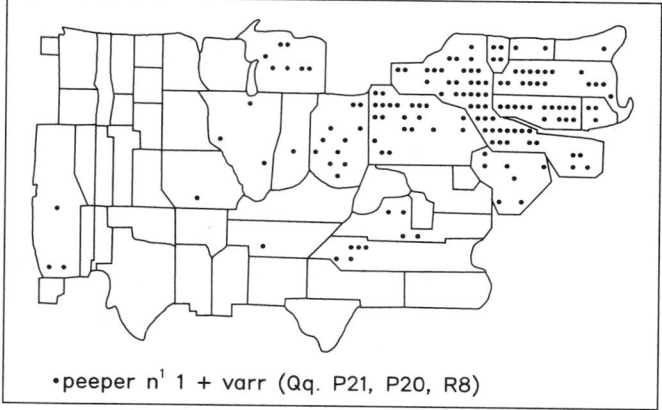

•*peeper* n[1] 1 + varr (Qq. P21, P20, R8)

2 A chorus frog (here: *Pseudacris triseriata*).

1919 *Copeia* 74.81 **NY**, *Pseudacris feriarum.* . . Swamp Cricket Frog. Peeper.

3 =**sanderling.**

1948 Pearson *Sea Flavor* 143 **NEng**, As the tide turns and a wave begins its rolling progress landward, the peepers scamper nimbly up the wet sand just ahead of it.

4 See **peep** n 3.

peeper n[2] [*peeper* eye]
1 A black eye.
   1967–68 *DARE* (Qu. X20, . . *A black eye*) Infs **MA**3, 27, Shiner, peeper; **MA**33, Peeper; [**MD**19, Black peeper].
2 pl: Eyeglasses. [*OED2* 1825 →] **scattered, but chiefly Sth, S Midl** See Map
   1942 Berrey–Van den Bark *Amer. Slang* 137.6, Spectacles. . . Peepers. **1965–70** *DARE* (Qu. X23, . . *Joking words* . . *for eyeglasses*) 28 Infs, **scattered, but chiefly Sth, S Midl**, Peepers; **NY**2, Peeper. [22 of 29 Infs male] **1968** *DARE* Tape **IN**9, [I'll get my peepers down looking at it right. **1979** *Capital Times* (Madison WI) 21 Apr 1/4, [Photo caption:] Miss Lillian's peepers.

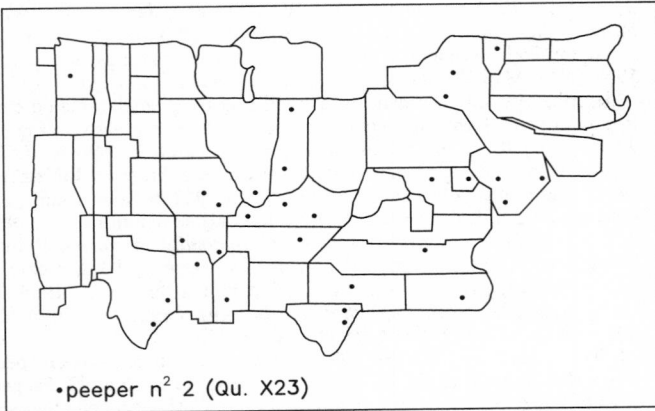

•peeper n[2] 2 (Qu. X23)

peeper frog (or toad) See **peeper** n[1] **1**

peep-eye n, v, exclam **chiefly Sth, S Midl**
The game of peekaboo; to play peekaboo; used as a call in the game.
   1887 *Harper's New Mth. Mag.* 76.79 **TN**, The baby. . . made futile efforts to play "peep-eye" with anybody jovially disposed in the crowd. **1945** Street *Gauntlet* 260 **MO** (as of 1920s), The child . . was more interested in their whiskers and tried to play peep-eye with Santa Claus. **1986** Pederson *LAGS Concordance*, 55 infs, **Gulf Region**, Peep-eye [*DARE* Ed: Typical explanatory comments are: "game with a baby (*or* small child, children)," "said by child (*or* call) from hiding."]; 1 inf, **neTN**, Peep-eyed = played peep-eye; 1 inf, **ceTN**, He's peep-eyeing = playing peep-eye. **1993** Mason *Feather Crowns* 322 **KY**, When a child in a chair up ahead tried to play peep-eye with her, she turned her face away.

peep frog See **peeper** n[1] **1**

peepie n See **peep** n **3, 4**

peepie(-peepie) exclam See **pee-pee** exclam

peeping frog See **peeper** n[1] **1**

peep of day n [*OED2* 1530 →]
Dawn, sunrise.
   1967–69 *DARE* (Qu. A1, . . *The time in the early morning before the sun comes into sight*) Inf **MD**31, Peep of day; **RI**1, Break of day, peep of day; (Qu. A2, *The time when the sun first comes into sight*) Inf **CO**7, Peep o' day—various points in mountains, too, given this expression. **1984** Wilder *You All Spoken Here* 60 **Sth**, Peep of day, morngloam: When the first streaks of dawn appear.

pee-pomp n Cf *DS* DD31
=**seesaw 1.**
   1949 *AmSp* 24.111 **seGA**, Pee-pomp. . . Seesaw.

peep-peep See **pee-pee** exclam

peep-squeak See **peep** n **2**

peep squirrel n Also *peep squirrel peep*
A children's game.
   c1937 in 1970 Yetman *Voices* 260 **NC** [Black], We chillen played de games of marbles, cat ball, and. . . At night we all played peep squirrel

in the house. **1940** Hench *Coll.* **ceVA**, Play peep-squirrel. **1945** FWP *Lay My Burden Down* 92 **AL** (as of c1865) [Black], We had a few little games we play, like Peep Squirrel Peep, You Can't Catch Me, and such like.

peep toad See **peeper** n[1] **1**

peepwink See **peewink**

peepy See **peep** n **3**

peer See **pear** v

peerie See **purie**

peerow See **pirogue**

peert adj See **peart** adj

peert adv See **peart** adv

peerten See **pearten**

peery See **purie**

peeteet See **peedee** 2

pee-the-bed See **piss-a-bed** 1, 3, 7

peetweet n [Echoic]
1 also *peeweet*: =**spotted sandpiper.**
   1834 Nuttall *Manual Ornith.* 2.162, Spotted Tatler, or Peet Weet. [*Ibid* 163, We hear the shores re-echo the shrill and rapid whistle of 'weet, 'weet, 'weet, 'weet, and usually closing the note, with something like a warble. . . The cry then again varies to 'peet, weet weet weet, beginning high and gradually declining into a somewhat plaintive tone.] **1844** DeKay *Zool.* NY 2.247, This is a familiar bird. . . It is known in the books under the names of *Spotted Sandpiper* and *Tatler*, but is better known among the people by the name of *Peet-weet*, in allusion to its notes. **1903** Dawson *Birds* OH 2.533, The Peet-weet's nest is usually a little removed from the water's edge. **1923** U.S. Dept. Ag. *Misc. Circular* 13.64, Spotted Sandpiper. . . Vernacular Names. . . In local use. . . peet-weet (R.I., N.Y., Md., Ont., Ind., Ala., Nebr., B.C.); pee-weet pewit (Pa.) **1938** Oberholser *Bird Life* LA 241, Spotted Sandpiper. . . Its note, which sounds very much like the syllables 'peet-weet', has given rise to one of its names. **1955** Forbush–May *Birds* 186, Spotted Sandpiper. . . *Other names.* . . Peet-weet, Perr-wipe, Pee-weet.
2 =**solitary sandpiper.**
   1932 Howell *FL Bird Life* 231, Eastern Solitary Sandpiper: *Tringa solitaria solitaria.* . . Other Names: Wood Tattler; Peet-weet.

peeve v
To complain, sulk, pout.
   1912 Ade *Knocking* 10 **NYC**, The Waiter peeved at being slipped a paltry $1.60. **1967–70** *DARE* (Qu. GG35a, *To sulk or pout: "It won't do any good to _____ about it."*) Infs **IL**4, **MD**34, 40, Peeve.

pee-wadding See **wadding**

peewee n[1]
1 See **pewee** n[1].
2 also sp *pewee*: In marble play: a small, usu cheap marble; a marble game (see quot 1958). [*EDD* pee-wee sb. 2]
   1848 Bartlett *Americanisms* 246, Pee-wee. The name given by boys to a little marble. **1905** *DN* 3.15 **cCT**, Peewee. . . A name given by boys to a small marble. *Ibid* 90 **nwAR**, Pee-wee. . . Marble of the smallest size. **1906** Lovett *Old Boston Boys* 42, A boy's stock of marbles was usually carried in a bag with a running string, and consisted of "Alleys," "Jaspers," "Chinees," "Pewees," "Agates," "Bulls' Eyes," and several other kinds. **1907** *DN* 3.215 **nwAR**, Peewee. . . Boys' name for a small marble. **1909** *DN* 3.357 **eAL, wGA**, Peewee. . . A small marble used as a 'stick-in' in playing for "keeps." **1942** McAtee *Dial. Grant Co.* IN 48 (as of 1890s), Peewee . . a small marble. Dial. **1949** *PADS* 11.9 **wTX**, Pee-wee. . . A small marble. *Ibid* 24 **CO**, Peewee. **1950** *WELS (Names and nicknames for different kinds of marbles: Small ones)* 8 Infs, **WI**, Peewees. **1950** *PADS* 14.51 **SC**, Peewee. **1951** *PADS* 15.67 **NH**, Peewee. . . Small clay marble. **1955** *PADS* 23.26 **cwAL**, Peewee. . . A small clay marble, not always perfectly round and always of less value than other marbles. **1958** *PADS* 29.38, Peewee. . . A marble game in which a series of holes were made perpendicular to the starting

line, and 4 feet apart; the marbles were rolled successively into hole 1, hole 2, hole 3, and then back again; the rules were as in croquet. **1965–70** *DARE* (Qu. EE6b, *Small marbles or marbles in general*) 212 Infs, **widespread,** Peewees; (Qu. EE6c, *Cheap marbles*) 13 Infs, **scattered,** Peewees; (Qu. EE6d, *Special marbles*) Infs **OK**1, 42, Peewees; (Qu. EE7, . . *Kinds of marble games*) Infs **IN**83, **OH**47, Peewee. **1969** *DARE* Tape **IN**83, [FW:] Do you know any games played with holes? [Inf:] No, I don't—yes. Peewee; we used to shoot and try to put a marble right in the hole there. **c1970** Wiersma *Marbles Terms, Pee wees*—the tiniest of the playing marbles. **1983** *MJLF* 9.1.50 **ceKY** (as of 1956), *Pee-wee* . . a small marble.

3 =**cat** n **3a, b.   esp Pacific   Cf peeny 2**

1945 Saxon *Gumbo Ya-Ya* 417 **LA,** Pee Wees the boys used to play a game with—those were little wooden pegs about two inches long that they'd stick in the ground, striking the other end with a broomstick. **1957–58** *Sat. Eve. Post Letters* **swCA,** *Pee Wee*—a competive [sic] game. Have a stick about 12 to 18 in. long—about thick as old broom handle—and a pee wee (a small stick about 3 to 4 in. long whittled to point on both ends)—object to hit small stick with long one on tip while on ground and when it flies up into the air hit it again for distance—furthest hit is Winner; **nwMT, ceWA,** One game I have enjoyed . . is called Pee Wee. Others call it Cricket. It is played with "three sticks and a hole." I learned it from some of my rural school pupils the school year of 1918–'19; **nwWA,** "Pee Wee", "Old Sow" and "Chuck the Wicket" called only for some sticks or clubs that could be quickly had at the nearest thicket or brush; **cwCA,** Peewee. . . Take a six-inch long . . stick . . put a blunt taper on each end. Dig a narrow trough in the earth about two inches deep. . . Place the stick in the trough lengthwise with one end lying partially out. . . The one at bat has to hit the nose of the stick in the trough and make it fly into the air and out into the playing field. . . If a player catches the little Peewee he stays at the same place at which it was caught and tries to hit the bat which has been laid across the center of the trough. He is then batter, if he hits it, but otherwise the same batter stays up. **1966–68** *DARE* (Qu. EE10, *A game in which a short stick lying on the ground is flipped into the air and then hit with a longer stick*) Infs **CA**9, **HI**9, **OR**15, **WA**16, Peewee; **HI**4, Peewee—3 pieces of broom handle, also 2 pieces of switch; dig hole, not played much now. **1998** *Capital Times* (Madison WI) 7 Dec sec A 8/2 **HI** (as of 1941), As a 6-year-old, I was more eager to get in a full day of "pee-wee"—a game using different lengths of an old broomstick.

pee-wee n² See **piss-a-bed 3**

pee-weed See **piss-a-bed 2**

peeweet See **peetweet 1**

pee-weezy n Cf **weasly**

1952 Brown *NC Folkl.* 1.575, *Pee-weezy.* . . A little dried-up person.—Nash county.

pee-willy See **willy**

peewink n Also *peepwink* **Cape Cod MA** Cf **pinkwink** =**spring peeper.**

1939 *LANE* Map 231 (*Frog*) **Cape Cod MA,** 1 inf, Peewinks, in swamps and brooks. 'I never see one; some say it's a small kind of frog'; 1 inf, Peewinks, in swamps. 'They're nothing but frogs, though'; 1 inf, Peepwinks, in swamps at night.

peewood See **peawood**

peezaltree adj Cf **peasly**

1953 Randolph–Wilson *Down in Holler* 270 **Ozarks,** *Peezaltree.* . . Inferior, uncultured, unsatisfactory. In McDonald County, Mo., one hears of *peezaltree* dances, *peezaltree* kinfolks, *peezaltree* clothing, and so forth. It is said to have started when a preacher in Pineville, Mo., mispronounced *psaltery,* and was henceforth known as the *"peezaltree preacher."* This mispronunciation is common in the South; Roark Bradford (*Collier's,* January 20, 1940) makes his characters say *p-saltree.* But I have never heard *peezaltree* used as an adjective except in southwest Missouri.

peg n, v Usu |pɛ(ɪ)g|; also **chiefly Sth, S Midl** |pe(ɪ)g|; occas |pæg|, |pɪg|; for addit varr see quots   Cf Pronc Intro 3.I.6.a
A Forms.

1934 *AmSp* 9.211 **Sth,** Some words with standard [ɛ] before [g] or [k] change [ɛ] to [eɪ] or [e]. This pronunciation is decidedly vulgar. . . *Beg,*

egg, . . neck, nutmeg, peg. **1936** *AmSp* 11.15 **eTX,** Before [g] the sound usually appears as [e], [eɪ], though sometimes as [ɛ]: *egg, keg, leg, peg.* **1941** *LANE* Map 481 (*Tuckered out*) 1 inf, **sME,** All [pegd] out; [pe^ɪgd] 1 inf, **sME,** [peɜɪgd] out. **1941** *AmSp* 16.5 **eTX** [Black], *Beg, peg,* are [bɛːg], [beɪg], [pɛːg], [peɪg]. **1942** Hall *Smoky Mt. Speech* 20 **wNC, eTN,** [æ] is common also in *beg, keg,* . . *peg.* **1943** *LANE* Map 521 (*Kicked the bucket*) 8 infs, **chiefly nNEng,** [pe^(^)gd] out; 2 infs, **sME,** [pe^(ˇ)ɪgd] out; 1 inf, **nwCT,** [pegd] out. *Ibid* Map 667 (*Threw*) 3 infs, **wCT,** [peɪgd]. **1961** *Mt. Life* Spring 8 **sAppalachians,** [peg] for peg. **1966–69** *DARE* Tape AL3, [p'ɛ^ɪg]; AL3A, [p'ɛe·g]; TN37, [p'ɛ^·e^g]. . . [p'ɛ·g]. . . [p'ɪ·ɛg]. **1970** *DARE* (Qu. L62, *A fence made of split logs*) Inf NC85, Peg fence [peɪg fɪns]. **1970** [see B4 below]. **1970** *DARE* Tape [see B1 below]. **1986** Pederson *LAGS Concordance Gulf Region* (*Died*) 7 infs, Pegged out [proncs of the type [p'ɛ(ɪ)gd, p'ɛəgd]]; 1 inf, [p'ɛ·ɜ^ɪg] out; 1 inf, He [p'ɪ^·gd] out; (*Worn-out*) 1 inf, All [p'ɪ^·gd] out; 1 inf, All [p'ɛgd] out.

B As noun.

1 Chiefly in tobacco farming: see quot 1966.   Cf **jobber, peg C1**

1966 *PADS* 45.19 **cnKY** [Tobacco word list], *Peg.* . . A pointed tool used to make holes in the soil for insertion of seedlings when setting by hand. . . "I've set many a plant with a peg." **1967** Key *Tobacco Vocab.* 263 **MD, NC, GA, TN.** **1970** *DARE* (Qu. L23, . . *Machinery* . . *used* . . *in putting in the seed*) Inf **KY**75, Peg—for replanting tobacco now; used to be only planting device they had; **KY**84, Peg—old-fashioned, tobacco; **VA**38, Planter peg. **1970** *DARE* Tape **VA**40, They'd go in the woods . . and they'd trim them a peg [p'e·ɪg]—what they call a peg [p'ɛ·ɪg]. . . They used to say we gonna peg [p'ɛ^·ɪg] tobacco. . . But they'd trim that peg [p'e·ɪg] really smooth . . so no splinters stick in your hand. And then the mud wouldn't stick to it. . . Before we pegged [p'ɛ·ɪgd] it, we would go there and use a hoe, what we called chop the hill.

2 A tooth, esp a baby tooth.   [*OED2* 1597–8 →]

1899 (1912) Green *VA Folk-Speech* 316, *Peg.* . . A tooth; children's teeth are often called "pegs." **1970** *DARE* (Qu. X13a, . . *Joking names* . . *for teeth*) Inf **VA**39, Pegs. **1982** *Smithsonian Letters* **FL,** Pegs = baby teeth. Term used primarily by black people in Leon and Gadsden Counties, Florida.

3 See **peggy** n¹.

4 =**husking pin.**   [Abbr for *husking peg* (at **husking pin**) or **shucking peg**]

1903 (1965) Adams *Log Cowboy* 74 **West,** The trustee of the township was shucking corn when I went to apply for the school. I simply whipped out my peg and helped him shuck out a shock or two. **1970** *DARE* Tape MI125, [MI125A:] Oh, you mean to husk the corn with? . . A husking peg [p'ɛˇɪg], usually. We got some yet. [FW:] The little knife with the leather straps you put around your hand. [MI125:] Yeah, I got a peg [p'ɛˇɪg] out here.

5 A playing marble.   [Cf **meg**]

1950 *WELS* (*Names and nicknames for different kinds of marbles: Small ones*) 1 Inf, **cWI,** Pegs. **1970** *DARE* (Qu. EE6d, *Special marbles*) Inf **NJ**68, Pegs [Inf doubtful].

6 A game similar to horseshoes in which a ring is tossed over a stake in the ground.   Cf **ring-a-peg**

1969 *DARE* (Qu. EE37, *The game where you try to throw metal rings or something similar over a stake in the ground*) Inf **MI**93, Peg—if a ring is used.

7 =**mumblety-peg.**   Cf **peg knife**

1968–70 *DARE* (Qu. EE5, *Games where you try to make a jackknife stick in the ground*) Infs **FL**48, **SC**65, Peg; **PA**247, Peg; I didn't use a knife, I used an ice pick. [All Infs Black]

8 in phr *not to budge* (or *move, turn*) *a peg* and varr: To make no effort or movement; not to cooperate in the least.   [*OED2* 1810 →]   **chiefly Sth, S Midl**

1851 (1852) Stowe *Uncle Tom's Cabin* 1.106 **KY,** You've got to fork over fifty dollars, flat down, or this child don't start a peg. **1858** Hammett *Piney Woods Tavern* 183 **TX,** Both they and the New Orleans volunteers refused to move a peg under any other commander than Gaines. **1859** Taliaferro *Fisher's R.* 56 **nwNC** (as of 1820s), I . . couldn't budge a peg. **1965–70** *DARE* (Qu. JJ23, *To refuse to give in or yield: "He tried to scare me off but I _____."*) Inf **VA**42, Didn't budge a peg; (Qu. KK19, *If a machine or appliance is temporarily out of order: "My sewing machine _____."*) Inf **MS**45, Just won't move a peg; (Qu. LL18, *To do no work at all, not even make any effort: "She hasn't _____ all day."*) Infs **GA**7, 28, 89, **LA**16, **IL**130, **NC**51, **TX**81, Moved (*or* turned) a peg.

9 in phr *on one's last peg(s):* Near death; worn out, decrepit. [Var of *on one's last legs*]

1966–68 *DARE* (Qu. BB54, *When a sick person is past hope of recovery . . he's [a] _____*) Infs **IL**5, **IN**3, **OH**23, 63, On his last peg(s); (Qu. KK20a, *Something that looks as if it might collapse any minute: "That old shed is certainly _____."*) Inf **AR**41, On its last pegs; (Qu. KK20b, *Something that looks as if it might collapse any minute: "Our old washing machine is _____."*) Infs **NM**9, **OH**40, On its last pegs.

C As verb.

1 In tobacco farming: to plant (seedlings) using a **peg B1.**

1966 *PADS* 45.19 cn**KY** [Tobacco word list], *Peg. . .* To use a peg for hand planting. . . "It's hard work to peg tobacco." **1967** *Key Tobacco Vocab.* 263 **MD, NC, GA, TN,** *Peg. Ibid* 262, **TN,** If it comes a wet spell . . you've got to go and peg 'em out. **1970** *DARE* Tape [see **B1** above].

2 To throw (something); to make a throw at, hit (with a thrown object); hence vbl n *pegging.*   [*OED2* a1700 →] **chiefly Nth**   Cf **peck** v[2]

[**1862** *NY Sun. Mercury* (NY) 13 July 6/1, Peter then pegged [=hit] the ball in good old style.] **1889** *Scribner's Mag.* 6.686, A wilful whippersnapper of eighteen, even, can peg stones at the family escutcheon. **1908** *German Amer. Annals* 10.38 se**PA,** Peg a stone at that bird. **1926** *AmSp* 1.369, He "pegs the bases" when he throws to the basemen. . . Any pitching or "pegging" arm is a "wing." **1942** Berrey–Van den Bark *Amer. Slang* 66.3, Throw; hurl. . . Peg (out). **1943** *LANE* Map 667 (*Threw*) w**CT,** 2 infs, Pegged; 1 inf, Pegged, as a boy. **1950** *WELS* **WI** (*To throw [for example, at a dog]: "He picked up a stone and _____ it at the dog."*) 6 Infs, Pegged; (*The children were _____ each other with snowballs*) 5 Infs, Pegging. **1957** *Sat. Eve. Post Letters* **NY,** There was also a game with the marbles propelled along the ground by knuckle power. I was a member of the "pegging" or "throwing" adherents, however. **1965–70** *DARE* (Qu. C24b, *"The dog wouldn't go away, so he took a stone/rock and . . _____ [it at it.]"*) Infs **NY**59, 66, 92, Pegged; **IL**98, Peg; (Qu. Y10, *To throw something . . "The dog came at him, so he picked up a stone and _____ it at him."*) 11 Infs, **chiefly Nth,** Pegged. **1966** *DARE* Tape **NM**9, [In marble play:] If you peg [p'e·g] and stick, you've got to shoot down. . . so that that taw'll stick where you want it. **1989** Mosher *Stranger* 14 n**VT** (as of 1952), The boy was pegging gravel at a utility pole across the road. **1998** *NADS Letters* n**AL** (as of c1945), Peg 'at ol' ball here, Jay Dubby [=J.W.] **1999** *Ibid* **OH,** I used to hear old people talk about pegging a rock at a rabbit, or pegging a rabbit with a rock. *Ibid* **WA,** I've heard "peg" as a word for throw or hit, as in, "I had an apple and I pegged it at the tree" or "I was throwing rocks and I pegged a bird." This from other kids in Bellevue, Wash. in the 70s.

3 See quots; hence ppl adj *pegged,* n *pegging.*

1898 (1899) Earle *Home Life* 262 **NEng,** A pair of double hooked and pegged mittens would last for years. Pegging, I am told, was heavy crocheting. **1898** *Boston Eve. Transcript* (MA) 16 Apr 14/5, To peg means [to crochet], . . but is oftener used in relation to mats made of rags or yarn drawn through bagging—burlap. *Ibid* 16 Apr 14/5, In my mother's time the work that we call crocheting now was called pegging or knitting with a hook.

4 Of a cow horse: to stop abruptly on the haunches in order to turn quickly or to resist the pull of the rope; hence vbl n *pegging;* nouns *pegger, peg horse, ~ pony* a horse skilled at doing this. **esp TX**

1936 in Lib. of Congress *Amer. Memory: WPA Life Hist.* (Internet) **TX,** I could just sit in the rocking chair pull a leaf out of the bible and roll a new lease on life out of my Bull Durham, while he was cutting a critter out of a herd. Now, talk about pegging, that hoss would turn like a top and on the same amount of ground. **1936** Adams *Cowboy Lingo* 83 **West,** A 'cutting horse' which possessed the talent of stopping short in his tracks when galloping in one direction, changing his direction, and instantly bounding off on a new course, was called a 'peg horse,' 'peg pony' or 'pegger.' **1937** in Lib. of Congress *Amer. Memory: WPA Life Hist.* (Internet) **TX,** I had a wise cuttin' hoss. The cuttin' hoss must be a pegger an' is the top hoss of the range. . . In peggin he could turn on a dime. *Ibid* **TX,** Everybody thought he had it in the bag for sure, because the hoss was a good pegger and had already sat down to keep the steer from jerking him over, and to throw the steer. *Ibid* **TX,** A properly trained hoss will peg as soon as the cow turns. That hoss will sit on

its hind legs and whirl. I mounted that hoss and started after a cow, and when I headed her and she turned, I set myself for the peg, but that hoss did not peg. **1938** *Ibid* **TX,** He roped a yearling, and his horse reared at something right when it should have pegged; that is, sat down.

pegatory See **purgatory**

pegged See **peg C3**

pegged out ppl adj phr [Often assoc with **peg out,** but the implied transitive sense, "to exhaust, wear out," is not attested for the verb phr.]

Exhausted, worn out, "done for."

1868 Fosdick *No Moss* 302, Here's the cap'n clean pegged out, a storm comin' up, . . an' only three of us left to make things safe. **1870** *Punchinello* 1.396, I was too pegged out to wash or fix, so I flung off my cowhides, jumped onto the bed and slept clean through till next day. **1914** [see **peg out**]. **1941** *LANE* Map 481 (*Tuckered out*) 1 inf, s**ME,** All pegged out; pegged; 1 inf, s**ME,** Pegged out. **1959** *VT Hist.* 27.152, *Pegged out. . .* Exhausted; worn out. Occasional. **1966–68** *DARE* (Qu. X47, . . *"I'm very tired, at the end of my strength"*) Inf **AR**28, Pegged out; (Qu. BB42, *If a person is very sick . . he's _____*) Inf **AR**52, About pegged out; (Qu. KK20b, *Something that looks as if it might collapse any minute: "Our old washing machine is _____."*) Inf **MD**26, About pegged out. **1986** [see **peg out**].

pegger See **peg C4**

pegger-back n Cf **peg C2, peggy** n[1]

1950 *WELS* (*Bat-and-ball games for a few players [when you don't have enough for a regular game]*) 1 Inf, c**WI,** Pegger-back.

pegging n See **peg C3**

pegging vbl n

1 See quots.

1941 Writers' Program *Guide WY* 464, *Pegging*—Holding one horn of steer in the ground to hold him down. **1944** Adams *Western Words* 114, *Pegging*—Ramming one horn of a downed steer into the ground to hold him down. This is not allowed in contests.

2 See **peg C2.**

3 See **peg C4.**

pegging awl n Also *peckinall, pegging awl loon* [Appar from the shape of the bill, but perh, if the *peg-* of **pegmonk** is of Algonquian origin, a folk-etym] Cf **peggy loon**

=**red-throated loon.**

1875 *Fur Fin & Feather* 119, The smaller species of loon I have heard variously called the spike-bill, the cape-race, the touch-monk, the gungreaser, the pegging-all [*sic*], etc. **1951** *AmSp* 26.90, The sobriquet *peggin'-awl loon* (Mass.), again for the red-throated loon, in reference to its long, pointed bill, is altered in the same State to *peckinall,* which may have a meaning, and to *pegmonk,* the significance of which is unknown. **1955** Forbush–May *Birds* 5, Red-throated Loon. . . *Other names:* Red-throated Diver . . Pegging Awl Loon [etc].

pegging string See **pigging string**

peggity n Also *peggity-wink* [Cf *peggotty* a children's board game played with pegs placed in holes, and **mumblety-peg**]

1968–69 *DARE* (Qu. EE5, *Games where you try to make a jack-knife stick in the ground*) Inf **RI**12, Peggity; **NJ**28, Peggity-wink [pɛgəti,wɪŋk].

peggy n[1] Also *peg(-stick), peggy bounce-out, ~-up, peggy on the bounce, ~ fly* [Brit dial: *EDD peg and stick* (at *peg* sb.[1] 2.(2)), *piggy; SND piggie* (at *pig* n.[1] 4); *OED2 piggy* sb.[1] 2; and *peggy* (see quot 1958 *WELS Suppl.* below); cf also *SND peg* n. 1 "The wooden block used as a ball in the game of *Shintie,*" *EDD peggy* n.[1] 5 "The game of hockey, played with a wooden ball"] **chiefly Nth, esp NEast** See Map Cf **peggyball, picky** n[2] **1, piggy move-up**

=**cat** n **3a, b.**

1903 *DN* 2.352 c**OH,** *Peggy. . .* A name for the 'cat' in the game of tip-cat. **1937** (1958) Levin *Old Bunch* 3 **Chicago IL,** Kids were playing peg. One of them slammed a peg that hit Harry's ankle. . . The kid doubled down and began to count the sticks. It had been a good long hit. **1950** *WELS* (*Bat-and-ball games for a few players [when you don't have* *enough for a regular game*]) 2 Infs, **WI**, Peggy; 1 Inf, **seWI**, Peggy—4 strikes allowed in peggy; 3 Infs, **WI**, Peggy on the bounce (*or* fly); 1 Inf, **csWI**, Peggy bounce-out. **1958** *Sat. Eve. Post Letters* **swMI** (as of c1915), In a sense, peggy is a condensation of baseball. . B holds the peggy, and the great object of his young life is to toss it into the circle C. But D is guarding the circle with his paddle, and the permanent object of *his* life is to bat the peggy clear out of sight. . . If the peggy lands in the circle the Pitcher is "up." . . If the Batter managed to hit the peggy the game went into a second phaze [sic]. The players quickly estimated the distance from the circle to the peggy. . . If it is fewer than thirty lengths [of the paddle] he's out. . . However, if the distance is greater than thirty lengths . . the game goes into the third phaze [sic]. . . Using the edge of his paddle he [=the Batter] taps the peggy on one of its tapered noses, the peggy jumps up into the air . . and the Batter swats it with the flat of the paddle. *Ibid* **Boston MA**, It went on to explain that this was a game that involved flipping a short stick into the air and whacking it with a longer stick. . . But in the suburban purlieus of Boston we called it "peggy." [**1958** *WELS Suppl.* **England,** I remember my father teaching me the game you were speaking of this morning played with a small stick or peg and a larger stick. He called the game "Peggy." We lived in a small Yorkshire village at the time, although my father is a native of Lancashire.] **1965–70** *DARE* (Qu. EE10, *A game in which a short stick lying on the ground is flipped into the air and then hit with a longer stick*) 11 Infs, **chiefly NEast**, Peggy; **MA71**, Peggy—it would be whittled at each end; you hit the end, then whacked it while it was in the air; **NY209**, One old cat or shinny—puck was pointed on each end like a peggy and hit on one end and then swatted when in the air; **RI3**, Peggy—a stick 9″ long, ends whittled down, longer stick hit the peggy, when it flipped up hit it with the big stick; **CT42, GA86, NC72, TN37, VT16**, Peg; **LA20**, Peg—the guy who owned the stick you hit had to run and drive it once in the ground while you drove yours three times into the ground; **PA1**, Peg-stick; (Qu. EE11, *Bat-and-ball games for just a few players [when there aren't enough for a regular game]*) Infs **KY73, MS65**, Peggy; **IL100**, Peggy bounce-up; **WI47**, Peggy on the bounce or fly. **1966–69** *DARE* Tape **AL3**, [Aux Inf:] I was thinking about that old game of peg. You have a piece of wood, cut with pointed end, and you dig a hole, and you put that peg in it and . . you have a stick. . . You knock that peg up, . . and it flies up, then you knock that peg as far as you can knock it. That person steps off the distance that the peg has gone, and calls it a certain number [of] steps. And somebody will challenge him and try to step that in that number of steps and if he can. . . he gets the points, but if he doesn't do it, that person that knocked it gets the number; **CT29**, [FW:] Can you tell me about the game called "peggy" that you mentioned? [Inf:] Well, this was a game that we played as youngsters that probably derived its name from one of the principal parts of the game, which was a piece of wood approximately . . six inches long and perhaps an inch in diameter that was sharpened to a point at both ends. This we used in conjunction with another stick which we used to hit one end of the peggy, so-called, to make it jump into the air, and then we attempted to hit it with the other stick to see how far we could knock it; **TN37**, Another game . . was called peg. This game was played with a broom handle stick . . with a little peg about four inches long, maybe five. . . We would set this peg down against a brick. . . With your peg stick . . you would tip the peg up and you hit it more or less like you would hit a baseball. . . We would step it off and count how far our peg went. . . The one that made 500 [feet] first in his different shots . . would be the winner. . . The one who was last had to do what they called chasin' the peg. **1975** Ferretti *Gt. Amer. Book Sidewalk Games* 192, Yet another baseball-type game is the South

•peggy n¹ + varr (Qq. EE10, EE11)

Boston game of Peggy, which uses a wooden clothespin (with the knob at the end whittled to a point) for the ball and a venetian blind slat for a bat. **1988** *DARE* File **MA** (as of 1940s), Peggy: a game we played with two pieces of broomstick. A short length, the peg or peggy, whittled down on both ends, was laid on the ground and hit on the back point with the longer length so that it flipped into the air and could be whacked as far as possible. **1991** *NADS Letters* **PA, NJ**, In Philadelphia and later in 1925 in Camden, N.J. . . it was really called, "peggy."

peggy n² Cf **ginny** n², **polly 2**
A chamber pot.
1967–68 *DARE* (Qu. F38, *Utensil kept under the bed for use at night*) Inf **IL23**, Peggies; **MD27**, Pot, peggy ['pɛɪgi]; **TN4**, Peggy, pot, chamber. **1968** *DARE* FW Addit **swVA**, Peggy—also called thunder mug, badger, jug, and pot.

peggyball n **seMA**
A game similar to **peggy** n¹ in which a wooden ball is used instead of a tapered peg.
1984 *Spinner* 3.170 **seMA**, Retired bowlawicket and peggyball players dot the map of Fall River. *Ibid* 171, Scoring peggyball is very strenuous, for each player tries to reach the struck ball in the fewest leaps. **1989** *Yankee* July 58 **seMA**, Players laid the riser on top of a stick so that the pointed end was up. The peggy-ball rested on the lower, wider end. The batter would strike the top end of the riser with the broomstick, and the ball would pop into the air to be hit like a baseball. The batter would then estimate how far he'd hit the ball and call out a number in increments of five. That was the number of leaps an opponent could take in an effort to reach the ball. The opponent would decide whether to accept the challenge. . . If he conceded and refused to jump, you got the points. Conversely, if the jumper covered the call, *his* team got the points. *Ibid* 59, Peggyball disappeared mysteriously and quietly in the mid-fifties, although there were sporadic revivals as late as 1960.

peggy bounce-out (or -up) See **peggy** n¹

peggy loon n Cf **pegging awl**
=**red-necked grebe.**
1951 *AmSp* 26.90 **NY**, Probably derivative also [from *pegging-awl loon*] is *peggy loon* for Holboell's grebe (Long Island, N.Y.)

peggy on the bounce (or fly) See **peggy** n¹

peg horse See **peg C4**

peg knife n [Prob **peg B7**]
1970 *DARE* (Qu. F39, *A large pocket knife with blades that fold in and out*) Inf **OK53**, Peg knife.

peg line n [**peg C2**]
In marble play: see quot.
1966 *DARE* (Qu. EE8, *The line toward which the players roll their marbles before beginning a game, to determine the order of shooting*) Inf **NM9**, Peg line—they call it "lagging."

pegmonk n [*peg-* of unknown origin + *-monk* of Algonquian origin (cf Ojibwa *ma·nkw* loon); cf **pegging awl, touchmonk**]
=**red-throated loon.**
1951 [see **pegging awl**].

peg out v phr
To die; to fail completely. Note: The sense "to get ill, become exhausted" given in some glossaries is not otherwise attested and seems to be due to confusion with **pegged out.**
1854 *Harper's New Mth. Mag.* 9.562, The gentleman, who had "the certain remedy for bronchial complaints," "pegged out" with the consumption. **1859** Taliaferro *Fisher's R.* 40 **nwNC** (as of 1820s), I got so I couldn't eat nuther turnip greens nur hog's gullicks, and like to a pegged out, and left poor Patsey a poor reflicted widder. **1869** *Scientific Amer.* 20.156, The *North American* says, "The new oil well at Franklin, which has been creating a sensation lately, has "pegged out," and is now only yielding two or three barrels daily.[*] **1896** Harris *Sister Jane* 290 **GA**, You and the rest of the niggers out there have got it in your heads that if Sally Beshears pegs out you 'll be free. **1914** *DN* 4.77 **ME, nNH**, Peg out. . . To get ill; die. "He's all pegged out." "He'll peg out 'fore snow flies." Also very tired; same as "beat." **1923** *DN* 5.217 **swMO**, Peg out. . . To become exhausted, to die. **1943** *LANE* Map 521

(Kicked the bucket) 11 infs, **chiefly nNEng,** Pegged out. **1956** McAtee *Some Dialect NC* 33, Peg out . . die. *Slang.* **c1960** *Wilson Coll.* **csKY,** Peg out. . . Become exhausted or even to die. **1986** Pederson *LAGS Concordance (Died)* 8 infs, **Gulf Region,** Pegged out; 1 inf, **ceGA,** Peg out; *(Worn-out)* 2 infs, **seAL, csTN,** All pegged out.

peg pony See **peg** C4

peg-stick See **peggy** n[1]

peg-tooth harrow n Also *peg-toothed harrow, peg-tooth (cultivator), ~ smoothing harrow*

A harrow with rigid, roughly cylindrical teeth.

1925 *Book of Rural Life* 4.2505, Smoothing Harrow (peg-tooth, or drag). **1968–69** *DARE* (Qu. L20, *The implement used in a field after it's been plowed to break up the lumps*) Infs **CA**161, **IN**30, Peg-tooth harrow; (Qu. L25, *The implement used to clean out weeds and loosen the earth between rows of corn*) Inf **NY**96, Peg-tooth cultivator—this had teeth like a harrow. **1973** Allen *LAUM* 1.218 **MN** (as of c1950), *Harrow.* . . For breaking up clods of earth after plowing. . . The oldest, once made entirely of wood, consists of pegs or spikes set in horizontal bars. . . pegtooth (harrow) [2 infs, **MN**]. **1986** Pederson *LAGS Concordance,* 2 infs, **cwGA, cLA,** Peg-tooth harrow(s); 1 inf, **ceAR,** Peg-tooth harrow—8′ single disc, horses and mules; 1 inf, **csTX,** Peg-tooth harrow—a lot of bars and pegs on it; 1 inf, **cnAR,** Peg-toothed harrow—on flatland, 8′ long, spikes.

pegwood n

A **burning bush 1** (here: *Euonymus atropurpureus*).

1890 *Century Dict.* 5835, *Spindle-tree.* . . It is so called from the use of its hard fine-grained wood in making spindles, and other uses have given it the names *prick-timber, skewer-wood,* and *pegwood.* . . The name is carried over to the American *E. atropurpurea,* the wahoo or burning-bush. **1930** Sievers *Amer. Med. Plants* 59, *Wahoo.* . . *Other common names.* . . Bitter ash, pegwood. **1971** Krochmal *Appalachia Med. Plants* 116, *Euonymus atropurpureus.* . . Common Names: Eastern wahoo, . . pegwood [etc.].

pehea oe phr **HI**

See quot 1938.

1938 Reinecke *Hawaiian Loanwords* 28, Pehea oe. . . How are you? How goes it with you?—a greeting. **1951** *AmSp* 26.21 **HI,** Pehea oe (how are you?) **1954–60** Hance et al. *Hawaiian Sugar* 6, Pehea oe . . ['pɛ'hɛɑ'oɛ]—How are you? **1984** Sunset *HI Guide* 85, Pehea 'oe—how are you?

pekan n Also *pekan marten, ~ weasel* Also sp *pekon* [Algonquian; see quot 1910]

A marten (here: *Martes pennanti*).

[**a1718** (1864) Perrot *Mémoire* 56, Et que dans les chasses éloignées, où ils ont costume d'aller, il y a des ours, des cerfs, des biches, des chevreüils, . . quelques peccans et des loutres. [=And in the distant hunting grounds, where they are accustomed to go, there are bears, stags, does, roebucks, . . pekans, and otters.]] **1760** Jefferys *Nat. & Civil Hist. French Dominions* 1.37, The fur of this animal, as also that of the Pekan, another creature of the wild-cat kind, . . are what is called the *Menuë Peleterie,* or lesser furs.] **1804** (1904) Lewis *Orig. Jrls. Lewis & Clark Exped.* 1.132 **NE,** [The Sioux] furnish *Beaver,* . . Pekon, *(pichou)* Bear & Deer Skins. **1838** MA Zool. & Bot. Surv. *Repts. Zool.* 24, Pekan Weasel, or Fisher Weasel. . . Is very troublesome on sable lines by robbing traps of the sable. It is found occasionally on the mountains in the neighborhood of Williamstown. **1843** (1940) Ferris *Rocky Mts.* 241 **NY,** During these rambles we sometimes saw an animal resembling an otter, in size, shape and color, called a pekan or fisher. **1886** Turner *Contribs. AK* 208, Mustela pennanti. . . *Pekan; Pennant's Marten; Fisher.* Occurs sparingly in the upper Yukon Valley. **1910** Hodge *Hdbk. Amer. Indians* 2.223, Pekan. A name of the fisher. . . came into English through Canadian French, where it occurs also as *pécan.* It seems to be of Algonquian origin, though not western, for the animal is called in Chippewa *otchig,* in Cree *otchek.* It is referred by some to an Abnaki *pékané.* **1961** Jackson *Mammals WI* 333, Fisher. . . *Vernacular names.*—Black cat, . . pekan, pekan marten, pekan weasel [etc.] **1968** *DARE* File **NY,** Pekan ['pikən]—Alternate names for fisher, a tree-dwelling member of the weasel family. These names are reportedly used in the Adirondacks.

pelado n Pronc-spp *paláo, pee-low* [Span] **chiefly SW** usu derog

A low-class Mexican; hence adj *pelado* low-class.

1848 (1855) Ruxton *Life Far West* 197 **NM,** The hunters have the floor all to themselves. The Mexicans have no chance in such physical force dancing; and if a dancing Peládo steps into the ring, a lead-like thump from a galloping mountaineer quickly sends him sprawling. [Footnote to *Peládo:*] A nickname for the idle fellows hanging about a Mexican town, translated into "Greasers" by the Americans. **1892** *DN* 1.192 **TX,** Peládo. . . The word is generally pronounced *palâo,* the first *a* being very much obscured or entirely slurred, and the *d* silent. The term is applied to Mexicans of the lower classes, the rabble, and is more generally used in the plural. **1929** Dobie *Vaquero* 44 **West,** Once, for instance, he killed three *pelados* (a contemptuous name used by many border gringos and resented by all Mexicans) on the north side of the Nueces [River]. *Ibid* 52, The Mexicans killed five citizens, turned a dozen *pelado* culprits out of jail. **1932** Bentley *Spanish Terms* 178, Pelado . . [pe'laðo and pe'la o]. . . A disparaging term applied to persons of the poorer class. . . By extension it is used to describe anything low class as for example "his language was pelado." *Pelado* is used with good effect where the significance of the word is generally understood. **1962** Atwood *Vocab. TX* 73, *Person of Mexican origin.* . . *Pelado* (7 [examples]) is concentrated in Southwest and South Central Texas. [Footnote:] Pronounced *pee-low. Ibid* 128, Pelado. Commonly used in Spanish with a derogatory meaning, implying that a person is ill-bred, unmannerly, or vulgar . . —a bum or a ruffian. . . [One informant] states that in the familiar speech of men it may often imply no more than a guy or fellow. It may have been the frequency of this latter usage that led to the adoption of the word in Southwest Texas.

pelay See **piler**

pelcher See **pilchard 1**

Pele's hair n Also *Pele's whiskers* [Calque of Haw *lauoho o Pele,* after the Hawaiian volcano goddess *Pele*] **HI** Cf **Pele's tear**

Naturally occurring threads of volcanic glass.

1840 in 1845 Wilkes *Narr. U.S. Explor. Exped.* 4.129 **HI,** One of the remarkable productions of this crater is the capillary glass, or, as it is here called, "Pele's hair." **1861** Bristow *Gloss. Mineralogy* 276 **HI,** Pélé's Hair. Lava blown by the wind . . into hair-like fibres. **1896** *Pop. Sci. Mth.* 48.355, The specimens are lavas from the volcano Mauna Loa, which the wind, lashing them before hardening, has reduced to fibers of extraordinary fineness. . . Pélé's hairs, or bald men's locks, as they are poetically called . . [are] similar to . . formations . . produced in furnaces. **1930** U.S. Geol. Surv. *Water-Supply Papers* 616.113, Threads of volcanic glass that look like spun glass are called Pele's hair. They are formed in large quantities during fountaining at Halemaumau and are often carried 5 or 10 miles by the wind. . . On the ends of some of the threads are little droplets of glassy lava, which are called Pele's tears. **1938** Reinecke *Hawaiian Loanwords* 28, Pele's hair. . . Threads of Volcanic glass that look like spun glass. **1941** Writers' Program *Guide UT* 285 **HI,** The process [of making rock wool] was copied from the volcano of Hilo in Hawaii, where a small amount of rock wool—called by the natives "Pele's whiskers"—forms during each eruption.

Pele's tear n [Calque of Haw *waimaka o Pele,* after the Hawaiian volcano goddess *Pele*] **HI** Cf **Pele's hair**

A droplet of volcanic glass.

1930 [see **Pele's hair**]. **1938** Reinecke *Hawaiian Loanwords* 28, Pele's tears. . . Little drops of glassy lava on the ends of some threads of Pele's hair. **1974** *DARE* File **HI,** Pele's tears—congealed lava droplets.

Pele's whiskers See **Pele's hair**

pelican flower n [From the shape of the flowers]

1 A **birthwort 1** (here: *Aristolochia grandiflora* or *A. serpentaria*).

[**1814** Lunan *Hortus Jamaicensis* 2.46, Pelican Flower, or Poison Hogweed. . . The flower is of a very singular structure.] [**1890** *Century Dict.* 4362, *Pelican-flower.* . . A plant of the birthwort family, *Aristolochia grandiflora* of Jamaica. The name is suggested by the pouch-like calyx.] **1953** Greene–Blomquist *Flowers South* 155, Pelican-Flower, Birthwort (*Aristolochia grandiflora*)—The humorist of plants, its bud caricatures a pelican, swan, or goose. **1971** Krochmal *Appalachia Med. Plants* 64, *Aristolochia serpentaria.* . . Common Names: Virginia snakeroot, . . pelican flower [etc.].

2 An **owl's clover** (here: *Orthocarpus erianthus* or *O. faucibarbatus*). **CA**

1906 (1918) Parsons *Wild Flowers CA* 54, During the spring the meadows about San Francisco are luxuriantly covered with snowy masses of the fragrant white pelican-flower. Dr. Kellogg saw in these queer little blossoms, with their large pouches and long beaks, something suggestive of the pelican. The name does not apply to all species of *Orthocarpus,* however, as all have not this aspect. **1915** (1926) Armstrong–Thornber *Western Wild Flowers* 498, Yellow Pelican Flower—*Orthocarpus faucibarbatus.* . . The flowers are about an inch long, with very clear bright yellow "pouches" and greenish "beaks" tipped with white. **1961** Thomas *Flora Santa Cruz* 318 **cwCA,** O[*rthocarpus*] *erianthus* Benth. var. *roseus* Gray. Pelican or Popcorn Flower.

pelick n

A **coot** n[1] **1** (here: *Fulica americana*).

1888 Trumbull *Names of Birds* 118 **CT,** To a majority of the gunners at Stratford, Conn., it [=the coot] is the *pelick.* **1955** Forbush–May *Birds* 168, American Coot. . . Other names . . Pelick [etc].

pellitory n Also *pellitory bark,* ~ *tree, pillentary tree, pillenterry* [Transf from its application to the herb *Anacyclus pyrethrum* of northern Africa and southern Europe (*OED2* pellitory sb. 1, 1533 →), whose root was used (like the bark of the prickly ash) as a remedy for toothache]

A **prickly ash 1** such as *Zanthoxylum clava-herculis.*

1716 Petiver *Petiveriana* 11, Pellitory-tree. From the Hotness of its Bark. **1731** Catesby *Nat. Hist. Carolina* 1.26, The Pellitory, or Toothach Tree. . . The leaves smell like those of Orange, which, with the Seeds and *Bark* is aromatic, very hot and astringent, and is used by the People inhabiting the Sea Coasts of Virginia and Carolina for the Toothach, which has given it its name. **1830** Rafinesque *Med. Flora* 2.113, *Xanthoxylon fraxineum.* Names . . Toothache Bush, Pellitory [etc]. **1876** Hobbs *Bot. Hdbk.* 87, Pellitory bark . . *Xanthoxylum fraxineum.* **1913** *Torreya* 13.231 **NC,** *Fagara clava-herculis* . . Pillenterry, Church's I[slan]d, N.C. **1946** *PADS* 6.23 **ceNC,** *Pillentary tree.* . . A small tree having rough bark, which is astringent. Grows near mouth of Neuse River. Pamlico. Occasional. **1960** Vines *Trees SW* 595, Vernacular names are Toothache, . . Pillenterry, and Wait-a-bit. **1974** (1977) Coon *Useful Plants* 239, *Zanthoxylum americanum*—Prickly ash, pellitory bark [etc].

pellow See **pillow A**

pelon See **pilon**

pelonce, peloncillo See **piloncillo**

pelota n Also *pelotaka* [Span] **esp sID, eOR**

A game played in a court with a ball and a wicker racket; see quot 1971.

1967 *DARE* (Qu. EE11) Inf **TX5,** Pelota [pɪˈlotə]—handball. **1967** *DARE* FW Addit **seOR,** Most of the people of Jordan Valley are of Basque descent, but few who are younger than 45 can speak the Basque language. . . The huge pelota court stands crumbling in the middle of the town. **c1971** Hall *Snake River Valley* **sID** (*Do you know a term for a very fast game played with a ball and a sickle-shaped basket which may be strapped to the wrist? The ball is hurled against a wall by one player and caught and hurled again by another*) 4 infs, Pelota; 1 inf, Pelota [FW sugg]; 1 inf, Pelotaka. **1977** Jones *OR Folkl.* 43, [Caption:] Pelota court in Jordan Valley. Pelota is a Basque hand-ball game. *Ibid,* Pelota is a traditional Basque hand-ball game. Many of the Basque people who settled in Eastern Oregon are Spanish Basques who came over here starting in the early 1900's, often on contract to work as sheepherders. **2000** Launspach *ID Dial. Project* 6 **seID,** (*A very fast game played with a ball and a sickle-shaped basket*) 3 infs, Pelota.

Pelsnickle See **Belsnickel**

pelter n **Nth**

A poor or worn-out horse.

1856 *Knickerbocker* 48.314 **seNY,** When his earthly tenement yields his soul no shelter,/ May it animate the corpse of an ancient pelter. **1892** *DN* 1.210 **seMA,** *Pelter:* an old, worn-out horse. **1896** (1898) Ade *Artie* 4 **Chicago IL,** It's like hitchin' up a four-time winner 'longside of a pelter. **1931** *AmSp* 6.231 **cnNE,** *Pelter.* A horse of little value, a nag; used humorously of any horse. "I see Henry has gone to feed his pelters." **1952** FWP *Guide SD* 84, *Pelter:* an old horse. **1958** *AmSp* 33.270 **eWA,** Horse. . . Hide, pelter.

pelter v [Engl dial; frequentative of *pelt;* cf *EDD* pelter v. 1] Cf **-er** affix **2**

1902 *DN* 2.41 **sIL,** *Pelter.* . . 1. To throw stones or other missiles at anything. 2. To clamor vociferously.

Peltsnickel, Pelznickel See **Belsnickel**

pemater See **tomato**

pembina n Also *pimbina* [CanFr *pimbina* < Cree *nipiminân;* see quot 1910 Hodge]

=**highbush cranberry.**

[**1760** Jefferys *Nat. & Civil Hist. French Dominions* 41 **Canada,** The *Pemine,* another plant peculiar to this country, is a different shrub, growing along the sides of rivulets, and in meadows, which also bears a clustering fruit of a very sharp and astringent taste.] **1824** Keating *Narrative* 2.52 **neND,** Of the plants observed in this neighbourhood, besides the Pembina, we can only mention the common hop. [**1910** Hodge *Hdbk. Amer. Indians* 2.223, *Pembina.* A Canadian name for the acid fruit of *Viburnum opulus,* the highbush cranberry, a plant growing in low ground, along streams, from New Brunswick, far westward, and s. to Pennsylvania. The word is a corruption of Cree *nipiminân,* 'watered berry,' i.e. the fruit of a plant growing in, or laved by, water; not 'waterberry,' as has been stated, since that would be *nipimin;* and besides, the fruit is not watery. The name of the fruit is derived from the habitat of the plant that bears it.] **1910** Graves *Flowering Plants* 368 **CT,** *Viburnum Opulus.* . . Cramp-bark. Pimbina. **1976** Bruce *How to Grow Wildflowers* 134, A variety (considered by some a distinct species) equally valuable for edible fruits but not so ornamental, being lower and more straggly, is *edule:* Mooseberry, Squashberry, or Pimbina.

pen n[1] Usu |pɛn|; also *esp Sth, S Midl* |pɪn|; for addit varr see quot 1989 Pronc-spp *pain, pin* Cf Pronc Intro 3.I.4, **pin** n[1] Note: Both of the homophonous *pen* nouns are treated together at **A** below.

A Forms.

1893 Shands *MS Speech* 8, The confusion of this sound [ɛ] with [ɪ] is very common indeed among the illiterate classes, and is heard quite often among the educated . . [pɪn] for *pen.* **1905** *DN* 3.103 **nwAR,** Abnormal vowels. . . [pɪn] (pen). **1927** Shewmake *Engl. Pronc. VA* 31, One also hears *pin* for *pen.* **1934** *AmSp* 9.210 **Sth,** Many words having standard [ɛn] become [ɪn] in the South. We have, for example, . . *pen* [pɪn]. **1936** *AmSp* 11.16 **eTX,** [Footnote:] *Bench, end, pen* (enclosure). . . (All these have [ɪ] in East Texas.) **1939** in 1944 *ADD* **wWV,** *Pen.* . . Pin. Current. 'This pin writes poorly.' **1961** Folk *Word Atlas N. LA* 56, The Southern tendency to raise the [ɛ] before nasals to [ɪ] was followed by every informant in such words as *pen, fence,* and *French harp.* **1962** Steinbeck *Travels* 202 **TX,** Our daughter, after a stretch in Austin, was visiting New York friends. She said, "Do you have a pin?" "Certainly, dear," said her host. "Do you want a straight pin or a safety pin?" "Aont [=I want] a fountain pin," she said. **1966–67** [see **B2** below]. **1974** Gilbreth *Dictionary* 13 **seSC,** *Pain:* A writing instrument mightier than the sword. **1989** Pederson *LAGS Tech. Index* 96 **Gulf Region,** [Of 953 exx of the pronc of *pen,* 361 were of the type [pɛn], 354 [pɪn], 26 [pin], 2 [pjɪn], and 1 [pjɛn].] **1998** *DARE* File **OK,** In Oklahoma, most people do not have the *pen-pin* distinction. One way of making clear what they are speaking of is to use the words *ink pen*—for "pen" and *straight pin*—for "pin."

B As noun. [*pen* a small enclosure]

1 An animal trap in the form of a log or rail enclosure—often in combs *bear pen, turkey* ~, *wolf* ~.

1647 in 1894 Watertown MA *Records* 1.12, The Towne gaue: to John Witherll: there Right in the palisado that inclosed the woulfe pen. **1657** in 1882 Southold NY *Town Rec.* 1.333, Such as are disposed to make a penn or penns to take wolves in. **1835** Parker *Trip to TX* 52 **NH,** A man on Fox river [IL] . . made a wolf pen over a cow that got accidentally killed, and caught twelve wolves in one week! **1843** *Amer. Pioneer* 2.57 **neOH,** In respect to turkey pens, as they were called, the more southern pioneers constructed them as above described. **1870** Nowland *Early Indianapolis* 43 **IN,** Turkeys were often caught by means of pens constructed for the purpose—a small log pen, about eight feet in length and four wide, something like a cabin, and covered tight. **1913** Rothert *Hist. Muhlenberg Co.* 115 **KY,** My grandfather . . had cleared a small field, in which he built a turkey-pen for the purpose of trapping wild turkeys. **1960** Hall *Smoky Mt. Folks* 20, The wild turkeys was about to eat it up, I built a pen to try to catch 'em. The pen was ten foot each way, and I covered over the top. Then I cut a ditch and run it into the pen and covered the ditch over with bark. I scattered corn in the ditch so as to draw the turkeys into the pen. *Ibid* 61, *Bear pen:* a deadfall bear trap. **1970** *Foxfire* 4.72 **nGA,** Some men also constructed large log pens in likely spots, and used green withes to set the trap. When the bear took the bait, the bear was caught for the gate fell behind him. *Ibid* 82 **nGA**, M'grandaddy had a bear in a trap—a pen they called 'em in them days, y'know. Made out'a wood split about six'r'eight feet long. Y'pegged'em t'gether an' made a top. **1986** Pederson *LAGS Concordance,* 1 inf, **swGA**, Pen—for catching wild hogs; 1 inf, **cnAR**, Pens—to trap wild hogs; 1 inf, **nwFL**, Pens—for trapping wild hogs; [1 inf, **swGA**, The dogs killed his calves so bad over there till they built some pen traps for [hi]m].

2 also *log pen:* A building or unit of a building built of horizontal logs interlocking at the corners; rarely, a smaller structure of the same sort forming the framework of a chimney.
Sth, S Midl   Cf **double-pen(ned)**

1789 in 1929 Weems *Mason Locke Weems* 3.418 **MD**, I lodged in a log-pen. **1835** [see **passage**]. **1843** (1969) Lewis *Odd Leaves* 147 **LA**, The house consisted of a double log cabin, of small dimensions, a passage, the full depth of the house, running between the "pens." **1846** (1973) Porter *Quarter Race* 24 **KY**, I went to town last night to the confectionary, [a whisky shop in a log pen fourteen feet square . .]. **1853** Hammett *Stray Yankee in TX* 124, When he'd nothing else to do, [he] lazed about anybody's log-pen that he pleased. **1922** (1926) Kephart *Highlanders* 305 **sAppalachians**, Ef you git yo' pen so almighty tight as that you won't git no fresh air. . *Ibid* 314, The mountain home of to-day is the log cabin of the American pioneer . . a pen that can be erected by four "corner men" in one day and is finished by the owner at his leisure. The commonest type is a single large room. **1950** Stuart *Hie Hunters* 114 **eKY**, The old double-log shack, with a dogtrot running between the two log pens, was just beyond the coal tipple of the worn-out coal mine. c**1960** Wilson *Coll.* **csKY**, Cat-and-clay. . . Said of a chimney made of a wooden pen covered with wisps of straw covered with mud. **1966–67** DARE (Qu. D23, *A house that is divided in two through the middle*) Inf **MS**1, Double-pen [pɪn] house; (Qu. M1, . . *Kinds of barns*) Inf **TN**14, Four-pen barn, two-pen barn. **1975** McDonough *Garden Sass* 34 **AR**, More elaborate than these simple homes was the dog-trot style of house, which consisted of two separate log pens with a covered breezeway between them. **1986** Pederson *LAGS Concordance*, 7 infs, **AL, GA**, Double pen (house); 2 infs, **AL, LA**, Double-pen log house; 1 inf, **LA**, Big-old double-pen house; 1 inf, **FL**, Double-pen barn; 1 inf, **AL**, Double-penned house—with breezeway; 1 inf, **GA**, Single-pen house; 1 inf, **GA**, Scrap pen—little room, on side, cookstove there; [1 inf, **AL**, Dog pen house]. **1987** *Hall Coll.* **eTN**, In the time of my father and grandfather, they built double pen log cabins and double pen barns near where I live today.

3 An enclosure or crib, often built of loosely stacked rails, used for storing fodder, corn, or other bulky commodities—often in combs *rail pen, shuck ~, corn ~*.   **chiefly Sth, S Midl**

1842 *Cultivator* 9.160, Buckwheat may be thrashed upon just such a rail pen, covered with rails, much better than upon the ground. **1844** *S. Lit. Messenger* 10.486, The neighbor aforesaid had the comforts of a shuck-pen, in which to console himself for the night. **1856** Davis *Farm Bk.* 64 (DA), Made 1 cotton Pen of rails. **1860** Claiborne *Life Dale* 26 **neGA** (as of 1783), We ran to the corn-pen, pulled down the rails, and let the high pile of corn slip down on the blazing shucks. **1895** *Scribner's Mag.* Dec 726 **GA**, As a matter of fact, Jeff, the little beagle, could have whipped a shuck-pen full of them. **1896** (1897) Hughes *30 Yrs. a Slave* 130 (as of 1862), The place where I stayed in the daytime was in a large shuck-pen—a pen built in the field to feed stock from, in the winter time. **1903** *DN* 2.325 **seMO**, Pen. . . Crib (for corn, etc.) **1907** *DN* 3.235 **nwAR**, Pen. . . Crib (for corn, etc.) **1909** *DN* 3.369 **cAL, wGA**, Shuck pen. . . A pen made of rails for holding shucks. **1938** Rawlings *Yearling* 278 **nFL**, Now you take down that tipply-tumbly pen, and build a coop to kiver the 'taters. **1959** *Hall Coll.* **wNC, eTN**, And they had apples put up in rail pen, shucks, fodder over the top of 'em. c**1960** Wilson *Coll.* **csKY**, Rail pen . . for corn that is hardly dry enough to put into the crib. **1966** Dakin *Dial. Vocab. Ohio R. Valley* 2.66, (Corn) pen (2 [infs]—Ind.; 1 [inf]—Ill.; 2 [infs]—K[entucky]) is used, sometimes at least, to designate a structure made of rails in contrast to one completely enclosed. Both Rush County, Indiana, informants made this distinction. **1966–70** DARE (Qu. M8, *The building where corn is kept*) Infs **IL**80, 114, **NC**85, Corn pen; (Qu. M12, *What do you keep food for the cattle in over winter?*) Infs **IL**50, **NY**198, **SC**9, **TN**34, Fodder pen; **TX**42, Cottonseed pen. **1986** Pederson *LAGS Concordance*, 1 inf, **AR**, Cotton pen—where cotton stored before baling; pen in barn, where hay was stored; 1 inf, **AR**, Cotton pen—for storing cotton; 1 inf, **MS**, Cotton pens; 1 inf, **GA**, A shuck pen; 1 inf, **TN**, Hay pen—back of the crib on ground level of barn; 1 inf, **TN**, Grain

pen; 1 inf, **LA**, A little pen—for holding coal; (The thing you put the food in for a hog) 1 inf, **AL**, We always called it pen.

4 A stack of pulpwood or fuelwood, each layer consisting of two pieces at right angles to those of the layer below; such a stack built to any of various standard dimensions; hence v *pen* to stack in this way.   **esp Sth**

1944 Society Amer. Foresters *Forestry Terminology* 52, Pen. A loose, rectangular stack of fuelwood or pulpwood in layers of two pieces each. **1955** (1956) Forbes *Forestry Hdbk.* 1.47, A *pen* of wood stacked in layers is used in the South as a pulpwood unit. . . Five pens, 6 ft. high, are considered equal to a cord (if of 4-ft. wood), or to a unit (if of longer wood—generally 5 ft., 3 in.). **1966** DARE (Qu. LL24, *To keep firewood neat you have to cut it, split it, and _____ it up*) Inf **GA**77, Rack it—stacked lengthwise; pin it—stacked crosswise; **SC**19, Pen—put it in an enclosure; it is put in crosswise to permit drying [FW illustr: pieces stacked in pairs at right angles]. **1986** Pederson *LAGS Concordance*, 1 inf, **ceTX**, Pen—¼ of a cord; 4′ x 8′.

pen v[1]   See **pen** n B4

pen n[2], v[2]   See **pin**

penaidie   See **panada**

penance   See **penence**

penance bench   See **penitent's bench**

pen barn n   Also *pen-type barn*   **MI, WI**   Cf **loafing barn**
A building with an undivided interior for the housing of farm animals.

1950 *WELS* (Names for barns according to the way they are built) 1 inf, **cnWI**, Pen barn. **1966–67** DARE (Qu. M1, . . *Kinds of barns . . according to their use or the way they are built*) Inf **MI**12, Pen-type barn—cows run loose in the barn, no stalls; **MI**27, Pen barn—just roof, sidewalls, no stalls, one open end; **MI**40, Pen barn—no stalls, one side open. **2001** *NADS Letters* seWI, Pen(-type) barn. . . It is a barn that doesn't have stalls, just trenches for the animals to drink out of. Other than that it is a normal barn. I know this because my godfather has one. **2001** DARE File WI, In my experience, pen barn refers to a barn where the cattle are allowed to roam loose within it. . . Again, in my experience pen barns were more often used to house beef cattle than dairy cattle. I've heard the term used in Wisconsin. In my travels around the country looking at barns, I did not hear the term used. But I didn't ask about it either.

pencil bean   See **pencil-pod bean**

pencil brush   See **pencil tree**

pencil cactus n   Cf **lead-pencil cactus**
Either of two cacti with slender stems, as:

a A **cactus B1** (here: *Rhipsalis baccifera*).

1933 Small *Manual SE Flora* 913, R[hipsalis] Cassutha. . . Plants in much-branched clusters . . the branches often very slender. . . Pencil-cactus, Mistletoe-cactus.

b A **prickly pear 1**; see quots.   Cf **pencil cholla**

1936 Whitehouse *TX Flowers* 77, The pencil cactus or tasajillo (*Opuntia leptocaulis*), conspicuous for its small stems and bright red fruits, is abundant in the state and Mexico. **1957** Jaeger *N. Amer. Deserts* 64, Some of these readily identifiable species are . . darning-needle or pencil cacti (*Opuntia*) with finger-sized stem-joints and very long, rigid gleaming spines. **1961** Wills–Irwin *Flowers TX* 160, The Tasajillo, Rat-tail Cactus, or Pencil Cactus, is one of the slenderest cacti known, often forming thickets with its curving spiny stems. **1974** Munz *Flora S. CA* 320, O[puntia] ramosissima. . . Pencil Cactus.

pencil cedar n   Cf **cedar pencil**

1 A **juniper 1** (here: *Juniperus bermudiana, J. silicicola,* or *J. virginiana*).

1876 Hobbs *Bot. Hdbk.* 183, Juniperus Virginiana, Red (pencil) cedar. **1892** (1974) Millspaugh *Amer. Med. Plants* 166–1, Red Cedar, Juniper, or Savin; Pencil Cedar. . The highly-colored and fragrant heart-wood is largely used in the manufacture of lead-pencils. **1908** Sudworth *Forest Trees Pacific* 183, It [=*Juniperus occidentalis*] is so similar to the wood of the eastern red-wooded pencil "cedars" (*J[uniperus] virginiana* and *J. barbadensis*) that it would serve excellently for lead-pencil wood. **1962** Harrar–Harrar *Guide S. Trees* 95, At one time this species [=*Juniperus* *virginiana*] was the principal pencil wood; hence the name *pencil cedar,* which still persists in some localities. **1974** Morton *Folk Remedies* 87 **SC,** Red Cedar; Southern Red Cedar; Pencil Cedar—*Juniperus salicicola* [sic]. . . Wood formerly much used for lead pencils.

2 =incense cedar.

[**1953** Peattie *Nat. Hist. W. Trees* 214, When the commercial supply of pencil wood from Eastern Red Cedar came to an end, half a century ago, it was to the Incense Cedar that the pencil-makers principally turned. The western tree has all the needed properties for a good pencil wood.] **1961** *W3, Incense cedar . . esp:* a tall tree (*L[ibocedrus] decurrens*) of the No. American Pacific coast . . called also *pencil cedar* [etc].

pencil cholla n Also *pencil-joint cholla*   Cf **cigarette cactus, pencil ~ b**

A **prickly pear 1** with slender stems; see quots.

1940 Benson *Cacti AZ* 31, Opuntia arbuscula. . . Pencil cholla . . branches cylindrical, the terminal ones 3/16 to 5/16 inch in diameter, the surface smooth . . the internal woody core almost a solid cylinder. **1949** Curtin *By the Prophet* 60 **AZ,** The fruit on both Deerhorn and Pencil cholla is always green. **1967** *DARE* (Qu. S26e) Inf **CA4,** Pencil cholla = cigarette cactus. **1971** Dodge *100 Desert Wildflowers* 58, Common along banks of washes and on desert flats, this cholla [=*Opuntia leptocaulis*], also called "tesajo," or "pencil cholla," is so slender-stemmed and sprawling in growth habit that it is easily overlooked. **1973** *AZ Highways* Mar 29, Other Chollas are not so spiny and less conspicuous, such as the Pencil Chollas and Cane Chollas. **1985** Dodge *Flowers SW Deserts* 65, Tesajo . . Pencil-Joint Cholla. . . *Opuntia leptocaulis. . . Opuntia ramosissima.*

pencil eel n

See quot.

1982 Sternberg *Fishing* 48, On eastern rivers, some anglers tip their jigs with 3- to 7-inch American eels, called *pencil eels.*

pencil-joint cholla See **pencil cholla**

pencil-pod bean n Also *pencil bean, pencil pod*   **esp Nth**

Prob a wax bean.

1950 *WELS* **WI** (*Beans that are eaten in the pod*) 1 Inf, Pencil beans; 1 Inf, Pencil-pod beans; (*Beans [that] have yellow pods*) 2 Infs, Pencil-pod beans; (*Other kinds of beans*) 1 Inf, Pencil beans; 1 Inf, Pencil-pod beans. **1966–69** *DARE* (Qu. I14, *Kinds of beans that you eat in the pod before they're dry*) Inf **MA6,** Pencil-pod beans; (Qu. I15, *Some of the beans that you eat in the pod have yellow pods; you call these* _____) Inf **MI110,** Pencil-pod beans; **VT9,** Pencil pods; (Qu. I20, . . *Kinds of beans*) Inf **NY70,** Pencil bean—long yellow pods; **MN12,** Pencil-pod bean—no big seed, more a round bean. **1973** Allen *LAUM* 1.310 (as of c1950), Singletons otherwise unattested are . . *pencil pod beans* [1 inf, **MN**].

pencil point n **chiefly NJ**

A piece of slender, tubular pasta; see quots.

1986 *DARE* File **cwNJ,** Pencil Points—A form of pasta found in Trenton, New Jersey and I think nowhere else. It is served like spaghetti or mostaccioli and is rice-like, looking like its name. **1996** Evanovich *Two Dough* 167 **NJ,** I watched the old folks beating their retreat over the blighted grass and hard ground. In a half-hour they'd all be at the Mayer house, eating pencil points and drinking highballs. **1998** *NADS Letters* **NJ,** I learned of "pencil points" while living in New Jersey in an area with a large Italian community. These were hollow, ribbed pasta shapes, about as round as a pencil, about 1½ inches long, with the ends being cut on a diagonal to resemble the point of a pencil. Pencil points are served with red sauce, pesto, or simply with butter, garlic and parmesan. *Ibid* **Trenton NJ,** Next time you're in the supermarket, go to the pasta section and find "penne rigate." That's pencil points. *Ibid* **NJ,** I think it [=pencil points] was what Ronzoni calls "Penne Rigate #76." *Ibid* **NJ,** Pencil points are still around. . . They are like small ziti, served in some restaurants as the pasta order when you order a meat entree [according to six students from NJ, one from Staten Island NY]. *Ibid* **NJ,** In Chambersburg (a largely Italian section of Trenton, NJ), as well as the surrounding area, pencil points most often applies to the pasta shape usually referred to as "penne."

pencil-tail See **pestle-tail**

pencil tree n Also *pencil brush*   [From obs *pencil* small paint-brush, in ref to the tufted fruit]

A **groundsel tree** (here: *Baccharis halimifolia*).

1830 Rafinesque *Med. Flora* 2.199, Baccharis halimifolia . . *Groundsel tree, Pencil tree.* **1876** Hobbs *Bot. Hdbk.* 49, Groundsel tree, Pencil tree, Baccharis halimifolia. **1910** Graves *Flowering Plants* 388 **CT,** Groundsel Tree. Pencil Tree. **1955** *S. Folkl. Qrly.* 19.232, The *Pencil Brush* (Baccharis halimifolia) bears heads of showy white bristles on stalked pencil-like clusters.

penco n Pronc-sp *pinco* [AmSpan]   **NM, sCO**

An orphan lamb.

1897 Lummis *King of Broncos* 57 **NM,** The lambs in his band were now five days old; and at that age a New Mexican *penco* is smart enough in body and impish enough in mind to undo Job himself. **1952** *CO Qrly.* 1.88, The terms [for orphan lamb] found in Colorado were "bum" or "bummer," "poddy," and "penco" (pronounced *pinco* by the non-Spanish). *Ibid* 90, That the word "penco" should be found with the meaning of orphan lamb in the Rio Grande Valley of New Mexico and then in southern Colorado is not surprising, since the route of the early sheep trails was up from Mexico and Texas through New Mexico into Colorado.

'pend See **spend A**

pender See **pinder**

penence n Also *penance* [Varr of *dependence;* cf Intro "Language Changes" I.7, 9]

Dependence; reliance.

1899 Chesnutt *Conjure Woman* 67 **csNC** [Black], Dey ain' much 'pen'ence ter be put on 'im. **1909** *DN* 3.356 **eAL, wGA,** Penance. . . Dependence. Also used in the sense of reliance.

penepne n

A **wild plum** (here: *Prunus umbellata*).

1950 *PADS* 14.51 **SC,** Penepne [pɪˈnɛpnɪ]. . . The hog plum or wild plum of the low country. Origin undetermined.

penetentiar, penetentir See **penitentiary**

peng n Also *panga, penga, penge(r), pengi* [Norw *peng(e),* usu pl *penger, pengar,* Sw (pl) *pengar*]

Money.

1894 in 1966 *AmSp* 41.66 **ND,** Eric Ramstead left for a six weeks visit in the southern States last Saturday. His objective point is Tennessee—where he expects to invest some good hard "panga." **1968** *DARE* (Qu. U19a, . . *Money in general: "He's certainly got the* _____") Inf **MN36,** Peng—Swedish for money; **AK1,** Penge—[pɛŋgɪ]; Norwegian. **1969** Sorden *Lumberjack Lingo* 84 **NEng, Gt Lakes,** Penger, panga, or penga—A Norwegian word for money or pay. *Pengi*—A Swedish word for pay.

pen handle See **handle** n **B1**

penhooker See **pinhooker**

penhooking See **pinhook** v **1**

Penitente n [Span]   **NM, sCO**

A member of a religious society of Flagellants.

[**1838** Ganilh *Mexico Versus TX* 79 **Mexico,** But this exhibition is rendered shocking and repulsive, by *penitentes,* who walk at the head of the *cortege,* naked from the waist upwards, and bare-legged, tottering under the weight of a huge piece of timber, to which their arms are fastened, in the form of a cross.] **1881** (1882) Chase *Editor's Run* 115 **NM,** At the lower end of the habitations [in the Cimarron] we found the Penitente church, a mud house. **1885** *Wkly. New Mexican Rev.* 9 April 4/6 (*DAE*), Albuquerque livery men ran excursion wagons to Los Gregorios when the penitentes tortured themselves. **1941** Cleaveland *No Life* 113 **NM,** It was the beginning of Holy Week and the Penitentes were 'out,' as we phrased it. **1942** *Colorado Mag.* 19.165, Many of the settlers in Colorado naturally belonged to the order of Penitentes, since they came from New Mexico. Some years members of the community reenacted the entire story of the capture, trial and crucifixion of Christ. **1949** *Natl. Geogr. Mag.* Dec 824 **NM,** Penitentes are a living counterpart of the santos [=carved and painted saints]. **1966** *DARE* Tape **NM5,** Penitentes are largely a political organization now. If you want to control the Spanish vote, you must be a Penitente. . . They were . . a religious group. . . About Easter time they would have their religious festivities and formerly, years ago, they crucified one of their members in commemoration of the crucifixion of Christ. But the government stopped that.

penitentiary v Also *penetentir, penetentiar, penitenture* **sAppalachians**

To send (someone) to prison.

1924 Raine *Land of Saddle-Bags* 135 **sAppalachians,** I wish I was on the jury, I'd penetentiar 'em every time. **1927** *DN* 5.469 **sAppalachians,** *Penetentir.* . . To put into a penitentiary. **1963** *Mt. Life* 39.2.51 **sAppalachians,** His pap, afore he was penitentured daown in Georgy, didn't hardly nuver work none to speak of. **1974** Fink *Mountain Speech* 19 **wNC, eTN,** *Penitentiary* . . send to prison. "They penitentiaried them for making licker." **1976** Garber *Mountain-ese* 67 **sAppalachians,** *Penitentiary* . . incarcerate, jail—If they ever ketch the thief they will penitentiary him for shore.

penitent's bench n Also *penance bench* Cf **repentant seat** =**mourners' bench.**

1929 (1951) Faulkner *Sartoris* 24 **MS** [Black], Sinner riz fum de moaner's bench,/ Sinner jump to de penance bench. **1983** *MJLF* 9.1.50 **ceKY** (as of 1956), *Penitent's bench* . . a mourner's bench.

penitenture See **penitentiary**

penknife n **chiefly N Midl, C Atl** See Map

Orig a small pocketknife used to make and mend quill pens; now a pocketknife of any size, but esp a small one.

1674 in 1878 *MA Hist. Soc. Coll.* 5th ser 5.3, My brother . . bought me an Hour-glasse and penknife. **1754** *Boston News–Letter* (MA) 23 May (*DAE*), Imported from London, . . pen knives, clasp-knives, butcher's knives. **1897** Howells *Open-Eyed Conspiracy* 25 **ceNY,** He took out his penknife and clicked open a blade to begin whittling. **1957** Battaglia *Resp. to PADS 20* **eMD** (*A large pocket knife with blades that fold in and out*) Penknife. **1965–70** *DARE* (Qu. F39, *A large pocket knife with blades that fold in and out*) 45 Infs, **chiefly N Midl, C Atl,** Penknife; **CT6, HI6, NY130,** Penknife—smaller; **CA54,** Penknife—a small one; **IL55,** Penknife—a little knife; **LA16,** The little one was a penknife; **NJ40,** Penknife—smaller, fancier; **TX31,** Penknife—regardless of size; **VA33,** Penknife—large or small. **1986** Pederson *LAGS Concordance,* 2 infs, **FL, GA,** (A) penknife; 2 infs, **AL, FL,** Penknives.

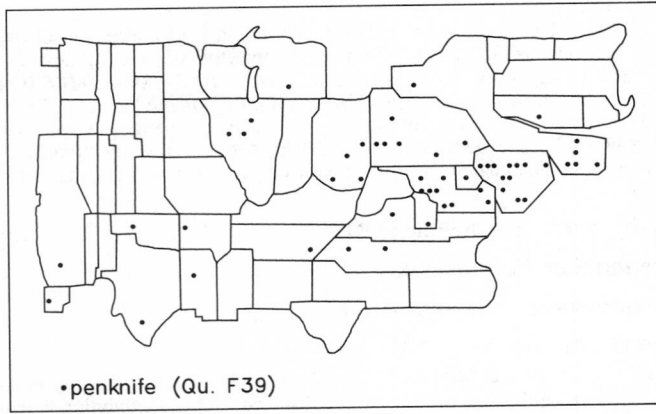

•penknife (Qu. F39)

penneroil See **pennyroyal**

pen-neumonia See **pneumonia**

penniwinkle See **pennywinkle**

Pennsylvania n Usu |ˌpɛn(t)səlˈvenjə, -nɪə|; also |ˌpɛnsəlˈven(j)ɪ, ˌpɛnsəˈvenjə|; for addit varr see quots Pronc-spp *Pennsylvany, Pensivania*
Std sense, var forms.

a1828 (1887) Bernard *Retrospections* 250, A "Pennsylvany hurricane," like a "Caroliny swamper," was, indeed, a common term, nearer home, for a sublime Munchausenism—vulgarly speaking, a long lie. **1848** Cooper *Oak-Openings* 49, My proper home is in Pennsylvany, on the other side of Lake Erie. **1891** *DN* 1.157 **cNY,** [pɛnslˈvenɪ]. **1907** *DN* 3.187 **seNH,** "He's in Pennsylvany, or one of them fur-off states." Older generation. **1942** Hall *Smoky Mt. Speech* 76 **wNC, eTN,** In the speech of most old people, of many middle-aged and young, both *-a* and *-ia* . . appear as [ɪ]. . . The words in which [ɪ] was heard . . Pennsylvania.

1950 (1965) Richter *Town* 36 **OH,** They said Pennsylvany, too, and Virginny. **1965** Carmony *Speech Terre Haute* 50, *Pennsylvania* [pˈɛˌnsɪˈveˈiˈnjə]. **1980** *LAMSAS* 1.106, [Throughout **NY, NJ, PA, OH, WV, KY, SC, GA, FL,** proncs of the type [pɛntslˈvenjə, -ˈvenjə, -ˈvenjɪ, -ˈvenjɪ] are widespread; 75 infs, 53 **PA, WV,** offered proncs of the type [pɛntslˈvenɪ, -ˈvenɪ]; 31 infs, [pɪntslˈvenjə]; 12 infs, [pɛnsəˈvenjə, pɪnts-]; [3 infs, **PA,** [pɛnslˈfɔnɪ, pɪ-]—PaGer form;] 1 inf, **OH,** [pɛnsɪlˈvenɪ].] **1981** Pederson *LAGS Basic Materials* **Gulf Region,** [10 infs offered proncs of the type [pˈɪˈnslˈveˈɪnjə; 5 infs, proncs of the type [pˈɛˈnsəˈvenjə]; 3 infs, proncs of the type [pˈɛ^ntsəˈve^ɪnjə]; 1 inf, [pˈɪntsləˈve^ɪnjə]; 1 inf, [ˌpɑntsaˈve^enjə]; 1 inf, [pˈɪnsɪˈvenjə]; 1 inf, [pˈɪnsɪˈve^ɪnjɪ]; 1 inf, [pˈɪˈnsɪˈve^·ɪnjɪ]; 1 inf, [pˈɛˈnsləˈve^ɪnjɐ].] **1982** McCool *Sam McCool's Pittsburghese* 27 **PA,** *Pensivania:* the state in which true champions find Pittsburgh.

Pennsylvanian sumac See **Pennsylvania sumac**

Pennsylvania sumac n Also *Pennsylvanian sumac*

A **smooth sumac** (here: *Rhus glabra*).

1785 Marshall *Arbustrum* 128, *Smooth Pennsylvanian Sumach.* . . grows naturally in several of the northern States. **1854** King *Amer. Eclectic Dispensatory* 806, *Rhus Glabrum* sometimes called Upland or *Pennsylvania Sumach,* is found in almost all parts of the United States. **1873** in 1976 Miller *Shaker Herbs* 241, Upland Sumach. Smooth Sumach. Pennsylvania Sumach. **1876** Hobbs *Bot. Hdbk.* 114, Sumach, Pennsylvania, *Rhus glabra.* **1930** Sievers *Amer. Med. Plants* 52, *Smooth Sumac.* . . *Other common names.* . . Pennsylvania sumac [etc]. **1958** Jacobs–Burlage *Index Plants NC* 11, *Rhus glabra* . . Pennsylvania sumach [etc].

Pennsylvany See **Pennsylvania**

penny n

A dollar.

1970 *DARE* (Qu. U26, *Names or nicknames . . for a paper dollar*) Inf **PA240,** Penny—if people I know ask me to lend them a penny or a nickel, they're referring to a dollar or five dollars. These are new expressions. **1972** Claerbaut *Black Jargon* 75, *Penny* . . a dollar; one-dollar bill.

penny after v phr Cf **penny-dog 2a**

2001 *NADS Letters* **PA,** A small child "pennys after" an older one, in a sense, a tagalong.

penny ante n, also attrib Also *penny-annie, ~-ant*

Std sense, var forms.

1966–67 *DARE* (Qu. DD35, . . *Card games*) Inf **ME16,** Penny-ant; penny-ant poker; (Qu. EE40, . . *Table games . . using dice*) Inf **AL32,** Penny-annie. **c1974** Jones *Ozark Hill Boy* 38 **AR** (as of c1930), They finally settled to a game of Penny-Annie on the floor and I stretched out on one of the seats & fell asleep.

penny bank n Cf **penny flower**

An **honesty** (here: *Lunaria annua*).

1959 Carleton *Index Herb. Plants* 90, *Penny bank* . . Lunaria annua.

penny berry n

Prob a **wintergreen;** see quots.

1980 in 1982 *Barrick Coll.* **csPA,** Penny berry—small ground plant with edible red berry. **2000** *NADS Letters* **cnPA,** Penny berry or ground berry—a small red berry, slightly bigger than a teaberry, starchier, closer to the ground, and less flavorful. Penny berries and teaberries often grow together and are picked together by children. In a handful of berries, the more abundant pennyberries or groundberries are the bulk, while the teaberries provide the flavor.

penny-ciders n [Folk-etym for **appendicitis**]

1940 in 1944 *ADD* 225 **swVA,** 'I've got penny-ciders' = appendicitis. [**1981** Pederson *LAGS Basic Materials* (Appendicitis) 1 inf, **swMS,** [ˌpˈɛnˈsa^də] = that's a penny inside of you.]

pennycress n

Std: a plant of the genus *Thlaspi,* esp *T. arvense.* Also called **penny grass, wild sweet alyssum.** For other names of *T. arvense* see **devil's-weed 5, fanweed, Frenchweed 2, garlic B, hedge mustard 3, Jim Hill mustard 3, mother schoolcraft, stinking mustard, stinkweed, treacle mustard, treaclewort**

penny-dog n [Scots, nEngl dial; attested only in similes such as "to follow one like a penny dog" and in the fig sense "toady"]

1 also *penny-feist:* A small dog—sometimes in phr *follow one around like a penny dog.* *sometimes derog*

  1930 Shoemaker *1300 Words* 45 **cPA Mts** (as of c1900), Penny-dog—A small hunting dog, or whiffet. **1939** in 1944 *ADD* **nWV,** Penny-feist. . . A small dog. **1960** Williams *Walk Egypt* 110 **GA,** He [=a hound] made a business of snuffling the chopping block, never looking at her, yet his neck was ready at her hand; for he was not a penny-feist or slinker-pup, loll-tongued and belly-up. He had affairs afoot. **2001** *NADS Letters* **csPA,** Penny dog. . . This is a term my mother (age 68) uses. She was born, raised, and still lives in south central Pennsylvania. . . "That boy loves you so much, he follows you around like a penny dog." . . She says she does not know the origins of it, but she remembers her grandmother . . using the term. This grandma is long deceased, but was born in 1884 in south central PA.

2 Fig:

a also *penny-pup:* A tagalong; a toady; hence v *penny-dog,* ~*-feist* to follow persistently; to pester; to toady.

  1914 *DN* 4.111 **cKS,** Penny-dog. . . To follow or fawn on. "He always expects some one to penny-dog after him." **1939** in 1944 *ADD* **nWV,** Penny-feist. . . Also v. = follow (one) around. **1953** *AmSp* 28.252 **csPA,** Penny-dog. . . A hanger-on, a servile follower. **1960** Wentworth-Flexner *Slang* 382, Penny-dog. . . To pester someone, usu. for money or an opinion; to curry favor; to follow. **1967–68** *DARE* (Qu. Y9, *Somebody who always follows along behind others: "His little brother is an awful _____."*) Infs **MD29, NJ3, PA27, 134,** Penny-dog; **MD27,** Penny-pup. **2000** *NADS Letters* **wPA,** Penny dog. . . I heard my mother use this term . . regarding her grandson who had followed his mother for no apparent reason [other] than that he thought he might be missing something.

b as *penny-feist:* See quot.

  1975 Gainer *Witches* 9 **sAppalachians,** To call one a penny-fice means that he is one who makes much noise that amounts to little. "The politician is nothing but a penny-fice."

c In mining and logging: an assistant foreman.

  1929 *AmSp* 4.368 **swPA** [Mining terms], *Assistant pit boss.* . . Assistant to the mine foreman. . . He is also called "penny-dog" because he gets all the blame when anything goes wrong. **1969** Sorden *Lumberjack Lingo* 86 **NEng, Gt Lakes,** *Penny dog*—An assistant foreman.

penny-dog v See **penny-dog** n **2a**

penny drink n

  1998 *DARE* File **MS** [Black], Here are . . words I know from the black people of Marks [MS]. . . penny drink—Koolaid.

penny duck n [*EDD* (at *penny* sb.[1] 1.(11)) "a mixture of pig's lights and blood, seasoned with herbs"]

  1981 Hachten *Flavor WI* 217 **csWI,** "Whenever a pig was butchered on the farm, the liver was ground and Penney [sic] Ducks were made," she reported. They were frequently served for breakfast. [Recipe calls for mixture of ground pork liver, ground pork, bread cubes, onions, and spices; small amounts are wrapped in bacon or pork skirting (stomach lining) and baked.]

penny-feist n See **penny-dog** n **1, 2b**

penny-feist v See **penny-dog** n **2a**

penny flower n [*OED2* 1578–1597; "*Obs.*"] Cf **penny bank**
An **honesty** (here: *Lunaria annua*).

  1900 Lyons *Plant Names* 231, *L[unaria] annua* . . Honesty, Penny-flower [etc]. **1923** *Amer. Botanist* 29.156, It [=*Lunaria annua*] is also known as "money-plant" and "penny-flower" in allusion to the large flat circular seed-pods. **1976** Bailey–Bailey *Hortus Third* 685, *[Lunaria] annua.* . . Silver-dollar, penny flower.

penny grass n
=**pennycress.**

  1906 Rydberg *Flora CO* 152, *Thlaspi* [spp] . . Penny-grass. **1937** U.S. Forest Serv. *Range Plant Hdbk.* W187, The genus *Thlaspi,* usually called pennycress, but also known locally as candytuft, pennygrass, and wild sweet-alyssum, is a member of the crucifer, or mustard family. **1964** *WV Folkl.* 14.46 **WV,** Also for cramps, boil the leaves of mother school craft (sometimes called penny grass) and drink.

penny lead pencil See **penny pencil**

penny-leaf See **pennywort 2**

penny night n

  1987 *DARE* File **swOH** (as of c1935), *Penny night* = "trick or treat." The Halloween celebration in Cincinnati, OH.

penny orchid n
A **tree orchid.** Cf **dollar orchid**

  1961 Douglas *My Wilderness* 147 **Everglades FL,** Lancewood, ironwood, inkwood, gumbo limbo—these were all new to me. So were the orchids that grow in them—grass pink orchid, cigar orchid, mule-ear orchid, butterfly orchid, shell orchid, penny orchid.

penny-over n, exclam Cf **Annie-over**
=**Antony-over A, B1.**

  1969 *DARE* (Qu. EE22, . . *The game in which they throw a ball over a building . . to a player on the other side*) Inf **PA**210, Penny-over; (Qu. EE23a, *In the game of andy-over . . what . . you call out when you throw the ball*) Inf **PA**210, Penny-over.

penny pencil n Also *penny lead pencil* **chiefly Sth, S Midl** See Map Cf **cedar pencil**
A cheap, eraserless lead pencil.

  1965–70 *DARE* (Qu. JJ10a, *Different kinds of pens and pencils*) 16 Infs, **esp Sth, S Midl,** Penny pencil; **KY**85, Penny pencil—old-fashioned; **LA**2, Penny pencil—same as cedar pencil; had no eraser; **MD**17, Penny pencil—eraser end sharpened like lead end—used in childhood; **MD**34, Penny pencil—sharpening kind; **OK**27, Penny pencil—old-fashioned, wooden, cost one cent; **OK**51, Penny pencil—very cheap, no eraser; **SC**40, Penny pencil—had no eraser; **OK**8, Penny lead pencils; **TN**4, Penny lead pencils—old-fashioned. [24 of 25 Infs comm type 4 or 5] [**1986** Pederson *LAGS Concordance,* 1 inf, **nwGA,** Them cedar pencils was a penny apiece.]

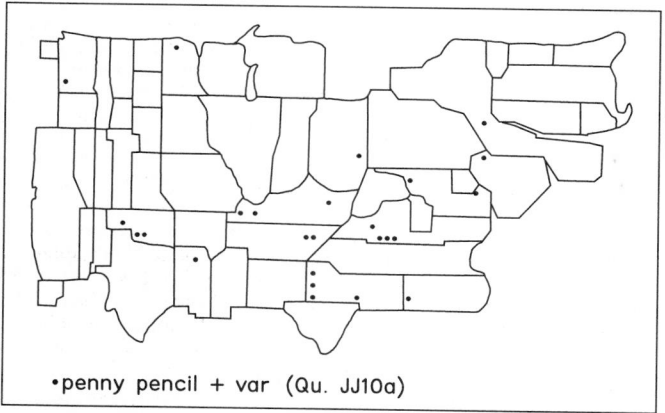

• penny pencil + var (Qu. JJ10a)

penny popper n Also *penny pooper*
A small firecracker.

  1966 *DARE* (Qu. FF14, . . *Kinds of firecrackers*) Inf **WA**33, Penny poppers. **1986** *DARE* File **MN** (as of c1905), *Penny-pooper* = small firecracker.

penny post n Cf **pennywort 1**
A **marsh pennywort** (here: *Hydrocotyle americana*).

  1896 *Jrl. Amer. Folkl.* 9.189 **West,** *Hydrocotyle Americana* . . penny post.

penny-pup See **penny-dog** n **2a**

pennyroyal n Pronc-spp *penneroil, pennyrial, pennyrile, pennyryal;* for addit varr see **A** below [*OED2* pennyroyal 1530 →, applied to the old-world plant *Mentha pulegium* and var other mostly related plants with aromatic leaves. Forms ending in -*ryal(l)* and -*rial(l)* are attested from the 16th and 17th cents.]
A Forms.

  1895 [see **pennyroyal hymn**]. **1908** [see **pennyroyal hymn**]. **1909** *DN* 3.356 **eAL, wGA,** Pennyryal. . . Pennyroyal. **1910** *DN* 3.454 **seVT,** Penny-rial. . . Corruption of penny-royal, an herb used for medicine. Very common. **1917** *DN* 4.397 **neOH,** Penny-royal. . . In the

'80's pronounced ['pɛnərɔɪl]. . . [pɛnɪ'raɪl] in Ashtabula Co. **1937** Thornburgh *Gt. Smoky Mts.* 32, Take pennyrile—that little green weedy thing with teeny weeny leaves that grows in the field—hit makes good tea for colds. **1939** *Hall Coll.* cwNC, ['pɛnɪ'raɪəl], the only pronunciation. **1965–70** [see **B1** below]. **1969** *DARE* FW Addit csKY, Pennyrile—the tops are boiled and sweetened. The resulting syrup is used for colds; cwNC, *Pennerol* ['pɛnɚˌɔˀl]—herb or weed. **1982** Slone *How We Talked* 116 eKY (as of c1950), "Penee-rile" or pennyroyal. **1983** *MJLF* 9.1.50 ceKY (as of 1956), *Pennyrile* . . a medicinal herb.

B Senses.

1 A plant of the genus *Hedeoma*, esp *H. pulegioides*. Also called **false pennyroyal 2, lemon mint 2, mock pennyroyal.** For other names of *H. pulegioides* see **mosquito plant 1, squaw mint, ~-weed, stinking balm, tickseed, tickweed;** for other names of var spp see **Mexican tea 3** Note: Some of these quots may refer instead to other senses below.

1630 Higginson *Nevv Englands Plantation* sig B3ʳ, Diuers excellent Pot-herbs grow abundantly among the Grasse, as . . Penyroyall, Wintersauerie, Sorrel [etc]. **1795** Winterbotham *Amer. U.S.* 3.398, Among the native and uncultivated plants of New-England, the following have been employed for medicinal purposes: . . Horsemint, spearmint, watermint, and pennyroyal. **1824** Bigelow *Florula Bostoniensis* 10, Cunila pulegioides. *Pennyroyal.* . . A well known pungent and strong scented plant. **1891** Jesup *Plants Hanover NH* 32, Hedeoma [spp] . . American Pennyroyal. **1912** Blatchley *IN Weed Book* 122, When the rambler through some old pasture in southern Indiana seats himself beneath the shade of oak or maple on a summer day the first thing to greet him is usually the odor of pennyroyal. **1931–33** *LANE Worksheets* CT, Pennyroyal and mountain mint—ingredients for a cure for headache. Take pennyroyal and mountain mint, steep and make drink; drink it hot. **1937** Sandoz *Slogum* 36 NE, She was the fifth of twelve children in a river-bottom family, with a mother who laid the cards and brewed tansy, pennyroyal, and like concoctions for luckless girls who were in need. **1965–70** *DARE* (Qu. I35, . . *Kitchen herbs . . grown and used in cooking around here*) Inf OH15, Pennyroyal, catnip—aren't for cooking, but tea; (Qu. S26a, . . *Wildflowers. . . Roadside flowers*) Inf KY5, Pennyrile— whip your legs with it to get rid of seed ticks or chiggers; GA46, Pennyroyal—blooms in the fall; (Qu. S26e, *Other wildflowers not yet mentioned;* not asked in early QRs) Inf OH47, Pennyroyal; OH82, Pennyroyal—used in home remedies and as herb; SC31, Pennyroyal—herb; (Qu. BB50a, . . *Favorite remedies . . for a cough*) Inf PA14, Pennyroyal tea; pennyroyal bush looked something like a mint; IL46, Penneroil— like a mint; WV7, Penderoil tea; (Qu. BB50d, *Favorite spring tonics*) Inf WV8, Pennyroyal tea for fevers; (Qu. BB51a, . . *Cures for corns or warts*) Inf IL55, Pennyroyal tea—also a wood herb. Don't know if it was a home remedy or just tasted good. **1968** *DARE* FW Addit neWV, Pennyroyal—when someone is ill you make tea and drench them with it. **1971** Krochmal *Appalachia Med. Plants* 138, Hedeoma pulegioides. . . Common Names: American pennyroyal, American false-pennyroyal, mock pennyroyal, pennyroyal, pennyroyal of America.

2 A **mountain mint 2** (here: *Pycnanthemum virginianum*).
1894 *Jrl. Amer. Folkl.* 7.96 MN, *Pycnanthemum lanceolatum* . . pennyroyal. **1900** Lyons *Plant Names* 210, *K[oellia] Virginiana.* . . Mountain Thyme, Pennyroyal [etc].

3 A plant of the genus *Monardella*. **esp CA** For other names of var spp see **balm B1c, mustang mint**
1897 Parsons *Wild Flowers CA* 324, Pennyroyal. Poléo. *Monardella villosa.* Ibid, *M. odoratissima* . . found abundantly in the Sierras, and known as "wild pennyroyal," is a bushy, many-stemmed plant. **1915** (1926) Armstrong–Thornber *Western Wild Flowers* 436 CA, Western Pennyroyal, Mustang Mint—*Monardella lanceolata.* **1941** Jaeger *Wildflowers* 223, Mohave Pennyroyal. *Monardella exilis.* Ibid, Rock Pennyroyal. *Monardella Robisonii.* . . often met with among rocks of the Little San Bernardino Mountains. **1961** Thomas *Flora Santa Cruz* 297 cwCA, *M[onardella] villosa* . . Pennyroyal, Coyote Mint. Fairly common in the Santa Cruz Mountains.

4 See **pennyroyal hymn.**

pennyroyal adj
Of livestock: common; inferior; transf; of a person: see quot 1912.
1864 OH State Bd. Ag. *Annual Rept. for 1863* 18.21, If the gentleman has any Pennyroyal cattle I hope to see them at the fair, and that a premium will be offered on them. [Laughter]. **1877** Bartlett *Americanisms* 458, Pennyroyal. Used as an adjective to designate very common stock,

as a *pennyroyal* steer or bull. Western. **1889** (1971) Farmer *Americanisms* 415, Pennyroyal. . . A Western term used adjectively to describe inferior stock. A *pennyroyal* horse is a poor, common beast. **1912** *DN* 3.585 wIN, Pennyroyal. . . Low; small-minded. "My guess is that he is pennyroyal stock."

pennyroyal hymn n Also *pennyroyal* **esp ME**
See quot 1850.
1850 Judd *Richard Edney* 274 ME, He sang one, popularly known as a pennyroyal hymn,—a measure that combines unction and vivacity. **1895** Wiggin *Village Watch-Tower* 115 ME, It was pennyrial hymns she used to sing mostly. **1905** *Methodist Rev.* 87.704, The attitude to take toward the sort of tune . . variously denominated, "gospel song," "spiritual song," "pennyroyal," has cost the Commission a good deal of vexation of the spirit. [*Ibid* 705, A taking melody will sometimes "cover a multitude of sins," and lead the thoughtless to sing lustily that which has perhaps little theology and little sense. . . Methodists should never . . encourage any poor sinner . . to base enthusiasm on a bubble, a rattle, or a jingle.] **1908** Day *King Spruce* 331 ME, Ben . . goes down past here, like he did a little while ago, swingin' his reins and singin' a pennyr'yal hymn? **1968** Coatsworth *ME Memories* 155, They call the more rollicking hymns like "Throw Out the Life Line" (usually sung at midweek services), "pennyroyal hymns."

pennyryal See **pennyroyal**

penny social n Also *penny supper* **esp NEast** Cf **dime-a-dip dinner**
See quots.
1968 *Liberty News* (NY) 13 June 5, Penny Social at Lake Huntington Presbyterian Church Hall at 8 p.m. Donation $1.00. **1968** *DARE* (Qu. FF1, . . *A kind of group meeting called a 'social' or 'sociable'. . . [What goes on?]*) Inf NJ6, Penny social—put out prizes, sell numbers, put numbers in cup next to prize you want to win; NY87, Penny social— charity. **1969** *DARE* Tape MA38, [At the Grange] they have penny socials. . . Everybody brings something and then you take chances on 'em, and if your number's drawn then you get it. You can get usually twenty-five tickets for twenty-five cents. There's little dishes or boxes or something beside of the article and you put the number, your number, in it if you think you'd like that special thing. **1983** *Greenfield Recorder* (MA) 5 Mar 9, Sometimes the church had a Penny Social held at somebody's home where the entertainment was furnished by the young people themselves. . . The refreshments were simple, and were actually served for 1 cent for each person. **1986** *DARE* File sIN (as of c1915), *Penny social*—Usually a church social. Admission was a penny for each letter in your name, or a penny for each year of your age. **1999** *Isthmus* (Madison WI) 19 Feb 33/1 neWI, One of the highlights of my Green Bay youth were the monthly potlucks in the basement of St. Willebrord's. . . These gustatory gatherings—we called them penny suppers—were a reprieve from daily Mass and boring classes.

penny-tree n
A **hop tree** (here: *Ptelea trifoliata*).
1931 Clute *Common Plants* 61, The wafer ash (*Ptelea trifoliata*) is not an ash, but the fuits [sic] are like wafers and may suggest other objects, as the name penny-tree clearly shows.

pennywinkle n Also *penniwinkle, pennywinkler, pennywrinkle, pinnywinkle* [*pennywinkle, pennyrinkle* Engl dial varr of **periwinkle** n²]
1 Any of var marine gastropod mollusks; rarely, a hermit crab.
1881 Ingersoll *Oyster-Industry* 246 **Atlantic,** Pennywinkle; Pennywinkler—the mollusks of the genera *Fulgur* and *Sycotypus,* interchangeably. **1899** (1912) Green *VA Folk-Speech* 317, Pennywinkle. . . A small, eatable, sea snail. **1930** *AmSp* 5.392 [Language of N Atl fishermen], Pennywrinkle. . . The periwinkle; also the hermit-crab which often inhabits the periwinkle shell. **1946** *PADS* 6.23 ceNC, Penniwinkle . . Periwinkle. Pamlico. Common. **1966** *DARE* Tape NC25, We used to walk and pick up little shells. . . little . . pennywinkles ['pɪnɪwɪŋkl̩z]. . . little tiny shells, you know—they were all colors. **1968–69** *DARE* (Qu. P2, . . *Kinds of saltwater fish caught around here . . good to eat*) Inf CA105, [In a list of shellfish:] pennywinkle; (Qu. P18, . . *Kinds of shellfish*) Inf RI8, Pennywinkles ['pɪnɪˌwɪŋkl̩z]. **1996** Horton *Island Out of Time* 241 **Chesapeake Bay MD,** Summers, we'd progue in the marsh for pennywinkles [Footnote: periwinkles].

2 also *pinnywinkle*: A freshwater or land snail; hence n *pinnywinkle fever*: see quot 1936. **esp Sth, S Midl**

1927 *DN* 5.476 Ozarks, *Pinnywinkle.* . . A snail, a periwinkle. The term is usually applied to the little black water-snail so common in the Ozarks, but sometimes refers to the big land-snail found along the limestone ledges. **1934** Vines *Green Thicket* 13 **cnAL,** Their bare feet were too much like leather for them to pay any mind to the thousands of pennywinkles they stepped on [in a stream]. **1936** *AmSp* 11.316 Ozarks, *Pinnywinkle fever.* . . A kind of summer flu, said to be acquired by swimming in water that contains pinnywinkles—little black water-snails. **c1940** Eliason *Word Lists FL* 10 **wFL,** *Pennywinkle:* A snail found in the small fresh water stream. **c1960** Wilson *Coll.* **csKY,** *Pennywinkle.* . . A small water snail, a periwinkle, penniwinkle. **1969–70** *DARE* (Qu. P18, . . *Kinds of shellfish*) Inf **GA1,** Pennywinkles [pɪnɪ'wiŋklz]; **KY53,** Mussels, pennywinkle; **KY68,** Pennywinkle—fasten themselves to rocks; ¼ to ½ inch across; more like a snail; circular shell; **TN56,** Pennywinkles—found in creeks, cold water; **TN65,** Pennywinkle, periwinkle—spiral shell, tiny (1 inch long), lives in creeks and rivers. **1983** *MJLF* 9.1.50 **ceKY** (as of 1956), *Pennywinkle* . . a water snail. **1986** Pederson *LAGS Concordance* (Oysters) 1 inf, **cnTN,** Pennywinkles—in the rivers, smaller than oysters.

3 =**periwinkle** n² **2.**

1966–67 *DARE* (Qu. P6, . . *Kinds of worms* . . *used for bait*) Inf **GA1,** Night crawler; [also] roller worms, stretchers, pennywinkle—found in wet decayed leaves; **OR3,** Pennywinkles—worm in shell under rocks; **WA8,** Pennywinkle, periwinkle, night crawler, grasshopper; **WA24,** Pennywinkle. **1999** *DARE* File **cwID** (as of 1940s), My goodness, your question about pennywinkles takes me back. That is just what we called them [=caddisfly larvae]. They make good trout bait. **2001** *NADS Letters* **nwMT** (as of 1940s), While growing up in Northwestern Montana we always referred to Caddis fly larva as Pennywinkles. . . They were most common in late June and early July. They grow to be about ¾″ long and have shells made from sand and, sometimes, wood splinters, or other debris. They are outstanding bait for trout fishing and never fail to generate interest when used. *Ibid* **cWA,** When fishing in the Cascades above Leavenworth, Washington (in the Wenatchee Valley) in the 1970s I heard local fishermen refer to using pennywinkles as bait for trout.

4 A **least sandpiper** or other small shorebird; see quot 1955.

1923 U.S. Dept. Ag. *Misc. Circular* 13.55 **VA,** *Least Sandpiper.* . . vernacular names. . . In local use . . pennywinkle. *Ibid* 57, *Semipalmated Sandpiper.* . . pennywinkle. **1955** *AmSp* 30.184 **eVA,** Small shore birds are called *bird bumblebees* and *penniwinkles* (=periwinkles or small sea snails) on the eastern shore of Virginia, in allusion to their tinyness.

pennywort n

1 =**marsh pennywort.** [*OED2* 1578 →]

1791 in 1793 *Amer. Philos. Soc. Trans.* 3.165, Hydrocotyle . . americana. Penny-wort. **1824** Bigelow *Florula Bostoniensis* 109, Hydrocotyle Americana . . *Pennywort.* **1876** Hobbs *Bot. Hdbk.* 181, Hydrocotyle vulgaris, Thick leav'd pennywort. **1901** Mohr *Plant Life AL* 649, Hydrocotyle verticillata. . . Whorled Pennywort. **1938** Baker *FL Wild Flowers* 158, *Hydrocotyle umbellata,* called pennywort from the shape of the small leaves has the more appropriate name in Florida of nickles and dimes, which takes note of their diversity in size. **1966** *DARE* (Qu. S21, . . *Weeds* . . *that are a trouble in gardens and fields*) Inf **FL16,** Pennywort. **1967** *DARE* Tape **GA30,** It's pennywort—dollar plant, lot of people call it, just has a little small, round—about the size of a dollar, the leaf is. **1972** Brown *Wildflowers LA* 125, Salt Pennywort—*Hydrocotyle bonariensis.* . . Also in Texas and Mississippi. *Ibid* 125, Pennyworts, Dollar-grass—*Hydrocotyle umbellata* . . *Hydrocotyle verticillata.*

2 also *penny-leaf:* A low perennial plant (*Obolaria virginica*). [See quot 1948]

1822 Eaton *Botany* 364, *Obolaria* . . *virginica* . . penny-wort. **1861** Wood *Class-Book* 587, *Obolaria* [sp] . . Pennywort. **1901** Mohr *Plant Life AL* 672, Obolaria virginica. . . Pennywort. . . Carolinian area. New Jersey to eastern Illinois, Tennessee south to Georgia. **1942** Hylander *Plant Life* 432, Pennywort (*Obolaria*) is a small purplish-green plant of moist thickets from New Jersey to Texas. **1948** Wherry *Wild Flower Guide* 103, Penny-leaf (*Obolaria virginica*). . . Flowers small, clustered toward stalk tip in axils of roundish bronzy-green bracts, to which the name refers. **1972** Brown *Wildflowers LA* 138, Pennywort—*Obolaria virginica.*

pennywrinkle See pennywinkle

penoche n Usu |pə'nučɪ, pə'nočɪ, pɪ'nučɪ|; for addit varr see quots Also *panocha, panoche, penuche, pinoche* [AmSpan *panoche* raw brown sugar] **chiefly NEast, N Cent, West** See Map

A fudge of which brown sugar is the chief ingredient.

1872 U.S. Bur. Indian Affairs *Rept. for 1871* 359, I doubt the good policy of issuing bread, and at times candy, (panoche,) to the pupils. **1920** Kander *Settlement Cook Book* 446 Milwaukee WI, *Penoche* . . brown sugar . . milk . . butter . . vanilla . . chopped nuts. *Ibid* 448, *Maple panoche* . . maple sugar . . light brown sugar . . butter . . water . . pecan nutmeats. **1952** Steinbeck *East of Eden* 226 **CA,** Faye twisted around in her chair to reach a piece of brown panocha studded with walnuts. When she spoke it was around a mouth full of candy. **1965** *Colonial Kitchens* 156, *Pinoche.* . . Brown Sugar . . white Sugar . . Salt . . Butter . . Milk. **c1965** Randle *Cookbooks* (Ask Neighbor) 1.5, *Panocha* . . brown sugar . . cream of tarter [sic] . . salt . . milk . . butter . . finely chopped nuts. **1965–70** *DARE* (Qu. H80, *Kinds of candy* . . *made at home*) 75 Infs, **chiefly NEast, N Cent, West,** Penoche; 11 Infs, **scattered, but esp NEast,** ['pʌnučɪ]; 10 Infs, **esp CA,** ['pʌnočɪ]; **MD50, NH6, NJ5, NY104, 107, PA67, WI47,** [pɪ'nučɪ]; **MI68, MA10, NY69, 88, 92,** [pə'nučɪ]; **CT29, MA65, PA131, 163,** [pɛnučɪ]; **CA22,** ['pʌn,nočɪ]; **CA99,** [pɪ'nočɪ]; **CO11,** ['pʌnočř]; **CO40,** ['pʌnučə]; **GA85,** [pə'noukɪ]; **MN6,** [pɛ'nou,kɪo]; **NC3,** [pə'noučɪjouw]; **MA6,** Penuche; (Qu. H82b, *Kinds of cheap candy* . . *sold years ago*) Inf **TX69,** Penoche. **1999** *DARE* File—Internet **eMA** [Boston Online *The Wicked Good Guide to Boston English*], Penuche—The fudge equivalent of mystery meat.

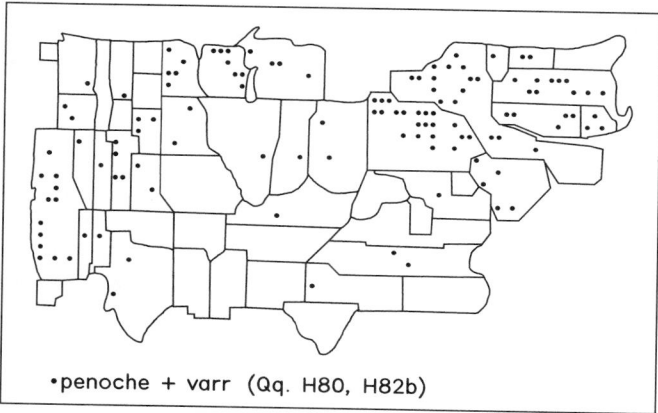

•penoche + varr (Qq. H80, H82b)

penola See pinole

Pensacola pullet n

=**gopher** n¹ **1a.**

1956 Rayford *Whistlin' Woman* 41 **AL,** This gopher . . is a highland, dry land tortoise. . . [F]or a long time you could go to most any market in Pensacola and give a gopher in trade for something else. And you always got a little gopher by way of change. So that gophers came to be known as "Pensacola pullets."

Pensacola snapper n

Either of two **snappers:** *Lutjanus griseus* or *L. blackfordi.*

1884 Goode *Fisheries U.S.* 1.396, Two other brilliant red species occur . . in the Gulf of Mexico—the Pensacola Snapper, *L[utjanus] Stearnsii,* and the Mangrove Snapper, *Rhomboplites aurorubens.* **1935** Caine *Game Fish* 130, Mangrove Snapper—*Lutianus griseus.* . . *Synonyms* . . Pensacola Snapper [etc]. *Ibid* 132, Red Snapper—*Lutianus blackfordii.* . . *Synonyms* . . Pensacola Red Snapper . . Pensacola Snapper. **1946** LaMonte *N. Amer. Game Fishes* 60, Pensacola Red Snapper. . . Center of abundance is the Gulf of Mexico. Found as far north as Long Island, N.Y. *Ibid* 62, Mangrove Snapper. . . Names: Gray Snapper, Pargo Prieto, Pensacola Snapper [etc].

Pensivania See Pennsylvania

pen staff See staff

pen stock See stock

pent road n Also *pentway* NEng, esp VT

A minor road that may be closed off by gates; hence v *pent* to close off (a road) with a gate.

1809 in 2001 *DARE* File—Internet **RI,** Likewise I reserve the privilege of a cartpath through said land from east to west for the purpose of accomodating [sic] the owner of the land lying east of the premises which cart path may be a pentway, so called. **1877** Bartlett *American-*

isms 458, *Pent-Way.* A road, not public, and generally kept closed. A few such ways remain in New England. 'A *pent-way* with a turn-stile and gate at each end.'—*Calkins, Hist. Norwich.* **1939** *LANE* Map 44 (*Side road; lane*) 12 infs, **VT,** Pent road; 1 inf, **csCT,** *A pent road* has gates; 2 infs, **seCT,** *Pentway,* from the main road to the house, with a gate or 'a pair of bars' at the entrance; 1 inf, **cwVT,** *Pent road,* through the meadows, with gates between lots, maintained by the town. **1999** *NADS Letters* **seCT,** The term "pentway" was in use in southeastern Connecticut at least into the early 1980's. I remember reading several articles in the New London Day about residents of one of the towns (Stonington?) trying to enlist the town's help in maintaining the pentways. **2001** *Ibid* **VT,** An older fellow from Boston, MA who lives up there said, "It's what the locals call a pentroad." He was talking of a roadway that he had stretched a rope across because it was on his property and [he] was wishing to limit access. **2001** VT Secy. of State *Opinions* Jan (Internet) **VT,** *Town may permit landowner to pent a road.* One landowner was unhappy because snowmobilers used the class four road in front of his house at all hours of the day and night, despite the fact that it was a privately maintained class four road that the board had not opened to snowmobiles. . . The board may grant the landowner permission to put up an unlocked gate across the road to deter recreational use of the road. . . (Pent roads were originally created to keep in farm animals where a landowner owned both sides of the road and let the animals graze freely.)

pen-type barn See **pen barn**

penuche See **penoche**

penuckle See **pinochle**

pe-ok n
=**flicker** n² **1.**
　1956 MA Audubon Soc. *Bulletin* 40.82 **MA,** Yellow-shafted Flicker. . . Pe-ok . . Sonic.

peola n *among Black speakers*
A light-complexioned Black person, esp a female.
　1942 *Amer. Mercury* 55.88 **Harlem NYC** [Black], Dat broad I seen you with wasn't no pe-ola. She was one of them coal-scuttle blondes with hair just as close to her head as ninety-nine to a hundred. *Ibid* 223, *Pe-ola*—a very white Negro girl. **1944** C. Calloway *Hepster's Dict. (OED2)*, *Peola*, a light person, almost white. **1960** Wentworth–Flexner *Slang* 382, *Peola.* . . A very light-complexioned Negro, esp. a girl or young woman. **1970** Major *Dict. Afro-Amer. Slang* 90, *Peola:* (rare) a light-skinned Afro-American girl.

peon n [Span "peasant"]
1 A Mexican or person of Mexican origin. **chiefly SW** *derog* Cf **cholo**
　[**1882** Chase *Editor's Run* 107 **NM,** Maxwell's force . . [consisted of two or three whites, a few Mexicans in his service, and a few pions, or Mexican young men bought and owned, according to a custom then [= in 1856] prevailing in the Territory.] **1956** Ker *Vocab. W. TX* 374, Two southwest words of Spanish origin for a Mexican, not glossed by the lexicographers . . are: *peon* . . and *paisano.* **1962** Atwood *Vocab. TX* 73, Persons of Mexican origin. . . Other nouns of less frequency are *Peon, Wetback, Hombre,* and *Bracero.* **1966–70** *DARE* (Qu. HH18, *Very insignificant or low-grade people*) Inf **CA66,** Peons—*cholo*—a low-grade Mexican; **TX72,** Peons—Mexican; (Qu. HH28, *Names and nicknames . . for people of foreign background: Mexican*) Infs **CA66, MS67, TX10, 72,** Peon; **CA24,** ['pionz]; **TX101,** [pi'onz]; [**MS67,** South Americans—['pe:ɑnz]]. **1970** Tarpley *Blinky* 258 **neTX,** Nicknames for Mexican people . . peons [rare]. **1971** Bright *Word Geog. CA & NV* 100, In the rural areas, the distribution of *peon* and *vacquero* is generally limited to the central and southern regions. *Ibid* 103, In response to: Mexican . . peon. **1981** Pederson *LAGS Basic Materials,* 1 inf, **csTX,** Greasers, Mexican wets, peon [p'iᵛ'jõˤn]. **1983** Allen *Lang. Ethnic Conflict* 63, Mexicans: . . peon. . . Especially offensive when pronounced "pee-on."
2 A gambling game played by American Indians; see quot 1959.
　1860 in 1948 *Western Folkl.* 7.14 **swCA,** [Los Angeles city ordinance:] The game of *Peon* is expressly prohibited, as also all reunions of Indians in the night time, within the corporate limits of the city. **1959** *Julian Apple Day* [13] **csCA,** As the shadows deepened, bonfires were lighted and invariably a Peon game was started. . . The vocalizing accompanying a game of Peon will never be mistaken for any other. To say "grunting with occasional cries" is far from a good description. One has

to hear it! The players [=American Indians] sit in two rows facing each other, with their counting sticks in hand, not seen however, since the action of the game goes on beneath a blanket which is usually held in the teeth of the players as they sway from side to side. The side in active play passes the small counting sticks back and forth under the blanket in a "button, button, who's got the button" manner until the leader of the opposite side suddenly steps away and grunting, drops the blanket and points dramatically to one of the opposite player [sic]. Has he rightly guessed which one holds the marked stick?

peon dog n Cf **rat dog 2b**
A Mexican Hairless.
　1892 *DN* 1.251 **TX,** *Peon dog* . . a name given sometimes to the hairless Mexican dog.

peonie See **peeny**

peony n¹ Usu |'piəni, -ɪ|; for varr see below
Std sense, var forms.
1 |'paɪ(ə)ni, -ɪ|; pronc-spp *pin(e)y, piony.* [*piony* remained in std use through the 18th cent, and both it and the syncopated *pin(e)y* are widespread in Brit dial; they represent expected outcomes of ME *pion(i)e* < OF *pion(i)e* (cf *violet* [vaɪ(ə)lɪt] < OF *violete*). The std sp and pronc have been re-fashioned on the basis of Lat *paeōnia.*] **chiefly Nth, Midl** See Map *old-fash* See also **piney rose**
　1771 in 1944 *Thomas Jefferson's Garden Book* 24, Hardy perennial flowers. . . Piony. **1828** Webster *Amer. Dict.,* Pi'ony, pe'ony. . . An herbaceous perennial plant of the genus Pæonia. **1858** Stearns *Practical Guide Pronc.* xxiv, Pronounce the following words in *three* syllables, and *not* in two. . . Say . . pĭ o nў *not* pī'ny. **1871** (1882) Stowe *Fireside Stories* 134 **MA,** He hung on till jest as the pinys in the front yard was beginnin' to blow out. **1873** Soule–Campbell *Pronc. Hdbk.* 67, *Piony,* pi'o-nĭ, *not* pi'nĭ; but *pe'o-ny* is a better spelling and pronunciation. **1899** (1912) Green *VA Folk-Speech* 323, *Piny.* . . Pl. pinies. A form of peony. **1904** *DN* 2.427 **Cape Cod MA** (as of a1857), *Piny.* . . Poeny [sic]. **1921** [see **3** below]. **1935** [see **2** below]. **1942** Warnick *Garrett Co. MD* 1 **nwMD** (as of 1900–18), *Piney* (peony). **1949** *WELS Suppl.* **cwWI,** *Peonies*—pineys only by older persons now. The usual however in my childhood. I never heard *peonies* until 35 years ago. **1950** *WELS WI* (*Give any other names used for . . peony*) 15 Infs, Pin(e)y; 1 Inf, Pinney; 1 Inf, [pini], [paɪni]. **1950** *WELS Suppl.* **csWI,** ['pi:əni]—most common; ['paɪni]—old-fashioned, but still going strong; ['pini] occasional. **1959** *VT Hist.* 27.152 **cn,cVT,** *Peony* ['paɪəni] and ['paɪni] . . pronc. Rare. Washington. **1965–70** *DARE* (Qu. S11) 208 Infs, **chiefly Nth, Midl,** Piney [proncs of the type ['paɪni, -ɪ, -ɨ]; comments were recorded from 32 Infs indicating that this was old-fashioned or that they knew it from the speech of grandparents or other older relatives; 4 indicated that it was amusing or was used as a joking term, and 3 that they heard it from other people.]; **IA38,** ['paɪni]—said by uneducated people; **MD23,** ['paɪni]—Inf's term; ['piəni]—greenhouse name; **MI69,** ['paɪni]—my grandfather always said, and I hear people still saying it; **SC2,** ['paɪni]—colored people; 11 Infs, **scattered, but esp IL,** [paɪəni, -ɪ, -ɨ]; **NJ45,** Not ['paɪəni], but I've heard it; 10 Infs, **scattered,** ['pani, 'pa(ə)ni, -ɪ, -ɨ]; **MD20,** Some people say ['paniᵛ]; **TN22,** ['panɪz]; ['piənɪ] is vulgar [FW: Inf explains that country people think it sounds too much like "pee."]; **VA15,** ['pæni]; **NY183, WI62,** ['paɪni] plant; **NC31, 35,** ['pa:ni] rose. **1968** *DARE* Tape **IN5,** Those are—I started to say pineys ['paɪnɪz] because that's what my mother always

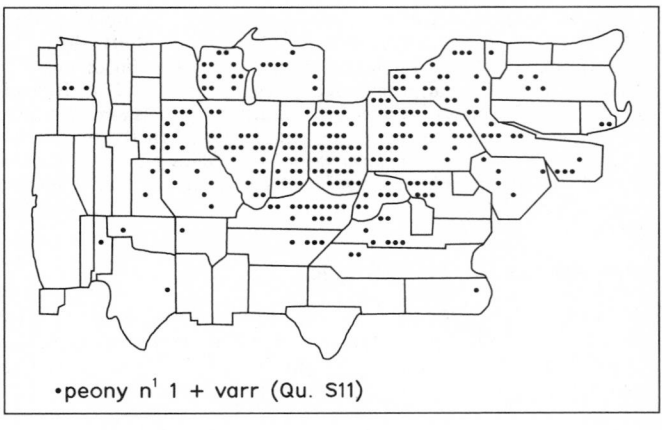
•**peony** n¹ **1** + varr (Qu. S11)

called them and . . it was for many years that I didn't know how that was spelled. I didn't know it was peonies ['piəniz], but round here many, many of the older people call them pineys. **1976** Garber *Mountain-ese* 68 **sAppalachians,** Don't mow down my piny flowers. **1979** *Greenfield Recorder* (MA) June 2, Our grandmother called their lovely double peonies, "pineys." **c1985** *Lutz Coll.* **neNJ,** In the early years of the 20th century the usual name for the common *peony* was *piney* in Ramsey. I have not heard that pronunciation for years, unless used in fun.

2 |ˌpiˈoni, -ɪ|; also |ˈpiˌoni, ˈpjoni, -ɪ|; for addit varr see quots. [Prob survival of 18th-cent learned proncs with "long *o*" in imitation of the Lat. Sheridan (1780) and Walker (1791) both imply /o/ for the *o* of *peony*, although they imply /ə/ for the corresponding syllable of the (presumably more popular) form *piony*.] **chiefly Cent, Mid Atl, S Midl, NEng** See Map *old-fash*

1906 *DN* 3.150 **nwAR,** *Peony*. . . Accented on the second syllable, [piˈonɪ]. **1935** *AmSp* 10.292 **NY,** Older people occasionally pronounce *peonies* as [pɪˈouniz], [ˈpaɪəniz], or [ˈpaɪniz]. **1940** in 1944 *ADD* **WV,** [piˈoni]. Reported. **1965–70** *DARE* (Qu. S11) 89 Infs, **chiefly Cent, Mid Atl, S Midl, NEng,** [Proncs of the type [ˌ(ˌ)piˈ(j)oni, -ɪ] comments were recorded from 6 Infs indicating that they considered this pronc old-fashioned and from 5 that they had heard it from others.]; **KY56,** [ˈpaɪni]—old-fashioned; [ˌpiˈoni]—some say now; **MD20,** [piˈoniˇ]—Inf says; some people say [ˈpaniˇ]; **MD39,** [piˈonɪ]; some people say [ˈpiənɪ]; **MO5,** [piˈouniz]; [Inf's wife:] Some people call 'em [ˈpiənɪz]; **MO13,** [ˈpaɪnɪ] years ago, [piˈouni] now; **MO15,** [piˈouniz]—some of 'em calls 'em [ˈpiənɪz]; **MO27,** [piˈouniz]—his pronunciation; he's heard [ˈpaɪnɪz] and [ˈpiənɪz]; **MS9, 19,** [piˈounə]; **LA12, NC8,** [ˈpjoni, -ɪ]; **AR49,** [ˈpjouni], occasionally [ˈpiənɪ]; 15 Infs, **scattered,** [Proncs of the type [ˈpiˌoni, -ɪ]]; **AZ9, ME7, 14, 20, OK1, WI58, 62,** [pi(j)oni] [stress not recorded]; **OK19,** Used to call it [paɪni], now it's [pijoni]; **WI64,** I've heard [pioni]. **1968** *DARE* Tape **IN14,** I have four different . . kinds of peonies [piˈoˇnɪz] that are just about gone. **1968** *DARE* FW Addit **cAR,** *Peony*—urban pronunciation is [ˈpiənɪz]; rural is [piˈouniz]. Joking rural term is *pee-on-you's* [ˈpiˌounjɪz]. **1982** *Barrick Coll.* **csPA,** *Peony*—pron[ounced] [piˈoni]. **1988** *DARE* File **ID, NV, UT,** *Peony* [piˈoni]—the standard pronunciation of the flower in the Intermountain West.

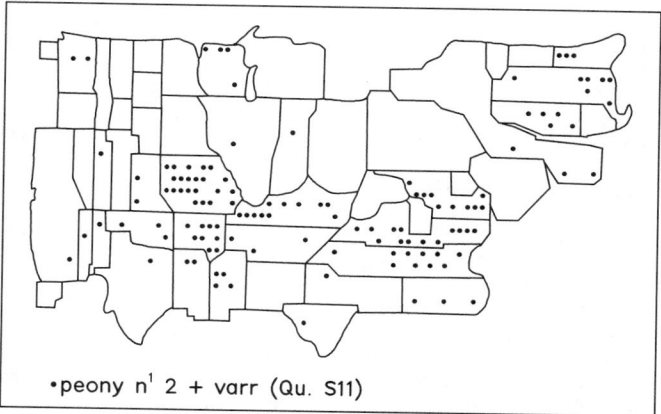

•peony n¹ 2 + varr (Qu. S11)

3 |ˈpini, -ɪ|; rarely |ˈpɪni|; pronc-spp *peeny, pinney.* [By syncope of the std pronc; cf *EDD*]

1921 *DN* 5.114 **CA,** *Peeny, piny*. . . Peony. **1941** in 1944 *ADD* **cnWV,** [ˈpini], not [paɪni]. **1950** *WELS* [see **1** above]. **1950** *WELS Suppl.* [see **1** above]. **1965–70** *DARE* (Qu. S11) 30 Infs, **esp Inland Nth, N Midl,** Peeny [proncs of the type [ˈpini, -ɪ]]; **IA32,** [ˈpiəni, ˈpini]—I call them by both names; **CO4,** [ˈpɪni]; **NE11,** [pini] plant.

4 |piˈonjə, piˈonji|; for addit varr see quots. Cf **piano plant**

1966–70 *DARE* (Qu. S11) Inf **AR51,** [piˌounjəz]; **GA77,** [pəˈounjə]; **NC37,** [piˈounjə]; **KY9,** [ˌpiˈouniz]; **VA40,** [ˌpiˈjonji]; **NH14,** [ˌpiˈjæni]; **1968** *DARE* FW Addit [see **2** above].

5 addit varr; see quots.

1966–69 *DARE* (Qu. S11) Infs **IN70, NY205,** [ˈpe(ɪ)əni]; **AR28,** [ˈpɛənɪ]; **TX71,** [ˈpoəˌnɪz].

peony n² See **peeny**

people n
A Gram form.

Pl: usu *people;* also *peoples.* [Cf Intro "Language Changes" II.3] *esp freq among Black speakers*

1927 in 1983 Taft *Blues Lyric Poetry* 64 [Black], I ain't got me nobody : carry my troubles to / I tell you peoples : I don't know what to do. **1945** FWP *Lay My Burden Down* 71 **GA** (as of c1865) [Black], You know, all the property and all the niggers belonged to Old Miss. She got all that from her peoples. **1953** Brewer *Word Brazos* 87 **eTX** [Black], Hit done lay so many low till de doctuhs an' de nusses calls a meetin' down to Calvert so dey kin tell de peoples how to teck keer. **1966** *DARE* Tape **AL14,** [FW:] What type of things would people put in their hope chest? [Inf:] Most peoples put jewelries in it . . valuable things; **MS61,** [FW:] Well, is there much demand for a blacksmith this day and age? [Inf:] Yes, . . but the peoples now . . they don't want to do it. **1968** *DARE* (Qu. HH28, *Names and nicknames . . for people of foreign background*) Inf **GA44,** White peoples. **1969** *DARE* FW Addit **ceNY,** *Peoples*—substituted for "people." **1981** Palmer *Deep Blues* 15 [Black], Peoples is awful funny. **1989** *DARE* File **cwWI,** Heard at the V.A. Hospital in Madison: a 62 year old white female, native of the Tomah–Sparta area said, in talking of her family relations, "We have peoples down in Madison." She said this twice. A doctor who is a native of LaCrosse was asked later if he was familiar with this usage and he said he had heard it frequently.

B Senses.

1 used predicatively of a single person: A person (of a specified type); a person of accepted standing.

1897 Lewis *Wolfville* 122 **AZ,** Texas [=a man] is good people, . . an' the last gent with which I thirsts to dig up the war-axe. **1931** (1991) Hughes–Hurston *Mule Bone* 133 **cFL** [Black], I was *people* in middle Georgy befo' I ever came to Floridy. **c1970** Pederson *Dial. Surv. Rural GA,* 1 inf, **seGA,** He's nice people. **1995** *Brophy Coll.* **swMO** (as of c1960), *People.* [A]s "he is awfully nice people."

2 also *peoples:* Members of one's family; relatives. **scattered, but chiefly Sth, S Midl** See Map Cf **folk C1a**

1945 [see **A** above]. **1950** *WELS Suppl.* **cWI,** *People.* . . One's family: "My father's people"; **csWI,** *People.* . . Family, relatives. "Her people are from Stoughton." **1959** Lomax *Rainbow Sign* 62 **AL** [Black], I thought he was some of our people—kin to us—he stayed there so much, but Mama said, "No, he's not any of our people. He just love to stay around here and we enjoys him." **1965–70** *DARE* (Qu. Z8, *General word for your own immediate family group*) 28 Infs, **scattered,** (My) people; (Qu. Z9, *General word for others related to you by blood*) 31 Infs, **scattered, but chiefly Sth, S Midl,** (My) people; **SC58,** All our people; **NY46,** His people. **1966–70** *DARE* Tape **CA100,** My people originally . . came with the gold rush days; **CA110,** We visited in Oklahoma, where my mother's people were living; **DC11,** My father's people are Southerners; **IA9,** My people were all railroad; my brothers were engineers and my father was a railroad man; **MI34,** Her people were born and raised there; **TX3,** They seemed more my people than my own. **1968** *DARE* FW Addit **NY68,** He fights most of the time with his own people. His father mostly. Once in a while he cuffs up his mother some. **1989** [see **A** above].

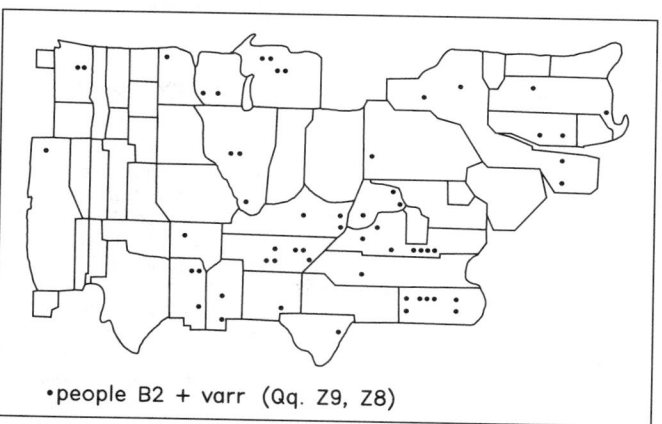

•people B2 + varr (Qq. Z9, Z8)

pep(e) See **pépère**

peperage See **pepperidge**

pépère n Also *pep, père* Pronc-sp *pepe* [Fr] **Fr settlement areas**

A grandfather—also used as a quasi-personal name.

1961 *PADS* 36.11 **sLA,** A small group of words that are positively confined to the informants of southern Louisiana. . . *Pepere* (Grandfather)—17.1 [percent of 70 informants]. **1967** LeCompte *Word Atlas* 264 **seLA,** Grandfather, usual term of affection . . *pe-père* [7 of 21 infs]. **1969** *DARE* (Qu. Z3, . . *'Grandfather'*) Inf **CT**23, Pepe—that's what French say; **RI**6, Pepé [pepe]; pep [pep]; **LA**23, Pere. **1969** Cagnon *Franco-Amer. Terms* 224 **RI,** *Pépère*. . . [pepeⁱɾ]ˑ [pë̆pɛ̈ⁱr]; [pœpeⁱr] Grandpa. "Where's pépère?" **1973** Allen *LAUM* 1.340 (as of c1950), *Grandfather*. . . pepère [2 infs, **MN, SD**]. **1983** *Reinecke Coll.* 8 **LA,** *Pépère, père*—n[oun] or term of address for a grandfather. As in La. Fr. [pɜª, pəpɜª]. **1986** Pederson *LAGS Concordance*, 1 inf, **seLA,** He calls grandfather pepere [p'ɛ^pɛ^ə; inf is a French speaker]. **1995** *DARE* File **wMA,** ['pepe], and occasionally [pə'pɛr], for 'grandfather,' are terms used affectionately and perhaps nostalgically even by non-French speakers.

peperidge See **pepperidge**

pepino See **chilipitin**

pepjinny See **pipjenny**

pepper n
1 See **hot pepper.**
2 See **pepper belly.**

pepperage See **pepperidge**

pepper-and-salt n
1 =**harbinger-of-spring.** [See quot 1861]
1861 Wood *Class-Book* 384, *Erigenia* . . Pepper-and-Salt. *Ibid* 385, *E. bulbosa*. . . white fl[ower]s, with dark purple or brownish anthers (hence the odd popular name). **1896** *Jrl. Amer. Folkl.* 9.189 **IN,** *Erigenia bulbosa,* Nutt., turkey pea, pepper and salt. **1916** Keeler *Early Wildflowers* 168, So white are the petals and so dark the anthers, that the country name, Pepper-and-Salt, is well deserved. **1951** *PADS* 15.17 **IN,** *Erigenia bulbosa*. . . Pepper-and-salt, Marion, Indiana. **1968** *DARE* (QR p128) Inf **PA**99, *Erigenia bulbosa* = harbinger-of-spring = pepper-and-salt.
2 A **biscuit root 1** (here: *Lomatium gormanii*). [See quot]
1937 St. John *Flora SE WA & ID* 291, Cogswellia Gormani . . *Pepper and Salt.* [*Ibid* 292, The purplish black anthers against the white petals look like pepper on salt.]
3 A **turkey pea** (here: *Orogenia linearifolia*).
1967 Harrington *Edible Plants Rocky Mts.* 191, May . . said that his brother's children near Steamboat Springs in northwestern Colorado are fond of eating the raw roots [of *Orogenia linearifolia*] and call the plant "pepper and salt."

pepperbark n
A **prickly ash 1** (here: *Zanthoxylum clava-herculis*).
1970 Correll *Plants TX* 910, *Zanthoxylum Clava-Herculis* . . Pepperbark, Hercules-club, prickly ash [etc]. **1979** Little *Checklist U.S. Trees* 298, *Zanthoxylum clava-herculis*. . . Other common names—pepperbark [etc].

pepper belly n Also *pepper (gut)* **chiefly TX** See Map *often derog* Cf **hot belly**
A Mexican or person of Mexican origin.
1944 Adams *Western Words* 114, Pepper-gut—Slang name for the Mexican. **1956** Ker *Vocab. W. TX* 373, Mexican (nicknames). . . pepperbelly. [11 of 67 infs] **1960** Wentworth–Flexner *Slang* 383, *Pepper.* . . [derog.] A Mexican. *Some use since c1945.* **1962** Atwood *Vocab. TX* 73, Person of Mexican origin. . . *Pepper-belly* (13[% of approx 270 infs]). **1965–70** *DARE* (Qu. HH28, *Names and nicknames* . . *for people of foreign background: Mexican*) 12 Infs, **chiefly TX,** Pepper belly; **CA**81, Pepper gut. **1970** *Current Slang* 4.3–4.22 [NM State Univ slang], *Pepper belly*. . . A mexican [sic] or a Mexican-American (derogatory). **1970** Tarpley *Blinky* 258 **neTX,** *Nicknames for Mexican people* . . pepper bellies [12 of 200 infs]. . . *Pepper bellies,* used predominantly in the city, . . [is] based on a knowledge of the Mexican's fondness for hot, spicy foods. **1981** Jenkins *Baja OK* 19 **TX,** "Beans and cheese and cornmeal is all it is." . . "Pepper bellies eat pepperbelly food but they don't know any better." **1986** Pederson *LAGS Concordance (Mexicans)* 3 infs, **TX,** Pepper bellies; 1 inf, **cwFL,** Pepper bellies; 1 inf, **cnGA,** Pepper bellies—used in California, very derogatory; 4 infs, **TX,** Pepper belly [2 infs characterize this as insulting.]; 1 inf,

csTX, Pepper gut—derogatory. **2000** Launspach *ID Dial. Project* 6 **seID,** *(Terms for Mexicans)* 1 inf, Pepper-bellies.

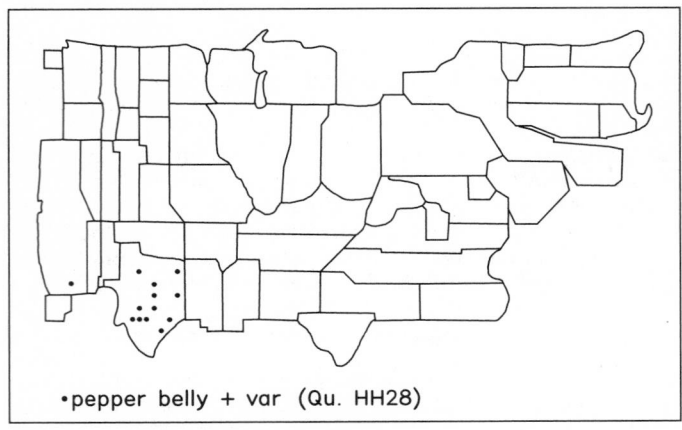

•pepper belly + var (Qu. HH28)

pepper berry See **pepper tree**

pepperbox n
=**partridge pea.**
1909 *DN* 3.356 **eAL, wGA,** *Pepper-box*. . . The name of a small leguminous plant and its fruit. When the seeds are dry the pod makes a tiny rattle if shaken. Also called *partridge (pottige)-pea,* and *rattle-box.*

pepperbush n
1 also *white pepper:* A **maleberry** (here: *Lyonia ligustrina*).
1842 Thompson *Hist. VT* 1.190, Andromeda . . *paniculata*. . . Pepper bush. Swamps, &c. **1860** Curtis *Cat. Plants NC* 96, Pepper bush. (*A[ndromeda] ligustrina,* Muhl.) **1900** Lyons *Plant Names* 400, *X[olisma] ligustrina*. . . White-bush, White Pepper. **1924** *Amer. Botanist* 30.61, I am at a loss to know why *Lyonia ligustrina* should be called "male-berry". Among its other names is "seedy buck-berry"[₁] "white wood", "white alder" and "pepper-bush". **1960** Vines *Trees SW* 811, He-huckleberry Lyonia, *L. ligustrina*. . . Also known under the vernacular names of Male-berry, pepper-bush [etc].
2 also *white pepper(bush):* A **fetterbush 3** (here: *Leucothoe racemosa*).
1784 in 1785 Amer. Acad. Arts & Sci. *Memoirs* 1.443, *Andromeda*. . . White Pepperbush. . . Common in swamps. . . It is generally called *Osier,* which is the *English* name of the *Salix viminalis* of Linnæus. **1830** Rafinesque *Med. Flora* 192, The *A[ndromeda] racemosa* or *White Pepperbush, White Osier,* is used for baskets and fish flakes. **1900** Lyons *Plant Names* 223, *L[eucothoe] racemosa* . . near Atlantic and Gulf sea-board . . is also called White Osier, White Pepper. **1960** Vines *Trees SW* 809, Sweet-bells Leucothoe. . . Vernacular names are White-osier and Pepper-bush.
3 =**sweet pepperbush.**
1860 Curtis *Cat. Plants NC* 100, Mountain Pepper Bush. . . Quite an ornamental shrub, 10 to 15 feet high, growing in the Mountains from Ashe to Cherokee. **1869** Fuller *Uncle John* 231 **NEng,** The other is a shrub that grows by Willow Brook. Father calls it a 'Pepper-bush'. . . Sweet Pepper-bush is the common name for the *Clethra,* a shrub with handsome glossy leaves and fragrant white flowers. **1901** Lounsberry *S. Wild Flowers* 375, With their intensely green and lustrous foliage and slender sprays of creamy flowers making the air heavy with a rich scent, there are through our woods hardly lovelier shrubs to be seen than these very pepperbushes. **1923** Pellett *Amer. Honey Plants* 256, *Pepperbush or White Alder (Clethra alnifolia)*. . . In Alabama, Georgia and north Florida, it is common in the coast plain, on swampy banks of streams and in low, wet thickets. **1972** Brown *Wildflowers LA* 127, Hairy Pepperbush . . *Clethra alnifolia*. . . Common in the cypress-black gum swamps around Lake Pontchartrain and in pineland sloughs of southeastern Louisiana. Also Texas and Mississippi.

pepper cabbage n Also *pepper slaw* **chiefly PA** See Map
A hot or cold salad consisting chiefly of cabbage and green pepper.
1935 Frederick *PA Dutch* 225, *Dutch Pepper Cabbage* . . cabbage . . celery . . peppers . . vinegar . . salt, pepper. Chop the cabbage, the peppers and the celery, add the seasonings and cook until tender. **c1965**

Randle *Cookbooks* (Plain Cookery) 3.6 **cOH**, *Pepper Cabbage* . . shredded cabbage . . salt . . green pepper, finely cut . . hot salad dressing (vinegar, oil, sugar). . . Mix well the cabbage, salt, and pepper. Stand for 1 hour or so. Drain off brine. . . Pour hot salad dressing, serve at once. **1965–70** *DARE* (Qu. H52, *Dishes made with fresh cabbage*) 12 Infs **PA**, Pepper cabbage; **PA2**, 150, Pepper slaw; **NJ5**, Pepper cabbage—with green peppers; **PA18**, Pepper cabbage—pickled with vinegar; **PA63**, Pepper cabbage—chop cabbage fine, pepper, pickle it; **MD27**, Pepper slaw—green pepper grated in, vinegar and sugar dressing; **PA136**, Pepper slaw—same as pepper cabbage; **PA176**, Pepper slaw—with green pepper.

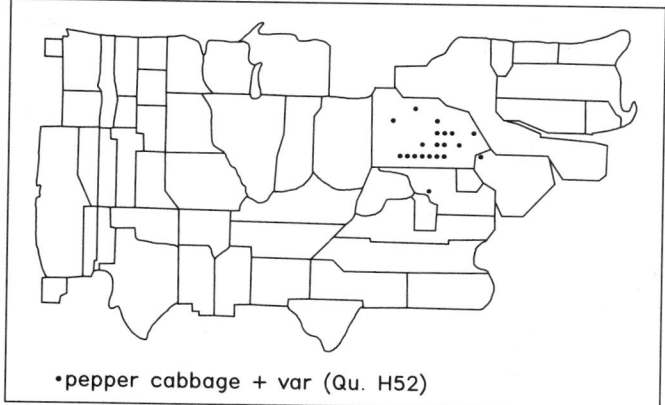

•pepper cabbage + var (Qu. H52)

peppercress n

A **peppergrass 1**, usu *Lepidium sativum* or *L. virginicum*.

1830 Rafinesque *Med. Flora* 2.237, Lepidium virginicum . . *Peppercress*. . . Eaten as cresses. **1876** Hobbs *Bot. Hdbk.* 186, Lepidium sativum, Pepper cress, Pepper grass. . . Lepidium Virginica, Wild pepper cress. **1900** Lyons *Plant Names* 220, L[epidium] sativum. . . Garden Pepper-cress. **1933** Small *Manual SE Flora* 554, Lepidium [spp] . . Pepper-grasses. Pepper-cresses.

pepper gnat n

See quot.

1970 *DARE* (Qu. R11, *A very tiny fly that you can hardly see, but that stings*) Inf **VA70**, Pepper gnat.

peppergrass n

1 A plant of the genus *Lepidium*. [From the peppery taste of the leaves and seeds] Also called **pepperweed 3, tongue grass**. For other names of var spp see **crow cress, peppercress, poor man's pepper, yellowseed** [Note: Some of these quots may refer instead to other senses below.]

1784 (1929) Filson *Kentucke* 24, The Shawanese sallad, wild lettuce, and pepper-grass, and many more, . . have excellent virtues. **1806** (1905) Lewis *Orig. Jrls. Lewis & Clark Exped.* 5.192 **MT**, Saw the common small blue flag and peppergrass. **1854** Wailes *Rept. on Ag. & Geol. MS* 347, Pepper-grass—Lepidium campistre [sic]. **1914** Georgia *Manual Weeds* 178, Field peppergrass—*Lepidium campestre.* . . A weed whose range is rapidly widening, mostly by the agencies of impure grass and clover seed. **1933** Cheley *Camping Out* 127, The camper should avail himself of water cress, yellow dock, lamb's quarters, pepper-grass, . . and any other edible plants which are to be found in the vicinity of the camp. **1938** in 1977 *Amer. Slave Suppl. 1* 1.420 **AL** [Black], She'd slip one of us chillun off ter hunt peppergrass to cook to help stretch de ration. **1945** Saxon *Gumbo Ya-Ya* 194 **LA**, Take pepper grass and bathe yourself all over with it. All your pains and aches gon' go away then. **1956** McAtee *Some Dialect NC* 33, *Pepper grass* . . any species of *Lepidium* of the mustard family. **c1960** Wilson *Coll.* **csKY**, Peppergrass. . . A kind of wild mustard (Lepidium) that grows in yards and gardens. **1966–69** *DARE* (Qu. I28a, . . *Kinds of things . . you call 'greens'*) Inf **AR27**, Peppergrass; (Qu. I28b, *Kinds of greens that are cooked*) Inf **MO13**, Peppergrass; (Qu. S21, . . *Weeds . . that are a trouble in gardens and fields*) Infs **FL4, GA84, NJ31, NC49**, Peppergrass; (Qu. S26d, *Wildflowers that grow in meadows*; not asked in early QRs) Inf **LA15**, Peppergrass; (Qu. S26e, *Other wildflowers not yet mentioned*; not asked in early QRs) Inf **CA87**, Peppergrass—a tiny white flower on a six- to ten-inch stalk, spicy taste; **LA15**, In plowed ground, peppergrass—often used for greens. **1972** in 1983 Johnson *I Declare* 145

nwFL, Take the taste: There's the sourwood tree . . and sourgrass . . and peppergrass. **1979** Spellenberg *Audubon Guide N. Amer. Wildflowers W. Region* 420 **West**, Yellow peppergrass, often so common it colors broad expanses of the desert yellow, has seeds with a peppery flavor.

2 =**shepherd's purse.**

1893 *Jrl. Amer. Folkl.* 6.137 **IA, MA**, Capsella bursa-pastoris, pepper grass. Del[aware] Co., Ia.; Concord, Mass.

3 A **blue-eyed grass 1** (here: *Sisyrinchium graminoides*).

1940 Clute *Amer. Plant Names* 148, S[isyrinchium] gramineum. Pepper-grass.

4 Perh a **smartweed**; see quot.

1968 *DARE* (Qu. S17, . . *Kinds of plants . . that . . cause itching and swelling*) Inf **LA20**, Peppergrass—found in the shade—has dark bluish-green leaves and burns the skin.

pepper gut See pepper belly

pepper head n [In ref to the small, tight curls in the hair of some Black people; cf *W3 peppercorn* adj 2]

A Black person.

1966 *DARE* (Qu. HH28, *Names and nicknames . . for people of foreign background: Negro*) Inf **SC26**, Pepper head. [Inf Black] **1966** *DARE* FW Addit **cSC**, Pepper head—a Negro. [Inf White]

pepperidge n Also *pep(p)erage, peperidge, pip(p)erage, piperidge* [Engl dial *pipperidge, pepperidge* the barberry or its fruit (*OED2* 1538 →)] **chiefly NEast**

Usu the **black gum 1**, but also the **tupelo gum.**

1689 in 1888 Huntington *NY Town Rec.* 2.56, A piperage tree marked faceing eastward and south ward. **1743** (1901) Hempstead *Diary* 1.406 **CT**, Wee Sawed of a pr Peperage wheels for my Stone Cart. **1810** Michaux *Histoire des Arbres* 1.30, Nyssa microcarpa. . . *Peperidge*, fréquemment usitée par Hollandois du New-Jersey. [=Nyssa microcarpa.] *Peperidge*, [name] frequently used by the Dutch of New Jersey.] **1828** Webster *Amer. Dict.*, The *piperidge* of New England is the *nyssa villosa*, a large tree with very tough wood. **1833** in 1834 Davis *Letters Downing* 145 **NY**, 'Why,' says the Gineral, gittin up and takin his Hickory, and givin it a whack on the floor—'if the Bank stands all that racket, Major, it's tuffer than a pepperage log.' **1871** (1882) Stowe *Fireside Stories* 127 **MA**, Old Black Hoss was about as close as a nut and as contrairy as a pipperidge-tree. **1968–70** *DARE* (Qu. T13, . . *Names . . for these trees*) Inf **MA78**, Tupelo = pepperidge ['pɛprɪj], sour gum; (Qu. T15, . . *Kinds of swamp trees*) Inf **CT13**, Bluegum—called a pepperidge ['pɛpərɪj] here; (Qu. T16, . . *Kinds of trees . . 'special'*) Inf **CT17**, Pepperidge ['pɛprɪj] tree—a breed of cat all of its own—the limbs grow straight out; **NJ29**, Peppridge [sic—FW sp]—turn red in fall.

peppernut n [Calque of pfeffernuss or its synonym in Finnish or one of the Scan languages] esp in Ger settlement areas =pfeffernuss.

1938 *Amer.–German Rev.* 5.1.41 [PaGer], *Pfeffernissen* or peppernuts are small Christmas cakes made by various formulas, which should include pepper. **1940** Brown *Amer. Cooks* 427 **MN**, Peppernuts ([Finnish] Piparpähkinöitä) [Recipe includes eggs, sugar, cream, cinnamon, cardamom, soda, flour, and butter.] . . It's interesting that the "pepper" in these Peppernuts consists of cinnamon and cardamom, and that half a cup of melted butter is characteristic of rich Finnish cooking. **1948** [see **pfeffernuss**]. **1957** Showalter *Mennonite Cookbook* 279, Peppernuts (Pfeffernusse). [Recipe includes shortening, sugar, flour, baking powder, salt, cream, milk, and peppermint extract.] . . These cookies are especially popular at Christmas time in many Mennonite homes.

peppernut tree n

=**California laurel.**

1902 U.S. Natl. Museum *Contrib. Herbarium* 7.350, All parts of the tree [=*Umbellularia californica*], including the wood, contain aromatic or fixed oils, the characteristic effect of which is more or less irritant and acrid, an effect which the early settlers compared with pepper and therefore called the tree pepperwood, or, on account of the general use of the nuts for food by the Indians, peppernut tree.

pepper plant See pepperweed 2

pepper pot (soup) n Also *Philadelphia pepper pot (soup)* [*OED2* 1698 → in ref to a similar West Indian dish] esp ePA

See Map on p. 98

A soup of tripe, meat, vegetables, and dumplings, seasoned with black pepper.

1794 *Thomas' MA Spy or Worcester Gaz.* (MA) 13 Mar [1]/2, A wag, in my neighbourhood, a lover of *pepper pots.* **1800** *Aurora Genl. Advt.* (Philadelphia PA) 14 Aug 1/4, The subscriber will have the above *soup* ready at 12 o'clock, on Wednesday's and Friday's during the season.— Also, *pepperpot* of a superior quality at 6 o'clock every evening. **1825** Paulding *John Bull* 160 **Philadelphia PA,** Whose principal trade consists in the exportation of Toughy and Pepper Pot. **1890** *Century Dict.* 4384 **PA,** *Pepper-pot.* . . Tripe shredded and stewed, to the liquor of which small balls of dough are added, together with a high seasoning of pepper. **1932** (1946) Hibben *Amer. Regional Cookery* 34, Philadelphia Pepperpot. **1940** Brown *Amer. Cooks* 706, *Pennsylvania-Dutch Soups.* . . That Dutch masterpiece, Philadelphia Pepper Pot Soup, was already on its way to being nationalized before the Campbell's Soup concern . . made it international by canning it. **1952** Tracy *Coast Cookery* 203 **PA,** Pepper Pot Soup. **1967–68** *DARE* (Qu. H36, *Kinds of soup*) Inf **NV**1, Pepper pot—a commercial soup with tripe and barley and vegetables, in tripe stock; **PA**171, Pepper pot; **PA**248, Pepper pot—Campbell's brand; **PA**49, 88, Philadelphia pepper pot; (Qu. H43, *Foods made from parts of the head and inner organs of an animal*) Inf **CA**59, Pepper pot soup; (Qu. H45, *Dishes made with meat, fish, or poultry that everybody around here would know, but that people in other places might not*) Inf **PA**41, Pepper pot.

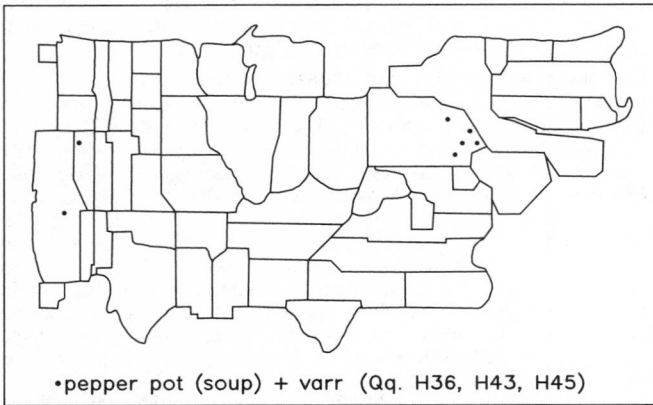

•pepper pot (soup) + varr (Qq. H36, H43, H45)

pepperroot n

1 A **toothwort,** usu *Cardamine concatenata* or *C. diphylla.*

1814 Pursh *Flora Americae* 2.439, *Dentaria* . . *diphylla.* . . In shady beech-woods, on high mountains: Pensylvania [sic] to Carolina. . . The roots of this plant . . are used by the natives instead of mustard; in the mountains it is generally known by the name of *Pepper-root.* **1843** Torrey *Flora NY* 1.58, *Dentaria diphylla* . . *Pepper-root.* . . The plant is well known on account of its singular and pungent rhizoma. **1897** Parsons *Wild Flowers CA* 4, *Dentaria Californica.* . . The little tubers upon the root often have a pungent taste, from which comes one of the other common names—"pepper-root." **1923** *Amer. Botanist* 29.155, "Pepper root" alludes to its pungent properties. It [=*Dentaria diphylla*] is well known to children who dig up the crisp, white underground parts and eat them. *Ibid, Dentaria lacinata* [sic] besides being known as "toothwort" and "pepper-root," is also called "crowfoot" and "crow-toes." **1966–68** *DARE* (Qu. S26c, *Wildflowers that grow in woods*) Inf **PA**99, Pepperroot, crinkleroot—same plant; **PA**104, Pepperroot—had a hot taste; (Qu. S26d, *Wildflowers that grow in meadows;* not asked in early QRs) Inf **ME**8, Pepperroot—root tastes good on sandwiches.

2 An **Indian poke 1** (here: *Veratrum viride*).

1940 Clute *Amer. Plant Names* 16, *V. viride.* . . Indian poke, pepperroot.

peppers See **hot pepper**

pepper-shinned loon n Also *pepper-shin* [See quot 1955]
=**red-throated loon.**

1925 (1928) Forbush *Birds MA* 1.28, *Gavia stellata* . . Pegging awl loon; pepper-shinned loon. **1955** MA Audubon Soc. *Bulletin* 39.309 **MA,** Red-throated loon. . . Pepper-shin, Pepper-shinned loon. . . From the speckled coloration of the legs.

pepper slaw See **pepper cabbage**

pepper tree n CA [See quot 1923 Pellett]
An ornamental evergreen tree of the genus *Schinus,* usu *S. molle;* hence *pepper berry* the red berry of this tree.

[**1848** (1850) Jenkins *Hist. War* 336 **Mexico,** The glossy leaves of the myrtle nestle close beside the pepper tree, whose scarlet berries cast a rich flush over its delicate foliage.] **1858** (1929) Hayes *Pioneer Notes* 183 **sCA,** When I was at San Bernardino last, I obtained two small fir trees and two pepper trees (a most beautiful evergreen). **1888** Lindley-Widney *CA of South* 175, The pepper-tree, the sycamore, and the acacia shaded their sidewalks. **1923** Dawson *Birds CA* 2.772, Where olives fail to tempt, or birds resist, the Christmas berry yields its yuletide cheer, and the unfailing pepper berry *(Schinus molle)* gives a palatable consolation. **1923** Pellett *Amer. Honey Plants* 256, The pepper-tree, a native of western South America, has been widely planted in California for ornament and shade. Its bright red berries are a substitute for pepper, hence the name. **1965** Teale *Wandering Through Winter* 26 **CA,** The feathery foliage of . . pepper trees swayed in green luxuriance. **1965–70** *DARE* (Qu. T5, . . *Kinds of evergreens, other than pine*) Infs **CA**10, 36, 65, Pepper (tree); **CA**22, Pepper tree—has red berries; (Qu. T16, . . *Kinds of trees* . . *'special'*) Infs **CA**20, 53, 79, 94, 185, 212, Pepper tree. **1970** *DARE* Tape **CA**185, I remember . . there were pepper trees all along Hollywood Boulevard on both sides of the street.

pepper turnip n

A **jack-in-the-pulpit 1** (here: *Arisaema triphyllum*).

1828 Rafinesque *Med. Flora* 1.67, *Arum triphyllum.* . . Vulgar Names—Indian Turnip . . Pepper Turnip. **1900** Lyons *Plant Names* 45, *A[risaema] triphyllum* . . Pepper-turnip. **1971** Krochmal *Appalachia Med. Plants* 62, Arisaema triphyllum. . . memory root, pepper turnip.

pepper vine n

A woody vine: usu *Ampelopsis arborea* but also **false grape 2.** For other names of *A. arborea* see **bird cherry 2, wild sarsaparilla**

1900 Lyons *Plant Names* 29, *A[mpelopsis] arborea.* . . Southeastern U.S. to Cuba. Pepper-vine. **1942** Hylander *Plant Life* 370, Pepper Vine *(Ampelopsis)* is a vine . . growing along river banks from Virginia southward and westward to the central states. **1964** Batson *Wild Flowers SC* 127, *A. cordata Michaux,* Pepper-vine.

pepperweed n

1 =**skunkweed 2.**

1914 Georgia *Manual Weeds* 329, Skunkweed. . . Other English names: Stinkweed, Pepperweed. . . A troublesome and most disagreeable weed, viscidly glandular and unpleasant to touch, very bitter to the taste, and emitting a strong, fetid odor.

2 also *pepper plant:* =**shepherd's purse.**

1920 *Torreya* 20.21 **IN,** *Bursa bursa-pastoris.* . . Hen pepper, pepperweed, Marion, Ind. **1940** Clute *Amer. Plant Names* 35, Shepherd's Purse. . . Pepper-plant, pepper-weed, hen pepper.

3 =**peppergrass 1.**

1947 (1976) Curtin *Healing Herbs* 131 **NM,** *Mostacilla*—Peppergrass[?] pepperweed. . . The people of Tularosa say that if one mashes the plant and mixes it with powdered lime, and then places the preparation in the wounds of animals, "it will kill the worms". **1967–70** *DARE* (Qu. S21, . . *Weeds* . . *that are a trouble in gardens and fields*) Infs **NJ**17, **TX**17, **VA**46, Pepperweed [*DARE* Ed: Some of these Infs may refer instead to other senses.]; (Qu. I28b, *Kinds of greens that are cooked*) Inf **CA**90, Pepperweed—a little tart. **1968** Barkley *Plants KS* 166, Lepidium campestre . . Field Pepperweed.

4 A **water parsnip** (here: *Sium suave*).

1966 *DARE* Wildfl QR Pl.149 Inf **NC**28, Pepperweed.

pepperwood n

1 =**California laurel. CA** [See quot 1902]

1856 *U.S. Naut. Mag. & Naval Jrl.* 5.228 **cwCA,** The timber used . . is pepper-wood. and was cut from the land close by the prison [=San Quentin]. **1858** in 1930 *CA Hist. Soc. Qrly.* 9.253 **CA,** Noticed the beautie's of the pep[p]er wood tree. **1897** *Jrl. Amer. Folkl.* 10.143 **CA,** *Umbellularia Californica* . . Pepper-wood. **1902** [see **peppernut tree**]. **1947** Chalfant *Gold* 25 **CA,** It was a small flat-topped point . . with a few nice trees standing together, among them a beautiful pepperwood—spice wood, we called it. **1961** Thomas *Flora Santa Cruz* 173 **cwCA,** California Laurel, California Bay, Oregon Myrtle, Oregon Pepperwood.

A common tree on canyons, mountain slopes, valleys, and occasionally in chaparral, San Francisco southward. **1968** *DARE* Tape **CA**100, It [= a valley] used to be covered with pepperwoods and brush and so forth in the early days and they slashed it and cleaned it off.

2 A **prickly ash 1:** usu *Zanthoxylum clava-herculis,* but also *Z. americanum.* [See quot 1908]

1884 Sargent *Forests of N. Amer.* 30, Toothache Tree. Prickly Ash. Sea Ash. Pepper Wood [etc]. **1908** Rogers *Tree Book* 348, The Negro in the South chews a piece of prickly ash bark to cure the toothache. "Sting-tongue" and "pepperwood" he calls it, for it produces a burning sensation and a copious flow of saliva. **1960** Vines *Trees SW* 594, Common Prickly-ash—*Zanthoxylum americanum.* . . Vernacular names in use are Angelica-tree, Northern Prickly-ash, Toothache, Suterberry, and Pepperwood. **1971** Krochmal *Appalachia Med. Plants* 278, Xanthoxylum clava-herculis. . . Pepper wood, pricklyash [etc].

per- pref¹ When unaccented: usu |pə(r)-|; also |prɪ-| Pronc-sp *pre-* See also **perambulator, perhaps, perspire, perspiration, pro-** Cf **pre-** pref¹
Std sense, var forms.

1787 (1936) Dewees *Jrl.* 4 **PA,** Crossed Sidling Hill and were the greatest part of the day in preforming the journey. **1837** Sherwood *Gaz. GA* 71, *Prevade,* for pervade. **1876** in 1969 *PADS* 52.54 **seIL,** There is to be a grand preformance at Elliott's Hall tonight. **1905** *DN* 3.58 **eNE,** *Metathesis,* especially of *r,* is very frequent: *prehaps, preform, prespiration, preceive.* **1937** *AmSp* 12.126 **Upstate NY,** Metathesis . . is common, especially when [r] is one of the affected sounds; thus: . . *persist* [prɪˈsɪst], *perform* [prɪˈfɔrm]. **1942** *AmSp* 17.152 **seNY,** Persist [pronounced with [ɚ] by] 111 [infs, with [ə] by] 89. . . *Persist* shows 5 instances of metathesized [prɪ-]. **1965–70** *DARE* (Qu. Y23, . . *To move yourself*) Inf **AR3,** Preambulate; (Qu. CC9, . . *Words or expressions for hell*) Infs **IL66, 69, 77, 85, TN31, 36,** Predition; (Qu. GG6, . . *"When she said she wouldn't go with him, he was quite _____."*) Inf **MO2,** Preturbed; (Qu. HH39, *A homosexual man*) Inf **IN32,** Prevert; (Qu. NN26b, . . *"Go to _____!"*) Inf **IL69,** Predition. **1976** Garber *Mountain-ese* 71 **sAppalachians,** We went to watch the magician preform at the school last night.

per- pref² See **pre-** pref¹

per- pref³ See **pro-**

per n Cf **hambone** n **4**
In marble play: see quot.

1957 *Sat. Eve. Post Letters* **cwKY** (as of 1930s), [In the marble game roly-holy:] Having made the circuit twice he could take a "per" which was a hambone and three spans.

perairie See **prairie**

perambulator n Also *perambular, perambulate* Also, by metath, *preambulator* [*OED2* 1856 →] **widespread, but less freq Sth, S Midl** See Map
A **baby carriage 1** or stroller.

1856 *Harper's New Mth. Mag.* 13.711, [Caption:] Every Lady Her Own Perambulator. **1893** Wiggin *Cathedral Courtship* 136, There are often two youngsters of a perambulator age in the same family at the same time. **1904** (1932) Rice *Sandy* 62, If Sandy had announced his intention of putting on baby clothes and being wheeled in a perambulator, Ricks could not have been more astonished. **1950** *WELS (Vehicles for babies and small children: that they can lie down in)* 6 infs, **WI,** Perambulator. **1963** *AmSp* 38.212 [Sears-Roebuck and Regional Terms], The catalog history of terms used for this item [=a baby buggy] . . reveals the sensitivity of copy writers to American regional terms. A number of variant names find their way in and out of the indexes; among them are *perambulator, cab, buggy,* and, the preferred trade term with Sears, *carriage.* **1965–70** *DARE* (Qu. N42, *Vehicles for a baby or small child—the kind it can lie down in)* 71 Infs, **chiefly Nth, N Midl,** Perambulator; **PA93,** Perambular; **PA134, WA20,** Preambulator; **NY37,** Perambulate; (Qu. N43, *Vehicles for a small child—the kind it has to sit up in)* 14 Infs, **scattered,** Perambulator; **CA11,** Preambulators. **1966** Dakin *Dial. Vocab. Ohio R. Valley* 2.431, Baby carriage. . . Seven scattered instances of *perambulator* are recorded [from 207 infs]. **1968** *PADS* 49.17 **Upper MW,** Two other terms, *(baby) cab* and *perambulator,* are relics. Both were offered by about 4.0% of the field informants, and neither term was offered by the students. **1970** Tarpley *Blinky* 106 **nwTX,** Ve-

hicle used to push baby in . . Perambulator [2 infs of 200]. **1973** Allen *LAUM* 2.341 **Upper MW** (as of c1950), Baby carriage. . . *Pram* is a distinct Canadianism, although the full word *perambulator* is found south of the border as well [9 infs out of a total of 203], where its use may be accompanied by a feeling that an infant wheeled in a perambulator is superior to one pushed around in a buggy. **1986** Pederson *LAGS Concordance (Baby carriage)* 18 infs, **Gulf Region,** Perambulator(s).

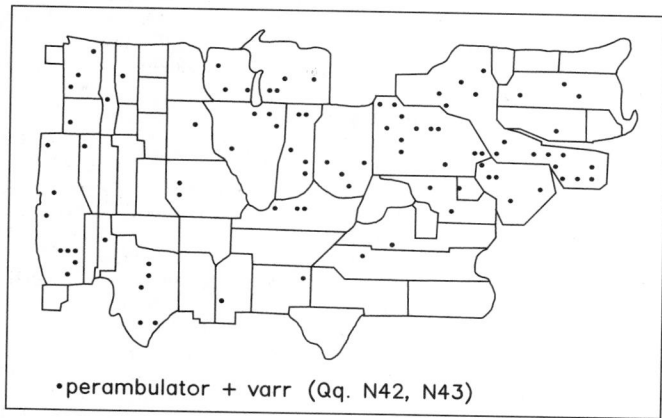

•perambulator + varr (Qq. N42, N43)

peratha See **parada**

perceivance n [*OED2* "*Obs. exc. dial.*"]
Heed, notice.

1916 Macy–Hussey *Nantucket Scrap Basket* 163 **seMA,** When a Nantucket woman of the old regime wishes to convey the idea that she scornfully ignored some slighting remark, she says with dignity: "Yes, I heard it, but I took no perceivance of it."

perch n¹ Usu |pɜ(r)č|; also **chiefly S Midl** |pɪrč, pɪrč, pjɝč|; for addit varr see quots Pronc-spp *pairch, pearch, peerch, pyetch* **A Forms.**

1634 Wood *New Engl. Prospect* 90, In frostie weater [sic] they [=Indians] cut round holes in the yce, about which they wil sit . . catching of Pikes, Pearches, Breames, and other sorts of fresh water fish. **1853** Simms *Sword & Distaff* 211 **SC,** Sp'ile a whole field of fine rice, jest flooded, to catch a few *pairch!* **1883** (1971) Harris *Nights with Remus* 104 **GA** [Black], Brer Fox 'low he gwine ter fish fer peerch fer de ladies. **1893** Shands *MS Speech* 49, Peerch. . . Negro and illiterate white for *perch,* meaning a certain kind of fish. This forms an exact parallel to the use of *peert* for *pert,* which is common in almost all parts of the United States. **1902** *DN* 2.241 **sIL,** Perch [pɪrč]. . . The perch, a fish. **1903** *DN* 2.290 **Cape Cod MA** (as of a1857), *Pairch* (= perch, a fish). *Ibid* 324 **seMO,** Perch. . . Pronounced pearch [pɪrč], a fish. **1906** *DN* 3.150 **nwAR,** Perch. . . Pronounced [pɪrč]. **1909** *DN* 3.356 **eAL, wGA,** *Pearch* [pɪrč]. . . Perch. Not uncommon. **1923** *DN* 5.217 **swMO,** Peerch. . . A perch, also a species of fish. **1928** *AmSp* 3.402 **Ozarks,** The long *e* replaces the short in such words as *pert* and *perch,* usually rendered *peert* and *peerch.* **1929** Sale *Tree Named John* 66 **MS,** Dem's goggle-eyes, feller, en eve'y udder kin' uv pyetch dey is in de worl'. **1937** *Hall Coll.* **ceTN,** Them's not perch [pɪɝtʃ]; them's bass. **c1960** *Wilson Coll.* **csKY,** Perch is still sometimes [pjɝtʃ]. **1965–70** *DARE* (Qu. P1) Infs **GA1, LA8, 12, 22,** (Goggle-eye *or* yellow) [pɜič]; **NY36,** [pɔič]; **IL95,** [pɪrč]; **KY34,** [pjɝs]; **SC9,** [peič]; (Qu. P14) Inf **NY151,** [perč]; **NY183,** [perč]. **1965–70** *DARE* Tape **FL21,** [FW:] What's the best fish you offer down here? [Inf:] Brim and perch [puɝč]; **LA8,** I like the way they eat. White perch [pɔič] and trout; **NJ67,** They get mackerels, bluefish, sea trout, . . perch [pɪrč], butterfish.
B Senses.

1 Std: a freshwater fish of the family Percidae, esp of the genus *Perca.* For other names of *Perca flavescens* see **yellow perch**

2 A **sunfish:** usu *Lepomis* spp, but also **flier 2.**
1772 in 1924 Phillips *Notes B. Romans* 123 **FL,** Those [=river fish] peculiar to America are three Species of the Bream, One of which is here Called Perch, the Striped Rock, and a kind of Fish . . on which there is not a Name yet fixed. **1887** Goode *Amer. Fishes* 67, Many other species [of *Lepomis*] . . abound in the fresh waters of the Mississippi Valley, and are known as "Sun-fish," "Bream" and "Perch." *Ibid*

68, *Centrarchus macropterus* has no name more distinctive than "Sunfish" or "Perch." **1903** *NY State Museum & Sci. Serv. Bulletin* 60.479, The long-eared sunfish has a very extensive range and is known under many common names, among which are . . perch, sun perch, red-bellied perch [etc]. **1931** Read *LA French* 101, Those persons who do not speak French refer to the sunfish by the erroneous term "perch." **1965–68** *DARE* Tape **FL21,** [FW:] What's the best fish you offer down here? [Inf:] Brim and perch; **GA35,** Our best fishing is what we call the perch fishing, is the warmouths, brim. **1967** *DARE* (Qu. P7, *Small fish used as bait for bigger fish*) Inf **AL28,** Perch—what we call a brim—but illegal; **AR51,** Perch—general term for all sunfish. **1984** Daigle *Dict. Cajun Lang.* 114 **LA,** Patassa. . . Sunfish, perch.

3 also *percher:* A **black bass 1. esp TX, LA, AR, OK**
[**1787** Gesellschaft Naturforschender Freunde *Schriften* 8.166, Oswego-Bass, oder Pertschen der innländischen Seen. [=Oswego-Bass, or perch of the inland lakes.]] **1815** *Lit. & Philos. Soc. NY Trans.* 1.146, *Basse;* is a Dutch word, signifying perch. **1884** Goode *Fisheries U.S.* 1.401, The Small-mouth [bass] shares with the Large mouth in the Southern States the names "Jumper," "Perch," and "Trout." **1911** U.S. Bur. Census *Fisheries 1908* 307, The small-mouth bass is generally found in clear running streams. . . In the Southern states it is also called "jumper," "perch," "trout," "mountain trout," etc. **1933** LA Dept. of Conserv. *Fishes* 313, None of our other fresh water fishes has been given so many popular names as our Black Bass . . It will be seen that such completely inaccurate designations as "Salmon," "Perch" and "Trout" have all been applied to this fine species. **1935** Caine *Game Fish* 3 **Sth,** Large-mouthed Black Bass. . . Synonyms. . . Perch. *Ibid* 7, Smallmouthed Black Bass. . . Perch. *Ibid* 10, Southern Small-mouthed Black Bass or Spotted Small-mouthed Black Bass. . . Perch. **1939** Hall Coll. **wNC,** Perch—same as bass. **1965–70** *DARE* (Qu. P7, *Small fish used as bait for bigger fish*) 26 Infs, 20 **TX, LA, OK, AR,** Perch; **CA111, OK25,** Little perch; **FL24,** Percher ['pɝ·čə]; **OK3,** Perches; **TX26,** Baby perch. [*DARE* Ed: Some of these Infs may refer instead to other senses.]

4 =freshwater drum.
1884 Goode *Fisheries U.S.* 1.370, *Haploidonotus grunniens.* . . In the Ohio River it is usually called "White Perch" or "Gray Perch," often simply "Perch." **1949** Caine *N. Amer. Sport Fish* 136, The fresh water drum is frequently called the white perch. . . Other names applying to this fish are: Bubbler . . Perch [etc].

5 Any of var **surfperch;** see quots. **Pacific**
1874 (1877) Hittell *Resources CA* 413, Embiotocoid fishes are. . . all marine fishes save one, which is found in fresh water. . . They are abundant in the market in all seasons of the year and are called "perch" by the fishermen, though they bear no relationship to the true perch. **1884** Goode *Fisheries U.S.* 1.276, The Surf-Fish Family—Embiotocidae. . . The general name "Perch" is applied to these fishes everywhere along the [Pacific] coast. This unfortunate misnomer came about from their resemblance to the sun-fishes or "perch" of the Southern States, and to the "white perch," *Roccus americanus,* of the East. . . About San Francisco, the name "Perch" is given to them all, as well as to *Archoplites interruptus,* and separate names for the different species are seldom heard. **1953** Roedel *Common Fishes CA* 102, The Surfperches, Family Embiotocidae. . . These fish are not true perches but form a distinct family. . . the six species most closely associated with surf are called "surfperch," those associated with the ocean, but not primarily with the surf, are "seaperch," while those of varying habitat are simply "perch." **1968–70** *DARE* (Qu. P2, . . *Kinds of saltwater fish caught around here* . . *good to eat*) Infs **CA36, 168, 191,** Perch; **CA65,** Perch—on the surf; **CA105,** Perch, smelt . . surf fish.

6 =cunner n¹ **1.**
1838 MA Zool. & Bot. Surv. *Repts. Zool.* 41, The *Crenilabrus burgall* too—*Marine perch*—or, as it is most commonly called, "Cunner," is for several months in the year, taken along our whole *sea-board,* . . and is one of the most common, as well as excellent species found in our waters. **1887** Goode *Amer. Fishes* 297 **Cape Cod MA,** At Provincetown they [=cunners] are called "Sea-Perch," and at the Isle of Shoals and occasionally on the adjoining mainland, "Blue-Perch" and "Perch." **1920** Packard *Old Plymouth* 163 **eMA,** In the beginning of things were the cunners, known before Massachusetts Bay mainly as perch.

7 Any of var other fish; see quots.
1906 NJ State Museum *Annual Rept. for 1905* 307, The White Perch. *Morone americana.* . . Perch. Peerch. White Perch. Yellow Perch. **1931** *Copeia* 2.49 **TX,** *Lagodon rhomboides* . . A "perch" . . taken in a cast net in a shallow lagoon on an island near Port Aransas. **1947** Caine *Salt Water* 50 **Gulf States,** Croaker . . are found along much of this coastline, . . sometimes swarming into passes. . . The perch can be caught in

shallow waters of open bays. **1947** Dalrymple *Panfish* 85, Here, my friend, are the various names by which you would address that little gamester, the Crappie, depending on where you happened to be at the moment: Bachelor, Bachelor Perch . . Perch [etc]. **1953** Roedel *Common Fishes CA* 93, California Sargo—*Anisotremus davidsoni.* . . Forms a small proportion of the Southern California "perch" catch. *Ibid* 114, Blacksmith—*Chromis punctipennis.* . . Forms a very small proportion of the Southern California "perch" catch. *Ibid* 119, Halfmoon—*Medialuna californiensis.* . . Formed about 40 percent of the Los Angeles "perch" catch in 1947.

perch n² Pronc-sp *pearch*
Std sense, var form.
1899 (1912) Green *VA Folk-Speech* 315, Pearch. . . Perch, a rod or pole serving as a roost for birds. . . An elevated seat or position.

perch bug n **chiefly NEast**
A **dragonfly** nymph; rarely, the adult.
1968 *DARE* FW Addit **ceNY,** Perch bugs—nymphs sold for fish bait. They hatch into devil's darning needles (dragonflies). [FW: from bait shop proprietress, North Granville, N.Y.] **1969** *DARE* (Qu. R2, . . *The dragonfly*) Inf **NY183,** Perch bug. **2000** *NADS Letters* **CT,** For sure, a perch bug is a dragonfly nymph, used as bait and sold as such in Connecticut when I was a kid (good for brookies). *Ibid* **ME,** My father, born 1918, Mapleton, ME used this term [=*perch bug*] for the dragonfly nymph we fished with in Maine and Connecticut. Never heard it related to adult. *Ibid* **NJ,** I learned the word [=*perch bug*] from my father who was an avid fisherman. We used the word as the name for dragonfly larvae which we raked out of ponds and swampy areas for fishbait. My father was born in Northern New Jersey in town of Riverdale on November 23 1919. He was an active outdoorsman most of his life, hunting, fishing, trapping in the tri-state area (NJ, NY, PA). . . Our family used this term, but we moved into Sullivan County in Southern New York State when I was 10 yrs old, and I have never heard the locals (except me, and no one knows what I am talking about) ever refer to the dragonfly larva by this name. . . As for your query we only used the word to refer to the larva in connection with fishbait, the adult was a dragonfly, or damselfly. **2001** *Daily Hampshire Gaz.* (Northampton MA) 6 Apr (Internet), Basically, this nymph is designed to imitate a dragonfly larva, what local fisherfolk know as "perch bugs."

percher See **perch** n¹ **3**

perchpike See **pike perch**

percipity See **precipitate**

percolator n Cf **shake** n¹ **2, skiffle**
=house-rent party.
1946 Blesh *Shining Trumpets* 303 **Chicago IL,** The great South Side institution of "rent party" (locally known as "skiffle", "shake", or "percolator"). **1956** Longstreet *Real Jazz* 126 **Chicago IL,** Depression came. . . You could always wrassel up a piano and get together to listen and charge a few coins and have a skiffle. Or, as some said, a rent party, or a shake, or a percolator. **1974** Foster *Ribbin'* 141, In Chicago, these parties [=rent parties] were called a 'parlour social', 'gouge', 'struggle', 'percolator', 'too terrible party', or the 'skiffle'.

percoon See **puccoon**

percosan, percossin See **pocosin**

perdiddle, perdiddo See **padiddle**

père See **pépère**

peregrine falcon n [*OED2* c1386 →]
Std: a falcon *(Falco peregrinus).* Also called **duck hawk, Mexican eagle-hawk**

perfect adj Pronc-spp *parfect, puffick* Similarly adv *parfectly, perfeckly, pufitly*
Std senses, var forms.
1815 Humphreys *Yankey in England* 107, Parfect, perfect. **1867** Lowell *Biglow* xix **'Upcountry' MA,** [Yankee] has clung to what I suspect to have been the broad Norman pronunciation of *e* . . in such words as *sarvant, parfect, vartoo,* and the like. **1903** *DN* 2.291 **Cape Cod MA,** In 1840 the younger and older generations differed most noticeably in their pronunciation of the vowels before *r* plus a consonant. Old folks

still pronounced *er* as *ar*. Thus they said *parfectly*, [etc]. **1904** Day *Kin o' Ktaadn* 208 **ME**, Puffick independence! That was Haines's creed. **1933** Rawlings *South Moon* 6 **nFL**, She's a perfeckly cur'ous young un. **1942** Hall *Smoky Mt. Speech* 42 **wNC, eTN**, [ɑɚ] for [ɝ] is rapidly becoming obsolete. Nevertheless, it is preserved in the speech of a few old people, who may use it in . . *perfectly.* **1959** Lomax *Rainbow Sign* 29 **AL** [Black], Since I got grown I can see that all my mama's whippin wus pufitly right.

perfectly adv

A Forms.

See **perfect.**

B Sense.

With a verb: Very much.

1933 Rawlings *South Moon* 68 **nFL**, "He'll perfeckly hate it," she said. "You jist as good to put a wildcat to the books."

perfume(d) pussy n Also *perfume kitty, ~ merchant joc*

A skunk.

1946 Peattie *Pacific Coast* 90, Shunned because of their mephitic odor and potentiality for malicious mischief, these animals are called by a number of humorous nicknames . . perfume merchant . . but a skunk by any other name! **1966–70** DARE (Qu. P26, *Names and nicknames . . for a skunk*) Infs **CA45, NJ21, PA234**, Perfume pussy; **NH10**, Perfumed pussy; **GA18**, Perfume kitty (not common).

perfume tree n

=catalpa B1.

1950 *WELS Suppl.* **WI**, Perfume tree—catalpa, [from the] strong smell of falling blossoms. Whole neighborhood, especially children, say it.

perhaps adv Usu |pə(r)ˈhæps|; also |pɚæps, præps| Pronc-spp *p'raps, prehaps, puhhaps;* aphet *'haps*

Std sense, var forms.

1815 Humphreys *Yankey in England* 107, Prehaps, perhaps. **1835** (1927) Evans *Exped. Rocky Mts.* 14.214 **IN**, On finding we were here and would prehaps interfere they thought it best policy to fire off their guns as a token of friendship. **1843** (1847) Field *Drama Pokerville* 102 **MO**, *Pre*haps there was the derndest *rise* all over that carpet. **1843** (1916) Hall *New Purchase* 146, Prehaps . . you know. **1853** Simms *Sword & Distaff* 539 **SC**, He's got other we'pons in that chist, prehaps. **1871** Eggleston *Hoosier Schoolmaster* 66 **sIN**, P'raps you'd like bed. **1884** *Anglia* 7.254 **Sth, S Midl** [Black], 'Haps (perhaps). **1890** DN 1.40 **csME**, Perhaps. . . [pərˈæps] *or* [prˈæps] *(two syllables)* and [pəˈhæps], *rather than* [præps]. **1899** (1912) Green *VA Folk-Speech* 334, Prehaps. . . Perhaps. **1905** DN 3.16 **cCT**, Prehaps. . . For perhaps. *Ibid* 58 **eNE**, Prehaps. **1914** DN 4.116, Not taken into account . . are syncopations, such as *p'raps.* **1922** Gonzales *Black Border* 320 **sSC, GA coasts** [Gullah glossary], Puhhaps—perhaps.

periagua n Also *pattyauguh, per(r)iauger, pettiauger, pettyauguh;* for addit varr see quots [Varr of Span *piragua,* ult of Cariban origin] **chiefly S Atlantic coast** *old-fash* Cf **pirogue**

A large, dugout canoe; an open, flat-bottomed, schooner-rigged vessel; see quot 1744.

1609 in 1846 Force *Tracts* 4.1.90 **FL**, The periagua ouerset. **1696** *S.C. Statutes at Large* II.105 (DAE), Any person . . [who] shall steal, take away, or let loose any . . perriaguer or canoe . . shall be liable to corporal punishment. **1716** Petiver *Petiveriana* 11, It's *Body* they scoop into *Canoes* and *Pereaugers.* **1733** *SC Gaz.* (Charleston) 28 July 4/2, To be sold. . . a plank Perriaugua, that will carry about 26 Cask of Rice. **1735** in 1940 *AmSp* 15.229 **NEng**, R. Gray caulked my periaugoe. **1744** in 1840 *GA Hist. Soc. Coll.* 112, These Periaguas are long flat-bottomed boats, carrying from twenty to thirty-five tons. They have a kind of a forecastle and a cabin; but the rest open, and no deck. They have two masts . . and sails like schooners. They row generally with two oars only. **1791** Bartram *Travels* 92 **neFL**, The trunks of these trees, when hollowed out, make large and durable pettiaugers and canoes. **1802** (1803) Ellicott *Jrl.* 189 **sLA**, They had a sufficient depth of water to float loaded periaguas and canoes. **1814** *Baltimore Patriot* 16 Jan 3/3 (Mathews Coll.), Port of New York, Jan. 13. Arrived, here yesterday, a petteauger schr of Rockaway. **1898** *Rudder* 407 (Mathews Coll.), A large periauger-rigged sharpie, called the Pirate. **1899** (1912) Green *VA Folk-Speech* 318, Periauger. . . A canoe made from the trunk of a single tree hollowed out, with built up sides. **1926** Smith *Gullah* 23 **sSC, GA coasts**, Me holleh one patty-augah [=I hollered to (or at) a piragua].

Ibid 31, *Popular Etymologies* . . *Petty-* or *pattyauguh* for piragua, pirogue.

perish v Pronc-spp *parish, persh*

1 To cause to die. [OED2 c1400 →; "Obs. or arch."]

[**1925** DN 5.338 **Nfld**, Perish. . . Cause to perish. "It'll perish you."]

1938 (1964) Korson *Minstrels Mine Patch* 195 **nePA**, Oh, a sudden flash and a deafening sound / Like a heavy storm or gale,/ Which perished those four miner boys / In the mines of Locust Dale.

2 with *out:* See below.

a To starve out, starve into submission.

1862 in 1953 Bryan *Confederate GA* 71, I am beginning to think we shall never be rescued or relieved and that we shall eventually be perished out and compelled to surrender.

b ppl adj phr *perished out:* Dead.

1884 *Anglia* 7.274 **Sth, S Midl** [Black], To be mos' pe'ish out = to be almost dead.

c To die out.

1894 in 1983 Zeigler *Lexicon Middle GA* 85 **cGA**, The most of 'em [=bees] 'll jes' give up, and not do one blessed thing, they'll drindle and they'll keep on a-drindlin' until they'll all perish out, jes' so.

3 in phr *perish to death:* To die a slow death; to waste away.

1940 (1941) Bell *Swamp Water* 41 **sGA**, You'd parish to death trying to git out by yourself. **1984** *Annals Internal Med.* 100.899 **cwAL**, To persh (perish) *to death* means the patient is starving and wasting away. **1986** Pederson *LAGS Concordance*, 1 inf, **swGA**, A cow would perish to death.

4 To consume (food). [Scots dial]

1927 Kennedy *Gritny* 215 **sLA** [Black], Mr. Amos endeavored to "perish" and "destroy" as much as was humanly possible. Because Felo was most pleased when he saw people "eat good."

5 foll by infin: To want desperately.

1863 in 1886 U.S. War Dept. *War of Rebellion* 1st ser 15.317 **MA**, But I would hazard all risks if it were within human power to accomplish the junction of our armies against the strong places of the enemy, for I am perishing to see a concentration of our armies at that point. **1875** (1876) Twain *Tom Sawyer* 162 **MO**, There was not an urchin in school but was perishing to have a glimpse of it. **1894** *Scribner's Mag.* 16.489 **Sth**, Because she was perishing to have Mr. March again begin where he had left off, she conversed with the Fairs longer than ever. **1966–70** DARE (Qu. GG17, *Other words for longing . . "She had been so lonely—she was really _____ [to see him]."*) Infs **CA110, MD20, NC31, NY166, TX39, VA73, WV16**, Perishing.

6 as ppl adj *perished:* Exhausted, esp by exposure to heat or cold; wasted, withered. Cf **famished**

[**1902** DN 2.241 **sIL**, Perish, v.i. To be exhausted with suffering.] **1921** DN 5.118 **KY**, Perished. . . Paralyzed. "They say the Kaiser has a perished arm." **1940** Harris *Folk Plays* 88 **NC**, I'll jes' keep on my circis jacket till I git warm. . . I'm a-goin' to have me a dip o' snuff. I'm near 'bout perished. **1941** LANE Map 482 *(Exhausted)*, The word *perished,* rarely offered in the meaning 'tired,' was incidentally recorded a number of times [DARE Ed: esp in **ME, NH**] in the meaning 'cold, frozen' (especially in the phrase *perished with the cold*), once in the meaning 'exhausted by heat'. **1942** *Sat. Eve. Post* 22 Aug 12, Her mother sat beside a low-burning fire, her perished-looking body hunched over. **1960** Williams *Walk Egypt* 102 **GA**, There were a few perished-by-dust blooms in the undergrowth along the road. **1971** Wood *Vocab. Change* 40 **Sth**, Fatigue. . . Least widely distributed . . *perished* (not reported in Mississippi, Florida, Louisiana).

perished out See **perish 2b**

perish out See **perish 2**

perish to death See **perish 3**

periwinkle n¹

Std: a plant of the genus *Vinca* or *Catharanthus roseus,* formerly included in that genus, but esp *Vinca minor.* Also called **myrtle** n¹ **B3**; for other names of *V. minor* see **blue myrtle 2, creeping ~, wintergreen**; for other names of *C. roseus* see **old maid 2**

periwinkle n² [By ext from *periwinkle* any of var marine gastropod mollusks, esp of the genus *Littorina* (OED2 1530 →)] Cf **pennywinkle**

1 A freshwater snail; see quots.

1806 (1905) Clark *Orig. Jrls. Lewis & Clark Exped.* 4.173, The Periwinkle both of the [Columbia] river and [Pacific] ocian are similar to those found in the same situation on the Atlantic. **1966–68** *DARE* (Qu. P7, *Small fish used as bait for bigger fish*) Inf **WA6**, Periwinkles (a mussel) or pennywinkle; (Qu. P18, . . *Kinds of shellfish*) Inf **IN22**, Mussels, periwinkle. **2000** *NADS Letters* **cnAL**, Periwinkle. . . Used in Huntsville, AL, to mean a small mollusc (snail) in fresh water streams. *Ibid* **wOR**, I grew up in western Oregon in the 1950's and when my father (who was from central Virginia) started to take me fishing, he used, among other things, what he called "periwinkles" for bait. My friends . . also used the term when we would play around in local streams. As I recall, they were very dark in color, rather small, and were either attached to or underneath rocks and boulders in the shallows near shore. I suspect they were larvae, although I also remember the term used for small fresh water snails that also attached themselves to stream boulders.

2 A caddis fly larva; rarely, another aquatic insect larva. [From the resemblance of the case of the caddis fly larva to a snail shell] **chiefly Pacific NW, CA**

1948 [see **rock worm**]. **1966–69** *DARE* (Qu. P6, . . *Kinds of worms . . used for bait*) Inf **CA120**, Periwinkles—find under rocks in streams—have little shells on them—take off the shells; **NV8**, Periwinkle—a sort of worm found on rocks—in a cocoon; **WA8**, Pennywinkle, periwinkle, night crawler, grasshopper; (Qu. R4, *A large winged insect that hatches in summer in great numbers around lakes or rivers, crowds around lights, lives only a day or so, and is good fish bait*) Inf **WA12**, Larva is periwinkle. [**1986** Pederson *LAGS Concordance,* 1 inf, **nwGA**, Periwinkle [no context]; *(Minnows)* 1 inf, **cGA**, A periwinkle; *(Earthworm)* 1 inf, **cGA**, Periwinkles—large worms or fish?] **1996** Hafele-Hinton *Guide Pacific NW Aquatic Invertebrates* 20 **OR**, Family: Limnephilidae *Genus:* 35+ in Oregon alone *Common Name:* Periwinkle, Cinnamon Sedge, Dark Sedge. . . *Habitat:* Lakes, ponds, sloughs, small and large streams and rivers. . . *Behavior:* True case makers. **1998** *NADS Letters* **wWA**, My dad called a local fresh-water larva "periwinkle." This creature was about an inch long, cream-colored body, black head, and built itself a full body-length cylindrical case out of cemented sand or small gravel particles. We found them in shallow water at the edges of fast-flowing streams. Used for bait. **1998** *Ibid* **ceCA**, We had periwinkles in the creeks in Bishop, California, east of the Sierra. They are little bug-like things that make their own tubes out of sand or other small bits from the stream (there were 2 kinds). Although we went fishing a lot, we didn't use these as bait. **1999** *DARE* File **ID**, My Dad remembers that fishermen called caddisfly worms "periwinkles" on the Salmon River when he was a kid in the 1920s and 30s. *Ibid* **eOR**, Periwinkle is used for any cased caddis larva. I'm sure I heard the term in the 1950s in eastern Oregon. *Ibid* **seWA**, Periwinkle, pennywinkle—The cased larva of the caddis fly. Peri- seems the preferred pronunciation in Washington. Commonly used as fish bait, the caddis larva makes a shell of accreted sand and debris. . . I have encountered an instance of the term being applied to the hellgrammite, which is the free swimming larva of the Dobson fly. I don't know if this was an error or an uncommon usage. **2001** *Ibid* **ceCA** (as of c1970), Two of the most fascinating (to me) creatures were periwinkles and heligramites. They are both similar, with some kind of insect living inside a self-made tube of tiny rocks. The heligramites . . had round tubes, and the rocks were larger than in the periwinkles, which I preferred. Periwinkles had a tapered, squarish case and the little rocks used were very tiny (sand-sized). They lived under rocks in the creek and we liked to pick them up and watch the creatures poke their heads out. *Ibid* **NW, OR, WA**, [Nine correspondents, 7 from WA, identify *periwinkle* as a caddis fly larva either explicitly or by description.]

perjinkety adj [Brit dial; cf *SND perfink, EDD perjinkety*] =**pernickety.**

1930 Stoney-Shelby *Black Genesis* 17 **seSC**, You is a ugly creeter nohow, for be so ungodly perjinkety 'bout yo' countenance!

perky Sue n **chiefly Desert SW**

A **bitterweed** (here: *Tetraneuris argentea*).

1967 Dodge *Roadside Wildflowers* 91 **AZ, NM**, Normally a flower of early spring, perky sue may blossom again following summer rains. It is particularly welcome in April after severe winters, when it covers hillsides. **1968** *DARE* FW Addit **CO7A**, Perky Sue.

perleau See **pilau** n[1]

perlice See **police**

---

perlite(ly) See **polite**

perloo, perlow See **pilau** n[1]

permanate See **promenade**

permeeter See **palmetto**

permillion n

A melon.

1963 Edwards *Gravel* 175 **eTN** (as of 1920s), Who cut up the water permillions? *Ibid* 176, Them's the same identical fellers that cut up the permillions!

perminade See **promenade**

permit n [Folk-etym for AmSpan *palometa*]

Either a **pompano 1** (here: *Trachinotus carolinus* or *T. goodei*) or the **round pompano.**

1884 Goode *Fisheries U.S.* 1.329, In the Gulf of Mexico it [=the pompano] is not unusual, being known at Key West as the "Permit." **1902** Jordan-Evermann *Amer. Fishes* 316, The permit is the largest of all pompanos. . . It occurs about Key West and is occasionally taken in Indian River. It should be remarked, however, that to the Indian River fishermen this species is not distinguished from the common pompano, and that the fish known to them as the "permit" is the round pompano (*T. falcatus*). **1911** U.S. Bur. Census *Fisheries 1908* 314, Other species [of *Trachinotus*] found on our eastern coast are the "old-wife," or "gafftopsail pompano," the "round pompano," or "Indian River permit." **1946** LaMonte *N. Amer. Game Fishes* 38, Common Pompano—*Trachinotus carolinus*. . . Names: Permit, Carolina Pompano [etc]. *Ibid*, Round Pompano—*Trachinotus falcatus*. . . Indian River Permit [etc]. *Ibid* Permit—*Trachinotus goodei*. . . Key West Permit. **1975** Evanoff *Catch More Fish* 197, Another fish of the flats that will break the surface of the water with its tail and dorsal fin is the permit.

pernady See **panada**

pernickety adj, hence n *pernicketiness* Also sp *pernicketty, pernickity, pernikety* [Scots, Ir, nEngl dial; cf *EDD pernickety*] **scattered, but chiefly Nth** *somewhat old-fash* Cf **persnickety**

Fussy, meticulous; crotchety.

1834 *Life Andrew Jackson* 232, Sich fellers are troubled with a vertigo in their consciences, and are never very pernikety how they steer it leads 'em tu profit. **1884** *Harper's New Mth. Mag.* 68.875 **NW**, It is necessary, however, to pick over the main body of the coal. . . any white man . . grows lame and impatient at such confining and pernickety work. **1884** *Pop. Sci. Mth.* 26.52, This I say for the benefit of those who otherwise might not understand what "pernickity" creatures astronomers are. **1890** *Century Dict.* 4408, Pernicketiness. . . The character of being pernickety. [Colloq.] Pernickety. . . [Also *pernicketty*. . .] 1. Of persons, precise in trifles. . . 2. Of things, requiring minute attention or painstaking labor. . . [Colloq. in both uses.] **1890** *DN* 1.62 **wPA**, Pernickely: cranky. [*DARE* Ed: Corrected to *pernickety* in 1892 *DN* 1.217.] **1905** [see **persnickety**]. **1914** *DN* 4.77 **ME, nNH**, Pernickety. . . Fussy, particular, crotchety. **1916** Macy-Hussey *Nantucket Scrap Basket* 141 **seMA**, "Pernickety"—A survival of old English speech, meaning fussy, particular, especially about trifles. **1928** *Sun* (Baltimore MD) 30 Nov np (Hench Coll.), I do, it is true, detest people who are always bubbling with merriment and brightening the corner where they are with sweet sunshine, and I am often told that I act as I do out of sheer pernicketiness. **c1950** Halpert Coll. 47 **wKY, nwTN**, Pernickety. . . = finicky, fussy, hard to please, meticulous about all things in general. "She's awful pernickety about her food." **1967–68** *DARE* (Qu. H12, *If somebody eating a meal takes little bits of food and leaves most of it on his plate, you say he _____*) Infs **CO27, NY49**, Pernickety; (Qu. HH11a, *Someone who is too particular or fussy—if it's a man*) Infs **NY48, 205**, Pernickety; (Qu. HH11b, *Someone who is too particular or fussy—if it's a woman*) Infs **NY12, 69**, Pernickety; (Qu. HH12, *A person who is always finding fault about unimportant things*) Inf **IN19**, Pernickety; (Qu. KK34, . . *Very neat and clean: "Her house always looks _____."*) Inf **PA22**, Pernickety. [7 Infs old, 1 mid-aged] **1986** *DARE* File **cMA** (as of 1970s), Pernickety.

pernt See **point A**

pero(a)gue See **pirogue**

perok See **pirok**

peroski See **piroshki**

perouge See **pirogue**

perriauger See **periagua**

perrie, perry See **purie**

persacitly, persackly See **prezactly**

persalm See **psalm**

perserve See **preserve**

persh See **perish**

persimmon n Also aphet *'simmern, 'simmon* Hist spp *per-simon, pirsimmon, pissimmond, posimon, pursimond;* for addit varr see quots at **A** below Pronc-spp *possimmun, priscimmon* [Of Algonquian origin]

A Forms.

  [**1606** in 1624 Smith *Genl. Hist. VA* 26, Plums there are of three sorts. The red and white are like our hedge plums, but the other which they [= Indians] call *Putchamins,* grow as high as a *Palmeta.*] **1626** in 1940 *AmSp* 15.294 **VA**, Extending Southerly . . towards the pursimond ponds. **1670** (1937) Denton *Brief Descr.* 3 **Long Is. NY**, The Fruits natural to the Island are Mulberries, Posimons, [etc]. **1676** in 1940 *AmSp* 15.334, There is a sort of fruit called a *Persimon* mentioned as most especially belonging to *Mary-Land.* [**1743** Catesby *Nat. Hist. Carolina* 2 [app] x, *Phishimons,* Whorts, and some other Fruit and wild Berries they [=Indians] also preserve for Winter.] **c1770** in 1833 Boucher *Glossary* 1 **MD**, I'd . . / Brown linen shirts, and cotton jackets wear,/ Or only *wring-jaw* drink, and *'simmon beer.* **1774** (1957) Fithian *Jrl. & Letters* 73, I gathered & eat some Pisimmonds from a large Tree which were exceeding sweet, & agreeable. **1804** in 1930 Dunbar *Life* 243 **MS**, Fruits of the forest, such as pirsimmons, grapes. **1843** (1973) Porter *Big Bear AR* 132 **MS**, They circled about among the . . priscimmon bushes. **1899** (1912) Green *VA Folk-Speech* 318, *Persimmon. . . Simmon.* The date-plum of a tree common in Virginia. **1909** *DN* 3.370 **eAL, wGA**, *Simmon. . . Persimmon.* **1922** Gonzales *Black Border* 319 **sSC, GA coasts** [Gullah glossary], *Possimmun*—persimmon, persimmons; the tree and fruit. **1927** Kennedy *Gritny* 49 **sLA** [Black], W'en de moon be riz/ An' come a-peepin' thoo de branches o' de 'simmon tree. **1931** Clute *Common Plants* 50, There are at least fifteen ways of spelling persimmon ranging from pessimin and pitchamin to pessimon, puchamine and parsemena. **1946** *PADS* 6.27 **ceNC** (as of 1900–10), 'Simmern beer. **1965–70** *DARE* (Qu. I46, *. . Kinds of fruits that grow wild around here*) 225 Infs, **chiefly Sth, Midl**, Persimmon(s); **FL**49, **KY**34, 42, 44, 77, **MD**12, **MI**68, **NC**50, **SC**66, **VA**69, 'Simmon(s); (Qu. R30, *. . Kinds of beetles*; not asked in early QRs) Inf **KY**6A, 'Simmon bugs. **1976** Garber *Mountain-ese* 82 **sAppalachians**, Pa picked a bushel uv simmons to make simmon brandy. **1986** Pederson *LAGS Concordance Gulf Region,* [*Persimmon* (alone and in combs) was recorded from 67 infs; *simmon* from 20.]

B Sense.

Std: a plant of the genus *Diospyros,* esp *D. virginiana,* native chiefly in the Sth and S Midl; also the fruit of such a plant. Also called **date plum, dog apple 2, huckleberry 8, Jove's fruit 2, Ozark date, possum wood 1, pucker tree, winter plum.** For other names of *D. texana* see **black persimmon**

persimmon beer n Also *persimmon and locust beer, persimmon buck, ~ wine* **chiefly Sth, esp SC** See Map Cf **buck** n⁴, **locust beer**

A fermented beverage made from persimmons, often with the admixture of other ingredients.

  1737 (1911) Brickell *Nat. Hist. NC* 38, The following are made in Country, viz. Cyder, Persimon-Beer . . Ceder-Beer. **c1770** [see **persimmon A**]. **1887** (1967) Harris *Free Joe* 77 **GA**, Permitted to sell ginger-cakes and persimmon-beer under the wide-spreading China-trees. **1909** *DN* 3.370 **eAL, wGA**, *Simmon. . . Persimmon. . .* "This simmon beer is powerful good." **1940** Harris *Folk Plays* 82 **eNC**, You women folks drawed off any 'simmon beer since dinner? **1942** (1960) Robertson *Red Hills* 179 **SC**, She made wine of anything that would ferment, blackberry wine, . . dandelion wine, persimmon and locust beer, a cordial of peaches. **1945** FWP *Lay My Burden Down* 66 **SC** (as of c1865)

[Black], 'Simmon beer was good in the cold freezing weather too. **1946** *PADS* 6.27 **ceNC** (as of 1900–10), 'Simmern beer. . . A beverage made of persimmons, water, and a few flavoring ingredients. **1950** *PADS* 14.51 **SC**, *Persimmon beer. . .* A beverage made from ripe persimmons. [Footnote:] One of the products of a culture that seems to be disappearing. **1965–70** *DARE* (Qu. DD28b, *. . Fermented drinks . . made at home*) 19 Infs, **chiefly Sth, esp SC**, Persimmon beer; **SC**26, Persimmon buck (beer); **KY**75, 84, **MO**15, Persimmon wine. **1986** Pederson *LAGS Concordance,* 1 inf, **cwGA**, Persimmon and locust beer.

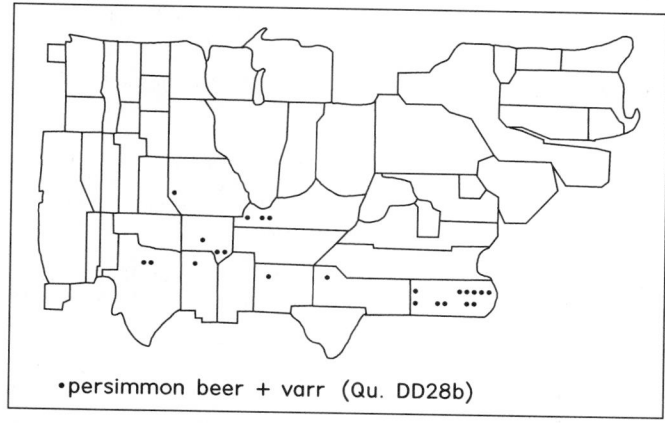

•persimmon beer + varr (Qu. DD28b)

persimon See **persimmon**

persnickety adj, hence n *persnicketiness* Also *persnickerty, persnickity* [Var of **pernickety**] **scattered, but more freq Nth, Midl** See Map

  1905 *DN* 3.63 **eNE**, *Persnickety, pernickety. . .* Disagreeable, or snippy. "They acted mighty persnickety." **1934** *AmSp* 9.213 **TX**, Examples of substitution and addition of sounds are. . . *persnickity* for *pernickety.* **1956** McAtee *Some Dialect NC* 33, *Persnickety. . .* meticulous. . . Colloq. **1959** *VT Hist.* 27.152, *Persnickety. . .* Snobbish; vain. Common. **1965–70** *DARE* (Qu. HH11a, *Someone who is too particular or fussy—if it's a man*) 89 Infs, **scattered, but more freq Nth, Midl**, Persnickety; **FL**28, Persnickety old maid; (Qu. HH11b, *Someone who is too particular or fussy—if it's a woman*) 67 Infs, **scattered, but more freq Nth, Midl**, Persnickety; **IA**9, **OK**1, Too persnickety; **FL**28, Persnickety old maid; **IL**92, Persnickety person; **OH**56, **WI**49, Persnickerty; (Qu. H12, *If somebody eating a meal takes little bits of food and leaves most of it on his plate, you say he* ___) Infs **CA**39, **IL**70, **MD**21, **OH**87, **PA**115, Persnickety; (Qu. U35, *. . Thrifty but not in a complimentary way: "She's not a bad housekeeper, but very* ___") Inf **OH**49, Persnickety; (Qu. GG14, *Names and nicknames for someone who fusses or worries a lot, especially about little things*) Inf **GA**67, Persnickety; (Qu. GG16, *. . Finding fault, or complaining: "You just can't please him—he's always* ___") Infs **MI**17, **MO**26, (So) persnickety; (Qu. GG18, *. . 'Obstinate': "Why does he have to be so* ___") Inf **CT**3, Persnickety; (Qu. GG19a, *When you can see from the way a person acts that he's feeling important or independent: "He surely is* ___ *these days."*) Inf **KY**70, Persnickety; (Qu. HH12, *A person who is always finding fault about unimportant things*)

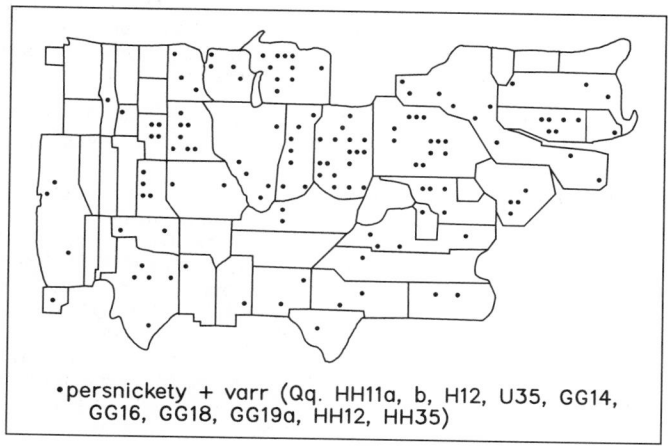

•persnickety + varr (Qq. HH11a, b, H12, U35, GG14, GG16, GG18, GG19a, HH12, HH35)

Infs **MA**89, **OH**87, **SC**54, Persnickety; (Qu. HH35, *A woman who puts on a lot of airs: "She's too _____ for me."*) Infs **DC**1, **IA**11, Persnickety. **1968** Kellner *Aunt Serena* 44 **IN**, As persnickety as she was about her health, she'd likely be with us forever, I thought gloomily. **1975** Gould *ME Lingo* 205, *Persnickety*—Petulant and hard to get along with. A *persnickety* person is fussy, opinionated, difficult, erratic, sometimes sulky and surly, and in general the opposite of what a proper person should be. **1976** Garber *Mountain-ese* 67 **sAppalachians**, *Persnickety . .* choosy. **1977** *Time* 17 Oct 106, Billy compensates for his brother's sweet-eyed psalm-singing and persnicketiness. **1986** Pederson *LAGS Concordance*, 1 inf, **seFL**, Persnickety—overly concerned with minor details; 1 inf, **ceTX**, Persnickety—neat, precise.

person n Pronc-spp *parson, porson, puss'n, pusson, pussun*
Similarly adv *puss'nully, pussonully, pussunully*
Std senses, var forms.

1760 in 1956 Eliason *Tarheel Talk* 315 **cNC**, Parson. **1795** Dearborn *Columbian Grammar*, *List of Improprieties. . . Parson* for Person. **1815** Humphreys *Yankey in England* 107, *Parson,* person. **1852** in 1956 Eliason *Tarheel Talk* 315 **cs,seNC**, Porson. **1901** Harben *Westerfelt* 13 **nGA**, I reckon a pusson kin manage to sort o' bear it better, after awhile. **1904** Day *Kin o' Ktaadn* 54 **ME**, He was goin' to flood that village—wa'n't a pusson to be spared. **1922** Gonzales *Black Border* 321 **sSC**, **GA coasts** [Gullah glossary], *Puss'n, pusson, pussun*—person, persons. *Puss'nully, pussonully, pussunully*—personally. **1930** *VA Qrly. Rev.* 6.247 **S Midl**, The hill man may say . . pusson for person. **1931** *PMLA* 46.1303 **sAppalachians**, Negro influence has crept in in such words as: . . *pusson,* person.

personate v [*OED2 personate* v. 8 →1662; "*Obs. rare.*"]
See quots.

1927 Randolph in *DN* 5.476 **Ozarks**, *Personate. . .* To call by name. "He personated me right out before all them 'ar furriners!" **1953** Randolph–Wilson *Down in Holler* 271 **Ozarks**, *Personate. . .* To call by name, to designate specifically. "That fool preacher done personated me right in meetin'! Said he was sorry I didn't come oftener!"

perspirate v Pronc-sp *prespirate* [Back-formation from *perspiration;* cf Intro "Language Changes" III.3]
To perspire.

1970 *DARE* (Qu. X56a, . . *Words for sweat*) Inf **KY**84, Prespiratin'. **1986** Pederson *LAGS Concordance* (*Sweated/ preterite form*) 1 inf **swGA**, Perspirate; 2 infs, **FL, LA**, Prespirated.

perspiration n Usu |ˈpə(r)spəˈrešən|; also |ˌpresp(ə)ˈrešən| Pronc-spp *perspriation, prespiration* Cf Intro "Language Changes" I.1
Std sense, var forms.

1899 (1912) Green *VA Folk-Speech* 334, *Prespiration. . .* Perspiration; sweat. **1905** *DN* 3.58 **eNE**, Prespiration. **1909** *DN* 3.359 **eAL, wGA**, Prespiration. **1910** *DN* 3.447 **wNY**, *Perspiration. . .* Often for *perspiration.* **1928** *AmSp* 3.406 **Ozarks**, Some consonants, particularly *l* and *r* are frequently shifted about by a kind of metathesis, producing such monstrosities as . . *prespiration.* **1936** *AmSp* 11.245 **eTX**, Perspiration . . *Plantation-Type* [=cultivated Southern speech] . . [pɔspəˈrešn]; *Hill-Type* [=spoken by most of the white inhabitants] . . [prespɚˈešn]. **1943** *LANE* Map 662 (*Sweated*) 1 inf, **swCT**, [presprešn]; 1 inf, **nwCT**, [presprešn]. **1968–69** *DARE* (Qu. X56a, . . *Words for sweat*) 226 Infs, **widespread**, Perspiration; **IA**45, **IL**99, Perspriation; (Qu. X56b, *Expressions about sweating very heavily*) Inf **MD**44, Wet with prespiration. **1976** Garber *Mountain-ese* 71 **sAppalachians**, *Prespiration . .* perspiration—Her dress was badly stained by prespiration.

perspire v Usu |pə(r)ˈspaɪr|; also |preˈspaɪr|; for addit varr see quots Pronc-sp *prespire* Cf Intro "Language Changes" I.1
A Pronc varr.

1909 *DN* 3.359 **eAL, wGA**, *Prespire. . .* To perspire. **1935** *AmSp* 10.306, *Prespire* and *perfesser . .* are common 'low colloquial' in America. **1943** *LANE* Map 662 (*Sweated*) 1 inf, **nwCT**, [prispɔɪrd]; 1 inf, **nwRI**, [prəspaɪəd]; 1 inf, **seMA**, [prɪspaɪəd]; 1 inf, **nwVT**, He gets to [prespaerɪn]. **c1960** *Wilson Coll.* **csKY**, *Perspire* becomes [ˌpresˈpaɪr] when some people try to "talk proper." **1965–70** *DARE* (Qu. X56a, . . *Words for sweat*) 20 Infs, **scattered**, Prespire; **GA**28, **MO**37, **NY**29, **WA**1, Prespiring; (Qu. X56b, *Expressions about sweating very heavily*) Inf **MO**8, Heavy prespired; **GA**28, Prespired; **CA**122, Prespiring freely; **MO**2, Prespiring heavily; **OK**11, Really prespiring; (Qu. OO47a, *Talking about horses sweating: "It was a warm day and the horses _____*

[*a lot].*") Infs **DE**3, **MD**43, Prespired. **1968** *DARE* FW Addit **GA**46, He prespired [ˈpresˌpard] sweat. **1970** Tarpley *Blinky* 277 **neTX**, Metathesis in . . the initial syllable of *perspired* produces *prespired,* which is heard more often than the standard form. *Prespired* is typically a non-city pronunciation found with greater frequency among informants over 50. . . Three non-city informants make the distinction that *sweat* is the past tense verb applying to men but *prespired* is the form referring (euphemistically) to women. **1976** Garber *Mountain-ese* 71 **sAppalachians**, *Prespire . .* sweat, perspire—It was so hot everybody started to prespire freely.
B Sense.
To cause (one) to sweat.

1969 *DARE* Tape **CA**158, They try to get you in a full soft and relaxed state in the first place and put you in a steam deal that prespires you.

perspriation See **perspiration**

persuade v esp **S Midl**
To urge, entreat; to plead.

1710 (1941) Byrd *Secret Diary* 169 **VA**, I returned to my chambers again and found above a girl who I persuaded to go with me into my chambers but she would not. **1903** *DN* 2.324 **seMO**, *Persuade. . .* To urge. 'He kept persuadin and persuadin till I told him flat-footed I wouldn't go anyhow.' **1907** *DN* 3.234 **nwAR**, *Persuade. . .* To urge. **1931** Hannum *Thursday April* 83 **wNC**, Thursday April persuaded Joe to buy him a fiddle. Joe fussed and fumed at such fritter-mindedness and said it was a sight of nonsense, but in the end he traded a man from Turkey Cove a lean pig for a fair instrument. **1969** *DARE* (Qu. OO43a, *About pleading with somebody: "She said she was afraid to be alone and _____ [with me to stay]."*) Inf **MO**39, Persuaded; (Qu. OO43b, *About pleading: "I wouldn't have stayed if she hadn't _____ [so hard]."*) Inf **MO**6, Persuaded.

pert- See **pretty A2b**

pertater See **potato A1**

perten See **pearten**

pertetter See **potato A1**

pertick(e)ler, pertic'lar See **particular**

pert night See **pretty near it**

perugy See **pirok**

peruse v [Scots, Engl dial] **Sth, esp SC, GA** *freq among Black speakers* Cf **bruise v 1, prog v 2, project v 2**
Also with *about, around:* To wander, saunter, prowl; to make (one's) way; fig, to be in tolerably good health.

1853 *S. Lit. Messenger* 19.89 **Gulf States**, I asked Nash, what he was doin perusin about the country, and Nash said he was just perusin about the country to see the climit. **1884** Smith *Bill Arp's Scrap Book* 41 **nwGA**, There [=the piney woods] no unfriendly soldier was perusing around and asking for papers. **c1885** in 1981 Woodward *Mary Chesnut's Civil War* 818 **SC** (as of 1865) [Black], "Stay where you are," say the Yanks. "We have nothing for you." And they sadly "peruse" the way. Now they have picked up the word, they use it in season and out. When we met Mrs. Preston's William [=a former slave]—"Where are you going?" "Perusing my way to Columbia." *Ibid* 829, Molly [=a Black woman] when she goes out to walk calls it "perusing the street." **1888** Johnston *Mr. Absalom Billingslea* 295 **GA**, Cynthy Stubblefield ain't a person to traipse and pe-ruse around a-huntin' for 'em [men]. **1893** Shands *MS Speech* 49, *Peruse. . .* Used by negroes to mean *to wander about;* as, "Yistiddy I was perusin' around in de woods." **1922** Gonzales *Black Border* 318 **sSC**, **GA coasts** [Gullah glossary], *Peruse*—to saunter, walk in a leisurely manner, as: 'Da' gal him bin peruse 'long de road en' 'e nebbuh study 'bout nutt'n'.' **1930** Woofter *Black Yeomanry* 54 **seSC**, *Peruse:* to saunter, walk leisurely. **1940** (1968) Haun *Hawk's Done Gone* 102 **eTN**, "How are you all getting along?" "We are perusing about. How are you and Mos?"

peruve n [Prob abbr for **Peruvian**; see quot 1892]
A **mountain ash 1** (here: *Sorbus americana*).

[**1892** (1974) Millspaugh *Amer. Med. Plants* 56–1, *American mountain ash. . .* The chemistry of the bark, so far as distinguished, is so much like that of the wild cherry (*Cerasus serotina,* D.C.) that its medical uses have been substitutive.] **1898** Sudworth *Forest Trees* 70 **TN,** *Pyrus americana.* . . names in use . . Rowan-berry; "Peruve" (mts., Tenn.)

Peruvian n [Prob from the medicinal use of its bark as a substitute for the *Peruvian bark* (cinchona bark, the source of quinine)] Cf **quinine cherry**
=**pin cherry 1.**

1883 Zeigler–Grosscup *Heart of Alleghanies* 58, The most ornamental of the trees of the firs [sic] forests is the Peruvian, with its smooth, slender trunk, and . . brilliant red berries. . . Its bark and berries taste like the kernel of a peach-pit, and are frequently mixed by the mountaineers in their whisky. **1913** Kephart *Highlanders* 54 **sAppalachians,** Beech, birch, buckeye, and chestnut persist to 5,000 feet. Then . . there begins a sub-arctic zone of black spruce, balsam, striped maple, aspen and the "Peruvian" or red cherry. **1917** Kephart in *DN* 4.407 **wNC,** Peruvian . . Wild red cherry.

Peruvian daisy n
A **galinsoga** (here: *Galinsoga quadriradiata*).
1968 Radford et al. *Manual Flora Carolinas* 1131, G[alinsoga] ciliata . . Peruvian Daisy. . . In gardens, fields, barnyards, pastures and waste places; common throughout the mts., local in the peid[mont] and c[oastal] p[lain] of N.C.

perzackly, perzactly See **prezactly**

pesce prétre See **pêche prêtre**

pestel See **pestle**

pestel-tail See **pestle-tail**

pesterous adj [*OED2* 1548 →]
Troublesome, given to pestering.
1806 (1970) Webster *Compendious Dict.* 223, Pesterous. . . Troublesome. [*DARE* Ed: This word was carried over from Webster's English model, though he has simplified the definition he found there: "encumbering, cumbersome, odious."] **1863** *Harper's New Mth. Mag.* 27.718, We have throughout the rich soil regions of the West . . a pesterous weed known as the "wild convolvulus." **1905** *DN* 3.90 **nwAR,** Pesterous. . . Teasing, mischievous. 'He's a pesterous boy.'

pestersome adj Cf **-some**
Troublesome, annoying.
1843 *Amer. Pioneer* 2.439 **NC,** All innocent enquiries, by infants and children . . should be indulged and encouraged, how pestersome soever they may seem. **1906** *DN* 3.150 **nwAR,** Pestersome. . . Bothersome, annoying.

pesticate v
1 To annoy, bother.
1905 *DN* 3.90 **nwAR,** Pesticate. . . 'Don't pesticate me.' Negroism. **1916** *DN* 4.278 **LA, NE,** Pesticate. . . To pester. **1942** McAtee *Dial. Grant Co. IN* 48 (as of 1890s), Pesticate . . pester, bother.
2 also with *about:* To wander idly; to prowl about; hence vbl nouns *pesticating (about).*
1916 *DN* 4.278 **LA, NE,** Pesticate . . to "nose around." "You just quit your pesticating about." **1997** Osgood *Paine Mt. Guidebook* 2 **VT,** One of my favorite ways of enjoying time on Paine Mountain is just to go "pesticating". This is a word you won't find in the dictionaries. I picked it up from my good friend and frequent companion, Douglas "The Iron Man" Wiggett. What pesticating means is simply to walk around with no particular objective in mind but to keep your eyes peeled for interesting sights along the way.

pestle n Usu |'pɛsḷ|; also |'pɛstḷ| Pronc-sp *pestel* Cf **apostle, epistle**
Std sense, var form.
[**1891** *PMLA* 6.166 **WV,** The *t* between *s* and *l* of words like *apostle, epistle,* etc., is sounded.] **1918** *DN* 5.19 **NC,** Pestel-tail, a mule. **1942** in 1944 *ADD* **Sth,** Pestle. . . The [pɛstḷ] in a mortar. **1944** Kenyon–Knott *Pronc. Dict.* 326, Pestle ['pɛsḷ, 'pɛstḷ]. **1999** *DARE* File **cwCA** (as of c1960), I remember being surprised when someone told me that the tool that went with a mortar was not a ['pɛstəl] but a ['pɛsəl].

pestle around v phr esp **VT** Cf **arsle 3**
To putter around, fuss about.
1937 Crane *Let Me Show You VT* 31 **VT,** To "pestle around," a phrase

plucked from the mortar-and-pestle days, was a common expression which I recall from the Black River Valley to describe a hasty, puttering activity. **1954** Forbes *Rainbow* 221 **VT,** This caused Burnap to lose his head— . . accusing wrong people of sheltering him, believing all false stories and refusing to take serious the true ones. He was getting laughed at plenty. . . Burnap was down to Windsor pestling around over that stolen church silver. **1959** *VT Hist.* 27.152, Pestle around. . . To putter around. Rare. **2000** *NADS Letters,* To pestle around. . . I heard it first when I was a child in Chicago. It must have been about 1938 when I was five years old. A friend of my parents . . used it a couple of times. I don't know where he got it. I don't remember exactly what Ivor said, but I remember something like, "Oh, I just like to pestle around." I suspect it had a naughty connotation because nobody would explain to me what Ivor meant. . . Basic Training in the Air Force, Pleasanton, Calif. Nov. 1954–May 55. A man going through basic training with me used it. He was from the Northeast, as is the person you quoted. My friend used to say, "We're just pestlin' around." This, when we were doing make-work.

pestle parsnip n [See quot 1925] **Pacific**
A **biscuit root 1** (here: *Lomatium nudicaule*).
1911 Jepson *Flora CA* 301, P[eucedanum] nudicaule . . Pestle Parsnip. **1925** Jepson *Manual Plants CA* 725, L[omatium] nudicaule . . Pestle Parsnip. . . Peduncles stoutish, arising from the base, conspicuously enlarged at summit (pestle-like). **1951** Abrams *Flora Pacific States* 3.268, Pestle Parsnip or Lomatium.

pestle-tail n Also *pestel-tail;* prob by folk-etym *pencil-tail* [*EDD* pestle-tail "a horse's tail denuded of hair."] esp **NC** Cf **broomtail, bushtail, fuzztail, hardtail 4, shavetail** n
A horse's tail that is relatively hairless; an animal (esp a mule) with such a tail; also fig.
1899 (1912) Green *VA Folk-Speech* 318, Pestle-tail. . . A horse's tail denuded of hair; also, applied to a person of an indifferent kind. "He is a pestle-tail anyhow." **1918** *DN* 5.19 **NC,** Pestel-tail, a mule. **1944** Adams *Western Words* 114, Pestle-tail—A wild horse with a brush or burr tail. **1952** Brown *NC Folkl.* 1.575, Pestle-tail. . . A mule; perhaps because the tail of the mule is trimmed to the shape of a wooden pestle, or small maul. **1970** *DARE* (Qu. K50, *Joking nicknames for mules*) Inf **NC87,** Pestle-tail. **1982** Powers *Cataloochee* 383 **cwNC** (as of a1940), A mule was also called a "pencil tail".

pet n
1 A scar or protuberance on the skin; see quots. **chiefly Sth, S Midl**
1899 (1912) Green *VA Folk-Speech* 318, Pet. . . A pit; a small depression or dent, such as left on the skin by the smallpox: his face is covered with *pets.* **1902** *DN* 2.241 **sIL,** Pet. . . A boil. **1903** *DN* 3.324 **seMO,** Pet. . . Often applied to boils, etc. Something that has to be carefully treated. 'I've got a pet on the back of my neck.' **1907** *DN* 3.234 **nwAR,** Pet. . . A boil or sore. "I have a pet on my thumb and can't cut wood." **1909** *DN* 3.356 **eAL, wGA,** Pet. . . A boil, carbuncle, or the like. **1912** *DN* 3.585 **wIN,** Pet. . . A boil, pimple, mole, or wart. "I have a pet on the leader of my neck." **1942** *AmSp* 17.130 **IN,** Pet (a boil). **c1960** Wilson *Coll.* **csKY,** Pet. . . A humorous reference to a sore or boil. **c1980** *DARE* File **nwNY,** Pet meaning a boil. . . I have heard this used for a cold sore by native of nwNY born 1888.
2 attrib; Of weather: unexpectedly mild. [Scots, Ir dial *pet(day)* a fine day in the midst of a spell of bad weather]
1954 *WELS Suppl.* **swWI,** I believe "weather breeder" is an old expression used by old "Yankees" and Irish around here. Another common expression, also I believe among the older Irish, is a "pet" day. A pet day seems to mean the same as "weather breeder." **1982** *Barrick Coll.* **csPA,** Pet weather—particular good weather early in the spring.

pet v, hence vbl n *petting* Also with *up* **scattered, but chiefly Sth, S Midl** See Map on p. 106
To pamper; to treat gently; to coax, cajole.
1828 Webster *Amer. Dict.,* Pet. . . To treat as a pet . . to indulge. **1899** (1912) Green *VA Folk-Speech* 319, Petted. . . Favoured; indulged. **1965–70** *DARE* (Qu. Z14a, *To give a child its own way or pay too much attention to it:* "Everyone _____ that child.") 51 Infs, **chiefly Sth, S Midl,** Pets; **GA82,** Pets it to death; (Qu. Z14b, *If a child expects to have its own way or have too much attention . . "That child is _____."*) Infs **AL46, GA7, MS1, NC24, SC34,** Petted; **GA44, 72,** Petted to death; **SC19,** Petted too much; **KY21,** Takes petting; (Qu. BB2, *If a person is careful not to put much weight on his injured leg, you might*

say he was _____ that leg) Infs **FL**33, **GA**74, 77, 84, **SC**10, Petting; **NC**41, A-petting. **1970** DARE Tape **VA**69, And sometimes if the teacher scolds 'em an' they cries, I'll take 'em over an' pet 'em an' get 'em straightened out. **1986** Pederson LAGS Concordance, 1 inf, **neLA**, Petted me up—cajoled her to do extra cooking.

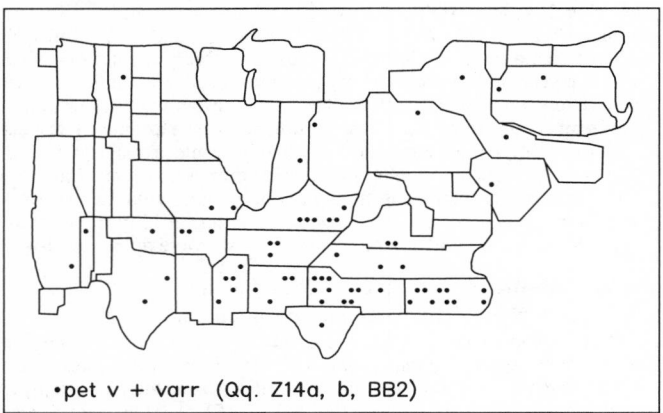

•pet v + varr (Qq. Z14a, b, BB2)

pet- adv See **pretty A2c**

petator, petatur See **potato A1**

Peter n
=**blue Peter 2.**
  1933 [see **Peter grass**].

Peter and Paul n
=**Jack and Jim.**
  1990 DARE File, I learned this [=Jack and Jim] (and have passed it on to children) as "Peter and Paul." The verse is: Two little dicky-birds sitting on a wall / One named Peter, the other named Paul;/ Fly away Peter, fly away Paul [change fingers],/ Come back Peter, come back Paul [change fingers]. Use middle fingers; it's less conspicuous than using index finger.

Peter bird n Also *Peter-Peter, peto (bird)* [Echoic] **chiefly S Midl**
The tufted **titmouse** (*Baeolophus bicolor*).
  1832 Nuttall Manual Ornith. 1.237, The *Peto*, as I may call this bird from one of his characteristic notes, and the Carolina Wren, were my constant and amusing companions during the winter, as I passed through the dreary solitudes of the Southern States. **1883** Nuttall Ornith. Club Bulletin 8.76 **wMD**, *Lophophanes bicolor* is the *Tufted* or *Crested Tit* or *Titmouse*. . . Mr. E.A. Small writes me that in Western Maryland it is called *Peter-bird*. **1910** KY Hist. Soc. Register 8.14, Tufted Titmouse, "Tomtit." Also known as "Peter-peter," in imitation of one of its notes. **1928** Skinner Guide Winter Birds NC 261, The whistled call of the "peto" bird is uttered all through the winter, but becomes more and more noticeable and insistent after the first of February. This "peto" note endlessly repeated over and over again is the song of the Titmice. **1952** Giles 40 Acres 158, Actually the peter-bird is a titmouse, and he has no song except that high, clear, ever-repeating cry, "Peter, peter, peter, peter." We also call him the tomtit. **1953** Randolph–Wilson Down in Holler 271 **swMO**, Peter-bird. . . The tufted titmouse (*Parus bicolor*). Ralph Bates tells me this name is common near Kissee Mills, Mo., where the bird cries *peter-peter-peter* all morning. **1983** MJLF 9.1.50 **ceKY** (as of 1956), Peterbird . . tufted titmouse.

Peter grass n [See quot]
=**ditch grass 2.**
  1933 Torreya 33.81 **NC**, *Ruppia maritima* . . Peter grass, Currituck Sound, N.C.; in allusion to the Peter, Blue Peter, or coot (*Fulica americana*).

Peter mudhole See **Peter's mudhole**

Peter-Peter See **Peter bird**

Peter Rabbit tooth See **rabbit tooth**

Peter's mudhole n Also *Peter ~, Pete's ~, Saint Peter's mudhole* [Perh in allusion to St. Peter] **GA, nFL**

An area of the horizon from which storm clouds typically approach or where threatening clouds are observed.
  1966–68 DARE (Qu. B9, . . Big clouds that roll up high before a rainstorm) Inf **GA**27A, Peter's mudhole—grandfather—where clouds come in from north; (Qu. B11, . . Other kinds of clouds that come often) Inf **GA**4, Peter mudhole—a cloud low near horizon in southwest which brings a storm. [Both Infs Black] **1986** Pederson LAGS Concordance (Heavy rain) 1 inf, **swGA**, (Be)cause it coming out of Peters' [sic] mudhole; (The wind's from the south) 1 inf, **neGA**, Out of Peter's mudhole—wind from south is. **2000** NADS Letters **cnFL**, Used in north central Florida to refer to clouds that come up from a particular direction known to bring rain. Down here it's called "Pete's mudhole." If a cloud comes up from another direction, there's no rain for the specific area. Ibid **swGA**, I recognize the term [=Peter's mudhole] from having grown up in southwest Georgia. The term as I know it refers to the place from which most rainfall comes. Most thunder heads in my area built and moved from southwest to northeast. Peter's mudhole was the southwest horizon from which one could expect lots of thunder in advance of rain. The term is still in general use in the area. Any farmer growing peanuts in the region will readily respond to its use. **2001** Ibid **swGA**, My mother remembers a gentleman who worked in the office with her in southwest Georgia would check St. Peter's Mudhole before planning his weekly golf game. He would look out the southwest window in the corner of the office and if the sky were cloudy he would say that it was raining in St. Peter's Mudhole and, therefore, would be raining on the golf course. If the sky were clear it was safe to plan the golf outing. This was in the 1940's and '50's. Mother says that most of the time his observance accurately predicted the weather as systems moved into the area, obviously, from the southwest.

Peterwort See **Saint-Peter's-wort**

Pete's mudhole See **Peter's mudhole**

peth(y) See **pith**

peticular See **particular**

'petigo See **impetigo**

petition n [Pronc-sp for *partition*]
  1795 Dearborn Columbian Grammar 137, List of Improprieties. . . Petition for Partition (of a house). **1813** (1927) Gerry Diary 108 **OH**, Behind him [=a horse working a treadmill] a petition is placed, and urges him on, when attempting to stop. **1915** DN 4.187 **swVA**, Petition. Variant of *partition*. **1919** DN 5.34 **seKY**, Petition. . . Partition (of a house). **1975** Gould ME Lingo 206, Petition—A wall between two rooms.

peto (bird) See **Peter bird**

Petoskey stone n [Ref to *Petoskey*, Michigan] **MI**
Finely textured limestone derived from coral; a piece of such stone.
  [**1911** Century Dict. Suppl., Petoskeyte. . . A name suggested by A.W. Grabau for limestones formed of fine calcareous muds, derived from coral reefs and deposited in water near their sources: illustrated by strata at Petoskey, Michigan.] **1968–70** DARE (Qu. C25, . . Kinds of stone . . about . . [. . size of a person's head], smooth and hard) Inf **MI**118, Petoskey stone; (Qu. C26, . . Special kinds of stone or rock) Infs **MI**94, 98, 118, 122, Petoskey stone(s). **1969** DARE Tape **MI**110, The [pɪˈtaˑˌski] stones we didn't find up there in Lake Superior because you find them along this shore of Lake Michigan. . . They're almost black and a lighter brown and they polish up very nicely. **1987** Bates–Jackson Gloss. Geol. 496, Petoskey stone. . . A waterworn fragment of Devonian colonial coral from the beach of Lake Michigan at Petoskey, Mich. It is the "state rock" of Michigan. **1998** DARE File, A friend from Michigan gave me a Petoskey stone. It's well polished by the water—like an agate—and has small but visible fossil pieces.

petrale sole n
A **sole** of the Pacific coast (here: *Eopsetta jordani*). Also called **English sole, flounder** n **B**
  1953 Roedel Common Fishes CA 59, Petrale sole. . . Alaska to the Coronado Islands, northern Baja California. **1998** DARE File **cwCA**, One finds petrale sole on the menu in seafood restaurants in the Bay Area, and for sale at upscale supermarkets.

petroleum (oil) n Also *petrol* [OED2 kerosene "Also commonly known as *petroleum*, which properly denotes the crude mineral oil from which kerosene is obtained."] *somewhat old-fash* Kerosene.

[**1872** Schele de Vere *Americanisms* 517, *Petroleum* takes in America the place of "rock oil" in Canada and England, but, when used for domestic purposes, appears almost universally as "kerosene."] **1889** *Scribner's Mag.* 6.192, A vessel of high-boiling petroleum-oil, like the well-known "astral oil." **1968–69** *DARE* (Qu. F45, . . *Fuel that's used in an ordinary lamp*) Inf **NJ**35, Kerosene; petrol; petroleum; **NJ**25, Petroleum [pə'trolim] oil; **OH**54, Coal oil; petroleum [pitroliəm] if you want to be fancy; **PA**70, Carbon oil; petroleum; kerosene. [All Infs old] **1986** Pederson *LAGS Concordance* (Kerosene) 1 inf, **csTX**, Petroleum. [Inf young]

petrushki n Also *patruskie, petrouski, petrushka, petruski* [Russ *petrushka* parsley] **swAK**
Sometimes used as a count noun: A **lovage** (here: *Ligusticum scoticum*).

1954 Winchell *Where Wind* 19 **swAK**, The children thought also of petruski, a small leafy plant that came up just as the snow was melting. They liked it and hunted for it. We teachers liked it too, and ate it raw in fish salad, or a little of it baked or boiled with fish. **1961** *AK Sportsman* Nov 29, Wild plants have been gathered in Alaska for many years to supplement the diet. There is the wild parsley, *petrushki*, which I think far excels the parsley from our gardens. **1977** in 1991 Tabbert *Dict. Alaskan Engl.* 173, We crawled about the fields digging up "patruskie" roots. **1980** in 1991 Tabbert *Dict. Alaskan Engl.* 173, Petruskies are good to eat also (wild parsley). **1985** AK Dept. Fish Game AK *Habitat Management Guide SW* 2.490, Beach celery, commonly call [sic] pushky, is a commonly used green, as is wild parsley, petrouski. Petrouski is a favored condiment used with salmon. **1991** Tabbert *Dict. Alaskan Engl.* 173, In Russian America the Russian word *petrushka* 'parsley' was borrowed by several Alaska Native languages . . , and it is used in English contexts in the Aleutian and Alaska Peninsula/Kodiak areas for this plant.

pettiauger See **periagua**

pettickler See **particular**

petticoat climber n
A **love grass** (here: *Eragrostis spectabilis*).
1950 Gray–Fernald *Manual of Botany* 126, E[ragrostis] spectabilis . . Tumble-grass, Petticoat-climber.

petticoat palm n [See quot 1960]
Either of two **fan palms**: *Washingtonia filifera* or *W. robusta*.
1960 McGeachy *Hdbk. FL Palms* 13, W[ashingtonia] robusta, species most commonly grown in Florida, is distinguished by its heavy growth, 80 to 100 feet when mature and untrimmed and usually covered with shaggy mass of dead leaves, like a huge skirt, giving its nickname "Petticoat Palm." **1980** Little *Audubon Guide N. Amer. Trees W. Region* 325, *California Washingtonia*. . . The largest native palm of the continental United States . . it is also known as "Desert-palm." Another name is "Petticoat-palm" from the shaggy mass of dead leaves hanging against the trunk. **1991** Leonard *Maximum Bob* 38 **FL**, Every morning . . he'd see her in the yard meditating: out there with her tiny dog Pokey, between the pair of Cuban petticoat palms she thought of as two women who'd been turned into trees.

petting See **pet** v

pettyauguh See **periagua**

petty morel n Also *petty morrel(l);* for addit varr see quots [Transf from earlier use in ref to *Solanum nigrum* (*OED2* 1450 →)]
A **spikenard** (here: *Aralia racemosa*).
1769 in 1909 Earle *Child Life* 8 **CT**, After you have dipt ye Child 3 Mornings Give it several times a Day ye following Syrup made of Comfry, Hartshorn, Red Roses, Hog-brake roots, knot-grass, petty-moral roots, sweeten ye Syrup with Melosses. **1778** Carver *Travels N. Amer.* 511, *Spikenard,* vulgarly called in the colonies Petty-Morrell. . . appears to be exactly the same as the Asiatick spikenard. **1795** Winterbotham *Amer. U.S.* 3.397 **NEng**, Pettimorrel, or life of man, Aralia racemosa. **1824** Bigelow *Florula Bostoniensis* 122 **MA**, Pettymorrel. Spikenard . . It is aromatic and in high estimation with people of the country. **1892** *Jrl. Amer. Folkl.* 5.97 **NH**, *Aralia racemosa,* Indian root; life of man; petty morrell. **1959** Gillespie *Compilation Edible Wild Plants WV* 91,

Petty Morrel. . . The rootstocks can be used as a starchy vegetable. **1971** Krochmal *Appalachia Med. Plants* 56.

petunia n *joc*
Used as a nickname for a **skunk**.
1968 *DARE* (Qu. P26, *Names and nicknames . . for a skunk*) Inf **MN**38, Petunia; **NJ**13, Called "Flower" or "Petunia" from Walt Disney. **1990** *DARE* File **cnIN**, As I was leaving my friend's house, she said, "You'll want to go out the front door. Petunia is on the back step." **1997** *Ibid* **seMN** (as of c1980), My college roommate's family referred to all skunks as "Petunia." If her father saw a dead skunk along the highway, he would invariably say, "Oh-oh—somebody hit Petunia." Her brother once wrote that the family dog had "had a run-in with Petunia."

pet up See **pet** v

peva See **pevo**

peverly bird See **peabody bird**

pevo n Also sp *peva* [Pol *piwo*]
Beer.
1968 *DARE* (Qu. DD25, . . *Nicknames . . for beer*) Inf **MI**76, Peva [pivə]—the Polish name, but they call it that; **WI**63, Pevo [pivo].

pewee n[1] Also *peewee*
1 also *pewee flycatcher:* A **flycatcher 1a:** usu of the genus *Contopus,* esp *C. virens,* but also a **phoebe.** [Echoic] Also called **gangling bird** Cf **pewit 1, wood pewee**
1810 Wilson *Amer. Ornith.* 2.78, Pewit Flycatcher. *Muscicapa nunciola*. . . The notes of the Pewee, like those of the Blue-bird, are pleasing. *Ibid* 81, Wood Pewee Flycatcher. *Muscicapa rapax*. . . The *Wood* Pewee . . is among the latest of our summer birds. **1823** James *Acct. of Exped.* 1.371, *Musicapa* [sic] *fusca*—Pewee fly-catcher. Wilson. **1832** Nuttall *Manual Ornith.* 1.286, The *Péwee* is a very expert and cautious flycatcher, and as if aware of the drowsiness of insects in the absence of the sun's broad light, he is on the alert at day-dawn after his prey. *Ibid* 288, Small Pewee. . . This is one of our most common summer birds in this part of New England, arriving from the South about the last week in April, and leaving us . . about the beginning of September, or sometimes a little later. **1839** Audubon *Ornith. Biog.* 5.299, Short-legged Pewee Flycatcher. *Muscicapa Richardsonii*. . . for a while, I thought it so nearly allied to our Common Pewee Flycatcher, as almost to render me indifferent to its notes [etc]. *Ibid* 424, Common Pewee Flycatcher. *Muscicapa fusca*. . is found in every portion of the United States. **1858** Baird *Birds* 189, *Contopus richardsonii,* Baird. Short-legged Pewee. **1894** Riley *Armazindy* 73 **IN**, Dad-burn climate out here [= "out West"] makes / Me homesick all Winter long,/ And when Springtime *comes,* it takes / Two pee-wees to sing one song,—/ One sings 'pee,'/ And the other one 'wee!' **1928** Aldrich *Lantern* 168 **NE**, One could hear . . the pee-wee calling his own name with plaintive patience. **1949** Sprunt–Chamberlain *SC Bird Life* 357, The Pewee arrives in the coastal area by mid-April and in the upper Piedmont about a week later, remaining until the end of October. **1964** Phillips *Birds AZ* 89, Pewees—Genus *Contopus*.
2 A **woodcock** (here: *Philohela minor*).
1888 Trumbull *Names of Birds* 153 **eVA**, The woodcock is known to some in the seaboard counties of Virginia as Night Partridge . . and also as pewee.
3 See quot. Cf **peep** n **3**
1936 *AmSp* 11.316 **Ozarks**, Peewee. . . A young wild turkey chick, still following the hen.
4 =**least sandpiper.**
1956 *AmSp* 31.184 **FL**, Names for birds that are small, or at least small of their kind, are numerous. . . Peewee—Least sandpiper.
5 A **swallow;** see quots. esp **S Midl**
1953 Randolph–Wilson *Down in Holler* 270 **Ozarks**, In some parts of the Ozarks, *peewee* means the bank swallow (*Riparia riparia*) or the rough-winged swallow (*Stelgidopteryx ruficollis*), as well as the species of the flycatcher family, the eastern wood pewee (*Contopus virens*), to which the name properly belongs in the Middle West. **1966–68** *DARE* (Qu. Q20, . . *Kinds of swallows and birds like them*) Inf **GA**18, Pewee; **NC**36, Tree swallow—called pewee. **1967** *Harder Coll.* **cwTN**, Pewee—The rough-winged swallow (*Stelgidopterys rufficollis*).
6 A **bluet 2** (here: *Houstonia caerulea*).
1967–69 *DARE* (Qu. S11, . . *Bluets*) Infs **KY**19, 34, Pewees.

pewee n[2] See **peewee** n[1]

pewee flycatcher See **pewee** n[1] **1**

pewink See **pewit 3**

pewit n

1 also *pewit flycatcher:* A **flycatcher 1a:** usu **wood pewee** or a **phoebe** (here: *Sayornis phoebe*). [Echoic] Cf **pewee** n[1] **1, wood ~**
    1791 Bartram *Travels* [289 *bis*] **PA,** Muscitapa [sic] nunciola, the pewit, or black cap flycatcher. . . M. rapax, the lesser pewit, or brown and greenish flycatcher. **1815** Lit. & Philos. Soc. NY *Trans.* 1.133, When the pewit or phebe, (muscicapa fusca), the first bird of passage which arrives in Philadelphia, in the spring, . . arrives, then pease, beans, and almost every kind of succulent garden seeds may be planted without danger of frost. **1832** Williamson *Hist. ME* 1.143, The Pewit, or Cheeweeh, lives in the summer months about barns and out buildings. **1874** Coues *Birds NW* 241, *Sayornis fuscus* . . Pewit Flycatcher; Phoebe-bird. **1923** Dawson *Birds CA* 2.867, Bridge Pewee. Pewit Flycatcher. Phoebe-bird. **1946** Hausman *Eastern Birds* 403, Acadian Flycatcher . . Other Names—Green Flycatcher . . Green Pewit, Small Pewit.

2 =**spotted sandpiper.**
    1923 U.S. Dept. Ag. *Misc. Circular* 13.64 **PA, RI,** Spotted Sandpiper. . . Vernacular Names. . . pewit.

3 also *pewink:* =**rufous-sided towhee.**
    1956 MA Audubon Soc. *Bulletin* 40.254, Towhee. . . Pewink (Mass., Conn.); Pewit (Maine. Sonic).

pewit flycatcher See **pewit 1**

pewter n, usu attrib
Used as a symbol of something worthless; see quots.
    1911 *DN* 3.542 **NE,** *Dinktum.* . . "The man is not worth a pewter dinktum." [**1939** *AmSp* 14.91 **eTN,** *Not worth a pewter's button.* Worthless or good for nothing. 'He's not worth a pewter's button.'] **1965–70** *DARE* (Qu. U29, *Names or nicknames . . for worthless money*) Infs **MO**37, **WA**11, Pewter; **TX**76, Pewter money; (Qu. HH20c, *Of an idle, worthless person . . "He isn't worth _____."*) Infs **IL**47, **MS**64, **PA**39, 104, 118, 138, Pewter damn; **OK**51, Pewter quarter. **1969** *DARE* FW Addits **KY**42, 44, *Not worth a pewter button*—not worth much.

pewter legs n
A **wood thrush** (here: *Hylocichla mustelina*).
    1897 *Oölogist* 14.27 **NC,** Wood Thrush, *Turdus mustelinus.* Commonly called . . by some "Pewter Legs" is both a summer and winter resident.

pewterwort n [*OED2* 1597 →]
A **horsetail 1** (here: either *Equisetum hyemale* or *E. arvense*).
    1890 *Century Dict.* 4431, Pewterwort. . . The scouring-rush, *Equisetum hyemale:* so called as being used for scouring dishes of pewter or other metal. **1974** (1977) Coon *Useful Plants* 131, *Equisetum arvense*—Scouring rush, . . pewterwort [etc]. [*Ibid* 132, The stems contain silica which once made them useful for scouring pewter, for brightening gun-stocks, and for kitchen scouring.]

peyote n Also *payote* [MexSpan *peyote* < Nahuatl *peyotl*]
A **cactus B1** (here: *Lophophora williamsii*); also the top of this cactus, used as a hallucinogen.   Also called **dry whiskey, dumpling cactus, mescal 3, ~ bean 2, ~ button, whiskey plant, ~ root**
    [**1754** Ortega *Apostolicos Afanes* 18, Porque los mas con el peyote y vino, que bebian, estavan incapazes de valerse de sus piernas, para mantenerse en pié [etc]. [=Since most of them, with the peyote and the wine which they were drinking, were unable to use their legs, to stay on their feet [etc].]] [**1859** (1968) Bartlett *Americanisms* 509, *Whiskey-root.* A plant of the Cactus species possessing intoxicating properties, which is thus described by a correspondent of the New Orleans Picayune: "It is what the Indians call Pie-o-ke. It grows in southern Texas, on the range of sand-hills bordering on the Rio Grande, and in gravelly, sandy soil."] **1885** U.S. Natl. Museum *Proc.* 8.521 **swTX,** It is principally as an intoxicant that the Peyote has become noted, being often added to "tizwin" or other mild fermented native drink to render it more inebriating. **1892** *DN* 1.193 **TX,** *Peyóte:* a plant of the cactus family, sometimes called "dry whiskey," as it is said to produce intoxication when chewed (*Mamillaria fissurata*, Engelm., or *Anhalonium fissuratum*, Lemaire). Probably of Mexican origin. **1920** *Scientific Amer.*

14 Feb 157, The peyote, often popularly miscalled "mescal," through confusion with the maguey cactus from which a fiery intoxicant is prepared, is a species of small cactus widely used for both medicinal and ceremonial purposes by the Indian tribes of the southwestern U.S. **1941** *Torreya* 41.50, *Lophophora williamsii.* . . The source of mescal buttons called by the natives in various localities payote, hikuli, and wokowi. **1945** Mathews *Talking Moon* 81 **neNM,** At same time he couldn't hardly see nothin' 'count too much peyote. **1968** *DARE* (Qu. BB50c, *Remedies for infections*) Inf **CA**65, Peyote poultice. **1997** *DARE* File **NY** (as of c1966), Peyote [peˈoti] makes me puke.

pfannkuchen n Also *pfannekuchen* [Ger]   **chiefly in Ger settlement areas**

1 A pancake, esp one that is served rolled up.
    1907 *Cosmopolitan* Mar 547 **NYC** [Yiddish speaker], Do you sometimes haf *pfannekuchen* for supper? **1910** Hart *Vigilante Girl* 84 **nCA,** He can even cook a German pancake, although he disapproves of it—the real *pfannkuchen*—thick, eggy, slab-like, buttery, delicious, yet not delicate. **1935** Frederick *PA Dutch* 208, *Dutch Egg Pfannkuchen*—4 eggs[,] 2 tablespoons milk[,] 1 teaspoon chopped parsley[,] 2 tablespoons butter[,] ½ teaspoon salt—Beat whites and yolks separately, add milk and parsley, mix, add salt. Melt butter in clean frying pan, pour in the batter, and when cooked, sprinkle with parsley. Serve rolled and hot. **1949** (1986) Leonard *Jewish Cookery* 125, *Pfannkuchen* (German Egg Rolls)—These have a definite German origin but have been adopted widely for their versatility. The most popular variation among Jewish cooks is what is perhaps better known as *blintzes* when cheese filled. . . Cut into 4 or 6 wedges, dust with confectioners' sugar and roll up each from outer edges. **1950** *WELS* (*Other names for pancakes in your neighborhood*) 1 inf, **ceWI,** Flapjacks, griddle cakes, "pfannkuchen."

2 also *Berliner pfannkuchen:* A doughnut; spec: a **Berliner.**
    1920 Kander *Settlement Cook Book* 365 **seWI,** Berliner Pfann Kuchen—Make a Kuchen Dough, . . cut into rounds with biscuit cutter. Place a piece of jelly or preserves in the center of one-half of them, . . cover with the other half. . . let raise very light and fry in deep fat until brown. . . Sprinkle with powdered sugar. **1935** Frederick *PA Dutch* 211, *Pfannkuchen.* . . Cut out [a rich yeast dough] with round cookie cutter. Place a half teaspoon of the jelly in the center of half of them and then lay the others on top. . . Fry until brown and double their size. **1967–68** *DARE* (Qu. H29, *A round cake, cooked in deep fat, with jelly inside*) Inf **WI**62, Berliner pfannkuchen; **IA**13, Pfannkuchen [fɑˈnkuken]. **1973** Allen *LAUM* 1.282, *Doughnut.* . . *Pfannkuchen*, reported by a southern Minnesota [sic] of New York and New Jersey parentage, here has a German dialect meaning; it originally referred to pancakes.

pfeffernuss n Also *pefferniss;* for addit varr see quots [Ger *pfeffernuss*, literally "peppernut," pl *pfeffernüsse;* PaGer *pefferniss*, pl *peffernissen*]   **chiefly in Ger settlement areas** Cf **peppernut**
A small, hard, highly spiced cookie.
    1920 Kander *Settlement Cook Book* 429 **seWI,** Cookies . . *Pfeffernuesse.* [Recipe includes syrup, molasses, butter or fat, brown sugar, flour, soda, cinnamon, cloves, citron, almonds, and lemon, rind and juice.] **1938** [see **peppernut**]. **1948** *AmSp* 23.107 **swIL,** German names having to do with foods and cooking are . . numerous. . . The following . . are frequently heard: *blitz kuchen* . . *pfeffernüsse* cookies . . *schwartemagen.* **1948** Hutchison *PA Du. Cook Book* 167, *Peffer Niss* (Pepper Nuts). [Recipe includes brown sugar, butter, eggs, flour, baking powder, cinnamon, cloves, and cardamom seeds.] **1961** Sackett-Koch *KS Folkl.* 232, *Pfeffernüsse*—[Recipe includes dark syrup or molasses, pepper, nutmeg, ginger, sugar, black coffee, lard, leavening, and other spices.] . . These last indefinitely. (This recipe is an old German recipe that was brought to America with our earliest pioneers. No Christmas is complete without them.) **1981** Hachten *Flavor WI* 299, Cookies. . . *Pfeffernüsse.* [Recipe includes lard, molasses, brown sugar, soda, flour, nutmeg, cinnamon, cloves, allspice, salt, freshly ground pepper, anise, and almonds.] **1999** *DARE* File **KS,** I didn't make them, but Grandma used to make Pfeffernuß [pfefəˈnɪs].

p.g. adj [Initialism for *pregnant*]   **chiefly west of Missip R, N Cent** See Map   *esp freq among mid-aged and young speakers*
    1965–70 *DARE* (Qu. AA28, . . *Joking or sly expressions . . women use to say that another is going to have a baby . . "She['s] _____."*) 74 Infs, **chiefly west of Missip R, N Cent,** P.g. [Of all Infs responding to the question, 36% were mid-aged or young; of those giving this response, 63% were mid-aged or young.] **1981** Spears *Slang & Euphem.* 296, *P.G.* . . "pregnant." . . U.S. colloquial euphemism, 1900s. **1988**

Hamilton *Book of Ruth* 199 **nIL,** "We're going to have a little baby." . . Then he told the waitress his wife was PG. **1998** *DARE* File **cwCA** (as of c1965), When I was in high school, if a girl got pregnant it was whispered that she was "p.g."

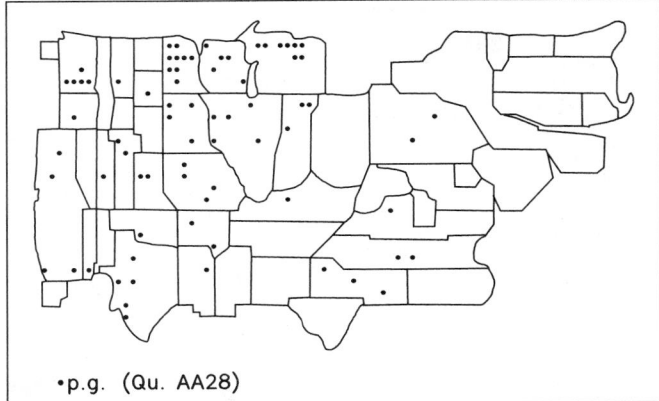

•p.g. (Qu. AA28)

phainopepla n
Std: a passerine bird *(Phainopepla nitens)* of the Desert Southwest. Also called **flycatcher 1e, flysnapper, Indian blackbird, Spanish mockingbird**

phalarope n
Std: a bird of the genus *Phalaropus.* Also called **harbor goose, sea ~ 1, whalebird.** For other names of var spp see **Jersey goose, mackerel ~, northern phalarope, red ~, Wilson's ~**

phantod See **fantod**

phantom orchid n Also *phantom orchis* [See quot 1934]
A saprophytic white orchid *(Cephalanthera austiniae)* of the western US. Also called **ghostflower 2, snow orchid**
1897 Parsons *Wild Flowers CA* 388, In Northern California and Oregon is occasionally found a rare and curious plant—the "phantom orchis," *Cephalanthera Oregana.* **1934** Haskin *Wild Flowers Pacific Coast* 65, Phantom Orchid. . In color the whole plant is a pure waxy white, except that within the throat of the flower there is a lovely spot of golden yellow. **1994** Guterson *Snow Falling* 153 **nwWA,** She knew where lady fern grew and phantom orchids and warted giant puffballs.

pharaoh n Also *ferro, pharaoh bug* [With ref to the plague of locusts afflicting Pharaoh's Egypt; cf Exodus 10:12–19]
chiefly sAppalachians
=locust 3 or **4.**
1913 Kephart *Highlanders* 295 **sAppalachians,** In some places . . the locust insect is known as a ferro (Pharaoh?) **1944** *PADS* 2.19 **sAppalachians,** Ferro. . . The locust. Variant of *Pharaoh?* **1966–70** *DARE* (Qu. R6, . . *Names . . for grasshoppers*) Inf **AR**41, Pharaoh bugs; (Qu. R8, . . *Kinds of creatures that make a clicking or shrilling or chirping kind of sound*) Inf **IL**126, Pharaoh bugs; [**KY**21, Bible bug—billions of 'em every 8–10 years, holler "Pharaoh" over and over]. **1975** *Appalachian Jrl.* 2.155 **wNC,** The most unusual word of all is *Pharaohs* for locusts. The explanation is that if one listens very carefully he will hear the locusts saying "Pharoah, Pharoah, let my people go, let my people go."

Pharaoh for meddlers n Also *faro for meddlers*
=layover(s) to catch meddlers.
1935 *AmSp* 10.282, Children and other inquisitive persons asking 'What is that?' are often silenced with the answer, 'Oh it's a so-and-so for meddlers.' And the so-and-so is called variously either a *laro,* a *lareo,* a *faro,* a *Pharaoh,* or a *marrow.*

phase, phaze See **faze**

Ph.D., get one's v phr For addit varr see quots [*Ph.D.* punning initialism for *petticoat hangs down*] *esp freq among women*
Cf **cotton 4**
See quots.

1966–68 *DARE* (Qu. W24a, . . *Expressions . . to warn a woman slyly that her slip is showing*) Infs **MN**6, **ND**2, **TN**3, 24, **TX**10, Got your Ph.D.; **IN**34, **MI**51, Ph.D.; **MI**78, She has a degree, a Ph.D.; [**SD**3, Got your P.D.; **WI**50, S.H.D. = slip hangs down]. [9 of 10 Infs White and female, 8 old.] **1985** *DARE* File **seWI,** Ph.D. meaning petticoat hanging down. Back when dresses were worn and before *slips* took over from the word, petticoat, we would warn a classmate, "You're a Ph.D. today." [Writer female]

pheasant n [Transf from its application to the old-world game bird *Phasianus colchicus* **(ring-necked pheasant),** which was not successfully introduced into the US until the end of the 19th cent]
1 A grouse, as:
a =**ruffed grouse.** [Note: Some of these quots may refer instead to *Phasianus colchicus* or to other senses below.] **chiefly Midl, esp PA, sAppalachians** Cf **partridge B2**
1625 Morrell *New Engl.* 15, The Fowles that in those Bayes and Harbours feede,/. . . / Are Swans and Geese, Herne, Pheasants, Duck & Crane. **1637** (1967) Morton *New English Canaan* 194, A kinde of fowles which are commonly called Pheisants, but whether they be pheysants or no, I will not take upon mee to determine. **1698** (1848) Thomas *Hist. & Geog. Acct.* 13 **PA,** There are an Infinite Number of Sea and Land Fowl, of most sorts. viz. *Swans . . Turkies . . Pheasants, Partridges* [etc]. **1791** Bartram *Travels* 290, T[etrao] tympanus, the pheasant of Pennsylvania. **1843** (1916) Hall *New Purchase* 306 **IN,** "Whi-i-i-irr!—what's that?" "A pheasant!" **1888** Trumbull *Names of Birds* 146, In the latter state [=Pennsylvania] and throughout the bird's southern range (to Georgia and Arkansas), it is the *Pheasant,* though in Virginia and the Carolinas we sometimes hear it referred to as the *Mountain Pheasant.* **1923** U.S. Dept. Ag. *Farmers' Bulletin* 1375.39 **WV,** *Open seasons:* . . Ruffed grouse (pheasant). **1930** Shoemaker *1300 Words* 46 **cPA Mts** (as of c1900), *Pheasant*—General term for the ruffed grouse, (Bonasa Umbellus), in Central Pennsylvania; called "partridge" further North in state. **1943** Peattie *Great Smokies* 251, On the side of Roan Mountain, near the central part of the Tennessee line, . . grouse aplenty feed on the mast. Grouse are called pheasant by the natives. **1955** MA Audubon Soc. *Bulletin* 39.443, *Ruffed Grouse.* . . Pheasant (Mass. Formerly the terms Partridge (north and east) and Pheasant (mountains and south) had rather definite distribution and stability. Since introduction of the Ring-necked Pheasant, the latter term is going out of use for the Ruffed Grouse.) **1982** Powers *Cataloochee* 475 **cwNC,** Grouse, known locally as pheasant, are also uncommonly good to eat.
b Any of var other American grouse; see quots.
1805 (1904) Lewis *Orig. Jrls. Lewis & Clark Exped.* 2.295, As I passed these mountains I saw a flock of the black or dark brown phesants. . . this bird is fully a third larger than the common phesant of the Atlantic states. **1806** (1905) *Ibid* 4.128, The large black and white pheasant is peculiar to that portion of the Rocky Mountain watered by the Columbia river. **1850** Houstoun *Hesperos* 1.245 *(DAE),* Another bird which our driver called a pheasant, but which, on making inquiry, we discovered to be a fowl possessed of much rarer qualities—namely the *prairie hen.* **1905** Townsend *Birds Essex Co. MA* 203, *Tympanuchus cupido.* . . Heath Hen; "Pheasant." Nuttall speaks of its being common on the "ancient bushy site of the city of Boston." **1955** MA Audubon Soc. *Bulletin* 39.443 **MA,** Heath hen. . . Pheasant, Prairie Hen.
2 See **pheasant duck 1.**
3 See **pheasant duck 2.**

pheasant berry n
A **partridgeberry 1** (here: *Mitchella procumbens*).
1933 *Torreya* 33.84 **VA,** *Mitchella repens* . . Pheasant berry, Fairfax County, Va.

pheasant duck n **chiefly Atlantic, esp N Atl**
1 also *pheasant, pheasant-tailed duck:* =**pintail 1.** [Because its long tail feathers resemble those of a pheasant]
1815 Lit. & Philos. Soc. NY *Trans.* 1.134, Latham says, that the American widgeon, (anas Americana,) or pheasant duck, as it is called at New-York, has been domesticated; its flesh is most excellent. **1888** Trumbull *Names of Birds* 38 **CT,** To the older gunners about Milford, this [=the pintail duck] is the *pheasant duck* or *pheasant.* **1925** (1928) Forbush *Birds MA* 1.222, American Pintail . . sprig tail; pheasant duck [etc]. **1955** *AmSp* 30.182, *Pheasant-tailed duck* (Calif.) and *pheasant duck* (Mass., Conn.) have reference to the extended, pointed tail of the ring-necked pheasant, as does the second term for the old squaw in

North Carolina. **1982** Elman *Hunter's Field Guide* 156, *Pintail.* . . Common & regional names . . pheasant-duck, water pheasant [etc].

2 also *pheasant (sheldrake):* **=merganser.**

1888 Trumbull *Names of Birds* 65 **ME,** Some of the older gunners there [=Milbridge] distinguish [the American Merganser] as the *pheasant. Ibid* 69 **MD,** At Crisfield, Md., [the red-breasted merganser is called] *pheasant. Ibid* 74 **NC,** At Morehead, N.C., [the hooded merganser is called] *pheasant duck,* and more commonly *pheasant.* **1923** U.S. Dept. Ag. *Misc. Circular* 13.6, *Red-breasted Merganser.* . . pheasant (Md.); pheasant sheldrake (Mass.) **1955** MA Audubon Soc. *Bulletin* 39.379, *American Merganser.* . . Pheasant (Maine. As a conspicuously colored bird.); Pheasant Sheldrake (Mass.) *Ibid,* Red-breasted *Merganser.* . . Pheasant Sheldrake . . (Mass.) **1968** *DARE* (Qu. Q5, . . *Kinds of wild ducks*) Inf **MD45,** Pheasant—kind of duck—dives for minnows.

3 **=old-squaw.**

1955 [see **1** above].

pheasant hawk n
=Cooper's hawk.

1890 Warren *Birds PA* 122, *Cooper's Hawk.* . . This much detested and commonly called "Long-tailed Chicken or Pheasant Hawk," is a common native.

pheasant sheldrake See **pheasant duck 2**

pheasant-tailed duck See **pheasant duck 1**

pheese, pheeze See **feeze**

phenagle See **finagle**

Philadelphia pepper pot (soup) See **pepper pot (soup)**

philippine v Cf **philopena 1a, philopene**

1968 *DARE* (Qu. II8, *When one person wants to share or divide something with another person* . . *"Let's _____ [on that]."*) Inf **NY105,** Philippine.

philopena n Also *filipino, fillipeen(er), phillerpener, phillipeener, phillipoenae, phillip(p)ina, philopaene, philopoena* [Although the custom is known by var similar names throughout northern Europe (cf Fr, Du *philippine,* Norw *filipine,* Ger *Vielliebchen, Phillipp(in)chen*), neither the ultimate origin nor the immediate source of the US borrowing is clear.]

1a A playful contest in which two people, by sharing the kernels of a double-kerneled nut, agree that whichever of the two fulfills a certain condition (as by being the first to say "Philopena!" on their next meeting) is entitled to a present from the other; such a present; a double-kerneled nut; hence v phr *eat a philopena* to engage in this game by eating one kernel of a double-kerneled nut.

1839 (1969) Briggs *Advent. Franco* 2.143, There would be [at the party]. . . scandal by the wholesale, besides sugar kisses, and phillipinas. **1848** Bartlett *Americanisms* 138, *Fillipeen* or *Phillipina.* . . There is a custom common in the Northern States at dinner or evening parties when almonds or other nuts are eaten, to reserve such as are double or contain two kernels, which are called *fillipeens.* If found by a lady, she give sone [sic] of the kernels to a gentleman, when both eat their respective kernels. When the parties again meet, each strives to be the first to exclaim, *Fillipeen!* for by so doing he or she is entitled to a present from the other. Oftentimes the most ingenious methods are resorted to by both ladies and gentlemen to surprise each other with the sudden exclamation of this mysterious word, which is to bring forth a forfeit. **1854** 'M. Harland' *Alone* ix *(DAE),* Will you eat a philopoena with me? **1857** Gunn *Physiology Boarding-Houses* 139, We remember her rashly volunteering a $100 wedding-dress . . in order to get off from paying a forfeit *philopoena.* **1859** (1931) DeLong *Jrls.* 10.48 **NY,** Eat and win a phillipoenae. **1860** *Knickerbocker* 56.365, Nella was hunting among the almonds to find a phillipeener. **1899** Champlin–Bostwick *Young Folks' Games* 677, *Philopena,* a game played by two persons with nuts, usually almonds. When a person finds one of these with two kernels in it, he may ask any one he chooses to eat a philopena with him. If the one asked consents, each eats one of the kernels, and whoever says the word "Philopena" first on meeting the other after a certain time (usually after the day on which the philopena is eaten) is entitled to a present from the other. A more common way of eating a philopena is called Give and

Take. If either of the players takes any object whatever from the other's hands, the giver is entitled to say "Philopena" and receive a present. This arrangement goes into force as soon as the philopena is eaten. **1912** Green *VA Folk-Speech* 319, *Philopena.* . . A nut with a double kearnel [sic].

b attrib: Won in a **philopena 1a.**

1847 (1946) Hammond *Remembrance Amherst* 59 **RI,** Received a beautiful lamp-mat as a philopæne present. **1857** *Knickerbocker* 49.180, The man . . settles down into quiet devotion, and the unostentatious charity of drives, bouquets, small fillipeener jewelry. **1893** *Harper's New Mth. Mag.* 86.609, She put on her ring again, using the philopena circlet as a guard.

c also attrib; Fig: a twin.

1890 *Harper's New Mth. Mag.* 80.715, Sisters is real lux'ries . . an' when you come to a twin, a kinder phillerpener sister, why, it's like a piece o' your own self. **1894** Twain *Pudd'nhead Wilson* 151, Boys, I move that he keeps still and lets this human philopena snip you out a speech.

d in comb *French philopena:* See quot.

1909 *DN* 3.357 **eAL, wGA,** *Philopena.* . . A variation of the regular game is called *French philopena,* in which one of the participants eats a bit of candy or a kernel of a nut from the other's mouth.

2 in phr *eat a filipino:* See quot.

1968 *DARE* (Qu. KK35, *When someone wants to pass on a compliment about you, in exchange for one about himself* . . *"I have a _____ for you."*) Inf **NJ20,** "Eat a filipino [fɪlɪpino] with you." Hook arms, act as if eating, and then swap compliments.

philopene v Cf **philippine**
To engage in the game of **philopena 1a** with.

1874 (1969) Coffin *Caleb Krinkle* 172 **MA,** Then they had apples and nuts, and philopened each other.

philopoena See **philopena**

phipsewa, phipsissiway See **pipsissewa**

phiz n Also *fiz(z), fizz(i)og, phiziog, phizog(omy), phizz, physcognamy, physmahogany* [Varr of *physiognomy*] **chiefly Nth, N Midl** See Map *somewhat old-fash*
The face; rarely, the mouth.

1774 in 1832 Sparks *Life Morris* 21 **NYC,** Grave phizes are grinned out of countenance. **1838** Kettell *Yankee Notions* 240, I [=a mosquito] have scratched the phizzes of all you see in the street here. **1858** Hammett *Piney Woods Tavern* 307, A kinder vacant smile beamin' on her smoke-dried old phizog. **1913** in 1983 Truman *Dear Bess* 115 **MO,** I've had a strenuous day you know, almost saw an osteopath, got my phiz snapped [=photographed], and did a half-day's real work. **1914** *DN* 4.125, My, what a dirty phiz! **1942** Berrey–Van den Bark *Amer. Slang* 121.25, *Face.* . . fiz, fizz. **1950** *WELS* **WI** (*Joking or uncomplimentary terms for a person's face*) 4 Infs, Fiz; 4 Infs, Fizzog; 1 Inf, Fizziog. **1965–70** *DARE* (Qu. X29) 38 Infs, **Nth, N Midl,** Phiz(og); **ME5,** Homely fizziog; **NY105,** Phiziog; **NY152,** Phizogomy; **RI15,** Physcognamy; **CT15,** Physmahogany; (Qu. X9, *Joking or uncomplimentary words for a person's mouth* . . *"I wish he'd shut his _____."*) Inf **WY2,** Phizog. [34 of 44 Infs old, 10 mid-aged] **1970** Major *Dict. Afro-Amer. Slang* 90 (as of 1940s), *Phiz* . . the face.

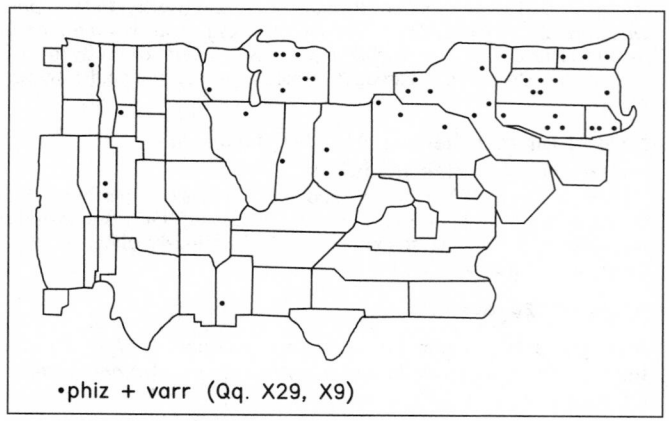

•phiz + varr (Qq. X29, X9)

phlegm n Usu |flɛm|; also |flʌm, flɪm, flem|; esp Sth, S Midl |flim| Pronc-spp *flame, phleem* [Proncs of the type [flim] represent an old var that survived in std Engl speech into the 18th cent.]
Std sense, var forms.

1835 Longstreet *GA Scenes* 211, It put him in a mighty fine sweat, and loosened all the *phleem,* and opened all his head. **1899** (1912) Green *VA Folk-Speech* 319, Phleem. . . A thick ropy matter secreted in the digestive and breathing passages, and thrown off by coughing or vomiting; bronchial mucus. **1903** *DN* 2.324 seMO, *Phlegm.* . . Pronounced phleem [flim]. **1906** *DN* 3.150 nwAR, *Phlegm.* . . Pronounced by the older generation [flim]. **1909** *DN* 3.357 eAL, wGA, *Phleem.* . . Phlegm. **1915** *DN* 4.187 swVA, *Phlegm* [flim]. **1936** *AmSp* 11.15 eTX, [fli:m] is the only pronunciation of *phlegm* that I have heard in East Texas. **1942** Hall *Smoky Mt. Speech* 21 wNC, eTN, *Phlegm* [flim] (usually; but in one area [flem] was said to be more common). **1952** Brown *NC Folkl.* 1.575, *Phlegm* [flim]. . . Central and east. **1966** *DARE* FW Addit OK25, *Phlegm*—[flim]. **1967–68** *DARE* (Qu. X16, . . *Mucus*) Inf AR52, Phlegm [flɛm]; NY81, Phlegm [flʌm]; TN24, Phlegm [flim]. **1976** Ryland *Richmond Co. VA* 371, *Flame*—phlegm. **1981** Pederson *LAGS Basic Materials,* 1 inf, cnMS, Phlegm [flɪ˞iˑm].

phlox n
Std: a plant of the genus *Phlox.* Also called **sweet William, wild ~.** For other names of var spp see **creeping phlox, Frenchman's buttons, mayflower 6, meadow phlox, moss ~, moss pink 1, mountain phlox 1, prairie ~, thrift**

phlug See **flug**

phoby cat See **hydrophobia skunk**

phoebe n
Std: a bird of the genus *Sayornis,* esp *S. phoebe* of the eastern US. For other names of *S. phoebe* see **barn pewee, bean bird, bridge pewee, dusky flycatcher, flycatcher 1a, house pewee, moss bird 3, pewee n¹ 1, pewit 1, preacher bird 1, spider ~, town ~, tickbird, water pewit, ~ pewee**

phthisic n Also with *the* Usu |ˈtɪzɪk|; for addit varr see quots Pronc-spp *tissic(k), tizic, tizzic(k), tizzy* [*OED2* phthisic 1340 →; "Now *rare*"]
Any of var conditions producing coughing or difficulty in breathing, esp asthma; rarely used as the name of an imaginary illness; hence adj *phthisicky,* pronc-spp *tiz(z)icky,* affected by such a condition; asthmatic, wheezy.

1806 (1970) Webster *Compendious Dict.* 224, Phthisic. . . a consumption, a shortness of breath. [*DARE* Ed: This entry was carried over from Webster's English model.] **1828** Webster *Amer. Dict.,* Phthisic. . . *tiz'zic.* A consumption. [Webster: *Little used.*] **1835** Crockett *Account* 15, We all got seated, and moved slowly off; the engine wheezing as if she had the tizzick. **1897** *Outing* 29.594, Diminutive and phthisicky mules, wheezing for breath. **1914** *DN* 4.81 ME, nNH, *Tizzicky.* . . Asthmatic, wheezy. **1929** *AmSp* 5.122 ME, A person had a "rising in the ear," the "phthisic" (asthma) or "salt rheum." **1942** Hall *Smoky Mt. Speech* 14 wNC, eTN, Phthisic [ˈtɪzɪk]. **1946** *PADS* 6.23 ceNC (as of 1900–05), *Phthisic.* . . Croup. **1947** (1964) Randolph *Ozark Superstitions* 94, Charley Cummins, veteran newspaperman of Springfield, Missouri, always called a severe cold a *tissic*—that's his own spelling. **1949** Arnow *Hunter's Horn* 23 KY, That ole tizic'ull leave you sure as shooten. **1954** Harder *Coll.* cwTN, *Tissick.* . . A cold, an infection of the throat or lungs. **c1960** Wilson *Coll.* csKY, *Phthisic* (or *tizzick*). Croup. . . Tissick. . . Phthisic. **1967–68** *DARE* (Qu. BB9, *A sickness in which you have a severe cough and difficult breathing*) Inf NJ39, Phthisic [tɪsɪk]; [(Qu. BB10, . . *Names or nicknames . . for tuberculosis*) Inf TX31, Phthisis [tɪsɛs]; CA65, Tísica [ˈtizɪkə]—Spanish;] (Qu. BB11, . . *A deep cough that you can't seem to get rid of*) Inf AL33, Phthisic [tɪzɪk]; (Qu. BB28, *Joking names . . for imaginary diseases: "He must have the _____."*) Inf MI65, Phthisic [tɪzɪk]. [All Infs old] **1967** *DARE* FW Addit KY34, "Take the tizzy": a wheezy cough—common childhood ailment. (Used in conversation.) **1973** *DARE* File swPA, *Tizicky.* . . Having a scratching sensation in the throat. **1975** Gould *ME Lingo* 292, *Tizzic*—Included here because somebody who didn't know how to spell it suggested it was a "good Maine word." Phthisic is in any good dictionary. Its peculiar orthography made it a

favorite in old-time spelling bees, and until spelling bees went out of style almost all Mainers could spell *phthisic.* **1982** Slone *How We Talked* 113 eKY (as of c1950), *Tissic*—Asthma. **1990** Cavender *Folk Med. Lexicon* 28 sAppalachians, *Phthisic*—[sometimes pronounced "tizzy"] a. congested lungs, wheezy breathing. b. asthma.

phumpher v [Yiddish *fonfen*]
To speak through the nose; to mumble.

1987 *Capital Times* (Madison WI) 24 July PM sec 35, "Hooten?" he says. . . "You are Hooten?" Lauren Hutton laughs merrily. "I am," she says. "I'm Hooten. I am. Nice to meet you. How do you do?" The guy phumphers out a fawning jumble of words, all to the effect of how stunningly lovely she is. [*DARE* Ed: According to the by-line, this story orig appeared in the *San Francisco Examiner.*] **1987** *DARE* File NYC (as of 1955), When I was growing up my mother would tell me "Don't phumpher!" or "Stop phumphering!" if I mumbled a reply which she couldn't understand.

phyce See **feist** n

physcognamy See **phiz**

physic root n
=**culver's root.**

1736 in 1894 *Documents Colonial & Post-Revol. Hist. NJ* 11.446, A Root call'd Physick Root, filarie or five leaf'd Physick. **1830** Rafinesque *Med. Flora* 2.20, *Leptandra purpurea.* Names. . . Vulgar . . Physic-root, Black-root [etc]. **1930** Sievers *Amer. Med. Plants* 26, *Culver's-physic.* . . tall veronica, physic-root, whorlywort.

physmahogany See **phiz**

P.I. n Also *pea-eye* [See quot 1975] ME
A Prince Edward Islander; broadly, someone from any of the Canadian Maritime Provinces.

1902 in 1924 Gray *Songs ME Lumberjacks* 50, Just look at that homespun / the lad is a-wearing! Is n't that enough to tell you / that he's a P.I.? [*Ibid* 51, On your little P.I./ a man can get drunk / And then sober up / under the shade of a tree.] **1902** Day *Pine Tree Ballads* 80 ME, [Footnote:] "P.I." is colloquial term for Prince Edward Islander. **1907** *DN* 3.248 eME, *P.I.* [pi aɪ]. . . A person from Prince Edward's Island (P.E.I.) or from Nova Scotia. "The P.I.'s come from Prince Edward's Island and Nova Scotia." An epithet of uncomplimentary connotation. **1914** *DN* 4.77 ME, nNH, *P.I.* . . A Prince Edward's Islander. **1966** *DARE* (Qu. HH28, *Names and nicknames . . for people of foreign background*) Infs ME9, 13, P.I.'s—Prince Edward Islander(s). **1966** *DARE* FW Addit ME14, P.I.'s—people from Down East (Canadian Provinces—New Brunswick, Nova Scotia). Originally for Prince Edward Islanders. **1975** Gould *ME Lingo* 204, *Pea-Eye*—This could just as well be entered as *P-I;* it derives from the initials of Prince Edward Island and it is the general term in the Maine woods for a *chopper* who originated in the Maritime Provinces, as distinguished from the French-speaking *Canuck.* . . Along the coast . . only the Prince Edward Islander was a *P-I.* The New Brunswicker was a *Herring-choker;* and the Nova Scotian was a *Bluenose.*

pia n Also sp *pya* [Haw *pia*] HI
The Polynesian arrowroot (*Tacca leontopetaloides*).

1852 *De Bow's Rev.* 13.462, The root of the pia, beaten to a pulp and washed repeatedly, and dried in the sun, forms a very nutritive substance, similar to arrow-root, and may in time become an imported article of commerce. **1858** Hogg *Vegetable Kingdom* 765 HI, *T[acca] oceanica,* a native of the Sandwich Islands, yields a similar product [= arrowroot], and is there called pya. **1888** Hillebrand *Flora Hawaiian Is.* 438, The Arrowroot-plant, "Pia", is found wild in the open woods of the lower regions and on grassy plains, principally on the island of Kauai. **1928** Pan-Pacific Research Inst. *Jrl.* 3.2.5 HI, Tacca, arrowroot or pia; a source of starch. **1933** Bryan *Hawaiian Nature* 83, The arrowroot, known as pia . . was formerly raised in small patches in open woodland. **1948** Neal *In Gardens* HI 193, Polynesian arrowroot or pia, the tubers of which are good food, high in starch, was probably introduced in ancient times . . by people migrating from southeastern Asia. **1976** Bailey–Bailey *Hortus Third* 1094, *Pia.* . . Once widely grown . . for its starchy tubers.

pial n, v Also *peal* [AmSpan *pialar, pealar* to lasso by the feet] West Cf **mangana**

A throw with a lasso, intended to catch an animal by its hind feet; to make such a throw.

1929 Dobie *Vaquero* 263 **West,** The *pial* is much more useful [as a method of roping than the *mangana*]. To *pial* an animal is to catch it by the hind feet. This throw is commonly used for "stretching out" a "cow critter"—never a horse—that has been roped around the head or neck. When adroitly cast, the loop turns so as to form a figure 8, and one hind foot is caught in one half of the figure and the other hind foot in the other half. Thus "twined," an animal cannot possibly kick itself loose if the rope is held at all tightly. **1944** Adams *Western Words* 113, *Peal* (pay-ahl´). . . To rope an animal by the hind foot.

pi-ank n [Prob echoic]
Either the **red-tailed hawk** or **Harlan's hawk**.

1916 *Times–Picayune* (New Orleans LA) 9 Apr mag sec 1, *Red-tailed Hawk*. . . "Pi-ank." . . *Harlan Hawk*. . . "Pi-ank."

piano n Usu |piˈæno, -ə|; also esp Sth, S Midl, NEast |paɪˈænə, piˈænɪ, piˈjænɚ| Pronc-spp *pee-anna, pianner, pian(n)y, pie-anna;* for addit pronc and sp varr see quots Cf Intro "Language Changes" IV.1.c, **-er 1, -y**
A Forms.

1843 (1916) Hall *New Purchase* 261 **IN,** That powerful pianne tune. *Ibid* 404, The body what could rattle the pianny. **1862** (1864) Browne *Artemus Ward Book* 141 **NEng,** She has just sot down to the piany. **1891** (1967) Freeman *New Engl. Nun* 95, She had a pianner. **1895** *DN* 1.375 **seKY, eTN, wNC,** *Pianer.* **1901** Harben *Westerfelt* 6 **nGA,** They say she's l'arned to play 'Dixie' on a pyanner. **1903** *DN* 2.324 **seMO,** *Piano* . . [piˈænɪ] or [paɪˈænɪ]. . . The usual pronunciation among old-fashioned people. **1906** *DN* 3.150 **nwAR,** *Piano*. . . Often pronounced [paɪˈænə]. **1928** Aldrich *Lantern* 187 **NE,** What you alwa's wishin' for a pianny for when you know you can't have it? **1936** *AmSp* 11.161 **eTX** [Black], In addition to the usual sound of [ə] in the final syllable, some . . words . . have [ɚ] in less literate speech. . . *piano*. **1949** Hedgecock *Gone Are the Days* 59 **swMO,** Speaking of Teague's piano reminds me of what a time we used to have pronouncing the word. We always pronounced it either *pee-anna* or *pie-anna*, and never with the *i* short and the long *o* sound at the end. **1967–68** *DARE* FW Addit **AR,** [ˈpjænə]; **GA25,** [ˈpiˌjænɚ]; **PA,** [paɪˈænəz]. **1968** *DARE* Tape **GA67,** I had a piano [piˈjænə] in those days. **1969** *DARE* (Qu. K8) Inf **NY209,** [ˈpjænə]; (Qu. N41a) Inf **MA47,** [pijænə]. **1973** *DARE* File **swPA** (as of 1920s), Piano [paɪˈænə]. **1976** Garber *Mountain-ese* 67 **sAppalachians,** *Pianner* . . piano. **1979** *NYT Article Letters* **sOH,** My uncle . . is now 73 and was raised in rural southern Ohio (that's "Ohi-uh," like "Cincinnat-uh" . . and "pie-an-uh"). **1997** *DARE* File—Internet **cePA** [CoalSpeak] 11, *Pie-anna.*

B Sense.
In phrr *play the piano(s)*: To milk a cow.

1968–69 *DARE* (Qu. K8, *Joking terms for milking a cow: A farmer might say, "Well, it's time to go out and _____."*) Inf **MN15,** Play the piano; **NY209,** Play the pianos.

piano box n, freq attrib [From its resemblance to the case of a square *piano*]
A buggy body having the shape of a shallow rectangular box.

1902 (1969) Sears *Catalogue* 367, Leather Quarter Top Buggy. . . *Body*—This handsome piano box body is made of selected wood, thoroughly seasoned, finished with rounded corners, convex risers. **1934** *Hanley Disks* **CT,** A piano box buggy came along in about—as I remember—1875, along in there. **1968** *Yankee* Apr 20 **NEng,** Can you tell me what a "piano-box buggy" was? . . *Answer: The side of the body was carried straight from the seat to the dasher with no downward sweep to favor the boarding passengers.* **1969–70** *DARE* (Qu. N41a, . . *Horse-drawn vehicles . . to carry people*) Inf **OH97,** Piano box; **MA47,** Piano-box buggy—narrow sides eight inches high, backs of seats had spindles on them. **1977** Berkebile *Amer. Carriages* 39, Introduced around the mid-1850s; the piano box buggy became the most popular horse-drawn vehicle in America, if not the world. It was comparable to the Model T Ford of a later era. **1986** Pederson *LAGS Concordance,* 1 inf, **swTN,** Piano-box buggy—slender box, high on wheels.

piano house n
1970 *DARE* Tape **TN60,** Colonel Wade, who had visited in France, had seen houses built with a courtyard and a room on either end. And while there were twenty-five or thirty houses built between 1850 and 1860 in Maury County, Tennessee, I've never seen them anywhere else. They are sometimes spoken of as piano houses because they look like the old-fashioned square piano with a keyboard like the porch and the two ends of it like rooms built at the ends.

piano plant n Also *piano rose* [By folk-etym from **peony;** cf *EDD piano, pyanno* (at *peony*)]
The peony.

1919 *DN* 5.57 **NW,** *Piano-plant.* Peony. **1966–70** *DARE* (Qu. S11, . . *Peony*) Inf **WV16,** Piano [ˈpaːænə] plant; **NC36,** Piano rose [ˈpaiænɚˌrouz].

pian queue See **paille-en-queue**

piany See **piano**

piazza n, also attrib Usu |piˈæzə|; also |paɪˈæzə, ˈpiæzə, piˈæzɚ| Pronc-spp *peazzer, piazzy, pizer, pyazzuh;* for addit pronc and sp varr see quots **chiefly NEast, S Atl** See Map *somewhat old-fash* Cf **gallery**
A covered porch; a veranda.

1724 (1865) Jones *Present State VA* 26, It is a lofty Pile of Brick Building adorn'd with a *Cupola*. . . [T]here is a spacious *Piazza* on the *West* Side, from one Wing to the other. **1809** (1890) Cutler *Life & Times* 100 **CT,** I judge it to be upward of a hundred feet in length, three stories below the roof . . and a piazza the full length of the building. **1817** (1890) Long *Jrl.* 57 **WI,** Piazzas are to be built in front of all the quarters. **1825** in 1956 Eliason *Tarheel Talk* 287 **cn,cNC,** I often think of the conversation we had on the piazza. **1829** in 1910 Buffalo Hist. Soc. *Pub.* 14.226 **NY,** The whole [hotel] is massive, built of hewn stone; and three successive piazzas will afford most beautiful places for promenading. **1833** in 1924 MA Hist. Soc. *Coll.* 57.253 **MA,** He went out on the piazza of the second story of the Public House and bowed to the crowd. **1853** Simms *Sword & Distaff* 422 **SC,** Even the dog lying down in the piazza . . seemed to enjoy dreams of a happier sort. **1871** (1892) Johnston *Dukesborough Tales* 90 **GA,** The onliest other place for a man to sleep at thar is the . . t'other side o' the pe-azer from Susan Temple's room. **1887** (1967) Harris *Free Joe* 89 **GA** [Black], He'd set out on de peazzer en sing. **1904** Day *Kin o' Ktaadn* 151 **ME,** Extry winders put in, a . . piazzy shifted to t' other side. **1922** Gonzales *Black Border* 321 **sSC, GA coasts** [Gullah glossary], *Pyazzuh.* **1926** *AmSp* 2.81 **ME,** *Piazza* is everywhere "piazzer" in Maine. **1927** Adams *Congaree* 96 **cSC** [Black], He went to de pizer where Louisa been layin' on a pallet. **1930** Stoney–Shelby *Black Genesis* 177 **seSC,** Dat House sho' is big! Br' Rabbit hafter walk a mile or mo' roun' to de back p'razza. **c1940** Eliason *Word Lists FL* 10 **wFL,** Piazza [paɪæzɚ, paɪɛzɚ, paɪzɚ]: [Eliason queries whether "ɚ" shouldn't be replaced by "ə" in the preceding transcriptions.] The front porch of the house. Rural. **1941** *LANE* Map 351 *(Porch)* Piazza usually denotes a long railed platform wide enough to sit on, often one that runs clear across the front of a house. It is so defined by 90 informants, mostly in Mass., Vt. and southern N.H. . . 1 inf, **ceRI,** [pəˈzærõ], jocular corruption of *piazza;* 1 inf, **ceMA,** [ˈpiˇˈJæz] heard from 'a queer old woman'; 1 inf, **cwVT,** [paɛˈæzə], modern pronc.; 1 inf, **nME,** [pãˀɪˈzæˀᵊrə], 'ignorant' pron. of *piazza*. **1941** *Language* 17.332 **WI,** [LANCS fieldwork], *Piazza*—2 [of 50 infs]. . . [1 inf] says it is still in use. The sister of [another inf] also remembers it. . . *Piazza* is a relic. **1946** *PADS* 6.23 **ceNC** (as of 1900–10), *Pizer.* . . *Piazza;* a one-story porch attached to a one-story house. **1949** Kurath *Word Geog.* 45, *Piazza* . . for a porch is in common use on the coast from the James to Georgia and in the piedmont of the Carolinas. Southern Maryland has relics of this term. (Note that *piazza* is also widely current in New England and the Hudson Valley but not in the Midland.) **1959** *VT Hist.* 27.152 **cwVT,** Piazza [paɪˈæzi] . . pronc. Rare. **1963** Watkins–Watkins *Yesterday Hills* 46 **cnGA,** [Pa] built a front piazzer where he could rest in the summer. **1965–70** *DARE* (Qu. D17, . . *The platform, sometimes with a roof, that's built on the front or the side of a house*) 59 Infs, **chiefly NEng, S Atl,** Piazza; **CT21, 29, NY88, 206, 230, NC62, PA115,** Piazza—old-fashioned; **CT5,** Piazza—older word; **TX35,** Used to call 'em [paɪæzɪz]; **NC1, 8, SC9, 20,** [ˈpaɪ(j)æzə]; **SC11, 38,** [ˈpiæzə]; **GA72, MD12,** [ˌpaɪˈæzə]; **AL52,** [ˌpaɪˈezə]; **NY53,** [piˈazə]; **SC19,** [paɪəzə]; **SC26,** [ˈpɛəzə]—used to call it; also uneducated rural Whites a generation ago; **SC29,** [pa-ˈæzə]; **SC34,** [paɪˈæzə]; **SC38,** [ˈpa-æzə]; **SC43,** [ˈpaɪæzə]; (Qu. D16, . . *Parts added on to the main part of a house*) Inf **NH10,** Piazza; **TN26,** [ˈpaɪˌeɪzɚ]. **1986** Pederson *LAGS Concordance* (*Porch*) 96 Infs, **chiefly AL, FL, GA,** Piazza. [*DARE* Ed: 32 infs characterized *piazza* as "old-fashioned," "an old word," "used by one's grandparents," "heard when young," "uncommon," or the like.] **1994** NC Lang. & Life Project *Dial. Vocab. Ocracoke* 14 **eNC,** *Pizer.* . . Porch. . . Used only by older speakers now.

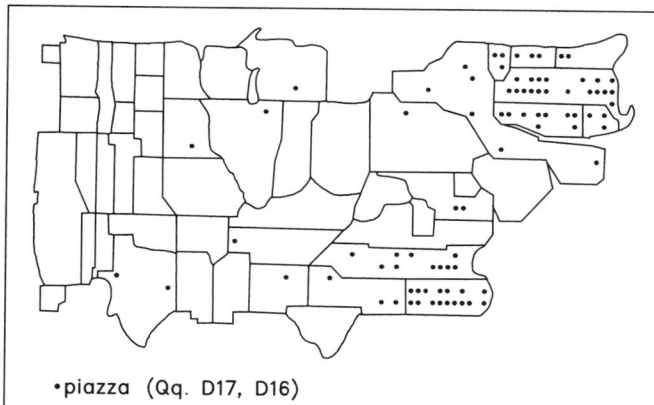

•piazza (Qq. D17, D16)

pic See **piccolo**

picacho n [Span] SW

An isolated mountain—also used as a place name.

1857 in 1864 Mowry *AZ & Sonora* 188, Between Tucson and the Gila . . is a well-known *picacho,* at the base of which water is often found in pools. **1877** Hodge *Arizona* 234, The southern portion of the Territory has numerous sugar-loaf mountains, which rise abruptly from the surface of the great plains and valleys to a height of hundreds and thousands of feet, and are called there picachos. **1892** DN 1.193 **TX,** *Picácho:* a large, isolated peak. **1906** *Out West Mag.* Feb 103 **AZ,** The Picacho [is] a huge, splintered, battle-ax-shaped peak of red sandstone, that was a landmark from Tucson to the Sonoran border. **1933** AmSp 8.3.8 **SW,** Then comes *picacho* for the solitary peak. **1946** Waters *Colorado* xi, The black volcanic picachos creep closer in the moonlight, baring their saw-tooth fangs. **1948** *So. Sierran* Jan. 3/1 *(DA),* Our first climb, on Saturday, was to Picacho on the California side of the river.

picanin(n)y, picanny See **pickaninny**

picayune n Also *pecune, pickayune* [Fr *picaillon* old copper coin] **esp LA** Cf **levy** n[1], **quartee**

Orig a Spanish half-real; hence, a five-cent piece, five cents; now esp in phr *not worth a picayune* and varr.

1804 J.F. Watson *Jrnl.* 4 Nov. in *Amer. Pioneer* (1843) II.228 *(OED2)* **LA,** One can't buy anything [at New Orleans] for less than a six cent piece, called a *picayune.* **1819** in 1824 Knight *Letters* 127 **New Orleans LA,** Near the green, is a horizontal fandango of four wooden horses. . . Upon these, children canter and circulate for exercise, by paying a half-bit, here called a *pécune.* **1834** in 1839 Townsend *Narr. Rocky Mts.* 17, We gave him a *pickayune* for his trouble, and went on. **1851** (1852) Stowe *Uncle Tom's Cabin* 2.52 **New Orleans LA,** From him she got many a stray picayune, which she laid out in nuts and candies. **1853** in 1976 Rose *Doc. Hist. Slavery* 502 **LA,** My master often received letters . . requesting him to send me to play at a ball or festival of the whites. He received his compensation, and usually I also returned with many picayunes jingling in my pockets. **1878** Hart *Sazerac Lying Club* 41 **NV,** Why, when I was back home my father bought a catfish from a nigger for a picayune, and when we come to open it thar was a gold watch and chain . . inside of it. **1903** Murrie *White Castle LA* 256, Liza . . danced with glee when she spied a Dago trudging along with his heavy burden, whether she had a picayune or not to buy any with. **1903** DN 2.325 **seMO,** Picayune. . . Sixpence; six and a quarter cents. Formerly a common coin and the smallest in circulation. 'He isn't worth a picayune!' Pennies are not used to any extent in the South, and formerly were almost unknown. **1909** DN 3.401 **nwAR,** Picayune. . . Five-cent-piece. **1916** DN 4.269 **New Orleans LA,** Picayune. . . Five cents. **1948** *Reader's Digest* Dec 148 **sIN,** Don't care a picayune how you waste that boy's time, do you? **1967–68** DARE (Qu. HH20b, *Of an idle, worthless person . . "He doesn't amount to _____."*) Inf **MD**28, A [ˌpɪkəˈjun]; **VA**31, A picayune; (Qu. HH20c, *Of an idle, worthless person . . "He isn't worth _____."*) Inf **MA**5, A picayune—parents' term; **NY**111, A picayune. **1983** Reinecke Coll. 8 **LA,** Picayune

[pɪkəjʉn] . . one sixteenth of a Span. silver dollar, half-a-bit, coin worth 6+ cents commonly circulating in early 19 c. La. Later transferred to a silver half-dime. . . The noun, like the coin(s) obsolete. From Fr. "picaillon" which in La. also meant a poor, shiftless individual. **1986** Pederson *LAGS Concordance,* 1 inf, **seLA,** Picayune—former name of a five-cent piece.

piccadilly n

A man's shoe with a pointed toe.

1968 DARE (Qu. W42a, . . *Nicknames . . for men's sharp-pointed shoes*) Inf **IA**17, Piccadillies; **IA**36, Piccadilly—years ago; **WI**59, Piccadilly—used to call them this.

piccalilli n Also *pickalilly, pickylilly* [OED2 1769 →] **widespread, but less freq Sth, S Midl** See Map

A usu spicy pickle of mixed vegetables.

1863 *Scientific Amer.* 9.163, Piccalilli is a mixture of all kinds of pickles. Select pickles, from the salt brine, of a uniform size and of various colors; as small cucumbers, button onions, small bunches of cauliflowers, carrots cut in fanciful shape, radishes, radish-pods, bean-pods, Cayenne-pods, mace, ginger, olives, limes, grapes, strips of horse-radish, &c. **1890** Blakeslee *Compendium* 146, Piccalilli. One peck of green tomatoes . . four green peppers . . slice all . . salt . . press dry through a sieve . . cover with vinegar . . one cup of sugar, a tablespoon of each kind of spice . . stew slowly. **1906** Gregory *Woman's Cookbook* 383, Piccalilli. Take two hundred small cucumbers, salt, one large head of cauliflower, two quarts of small white onions, one-quarter of a peck of green tomatoes, one bunch of celery; salt over night. Next day put all in boiling water and have it come up to a boil twice. Drain and put in a jar. Put all kinds of spice in a muslin bag and put into vinegar and boil. **1922** (1926) Cady *Rhymes VT* 145, Making Vermont Piccalilli. . . We always used the biggest bowl / To chop the green tomaters;/. . . / We salted 'em like sixty next / And set 'em off for dreening;/. . . / And then we cut the smarty things,/ The peppers, jest a-turning,/ And that there white horse radish root / Precisely just as burning;/. . . / Then next come in the cooking part,/ Which took the stove and kittle;/. . . / Then back inside the bowl it went / To get them fixings fiery,/ And sugar, cloves and mustard seed/. . . / The vinegar was last to add,/ Which made it pickle proper. **1925** Dargan *Highland Annals* 44 **cwNC,** You don't eat pickle either—tomato-pickle, cabbage-pickle, beet-pickle, pickylilly, onion-pickle, pickle everything. **1960** Criswell *Resp. to PADS 20* **Ozarks,** Pickalilly. . . A condiment made of green tomatoes, spices, etc. to eat with meat. Always common. **1965–70** DARE (Qu. H57, *Tasty or spicy side-dishes served with meats*) 171 Infs, **widespread, but less freq Sth, S Midl,** Piccalilli; (Qu. H56, *Names for . . pickles*) 11 Infs, **scattered, esp Nth, N Midl,** Piccalilli. **2000** DARE File **NEng,** We used to make it every year in Maine—green tomato piccalilli—never had it with any hot spices in it. My great grandmother and other relatives have always made it—sometimes with a little horseradish but not "hot spices."

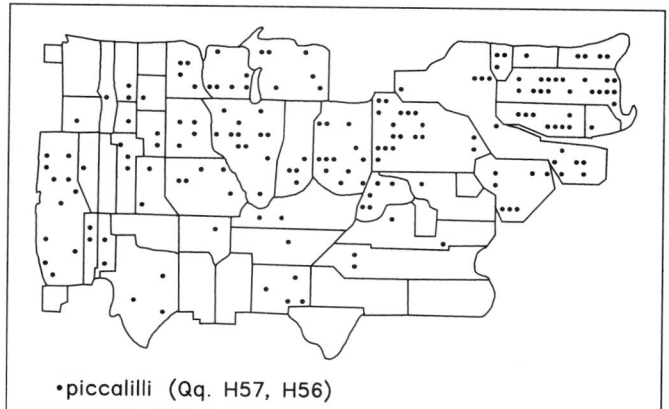

•piccalilli (Qq. H57, H56)

piccaninny See **pickaninny**

piccolo n Also *pic, piccolo box* **chiefly S Atl; also NYC** chiefly among Black speakers Cf *jook organ* (at **jook** n 3)

A coin-operated automatic musical instrument; a jukebox; hence comb *piccolo joint* a *jook joint* (at **jook** n 2).

c1937 in 1976 *Weevils in the Wheat* 283 **seVA,** De "piculous" [sic] [*Weevils* Ed: nickelodeons?] playin' all de night long right over my head,

I jes' can rest heah, can't even sleep a wink. **1938** *NY Amsterdam News* (NY) 12 Mar 17/2, The Harlem Hamfats grind out the tune on myriad Harlem piccolos. **c1938** in 1970 Hyatt *Hoodoo* 2.1106 **SC**, Tuh make a success in de sto' or *piccolo joint*. . . (What kind of a *joint?*) Where yo's havin' a beer garden or a *piccolo joint*—where a beer garden or any kinda music machines. (What does *piccolo* mean?) It's somepin on de order of a Victrola fo' music. . . An' yo' put it in yore beer garden or whatevah. **1939** in Lib. of Congress *Amer. Memory: WPA Life Hist.* (Internet) **csSC**, "One of them piccolo joint right near home. I hear the bang-bang music from here. You don't catch me visit um though, not July Geddes." . . He is not strict with the children however. They can go to dances when they wish and "throw 'way nickels on the piccolo, if they got nickel to throw 'way." **1941** Writers' Program *Guide SC* 358 **nwSC**, Along the road are 'piccolo joints,' where city and mill village youths gather for dancing. **1942** Kennedy *Palmetto Country* 186 **FL**, A jook is an establishment that is usually crude but sometimes sumptuous; . . music is provided by a jook organ (called a *piccolo* by Negroes) or jook band (ensemble of rhythm instruments); girls . . are available for dancing without charge. **1944** *AN&Q* 4.183 **NYC**, Piccolo Box: Harlemese for *juke box*. **1950** *PADS* 14.52 **SC**, Piccolo. . . An automatic music box, worked by a nickel slot machine. Origin undetermined. **1970** Major *Dict. Afro-Amer. Slang* 91, Pic, piccolo: (1930's–40's) juke box. **1972** Bowers *Encycl. Automatic Musical Instruments* 969, Piccolo. . . A coin piano or orchestrion. [Bowers: slang, southern United States usage] **1992** *DARE* File, Dad, 74 yrs. old from nwSC, always calls a 'jukebox' a *piccolo,* pronounced ['pɪkə,low]. He says: 'Why don't you put a quarter in the *piccolo,* and don't play that hippie stuff.' It isn't that he doesn't use *jukebox,* just that he uses *piccolo* more often. **1994** NC Lang. & Life Project *Dial. Dict. Lumbee Engl.* 9 **seNC**, Piccolo. . . Jukebox. *I found that old piccolo at a yard sale, and it still plays.*

pichtel See **pightle**

picitail See **picket-tail**

pick v

1 To prick; to pierce. **scattered, but esp nMI** See Map Cf **pick** n³, **picker**, **pick tree**, **picky** adj, n¹

1890 James *Mother James' Cooking* 505, If nutmegs are good, when picked with a pin oil will instantly ooze out. **1950** *WELS Suppl.* ("She _____ herself with a needle.") 1 Inf, **cwWI**, Picked. **1965–70** *DARE* (Qu. Y46b, *To get hurt with something sharp . . "She _____ herself with a needle."*) 20 Infs, **scattered, but esp nMI**, Picked; (Qu. Y46a, *To get hurt with something sharp . . "He _____ a thorn into his hand."*) Inf **AZ1**, Picked; (Qu. BB51b, . . *'Magical' cures for corns or warts*) Inf **MO39**, Pick warts with pen, [etc]; [**KY6, SC32**, Pick till it bleeds, [etc]; **AR27, LA2**, Pick wart, [etc]; **NC52, VA35**, Pick it (open), [etc]; **GA72**, Pick them till they bleed [*DARE* Ed: It is not clear that these Infs mean "prick" rather than "pull at with the fingernails."]]. **1996** *DARE* File **wMA**, I usually get "scratched" by pickers [=brambles], but I could get "picked" too.

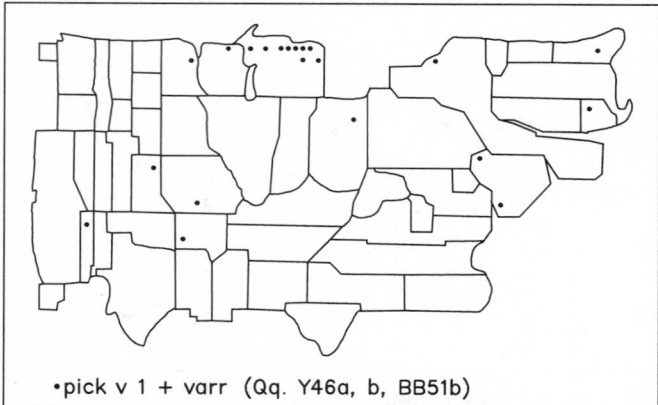

•pick v 1 + varr (Qq. Y46a, b, BB51b)

2 with var advs (see below): To incite to anger, nag at, tease. Note: *Pick on* in this sense is std and is not illustrated here. Cf **peck** v¹ **2**

a with *at.* [*OED2* a1670 →; "Now only *dial.,* U.S., and *Austral.*"] **chiefly Sth, S Midl** See Map

1786 in 1853 Jefferson *Writings* 1.605, The Emperor, the Empress, and the Venetians seem all to be picking at the Turks. **1884** Roe *Na-*ture's Serial Story* 62, When the papers have nothing else to find fault with they pick at West Point. **1893** [see **2b** below]. **1896** *Cosmopolitan* 20.430 **cwPA**, I'm always being picked at. I wish I was dead. **1899** (1912) Green *VA Folk-Speech* 319, Pick at. . . To quarrel with. They are always picking at each other. **1909** *DN* 3.357 **eAL, wGA**, Pick at one. . . To irritate one, stir one up as to a fight. "He picked at me all day." **1965–70** *DARE* (Qu. Y7, *When one person never misses a chance to be mean to another or to annoy another: "I don't know why she keeps _____ me all the time!"*) 25 Infs, **scattered, but more freq Sth, S Midl**, Picking at; (Qu. GG3, *To tease: "See those big boys trying to _____ [that little one]."*) Infs **FL48, GA13, LA2, 14, SC7, 26, 40, 58**, Pick at; (Qu. GG16, . . *Finding fault, or complaining: "You just can't please him—he's always _____."*) Inf **MI9**, Picking at you; (Qu. II33, *To get an advantage over somebody by tricky means: "I don't trust him, he's always trying to _____."*) Inf **MO35**, Pick at me. **1968–69** *DARE* FW Addit **sLA**, He could play good till them boys got to picking at him, calling him sissy and all that; **seGA**, They'll fight "if you pick at them"—said of alligators. **1986** Pederson *LAGS Concordance,* 1 inf, **cnAR**, Go to picking at you; 1 inf, **nwAR**, Picking at her = teasing her; 1 inf, **csTX**, Mexicans, Whites might say picking at me [for *playing the dozens*].

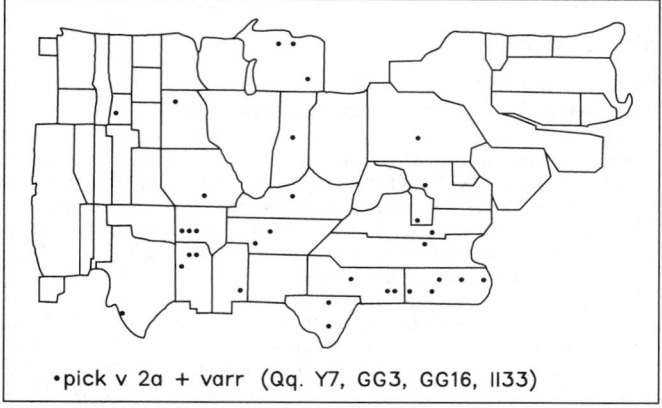

•pick v 2a + varr (Qq. Y7, GG3, GG16, II33)

b with *onto, upon, with.*

1893 *KS Univ. Qrly.* 1.141 **KS**, Pick (onto or at): to tease, to talk overbearingly, as 'Pick onto one of your size;' 'He's always picking at me to sell out.' **1899** (1912) Green *VA Folk-Speech* 320, Pick-upon. . . To annoy; the other boys always pick upon this one. **1946** McCullers *Member* 30 **AL**, I warned you to quit picking with me.

3 To pick up; spec:

a To collect and remove (stones or other undesirable material) from an area; to remove such material from (an area); hence vbl n *picking.*

1850 *N. Eng. Farmer* II.164 *(DA),* Sometimes the number of stones is so great, and the size so small, that the labor of 'picking,' . . is either neglected, or but imperfectly done. **1891** *Scribner's Mag.* 9.520 **NY**, I drive the horses and put up the Cows and clean out the Cow Stable i am all well i pick stones and i have an apple tree 6 Feet High. **1896** *DN* 1.421 **wCT, wNY**, Pick: "To pick stone," to gather them from the field. **1898** *New Engl. Mag.* 24.728, Should he harvest what the worms had left of the cabbages? Should he pick stones? **1950** *WELS Suppl.* **cWI**, Stone-picking vacation—In Waupaca County, every spring the school closed in certain districts to allow the children to clear fields of stone. They walked down the field on each side of a horse and stone-boat and tossed the stones into it. **1953** Van Wagenen *Golden Age* 144 **NY**, Now, "picking the crick" was merely the spring chore of cleaning up the ford by disposing of any boulders that might have been rolled in by the spring floods. **1957** *Eaton Coll.* **Washington Is. WI**, Picking rock . . cleaning unwanted stones from land by hand, with stone boat. **1963** Burroughs *Head-First* 188 **CO**, Mother . . went to the field to "pick brush"; that is, she wrestled the buck and sage and serviceberry bushes out of the newly plowed field, shook the dirt from their roots, and heaped them up to be burned when they had dried out sufficiently. **2000** *DARE* File **neWI**, Many farmers pick stones in their fields and in order to do that they must have a "strong back and a weak mind." But the rationale behind picking stones each spring is to save the "wear and tear" on all of the equipment.

b To collect from the ground and save (desirable items).

1942 *AmSp* 17.172 **sIL**, Phrases involving unusual uses of verbs may be mentioned: . . *to pick the eggs* (for 'to gather the eggs'). **1966** *DARE* Tape **OK**30, We burned chips in those days, cow chips. . . They'd pick chips while I was gone. **1975** Gould *ME Lingo* 206, *Pick*—For *pick* up, the Maine word for gathering potatoes after the mechanical digger has left them lying in rows. Men go to Aroostook in the fall to *pick* potatoes. **1985** Ehrlich *Solace* 19 **WY**, Men and women from the surrounding ranches and towns were hired to work in the sheds. Some did nothing but fill water troughs all day; others "picked drop"—pulled newborn lambs inside [the sheds] from the drop corrals.

c In logging: =**sack** v 1a—usu in phr *pick the rear*.

1905 U.S. Forest Serv. *Bulletin* 61.43 [Logging terms], *Pick the rear, to. See* Sack the rear, to. **1913** [see **rear** n¹ 1]. **1975** Gould *ME Lingo* 207, *Picking the rear*—This suggestive Maine-ism refers only to cleaning up the stray logs after a river drive. After the main drive has passed down, eddies and *logans* are *picked* and the stragglers thrown back into the channel. Since the term is regularly applied to the boss of the crew rather than to the men in general, the term has a bounce when strangers first hear it: "Where's Arthur Bessey?" "He's over on the South Branch picking his rear."

4 also with *up:* To shred or flake (fish); hence ppl adj *picked* of fish: shredded, flaked. [*OED2 pick* v. 11.a "To separate by picking, to pull or comb asunder" (usu in ref to oakum or textile fibers); 1536 →] **chiefly NEng**

1847 (1852) Crowen *Amer. Cookery* 35 **NY**, Scald some soaked cod . . ; then scrape it white, pick it in flakes, and put in a stew-pan. **1886** *Century Illustr. Mag.* 32.512 **MA**, She drew him a cup of Japan tea, and made him some milk-toast and picked-fish. **1890** *Century Dict.* 4472, To *pick up* codfish (in cookery). **1890** *New Engl. Mag.* 8.694 e**MA**, To-day is Friday, and the bill of fare is:—Breakfast: picked fish in cream, potatoes, bread and butter, pickles, coffee. **1891** *Atlantic Mth.* 67.795 **NEng**, She soon followed her sister, guided by savory odors of hot biscuit, "picked" codfish, and wild strawberries. **1896** (c1973) Farmer *Orig. Cook Book* 160 e**MA**, Pick salt codfish in long thin strips. **1939** Wolcott *Yankee Cook Book* 29, Soak codfish in cold water ½ hour; drain and "pick up" (flake). *Ibid* 32, *New England salt fish dinner.* . . "Picked Fish"—it's sometimes called.

5 See quots.

1902 *DN* 2.241 s**IL**, *Pick.* . . To graze, as a horse or cow. **1907** *DN* 3.225 nw**AR**, *Pick.* . . To graze (used of a horse or a cow).

6 To imitate or alter (a cattle brand) by plucking out the hair and sometimes scarring the hide with a knife; hence n *picked brand* a brand made in this way. **West**

1908 *Pacific Mth.* Mar 309 **OR** (as of c1865), Well we got on the track of a fellow that had been sellin' a heap of horses that had picked brands or the frying-pan brand so we started to round him up. **1936** Adams *Cowboy Lingo* 130 **West**, A 'picked brand' was accomplished by picking out tufts of hair in the lines desired by the aid of a jackknife. It was seldom used except by dishonest men until they could get the animal out of the country, as it was only temporary. [**1938** in Lib. of Congress *Amer. Memory: WPA Life Hist.* (Internet) **TX**, Some men started in the cattle business by branding the unbranded critters and never paid out a dollar for cattle. . . Then later some went further and worked brands over. There were several methods used. One we had was picking the hair, another was using the sap of the milkweed which would cause the hair to die where it was applied.] **1957** *Western Horseman* 22.4.80 **TX**, Rustlers would come across a large unbranded calf following its mother, and they would "pick" the brand carried by the mother on the calf by pulling the long hair out of the skin in such a way that it appeared to be branded. **1958** *AmSp* 33.267 e**WA**, The term *picked brand* does not seem to have been described adequately. This type of brand may be made in two ways. In the first, a quantity of hair is plucked to describe an outline of the desired brand. A brand made in this way lasts only a short time. In the second, after an outline has been traced by picking, the skin is lacerated with the point of a knife. When the hair grows back, it will have a slightly curly appearance, and a brand so made will last the life of the animal. Both are used as temporary or auxiliary markings and do not constitute legal brands because they do not show through the hide when the animal is skinned.

pick n¹

In phrr *have a pick at* (or *on*) *someone:* To hold a grudge against one, feel enmity or ill will towards one; to give one a hard time. [Scots, nIr dial < *pick* dial var of *pique*]

1834 *Life Andrew Jackson* 39, The Gineral and they had a pick at one another. . . The Gineral soon had vengeance. **1878** *Scribner's Mth.*

16.686, The youths plowing in the fields beside the way halloo at them saucily, and even the dogs of the residents have a pick at the superannuated-looking curs that follow the wagon. **1912** *DN* 3.577 w**IN**, Charley seems to have a pick at him. **1930s** in 1944 *ADD* e**WV**, To have a pick on someone = to pick on someone. 'She's got a pick on me.' **1940** Cather *Sapphira* 45 **VA** (as of 1856), I knows that fat Lizzie's at the bottom of it, somehow. She's always got a pick on me. **1967** *DARE* File, *Pick*—antagonism expressed through being strict or demanding. "She [= a teacher] have a little pick on him." Said of her son by a Milwaukee Negro mother from Memphis, Tennessee.

pick n² [Prob var of *peak*]   Cf **picked** adj ¹

The tip (of the ear).

1904 Day *Kin o' Ktaadn* 152 **ME**, Ase Dodge friz' the pick of his ear.

pick n³ [Prob var of *prick*]   Cf **pick** v 1, **picker**

See quot.

1970 *DARE* File ne**MI**, Pick . . an inoculation. "I've got to go for a pick." Said by young people of Polish language background in Rogers City (Presque Isle Co.), Michigan.

pickaback (plant) See **piggyback plant**

pickalilly See **piccalilli**

pickaninny n Also *picanny, picaninny, piccaninny, pickaniny, pickney* [W Afr and W Indian Creoles, of Span or Port origin; *OED2* 1657 →] **chiefly Sth**

A Black or other non-White child; rarely, a White child; also fig.

c1770 in 1833 Boucher *Glossary* xlix **MD, VA**, A *Pickaninny;* a male infant: probably from the Spanish *picade nino, pequeno nino.* [**1826** (1918) Rogers *Jrl.* 221 **CA**, The women here are very unchaste. . . [O]ne came to my lodgings last night and asked me to make her a blanco Pickanina, which, being interpreted, is to get her a white child.] **1848** Bartlett *Americanisms* 249, *Pickaninny.* A Negro or mulatto infant. Used in the Southern States. **1875** *Appletons' Jrl.* 14.171, My guide, a host of pickaninnies [=Seminole children], eleven dogs, a colt, and a hog or two, came next. **1887** Amer. Philol. Assoc. *Trans. for 1886* 17.35 **Sth**, A gentleman from Ohio . . has attempted to indicate for me the words that were imported during or after the war from the South into Southern Ohio. . . He mentions as recently imported . . *pickaninny* (negro child). **1894** *Century Illustr. Mag.* 47.852 **SC**, Newcomers . . called a negro child a "piccaninny," from the Spanish *pequeño nino,* now shortened in South Carolina to "pickney." **1898** Lloyd *Country Life* 41 **AL**, I didn't want to lose our little picaninny that a way. [*DARE* Ed: *Picaninny* refers here to a White child.] **1903** *DN* 2.324 se**MO**, *Pickaninny.* . . A negro child. **1909** *DN* 3.357 e**AL**, w**GA**, *Pickaniny.* . . A negro child: this is not a colloquialism in east Alabama. The term is known only in 'coon' songs. **1926** in 1942 Handy *Father of Blues* x **Sth** [Black], I would think it hardly necessary, inopportune to use the word "pickaninny" in referring to my school-mates who include such men as Dr. Lewis Moore, former Dean of Howard University. . . Southern children of our times and locality never had themselves referred to as "pickaninnies", and the term is used by Northerners inadvisedly. **1937** in 1976 *Weevils in the Wheat* 73 **VA** [Black], Dis ole white 'oman use to slip Cinda food. Say, "Cinda, heres something to eat fer you and your little picannies." **1944** *AmSp* 19.174 **MD**, In the Baltimore of my youth *pickaninny* was not used invidiously, but rather affectionately. **1945** FWP *Lay My Burden Down* 61 **NC** (as of c1865) [Black], Every evening at three o'clock Old Mistress would call us litsy bitsy children in, and we would lay down on pallets and have to go to sleep. I can hear her now singing to us pickaninnies. **1966–70** *DARE* (Qu. HH28, *Names and nicknames . . for people of foreign background*) Inf **IA**22, Pickaninny—Negro child; **SC**26, Pickaninny—fanciful, literary? **SC**44, Pickaninny—Negro child, not used in years; **VA**42, Pickaninny—Negro; that's a chap now—a child; **MS**73, Pickaninnies. **1968** *Foxfire* Fall–Winter 40 n**GA**, As one moonshiner said, "I never gave an officer trouble except catchin' me. After I 'uz caught, I 'uz his pickaninny." **1986** Pederson *LAGS Concordance* **Gulf Region**, [12 infs used *pickaninny/pickaninnies*, 6 specifically in ref to Black children; 2 regarded it as derogatory, 1 as a term of endearment, and 1 as referring to a White person.] **1993** Delany–Delany *Having Our Say* 74 c**NC** [Black], When I was a child, the words used to describe us most often were colored, Negro and nigger. I've also been called jiggerboo, pickaninny, coon—you name it, honey.

pick at See **pick** v 2a

pickaway anise n

A **hop tree** (here: *Ptelea trifoliata*).

1876 Hobbs *Bot. Hdbk.* 89, Pickaway anise, Wafer ash, Ptelea trifoliata. **1900** Lyons *Plant Names* 309, Pickaway Anise. . . *Bark* of *root* tonic, febrifuge, stomachic. **1958** Jacobs–Burlage *Index Plants NC* 195, *Ptelea trifoliata.* . . Pickaway anise; . . Pickaway-anixe [sic]. This grows from New York to Florida and west to Minnesota and Texas. **1960** Vines *Trees SW* 593, *Ptelea trifoliata.* . . Vernacular names are . . Pickaway-anise . . and Wingseed. All parts of the plant emit a disagreeable odor. The fruit was once used as a substitute for hops in beer brewing.

pickaxe (sheldrake) n

=**hooded merganser.**

1888 Trumbull *Names of Birds* 73 **ME,** Hooded Merganser. . . At Bath, Me., *Pickaxe Sheldrake* (the bill being the pointed end of the pickaxe, I suppose; the crest, its wide transverse edge). **1923** U.S. Dept. Ag. *Misc. Circular* 13.6 **ME,** *Hooded Merganser.* . . *In local use.* . . Pickaxe, pickaxe sheldrake. **1982** Elman *Hunter's Field Guide* 228, *Hooded Merganser.* . . *Common & Regional Names* . . pickaxe.

pickayune See picayune

picked adj[1] |ˈpɪkɪd| Pronc-sp *pickid* [*OED2 picked* a. c1430 →; *"Obs."*] esp nNEng Cf peaked, picketty

Sharp-pointed.

1791 [see **savannah cricket**]. **1904** Day *Kin o' Ktaadn* 151 **ME,** A cupoly made pickeder. **1907** *DN* 3.196 **seNH,** Picked [ˈpɪkɪd]. . . Pointed. "He drove a picked stick into the ground." **1914** *DN* 4.78 **ME, nNH,** *Pickid.* . . Sharp-pointed. **1939** *LANE* Map 115 (*Picket fence*) 1 inf, **neMA,** [pɪks] are [pɪk̇ɪd]; 1 inf, **neMA,** The rungs are [pɪx̌ɪd] on top; 1 inf, **seNH,** [pɪkɪʔts] are [pɪkɪd]; 1 inf, **sME,** The *pick fence* has [pɪkɪd stɪks]; 2 infs, **sME,** The slats of the *pick fence* are [pɪkɪd]; 1 inf, **sME,** The [pɪkɪts] are [pɪkɪd]. [Exx of the type [pɪkɪd fɛnts] occur occas on the map, esp in **nNEng.**] **1966–69** *DARE* (Qu. O1) Inf **ME6,** Peapod—used for a saltwater boat pickèd at both ends; (Qu. W42a, . . *Nicknames . . for men's sharp-pointed shoes*) Infs **ME22, NH14,** Picked [ˈpɪkɛd]-toed. **1979** Lewis *How to Talk Yankee* [26] **nNEng,** *Pick-ed.* Adj. (two syllables), pointed. "You give that heifer the pick-ed end of the stick an she'll move."

picked adj[2] See peaked

picked ppl adj See pick v 4

picked brand See pick v 6

picked-up adj phr Also *pick-up;* also used absol chiefly Nth, esp NEng

Of a meal: consisting of leftovers.

1771 (1961) Adams *Diary* 31 **NEng,** We had a picked up Dinner. **1848** Bartlett *Americanisms* 249, A *pick-up* or *a pick-up* dinner, is a dinner made up of such fragments of cold meats as remain from former meals. The word is common in the Northern States. **1867** Hill *Homespun* 126 **NEng,** A sort of "picked-up" dinner is set before them. **1878** (1977) Stowe *Poganuc People* 231 **CT,** We shall just have a pick-up dinner. **1905** *DN* 3.15 **cCT,** *Pick-up.* . . A pick-up dinner. **1910** *DN* 3.446 **cwNY,** *Pick-up-dinner.* . . A warmed-over dinner. **1913** *DN* 4.3 **ME,** *Always around like a picked up dinner.* . . Easily at hand. **1927** *AmSp* 2.351 **WV,** *Come like a picked-up dinner* . . to convey that a dinner of scraps on washing day will always bring an unexpected guest. "The minister came like a picked-up dinner." **1934** Carmer *Stars Fell on AL* 94, Candles in hurricane glasses still gleam on silver goblets and still a ham and a chicken and a roast are served with corn and okra and . . a watermelon, for just a "pick-up potluck dinner." **1941** *LANE* Map 313 (*Warmed over*), Food that is left over from one meal and is heated to be served again. . . A picked-up dinner (a pick-up dinner) [3 infs **CT,** 3 **MA,** 1 **VT,** 1 **NH**]. **1968** *DARE* (Qu. H3, *The meal that people eat at the end of the day*) Inf **VA26,** Pick-up supper; (Qu. LL13, *Not full or sufficient: "She gave us a _____ meal."*) Inf **MA38,** Pick-up; **MN3,** A pick-up meal—a light lunch, not a full meal. **1968** *DARE* Tape **WI13,** Christmas Eve was always a hectic day. . . so we had what my mother would call a pick-up supper, meaning more or less of a cold meal. **1975** *DARE* File **cwMA** (as of c1920), Pick-up dinner.

pick eggs v phr, hence vbl n *picking eggs* Also *peck eggs*

To engage in **egg picking.**

1835 Longstreet *GA Scenes* 77 (as of 1790), It was a common custom of those days with boys, to dye and peck eggs on Easter Sunday, and for a few days afterwards. . . Our "young operatives" sallied forth to stake the whole proceeds of their *"domestic industry"* upon a peck. Egg was struck against egg, point to point, and the egg which was broken was given up as lost to the owner of the one which came whole from the shock. **1869** in 1953 *PA Dutchman* April 11 (*Mathews Coll.*), The juveniles had their usual privilege and enjoyment of shouting out their *nary eggs* along the streets, and hundreds of them were duly picked and broken. **1895** *DN* 1.392 **DC,** *Pick eggs:* to rap one egg against another till one cracks. The owner of the egg cracked loses it. (Boys.) **1912** Green *VA Folk-Speech* 316, *Peck.* . . At Easter boys peck eggs by knocking the small ends together, the broken egg is won by the whole one. **1953** *PA Dutchman* April 11 (*Mathews Coll.*), We come now to the universal Easter custom—picking eggs. Children tested the strength of the shells by striking the smaller end of the eggs together. **1964** Smith *PA Germans* 113 **cnVA, sWV,** A popular Easter game among the young people was called "picking" eggs or egg "fighting." A person selected what he considered to be his strongest egg and challenged someone else to "pick" against him. The eggs were tapped against each other until one of the egg shells cracked, then the owner of the other egg claimed the cracked one as prize.

picker n

1 also *picky:* A burr, bramble, prickle; hence adj *pickery* stickery. **chiefly NEast, N Cent** Cf pick v 1, **pricker, sticker**

1950 *WELS* **WI** (*A large round weed seed that clings to your clothing*) 1 Inf, Burr, picker; (*Small, flat weed seeds with two prongs that cling to clothing*) 1 Inf, Pickies; 1 Inf, Picker; 1 Inf, Sticktights—pickers. **1966–68** *DARE* (Qu. S13, . . *A common wild bush with bunches of round, prickly seeds; when they get dry they stick to your clothing*) Inf **NY21,** Burrs, pickery burrs; burdock; (Qu. S14) Inf **NJ6,** Sandburrs—round, small, light-colored, with "pickers," hooks; (Qu. S15, . . *Weed seeds that cling to your clothing*) Inf **MI15,** Small burrs—called "pickers"; (Qu. Y44) Inf **CA59,** Pickers—a thorny part of a sandburr. **1996** *DARE* File **seWI** (as of c1948), My little brother came home covered with brown burrs and crying that he had fallen in the "pickers." Children and some adults in our neighborhood used this word or "prickers" to refer to any burr or beggar ticks that stuck to clothing and shoelaces. *Ibid* **csWI** (as of c1960), Pickers or prickers were the words we used for the flat brown two-pronged weed seeds that stuck to our clothes. *Ibid* **wMA,** "Don't pick it [=a squash] up by the stem—it has pickers on it." [The speaker added that she usually uses the term *pickers* for brambles:] "Is there any way out of these pickers?" *Ibid* **ceNY** (as of 1960s), You'll get all scratched up in those pickers. There are lots of pickers in the puckerbrush. Stickers are burrs like burdock and beggar's lice that stick on your clothes. **1997** *Ibid* **nwMA,** I still call blackberry patches picker bushes.

2 See quot.

1976 *DARE* File **Isle Royale MI,** Picker—A device, usu a piece of wood 5–6″ long with a nail through one end, used to break the air bladder in *Coregonus hoyi,* a species of lake trout, which expands when the fish is brought up from deep water (250–300′).

pickerel n Cf pike

1 A freshwater fish of the genus *Esox.*

1709 (1967) Lawson *New Voyage* 162 **NC, SC,** The Jack, Pike, or Pickerel, . . are very plentiful with us in *Carolina.* **1794** Williams *Nat. & Civil Hist.* **VT** 122, The *Pike* or *Pickerel* abounds much in Lake Champlain. It is there called by the name of Muschilongoe. **1865** Norris *Amer. Angler's Book* 130, The term "Pickerel," is applied to all fish of this genus [=*Esox*], with the exception of the Mascalonge, by the people of New York and the Eastern States. **1905** U.S. Bur. Fisheries *Rept. for 1904* 595, Nor do I know of any specific complaints of damage to the herring (*Argyrosomus*), sturgeon, or the true pikes (*Esocidae,* "pickerel" of the inland waters). **1913** *Auk* 30.488 **Okefenokee GA,** Some of the characteristic vertebrate forms of the water courses are the pied water snake, . . two pickerels (*Esox americanus* and *E. reticulatus*), and various catfishes . . and killifishes. **1927** Weed *Pike* 38, In Chicago, a fisherman speaking of. . . "Pickerel" . . generally means *Esox lucius* . . , but may mean *Stizostedion, Esox niger* . . or *Esox americanus.* If such a fisherman should tell of catching "Pickerel" and "Pike" he would probably refer to *Esox lucius* and *Stizostedion. Ibid* 44, *[Esox lucius:]* Pickerel; northern United States. *Ibid* 45, *Esox niger.* . . Pickerel; general. . . *Esox ohioensis* [=*E. masquinongy*]. . Pickerel; western New York. **1947** Dalrymple *Panfish* 271 *(DA),* Any one species [of *Esox*] may be a Jack, a Pickerel, a Pike, a Green Pike, Blue Pike, Grass

Pike, and so on for pages. **1965–70** *DARE* (Qu. P1, . . *Kinds of freshwater fish . . caught around here . . good to eat*) 134 Infs, **chiefly NEast, Gt Lakes,** Pickerel [*DARE* Ed: Some of these Infs may refer instead to other senses below.]; NY74, Pickerel—all are grass pickerel; FL4, NC15, NY74, Grass pickerel; (Qu. P3, *Freshwater fish that are not good to eat*) Infs **ME**10, NY71, Pickerel. **1968** *DARE* Tape **GA**35, We have pickerel, a good many pickerel, in the [Okefenokee] Swamp at this time. . . We catch a good many bass and pickerel on in the fall and winter. **1975** Evanoff *Catch More Fish* 86, There are three kinds of pickerel found in United States waters, but two of them [=*Esox americanus americanus* and *E. a. vermiculatus*] . . are too small and too limited in range to be important. The one usually caught and sought is the chain pickerel *(Esox niger)*. *Ibid* 87, Pickerel are usually found . . along shorelines with weeds, logs, brush, rocks, and other obstructions. **1983** Becker *Fishes WI* 393, *Grass Pickerel—Esox americanus vermiculatus.* . . Pickerel.

2 Spec:

a =northern pike 1. chiefly Gt Lakes, AK

1792 Belknap *Hist. NH* 3.179, Pickerel, or Pike, *Esox lucius.* **1819** Thomas *Travels W. Country* 212 **IN**, The *Jack pike* or *pickerel* is an excellent fish, and weighs from six to twenty pounds. **1899** Garland *Boy Life* 124 **nwIA**, A freshet in June brought large numbers of fish up the rivers from the Mississippi, and one day the boys organized a night expedition for spearing pickerel. **1903** NY State Museum & Sci. Serv. *Bulletin* 60.299, The name pickerel [for *Esox lucius*] is used in Vermont and around Lake George, N.Y. **1927** [see **1** above]. **1943** Eddy–Surber *N. Fishes* 168, In Minnesota and parts of Wisconsin the northern pike is often called "pickerel" or "great northern pike." **1946** Dufresne *AK's Animals* 250, While there has been a tendency on the part of some Alaska residents to miscall this fish a "pickerel" or a "muskellunge," it can be very definitely stated that the Great Northern pike is the only member of the genus found in Alaska. **1950** *WELS* **WI** (*Kinds of fish that are good to eat, commonly caught in your neighborhood)* 20 Infs, Pickerel; 1 Inf, Northern pike (often called pickerel). **1952** Giddings *Arctic Woodland* 3 **nwAK**, Pickerel [=*Esox lucius*] and lingcod ("mudshark"), as well as the trout-like grayling, furnish an off-season supply of fish to be caught under the ice. **1965–70** *DARE* (Qu. P1, . . *Kinds of freshwater fish . . caught around here . . good to eat*) Inf **MI**84, Pickerel; **MI**103, Pickerel—also called "snakes"; **MN**2, Pickerel—more of a snake, longer snout than northern; **WI**38, Pickerel—really northern pike; **WI**66, Northern pickerel; **MN**29, Snake pickerel; (Qu. P14, . . *Commercial fishing . . what do the fishermen go out after?*) Infs **MI**27, 80, **OH**20, 22, 29, 67, Pickerel; **MI**84, [Inf's] father sold pickerel once in a while. **1967** *DARE* Tape **IA**15, [FW:] They get pike in the river? . . What types? [Inf:] Walleye pike. There are some northern. We call them pickerel. **1983** Becker *Fishes WI* 398, *Northern Pike—Esox lucius.* . . Pickerel. **1996** *DARE* File **WI**, A pickerel is like a northern pike, but smaller. It has yellow speckles or blotches and no marks on the fins. Some people call northerns "pickerel," but that's incorrect—a pickerel is a different fish.

b =chain pickerel. chiefly NEast

1838 MA Zool. & Bot. Surv. *Repts. Zool.* 42, The *Esox reticulatus*—pickerel—a very common species, is by many considered a great treat. **1896** Robinson *In New Engl. Fields* 122, They were only pickerel at best, though some of them, bearing their spots on a green ground, are honored with the name of "maskalonge" by our fishermen. A scratch of the finger-nail across the scaly gill-cover gives proof enough to convince even a blind man of the worthlessness of this claim to distinction. **1913** [see **1** above]. **1927** [see **1** above]. **1968** *DARE* (Qu. P1, . . *Kinds of freshwater fish . . caught around here . . good to eat*) Inf **PA**176, Pike—some call them pike—they're really pickerels; **GA**25, Eastern pickerel. **1968** *PA Game News* Jan 3 **PA**, A solitary pickerel lounging beside a sunken log waited for a school of suckers to come within striking distance. **1976** Tryckare et al. *Lore of Sportfishing* 78, Chain Pickerel . . *Esox niger.* . . Often known simply as pickerel in some locales. . . A popular sport fish and ice-fished winter in the New England states. **1996** [see **2a** above].

3 A freshwater fish of the genus *Stizostedion*. chiefly Gt Lakes Cf **pickering**

1838 Geol. Surv. OH *Second Annual Rept.* 168, *Lucio-Perca Americana.* . . Pickerel of the Lake. [*Ibid* 190, *L[ucioperca] americana.* The . . *pike of the lake.* . . is one of the most valuable fishes for the table found in the western waters, and sells readily at a high price in the markets of the towns on the banks of the Ohio. Those taken in Lake Erie are less esteemed. Two varieties are discoverable among them, which I suppose to be a mere sexual difference, though many fishermen, and market

people consider them distinct species.] **1842** DeKay *Zool. NY* 4.18, This [=*Stizostedion vitreum vitreum*] is the *Common pike, Pickerel, Pickering, Glass-eye* and *Yellow Pike* of the Great Lakes, and of most of the streams and inland lakes in the western part of the State. **1850** *Family Visitor* (OH) 3 Jan 1, Large numbers of Pike, Pickerel and white Perch visited the upper waters of the Mahoning during Spring and Summer. **1884** Goode *Fisheries U.S.* 1.419, In the fishing grounds comprised between Little Traverse Bay (passing north and east through the Straits of Mackinaw as far down the western shore of Lake Huron as Hammond's Bay) and Adams Point the name "Pickerel" is given to this species [=*Stizostedion vitreum vitreum*]. *Ibid* 420, The "Pickerel" is the most abundant and important fish in Saginaw Bay. *Ibid* 421, At all the fishing points between Ottawa City . . and the Huron fisheries, . . the greater part of the "Pickerel" are called "Gray Pickerel," and many say that they are totally different from the "Yellow" or "Blue" Pickerel. *Ibid* 424, *Stizostedium canadense.* . . The "Sauger," known also as the "Gray Pike," . . "Pickerel," and "Horse-fish," has its habitat . . in the Saint Lawrence River, Great Lake region, Upper Mississippi, and Upper Missouri Rivers, also in the Ohio. **1902** Jordan–Evermann *Amer. Fishes* 361, *Wall-eyed Pike.* . . Among the Great Lakes it is called . . pickerel in places where the true pike *(Esox lucius)* is found. **1927** [see **1** above]. **1932** OH Bur. Scientific Research *Bulletin* 23.2, The species known locally as Wall-eyed Pike, Jack Salmon, White Pike or Pickerel. . . should be stocked only in the largest tributaries of the Muskingum. **1949** Caine *N. Amer. Sport Fish* 117, *Stizostedion canadense.* . . Frequently confused with the walleye it is also known as . . Pickerel, Pickering, Pikeperch and Sand Pike. **1968** *DARE* (Qu. P1, . . *Kinds of freshwater fish . . caught around here . . good to eat*) [Inf **MN**38, Walleyed pike—or pickerel—in Canada;] **PA**136, Rockfish—dark, stripes—I call them pickerel. **1983** Becker *Fishes WI* 871, *Stizostedion vitreum vitreum.* . . Yellow walleye, pickerel [etc].

4 Fig, in ref to the narrow, pointed shape of the fish, as:

a also *pickerel sled:* A kind of coasting sled.

1943 *LANE* Map 573–74, 1 inf, neCT, Pickerel [="a low sled with solid sides coming to a point in front, often home-made"]; 1 inf, **csMA**, *Pickerel sled,* low, 'round shod', steered by a cross-bar [="a frame sled with post supported seat and a device for steering"].

b in comb *pickerel snowshoe:* See quots.

1965 Teale *Wandering Through Winter* 325 **ME**, The ones we buckled on Nellie's feet were long and slender, pickerel snowshoes. . . [He] first fitted her out with bearpaws. Then he decided that Ann's pickerel snowshoes would suit her better. **1997** *DARE* File **nwMA**, Now, about pickerel snowshoes: They are the long, skinny ones, that are shaped like a pickerel, sort of. They are not the snowshoe of choice around here where the terrain is irregular and brushy. . . Grandpa looked on them as foreign curiosities, and regarded them as cumbersome and clumsy.

c in comb *pickerel-toed:* Of a shoe: having a sharp-pointed toe.

1968 *DARE* (Qu. W42a, . . *Nicknames . . for men's sharp-pointed shoes*) Infs **IN**13, **MD**13, Pickerel-toed.

pickerel flower See **pickerelweed**

pickerel frog n [From the markings; see quot 1928]

A frog *(Rana palustris)* native to much of the eastern US. Also called **grass frog a, leopard ~, marsh ~ 1, pisser 3, spring ~, swamp ~, tiger ~, yellowlegs**

1838 Geol. Surv. OH *Second Annual Rept.* 168, *Rana palustris* . . , Pickerel Frog. **1867** *Amer. Naturalist* 1.109 **MA**, The other species of Frogs found in Massachusetts. . . are the Spotted Frog, Marsh Frog, or Pickerel Frog *(Rana palustris* . .) [etc]. **1891** Jesup *Plants Hanover NH* 62, R[ana] palustris. . . Pickerel Frog. Rather common. **1915** *Copeia* 19.13 **csWI**, During the early fall of 1914, three specimens of *Rana palustris* . . were found in a small stream entering the south side of Lake Wingra. . . Frequent and diligent search throughout the year previous had failed to disclose any pickerel frogs. **1928** Pope–Dickinson *Amphibians* 39, Pickerel Frog. . . Two rows of dark, squarish spots on back. **1949** Palmer *Nat. Hist.* 457, Pickerel Frog. . . Legs sometimes used as food and are considered poisonous by some persons. . . Will take a red-flannel-baited hook readily. **1985** Clark *From Mailbox* 45 **ME**, The leopard frog's mating song has a quality of a snore about it while the pickerel frog maintains a prolonged note.

pickerel lily See **pickerelweed**

pickerel sled See **pickerel 4a**

pickerel snowshoe See **pickerel 4b**

pickerel-toed See **pickerel 4c**

pickerelweed n Also *pickerel flower,* ~ *lily* [*OED2* 1653 →
for *Potamogeton* or other aquatic plant] **esp NEast, N Cent**
An aquatic plant *(Pontederia cordata)* native chiefly to the
eastern half of the US. Also called **alligator wampee, bull
tongue 4, cooter wampee 1, cow** ~, **dog's tongue 4, dogtongue wampee 1, Indian root 3, moosehead plant, prickler
weed, rattail 4, wampee, water hyacinth, wild gentian**
1784 in 1785 Amer. Acad. Arts & Sci. *Memoirs* 1.433, *Pontederia. . .
Pickerelweed. Blue Spike.* Blossoms blue. Common on the borders
of ponds and rivers. July. **1814** Bigelow *Florula Bostoniensis* 79,
Pontederia cordata. . . Pickerel-weed. . . During the month of July, the
tall blue spikes . . are very conspicuous on the borders of ponds and
rivers of deep water and muddy bottoms. **1842** in 1874 Hawthorne *Passages Amer. Note-Books* 2.64, The pickerel-weed . . grows just on the
edge of the water, and shoots up a long stalk crowned with a blue spire,
from among large green leaves. **1867** Emerson *May-Day* 44 neNY,
Through gold-moth-haunted beds of pickerel-flower. **1880** *Harper's
New Mth. Mag.* 61.70 **NEng,** We see the frog pond, with lush growth of
arrow leaves and pickerel weed. **1896** Robinson *In New Engl. Fields*
69, The pickerel weeds have struck their blue banners. **1901** Eckstorm
Bird Book 4 **ME,** Clumps of tall *pontederia,* which in Maine we call
both "pickerel-weed" and "moose-ear." **1944** Holton *Yankees* 147
(DA), Pink lady's slippers grew in abundance among the rosy needles,
and thence through a pasture along the pond shore, smelling of pickerel
weed, and so to the familiar swamp again. **1967–70** *DARE* (Qu. S26b,
Wildflowers that grow in water or wet places) Inf **LA**14, Pickerel lilies;
GA35, **PA**89, **RI**15, **VA**52, Pickerelweed; **MI**42, Pickerelweed—a colorful blue flower; **PA**49, Pickerelweed—spike of lavender flowers,
comes up out of water. **1968–69** *DARE* Wildfl QR Pl.8 Infs **MI**7, 31,
57, **WI**80, Pickerelweed; **OH**14, Pickrel [*sic*] weed. **1987** Hiaasen
Double Whammy 19, It looks like pickerel weeds, hair does. . . In the
water it looks like weeds.

pickering n Cf **pickerel 3**
Either a **walleye** (here: *Stizostedion vitreum vitreum*) or a
sauger n[1] (here: *S. canadense*).
1842 [see **pickerel 3**]. **1927** Weed *Pike* 46 **Gt Lakes,** Pickering [for
Stizostedion spp.] **1949** Caine *N. Amer. Sport Fish* 117, *Stizostedion
canadense. . .* Frequently confused with the walleye it is also known as
Eastern Sauger, . . Pickering, . . and Sand Pike. **1983** Becker *Fishes WI*
880, *Sauger. . .* Other common names . . pickering, jackfish, jack
salmon.

picker stick n [Transf from *picker stick* a bar that imparts motion to the shuttle of a loom]
Fig: a very thin person.
1999 *DARE* File **SC** (as of 1960s), If you saw an extremely thin
woman, you might say "She's a picker stick." This was in the Piedmont
area of South Carolina where textile mills were very common.

pickery See **picker 1**

picket See **picket pin 1**

picket house n Also *picket hut,* ~ *shack* **chiefly SW**
A house constructed of poles set upright in the ground.
[**1834** (1847) Lundy *Life & Travels* 102 **sTX,** All the houses [of Irish
living in Texas] but one are composed of pickets, thatched with bul-
rushes.] **1844** Gregg *Commerce* 1.206, Wood buildings of any kind or
shape are utterly unknown in the north of Mexico, with the exception of
an occasional picket-hut in some of the ranchos and mining-places.
1863 *Rio Abajo Weekly Press* (Albuquerque NM) 20 Jan 3/2, A certain
lot situated in the town of Mesilla . . on which is erected a picket house.
1884 Aldridge *Ranch Notes* 171 **TX,** Beyond that was a picket-house,
where the men slept. **1925** Hunter *Trail Drivers TX* 557 (as of c1860),
We lived in picket houses, covered with sod and dirt, and the flooring
with buffalo hides. **1927** Siringo *Riata* 80 **TX,** At midnight our crowd
ushered in the new year of 1881, in front of our picket shack. **1943**
Hamner *Short Grass* 6 **TX** (as of 1870s), Along the creeks, picket
houses of slender poles, set in a trench, with mud daubed between the
pickets, were used. **1967** *DARE* Tape **TX**24, There wasn't no house on
it, only a little old picket house when he bought it. . . Take poles and
stand 'em up and chink in between 'em. That's a picket house—where

they're stood up. . . and a log house, they lay 'em flat. **1986** Pederson
LAGS Concordance, 1 inf, **swMS,** Picket house—old-time house.

picket night n
=**cabbage night.**
1977–78 Foster *Lexical Variation* 35 **NJ,** In Central and North Jersey,
five Mischief Night names are found: *Picket Night* in Sayreville and
South River (Middlesex). *Ibid* 76, *Picket Night,* so called from the custom of producing noise by running a stick along a picket fence.

picket pin n [See quot 1893 at **1** below] **West**
1 also *picket, picket-pin gopher,* ~ *(ground) squirrel:*
=**ground squirrel b.**
[**1893** U.S. Dept. Ag. Div. Ornith. *Bulletin* 4.32, Throughout the prairies of the Mississippi Valley the little Striped Spermophile . . is seen
standing upright on its hind feet, straight and motionless as a stick. . . At
a little distance it is impossible to distinguish it from an old picket pin or
tent stake.] **1901** Seton *Lives of the Hunted* 214, The darling ambition
of his life . . was to catch one of the Picket-pin Gophers. . . These little
animals have a trick of sitting bolt upright on their hind legs, with their
paws held close in, so that at a distance they look exactly like picket-
pins. **1906** Stephens *CA Mammals* 71, Belding Ground Squirrel. . .
They often sit up very erect, with the forefeet held close to the breast.
This habit has given them the name of "Picket-pin," from the resemblance to a stake driven in the grass. **1936** AZ Univ. *Genl. Bulletin*
3.79, Last of the ground squirrels to be mentioned are the small ones . .
variously known over the West as spermophiles, picket-pin gophers, or
simply ground squirrels. **1941** Writers' Program *Guide WY* 413, In this
vicinity are 'picket-pin' ground squirrels, pine squirrels, and chipmunks.
1949 *PADS* 11.24 **CO,** *Picket pin. . .* A gopher. "A picket-pin gopher."
1964 Jackman–Long *OR Desert* 186, There are numerous rodents on the
desert. Some of them are mice, . . picket pin squirrels, . . pocket gophers.
1967 *DARE* (Qu. P27, . . *Kinds of squirrels*) Inf **OR**13, Picket; **WY**1,
Picket pin—so called because he sits up like a stake in the ground.
1973 Allen *LAUM* 1.322 **NE** (as of c1950), The most common . . species is the thirteen-striped ground squirrel. . . Its appearance leads to
such epithets as . . *streaked* and *striped squirrel,* and, once in Nebraska,
striped picket pin. **1980** [see **2** below].
2 A **marmot a** or a **prairie dog** (here: *Cynomys* spp).
[**1975** Zwinger *Run River* 39 **UT,** The immaturity of the soil also
shows in the pale tan rims of white-tailed prairie-dog holes which
abound along the bank. Locally called "gophers," they stand picket-pin
fashion on their haunches, stationed at the edges of their burrows, chir-
ruping like birds.] **1980** Whitaker *Audubon Field Guide Mammals* 371,
Ground squirrels, prairie dogs, the Woodchuck, and marmots are all
sometimes called "picket pins" because of the way they sit bolt upright
to survey their domain.

picket-pin gopher (or ground squirrel, squirrel) See **picket
pin 1**

picket shack See **picket house**

picket-tail n Also *picitail* [In ref to the long, pointed tail; perh
from **picked** adj[1] rather than *picket*]
A **pintail 1.**
1844 Giraud *Birds Long Is.* 394, [Index:] Duck, Picitail—310. . .
Duck, Pin-tail—310. **1888** Trumbull *Names of Birds* 38, [*Anas acuta:*]
At Milford, Conn., *Picket-tail;* this being probably the original form of a
Long Island name, which I find spelled "picketail" in my note book, and
which Giraud gives us as "Picitail" in the index to his Birds of Long Island. Several old duckers conversed with at Shinnecock Bay, Moriches,
Bellport, etc., consider this a corruption of *peaked-tail,* but I imagine
they are a little off the track. **1925** (1928) Forbush *Birds MA* 1.222,
American Pintail. . . Picket-tail. **1982** Elman *Hunter's Field Guide* 156,
Anas acuta . . picket-tail. [*Ibid* 158, The tail feathers are mostly brownish gray . . , but the two central tail feathers are black, pointed, strikingly
elongated.]

picketty adj [Prob pronc-sp for **picked** adj[1] + *-y;* cf Intro "Language Changes" III.1]
Of the sea: choppy.
1968 Coatsworth *ME Memories* 155 **cME coast,** They exclaim, "Want
to know!" at a piece of news, or say that choppy water is "picketty."

pickety adj [Prob frequentative of *picky,* but cf Intro "Language
Changes" III.1, **crinklety**]

Fussy, hypercritical.

1966–70 *DARE* (Qu. H12, *If somebody eating a meal takes little bits of food and leaves most of it on his plate, you say he _____*) Infs **AL**60, **DC**1, **SC**7, 21, Pickety (eater); (Qu. HH12, *A person who is always finding fault about unimportant things*) Inf **WA**25, Pickety.

pickety hop n [Perh rel to Scots, Ir dial *pickie(s)* hopscotch] Cf **hippety-hop**, *DS* EE19

1957 *Sat. Eve. Post Letters* nwMI (as of early 1900s), We called hopscotch 'pickety hop'.

pickey See **picky** n² 1

pick-handle n

Homemade whiskey.

1968 *DARE* (Qu. DD21c, *Nicknames for whiskey, especially illegally made whiskey*) Inf **WV**7, Pick-handle. [FW: Inf doesn't know why it's called this.] **1973** *DARE* File swPA, Illegal homemade whiskey. . . "pick handle". . . used during the ascendancy of the mining and coking industry of this western Pennsylvania bituminous coal region. I cannot explain . . this . . but I always imagined that the miners might have stirred the mash with a pick handle. . . Latrobe, PA. **1998** *NADS Letters* seKY, Pick-handle—Leslie County, Kentucky, 1946. I heard it as a term for moonshine. I remember asking a still-owner/bootlegger why it was called that; he said words to the effect that "because it hits you over the head like a pick-handle"; nwSC, Pick handle. . . homemade whiskey. Named so because when you wake up in the morning, you feel like you've been hit in the head with a pick handle. I've also heard it called "Axe-handle." This is from my grandfather, an old ridge runner from way back.

pickid adj¹ See **picked** adj¹

pickid adj² See **peaked**

pickie See **picky** n² 1

picking See **pick** v 3a

picking bow n

=**mouth bow.**

1975 McDonough *Garden Sass* 230 **AR**, Many Ozark musicians have gone on to make some of the loveliest and most unusual musical instruments in the land. Probably the simplest one is the unique mountain picking bow. . . This instrument is simply a strip of wood about thirty-eight inches long and three inches wide, curved into an arc, with a string and a key.

picking eggs See **pick eggs**

pickle n

1 A fresh cucumber *(Cucumis sativus).* **widespread, but chiefly Nth, N Midl** See Map

1950 *WELS* WI (*Names or nicknames for cucumbers*) 23 Infs, Pickles; 1 Inf, Pickles—occasionally; 1 Inf, Pickles (by those who raise them on contract); 1 Inf, Pickles—surprising to hear adults and children call [cucumbers] "pickles" in the field; 1 Inf, The common name for them is pickles—they are picked and hauled to a pickle station to be sold; 1 Inf, Patch of pickles. **1951** *PADS* 15.58 neIN (as of c1890), Pickle-vine. . . Cucumber plant. **1965–70** *DARE* (Qu. I25, *Names or nicknames for cucumbers [growing]*) 182 Infs, **widespread, but chiefly Nth, N Midl**, Pickles; **NY**79, Fresh pickles; **IL**31, Pickle patch. **1968** *DARE* Tape **IN**35, We grow onions and green beans and yellow beans and beets, carrots, tomatoes, cabbage, pickles; **WI**7, [Inf:] What we handle in the factory down here is a green cucumber. [FW:] But would you talk to somebody. . . Would you say, "How's your cucumbers?" [Inf:] No, no. "How're the pickles?" They call them pickles. . . They are cucumbers, but that's the trade—pickles. And the contract's written for pickles. . . Some of them [=contracts] mention cucumbers; **WI**34, We always called them cucumbers when they were growing and pickles when you ate them out of the can, but I kind of remember when the change came and then everybody just said pickles no matter what they were doing. And I knew it was hard to get used to, but now I guess I call—"There's a bunch of pickle plants over in the field." **1976** *DARE* File, Pickle = a large fresh cucumber . . in Millins [Market], Madison, WI. I have seen small (2–3 inch) cucumbers (to make pickles from) labeled *pickles* in Cleveland [OH] markets, but not large ones. **1996** *Ibid* seWI (as of c1960), When I was a boy we called small cucumbers "pickles" even before they were pickled.

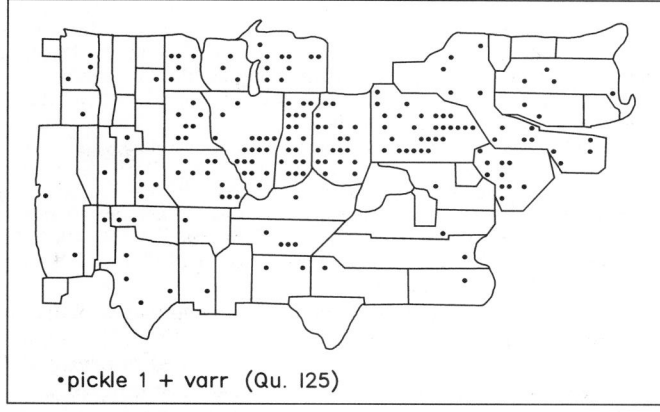

•pickle 1 + varr (Qu. I25)

2 pl: =**desert trumpet.**

1920 Saunders *Useful Wild Plants* 123, Some members of this genus [=*Eriogonum*] are prized by Indians and children for the refreshing acidity of the young stems. . . Among such is *Eriogonum inflatum*, . . the so-called "Desert Trumpet" or "Pickles," found abundantly on the southwestern desert as far north as Utah and eastward to New Mexico. It is remarkable for its bluish-green, leafless stalks, hollow and puffed out like a trumpet. . . The stems before flowering are tender and are eaten raw.

3 pl: A **wood sorrel.**

c1970 *DARE* File swIN (as of c1910), Pickles—yellow sorrel, from the shape and taste of the fruit, which children ate.

4 also *pickle card:* A pull-tab lottery ticket. **NE**

2000 Metcalf *How We Talk* 113 **NE**, The Nebraska *pickle* or *pickle card* is a printed card used in a lottery. You peel the tabs from the pickle to look for winning symbols. The pickle gets its name from the former practice of selling the cards from pickle jars at bars. **2001** *DARE* File **NE**, In a telephone conversation with the Charitable Gaming Analyst in the Nebraska Department of Revenue, the following passage was quoted to me from a Legislative report of August, 1988 entitled *The Evolution of Gambling in Nebraska:* "In the early 1970s a new gambling device called pickle cards began to appear." A canvas by the Analyst of her coworkers failed to turn up any recollection of the term before the early '70s.

picklebush See **pickleweed** 2

pickled rats n

A **unicorn plant** (here: *Proboscidea louisianica*).

1894 *Jrl. Amer. Folkl.* 7.96 **NY**, *Martynia proboscidea*, . . pickled rats. . . Name apparently transferred from the fruit, as seen pickled, to the entire plant.

pickle grass See **pickleweed** 1

picklement n [*pickle* + *-ment* B]

A difficult or awkward situation.

1945 FWP *Lay My Burden Down* 20 **TX** (as of c1865) [Black], I was too young to git in no picklement with the Klux. **1948** Manfred *Chokecherry* 56 nwIA, What a picklement I've gotten myself into. **1951** *DE Folkl. Bulletin* 1.7, Picklement (predicament). **1995** Brophy *Coll.* 55 swMO (as of c1960), Picklement. [A] predicament.

pickle plant See **pickleweed** 1

pickles See **pickle** 2, 3

pickleweed n

1 also *pickle grass*, ~ *plant*, *pickly-weed:* =**glasswort.** [See quot 1910; *EDD* pickle plant (at *pickle* sb.² 1)]

1898 Britton–Brown *Illustr. Flora* 3.577, Pickle-plant [=*Salicornia herbacea*]. **1901** Jepson *Flora CA* 182, S[alicornia] ambigua. . . Pickle-weed. . . Very abundant in salt marshes about San Francisco and Suisun Bays. **1910** Graves *Flowering Plants* 168 **CT**, *Salicornia Bigelovii*. . . Pickle Plant. Frequent on salt marshes along the coast. . . Sometimes gathered for pickling. *Salicornia europaea*. . . Pickle Plant. . . Frequent or common on salt marshes and shores. . . Often gathered for pickling. **1916** *Torreya* 16.237 **VA**, *Salicornia* spp.—Pickle grass, . . Revels I[slan]d, Va. **1939** Medsger *Edible Wild Plants* 163, Pickle Plant, Salicornia europaea. Found in salt marshes from Nova Scotia to Georgia, also about salt springs in central New York (where it is much used for pickling) and in salty soil from Manitoba to British Columbia, south to Kansas and Utah. . . Another Glasswort, *Salicornia ambigua,* which grows in salt marshes along the Pacific coast and also along the Atlantic coast is sometimes used for pickling. **1958** Jacobs–Burlage *Index Plants NC* 38, *Salicornia ambigua.* . . Pickly-weed. . . The plant grows in salt marshes of eastern North Carolina. . . The stems of this plant are used for pickling and as a food. **1964** Munz *Shore Wildflowers* 88 **CA,** Inhabiting salt marshes and low alkaline places . . is a plant with jointed leafless stems, *Pickleweed* . . *(Salicornia subterminalis).* **1973** Hitchcock–Cronquist *Flora Pacific NW* 100, Salt marshes and beaches along coast; Alas[ka] to Baja Cal[ifornia]; pickleweed . . S[alicornia] *virginica.*

2 also *picklebush:* A shrub *(Allenrolfea occidentalis)* native to alkaline desert areas of the western US. [From the appearance of the stems; see quot 1941] Also called **burroweed 1, greasewood 2e, inkweed 1, iodine bush 1, samphire 2**

1931 U.S. Dept. Ag. *Misc. Pub.* 101.36, Burroweed, or pickleweed *(Allenrolfea occidentalis)* . . is a fleshy, jointed, and practically leafless undershrub of the Great Basin and Southwest. **1941** Jaeger *Wildflowers* 48 **Desert SW,** Picklebush, pickleweed. . . Pickleweed is unique because of its almost leafless, cylindrical stems, made up of joints which appear like elongate green beads. **1960** Vines *Trees SW* 235, Pickleweed. . . is browsed by livestock only in times of great want. **1981** Benson–Darrow *Trees SW Deserts* 174, Pickleweed. . . tolerates more alkali than any other desert shrub.

3 A low-growing maritime shrub *(Batis maritima)* of the southeastern US, California, and Hawaii. [See quot 1929] Also called **saltwort**

1929 Neal *Honolulu Gardens* 108 **HI,** Akulikuli (*Batis maritima* . .). . . When broken open these [=leaves] were found to contain much salty-tasting juice, which has won for the plant the local name of "pickle-weed." In the neighborhood of patches of *akulikuli* is a strong odor also resembling that of pickles. **1967** Will *Dredgeman* 66 **FL,** The ground is now covered by the sickly, yellowish green, ground hugging shrub called batis or pickle weed. **1968** *DARE* (Qu. S26b, *Wildflowers that grow in water or wet places)* Inf **GA20,** Pickleweed.

pickly-weed See **pickleweed 1**

pick-me-up n [Prob echoic]
=**kittiwake.**
　1917 (1923) *Birds Amer.* 1.39, Kittiwake. . . Other names . . Pick-me-up.

pick needle n Cf **pick** v **1**
A **storksbill** (here: *Erodium moschatum*).
　1900 Lyons *Plant Names* 150, E[rodium] *moschatum.* . . Ground-needle, Pick-needle.

pickney See **pickaninny**

pick onto See **pick** v **2b**

pickry See **picry**

picks n, exclam Also sp *pix*
In marble play: a situation in which a marble is obstructed; a call allowing a player to clear away the obstruction or relocate the marble.
　1922 *DN* 5.187 **KY,** Picks. . . A case where an obstruction prevents shooting at a taw. . . If he cried out "Picks," he may clear it away, unless his opponent first calls, "Vence ye picks." **1942** Whipple *Joshua* 376 **UT** (as of c1860), Always shooting 'chinies' with the Peabody boys in the dooryard during Kissy's afternoon nap. ('Putcha on a pix!'—'You fudged!'—'I never!') **1966** *DARE* Tape **OK42,** If a marble happens to be in a little hole out there, we say "picks"—and you get to put that little marble up on a little knoll of dirt there. You put it up there and set that marble, you shoot at it that way. But if you say "venture picks" before I say "picks," I don't get to do it. I just got to shoot at it like it is. **1983** *MJLF* 9.1.51 **ceKY** (as of 1956), Pix . . the call which enables rearranging the object marbles within the square.

pick the rear See **pick** v **3c**

pick tree n Cf **pick** v **1**
=**Hercules'-club 1.**
　1898 Britton–Brown *Illustr. Flora* 3.577, Pick-tree [=*Aralia spinosa*].

1960 Vines *Trees SW* 792, Vernacular names are Hercules' Club, . . Picktree, Pigeon-tree, and Toothache-tree.

pick up v phr
1 To tidy up (a room or house), clear (a table); to do tidying. **chiefly NEast, N Cent, West** See Map
　1864 *Continental Mth.* 6.248, Thursday I picks up the house. **1889** (1971) Farmer *Americanisms* 419, *To pick up a room* is a New England phrase for putting it in order. **1941** *LANE* Map 336 *(She cleans up every morning),* 20 infs, **scattered NEng,** Pick(s) up; 1 inf, **cwMA,** Picks up the room; 1 inf, **csCT,** Pick it up. **1957** *Sat. Eve. Post Letters* **MA,** Back in Boston, we'd "pick up" the room while in Worcester they "tidy up" or "clean up." **1965–70** *DARE* (Qu. E21, . . *About a room that needs to be put in order* . . "*I'm just going to _____ this room.*") 31 Infs, **chiefly NEast, N Cent, West,** Pick up; **CA**182, **FL**11, **MI**61, **NY**206, **OH**87, **RI**3, Pick it up [19 of 36 total Infs young or mid-aged]; (Qu. G10, *When the meal is all over, what do you have to do to the table?)* Infs **CA**31, **NH**15, **NY**28, Pick it up; **NY**92, Pick up the table; (Qu. KK34, . . *Very neat and clean:* "*Her house always looks _____.*") Inf **IL**30, Picked up; (Qu. KK49, *When you don't have the time or ambition to do something thoroughly:* "*I'm not going to give the place a real cleaning, I'll just _____.*") Infs **CA**93, 183, **KS**15, **WI**52, Pick it up; **MO**20, Pick up the middle. **1968** *DARE* FW Addit **LA**25, Pick up the table—what you do after eating; this usage common among French, considered quaint by Inf. **1986** Pederson *LAGS Concordance (She cleans up [every morning])* 1 inf, **seMS,** Pick it up; 1 inf, **csTN,** Pick up the house—term used in family; 1 inf, **seMS,** She has heard pick up house; 1 inf, **seAL,** Pick up the house; 1 inf, **swAL,** Picking up your room. **2000** *DARE* File **cwCA** (as of c1965), What a mess! We'd better pick up around here.

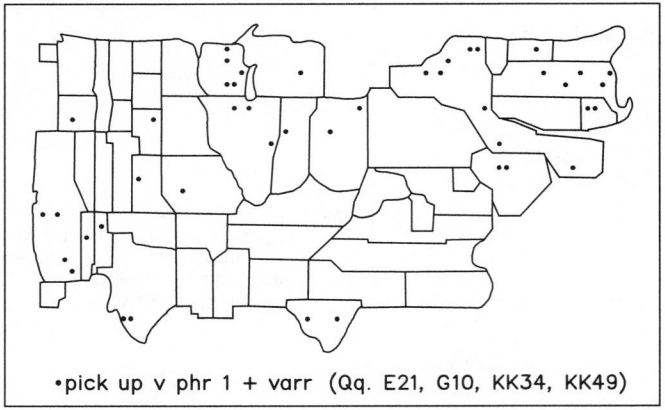

•pick up v phr 1 + varr (Qq. E21, G10, KK34, KK49)

2 See **pick** v **4.**

pickup n Cf **drop** C4
　1943 *AmSp* 18.75 **swWI** [Apple-picking terms], Those picked up off the ground. . . are officially known as *windfalls* . . and colloquially as *falls, drops,* or (once gathered) *pick-ups.*

pick up adj phr See **picked up**

pick upon (or with) See **pick** v **2b**

picky adj Cf **pick** v **1**
Prickly, thorny.
　c1970 *DARE* File **MI,** *Picky*—prickly, scratchy. "That coat is picky, especially around the collar." Rural Saginaw Co. MI; German-background farm wife, old generation. **1997** *DARE* File **nwMA,** And we'd have to wear shoes, because they [=dewberries] were picky. The vines had pickers on them.

picky n[1]
1 See **picker 1.**
2 A pine needle.
　1966 *DARE* (Qu. T6, *The pointed leaves that fall from pine trees)* Inf **MI**2, Pickies.

picky n[2]
1 also sp *pickey, pickie:* =**cat** n **3a, b. swMA** Cf **peggy** n[1], **piggy move-up**

1901 *DN* 2.145 **swMA**, *Pickie.* . . Name of a game. *Ibid* 137, *Cat.* . . A game like pickie, . . but more elaborate. **c1915** *Springfield Republican* (MA) (*W3* File), The picky is and always has been a piece of broomstick about seven inches long, whittled at both ends so as to allow it to bounce up into the air when either of those ends is hit. The propelling instrument is another piece of broomstick about 3½ feet long. The old game of picky was played with a ring about six feet in diameter. The boy who was "in bats" stood in front of this ring and was pitched to by the other boy. If the "pitch" landed in the ring the boys changed positions. Otherwise the first named remained at bat. He then took three raps at the picky, after which he estimated the distance that he had driven it. **1957** *Sat. Eve. Post Letters* **swMA** (as of c1920), *Pickey*—A broomstick piece about 4 inches long was sharpened at both ends. A broomstick piece was used as a bat to pound this, making it bounce in the air. It was then struck for distance three times. . . This game was also played where man at bat hit the pickey once. Opponent could get him out and go to bat by catching pickey in the air or failing this shoot it at the handle and hit it where it was laid down on the ground as a target. **1969** *DARE* (Qu. EE10, *A game in which a short stick lying on the ground is flipped into the air and then hit with a longer stick*) Inf **MA42**, Peggy, picky—Inf not sure of name, but knows the game.

2 in phr *picky ball:* See quot.
c1915 *Springfield Republican* (MA) (*W3* File), With picky ball the . . picky and bat remained substantially the same [as in quot c1915 at **1** above], but in every other respect the action was quickened. Instead of two boys playing the game there were at least six on a side. A diamond was laid out. . . There were first, a second and third baseman. There were two outfielders [as well as a man on a line between first and third bases].

picky-diddle conkle n Cf **conkle**
See quot.
1966 *DARE* Tape **ME24**, [FW:] What do you haul up besides lobsters in your traps? [Inf:] Oh, we get conkles and—[FW:] What kind of conkles? [Inf:] Crab conkles, and then there's some kind you can eat, and there's whore's eggs and sculpins—and we get any kind of—codfish, crabs. . . [FW:] What do you call these conkles, now? [Inf:] Crab conkles. [FW:] No, there's another kind. [Inf:] Picky-diddle conkles!

pickylilly See **piccalilli**

picnic n **WI**
A large bottle of beer.
1991 *DARE* File **seWI** (as of 1940s), A picnic of beer? Sure, we always had that—it was just the right size for me and my buddies to drink. *Ibid* **csWI** (as of 1940s), We always got a picnic of beer whenever a group was getting together. A big bottle (64 oz. or so) of beer was called a picnic of beer by everybody in Madison in the '40s. **1997** *WI State Jrl.* (Madison) 18 May sec G 1/1 **swWI**, She said the bottle in question was a "picnic," or one of the large bottles of beer large enough to serve everyone at a (small) picnic.

picnic ant n
See quot.
1969–70 *DARE* (Qu. R17, *. . Names . . for the big black ants that sting*) Inf **MA122**, Common picnic ant; **MO37**, Picnic ant; (Qu. R18, *. . Kinds of ants*) Inf **TN65**, Picnic ant.

picnic beetle n Also *picnic bug* [See quot 1972]
A beetle of the genus *Glischrochilus.*
1969 *DARE* (Qu. R30, *. . Kinds of beetles;* not asked in early QRs) Inf **IL41**, Picnic bugs. . . size of ladybugs, black hard shell, especially like beer and bread at picnics. **1972** Swan–Papp *Insects* 398, *Glischrochilus* spp. are sometimes called picnic beetles because of their intrusions into picnic grounds and barbecues; they are often a problem around fruit stands, can be dealt with effectively in small areas by luring with fermenting fruits and trapping. **1996** *Capital Times* (Madison WI) 5 Apr sec A 4, Oak wilt. . . is caused by a fungus that usually invades the root system but can also be transmitted to the leaves by picnic beetles.

picque bois See **pique bois**

picry n Also sp *pickry*
A **poison ivy 1** (here: *Toxicodendron radicans*).
1896 *Jrl. Amer. Folkl.* 9.185 **ME**, *Rhus toxicodendron* . . mercury (marc'ry), picry, Hartford, Me. **1935** (1943) Muenscher *Weeds* 329, Poison ivy, Poison oak, Poison creeper, Three-leaved ivy, Picry, Mer-

cury. **1959** Carleton *Index Herb. Plants* 91, *Pickry:* Rhus toxicodendron [sic].

picture n Usu |ˈpɪkčə(r)|; also |ˈpɪčə(r), pi-, ˈpɪktə(r)| Pronc-spp *picter, pictur, pitcher, pitch(t)ure, piture, pixture* Cf **nature**
A Forms.
1843 (1916) Hall *New Purchase* 104 **IN**, Picters to match. **1845** Thompson *Chron. of Pineville* 181 (*DAE*) **GA**, Drat your infernal picters. **1861** Holmes *Venner* 1.119 **NEng**, Jest look at the picters! **1884** *Anglia* 7.278 **Sth, S Midl** [Black], To have de picter took = to have one's picture taken. **1905** *DN* 3.57 **eNE**, An *s* is added medially after *k* in the occasional *pixture.* . . Substitution only (*t* for *k*) in *pitcher* for *picture.* **1913** Kephart *Highlanders* 120 **sAppalachians**, The women folks's seed his pictur. **1915** *DN* 4.228 **wTX**, *Pitchture.* . . Picture. **1923** *DN* 5.217 **swMO**, *Pi'ture.* . . Picture. **1928** *AmSp* 3.406 **Ozarks**, *Picture* becomes *pitcher.* **1936** *AmSp* 11.312 **Upstate NY**, In . . *picture*, [k] is occasionally lost. **c1938** in 1970 Hyatt *Hoodoo* 1.22 **seVA**, He draws his pitchure on de ground—de other man pitchure. **c1940** Eliason *Word Lists FL* 13 **wFL**, *Picture:* Common in some places. **1942** Hall *Smoky Mt. Speech* 96 **wNC, eTN**, *Picture* . . [ˈpɪktɚ]. **1953** *PADS* 19.5, The Pennsylvania German. . . pronunciation of *picter* for "picture," . . is attested not only in early American speech, but also extensively in the dialects of northern England. **1966–70** *DARE* (Qu. FF25, *Joking names for motion pictures*) Infs **OH61, TX9**, Moom pitchers; **IN5, NY205**, Moom pitchers [FW sugg]; **KY81**, I don't [have] any joking names for [ˈmuəm] pitchers; **ME15, MI18, NC60**, Moving pitchers; **MI120**, Pitchers. **1982** *Barrick Coll.* **csPA**, *Picture* . . pitcher. **1982** Slone *How We Talked* 30 **eKY** (as of c1950), *Pitcher*—picture. **1989** Karni–Jarvenpa *Sampo* 37 (as of 1919), We used to think we could get married, have our pitchers took, an' then life would start.

B Sense.
Fig: a signature.
1965–70 *DARE* (Qu. JJ13, *. . Joking words . . for a name signed to a paper: "I'll put my _____ on that.")* 10 Infs, **scattered**, Picture; **NC33**, Draw my picture on it; **OK6**, Paint my picture.

pictured-bill n [See quot 1955]
=**surf scoter.**
1888 Trumbull *Names of Birds* 103, In Massachusetts at Salem, Pictured-bill. **1917** (1923) *Birds Amer.* 1.151, *Surf Scoter.* . . *Other Names* . . Butterboat-billed Coot . . Speckle-billed Coot, Blossom-billed Coot . . Pictured-bill; Plaster-bill [etc]. **1955** MA Audubon Soc. *Bulletin* 39.377, Pictured-bill (Mass. The bill is "singularly variegated in color.")

picture elm n
Prob the English elm (*Ulmus procera*).
[**1950** Peattie *Nat. Hist. Trees* 245, Some of the . . [English] Elms produce abnormal lumpy growths on the trunk, called burls, which when sliced by the veneer knives reveal fancy figures that . . pleased the public taste.] **1967** *DARE* (Qu. T11, *. . Kinds of elm trees*) Inf **NY22**, Slippery elm, picture elm, swamp elm.

picture house n Also *picture-show house;* rarely *picture saloon old-fash*
A motion picture theater.
1908 *Variety* 23 May 12, Any time during the day you may see hundreds seated in a picture house who have settled themselves comfortably, and watch with cooling brows the reels run off. **1943** *LANE* Map 542 *(Motion picture theater)*, [Scattered exx of *picture house* occur, **chiefly in nNEng.**] 1 inf, **cNH**, Picture saloon. **1950** *WELS* (The place where you go to see a motion picture) 1 Inf, **seWI**, Picture house—by grandmother. **1966–69** *DARE* (Qu. FF24, *The place or building where people go to see motion pictures*) Infs **ME19, MN3, MT2, NJ8, NY219, VA6**, Picture house; **NC33**, Picture-show house. [6 of 7 Infs old] **1969** *DARE* Tape **IL68**, When people want to go to a show here, they either . . go to that drive-in or they go to Sparta for the show. Or to Steeleville—they have a picture house at Steeleville.

picture jasper See **picture rock 2a**

picture rock n
1 also *picture ore:* Ore in which gold or silver is plainly visible and easily processed. Cf **blossom rock**
1894 *Overland Mth.* 23.410, Siskiyou makes a fine showing of coal, gold, silver, cinnabar, asbestos, and clay; also . . four rare specimens of

detritus or picture rock. **1941** Writers' Program *Guide CO* 56, During the initial boom, ore had to be "picture rock" to attract prospectors and investors; it had to be amenable to treatment by simple processes; if gold and silver could not be seen with the naked eye, there was little enthusiasm for the "diggings" from which it came. **1950** Williams *Rocky Mts.* 169 **CO**, Picture rock and blossom rock, rich quartz with the gold just lying in an open seam to be melted down. **1968** Adams *Western Words* 130, *Gossan*—In mining, the outcrop of a lode, usually colored by the decomposition of iron. Picture ore of a very rich grade.

2 A chalcedonous mineral that, when sliced, reveals picture-like patterns; spec:

a also *picture jasper:* Jasper. [See quots]

1996 *DARE* File **eOR**, In Wild Horse Canyon in the desert of eastern Oregon, rock hounds search for picture rock—jasper that, because of its chemical composition, has brown, yellow, red, and blue colors. When sliced, the rock yields pieces that look like paintings of mountains and deserts. *Ibid* **WI**, People often come in to buy picture rock. It's also called picture jasper because the layers of colors, after cutting, look like landscapes. Although found in different places, picture rock most often comes from Montana or Wyoming.

b Perh moss agate; see quots. [From the dendritic patterns]

1966 *DARE* (Qu. C26, . . *Special kinds of stone or rock*) Inf **MT2**, Picture rock—has fern fossils on it. [**1978** Chesterman *Audubon Field Guide Rocks* 504, *Chalcedony*. . . In several varieties as . . *carnelian* and *sard* . . and . . *moss agate,* with mosslike or treelike inclusions.]

picture saloon See **picture house**

picture show n **widespread, but less freq NEast, C Atl, Pacific** See Map

The exhibition of a motion picture; a motion picture theater.

1908 *Variety* 16 May 11, A new picture show opened in the Hague building, Huntington, Ind., by the Reno Theatre Company. **1925** *Scribner's Mag.* 78.430 **ME**, There's young people, and parties, and a picture-show every night. **1940** Chandler *Farewell* 194, Folks took me to the picture show. **1942** Faulkner *Go Down* 159 **MS**, I'm going to the picture show. **1943** *LANE* Map 542, Terms denoting primarily a motion picture play or performance . . *Picture show* [7 infs **ME**, 4 **MA**, 2 **VT**]. **1958** Humphrey *Home from the Hill* 125 neTX, The picture-show lets out. **1965–70** *DARE* (Qu. FF24, *The place or building where people go to see motion pictures*) 115 Infs, **widespread, but less freq NEast, C Atl, Pacific,** Picture show; 7 Infs, **scattered,** Moving-picture show (house); **IN69**, Motion-picture show; **AL6**, Outdoor picture show; (Qu. FF25, *Joking names for motion pictures*) 26 Infs, **scattered, but esp Sth, Lower Missip Valley,** Picture show; **MO3, WA6,** Moving-picture show. **1966–70** *DARE* Tape **AL13**, We had a picture show we'd go to after school; you had a silence [sic] picture you went to see, but it didn't talk, it just show you the pictures; **CA185**, The picture shows in Hollywood were not fancy ones. . . Then we'd walk over to Clue's picture show and see it; **MI14**, We didn't have picture shows or anything else to go to. And . . no radio or television or anything of that sort. **1983** *MJLF* 9.1.50 ceKY (as of 1956), *Picture show* . . a movie theatre. *Picture show* . . a moving picture. **1986** Pederson *LAGS Concordance* **Gulf Region** *(Theater)* 94 infs, Picture show(s); 2 infs, Picture show—older term; 2 infs, Picture show—older name; 1 inf, Picture show—former name; 1 inf, Picture show—old-fashioned; 4 infs, Picture show—(for a) movie; 2 infs, Picture show—(for) movies; 1 inf, Picture show—for a play or movie; 1 inf, Picture shows—the films not the buildings; 1 inf, Picture shows—shows, not the name for the building; 1 inf, Picture shows—movies, not the building.

picture-show house See **picture house**

picuda n [Span]

A **barracuda** (here: *Sphyraena barracuda*).

1882 U.S. Natl. Museum *Bulletin* 16.412, *S[phyraena] picuda* . . Picuda; Barracuda. . . West Indies, north to Florida. **1896** *Ibid* 47.823, *Sphyrena picuda* . . Great Barracuda; Picuda; Becuna. **1902** Jordan–Evermann *Amer. Fishes* 259, Great Barracuda; Picuda. **1946** LaMonte *N. Amer. Game Fishes* 15, Great Barracuda. . . *Names:* Picuda, Becuna, Tiger of the Sea [etc].

piddle v

1 also with *about, along, around;* rarely *piss-piddle:* To dawdle, putter; to concern oneself with trifles; with *away:* to waste by trifling; hence n *pidd(e)ler* a trifler or worthless person; vbl n *piddling* trifling. [*OED2* 1545 →] **widespread, but less freq Nth, esp NEast** See Map Cf **diddle** v 5

1774 (1957) Fithian *Jrl. & Letters* 149 **NJ**, I piddled at my Exegessis [sic]. **1779** in 1854 Adams *Works* 9.490, If this was not the *piddler,* it might be the *oddity* of Virginia. **1899** (1912) Green *VA Folk-Speech* 320, *Piddle.* . . To deal in trifles; spend time in a trifling way or about trifling or unimportant matters; attend to trivial concerns, or to take the small parts rather than the main; trifle. . . *Piddler.* . . One who piddles; a mere trifler or good-for-nothing. *Piddling.* . . Trifling. **1902** *DN* 2.241 sIL, *Piddle.* . . To potter or perform seemingly unnecessary details in perfecting any work. **1903** *DN* 2.324 seMO, *Piddle.* . . To potter. To do light work. **1905** *DN* 3.90 nwAR, *Piddle.* . . 'He's just piddlin' around.' Universal. **1906** *DN* 3.122 sIN, *Piddle.* . . To chore, do light work. **1907** *DN* 3.225 nwAR, *Piddle.* . . To potter. **1909** *DN* 3.357 eAL, wGA, *Piddle.* . . To waste one's time at trifles, do small jobs about the house. Universal. *Ibid* 401 nwAR, *Piddle.* . . To waste time. "When I was a boy I piddled my time away. I was a piddeler from Piddelerville." *Piddle* in the sense of *waste time* is used by both sexes and all classes. **1912** *DN* 3.585 wIN, *Piddle.* . . To waste one's time in trifles. **1927** *DN* 5.476 Ozarks, *Piddle.* . . To potter about, to be occupied with small tasks of no great consequence. **1943** *LANE* Map 568 *(Loafing)* 1 inf, **CT**, Piddling; 2 infs, **ME**, Piddlin' round. **1949** Hedgecock *Gone Are the Days* 64 swMO, We'd piddle along on the way home from school. **1959** *VT Hist.* 27.152, *Piddle around.* . . To putter around; to waste time. Common. **1965–70** *DARE* (Qu. A10, . . *Doing little unimportant things: . . "What are you doing?" . . "Nothing in particular—I'm just _____."*) 170 Infs, **widespread, but less freq Nth, esp NEast,** Piddling (around); (Qu. KK31, *To go about aimlessly looking for distraction: "He doesn't have anything to do, so he's just _____ around."*) 28 Infs, **chiefly Midl, Sth,** Piddling; (Qu. A9, . . *Wasting time by not working on the job*) 14 Infs, **scattered, but esp Midl, Sth,** Piddling (around); **DC12**, Piddler; **IN3**, Piddling your time away; (Qu. A11, *When somebody takes too long about coming to a decision . . "I wish he'd quit _____."*) Infs **AR34, CO17, MS2, NY233, TX35**, Piddling (around); **DE4**, Piss-piddling; (Qu. A12, *When somebody keeps you waiting . . "Hurry up! I don't have all day to _____ you!"*) Inf **CA101**, Piddle around; (Qu. Y21, *To move about slowly and without energy*) Infs **MN28, MO15**, Piddle (around); (Qu.

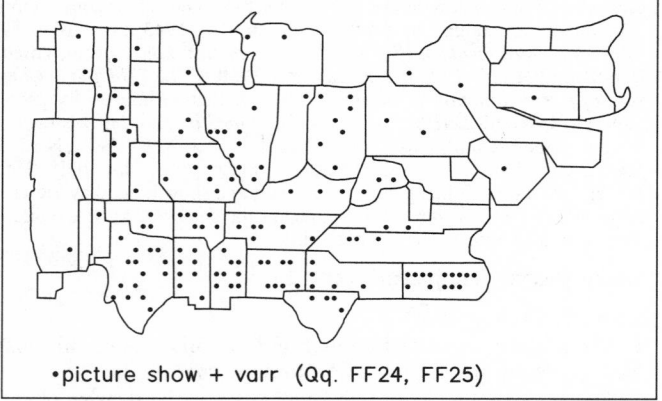

•picture show + varr (Qq. FF24, FF25)

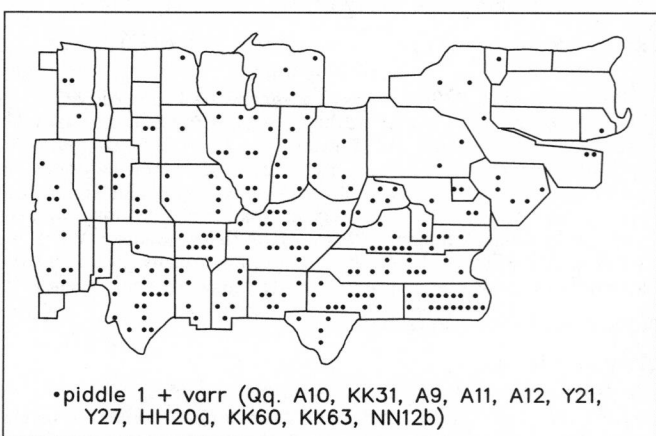

•piddle 1 + varr (Qq. A10, KK31, A9, A11, A12, Y21, Y27, HH20a, KK60, KK63, NN12b)

Y27, *To go about aimlessly, with nothing to do:* "He's always _____ around the drugstore.") Infs **FL**33, **GA**13, **LA**23, 25, **MO**27, **TX**23, **VA**31, Piddling; (Qu. HH20a, *An idle, worthless person:* "He's a _____.") Inf **AR**39, Piddler; (Qu. KK60, *Having nothing in particular to do:* "I'd just as soon go with you this afternoon—I'm anyway.") Infs **GA**31, **SC**32, 59, (Just) piddling around; (Qu. KK63, *To do a clumsy or hurried job of repairing something:* "It will never last—he just _____.") Inf **TX**27, Piddled around with it; (Qu. NN12b, *Things that people say to put off a child when he asks, "What are you making?")* Inf **VA**2, Just piddlin'. **1976** Garber *Mountain-ese* 68 **sAppalachians,** Uncle Penn kaint do much these days except to piddle about. **1992** Hunter-Gault *In My Place* 63 **GA** [Black], By the time he got back, Momma Hunter would be up and piddling around the kitchen.

2 To eat slowly with small bites or morsels.
   1902 *DN* 2.241 **sIL,** Piddle... To eat daintily, or as one with poor appetite. **1907** *DN* 3.225 **nwAR,** Piddle... To eat daintily.

3 See quot. Cf **diddle** v 3
   1912 *DN* 3.585 **wIN,** Piddle... To fornicate.

piddle about (or along, around, away), piddler, piddling See **piddle** v 1

pided See **pieded**

pidgin See **piggin** 1

pie n[1] Also *pie tag* Cf **cut the pie** 1
=**fox and geese** 2.
   1969 *DARE* (Qu. EE26, .. *Games .. children play in the snow*) Inf **IL**47, Pie—mark a big circle or pie and cut it in sections; one person is it and he has to tag another. The ones being chased have to stay within the pie sections. **1988** *DARE* File **csMN,** Pie tag is a game played in the winter time by children. We would find an open area .. and walk in a large circle about twenty feet across, making a path. Once we had a circle made in the snow we would make paths across it so it would resemble a large pie. In one of the 'slices' we would make a path half way to the center of the pie, where all the paths met. This would be gool. You could go to this spot and be safe, you couldn't be tagged... The whole time, all the players had to stay on the paths of the pie. A variation was instead of having a gool, a jail could be made instead... This could also be played on ice with skates.

pie n[2] See **paisano** 1a

pie-and-ice-cream social See **ice-cream social**

pie-anna See **piano**

pie-billed grebe See **pied-bill(ed) grebe**

piece n

1 A part (of a measure or an abstract whole)—freq in combs *piece of a load* (and varr) a part of a load, partial wagonload; *piece of the way, piece of (the) ways* a part of the way. **chiefly Sth, S Midl** See Map
   1755 in 1889 Washington *Writings* 1.161 **VA,** After waiting a day and piece in Winchester. **1890** *Century Illustr. Mag.* 41.299, [They] were escorted a piece of the way down the mountain by Spurlock and some of the others. **1927** *DN* 5.476 **Ozarks,** Piece of the ways... A part of the distance. "Maw she come a piece o' th' ways with me." **1954** Harder

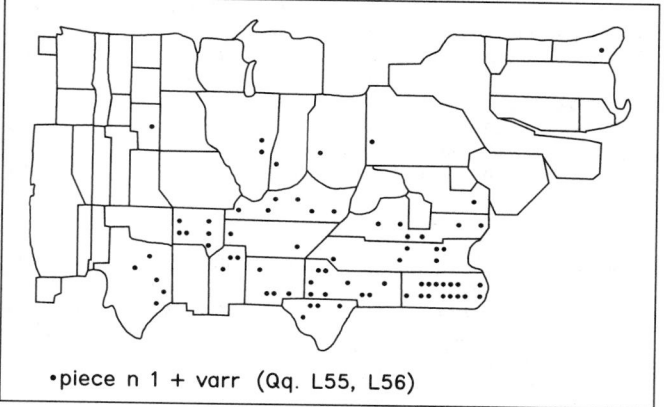

•piece n 1 + varr (Qq. L55, L56)

Coll. **cwTN,** If it's part full, we say *part of a load,* but mostly it's *piece of a load.* **1965-70** *DARE* (Qu. L55, *If the wagon was only partly full .. he had a _____*) 47 Infs, Midl, Sth, Piece of a load; 25 Infs, **Midl, Sth, S Midl,** Piece of (*or* a) load; **AL**7, **AR**40, **FL**12, Piece load; (Qu. L56, *The amount of wood a person can carry in both arms:* "We're out of firewood—I'll just get in a _____.") Inf **NC**54, Armful, few sticks, piece of a armful. **1966** Dakin *Dial. Vocab. Ohio R. Valley* 2.297, A number of Kentuckians indicate the use of *a short piece* and several speakers in the southern Mountains say *a piece o'ways.* **1967** *DARE* FW Addit **neLA,** Piece load = less than a full load. **1986** Pederson *LAGS Concordance* **Gulf Region,** 15 infs, Piece of a load; 6 infs, Piece a load; 3 infs, Piece of load. [*DARE* Ed: Defined by many as "a partial load," "half a load," or "half a wagonload."]

2 A poor specimen (of something); a kind or sort (of a). [*OED2 piece* sb. 2.e "one who partakes to some extent of the character mentioned. *Obs.*"; 1581–1768] **chiefly Sth, S Midl**
   1764 in 1950 Jefferson *Papers* 1.16 **VA,** Now Will, as you are a piece of a limner I desire that you will seat yourself immediately before your lookingglass and draw such a picture of yourself as you think proper. **1837** *S. Lit. Messenger* 3.176 **VA,** Really, from my love to the water one might take me for a piece of a poet. **1884** *Harper's New Mth. Mag.* 69.303 **eMA,** The spirit which animated her father when he went to housekeeping in a piece of a house without any front window blazed up within her. **1938** in Lib. of Congress *Amer. Memory: WPA Life Hist.* (Internet) **FL,** So I built us this little ole piece-a trailer, an we lit a shuck fer Floridy. **1966** *DARE* Tape **GA**9, A coon is a cunning rascal... He'll fool you if you just got a piece of dog. **1967** Williams *Greenbones* 227 **GA,** Nin broke in. "Let's stop for the night. Yonder's a piece of cabin." .. The old man stopped. He followed Nin into a moldy, smelly shack, tumbled down until only owls would have it. **1967-70** *DARE* (Qu. D21, *A small, poorly-built house, or one in rundown condition*) Inf **FL**49, Piece of house [laughter]; (Qu. LL13, *Not full or sufficient:* "She gave us a _____ meal.") Inf **LA**7, Piece of a. **1972** Hall *Sayings Old Smoky* 107 **eTN** (as of 1937), One day I asked Pettibone Gunter if he was sheriff of Cosby. He replied, "A piece of one," perhaps suggesting by this that he was the constable, not the sheriff, but possibly referring to his old age. **1986** Pederson *LAGS Concordance,* 1 inf, **ceGA,** Piece of a doctor—unqualified. **1996** *DARE* File **eKY** (as of 1972), My man had a piece of a mine—he war a piece of a miner, leastways till hit fell on him.

3 A quantity (of money).
   1925 *AmSp* 1.153 **West,** "A little piece of change" is a locution that means not so much a stake as a bit of surplus money to make a man feel more safe and stable. **1947** Steed *KY Tobacco Patch* 96, Well, we got a little piece of money ahead and I bought another horse. **1966-70** *DARE* (Qu. U8a, .. "It cost me ten dollars.") Inf **CA**106, Set me back a piece; (Qu. U38a, .. *A great deal of money:* "He's got _____.") Inf **PA**175, Nice piece of change; (Qu. U38b, .. *A great deal of money:* "He made a _____ [of money].") Infs **OH**102, **WA**6, (Nice) piece. **1986** Pederson *LAGS Concordance,* 1 inf, **cnAL,** Good piece of money.

4 A (small) portion or quantity not forming a single mass; also fig: a bit, the smallest amount. *esp freq among Gullah speakers*
   1926 Roberts *Time of Man* 356 **cKY,** A little piece of greens for my dinner, a little mess. **1949** Turner *Africanisms* 277 **seSC** [Gullah], If you give that old lady a piece of milk .. , that old lady is go from her. **1966** *DARE* (Qu. LL6a, *A small, indefinite amount* .. "I'll take just a _____ of cream in my coffee.") Inf **SC**9, Small piece. [Inf Black, Gullah speaker] **1971** Cunningham *Syntactic Analysis Gullah* 25, That boy there ain't got a piece of manners.

5 also *piece of fire:* A burning coal, firebrand. Cf **chunk of fire**
   1928 Peterkin *Scarlet Sister Mary* 93 **SC** [Gullah], Whyn' you bank de fire last night? E's dead as a wedge. Now I got to go borrow a piece from somebody. **1949** Turner *Africanisms* 276 **seSC** [Gullah], If you give that old lady .. a piece of fire, that old lady is go from here.

6 An extent of time; a while. [*OED2* a1300 →; "Now *dial.*"]
   1848 Bartlett *Americanisms* 249, Piece. A little while. 'Stay a piece.' **1858** Hammett *Piney Woods Tavern* 42 **TN,** We found what we wanted arter a piece. **1931** Hannum *Thursday April* 101 **wNC,** She studied about it for a good little piece. **1938** Liebling *Back Where* 34 **seNY,** After a piece an old feller come along. **1984** Wilder *You All Spoken Here* 73 **Sth,** No piece a-tall: About as long as flavor lasts in chewing gum.

7 An indefinite, often short, distance of travel; a (longer or shorter) ways; occas fig. [*OED2* 1612 →; "Chiefly *dial.*"] **widespread, but more freq Sth, Midl, TX** See Map Cf **far piece 1, pieceway(s)**

1776 *Battle of Brooklyn* 20, We was standing by the end of a side of an Indian cornfield, up yonder a-piece. **1794** (1936) Parry *Jrl.* 34.387 **PA,** On the former of these streams, on both sides of it, for a piece, it is but 2nd rate land. **1810** (1912) Bell *Journey to OH* 29 **MA,** We came but a little peice as the Dutchmen say. **1858** in 1983 *PADS* 70.45 **ce,sePA,** We left the cars and stepped into an omnibus. . . and rode quite a good piece. **1902** *DN* 2.241 **sIL,** Piece. . . A short distance. **1906** *DN* 3.122 **sIN,** I went a little piece ahead. **1907** *DN* 3.225 **nwAR,** Piece. . . A short distance. **1909** *DN* 3.357 **eAL, wGA,** Piece. . . Distance. Universal. "It's a good piece to town. Come and go a little piece with me." **1912** *DN* 3.568 **cNY,** It's quite a piece from here. **1914** *DN* 4.78 **ME, nNH,** Piece. . . A distance. **1915** *DN* 4.187 **swVA,** Piece. . . A short, indeterminate distance. **1916** *DN* 4.346 **KS, LA,** Piece. . . A short distance. **1923** *DN* 5.217 **swMO,** He went down the big road a piece. **1927** *AmSp* 2.361 **cwWV,** Can I go a piece with the girls? **1931** *AmSp* 7.20 **swPA,** I will go a piece with you. **1944** *PADS* 2.11, Piece. . . Part of the way. *Go* (*walk*) *a piece with* (someone): accompany (someone) part of the way. Deep South, parts of Mo. . . Popular. **1945** *PADS* 3.11 **cwNY,** Piece. . . From earliest childhood I have been familiar with this expression. **1945** *PADS* 3.11 **cwNY,** Piece. . . From earliest childhood I have been familiar with this expression. **1948** *WELS Suppl.* **csWI,** I had the pleasure of meeting some people that reveled in the fact that they sprung from down east stock. . . If they invited themselves to go along with you as they frequently did they would say "I'll go a piece with you." **1949** Kurath *Word Geog.* 66, In the greater part of the Midland, however, many are more apt to say *a little piece* instead of *a little way(s)*. This expression is also in common use in Delmarvia and between the Cape Fear and the Peedee. . . Pennsylvania is clearly the original home of this expression. Whether the German expression *ein klein(es) Stück* had something to do with the preservation of it in the Midland is not clear. **1965–70** *DARE* (Qu. MM25, . . *'A long distance'*: *"Texas is a _____ [from here]."*) 134 Infs, **scattered, but more freq Sth, Midl, TX,** Fur (*or* far) piece; 26 Infs, **chiefly Sth, Midl,** Good piece; 23 Infs, **scattered,** Big (*or* damn fur, deal of a, great, etc) piece; (Qu. MM24, . . *'A short distance'*: *"The river is just a _____ from the house."*) 38 Infs, **chiefly Sth, S Midl, TX,** Little piece; 24 Infs, **scattered,** Short piece; 24 Infs, **scattered,** Piece; 9 Infs, **scattered,** Small piece; **MO7, NJ44,** Down the road a piece; **TX37,** No piece; **MO20,** Piece away; (Qu. MM4, . . *A short distance past* . . *"The mail box is just _____ the pine tree."*) 24 Infs, **chiefly Sth, Midl, TX,** A little piece past (*or* beyond, etc); **IN5, KS2, 19, NY191, OH56, WI48,** A piece past (*or* beyond, aways from); **CT29,** A piece past—not a far [fɝ] piece, a short piece; **IL119,** A short piece past; **IN22, MO3, NY109,** Down the road a piece; (Qu. LL33, *A longer distance: New York or California—which is _____ from here?*) Inf **ME13,** A far piece; **TN23,** It's a fur piece; (Qu. MM1, . . *"The shed is _____ the barn."*) Inf **VA99,** Not a fur piece; (Qu. MM5, *When you're pointing out a house that's not far away: "The house is over _____."*) Infs **CA114, DC13, NY226,** A piece; **IN68, MO13,** (Just) a little piece; **LA17, NY94,** (Just) down the road a piece; **IN61,** There a piece; (Qu. MM6, . . *'Very close' or 'only a short distance away': "The house is _____ the park."*) Infs **KY19, MS6,** A little piece (away) from; **NM9, TX92,** (Back) a piece from; **NY109,** A short piece; **SC54,** Just a short piece from. **1965–70** *DARE* Tape **IN20,** We got up the road a little piece; **IN69,** How far do you live from Noblesville? . . Quite a little piece; **KY1,** This is mine. It goes above the hill a piece and then another party owns it; **TN44,** A ridge . . runs a good piece down the valley here. **1966** Dakin *Dial. Vocab. Ohio R. Valley* 2.295, *A little way.* . . The midland expression *a little piece* is commonly used everywhere and at all social levels in Kentucky. . . Above the Ohio River *a little piece* is common in Ohio from the Muskingum eastward, along the line of Zane's Trace, and westward along the National Road. . . West of Ohio *a little piece* appears with decreasing frequency. . . Especially in Kentucky, the reduced expression *a piece* (down the road) is fairly common. *Ibid* 297, *A long way.* . . Among those speakers who say *a little piece,* the expressions *a long piece, a good piece, quite a piece, a far piece,* and *a right smart piece* are fairly common. It is quite evident, however, that many speakers who use *piece* in reference to a short distance restrict the word to that usage and say *way(s)* when speaking of a longer distance. **1973** Allen *LAUM* 1.270 **Upper MW** (as of c1950), *A little way(s).* . . The Midland variant, *a little piece,* survives feebly with a 6% frequency in Iowa and 5% in Nebraska. For various reasons the latter locution is clearly dying out. . . *A long ways.* . . Still fewer (6, only 3%) report the declining Midland and South Midland *piece* as either used or overheard locally.

1989 Pederson *LAGS Tech. Index* 144 **Gulf Region** (*A little way*) 206 infs, Little piece (away / off / over); 47 infs, A piece (away); 18 infs, Short piece; 2 infs, Small piece; (*A long way*) 43 infs, Far piece; 39 infs, Good piece; 16 infs, Pretty good (little) piece; 5 infs, Good little piece; 10 infs, A piece (further); 6 infs, Quite a (little) piece; 9 infs, Long (*or* right smart, etc) piece.

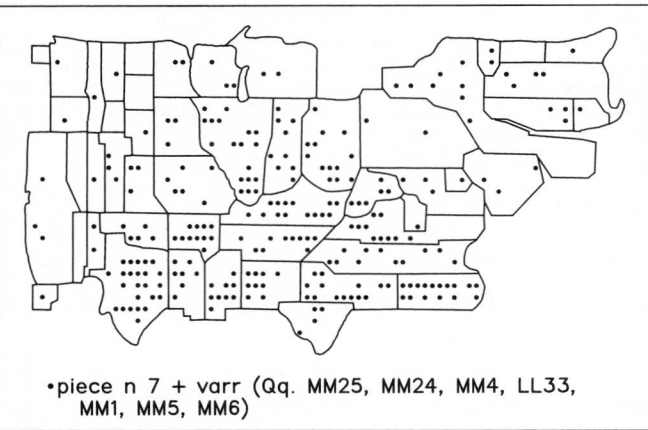

•piece n 7 + varr (Qq. MM25, MM24, MM4, LL33, MM1, MM5, MM6)

8 A slice of bread, usu with some topping; a snack or light meal. [Scots, Ir, Engl dial] **chiefly N Midl, West** See Map *old-fash* Cf **piece meal**

1847 Büttner *Briefe Nordamerika* 1.2 **OH,** In welchem [Wirthshause] wir unser "kaltes Stück" (cold piece) zu uns nahmen. [=In which [inn] we took our "cold piece."] **1870** *Nation* 28 July 56 **sePA,** "It's time to get piece" was the way of saying it was time to prepare luncheon, "piece" being still the term for a child's luncheon in the north of Ireland. **1887** Kirkland *Zury* 538 **IL,** Piece. . . A luncheon. **1907** (1970) Martin *Betrothal* 111 **sePA,** If you feel for some more supper, go to the cupboard and get a piece. Don't eat them snits. **1930** Shoemaker *1300 Words* 47 **cPA Mts** (as of c1900), Piece—A large slice of bread spread with apple butter or jelly. **1938** *Amer.–German Rev.* 5.1.41 [PaGer], Other favorite dishes included . . *Schtreivelin,* or a whorl of doughnut batter, made with a funnel pouring into hot fat, these being popular as nine o'clock pieces. **1942** Warnick *Garrett Co. MD* 12 **nwMD** (as of 1900–18), Piece . . a light lunch. **1944** in 1946 *AmSp* 21.52 **nwMN,** As children we asked, 'May we have a piece?' which meant a between-meal snack of bread and butter (usually superimposed with brown sugar, jelly, peanut-butter or anything available, the thicker the better), or a doughnut, a cookie, or a piece of pie or cake. **1946** *PADS* 5.31 **VA,** Piece. . . A lunch eaten between meals; in the Blue Ridge south to the James. **1948** *WELS Suppl.* **seWI,** The word "piece" for between meals lunch was in use in our family—My mother (91) says it was used by her mother who came from near Rochester N.Y. My husband who came from western Penna. says it was a commonly used term in his family. We must have abandoned use of the word as it is not in the vocabulary of our children. **1948** Davis *Word Atlas Gt. Lakes* 83, North Midland words . . are usually most frequent in Pennsylvania. Generally common to this area are the expressions *smearcase* and *eat a piece.* . . The expression *eat a piece* is . . concentrated in northern Indiana (north of the National Road) and in Ohio. It is rather rare in Illinois. *Ibid* 89, Certain North Midland terms set off Ohio and northern Indiana from southern Indiana (eat a *piece* is a good example). **1949** Kurath *Word Geog.* 72, *Piece* is in general use in all of Pennsylvania except for Philadelphia and its immediate vicinity, in northern West Virginia, and in the Ohio Valley. It is less common in the Shenandoah Valley and rather rare on the Kanawha, where the Southern *snack* has become established. . . *Piece* is not uncommon in the New England counties of Pennsylvania, in parts of Upstate New York, and on the Jersey side of the upper Delaware. Since Pennsylvania expressions rarely spread to these sections and since the word is not current in New England, *piece* may here have a Dutch background. **1954** *PADS* 21.33 **SC,** Morning piece. . . A layout of coffee, tea, or other beverage with crackers, cookies, or sandwiches offered to morning callers. *Evening piece* is a similar offering in the afternoon or evening. **c1955** Reed–Person *Ling. Atlas Pacific NW,* [A snack:] 6 [of c50] infs, Piece. **1965–70** *DARE* (Qu. H5, . . *A small amount of food eaten between regular meals*) 40 Infs, **chiefly Inland Nth, N Midl, SW,** Piece. [39 of 40 Infs old] **1966** Dakin *Dial. Vocab. Ohio R. Valley* 2.348, *Piece* . . is clearly the predominant oldest term everywhere in Ohio except in the lower Virginia Military District and the Zane's Trace counties west of the Muskingum where *snack* was established early. . . [T]he verb usages *piecing, snacking* = "eating between meals" are commonly noted.   **1967** Faries *Word Geog. MO* 106, *Piece* . . is concentrated north of the Hannibal and St. Joseph Railroad and is in scattered use throughout Southwest Missouri, especially in the Southwest Plains.   **1971** Bright *Word Geog. CA & NV* 180, A *snack*. . . *Piece / piecing / piecemeal(ing)* 14% [of 300 infs] Scattered.   **1982** *Barrick Coll.* **csPA,** *Piece*—a spread slice of bread, or a sandwich made from a single slice . . as in *butter piece, molasses piece* . . , *baloney piece.*

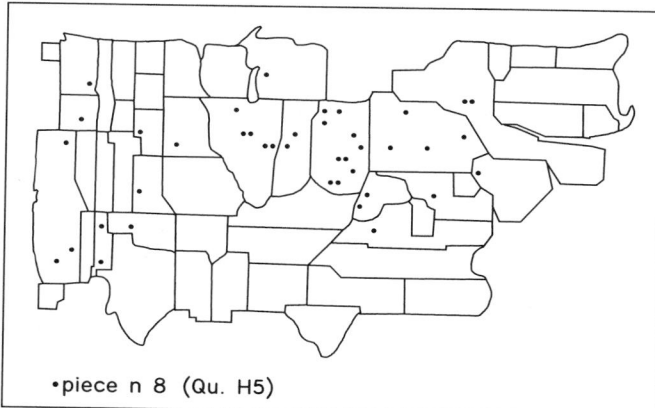

• piece n 8 (Qu. H5)

piece v

1 also with *along, around:* To snack; to eat between meals; hence vbl n *piecing* snacking; n *piecer* one who snacks. **[piece n 8]   chiefly N Midl, West   See Map   *old-fash***

1908 *German Amer. Annals* 10.38 **sePA,** *Piecing.* Eating between meals. "That child's always piecing."   **1912** *DN* 3.585 **wIN,** *Piece.* . . To eat between meals. "My children want to piece all the time."   **1941** in 1980 Welty *Coll. Stories* 53 **MS,** "So that's the way the land lies," says Uncle Rondo. There he was, piecing on the ham.   **1944** Holton *Yankees Were Like This* 242 **Cape Cod MA** (as of c1890), It was baking day and wives and mothers were usually too busy stocking the pantry shelves with a week's supply of pastry to get a regular meal at noon as on other days. So the family was encouraged to "piece around" with fresh pies, cakes and doughnuts, "staying their stomachs" until time for the baked bean supper.   **1959** Robertson *Ram* 41 **ID** (as of c1875), She could always dig a sandwich out of the box for me as we rode along, even as she scolded me for "piecing" between meals.   **1959** *VT Hist.* 27.152, *Piece.* . . To eat between meals. . . Common.   **1966** [see **piece n 8**]. **1966–70** *DARE* (Qu. H5, . . *A small amount of food eaten between regular meals*) Infs **IN**60, **OR**13, **WA**1, Piecing; **CA**97, He was piecing; **CO**7, That would be piecing; **CO**11, Mother said, "Quit piecing"; **CO**35, Piecing—eating between meals; **IA**9, Piecing between meals; **IA**22, I want you to quit piecing between meals; **IL**134, Piece or piecing; **OK**32, Piecing in between meals; **PA**242, Piecing—snacking; (Qu. H9, *If somebody always eats a considerable amount of food, you say he's a _____*) Inf **IN**30, Piecer. [12 of 13 Infs old]   **1968** Kellner *Aunt Serena* 78 **cIN** (as of 1910s), The boy was inclined to fat (also, I soon learned, to piecing on cake and candy).   **1968** *DARE* FW Addit **cIA,** *Piecing*—eating between meals. Heard. *Ibid* **cwIN,** *Piecing*—eating, nibbling between meals.   **1993** *DARE* File **nIN, nIL,** My grand-

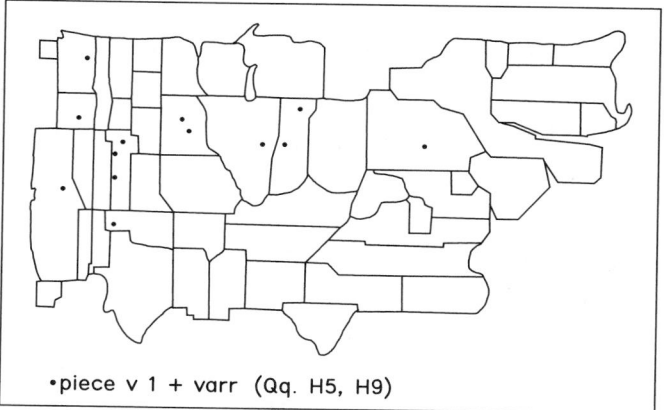

• piece v 1 + varr (Qq. H5, H9)

mother, commenting on the domestic arrangements of her recently married great-granddaughter, remarked that she thought they didn't eat a lot of regular meals, but "kind of pieced along."   **1997** *DARE* File **cnIN,** We would say piecing for eating between meals. We never called it snacking.

2 See quot. [Cf *OED2 piece* v. 3 "to come to an agreement, agree. . . *Obs.*"]

1931 *AmSp* 7.20 **swPA,** *Piece.* Agree, get on well, prosper. "Do your children piece to-day?"

3 with *along;* Fig: to make do, get along.

1979 Lewis *How to Talk Yankee* [29] **nNEng,** Well, the regular one [= a fan belt] busted and I made up one out of a piece of harness. Guess I can piece along with it till I get a new one.

piece along See **piece** v 1, 3

piece ant See **pissant** 1

piece around See **piece** v 1

piece bag n **Nth, esp NEng   *old-fash***

A bag for fragments of cloth such as those used in piecing quilts.

1869 Alcott *Little Women* 2.11 **MA,** So rich a supply of dusters, holders, and piece-bags.   **1886** Bates *Old Salem* 94 **MA,** We were allowed to play with the curious ivory chessmen which her great-uncle Joseph had brought from Calcutta; she let us look over her piece-bags, and choose one bit of silk or satin for ourselves.   **1900** Dix *Deacon Bradbury* 251 **VT,** His wife . . was upstairs sorting over her piece-bag.   **1926** Lowell *East Wind* 177 **seMA,** She would frame them / with bits of silk and ribbon from her piece-bag / and hang them in her bedroom.   **1945** *Eaton Coll.* **Milwaukee WI** (as of 1915), Piece bag . . a bag in which a housewife kept usable cloth scraps.   **1954** *WELS Suppl.* **seWI,** *Piece bag*—scraps of material (new) left over from sewing, suitable for mending, quilt making, appliqueing.

piece meal n [**piece n 8**]   **esp NC, VA, WV, Ohio Valley**

A snack or light meal; hence v phr *piece meal* to have a snack.

1946 *PADS* 5.31 **VA,** *Piece, piece meal.* . . A lunch eaten between meals; in the Blue Ridge south to the James.   **1949** Kurath *Word Geog.* 72, Scattered instances of *piece meal* . . have been recorded in the Blue Ridge [in VA, NC] and on the Kanawha [in WV].   **1966** Dakin *Dial. Vocab. Ohio R. Valley* 2.349, *Check* and *piece meal,* both of which are used along the Kanawha, are known across the river in Ohio, and the latter term is used in the White River Valley . . in Indiana.   **1967** Faries *Word Geog. MO* 106, The South Midland term *piece meal* (47 occurrences [from 700 infs]) is virtually absent from all of the southern and eastern portion of the state as far north as the Salt River and as far west as the Osage River.   **1968** *DARE* (Qu. H5, . . *A small amount of food eaten between regular meals*) Infs **WV**4, 13, Piece meal.   **1971** [see **piece n 8**].

piecen out v phr [*piece* v + *-en* suff[5]; cf *OED2 piecen* "local or techn."; 1835 →]   **esp ME   Cf piece v 3**

To extend; to eke out; to supplement, fill out something.

c1900 in 1974 *AmSp* 49.63 **sME coast,** We piecened out our bait. **1907** *DN* 3.249 **eME,** *Piecen out.* . . Piece out.   **1909** *DN* 3.421 **Cape Cod MA** (as of c1857), *Piecen out.* . . To piece out.   **1975** Gould *ME Lingo* 208, *Piecen out*—To round out the sum total: "He ate enough for a horse, and then piecened out with two slabs of pie!"

piece of a load See **piece** n 1

piece of fire See **piece** n 5

piece of the way(s), piece of ways See **piece** n 1

piecer See **piece** v 1

pieces-of-eight bird n

Prob a **wood pewee** (here: *Contopus sordidulus*) or similar **flycatcher 1a.**

1968 *DARE* (Qu. Q14) Inf **CA**87, Pieces-of-eight birds—a brush bird, lives here all year, bigger than a sparrow, grayish-brown. His call sounds like "pieces of eight."

pieceway(s) n [Prob survival of Scots idiom in which *of* is regularly omitted after *piece;* in PA perh reinforced by PaGer *schtick wegs* a part of the way]   **Cf piece** n 1, 7

A part of the way; an indefinite distance.

1886 *Amer. Philol. Assoc. Proc.* 17.xiii **ePA**, "Piece-way" of course signifies a part of the way. **1908** *German Amer. Annals* 10.38 **sePA**, *Piece-way.* Part of the way. "Won't you go with me a piece-way?" **1932** Faulkner *Light in August* 9 **MS**, I was trying to get up the road a pieceways before dark. **1944** *PADS* 2.11, *Piece.* . . Part of the way. . . In some Southern states: *a piece-ways.* **1948** in 1958 Brewer *Dog Ghosts* 32 **TX** [Black], A li'l' ole fishin' hole piece-ways down de main road. **1966–67** *DARE* (Qu. MM4, . . *A short distance past* . . *"The mail box is just _____ the pine tree."*) Inf **PA**50, A pieceways past; (Qu. MM24, . . *'A short distance':* "*The river is just a _____ from the house."*) Inf **MS**71, Piece of the way, little piece. **1967** Faries *Word Geog. MO* 97, *Piece way, a short piece,* and *a piece* are listed by a few [of 700] informants. **1971** *Today Show Letters* **sePA** [PaGer], The way a country or Dutchified person would give directions. Stop and ask one of these "How far is it to Mohnton?" and the reply might be "Chust a piecevays down the road."

pie cherry n
=sour cherry.

1817 Coxe *View of Cultivation* 249, *Kentish Red,* or *Pie Cherry* . . Is a tree of small growth, very much cultivated for pies. The flesh and juice are of a light colour, and too acid for eating in an uncooked state: the size is small and round: ripens late in June. **1845** (1847) Downing *Fruits Amer.* 166, *Morello cherries.* The common Kentish or pie cherry, and the Morello, are well known types of this class. The fruit is mostly round, with thin skin, juicy, tender, and quite *acid,* being chiefly valued for cooking, preserving, and various culinary purposes. **1908** Rogers *Tree Book* 330, The *Sour, Pie Cherry* . . which often escapes from old gardens and spreads by suckers into roadside thickets, is a European immigrant. It is believed to be the parent of our cultivated sour cherries. **1928** Rosendahl–Butters *Trees MN* 227, Sour, Pie, or Morello Cherry. **1980** Little *Audubon Guide N. Amer. Trees E. Region* 497, *Sour Cherry—"Pie Cherry." Ibid* 498, The widely cultivated common "Pie Cherry" has several ornamental varieties. **1989** Whealy *Fruit Inventory* 108, *Montmorency*—The standard for pie cherries. Medium large, bright red fruits with firm, yellow flesh and clear juice. Rich, tart, tangy flavor.

piecing See piece v 1

pie-crust squash n Also *pie-pan squash*
=pattypan squash.

1968–69 *DARE* (Qu. I23, . . *Kinds of squash*) Inf **OH**49, Pie-crust squash; **PA**210, 213, Pie-pan squash.

pied-bill See pied-bill(ed) grebe

pied-bill(ed) dabchick n Also *pied-bill dobchick, ~ dopchick*
=pied-bill(ed) grebe.

1731 Catesby *Nat. Hist. Carolina* 1.91, The Pied-Bill Dopchick. This Bird weighs half a pound. The Eyes are large, encompassed with a white Circle: the Throat has a black spot; a black list crosses the middle of the Bill. . . These Birds frequent fresh water-Ponds in many of the inhabited parts of *Carolina.* **1789** Morse *Amer. Geog.* 59, The . . Pied bill Dobchick. **1834** Nuttall *Manual Ornith.* 2.259, The Pied-Bill Dobchick is an exclusive inhabitant of the North American continent. **1844** Giraud *Birds Long Is.* 382, Pied-bill Dobchick, or Grebe. **1898** (1900) Davie *Nests N. Amer. Birds* 5, Pied-bill Dabchick, Dipper, Water-witch, "Devil-diver," and "Hell-diver" are some of the names applied to this Grebe. **1917** (1923) *Birds Amer.* 1.7, Pied-billed Grebe. . . Other Names . . American Dabchick; Pied-billed Dabchick [etc]. **1946** Hausman *Eastern Birds* 68, Pied-billed Grebe. . . Other Names . . Dipper, Pied-billed Dabchick [etc].

pied-bill(ed) grebe n Also *pie-billed grebe, pied-bill* [See quot 1955] See also **high diver**

A grebe (here: *Podilymbus podiceps*). Also called **chicken-billed grebe, dabchick, devil-diver 1, didapper 1, dipper 3a, diver, frog-in-throat, ghost duck 2, gray pond-hen 1, hell-borer, hell-diver 1, hell-hen, henbill 2, little diver, mud hen 2e, no-tail, pied-bill(ed) dabchick, plongeur, sac-a-plomb, spirit duck, tad, water witch, witch-diver**

1785 Pennant *Arctic Zool.* 2.497, *Pied-bill grebe.* . . Columbus podiceps. . . Inhabits from *New York* to *South Carolina:* is called in the first, the *Hen-beaked Wigeon,* or *Water Witch.* **1824** Latham *Genl. Hist. Birds* 10.35, *Pied-billed Grebe.* . . Columbus Podiceps. . . is common in the rivers and ponds about Savannah, in Georgia . . [and] called Didap-

per, or Water Witch. Found as far north as New York . . called there the Hen-beaked Wigeon. **1858** Baird *Birds* 898 **West**, The Pied-Bill Grebe. **1879** Rathbun *Revised List Birds* 42 **NY**, Pied-billed Grebe; *Dabchick.* A common Spring and Autumn migrant. A few breed. **1898** (1900) Davie *Nests N. Amer. Birds* 5, [Caption:] Pie-Billed Grebes and Nest. **1916** *Times–Picayune* (New Orleans LA) 26 Mar mag sec 1/3, *Pied-billed Grebe.* . . A resident of Louisiana, but in greater numbers during the winter. **1955** MA Audubon Soc. *Bulletin* 39.310, *Pied-billed Grebe.* . . Pied-bill (Mass. The beak is parti-colored.) **1967–68** *DARE* (Qu. Q5, . . *Kinds of wild ducks*) Inf **TN**11, Pied-bill grebe, didapper; (Qu. Q9, *The bird that looks like a small, dull-colored duck and is commonly found on ponds and lakes*) Inf **IA**3, Grebe, pied-bill grebe; (Qu. Q10, . . *Water birds and marsh birds*) Inf **MN**18, Hell-diver or pied-bill grebe. **1977** Udvardy *Audubon Field Guide Birds* 478, *Pied-billed Grebe.* . . black bill ring and throat in summer, white throat and bill in winter.

pied brant n
=white-fronted goose.

1888 Trumbull *Names of Birds* 11, *Pied Brant.* Known in various parts of the West as *Prairie Brant, Speckled Belly,* and *Speckled Brant.* **1895** Elliot *N. Amer. Shore Birds* 47, Although the name by which this species is generally known to the gunners of the west is Brant, it has also various others in different parts of its dispersion. Some of these are . . Gray Goose, Pied Brant [etc]. **1923** U.S. Dept. Ag. *Misc. Circular* 13.35 **LA**, *White-fronted Goose.* . . pied brant. **1931** Read *LA French* 53, *Oie Câille.* . . Other English names of this wild goose are *Speckle-Belly, Pied Brant,* and *Gray Brant.* **1982** Elman *Hunter's Field Guide* 295, *White-fronted Goose* . . *Common & Regional Names* . . speckled brant, pied brant [etc].

pied cat n Also *pieded cat, yellow pied catfish*
=flathead catfish 1.

1902 Jordan–Evermann *Amer. Fishes* 32, In the South it [=the flathead catfish] is known as the "pieded cat," Opelousas cat, and mud cat, the last of these being also generally used in the North, where it is also called granny cat. **1911** *Century Dict. Suppl., Opelousas cat,* the long-jawed catfish, *Leptops olivaris.—Pied cat.* Same as *Opelousas cat.* **1973** Knight *Cook's Fish Guide* 377, Catfish . . yellow-pied—Flathead. **1983** Becker *Fishes WI* 728, *Flathead Catfish.* . . Appaluchion, pied cat, Opelousas cat, granny cat.

pieded adj Usu |ˈpaɪdɪd|; for varr see quot 1966–70 Also *pided, piedied, pieted* chiefly **Sth, S Midl** Cf Intro "Language Changes" II.5, **piedidy, piedy**
Pied, spotted, mottled.

1757 *SC Gaz.* (Charleston) 23 June [4]/2, A black and white pided cow . . A red and white pided heifer. **1845** (1969) Hooper *Advent. Simon Suggs* 144 **AL**, The ole feller looked as pided as a rattle-snaik. **1855** in 1956 Eliason *Tarheel Talk* 287 **c,csNC**, Pided cow. **1867** Harris *Sut Lovingood Yarns* 252 **TN**, Wirt wer bilin hot; nobody tu gainsay him, hed made him piedied all over; he were plum pizen. **1902** *DN* 2.241 **sIL**, *Pided* [ˈpaɪdɪd]. . . Pied. **1903** *DN* 2.324 **seMO**, *Pided.* . . Pied; spotted. 'The cow is pided all over.' **1905** *DN* 3.90 **nwAR**, *Pieded.* . . Mottled. 'Her face is pieded when she has a cold.' Common. **1917** *DN* 4.415 **wNC**, *Pieded.* . . Pied; piebald. **1921** *DN* 5.116 **KY**, *Pieded,* pied. Variegated. "A pieded cow jumped in the field." **1927** *AmSp* 2.361 **cwWV**, *Pieded.* **1927** *DN* 5.476 **Ozarks**, *Pieded-like.* . . In poor health, of an unhealthy complexion. "Lizzie looks kinder pieded-like lately." The word really means spotted, or pied. **1930** Raine-Barnes *Cattle* 300, I just seen that old pieded . . steer we lost out of the herd last fall. **1931** *AmSp* 7.91 **eKY**, *Pieded,* spotted in color. . . "That pieded heifer gives the most milk." **1933** Rawlings *South Moon* 6 **nFL**, There was oncet hundreds o' wolves, quare-lookin' and pieded. **c1938** in 1970 Hyatt *Hoodoo* 1.228 **Mobile AL**, Den it became pi-ded . . jest like a snake—brown and clar-water-looking—pided. **1944** *PADS* 2.47 **NC**, *Pieded* [ˈpaɪdɪd]. . . Spotted. **1954** *Harder Coll.* **cwTN**, *Pieded.* . . A cow that is "black and white striped." **1966–70** *DARE* (Qu. J5, *A cat with fur of mixed colors*) Inf **GA**19, [ˈpaɪdɪd] (predominantly one color); **KY**84, [ˈpaɪdɪd] cat; (Qu. K37, . . *A horse of mixed colors*) Infs **FL**32, 34, [ˈpaɪdɪd]; **GA**7, [ˈpaɪdɪd]; **GA**22, 39, [ˈpa(ɪ)dɪd] horse; **GA**46, [ˈpadɪd] [laughter]—old-fashioned. **1984** *Annals Internal Med.* 100.899 **wAL**, I saw a patient with a blotchy, purplish discoloration of the skin from circulatory insufficiency who was said to be *purple pieted.* **1986** Pederson *LAGS Concordance,* 1 inf, **nwFL**, Pieded—speckled butter bean. **1990** Cavender *Folk Med. Lexicon* 28 **sAppalachians**, *Pieded*—skin or wound having a variegated, blotchy appearance: "My leg swelled up and got pieded." **2001** House *Clay's Quilt* 117 **eKY,** My Baby. . . You are little as I write this. You're sleeping on the pallet across the room from me, all little hands and pieded skin.

pieded cat See **pied cat**

pieded curlew n [See quot]
=**white ibis.**

  1913 *Auk* 30.491 **Okefenokee GA,** The natives speak of 'Brown Curlews' which often fly and feed apart from the white forms. They also designate some brown and white ones as 'Pieded Curlews' or 'Black-pieded Curlews,' which roost with the other two.

pied gray duck See **gray duck c**

piedidy adj Cf Intro "Language Changes" III.1, **fadedy**
=**pieded.**

  1963 Watkins–Watkins *Yesterday Hills* 47 **cnGA,** The hot fire baked the blood in the front of the girls' legs, and they looked bloodshotten or piedidy.

piedied See **pieded**

pied jaune n Also *patte jaune* [LaFr, literally "yellow-foot"]
A **yellowlegs** (here: either *Totanus flavipes* or *T. melanoleucus*).

  1897 *Auk* 14.288 **LA,** *Greater Yellowlegs.*—Known as *Pied jaune.*
1916 *Times-Picayune* (New Orleans LA) 2 Apr mag sec 8/1, *Greater Yellow-legs.* . . Klook-klook. Pied Jaune.—The very long and slender chrome-yellow legs characterize this bird, and explains [sic] its common name. *Ibid, Lesser Yellow-legs.* . . Pied jaune. **1923** U.S. Dept. Ag. *Misc. Circular* 13.60 **LA,** The two species of yellowlegs share a number of names. . . *In local use* . . patte jaune, pied jaune (yellowlegs). **1996** *DARE* File **sLA,** These names, *pied jaune* and *patte jaune,* are still used in French and to a lesser degree perhaps in English just as we still use gros-bec in English for another bird. The pronunciation would be . . [pje žon] . . and [pɑt žon].

pie dock n [See quots]
=**canaigre.**

  1923 in 1925 Jepson *Manual Plants CA* 292, *R[umex] hymenosepalus* . . *Canaigre.* . . The stem is used as a substitute for rhubarb, whence the names Wild Rhubarb, Pie Dock, and Sour Dock. **1945** Wodehouse *Hayfever Plants* 94, The canaigre. . . is a coarse perennial herb growing naturally in dry sandy washes from California eastward to New Mexico. It is also cultivated for its large fleshy dahlia-like roots which are used for tanning leather, and its juicy stem which is used as a substitute for rhubarb. As a consequence of these uses it is sometimes known in these regions as pie or sour dock, and wild rhubarb.

pied sheldrake n [Cf quot 1888 at **pied whistler**] **esp NY**
Usu the **red-breasted merganser,** but also the **hooded merganser.**

  1792 Belknap *Hist. NH* 3.168, Pyed Sheldrake, *Mergus castor?* **1844** DeKay *Zool. NY* 2.319, The Red-breasted Sheldrake. . . This species is also called the *Sawbill, Whistler,* and *Pied Sheldrake,* in this State. **1844** Giraud *Birds Long Is.* 343 **NY,** This species [=*Mergus serrator*] is called by our gunners "Pied Shell Drake." **1910** Eaton *Birds NY* 1.180, The Red-breasted merganser, Sawbill, Indian, or Pied sheldrake, as this species is called, is one of the most abundant ducks along the coast and on the inland waters. **1923** U.S. Dept. Ag. *Misc. Circular* 13.7, *Hooded Merganser.* . . pied sheldrake (N.H., Long I[slan]d, N.Y.) **1982** Elman *Hunter's Field Guide* 230, Red-breasted Merganser . . *Common & Regional Names* . . Long Island sheldrake, pied sheldrake [etc].

pie duck n
=**goldeneye 1.**

  [**1923** U.S. Dept. Ag. *Misc. Circular* 13.22, *Goldeneye.* . . *Vernacular Names.* . . *In local use.* . . Pie duck (N[ew]f[oundlan]d).] **1982** Elman *Hunter's Field Guide* 218, *American Goldeneye* . . Common & Regional Names . . pie duck, pied whistler [etc]. *Ibid* 221, *Barrow's Goldeneye* . . whistle-wing, pie duck [etc].

pied wamp See **wamp**

pied whistler n Cf **whistler**
The male **goldeneye 1.**

  1888 Trumbull *Names of Birds* 78 **swCT, Long Is. NY,** At Milford, Conn., and Shinnecock, the adult drake, though recognized by all as of the same species [=*Glaucionetta clangula americana*] with the rest, is commonly referred to as the "pied Whistler." [Footnote to *pied whistler:*] The word "pied" is peculiarly popular on Long Island, where the gunners prefix it to local names to designate the "full dressed" male of any species whose plumage *is* pied or showily variegated, and when I asked an old ducker if he did not think the present species particularly handsome, he said, "Yes, the *pied* ones are very handsome." **1923** U.S. Dept. Ag. *Misc. Circular* 13.22, *Goldeneye* . . Vernacular Names. . . pied whistler (Conn., Long I[slan]d, N.Y.) **1955** MA Audubon Soc. *Bulletin* 39.316, *American Golden-eye.* . . Pied Whistler (Conn. In allusion to the whistling sound made by the wings in flight.) **1982** [see **pie duck**].

pied widgeon n
The female **pintail 1.**

  1917 (1923) *Birds Amer.* 1.128, *Pintail.* . . *Other Names.* . . *Female:* Gray Duck; Pied Gray Duck, Pied Widgeon.

pied-winged coot n [See quot 1955]
=**white-winged scoter.**

  1888 Trumbull *Names of Birds* 99 **seNH, neMA,** At Portsmouth, N.H., and at Rowley and Salem, Mass., [the white-winged scoter is called] *pied-winged coot.* **1929** Forbush *Birds MA* 1.274, *White-winged Scoter. Other names:* Black White-wing . . Pied-winged Coot [etc]. **1955** MA Audubon Soc. *Bulletin* 39.376, White-winged Scoter. . . Pied-winged Coot (N.H., Mass. The speculum is white.)

pied-winged curlew n Also *pied-wing curlew* [See quots 1925, 1956] **esp MA**
=**willet.**

  1888 Trumbull *Names of Birds* 164 **neMA,** *Semipalmated Snipe.* . . Mr. Raymond L. Newcomb tells me of hearing it also called, at Salem, the *Pied-winged curlew.* **1925** (1928) Forbush *Birds MA* 1.443, *Willet. Other names:* humility; pied-wing curlew; white-wing. . . When it flies or even raises its wings the unmistakable long, wide, white patches up both upper and under surfaces of blackish wing identify it; no other bird like it on our coast except its sister variety, the Western Willet. **1956** MA Audubon Soc. *Bulletin* 40.18, *Willet.* . . Pied-wing Curlew (Mass. When lifted, the wings have a percurrent white band bordered on each sade [sic] by blackish; "Curlew" is a technical misnomer, although possibly of independent sonic origin for this species.)

piedy adj **S Midl**
=**pieded.**

  1895 *DN* 1.373 **seKY, eTN, wNC,** *Piedy:* spotted. "A sort of piedy cow." **1909** *DN* 3.401 **nwAR,** *Piedy.* . . Spotted. **1924** Raine *Land of Saddle-Bags* 98 **sAppalachians,** Caliban's *pied ninny,* as also Milton's "meadows trim with daisies pied," come to mind when we hear a boy praise his *piedied* (or *piedy*) cow. **1927** *DN* 5.476 **Ozarks,** *Piedy.* . . Spotted. "I shore caint abide thet 'ar piedy hoss." **1952** Brown *NC Folkl.* 1.576 **cwNC,** *Piedy.* . . Same as *pieded.* **1954** *Harder Coll.* **cwTN,** *Piedy.* . . Spotted. **1981** Pederson *LAGS Basic Materials,* 1 inf, **cMS,** ['pʻaˑ·dɪˆ ,mɑˈkəsn̩] [=piedy moccasin, a snake].

pie elder n
An **elder 2** (here: *Sambucus canadensis*).

  1960 Vines *Trees SW* 942, It [=the American Elder] is also known under the local names of Elderberry, Common Elder, Sweet Elder, Pie Elder, and Elder-blow. . . The fruit is made into pies, wines, and jellies.

piemarker n Also *pieprint* [See quots 1899, 1948]
A **velvetleaf** (here: *Abutilon theophrasti*).

  1896 *Jrl. Amer. Folkl.* 9.183 **MO, OH,** *Abutilon Avicennæ,* . . pie-print, S.W. Mo.₍₃₎ pie marker, . . Sulphur Grove, Ohio. . . Used to stamp pie-crust. **1899** Bergen *Animal Lore* 120 **OH, IL, IA, MO,** *Abutilon Avicennæ* is called "butter-print," "pie-print," and "pie-marker," because its pods are used to stamp butter or pie-crust. **1924** *Amer. Botanist* 30.108, *Abutilon Theophrasti.* . . The seed-pod is a curious affair with radiating points at the top. . . From the appearance of this pod has come such names as "piemarker," "pie-print." **1948** Stevens *KS Wild Flowers* 83, *Abutilon theophrasti.* . . 'Piemarker' because of the resemblance of the fluted [fruit] capsule to that implement. **1967** *DARE* (Qu. S21, . . *Weeds . . that are a trouble in gardens and fields*) Inf **IL19,** Cottonweed, buttonweed, piemarker, velvetweed—all same.

pie melon n **chiefly Sth, S Midl, SW** See Map on p. 128 *old-fash*
=**citron melon.**

1860 MI State Ag. Soc. *Trans. for 1858* 10.623, Best pie melon, H.T. Young. . . [\$0.]50. **1888** Hillebrand *Flora Hawaiian Is.* 134, To the latter species [=*Citrullus Citrullus*] has to be referred as a variety the much esteemed Pie-melon. **1948** Wolfe *Farm Gloss.* 312, Stockmelon—Practically the same as citron melon and is sometimes called pie melon. A kind of non-saccharine watermelon planted usually in corn fields for livestock and for making preserves. **1957** Battaglia *Resp. to PADS 20* **eMD** (*Kinds of pumpkins that grow in your neighborhood*) Pie melons, cow pumpkin. **1966–70** *DARE* (Qu. I26, . . *Kinds of melons*) Infs **AR**51, **KS**6, **KY**56, 66, **SC**29, Pie melon(s); **CA**36, Pie melon—a citron, really; **NC**87, Pie melon—like a small watermelon—light green or striped, yellow inside, good only for cooking and pies; **OK**18, Pie melon—good only for preserves; **SC**22, Pie melon—like a small watermelon, but they're too hard to cut or eat, so they're fed to hogs; **TX**11, Pie melon—grows wild; **TX**42, Pie melon—livestock eat them; make preserves out of them; **TX**67, Pie melon—not grown anymore. [All Infs old] **1986** Pederson *LAGS Concordance,* 1 inf, **cAL**, Pie melon = citron melon, not very sweet; 1 inf, **seAL**, Pie melon; 1 inf, **seAL**, Pie melon = pumpkin [melon]; 1 inf, **seAL**, Pie melon—small watermelon; 1 inf, **csAL**, Pie melons—mother made preserves of them—hard; 1 inf, **csAL**, Pie melons—look like watermelons, no good, hard; 1 inf, **nwAL**, Pie melon—similar to watermelon, not edible; 1 inf, **ceFL**, Pie melon—large, 40–50 pounds, open with hatchet; 1 inf, **nwFL**, Pie melons—make pies out of them; 1 inf, **seGA**, Pie melon—smaller than pumpkin, used in pies; 1 inf, **csLA**, Pie melon—a kind of melon you make a pie from; 1 inf, **cwLA**, Pie melons; 1 inf, **cMS**, Pie melon—green skin, meat, used in pies; 1 inf, **ceMS**, Pie melon—real good but there ain't much to it; 1 inf, **seMS**, Pie melon—looks just like a little watermelon; 1 inf, **seMS**, Pie melon—round, white; 1 inf, **csMS**, Pie melon; 1 inf, **swMS**, Pie melon—very hard, looks like watermelon; 1 inf, **swTN**, Pie melon = cue melon—for preserves; 1 inf, **cTX**, Pie melon; 1 inf, **csTX**, Pie melon—tough skin. [15 of 21 infs old]

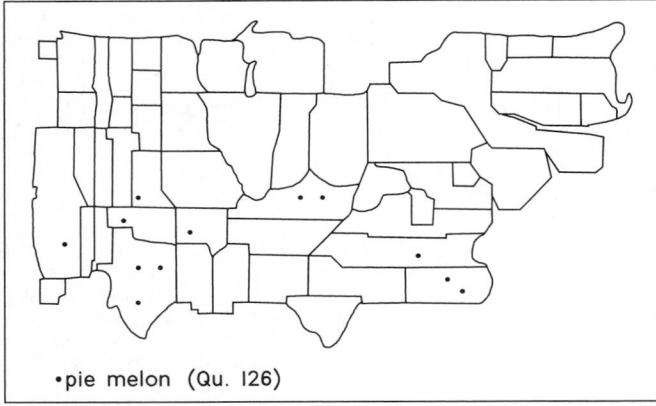

•pie melon (Qu. I26)

pie-pan squash See **pie-crust squash**

pieplant n **widespread exc Sth** See Map Cf **wild pieplant** =**rhubarb B.**

1838 *Youth's Mag.* July 91, Half a dozen roots of the pie-plant [rhubarb] will furnish abundant materials for pies and tarts. **1864** Lowell *Fireside Travels* 26 **MA**, His *pie-plants* . . blanched under barrels, each in his little hermitage, a vegetable Certosa. **1884** Nye *Baled Hay* 207, Afterward pulverize and spread over the pie plant bed. **1892** *Jrl. Amer. Folkl.* 5.102, *Rheum Rhaponticum*, pie-plant. General in Middle States and westward. **1896** *Daily News Cook Book* 227 **MN**, Baked Pie-plant—Wash and wipe dry one bunch of pieplant. Cut in inch bits without peeling. **1907** *DN* 3.196 **seNH**, *Pie-plant.* . . Rhubarb. **1908** (1911) Gale *Friendship Village* 45 **cWI**, Mis' Mayor Uppers tapped at my back door, with . . a jar of pineapple and pie-plant preserves "to chink in." **1910** *DN* 3.446 **cwNY**, *Pie-plant.* . . Rhubarb. **1927** *AmSp* 2.361 **cwWV**, *Pieplant pie* . . rhubarb pie. **1935** Sandoz *Jules* 71 **wNE** (as of 1880–1930), Often, too, there was a glass of wine, pieplant at first, currant later in the summer. **1950** *WELS* (*Other names for rhubarb*) 52 Infs, **WI**, Pieplant. **1962** Dykeman *Tall Woman* 181 **NC** (as of c1860), This was the first year since she had planted the roots Robert brought her from town that she had had enough rhubarb, or pieplant, to make a decent dish. **1965–70** *DARE* (Qu. I30, *Other names for rhubarb*) 474 Infs, **widespread exc Sth**, Pieplant; **MI**1, Pieplant [FW sugg]; some call it raspberry pieplant; (Qu. BB22, . . *Home remedies . . for constipation*)

Inf **WI**12, Pieplant juice; (Qu. BB50d, *Favorite spring tonics*) Inf **IL**9, Pieplant; (Qu. DD28b, . . *Fermented drinks . . made at home*) Inf **WI**12, Pieplant wine. **1967** Fetterman *Stinking Creek* 84 **seKY**, I have seen pie plants—some call them rhubarb—big as your arm. **1982** Slone *How We Talked* 26 **eKY** (as of c1950), *Pie plant*—rhubarb. **1985** Clark *From Mailbox* 58 **ME**, Probably because sugar was a scarce commodity in rural New England, it was after 1800 that rhubarb gained the Yankee name "pieplant." **1986** Pederson *LAGS Concordance,* 3 infs, **TN**, Pieplant; 1 inf, **nwAR**, Pieplant. **1991** *DARE* File **seWI**, We used to always call rhubarb, pie plant!

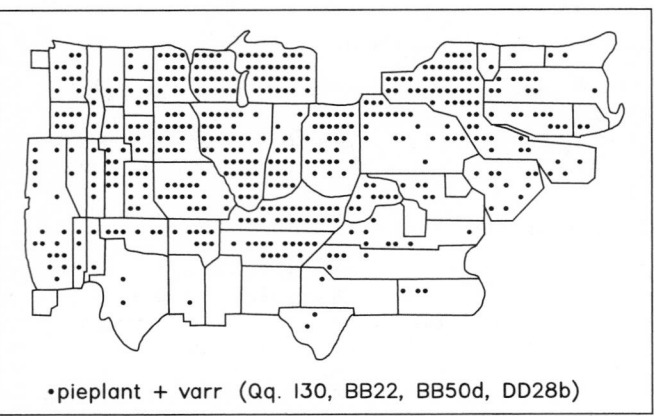

•pieplant + varr (Qq. I30, BB22, BB50d, DD28b)

pieprint See **piemarker**

pie pumpkin n Cf **pie squash, sugar pumpkin**

A **pumpkin** n[1] **B1,** usu a cultivar of *Cucurbita pepo,* used for pies; see quots.

1907 *DN* 3.248 **eME**, *Pie punkin.* . . Small round pumpkin which makes excellent pie. **1925** *Book of Rural Life* 4552, There are several varieties of pumpkins, which fall into two groups, the ordinary field pumpkins and the various sweet or pie pumpkins that have been bred up from the common stock. **1949** Arnow *Hunter's Horn* 282 **eKY**, But here and yonder on the floor would be a big warty cushaw or a pile of little red-gold pie pumpkins. **1950** *WELS* **WI** (*Kinds of pumpkins that grow in your neighborhood*) 22 Infs, Pie pumpkin; 5 Infs, Pie pumpkin(s)—small; 3 Infs, Pie pumpkin—small, sweet; 1 Inf, Pie pumpkin—small, orange; 1 Inf, Only kind I'm familiar with is just the yellow pie pumpkin; 1 Inf, Pie pumpkin—small, flat; 1 Inf, Little round orange sweet pumpkins are sugar pumpkins, but most everyone says "pie pumpkins"; 1 Inf, Pie pumpkin—small, tender, yellow; 1 Inf, Pie pumpkin—sweet, more firm flesh; 1 Inf, Pie pumpkin—smaller in size [than field pumpkin] and slightly sweet; 1 Inf, Pie pumpkin—small, yellow; 1 Inf, Pie pumpkin—small and tender; 1 Inf, New England pie pumpkin. **1965–70** *DARE* (Qu. I24, . . *Kinds of pumpkins;* total Infs questioned, 75) Infs **AR**39, **FL**6, 8, 9, 17, 26, **MS**1, 16, **OK**49, Pie pumpkin(s); **FL**11, Pie pumpkins—medium-sized, round orange ones; **FL**19, Pie pumpkins or butternut pumpkins—small ones; **FL**27, A few raise . . the little pie pumpkins; **MS**59, Miniature pie pumpkins; **NM**2, Pie pumpkin—most commonly grown, small, yellow, round, flat top; **OK**3, Pie pumpkin—deep yellow; **OK**27, Pie pumpkin—small, round, rich, golden orange; **OK**32, Pie pumpkin—round, yellow, get up to 100 pounds, kind of a golden color; **OK**43, Pie pumpkin—small, round, orange flesh; **AR**27, Pie punkins; (Qu. I23, . . *Kinds of squash*) Infs **CO**3, Pie pumpkin—large and small; **IN**7, Pie pumpkin. **1975** Olds Seed Co. *Seeds* 21, The famous New England Pie Pumpkin. A rather small, round but flattened variety about 8 by 10 inches, fine grained and high in sugar content. . . Color, deep orange-yellow. **1986** Pederson *LAGS Concordance* (*Pumpkin*) 1 inf, **cnAR**, Pie pumpkin; 1 inf, **ceTN**, Pie pumpkin. **1988** Whealy *Garden Seed Inventory* (2d ed) 343, Squash (Pepo). . . Luxury Pie Pumpkin. . . Nearly globe, 10 in. dia., finely netted golden russet skin which is a sign of finest quality. *Ibid* 344, Squash (Pepo). . . Small Sugar (New England Pie Pumpkin, Northeast Pie, Boston Pie [etc]) . . Classic pie pumpkin, small round slightly flattened light-ribbed orange globes, 7–9 x 8–12 in. dia., 5–8 lbs., fine-grained stringless sweet thick yellow flesh, widely believed to be the best for canning or pies. **1996** *DARE* File **NEng**, To make a really good pumpkin pie you have to use pie pumpkin. I've found that in the Midwest people use cow or field pumpkins for pie. The flavor and texture just don't compare to

New England pie pumpkins. They're smaller than a jack-o'-lantern and round. Sometimes there are green streaks in the orange color.

pierogi n Also sp *pierogie, pirogi;* pronc-spp *padogie, pirohi, pirotti* [Polish *pierogi* pl of *pierog* dumpling] **chiefly in Polish settlement areas, esp PA** Cf **pirok, piroshki**
A filled dumpling, usu boiled; see quots.

1948 (1949) *Treasured Pol. Recipes* 114, *Pierogi*—2 eggs[,] ½ cup water[,] 2 cups flour[,] ½ t salt[.] Mound flour on kneading board and make hole in center. Drop eggs into hole and cut into flour with knife. Add salt and water and knead. . . Cut circles. . . Place a small spoonful of filling . . on each round . . and press edges together firmly. . . Drop *pierogi* into salted boiling water. **c1965** Randle *Cookbooks* (Ask Neighbor) 1.53, *Polish Pierogi.* **1968** *Amherst Rec.* (MA) 27 Nov 6, The meal includes: Pierogi with filling of cabbage, prunes, and potatoes and cheese. **1968–69** *DARE* (Qu. H45, *Dishes made with meat, fish, or poultry that everybody around here would know, but that people in other places might not*) Inf **MA**48, Pierogi; **PA**110, Pierogi—dough, mashed meat . . potato, cheese, prunes, meat pies; (Qu. H49, *Dishes made by boiling potatoes with other foods*) Inf **PA**176, Padogies [pəˈdogiz]— mashed potatoes mixed with melted cheese; roll out potpie dough, make into triangles, put potatoes in dough, press down edges and drop in boiling water; serve buttered; (Qu. H65, *Foreign foods favored by people around here*) Inf **MA**48, Pierogi; **NY**49, Pieregi (Polish)—like dumplings stuffed with meat; **NY**199, Pierogi; **PA**225, Pierogis; **PA**67, Pirotti—triangle of dough filled with potatoes, cheese, sauerkraut, sweet cabbages. Use with sour cream dip. Cooked in boiling water or baked; **PA**176, Padogies. **1985** *Capital Times* (Madison WI) 24 July 12/6 **Chicago IL,** Do you think that in Russia any newsman would ever have an opportunity to make that much money by biting into a pirogi? **1989** *Valley Advocate* (Hatfield MA) 10 Apr 33/1, Father Snieziak went on to explain that the two big times for traditional Polish food are Christmas and Easter. At Christmastime, soup and pierogi ("giant tortellini stuffed with fried cabbage, or cheese or other fillings") are served. **1995** *Daily Hampshire Gaz.* (Northampton MA) 6 Jan Suppl 6 **CT,** A parishioner who ran a baking business offered to donate $1,000 worth of homemade pierogis to the cause. The "Holy Pierogies," as they're called, proved so popular that the pastor . . decided to make them a permanent fund-raiser. . . The stuffed pastries come in four flavors—cheese, potato and cheese, cabbage, and cabbage and mushroom. **1996** *Capital Times* (Madison WI) 1 Apr sec A 3/2, Pirogis—potato-filled pockets of pasta— . . were part of the program Sunday during the 16th Polish Spring Festival. **1997** *DARE* File ce**PA**, *Padogies* is a variant of *pierogies.* I'm from the Coal Region of East-Central PA, and many people refer to pierogies this way. . . Pierogies are semi-circular potato-filled pasta pocket[s]. *Ibid* w**PA**, Being also of Polish ancestry, I've had my share of pierogies. . . In the Polish language R's are rolled. Thus, if the word pierogie is spoken quickly, it's likely that . . [it] would sound like . . padogie. . . I've also heard people use the word pirohi (pronounced peroh-hee). *Ibid* w**PA**, My former roommate . . pronounces the word pirogi with the . . 'd' sound instead of the actual 'r' sound. This pronunciation seems to be preferred in the area south of Pittsburgh, where a large majority of the population is of Polish descent. *Ibid* **CT,** My Polish grandfather used to make padogies for dinner all the time. It wasn't until years later that I found out they were also called pirogis. **1998** *DARE* File cw**MA**, Pierogi [pɪrogi].

piert See **peart** adj

pie safe See **safe 1**

pie social n **esp Nth, N Midl** See Map Cf **cake social, pie supper**
A social gathering at which pies are sold or auctioned off, esp for a charitable purpose.

1929 *Randolph Enterprise* (Elkins, W. Va.) 14 Mar 1/5 *(DA),* There will be a pie social at the Ivy Hill School House. . . The proceeds will go for the benefit of the school. **1939** in Lib. of Congress *Amer. Memory: WPA Life Hist.* (Internet) **NE,** For entertainment one of the neighbors brought an old organ to the schoolhouse and we practiced singing, and had literaries, basket suuppers, pie socials, spelling bees. **1947** *Steamboat* (Colo.) *Pilot* 30 Jan. 4/2 *(DA),* There will be a pie social at the Pleasant View school house. **1950** *WELS* (Do you have in your community a kind of gathering called a "social" or a "sociable"?) 6 Infs, **WI,** Pie social. **1965–70** *DARE* (Qu. FF1, . . *A kind of group meeting called a 'social' or 'sociable'. . . [What goes on?]*) 10 Infs, **Nth, N Midl,** Pie social; **OH**44, 70, Pie social—old-fashioned; **MD**23, Pie so-

cial—pies sold, money goes to church; **ME**4, Pie social—all cook a pie and someone buys it, bidding on it; **MN**28, Pie social—buy the pie by bidding; **OR**14, Pie social—every woman brings pie and the men choose pies and eat lunch with she who bakes the chosen pie; **MN**6, Cake and pie social; (Qu. FF2, . . *Kinds of parties*) Inf **PA**71, Box social, pie social—when I was a boy. **1997** *Parade* 13 July 12 e**OR,** [She] is on her way to Ukiah, Ore. (pop. 250), where she is the featured guest at the community's pie social.

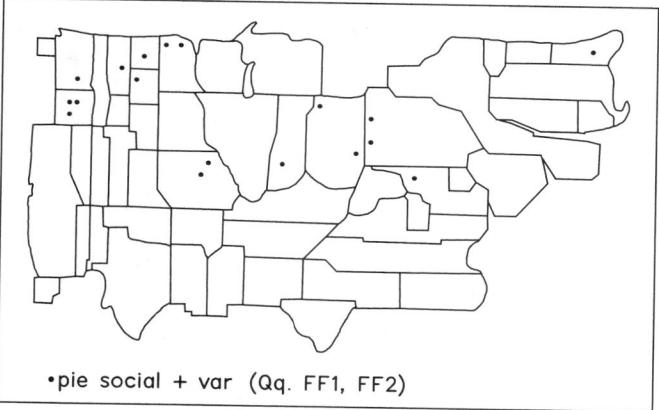

•pie social + var (Qq. FF1, FF2)

pie squash n **chiefly Midl** See Map
Either a **pie pumpkin** or a squash such as **pattypan squash.**

1886 *Colo. Springs Republican* 21 Oct. 1/2 *(DA),* It reports the gift of forty pie squash. [**1911** *Century Dict.* 5878, The winter squash is boiled or roasted; . . in America often made into pies.] **1950** *WELS* **WI** (*Kinds of squash that grow in your neighborhood*) 1 Inf, Pie squash— large, round; 1 Inf, Pie squash. **1965–70** *DARE* (Qu. I23, . . *Kinds of squash*) Infs **DE**1, **IN**52, **KS**1, **MO**1, 32, **PA**143, We call small pumpkins pie squash; **DE**3, Pie squash—a round, kind of flat squash scalloped ['skɑləpt] around the edge; **IA**22, Pie squash—like a pumpkin, only green; **IL**5, Pie [squash]—flat, white, has fluted edges; **IL**13, Pie [squash]—flat with fluted edges; **IN**23, Pie squash—a small, round squash that you boil; **KY**62, Pie squash—small, round, yellow squash; **KY**71, Pie squash—round, different colors some squash—green and orange; **MD**17, Pie squash—sweet pumpkin used for pie, called squash here; **NJ**3, Flat squash (pie squash); **OH**82, Pie squash—orange or tan; **SD**2, Pie squash—like yellow pumpkin; **VA**13, Pie squash—like a pumpkin but longer—1' high, 2' long. **1968** *DARE* Tape **IN**32, [FW:] Which kind do you use, of squash [to make squash cake, cookies, puddings, and pies]? [Inf:] The pie squash. The little green squash. . . They look like a little basket. **1983** *MJLF* 9.1.50 ce**KY** (as of 1956), *Pie squash* . . a type of squash pies are made from.

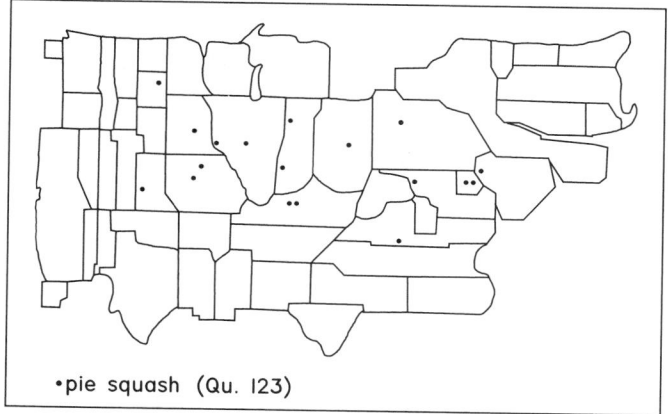

•pie squash (Qu. I23)

pie stem n
=**rhubarb B.**

1969 *DARE* (Qu. I30, *Other names for rhubarb*) Inf **IL**56, Pie stem— uncle's word for it.

pie supper n **chiefly W Midl** See Map on p. 130
=**pie social.**

1892 *Atlantic Mth.* 69.379 **nNEng,** Eunice Emery ain't fit to house-keep for a cat. The pie she took to the pie supper at the church was so tough that even Deacon Dyer could n't eat it. **1906** Johnson *Highways Missip. Valley* 140 **Ozarks,** "I like the pie suppers best," said Mrs. Doten. "Each lady brings a pie with her name on the bottom, and the pies are sold for ten cents apiece. There's all kinds—apple, peach, black-berry, sorrel, pumpkin, sweet potato, and I don't know what." **1937** in Lib. of Congress *Amer. Memory: WPA Life Hist.* (Internet) **NM,** The equipment for these schools was purchased by money made from pie suppers, tackey parties and festivals common in this state. **1948** *Daily Oklahoman* (Oklahoma City OK) 31 Oct D6/1, They sent the price of pie skyrocketing at a pie supper to raise money for horns and drums. **1949** Hedgecock *Gone Are the Days* 80 **swMO,** About once a year or such a matter, we'd have to raise a little money to buy coal oil for the lamps, and a few such incidentals. An easy pleasant way to do it was to have a pie supper. **1954** *Harder Coll.* **cwTN,** *Pie supper. . .* A supper at which pies are auctioned off for benefit of a church. **1965–70** *DARE* (Qu. FF1, *. . A kind of group meeting called a 'social' or 'sociable'. . . [What goes on?]*) 23 Infs, **chiefly W Midl,** Pie supper; **WV4, 5, 13,** Pie supper—old-fashioned; **AR56,** Pie supper—women and girls brought pies; pies were auctioned off to the men; money went to the church; **KY19,** Pie supper—pies sold to raise money; gentleman ate with the girl who made the pie; **KY75,** Pie supper—winter; pies auctioned off; you ate it with the one who bought your pie; to make money for school or church; **TN30,** Pie supper—same as box supper except that girls bring only pies or cakes; **TN56,** Pie supper—country schools; used to be more frequent than today; (Qu. FF2, *. . Kinds of parties*) Infs **KY5, MO34,** Pie suppers. **1966** *DARE* Tape **OK31,** Sometimes we would have pie suppers where the women would bring in pies and the men would bid on them and buy them and then they'd have to eat pie . . with whoever they bought. **1968** Allen *It Happened* 222 **sIL** (as of c1900), Pie suppers along with some similar affairs called box suppers were an-nual events. **1976** Lynn–Vecsey *Loretta Lynn* 38 **eKY,** Since I was thir-teen years old, the teacher let me help arrange the programs for the pie supper. . . Whoever bought a girl's pie got to take her home. **1982** Slone *How We Talked* 79 **eKY** (as of c1950), Box supper (sometimes called a "pie supper")—Held when they needed to raise money for something extra for the school or Christmas presents for the students. **1983** *MJLF* 9.1.50 **ceKY** (as of 1956), *Pie supper . . :* a party to which the ladies bring pies they have baked. The men bid on the individual pies, and the highest bidder gets to eat the pie with the lady, sometimes at a secluded spot. **1985** *NC Folkl. Jrl.* 33.46 **wNC** (as of c1920), Pie suppers and box suppers were great fun in those days. Every girl of "courting" age was expected to bring a box lunch or bake a pie to be auctioned off to the highest bidder. **1986** Pederson *LAGS Concordance,* 1 inf, **cTN,** Pie suppers—girls' pies sold to highest bidder.

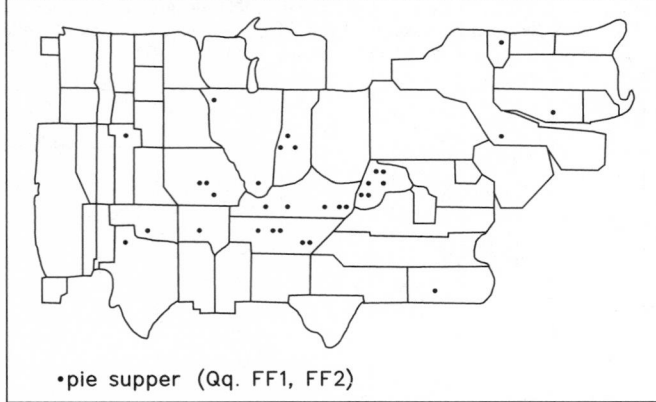

•pie supper (Qq. FF1, FF2)

pie tag See **pie**

pieted See **pieded**

pieu n, also attrib Rarely sp *pu* [Fr *pieu,* pl *pieux* stake, post] **LA, eTX**

A split post, board, rail, or picket used to make a fence; rarely, a fence made of split boards—often in combs *pieu(x) fence.*

1872 U.S. Dept. Ag. *Rept. of Secy. for 1871* 503 **LA,** In the Creole section, a fence made of cypress, and known as *Pieux* fence, is the pre-vailing style. . . It is 5 to 5½ feet high. Slabs of cypress, 9 feet in length, are split from the circumference of the log, in size about 10 by 2 inches,

one of which is morticed as a post, for every four tenoned, to be used as boards, making a rough but strong and durable board-fence. **1917** *DN* 4.420 **LA,** *Pieu* [pju]. . . A fence built of split boards. Also *pu.* La Salle and Catahoula Parishes, La. **1967** *DARE* (Qu. L62, *A fence made of split logs*) Inf **TX35,** Pieu [pjuɣ] fence; (Qu. L65, *. . Kinds of fences*) Inf **LA2,** Pieu fence—pieus split out of logs and nailed onto posts—usually used to enclose barn lots and smaller fields and patches. **1986** Pederson *LAGS Concordance* (Picket fence), 4 infs, **LA,** Pieu fence(s); 1 inf, **cLA,** Cypress pieu; 1 inf, **cwLA,** Pieu fence—post fence; 1 inf, **swLA,** Pieu fence—post and rail fence, pieux are rails; 1 inf, **swLA,** Pieu fence—boards [from] willow trees are used; 1 inf, **ceTX,** Pieu fence—pew [sic] split to make pickets, nailed; (Rail fence) 1 inf, **swLA,** Pieu fence; 1 inf, **cnLA,** Pieu fence—wood from pin oak trees; 1 inf, **swLA,** Pieu fence—split cypress tree; posts, not zigzag; 1 inf, **csLA,** A pieu fence—straight, holes in posts for planks; 1 inf, **ceTX,** Two kinds, rail and pieu—pieu is center of log; 1 inf, **cwLA,** The pieu—the fence post; 1 inf, **swLA,** Pieux—also for picket fences; upright, pointed.

pie wagon n **chiefly NYC area**

A police patrol wagon.

1904 Number 1500 *Life in Sing Sing* 257, Pie Wagon. Patrol wagon. **1960** Rockwell *Adventures* 31 **NY** (as of c1900), When the police ar-rived in the pie wagon to take the body away we were gathered around, Ewald among us. **1967–68** *DARE* (Qu. N3, *The car or wagon that takes arrested people to the police station or to jail*) Inf **CT2,** Pie wagon; **NJ1,** Pie wagon—archaic; **NY51,** Pie wagon—wagons shaped like pie-delivery wagons; **NY82,** Patrol wagon; pie wagon.

pifflicated adj Also *piffed, pifficated, piffled* Cf **spifflicated**

Tipsy; drunk.

1900 *DN* 2.48 **RI, MI, NY** [College slang], *Piffed.* . . Intoxicated. *Ibid* **RI, MI, NH, CT,** *Pifficated.* . . Intoxicated. **1905** *DN* 3.15 **cCT,** *Pifficated.* . . Slang. . . Drunk. **1912** *DN* 3.585 **wIN,** *Pifflicated.* . . Drunk. "He is completely pifflicated to-night." **1929** *AmSp* 4.440, 'Pifflicated. *Ibid* 5.441, Slang equivalents for "drunk," . . are too inter-esting to be omitted from the record: piffed[,] piffled[,] pifficated. *Ibid* 5.128 **ME,** An intoxicated man was . . "pifflicated." **1950** *WELS Suppl.* **seWI,** *Pifflicated*—Drunk. To be refined, said with *slightly.* Inf heard word from Milwaukee woman. **1967–69** *DARE* (Qu. DD13, *When a drinker is just beginning to show the effects of the liquor . . he's _____*) Inf **IA5,** Pifflicated; (Qu. DD14, *When a person is partly drunk, "He's _____."*) Inf **IN80,** Pifflicated; (Qu. DD15, *A person who is thoroughly drunk*) Inf **NY196,** Pifficated ['pɪfə,ketəd].

pifine See **paille fine 1**

pig n[1] Usu |pɪg|; also |pɛg| and, esp in animal calls, |pɪg| Pronc-sp *peeg*

A Forms.

1914 *DN* 4.160 **eVA,** *Peeg.* . . Pig. "Ah'm gwine tuh call them peegs. Pee-ee-g, pee-ee-eg, pe-e-o-o-e-eg!" **1926** Roberts *Time of Man* 187 **KY,** Ho-eee, peeg, peeg, peeg, peeg. **1934** *AmSp* 9.210 **Sth,** A great many words having standard [ɪ] before [g] . . change [ɪ] to [i]. This prac-tice is very common. . . *pig; shote).* **1939** *LANE* Map 205 (*Pig; shote*), [The prevailing pronc **throughout NEng** is [pɪg]; there are scattered in-stances of [pɪˆg], [pɪˇg], and [pɪˀg]; occasional examples of [pɪˀg], [pʰɪg].] *Ibid* Map 226 (*Calls to pigs*), [The most common pronc is [pɪg]; there are scattered instances of [pɪˆg], [pɪˇg], [pɪˀg], [pig], [pɪˀg], [pʏg], and [pɪg].] **1942** Hall *Smoky Mt. Speech* 15 **wNC, eTN,** Laxer and lowered varieties of [ɪ], often reaching [ɛ], may frequently be heard . . *whistlepig* . . ['hwɪsl̩,pɛˆg]. **1968** *DARE* (Qu. K84, *The call used . . to get the pigs in at feeding time*) Inf **PA71,** Peeg.

B Senses.

1 A swine of any age, but esp a young one; see quots. Cf **hog B1a**

1634 in 1884 ME Hist. Soc. *Doc. Hist.* 3.31, The pigs ar growen to som bignes. **1903** *DN* 2.316 **seMO,** 'Pig' is only applied to sucklings, while in the North it is generic. **1939** *LANE* Map 110 **NEng,** [355 re-sponses, Pig pen (*or* shed, etc); this contrasts with 151 responses, Hog pen (*or* shed, etc).] *Ibid* Map 205, Both *pig* and *shote* are commonly applied to young animals of the swine family, the usual distinction . . be-ing that *pig* is used of a very young animal, *shote* of a somewhat older one. . . The term *pig* may have also the generic meaning 'any member of the swine family'. . . and is doubtless familiar to many who mention only the specific meaning. . . Some informants qualify the word in its specific sense by some adjective as *young* or *little.* **1941** *Ibid* Map 301 (*Salt pork*) 1 inf, **ceCT,** Pig pork, from a young animal; hog pork, from an old one. **1960** Criswell *Resp. to PADS 20* **Ozarks,** A pig. A shoat. A hog. . . [refers to] young pig . . half-grown pig . . full-grown pig. **1965–70** *DARE* (Qu. K51, . . *Pigs, a very young one*) 275 Infs, **widespread, but less freq NEast, Pacific,** Pig; 267 Infs, **widespread,** Little (*or suckling, baby, etc*) pig; (Qu. K55, *A pig that doesn't grow well and is not worth keeping*) 74 Infs, **scattered,** Scrub (*or stunted, runty, etc*) pig; (Qu. K58, *A castrated pig*) 37 Infs, **scattered,** Cut (*or marked, altered, etc*) pig; 13 Infs, **scattered,** Pig; (Qu. K52, *A male pig kept for breeding*) 23 Infs, **scattered,** Male (*or boar, papa, etc*) pig; (Qu. K60, *When somebody is going to give the pigs food . . "I'm going to _____."*) Infs NC79, VA40, Feed (*or slop*) the pig; (Qq. M1, 13, 15, 22) 150 Infs, **widespread, but less freq Pacific,** Pig lot (*or pen, house, etc*). **1966** *DARE* Tape **SC15,** One day, catch a little one, a pig. . . We kept that pig . . called him a boar hog. . . Got tush-hook that long. And we run, run up the tree and we drop the pig. **1973** Allen *LAUM* 1.249 **Upper MW** (as of c1950), The male of swine is commonly designated with the term *boar* in the U[pper] M[idwest], with a variant *boar pig* chiefly in Minnesota and North Dakota. The element *pig* appears in several other compounds as well, all of which are characteristically found in Northern speech areas. . . [S]uch expressions as . . *male pig* and *gentleman pig* are primarily women's terms. . . bull pig [1 inf, **IA**] . . gentleman pig [1 inf, **MN**] . . he pig [1 inf, **MN**] . . male pig [5 infs, **MN, IA, ND**]. *Ibid* 1.250, Despite the technical distinction between *pig* and *hog* based upon age and the arbitrary weight of 120 pounds, most infs. employ either one term or the other as a generic. . . *Pig,* less frequent [than *hog*] but also widespread and perhaps with a slight Northern orientation, is more likely to be used by infs. without a farm background. *Ibid,* You feed 'pigs' but sell 'hogs' [1 inf, **MN**]. *Ibid,* Female hog . . sow pig [3 infs, **MN, IA**] . . *sow pig:* A young sow [1 inf, **IA**]. *Ibid,* Young hog [is a] pig [51 infs, **chiefly MN, IA**] . . baby pig [1 inf, **NE**] . . little pig [1 inf, **NE**] . . young pig [1 inf, **ND**] . . *feeding pig:* A half-grown hog [1 inf, **IA**]. **1986** Pederson *LAGS Concordance* **Gulf Region,** [181 infs respond that a pig is "young" or a "young hog" or "a baby," or "until weaned" or "first born" or similar expressions; 9 infs say that it is equivalent to hog, 3 infs that it is a pig until grown or it becomes a hog.]

2 also *pig meat* (or *pork*): Pork; sometimes spec bacon or salt pork; see quots. Cf **hog B3, hog meat**

1846 Farnham *Life in Prairie Land* 358, She nevertheless stirred about with a right hearty zeal, setting on her quail, chicken, pig, dodger, and biscuit. **1941** in 1957 *Old Farmer's Almanac Sampler* 79, You remove the [bean pot] cover; take a large spoon; stand up; break gently the crispy black surface of the covering of pig-pork. . . With each helping, you give out a fine piece of pork. **1941** [see **B1** above]. **1943** *AmSp* 18.308 **wLA, eTX** [Cafe terms], *Juicy pig.* Barbecued pork sandwich. **1968** *DARE* (Qu. H38, . . *Words for bacon [including joking ones]*) Inf **NY36,** Pig meat; [**PA234,** Pig bacon]. **1968** *DARE* Tape **MD3,** We bought our beef on Saturday. . . We did not have pig meat or anything like that because it disagreed with the whole family. . . We could get some ham but we didn't have too much meat to eat. **1972** Claerbaut *Black Jargon* 75, *Pig.* . . pork: *I had some bad pig tonight.* **1997** *DARE* File **csWI,** The Village Green Bar & Grill in Middleton serves Georgia Pig every Weds. (one day every week anyway). It is a distinctive way of preparing the meat and a special BBQ-type sauce.

3 =**jabalina.**

1917 Anthony *Mammals Amer.* 61, *Pecari angulatus.* . . This animal is the only native "pig" found in the United States. *Ibid* 63, The Peccaries showed no sign of leaving. . . I was getting tired of being treed. . . Some of the pigs would feed while others stood guard. . . I was so tired. I . . buckled myself to the tree, so that I would not fall out.

4 A **marmot a.** Cf **whistlepig**

1968 *DARE* (Qu. P31, . . *Names or nicknames . . for the groundhog*) Inf **CA72,** Pig.

5 also *pigboat:* A lake steamship. [From the rounded deck] Cf **whaleback**

1898 *N. Amer. Rev.* 166.723, Some of the tow barges are built of steel, and all of the whalebacks, or "pigs," as the lake sailors call them, are so constructed. **1944** Landon *Lake Huron* 356, The whaleback or "pig," as it became known in the slang of the sailors, was the most radical departure in ship design since the time when the first iron vessel appeared on the lakes. **1949** *Sat. Ev. Post* 16 April 162/2 (*DA*), Called whalebacks, they had pointed prows and rounded sides, and quickly earned the name 'pigboat' from sailors.

6 also *pigboat;* In logging: a crude sled used to haul tools and equipment.

1905 U.S. Forest Serv. *Bulletin* 61.43 [Logging terms], *Pig.* . . See

Rigging sled. [*Ibid* 44 **Pacific NW,** *Rigging sled.* A sled used to haul hooks and blocks on a skid road.] **1957** Perrin *Coll.* **WA,** Years ago logging equipment included a sled called a "pig" which carried tongs and tools between the "donkey engine" and the rigging crews out in the woods. The man who rode this sled, and attended to it, was called— when ladies were present—the pig feeder. **1958** McCulloch *Woods Words* 134 **Pacific NW,** *Pig*—A hollowed log which was used on fore-and-aft roads to bring the dogs and other tools back to the woods or yarder donkey. It was dogged to the last log of an incoming turn, and when the logs were unfastened at the landing, the dogs were thrown in the pig for return to the woods. Pigs were used both in the Idaho white pine and the Douglas fir regions. *Pig boat*—Another name for the pig.

7 A railroad locomotive. Cf **hog B6**

1931 *Writer's Digest* 11.42 [Railroad terms], *Pig*—Locomotive. **1945** Hubbard *Railroad Ave.* 355, *Pig*—Locomotive. *Pig-mauler* is locomotive engineer; *pigpen* locomotive roundhouse.

8 An old truck or car.

1961 *AmSp* 36.273 **NW, West** [Truck drivers' language], *Pig.* . . An old truck. **1967** *DARE* (Qu. N5, *Nicknames for an automobile, especially an old or broken-down car*) Inf **MA1,** Pig. **1969** *AmSp* 44.207 [Truck drivers' jargon], *Pig.* . . Tractor with little power. **1977** Dillard *Lexicon* 65, *Pig* is also the inner city's derogatory term for last year's Cadillac (i.e., a "hog" that does not quite make it anymore).

9 The horn of a saddle.

1940 Writers' Program *Guide NV* 75, The horn of the saddle, called the *biscuit, grandma, old Susie,* the *handle,* or the *pig,* all indicative of the contempt of true cowhands for the flat-heeled *peeler* who must *pull leather* (grasp the saddle horn) in order to remain with his mount. **1944** Adams *Western Words* 115, *Pig*—Nickname for the saddle horn.

10 also *pig's ear, pig's eye:* =**blind tiger 1.** Cf **blind pig 1, piggery 2**

1930 Shoemaker *1300 Words* 45 **cPA Mts** (as of c1900), *Pigs ear*— An unlicensed liquor store. **1934** (1940) Weseen *Dict. Amer. Slang* 281, *Pig*—A place where liquor is sold illegally. **1967–69** *DARE* (Qu. DD30, *Joking names for a place where liquor is [or was] sold and consumed illegally*) Infs **MI64, 76,** Pig; **NY148, OR1,** Pig's eye; **NY101,** Pig's ear. **1982** Barrick *Coll.* **PA,** *Pig's ear*—Place where liquor could be purchased. More common in northern Penna. than southern. [**1997** *NADS Letters* **sCA,** There is a bar in San Bernardino called "The Pig's Ear."]

11 A miser, stingy person. Cf **hog B4**

1951 Johnson *Resp. to PADS 20* **DE** (*Words and expressions about greedy people:* "He's an awful _____.") Pig. **1960** Bailey *Resp. to PADS 20* **KS,** [A greedy man is a] pig, nickel-grabber, hog. **1965–70** *DARE* (Qu. U36a, . . *A person who saves in a mean way or is greedy in money matters:* "He's an awful _____.") 21 Infs, **scattered,** Pig; **VA16,** Big pig; (Qu. U33, *Names or nicknames for a stingy person*) Inf **VA31,** Pig.

12 A forfeit in the game of **hat ball.** Cf **pigtail** exclam

1946 Wilson *Fidelity Folks* 145 **sKY,** In Hat Ball we "nailed to the cross" the loser, that is, the one who got the most forfeits or "pigs."

13 A segment of an orange or tangerine. [*EDD pig* sb.[1] "A segment of an apple or orange."]

1994 *DARE* File **NEng,** I'm stunned to discover that 'pigs' meaning orange or tangerine sections is not a family word. I've never heard it anywhere but at home. I grew up in New England (mostly R.I.)

14 =**long john 2.** Cf **pig's ear 2**

1997 *NADS Letters* **neMN,** I first heard of "pigs" as long johns on the Iron Range, particularly in Virginia, Minnesota. It apparently can be traced to a Slovenian bakery and spread from there. They are frosted and can be filled.

15 also *pig plant, pigs, piggy:* A **wild ginger** (here: *Asarum* spp) or its flower. **esp sAppalachians**

1956 McAtee *Some Dialect NC* 57 **cwNC,** *Piggies:* . . that is pygmies, the little, brown, almost, subterranean flowers of wild ginger (*Hexastylis*). Marshall [NC]. **1959** Carleton *Index Herb. Plants* 92, *Pigs:* Asarum canadense. **1964** Campbell et al. *Gt. Smoky Wildflowers* 36, *Little Brown Jug*—*Asarum arifolium.* . . Often hidden by the leaves, the interesting jugs occur at ground level. . . Other names include *pigs, wild ginger,* and *heart-leaf.* **1966** *DARE* Wildfl QR Pl.46 Inf **SC41,** Pig plant. **1979** *Our Smokies Heritage* May 60 **wNC, eTN,** The jugs (known as a calyx) grow to roughly an inch in length, and clustered together, they look like piglets with open mouths waiting for supper. Little Brown Jugs were thus quite often called "pigs" by the local people.

16 in phr *sweat like a pig* and var: To sweat profusely. **chiefly Nth, esp NEast** See Map Cf *sweat like a mule* (at **mule** n[1] **6**)

1965–70 *DARE* (Qu. X56b, *Expressions about sweating very heavily*) 20 Infs, **chiefly Nth, esp NEast,** Sweat (*or* sweating) like a pig; **CT**40, **MI**70, **WY**5, (Sweat) like a stuck pig; **MA**3, Sweats like a pig. **1997** *DARE* File, My husband, from southern California, has used the phrase *sweat like a pig* for at least 25 years, but he doesn't know where he picked it up.

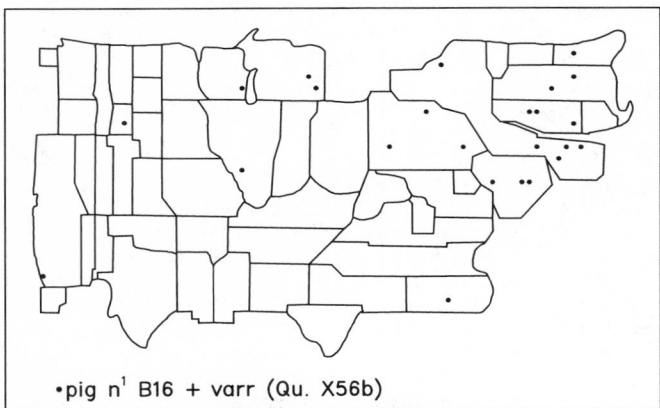

•pig n[1] B16 + varr (Qu. X56b)

pig n[2] [Scots, nEngl dial < *pig* earthenware vessel]
Also in combs *china pig, hot ~:* A ceramic hot-water bottle, heated brick, or similar object used to apply heat to the body.

1976 *WI Then & Now* Dec 2, Brightly-colored quilts and beautifully woven throws were tucked around laps and over soap stones heated on the stove, "china pigs" filled with hot water, or Clark heaters stuffed with live coals. **1984** Ehle *Last One Home* 162 **NC** (as of c1900), "I would curl up under the quilts with the hot brick clutched to my belly, . . and I would go to sleep with that hot pig. . . " "Hot pig?" he said softly. She looked over at him. . . "That's what we call them, anything hot, whether a hot-water bottle, or the clay water bottle mama used, or the bricks, or a bag of creek sand my brother used till the cloth broke. We called them hot pigs." **1995** Rogers *Other Words* 82 **cnCO,** I had an earthenware thing called a pig. It was round, and it had a little snout kind of like a pig that you filled the hot water in. . . That would stay all night long, not like a hot water bottle that cools off. **2001** *NADS Letters* **IA,** Though I am a little dubious, I think that my grandmother used the word "pig" for the gray ceramic hot water bottle she used to put in her bed. . . I am encouraged to send the information because I think I can remember making a joke (probably only in my head) that my grandmother slept with a pig. She lived in Huron Township, Iowa. Her father was of Pennsylvania German stock, but her mother had Scottish ancestry.

Pig Alley n
1967–69 *DARE* (Qu. C35, *Nicknames for the different parts of your town or city*) Infs **IL**15, **KS**5, **NY**137, Pig Alley; (Qu. II25, *Names or nicknames for the part of a town where the poorer people, special groups, or foreign groups live*) Infs **CT**23, **MI**68, **NY**139, Pig Alley.

pig bean n
=**lima bean.**
c1955 Reed–Person *Ling. Atlas Pacific NW,* 1 inf, Pig beans. **1997** *NADS Letters* **neTN,** I . . have heard of pig beans, and unfortunately eaten them, all my life. You ask "why pig." . . Newborn pigs are large, relatively flat, yellow, and of course not in pods. . . My grandparents regularly referred to butter beans as pig beans . . [as] their grandparents before them had. *Ibid* **cTX,** As for the term "pig beans," I've heard butter beans referred to as such in San Antonio. I was told that they're called pig beans because of their size.

pigberry n
A **deerberry a** (here: *Vaccinium stamineum*).
1899 *Plant World* 2.199 **PA,** Pigberry for *Vaccinium stamineum.* . . Fruit fit for pigs?

pig blanket n
=**pallet.**
1998 *DARE* File **TX,** The Dallas informant born in 1954 uses the word

pig blanket for what he also calls *pallet*—a blanket spread on the floor for small children.

pigboat See **pig** n[1] **B5, 6**

pig corn n Cf **hog corn**
A field var of **Indian corn 1.**
1966–68 *DARE* (Qu. I34, *If you don't have sweet corn, you can always eat young _____*) Infs **CA**94, **OH**80, **WA**15, Pig corn.

pig ears n Also *pig's ears*
1 also *pig-ear cup:* Any of var **mushrooms B1,** but freq a chanterelle (here: *Gomphus clavatus*). Cf **human ear**
1958 Smith *Mushroom Hunter's Field Guide* 64, Some collectors know this [=*Gomphus clavatus*] as "pig's ears." Young material should be sliced for cooking. **1967** *DARE* (Qu. S19, *Mushrooms that grow out like brackets from the sides of trees*) Inf **WA**30, Pig ears. **1981** Lincoff *Audubon Field Guide Mushrooms* 331, Pig's Ears—*Discina perlata.* . . Brown to tannish, wrinkled, cup- or ear-shaped fungus, sometimes with short, stout stalk. [*Ibid* 396, Pig's Ear Gomphus—*Gomphus clavatus.* . . The wavy cap sometimes resembles a pig's ear, but this common name is also used of entirely unrelated mushrooms, such as *Discina perlata.*] **1987** McKnight–McKnight *Mushrooms* 56, Pig-ear Cup—*Peziza badioconfusa.* . . Pig-ear Cup is most readily recognized by the surface pattern on its spores, as seen highly magnified by a microscope. *Ibid* 86, Pig's Ears—*Gomphus clavatus.* . . Coast to coast, southern Canada and northern U.S. . . Edible.
2 A **plantain** or similar plant. Cf **hog-ear leaf**
1966–68 *DARE* (Qu. S21, . . *Weeds . . that are a trouble in gardens and fields*) Inf **PA**1, Plantain = pig ears; **PA**111, Pig ears; **OH**80, **PA**22, Pig's ears. **1997** *DARE* File **neOH,** Pig's ear or pig ears. . . The only place I ever heard this was in northeast Ohio. It was a type of weed that people hated to have in their yards. . . The plant grows only about 5″ in height, and the leaves look like pig ears. They can take over the lawn.

pigeon n
=**ruddy turnstone.**
1897 *Auk* 14.289 **LA,** *Arenaria interpres.* Turnstone.—Commonly known as Pigeon. An abundant resident, on the coast.

pigeonbark n
=**coffeeberry 2a(1).**
1902 [see **pigeonberry 7**].

pigeonberry n
Any of var plants with berries said to be attractive to pigeons or other birds, as:
1 also *pigeonberry bush:* =**pokeweed 1a.**
1759 in 1775 Burnaby *Travels* 7 **VA,** Tobacco and Indian corn are the original produce of the country; likewise the pigeon-berry and rattlesnake-root. **1778** Carver *Travels N. Amer.* 518, *Gargit* or *Skoke* is a large kind of weed. . . [The] red berries . . hang in clusters in the month of September, and are generally called pigeon berries, as those birds then feed on them. **1792** Belknap *Hist. NH* 3.134, About the second or third year, another weed, called pigeon-berry, succeeds the fireweed, and remains till the grass overcomes it. It rises to the height of three feet, spreads much at the top, and bears bunches of black berries, on which pigeons feed. **1830** Rafinesque *Med. Flora* 2.251, *Phytolacca decandra,* Poke, Pocan of Virginia tribes, *Coakum* of northern tribes, *Garget* or *Pigeon berries* in N. Engl. . . Berries sweetish, nauseous, subacrid, eaten by birds and fowls, give bad taste to their flesh. **1832** Williamson *Hist. ME* 1.115, The *pigeon-berry bush* is as tall as that of a blackberry, bears abundance of small purple berries, the chief food of pigeons. **1859** (1880) Darlington *Amer. Weeds* 270, *P[hytolacca] decandra.* . . Poke. Poke-weed. Pigeon-berry. . . used by the pastry cook in making pies of equivocal merit. **1897** *Jrl. Amer. Folkl.* 10.54 **West,** *Phytolacca decandra,* . . pigeon berry. **1910** Graves *Flowering Plants* 171 **CT,** Common Pokeweed, Pike or Scoke. Garget. Pigeon Berry. . . Woods, fields and waste places. **1953** Greene–Blomquist *Flowers South* 30, Our common pokeweed or pigeon-berry (*Phytolacca americana*).
2 A **dogwood 1,** usu *Cornus alternifolia*. [*DCan* 1822 → for *Cornus canadensis* and other berries] Cf **pigeonbrush**
1897 Sudworth *Arborescent Flora* 310 **NY,** *Cornus alternifolia* . . Pigeonberry. **1940** Clute *Amer. Plant Names* 97, Blue dogwood, purple dogwood, umbrella-tree, pigeon-berry. *Ibid* 257, *Cornus paniculata.*

Gray-barked dogwood, pigeon berry. **1942** W.R. Van Dersal *Ornamental Amer. Shrubs* 183 *(OED2)*, The plant (sc. *Cornus alternifolia*) has a number of common names, including . . purple dogwood, pigeon-berry, umbrella tree, and pagoda cornel. **1967–68** *DARE* (Qu. S26c, *Wildflowers that grow in woods*) Inf **MI**53, Bunchberry or pigeonberry; (Qu. T16) Inf **NY**71, Pigeonbrush or pigeonberry.

3 A sarsaparilla B2 (here: *Aralia hispida*).

1894 *Jrl. Amer. Folkl.* 7.89 **ME**, *Aralia hispida* . . pigeon-berry, Buckfield, Me. **1896** *Ibid* 9.189 **ME**, *Aralia hispida* . . pigeon berry, Oxford County, Me. **1940** Clute *Amer. Plant Names* 96, *Bristly Sarsaparilla* . . pigeon-berry.

4 =partridgeberry 1.

1889 (1971) Farmer *Americanisms* 419, *Pigeon-berry*—A New England name for the *partridge-berry*. **1896** *Jrl. Amer. Folkl.* 9.190 **MA**, *Mitchella repens*. . . pigeon berry. **1911** Henkel *Amer. Med. Leaves* 34, *Squaw Vine*. . . Other common names. . . oneberry, pigeonberry, snakeberry [etc].

5 A raspberry B (here: *Rubus pubescens*).

1896 *Jrl. Amer. Folkl.* 9.187 **West**, *Rubus triflorus* . . running raspberry, . . pigeon berry. **1940** Clute *Amer. Plant Names* 8, *R[ubus] triflorus*. Swamp Raspberry. Running raspberry . . pigeon-berry.

6 A serviceberry, usu *Amelanchier alnifolia*.

1897 Sudworth *Arborescent Flora* 214 **sOR**, *Amelanchier alnifolia*. . . Common Names. Pigeon Berry. **1931** U.S. Dept. Ag. *Misc. Pub.* 101.60, Common serviceberry . . known variantly as saskatoon, alderleaf sarvisberry, western juneberry, and pigeon berry . . is normally a shrub 3 to 10 or occasionally 15 feet high. **1940** Clute *Amer. Plant Names* 218, *Amelanchier spicata*. Pigeon berry. **1971** Kieran *Nat. Hist. NYC* 183, It [=*Amelanchier arborea*] is often called "Serviceberry," but more scientifically Downy Juneberry. Pigeonberry is another name for the group.

7 A buckthorn: usu **coffeeberry 2a(1)**, but also **cascara 1. CA**

1897 Parsons *Wild Flowers CA* 67, In Monterey County it [=cascara sagrada] is known as "yellow-boy" or "yellow-root," and in Sonoma County it becomes "pigeon-berry," because the berry is a favorite food of the wild pigeons, and lends to their flesh a bitter taste. **1902** U.S. Natl. Museum *Contrib. Herbarium* 7.368, *Rhamnus californica*. . . It grows on rocky hillsides and near streams throughout the region and is well known there, together with *Rhamnus tomentella*, as pigeon berry and pigeon bark. Wild pigeons eat the berries. **1937** U.S. Forest Serv. *Range Plant Hdbk*. B127, *California buckthorn*. . . is variously known as coffeeberry, pigeonberry, yerba-del-oso, and cascara sagrada. **1960** Vines *Trees SW* 704, *[Rhamnus californica]* is also known under the names of California Coffee-berry, Coast Coffee-berry, and pigeon-berry. The fruit is eaten by at least 7 species of birds, including the band-tailed pigeon. **1979** Little *Checklist U.S. Trees* 246, Coffeeberry, California coffeeberry, coast coffeeberry, Sierra coffeeberry, pigeonberry.

8 A crowberry 1 (here: *Empetrum nigrum*).

1916 *Torreya* 16.238 **ME**, *Empetrum nigrum* . . Pigeon berry, heath, Matinicus I[slan]d, Me. **1940** Clute *Amer. Plant Names* 125, *E[mpetrum] nigrum*. . . crow-pea, curlew-berry, pigeon-berry.

9 A winterberry (here: *Ilex verticillata*).

1916 *Torreya* 16.238 **ME**, *Ilex verticillata* . . Dog Berry, pigeon berry, white alder, Matinicus I[slan]d, Me. **1940** Clute *Amer. Plant Names* 127, *I[lex] verticillata*. Black Alder. Winterberry, . . pigeon-berry [etc].

10 =rouge plant 1. TX

1946 Reeves–Bain *Flora TX* 107, *R[ivina] humilis* . . (Pigeon Berry.) **1961** Wills–Irwin *Flowers TX* 108, The Pigeonberry or Small Pokeweed is found rather commonly, in places abundantly, in woods in the rolling hills of Central Texas, south to the Rio Grande, west to the Trans-Pecos. **1967** *DARE* Wildfl QR (Wills-Irwin) Pl.8D Inf **TX**44, Pigeonberry. **1970** Correll *Plants TX* 601, *Rivina humilis* . . Pigeon-berry, rouge-plant, coralito.

11 =bearberry honeysuckle.

1960 Vines *Trees SW* 955, Bearberry Honeysuckle. . . is also known under the vernacular names of Twinberry Honeysuckle, Fly Honeysuckle, Black Twinberry, Pigeonberry, and Inkberry. The fruit of Bearberry Honeysuckle is known to be eaten by at least 6 species of birds.

12 =golden dewdrop.

1960 Vines *Trees SW* 894, Creeping Skyflower—*Duranta repens*. . . Vernacular names are Golden Dewdrop, Violet Duranta, Pigeon-berry [etc]. **1970** Correll *Plants TX* 1338, *Duranta repens* . . Espina de paloma, fruta de iguana, . . pigeonberry.

13 A wintergreen (here: *Gaultheria procumbens*).

1971 Krochmal *Appalachia Med. Plants* 128, *Gaultheria procumbens* . . *Common Names:* . . partridge berry, pigeonberry [etc]. **1974** (1977) Coon *Useful Plants* 135, Partridgeberry, wintergreen, checkerberry, pigeon berry, clink, tea of Canada, and a host of other names.

pigeonberry bush See **pigeonberry 1**

pigeonbrush n Cf **pigeonberry 2**

A **dogwood 1**; see quot.

1968 *DARE* (Qu. T16) Inf **NY**71, Pigeonbrush or pigeonberry. Good rabbit cover—low bush. Grows in fairly damp ground; seldom grows over six foot high. Has little ivory-colored berries a little less than a half inch in diameter—about three-eighths.

pigeon cherry n

=pin cherry 1.

1850 *New Engl. Farmer* 2.160 **MA**, The small, red wild cherry, often called the *pigeon* cherry . . very much resembles some of our cultivated varieties. **1884** Sargent *Forests of N. Amer.* 66, *Wild Red Cherry. Pin Cherry. Pigeon Cherry*. . . Common in all the northern forests, in northern New England taking possession of ground cleared by fire of the coniferous forests. **1897** Sudworth *Arborescent Flora* 240 **NH, NY, ND, RI, VT, Ontario Canada**, *Prunus pennsylvanica*. . . Pigeon Cherry. **1908** Britton *N. Amer. Trees* 499, *Wild Red Cherry—Prunus pennsylvanica*. . . Also called Bird, Pigeon, or Pin cherry, this tree grows in open woods and clearings from Newfoundland to British Columbia, south to Georgia, Tennessee and Colorado. **1979** Little *Checklist U.S. Trees* 215, Northern pin cherry, pigeon cherry, bird cherry [etc].

pigeon de mer n **LA**

1 also *pigeon mer*: A small **tern**; see quots.

1916 *Times–Picayune* (New Orleans LA) 26 Mar mag sec 1/5, *Forster Tern* (*Sterna fosteri* [sic])—Sea Swallow; Pigeon Mer. (a name applied to all the small terns). **1931** Read *LA French* 58, *Pigeon de Mer* . . Cabot's Tern (*Sterna sandivicens* [sic] *acuflavida* Cabot). The same name, which signifies "sea pigeon," is given to Forster's Tern (*Sterna forsteri* . .).

2 Either the **black-bellied plover** or the **golden plover**.

1923 U.S. Dept. Ag. *Misc. Circular* 13.68 **LA**, *Black-bellied Plover*. . . Vernacular Names. . . pigeon de mer (sea pigeon). *Ibid* 69 **LA**, *Golden Plover*. . . pigeon de mer.

pigeon diver n [*OED2* (at *pigeon* sb. 6.a) 1694]   Cf **little pigeon**

=dovekie.

1834 Nuttall *Manual Ornith.* 2.531, *Little Auk*, or *Sea Dove*. . . This neat and singular little bird, with a quaint resemblance to the Columbine tribe, is known to mariners by the name of the Greenland Dove; and in this vicinity it is also called the Pigeon Diver. **1844** DeKay *Zool. NY* 2.281, *Mergulus alle*. . . This little *Sea Dove, Sea Pigeon, Greenland Dove, Pigeon-diver*, or *Ice-bird*, is but rarely seen on our coast. The specimen represented in the plate was shot on Long island. **1955** *AmSp* 30.181 **MA**, General form, or some detail of physique, also is pointed out in some of the folk names incorporating those of birds. Illustrations include, for general appearance . . *pigeon diver* (dovekie, New Brunswick, Mass.) [etc].

pigeon duck See **pigeontail**

pigeon falcon n

A **pigeon hawk 1** (here: *Falco columbarius*).

1839 Audubon *Synopsis Birds* 16, Falco columbarius . . Pigeon Falcon.—Pigeon Hawk. **1917** (1923) *Birds Amer.* 2.89, *Pigeon Hawk*. . . Other Names.—Pigeon Falcon; American Merlin; Bullet Hawk; Little Blue Corporal. **1946** Hausman *Eastern Birds* 204, *Eastern Pigeon Hawk*. . . Other Names—Pigeon Falcon [etc].

pigeon foot See **pigeon's foot**

pigeon grape n

Either a **summer grape** (here: *Vitis aestivalis*) or a **winter grape** (here: *V. cinerea*).

1830 Rafinesque *Med. Flora* 2.131, *V[itis] columbina* . . Pigeon Grape. . . Large vine, growing from New York to Louisiana, in woods, . . berries small, blackish, sweetish, eaten by the wild pidgeons like many others. **1907** *DN* 3.196 **seNH**, *Pigeon grape*. . . A tiny wild grape. "There are pigeon grapes hanging in that tall tree." **1942** Hylander *Plant Life* 371, The Summer or Pigeon Grape differs from the

Downy Grape in the rusty red hairy covering of the undersurface of the leaves; it is a tall climbing vine with black berries which vary in taste. **1950** Gray–Fernald *Manual of Botany* 997, *V[itis] aestivalis* . . Summer- or *Pigeon-G[rape]*. . . Dry woods and thickets. . . *V. cinerea . . Graybark-* or *Pigeon-G.* . . Grapes 4–9 mm. in diameter, blackish, with slight bloom, finally sweet. . . Rich low thickets, bottoms and banks of streams. **1973** Wharton–Barbour *Trees KY* 548, *Vitis cinerea.* . . Early settlers called it pigeon grape before the extinction of the passenger pigeon.

pigeon grass n

1 A **bristlegrass 1,** usu *Setaria glauca* or *S. viridis*.

1838 MA Ag. Surv. *Rept. for 1837* 128, There were several patches of black or pigeon grass when the dyke was built. **1881** Phares *Farmer's Book of Grasses* 108, *S[etaria] setosa*, Texas Millet, Pigeon grass, Bristle grass. **1887** (1895) Robinson *Uncle Lisha* 129 **wVT**, The pumpkins trailed their dark vines overhung by their own drooping leaves, pigeon grass and rag-weed. **1889** Vasey *Ag. Grasses* 30, *Setaria glauca* and *Setaria viridis*. These two kinds, called pigeon grass, are very common in cultivated fields, especially among stubble after the cutting of grain. **1925** *Book of Rural Life* 4.2190, *Foxtail grass*, or *Pigeon . . Grass*. There are two common species of weedy foxtails—the yellow foxtail *(Setaria glauca)* and the green foxtail *(S. viridis)*. **1950** WELS *(Other kinds of grass that are hard to get rid of)* 7 Infs, **WI,** Pigeon grass. [*DARE* Ed: Some of these Infs may refer instead to **2** below.] **1965–70** DARE (Qu. S9, . . *Kinds of grass that are hard to get rid of*) 18 Infs, **chiefly Gt Lakes, Upper MW,** Pigeon grass; (Qu. S21, . . *Weeds . . that are a trouble in gardens and fields*) Infs **MN**6, 16, 23, Pigeon grass. [*DARE* Ed: Some of these Infs may refer instead to **2** below.]

2 A **crabgrass 1** (here: *Digitaria sanguinalis*).

1894 *Jrl. Amer. Folkl.* 7.104 **IA,** *Panicum sanguinale* . . pigeon-grass, Hopkinton, Iowa. **1935** (1943) Muenscher *Weeds* 152, *Digitaria sanguinalis*. . . Large crab-grass . . Pigeon-grass. **1945** Wodehouse *Hayfever Plants* 56, Crabgrass . . also called hairy finger grass, crowfoot or pigeon grass.

pigeon guillemot n [See quots 1904, 1949]

A guillemot *(Cepphus columba)* native to the Pacific coast. Also called **sea pigeon a**

1872 Coues *Key to N. Amer. Birds* 345, Pigeon Guillemot. . . N. Pacific. **1886** Turner *Contribs. AK* 121, *Cepphus columba* . . Pigeon Guillemot. . . It frequents the small islets off shore and is rather shy, permitting no reasonable approach. The only way I could obtain them was to watch from the top of some bluff and shoot them as they sat below. **1904** (1910) Wheelock *Birds CA* 12, The Pigeon Guillemot, "so like a guillemot and so like a pigeon," is very abundant on the Farallones. **1949** Kitchin *Birds Olympic Peninsula* 128, In spring or summer, as one walks the beaches along the Strait or Puget Sound, he may frequently observe a pair of small duck-like birds on the water near shore. They will likely be a mated pair of pigeon guillemots. [*Ibid* 129, At this close range it was easy to understand why it is called a pigeon-like bird. The soft immaculate coat was smooth, like the dove, and the bird lay in my hand offering no resistance.] **1953** Jewett *Birds WA* 320, The pigeon guillemot is a friendly species, known to many who love the water as the sea pigeon. **1982** *AK Geographic* 9.2.33, Glaucous-winged gulls, pigeon guillemots and others inhabit the sea cliffs [of St. Lazaria Island].

pigeon gull n [EDD (at pigeon sb. (5)) "a young gull"]

The young of the **black tern.**

1917 *Wilson Bulletin* 29.2.76 **VA,** *Hydrochelidon nigra surinamensis*.—Adult is black striker, young, pigeon gull, Wallops I[slan]d, Va.

pigeon hawk n [See quot 1954 at 2 below]

1 A small falcon *(Falco columbarius).* Also called **bird hawk 1, blue bullet 1, bullet hawk, chicken ~ 1, hen ~, little corporal, merlin, mouse hawk 1d, pigeon falcon, privateer**

a1782 (1788) Jefferson *Notes VA* 72, *Falco columbarius* . . Pigeon hawk. **1792** Belknap *Hist. NH* 3.165, Pigeon Hawk, *Falco columbarius*. **1810** Wilson *Amer. Ornith.* 2.107, *Pigeon Hawk. Falco columbarius*. . . Small birds and mice are his principal food. . . The flocks of Robins and Pigeons are honored with. . . attentions from this marauder. **1858** Baird *Birds* 9, *Falco columbarius*, Linnaeus. *Pigeon Hawk.* . . This little hawk inhabits the entire coast of the possessions of the United States on the Pacific ocean. Being, also, one of the most abundant species of its family in the States on the Atlantic, its locality may be stated

as the whole of temperate North America. **1874** NY Acad. Sci. *Annals Lyceum Nat. Hist.* 10.9 **UT,** *Hypotriorchis columbarius* . . Pigeon Hawk. Rather frequent. Generally distributed. Resident. *Ibid* 379 **IL,** *F[alco] columbarius* . . American Merlin; Pigeon Hawk. **1899** in 1900 LA Soc. Naturalists *Proc.* 100, *Falco columbarius* . . *Pigeon Hawk.* A winter resident, but never as common as the other hawks. **1923** Dawson *Birds CA* 4.1630, There is an air of indefinable quality and power about the diminutive Pigeon Hawk which does not pertain to his less spirited cousin. . . Himself not larger than a full-sized pigeon, the Hawk sometimes pursues a Mourning Dove with relentless fury, and easily overtakes this fleet bird, unless it finds cover or the protection of man. **1950** WELS *(Kinds of hawks in your neighborhood)* 2 Infs, **cwWI,** Pigeon hawk. [*DARE* Ed: These Infs may refer instead to **2** below.] **1965–70** DARE (Qu. Q4, . . *Kinds of hawks*) 35 Infs, **chiefly NEast, N Cent,** Pigeon hawk; **IL**4, Pigeon hawk—smaller than a chicken hawk; **MA**42, Pigeon hawk—about size of dove; **NJ**22, Bird hawk—merlin or pigeon hawk; **NY**97, Pigeon hawk—larger than sparrow hawk; **PA**10, Chicken hawk = pigeon hawk; **WI**32, Pigeon hawk—faster than hell. [*DARE* Ed: Some of these Infs may refer instead to **2** below.] **1977** Bull–Farrand *Audubon Field Guide Birds* 682, This northern species, formerly called "Pigeon Hawk," is best known as a migrant along our larger rivers and coastal marshes.

2 Any of several other accipiters, but esp **Cooper's hawk** or the **sharp-shinned hawk; see quots.**

1731 Catesby *Nat. Hist. Carolina* 1.3, *Accipiter palumbarius* [=*A. gentilis*]. *The Pigeon-Hawk.* . . It is a very swift and bold Hawk, preying on Pigeons and wild Turkeys while they are young. **1831** Audubon *Ornith. Biog.* 1.85, The French and Spaniards of Louisiana have designated all the species of the genus Falco by the name of *"Mangeurs de Poulets;"* and the farmers in other portions of the Union have bestowed upon them, according to their size, the appellations of "Hen Hawk," "Chicken Hawk," "Pigeon Hawk," &c. **1844** DeKay *Zool. NY* 2.14, It [=*Falco peregrinus*] is frequently taken in various parts of the State, and known under the various popular names of *Hen Hawk, Chicken Hawk* and *Pigeon Hawk*. **1872** Coues *Key to N. Amer. Birds* 212, Sharp-shinned Hawk. "Pigeon Hawk." **1898** (1900) Davie *Nests N. Amer. Birds* 202, *Sharp-shinned Hawk.* . . This spirited little Hawk is distributed at large throughout North America. . . Known as Pigeon Hawk, but it should not be confounded with *Falco columbarius.* **1923** WV State Ornith. *Birds WV* 14, *Cooper's Hawk.* . . *Common names*—Blue darter, Bullet hawk, Chicken hawk, Quail hawk, or Pigeon hawk. **1932** Bennitt *Check-list* 22 **MO,** *Sharp-shinned hawk*. . . Little blue darter; chicken hawk; pigeon hawk. **1954** *AmSp* 29.233, Because they preyed, or were thought to prey, upon the wild pigeon, a number of kinds of hawks received the name *pigeon hawk*. Those coming to my notice are: the Mississippi kite, the peregrine falcon, and the broad-winged, Cooper's, marsh, sharp-shinned, and sparrow hawks, besides one small bird hawk, which to the present day bears the standard name of *pigeon hawk.* Hearing that appellation now, one may think that it denotes a predator upon the familiar blue-rock or domestic pigeon, but, no, the name roots in the past and stems from that of an American bird, which though seen in greater numbers than any other, has not had a living representation in the wild for nearly half a century. **1955** MA Audubon Soc. *Bulletin* 39.442 **NH, MA, RI,** *Sparrow hawk.* . . Pigeon Hawk (. . Probably from its size and form, as very rarely does it prey upon so large a bird as a pigeon.) **1967** DARE (Qu. Q4, . . *Kinds of hawks*) Inf **MI**53, Sparrow hawk—some call it the pigeon hawk; **MI**65, Pigeon hawk—maybe the same as the sparrow hawk. I don't know.

pigeon mer See pigeon de mer 1

pigeon millet n Cf pigeon grass 1

A **bristlegrass 1** (here: *Setaria viridis*).

1948 Blomquist *Grasses NC* 186, One species (*S[etaria] viridis*) known as "pigeon millet" or "foxtail" is an obnoxious weed in cultivated ground in some of the Northern states.

pigeon murre n Cf murre 1

The black guillemot *(Cepphus grylle)*.

1956 MA Audubon Soc. *Bulletin* 40.80 **ME,** Black Guillemot. . . Pigeon Murre.

pigeonnier n [Fr] LA

A dovecote.

1941 Writers' Program *Guide LA* 691, *Pigeonnier*—Fr. *pigeon*, pigeon—Pigeon-house, dovecote. **1961** *PADS* 36.12 **sLA,** Other such terms . . are . . *pigeonnier* for a pigeon roost. . . Sometimes we may . . say that . . certain usages are confined to the rural parishes as against New Orleans. Among these are . . *pigeonnier.* **1981** Pederson *LAGS Basic Materials,* 1 inf, **nwLA,** [ˌpˈɪˈdʒn̩ˈæˈ·ɚ]—house on stilts for raising pigeons (to be eaten).

pigeon oak n
=**chinquapin oak 1.**

1921 Deam *Trees IN* 107, In White County a pioneer was found who knew the tree [=*Quercus muhlenbergii*] only by the name of pigeon oak. He said it received this name from the fact that the wild pigeons were fond of the acorns.

pigeon owl n
A **screech owl 1** (here: *Otus asio*).

1939 *LANE* Map 230 (*Screech owl*) 1 inf, **swNH,** Pigeon. **1950** *WELS,* 1 Inf, **ceWI,** Pigeon owl—shivering, whispering owl. **1969** *DARE* (Qu. Q1, . . *Kind of owl that makes a shrill, trembling cry*) Inf **IL33,** Pigeon owl.

pigeon pea n
1 A shrub (*Cajanus cajan*) grown for its edible seed and as a cover crop; also the seed of this plant. [*DJE* 1696 →] **chiefly FL**

[**1889** *Century Dict.* 756, *Cajanus.* . . furnishes a sort of pulse. . . It is a shrub . . and a native of the East Indies. . . The plant is called cajan, *pigeon-pea* [etc.].] **1925** *Book of Rural Life* 7.4319, In the United States, pigeon peas are cultivated sparingly in Florida. **1929** Neal *Honolulu Gardens* 163 **HI,** According to the botanist, Hillebrand, the pigeon pea was brought in early days to Hawaii. Not until about 1908 was it grown extensively as feed for horses, cows, and poultry. The green crop is used for pasturage, and the hay and seeds are ground up for meal. **1946** FL Dept. Ag. *Qrly. Bulletin* ns 77.11, The Conch liked his sea-food and pigeon-peas. **1966** *DARE* (Qu. I20, . . *Kinds of beans*) Inf **FL3,** Pigeon pea. **1981** Pederson *LAGS Basic Materials,* 1 inf, **csFL,** Lima beans, black-eyed peas, pigeon peas, white beans, black beans. **1988** Whealy *Garden Seed Inventory* (2d ed) 413, *Pigeon Pea*—Cajanus cajon [sic], . . perennial legume, one plant will supply a family.
2 =**black-eyed pea.**

1946 McDavid *Coll.* **Beaufort SC,** Pigeon peas = blackeyed peas.

pigeon plum n
1 A **sea grape** (here: *Coccoloba diversifolia*) native to southern Florida. [See quot 1743] Also called **dove plum, tietongue**

[**1743** Catesby *Nat. Hist. Carolina* 2.94 **Bahamas,** *Cerasus latiore folio.* . . *Pigeon-Plum.* This is a large Tree, with a smooth light coloured Bark. . . The Fruit is round, and grows in Bunches, like Currans, but larger, and of a purple Colour, with a single Stone in the Middle: In *December* the Fruit is ripe, and is the Food of Pigeons and many wild Animals.] **1837** (1962) Williams *Territory FL* 99, Pigeon plum. **1884** Sargent *Forests of N. Amer.* 117, *Pigeon Plum.* . . A tree 15 to 18 meters in height. . . The edible and abundant grape-like fruit, ripening in February and March, is eagerly devoured by raccoons and other animals. **1897** Sudworth *Arborescent Flora* 192 **FL,** *Coccolobis laurifolia.* . . *Common Name.* Pigeon Plum. **1945** Dickinson *Jrl.* 152 **FL,** They obtained their food . . from aquatic plants and berries—the last named chiefly clusters of . . pigeon plums. **1961** Douglas *My Wilderness* 148 **Everglades FL,** I recognized the royal palm and the live oak and the mahogany tree, now almost extinct in Florida. But the pigeon-plum tree was new. **1991** Hiaasen *Native Tongue* 166 **FL,** He parked on the side of the road and watched a pair of mustard-colored bulldozers plow a fresh section of hammock, creating a tangled knoll of uprooted tamarinds, buttonwoods, pigeon plums and rougeberry. **1996** *Audubon Mag.* Nov-Dec 18 **FL,** [On] Lignumvitae Key. . . there is also the gumbolimbo tree . . and pigeon plum, mastic, and poisonwood.
2 =**partridgeberry 1. NEng**

1775 *Mass. Hist. Soc. Coll.* 2 Ser. II. 287 [sic *DAE*—quot not found], I had nothing to assist Nature with, but a Tea of Piggen plumb Roots, and Spruce. **1898** *Jrl. Amer. Folkl.* 11.228 **ME,** *Mitchella repens.* . . pigeon plum, South Berwick, Me. **1966** *DARE* (Qu. S26a, . . *Wildflowers.* . . *Roadside flowers*) Inf **ME7,** Checkerberries—also called pigeon plums.

pigeon roost n Also *pigeon's roost* Cf **roost 1**
The balcony of a theater.

1905 *DN* 3.90 **nwAR,** Pigeon roost. . . Theatre balcony. **1966–69**

DARE (Qu. D40, *Names and nicknames . . for the upper balcony in a theater*) Infs **AR38, IN82, OH31,** Pigeon roost; **AR52,** Pigeon's roost; **MO38,** The pigeon roost.

pigeon root n
A **spring beauty** (here: *Claytonia lanceolata*).

1900 Lyons *Plant Names* 106, *C[laytonia] lanceolata* . . of the west is called also Pigeon-root.

pigeon's foot n Also *pigeon foot* [From the shape of the leaf]
A **glasswort:** usu *Salicornia europaea,* but also *S. bigelovii.*

1814 Bigelow *Florula Bostoniensis* 2, *Salicornia herbacea.* . . Pigeons foot. **1843** Torrey *Flora NY* 2.140, *Salicornia mucronata.* . . This and the preceding species [=*S. herbacea*] are sometimes made into pickles. They are often called *Samphire,* or *pigeon's-foot.* **1950** Gray–Fernald *Manual of Botany* 599, *S[alicornia] europaea* . . Chicken claws, Pigeonfoot.

pigeon's roost See **pigeon roost**

pigeontail n Also *pigeon duck* [See quot 1955]
A **pintail 1.**

1849 Herbert *Frank Forester's Field Sports* 1.128, Pintail Duck. . . Winter Duck, Sprigtail, Pigeontail. **1898** Elliot *Wild Fowl* 125, This duck [=*Anas acuta*] is known in various parts of our country as Spiketail, Spindletail, Spreettail, Pigeontail [etc.]. **1917** (1923) *Birds Amer.* 1.128, Pintail. . . Other names.—Male: Sprig-tail . . Pigeon-tail. **1955** *AmSp* 30.182, The elongated tail feathers of the pintail duck have stimulated the invention of numerous names, some of which carry comparisons with other birds. . . *pigeontail* (Fla., Mich., Ill., Minn.) and *pigeon duck* (Iowa) doubtless trace to the extinct passenger pigeon, which had a long tail.

pigeon-tailed gull n
=**parasitic jaeger.**

1954 *AmSp* 29.233, *Pigeon-tailed gull.* **1955** *AmSp* 30.182 **NY,** *Pigeon-tailed gull* for the parasitic jaeger (N.Y.) is an interesting allusion to resemblance in form to the wild pigeon [=the passenger pigeon]—a bird that was extirpated years ago.

pigeon tree n [See quot 1830] Cf **pigeonberry 3, pigeonweed 1**
=**Hercules'-club 1.**

1830 Rafinesque *Med. Flora* 2.194, *Aralia spinosa,* L. *Prickly Elder, Shot Bush, Pigeon Tree, &c.* . . The berries are said to be a certain cure for spring intermittents, . . and are eaten by wild pigeons [=passenger pigeons]. **1876** Hobbs *Bot. Hdbk.* 89, Pigeon tree, Prickly elder, Aralia spinosa. **1900** Lyons *Plant Names* 42, *A[ralia] spinosa* . . Gulf States to New York. . . Pigeon-tree. **1950** Peattie *Nat. Hist. Trees* 493, Hercules'-club . . Other Names . . Toothache-tree. Shotbush. Pigeontree. **1960** [see **pick tree**].

pigeonweed n
1 A **spikenard:** either *Aralia racemosa* or **Hercules'-club 1.** Cf **pigeonberry 3, pigeon tree**

1784 in 1785 Amer. Acad. Arts & Sci. *Memoirs* 1.431, *Aralia.* . . *Shot Bush. Pigeon Weed.* Blossoms white. Berries black. Common in new plantations. **1892** (1974) Millspaugh *Amer. Med. Plants* 69-1, *Aralia racemosa.* . . American Spikenard, Pettymorrel, Life-of-man, Pigeonweed [etc.]. **1974** (1977) Coon *Useful Plants* 68, *Aralia racemosa* . . old man's root, spignet, pigeon weed.
2 The corn **gromwell** (*Lithospermum arvense*).

1848 in 1850 Cooper *Rural Hours* 106 **ceNY,** The pigeon-weed of the grain-fields; the darnel, yarrow, wild parsnip. **1855** MI State Ag. Soc. *Trans. for 1854* 468, A still more troublesome pest, the "Pigeon Weed," . . is making its appearance among us. **1898** *Jrl. Amer. Folkl.* 11.275, *Lithospermum arvense* . . pigeon-weed. **1912** Blatchley *IN Weed Book* 114, Corn Gromwell. Wheat Thief. Pigeonweed. **1935** (1943) Muenscher *Weeds* 384, *Lithospermum arvense* . . Stone seed, Puccoon, Pigeon-weed.
3 =**Mexican clover.**

1874 in 1889 Vasey *Ag. Grasses* 104 **AL,** The plant is known here by the name of "Mexican clover," "poor toes," or "pigeon weed." **1881** Phares *Farmer's Book of Grasses* 14, *Richardsonia scabra. Mexican Clover.* This is a native of Mexico and South America. It has become naturalized in Florida and the southern parts of other southern States. It is called Mexican Clover, Spanish Clover, Florida Clover, water pursley, bellfountain, poor Joe, pigeon-weed etc.

pigeon wheat n Also *pigeonwheat moss*

=**haircap moss.**

1942 Hylander *Plant Life* 98, Among the erect mosses with terminal spore capsules we find the Hairy Cap Moss (*Polytrichum*), also known as Bird Wheat or Pigeon Wheat. **1947** Grout–Howe *Mosses & Liverworts* 39, The Hair-Cap Mosses, called Bird Wheat or Pigeon Wheat in many localities, are the largest and in some respects most highly developed of all our mosses. **1956** Conard *Mosses* 38, *Polytrichum commune.* . . The Haircap or Pigeonwheat Mosses grow in beds often 100 ft. across, and up to 6 in. tall. **1987** Case *Orchids* 189, Perhaps the most frequent plant companion observed is the moss *Polytrichum*, commonly called pigeon-wheat.

pigeon-wings n

=**butterfly pea a.**

1933 Small *Manual SE Flora* 722, *Martiusia* [spp]. . . Butterfly-peas. Pigeon-wings. **1970** Correll *Plants TX* 878, *Clitoria* L. Pigeon-wings. Butterfly Pea. **1979** Ajilvsgi *Wild Flowers* 175 **eTX**, Pigeon-wings . . *Clitoria mariana.* . . *Flower:* bluish or lavender with darker markings.

pigeonwood n

A blolly, usu *Guapira longifolia*, native to Florida.

1884 Sargent *Forests of N. Amer.* 117, *Pisonia obtusata.* . . Pigeon Wood. Beef Wood. Cork Wood. Pork Wood. Semi-tropical Florida, cape Canaveral to the southern keys; through the West Indies. **1898** Sudworth *Forest Trees* 64 **FL**, *Pisonia obtusata.* . . Names in use.—Pigeon-wood . . ; Beef-wood [etc]. **1979** Little *Checklist U.S. Trees* 141, *Guapira discolor.* . . *Other common names*—Brace blolly, roundleaf blolly, beeftree, beefwood, porkwood, pigeonwood.

pigeon woodpecker n

1 also *pitchin' woodpecker:* A **flicker** n[2] **1.** [See quot 1882] **chiefly NEng** Cf **flying auger, looping bird**

1844 DeKay *Zool. NY* 2.192, This species [=*Picus auratus*], from the extreme beauty of its plumage, has attracted general attention, and received many popular names in different districts. It is called *High-hole, Yucker, Flicker, Wake-up,* and *Pigeon Woodpecker,* and usually *Clape* in this State. **1848** *Union Mag.* (NY NY) 3.73 **ME**, The roar of the rapids, the note of a whistler-duck on the river, of the jay and chickadee around us, and of the pigeon-woodpecker in the openings, were the sounds that we heard. **1882** Ingersoll *Birds'-Nesting* 69, As for "pigeon woodpecker," I think it arises from the peculiar pigeon-like attitude of this species, in perching *across* the branch, instead of along it as do other genuine woodpeckers. **1900** *Wilson Bulletin* 31.9, The Flicker. . . Pigeon Woodpecker. New England; New York; Minnesota. **1927** Forbush *Birds MA* 2.292, Flicker; Golden-winged woodpecker; Pigeon woodpecker [etc]. **1956** MA Audubon Soc. *Bulletin* 40.82 **ME, MA, NH, RI**, Yellow-shafted Flicker. . . Pigeon Woodpecker. . . The bird is plump, often perches crosswise on branches like a pigeon—but unlike its fellow woodpeckers—and was long killed as game. **1969** *DARE* (Qu. Q17, . . *Kinds of woodpeckers*) Inf **MA**68, Pigeon woodpecker—same as yellowhammer and flicker; **RI**4, Pitchin' woodpecker—flies like this [FW illustr: a wavy line]; same as red-headed woodpecker—big, red on wing when flies, lives near barns and buildings.

2 =**pileated woodpecker B.** [See quot]

1955 *AmSp* 30.181 **CT**, Of bird names given for size, consider . . *pigeon woodpecker* (pileated woodpecker, Conn.)

pig eye n

A marble game; see quot 1967.

1940 *Recreation* (NY) 34.110, A list of the many games of marbles played throughout the country follows: . . Pig eye. **1966–70** *DARE* (Qu. EE7, . . *Kinds of marble games*) Infs **GA**93, **SC**26, 32, 68, Pig eye. **1967** *DARE* Tape **SC**32, [FW:] How'd you play pig eye? [Inf:] You'd draw out . . it wasn't exactly round, it was just like a circle pushed in. And then you'd have a big circle, then the little circle. . . It was just a circle, just like it'd been pushed in. It wouldn't be too big, be—oh, six, eight inches across one way, and it'd be ten or twelve the other way. . . [FW:] And how'd you go about winning another fellow's marbles? [Inf:] Well, you'd have to knock them . . out of that ring. . . You'd have a line drawed around that, and you'd have to shoot from that line every time.

pig-eyed adj Cf **hog-eyed**

Of a person: see quot.

1966–69 *DARE* (Qu. X21a, . . *Words . . used to describe people according to their eyes . . if they stick out*) Infs **CA**36, **FL**39, **MO**9, **TX**18, Pig-eyed; (Qu. X21b, *If the eyes are set back in head*; (Qu. X21b, *If the eyes are very sharp or piercing*) Inf **GA**89, Pig-eyed—for squinty eyes; **IL**25, Pig-eyed; (Qu. X21c, *If the eyes are very round*) Inf **CA**87, Pig-eyed—if set close together; **NE**3, Pig-eyed.

pigfish n [From the piglike sound made by the fish]
Any of var saltwater fish of the Atlantic or Gulf coasts; see below.

a A **sculpin 1,** usu *Myoxocephalus octodecemspinosus.*

1807 in 1846 *MA Hist. Soc. Coll.* 2d ser 3.56 **seMA**, The pig-fish is of the size and form of a sculpion, but with a head not so large and bony. **1814** in 1815 *Lit. & Philos. Soc. NY Trans.* 380, Eighteen-spined Bullhead. (*Cottus octodecem-spinosus*). . . Called *pig-fish,* from the squeaking noise he makes immediately on being taken out of the water. Another of his names is *sculpin.* **1842** DeKay *Zool. NY* 4.52, It [= *Myoxocephalus octodecimspinosus*] is known under the various popular names of *Sculpin,* . . *Sea Robin, Bull-head, Sea Toad,* and *Pig Fish;* the latter from its croaking noise when drawn from the water. **1884** Goode *Fisheries U.S.* 1.258, On our Atlantic coast are found several species of this family [=Cottidae], known by the name "Sculpin," and also by such titles as . . "Pig-fish." . . The most abundant species is the Eighteen-spined Sculpin, *Cottus octodecimspinosus,* which. . . is usually associated with a much smaller species, *Cottus æneus.* **1911** U.S. Bur. Census *Fisheries 1908* 315, Sculpin. . . Those on the Atlantic [coast] are called . . "bull-head," . . "pigfish," "sea-raven," etc.

b A **sea robin 1a** (here: either *Prionotus carolinus* or *P. evolans*). Cf **grunter** n[1] **1**

1859 (1968) Bartlett *Americanisms* 389, *Sea-Robin.* (*Prionotus lineatus*). . . From the croaking or grunting noise it makes when caught, it is sometimes called Pig-Fish. **1905** *NJ State Museum Annual Rept. for 1904* 380, *Prionotus carolinus.* . . Pig Fish. Rock Pig Fish. *Ibid* 382, *Prionotus evolans strigatus.* . . Sand Pig Fish. Pig Fish. . . This is a most abundant species on our coast in shallow or deep water alike.

c A **grunt** n **1,** esp *Orthopristis chrysoptera;* hence n *pigfisherman.* For other names of *O. chrysoptera,* see **hogfish d, nigger-knocker, piggy** n[1] **1, porkfish, redmouth, sailor's choice 1a, whiting**

1882 U.S. Natl. Museum *Proc.* 5.277 **Gulf coast**, *Pomadasys fulvomaculatus* [=*Orthopristis chrysoptera*]. . . Pig-fish. . . A common shore fish of small size and good quality. **1884** Goode *Fisheries U.S.* 1.398, From their [=fishes of the genus *Haemulon*] habit of uttering a loud, rather melodious sound when taken from the water they have acquired the name of "Grunt" and "Pig-fish." . . In many localities they are in high favor as a food fish. . . A species belonging to a closely related genus is the Hog-fish, or Grunt, of the Chesapeake, called also "Pig-fish" or "Grunt" in the Gulf of Mexico, *Pomadasys fulvomaculatus.* **1931** *Copeia* 2.48 **csTX**, *Orthopristis chrysopterus.* . . Three "pigfish" . . from Port Aransas, July 9, 1928. **1933** LA Dept. of Conserv. *Fishes* 70, *Orthopristis chrysopterus.* . . The Pigfish . . occurs commonly along the Gulf Coast. Its "grunt" can often be heard before the fish that has been hooked is landed. **1937** Pearson *Adventures* 333 **FL**, They were mullet, pig fish, pin fish and cravalle. **1946** LaMonte *N. Amer. Game Fishes* 64, *Haemulon macrostomum.* . . Pigfish. . . North to Florida; not abundant. . . Feeds at night on small fishes, crabs, starfish, sea urchins. *Ibid* 66, Pigfish—*Orthopristis chrysopterus.* . . Long Island (or north); common in Florida, Chesapeake Bay, Virginia, and Texas. **1951** Taylor *Surv. Marine Fisheries NC* 132, *Orthopristis chrysopterus.* . . Known as pigfish, this species is one of the most common food fishes of the North Carolina coast. . . Most of the catch is sold fresh, but small quantities are salted for local consumption. **1968–70** *DARE* (Qu. P2, . . *Kinds of saltwater fish caught around here . . good to eat*) Inf **MD**36, Pigfish—like [spot], but no spot and yellow stripes instead of black; **VA**55, Pigfish; (Qu. P14, . . *Commercial fishing . . what do the fishermen go out after?*) Inf **VA**55, Pigfish. **1968** *DARE* FW Addit **DE**, Pigfish—this name is used in Delaware Bay for the fish called *grunt* by fishing-boat captains out of Clearwater, Florida. **1969** Lyons *My Florida* 123, The squidder. . . felt himself to be far above the cane-pole poppers, the pigfishermen and the live-mullet-for-bait men. With all those he shared just one thing, a detestation for sport fishermen.

d =**pinfish 1a.**

1902 Jordan–Evermann *Amer. Fishes* 440, *Lagodon rhomboides,* the . . pigfish, or bream, [is] a small species . . very abundant on our east coast from Cape Cod to Cuba and Texas. Though small, it is a most excellent pan-fish, and is highly prized wherever found. **1935** Caine *Game Fish* 55, *Lagodon rhomboides*. . . Pigfish.

pigfisherman See **pigfish c**

pig frog n [See quot 1914]
A **bullfrog 1** (here: *Rana grylio*) native to the southeastern US. Also called **granddaddy 5, grunter** n[1] **4, Joe Brown frog, lagoon ~**

[**1791** Bartram *Travels* 276, The largest frog known in Florida and on the sea coast of Carolina, is about eight or nine inches in length from the nose to the extremity of the toes; . . they live in wet swamps and marshes, on the shores of large rivers and lakes; their voice is loud and hideous, greatly resembling the grunting of a swine, but not near as loud as the voice of the bull frog of Virginia and Pennsylvania, neither do they arrive to half their size.] **1914** *Copeia* 5.3 neFL, *Rana grylis* [sic] . . is called the "Pig-frog" owing to its loud grunting call, repeated three or four times. . . The call is heard at any time, day or night, from deeply wooded bayous, oftenest in March, April and May. **1932** Wright *Life-Hist. Frogs* 364 **Okefenokee GA**, *Rana grylio*. . . Common Names—Southern Bull-frog, . . Pig-frog. **1938** Matschat *Suwannee R.* 59 neFL, seGA, He sat with his back against the trunk, listening to the monotonous grunt of the pig-frog. **1967** *LA Conservationist* 19.7–8.9 **LA**, There are two species of frogs in Louisiana of significant sport and commercial value. These are the bullfrog and the pig frog or grunter. . . The smaller pig frog is confined generally to southern portions of the State. **1975** Natl. Audubon Soc. *Corkscrew* 17 **FL**, The Pigfrog (*Rana grylio*). . . is the largest frog in the swamp [and]. . . provides most of the frog legs of commerce. . . Its calls are so loud many people mistake their grunting for alligators. **1982** Sternberg *Fishing* 112, Pig frogs and river frogs are almost identical to bullfrogs and live in similar habitat. Pig frogs have pointed snouts, while river frogs are dark with white spots on their lips. Both types are found in the southeastern United States. **1996** *DARE* File, Pig frog—A small frog found in southwestern Florida. I know it from Ding Darling Nature Preserve. It makes a sound like "oink"—loud. Lives in the creek.

pigged adj Cf **pigging string**
1949 *PADS* 11.24 **CO**, Pigged: . . Helpless, bound hand and foot.

piggery n Usu |ˈpɪgɚi, ˈpɪgəri|; less freq |ˈpɪgri|
1 A place where pigs are kept; a pigsty. [*OED2* 1781 →] esp **NEast** See Map *old-fash*
1828 *N. Amer. Rev.* 27.352, The stercorary and piggery are next resorted to by these insects [=bees]. **1845** in 1857 Webster *Private Corresp.* 207 eMA, I wish him to . . go carefully over the whole field round the piggery, and scatter the [bone-]dust and sow the seed, on every bare spot. **1849** Willis *Rural Letters* 184 **NEast**, You can easily calculate the distribution of the remainder, upon the flower-garden . . and piggery. **1860** Hundley *Social Relations S. States* 341, Each family of negroes has a house or cabin of its own, generally with sufficient garden-ground, piggery, hennery, and so forth. [*DARE* Ed: quoted from "a Northern writer"] **1883** *Wheelman* 1.245 **NEng**, A milk-house, with running-water troughs to convey the refuse milk to the piggery. **1913** London *Valley of Moon* 336 **CA**, They were shown over the cattery, the piggery . . and the kennelry. **1939** *LANE* Map 110 (*Pig pen; hog house*), [47 infs, **NEng**, Piggery; usu proncs of the type [ˈpɪgəri]; less freq, proncs of the type [ˈpɪgrɪ].] **c1955** Reed–Person *Ling. Atlas Pacific NW*, 1 inf, Piggery. **1965–70** *DARE* (Qu. M15, *The place out-*

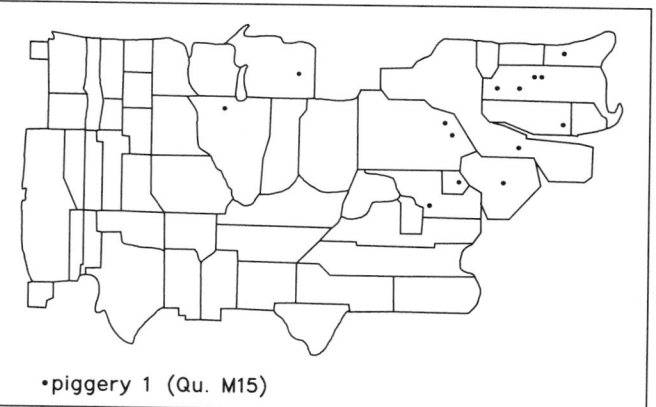

•piggery 1 (Qu. M15)

doors where pigs are kept) Infs CT39, **ME14, MD3, MA6, MI67, NY66, PA59, 127,** Piggery; **DE1,** Piggery—where sows are kept for farrowing; each one has a narrow pen so the pigs are born safely where she can't roll over on them; **IL31,** [ˈpɪgəˌriˇ]; **MA37,** [ˈpɪgəri]; **MA47,** [ˈpɪgɚi]—an acre or two; **MA66,** [ˈpɪgəˈi], [ˈpɪgri]; **NJ65,** Piggery—not a pigsty. [All Infs old] **1967** *DARE* Tape **MI42**, I took care of the pigs. I worked in a piggery [ˈpɪgəri] they called it, out there. Kind of a smelly job, but it wasn't that bad. [**1973** Allen *LAUM* 1.188 **Upper MW** (as of c1950), *Piggery*, though found in New England, has survived only with Canadian speakers except for the one response by an aux. mid-Minnesota inf. who was born in Norway.]
2 =**blind tiger 1.** *obs* Cf **blind pig, blind-pigger, pig** n[1] **B10, striped pig**
1854 *Alta Californian* 7 Jan (*DAE*), A number of persons were. . . charged with keeping a nuisance in the shape of piggeries, on the corner of Turk and Jones streets.

piggie See **piggy** n[1] **1**

piggie move-up See **piggy move-up**

piggin n
1 rarely *pidgin*: A wooden bucket or dipper with one stave extended as a handle; by ext, an indefinite quantity. [*OED2* 1554 →; "Chiefly *dial.*"] **chiefly NEng, Sth, S Midl** *old-fash* Cf **cannikin 1, firkin**
1653 in 1909 *Mayflower Descendant* 11.101, 2 bowles and 3 piggens. **1684** (1977) Mather *Essay Providences* 147, The man tried to save the Milk, by holding a Piggin side-wayes under the Cowes belly. **1737** (1901) Hempstead *Diary* 17 Aug 323 seCT, I was at home al Day underpining & putting a New bottom in to a pail & piggan. **1839** (1863) Kemble *Jrl. Georgian* 52 **GA**, A very small cedar pail—a piggin as they termed it. **1865** Byrn *Advent. Fudge Fumble* 38 **TN**, I . . knocked over the piggin of water. **1887** Amer. Philol. Assoc. *Trans. for 1886* 17.41 **Sth**, Piggin. . . It is still common in country districts all over the South. **1899** (1912) Green *VA Folk-Speech* 281, *Milk-piggin*. . . A small, wooden vessel with an upright handle formed by continuing one stave above the rim, used for milking. **1916** Macy–Hussey *Nantucket Scrap Basket* 141, "Piggin"—Another good old word, still used to some extent. It means a small wooden tub, with hoops, and one stave projecting above the rim to form a handle; used as a receptacle for flour, meal or other material. It differs from a cannikin tub, in having the long stave and no cover. **1927** Mason *Lure Great Smokies* 166 eTN, Thar was many a feller thet come with a "piggin' full o' expectation," as the sayin' goes, and went away empty-handed. **1937** (1963) Hyatt *Kiverlid* 30 **KY**, Watching Marthy Lou come down the path from the draw-bars with her piggin and pail brimming with foaming milk. **1939** *LANE* Map 129 (*Pail; bucket*), Piggin, made of staves, holding about 4 quarts, with one or two long staves for handle(s) [4 infs, **MA, ME**]. **1950** *PADS* 14.52 **SC**, Piggin: . . A small wooden tub with one of the staves extending a few inches above the rim and used as a handle. Formerly used as a milk pail and called a *milk piggin*. **1953** *PADS* 19.12 **sAppalachians**, *Pidgin*: . . Piggin, a small wooden vessel kept near the stove for storing salt or soda. **1966** Dakin *Dial. Vocab. Ohio R. Valley* 2.111, In southeastern and south-central Kentucky . . the old name *piggin* is still commonly used for the wooden pail with one long stave. In this region *pail* and *piggin* stand side by side with about equal frequency. **1966** *DARE* Tape **SC9**, Make peeling one time back, make box, make piggin. My grandpa made all them things one time. **1967** *DARE* (Qu. F31, . . *Bucket*) Inf **MA72**, Piggin—small bucket with an upright handle. **1968** *DARE* FW Addit **VA**, Piggin—wooden measuring bucket; about a gallon. "So much a piggin." **1975** Gould *ME Lingo* 208, Piggin—Originally a *piggin* was a small wooden pail with one longer stave for a handle. It came to mean a quantity or amount, and now it means a dipperful or a ladleful. A *piggin* of blueberries might be just enough for one pie. **1986** Pederson *LAGS Concordance (Bucket)* 1 inf, cGA, Piggin; 1 inf, ceTN, Piggin—wood, long stave for handle, for milking; 1 inf, ceTN, Piggin—one long stave, one handle up; 1 inf, cTN, Piggin—made of cedar with a handle; 1 inf, nwFL, Piggin—holds water; not sure what it is; 1 inf, cTN, Piggins—long ago; 1 inf, cnAR, Piggins—small buckets used in milking.
2 See quot.
1952 Brown *NC Folkl.* 1.576, Piggin. . . A skillet. The word is, of course, also used in its usual sense.—Central and east.

pigging string n Also *pegging string, piggin ~* **chiefly West** Cf **hogging rope,** *hog-tie*

A short length of rope used for tying an animal by the feet.

1924 James *Cowboys N. & S.* 90, At the first sign of a strong wind, . . you could see Bob getting his "piggin' string," unlimbering his ropes and testing his acid. **1929** Dobie *Vaquero* 264 **West,** If he did not have a "piggin string"—a short rope used for tying down animals—he tied the calf's legs together with the bandana. **1940** (1966) Writers' Program *Guide AZ* 446, When we got to the ranch we went into the corn crib to watch Swede put a collar and chain on the varmint. But the lion had chawed the piggin string in two and he was plumb loose when Swede shook him out of the sack. **1940** *Cattleman* 26.12.28 **West,** Put the noose of your tie rope, pegging string, piggin' string, or hoggin' rope (depending upon what you wish to call [the] piece of soft cord about four feet in length which you have with you) around the right front foot. **1946** *NYT Mag.* 20 Oct 35 [Rodeo lingo], *Piggin' string:* rope or thong used to tie three of the calf's feet in bulldogging. **1958** *AmSp* 33.271 **eWA** [Ranching terms], *Pigging string.* Any short length of rope of small diameter, but particularly the rope used to tie an animal's legs. **1960** Hall *Smoky Mt. Folks* 63, As tough as a pigging string . . said to be a rawhide string often used in tying the legs of a pig together before carrying it. **1981** *KS Qrly.* 13.2.69, *Piggin' string* . . short piece of manila rope with an eye in one end used for hogtying calves in roping contests. **1999** Proulx *Close Range* 67 **WY,** My granddad Bitts did most of his ropin at Huntsville. . . That bad old cow-hand had a tattoo of a rope around his neck and piggin strings around his wrists.

piggle v [Engl dial]
1936 *AmSp* 11.191 **seWY,** To *piggle.* To pull or tug nervously. 'The baby kept piggling at my ear.' 'She piggles at her buttons till they come off.'

piggo(o), piggooey See **pigoo**

piggy n[1]
1 also *piggie:* A **pigfish** c (here: *Orthopristis chrysoptera*).
1946 LaMonte *N. Amer. Game Fishes* 66, *Pigfish. . . Names:* Piggie, . . Hogfish. **1967** *DARE* (Qu. P4, *Saltwater fish that are not good to eat*) Inf **TX**14, Piggy. **1973** Knight *Cook's Fish Guide* 386, Piggie— Pigfish.
2 See **pig B15.**

piggy adj
Of a sow: pregnant; also transf.
1937 *AmSp* 12.104 **eNE** [Farm terms], A sow that is giving birth to a litter is said to be *piggin'*, and one that is conspicuously pregnant is *piggy.* **1953** Randolph–Wilson *Down in Holler* 114 **Ozarks,** If no women are about, a hillman may remark to a comparative stranger that his wife is . . *lookin' piggy.* **1979** *DARE* File **nwKS,** [A] piggy sow is one still carrying babies. They also refer to piggy heifer the same. *Ibid* **cwIL,** [From an unidentified shopping flier:] *For Sale:* 3 piggy sows, will farrow any day. *Ibid* **NE,** *Piggy* means 'pregnant.'

piggy n[2] See **piggy move-up**

piggyback plant n Also *pickaback (plant), pig-a-back plant, piggyback* [See quot 1976]
=youth-on-age.
1946 (1948) Free *All about House Plants* 275, The Picka-back Plant has become very much to the fore as a house plant. It is native to the Pacific coast from Alaska to California. . . The culture of Picka-back does not present any special problems. **1959** Carleton *Index Herb. Plants* 91, *Pickaback-plant:* Tolmiea menziesi. *Ibid* 92, *Piggy-back-plant:* Tolmiea menziesi. **1967** *DARE* Wildfl QR **WA**30, Piggyback— pickaback. **1970** GA Dept. Ag. *Farmers Market Bulletin* 30 Dec 8/1, Piggyback plant—Tolmiea menziesii, also called Youth on Age, is a perennial herb of the Saxifragaceae Family. It is a hardy and somewhat sticky-hairy herb with greenish brown flowers and narrow petals. **1973** Hitchcock–Cronquist *Flora Pacific NW* 199, Pig-a-Back-Plant. . . *T[olmiea] menziesii.* . . Alas[ka] s, from coast to w side Cas[cades], through W[ashingto]n and Ore to Cal. **1976** Bailey–Bailey *Hortus Third* 1117, Pickaback plant, piggyback plant. . . Reproduces vegetatively by buds that develop and form new plants at base of lf. blades. Useful in the shaded rock garden but also grown as a house plant.

piggy move-up n Also *piggie move-up, piggy* **esp Chicago IL** Cf **move-up, peggy** n[1]
Any of var bat-and-ball games; see quots.
1945 Boyd *Hdbk. Games* 65, *Piggie Move Up*—This is a form of baseball in which there is no base running. A pitcher, a catcher, and a batter

are selected, and all the other players are fielders. The batter bats the ball, and whoever catches it on the fly is the next to bat. . . The players decide whether the batter gets one or two strikes. Everything is a strike. There are no fouls. If the batter fans out, he becomes a fielder; the catcher becomes batter; and the pitcher becomes catcher. Instead of the fielders volunteering to pitch, they may be numbered and pitch in turn. **1958** *Sat. Eve. Post Letters* **Chicago IL,** We played "Piggy Move Up" which was 4 player baseball. *Ibid* **Chicago IL,** "Piggy" was a miniature game of baseball played in the brick street and allowed only bunting of the ball. **2001** *DARE* File **Chicago IL** (as of 1940s), Two kinds of baseball games were Piggy Move Up and Bounce or Fly.

piggy perch n Cf **perch 7, pigfish d**
=pinfish 1a.
1998 *Houston Chron.* (TX) 28 June 19 (Internet), Live 3- to 4-inch baitfish such as croakers and pinfish ("piggy perch") are increasingly being used for summer specks.

piggy-piggy come in free exclam
=all (in) free.
1967 *DARE* (Qu. EE15, *When he has caught the first of those that were hiding what does the player who is 'it' call out to the others?*) Inf **KS**4, Piggy-piggy come in free.

piggytail See **pigtail** exclam

pig hash See **hash** n 2

pig, hem a See **hem** v B2

pig hickory n esp **Missip-Ohio Valleys** Cf **pignut 1**
=bitternut 1.
1897 Sudworth *Arborescent Flora* 111 **IL,** Bitternut. . . Pig Hickory. **1932** Randolph *Ozark Mt. Folks* 114, Black-oak bark'll make a purty good yaller if you set it with alum—if you set it with copperas it gives a kinder greenish-lookin' brown, like a puddle-duck's neck. Pig-hick'ry works th' same way, but not so good as black-oak. **1950** Peattie *Nat. Hist. Trees* 146, *Carya cordiformis.* . . Swamp or Pig Hickory. **1967–68** *DARE* (Qu. T16, . . *Kinds of trees . . 'special'*) Infs **MN**36, **OH**6, Pig hickory. **1982** *Smithsonian Letters* **cMI,** Pig hickory is the name used for the hickory tree that has bitter nuts, in the area I grew up—Midland County, Michigan. I could not find out if the bark or wood is also bitter. **1986** Pederson *LAGS Concordance,* 1 inf, **cwGA,** Pig hickory nut.

pig hip n Also *pig's hip*
Ham; a ham.
1979 *New Yorker* 5 Mar 97 **Amarillo TX,** Sign: *Pig Hip Sandwiches.* **1990** *NY Times* (NY) 8 Mar sec A 12/1 **cIL** (as of c1940), "All right, what'll you have?" the waitress asked. "A pig's hip on bread," the farmer said, pointing to a ham on the counter. That was about 50 years ago.

pig house n
1 **=hog house 1a. esp N Cent, Upper MW**
1842 in 1845 Cist *Cincinnati Misc.* 1.186, A stout looking fellow set his gun leaning on a pig house, and jumped in to catch some fowls. **1939** *LANE* Map 110 (*Pig pen; hog house*), [Occas, esp in **sNEng,** Pig house.] **1950** *WELS* (*Building where pigs are kept*) 5 infs, **WI,** Pig house. **1960** Bailey *Resp. to PADS* 20 **KS** (*Building for holding pigs*) Pig house. **1966** Dakin *Dial. Vocab. Ohio R. Valley* 2.84, (*Pig, hog*) *pen* is common throughout the Valley and is the usual term in Kentucky. North of the Ohio River (*pig, hog*) *house* occurs with about equal frequency. **1966–69** *DARE* (Qu. M15, *The place outdoors where pigs are kept*) Inf **CT**36, Pig house; (Qu. M22, . . *Kinds of buildings . . on farms*) Infs **IL**70, **MI**23, **MN**33, Pig house. **1973** Allen *LAUM* 2.189 **Upper MW** (as of c1950), Shelter or building only [for hogs and pigs]. . . [7 infs, 3 **MN,** 2 **ND,** 2 **SD**]. **1986** Pederson *LAGS Concordance* (*Hogpen; shelter and enclosure for hogs and pigs*) 3 infs, **TN,** Pig house; 1 inf, **cTX,** Pig houses.
2 **=hog house 2.**
1970 *DARE* (Qu. V11, . . *Joking names . . for a county or city jail*) Inf **MO**29, Pig house.

pightle n Also sp *pichtel, pightel* Pronc-spp *pike'l, pikle, pitle, pykle, pytel* [*OED2* pightle a1210 →; "local"] **Long Is. NY** relic
A yard, barnyard, or cow pen.
1860 *N&Q* 2d ser 9.443 **NY,** *Pightel,* or *pikle,* is a word very nearly

obsolete. . . *Pightel* signifies an enclosure surrounding a dwellinghouse, and is sometimes synonymous with *lawn.* **1895** *DN* 1.392 **Long Is. NY,** *Pykle:* small enclosed field or yard. Patchogue, L.I. **1939** *LANE* Map 113 *(Barnyard)* 4 infs, **eLong Is. NY,** Pightle [pɛˑʏ̆kɫ, pɛˑʏ̆ɫ̩, pɛˑʏ̆ɫ̩, pɑˑɪ̆ɫ]. **1949** Kurath *Word Geog.* 27, Scattered relics . . *pightle . .* for a cow pen, on eastern Long Island. *Ibid* 55, In the North only Eastern New England and eastern Long Island have local expressions for the cowpen, the former *cow yard,* the latter *pightle* (riming with *title*). In all the vocabulary gathered for the Linguistic Atlas *pightle* is the only expression that is confined to Long Island. **1973** *DARE* File **seNY** (as of c1900), *Pightle. .* The second word referred to his grandparents *pitle . .* or *pytel . .* and meant barnyard. . . **c1900,** by native of eastern Long Island; never heard otherwise. **1991** *DARE* File **seNY,** *Pichtel* = *pightle.* Pronounced *pike*'l. The area enclosed by house, barns and other outbuildings to form a sort of courtyard. The center of farm life and activity. I loved this word. Still in use among a few.

pig in a bag n Also *pig in a sack, pig in the bag* **chiefly Atlantic** See Map Cf **cat in a bag**
=**pig in a poke 1.**

1942 Berrey-Van den Bark *Amer. Slang* 545.4, Pig in a poke *or* bag . . a blind exchange. **1965–70** *DARE* (Qu. U13, *When buying or exchanging something that you have not seen . . you're getting it* _____) 38 Infs, **chiefly Atlantic,** Pig in a (*or* the) bag; 9 Infs, **chiefly SE,** Pig in a sack; **ME4, MA72, NJ11, NY10,** (Buying) a pig in a bag; (Qu. U14, . . *Exchanging with somebody when neither one has seen what the other has*) Inf **PA248,** Pig in the bag. **1965** Bradford *Born with the Blues* 115 [Black], I know what the results will be and Columbia [Record Co.] won't be buying a 'pig in the bag,' for I played for her . . in 1912 where she stopped the show at every performance singing jazz songs.

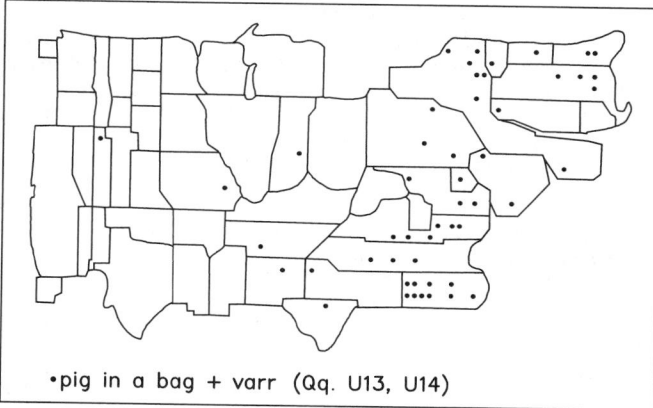

•pig in a bag + varr (Qq. U13, U14)

pig in a blanket n Also *pig in the blanket;* for addit varr see quots

1 Usu a sausage or wiener wrapped in dough or batter and cooked; occas a sausage wrapped in bread or a bun.

[**1935** Frederick *PA Dutch* 122, *Dutch Pigs-in-Blankets* [*DARE* Ed: = diced boiled potatoes wrapped in noodle dough and simmered in broth].] **1965–70** *DARE* (Qu. H14) Inf **PA66,** Pig in a blanket—hot dog wrapped in dough; (Qu. H32, . . *Fancy rolls and pastries*) Inf **CT6,** Pig in the blanket—sausage twisted in dough; **WA18,** Pigs in the blanket—pork in dough; (Qu. H40, *A small sausage that is put into a long roll or bun to make a sandwich*) Inf **CT6,** Pig in a blanket; **MA57,** Pigs in a blanket— heard but not common here; **NY130,** Pig in a blanket—hors d'oeuvres; **NY240,** Pig in a blanket; **WA22,** Pig's blanket—dough with little pigs— wienies—inside; (Qu. H45, *Dishes made with meat, fish, or poultry that everybody around here would know, but that people in other places might not*) Inf **NY39,** Pigs in the blanket—sausage wrapped in dough; (Qu. H82b) Inf **MI102,** Pigs in the blanket—pork or veal ground up and cooked with a pie crust on the outside; often eaten as snack or at lunch. **1995** *DARE* File, Pancake chains now call breakfast sausages wrapped in pancakes pigs in blankets. *Ibid,* A pig-in-a-blanket is a vienna sausage wrapped in a canned biscuit held together with a toothpick and baked. *Ibid* **cwCA** (as of 1950s), When I went to summer camp, we would skewer a hot dog lengthwise on a sharpened stick, wrap the hot dog with biscuit dough, and toast it over an open fire. This was a pig in a blanket. *Ibid* **MS,** Pigs in a Blanket are vienna sausages in bread with mustard. *Ibid* **TX,** Pigs in a Blanket . . were horrible store-bought dough wrapped around hot dogs and baked. [**2001** *Ibid* **seOH,** In Mor-

gan County, . . *[pig in a blanket]* is a pork casserole with a biscuit topping.]

2 A cabbage leaf wrapped around a filling of ground meat and simmered in a sauce. Cf **holishkes**

1965–70 *DARE* (Qu. H45, *Dishes made with meat, fish, or poultry that everybody around here would know, but that people in other places might not*) Inf **NM9,** Pig in a blanket—wrap cooked sausage in a cabbage leaf, add tomatoes, rice, etc, and simmer; **NY70,** Pig in the blanket—rice and hamburger rolled up in cabbage leaves; Polish dish; **NY86,** Stuffed cabbage; pig in a blanket; Hungarian goulash; **PA206,** Pig in the blanket—hamburger, rice, and tomato sauce wrapped in cabbage leaves; (Qu. H52, *Dishes made with fresh cabbage*) Inf **NY188,** Pigs in a blanket; **PA159,** Pigs and blankets; **PA134,** Pigs in the blanket—cabbage leaf with meat, etc, inside; (Qu. H65, *Foreign foods favored by people around here*) Inf **NE7,** Pigs in a blanket; **PA176,** Pig in a blanket—same as halupki. **1995** *DARE* File, Stuffed Cabbage . . I have heard . . called Pigs in a Blanket. **1996** *Ibid* **seWI** (as of 1950s), For us pigs in the blanket was meat balls and cabbage simmered in tomato soup. **2001** *Ibid* **seOH,** Some of my students confirmed . . [that] in elementary school, "pigs in a blanket" would be written on the lunch menu, and it would be cabbage rolls.

3 A thin slice of meat wrapped around a filling; a roulade; see quots.

1889 *Culinary Nuggets* 39 **cwNY,** *Little Pigs In Blankets.* Season large oysters with salt and pepper, cut fat English bacon in very thin slices, wrap an oyster in each slice of bacon and fasten with small wooden toothpicks, heat a frying pan and put in the little pigs; cook just long enough to crisp the bacon; place on small slices of toast. **1939** Wolcott *Yankee Cook Book* 55, Pigs in blankets [*DARE* Ed: =oysters wrapped in bacon]. **c1965** Randle *Cookbooks* (Ask Neighbor) 38, *German pigs in blanket* [*DARE* Ed: =a roulade of salt pork wrapped in a steak strip]. **1966** *DARE* (Qu. H45, *Dishes made with meat, fish, or poultry that everybody around here would know, but that people in other places might not*) Inf **MA6,** Pigs in blankets—hunk of bacon wrapped around hot dog. **1995** *DARE* File **seWI,** Back in the 40s, my mother made pigs in blankets. They were what the Germans call Rouladen—that is, some thinly sliced round steak wrapped around some bacon and a pickle and tied with string or thread.

4 =**pig in a poke 1.**

1967–70 *DARE* (Qu. U13, *When buying or exchanging something that you have not seen . . you're getting it* _____) Inf **MO29,** Pig in a blanket; pig in a sack; **VT16,** Sight unseen; blindfolded; a pig in a blanket; (Qu. U14, . . *Exchanging with somebody when neither one has seen what the other has*) Inf **OH18,** Pig in a blanket.

pig in a pen See **pig in the pen**

pig in a poke n Also *pig in the poke* [**poke** n[1] **1a**]

1 Something one cannot see or evaluate before deciding to accept or purchase it. [*OED2* 1562 →] Cf **cat in a bag, pig in a bag**

1788 in 1939 Washington *Writings* 30.144 **VA,** I am not fond of buying a Pig in a Poke (as the phrase is). **1872** Schele de Vere *Americanisms* 521, "To buy a pig in a *poke,*" is often heard in England and in the United States, and shows how old, obsolete words survive in proverbial sentences. **1903** *DN* 2.325 **seMO,** Pig in a poke. **1927** *AmSp* 3.140 **eME,** Don't buy a pig in a poke. **1950** *WELS,* 11 Infs, **WI,** (Buying a) pig in a poke. **1957** *Sat. Eve. Post Letters* **sIN** (as of 1910–20), That's sure a pig in a poke. **1965–70** *DARE* (Qu. U13, *When buying or exchanging something that you have not seen . . you're getting it* _____) 215 Infs, **widespread,** (Buying a *or* like a) pig in a poke; **GA13, KY5,** 59, **MS1, NC55,** 76, **NY233, SC69,** (Buying a) pig in the poke; (Qu. U14, . . *Exchanging with somebody when neither one has seen what the other has*) 30 Infs, **scattered,** (Trading a) pig in a poke; **GA9,** 15, **OK20, SC11, VA23,** Pig in the poke; [[(Qu. HH14, *Ways of teasing a beginner or inexperienced person—for example, by sending him for a 'left-handed monkey wrench':* "Go get me _____.") Inf **NY35,** A pig in a poke]. **1985** Ladwig *How to Talk Dirty* 36 **Ozarks,** He bought a pig in a poke . . bought it sight unseen. **1986** Pederson *LAGS Concordance* **Gulf Region,** 1 inf, Pig in a poke—buying. . . you don't know what; 1 inf, Pig in a poke—only use of "poke"; 1 inf, Pig in a poke—inf has heard.

2 also *pigs in a poke:* A children's game; see quot.

1967–69 *DARE* (Qu. EE13a, *Games in which every player hides except one, and that one must try to find the others*) Inf **WA22,** Pigs in a poke; (Qu. EE18, *Games in which the players set up a stone, a tin can,* *or something similar, and then try to knock it down)* Inf **PA**181, Pig in the poke.

pig in a sack, pig in the bag See **pig in a bag**

pig in the blanket See **pig in a blanket**

pig in the parlor n
Any of var games or dances; see quots.

1933 *AmSp* 8.4.48 **NE** [Pioneer vocabulary], Popular *play-party games* were . . Pig in the Parlor, Skip to my Lou. [Footnote:] I saw these dances or *games,* so common in the pioneer era, *played* in Brown County two years ago (1931). **1965–68** *DARE* (Qu. EE1, . . *Games . . children play . . in which they form a ring, and either sing or recite a rhyme)* Infs **SC**46, **WI**66, Pig in the parlor; (Qu. EE2, *Games that have one extra player—when a signal is given, the players change places, and the extra one tries to get a place)* Infs **OK**1, **SC**46, **WV**7, Pig in the parlor. **1967** *DARE* Tape **OH**6, They'd play kitchen games. We'd sing and have certain steps to the music. They provided their own music by singing—folk dances, really. . . They didn't call it dancing, really, called it playing games, but that's what it was. . . I can remember the titles of some of them, but I can't remember all the words. One was pig in the parlor.

pig in the pen n Also *pig in a pen*
Any of var children's games; see quots.

1901 *DN* 2.146 **neNY**, Ring alevio. . . in Essex Co., N.Y., pig in the pen. **1966** *DARE* (Qu. EE2, *Games that have one extra player—when a signal is given, the players change places, and the extra one tries to get a place)* Inf **NC**4, Pig in a pen; **FL**14, Pig in the pen—one is in the middle, he grabs what they drop and gets out; (Qu. EE33, . . *Outdoor games . . that children play)* Inf **PA**177, Pig in the pen.

pig in the poke See **pig in a poke**

pig Irish See **pigpen Irish**

pig Latin n
=**hog Latin 2.**

[**1934** (1940) Weseen *Dict. Amer. Slang* 379, *Pig Latin*—An invented language used by children in which Latin case endings are added to English words. Also called *Hog Latin.*] **1937** *Dime Detective Mag.* Nov 50, Don't give me any more of that pig Latin. **1938** in 1963 Fitzgerald *Letters* 22, But when anything, Latin or pig latin, was ever put up to me . . I could always rise to meet that. **1955** McAtee *Dial. Grant Co. IN Suppl.* 6 [2], *Pig-latin:* . . a jargon made by dividing words, and adding a meaningless syllable to each. I have known persons who could both utter, and understand it readily. It served well to guard their conversation from the uninitiated. Sample: "Ixnay, ehay illway eesay ouyay" (Nix, he will see you). **1975** Ferretti *Gt. Amer. Book Sidewalk Games* 127, *I'm Going to Boston.* . . The player chosen begins by saying, "I'm going to Boston, and I'm taking my brother." . . The next player then has to say, "I'm going to Boston, and I'm taking my brother and his fiddle." The next player has to add to the verbal chain. . . [I]n the Queens section of New York City, the game is played in pig Latin . . for example, by the time the sentence reaches the third player, it sounds like this: "I'mgay oingay ootay ostonbay ithway ymay rotherbay nday ishay iddlefay nday ymay etpay oatgay." **1980** Pearl *Jonathan David Slang* 117, *Pig Latin* . . a verbal amusement, popular in the 1920s, in which words are formed by displacing the first letter or letter grouping of a word to the end of it and adding the sound "ay," so that bank, for example, becomes ankbay, and strum becomes umstray.

pig laurel n
A **sheep laurel** (here: *Kalmia angustifolia*).

1950 Gray–Fernald *Manual of Botany* 1121, *K[almia] angustifolia . . Pig-* or *Dwarf l[aurel]. . .* Old pastures and barrens. **1976** Bailey–Bailey *Hortus Third* 623, Pig l[aurel]. . . Slender shrub, to 3 ft. . . Early summer. E. N. Amer.

pig leaf n
Prob a **pigweed.**

1967 *DARE* (Qu. S21, . . *Weeds . . that are a trouble in gardens and fields)* Inf **PA**18, Pig leaves.

piglin n
The American **egret** *(Casmerodius albus).*

1917 *Wilson Bulletin* 29.2.78 **swKY**, *Herodias egretta.*—White crane, piglin, Hickman, Ky.

pigling n
A piglet.

1968–70 *DARE* (Qu. K51, . . *Pigs, a very young one)* Infs **MO**20, **NJ**44, **NY**79, **PA**56, Pigling; **PA**235, ['pɪglən]. **1986** Pederson *LAGS Concordance* (Hogs . . young) 1 inf, **cnAR**, Not a pigling.

pig lot See **lot** n **1b(2)**

pig maw n Also *pig's maw* esp **PA**
=**hog maw.**

1934 *Language* 10.4 **cPA**, Names of dishes which are peculiar to the Dutch: *pig's maw* (where the word *maw* is no doubt not the English word, since this is not used in colloquial English, but the German word *Magen*). **1948** Hutchison *PA Du. Cook Book* 50, Stuffed pig's maw. **1969** *DARE* File **sePA**, *Pig maw* [mɑ] . . pig stomach stuffed with potatoes, sausage, & onion—you don't eat the stomach itself, however.

pig meat See **pig** n¹ **B2**

pigmy cedar See **pygmy cedar**

pigmy owl See **pygmy owl**

pigmy rattler (or rattlesnake) See **pygmy rattlesnake**

pignut n
1 also *pignut hickory,* ~ *tree:* Any of several **hickories** n **B1,** but usu *Carya glabra* or, less freq, **bitternut 1;** also the nut of such a tree. [See quot 1968] Also called **hickory nut 1.** For other names of *C. glabra* see **bitternut 2, broom hickory, hard-bargain hickory nut, hard-shell hickory, hognut 1, hog walnut, pig** ~, **red hickory a, smoothbark** ~, **swamp** ~, **sweet pignut, switch-bud hickory, white** ~, **walnut;** for other names of *C. ovalis* see **balsam hickory, false shagbark, red hickory a, shagbark** ~, **shellbark** ~, **sweet pignut;** for other names of *C. texana* see **bitter pecan, Texas** ~

1666 in 1926 Warwick RI *Early Rec.* [323], Upon a straight Lyne from ye pond to a pignut tree standing upon a hill. **1705** Beverley *Hist. VA* 2.16, There are also several Sorts of Hickories, call'd Pig-nuts, some of which has as thin a Shell as the best *French* Walnuts. **1730** Royal Soc. London *Philos. Trans.* 36.430 **NC, SC,** *Juglans Carolinensis,* . . the Pig-nut. **1785** Marshall *Arbustrum* 1.68, *Juglans alba minima* [=*Carya cordiformis*]. *White, or Pig-nut Hickery. . .* The shell of the nut is also very thin, and easily cracked with the teeth; the kernel plump and full but very bitter. **1830** Rafinesque *Med. Flora* 2.228, The *Pignut hickories,* such as *H[icoria] amara, H. porcina* and *H. aquatica* have bitter nuts, their bark is styptic. **1848** in 1870 Drake *Pioneer Life* 73 **KY,** Of the whole forest the red or slippery elm was the best; next to that the white elm, and then the pig-nut or white hickory. **1850** Emerson *Rept. Trees & Shrubs* 197 **MA,** Although the pignut hickory [= *Carya glabra*] occurs more frequently than any other species, yet the name is often made to include the mockernut and the bitternut. **1897** Sudworth *Arborescent Flora* 111, *Hicoria minima. . .* Pig Nut (N.Y., W. Va., Mo., Ill., Iowa, Kans.) . . Bitter Pig Nut (N.Y., N.J.) *Ibid* 115, *Hicoria glabra. . . Pignut (Hickory). . .* Pignut (N.H., Vt., Mass., Conn., R.I., N.Y., N.J., Pa., Del., W. Va., N.C., S.C., Fla., Ala., Miss., La., Tex., Ark., Ky., Mo., Ill., Ind., Wis., Iowa, Kans., Nebr., Minn., Ohio, Ont.) **1906** *DN* 3.150 **nwAR,** *Pignut.* . . A kind of nut with a bitter kernel and with outside and inside shells so thin that it can be cracked with the teeth. **1913** (1980) Hardy *OH Schoolmistress* 76, We found a big black snake in the woods. . . stretched at length near a favorite log of ours, on one side of which grew a pig-nut tree, where we were looking for nuts. **1938** Van Dersal *Native Woody Plants* 81, *Carya glabra. . . Pignut hickory. . .* A large tree. *Ibid* 338, [Hickory,] Pignut *(Carya cordiformis, Carya glabra, Carya leiodermis, Carya pallida, Carya villosa).* **1950** *WELS* **WI** *(Nuts that grow wild in your neighborhood)* 1 Inf, Pignuts—resembling the hickory in many ways, are bitter and not good to eat; *(Nut-bearing trees in your neighborhood)* 1 Inf, Pignut; 1 Inf, Hickory nut—same as pignut. **1958** Babcock *I Don't Want* 126 **eSC,** He . . could shoot a snake through the head or topple a big red fox squirrel from the tallest pignut tree. **1960** Vines *Trees SW* 131, *Carya aquatica. . .* Vernacular names are Bitter Pecan, Swamp Hickory, and Water Pignut. *Ibid* 133, *Carya cordiformis. . .* Vernacular names are . . Swamp Hickory, . . Pignut Hickory. *Ibid* 134, *Carya texana. . .* Some of the vernacular names for it are Buckley Hickory and Pignut Hickory. *Ibid* 136, Pignut Hickory—*Carya glabra.* **1965–70** *DARE* (Qu. I43, *What kinds of nuts grow wild around here?)* 49 Infs, **scattered, but rare West,** Pignut(s); (Qu. T16, . . *Kinds of* trees . . 'special') 27 Infs, **scattered exc West**, Pignut (hickory). **1968** *DARE* FW Addit **VA**, *Pignut hickory*—mountain people turn their pigs loose and they eat these small hickory [sic]. **1969** *DARE* Tape **KY**50, [FW:] Do you have the small ones that taste bitter? [Inf:] Yeah, that's pignuts we call them, but they don't gather them. Nothing eats that but a hog.

2 A **groundnut B1** (here: *Apios americana*).

1891 *AN&Q* 6.178 **MA**, Another article of savage diet, that we boys of long ago used to collect and eat, was the fleshy tubers of a wild vine, the *Apios tuberosa,* or pig-nut. . . Some called them Indian potatoes. They were very small; but roasted, they were sweetish and not unpleasant. **1899** (1912) Green *VA Folk-Speech* 321, *Pig-nut.* . . earth-nut, ground-nut, a small nut growing in the ground, dug up and eaten by children.

3 =**jojoba.**

1897 *Jrl. Amer. Folk.* 10.143 **AZ**, *Simmondsia Californica,* . . pig-nut. **1931** U.S. Dept. Ag. *Misc. Pub. 101* 94 **West**, *Jojoba* . . , known by a variety of vernacular names, including . . pignut, . . is a bushy-branched and spreading shrub. . . The seeds of jojoba have an agreeable nutty flavor. **1995** Brako et al. *Scientific & Common Names Plants* 203, Pig-nut—*Carya cordifformis, Hoffmannseggia glauca, Simmondsia chinensis.*

4 =**Jerusalem artichoke.**

1959 Carleton *Index Herb. Plants* 92, *Pig-nut:* . . Helianthus tuberosa.

5 =**peanut 1.**

1959 Carleton *Index Herb. Plants* 92, *Pig-nut:* Arachis hypogaea.

6 =**hog peanut 1.**

1966 *DARE* Wildfl QR Pl.118A Inf **OH**14, Pignut.

7 A **rush pea** (here: *Hoffmannseggia glauca*).   Cf **hog potato 4**

1995 [see **3** above].

pignut hickory (or tree)   See **pignut 1**

pigoo exclam, sometimes repeated   Also *piggo(o), piggooey;* for addit varr see quots   **chiefly OH Valley, Gulf States, S Atl** See Map   Cf **goop v¹**

Used as a call to pigs; see quots.

c1937 in 1972 *Amer. Slave* 2.1.242 **SC** [Black], We called . . de hogs and pigs, 'pig-oo, pig-oo.' **1949** Kurath *Word Geog.* 44, The Carolinas have their own range of hog calls: *goop!, woop!,* and *piggoop! Ibid* 65, In North Carolina south of the Neuse, in South Carolina, and in Georgia entirely different calls are in regular use: *goop!, piggoop!* (with the vowel of *loop*), and *woop!, woopie!* **1965–70** *DARE* (Qu. K84, *The call used . . to get the pigs in at feeding time*) Infs **MO**19, 24, **TN**14, Piggo; **LA**40, Piggoo; **GA**72, Piggoo pig; **MO**34, Piggoo piggo; **SC**57, Piggoo piggoo; **GA**17, Piggoo piggy pig pig; **IN**8, 32, **KY**43, **MO**4, **TN**2, Piggooey; **AL**2, Piggy piggy piggo; **KY**84, Piggy ['pɛɪgi] piggy piggoo ['pɛɪgu:]; **SC**47, Woo piggoo. **1966** Dakin *Dial. Vocab. Ohio R. Valley* 2.282, *Calls to pigs.* . . Some residents of the Mountains region also use the call which occurs most frequently as *pig-oo-(w)ie!* (also *pi-goo-(w)ie!, pi-gwoo-(w)ie!, pi-go-(w)ie!, pi-goo!, pig-oo!*). This call, which unquestionably was brought into Kentucky from the southeast and carried northwest into Indiana and Illinois, would seem to be derived from the *piggoop!* of the Carolinas. . . *Pig-oo-ie!* is fairly common in the Mountains south of the Kentucky River, in the southern Pennyroyal, and in the Wabash Valley in Indiana and Illinois. . . Several eastern Indiana speakers use this call, but it is unknown in Ohio. **1967** Faries *Word*

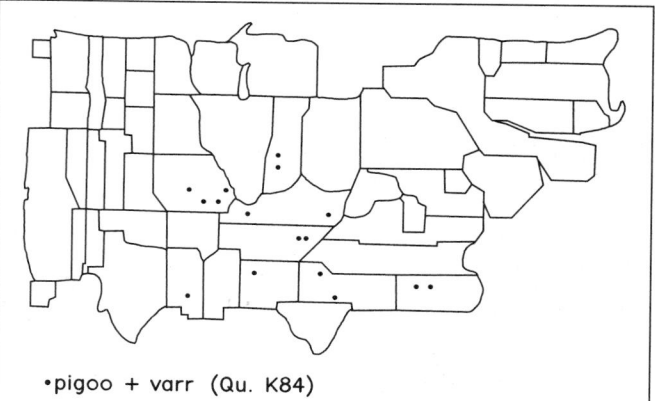

•pigoo + varr (Qu. K84)

Geog. MO 93, *Call to pigs. . . piggoie!* (35 occurrences [out of c700 infs]). **1973** Allen *LAUM* 1.266, Calls to pigs at feeding time. . . pigooie [1 inf, **IA**]. **1986** Pederson *LAGS Concordance (Calls to pigs)* 1 inf, **ceAR**, Piggo—single call, falsetto; 1 inf, **cnGA**, Piggo, pig, ooey (x2)—to hogs, not to scatter; 1 inf, **seTN**, Piggo, pig, pig—falsetto; 1 inf, **nwFL**, Piggo, piggo, pig (x2)—falsetto; 1 inf, **cwGA**, Piggo, piggy, pig (x3)—falsetto; 1 inf, **seGA**, Piggo, pig (x2), erp (x2)—falsetto; 1 inf, **nwFL**, Piggo, pig (x2), piggo—falsetto; 1 inf, **nwAR**, Piggooee; 1 inf, **cGA**, Piggoo—high pitch, rising at end; 1 inf, **ceAR**, Piggoo—single call, falsetto; 1 inf, **cnAL**, Piggoo (x2), pig (x2)—first two elements falsetto.

pig oyster n   Cf **mountain oyster, oyster B3, prairie oyster 1**

A pig's testicle, esp as an article of food.

1991 Still *Wolfpen Notebooks* 78 **sAppalachians**, When I was a shirt-tail boy my Pap used to kill us a mess of snowbirds for supper in the winter time. A bite to a bird. Tasty as pig oysters.

pig parlor   See **parlor B2**

pigpen brand n   Also *hogpen, pigpen*

A livestock brand; see quot 1936.

1890 *Stock Grower & Farmer* (Las Vegas NM) 15 Mar 6/2, On all the horses recovered their hat brand was changed to a "Pig Pen." **1936** Adams *Cowboy Lingo* 126, Every conceivable symbol was used in brands. Triangles, bells, pots, kettles, . . and countless others. . . [T]here were many that even a cowboy would be at a loss to call correctly. . . Brands coming under this class were the 'Two-Pole Pumpkin,' . . the 'Hog-Pen,' and the 'Porcupine.' [Illustr shows two sets of parallel lines crossing at right angles.] **1964** Jackman–Long *OR Desert* 19, The summer I was twelve, Denny O'Connor bought one of the nicest little horses you ever seen, a little buckskin with black stripes around his legs and a dark stripe down his back. He had a pigpen brand on the right shoulder.

pigpen Irish n   Also *pig Irish, pigshit (Irishman)* =**shanty Irish.**

1932 Farrell *Young Lonigan* 31 **Chicago IL** (as of 1916), They were always calling him names, pigpen Irish, shanty Irish. *Ibid* 239, Well if you ask me, Barney is a combination of eight ball, mick, and shonnicker, said McArdle, one of the corner topers. And the Irish part is pig-irish, said Studs. **1967** *DARE* File **cwOR**, Pigpen Irish—same as shanty Irish. **1968–69** *DARE* (Qu. HH28, *Names and nicknames . . for people of foreign background: Irish*) Inf **PA**199, Pigshit; **PA**94, Pigshit Irishman.

pigpens n =**evening-snow 1.**

1898 *Jrl. Amer. Folk.* 11.275 **CA**, *Gilia dichotoma,* . . pig-pens, Kern Co.

pig picking n   **chiefly S Atl**

A social gathering at which a pig is barbecued, esp an event where the guests help themselves to the food.

1979 *News & Observer* (Raleigh NC) 30 Jan np **ceNC**, Pig pickin'. A social event at which a whole pig or more is cooked over coals (a barbecue up North) and is consumed self-service style. Generally large gatherings with lots of slaw, hush puppies, salat, butter beans and black-eyed peas to accompany the pig. **1980** *Chatham Rec.* (Pittsboro NC) 16 Oct np, The Piedmont Horseman's Association will hold a Flea Market, Pig Pickin', Futurity Class and Stud auction. . . The public is invited. **1980** *DARE* File **Fayetteville NC**, We have a pig-picking when we want to discuss political matters. **1995** *Ibid*, Pig pickin' is used widely (perhaps generically) in South Carolina for a barbecue. I have also heard the term used in the two communities of Columbus, Indiana, and Marion, Ohio. *Ibid*, I've been to pig-pickin's, so called, in North Georgia. . . But not just any barbecue is a pig-pickin': only the real ones, where you go whole hog, splitting the hog flat and cooking it between two grills. Then you pick off bites without burning your fingers.

pig pile n   Cf **dog pile, monkey pile, nigger pile**

A game in which children pile themselves on one another; a pile of people formed in or as if in this way—also used as a call in this game.

1955 Hobson *Nothing Too Good* 227, There must have been fifty Indians of all sizes, generations, and varying degrees of talent pulling on the rope. . . We went down twice in a pig-pile. **1994** *DARE* File **OR** (as of 1970s), A bunch of kids jumping on each other is a "pig pile." *Ibid*

WA, OR, Pig-pile. *Ibid* **Portland OR** (as of 1950s), "Pig-pile" e.g. in "Pig-pile on [insert name of victim here]." *Ibid* **Boston MA,** All kids pile on yelling, "Pig pile! Pig pile!" It is called "pig pile." **1997** *Ibid* **nwMA** (as of 1940s), If someone was on the ground, intentionally or unintentionally, it was fair game for everyone to pile on top of him, if someone yelled, "Pig pile!" **1998** *Ibid,* I grew up and live in Connecticut. . . I and those I have grown up with have called to action such incoming attacks by yelling "Pig pile on [victim]." . . When I did this at school, a friend (who is from and grew up in Texas) said "What's a pig pile?" When I explained, she said, "No, that's a dog pile." . . Others from New Jersey and Maine sided with me, while Californians and still more Texans favored the seemingly midwest version. Then I had the opportunity to spend time with a cousin who lives in Washington, DC. His parents grew up in Connecticut, minutes from where I live today. . . The fellow from Boston agreed with me, but to my bewilderment, my cousin favored dog piles.

pig plant See **pig B15**

pig plum n
=**hog plum 1.**
  1859 (1968) Bartlett *Americanisms* 320, *Pig-Plum.* See *Hog-Plum.* **c1902** Clapin *New Dict. Amer.* 229, *Hog plum* (Ximenia americana). A tall shrub of South Florida, bearing a fruit in size and shape like a plum, and pleasant to the taste. Also, *pig-plum.*

pig pork See **pig B2**

pig potato n
  1 A **groundnut B1** (here: *Apios americana*).
  1896 *Jrl. Amer. Folkl.* 9.185 **West,** *Apios tuberosa,* . . pig-potato. **1922** *Amer. Botanist* 28.75, *Apios tuberosa.* . . is . . frequently known as "ground-nut" in allusion to the rounded tubers . . which. . . are edible. . . A considerable number of other names allude to these tubers among which are . . "Indian potato," "pig potato." **1959** Carleton *Index Herb. Plants* 92, *Pig-potato:* Apios tuberosa; Oxypolis rigidor [sic].
  2 A **cowbane 2** (here: *Oxypolis rigidior*).
  1898 Britton–Brown *Illustr. Flora* 3.577, *Pig-potato* [=*Oxypolis rigidior*]. **1933** Small *Manual SE Flora* 986, *O[xypolis] rigidior.* . . Pig-potato. **1959** [see **1** above].
  3 also *pig's potato:* An undersized **white potato.** [*OED2* 1796 →] **esp NEng**
  1966–70 *DARE* (Qu. LL2, . . *Too small to be worth much: "I don't want that little _____ potato."*) Infs **CT22, 25, MA68, NJ51,** Pig (potato); **RI3,** Pig—only applies to potatoes; so small to eat they're given to pigs; **MA98,** Pig potatoes; **ME6,** Pig's potato—used to be fed to pigs.

pigroot n
A **blue-eyed grass 1** (here: *Sisyrinchium angustifolium*).
  1898 Britton–Brown *Illustr. Flora* 3.577, *Pig-root* [=*Sisyrinchium angustifolium*]. **1959** Carleton *Index Herb. Plants* 92, *Pig-root:* Sisyrinchium (v.).

pigs n
  1 A **cockleburr 1** (here: *Xanthium strumarium*).
  1898 *Jrl. Amer. Folkl.* 11.230 **CA,** *Xanthium strumarium,* . . pigs.
  2 See **pig n¹ B15.**

pig's ear n
  1 See **pig n¹ B10.**
  2 A type of pastry; see quots. [Cf Fr *oreille de cochon,* Ger *Schweinsohr* in ref to pastries] Cf **elephant's ear 9**
  1979 *Cuisine* Sept 88, *Oreilles de cochon.* . . Slide 1 dough circle into [hot] shortening; when dough returns to surface, pierce center with roasting fork; lift and twist fork slightly, folding pastry over on itself to form ear shape. . . Remove pig's ear with tongs. **1996** *DARE* File **sNJ,** In southern Jersey . . , "pig's ears" are a kind of pastry made out of a light, flaky (like filo) dough and having a large shape. . . Some people also call them "elephant's ears." *Ibid* **sLA,** I am in south Louisiana, Cajun country, and here pig's ear is a sweet usually breakfast food dish. Actually it's a French dish, Oreille de Cochon, literally 'pig's ears.' It's a fried pastry similar to a donut but shaped like pigs ears and usually served with powdered sugar and/or syrup coating. . . This dish is traditional and popular among Cajuns. Available in some few restaurants but probably mostly a treat within families. **1997** *Ibid* **Madison WI,** For several years now, I've noticed bakery signs referring to a fairly large

puff pastry, honey-glazed cookie as a "pig's ear." This cookie looks more like a heart than a pig's ear. *Ibid* **sePA,** Pig's ears—a Swiss-type pastry, flat and shaped in the form of two small connected wheels. *Ibid* **TX,** I remember seeing in Austin, TX, in a Bavarian bakery, a pastry called Pig's Ear. It consisted of layered strips of dough wrapped around each other, . . resembling an ear (somewhat).
  3 See **pig ears 2.**

pig's ears See **pig ears**

pigs et up my little brother, since the See **hogs ate my brother up, since the**

pig's eye n
  1 =**trillium.**
  1923 *DN* 5.245, "Oh," said one member of the class [at the University of Washington], "in Minnesota we always called the *trillium* the *pig's eye.* I never knew it had another name until I left there." Several other members of the class knew the trillium by the same name.
  2 See **pig n¹ B10.**

pig's foot See **pigtoe**

pig shave n
A crew or other very short haircut.
  1950 *WELS* (*Names for different kinds of men's haircuts*) 2 Infs, **WI,** Pig shave. **1960** Wentworth–Flexner *Slang* 389, *Pig shave*—A crew-cut haircut. *Not common.* **1966–67** *DARE* (Qu. X5, . . *Different kinds of men's haircuts*) Infs **WA22, 30,** Pig shave; **WA17,** Pig shave—all cut off.

pig's hip See **pig hip**

pigshit (Irishman) See **pigpen Irish**

pigs in a poke See **pig in a poke 2**

pigs in blankets See **pig in a blanket**

pig's maw See **pig maw**

pig squealer n
=**tulip tree.**
  1968 *DARE* (Qu. T13, . . *Names . . tulip tree*) Inf **GA20,** Tulip gum—what we call a "pig squealer."

pig-stabber n
  1 See quot. Cf **snake kicker, toad-stabber**
  1968 *DARE* (Qu. W42a, . . *Nicknames . . for men's sharp-pointed shoes*) Inf **PA167,** Pig-stabbers.
  2 See **pigsticker 1.**

pig's tail See **pigtail exclam**

pigsticker n
  1 also *pigstabber:* A homemade sled with a pointed front; see quots. **esp wCT, wMA** Cf **double-ripper, pickerel 4a**
  1889 *Scribner's Mag.* 6.716 **NEng,** About eight o'clock, when the school-boys' "pig-stickers" had mostly disappeared from the slide, a new party arrived. **1943** *LANE* Map 573–574 (*Sled; sleigh*) [Of the 16 infs who responded with "pigsticker," 13 were located in wCT and wMA. One inf described it as "a little hand-made sliding-sled," and another as "low, long, with solid runners."] **1966–68** *DARE* (Qu. N40c, *Other kinds of sleighs*) Inf **CT2,** Pigsticker—original sleds for sledding were pigstickers—had a sharp point on front; (Qu. EE24a, *When there's snow, children go down the hill on a _____*) Inf **CT5,** Pigsticker—used to be; **CT12,** Double ripper = two pigstickers, side by side, with a board between; old-fashioned; **MI24,** Pigstabber—made of barrel staves, the front of the runners are sort of sharp.
  2 A knife, now esp a large folding knife. Cf **frogsticker (knife)**
  1870 Leland *Hans Breitmann in Church* B127, Den out he flashed his pig-sticker. **1871** Leland *Breitmann Ballads* 285, *Pig-sticker*—Bowie-knife. **1895** *Funk's Stand. Dict.* (*OED2*), *Pigsticker.* . . 4. (Slang.) A large pocket-knife. **1941** Smiley *Hash House Lingo* 43, *Pig sticker*—carving knife. **1951** *PADS* 15.67 **NH,** *Pigsticker.* . . Pocket knife. **1954** *Harder Coll.* **cwTN,** Pigsticker. . . Pocket knife. Slang or colloquial. **1968–69** *DARE* (Qu. F39, *A large pocket knife with blades that fold in and out*) Infs **AL43, CT2, 32, GA36, 46,** Pigsticker. **1980**

DSNA Letters **AL**, *Pig-sticker* in these parts . . is the slang name for a folding (pocket) knife which has an unusually long (narrow) blade—including switch-blade knives of large size. **2000** *NADS Letters*, When I was in 3rd grade (in Santa Barbara, CA) I'd brought a switchblade (actually a comb, but made to look like a knife) to class and it fell out [of] my pocket. Our teacher, Mr. Jenkins, who I believe was from Arkansas, asked me, "Boy, where'd you get that pigsticker?"

pigsty daisy n [See quot 1931]
=dog fennel 1.

1892 *Jrl. Amer. Folkl.* 5.98 **MA**, *Anthemis cotula.* . . Pigsty daisy. Ipswich, Mass. **1929** *Torreya* 29.151 **ME**, Anthemis Cotula was *"Stink weed," "Pig-sty Daisy."* **1931** Harned *Wild Flowers Alleghanies* 591, *Anthemis Cotula.* . . Various appellations have been generously assigned to this common plant, such as . . "Pig-sty daisy." . . The odor of the foliage is strong and unpleasant.

pig's weed See **pigweed 4**

pigtail n

1 also *pigtail tobacco, pigtwist auger:* Tobacco twisted into a rope. [From the shape] Cf **ladies' twist**

1733 *SC Gaz.* (Charleston) 21–28 Apr 4/2, To be sold . . very good cut Tobacco, Scotch Snuff, and Pig-tail. **1779** in 1906 *Documents Revol. Hist. NJ* 3.191, Plugg and pigtail tobacco by the barrel. **1825** Neal *Brother Jonathan* 2.81 **CT**, Wiping the offered pig tail on his cuff, he . . bit off three large mouthfuls. **1860** *De Bow's Rev.* 28.194, I may venture to say that more tobacco is manufactured in Richmond, than in any other place in the world. Such vulgar terms as *"negro-head and pigtail"* are discarded, and the most fanciful ones substituted. **1870** Nowland *Early Indianapolis* 169, The plaits . . resembled very much the "pigtail" tobacco so much used at that time. **1871** Eggleston *Hoosier Schoolmaster* 41 **sIN**, Old Jack, having bit off an ounce of "pigtail," returned the plug to his pocket. **1876** Miller *First Fam'lies* 87, A Missourian . . lay in his bunk . . smoking his pipe of 'pigtail.' **1899** (1912) Green *VA Folk-Speech* 321, Pigtail. . . Tobacco twisted into a rope or coil. **1960** Heimann *Tobacco* 136, Burley twist . . , popularly known as "pigtail," evolved from the old Spanish tobacco rope, was first woven or spun, then compressed. **1984** Wilder *You All Spoken Here* 195 **Sth**, *Pig-twist auger:* A twist of chewing tobacco. The imagery relates to the twist in a pig's tail and the turns in an auger.

2 A Chinese person; also used as a nickname.

1870 *Punchinello* 1.350, Late advices from China convey the intelligence that the American–Chinese General Ward . . has been postmortuarily brevetted to the rank of a "major god," and is now regularly worshipped as such by *John Pigtail.* **1942** Berrey–Van den Bark *Amer. Slang* 385.20, Chinese . . pigtail. **1964** *PADS* 42.31 **Chicago**, Chinese, *Chink* and *Chinaman*, with a single occurrence of the relic *pigtail.*

3 In baseball: one who fetches out-of-bounds balls; also v *pigtail* to fetch such balls. Cf **pigtail** exclam

1897 *KS Univ. Qrly.* (ser B) 6.90 **KS, MO**, *Pig tail:* a small boy who stands behind ball players and chases the ball. Also as verb. **1906** *DN* 3.150 **nwAR**, *Pig-tail.* . . Boy who stands behind the catcher in a baseball game, runs after the ball, if it passes out of bounds, and returns it to the catcher. "Who'll be pig-tail?" *pig-tail.* . . To run after a ball which has passed out of bounds, and throw it back to a player. "I'll pig-tail for you." **c1970** *DARE* File **wTN**, *Pigtail* 'a baseball player stationed *behind* the catcher to serve as a sort of human backstop.' The player was a feature of baseball games played in pastures and on schoolyards in West Tennessee until 1950 (at least that long). In all games the pigtail batted last. He was (generally) the *least* adept player.

4 A tagalong; also v *pigtail* to tag along; to follow.

1942 Berrey–Van den Bark *Amer. Slang* 8.4, Follow . . pigtail, put a tail on, . . tag along *or* after. **1967–68** *DARE* (Qu. Y9, *Somebody who always follows along behind others:* "His little brother is an awful _____.") Infs **CA**9, **LA**3, 31, **MO**3, 35, Pigtail.

5 The person at the end of the line in a game of crack-the-whip.

1967 Jacobs *Rejoicing* 121 **cIN** (as of c1930), "Have you ever played whipcracker? . . Everybody line up—Jacobs is pigtail." About ten boys lined up abreast, hands locked, Marvin at one end of the line and me at the other. . . The line lunged forward. I could hardly keep up. . . They dragged me along. The left side of the charging line suddenly halted. The right side was carried on by the momentum. No one broke hands, but the line turned, cracking like a whip. I was at the end, and I could

not hold on with one hand. I went tumbling end over end. As I rolled I heard the other kids laughing. As a pigtail I had performed perfectly.

6 A curlicue.

1966–69 *DARE* (Qu. JJ12, *Little flourishes that some people put on their handwriting or signature to make it look fancy*) Infs **FL**19, **IL**28, **LA**11, **MO**18, 27, **UT**4, Pigtails.

pigtail v See **pigtail** n 3, 4

pigtail exclam Also *piggytail, pig's tail, pigtail back* Cf **pig** n[1] **12, pigtail** n 3

In the game of **Antony-over:**

a The phr that the thrower calls out if the ball fails to go over the building. **scattered, but less freq NEast, S Atl** See Map

1947 *WELS Suppl.* **swWI**, If the ball didn't go over, we called "Back Ball"—or "Pig Tail" was just as acceptable. **1948** *Ibid* **WA**, We said "Aunty-I-over" and also "Pigtail." *Ibid* **cwWI** (as of c1900), I never heard of "backball," but "pigtail" sounds familiar. *Ibid* **swWI**, Pigtail back. **1965–70** *DARE* (Qu. EE23b, *In the game of andy-over . . if you fail to get the ball over the building and it rolls back, what . . you call out*) 83 Infs, **scattered, but less freq NEast, S Atl**, Pigtail; 11 Infs, **chiefly Upper MW**, Pig's tail; **IA**29, 46, **MN**28, **SD**2, Pigtails; **WV**1, 3, 4, 12, Piggytail. **1991** *NADS Letters* **ceWA** (as of 1940s), We said "pigtail" when the ball failed to clear the top of the house or garage. . . Both structures had a sloped roof, . . so the ball did execute a curly-cue when it failed to reach to [sic] top of the building.

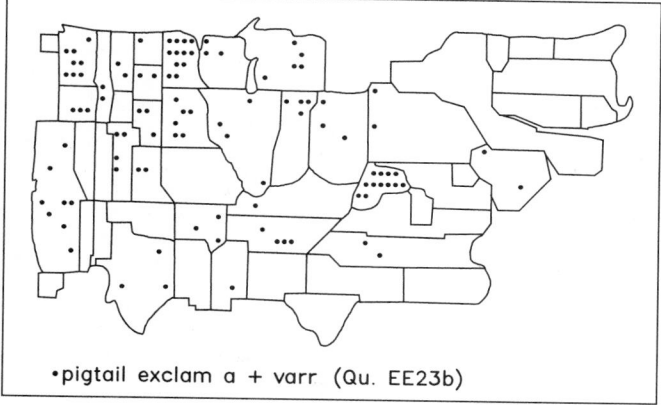

•pigtail exclam a + varr (Qu. EE23b)

b See quot.

1968 *DARE* (Qu. EE23a, *In the game of andy-over . . what do you call out when you throw the ball*) Inf **IA**43, Pig's tail.

c See quot.

1949 *PADS* 11.17 **CO**, If the ball is not caught, the players yell "Pigtail" or "Pig's tail."

pigtail tobacco See **pigtail** n 1

pig thrasher n
=brown thrasher.

1955 *Oriole* 20.1.11 **GA**, Brown Thrasher. . . *Pig Thrasher* (probably because it "roots" among fallen leaves for food).

pig-tight adj Cf **bull-strong**
=hog-tight.

1853 in 1855 Willis *Out-doors at Idlewild* 66 **seNY**, "Yes, sir," said he, after looking at it [=plans for a gate] a moment, *"but it isn't pig-tight!"* **1859** *Harper's New Mth. Mag.* 19.712, A Buncombe fence . . is bull strong, horse high, and pig tight! **1873** Beadle *Undeveloped West* 40 **IA**, A 'lawful fence' required five [strands of wire], which . . will make it 'horse-high, bull-strong, and pig-tight.' **1895** in 1950 *PADS* 13.12 **AL**, An old man had a mortgage on his land that was 'bull-proof and pig-tight.' **1935** *Ada* (O.) *Herald* I Nov. *(DA)*, The specifications for a good stake-and-rider line, or road-side fence were that it should be 'pig tight, horse high and bull strong.' **1942** (1960) Robertson *Red Hills* 209 **SC**, "Boys," he shouted, "you got to keep your fences horse-high, bull-strong, and pig-tight." **1954** *Harder Coll.* **cwTN**, Bull-proof and pig-tight. **1967** *DARE* (Qu. L63, *Kinds of fences made with wire*) Inf **OR**1, Pig-tight fence. **1984** Wilder *You All Spoken Here* 58 **Sth**, Bull-proof and pig-tight: Secure; impregnable.

pigtoe n Also *pig's foot* esp Upper Missip Valley Cf **Ohio River pigtoe**

A **freshwater clam** of the genus *Fusconaia* or *Pleurobema*, esp *Fusconaia flava.*

1938 FWP *Guide IA* 327, The fisherman's haul usually contained a wide assortment of shells: the niggerhead . . commanded the highest price; others, all salable, were the . . pig toe, maple leaf, and elephant's ear. **1953** (1977) Hubbard *Shantyboat* 211 **Missip-Ohio Valleys,** We learned that there are many classes of shells, of different value. Those called sand and niggerhead shells bring the highest price; then muckets and pigtoes. **1979** *WI Week-End* Apr 6, Such shellfish as the elephant's ear . . and pig's foot go right on living their private lives in the quiet waterways of the Mississippi. **1982** *WI State Jrl.* (Madison) 22 Aug sec 7 3, The clams that may be found in Wisconsin rivers include . . pig-toe. **1982** U.S. Fish & Wildlife Serv. *Fresh-Water Mussels* [Wall chart] **Upper Missip Valley,** Pigtoe. Historically widespread and abundant; currently somewhat less widespread, common. Hosts: several widespread, common fishes. **1991** IL Nat. Hist. Surv. *Biol. Notes* 137.11, *Fusconaia flava* . . Wabash pigtoe. Though declining in some Illinois streams because of siltation . . , the Wabash pigtoe appears to be holding its own in the Sangamon River basin. **1992** Cummings–Mayer *Field Guide Freshwater Mussels MW* 44, *Fusconaia subrotunda.* . . Pigtoe. . . . Similar species . . pigtoes (*Fusconaia* and *Pleurobema*).

pig tracks n pl chiefly Sth, S Midl

Used in var compar phrr in ref to what is plentiful, frequent, or vulgar, esp *common as pig tracks* vulgar, ill-bred; hence *pigtracks* fig: a vulgar, ill-bred person.

1853 (1854) Baldwin *Flush Times* 307 **MS,** Since the penitentiary has been built, they are got quare ways of doing things,—they are sending gentlemen there as regular as pigtracks. **1870** (1935) Duval *Advent. Big Foot* 66 **TX,** We found Indian "signs" as plentiful as pig-tracks around a corn crib. *Ibid* 302, And no wonder, neither, for the people are 'piling in' here as thick as pig-tracks around a corn-crib door. **1942** (1960) Robertson *Red Hills* 111 **SC,** Don't you marry a Yankee. They are just pigtracks. **1952** *Argosy* (NY) June 100, In his [=a type of dog's] breeding and appearance he may be "common as pig tracks." **1966–67** *DARE* FW Addit **AR55,** *Common as pig tracks:* exceedingly common; **MS,** *Common as pig tracks:* denoting the idea that something is very ordinary (used primarily by Negroes). **1978** *AP Letters* **cGA** (as of c1890), My mother, born in 1859, would describe no-good white folks as "common as pig tracks." *Ibid* **GA,** Sayings attributed to Texans that I say belong to all of the southland . . "He's as common as pig tracks." **1985** Ladwig *How to Talk Dirty* 22 **Ozarks,** She's as common as pig tracks. **1986** Pederson *LAGS Concordance (Common)* 1 inf, **csTN,** Common as pig tracks—of character, derogatory; 1 inf, **csTX,** Common as pig tracks, common as gully dirt. **1986** *DARE* File **AL** [Black], In an interview, Rosa Parks, whose refusal to give up her "White" seat in a segregated bus precipitated the Montgomery, Alabama bus boycott, spoke of certain White politicians as being "common as pig tracks."

pigtwist auger See **pigtail** n 1

pig ulua n

An **ulua** (here: *Caranx cheilio*).

1960 Gosline–Brock *Hawaiian Fishes* 177, *Caranx cheilio* . . Pig ulua. . . The conical, pointed snout and the slight concave depression in the profile above the eyes make this ulua easy to identify.

pig walnut n chiefly sNEng Cf **hog walnut**

Either **bitternut 1** or a **pignut 1** (here: *Carya glabra*).

1897 Sudworth *Arborescent Flora* 111 **NH,** *Hicoria minima* [=*Carya cordiformis*]. . . Pig Walnut. **1931–33** *LANE Worksheets* **CT,** Pig walnuts. . . Poorer nuts than shagbark walnuts. *Ibid* **RI,** Pig walnuts. . . Pignuts. **1938** Damon *Grandma* 64 **CT** (as of late 1800s), We made out with the pig-walnuts or spice-bush blossoms or what not. **1941** *LANE* Map 277 *(Walnut shell)* **NEng,** The walnut proper . . is not native to New England. The term *walnut* is most commonly used here to denote a hickory nut . . Hicoria glabra (Carya porcina). . . 6 infs, **sCT, RI, sMA,** Pig walnut(s); 1 inf, **csCT,** Pig walnut, smooth-shelled; 1 inf, **csCT,** Pig walnut, hardshelled; 1 inf, **neCT,** Pig walnut, inferior kind; 1 inf, **csMA,** Pig walnut, the most common kind of walnut. **1950** Peattie *Nat. Hist. Trees* 146, Bitternut Hickory. . . Pig . . Walnut. *Ibid* 147, *Fruit* nearly round, . . with scaly, thin husk splitting by four sutures halfway down. **1966–69** *DARE* (Qu. I43, *What kinds of nuts grow wild around here?*) Infs **CT2, MA5,** 6, Pig walnut(s); **MA37,** Pig walnuts—bitter.

pigweed n Cf **Russian pigweed, winged ~**

1 =**goosefoot,** esp *Chenopodium album.* Cf **hogweed 3**
Note: *Pigweed* is more commonly used for goosefoot in the Northeast and for amaranth in the West; see **2** below.

c1801 Fessenden *Orig. Poems* (1806) 17 *(DAE),* The hyacinth and daffodil, With now and then a big weed Of purslain and of pigweed. **1820** in 1832 MA Hist. Soc. *Coll.* 2d ser 9.148 **cwVT,** Chenopodium album, . . Pig-weed. **1822** Eaton *Botany* 235, *[Chenopodium] album* (pigweed . .). *[C.] ambrosioides* . . (sweet pigweed . .). *[C.] maritimum* (sea pigweed . .). **1850** (1852) Hawthorne *Scarlet Letter* 54 **NEng,** A grassplot, much overgrown with burdock, pigweed, apple-peru, and such unsightly vegetation. **1886** Ebbutt *Emigrant Life* 75 **KS,** There were great bushy plants called "pigweeds," which grew five or six feet high, which it was impossible for any one to pull up. **1899** MacMillan *MN Plant Life* 259, The fourteenth order includes the goosefoots or pigweeds, and the amaranths, known also as pigweeds, redroots or tumbleweeds. **1910** Graves *Flowering Plants* 166 **CT,** *Chenopodium album.* . . Pigweed. . . . Sometimes troublesome as a weed. Occasionally used as a pot-herb. **1929** Bell *Some Contrib. KS Vocab.* 185, Pigweed. . . A kind of rank weed, having a reddish stem, and growing to a height of several feet. **1950** WELS **WI** (*What do you include under the word "greens" in your neighborhood?*) 3 Infs, Pigweed; 1 Inf, Pigweed = lamb's quarters; (*Other weeds common in your locality*) 3 Infs, Pigweed or lamb's quarters; 1 Inf, Pigweed. [*DARE* Ed: Some of these Infs may refer instead to senses below.] **1965–70** *DARE* (Qu. S21, . . *Weeds . . that are a trouble in gardens and fields*) 189 Infs, **widespread, but chiefly Nth, West,** Pigweed(s) [*DARE* Ed: Some of these Infs refer instead to senses below.]; **CT2, MI9,** 116, **NY122, ND9, SD8, WI72,** Pigweed—also called (*or same as*) lamb's quarters; **IA13,** Pigweed—both prostrate and upright; (Qu. I28b, *Kinds of greens that are cooked*) Infs **CA90, ID4, MA58, NM9, NY28,** 106, **PA221, RI16, VT13,** Pigweed(s); **WY3,** Pigweed greens [*DARE* Ed: Some of these Infs refer instead to senses below.]; **CO11, MI53, NM9, WI72,** Pigweed—also called (*or same as*) lamb's quarters; (Qu. I28a, . . *Kinds of things . . you call 'greens' . . [Those that are eaten raw]*) Infs **CA205, NY146,** Pigweed; **WA13,** Pigweed—same as lamb's quarters; (Qu. S8, *A common kind of wild grass that grows in fields: it spreads by sending out long underground roots, and it's hard to get rid of*) Inf **PA92,** Pigweed; (Qu. S26d, *Wildflowers that grow in meadows;* not asked in early QRs) Inf **IA18,** Pigweed—like a little tiny daisy; (Qu. BB50d, *Favorite spring tonics*) Inf **MA51,** Pigweed cooked and served with a cream sauce; (Qu. OO23a, *About a child growing: "Billy has to have new clothes—during the summer he _____ [two inches]."*) Inf **MA58,** Grew like pigweed in a manure pile.

2 =**amaranth,** esp *Amaranthus retroflexus.* Cf **hogweed 1**
See note at **1** above.

1835 Ingraham *South-West* 2.110 **MS,** A weed not unlike the common pigweed. **1859** (1880) Darlington *Amer. Weeds* 275, *A[marantus] hybridus.* . . Hybrid Amarantus. Green Amaranth. Pigweed. **1868** (1870) Gray *Field Botany* 286, *Green Amaranths* or *Pigweeds,* flowers and leaves green or greenish. **1898** *Jrl. Amer. Folkl.* 11.277 **KS,** *Acnida* [=*Amaranthus*] *tuberculata,* . . pigweed, red-root. . . *Amaranthus blitoides,* . . pigweed. **1923** in 1925 Jepson *Manual Plants CA* 334, *A[maranthus] retroflexus.* . . Rough Pigweed. . . Very common in orchards, gardens and waste lands. **1942** Whipple *Joshua* 19 **UT** (as of c1860), 'It's their victuals, mostly,' said Willie. 'Pigweed greens. They git the scours hand hit dries up their blood.' *Ibid* 213, The family were eating supper. . . Last night it had been dandelion greens, and the night before pigweed greens. **1950** WELS **WI** (*Other weeds common in your locality*) 3 Infs, Pigweed; 2 Infs, Pigweed [same as] redroot (pigweed). **1951** West *Witch Diggers* 25 **IN,** Uncle Wes . . told him to get the purslane and pigweed out from between the corn rows. **c1960** *Wilson Coll.* **csKY,** Pigweed. . . . Amaranthus. . . commonly called careless weed. **1965** Will *Okeechobee Boats* 150 **FL,** Custard apple trees, head high elders, and in summer, pigweeds twenty feet in height. **1965–70** *DARE* (Qu. S21, . . *Weeds . . that are a trouble in gardens and fields*) Infs **AL2, KY74, NJ10, WI37,** Pigweed—same as hogweed; **CO4, NY160, PA165, VA82,** Pigweed—same as redroot; **IA13,** Pigweed—both prostrate and upright; **ND3,** Pigweed—tumbling weed; **WA12,** Pigweed; (Qu. S20, *A common weed that grows on open hillsides: It has velvety green leaves close to the ground, and a tall stalk with small yellow flowers on a spike at the top*) Inf **IL52,** Pigweeds—but that spike doesn't really have flowers, it has seedy stuff like very little fibers; **ND1,** Pigweed. **1966** *DARE* FW Addit **WA12,** Pigweeds—all tumbleweeds—bloom doesn't amount to anything. Can be cooked for spinach. **1974** *WI Acad. Rev.* Summer 18, Green Amaranth (*Amaranthus* *retroflexus*) Pigweed. **1995** Brako et al. *Scientific & Common Names Plants* 6, *Amaranthus . . albus . .* white pigweed. . . *[A.] fimbriatus . .* fringed pigweed. . . *[A.] graecizans . .* prostrate pigweed. . . *[A.] hybridus . .* pigweed. . . *[A.] retroflexus . .* pigweed. . . *[A.] spinosus . .* spiny pigweed.

3 =Russian thistle.

1899 MacMillan *MN Plant Life* 260, Another variety of pigweed, not native to the state, . . has excited a great deal of attention on account of its rapid development in the wheat fields of the Red river valley. This is the Russian thistle.

4 also *pig's weed:* A **purslane 1,** usu *Portulaca oleracea.* [*OED2* 1911 →]

1929 Neal *Honolulu Gardens* 111 **HI,** Pigweed, purslane, pusley, wild *portulaca . .* (*Portulaca oleracea*)*. .* Pigweed is abundant. . . on lawns and in gardens . . in Honolulu. . . Pigweed has some value, for. . . livestock eat it readily. **1940** Clute *Amer. Plant Names* 144, *P[ortulaca] retusa. .* Western purslane, (pigweed). **1968–69** *DARE* (Qu. S21, . . *Weeds . . that are a trouble in gardens and fields*) Infs **MD**29, **RI**12, 17, Pigweed—also called (*or* same as) pusley; **MN**12, Pigweed—small waxy plant. **1970** Anderson *TX Folk Med.* 75 ceTX, Tonics—A good spring tonic is pig's weed [pigweed, i.e., purslane] tea. *Brazos* [Co.] **1973** *Foxfire 2* 69 nGA, *Portulaca oleracea . .* (pussley, pigweed)—A common weed in gardens or cultivated fields. **1974** *WI Acad. Rev.* Summer 20, Purslane . . pigweed.

5 =alligator grass.

1937 *Torreya* 37.96 **SC,** *Alternanthera philoxeroides. . .* Pigweed, throughout lower South Carolina.

pigwick n Also *pigwitch* **MD**
=horned grebe.

1877 Bartlett *Americanisms* 464, Pigwick. A small species of duck, very numerous in the coves and rivers of the eastern shore of Maryland. It has remarkably red eyes, feeds on fish, keeps near the shore, and is a great diver. **1959** *Names* 7.111, The horned grebe is known . . in Maryland. . . [as] pigwick and pig witch. . . "Wick" is an old form of witch but what the syllable, "pig", signifies is a question. **1968** *DARE* (Qu. Q9, *The bird that looks like a small, dull-colored duck and is commonly found on ponds and lakes*) Inf **MD**42, Pigwitch; coot [is] not the same.

pig wire n, also attrib
=hog wire.

1967–69 *DARE* (Qu. L63, *Kinds of fences made with wire*) Infs **NY**93, **RI**15, Pig wire fence; **MN**7, Page wire or pig wire, a woven fence; **MA**51, Pig wire fence—square 3 to 4 inches; [**PA**191, Pig fence]. **1986** Pederson *LAGS Concordance* (Barb(ed) wire fence) 1 inf, swGA, Pig wire.

pigwitch See **pigwick**

pig yard n **chiefly Nth** See Map Cf **hog yard, piggery 1**
An outside enclosure for pigs.

1949 *WELS Suppl.* csWI, A *pig yard* or *pig lot* is an exercising lot adjacent to the pen—the pasture is something else again. **1950** *WELS* (*The place outdoors where pigs are kept*) 5 Infs, **WI,** Pig yard. **1965–70** *DARE* (Qu. M15) 31 Infs, **scattered Nth,** Pig yard. **1973** Allen *LAUM* 1.188 (as of c1950), Shelter and enclosure for hogs and pigs. . . pig yard [5 infs, **MN, ND**]. *Ibid* 189, Enclosure only. . . pig yard [2 infs, **ND**].

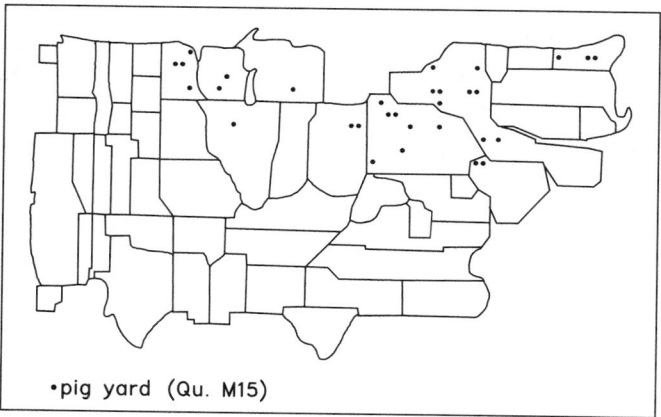

•pig yard (Qu. M15)

pika n Usu |'paɪkə| [From the native name in Siberia for another species of this genus]
A small social animal (*Ochotona collaris* or *O. princeps*) with rounded ears and no visible tail, native to western North America. Also called **coney** n[1] **1, little chief hare, piping ~, rock cony, ~ rabbit 1, squeaker, whistling hare**

1869 (1911) Muir *First Summer* 207 cCA, I caught sight, for the first time, of the curious pika, or little chief hare, that cuts large quantities of lupines and other plants and lays them out to dry in the sun for hay. **1889** *N. Amer. Fauna* 2.11, Description of a new species of pika (*Lagomys schisticeps*) from the Sierra Nevada Mountains in California. **1917** Anthony *Mammals Amer.* 272, The Pikas. . . are curious little creatures whose appearance is something between that of a Guinea-pig and a Rabbit. **1940** Writers' Program *Oregon* 426, Coneys or Pikas, tiny cousins of the rabbit, are among the smaller creatures that inhabit the slide rocks along the canyon rims [near Hart Mountain]. **1941** Writers' Program *Guide CO* 20, Perhaps the most interesting of the small mammals is the diminutive cony, or pika, an odd rabbit-like creature found only in rock slides above timberline. **1955** U.S. Arctic Info. Center *Gloss.* 60, Pika. . . [Pronounced "peeka".] . . Pikas usually live in colonies and build corridor homes under rocks. . . Their call note is a sharp, short, clear whistle. **1958** Barnes *Nat. Hist. Wasatch Autumn* 29 **UT,** Mammals sometimes select strange habitats, . . [such as] the high mountain slide-rock chosen by the pika. . . With voices like toy trumpets they live in small colonies. . . [and] build bushelsize haystacks. **1980** Whitaker *Audubon Field Guide Mammals* 343, The name "pika". . . was originally pronounced *peeka* but has been Americanized to *pie-ka.* **1996** *DARE* File CO, The Pika Bagel Bakery of Breckinridge is named for the pika ['paɪkə], a small furry creature locally at home in the Colorado Rockies.

pikake n |'pikɑki| [See quot 1948] **HI**
The Arabian jasmine (*Jasminum sambac*).

1948 Neal *In Gardens HI* 599, *Jasminum sambac. . .* In Hawaii, where they are popular for leis, they were named pikake, meaning "peacock," because Princess Kaiulani was very fond both of this flower and of peacocks. . . Single-flowered forms are called pikake lahilahi; double-flowered forms, pikake pupupu. **1967** *DARE* (Qu. S26e, *Other wildflowers not yet mentioned;* not asked in early QRs) Inf **HI**11, [pikɑki] (jasmine)—used in leis. **1984** Sunset *HI Guide* 85, Pikake—jasmine.

pike n[1]

1 A freshwater fish of the genus *Esox;* see below. Cf **jack** n[1] **24a(1), jackfish 1a, pickerel 1**
a Std: **=northern pike 1.** [*OED2* 1314 →]
b Any other fish of this genus: **chain pickerel, grass ~ 1, redfin ~,** or **muskellunge 1.**

1637 (1972) Morton *New English Canaan* 91, There are in the rivers, and ponds, very excellent Trouts, Carpes, Breames, Pikes. **1709** (1967) Lawson *New Voyage* 162 **NC, SC,** The Jack, Pike, or Pickerel. . . are very plentiful with us in Carolina. **1794** Williams *Nat. & Civil Hist. VT* 122, The *Pike* or *Pickerel* abounds much in Lake Champlain. It is there called by the name of Muschilongoe. **1820** Rafinesque *Ohio R. Fishes* 70, Pike. Esox. . . There are several species of Pikes in the Ohio, Mississippi, Wabash, Kentucky, &c. . . The American settlers [call them] Pikes or Pickerels. **1838** Geol. Surv. OH *Second Annual Rept.* 194, *E[sox] reticulatus* [=*E. niger*]. . . The Pike is common both to the waters of the lake and the Ohio. As the names pike, pickerel, and muskallonge are used rather indiscriminately, the *E. estor* [=*E. lucius*] and *reticulatus,* and the *Lucioperca Americana* [=*Stizostedion canadense* or *S. vitreum*] are very likely to be mistaken one for the other. **1865** Norris *Amer. Angler's Book* 130, All fish of this genus [=*Esox*]. . . in the Middle States . . are called "Pike," and in Virginia and further South they go by the name of "Jackfish." **1884** U.S. Natl. Museum *Bulletin* 27.469, *Esox americanus. . . Banded Pickerel; Pike. . .* In length this pickerel seldom exceeds one foot. **1906** NJ State Museum *Annual Rept. for 1905* 174, *Esocidae.* The Pikes. . . Fresh-water fishes reaching some size and of value as food. . . The pike is noted for its voracity, aptly quoted from Thoreau as "mere machines for the assimilation of other organisms." **1927** Weed *Pike* 29, *Esox ohioensis* [=*E. masquinongy ohioensis*]. . . In the southern streams . . this fish is called "Pike." *Ibid* 42, *Esox americanus. . .* Pike: this seems to be a fairly well distributed common name from eastern Maryland to Florida. *Ibid* 45, *Esox niger. . .* Pike: general. . . *Esox ohioensis. . .* Pike: Ohio River valley. **1950** *WELS* (*Kinds of fish that are good to eat, commonly caught in your neighbor-*

hood) 26 Infs, **WI**, Pike. [*DARE* Ed: Some of these Infs may refer instead to **1a** above or to **2** below.] **1957** Trautman *Fishes* 220 **OH**, Until recently this Muskellunge [=*Esox masquinongy ohioensis*] was almost universally known as the "Pike." . . I saw . . barns . . upon whose sides were nailed the heads of 5–25 "Pikes." **1965–70** *DARE* (Qu. P1, . . *Kinds of freshwater fish . . caught around here . . good to eat*) 125 Infs, **widespread exc NEng, West**, Pike; **AL**17, **GA**16, 65, **SC**99, **VA**43, Pike—jack(fish); **DE**1, Pike [FW: I believe this refers to chain pickerel—description of size fits, but I did not get to examine a fish to check gill covers for proper identification.]; **MI**44, Pike—both the grass and the northern; **LA**15, Pike—they're called this up the road (North); we call them "jackfish"; **MN**22, Pike, pickerel—alternate names; **MA**6, Pike—more scales than pickerel; **NY**71, Pike or walleye pike; **NC**49, Pike, jackfish, redfin pike; **PA**176, Pike—some call them pike—they're really pickerel; **SC**40, Pike—in eddy lakes; (Qu. P3, *Freshwater fish that are not good to eat*) Infs **LA**2, **NC**80, Pike; **FL**27, Jack—a pike; **GA**65, Pike, jack—not very good eating; (Qu. P14, . . *Commercial fishing . . what do the fishermen go out after?*) Infs **MN**2, **MO**38, **NY**12, 142, 177, **WI**54, Pike. [*DARE* Ed: Some of these Infs may refer instead to **1a** above or to **2** below.] **1967** *DARE* Tape **MI**32, The biggest fish we got up around here is pike. . . They had one last year of forty-six inches. Went right around nineteen pounds. . . and some are bigger. **1968** *DARE* FW Addit **DE**3, Branch pike = smaller than regular ones—live in small streams. [FW: From Inf's descriptions, *pike* refers to chain pickerel and *branch pike* to one of its smaller cousins, perhaps the grass pickerel.] **1983** Becker *Fishes WI* 391, *Esocidae*. . . All pike are fish eaters and highly predacious; the stomachs are long and the intestines short.

2 A freshwater fish of the genus *Stizostedion*. **chiefly Gt Lakes** Cf **pickerel 3**

1838 [see **1b** above]. **1838** Geol. Surv. OH *Second Annual Rept.* 190, *L[ucioperca] americana* [=*Stizostedion canadense* or *S. vitreum*]. The . . *pike of the lake*. . . is one of the most valuable fishes for the table found in the western waters, and sells readily at a high price in the markets of the towns on the banks of the Ohio. Those taken in Lake Erie are less esteemed. Two varieties are discoverable among them, which I suppose to be a mere sexual difference, though many fishermen, and market people consider them distinct species. **1875** Scott *Fishing Amer. Waters* 289 **NY**, The glass-eyed pike of the rivers in New York is very satisfying game to the angler. **1884** Goode *Fisheries U.S.* 1.417, In the Upper Lakes, where the true Pike (*Esox lucius*) is known as 'Pickerel,' the Wall-eyed Pike becomes simply 'Pike.' **1911** U.S. Bur. Census *Fisheries 1908* 313, Pike (*Esox lucius*).—A food fish found in the Great Lakes region; also called "pickerel." . . The name "pike" is also applied to the wall-eyed pike or pike perch (*Stizostedion vitreum*) in the upper lakes, and to the Sacramento pike (*Ptychocheilus oregonensis*) in the Columbia and Sacramento Rivers. "Gray pike," "sand pike," "ground pike," etc., are names for the sauger (*Stizostedion canadense*). **1927** Weed *Pike* 38, In Chicago, a fisherman speaking of. . . catching "Pickerel" and "Pike" . . would probably refer to *Esox lucius* and *Stizostedion*. *Ibid* 46, *Stizostedion*—Common names of this group are so confused that no attempt has been made to separate names belonging to the Saugers from those belonging only to the Walleye. It is probable that practically all the names are applied to either. . . Pike; general. **1933** John G. Shedd Aquarium *Guide* 85, *Stizostedion vitreum*. . . The practice of calling this fish Pike should be discouraged. Except for the general shape of the body, it has nothing in common with the true pikes, which are soft finned fishes. **1965–70** *DARE* (Qu. P1, . . *Kinds of freshwater fish . . caught around here . . good to eat*) Infs **CO**4, **NM**6, **UT**3, Pike; **NY**177, **NC**53, Pike (walleyed); **WI**17, Pike (walleye); **IL**6, Pike (walleyed pike); **IN**18, Pike—walleye; **NY**92, Pike—this applies to walleyes; **NY**183, Pike—walleyed variety; **ND**1, Pike—northern, . . walleye, . . sand pike; **WI**45, Pike—northern, walleyed. **1967** *DARE* Tape **IA**15, [FW:] They get pike in the river? . . What types? [Inf:] Walleye pike. There are some northern. We call them pickerel.

3 =**squawfish** (here: *Ptychocheilus* spp). Cf **Sacramento pike**

1882 U.S. Natl. Museum *Bulletin* 16.226, *P[tychocheilus] oregonensis*. . . Sacramento "Pike". . . Rivers of the Pacific slope, chiefly west of the Sierra Nevada. *Ibid* 227, *P. lucius*. . . Colorado "Pike". . . Colorado River; abundant. **1884** Goode *Fisheries U.S.* 1.616, *Ptychochilus oregonensis*. This species abounds in the Columbia and Sacramento Rivers and their tributaries, where it is usually known as the "Pike." **1890** *Century Dict.* 4484, Pike. . . A cyprinoid fish, *Ptychochilus lucius*, of slender form with a long snout, inhabiting the Sacramento river and other streams of the Pacific coast. [*Century* Ed:

California.] . . Another cyprinoid fish, *Gila grandis* [=*Ptychocheilus grandis*]: a misnomer in the San Francisco market. **1911** [see **2** above]. **1967–70** *DARE* (Qu. P3, *Freshwater fish that are not good to eat*) Inf **CA**25, Pike—very bony; **CA**136, Pike—not the kind you eat; **CA**160, Pike or squawfish; **CA**211, Pike.

4 A **snook** (here: *Centropomus undecimalis*).

1931 *Copeia* 2.48 **TX**, *Centropomus undecimalis*. . . Locally called "pike" or "robalo." . . On July 21 the same fishermen secured another "pike" in the Gulf surf.

pike n[2] Also *pike road* [Abbr for *turnpike*] **scattered, but esp OH, PA, KY** Cf **pike** v[1]

A highway or other, usu hard-surfaced, road; a toll road.

1836 O'Bryan *Narr. Travels U.S.* 69 **csPA**, Being informed that instead of going on the 'pike, as they call it, I could save ten miles by crossing the Blue mountain the pine way, I took the latter road. **1851** (1852) Stowe *Uncle Tom's Cabin* 1.92 **KY**, The road . . had formerly been a thoroughfare to the river, but abandoned for many years after the laying of the new pike. **1864** (1922) Jackson *Col.'s Diary* 105 **PA**, The pike is a hard road to march on. **1897** *Outing* 30.132 **VA**, We found greater comfort in the well-kept pike road, with ridable grades. **1903** *DN* 2.325 **seMO**, Pike. . . Turnpike; levee road. **1922** (1926) Cady *Rhymes VT* 110, It's hemlock, maple, beech and spruce,/ From 'way below the schoolhouse sluice / To where the pike gets hard. **1931** *AmSp* 7.20 **swPA**, Pikes. All main-traveled roads. **1934** Carmer *Stars Fell on AL* 197, Pap Haines lives . . on the old winding road that they don't keep up any more since the straight clay pike was built. **1937** *AmSp* 12.203 [Engl of PaGer area], The doctor, lawyer, or professor in a Pennsylvania German community. . . will, however, use words like 'machine' (automobile), 'pike' (highway), . . and many another word which might startle his colleagues from other parts of the nation. **1937** *Hall Coll.* **ceTN**, Pike, a "rocked" country road, not a highway. **1939** *LANE* Map 42 (*Turnpike*), Most of our informants no longer use *turnpike* and *pike* as common nouns, but only in the names of particular roads. . . **seMA**, Turnpike regarded as older term for pike; 1 inf, **csMA**, Pike familiar only in the phrase *down the pike*; 1 inf, **csMA**, Pike, rare; 2 infs, **sNH**, Pike not common. **1942** McAtee *Dial. Grant Co. IN* 48 (as of 1890s), *Pike* . . a highway to which some road-metal had been applied; others were dirt roads. **1947** *WELS Suppl.* **OH**, I noticed also out there that automobiles were "machines" and a hard road was a "pike," both of which were not used here [=**csWI**]. **1956** Sorden–Ebert *Logger's Words* 25 **Gt Lakes**, Pike, see tote-road. [*Ibid* 38, Tote-road, A supply road to camp. Same as pike, portage-road.] **1957** *Mathews Coll.* **OH** (as of 1880s), He had a good team of horses and would be away most all week hauling gravel to make pikes. In Ohio where we lived the highways today are still called pikes, although they are all paved. **1959** *VT Hist.* 27.152, *Pikes*. . . Toll roads. Occasional. **1965–70** *DARE* (Qu. N16a, *Names for a highway with two lanes on each side and a separation down the middle*) Inf **OH**72, Pike; (Qu. N16b, *Names for a highway . . if you have to pay to drive on it*) Infs **MA**6, **OK**15, 20, **OR**3, **VA**33, Pike; **CT**29, Mass [=**Massachusetts**] pike or thruway; (Qu. N21, *Roads that are surfaced with smooth black pavement*) Inf **OH**82, Pike; (Qu. N27a, *Names . . for different kinds of unpaved roads*) Inf **MD**48, Pike—rolled stone, also called hard surface; **PA**29, Pike road; (Qu. N29, . . *Names . . for a less important road running back from a main road*) Inf **OH**34, Pike; (Qu. C33, . . *Joking names . . for an out-of-the-way place, or a very small or unimportant place*) Inf **OH**65, Down the pike; (Qu. Y19, *To begin to go away from a place: "It's about time for me to _____."*) Inf **PA**66, Get down the pike. **1966** Dakin *Dial. Vocab. Ohio R. Valley* 2.214, The old name *turnpike*, most frequently used as the simplex *pike* and occasionally *pike road*, is quite common in Ohio and Kentucky—and some speakers say only pike for any kind of improved or paved road. . . It is significant, however, that neither of McDavid's Indiana records record this usage which he regularly noted, and its absence in Illinois must be interpreted to mean that *pike* is not used there. The frequency of the use of this term undoubtedly reflects the extent of the nineteenth century turnpike construction, much greater in Ohio and parts of Kentucky than farther west. **1966–67** *DARE* Tape **MI**67, And of course Michigan Avenue was called the Michigan tollroad to Chicago—the pike, as it was called, to Chicago; **PA**29, Those roads were all laid out beforehand. . . Therefore they keep those roads, but if they're building a new road they would build it straight. . . At one time they were called dirt roads or pike roads; **PA**30, Because of the location of their church, being right along the 322 pike, they're called Pikers. **1967–68** *DARE* FW Addit **TN**17, Pike—any paved road. (I asked the Inf what he meant by "pike," when he mentioned the "pike down yonder"—though I think townspeople only call a major road a "pike.");

sNJ, Names for major highways—the pike. "Drive up the pike," etc. **1976** Garber *Mountain-ese* 68 **sAppalachians,** *Pike* . . public road— You kaint miss us, the big pike runs right by our house.

Pike n[3] See **Piker** n[1]

pike v[1]

To improve or pave (a road); spec to crown (it); hence n *piker* one who so improves roads; adj *piked.*

1871 Hutchinson *Resources KS* 56, Those who manage the public highways often make the same mistake here that is made elsewhere, by attempting to round or "pike" up with dirt, or fill in with stone at bad places, without *first* cutting ditches to carry off the water. **1872** Huntington *Road-Master's Asst.* 60, How often do we see a piece of track at the foot of a steep grade, on a high embankment, *piked up* as far as possible. **1942** McAtee *Dial. Grant Co. IN* 48 (as of 1890s), *Pike* . . to add road metals to a road; "Nine of the 34 miles were piked." **1951** *DE Folkl. Bulletin* 1.7, *Pike* (to improve, or to hard-surface, a road). **1957** *Mathews Coll.* **OH** (as of 1880s), If it wasn't zero or snow it was plain stick mud, and how to this day I hate mud. Although my father was a piker, he never seemed to have piked any of the roads where we went to school. **1967** *DARE* (Qu. N27a, *Names . . for different kinds of unpaved roads*) Inf **PA34,** Piked road—made with stone. **1975** *DARE* File **cPA,** *To pike a road* = to surface it with macadam (in contrast to building a new concrete highway). **1996** *DARE* File **WI** (as of c1950), I recall that a man mentioned improving a road: "They piked it up," meaning that they made it level, filling in the low places of the original track with stone and other solid stuff.

pike v[2]

1 To gamble, esp in a small way; to gamble at. [*piker* a petty gambler] **chiefly West**

1889 (1971) Farmer *Americanisms* 420, To *Pike* (Cant).—To play cautiously and for small amounts, never advancing the value of the stake. . . Those who gamble in this fashion are called *Pikers.* **1903** (1965) Adams *Log Cowboy* 200 **West,** We made the rounds of the gambling houses, looking for our crowd. We ran across three of the boys piking at a monte game, who came with us reluctantly. **1910** *Sat. Eve. Post* 7 May 10 **Pacific,** I pike a dollar now and then, just for the excitement. **1920** Hunter *Trail Drivers TX* 178 (as of c1880), One of the cowboys on a Southwest Texas ranch . . decided to go up to San Antonio for a few days . . and incidentally "pike" a little at the Bull's Head or the White Elephant gambling tables. *Ibid* 190, Piked at monte some. **1929** Dobie *Vaquero* 100 **swTX,** "We had a negro cowboy named George," says an old time Plains cowman, . . "who was not very well clad because he liked to pike at monte too well to buy clothes." *Ibid* 268, I have spoken of piking monte and I have mentioned Monterrey. Perhaps I had as well admit that I at times played cards pretty hard and drifted down to Monterrey—the monte capital of the two republics—every once in a while. **1968** Adams *Western Words* 226, *Piking*—In faro, making small bets all over the layout; see *piker.*

2 See quot.

1916 *DN* 4.327 **KS,** *Pike.* . . To back down; to fail or refuse to go with the crowd.

pike v[3], n[4] [Prob *EDD pike* v.[2] 9 "To look closely and curiously"]

To snoop, pry; a snoopy person; hence adj *pikey* snoopy.

1959 *AmSp* 34.306 **sLA,** In New Orleans, almost any native or long-term resident will recognize the verb *pike,* . . meaning 'to be nosy, to pry, to look or watch with great curiosity.' . . The word also exists as a noun, and an adjective has been made from it. For example, one might say to such a busybody, 'Oh, don't be such a pike!' Or he might comment, 'I wonder what those pikey neighbors are looking at.' . . [E]very New Orleanian I have spoken to, including one past eighty, has readily defined the term, and some attempt to specify the exact neighborhood— usually 'downtown' (down river from Canal Street)—where the word is most common.

pike v[4] See **play like**

piked See **pike** v[1]

pike'l See **pightle**

pike perch n Also *perchpike*

A fish of the genus *Stizostedion.* **chiefly NEast, N Cent** Also called **golden trout 3, jack** n[1] 24a(2), **pickerel 3, pike**

n[1] **2, rock pike.** For other names of var spp see **Ohio pike, sauger** n[1], **walleye**

1842 DeKay *Zool. NY* 4.18, The Pike-perch [=*Stizostedion vitreum*] is exceedingly voracious, and is highly prized as food. **1876** *Fur, Fin, & Feather* Sept. 163/1 (*DAE*), All along the Minnesota Division are numerous clear lakes and ponds, teeming with . . 'wall-eyes' or pike-perch, tarred-perch [etc]. **1892** *VT State Bd. Ag. Rept. for 1891– 92* 157, Our waters abound in a great variety of fish, the leading ones being . . pike, pike perch, and pickerel. **1896** Robinson *In New Engl. Fields* 82, The bass comes to his river in May to spawn, the pike-perch for food. **1901** Stillman *Autobiog.* 1.28 **NY,** I can see vividly the banks of the Mohawk, where we used to fish for perch, bream, and pike-perch. **1908** Forbes–Richardson *Fishes of IL* 274, The pike-perch is said to spawn in April in Lake Erie. **1927** Weed *Pike* 46, *Stizostedion*—Common names of this group are so confused that no attempt has been made to separate names belonging only to the Saugers from those belonging only to the Walleye. It is probable that practically all the names are applied to either. . . Perch Pike: Eastern States. . . Pike Perch: Eastern States. **1939** Natl. Geogr. Soc. *Fishes* 134, This latter fish [= *Stizostedion vitreum glaucum*] is called the blue pike and occurs in the Great Lakes in abundance, helping make up part of the commercial catch of pike-perches. **1956** Harlan–Speaker *IA Fish* 143, *Walleye* . . *Other Names*—Pike-perch, walleyed pike. . . The population of this much-prized fish is never static and goes through "booms and depressions", especially in rivers. **1983** Becker *Fishes WI* 871, *Walleye.* . . Other common names . . perchpike, . . walleyed pikeperch. *Ibid* 880, *Sauger.* . . Other common names . . blue pikeperch.

pike plant n

=curled dock.

1973 *Foxfire 2* 61 **sAppalachians,** Dock (*Rumex crispa*) . . (pike plant, curled dock . .). A common weed. . . It is about knee-high, and has leaves. . . [with] crinkled edges.

Piker n[1] Also *Pike* [*Pike* County, Missouri] **chiefly Pacific Coast, esp CA** *old-fash* Cf **Okie**

A person from Missouri; by ext, a poor White person; a good-for-nothing.

1854 *Pioneer* (San Francisco CA) Apr 1.252, "Pike" is a genius. He is wrapped up, body and soul, in the State of Missouri. . . "Pike, O! Pike, it is my name,/ Missourer is my nation,/ Pike County is my dwelling place,/ and Pike is my salvation." **1856** *Harper's New Mth. Mag.* 13.588, An inhospitable coast is that of California and Oregon. . . Crescent City is . . inhabited by several hundred traders, packers, Indians, dogs, and mules. . . The men were mostly "Pikes" of an exceedingly rough cast. **1859** in 1941 Hafen *CO Gold Rush* 318, An extra train of [returning] "Pikers" came in [to Hannibal MO] about 2 o'clock yesterday afternoon. **1872** (1873) Nordhoff *California* 138, The true "Pike," however, in the Californian sense of the word, is the wandering gypsy-like Southern poor white. **1873** Beadle *Undeveloped West* 763 **OR,** These old Pikers don't want the country fenced up and the game scared off. **1907** Stewart *Partners* 228, "I'm from Missouri," I says. "Oh! then you are a Piker." **1946** *St. Louis* (Missouri) *Globe-Democrat* 17 Nov E 2/6 (*OED2*), The term 'Pike' or 'piker', in the sense of a worthless, lazy, good-for-nothing person arose first in California in the days of the Forty-Niners. **1996** Simpson *Reg. Guy* 109 **nCA,** I wonder what California would be like if it had just been the Spaniards and then the Asians. If the—what did they call them?—the Okies and Pikers and Hoosiers never came. **1997** *DARE* File **sCA** (as of c1940), Southern California had lots of immigrants from Arkansas, Oklahoma, and Missouri. They were known as Arkies, Okies, and Pikers. *Ibid* **MO,** I use 'piker' [for a Missourian] myself, but I don't know whether younger people do.

piker n[2] See **pike** v[1]

pike road See **pike** n[2]

pike shiner n

A **dace** (here: *Clinostomus funduloides*).

1905 NJ State Museum *Annual Rept. for 1904* 134, *Leuciscus vandolsulus.* . . Rosy Dace. Pike Shiner. . . It has a wide mouth and small scales, and the males are brilliantly colored during the breeding-season.

piket See **P.K.**

piketail n

1 =**pintail 1.**

1888 Trumbull *Names of Birds* 38 **IL**, *Pin-tail*. . . At Chicago, *spike-tail*, and less commonly *pike-tail*.

2 also *piketail grouse:* =**sharp-tailed grouse.**

1946 Hausman *Eastern Birds* 217, *Pedioecetes phasianellus phasianellus*. . . *Other Names* . . Piketail, and these terms combined with the name Grouse. . . A pale grouse with a very short pointed tail.

pike up See **pike** v[1]

pikey See **pike** v[3], n[4]

piko n |'piko| [Haw] **HI**
The navel.

1938 Reinecke *Hawaiian Loanwords* 29, *Piko* ['piko]. . . The navel. F[requent]. **1967** *DARE* (Qu. X34, *. . Names and nicknames for the navel*) Inf **HI**1, ['pikoʊ]; **HI**8, ['piko]; **HI**9, Piko.

pilated woodpecker See **pileated woodpecker**

pilau n[1] Usu |pəˈlo, ˈpɪlo, ˈpɜ(r)lo, ˈpɜ(r)lu|; for addit varr see quots Note: Proncs of the type |pɪˈlau, -ˈlɑf| are not treated here. Pronc-spp *pearlo, perleau, perloo, perlow, pillo(e), purloo* [Ult from Persian *pilāw*, but Engl borrowings (beginning in the 17th century) have often been through var intermediaries. The US forms illustrated here appear to be immediately from Fr *pilau;* for the forms ending in [-u] cf analogous *pull-doo* (at **poule d'eau**) and *cahoo* (at **cahot**).] **chiefly SC, GA, FL** See Map

A dish of meat or vegetables and rice usu cooked together—often in combs indicating the main ingredient. Note: *Pilau* is treated here only as it appears to belong to an established American folk tradition; no account is taken of *pilau* (or *pilaf(f)*) as a foreign dish.

1791 Bartram *Travels* 63, We were not altogether unsuccessful, having taken three young racoons . . which are excellent meat: we had them for supper, served up in a pillo. *Ibid* 249, They [=young waterfowl] were almost a lump of fat, and made us a rich supper; some we roasted and made others into a pilloe with rice. **1847** (1979) Rutledge *Carolina Housewife* 83 **SC**, *Carolina pilau.* Boil one and a half pounds of bacon. When nearly done, throw into the pot a quart of rice. . . Then put in the fowls (one or two, according to size), and season with pepper and salt. **1890** McAllister *Society* 314 **Sth**, Some features of the everyday Southern dinner were *pilau,* i.e. boiled chickens on a bed of rice, with a large piece of bacon between the chickens. **1930** *DN* 6.83 **cSC**, *Pilau.* . . ['pərlo]. A dish in which some meat or vegetable is cooked with rice, such as chicken pilau, tomato pilau, shrimp pilau. **1931** (1991) Hughes–Hurston *Mule Bone* 61 **cFL** [Black], Now I reckon you can't even drink lemonade and eat chicken perlow wid us. **1935** Hurston *Mules & Men* 31 **FL**, There are plenty of chicken perleau. **1939** McGuire *FL Cracker Dial.* 162, *Pilau:* [pɜlu]. . . This word is found elsewhere also pronounced [pəlo] as in the French; and more commonly, [pɜlo]. **1942** Rawlings *Cross Creek Cookery* 131 **FL**, *Pilaus.* . . We pronounce the word "pur-loo." It is any dish of meat and rice cooked together. **1949** Botkin *Treas. S. Folkl.* 552, South Carolinians [grow lyrical] over rice, calibash, and pilaus (pronounced pé-los, púr-loos). **1952** Brown *NC Folkl.* 1.576, *Pilau* ['pɪlo, -ɔ]; in Sumter county, S.C. ['pɜ˞lo]. **1965–70** *DARE* (Qu. H45, *Dishes . . that everybody around here would know, but that people in other places might not*) Inf **FL**11, Shrimp ['pɜ˞luw]—shrimp, rice, cooked with tomato; **FL**18, Chicken perloo—chicken and rice cooked outside in a big pot for a crowd; **FL**19, [pəˈlow]—chicken with rice, celery, maybe tomatoes; **FL**31, ['pɜˈlou]—chicken and rice; **FL**33, ['pʌlou raɪs]—chicken and rice; **FL**36, Backbone and ['pʌlou]; **FL**49, Chicken perloo, shrimp perloo; **FL**51, Shrimp [pɜloz]—chopped boiled shrimp cooked with rice, seasonings—can also have chicken perlow; **GA**11, ['pɜ˞lo]; **GA**15, Shrimp [pəˈlu]; **GA**24, Chicken perloo; **MS**23, [pəˈlo]—chicken and rice cooked together; **NC**34, Chicken perloo; **OH**93, Chicken [pəˈlo]—[FW:] Inf says this was brought in from Florida; **SC**4, [pɜrlo]—meat and rice, e.g., shrimp, chicken; **SC**9, Chicken [preˈlo]; **SC**11, Chicken ['perlo]; **SC**19, Chicken [perlo], beef perlow, pork perlow; **SC**21, Shrimp [perlu], ['prelo], ['perlo]; **SC**22, Chicken ['pɛrlo], sausage perlow; **SC**26, Chicken ['pɛrlo]; **SC**38, Chicken [pɜrlo]—chicken and rice cooked together; bird perlow, sausage perlow; **SC**43, [pɜɜˈlo]—chicken, pork, cooked together with rice; **SC**46, Chicken [paˈlo]—what low-country people call it; ['pɜ˞lo]—what up-country people call it; not correct pronunciation; **SC**51, Chicken, beef, pork, shrimp [pɜɜˈlo]; **SC**62, Tomato pilau—also called red rice; **SC**67, Okra and tomato ['pɪlo]; (Qu. H49) Inf **AL**15,

Chicken ['pɔlo]; (Qu. H65, *Foreign foods favored by people around here*) Inf **MS**23, [pəˈlo]—Italian; (Qu. FF2) Inf **GA**23, Chicken ['pɜ˞lo]—steal somebody's chicken and go out and cook him. **1975** Newell *If Nothin' Don't Happen* 46 **FL**, So we had to settle for squirrels and I tried my hand at makin' up purloo. . . I skinned out six or eight squirrels, cut 'em up and put 'em in a kettle with some water. When it got to boilin' good I dumped in the rice and some salt and pepper and put on the lid. **1977** Anderson *Grass Roots Cookbook* 118 **sSC**, *Chicken Purloo.* . . Here's one of Mary's favorite ways to use up leftover roast chicken (the recipe works equally well with leftover roast turkey). "Purloo," by the way, is how "pilau" is pronounced in the South Carolina Low Country. This isn't a true pilau—the chicken mixture is ladled over the rice instead of being mixed with it. But it's delicious nonetheless. **1981** Pederson *LAGS Basic Materials* 1 inf, **neFL**, Chicken ['pˈɜ˞ˌloʊ]; 1 inf, **neFL**, Gopher ['pˈɜ˞loˈᵁ<]; 1 inf, **ceGA**, ['pˈɜˈ˞ˌloˈ̆ʊ]—dish made with shrimp, tomatoes and rice; 1 inf, **cFL**, ['pˈɜ˞ˌloˈ<·ᵁ]—turtle meat cooked with rice. **2000** *DARE* File—Internet **seGA**, You are very Wiregrass if . . your family called the annual family reunion "The Chicken Pearlo."

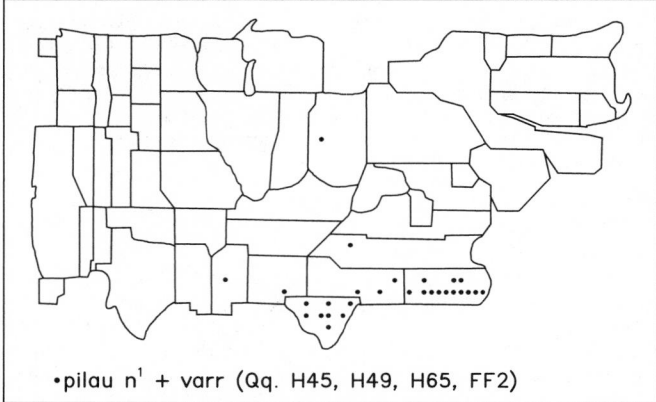

•pilau n[1] + varr (Qq. H45, H49, H65, FF2)

pilau n[2], v, adj Usu |ˈpilau|; see quots for var stress patterns [Haw]
See quot 1967 Reinecke–Tsuzaki.

1934 *AmSp* 9.128 [Engl dial of HI], The adjective is placed ahead of article and noun when the speaker desires to call attention to the quality: *Pilau* [=stinking] *the smell!* **1967** Reinecke–Tsuzaki *Hawaiian Loanwords* 86, *Pilau* is widely used by non-Hawaiians, to whom it offers a serviceable euphemism for "stink" and related ideas; but native Hawaiians use it little, as it is an impolite or even indecent word in their language. *Ibid* 109, *Pilau;* /ˈpilau/; . . 1. To stink; stinking; a stench; a stinker, all either literally or figuratively. 2. Disagreeable to the taste or any other of the senses; dirty; filthy; nasty; "no good": a blanket word expressive of strong disapproval and/or disgust. . . 3. Fertilizer. **1967** *DARE* (Qu. K14, *Milk that has a taste from something the cow ate in the pasture . . "That milk is _____."*) Inf **HI**2, Pilau [ˌpiˈlau]; local word—used of many things; = stink; [(Qu. BB37, *When yellowish stuff comes out of a person's ear, he has a _____*) Inf **HI**4, Pepeiau pilau—stink ear;] (Qu. NN23, *Exclamations when people smell a very bad odor*) Inf **HI**1, Pilau ['piˈlau]. **1969** *DARE* File **HI**, *Pi-lau* ['pilau]—smelly. **1981** *Pidgin To Da Max* np **HI**, [Drawing of two girls talking:] . . So den Jimmy wen da kine me, you know, wit' his da kine!" "Hoo, Chahlene! You get one pilau mout'!" **1997** *NY Times* (NY) 2 Mar sec F14/4 **HI**, "Auwe! Away from Waikiki, dese haoles dey all pau, brudda," a friend used to say, cranking up his pidgin. "Dey make every people huhu talkin' pilau." . . In other words, when you travel outside the tourist spots, you're finished (pau), and can make people very angry (huhu) if your knowledge of their ways leaves something to be desired—that is if it stinks (pilau).

pilchard n [*OED2* 1530 → for the old-world *Sardina pilchardus*]

1 also *pelcher, pilcher:* A **menhaden 1** (here: *Brevoortia tyrannus*).

1637 (1972) Morton *New English Canaan* 90 **NEng**, There are greate store of Pilchers. **1775** (1905) U.S. Continental Congress *Jrls.* 3.503, Indian corn and fish are not to be had . . except pilchards. **1884** Goode *Fisheries U.S.* 569, The Menhaden has at least thirty popular names. . . In Delaware Bay, the Potomac, and the Chesapeake, we meet with the

"Alewife," "Bay Alewife," "Pilcher" (Pilchard), and "Green-tail." **1911** U.S. Bur. Census *Fisheries 1908* 312, Menhaden. . . It is known by a great number of local names, the most common being "pogy," "hardhead" . . "pilcher" [etc]. **1927** *AmSp* 3.136, "Pelcher" of "deader than a pelcher," still common on the Maine coast, appears in the *English Dialect Dictionary* as "pilchard, pilcher," "killed as dead as a salt pilcher."

2 =sardine 1c.

[**1759** Venegas *Hist. CA* (transl. Anon.) 1.47, Both in the Pacifick ocean and the gulf of California, the multitude and variety of fishes are incredible. Father Antonio de la Ascencion, speaking of the bay of San Lucas [Lower California], says, "With the nets which every ship carried, they caught a great quantity of fish of different kinds, and all wholesome and palatable: particularly holybuss, salmon, turbots, skates, pilchards [etc]."] **1890** *Century Dict.* 4485 **CA,** *Pilchard.* . . A fish, *Clupea sagax*, closely related to the pilchard. **1939** Natl. Geogr. Soc. *Fishes* 244, Called pilchard in Washington and British Columbia, and California sardine in California, this fish belongs to the great group of herring and shad classified in the family Clupeidae. *Ibid*, The most northerly record of the pilchard is off the Queen Charlotte Islands, and the most southerly in the Gulf of California. Throughout this area it occurs in large schools. **1948** Wolfe *Farm Gloss.* 283, *Sardine Oil*—Product obtained by the extraction of part of the oil from the whole Pacific sardine or pilchard. **1955** Zim–Shoemaker *Fishes* 38, Pacific Sardines, often called Pilchards or California Sardines, are most familiar in cans. **1991** Amer. Fisheries Soc. *Common Names Fishes* 158, Pilchard—see Pacific sardine.

pilcher See **pilchard 1**

pile v [By ext from *pile* to form into a heap]
Esp of a horse: to throw (one) down.

1917 *Munsey's Mag.* 61.658 **West,** As the horse flashed past, the young man's wrist flipped outward and downward. . . Forefooted [= caught by the front feet], the horse stood on his nose and piled his rider. *Ibid* 62.345, I've loved yuh ever since that day when I piled yuh, not knowin' yuh were a girl. **1934** (1943) *W2, Pile.* . . To throw (one) down. *Local, U.S.* **1939** (1973) FWP *Guide MT* 415, *Pile*—To throw. "That horse piled me." **1944** Adams *Western Words* 115, *Piled*— Thrown from a horse. c**1960** Mathews Coll. **AL** (as of c1900), *Pile* . . to throw (one) down. This is in Web. 1934, as local U.S. . . It was well known to me as a boy c1900 in Alabama. **1970** *DARE* (Qu. OO30b, *Talking about a horse throwing the rider: "Last week the same horse* _____ *[his brother]."*) Inf **IL**142, Piled him. **1984** Doig *English Creek* 185 **nMT,** The mare piled the contestant [in a rodeo], some guy from Shelby, with its third jump.

pileated woodpecker n Usu |ˈpaɪliˌetɪd, ˈpɪliˌetɪd|; also freq |ˈpaɪˌletɪd|, less freq |ˈplitɪd| Pronc-spp *pilated woodpecker, pleated ~*; for addit pronc and sp varr see quots

A Forms.

1965–70 *DARE* (Qu. Q17) 62 Infs, **scattered exc West,** Pileated woodpecker; 28 Infs, **scattered, but esp Inland Nth, PA,** Pilated woodpecker [in 15 instances FWs recorded proncs of the type |ˈpaɪˌletɪd|]; **MI**2, 104, **NY**148, Pleated woodpecker; **CA**105, |ˈpaɪlitəd, ˈplitəd| woodpecker; **MI**53, |pɪˈletəd| woodpecker; **VA**110, |ˈpɪletɪd| woodpecker; **PA**147, Pellated woodpecker; **VT**10, |ˈpaɪjaletɪd| woodpecker—Inf uncertain. **1981** Pederson *LAGS Basic Materials* **Gulf Region,** [Of 12 infs who gave the response *pileated (woodpecker)*, 4 used proncs of the type |ˈpa(ɪ)lietɪd|, 4 |ˈpa(ɪ)letɪd|, one |ˈpaᵊlitɪd|, one |ˈpɪlieɪtɪd|, one |ˈpilieɪtɪd|, and one |flitɪd| [sic]. One inf said that |ˈpileʒɪt| is the formal name.]

B Sense.

Std: A **woodpecker** (here: *Ceophloeus pileatus*). Also called **black-billed logcock, black woodcock, ~ woodpecker 1, carpenter, cock of the woods, crow woodpecker 2, Doctor Jesus, do Lord, English woodpecker 2, French peckerwood, good god 1, great god, hen bird, Indian crow, ~ head 3, ~ hen 3, johnny cock, Kate, laughing woodpecker, logcock 1, log god 2, lord ~ 1, peckerwood 1, pigeon woodpecker 2, rain crow 1d, red-headed woodcock, ~ woodpecker 4, stump-breaker, swamp woodpecker, weathercock, womacock, woodchuck, woodcock, wood god, ~ hen**

pile driver n

1 =bittern. [See quot 1959] Cf **post driver, stake ~, stump-~**

1857 Hammond *Wild N. Scenes* 177 **NY,** [A bird] known in these parts as the 'Pile-driver'. . . is about the homeliest creature in these woods. It is a small grey heron. **1959** *Names* 7.119 **FL, Ontario,** Names suggested by resemblance of the bittern "music" to resonant pounding include . . pile-driver. **1966–68** *DARE* (Qu. Q8, *A water bird that makes a booming sound before rain and often stands with its beak pointed almost straight up*) Inf **MI**10, Bittern—nickname shitepoke—other names . . pile driver (more commonly stump driver); **NJ**39, Pile driver, shitepoke.

2 A horse that attempts to dislodge its rider by leaping vertically in the air and landing stiff-legged. **West** Cf **buckjump** v, n

1936 Adams *Cowboy Lingo* 99, A 'pile-driver' was a horse that humped his back and came down with all four legs as stiff as ramrods. **1937** *DN* 6.619 **swTX,** [A horse] is a *pile driver* when he jolts his rider by coming down with all four feet closely grouped and legs as stiff as ramrods. **1946** Mora *Trail Dust* 119 **West,** A big twelve- or thirteen-hundred-pound bronco that's a "pile-driver"; the kind that go straight up and come down on all fours stiff-legged at one time.

pile it n

A **shoveler** (here: *Anas clypeata*).

1945 McAtee *Nomina Abitera* 31, Shoveller (*Spatula clypeata*) . . shit-digger. . . The names "chambermaid" . . from Medicine Lake, Montana . . and "pile it" from Wisconsin . . doubtless have allied meanings.

pile perch n [See quot 1953]

A **surfperch,** usu *Rhacochilus vacca*.

1928 Pan-Pacific Research Inst. *Jrl.* 3.3.13 **OR, WA,** *Damalichthys argyrosomus* . . Pile perch. **1953** Roedel *Common Fishes CA* 107, *Rubberlip perch* . . *Unauthorized Names:* Pile perch, porgy, niggerlip. *Ibid* 108, *Pile perch.* . . Common along both sandy and rocky shores, around kelp, and around pilings. **1983** Audubon Field Guide N. Amer. *Fishes* 643, Pile Perch (*R[hacochilus] vacca*) with lips not fleshy or pink. **1991** Amer. Fisheries Soc. *Common Names Fishes* 57, *Rhacochilus vacca* . . pile perch.

piler v Pronc-spp *pe(a)lay*

See quot 1983.

1916 *DN* 4.269 **New Orleans LA,** *Pelay.* . . "He pelayed on the jump." **1983** Reinecke Coll. 8 **LA,** *Piler, pea-lay.* . . to hit, strike, or to "fudge," cheating by crossing the shooting hand over the base-line in "chinies." [**1984** Daigle *Dict. Cajun Lang.* 2.117, *Piler* . . To pound, to crush, to tamp. . . To cheat, to fudge.]

pileweed See **pilewort 1**

pilewort n

1 also *pileweed*: A **fireweed c** (here: *Erechtites hieracifolia*).

1876 Hobbs *Bot. Hdbk.* 89, Pilewort, Fireweed, Erechtites hieracifolius. **1935** (1943) Muenscher *Weeds* 482, *Erechtites hieracifolia* . . Fireweed, Pilewort. **1940** Clute *Amer. Plant Names* 222, *Erechtites hieracifolia.* Pile-weed. **1963** Zimmerman–Olson *Forest* [197], Pilewort (Erechtites hieracifolia).

2 A **figwort 1** (here: *Scrophularia marilandica*). [From its reputed efficacy in treating "piles" (hemorrhoids)]

1914 Georgia *Manual Weeds* 380, Pilewort, Heal-all. . . The knotted roots of this plant have long been reputed a cure for scrofula, piles, and other diseases, and are salable in the drug-market. **1923** *Amer. Botanist* 29.61, The name "scrofula-plant", like the generic term [= Scrophularia], alludes to the reputation of the plant in the cure of other ills and "pile-wort" is of the same nature. **1971** Krochmal *Appalachia Med. Plants* 230, Scrophularia marilandica . . Common Names: Maryland figwort, . . great pilewort, . . pilewort [etc]. **1974** (1977) Coon *Useful Plants* 246, Figwort, healall, pilewort, Scrophula plant, etc. . . The many names of "wort" indicate long-known medicinal values, which include such uses as diuretic, diaphoretic, tonic, and especially reducing hemorrhoids.

pilfer v Also *pilf*; also with *around* **S Midl**
To loaf, loiter; to meddle, snoop.

1919 DN 5.34 **KY,** Pilfer. . . To loaf, loiter. Knott Co. **1953** Randolph–Wilson Down in Holler 271 **Ozarks,** Pilfer round. . . To examine or disturb property belonging to another; perhaps to look about with the intention of stealing something. Apparently it does not mean the act of stealing. **1968** DARE (Qu. Y27, To go about aimlessly, with nothing to do: "He's always _____ around the drugstore.") Inf **NC49,** Pilfing ['pɪlfɪn]. **1974** Fink Mountain Speech 19 **wNC, eTN,** Pilfering around . . idly wandering, not necessarily to steal. "Them boys were jest pilfering around." **1976** Garber Mountain-ese 68 **sAppalachians,** Pilfer . . wander idly about—Don't you youngens pilfer about the house while we are away. **1986** Pederson LAGS Concordance, 1 inf, **neMS,** Pilfering around = just looking.

pilgrim n

1 One who has come from elsewhere, spec:

a An emigrant, migrant, or visitor; a greenhorn, tenderfoot. **esp West**

1867 (1868) Meline 2000 Miles 22, [Footnote:] The term Pilgrims for emigrants first came into use at the period of the heavy Mormon travel—the Mormons styling themselves "Pilgrims to the promised land of Utah." The word has been retained on the Plains, and applied indiscriminately to all emigrants. **1877** Wright Big Bonanza 556 **NV,** Newcomers—known as "pilgrims" or "greenhorns"—are much more likely to do real work when on a prospecting trip than any of the old miners. **1887** Amer. Field 27.62, I have seen "pilgrims" inveigled into riding "bucking cayuses," either for the sake of novelty or because they wanted a mount and there was no other to be had. **1887** [see **1b** below]. **1890** Langford Vigilante Days 1.221, Some of the companies were composed entirely of "pilgrims," a designation given by mountain people to new comers from the States. **1933** AmSp 8.4.51 **NE** [Pioneer vocabulary], Pilgrims was the name given to emigrants by the old settlers on the Plains. **1936** McKenna Black Range 105 **NM** (as of 1880s), Among the pilgrims, as all newcomers were called, were two young men from the hard-coal regions of eastern Pennsylvania. **1941** Writers' Program Guide WY 464, Pilgrim—A newcomer. **1950** Western Folkl. 9.119 **nwOR** [Logger speech], Pilgrim. A migratory worker; one who is from another section of the United States. **1956** Almirall From College 22 **CO,** "Right, pilgrim," she said. "You know, I believe you'll get on out in this country." Ibid 24, I felt that he was probably thinking, "Looks like I took on a real pilgrim," because at that time I sure looked and felt like a tenderfoot. **1958** McCulloch Woods Words 135 **Pacific NW,** Pilgrim—a. A short-stay logger, who works little time in any one camp. b. A visitor to camp. **1968–69** DARE (Qu. HH28, Names and nicknames . . for people of foreign background) Inf **NC82,** Foreigner, pilgrim; (Qu. HH31, Somebody who is not from your community, and doesn't belong) Inf **PA199,** Pilgrim, stranger. **1975** Gould ME Lingo 208, Pilgrim—A lovely Pine Tree State term . . for a tourist.

b also attrib: A cow recently imported to a range.

1884 Prairie Farmer 17 May 308/3 **NW,** The losses were among old cattle in poor condition, the young stock sent to the ranches last fall—known as 'pilgrims' on the ranges—and untimely calves. **1885** U.S. Bur. Indian Affairs Report 120 **MT,** This, we think, is a very fair crop of calves considering the fact that the cattle were what is called "pilgrim" cattle (cattle for the States that had never passed through a winter before being housed and fed). **1887** Scribner's Mag. 2.508 **West,** "Pilgrim" and "tenderfoot" were formerly applied almost exclusively to newly imported cattle, but by a natural transferrence [sic] they are usually used to designate all new-comers, tourists, and business-men. **1888** Century Illustr. Mag. 35.509 **West,** Those herds consisting of "pilgrims" . . animals driven up on to the range from the south, and therefore in poor condition. **1942** Henry High Border 170 **nRocky Mts,** Thereafter the Montana cow bonanza boomed for a few years until the terrific setback of the winter of 1886–87, when hundreds of thousands of head of soft "pilgrims" from the South, unable to endure the cold of the northern plains, froze to death.

2 See quot.

1964 Jackman–Long OR Desert 394, Pilgrim—horse once good, now too old.

pili n Also pili grass [Haw pili] **HI**

A **tanglehead** (here: Heteropogon contortus).

[**1888** Hillebrand Flora Hawaiian Is. 508, Andropogon contortus. . . Common on all islands, the "Pili" of the natives, very troublesome on account of the awns, which get entangled in the wool of sheep.] **1929** Neal Honolulu Gardens 25 **HI,** Pili is a forage grass . . common in some locations in Hawaii. **1934** Frear Lowell & Abigail 94 **HI,** It was easy to

accept the Hawaiian roof of thatch, using what was obtainable, ti leaf where pili grass was not to be had. **1955** Day HI People 296, Thatching of pili grass . . was tied in bundles and lashed to battens. **1967** DARE (Qu. S26e, Other wildflowers not yet mentioned; not asked in early QRs) Inf **HI4,** Pili grass—best against mouth ulcers when reduced to ashes. **1972** Carr Da Kine Talk 116 **HI,** Pili grass. . . A grass known in many warm regions. [F]ormerly used for thatching houses in Hawaii, and, mixed into clay, for making adobe walls. **1994** Stone–Pratt Hawai'i's Plants 109, One of the few common lowland grasses thought to be native to Hawai'i, pili . . is abundant at only a few sites.

pilikia n, adj **HI**

Trouble; a difficulty; troublesome.

1873 in 1966 Bishop Sandwich Is. 71 **HI,** There is one native word in such universal use that I already find I cannot get on without it, pilikia. It means anything, from a down-right trouble to a slight difficulty or entanglement. "I'm in a pilikia," or "very pilikia," or "pilikia!" A revolution would be "a pilikia." **1938** Reinecke Hawaiian Loanwords 29, Pilikia. . . A difficulty; a hindrance. . . A blanket word, which can be applied to any trouble from the least to the greatest. . . The phrase "no pilikia" means approximately, "Don't mind; it's no bother." **1955** Day HI People 212, The result was pilikia—trouble. **1965** Krauss–Alexander Grove Farm 12 **HI,** Sailors smoke and drink and make plenty pilikia sometimes. **1969** DARE File **HI,** Pilikia—[ˌpɪləˈkiə]; trouble. **1972** Carr Da Kine Talk 116 **HI,** No pilikia! (English + Hawaiian). 'That's all right!' 'It's no trouble!' Pilikia means 'trouble'—of any kind, great or small. **1984** Sunset HI Guide 85, Pilikia—trouble.

pill n

1 also cancer pill, pill of death: A cigarette. **scattered, but chiefly NCent, Cent, West** See Map old-fash; esp freq among male speakers

1904 NY Eve. Jrl. (NY) 1 July 10 (Zwilling Coll.), [Cartoon:] "Well, I guess you'll have to give me a ticket on Fitz again," said the old sport last night as he pulled away on a new pill. **1914** DN 4.164 **NW,** Pill. . . A cigarette. **1915** DN 4.207, Pill-smoker, cigarette fiend. "Thomas has become a pill-smoker too." Ibid 234 **neOH** [College slang], Pill. . . A cigarette. **1916** DN 4.279 **NE, MA, KS,** Pill. . . Cigarette. "A lot of boys, buying the deadly pills." **1927** AmSp 2.281 [Prison lingo], Pill. . . Cigarette. **1937** Writer 50.239 **neOH** [Black], Pills—cigarettes. **1965–70** DARE (Qu. DD6b, Nicknames for cigarettes) 31 Infs, **scattered, but chiefly N Cent, Cent, West,** Pill; **OK1,** Some call them pills; **PA27,** Pill—rare; **CA27, ND3,** Pill [FW sugg]; **MN35,** Cancer pill; **WI44,** Pill of death. [34 of 37 Infs male, 33 old]

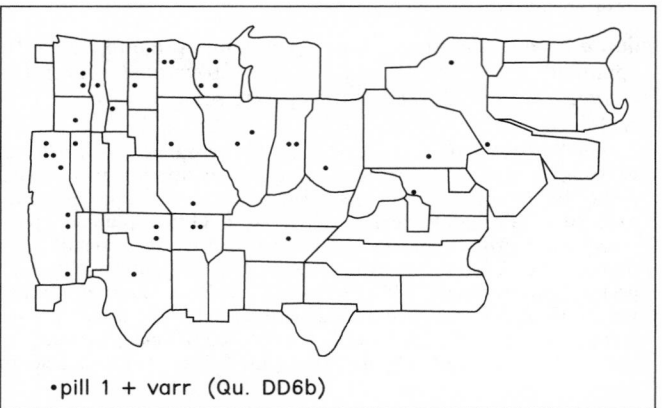

•pill 1 + varr (Qu. DD6b)

2 A pellet of animal dung. **esp Sth, S Midl** Cf **nanny** n[2] **2**

1938 Stuart Dark Hills 342 **eKY,** I heard he hit a teacher in the face with a dry horse pill. **1940** (1978) Still River of Earth 22 **KY,** Fletch squalled until he was hoarse, the eggs and tears mixing on his face. I had to find him a pocketful of rabbit pills to get him to stop. **1945** Saxon Gumbo Ya-Ya 531 **LA,** Measles. Medicine: . . sheep pills (dung) are widely employed. **1970** Anderson TX Folk Med. xviii, Sheep provided . . manure for "sheep pill" tea. **1984** Burns Cold Sassy 66 **nGA** (as of 1906), He and I had us a great manure war then, throwing dried cow cushions and sheep pills and horse biscuits at each other and dying laughing.

pillar See **pillow**

pillar poplar n
=**tulip tree.**

   1968 *DARE* (Qu. T13, . . *Names . . for . . tulip tree*) Inf **PA**118, Pillar poplar. [**1997** *NADS Letters* **CT**, [Re *pillar poplar*:] I'm sure "pillar" is in reference to the very tall and straight growth of these trees. We have one in our yard, and it is remarkably tall and straight. The tulip is also called the yellow poplar, hence the poplar part.]

pill bug n [See quot 1844; cf **pill 2**]
=**sow bug.**

   1844 DeKay *Zool. NY* 6.52, *Armadillo pillularis.* . . This is known under the name of *Pill-bug,* from its form, in a contracted state, completely resembling a pill. **1899** Bergen *Animal Lore* 64, Pill-bug, genus *Asellus.* **1926** Essig *Insects N. Amer.* 2, The pillbugs . . of the Family *Oniscidae* are occasionally injurious. **1933** Bryan *Hawaiian Nature* 156 **HI**, Pill-bugs . . roll themselves up into a ball like little armadillos. **1954** Borror–DeLong *Intro. Insects* 772, Some of the sowbugs (often called pillbugs) are capable of rolling up into a ball. **1970** Anderson *TX Folk Med.* 40, Hiccups—Put a bunch of pill bugs (sometimes called sow bugs) in a sack and tie it around the neck with a string. This is also useful for preventing hiccups. *Harris* [County]. *Ibid* 59, Rheumatism— Collect some pill bugs and fry them, then eat them. *Brazos* [County]. **1997** *DARE* File **cwCA** (as of c1955), We had lots of sow bugs in our garden. Some people called them pill bugs. **2000** Launspach *ID Dial. Project* 5 **seID**, (*The little black insect that curls up when you touch it*) 16 infs, Pill bug. **2000** *NADS Letters*, There are these little bugs that are common at least here on the east coast. If you touch them they roll into a little ball. My wife who is from New York calls them "pill bugs," as is common up there.

pill clam n
=**pea clam.**

   1992 Cummings–Mayer *Field Guide Freshwater Mussels MW* 172, *Fingernailclams* and *Peaclams* (Family Sphaeriidae) *Musculium, Piscidium,* and *Sphaerium.* . . *Other common names* Pillclams, nutclams. . . Shell rounded to slightly oval and inflated.

pillentary tree, pillenterry See **pellitory**

piller See **pillow**

pillibear case See **pillow beer**

pillo(e) See **pilau** n[1]

pill of death See **pill 1**

pillow n Usu |ˈpɪlo|; also, **esp S Midl**, |ˈpɪlə(r)| Pronc-spp *pellow, pillar, piller*

   A Proncs.

   1812 in 1956 Eliason *Tarheel Talk* 315 **c,cnNC**, Pillar. **1831** *Ibid* 315 **nw,cwNC**, Piller. **1837** Sherwood *Gaz. GA* 71, *Pillar,* for pillow. **1861** Holmes *Venner* 1.119 **NEng**, Ruffles all round the piller. *Ibid* 2.142, Right back on her piller. **1864** (1868) Trowbridge *3 Scouts* 26 **TN**, Nor even a straw-tick, to spare, say nothing of pillers and comforters! **1892** *DN* 1.233 **KY**, Pillow pronounced like *pillar,* as [pɪlə]. **1894** Riley *Armazindy* 25 **IN**, Wher' Sleep bared her breast as a piller fer them. **1899** (1912) Green *VA Folk-Speech* 321, *Piller.* . . Pillow. **1932** [see **pillow beer**] **1937** *AmSp* 12.287 **wVA**, Final [o] sounds become [ə] in . . *pillow.* **1942** McAtee *Dial. Grant Co. IN* 49 (as of 1890s), *Piller* . . pillow. **1966** *DARE* File **cwNC**, Pillow . . [ˈpɪlɚ]. **1976** Garber *Mountain-ese* 68 **sAppalachians**, We made new pillers fer the bed out uv goose feathers. **1998** *DARE* File—Internet **cePA** [Language of the Hayna Valley], *Pellow*—Where you put your head when you sleep.

   B Senses.

   1 also *kiss the pillow, pillow and key, pillows and keys*: A kissing game; see quots.

   1894 Frederic *Marsena* 9 **nNY**, He never shrank from bearing his part in "pillow," . . or in whatever other game was to be played, and he went through the kissing penalties and rewards involved without apparent aversion. **1897** Stuart *Simpkinsville* 35, "Spinning the plate," "dumb-crambo," "pillow," "how, when and where," such were the innocent games that composed the simple diversions of the evening. **1899** Champlin–Bostwick *Young Folks' Games* 533, *Pillows And Keys, or Pillow And Key.* . . All sit in a circle, and a boy taking a cushion or pillow, lays it at the feet of any girl he chooses and kneels on it. The girl must kiss him, and then, taking the cushion, places it in like manner before

any boy. **1907** *DN* 3.248 **eME**, *Pillow.* . . An indoors game. **1932** Farrell *Young Lonigan* 92 **Chicago IL** (as of 1916), They changed to kiss-the-pillow. Everyone got into the spirit of the game, even Weary. He found it wasn't so goofy kissing girls. [*Ibid* 94, The game went on. Studs dropped the pillow, by accident, in front of Helen. They looked meanly at each other . . until everybody yelled at them to play the game square, so they knelt down, each at an edge of the pillow, peck-kissed each other, and deepened their mutual hatred.] **1953** Brewster *Amer. Nonsinging Games* 155 **SC**, *Pillow.* . . [A]ll the girls are seated in a rough semicircle. Each of the boys in turn carries a pillow or a cushion, which he lays at the feet of his favorite. He then kneels upon it. If the girl likes the boy, she kneels facing him and they kiss each other. **1966** *DARE* File **NE**, Kiss the pillow—a type of children's game.

   2 See **pillow cloud.**

pillow and key See **pillow B1**

pillow beer n Also *pillow bear,* ~ *bere,* ~ *bier;* rarely, redund *pillibear case* [*OED2 pillow-bere* c1386 →] **obs**
   A pillowcase.

   1638 in 1887 *Archives of MD* 4.46, Item 4. towels & 1. pillower. **1721** in 1882 *MA Hist. Soc. Coll.* 5th ser 7.281, I gave Mr. Lewis a Lac'd Pillow-beer. **1758** in 1900 Shelton *Salt-Box House* 298 **CT**, 12 Pair pillibear cases. **1859** (1968) Bartlett *Americanisms* 321, *Pillowbier* and *Pillow-slip* are used in New England to signify a pillow case. **1896** (1968) Earle *Colonial NY* 108 (as of 1690), One of the early mayors of New York, had, at the time of his death, in the year 1690, fifty-six diaper napkins, . . fifty-one "pillow-bears," . . ten checked "pillowbears." **1899** (1912) Green *VA Folk-Speech* 321, *Pillowbear.* . . A cover to draw over a pillow. *Pillowbeer. Pillowbier. Pillowbere.* **1932** *DN* 6.283 **swCT**, *Piller bier* or *pillow bier.* Heard as late as 1916 instead of pillow case or pillow slip.

pillow cloud n Also *pillow* Cf **ice-cream soda (cloud)**
   A cumulus cloud.

   1967–68 *DARE* (Qu. B10, . . *Long trailing clouds high in the sky*) Inf **PA**134, Pillows; (Qu. B11, . . *Other kinds of clouds that come often*) Inf **IA**4, Pillow clouds—billowy, medium-sized white clouds, separated from each other, not on overcast [days].

pillow pigeon n
   The bedbug (*Cimex lectularius*).

   1968 *DARE* (Qu. R24, . . *Names . . for a bedbug*) Inf **OH**47, Pillow pigeons.

pillows and keys See **pillow B1**

pillow sham n Also *sham* somewhat old-fash; *esp freq among women*
   A decorative covering placed over a pillow or bolster when not in use.

   1873 *Appletons' Jrl.* 10.815 **NYC**, There was a "pillow-sham" which Pet had worked while in bed under the full influence of chills-and-fever. **1886** *Century Illustr. Mag.* 31.505, If his wife had dropped the pillow-sham . . Sewell could have borne; but she only went on tying the sham on the pillow, without a word. **1899** (1912) Green *VA Folk-Speech* 379, *Sham.* . . A false pillow-cover; a pillow-*sham.* **1902** (1969) Sears Catalogue 924, *Pillow Shams Stamped.* . . Good quality muslin shams. Stamped in assorted designs. A very desirable sham. [*DARE* Ed: In the 1927 ed of the above catalogue, pillow shams are no longer offered.] **1914** Dickinson *WI Plays* 23, Run for Mis' Trot and be don't lettin' me let my spare room pillow shams dry. **1946** Thompson *Amer. Daughter* 19 **IA**, I took Sue's tiny room with its magazine pictures pasted on the walls and embroidered shams over the pillows. **1962** Dykeman *Tall Woman* 133 **NC** (as of c1860), Its wingspread seemed wide as a pillow sham fluttering in the wind whenever it sailed past me there in the half-light with a whispery rush. **1965–70** *DARE* (Qu. E17, *The removable cover for a bed pillow*) 104 Infs, **widespread**, Pillow sham; 37 Infs, **scattered**, Sham. [Of all Infs responding to the question, 70% were old, 69% women; of those giving these responses, 80% were old, 92% women.] **1967** *DARE* Tape **NY**34, The things that received starch, heavy starch, were such things as the pillow shams with their ruffled edges that were used on all the beds in the house. **1984** Burns *Cold Sassy* 45 **nGA** (as of 1906), It gave me the creeps, helping Grandpa slip his pillow sham of roses under Granny's head. **1986** Pederson *LAGS Concordance* **Gulf Region**, 38 infs, Pillow sham(s); 1 inf, Pillow sham—mother used; 1 inf, Pillow sham—old term for pillowcase; 1 inf,

Pillow sham—older term; 1 inf, Pillow sham—roll; twice as long as pillow; 1 inf, Pillow sham—all the way across; 10 infs, Sham(s); 1 inf, Shams—were ornamental—covers over bolsters; 1 inf, Shams—for bolsters; 1 inf, Shams—coverings for long, continuous pillows. [Of 56 infs, 51 were women, 5 men; 42 were over 60, 12 between 40 and 60; 2 under 40.]

pill-pill n

A **yellowlegs** (here: either *Totanus flavipes* or *T. melanoleucus*).

1956 MA Audubon Soc. *Bulletin* 40.18 **MA,** *Greater Yellow-legs. . . Lesser Yellow-legs. . .* Pill-pill (Mass. . . Sonic.)

pill-willet n Also *will-willet* [Echoic]

1 also *bill-willie, billy-will, pill-will-willet:* =**willet.**

1709 (1967) Lawson *New Voyage* 151 **NC, SC,** *Will Willet* is so called from his Cry, which he very exactly calls *Will Willet*, as he flies. His Bill is like a Curlue's, or Woodcock's, and has much such a Body as the other, yet not so tall. He is good Meat. **1843** *Amer. Jrl. Science* 44.266 **CT,** Pill-will-willet, Stratford. . . The pill-willet, the green-rump tattler, . . and Bartram's tattler, all breed here. **1888** Trumbull *Names of Birds* 164, In Florida it [=the willet] is occasionally termed the *Bill-willie. . .* Elsewhere . . *Pill-willet. . .* Imitative of the bird's shrill cries. **1917** (1923) *Birds Amer.* 1.246, *Willet. . . Other Names. . .* Will-willet; Pill-will-willet; Billy-will. **1923** U.S. Dept. Ag. *Misc. Circular* 13.62 **NC, SC,** *Willet. . . Vernacular Names. . . In local use. . .* Will-willet. **1949** Sprunt–Chamberlain *SC Bird Life* 231, *Catoptrophorus semipalmatus semipalmatus. . . Local Names . .* Will-willet. . . The shrill, incessantly repeated notes which give it the name are certainly the characteristic sound of the summer marshes. The words "pill-will-willet" give a reasonably good impression of the sound, though the bird does have other calls. **1955** Lowery *LA Birds* 253, The local names of this large shore bird [=the willet], *vire-vire* and "pill-will-willet," are derived from two of its call notes. **1956** MA Audubon Soc. *Bulletin* 40.18 **CT,** *Willet. . .* Pill-willet, Pill-will-willet. **1969** Longstreet *Birds FL* 63, *Willet—Other names . .* Bill-willie. . . During nesting season the birds discourage intrusion by flying close to the trespasser and uttering loud cries of *pill-will-willy.*

2 An **oyster-catcher** (here: *Haematopus palliatus*).

1791 Bartram *Travels* 296 **S Atl,** Hematopus ostrealegus, the will willet or oister catcher. **1888** Trumbull *Names of Birds* 165 **TX,** Mr. Dresser . . speaks of this name "Pill-willet" being applied by his boatman in Galveston Bay to the American Oyster-catcher—a bird seldom found north of New Jersey. **1923** U.S. Dept. Ag. *Misc. Circular* 13.72 **TX,** American Oyster-catcher. . . Vernacular names. . . Pill-willet.

pill-will-willet See **pill-willet 1**

pilon n Usu |piˈlon|; for varr see quot 1965–70 Also *pelon, pilone* [MexSpan] **chiefly TX** See Map *old-fash* =**lagniappe;** also fig.

1883 Sweet–Knox *Mexican Mustang* 348 **TX,** *Pelon* was nothing more nor less than any little trifle thrown in,—a kind of voluntary commission to the customer. **1892** *DN* 1.251 **TX,** *Pilón . .* the gratuity given by merchants to customers, whenever accounts are settled. **1903** (1965) Adams *Log Cowboy* 125 **NM,** McCann had talked the storekeeper at Doan's, where we got our last supplies, out of some extras as a *pelon.* **1939** *AmSp* 14.96, The Río Grande valley . . uses the Mexican *pilón.* **1942** Perry *Texas* 137, Anything that is free we call a *"pilone,"* which is what the Mexicans call the little free sack of candy our border grocers still give a Mexican family which has bought a substantial order of groceries. **1947** Bedichek *Advent. TX Naturalist* 75, [The yaupon] stands drought, resents coddling, and throws in, as a *pilon* to its domesticator, decorative red berries in the fall and winter. **1962** Atwood *Vocab. TX* 68, The custom of giving something extra with a purchase (or when a bill is paid) is firmly established in the United States. . . Most areas lack a specific word for this sort of gift. In the Southwest, the West, and part of Central Texas *pilón . .* is very well known and widely used. *Ibid* 128, Modern stores are becoming less and less inclined to give *pilón.* **1965–70** *DARE* (Qu. U15, *When you're buying something, if the seller puts in a little extra to make you feel that you're getting a good bargain)* Infs **TX**28, 29, 31, 43, [piˈlo(ʊ)n]; **TX**11, 26, 54, [prˈlo(ʊ)n]; **TX**3, 13, 23, [pəˈlon]; **TX**1, [prˈloun]; **TX**4, [piˈlon]—rare now, but Mexican old women will stick out hands and say, "Pilon? Pilon?"; **TX**103, [piˈon]—in Mexican; a gift; **CA**65, For [ˈpilon]—Spanish; common here. [12 of 14 Infs old] **1969** O'Connor *Horse & Buggy West* 185 **AZ,** I always asked for the privilege of going

up to pay the bill because Moe always came through with a generous *pelon*—a Spanish word for a gift thrown in free with a purchase or with the payment of a bill. **1986** Pederson *LAGS Concordance (Lagniappe; bonus or gift when a bill is paid)* 30 infs, **ce,csTX,** Pilon. [*DARE* Ed: Many infs described the gift of a *pilon* (piece of candy) as an obsolete custom.]

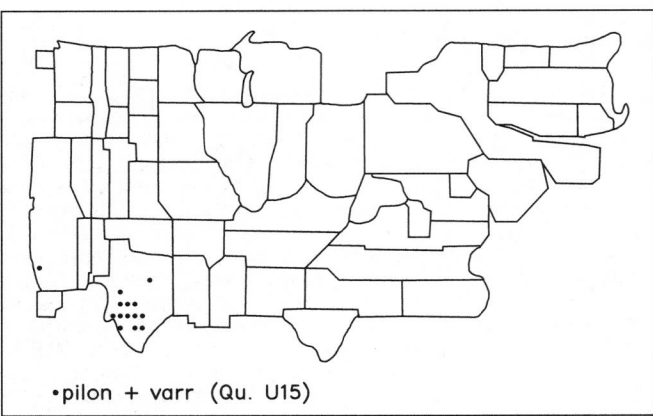

•pilon + varr (Qu. U15)

piloncillo n |ˌpilonˈsiə| and varr; see quots 1967, 1981 Also *pelonce, peloncillo, pilonce, pilonci, pilonsillo* [MexSpan; dimin of *pilon* a loaf of sugar] **chiefly TX**

Unrefined sugar, usu in the form of a cone or loaf.

1844 Gregg *Commerce* 1.173 **NM,** When short of means they often support themselves upon only a *real* each per day, their usual food consisting of bread and a kind of coarse cake-sugar called *piloncillo.* **1845** Green *Jrl. Texian Exped.* 264, Our cook brings us in . . two and a half pounds of brown sugar, 'pilonci.' **1854** (1932) Bell *Log TX–CA Trail* 35.310, Gathered some quinces and stewed them with Pelonce or Mexican sugar. **1875** *Fur Fin & Feather* 108 **NM,** You are all the nights at fandangoes, and all the days eating *piloncillo* and learning Spanish with the senorites [sic]. **1892** *DN* 1.193 **TX,** *Pilón:* a loaf of sugar. The usual forms in Texas are *pilonce* and *piloncillo;* they are applied to small loaves of unrefined Mexican sugar in the form of a truncated cone three or four inches high, which come generally wrapped in yucca or palm leaves. They taste very much like maple sugar. **1898** Canfield *Maid of Frontier* 207 *(DA),* 'Peloncillo,' crude brown sugar, in a stick. **1940** Writers' Program *Guide AZ* 206 **cAZ,** In the show cases are Mexican candies: *Pilonsillos*, brown, cone-shaped, and made from pure cane sugar. **1967** *DARE* (Qu. H82b, *Kinds of cheap candy that used to be sold years ago)* Inf **TX**5, Piloncillo [ˌpilonˈsio]—raw sugar (unrefined) in shape of cone with stick in it; **TX**11, Piloncillo [ˌpilonˈsijə]—dregs from sugar mill formed into a cone. **1981** Pederson *LAGS Basic Materials,* 1 inf, **csTX,** [ˈpʼiᵻlnˈsiˑəl]—Made from boiling sugar cane and molding it into cones. It's brown, like brown sugar. Used for sweetening by chipping off pieces for coffee, lemonade, etc; 1 inf, **csTX,** [ˈpʼɛˊˑlənˌsiˇˑəˌz̩]—Piloncillos = unrefined sugar loaves. **1985** Fierman *Guts & Ruts* 68 **NM** (as of c1850), Chocolate is a very popular drink of the affluent. Sugar is used, but not the refined variety; rather, coarse brown sugar is molded into cakes called *peloncillo.*

pilone See **pilon**

pilonsillo See **piloncillo**

pilot n

1 See **pilot snake.**

2 =**black-bellied plover.** [See quot 1880]

1880 *Forest & Stream* 15.4, Black-bellied plover. . . On the coast of Virginia, about Cobb's Island, the name of pilot has been given, as it is always seen leading the large flights of birds which the rising tides drive from the shoals and oyster rocks, and it is supposed to direct the flocks "to pastures new." **1917** (1923) *Birds Amer.* 1.256, *Black-bellied Plover. . . Other Names. . .* Pilot.

3 See **pilot fish.**

pilot biscuit See **pilot bread**

pilot black snake n [See quots 1951, 1981]

A **rat snake 1** (here: *Elaphe obsoleta obsoleta*). Also called

black snake 2, chicken ~ 1, mountain black ~, pilot ~ 2, racer 1b

1842 DeKay *Zool. NY* 3.37, The Pilot Black-snake appears to select in preference elevated rocky situations, for it is found along the Allegany mountains as far south as Virginia. It has hitherto been confounded with the ordinary Black Snake, but is at once distinguished from that species by the carinated scales. **1879** Smith *Catalogue Reptilia MI* 6, *Coluber obsoletus.* . . Pilot Black Snake. **1935** *Copeia* 1.42, The pilot blacksnake . . has several times been noted on the islands of the St. Lawrence River. **1951** Conant *Reptiles OH* 59, In many parts of its range the pilot black snake was found in association with the copperhead and timber rattlesnake. A superstition maintains that it "pilots" these venomous snakes to safety in times of danger. **1967** *PA Game News* Aug 4 **PA**, It's a good thing, pilot black snakes aren't poisonous, for they certainly have bad tempers. **1968** *Ibid* May 51 **PA**, Pilot blacksnakes are absolutely unpredictable in their reactions to humans. . . I've met two blacksnakes . . that let me ease a camera within a foot of their faces to take their picture. **1970** *DARE* (Qu. P25, . . *Kinds of snakes*) Inf **OH92**, Pilot black snake. **1981** Vogt *Nat. Hist. WI* 137, The name "pilot blacksnake" stems from a folk tale that black rat snakes lead timber rattlesnakes back to their dens in the fall. There is no evidence to give credence to this fable.

pilot bread n Also *pilot biscuit, ~ cracker*
=hardtack 1a.

1788 *MD Jrl. & Baltimore Advt.* (MD) 7 Mar [4]/2, The subscriber has just begun to bake *Ship, Pilot,* and *Cag Bread.* **1858** in 1966 Boller *MO Fur Trader* 121 **MO**, Our lunch consisted of a piece of Pilot bread and a slice of raw bacon. **1862** (1922) Jackson *Col.'s Diary* 65 **PA**, I was glad to borrow a piece of pilot bread and to find a haversack containing a fine, large piece of mess pork. **1880** *Scribner's Mag.* 20.128, Flour is more portable than pilot biscuit; therefore warm, light bread . . has gratefully succeeded hard-tack in all mining and mountain camps. **1880** *Harper's New Mth. Mag.* 60.224 **NYC**, Rhene . . watches the pilot crackers shovelled out, two to each boy. **1899** (1912) Green *VA Folk-Speech* 322, *Pilot-bread.* . . Dry, hard bread made for use at sea. **1932** Wasson *Sailing Days* 107 **cME coast**, Soon there appeared round pilot biscuit, slabs of cheese, pickles. **1939** Wolcott *Yankee Cook Book* 26, A clam-cake in the left hand and a spoonful of chowder thickened with pilot bread (a flaky hard cracker of nutty flavor) in the right is the proper procedure. **1946** Gould *Yankee Storekeeper* 29 **NH**, Take my word. I want . . five pounds of pilot bread. **1968** *DARE* Tape **AK11**, [Inf:] Do you know what the saloon pilot bread is like? . . They just used to call it crackers. . . [FW:] What were these crackers made of . . ? [Inf:] Well, they were just a big—you've seen them—a big round crackers and thick, hard. **1972** *River Times* (Fairbanks AK) Aug 5/3, The picnics with smoked salmon and pilot bread will always be remembered by the Native people as an old custom. **1989** *Yankee* Aug 21 **CA**, I'm trying to locate a source for the cracker of my youth, *Pilot Crackers.* Originally round, then rectangular, they have disappeared from the Los Angeles markets. **1997** *DARE* File **AK**, We use pilot crackers for our backpacking lunches. They are filling and sturdy—don't crumble in the pack like regular crackers would; **coastal ME**, When people in coastal and island communities in Maine found out that pilot crackers were no longer going to be available, their first reaction was to stockpile all the boxes they could get. Their second reaction was organized outrage at Nabisco.

pilot fish n Also *pilot*

1 Std: a slender **jack** n[1] **24b(1)** (here: *Naucrates ductor*) of warm seas, reputed to guide sharks. Also called **shark pilot 2**
2 =rudderfish b.

1880 *Harper's New Mth. Mag.* 61.503 **ME**, The tiny pilot-fish, perhaps a kind of fugleman for the mackerel, but more likely his prey. **1903** NY State Museum & Sci. Serv. *Bulletin* 60.415, The banded pilot is found on our east coast from Cape Ann to Cape Hatteras. . . The young are very common as far north as Cape Cod. **1919** *Copeia* 71.57 **Long Is. NY**, *Seriola zonata*. Pilotfish. . . When two young dusky sharks were trapped, not less than fifty pilotfishes were taken ranging from 6 to 8 inches in length. It is interesting to study these accompanying the sharks around in the trap a couple of feet beneath the surface, the pilots copying every turn of the sharks. **1933** John G. Shedd Aquarium *Guide* 83, *Seriola zonata*—Pilotfish; Rudderfish. This fish, which is restricted to the Atlantic coast of the United States, resembles the Shark-pilot [= *Naucrates ductor*]. **1966** *DARE* (Qu. P4, *Saltwater fish that are not good to eat*) Inf **DC8**, Pilot fish.
3 =round whitefish.

1882 U.S. Natl. Museum *Bulletin* 16.298, *C[oregonus] quadrilateralis* [=*Prosopium cylindraceum*]. . . Pilot-fish; Menominee White-fish . . Lakes of New Hampshire, Upper Great Lakes, northwestward to Alaska; abundant in cold, deep waters. **1902** Jordan–Evermann *Amer. Fishes* 122, *Menominee Whitefish.* . . is known as . . pilotfish (Lake Champlain). **1927** in 1929 U.S. Dept. Commerce Bur. Fisheries *Document* 1048.552, Thus all the records indicate that the pilot begin to move inshore in numbers on honeycomb rock and gravel about the middle of October. . . Since few gill nets of a mesh suitable for pilot are set in the spring, not much is known about the offshore movement. **1946** LaMonte *N. Amer. Game Fishes* 122, *Pilot.* . . Dorsal fin and portion of the tail brown. Sometimes there are bright pink splotches on the other fins. **1974** WI Univ. *Fish Lake MI* 31, *Prosopium cylindraceum*. . . Pilot fish. . . When smoked, they are prized as a fine table food. **1983** Becker *Fishes WI* 372, *Round Whitefish.* . . Other common names: the pilot, the pilot fish.

pilot plant See **pilot weed**

pilot rattlesnake See **rattlesnake pilot 1**

pilot snake n Also *pilot* Cf **rattlesnake pilot, water ~**

1 also *copperhead pilot:* **=copperhead snake 1.** [See quot 1818] Cf **ground pilot**

1782 Crèvecoeur *Letters* 236, The most dangerous one is the *pilot,* or *copperhead.* **1789** in 1793 Amer. Philos. Soc. *Trans.* 3.xx, *Poor Robins plantain* . . [is] said to frustrate the bite both of the rattle snake, and of his supposed precursor the *pilote-snake.* **1818** *Amer. Jrl. Science* 1.84 **NY**, *Scytalus Cupreus, or Copper-head Snake* . . has been called sometimes *pilot-snake,* on a false supposition that he was the pilot or guide of the rattlesnake. **1859** Van Buren *Jottings* 197 **MS**, The pilot-snake . . gets so full of poison in the fall that it grows blind. **1860** *Harper's New Mth. Mag.* 20.584 **NJ**, They had been cautioned against getting into the swamps, as the deadly rattlesnake, and still more fatal "pilot," were frequently found in those localities. **1890** *Century Illustr. Mag.* 40.615, I killed two large snakes called the "pilot-snake," from the fact that they are generally found in the vicinity of rattlesnakes. **1903** *Scientific Amer.* 14 Feb 118, The Copperhead, also known in different localities by the names Upland Moccasin, Chunkhead, Deaf Adder, Pilot Snake, etc., is perhaps to be more dreaded than any other American snake. **1916** Seton *Woodcraft Manual Girls* 320, The Copperhead . . is the Highland, or Northern Moccasin or Pilot Snake, found from Massachusetts to Florida and west to Illinois and Texas. **1956** Klauber *Rattlesnakes* 2.1244, Another phase of the myth is that pilot snakes are crosses between rattlesnakes and bull snakes. **1958** Conant *Reptiles & Amphibians* 185, The Copperhead [=*Agkistrodon contortrix mokeson*] has many aliases—"chunkhead," "highland moccasin," "pilot," "adder," etc. **1965–70** *DARE* (Qu. P25, . . *Kinds of snakes*) Infs **NJ3, SC3, 66, TX36**, Pilot(s); **SC19, 26**, Copperhead = pilot; **AL7**, Pilot—around rattlers; **GA80**, Pilot—poisonous; **PA121**, Copperhead or pilot—same snake; **NJ1**, Copperhead pilot; **NJ8**, Copperheads or copperhead pilots; **NC41**, Copperhead pilots; **NJ56**, Pilot snake—follows rattlesnake; **SC32**, Pilot snake—colored like rattler, but no rattles; **SC57**, Pilot snake. [*DARE* Ed: Some of these Infs may refer instead to other senses below.] **1986** Pederson *LAGS Concordance*, 1 inf, **seAL**, Pilots—local snakes.

2 A rat snake 1: esp *Elaphe obsoleta,* but also **corn snake** and **fox snake.** Cf **pilot black snake**

1842 DeKay *Zool. NY* 3.37, It [=the pilot black snake] is manifestly the snake which has been frequently described to me, of great length and prodigious velocity, and to which they gave the name of *Racer* and *Pilot.* As these names are also frequently applied to the Black Snake [= *Coluber constrictor*], I had supposed that species to have been intended by their descriptions. **1854** Wailes *Rept. on Ag. & Geol. MS* 329, *Scotophis guttatus* [=*Elaphe guttata*]. Black pilot snake. **1891** in 1895 IL State Lab. Nat. Hist. Urbana *Bulletin* 3.290, *Pilot Snake. Black Snake. [Elaphis obsoletus]* Var. *Obsoletus.* . . [E. o.] Var. *Lindheimeri. Ibid* 291, This [=*Elaphe obsoleta var lindheimeri*] is a fine large species which bears a superficial resemblance to the common black snake (*Coluber constrictor*) and this latter species is occasionally credited with traits which belong to the pilot snake. The pilot snake is said to climb trees in search of birds' nests as does the true black snake. **1892** IN Dept. Geol. & Nat. Resources *Rept. for 1891* 499, The Fox-snake appears to be moderately common in some localities. It is often known as the "Pilot-snake," and is supposed to have some mysterious connection with the rattlesnake. **1908** Biol. Soc. DC *Proc.* 21.74 **TX**, *Coluber spiloides* [=*Elaphe obsoleta spiloides*]. . . Texas Pilot Snake. Abundant wherever there are wooded tracts and . . on account of their expertness in climbing trees, they annually destroy large numbers of young birds. . .

Coluber obsoletus lindheimeri. . . Lindheimer's Pilot Snake. My friend . . presented me with a fair sized specimen of this bright colored pilot snake. **1913** *Auk* 30.489 **Okefenokee GA,** Some of the characteristic . . forms of the water courses are the pied water snake, pilot snake *(Coluber obsoletus),* . . and various catfishes. **1919** *Copeia* 67.11 **NY,** *Elaphe obsoleta. . . Pilot Snake. . . Natrix sipedon. . .* This like the pilot and racer is called indiscriminately "black snake." *Ibid* 69.28 **PA,** A pair of pilot snakes. . . had the habit of lying on the surface or burying themselves in an old sawdust pile. **1926** *TX Folkl. Soc. Pub.* 5.76, Almost any Texas farmer boy can relate instances where the gray pilot [= *Elaphe obsoleta spiloides*] or chicken snake has entered his father's hen house and disposed of eggs. **1928** *Baylor Univ. Museum Contrib.* 16.15 **TX,** *Elaphe obsoleta confinis. . .* The Gray Pilot Snake is abundant throughout eastern Texas. *Ibid* 16, Emory's Pilot Snake *(Elaphe laeta . .).* **1966** *DARE* (Qu. P25, . . *Kinds of snakes*) Inf **FL**27, Pilot snake.

3 =**racer 1a.**

1842 DeKay *Zool. NY* 3.36, The Black Snake [=*Coluber constrictor*] is a bold, active, wild and untameable animal. . . In various parts of the State they have the popular names of *Racer, Pilot* and *Black Snake.* [**1891** in 1895 IL State Lab. Nat. Hist. Urbana *Bulletin* 3.286, The pilot snakes [=*Elaphe obsoleta* varr *lindheimeri* and *obsoleta*] and this species [=*Coluber constrictor*] are not commonly discriminated, and accounts of the habits of the black snake as frequently refer to one as to the other.] **1981** Hardeman *Shucks* 65, Here a mole and there a field mouse, and occasionally a stunned, writhing six-foot "pilot" snake (black snake), a corn snake, or perhaps a lethal copperhead that had taken refuge in a mole tunnel.

4 Any of var other snakes such as the **bull snake** or a **milk snake 1** (here: *Lampropeltis triangulum*).

1852 in 1854 U.S. War Dept. *Explor. Red River* 211 **LA,** *Pituophis,* Holbr. . . The names of Bull, Pine, and Pilot snake, are commonly given to different species of this genus. **1907** NJ State Museum *Annual Rept. for 1906* 198, Like most all snakes in this region they [=*Lampropeltis triangulum*] are locally known as the "pilot."

pilot tree n

=**Texas ebony.**

1951 *PADS* 15.33 **TX,** *Zygia flexicaulis* [=*Pithecellobium flexicaule*]. . . Texas ebony, pilot tree (as an indicator of fertile soil).

pilot weed n Also *pilot plant* [See quot 1914]

A **rosinweed 1** (here: *Silphium laciniatum*).

1847 in 1848 Emory *Notes Reconnoissance* 11 **KS,** On the uplands . . occasionally is found the wild tea, . . and pilot weed, (silphium lacinatum [sic] . .). **1885** *Girl's Own Paper* Jan. 171/1 (*OED2*), The compass plant—variously known, also, as the pilot weed, polar plant, and turpentine weed—is a vigorous perennial. **1901** Lounsberry *S. Wild Flowers* 517, *S[ilphium] laciniatum,* pilot, polar or compassplant, . . is familiar from the prairies of Ohio southward to Alabama and Texas. **1914** Georgia *Manual Weeds* 447, *Silphium laciniatum. . . Pilotweed. . .* Many a traveler of the pioneer, roadless days of "going west" found this plant a very serviceable compass, for its large leaves are held nearly erect with their edges directed north and south. **1939** Medsger *Edible Wild Plants* 232, *Compass Plant,* or *Pilotweed—Silphium laciniatum.* **1976** Bruce *How to Grow Wildflowers* 236, Its botanical name is *Silphium laciniatum;* its colloquial, Compass-plant or Pilot-weed.

pimbina See **pembina**

pime-blank See **point-blank A3**

pimento n [See quots] Cf **wild pimento**

=**Carolina allspice.**

[**1830** Rafinesque *Med. Flora* 203, *Sweet Shrub, Allspice. . .* Much esteemed for the blossoms, smelling like Pine-apple. . . The seeds taste like Pimento [=*Pimenta dioica*].] **1872** Schele de Vere *Americanisms* 413, In like manner they appropriate the name of the tropical Pimento [=*Pimenta dioica*] to a sweet-scented shrub (Calycanthus floridus), the bark and wood of which have quite a spicy flavor. At times, a more careful distinction is attempted, by calling it the *Carolina Allspice,* from the State, in which it is quite abundant.

pime-plank See **point-blank A3**

pimgenet, pimjimmy See **pipjenny**

pimp n[1] [Cf *OED2* pimp c. (a) "Austral. and N.Z. slang, an informer, tell-tale"; a1885 →; (b) "Welsh dial., one who spies on lovers, a peeping Tom."] **formerly widespread, now chiefly Sth**

A toady, apple-polisher; a spy, informer.

1791 in 1988 Maclay *Diary* 390 **PA,** He has acted in a Strange kind of Capacity half pimp half envoy, or perhaps more properly a kind of Political Eavedropper about the British Court. **1844** *N. Amer. Rev.* 59.272, It [=the practice of tarring and feathering] was confined principally to obnoxious custom-house officers, pimps, and informers. **1865** *Old Guard* 3.429, Almost all the witnesses were the hired pimps and spies of Stanton's department—a set of vagabonds and thieves!—common liars! **1866** *N. Amer. Rev.* 102.179, He [=Andrew Jackson] was reconciled with General Winfield Scott, whom, in 1817, he had styled . . an "intermeddling pimp and spy of the War Office." **1873** Bear *Life & Travels* 237, They reported there that there were a number of officers unnecessarily employed in the Custom House and finally got one of Johnson's pimps sent over to investigate the matter. **1968–69** *DARE* (Qu. II20a, *A person who tries too hard to gain somebody else's favor: "He's an awful _____."*) Inf **SC**10, Pimp; (Qu. JJ3b, *When a school child makes a special effort to 'get in good' with the teacher in hopes of getting a better grade: "She's an awful _____."*) Inf **GA**9, Pimp; (Qu. JJ4, *A child who is always telling on other children*) Infs **GA**86, **LA**46, Pimp. **1986** Pederson *LAGS Concordance* **chiefly coastal Gulf Region** *(Tattletale)* 13 infs, Pimp [*DARE* Ed: Some infs qualify this by saying that it refers to an adult.]; 1 inf, Pimp—an informer, one who tells on another; [also] to pimp on him; 1 inf, Pimp—an informer, in the past; 1 inf, Pimp—adult who carries information; 1 inf, Pimp—takes tales to the boss, an informant; 1 inf, Pimp—like tattletale, will "go and tell"; 1 inf, Pimp—"snoops around"; 1 inf, Pimp—informer; 1 inf, Pimp—gossip; 1 inf, Pimp—tattletale to police; commonly used locally; 1 inf, Pimp—tattletale, one who tells on criminals; 1 inf, Pimp—excessive tattling, usually undercover; 1 inf, Pimp—man who tells police what's going on; 1 inf, Pimp—will tell anything they know; 1 inf, Pimp—tattletale; 1 inf, He was a pimp (=informer) for a prohibition man; 1 inf, Pimp means teacher's or parent's "pet"; 1 inf, A pimp—childhood term—seeker of favor and praise; 1 inf, A pimp—an adult who seeks praise.

pimp v[1] [**pimp** n[1]]

To snoop, sneak, tattle, inform (on).

1851 Hall *College Words* 231, *Pimp.* To do little, mean actions for the purpose of gaining favor with a superior, as, in college, with an instructor. **1855** *U.S. Democratic Rev.* 35.432, We went on swimmingly in this course, and should have gone on still more so, had it not been for . . a busy pragmatical Comptroller, who took it into his head to set up for an honest man, and was perpetually pimping into our private affairs under pretense of taking care of the public money. **1865** *Atlantic Mth.* 16.53 **sePA,** I thought that was what you were going at. . . That's what your pimping about us comes to. Want to ruin our business, do you, and have strawberries of your own to sell to our customers? **1942** Hurston *Dust Tracks* 192 **FL** [Black], Unless some strange, low member of your own race has gone and pimped to the white folks about something getting hurt. **1976** *DARE* File **Baton Rouge LA** [Black], He was a pimp for the police. **1986** Pederson *LAGS Concordance* **coastal Gulf Region,** 2 infs, To pimp on (him); 1 inf, Pimp on me = tattle; 1 inf, He's a-pimping on you; 1 inf, So-and-so pimped on him—informing to the police; 1 inf, Pimping—tattling. **1989** Flynt *Poor But Proud* 112 **ceAL,** Well, I got fired. . . two or three times on account of it. . . they's some of them. . . usually pimp on you, tell everything that happened.

pimp v[2] See **pimping**

pimp n[2] [Abbr]

1 A pimple.

1969 *DARE* (Qu. X59, . . *The small infected pimples that form usually on the face*) Infs **NY**221, **VT**12, Pimps.

2 See quot.

1958 *Sat. Eve. Post Letters* **ceWI,** Regarding the "pimps," . . they were a small glazed marble, and as this glaze coating dried, the marbles were evidently touching each other, causing a small blister, crater, or pimple to form on the outside of the marble in 3 or 4 spots.

pimp n[3] See **pimp stick**

pimping adj Also *pimpy* [*OED2* 1687 →] **scattered, but esp NEng**

Puny, sickly; petty, mean; hence v *pimp* to droop, languish.

1792 in 1891 Washington *Writings* 9.105 **VA,** He found matters were likely to be conducted upon so pimping a scale, that he would not hazard his character or reputation on the event. **1845** Judd *Margaret* 19 **NEng,** "Was I so little?" asked Margaret. "Yes, and pimpin enough. . . Ye was thin and poor as a late chicken." **1884** Baldwin *Yankee School-Teacher* 36 **VA** [Black], Miss Lucy done los' mos' all her chick'ns. Dis yer ole feller was a pimp'n roun' all las' week; him was de las' one Miss Lucy hab, an' sh' done hate f'r t' see him waste 'way. **1905** *DN* 3.16 **cCT,** *Pimping.* . . Petty. **1941** *LANE* Map 459 *(Emaciated, peaked)* 3 infs, **CT, MA,** Pimping. **1967** *DARE* (Qu. X52, *. . A person . . who had been sick and was looking* _____) Inf **MA5,** Pimping; (Qu. BB38, *When a person doesn't look healthy, or looks as if he hadn't been well for some time . . "He looks* _____.") Inf **MA5,** Pimping. **1997** *NADS Letters* **sCA** (as of 1960s), I've never run across pimping [in the sense "puny, sickly"], but regularly use pimpy to have the same meaning. . . This seemed to be in common usage when I was a child. . . I am 40, and grew up in Southern California. **2000** *Ibid* **neIL** (as of c1965), In my youth in Oak Lawn, a suburb of Chicago, it was common to say that that scrawny, puny kid was a "pimpy little guy."

pimpjennet, pimpjenny See **pipjenny**

pimpleback n Cf *purple pimpleback* (at **purple wartyback**)
A **freshwater clam:** usu *Quadrula pustulosa,* but also *Q. nodulata, Cyprogenia stegaria,* or *Pelthobasus cooperianus.*

1941 *AmSp* 16.156 **Missip Valley,** The following list gives the common names [of freshwater clams] as applied by the cutter and fisher of shells. . . Egg-shell[,] Elephant Ear[,] . . Pimple-back. **1979** *WI Week-End* Apr 6 **Missip Valley,** The thick shelled varieties such as pimple backs and hacklebacks were the most valuable during the decades of the pearl button industry. **1982** U.S. Fish & Wildlife Serv. *Fresh-Water Mussels* [Wall chart] **Upper Missip Valley,** Pimpleback. . . Few to many rounded tubercules, arranged without pattern. *Ibid,* Pimpleback. . . Common to abundant. . . Hosts: several widespread, common fishes, mostly catfishes. **1991** IL Nat. Hist. Surv. *Biol. Notes* 137.14 **IL,** *Quadrula pustulosa.* . . The pimpleback has noticeably declined in numbers. **1992** Cummings–Mayer *Field Guide Freshwater Mussels MW* 36, *Quadrula nodulata.* . . Winged pimpleback, pimpleback. . . Rounded shell with two rows of paired knobs or pustules on the posterior half of the shell. *Ibid* 38, Pimpleback—*Quadrula pustulosa.* . . Rounded shell . . usually densely covered with pustules. *Ibid* 54, Orange-foot pimpleback—*Plethobasus cooperianus. Ibid* 102, Fanshell—*Cyprogenia stegaria.* . . Other common names . . pimpleback.

pimple ball n
A small, rubber ball with protuberances on the surface.

1967 *DARE* (Qu. EE33, *. . Outdoor games . . that children play*) Inf **MA33,** Half-ball—a pimple ball cut in half. . . Hit off the step—you throw a pimple ball off the nosing or the aisle on a step. **1999** *DARE* File—Internet **eMA** [Boston Online *The Wicked Good Guide to Boston English*], Game similar to punchball, except the ball had to first bounce in the "infield." Played with "pinkies" or "pimple balls"—soft, small, white balls. **2001** *DARE* File—Internet, Pimple balls were used in Philly, Boston and some other Northeastern cities for Wallball, Handball, Boxball, Points, Wireball, Stickball, Hit the Penny and some other games. If they were severely exposed to the elements (down a sewer or over the roof) they usually did not bounce as well so they were cut into halfballs. And if you had the dough, you might even cut up a new pimpleball for a game of Halfball. **2001** *DARE* File **eMA,** A "pimple ball" is a hollow, white, rubber ball, slightly smaller than a golf ball. I would describe the surface of a pimple ball as the opposite of a golf ball's: A golf ball's surface has indentations; a pimple ball's has small bumps (whence, I assume, the name). When I used them (in Boston in the late 50's and early 60's) it was primarily for stickball. . . I asked two of my teenaged kids, both native, life-long Bostonians, if they knew what a "pimple ball" was. They didn't.

pimp stick n Also *pimp* esp **Nth, West** See Map Cf **pill 1**
A cigarette.

1925 *AmSp* 1.138 **Pacific NW,** Some loggers smoke the "paper collar stiff's" cigarette, but it is still called a "pimp stick" in the bunkhouses. **1937** *Writer* 50.239 **neOH** [Black], *Pimp stick*—an odd name for cigarettes. **1965–70** *DARE* (Qu. DD6b, *Nicknames for cigarettes*) 12 Infs, esp **Nth, West,** Pimp stick; **CA105, MN15,** Pimp stick—old-fashioned; **CA36,** Pimp stick—goes back to before it became common among

women; the prostitutes and pimps smoked; a pimp-stick shooter = a smoker; **MI2,** Pimp stick; anybody who smoked was said to be a pimp; **MI107,** Pimp stick—heard in the lumber camps; people who smoked them were held in contempt; **NM11,** Pimp stick—used by non-smokers; **PA11, 71,** Pimp; [**NY42,** Pip stick—family usage]. [16 of 20 Infs male] **1969** Sorden *Lumberjack Lingo* 87 **NEng, Gt Lakes,** *Pimp sticks*—Cigarettes. Loggers and lumberjacks despised men who smoked cigarettes, and many foremen would not hire them. Their other names for cigarettes are unprintable.

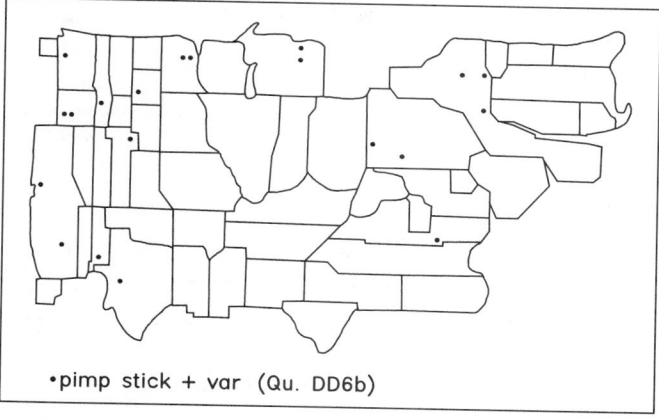

•pimp stick + var (Qu. DD6b)

pin n[1], v Usu |pɪn|; also esp **Sth, S Midl** |pɛn|; for addit varr see quot 1989 Pronc-sp *pen* Cf **pen** n[1]
A Forms.

1893 Shands *MS Speech* 10, Short *i* . . is very frequently pronounced by all classes of people as short (e): as, (pen) for *pin.* **1899** (1912) Green *VA Folk-Speech* 317, *Pen-feather.* **1942** Hall *Smoky Mt. Speech* 16 **wNC, eTN,** *Pin* and *pen* may be homophones. **1966–69** *DARE* (Qu. T6, *The pointed leaves that fall from pine trees*) Inf **AR5,** Pine pens; (Qu. BB51b, *. . 'Magical' cures for corns or warts*) Inf **MO39,** Pick warts with pen, give pen to somebody else; **UT7,** Rub a pen on the wart and never give pen away; **SC46,** Stick into it with a pen. **1989** Pederson *LAGS Tech. Index* 96 **Gulf Region,** [Of 724 exx of the pronc of *pin,* 564 were of the type [pɪn], 120 [pɛn], 39 [pɪn], and 1 [pjɪn].]
B As noun.
=**needle 1.**

1941 *Nature Mag.* 34.139, At about the middle of the coast of Maine, I have heard the word pins used fittingly for leaves of the genus *Pinus.* **1942** in 1944 *ADD* (at *diddledees*), What you call pine leaves all depends on the section of the country in which you live. They are known as needles, spills, pins, twinkles, diddledees, straws, tags, and shats. **1966** *DARE* (Qu. T6, *The pointed leaves that fall from pine trees*) Inf **AR5,** Pine pens.

pin n[2] See **pen** n[1]

pinacate bug n Also *pinacate (beetle);* prob by folk-etym *pity cardy* [MexSpan *pinacate* < Nahuatl *pinacatl*] **SW**
Any of several darkling beetles of the genus *Eleodes.* Also called **circus beetle, stink ~**

1895 Comstock–Comstock *Manual Insects* 584, The most common species [of *Eleodes*] are large, smooth, club-shaped beetles . . commonly known as Pinacate-bugs. **1905** Kellogg *Amer. Insects* 288, The most familiar of them [=darkling beetles] on the Pacific coast are large, awkwardly moving, shining black pinacate bugs, Eleodes . . , which, when disturbed by the turning over of their covering stone, stand on their fore legs and head and emit an ill-smelling fluid from the tip of the abdomen. **1924** *Century Illustr. Mag.* 108.389 **AZ,** Usually, however, you will see the *corredor del camino* catching lizards or picking up black pinacate-beetles. **1936** AZ Univ. *Genl. Bulletin* 3.115, Probably the best known beetle of the state is the Pinacate or the beetle that stands on its head. **1965** Teale *Wandering Through Winter* 21 **CA,** Advancing laboriously over the bare ground moved a swollen, jet-black beetle. . . Disturbed, it stopped, lifted its body almost vertically in the air, balanced itself on long, katydid-like hind legs and stood on its head in the sand. We were seeing the famed circus or pinacate beetle of the dry Southwest. **1967–68** *DARE* (Qu. R30, *. . Kinds of beetles; not asked in early QRs*) Inf **CA12,** Pity cardy [ˌpɪtiˈkɑrdi]; **CA87,** Stink bug or [ˈpɪnəkɑrtɛɪ] [sic].

pinao n |pi'nau| **HI**
=**dragonfly.**
 1933 Bryan *Hawaiian Nature* 172, There are five kinds of dragonflies, or *pinao,* in these islands, besides a number of smaller kinds, called damsel flies. **1967** *DARE* (Qu. R2, . . *The dragonfly*) Inf **HI**4, Pinao [pi'nau]. **1994** Stone–Pratt *Hawai'i's Plants* 225, The giant aeshid *Anax strenuus* with a wingspan of up to 6 in., . . known as pinao to Hawaiians, is the largest native Hawaiian insect and the largest insect in the United States.

pinawinda n Also *pindawinda, piny windy* [Pronc-spp for **pride of India 1**]
=**Chinaberry 1.**
 1950 *PADS* 15.52 **SC**, *Piny windy*. . . The *pride of India*. Negro folk etymology. **1974** Morton *Folk Remedies* 95 **SC**, *Chinaberry Tree; "Pinawinda;" "Pindawinda."* . . *Melia azedarach.* . . Commonly grown in yards; generally planted very close to rural dwellings.

pinback n
The horn shark *(Heterodontus francisci).*
 1970 *DARE* (Qu. P4, *Saltwater fish that are not good to eat*) Inf **CA**191, Pinback—type of shark. [**1983** *Audubon Field Guide N. Amer. Fishes* 331, *Horn Shark.* . . *Each dorsal fin preceded by spine.* . . Divers off southern California find them easy to approach and thus good photographic subjects.]

pinball n [From the form and shape of the flower head]
=**buttonbush 1.**
 1892 *Jrl. Amer. Folkl.* 5.97 **NH**, *Cephalanthus occidentalis,* pin-ball. **1960** Vines *Trees SW* 938, Vernacular names for the shrub [= *Cephalanthus occidentalis*] are . . Pinball . . and Crouper-brush.

pin-basket n Also *pincushion* [Engl dial]
The youngest child in a family.
 1813 in 1833 *New Engl. Mag.* 5.265 **VA**, I was left by my father an orphan, when too young to be sensible of my loss. The first thing that I can remember, is, finding myself in my mother's family, the *pin-basket* of the whole house. **1899** (1912) Green *VA Folk-Speech* 322, *Pin-basket.* . . The youngest child of a family. **1912** *Ibid* 322, *Pincushion.* . . A small cushion on which pins are stuck. The youngest child and pet of the parents: "Mammy's pincushion."

pin birch n
=**gray birch a.**
 1894 *Jrl. Amer. Folkl.* 7.98 **ME**, *Betula populifolia,* . . pin-birch, Penobscot Co., Me. . . A name given especially to the young trees, an inch or more in diameter, which are cut into hoop-poles, etc. **1940** Clute *Amer. Plant Names* 161, *B[etula] populifolia.* . . Pin birch.

pincers n Cf **pilchard**
A **herring** n[1] **1** (here: *Harengula humeralis*).
 1896 U.S. Natl. Museum *Bulletin* 47.431, *Sardinella humeralis.* . . *Pincers.* . . Abundant from Pensacola and Cedar Keys southward.

pinch ant n Also *pincher, pinching ant* Cf **piss ant** n **1**
See quot.
 1967–69 *DARE* (Qu. R17, . . *Names . . for the big black ants that sting*) Infs **CA**136, **NJ**2, Pinchers; **KY**35, Piss ants or pinch ants; **MO**15, Pinchin' ant.

pinch bug n Also *pincher (bug), pinching beetle,* ~ *bug* chiefly **N Midl, N Cent** See Map
Usu =**stag beetle;** occas another large beetle.
 1850 Garrard *Wah-to-yah* 253 **West**, Noah was so hurried to git the yelaphants, pinchin bugs, an' sich varment aboard. **1875** (1876) Twain *Tom Sawyer* 57 **MO**, It was a large black beetle with formidable jaws—a "pinch-bug," he called it. **1877** Burdette *Rise & Fall* 77 **IA**, That Bilderback boy. . . put a pinching-bug as big as a postage-stamp down a boy's back. **1909** Wason *Happy Hawkins* 183 *(DAE)*, You'll have to do a master job of painting to make that William goat look like a pinchin' bug. **1915** Bryan *Nat. Hist. HI* 417, The stag-beetles or pinch bugs, so called on account of their large mandibles. **1928** Metcalf–Flint *Destructive & Useful Insects* 16, A certain amount of pain may result from mere mechanical injury by insects as when a boy finds a "pinching bug" for the first time. **1942** McAtee *Dial. Grant Co. IN* 49 (as of 1890s), *Pinch-bug* . . the large black beetle *(Passalus cornutus)* found in rotten logs. **1950** *WELS* **WI** *(Big brown beetle that comes out in large num-*

bers *between spring and summer and flies with a buzzing sound)* 3 Infs, Pinch bug(s); 1 Inf, Stag beetle, pinch bug; 1 Inf, Pinch bugs same as June bug. **1954** Borror–DeLong *Intro. Insects* 381, Family *Lucanidae.* . . These large brownish beetles are sometimes called pinchingbugs because of the large mandibles of the males. **c1960** *Wilson Coll.* **csKY**, Pinch-bug (or pinching-bug). . . Any large beetle. **1965–70** *DARE* (Qu. R5, *A big brown beetle that comes out in large numbers in spring and early summer, and flies with a buzzing sound*) 23 Infs, **chiefly Missip-Ohio Valleys, N Midl, MI**, Pinch bug; **IL**4, Pinch bug—bigger than a June bug; **MD**3, Pinch bug—this has pincers in front to pinch its enemies—like a roach—about one inch long—blackish color—quite different from June bug; **MO**1, The pinch bug is a little different from them [=June bugs], aren't they? They have more of a pincer up near the snout; **NY**223, Pinch bug—different from June bug; **PA**17, June bug flies—pinch bug on the ground, black; **OH**84, Pinch bug—same as June bug; **DE**4, June bug—kids call these pinchers; **NJ**2, **OH**45, 65, **PA**1, Pinching bug; (Qu. R30, . . *Kinds of beetles;* not asked in early QRs) Infs **IA**14, **IN**17, 67, **KS**20, **OH**28, 60, 67, **PA**213, Pinch bug; **IA**29, Pinching bug or pinch bug—have a pincher; **MI**14, Pinch bugs—could bite pretty hard; **MI**65, Pinch bug—have those big jaws; **WI**37, Pinch bug—large, black, clawlike things in the front; **KY**16, Pincher bug; **MO**20, Pinching beetle; **IL**21, 119, **IN**62, **MI**101, Pinching bug; **IL**14, Pinching bug—large black clawed beetle—looks like a crawdaddy; (Qu. HH22b, . . *A very mean person* . . *"He's meaner than _____."*) Inf **OH**42, Pinchin' bug. **1980** Milne–Milne *Audubon Field Guide Insects* 552, Because adults [of the family Lucanidae] sometimes pinch with their mandibles, they are also called pinching bugs.

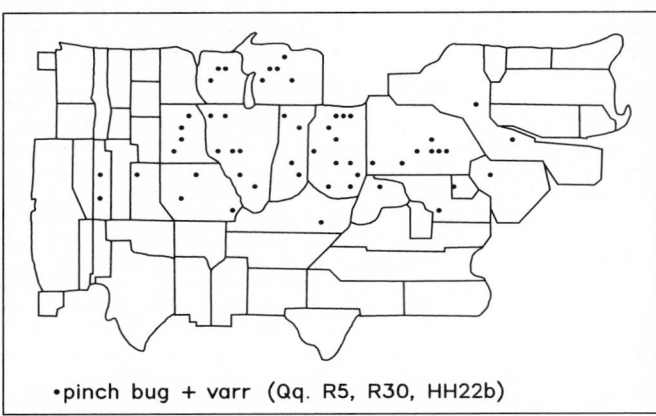

•pinch bug + varr (Qq. R5, R30, HH22b)

pincher n
1 See **pinch ant.**
2 See **pinch bug.**

pincher bug n
1 See **pinch bug.**
2 An earwig (Dermaptera).
 1968 *DARE* FW Addit **LA**23, *Pincher bug*—another name for earwig.

pin cherry n
1 A small, often shrubby cherry tree *(Prunus pensylvanica);* also the fruit of this tree. **Nth, esp MI, MN, WI** See Map
Also called **bird cherry 1b, dogwood 8, fire cherry, Peruvian, pigeon cherry, red** ~ **1, wild** ~
 1884 Sargent *Forests of N. Amer.* 66, *Prunus Pennsylvanica.* . . Pin Cherry. [*Ibid* 67, The small fruit used domestically and by herbalists in the preparation of cough mixtures, etc.] **1897** Sudworth *Arborescent Flora* 240, *Prunus pennsylvanica.* . . *Common Names.* . . Pin Cherry (N.H., Vt., N.Y., Mich., Ohio, Iowa, N. Dak.) **1913** Otis *MI Trees* 159, *Pin Cherry.* . . Abundant on sand-lands; roadsides; burned-over lands; clearings; hillsides. . . Rapid of growth. Short-lived. **1928** Rosendahl–Butters *Trees MN* 226, *Pin Cherry.* . . Fruit . . light red, . . its flesh thin and sour. **1950** *WELS* **WI** *(Fruits that grow wild in your neighborhood)* 5 Infs, Pin cherry; *(Different kinds of wild cherries in your neighborhood)* 23 Infs, Pin cherry (*or cherries*). **1961** Douglas *My Wilderness* 284 **nME**, Pin cherries by the dozens also had their white blossoms on display. **1965–70** *DARE* (Qu. I46, . . *Kinds of fruits that grow wild around here*) 28 Infs, 23 **MI, MN, WI**, Pin cherries; (Qu. I44, *What kinds of berries grow wild around here?*) Infs **MN**6, **MA**6, Pin cherries;

(Qu. T16, . . *Kinds of trees* . . *'special'*) Infs **MI**14, **WI**78, Pin cherry. **1972** Evers–Link *Poisonous Plants MW* 77, Pin cherry. . . grows in dry or moist woods and in recent burns and openings.   **1989** Mosher *Stranger* 266 **nVT** (as of 1952), I came out of the blackberry cane patch by a pin cherry tree growing on the very brink of the quarry.

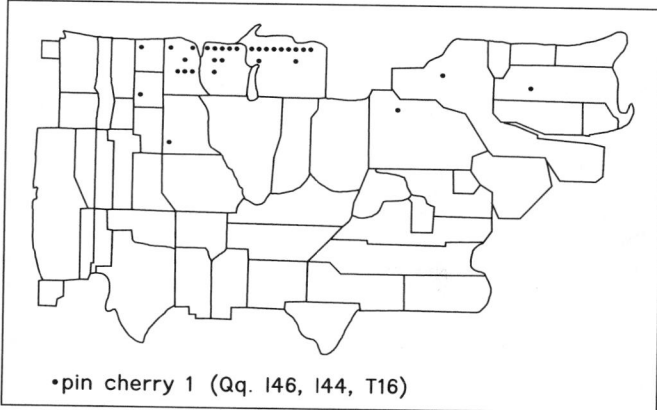

•pin cherry 1 (Qq. l46, l44, T16)

2 The bitter cherry (*Prunus emarginata*).

1931 U.S. Dept. Ag. *Misc. Pub.* 101.69, *Bitter cherry (P[runus] emarginata)*, known also as bird cherry, . . pin cherry, and quinine cherry, is perhaps the commonest and best known of the native western true cherries. . . It is frequently claimed to be poisonous, but probably because it has been confused with the chokecherries.   **1966** *DARE* (Qu. 146, . . *Kinds of fruits that grow wild around here*) Inf **WA**13, Pin cherry.

pinchers n pl, sometimes constr as sg **widely scattered, but esp freq Nth, Midl, TX**   See Map
Pincers, pliers, or a similar tool.

1820 in 1956 Eliason *Tarheel Talk* 315 **nw,cnNC**, Pinchers.   **1848** *Scientific Amer.* 4.27, The soldering of two pieces of scale [of tortoise shell] is easily effected, by placing their edges together . . and then squeezing them between the long flat jaws of hot iron pinchers.   **1861** Holmes *Venner* 2.182 **NEng**, Bring down a pair of pinchers and a file.   **1876** Knight *Amer. Mech. Dict.* 3.1706, *Pinchers*. An instrument having two handles and two grasping jaws, formed of two pieces pivoted together. . Pinchers are adapted for special work, such as drawing nails, for shoemakers' work. . . common pinchers. . . lasting-pinchers. . . shoemakers' pinchers. . . cutting pinchers.   **1899** (1912) Green *VA Folk-Speech* 322, *Pinchers*. . . A metal implement for seizing and holding. Pincers.   **1909** *DN* 3.357 **eAL, wGA**, *Pinchers*. . . Pincers. The latter form is rarely if ever heard.   **1912** *DN* 3.585 **wIN**, *Pinchers*. . . Pincers, which is never heard.   **1915** *DN* 4.187 **swVA**, *Pinchers*. . . Has completely replaced *pincers*.   **1937** *AmSp* 12.103 **eNE** [Farm terms], The farmer commonly pronounces the word *pincers* as *pinchers*.   **1965–70** *DARE* (Qu. F33, *A small tool that you hold in one hand, with 'jaws' for gripping things*) 103 Infs, **widespread, but less freq S Midl, Gulf States, CA**, Pinchers; **MO**8, Wire pinchers; **NY**34, Pair of pinchers; **MI**68, **WI**76, Pincher; (Qu. K70, *Words used* . . *for castrating an animal*) Inf **IL**62A, Use pinchers or emasculators.   **1969** *DARE* Tape **CT**36, I would always busy myself [in a blacksmith's shop]. . . I'd . . put the pinchers on the mean horse's nose and hold the pinchers.

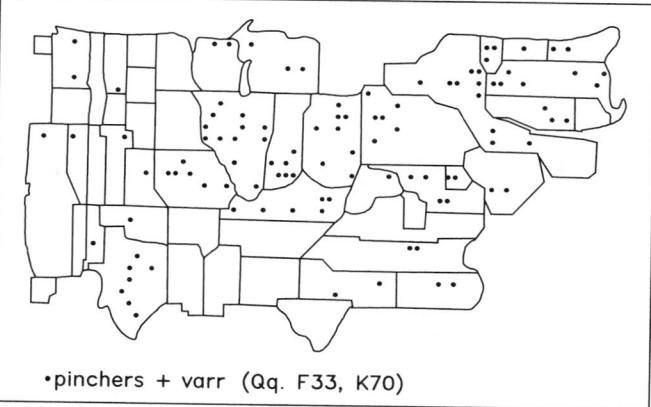

•pinchers + varr (Qq. F33, K70)

pinching ant   See **pinch ant**

pinching beetle   See **pinch bug**

pinching bug n
1 See **pinch bug**.
2 =**hellgrammite 1.**
   1890 *Century Dict.* 4495 **wPA**, *Pinching-bug*. . . The dobson or hellgrammite.

Pinchot (road) n |ˈpɪnčo| [Gifford *Pinchot*, governor of Pennsylvania 1923–27]   **PA**
=**macadam** n **1**; hence v *pinchot* to **macadamize** a road.
   1935 *AmSp* 10.172, A recent governor of Pennsylvania has given his name to a type of road new in the state. Many miles of road made of light surface macadam were built during the administration of Governor Gifford Pinchot. While these roads are not officially so called, they are universally known as *Pinchot roads* and are seldom referred to in any other way. The verb is *to pinchot*.   **1967–68** *DARE* (Qu. N21, *Roads that are surfaced with smooth black pavement*) Inf **CO**7, Pinchot—in Pennsylvania called after a Governor Pinchot; Pinchot "got the farmers out of the mud"; **PA**165, Pinchot [ˈpɪnčo] roads; (Qu. N23, *Other kinds of paved roads*) Inf **PA**27, Pinchot—he was a governor—he said he will get the farmer out of the mud. Named (hard) road after him.   **1979** *DARE* File **wPA**, You'd drive up the hill on the Pinchot, then turn off on the red dog.   **1980** *Ibid* **wPA**, A Pinchot road was made with a shale and clay bottom, blacktopped. The purpose was to help farmers to get their crops to market where roads had been very bad before.   **1981** *Ibid* **nwPA**, As an aid to the farmers they pinchoted the roads.

pinchy adj [Var of *pinching*]
1 Stingy, niggardly.   Cf **chinchy**
   1966–67 *DARE* (Qu. U33, *Names or nicknames for a stingy person*) Inf **OK**18, Uncle Pinchy; (Qu. U34, . . *'Stingy,' especially when a person saves money in a mean way*; total Infs questioned, 75) Inf **OK**18, Pinchy; (Qu. U36b, . . *A person who saves in a mean way or is greedy in money matters: "She certainly is _____."*) Infs **IL**12, **KS**2, Pinchy.   **1996** *DARE* File **sTX**, A related form [to *chinchy* "stingy"] . . is "pinchy," usually pronounced with a somewhat Hispanicized raised /iy/.
2 Of the weather: cool, chilly.
   1984 Wilder *You All Spoken Here* 140 **Sth**, *Pinchy*: Biting cold.   **1986** Pederson *LAGS Concordance* (*It's rather snappy this morning*) 2 infs, **AL**, 1 inf, **MS**, Pinchy; 1 inf, **csTN**, Pinchy—a little cold; 1 inf, **cwAL**, It's a little pinchy (=cool) this morning.

Pinckster   See **pinkster 1**

pin clover n [From the slender, pointed fruit; cf **needle n 2**]   **esp CA**   Cf **pin grass 1, pinweed 2**
A **storksbill** (here: either *Erodium cicutarium* or *E. moschatum*).
   1884 Miller *Dict. Engl. Names of Plants* 106, *Pin-grass*, or *Pin-clover*, of California. *Erodium cicutarium*.   **1889** Vasey *Ag. Grasses* 102, *Erodium cicutarium* (Alfilaria). . . is known as storksbill, pin clover, pin grass, and filaree; it is neither a grass nor a clover, but belongs to the geranium family.   **1896** *Jrl. Amer. Folkl.* 6.183 **CA**, *Erodium cicutarium*, . . pin clover. . . *Erodium moschatum*, . . pin clover.   **1911** CA Ag. Exper. Sta. Berkeley *Bulletin* 217.1002, *Erodium cicutarium*. . . *Erodium moschatum*. . . Pin clover and pin grass apply to either species. . . No distinction has been drawn between [these] . . as to their honey producing merits.   **1961** Wills–Irwin *Flowers TX* 141, With very similar fruits but much smaller pink flowers and larger finely dissected leaves [than *Erodium texanum*] is Filaree or Pin-clover, *E. cicutarium*.

pinco   See **penco**

pincushion n
1 Any of var plants, as:
a also *pincushion flower, pincushions*: =**mourning bride**. [*OED2* 1856 →; see quot 1993]
   1890 *Century Dict.* 4495, *Pincushion*. . . A plant of the genus *Scabiosa*, the scabious: so called with reference to the soft convex flower-head.   **1901** Jepson *Flora CA* 476, *S[cabiosa] atropurpurea*. . . *Mourning Bride*. . . Called "Pin Cushion" by children at East Oakland.   **1917** Bailey *Std. Cyclop. Horticul.* 6.3564, *Scabiosa atropurpurea*.—The mourning bride or pin-cushion flower.   **1940** Clute *Amer. Plant*

Names 105, *S[cabiosa] arvensis.* . . Pincushions. *S. australis.* Pincushion flower. **1961** Thomas *Flora Santa Cruz* 327 **cwCA,** *S[cabiosa] atropurpurea.* . . Pincushion. Becoming increasingly common along roads and highways . . ; probably flowering the year around. **1976** Bailey–Bailey *Hortus Third* 1014, *[Scabiosa] atropurpurea.* . . *Pincushions.* . . Naturalized in Calif. **1993** Comstock Ferre *1993 Seed Catalog* 23, *Pincushion Flower (S[cabiosa] atropurpurea).* . . Plant . . bearing rounded flowers with floral parts resembling pins in a pincushion.

b A **cudweed 1** (here: *Gnaphalium obtusifolium*).

1892 *Garden and Forest* 5.614 **MA,** The omnipresent Life-everlasting. . . Here in Hingham many people call them Pincushions, from their round ball-like effect, with tiny black spots like the heads of pins scattered over them.

c pl: =**devil's bit.**

1896 *Jrl. Amer. Folkl.* 9.190 **OH,** *Scabiosa succisa* [=*Succisa pratensis*], pin cushions, Sulphur Grove, Ohio.

d also *pincushion flower, ~ plant:* =**morning brides. West**

1933 *Torreya* 33.59 **nAZ,** In this world of picturesque grandeur. . . [is] the pure white *pincushion flower (Chaenactis douglasii).* **1941** Jaeger *Wildflowers* 298, Mohave Pincushion. *Chaenactis macrantha.* . . A low annual, with reddish-brown stems, pink-tipped florets, and whitish bracts, which appear as if covered with flour. **1960** Abrams *Flora Pacific States* 4.245, *Chaenactis fremontii.* . . Fremont Pincushion. . . Open desert. **1964** Munz *Shore Wildflowers* 22, *Pincushion Flower (Chaenactis glabriuscula)* . . ; its many yellow florets are arranged in a compact head, but all of them are tubular, the outer somewhat enlarged. . . It occurs in the interior and coastal regions of much of California. **1971** Dodge *100 Desert Wildflowers* 94, Both [=*Chaenactis fremontii* and *C. glabriuscula*] are spring flowering annuals and, in common with other members of the genus, sometimes called "pincushion plants." **1979** Spellenberg *Audubon Guide N. Amer. Wildflowers W. Region* 353, *Esteve's Pincushion (Chaenactis stevioides).* . . A small, openly branched plant with heads of *white disk flowers,* those around the edge larger and somewhat ray-like. **1995** *Smithsonian* Mar 80 **AZ,** A few desert basins have been freckled with white dots of pincushion flowers.

e See **pincushion tree.**

f See **pincushion cactus.**

2 also *pincushion fish:* A **burfish** (here: *Chilomycterus schoepfi*).

1882 U.S. Natl. Museum *Proc.* 5.619 **SC,** *Chilomycterus geometricus.* . . Pin-cushion. Very abundant. Very young specimens have the body soft and flabby, with the spines admitting of considerable movement because of the looseness of the skin; . . the belly is often of purplish black, with pink spines. **1966–70** *DARE* (Qu. P4, *Saltwater fish that are not good to eat*) Inf **GA11,** Pincushion; **SC69,** Blowfish—called pincushion; **SC63,** Pincushion fish.

3 also *needle cushion, walking pincushion:* =**porcupine.**

1968 *DARE* (Qu. P31, . . *Names or nicknames* . . *for the* . . *porcupine*) Infs **NJ13, NV8,** Pincushion; **CA80,** Walking pincushion; **NY76,** Needle cushion.

4 See **pin-basket.**

pincushion cactus n Also *pincushion*

1 A **cactus B1** of the genus *Mammillaria.* Also called **finger cactus,** *fishhook cactus* (at **fishhook 1**), **nipple cactus, strawberry ~.** For other names of var spp see **devil's-head 1, pitayita, sunset cactus**

1882 *Bot. Gaz.* 7.9 **AZ,** The way was along a sandy creek wash, with patches of boulders and occasional steep ascents, the whole way beset with cacti of varied degrees of formidable armature, from the innocent pincushion cactus, that only catches to your feet and clothing with its fishhook spines while the other straight spines tickle you, to the horrid, wide-branching tree cactus. **1896** *Jrl. Amer. Folkl.* 9.188 **AZ,** *Mammillaria Grahami,* . . pin-cushion cactus. **1898** Davidson *CA Plants* 244, *Mammillaria.* Pincushion Cactus. Small, more or less globose plants with spines borne on oval or conic tubercles which cover the plant. **1915** (1926) Armstrong–Thornber *Western Wild Flowers* 310, *Pincushion Cactus.* . . Sometimes we see one of these prickly little balls peeping from under a rock and again we find them growing in a colony, looking much like a pile of sea-urchins. **1942** Hylander *Plant Life* 322, Some of the Pincushions range north of Texas into the plains area. **1961** Douglas *My Wilderness* 82 **AZ,** The century plant, the prickly-pear cactus, and the delicate pincushion cactus are scattered over

the entire lower slopes. **1968** *DARE* (Qu. S26e, *Other wildflowers not yet mentioned;* not asked in early QRs) Inf **CA91,** Pincushion cactus. **1970** Correll *Plants TX* 1100, *Pin-cushion Cactus.* . . Perhaps 100 species from California to Nevada, Utah, New Mexico, Oklahoma and Texas. **1985** Dodge *Flowers SW Deserts* 52, Pincushion Cactus. . . the little *Mammillarias.* . . Being small and forming low clumps, or with single pincushion like stems, they often escape attention except when glorified with bright, comparatively large flowers, which frequently form a crown around the top of the plant.

2 also *cushion cactus:* =**barrel cactus.** Cf **devil's pincushion 1**

1924 Austin *Land of Journeys' Ending* 127 **AZ,** There are scores of variations of the bisnaga type, "niggerhead," "fish-hook," and "cushion" cacti, running to fat button shapes or short thickened cylinders, widely distributed through the Southwest. **1939** Tharp *Vegetation TX* 63, Pincushion Cacti (*Echinocactus* spp.) are widespread westward.

3 also *cushion cactus:* A **cactus B1** of the genus *Coryphantha.* Also called **nipple cactus.** For other names of *C. vivipara* see **foxtail cactus, snowball ~**

1940 Benson *Cacti AZ* 121, *Arizona pincushion.* (*Coryphantha arizonica* . .). This plant occurs in northern Arizona and in the mountains somewhat to the southward. **1942** Hylander *Plant Life* 322, The Missouri Pincushion [=*Coryphantha missouriensis*] grows solitary or in masses to a foot in diameter among the grasses from Texas and Missouri to Montana and Kansas. **1967** *DARE* Tape IA8, You get out there in Nebraska in the middle of the summer. . . He'd . . clear off a place for the tent, shovel off the cactus . . so much of . . the pincushion cactus. **1973** Hitchcock–Cronquist *Flora Pacific NW* 301, Cushion c[actus] . . *C[oryphantha] vivipara.* **1973** *AZ Highways* 20, The Arizona Pincushion (*Coryphantha vivipara*) prefers the cooler, wetter climate near Sedona.

4 A **hedgehog cactus 3** (here: *Echinocereus triglochidiatus* var *melanacanthus*).

1940 Benson *Cacti AZ* 119, *Mammillaria aggregata* [=*Echinocereus triglochidiatus* var *melanacanthus*]. . . Common pincushion. . . Low-growing cactus with stems often forming mounds several inches to 2 feet high and up to 2 feet in diameter; stems usually clustered . . , the stem surface obliterated by spines. **1967** Dodge *Roadside Wildflowers* 46, *Arizona pincushion.* . . This small, globular representative of the pincushion cactus group blossoms in May and June. . . *Mammillaria aggregata* [=*Echinocereus triglochidiatus* var *melanacanthus*].

5 A **cactus B1** of the genus *Pediocactus.* For other names of *P. simpsonii* see **snowball cactus**

1952 Davis *Flora ID* 481, *Pediocactus.* . . Pincushion Cactus. **1953** Nelson *Plants Rocky Mt. Park* 107, *Pediocactus simpsonii* var. *minor.* . . The most common cactus in this region most aptly described by the name "pincushion." **1957** Roberts–Nelson *Wildflowers CO* 25, *Echinocactus simpsonii.* . . The body of this plant is a round ball about 3 to 6 inches in diameter covered with cone-shaped tubercules in a spiral arrangement, each of these tipped with a cluster of spines. . . The term "pincushion" is given to many cacti of this type and larger but this is the perfect one for the name as it might go into a large sewing basket.

pincushion daisy n

A **gaillardia B** (here: *Gaillardia suavis*).

1961 Wills–Irwin *Flowers TX* 241, *Pincushion Daisy—Gaillardia suavis. Ibid* 242, Pincushion Daisy makes up for lack of visual attraction by its odor, rather suggestive of that of gardenias.

pincushion fish See **pincushion 2**

pincushion flower n

1 See **pincushion 1a.**

2 See **pincushion 1d.**

3 A **buttonbush 1** (here: *Cephalanthus occidentalis*). Cf **Spanish pincushion**

1974 Morton *Folk Remedies* 39 **SC,** *Pincushion Flower* . . *Cephalanthus occidentalis.* . . Flowers heavily fragrant, white, slim, tubular, with prominent stamens, massed in spherical "pincushion" heads to 1½ in. wide.

pincushion moss n

=**white moss** (here: *Leucobryum* spp).

1942 Hylander *Plant Life* 96, The Pin Cushion Moss (*Leucobryum*) . .

forms hemispherical cushions at the base of trees in damp woods. The compact habit of the closely growing Pin Cushion Mosses is very different from the loose and spongy mass of Sphagnum plants. *Ibid* 641, Pin-cushion Moss—Leucobryum glaucum. **1961** Douglas *My Wilderness* 242 **ME,** A pincushion moss made a sturdy stand in dry gravel.

pincushion plant See **pincushion 1d**

pincushions See **pincushion 1a**

pincushion tree n Also *pincushion* [*EDD* 1896]
=**highbush cranberry.**

 1890 *Century Dict.* 4495, Pincushion. . . Also applied locally to various other plants, as the snowball, *Viburnum Opulus,* sometimes called *pincushion-tree.* **1960** Teale *Journey into Summer* 10, A cranberry tree spread its broad, three-pointed leaves. This north-country viburnum, *Viburnum opulus* [here: =*V. edule*], is variously known as the squaw bush, the water elder, the high-bush cranberry and the pincushion tree.

pinda, pindar (pea) See **pinder**

pindawinda See **pinawinda**

pinder n Also *pender, pinda, pindar (pea), pindor, pinduh* [Kongo *mpinda; OED2* 1692 →] **chiefly S Atl, Gulf States** See Map
=**peanut 1.**

 [**1830** Rafinesque *Med. Flora* 2.194, *Arachis hypogaea.* . . *Ground Nut, Pea Nut.* Cultivated from Maryland to Florida. . . Called *Pindars* in the West Indies.] **c1840** in 1976 Rose *Doc. Hist. Slavery* 353 **SC,** A field of suitable size shall be planted in pindars, & cultivated in the same manner as the general crop, the produce of which is to be divided equally among the work-hands. **1848** U.S. Patent Office *Annual Rept. for 1847* 190, The *ground pea* of the south, or . . the *gouber* or *pindar pea,* is highly recommended in the Tallahassee Floridian. **1867** *De Bow's Rev.* 3.365 **Sth,** Make on the plantation everything that can be made suitable for man and beast . . peas of all kinds, especially the Pindor. **1869** Porcher *Resources* 227 **Sth,** *Groundnut; Pindar; Peanut; Goobernut.* . . Brought by the Negroes from Africa. . . The fruit preserves its germinative powers for forty years. **1888** Jones *Negro Myths* 60 **GA coast,** Groun-mole . . bin er root up de tetter patch, an stroy pinder. **1893** Shands *MS Speech* 50, Pinder ['pɪndə]. The common name for *peanut* in the southern and central portions of the State. **1897** (1952) McGill *Narrative* 15 **SC,** It is asserted that boys, like him, could not be kept from eating raw turnips, potatoes and pinders. **1906** *DN* 3.150 **nwAR,** Pindar [pɪndə]. . . Peanut. **1909** *DN* 3.317 **eAL, wGA,** Groun(d)-pea. . . The peanut, goober, pinder. All four words are used, but perhaps *goober* is the favorite. **1917** *DN* 4.421 **LA,** Pender ['pɛndə]. . . Peanut. **1922** Gonzales *Black Border* 318 **sSC, GA coasts** [Gullah glossary], Pinduh—pindar. **1926** TX Folkl. Soc. *Pub.* 5.56, In the valleys of the Red River of Louisiana and the Sabine River of Louisiana and Texas, are to be found negroes who use many African words, the inheritance of their ancestors. . . A ground-nut (peanut) is a "pinda." **1940** *Sat. Eve. Post* 6 Apr 17 **Sth,** [They] did field work . . , shaking penders and pulling fodder. **1949** Turner *Africanisms* 199 **sSC, GA coasts** [Gullah], [Words used in conversation:] ['pɪnda ('pɪnə)] 'peanut.' **1956** McAtee *Some Dialect NC* 57 **SC,** Pinder . . peanut, especially the one-seeded Spanish peanut. "Boiled pinders." Bamberg County, S.C. **1965–70** *DARE* (Qu. I42, . . *Names or nicknames . . for peanuts*) 50 Infs, **chiefly S Atl, Gulf States,** Pinders; **FL19, NJ69, NC38,**

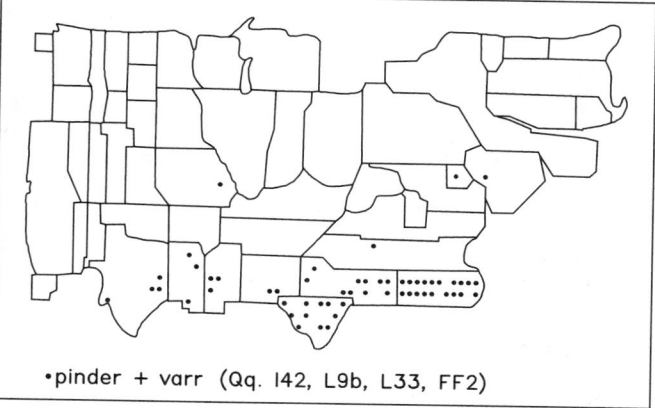

•pinder + varr (Qq. I42, L9b, L33, FF2)

['pɛndəz]; **GA1,** ['pɛndəz]; **LA24,** ['pɪndəz]; (Qu. L9b, *Hay from other kinds of plants [not grass];* not asked in early QRs) Inf **GA19,** Pinder tops; (Qu. L33, *How is the grain separated from the straw nowadays?*) Inf **FL50,** Pinder sheller; (Qu. FF2, . . *Kinds of parties*) Inf **SC26,** Pick pinders. **1966** *Greenville Advocate* (AL) 3 Nov 2/1, In Greenville, the peanut might be *goober, ground pea* or *pender,* but never *peener*—not even when combined with butter. **1968** *DARE* FW Addit **GA22,** A "pinder" has only one nut in it; a "goober" has two; **NC,** Pinda—pronounced ['pɪndə]; a peanut. **1986** Pederson *LAGS Concordance* **Gulf Region,** 135 infs, Pinder(s); 2 infs, Pinder field; 2 infs, Pinder nut(s); 1 inf, Pinder patch.

pindle v [Prob ult < *pine* + *-le* frequentative suffix; cf *EDD* *pindling* "Fretful, fractious, tiresome" and *pinder* "To waste away; to pine," *pindered* "Puny, ill-developed"] Cf **pindling** To waste away, dwindle, languish.

 1893 Owen *Voodoo Tales* 13 **MO** [Black], Ef yo' don't tell de bees 'bout all de bornin's an' weddin's an' fun'als dey gwinter (going to) cl'ar out or else sorter pindle (pine) an' die. **1898** Westcott *Harum* 324 **nNY,** Her health wa'n't jes' right, an' she showed it in her looks. I noticed that she'd pined an' pindled some, but I thought ther' was some natural crisscrossedniss mixed up into it too. **1931** *AmSp* 7.92 **eKY,** Poor Cora pindled along for a year after Jim was took with the breast-complaint afore she died.

pindling adj [**pindle**] **chiefly NEng, S Midl** Puny, sickly; also fig.

 1862 (1882) Stowe *Pearl of Orr's Is.* 25 **ME,** [The baby is] such a pindlin' little thing. **1887** Freeman *Humble Romance* 110 **NEng,** She was a quietly strong-minded, conscientious girl; but she was too delicate. . . "Seems to me Leviny's lookin' kinder pindlin', ain't she?" . . Marm Lawson sat up straighter and knitted firmly. "I don't see any reason why Leviny ain't well. She allers looks pale; it's her nateral color." **1902** (1904) [see **peaking**]. **1913** *DN* 4.5 **ME,** Pindling. . . Delicate; weak and sickly. "He was a pindlin' baby." **1914** *DN* 4.79 **ME, nNH,** Pindlin'. . . Weak, frail. **1914** Furman *Sight* 42 **KY,** And these few pindling present-day district-schools scattered here and yan they only spiles the young uns for work. **1923** *DN* 5.236 **swWI,** Pindlin'. **1926** *AmSp* 5.80 **ME,** A frail person is denoted as "pindlin." **1926** *DN* 5.402 **Ozarks,** Pindlin'. . . Weak, puny. "Them Injun young-uns is all kinder pindlin', 'pears like." **1936** Morehouse *Rain on Just* 13 **NC,** Dolly was a smart young un, . . for all her pindling size, her puny ways. **1941** *LANE* Map 459 *(Emaciated, peaked)* 5 infs, **ME, MA, NH, RI,** Pindling. **1942** (1971) Campbell *Cloud-Walking* 246 **seKY,** I told her they's a pindling chance it might do some good. **1944** *PADS* 2.20 **sAppalachians,** Pindling ['pɪndlɪŋ]. . . Ailing, weak; said of children. **1969** *DARE* (Qu. BB38, *When a person doesn't look healthy, or looks as if he hadn't been well for some time . . "He looks _____."*) Inf **MA69,** Pindling. **1978** Massey *Bittersweet Country* 207 **Ozarks,** Pindling (weakling): She was a pindling child. **1979** *DARE* File **cnMA** (as of c1915), When I was a child I used to hear women refer to children as *pindling,* meaning puny. A woman might have a frail or delicate child of her own, but other people had pindling children. "I saw her on the electric car the other day with that pindling little girl of hers." **1990** Cavender *Folk Med. Lexicon* 29 **sAppalachians,** Pindling—ailing and weak; child specific: "That boy was born pindling."

pindly adj
=**pindling.**

 1959 *VT Hist.* 27.152, Pindly. . . Thin; sickly; puny; trifling. . . Occasional. Bennington. **1968** Kellner *Aunt Serena* 148 **cIN** (as of c1920), Zeburn was small and pindly . . on account of her sister went and cut his hair . . before he was a year old, and stunted his growth. **1984** Wilder *You All Spoken Here* 201 **Sth,** Drinlin': Puny; pindly; frail; in old age and decay; has seen best days.

pindor, pinduh See **pinder**

pine n

 1 Std: a tree of the genus *Pinus.* For other names of var spp see **bastard pine, bigcone ~, bishop ~, black ~, book ~, Boston ~, bristlecone ~, brush ~, buckwheat ~, buffalo ~, bull ~, Caesar ~, candy ~, clabber ~, digger ~, fat ~ 1, forest ~, foxtail ~, glacier ~, gray ~, hard ~, hog ~, jack ~, Jefferson ~, Jeffrey ~, Jersey ~, knobcone ~, limber ~, loblolly ~, lodgepole ~, longleaf ~, long-needle ~, longtag ~, meadow ~ 1, Mexican white ~, Monterey ~, mountain**

~, **Norway** ~, **nut** ~, **ocote, piñon, pitch pine, pond** ~, **ponderosa** ~, **sand** ~, **shortleaf** ~, **slash** ~, **soft** ~, **spruce** ~, **sugar** ~, **Table Mountain** ~, **Torrey** ~, **white** ~, **whitebark** ~ Cf **lightwood** n[1]

2 The pineapple (*Ananas comosus*). [*DJE* 1657 →] **chiefly HI** Cf **wild pine**

[**1889** (1971) Farmer *Americanisms* 421, *Pine.*—A West Indian contraction for *pine-apple*—now generally adopted in England.] **1955** Day *HI People* 248, The value of the annual "pine" crop has risen. **1966–67** *DARE* Tape **FL30**, The man who picked the pines could walk down the row between these long sections; **HI2**, [FW:] Do they say pineapple regularly, or do they say pine? [Inf:] Well, they say both. More often maybe pine. **1972** Carr *Da Kine Talk* 144 **HI**, In Hawaii, the word *pine* usually refers to a pineapple rather than to a coniferous tree—a usage which frequently startles, and sometimes confuses, visitors to the Islands.

3 See **pineapple clip**.

pineapple cactus n

A **cactus B1** (here: *Sclerocactus polyancistrus*).

1858 (1935) Reid *Reid's Tramp* 91 **TX**, Here we first saw the globular and pineapple cacti. **1941** Jaeger *Wildflowers* 168 **Desert SW**, *Mohave Fishhook, Pineapple Cactus.* . . 8–12 in. high, shaped much like a pineapple. **1947** *So. Sierran* May 4/2 (*DA*), And last, rare and very beautiful, the Mohave Fishhook or Pineapple Cactus, Echinocactus Polyancistrus, with clustered iridescent magenta-pink blossoms, [was] seen in considerable number.

pineapple clip n Also pineapple (cut), ~ shave esp NEng

See quots.

1908 in 2001 Rompkey *Jessie Luther* 140 **RI**, He says it is a "lovely cut" I gave him, and I really begin to feel like a professional. I have not yet attempted a "pineapple" but imagine that would be easy, as one would not have to consider delicate gradations of length. **1967** *DARE* File **csMA** (as of c1945), *Pineapple clip, pineapple shave*—for "close haircut" or "butch haircut." **1969** *DARE* (Qu. X5, . . *Different kinds of men's haircuts*) Inf **CT23**, Pineapple clip—short all over; old-fashioned; **MA40**, Pineapple clip—hair cut short all around about a ¼″; **RI17**, Pineapple cut—all short.

pineapple palm n [See quots]

The Canary Island date palm (*Phoenix canariensis*).

1960 McGeachy *Hdbk. FL Palms* 21, *Phoenix canariensis.* . . This palm is often called the Pineapple Palm because of its pineapple-shaped trunk. **1980** Little *Audubon Guide N. Amer. Trees W. Region* 324, This popular street tree [=*Phoenix canariensis*]. . . is sometimes called "Pineapple-palm" from the resemblance of its trunk to that fruit.

pineapple plant n Also pineapple shrub

=**Carolina allspice**.

1898 *Jrl. Amer. Folkl.* 11.221 **eMA**, *Calycanthus floridus*, . . pine-apple plant. **1995** Brako et al. *Scientific & Common Names Plants* 205, Pineapple-shrub—*Calycanthus floridus*.

pineapple shave See pineapple clip

pineapple shrub See pineapple plant

pineapple weed n

A **wild chamomile** (here: *Matricaria matricarioides*) native to the Pacific states, but now widely naturalized elsewhere. Also called **manzanilla 1, wild marigold**

1908 Gray *New Manual Botany* 847, *Pineapple-weed.* . . odor of the bruised plant suggesting pineapple. **1931** Harned *Wild Flowers Alleghanies* 593, *Rayless Camomile.* . . Sometimes called Pineapple-weed, the bruised leaves yielding an odor resembling Pineapple fruit. . . Roadsides and old fields. **1961** Thomas *Flora Santa Cruz* 371 **cwCA**, Pineapple Weed. Very common throughout the Santa Cruz Mountains. **1987** Hughes–Blackwell *Wildflowers SE AK* 47, Pineapple Weed. . . flower heads are knob-like with only disk flowers. Leaves are dissected and lacy.

pine ball n

=**pinecone 1**; hence n *pineballer* one who gathers pine cones.

1968 *DARE* Tape **NJ53**, The little old pines is where they break the pine balls. And there's a place up here to Whiting's that's the biggest places I know of where they buy the pine balls and the . . different shrubs and everything. **1968** McPhee *Pine Barrens* 46 **NJ**, People who specialized in pine cones became known as pineballers, and the term is still used. The Christmas business continues to be an important source of income in the pines.

pine-bark stew n [See quots 1872, 1951] NC, SC

A fish stew.

[**1872** *Atlantic Mth.* 29.748, In these packages were strips of white pine bark, which in its dried state gives out the flavor of nutmegs—slightly bitter and fragrant.] **1940** Brown *Amer. Cooks* 49 **SC**, From the Up Country comes the famous Pine Bark Stew that has as many variations as has the Brunswick Stew and the Kentucky Burgoo. **1941** Writers' Program *Guide SC* 369 **neSC**, Bream and mollies are made into 'pine-bark stew,' and tall tales recounted around the bonfire. **1951** Brown *Southern Cook Book* 159, Pine Bark Stew, a fish stew with a dark brown color and pungent flavor, is a South Carolina Pee Dee River dish. . . Some sources state that the stew derives its name from the chocolate-like color similar to pine bark; others, from the pine bark used to kindle the open fire over which the stew is cooked. From *The Pee Dee Pepper Pot*, Darlington, South Carolina, is a third explanation: "Since seasonings were unobtainable during Revolutionary War days, the tender small roots of the Pine tree . . were used for flavoring (the stew). With homemade ketchup as a base, the only other seasoning was red pepper." **1952** Brown *NC Folkl.* 1.576, *Pine-bark stew.* . . Fish and vegetables stewed together.—Central and east. **1966** *DARE* (Qu. H45, *Dishes made with meat, fish, or poultry that everybody around here would know, but that people in other places might not*) Inf **NC3**, Pine-bark stew—cook vegetables with strip of lean, strip of fat, add fish (flounder), let cook several hours slow.

pine barren n, usu pl exc as attrib C and S Atl Cf piney woods 1

A region of poor, usu sandy, soil covered with pine forest.

1731 *PA Gaz.* (Philadelphia) 29 Apr–6 May 1/2, At our first setting out we had a sandy Pine Barren to walk in, which was covered pretty thick with large Pine Trees. **1743** Catesby *Nat. Hist. Carolina* 2 [app] iv, The third and worst kind of Land is the *Pine barren Land*, the Name implying its Character. The Soil is a light sterril Sand, productive of little else but Pine-Trees. **1775** (1962) Romans *Nat. Hist. FL* 15, First the pine land, commonly called pine barren, which makes up the largest body by far, the Peninsula being scarce any thing else. *Ibid* 117, These even overlooked the most useful places there, and planted their baronies in the pine barrens. **1810** Lambert *Travels* 3.2, The road which I had to travel lay through a dreary and extensive forest of pine trees, or as it is termed by the Carolinians, a *pine barren*, where an habitation is seldom seen, except at intervals of ten or twelve miles. **1860** in 1953 McMullen *Topog. Terms FL* 166, The poorest pine barren lands of Florida, will produce without manure, a luxuriant crop of Sisal Hemp. **1883** *Harper's New Mth. Mag.* 66.418 **NC**, Huge pine-barrens near the coast hindered the first efforts of the planter. **1968** *Atlantic Co. Rec.* (Mays Landing NJ) 8 Aug 8, [Headline:] Legislation Seen for Preserving of Pine Barrens. **1968** McPhee *Pine Barrens* 5 **NJ**, Settlers in the seventeenth and eighteenth centuries found these soils unpromising for farms, left the land uncleared, and began to refer to the region as the Pine Barrens. People in New Jersey still use the term. **1969** *DARE* FW Addit **swNJ**, *Pine barrens*—section of coastal plain of New Jersey where scrub pines grow; no good for farming.

pine-barren beauty n

1 =**pyxie moss**.

1883 W. Robinson *Eng. Flower Garden* 237/2 (*OED2*), Pine Barren Beauty . . is an evergreen shrub, yet smaller than many Mosses. **1901** Lounsberry *S. Wild Flowers* 406, Blossoms! Blossoms! fairly is this little pine-barren beauty covering itself with them. **1901** Bailey *Cyclop. Horticult.* 3.1475, The *Pyxie, Flowering Moss,* or *Pine-barren Beauty* is a pretty little creeping plant, native only to New Jersey and North Carolina. **1941** Writers' Program *Guide SC* 15, Here and there is found one of the loveliest little plants in the State—the pyxie, also known as flowering moss and pine barren beauty. **1976** Bailey–Bailey *Hortus Third* 932, [*Pyxidanthera*] *barbulata.* . . *Pine-barren-beauty.* . . Spring. N.J. to S.C.

2 =**galax**.

1959 Carleton *Index Herb. Plants* 92, *Pine-barren-beauty:* Galax aphylla; Pyxidanthera barbulata.

pine-barren crow n

The common crow (*Corvus brachyrhynchos*).

1955 *Oriole* 20.1.11 **GA**, Common Crow. . . Pine-barren Crow.

pine-barren gentian n Also *pine gentian*

A **gentian** (here: *Gentiana autumnalis*).

   1911 NJ State Museum *Annual Rept. for 1910* 640, *Pine Barren Gentian*. . . Damp sand of the Pine Barrens, frequent, and occasional in the southern part of the Cape May peninsula. **1946** Tatnall *Flora DE* 207, *G[entiana] Porphyrio*. . . Pine Barren Gentian. **1948** Wherry *Wild Flower Guide* 101, *Pine Gentian (G. porphyrio)*. . . One of the most beautiful of late-season flowers. **1968** Radford et al. *Manual Flora Carolinas* 840, *Pine-barren G[entian]*. . . Pocosins, savannahs and pine barrens.

pine-barren heather n

A **beach heather** (here: *Hudsonia ericoides*).

   1911 NJ State Museum *Annual Rept. for 1910* 561, *Hudsonia ericoides*. . . Pine Barren Heather. . . This is the "Heather" of the Pine Barrens; the characteristic species in the patches of open white sand. **1946** Tatnall *Flora DE* 178, *H[udsonia] ericoides*. . . *Pine Barren "Heather"*. . . Mid-May, early June. *H. tomentosa*. . . Beach "Heather".

pine-barren milkwort n

A **milkwort** (here: either *Polygala cymosa* or *P. ramosa*).

   1901 Lounsberry *S. Wild Flowers* 294, *Tall Pine-barren Milkwort*. . . *Polygala cymosa*. . . Two to four feet high. . . *P. ramosa*, low pine-barren milkwort, becomes when in bloom a most attractive individual and is very similar in growth to the above species, although altogether smaller. [*Ibid* 296, In low pine-barrens near Jacksonville, Fla. it [=*P. ramosa*] is often abundant.] **1946** Tatnall *Flora DE* 165, *P[olygala] ramosa*. . . Pine-barren Milkwort. . . *P. cymosa*. . . Tall Pine-barren Milkwort. **1949** Moldenke *Amer. Wild Flowers* 51, Quite showy are *P[olygala] cymosa* and *P. ramosa*, the *tall* and *low pinebarren-milkwort*, respectively, which inhabit low pinebarrens from Delaware to Florida and westward to Louisiana.

pine-barren rooter See **piney-woods rooter**

pine-barren terrapin n

=**box turtle.**

   1829 in 1836 NY Acad. Sci. *Annals Lyceum Nat. Hist.* 3.124, *Testudo clausa*. . . *Terrapene carolina*. . . Land turtle of the northern states; Pine-barren tarapin of the southern. **1884** Goode *Fisheries U.S.* 1.158, *The Carolina Box Turtle*. . . in the Southern States . . is known as the "Pine-barren Terrapin," and is also called "Cooter" by the negroes. It lives almost entirely on land.

pine-blang, pine-blank See **point-blank A2**

pine bluegrass n Cf **pine grass 1c**

A **bluegrass 1**: usu *Poa scabrella*, but also *P. secunda*.

   1937 U.S. Forest Serv. *Range Plant Hdbk.* G95, Many of the native bluegrasses, such as . . pine bluegrass *(P[oa] scabrella . .)*, . . are important range plants because they furnish an abundance of tender and nutritious forage. **1952** Davis *Flora ID* 123, *Pine Bluegrass*. . . Mont. to Wash., to Calif. **1961** Thomas *Flora Santa Cruz* 81 **cwCA**, Pine or Malpais Bluegrass. Rocky grassland and serpentine soils. **1973** Hitchcock–Cronquist *Flora Pacific NW* 663, From near sea level in Cal. to 10,000 ft in the R[ocky] M[ountains] . . pine b[luegrass].

pine bullfinch n

=**pine grosbeak.**

   1828 Bonaparte *Amer. Ornith.* 3.17, The female Pine Bullfinch is eight and a half inches long. **1844** DeKay *Zool. NY* 2.181, In this country [=the U.S.], the Pine Bulfinch ranges from the highest northern latitude to the 40th parallel. **1917** (1923) *Birds Amer.* 3.3, *Pine Grosbeak*. . . *Other Names*. . . Pine Bullfinch. **1946** Hausman *Eastern Birds* 579, Pine Bullfinch. . . A short, heavy, stout bird with a stout blackish bill.

pine burr n **chiefly Sth, S Midl** Cf **burr n¹ 2b**

=**pinecone 1.**

   1804 (1904) Clark *Orig. Jrls. Lewis & Clark Exped.* 1.149 **VA**, They Saw as well as my self Pine *burs* & Sticks of Birch in the Drift wood up [the White River]. **a1816** in 1848 GA Hist. Soc. *Coll.* 3.1.77, They collect old corn cobs and pine burs. **1836** Simms *Mellichampe* 1.186, You should be pelted with pine-burs, and I will undertake your punishment before the day is well over. **1899** (1912) Green *VA Folk-Speech* 322, *Pine-burr*. . . The cone of the pine-tree. **1966–67** DARE (Qu. T6) Inf **AR**48, Pine burrs [FW: =cones]; **SC**4, Cone—on the tree—(pine) burrs—on the ground. **1967** DARE FW Addit **AR**55, Pine burrs = pine

cones. **1969** *DARE* Tape **CA**165, [FW:] One house we went to put old branches from their juniper tree in the fireplace. [Inf:] Somebody puts pine burrs all inside, looks pretty that way.

pine bush n

A **rabbit brush 1b** (here: *Ericameria pinifolia*) native to California.

   1960 Abrams *Flora Pacific States* 4.286, *Haplopappus pinifolius*. . . Pine-bush. . . Stout shrub. . . Dry slopes and washes. **1981** Benson–Darrow *Trees SW Deserts* 330, *Pine Bush*. . . Leaves filiform, reminiscent of pine needles, with glandular dots. . . Most abundant in the disturbed soils of washes in the California Chaparral.

pine cheat See **pineweed 2**

pinecone n

   1 Std: the fruit or strobilus of a **pine 1**. Also called **burr n¹ 2b, comb B7, pine ball, ~ burr**

   2 also *pinecone fungus*: A **morel n²** or its cap. Cf **pinecone mushroom**

   1972 Miller *Mushrooms* 214, *Morchella—The True Morels*. . . The "head" or brown top of the fungus resembles a pine cone and often is referred to by that name. **1980** Marteka *Mushrooms* 68, *Morchella esculenta*. . . *Common Names* . . pine cone fungus. . . *Cap* . . oval to almost cone shaped, yellow-brown to other shades of brown.

pinecone fungus n

   1 See **pinecone 2.**

   2 See **pinecone mushroom.**

pinecone lily n

A **ginger 1** (here: *Zingiber zerumbet*).

   1955 *S. Folkl. Qrly.* 19.232 **FL**, *Old Maid's Pins* (Bidens leucantha) . . and *Pine Cone Lily* (Zingibar [sic] zerumbet) are named from the objects they most resemble.

pinecone mushroom n Also *pinecone fungus*

   1 A **mushroom B1** of the genus *Strobilomyces*, usu *S. floccopus*. Also called **old-man-of-the-woods**

   1939 Medsger *Edible Wild Plants* 234, Pine Cone Mushroom—*Strobilomyces strobilaceus*. **1972** Miller *Mushrooms* 159, *Strobilomyces floccopus*. . . The "Pine Cone Fungus" or "Old Man of the Woods" is very distinctive . . but its taste is not outstanding. **1980** Smith–Weber *Mushroom Hunter* 113, *Strobilomyces* pertains to a pine cone, hence the species has been called the "pine cone fungus."

   2 also *pinecone tooth*: A **mushroom B1** (here: *Auriscalpium vulgare*).

   1972 Miller *Mushrooms* 186, *Auriscalpium vulgare* . . "Pine Cone Fungus". . . Single or in nearly cespitose clusters *always on pine cones* in S[ummer] and F[all]. . . This fungus has a unique appearance and a unique habitat on pine cones. **1981** Lincoff *Audubon Field Guide Mushrooms* 426, Pinecone Tooth—*Auriscalpium vulgare*. **1987** McKnight–McKnight *Mushrooms* 87, Pinecone Mushroom. . . On partially buried, decaying pine cones or on litter under pines. Throughout U.S. and Canada. . . As a scavenger on pine cones and other debris (it has also been found on corncobs!), it illustrates the important role of many mushrooms in forest ecology.

pine creeper n Also *pine-creep, pine-creeping warbler*

=**pine warbler.**

   1731 Catesby *Nat. Hist. Carolina* 1.61, The Pine-creeper Weighs eight Penny-weight and five Grains. . . They creep about Trees; particularly Pine and Fir-Trees; from which they peck Insects and feed on them. **1791** Bartram *Travels* 289, C[erthia] pinus, the pine creeper. **1811** Wilson *Amer. Ornith.* 3.25, Pine-Creeping Warbler. *Sylvia pinus*. . . inhabits the pine woods of the Southern states. **1844** Giraud *Birds Long Is.* 52, The Pine-creeping Warbler—so called from its habit of creeping up the trunks of pine-trees in search of the larvae of insects—is quite a common species, and one of the first that arrives in the spring. **1895** Minot *Land-Birds New Engl.* 122, *Pine-creeping Warbler ("Pine Creeper")*—A common summer resident in the pine tracts of Massachusetts. . . The distribution . . in New England is practically if not very strictly coextensive with that of the pitch pine *(Pinus rigida)*. **1913** Bailey *Birds VA* 299, Pine Creeper. . . Many birds winter with us; these I judge to be the first to lay. **1946** Hausman *Eastern Birds* 524, *Dendroica pinus pinus*. . . Pine-creeping Warbler, Pine Creeper, Pine-Creep. . . Seldom found in any but pine woods, Pitch Pine being preferred. **1955** Forbush–May *Birds* 437, Pine-creeping Warbler.

pine crow n

=nutcracker a.

1953 Jewett *Birds WA* 472, *Nucifraga columbiana*. . . Pine Crow. . . *Nest:* In conifers, usually 8 to 40 feet from the ground. [*Ibid* 473, Individuals may sometimes be observed pounding pine cones to extract the seeds.]

pine devil n Cf hickory horned devil

The larva of a royal moth *(Citheronia sepulchralis);* hence *pine-devil moth* the adult moth.

1980 Milne–Milne *Audubon Field Guide Insects* 773, The Pine Devil Moth (*C[itheronia] sepulchralis*) . . has dull gray-brown wings and its caterpillars feed on pines from Massachusetts to Georgia. **1984** Covell *Field Guide Moths* 46, Pine-devil Moth. . . Wingspan 7–10 cm. . . Larva (Pine-devil) feeds on pines, including Caribbean, pitch, and white pines. . . Common southward.

pinedrops n

A saprophytic plant *(Pterospora andromeda).* Also called **Albany beechdrops, dragonclaw, dragonroot 2, fall-bird's nest, false crawley, feverroot 3, gall of the earth 4, giant bird's nest**

1848 Gray *Manual of Botany* 274, Pine-drops. . . *P[terospora] Andromedea*. . . Hard clay soil, parasitic on the roots apparently of pines. **1898** *Jrl. Amer. Folkl.* 11.273 **CA**, *Pterospora Andromeda*, . . pine drops. **1941** Writers' Program *Guide CO* 17, The coral-root orchid is frequently found in the woods, as are the peculiar pine drops of the Indian pipe family. **1961** Douglas *My Wilderness* 20 **CO**, Pine-drops, which are a fleshy red in Summer, are a dry brown stalk by Fall, hoarding a host of seeds for birds. **1966** *DARE* Wildfl QR Pl.153A **OR**12, Similar to pinedrops.

pine duck n

=pileated woodpecker B.

1956 *AmSp* 31.182, *Pine duck* (pileated woodpecker, Fla.) refers to a bird nearly as large as a duck (and doubtless eaten as readily as if it were one) that inhabits pinelands.

pine finch n

Any of three related birds:

a =pine siskin.

1810 Wilson *Amer. Ornith.* 2.133, [The] Pine Finch. *Fringilla pinus*. . . seeks the seeds of the black alder, on the borders of swamps, creeks and rivulets. **1844** DeKay *Zool. NY* 2.167, *The Pine Finch*. . . This modest colored little species. . . has been observed from Maine to Georgia, during the autumn and winter. . . They feed on the seeds of the thistle, pine, larch, etc. **1871** Burroughs *Wake-Robin* 78 **NY,** I observed several pine finches—a dark brown or brindlish bird, allied to the common yellowbird. **1890** Warren *Birds PA* 231, The Pine Finch is a common winter resident in Pennsylvania. . . As its specific name would indicate it delights especially to dwell in pine forests. **1904** Wheelock *Birds CA* 211, *Pine Finch*. . . Upper parts grayish or brownish. **1929** Forbush *Birds MA* 3.29, *Pine Finch*. [*Ibid* 31, Frequents pines (especially pitch pines) and spruces of various kinds.] **1959** Barnes *Nat. Hist. Wasatch Winter* 72 **UT,** Most gregarious of birds is the pine siskin or pine finch. **1964** Phillips *Birds AZ* 186, *Pine Finch*. . . Common summer resident. . . Winters more or less commonly in weedy fields and river valleys almost throughout the state.

b =pine grosbeak.

1839 Audubon *Synopsis Birds* 127, Corythus Enucleator. . . Common Pine-finch. . . From Pennsylvania and New Jersey, in winter. **1956** MA Audubon Soc. *Bulletin* 40.254 **MA,** Pine Grosbeak. . . Pine Finch.

c =pinewoods sparrow.

1917 (1923) *Birds Amer.* 3.49, *Peucaea aestivalis aestivalis*. . . and . . [the] Bachman's Sparrow, or Southern Pine Finch *(Peucaea aestivalis bachmani)* are striped sparrows that are distinctly southern birds.

pine fly n esp NJ

Prob a fly of the family Tabanidae; see quots.

1913 Johnson *Highways St. Lawrence to VA* 213 **ceNJ**, "What troubles me most is the pine flies," Emma said. "They're no larger than a house fly, but when they get onto you they're enough to make you say your prayers the other way; and they're awfully tormentin' to the animals." **1968–69** *DARE* (Qu. R12, . . *Other kinds of flies*) Infs **NJ**31, 52, 55, Pine fly.

pine gentian See pine-barren gentian

pine grass n

1 Any of several grasses; see below. **West**

a Any of var **reedgrasses a,** but esp *Calamagrostis rubescens.* Cf **meadow pinegrass, marsh ~**

1911 *Century Dict. Suppl.*, *Grass*. . . *Pine-grass*, one of the bluejointgrasses, *Calamagrostis Suksdorfii* [=*C. rubescens*], common in the extreme northwestern United States in low pine woods and on moist mountain slopes. It presents the qualities of a good hay or pasture grass. **1937** U.S. Forest Serv. *Range Plant Hdbk.* G40, Purple pinegrass (*C[alamagrostis] purpurascens*) . . is an erect, densely tufted grass . . with dense, spikelike, pale or often purplish flower heads. *Ibid* G42, Pinegrass [=*Calamagrostis rubescens*], so named because of its intimate association with ponderosa pine and lodgepole pine forests, is. . . widely distributed from British Columbia and Manitoba southward to northern Colorado and central California. **1953** Nelson *Plants Rocky Mt. Park* 41, *Calamagrostis purpurascens* . . Purple reedgrass or purple pinegrass. **1961** Thomas *Flora Santa Cruz* 95 **cwCA,** *C[alamagrostis] rubescens*. . . Pine Grass. Usually growing in redwood forests, occasionally in shaded woods. *Ibid* 96, *C. koelerioides*. . . Tufted Pine Grass. Open areas in redwood-Douglas fir forests, edges of brush-covered slopes, and in rocky grasslands.

b A **fescue** (here: *Festuca arizonica*).

1937 U.S. Forest Serv. *Range Plant Hdbk.* G57, Arizona fescue, often called pinegrass or mountain bunchgrass, is. . . very abundant throughout the open ponderosa pine types, on slopes, mesas, and in open parks, chiefly in southern Colorado, New Mexico, and Arizona. **1950** Hitchcock–Chase *Manual Grasses* 75, *Festuca arizonica*. . . Often called pinegrass.

c =bluegrass 1. Cf **pine bluegrass**

1937 U.S. Forest Serv. *Range Plant Hdbk.* G95, *Poa spp*. . . The bluegrasses are often called speargrasses, and sometimes also pinegrasses and greengrasses.

2 A **horsetail 1** (here: *Equisetum arvense*). Cf **meadow pine 2, pine top 4**

1914 Georgia *Manual Weeds* 20, *Equisetum arvense*. . . Pine Grass. . . In early spring one may note large colonies . . of these plants. **1935** (1943) Muenscher *Weeds* 129, *Equisetum arvense*. . . Pine-grass. . . When horses or cattle are fed on hay containing large quantities of this weed they become sick.

3 A **squaw grass** (here: *Xerophyllum tenax*). Cf **pine lily 1**

1936 Thompson *High Trails* 86 **nwMT,** The bear grass flower . . is also listed as pine grass, moose grass, Indian basket grass, and turkey beard. **1949** Peattie *Cascades* 248, In days gone by the Indians used its tough leaves in their baskets, which accounts for its common names of squaw-grass and Indian basket-grass. It is so conspicuous and attractive that it has a number of other popular names, some of which are bear-grass, elk-grass, pine grass, pine lily, and mountain lily.

4 also *pine sedge:* A **sedge B1** (here: *Carex geyeri*).

1937 U.S. Forest Serv. *Range Plant Hdbk.* GL6, *Carex geyeri*. . . Elk sedge, sometimes known as . . pine sedge, or unfortunately pinegrass and elkgrass, is a grasslike plant belonging to the sedge family. . . This species, on account of its range, appears typically in open ponderosa pine and lodgepole pine stands, frequently being intermixed with pinegrass (*Calamagrostis rubescens*). . . Elk sedge and pinegrass are sometimes confused, perhaps because they grow in similar sites and have somewhat similar leaves. When flower or seed heads are in evidence, the sedge . . is not readily mistaken for the grass.

pine grosbeak n

A **grosbeak** (here: *Pinicola enucleator*). Also called **pine bullfinch, ~ finch b, ~ robin, winter robin**

[**1772** Royal Soc. London *Philos. Trans.* 62.402, [The] Pine Grosbeak. . . visits the Hudson's Bay settlements in May, on its way to the north, and is not observed to return.] **1808** Wilson *Amer. Ornith.* 1.80, [The] Pine Grosbeak. *Loxia Enucleator*. . . is perhaps one of the gayest land birds that frequent the inhospitable regions of the north. **1858** Baird *Birds* 410 **West,** Pine Grosbeak. . . Bill and legs black. General color carmine red. **1890** *Atlantic Mth.* 66.255 **NH,** I . . saw with perfect distinctness . . two pine grosbeaks in bright male costume,—birds I had never seen before except in winter. **1917** Eaton *Green Trails* 104 **MA,** This same deep snow . . brought down to New England and New York . . flocks of the rare pine grosbeaks. **1942** Rich *We Took to Woods* 278 **ME,** I saw a pine grosbeak in a little poplar tree. **1959** Barnes *Nat. Hist. Wasatch Winter* 58 **UT,** The finches, however, are a hardy lot; for among this great family are included such storm-resisting birds as . . the pine grosbeak. **1963** Murie *Birds Mt. McKinley* 79 **AK,** The mature male pine grosbeak is rosy red with blackish wings and tail and two white wing bars. The female is gray with a dull golden crown and rump patch. **1977** Bull–Farrand *Audubon Field Guide Birds* 698, *Pine Grosbeak.* . . Habitat: coniferous forests; in winter, spreading to mixed woodlands and wherever fruiting trees are found.

pine grouse n
=dusky grouse.

1853 Schoolcraft *Indian Tribes U.S.* 3.112 **nwCA,** The pine grouse and quail, geese, ducks, and cranes, abound in their proper season. **1859** Cooper–Suckley *Nat. Hist. WA Terr.* 3.220, This bird, called generally in Oregon the *blue* grouse, also known as pine grouse, dusky grouse, &c., I met, for the first time, when our exploring party reached the main chain of the Rocky mountains, where we found it exceedingly abundant, but not more so than in the Blue mountains of Oregon, Cascade mountains, and in all the timbered country between the last mentioned range and the Pacific coast. **1874** Coues *Birds NW* 395, *Dusky Grouse; Blue Grouse; Pine Grouse.* . . Dwelling in remote mountainous regions not often visited by the sportsman, . . [it] is not yet a well-known bird. **1918** Grinnell *Game Birds CA* 546, The Sierra Grouse has been called by a variety of names. . . The name Pine Grouse suggests the nature of its preferred habitat. **1953** Jewett *Birds WA* 196, Pine Grouse. . . While ordinarily not observed in swamps or heavy timber, and rarely noted in the hemlock and cedar woods of the coastal country, the grouse is a denizen of the Douglas fir belt; it is often seen in burned-over areas, and is particularly fond of thick second-growth timber. [**1977** Udvardy *Audubon Field Guide Birds* 690, In winter this grouse [=*Dendragapus obscurus*] feeds exclusively on pine needles; its summer diet consists of insects, seeds, and berries.]

pine hackee n [hackee]   Cf ground hackee
A chipmunk (here: *Tamias striatus*).

1997 *DARE* File **cPA,** A "P" word that I've always loved—"pine-hacky". It means "chipmunk" in Perry County, PA. . . I've heard the term in common usage around Loysville and Newport, PA. Twenty miles west, in Lewiston, they've never heard of it.

pine ham n   Cf ham n[2]
=needle 1.

1976 Ryland *Richmond Co. VA* 375, Pine hams—pine needles.

pine, hemlock spruce   See hemlock 2

pine hen n
=dusky grouse.

1883 *Harper's New Mth. Mag.* 67.711 **UT,** A strapping young fellow with a gun in his hand came up to me and asked me if I would like to have a shot at a "pine hen." **1917** (1923) *Birds Amer.* 2.13, The Dusky Grouse is a western bird. . . known locally by several expressive and descriptive names, the most common of which are Blue Grouse, . . Pine Hen, and Fool Hen. **1953** *AmSp* 28.282 **OR, NV, UT, WA,** Pine hen— Dusky grouse. **1961** Douglas *My Wilderness* 62 **UT,** A pine hen, feeding on the nuts of the piñon, ran hastily for cover. **1968** *DARE* (Qu. Q7, *Names and nicknames for . . game birds*) Infs **UT4, 5,** Pine hen. **1982** Elman *Hunter's Field Guide* 15, Pine hen.

pine hyacinth n
A virgin's bower (here: *Clematis baldwinii*) native to Florida.

1903 Small *Flora SE U.S.* 439, *Viorna Baldwinii.* . . In pine lands or hammocks, peninsular Florida. Spring to fall. *Pine Hyacinth.* **1938** Baker *FL Wild Flowers* 75, *V[iorna] Baldwinii.* . . The local name of pine hyacinth reveals as much imaginative genius as does the Florida custom of calling the common tortoise a "gopher," and the equally bizarre usage that names our true gophers "salamanders," but as the word hyacinth holds suggestions of beauty it is not altogether inappropriate. **1979** Niering–Olmstead *Audubon Guide N. Amer. Wildflowers E. Region* 732, *Pine Hyacinth.* . . Long stalks each bear a solitary, *nodding, pink to bluish-lavender, bell-shaped flower.* . . Wet areas or pinewoods.

pine jay n
1 See **piñon jay.**

2 =Steller's jay.
1917 (1923) *Birds Amer.* 2.219, *Cyanocitta stelleri stelleri.* . . Pine Jay. [*Ibid* 220, *Distribution.* Coniferous forests of northern Pacific Coast district.]

pine keg n [Etym uncert; perh erron for *key;* cf **key** n **2, 6**]
=needle 1.

1976 Ryland *Richmond Co. VA* 375, Pine kegs—pine needles (nearly obsolete).

pine knot n
1 also *(pine) knotty:* **=dovekie.   esp MA, ME**

1925 (1928) Forbush *Birds MA* 47, The fishermen call Dovekies "Pine Knots" or "Knotties" to indicate their extreme hardiness, for they are indeed as "tough as a pine knot." **1928** Beston *Outermost House* 105 **Cape Cod MA,** On the Cape, these auks are known as "pine knots"—a term said to be derived from the creature's tough compactness—or as "dovekies." They have always been "aukies" to me. **1946** Hausman *Eastern Birds* 337, *Dovekie.* . . *Other Names* . . Pine Knot, Knotty. . . The smallest of the sea birds along our winter coasts. **1956** MA Audubon Soc. *Bulletin* 40.80, *Dovekie.* . . Pine-knot (Maine, Mass. From its hardiness, especially with respect to cold . .); Pine-knotty (Mass.)

2 =old-squaw.
1956 *AmSp* 30.182, Toughness of flesh has been commemorated in the term *pine knot* for . . the oldsquaw.

3 See **pine top 2.**

pine knotty   See **pine knot 1**

pineland daisy n
A sunbonnets (here: *Chaptalia tomentosa*).
1938 Baker *FL Wild Flowers* 232, *Chaptalia tomentosa.* Pineland daisy. . . Low pinelands. Winter, spring. Fla. to Tex. and N.C.

pineland ginseng n
A composite plant (*Tetragonotheca helianthoides*) native to the southeastern US.
1933 Small *Manual SE Flora* 1418, *T[etragonotheca] helianthoides.* . . *Pineland-ginseng.* . . Pinelands and woods, Coastal Plain and adj. provinces, Fla. to Miss. and Va. **1953** Greene–Blomquist *Flowers South* 138, *Pineland-Ginseng.* . . Although it resembles a sunflower, it is more closely related to the rosin-weeds (*Silphium*).

pineland woodcock n
=pileated woodpecker B.
1953 *AmSp* 28.284 **GA,** [Pileated woodcock:] *Pineland woodcock* in Georgia.

pine leaf   See **leaf** n[1] **B1**

pine lily n
1 A squaw grass (here: *Xerophyllum tenax*).   Cf **pine grass 3**

1911 *Century Dict. Suppl.* **ID,** *Grass.* . . *Bear-grass.* . . *(c)* In the northwestern United States, *Xerophyllum tenax.* . . Also called . . in Idaho, *pine-lily.* **1949** Peattie *Cascades* 248, It [=*Xerophyllum tenax*] is so conspicuous and attractive that it has a number of other popular names, some of which are bear-grass, elk-grass, pine grass, pine lily, and mountain lily. **1967** Gilkey–Dennis *Hdbk. NW Plants* 46, *Pine Lily.* . . Densely covered with minute flowers. . . Open woods in the Coast Range and Cascades. **1979** Spellenberg *Audubon Guide N. Amer. Wildflowers W. Region* 595, *Bear Grass.* . . Indians . . ate the roasted rootstock. . . Other common names are . . Bear Lily, and Pine Lily.

2 =red lily b.
1933 Small *Manual SE Flora* 291, *L[ilium] Catesbaei.* . . *Pine-lily.* Coastal Plain, Fla. to La. and N.C. **1949** Moldenke *Amer. Wild Flowers* 323, A great favorite in the Southeast is the *leopard lily* or *pine lily.* . . This species differs . . in having its bright red flower segments very long-pointed. **1964** Batson *Wild Flowers SC* 30, *Pine Lily.* . . This disappearing species is native to low pinelands and blooms in summer. **1976** Bruce *How to Grow Wildflowers* 181, Related to the Wood Lily is a species from the Southeast, *Lilium catesbaei*, the Southern Red or Pine Lily.

pine linnet n
=pine siskin.
1839 Audubon *Synopsis Birds* 115, Pine Linnet. . . Wanders during

winter to South Carolina, Louisiana, and Kentucky. **1844** Giraud *Birds Long Is.* 115 **NY,** *Pine Linnet.* . . At some seasons, this species is very abundant with us. . . During winter it resorts to the Pines, the seeds of which, at that season it feeds on. **1872** Coues *Key to N. Amer. Birds* 131, *Pine Linnet.* . . Ranging throughout most of the United States, in flocks, in the winter; abundant. **1899** Going *Field Flowers* 269 **NEast,** The brooding silence of the evergreen woods is broken . . by the tremulous whistle of the pine-linnet, or the bell-like notes of the hermit-thrush. **1917** *DN* 4.429 **LA,** *Pine linnet.* The pine finch (Spinus pinus). **1949** Sprunt–Chamberlain *SC Bird Life* 519, In the pine trees they [=*Carduelis pinus*] cling to the cones, sometimes upside down, as they extract the seeds. . . The notes of the Pine Linnet, as these birds are sometimes called, are similar to those of the Goldfinch. **1955** Forbush–May *Birds* 497, Pine Linnet. . . Frequents pine trees (especially pitch pines) and spruces of various kinds.

pine lizard n Also pine-tree lizard

Usu a **fence lizard 1** (here: *Sceloporus undulatus*); occas a related **swift** such as *S. graciosus* or *S. woodi.*

1842 DeKay *Zool. NY* 3.33, It [=*Sceloporus undulatus*] inhabits in preference sandy and rocky situations; and from its abundance in pine forests, has obtained the name of *Pine Lizard.* **1883** WI Chief Geologist *Geol. WI* 1.423, *Sceloporus undulatus.* . . Pine Tree Lizard. **1892** IN Dept. Geol. & Nat. Resources *Rept. for 1891* 541, In the South they [=*Sceloporus undulatus*] are most abundant in the pine forests. On this account they have received the name of "Pine-tree Lizard." **1895** *Outing* 26.34 **NJ,** A pine lizard ran up the trunk of a cedar tree. **1920** *Copeia* 85.74 **CT,** Pine lizard, *Sceloporus undulatus.* **1928** Baylor Univ. Museum *Contrib.* 16.11, Sceloporus undulatus. . . is abundant in the timbered regions of extreme eastern Texas. Here it is known as the *Pine Lizard* [etc]. **1953** Schmidt *N. Amer. Amphibians* 129, *Sceloporus graciosus gracilis.* . . Sierra pine lizard. . . *Sceloporus graciosus vandenburgianus.* . . Van Denburgh's pine lizard. **1955** Carr–Goin *Guide Reptiles* 258 **FL,** *Sceloporus woodi.* . . The Scrub Pine Lizard is known by its rough, overlapping scales. . . Distributed in scattered sand pine and rosemary scrub areas. **1958** Conant *Reptiles & Amphibians* 86, *Sceloporus undulatus.* . . Often called "pine lizard" because of its frequent occurrence in open pine woods. . . *Range:* Se. New York to cent. Florida; west to e. Kansas and cent. Texas.

pinely See pointedly

pine marten n [DCan 1772 →] Cf fisher 1

A marten *(Martes americana)* native to North America.

1826 Godman *Amer. Nat. Hist.* 1.201, The pine marten resembles the ermine weasel in habits and disposition. **1838** Geol. Surv. OH *Second Annual Rept.* 160, Mustela martes . . *Pine Martin* [sic]. **1879** U.S. Natl. Museum *Bulletin* 14.3, *Mustela americana.* . . *Pine Martin* [sic] or *American Sable.* Northern United States. **1917** Anthony *Mammals Amer.* 115, Though frequently called Pine Marten, like its European relative, it does not appear to be particularly attached to coniferous woods. **1961** Jackson *Mammals WI* 328, *Pine marten.* . . Forests and heavy woodland, particularly of old and dense conifer growth, sometimes wandering short distances into brushland and meadows in summer. **1968** *DARE* Tape **CA**100, That's pine marten—them's furs, you know, very pretty furs. **1969** *DARE* (Qu. P32, . . *Other kinds of wild animals*) Inf **CA**145, Fisher—like a pine marten but three times as big. **1980** Whitaker *Audubon Field Guide Mammals* 569, "Pine Marten". . . Range . . in the West, south to n California through Rocky Mountains; in the East, to n New England and n New York.

pinemat n

1 See **pinemat manzanita.**

2 A **bluebrush** (here: *Ceanothus diversifolius*).

1951 Abrams *Flora Pacific States* 3.70, *Ceanothus diversifolius.* . . Pine-mat. . . Prostrate shrubs with reddish or green . . branchlets. . . Open coniferous forests. **1959** Munz–Keck *CA Flora* 981, *Pine Mat.* . . Low trailing shrub . . with long flexible villous branches forming extensive mats.

pinemat manzanita n Also pinemat

A **manzanita 1** (here: *Arctostaphylos nevadensis*).

1925 Jepson *Manual Plants CA* 748, *A[rctostaphylos] nevadensis.* . . *Pine-mat Manzanita.* Plants gregarious and roughly carpeting the forest floor. **1937** U.S. Forest Serv. *Range Plant Hdbk.* B15, Pinemat *(A. nevadensis)* and bearberry are low forms with trailing stems that seldom become more than a foot high. **1951** Abrams *Flora Pacific States* 3.312, Pinemat Manzanita. . . Leaves . . bright green on both surfaces. . .

Fruit . . with copious acid pulp. **1973** Hitchcock–Cronquist *Flora Pacific NW* 342, Mont[ane], W[ester]n Cas[cades] to Cal, e to Blue Mts, Ore; pinemat m[anzanita].

pine mouse n

A **meadow mouse** (here: *Microtus pinetorum*). Also called **mole mouse 3**

1851 Audubon–Bachman *Quadrupeds* 2.216, *Arvicola Pinetorum.* . . Leconte's Pine-Mouse. . . This species bears some resemblance to Wilson's Meadow Mouse. **1885** *Amer. Naturalist* 19.895, On the 13th of June, 1884, at my home in Lewis county, New York, I caught a female pine mouse. **1907** NJ State Museum *Annual Rept. for 1906* 69, The meadow mouse. . . very rarely disturbs seeds, fruits, tubers, roots or vegetables during the growing season, . . most of the ravages in these cases being the work of the pine mouse *(Microtus pinetorum).* **1927** Boston Soc. Nat. Hist. *Proc.* 38.7.267 **Okefenokee GA,** It might be questioned whether all of the reported damage is actually done by these animals [= moles], and not rather by Pine Mice (Pitymys pinetorum pinetorum) while trespassing in the runways of the former. **1950** Peattie *Nat. Hist. Trees* 343, It is under the Hawthorn that the pine mouse often passes his obscure life in tunnels around the roots, on the bark of which he nibbles all winter under ground. **1961** Jackson *Mammals WI* 240, *Microtus pinetorum scalopsoides.* . . Where recognized in Wisconsin commonly called pine mouse. . . The pine mouse is a small, thickset burrowing microtine with short legs, very short tail, and small eyes and ears.

pine mushroom n

A **mushroom B1** (here: *Armillaria ponderosa*). Also called **piney** n[1] **2, steelie**

1975 Smith *Field Guide W. Mushrooms* 146, *Armillaria ponderosa* (Pine Mushroom). . . It fruits in the fall season on the pine covered sand dunes of the coastal region. The fungus can be found throughout the pine areas of the region.

pine needle n

=**storksbill** (here: *Erodium* spp).

1900 Lyons *Plant Names* 149, E[rodium] Cicutarium. . . Pine-needle. **1903** Small *Flora SE U.S.* 660, *Erodium.* . . Stork's-bill. Pine Needle. **1936** Whitehouse *TX Flowers* 59, Pine Needle *(Erodium texanum)* has fruits similar to the Texas geranium, but the beaks are much longer, 1–2 in. long.

pine nut n West

The edible seed of any of several **pines 1.** Also called **Indian nut, piñon ~**

1845 Frémont *Rept. Rocky Mts.* 222, A party of twelve Indians came down from the mountains to trade pine nuts, of which each one carried a little bag. **1871** U.S. Dept. Ag. *Rept. of Secy. for 1870* 411, *Pine nuts, (Pinus Sabiniana, P. monophylla, P. Parryana, P. Lambertiana flexilis, P. Coulteri.)*—These trees grow in the mountains of the western Territories, and the seeds are commonly called pine nuts, and are used as an article of food by all the Indians inhabiting the regions in which they grow. The seeds are oily, of a very disagreeable flavor, but highly nutritious. **1898** Harte *Stories in Light* 51 **West,** We had to grub on pine-nuts and jackass rabbits. **1965–70** *DARE* (Qu. I43, *What kinds of nuts grow wild around here?*) Infs **AZ**8, **CA**118, 126, 136, 151, 162, 165, 210, **NV**5, **OR**1, **UT**4, 8, 13, **WY**3, Pine nuts; **CA**136, Sugar pine nuts, digger pine; (Qu. T17, . . *Kinds of pine trees;* not asked in early QRs) Inf **NV**8, Pine nut. **1976** Elmore *Shrubs & Trees SW* 14, They are some of the largest nuts produced by any of our pines and are sold throughout the country as pinyon or pine nuts, Indian nuts, or Christmas nuts. **1980** Little *Audubon Guide N. Amer. Trees W. Region* 283, The large, edible, mealy seeds [of *Pinus monophylla*] are sold locally as pinyon or pine nuts and used as a staple food of Indians in the Great Basin region.

pine nuthatch n

The brown-headed **nuthatch** *(Sitta pusilla).*

1964 Phillips *Birds AZ* 114, *Pine Nuthatch . . Sitta pusilla.* . . This noisy, gregarious little nuthatch is almost entirely restricted to ponderosa pines in Arizona.

pine oak n

1 Prob a **white oak** (here: *Quercus alba*).

1835 Irving *Crayon Misc.* 184 **Upper MW,** There is a pine-oak which produces an acorn pleasant to the taste, and ripening early in the season. **1885** Thompson *By-Ways* 102 **sIN,** I cannot understand the taste of those who do not like the rich oily kernels of the butternut, the hickory nut, and the sweet acorns of the pine oak.

2 =laurel oak 2.

1849 Bracht *Texas* 69, Die Fichteneiche (pine oak) mit ihrem engen zackigen Blatt habe ich nur in den östlichen Texas angetroffen. [=I have met with the pine oak with its narrow, bristled leaf only in eastern Texas.] **1960** Vines *Trees SW* 182, *Quercus obtusa* [=*Q. laurifolia*]. . . is also known as . . Swamp Laurel Oak, Pine Oak, . . and Laurel-leaved Oak.

pine pheasant n Cf pheasant 1a

=ruffed grouse.

[**1957** Natl. Museum Canada *Bulletin* 149.24, Ruffed Grouse . . [is also called] pheasant (N.B., "Keewatin", Sask., B.C.); pine pheasant (Eastern Canada).] **1968** *DARE* (Qu. Q7, *Names and nicknames for . . game birds*) Inf **NJ52**, Pine pheasant—old-fashioned pheasant.

pine rat See piney n¹ 1

pine rattler n

=timber rattlesnake.

1968 *DARE* (Qu. P25, . . *Kinds of snakes*) Inf **GA65**, Pine rattler (same as timber rattler).

pine robin n

=pine grosbeak.

1956 MA Audubon Soc. *Bulletin* 40.254 **MA**, Pine Grosbeak. . . Pine Robin.

pine root n

=sweet flag.

1958 Jacobs–Burlage *Index Plants NC* 15, *Acorus Calamus*. . . Pine root. . . The infusion is made with 1 ounce of the drug to 1 pint of water and the dose is a wineglassful. **1971** Krochmal *Appalachia Med. Plants* 32, *Acorus calamus*. . . *Common Names*: Sweet flag, beewort, . . pine root. **1974** (1977) Coon *Useful Plants* 65, Pine root. . . As a food plant, the rhizomes have been cut into, sliced, and candied.

pine rooter See piney-woods rooter

pine-root skinner n

=piney-woods rooter.

1968 *State* (Raleigh NC) 15 Oct 13/1 *(Mathews Coll.)*, And "razor-back" hogs, also called pine root skinners, went scurrying with a frightened snort for the protection of the gallberry thickets.

pinery n Pronc-sp pinry

A pine forest; a region characterized by pine forests.

1818 in 1920 *WI Mag. Hist.* 3.358 **VT**, Mr J. Shaw's brother arrives from St Louis with several men going to the Pinery for rafting timber. **1819** *Ibid* 453, Retrace our steps 2 or 3 miles to a noble pinry. **1897** Lummis *King of Broncos* 168 **NM**, Even without the noble pineries and the old volcanoes and the cañons which endear that lonely spot to all who can feel the love of Nature. **1899** Garland *Boy Life* 152 **nwIA** (as of c1870s), He stayed till snow fell, then went away to the pinery, and was seen no more. **1910** in 1914 Stewart *Letters* 106 **WY**, Soon we came to the pineries, where we traveled up deep gorges and cañons. **1926** *AmSp* 2.100, The lumberjacks have found anthologists who appreciate the charm of the pinery songs. **1933** *AmSp* 8.1.51 **Ozarks**, *Pineries*. . . Pine forests. The singular form is rarely heard. **1956** Sorden–Ebert *Logger's Words* 25 **Gt Lakes**, *Pinery*, The area in Northern Wisconsin and Michigan where there was a heavy growth of pine trees.

pinesap n Cf sweet pinesap

A saprophytic plant of the genus *Monotropa*, usu *M. hypopitys*. Also called **bird's nest 6**. For other names of *M. hypopitys* see **beechdrops 4, false beechdrops, fir-rape 2, Indian pipe 2**; for other names of var spp see **Indian pipe 1**

1824 Bigelow *Florula Bostoniensis* 176, *Monotropa lanuginosa*. . . *Pine sap*. . . The root . . consists of a mass of agglomerated brownish fibres, said to be parasitic on the roots of trees. **1861** Wood *Class-Book* 495, *Monotropa*. . . Indian Pipe. Pine Sap. . . Low, parasitic herbs, of a white or tawny color, furnished with scale-like bracts instead of leaves. . . *M. Hypopytis* [sic]. . . Pine Sap. . . The whole plant is of a tawny white or reddish color. **1899** Going *Flowers* 260 *(DA)*, In July pine-roots give a home and a maintenance to some curious parasitic plants—"pine-drops," "pine-sap," and "Indian pipe" or "ghost-flower." **1924** *Amer. Botanist* 30.63, *Monotropa hypopitys* . . has several flowers on a stem and. . . is usually called "pine sap" from the idea that it

grows on the roots of coniferous trees. **1966–67** *DARE* Wildfl QR Pl.153A Infs **MI7, SC41**, Pinesap(s). **1979** Niering–Olmstead *Audubon Guide N. Amer. Wildflowers E. Region* 634, Pinesap . . (*Monotropa hypopitys*). . . does not carry on photosynthesis but obtains its nourishment from fungi associated with roots, often those of oaks or pines.

pine sawyer See sawyer 1

pine sedge See pine grass 4

pine siskin n Also *siskin*

A **goldfinch 1** (here: *Carduelis pinus*) which nests in conifers. Also called **gray linnet 1, linnet 1, pine linnet, ~ finch a**

1887 Ridgway *N. Amer. Birds* 400, Northern North America, breeding from northern United States northward, and south in Rocky Mountains; south, in winter, to Gulf States and Mexico. . . Pine Siskin. **1895** Minot *Land-Birds New Engl.* 186, Pine Finch. "Siskin." . . So irregular are the habits of the American "Siskins" that I have never clearly understood their distribution and annual movements. **1929** Forbush *Birds MA* 31, The Pine Siskin frequents pines (especially pitch pines) and spruces of various kinds. Siskins are very active birds. **1946** Kopman *Wild Acres* 185 **LA**, A small finch, the pine siskin, or linnet, enters the lowlands and other country near the coast during or following the colder weather. **1961** Ligon *NM Birds* 278, In summer the Pine Siskin is a common resident throughout all principal mountainous sections, . . dropping lower into adjacent foothills and valleys in winter and spring, and often collecting in large flocks. . . Siskins evidently are rather late nesters. **1965** *Bee* (Phillips WI) 19 Aug [3/2], The pine siskins are back at the feeders, They've brought their families with them. **1977** Bull–Farrand *Audubon Field Guide Birds* 714, The Pine Siskin is another of the northern finches whose winter visits to the United States occur mainly in years when the seed crop has failed in the boreal forests.

pine snake n

1 =bull snake. [See quot 1894] chiefly **Mid and S Atl, Cent**

1791 Bartram *Travels* 276 **S Atl**, The pine or bull snake is very large and inoffensive with respect to mankind, but devours squirrels, birds, rabbits and every other creature they can take as food. **1837** (1962) Williams *Territory FL* 67, The Pine Snake is long and slender also, and chequered with black, on a light ground, the cheques are scarcely a twelfth [sic] of an inch square. It is innocent. **1883** WI Chief Geologist *Geol. WI* 1.424, *Pityophis Sayi*. . . Western Pine Snake. A large species. In early days it was common in the western part of the state. **1894** U.S. Natl. Museum *Proc.* 17.328 **FL**, From its loud hissing it is called "bull snake," and "pine snake" from its living in the pine woods. **1916** *Copeia* 26.7 **NJ**, A Pine Snake, *Pityophis melanoleucus*. . . at the time of capture was said to have measured seven feet, four inches. **1934** *Natl. Geogr. Mag.* 65.612 **Okefenokee GA**, Of temporary guests [in the burrow of a gopher turtle], I have noted the cottontail rabbit, the six-lined lizard, . . and the pine snake. **1950** *WELS* (*Kinds of snakes found in your neighborhood*) 1 Inf, **WI**, Pine or bull snake. **1952** Ditmars *N. Amer. Snakes* 43, Extending into the pine barrens of New Jersey, where it is common. . . the Pine Snake has an alarming habit of taking a deep breath, opening the mouth slightly and, by means of a voluntarily erectile appendage in front of the breathing passage or glottis, is able to eject the air, in a loud hissing sound. . . When thus bluffing, it vibrates its tail. **1965–70** *DARE* (Qu. P25, . . *Kinds of snakes*) 13 Infs, 8 **NJ**, Pine snake; **NJ53**, Pine snake [same as] bull snake. [*DARE* Ed: **pine snake 2** is not found in this region.] **1974** Shaw–Campbell *Snakes West* 114, Kennedy captured a snake near Livington, . . Texas, in an area between populations of the pine snake . . and the bullsnake.

2 =fox snake. esp MI, WI

1949 Dickinson *Lizards & Snakes WI* 36 **WI**, The fox snake is often called "pine snake." **1950** *WELS* (*Kinds of snakes found in your neighborhood*) 19 Infs, **WI**, Pine snake(s). **1958** Conant *Reptiles & Amphibians* 157, Fox Snake. . . A serpent with many aliases—a "timber snake" in Ohio and parts of Michigan, a "pine snake" in Wisconsin and adjacent states. **1965–70** *DARE* (Qu. P25, . . *Kinds of snakes*) 18 Infs, 15 **MI, WI**, Pine snake. [*DARE* Ed: **pine snake 1** is not generally found in this region.] **1981** Vogt *Nat. Hist. WI* 138, Residents of north and central Wisconsin refer to fox snakes as pine snakes presumably because they are often seen in pine woods.

3 A green snake (here: *Opheodrys vernalis*). Cf **green tree snake**

1966 *DARE* (Qu. P25, . . *Kinds of snakes*) Inf **AL7**, Pine snake—small, green.

pine squirrel n

1 also *piney:* =**red squirrel 1.**

1812 Henry *Campaign Against Quebec* 44, The sterility of the country . . had afforded us no game, . . nothing in short, but the diver, and a red pine squirrel, which was too small and quick to be killed by a bullet. **1857** U.S. Patent Office *Annual Rept. for 1856: Ag.* 67, This pretty and active little animal is well known through the Northern States, under the names of "Red Squirrel," "Chickaree," "Pine Squirrel," and, sometimes, "Mountain Squirrel." **1873** Miller *Modocs* 187 **nCA,** Little foxy-looking pine squirrels with pink eyes, stopped from their work of hoarding them [=pine nuts] for winter, to look or chatter at us. **1897** *Outing* 30.456 **AZ,** The nimble pine-squirrel has his home in a tufty bough of the tallest, most tapering pine-tree. **1941** Writers' Program *Guide WY* 413, In this vicinity are 'picket-pin' ground squirrels, pine squirrels, and chipmunks. **1961** Douglas *My Wilderness* 22 **CO,** Pine squirrels with dark bodies and black tails chatter most of the way to the 11,000–11,500-foot zone that marks the end of the tree line. **1965–70** *DARE* (Qu. P27, . . *Kinds of squirrels*) 15 Infs, 12 **West,** Pine squirrel; **CO**47, Pine squirrel—little gray one with bushy tail, a little bigger than a chipmunk; **MD**26, Pine squirrel—very small, brown; **PA**168, Red squirrel, also [called] pine squirrel, little bigger than a chipmunk; **IN**22, Piney—a little tiny squirrel like a rat; **IN**58, Piney—small, black, ornery. **1968** *Hungry Horse News* (Columbia Falls MT) 20 Dec 18/3, Six orphanned pine squirrels were afraid of trees and liked to climb on people. **1980** Whitaker *Audubon Field Guide Mammals* 419, "Pine Squirrel" . . *(Tamiasciurus hudsonicus). Ibid* 421, "Pine Squirrel" . . *(Tamiasciurus douglasii)*. . . It eats new shoots of conifers, green vegetation, acorns, nuts, mushrooms, fruits, and berries.

2 also *pine-tree squirrel:* =**fox squirrel.**

1837 (1962) Williams *Territory FL* 63, There are two kinds of squirrel;—the small grey, and the pine squirrel. The latter is a beautiful animal. His body is usually of a rich, glossy, brown color, and his head black, and very often one half of his face white. **1967** *DARE* (Qu. P27, . . *Kinds of squirrels*) Inf **SC**31, Pine-tree squirrel.

pine straw See **straw**

pine tag See **tag**

pine tassel n Cf **pineweed 1**

A **Saint-John's-wort** (here: *Hypericum gentianoides*).

1903 Small *Flora SE U.S.* 791, *Sarothra gentianoides* [=*Hypericum g.*] . . In sandy soil and on rocks. . . Pine-tassle [sic]. **1940** Clute *Amer. Plant Names* 225, *Hypericum gentianoides*. Pine tassel.

pine thorn n Cf **pin thorn**

=**cockspur thorn.**

1950 Peattie *Nat. Hist. Trees* 364, *Crataegus Crus-galli*. . . Newcastle or Pine Thorn. Thorn Plum.

pine top n

1 A shoot of new growth on a pine or other evergreen, often brewed for tea. **chiefly Sth** Cf **candle 3, tassel**

1876 Hobbs *Bot. Hdbk.* 90, [Common:] Pine . . tops, [English:] Hemlock leaves, [Botanical:] Pinus . . (abies) Canadensis. **1937** in 1977 *Amer. Slave Suppl. 1* 1.39 **AL,** Us had mullen an' pine top tea fer colds and fever. **1958** Browne *Pop. Beliefs AL* 84, A tea made by boiling tender pine tops is used for every pain. Crush the buds, boil and give one cupful every three or four hours. **1966–68** *DARE* (Qu. F36, . . *Kinds of brooms*) Inf **MS**72, Broom sage, pine tops—used in house; (Qu. BB50a, . . *Favorite remedies . . for a cough*) Inf **AR**18, Cough syrup of pine tops and mullein and catnip; (Qu. DD21c, *Nicknames for whiskey, especially illegally made whiskey*) Inf **VA**15, Pine top—a type of bootleg; pine tops put in for flavor. **1968** Harris *S. Home Remedies* 84 **SC,** Pine top tea, boil pine needles to make tea, "drink off it" as needed for colds. **1974** Morton *Folk Remedies* 111 **SC,** Longleaf Pine . . *Pinus palustris*. . . The whitish new shoot ("tip," "bud," or "tassel") at the tip of the pine branch is boiled to make a "tea," though, more often, the new shoot and the surrounding needles are clipped off together and called "pine tops;" the decoction is drunk as a beverage. *Ibid* 112, Young green needles of pine tops may be plucked off and boiled. . . It is a superstitious belief that pine tops should be collected from the "sunrise side" and the "sunset side" of the house and not from the north or south. **1986** Pederson *LAGS Concordance,* 1 inf, **cAL,** Pine-top tea—made from tops of pine trees; 1 inf, **cwAR,** Pine top; 1 inf, **swGA,** Pine top—boiled with mullein and rabbit tobacco; 1 inf, **seMS,** Old pine tops—used for brooms.

2 also *pine knot:* Whiskey flavored with **pine tops 1;** any cheap liquor. **scattered, but chiefly Sth**

1817 in 1994 Martin *Mr. Jefferson's Business* 158 **VA,** I perchased of John Fagg pine top. **1858** *S. Lit. Messenger* 27.463 **OH** (as of c1805), A rough, but hearty frolic . . with rustic "jigs" and "hoedowns," and profusion of "pine-top" succeeded, and numbers of the hardy and adventurous youth of the country round-about, exhilarated by the frolic and the whiskey . . gladly enrolled themselves. **1869** *Overland Mth.* 3.130 **NC,** "Pinetop" is a kind of mean turpentine whisky of North Carolina. **1899** (1912) Green *VA Folk-Speech* 322, Pinetop. . . Cheap, adulterated whiskey, said to be made of pinetags. **1927** *AmSp* 3.25 **eTX** [Sawmill talk], The liquor on tap at these dances is called "pine-top," "Shinny," "white mule," or "corn." **1931** *AmSp* 7.50 **Sth, SW** [Lumberjack lingo], There are plenty of native liquors "on tap" for the refreshment of the men. The "drinks" are "pine-top," "white mule," "mountain dew," "honey dip," and "red eye." **1965–68** *DARE* (Qu. DD21c, *Nicknames for whiskey, especially illegally made whiskey*) Infs **MS**64, **TX**36, 37, Pine top; **VA**15, Pine top—a type of bootleg; pine tops put in for flavor; **MS**64, Pine knot. **1969** Sorden *Lumberjack Lingo* 87 **NEng, Gt Lakes,** *Pine top*—Intoxicating liquor. **1974** Dabney *Mountain Spirits* 25 **sAppalachians,** Francis Lynde, writing in the *Century Magazine* in 1929, quoted an old-time North Carolinian as saying: . . There was the time when Jim Layne got hisself killed in that there *argymint* with Jud Byars. They'd both of 'em been fillin' up on *pine top*. . . Now that's a name for corn whiskey you don't hear about these days—"pine top." **1985** Wilkinson *Moonshine* 28 **neNC,** "After that they'd serve you North Carolina Corn." It is called . . pine top.

3 See quot 1958.

1949 Peattie *Cascades* 165 **Pacific NW,** Forestry practices in logging on the piney eastern slopes of the Cascades have progressed there as well as on the Douglas fir side. It does our hearts good, it is a sight for sore eyes among all of us old pinetops and fir conks of these parts. **1958** McCulloch *Woods Words* 135 **Pacific NW,** *Pinetop*—An old timer in the pine woods.

4 A **horsetail 1** (here: *Equisetum arvense*). Cf **meadow pine 2, pine grass 2**

1914 Georgia *Manual Weeds* 20, *Equisetum arvense*. . . Pinetop.

pine tree frog See **pinewoods tree frog**

pine-tree lizard See **pine lizard**

pine-tree squirrel See **pine squirrel 2**

pine tree toad See **pinewoods tree frog**

pine tulip n

A **pipsissewa** (here: *Chimaphila umbellata*).

1876 Hobbs *Bot. Hdbk.* 90, Pine tulip, Pipsissewa, Chimaphila umbellata. **1911** Henkel *Amer. Med. Leaves* 16, *Chimaphila umbellata*. . . Pine tulip. . . From about June to August the pipsissewa may be found in flower, its pretty waxy-white or pinkish fragrant flowers, consisting of five rounded, concave petals, each one with a dark-pink spot at the base, nodding in clusters from the top of the erect stem. **1958** Jacobs–Burlage *Index Plants NC* 82, Pine tulip. . . The leaves especially are used as a diuretic, tonic, astringent, appetizer [etc]. **1971** Krochmal *Appalachia Med. Plants* 90, Pine tulip. . . Coniferous and hardwood forests, and acid woodlands.

pine violet n esp CA

A **violet:** usu *Viola lobata,* but also *V. purpurea.*

1901 Jepson *Flora CA* 233, *V[iola] lobata*. . . Pine Violet. . . Coast Ranges north of San Francisco Bay, often under Yellow Pine. **1951** Abrams *Flora Pacific States* 3.125, *Viola lobata*. . . Pine Violet. . . Open coniferous forests. **1976** Bailey–Bailey *Hortus Third* 1160, *[Viola] purpurea*. . . Pine v[iolet]. . . Mts., Calif. and Ore.

pine warbler n

A **warbler** (here: *Dendroica pinus*) native to much of the US east of the Mississippi River. Also called **pine creeper**

1831 *New Engl. Mag.* 1.330 **eMA,** The stillness of the scene is only broken by the shrill note of the Pine-warbler, who, now and then from the dark leaves of the evergreens, trolls forth a rattling cry. **1839** MA Zool. & Bot. Surv. *Fishes Reptiles* 310, The Pine Warbler, *Sylvia pinus*, is . . not much known, because it resides in deep, evergreen forests. **1889** Ridgway *Ornith. IL* 152, Pine Warbler. [*Ibid* 153, In the Mississippi Valley, where its breeding range is probably pretty general, conifers of any species are comparatively rare and exceedingly local.] **1905** Townsend *Birds Essex Co. MA* 295, There are many groves of pitch pines in Essex County, some of these, as at Magnolia, close to the sea, and here it is that the Pine Warbler makes its home. **1938** Oberholser *Bird Life LA* 546, In almost any pine woods in Louisiana one may be reasonably sure of hearing the monotonous rather unmusical trilling song of. . . the Pine Warbler. **1977** Bull–Farrand *Audubon Field Guide Birds* 686, *Pine Warbler*. . . Unstreaked olive above with yellow throat and breast.

pineweed n

1 A **Saint-John's-wort**: usu *Hypericum gentianoides*, occas also *H. drummondii*.

1814 Bigelow *Florula Bostoniensis* 73, *Sarothra gentianoides* [= *Hypericum g.*] . . *Pine weed*. . . A small, erect, branching plant. **1843** Torrey *Flora NY* 1.89, *Hypericum Sarothra*. . . *Pine-weed*. . . Sandy fields and roadsides; common. **1901** Lounsberry *S. Wild Flowers* 344, *Sarothra gentianoides*, pine-weed . . , is the wiry, grass-like looking little plant with minute leaves. **1940** Gates *Flora KS* 154, *Hypericum drummondii*. . . Pineweed. . . Southeast twelfth [of the state of Kansas]. **1979** Niering–Olmstead *Audubon Guide N. Amer. Wildflowers E. Region* 559, Pineweed (*Hypericum gentianoides*). . . Small, yellow, nearly stemless flowers are on the *wiry, ascending branches* of this bushy plant. . . Height 4–20″.

2 also *pine cheat:* Corn spurry (*Spergula arvensis*).

1891 *Jrl. Amer. Folkl.* 4.148 **MA**, Spergula arvensis was very fittingly named *Pine Weed*. **1900** Lyons *Plant Names* 353, *S[pergula] arvensis*. . . *Pine-cheat*. . . *Plant* occasionally grown for fodder. **1974** (1977) Coon *Useful Plants* 92, Pine cheat. . . A weed from East to West.

pinewoods grape n Also *pinewood grape*

A **grape** (here: *Vitis lincecumii*).

1826 Flint *Recollections* 255, They are common through the pine-woods of Louisiana, and known by the name of the pine-woods grape. **1862** U.S. Patent Office *Annual Rept. for 1861: Ag.* 485, "Post-oak grape," "Pine-wood grape," *Vitis Linsecomii* [sic], (new species.) . . grows in eastern and middle Texas and western Louisiana. **1938** Van Dersal *Native Woody Plants* 288, Pinewoods grape. . . Fruit often eaten by . . turkeys before ripening. **1960** Vines *Trees SW* 723, Pinewoods Grape. . . Berries . . purplish black or black, with a thin bloom.

pinewoods hog See **piney-woods rooter**

pinewoods lily n

A plant (*Eustylis purpurea*) native to Louisiana and Texas.

1972 Brown *Wildflowers LA* 29, Pinewoods-Lily. . . Flower opens in the morning and closes in the afternoon, with a succession of new ones each day. **1979** Niering–Olmstead *Audubon Guide N. Amer. Wildflowers E. Region* 566, Pinewoods Lily. . . From a black, scaly bulb rise long, narrow leaves and a tall floral stalk with light to deep purplish-blue . . flowers. . . Habitat: Pinewoods. Range: Louisiana, Texas.

pinewoods rooter See **piney-woods rooter**

pinewoods sparrow n Also *pinewood sparrow* [See quot 1977]

Bachman's sparrow (*Aimophila aestivalis*). Also called **chee-dee, gentle sparrow, grass ~ d, pine finch c, stinkbird, summer sparrow**

1894 Torrey *FL Sketch-Book* 6, One of the three novelties which I knew were to be found in the pine lands . . [was] the pine-wood sparrow. **1910** Wayne *Birds SC* 126, The Pine-woods Sparrow is known to breed from Savannah, Georgia, coastwise to southern Florida. **1934** *Natl. Geogr. Mag.* 65.597 **Okefenokee GA**, I love to recall. . . the pine-woods sparrow chanting its vespers. **1955** Lowery *LA Birds* 490, One of the most melodious sounds to be heard anywhere is the clear ethereal medley that resounds through our pine forests when the Pine-woods Sparrow pours forth its song. **1967** *DARE* (Qu. Q21, . . *Kinds of sparrows*) Inf **TN21**, Pinewoods sparrow. **1977** Bull–Farrand *Audubon Field Guide Birds* 594, In the southern parts of its range, its older name, "Pine-woods Sparrow," is more appropriate since it dwells in open stretches of pines with grass and scattered shrubs for ground cover.

pinewoods tree frog n Also *pine tree frog, ~ tree toad, pinewoods tree toad, piney-woods tree frog* [See quot 1915]

A **tree frog** (here: *Hyla femoralis*).

1909 Biol. Soc. DC *Proc.* 22.133 **NC**, *Hyla femoralis*. Pine Treefrog.

Three taken along the edge of the north canal in May. **1915** *Copeia* 18.3 **eFL**, *Hyla femoralis* . . is called the Pine tree toad, from its habit of frequenting the tops of pine trees almost exclusively, during the summer months. **1932** Wright *Life-Hist. Frogs* 272, *Hyla femoralis*. . . *Common Names* Pine Woods Tree Frog. Pine Woods Tree Toad. Pine Tree Frog. Pine Tree Frog. . . In the piney woods we have more notes on it than any other Hylid (except *Acris*) it was so abundant. . . At times it betakes itself into the high pines and is hard to get. **1957** Blair et al. *Vertebrates U.S.* 256, Piney Woods tree frog. . . Arboreal. Eastern Louisiana to Maryland in coastal plain; not in southern Florida. **1979** Behler–King *Audubon Field Guide Reptiles* 407, Pine Woods Treefrog. . . Nocturnal. It is difficult to observe because of its treetop habitat and its mottled appearance, which blends well with pine tree bark.

piney n[1]

1 also *pine rat:* An inhabitant of the New Jersey **pine barrens**. esp **NJ** *occas derog*

[**1892** Johnston *Mr. Billy Downs* 121 **GA**, People, especially women, not only piney, but oaky, went into the canvass.] **1913** *Survey* (E. Stroudsburg PA) 4 Oct 7 **NJ**, In the heart of this region scattered in widely separated huts over miles of territory exists today a group of human beings so distinct in morals and manners as to excite curiosity and wonder in the mind of any outsider brought into contact with them. They are known as the "Pineys" or "Pine Rats." **1939** FWP *Guide NJ* 605 **csNJ**, Northwest of Batsto . . is the heart of the Jersey Pines, a deep scrub forest threaded by occasional trails and a few wretched roads. . . The inhabitants are called the Pineys. **1940** Weygandt *Down Jersey* 138 **sNJ**, I have met his like, though, among "pineys," as the farmers on the brown soil call their neighbors in the pines to the eastward. **1963** Berry *Almost White* 23 **NJ**, In Burlington and adjacent counties, there are the Pineys, a forsaken people who make their living by picking cranberries, weaving baskets, and working at odd jobs. **1968** *DARE* (Qu. HH1, *Names and nicknames for a rustic or countrified person*) Inf **NJ39**, Piney. **1969** *DARE* File **sNJ**, The Pineys—originally Hessian soldiers who moved into pine woods . . and intermarried—supposed to be a degenerate closed community. **1979** *Ibid* **c,nNJ** (as of 1965–70), *Piney*—A person who lives in the Jersey Pine barrens.

2 =**pine mushroom.**

1968 *PA Game News* Nov 14 **PA**, Steve stopped in with a mess of mushrooms today—pale yellow fungi called equestrian tricholomas. Squatty plants, they grow in hard pine woods and often do not quite protrude through the pine needles and leaves. They are abundant in the fall, usually free of insects, and are tops in flavor and texture. Folks in many areas have fondly nicknamed them "pineys." **1992** *NYT Mag.* 16 Feb 67 **PA**, As a child, he would shimmy up a . . hillside on his stomach, following a vein of tricholoma (called "steelies" or "pinies [sic]" in his part of the country), . . a basket on his wrist.

3 See **pine squirrel.**

piney n[2] See **peony** n[1] 1

piney rooter See **piney-woods rooter**

piney rose n [Cf Scots, nIr *peony-rose* and varr (*EDD* at *peony*) and **peony** n[1] 1] Cf **piano plant**

The peony.

1833 *New Engl. Mag.* 5.314 **CT**, She had cheeks like a piony rose. **1937** (1963) Hyatt *Kiverlid* [6] **KY**, The old-fashioned "piney-rose" (peony). **1944** *PADS* 2.35 **NC**, Piny rose ['paɪnɪ]. . . The peony. **1966** *DARE* (Qu. S11) Infs **NC31, 35**, Piney rose.

piney-wood See **piney woods 2**

piney-wood hog (or rooter) See **piney-woods rooter**

piney woods n pl Also sp *piny woods* **chiefly Sth, S Midl**

1 A region of pine forest; a backwoods area.

1791 in 1956 Eliason *Tarheel Talk* 288 **NC**, Piney woods. **1843** Thompson *Major Jones' Courtship* 14 **GA**, Sich larnin as we had thar dont grow in the piny-woods, I tell you. **1903** *DN* 2.325 **seMO**, Pineywoods. . . Pine woods; pinery. **1909** *DN* 3.357 **eAL, wGA**, Pineywoods. . . The common expression for *backwoods*. **1916** *DN* 4.269 **New Orleans LA, NC**, Piney woods. . . The forests in the eastern part of the state [=LA]. "They went to the piney woods for the summer." **1926** *AmSp* 1.407 **Okefenokee GA**, Islands . . were covered a few years ago with open, sunny forests of longleaf pine—the 'piney woods' beloved of Georgia country folks. **1942** *Sat. Eve. Post* 68 **eGA, eSC**, And if in the piney woods and on the sea islands the Negro stops singing them and forgets them, many spirituals will be lost. **1966–69** *DARE* (Qu. T2b, . . *A piece of land covered with trees . . a large acreage*) Inf **MS**72, Piney woods; (Qu. II21, *When somebody behaves unpleasantly or without manners: "The way he behaves, you'd think he was _____."*) Inf **GA**77, Raised in the piney woods. **1966** *DARE* Tape **FL**39, We're extremely fortunate . . to come back to our piney woods and lowlands. **1976** Garber *Mountain-ese* 68 **sAppalachians**, Jeb went squirrel huntin' up in the piny woods back uv the house. **1986** Pederson *LAGS Concordance*, 1 inf, **cAL**, Piney woods—50 miles south of Montgomery; 1 inf, **ceAL**, He's from the piney woods [=a rustic]; 1 inf, **cwAL**, Piney woods—remote areas; 1 inf, **csAL**, Piney woods—locally no other vegetation; 1 inf, **swAL**, Piney woods—six miles south; 1 inf, **cLA**, Piney woods—local subregion; 1 inf, **csMS**, Piney woods—local region; 1 inf, **ceTX**, Way back in the piney woods—remote country; 1 inf, **csTX**, The piney woods—AR/LA/TX; 1 inf, **csTX**, Piney woods—East Texas.

2 attrib; rarely *piney-wood:* Consisting of, belonging to, or dwelling in such a region; rustic, backwoods, primitive; hence used absol, a rustic. See also **piney-woods rooter**

1809 (1814) Weems *F. Marion* 132, Had this savage spirit appeared among a few poor British *cadets* or *piney wood* tories, it would not have been so lamentable. **1840** (1847) Longstreet *GA Scenes* 128, *He* could not be reconciled, until he fretted himself into a pretty little *piney*-woods fight, in which he got whipt; and then he went home perfectly satisfied. **1844** Thompson *Major Jones's Courtship* 165 **GA**, We had . . more vials of medicine than would fill a piny woods doctor's shop. *Ibid* 179, Who could expect better from a piny-wood's fool? **1860** *Russell's Mag.* 6.394, I see no reason to doubt the truth of your "Piney Wood's Story," though you seem yourself, willing to take it with some grains of allowance. **1872** *KS Mag.* Mar 238, Who that has seen the "clay-eater," the "sandhiller," or the "piney woods cracker" of the South, does not know that it is impossible to exaggerate the sinfulness which looks out through the loop-holes of his red apologies for eyes? **1884** *Anglia* 7.278, Piny woods niggers (term of contempt) = pine-woods negroes. **1888** *Century Illustr. Mag.* 36.799, If Mr. Catlett will come to Georgia and go among the "po' whites" and "piney-wood tackeys," he will hear the terms "we-uns" and "you-uns" in every-day use. **1892** Johnston *Mr. Billy Downs* 105 **GA**, It was in that section of the country next from ours across the Ogeechee River, known as Dooly District, wherein were large bodies of piney-woods land. **1935** Hurston *Mules & Men* 113 **FL**, They looked so trashy he figgered they was piney woods crackers. **1949** *Time* 7 Mar 28, The unit-voting system makes it possible for Hummon's beloved piney-woods counties to outvote their city neighbors. **1950** Corliss *Main Line* 416, Up to that time the cattle herds in Mississippi were almost entirely of the scrub varieties, commonly known as piney woods cows. **1966–68** *DARE* (Qu. K15, *A thin, bony, or poor-looking cow*) Inf **GA**33, Piney-woods scrub; (Qu. HH1, *Names and nicknames for a rustic or countrified person*) Inf **AR**33, Piney-wood tick. **1967** Will *Dredgeman* 28 **FL**, This here is tonsil oil! Cape Sable aguardient! Piney woods champagne! **1986** Pederson *LAGS Concordance (A rustic)* 1 inf, **cLA**, Piney wood; 1 inf, **ceTX**, Piney woods; 1 inf, **csLA**, Piney woods peckerwood; 1 inf, **csGA**, Piney woods people; [1 inf, **cAL**, Piney-woodsy;] *(Poor whites)* 1 inf, **cLA**, Piney woods; *(Cow)* 1 inf, **seMS**, Regular piney-wood cows; 3 infs, **sGA, nFL**, Piney-woods cow(s).

piney-woods rooter n Also *pine(-barren) rooter, pinewoods hog, ~ rooter, piney(-wood) ~, piney-wood(s) hog;* for addit varr see quot 1986 **S Atl, Gulf States**
=**razorback hog.**

1872 McClellan *Golden State* 204, These hogs . . are somewhat like the North Carolina pine-woods hogs. **1934** Hurston *Jonah's Gourd Vine* 155 **AL** [Black], Almost home he remembered the empty meal-barrel and swerved off into the Weens' wood lot where droves of piney wood rooters nosed for ground nuts. **1938** Matschat *Suwannee R.* 76 **neFL, seGA**, One of the most dangerous cannibals in the swamp country is the wild hog, or piney woods rooter. . . Rooters are huge, grayish creatures, utterly wild and savage, that haunt the fastnesses of the moss-draped swamp thickets. . . For tidbits they dig up and eat the roots of young pines, which explains their local name. **1940** Writers' Program *Guide TX* 407 **ceTX**, Occasional signs warn the motorist to *Watch Out for Hogs.* The reference is to razorbacks that roam the east Texas woods—angular, vicious descendants of hogs brought more than two centuries ago by the Spaniards—and known in this area as "piney rooters." **1941** Street *In Father's House* 65 **MS**, Her hogs run wild in the swamps and root on the piney ridges. We call such hogs "pineywoods rooters." **1952** Brown *NC Folkl.* 1.576, Piney-woods rooter. . . A com-

mon pig or hog.—Central and east. **1954** *PADS* 21.34 **SC**, *Piney woods rooter, pine rooter. . .* A hog turned out to find his living by *rooting* in the woods, long-snouted, thin, razor-backed. **1956** *Hall Coll.* **cwNC**, Pine rooters—people didn't have to fatten hogs in the old days. They'd turn 'em out and let 'em eat mast. **1956** McAtee *Some Dialect NC* 33, *Pine-rooter . .* a hog turned out to get its living in the woods: a razorback. **1967** *DARE* Tape **NC**41, [FW:] What breed were those that never got very heavy? [Inf:] Oh, that was the piney-woods rooter. . . They'd go around and root for a living, eating roots and things. **1968** *DARE* FW Addit **LA**22, Pine rooter—feral hog. **c1970** Pederson *Dial. Surv. Rural GA* **seGA** (*What do you call a long-legged hog that has a thin body and a long snout?*) 13 infs, Pineywood rooter; 11 infs, Pineywoods rooter; 1 inf, Pinewoods rooter; 1 inf, Pine rooter; 1 inf, Pine barren rooter; 2 infs, Pineywood hog; 2 infs, Pineywoods hog. **1975** Newell *If Nothin' Don't Happen* 139 **nwFL**, I'll swear that old piney-woods rooter's head was near 'bout as long as his body. He could have stuck his nose two feet in the ground and then been lookin' right straight at you! **1986** Pederson *LAGS Concordance* **Gulf Region**, 57 infs, Piney-woods rooter(s); 27 infs, Piney-wood rooter(s); 15 infs, Pine rooter(s); 6 infs, Piney rooter(s); 2 infs, Pinewood(s) rooters; 2 infs, Pine-hill rooter(s); 1 inf, Pine-ridge rooter; 6 infs, Piney-woods hog(s); 2 infs, Piney-wood hogs; 2 infs, (A) piney woods.

piney-woods tree frog See **pinewoods tree frog**

piney-woods violet n
=**bird's-foot violet 1.**

1951 *PADS* 15.36 **TX**, *Viola pedata.* . . Piney-woods violet. **1966** *DARE* Wildfl QR Pl.133 Inf **TX**34, Some kind of violet—could be piney-woods or bird's-foot violet.

pinfish n

1 Either of two fishes of the family Sparidae:

a A fish *(Lagodon rhomboides)* of the Atlantic and Gulf coasts. [See quot 1983] Also called **bream B2, chopa spina, hogfish g, ladyfish 4, perch 7, pigfish d, porgy** n[1] **1b(3), robin 3, sailor's choice 2, saltwater bream 1, sargo 1, scup 2, shiner 2d, spot, squirrelfish, yellowtail**

1878 *U.S. Natl. Museum Proc.* 1.378 **NC**, *Lagodon rhomboides.* . . Robin; Pin-fish. Taken by the thousands by boys with hook and line, from the wharves. **1933** *LA Dept. of Conserv. Fishes* 195, Smaller in size are several other Porgies which like the Sheepshead are good food fishes. The most common of these is the Pinfish . . , *Lagodon rhomboides.* **1955** Carr–Goin *Guide Reptiles* 103 **FL**, Pinfish. . . A strongly compressed fish with protuberant teeth, a spot on the shoulder, and 3 or 4 vertical dark stripes on the sides. Length about 6 inches. **1968** *DARE* (Qu. P1, . . *Kinds of freshwater fish . . caught around here . . good to eat*) Inf **NC**80, Pinfish. [*DARE* Ed: This Inf may refer instead to **1b** below.] **1969** *DARE* FW Addit **NC**, Pinfish—also called bream and spot. [*DARE* Ed: This quot may refer instead to **1b** below.] **1983** *Audubon Field Guide N. Amer. Fishes* 615, Pinfish. . . Pectoral fins long; dorsal fin single, *forward-directed spine at origin.* **1991** Amer. Fisheries Soc. *Common Names Fishes* 54, *Diplodus holbrooki* . . A[tlantic] . . spottail pinfish. *Lagodon rhomboides* . . A[tlantic]-F[reshwater] . . pinfish.

b also *spot-tail(ed) pinfish:* A similar fish *(Diplodus holbrooki)* of coastal waters from North Carolina to Texas. [See quot 1878] Also called **bream B2, jimmy 2, spot**

1878 *U.S. Natl. Museum Proc.* 1.379 **NC**, *Sargus holbrooki.* . . Spot-tailed Pin-fish. Extremely abundant everywhere along the Beaufort shore. . . This species . . wants the recumbent dorsal spine. Its color is bright silvery, with a large black blotch on the upper part of the caudal peduncle. . . The fishermen call it Pin-fish, and as such it is beneath their notice. Most of the fishermen, indeed, did not distinguish it from *Lagodon rhomboides.* **1902** Jordan–Evermann *Amer. Fishes* 444, The pinfish or spot, *Diplodus holbrooki.* . . is found on our South Atlantic and Gulf coasts from Cape Hatteras to Cedar Keys. **1955** Carr–Goin *Guide Reptiles* 104 **FL**, *Diplodus holbrooki* . . Spot-tail Pinfish. . . A strongly compressed fish with protuberant teeth and a black saddle across the base of the tail. **1983** *Audubon Field Guide N. Amer. Fishes* 615, Spottail Pinfish *(Diplodus holbrooki)* has dark blotch on caudal peduncle. **1991** [see **1a** above].

2 A **sunfish** such as the **bluegill 1.**

1911 *Century Dict.* 4498, Pinfish. . . A small sunfish of the United States, as the copper-nosed bream, *Lepomis pallidus.*

3 A **stickleback** (here: either *Culaea inconstans* or *Pungitius pungitius*). Cf **needlefish 4**

1983 Becker *Fishes WI* 777, *Brook Stickleback—Culaea inconstans.* . . Other common names . . pinfish. . . Dorsal spines 4–6, separate, and . . followed by dorsal fin. *Ibid* 782, *Ninespine Stickleback—Pungitius pungitius.* . . Other common names . . pinfish. . . Dorsal spines 9 (8–11), separate, and . . followed by dorsal fin.

pinginnet See **pipjenny**

pin grass n

1 A **storksbill** (here: either *Erodium cicutarium* or *E. moschatum*). [See quot 1874] **West** Cf **pin clover, pinweed 2**
1847 *Californian* (San Francisco) 10 July 3/3, Quality of Pasture—Bunch Grass; Clover; Wild Oats and Pin Grass, all in abundance. **1874** (1877) Hittell *Resources CA* 369, *Erodium cicutarium.* . . is succulent, sweet, hardy, bearing clusters of spikes, which are an inch and a half long, and have given it the name of pin grass. **1891** Coulter *Botany W. TX* 51, *E[rodium] cicutarium.* . . Southern and western Texas. Known by various popular names, as "alfilaria," . . "pin-grass," and valuable as a forage plant. **1911** CA Ag. Exper. Sta. Berkeley *Bulletin* 217.1002, *Erodium cicutarium.* . . *Erodium moschatum.* . . Pin clover and pin grass apply to either species. . . No distinction has been drawn between [these] . . as to their honey producing merits. **1976** Bailey–Bailey *Hortus Third* 443, *[Erodium] cicutarium.* . . *Pin grass.* . . A weedy plant, valuable for forage.

2 A **needlegrass 1** or similar plant; see quots.
1871 U.S. Dept. Ag. *Rept. of Secy. for 1870* 419, *Wild oat, (Avena fatua.)* . . Some of the early travelers call this plant pin grass. **1966–70** DARE (Qu. S14, . . *Prickly seeds, small and flat, with two prongs at one end, that cling to clothing*) Inf **OK**52, Pin grass or needle grass—sticks to socks, etc; (Qu. S15, . . *Weed seeds that cling to clothing*) Infs **AL**25, **KY**93, Pin grass.

pingree n
A **wolfberry** (here: *Symphoricarpos occidentalis*).
1920 *Torreya* 20.25 **ND**, *Symphoricarpos occidentalis.* . . Pingree, Binford, N. Dak.

pingue n Also *pinguay weed, pinguey, pinhue* [See quot 1937]
A rubber-yielding composite plant *(Hymenoxys richardsonii)* native chiefly to the Southwest and toxic to livestock; hence, the livestock disease caused by eating it. Also called **bitterweed, pingwing, rubber plant 1, rubberweed 1**
1906 in 1913 U.S. Congress *Serial Set* 6166 Doc 719 3.166 **CO,** The Secretary of the Interior is hereby authorized, directed, and empowered to lease . . an experimental farm on which to plant, improve, and harvest the plant known as the pinguay weed, or similar rubber producing plants. **1909** *Springfield W. Republican* 24 June 14 *(DA)*, The disease known as 'pingue,' which for several years has been disastrous on the sheep ranches of the Southwest. It is supposed to afflict sheep as a consequence of their eating the leaves or the roots of the so-called rubber plant. **1913** (1979) Barnes *Western Grazing* 269, *Pingue* . . *(Hymenoxys floribunda).*—In northern New Mexico and southern Colorado in the upper Rio Grande region there has been for several years past more or less loss from some disease known locally among the sheepmen as "pingue," from the Spanish name of the plant which is presumed to be responsible for the trouble. **1937** U.S. Forest Serv. *Range Plant Hdbk.* W7, Pingüe, pronounced peeng'gway, the widely established and generally used common name of this species, is a Spanish word meaning oily, referring, undoubtedly, to the oily, resinous leaves. **1947** Curtin *Healing Herbs* 154 **NM,** The *pinhué* only grows about one foot high at best. . . Likewise *pingué* is dangerous to sheep as it will form balls of rubber in their stomachs. **1968** Schmutz et al. *Livestock-Poisoning Plants AZ* 46, The toxic principle of pingue is unknown. . . It is most poisonous to sheep, though cattle and goats also are affected. . . There is no specific medicinal treatment for pingue-poisoned animals. **1971** Green *Village Horse Doctor* 200 **cwTX** (as of 1940s), I telephoned the agent and explained to him that my suspicions were that pinguey was the weed that had caused the trouble [=a die-out of sheep] at Hubble.

pingwing n
=**pingue.**
1949 Moldenke *Amer. Wild Flowers* 203, The *fragrant bitterweed,* . . and *Pingwing, A[ctinea] richardsonii,* are poisonous to cattle and other livestock, . . but are eaten only when other forage is scarce. **1967** Dodge *Roadside Wildflowers* 90 **SW,** Pingwing is a tufted perennial with a woody crown and branched stems 6 to 18 inches tall. . . The root bark is used by Indians as a substitute for chewing gum.

pinhead n
1 =**pintail 1.**
1940 Trautman *Birds Buckeye Lake* 179 **OH,** *Anas acuta.* . . The "pin head" as it was called, was a favorite with sportsmen, for it was more easily decoyed to "wooden blocks" and live decoys than were most puddle ducks, especially in spring. **1965** DARE (Qu. Q5, . . *Kinds of wild ducks*) Inf **OK**46, Pinhead—not numerous.

2 Appar a **croaker** n[1] **1a(1)** (here: *Micropogon undulatus*).
1970 DARE (Qu. P2, . . *Kinds of saltwater fish caught around here . . good to eat*) Inf **VA**55, Pinhead; (Qu. P14, . . *Commercial fishing . . what do the fishermen go out after?*) Inf **VA**55, Pinhead. **1984** DARE File **Chesapeake Bay** [Watermen's vocab], Croaker / grumbler / growler / hard head / pin head / kingbilly / roundhead.

3 A **minnow B1**; see quot.
1974 McClane *McClane's New Std. Fishing Encycl.* 555, Tiny minnows, usually called "pinheads," are best for panfish, and they are excellent for use on the trout of small streams.

pinhook adj Also *pinhookish* [*pinhook* a bent pin used as a fishhook]
Petty, small-time.
1834 Crockett *Narrative* 110 **TN,** I was hunted down like a wild varment, and in this hunt every little newspaper in the district, and every little pin-hook lawyer was engaged. **1971** DARE File **AL,** That's too pinhookish ['pɛn,hʊkɪš] to bother with.

pinhook v [Prob back-formation from **pinhooker**] **chiefly S Midl**
1 To act as a **pinhooker**; hence vbl n *pinhooking,* pronc-sp *penhooking.*
1944 PADS 2.68 **S Midl,** *Pin-hook.* . . To buy privately, usually small crops and at bargain prices, tobacco in the barn or at the warehouse [PADS Ed: and sometimes in the field [in sVA]]. **1966** PADS 45.19 **cnKY,** *Pinhook.* . . To speculate in tobacco by buying from the farmer and reselling at auction on low profit margins. These transactions often take place just outside a warehouse, and the pinhooker will attach his sales tag to a lot of tobacco waiting to be received by the warehouse workers. . . "If you want to start pinhooking, you have to really know tobacco." **1980** Banks *First-Person America* 142 **NC** (as of c1939), That was when speculators used to pinhook by buying right in the fields. **1983** Montell *Don't Go Up* 46 **csKY, cnTN,** Today, some area residents . . earn comfortable livings farming part-time and "pen-hooking" the rest of the time. They roam from farm to farm and from community to community, hoping to buy one or more head of livestock in order to turn a quick dollar. They may haul the stock to market and take their chances of prices there, or they may sell to another jobber without ever loading up the animals in their own trucks. In classic form, the penhooker hangs around the regional livestock markets . . ; he jumps onto trucks loaded with hogs or cattle and offers the owner "top dollar" for his cargo before he has the chance to yard the animals. *Ibid* 200, *Penhooking.* Practice of visiting local farms and communities seeking to buy livestock and, in turn, to sell the stock for a quick profit. **1997** Roberts *Man Who Listens* 165, From the mid-1970s until 1989 . . I bought yearling Thoroughbreds at one public auction, in Kentucky, say, and then sold them as two-year-olds at another public auction, perhaps in California. It's called "pinhooking."

2 To sell (something) to a **pinhooker;** to avoid a middleman in a crop sale.
1976 Garber *Mountain-ese* 68 **sAppalachians,** *Pin-hook* . . buy or sell secretly—Lonnie decided to pin-hook his backer crop fer a shore amount. **1983** MJLF 9.1.50 **ceKY** (as of 1956), *Pinhook* . . to sell a tobacco crop directly to a buyer rather than auctioning it.

pinhooker n Pronc-sp *penhooker;* abbr *hooker* **S Midl** Cf **pinhook** adj, v
A small-time speculator in farm products, esp tobacco; esp one who buys directly from farmers.
1936 *AmSp* 11.276 **eTN,** *Pin-hooker.* Dishonest tobacco buyer. 'He is a pin-hooker.' **1939** Writers' Program *Guide KY* 352, At the old tobacco house in Pinhook, an early settlement in Robertson County, originated the term "pinhooker," which is applied to the tobacco brokers who refuse to buy until the prices are low and the farmers are at their mercy, then resell to the warehouse for a higher price. **1940** *AmSp* 15.134 [Tobacco market language], *Pinhooker.* A speculator in tobacco. **1942** *Sun* (Baltimore) 23 Sept. 7/2 *(OED2)*, 'Pinhookers', who make small pur-

chases in auction markets and then resell them in the same markets also are exempt from price control. **1944** *PADS* 2.68 **S Midl**, *Pin-hooker. . .* A dealer who pin-hooks. **1949** Arnow *Hunter's Horn* 79 **eKY**, Nunn said nothing. He never could make up his mind to deal with penhookers like these or sell it in the auction ring. Everybody said that either way a man was liable to get cheated out of his eyeteeth. John dealt with the hookers, but Preacher Samuel never would. *Ibid* 83, He sold the pigs to a penhooker. **1949** Botkin *Treas. S. Folkl.* 652 **NC**, There's Carroll, Jones, and Mallory for the Big Three . . buyers from the four large independents who are on this market, and seven or eight pinhookers. **1966** *PADS* 45.20 **cnKY**, *Pinhooker. . .* One who practices pinhooking. **1969** *DARE* Tape **KY**60, What we used to have was pinhookers would come out [to market] and they'd catch a farmer . . half-drunk and didn't know the value of his tobacco. They'd buy his 'bacca, tobacco, and if it hadn't been handled correctly they'd hire people to rehandle it. They'd put it on the floor and make some money out of it. But that has practically passed now. **1983** [see **pinhook** v 1]. **1987** Kytle *Voices* 266 **NC**, A pin hooker goes to the tobacco market, comes along after the big tobacco company buyers. He finds farmers whose tobacco wasn't sold to these buyers. Sometimes he finds tobacco that he thinks isn't properly graded. Grading isn't easy, and it's not everybody who can do it, but a pin hooker knows all about tobacco. Because the farmers don't have money enough to hold on to their tobacco, the pin hooker can buy it for next to nothing. He regrades it, packs it, and sells it. **1993** Mason *Feather Crowns* 301 **KY** (as of c1900), The tobaccer's bad with them worms, and them pinhookers that come around won't offer the price it takes to raise it.

pinhooking See **pinhook** v 1

pinhookish See **pinhook** adj

pinhue See **pingue**

pinion See **piñon** 1

pinjinnet See **pipjenny**

pink n[1] See **pinkie** n[1]

pink n[2]

1 Std: a plant of the genus *Dianthus.* For other names of var spp see **cemetery pink, clove ~, everlasting** n **1, grass pink 3, Indian ~ 10, spice ~, sweet William**

2 Any of var other plants; see quots.

1883 Zeigler–Grosscup *Heart of Alleghanies* 187, What is locally known as the Pink [=rhododendron] Beds, in the northwestern part of Transylvania, a dense forest plateau, is an absolute wilderness in which a lost traveler might wander for days. **1898** *Jrl. Amer. Folkl.* 11.274 **CA**, *Dodecatheon* (sp.), . . pinks. *Ibid* 275 **WI**, *Phlox* (all species), pinks, Monroe, Wis. **1948** Pearson *Sea Flavor* 54 **NH**, Anyone who walks on the salt meadows in midsummer knows the friendly rosy faces of. . . *Sabbatia* [sic] *stellaris.* . . The pinks' small faces, perhaps ½ inch across, are divided into five petals. **1950** Correll *Native Orchids* 139, On forested slopes overlooking the "pink beds," a mountain basin filled with Rhododendron near Brevard, North Carolina, I have seen this little orchid growing profusely. **1968–69** *DARE* (Qu. S11, . . Bachelor's button) Infs **MO**37, **NY**115, Pinks. **1968** *DARE* FW Addit **VA**15, Pink = cornflower . . *Centaurea maculosa.*

3a A society belle; a girl or woman of the social elite.

1830 in 1956 Eliason *Tarheel Talk* 155 **se,ceNC**, I visited Pa's old faded pink . . his old withered belle. **1983** *NADS Letters* **GA**, Atlanta pink (girl or woman who grew up with all the seeming necessities of society: cashmere sweaters, pearls—whatever was "in"). **1993** *Atlanta Jrl.–Constitution* (GA) 22 Sept sec B 1 **Atlanta GA**, When I came to Atlanta in the 1940s I was fully grown and only heard about "pinks" as that group of teenage girls who gathered at the Palace of Sweets on Broad Street when they changed streetcars on their way home from Girls High after school.

b A White person, esp an attractive girl or woman; hence n *pink chaser* a Black person who seeks the company of White people. *among Black speakers*

1926 Van Vechten *Nigger Heaven* 157, Funny thing about these pink-chasers, the ofays never seem to have any use for them. **1945** L. Shelly *Jive Talk Dict.* 16 *(OED2), Pink,* pretty white girl. **1964** *PADS* 42.31 **Chicago IL** [Black], Names for Caucasians. . . *pink.* **1970** Major *Dict. Afro-Amer. Slang* 91, *Pink:* (1900's–40's) white person. *Pink chasers:* (1900's–40's) black people who deliberately cultivate friendships with

white people. **1980** Folb *Runnin' Down* 60 **cwCA** [Black], The single most descriptive attribute young blacks focus on in their labeling of whites is color . . such as *whitey, . . gray boy, pinks.*

c also *pinkie, pinky:* A light-skinned Black girl or woman.

1934 *AmSp* 9.288 **PA** [Black student slang], *Pinkie.* A very attractive light-skinned colored girl. **1970** Major *Dict. Afro-Amer. Slang* 91, *Pinky:* (1940's) Afro-American girl who looks white; term popularized by the movie *Pinky,* starring Jeanne Crain. **1983** Mebane *Mary Wayfarer* 62 **NC**, Light-skinned black women, incidentally, were often called "red-bones" by black males, less often "pinks," sometimes the grossly inelegant "yellowhammers," as in "I've got me a yellowhammer."

4 See **pink salmon 1.**
5 See **pink bird.**

pink v Also with *up* [*EDD pink* v.[4] 4 "To pitch at a mark in order to settle precedence in any game."] Cf **pink** n[3]
In marble play: =**lag** v[1] **1a, b;** also used as a call.

1963 *KY Folkl. Rec.* 9.63 **eKY**, When a marble is tossed by a player toward a line to decide the order of play: . . pinks-up [used in four counties] . . pink-up [used in one county]. *Ibid* 64, Request to toss marble into ring in order to be closer for next shot. The turn to shoot is forfeited when this is done and permission is granted: . . pink-up [used in three counties]. **c1970** Wiersma *Marbles Terms, Pink the line:* . . game; rolling marbles, attempting to get as close as possible to a line in the dirt (old term).

pink n[3] [**pink** v]
In marble play:

a =**lag** n[1] **1b;** hence n *pink line* =**lag line.**

1895 *Searcher* 1.7 **CT**, In Connecticut, where I was "brought up," or "raised," we played the game of marbles . . with the aid of . . "knuckle down," "last pink," (claiming the right to the last toss at the "bar" to determine which of the players should "shoot" first at the marbles). **1963** *KY Folkl. Rec.* 9.64 **eKY**, The line which one tosses marbles toward: . . pink-line [used in three counties].

b A ring on the ground into which marbles are placed, and out of which marbles are shot; hence n *pinks* a game involving such rings.

1958 *Sat. Eve. Post Letters* **swMO** (as of 1914), How the game of "pinks" was played with marbles [*DARE* Ed: drawing of four rings (designated *pinks*) in a row, with 6 feet between them]. . . The object . . was to knock as many marbles out of the pink as possible. . . If the first player knocked all marbles out before missing, then all other players had the opportunity to shoot at his taw . . in the first pink. Any player knocking it out took all the marbles. . . I have . . seen good players make a stand in each pink and go right through all pinks . . leaving only one in the last pink.

pink n[4] See **pinkie** n[1]

pink and blue ladies n Cf **languid lady**
A **bluebell 1g** (here: *Mertensia virginica*).

1899 (1909) Earle *Child Life* 384 **NEng**, Mertensia, or lungwort, we termed "pink and blue ladies." The lovely blossoms, which so delighted the English naturalist Wallace, and which he called "drooping porcelain-blue bells," are shaped something like a child's straight-waisted, full-skirted frock. If pins are stuck upright in a piece of wood, the little blue silken frocks can be hung over them, and the green calyx looks like a tiny hat.

pink Annie n
A cultivated bean (*Phaseolus vulgaris* var).

1982 *Smithsonian Letters* **csWV**, Pink Annies—a light yellow bean that turns pink when ripe (Lewisburg, WV).

pink azalea n Cf **pink-shell azalea**
A **rhododendron:** usu *Rhododendron nudiflorum,* occas another **rhododendron;** see quots.

1901 Lounsberry *S. Wild Flowers* 378, A[zalea] nudiflora, . . pink azalea, . . grows . . through woods and thickets and opens its bloom at the same time, or a little before its leaves. Its pink and white flowers have not as intense a fragrance as those of the swamp honeysuckle. **1911** NJ State Museum *Annual Rept. for 1910* 612, *Azalea nudiflora.* . . Pink Azalea. . . Common in woodlands of the Northern and Middle districts, occasional in the Cape May peninsula, and very rare in the Pine Barrens. **1924** *Amer. Botanist* 30.59, *Azalea nudiflora.* . . Among names derived from its color are "pink azalea," "swamp pink" [etc]. **1936** Whitehouse *TX Flowers* 92, Thickets of the pink azalea . . *(Azalea nudiflora)* occur in a few places in East Texas. **1952** Taylor *Plants Colonial Days* 67 **VA,** *Rhododendron nudiflorum.* . . Pink azalea . . is a native shrub, usually under 5 feet. **1963** IL Nat. Hist. Surv. *Biol. Notes* 22 **swIL,** The forest is a mixed deciduous type, with southern yellow pine and pink azalea as unusual species. *Ibid* 31, Azalea, pink—*Rhododendron roseum.* **1964** Batson *Wild Flowers SC* 83, *Pink Azalea: Rhododendron nudiflorum.* . . This is a hardy wild flower. . . Vermont to South Carolina. *Ibid* 84, *Hoary Pink Azalea: Rhododendron canescens.* . . Deciduous shrub resembling preceding species except that the leaves, particularly the young ones, are whitened with a gray or hoary pubescence. . . Delaware to Florida. **1973** Wharton–Barbour *Trees KY* 557, *Rhododendron nudiflorum.* . . Pink Azalea. . . Scattered throughout the Cumberland Plateau and Cumberland Mountains but is infrequent.

pink bat n

A brown bat (here: *Myotis sodalis*).

   1961 Jackson *Mammals WI* 83, *Myotis sodalis.* . . *Vernacular names.*—Cave bat, . . pink bat. . . Below, the fur is slaty basally, the hairs with grayish white tips, washed more or less heavily with cinnamon-brown, particularly at the flanks. . . The general effect is a pinkish white below and a dull chestnut gray above.

pink bean n esp CA   See Map   Cf **Mexican bean 1, frijole**

A cultivated bean (*Phaseolus vulgaris* var) similar to a kidney or **pinto bean** and used in chili, soups, and similar fare.

   1900 *Land of Sunshine* 13.435 **CA,** All this land is most fertile, yielding with very great abundance all that is planted in it—corn, wheat, pink beans [Author: *frijoles*], lentiles, peas [etc]. **1965–70** *DARE* (Qu. I17, *Beans . . that are dark red when they are dry*) Infs **CA**4, 11, 22, 36, 63, 87, 90, **GA**75, **WA**8, Pink beans; **CA**24, Pink beans or Mexican pink beans or frijoles; **CA**77, Pink bean—the Sacramento pink; **CA**17, California pink beans; (Qu. I20, . . *Kinds of beans*) Infs **CA**36, 63, 126, 138, 212, Pink beans; **CA**90, Pink beans [same as] California strawberries; **CA**162, California pink beans; (Qu. H50, *Dishes made with beans, peas, or corn that everybody around here knows, but people in other places might not*) Infs **CA**22, 24, 32, Pink beans; **CA**59, California pink beans [same as] Mexican beans; (Qu. I18, *The smaller beans that are white when they are dry*) Infs **CA**139, 210, Pink beans. **1968** *DARE* Tape **CA**63, [FW:] You raised a lot of beans out here in California . . mostly the pink bean though, I hear. [Inf:] Mostly the pink bean, yeah. *Ibid* **CA**90, On my board was, all it was, was Mexican tortillas, if you know what they are, and good old-fashioned pink beans, what we called California strawberries. **1971** Bright *Word Geog. CA & NV* 184 **CA,** *Pinto bean . . pink beans* 17% [of 300 infs]. **1990** *Seed Savers Yearbook* 42, *Pink.* . . Very prolific dry weather bean, seeds are really pink, twining, good chili or soup bean.

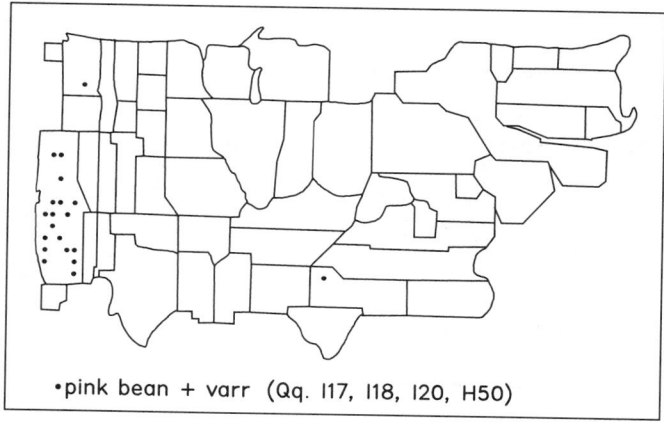

•pink bean + varr (Qq. I17, I18, I20, H50)

pink bell n

A **fritillary** (here: *Fritillaria pluriflora*).

   1959 Carleton *Index Herb. Plants* 93, Pink bell: Fritillaria pluriflora.

pink-bellied racer n Also *pink-bellied whipsnake* Cf **pink racer**

A **coachwhip snake** (here: *Masticophis flagellum* subsp *piceus*).

   1952 Ditmars *N. Amer. Snakes* 182, *Pink-bellied Racer, Pink-bellied*

Whipsnake, *Masticophis piceus* [*M. flagellum p.*] . . *Coloration:* Uniform dark reddish brown to satiny blue black above. Pink or pinkish red beneath. . . Southern Arizona and Lower California. . . A very active, desert reptile.

pink belly n

=**redbelly 9.**

   1975 Ferretti *Gt. Amer. Book Sidewalk Games* 213 **NYC** (as of 1940s), Involved [in the game "Gestapo"] were such things as . . pulling up his shirt and giving him a "pink belly" (creating a bright red stomach area by constant pat-pat-patting on the stomach). **1997** *DARE* File **swCA** (as of c1950), We used to call it [=pushing a kid to the ground and rubbing his belly on the grass] pink belly. **1999** *Ibid* **Bronx NYC** (as of c1955), A group of boys would secretly decide to give one of their number a pink belly. We used the verb "to woof" to mean "to give someone a pink belly," and the signal to commence the operation was, as I recall, "OK, let's woof'm." To give a kid a pink belly as "played" by us in the projects, was for a group to grab the victim, drag him into a stairwell, hold him down, raise his shirt, and slap his belly until red.

pink bird n Also *pink (flamingo)*

=**roseate spoonbill.**

   1938 Oberholser *Bird Life LA* 81, *Roseate Spoonbill.* . . Its color has given rise to most of its names, and it is known popularly often as 'pink curlew', or simply 'pink bird'. **1943** Gabrielson *Wildlife Refuges* 229, The nineteen Texas [National Audubon Society] refuges are largely islands lying in shallow lagoons along the coast. . . There are two large colonies of spoonbills or "pinks." **1950** Writers' Round Table *Padre Is.* 120 **csTX,** Miss Maggie Benson, of Corpus Christi, told that she and her mother found "pink flamingoes" (roseate spoonbills) which had been beaten to death by a severe hurricane. They dressed the wing feathers and used them for fans. **1954** Sprunt *FL Bird Life* 47, *Ajaia ajaja.* . . *Local Names:* Pink Curlew; Pink. . . Breast white; rest of body and wings pale rose-pink, the shoulders and tail coverts splashed with carmine. **1962** Imhof *AL Birds* 110, *Roseate Spoonbill.* . . *Other name:* Pink. **1969** Longstreet *Birds FL* 30, Roseate Spoonbill—Other names: . . Pink Bird.

pink bloom n

A **marsh pink 1** (here: *Sabatia angularis*).

   1894 *Jrl. Amer. Folkl.* 7.94 **WV,** *Sabatia* [sic] *angularis,* . . pink bloom. **1959** Carleton *Index Herb. Plants* 93, *Pink-bloom:* Sabatia [sic] angularis.

pink bottom n Also *pink undies* Cf **pink crown, ~ gills**

A **field mushroom** (here: *Agaricus campestris*).

   1972 Miller *Mushrooms* 129, *Agaricus campestris.* . . "Meadow Mushroom" or "Pink Bottom". . . One must note the characteristic pink, free gills which soon turn chocolate-brown from the maturing spores. **1980** Marteka *Mushrooms* 113, *Agaricus campestris* . . *common names* . . pink bottom, . . pink undies. **1985** Weber–Smith *Field Guide S. Mushrooms* 221, *Pink Bottom.* . . can be recognized by the . . bright rosy pink young gills. . . Edible and one of the most popular mushrooms.

pink-bottom turtle n

Prob a **red-bellied turtle.**

   1969 *DARE* (Qu. P24, . . *Kinds of turtles*) Inf **OH**89, Pink-bottom turtle.

pinkbud n

A **redbud** (here: *Cercis canadensis*).

   1970 *DARE* (Qu. T16, . . *Kinds of trees . . 'special'*) Inf **KY**80, Pinkbud [same as] redbud.

pink chaser See **pink** n[2] **3b**

pink clover n

=**alsike.**

   1929 *Torreya* 29.150 **ME,** T[rifolium] hybridum, *"Pink Clover."* **1945** Wodehouse *Hayfever Plants* 115, Several clovers (*Trifolium*) have attracted attention as possible causes of hayfever. . . One . . is . . *T. pratense.* . . Often associated with it is the pink or alsike clover (*T. hybridum* L.) **1969** *DARE* (Qu. S26d, *Wildflowers that grow in meadows; not asked in early QRs*) Infs **RI**1, **VT**16, Pink clover; (Qu. S26a, . . *Wildflowers . . Roadside flowers*) Inf **IL**17, Pink clover.

pink crane n

=**roseate spoonbill.**

1916 *Times–Picayune* (New Orleans LA) 2 Apr mag sec 5/1, *Roseate spoonbill (Ajaia ajaja). . .* Pink "Crane."

pink crown n Cf **pink bottom**

A **mushroom B1** (here: *Sarcosphaera crassa*).

1972 Miller *Mushrooms* 220, *Sarcosphaera coronaria* [=*S. crassa*] . . "Pink Crown". . . Most abundant in P[acific] N[orth]W[est]. . . I have eaten this and like it, but it requires much cleaning. **1981** Lincoff *Audubon Field Guide Mushrooms* 346, *Pink Crown—Sarcosphaera crassa. . .* Common in Rocky Mountains and Pacific NW; also reported in Michigan and New York. . . Because it usually grows just beneath the surface . . , it resembles a pinkish-violet hole in the ground.

pink curlew n [See quot 1955]

=**roseate spoonbill.**

1884 Henshall *Camping in FL* 74, Among the number the beautiful roseate spoonbill *(Ajaja rosea),* called by Floridians the "pink curlew." **1913** *Auk* 30.503 **Okefenokee GA,** *Ajaia ajaja. . .* 'Pink Curlew.'—Col. A.B. Perram, of Waycross, informed us that some years ago a well-known hunter . . brought to his office some 'Pink Curlew' feathers from the Okefinokee. **1917** (1923) *Birds Amer.* 1.175, Formerly the Spoonbills, or "Pink Curlews," as the Florida hunters know them, were extensively shot and their feathers shipped to Jacksonville where they were made into fans to sell to winter tourists. **1938** [see **pink bird**]. **1955** *Oriole* 20.1.3 **GA,** *Roseate Spoonbill—Pink Curlew* (general; the full plumage has much tincture of pink to rose; "curlew" from affinity with the ibises, which are commonly miscalled curlews). **1967** Will *Dredgeman* 149 **FL,** Now one may even, on occasions, see the spoonbill or "pink curlew". **1969** Longstreet *Birds FL* 30, Roseate Spoonbill— Other names: Pink Curlew.

pink daisy n **AK** Cf **daisy 2b**

A **fleabane** (here: *Erigeron peregrinus*).

1966 Heller *Wild Flowers AK* 38, *Pink Daisy—Erigeron peregrinus. . .* Flowers in solitary terminal heads, outer ray flowers pink. . . Coastal meadows from Ketchikan north to Prince William Sound area, west to Aleutians. **1982** *AK Geographic* 9.3.28, The wild geranium . . grows only at Whitney Pond [on Saint Paul Island in the Pribilofs] . . , just as does a single clump of coastal fleabane or pink daisy *(Erigeron peregrinus).* **1996** *DARE* File **AK,** While I was in Unalaska last summer, a local resident called my attention to a number of bright "pink daisies" in bloom.

pink elephants n Also *little pink elephants*

An **elephant's head** (here: *Pedicularis groenlandica*).

1959 Carleton *Index Herb. Plants* 75, *Little-pink-elephants:* Pedicularis groenlandica. *Ibid* 93, *Pink elephants:* Pedicularis groenlandica. **1963** Craighead *Rocky Mt. Wildflowers* 176, When you see a dense spike of small reddish-purple to pink flowers, each unmistakably resembling an elephant's head with the trunk curving out and up, you are . . seeing pink elephants. **1973** Hitchcock–Cronquist *Flora Pacific NW* 432, Pink elephants, elephant's head . . *P[edicularis] groenlandica.*

pinkets n **West**

A **storksbill** (here: *Erodium cicutarium*).

1915 (1926) Armstrong–Thornber *Western Wild Flowers* 276, *Erodium cicutarium.* . . Filaree is a corruption of the Spanish Alfilerilla. . . Other names are Pinkets [etc]. **1959** Barnes *Nat. Hist. Wasatch Winter* 39 **UT,** Alfilaria *(Erodium cicutarium).* Locally it is called . . "pinkets", or "May flower". **1963** Craighead *Rocky Mt. Wildflowers* 105, *Erodium cicutarium.* . . Pinkets. . . A prostrate, mat-forming plant with 2 to 10 small pink flowers. . . Seed pods strikingly resemble stork heads.

pinkey n[1] See **pinkie** n[1]

pinkey n[2] See **pinkie** n[3]

pinkeye n Also *pinkeye pea* [See quot 1990] Cf **pinkeye soldier**

A var of the **black-eyed pea** (here: *Vigna unguiculata* subsp *unguiculata*).

1965 *DARE* (Qu. I20, . . *Kinds of beans*) Inf **FL18,** Pinkeye peas—like blackeye, but have a pink eye. **1988** Whealy *Garden Seed Inventory* (2d ed) 164, Pinkeye. **1990** *Seed Savers Yearbook* 104, *Purple Hull Pinkeye. . .* Compact bush or plant, young elongated white seeds with pink or purple eyes, delicious heavy-yielding field pea, . . can produce 2 crops per season with favorable weather conditions. **2000** *NADS Letters* **cnAL,** There is a pea very similar to the black-eye peas called a

"pink-eye pea". Grown in the South and cooked like black eye peas and just as popular. I can buy them at the farmers market. The "eye" of the pea is reddish or pinkish instead of black.

pink-eyed diver n

=**horned grebe.**

1910 Eaton *Birds NY* 1.95, This bird [=*Podiceps auritus*] called also Hell-diver, Pink-eyed diver, Dipper, . . is a common migrant in every county of the State. **1917** (1923) *Birds Amer.* 1.5, *Horned Grebe. . . Other Names.* . . Pink-eyed Diver. **1946** Hausman *Eastern Birds* 67, Pink-eyed Diver. . . Large lakes, bays, and open water generally.

pink-eyed snake n Also *pink-headed snake*

Prob =**fox snake.**

1969 *DARE* (Qu. P25, . . *Kinds of snakes*) Inf **KY6,** Pink-eyed snake or pink-headed snake. [**1981** Vogt *Nat. Hist. WI* 138, Fox snakes are regularly but needlessly killed by misinformed people who believe them to be poisonous copperheads because of their reddish-brown heads.]

pinkeye pea See **pinkeye**

pink eyes n

=**bird's eye 2.**

1911 Jepson *Flora CA* 331, *G[ilia] tricolor. . .* Also called "Pink Eyes" near Vallejo.

pinkeye soldier n Cf **pinkeye**

A cultivated bean (*Phaseolus vulgaris* var).

1978 *Wanigan Catalog* 16, *Pink Eye Soldier. . .* From Utah, this . . white seed has a red figure in a broad area at hilum. Carried West by pioneers from Illinois. Midseason baking bean. **1979** *UpCountry* Jan 20 **neMA,** The commodity is beans . . Pink Eye Soldier and hundreds of other varieties of shell beans.

pinkey-stern schooner See **pinkie** n[1]

pink fairies n

A **farewell-to-spring** (here: *Clarkia pulchella*).

1915 (1926) Armstrong–Thornber *Western Wild Flowers* 322, *Pink Fairies. . .* The flowers are fantastic in form, the airiest and most fairy-like blossoms that can well be imagined. **1963** Craighead *Rocky Mt. Wildflowers* 120, *Clarkia pulchella. . .* Pink-fairies. . . This attractive annual has clusters of deep rose-lavender blossoms 1/2–1 in. broad that superficially resemble a cluster of miniature oak leaves.

pinkfish n

The blind goby *(Typhlogobius californiensis).*

1898 U.S. Natl. Museum *Bulletin* 47.2262, *Typhlogobius californiensis. . . Pink-fish. . .* Color uniform light pink. . . From San Diego southward to Cerros Island; an extraordinary fish, found attached to the lower side of rocks in shallow water or surf.

pink flamingo See **pink bird**

pink flamingo snake n [See quot]

A **water snake** (here: *Nerodia fasciata* subsp *confluens*).

1958 Conant *Reptiles & Amphibians* 119, *Broad-banded Water Snake—Natrix sipedon confluens* [=*Nerodia fasciata c.*] . . In some parts of range, either the yellow or red [coloration] may be exceptionally prominent, as is reflected in such colorful local names as . . "pink flamingo snake." . . Occurs to very edge of salt or brackish water along Gulf Coast.

pink-flowered acacia n

=**fairy duster.**

1960 [see **pink mimosa 2**].

pink gills n Also *pink-gilled mushroom* Cf **pink bottom**

A **field mushroom** (here: *Agaricus campestris*).

1908 Hard *Mushroom Edible* 307, *Agaricus campestris.* . . is perhaps the widest known of all mushrooms, familiarly known as the "Pink-gilled mushroom." **1925** *Book of Rural Life* 2.3722, The cultivated mushroom is simply a variety of the common *field,* or *pink-gilled, mushroom.* . . The delicate pink-tinted gills become brownish on maturity. **1955** Adams *Grandfather* 200 **NY** (as of 1830s), The ground here was dotted with pink-gills, the flavorsome and meaty field mushrooms.

pink-headed snake See **pink-eyed snake**

pinkie n[1] Also *pink (stern)*, *pink(ey)-stern schooner* Also sp *pink(e)y* [Du *pink* and its dimin *pinkje*. Pink was borrowed into English early (*OED2* 1471 →), but *pinkie* (and varr) occur first and nearly exclusively in North America.] **NEng**
A small sailing vessel with a sharp stern.

1636 in 1865 MA Hist. Soc. *Coll.* 4th ser 7.54, When the pinckes comes downe I hope the will bringe hay. **1690** (1892) Hammond *Diary* 156 **MA**, A Pink . . was fired & burnt to ye water. **1705** *Boston News-Letter* (MA) 23–30 Apr [2]/1, On the 15th Instant, arrived here William Card in a Pink from Boston. **1840** *Niles' Natl. Reg.* 15 Aug 376, Chebacco boats and small schooners are known to him as *"pinkies," "pogies,"* and *"jiggers."* **1851** *NY Jrl. Commerce* 22 Dec 1/3 **Boston MA**, A pink stern schooner of about 50 tons, belonging to Millbridge . . went ashore near Philip's Cove. **1891** Cooke *Huckleberries* 234 **RI**, I'd ruther sail a pinky round Pint Judy pint in a sou'easter. **1902** (1904) Rowe *Maid of Bar Harbor* 188 **ME**, An' a pinkie all 'er own, painted green. **1903** *DN* 2.295 **Cape Cod MA** (as of a1857), Pinkey, or pink-stern. . . A small vessel with a sharp stern above water. **1903** *N.Y. Tribune* 25 Oct. 14 (*OED2*), On another occasion the Houghton ran into a pinkey-stern schooner. **1932** Wasson *Sailing Days* 113 **cME coast**, True smacks were often sharp-sterned craft called pinkys, with rail rising aft to a high peak, ending in a crotch for holding the main boom when sail was lowered. Pinkys, often known as "pinks", were noted for their seagoing qualities and were, above all others, of purely New England origin. **1937** FWP *Guide ME* 231, A boat once frequently seen along the Maine coast and still occasionally found in some of the fishing villages of Nova Scotia is the pinky. . . These boats, pointed at both ends, have wide gunwales rising to meet in a stern overhang. **1975** Gould *ME Lingo* 209, Pinky—A distinctive small schooner with sharp or "pinked" stern. Designed in Massachusetts, they had a vogue in Nova Scotia and were common along the Maine coast in short-haul trading. An occasional *pinky* is seen today in the summer fleet, preserved by someone who cares.

pinkie n[2] See **pink** n[2] **3c**

pinkie n[3] Also *pinkie finger* Also sp *pink(e)y* [Either directly from Du *pink(je)* or through Scots *pinkie* (*SND* at *pink* n.[2] 2 1808 →)]
The little finger.

1848 Bartlett *Americanisms* 406 **NY**, Pinky. (Dutch, *pink*.) The little finger. A very common term in New York, especially among small children, who, when making a bargain with each other, are accustomed to confirm it by interlocking the little finger of each other's right hands and repeating the following doggerel: *Pinky, pinky, bow-bell,/ Whoever tells a lie,/ Will sink down to the bad place,/ And never rise up again.* **1934** (1939) Miller *Tropic of Cancer* 64 **NYC**, Ever since I left Mona I had worn the ring on my pinkie. **1941** *Sun* (Baltimore MD) 13 Oct 8 (Hench Coll.), [Cartoon caption:] Pinkey Straight Up, That's The Class Way To Drink Tea, Pal! **1950** WELS **WI** (*Nicknames for the . . little finger*) 4 Infs, Pinkie. **1955** *AmSp* 30.295, The assumption of these users of the word in the New York area seems to be that *pinkie* is known the length and breadth of the land. . . My own investigations, however—so far as they have gone—reveal vast stretches of the continent in which *pinkie* 'little finger' is known to very few. It has a considerable degree of currency in Connecticut and Massachusetts, and it seems to be known in some parts of upper New York State as well as in the Hudson River region; but to the west and south of New York State there are few areas, with the exception of central and northern Michigan, where it passes current. **1962** *Hand Coll.* **neOH**, When two people say the same thing at the same time, they should say nothing, link their pinkies, i.e., their little fingers, and make a wish. . . Variant: they should link their pinky fingers. **1968** *Atlantic City Press* (NJ) 8 Aug 27/2, *$6,450 in Gems Stolen As Theft Wave Continues.* . . A $200 white gold pinky ring. **2000** *DARE* File **neIL, csWI**, "Pinkie swear?" Spoken in reply to a promise; an affirmative response is followed by the discourse participants linking their pinkies with the rest of the fingers in a fist.

pink in v phr [Engl dial; ult < Du *pinken* to shut the eyes] **NC** Cf **pink of the evening**
Of the day: to grow dark; hence n *pinking in of the day* early dusk.

1939 FWP *Guide NC* 98, The speech of the countryman is full of imaginative phrases. . . Late afternoon is "the pink of the evenin'" or "day down," or the time when "evenin' is a-pinkin' in." **1952** Brown *NC Folkl.* 1.576, *Pinking in of the day:* . . The time just before dusk.—

Central and east. **1972** Cooper *NC Mt. Folkl.* 95, *Pinked in*—late afternoon came.

pinkish adj Also *pinky* [Perh folk-etyms for *peakish, peaky*]
1965–68 *DARE* (Qu. X52, . . *A person . . who had been sick was looking* _____) Inf **DC8**, Pinkish [FW: Inf repeated resp]; [**GA23**, Pink around the gills;] (Qu. BB38, *When a person doesn't look healthy, or looks as if he hadn't been well for some time . . "He looks* _____.") Inf **GA23**, Pinkish; **FL22**, Pinky.

pink ladyfingers See **ladyfinger 5**

pinkletink n **Martha's Vineyard, Nantucket MA** Cf **pinkwink, tinky**
=spring peeper.

1918 *DN* 5.16 **Martha's Vineyard MA**, Pinkletink. . . Young frog. "I could hear the pinkletinks out in the swamp." **1931–33** LANE Worksheets **Martha's Vineyard MA**, Pinkletink. . . A peeper (frog). **1951** Hough *Singing in Morning* 15 **Martha's Vineyard MA**, Someone says that the frogs are going it on Cape Cod, and that "many natives call them pinkwinks." . . Over here on the Vineyard what we have is pinkletinks, and they are *Hyla crucifer,* tree toad now and forever. **1967** Borland *Hill Country* 107 **Nantucket MA**, On Nantucket the peepers are called pinkletinks, a name that sounds to me much like the sound the peepers make. **1980** *NYT Article Letters* **Martha's Vineyard MA**, Pinkletink—Used *only* on Martha's Vineyard. The spring-peeper or tiny tree frog.

pink line See **pink** n[3] **a**

pink liner See **pink sign**

pink matweed n
A sand spurry (here: *Spergularia rubra*).
1967 Gilkey–Dennis *Hdbk. NW Plants* 114, *Spergularia rubra. . . Pink mat-weed.* . . Prostrate herbs forming mats 1–4 dm. in diam. . . Common in dry hard ground.

pink milkwort n
A **milkwort** (here: *Polygala incarnata*).
1900 Lyons *Plant Names* 299, *P[olygala] incarnata* . . Pink Milkwort. **1911** NJ State Museum *Annual Rept. for 1910* 522, Pink Milkwort. . . Late June to mid-September. **1930** OK Univ. Biol. Surv. *Pub.* 2.69, *Polygala incarnata. . .* Pink Milkwort. **1946** Reeves–Bain *Flora TX* 79, Pink Milkwort. . . Flowers nearly white, pink, or purple. . . Subterranean flowers none. **1968** Barkley *Plants KS* 217, *Polygala incarnata. . .* Pink Milkwort. Sandy soil.

pink mimosa n
1 A **mimosa 1** (here: either *Mimosa borealis* or *M. microphylla*).
1936 Whitehouse *TX Flowers* 46, Pink Sensitive Brier (*Leptoglottis uncinata*) is also called pink mimosa. . . The small, fragrant pink flowers are borne in dense heads. **1938** Van Dersal *Native Woody Plants* 344, Mimosa[,] . . Pink (*Mimosa dysocarpa*). **1970** Correll *Plants TX* 778, *Mimosa borealis. . .* Pink mimosa. Rounded much-branched shrub about 1 m. tall. . . Flowers in pink globes.
2 =fairy duster.
1960 Vines *Trees SW* 502, *C[alliandra] eriophylla. . .* is also known under the names of Fairy Duster, Pink Mimosa, Pink-flowered Acacia [etc]. . . It is considered to be a valuable browse for livestock and deer, being tolerant of grazing.

pink mint n
A **hedgenettle** (here: *Stachys drummondii*).
1970 Correll *Plants TX* 1362, *Stachys Drummondii. . .* Pink mint. . . Corolla lavender or pink. . . In clayey soils, sandy or gravelly loam in chaparral, open woods, palm groves and brushlands in s. and coastal Tex.

pink of the evening n Cf **pink in**
Evening twilight.
1939 [see **pink in**]. **1946** Campbell *Folks Do Get Born* 212 **sGA**, I like to have some time to sit on my own front porch and enjoy the pink of the evening with my friends passing by, and my flowers about me. **1952** Brown *NC Folkl.* 1.576, *Pink of the evening:* . . Early twilight.—Central and east.

pink plumes n

1 A **prairie smoke 1** (here: *Geum triflorum*).

1953 Nelson *Plants Rocky Mt. Park* 93, Pink plumes . . *(Geum triflorum)*. . . Styles very long, becoming conspicuously plumose in fruit. **1954** Sharpe *101 Wildflowers* 29 **nwWA,** Pink Plumes . . Flowers purplish pink to reddish, nodding. . . Fruiting head an erect, feathery plume. . . Common in the northeast Olympics. **1975** Zwinger *Run River* 31 **UT,** Three-flowered avens or pink plume [sic] *(Geum triflorum)*.

2 A **bistort** (here: *Polygonum bistorta*).

1966 Heller *Wild Flowers AK* 30, Pink Plumes . . *Polygonum bistorta*. . . Flowers small, pink to rose-red, in showy, compact, terminal spikes. . . Most commonly in moist alpine meadows throughout interior Alaska north to the Arctic.

pink queen n

A **spiderflower** (here: *Cleome hassleriana*).

1970 Correll *Plants TX* 710, *Cleome Hassleriana*. . . *Spider plant, spider flower, pink queen*. . . Petals large, showy, pink to purple (rarely white).

pink racer n Cf **pink-bellied racer**

A **coachwhip snake** (here: *Masticophis flagellum* subsp *testaceus*).

1928 Baylor Univ. Museum *Contrib.* 16.15, *Masticophis flagellum flavigularis* [=*M. f. testaceus*]. . . In Trans-Pecos Texas, the names *Pink Racer* and *Red Racer* are applied to specimens in nuptial coloration whose upper and under surfaces have either a pinkish or deep reddish coloration.

pink rattler n Also *pink rattlesnake*

=**rock rattlesnake b.**

1974 Shaw–Campbell *Snakes West* 223, In the Chisos Mountains, near the Big Bend of Texas, where a reddish igneous rock is found, the rock rattlesnake is known locally as the "pink rattler" because its ground color is pinkish. **1997** *USA Today* (Arlington VA) 10 Jan sec A 12 **AZ,** The environment of the [Grand] canyon could be breathtakingly still, muted enough to hear the scales of a pink rattlesnake glide across stone.

pink rim See **pink sign**

pinkroot n

1 A plant of the genus *Spigelia,* esp **Indian pink 1.** Also called **worm grass**

1764 *Annual Reg. for 1763* 54, Produce of South Carolina. . . Pinkroot, 1 cask. **1795** Winterbotham *Amer. U.S.* 3.399 **NEng,** The following have been employed for medicinal purposes: . . Pink root . . Senna [etc]. **1830** Rafinesque *Med. Flora* 2.89, *Spigelia marilandica. Names*. Common Pinkroot. [*Ibid* 90, The root is the officinal part. . . It has chiefly attracted notice as a vermifuge and for diseases of children, convulsions, worm fever, &c.] **1854** Wailes *Rept. on Ag. & Geol. MS* 347, [*Plants Useful, Medicinal, and Ornamental:*] Pink-root, Spigelia marilandica. **1892** Coulter *Botany W. TX* 271, *Spigelia*. . . Pink-root. . . Flowers showy, . . corolla red or pink. **1933** Small *Manual SE Flora* 1046, *S[pigelia] marilandica*. . . *Pink-root*. . . Rich woods and hillsides, Fla. to Tex., Ind. and Md. (or N.J.) **1941** Walker *Lookout* 54 **TN,** Found growing in the mountain's rich woods . . is pink-root. . . Root-diggers once sought this plant so persistently that its numbers were greatly reduced. **1954** *Harder Coll.* **cwTN,** Pinkroot. . . (Spigelia)—A plant whose roots are valued for medicinal uses. **1969** *DARE* (Qu. S2) Inf **KY**21, Pinkroot; (Qu. S26e, *Other wildflowers not yet mentioned;* not asked in early QRs) Inf **KY**21, Pinkroot.

2 =**redroot c.**

1942 U.S. Natl. Park Serv. *Fading Trails* 173 **FL,** The prairie plant locally known as "pink-root" is a favorite item [of food for cranes], together with grasshoppers, lizards, and other small animal life. **1951** Teale *North with Spring* 41, The Kissimmee cranes are specialists at finding the underground tubers of *Gyrotheca tinctoria*, the pinkroot, bloodroot, Indian root, or painroot [sic for *paintroot*] of the prairie. **1969** *DARE* File **Okefenokee GA,** Pinkroot—an Okefenokee prairie plant; sandhill cranes feed on the roots.

pinks See **pink** n[3] **b**

pink salmon n chiefly **AK**

1 also *pink:* =**humpback salmon.** [See quot 1991]

1897 in 1900 U.S. Congress *Serial Set* 3852 Doc 153 24 **AK,** Pink or humpback. **1905** U.S. Bur. Fisheries *Rept. for 1904* 91 **AK,** The humpback salmon . . is known . . to the trade as pink salmon. *Ibid* 97, This establishment [=a cold-storage plant at Taku Bay AK] also salts a good many humpback and dog salmon bellies. . . The dog salmon bellies are cut small, to conform in size to the humpbacks, and all are sold as "pinks." **1925** *Book of Rural Life* 4868, Humpback salmon, often marketed as *Alaska pink* salmon. **1935** *Anchorage Daily Times* (AK) 24 July 1 (Tabbert *Dict. Alaskan Engl.*), Pinks prevail with chums, red and cohoes and kings in the order named. **1946** Dufresne *AK's Animals* 279, The pink salmon . . may also occasionally strike a lure in either salt or fresh water. **1968** *DARE* (Qu. P1, . . *Kinds of freshwater fish* . . *caught around here* . . *good to eat*) Inf **AK**1, There are light-meated (white) pink salmon, too; (Qu. P2, . . *Kinds of saltwater fish caught around here* . . *good to eat*) Inf **AK**9, Pink salmon. **1978** *AK Fishing Guide* 58, *Pink Salmon—Oncorhynchus gorbuscha:* Smallest of the Pacific salmon. *Ibid* 60, Pink salmon change rapidly when they arrive in fresh water, and within a week of their arrival are slab-sided, thin. . . Pinks that are bright and fresh from the sea are fairly scrappy. **1979** *Anchorage Daily News* (AK) 5 May sec C 3 (Tabbert *Dict. Alaskan Engl.*), There will be no pink salmon run this summer, since the Bristol Bay pinks come in two-year cycles. **1991** Tabbert *Dict. Alaskan Engl.* 134, The "official" common name *pink salmon* derives from the color of the soft, tasty flesh. The term is often shortened to *pink*, especially in the plural.

2 =**chum salmon.**

1905 [see **1** above]. **1955** U.S. Arctic Info. Center *Gloss.* 61, Pink salmon. 1. A small salmon, *Oncorhynchus gorbuscha*, which ascends Pacific coastal rivers. . . . 2. A misleading name for the chum salmon in parts of Alaska.

pink-shell azalea n Cf **pink azalea**

A **rhododendron** (here: *Rhododendron vaseyi*) native to North Carolina.

1938 Van Dersal *Native Woody Plants* 227, *Rhododendron vaseyi*. . . *Pinkshell azalea*. . . A small to large shrub. **1966** Grimm *Recognizing Native Shrubs* 215, *Pink-shell Azalea*. . . North Carolina. Beautiful flowering shrub of very limited natural distribution.

pink sign n Also *pink liner, ~ rim* [See quot 1976] Cf **peeler crab, red sign (crab), second, shedder, snot, white sign**

A blue crab (*Callinectes sapidus*) that is a week or less away from shedding.

1970 *DARE* Tape **VA**112, There's three stages of 'em. . . Now at first if there's a green crab . . and he will one day turn around and make a soft shell, he'll have a white sign. . . Where a rainbow is pink he'll have a white rim streak crawlin' around that back fin that he paddles with. . . And then the next one will come along, he's at a different stage, he'll have a pink rim. . . Now the pink rim won't bother each other, they can shed right in there together. **1976** Warner *Beautiful Swimmers* 27 **eMD,** Mike reads these crabs by examining the translucent next-to-last segment of their swimming legs. Some will be "white sign" crabs, . . which have about two weeks or less to moult. Others will be "pink signs" or "seconds," which will do it within a week. **1984** *DARE* File **Chesapeake Bay** [Watermen's vocab], Pink rim, pink liner, pink sign, second, medium.

pink snakeroot n Cf **pinkroot 1**

Prob =**Indian pink 1.**

1983 *MJLF* 9.1.50 **ceKY** (as of 1956), *Pink snakeroot* . . a medicinal herb.

pink snowbird n

The gray-crowned rosy finch (*Leucosticte tephrocotis*).

[**1928** Bailey *Birds NM* 699, Although there are only small snowbanks on the highest of these mountains in midsummer, the beautiful Rosy Finches are generally found in the region of large bodies of snow.] **1936** Roberts *MN Birds* 2.360, *Leucosticte tephrocotis littoralis*. . . "Pink Snowbird." . . Dark brown . . with a black cap, more or less gray about the head, and most of the plumage suffused with rose-color. **1957** Pough *Audubon W. Bird Guide* 305, Pink snowbird. See Gray-crowned rosy finch.

pink-spot n

A **gilia** (here: *Linanthus maculatus*).

1941 Jaeger *Wildflowers* 192 **Desert SW,** *Pygmy Pink-spot*. . . Corolla white, with pink spot on each lobe. Rare in sandy washes of the Morongo Pass area; also near Palm Springs.

pink star n Cf **sea star, Texas ~**

A **marsh pink 1** (here: *Sabatia angularis*).

1948 Wherry *Wild Flower Guide* 100, Upland Pinkstar (*Sabatia angularis*)... Flowers starry;.. pink with yellow basal spot... Southern states and lower half of our area [=NEast, Midl].

pinkster n Also *pinxter* [Du *Pinkster* Pentecost]

1 usu cap; also *Pinckster, Pinkster Day:* A holiday orig observed at Whitsuntide; see quots. **chiefly NY** *hist*

1797 in 1930 Dunlap *Diary* 1.65 **NJ**, The settlements along the river are dutch, it is the holiday they call pinkster & every public house is crowded with merry makers. **1821** Cooper *Spy* 2.188 **NY**, Upon my word you'd pass well at a pinkster frolic. **c1831** in 1875 Furman *Antiquities* 265 **NY**, The first Monday in June, or as the Dutch call it, *Pinckster,* was formerly considerable of a festival among the Dutch inhabitants of Long Island... But now poor *Pinckster* has lost its rank among the festivals, and is only kept by the negroes; with them, however, especially on the west end of this island, it is still much of a holiday. **1856** *Frank Leslie's Illustr. Newsp.* 24 May 382/3, The feast of Pinxter—answering to the English Whitsuntide—was celebrated May 12, by the German population of New York. **1881** *Harper's New Mth. Mag.* 62.526 **ceNY** (as of a1822), The Pinkster festivities commenced on the Monday after Whitsunday, and now began the fun for the negroes, for Pinkster was the carnival of the African race. The venerable "King of the Blacks"... originally came from Africa... [He was] the purchased slave of one of the most.. respectable merchant princes of the olden time... During Pinkster-day the negroes made merry with games and feasting, all paying homage to the king, who was held in awe and reverence as an African prince. **1895** *DN* 1.383 **NJ**, *Pinxter:* Whitsuntide. *Ibid* 392, *Pinxter:* Easter. Negroes in N.Y. **1896** (1968) Earle *Colonial NY* 195, There was one old-time holiday beloved of New Yorkers whose name is now almost forgotten,—Pinkster Day. **1945** *AN&Q* 5.121, Pinkster... I believe the celebration was on "Pink Monday." Traces of it survived into the early twentieth century; at least my great-aunt, born about 1860, used to mention the festival as late, say, as 1910. She made, I think, a special kind of cake for the day, and gave me, a small boy, some slight present. The Biblical descriptions of Pentecost suggest that the feast was modeled on stories from the Bible... I cannot recall ever hearing it mentioned by anyone else.

2 also *pinkster flower, pinxter bloom,* and varr: A **rhododendron,** usu *Rhododendron periclymenoides.* [Du *pinksterbloem,* dimin *pinksterbloemetje,* from its time of flowering] **chiefly NEast, esp NY, NJ** Cf **pinkster apple** For other names of *R. periclymenoides* see **election pink, honeysuckle 3, June apple 2, mayflower 2, mountain pink 4, pink azalea, swamp apple, ~ honeysuckle, wild azalea, ~ honeysuckle**

[**1739** (1946) Gronovius *Flora Virginica* 21, Azalea... Caprifolio simili... *Pinxterbloem.* [=*Azalea.* . . resembling honeysuckle... *Pinxterbloem.*]] [**1822** Eaton *Botany* 149, [*Azalea*] nudiflora [=*Rhododendron periclymenoides*],.. pinxter blomache... Flowers abundant not viscous.] **1833** *NY Mirror* 2 Feb 242 **NYC**, He.. plucked for her the most beautiful pinkster blossoms. **1848** Gray *Manual of Botany* 268, *A[zalea] nudiflora...* Pinxter-flower. **1859** (1968) Bartlett *Americanisms* 322, *Pinxter blumachies...* A familiar name in the State of New York for the Swamp Honeysuckle and other early flowers. **1869** Fuller *Uncle John* 60 **NY**, Another species of Azalea, the *calendulaceum,..* is found in some parts of Pennsylvania and Ohio, and still further south. The flowers are a reddish yellow, so bright it is often called the *Flaming pinxter.* **1881** *Harper's New Mth. Mag.* 62.526 **NY** (as of a1822), The Pinkster king.. and his followers were covered with Pinkster *blummies*—the wild azalea, or swamp-apple. **1895** *DN* 1.383 **NJ**, *Pinxterblossoms:* azalea (Albany Co.) **1913** *Torreya* 13.26 **NY**, By the middle of May the pinxter flower (*Azalea nudiflora*) is in bloom. **1924** *Amer. Botanist* 30.59, *Azalea nudiflora...* From the fact that it blooms at Whitsuntide it is known as "pinkster" and "pinkster-flower," the Dutch name for the season being Pinxter... *A. calendulacea..* has larger showy red or yellow flowers and is known as.. "flaming pinxter." **1939** FWP *Guide NJ* 18, Wild azalea... is known also as the pinxter-bloom because it is seen on Whitsunday, for which the Dutch word is *Pinxter.* **1948** Peattie *Berkshires* 46 **wMA**, Sometimes called June pinks or Pinxters, this shrub [=the azalea] is quite common throughout the region. **1965** *Native Plants PA* 11, *Rhododendron roseum...* Downy Pinxterbloom. **1968–69** DARE (Qu. S2) Inf **NY**195, Pinkster; (Qu. S4) Inf **NJ**29, Pinkster, wild azalea; (Qu. S26b, *Wildflowers that grow in water or wet places*) Inf **NY**92, Pinksters—three to six feet

high—on a bush, are in clusters like bougainvillea; (Qu. S26c, *Wildflowers that grow in woods*) Inf **NY**186, Wild pinksters; (Qu. S26d, *Wildflowers that grow in meadows; not asked in early QRs*) Inf **NY**48, Pinkster; **NJ**29, Pinksters—they're mayapples; (Qu. S26e, *Other wildflowers not yet mentioned; not asked in early QRs*) Inf **PA**231, Pinkster; **NY**223, Pinksters—wild azalea, also called "mayflower." **1969** *DARE* Tape **NY**223, Pinksters.. grow on a low bush, and they're very pink; they have long tongues, stamens. It really is a wild azalea... Some of.. the older ones in the family called those mayflowers. **c1985** *Lutz Coll.* **neNJ**, As a child in grade school, I learned the name *pinxter* for our wild azalea. I did not know I was using a Dutch word and that the name was really *pinxter bloom* or *pinxter flower.* I thought the name came from the color—pink.

pinkster apple n Cf **mayapple 3**

A **swamp apple** (here: *Exobasidium* spp).

1867 De Voe *Market Asst.* 379 **NYC**, There is.. [a] peculiar-looking fruit, which, some forty years ago, became known to me, and, in fact, to many boys of my acquaintance, as the *May-apple.* However, afterwards, I found it generally known as *pinkster-apple,* and *hog-apple.* **1962** *Natl. Geogr. Mag.* July 89 **eTN**, The azaleas had watery growths on them, some of them half the size of a lemon. They are known as leaf galls, or "pinkter apples"; we used them to quench our thirst.

Pinkster Day See **pinkster 1**

pinkster flower See **pinkster 2**

pink-stern (schooner) See **pinkie** n[1]

pink three-flower n [See quot 1985]

An **umbrellawort** (here: either *Allionia incarnata* or *Oxybaphus pumilus*).

1941 Jaeger *Wildflowers* 62 **Desert SW**, Pink three-flower. *Allionia pumila* [=*Oxybaphus pumilus*]... The small flowers wilt quickly, remaining open but for a brief period. **1985** Dodge *Flowers SW Deserts* 43, Pink Three-Flower... *Allionia incarnata...* "Flower" really three separate flowers... Blossoms are usually showy and colorful.

pinkthroat n

=**flicker** n[2] **1.**

1900 *Wilson Bulletin* 31.9 **MI**, Pink-throat. Mackinac Island, Michigan. In certain lights the pinkish-cinnamon of the neck appears to advantage.

pinktop smartweed n Cf **smartweed**

A **marsh fleabane 1** (here: *Pluchea camphorata*).

1913 *Torreya* 13.234 **NC**, *Pluchea camphorata...* Pink-top smartweed, Church's Island, N.C.

pink undies See **pink bottom**

pink up See **pink** v

pink vine n

=**coral vine 3.**

[**1953** Greene–Blomquist *Flowers South* 155, Coral vine is at home over the lower South into Calif. Its clusters of tiny rose-pink flowers are borne in huge festoons.] **1959** Carleton *Index Herb. Plants* 93, *Pink-vine:* Antigonon leptopus. **1976** Bailey–Bailey *Hortus Third* 86, *Pink vine...* Climbing, to 40 ft.;.. fl[ower]s bright pink in axillary racemes.

pinkweed n

1 Std: a **knotgrass 1** (here: *Polygonum aviculare*). [*OED2* 1657 →]

2 A related **smartweed** (here: *Polygonum pensylvanicum*).

1933 Small *Manual SE Flora* 456, P[ersicaria] pennsylvanica [= *Polygonum pennsylvanicum*]... Pinkweed... Fla. to Tex., Minn., and N[ova] S[cotia]. **1950** Gray–Fernald *Manual of Botany* 582, *P. pensylvanicum..,* Pinkweed... Spikes [of flowers] dense, erect pink to purplish. **1961** Thomas *Flora Santa Cruz* 147 **cwCA**, *Polygonum pensylvanicum* L., Pinkweed, has been reported from San Francisco.. and is known from other parts of California as an introduced weed from the eastern part of the United States. **1972** Courtenay–Zimmerman *Wild Flowers* 63 **Gt Lakes**, Pinkweed, *P. pensylvanicum.* . . Disturbed ground, often wet. **1974** Morton *Folk Remedies* 115 **SC**, *Pinkweed...* *Polygonum pensylvanicum.* . . People wet the plant with vinegar and wrap around head to relieve headache.

3 The fourwing **saltbush 1** (*Atriplex canescens*).

1923 *Amer. Botanist* 29.70 **ID**, *Atriplex laciniata* [=*A. canescens* var *laciniata*]. . . is well established here (Pocatello, Idaho). . . This plant is called locally "pink weed".

pinkwink n **Cape Cod MA**   Cf **peewink, pinkletink, tinky** =**spring peeper.**

1913 *DN* 4.56 **Cape Cod MA**, *Pink-wink*. . . A tadpole,—especially referring to the noise they make on spring evenings. "Just listen to them pink-winks! They must be millions of 'em." **1939** *LANE* Map 231 (*Frog*) **Cape Cod MA**, 1 inf, *Pinkwink*, 'a species of little bullfrog'; 1 inf, *Pinkwinks*, in swamps. 'I don't know if they're frogs or not.' **1951** Hough *Singing in Morning* 15 **Cape Cod MA**, Someone says that the frogs are going it on Cape Cod, and that "many natives call them pinkwinks." **1963** *PADS* 39.14 **Cape Cod MA**, For the spring frog, . . "natives think this term [=*spring peepers*] too classy; they say *pinkwink*." **1969** *DARE* (Qu. P20, *Very young frogs—when they still have tails but no legs*) Inf **MA**55, Pinkwinks; (Qu. P21, *Small frogs that sing or chirp loudly in spring*) Inf **MA**55, Pinkwinks. **1988** Nickerson *Days to Remember* 159 **Cape Cod MA**, In late March on a mild evening are heard the first tentative pipings of a scattered few "peepers" or "pinkwinks." These little frogs abound at this season in every wetland puddle.

pink worm n   Cf **Louisiana pink worm, redworm 1**
See quot.

1969 *DARE* (Qu. P6, . . *Kinds of worms . . used for bait*) Inf **GA**84, Pink worm—6 to 8 inches, pink.

pinky n[1]   See **pinkie** n[1]

pinky n[2]   See **pinkie** n[3]

pinky n[3]   See **pink** n[2] **3c**

pinky adj   See **pinkish**

pinky-winky n
=**shooting star.**

1898 *Jrl. Amer. Folkl.* 11.274 **CA**, *Dodecatheon* (sp.), . . pinky-winky.

pin minnow See **minnow B2e**

pin needle n
1 A **beggar ticks 1.**
1970 *DARE* (Qu. S14, . . *Prickly seeds, small and flat, with two prongs at one end, that cling to clothing*) Inf **VA**38, Pin needles.
2 A **storksbill** (here: *Erodium moschatum*).   Cf **pine needle**
1974 (1977) Coon *Useful Plants* 144, *Erodium moschatum* . . pinweed, pin-grass, pin needle. . . The sharp pointed outgrowths of the seeds may possibly cause injury for tender skins.

pinney See **peony** n[1] **3**

pinnie n
=**pintail 1.**
1923 U.S. Dept. Ag. *Misc. Circular* 13.15, *Dafila acuta*. . . *Vernacular Names. In general use*. . . Pintail, sometimes pintail duck, or pinnie. **1982** Elman *Hunter's Field Guide* 156, *Pintail*. . . *Common & Regional Names*: pinnie.

pinny owl See **pinyole**

pinnywinkle See **pennywinkle 1, 2**

pinnywinkle fever See **pennywinkle 2**

pin oak n   Note: It is not always possible to be certain which species the *DARE* and *WELS* Infs are referring to. Assignments have been made on the basis of Inf comments whenever possible, and on the natural range of the tree in other cases.
1 Any of var **oaks** native chiefly to much of the eastern US, as:
a An **oak** (here: *Quercus palustris*) native esp from the central Mississippi and Ohio Valleys eastward to the Central and North Atlantic states. [See quots 1917, 1921]   Also called **piss oak, red ~ 2d, Spanish ~, swamp ~, swamp Spanish ~, turkey ~, water ~**
1812 Michaux *Histoire des Arbres* 2.123, Dans le bas de l'Etat de

New-York, dans le New-Jersey, et probablement aussi dans le Connecticut, cette espèce de Chêne est connue sous le seul nom de *Pine* [sic] *oak, Chêne à épingles ou à chevilles*. [=In lower New York State, New Jersey, and probably also Connecticut, this species of oak [=*Quercus palustris*] is known exclusively by the name *pine* [sic] *oak*, [that is,] pin or peg oak.] **1813** Muhlenberg *Catalogus Plantarum* 87, [*Quercus*] palustris—swamp oak, pin o[ak]. **1894** Coulter *Botany W. TX* 417, *Q*[*uercus*] *palustris*. . . (*Swamp Spanish* or *Pin Oak*.) Leaves deeply pinnatifid, with divergent lobes and broad rounded sinuses. **1897** Sudworth *Arborescent Flora* 172, *Quercus palustris*. . . *Common Names*. Pin Oak (Mass., Conn., R.I., N.Y., Pa., Del., Va., Md., Ark., Mo., Ill., Wis., Iowa, Kans.). **1906** *DN* 3.124 **nwAR**, *Pin-oak*. . . A kind of oak with small, deeply serrated leaves. **1917** (1923) Rogers *Trees Worth Knowing* 60, The pin oak earns its name by the sharp, short, spurlike twigs that cluster on the branches, crowding each other to death and then persisting to give the tree a bristly appearance. . . On the winter twigs, among the characteristic "pins," are the half-grown acorns that proclaim the tree an oak beyond a doubt. **1921** Deam *Trees IN* 123, *Quercus palustris*. . . Found in every county of Indiana. . . The stumps of the dead branches which penetrate to the center of the tree have given it the name of pin oak. **1949** MO Bot. Garden *Bulletin* 37.92, Pin oak (*Quercus palustris*) . . [is] a very good tree for city planting. **1950** Peattie *Nat. Hist. Trees* 228, In outline, as it stands winter-naked, the Pin Oak is remarkable for having as a rule a single, mast-like shaft of a trunk going right up through the center of the tree. **1965–70** *DARE* (Qu. T10, . . *Kinds of oak trees*) 250 Infs, **chiefly NEast, N Midl, Gt Lakes, Missip-Ohio Valleys**, Pin oak [*DARE* Ed: Some of these Infs may refer instead to other senses below.]; **DE**5, Pin oak—he grows down the water hole; **NY**52, Piss oak—has a lot of little fine branches—another name is "pin oak"; leaves almost the same as other oaks; **NY**66, Pin oak—in swamps; **RI**15, Cultivate pin oak; (Qu. T15, . . *Kinds of swamp trees*) Infs **AR**28, **IN**35, **MO**19, **OH**72, Pin oak; (Qu. T16, . . *Kinds of trees . . 'special'*) Infs **IA**8, **IL**143, **KS**16, **MO**13, Pin oak. **1980** Little *Audubon Guide N. Amer. Trees E. Region* 403, *Pin Oak*. . . Straight-trunked tree with spreading to *horizontal branches*, very slender *pinlike twigs*, and a broadly conical crown. *Ibid* 404, Named for the many short side twigs or pinlike spurs. . . Pin Oak is hardy and easily transplanted.

b =**burr oak.** [See quot 1850]
1850 Emerson *Rept. Trees & Shrubs* 133 **MA**, It [=*Quercus macrocarpa*] is called pin oak, in Stockbridge and Sheffield, from its use in making wooden pins or treenails, for which purpose it is preferred to every other material. **1967–69** *DARE* (Qu. T10, . . *Kinds of oak trees*) Infs **NE**3, 6, 8, 11, Pin oak; **CT**13, Pin oak—kind of a scrub; **MI**10, Pin oak—limited amount, also called "scrub" oak; **MA**37, Pin oak—a scrub kind of thing; **WI**37, Pin oak—small trees.

c =**chinquapin oak 1.**
1897 Sudworth *Arborescent Flora* 172 **KS**, *Quercus acuminata* [=*Q. muhlenbergii*]. . . *Common Names*. Pin Oak. **1908** Britton *N. Amer. Trees* 328, The wood is hard, very strong, close-grained. . . It [=*Q. muhlenbergii*] is also called . . Pin oak. **1960** Vines *Trees SW* 152, *Quercus . . muhlenbergii*. . . Other vernacular names are Pin Oak [etc]. **1968** *DARE* (Qu. I43, *What kinds of nuts grow wild around here?*) Inf **VA**24, Pin oak acorns; (Qu. T10, . . *Kinds of oak trees*) Inf **VA**24, Pin oak acorns look like a chinquapin [=*Castanea pumila*].

d =**shingle oak.**
1897 *Jrl. Amer. Folkl.* 10.144 **swMO**, *Quercus imbricaria*, . . swamp oak, pin oak. **1940** Clute *Amer. Plant Names* 269, *Quercus imbricaria*. Pin oak, willow oak. **1968** *DARE* (Qu. T10, . . *Kinds of oak trees*) Inf **TN**24, Pin oak has little narrow leaves, the end will almost stick you on the end [sic]; grow in swamps; **TN**26, Pin oak—little old pin-shaped leaves. [**1980** Little *Audubon Guide N. Amer. Trees E. Region* 391, *Quercus imbricaria*. . . Leaves. . . Oblong or lance-shaped, short-pointed or rounded at ends; bristle-tipped.]

e =**jack oak d.** [See quot 1913]
1913 Otis *MI Trees* 115, *Northern Pin Oak . . Quercus ellipsoidalis*. . . Many small, drooping branches are sent out near the ground, which eventually die; and it is to the stubs or pins which persist about the trunk that the appellation Pin Oak is due. **1928** Rosendahl–Butters *Trees MN* 109, *Quercus ellipsoidalis*. . . *Northern Pin Oak*. *Ibid* 110, *Quercus palustris*. . . the true pin oak, is rarely planted in Minnesota. **1938** Van Dersal *Native Woody Plants* 346, Northern Pin [Oak] (*Quercus ellipsoidalis*). . . Pin [Oak] (*Quercus laurifolia, Quercus palustris, Quercus phellos*). **1950** *WELS* (*Different kinds of oak trees in your locality*) 8 Infs, **WI**, Pin oak. [*DARE* Ed: These Infs may refer instead to other senses above.] **1952** Blackburn *Trees* 227, *Q. ellipsoidalis* (e[ast] c[entral] N America) . . *northern pin oak*. **1968** *DARE* (Qu. T10, . . *Kinds*

of oak trees) Infs **WI**8, 23, 43, 58, Pin oak. **1980** Little *Audubon Guide N. Amer. Trees E. Region* 387, *Northern Pin Oak.* . . Tree with short trunk, many small branches, and a narrow crown. *Ibid* 388, This Lake States species resembles Pin Oak and Scarlet Oak, which have more southern ranges.

2 Any of several **oaks** native chiefly to the southern US, as:

a =**Durand oak** or its var *Q. durandii breviloba.* **esp TX, OK**

1897 Sudworth *Arborescent Flora* 159 **TX**, *Durand Oak.* . . *Common Names.* Pin Oak. **1901** Mohr *Plant Life AL* 100, On these rich uplands [of **cwAL**] the Texas white oak *(Quercus breviloba)* [=*Q. durandii* var *breviloba*], commonly known in this section as pin oak, is found most frequent and in the same perfection as in the rich bottom lands of southern Texas, rivaling in size the common white oak. *Ibid* 470, *Quercus brevilobata.* . . *Pin Oak.* . . Frequently 80 feet high and 2 feet in diameter. **1908** Britton *N. Amer. Trees* 318, *Quercus breviloba* [=*Q. durandii* var *b.*] . . is also called White oak, Pin oak, and Shin oak. *Ibid* 325, *Quercus austrina* [=*Q. durandii*]. . . A rough-barked tree of river borders in Georgia and Alabama, . . it is also called Pin oak and Bastard oak. **1933** Small *Manual SE Flora* 426, *Q. Durandii.* . . *Pin-oak.* . . Hills and stream-banks, . . Coastal Plain, Ga. to Tex. and Ark. **1960** Vines *Trees SW* 157, *Quercus durandii.* . . Also known by the vernacular names of Bluff Oak, Pin Oak, . . and Basket Oak. Wood used for making splint cotton baskets in early times. **1965–70** *DARE* (Qu. T10, . . *Kinds of oak trees)* 18 Infs, 14 **TX**, Pin oak. [*DARE* Ed: Some of these Infs may refer instead to other senses below.] **1967** *DARE* Tape **TX**47, We had pin oak, post oak, and live oak. That was the three main timbers. . . hogs . . they didn't like pin oak acorns very well, and they were bitter acorns. The ducks came in those marshes, pin oak marshes, and picked up those pin oak acorns and whatnot.

b A **willow oak** (here: *Quercus phellos*). [See quot 1947]

1908 Britton *N. Amer. Trees* 302, The Willow oak [=*Q. phellos*] is extensively planted as a shade and street tree from Philadelphia southward. . . It is also known as . . Pin oak. **1938** Faulkner *Unvanquished* 13 **MS**, We worked fast, felling the saplings—the willow and pin oak, the swamp maple and chinkapin—and . . dragging them behind the mules . . to where Father waited. **1947** Collingwood–Brush *Knowing Trees* 198, *Willow Oak.* . . The abundant short spurlike branchlets on the lower branches have led to wide use of the name pin oak. **1950** Grimm *Trees PA* 172, The prevalence of short spiky branchlets reminds one of Pin Oak, and this name is sometimes erroneously applied to the Willow Oak. **1950** Moore *Trees AR* 57, *Quercus phellos.* . . Local Names: Pin and Swamp Willow Oak. . . Stands [of *Q. phellos*] on flat, poorly drained soils with southern red, post, or water oaks are termed "pin-oak flats." **1966–68** *DARE* (Qu. T10, . . *Kinds of oak trees)* Infs **DC**2, 5, 8, Pin oak; **DE**3, Pin oak—little narrow leaves; **LA**2, 15, Pin oak—leaves . . like this [=FW illustr: willowlike leaf]; **LA**3, Pin oak—leaves shaped like willow leaves; **LA**7, Pin oak—very small leaves; **LA**13, Pin oak—little narrow leaves, not very scalloped; **LA**40, Pin oak—a narrow leaf, oblong and pointed at the end. **1980** Little *Audubon Guide N. Amer. Trees E. Region* 404, *Willow Oak*—"Pin Oak." *Ibid* 505, Widely planted in Washington, D.C., and southward. . . While superficially the foliage resembles that of willows, it is recognized as an oak by the acorns and the tiny bristle-tip. **1986** Pederson *LAGS Concordance,* 61 infs, **Gulf Region**, Pin oak(s) [*DARE* Ed: Some of these infs may refer instead to other senses.]; 1 inf, **neAR**, Pin oak = red oak; 1 inf, **nwLA**, Pin oak—pin-shaped leaf; 1 inf, **ceTX**, Pin oak—smaller, narrow leaves.

c =**laurel oak 2.**

1913 Torreya 13.229 **LA**, *Quercus laurifolia.* . . Red, pin or water oak, Abbeville, La. **1938** [see **1e** quot]. **1966–70** *DARE* (Qu. T5, . . *Kinds of evergreens, other than pine)* Infs **TX**9, 37, 91, 101, Pin oak; (Qu. T10, . . *Kinds of oak trees)* Infs **TX**9, 37, 91, Pin oak.

d A **water oak** (here: *Quercus nigra*).

1933 Small *Manual SE Flora* 428, *Q[uercus] nigra.* . . *Pin-oak.* . . Sandy soil, swamps, and river-swamps. **1939** Tharp *Vegetation TX* 52, Southern Pin Oak *(Q. nigra).* **1950** Moore *Trees AR* 56, *Quercus nigra.* . . Local Names . . Pin Oak. . . *Leaves* variable in shape, always bristle-tipped. . . Distinctly southern, including eastern Texas, southern and eastern Arkansas, the Gulf states, eastern Tennessee, Atlantic states to Virginia. **1960** Vines *Trees SW* 181, *Quercus nigra.* . . Vernacular names are Bluejack Oak, . . Pin Oak [etc]. . . Extensively planted as a shade tree in the South and . . subject to attack by mistletoe. **1966–70** *DARE* (Qu. T10, . . *Kinds of oak trees)* Inf **NJ**58, Pin oak—same as black oak; **NC**72, Pin oak—same as water oak; **TX**96, Pin oak—mistletoe grows on it; (Qu. T16, . . *Kinds of trees . . 'special')* Inf **MS**1, Pin or water oak.

e =**Texas oak.**

1960 Vines *Trees SW* 198, Nuttall Oak is easily confused with the Northern Pin Oak, *Q[uercus] palustris.* . . Other names for it [=*Q. nuttallii*] are Smooth-bark Red Oak . . and Pin Oak. **1965–70** *DARE* (Qu. T10, . . *Kinds of oak trees)* 9 Infs, 8 **AR**, Pin oak . . a pinnate leaf, not willowlike. **1980** Little *Audubon Guide N. Amer. Trees E. Region* 402, *Nuttall Oak* . . "Pin Oak". . . The foliage resembles Pin Oak [=*Quercus palustris*]; the ranges overlap in Arkansas, but Pin Oak has smaller rounded acorns with a shallow cup.

3 =**Gambel oak.**

1897 Sudworth *Arborescent Flora* 172 **AZ**, *Quercus gambelii.* . . *Common Names.* Pin Oak.

4 =**canyon oak 1.**

1910 Jepson *Silva CA* 223, "Iron Oak," "Pin Oak," and "Hickory Oak" are names which, like Maul Oak, speak the respect of the ranch man for its wood [=that of *Quercus chrysolepis*].

pinoche See **penoche**

pinochle n Also *peanukle, penuckle* [Swiss Ger *Binokel*] **widespread, but less freq Sth, S Midl** See Map
Any of var card games played with two decks of cards from which all cards below the 9 have been removed and in which points are made by melding combinations of cards and taking tricks.

1864 Dick *Amer. Hoyle* 127, Bezique. . . is known among our German brethren as *Peanukle.* **1875** *Chicago Tribune* (IL) 14 Oct 2/2, If . . he could . . take a hand at penuckle or sixty-six, his chances could be infinitely increased. **1944** *Sat. Eve. Post* 25 Nov 26, The card games America plays today . . Rummy . . pinochle . . zioncheck. **1965–70** *DARE* (Qu. DD35, . . *Card games)* 433 Infs, **widespread, but less freq Sth, S Midl**, Pinochle; **PA**110, Double pinochle; (Qu. DD37, . . *Table games played a lot by adults)* Inf **PA**247, Pinochle; (Qu. FF1, . . *A kind of group meeting called a 'social' or 'sociable'.* . . *[What goes on?])* Inf **CA**145, Pinochle social; (Qu. FF2, . . *Kinds of parties)* Infs **MO**21, **MT**5, **WA**13, 28, Pinochle parties; **ID**5, Pinochle and bridge parties; (Qu. FF22a, . . *Clubs and societies . . for women)* Inf **UT**4, Pinochle club. **1986** Pederson *LAGS Concordance,* 1 inf, **csTX**, Pinochle.

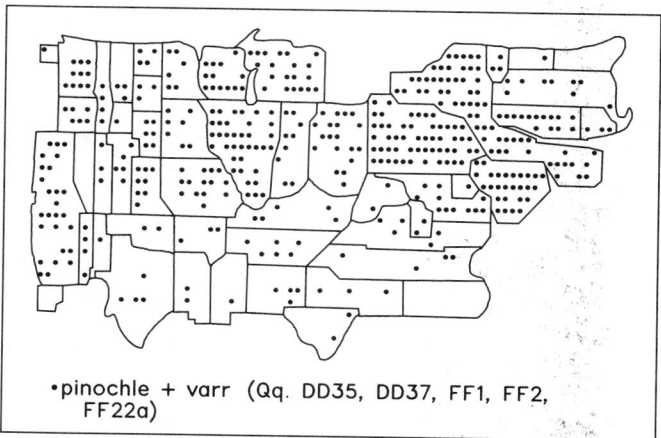

•pinochle + varr (Qq. DD35, DD37, FF1, FF2, FF22a)

pinole n Also *penola, pinola* [AmSpan] **SW**
Finely ground flour of maize or other edible seeds, often mixed with sugar and other flavorings; a beverage made by mixing this material with water.

1842 Ganilh *Ambrosio* 1.91, Pinole is made with fine corn meal, pounded almonds, sugar and various spices. **1844** Gregg *Commerce* 1.149, The aliment of these Indians [=the Pueblos] is, in most respects, similar to that of the Mexicans. . . The *tortilla,* the *atole,* the *pinole,* and many others, . . are from the Indians. Some of the wilder tribes make a peculiar kind of *pinole,* by grinding the bean of the mezquite tree into flour, which is then used as that of corn. **1846** in 1942 *CA Hist. Soc. Qrly.* 21.216, They had nothing to eat but penolas & corn mush. **1856** in 1948 *Western Folkl.* 7.14 **AZ**, Their only food is pinola. **1869** Browne *Adventures* 30 **AZ**, A jewel of a White is he in his native element of sage-deserts and Indians, pork and beans, adobe hovels and pinole. **1892** *DN* 1.193 **TX**, *Pinóle:* parched corn ground and mixed with honey or sugar. **1919** Chase *CA Desert* 78, Mixed with flour it [=chia seed] becomes the famous *pinole* of the Mexicans, the staff of life of the common people. **1976** Elmore *Shrubs & Trees SW* 37, *Atriplex canescens.* . . The Indians and Spanish-Americans grind its parched seeds and mix them with sugar and water for a drink called pinole. **1977** *New Yorker* 20 June 49 **AK,** His own food is dried moose or bear meat and pinole—ground parched corn, to which he adds brown sugar. **1980** Little *Audubon Guide N. Amer. Trees W. Region* 484, Catclaw [= *Acacia greggii*]. . . Indians once made meal called "pinole" from the seeds.

pinole clover n Cf **pinole**

A clover (here: *Trifolium bifidum*).

1925 Jepson *Manual Plants CA* 541, *T[rifolium] bifidum.* . . *Pinole Clover.* . . Open hills and valleys. **1961** Thomas *Flora Santa Cruz* 215 **cwCA,** Pinole Clover. Grassy slopes and openings in woods. . . San Francisco southward. **1973** Hitchcock–Cronquist *Flora Pacific NW* 276, Mostly w Cas[cades], . . W[ashingto]n, s to s Cal; Pinole c[lover].

piñon n

1 also *piñon pine* (or *tree*); also sp *pinion, pinone, pinyon:* Any of var **pines 1** native chiefly to the southwestern US which produce edible seeds, but usu *Pinus cembroides, P. edulis, P. monophylla,* or *P. quadrifolia.* Also called **nut pine a.** For other names of *P. cembroides* see **Mexican piñon, ocote, stone pine, stoneseed piñon;** for other names of *P. monophylla* see **gray pine c, stone ~**

[**1831** (1973) Pattie *Personal Narr.* 43 **NM,** A nut of the shape and size of a bean . . grows on a tree resembling the pine, called by the Spanish, pinion.] **1839** Leonard *Narr. Advent.* 35 **West,** Its top is covered with the pinone tree. **1844** Gregg *Commerce* 1.158 **NM,** A kind of scrub pine called *piñon* . . grows generally to the height of twenty or thirty feet, with leaves ever-green and pine-like, but scarcely an inch long. **1848** (1962) U.S. Army Corps Topog. Engineers *Abert's NM Rept.* 29, The banks were composed of high, rugged sandstone rocks, covered with a dense growth of cedar and pinyon, (pinus monophyllus). **1851** (1854) Bartlett *Personal Narr.* 1.234 **NM,** Several pines, among them the *Pinus edulis,* or piñon pine. **1892** *DN* 1.193 **TX,** *Pinión:* a species of pine tree, also the fruit or nuts of the tree, which are sweet and nourishing. This is the Texas form of Spanish *piñon.* **1897** Lummis *King of Broncos* 8 **NM,** Over ridge after ridge they trotted, ducking under stubborn branches of the piñon. **1920** Saunders *Useful Wild Plants* 75, The Two-leaved Pine (*Pinus edulis* . .), a low, round-topped tree . . [is] generally known by its Spanish name *piñon* and common from Southern Colorado to Texas and westward to Arizona and Utah. **1962** Balls *Early Uses CA Plants* 28, Several species of Pine are know [sic] by the name Pinyon, but in southern California the most common is *Pinus monophylla.* *Ibid* 29, Much less generally known are some of the other uses served by the Pinyon Pine. The gum or resin . . was collected in quantity and used medicinally. **1965–70** *DARE* (Qu. T17, . . *Kinds of pine trees;* not asked in early QRs) 26 Infs, **chiefly SW,** Piñon (pine); **CA113,** Piñon [pinˈjoʊn] pine; (Qu. T5, . . *Kinds of evergreens, other than pine*) Infs **CO22, NM6, 9, 13,** Piñon (pine); (Qu. T16, . . *Kinds of trees* . . '*special*') Infs **CA207, NM6, 13,** Piñon (pine); (Qu. BB50c, *Remedies for infections*) Inf **UT12,** Pitch from the piñon pine tree—lard was put with it to make it spread easily. **1970** Kirk *Wild Edible Plants W. U.S.* 218, *Pinus edulis, monophylla, quadrifolia* . . Pinon Pine. . . Many of the species of this genus produce delicious nuts, but the three named above are the best. **1995** Brako et al. *Scientific & Common Names Plants* 205, Pinyon. Colorado pinyon—*Pinus edulis.* Mexican pinyon—*Pinus cembroides.* Parry's pinyon pine—*Pinus quadrifolia.* Pinyon pine—*Pinus edulis.* . . Single-leaf pinyon pine—*Pinus monophylla.*

2 See **piñon nut.**

pinone See **piñon 1**

piñon jay n Also *pine jay, piñonero (blue jay), piñon squawker*

A gray-blue corvine bird (*Gymnorhinus cyanocephalus*) native to much of the western US, which commonly feeds on **pine nuts.** Also called **nutcracker b**

1887 in 1949 Denton *Pages from a Diary* 115 **NV,** We started off for the piñon hills after the piñon jays. **1897** Lummis *King of Broncos* 76 **NM,** Only the deep breath of the pines, the sudden screech of the piñonero blue jay, ever break it [=the silence] now. [Footnote to *piñonero blue jay:*] A large and brilliant blue jay, which lives largely on the delicious little nuts of the piñon. **1898** (1900) Davie *Nests N. Amer.*

Birds 336, The region between and including the Rocky Mountains and the eastern slope of the Sierra Nevadas, wherever grows the yellow pine, the pinon and the juniper, the Blue Crow, . . or Pinon Jay makes its home. **1917** (1923) *Birds Amer.* 2.234, *Cyanocephalus cyanocephalus.* . . *Other Names.*—Blue Crow; Piñonero. *Ibid* 235, The Piñon Jay is a loosely clothed, fluffy bird that combines the form of a Crow with the color and habits of a Jay. . . The nuts of the piñon pines are the natural food of these birds. **1923** Dawson *Birds CA* 1.28, Pinyon Jay. . . *Synonyms.*—Blue Crow. . . Pine Jay. *Ibid* 29, The range of the Pinyon Jay is normally coextensive with that of the pinyon (*Pinus monophylla*) plus that of the juniper (*Juniperus occidentalis*). **1940** Fergusson *Our Southwest* 121, The Mesa Verde National Park. . . is a high plateau, where . . piñon-jays scream, and fluffy-tailed squirrels scold heatedly. **1966–68** *DARE* (Qu. Q16, . . *Kinds of jays*) Infs **CO7, NE4, NV6, NM13,** Piñon jay; **CO11,** Piñon squawker. **1977** Udvardy *Audubon Field Guide Birds* 615, Although they sometimes pull up earthworms from lawns in the fashion of Robins, Pinyon Jays feed principally on pine nuts. . . Their local abundance varies from year to year with the success of the nut crop.

piñon mouse n [See quot 1980]

A **white-footed mouse** (here: *Peromyscus truei*).

1886 U.S. Natl. Museum *Proc. for 1885* 408 **NM,** True's piñon mouse differs then from the common white-footed mouse, *H[esperomys] leucopus,* in the fact that it chooses a different character of the country where it is found, as its home; in its more robust form; in its extraordinary large ears. **1952** Burt *Field Guide Mammals* 109, Piñon mouse. . . This *large-eared* mouse, *grayish-brown,* . . is characteristic of the lower slopes of the mountains where there are *rocks* and *piñon pines, junipers,* or their equivalents. **1980** Whitaker *Audubon Field Guide Mammals* 476, *Peromyscus truei.* . . Southwestern Oregon and California east to Colorado, New Mexico, extreme w Oklahoma. . . Piñon mice live in hollow juniper trunks, or under rocks. . . Agile climbers, these mice often forage in trees for the piñon nuts and juniper seeds that are their staple diet.

piñon nut n Also *piñon (pine nut)* **SW** =**pine nut.**

1846 (1848) Bryant *What I Saw in CA* 236, The burrs of the pine, which have fallen to the ground, . . contain a nut, (*piñon,*) which, although it is said to be nutritious, is not agreeable to the taste. **1848** (1962) U.S. Army Corps Topog. Engineers *Abert's NM Rept.* 46, The markets have . . great quantities of . . "uvas" or grapes, and "piñones," nuts of the pine tree, (pinus monophyllus). **1864** *Rio Abajo Weekly Press* (Albuquerque NM) 9 Feb 3, Two [Navajo] women . . had been ten days travelling, during which time their food was cedarberries and piñon nuts. **1892** [see **piñon 1**]. **1905** *Eve. Post* (NY NY) 24 June 7/4, Fattening hogs on pinon nuts is the latest money-making method in Colorado. **1920** Saunders *Useful Wild Plants* 20, The Piñon or Pine-nut . . [is] the plump, oily seed of certain species of the Far Western pines. . . Under the name of *piñons* they are sold in town throughout the Southwest as well as Mexico. **1947** *Desert Mag.* Dec 33 **SW,** High prices are being paid for pinyon pine nuts this year. **1965–70** *DARE* (Qu. I43, *What kinds of nuts grow wild around here?*) Infs **AZ2, 8, CO11,** Piñon(s); **CA1, 9,** Piñon(s)—in mountains; **CA6, 210, CO30,** Piñon nuts; **CA113,** Piñon [ˈpinjoʊn]—from a pine tree; **CO3,** No piñon nuts here; **CO27,** Piñons—gathered in fall; **NM12,** Piñon—grow on a pine tree, small and rich; **CA36, NV5,** Piñon pine (nut); **NM5,** We have [pɪnjonɪz]—the nut of the [pɪnjən] tree. **1980** Little *Audubon Guide N. Amer. Trees W. Region* 273, The hard seeds [of *Pinus cembroides*] are the main commercial pinyon nuts (*piñones*) of Mexico. However, in the United States . . other species . . are more common. *Ibid* 283, The large, edible, mealy seeds [of *Pinus monophylla*] are sold locally as pinyon or pine nuts and used to be a staple food of Indians in the Great Basin region. **1990** *Plants SW* (Catalog) 70, *Pinus edulis.* . . Bears large seeds which are eaten off the tree or used in cooking. Odorless Piñon nut oil is also valuable in cosmetics.

piñon pine See **piñon 1**

piñon pine nut See **piñon nut**

piñon squawker See **piñon jay**

piñon tree See **piñon 1**

pin pear n [Prob from the shape]

A pincushion.

1940 (1978) Still *River of Earth* 217 **KY,** A beeswax candle, a fox horn, and a pin pear lay upon the [mantel] board.

pin-point clover n Also *pin-pointed clover* [See quot 1911]
A clover (here: *Trifolium gracilentum*).

1911 Jepson *Flora CA* 226, *T[rifolium] gracilentum*. . . Pin-point Clover. . . Heads numerous, small, . . reflexed in fruit, the rachis projecting. . . Very common throughout the coast counties. **1941** Jaeger *Wildflowers* 99 **Desert SW,** *Pin-pointed clover*. . . A handsome, dainty clover, found frequently in coastal southern Calif. and occasionally on the western Mohave D[esert], . . to Wash. **1961** Thomas *Flora Santa Cruz* 216 **cwCA,** Pin-point Clover. Common on grassy slopes . . [and] in fields.

pin-pricker n
A man's sharp-pointed shoe.

1954 *WELS Suppl.* **seWI,** One elderly retired salesman told me that the pickerel toed shoe was also called "pin-pricker." **1966–67** *DARE* (Qu. W42a, . . *Nicknames . . for men's sharp-pointed shoes*) Infs **AR4, MA4,** Pin-prickers.

pinquin(t) n
=**red-necked grebe.**

1917 *Wilson Bulletin* 29.2.74 **VA,** *Columbus holboelli*. . . Pinquin, pinquint, Wallops Id., Va.

pinry See **pinery**

pin snipe n
Any of three **sandpipers:** the **least, spotted** or **white-rumped sandpiper.**

1923 U.S. Dept. Ag. *Misc. Circular* 13.64 **TX,** *Spotted Sandpiper*. . . *Vernacular Names*. . . *In local use*. . . Pin snipe. **1950** *AmSp* 27.75, In a bird name, *pin snipe* reported from Texas for three different species, the term *pin* surely means small. The birds are the spotted, white-rumped, and least sandpipers.

pin sucker n Cf *pin minnow* (at **minnow B2e**)
A **chubsucker 1** (here: *Erimyzon sucretta*).

1951 Harlan–Speaker *IA Fish* 68, *Western Lake Chubsucker*. . . *Other Names*—Chubsucker and pin sucker. . . Of little or no importance to the angler. **1983** Becker *Fishes WI* 646, *Lake Chubsucker*. . . Other common names: chubsucker, pin sucker.

pint n, v[1] See **point A**

'pint v[2] See **appoint**

pintado n [Span "painted"; see quot 1976]
A **Spanish mackerel:** usu *Scomberomorus regalis*, occas also *S. cavalla*.

1896 U.S. Natl. Museum *Bulletin* 47.875, *Scomberomorus regalis*. . . Pintado. . . Not very common on our Atlantic coast. **1902** Jordan–Evermann *Amer. Fishes* 286, *Pintado* . . *Scomberomorus regalis*. . . This fine fish is found from Cape Cod to Brazil, but it is not common anywhere except about Florida and Cuba. **1946** LaMonte *N. Amer. Game Fishes* 28, *Scomberomorus regalis*. . . Pintado. . . The fish is silvery, with spots. . . It also often has a narrow, brownish stripe from the pectoral fin to the caudal. **1976** Tryckare et al. *Lore of Sportfishing* 122, *Scomberomorus regalis*. . . Pintada [sic]. . . Deep blue on upper half of first dorsal fin. Dark blue-green above shading to silver below. A dark brown stripe runs from just behind each pectoral fin to caudal peduncle. . . Rows of oval, yellow orange spots on sides. . . A very popular small game fish.

pintail n
1 also *pintail duck, pin-tailed* ~, *pintail widgeon:* A widely distributed, slender-necked duck (*Anas acuta*) with long, pointed central tail feathers. [*OED2* 1768 →] Also called **bull sprig, English duck 2, fall** ~, **gray** ~ **c, gray widgeon 2, kite-tailed** ~, **long gray, longneck 3, paille-en-queue, pheasant duck 1, picket-tail, pied widgeon, pigeontail, piketail 1, pinhead 1, pinnie, sea widgeon 1, sharp-tail 3, smoker, spike, spiketail, spindletail, splittail, sprig, sprigtail, springtail, sprittail, tinpail, trilby duck, widgeon, winter duck**

1814 Wilson *Amer. Ornith.* 8.72, The Pintail, or . . the Sprigtail, is a common . . duck in our markets, much esteemed for the excellence of its flesh. **1823** James *Acct. of Exped.* 1.374 **NE,** *Anas acuta*—Pin-tailed

duck. **1844** Giraud *Birds Long Is.* 311, *Pintail Duck*. . . Two middle feathers [of the tail] black, with green reflections, narrow, and about three inches longer than the rest. **1891** *Leighton News* (AL) 14 Feb np **nwAL,** The Pintail . . is some thirty inches in length . . due to the two long central tail feathers from which the bird takes its name. **1913** *Pacific Coast Avifauna* 9.17 **CA,** Pintail. . . A very common and much sought-for duck, occurring through the winter in large flocks. **1947** *Jrl. Wildlife Management* 2.51 **Missip R Delta,** Geese make available to pintails, baldpates, mallards and canvasbacks, rhizomes that these ducks could not otherwise get. **1955** MA Audubon Soc. *Bulletin* 39.314, Pintail (General . .); Pintail Widgeon (Conn . .). **1965–70** *DARE* (Qu. Q5, . . *Kinds of wild ducks*) 139 Infs, **widespread,** Pintail (duck) [*DARE* Ed: Some of these Infs may refer instead to other senses below.]; **AZ2, CA130, 145, IL32, IA22, OR5,** Pintail—also called (*or same as, or*) sprig. **1989** (1990) Baden *Maryland's E. Shore* 68, The pintails, the goldeneye, the black duck . . gathered by the thousands in the endless creeks and inlets of the [Chesapeake] Bay.

2 =**ruddy duck.** [See quot 1923]

1888 Trumbull *Names of Birds* 112 **DE, MD,** At St. Georges, Del. (Delaware and Chesapeake Canal), and to some at Havre de Grace, [*Oxyura jamaicensis* is called] *Pin-tail* (the Pin-tail duck [=*Anas acuta*] . . being the "Sprig-tail" in these localities). **1913** *Pacific Coast Avifauna* 9.18, The duck [=the ruddy duck] is often called "pintail" by the hunters. **1923** Dawson *Birds CA* 4.1841, The Ruddy Duck . . Their. . . saucy tails are composed of stiff, spiny feathers, having shafts denuded toward the tips, more or less, according to season, so that the birds are popularly known as Pintails, . . in confusion with *Dafila acuta tzitzihoa* [=*Anas acuta*], which owes its common name not to the stiffness but to the graceful length of its caudal appendage. **1940** Gabrielson *Birds OR* 171, Ruddy Duck; . . Pintail: *Erismatura jamaicensis rubida*. **1955** Forbush–May *Birds* 88, *Ruddy Duck*. . . Other names: Butter-ball; . . Pintail [etc].

3 =**old-squaw.**

1904 Carnegie Museum *Annals* 2.524 **PA,** The species [=*Clangula hyemalis*] is called "Pintail" or "Coween" by the local gunners, and exhibits a great variety of plumages in the transition from the winter to the summer dress, and *vice versa*. **1923** U.S. Dept. Ag. *Misc. Circular* 13.24 **MI, PA,** Old-squaw. . . *Vernacular Names*. . . *In local use*. . . Pintail.

4 See **pin-tailed grouse.**

pintail chicken See **pin-tailed grouse**

pin-tail(ed) duck See **pintail 1**

pin-tailed grouse n Also *pintail (chicken)*, ~ *grouse* [*DCan pintail grouse* 1819 →]
=**sharp-tailed grouse.**

1876 Bourke *Diary* 13 Mar **MT,** On one occasion during our march, a small covey of "pin tailed grouse" flew across our path. **1888** Trumbull *Names of Birds* 138, Pin-tailed grouse, or Pin-tail: . . Pin-tail chicken. **1894** *Outing* 24.385, We found the pin-tails more frequently on the sides of hills, about the coolies in the rolling prairie. **1907** Anderson *Birds IA* 236, *Pediocoetes phasianellus campestris*. . . The "Pintail Chicken" of the Northwest. **1936** Roberts *MN Birds* 1.395, *Prairie Sharp-tailed Grouse*. . . Other names: Pintail Grouse, . . Sharp-tail. **1953** Jewett *Birds WA* 212, Pin-tailed Grouse. . . Permanent resident . . throughout eastern Washington. **1963** Gromme *Birds WI* 216, Pintail . . (Sharp-tailed Grouse). **1966–68** *DARE* (Qu. Q7, *Names and nicknames for . . game birds*) Infs **MI36, MN29,** Pintail grouse. **1982** Elman *Hunter's Field Guide* 26, *Common & regional names*. . . For sharp-tailed grouse . . *pintail grouse*.

pintail whistler n Cf **pintail**
=**bufflehead 2.**

1955 MA Audubon Soc. *Bulletin* 39.316 **ME,** *Buffle-head*. . . Pintail Whistler (Maine. The tail is moderately pointed; "whistler" probably from association with the golden-eyes; this species makes no special whistling sound.)

pintail widgeon See **pintail 1**

pint-blank See **point-blank A1**

pintedly See **pointedly**

pin thorn n
=**cockspur thorn.**

1897 Sudworth *Arborescent Flora* 216 **WV,** *Crataegus crus-galli. . .*
Pin Thorn. [**1980** Little *Audubon Guide N. Amer. Trees E. Region*
469, The common and Latin species names [=cockspur hawthorn and
Crataegus crus-galli] both describe the numerous and extremely long
spines, which are used locally as pins.]

'pintment See **appoint**

pinto adj, freq used absol [AmSpan "spotted, painted"] **orig
SW; now widespread, but more freq West** See Map Cf
paint
Usu of a horse or pony: piebald, spotted; absol: a piebald animal; anything that is spotted or multicolored.

  1860 *Marysville* (Calif.) *Appeal* 9 Feb. 3/1 *(DA),* The struggle. . .
ended in the success of the black horse, which came out some twenty-
five feet in advance of the 'Pinto.' **1865** B. Harte in *Californian* 15 Apr.
4/1 *(OED2),* The devil in the shape of a fleet pinto colt. **1892** *DN* 1.193
TX, *Pinto:* painted, mottled, light red. In speaking of horses it has been
translated in the Southwest into *paint . . , i.e.* piebald. As a noun, a piebald horse. This word is frequently found in names of places, as *Palo
Pinto, i.e.* painted pole, the name of a county in Texas. **1903** (1965)
Adams *Log Cowboy* 14 **SW,** There were, as it happened, only three
pinto horses in the entire saddle stock. **1929** *AmSp* 5.66 **NE** [Cattle
country talk], "Pinto," "painted," "calico," "flea-bit," and "buckskin" are
names descriptive of the color and color pattern of the "pony." **1933**
AmSp 8.1.28 **nwTX** [Ranch diction], *Pinto.* Piebald; a *paint* pony. **1941**
Writers' Program *Guide WY* 464, *Pinto*—A spotted pony. **1958**
McCulloch *Woods Words* 135 **Pacific NW,** *Pinto*—Originally a horse
with patches of different color on his hide; applied to anything which
has two or more colors. **1958** *Sat. Eve. Post Letters* **swMO** (as of
1912–16), Pinto marbles no doubt received their name from the pinto
pony which became popular about that time. The marble was very hard,
glazed and had brown spots on a dull white. **1965–70** *DARE* (Qu.
K37, *. . A horse of mixed colors*) 272 Infs, **widespread,** Pinto; (Qu.
K39, *. . Names . . for horses according to their colors*) 25 Infs, **scattered,** Pinto. **1968** *DARE* Tape **CA90,** He gave me a pinto pony.
c1970 Wiersma *Marbles Terms* **MS,** *Pinto . .* a speckled marble.

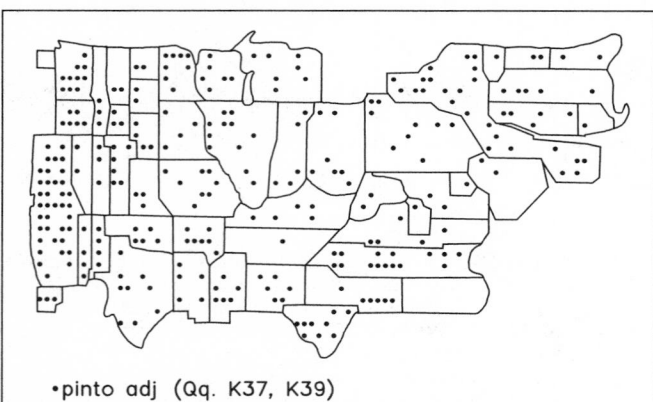

•pinto adj (Qq. K37, K39)

pinto n[1] See **pinto bean**

pinto n[2] Also *bento, pinto box* [See quot 1949] **chiefly SC,
GA** *chiefly among Gullah speakers*
A coffin, esp a homemade or inexpensive one; hence *pinto funeral* an inexpensive funeral.
  1949 Turner *Africanisms* 190 **SC, GA coasts** [Gullah], ['bɛnto] 'a
wooden box in which a dead person is buried'—Tem[ne], *bento* (*bentro*)
'a rafter bier made of sticks on which a corpse is carried.' **1951** *AmSp*
26.13 **S Atl,** *Pinto,* 'coffin,' has been recorded sporadically from the
Pedee River to Savannah—chiefly from Negroes, but sometimes offered
by white informants as a characteristic 'Negro word.' *Ibid* 14, [Foot-
note:] *Pinto* is used chiefly for the old-fashioned hexagonal coffin (occasionally pentagonal, with the omission of the footboard); informants often explain the name by commenting that the narrowness of the coffin
pins the corpse's toes together—a spurious etymology which was seldom questioned prior to Turner's investigations. **1966** *DARE* FW Addit
SC [Black], *Pinto*—casket—of boards—the cheapest. *Pinto funeral*—
the most inexpensive sort of burial. Known (and occasionally used) by
morticians as well as their public. **1970** Major *Dict. Afro-Amer. Slang*
91, *Pinto:* (African term) a coffin. **1986** Pederson *LAGS Concordance*

(Casket) 1 inf, **cnGA,** Pinto—a little-old sharp box. . . cheap; 1 inf,
ceGA, Pinto—very cheap casket; 1 inf, **seGA,** A pinto box—old style;
homemade coffin. [All infs Black] **1987** Jones-Jackson *When Roots
Die* 137 **sSC coast** [Gullah], There are a host of African-derived words
in Gullah, some of which are generally unknown to inland black speakers, for example: . . *pinto, bento,* "coffin": Temne.

pinto bean n Also *pinto* **orig chiefly SW, but now widely
scattered exc NEast** See Map
A buff and reddish-brown, mottled seed of the bean *Phaseolus
vulgaris;* the plant itself. Also called **brown bean, frijole,
Mexican bean 1, red ~**
  1916 Sinclair *Phantom Herd* 46 **West,** A girl gave me a handful of
pinto beans. **1925** Raine *Troubled Waters* 267 **WY,** Pinto beans . . were
no sooner cut and stacked than the men were hard at it putting in winter
wheat. **1936** in 1943 *Colorado Mag.* 20.183 **NM** (as of 1850s), Massive Indian jars stood there, filled to the brim with pinto or Mexican
beans. **1950** *WELS* **WI** (*Flat beans that are striped or speckled with
red*) 1 Inf, Pinto beans; (*Beans . . that are dark red when they are dry*) 1
Inf, Pinto beans. **1962** Atwood *Vocab.* **TX** 60, The commercial term
pinto beans is current all through the state. **1963** in 1970 Johnson
White House Diary 26, There were beans (pinto beans, always), delicious barbecued spare ribs. **1965–70** *DARE* (Qu. I20, *. . Kinds of
beans*) 133 Infs, **widespread exc NEast,** Pinto bean(s) (*or* pinto(s)); **CA1,** Pinto beans—pink; **CA2,** Pinto beans—tan with brown specks;
CA15, Pinto beans—smaller than kidney [beans]; pink; **CO11,** Pinto
beans—speckled; **CO30,** Pintos—Mexican beans . . brown and spotted;
DC8, Pinto bean—like a pinto horse—with small spots, has yellow eye;
GA79, Pintos—dark, smaller than great northern bean, speckled; **IL134,**
Pinto beans—speckled—twice the size of navy [beans]; **NC79,** Pinto
beans—kind of spotted; **NM8,** Pinto beans—Mexican beans (same);
OK43, Pinto beans—have little specks; (Qu. I17, *Beans . . that are dark
red when they are dry*) 50 Infs, **scattered exc NEast,** Pinto bean(s) (*or*
pinto(s)); **NH14,** Mexican pinto; **AR55,** Pintos are speckled; **LA28,**
Pintos—spotted, not smooth red; **MI68,** Pinto beans—smaller, mottled;
NM12, In English a frijole is a pinto bean; **TX52,** Pintos—speckled
brown and white; (Qu. H25, *. . Names or nicknames . . for fried cornmeal*) Inf **NC44,** Lye hominy—don't fry it, rinse twice, put pinto beans
under, put one cup black walnuts, boiling; (Qu. H50, *Dishes made with
beans, peas, or corn that everybody around here knows, but people in
other places might not*) Infs **TX4,** 11, Pinto beans; (Qu. H65, *Foreign
foods favored by people around here*) Inf **NM5,** Pinto beans; (Qu. I14,
Kinds of beans that you eat in the pod before they're dry) Inf **TX77,**
Pinto; (Qu. I18, *The smaller beans that are white when they are dry*) Infs
CA118, GA88, MO19, PA239, Pinto bean(s); **FL8,** Pinto; (Qu. I19)
Infs **CA196, IL31, IN39, PA66,** Pinto bean(s); **IL63,** 142, **MO1, NJ3,**
Pinto; (Qu. L34, *. . Most important crops grown around here*) Infs
CO22, MN16, Pinto beans. **1967–70** *DARE* Tape **AZ8,** He had done
some dry farming—had quite a large crop of corn, and squash, and pinto
beans in when the scouts arrived here; **CA192,** I, at home, cooked beans,
the regular pinto beans which were so popular with the fellas. **1969**
Madill Rec. (OK) 20 Feb 4/2, *School menu. . .* Pinto beans. **1971**
Bright *Word Geog. CA & NV* 184 **CA,** Pinto beans 33% [of 300 infs]
S[cattered]. **1988** Whealy *Garden Seed Inventory* (2d ed) 34, *Bean. . .
Pinto . .* good for Southwestern dryland conditions, snap/green shell/dry/
refried, short broad oval pods with 5–6 broad oval light-buff seeds
speckled brown.

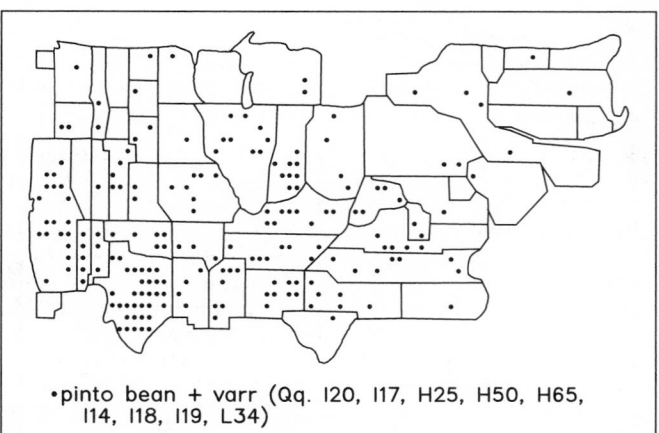

•pinto bean + varr (Qq. I20, I17, H25, H50, H65,
I14, I18, I19, L34)

pinto box See **pinto** n[2]

pin-toe n
   1968–70 DARE (Qu. W42a, . . Nicknames . . for men's sharp-pointed shoes) Infs **IA**22, **OH**43, **SC**70, Pin-toes.

pin-toed adj esp Delmarva
   Pigeon-toed.
   1946 PADS 6.23 **eNC**, Pin-toed. . . Pigeon-toed. . . Common. **1958** DE Folkl. Bulletin 1.32, Pin-toed—(pigeon-toed). **1968** DARE (Qu. X37, . . Words . . to describe people's legs if they're noticeably bent, or uneven, or not right) Infs **MD**35, 36, 39, 44, Pin-toed—toes point (or turn) in.

pinto funeral See **pinto** n[2]

pinto oak n
   Perh a **spotted oak**.
   1968 DARE (Qu. T5, . . Kinds of evergreens, other than pine) Inf **GA**35, Pinto oak.

pinto pepper n
   See quot.
   1968 DARE (Qu. I22a, . . Peppers—small hot) Inf **LA**15, Pinto pepper—little slim green pepper about an inch long.

pinweed n
   1 A plant of the genus Lechea, native chiefly to the eastern half of the US. [Prob from the resemblance of the flowers or capsules and their pedicels to the ball-headed pins used in dressmaking]
   1814 Bigelow Florula Bostoniensis 29, Lechea major. . . Large Pin weed. . . Flowers small, obscure, crowded upon the ends and sides of the branches, followed by roundish capsules of the size of a large pin head. **1854** (1969) Thoreau Walden 331 **MA**, Golden-rods, pinweeds, and graceful wild grasses. **1892** Torrey Foot-Path Way 72 **Cape Cod MA**, Acres and acres of horseweed, pinweed, stone clover, poverty grass, . . and bearberry! **1931** Harned Wild Flowers Alleghanies 301, Pinweed (Lechea minor L.) A very small, rather insignificant, fine hairy perennial. . . Capsule about the size of a pin head. **1950** Stevens ND Plants 207, Lechea stricta. . . Pinweed. . . Flowers greenish, . . in dense, slender, terminal clusters. **1968** Barkley Plants KS 240, Lechea tenuifolia. . . Pinweed. . . Lechea villosa. . . Pinweed. **1972** Courtenay-Zimmerman Wild Flowers 36 **Gt Lakes**, Pinweed, Lechea intermedia / July–Sept. / 6″–24″ / Inland sands, open dry woods, rocks.
   2 A storksbill (here: Erodium cicutarium). Cf **pin clover**, ~ **grass 1**, ~ **needle 2**
   1876 Hobbs Bot. Hdbk. 90, Pin weed, . . Erodium cicutarium. **1914** Georgia Manual Weeds 258, Alfilaria or Filaree—Erodium cicutarium. . . Pin Weed. . . Spirally twisted and bearded awns or beaks with sickle-bent tips. **1974** (1977) Coon Useful Plants 144, Erodium cicutarium . . Pin-weed. . . The sharp pointed outgrowths of the seeds may possibly cause injury for tender skins.

pinxter See **pinkster**

pinxter bloom, pinxter flower See **pinkster 2**

piny See **peony** n[1] **1**

pinyole n Also pinny owl
   The black-legged **kittiwake** (Rissa tridactyla).
   1882 Nuttall Ornith. Club Bulletin 7.125 **neMA**, The Kittiwakes—or "Pinny Owls". . . are annually taken by the fishermen, who either skin and stew them or use the flesh for bait. I was assured that a "Pinny Owl" stew is by no means an unpalatable dish. **1884** U.S. Bur. Fisheries Rept. for 1882 330, Larus tridactylus. . . Of all the birds which visit the fishing-banks the kittiwake gull (. . "pinyole," . . of the fishermen) is . the most abundant. . . I have seen them along the coast of New Jersey, and thence to the eastern coast of Newfoundland. **1905** Townsend Birds Essex Co. MA 88, Buckets of bait . . are thrown out to attract the fish. . . Of this custom the Kittiwakes—or 'Pinny Owls,' as these men [=fishermen of Swampscott MA] invariably call them—are well aware. **1955** Forbush-May Birds 225, Pinny Owl or Pinyole. . . Winters from the Gulf of St. Lawrence south to New Jersey.

pinyon See **piñon 1**

piny windy See **pinawinda**

piny woods See **piney woods**

piojo n |'pjo₁ho| [Span] esp TX
   A **louse B1** (here: either Pediculus humanus or Pthirus pubis).
   1967–69 DARE (Qu. R25, Joking names for a head louse, or body louse) Inf **TX**1, Piojos ['pjou₁hǝs]; **TX**4, Piojos ['pjo₁hǝz]; **TX**29, Piojos [pjohos]; **CA**65, Piojos—old Spanish name for head louse; **TX**66, ['piɛho]—Mexican for louse.

pioneer violet n
   A **violet** (here: Viola glabella).
   1954 Sharpe 101 Wildflowers 6 **nwWA**, Pioneer Violet. . . Most commonly found in the moist shaded forests or boggy meadows. **1973** Hitchcock–Cronquist Flora Pacific NW 299, Petals all clear yellow on both surfaces. . . Pioneer v[iolet] . . V[iola] glabella.

piony See **peony** n[1] **1**

pip n[1] Also with the; also pips [Transf from pip any of var nonspecific disorders] esp Mid Atl See Map
   Menstruation.
   1965–70 DARE (Qu. AA27, . . A woman's menstruation) 9 Infs, esp **Mid Atl**, Pip; **GA**89, **NC**62, **PA**161, **SC**46, (She's) got the pip; **PA**44, **VA**42, The pip; **SC**26, Pips. **1975** King S. Ladies & Gentlemen 172 **Sth**, The wedding is set for the end of the month. It would've been sooner, but Puddyface got the pip. You know how women are. Ibid 212, Flossie, are you gettin' the pip? **1990** Cavender Folk Med. Lexicon 29 **sAppalachians**, Pip—menstruation.

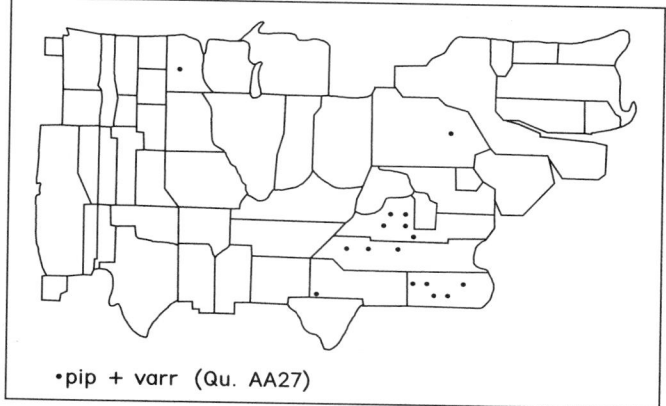

•pip + varr (Qu. AA27)

pip v
   1 Of a young bird: to crack (the shell of the egg) as a first step in hatching; rarely of an egg: to become cracked by the chick; also fig; hence ppl adj pipped, vbl n pipping.
   1879 (1880) Tourgée Fool's Errand 266, I only hope it is a hole that will let light in upon the thing. I have always supposed it would come, and have known, that, if one ever pipped the shell, a thousand would try to be the first to get their heads out. **1899** (1912) Green VA Folk-Speech 323, Pip. . . To crack the egg in hatching. "The chickens will be out tomorrow, the eggs are all pipped." **1901** Century Illustr. Mag. 61.442 **West**, She's welcome to all she gets out o' me. . . I pipped my shell as many as two seasons ago. **1901** Chambers's Jrl. Nov. 717 (OED2), Gigantic incubators . . literally vomiting forth their flocks of twittering little creatures at pipping-time. **1959** Lahey-Hogan As I Remember It 109 **swKS**, She replied, "Why, how could that be? Wasn't it hatching today?" He said, "No, it [=a turkey egg] was hatching tomorrow, but I thought it might be pipped, so I looked and it's gone entirely." **1970** WI Conserv. Bulletin 35.5.19 **WI**, It was a small brood—only five chicks—and her total clutch on this second attempt was only seven eggs. Two eggs never "pipped." **1972** Scientific Amer. Aug 30 **MD**, The ducklings begin to pip their eggs. . . As the eggs are being pipped the female clucks. . . When the pipping is completed, she drops back to . . four calls per minute.
   2 Of a grain of rice: to sprout; hence vbl n pipping. Cf **pip** n[2] **2**
   1936 Smith–Sass Carolina Rice 27 **SC coast** (as of 1850s), On the following tide the field was flowed from the river, and kept on from three to six days, as the weather demanded, until the rice "pipped," or sprouted. **1937** Heyward Madagascar 36 **sSC coast**, Each morning the water-

minder would grapple under the water for a few of the grains, and just as soon as they began to "pip", the inner doors or the trunks would be lifted. **1967** [see **pip** n[2] **2**].

3 in phr *pip eggs:* =**pick eggs.** [Perh var of **pick eggs,** infl by **1** above] Cf **pip** n[2] **1**

1952 Brown *NC Folkl.* 1.231, [Easter] egg hunts are the usual thing, and at these the children "pip" eggs with each other. Each takes an egg and they crack the eggs together to see which will not get broken.

pip n[2]

1 =**egg picking.** Cf **pip** v **3**

1914 *DN* 4.156 seMA, *Pip.* . . A game played as early as 1860 at shearing time when crowds had gathered for several days on the Nantucket moors or commons. It consisted merely in striking hard-boiled eggs on end; the one whose shell first yielded lost it. A guinea hen's egg usually endured best.

2 The emerging sprout of a rice grain. Cf **pip** v **2**

1967 *DARE* Tape **TX**8, [Inf:] You either plant your seed that's sprouted . . or plant it dry and watch the seed; as soon as it makes a pip and starts to sprout, . . you cut your water off. . . [FW:] You say when the pip shows up, you say that's pipping then? [Inf:] Pipping, yes; that's pipping or making a sprout.

pipebill n

=**shoveler.**

1955 *Oriole* 20.1.4, *Shoveler.* . . In allusion to the spatulate bill . . Pipe-bill.

pipe elder n Cf pipestem

An elder (here: *Sambucus canadensis* var *laciniata*).

1938 Rawlings *Yearling* 331 **nFL,** A low place where pipe-elders grew.

pipefish n [From the elongate shape]

1 Std: a fish of the family Syngnathidae. For other names of var spp see **needlefish 2**

2 also *tobacco-pipe fish:* A cornetfish (here: *Fistularia tabacaria*).

1839 MA Zool. & Bot. Surv. *Fishes Reptiles* 80, *F[istularia] serrata.* . . The Tobacco-pipe Fish. **1842** DeKay *Zool. NY* 4.232, *The American Pipefish. Fistularia serrata* [here: =*F. tabacaria*]. . . Body cylindrical, elongate. *Ibid* 233, *The Spotted Pipefish. Fistularia tabacaria.* . . Body rounded, slender; its depth less than its thickness. **1862** *Acad. Nat. Sci. Philadelphia Proc. for 1861* 38, *Solenostomus tabacarius* [=*Fistularia t.*] . . "Pipe Fish." **1905** NJ State Museum *Annual Rept. for 1904* 229, *Fistularia tabacaria.* . . Pipe Fish. . . Body very long, slender, depressed.

pip eggs See pip v 3

pipe organ cactus See organ-pipe cactus

pipe organ mud dauber See organ-pipe mud dauber

pipe plant n [See quot 1924]

=**Indian pipe 1.**

1830 Rafinesque *Med. Flora* 2.243, *Monotropa uniflora.* . . Pipeplant. . . Used by Indians and herbalists, juice mixt with water deemed specific lotion for sore eyes. **1854** King *Amer. Eclectic Dispensatory* 640, *Monotropa uniflora.* . . found in various parts of the Union from Maine to Carolina, and westward to Missouri. . . The flowers are inodorous, and . . their resemblance to a pipe has given rise to the names *Indian Pipe,* or *Pipe-plant.* **1924** *Amer. Botanist* 30.62, *Monotropa uniflora.* . . The urn-shaped single flowers on scaly stems bend toward the earth in exact similitude to a small white pipe. The derivation of such names as "pipe plant," . . is apparent. **1966** *DARE* (Qu. S26e, *Other wildflowers not yet mentioned;* not asked in early QRs) Inf **MA**6, Dutchman's pipe, pipe plant.

piper n Also piping (tree) frog Cf peeper

A **tree frog** such as *Hyla crucifer.*

1891 in 1895 IL State Lab. Nat. Hist. Urbana *Bulletin* 3.348, *Hyla pickeringi* [=*H. crucifer*]. . . Piping Tree-frog. [*Ibid* 349, Though so delicate in appearance this tree-frog is really one of the most hardy of our frogs. . . The note is a clicking or piping noise.] **1911** *Century Dict. Suppl., Piping-frog.* . . A small North American tree-frog, *Hyla pickeringi.* **1966** Dakin *Dial. Vocab. Ohio R. Valley* 2.388, In addition to

the names [for *tree frog*] mentioned, these are recorded in Ohio: *kweequacks,* . . and *pipers.*

piperage, piperidge See pepperidge

pipes n Cf ghost pipe 2

A **broomrape 1** (here: *Orobanche uniflora*).

1898 *Jrl. Amer. Folkl.* 11.276 **ME,** *Aphyllon uniflorum,* . . pipes, South Berwick, Me.

pipestem n Cf pipestem wood

Any of several plants with slender stems, as:

a A **staggerbush** (here: *Lyonia lucida*). Cf **pipewood 2**

[**1821** Elliott *Sketch* 1.487, The upright younger branches [of *Lyonia lucida*] are very straight, and when deprived of their pith make good pipe stems.] **1830** Rafinesque *Med. Flora* 2.191, *A[ndromeda] nitida* [=*Lyonia lucida*] . . *Pipestem,* is equivalent of *Kalmia* for the itch. **1876** Hobbs *Bot. Hdbk.* 90, Pipe stem, Andromeda nitida. **1924** *Amer. Botanist* 30.61, *Lyonia nitida* [=*L. lucida*]. . . is also called "pipe-stem" probably from its hollow stems. **1960** Vines *Trees SW* 811, *Lyonia lucida.* . . Other local names are Pipe-stem and Stagger-bush.

b A **virgin's bower,** usu the two Western species *Clematis lasiantha* and *C. ligusticifolia.*

1901 Jepson *Flora CA* 197, *C[lematis] lasiantha.* . . Pipe-stem. **1920** Rice–Rice *Pop. Studies CA Wild Flowers* 79, A local name for *C. lasiantha,* in some localities, is Pipe Stem. **1932** Rydberg *Flora Prairies* 336, *Virgin's Bower, White Clematis, Traveler's Joy, Pipe-stem.* . . *C[lematis] ligusticifolia.* . . Copses and cañons among bushes. **1963** Craighead *Rocky Mt. Wildflowers* 58, *Clematis ligusticifolia.* . . Virgin's Bower, Pipestem. . . The feathery seed tails, when bunched together, form a "fuzz". . . A hunter whose feet are cold will experience immediate relief if he stuffs this insulating fuzz into his boots. **1979** Spellenberg *Audubon Guide N. Amer. Wildflowers W. Region* 710, *White Virgin's Bower; Pipestems; Traveler's Joy (Clematis liguisticifolia* [sic]). . . A woody vine which clambers over other vegetation and, when in bloom, is covered with *hundreds of cream flowers.*

c also *Indian pipeshank:* A **spirea** (here: *Spiraea alba*).

1837 Darlington *Flora Cestrica* 299 **sePA,** *S[piraea] salicifolia* [=*S. alba*]. . . Ind[ian] Pipe-shank. . . *Stem* 3 to 6 feet high, somewhat branched; branches . . mostly dark purple, filled with pith. **1952** *Castanea* 17.64 **WV,** In Summers Co., W. Va., there is a creek, district, and post office called Pipestem. . . These were obviously named for some plant. . . Two elderly gentlemen who had lived all their lives in the Pipestem community. . . said the shrub was used extensively for stems for the clay pipes that were used almost exclusively at that early date [= c1880]. They said the canes were also used for stems for corncob pipes. . . I gathered some of the "pipestem" shrubs which proved to be *Spiraea alba.* **1953** Strausbaugh–Core *Flora WV* 462, *S[piraea] alba.* . . Pipestem. . . Abundant, especially on the western slopes of the mountains.

pipestem wood n Cf pipewood 1

The Florida **hobblebush** (*Agarista populifolia*).

1791 Bartram *Travels* 24, I observed, growing on the banks of this sequestered river, . . the great evergreen Andromeda of Florida, called Pipe-stem Wood, to which I gave the name of Andromeda formosissima [=*Agarista populifolia*], as it far exceeds in beauty every one of this family. **1813** Muhlenberg *Catalogus Plantarum* 43, [*Andromeda*] *acuminata* [=*Agarista populifolia*] . . (pipe-stem wood).

pipestone n Also Indian pipestone [See quot 1833]

Catlinite.

1804 (1905) Lewis *Orig. Jrls. Lewis & Clark Exped.* 1.115 **swMN,** Mr. Durrien our Soues intptr says. . . below the falls a Creek coms in which passes thro Clifts of red rock which the Indians make pipes of. *Ibid* (1905) 6.44, The third is called *red pipe stone river,* which heads with the waters of the River St. Peters. **1809** Henry *Travels Indian Terr.* 24 (as of 1761), We had reached the Portage du Grand Calumet, . . which name is derived from the *pièrre à calumet,* or pipe-stone, which here interrupts the river. **1833** in 1841 Catlin *Letters Indians* 1.234 **MT,** The bowls of these [=pipes] are generally made of the red steatite, or "pipe-stone." **1855** in 1878 Longfellow *Poems* 142, On the Mountains of the Prairie,/ On the great Red Pipe-stone Quarry. **1868** (1869) *Amer. Naturalist* 2.648 **SD,** At Sioux Falls . . a layer of Pipestone occurs intercalated with the quartzite. **1902** *Jrl. Amer. Folkl.* 15.110, *Indian pipestone.* A name for catlinite. **1938** FWP *Guide MN* 100, Not important economically, but of great interest to the student of American history, is the pipestone or catlinite, a dull red or flecked indurated clay of variable composition.   **1963** Schwartz–Thiel *Minnesota's Rocks* 287 **swMN,** The town of Pipestone took its name from the place where for hundreds of years the Indians had quarried the soft rock called pipestone to make their ceremonial peace pipes.   **1968** *DARE* (Qu. C26, . . *Special kinds of stone or rock*) Inf **MN**38, Pipestone—one of the few in the world.

pipe, take the v phr   Also *take the gas pipe*   esp NYC, C Atl   See Map

To commit suicide.

1951 in 1993 Burroughs *Letters* 78, Yes, I remember Bozo who took the gas pipe.   **1962** Brosnan *Pennant Race* 19, Three games I've pitched in this park. Two to one, two to one, and one to nothing. Enough to make a guy take the pipe.   **1968–70** *DARE* (Qu. BB57, *If someone committed suicide . . he* _____) Infs **MD**9, **NJ**18, **NY**79, 90, 186, **PA**245, Took the pipe; **NJ**35, **NY**36, 37, Took the gas pipe. [8 of 9 Infs male, 8 old]   **1971** Landy *Underground Dict.* 181, *Take the pipe. . .* Commit suicide.   **1992** *Newsweek* 8 June 68/2, In 1976, Jimmy Carter's head campaigner, Hamilton Jordan, avowed that he would take the pipe if Northeast establishment types . . turned up in a Carter government.   **1997** *DARE* File **NYC,** I remember that in the 1987 film *Radio Days,* a character says, "If you don't like it, take the gas pipe!"

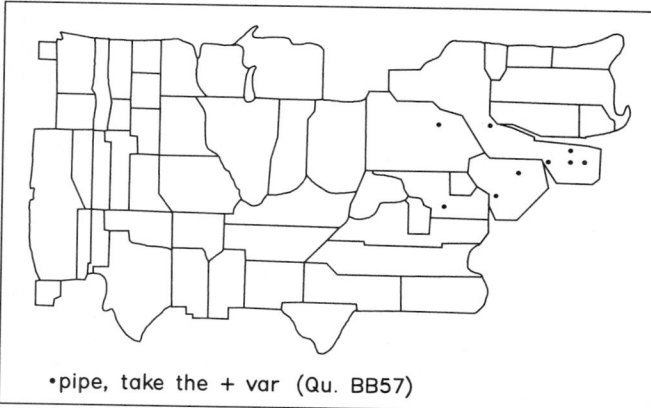

•pipe, take the + var (Qu. BB57)

pipe tree n

1 A **catalpa B1.**   Cf **Indian pipe 4**

1899 (1912) Green *VA Folk-Speech* 323, *Pipe-tree. . .* The catawba. Catalpa. The long pods are smoked by the children.

2 The common lilac (*Syringa vulgaris*).   [*OED2* 1629 →]

1930 Shoemaker *1300 Words* 47 **cPA Mts** (as of c1900), *Pipe tree*—The Lilac tree.

pipe vine n

1 =**birthwort 1.**   [See quot 1940]

1859 (1880) Darlington *Amer. Weeds* 268, Another species . . , the Pipe Vine, or Dutchman's Pipe, is a native of the West and South.   **1869** U.S. Dept. Ag. *Rept. of Secy. for 1868* 204, Pipe vine, (*Aristolochia sipho.*) . . The peculiar shape of the flowers gives it the name of the Dutchman's pipe, to which they have a very strong and remarkable resemblance.   **1886** *Century Illustr. Mag.* 32.237 **MA,** Professor Gray's modest house, where wistaria, forsythia, and pipe-vine intertwine their varying greenery.   **1901** Lounsberry *S. Wild Flowers* 150, *A*[*ristolochia*] *tomentosa,* woolly pipe-vine, bears a specific . . name suggested, no doubt, by the dense white tomentum which covers its every part. Aside from this trait it is a similar vine to the Dutchman's pipe [=*A. macrophylla*] although its flowers and leaves are smaller.   **1906** (1918) Parsons *Wild Flowers CA* 380, *Dutchman's Pipe. Pipe-vine. Aristolochia Californica. . .* Before the flowers are fully open, the buds resemble ugly little brown ducks hanging from the vine.   **1940** Steyermark *Flora MO* 158, *Pipe Vine* (*Aristolochia tomentosa*). . . Flowers with an abruptly curved long yellow-green tube expanded at the top into 3 dark purple lobes, its shape suggesting a Dutchman's pipe.   **1970** Correll *Plants TX* 508, *Aristolochia tomentosa. . . Pipe-vine.* A high-climbing woody twining vine.   **1981** Pyle *Audubon Field Guide Butterflies* 325, *Pipevine Swallowtail . .* (*Battus philenor*). . . Host plants are chiefly pipevines, Dutchman's pipe (*Aristolochia macrophylla*) or Virginia snakeroot (*A. serpentaria*) in East and 2 other species (*A. californica* and *A. longiflora*) in West.

2 A **virgin's bower** (here: *Clematis texensis*).   Cf **Dutchman's pipe 3, granddaddy's ~, Indian ~ 3, pipestem c**

1960 Vines *Trees SW* 263, *Clematis texensis. . .* Also known under the vernacular names of Leather-flower and Pipe-vine.

pipe-vine swallowtail n

A butterfly (*Battus philenor*) that feeds chiefly on **pipe vine 1.**

1902 Holland *Butterfly Book* 315, The Pipe-vine Swallowtail. . . flashes all summer long in the sunlight about the verandas over which the *Aristolochia* spreads the shade of its great cordate leaves. . . The caterpillar feeds upon the leaves of *Aristolochia sipho* (the Dutchman's-pipe) and *Aristolochia serpentaria,* which abound in the forest lands of the Appalachian region.   **1926** Essig *Insects N. Amer.* 633, The pipevine swallowtail . . is beautiful glossy blue-green. . . The caterpillars feed on the wild dutchman's pipe or pipevine which grows abundantly along the Sacramento River and elsewhere in California.   **1972** Harris *Butterflies GA* 158, In central and northern Georgia, it is usually March before the Pipe-vine Swallowtail first appears.   **1981** [see **pipe vine 1**].   **1985** Sedman–Hess *Butterflies W. Cent. IL* 34, The Pipevine Swallowtail occurs throughout much of our area. . . The adults are apparently distasteful to certain predators and there are a number of palatable butterflies which appear to mimic the Pipevine. . . Its larval hostplant [= *Aristolochia*] has not been observed in west central Illinois but possible suitable species in our area include wild ginger and Virginia snake-root.

pipeweed n

A **pipewort.**

1966 *DARE* (Qu. S26b, *Wildflowers that grow in water or wet places*) Inf **MI**31, Pipeweed.   **1966** *DARE* Wildfl QR Pl.6A Inf **MI**31, Pipeweed.

pipewood n Sth

1 The Florida hobblebush (*Agarista populifolia*).   [See quots] Cf **pipestem wood**

1861 Wood *Class-Book* 488, *A*[*ndromeda*] *acuminata* [=*Agarista populifolia*]. . . *Pipe-wood. . .* The stems are used by smokers in pipe-making.   **1901** Lounsberry *S. Wild Flowers* 391, *L*[*eucothoe*] *acuminata,* pipe-wood, . . inhabits the swamp margins from eastern Florida to the Carolinas. . . This species, on account of its long hollow stems, furnishes many people an industry, in collecting them for pipes.

2 A **staggerbush;** see quot.   Cf **pipestem a**

1924 *Amer. Botanist* 30.61, "Fetterbush" is *Lyonia lucida.* . . A southern species [of *Lyonia*] is known as "pipe-wood" because its hollow stems are used by smokers.

pipewort n   [*OED2* 1806 →]

A plant of the genus *Eriocaulon.*   Also called **buttonrod, everlasting n 2, hardhead 6d, hatpins, pipeweed, white buttons.**   For other names of var spp see **duck grass 4, water daisy**

1814 Bigelow *Florula Bostoniensis* 215, *Eriocaulon pellucidum. . . Transparent Pipewort. . .* Found in ponds, growing under water, a part of the stem only projecting above the surface, and supporting a small, flat head of obscure flowers.   **1861** Wood *Class-Book* 729, *Eriocaulon. . . Pipewort. . . L*[*ea*]*v*[*e*]*s* grasslike, flat, tufted at the base of the slender, simple, one-headed, fluted scape.   **1894** Torrey *FL Sketch-Book* 30, Beside the railway track were blue-eyed grass and pipewort.   **1915** *Copeia* 23.47, Finally, on Fletcher Lake, September 1, we found them [=mink frogs] in the shallow, sandy shores amongst pipeworts (*Eriocaulon articulatum*).   **1951** Teale *North with Spring* 40 **FL,** Pipeworts lifted white button flowers from pools of standing water and across acres of drenched plains.   **1969** *Milwaukee Jrl.* (WI) 19 Jan Picture Journal sec 8 **nFL,** He . . described the large cell structure in the onionlike leaves of the buttonrod or pipewort plant.   **1979** Niering–Olmstead *Audubon Guide N. Amer. Wildflowers E. Region* 511, *Eriocaulon septangulare. . .* is the most common and widespread of several species of Pipeworts.

piping frog See **piper**

piping hare n Cf **squeaker, whistling hare**

=**pika.**

1890 *Century Dict.* 4507, *Piping-hare. . .* A pika or calling-hare.   **1980** Whitaker *Audubon Field Guide Mammals* 343, *Pika . .* "Piping Hare" (*Ochotona princeps*).   [*Ibid* 344, The naturalist Thomas Nuttall described the call as "a slender, but very distinct bleat, so like that of a young kid or goat," that he was astonished when "the mountains brought forth nothing much larger than a mouse."]

piping plover n

A small North American **plover** (*Charadrius melodus*) native chiefly to Atlantic coastal areas.   Also called **beach flea, butterbird 2, feeble, gunwad, mourning bird, oxeye 1b, quill-toot, ringneck 3, ring plover, stone runner, tee-o**

1826 in 1828 NY Acad. Sci. *Annals Lyceum Nat. Hist.* 2.296, *Ringed Plover . . and Piping Plover. . .* common all along the eastern sea coast of North America. **1880** *Forest & Stream* 17.226 **NEng,** The spring season is ushered in by the soft plaintive note of the piping plover . . and the shrill tones of the ring-neck. **1921** LA Dept. of Conserv. *Bulletin* 10.85, Two other species found in Louisiana are the piping plover . . and the snowy plover . . , the former rather common, the latter rare. **1954** Sprunt *FL Bird Life* 157, The Piping Plover. . . is rarely seen on mud flats or indeed anywhere except the ocean beaches, . . [and] is one of the palest of the beach birds, its soft grays and whites matching the sand beautifully. **1977** Udvardy *Audubon Field Guide Birds* 374, *Piping Plover. . .* Voice: Clear, whistled *peep-lo.* **1987** *Nature Conserv. News* 37.3.30 **ND,** Piping plovers . . find the lakes' wide, gravel-covered beaches ideal for breeding and nesting. **1994** *USA Today* (Arlington VA) 13 June sec A 11 **DE,** Four piping plover chicks that hatched this year have vanished and are believed to have been eaten by predators. . . The chicks' parents may be trying to start a new nest.

piping tree frog See **piper**

pipit n
Std: a bird of the genus *Anthus.*   For other names of *A. spragueii* and *A. spinoletta* see **lark** n[1] **2, skylark 2, titlark;** for other names of *A. spragueii* see **Missouri skylark;** for other names of *A. spinoletta* see **brown lark, peedee 1, red lark, wagtail, water pipit**

pipjenny n Also *pepjinny, pimpjennet, pinjinnet;* for addit varr see quots [*OED2 pimgenet* "*slang* or *dial. Obs.*" Cf *EDD pip* sb.[1] 5 "A small spot on the skin"] esp **Delmarva, S Atl** See Map
A pimple; also transf.

1899 (1912) Green *VA Folk-Speech* 323, *Pipjinny. . .* Pimgenet. A pimple; a small bile. Pustule. **1912** *Ibid* 323, *Pinginnet. . .* A pimple on the face. **1952** Brown *NC Folkl.* 1.576, *Pimpjennet, pimpjenny. . .* A pimple.—Central and east. *Ibid, Pipjenny. . .* A pimple.—Chapel Hill. **1965–70** DARE (Qu. X59, *. . The small infected pimples that form usually on the face*) Infs **DE2, VA74,** Pipjennies; **NC6,** Pipjenny—little hickies; **VA73,** Pepjinnies ['pɛpˌjɪnɪz]; **MD36,** Pimjinnets ['pɪmˌjɪnɪts]; **MD15,** Pimjimmies ['pɪmˌjɪmɪz]; **DE3,** Pinjinnets ['pɪnˌjɪnɪts]—I got some on my face now; **MS86,** Pipjinnies; (Qu. BB25, *. . Common skin diseases around here*) Inf **GA3,** Pipjennies—small, infected risings on skin from heat; little fester bumps; (Qu. BB33a, *. . A swelling under the skin, bigger than a pimple, that comes to a head*) Inf **FL49,** Pipjenny—smaller than a rising; **VA69,** Pipjinny [pɪpˈjɪnɪ] is smaller than a rising, but contains white pus and comes to a head. **1968** McDavid Coll. **GA,** 1 inf, Pipjinnit; 1 inf, Pipginnies. **1981** DARE File **GA,** My maid left me a note that the pip jenny had come off the vacuum cleaner. Baffled, I sought help from friends. One of them said it is a lump (hump? mump?) on the skin. **1986** Pederson *LAGS Concordance (Boil)* 1 inf, **swAL,** Pip jennies; 1 inf, **ceGA,** Pip jennies—small ones; 1 inf, **swGA,** Pip jenny—a rising; 1 inf, **swMS,** Pip jenny; 1 inf, **cGA,** A pip jenny—called this when they're small; 1 inf, **swGA,** A pip jenny.

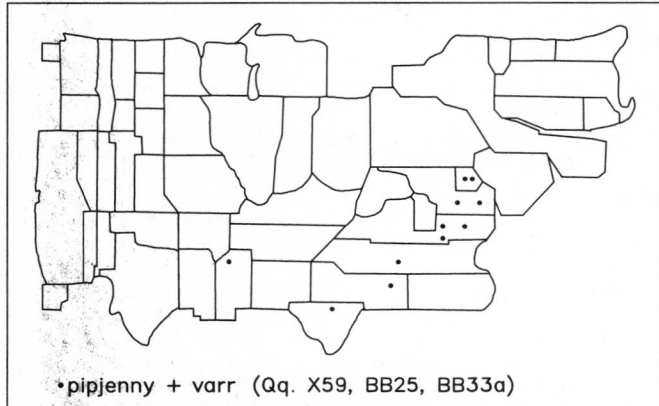

•pipjenny + varr (Qq. X59, BB25, BB33a)

pipped See **pip** v 1

pipperage See **pepperidge**

pippin n esp **NEng**
The shoot or young leaf of a **wintergreen** (here: *Gaultheria procumbens*).

1891 *Jrl. Amer. Folkl.* 4.149 **NH,** Gaultheria procumbens seems to have an almost endless variety of epithets. . . My daughter tells me that her cousins and other young people at Gilsum now call the young shoots *Pippins,* though I never heard it formerly. **1892** *Ibid* 5.100 **MA, NH,** *Gaultheria procumbens. . .* Pippins. Stratham, N.H.; Central Mass. . . Young leaves [are so called]. **1981** DARE File **cMA** (as of c1920), When I was a child we called the young wintergreen leaves pippins (and ate them). **1997** DARE File **nwMA,** Well, in spite of my assertion earlier in the summer that no one around here had heard of the word pippin in association with wintergreen, (and I had asked everyone, grandma included) this time both she and Aunt identified pippins as the tender young leaves of a checkerberry, which are chewed to extract the flavor before the berries appear.

pipping See **pip** v 1, 2

pips See **pip** n[1]

pipsissewa n Also *phipsewa, phipsissiway, pipsiseva, pipsiseway, pipsissaway, pipsissiwa* [Cree; see quot 1910]
A plant of the genus *Chimaphila,* esp *C. umbellata.*   Also called **lion's tongue, prince's pine 1, waxflower, wintergreen.**   For other names of *C. maculata* see **spotted wintergreen;** for other names of *C. umbellata* see **bittersweet, bitter wintergreen, false ~ 2, fragrant ~, ground holly 2, king's cure, love-in-winter, mayflower 14, noble pine, pine tulip, ratsbane 1, rheumatism weed a**

1789 in 1793 Amer. Philos. Soc. *Trans.* 3.xvii, An infusion of the plant Pyrola *maculata* has been frequently used for some years in Pennsylvania, under the name of *pipsiseva.* **1814** Bigelow *Florula Bostoniensis* 106, *Pyrola umbellata. . . Umbelled Winter Green. . .* [is] known by the names of *Rheumatism weed, Phipsewa* or *Wipsewog, &c.* **1818** *Thomas' MA Spy or Worcester Gaz.* (MA) 25 Feb [4]/5, On the Schuyl-kill, . . they [=Indians] procured the herb called by them Phipsissiway, in great plenty. . . I informed him we had given Phipsissiway tea, very strong, and as hot as he could drink. **1848** in 1850 Cooper *Rural Hours* 433, We contributed a basket-full of ground-pine . . with some glittering club-moss, and glossy pipsissiwa, for our share. **1896** *Garden and Forest* 9.292, *Pipsissewa,* or *Pipsiseway. . .* is a word of Cree (Algonk.) origin, . . *pisisiwayoo.* **1910** Hodge *Hdbk. Amer. Indians* 2.260, *Pipsissewa. . .* The plant once enjoyed a great reputation as a lithontriptic among some of the Wood Cree, who raised it to the dignity of an animate object and spoke of [it] as *pipisisikweu,* 'it reduces it (stone in the bladder) to very fine particles.' **1915** (1926) Armstrong–Thornber *Western Wild Flowers* 356, *Pipsissewa—Chimaphila Menziesii. . .* has a delicious fragrance, like Lily-of-the-valley, and grows in pine woods in the Sierra Nevada and Coast Ranges. **1940** (1948) Seton *Trail of Artist* 121, I drank pipsissewa tea from time to time, but I fear it had little virtue. **1966–70** DARE (Qu. S26c, *Wildflowers that grow in woods*) Infs **MI31, MA100, NJ29,** Pipsissewa; **CT30,** White waxy pipsissewa; (Qu. S26a, *. . Wildflowers. . . Roadside flowers*) Inf **MA5,** Pipsissewa; (Qu. S26e, *Other wildflowers not yet mentioned;* not asked in early QRs) Inf **SC46,** Pipsissewa; (Qu. BB50a, *. . Favorite remedies . . for a cough*) Inf **NJ34,** Pipsissewa; (Qu. BB50b, *Remedies for chest colds*) Inf **WV13,** Pipsissewa. **1966–68** DARE Wildfl QR Pl.152A Infs **MI7, 57, MN15, WA10,** Pipsissewa; **NH4,** Pipsissaway; **WA30,** Pipsissewa.

pique bois n Also sp *picque bois* [LAFr < Fr *pic* "woodpecker"] **LA**
Also with modifiers: Any of several **woodpeckers;** see quots.

1844 DeKay *Zool. NY* 2.192 **LA,** The Clape, or Golden-winged Wood-pecker. . . It is called. . . in Louisiana, *Pique-bois jaune.* **1887** *Forest & Stream* 28.248 **LA,** *Colaptes auratus. . .* Pique-bois-jaune. **1900** *Wilson Bulletin* 31.9 **LA,** *Picque-bois-jaune.* Louisiana. French. Yellow Wood-pecker. **1916** *Times–Picayune* (New Orleans LA) 16 Apr mag sec 9, *Flicker. . .* Pique Bois Dore. *Ibid, Ivory-billed woodpecker. . .* Pique bois. . . *Southern hairy woodpecker. . .* Pique bois (a local name for all woodpeckers). . . *Red-headed woodpecker. . .* Pique Bois Tete Rouge. This familiar 'pique-bois,' a local name applied to all of the woodpeckers by the French-speaking people of Louisiana, can be recognized at a glance by its bright red head. [**1931** Read *LA French* 59, *Pique-bois. . .* Woodpecker (family Picidae). Charlevoix, writing in April, 1721, mentions the great beauty of birds that he calls . . *Picque-bois.* The local name for a woodpecker is now almost always *pique-bois. . .* Thus the Red-headed Woodpecker . . is *Le Pique-bois Tête Rouge;* the large

Ivory-billed Woodpecker . . , which is not yet extinct in Louisiana, is . . *Le Grande Pique-bois*. . . *Pique-bois* is composed of the imperative of *piquer*, "to pierce," "to stick," and the object-noun *bois*, "wood." *Ibid*, *Pique-bois Doré*. . . "Golden Woodpecker." This is the name of the . . Flicker. . . *Le Pique-bois Jaune*, "the yellow woodpecker," is another name for this bird.]

piquin See **chilipitin**

piramidig n [*DJE* 1847]

A **nighthawk 1** (here: *Chordeiles minor*).

1874 Coues *Birds NW* 263, *Chordeiles virginianus* [=*C. minor*]. . . Night-hawk; Bull-bat; . . Piramidig. **1946** Hausman *Eastern Birds* 367, *Chordeiles minor minor*. . . Piramidig. . . The vocal notes are sharp, musically nasal in quality, sounding like the syllable *peeent* or *beans*.

piraski See **piroshki**

pirate See **pirate perch**

pirate bird n

=**man-o'-war bird**.

1962 Imhof *AL Birds* 79, *Fregata magnificens*. . . Pirate Bird. . . It eats various kinds of marine life snatched from the surface of the sea or from other seabirds. It can swoop down on another bird which is carrying food and . . force it to drop or disgorge its burden . . [and] scoop up the food before it hits the water.

pirate bug n

=**assassin bug**.

1901 Howard *Insect Book* 293, *Assassin Bugs*. . . are predatory in their habits and feed on other insects which they pierce and whose blood they suck by means of their strong, sharp beaks. From this food some of the subfamilies are known as "cannibal bugs" or "pirate bugs." **1926** Essig *Insects N. Amer.* 355, *Reduviidae*. . . Pirate Bugs. . . The food consists . . [of] any living thing small enough for them to overpower.

pirate perch n Also *pirate* [See quot 1908]

A freshwater fish (*Aphredoderus sayanus*) native chiefly to the Atlantic and Gulf coasts and the Mississippi Valley.

1870 *Amer. Naturalist* 4.101, In the Assunpink Creek, where these 'pirates' it would seem must have gone to, we have also carefully searched. *Ibid* 107, Pirate Perch (*Aphrodedurus* [sic] *Sayanus*). . . The adult fish, measuring five inches in length, has been seen frequently to swallow one of its own kind measuring an inch. **1883** WI Chief Geologist *Geol. WI* 1.429, *Aphredoderus sayannus* [sic]. . . Pirate Perch. Found in Fox river. **1905** NJ State Museum *Annual Rept. for 1904* 275, Pirate Perch. Pirate. Mud Perch. . . Very abundant in tide-water in the lower Delaware. **1908** Forbes–Richardson *Fishes of IL* 230, It [=*Aphredoderus sayanus*] was named the "pirate-perch" by Dr. C.C. Abbott, because it ate only fishes when confined in his aquarium. **1956** Harlan–Speaker *IA Fish* 158, The pirate perch. . . is bass-like in appearance and feeds largely on aquatic insects. **1983** *Audubon Field Guide N. Amer. Fishes* 482, The Pirate Perch hides in aquatic vegetation by day and emerges in darkness to feed.

pirie See **purie**

pirogi See **pierogi**

pirogue n Usu |'pi,roʊ(g)|; for varr see quots 1916, 1965–70 Also *pero(a)gue, perouge;* pronc-sp *peerow* [Fr < Span *piragua*, of Cariban origin] **chiefly Missip Valley; now esp MS, LA** See Map Cf **periagua**

Orig a dugout canoe; later any of var small, canoe-like boats.

1810 Pike *Expeditions* 8 **Upper Missip Valley,** Met two peroques [sic] full of Indians. **1813** in 1932 *OH Archeol. & Hist. Qrly.* 41.64 **cwOH,** Three Men that we Dispatch'd Early in the morning Down the River to bring up A Perouge Did not return until evening. **1817** (1890) Long *Jrl.* 10 **IA,** It [=the Yellow River] is navigable for pirogues, in time of high water, about fifty miles from its mouth. **1826** Biggs *Narrative* 14 **IL** (as of 1788), They [=Indians] put all their property into a large Perouge and moved by water up the Wabash river. **1834** (1928) Underwood *Jrl.* 32.127 **TX,** I proceeded up the river as far as Bell's landing in a perogue, a kind of boat dug out of a large logue. **1882** in 1883 Twain *Life on Missip.* (Boston) 595, A pirogue sometimes flits from the bushes and crosses the Red River on its way out to the Mississippi. **1916** *DN* 4.269 **New Orleans LA,** Pirogue. . . Pronounced ['pɪrəg]. **1921** in 1942 McAtee *Dial. Grant Co. IN* 79 (as of 1890s), Perogue. **1945** Saxon *Gumbo Ya-Ya* 199 **LA,** A pirogue is a frail shell of a boat, hewn

out of a single log, averaging thirteen feet in length and twenty-two inches in width. **1946** Kopman *Wild Acres* 160 **LA,** These are mere ditches in which only the shallowest pirogue may be propelled by a pole. . . At some points these ditches are too shallow to float the pirogue, and only vigorous pushing will keep it moving over the . . ooze. **1953** (1977) Hubbard *Shantyboat* 276 **Missip-Ohio Valleys,** Always on the lookout for new words, we heard bateau and pirogue, which Old Sam called peerow. **1961** *PADS* 36.10 **sLA,** We might begin with a small group of words that are positively confined to the informants of southern Louisiana. . . *pirogue* (small river boat)—71.4 [percent of 70 infs]. **1961** Douglas *My Wilderness* 259 **ME,** When the Old Guide first came to the river as a boy, people used the pirogue. It was hollowed out of a white pine with an adze. . . These pirogues were thirty feet long. They drew about three inches of water and carried three people. In those days the river was used in lumber operations. Pirogues took supplies upstream to the camps. **1965–70** *DARE* (Qu. O1, . . *A small rowboat, not big enough to hold more than two people*) Infs **IN**42, **MS**16, 32, 72, 73, ['pi,ro]; **LA**34, 37, ['pi,roʊg]; **LA**20, 26, ['pi,rog] [FW illustr: double-ended boat]; **LA**10, ['pi,ru]—pointed at both ends; **LA**23, ['pi,roʊg]—small, pointed boat for hunting and fishing; **LA**31, ['pi,roʊg]—a double-ender; **LA**2, ['pi,roʊ]—used in marshes, pushed with sticks; **LA**3, ['pi,roʊ]—mostly used in swamps, narrow, very easy to turn over; **LA**8, ['pi,roʊ]—slender, room for only two; **LA**45, ['pi,roʊ]—used in the swamps; **MI**108, [,pɪ'rɑg]; **TX**9, ['pi,rag]. **1968** *DARE* FW Addit **sLA,** *Pirogue* ['pi,rog]—Narrow, shallow boat for swamps. Older ones . . were made from a single cypress log; newer ones are made of cypress boards. **1979** Hallowell *People Bayou* 42 **sLA,** Trappers now rely on motorboats rather than working the marsh by foot or pirogue, the name first given a dugout canoe used by Indians but now more often applied to a double-ended, narrow-beam dory nailed together out of plywood and cypress. **1986** Pederson *LAGS Concordance (Rowboat)* 127 infs, **chiefly LA, MS,** Pirogue. [*DARE* Ed: Typical descriptions of the pirogue include "shaped like a canoe," "narrow," "flat bottomed" and "sharp on both ends" or "both ends pointed."] **1992** Scott *Cajun Vernacular Engl.* 49, Resembling a canoe with a flat bottom, pirogues are commonly handmade and continue to be a preferred mode of transportation among Cajuns on shallow or slow-moving waterways. C[ajun] V[ernacular] E[nglish] speakers will frequently call ordinary canoes pirogues as well: (overheard at a Lafayette sporting shop) "Cher, you'd never get me in one of them funny-looking pirogues. How you gonna get that over the dam? The bottom ain't flat." **1995** Karr *Liars' Club* 82 **eTX,** They ran film clips . . with Cattleman Bill bragging that he had personally rowed a pirogue—a kind of Cajun kayak—up Main Street.

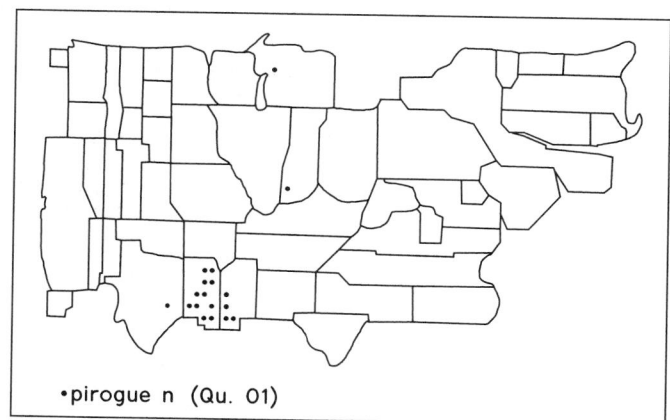

•pirogue n (Qu. O1)

pirohi See **pierogi**

pirok n Also *perok, perugy* [Russ *pirog* pie] **AK** Cf **piroshki**

A main-dish pie, frequently containing fish and rice.

1945 *AK Sportsman* Feb 32, They made a fish pie, or pirok, that was a full one-dish meal. **1968** *DARE* (Qu. H45, *Dishes made with meat, fish, or poultry that everybody around here would know, but that people in other places might not*) Inf **AK**3, Pirok—salmon, rice, cabbage, onion, and hard-boiled egg chopped; a pie with crust top and bottom, meal in itself; (Qu. H52, *Dishes made with fresh cabbage*) Inf **AK**3, Cabbage pirok—shred cabbage and some onions, saute in olive oil or butter. Use ground cold roast—cooked meat—add to make a sort of hash, much butter, etc. **1979** *Theata* 44 **AK,** Pirok is a main dish that contains fish and another name for it is Russian pie or Fish pie. **1986** McClanahan *Our Stories* 48 **AK,** Perok. Meat perok. Made out of moosemeat and rice and baked between two crusts. **1988** Oliver *Jrl. Aleutian Yr.* 198 (as of 1946–47), Pari Lokanin sent Mike down with a delicious *perugy*, a rice and salmon pie, for my dinner.

piroot v Often with *around* [Prob var of *pirouette*, infl by *root* v] **chiefly Sth, SW** Cf **rootle**

To whirl around; to gambol, dash about; to prowl, nose around.

   1858 *S. Lit. Messenger* 27.201 **VA**, She went a skippin and a hoppin and a pirootin aroun on the flatform uv the stage. **1863** Massett *Drifting About* 242 **cnCA**, The streets were almost impassable from the mud and slush, and . . the "ladies" . . would find it impossible to "piroot" thither. **1866** Smith *Bill Arp* 116 **Sth**, For four years the Confederate Horse-Stealing Cavalry have been pirooting around, preparing themselves for the frightful struggle that is to come. **1878** Hart *Sazerac Lying Club* 91 **NV**, One day his [=George Washington's] old man went to town and bought him a hatchet for a birthday. When George got the hatchet he went pirootin' round the ranch, cuttin' and slashin' at everything in sight. **1883** (1971) Harris *Nights with Remus* 302 **GA** [Black], W'en you see dat ar 'Tildy gal pirootin' 'roun' I boun' you ole Brer Affikin Jack aint fur off. **1909** *DN* 3.357 **eAL, wGA**, *Piroot* ['paɪrut]. . . To root or nose about. "What do you come pirootin' around here for?" **1910** Raine *Bucky O'Connor* 30 (*DAE*), I've been pirootin' around this country, boy and man, fifteen years. **1923** *DN* 5.244 **LA**, *Pirooting* [paɪrutɪn]. . . 1. Romping like children. 2. Going about aimlessly. 3. Rooting about like a pig. **1936** White *My TX* 154, What does this Bostonese woman do but get to pirootin' around down in Chihuahuita. **1964** Will *Hist. Okeechobee* 227 **FL**, Three of the young bucks of the settlement had been pirooting around for to see what kind of devilment they might discover or even maybe, initiate. **1985** *DARE* File **AL**, *Piroot*. . . To lollygag, fool around. **1986** Pederson *LAGS Concordance*, 1 inf, **neTX**, *Piroot*—to stir around, go visiting.

piroshki n sg or pl Also sp *peroski, piraski, pirozhki* [Russ *pirozhki*, pl of *pirozhok*, dimin of *pirog*; cf **pirok**] Cf **pierogi**

A small pocket of dough with a meat or fish filling.

   1949 (1986) Leonard *Jewish Cookery* 163, *Piroshki*—Use well-kneaded yeast dough or any of the pie crust doughs. . . Cut into 3-inch rounds . . and place a spoonful of chopped cooked meat, liver, lung, chicken or kasha in the center and pinch edges together securely. . . [Bake] . . for 20 to 30 minutes. **1957** Showalter *Mennonite Cookbook* 64 **KS**, *Meat Tarts (Piroshki)*. . . [F]lour . . sour cream . . egg yolk . . butter . . fresh or leftover meat, chopped . . onion . . salt. . . Roll out [dough]. . . Cut with a round biscuit cutter. Place a spoonful of filling in center and close tightly by pinching into an oblong shape. . . [B]ake. **1980** *AK Geographic* 7.3.184, Russian recipes remain favorites . . *pirozhkies*, deep-fried pastries stuffed with meat. **1981** *Alexandrovsk: English Bay in its Traditional Way* (high-school publication) 57 (Tabbert *Dict. Alaskan Engl.*), *Piraskies*—A popular food and the same as "Fish Pie", it is made into smaller pies and fried 'till brown. **1982** *Fireweed Cillqaq: Life and Times in Port Graham* (high-school publication) 39 (Tabbert *Dict. Alaskan Engl.*), *Peroskies*. . . [B]acon . . salmon . . onion . . oil . . rice. . . Bread dough. . . Roll dough and cut into squares. Put 1 Tbsp. salmon-rice mixture on each square, fold and deep fry in hot skillet till golden brown.

pirotti See **pierogi**

pirozhki See **piroshki**

pirsimmon See **persimmon**

pis ant See **piss ant** n

pis-au-lit See **pissenlit**

Piscopal(ian) adj, n Also *Piscalopian, Piscobal, Pishopaligan, Piskie, Piskubble* [Aphet forms of *Episcopal(ian)*]

1 Episcopalian; an Episcopalian.

   1922 Gonzales *Black Border* 319 **sSC, GA coasts** [Gullah glossary], *'Piskubble*—Episcopal, Episcopalian. **1936** Reese *Worleys* 37 **MD** (as of 1865) [Black], I's a Baptis' preachah, I is, an' dese heah is Pishopaligans. **1954** in 1958 Brewer *Dog Ghosts* 83 **TX** [Black], He goes to de bigges' white 'Piscopal chu'ch in Eas' Texas. **1965–70** *DARE* (Qu. CC2, . . *Predominant religious denominations*) Inf **VA85**, Piscopal; **FL22, 26**, Piscopalian(s); (Qu. CC3, . . *Religions that have come in recently . . or are a bit different from the common ones*) Inf **NC23**, Piscopalians; (Qu. CC4, . . *Nicknames . . for various religions or religious groups*) Infs **MA59, OH37, VT16, WA17**, Piscalopian; **CT3**, Piscobals; **MN33**, Piskies.

2 as noun: See quot.

   1968 *DARE* (Qu. BB20, *Joking names or expressions for overactive kidneys*) Inf **WV2**, Piscopalians.

pis-en-lit See **pissenlit**

pishaug n [Of Algonquian origin; see quot 1910]

The female or immature **surf scoter.**

   1888 Trumbull *Names of Birds* 104 **MA**, The females and young males [of *Melanitta perspicillata*] are, by many, regarded as a species distinct from the adult drakes; the two former being known on Buzzard's Bay, from New Bedford to Westport, by the name *Pishaug*. **1910** Hodge *Hdbk. Amer. Indians* 2.262, *Pishaug*. . . apparently identical with the Massachuset *a'pishaug*, widgeons, given by Trumbull (Natick Dict., 249, 1903). **1955** MA Audubon Soc. *Bulletin* 39.377 **MA**, *Surf Scoter*. . . Pish-aug. . . The female and young. A Pequot Indian term meaning duck.

Pishopaligan See **Piscopal(ian)**

pisk n

A **nighthawk 1** (here: *Chordeiles minor*).

   1834 Nuttall *Manual Ornith.* 2.609, *Night-Hawk*, or *Pisk*. . . This well known bird ranges in summer throughout the fur-countries, and to the remotest Arctic islands. **1874** Coues *Birds NW* 263, *Chordeiles virginianus* [=*C. minor*]. . . Pisk. **1917** (1923) *Birds Amer.* 2.172, Pisk. . . Breeds . . South to northern parts of Gulf States and west to edge of Plains from Minnesota to northeastern Texas. **1946** Hausman *Eastern Birds* 367, *Eastern Nighthawk*. . . *Other Names* . . Pisk. . . Often seen hawking over towns and cities, calling as it goes.

Piskie, Piskubble See **Piscopal(ian)**

pismire n Usu |'pɪs,maɪə(r)|; also |'pɪsə-, 'pɪz-|; for addit varr see quot 1965–70 at **1** below   Pronc-spp *piss(a)mire*

1 An ant.   [*OED2* c1386 →]   **chiefly NEast**   See Map   Cf **piss ant** n **1**

   1834 *New Engl. Mag.* 7.448, We often lost sight of it [=a small boat] for several minutes—it was like an egg-shell afloat in a mill-pond, with five pismires. **1863** *S. Lit. Messenger* 37.600 **VA**, It is a fine thing . . to sit under these noble trees . . until a caravan of gigantic black or red pismires begin a pilgrimage up your backbone. **1904** *DN* 2.427 **Cape Cod MA** (as of a1857), *Pismire*. . . The large black ant. **1907** *DN* 3.196 **seNH**, *Pismire*. . . An ant. Usually applied to the red ant common on country sidewalks. **1930** Shoemaker *1300 Words* 41 **cPA Mts** (as of c1900), [*Meyer* [sic]—An ant.] *Ibid* 47, *P—ss meyer*—A winged ant, commonly supposed to be the male of the species. **1950** *WELS* (*Other kinds of ants*) 5 Infs, **WI**, Pismire. **1965–70** *DARE* (Qu. R17, . . *Names . . for the big black ants that sting*) 11 Infs, **esp NEast**, Pismire; **ME3**, ['pɪs,maɪjə]; **ME8**, [pɪsəmaɪə]—don't sting; when females are flying, some call them piss ants; **ME12**, [pɪsmaɪə]; **MI65**, He [=a dog] ran all around a mullein stalk and treed a big [,pɪs'maɪə]; **NY105**, [pɪsmaɪə]; **NJ39**, Pismire—these are little; **NY133**, Pismire—seldom around here; [**NY227**, Pismire—thousand legs;] **PA246**, Pismire—old-fashioned; (Qu. R18, . . *Kinds of ants*) Inf **NY68**, Pismire; **NJ16, NY75**, Pismire—small (ones); **NJ4**, Pismire—tiny red ones; **CA15**, Pismires [FW: [pɪz-]]; **ME6**, ['pɪsə,maɪə]; **MA37**, ['pɪsəmaɪjəz]—small; **NH14**, ['pɪsə,maɪjə]. [21 of 27 Infs male] **1968** McPhee *Pine Barrens* 123 **NJ**, "This ground is so poor a pismire can't live on it," he said. "If you found a pismire here, he'd be half starved to death."

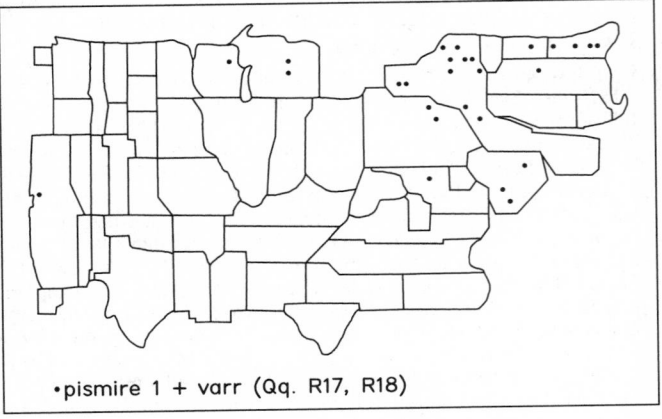

•pismire 1 + varr (Qq. R17, R18)

2 Transf: a contemptible person. [*OED2* →1818] Cf **piss ant** n **2**

1870 *Punchinello* 1.123, Mr. *Schenk* intimated that Mr. *Logan* was an insect. At first he said he was a pismire, but the Speaker said pismire was not parliamentary, and he modified it to grasshopper. **1935** *N&Q* 169.366 [Animal names applied to persons], Pismire—A useless and contemptible little thing. An insignificant ant but without the idea of activity. **1959** *VT Hist.* 27.152, Pissamire. . . (A corruption of the word *pismire,* 'an ant'). A sniveling, petty person. Heard in southeastern Vermont, specifically from an old carpenter in Brookline and a farmer (75) and school children in Marlboro. Windham Co.

3 =**oxeye daisy 1.** [Cf *EDD* pissimire for *Taraxacum officinale*] Cf **piss-a-bed 2**

1892 *Jrl. Amer. Folkl.* 5.98 **MA**, *Chrysanthemum leucanthemum,* pismire. East Weymouth, Mass.

4 A **bluet 2** (here: *Hedyotis caerulea*). Cf **piss-a-bed 3**

1969 *DARE* (Qu. S11, . . *Bluets*) Inf **MA**25A, Known in Maine as [ˈpɪsəmaɪjəz].

Pismo clam n [*Pismo* Beach, California]

An edible bivalve mollusk (*Tivela stultorum*) native to the southern California coast. Also called **hen clam 2**

1911 Keep *West Coast Shells* 77 **CA**, The Tivelas live from Santa Cruz southward, and they burrow but slightly. Sometimes at low tide the farmers come down with a plow and run furrows in the sand, turning the mollusks out like potatoes. They are highly esteemed by lovers of a good clam chowder, and occasionally they get into the city markets, where they are called Pismo clams. **1952** Morris *Field Guide Shells* 43 **CA**, *Tivela stultorum* . . (Pismo Clam). . . An important commercial clam in parts of California where it is sufficiently abundant. **1967–70** *DARE* (Qu. P18, . . *Kinds of shellfish*) Inf **CA**25, Pismo clams—have to be 4½ inches across to be kept; **CA**191, Pismo clams. **1981** Rehder *Audubon Field Guide Seashells* 796 **CA**, *Pismo Clam.* . . This large clam was once extensively dug for in California. . . [N]ow there is . . a catch limit of 15 clams a day per person; no commercial digging is allowed.

pison See **poison**

pis out v phr Cf **dog** v **7**

In marble play: see quot.

1922 *DN* 5.187 **KY**, Pis out. . . =dog up. [*Ibid* 186, Dog up. . . To shoot a taw not at the ring but away from it or nearer to it.]

piss-a-bed n

1 also *pee-the-bed, piss-bed, piss-the-bed, piss-weed, pissy-bed, pissy-pee:* =**dandelion 1.** [*OED2* 1597 →; cf Fr *pissenlit* 1545 (*OED2*)] **chiefly C and N Atl exc NEng** See Map

1830 Rafinesque *Med. Flora* 2.18, *Leontodon taraxacum.* . . Names. Common Dandelion. . . *Vulgar.* Pissabed, Puffball, &c. **1899** (1912) Green *VA Folk-Speech* 324, Pissabed. . . The dandelion flower. Children are warned not to pull it under the penalty of wetting their beds at night. **1940** in 1966 Goldstein–Byington *Two Penny Ballads* 143 **PA**, If you smell a dandelion, you are going to piss the bed; so the flowers are called "piss-the-beds." **1945** McAtee *Nomina Abitera* 15, Dandelion (*Taraxacum taraxacum*). . . Pissabed (Pissybed) has been noted in spoken use in Ontario, Pennsylvania and Virginia. **1965–70** *DARE* (Qu. S11, . . *Dandelion*) 20 Infs, **chiefly C and N Atl exc NEng**, Pissy-

bed(s); **LA**43A, Pissy-bed—they say if you play with them flowers, you pee in the bed; **CT**11, **NJ**21, 39, 52, 56, **NY**65, **SC**27, Piss-a-bed; **NJ**31, Piss-a-bed—Inf was told as a boy that if he picked some, he would piss a bed; **NY**44, 45, **PA**225, Pee-the-bed(s); **NJ**1, **OH**82, Piss-bed; **PA**162, Pissy-pee; **PA**245, Piss-the-bed, piss-weed; (Qu. I28a, . . *Kinds of things . . you call 'greens' . . [Those that are eaten raw]*) Inf **OH**82, Piss-bed. **1971** *Hand Coll.* **UT**, Dandelions = "pee-the-bed," "pissabed." . . The flower was sometimes called by that name. **1982** Brooks *Quicksand* 9 **swUT** (as of c1905), We set ourselves to gathering the hill flowers to take home—plenty of buttercups, and miniature hollyhocks, blue bells, piss-a-beds, rare sego lilies.

2 also *pee-bed, pee-weed, piss-(in-)the-bed, pissy-bed, wet-the-bed:* Another composite plant, usu **oxeye daisy 1, dog fennel 1,** or a **tansy.** Also called **pissenlit** Cf **pismire 3** Note: These plants often have an unpleasant odor; LA quots apparently refer to **dog fennel 1.**

1790 Deane *New Engl. Farmer* 313, Of the upland-weeds those which have proved to be the most troublesome are . . the greater-daisy, ox-eye, or piss-abed. **1842** (1878) Aime *Plantation Diary* 81 **LA**, Through cutting pisabeds [sic], in pastures, on the 21st. . . It took seven days, with whole gang, to cut, pile up, and burn, everywhere on the plantation, "Pisabeds". **1890** *DN* 1.56 **MA**, On Cape Cod, piss-abed is used for the "field-daisy," "white-weed [=*Leucanthemum vulgare*]." **1892** *DN* 1.212 **MA**, Piss-abed for the "white-weed [=*Leucanthemum vulgare*]." **1945** McAtee *Nomina Abitera* 15 **MA**, Dog Fennel (*Anthemis cotula*)—Piss-the-bed; children playing with it will be so affected. **1960** Williams *Walk Egypt* 103 **GA**, Children lagging to school, rebellious and aching for summer, would point to the yellow tansy and the orange coneflowers with their bulging brown centers. "Pee weed," they would shrill. "Shit weed!" **1966–70** *DARE* (Qu. S11) Inf **CT**26, Piss-a-bed—white and yellow, grow in a wet place, small blossoms; **SC**67, Pee-bed; (Qu. S7) Inf **SC**11, Wet-the-bed flower—about 1 foot high—if you pick them, so they said, you'll wet the bed; (Qu. S21, . . *Weeds . . that are a trouble in gardens and fields*) Inf **LA**43, Piss-in-the-beds—wild daisies, not dandelions; (Qu. S26d, *Wildflowers that grow in meadows;* not asked in early QRs) Inf **SC**67, Pee-bed—at least a foot tall, tiny flower, smells bad, a head . . similar to a dandelion; (Qu. S26e, *Other wildflowers not yet mentioned;* not asked in early QRs) Inf **NH**16, Pissy-beds—doesn't associate with any other flowers—little white flowers. **1983** [see **pissenlit**].

3 also *pee-(in-)the-bed, pee-wee, piss-(in-the-)bed, piss-pants, piss-the-bed, pissy-bed, wet-the-bed:* A **bluet 2** (here: *Hedyotis caerulea*). [*EDD* 1897] **chiefly sNEng, esp MA** See Map Cf **piss-ant grass**

1954 McAtee *Suppl. to Nomina Abitera* [4] **NH**, Bluets (*Houstonia caerulea*)—Pissabed. **1965–70** *DARE* (Qu. S11, . . *Bluets*) Infs **CT**23, 30, **MA**6, 14, 29, 71, **NY**94, Piss-a-bed; **MA**42, Piss-beds; **CT**40, Piss-the-bed; **MA**58, Pissy-bed; **MA**78, Wet-the-beds; **KY**18, 34, Pee-wees; (Qu. S23, *Pale blue flowers . . in March or early April*) Inf **NY**183, Pissy-beds; (Qu. S26e, *Other wildflowers not yet mentioned;* not asked in early QRs) Inf **SC**27, Pee-the-bed—tiny blue flowers that appeared in spring in open fields. **1968** *DARE* FW Addit **AR**, "Piss-in-the-beds"—the tiny blue four-petaled flowers that come up early in spring on lawns. "Pee-in-the-beds" is a euphemism. **1982** *DARE* File **cwMA**, For "bluet" I have heard "piss-pants" in Mass. from a woman 65–70 [years old]. Stepping on the plant is said to have a diuretic effect. **1988** *Ibid* **csMA** (as of 1940–50), Piss-a-beds: bluets.

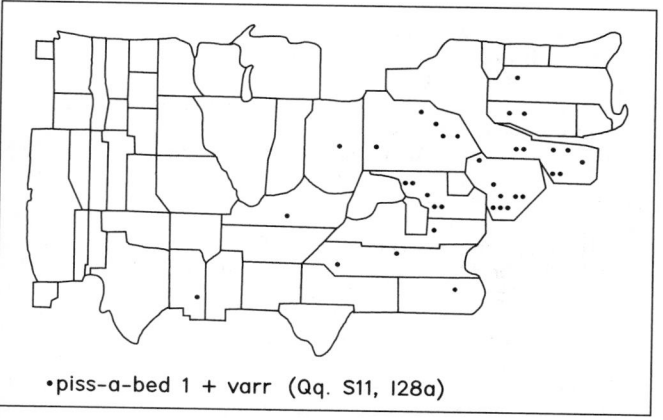

•piss-a-bed 1 + varr (Qq. S11, I28a)

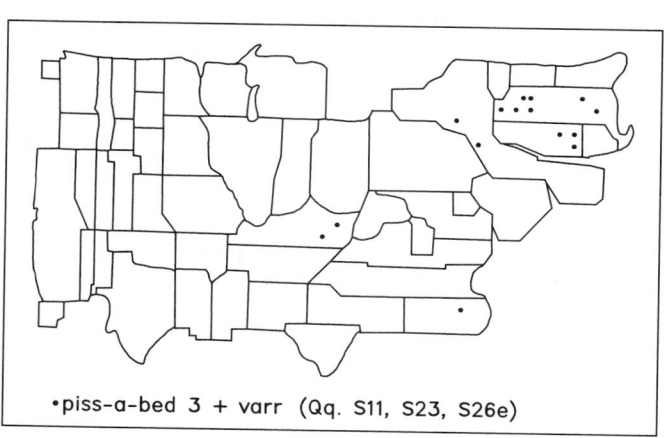

•piss-a-bed 3 + varr (Qq. S11, S23, S26e)

4 as *pissy-bed:* A **trillium.** Cf **stinking benjamin, wildcat piss**

1969 *DARE* (Qu. S2, . . *The flower that comes up in the woods early in spring, with three white petals that turn pink as the flower grows older*) Inf **KY**18, Pissy-bed.

5 A chaff-flower (here: *Alternanthera sessilis*).

1974 (1977) Coon *Useful Plants* 55, *Telanthera polygonoides* [= *Alternanthera sessilis*]—Piss-a-bed. Given this common name it should hardly be necessary to indicate its use.

6 as *pee-in-the-bed:* Prob either **arbutus** or a **wintergreen** (here: *Gaultheria procumbens*), but see quot. Cf **gravel plant, mountain tea 1**

1991 Still *Wolfpen Notebooks* 88 s**Appalachians,** Here's an herb that's good for kidney trouble. If you have to get up in the night more than once, go to the woods and find you a few runners of it and brew them into a tea. We call it 'pee-in-the-bed.'

7 as *pee-the-bed:* See quots. *derog*

1937 (1977) Hurston *Their Eyes* 141 **FL,** Lemme know when dat ole pee-de-bed is gone and Ah'll be right back. **1971** *Hand Coll.* **UT,** If the milk from the dandelions left a brown stain, one was jeered as a "pee-the-bed."

pissamire See **pismire**

piss ant n Also *pis ant, pissy ant*

1 also *piece ant, pizzy* ~: An ant (Formicidae). [*OED2* 1661 →] **widespread, but somewhat less freq NEast, Gulf States** See Map *esp freq among male speakers* Cf **horse ant, pee ant, pismire 1**

1770 in 1917 *MD Hist. Mag.* 12.362, It seems the Pissants eat a great deal of Corn in the ground. **1846** (1973) Porter *Quarter Race* 84 **KY,** The galls . . come pourin out of the woods like pissants out of an old log when tother end's afire. **1867** Harris *Sut Lovingood Yarns* 32 **TN,** I felt like I'd crowded intu an ole bee-gum, an' hit all full ove pissants. **1899** (1912) Green *VA Folk-Speech* 324, Piss-ant. . . An ant. **1904** *DN* 2.420 nw**AR,** Pis-ant. . . Pismire. "The holler of her foot would kill a pis-ant." **1909** *DN* 3.357 e**AL,** w**GA,** Pis-ant. . . The pismire, a small black or red ant with a strong odor. This species does not sting so readily as the common or stinging ant. The word is felt as a vulgarism. **1912** *DN* 3.525 w**IN,** Pis-ant. . . Any kind of ant. In some sections of the country the word has a vulgar connotation. **1916** *DN* 4.346 **LA,** Piece ant ['pis ænt]. Same as *piss ant*, pismire. **1942** Whipple *Joshua* 100 **UT** (as of c1860), "Men's men," she stated, "just like piss-ants is piss-ants." **1949** *PADS* 11.9 **TX,** Pissant. . . A small red ant. Also called *sugar ant.* **1950** *WELS* (Other kinds of ants) 2 Infs, **WI,** Piss ant. c**1960** Wilson *Coll.* cs**KY,** Pissant. . . An ant of any kind: men's language; women and children say ant. **1965–70** *DARE* (Qu. R17, . . *Names . . for the big black ants that sting*) 141 Infs, **widespread, but somewhat less freq NEast, Lower Missip Valley,** Piss ant; **PA**176, Pissy ant [Of all Infs responding to the question, 61% were male; of those giving these responses, 73% were male.]; (Qu. R18, . . *Kinds of ants*) 44 Infs, **scattered, but more freq Sth, TX, OK,** Piss ant; **CA**136, Black piss-ant; **NC**49, Flying piss-ant; **MD**9, Pizzy ant [41 of 47 Infs male]. **1967** LeCompte *Word Atlas* 199 se**LA,** Big black ants that sting. . . piss ant [1 of 21 infs]. **1983** *MJLF* 9.1.51 ce**KY** (as of 1956), Piss ant . . an ant, not an objectionable term to the informants [=2 older men]. **1991** Still *Wolfpen Notebooks* 162 s**Appalachians,** Piss ant: large black ant (small black ant called *anty-mar*).

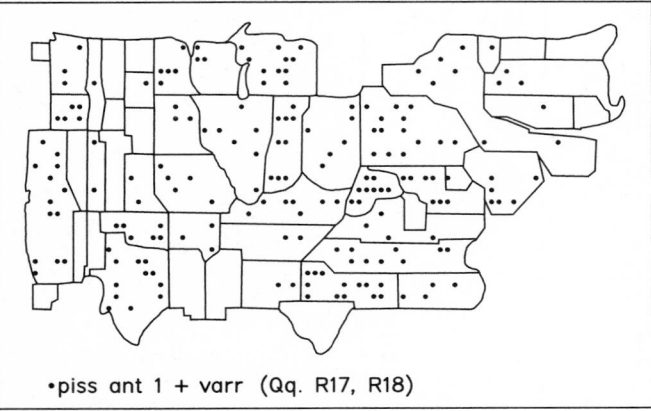

•piss ant 1 + varr (Qq. R17, R18)

2 Transf: a mean or contemptible person; also attrib: petty, insignificant. **scattered, but esp West** Cf **pismire 2**

1935 Davis *Honey* 263 **OR,** Anybody who called owning horses disorderly conduct was a liar and a pissant. **1946** (1972) Mezzrow–Wolfe *Really Blues* 337, Piss-ant: a nobody, small fry. **1970** *DARE* (Qu. GG38, *Somebody who is usually mean and bad tempered:* "He's an awful _____.") Inf **CA**192, Piss ant. **1971** Jennings *Cowboys* 68 **MT, WY** (as of 1877), You'd lose all their respeck sticking your nose in their little pissy-ant doings. **1973** Heinlein *Time* 522, Not on your tintype . . you pusillanimous piss-ant. **1978** *Guardian Weekly* 25 June 18/4 (*OED2*), That pissant [California Governor] Brown. **1978** (1979) Hailey *Overload* 237, All you do now is let off some pissant firecrackers, then laze around here for a goddam month's vacation. **1984** Erdrich *Love Medicine* 159 **ND,** Only three things made her angry. . . Number three was a piss-ant. . . "A piss-ant," she said, "is a man with fat buns who tries to sell you things. A Jaycee, an Elk, a Kiwanis." **1984** Weaver *TX Crude* 120, Pissant. . . Of little or no consequence. "Son, don't let one little pissant punch in the nose stop you." *Pissant.* . . One small of stature, physical or social. "Yeah, I know he's a sawed-off little ol' pissant, but you call him 'Shorty' and he'll stop your heart!"

pissant v

To move (a heavy object) by brute force.

1953 Randolph–Wilson *Down in Holler* 117 **Ozarks,** Piss-ant is a common Ozark verb, since the backwoods lumberman often piss-ants his logs down to the river; that is, he pulls and pushes and prizes them down without the use of wheels. **1984** Weaver *TX Crude* 121, Pissant. . . To carry, tote, lug. . . "The danged ol' forklift is cratered [*DARE* Ed:=broken down], and y'all are goin' to have to pissant the bricks over to the jobsite."

piss-ant grass n Cf **piss-a-bed 3**

A **bluet 2** (here: *Hedyotis caerulea*).

1968 *DARE* (Qu. S11, . . *Bluets*) Inf **VA**15, Piss-ant grass.

piss ash n Cf **piss elm, ~ maple, ~ oak, ~ willow**

=**green ash.**

1897 Sudworth *Arborescent Flora* 329 **VT,** *Fraxinus pennsylvanica.* . . Piss Ash.

piss ball n

A sea squirt (here: *Molgula pellucida*); see quot.

1945 McAtee *Nomina Abitera* 19 e**MD,** Ascidian (*Molgula pellucida*)—Piss-ball.

piss-bed See **piss-a-bed 1, 3**

piss-burnt brown adj phr Cf **pisser-legs**

1961 Seeman *In Arms of Mt.* 158 e**TN,** Brownie [=a pet woodchuck] has . . brindled fur that is rusty red underneath—called "piss-burnt brown" in the hills.

piss cat n Also *pisser, piss kitty*

=**skunk.**

[**1924** Lambert *PA Ger. Dict.* 28, Bisskatz . . skunk.] [**1966** Dakin *Dial. Vocab. Ohio R. Valley* 2.399, One instance of Pennsylvania German *Pisskatz* [for *skunk*] is recorded as an "old name" in Tuscawaras County, Ohio.] **1966–69** *DARE* (Qu. P26, *Names and nicknames . . for a skunk*) Infs **GA**72, **LA**7, **MI**47, **OH**82, **PA**1, Piss cat; [**PA**157, ['bɪs,kats]—literally, piss cat;] **MA**15, Piss kitty; **PA**245, Pisser.

piss clam n Also *pisser*

=**soft-shell clam.**

1788 Schöpf *Reise Staaten* 1.8 se**NY,** Die *Austern,* Clams (Venus mercenaria L.) und *Pissers* (*Myae Species*) sind die gewöhnlichsten Schaaltiere, die man in hiesigen Gegenden zu Markte bringt und speisst. [Footnote to *pissers:*] Wenn man sie gelinde drücket, sie ein klares Wasser mit ziemlichen Nachdruck von sich sprissen. [=The *oysters, clams* (Venus mercenaria L.) and *pissers* (*Myae species*) are the most usual shellfish brought to market in these regions and eaten. [Footnote to *pissers:*] If one presses them slightly, they spurt forth a clear water with considerable force.] **1811** in 1965 *AmSp* 40.199 **NYC,** Went for piss Clambs found a black fish. **1814** in 1815 Lit. & Philos. Soc. NY *Trans.* 1.401, The common bait for black-fish is the soft clam or pisser, (mya.) **1843** DeKay *Zool. NY* 5.240, It [=*Mya arenaria*] is known under the various appellations of *Long Clam* and *Piss Clam* to distinguish it from the common *Round Clam.* **1859** (1968) Bartlett *Americanisms* 84, The Soft Clam . . has a long, extensible, cartilaginous snout, or proboscis, through which it ejects water; whence it is also called Stem-clam and

Piss-clam. **1899** (1912) Green *VA Folk-Speech* 324, *Piss-clam.* . . So called from its squirting. **1967–68** *DARE* (Qu. P18, . . *Kinds of shellfish*) Inf **DE**4, Piss clam—they squirt water; **MA**72, Piss clams. **1984** *DARE* File **Chesapeake Bay** [Watermen's vocab], Piss clams.

piss-cutter n Cf cutter n¹ 3, piss-ripper

Something or someone remarkable for its kind; also used ironically.

1942 Berrey–Van den Bark *Amer. Slang* 29.2, *Something excellent.* . . piss-cutter. *Ibid* 432.2, *Capable person; expert.* . . piss-cutter. **1956** *AmSp* 31.192 [US Marine Corps slang], His [=a Marine's] garrison cap is a *pisscutter* (also used as a cynical description, i.e., 'He's a pisscutter, he is!'). **1967** *DARE* FW Addit **MI**42, Piss-cutter—"That's a real piss-cutter," meaning, it's tough, or terrible, or out of the ordinary. "A piss-cutter of a storm." **1968** Buckler *Ox Bells* 206, Gus Jordan's got a new rowboat. It's a real pisscutter. **1969** *AmSp* 44.259 [Railroad terms], *Piss-cutter*—Freight train that works long hours without rest time. **1975** Gould *ME Lingo* 209, *Piss-cutter*—A word not tossed off in genteel company, but very much used throughout Maine as a term for somebody putting on a bit of a show of excellence. . . A young man who is all dressed up to go and make an impression on his girl-friend may elicit from his rougher cronies, "Boy-o-boy! Ain't you the piss-cutter!" **1977** *Maledicta* Summer 13, A clever person is sometimes called a *piss-cutter.*

piss elm n Also *piss ellum* chiefly N Cent, Missip Valley, Upstate NY See Map Cf piss ash, ~ maple, ~ oak, ~ willow

An elm, usu a **slippery elm** (here: *Ulmus rubra*).

1914 *DN* 4.106 **KS**, *Piss-elm.* . . A water elm. When burnt green, the sap steams out and hisses. **1923** *DN* 5.206 **swMO**, *Ellum.* . . Elm. Piss elm, a variety of elm that carries a large amount of sap. **1942** McAtee *Dial. Grant Co. IN Suppl. 1* 7, *Piss-ellum* . . the slippery elm (*Ulmus fulva*). **1945** McAtee *Nomina Abitera* 11 **IN, KS, WI**, The Slippery Elm (*Ulmus fulva*)—This species is called piss-elm in the Midwest. **1950** *WELS* **WI** (*Different kinds of elm trees*) 6 Infs, Piss elm; 1 Inf, Piss elm—because it throws off a sticky juice; 1 Inf, Piss elm—full of moisture; when cut down, it would flow out; 1 Inf, Piss elm—full of sap—leave 'em lay for a long time before could cut them up. **1965–70** *DARE* (Qu. T11, . . *Kinds of elm trees*) 35 Infs, chiefly N Cent, Missip Valley, Upstate NY, Piss elm; **AR**5, **IA**8, **OK**1, Water elm, piss elm—same; **OK**7, **TX**35, Piss elm—same as white elm; **MI**26, Some people speak of "piss elm," but I just called them "elm"; **MI**27, The ordinary elm . . that's called the piss elm; **WI**12, "Slippery elm" not used; all called "piss elm." [35 of 43 Infs male] **1986** Pederson *LAGS Concordance*, 1 inf, neAR, Piss elm; 1 inf, ceTX, Piss elms = American elms. **1994** *DARE* File csWI, Some Winnebago women in this area use the term *piss elm* for slippery elm. **2001** *DARE* File, How about "piss-elm"? My dad used that one, amused that I was planning to burn Chinese elm in the fireplace. Again, the "piss" element seems to have referred to the urine-like smell of the burning wood. . . as I found out.

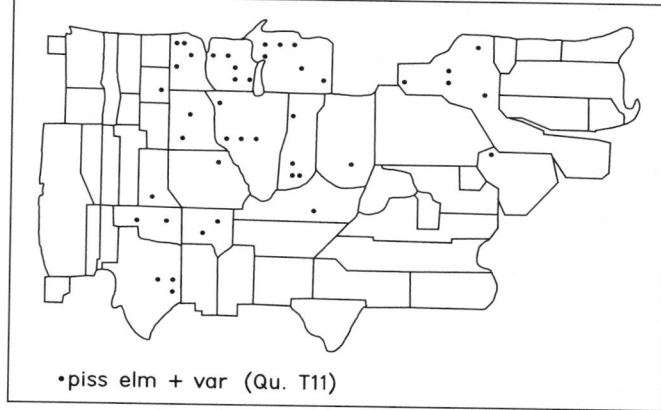

•piss elm + var (Qu. T11)

pissenlit n Also *pis-au-lit, pis-en-lit* [Fr; see quot 1967] esp LA

=**piss-a-bed 2.**

[**1850** *De Bow's Rev.* 9.289 **LA**, The forests are covered with a great number of varieties of the wild onion plant, . . the pompier and coco grass, . . the pisantlits, an exotic grass.] **1967** LeCompte *Word Atlas* 235 seLA, Pis-en-lit [10 of 21 infs]. . . *pis-au-lit* [7 of 21 infs]. . . *Pis-en-lit* means, literally, "urinate in the bed." This awkward name is given

to one of the more beautiful wild flowers which grow profusely in South Louisiana. The name stems from the legend that if a child picks the blossoms, he will wet the bed that night. Few people pick them. [**1969** *DARE* (Qu. S11, . . *Dandelion*) Inf **VT**16, Pissenlit [pɪsẽli]—French.] **1983** *Reinecke Coll.* 8 **LA**, *Pissenlit* . . ['pisɔ̃ˌli]—wildflower of aster type growing on roadsides or ditches, yellow or purplish white with yellow center, reputed to cause bedwetting if children handle them. Also pissybed [pɪsɪbed]. This is Eu[ropean] Fr[ench] word for dandelion, not so called in La.

pisser n

1 See **piss clam.**

2 See **piss cat.**

3 =**pickerel frog.**

1945 McAtee *Nomina Abitera* 21, Pickerel Frog (*Rana palustris*)—Although frogs in general and even toads may eject urine in a noticeable jet when suddenly flushed, the name "Pisser" was more or less fixed on this species in Grant County, Indiana, possibly because of its orange thighs and underparts, suggesting staining and also because of its unpleasant odor.

pisser-legs n

=**gray fox.**

1945 McAtee *Nomina Abitera* 49, Gray Fox (*Urocyon cinereoargenteus*)—Pisser-legs, from the rufous color suggesting stain on its hind legs.

pisser's flower n Cf woodman's Charmin

=**skunk cabbage 1b.**

1945 McAtee *Nomina Abitera* 8 **NW**, Western Skunk Cabbage (*Lysichiton camtschatcense*)—Pisser's flower.

piss fir n [From the odor] Cf stinking fir

Either the **grand fir** or a **white fir** (here: *Abies concolor*).

1956 *AmSp* 31.151 **nwCA**, *Piss fir.* . . White fir or lowland white fir. Called thus because of its strong odor. **1968–69** *DARE* (Qu. T5, . . *Kinds of evergreens, other than pine*) Inf **CA**120, Piss fir—stinks; (Qu. T17, . . *Kinds of pine trees; not asked in early QRs*) Infs **CA**105, 120, Piss fir. **1979** *Oregonian Article Letters* csOR, Piss Fir is slang for the trees Abies Concolor (white fir) and Abies Grandis (lowland white fir). . . White-fir gets its nickname from the water and sap it contains. The odor of this mixture smells like an uncleaned toilet.

‡piss fuzz n

1967 *DARE* File TX, Piss fuzz—balls or rolls of dust and lint that gather under beds and other furniture.

piss-hole in the snow n Also *piss in the snow;* euphem *hole in the snow*

In var phrr signifying an unimportant or insignificant person; see quots.

1967–70 *DARE* (Qu. HH20b, *Of an idle, worthless person* . . *"He doesn't amount to _____."*) Infs **MA**71, **NJ**53, Piss-hole in the snow; **TX**81, Piss in the snow. **1975** Gould *ME Lingo* 134, *Hole in the snow*—Worthless; not worth a hole in the snow. (It is a certain kind of a hole, however.)

piss horse See piss mare

pissimmond See persimmon

piss-in-the-bed See piss-a-bed 2, 3

piss in the snow See piss-hole in the snow

pissitis See -itis

piss kitty See piss cat

piss maple n Cf piss ash, ~ elm, ~ oak, ~ willow

A **red maple** (here: *Acer rubrum*).

1966 *DARE* (Qu. T14, . . *Kinds of maples*) Inf **ME**8, Red maple—also called piss maple.

piss mare n Also *piss horse*

A **praying mantis B** or similar insect.

1966–69 *DARE* (Qu. R9a, *An insect from two to four inches long that lives in bushes and looks like a dead twig*) Inf **GA**3, Piss horse; **FL**35, Piss mares—he'd spit in your eye and blind you—throw musk that burns eye; **GA**72, Piss mare; (Qu. R9b, *An insect that holds up its front* *feet as if saying a prayer;* not asked in early QRs) Inf **GA**72, Praying mantis—also called piss mare.

pissmire See **pismire**

piss oak n **chiefly NEng, NY**   See Map   Cf **piss ash, ~ elm, ~ maple, ~ willow**

A **pin oak 1a** or similar **red oak.**

1945 McAtee *Nomina Abitera* 11, *Pin Oak (Quercus palustris)*—In Dr. B.S. Barton's Journal (early 1800's) the name of "piss oak" is noted from the Genesee River district, New York. He further writes, "I know not why this last receives its name unless from the circumstance of its abounding in a large quantity of sap." **c1960** *Wilson Coll.* **csKY,** Piss oak . . probably the water oak. **1965–70** *DARE* (Qu. T10, . . *Kinds of oak trees*) Infs **NH**16, **NY**86, **RI**4, Piss oak; **MA**6, Piss oak—tall, straight, wood smells bad when burned; **MA**25, Piss oak, red oak— same; **MA**47, Piss oak—about impossible to burn the stuff—might be the red oak; **NY**52, Piss oak—has a lot of little fine branches—another name is pin oak; leaves almost the same as other oaks; **NY**68, Piss oak—that's red oak; **NY**93, Piss oak—a little red oak that grows in cold rocky places. [8 of 9 Infs male, 7 old] **2000** *Duckworks Mag.* Dec (Internet) **CA,** The pièce de résistance was the bottom which was cross-planked with ¾″ thick boards. To me, the wood looked a lot like piss-oak robbed from forklift pallets.

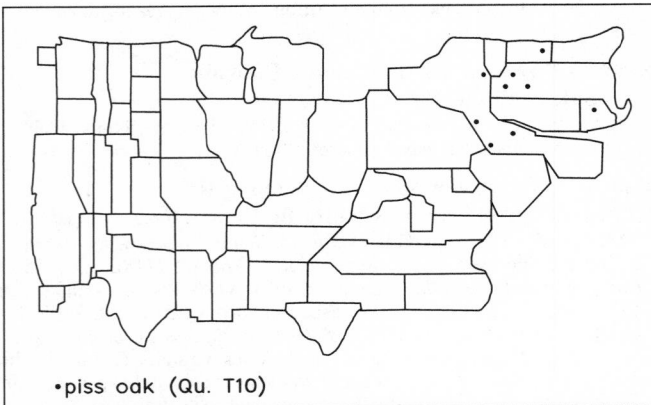

•piss oak (Qu. T10)

piss out of a boot, pour See **pour piss out of a boot**

piss-pants See **piss-a-bed 3**

piss-piddle See **piddle** v 1

piss-ripper n Cf **piss-cutter, ripper 1**

1966 *DARE* (Qu. HH27a, *A very able and energetic person who gets things done*) Inf **GA**13, Piss-ripper.

piss tail n

Prob a **musk turtle 1** (here: *Sternotherus odoratus*).

1968 *DARE* (Qu. P24, . . *Kinds of turtles*) Inf **DE**4, Piss tail—a trash turtle no good for anything. [**1979** Behler–King *Audubon Field Guide Reptiles* 445, *Sternotherus odoratus*. . . When disturbed, it secretes a foul-smelling, yellowish fluid from 2 pairs of musk glands under the border of the carapace.]

piss-the-bed See **piss-a-bed 1, 2, 3**

piss toad n Cf **pisser 3**

Perh Fowler's **toad** (*Bufo woodhousei fowleri*).

1968 *DARE* (Qu. P23, *Names for the animal similar to the frog that lives away from water*) Inf **NY**75, Warty toad [and] piss toad [are] different types; [piss toads] live nearer the water, squirt water when they're frightened.

piss uncle n [By joc analogy with *piss ant* understood as *piss aunt*]

=**piss ant** n **1.**

1969 *DARE* (Qu. R17, . . *Names . . for the big black ants that sting*) Inf **GA**72, Piss ant; piss uncle.

piss-weed See **piss-a-bed 1**

piss willow n Cf **piss ash, ~ elm, ~ maple, ~ oak**

An unidentified **willow.**

1966–70 *DARE* (Qu. T15, . . *Kinds of swamp trees*) Infs **AL**11, **AR**56, **TN**46, Piss willow; (Qu. CC13a, . . *A forked stick that's used to show where there's water underground. . . [What kind of wood?]*) Inf **MS**1, Piss-willow stick.

pisswood See **peawood**

pissy ant See **piss ant** n

pissy-bed See **piss-a-bed 1, 2, 3, 4**

pissy-pee See **piss-a-bed 1**

pistachio n Also sp *pistachoe* [See quot 1828]

A **witch hazel** (here: *Hamamelis virginiana*).

1828 Rafinesque *Med. Flora* 1.227, *Hamamelis virginica.* . . *Vulgar Names*—Witch hazel, . . Pistachoe nut, &c.   *Ibid* 229, The fruits stand [sic] on the whole year, till next fall, and then explode successively with a noise, . . scattering the seeds around. These seeds . . in the South . . are called erroneously Pistachoe nuts, although quite unlike the *Pistacia vera* or true Pistachoe of the Mediterranean. They are similar in shape to the esculent Pine seeds of *Pinus picea,* cylindrical, shining black outside, white and farinaceous inside, rather oily and palatable. **1876** Hobbs *Bot. Hdbk.* 91, Pistachio, Witch hazel, Hamamelis Virginica. **1971** Krochmal *Appalachia Med. Plants* 136, *Hamamelis Virginiana.* . . *Common Names:* Witch hazel, . . long boughs, pistachio. **1979** Erichsen-Brown *Med. N. Amer. Plants* 177, *Witch hazel.* . . The capsules contain two hard shiny seeds which ripen a year later. . . *Common names.* . . Pistachio, winter bloom.

pistol n

1 See quots.

1944 Adams *Western Words* 116, *Pistol*—A young rider, inexperienced hand. **1973** Allen *LAUM* 1.408 (as of c1950), 1 inf, **SD,** Pistol. The last cowpuncher to catch his horse in the morning.

2 A **lobster B1** that is missing one or both claws.

1966 *DARE* Tape **ME**24, [FW:] Any names for a lobster that's got only one claw, one big claw? [Inf:] Well, . . one with no claws we call pistol. . . dummies or pistols. **1975** Gould *ME Lingo* 210, *Pistol*—A Maine lobster which has lost a claw, regrettably—or more regrettably— both claws.

pistol-cap tree n

A **hop tree** (here: *Ptelea trifoliata*).

1946 *Nat. Hist.* 55.143, *Ptelea trifoliata.* . . [Y]oungsters call it Pistol Cap Tree, pretending that the seeds are "caps" for toy guns.

pistol crab n Also *pistol shrimp* [See quot 1915]

A snapping shrimp (family Crangonidae).

1915 *Nature & Sci.* 128 **sCA,** The collecting grounds at San Diego are rich and varied. . . On the mud and sand flats exposed at low tides are found . . burrowing white alpheid crustaceans which are called pistol crabs from their habit of snapping their claws. **1981** Meinkoth *Audubon Field Guide Seashore* 614, *Brown Pistol Shrimp (Alpheus armatus).* . . The red-and-white-banded antennae make this species easy to distinguish from other species of pistol or snapping shrimps.

pistolet n Also *pistolette* [Appar LaFr; cf *OED2 pistolet* sb.[1] 2 "Esp. in Belgium, a small bread roll"]   **New Orleans LA**

A small bread roll.

1983 Reinecke Coll. 9 **LA,** Pistolet . . ['pɪstəlɛt]—a small crusty bread-roll, no longer shaped like a pistol. Smaller, but much like a frog. Word now commoner than it was, because distributed by major bakers. **1984** Stall *Proud New Orleans* 7, Since . . the little short French roll looked something like a small pistol, the mini-bread became known as a *pistolette.* **1986** Pederson *LAGS Concordance,* 1 inf, **New Orleans LA,** Pistolets. **1997** *DARE* File **sLA,** I asked a Cajun friend more about pistolet. It is bread, as I said, though she thought smaller than a goose egg, but they do stuff them. Interestingly a major ingredient is cabbage and inside that shrimp, crawfish, ground beef, whatever is around.

pistolgrip n

1 =**buckhorn 9.**

1941 *AmSp* 16.155, The following list gives the common names [of freshwater clams] as applied by the cutter and fisher of shells. . . Pistol Grip [etc]. **1982** U.S. Fish & Wildlife Serv. *Fresh-Water Mussels* [Wall chart], *Buckhorn.* Pistolgrip. Historically widespread, common. **1991** IL Nat. Hist. Surv. *Biol. Notes* 137.15, *Tritogonia verrucosa* . . pistol-grip. . . Parmalee (1967) stated that the pistolgrip was "common, although of local occurrence, in most rivers throughout the state." . . Matteson collected 39 pistolgrips in 1956–60. . . In the current study . . this species . . ranked 17th in abundance.

2 See quots.

1958 McCulloch *Woods Words* 136 **Pacific NW,** *Pistol grip*—A tree with a sharp crook near the butt; often caused by snow pressure. **1967** *DARE* FW Addit **WA**20, *Pistolgrip*—a tree that grows along the ground (parallel to the ground) before rising; area of the trunk where the tree rises is the pistolgrip.

pistol gun n [Redund; cf Intro "Language Changes" I.4] Cf **rifle gun**

See quots.

1974 Fink *Mountain Speech* 19 **wNC, eTN,** *Pistol-gun* . . pistol. **1976** Garber *Mountain-ese* 68 **sAppalachians,** Lemuel took his pistol gun along when he went coon huntin'.

pistol shrimp See **pistol crab**

pit n¹ Cf **hole** n 4, **pot** n 6

A marble game; see quots.

1958 *PADS* 29.39 **WI,** *Pit.* . . A marble game in which a pit is dug and marbles are rolled into it. **c1970** Wiersma *Marbles Terms, Pit:* . . Game in which the player tries to throw his marble into a small hole. Closest one wins.

pit n²

1 The hard center of a fruit, as: see below. Cf **cobble** n¹ **2, heart** n¹ **B1c, kernel** n 1, **seed** n 1, **stone**

a Of a cherry. **widespread, but somewhat less freq Mid and S Atl, W Midl** See Map

1847 *Yankee Doodle* 10 July 139 **NYC,** We ate cherry pie and flung the pits at old codgers passing in the streets. **1848** Bartlett *Americanisms* 252, *Pit.* (Dutch, *pit,* a kernel.) The kernel or nut of fruit; as, a cherry-*pit.* Peculiar to New York. **1866** [see **1c** below]. **1941** *LANE* Map 269 *(Cherry stone)* **NEng,** [*Stone* is the predominant term throughout the region, with *pit* scattered but strongest in the southwest.] **1965–70** *DARE* (Qu. I48, *The hard center of a cherry*) 622 Infs, **widespread, but somewhat less freq Mid and S Atl, W Midl,** Pit. **1966** Dakin *Dial. Vocab. Ohio R. Valley* 2.357, In Indiana and in the Illinois Wabash Slope as well as in all of Kentucky, . . both *stone* and *pit* are scattered throughout. . . In the western Illinois counties and in Ohio north and west of Zane's Trace *seed, stone,* and *pit* are used with about equal frequency. *Stone* and *pit* . . predominate as the regular usage only in greater Cincinnati and the lower Miami Valley. Both *stone* and *pit* . . are in general more common in the speech of the younger generation of speakers, but there seems to be no evidence that either is spreading rapidly or that *seed* is apt to be supplanted. **1970** Tarpley *Blinky* 187 **nwTX,** As in the case of peaches, *seed* is the name given most often to the hard center of a cherry. *Pit,* a word unknown to the least educated and rare in rural communities, is used by 19.5% of the [200] informants, many of whom indicate they learned it from labels on cans of cherries. **1971** Bright *Word Geog. CA & NV* 182, Pit /of a cherry/ 83% [of 300 infs]. **1972** *PADS* 58.21 **cwAL,** Cherry *pit.* Northern *(cherry) pit* (7 [of 27 infs]) is less common than *(cherry) seed* (17); *cherry stone* (2) also occurs. *Pit* is generally restricted to educated usage (5 of the 7 occurrences). **1973** Allen *LAUM* 1.304 (as of c1950), *Seed* (of a cherry). . . *Pit* not only . . dominates all the U[pper] M[idwest] but appears to be gaining in popularity, since the proportion increases from 69% in Type I [=old, with lit-

tle educ] . . to 94% in Type III [=mid-aged, with coll educ]. **1989** Pederson *LAGS Tech. Index* 180 **Gulf Region** *(Cherry seed)* 287 infs, Pit; 5 infs, Cherry pit.

b Of a plum. **widespread, but somewhat more freq Inland Nth, Pacific** See Map

1828 *Evangelical Mag.* (Utica NY) 17 May 31 **ceNY,** In August, 1826, a Mr. Robert Martin, of Blenheim, in this county, ate a quantity of plumbs, and under the impression that they would be less liable to injure him, swallowed pits and all. **1851** Turner *Hist. Pioneer Settlement* 221 **NY,** The first settlers of Farmington, bringing with them apple seeds, and peach and plum pits, were early fruit growers. **1866** [see **1c** below]. **1965–70** *DARE* (Qu. I49, . . *The hard center of a plum*) 389 Infs, **widespread, but somewhat more freq Inland Nth, Pacific,** Pit.

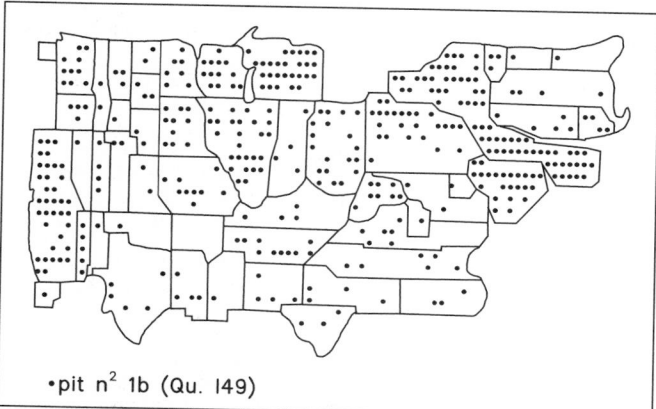
•pit n² 1b (Qu. I49)

c Of a peach. **chiefly Inland Nth, Pacific** See Map

1841 in **1848** Bartlett *Americanisms* 252, You put an apple-seed or a peach-pit into the ground, and it springs up into the form of a miniature tree. **1851** [see **1b** above]. **1866** Bridgeman *Amer. Gardener's Asst.* 1.22, If . . the pits of the Apricot, Cherry, Peach, and Plum, were not planted in autumn, let it be done as soon as the earth can be brought into tillable condition in the spring. **1941** *LANE* Map 268 *(Peach pit)* **NEng,** [*Stone* predominates throughout the region; *pit* is also found scattered throughout, occurring most frequently in the southwest, least frequently in ME.] **1965–70** *DARE* (Qu. I50, . . *The hard center of a peach*) 290 Infs, **chiefly Inland Nth, Pacific,** Pit; (Qu. I52) Inf **NY**70, Clinging-pit peach. **1966** Dakin *Dial. Vocab. Ohio R. Valley* 2.357, *Stone (of a peach).* . . Scattered speakers in Ohio north and west of Zane's Trace say *peach pit,* but this name is relatively uncommon. Outside of Ohio *pit* is extremely rare with reference to a peach. **1967** LeCompte *Word Atlas* 314 **seLA,** *Hard center of a peach.* . . pit [1 of 21 infs]. **1968** *PADS* 49.16 **Upper MW,** Vocabularies sometimes change because a word from one dialect appears to have more prestige than that of another dialect. . . The Midland *peach) seed* appears to be replacing the Northern *peach) stone; peach) pit,* another Northern term is perhaps also on the increase (field informants, 31%; students, 49%). **1970** Tarpley *Blinky* 185 **nwTX,** The hard center of a peach is regularly called a seed. . . *Pit* is a non-rural term found only among the highest educational bracket. **1971** Bright *Word Geog. CA & NV* 182, Pit /of a peach/ pit 60% [of 300 infs]. **1973** Allen *LAUM* 1.305 (as of c1950), *Stone* (of a peach). . . *Pit* . . is quite evenly spread throughout the U[pper] M[idwest], being favored by one-third to one-half of all speakers of all

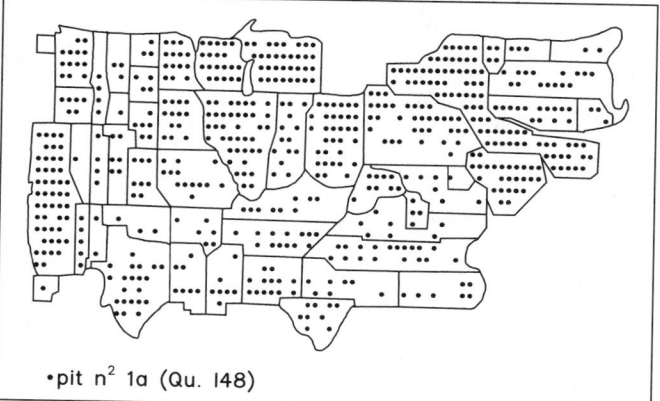
•pit n² 1a (Qu. I48)

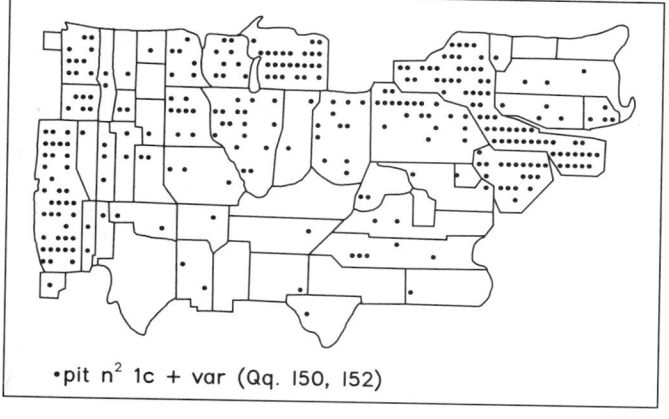
•pit n² 1c + var (Qq. I50, I52)

types. **1989** Pederson *LAGS Tech. Index* 180 **Gulf Region** *(Peach seed)* 101 infs, Pit; 8 infs, Peach pit.

2 The green leaves at the top of a strawberry.   Cf **hull** n **B1**

1967–68 *DARE* (Qu. I47, *When you pull the stem out of a strawberry, what do you call the green part that comes off with the stem?*) Infs **CA**6, **CT**11, **PA**63, Pit.   **1996** *DARE* File ceKS, My mom would call the top of a strawberry a pit, especially in older strawberries because when you pull the stem off, you also get some meat from the center out along with it.

pit v   See **put** v

pitahaya n [AmSpan < Taino *pitahaya*]   Also *pitajaya*   **SW**   Cf **pitayita**

1 less freq *pitaya*: A **cactus B1** of the genus *Cereus*, usu **organ-pipe cactus** or **saguaro**; also the fruit of such a cactus.   Cf **Indian fig 2, pitahaya dulce**

[**1759** Venegas *Hist. CA* (transl. Anon.) 1.43, The fruit is like a horse chestnut, and full of prickles: but the pulp resembles that of a fig, only more soft and luscious. In some it is white, in some red, and in others yellow; but always of an exquisite taste: some again are wholly sweet; others of a grateful acid. And as the pitahaya is very juicy, it is chiefly found in a dry soil.]   **1846** in 1847 U.S. Congress *Serial Set* 7 Doc 158, It is called in California *pitahaya*, but it appears that the Mexicans call by that name all large columnar cacti, the fruit of which is edible. . . I propose for it the name *Cereus gigantens*.   **1864** *Alta California* (S.F.) 16 Jan. 1/4 (*DA* at dome), On the road to Castle Dome, we had passed some fine specimens of that gigantic species of cactus known as the *petahaya* [sic].   **1874** (1877) Hittell *Resources CA* 372, Many varieties of cactus are found in the southern parts of the State. . . Most of the wild cacti bear insipid edible fruits, and yet are prized by the Indians and travelers for their abundant moisture. The dried pitahaya resembles a fig in taste.   **1892** *DN* 1.193 **TX**, Pitaháya, pitáya: the fruit of certain cacti. The fruit of almost any cactus, except *opuntia*, is called thus by the Mexicans, almost without discrimination, although it is generally the fruit of some *echinocereus*. In Arizona and Sonora the fruit of *Pilocereus giganteus* and *giganteus Thurberii* goes also by this name. Probably of native origin.   **1920** Saunders *Useful Wild Plants* 111 **SW**, The fruit [of *Cereus gigantea*] commonly goes by its Mexican name, *pitahaya*. It ripens in June and July, and somewhat resembles the tuna in form, with a juicy, seedy, crimson pulp. . . The pitahayas are gathered with a twenty-foot pole, made of the rod-like ribs of some dead sahuaro lashed together and having a hook affixed to the tip, with which the fruit is dislodged.   **1940** Benson *Cacti AZ* 76, *Cereus Thurberi*. . . Organ Pipe cactus or *pitahaya*. . . The fruit is palatable and is gathered in quantity by the Papago Indians, who move into the Pitahaya areas for the harvest.   **1942** Castetter-Bell *Pima & Papago Ag.* 59 **SW**, Pitajaya or pitaya here refers to the fruit of either or both *Carnegiea gigantea* [=*Cereus gigantea*] and *Lemaireocereus Thurberi* [=*Cereus thurberi*].   **1960** Vines *Trees SW* 768, *Acanthocereus pentagonus* [=*Cereus pentagonus*]. . . Vernacular names are Pitahaya [etc].   **1971** Dodge *100 Desert Wildflowers* 52, The term *pitaya* or *pitahaya* is commonly applied along the Mexican border to cactuses bearing edible fruits. In Texas the term refers to the low-growing floral hedgehogs; in Arizona to the columnar cactuses.

2 now more freq *pitaya*, also sp *pitalla*: =**hedgehog cactus 3**; also its fruit.   **esp TX**

1886 Havard *Flora W. & S. TX for 1885* 519, *Cereus stramineus* [=*Echinocereus enneacanthus*]. . . (Strawberry Cactus; Pitahaya.) Very common west of the Pecos. . . The ripe fruit is red, 1½ inches long, 1 inch thick, with thick skin bearing but few spines and easily peeled off. It is equal or superior, in quality and flavor, to the best strawberry.   **1892** [see **1** above].   **1895** *Jrl. Amer. Folkl.* 8.47 swTX, The Alicóchis [=*Echinocereus pentalophus*], to which many people persist in giving the name of Pitahaya, is a cactus. . . It yields, in the early days of summer, a fruit the size of a small plum, green in color, filled with fine black seeds; the skin is quite thin. This is generally regarded as the most delicious of all the wild fruits.   **1906** NM Ag. Exper. Station *Bulletin* 60.116, Pitalla. . . *Echinocereus enneacanthus*. . . This is a low plant. . . exceedingly abundant in the valley of the Rio Grande in Texas and adjacent Mexico. Its application in feeding stock is very limited.   *Ibid* 118, Pitalla. . . *Echinocereus Mojavensis* [=*E. triglochidiatus* var *mojavensis*]. . . This is a somewhat conspicuous species . . having much the same general habit as *Echinocereus enneacanthus*.   **1942** Hylander *Plant Life* 324, Many of the sixty species of *Echinocereus* are native to Texas and the adjacent states. . . Brown-flowered Pitaya [=*Echinocereus chloranthus*] is . . [a] cylindrical unbranched cactus. . . The Green-flowered

Pitaya [=*E. viridiflorus*] is the common cactus of the plains.   **1947** Curtin *Healing Herbs* 157 **NM**, Pitajaya . . pitahaya . . pitaya. . . The cactus that is usually called *pitajaya* in New Mexico is Echinocereus paucispinus [=*Echinocereus triglochidiatus* var *paucispinus*], although it is certain that the same name would be given to any species of Echinocereus. There are several of them in the state.   **1967–69** *DARE* (Qu. I44, *What kinds of fruits grow wild around here?*) Inf **TX**29, Pitaya [pɪ'tajə]; (Qu. I46, . . *Kinds of fruits that grow wild around here*) Inf **TX**28, Edible cacti: tuna ['tunə], pitaya [pɪ'taja], [ɑ'nɑkwə]; **TX**69, Pitaya [pə'taɪjə].   **1971** [see **1** above].   **1985** Dodge *Flowers SW Deserts* 128, *Echinocereus*—Hedgehog Cactus. . . Fruits (called "pitayas" in Texas) are dark mahogany red, juicy, rich in sugar, and may be eaten like strawberries.

3 A **prickly pear 1** (here: *Opuntia imbricata*).

1947 Curtin *Healing Herbs* 79 **NM**, Opuntia arborescens. . . Pitajaya.

pitahaya dulce n [*pitahaya* + Span *dulce* sweet]   **SW**   =**organ-pipe cactus**; also its fruit.

1920 Saunders *Useful Wild Plants* 111 **SW**, To civilized tastes, the fresh fruit [of *Cereus gigantea*] is rather mawkish, less sweet than that of the related *pitahaya dulce*, which . . is borne by *Cereus Thurberi*.   **1925** Bryan *Papago Country* 46 **AZ**, The pitahaya dulce or organ-pipe cactus (*Cereus thurberi*) consists of a clump of columns, each 3 to 4 inches in diameter and 3 to 8 feet high.   **1957** Jaeger *N. Amer. Deserts* 234, *Pitahaya dulce. Lemaireocereus thurberi* [=*Cereus thurberi*]. . . Stout-stemmed cactus branching from the base and growing up to 20 feet high. The fruits are prized for their sweetness. . . Southwestern Arizona to Baja California and Sonora.   **1971** Dodge *100 Desert Wildflowers* 48, Organpipe cactus. . . The fruits are locally called *pitahaya dulce*, or sweet cactus fruit.   **1985** Dodge *Flowers SW Deserts* 51, Organpipe Cactus—Senita, Pitahaya Dulce.

pitajaya   See **pitahaya**

pitalla   See **pitahaya 2**

pitaya   See **pitahaya 1, 2**

pitayita n [Dimin of *pitaya*]   Cf **pitahaya**

A **pincushion cactus 1** (here: *Mammillaria dioica*).

1951 Abrams *Flora Pacific States* 3.162 **CA**, *Mammillaria dioica*. . . Strawberry Cactus or Pitayita. . . Fruit scarlet, . . seeds black, shining, minutely pitted. . . San Diego County, California, southward along the western side of the mountains to . . Lower California.

pitch n[1] [*OED2* 1398 →]   **chiefly Nth, N Midl, West**   See Map   Cf **rosin B1a, turpentine**

The resinous material that exudes from and sometimes impregnates the wood of var conifers; hence adj *pitchy* resinous.

1792 Belknap *Hist. NH* 3.90, A lighted pitch-knot is placed on the outside of a canoe.   **1808** *Thomas' MA Spy or Worcester Gaz.* (MA) 9 Nov [3]/4, A pine post, fat with pitch, had taken fire.   **1825** Neal *Brother Jonathan* 1.58 **CT**, The fire-place, within which, two or three lighted pitch knots, a substitute for candles, were burning.   **1905** U.S. Forest Serv. *Bulletin* 61.43, *Pitch pocket.* A cavity in wood filled with resin. (P[acific] C[oast] F[orest], R[ocky] M[ountain] F[orest]). *Pitch streak.* A seam or shake filled with resin. (Gen[eral]).   **1913** Bryant *Logging* 94, Coniferous species, like western larch, are often so pitchy in the butt that from 4 to 6 feet must be left in the stump.   **1950** *WELS* **WI** (*The sticky stuff that comes out of pine trees*) 35 Infs, Pitch; 1 Inf, Pitch or pine pitch; 1 Inf, Pine pitch.   **1958** McCulloch *Woods Words* 136 **Pacific NW**, *Pitch butt*—A pitch-soaked bottom log in a tree.   **1965** Will *Okeechobee Boats* 18 **FL**, They was made to order for this river trade, little and shallow draft and burning fat pitchy pine for fuel.   **1965–70** *DARE* (Qu. T7, *The sticky stuff that comes out of pine trees*) 260 Infs, **chiefly Nth, N Midl, West,** Pitch; **CT**31, **MN**14, **NH**14, **NY**205, 209, **VT**13, Pine pitch; (Qu. T8, *Joints of pine wood that burn easily and make good fuel*) 28 Infs, **chiefly Nth, West,** Pitch knots; 9 Infs, **scattered,** Pitch; **FL**29, **KY**16, **ME**12, **MD**24, **MA**5, **NJ**6, **NM**6, **NY**101, Pitch pine (knots); **ME**5, **NV**8, **WA**24, Pitch wood; **CO**39, Pitch nuts; **WA**11, Pitchy knots; **CA**136, Pitchy wood; (Qu. BB50c, *Remedies for infections*) Infs **NY**23, **PA**133, **WI**30, Pine pitch; **CO**14, 33, Pitch salve; **MT**4, Balsam pitch; **NY**75, Pitch; **UT**12, Pitch from the piñon pine; **CO**14, Pitch plasters; (Qu. BB50a, . . *Favorite remedies . . for a cough*) Inf **CO**14, Chew pitch; **MT**4, Balsam pitch; (Qu. BB51a, . . *Cures for corns or warts*) Infs **MN**15, **MT**4, Balsam pitch; **NY**191, Pine pitch for corns.   **1968** *DARE* FW Addit neNY, Pine pitch—that from white pine is used as a poultice. "It will draw a sliver right out of your finger."

1969 Sorden *Lumberjack Lingo* 87 **NEng, Gt Lakes,** *Pitch*—Sticky, resinous material found in coniferous trees. Woodsmen often used it medicinally.

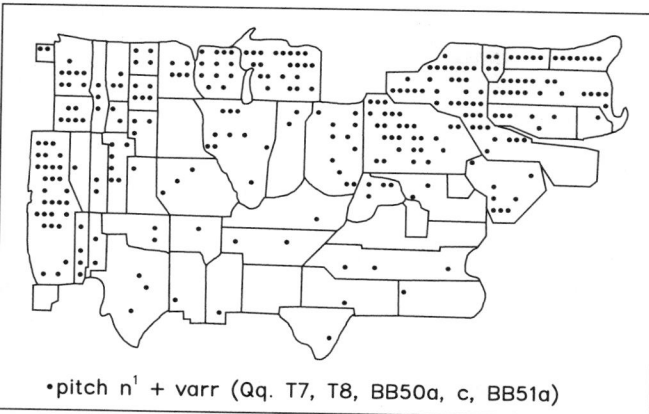

•pitch n¹ + varr (Qq. T7, T8, BB50a, c, BB51a)

pitch v

1 To plant (a crop). **Sth, S Midl**

1688 in 1694 Royal Soc. London *Philos. Trans. for 1693* 17.980 **VA,** The Gentlewoman where I lived, was a very Acute Ingenious Lady; who one day Discoursing the Overseer of her Servants, about pitching the ensuing Year's Crop. **1772** in 1919 *MD Hist. Mag.* 14.273, We have pitched above 9 tenths of our Crop. **1800** in 1969 Herndon *Wm. Tatham Tobacco* 122 **VA,** After your crop is *pitched*, or planted . . it will require your closest attention. **1880** Tourgée *Fool's Errand* 194 **Sth,** The sons were enabled to pitch a crop . . upon their own account. **1899** (1912) Green *VA Folk-Speech* 324, *Pitch*. . . To plant. "I have already pitched my crop." [**1903** *DN* 2.325 seMO, *Pitch*. . . In expression *pitch a crop*, to plan the distribution of ground for a season's crop. 'I haven't pitched my crop fully, but I aim to plant ten acres, at least, in cotton.'] **1923** *DN* 5.217 swMO, *Pitch a crap*. . . To plant and cultivate a crop. **1940** Writers' Program *Guide TX* 383 **ceTX,** *Pineland* . . is a lumbermill town in the piney woods. . . These people, who are highly individualistic, are largely of old English stock and speak a dialect that contains odd idioms. They "pitch" a crop when they plant it. **1944** *PADS* 2.48 **wNC, sVA,** *Pitch a crop*. . . To plant a crop. **1946** *PADS* 6.23 **eNC** (as of 1900–10), *Pitch a crop*. . . To plant a crop. . . Old farmers. Obsolete. **1952** Brown *NC Folkl.* 1.576, *Pitch a crop*. . . To plant a crop. . . General. **1984** Wilder *You All Spoken Here* 134 **Sth,** *Pitch a crop:* Plant a crop.

2 Of a bird or other flying creature: to settle, alight. [*OED2* 1609 →; "Now *rare* or *arch.*"]

1899 (1912) Green *VA Folk-Speech* 324, *Pitch*. . . To sit down; to light. "I saw the wild geese pitch in the wheatfields." **1970** *DARE* FW Addit **ceVA,** A bunch a ducks ready to pitch and they don't get to shoot at 'em. **a1975** Lunsford *It Used to Be* 162 **sAppalachians,** That hawk pitched in a dead chestnut. That is, he flew to a dead chestnut tree and was there on its perch. **1981** Harper–Presley *Okefinokee* 70 (as of 1930), **seGA,** But it pitched right on my head . . and I found it was a bird of some description. **1991** *DARE* File **eVA,** When my mother wanted a flying insect to land so she could swat it, she'd order it to "pitch." **1996** Horton *Island Out of Time* 135 **Chesapeake Bay MD,** A lone swan pitched over across from Rhodes Point.

3 Usu of a horse: =**buck** v¹ **A1a;** hence n *pitcher;* vbl n, also attrib, *pitching.* **chiefly West** Cf **buck** v¹ **A1, bucking** vbl n¹

1840 in 1965 *AmSp* 40.131, He rared and pitched but he couldn't make a jump. **1844** *Ibid,* De ole hoss he did rare and pitch. **1865** (1932) Pike *Scout & Ranger* 70, I had scarcely touched his back, when he began that species of rearing and plunging, known in Texas as "pitching"; in California as "spiking," and in this country [=what is now central Texas] as "bucking." **1889** *Century Illustr. Mag.* 37.335, A Texas pony. . . does not break his legs or fall over backwards in the "pitching" process as does the "cayuse" of the North-west. **1892** Duval *Young Explorers* 57 **TX,** He had a Roman nose, white eyes and protuberant stomach, and was a most expert "pitcher" whenever he wanted to get rid of his rider. **1900** Garland *Eagle's Heart* 98 **West,** A horse that reared and leaped to fling its rider was said to "pitch." **1929** *AmSp* 5.61 **NE** [Cattle country talk], "Swells" are projections in the leather on either side and below the "horn" or "safety grip." The rider can hook his knees under the "swells" if the horse happens to "pitch." **1940** Writers' Program

Guide NV 76, The horse that bucks . . *pitches.* **1948** *Sat. Review* 28 Aug 37, Bucky Durant calmly rolled a cigarette as he sat atop the pitching bronc. **1962** Atwood *Vocab. TX* 56, When a bronc wants to dislodge the rider, he is usually said to *pitch* . . or to *buck.* **1967** *DARE* Tape **TX**24, Brother Jim and I were both riding gentle horses. And Jim said to me, said, "Now when he comes out of the gate, you get on one side and I'll get on the other." We'd kinda see if we can keep him from pitching, but he—that son-of-a-bitch come out of there slamming his head.

4 To engage in (some manifestation of unrestrained behavior); to throw (a fit), go on (a spree), have (a party). **chiefly Sth, S Midl** See Map

1934 *AmSp* 9.289 **PA** [Black student slang], *Pitch a ball.* To have a riotous time at any social gathering. **1959** Lomax *Rainbow Sign* 102 **AL** [Black], I close the doors and shut the windows down tight and we'd pitch a party. **1965–70** *DARE* (Qu. DD16, *To have a drinking bout and get drunk*) Inf **LA**14, To pitch a drunk or to pitch a (real) drunken spree; (Qu. FF18, *Joking words . . about a noisy or boisterous celebration or party: "They certainly _____ last night."*) Inf **FL**51, Pitched one; **NC**37, Pitched a drunk; (Qu. KK11, *To make great objections or a big fuss about something: "When we asked him to do that, he _____."*) Infs **KY**60, **NC**47, **SC**3, Pitched a fit; **KY**60, Pitched a duck-fit; **NY**98, Pitched a bitch; **TX**33, Pitched a hissy-fit; [(Qu. KK19, *If a machine or appliance is temporarily out of order: "My sewing machine _____."*) Inf **GA**84, Pitchin' fit.] **1972** Cooper *NC Mt. Folkl.* 95, *Pitch a fit*—to fuss or rave in anger. **1973** *Patrick Coll.* **AL,** *Pitch a fit*—throw a fit, become much excited. Montgomery, AL, after 1946. **2000** *NADS Letters* s**UT,** "Pitch a fit" meaning to have a fit for no good reason, like a small child has a fit over something trivial.

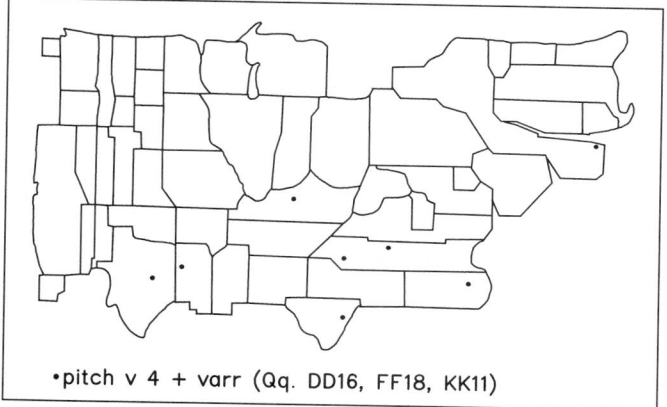

•pitch v 4 + varr (Qq. DD16, FF18, KK11)

pitch n²

1 A card game similar to **high-low-jack** in which the suit of the first card played determines trump. **chiefly NEng, Upstate NY, Delmarva, Missip Valley, Cent** See Map Cf **buck pitch, pedro**

1860 Geo. T. Clark *Diary* (MS.) 10 (*DAE*), Had a game of pitch in our tent today. **1874** *Northern Vindicator* (Estherville, Iowa) 7 March (*DA*), He can find good quarters with a jolly crowd who know how to play 'pitch.' **1940** Stong *Hawkeyes* 36 **IA,** His enjoyments—soda pop, pipe

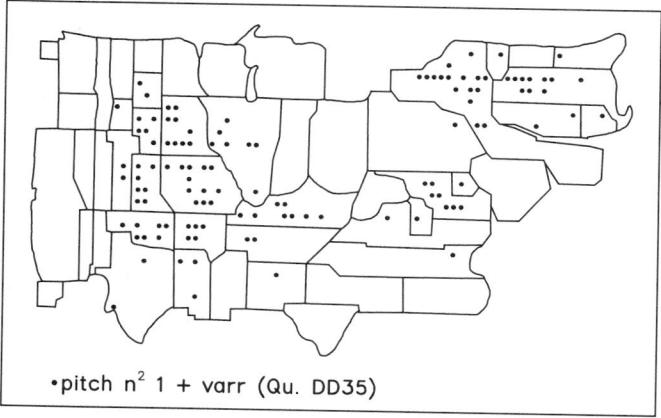

•pitch n² 1 + varr (Qu. DD35)

tobacco, his comfortable home, provision for his son and a card game called "pitch." **1965** Guthrie *Blue Hen's Chick* 245 **MT**, We were playing pitch, but George's thoughts weren't on the cards. **1965–70** DARE (Qu. DD35, . . *Card games*) 113 Infs, **chiefly NEng, Upstate NY, Delmarva, Missip Valley, Cent,** Pitch; **KY70,** 72, Buck pitch; **DE3,** Auction pitch; **NY96,** Chicago pitch; **MO3,** Draw pitch; **NY213,** Polack pitch; **KY11,** Sale pitch. [Of all Infs responding to the question, 70% were comm types 4 and 5, 28% gs educ or less; of those giving these resps 83% were comm types 4 and 5, 43% gs educ or less.]

2 A children's game in which a ball is tossed and caught; the game of catch.

1968 DARE FW Addit **GA25,** *Pitch* [pɪč]—children's game of tossing a ball to each other (called "catch" in Michigan). "Let's play pitch." **1992** Kincaid *Crossing Blood* 146 **nwFL,** Some kids we didn't hardly know or like were playing pitch with gumballs off our gumball tree.

3 See quot.

1967–70 DARE (Qu. EE18, *Games in which the players set up a stone, a tin can, or something similar, and then try to knock it down*) Infs **LA3, MO37, SC40, VA90,** Pitch; **LA2,** Pitch—if you set a bottle on a post and then throw at it.

4 See **pitch hole 1.**

pitch exclam Cf **high-pitch**

1965–70 DARE (Qu. EE23a, *In the game of andy-over . . what . . you call out when you throw the ball*) Infs **FL22, NJ8, VA65,** Pitch.

pitcher n¹ See **pitch v 3**

pitcher n² See **picture**

pitcher plant n

1 A plant of the genus *Sarracenia.* Also called **bog bugle, devil's boots, Eve's cup, flycatcher 4a, flytrap n 2, forefather's cup, frog bonnet(s), hen and biddies 1, Indian cup 2, ~ pitcher, jack-in-the-pulpit 2e, sidesaddle flower, trumpet, trumpet-leaf;** for other names of *S. purpurea* see **Adam's cup, ~ pitcher, blob n 2, carrion flower 2, clock dials, cup plant 2, dumb watches, foxglove 3, huntsman's cup, ~ horn, Indian jug, ~ teakettle, meadow cup 1, skunk cabbage 3, smallpox plant, sweet pitcher ~, watches, watercup, whippoorwill's shoes;** for other names of var spp see **biscuits, fiddler's trumpet, frog belly, huntsman's horn, smallpox plant, sweet pitcher ~, watches, watercup**

1843 Torrey *Flora NY* 1.42, The genus *Sarracenia* . . is remarkable for its hollow, pitcher-form leaves. . . . *S. purpurea* is, in some parts of the State, known by the name of the *American Pitcher-plant.* **1857** Gray *First Lessons* 179, *S[arracenia] purpurea.* . . *Pitcher-Plant.* . . Common from N. England to Wisconsin, and southward east of the Alleghanies. . . . The curious leaves are usually half filled with water and drowned insects. **a1862** (1864) Thoreau *ME Woods* 310, The characteristic flowers in *swamps* were: *Rubus triflorus* (dwarf raspberry), *Calla palustris* (water-arum), and *Sarracenia purpurea* (pitcher-plant). **1899** Going *Field Flowers* 300, The pitcher-plant . . beguiles the hapless fly to his drowning in its vase-shaped leaves, baited on the outside with nectar-bearing glands, and filled with water. **1938** Rawlings *Yearling* 87 **nFL,** The bitter brew she made from pomegranate peelings, or that from pitcher-plant root, was infinitely worse. **1944** Nute *Lake Superior* 322 **MI, WI, MN,** Late June and early July find the swamps full of magnificent pitcher plants, sundews and orchids in bloom. **1965–70** DARE (Qu. S26b, *Wildflowers that grow in water or wet places*) Infs **GA20, MI31,** 42, 53, 67, **NJ39, PA99,** 223, Pitcher plant; **GA80,** Pitcher plant—green flowers [sic], pitcher-shaped; **MI2,** Pitcher plant—one of the flytrap plants; **MA42,** Pitcher plants—shaped like a cupped hand, will hold water; **NY134,** Picture [sic] plant; (Qu. S1, . . *Jack-in-the-pulpit*) Infs **FL16, NC3,** Jack-in-the-pulpit or pitcher plant; **AL15, GA35, NC41, PA245,** Pitcher plant; (Qu. S22) Inf **PA191,** Pitcher plant; (Qu. S26c, *Wildflowers that grow in woods*) Inf **PA104,** Pitcher plant—called flycatchers; (Qu. S26d, *Wildflowers that grow in meadows; not asked in early QRs*) Infs **MI45, MA71,** Pitcher plant(s); (Qu. S26e, *Other wildflowers not yet mentioned*; not asked in early QRs) Inf **MA58,** Pitcher plant ("flycatcher"); **NY205,** Pitcher plant—like jack-in-the-pulpit, holds water; **SC31,** Pitcher plant.

2 =**California pitcher plant.**

1897 Parsons *Wild Flowers CA* 390, *Darlingtonia Californica.* . . Our pitcher plant is one of the most wonderful and interesting of all the

forms that grow. **1951** Writers' Program *Oregon* 20, Along the sea beaches and on the wave-cut bluffs are. . . watery sphagnum bogs lush with the cobra-leaved pitcher plant and the delicate sundew. **1967** Gilkey–Dennis *Hdbk. NW Plants* 172, *Pitcher plant.* Leaves . . tubular, enlarged above, hood-like, with an opening beneath somewhat hidden. . . Bogs of south-western Oregon. **1979** Spellenberg *Audubon Guide N. Amer. Wildflowers W. Region* 733, Insects, or other small organisms, attracted to the nectar . . , enter the hole beneath the hood. Once inside, . . they are decomposed by microorganisms in the fluid in the tubular base. Nutrients thus released are absorbed by the Pitcher Plant.

3 A **water hyacinth** (here: *Eichhornia crassipes*).

1900 Lyons *Plant Names* 288, *P[iaropus] crassipes* [=*Eichhornia c.*] . . Nat[uralized] in Florida, where it impedes navigation of rivers. Water Hyacinth, Pitcher-plant.

4 =**lady's slipper 1.**

1920 *Torreya* 20.20 **MI,** *Cypripedium* spp.—Pitcher plant, Traverse City, Mich. **1924** *Amer. Botanist* 30.153, The "stemless Lady's slipper" (*C[ypripedium] acaule*). . . has been called "pitcher-plant" also, but this is doubtless due to sheer ignorance.

5 =**cup plant 1.**

1943 *Torreya* 42.166 **KS,** *Silphium perfoliatum.* . . Pitcher-plant, Allen County, Kansas.

pitchers n Also *dull meadow pitchers* [Prob from the urn-shaped hypanthium; see quot 1979]

A **meadow beauty 1** (here: *Rhexia mariana*).

[**1979** Niering–Olmstead *Audubon Guide N. Amer. Wildflowers E. Region* 631, Members of this genus [=*Rhexia*] have a distinctive urn-shaped fruit that Thoreau once compared to a little cream pitcher.] **1995** Brako et al. *Scientific & Common Names Plants* 206, Pitchers, dull meadow pitchers—*Rhexia mariana.*

pitcher sage n CA

1 An aromatic plant of the genus *Lepechinia,* usu *L. calycina.* [See quot 1920] For other names of *L. calycina* see **wood balm**

1897 Parsons *Wild Flowers CA* 42, *Sphacele* [=*Lepechinia*] *calycina.* . . The dwellers among our southern mountains, with that happy instinct possessed by those who live close to the heart of nature, have aptly named this "pitcher-sage." After the flowers have passed away, the large inflated, light-green calyxes, densely crowded upon the stems, become quite conspicuous. **1920** Rice–Rice *Pop. Studies CA Wild Flowers* 104, *Sphacele calycina.* . . Pitcher Sage it is called, because the flowers resemble in miniature a white porcelain pitcher, and the name Sage is suggested by its fragrance. **1959** Munz–Keck *CA Flora* 707, *Lepechinia.* . . *Pitcher Sage.* Shrubby or suffrutescent, aromatic. **1961** Thomas *Flora Santa Cruz* 300 **cwCA,** *L. calycina.* . . Pitcher Sage. Chaparral and brush-covered slopes throughout the Santa Cruz Mountains. . . San Francisco southward.

2 A **sage 1** (here: *Salvia spathacea*).

1959 Munz–Keck *CA Flora* 704, *S[alvia] spathacea.* . . Pitcher Sage. Coarse perennial herb with creeping rhizomes. **1976** Bailey–Bailey *Hortus Third* 1000 **CA,** [*Salvia*] *spathacea.* . . Pitcher s[age]. . . Corolla . . purplish-red.

pitchfork n

1 The usu two-pronged seed of **beggar ticks 1;** hence nouns *pitchforks, pitchfork weed* the plant itself. **chiefly Nth** See Map Cf **devil's-pitchfork(s)**

1896 *Jrl. Amer. Folkl.* 9.191 **ME,** *Bidens frondosa,* . . *cernua,* . . and *coronata,* . . pitchforks, Rumford, Me. **1909** DN 3.421 **Cape Cod MA** (as of a1857), *Pitchforks.* . . Fork-shaped seeds of a weed that sticks to clothes. Called in some places *sticktights* or *beggar lice.* **1912** Blatchley *IN Weed Book* 160, *Bidens connata.* . . is one of 8 or 10 species of troublesome weeds occurring in the State and known as . . pitch-forks, devil's bootjacks, etc. **1914** Georgia *Manual Weeds* 473, *Beggarticks—Bidens frondosa.* . . Pitchfork Weed. . . Achenes wedge-shaped, black, flat, . . the apex bearing two diverging downwardly barbed awns. **1949** WELS Suppl. **seWI,** With us the 2 pronged seeds are pitchforks or sticktights and the little round ones, beggar's lice. *Ibid* **seWI,** Pitchfork [is the] only name I ever heard. **1950** WELS **WI** (*Small, flat weed seeds with two prongs that cling to clothing*) 2 Infs, Pitchfork(s); 1 Inf, Jane called them pitchforks. **1963** Zimmerman–Olson *Forest* [197], Pitchforks (Bidens vulgata). **1965–70** DARE (Qu. S14, . . *Prickly seeds, small and flat, with two prongs at one end, that cling to clothing*) 33

Infs, **chiefly Nth,** Pitchforks; (Qu. S15, . . *Weed seeds that cling to clothing*) Inf **OH**80, Pitchforks.

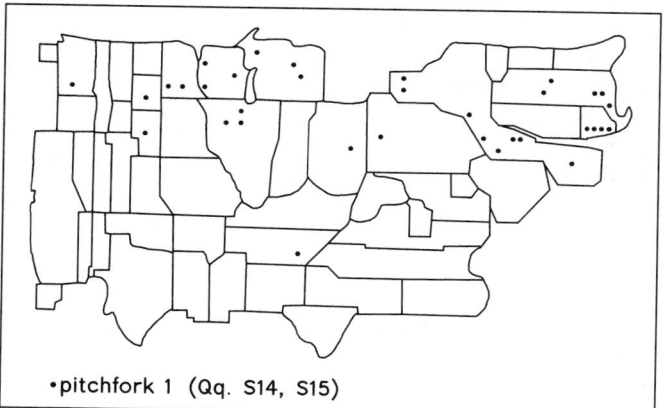

•pitchfork 1 (Qq. S14, S15)

2 A composite plant *(Dicranocarpus parviflorus)* native to western Texas. [See quot]

1970 Correll *Plants TX* 1665, *Dicranocarpus parviflorus. . . Pitchfork. . .* Ray pappus of 2 widely divergent persistent stout awns. Infrequent in gypseous soil in the Trans-Pecos, Sept.–Oct.

3 pl; In var phrr referring to a heavy rain, spec:

a *rain pitchforks (tines downwards)* and varr.

1815 Humphreys *Yankey in England* 55, I'll be *even* with you, if it rains pitchforks—tines downwards. [**1856** Cary *Married Not Mated* 295 **OH,** As soon as the rain should stop falling in pitch-forks.] **1883** (1884) Howe *Story Country Town* 27 **West,** He said it would probably come about when the sky rained pitchforks on the roof of Jo Erring's mill. **1901** *DN* 2.145 **ceNY,** *Pitch-forks. . .* In phrase, 'It rained pitchforks.' . . [O]f an especially heavy rain. **1909** *DN* 3.363 **eAL, wGA,** *Rain pitchforks. . .* To rain heavily. **1910** *DN* 3.447 **cwNY,** *Rain pitchforks. . .* To rain in torrents. **1915** *DN* 4.188 **swVA,** *Rain pitchforks. . .* To pour with extreme violence. [*DN* Ed: Used in New England.] **1927** *AmSp* 2.362 **cwWV,** *Rain pitchforks . .* a short, hard rain. "It rained pitchforks about three o'clock." *Rain pitchforks with the tines on both ends . .* a very hard storm of rain and wind. "It rained pitchforks with the tines on both ends before daylight this morning." **1954** *Harder Coll.* **cwTN,** It's a-raining pitchforks. **1965–70** *DARE* (Qu. B26, *When it's raining very heavily . . "It's raining _____."*) 114 Infs, **widespread,** Pitchforks; **AL**30, **NC**87, Down pitchforks; [**NH**16, Harder than pitchforks; **CA**129, Like pitchforks;] **ME**5, Pitchforks and tines down; **WI**13, Pitchforks tines downward; **PA**233, Pitchforks with the tines down; (Qu. B25, . . *Joking names . . for a very heavy rain. . . "It's _____."*) Inf **TN**14, Raining pitchforks. [**1969** *DARE* FW Addit **cwMA,** You say "It's raining like a pitchfork" when it's raining very heavily. [Inf old]] **1984** *DARE* File **UT,** (When it's raining very heavily, you say, "It's raining _____.")

b *rain pitchforks and hammer handles* (or *hammerheads, hoe handles, peavey handles*) and varr. **chiefly NEast, Gt Lakes** See Map

1901 *DN* 2.145 **cNY,** It rained pitch-forks and hammer handles.

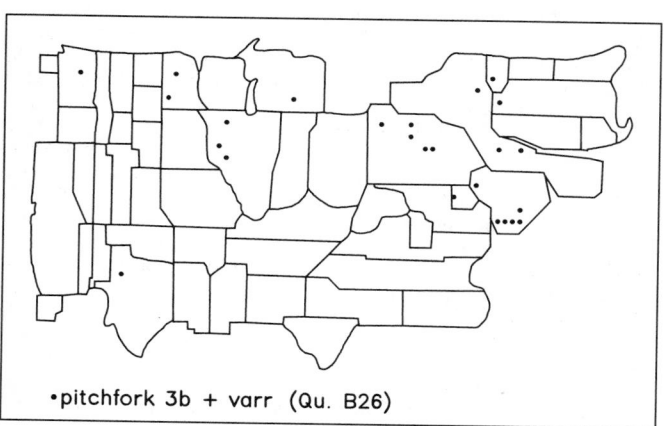

•pitchfork 3b + varr (Qu. B26)

[**1912** *DN* 3.587 **wIN,** *Rain pitchforks with sawlogs for handles. . .* To rain in a great downpour.] **1965–70** *DARE* (Qu. B26, *When it's raining very heavily . . "It's raining _____."*) 20 Infs, **chiefly NEast, Gt Lakes,** Pitchforks and hammer (*or* hoe) handles; **MI**112, Pitchforks and hammerheads; **WA**21, Pitchforks and peavey handles; **PA**72, Pitchforks and sawed handles; **MA**15, Hammer handles and pitchforks.

c *rain pitchfork(s) and nigger babies* and varr. **chiefly N Cent, Missip Valley, Cent** See Map Cf **nigger baby 3**

1906 *DN* 3.152 **nwAR,** *Rain pitchforks and nigger-babies. . .* To rain copiously. "I can't go out; it's raining pitchforks and nigger-babies." **1912** *DN* 3.587 **wIN,** *Rain pitchforks and nigger babies. . .* To rain heavily. **c1950** *Halpert Coll.* 52 **wKY, nwTN,** It's raining (rainin') pitchforks and nigger babies. **1954** *WELS Suppl.* **nwMO,** The saying I am familiar with, have used it all my life, is raining 'pitchforks and nigger babies.' I asked my husband, whose parents were born in Osceola, Iowa, and Monmouth, Ill., . . what expression his mother used and it was the same. **1965–70** *DARE* (Qu. B26) 30 Infs, **chiefly N Cent, Missip Valley, Cent,** Pitchforks and (little) nigger babies; **MI**98, Nigger babies and pitchforks; (Qu. B25) Inf **AR**47, Raining pitchforks and nigger babies. **1986** Pederson *LAGS Concordance* (Heavy rain) 2 infs, **ceMS, ceTX,** Raining pitchfork(s) and nigger babies. **1986** *DARE* File **swCA,** When it's raining really hard Ruby [who grew up in Tennessee] still says it's raining pitchforks and nigger babies. Then she adds, oh, I shouldn't say that any more.

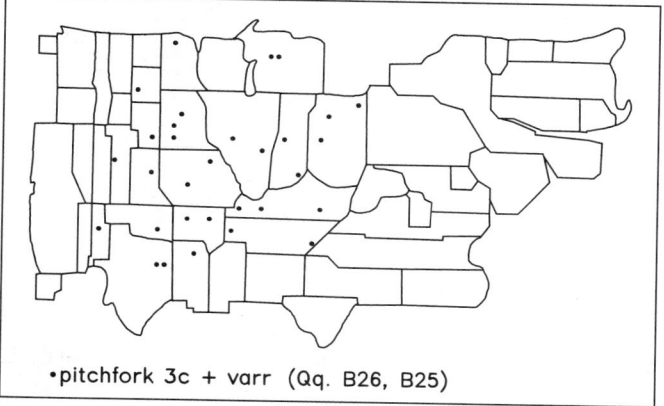

•pitchfork 3c + varr (Qq. B26, B25)

d in var other phrr: See quots.

1890 *Catholic World* 51.664 **NYC,** It rained pitchforks and pineapples, but the hall, a large one, was completely filled. **1913** *DN* 4.5 **ME,** *Rain pitchforks and darning needles,* or *pitchforks and chicken coops. . .* To rain in torrents. Penobscot Co. **1940** M. Fishback *Time for Quick One* 77 *(OED2),* It's raining cats and dogs. And pitchforks and assorted frogs. **1965–70** *DARE* (Qu. B26, *When it's raining very heavily . . "It's raining _____."*) Infs **MO**19, **MT**5, **PA**78, **TN**23, Pitchforks and bullfrogs; **IL**15, 114, **MI**47, **PA**134, Pitchforks and sawlogs; **AL**6, **OH**78, Pitchforks and darning needles; **NC**67, **PA**188, Pitchforks and grindstones; **FL**35, Devil and pitchforks; **MN**15, Pitchforks and angleworms; **ME**16, Pitchforks and barn shovels; **MN**12, Pitchforks and brimstone; **TX**1, Pitchforks and bull yearlings; **KY**10, Pitchforks and hay bales; **OH**89, Pitchforks and sawhooks; **KY**83, Pitchforks and shovels; **MO**15, Pitchforks and something else; **NC**62, Pitchforks and tadpoles; **MO**39, Toads and pitchforks; (Qu. B25, . . *Joking names . . for a very heavy rain*) Inf **IL**114, Rained pitchforks and sawlogs. **1979** *Reader's Digest Letters* **MA,** My mother used to say "It's raining pitchforks and darning needles."

pitchforks See **pitchfork 1**

pitchforks (and hammer handles, etc), rain See **pitchfork 3**

pitchfork weed See **pitchfork 1**

pitchhole n

1 also *pitch:* A depression or defect in the surface of a road; a pothole. **Nth** Cf **chuckhole 1**

1861 Burton *City Saints* 18, As we sped onward we soon made acquaintance with a traditionally familiar feature, the "pitch-holes," or "chuck-holes" . . which render traveling over the prairies at times a sore

task. **1874** VT State Bd. Ag. *Report* 2.659, The highways leading to our larger villages . . are frequently so full of pitchholes . . as to render them totally unfit for travel. *Ibid* 661, Pitch holes . . in winter roads, are a dangerous nuisance. **1893** Frederic *Copperhead* 92 **nNY,** It was a matter of lashing the panting teams through seas of mud punctuated by abyssmal [sic] pitch-holes, into which the wheels slumped over their hubs. **1950** *WELS (A sudden, short dip in the road)* 2 Infs, **WI,** Pitchhole. **1966–69** *DARE* (Qu. N27b, *When unpaved roads get very rough, you call them* _____) Inf **NY**97, Pitchholes; (Qu. N30, . . *A sudden short dip in a road)* Infs **NY**219, **WA**12, Pitch; **WI**51, Pitchhole. **1973** Allen *LAUM* 1.400 (as of c1950), Hole in a road. . . Infrequent . . *Pitch hole* [1 inf **IA,** 1 inf **ND**]. **1980** *NYT Article Letters* **wNY,** *Thank-you maam,* (also called *pitch-hole,*) a melted area in unploughed snow on back country road so that sleigh dipped down while descending into it and tilted back while coming out making the sleigh-riders nod.
2 also *pitching hole:* =**hay chute.** [Cf *OED2 pitch-hole* quot 1805] **NEng, neNY** See Map
1966–69 *DARE* (Qu. M5, . . *The hole for throwing hay down below)* Infs **ME**14, **MA**58, **NY**27, Pitchhole; **ME**19, **NY**23, 32, **VT**12, Pitching hole. **1998** *DARE* File **sWI** (as of 1940s), Pitch-hole—In use in southern Wisconsin, middle to late 1940s.

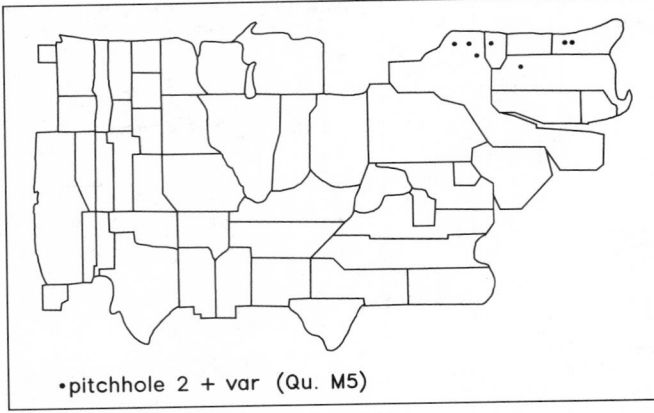

•*pitchhole 2 + var* (Qu. M5)

pitch-in dinner n Also *pitch-in (picnic),* ~ *supper* **chiefly IN;** **also MT** See Map Cf **covered-dish meal**
A potluck meal.
1965–70 *DARE* (Qu. H70, *When people bring baked dishes, salads, and so forth to a meeting-place and share them together, that's a _____ meal)* Infs **IN**19, 34, 54, 76, 82, Pitch-in; **IN**16, 30, 52, Pitch-in dinner; **IN**7, 41, Pitch-in supper; (Qu. FF1, . . *A kind of group meeting called a 'social' or 'sociable'. . . [What goes on?])* Inf **IN**19, Pitch-in dinners; (Qu. FF2, . . *Kinds of parties)* Inf **IN**82, Pitch-in dinners; (Qu. FF16, . . *Local . . celebrations)* Inf **IN**30, Pitch-in suppers. **1973** *WI State Jrl.* (Madison) 7 Oct (Parade Suppl.) 26, The answers were as varied as the food at a large pitch-in picnic. **1976** *Laurel* (Montana) *Outlook* 16 June 9/1 *(OED2),* The Park City Garden Club guest night was held at the civic center with a pitchin dinner. **1976** *Columbus* (Montana) *News* 17 June 6/3 *(OED2),* Mr. and Mrs. Charles Wark were hosts at a pitch-in picnic for members and their families. **1979** *DARE* File **IN,** Pitch-in—a potluck dinner. **1982** *Smithsonian Letters* **MT,** The term "pitch in" is the commonly used term in Broadus, *Montana.* I served a parish there for three years, and that was the only name potluck dinners went by. *Ibid* **MT,** You list the term "pitch-in" as indigenous only to southern Indiana. Please tell your computer to include western Montana, as it was in common use in the 30's and early 40's when I was growing up in Bozeman, Montana. The distinction was that an organization held a potluck supper, while individual friends or neighbors had a pitch-in dinner. **1997** *DARE* File **c,seIN,** In central and southeastern Indiana, we called such events "pitch-ins"—I guess because everyone pitches in and brings something. This was a very common term when I was a child in Indiana—in the mid-1960s and early 1970s. In 1977, my family moved to Cincinnati, Ohio—only 45 miles away . . , but even that short distance transformed "pitch-ins" into "pot-lucks." . . I'm still on the mailing list for the church newsletter . . , and they definitely still have "pitch-ins" every month. **1999** in 2000 *DARE* File—Internet **IN,** Aunt Maude's beans are excellent for canning . . and are always popular at pitch-in dinners.

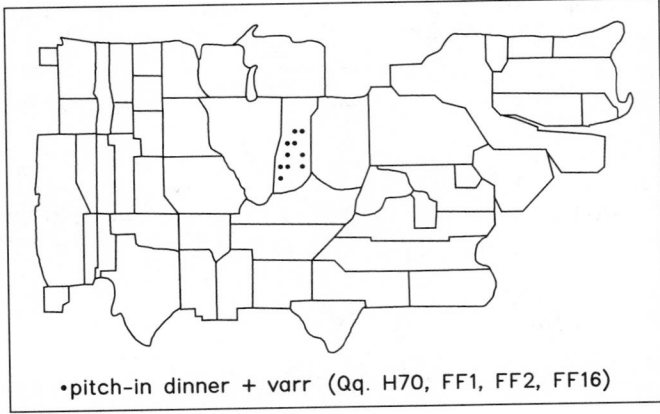

•*pitch-in dinner + varr* (Qq. H70, FF1, FF2, FF16)

pitching See **pitch** v 3

pitching gig n
A short **gig** n[2] **1** designed to be thrown beyond the user's reach; similarly *pitch gigger* one who uses such a gig.
1931 Randolph *Ozarks* 263, A few of the hill people to the southwest of us use a much shorter and lighter spear with a single slender prong, the handle being fastened to the wrist with a long cord. These spears are seldom more than five or six feet long, and are called "pitchin'-gigs." It is said that they are modelled after the fishspears used by the Osage Indians. . . The pitchin'-gig . . enters the water almost without a sound or a splash, and it is really a pleasure to watch an expert pitch-gigger kill fish with it.

pitching hole See **pitchhole 2**

pitch-in picnic (or supper) See **pitch-in dinner**

pitchin' woodpecker See **pigeon woodpecker 1**

pitch out v phr Also *pitch off*
To make an abrupt start.
1909 *DN* 3.357 **eAL, wGA,** Pitch-out. . . To start suddenly. "He pitched out for home." **1952** Brown *NC Folkl.* 1.576, Pitch out. . . To begin. Generally followed by a gerund or *and* plus another verb. "He pitched out dancing." "He pitched out and ran."—Central and east. **1975** Gainer *Witches* 14 **sAppalachians,** *Pitched off* (v.), left hurriedly. "When it began to rain, he pitched off for home." **1985** Clark *From Mailbox* 272 **ME,** To change, to pitch out and make a fresh start.

pitch pine n
Any of var esp resinous spp of **pine 1,** as:
a A **pine 1** native chiefly to the northern US:
(1) A **pine 1** *(Pinus rigida)* native from Maine and New York south mostly through the mountains to Georgia. Also called **black pine 1c, candlewood 1, fat pine 1, hard** ~ **2, jack** ~ **2b, lightwood** n[1]**, longleaf pine 2, longshat** ~**, old Jersey bull** ~**, sap** ~**, torch** ~**, yellow** ~
1676 in 1920 Essex Inst. *Coll.* 56.306 **MA,** 4 ¾ acres of land . . bounded by a pitch pine, small heap of rocks [etc]. **1736** in 1885 Boston Registry Dept. *Records* 150 **MA,** Add to the South East Side Ten foot, To be Built of Square Pitch Pine Timber. **1771** in 1914 MA Hist. Soc. *Coll.* 71.138, The floor of the Peazas except that next the Kitchen should be Pitch Pine. **1792** Belknap *Hist. NH* 3.108, The *Pitch Pine* . . is the hardest and heaviest of all the pines; . . at present the principal use of it is for fewel. When burnt in kilns, it makes the best kind of charcoal; its knots and roots being full of the terebinthine oil, afford a light surpassing candles. **1832** Williamson *Hist. ME* 2.136, They left [their packs] . . in a pitch-pine plain, where the trees were thin, and the brakes at that time of the year small. **1857** (1930) DeLong *Jrls.* 9.169 **NY,** 200 feet in length and some of the top broke off at that six feet through at the butt, pitch pine. **1901** Lounsberry *S. Wild Flowers* 4, *P[inus] rigida,* pitch pine, before it became supplanted by the richer pines of the south, was greatly valued for the large amount of pitch contained in its wood. . . In appearance it is irregular and rough, quite awkward, in fact, as are many of the pitch pines. . . The tree forms a great part of "the pines" of New Jersey and covers considerable tracts of land

along the New England coast. From New Brunswick it extends to Virginia and Kentucky, and is found in the mountains of North Carolina and Tennessee. **1906** *Atlantic Mth.* 98.212, He could tell a white pine (*strobus*) from a pitch pine (*rigida*) by just a cone and a bundle of needles,—one has five, the other three, to the bundle. **1965–70** *DARE* (Qu. T17, . . *Kinds of pine trees;* not asked in early QRs) 12 Infs, **NEast,** Pitch pine; **ME5,** Hard pine—also called pitch pine—not good lumber; (Qu. T8, *Joints of pine wood that burn easily and make good fuel*) Infs **KY16, ME12, MA5, NJ6, NY101,** Pitch pine. [*DARE* Ed: Some of these Infs may refer instead to other senses below.] **1980** Little *Audubon Guide N. Amer. Trees E. Region* 294, Now used principally for lumber and pulpwood, Pitch Pine was once a source of resin. . . The common name refers to the high resin content of the knotty wood.

(2) Another northern **pine 1** such as **jack pine 1** or **Norway pine.**

1908 Rogers *Tree Book* 32, The Pitch Pines. . . *P[inus] resinosa. . . P. divaricata* [=*P. banksiana*]. **1966–69** *DARE* (Qu. T17, . . *Kinds of pine trees;* not asked in early QRs) Infs **MA40, MI18,** Pitch pine, soft pine—same; **MA68,** Pitch pine, scrub pine—same.

b A **pine 1** native chiefly to the southern US, as:

(1) =**loblolly pine 1.**

1709 (1967) Lawson *New Voyage* 97 **NC, SC,** Ever-Greens are here plentifully found, of a very quick Growth, and pleasant Shade: Cypress, or white Cedar, the Pitch Pine, the yellow Pine, the white Pine with long Leaves. *Ibid* 104, The Pitch-Pine, growing to a great Bigness, . . affords the four great Necessaries, Pitch, Tar, Rozin, and Turpentine. **1743** Catesby *Nat. Hist. Carolina* 2.xxii, There are in Carolina four Kinds of Pine Trees. . . The *Pitch-Pine* is the largest of all the Pine Trees, and mounts to a greater Height than any of them; its Leaves and Cones are also larger and longer than those of the other Kinds; the Wood is yellow, the Heart of it so replete with Turpentine, that its Weight exceed [sic] that of *Lignum Vitae.* **a1782** (1788) Jefferson *Notes VA* 39, Black, or pitch-pine, *Pinus taeda.* **1854** Wailes *Rept. on Ag. & Geol. MS* 343, Pine, pitch. Pinus taeda. **1908** Rogers *Tree Book* 21, "Pitch pine" is a term applied to species whose wood is rich in resin. Chief among these is *P[inus] palustria* [sic]. It includes the other Southern lumber pines [=*Pinus echinata, P. elliottii,* and *P. taeda*] and *P. rigida* in the Eastern States.

(2) also *Georgia pitch pine:* =**longleaf pine 1.**

[**1754** in 1845 Gt. Brit. Pub. Rec. Office *Rept. Deputy Keeper* App. ii.128, Preparing from the Glutinous Juices of the American Pitch Pine Tree a Varnish of Pine for paying Ships' Sides.] **1795** Winterbotham *Amer. U.S.* 3.199 **NC,** The large natural growth of the plains in the low country is almost universally pitch pine, which is a tall, handsome tree, far superior to the pitch pine of the northern States. This tree may be called the staple commodity of North-Carolina. It affords pitch, tar, turpentine, and various kinds of lumber, which together constitute at least one half of the exports of this State. This pine is of two kinds, the common and the long-leaved. The latter has a leaf shaped like other pines, but is nearly half a yard in length, hanging in large clusters. **1810** Michaux *Histoire des Arbres* 1.64, *P[inus] palustris.* . . Dans le pays où il croît, . . il est connu . . sous le noms de *Long leaved pine,* . . de *Yellow pine,* . . de *Pitch pine,* . . et de *Broom pine. . .* Les noms de *Yellow pine* . . et de *Pitch pine,* . . qui lui sont peut-être plus universellement donnés, servent dans les Etats du milieu à désigner deux autres espèces très-distinctes et . . très-répandues. [=In the area where it grows, . . it is known . . under the names of *Long leaved Pine,* . . of *Yellow pine,* . . of *Pitch pine,* . . and of *Broom pine. . .* The names of *Yellow pine* . . and of *Pitch pine,* . . which perhaps are most generally given to them, are used in the middle States to designate two other quite distinct and . . widespread species.] **1842** Buckingham *Slave States* 1.177, The Georgia pitch pine is abundant, and it is a highly valuable tree. This is called by a great variety of names, such as the southern, the red, the brown, the yellow, and the long-leaved pine; but they all indicate the same kind of tree. **1859** Perry *Turpentine Farming* 26, Among the various qualities of pines, we may distinguish four in particular, viz.: common short-straw pine; rosemary, or what some call spruce pine; pitch, or long-straw pine, and the white pine of Mississippi. *Ibid* 160, Pitch pine . . its straw is the largest, longest and stiffest of any pine, and has a close glass-work surface. **1896** Mohr–Roth *Timber Pines* 28, *Pinus palustris.* . . Pitch Pine (Atlantic region). . . Georgia Pitch Pine (Atlantic region). **1933** Small *Manual SE Flora* 4, *P[inus] palustris.* . . *Pitch-pine.* . . A timber tree of the first importance, and the principal source of rosin and turpentine in the U.S. **1946** *PADS* 6.23 **cNC** (as of 1900–10), *Pitch pine.* . . The longleaf pine. **1965–70** *DARE* (Qu. T8, *Joints of pine wood that*

burn easily and make good fuel) Inf **MD24,** Pitch pine; **FL29,** Pitch pine knots; (Qu. T17, . . *Kinds of pine trees;* not asked in early QRs) Infs **MD24, NC8, VA47, 79,** Pitch pine. [*DARE* Ed: Some of these Infs may refer instead to other senses.] **1979** Little *Checklist U.S. Trees* 195, *Pinus palustris.* . . Pitch pine. . . Coastal Plain from se. Va. to c. Fla. and w. to e. Tex.

(3) A **shortleaf pine 1** (here: *Pinus echinata*).

1806 in 1852 U.S. Congress *Debates & Proc.* 9th Cong 2nd sess. app 1115, The short-leaved, or pitch pine . . is always found upon arid lands, and generally in sandy and lofty situations. **1897** Sudworth *Arborescent Flora* 29 **MO,** *Pinus echinata.* . . Pitch Pine. **1908** Britton *N. Amer. Trees* 33, Short-leaved Pine. . . The wood is hard, strong, coarse-grained, dark yellow or light brown and resinous. . . It . . is known under many common names . . as Yellow Pine, . . Pitch Pine [etc]. **1960** Vines *Trees SW* 25, *Pinus echinata.* . . Vernacular names are Yellow Pine, . . Pitch Pine. . . The wood is valuable because of its softer and less resinous character.

(4) A **slash pine** (here: *Pinus elliottii*).

1896 Mohr–Roth *Timber Pines* 74 **FL,** *Pinus elliottii.* . . Pitch Pine. **1908** Britton *N. Amer. Trees* 37, It [=*Pinus elliottii*] is also considered the handsomest of the southeastern pines. . . Also called Swamp pine, . . Pitch pine. **1970** Correll *Plants TX* 72, *Pinus elliottii.* . . Pitch pine. . . Tree to 35 m. tall, with a tall tapering trunk to 1 m. in diameter and horizontal branches to form a rounded crown. **1979** Little *Checklist U.S. Trees* 192, *Pinus elliottii.* . . Yellow slash pine, . . pitch pine. . . Coastal Plain from s. S.C. to s. Fla., also Lower Fla. Keys, and w. to se. La.

(5) Any of var other **pines 1,** such as **sand pine 1,** a **spruce pine** (here: *Pinus glabra*), **Table Mountain pine,** a **pond pine 1,** or **Jersey pine.**

1908 Rogers *Tree Book* 32, The Pitch Pines. . . *(P[inus] serotina)* Pond pine. . . *(P. pungens)* Table-Mountain pine. . . *(P. clausa)* Sand pine. . . *(P. glabra)* Spruce pine. . . *(P. Virginiana)* Jersey pine.

c A **pine 1** native to the western US, as:

(1) =**ponderosa pine 1.**

1894 *Jrl. Amer. Folkl.* 7.100, *Pinus brachyptera* [=*P. ponderosa*]. . . Called pitch pine in some regions. **1908** Britton *N. Amer. Trees* 25, The wood [of *Pinus ponderosa*] is hard, strong, but brittle, close-grained, light reddish and very resinous in conspicuous bands. . . It is also called Yellow pine, . . Pitch pine, . . and Heavy wooded pine. **1966–67** *DARE* (Qu. D34, . . *The small pieces of wood and other stuff that are used to start a fire*) Inf **NE7,** Pitch pine; (Qu. T8, *Joints of pine wood that burn easily and make good fuel*) Inf **NM6,** Pitch pine.

(2) =**whitebark pine.**

1897 Sudworth *Arborescent Flora* 16 **MT,** *Pinus albicaulis.* . . Pitch Pine. **1908** Britton *N. Amer. Trees* 13, White Bark Pine. . . has received many names, among them . . Pitch pine.

(3) The Coulter **pine 1** (here: *Pinus coulteri*). **CA**

1908 Britton *N. Amer. Trees* 39, *Coulter's Pine.* . . is also known as Pitch pine. [*Ibid* 40, The wood is soft, weak, brittle, coarse-grained, light red, with wide conspicuous resin bands and very large resinducts. . . It is sometimes used as fuel.] **1922** Sargent *Manual Trees* 21, *Pinus Coulteri.* . . Pitch Pine. . . A tree, 40° to 90° [=feet] high. **1980** Little *Audubon Guide N. Amer. Trees W. Region* 275, *Coulter Pine* . . "Pitch Pine". [*Ibid* 276, The lightweight, soft wood serves for rough lumber and fuel.]

(4) =**lodgepole pine.**

1908 [see c(7) below]. **1910** Jepson *Silva CA* 83, It [=*Pinus contorta* subsp *murrayana*] is also called . . Pitch Pine, and in the Uinta Mountains of Utah, Red Pine.

(5) =**bishop pine. CA**

1908 [see c(7) below]. **1910** Jepson *Silva CA* 99, It [=*Pinus muricata*] is often called . . "Prickle-cone Pine" because of its muricate cones, . . "Pitch Pine" because of its free yield of resin.

(6) =**limber pine.**

1966 Barnes–Jensen *Dict. UT Slang* 34, *Pitch Pine* . . a name sometimes given in northern Utah to the Limber Pine (*Pinus flexilis*). **1967** *DARE* (Qu. T17, . . *Kinds of pine trees;* not asked in early QRs) Inf **CO31,** Pitch pine.

(7) Any of var other **pines 1,** such as **digger pine, knobcone ~, Monterey ~,** or **Torrey ~.**

1908 Rogers *Tree Book* 32, The Pitch Pines. . . *(P[inus] Torreyana)* Torrey's pine. . . *(P. Sabiniana)* Digger pine. . . *(P. attenuata)* Knob-cone pine. . . *(P. radiata)* Monterey pine. . . *(P. muricata)* Prickle-cone pine. . . *(P. contorta)* Scrub pine.

pitchpole v Also sp *pitchpoll* [Engl dial; cf *OED2* pitchpoll, -pole sb. 1 "A somersault"; a1661 →, and *EDD* pitchpoll v. 1 "To turn head over heels."] **chiefly NEng**

1 To be upended, turn a somersault; to gambol; now esp of a boat: to pitch severely; to capsize bow first.

1857 (1861) Bates *Incidents* 190 **MA**, As a party of emigrants . . were descending in an ox-team, the wagon pitch-poled. **1861** *Harper's New Mth. Mag.* 23.481 **NEng**, Some servant seemed to have snatched from one of the dogs, as they came pitchpolling toward the house, a little silk handkerchief. **1892** *Century Illustr. Mag.* 44.22, It did actually capsize in a very disagreeable and unseemly manner, kicking up its heels and plunging nose down, as a cat-boat will sometimes "pitch-pole," thus turning a porpoise-like somersault, and disgracing both itself and its master. **1903** Wasson *Cap'n Simeon's Store* 44 **ME**, Ain't it hard lines enough for a sickly ole feller same's him having to go outside here late in the fall o' the year and pitch-pole around into a punky ole ark. **1926** Ashley *Yankee Whaler* 137, *Pitch-pole, to:* . . Said of a whale when he stands vertically with his head out of water bobbing up and down. **1945** Colcord *Sea Language* 142 **ME, Cape Cod, Long Island**, *Pitchpole.* To turn over end for end, as a small boat in the breakers, or a whale in breaching. Alongshore, it means to turn a somersault. **1962** Morison *One Boy's Boston* 1 **MA**, He . . beheld a baby carriage, unattended, bouncing down the stone steps. Upon hitting the sidewalk it pitchpoled, hurling the contents . . into Brimmer Street. **2001** *DARE* File **NEng** (as of 1970s), I didn't think that skier would survive his fall, seeing him go pitchpoling down the mountain, end over end like that.

2 To cause it to turn end over end; spec to hurl (a whaling lance or harpoon) in a high arc so that it descends nearly vertically; hence vbl n *pitchpoling*, n *pitchpoler.*

1851 (1976) Melville *Moby-Dick* 364 **NEng**, The harpoon may be pitchpoled in the same way with the lance, yet it is seldom done. *Ibid,* Look now at Stubb; a man who . . was specially qualified to excel in pitchpoling. . . Then holding the lance full before his waistband's middle, he levels it at the whale; when, covering him with it, he steadily depresses the butt-end in his hand, thereby elevating the point till the weapon stands fairly balanced upon his palm, fifteen feet in the air. . . Next moment with a rapid, nameless impulse, in a superb lofty arch the bright steel spans the foaming distance, and quivers in the life spot of the whale. *Ibid* 365, The pitchpoler, dropping astern, folds his hands, and mutely watches the monster die. **1880** *Scribner's Mth.* 19.326, The sea behind is liable, in spite of the efforts of the steersman, to turn it to the right or left, causing it to "broach to" and capsize, or, if this be avoided, perhaps to be "pitch-poled," end over end. **1926** Ashley *Yankee Whaler* 137, *Pitch-pole, to:* . . To dart an iron a long distance by tossing it upward and allowing it to describe a considerable arc before striking. **1997** Junger *Perfect Storm* 137 **NEng**, A single *breaking* wave, though, would flip a ship end over end if it was higher than the ship was long. . . This is called pitch-poling; Ernie Hazard was pitch-poled on Georges Bank.

pitchpole adv

Headlong, head over heels.

1969 *DARE* Tape **MA**56, They get a little careless and try to do something—go pitchpole. . . That means . . it [=a boat] goes down head first. **1975** Gould *ME Lingo* 210, *Pitchpole.* . . A youngster turning head over heels downhill is said to be "going pitchpole down;" sometimes "down pitchpole."

pitch-pole fence n Cf **backbone fence, buck ~, herringbone ~, ripgut ~, shadback ~, stake-and-rider ~**

A type of rail fence; see quot 1938.

1868 Brackett *Farm Talk* 118 **ME**, Pitch-pole fence ain't of much account. **1887** *New Engl. Mag.* 5.357 **ME**, On the top of a pitch-pole fence that extends some distance off shore, my friend creeps out to clearer water, and fills the kettle. **1938** *Rotarian* 55 **NEast**, The pitchpole fence was one of my first discoveries. It is a fence with the rails laid at a pitch—an angle—one end resting on the ground, the other supported at the desired height by cross stakes. It is disappearing from Maine, but I have photographed it in Pennsylvania. **1942** Giese *Farm Fence Hdbk.* 10, [Caption:] A pitch pole fence.

pitchpoll See **pitchpole** v

pitch(t)ure See **picture**

pitchy See **pitch** n[1]

pith n, hence adj *pithy* Also **widespread, but less freq Nth, West** (See Map) *peth(y)* Cf **corky, woody**

A Forms.

1856 *Harper's New Mth. Mag.* 13.860 **cwNY, W'al** . . it is pretty hard eatin', but I *kinder like the peth on't!* **1873** Beadle *Undeveloped West* 175, They [=California apples] seem to me overgrown, lacking in piquancy, cloying and "filling" to an extreme, and what we, when boys, used to call "pethy." **1895** *DN* 1.398 **NYC**, *Peth* [pɛθ] . . for *pith.* **1899** (1912) Green *VA Folk-Speech* 318, *Peth.* . . A form of pith. The *peth* of a tree. The marrow in an animal's backbone. *Ibid* 319, *Pethy.* . . Dry, spongy and tasteless. "These apples are not good; they are pethy." **1899** Chesnutt *Conjure Woman* 208 **csNC** [Black], Aun' Peggy gun 'im a baby doll, wid . . a head made out'n elderberry peth. **1909** *DN* 3.357 **eAL, wGA**, *Peth.* . . Pith. *Pethy.* . . Pithy. **1912** *DN* 3.585 **wIN**, *Peth.* . . Almost universal. *Pethy.* . . Pithy. **1914** *DN* 4.77 **ME, nNH**, *Peth.* . . Pith, marrow. **1915** *DN* 4.187 **swVA**, *Peth, pethy.* Variant of *pith, pithy.* **1923** *DN* 5.217 **swMO**, *Peth.* . . Pith. **1928** *AmSp* 3.403 **Ozarks**, The short *i* sound is sometimes replaced by short *e.* . . the Ozarker always says *sperrit* and *peth.* **1942** Warnick *Garrett Co. MD* 1 **nwMD** (as of 1900–18), *Pethy* (pithy). **1946** *PADS* 6.23 **ceNC** (as of 1900–10), *Pethy.* . . *Pithy* (wood). . . Common. **1947** *PADS* 8.20 **seIA**, *Pethy.* **1960** Criswell *Resp. to PADS* 20 **Ozarks**, *Pithy.* . . pethy only pr[onunciation] I ever heard here. **1965–70** *DARE* (Qu. I8, *When root vegetables get old and tough and are not good to eat, you say they are _____*) 307 Infs, **widespread, but less freq Nth, West**, Pethy; [**KY**28, Pethified;] (Qu. I39, . . *The thick outside covering of a walnut*) Inf **LA**12, Peth; (Qu. I47, . . *The green part that comes off with the stem [of a strawberry]*) Inf **MO**38, Peth; (Qu. I48, *The hard center of a cherry*) Inf **OK**43, Peth; (Qu. KK7, *When wood . . is starting to decay inside*) Infs **CA**87, **KY**77, Pethy; (Qu. KK24, *Something that breaks easily: "She broke her arm again: Her bones must be _____"*) Inf **KY**85, Pethy; (Qu. LL3a, *Shrunk, dried up: "These apples are all _____."*) Infs **NM**12, **OH**89, **TX**102, **VA**54, Pethy; [**NE**6, Peffy]. **1976** Garber *Mountain-ese* 67 **sAppalachians**, Punch the peth out uv a reed to make a real good pea shooter. **1983** *MJLF* 9.1.50 **ceKY**, *Pethy* . . tough, fibrous, as in old root vegetables. **1994** NC Lang. & Life Project *Harkers Is. Vocab.* 9 **eNC**, Mama wanted me to finish up those old, pethy apples.

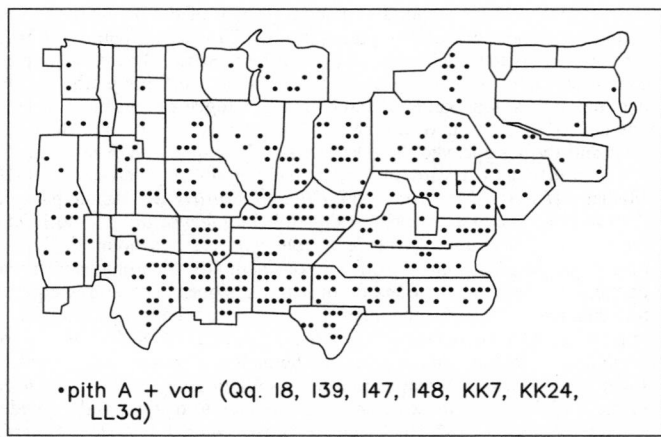

•pith A + var (Qq. I8, I39, I47, I48, KK7, KK24, LL3a)

B As noun.

1 =**pit** n[2] **1.**

1966 *DARE* (Qu. I48, *The hard center of a cherry*) Inf **OK**43, Pit, peth, stone. **c1970** Pederson *Dial. Surv. Rural GA* (*What do you call the hard thing in the middle of a cherry?*) 1 inf, **seGA**, [p'ɛ·ə<θ]. **1981** Pederson *LAGS Basic Materials* (*Seed of a cherry*) 1 inf, **nwGA**, [p'ɛ>əθ]; 1 inf, **cnGA**, [p'ɪˇɪ^θ], seed; (*Seed of a peach*) 1 inf, **cnGA**, Seed, [p'ɪˇɪ^θ].

2 See quot.

1967 *DARE* (Qu. I39, . . *The thick outside covering of a walnut*) Inf **LA**12, Peth; (Qu. I47, . . *The green part that comes off with the stem [of a strawberry]*) Inf **MO**38, Peth.

pitle See **pightle**

‡**pittum** n Cf *DS* E20

   1980 *DARE* File **Chicago IL**, My husband, who is also from Chicago, calls dust balls "pittums," while I call them "moozies."

pitty-pat n *among Black speakers* **Sth, S Midl**
A card game in which the object is to make pairs.

   1947 *Sat. Eve. Post* 15 Feb 60 **MS** [Black], While still in knee breeches he became a master at dice, cooncan, pitty pat and all the other Negro gambling games. **1957** *Ibid* 26 Jan 98 [Black], Pitty-pat is a card game in which the players merely match cards into pairs. **1965–70** *DARE* (Qu. DD35, . . *Card games*) 11 Infs, **Sth, S Midl**, Pitty-pat; **AL6**, Pitty-pat—Negroes; (Qu. DD37, . . *Table games played a lot by adults*) Inf **DC12**, Pitty-pat. [12 of 13 Infs Black] **1987** *Newsweek* 23 Mar 66 **Chicago IL** [Black], She was expected to tolerate his vices. He was unforgiving of hers. Her worst, in his eyes, was pitty-pat, a card game she appeared to like better than she played it. **1996** *DARE* File, I played pitty-pat when I was younger. I know it involved finding pairs. I believe each player was dealt five cards. Then each player took turns plucking cards from the deck. If the card could be used (paired with a card held in the hand), the card could be taken, and the pair spread in front of the player. If the card couldn't be used by the first player, the next person had a chance at it and so on until the card was either used or placed in the discard card [sic]. I believe that players who used the card had to discard a card from their hand, and that the card was also available to others (it gets a little vague here). . . The winner was the person who managed to make three pairs first, thus going "out." My husband and I agree that it is often played by females, and I can remember it as a "beginner" card game similar to "war," but I've heard from others that some gamblers played it seriously and bet money on the outcome. (I am an African American female who played this game in the forties and fifties in New Jersey and Chicago). *Ibid*, I played pitty-pat as an African American growing up in Lynchburg, VA in the early 60's. It was very popular then.

piture See **picture**

pity cardy See **pinacate bug**

pitysake n [By reanalysis of the phr *for pity's sake*]
In phr *take (a) pitysake on:* to have mercy on.

   1952 Brown *NC Folkl.* 1.576, *Pity-sake, to take _____ on: phr.* To take pity on. "He took pity-sake on me and give me some work."—West. **1961** Seeman *In Arms of Mt.* 55 **eTN**, Tracy's as cold as a rock-fence lizard—and twict as poison. He wouldn't take a pitysake on nobody.

piunkum See **unkum**

pivet bush n Also *pivy bush* [Perh for *privet*]
See quots.

   1965 *DARE* (Qu. S10, *A shrub that gets covered with bright yellow, spicy-smelling flowers early in spring; total Infs questioned, 75*) Inf **FL22**, Pivet bush. **1982** Slone *How We Talked* 107 **eKY** (as of c1950), Another cure was to chew on the bark of the "pivy" bush (an evergreen hedge).

pix See **picks**

pixie eyes n Also sp *pixy eyes*
A primrose (here: *Primula cuneifolia*) native to Alaska.

   1938 (1958) Sharples *AK Wild Flowers* 112, *P[rimula] cuneifolia*. . . Sometimes aptly called "Pixy Eyes." **1952** Williams *AK Wildfl. Glimpses* 41, Pixy Eyes, that I mention on the Mt. Roberts trail at Juneau, is a very low-growing plant found only in Alaska. **1974** *AK–Yukon Wild Flowers Guide* 122, Pixie Eyes. . . This most attractive little primrose often appears stemless when first in bloom.

pixie moss See **pyxie moss**

pixture See **picture**

pixy eyes See **pixie eyes**

pizen See **poison**

pizer See **piazza**

pizon See **poison**

pizzy ant See **piss ant** n 1

P.K. n Also *piket* [Perh joc abbr for **polecat 1** or **piss cat**]
=skunk.

   1921 *DN* 5.114 **CA**, *P.K.,* or *piket,* n. Pole cat. Sierra Nevada.

place back(s) exclam Also abbr *p.b.* Cf **-s** suff[2]
Used as a preemptive assertion of one's right to reclaim a seat or place in line after leaving for a short time.

   1971 Brunvand *Guide Folkl.* UT 30, "Place backs" is what my cousins call out when they leave their chairs for some reason, and want to return to the same chair. If they do not call "place backs," then anyone else in the room may take their place. **1998–99** *DARE* File **IA**, The term *place backs* is very, very common among the youth of the Midwest. Any time a group of kids is watching TV and one gets up to go to the restroom, he'll call *place backs!* And it's respected; the other kids won't go take his seat; **CO** (as of 1980s), You could use it [=*place backs*] if you wanted to leave a line . . temporarily and then come back, but it was more often used to make sure you got your favorite chair back, or your place at the table; **nIN, MT, West**, Place backs! **MN**, *Place back* . . was used to reserve your chair, or couch space, or floor space when you needed to leave the room . . and wanted to go right back to where you were; **NH**, My 16 and 19 year old boys use *place back* regularly to "reserve" the place where they were sitting. . . My 16 year old . . said that it is a regular expression for kids his age. It is also strangely honored, as if invoked as a spell; **nIN** (as of 1970s), **wKY, NH** (as of 1940s), Place back! **2000** *NADS Letters* sePA (as of 1970s), Place-backs. *Ibid* **AL** (as of 1949), Place backs. *Ibid* **MO** (as of c1980), Place backs! . . My husband, who is from California doesn't remember this. *Ibid* **AZ** (as of 1960s), Place backs! . . I remember being confronted with puzzlement and guffaws when we moved to California in 1968 and I tried to use it. *Ibid* **swWA**, Place backs. . . Here people also will knock on the seat as they get up and say "Tap, tap, place backs." **2001** *DARE* File **csWI**, My friend's two sons were watching television. Ben got out of his chair to get a drink of water. "P.b., Donald!" he admonished his brother. When I asked about the expression, the boys told me that all the children at their day-care center used it. "Everybody knows it means 'place back,'" Ben explained, "but we just say 'p.b.'"

place down below n Cf **down below 2**

   1966 *DARE* (Qu. CC9, . . *Words or expressions for hell: "That man is headed straight for _____."*) Infs **FL2, 10, 14, 15, 28, 36**, Place down below.

place-eyed pea n
Perh a **black-eyed pea.**

   1938 Stuart *Dark Hills* 210 **KY**, Where the black shoe-makes grow, the land won't sprout place-eyed peas.

placer n |ˈplæsɚ| [AmSpan *placer* a deposit] **West**
A deposit of sand or gravel where particles of gold are found; the gold itself—freq attrib, esp in comb *placer mining* a method of extracting gold by washing; see quots. For addit combs cf *DA, DAE*

   [**1842** *Niles' Natl. Reg.* 8 Oct 96/1 **CA**, They have at last discovered gold. . . Those who are acquainted with these "placeres," as they call them, (for it is not a mine), say it will grow richer, and may lead to a mine.] **1844** (1954) Gregg *Commerce* 117 **NM**, From the peculiar character of the place and the remains of the cisterns still existing, the object of pursuit in this case would seem to have been a *placer,* a name applied to mines of gold-dust intermixed with the earth. *Ibid* 123, As some of the natives have justly remarked, New Mexico is almost one continuous *placer;* traces of gold being discoverable over nearly the whole surface of the country. **1848** *Californian* (S.F.) 29 May 1/2 *(DA)*, Those who find it necessary to have the correct standard can be accommodated by the subscriber, who will take Placera [sic] Gold in payment. **1863** Hittell *Resources CA* 383, *Placer,* from the Spanish, a place where gold is found in dirt near the surface of the ground. **1907** White *AZ Nights* 232, We made a little on our placer—just enough to keep interested. **a1922** (1953) Brooks *Blazing* 361 **AK**, An experienced placer miner could also obtain leases, or "lays" as they were called. **1932** Bentley *Spanish Terms* 183, The fact that one of the best known mines of New Mexico in the early nineteenth century was known as *El Placer* may account in part for the general currency of *placer* in mining circles. **1933** *Anchorage Daily Times* (AK) 24 Oct 2 (Tabbert *Dict. Alaskan Engl.*), As the placer season draws near to the close all those who have been sniping pay on the Kenai river bars. **1940** Writers' Program *Guide NV* 61, A *placer miner* or *gravel miner* works in superficial gravel deposits. **1967–69** *DARE* Tape **AZ**4, There was lots of placer ['plæsɚ] mining around this country. I had a cousin. . . A fella got him to go in with him and they . . done a lot of placer mining, brought a lot of machinery up there; **CA**120, That's placer ['plæsɚ] mining. . . Placer is different; that's gold that's been washed out of the hard rocks from water and . . corrosion. . . Sometimes you can find a big, flat bar of gravel where the river really slowed down and it just spread out; that's mostly the place where you find large quantities of placer gold. **1969** *DARE* FW Addit **CA**114, *Placer gold*—gold that's separated from the quartz and has washed down into streams. The gold that is panned out of streams. Also called *free gold*. **1970** [see **placer** v].

placer v, hence vbl n *placering*

To extract gold from sand and gravel by washing.

　　1901 *Land of Sunshine* 14.116 **CA**, Gold scales used for dust and nuggets which were being "placered" in Los Angeles county more than a decade before Marshall's "discovery" of California gold on Sutter Creek. **1970** *DARE* Tape **CA**200, They did lots of placering ['plæsɚɪn] in the county. . . Placer mining. That's a wash . . in the creek beds. . . The water runs in and washes the rocks, and the gold settles on the crosspieces.

placer mining See **placer** n

placings n, exclam

In marble play: the right to reposition one's marble; used as a call to claim this right.

　　1876 *N&Q* 54.348, *Fen (or Fend?)*.—Boys in all parts of the United States employ this word, especially when playing marbles, to prevent any change in the existing conditions of the game, as, for instance, *fen-placings,* to prevent an alteration in the position of the marbles. **1950** *WELS* (*Cries or calls used in playing marbles . . to get the right to do something*) 1 Inf, **ceWI**, Placings.

‡placket house n [*placket* an opening or slit in a garment]　Cf *DS* M21a, b

An outdoor privy.

　　1960 Criswell *Resp. to PADS 20* **Ozarks**, *Placket house*—Privy, the commonest term. (I knew one old lady who called it a *placket house*).

plag-gone See **plague-gone**

plague n, v Usu |ple(ɪ)g|; also **scattered, but esp freq S Midl** |plɛg|; infreq |plæg|　Cf Pronc Intro 3.I.6.a　Similarly ppl adj, adv *plagued* Usu |ple(ɪ)gd|; also freq |'plɛgɪd, 'plegɪd|; also |plɛgd, plægd|　Infreq ppl adj *plaguing* |'plægɪn|　Pronc-spp *pleg(ged), pleggid*

A Forms.　For addit quots see **B** and **C** below

　　1887 (1895) Robinson *Uncle Lisha* 95 **wVT**, Seems 's' ough the pleggid foxes had ort tu git some scacer. **1887** (1967) Harris *Free Joe* 101 **GA**, That pleggëd old cat's a-tryin' to drink out'n the water-bucket. Fling a cheer at 'er! *Ibid* 156, A man can't afford to be too plegged particular. **1890** *DN* 1.69 **KY**, *Plagued*. Pronounced [plɛgd]. **1891** *PMLA* 6.175 **TN**, *Plague* is generally given with the short e-sound, *pleg*. **1893** Shands *MS Speech* 50, *Pleg* [plɛg]. Common pronunciation of *plague*, especially in the expression, "Pleg take it!" a euphemistic form of swearing. The same pronunciation is used in Tennessee. **1905** *DN* 3.56 **eNE**, *Plague* (pronounced *pleg*). *Ibid* 103 **nwAR**, [plɛg] *plague*. **1942** Hall *Smoky Mt. Speech* 18 **wNC, eTN**, *Plague* . . heard only with [æ]. **1942** Warnick *Garrett Co. MD* 1 **nwMD** (as of 1900–18), *Plegged* (plagued). **1965** [see **C2** below]. **1965–70** [see **C1** below. **1966** [see **C1** below]. **1975** Gould *ME Lingo* 211, *Plague*—Pronounce "pleg"; to tease, even to the point of downright meanness. **1979** Lewis *How to Talk Yankee* [26] **nNEng**, *Pleg-ged*. . . "I had to quit pulling weeds because of them pleg-ged minges."

B As noun.

1 in phrr *plague on* (or *plague take*) (*someone* or *something*): Used as a mild oath. **chiefly Sth, S Midl; also NEast**　See Map　*somewhat old-fash*　Cf **plague-gone, plague-taked**

　　1871 Eggleston *Hoosier Schoolmaster* 212 **sIN**, Dr. Small's trying to git out, plague take him. **1893** [see **A** above]. **1902** *DN* 2.241 **sIL**, *Plague on*. . . An expletive. *Plague take*. . . An expletive. **1906** *DN* 3.122 **sIN**, *Plague on*. . . A mild oath. *Plague take*. . . A mild oath. **1907** *DN* 3.225 **nwAR**, *Plague on*. . . An expletive. **1909** *DN* 3.358 **eAL, wGA**, *Pleg*. . . 'Pleg take it!' *Ibid* 401 **nwAR**, *Plague on*. . . A mild oath. **1910** *DN* 3.446 **wNY**, *Plague take*. . . A mild oath. **1952**

Brown *NC Folkl.* 1.577, *Plague take (one)*. . . A mild imprecation = *may the plague take you*. **1962** Atwood *Vocab. TX* 70, *Exclamations of disgust*. . . Some of those of less frequency . . all occur more than once. . . *plague take it*. **1965** *West Time Was* 235 **nwNC**, "Plague-gone [sic] her!" Vi muttered. "She's gone and run off some'ers and tuck that pore chile with her." **1965–70** *DARE* (Qu. NN8b, . . *"This jar won't come open, _____ it."*) 13 Infs, **chiefly Sth**, Plague take; (Qu. NN9b, . . *"He's run off with my hammer again, _____!"*) Infs **AL**6, **CT**16, **NY**42, **PA**234, **SC**59, **WV**3, 5, Plague take him; **NC**40, **WV**4, 18, Plague take his skin; **MD**30, Plague take it; (Qu. NN8a, . . *"Oh _____. I've lost my glasses again."*) Infs **IA**5, **WI**44, Plague take it; (Qu. NN9a, . . *"_____. The electric power is off again."*) Infs **IA**5, **VA**69, 71, Plague take it; (Qu. NN25a, *Weakened substitutes for 'damn' or 'damned': "_____ it all!"*) Inf **WA**11, Plague take. [20 of 27 total Infs old] **1986** Pederson *LAGS Concordance*, 1 inf, **neTN**, Plague on it—great grandmother's expression; 1 inf, **cwGA**, Plague on it.

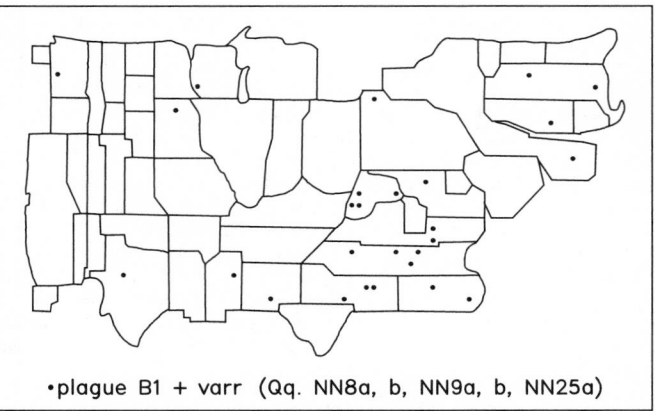

•plague B1 + varr (Qq. NN8a, b, NN9a, b, NN25a)

2 usu with *the*: Menstruation.

　　1969 *DARE* (Qu. AA27, . . *A woman's menstruation*) Inf **PA**184, The plague. **1990** Cavender *Folk Med. Lexicon* 29 **sAppalachians**, *(The) plague*—menstruation.

C As verb.

1 To bother, annoy, torment; to damn—used as a mild oath; hence ppl adj *plagued*, rarely *plaguing* troublesome, annoying; damned; also adv *plagued* damned, extremely.　*somewhat old-fash; esp freq in rural areas*　Cf **plaguey** adj, adv

　　1851 Hooper *Widow Rugby's Husband* 95 **AL**, I tho't I'd plague her some. **1899** (1912) Green *VA Folk-Speech* 325, *Plague*. . . To vex; harrass [sic]; trouble; annoy; tease. *Ibid* 326, *Plegged*. . . Troublesome; annoying. **1909** *DN* 3.358 **eAL, wGA**, *Pleg*. . . 'Pleg your time!' This pronunciation is used only in an exclamatory way. *Plegged*. . . Plagued, darned. "You plegged rascal." **1917** *DN* 4.398 **neOH**, *Pleg*. . . "You children stop plegging one another." "They plegged him about his girl." General. *Plegged* [plɛgɪd]. . . Annoying, -ly. "I can't get this plegged boot on." "He's too plegged mean for anything." General. **1942** McAtee *Dial. Grant Co. IN* 49 (as of 1890s), *Plegged* . . plaguy of the dictionary in its intensive sense; it usually meant "very"; "so _____ mean", "_____ long-legged." (Ala., Md., N.Y., Va.) **1965–70** *DARE* (Qu. GG3, *To tease: "See those big boys trying to _____ [that little one]."*) 22 Infs, **chiefly Nth, N Midl**, Plague; (Qu. NN17, . . *"That _____ fly won't go away."*) Infs **FL**19, **GA**7, 9, **NY**7, ['plegɪd, -əd]; **NY**75, **SC**39, ['plɛgɪd]; **OH**41, **VA**46, Plegged; **LA**32, Plegged—old-fashioned; (Qu. Y2, . . *"Losing all that money didn't seem to _____ him a bit."*) Inf **MA**68, Plague; (Qu. Y5, . . *"Johnny wouldn't have tried that if the other boys hadn't _____."*) Inf **IL**72, Plagued him; (Qu. Y7, *When one person never misses a chance to be mean to another or to annoy another: "I don't know why she keeps _____ me all the time!"*) Infs **FL**19, **NJ**56, **NY**33, 92, 100, **PA**55, **WA**1, Plaguing; (Qu. CC12b, . . *If a person has a lot of bad luck . . "He's been _____."*) Inf **NY**88, [pleɪgɪd]; (Qu. GG13a, *When something keeps bothering a person and makes him nervous . . "It _____ me."*) Infs **MA**100, **NY**166, **OH**18, Plagues; (Qu. NN8b, . . *"This jar won't come open, _____ it."*) Infs **NJ**9, **TX**45, **VA**24, **WI**26, Plague; **TX**40, [plɛgɪt]. [34 of 44 total Infs old, 34 comm type 4 or 5] **1966** *DARE* FW Addit **AR**, That plaguing ['plægɪn] pump keeps going off before the tank is full; **ME**14, I used to plague (tease) him about that. **1975** [see **A** above]. **1975** *DARE* File **csGA**, Plagued ['plɛgɪd]—bothersome, annoying; a very weak curse-word; =cotton-pickin'. **1979** [see **A** above].

2 To embarrass; hence ppl adjs *plagued (out)* embarrassed. **chiefly S Midl**

1923 *DN* 5.217 **swMO**, *Plague.* . . To embarrass, to annoy, to confuse. **1924** (1946) Greer-Petrie *Angeline Gits an Eyeful* 24 **csKY**, I stept into a great big room that had a body of warter in hit . . , and I hope to my die, if all them folks wan't in a *a-warshin'*, men and wimmen, and you couldn't tell one from t'other in them little, bitty, short, tight suits they had on. Why Jeemses River, I never wuz *so plagued* in my life. **1942** McAtee *Dial. Grant Co. IN* 49 (as of 1890s), *Pleg* . . embarrass; "I was so plegged I didn't know what to do". **1956** McAtee *Some Dialect NC* 34, *Pleg:* . . i.e., plague, embarrass. **1965** *DARE* (Qu. GG9, *To suddenly embarrass somebody and throw him off balance: "When they told him what she had said about him, it certainly did _____ him."*) Inf **OK9**, [plæg]; he was sure [plægd] out. **1976** Garber *Mountain-ese* 69 **sAppalachians**, *Plague* . . embarrass—It shore did plague him when he heard his trousers tear. **1982** Slone *How We Talked* 33 **eKY** (as of c1950), *Plagued*—embarrassed.

plagued ppl adj See **plague C1, 2**

plagued adv See **plague C1**

plagued out See **plague C2**

plague-gone adj phr, adv phr Also *plag-gone, plague-on(ed)* [*plague on (something)* (at **plague B1**)] **Sth, S Midl** euphem
Darned, damned.

1884 *Anglia* 7.258 **Sth, S Midl** [Black], There are many peculiar intensives in the Negro dialect designed to give emphasis to an assertion: . . Plag-gone: *to be er plag' gone ape* (plague-so-on). **1929** *W. Va. Rev.* Nov. 44 *(ADD)*, I could make one myself ef I didn't have so plague-oned much else on han' to do. **1953** Goodwin *It's Good* 126 **sIL** [Black], If niggers knowed anything, whyn't they conjured some o' them plague-gone mean white folks in slavery time. **1966** *DARE* (Qu. NN17, *Something that keeps on annoying you—for example, a fly that keeps buzzing around you: "That _____ fly won't go away."*) Inf **MS73**, Plague-on.

plague on (someone or something) See **plague B1**

plague-taked ppl adj phr, adv phr Pronc-spp *plague-take-it, plegtated* [*plague take (something)* (at **plague B1**)] **chiefly Sth, S Midl**
=**plague-gone.**

1924 (1946) Greer-Petrie *Angeline Gits an Eyeful* 3 **csKY**, I be consarn my skin if them men wan't too plague-taked lazy to tote them canvas bags theirse'ves. **1938** Rawlings *Yearling* 287 **nFL**, You're a plague-taked ninny, that's what you be. **1941** Ward *Holding Hills* 162 **IA** (as of early 20th cent), Joe Egbert said a day or two afterwards that he danced "so plague take it much" that he couldn't walk for a week. **1942** Perry *Texas* 54, It takes nearly as much time keeping those plague-taked kids on the job. **1947** *AmSp* 22.75, Wentworth's *American Dialect Dictionary* records the dialect expression *plague take it* but does not mention its use as an adjective. In west central Wisconsin I have often heard the entire phrase combined into one adjective and pronounced ['plɛgtetɪd]. For example, 'We can't get to town with this plegtated ice on the roads.' Those users of the word whom I questioned did not know its origin. **1949** Perry *Granny Van* 128 **TX**, I'm tired of being imposed on by those plague-taked chickens. **1952** Giles *40 Acres* 70 **KY**, "This dad-ratted dress," she fumed, "I'd ort to know hit was sleazy! . . Crept up two, three inches at a time. I says to myself the plague-taked thing is goin' plumb to my knees!" **1963** Edwards *Gravel* 20 **eTN** (as of 1920s), Now since you're so plague-taked interested in that candy you wouldn't mind playing a little for it wouldje? **1970** *DARE* (Qu. LL37, . . *"I could have wrung her neck, I was so _____ mad."*) Inf **VA69**, Plague-take-it; (Qu. NN17, . . *"That _____ fly won't go away."*) Inf **VA42**, Plague-take-it.

plague take (someone or something) See **plague B1**

plaguey adj Also sp *plag(u)y, pleggy* [**plague C1**]
Annoying, vexatious; damned.

1834 *Life Andrew Jackson* 82, His men knew the law tu well for him tu cheat 'em, and were plaguy sticklers for it. **1844** Thompson *Major Jones's Courtship* 65 **GA**, It wasn't no easy ways to hawl things, but then you know it's such a plagy job. **1859** Taliaferro *Fisher's R.* 30 **nwNC** (as of 1820s), He had, moreover, a fund of sharp, provoking wit running into satire when necessary, which Johnson maintained "were worth more than all yer college lingo, a plaguy sight." **1899** (1912)

Green *VA Folk-Speech* 325, *Plaguy.* . . Troublesome; vexatious; annoying. **1903** *DN* 2.300 **Cape Cod MA** (as of a1857), *Plaguey.* . . Bothersome. 'There comes that plaguey pedler again.' **1905** *DN* 3.16 **cCT**, *Plaguey sight.* . . A great deal. 'I'd a plaguey sight rather go than stay here.' **1907** *DN* 3.207 **nwAR**, *Plaguey.* . . Bothersome. **1922** (1926) Cady *Rhymes VT* 58, It wan't a pleggy bit too soon. **1963** Owens *Look to River* 14 **TX**, He had never heard of anything as plaguy as blackbirds. **1967** (Qu. NN8b) Inf **MA5**, The plaguey [plɛgɪ] thing has stopped; (Qu. NN17, *Something that keeps on annoying you—for example, a fly that keeps buzzing around you: "That _____ fly won't go away."*) Inf **MA5**, Plaguey.

plaguey adv Also *plaguy*
Annoyingly, vexatiously; very, darned, damned.

1815 Humphreys *Yankey in England* 107, *Plaguy*, as a degree of comparison—very—to enhance the force of the word with which it is connected. **1834** Davis *Letters Downing* 39, I was plaguy fraid I was the only one. **1834** *Life Andrew Jackson* 13, The debates was plaguy warm. **1838** Kettell *Yankee Notions* 123, Hannah 's a nice gal, but somehow or other I feel plaguy queer about it. **1843** (1916) Hall *New Purchase* 162 **IN**, Here we rested and blowed, uttering between the puffs—"plaguey heavy!" **1848** Bartlett *Americanisms* 253, *Plaguy.* In the United States used adverbially, in the same sense as *plaguily.* **1858** Hammett *Piney Woods Tavern* 32, He always keeps to the windard of the law, but I guess he'll sail plaguy nigh the wind. **1899** (1912) Green *VA Folk-Speech* 325, *Plaguy.* . . Vexatiously; deucedly: as, plaguy hard. **1905** *DN* 3.16 **cCT**, *Plaguey.* . . Horribly. 'He looks plaguey suspicious.' *Ibid* 65 **eNE**, *Plaguey.* . . Very, or annoyingly. "He's plaguey selfish." **1907** *DN* 3.215 **nwAR**, *Plaguey.* . . Horribly. **1916** Lincoln *Mary-'Gusta* 104 **MA**, "Don't be so foolish, Zoeth," he protested. "You know plaguey well I never meant anything else." **1959** *VT Hist.* 27.153, *Plaguey.* . . Vexatiously. Occasional. [**1981** Pederson *LAGS Basic Materials* (*It's almost midnight*) 1 inf, **neTN**, It's [plɛˬg naˬⁱ]. . . "Plague nigh" was one of her great-grandmother's expressions.]

plaguing ppl adj See **plague C1**

plaguy adj See **plaguey** adj

plaguy adv See **plaguey** adv

plagy See **plaguey** adj

plaik See **play like**

plain adj **chiefly PA**
Being or belonging to a conservative religious organization such as the Mennonites (esp the Amish) or the Brethren, which emphasizes simplicity and separation from the dominant culture—esp in comb *plain people.*

[**1852** in 1983 *PADS* 70.46 **ce,sePA**, *Plain,* adv. "the woman was dressed plane rather she gave me a apple."] **1866** *Ibid,* Had to wait till seven for the Lehigh Lackawanna & Western RR those plain persons went there too. **1904** Martin *Tillie* 113 **PA**, But can't you see the inconsistentness of the plain people [=Mennonites]? **1929** *Sat. Eve. Post* 23 Mar 165 **PA**, You found it in your heart for to join the Plain People [=Amish]? **1948** *Chicago Daily Tribune* (IL) 25 Jan sec 4 5/4, The Plain People [=Amish], as they are known, won't use automobiles or tractors, have no telephones, plumbing or political parties. **1951** Swetnam *Pittsylvania Country* 5 **wPA**, No one is surprised to see the garb of the "plain people"—Amish or Mennonite. **1952** *PA Dutchman* July 3/1 *(Mathews Coll.)*, And many of the families still belong to the "plain" churches—Mennonite, Brethren, and Brethren in Christ. **1953** *Reading Times* (PA) 9 Dec 36/3 *(Mathews Coll.)*, Levi Gibble, a heavily bearded member of one of the "plain" sects, appealed an increase. **1964** *Ferhoodled Engl.* [21] *[PaGer]*, A teacher of a small Lancaster County school told about a little girl from a "plain" family who was taken on a trip to Florida. **1966** *DARE* (Qu. CC4, . . *Nicknames* . . *for various religions or religious groups*) Inf **PA1**, Plain folk—Amish, Mennonites, Dunkards, etc. **1967–70** *DARE* Tape **PA30**, By the plain person's standard, I am gay, I am dressy. And they are plain. . . You can go into the Mennonite person who does not abide by the plain dress—the collarless coat, the broad-rimmed hat—and he's still considered to be a gay individual, he's still not a plain person; and if you were to talk to him, he would refer to plain people . . and he'd talk about the Amish and the team Mennonites. . . A black-bumper person will refer to the team person as a plain person, meaning he feels he is no longer plain. . . If you belong to a horse-and-wagon or a team church, then you are plain. Anything above that is not necessarily plain anymore; **PA184**, There's a quite good size Amish community down . . between Volant and New

Wilmington. And there's another smaller one up near the town of Fredonia. . . They're a plain folk. That's another name, I believe, for them is plain folk; **PA**242, I remember as a child . . the total social life was centered around the church. And I remember that we were among the plain people of Lancaster County. I'm no longer with the plain people, but my family and my parents raised me in this tradition; **PA**249, My father and mother were plain people [*DARE* Ed: here =United Brethren]. They were very religious people and we had family worship every morning, where father would read the Bible and we'd all gather round in the living room, and we'd have our morning prayers and morning devotions. **c1970** *DARE* File **neOH**, *Plain People*—It is frequently used in northern Ohio in speaking of Amish, Mennonites, etc. **1975** *Budget* (Sugarcreek, Ohio) 20 Mar. 8/5 *(OED2)*, Both Bro. David Wagler and his wife are plain people. They work helping this organization to distribute Bibles, hymn books and concordances behind the Iron Curtain.

plain bread n Also *plain brick,* ~ *dodger* **Sth, S Midl** Cf **bread** n B1, **dodger** n[1] 1
Basic corn bread.
   1906 *DN* 3.151 **nwAR**, *Plain bread.* . . Corn bread made of meal, salt, and cold water. "Plain bread and cold water bread are the same." **1909** *DN* 3.401 **nwAR**, *Plain dodger.* . . Corn-bread, the meal of which is made up with cold water into pones. **1968** *DARE* (Qu. H14, *Bread that's made with cornmeal*) Inf **LA**16, Plain bread [FW: stress on *plain*]—just a scalded bread without any fancy doin's to it. **1986** Pederson *LAGS Concordance,* 4 infs, **GA, TN, AL**, Plain bread—(made with only) cornmeal, salt, water; 1 inf, **csAL**, Plain bread—basic corn bread; 1 inf, **cwTN**, Plain bread—cornmeal, salt, water; dished from pan; 1 inf, **neAR**, Plain bread [or] plain brick = corn dodger, hoecake.

plain out adv phr **Sth, Midl**
Plainly, simply.
   1965–70 *DARE* (Qu. B34, *When a pond . . becomes entirely covered with ice . . it is* _____) Inf **MO**36, Just plain out frozen; (Qu. KK51, *Very plainly or abruptly: "I asked him _____ what he meant by that."*) Infs **IL**131, **MD**17, **MO**1, 19, **PA**150, **TX**32, Plain out; **MD**26, Right plain out; (Qu. KK55c, . . *Expressions of strong denial*) Inf **MO**19, Plain out "no." [7 of 8 total Infs old] **1970** *Thompson Coll.,* He jus plain-out said what he really thought. **1975** Newell *If Nothin' Don't Happen* 6 **nwFL**, Some crazy happenin' that'll plain-out tickle the fire out of you. **1981** Pederson *LAGS Basic Materials (It's rather cold)* 1 inf, **seTN**, Pretty plain out [cold]; kinda [cold].

plain people See **plain**

plains hare See **prairie hare**

plain view n
=**I spy 2.**
   1906 *DN* 3.151 **nwAR**, *Plain view.* . . A house game. An object is hidden where it can be seen. One person is then called in and searches for it.

plait v, hence ppl adj *plaited,* vbl n *plaiting* Usu |plæt|; also |plet| Pronc-spp *plat, platted, platting* **chiefly Sth, Midl, SW**
See Map
To braid.
   1899 (1912) Green *VA Folk-Speech* 325, *Plat.* . . To interweave; make or shape by interweaving. **1900** Harris *Reminiscences* 4.100 **TX** (as of 1834), I soon learned to plat straw and ropes. **1902** *DN* 2.241 **sIL**, *Plait* (pronounced [plæt]). . . To braid or plait. The word braid is not used. **1907** *DN* 3.225 **nwAR**, *Plait.* . . Pronounced [plæt]. **1912** *DN* 3.585 **wIN**, *Plait.* . . Pronounced . . *plat* when applied to dressing the hair, or weaving the strands of a leather chain or whip. **1923** *DN* 5.217 **swMO**, *Plat.* . . To plait or braid, as the hair or strips of bark. **1930** *AmSp* 5.202 [Ozark dialect], Shakespeare's line about Mab who "*plats* the manes of horses" is still good English in the Ozarks, although the ordinary American usage is *plait,* with a long *a* sound. **1965–70** *DARE* (Qu. X2, *When a woman divides her hair into three strands and twists them together . . she is* _____ [*her hair*]) 316 Infs, **chiefly Sth, Midl, SW**, Platting; **MA**5, **SC**3, 11, 24, 55, Plat; **AL**26, Plats; **NC**55, French platting; **MO**3, Platted; 34 Infs, **scattered, esp Midl, Sth**, Plaiting [no pronc given]; **KY**85, ['pletn]—Negro usage; **PA**162, Braiding; used to say ['pletɪŋ]; (Qu. H28, *Different shapes or types of doughnuts*) Inf **PA**110, Plaited ones; (Qu. L65, . . *Kinds of fences*) Inf **SC**57, Platted fence—split. **1966–67** *DARE* Tape **FL**24, It's a piece of rope, . . it's rope that's platted; **AL**20, They would gather these fronds . . and strip 'em off like

that and dry it and [plæt] 'em and then sew it together to make 'em hats. **1975** Gould *ME Lingo* 211, *Plat*—Maine way to pronounce plait; to braid, whether for *platting* the hair or *platting* rugs. **1983** *MJLF* 9.1.51 **ceKY**, *Plat* . . to braid, plait. **2001** [see **plait** n].

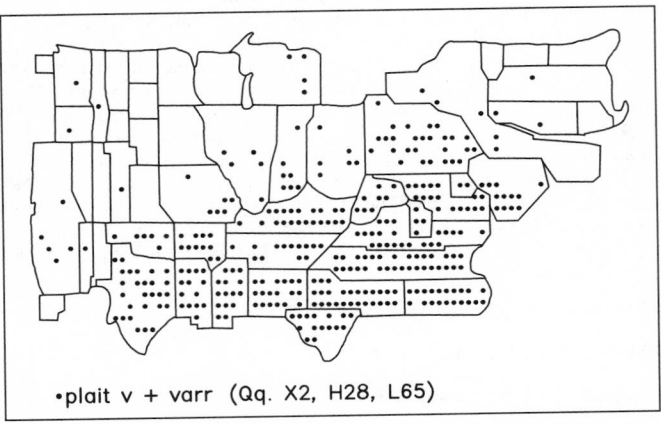

•plait v + varr (Qq. X2, H28, L65)

plait n Usu |plæt| Pronc-sp *plat* **chiefly Sth, S Midl** Cf **plait** v
A braid; also transf.
   1899 (1912) Green *VA Folk-Speech* 325, *Plat.* . . A platted or braided thing, something produced by platting or interweaving: as, a straw *plat* for hats; a *plat* of hair. **1903** *DN* 2.325 **seMO**, *Plat* (plait). . . Braid. 'She wears her hair in two plats.' **1906** *DN* 3.123 **sIN**, *Plat.* . . Braid, plait. **1909** *DN* 3.358 **eAL, wGA**, *Plait.* . . Universally pronounced [plæt], never [plet]. *Braid* is rarely or never heard. *Ibid* 401 **nwAR**, *Plat.* . . Braid, plait. **1966–70** *DARE* (Qu. H28, *Different shapes or types of doughnuts*) Inf **DE**4, Plats—three strips platted together, then fried in deep fat; (Qu. K27, . . *The sharp-pointed stick used to get oxen to move*) Inf **RI**4, Four-plat whip; (Qu. X1b, *False hair worn by women*) Inf **SC**2, False plaits; (Qu. X3, *When a woman puts her hair up on her head in a bunch*) Inf **TN**52, French plait. **1976** Ryland *Richmond Co. VA* 375, *Plat*—braid. **2001** *DARE* File **seIA** (as of c1940), My sister used to wear her hair in two plats. Mom would plat it for her every morning before we went to school.

plaited, plaiting See **plait** v

plan'ation See **plantation**

plane See **plane tree**

planeleaf willow n
Std: a northern shrubby willow *(Salix planifolia).* Also called **diamond-leaf willow, mountain** ~, **tealeaf** ~

planer tree n
Std: an elmlike tree *(Planera aquatica)* of the southern Atlantic and Gulf states. Also called **hornbeam 4, water elm**

plane tree n Also *plane*
1 A **sycamore,** esp *Platanus occidentalis.* [*OED2* *plane* sb.[1] 1 1382 →, *plane-tree* sb. a 14.. →]
   1640 Parkinson *Theatrum Botanicum* 1427, *Platanus Occidentalis aut Virginensis.* The Plane tree of the West parts or *Virginia.* **1731** Catesby *Nat. Hist. Carolina* 1.56, The Western Plane-Tree. This Tree usually grows very large and tall. . . In Virginia they are plentifully found in all the lower Parts of the Country. **1813** Michaux *Histoire des Arbres* 3.184, Sur les bords de l'Ohio, dans le Kentucky et le Tennessée, le nom de *Sycamore* est plus en usage; quelques personnes le connoissent aussi sous celui de *Plane tree.* [=On the banks of the Ohio, in Kentucky and in Tennessee, the name *Sycamore* is more in use; some people know it also under that of *Plane tree.*] **1897** Sudworth *Arborescent Flora* 206, Sycamore. . . Common Names. . . Plane Tree (R.I., Del., S.C., Kans., Nebr., Iowa.) **1966–69** *DARE* (Qu. T13, . . *Names . . for . . sycamore*) Infs **GA**25, **NJ**39, **WA**6, Plane tree.
2 also *planetree maple:* A **maple** such as **box elder, red maple,** or **sycamore** ~. [*OED2* *plane-tree* sb. b 1778 →, *plane* sb.[1] 2 18.. →, for *Acer pseudoplatanus* in Scotl and nEngl]
   a1857 (1916) Champlain Soc. Toronto *Pub.* 12.276 **cnMN** [Author from **Canada**], The Plane Tree also makes a good sugar. **1913** *Torreya*

13.232 **LA**, *Acer drummondii.* . . plane, Avoyelles Parish, La. **1979** Little *Checklist U.S. Trees* 39, Cultivated species of *Acer* have been recorded as escaping and becoming established locally in eastern United States. . . These include . . *A[cer] pseudoplatanus,* L., planetree maple (sycamore maple).

planker n

=float n 5.

1925 *Book of Rural Life* 7.4334, *Planker,* a homemade implement used to smooth the surface of the ground in preparing a seed bed, and for crushing clods which may be on the surface. A common style is made of three planks . . lapped slightly and held together with crosspieces bolted to the top side. **1950** *WELS Suppl.* WI, *Planker*—For smoothing fields. Planks bolted together into strips, with edges overlapping slightly. **1967–68** *DARE* (Qu. L20, *The implement used in a field after it's been plowed to break up the lumps*) Infs **NY**105, **OH**68, **WI**51, Planker; **MI**40, Planker—following a harrow.

plank fence n Also *plank fencing* **chiefly Sth, S Midl** See Map

A board fence.

1840 in 1841 *Spirit of Times* 2 Jan 523/1 AR, The race course is. . . enclosed with a good plank fence. **1879** (1880) Twain *Tramp Abroad* 386, Every few hundred yards, . . one came across a panel or so of plank fencing. **1885** U.S. Bur. Indian Affairs *Report* 167 OR, We have . . 2 miles of plank fencing. **1892** Allen *Blue-Grass Region* 28 *(DA),* Some [limestone fences] being torn down and superseded by plank fences or post-and-rail fences. **1965–70** *DARE* (Qu. L64, *The kind of wooden fence that's built around a garden or near a house*) 38 Infs, **chiefly Sth, S Midl,** Plank fence; MS4, Kentucky plank fence; (Qu. L65, . . *Kinds of fences*) 17 Infs, **Sth, S Midl,** Plank fence; (Qu. L61, *Fences made of solid logs, now or in the past*) Inf **AL**11, Plank fence; (Qu. L62, *A fence made of split logs*) Inf **TN**53, Plank fence. **1966** Dakin *Dial. Vocab. Ohio R. Valley* 2.97, *Picket fence.* . . *Plank fence* and *board fence* appear less commonly but are used by some informants as apparent synonyms for *picket/paling fence.* **1966** *DARE* Tape DC10, Them plank fences which are on the road. **1986** Pederson *LAGS Concordance* **Gulf Region,** 75 infs, (A) plank fence; 2 infs, Plank fencing.

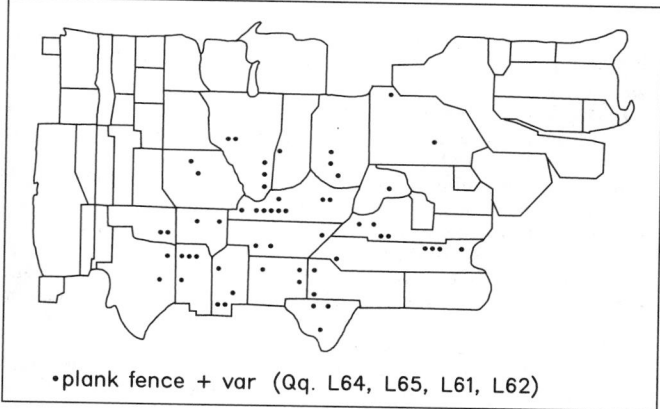

•plank fence + var (Qq. L64, L65, L61, L62)

plank float See **float n 5**

plank road n [*DCan* 1839 →] **scattered, but more freq Nth, N Midl** *old-fash*

A road built of planks laid side by side transversely, esp over swampy ground.

1847 *Scientific Amer.* 20 Feb 172 NY, Positions are before the Legislature for plank roads from Rochester to Greece. **1848** in 1882 MI *Laws Genl. Statutes* 1.914, All corporations hereafter created for the purpose of constructing plank roads, shall be subject to the provisions hereinafter contained. **1850** in 1927 Jones *FL Plantation Rec.* 61 nwFL, The subscribers to stock for a plank road have met and formed a company to be called the "Florida and Georgia" "Plank Road Company." **1865** (1922) Jackson *Col.'s Diary* 195 PA, Shortly after midnight we struck an old plank road. **1906** *DN* 3.151 nwAR, *Plank-road.* . . A road in a swampy district made by laying planks horizontally after the fashion of corduroy roads. **1942** McAtee *Dial. Grant Co. IN* 77 (as of 1890s), *Plank road* . . a road of heavy oak planks, the ends of which were fastened to sills; at first an improvement over corduroy, they caused endless trouble as they got out of repair and proved impractical. **1956** McAtee *Some*

Dialect NC 33, *Plank road* . . a road covered with planks, which retained the name after the planks had worn out and disappeared. **1958** McCulloch *Woods Words* 136 Pacific NW, *Plank road*—A wooden truck road, varying from makeshift planks thrown on the ground to costly decked roads built almost to railroad standard. **1965–70** *DARE* (Qu. N27a, *Names . . for different kinds of unpaved roads*) Infs NY2, WA19, WI48, Plank road; IL4, Plank road—used to be many here; IL46, Plank road—used to have them in wet land; none anymore, but still call them plank roads even though they're now macadam; IN3, Plank road—used to be one from Corydon to Salem; IN19, Plank road—same as corduroy road; MI49, Plank road—old-fashioned; NJ56, Plank road—just oak planks laid down. [7 of 9 Infs old] **1968** *DARE* Tape MI96, It was a plank road in the first place. Planks on the west side and the sand road on the other, and you went downhill on the sand road and uphill on the plank road. **1969** Sorden *Lumberjack Lingo* 88 **NEng, Gt Lakes,** *Plank roads*—Roads around the sawmill and near towns and cities or between towns. Made from rough-sawed heavy lumber of inferior species. **1986** Pederson *LAGS Concordance,* 1 inf, ceTX, Plank road—in Civil War times; 1 inf, neLA, A plank road.

plank-stretcher See **stretcher**

planned-overs n pl

Intentional leftovers.

1968 *DARE* (Qu. H67, *Food that was not finished at one meal but saved for another*) Inf WI47, Planned-overs—if thought through beforehand. **2000** *DARE* File csWI, A friend intentionally makes more than enough food for a meal, calling the leftovers "planned-overs." She thinks she learned the term in Minnesota.

plannuhtation See **plantation**

plant v

1 To bury (a dead person); hence n *planting* a burial; n *planting ground* and varr, a cemetery. *joc* or *euphem*

[**1855** *Harper's New Mth. Mag.* 12.37, Let it [=yellow fever] catch hold of a crowd of 'Johnny come latelys,' and it plants them at once.] **1897** *KS Univ. Qrly.* (ser B) 6.90, *Plant:* bury.—General. **1898** Canfield *Maid of Frontier* 186 TX, They planted Chisolm in the little cemetery. **1913** Kephart *Highlanders* 78 sAppalachians, I disremember which buryin'-ground they-all planted ye in. **1936** *AmSp* 11.199 [Euphemisms for dying], Planted. (Pioneers' slang.) *Ibid* 201 [Euphemisms for the funeral], Planting. *Ibid* [Euphemisms for the coffin], Planting crate. **1949** Emrich *Wild West Custom* 170 **West,** The Westerner rarely "died." Nor was the problem of death a matter about which he talked other than casually. . . The funeral service was a *send-off* and the burial itself a *planting.* **1966–70** *DARE* (Qu. BB56, *Joking expressions for dying: "He _____."*) Inf MI96, They planted him in the city of death; (Qu. BB61b, . . *Joking names for a cemetery*) Infs FL51, PA175, SC21, VT16, VA13, Planting ground(s); NY123, Planting spot; OR6, Where you plant a stiff. **2001** *DARE* File csWI (as of early 1970s), When we were in junior high, a friend of mine used to horrify his mother by answering their home phone as follows: "John's Mortuary—you plug 'em, we plant 'em."

2 To stock (a body of water) with fish; to put (fish) in a body of water; hence vbl n *planting;* n *planter* a fish so introduced. **esp West**

1871 PA *Laws Laws Genl. Assembly* 276, Fishes planted and retained in private ponds shall be at the disposal of their owners. **1945** *Jefferson Co. Republican* (Golden, Colo.) 2 May 1/5 *(DA),* Clear Creek, in the Golden region, is on our schedule for planting trout this year. **1966** *Pullman News–Rev.* (WA) 2 Nov 5/1, Idaho's general trout season closed Sunday. . . Even thought [sic] the fish were all "planters," don't think we've ever seen a little pond that produced like Spring Valley [R]eservoir. **1970** *DARE* Tape CA181, [FW:] Is there any fishing in this area: [Inf:] Only on rare occasions. They do plant the stream up above the park. **1998** *DARE* File NV, In Nevada, they plant fish rather than stocking them. **2000** *Ibid* swID, The people who put new fish in the water I would say are planting the fish. That's the word that first comes to mind. If I reflect upon it a bit, I would use the synonym "stocking." . . Black Lake had been planted with trout and grayling. . . When a planted (or stocked) fish has been caught . . the fisherman may say, "I caught this big planter." . . He would not say, "I caught this big stocker." *Ibid* ceNY (as of 1950s–60s), Most of the Brook Trout we caught in High Falls Creek were planted fish. There was a big program to stock fish in the mountain creeks.

3 To place (shellfish, or material for shellfish to grow on) in artificial beds; hence vbl n *planting;* n *plant* a shellfish so placed.   **esp N and C Atl coast**

1870 *Scribner's Mth.* 1.58, He went on for a while, calculating silently how many oysters would be needed for planting. **1884** U.S. Natl. Museum *Bulletin* 27.224 **CT**, More attention is given to "planting" shells and other suitable cultch than in Rhode Island. *Ibid* 226 **DE**, Citizens of the State alone are permitted to "plant" oysters. . . The natural beds are worked continuously for "seed," but the majority of the "planted" oysters come from the Chesapeake. **1899** (1912) Green *VA Folk-Speech* 325, *Plants*. . . Oysters that have been taken from the rocks and planted to grow and fatten. **1949** *Fishing Gaz.* Aug. 80 *(DA),* The clams were seeded over 15 acres in the Maquoit Middle Bay section to make the first time that shellfish planting has been done in this country from a plane. **1968** *DARE* Tape **MD**37, You take your shells that you shuck the oysters out of, and they're rolled out onto a pile. The state comes and gets 'em and hauls 'em away. Those shells are replanted. . . Those shells do have to be planted so that spat will form by way of nature or whatever is in the water and more oysters will grow in years to come. **1976** Ryland *Richmond Co. VA* 375, *Plants*—oysters taken from rocks and planted to grow elsewhere.

plantain n

Std: a plant of the genus *Plantago*.   Also called **fleaseed, Indian plantago, ribgrass, ribwort.**   For other names of var spp see **buckhorn plantain, devil's shoestring 15, dooryard plantain, goose tongue, ~ greens, healing herb 2, hen plant, hog-ear leaf, Indian wheat 3, liar weed, monkey tail, pig ears 2, rabbit plantain, tallowweed, whiteman's foot** Cf **Doctor Walker**

plantation n Usu |ˌplænˈte(ɪ)šən|; also **chiefly Gulf States** |ˌplæntˈe(ɪ)šən| Pronc-spp *plan'ation, plannuhtation*

A Forms.

1906 *DN* 3.151 **nwAR**, *Plant-ation (t* being distinctly pronounced with the first syllable). **1953** Brewer *Word Brazos* 11 **eTX** [Black], He runned off from de plannuhtation time an' time again. **1966** *DARE* Tape **MS**78, This is a plantation [ˌplæ·ntˈeɪšən] desk. **1968** *DARE* FW Addit **cLA**, Plantation—[ˌplætˈeɪšən] competes with [ˌplænˈteɪšən]; **neLA**, [ˌplætˈeɪšn]. **1984** Wilder *You All Spoken Here* 82 **Sth**, *Plan'ation fare:* Chicken every Sunday. **1993** *DARE* File **ceAL**, I was surprised to hear people from Anniston say [ˌplæntˈešən] rather than [ˌplænˈtešən]. **2000** *DARE* File **Gulf States**, On the radio I heard someone from Mississippi or Alabama talking about [ˌplæntˈešənz].

B Senses.

1 Orig a settlement; now an administrative unit of local government.   **NEng, esp ME**

1636 in 1850 CT (Colony) *Pub. Rec.* 1.2 **MA**, Geo. Hubberd shall [survey] the breadth of the plantaçon of Dorchester. **1780** in 1950 *AmSp* 25.21 **MA**, The plantation meetings for that purpose shall be held annually on the first Monday in April. **1832** Williamson *Hist. ME* 1.53, The *Sagadahock plantations,* or settlements, must be called the "Ancient Dominions" of Maine. **1891** *AN&Q* 6.264, When the Maine township becomes settled, it receives a name, and organizes a local "plantation" government of a simple kind and with limited powers. . . There are, however, some named plantations which have gone back in population and now have no local government. **1945** *Natl. Geogr. Mag.* Sept 289, Some of the islands are "plantations." This term goes back to colonial times, but means in Maine today a minor civil division or unit of local government having a status between that of an organized township and an incorporated town. **1946** Attwood *Length ME* 15 [Geographical terms], *Plantation*—A civil division of the State of one of the three following classes: One having, in effect, the same form of government as a town; one organized for tax purposes only; one which is unorganized, taxes being assessed and collected by the State. **1966** *Bar Harbor Times* (ME) 9 June 7/6, Willard Roscoe Fletcher, 68, of Plantation 8 died Friday at a Bangor hospital after a brief illness. **1966** *DARE* Tape **ME**1, [FW:] Allagash is a plantation . . what's a plantation? [Inf:] Well, there's people all settled down . . every town meeting they collect the taxes on every person that pays a tax, but they never made a town of it, . . so they left it just a plantation. We don't get no help from the state, but we get help from the landlords. They pay all the taxes in here. . . So that gives us money enough to run our schools and build our roads and bridges and stuff. **1966** *DARE* FW Addit **ME**, *Plantation*—an unorganized township (Garfield Plantation, Nashville Plantation, etc). **1995**

ME Atlas & Gaz. 4, *Legend of Abbreviations and Land Grant Designations—Plt*—Plantation; *Twp*—Township.

2 A foot, esp a large one.

1907 *DN* 3.196 **seNH**, *Plantations.* . . Feet. Jocose. "Get your old plantations out of the way." **1909** *DN* 3.421 **Cape Cod MA** (as of a1857), *Plantations.* . . Feet. "Get your great plantations off." **1931** (1991) Hughes–Hurston *Mule Bone* 94 **cFL** [Black], Well. . . you can just lift your big plantations out of my shoes. You can just foot it home barefooted. **1967–68** *DARE* (Qu. X38, *Joking names for unusually big or clumsy feet*) Infs **LA**25, **NJ**1, Plantations.

‡plantation biscuit n

1967 *DARE* FW Addit **SC**19, *Plantation biscuit*—a big biscuit with a hole punched in it to hold syrup—hole made in the side.

plantation dog n

A watchdog.

1803 Davis *Travels* 392 **VA**, His son, repugnant to my express commands, has brought his father's two plantation dogs to the Academy. **1839** *S. Lit. Messenger* 5.377 **seGA**, Tommy King . . followed by several lean, plantation dogs, brought up the rear. **1853** Stowe *Key Uncle Tom* 186, The leaders of the community . . keep this blind, furious monster . . very much as an overseer keeps plantation-dogs, as creatures to be set on to any man or thing whom they may choose to have put down. **1858** (1859) Presbury *Mustee* 279 **sLA**, Bill shouted "It's a start!" When the plantation dogs were let loose, and taking the scent, they followed with full voice. **1970** *Foxfire* 4.13 **nGA**, The mountain people kept several different kinds of dogs around their homes. Many had at least one "plantation dog" whose whole job was to keep the hogs and cows out of the corn.

plantation match n Cf **farmer match**

A wooden match that can be struck on any rough surface.

1970 *DARE* (Qu. F46, *. . Matches you can strike anywhere;* not asked in early QRs) Infs **NC**88, **SC**70, Plantation matches. [Both Infs Black]

plant corn afore the fence is built See **plant one's corn before one builds the fence**

planter n

1 A tree or branch lodged rigidly in a river bed and constituting a hazard to navigation.   **esp Missip-Ohio Valleys** Cf **sawyer 4**

1802 (1803) Ellicott *Jrl.* 123 **Missip Valley**, From the mouth of the Ohio, down to the Walnut Hills, it is not safe to descend the river in the night . . on account of the sawyers and planters. . . The latter are more dangerous, being firmly fixed or planted in the bottom. **1843** (1916) Hall *New Purchase* 43 **Ohio Valley**, A *planter* is the trunk of a tree, perpendicular or inclined, with one end fixed or planted immoveable in the bottom of the river, and the other above or below the surface, according to the state of the water. **1884** *Harper's New Mth. Mag.* 69.125 **Missip-Ohio Valleys**, Their talk was of the dangers of the river; of "planters and sawyers," meaning tree trunks imbedded more or less firmly in the river. **1953** (1977) Hubbard *Shantyboat* 268 **Missip-Ohio Valleys**, Some of the trees were leaning, and disappeared under the surface and rose above it with a slow rhythm as if worked by a giant machine. These are called sawyers; the stationary ones are called planters. **1985** Madson *Up River* 45 **Upper Missip Valley**, There were the "planters," whole trees that had become solidly embedded in the river bottom and anchored there with tons of silt.

2 See **plant 2.**

planter bird See **planting bird**

‡planter's nose n

1967 *DARE* (Qu. X15, *. . Kinds of noses, according to shape or size)* Inf **OR**1, Planter's nose—humped.

planting vbl n See **plant 2, 3**

planting n See **plant 1**

planting bird n Also *planter bird* [See quots]
=**brown thrasher.**

1925 (1928) Forbush *Birds MA* 3.329, He [=the thrasher] pays little attention, however, to the plowman or the busy farmer, for at planting time he sits nearby on some tree-top and sings—at least so the country people say—"drop it, drop it, cover it, cover it, I'll pull it up, I'll pull it up," and so some of the country people call the singer the "Planting Bird." **1936** Roberts *MN Birds* 2.109 (as of 1885), Forbush says, in his *Useful Birds,* that the Thrasher is known in some parts of New England as the "Planting Bird," and Prof. F.L. Washburn states that while on a trip to Mille Lacs in 1885, he encountered a farmer who used the same name for it. **1950** *WELS* (Brown thrasher) 1 Inf, **swWI,** Planter bird. **1967** *DARE* (Qu. Q14, . . *Names . . for . . brown thrasher*) Inf **MA5,** Planting bird. Song: "Pick it up, pick it up; quick, quick, quick; plant it, plant it." **1968** *DARE* File c**MA,** One day I heard a brown thrasher singing so beautifully I called Grandma Pierce [born c1830] to hear it, and she exclaimed, "Why, that's a planting bird, the farmers always used to say he told them, 'Drop it, drop it, cover it up, quick, quick, quick.'"

planting ground See **plant 1**

plant one's corn before one builds the fence v phr For varr see quots **Sth, S Midl** *euphem*
Of a couple: to conceive a child before getting married.

1935 Sheppard *Cabins* 172 **NC,** Perhaps he overpersuades her and they "plant their corn before they build their fence." **1947** (1964) Randolph *Ozark Superstitions* 202, "Caint fool me," said one old woman. "Them young-uns planted their corn 'bout six weeks 'fore they built their fences. I *seen* fingernails on that baby!" **1970** *DARE* (Qu. AA20, *A marriage that takes place because a baby is on the way*) Inf **TX103,** They planted the corn before they built the fence. **1982** Slone *How We Talked* 9 e**KY** (as of c1950), "Planting the crop before building the fence"—getting pregnant before getting married, yet getting married before the baby is born. **1984** Wilder *You All Spoken Here* 98 **Sth,** They planted corn a-fore the fence was built: They had a baby in progress before they married.

plarine See **praline**

plash n, hence adj *plashy* [OED2 963 →]
A shallow, stagnant pool.

1709 in 1940 *AmSp* 15.295 **VA,** Along the said Path to the Plash. **1790** *Ibid,* To a Gum in the head of a Plash. **1853** *Putnam's Mag.* 2.465 **MA,** Their camp was near, and our two hunters set out for it, leaving us seated in the birch on the plashy border of the pond. **1899** (1912) Green *VA Folk-Speech* 325, *Plashy. .* . Watery; full of puddles; wet. **1909** *DN* 3.421 **Cape Cod MA** (as of a1857), *Plashes. .* . A swampy place in the town of Dennis is called The Plashes. **1930** Shoemaker *1300 Words* 45 c**PA Mts** (as of c1900), *Plash*—A dead water, or pool in a mountain stream.

plaster See **shin plaster**

plastered adj **widespread, but less freq W Midl, West** See Map
Drunk, intoxicated.

1912 *DN* 3.585 w**IN,** Plastered. . . Very drunk. **1928** *AmSp* 4.102 [Slang synonyms for "drunk"], Plastered. **1929** *AmSp* 5.128 **ME,** An intoxicated man was "pickled" or "plastered" (the latter also referred to venereal disease). **1931** *AmSp* 7.88 [Prohibition terms], Terms referring to the state of intoxication. . . Plastered. **1932** *AmSp* 7.335 [Johns Hopkins jargon], *Plastered*—intoxicated. **1965–70** *DARE* (Qu. DD15, *A person who is thoroughly drunk*) 120 Infs, **chiefly Nth, N Midl,** Plastered [Of all Infs responding to the question, 65% were old, 10% young; of those giving this response, 56% were old, 17% young.]; (Qu. N13, *If*

someone has been drinking and then drives a car, he may be arrested for _____) Inf **PA163,** Being plastered; (Qu. DD12, . . *A person who drinks steadily or a great deal*) Inf **MI44,** Plastered all the time; (Qu. DD13, *When a drinker is just beginning to show the effects of the liquor . . he's* _____) Infs **GA82, NY76,** Getting plastered; (Qu. DD14, *When a person is partly drunk, "He's* _____.") Inf **NY122,** Partly plastered. **1966** Barnes–Jensen *Dict. UT Slang* 23, He's plastered . . drunk. **1977** Adams *Lang. Railroader* 115, *Plastered:* Drunk.

plat v See **plait** v

plat n See **plait** n

plate cake See **plate pie**

plate meat n Also *side-plate meat* Cf **fat meat** =**side meat.**

1966 *DARE* (Qu. H38, *Other words for bacon*) Inf **AL24,** Fat meat or plate meat—if mostly fat. **1986** Pederson *LAGS Concordance (Salt pork)* 1 inf, **swMS,** Plate meat—old name [for] fat salt meat; *(A side [of] bacon])* 1 inf, **swMS,** Side-plate meat.

plate pie n Also *plate cake* Cf **deep-dish pie**
A shallow pie.

1939 Wolcott *Yankee Cook Book* 192 **NH,** New Hampshire "Plate Cake"—Fill a pie tin with any fresh fruit. . . Sprinkle with sugar. Cover with a biscuit crust. . . Bake. . . Loosen the crust around the edge, invert the dish and serve upside down. **1966** *Good Old Days* Apr 2 nw**TX** (as of 1918–23), I can't remember ever serving plate pies to the threshing crew. It would take too many. We made huge cobblers using gallon cans of fruit. **1966** *DARE* FW Addit **SC,** *Plate pie*—a round, thin one with dough in bottom—as opposed to a cobbler, which is 2–3 inches deep. **1967** *DARE* Tape **TX32,** I like to fix a couple vegetables, and some meat, and something for dessert. Maybe it might be a cobbler or a plate pie. **1986** Pederson *LAGS Concordance ([Apple] cobbler/baked in a deep dish)* 2 infs, **AL,** (A) plate pie; 1 inf, ce**TX,** Plate pies.

plat-eye n Also sp *platt-eye* [Etym unknown] **SC** *among Black speakers*
A hobgoblin; hence n *platt-eye prowl* the time of night when it is said to roam.

1908 *S. Atl. Qrly.* 7.342 [Gullah], [Terms for times of day include] *platt-eye prowl.* [Footnote:] Presumably midnight, when graves give up their dead and the spirits of the damned howl abroad . . : . . platt-eyes [are] diabolical spirits of the mist. **1928** Peterkin *Scarlet Sister Mary* 278 **SC** [Black], A ghost must be walking around under the house. . . Maybe a plat-eye was outside, screech owls and whippoorwills had both been crying. She had put the shovel in the fire to stop them. **1930** Woofter *Black Yeomanry* 54 se**SC,** African words which are more or less confined to the low country are *buckra* . . and *plat-eye* (a ghost). **1941** Writers' Program SC *Folk Tales* 52 [Gullah], Den yuh go out an kill one ob yuh enemy an cut he haid off. Yuh bury dat haid in de hole w'en yuh bury de treasure. After dat, ef anybody come sarchin' round, uh plat-eye rise out ob de hole an scare de pusson off. Plat-eye tek all kind ob form—hunchback hog, fibe foot cow, double-haid dog an sech. **1941** Writers' Program *Guide SC* 169 cs**SC** [Black], Strange folklore and folk customs persist; the last articles used by the deceased are placed on his grave and never disturbed for fear of 'plat-eye.' **1966–67** *DARE* (Qu. CC16, *A small light that seems to dance or flicker over a marsh or swamp at night*) Inf **SC5,** Plat-eye. Negro—their window and door frames are painted blue to keep him away; (Qu. EE41, *A hobgoblin that is used to threaten children and make them behave*) Inf **SC44,** Plat-eye—darky superstition. **1984** Joyner *Down by Riverside* 150 **SC coast** (as of a1866), Hags, haunts, and plat-eyes—malevolent, shape-changing spirits—persisted in a parallel stream of belief. *Ibid* 152, Perhaps the most hideous and most malevolent of the occult creatures of this stream of African cosmology was the plat-eye, a malign spirit that took various shapes in order to lure its victims into danger and rob them of their wits.

platform n Cf **plantation B2**
A large foot.

1968–69 *DARE* (Qu. X38, *Joking names for unusually big or clumsy feet*) Inf **MO20,** Platform; **TN24,** Platforms [laughter].

platform wagon n
An unenclosed four-wheeled horse-drawn vehicle with an elevated decklike flooring on which freight or passengers are carried.

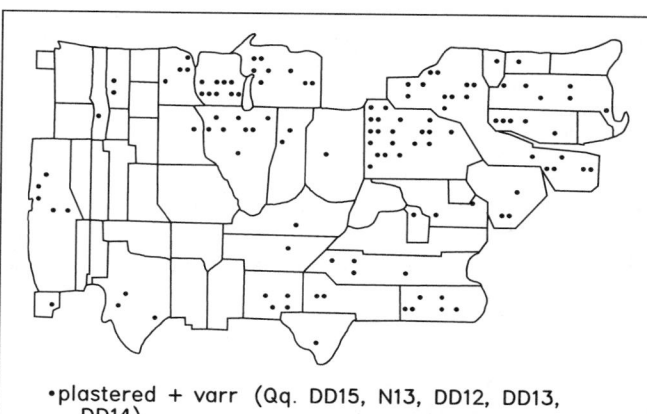

•plastered + varr (Qq. DD15, N13, DD12, DD13, DD14)

1865 (1866) Barnum *Humbugs* 40, A band of music preceded a procession of animal-cages . . ; Old Adams . . heading the line, with a platform wagon on which were placed three immense grizzly bears. 1876 McCracken *Michigan* 168, A pyramidal platform wagon carried representatives of all the states in the union. 1902 (1969) Sears *Catalogue* 376, *Our $35.95 combination platform spring wagon. . . $59.60 heavy three-seat full platform wagon. . .* We have a large demand for these wagons among liverymen, who use it for carrying six or more passengers, or for carrying one or two passengers with several trunks or sample cases. It is also used very largely in the far West. 1948 Rittenhouse *Amer. Horse-Drawn Vehicles* 15, Side-seated Platform Wagon. Used by hotels and resorts to convey guests from railroad "depots." Also frequently used at funerals. Body was 9 by 3 feet. . . It was equipped with . . removable seats. *Ibid* 19, Three-Seat Platform Wagon. A vehicle used chiefly in rural districts, where it was often "hired out" by livery stables. It had . . a body nine feet long by three feet wide. Also made 10 ½ feet long, with four seats. 1967–69 *DARE* (Qu. N41a, . . *Horse-drawn vehicles . . to carry people*) Inf NY224, Platform wagon; (Qu. N41b, *Horse-drawn vehicles to carry heavy loads*) Infs NY24, 209, OH56, Platform wagon; (Qu. N41c, *Horse-drawn vehicles to carry light loads*) Infs NJ1, NY148, 224, Platform wagon; [(Qu. L57, *A low wooden platform used for bringing stones or heavy things out of the fields*) Inf IL59, Platform wagon? Stone boat [FW sugg]—yeah, that's the proper name].

platted See **plait** v

platter-leaf n
A **sea grape** (here: *Coccoloba uvifera*).
1933 Small *Manual SE Flora* 461, *C[occoloba] uvifera. . . Platter-leaf.* 1953 Greene–Blomquist *Flowers South* 28, Sea-Grape, . . Platter-Leaf (*Coccoloba uvifera*). . . The reddish, berry-like fruits . . are edible and used for jelly when enough remain after certain crabs come up from the ocean at night and devour them.

platter stool n Cf **footstool 2**
1967 *DARE* FW Addit LA10, Platter stool—a large toadstool; mainly used by younger people.

platt-eye See **plat-eye**

platting See **plait** v

play n
1a rarely *play-game:* A game, esp an active or dance-like game; a party devoted to such games. Cf **play-party**, **play song**
1841–44 Emerson *Ess., Experience* Wks. (Bohn) I.178 (*OED2*), The plays of children are nonsense, but very educative nonsense. 1850 in 1934 Frear *Lowell & Abigail* 200 MA, We went into town . . to Mrs. John Ladd's and drank tea and passed the evening. We enjoyed it very much. Eddy and I had a grand play. 1890 (1972) Howells *Boy's Town* 84 sOH, The other plays which involved running, like . . tag. 1899 (1912) Green *VA Folk-Speech* 325, Play-game. . . Sport; child's play; a play of children. 1922 Talley *Negro Folk Rhymes* 262, Since the Play [=Goosie-gander] has probably passed from the memory of most persons, I shall tell how it was played. 1937 in 1996 *Montgomery Coll.* eTN, An evening devoted to party-games was called a "play". . . The fun began when the two oldest women of the group requested leadership of the first "play." 1972 Jones–Hawes *Step it Down* xii GA [Black], I remember a hundred games, I suppose. . . We had all kinds of plays; we had house plays, we had outdoor plays. Some of the plays have songs, some have just plays—you know, just acts or whatnot. *Ibid* xiv, I discovered that Mrs. Jones did indeed use the nouns "play," "game," and "dance" to refer to different items in her repertoire. . . She referred to abstract (nonmimetic) movement patterns, especially when performed by couples, as "dances." . . The term "game" she reserved not exactly for competitive but rather for conditional sequences of actions. . . By far the bulk of her repertoire, however, she called "plays."
b in comb *ring play;* Spec: a circle game with singing and dance-like motions. *among Black speakers*
1937 (1977) Hurston *Their Eyes* 22 FL [Black], So she would pick at me all de time and put some others up tuh do de same. They'd push me 'way from de ring plays and make out they couldn't play wid nobody dat lived on the premises. 1942 (1965) Parrish *Slave Songs* 13 GA coast, There are also the ring-play dances, which appear to be a combination of African play songs and the old English play-party or ring

games. *Ibid* 93, Of the ring-play, dance, and fiddle songs, only those accompanying ring-play were countenanced by the church. 1959 Lomax *Rainbow Sign* 125 LA [Black], On Saturday evenings we had old-time square dances and what we called "ring plays." They'd be skippin and goin round and round, something like you see children do now on the school ground. They'd turn you out of church for dancin, but they didn't bother us about ring plays. 1966 *DARE* (Qu. EE1, *What games do children play around here in which they form a ring, and either sing or recite a rhyme*) Inf FL2, Ring plays. [Inf Black] 1972 Jones–Hawes *Step it Down* 88 GA [Black], The "ring play," as the term is used here, consists of a group standing in a circle, clapping, singing, and musically supporting a single central character who acts out his own brief drama on center stage, as it were, before he chooses another to take his place. 1986 Pederson *LAGS Concordance,* 1 inf, **cnGA**, Played ring plays. [Inf Black]
2 =**play-party**.
1916 *DN* 4.347 TX (as of 1896), *Play. . .* Entertainment (without dancing); 'sociable.' 1930 *DN* 6.83 cSC, *Play. . .* A party in a private house, with dancing. A negro and po' buckra word. 1941 *Jrl. Amer. Folkl.* 54.68 eTN, An evening devoted to party-games was called a "play" on Cosby Creek, Cocke County, Tennessee. . . The games played upon that occasion were known by the names: "Disease and Cure," [etc]. . . No games were played in which singing or dance-forms were featured. 1955 Ritchie *Singing Family* 119 **seKY**, I got some [=songs] from other singers too, and pretty soon folks began asking me to plays just on account of that. 1974 Fink *Mountain Speech* 19 wNC, eTN, *Play . .* square dance. 1976 Garber *Mountain-ese* 69 sAppalachians, *Play . .* jamboree, party—I took Lucy to the play in town.

play v Cf **play** n **1**, **play-party**, **play song**
To engage in dancing or a dance-like game; hence vbl n *playing games* dancing.
1917 Campbell–Sharp *Engl. Folk Songs* xv sAppalachians, I have no doubt that religious scruples have also been a contributory cause [of the decadence of dancing]—I noticed that in reply to my enquiries on this subject the euphemism "playing games" was always substituted for "dancing" by my informants. 1934 Carmer *Stars Fell on AL* 47, "Come on 'nd play, perfesser. You know how to play." . . "Ain't what she means play," said Henry. "She means dance with her." 1967 *DARE* Tape OH6, They didn't call it dancing, really, they just called it playing games, but that's what it was. 1972 Jones–Hawes *Step it Down* 143 GA [Black], No, the ring plays are not exactly like the ring shouts, because you are *playing. . .* Some ring plays seem just like a shout in some ways but they are plays. . . You see, if you're going to play, you *play,* and if you're going to shout, you *shout.*

play adj *esp freq among Black speakers*
Pretend, surrogate—used in combs denoting quasi-familial relationships; see quots.
1969 *DARE* File **St. Louis MO** [Black], A play daughter or play son is a child that someone who has financial means looks after and helps take care of. The child is not adopted and it is not a foster child. The people who have a play daughter or son take them to movies, ball games, etc; buy them clothes, have them for dinner, etc. They more or less provide things the children's own parents cannot afford. This may be a ghetto term. 1986 Pederson *LAGS Concordance* (Surrogate parent) 6 infs, **AL, FL, GA, TN, TX**, Play daddy; 1 inf, **swAL**, Play daddy—heard in early childhood; 1 inf, **ceTX**, Play daddy—not as old as real father; 4 infs, **AL, LA, MS**, Play father; 1 inf, **cnGA**, Play father—less formal role; 1 inf, **cnGA**, Play father—adult friendly to children; 7 infs, **AL, AR, LA, TN**, Play mother; 1 inf, **ceTX**, Play mother—friend of her mother; 1 inf, **csTX**, Play mother—an adult who is close to the child; 1 inf, **seFL**, Play mothers; 6 infs, **FL, GA, TX**, Play mamma; 1 inf, **swAL**, Play mamma—when you're coming up young; 1 inf, **cAR**, Play mamma—could be mother's close friend; 1 inf, **nwFL**, Play mamma—heard on television; 1 inf, **cnGA**, Play mamma—adult friendly to children; 1 inf, **ceTX**, Play mamma—someone older who likes you as [a] child; 1 inf, **cAR**, Play sister; 1 inf, **ceTX**, Play daughter—adopted by senior girls in college; (Best friend) 1 inf, **cnGA**, Play brother; 1 inf, **cnGA**, Play sister; 1 inf, **ceTX**, Play sister—has heard among Blacks. [All but 1 inf Black]

playa n Also *playa lake* [Span *playa* a beach] **West, esp SW**
A dried-up lake or lagoon.
1851 (1854) Bartlett *Personal Narr.* 1.246, The playas . . seemed to have an extent of twenty-five or thirty miles. 1856 (1928) Jaeger *Diary Fort Yuma* 124 sCA, Then pushed on to the playa . . arrived at 1½

o'clock at the playas. **1892** *DN* 1.193 **TX**, *Pláya:* properly a beach. In Texas the dried-up bed of some shallow lake or lagoon. **1932** *DN* 6.232 **West**, *Playa.* A salt lake which has gone dry, leaving a level bit of territory, generally encrusted with salt. As such places exist only here and there in the West, the word is not widely used; but it may be heard in California, Nevada, and Utah. **1933** *AmSp* 8.3.9 **SW**, For the flattened roundish space at the bottom of a shallow dip where the runoff of the rain collects and shortly dries, the term *playa* (beach) is used. **1944** (1967) McNichols *Crazy Weather* 82 **SW**, They slept that night in the middle of a little playa at the far end of the Snake lagoon. **1946** Waters *Colorado* 95, Large alluvial fans gracefully spread out at the mouth of cañons and vast dry lake beds called playas record one effort, as equally vast lava flows, numerous cinder cones and sharp volcanic picachos attest another. **2000** *DARE* File **nTX**, *Playa lake* in [the] Texas panhandle is a temporary lake.

play-diddle n

A piece of playground equipment.

1991 Still *Wolfpen Notebooks* 47 **sAppalachians**, The trouble with the schools nowadays is they got all them play-diddles in the yard. Young'uns can't think about their text books for wanting to get to the swings and ridey-horses.

play-dolly See **play-toy**

play ducks and drakes with See **ducks and drakes 2**

play-game See **play** n **1a**

playing games See **play** v

play in the family v phr

=*play the dozens* (at **dozen** n **B1**).

1942 Hurston *Dust Tracks* 195 **FL** [Black], If you are sufficiently armed . . it is all right to go to the house of your enemy, put one foot on his steps, rest one elbow on your knee and play in the family. That is another way of saying play the dozens, which also is a way of saying low-rate your enemy's ancestors and him.

play like v phr Pronc-spp *pike, plaik, playk, plike* **chiefly Sth, S Midl, TX** See Map Cf **make like**

To pretend; to play in imitation of.

1916 in 1944 *ADD* **OK**, *Play like* [paɪk]. 'Let's pike we're Indians.' **1927** Ruppenthal *Coll.* **KS**, *Let's plaik* or *playk* (let us play like). . . Pron[ounced] nearly plike—child's term. . . Let's playk we're actors. **1928** *Ibid* **KS**, *To play like*. . . We'll play like circus. They play like herding cattle. **1942** McAtee *Dial. Grant Co. IN* 49 (as of 1890s), *Play like* . . pretend, let on. **1944** *PADS* 2.11 **AL, SC**, *Play like* ['pleˈlaɪk, plaɪk]. . . A child's word. To play. ((To pretend.)) Used of imaginative games without rules. "Let's play like we're Indians." **1949** *PADS* 11.24 **CO**, *Play like*. . . To pretend. "The children play like they are giants." **1954** Harder *Coll.* **swTN**, *Play like*. . . To pretend. **1956** McAtee *Some Dialect NC* 33, Play like we don't see them. **1965–70** *DARE* (Qu. JJ46, *. . To pretend: "Let's _____ we don't know a thing about it."*) 132 Infs, **chiefly Sth, S Midl, TX**, Play like; **LA**12, 17, Plike; (Qu. BB27, *When somebody pretends to be sick*) Inf **MS**1, Play like. **1968** *DARE* FW Addit **LA**, *Plike* = "play like," telescoped; to pretend. Common among children; also used playfully by adults. **1984** Head *Brogans* 116 **eKY, eTN**, Other terms [used here] are . . "play like" for pretend; . . etc.

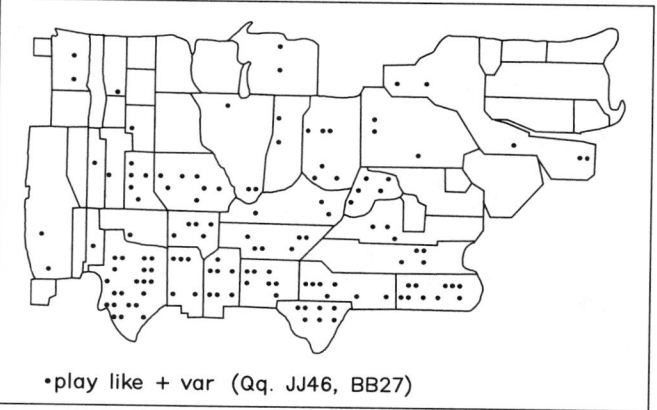

•play like + var (Qq. JJ46, BB27)

playment n Cf **-ment B**

1936 *AmSp* 11.316 **Ozarks**, *Playment*. . . A toy, a plaything. The word *play-purty* is also common.

play off v phr

1 To shirk responsibility; esp, to evade work; to absent oneself or escape (from some responsibility) without adequate excuse—often used in phr *play off sick* to do this on the pretext of illness. **esp Midl, Sth** See Map

1783 (1922) U.S. Continental Congress *Jrls.* 25.886, She [=the state of Virginia] had paid the paltry sum only of 35,000 Drs. and was notwithstanding endeavouring to play off from further contributions. **1836** Howard *Hist. Virgil A. Stewart* 140 **GA**, I stay mostly in the neighbourhood of Commerce at present, and sometimes work, to prevent being suspected, I play off occasionally. **1870** [see **shavetail** n **2**]. **1935** Hurston *Mules & Men* 154 **FL**, 'Tain't a thing de matter wid him. He's jus' playin' off sick. **1945** FWP *Lay My Burden Down* 72 **GA** (as of 1860s) [Black], Howsomever, it was hard sometimes to get her to believe you sick when you tell her that you was, and she would think you just playing off from work. **1950** *WELS* (*When someone is pretending to be sick [usually to get out of doing something] you might say: "He is _____."*) 2 Infs, **WI**, Playing off. **1965–70** *DARE* (Qu. BB27) 60 Infs, **chiefly Midl, Sth**, Playing off; **GA**8, **IL**118, **KY**11, **MD**37, **NY**8, **PA**164, **TN**37, Playing off sick; **IA**11, Playing off on you; **MA**69, Playing it off; **TX**51, Played off; (Qu. BB41, *Not seriously ill, but sick enough to be in bed: "He's been _____ for a week."*) Inf **IA**11, Playing off; (Qu. JJ6, *To stay away from school without an excuse*) Inf **TX**32, Play off. [57 of 70 Infs old]

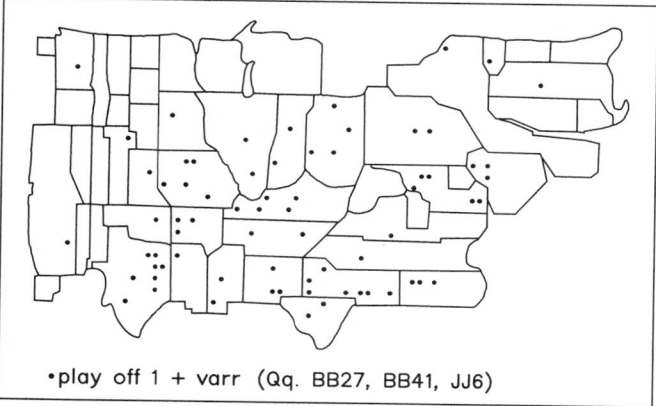

•play off 1 + varr (Qq. BB27, BB41, JJ6)

2 with *on:* To deceive, fool, or trick.

1863 in 1903 Norton *Army Letters* 135 **PA**, If I did want one [=a discharge], I fancy . . I could play off on the doctors and get it. **1865** (1922) Jackson *Col.'s Diary* 194 **PA**, I did not enlighten her that some fellow had played off on them. **1939** Hall *Coll.* **wNC**, Me and Mark Cathey we played off on 'em. We let them go and we took up Nettle Creek. **1942** McAtee *Dial. Grant Co. IN* 49 (as of 1890s), *Play off on* . . go back on a promise, disappoint; "Don't you _____ me." **c1960** Wilson *Coll.* **csKY**, *Play off on*. . . To deceive. **1967** *DARE* (Qu. BB27, *When somebody pretends to be sick . . he's _____*) Inf **IA**11, Playing off on you.

play off sick See **play off 1**

play-party n chiefly W Midl, TX See Map on p. 208 Cf **kitchen game**

A party featuring lively games, dancing, or quasi-dancing, usu without instrumental music.

1889 *Harper's New Mth. Mag.* 79.127 **S Midl**, At every chance meeting at "play party," "meetin'," or spelling match, there had come to them . . a strong mutual consciousness that was in itself complete assurance of each other's constancy. **1893** (1958) Wister *Out West* 151, Many families here are so religious that they cannot possibly dance. But they have assemblings of young men and maidens that are called Play Parties. At these a song is sung, quite harmless throughout. **1902** *DN* 2.241 **sIL**, *Play-party*. . . A party at which old-fashioned games are played. **1905** *DN* 3.91 **nwAR**, *Play-party*. . . A party at which games are played. **1913** Kephart *Highlanders* 264 **sAppalachians**, In homes where dancing is not permitted, and often in others, "play-parties" are held, at which social games are practiced with child-like abandon: Roll the Platter, Weavilly Wheat, Needle's Eye, . . and many others of a rollicking, half-dancing nature.   **1923** *DN* 5.217 **swMO,** *Play party.* . . A social gathering where the chief entertainment is the playing of games.   **1923** (1946) Greer-Petrie *Angeline Doin' Society* 6 **csKY,** We've giv' up dancin' and tuck to havin' play parties instid.   **1927** *AmSp* 2.362 **cwWV,** *Play party* . . a social gathering where games are played, but no dancing is allowed.   **1931** *AmSp* 7.94 **eKY,** We play games, sing song-ballets, 'n' do the Virginia reel at most play-parties.   **1933** *AmSp* 8.1.51 **Ozarks,** *Play-party.* . . A dance at which there is no instrumental music; the players sing game-songs or *swing-arounds* as they go through the complicated figures.   **1947** Lomax *Advent. Ballad Hunter* 71, I have often heard the song among West Texans where "play-parties" yet flourish instead of dances, fiddle music being thought sinful while the same tunes with dance music and precisely the same dance movements are not frowned upon by the churches.   **1965–70** *DARE* (Qu. FF2, . . *Kinds of parties*) 32 Infs, **chiefly W Midl, TX,** Play-parties; (Qu. FF1, . . *A kind of group meeting called a 'social' or 'sociable'*) Infs **AR**41, **MO**39, **OK**6, **TX**42, Play-party; (Qu. FF3, . . *'Showers' or 'gift parties'*) Inf **TX**32, Play-party; (Qu. FF4, . . *Different kinds of dancing parties*) Infs **KY**65, 75, **MI**67, **OH**41, **TX**40, Play-party. [30 of 38 Infs old]   **1967–70** *DARE* Tape **IL**113, There used to be folk dances, what they call play-parties. . . where they played games. They used to play kissing games, you know; **IN**30, I had been to one or two play-parties where we sang our own songs; **KS**1, We always had play-party games at the schoolhouse or the neighbor's home. . . There wasn't any instrumental music; we had to do our own music-making by singing these songs which gave the actions; **KY**75, In the summer we'd have play-parties, mostly out in the yard. . . Usually we'd have someone a-playing a violin and a guitar and some string music. It was a form of dancing, but it wasn't called that; **TX**89, For entertainment about all we had was the little play-parties on the weekend; **TX**96, Mostly [we had] what they called play-parties. We didn't indulge in the dancing too awful much. . . but they would play different—ring-around-the-rosy—and games along that particular line.   **1986** Pederson *LAGS Concordance,* 3 infs, **AR, TN,** Play parties; 1 inf, **csAR,** Play parties—games played, no dancing; 1 inf, **cwAR,** Play parties—square dances; 1 inf, **ceTX,** Play parties—we had no music; sang and danced; 2 infs, **AR, LA,** Play party.   **1993** Mason *Feather Crowns* 155 **KY** (as of c1900), At a play-party, the young people played singing games so they could dance when musical instruments and dance leaders couldn't be found in a hurry.

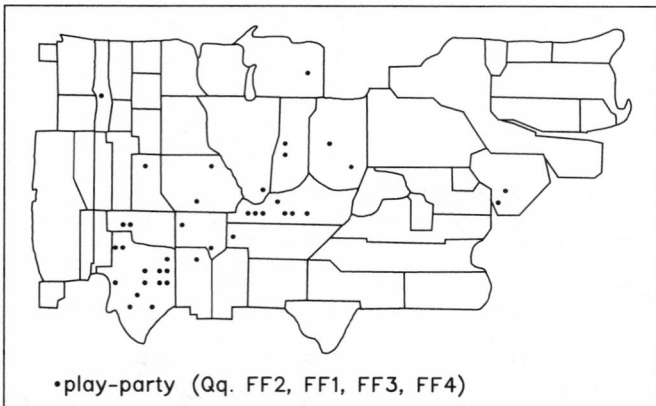

•play-party (Qq. FF2, FF1, FF3, FF4)

play-pretty n **chiefly Sth, S Midl, TX, OK**   See Map   Cf **pretty D**

A child's plaything; a toy; also transf.

1902 *DN* 2.241 **sIL,** *Play-pritty.* . . A toy; plaything.   **1905** *DN* 3.90 **nwAR,** *Play-pretty.* . . Toy. 'The children want some play-pretties for Christmas.' Common.   **1913** Kephart *Highlanders* 259 **sAppalachians,** The children have few toys other than rag dolls, broken bits of crockery for "play-purties," and such "ridey-hosses" and so forth as they make for themselves.   **1929** (1931) Faulkner *Sound & Fury* 36 **MS,** Ain't you shamed of yourself. Taking a baby's play pretty.   **1931** Hannum *Thursday April* 150 **wNC,** She had the feeling that they were twirling her about joyously like a play-pretty on a red string.   **1936** [see **playment**].   **1944** *PADS* 2.59 **MO, VA, NC, TN,** *Play-pretty.* . . A toy, perhaps a home-made toy.   **1946** *PADS* 6.23 **ceNC** (as of 1900–10), *Play-pretty.* . . A plaything. . . Common.   **1956** Algren *Walk on the Wild Side* 75 **wTX,** I love you, baby. . . I'll buy you play-pretties and posey-flowers.   **1960** Williams *Walk Egypt* 4 **GA,** I'll name her Toy, that's

what, 'cause she's going to be my little play-pretty, ain't you, sugarpie?   **1965–70** *DARE* (Qu. EE34, . . *A child's toy*) 94 Infs, **chiefly Sth, S Midl, TX, OK,** Play-pretty.   **1969** (1970) Angelou *Caged Bird* 51 **AR,** You think your momma and poppa went to all the trouble to send you these nice play pretties to make you . . cry?   **1978** Massey *Bittersweet Country* 207 **Ozarks,** The baby lost his play pretty.   **1983** *MJLF* 9.1.51 **ceKY** (as of 1957), *Play purty* . . a plaything.   **1986** Pederson *LAGS Concordance* **Gulf Region,** 262 infs, (A) play-pretty; 135 infs, Play-pretties.

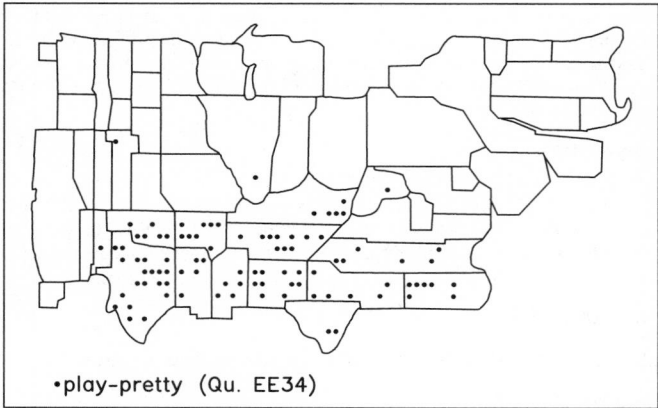

•play-pretty (Qu. EE34)

play shut-mouth   See **shut-mouth**

play song n [**play** n **1a**]

A song used to accompany an active game or dance.

1898 Harris *Tales Home Folks* 19 **GA,** The negroes made the night melodious with their play-songs.   **1899** Woerner *Rebel's Daughter* 234 **Ozarks,** Leslie, noticing the constraint that kept the young people apart, determined to break the ice for them. An old-fashioned "play-song" he knew to be . . efficient to bring together a room full of people anxious to be sociable. . . He beckoned to Ralph Payton, requesting him to choose a partner and lead off.   **1922** Talley *Negro Folk Rhymes* 270, These simple little songs . . are typical Negro Play Songs. I shall not describe the simple play that accompanied them.

play street n **NYC**

A street closed to traffic to allow children to play in it.

1915 *NY Tribune* (NY) 17 May 6/3, In the establishment of what are called "play streets" the avowed endeavor of the People's Institute is to give "as free rein as possible to the individuality of the child."   **1936** in Lib. of Congress *Amer. Memory: FSA/OWI* (Internet) **NYC,** [Caption:] Background photograph for Hightstown project. Play street for children. Sixth Street and Avenue C, New York City.   **2000** *DARE* File **NYC,** During the summer, some streets are closed off so children can play. Some people read the permanent signs, don't see the temporary "Play Street" signs, and eventually come to me [=a judge in traffic court]; **NYC** (as of c1950), I distinctly remember the stanchions with the legend "Play Street" that would appear on the streets of the Lower East Side in the summertime.

play the dozens   See **dozen** n **B1**

play the numbers, you   See **numbers 3**

play the piano(s)   See **piano B**

play-toy n **scattered, but chiefly NEast, Sth, S Midl**   See Map *esp freq among Black speakers*   Cf **play-pretty**

A plaything; a child's toy; also fig; similarly n *play-dolly* a doll.

1875 Smith *Marvels Prayer* 348 **NEast,** Our shoes were brushed; . . our play-toys hidden, and all entertaining books—few indeed at best—were locked up.   **1880** *Scribner's Mth.* 20.814 **LA** [Black], 'Tain' nutt'n' nowhow but a lill play-toy.   **1895** *Overland Mth.* 26.121, Contrary to what might be expected, the cèlèrifère [=an early bicycle] . . was not to be used as a play toy for the Democratic, but was reserved for the aristocratic and the Beau Brummels.   **1935** Hurston *Mules & Men* 19 **Sth** [Black], The white man is always trying to know into somebody else's business. All right, I'll set something outside the door of my mind for him to play with and handle. He can read my writing but he sho' can't read my mind. I'll put this play toy in his hand, and he will seize it and go away. Then I'll say my say and sing my song. **c1938** in *Lib. of Congress Amer. Memory: WPA Life Hist.* (Internet) **RI**, The seine is seven hundred and fifty feet from tip to tip so you see she's no play toy. **1938** Rawlings *Yearling* 318 **nFL**, You cain't carry him places like a gal would a play-dolly. **1942** (1971) Campbell *Cloud-Walking* 204 **seKY**, How foolish folks would say it for a woman growed and married to get such a notion for a play-toy. **1965–70** *DARE* (Qu. EE34, . . *A child's toy*) 51 Infs, **scattered, but chiefly NEast, Sth, S Midl**, Play-toy. [Of all Infs responding to the question, 6% were Black; of those giving this response, 33% were Black.] **c1970** Pederson *Dial. Surv. Rural GA* (*What do you call anything that a child likes to play with?*) 7 infs, **seGA**, Play-toy(s). [6 of 7 infs Black] **1986** Pederson *LAGS Concordance* (*A toy*) 41 infs, **Gulf Region**, Play toy(s). [14 infs Black]

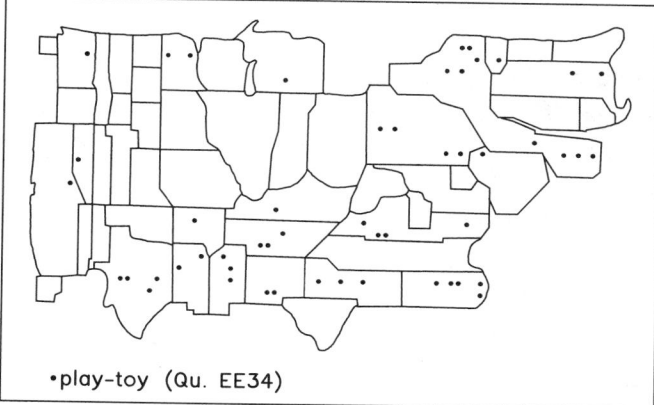

•play-toy (Qu. EE34)

plaza n [Span] **chiefly SW** Cf **common** n **2**
A public square.

1835 in 1952 Green *Samuel Maverick* 41 **cTX**, He was siezed by the picket guard and carried to the jail of the Plazas. **1854** (1932) Bell *Log TX–CA Trail* 35.304, Scatered about the plaza are several peices of stone mortars. **1858** (1930) DeLong *Jrls.* 9.258 **CA**, Came down to the Plaza, to attend a public meeting. **1859** (1968) Bartlett *Americanisms* 327, *Plaza*. (Span.) A public square. A term used in California and other countries recently acquired from the Mexicans. **1892** *DN* 1.193 **TX**, *Pláza*: a public square . . sometimes planted with trees. It is the representative of the Southern court-house square, and no village with self-respect is without at least one. **1907** Mulford *Bar-20* 110 **West**, He clattered across the stone-paved plaza and threw his mount back on its haunches as he stopped before a house. **1948** Weston *Mother Lode* 74, Like so many camps of the Southern Mines section, it was built around a plaza. **c1955** Reed–Person *Ling. Atlas Pacific NW*, 1 inf, Plaza [=town square]. **1958** *AmSp* 33.105, The third word, *plaza*, is one of the most circumscribed terms in the Rocky Mountain area in one sense. It is a Spanish word . . for a town square and is limited to localities with Spanish speech traditions. . . The Rocky Mountain map shows that the usage chiefly centers along the old Spanish trails where Spanish settlement occurred and where there are still plazas even though Anglo-American cities have developed around them. **1986** Pederson *LAGS Concordance* (*Public square*) 11 infs, 6 **TX**, Plaza.

please v
A Forms.
Pret and past pple: usu *pleased;* rarely *plead, pleaged.*
1891 Page *Elsket* 127 **VA** [Black], He teck off he hat kine o' flourishy 'whurr,' an' say, 'Good mornin', pa an' ma.' He mammy . . monsus pleaged [=monstrous pleased] wid dem manners. **1910** Univ. NC *Mag.* 40.3.8 **Hatteras Is. NC**, The pronunciation of words with the omission of certain letters; as, . . plead (pleased).
B Senses.
1 with *up:* To treat with special care; to make happy. Cf **praise up**
1884 Jewett *Country Dr.* 15 **ME**, She found his folks felt put out and hurt, and instead of pleasing 'em up and doing the best she could, she didn't know no better than to aggravate 'em. She was wrong there, but I hold to it that if they'd pleased her up a little and done well by her, she'd ha' bloomed out, and fell right in with their ways. **1913** *DN* 4.1 **ME**, I guess that will please him up.

2 To amuse.
1917 *DN* 4.397 **neOH**, *Please, be pleased.* . . Amuse, be amused, affected humorously. "I was pleased to hear him brag." "It pleased me so, I could hardly keep from laughing." . . Also N. Eng., Ky.

please interrog exclam **chiefly N Cent, esp OH**
Used to elicit a repetition of something imperfectly heard or understood; see quots.

1967–68 *DARE* (Qu. X18, . . *When one person doesn't quite hear what another person said, what does he say?*) Infs **KS4, MI67, MN12, PA66, TX28**, Please. **1973** *DARE* File **swOH**, Please. . . Interrogative expr[ession] meaning "Will you please repeat that?", Cincinnati OH, some time in the past. **1980** *Ibid* **OH**, My Aunt had a friend from Ohio who used the word "please?" when I would say "Pardon me?" when not understanding someone fully. **1980** *NYT Article Letters*, I [=a Westerner] say "Excuse me" (as in "would you please repeat that") [but] Rhode Islanders say "Please?" **1981** *Seventeen Letters* **swOH**, When someone has said something that you didn't hear or don't understand instead of saying Pardon we here in Cincinnati say Please; **swOH**, In the Cincinnati area, I, among others, say, "please" when asking someone to repeat what he has just said. **1982** Chaika *Speaking RI* [7], *Please* = "what did you say?", "excuse me." **1995** *DARE* File **seWI**, A friend of mine went to a restaurant in Milwaukee and said, "I'd like a turkey sandwich". The waitress said, "Please?" Miffed at being corrected, he said, "OK, I'll have a turkey sandwich, *please*!" In this Germanic town, people sometimes use "please" as the Germans use "bitte"—as a way of saying "Please say that again, I didn't hear you the first time".

pleased or displeased n Also *please and displease*
=**fine or superfine.**
1931 in 1996 Horton *Island Out of Time* 115 **Chesapeake Bay MD**, There are only a few boys around, so they came and we played Blind Man's Bluff, Heavy, Heavy; Pleased or Displeased, Clap in Clap out, and Poor Puss. **1968** *DARE* (Qu. EE33, *Other outdoor games*) Inf **AL39**, Pleased or displeased—one person gets to make another perform a job like turn a flip. **1982** Slone *How We Talked* 95 **eKY** (as of c1950), They also played kissing games: "Please and Displease"—one person passed a hat or basket and each player dropped into it some personal item as a forfeit. . . Another person sat in a chair while someone else held over his head one of the forfeits one at a time saying, "heavy, heavy, over your head." The one sitting in the chair asked, "Fine or superfine?" ("fine" meant the object belonged to a boy, "superfine" meant it was a girl.) "Pleased or displeased?" he was asked. If he said "Pleased." he was asked what it would take to please him any better, and he would say the person to whom the forfeit belonged must do something.

please up See **please** v **B1**

pleasure n, v Usu |'plɛžə(r)|; also *esp freq among Black speakers* |'plɛjə(r)| Pronc-spp *pledger, pledjuh(r), pledjur* Cf Pronc Intro 3.I.18, **measure**
A Forms.
1888 [see **B1** below]. **1922** Gonzales *Black Border* 319 **sSC, GA coasts** [Gullah glossary], *Pledjuh*—pleasure, pleasures. *Ibid* [see **B1** below]. **1930** Stoney–Shelby *Black Genesis* 6 **seSC**, Mebbe dis t'ing is goin' to gib you mo' o' trouble dan pledjur, but I is jis' bleege to cut you a mout'. *Ibid* 30, God come in de garden for walk 'bout, an' see how eberyt'ing stan', an' pledjur heself. **1937** (1977) Hurston *Their Eyes* 67 **FL** [Black], It's uh pledger fuh her tuh be heah amongst us.
B As verb.
1 To please; to indulge (someone). **chiefly Sth, S Midl**
1888 Jones *Negro Myths* 51 **GA coast**, Eh lib day, eh eat, eh sleep, eh pledjur ehself. **1922** Gonzales *Black Border* 319 **sSC, GA coasts** [Gullah glossary], *Pledjuhr'um*—please, give pleasure to him, her, it, them. **1924** Raine *Land of Saddle-Bags* 81 **sAppalachians**, I did bring on a leetle table-stand that were kindly purty to pleasure my woman. **1927** Adams *Congaree* 79 **cSC** [Black], He fly up on de high rocks and rest he-self, an' pleasure he-self. **1927** *DN* 5.469 **Appalachians**, *Pleasure.* . . To please. **1933** Rawlings *South Moon* 265 **FL**, Your mother's eyes is got to be so bad, I reckon it'll pleasure her to set and listen to a radio. **1937** (1963) Hyatt *Kiverlid* 38 **KY**, Hit pleasures me a heap to see you better. **1942** Hurston *Dust Tracks* 122 **FL** [Black], My stepmother had lost her point. She never was pleasured to rack her bones on Mama's featherbed again. **1944** *PADS* 2.48 **wNC**, Pleasure. . . To

please. "Hit'll pleasure us to have you eat at our house." **1959** Lomax *Rainbow Sign* 112 **AL** [Black], I told him, if it would pleasure him, I would go. **1960** Williams *Walk Egypt* 94 **GA,** Everything choked her. Everywhere she looked people pleasured themselves. **1963** Owens *Look to River* 105 **TX,** What can you do to pleasure the Cap'n? **1967** Will *Dredgeman* 120 **FL,** This pleasured Jim greatly. He could talk of nothing else. **1968** *DARE* (Qu. X43b, *If you sleep later than usual one day on purpose . . "I _____."*) Inf **GA**54, Pleasuring myself. **1979** Carpenter *Walton War* 170 **sAppalachians,** Hit pleasures me to look at a good fat hog in the pen.

2 To take pleasure. **Sth, S Midl**

1924 (1946) Greer-Petrie *Angeline Gits an Eyeful* 19 **eKY,** I couldn't a-pleasured none in w'arin' all them dimunts and fine clothes with my young'un in a manner naiked. **1928** Peterkin *Scarlet Sister Mary* 94 **SC** [Black], How-come you duh scour when evybody else is pleasurin? **1942** Faulkner *Go Down* 187 **MS,** Plenty of places still unchanged from what they were when the blood used and pleasured in them while it was still blood? **1957** in 1996 *Montgomery Coll.* **eTN,** It wasn't worth anything, only just to pleasure, look at.

pleasure-bent adj phr [From the position of a woman's legs in sexual intercourse, with pun on *pleasure-bent* bent on pleasure] *joc*

Bowed, bent—usu of a woman's legs.

1965 Davis *Summer Land* 57 **cnNC,** "I do my best," Papa said. "I don't get so many chances." "Well, it looks like to me you don't half try to stand up straight." "We've all got some little defects of character. I can't help it if mine settled in my legs. God knows they ain't pleasure-bent, anyway." Mama hissed like she was scandalized. **1965–70** *DARE* (Qu. X37, *. . Words . . to describe people's legs if they're noticeably bent, or uneven, or not right*) Infs **IN**42A, **MN**10, 42, **NY**10, Pleasure-bent legs; **AL**26, Pleasure-bent bow legs—couldn't stop a hog in a one-man ditch; **CO**47, Pleasure-bent legs—of a bow-legged woman; **CT**6, Pleasure-bent—in referring to women; **CT**30, Pleasure-bent—of females; **MI**24, Pleasure-bent—in a woman, real bow-legged; **MI**120, Pleasure-bent [laughter]; **MN**2, Pleasure-bent legs—slightly bent, women only; **MA**6, Pleasure-bent [FW illustr: bowed legs]; **NY**52, Pleasure-bent—if they're bent out [laughter]; **OR**3, Pleasure-bent—if a woman; **VT**16, Pleasure-bent—she's got legs a pig could run through. **1996** *DARE* File **cWI,** "Pleasure-bent" means "bow-legged." It's only used in reference to women, and I've known and heard the term at least since I was in high school (c1924).

pleated woodpecker See **pileated woodpecker**

pledger, pledjuh(r), pledjur See **pleasure**

pleg(ged), pleggid See **plague**

pleggy See **plaguey** adj

plegtated See **plague-taked**

pleurisy root n
=**butterfly weed 1.**

a1782 (1788) Jefferson *Notes VA* 36, Pleurisy root. Asclepias decumbens. **1828** Rafinesque *Med. Flora* 1.74, Orange Swallow-wort. . . Vulgar Names—Pleurisy root, Butterfly weed [etc]. **1877** Still *Early Recoll.* 187 **cwNJ,** At the same time drink freely of warm catnip or pleurisy-root tea. **1911** Porter *Harvester* 418 **IN,** When they came to the large beds of orange pleurisy root the Girl cried out with pleasure. . . "The Bird Woman calls it butterfly flower." **1948** Stevens *KS Wild Flowers* 179, Butterfly Milkweed (Pleurisy-root). . . Our own physicians in pioneer days used the powdered root for disorders requiring sweating, free expectoration, or a mild purgation; especially they found preparations of the root efficient in the treatment of pleurisy—hence the name 'pleurisy root.' **1967** *DARE* Tape **TX**1, [FW:] Did you ever hear of golden seal . . ? [Inf **TX**1A:] Yeah, and pleurisy root.

pliam-blank See **point-blank A4**

pliers man n [From the pliers carried by a cowboy for the repair of wire fencing]
=**fence rider 1.**

1897 Hough *Story Cowboy* 207 **West,** Of later times the faithful cowboy who works on a fenced ranch is sometimes called contemptuously a "pliers man" by the [*"*]rustlers" who have no fences of their own. **1969** Furnas *Americans* 688 **West,** The cowhand became primarily a fence inspector, a pliersman, riding and riding to check and repair wire.

plike See **play like**

plime adv Cf *plime-blank* (at **point-blank A4**)
=**plumb** adv **2.**

2000 *NADS Letters* **seKY,** They used plime as plumb . . occasionally as in "he's plime crazy."

plime-blank, pline-blank See **point-blank A4**

p'lite See **polite**

plogger n Cf **progger**

1989 (1990) Baden *Maryland's E. Shore* 68, Poachers, who were called "ploggers" got into the market and could bring down fifty thousand ducks a year. . . The despicable "ploggers" pillaged to extinction the ducks on the Eastern Shore.

plogue See **ploye**

plongeon See **plongeur**

plongeur n Also *plongeon* [Fr "diver, diving bird"] **LA**
Any of var diving birds, as **hooded merganser, horned grebe,** or **pied-bill(ed) grebe.**

1916 *Times–Picayune* (New Orleans LA) 26 Mar mag sec 1/3, Pied-billed Grebe (Podilymbus podiceps); Hell Diver; Sac-a-plomb; Di-dipper; Plongeur—A resident of Louisiana, but in greater numbers during the winter. **1917** *Wilson Bulletin* 25.2.76 **LA,** Lophodytes cucullatus.—Zin-zin, plongeon, diver, Marksville, La. [**1931** Read *LA French* 60, The name *plongeur,* "diver," is applied to several species of diving birds—the Horned *Grebe . . ,* the Pied-billed Grebe . . , and a duck known as the American goldeneye.] **1967** LeCompte *Word Atlas* 206 **seLA,** In Louisiana the Horned Grebe is usually referred to as a *plongeon* or *plongeur.*

plotched See **plotzed**

Plott hound n Also *Plott,* ~ *(bear) dog* [Jonathan *Plott,* 18th-cent Amer dog breeder] **sAppalachians**
A breed of dog used esp in bear hunting.

1913 Kephart *Highlanders* 80 **sAppalachians,** "I've been told that the Plott hounds are the best bear dogs in the country." "Tain't so," snorted John. "The Plott curs are the best: that is, half hound, half cur." **1914** Arthur *Western NC* 254, The Plott dog . . was said to be the finest bear dogs in the State. **1939** *Hall Coll.* **eTN,** We had two pretty severe dogs with us, Plott hounds. **1949** *Ibid* **eTN,** Plott hounds are used for coon-huntin', about any kind of huntin'. . . It ain't been over twenty year ago we didn't have that name. **1953** *Ibid* **wNC,** And when my great grandfather came home he brought about six dogs, of what is known now as our Plott bear dog. **1954** *Sportsman* 2.4.64, A better known dog, is the Plott of western North Carolina. Old Jonathan Plott brought his first hounds to this country from Heidelberg, Germany, in 1750. Some 30 years later, his son, Henry, bred mongrels into the line adding a fierce fighting strain. He developed a formidable bear hunter. **1958** Humphrey *Home from the Hill* 48 **neTX,** He kept a pack of about fifteen foxhounds, and he liked to have one or two of all breeds on a chase for the harmony of their differently pitched voices. He had Black and Tans, Redbones, Goodmans, Blueticks and Redticks, Walkers, Triggs, a pair of Plott hounds that he had sent Chauncey after all the way to North Carolina. **1960** Hall *Smoky Mt. Folks* 61, *Plott hound:* a strong, rugged bear hound locally bred by the Plott family.

plotz v [Ger *platzen,* Yiddish *platsn* to burst]
Fig: to burst (from anger, pleasure, or annoyance); to split one's seams; to die (from laughter, etc).

1967 P. Welles *Babyhip* iii.46 (*OED2*), 'You're not smoking that filthy thing in here. I'll *plotz*,' Mrs Green said. **1967** *DARE* (Qu. GG31, *To laugh very hard: "I thought I'd _____."*) Inf **MA**2, Plotz [plʌts]. [Inf Jewish] **1970** Feinsilver *Yiddish* 367, Plotzing. . . A recent ad for a Yiddish revue read: "In Miami they're plotzing"—meaning "They're still howling over the preview." **1982** Rosten *Hooray for Yiddish* 258, Plotz. . . Bust, burst, explode. ("I laughed so hard I thought I'd plotz!") . . ("He was so furious he almost plotzed!") **1998** Kahn *Fax Bagel* 225 **TX,** I have to laugh after we hang up. She had me plotzing when she first called—thinking I'd really blown it with both of them. Now she seems to be putting it out of her mind. **2000** *DARE* File **csWI** (as of early 1970s), I learned the word "plotz" from my grandmother, who was of German descent. It meant to overreact, carry on, or cause a fuss; for example, "Mrs. Johnson will just plotz when she hears about this." One of the characters in our sixth-grade class musical (written by a local music teacher and professionally published) was named Agnes Plotz; she provided comic relief by overreacting to situations.

plotzed adj Also *plotched* [Perh < **plotz**, infl by **plowed**, *polluted*]

Drunk; intoxicated.

1950 *WELS Suppl.* **ceWI,** *Plotched*—drunk; occasional. **1962** J.D. MacDonald *Key to the Suite* (1968) ii.16 *(OED2),* If one of our boys gets plotzed, we run him off the team fast before any damage is done. **1974** Allen *Super Tour* 175, She was so loaded I had to put her to bed, and I know from my own experience that when I'm plotzed I go out for the night.

plough See **plow**

ploughed (under) See **plowed**

ploughline See **plowline**

plover n

Std: a shore or upland bird, usu of the family Charadriidae. For other names of var of these birds see **black-bellied plover, golden ~, killdeer, mountain plover, piping ~, ruddy turnstone, semipalmated plover, snowy ~, upland ~, Wilson's ~, yellowlegs**

plow n, v Usu |plau| and varr (see Pronc Intro 3.II.14); also infreq esp S Midl |plaɪ| Also sp *plough*

A Std senses, var forms.

1967 *DARE* (Qu. L18, *Kinds of plows*) Inf **KY34,** Garden [plaɪ:^]; (Qu. L25) Inf **KY34,** [plaɪ:^]. **1967** *DARE* FW Addit **KY31,** [plaɪ], [haɪs]—typical of mountain speech of older and illiterate speakers. **1981** Pederson *LAGS Basic Materials,* 1 inf, swGA, [plaɪⁱᵛ]; 1 inf, cGA, [plaᵊ˸ɪ]; 1 inf, swAL, [plạˢ˗ɪ].

B As verb.

1 To cultivate (a crop), esp corn; hence vbl n *plowing.*

1937 *AmSp* 12.106 **eNE** [Farm terms], Cultivating corn is usually called *plowing* it. **1941** Smith *Going to God's Country* 131 **MO** (as of 1890), I thought that I would have time to get one good breath. I was mistaken. For then the coton [sic] was to plow. **1950** *WELS Suppl.* **ceIA,** Plow. . . To cultivate a crop, as corn. **1967** *DARE* Tape **IA6,** We never plow any corn after the first of July. **1986** Pederson *LAGS Concordance,* 1 inf, seAL, Plow—what you do after crops come up; 1 inf, neAR, Plowing cotton—keeping it cultivated; 1 inf, neMS, Plowing—cultivating. **1989** *DARE* File **csWI,** A Wisconsin farmer *cultivates* his corn and the Arkansas farmer *plows* his. It's the same job with a different name for the task and the implement used.

2 To drive (an animal) in plowing. **Sth, S Midl**

1930 *VA Qrly. Rev.* 6.248 **S Midl,** "You plowed the field, I suppose?" "Wal no, my mule Tim plowed the field. I plowed Tim." **1939** *Hall Coll.* **wNC,** I plowed a steer there for seven year until I got ready to have a horse. **1940** Stuart *Trees of Heaven* 226 **eKY,** Anse plows behind the young mules. He plows Dick and Murt on the old ground slopes. **1966** *DARE* Tape **FL41,** She said, "Oh, you should never gotten rid of . . that donkey." . . But Dad got the place he couldn't use him. He used to plow, he used to plow him, you know, and he'd do quite a bit of work. **1971** *Foxfire* 5.18 **nGA,** My daddy plowed th'steers, and when th'ground got too wet t'plow, used t'go fishin'. **1986** Pederson *LAGS Concordance,* 1 inf, cnGA, When you was plowing them mules; 1 inf, cwGA, We'd plow the mules; 1 inf, nwLA, Used to plow mules; 1 inf, cMS, I plowed a mule to them with; 1 inf, cMS, Plowed steers; 1 inf, seMS, They used to plow mule (=with a mule); 1 inf, seMS, Plow them (=plow with them); 1 inf, nwTN, If you was plowing him (of a mule); 1 inf, ceAL, I plowed a plow stock and a mule and a pony turner a-many a day, son.

plow bone n [Abbr for *plowshare bone;* *OED2* (at *ploughshare* sb. 3) 1831 →]

The pygostyle or tailbone of a bird.

1937 *AmSp* 12.104 **eNE** [Farm terms], The *wish bone* and *plow bone* of a fried chicken are well known.

plowboy, plow chaser See **plow jockey**

plowed adj Also *ploughed (under)* **esp Nth**

Drunk.

1934 (1940) Weseen *Dict. Amer. Slang* 281, *Ploughed*—Intoxicated. **1942** Berrey–Van den Bark *Amer. Slang* 106.7, *Drunk. . .* ploughed (under). **1955** *AmSp* 30.303 **seMI** [Univ slang] *Gassed; ploughed; schnockered. . .* Drunk. **1965–70** *DARE* (Qu. DD14, *When a person is partly drunk, "He's _____."*) Inf **WI48,** Half-plowed; (Qu. DD15, *A person who is thoroughly drunk*) Infs **MN21, 42, MO26, MA1, 9, PA202,** Plowed; **MI118,** Pretty well plowed. [7 of 8 Infs young or mid-aged, 5 coll educ]

plowed flesh (or fresh) See **proud flesh**

plow, furrowing-out See **furrow out**

plowing See **plow B1**

plow jockey n Also *plowboy, plow chaser,* ~ *jock,* ~ *pusher*

A farmer; a rustic.

1927 *AmSp* 2.387 [Vagabond argot], The farmer is christened by the vag with many nicknames,—*John Farmer, hay-shaker, plough-jockey* [etc]. **1935** Safford *Bennington Mob* 252 **VT,** Benedict Arnold had those farmers who had never seen salt water believing that they could beat the flower of the British Navy. . . And how that hard-faced slave-driver did rig them! " 'Vast there, ye clumsy-fisted plow-pushers! . . Get a move on ye." **1942** *AmSp* 17.104 [Truck driver lingo], *Plow jockey.* Cheap driver, just off the farm. **1950** *WELS* (A city person's names and nicknames for a country person) 1 Inf, csWI, Plowboy; 1 Inf, cwWI, Plow jock. **1965** *PADS* 43.27 **seMA,** A rustic. . . 1 [of 9 infs] *plow jock* or *plow jockey.* **1966–70** *DARE* (Qu. HH1, *Names and nicknames for a rustic or countrified person*) Infs **CA117, MS88,** Plowboy; **NY42, 156,** Plow jockey; **FL1,** Shirttail plowboy; **WA11,** Plow pusher; (Qu. HH42, *Names and nicknames for a common laborer;* total Infs questioned, 75) Inf **FL7,** Plowboy. **1966** *Julian Apple Day* [1] **csCA,** If a hick is a bumpkin, a clod, a plow-jockey who follows horses' behinds over the fields . . well, maybe we'd better let them go on thinking that way. **1971** Jennings *Cowboys* 135 **MT, WY** (as of 1877), You can try to reason with them if you want to. You talk like a real plow chaser, Charlie Schwartz. I've seen what redskins do when they're riled, and I know the only thing that'll stop them. **1977** Adams *Lang. Railroader* 116, *Plow jockey:* A cowboy with a cattle shipment.

plowline n Also sp *ploughline*

1 A rein, usu of rope, used for guiding a plow animal; also fig. **chiefly Sth, S Midl**

1777 in 1901 *Documents Revol. Hist. NJ* 1.516, Halters, Plough-Lines, Bed-Lacings . . Sold by *Edward Pole.* **1853** Simms *Sword & Distaff* 70 **SC,** The girl was already slashing away at the ploughlines which had been used to secure the mistress. **1899** (1912) Green *VA Folk-Speech* 326, *Plough-lines. . .* The cord used as reins by which a ploughman drives and guides his horses. **1935** Hurston *Mules & Men* 54 [Black], Y'all lady people ain't smarter *than* all men folks. You got plow lines on some of us, but some of us is too smart for you. **1940** Faulkner *Hamlet* 8 **MS,** One afternoon he was in the store, cutting lengths of plow-line from a spool of new cotton rope. **c1960** Wilson *Coll.* **csKY,** *Plow-lines. . .* Ropes used to guide a horse or mule that is being used to draw a plow. **1967–70** *DARE* (Qu. L51, *The leathers or ropes that a driver holds to guide a horse*) Infs **AR51, KY29, MS81, TN58, VA40,** Plowlines. **1976** Garber *Mountain-ese* 69 **sAppalachians,** *Plow-line . .* guiding strap—Lance tied his plow-line to a tree and went to sleep in the shade. **1986** Pederson *LAGS Concordance* (Lines . . for plowing) 126 infs, **Gulf Region,** Plowline(s).

2 Transf: a **funnel cake.**

1957 Showalter *Mennonite Cookbook* 345 **MD, PA,** *Plowlines or Funnel Cakes. . .* This batter should be thin enough to run through a small funnel. Drop from funnel into hot deep fat. . . Fry until a golden brown. **1965** *Woman's Day Encycl. Cookery* 9.1357 **sePA,** *Funnel Cakes or Plowlines. . .* Holding the opening of a funnel, fill the funnel with batter. Open the end of the funnel and allow dough to run out in a stream into deep hot fat. . . Sprinkle with confectioner's sugar.

plowman's wort n Also *plowmanwort* [Cf *OED2 ploughman's spikenard* (for *Inula conyza*) 1597 →]

A **marsh fleabane 1** (here: *Pluchea camphorata*).

1822 Eaton *Botany* 249, [*Conyza*] *camphorata . .* marsh fleabane, plowman's wort. **1830** Rafinesque *Med. Flora* 2.212, *Conyza . . Plowmanwort.* Several species, with strong balsamic smell. **1876** Hobbs *Bot. Hdbk.* 58, Plowman's wort, Marsh fleabane, Conyza Marilandica. **1940** Clute *Amer. Plant Names* 86, P[luchea] *camphorata.* Salt-marsh Fleabane. Spicy fleabane, plowman's wort.

plow pan n Also *plow sole*
=**hardpan 1.**
    1921 *DN* 5.110 **CA,** *Plough-pan.* . . Hard earth just beyond the reach
of an ordinary ploughshare. San Joaquin Valley.   **1937** *AmSp* 12.105
eNE [Farm terms], The *plow-sole* is the *pan* or hard surface created by
plowing often at a certain depth.

plow pusher See **plow jockey**

plow shoe n
=**brogan 1.**
    1937 *AmSp* 12.102 **eNE** [Farm terms], The term *breeches* can be used
to mean any kind of trousers and work shoes are sometimes called *plow
shoes.*   **1950** *WELS* (*Men's low, rough work shoes*) 3 infs, **WI,** Plow
shoes.   **1954** *Harder Coll.* **cwTN,** *Plow shoes.* . . brogans.   **1965–70**
DARE (Qu. W11) 9 Infs, **scattered,** Plow shoes; **IN70,** Plow shoes—for
farmers; **KY84,** Plow shoes—old-fashioned—same as brogans; **SC3,**
Brogans; plow shoes—older name.   **1986** Pederson *LAGS Concordance,* 1 inf, **neMS,** Plowshoes—type of brogan; durable.

plow sole See **plow pan**

plow the back forty See **back forty, the 2**

ploye n Also *plogue* [Canadian (esp Acadian) Fr]   **chiefly
nME**
    A buckwheat pancake.
    1959 Tallman *Dict. Amer. Folkl.* 230, *Plogues*—This was the name
given to the buckwheat cakes introduced by the French-Canadians in the
early Aroostook timber camps.   **1983** Rich *Baked Bean* 34 **ME,** "My
specialty is the *plogues,*" Giselle said modestly, giving the word the
French-Canadian pronunciation, *ployes.* "My Louis says they deserve 3
stars."   **1988** *NY Times* (NY) 12 Oct Sec C 10 **nME,** And what made
buckwheat possible was Mrs. Bouchard's idea to market a mix for ploye,
the unusual pancake that is a staple in the diet of the deeply traditional
inhabitants of the St. John River Valley. . . The ploye is a griddle cake
made of roughly equal parts of buckwheat and whole-wheat flour, with a
little baking powder for leavening. No eggs, no milk, no cream. . . Odile
Pelletier, 88, . . reminisced about making ployes for her family and the
five or six hired hands who came by during potato harvest.   **1996** *DARE*
File **nME,** [Box label:] For generations the Bouchard Family has been
milling a unique light buckwheat flour in order to prepare Ployes
(rhymes with 'boys').   **2000** *NADS Letters* **cnME,** Ployes. . . In my
memory, growing up in north central Maine in the 1970s, they were a
thinnish buckwheat pancake made principally by French Canadian people. . . I seem to remember the word was pronounced to rhyme with
"toys" but this would be by principally non-Francophone people. *Ibid*
ME, I have heard mention of ploye, however it was not pronounced the
way it is spelled. Whenever I heard it mentioned it sounded like ployeg.
Ibid **neNY,** Can't help with the pronunciation of ploye but can tell you
that it is on the menu of the Mirror Lake Inn in Lake Placid, New York.
2001 *Ibid* **nME,** I'm still looking into "ploye." So far, two people have
told me that they have never heard it pronounced with final /g/, and three
have told me that they have.   **2001** *DARE* File—Internet **nME,** The
plogue (pronounced 'ploye' and sometimes spelled this way as well) is
the staple of any meal along the St-John River in Maine and New Brunswick. Many claim it to be an Acadian food as opposed to a French-Canadian food. But I asked about plogues in the Baie Ste-Marie area of
Nova Scotia, and the Acadians there have never heard of it.

pluck n
1 Usu the heart, liver, and lungs of a butchered animal; sometimes other visceral parts or viscera in general; a prepared dish
of such parts.   **esp NEast, C Atl**   *old-fash*   Cf **haslet, lights,
melt 2**
    1772 (1894) Winslow *Diary* 45 **MA,** One [dish] contain'd three calves
heads (skin off) with their appurtinencies anciently call'd pluck.   **1895**
DN 1.392 **CT,** *Pluck:* the heart, liver, lungs, etc., of a slaughtered animal. . . The "head and pluck" are sometimes the perquisite of the
butcher.   **1899** (1912) Green *VA Folk-Speech* 326, *Pluck.* . . The heart,
liver, and lights or lungs of a sheep, ox, or other animals used as butch-
ers' meat: also, used figuratively or humourously of the like parts in a
human being.   **1939** *LANE* Map 209 (*Pluck, haslet*) **NEng,** The *pluck*
may include the heart, liver, lights (i.e. lungs) and tongue, [1 inf] . . [or]
without the tongue . . [13 infs], the heart, liver and tongue . . [3 infs], the
heart and liver . . [1 inf], the heart and tongue . . [1 inf], the liver and
tongue . . [1 inf], or the liver and lights . . [5 infs]; or *pluck* may denote a
single organ . . usually the liver.   **1946** *PADS* 5.32 **VA,** *Pluck.* . . The
heart, liver, and lights of a sheep, ox, or other animal; east of the Blue

Ridge, not common.   **1949** Kurath *Word Geog.* 64, *Pluck* is current, in
uneven distribution, from New Hampshire to Virginia. It is common in
Rhode Island, Connecticut, western Vermont, and the New York counties east of the Hudson; also in the New England settlements on the upper Susquehanna, on Delaware Bay, and in Maryland west of the Bay.
1958 *PADS* 29.14 **TN,** *Pluck:* A food. "At hog killing time we had pluck
for dinner, made of the liver, lights, and melts, and sometimes sweetbreads."   **1966** Dakin *Dial. Vocab. Ohio R. Valley* 2.261, *Pluck* appears
only three times, all in the Bluegrass, but two of the speakers who mention it are uncertain what it means and one says *pluck, liver, 'n lights.*
1967–70 *DARE* (Qu. H43, *Foods made from parts of the head and inner
organs of an animal*) Infs **OH**15, **VA**39, Pluck; **MA**38, Calf's head and
pluck; (Qu. X8, . . *General words* . . *for the organs inside the body*) Inf
MA30, Pluck.   **1967** Faries *Word Geog.* **MO** 137, Pluck . . 3 [of c700
infs].   **1970** *DARE* FW Addit **VA**46, *Pluck*—heart, liver, lungs, and
windpipe of a butchered hog.   **1973** Allen *LAUM* 1.257 **Upper MW** (as
of c1950), *Pluck* . . is actually used by a Duluth inf., and is remembered
as old-fashioned by three other Minnesota infs.

2 also *plug:* Cheap or inferior wine.   *esp freq among Black
speakers*
    1904 Day *Kin o' Ktaadn* 33 **ME,** And the brand of pluck they sell at
bars.   **1968–70** *DARE* (Qu. DD27, . . *Nicknames . . for wine*) Infs **FL**52,
OH102, **PA**66, Pluck. [All Infs Black]   **1970** Major *Dict. Afro-Amer.
Slang* 92, *Pluck (plug):* wine, especially cheap wine.   **1980** Folb *Runnin' Down* 187 **cwCA** [Black], There are many vernacular terms for
wine—*the grapes, . . pluck, smash.*   **1986** Pederson *LAGS Concordance*
(*Wine*) 1 inf, **csTX,** Pluck; 1 inf, **seFL,** Pluck—wine; grapes, berries.
[Both infs Black]   **1988** *AmSp* 63.131 **CO** [Prison talk], Prison home-
brew is called *julep* or *jack* and is made from sugar, plus anything else
that will ferment. . . (In Colorado . . this concoction is called *stew* or
pluck.)   **1994** Smitherman *Black Talk* 183, *Pluck*—Wine. Possibly derived from *pluck,* meaning "courage"; in earlier years, wine was often
drunk before gang fights.

pluck v, **plucks** See **plug** v 2

pluff adj Also *pluffy* [swEngl dial *pluff(y)* soft, spongy]
1 Of mud: of a fine, silty texture.   **chiefly SC**
    1853 *S. Qrly. Rev.* 7.513 **SC,** At the depth of thirteen feet the blue, te-
nacious, pluff-mud and shells of a more ancient geological epoch are
reached.   **1941** Writers' Program *Guide SC* 326 **csSC,** As the highway
nears the sea, the air is odorous with sweet myrtle and, at low tide, with
the pluffy mud of the salt marshes.   **1950** *PADS* 14.53 **SC,** *Pluff mud.* . .
The soft, rich, sedimentary mud of the marsh lands in the coastal area.
1956 *Holiday* Dec 77 **SC,** The crab are especially plentiful, and you can
laze in a boat and bring them up on a drop line or rake them out of the
"pluff" mud in the marshes at low tide.   **1982** *NADS Letters,* Do you
know the term *pluff mud?* . . It has been described to me as the kind of
mud that "goes 'pluff'" when you drop a rock into it. It is fine and silty,
not clayey or sticky, so it splashes up around the sides of the rock that
lands in it.   **1990** Simpson *Gt. Dismal* 63 **nNC, sVA,** The border party
pressed on. They ran aground in Currituck Sound, waded in the pluff
mud of the marshes.

2 as *pluffy;* Of vegetables: spongy, pithy.
    1966 *DARE* (Qu. I8, *When root vegetables get old and tough and are
not good to eat*) Inf **MI**23, Pluffy—when they get soft.

pluffer n [nEngl, Scots dial; cf *EDD* *pluffer* (at *pluff* v.)]   **S Atl**
    A homemade popgun.
    1950 *PADS* 14.53 **SC,** *Pluffer.* . . A popgun, made from an elder joint
with the pith thrust out, fitted with a plunger not quite the length of
the popgun barrel. Green chinaberries are used as ammunition.   **1982**
DARE File Savannah **GA** (as of 1937–41), *Pluffer*—a homemade,
hand-operated air gun using chinaberry ammunition and consisting of a
wooden tube (elderberry or boxwood stem) 6–10 inches long and a
wooden piston. The hard, spherical berry is tamped into one end of the
tube, then the piston is quickly rammed at the other end, compressing air
and expelling the load with force enough to sting a human target 10–12
feet away. The name of the device may well relate to the soft-explosive
sound made by firing it. . . The device seems to have been well known
as a "pop gun" in other parts of Georgia and in North Carolina.   **1986**
Pederson *LAGS Concordance,* 1 inf, **ceGA,** Pluffers—child's toys, guns.
2000 *DARE* File **ceGA,** As a child in Savannah, GA (65 years ago) we
kids used to take an elder (I think) stalk, hollow it out as the barrel. It
was about 10 inches long. We would then whittle down a broomstick, or
other piece of wood, to make a plunger, about 8 inches long. . . Then,
we'd put a chinaberry in and push it in to the full length of the plunger.
Now, by inserting a second chinaberry, and holding the plunger handle

to our stomach, then vigorously shoving the barrel so as to shove the plunger in abruptly, there would be a loud POP and the first chinaberry would be shot out with great force as a missile. . . We called it a *Pluffer.*

pluffy See **pluff**

plug n[1]

1 A mule. [Transf from *plug* an inferior horse]
1965–69 DARE (Qu. K50, *Joking nicknames for mules*) Infs **AR**55, **KY**23, **MS**60, Plug; **SC**30, Old plug; [**NC**3, Plug mule].
2 also *plug run,* ~ *train:* A small, local railroad line or train.
1916 DN 4.327 **KS**, *Plug.* . . Used attributively as not the best or highest of its kind; common; ordinary; as . . a *plug* (local) train. General. **1931** *Writer's Digest* 11.42 [Railroad terms], *Plug*—One horse passenger train. **1945** Hubbard *Railroad Ave.* 355, Local passenger trains are sometimes referred to as *plug runs.* **1968–70** DARE (Qu. N37, *Joking names for a branch railroad that is not very important or gives poor service*) Infs **IL**135, **MI**76, Plug; **IA**36, Old plug.

plug v

1 To throw, fling. **esp NEng**
1911 Shute *Plupy* 16 **NH**, The green apples were just large enough to throw with an elastic switch. . . "Kin I plug some green apples with a stick?" "Why, y-e-e-s . . ," his mother replied . . , "don't throw them at people and don't break any windows." **1943** LANE Map 667 *(Threw)* 3 infs, **wCT, ceMA,** Plugged; 1 inf, **swCT,** Plugged, 'I never liked it; I always tried to avoid slang.'; 1 inf, **ceMA,** Plugged = *threw hard; chucked = tossed.* **1965** DARE File **UT,** Plug = throw (e.g. a stone). *Ibid* **eMA** (as of 1955), Plug = throw. **1969** DARE (Qu. BB51b, . . *'Magical' cures for corns or warts*) Inf **RI**12, Rub with salt pork, then plug it through the window.
2 usu *pluck;* In marble play: =**plump;** hence n *plucks* a marble game played by tossing a marble. **esp S Midl**
1955 PADS 23.27 **cwTN,** *Plug.* . . To toss the marble or taw through the air towards the defensive marble or marbles. . . *Plunk.* . . Same as *plug.* **1966** DARE (Qu. EE7, . . *Kinds of marble games*) Inf **DC**7, Pluck for five [or] the number of marbles for which the game is played; plucks—played as two players walk along—shooting at each other's taws. **1968** DARE Tape **DE**3, You made a small ring . . and placed the marbles around it . . and you shot from these two lines. . . If you wanted to, what we call pluck, where you had to, you took the first line and you held your hand off the ground to pluck. **1983** *MJLF* 9.1.51 **ceKY,** *Pluck* . . to shoot the taw so as to hit the object marble on the fly.

plug n[2] See **pluck** n 2

plug run (or train) See **plug** n[1] 2

plum n **NEng**
Any of var round, smooth, edible berries; hence vbl n *plumming* picking such berries; n *plummer* one who picks them.
1872 Schele de Vere *Americanisms* 520, *Plum,* in the New England States, serves as a generic name for all berries, and thus is used for the brilliant berries of the *Diacæna borealis,* an elegant forest-plant bearing a few acid blueberries, the partridge-berries, the mountain-cranberries, and some other species. **1890** *AN&Q* 5.250 **eMA,** In Eastern Massachusetts many kinds of berries are called *plums.* To go berrying is termed *plumming.* A huckleberry is sometimes called a huckleberry-plum; a blueberry, a blueberry-plum. But I do not feel sure that a raspberry, or any kind of berry not of a round or spheroidal shape, would be called a *plum.* **1895** DN 1.392 **neMA,** To go plumming = to go huckleberrying. **1905** Wasson *Green Shay* 103 **NEng,** I won't make no account of the young fry that's drifted in here to spark the gals and go plummin' [Footnote: Berrying] summer-times. **1907** DN 3.196 **seNH,** *Plum.* . . Used generically of the blueberry. "I want to pick some plums in your pasture." *Plumming.* . . Gathering blueberries. "I liked nothing better than to go plumming." **1932** Wasson *Sailing Days* 119 **cME coast,** On many parts of Isle au Haut, blueberries flourished in great quantities, and commonly known as "plums," were gathered and used in the homes of the islanders. . . Large parties of blueberry-picking men, women and children came from towns far up bay and river. . . Beyond getting a little milk at convenient houses, "plumming" parties were of little benefit, and generally were regarded with slight favor. Hence it is significant that the earliest of summer visitors to the island were often spoken of as mere "plummers." **1975** Gould *ME Lingo* 212, *Plummin'*—Berrying, and in particular going after the Maine wild blueberry. . . *Rakin'* is the term for gathering blueberries commercially; *plummin'* is done by housewives, children, and *summercaters* by hand.

plum adv See **plumb** adv

plum adj See **plumb** adj

plumas brush n
A **bluebrush** (here: *Ceanothus lemmonii*).
1938 Van Dersal *Native Woody Plants* 88, *Ceanothus lemmonii* Parry. *Plumas-brush.* . . A small, spreading shrub; flowers April–May.

plumb adv Also sp *plum*

1 with adv (phr): All the way, directly, right. **scattered, but chiefly Sth, S Midl**
1843 (1969) Lewis *Odd Leaves* 51 **MS,** His breeches split plum across with the strain. **1862** Winthrop *John Brent* 296, I paid their ticket plum through to York. **1884** *Anglia* 7.268 **Sth, S Midl** [Black], *Plum down ter* = as far as, quite to. **1899** (1912) Green *VA Folk-Speech* 327, *Plumb.* . . Exactly . . as, hit him *plumb* on the nose. *Plumb.* . . Altogether; all the time. "He was there plumb to Sunday." **1905** DN 3.16 **cCT,** *Plumb.* . . Straight. 'I shot him plumb through the heart.' **1932** Randolph *Ozark Mt. Folks* 37, He . . never stopped a-runnin' till he got plumb home. **1936** *Esquire* Nov 226 **KY,** Killed it plum over yander at that rock on tother hill. **1946** PADS 5.32 **VA,** *Plum (across).* . . Entirely (across); in the southern part of the Blue Ridge. **1961** *AmSp* 36.269 **CO,** Such expressions as *(eat a) piece, whiffletree, nigh horse,* and *plum across* seem to be relics because they are both old-fashioned and scattered. **1965–70** DARE (Qu. LL26a, . . *'All the way': "He drove _____ to the end of the road."*) 91 Infs, **chiefly Sth, S Midl,** Plumb; **TN**23, Plumb all the way; **TN**46, Plumb clean; **MO**19, Plumb out, plumb past; **GA**68, Plumb slap; (Qu. KK53, *When one thing suddenly hits hard against something else: "He ran _____ into a car."*) 22 Infs, **scattered,** Plumb; **MO**16, Plumb wild; (Qu. LL26b, . . *'Entirely'—for example, "He's Irish _____."*) Inf **GA**9, Plumb through. **1968** DARE Tape **GA**30, It [=the county line] runs on down just a little ways and then curves back and goes plumb back out and goes through the swamp. **1972** PADS 58.16 **cwAL,** *Clear across.* Most of the informants avoided regional usage with *all the way;* however, *clear* (2 [of 27 infs]), South Midland *plum,* and Southern *clean* were given. **1995** Williams *Gt. Smoky Mts. Folklife* 116 **wNC, eTN,** That hog had cut him plumb to the heart on both sides.
2 Entirely, quite, very, downright.
1858 *Olympia Pioneer* 26 Feb (1912 Thornton *Amer. Gloss.*), He wur plum crazy. **1884** Murfree *TN Mts.* 258, I war plumb glad when they got that woman under ground. **1902** DN 2.241 **sIL,** *Plum.* . . Completely; quite. 'The box is plum full.' **1903** DN 2.325 **seMO,** *Plumb.* . . Entirely; absolutely. 'My corn crop is plumb ruint.' 'The house was plumb empty.' **1905** DN 3.64 **eNE,** He's plumb crazy. *Ibid* 90 **nwAR,** It's plumb good. **1906** DN 3.122 **sIN,** My crop is plumb ruined. **1907** DN 3.225 **nwAR,** *Plum.* . . Complete(ly). **1909** DN 3.358 **eAL, wGA,** *Plum(b).* . . Entirely. **1910** DN 3.456 **seKY,** I was so plumb tired out that I forgot all about it. **1918** DN 5.19 **NC,** *Plum,* entirely. **1923** DN 5.217 **swMO,** *Plumb.* . . Completely. May be used to modify any adjective. **1925** Hunter *Trail Drivers TX* 553 (as of 1916), Now this Chisholm trail, where it started and where it ended and when it was blazed, we're not plum sure of it an' I'd like to find someone that is. **1938** Rawlings *Yearling* 59 **nFL,** He takened us plumb by surprise. **1959** VT Hist. 27.153, *Plumb full.* . . Completely or absolutely full. Common. **1965–70** DARE (Qu. LL28, . . *Entirely full: "The box of apples was _____."*) 115 Infs, **widespread, but somewhat less freq NEast, C Atl,** Plumb full; (Qu. JJ30a, *Other words or expressions for forgetting something: "I _____."*) 20 Infs, **scattered,** Plumb forgot (it); **KY**21, **TN**4, (Just) plumb forgot that; **NJ**55, Plumb forget it; (Qu. LL17, . . *There's no more of something: "The potatoes are _____."*) Infs **FL**48, **GA**72, **IN**38, **MN**16, **MS**1, **NC**31, **TN**36, **VT**12, Plumb out; **TX**13, Plumb gone; (Qu. V3, . . *A thoroughly dishonest person . . "He's a _____."*; total Infs questioned, 75) Inf **OK**1, Plumb dishonest; (Qu. W20, *If somebody has no clothes on at all*) Infs **CA**65, **IL**126, **IN**66, **LA**40, **MN**33, **SC**56, Plumb naked; (Qu. X19b, . . *If a person's hearing is very bad . . he's _____*) Infs **IN**9, **ND**5, **TX**76, 98, **VA**35, Plumb deaf; **TN**52, Plumb deef; (Qu. X47, . . *"I'm very tired, at the end of my strength"*) Infs **GA**15, **IL**135, **WV**4, 12, 18, Plumb tuckered (out); **CO**7, Plumb fagged; (Qu. AA8) Inf **SC**34, They're plumb silly; (Qu. BB39, *On a day when you don't feel just right, though not actually sick . . "I'll be all right tomorrow—I'm just feeling _____ today."*) Inf **KY**24, Plumb trifling and sorry; (Qu. BB47) Inf **TX**6, Plumb full of shit; (Qu. DD15, *A person who is thoroughly drunk*) Infs **KY**24, **VA**111, Plumb drunk; (Qu. DD24, . . *Diseases that come from continual drinking*) Inf **LA**6, Will eat your liver plumb up; (Qu. HH6, *Someone who is out of his mind*) Inf **LA**32, Plumb crazy; **OK**45, Plumb out of his mind;

(Qu. HH9, *A very silly or light-headed person*) Inf **TX**13, Plumb silly; (Qu. KK20b, *Something that looks as if it might collapse any minute: "Our old washing machine is _____."*) Inf **SC**8, Plumb wore out; **OK**6, Wore plumb out; (Qu. KK22, *. . Completely shattered: "The jug fell out of the window and was _____."*) Inf **LA**14, Plumb busted; (Qu. KK27, *A very lively, active old person: "For his age, he's _____."*) Inf **VA**15, Plumb pert; (Qu. KK53, *When one thing suddenly hits hard against something else: "He ran _____ into a car."*) Inf **MO**16, Plumb wild; (Qu. KK68, *When people don't think alike about something: "We agree on most things, but on politics we're _____."*) Inf **KY**85, Plumb crossways about it; (Qu. KK70, *Something that has got out of proper shape: "That house is all _____."*) Inf **AK**8, Plumb out of line; **FL**35, Plumb out of shape; (Qu. LL14, *None at all, not even one: "This pond used to be full of fish but now"*) Inf **OR**10, It's plumb empty; (Qu. LL30, *. . 'Nearly' or 'almost': "He fell off the ladder and _____ [broke his neck]."*) Infs **MN**42, **TX**92, Plumb near; (Qu. LL35, *Words used to make a statement stronger: "This cake tastes _____ good."*) Infs **MS**7, 42, **TN**23, **TX**19, **VA**11, Plumb; (Qu. NN13, *When you think that the thing somebody has just said is silly or untrue: "Oh, that's a lot of _____."*) Inf **OR**10, Plumb full of crap. **1991** Still *Wolfpen Notebooks* 11 s**Appalachians,** Some of that attitude rubbed off on me. Few people were ever able to suit me plumb in my own [garden].

plumb adj Also sp *plum* **chiefly Sth, S Midl**

Complete, total; entire.

1887 *Scribner's Mag.* 2.477 **AR,** *He* wuz a-cussin' an' a sw'arin' the plum' w'ile. **1902** *DN* 2.241 s**IL,** *Plum, adj.* Complete; consummate, as 'He's a plum idiot. . . ' 'It's plum sundown.' **1907** Wright *Shepherd* 23 **Ozarks,** Hit's a plumb shame. **c1920** in 1993 Farwell–Nicholas *Smoky Mt. Voices* 125 s**Appalachians,** You're a plumb fool. . . You plumb rogue. **1921** Haswell *Daughter Ozarks* 22 (as of 1880s), I seen his back up yander at the deepo, and hit were a plumb sight, cut up raw as a beef steak, hit were. **1923** *DN* 5.236 sw**WI,** *Plumb-buster.* . . A very powerful man physically; intensive of *buster.* (Complimentary.) "Strong? I should say he was! Why, he's a plumb-buster!" **1930** *VA Qrly. Rev.* 6.249 **S Midl,** The gentleman of the backwoods . . can testify perhaps that he is a plumb fool about turnip greens. **1932** (1974) Caldwell *Tobacco Road* 169 **GA,** It was a plumb shame that she was so bad about wanting to stay by herself all the time. **1966–70** *DARE* (Qu. E22, *If a house is untidy and everything is upset . . "It's a _____!" or "It looks like _____."*) Inf **MS**72, Plumb wreck; (Qu. V6, *. . Words . . for a thief*) Inf **TX**106, Plumb rogue; (Qu. LL36, *To make a statement much stronger: "Poor fellow. I think it's a _____ shame."*) Inf **TN**23, Plumb. **1969** *DARE* Tape **GA**51, I found the little fellers [=turtles]; just a plumb string of them.

plumbings See **plummy**

Plumb Nearly n Also *Plum(b) Nellie,* ~ *Nelly* **Sth, S Midl**
Cf **poke and plumb town**

Used as a name or nickname for an out-of-the-way place; hence adv phr *plumb nellie* (and varr) in a remote place; see quots.

1941 in 1944 *ADD* **LA,** Because he liked large places, & had to get them cheap, they were invariably located 'plumnelly,' as the Negroes on the farm in La. had put it—meaning plum out of the city & nelly out of the country. **1942** *Ibid,* [Radio:] There's a town down there [near Bluefield, W.Va.] called Plumbnearly, isn't there?—*Plumb* down in W.Va., & *nearly* in Va. **1952** Brown *NC Folkl.* 1.577, *Plum(b) nellie. . .* Completely out of town; nearly in the country. **1969–70** *DARE* (Qu. C33, *. . Joking names . . for an out-of-the-way place, or a very small or unimportant place*) Inf **GA**80, This is Plumb Nearly—it's plumb out of town and nearly out of the country [laughter]; **SC**66, Plumb Nelly—plumb out of the city and nearly out of the country; **SC**69, Plumb Nelly—plumb out of the country and nearly out of the world. **1981** Pederson *LAGS Basic Materials,* 1 inf, ce**AR,** Says she lives in "Plum Nelly," which is plum in the country, nelly out of town. **1984** Wilder *You All Spoken Here* 65 **Sth,** *Plum' nelly:* Plumb nearly; almost. In Dade County, Georgia's northwesternmost country, is Plum Nelly—"plum' out of Tennessee and nelly out of Georgia"—a craft center noted for its annual "clothes line" art show. **1986** Pederson *LAGS Concordance,* 1 inf, nw**GA,** Plum Nelly—town in Georgia. **1995** Brophy Coll. 56 sw**MO** (as of c1960), *Plumb nearly . .* [A] name given to a road which was "plumb out of town and nearly out of the county."

plumb peach See **plum peach**

plume bird n **FL, GA**
Any of var birds once hunted extensively for their feathers, esp the American **egret** or **snowy egret.**

1898 (1910) Willoughby *Across Everglades* 111 s**FL,** We saw the white egret (plume birds) in every direction. **1913** *Auk* 30.491 **Okefenokee GA,** *Herodias egretta.* Egret; 'Plume-bird'; 'Big White Plume-bird' . . Formerly common. *Ibid* 503, Snowy Egret; 'Egret.'—A plume-bird, called the 'Egret,' was found in the swamp twenty years ago. **1955** *Oriole* 20.1.2, American Egret.—*Plume Bird* (as a bird formerly sought by hunters of plumes, or aigrettes, for millinery trade). **1964** Will *Hist. Okeechobee* 93 **FL,** This lake was the last refuge of the plume birds. . . [T]he really dressed-up high toned lady must have her hat trimmed with "aigrettes". These snow white, curved and lacy plumes were the swellest thing for style. . . These plumes could be got only from certain of the egret family and they grew only during the nesting season. . . It took only a few years to kill off all the plume birds on Okeechobee. **1966–68** *DARE* (Qu. Q10, *. . Water birds and marsh birds*) Inf **FL**35, Plume bird; **GA**20, A lot of those egrets and herons are called plume birds.

plumed quail n
=**mountain quail 1.**

1874 (1877) Hittell *Resources CA* 402, The plumed quail, *(Oreortyx pictus)* likewise called the "mountain quail," . . is peculiar to this Coast. . . Its head is surmounted by a crest of two straight feathers, three and a half inches long, which hang backward, one immediately over the other. **1982** Elman *Hunter's Field Guide* 92, *Mountain quail*—plumed quail, painted quail, San Pedro quail, mountain partridge.

plume grass n [Because the panicles have a feathery appearance]
A grass of the genus *Erianthus,* found chiefly in the southeastern US.

1861 Wood *Class-Book* 807, *Erianthus . .* Plume Grass. . . Stout, erect grasses, remarkable for their large woolly or silky, tawny panicles. **1901** Mohr *Plant Life AL* 334, *Erianthus* [spp]. . . Plume Grass. . . Atlantic North America. **1948** Blomquist *Grasses NC* 195, *Erianthus alopecuroides.* . . Silver plumegrass. . . Not common; from the upper to the lower Piedmont. New Jersey to southern Indiana, southern Missouri, and Oklahoma, south to Florida and Texas. **1968** McPhee *Pine Barrens* 46 c**NJ,** In December, . . shiploads of holly, laurel, mistletoe, ground pine, greenbriar, inkberry, plume grass, and boughs of pitch pine were sent to New York for sale as Christmas decorations.

plume lily n
A **false Solomon's seal** (here: *Smilacina racemosa*).

1952 Strausbaugh–Core *Flora WV* 240, S[milacina] racemosa . . Plumelily. False Spikenard. False Solomon's Seal. **1959** Gillespie *Compilation Edible Wild Plants WV* 24, Plume Lily. . . The slightly bitter berries are highly laxative when eaten in abundance, so they should be eaten only as an emergency food.

plume locust n Cf **locust B1**
=**false indigo 1.**

1933 Small *Manual SE Flora* 688, *Amorpha* [spp]. . . About 20 species, North American.—Lead-plants. Plume-locusts. **1953** Greene–Blomquist *Flowers South* 56, Indigo-Bush, Plume-Locust, Lead-Plant. . . Many of these [species] are so hairy as to give them a grayish appearance. **1966** Grimm *Recognizing Native Shrubs* 152, Plume-Locust—*Amorpha herbacea . .* a shrub 1 to 3 feet high; growing in open sandy woods and pinelands.

plume moss n [See quot 1947]
A **moss** n 1 (here: *Hypnum crista-castrensis*).

1907 Marshall *Mosses* 297, The Knight's Plume Moss, *Hypnum crista-castrensis.* **1942** Hylander *Plant Life* 98, The Plume Moss *(Hypnum)* is also appropriately known as the Feather Moss. Its flattened branches, looking like the sprays of some miniature evergreen tree, cover logs and stumps in the cool woods with raiment of deep green. **1947** Grout–Howe *Mosses & Liverworts* 185, The Plume Moss . . is common on decayed wood and stumps in cool moist woods. . . The shoots are ascending and as regularly pinnate as any feather.

plume of Navarre n
A **fringed orchid** (here: *Platanthera blephariglottis*).

1950 Correll *Native Orchids* 57, *Habenaria blephariglottis.* . . Common names: White Fringed-Orchid, Snowy-orchid, Plume-of-Navarre.

plume-royal n

A **fringed orchid** (here: *Platanthera psycodes*).

1933 Small *Manual SE Flora* 370, B[lephariglottis] grandiflora. . . *Plume-royal. Purple-fringe-orchid.* **1950** Correll *Native Orchids* 99, *Habenaria psycodes* var *grandiflora. . . Common names:* Large Purple Fringed-orchid, Large Butterfly Orchid, Plume-royal [etc].

plume tree n

A **mountain mahogany 2** (here: *Cercocarpus montanus* var *glaber*).

1961 Peck *Manual OR* 440, C[ercocarpus] betuloides . . Plume Tree. . . Dry thickets, Umpqua Valley and southward to Calif. **1979** Little *Checklist U.S. Trees* 84, *Birchleaf cercocarpus.* . . Other common names . . hardtack, plume-tree.

plumgranate, plumgranite, plumgranny See **pomegranate**

plum grape n Also sp *plumb grape*
=**fox grape 1.**

1822 Eaton *Botany* 515, [Vitis] labrusca (plum grape. Y[ale] C[olumbia College] P[ennsylvania] T[roy Lyceum] Catskill.) **1830** Rafinesque *Med. Flora* 2.126, V[itis] latifolia. . . Fox Grape. . . Many varieties [including] *Pruniformis,* as large as a plumb, or a deep purple, fleshy when ripe, called Elkton or Plumb Grape. **1939** Medsger *Edible Wild Plants* 53, Northern Fox Grape, or Plum Grape. **1960** Vines *Trees SW* 722, Fox Grape. . . Also known under the names of Northern Fox Grape, Plum Grape [etc].

plumis See **plummy**

plummer See **plum** n

plummies See **plummy**

plumming See **plum** n

plummy n Also *plumbings, plumis, plummies* [Varr of **pomace**]

1949 Webber *Backwoods Teacher* 140 **Ozarks,** Lonnie Haskins had taken out the horse which pulled the sweep, and was now forking "plummy" (pomace, the crushed cane stalks) to one side so it wouldn't be in the way. **1971** *NY Times* (NY) 17 Oct sec 10 7/2 **cNY,** In the shredder the apples are reduced to a pulpy mass which Harold calls "plumis." **1974** *Bittersweet* 1.3.25 **Ozarks,** The stalks [of sorghum] flattened by the three rollers go on through the mill and come out on the other side as plummies. These plummies can then be used as feed or compost. **1981** Pederson *LAGS Basic Materials,* 1 inf, **cnAL,** Juice from cane mashed out—plumbings ['plʌ⁔mɪˑⁱŋz] left; 1 inf, **cnLA,** ['plʌ⁔mɪnz, 'pɫʌmɪnz]—foamy stuff left over from making cane syrup; used to make sheetrock. **1984** *DARE* File **csPA** (as of 1983), Plummies—pomace.

Plum Nellie (or Nelly) See **Plumb Nearly**

plump v, hence vbl n *plumping* [Engl dial] Cf **plug** v **2, plumpers**

To project (a playing marble) through the air; hence n *plumps* a game played by so doing.

1890 *DN* 1.24 **KY,** The following specimens are words used in playing at marbles . . "plunk" or "plump." **1899** (1912) Green *VA Folk-Speech* 328, Plumps. . . A game of marbles where the marble shot must hit the one shot at without striking the ground. **1909** *DN* 3.358 **eAL, wGA,** Plump. . . To shoot (a marble) through the air so as to hit another marble before touching the ground. **1916** *DN* 4.346 **LA,** Plump. . . In playing marbles, to shoot through the air instead of along the ground. **1957** *Sat. Eve. Post Letters* **OK** (as of c1895), To loft a taw . . so it did not contact the ground for a considerable distance from a knux position, was called plumping. When I got to be a good sized boy, I could knuckle down and plump an agate taw twenty five feet.

plump Boston n Cf **plump, plumpers**

A var of **Boston 2;** see quot.

1957 *Sat. Eve. Post Letters* **Seattle WA** (as of c1900), The other game was Boston. . . Since it required considerable effort to propel [sic] a marble with sufficinet [sic] force to knock the 'centered' marbles out of the ring the hand was not obliged to hug the ground consequently the game was often known as "Plump Boston."

plum peach n Also sp *plumb peach* Also *plum-seed peach, plum-stone ~* **chiefly Sth, S Midl** See Map Cf **press peach** =**clingstone.**

1705 Beverley *Hist. VA* 4.78, The best sort of these [=peaches and nectarines] cling to the Stone, and will not come off clear, which they call Plum-Nectarines, and Plum-Peaches, or Cling-Stones. **1859** Taliaferro *Fisher's R.* 85 **nwNC** (as of 1820s), Thar was two grate big plum-peach trees. **1899** (1912) Green *VA Folk-Speech* 327, Plum-peach. . . A peach the meat of which does not leave the seed. **1903** *DN* 2.325 **seMO,** Plumb-peach. **1907** *DN* 3.234 **nwAR,** Plum-peach. **1909** *DN* 3.358 **eAL, wGA,** Plum-peach. **1915** *DN* 4.187 **swVA,** Plum peach. **1949** Kurath *Word Geog.* 72, *Plum peach* is the Virginia Piedmont term which has spread in a southwesterly direction into southwestern Virginia, southern West Virginia, and the western parts of the Carolinas, where it is in competition with the Midland word *cling-(stone) peach.* It does not occur north of the Rappahannock. **1965–70** *DARE* (Qu. I52, *The kind of a peach where the hard center is tight to the flesh*) 34 Infs, **chiefly Sth, S Midl,** Plum (peach); MS60, 87, Plum-seed peach. **1966** Dakin *Dial. Vocab. Ohio R. Valley* 2.360, Kentuckians in the Knobs and in the Mountains south of the headwaters of the Licking more commonly use the Southern *plum peach* and this term is regular in the Pennyroyal and the Purchase. . . Several speakers in the transition area between the more common *cling-stone peach* of the Bluegrass and the more common *plum peach* of southeastern Kentucky say *plum-stone peach.* **1971** Wood *Vocab. Change* 42, East of the Mississippi a second preference [after *cling* and *varr*] is *plum peach* in Tennessee, Alabama, and Mississippi; this word is unreported in Florida and Louisiana, but is close to second preference in Arkansas. **1972** *PADS* 58.21 **cwAL,** *Clingstone peach.* Northern and Midland *cling(stone) peach* (13 [of 27 infs]) is most frequent. Virginia Piedmont *plum peach* (7) also occurs, but Coastal Southern *press peach* does not. **1983** *MJLF* 9.1.51 **ceKY** (as of 1956), *Plum peach.*

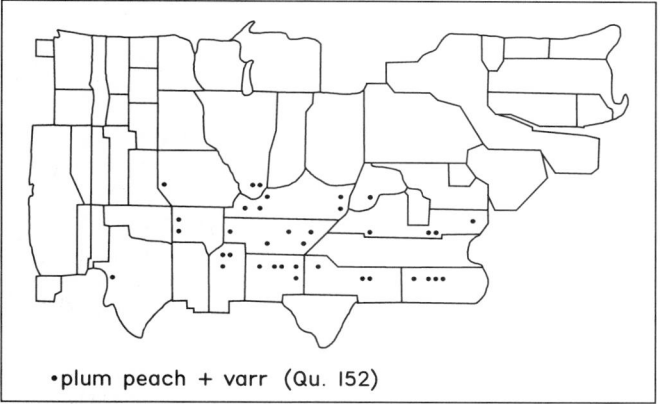

•plum peach + varr (Qu. I52)

plumper n

A shameless lie; a whopper.

1812 *Salem Gaz.* (MA) 26 Nov 3/3, A Plumper. . . A more barefaced falshood [sic] never was published. **1828** Webster *Amer. Dict.,* Plumper. . . A full unqualified lie. *[In vulgar use.]* **1899** (1912) Green *VA Folk-Speech* 327, Plumper. . . An unqualified lie; a downright falsehood.

plumpers n Cf **plump Boston**
=**chase** n **1.**

1973 Ferretti *Marble Book* 66 **MA,** In the United States it [=*boss-out*] is called *chasies* but is also known as *trails* or *trailing, bomber, curb, span* and, in Massachusetts, *plumpers.*

plumping, plumps See **plump**

plum pudding n

1 =**bittern.** [Echoic] Cf **drink pudding, plunket(t) 1**

1897 *Oölogist* 14.81 **IL,** The notes much resemble the words *plum pud'n* accent on *pud,* and for this reason the oddity has been given the name of Plum Pudding among the many other appellations with which this peculiar bird [=the great bittern] is favored. **1917** *Wilson Bulletin* 29.2.78 **MI,** Nicknames for the bittern . . plum-pudden [etc]. **1959** [see **plunket(t) 1**]. **1970** *DARE* (Qu. Q8, *A water bird that makes a booming sound before rain and often stands with its beak pointed almost* *straight up*) Inf **MI**116, Plum-pudding—because of the sound they make.

2 See quot.

1966 *Good Old Days* 2.11.27 **cIL** (as of 1907), The pupils always looked forward to the Christmas season and the "Treat." I gave them. . . a "Plum Pudding." This consisted of a large washtub filled with oats in which was hidden a ten cent toy for each child. They would come to the front in turn, reach down in the oats and bring up a toy.

plum-seed (or -stone) peach See **plum peach**

plunder n [Ger dial *Plunder* household goods, junk]

1 Baggage, gear. **orig chiefly Sth, S Midl; now more widespread**

1805 (1904) Lewis *Orig. Jrls. Lewis & Clark Exped.* 2.220 **VA**, I dispatched Sergt. Ordway with 4 Canoes and 8 men to take up a load of baggage as far as Capt. Clark's camp and return for the remainder of our plunder. **1815** in 1947 *AmSp* 22.284, *Plunder.* Baggage &c. When a traveller arrives at an Inn, he is asked by the Landlord or servant, 'What shall I do with your plunder?' meaning his travelling baggage. This is sometimes used in Kentucky & Ohio, though very rarely. I heard it two or three times, & several Gentlemen told me [=an Englishman] it was common. Probably cant. **1823** *Natl. Intelligencer* (DC) 1 May (*DN* 4.47), *Plunder.* . . Personal property. **1827** in 1956 Eliason *Tarheel Talk* 134 **cnNC**, Scipeo will carry the Carriage for you, you can bring your trunk & plunder all very conveniently. **1837** Sherwood *Gaz.* GA 71, *Plunder*, for . . effects. **1899** (1912) Green *VA Folk-Speech* 328, *Plunder.* . . Household or personal effects; baggage; luggage. **1946** [see **2a** below]. **1958** McCulloch *Woods Words* 136 *Pacific NW*, *Plunder.* . . The personal gear which a logger totes into camp. **1961** Adams *Old-Time Cowhand* 149 **West**, When camp was moved, he [=a wrangler] helped pack the camp plunder and load the wagon. **1975** Gould *ME Lingo* 212, *Plunder* . . the esoteric woods term for whatever is in the packsack or *kennebecker*. To describe taking off down the trail, Gerald Averill wrote, "I horsed my plunder on my back and lit out."

2a Household furnishings and effects. **chiefly Sth, S Midl**

1858 Hammett *Piney Woods Tavern* 61 **TX**, I was expectin' some plunder in the waggons from Augusty [=Augusta]. **1899** [see **1** above]. **1902** *DN* 2.241 **sIL**, *Plunder.* . . General term for household goods and utensils, and farm implements. **1903** *DN* 2.325 **seMO**, *Plunder.* . . Effects; household goods. 'They left some chairs and other plunder in the house when they moved out.' **1909** *DN* 3.359 **eAL, wGA**, *Plunder.* . . Household goods. **1934** *AmSp* 9.320 **IN, Ohio Valley**, *Plunder*. From Pennsylvania, exactly equivalent to German word *plunder*, in sense of household effects. **1946** *PADS* 5.32 **VA**, *Plunder*: Household or personal effects, baggage; common everywhere except the Northern Neck and the Eastern Shore. **1976** Garber *Mountain-ese* 69 **sAppalachians**, *Plunder* . . household goods—They loaded all their plunder on a truck and headed fer a new home. **1982** Slone *How We Talked* 33 **eKY** (as of c1950), *Plunder*—household goods; household furnishing. **1986** Pederson *LAGS Concordance* **Gulf Region** (*Furniture*) 7 infs, Plunder; 2 infs, Plunder = furniture; 1 inf, Plunder and house fixings are old terms; 1 inf, Plunder—old-time word for furniture.

b esp in combs *house(hold) plunder.* **esp KY, NC**

1950 Stuart *Hie Hunters* 26 **KY**, My terbacker, cattle, mules, and corn are in that barn. About everything I've got but my fambly and the house plunder's out there. **1952** Giles *40 Acres* 4 **KY**, Here there is a pocket of pure Appalachianism and our older people still speak the tongue. . . Livestock is called "property" and house furnishings are "house plunder." **1954** Roberts *I Bought Dog* 7 **KY**, I left my father and mother and brother Bill down yander with our wagon and house plunder. We was movin out of this country. **1962** Dykeman *Tall Woman* 17 **NC** (as of c1860), But when your papa came from the Low Country, up into these mountains, and the load in the wagon had to be lightened, he threw out the household plunder and kept his box of books. **1971** in 1982 Powers *Cataloochee* 91 **cwNC**, The last trip out of there I drove a wagon with a team and had some chicken coops on it. And Daddy had hired a fellow with a truck to haul the household plunder. **1972** Cooper *NC Mt. Folkl.* 93, *House plunder*—furniture for the home. **1982** Slone *How We Talked* 5 **eKY** (as of c1950), Most often they lived with their parents for the first months, until they got together enough "house plunder." **1986** Pederson *LAGS Concordance* **Gulf Region** (*Furniture*) 6 infs, House plunder; 1 inf, House plunder—includes chairs, beds, trunks, etc.

3 Disused or discarded articles that are kept around; junk; hence *plunder room, ~ house, ~ porch* a place to store such articles. **chiefly Sth, S Midl, esp SC** Cf **lumber** n¹ **1, lumber room**

1843 Thompson *Major Jones' Courtship* 32 **GA**, I never thought ther was so much plunder bout our house til we come to move. . . Mother's allways got more old washin-tubs and fat-gourds, and spinnin-wheels, and quiltin frames, and sich fixins than would fill Noar's ark. **1905** *DN* 3.90 **nwAR**, *Plunder.* . . Household goods, baggage, belongings. 'My garret's full of plunder.' Rare. **1931** Goodrich *Mt. Homespun* 41 **sAppalachians**, It's got six rooms in it and some other little rooms where she keeps her plunder; calls 'em closets. **1939** FWP *Guide NC* 98, Common phrases of the household may be quaint and humorous. . . The . . storeroom a "plunder room." **1949** Kurath *Word Geog.* 42, *Lumber room* . . is current for a storeroom in rather large parts of the South. . . In the Carolinas *plunder room* predominates, a term that has also a degree of currency in Virginia. **1952** Brown *NC Folkl.* 1.577, *Plunder.* . . Trash, worthless odds and ends. "I've got a lot of plunder in my garage that ought to be thrown away." . . *Plunder-room.* . . A store room; a room in which to store "plunder." **1965–70** *DARE* (Qu. D4, *The space up under the roof, usually used for storing things*) Infs **SC**42, 46, 51, 56, Plunder room—a spare room used for storage; **NC**46, Plunder room; **SC**19, 22, Plunder room—on the main floor; **SC**26, Plunder room—can be on the main floor if you have a big house; **SC**29, Plunder room—could be on any floor—used to put "plunder" in; a full-sized spare room; **WV**14, Plunder room—storage room built onto house; (Qu. D7, *A small space anywhere in a house where you can hide things or get them out of the way*) Infs **MS**1, 72, **SC**1, **TX**84, 99, **VA**94, Plunder room; **SC**6, Plunder room—spare room for odds and ends. **1968** Haun *Hawk's Done Gone* 184 **TN**, We never did use that little back room for anything save plunder. **1986** Pederson *LAGS Concordance* **Gulf Region** (*Junk*) 60 infs, Plunder; 4 infs, Old plunder; 1 inf, Plunder—furniture you don't use anymore; 1 inf, Mother called almost everything plunder; 1 inf, Plunder—old furniture; 1 inf, Plunder—in kitchen, usually means old furniture; 1 inf, One person's plunder is another's pleasure; 1 inf, Plunder—worthless, worn-out things; 1 inf, Plunder—just stuff we don't use; (*Furniture*) 1 inf, Plunder = old furniture; 1 inf, Plunder—outdated furniture that's in the way; 1 inf, Plunder—if it was junky; 1 inf, Plunder—just things in the way; 1 inf, Plunder—when it gets kind of old; 1 inf, Plunder = junk; she throws it away; (*Junk room*) 47 infs, Plunder room; 10 infs, Plunder house; 1 inf, Plunder room—not for junk; 1 inf, Plunder room—for things not used daily; 1 inf, Attic is used for a plunder room; 1 inf, Plunder room—separate building, house, in yard; 1 inf, Plunder room—in barn, stores old furniture; 1 inf, Plunder room—mother kept canned goods, clothes; 1 inf, Plunder porch; (*Shed*) 1 inf, Plunder house; 1 inf, A plunder house—wood and junk, also tools.

plunder v¹ Also *plunder about* Cf **lumber** v¹

To proceed in a clumsy or heavy manner.

1912 Green *VA Folk-Speech* 328, *Plunder.* . . To plunge; flounder: "What are you doing plundering about in the water like that?" **1942** Hench Coll. **cVA**, She told me of a man whose wife died leaving a houseful of children and they just "rummaged, ranched and rambled about"—sometimes she would say children plundered about. **1966** *DARE* (Qu. Y25, *To walk heavily, making a lot of noise: "He came _____ into the house."*) Inf **AL**3, Plundering.

plunder v² Also *plunder up* **chiefly S Midl**

1 also with *around*: To rummage around; to search for something; to ransack. [Cf **plunder** n **3**]

1952 Brown *NC Folkl.* 1.577, *Plunder.* . . To hunt around for something. "He's plundering in the loft for something to fish with."—Central and east. **1953** Randolph–Wilson *Down in Holler* 272 **Ozarks**, *Plunder.* . . To search, to ransack. . . An old woman in Galena, Mo., returned from picking a mess of wild greens, and she was very tired. "It just kills me any more," she said, "to git out an' plunder around that-a-way." **1966** *DARE* (Qu. Y48, *To look in every possible place for something you've mislaid.* . . *"I've _____ [the house looking for them]."*) Inf **GA**6, Plundered up. **1982** Slone *How We Talked* 33 **eKY** (as of c1950), *Plunder*—ramble or look through; "I plundered through that old trunk." **1986** Pederson *LAGS Concordance*, 1 inf, **cnGA**, Plundering—rummaging through long-stored things; 1 inf, **cnAR**, Rattle and plunder—children, rummaging in woods.

2 with *up*: To heap or put together carelessly. Cf **lumber** v² **1**

1969 *DARE* (Qu. Y37, *To make a place untidy or disorderly: "I wish they wouldn't _____ the room so."*) Inf **GA**77, Plunder up; (Qu. KK63, *To do a clumsy or hurried job of repairing something: "It will never last—he just _____."*) Inf **GA**77, Plundered it up.

plunder about See **plunder** v[1]

plunder around See **plunder** v[2] **1**

plunder house (or porch, room) See **plunder** n **3**

plunder up See **plunder** v[2]

plunge n Also *plunge bath* **West**
A swimming pool.
   c1905 in Lib. of Congress *Amer. Memory: Detroit Pub.* (Internet) **CO**, [Caption:] News Tribune newsboys' plunge bath. [*DARE* Ed: Photo shows indoor swimming pool.] **1908** in Lib. of Congress *Amer. Memory: Panoramic Photos* (Internet) **Santa Cruz CA**, [Panoramic photograph of a large public swimming pool called] The Plunge. **1982** *Grit* (Williamsport PA) 4 July 17 **nWY**, Ready to take the plunge? If you do it in northern Wyoming it'll be in just that—a plunge. That's the word used to refer to a swimming pool. **2000** *DARE* File **cwID** (as of c1960), When my family vacationed in Idaho we used to see signs advertising various "plunges," or, as we discovered, swimming pools. *Ibid* **ID**, Yes, indeed, "plunge" was a very common equivalent for swimming pool. . . There was a plunge at Starkey, . . there used to be a plunge on the South Fork of the Payette River . . and I think there was a plunge at . . Ontario, Oregon, before the days of that city's modern pool. *Ibid* **csID** (as of c1918), When I was a kid we went to a plunge near Ketchum that was fed by a hot spring, where the water was diluted with cool water so that it wasn't too hot. The plunge was a concrete pool, complete with dressing rooms around the sides.

plunk v, hence vbl n *plunking* [Engl dial] Cf **plunk** n **2**, **plunker 1**
=**plump**.
   1890 [see **plump**]. **1955** *PADS* 23.27 **cwTN**, *Plunk.* . . Same as *plug.* **1958** *Resp. to PADS 29*, Here are a few more marble terms. . . Plumping—We called it plunking. **1967** *DARE* (Qu. EE7, . . *Kinds of marble games*) Inf **MN2**, Plunking—set up marble and plunk at it.

plunk n
1 also *plunker:* A dollar, esp a silver dollar. [From the sound when dropped or set down] *old-fash*
   1891 Maitland *Amer. Slang Dict.* 207, *Plunk* (Am.), a dollar. **1893** *KS Univ. Qrly.* 1.141 **KS**, *Plunk:* dollar, as 'I drop ten plunks,' i.e., lose ten dollars. **1900** *DN* 2.51 [College slang], *Plunk.* . . A dollar. **1901** Hobart *John Henry* 9 **NYC**, When a guy can buy a couple of cosy-corners in a dead swell theatre for fifty cents per coze, he's a mark to blow four plunks to squeeze into one of those joints. **1909** *DN* 3.358 **eAL, wGA**, *Plunk.* . . A silver dollar, money: usually in the plural. "He's got the plunks." **1912** *DN* 3.585 **wIN**, *Plunk.* . . A silver dollar. In the plural the word is applied to money in general. "He'll put up the plunks, all right." **1919** *DN* 5.67 **NM**, My new hat cost me five plunks in Mexican money. **1929** *AmSp* 4.343 [Vagabond lingo], *Plunk*—One dollar. **c1960** Bailey *Resp. to PADS 20* **KS**, Smackers/bucks/simoleons/cartwheels/plunkers. **1967** *DARE* (Qu. U20, . . *Dollars* . . "*It cost a hundred _____.*") Inf **CA15**, Plunkers; **MN29**, Plunks.
2 In marble play: a game in which the **taw** is shot or tossed through the air at the target marble. Cf **plunk** v
   1966 *DARE* (Qu. EE7, . . *Kinds of marble games*) Inf **WA16**, Plunk—where you stand up outside the circle.

plunk-a-lunk See **plunket(t) 1**

plunker n
1 A type of marble; see quot. [Engl dial] Cf **plump**
   1968–69 *DARE* (Qu. EE6a, . . *Different kinds of marbles—the big one that's used to knock others out of the ring*) Inf **MD34**, Plunker; (Qu. EE6b, *Small marbles or marbles in general*) Inf **VT16**, Plunkers; (Qu. EE6d, *Special marbles*) Inf **LA17**, Plunker—for tossing from the lag line—an extra big, heavy marble.
2 See **plunk** n **1**.

plunket(t) n [Echoic]
1 also *plunk-a-lunk, plunk-puddle:* =**bittern.** Cf **plum pudding 1**
   1852 in 1876 *Forest & Stream* 7.212 **eMA**, List of Gunner's Names . . obtained in Plymouth Bay, Mass.: . . *Botaurus leutiginosus* [sic]. Plunkett. **1959** *Names* 7.120, The true sound names [of the American Bittern] range almost from "a" to "z": Bill-gudgeon . . plum-pudd'n (Mass.,

N.Y., Ont., Mich., Ill.), plunk-a-lunk (Pa., Va.), plunkett (Mass.) . . plunk-puddle (Mich.) [etc].
2 =**black-crowned night heron.**
   1946 Hausman *Eastern Birds* 108, Black-crowned Night Heron. . . Other Names . . Buttermunk, Plunket [etc].

plunking vbl n See **plunk** v

plunking n Cf *DS* P17
See quot 1975.
   1967 *DARE* (Qu. P13, . . *Ways of fishing . . besides the ordinary hook and line*) Inf **MI67**, Plunking—bobbing the bait up and down by hand; (Qu. P17, . . *When . . people fish by lowering a line and sinker close to the bottom of the water*) Infs **WA20, 24**, Plunking. [All Infs old] **1975** Evanoff *Catch More Fish* 9, One of the best ways to catch a steelhead along the West Coast . . is by still fishing. Called "plunking," it is simply another form of bottom fishing, with a sinker and hook rig to keep the bait down deep. Up to 5 or 6 ounces of lead may be needed to hold bottom in swift or strong currents. The best bait for plunking are salmon eggs.

plunk-puddle See **plunket(t) 1**

plunkus n Cf **dingmaul**
An imaginary beast; see quots.
   1907 *DN* 3.248 **eME**, *Plunkus.* . . A mythical creature of Maine woodsmen's lore, thus described in the *Bangor Commercial:* "The plunkus is about as large as a six months' old hog and its body is shaped considerably like that of a hog. The head resembles that of an otter and it has wicked looking teeth. The most important item in the make-up of the plunkus, however, is the tail. This appendage is about six feet long and as thick through as a man's arm. At the end of this tail is a huge lump of bony gristle as large as an ordinary football. This is the plunkus' chief weapon of defence. This ball of gristle is as hard as gutta percha and when wielded with all the strength of the powerful tail is a dangerous weapon." Formerly called *ding-maul.* **1939** Tryon *Fearsome Critters* 15, *The Dingmaul (The Plunkus).* . . [is] cat-like, being long, slim, slick, sorry-looking . . having wolf-like pelts. . . The tail is very long . . the California variety carries a medium-sized bony ball on the end. . . This is used to keep off flies, to pound on dead trees . . and, in the mating season, to beat on the male's chest to call his mate. The female also wears a ball a shade bigger than the male's.

pluvier à cou blanc See **cou blanc**

plyg See **polyg**

Plymouth gentian n
A **marsh pink 1** (here: *Sabatia kennedyana*).
   1950 Gray–Fernald *Manual of Botany* 1156, *S[abatia] Kennedyana* . . Plymouth Gentian.

pneumonia n Usu |n(j)ʊ'monjə, nɪʊ-, nu-, nə-, -iə|; also **chiefly S Midl, Sth** |nu'moni|; for addit varr see quots Pronc-spp *n(e)umony, new money, new mon(i)er, newmounie, pen-neumonia, pneumoni(e), pneumony, remonia;* for addit varr see quots
Std sense, var forms.
   1828 Webster *Amer. Dict., Pneumonia, Pneumony.* **1852** in 1956 Eliason *Tarheel Talk* 316 **cnNC**, New monier. . . new moner. **1855** in 1927 Jones *FL Plantation Rec.* 125 **nwFL**, Severl of the people have had a tact of it and New money [i.e., pneumonia] to gether. **1856** *Ibid* 153 **nwFL**, Aafter you left Harry and Lucy bouth war take with Newmony. **1887** (1967) Harris *Free Joe* 90 **GA** [Black], He had fever, he had pneumonia. **1903** *DN* 2.325 **seMO**, *Pneumonia.* . . Pronounced numony [nu'monɪ]. Numony-fever also used. **1907** *DN* 3.234 **nwAR**, *Pneumoni'* (fever). . . Pneumonia. **1912** *DN* 3.585 **wIN**, *Pneumonia.* . . Sometimes pronounced *pen-neumonia.* **1921** Haswell *Daughter Ozarks* 27 (as of 1880s), I kin jest nacherly knock the hind sights offen cases of our old-fashioned Missouri pneumony. **1922** Gonzales *Black Border* 244 **sSC, GA coasts** [Gullah], *Remonia*—pneumonia. My lady, w'ich dead en' las' Augus', had de consumpshus en' de remonia. **1928** *AmSp* 3.402 **Ozarks** (as of 1916–27), Words like *pneumonia* and *malaria* . . are nearly always pronounced *neumony* and *malary.* **1938** Rawlings *Yearling* 232 **nFL**, Now you be peert and git back in here or you'll die o' the pneumony. **1942** Hall *Smoky Mt. Speech* 76 **wNC, eTN**, [nu'moʊnɪ]. **1950** *PADS* 14.56 **SC**, *Remonie:* . . Pneumonia. An illiterate corruption. **1954** *Harder Coll.* **cwTN**, Pneumonia [nʊ:monɪ].

1957 *Julian Apple Day* [11] **csCA,** It was raining all the time, and the water was wetter then, and the old boy came down with pewmony, and didn't get better. **1960** [see **pneumonia fever**]. **1965–70** *DARE* (Qu. K28) Inf **NY200,** ['monjə]; (Qu. K78) Inf **GA87,** [nu‹ˈmoʉnɨ]; (Qu. BB9) Infs **AR47,** 51, [ˌnjuˈmoun(j)ɪ]; **KY21,** [ˌnjuˈmoni]; (Qu. BB49) Inf **GA1,** [ˌnɪuˈmoni]; **KY44,** [ˌnuˈmoni]. **1967** *DARE* Tape **TX1A,** Lobelia was . . the way he treated [ˌnɪʉˈmonjɨ]. **1970** *NC Folkl.* 18.27, For "pneumony," drink strong tea of onions and lobelia flowers. **1982** [see **pneumonia fever**].

pneumonia fever n [Redund]   S Midl

Pneumonia.

    1903 [see **pneumonia**]. **1907** [see **pneumonia**]. **1915** *DN* 4.242 **eTN,** *Pneumonia fever.* . . Pneumonia. **1938** Stuart *Dark Hills* 39 **neKY,** My youngest brother was the victim of pneumonia fever and lasted only a few days. **1960** Hall *Smoky Mt. Folks* 61, *Pneumonie fever:* pneumonia. **1967–70** *DARE* (Qu. K28, . . *Chief diseases that cows have*) Inf **TN1,** Pneumonia fever; (Qu. BB49, . . *Other kinds of diseases*) Infs **IL118, MO5, TN14,** Pneumonia fever. **1969** *DARE* Tape **IL66,** My dad had had pneumonia fever three different times. . . Those days, you know, when you got pneumonia fever and pulled through once, you done pretty good. 'Course today they, the new treatments they have now, they knock pneumonia fever in just a few days. **1973** Van Noppen–Van Noppen *Western NC* 105 (as of 1880s), Other well-known diseases of the area, in the vernacular, were "pneumony fever," "side pleurisy," "joint rheumatism[,]" "jumpin' toothache," the "bloody flux" (dysentery), and "gallopin' consumption." **1975** Chalmers *Better* 44 **wNC, eTN,** Onion poultices are good for pneumony-fever. **1982** *Smithsonian Letters* **AR,** First he had the flu, then he had newmounie fever (as she said it), then he had a rizin' in the head.

pneumonia plant n

=**sweet flag.**

    1945 Saxon *Gumbo Ya-Ya* 531 **LA,** *Pneumonia.* Medicine: A strong tea of the roots of wild iris (pneumonia plant).

pneumonie, pneumony See pneumonia

po n See popo

po exclam Also *poo;* for addit varr see quots   Cf **poig, pooey, poo-gee, poy**

Used as a call to pigs.

    1966–67 *DARE* (Qu. K84, *The call used . . to get the pigs in at feeding time*) Inf **AR40,** Po [po:]; **OH4,** Poo poo poo. **1981** Pederson *LAGS Basic Materials* **Gulf Region,** 1 inf, Piggy poo ['pʼɪ˺ɡɪ,pʼʊʉ] (falsetto); 1 inf, Piggy piggy po ['pʼoʉ‹].

po' adj See poor

poach v, hence ppl adj *poached* Usu |po(ʊ)č|; for varr see **A** below

A Forms.

1 |porč|; pronc-spp *po(a)rch.* [Cf Intro "Language Changes" I.8]   **chiefly Sth, S Midl** See Map *esp freq among speakers with gs educ or less and among women*

    1802 in 1922 *PA Mag. Hist. & Biog.* 46.129 **PA,** Our breakfast today at a public Inn consisted of Coffee,—Venison Stake, porcht eggs. a roast chicken, honey, raddishes. **1934** *AmSp* 9.94 **NEng,** The form *porched,* with an intrusive *r,* is widespread. . . [I]n a few cases we find [pɔrʃt]. . . The majority of cases . . are of the type [porʧt]. [*DARE* Ed: *LANE* Map 295, which shows the results of the same fieldwork, shows few exx of intrusive [r], but numerous exx of the type [poətʃt].] *Ibid,* [Footnote:] Intrusive *r* in *poached* occurs outside New England in three out of four sample records from Kentucky, and in the samples from Roanoke County, Va., Bland Co., Va., and Florence County, S.C. *Ibid* 213 **TX,** *Poarched egg* for *poached egg.* **1948** McDavid *Coll.* **ceNY,** Poached [porʧt] eggs—fried. [Inf] Male, 74 [years old], farmer. **1954** Harder *Coll.* **cwTN,** Poached /pórčt/. . . An egg that is taken out of the shell and cooked in boiling water. **1960** Criswell *Resp. to PADS 20* **Ozarks,** *Porched* . . of an egg. Once heard often. **c1960** Wilson *Coll.* **csKY,** Poached eggs—fairly commonly eaten as food. Often /porʃt/. **1965–70** *DARE* (Qu. H35, *When eggs are taken out of the shells and cooked in boiling water, you call them _____ eggs*) 71 Infs, **chiefly Sth, S Midl,** Porched [proncs of the type [poɚčt, poətʃt]]; **LA11,** Poached; porched—old-fashioned; **LA14,** Poached; porched—most people say this; **TX91,** Poached; porched—old-fashioned, but still used. [Of all Infs responding to the question, 26% were gs educ or less, 72% women; of those giving

this response, 54% were gs educ or less, 84% women.] **1966–68** *DARE* FW Addits **CT2C, WA1A,** Porched [eggs]. **1976** Allen *LAUM* 3.256 **Upper MW** (as of c1950), Three U[pper] M[idwest] infs. have /paučt/ . . . A pronunciation with intrusive /r/, either /porčt/ or /pɔrčt/. . . persists in the U[pper] M[idwest] with five examples—in each state but Nebraska. One . . North Dakotan [old, with little educ] has the unusual form /pɚčt/, and one Iowan has [ʊˇ], which in this instance may simply be a variant of /o/. **1981** [see **A4** below]. **1983** *MJLF* 9.1.51 **ceKY,** *Poarch* . . to poach.

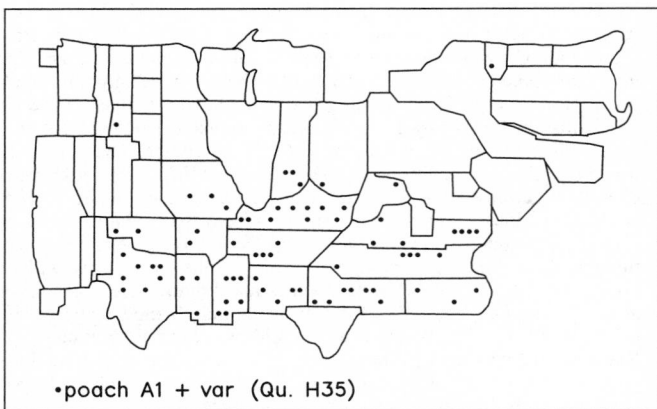

• poach A1 + var (Qu. H35)

2 |proč| and varr; pronc-sp *proach.* [Cf quot 1934 and Intro "Language Changes" I.8]   **chiefly Sth** See Map *esp freq among Black speakers*

    1934 *AmSp* 9.95 **NEng,** The form *proached eggs* is probably due to metathesis, which may have resulted from a contamination of the two forms *poached* and *porched.* It occurs in . . [3 Conn. communities]; also, outside New England, in Southampton, Long Island; . . and the counties of Albemarle and Rockbridge, Virginia. **1965–70** *DARE* (Qu. H35) 9 Infs, **chiefly Sth,** Proached [pro(ʊ)čt]; **AR26, FL49, SC26,** 67, 70, Proach [proč]; **MS60,** [proəčt]; **AL11,** [pračt]. [10 of 16 Infs Black]. **1981** [see **A4** below]. **1983** *MJLF* 9.1.52 **ceKY,** *Proach* . . to poach.

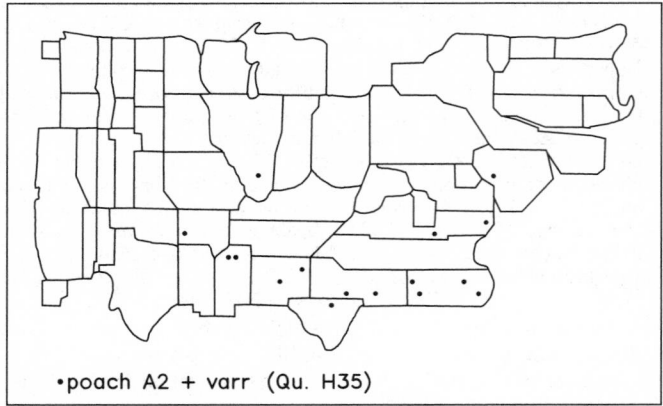

• poach A2 + varr (Qu. H35)

3 |pauč|; rarely |pauš|; pronc-sp *pouch.* [Perh by folk-etym]

    1934 *AmSp* 9.94 **NEng,** The word *poached* . . has several interesting phonetic variations. *Pouched* [pauʧt] is the form used by informants in Milford [CT] . . and on Martha's Vineyard; *pooched* [puʧt] occurs in Marblehead [MA] . . , and *polched* [pɔłtʃt] in Billerica [MA]. **1966–69** *DARE* (Qu. H35) Infs **NC44,** 60, **PA29,** 63, Pouched [paučt]. **1976** [see **A1** above]. **1981** [see **A4** below].

4 Addit varr; see quots.

    1934 [see **A3** above]. **1976** [see **A1** above]. **1981** Pederson *LAGS Basic Materials,* 1 inf, **cGA,** [pʼoˇčtʃt] [*LAGS* Ed: r color]; 1 inf, **swGA,** [pʼʊˑɪ̆tʃt]—laughing; [pʼɵᵘtʃtʼ]—what *he* says; 1 inf, **csGA,** [kɹoˍᵘtʃənəm]; [pʼoˍˑᵘtʃəm]—corrects herself; 1 inf, **ceAL,** [pʼoˑɪ̆tʃt] [*LAGS* Ed: 2 syllables?]; 1 inf, **ceMS,** [pʼo̞ʂətʃt]; 1 inf, **swMS,** [pʼoʂuˍstɪd]; 1 inf, **seLA,** [pʼʊʂɪ̆tʃ], [pʼɵˑɪ̆tʃ]; 1 inf, **cTX,** [pʼoˍˑɚtʃ] [pʼoˍˑ˗ətʃ] [Inf Black]; 1 inf, **ceTX,** [pʼrɵˍ˗utʃtɛ^ˍɪɡ] [Inf Black]; 1 inf, **cTX,** [pʼʉ̯ʉtʃt], [pʼʉ̯ʉʃ], [pʼaˍʊʃ] [*LAGS* Ed: Unsure of pronunciation of *poached*].

B Sense.

To scramble or fry (an egg). [Prob by semantic differentiation from **dropped egg,** widely used in New England for "poached egg," but cf *OED2 poach* v.[2] 1 "To push or stir (anything) *with* the point of a stick, a finger, a foot, etc."]

1933 Hanley *Disks* neMA, Poached egg. . . Eggs and milk and butter beat up together and fried. **1934** *AmSp* 9.90 NEng, In eastern and northern New England *poached eggs* . . usually means scrambled eggs. *Ibid,* [Footnote:] Usually the term *poached eggs* seems to be used of eggs mixed with milk before being put into the frying pan, while *scrambled eggs* denotes eggs stirred up in the pan without milk. **1948** [see A1 above].

poachard See **pochard**

poached See **poach**

poacher n

1 =**baldpate 1.** [See quot 1888] Cf **robber duck, pochard**

1888 Trumbull *Names of Birds* 20, To some of the gunners of Detroit it [=the American widgeon] is the *poacher,* being so called from its well-known habit of foraging upon the food for which other ducks have dived. **1905** Townsend *Birds Essex Co. MA* 130, The Baldpate, being unable to dive, makes use of diving Ducks to obtain food in deep water, and has therefore received in some places the name of "Poacher." [**1929** Forbush *Birds MA* 1.208, I have seen a flock of five Baldpates eagerly following half a dozen American Coots that were frequently diving in a pond and bringing up weeds from the bottom. The Baldpates . . helped themselves to the spoils, tipping up occasionally to catch some sinking weed. . . The Coots appeared to take the pilfering as a matter of course; in fact they pilfered from each other, and continued to work for themselves and the poachers.]

2 A marine fish of the family Agonidae.

1890 *Century Dict.* 4576, Poacher. . . The sea-poacher, a fish. **1983** *Audubon Field Guide N. Amer. Fishes* 734, Poachers—(Family Agonidae). . Poachers are often confused with juvenile sturgeons. . . This entirely marine family has 29 North American species. **1991** Amer. Fisheries Soc. *Common Names Fishes* 43, Agonidae—poachers.

poarch See **poach** A1

po'boy See **poor boy**

pocan n Also *pocan bush, pocum* [Algonquian] Cf **coakum** =**pokeweed 1a.**

c1612 (1849) Strachey *Hist. VA Britannia* 64, Their heads and shoulders they paint oftennest, and those red, with the roote pochone, brayed to powder, mixed with oyle of the walnutt, or bear's grease. [**1830** Rafinesque *Med. Flora* 251, *Phytolacca decandra,* Poke, Pocan of Virginia tribes.] **1897** *Jrl. Amer. Folkl.* 10.54 West, *Phytolacca decandra* . . cocum, pocum, pigeon berry. **1931** Clute *Common Plants* 24, No such doubt exists regarding the derivation of poke-weed *(Phytolacca decandra).* . . This plant is certainly the pocan of the Indians and the pocan-bush of the whites. **1971** Krochmal *Appalachia Med. Plants* 190, Pokeweed, . . pocan, pocan bush, poke, pokeberry, pokeroot [etc].

Pocatello yardmaster n [See quot 1940]

In railroading: a **boomer** n[2]; by ext, a fraud or blowhard.

1940 *RR Mag.* Apr 50, Pocatello Yardmaster—Derisive epithet for *boomer,* all of whom presumably claimed to have held, at some time, the tough job of night yardmaster . . at Pocatello, Idaho. An extra switchman was used to deliver switch lists at Pocatello. Because he was delivering the work he was sarcastically called "the yardmaster." Most of the extra men working there sooner or later caught the job, hence the plethora of *Pocatello Yardmasters.* **1947** Beebe *Mixed Train* 359, [Glossary:] *Pocatello Yardmaster:* Boomer. Many old-time boomers claimed to have had experience in this capacity, hence it became a derisive term for a fraud or four-flusher.

pochard n Also *American pochard, poachard* [*OED2* 1552 → for the Old World species *Aythya ferina*] =**redhead 1a(1).**

1824 Latham *Genl. Hist. Birds* 10.332, Pochard Duck. Anas ferina [here: =*Aythya americana*]. . Is well known in America, in winter as low as Carolina, and . . sometimes seen in the rivers and ponds about Georgia, . . is known there by the name of Brown-headed Duck and Sheldrake. **1834** Nuttall *Manual Ornith.* 2.435, The Pochard dives and swims with great agility. . . They are said to walk awkwardly and with difficulty. **1872** Coues *Key to N. Amer. Birds* 289, Red-head. Pochard.

1898 (1900) Davie *Nests N. Amer. Birds* 86, The Redhead or Poachard, so frequently confounded with the Canvas-back, is a common duck throughout North America. . . It nests in suitable localities of various northern states, Maine, Michigan, Wisconsin, Minnesota and Dakota. **1923** Dawson *Birds CA* 4.1800, Redhead. . . Synonym.—American Pochard. **1953** Jewett *Birds WA* 131, Redhead. . . Pochard; American Pochard. **1982** Elman *Hunter's Field Guide* 195, *Aythya americana.* . . Pochard.

po'ch chile See **porch child**

Pochuck n [Perh < **Podunk** infl by *Pochuck* Mt., NJ] Cf **Podock, Podunk 1**

Used as a nickname for a small, out-of-the-way, or unimportant place; hence n *Pochucker* one who resides in such a place.

1968 *DARE* (Qu. C33, . . *Joking names* . . *for an out-of-the-way place, or a very small or unimportant place*) Inf **PA**115, Pochuck; (Qu. C35, *Nicknames for the different parts of your town or city*) Inf **NY**80, Pochuck ['po·čək]; (Qu. HH18, *Very insignificant or low-grade people*) Inf **NY**80, Pochucker [po'čəkɚ].

pock n [Var of *pox;* cf *OED2 pock* sb. 2.β "Now *dial.* or *vulgar*"; *SND pock* n.[1] 1]

1845 Judd *Margaret* 284 swME, Glad you got through with the pock so well—it takes a second time, some say. **1917** *DN* 4.415 wNC, Pock. . . Pox. Also W[estern] Res[erve OH] (rare), Ill. **c1920** in 1993 Farwell-Nicholas *Smoky Mt. Voices* 125 sAppalachians, He had the pock. **1968** *DARE* (Qu. BB49, . . *Other kinds of diseases*) Inf **GA**23, Pock—syphilis, old-fashioned.

pock v [LaFr *pâquer* < Fr *Pâques* Easter] Cf **egg picking**

1983 Reinecke *Coll.* 9 LA, Pock [pɑk]. . . To strike the small end of one's hardboiled Easter Egg against that of another child, so that his whose egg is least damaged keeps both eggs. Custom still extant in some "Cajun" w. bank suburbs of N[ew] O[rleans].

pocket n

1 A bag or sack. [*OED2 pocket* sb. 1 1280 →] Cf **poke** n[1] **1a, saddle pocket**

1806 (1970) Webster *Compendious Dict.* 228, Pocket . . a small bag. [*DARE* Ed: This entry was carried over from Webster's English model.] **1881** *Harper's New Mth. Mag.* 63.728 Sth, There is not a process to which the lint is submitted after it is thrown from the negro's "pocket" that does not act directly on the quality of the cloth that is finally produced. **1953** *PADS* 19.12 nwNC, Paper pocket. . . Paper sack.

2 in phrr *in one's* (or *one another's*) *pocket* and varr: Close to or in close proximity to someone; on very friendly terms with one another; in someone's way. [*OED2 pocket* sb. 3.d 1812 →]

1909 (1910) *WNID* 1661, In one's pocket. . . Very close to one; as, to sit *in one's pocket.* **1913** *Funk & Wagnalls Dict.* 1911, In one's p[ocket]. . . On terms of intimacy as close to one as one's pocket. **1968–69** *DARE* (Qu. II3, *Expressions to say that people are very friendly toward each other: "They're _____."*) Infs **CA**110, **PA**151, Live in (*or* living out of) each other's pockets; **CT**8, [They're] in one another's pocket. [All Infs old] **1995** *DARE* File **TX**, "Since he's retired, he's really in her pocket all day long." To be "in one's pocket" meaning "underfoot" is a common expression to me.

3 in var phrr: See below. **chiefly Sth, S Midl**

a in phrr *out of (the) pocket:* Unavailable, absent, out of place.

1967 *DARE* (Qu. MM11, *When you're trying to find something—you don't know where it is* . . *"I must have left it _____."*) Inf **AL**37, Out of pocket. **1972** *DARE* File neTX, Out of pocket. . . whereabouts unknown. "Where's X_____?" "He's out of pocket." **1974** *Anderson Independent* (SC) 20 Apr sec A 1/1, If you . . have ever been sick and the only doctor is out of pocket for the weekend, then you know we need more doctors. **1983** *DARE* File **TX**, Out of pocket—away from your usual place. "I called you at home yesterday, but you were out of pocket." **1986** Chapman *New Dict. Amer. Slang* 310, Out of pocket (or the *pocket*) . . esp Southern and Southwestern Absent or otherwise unavailable: *I'm out of the pocket for a bit, but I'll get back at ya*—Rolling Stone / *The station chief was out of pocket*—WT Tyler. **1991** Still *Wolfpen Notebooks* 162 sAppalachians, Out of pocket: missing. **1995** *DARE* File **TX**, "I'll probably be out of pocket for a few days, but you can leave any messages for me on my answering machine." . . I use "out of pocket" to mean a *person* being unavailable. Don't think I'd ever use it to mean some*thing* misplaced. "My watch is out of pocket?" No! But I'll bet this might be where the expression originated. **1996** *Ibid,* My father from Hannibal, Missouri . . and my mother, who's from Omaha, Nebraska, use the term to mean "not being where one is supposed to be," as in "I'm sorry we couldn't be there but we were out-of-pocket." *Ibid* **TX, MS.**

b in phr *in pocket:* Available, in the usual place.

1995 *DARE* File **TX,** We called to tell her that we are going to be in Texas over the Christmas break and want to come by to visit. Her reply was, "Sure, y'all come on by. We'll be in pocket then."

4 often attrib; In mining: a small cavity in the earth filled with gold or other ore; a small compact deposit of rich ore; also v *pocket* of a vein of ore: to expand or bulge out into such a deposit. **West, esp CA, NV**

1847 in 1848 U.S. Congress *Serial Set* 505 Doc 41 451, The sides of the passage worn into deep rounded fissures that our host calls pockets; . . in them the richest ores are found. **1850** (1968) Taylor *Eldorado* 1.89 **CA,** We found many persons at work . . searching for veins and pockets of gold. **1872** Twain *Roughing It* 436 **cCA,** In that one little corner of California is found a species of mining which is seldom or never mentioned in print. It is called "pocket mining" and I am not aware that any of it is done outside of that little corner. The gold is not evenly distributed through the surface dirt, as in ordinary placer mines, but is collected in little spots, and they are very wide apart, and exceedingly hard to find, but when you do find one you reap a rich and sudden harvest. *Ibid* 437, Pocket hunting is an ingenious process. You take a spadeful of earth from the hill-side and put it in a large tin pan and dissolve and wash it gradually away till nothing is left but a teaspoonful of fine sediment. *Ibid* 443, At the end of two months we had never "struck" a pocket. **1873** Beadle *Undeveloped West* 336, A vein . . "pinching" and "pocketing" alternately towards the interior. **1873** Raymond *Silver & Gold* 47 **CA,** Although many so-called pocket-veins exist near to and parallel with the Mother lode, . . it is generally believed they are outlying "stringers" of the main lode. **1877** Bartlett *Americanisms* 476, *Pocket diggings.* A term used by gold-miners to denote hollow places where gold is concentrated as in a pocket. **1903** (1950) Austin *Land of Little Rain* 24 **neCA,** I suppose no man becomes a pocket-hunter by first intention. . My friend had been several things of no moment until he struck a thousand-dollar pocket in the Lee district. . . A pocket, you must know, is a small body of rich ore occurring by itself, or in a vein of poorer stuff. **1914** *DN* 4.164 **NW,** *Pocket-hunter.* . . A prospector. **1940** (1942) Clark *Ox-Bow* 13 **NV,** A couple of young fellows from Sacramento found loose gold in Belcher's Creek, up at the north end, and traced it down to a pocket. **1947** Peattie *Sierra Nevada* 278 **CA,** It has been the custom for ninety years to believe that pocket miners invariably wrest fortune from Jackass Hill. **1969** *DARE* Tape **CA120,** If you see color, why, you just keep followin' it and hope that it'll make a pocket. **1979** *Oregonian Article Letters* **Pacific NW** [Mining terms], Pocket hunter: prospector who looks for rich pockets of gold.

5 Any of var topographic formations, as:

a A cove n[1] **3** or **coulee 1c.**

1745 in 1915 NH *Prov. & State Papers* 33.293, I also give to my said Son Samuel the Marsh called the Little Pocket & all the flats facing or Lying against the Same. **1860** *Harper's New Mth. Mag.* 21.604 **ND,** One Saturday afternoon we brought up in a "pocket" near the Lac de Gros Butte, where we were protected on two sides by water, and on one side by an impassable marsh. **1874** Long *Wild-Fowl* 215 (*DAE*), High cypress timber. . . bordered the little coves (or pockets as they are called by the natives). **1885** (1891) Roosevelt *Hunting* 136 **MT, WY,** In many of the pockets or glens in the sides of the hills the trees grow to some little height. **1886** Ingersoll *To the Shenandoah* 48 **VA** (*AmSp* 15.296), Scattered here and there in all directions, nestling in the intervals and pockets of the ranges, are the log cabins of the mountaineers. **1928** *AmSp* 4.126 **cnNE,** The depressions among the hills are called "pockets," and after the spring rains many of these "pockets" are tiny lakes called "water pockets." **1934** Vines *Green Thicket* 65 **cnAL,** They rode a few miles down the Big River's way and drew up at a pocket between two ridge prongs where a branching hollow started for a near-by main hollow. [**1947** *PADS* 7.19 **csWI,** Pocket seems to be still in the stage of metaphor here, appearing in the *Devil's Pocket* (alias the *Devil's Washbowl*). *Ibid* 101, *Devil's Pocket, The*—Subjectively descriptive: a very sharp ravine where two branch ravines meet.] **1968** *DARE* (Qu. C19, . . *Low land running between hills [With and without water]*) Inf **NY92,** Pocket—down the side of a mountain. **1973** Allen *LAUM* 1.232 (as of c1950), *Pocket:* Low grassland in hills or on the prairie [1 inf, **swSD**]. *Ibid* 235, *Coulee.* . . pocket [1 inf, **csNE**].

b A **bayou 3.**

1967–68 *DARE* (Qu. C14, *A stretch of still water going off to the side from a river or lake*) Inf **LA15,** Pocket; **KS5,** Side pocket; (Qu. C34, *Nicknames for nearby settlements, villages, or districts*) Inf **MO9,** The devil's pocket—it used to be so swampy. **1981** Pederson *LAGS Basic Materials,* 1 inf, **seAR,** Pockets—little places where river moves in and works out the land; 1 inf, **seAR,** Pocket—behind sandbar; [1 inf, **ceTX,** Devils Pocket—NE Newton County].

c See quot.

1946 Attwood *Length ME* 15 [Geographical terms], *Pocket*—A cove. Squirrel Pocket. [*Ibid* 14, *Cove*—A comparatively small sheltered inlet from the sea or other body of water.]

6 In commercial fishing: the trap of a weir or other fishing net.

1884 Knight *New Mech. Dict.* 698, *Pocket Net.* (Fishing.) One with a relatively small compartment in which the fish are collected. . . *Trap Net.* . . *Trammel Net.* **1890** *Century Dict.* 4576, *Pocket.* . . The trap of a weir, in which the fish are retained or caught. The fish pass from the little pound into the pocket, which is a frame about 16 feet long and 10 feet wide, with sides of netting and a board floor. The fish are left in the pocket by the receding tide, and are taken out at low water. In a deep-water weir the fish are not left by the tide, but must be lifted out with a seine or purse-net. **1947** *Richmond Times–Dispatch* (VA) 3 Sept 6/1 (*Hench Coll.*) **ceVA,** The only opening they [=fish] find out of that one goes into the pound, which has a bottom raised up off the bay bottom, and is just a big 50-foot cage. Then they go into the 30-foot pocket, and that's where the fisherman takes 'em out. **1966–70** *DARE* Tape **ME17,** A pocket of a seine is the, after you run . . a piece of twine, clear across a cove, why, you put a pocket on it which is an eighty-fathom twenty fathoms square with four kegs on it, so the carrier [=a boat that removes fish from nets] can come to it and take your fish out; **NC58,** There was a large net that was . . called a pocket, and it had a trap or a door in it. The mouth of this door was a big iron square shape with the net hung to it and open out into the water, and the back of this was tied with a rope to a stake over in one corner, and that would let the fish in. And when the fisherman went to fish the net he would untie this and that would close the door or trap so that the fish could not get out so that he could put the net over the side of his boat; **VA55,** Then they put the pocket overboard. You fasten the pocket—the end of the seine to the ring on the pocket, and then they lower it, get it all in and walk it right around and a man standing overboard with the other end of it right against the seine, keep the fish from going by. After you get it all in, you run 'em right in the pocket and raise the pocket up, tie it up. [**1981** Pederson *LAGS Basic Materials,* 1 inf, **nwFL,** A long pocket—speaking of the seine net, making a long pocket.]

7 In logging: see quot 1958.

1958 McCulloch *Woods Words* 136 **Pacific NW,** *Pocket.* . . An area into which logs are stowed before making up a boom. **1968** *DARE* Tape **NY96** (as of c1920), When these logs came in, came down the river, a man stood at what they call the mouth of the boom. . . Whatever name was on the log, it went in the mill owner's boom. . . They yard these logs all in one pocket, different owner's pocket in the water.

8 In marble play: see quot.

c1970 Wiersma *Marbles Terms* **swMI,** *Pocket* . . hole in center of marked off circle—to gain points you must get your marbles into this hole.

9 in phr *put (a slave) in one's pocket:* To convert (a slave) into money. *hist*

1857 Long *Pictures Slavery* (2d ed) 183 **MD,** He deserved hanging, or the penitentiary for life. But his master simply took him to the slave-pen in Baltimore, and—*put him in his pocket!* **c1937** in 1970 Yetman *Voices* 189 **MS** (as of a1865) [Black], Another rule on dat place was dat if a man [=a slave] got dissatisfied, he was to go to de marster and ask him to "put him in his pocket." Dat meant he wanted to be sold and de money . . put in de marster's pocket. **1937** in 1976 *Weevils in the Wheat* 215 **VA** (as of c1850) [Black], Marser Riles was a mean man. . . Ole Marser git cross an' he "put you in his pocket." Dat what dey say when dey mean he give you to a mean man to wuk fer.

pocket v See **pocket** n **4**

pocket bird n
=scarlet tanager.

1917 *Wilson Bulletin* 29.2.83 **swKY,** *Piranga erythromelas.*—Fire bird, pocket-bird, black-winged redbird, redbird, Hickman, Ky.

pocketbook n

1 also *pocketbook clam*; A **freshwater clam:** usu *Lampsilis ovata*, but also *L. cardium, L. ventricosus, Potamilus capax,* or *P. purpurata.* Cf **rock pocketbook**

1911 *Century Dict. Suppl., Pocket-book. . . A fresh-water mussel, Lampsilis capax* or *L. ventricosus,* which has round valves of great depth. **1935** Pratt *Manual Invertebrate Animals* 657, *L[ampsilis] ventricosa . . Pocket-book clam . .* valleys of the Mississippi and St. Lawrence; in large streams and lakes; common; used in button making. **1938** FWP *Guide IA* 327, The niggerhead . . commanded the highest price; others, all salable, were the warty black, yellow back, mucket, washboard, pocketbook [etc]. **1941** Writers' Program *Guide AR* 207 **neAR,** Dredging the White River and its tributaries for fresh-water mussels used for button making affords farmers a part-time occupation. . . Payment, made by the ton, varies according to the type of shell, "grandmaws," "pocketbooks," and "cucumbers" bringing less than "elephant ears" and "niggerheads." **1982** U.S. Fish & Wildlife Serv. *Fresh-Water Mussels* [Wall chart], Pocketbook . . *Lampsilis ovata ventricosa. Ibid,* Purple Pocketbook. . . *Proptera [Potamilus] purpurata. Ibid,* Fat Pocketbook . . *Proptera [Potamilus] capax.* **1991** IL Nat. Hist. Surv. *Biol. Notes* 137.11 **IL,** *Lampsilis cardium . .* plain pocketbook. Currently the most common species in the Sangamon River drainage. **1992** *Nature Conserv. Mag.* Nov/Dec 18 **swVA,** Neves, an aquatic biologist . . in Blacksburg, Virginia, raises a stream of varied forms and colorful appellations from Pendleton's mussel bed: pheasantshell, kidneyshell, rabbitsfoot, pigtoe, monkeyface, heelsplitter, pimpleback, pocketbook.

2 in phr *take out one's pocketbook*; Of a **green lizard 1** (here: *Anolis carolinensis*): see quot. Cf **money 2**

1930 *Copeia* 4.154 **swGA,** One of the residents said that when this lizard distends its pink throat, they speak of its 'taking out its pocketbook.'

3 The female genitals.

1969 (1970) Angelou *Caged Bird* 71 **AR** [Black], Mr. Freeman pulled me to him, and put his hand between my legs. He didn't hurt, but Momma had drilled into my head: "Keep your legs closed, and don't let nobody see your pocketbook." **1977** Dillard *Lexicon* 33 [Black], Frequently attested [for the female sex organs] . . is *pocketbook.* **1980** *DARE* File **Columbia SC,** Pocketbook = vagina. A physician reported that an elderly black patient asked him diffidently if he was "going to look in my pocketbook." **1990** Cavender *Folk Med. Lexicon* 29 **sAppalachians,** *Pocketbook*—vagina. **1992** Ayto–Simpson *Oxford Dict. Mod. Slang* 172 (as of 1942), *Pocketbook . .* U[nited] S[tates] The female genitals.

4 See **pocketbook roll.**

5 A type of turnover or filled pastry; see quots. Cf **pocketbook roll**

1920 Kander *Settlement Cook Book* 356, *Turnovers, Kipfel* or *Pocketbooks.* Make a Kuchen Dough . . or Cookie Dough. . . and place . . preserves . . in center. . . and fold . . forming a three cornered little pie, or place filling on lower half of square and fold over the other half, pinch the edges well together. **c1965** Randle *Cookbooks* (Ask Neighbor) 1.7, *Petite Pocketbooks. . .* Cut [dough] into 3″ squares. . . Fold so corners overlap in center of each square to enclose filling.

pocketbook clam See **pocketbook 1**

pocketbook roll n Also *pocketbook, pocket roll* **chiefly east of Missip R, esp PA** See Map

A type of yeast roll formed by cutting the dough, then folding or rolling it; see esp quot 1965–70.

1879 (1965) Tyree *Housekeeping in Old VA* 33, *Pocketbook Rolls. . .* Mix up . . ingredients with warm water. . . Roll out the dough in strips as long and wide as your hand, spread with butter and roll up like a pocketbook. **1885** *Cuisine Creole* 134 **New Orleans LA,** When it [=the dough] is risen it is ready to form into shapes, called pocket-books. **1890** James *Mother James' Cooking* 175, *Pocketbooks.* **1950** *WELS* **WI** (*Kinds of fancy home-baked rolls*) 2 Infs, Pocketbook [rolls]; 1 Inf, Parker House [rolls], also called pocketbook [rolls]; 1 Inf, Pocketbooks; pocketbook [rolls]—old-fashioned; like Parker only larger. **1951** Johnson *Resp. to PADS 20* **DE,** Pocketbook rolls. **1965–70** *DARE* (Qu. H32, . . *Fancy rolls and pastries*) 47 Infs, **chiefly east of Missip R, esp PA,** Pocketbook rolls; **MS79, NJ40,** 53, **OH44, TN52,** Pocketbook rolls [FW sugg]; **AL6,** Pocketbook rolls—rolls were folded over, seam on one side; **LA19,** Pocketbook rolls—a folded-over roll; **MA6,** Pocketbook rolls—rolled out square, turn flap like envelope; **MA98,** Pocketbook rolls—fold over; **NE9,** Pocketbook rolls—they're the same as

Parker House rolls; **NC51,** Pocketbook rolls—made by folding over the dough before cooking; **OH55,** Pocketbook rolls—old-fashioned; same as Parker House rolls; **OH98,** Pocket rolls; **PA49,** Pocketbook rolls— like a Parker House roll; [(Qu. H19, *What do you mean by a biscuit? How are they made?*) Inf **PA67,** Pocketbook [biscuit]—piece of dough folded over]. [60 of 61 total Infs mid-aged or old, 52 female]

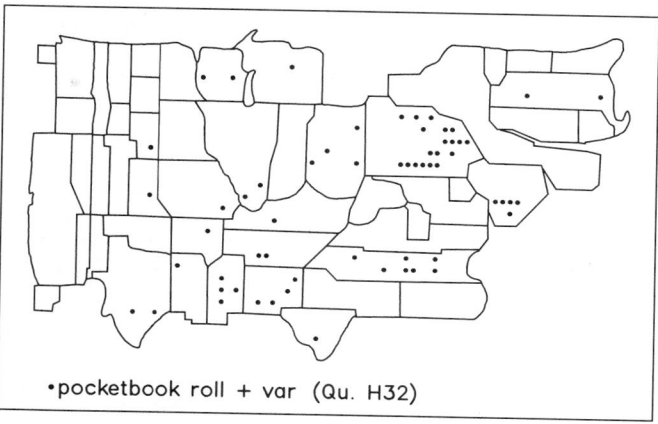

•pocketbook roll + var (Qu. H32)

pocket dipper n
=**bufflehead 2.**

1955 MA Audubon Soc. *Bulletin* 316 **MA,** *Buffle-head. . .* Pocket Dipper. . . That is, small diver.

pocket gopher n

1 A rodent of the family Geomyidae, native to the Mississippi and Ohio Valleys and westward and in the Gulf States. [See quot 1917] Also called **gopher** n[1] **2a, sand rat.** For other names of *Geomys* or of var spp of this genus see **ground gopher 3, ~ rat 1, pouched gopher, ~ rat, salamander 2;** for other names of *Thomomys* or of var spp of this genus see **camas rat, pouched gopher, ~ rat**

1873 Eggleston *Mystery* 37 **MN,** She would . . explain how the pocket-gophers built their mounds. **1899** Garland *Boy Life* 85 **nwIA** (as of c1870s), The "pocket gopher" was considered a sort of mole or rat and not really a gopher. **1917** Anthony *Mammals Amer.* 266, The Pocket Gophers. . . receive their distinctive name "pocket," from the presence of large, fur-lined cheek pouches opening outside the mouth. These are used as genuine pockets for carrying things of quite as much value to the Gopher as the contents of their pockets are to small boys. **1947** Cahalane *Mammals* 425, The pocket gopher. . . [has] complete pouches, not merely bulging cheeks outside the molars like those of the chipmunk. **1961** Jackson *Mammals WI* 184, *Geomys bursarius bursarius. . .* In Wisconsin generally called pocket gopher. **1965–70** *DARE* (Qu. P29, . . *'Gophers' . . other name . . or what other animal are they most like*) 21 Infs, **chiefly West, Upper MW,** Pocket gopher; **CA23,** Pocket gopher—has pockets like a chipmunk—stays underground; gophers called pocket gophers here; **CA36,** Gopher . . also called pocket gopher—has the pouch on each side of the jaw; **CA117,** Pocket gopher—regular gopher—light brown, no stripes; **FL16,** Pocket gopher or salamander; **KS20,** Pocket gopher—bigger than a mole, shovel-like teeth; mounds up the ground. [*DARE* Ed: Some of these Infs may refer instead to **2** below.] **1987** *Nature Conserv. News* 37.3.28 **IN,** This . . dune and swale community . . supports populations of plains pocket gopher and paper birch. **1992** Martone *Townships* 74 **swMN,** Every farm was ringed by a little greenway, in which . . ground squirrels, pocket gophers, and badgers burrowed.

2 A **ground squirrel b,** usu *Spermophilus tridecemlineatus.* **Upper MW**

1970 *DARE* (Qu. P29, . . *'Gophers' . . other name . . or what other animal are they most like*) Inf **IA14,** Pocket gopher—striped gophers; **IL38,** Pocket gopher—carry food in cheeks; they call them pocket gophers south of the [Illinois] River and ground squirrels north of the river; **MN7,** Pocket gopher—striped gopher; **WI6,** Pocket gophers—yellow-and-black striped. **1970** *Western Folkl.* 29.172 **Upper MW,** Pocket gopher . . and striped squirrel are names for the thirteen-lined ground squirrel. **1973** Allen *LAUM* 1.323 (as of c1950), 2 infs, **MN, ND,** Pocket gopher.

pocket mouse n [From the external cheek pockets]

Usu a small burrowing rodent of the genus *Perognathus* native to the western US, but also the related *Liomys irroratus* of extreme southern TX. Also called **pocket rat 2.** For other names of the former see **kangaroo mouse 2b;** for other names of the latter see **spiny mouse**

1884 *Cassell's Nat. Hist.* 3.124, The *Heteromyinæ* (forming the family Saccomyidæ of Dr. Coues . .). . . Like the Geomyinæ, these animals are confined to America, and chiefly limited to the Southern United States and Central America, although some of the species occur as far north as the Columbia River and Hudson's Bay. . . By American writers they are called "Pocket Mice." *Ibid,* The *Yellow Pocket Mouse* and the *Least Pocket Mouse* (*Cricetodipus flavus* and *parvus*) are very minute creatures. . . These species are found in the Rocky Mountains and the region west of that range to the Pacific, the latter being inhabited by the second of the above species. **1917** Anthony *Mammals Amer.* 257, Pocket mouse—*Perognathus fasciatus.* . . A small Mouse with a large head, external cheek pouches, and rather a long tail. **1947** *S. Sierran* March 3, This mouse is about one inch longer than the Pocket Mouse. **1957** Barnes *Nat. Hist. Wasatch* Summer 67 **UT,** The Great Basin pocket mouse . . , being nocturnal, . . is seldom seen, though its little earth mounds about bushes often attract one's attention. **1980** Whitaker *Audubon Field Guide Mammals* 436, Pocket mice, smaller than kangaroo mice, look more mouselike and have only moderately long tails . . ; they are poor jumpers.

pocket peddler n

See quots.

1892 *Nation* 28 July 66, The liquor traffic. . . is now largely conducted by men called pocket-peddlers—men who stand on the street corners with a bottle in one pocket and a glass in the other, and will sell you a drink in a doorway or a horse-shed. **1909** *DN* 3.414 **nME,** *Pocket peddler.* . . A person who carries about bottles of distilled liquor for illicit selling. **1965–69** *DARE* (Qu. DD32, *A person who sells illegal liquor*) Inf **ME**19, Pocket peddler—he carries liquor in [his] pocket; sold pints or half-pints in alleys; **MS**59, Pocket peddler; **TN**30, Pocket peddler—small-time bootlegger, carries a bottle in his pocket to sell; **TN**37, Pocket peddler—a small-time bootlegger. [3 of 4 Infs old]

pocket purse n

A coin purse.

1966 Dakin *Dial. Vocab. Ohio R. Valley* 2.190, The most common name for a container for coins is *purse,* regular throughout the Valley and frequently given as *coin purse, money purse, change purse, pocket purse.* **1986** Pederson *LAGS Concordance* **Gulf Region** (*Purse for coins*) 2 infs, Pocket purse; 1 inf, Pocket purse—men carried change in this.

pocket rat n [From the external cheek pockets]

1 =**kangaroo rat 1.**

1906 Stephens *CA Mammals* 150, A singular characteristic of Pocket-Rats and Pocket-Mice is their ability to go without water and if necessary without eating moist food. Most species inhabit arid regions or deserts, though a few species are found in regions of moderate rainfall. **1917** Anthony *Mammals Amer.* 257, Pocket Rats are. . . an interesting group of small rodents characterized, like the Pocket Gophers, by cheek pouches which are used for carrying food. . . They include the Pocket Mice, which are usually plains-loving animals, and the Pocket, or Kangaroo Rats, characterized by enormously developed hind legs.

2 =**pocket mouse.**

1906 Stephens *CA Mammals* 162, *Perognathus panamintus.* . . Panamint Pocket-Rat. . . Panamint Mountains, California, eastward to St. George, Utah. **1917** [see **1** above]. **1928** Anthony *N. Amer. Mammals* 297, *Liomys irroratus texensis* . . *Names.*—Texas Spiny Mouse; Texas Spiny Pocket Rat. . . A large Mouse or small Rat with fur-lined cheek-pockets and pelage composed of normal hairs mingled with stiff bristles or spines.

3 =as *dwarf pocket rat, pygmy* ~: =**kangaroo mouse 2c.**

1917 Anthony *Mammals Amer.* 259 **cNV,** Pygmy Pocket Rat.— *Microdipodops megacephalus.* **1928** Anthony *N. Amer. Mammals* 325, *Microdipodops megacephalus* and related forms. . . Dwarf Pocket Rat.

pocket roll See **pocketbook roll**

pock-leg n [Cf *EDD pock* v.[2] 2 "To shove, push."]

1918 *DN* 5.19 **NC,** *Pock-legs,* legs to be driven in, as in a bench or chair.

poco pronto adv phr Pronc-sp *poky pranto* [Pseudo Span]

At once, quickly, immediately.

1907 White *AZ Nights* 174, The Mexican was only too glad to get off so easy. I don't know whether he'd really won the coat at monte or not. In any case, he flew *poco pronto,* leaving me and my friend together. **1922** Knibbs *Saddle Songs* 36 (Carlisle *Southwestern Dict.*), We locked the door on vain regret and, poco pronto, lost the key. **1933** *AmSp* 8.1.32 **nwTX,** *Poco pronto* (pronounced *poky pranto*). Very soon. **1934** (1940) Weseen *Dict. Amer. Slang* 104 [Cowboys' and Westerners' slang], *Poco pronto*—Very quickly; immediately.

pocosin n Usu |pə'kosn̩, 'pokəsən| Also *pocoson, poquoson* Pronc-spp *percosan, percossin, pocoshun;* for addit pronc and sp varr see quots and *DA(E), OED2* [Algonquian] **chiefly NC, VA, MD** Cf **bay** n[1] 3, **pokelogan**

1 A swamp, marsh, or low-lying area—also used in place-names.

1631 in 1940 *AmSp* 15.296 **VA,** Which. . . lyeth upon a river called the Pocoson river. **1643** *Ibid* **VA,** Runing for length North by East three hundred and twentie pole something nigh unto a reedy Swampe or Poquoson. **1709** (1967) Lawson *New Voyage* 32 **NC, SC,** The Swamp I now spoke of, is not a miry Bog, . . but you go down to it thro' a steep Bank, at the Foot of which, begins this Valley. . . The Land in this Percoarson, or Valley, being extraordinary rich, and the Runs of Water well stor'd with Fowl. *Ibid* 63, We lay in a rich *Perkoson,* or low Ground. **1713** in 1886 NC *Colonial Rec.* 2.69, A certaine parcell of Land . . begining at a Gume [=a gum tree] by ye side of a great Swamp . . running . . to ye pocosson. **c1738** (1929) Byrd *Histories* 50 **VA,** We row'd up an Arm of the Sound. . . There we were stoppt by a Miry Pocoson . . thro' which we were oblig'd to daggle on foot, . . up to the Knees in Mud. **c1770** in 1833 Boucher *Glossary* 1 **MD,** Strolling, last *fall,* by yon *pacosen* side,/ Coil'd in a heap, a rattle-snake I spied. [Footnote: *Pacosen;* an Indian term for a swamp, or marsh.] **1784** Smyth *Tour U.S.A.* 1.106 **NC,** Rode along upon a wooden causeway, through a marsh, which is here called a poccoson. **1859** Perry *Turpentine Farming* 161 **NC,** Common short-straw pine. . . will thrive near ponds, rivers and percosans, where the surface is flat and wet. **1899** (1912) Green *VA Folk-Speech* 330, *Poquoson.* . . A wet, swampy piece of ground. Pocoson. Pawquoson. **1910** Hodge *Hdbk. Amer. Indians* 2.287, *Poquoson.* A name applied in eastern Maryland, Virginia, and North Carolina to a low wooded ground or swamp, which is covered with shallow water in winter and remains in a miry condition in summer. . . The name is spelled also *poaquesson, poquoson, pocoson, perkoson.* *Ibid* 270, Pocosan, Pocosin, Pocoson. See *Poquoson.* **1925** in 1940 *AmSp* 15.296 **VA,** There is an accumulation of humus on some of the upland flats, which are known as pocosins. **1939** in 1944 *ADD* **NC, VA,** Percossin = low, yellow marsh land. **1939** FWP *Guide NC* 9, These swamplands, locally known as "dismals" and "pocosins." **1940** *AmSp* 15.296 **VA,** *Pocosin* (*pocoson, poquoson*). Pronounced [po·'ko:sn], ['po:kəsn]. **1942** McAtee *Notes Thornton's Gloss.* [3], There are several well recognized pocosins in Maryland; Patuxtent [sic] Valley people pronounce the word pocoshun. **1966–70** *DARE* (Qu. C6, . . *A piece of land that's often wet, and has grass and weeds growing on it*) Inf **NC**15, [pə'kousən]—used in old deeds; not sure of its meaning, but it's wet lowland or meadowland; old-fashioned; **VA**44, [pə'kosn̩]—poor drainage, high and dry enough to grow trees, but water level high in ground and floods quickly in spring; Poquoson—place-name in York County, Virginia; (Qu. C7, . . *Land that usually has some standing water with trees or bushes growing in it*) Inf **NC**5, [pə'kousn̩]—a swamp; old-fashioned; **NC**11, [pɚ'koušn]—old-fashioned; (Qu. C11) Inf **NC**17, [pə'kousn̩]—a wet, marshy area. [4 of 5 Infs old, 1 mid-aged] **1976** [see **2** below]. **1981** Pederson *LAGS Basic Materials,* 1 inf, ceAL, [ðɪᵛ pˑɪᵛ'ko⁺ʃŋz]—area in Pike County where plants stay green year-round; 1 inf, seAL, [ðə ˌprə'ko⁺ʊsŋz]—a place perennially green, written up in National Geographic. **1994** NC Lang. & Life Project *Dial. Dict. Lumbee Engl.* 9 **seNC,** Pocosin. . . Big swamp. *In the old days, they would hide out in the middle of the pocosin, and no one would ever find them.*

2 also *pocosin canoe:* A type of **log canoe;** see quots.

1906 *Forest & Stream* 67.898 **Chesapeake Bay,** Why should not a bugeye, a bugeye with a bustle, a three-log canoe, a five-log one, a Pocosin, a maulhead, a jigger rig, a spanker rig, and all the other small boat rigs of Chesapeake Bay be hung as they are rigged for the edification of the near generation which will have forgotten these strange craft? **1907** *Ibid* 68.212, Our canoe was a maulhead—wide at the bow and tapering aft like a tadpole. The Pocosin model tapers forward from the broad stern, and is a much faster boat under sails, it is claimed. A built-up boat would have been much lighter, and, on the whole, much more satisfactory, although the canoe will last 50 years, and the plank boat only half as long. **1951** Chapelle *Amer. Small Sailing Craft* 292 **eVA,** The Poquoson. . . The double-ended hull, variously rigged, usually had straight stem and stern posts set at moderate rake. In the late 1850's, the boats were often two-masted leg-of-mutton-rigged, without a bowsprit or jib, but later most were one-masted and many had jibs. **1963** Brewington *Chesapeake Bay Canoes* 7 **eVA,** Canoes built near the Poquoson River have long been the most famous, and the custom of calling all Virginia-built craft "Poquoson canoes" will be followed hereafter. **1976** Warner *Beautiful Swimmers* 141 **eMD,** Before the advent of crab pots, mud-larking was practiced rather widely around Poquoson on Virginia's Lower Neck. Poquoson (pronounced Puh-*ko*-son) is famous for two things. The first is the Poquoson canoe . . , the last made and best of workboat forms of the log sailing canoe.

pocosin pine n
=**pond pine 1.**

   1950 Peattie *Nat. Hist. Trees* 24, Pocosin Pine. . . Pocosin, in the language of the Delaware Indians and other Algonquin tongues, means a small but deep pond or bog, and that is the place to look for this curiously aquatic Pine. **1980** Little *Audubon Guide N. Amer. Trees E. Region* 295, Pond pine—"Marsh Pine" "Pocosin Pine"—*Pinus serotina.*

pocoson See **pocosin**

pocum See **pocan**

pod n

1 The outer covering of a pea or bean. [*OED2 pod* sb.[2] 1 1688 →] **widespread, but less freq Sth, S Midl** See Map and Map Section   Note: The phr *like two peas in a pod* and varr are not regional and thus not included. Cf **hull** n **B2a(3), husk** n **B3, pod** v **1**

   1806 (1970) Webster *Compendious Dict.* 228, Pod . . a case of seeds. [*DARE* Ed: This entry was carried over from Webster's English model.] **1828** Webster *Amer. Dict.,* Pod. . . In popular language, *pod* is used for the legume as well as for the silique or siliqua. In New England, it is the only word in popular use. **1871** Bagg *4 Yrs. at Yale* 245, Whenever peas were to be boiled for dinner, all undergraduates were summoned to assist in shelling them, and if any man was absent, the rest collected the pods and threw them, without ceremony into the delinquent's room. **1925** *Book of Rural Life* 7.4387, The most familiar examples of pods are those belonging to the pulse, or leguminous family—the peas and beans. **1950** WELS **WI** (*The outside covering that you break open to take the peas out*) 49 Infs, Pod; (*The outside covering of dry beans*) 32 Infs, Pod. **1951** Johnson *Resp. to PADS 20* **DE,** I think of them as pods when containing peas. **1957** Battaglia *Resp. to PADS 20* **eMD,** Pod. **1960** Bailey *Resp. to PADS 20* **KS,** Pod—widely used. **1965–70** *DARE* (Qu. I10) 582 Infs, **widespread, but less freq Sth, S Midl,** Pod; **ME1,** Pea pod; (Qu. I12) 339 Infs, **widespread, but less freq Sth, S Midl,** Pod; (Qu. H50, *Dishes made with beans, peas, or corn*) Inf **HI1,** Peas in pods; **MN16,** Buttered peas in the pod—young ones; (Qu. I11, *When somebody takes peas out of the covering . . . "She's _____ peas."*) Inf **MO14,** Breaking (*or opening*) the pod; **PA176,** Taking them out of the pod; **PA245,** Shelling the pod; (Qu. BB51b, . . *'Magical' cures for corns or warts*) Inf **MA38,** If you take five pods of shell beans and plant them;

(Qu. JJ15b, *Sayings about a person who seems to you very stupid: "He doesn't know _____ ."*) Inf **OH78,** Beans when the pod's open; **SD3,** Beans from peas when the pods are open.

2 =**hull** n **B2a(1).**   Cf **husk** n **B2a**

   1968–69 *DARE* (Qu. I39, . . *The thick outside covering of a walnut*) Infs **NY87, PA77, WI72,** Pod; **NC76,** Pod, I reckon; **PA167,** Pod [FW: Inf queries]. **1973** Allen *LAUM* 1.307 (as of c1950), The green outer covering of a walnut or hickory nut. . . pod [1 inf, **neSD**].

3 A paunch, potbelly; hence adj *poddy* paunchy, stout. [*OED2 pod* sb.[2] 3 a1825 →; "*dial.*"; *EDD pod* sb.[1] 2] **chiefly Nth, esp NEng**   Cf **pod** v **2, poddy** n

   1858 *Harper's New Mth. Mag.* 18.139, The venerable President [of Dartmouth College] was observed jogging out of the village on his little *poddy* black horse. **1909** (1910) *WNID,* Pod. . . Anything resembling a pod or pouch; specif., a large protuberant belly. *Dial. or Vulgar.* **1920** in 1954 Weingarten *Amer. Dict. Slang* np, Poddy. . . Stocky; thick-set. **1929** *AmSp* 5.129 **ME,** A fat man was "consid'able pus-sy" or "had quite a pod." **1941** *LANE* Map 458 (*Stout, paunchy*) [1 inf, seMA, [hi̯z ə 'pɒd bɛlɪ]]; 1 inf, ceMA, He has a [pɒd]; 1 inf, cwVT, He's got a big [pɑd]; 1 inf, ceVT, He has a ['pɒ^d] on him; 1 inf, swNH, He has a [pɒdɪ]; 2 infs, c,eMA, [pɒdɪ]; 1 inf, swMA, [pɑdɪ]; 1 inf, csNH, [pɒˑdɪ̇ˑ]. **1950** WELS (*An oversize stomach*) 6 Infs, WI, Pod. **1952** WELS Suppl. cwWI, Poddy. . . Pursy. . . Said of a goldfish. **1953** Randolph–Wilson *Down in Holler* 272 **Ozarks,** Pod. . . Belly, paunch. Of a very fat man in McDonald County, Mo., a neighbor remarked: "It looks like Lon's pod is about to bust on him." **1965** *DARE* File cnMA (as of c1920), "I hadn't seen Mr. Whitacre for three or four years. He's developed quite a pod." I think it [=the word] was used only of men. **1967–70** *DARE* (Qu. X53a, . . *An oversize stomach*) Infs **MI63, MN39, MA98, NY7, RI17,** Pod; (Qu. X53b, *An oversize stomach that results from drinking*) Inf **RI15,** Pod.

4 also *pod sleigh:* A kind of sleigh; see esp quot 1976. [Cf *EDD pod* sb.[1] 4 "The body of a cart."] **esp NEng** *hist*

   1915 Dunbar *Hist. Travel* 1.50 (as of 18th cent), The people of New England . . called a sleigh either a pung or a pod. . . A pung was drawn by two horses; a pod by one. **1942** Rawson *NH Borns a Town* 227, Many a long pod sleigh went ringing along to the jingle of its sleighbells, well laden with frozen hides and hogs or whatever the farm or mill or shop had to send "off." **1976** *WI Then & Now* Dec 3 (as of c1822), Carioles, mounted on runners in winter, resembled dog or goat carts, and were pulled by one horse. Pods were copies of carioles and were early models of the low-cut, "one-horse open sleigh."

pod v

1 also rarely *unpod:* =**hull** v **1.** [*OED2 pod* v.[1] 3 1902] **chiefly Inland Nth, N Midl** See Map   Cf **pod** n **1**

   1866 *Scientific Amer.* 15.132, I have found that, by gathering peas when young, . . then podding and scalding, and drying thoroughly . . they will keep almost any length of time. **1909** (1910) *WNID,* Pod. . to hull or shell, as peas. **1941** *LANE* Map 260, 2 infs, **VT,** Pod the beans; 1 inf, **VT,** Have you got those beans podded? 1 inf, cnMA, Pod the peas. **1948** Davis *Word Atlas Gt. Lakes* app qu 44, 22 (of 233) infs, **esp MI,** Pod. **1950** WELS (*When you take the peas out of the covering, you are _____ them*) 3 Infs, **WI,** Podding. **1965–70** *DARE* (Qu. I11, *When somebody takes peas out of the covering . . "She's _____ peas."*) 23 Infs, **chiefly Inland Nth, N Midl,** Podding; **PA70,** Unpodding; (Qu. I13, *When you take dry beans out of the cover you are*

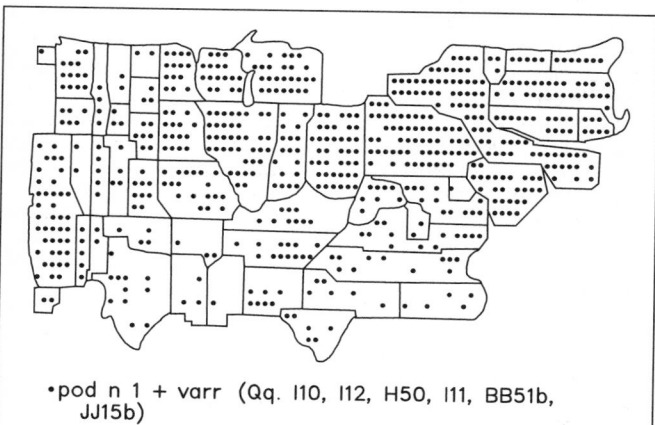

•pod n 1 + varr (Qq. I10, I12, H50, I11, BB51b, JJ15b)

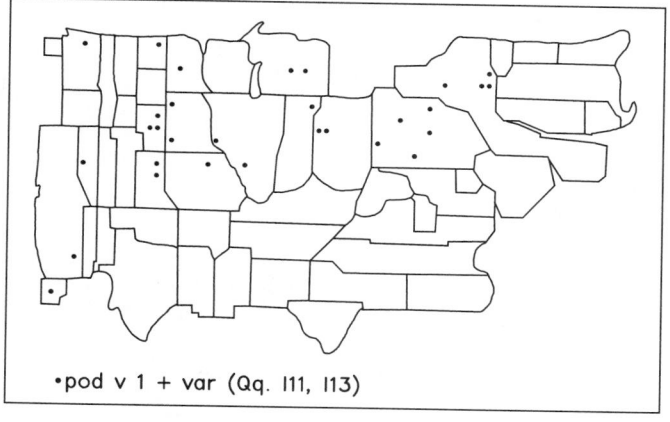

•pod v 1 + var (Qq. I11, I13)

_____ *them*) 9 Infs, **chiefly Inland Nth, N Midl,** Podding; **PA70,** Unpodding. **1971** Wood *Vocab. Change* 42 **Sth,** When a housewife removes beans from their pods. . . Scattered instances of *to pod* . . are reported. [Offered by 17 of 1000 infs] **1973** Allen *LAUM* 1.309 **Upper MW** (as of c1950), To *shell* beans or peas. . . *Pod* . . by *LANE* reported twice in Vermont, has gained proportionately in its westward extension, with instances in all states but South Dakota. **1973** Gawthrop *Dial. Calumet* 73 **nwIN,** *Of beans:* . . to pod 11 [of 125 infs]. **1981** *PADS* 67.35 **Mesabi Iron Range MN,** To *shell* beans. . . Both Iron Range and other Minnesota informants have *shell* as their usual term. . . The only other word recorded on the Mesabi is *pod,* occurring twice.

2 also with *out:* To bulge, swell out; hence ppl adj *podded,* vbl n *podding* (in ref to a pregnant woman). [Cf *OED2 in pod* pregnant (at *pod* sb.[2] 1.b)] Cf **pod** n **3**

1806 (1970) Webster *Compendious Dict.* 228, *Pod* . . to fill, swell. [*DARE* Ed: This entry was carried over from Webster's English model.] **1890** *Columbus Dispatch* 9 July (*DAE*), Immediately twelve intelligent eyes podded until one could have snared them with grape vines. **1949** McDavid *Coll.* **cNY,** *Pod out*—[to] bulge, as pockets. [Inf old] **1959** *Moosehead Gazette* (Dexter ME) Feb (Hench *Coll.*), Paul clutched Juan Innuendo by the larynx, causing Juan's neck to elongate into a stalk the length of a peavy handle, whilst the evil one's eyes podded outward from his skull. **1967** Stegner *Little Live Things* 96 **cwCA,** She chatted in the fluty, hyperthyroid voice, a thin girl in a faded denim skirt that showed no slightest sign of podding under its wide pocket. **1987** Stegner *Crossing* 52, There sit our two podded wives close together on the couch, whispering and intimate, two months away, rosy with the heat of indoors.

pod auger n Also sp *pod augur* [From the simple boring tool of this name, largely superseded in the 19th cent by more complicated and efficient types; see quot a1890 at **b** below] **NEng**
Used fig as a type of something that is obsolete and inefficient, as:

a See quot. Cf **pod auger** v

1905 Wasson *Green Shay* 105 **NEng,** Now bein' as she's nothin' only a poor wrack anyways, you may figger that most any old pod-auger [Footnote: A superannuated workman] of a feller same's I be is plenty good enough to tinker her up so's she'll be some good to ye once more.

b in phrr *pod-auger days,* ~ *times:* Older and simpler days. Cf *DNE*

1863 *Continental Mth.* 3.12, They will sing *rondinelle* bearing severely on the *forestieri* who have ruined the good old pod-augur days when they made *vendetta* without trouble. **1882** *Boston Jrl. Commerce* (MA) 7 Oct 246/1, Who would like to go back to the "old pod-auger days?" **a1890** (1944) Robinson *Hist. Morrill* 135 **csME,** Before 1800 almost all of the boring was done with Pod augurs, but few of this generation can remember of ever having seen one, but old times, before the invention of machinery are sometimes referred to as "Pod Augur" days. **1932** Wasson *Sailing Days* 112 **cME coast,** Later, . . factory-made ash oars and iron rowlocks gradually worked into common use, and cross-handed rowing with tholepins was laughed at as reminiscent of old "pod-augur" days. **1939** Linscott *Folk Songs Old New Engl.* 251, *Old Pod-auger Times.* . . This very popular ballad of the last century was composed by Comical Brown, an itinerant entertainer who traveled through the East giving a one-man show. **1975** Gould *ME Lingo* 212, In Maine, *pod-auger* days is equivalent to The Good Old Days; Holman Day celebrated them in his rhyme "Pod-Auger Days." **1996** *DARE* File **nwMA,** A pod-auger is a long-shanked auger that was used to hollow out the logs that were used as water pipe before metal pipes became common. . . Pod-auger times or days is another way of saying the good old days. One of the songs that I sing at the nursing homes has that name: Old Pod-Auger Times.

pod auger v [**pod auger** n] Pronc-sp *pawdogger* Cf *DNE,* *DS* Y27, KK31
See quots.

1912 *DN* 3.585 **wIN,** *Pod-auger.* . . To live along aimlessly without working very hard at anything. It was difficult to make much real progress with the pod-auger. "He just pod-augers around all the time." **1959** *VT Hist.* 27.151 **cnVT,** *Pawdogger.* . . To hurry. Rare. [*DARE* Ed: This def may be erroneous.]

pod-auger days (or times) See **pod auger** n **b**

pod augur See **pod auger** n

podded, podding See **pod** v **2**

poddishaw n [Pronc-sp for Fr *patte-de-chat* cat's paw; cf **paddybass**]
A type of purple **grape.**

1947 Ballowe *The Lawd* 117 **LA,** "Look whut Ah brunged you, ma'am: poddishaws." "Thank you. Here is some money. Take the grapes to the back door and give them to the maid." . . Patte-de-chat grapes were a special weakness of the chatelaine of Effingham.

poddy adj See **pod** n **3**

poddy n Also *potty* [*OED2 poddy* sb. B.1 "(Austral.) . . An unbranded calf. . . A calf . . lamb or foal . . fed by hand"; 1893 →] Cf *poddy* at (**pod** n **3**)
An orphan calf or lamb; see quots.

1944 Adams *Western Words* 117, *Poddy*—An occasional name for an orphan calf, usually big-bellied and undernourished. **1952** *CO Qrly.* 1.89, Very few instances of "poddy" were found, one in northeastern Colorado, two in western Colorado near the Utah border. *Ibid* 94, A poddy is the orphan lamb brought up on a bottle. It is fed skim milk until its body gets puffed up like a pod. The people who use the word explained that poddies were the potbellied lambs brought up by hand. **1964** O'Hare *Ling. Geog. E. MT* 148, A motherless lamb. . . [3 of 12 infs] potty.

podge See **pudge** v **1, 4**

podging See **pudge** v **4**

podna, podner See **partner**

Podock n [Prob blend of **Podunk** 1 + **boondock** n 1] =**Pochuck.**

1971 *DARE* File **csWI,** [He] lives in Podock. [That's] some Podock town. [Used by a 28-year-old woman]

pod out See **pod** v **2**

pod pepper n
A pepper (*Capsicum* spp) or the fruit of such a plant.

1889 *Century Dict.* 809, Cayenne or red pepper consists of the ground pods of various species, especially of *C[apsicum] fastigiatum,* the African or Guinea pepper, or spur-pepper, and of the common red pepper of the garden, *C. annuum.* The pods of both of these species are also known as *chillies,* and before they are ground as *pod peppers.* **1966–70** *DARE* (Qu. I22a, . . *Peppers—small hot*) Inf **AR47,** Red pepper, pod peppers; **MO22,** Pod pepper; (Qu. I22b, . . *Peppers—large hot*) Inf **FL1,** Pod pepper; (Qu. I22d, . . *Peppers—large sweet*) Inf **MS1,** Long pod peppers; **TN13,** California sweet pod peppers. **1986** Pederson *LAGS Concordance,* 1 inf, **cwAR,** Pod pepper.

podridge See **partridge A1**

pod sleigh See **pod** n **4**

Podunk n [From the name given in colonial times to a number of meadows, ponds, and streams in southern New England and New York, appar from an Algonquian place name meaning "marshy place"; see 1939 *AmSp* 14.99–108]

1 also *Podunk Center,* ~ *Hollow,* ~ *Junction, Podunkia, Podunkville:* Used as a nickname for a small, unimportant, remote, or backward place. **scattered, but less freq C and S Atl, West** See Map Cf **Pochuck, Podock**

1840 *Token* 109, *The Politician of Podunk.* Solomin Waxtend was a shoemaker of Podunk, a small village of New York, some forty years ago. **1877** *Catholic World* 25.726, We cannot very well imagine a leading Congressman summoning Horace to enforce his argument, say, on the vital necessity to the nation of repealing the Seventh Commandment until such time as his constituents at Podunk can get enough of their neighbors' currency to make resumption and patriotism convertible terms. **1901** *Harper's Weekly* 7 Sept 903, He [=Mark Twain] might just as well have been John Smith, of Podunk Centre. **1916** *DN* 4.279 **NE, PA, KS,** *Podunk.* . . Name for a back country town, the name of which is not readily recalled, or is unknown. "Where did he come from?" "Probably from Podunk." "So he took up his dwelling place somewhere in Podunk." . . Also *Podunkia, Podunkville.* **1917** *DN* 4.437 **NE, NY,** *Podunk.* **1928** Ruppenthal *Coll.* **KS,** *Podunk* . . any place of small size, limited vision. ["It is immaterial whether the records got to

Washington or got to Podunk.[⁹] **1934** *Sun* (Baltimore MD) 16 Feb 10/3 (Hench Coll.), *Advocates of sound improvements were compelled to accept unsound ones as the price of passage of an appropriation measure. Podunk creek was linked with important harbor developments essential for promotion of foreign commerce.* **1950** *WELS* (*An out-of-the-way place or an unimportant village*) 1 Inf, **seWI**, *Podunk.* **c1960** *Wilson Coll.* **csKY**, *Podunk.* . . Nickname for some inconsequential place. **1965–70** *DARE* (Qu. C33, . . *Joking names* . . *for an out-of-the-way place, or a very small or unimportant place*) 20 Infs, **scattered, but less freq C and S Atl, West,** *Podunk;* **AL**54, **IL**113, **MA**10, **MI**49, **TN**42, *Podunk* [FW sugg]; **MO**11, *Podunk Center;* (Qu. C34, *Nicknames for nearby settlements, villages, or districts*) Infs **AL**49, **IL**134, **MI**109, 115, **MA**30, **NY**75, *Podunk;* [(Qu. C35, *Nicknames for the different parts of your town or city*) Inf **CT**36, *Podunk—actual section of a Connecticut town;* (Qu. N37, *Joking names for a branch railroad that is not very important or gives poor service*) Inf **WI**39, *A podunk;*] (Qu. II21, *When somebody behaves unpleasantly or without manners: "The way he behaves, you'd think he was _____."*) Inf **WA**3, *From Podunk.* [30 of 32 total Infs hs or coll educ, 26 old] **1979** *NY Times* (NY) 24 May sec B 2/2, *The really sad thing about the court's decision is that in some jail in East Podunk there could be really bad conditions, and the inmates would lose a case.* **1986** Pederson *LAGS Concordance* **esp AR, MS, eTX,** 3 infs, *Podunk;* 2 infs, *Podunk Junction;* 1 inf, *Podunk—has heard of;* 1 inf, *Podunk—small town;* 1 inf, *Podunk—of any rural town;* 1 inf, *Podunk—small, culturally backward town;* 1 inf, *From Podunk—has heard;* 1 inf, *From Podunk—not used much;* 1 inf, *Do you go to Podunk High School?—backcountry;* 1 inf, *Podunk Hollow;* 1 inf, *A podunk town—small town;* 1 inf, *Podunk U—university with bad academic reputation.*

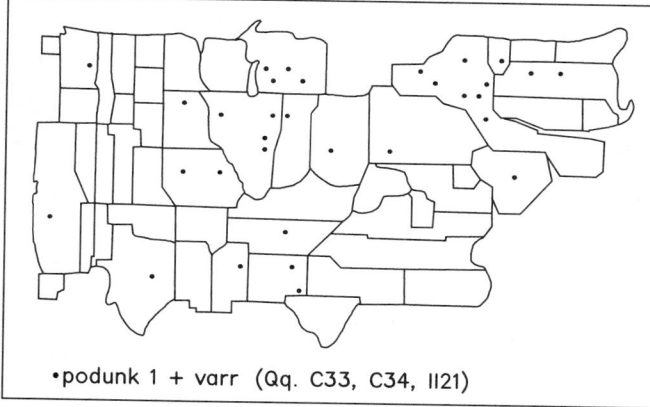

•**podunk 1 + varr** (Qq. C33, C34, II21)

2 By ext: a person from **Podunk 1;** a rustic.
1916 *DN* 4.279 **NE,** *Podunk.* . . Used also with reference to persons. "Come on, Podunk, let's see the city." [**1976** *AmSp* 51.108 **ceTX,** *Although it's probably your fault, but then your parents could turn around and sue the company for an undeterminate* [*sic*] *amount of money. And then what would happen is you'd have a bunch of poor dunks* [pᵿə'dʌŋks]; *they would get on that jury, and they be* [*sic*] *so prejudice* [*sic*] *against that, 'cause that company's a company, that they'd just say, "Sure give it to 'em."*] **1986** Pederson *LAGS Concordance* (*A rustic*) 1 inf, **csGA,** *Podunk—someone from small town;* 1 inf, **ceTX,** *A podunk—person.*

3 See quots.   Cf **bohunk 1, Polack**
1969 *DARE* (Qu. HH28, *Names and nicknames* . . *for people of foreign background*) Inf **VT**12, *Podunk—Polish.* **1969** *DARE* Tape **MA**58, *Here's other names for immigrants: Polank or Podunk for Polish.*

4 See quot.
1916 *DN* 4.279 **seWY,** *Podunk is also jocular for house or home.* "I spent the afternoon at Bob's podunk."

Podunk Center See **Podunk 1**

podunker n [Echoic, but also infl by **Podunk 1**]   Cf **bull paddock, paddock**
A frog.
1857 Hammond *Wild N. Scenes* 30 **neNY,** *There, hear that venerable podunker off to the right, with his deep bass.* **1947** Adams *Banner* 135 **NY** (as of 1817–47), *Booms like a basso podunker in a marsh. Ibid* 255, *A solo concert which left him hoarse as a bull podunker.*

Podunk Hollow, Podunkia, Podunk Junction, Podunkville See **Podunk 1**

poe See **poi**

po-ee See **poy**

poem n Pronc-sp *pome*   Cf **poetry**
Std sense, var form.
c1820 in 1941 *AmSp* 16.157 **NYC** [New York dialect], *Pome—poem.* **1829** Kirkham *Engl. Grammar* 194, [Improper:] *pome—*[pronounced:] *po em.* **1897** *KS Univ. Qrly.* (ser B) 6.90 **neKS,** *Pome* or *Po-um:* poem. **1936** (1947) Mencken *Amer. Lang.* 341, *In the vulgar speech* . . *poem* . . *pome.* [**1936** *AmSp* 11.161 **eTX,** *Poem, is always* ['poɪm] *or* ['poɪᵛm], *never* ['poəm] *or* [po:m].] **1976** Garber *Mountain-ese* 70 **sAppalachians,** *I had to write a pome in school fer my english assignment.* **1996** *DARE* File **cwCA** (as of 1950s), *When I was growing up, people used the word* poem *for serious poetry, but said* pome *with regard to doggerel or unsophisticated verse, or with self-deprecation applied to one's own work.*

poetry n Pronc-spp *po(r)try, pottery*
Std sense, var forms.
c1820 in 1941 *AmSp* 16.157 **NYC** [New York dialect], *Potry—poetry.* **1848** Lowell *Biglow* 2 **'Upcountry' MA,** *Zekle, ses she, our Hosee's gut the chollery or suthin anuther ses she, don't you Bee skeered, ses I, he's oney amakin pottery ses i* . . *and shure enuf, cum mornin, Hosy he cum down stares* . . *to go reed his varses to Parson Wilbur.* **1916** *DN* 4.279 **NE,** *Po-try. Frequent for* poetry. "I shall not speak to you long concerning the various theories of po-try." **1963** Mencken–McDavid *Amer. Lang.* 448, *Portry.*

pog See **pogy 1**

poganate v   Cf **DS Y18**
1923 *DN* 5.236 **swWI,** *Poganate.* . . To depart hurriedly or quickly. "Here, now, you poganate!"

poganip See **pogonip**

pogey n See **pokey** n¹ **1**

pogey v, hence vbl n *pogeying*
=**hooky bob.**
2000 *NADS Letters* **cwNY,** *I grew up on the north side of Buffalo in the 1960's.* . . [T]o "pogey" was to grab onto the rear bumper of a car or bus going down a slippery, snow-covered street, and kind of surf along behind it in a crouching position. . . "Pogey" was always a verb or a verbal noun ("pogeying"). **2001** *Ibid* **cwNY,** "Pogey"—the action of "foot-surfing" . . along a snowy street while hanging onto the rear bumper of a vehicle. . . [This term was] in completely common usage among children and older adolescents throughout the northern suburbs [of Buffalo] from at least the late 1960s through the mid 1970s.

poggie See **pogy 1, 4, 6**

poggle See **puggle**

poggy See **pogy 1, 2**

poghaden See **pauhagen**

pogie See **pogy 2, 4**

pogonip n Also *pogonip fog, ~ frost* Also sp *poganip;* for addit varr see quots [Paiute] **chiefly NV** Cf **tule fog**
A dense, icy fog; formerly also a severe snowstorm.
[**1865** (1973) Stuart *Montana as it Is* 29, [Snake Indian words:] *Fog—Pag'-in-up.*] **1869** *Overland Mth.* 3.212 **NV,** *Pogonip Flat offers no shelter whatever from the fury of the bleak, cutting blasts* . . ; *and here, too, it is that the dense piercing fog hangs from hour to hour in the dull dreary days of the winter. Hence "Pogonip" is now the conventional term for a roaring, piercing, cutting, bleak, merciless snow-storm, with all the furies of Boreas cut loose and filling the air with hideous noises.* **1892** *Scientific Amer.* 16 Apr 240, *The pogonip fog is peculiar to elevated altitudes in the Nevada Sierras.* **1910** Hodge *Hdbk. Amer. Indians* 2.272, *Pogonip. A Shoshonean term used in Nevada to designate a peculiar fog that occasionally visits the mountain country in winter. The sun is obscured, usually during the entire day, and sometimes for days, while the air is charged with a heavy fog in which fine particles of snow seem to be flying. Although the temperature may not be low, intense cold is*

felt on account of the unusual humidity that prevails. **1940** Writers' Program *Guide NV* 10, A most unusual dense fog, known as pogonip, appears at times during the winter, covering everything with beautiful radiating frost crystals. **1957** *AmSp* 32.310, *Pogonip,* a Shoshonean word, means an icy fog. . . The word lives also in the name of the Pogonip Golf Club. This club is just outside the little coastal town of Santa Cruz, California. The chilling fog is well known in the area. **1968** *DARE* FW Addit **NV,** Pogonip . . ['pɑgənɪp]—A fog that freezes onto trees and bushes. When you see a fog in the mountains in winter, "there will be pogonip in the morning." Only during very cold weather (for Nevada). Same phenomenon as very heavy frost in Wisconsin, etc. **1971** Bright *Word Geog. CA & NV* 110, [Indian terms:] [Poganip—1 response for 'warm wind in winter'. "Used by older brother and other folks."] . . poganip frost—4 responses. (One informant used the [k] sound instead of the [g].) "So called by the Paiute Indians." "Very severe." . . pogalip—1 response. "Very heavy foggy weather—an Indian term."

pogy n Usu |'pogi, -ɪ|; also |'pɔgi, -ɪ|; for addit varr see quots [In senses **1** and **2** appar < Narraganset *mishcùppaûog,* pl of *mishcup* < *mishe* large + *cuppe* scale, in ref to the closely imbricated scales; cf **pauhagen, scuppaug, skippaug.** Possibly of independent origin for other senses; cf **porgy** n[1]]

1 also *paugy, pog(gie), poggy:* =**menhaden 1.** chiefly **nNEng, S Atl, Gulf States**
1840 *NY Mirror* 5 Sept 87/2, Perhaps we may all of us live to see a Paulding paugy boat. **1858** ME Bd. Ag. *Ag. ME for 1857* 69, The fish known as menhaden, and often called along shore "hard-heads" and "poggies," . . after being boiled, are pressed . . to extract an oil . . ; what remains after extracting the oil, is called "poggy chum," and sells at twenty cents per barrel. **1863** U.S. Dept. Ag. *Rept. of Secy. for 1862* 57 **ME,** The article which he puts up is prepared from "pogy chum" by simply drying it in the sun. **1887** Goode *Amer. Fishes* 385, North of Cape Cod the name "Pogy" is almost universally in use, while in Southern New England the fish is known only as the "Menhaden." **1902** *Jrl. Amer. Folkl.* 15.248, In Massachusetts, Rhode Island, etc., the name *menhaden* is the more common one; in New York, mossbunker and *skippaug;* in other regions *pauhagen* . . , sometimes cut down to *poggie, poggy,* or *pog.* **1911** U.S. Bur. Census *Fisheries 1908* 313, *Pogy.*—A name applied to the menhaden *(Brevoortia) tyrannus* north of Cape Cod, to the moonfish *(Chaetodipterus faber)* and the scup *(Stenotomus chrysops)* along the southern coast, and to the surf-fish *(Damalichthys argyrosomus)* on the coast of Oregon. **1913** *Oysterman & Fisherman* 10 July 31 *(Mathews Coll.),* The new pogy steamer E.B. Thomas the largest ever built for the menhaden industry made her official trip off Portland Monday. **1939** *LANE* Map 233 *(Porgy; pogy),* Brevoortia tyrannus (a clupeoid), a commercially important fish found from Maine to Florida. . . This fish is called *pogy* |poʊgɪ, poˢˑgɪ, pɔˢˑgɪ| from Maine to Narragansett Bay; *menhaden* from Cape Cod westward . . ; *bony-fish* from Narragansett Bay westward. **1942** Kennedy *Palmetto Country* 240, A peculiar lot are the Negroes who man the pogy (menhaden) fishing boats—some are Geechees from South Carolina, while others are from the West Indies. **1948** Hanna–Hanna *Lake Okeechobee* 196 **FL,** He took to market a boatload of inedible, bony fish commonly used as bait. "Why, them's pogies!" derided the boys at the water front. **1949** Kurath *Word Geog.* 21, Along the coast from Block Island and Nantucket to eastern Maine, *pogy* . . is the name of a herring that is known as a *menhaden* on Long Island Sound. *Pogy* rimes with *stogy* and is not to be confused with the Connecticut *poggy,* which rimes with *foggy,* and denotes an entirely different fish the *scup* or *scupaug* of southeastern New England. **1965–70** *DARE* (Qu. P2, . . *Kinds of saltwater fish caught around here . . good to eat)* Inf **CT**13, ['pɑgɪz]; **LA**44, Pogy; **MA**55, Pogy ['pogi]; **MA**97, Pogy ['pogi]—has oil; **NC**12, Other names for menhaden—['poʊgi], bunker; **NJ**19, **NY**40, Pogy [pɔgɪ]; **SC**66, Pogy ['pogɪ]; **SC**69, Pogies ['pogɪz]; (Qu. P4, *Saltwater fish that are not good to eat)* Inf **CT**39, Pogies ['pogɪz]; **LA**31, Menhaden or pogy; **RI**8, Menhaden—we call 'em pogies ['pogiz]; (Qu. P14, . . *Commercial fishing . . what do the fishermen go out after?)* Inf **LA**31, Menhaden or pogies; **LA**44, Pogy; **MA**55, ['pogi]; **MS**73, Menhaden or pogy fish for fertilizer. [*DARE* Ed: Some of these Infs may refer instead to other senses below.] **1968** *Cameron Pilot* (LA) 29 Feb 2/1, What are menhaden? The adult Gulf menhaden is a herring or shadlike fish that inhabits estuarine and coastal waters bordering the Gulf of Mexico. They are generally found in large schools. In Louisiana, most fishermen call them "pogies." **1969** *DARE* Tape **NC**65, We used to fish on them pogy boats . . for them fatbacks for fertilizer. **1975** Gould *ME Lingo* 213, The *pogy* is the menhaden, an inferior fish yielding an oil once important in making paint. Pogy-oil paint was an excellent preservative, but until suitable driers were developed it required about fifty-five years to

dry. **1978** Mullen *Old Fishermen* 85 **seTX,** Menhaden fish, better known as "pogies" to the fishermen, travel in schools in nearshore salt water. They are processed at a plant in Sabine into fertilizer, fish oil, and additive for poultry and livestock feed. **1981** Pederson *LAGS Basic Materials* **FL, LA, MS,** 2 infs, Pogy ['poˑʊgɪ]; 2 infs, Pogy ['poˢʊgɪ]; 1 inf, Pogies ['poˢʊgɪ]; 1 inf, Pogy ['poʊgɪ] boats—big shrimpers or trawlers; 1 inf, Pogy ['pɔˢʊˑgɪ] fish; 1 inf, Pogy ['pɔˢˑgɪ] fish; 1 inf, Pogy ['poˢʊgɪ] fish.

2 also *paugie, paugy, poggy, pogie:* =**scup 1.** esp **NY, sNEng**
1848 Bartlett *Americanisms* 257, *Porgy,* or *Paugie.* . . (Indian, *scuppaug.*) A fish of the *sparus* family, common in the waters of New England and New York. . . It is singular that one half the aboriginal name, *scup,* should be retained in Rhode Island for this fish, and the other half, *paug,* changed into *paugie* or *porgy,* in New York. **1872** Schele de Vere *Americanisms* 67, The *Porgy* (Pagrus argyrops) from the imperfect pronunciation of *r* by Americans also frequently called *Paugy* and *Poggy* . . has a curious history connected with its Indian name. . . *paug* has been lengthened into *paugie* or altered into *porgie,* and thus furnished the name by which the fish is known in New York. **1884** Goode *Fisheries U.S.* 1.386, In New England it is generally called "Scup," while about New York the second syllable of the abbreviated Indian name has been lengthened into "Paugy" or "Porgy." **1902** *Jrl. Amer. Folkl.* 15.254, *Porgy* (paugy, pogie). The porgy is the *Stenotornus* [sic] *argyrops* of the *Sparus* family. *Porgy* (pogie, paugie, etc.) is a "reduction" of the Indian word seen in Narragansett *scuppaug,* Abnaki *scuppauog.* **1911** U.S. Bur. Census *Fisheries 1908* 315, Scup (Stenotomus chrysops).—This fish is found along the Atlantic coast from Cape Cod to South Carolina; abundant North. Common local names are "scuppaug," "paugy," "porgy," "pogy," "fair maid," etc. **1939** *LANE* Map 233 (Porgy; pogy), Stenotomus argyrops (a sparoid), a common food fish found from Cape Cod southward. . . is closely related to the sheepshead, flat and high-backed (sometimes described as shaped like a pumpkin seed), attaining a length of 1 ½ feet. This fish is called *porgy* [pɔrgɪ] or *poggy* [pɑgɪ] in Conn. **1949** [see **1** above]. **1967** *DARE* (Qu. P2, . . *Kinds of saltwater fish caught around here . . good to eat)* Inf **MA**8, Pogy [pɔ:gi]—flat like a flounder—large—about a foot in length. **1976** Tryckare et al. *Lore of Sportfishing* 103, Scup. . . Other common names . . paugy. . . Ovate-elliptical body much compressed laterally. . . An important commercial species in eastern North America. An excellent table fish.

3 A **spadefish** (here: *Chaetodipterus faber).*
1878 U.S. Natl. Museum *Proc.* 1.380 **ceNC,** Parephippus faber . . *Porgee; Pogy.* **1911** [see **1** above].

4 also *pog(g)ie:* Any of several **surfperches;** see quots. [See quot 1884] **Pacific**
1884 Goode *Fisheries U.S.* 1.276 **OR,** On the coast of Oregon the large species [of the surf-fish family] (especially *Damalichthys argyrosomus*) are called "Pogy" or "Porgee," in allusion to their undoubted resemblance to the scup or porgee of the East. **1911** [see **1** above]. **1913** London *Valley of Moon* 235 **cwCA,** An' we used to go out on the Rock Wall an' catch pogies an' rock cod. **1928** Pan-Pacific Research Inst. *Jrl.* 3.3.12 **nwWA,** Tocichthys ellipticus [=Hyperprosopon ellipticum] . . Silver pogie. . . Taken by us north to Clallam County, Washington; usually called by the latter name. *Ibid* 13 **nwWA,** Holconotus rhodoterus [= Amphistichus rhodoterus] . . Pogie. . . Occurs north to Cape Flattery. **c1955** Reed–Person *Ling. Atlas Pacific NW,* 1 inf, **nwWA,** Pogies. **1991** Amer. Fisheries Soc. *Common Names Fishes* 159, Poggie—see shiner perch [=Cymatogaster aggregata]. . . Pogy—see redtail surfperch [=Amphistichus rhodoterus].

5 also *pogy trout:* =**cutthroat trout.** **ceCA, cwNV**
1902 Jordan–Evermann *Amer. Fishes* 180, Lake Tahoe Trout; Truckee Trout; "Pogy"; "Snipe" . . *Salmo henshawi.* **1904** *Salmon & Trout* 234, There is another form of the Lake Tahoe cutthroat, known technically as *Salmo clarkii henshawi,* and locally as the "pogy" when mature, and as the "snipe" when young. *Ibid* 210, The Lake Tahoe, Truckee, or "pogy" trout. **1968** *DARE* (Qu. P1, . . *Kinds of freshwater fish . . caught around here . . good to eat)* Inf **NV**8, Pogy—the natural trout of Tahoe; nearly gone now.

6 also *poggie:* =**greenling.** **AK**
1948 *AK Sportsman* Aug 12, [Caption:] Sometimes we caught other things, like the strange greenish-colored fish shown below. The natives of Kodiak Island call it a pogy fish). **1956** Bank *Birthplace of the Winds* 101 (Tabbert *Dict. Alaskan Engl.),* Trout, salmon, poggie, and halibut form the basis for all three meals of each day. **1991** Tabbert *Dict. Alaskan Engl.* 149, In Alaskan usage *pogy* has been used to name greenlings of the genus *Hexagrammos,* four species of which occur in Alaskan waters: kelp greenling *(H. decagrammus),* rock greenling *(H. lago-*

cephalus), masked greenling *(H. octogrammus)*, and whitespotted greenling *(H. stelleri)*.

pogy trout See **pogy 5**

poha n [Haw] **HI**

A **ground-cherry** (here: *Physalis peruviana).*

1900 Lyons *Plant Names* 286, *P[hysalis] Peruviana* . . Poha or Paina of Hawaiian Islands. **1930** Degener *Ferns of HI* 257, The Cape gooseberry . . , known locally by the Hawaiian name of *poha,* is botanically *Physalis peruviana.* . . It is not a gooseberry but a member of the Solanaceae or Nightshade Family. **1967** *DARE* (Qu. I44, *What kinds of berries grow wild around here?)* Inf **HI**3, [ˌpoˈha]—ground-cherry; (Qu. S21, . . *Weeds . . that are a trouble in gardens and fields)* Inf **HI**2, [ˈpoˌha] (round berry) = ground-cherry—is eaten raw or in jam. **1991** Saiki *From the Lanai* 84 **HI,** She spent her afternoon making poha jam, ten golden glassfuls topped with paraffin. **1994** Stone–Pratt *Hawai'i's Plants* 167, The presence of fruiting bushes such as . . pohā . . provides some nutrients for adult nēnē.

pohagen See **pauhagen**

pohaku n, adj [Haw] **HI**

See quots.

1938 Reinecke *Hawaiian Loanwords* 30, *Pohaku* [ˈpoːˈhaːku]. . . A stone; a rock. . . Slang for one dollar. . . Slang for hard-hearted. . . F[requent]. **1954–60** Hance et al. *Hawaiian Sugar* 6, *Pohaku* [ˈpoˈhaku]—stone, rock. **1967** *DARE* [(Qu. C22, *A piece of stone too big for one person to move easily)* Inf **HI**4, [poˈhaku]—stone; (Qu. C24a, *A small piece of stone that you could easily throw)* Inf **HI**4, [poˈhaku] liilii—little;] (Qu. GG18, . . *'Obstinate': "Why does he have to be so _____."*) Inf **HI**1, Such a [poˈhaku]—rock. **1984** Sunset *HI Guide* 85, *Pohaku*—rock, stone.

pohegan See **pauhagen**

poho n, v, adj, intj [Haw] **HI**

See quots.

1938 Reinecke *Hawaiian Loanwords* 30, *Poho* [ˈpoːˈhoː]. . . Loss or damage in any transaction. . . To lose; to suffer loss or damage. . . Lost. . . Out of luck in any way—sometimes used as an interjection, like "Hang it!", "Darn the luck!" V[ery] F[requent]. **1951** *AmSp* 26.23 **HI,** Common Hawaiian words. . . *poho* (loss, damage). **1954–60** Hance et al. *Hawaiian Sugar* 6, *Poho* [poˈho]—To lose, lost (as money). **1968** *Jrl. Engl. Ling.* 2.83 **HI** [Common Hawaiian loanwords], *Poho.* . . Loss, waste, or damage. . . To waste, to suffer loss or damage. . . Lost, wasted, damaged. **1969** *DARE* FW Addit, *Poho* [pouˈhou]—to have bad luck in fishing, e.g., "I really poho." . . Not common among the haole (white) Hawaiians because *they* don't fish, but common among Hawaiians that do fish. **1972** Carr *Da Kine Talk* 88 **HI,** *Hawaiian Words Commonly Heard In Hawaii's English.* . . *Pohō.* Out of luck.

pohuehue n [Haw] **HI**

A **railroad vine 1** (here: *Ipomoea pes-caprae).*

1929 Pope *Plants HI* 173, Beach morning glory, Pohuehue. **1933** Pan-Pacific Research Inst. *Jrl.* 8.11 **HI,** The wild morning-glory, or convolvulus, . . grows from sea level . . up to the foot-hills. One of the varieties, growing near the sea, the *Pohuehue,* has long, vigorous runners reaching to high tide mark, heart shaped leaves and deep pink flowers. **1965** Neal *Gardens HI* 709, Beach morning-glory, Pohuehue. . . Hawaiians still use the vines for driving fish into nets, and formerly they whipped the sea with them when they wished to have high waves for surf-riding. **1979** Bushnell *Stone of Kannon* 279 **HI,** He had chosen to take his charges by the shorter and cooler way, first along the shore, across the patches of green grass and the tangled pohuehue vines, then inland on the dirt road. **1994** Stone–Pratt *Hawai'i's Plants* 66, Pōhuehue *(Ipomoea pes-caprae* subsp. *brasiliensis). Ibid* 67, The pōhuehue or beach morning glory . . primarily grows on or near sandy beaches. This robust vine often forms thick mats of trailing reddish stems just above the high-water mark.

poi n Formerly sp *poe* [Haw] **HI**

A food made of cooked taro root pounded into a paste, mixed with water, and sometimes allowed to ferment.

1823 (1970) Stewart *Jrl. Sandwich Is.* 133 **HI,** This immense bulk of person is supposed to arise . . from the abundance and nutritious quality of their food, especially that of poe, a kind of paste made from the taro, an esculent root, a principal article of diet. **1826** Ellis *Narrative HI* 284, A native girl sat beside it, . . holding a cocoa-nut shell in her hand, con-

taining a little poë. **1833** in 1934 Frear *Lowell & Abigail* 72 **HI,** Their [=the Hawaiians'] "staff of life" is poi, which is made by baking taro in the ground and pounding to the consistency of thin flour paste. After it has fermented, they eat it with their fingers out of a calabash. A whole family gather around one common dish which is placed on the ground, and themselves seated in the same posture, enjoy their social repast. **1873** in 1966 Bishop *Sandwich Is.* 18 **HI,** Poi, the national Hawaiian dish, a fermented paste made from the root of the *kalo,* or *arum esculentum.* **1938** Reinecke *Hawaiian Loanwords* 30, *Poi* [ˈpoː-i] [ˈpɔɪ]. . . A thick paste of taro root pounded (in modern times ground by machinery) with water, eaten cold as the staple food of the Hawaiians. V[ery] F[requent]. **1954** *Ellery Queen's Mystery Mag.* 4.35 **HI,** We ate with the Hawaiian family Troy had been living with, a meal consisting of *laulaus* (salt salmon, butterfish, and pork wrapped in *ti* leaves), *poi,* and coconut pudding. **1967** *DARE* (Qu. G6, . . *Dishes that you might have on the table for a big dinner or special occasion)* Inf **HI**1, Poi bowl. **1972** Carr *Da Kine Talk* 117 **HI,** Poi Belt (Hawaiian + English). A phrase noted in the *Honolulu Advertiser,* July 2, 1968, analogous to "Bible Belt." **1991** Saiki *From the Lanai* 11 **HI,** You rent the Kikuchi's back apartment on Hanapopo Street, next door to the poi factory.

poick See **poig**

poi dog n [poi] **HI**

A dog of a native Hawaiian breed; a mutt, mongrel; transf: used as a derog term for a person of native Hawaiian ancestry.

1938 Reinecke *Hawaiian Loanwords* 30, *Poi dog.* . . A native Hawaiian dog—now extinct. . . Any nondescript cur. . . Used in anger as an epithet for a Hawaiian. *Dogeater* is another common epithet. F[requent]. **1951** *AmSp* 26.23 **HI,** Other common Hawaiian words are . . *poi* dog (a nondescript cur; formerly the native breed of dog was fattened on 'poi' and served at feasts). **1965** Krauss–Alexander *Grove Farm* 20 **HI,** What's the matter, ye lose that poi dog of yours again? **1967** *DARE* (Qu. J1, . . *A dog of mixed breed)* Inf **HI**1, [ˈpɔɪ ˌdɒg]—in Hawaii; **HI**12, [ˈpɔɪ ˌdɔg]. **1967** *DARE* Tape **HI**4, [Inf:] That was the poi dog. The dog what they feed—small dog, the pup; they feed 'em. And then when they ready to eat, then they—[laughter] that's why they call it poi dog. [FW:] The dog that is ready to be eaten. [Inf:] Yeah. **1968** *Jrl. Engl. Ling.* 2.83 **HI** [Common Hawaiian loanwords], *Poi dog.* . . [Poi + Eng. *dog.*] . . Any nondescript cur. . . An extinct native Hawaiian dog. **1969** *DARE* FW Addit **Honolulu HI,** Poi [pɔɪ] dog. . . mongrel, probably because poi is a mixture just like a mongrel is. **1972** Carr *Da Kine Talk* 111 **HI,** The small Polynesian dog, brought to the Islands by the early Hawaiians, is now sometimes referred to as the *poi dog.* He has a pedigree of his own making, because no other dog can equal him in hunting wild pigs in the mountain undergrowth. He has a past, too, since he was sometimes served up, along with *poi,* at the feasts of the ancient Hawaiians. The term is now commonly used in the Islands to mean any dog of mixed or uncertain breed. **1981** *Pidgin To Da Max* np **HI,** Poi dog—Local mixture.

poig exclam |pɔɪg, ˈpu(w)ɪg|; also esp **WI** |pɔɪk, puik| Pronc-sp *pooig;* for addit pronc and sp varr see quots [Cf *EDD poo-ik* int. "A call to pigs"] **scattered, but esp WI, MI, MN** See Map Cf **hoog, po** exclam, **pooey, poo-gee, poy**

Used as a call to pigs.

c1950 *Atlas Checklists* **csWI,** *Call to hogs at feeding time . .* poo-week. **1950** *WELS* **WI,** 5 Infs, Poig—repeated; 2 Infs, Poi(c)k—repeated; 2 Infs, P(o)uig—repeated; 1 Inf, Pig poigh; 1 Inf, [pwɪk]—repeated; 1 Inf, Poo-week—repeated. **1951** *NY Folkl. Qrly.* 7.186, The

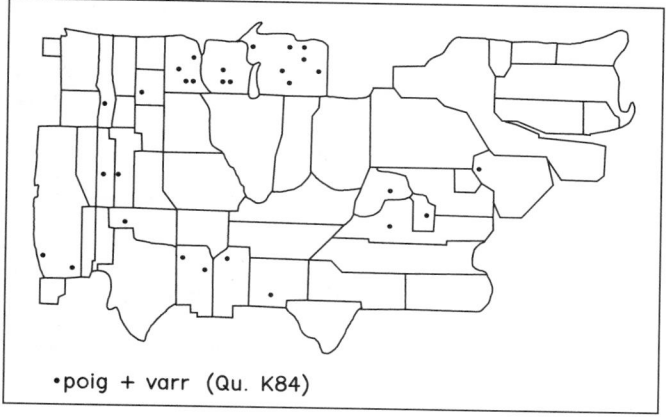

•poig + varr (Qu. K84)

Finger Lakes area has . . the Pittsburgh and New Jersey hog call *poo-ig!* or *pwig!* **1965–70** *DARE* (Qu. K84, *The call used . . to get the pigs in at feeding time*) 18 Infs, **scattered**, Poig (sometimes repeated); **DC5**, **LA18**, [puɪg] (sometimes repeated); **WI16**, [puik]—repeated; **MI2**, ['puwɪg]—repeated; **MI11**, [pu'ɪg]—repeated [FW sugg]; **MI47**, Just a yell—[pɔɪg] [FW: long, drawn-out, like a junior-size ambulance siren]; **MI83**, [pɔɪg]; **MI87**, ['puwɪg]—repeated; **WV2**, [pu:ig] [FW: repetitions have shorter vowels]; **WI6**, [poɪk]—repeated; **WI21**, [pɔɪk kəm pɔɪk]—repeated [FW: higher pitch on [kəm], lower on [pɔɪk]]. [25 of 29 Infs old, 22 male] **1966** [see **pooey** exclam]. **1973** Allen *LAUM* 1.266 **Upper MW** (as of c1950), Calls to pigs at feeding time. . . pooig [9 infs].

poinciana n [*OED2* 1731 →] Cf **yellow poinciana**
Either a plant of the genus *Caesalpinia* or the related **royal poinciana.** For other names of var spp of *Caesalpinia* see **camote, pride of Barbados**

1929 Neal *Honolulu Gardens* 149, *Dwarf poinciana* [*Caesalpinia pulcherrima* . .]. A bush or small tree. . . popular because of its beauty. . . The flower yields honey and is not unlike that of a poinciana [=*Delonix regia*] in shape. **1948** Neal *In Gardens HI* 377, *Delonix regia*. . . One of the showiest and best loved trees in Hawaii is the poinciana, especially in the flowering season. *Ibid* 379, A rarer poinciana (*P[oinciana] gilliesii*) . . differs . . in having . . flowers light yellow with bright-red stamens. **1949** Moldenke *Amer. Wild Flowers* 242, In our cultivated flower gardens everyone knows how popular red cannas . . and poinciana are with hummingbirds. **1960** Vines *Trees SW* 543, *Caesalpinia pulcherrima*. . . Other vernacular names are . . Barbados-Pride, Flame-tree, and Dwarf Poinciana. . . Poincianas [=*Caesalpinia* spp] are easily grown from seed. *Ibid* 544, The Flamboyant-tree [= *Delonix regia*] is often confused with the tropical American poincianas. The propagation methods are the same as those of the poincianas. **1967** *DARE* (Qu. T16, . . *Kinds of trees* . . '*special*') Inf **HI11**, Poinciana—shade tree. **1979** Little *Checklist U.S. Trees* 68, *Caesalpinia gilliesii*. . . Paradise poinciana. . . *Caesalpinia pulcherrima*. . . Dwarf poinciana, poinciana. **1986** Pederson *LAGS Concordance*, 2 infs, **sFL**, Poinciana trees. **1996** *DARE* File **sFL**, Hazel called the other day to invite me for brunch at the Poinciana Country Club, where she said all the poincianas were in bloom and "just lovely."

poinsettia n Usu |pɔɪn'sɛtə|; also |pɔɪn'sɛtiə| Pronc-sp *poin-setta;* for addit pronc and sp varr see **A** below
A Forms.
1937 in 1944 *ADD*, Poinsetta. . . Established mispron. **1940–44** *Ibid* **eUS**, Poinsetta. . . Common. **1950** *WELS Suppl.* **WI**, [pɔɪn'sɛtə]. Nobody says [pɔɪn'sɛtiə]. *Ibid*, Poinsetta [pɔɪnsɛtə] or [pɔɪnzɛtə]. The usual pronunciation for poinsettia. Only florists pronounce it correctly here. **1966** *DARE* Tape FL41, Then we have the redbud, and we have the ['pɑn'sɛtəz]. [Inf Black] **1981** Pederson *LAGS Basic Materials* **Gulf Region**, 4 infs, [Proncs of the type [p'ɔɪn'sɛtə]]; 1 inf, ['p'ʌnt,sɛtə]; 1 inf, ['p'ɑ.n,sɛ˞təz]. **1982** Barrick *Coll.* **csPA**, Poinsettia—pron. [pʌn'sɛtə]. **1995** *DARE* File **NYC** (as of 1940s–present), My whole family pronounces pointsetta with a "t" and no second "i."
B Senses.
1 Std: a **spurge** (here: *Euphorbia pulcherrima*). Also called **Christmas flower 2, ~ tree 6, Mexican flameleaf** Cf **summer poinsettia, white ~, wild ~**
2 Transf: a person who attends church chiefly at Christmas. Cf **Easter lily 5**
1967 *DARE* (Qu. CC7, . . *A person who goes to church very seldom or not at all*) Inf **TX5**, Poinsettas.

point n, v Usu |pɔɪnt|; also **chiefly Sth, S Midl, formerly also NEng** |paɪnt| See Pronc Intro 3.I.11 Pronc-sp *pint;* for addit pronc and sp varr see **A** below
A Forms. [Cf *OED2* point sb.[1], headnote; *pint* sb.[2] "a vulg. and dial. (esp. U.S.) pronunc."] Cf **appoint**
1773 in 1967 *PADS* 48.39 **NC**, Pint [for *point*]. **1813** (1939) Hartsell *Memora* 11.101 **PA**, Received of Capt Jacob Hartsell, one six and halfe pint blanket. **1848** Lowell *Biglow* 145 '**Upcountry' MA**, Pint, *point*. **1860** Hundley *Social Relations S. States* 36 **MA**, One of whom . . descanted in a . . maudlin way on the *pup's pints*. **1871** Eggleston *Hoosier Schoolmaster* 76 **sIN**, He could p'int out somebody as know'd a blamed sight more'n they keer'd to tell. **1872** Schele de Vere *Americanisms* 518, *Pint*, instead of point . . quite common in New England and in

some of the Southern States, where the old English pronunciation has been preserved. **1893** Shands *MS Speech* 50, Pint [paɪnt]. Negro and illiterate white for *point*. **1901** *DN* 2.183 **neKY** [Black], Point—pint. **1903** *DN* 2.291 **Cape Cod MA** (as of a1857), [paɪnt] for *point*. **1905** Wasson *Green Shay* 139 **NEng**, Down to the top o' the P'int [Footnote: End of the point]. **1909** *DN* 3.357 **eAL, wGA**, Pint. **1923** *DN* 5.217 **swMO**, P'int. **1930** *AmSp* 5.204 **Ozarks**, The *oi* in such words as *boil* and *join* is always given the long *i* sound in the Ozarks, so that the words sound like *bile* and *jine*. . . The same vowel substitution occurs in *point*, and both *pint* and *disappint* are survivals of a good old English pronunciation. **1931** (1991) Hughes–Hurston *Mule Bone* 133 **cFL** [Black], "Dat ain't de point, Brother Hambo." . . "It's jes' as good uh pint as any." **1933** *AmSp* 8.1.24 **sAppalachians**, *Pint* for point is still heard, chiefly among the old folk. **1934** in 1944 *ADD* **Brooklyn NYC**, [p(ɜ)ɪnt]. Supposedly refined. **1937** (1963) Hyatt *Kiverlid* 31 **KY**, The set o' them horns p'ints that she'll be a pow'ful fine milker when she fetches a calf. **1940** in 1944 *ADD* **NYC**, Point—[ɔɪ], [ʌɪ]. Less educated. **1941** *Ibid*, [pɜnt]. D'y get my pernt? Radio song. **1960** Criswell *Resp. to PADS* 20 **Ozarks**, Point. . . pronounced *pint*, even up to this time by many. **1960** *VT Hist.* 28.130, It ain't the matter of fact; it's the pernt of view. **c1960** Wilson *Coll.* **csKY**, Point /paɪnt/ older pron. **1967–69** *DARE* FW Addit **KY31**, [paɪnt] . . used by older speakers; **LA8**, Point [pɔɪnt]. **1976** Garber *Mountain-ese* 68 **sAppalachians**, Mandy got stuck with the pint uv her needle while she was sewin'. Don't pint that gun at people. **1991** *Macoupin Co. Enquirer* (Carlinville IL) 6, [From a 1961 issue quoting "oldsters":] Men also pinted out objects.

B As noun.
1 Either of the two positions abreast of the head of a moving herd of cattle; rarely, a cowboy who occupies this position; hence combs *point man, ~ rider*. **West** Cf **C1** below, **pointer 2, ride** v **6**
1880 (1883) U.S. Census Office *Rept. Ag.* 974 **TX**, On each side of the lead rides a man on "point", that is, to direct the column. Back where the line begins to swell ride two more at "swing", further back ride two at "flank", and the remainder are on "drag", *i.e.*, about the rear), to push on the march. These positions give *cowboy rank*. **1903** (1965) Adams *Log Cowboy* 28 **West**, Two riders, known as point men, rode out and well back from the lead cattle, and by riding forward and closing in as occasion required, directed the course of the herd. **1916** [see **ride** v **6**] **1920** [see **C1** below]. **1922** Rollins *Cowboy* 253 **West**, The foremost one of the punchers in each of these lines was slightly more advanced than the van of the herd and was called a "point man" or "lead rider." **1929** *AmSp* 5.72 **NE** [Cattle country talk], Two "hands" "heading" the side lines guarding the cattle on march, are "lead riders" or "point men," and those riders behind them at long intervals are "swing men" or "flank riders." **1946** Mora *Trail Dust* 147 **West**, The herd would be strung out into more of a marching formation. A couple of the cowboys, one on each side, near the head of the column guided the movement and direction of the leaders. These were called the "point riders." **1956** [see **ride** v **6**]. **1966–67** *DARE* Tape CO4, The lead men and point men, was generally one on each side, the lead men on the side, well, they called them the point men; OK30, They'd have two men on the point to point 'em. **1981** *KS Qrly.* 13.2.69, Point . . a rider at the head of the herd on a cattle drive. **1985** Ehrlich *Solace* 67 **WY**, On a long circle, cowboys are assigned positions and work like traffic cops directing the cattle. Those that "ride point" are the front men. They take charge of the herd's course, turning the lead down a draw, up a ridge line, down a creek, galloping ahead to chase off steers or bulls from someone else's herd, then quickly returning to check the speed of the long column.
2 A street corner, often one formed by two streets meeting at less than a ninety-degree angle; also used in place-names; by ext, a fork in a road.
1832 *Boston Eve. Transcript* (MA) 5 Jan 2/3, The stern censors of New York have decreed in council, that the *Five Points* shall be no more; that interesting triangle is to be hurled from its height of fame, and buried in the bosom of a public *square*. **1860** *Vanity Fair* 14 July 30 **NYC**, The best thing for the Avenue [=Fifth Avenue] to do . . is to shake hands with the Points [=Five Points] . . , for after all there is but little difference between a Wall-street Broker and a Baxter-street Cracksman. **1904** *Eve. Post* (NY NY) 14 Oct 12/1, "Where were you brought up, at Five Points?" the New York mother of a generation ago would say when her child forgot to say "Thank you." **1935** Horwill *Mod. Amer. Usage* 134, In N.Y. the spot where Worth, Baxter, and Park Streets intersect is popularly called *Five Points*. The number is five, not six, because originally Worth Street only met the other two streets and did not run across

them. At one time the Five Points district was proverbial for rowdyism and vice. **1966–70** *DARE* (Qu. C35, *Nicknames for the different parts of your town or city*) Infs **NC**10, **WI**62, Five Points; (Qu. N20, . . *A circular arrangement on one level at a big intersection, where cars can go around till they come to the road they want*) Inf **FL**48, Four-point, five-point, etc, depending on how many streets turn off the circle; (Qu. N32, *A place where roads cross at right angles*) Inf **NJ**60, A corner [is] sometimes called a point; (Qu. II25, *Names or nicknames for the part of a town where the poorer people . . live*) Inf **PA**104, Five Points. **1968** McPhee *Pine Barrens* 59 **cNJ**, A point is a place where a road forks. **1969** *DARE* FW Addit **swNJ**, *Point*—a street corner, but more angled (sharper, narrower) than a corner at a four corners. **1996** *DARE* File **Philadelphia PA**, Near my folks' home in Philadelphia, there is an area where five streets come together called, for as long as I can remember, "Five Points."

3 In phr *in good point:* See quot.   [*OED2 point* sb. 25 1297–1732; "*Obs.*"]
1958 *AmSp* 33.270 **eWA** [Ranching terms], *Good point, in.* Fat, or in good condition. Often applied to a man ironically.

4 See quot.
1958 *AmSp* 33.267 **eWA**, I have never found all the positions of a ten-horse team named. The first pair is called the *lead,* the second the *point,* the third the *swing,* the fourth the *block,* the fifth the *wheel.*

5 pl: A children's ball game; see quot.   Cf **off-the-point**
1967–68 *DARE* (Qu. EE33, . . *Outdoor games . . that children play*) Inf **MA**27, Points—throw ball at steps; player got a point if he caught it on the fly. Soft rubber ball was used; **PA**172, Points—throwing a ball against a step; if it pops up, player gets a point.

C As verb.

1 Of a cowboy: to guide (a herd of cattle); to drive a herd (in a specifed direction).   **West**   Cf **B1** above, **pointer 2**
1903 (1965) Adams *Log Cowboy* 43 **West**, Priest sent Officer to the left and myself to the right, to point in the leaders in order to keep the herd from splitting or scattering. **1916** Sinclair *Phantom Herd* 244 **West**, You're trying to point the herd then. **1920** Hunter *Trail Drivers TX* 314 (as of c1880), In swimming across he had taken the left point (or lead) to point the cattle across. . . This brought up the question to us. Who would venture to point our herd across; and what would it cost to have them pointed? **1925** Hunter *Trail Drivers TX* 566 (as of 1869), When we came to the Smoky River, Jack Kyle pointing the herd, I was riding a little mule. **1937** Sandoz *Slogum* 32 **NE**, A lone rider pointed the lean, horn-weary herd, two shambled along each side, and the trailer, the dirt eater, limbered up the drags with voice and knot-ended rope. **1938** in Lib. of Congress *Amer. Memory: WPA Life Hist.* (Internet) **TX** (as of 1893), On the morning of March 15th, Cockrell said: 'Point 'em towards the North Star by way of Midland and Amarillo.' . . After leaving Amarillo, we pointed towards Colorado. . . From there, we pointed towards Lusk, Wyo. **1966–67** [see **B1** above].

2 In fishing: to bait (a hook).
1988 Nickerson *Days to Remember* 190 **Cape Cod MA** (as of c1900), If we were lucky enough to catch gudgeons (minnows) or small frogs, we sometimes "pointed" the hook with them.

point-black See **point-blank A5**

point-blank adv, adj Usu |ˈpɔɪnt ˈblæŋk|; for varr see **A** below
A Forms.

1 |paɪnt|-*blank;* pronc-sp *pint-blank.*   **chiefly S Midl**   Cf **point A**
1845 [see **C1** below]. **1887** [see **B** below]. **1902** *DN* 2.241 **sIL**, *Point-blank* [paɪnt-] or [paɪn-]. **1903** *DN* 2.325 **seMO**, *Point-blank* or *pint-blank.* **1907** *DN* 3.225 **nwAR**, *Point-blank* [paɪn(t)-]. **1909** *DN* 3.358 **eAL, wGA**, *Point-blank.* . . Often pronounced [paɪnt-]. **c1920** in 1993 Farwell–Nicholas *Smoky Mt. Voices* 123 **sAppalachians**, P'int-blank. **1924** (1946) Greer-Petrie *Angeline Gits an Eyeful* 9 **csKY**, P'int-blank. **1927** *AmSp* 2.360 **cwWV**, Pint blank. **c1950** *Hall Coll.* **wNC, eTN**, [paɪnt blæŋk]. **1976** Garber *Mountain-ese* 68 **sAppalachians**, *Pint-blank.*

2 |paɪn|-*blank;* pronc-spp *pine-blank,* ~-*blang.*   **chiefly S Midl, esp sAppalachians**
1872 Schele de Vere *Americanisms* 624, *Pineblank* is the popular pronunciation of *pointblank.* **1887** (1967) Harris *Free Joe* 87 **GA** [Black], I des put it at Mistiss right pine-blank. **1888** Johnston *Mr. Absalom Billingslea* 207 **cGA**, When I starr'd at her pine blang. **1899** (1912) Green *VA Folk-Speech* 322, *Pine-blank.* **1902** [see **A1** above]. **1907**

[see **A1** above]. **1909** *DN* 3.357 **eAL, wGA**, *Pine-blank.* *Ibid* 358, *Point-blank.* . . sometimes [paɪn-blæŋk [sic]]. **1915** *DN* 4.187 **swWA**, *Pineblank.* Variant of *pointblank.* Also *paimblank* [sic]. **1933** *AmSp* 8.1.24, *Pine blank* for *pint* (point) *blank* is heard in sections of North Carolina, Tennessee and Virginia, and in some places in West Virginia and Kentucky. **1940** (1978) Still *River of Earth* 26 **KY**, He grinned at us and I thought, looking hard at him, that he had a face pine-blank like a 'possum's. **1942** (1971) Campbell *Cloud-Walking* 29 **seKY**, Yankee John knew pine-blank how it ought to be done. **1954** *PADS* 21.34 **SC**, *Pine blank.* **1956** McAtee *Some Dialect NC* 33, *Pine-blank.* **1965–68** *DARE* (Qu. KK51, *Very plainly or abruptly: "I asked him _____ what he meant by that."*) Infs **FL**26, **MS**56, **VA**15, Pine blank.

3 |paɪm|-*blank;* pronc-spp *pime-blank,* ~-*plank.*   **chiefly sAppalachians, esp eKY**
1911 *DN* 3.539 **eKY**, *Pīme* (prīme-, plīme-) blank. . . Point-black. **1915** [see **A2** above]. **1931** *AmSp* 7.94 **eKY**, *Pime-blank.* **1972** Cooper *NC Mt. Folkl.* 95, *Pimeblank.* **1976** Garber *Mountain-ese* 68 **sAppalachians**, The young Smith boy is pime-blank like his pa wuz at his age. **1977** Norman *Kinfolks* 43 **eKY**, I think he's in his second childhood. Gone back to wanting attention pime blank like a four-year old. **1982** Slone *How We Talked* 28 **eKY** (as of c1950), *Pime plank*—true or exactly; "That's just plime plank how it looked." *Ibid* [see **A4** below].

4 pronc-spp *pliam-blank, plime-~, pline-~, prime-~.*   **chiefly sAppalachians, esp eKY**
1911 [see **A3** above]. **1940** Stuart *Trees of Heaven* 188 **eKY**, Son, you act pliam-blank like a spring redbird buildin a nest. **1942** Hall *Smoky Mt. Speech* 93 **wNC, eTN**, [l] is intrusive in the reported [plaɪm blæŋk] *point-blank* (usually [paɪm blæŋk]), possibly through the influence of the much-used intensive *plumb.* **1963** *Mt. Life* 39.2.51 **sAppalachians**, Who's that gimlet-ended shikepoke a-baouncin' up 'n' daown on that old rack o' bones jis' zackly and plime blank like a peckerwood on a rotten fence post? **1966** *DARE* (Qu. KK51, *Very plainly or abruptly: "I asked him _____ what he meant by that."*) Inf **FL**19, Pline-blank [plaɪn blæŋk]. **1982** Slone *How We Talked* 35 **eKY** (as of c1950), *Pime blank* (also plime blank)—exact; "That is just plime blank how it was." **1991** Still *Wolfpen Notebooks* 96 **sAppalachians**, That's plime-blank what happened to me last fall. *Ibid* 122, A boy is plime-blank like a mule. If you don't give him something to do, he's into something.

5 *point-black.*   [Perh by folk-etym]
1967 *DARE* (Qu. KK51, *Very plainly or abruptly: "I asked him _____ what he meant by that."*) Inf **CO**4, Point-black [FW: sic].

B As adv.
Absolutely, completely, exactly, simply.   For addit quots see **A2, 3, 4** above   [Cf *OED2 point-blank* a., sb., and adv. C.2.b 1621–1756; "Now *rare* or *Obs.*"]   **S Midl, esp sAppalachians**
Note: In the sense "directly, bluntly, unequivocally," *point-blank* is widespread throughout the US.
1851 Hooper *Widow Rugby's Husband* 69 **AL**, That was pint-blank agin Clay's Digest. **1887** *Scribner's Mag.* Oct 476 **AR**, Jeff looked . . p'int blank gashly. **1901** Harben *Westerfelt* 242 **nGA**, They are every one p'int-blank alike. **c1920** in 1993 Farwell–Nicholas *Smoky Mt. Voices* 123 **sAppalachians**, That beer tastes p'int-blank [exactly] like a mad bumblebee smells. **1924** (1946) Greer-Petrie *Angeline Gits an Eyeful* 9 **csKY**, I know'd 'twan't no sweet-art, from the way he order'd her around (p'int-blank like she wuz his wife). **1924** Raine *Land of Saddle-Bags* 207 **sAppalachians**, I'm pint-blank drug out, but I shan't keer nary grain if Sally Ann's baby lives. **1926** Roberts *Time of Man* 304 **cKY**, You must have that room. . . You just pintblank need it, I know. **1927** *AmSp* 2.360 **cwWV**, They say I look pint blank like my brother. **1931** *AmSp* 7.94 **eKY**, *Pime-blank,* absolutely. "Sherm knowed pime-blank he wuz on a slip." **1937** (1963) Hyatt *Kiverlid* 14 **KY**, I knowd then, p'int-blank what was up atwixt you two. **1943** Stuart *Taps* 177 **eKY**, "It's pint-blank right," Grandma said. **1977** [see **A3** above]. **1982** [see **A3** above].

C As adj.

1 Absolute, unqualified, out-and-out.   **S Midl**
1845 Thompson *Pineville* 114 **cGA**, I always thought you wasn't none too good to steal, but now I've got pint blank proof agin you. **1902** *DN* 2.241 **sIL**, He said he was a pint-blank liar. **1903** *DN* 2.325 **seMO**, He told a point-blank lie. **1928** Chapman *Happy Mt.* 79 **seTN**, Never in all his life long had Virgil Howard given out what he did nor why—least of all to a point-blank stranger. **c1950** *Hall Coll.* **wNC, eTN**, "Point blank proof" means complete, incontrovertible proof. **1954** *PADS* 21.34 **SC**, A *pine blank* lie or liar.

2 See quot.

2000 *NADS Letters* **seKY**, When people would see us as little boys they would say "Them boys is plime blank." Which meant that we looked just alike. Or if two companions were always together, or doing the same thing, or getting into trouble together, they were plime blank. The same as "two peas in a pod."

pointedly adv Pronc-sp *pintedly*; also *appointedly, appintedly*; for addit varr see quots [Cf *SND* pointedly, pintitly adv (at *point* n., v. II.4)] **chiefly S Midl** Cf **point A, point-blank B** Certainly, thoroughly, absolutely, simply.

a1883 (1911) Bagby *VA Gentleman* 307, The man asked me the number of my room, and I told him, 'Hot music on the half-shell for two!' I pintedly did. **1887** (1967) Harris *Free Joe* 83 **GA** [Black], I tell you dat p'intedly. **1891** Page *Elsket* 134 **VA**, I tolt her hit wuz p'intedly oudacious. **1903** *DN* 2.305 **seMO**, *Appointedly*, often *appintedly*. . . 'I told him appintedly what he might expect.' **1913** Kephart *Highlanders* 213 **sAppalachians**, I allers did hold that a fat woman was bad enough, but a fat man ort p'intedly to be led out and killed! **1915** *DN* 4.180 **swVA**, I appintedly aint goin' to do it. **1921** Haswell *Daughter Ozarks* 31 (as of 1880s), I pintedly don't never 'low to git ketched no more without a box of 'Doctor Ezry's Compound Excentric Pills' in my saddle bags! **1923** (1946) Greer-Petrie *Angeline Steppin'* 36 **csKY**, Mr. Seelback was p'intedly a-makin' that big fiddle talk. . . [H]e shines 'em up till they are p'intedly hard to beat. **1927** *AmSp* 2.361 **cwWV**, I pintedly believe that he did it. **1938** *AmSp* 13.6 **seAR**, 'He is pintly able to play football.' 'She is pintly dressed.' **1939** *Esquire* July 38 **eKY**, They piantly laid it on me last night. **1947** Ballowe *The Lawd* 196 **LA**, Ah got jess whut hit takes; but Ah p'intedly hates to use it on Donis. . . he like a son to me. **1963** *Mt. Life* 39.2.52 **sAppalachians**, The outsider might be pronounced "so pinted ugly a glance from her eye would stop the clock." **1976** Garber *Mountain-ese* 68 **sAppalachians**, John most pintedly won the contest. **1986** Pederson *LAGS Concordance*, 1 inf, **cwMS**, They pinely are; 1 inf, **neTN**, They'd be so shook . . [they'd] just pinely, just get a-shaking.

pointer n
1 In a draft team of at least three pairs: one of the animals directly in front of the **wheelers. esp West**

1866 in 1932 *NE Hist.* 13.146, It was no easy task to go into a corral crowded with some 300 oxen, ramming and butting each other about; pick out your "wheelers" and then your "leaders," "swing cattle," and "pointers"—twelve oxen in all and make no mistakes. **1955** Sharp *Whoop-Up Country* 189 **MT** (as of 1865–85), Ahead of the "wheelers" were the first "pointers," while the next pairs were called first, second, and third "swings." **1967–69** *DARE* Tape CA160, [Inf:] You had your leaders, your swing team, your pointers, and your wheelers—that was eight. [FW:] What was the swing team? [Inf:] Well, they was right back of the leaders—now I don't know why. But the pointers, in some of these crooked roads, they were hooked on the end of the tongue, see, and one of them, they'd pull him off sideways and he'd pull that tongue over and guide the wagon the way you wanted to. . . That's why they would call those pointers; LA2, [Inf:] The one next to the leaders is a swing steer and the ones next to the tongue steers were the pointers. . . and then the tongue steers. [FW:] Tongue steers were closest to the wagon? [Inf:] Yeah; NV2, The next horses [after the wheelers]—the pointer. . . On the team there are pointers. Then next is the six and then the eights, you see. It didn't go much above the eights. [All Infs old] **1968** Adams *Western Words* 231, *Pointers*—In freighting, the animals placed between the wheelers and the leaders. **1976** Sublette Co. Artist Guild *More Tales* 158 **WY** (as of c1900), The horses, except the "wheelers" were all driven with one line called a "Jerk Line." This rope, about a one-half inch, ran from the left side of the lead wagon through the hame ring of all the left, or near, horses except the "pointer".

2 A cowboy who helps guide a herd of cattle, esp one who rides near the head of the herd. **West** Cf **point B1, C1**

1869 *Overland Mth.* 3.126 **TX**, On the march the mighty herd sometimes strings out miles in length, and then it has "pointers," who ride abreast of the head of the column. **1938** in Lib. of Congress *Amer. Memory: WPA Life Hist.* (Internet) **TX**, We divided the critters into three herds and worked 12 waddies with each bunch. Each crew had a cook, hoss wrangler, who looked after the hosses, trail boss who picked the route and the rest were pointers. *Ibid* **TX**, The crew always consisted of a cooky, hoss wrangler, trail boss and nothing less than six pointers. . . With a herd of 3000 to 3500, ten pointers can handle the herd easily. *Ibid* **TX** (as of 1888), On the drive, we used about 14 waddies. Besides

the cook, two wranglers and the trail boss, all the waddies worked as pointers. The term pointer is applied to the men who ride at either side of the herd and keep the critters herded in the proper direction, and also to regulate the speed. **1943** Hamner *Short Grass* 50, Two men, his best, were put near the front of the line . . these were the pointers. **1952** *FWP Guide SD* 84, *Pilot or pointer:* rider preceding the herd to show the way.

3 also *pointer-man, point finger:* The index finger. [*SND* pointer (at *point* n., v. II.1.(1))]

1975 *DARE* File **neMN**, Pointer, point-finger. **1987** *NADS Letters* **cUT**, [From a children's song, "Thumbkin Says":] Pointer-man says "I'll dance."

4 also *pointer sled:* A type of sled; see quots. Cf **point A**

1913 (1919) *WNID*, Pointer. . . A clipper sled. *U.S.* **1943** *LANE* Map 573–74, A low sled with solid sides coming to a point in front, often home-made. . . 1 inf, **csRI**, [paɪntə] . . a low [paᵊɪntə] sled; 1 inf, **seMA**, [poɪntə], boy's sled; 1 inf, **swVT**, [pɔč̬ᵛntə]; 1 inf, **swVT**, [poɪntə]. [3 of 4 infs old]

5 =**daddy longlegs 1.** [See quots]

[**1899** Bergen *Animal Lore* 89, "Daddy-long-legs" will point out with one leg, if held by another leg, where the cows are. *General in the United States.*] **1942** McAtee *Dial. Grant Co. IN* 49 (as of 1890s), *Pointer* . . granddaddy longlegs, harvestman, or phalangid, so-called because used by children to point out with one of its extra-long legs the location of a lost object. **1956** McAtee *Some Dialect NC* 34, *Pointer* . . grandaddy longlegs or phalanigd [sic] spider; so-called because children thought its long legs or pointers would indicate where to look for a lost object.

pointer-man See **pointer 3**

pointer sled See **pointer 4**

point finger See **pointer 3**

point loco See **pointvetch**

point man (or rider) See **point B1**

point row n [Cf *SND* point n. I.5 "The tapering part of a field which is not completely rectangular; the furrows or drills which are shortened thereby"]
See quots.

1916 *DN* 4.328 **KS**, Point row. . . In fields other than rectangular, one of the short rows. "We have husked all the full rows of corn but have the point rows left yet." **1927** *AmSp* 2.362 **cwWV**, Point row . . a short row furrowed to straighten the rows in the corn field. "You are hoeing a point row." **1954** *Harder Coll.* **cwTN**, Point row. . . A short row at the end of a field.

pointsetta See **poinsettia**

pointvetch n Also *point loco* [See quot 1964] =**locoweed** (here: *Oxytropis* spp).

1937 U.S. Forest Serv. *Range Plant Hdbk.* W138, In North America crazyweeds and pointvetches extend from sea level in Alaska to elevations of about 11,000 feet in Colorado and 12,000 feet in California. **1964** Kingsbury *Poisonous Plants U.S.* 306, In . . [*Oxytropis*] the keel (lowermost petal) is prolonged into a long, distinct point (whence the common name, point vetch or point loco). **1968** Schmutz et al. *Livestock-Poisoning Plants AZ* 26, Point loco (*Oxytropis lambertii*).

poison n, v, adj, adv Usu |ˈpɔɪz(ə)n|; also occas |ˈpɔɪs(ə)n|; also **chiefly Sth, S Midl, occas NEast** *esp freq among older speakers* |ˈpaɪz(ə)n| (see Pronc Intro 3.I.11); also **Sth, S Midl** |ˈpɒz(ə)n| (see Pronc Intro 3.II.15) Pronc-spp *pizen, pison;* for addit pronc and sp varr see **A** below Cf **hoist**
A Forms.

1721 [see **poison tree 1**]. **1833** Neal *Down-Easters* 1.81 **NEng**, [I] hate a sharper as I do pyz'n. **1834** Caruthers *Kentuckian* 1.63, It was as strong as *pison*. **1834** *Life Andrew Jackson* 105, Pisen. *Ibid* 257, He'll cling to you like a pizin vine. **1843** (1916) Hall *New Purchase* 221 **IN**, [He] hates poor folks like pisin. **1851** Hooper *Widow Rugby's Husband* 23 **AL**, A true-hearted Union man . . that's worth a drop of pizen of treason in his veins! **1870** (1871) Shaw *Josh Billings' Farmer's Allminax for 1871* [17] **NEng**, Oh, don't go ni the tarnal kritters [=hornets]!/ For they are sure, and pizon hitters. **1890** *DN* 1.69 **KY**, Pizin [paɪzn]: for *poison*. In all words with an "oi" in them the "oi" was formerly pronounced *ai*. Now growing rare. [*DN* Ed: So too in New England.] **1892** *DN* 1.210 seMA, *P'ison* [paɪzn̩]. **1893** Shands *MS Speech* 50, *Pizin* [paɪzn̩]. Negro for *poison*. **1899** Garland *Boy Life* 201 **nwIA** (as of c1870s), Never mind the chaff, sonny—it ain't pizen. **1903** *DN* 2.291 **Cape Cod MA** (as of a1857), *Paison* for *poison*. **1904** Day *Kin o' Ktaadn* 194 **ME**, Jest 'cause they're afraid to pizen themselves by bitin' you is no sign other folks don't taste good to 'em. **1905** *DN* 3.57 **eNE**, For *oi, ai* is very common; . . *poison*. **1909** *DN* 3.358 **eAL, wGA**, *Pizen*. *Ibid* 401 **nwAR**, *Pizn*. . . This pronunciation is growing rare. **1916** *DN* 4.344 **seSC**, *Poison* [paɪzn̩]. **1917** *DN* 4.415 **wNC**, *Pizen vine*. **1923** *DN* 5.217 **swMO**, *Pizen*. **1934** Smiley *Gloss. New Paltz* **seNY**, A pison wind. **1937** *Hall Coll.* **eTN**, *Poison*. . . Usu. /paɪzn/ in older, untutored speakers. . . Ivy /paɪznz/ them. **c1938** in 1970 Hyatt *Hoodoo* 1.326 **eNC**, She vure . . *pyzon* . . on branch vatah. [=She were poisoned on branch water.] **1940** in 1944 *ADD* **NYC**, *Poison*. . . [pəɪ]-, [pʌɪ]-. Less educated. **1941** *LANE* Map 251, [[paɪzn, pɛɪzn] and similar proncs found **throughout NEng**, are labeled obsolete or old-fashioned by infs.] **1942** *New Yorker* 11 July 18, Why, this stuff is positively perzin! **c1960** *Wilson Coll.* **csKY**, *Poison*, pronounced /ˈpaɪzn/. **1965–70** *DARE* (Qu. S16) 506 Infs, **widespread**, proncs of the type [ˈpɔɪz(ə)n]; 42 Infs, **scattered**, proncs of the type [ˈpɔɪs(ə)n]; 18 Infs, **Sth, S Midl,** proncs of the type [ˈpɔz(ə)n]; 9 Infs, **Sth, S Midl,** proncs of the type [ˈpaɪz(ə)n] [8 of 9 Infs old]; **MI**34, 45, **NY**65, [pɔɪz(ə)n]; **MS**6, [pɑɔzn], **NY**45, [pəɪzən]; (Qu. S17) 42 Infs, **scattered**, proncs of the type [ˈpɔɪz(ə)n]; **CT**8, **MA**3, **MS**86, **NE**3, **PA**70, 204, proncs of the type [ˈpɔɪs(ə)n]; **AR**10, [ˈpɒzn]; **MI**45, [paɪzn]; **VA**15, [ˈpaɪzn]; (Qu. I38) 39 Infs, **scattered**, proncs of the type [ˈpɔɪz(ə)n]; **IL**85, **NC**60, **PA**143, **TN**36, proncs of the type [ˈpɔɪsən]; **GA**32, **VA**83, [ˈpɔzɪn]; **IN**39, [ˈpaɪzn]; (Qu. HH22b) Inf **MA**5, *Pizen*. **1966–69** *DARE* FW Addit **AR**55, Negro pronunciation is [ˈpaɪzn]; White, both standard and poor, is [ˈpɔɔzn]; **neNC**, [ˈpɑˆɪzn] . . reported as said with the old brogue; **swNC**, [ˈpazn]. **1985** [see **B2** below]. **1989** Pederson *LAGS Tech. Index* 222 **Gulf Region**, [Proncs of the type [ˈpɔɪz(ə)n] occur most frequently; proncs of the types [ˈpaɪzən, ˈpɔzən] occur occasionally; those of the types [ˈpɔɪsən, ˈpɔɪʒən, ˈpɔɪzən] occur rarely.]

B As noun.

1 In var children's games:

a An imaginary quality that is held to be transmitted from one player or object to another by contact and that affects the role or status of the other player or object in the game; a person or object having this quality; hence adjs *poison(ed)* held to possess this quality—often used as a call in games.

1909 (1923) Bancroft *Games* 148, *Poison*—A circle is marked . . smaller than an outer circle formed by the players. . . Each player tries, by pulling or pushing, to induce the others to step within the smaller circle. . . Any one who touches the ground within the inner circle . . is said to be poisoned. . . [T]he other players shout "Poisoned!" . . and run for safety, which consists in standing on wood. **1923** Acker *400 Games* 26, *Poison*. . . a circle of . . players. . . This object in the center is "poison." The players . . try by pushing and pulling to cause members of the circle to touch . . the "poison." When one has done that, he is poisoned and must leave the ring. **1952** [see **B1b(1)** below]. **1957** *Sat. Eve. Post Letters* **ceWI** (as of 1890s), Poison: Parlor Game. All sit in a circle. One person stands in the middle of the ring. He tosses a handkerchief or cloth at the circle. The cloth is *poison*. When it alights on a person, that person must toss it upon some one else. . . The person in . . the circle endeavors to pin the poison with his hand on the person whom *poison* is touching. *Ibid* **Bronx NYC** (as of c1945–51), *Pussy-in-the-corner*—where you arranged yourself on a square on the sidewalk and joined hands with someone on an opposite or diagonal corner. The "Pussy" stood in the middle and tried to step on a vacant corner before you did. If there was a free corner, it was declared "poison" and no one used it. **1966–70** *DARE* Tape **CA**190, Once they go through the last one they're poison and they shoot at the other player's marbles and once they hit them, the player's out of the game. *Ibid* **MS**76, [FW:] What was this game called Poison that you were telling me about? [Inf:] Oh, yes, well, Poison . . they get in a ring. . . And we all run around, try to keep him [=the one in the middle] from getting out. . . When he get out, he runned. If you catch him, touch him before he get on the wood, he'd be poison. . . When he'd get poison, then he'd had to come out and catch the others. *Ibid*, We played we'd had to stand on wood. . . If he put his hands on you before you got on the wood, you's poison. You couldn't play no more. **1967–69** *DARE* (Qu. EE17, *In a game of tag, if a player wants to rest, what does he call out so that he can't be tagged?*) Infs **GA**80, **PA**49, Poison. [Both Infs old] **1974** [see **B1b(1)** below]. **1975** [see **B1b(1)** below]. **1985** Runyan *Knuckles Down* 14, If the taw or shooter

lands in the hole, that player is poison and can begin to eliminate other players by hitting their marbles on his turn.

b Used in the names of games, as:

(1) *poison, poison(ed) circle, poison rag,* ~ *snake,* ~ *spot,* ~ *stick:* Any of var games in which players try to force another player into contact with something deemed "poison" while avoiding it themselves, often as the preliminary to a game of tag.

1865 *Harper's New Mth. Mag.* 30.608 **CT** (as of c1815), On the very school-ground where I used to play ball are now visible the foot marks of the same old games: "one old cat," and "two old cat," and "base ball," and "prison base," and "pison," and "gould," and "tag," and "I spy." **1909** [see **B1a** above]. **1923** [see **B1a** above]. **1940** Harbin *Fun Encycl.* 181, *Poisoned circle*. . . form a ring around a circle. . . The object of the game is to keep out of the poisoned circle and to try to pull some of the other players into it. **1946** TN Folk Lore Soc. *Bulletin* 12, Some of the mixed games required a good deal of running as. . . poison stick. **1952** Brown *NC Folkl.* 1.72 **cNC** (as of 1924), *Poison Stick*. . . All the children join hands and form a circle. A stick about a foot long is stuck upright in the center. All the players pull and try to make someone knock the stick over. The one who knocks it over must try to catch the others, who cannot be caught while they are stooping down. When one player is caught, he must help to catch the rest. *Ibid* **c,eNC** (as of 1926–28), *Poison Stick*. . . All join hands in a circle and try by pulling and pushing to cause some player . . to touch a stick which has been stuck up in the center. The player who knocks it over must then try to touch the others with the "poison stick." Players touching wood are safe. **1953** Brewster *Amer. Nonsinging Games* 34 **KS**, Poison. . . Other names given this game are Poison Circle, Poison Spot, Poison Snake. **1966** *Good Old Days* 2.10.8 **seWI**, Perhaps they were already planning tomorrow's games. How about "Poison Rag" or jump rope? **1966–70** *DARE* (Qu. EE1, . . *Games . . children play . . in which they form a ring, and either sing or recite a rhyme*) Inf **IN**10, Poison [FW sugg]; (Qu. EE18, *Games in which the players set up a stone, a tin can, or something similar, and then try to knock it down*) Inf **IN**16, Poison stick; (Qu. EE33, . . *Outdoor games . . that children play*) Inf **GA**8, Poison stick— put a stick in center of a ring and try to pull each other over it; **IL**143, Poison—form a circle around stick, pull someone to touch it. **1974** Betts–Walser *NC Folkl.* 3, *Poison*. A stick is driven into the ground, and the players join hands and form a circle around it. They then pull and scramble, in order to make one of them touch the stick, which is poison. The one who is poisoned becomes *It*. *It* then tries to poison all the others by touching them. If a player can place both hands on the ground, he is "vaccinated," and the poison will not take. **1975** Ferretti *Gt. Amer. Book Sidewalk Games* 211, *Poison*. A group of players joins together by placing their arms over and under the shoulders of their neighbors and form a circle. A ball, usually a basketball, is put on a manhole cover, and the circle surrounds it. At a signal, everyone tries to force his neighbor against the ball, hoping to force the neighbor to nudge it, kick it, even fall on it. Whoever ultimately does so is Poison, or "It," and a game of Tag ensues.

(2) *poison oak, poison(ed) penny,* ~ *seat:* Any of var games similar to **musical chairs** in which players are progressively eliminated by contact with a "poison" object.

1932 (1953) Smith *Games* 284, *Poisoned seat*. . . [The] teacher poisons two or more seats by placing a book upon each one. The children march around the room. . . Suddenly, the music stops and every one rushes for a seat. All players who get poisoned seats keep them, and they are not permitted to continue the march. **1940** Harbin *Fun Encycl.* 714, *Poison penny*—Pass article or articles to right. . . When the music stops or the whistle blows players holding the "poisoned pennies" drop out of the circle. **1947** Webb *Games* 41, *Poisoned penny*—The children sit in a circle while music is played. The leader starts a penny around the circle, each child passing the penny as rapidly as possible. The music stops suddenly and whoever holds the penny drops out of the circle. **1966–70** *DARE* (Qu. EE2, *Games that have one extra player—when a signal is given, the players change places, and the extra one tries to get a place*) Infs **NC**88, **WV**1, Poison seat; **MS**21, Poison oak; (Qu. EE3, *Games in which you hide an object and then look for it*) Inf **CA**133, Poison penny.

(3) *poison, poison pit,* ~ *ring, five-pot poison:* Any of var marble games involving a hole or holes in the ground.

1963 *KY Folkl. Rec.* 9.3.59 **eKY**, *Game played through a series of holes . . poison*. *Ibid* 60 **eKY**, *Game played by shooting at opponent's marble, his shooter, no boundaries . . poison*. **1967** *DARE* (Qu. EE7, . . *Kinds of marble games*) Inf **OR**10, Five-pot poison. **c1970** Wiersma

Marbles Terms **seMI** (as of 1960), *Poison Pit.* . . The name of a marble game and the name of the hole(s) dug in the playing surface of this game. The object of the game is to hit an opponent's marble which is in the circle without putting the shooter into a poison pit. If the shooter falls into a pit it is lost. *Ibid, Poison*—pot or circle. **1976** Knapp–Knapp *One Potato* 40, *Poison:* Holes are dug in three of the corners of a ten-foot square. Each player tries to put his marble around the course, sinking it in each hole. When a marble gets back "home" it is "poison" and can "kill" the other marbles. Killed marbles belong to the player who kills them. **1985** Runyan *Knuckles Down* 13, *Poison ring.*

2 The supposed causative agent of var diseases and infections; the discharge from an infected site.

1935 Hyatt *Folkl. Adams Co. IL* 262, Take a chicken and cut it in two and leave all the entrails in, and put your foot right in the chicken and it will take all the rheumatism you have in your body. The poison will go into the chicken. *Ibid* 282, You will never have boils, if you don't wash your feet; for if you don't wash your feet, the poison will all stay in your feet. *Ibid* 283, The next day the boil broke and all the poison came out, and the woman got well. *Ibid* 287, If you have a social disease, let someone put you in a manure pile and cover you all up but your head. . . The manure will draw out all the poison in your body. **1968–69** *DARE* (Qu. BB35, *The yellowish stuff that comes out of a boil when the head breaks*) Infs **NY**82, **VT**3, Poison; (Qu. BB36, *When there's an open sore and this yellowish stuff is coming out of it*) Inf **VT**16, Poison working out; **MD**20, The poison's coming out; (Qu. BB50c, *Remedies for infections*) Inf **CA**118, Rub a nickel on it and it will draw the poison. **1985** *Amer. Jrl. Med.* Feb 183 **eTN**, *Piezin* . . an ill humour such as that one causing arthritis—"Those golden shots sure drove the piezin out." **1986** Pederson *LAGS Concordance* **Gulf Region** (*Pus*) 7 infs, Poison; (*Water in a blister*) 1 inf, Poison.

3 See **rain poison**.

C As adj.

1 See **B1a** above.

2 as pred adj: Poisonous.

1913 Johnson *Highways St. Lawrence to VA* 69 **seNY**, But a rattlesnake is ten times more p'isener. **1921** Haswell *Daughter Ozarks* 53 (as of 1880s), That feller's jist as pizen as a rattlesnake. **1935** Hurston *Mules & Men* 206 **FL** [Black], Dat snake dat was so poison tell he bit de railroad track and killed de train. **1940** (1978) Still *River of Earth* 29 **KY**, They're poison as rattlesnake spit. **1950** *WELS* (*If berries are not good to eat, you say they are* _____) 14 Infs, **WI**, Poison. **c1960** *Wilson Coll.* **csKY**, It is poison. . . *Poisonous* is rare. **1965–70** *DARE* (Qu. I45, *If berries are not safe to eat* . . *"Don't eat those berries, they're* _____"; total Infs questioned, 75) 35 Infs, **scattered**, Poison; [19 Infs, **scattered**, Poisonous]. **1967** *DARE* Tape **AZ**1, They know snakes are poison, and they'll just die from fright instead of from the real poison. **1971** Bright *Word Geog. CA & NV* 190, Some berries are . . *poison* 40% [of 300 infs]. **1975** Allen *LAUM* 2.58 (as of c1950), In predicative position two adjectivals occur, *poisonous* and *poison*. . . In New England *poison* is general; *poisonous* is largely confined to the southern half, i.e., Massachusetts, Rhode Island, and Connecticut. For the U[pper] M[idwest] a possible regional weighting appears in the slightly higher incidence of *poisonous* in the Northern speech territory. But a marked social pattern emerges from the field data. Although only one college graduate uses the simple *poison*, one-third of the type II infs [=mid-aged, with approx hs educ], and more than one-half of those in type I [=old, with little educ] have this form. *Poisonous*, conversely, is strongly favored by the more-educated speakers. **1982** Slone *How We Talked* 49 **eKY** (as of c1950), *Nightshed*—Very poison.

3 Mean, hateful, vicious; extreme. [*EDD*] **esp S Midl**

1834 *Life Andrew Jackson* 105, Had you bin a leetle more pisen, and lambasted the Inglish afore they giv'd up, . . nothin in nature cou'd've kept you from bein president. **1839** (1969) Briggs *Advent. Franco* 18 **NEast**, "I presume there's no occasion for hurrying," said the driver. "Yes there is though, you pisen critter," said another passenger. **1871** (1882) Stowe *Fireside Stories* 165 **MA**, Then they burnt all the houses in Groton, meetin'-house and all; and the pisen critters they hollared and triumphed over the people. **1885** Twain *Huck. Finn* 249 **MO**, The old man. . . was on hand and looking his level pisonest. **1913** Kephart *Highlanders* 171 **sAppalachians**, Oh, sometimes hit's some pizen old bum who's been refused credit. [**1916** *DN* 4.344 **seSC**, *Poison.* . . Meanness of disposition.] **1924** Raine *Land of Saddle-Bags* 135 **sAppalachians**, Possibly a majority of the women *of his own age* in that district might take a drink, but . . he himself was known to be "mighty pizen agin whiskey." **1942** McAtee *Dial. Grant Co. IN* 49 (as of

1890s), *Pizen* . . no good, treacherous; "He's _____". **c1960** *Wilson Coll.* **csKY**, *Poison.* . . Treacherous.

D As adv.

1 with adj: Extremely; unpleasantly, viciously. **esp S Midl** Cf **powerful C**

1840 Hoffman *Greyslaer* 1.61 **Upstate NY**, The night was pison cold, I tell ye. **1894** Twain *Pudd'nhead Wilson* 194 **MO**, You's got to be pison good, en let him see it. **1932** Randolph *Ozark Mt. Folks* 152, They got well finally, but from then on Charley was pizen mean, an' Bud he was a dummy. **1937** in 1976 *Weevils in the Wheat* 95 **VA** [Black], Dese here chillun what is now comin' up is too pisen brazen fer me. **1941** *LANE* Map 251, 1 inf, **wCT**, A mean dog is said to be [pɑɪzn mi·n]. **1942** (1971) Campbell *Cloud-Walking* 51 **seKY**, One [book] was . . about which kings were pizen mean and who beat when they fit battles. **1947** Ballowe *The Lawd* 66 **LA**, He pizen mean an' pow'ful. **1968** *Foxfire* Fall-Winter 111 **NC**, "Who's been messing around my still?" he cries, poison mad.

2 esp in comb *poison-neat:* See quots. **chiefly NEng** Cf **nasty-neat**

1877 *Scribner's Mth.* 13.344 **MA**, P'ison neat was the only phrase to express her views of housekeeping; and lest even a grasshopper . . should take her unawares, every door was locked. **1892** *DN* 1.210 **seMA**, P'ison neat . . extremely neat. **1926** *AmSp* 2.80 **ME**, A housewife who takes a bit too much pride in her art with the broom and mop is dubbed "pizen-neat," a term which we would regard as complimentary, rather than otherwise. **1926** *DN* 5.388 **ME**, *Pizen-neat.* . . Overneat; sometimes used in a complimentary sense. Common. **1956** *VT Hist.* 24.289 (as of 1800s), A person was "pizen neat" when she spent all of her time cleaning and nagged the family if anything was misplaced or soiled. **1959** *Ibid* 27.153, *Poison-neat.* . . Usually, pizen . . neat. Vexatiously neat. Common; Addison; Essex. **1965** *DARE* File **cVT** (as of c1880), Neat—pizen (poison) neat. **1966–69** *DARE* (Qu. HH11b, *Someone who is too particular or fussy—if it's a woman*) Infs **ME**16, **MA**73, Poison-neat; (Qu. KK34, . . *Very neat and clean: "Her house always looks* _____.") Infs **MA**5, **TN**12, Pizen-neat. [All Infs old] [**1967** *DARE* FW Addit **PA**, A very clean house—her house looks as clean as poison.]

E As verb.

1 In hoodoo: to harm by means of magic; see quots.

1931 *Jrl. Amer. Folkl.* 44.416 **Sth** [Black], When a conjure doctor tells one of his patients, "Youse poisoned nearly to death," he does not necessarily mean that poison has been swallowed. He might mean that, but the instances are rare. He means that something has been put down for the patient. **c1938** in 1970 Hyatt *Hoodoo* 1.7 **seNC** [Black], Well, I know of a lady tryin' to *poison* someone else. An' so I wus told by a gentleman . . that—she goes to work an' takes a tahrahpin [=terrapin], a water tahrahpin, cooks this . . up, takes this grease of it an' greases the other lady's husband in order to *poison* this lady. *Ibid* 150 **seSC**, You see, I was *poisoned*. . . I use to been smart . . and working, going all de time, and dey didn't like dat—they *fixed* something you see to take all of my strength away from me. *Ibid* 2.1099 **cSC**, Then if de person's *poisoned* an' yo' put dat dime in dat shoe to tell whether she or he is *poisoned*, de pores of her skin will run dat *poison* in dat hole in de dime an' turn de dime black jes' three times as quick.

2 In children's games: to transmit **poison B1a** to (someone or something).

1932 [see **B1b(2)** above]. **c1970** Wiersma *Marbles Terms*, When you have gone to all five [pots] you are poison and you can poison the pots you go into. **1974** [see **B1b(1)** above].

3 To affect with passion or enthusiasm; hence ppl adj phr *poisoned on* smitten by, in love with.

1893 Twain in *St. Nicholas* **MO**, Do you reckon Tom Sawyer was satisfied after all them adventures? . . No, he was n't. It only just p'isoned him for more. **1967** *DARE* (Qu. AA1, *When a man goes to see a girl often and seems to want to marry her, he's* _____ *her*) Inf **OR**3, Poisoned on; (Qu. AA10, *A very special liking that a boy may have for a girl [or the other way round]*) Inf **OR**3, Poisoned on.

4 in phr *poison up on:* To come to dislike or mistrust.

1933 Williamson *Woods Colt* 83 **Ozarks**, If you want to do somethin' bright, you git shet of them. . . I pizened up on that bunch long time ago, an' you better do the same thing.

poison adder n Cf **adder 1**
=**hognose snake**.

1981 Pederson *LAGS Basic Materials,* 1 inf, **swAL,** Spreading adder, poison adder.

poison alder n CT   Cf **poison elder 1**
=**poison sumac.**

1941 *LANE* Map 250 *(Sumach),* 1 inf, **csCT,** White poison = poison sumach = poison alder; 1 inf, **csCT,** Poison sumach = poison alder, has silvery berries, grows in swamps and along roads. **1968** *DARE* (Qu. S17, . . *Kinds of plants . . that . . cause itching and swelling*) Inf **CT**17, Poison alder—same as poison sumac.

poison apple n   Cf **paradise apple**
The **tomato** *(Lycopersicon lycopersicum).*

1950 *WELS (Names or nicknames for tomatoes)* 1 Inf, **csWI,** Love apple, poison apple. **1996** *DARE* File **WI** (as of c1940), I heard elderly people refer to tomatoes as "poison apples."

poison arum n
An **arrow arum** (here: *Peltandra virginica).*

1933 Small *Manual SE Flora* 246, *P[eltandra] virginica. . . Virginia Wake-robin, Poison-arum. . .* Swamps and shallow water, various provinces, Fla. to La. **1974** (1977) Coon *Useful Plants* 67, Arrow arum, Virginia tuckahoe, Indian bread, poison arum. . . Much used by many Indians as a food plant after extracting the acrid principle with heat, it is not, however, recommended as a "quickie-wayside-food."

poison ash n

1 A **poison ivy 1,** usu a **poison sumac** (here: *Toxicodendron vernix).*

1760 J. Lee *Introd. Botany* App. 323 *(OED2),* Poison Ash, Rhus. **1763** Lewis *Commercium* 330, Mr. Catesby, in his history of Carolina, describes one, called there the poison-ash. **1785** Marshall *Arbustrum* 1.130, *Rhus-Toxicodendron Vernix.* Varnish-Tree, or Poison Ash. . . This tree ought to be handled with caution, as it is very poisonous to many people. **1822** Eaton *Botany* 428, *[Rhus] toxicodendron . .* poison vine, poison ash. . . The sap of this species is an excellent marking ink for linen. **1839** in 1856 MI State Ag. Soc. *Trans. for 1855* 7.417, Rhus . . toxicodendron. . . Poison ash. **1855** Davis *Farm Book* 141 **AL** *(DA),* Sunday a warm day—I was laid by handling the poison ash. **1896** *Jrl. Amer. Folkl.* 9.185 **VT,** *Rhus venemata* [=*Toxicodendron vernix*] . . , poison ash. **1901** Lounsberry *S. Wild Flowers* 308, *R. Vernix,* poison sumac, elder, ash or dogwood . . is thought by many to be the strikingly beautiful member of the genus. **1920** *Torreya* 20.22 **PA,** *Toxicodendron radicans . .* Poison ash, Mercersburg, Pa. **1986** Pederson *LAGS Concordance* **Gulf Region,** 3 infs, Poison ash; 1 inf, Poison ash, a tree-like plant. . . all of these trouble the skin.

2 =**fringe tree.**

1900 Lyons *Plant Names* 96, *C[hionanthus] Virginica* L. Delaware to Florida and Texas. . . Poison Ash. . . *Root bark* tonic, febrifuge, laxative, reputed narcotic. **1930** U.S. Dept. Ag. *Misc. Pub.* 77.30, Fringe-tree. . . Poison ash. **1960** Vines *Trees SW* 850, Poison ash. . . The tree is cultivated to some extent for the fragile panicles of flowers in spring and for the dark green foliage. **1971** Krochmal *Appalachia Med. Plants* 92, *Chionanthus virginicus. . .* poison ash. . . In Appalachia a liquid of boiled root bark is applied to skin irritations.

poisonball tree n [From the poisonous fruit]   Cf **Chinaball, poisonberry 1**
Prob =**Chinaberry 1.**

1941 O'Donnell *Great Big Doorstep* 85 **sLA,** The poisonball tree before the post office had not been burned by frost. *Ibid* 64, The most valuable lumber. . . oak, ash, and elder and the poisonball tree.

poison bay n
=**Florida anise-tree.**

1866 Lindley–Moore *Treas. Botany* 619, In Alabama . . [the leaves of *Illicium] floridanum* have . . acquired the name of Poison-bay. **1900** Lyons *Plant Names* 200, *I[llicium] Floridanum . .* Florida to Louisiana, Poison Bay. . . *Leaves* and *fruit* have poisonous properties. **1938** Van Dersal *Native Woody Plants* 324, Bay, Poison *(Illicium floridanum).* **1960** Vines *Trees SW* 278, Florida Anise—*Illicium floridanum. . .* Other vernacular names are Polecat-tree, Poison Bay [etc.]. . . The leaves are reported as being poisonous to stock.

poison bean n
A **rattlebox 1h** (here: *Sesbania drummondii).*

1934 (1943) *W2,* Poison bean. The seed of a shrub *(Daubentonia*

drummondii) . . , of the southern United States, poisonous to stock; also, the plant itself. **1964** Kingsbury *Poisonous Plants U.S.* 353, *Sesbania spp.* Coffeeweed, coffeebean, bagpod, rattlebush, rattlebox, sesbane, poison bean. **1970** Correll *Plants TX* 836, *Sesbania Drummondii. . .* Poison Bean. . . The seeds, if eaten, are known to be poisonous to sheep and goats.

poisonberry n

1 also *poisonberry tree:* =**Chinaberry 1.** **SC**   Cf **poisonball tree**

1803 Davis *Travels* 79 **SC,** The mocking bird. . . was warbling, close to my window, from a tree called by some the Pride of *India,* and by others the Poison-berry Tree. **1968–70** *DARE* (Qu. T16, . . *Kinds of trees . . 'special'*) Inf **SC**4, Poisonberry—same as Chinaberry; **SC**67, Chinaberry—also called poisonberry.

2 =**red baneberry.**

1876 Hobbs *Bot. Hdbk.* 91, Poison berry, Red cohosh, Actaea rubra. **1900** Lyons *Plant Names* 14, *A[ctaea] rubra . .* Red Cohosh, Red Baneberry, Coral-and-Pearl, Poison-berry [etc.]. **1933** Small *Manual SE Flora* 513, *A[ctaea] rubra . .* Coralberry, Poisonberry [etc.].

3 A **nightshade 1:** usu **deadly nightshade,** but also a **bittersweet** (here: *Solanum dulcamara).*

1900 Lyons *Plant Names* 349, *S[olanum] Dulcamara. . .* Poison-berry, Pushion-berry. **1914** Georgia *Manual Weeds* 363, *Bittersweet Nightshade. . . Other English names . .* Felonwort, Poison Berry. . . The fruits of this plant are not dangerously poisonous, but are sufficiently so to bring on unpleasant sensations of nausea and cramp, particularly if the seeds are well ripened. *Ibid* 364, *Common, or Black, Nightshade. . . Other English names:* Deadly Nightshade, Duscle, Poison Berry [etc.]. . . Some housewives boldly make pies of the fruit—occasionally with unpleasant consequences. **1935** (1943) Muenscher *Weeds* 411, *Solanum Dulcamara . .* Poison berry. . . There is still some difference of opinion concerning the poisonous properties of the berries, some maintaining that they are poisonous while others claim that they are harmless. *Ibid* 413, *Solanum nigrum* L. Black nightshade, Deadly nightshade, Poison berry. . . Poisonous when eaten, although certain cultivated forms are grown, under such names as "garden huckleberry" or "wonder berry", for the berries which are used in preserves. **1963** Craighead *Rocky Mt. Wildflowers* 167, *Black Nightshade. . .* Other names: Deadly Nightshade, Poisonberry. **1967** *DARE* (Qu. I44, *What kinds of berries grow wild around here?*) Inf **MI**69, Poisonberries—a red berry, grew on a vine; it's a weed, really.

poisonberry tree   See **poisonberry 1**

poison bitterweed n
A **bitterweed** (here: *Hymenoxys odorata).*

1961 Wills–Irwin *Flowers TX* 239, Poison Bitterweed—*Hymenoxys odorata.* [*Ibid* 240, As the common name suggests, this is a poisonous plant, sheep being the most severely affected.] **1969** *DARE* Wildfl QR (Wills–Irwin) Pl.60D Inf **TX**44, Poison bitterweed.

poison bush n
=**poison sumac** or a similar plant.

1950 *WELS (Trees that are found in your neighborhood . . sumac)* 1 Inf, **cWI,** Poison bush. **1956** Ker *Vocab. W. TX* 88, *Poisonous vine that makes the skin break out. . .* poison bush. [2 of 67 infs]

poison camas n Also sp *poison camass*   **West**
=**death camas.**

1900 U.S. Natl. Museum *Contrib. Herbarium* 7.321, On account of its poisonous qualities and its resemblance to the true camas (Quamasia) a most highly esteemed food plant, this is known throughout the West as "poison camas" or "death camas." **1911** *Century Dict. Suppl., Camass. . . Poison camass, white camass,* the death camass, *Zigadenus venenosus,* a plant which causes severe losses of sheep in Montana and elsewhere. **1937** U.S. Forest Serv. *Range Plant Hdbk.* W209, Death-camases, sometimes known as poison-segos, poison-camases, poison-soaproots, and erroneously called lobelias, are herbaceous perennials of the bunchflower family. **1963** Craighead *Rocky Mt. Wildflowers* 32, *Mountain Death-Camas—Zigadenus elegans . .* Other names: Poison Camas [etc.]. **1995** Brako et al. *Scientific & Common Names Plants* 209, Poison camass—*Zigadenus nuttallii.*

poison catfish n
A **stonecat** (here: either *Noturus gyrinus* or *N. insignis).*

1906 NJ State Museum *Annual Rept. for 1905* 171, Schilbeodes

[=*Noturus*] *gyrinus*. . . Stone Cat. Little Cat Fish. Poison Cat Fish. Mud Cat Fish. . . These small cat fish are dangerous to handle, as their small spines are capable of inflicting painful wounds. The pectoral spines are also furnished with a poison apparatus to increase distress. *Ibid* 173, *Schilbeodes insignis*. . . Mud Cat Fish. Poison Cat Fish. Stone Cat.

poison cedar n Cf **cedar 1, ~ fever**
A **juniper 1** which causes contact dermatitis.
1966 *DARE* (Qu. S17, . . *Kinds of plants . . that . . cause itching and swelling*) Inf **MI2**, Poison oak, poison cedar; [**MI9**, Some people get cedar poisoning].

poison chickweed n
=**scarlet pimpernel.**
1897 *Jrl. Amer. Folkl.* 10.49 **CA**, *Anagallis arvensis* . . poison chickweed.

poison circle See **poison B1b(1)**

poison clover n
A **saltbush 1** (here: *Atriplex corrugata*).
1960 Vines *Trees SW* 238, *Mat Saltbush—Atriplex corrugata*. . . New Mexico, Arizona, Colorado, and Utah. . . The plant is also known under the vernacular name of Poison Clover. It is occasionally grazed by sheep, but some ranchers consider it to be poisonous.

poison creeper n
=**poison ivy 1.**
1898 U.S. Dept. Ag. Div. Botany *Bulletin* 20.35, *Poison Ivy. Rhus radicans* . . *Other names:* Poison oak; poison vine; three-leafed ivy; poison creeper. **1914** Georgia *Manual Weeds* 274, *Poison ivy*. . . *Other English names:* Poison Oak, Poison Creeper, Three-leaved Ivy [etc]. **1935** (1943) Muenscher *Weeds* 329, Poison ivy, Poison oak, Poison creeper. **1974** (1977) Coon *Useful Plants* 58, *Rhus radicans*—Common poison ivy, three-leaved ivy, poison creeper [etc]. . . This is the eastern low-growing poison ivy.

poison daisy n
=**dog fennel 1.**
1900 Lyons *Plant Names* 37, *A[nthemis] Cotula*. . . Pig-sty or Poison Daisy. **1940** Clute *Amer. Plant Names* 251, *Anthemis cotula* . . poison daisy, dog banner, jay-weed. **1974** (1977) Coon *Useful Plants* 102, *Anthemis cotula*—Mayweed, dog-fennel, poison daisy, chiggy weed, fetid chamomile. A plant used medicinally for its "irritating properties" . . overuse may cause blisters on the skin and an infusion may cause vomiting.

poison darnel n Also *poisonous darnel*
A **ryegrass 1** (here: *Lolium temulentum*).
1847 Wood *Class-Book* 620, *L[olium] Temulentum. Poisonous Darnel*. . . Remarkably distinguished from all other grasses by its poisonous seeds. N. Eng. to Penn. July. **1889** Vasey *Ag. Grasses* 75, *Lolium temulentum* (Poison Darnel). . . The seeds have long enjoyed a reputation of being poisonous to stock, and also to mankind when mixed in large quantity with the wheat or rye used in the making of bread. **1940** Gates *Flora KS* 130, Lolium temulentum . . Darnel, Poison Darnel. Introduced in fields and waste ground.

poison dock n
A **dock** n[1] (here: *Rumex obtusifolius*).
1897 *Jrl. Amer. Folkl.* 10.54 **OH**, *Rumex obtusifolius* . . sour dock, poison dock, Sulphur Grove, Ohio.

poison dogwood n
1 =**poison sumac** (here: *Toxicodendron vernix*).
1814 Bigelow *Florula Bostoniensis* 72, *Rhus Vernix. Poison dogwood. Swamp Sumach*. . . Berries white. **1870** *Galaxy* 10.704, The *rhus vernix*, which is commonly called poison tree, poison wood, poison ash, and in Massachusetts poison dogwood, is a handsome tree. **1897** Sudworth *Arborescent Flora* 276, *Poison Sumach*. . . Poison Dogwood (N.H., Vt., N.J., Pa., D.C., Mo., Mich., Minn.) **1931** Otis *MI Trees* 275, *Poison Sumac*, also known as *Dogwood* or *Poison Dogwood, Rhus vernix* L., is an upright shrub or small tree, sometimes 15–20 feet in height. . . A beautiful plant in its native habitat, but it should not be planted for ornamentation. **1970** Correll *Plants TX* 990, *Rhus vernix* . . *Poison sumac, poison elder, poison dogwood*. . . The plant, at all seasons, is virulently poisonous to the touch.
2 A **red osier** (here: *Cornus sericea*).

1960 Vines *Trees SW* 796, *Redosier Dogwood*. . . Also known as Harts Rouges or Poison Dogwood.

poisoned See **poison B1a**

poisoned circle See **poison B1b(1)**

poisoned oak See **poison oak 1**

poisoned on See **poison E3**

poisoned penny (or seat) See **poison B1b(2)**

poison elder n
1 also *poisonous elder:* =**poison sumac** (here: *Toxicodendron vernix*). Cf **poison alder**
1778 Carver *Travels N. Amer.* 507, The *Alder* or *Elder,* termed the poisonous elder, nearly resembles the other sorts in its leaves and branches, but it grows much straiter, and is only found in swamps and moist soils. **1822** Eaton *Botany* 428, *[Rhus] vernix* (poison sumach, poison elder). . . Very poisonous. **1848** Gray *Manual of Botany* 79, *R[hus] venenata* . . Poison Sumach. . . The most poisonous species, even the effluvium affecting many persons. It is also called, inappropriately, *Poison Elder* and *Poison Dogwood*. **1892** (1974) Millspaugh *Amer. Med. Plants* 37-1, *Rhus venenata*. . . Com. Names.—Poison or Swamp Sumach, Poison Elder, Poison or Swamp Dogwood, Poison Ash, Poison Tree, Poison Wood. **1931–33** *LANE Worksheets* seCT, Poison elder—has silver berries. **1935** (1943) Muenscher *Weeds* 332, *Rhus Vernix*. . . Poison elder [etc]. **1950** *WELS* (Trees that are found in your neighborhood) 1 Inf, **cWI**, Poison elder—sumac. **1966–69** *DARE* (Qu. S17, . . *Kinds of plants . . that . . cause itching and swelling*) Infs **CT12, GA7,** 20, Poison elder; (Qu. T13) Inf **GA20**, There's a poison elder and a tame elder; (Qu. T15, . . *Kinds of swamp trees*) Inf **CT28**, Poison elder—grows in swamp; (Qu. BB25, . . *Common skin diseases around here*) Inf **GA8**, Poison oak, poison elder. **1981** Pederson *LAGS Basic Materials* sGA, 2 infs, Poison elder; 1 inf, Poison elder is probably twice as worse [FW: as poison ivy or poison oak].
2 An elder (here: *Sambucus callicarpa*).
1896 *Jrl. Amer. Folkl.* 9.189 **ME**, *Sambucus pubens*, poison elder, Oxford County, Me.

poison fern n
A **cliff brake** (here: *Pellaea mucronata*).
1923 in 1925 Jepson *Manual Plants CA* 33, *P[ellaea] ornithopus*. . . Sometimes called Tea Fern; also Poison Fern and Black Fern, since causing death to sheep.

poison fish n
A **sculpin 1** (here: *Cottus carolinae*).
1933 Randolph in *AmSp* 8.1.51 **Ozarks**, *Pizen fish*. . . A little brown mottled fish. Never more than four or five inches long, it has the form and markings of a hogmolly, but lacks the characteristic sucker mouth. **1953** Randolph-Wilson *Down in Holler* 272 **Ozarks**, *Poison fish*. . . A little brown mottled sculpin or muddler *(Cottus carolinae)*. Most hillmen know that these creatures are not poisonous, but they call 'em *p'izen fish* anyhow.

poison flag n Also *poison flagroot*
An **iris B1**, usu *Iris versicolor.*
1840 MA Zool. & Bot. Surv. *Herb. Plants & Quadrupeds* 194, *I[ris] versicolor* . . Blue or Poison Flag. Common on wet grounds, and about sluggish waters, or stagnant pools. **1876** Hobbs *Bot. Hdbk.* 91, Poison flag, Blue flag, Iris versicolor. **1894** *Jrl. Amer. Folkl.* 7.101 **MA**, *Iris prismatica*, . . *Iris versicolor* . . poison flag-root, Concord, Mass. **1972** GA Dept. Ag. *Farmers Market Bulletin* 19 Apr 8/1, *Southern Blue Flag*. . . This member of the iris family is a common sight along roadways and swamps from South Carolina to Florida and west to Missouri. Its close cousin travels north as far as New England and Minnesota. . . Because of the presence in the rootstock of a bitter resinous substance which causes intestinal upsets, this species is also known in some localities as Poison Flag.

poison flax n [Because it may be poisonous to livestock]
A **flax** (here: *Linum rigidum*).
1951 *PADS* 15.35 **TX**, *Linum rigidum*. . . Poison flax.

poison flower n
1 A bushy composite plant *(Porophyllum gracile).*

1894 *Jrl. Amer. Folkl.* 7.92, *Porophyllum gracile* . . poison flower, Colorado River.

2 A **bittersweet** (here: *Solanum dulcamara*).

1900 Lyons *Plant Names* 349, *S[olanum] Dulcamara* . . Poison-berry, Pushion-berry, Poison-flower [etc.]. **1940** Clute *Amer. Plant Names* 51, Bittersweet . . poison-flower.

poison grass n

A **death camas** (here: *Zigadenus venenosus*).

1934 Haskin *Wild Flowers Pacific Coast* 35, As a stock poisoning plant death camas is one of the worst. . . Other names locally applied to this plant are lobelia, poison sego, poison grass, alkali grass, water lily, and soap-root.

poison haw n

An **arrowwood a** (here: *Viburnum molle*).

1861 Wood *Class-Book* 398, *V[iburnum] pubescens*. . . Poison Haw. Tenn. to Ga. . . and La. **1940** Clute *Amer. Plant Names* 56, *V[iburnum] molle. Soft Arrow-wood.* Poison-haw.

poison hemlock n

1 A naturalized plant *(Conium maculatum)* known for its toxic properties. Also called **badman's oatmeal, beaver poison, bunk n¹ 1, cashes, heck-how, poison parsley, snakeweed, spotted cowbane, ~ hemlock, ~ parsley, stinkweed, wild hemlock**

1822 Eaton *Botany* 247, *Conium maculatum*, poison hemlock. Stem very branching. **1840** MA Zool. & Bot. Surv. *Herb. Plants & Quadrupeds* 16, *C[onium] maculatum* . . Poison Hemlock. . . In the time of flowering especially, it fills the air with nauseating effluvia. **1902** (1909) Mathews *Field Book Amer. Wild Flowers* 312, *Poison Hemlock—Conium maculatum*. . . from which is obtained a virulent poison, used in medicine. **1935** (1943) Muenscher *Weeds* 350, According to tradition the poison-hemlock is the plant which furnished the "cup of death" given to Socrates in ancient Greece. It was formerly grown in the United States as a drug plant. **1964** Kingsbury *Poisonous Plants U.S.* 379, Poison hemlock was introduced from Europe many years ago and now is found throughout the United States and southern Canada, especially in the northeastern, north- central, and Pacific northwestern states and adjacent Canada as a luxuriant weed of roadsides, ditches, edges of cultivated fields, waste areas, and the like. **1968–69** DARE (Qu. S17, *Kinds of plants . . that . . cause itching and swelling*) Infs **NY**75, 191, Poison hemlock. [DARE Ed: These Infs may refer instead to **2** below.]

2 A **water hemlock**, usu *Cicuta maculata*.

1900 Lyons *Plant Names* 101, *C[icuta] maculata*. . . Musquash-poison, Poison Hemlock, Poison Snakeweed. **1932** Rydberg *Flora Prairies* 598, *Cicuta [spp]* . . Cowbane, Poison or Water Hemlock. **1948** Wherry *Wild Flower Guide* 91, American Poison Hemlock. . . arising from a cluster of fleshy roots containing a deadly poisonous principle. . . Eastern half of the United States and adjacent Canada. **1963** Craighead *Rocky Mt. Wildflowers* 124, *Water-hemlock—Cicuta douglasii* . . Other names: Poison-hemlock, Cowbane. **1975** Hamel–Chiltoskey *Cherokee Plants* 31, Poison Hemlock, water hemlock. . . Suicide to eat large quantities. . . Corn is soaked in a root tea before planting to repel insect pests.

3 =**dog hobble 1**. [See quot 1901] Cf **hemlock 3**

1901 Lounsberry *S. Wild Flowers* 389, *Catesby's Leucothoë. Dog Hobble*. . . The mountain people also call it "poison hemlock" knowing that it is poisonous to both cattle and sheep. **1924** *Amer. Botanist* 30.62, The plant most commonly called "fetter- bush" is probably Leucothoe Catesbaei. This is also the "dog-hobble," the name given for the same reason that "fetter-bush" is. It has poisonous properties and from this circumstance it is known as "poison hemlock." **1932** *Country Life* 62.66, Catesby's Leucothoe, called also Dog-hobble or Poison-hemlock, is found most often along the borders of cool trout streams.

poison hyacinth n Cf poison grass

A **death camas** (here: *Zigadenus nuttallii*).

1951 *PADS* 15.28 **TX**, *Toxicoscordion nuttallii*. . . Easter candle; wild hyacinth; poison hyacinth.

poisoning oak See poison oak 1

poison ivy n

1 also *poisonous ivy, poison(ous) ivory*: Any of several plants of the genera *Rhus* and *Toxicodendron*, esp *T. radicans*, which may cause severe skin irritation; also such dermatitis itself. **widespread, but less freq Pacific** See Map For other names of *Toxicodendron* spp see **cowitch 3, ground ivy 2f, itchweed 3, ivy 5, ivy poison, markweed, mercury 1, picry, poison ash 1, ~ creeper, ~ oak 1, ~ sumac, ~ vine 1, running ivy, three-leaved ~, shoestring weed 1;** for other names of *Rhus* spp see **sumac** Cf **ivory n², ivy poison**

1784 in 1785 Amer. Acad. Arts & Sci. *Memoirs* 1.422, *Hedera foliis ovatus lobatisque.* Syft. Nat. *Hedera trifolia Canadensis.* Com. Poison Ivy. . . produces the same kind of inflammations and eruptions . . as the poison wood tree. **1824** Bigelow *Florula Bostoniensis* 120, *Rhus radicans. Poison Ivy*. . . A hardy climber, frequently seen running up trees to a great height. . . The berries are roundish, and of a pale green colour, approaching to white. **1850** Emerson *Rept. Trees & Shrubs* 506 **MA**, *The Poison Ivy*. . . When climbing over rocks or on the trunks of trees, it seems to have been considered *R[hus] radicans*; when standing by itself, and forced to erect a portion of its stem, *R. toxicodendron*. **1874** (1877) Hittell *Resources CA* 365, The poison oak, or poison ivy [=*Rhus diversiloba*] . . grows abundantly in the valleys, the Coast Mountains, and the Sierra. . . One of the first lessons of the new-comer in California, should be to learn to distinguish and avoid this useless and dangerous plant. **1903** DN 2.318 seMO, He ran into a poison ivory vine. **1903** Small *Flora SE U.S.* 726, *Rhus*. . . Shrubs, trees, or vines, with a caustic and often very poisonous resinous sap. . . *Poison Ivy. Poison Oak.* **1924** Hawkins *Trees & Shrubs* 78 nwWY, *Poison Oak* or *Poison Ivy* (Rhus Rydbergii). . . A little upright shrub less than four inches high. . . The leaves . . grow in threes and are highly colored. **1950** WELS **WI** (*A low, three-leaved plant that makes people's skin itch and swell*) 51 Infs, Poison ivy; 1 Inf, Poisonous ivy; (*Common itching diseases, other common skin diseases*) 7 Infs, Poison ivy; (*Other kinds of plants that will cause itching and swelling*) 1 Inf, Poison ivy. **1950** WELS Suppl. **cWI**, Poisonous ivy—jocular and occasional. **1965–70** DARE (Qu. S16, *A three-leaved plant that grows in woods and countryside and makes people's skin itch and swell*) 818 Infs, **widespread, but less freq Pacific**, Poison ivy; **AR**41, Poison ivy vine; 19 Infs, **scattered**, Poisonous ivy; 35 Infs, **scattered, but more freq Sth, S Midl, NEast**, Poison ivory; **DC**5, Poisonous ivory; (Qu. BB25, . . *Common skin diseases around here*) 77 Infs, 76 **east of Rocky Mts**, Poison ivy; **MD**17, **OK**51, Poison-ivy rash; **MO**1, Poison ivory; (Qu. S17, . . *Kinds of plants . . that . . cause itching and swelling*) 10 Infs, 7 **east of Missip R**, Poison ivy; (Qu. BB24, . . *A rash that comes out suddenly—from hives or something else:* "He's got some kind of _____ all over his chest.") Inf **GA**33, Poison ivy. **1973** Allen *LAUM* 1.334 **Upper MW** (as of c1950), Any of various low shrubs or vines having three-lobed leaves and a highly irritant sap is known as *poison ivy*. . . Some infs. use *poison oak* to distinguish the shrub from the vine, although the reverse distinction also appears. . . *Poison ivory* . . is used by four older speakers in the Dakotas and by one in Iowa. It seems to be declining. **1989** Pederson *LAGS Tech. Index* 220 **Gulf Region**, 545 infs, Poison ivy; 52 infs, Poison ivory. **1995** Brako et al. *Scientific & Common Names Plants* 209, Poison-ivy—*Toxicodendron pubescens, T. radicans*. . . Western poison-ivy—*Toxicodendron rydbergii, T. vernix*.

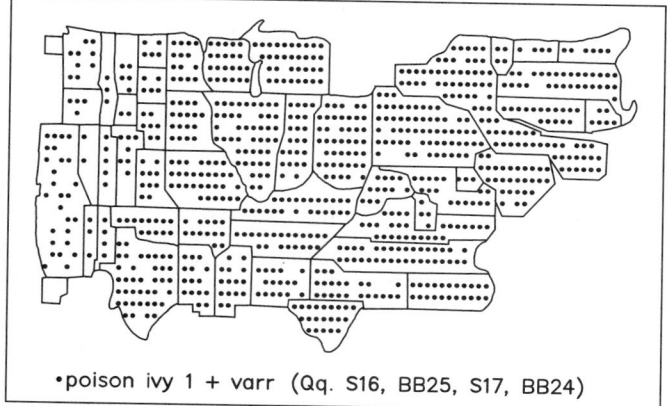

•poison ivy 1 + varr (Qq. S16, BB25, S17, BB24)

2 =**calico bush 1**. Cf **mountain ivy**

1861 in 1863 Porcher *Resources* 381, Upon the authority of Mr. Charles Foster, long known as a wood engraver at Nashville, Tennessee, many years since, I can state that the wood of the *maximum* or mountain laurel, as well as its *confrère, Kalmia latifolia*, known by every farmer as poison ivy, are equalled only by the best boxwood. **1897** Sudworth *Arborescent Flora* 315 **TN, AL,** *Kalmia latifolia.* . . Poison Ivy. **1924** *Amer. Botanist* 30.58, *Kalmia latifolia.* . . is occasionally called "small laurel" and "wood laurel" and in the southern part of its range is known as "ivy," "big-leaved ivy," "ivy-bush" or even "poison ivy." **1950** Peattie *Nat. Hist. Trees* 523, *Mountain Laurel.* . . Big-leaved or Poison Ivy. [*Ibid* 525, Amongst Southerners there is a well-founded belief that the honey from Laurel nectar is poisonous. . . The leaves of Mountain Laurel are likewise poisonous.]

poison larkspur n chiefly Pacific Cf **cow poison**
A **delphinium**, usu *Delphinium trolliifolium.*

1908 Sweetser–Kent *Key & Flora* 52 **OR,** D[elphinium] trolliifolium . . (Poison Larkspur). **1951** *PADS* 15.31 **TX,** *Delphinium* spp. . . Poison larkspur. Said to be poisonous to all forms of livestock; the animals do not eat the plant when in bloom, but gather the young ones in, with other weeds and grass, in early spring. **1961** Peck *Manual OR* 345, D[elphinium] trolliifolium . . Poison Larkspur. . . Moist woods, Cascade Mts. and westward, from Columbia River to Calif. **1973** Hitchcock–Cronquist *Flora Pacific NW* 130, Poison l[arkspur], Columbia l[arkspur] . . D[elphinium] trolliifolium.

poison laurel n
=**calico bush 1.**

1897 Sudworth *Arborescent Flora* 315 **AL,** *Kalmia latifolia.* . . Poison Laurel. **1901** Mohr *Plant Life AL* 89, Box elder, . . farkleberry, and the poison laurel *(Kalmia latifolia)* shade the rocky banks of the swift mountain streams. **1950** Peattie *Nat. Hist. Trees* 523, *Mountain Laurel.* . . Sheep, Poison, or Wood Laurel. [*Ibid* 525, The leaves of Mountain Laurel are likewise poisonous.] **1971** *Today Show Letters* seNY, *Pizen laurel*—this is the way Mr. John Stokes, the previous owner of Mohonk, referred to the mountain laurel in talking with my ancestors in 1869. This is the mountain laurel *(Kalmia latifolia).*

poison lily n
=**fly poison 1.**

1948 Wherry *Wild Flower Guide* 8, *Poison-lily (Amianthium muscaetoxicum).* . . The tissues of this plant contain a very poisonous alkaloid, and cattle are often killed by eating the leaves.

poison lizard n [See quot]
The collared **lizard 1** *(Crotaphytus collaris).*

1928 Baylor Univ. Museum *Contrib.* 16.10, This [=the collared lizard] is one of the largest and most strikingly colored lizards inhabiting the Southwest. It is generally considered to be poisonous and many persons in West Texas, mistaking it for the *Heloderma suspectum* . . call it either Gila Monster or Poison Lizard.

poison milkweed n
A **milkweed 1** (here: *Asclepias subverticillata).*

1935 (1943) Muenscher *Weeds* 366, *Asclepias galioides.* . . Poison milkweed or Whorled milkweed, a native perennial of the ranges and dry hillsides from Colorado and Utah southward into Mexico. . . This weed causes poisoning when eaten by livestock. **1967** *DARE* (Qu. S21, . . *Weeds . . that are a trouble in gardens and fields*) Inf **CO**15, Milkweed, poison milkweed. **1968** Barkley *Plants KS* 275 **nwKS,** *Asclepias subverticillata* . . Bedstraw milkweed. Whorled milkweed. Poison milkweed.

poison-neat See **poison D2**

poison nettle n
1 =**nettle 1.**

1867 Lowell *Biglow* 14 'Upcountry' **MA,** But *I* tell *you* my other leg hed larned wut pizon-nettle meant,/ An' var'ous other usefle things, afore I reached a settlement. **1969** *DARE* (Qu. S16, *A three-leaved plant that grows in woods and countryside and makes people's skin itch and swell*) Inf **IN**83, Poison nettle. **1997** *NADS Letters* NE, Poison nettles (also stinging nettles) are found throughout Nebraska. *Ibid* **Upstate NY,** I recall using "poison nettles" to refer to a shorter variety of the plant in Port Edward, New York. Circa 1960–61 my older sister and I would play in the yard of friends in the neighborhood that had "poison nettles." These were small leafed nettle plants that grew to about 3 feet max. *Ibid* **TX,** Poison nettle is occasionally used in the Central Texas hill country . . for stinging nettle or nettle. A small group of Old Whites whose ancestors were 16th and 17th [century] immigrants to N. America from Britain, locally characterized as cedar choppers, tends to use the term. The term seems to be used more by those over 50. *Ibid* **VT,** A

poison nettle is a plant normally known as a stinging nettle, that hurts a lot when you touch it. Common in Vermont. Used as far back as I can recall. Still used.

2 =**stinging nettle.**

1998 *NADS Letters* **VA,** In the area around Deltaville, VA where I spent time as a youth, the small jellyfish that come into the Chesapeake Bay in summer are called "stinging nettles" or sometimes "poison nettles."

poison oak n
1 also *oak-leaf poison, oak poison(ing), poisoned oak, poisoning ~, poisonous ~:* =**poison ivy 1,** esp *Toxicodendron pubescens* and *T. vernix* in the eastern half of the US and *Rhus diversiloba* on the Pacific coast. **widespread, but slightly less freq NEast** See Map Cf **poison sumac**

1743 (1946) Gronovius *Flora Virginica* 33, *Rhus.* . . Toxicodendron. . . folio querciformi. *Poison-Oak.* **1822** Eaton *Botany* 428, [*Rhus*] toxicodendron . . Var. *Quercifolium* (poison oak) erect, low: leaflets variously sinuate-lobed. **1851** Woods *16 Months* 103 **CA,** Captain W. is sorely afflicted with an eruption, which covers his whole body, probably the effects of having handled "poison oak." **1888** Lindley–Widney *CA of South* 172, Poison-oak grows luxuriantly in places, . . and is almost the only shrub that shows red leaves at the approach of autumn. **1897** Sudworth *Arborescent Flora* 276 **LA,** Poison Sumach. . . Poison Oak. **1903** Small *Flora SE U.S.* 727, *Rhus vernix.* . . In swamps, Ontario to Minnesota, south to Florida and Louisiana. Spring. *Poison Sumac. Poison Oak. Poison Elder. Poison Dogwood. Thunder-wood.* **1922** Gonzales *Black Border* 319 **sSC, GA coasts** [Gullah glossary], *Pizen-oak*—poison-oak, or poison ivy. **1934** Haskin *Wild Flowers Pacific Coast* 207, The result of touching poison oak [=*Rhus diversiloba*] largely depends on the physical condition of the individual. . . A thorough washing . . in a solution of baking soda is an almost sure preventive of oak poisoning. **1950** *WELS* **WI** (*Plants that will cause itching and swelling*) 31 Infs, Poison oak; (*A low, three-leaved plant that makes people's skin itch and swell*) 3 Infs, Poison oak [*DARE* Ed: All 3 Infs gave this response in addition to *poison ivy.*] **1965–70** *DARE* (Qu. S16, *A three-leaved plant that grows in woods and countryside and makes people's skin itch and swell*) 335 Infs, **chiefly Sth, S Midl, Pacific,** Poison oak; **AL**2, Poison oak—same as poison ivy; **AR**41, Poison oak bush; **AR**49, Poison ivy, poison oak—same stuff, two names; **DC**5, Poisonous oak—same as poisonous ivory; **FL**48, Poison oak, poison ivy—different—don't bother many Negroes—mostly gets White folks; **GA**3, 9, Poisonous oak; **IN**58, Poison oak [FW: There is no such thing as poison oak, according to Inf. It is a poison ivy vine on an oak tree or stump.]; **IN**67, Oak poisoning, poison ivy; **MO**38, Poisoned ivy, poisoned oak—same thing; **SC**27, Poison oak—usu; poison ivy—more "learned"; **TN**13, Poison vine—same as poison ivy; poison oak—about the same difference as poison vine; **TN**39, Poison ivy, poison oak—different plants—leaves arranged differently; **VA**71, Poison oak, poison ivory are not synonyms for the same plant; both cause a rash; (Qu. S17, . . *Kinds of plants . . that . . cause itching and swelling*) 190 Infs, **chiefly Nth, N Midl,** Poison oak; **DE**2, Poison oak—not certain whether this is the same as [poison ivy]; **KY**56, Poison oak—similar to poison ivy; **LA**31, Poison oak—a little difference in the leaf from poison ivy; **PA**211, 213, Oak poison; **PA**206, Oak-leaf poison; **VT**4, Poison oak—this may be the same as poison ivy; (Qu. BB25, . . *Common skin diseases around here*) 23 Infs, **scattered,** Poison oak; **MD**17, **OK**51, Poison-oak rash; **AR**12, Infection from poison oak; **ME**10, **WI**76, Oak poisoning; (Qu. S26d, *Wildflowers that grow in meadows;* not asked in early QRs) Inf **MA**6, Poison oak—even smoke is dangerous; (Qu. T13, . . *Names . . for these trees: . . sumac*) Inf **MI**67, Sometimes called poison oak; **MO**22, Poison oak, poison sumac; (Qu. BB24, . . *A rash that comes out suddenly—from hives or something else:* "He's got some kind of _____ all over his chest.") Inf **GA**28, Poison oak, elder; (Qu. BB51a, . . *Cures for corns or warts*) Inf **CA**31, Poison-oak juice on it. **1970** Tarpley *Blinky* 66 **neTX,** 68 infs, Poison oak. *Ibid* 67, The majority of informants refer to a poisonous vine that makes the skin break out as either *poison ivy* or *poison oak,* and some use both expressions. *Poison oak* has a higher occurrence in the eastern part of the region where oak trees are more plentiful. . . The highest percentage of informants using *poison oak* is among males and the lowest educational class. **1972** Brown *Wildflowers LA* 102, *Poison Oak—Rhus quercifolia* . . A small shrub 12 to 18 inches tall. . . The 3-foliolate leaves are . . suggestive of oak leaves, and toxic. *Ibid* 103, *Poison Ivy—Rhus radicans.* . . A variable plant. . . Incorrectly called "poison oak." A contact poisonous plant. **1973** Allen *LAUM* 1.334 **Upper MW** (as of c1950), 47 infs, Poison oak; 1 inf, Poisoned oak. *Ibid* [see **poison ivy 1**]. **1986** Pederson *LAGS Concor-*

dance **Gulf Region,** 590 infs, Poison oak; 3 infs, Poison oak—worse than poison ivy; 1 inf, **cwGA,** Poison oak—different from poison ivy— thunderwood; 1 inf, **seAL,** Poison oak—thunderwood; 1 inf, **swGA,** Poisoning oak.

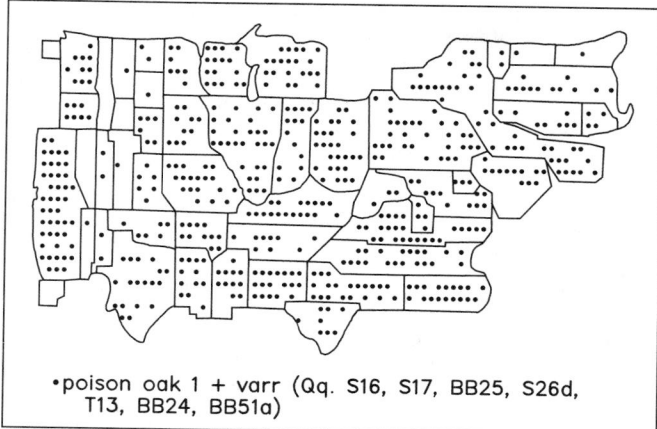

•poison oak 1 + varr (Qq. S16, S17, BB25, S26d, T13, BB24, BB51a)

2 See **poison B1b(2).**

poison-oaker n esp **CA**

A rustic; see quots.

1930 Williams *Logger-Talk* 27 **Pacific NW,** *Poison-oaker:* A native Northern Californian. **1969** *DARE* (Qu. HH1, *Names and nicknames for a rustic or countrified person)* Infs **CA**110A, 120, Poison-oaker; (Qu. HH28) Inf **CA**158, Poison-oakers—from Oklahoma. **1969** *DARE* FW Addit **cCA,** *Poison-oaker*—a mountaineer, like me.

poisonous darnel See **poison darnel**

poisonous elder See **poison elder 1**

poisonous iv(or)y See **poison ivy 1**

poisonous oak See **poison oak 1**

poisonous sumac See **poison sumac**

poison parsley n

=**poison hemlock 1.**

1828 Rafinesque *Med. Flora* 1.118, *Conium maculatum. . . Vulgar Names*—Poison Parsley, Spotted Parsley. **1892** (1974) Millspaugh *Amer. Med. Plants* 68-1, Wild or Poison Hemlock, Stinkweed, Spotted Poison Parsley [etc]. **1968** Schmutz et al. *Livestock-Poisoning Plants AZ* 74, *Poison hemlock, . . poison parsley (Conium maculatum). . . The plant is a leafy herb of the carrot family. . . Leaves are . . pinnately divided. . . All parts . . are poisonous to all livestock and humans.*

poison parsnip n Cf **cow parsnip, wild parsnip**

A **water hemlock** such as *Cicuta douglasii.*

1938 (1958) Sharples *AK Wild Flowers* 36, *C[icuta] Douglasii.* "Water Hemlock," "Poison Parsnip." **1968** Schmutz et al. *Livestock-Poisoning Plants AZ* 34, *Douglas Waterhemlock,* poison parsnip *(Cicuta douglasii). . .* Probably the most violently poisonous plant in the United States and even a small fragment of the root may be lethal. . . Most poisoning occurs from eating exposed or pulled-up roots. **1969** *DARE* (Qu. S17, . . *Kinds of plants . . that . . cause itching and swelling)* Inf **NY**195, Poison parsnip. **2001** *DARE* File **swWI,** I heard a farmer . . refer to a common plant on the farm as poison parsnip. When I came in contact with the plant, I developed redness, then blisters.

poison penny See **poison B1b(2)**

poison pie n [See quot 1987]

A **mushroom B1** (here: *Hebeloma crustuliniforme).*

1981 Lincoff *Audubon Field Guide Mushrooms* 624, *Poison Pie— Hebeloma crustuliniforme. . .* Cream, slimy cap with cinnamon-buff center, pale brownish gills, and strong, radishlike odor. **1987** McKnight– McKnight *Mushrooms* 300, *Poison Pie. . .* Medium to large, *rounded, cream-colored* to *brownish cap; surface smooth. . . Cap:* Convex, with an inrolled margin at first, later broadly rounded to flat, often with a low, rounded hump.

poison pit See **poison B1b(3)**

poison rag See **poison B1b(1)**

poison ring See **poison B1b(3)**

poison sage n Cf **poison sego**

A **death camas** (here: *Zigadenus paniculatus).*

1957 Barnes *Nat. Hist. Wasatch Spring* 64 **UT,** The greenish white flowers of the poison sage or death camas *(Zigadenus paniculatus)* are in bloom.

poison seat See **poison B1b(2)**

poison sego n

=**death camas.**

1914 Georgia *Manual Weeds* 76, *Death Camas—Zygadenus venenosus . . Other English names:* Poison Camas, Poison Sego [etc]. **1937** U.S. Forest Serv. *Range Plant Hdbk.* W209, Deathcamases, sometimes known as poison-segos [etc]. . . At certain stages of plant growth, it is very difficult to distinguish deathcamas from such related but harmless plants as . . mariposa, including sego-lily. **1966** Barnes–Jensen *Dict. UT Slang* 34, Poison Sego . . a name often given to the Death Camas *(Zigadenus paniculatus).* **1970** Correll *Plants TX* 381, *Zigadenus* [spp] . . Death Camas, Poison Sego.

poison shoemack (or shoemake, shoemate) See **poison sumac**

poison snake See **poison B1b(1)**

poison snakeweed See **snakeweed**

poison soaproot n Cf **soaproot**

=**death camas.**

1937 U.S. Forest Serv. *Range Plant Hdbk.* W209, Deathcamases, sometimes known as poison-segos, poison-camases, poison-soaproots, and erroneously called lobelias.

poison spot (or stick) See **poison B1b(1)**

poison stickerweed n Cf **itchweed 1**

Perh a **false hellebore 1;** see quot.

1967 *DARE* (Qu. S17, . . *Kinds of plants . . that . . cause itching and swelling)* Inf **LA**10, Poison stickerweed—purple stalks and dark leaves—makes you sting for hours.

poison sumac n Also *poisonous sumac;* for var forms of the second element see **sumac** chiefly **NEast, N Cent, W Midl** See Map on p. 238 Cf **poison oak 1**

Usu a shrub or small tree *(Toxicodendron vernix)* with a pinnately compound leaf; occas another **poison ivy 1.** For other names of *T. vernix* see **dogberry b, dogwood 3, mercury 1, poison alder, ~ ash 1, ~ bush, ~ dogwood 1, ~ elder 1, ~ ivy 1, ~ oak 1, ~ tree 1, poisonweed 4, poisonwood 1, sumac, swamp dogwood, ~ sumac, white poison, ~ sumac, thunderwood**

1772 Kalm *Travels N. Amer.* (transl. Forster) 1.53 **sePA,** the poisonous Sumach, in wet places. **1817** Eaton *Botany* 34, *Rhus . . vernix,* (poison sumach) glabrous panicle few-flowered. **1843** (1844) Johnson *Farmer's Encycl.* 949, The juice of *R[hus] radicans,* poison or swamp sumach, and *R. toxicodendron,* poison vine or poison oak, is milky, stains black, and is extremely poisonous. **1872** VT State Bd. Ag. *Report* 1.276, *Rhus venenata,* Poison Sumac of swamps . . should be known to all. **1897** Sudworth *Arborescent Flora* 276, *Rhus vernix. . . Common Names.* Poison Sumach (Vt., N.H., Mass., R.I., Conn., N.Y., N.J., Del., N.C., S.C., Ala., Miss., La., Mo., Iowa, Wis., Mich., Minn., Ohio, Ont., Nebr.) **1898** U.S. Dept. Ag. Div. Botany *Bulletin* 20.36, *Rhus diversiloba. . .* California poison sumac. **1912** Blatchley *IN Weed Book* 95, In the tamarack and other marshes of northern Indiana the . . poisonous sumac *(R[hus] vernix* L.) grows in abundance. It is . . , if anything, more poisonous than the 3-leaved ivy. **1950** *WELS* **WI** *(Other kinds of plants that will cause itching and swelling)* 13 Infs, Poison sumac; *(Common itching diseases, other common skin diseases)* 2 Infs, Poison sumac. **1960** Vines *Trees SW* 638, *Toxicodendron quercifolium* [=*T. pubescens*]. . . Also known locally as Poison-wood, Poison-weed, Scratch-ivy, Poison-ivy, and Poison Sumac. **1965–70** *DARE* (Qu. S17, . . *Kinds of plants . . that . . cause itching and swelling)* 196 Infs, **chiefly NEast, N Cent, W Midl,** Poison sumac *(or shoemack, shoe-*

make); **MS**31, Poison shoemate ['šu͵meɪt]; (Qu. T13, . . *Names . . for . . sumac*) 12 Infs, **scattered east of Missip R,** Poison sumac; **ME**5, Poison shoemake; (Qu. S16, *A three-leaved plant that grows in woods and countryside and makes people's skin itch and swell*) Infs **GA**84, **IA**3, **WI**32, Poison shoemack; (Qu. T15, . . *Kinds of swamp trees*) Infs **CT**2, **MI**65, Poison sumac; (Qu. BB25, . . *Common skin diseases around here*) Infs **MI**62, **NJ**64, **NY**36, Poison sumac. **1986** Pederson *LAGS Concordance* **Gulf Region** *(Sumac)* 32 infs, Poison sumac; 1 inf, Poisonous sumac; *(Poison ivy)* 33 infs, Poison sumac.

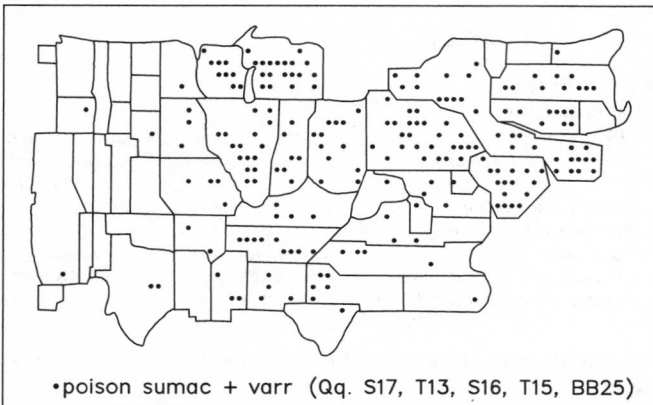

•poison sumac + varr (Qq. S17, T13, S16, T15, BB25)

poison tobacco n [See quot 1828]

Black henbane *(Hyoscyamus niger).*

1828 Rafinesque *Med. Flora* 1.255, *Hyosciamus niger. . . Vulgar Names*—Henbane, Poison-Tobacco, Stinking Nightshade, &c. [*Ibid* 257, The smell is virose, rank, strong, fetid, pernicious and narcotic, which, however, is lost by exsiccation: when burnt it smells like Tobacco.] **1892** (1974) Millspaugh *Amer. Med. Plants* 126-1, *Hyoscyamus. . .* Com. Names . . Stinking Nightshade. Poison Tobacco. **1974** (1977) Coon *Useful Plants* 249, *Hyoscyamus niger*—Henbane, stinking nightshade, poison tobacco.

poison tree n

1 A **poison sumac** (here: *Toxicodendron vernix*).

1721 Royal Soc. London *Philos. Trans.* 31.147, The Poyson-Tree grows to the bigness of Elder. **1756** Kalm *Resa* II.211 *(DA),* Poyson-tree, d.ä. det forgifftiga trä, kallades af Ångelsmän och Svänskar en art af *Rhus.* [*DARE* Ed: =Poyson-tree, that is, the poison tree, a kind of *Rhus* so called by English and Swedes.] **1828** Webster *Amer. Dict.* np, *Poison-tree. . .* This name is given to a species of Rhus or sumac, the *Rhus vernix* or *poison ash,* a native of America. **1892** (1974) Millspaugh *Amer. Med. Plants* 37-1, *Poison sumach. . .* Poison Ash, Poison Tree, Poison Wood. **1950** Peattie *Nat. Hist. Trees* 439, *Poison Sumac. . .* Other Names . . Poison Ash, Poisontree, Poisonwood. **1986** Pederson *LAGS Concordance,* 2 infs, **sGA,** Poison tree.

2 also *Florida poison tree:* =**poisonwood 2.**

1775 (1962) Romans *Nat. Hist. FL* 28, Shumac or poison tree, with winged leaves, and a rhomboidal fruit. **1897** Sudworth *Arborescent Flora* 274, *Rhus metopium. Poisonwood. . . Common names* [include]. . . Bumwood, Hog Plum, Doctor Gum. **1946** West–Arnold *Native Trees FL* 112, The Florida poisontree occurs in pinelands, hammocks, and sand dunes from Martin County southward. . . All parts of this tree act as a contact skin-poison to many people. **1962** Harrar–Harrar *Guide S. Trees* 435, *Florida Poisontree—Metopium toxiferum. . .* The sap exudations are extremely poisonous to the touch, and actual contact with this species should be avoided. **1979** Little *Checklist U.S. Trees* 173, *Metopium toxiferum . . Florida poisontree. . .* the sap causing skin irritation similar to that produced by its relative poison-ivy.

poison up on See poison E4

poison vetch n Cf locoweed

A **milk vetch** poisonous to animals; see quots.

1937 U.S. Forest Serv. *Range Plant Hdbk.* W36, Timber poisonvetch, also called greenvetch, timber milkvetch, and timber loco, . . is poisonous in many areas and responsible for heavy losses of cattle, sheep, and horses, but in other areas is grazed without injurious results. *Ibid,* There is an extensive local lingo for the cumulative symptoms caused by timber poisonvetch, including such terms as alkali disease, blind staggers, cracker-heel, knocking disease, mountain fever, roaring disease,

timber paralysis, and timber trouble. **1948** Stevens *KS Wild Flowers* 296, A harmless species [of *Astragalus*] is a milk-vetch; one that causes only mild symptoms of poisoning is a poison-vetch, while one that can seriously derange the functioning of the nervous system, with loss of muscular control, and, in extreme cases, emaciation and death, is a loco. **1964** Kingsbury *Poisonous Plants U.S.* 305, Many closely related species of *Astragalus* . . possess the ability to accumulate selenium. . . The common name, poisonvetch, has been suggested for the seleniferous species of *Astragalus* to distinguish them from locoweeds. **1967** Dodge *Roadside Wildflowers* 34 **SW, sRocky Mts,** *Straightstem loco—Poison vetch, Loco, Locoweed, Rattleweed*—One of the first roadside flowers to bloom in the spring, this bushy Astragalus [=*A. praelongus*] is noted for its early appearance.

poison vine n

1 =**poison ivy 1,** esp *Toxicodendron radicans.* **chiefly Midl** *old-fash*

1709 (1967) Lawson *New Voyage* 107 **NC, SC,** The Poison Vine is so called, because it colours the Hands of those who handle it. What the Effects of it may be, I cannot relate. . . The Juice of this will stain Linnen, never to wash out. It marks a blackish blue Colour. **1804** *Philadelphia Med. & Phys. Jrl.* 1.1.35, A decoction of the vines of the Rhus Radicans, known by the names of Poison Vine, Cow-itch, Mercury, &c., has lately been employed. . . in the Pennsylvania Hospital. **1830** Rafinesque *Med. Flora* 2.257, *R[hus] vernix, pumilum, radicans* and *toxicum,* called *Poison wood* or *vines,* are poisonous even by handling, or exposure to the effluvia in some persons, causing a distressing cutaneous disease or eresypela: remedy rest, evacuations and parsley poultice, ice and lead. **1894** Riley *Armazindy* 49 **IN,** Flick me with a pizenvine / And yell *"Yip!"* and lem me loose! **1912** Green *VA Folk-Speech* 328, Poison-vine. . . The *rhus toxicodendron.* **1917** *DN* 4.415 **wNC,** Pizen vine. Poison ivy. [*DN* Ed: In Ill., also *poison-vine.*] **1935** *Yale Rev.* 25.174 **KY,** I hear the hoof-beats of the racin' horses. I hear them snortin' up the land where the pizen-vines grow around the sycamore stumps. **1948** Davis *Word Atlas Gt. Lakes* 83, With few exceptions, general Midland terms . . have become the prevailing terms of Areas II and III [=central and southern IL, IN, OH]. . . Only a few forms have become obsolescent: *poison vine,* for example, is being abandoned in favor of the literary term, *poison ivy.* **1954** Harder *Coll.* **cwTN,** Poison vine. . . A low, three-leaved plant that makes people's skin itch and swell. **1965–70** *DARE* (Qu. S16, *A three-leaved plant that grows in woods and countryside and makes people's skin itch and swell*) Infs **KY**34A, 40, 47, **MS**63, **PA**135, Poison vine; **OH**78, **TN**13, Poison vine—same as poison ivy; **TN**22, Pizen vine. (Qu. S17, . . *Kinds of plants . . that . . cause itching and swelling*) Inf **NC**14, Poison vine—not the same as poison ivy. [8 of 9 Infs old] **1966** Dakin *Dial. Vocab. Ohio R. Valley* 2.409, Although still commonly used, *poison vine* is clearly the oldest name. Most speakers of the younger generation have adopted *poison ivy,* which seems well on its way to becoming the national name. . . Some, it appears, have adopted *poison ivy* (or *ivy poison*) as the name for the skin eruption . . , but still call the plant itself a *poison vine.* **1969** *DARE* FW Addit **neNC,** Poison vine ['paɪzɪn wɑˀɪn] (reported as said with the old brogue)—poison ivy. **1982** Slone *How We Talked* 47 **eKY** (as of c1950), Sour vine—resembles the poison vine, except it has five leaves in a cluster; the poison variety has only three. **1986** Pederson *LAGS Concordance,* 28 infs, 17 **TN,** Poison vine; 1 inf, **neTN,** Poison vine—same as poison oak; 1 inf, **ceTN,** Poison vine—same as poison ivy; 1 inf, **neTN,** Five-leaf poison vine, four-leaf poison vine, three-leaf poison vine; 1 inf, **neTN,** Five-leaf poison vine—poisons worse than 3-leaf.

2 =**Carolina jasmine.**

1946 *PADS* 6.23 **ceNC,** Poison vine. . . A variety of yellow jessamine. Thought to be poison.

poison viper n

A **hognose snake** (here: *Heterodon platyrhinos*).

1928 Pope–Dickinson *Amphibians* 50, Hog-nosed Snake. . . This snake is also known under various names in different localities, such as, Puffing Adder, Spreading Adder, Blowing Adder, Sand Viper, Poison Viper and Blow Snake. . . The Hog-nosed Snake . . has a very alarming way of taking in a deep breath and expelling it in a long, loud explosive hiss, and flattening its head at the same time in a manner similar to that of the famous Indian Cobra. Unlike the Cobra, however, it is perfectly harmless.

poisonweed n

1 A **delphinium;** see quots. **West** Cf **cow poison, poison larkspur**

[1856 (1928) Jaeger *Diary Fort Yuma* 128 **Desert SW**, 2 of the mules died also at the Tinajas Altas—I think they ate some of the poison weed also.] **1918** U.S. Dept. Ag. *Farmers' Bulletin* 988, Larkspur or Poison Weed [title]. **1949** Moldenke *Amer. Wild Flowers* 12, Very abundant on the plains in the Rocky Mountain area is the *poisonweed, D[elphinium] geyeri.* . . All larkspurs contain a poisonous principle, and this particular species is very dangerous to cattle. **1967** *DARE* (Qu. S26e) Inf **WY**5, Larkspur [sic]—poisonweed (poisonous to cattle). **1995** Brako et al. *Scientific & Common Names Plants* 209, Poison-weed—*Delphinium menziesii.*

2 =**mule-ear 2.**

1897 Parsons *Wild Flowers CA* 157, Californian Compass-plant. Sunflower. . . This plant is used as a common domestic remedy for coughs and colds by Californian housewives, and goes under the unmerited name of "poison-weed."

3 A **nightshade 1**; see quots. Cf **poisonberry 3, poison flower 2**

1940 Clute *Amer. Plant Names* 272, *Solanum dulcamara.* Poisonweed, wolf-grape [etc]. **1951** *PADS* 15.39 **TX**, *Solanum nigrum* . . Deadly nightshade; poison weed; trompillo. *Ibid, Solanum triquetrum* . . Hierba mora; poison or fence-corner weed. *Ibid, Solanum eleagnifolium* . . Purple, prickly, or Mexican, nightshade; poison weed.

4 A **poison ivy 1**; see quots.

[**1624** Smith *Genl. Hist. VA* 170, The poysoned weed is much in shape like our English Iuy, but being but touched, causeth rednesse, itching, and lastly blisters, the which howsoeuer after a while passe away of themselues without further harme, yet because for the time they are somewhat painfull, it hath got it selfe an ill name, although questionlesse of no ill nature.] **1958** Jacobs–Burlage *Index Plants NC* 12, *Rhus vernix.* . . Poison wood; poison ash; poison dogwood; poisonweed. [*Ibid* 13, The plant produces flushing and itching of the skin.] **1960** Vines *Trees SW* 638, *Toxicodendron quercifolium.* . . Also known locally as Poison-wood, Poison-weed [etc].

poison wind n Cf poison C3

See quots.

1934 Smiley *Gloss. New Paltz* **seNY**, "A pison wind" means a raw, mean, rough wind. **1965–69** *DARE* (Qu. B18, . . *Special kinds of wind*) Inf **GA**77, Poison wind—comes from east, gives you health trouble; (Qu. O20, *Winds from particular directions;* total Infs questioned, 75) Inf **MS**60, East wind—this is poison wind.

poisonwood n

1 also *poisonwood tree:* =**poison sumac**, usu *Toxicodendron vernix.*

1721 Royal Soc. London *Philos. Trans.* 31.145, The Poyson-Wood-Tree grows only in Swamps, or low wet Grounds, and . . is by some called the *Swamp Sumach.* **1830** [see **poison vine 1**]. **1876** Hobbs *Bot. Hdbk.* 91, Poison wood, Poison sumach, Rhus vernix. **1892** (1974) Millspaugh *Amer. Med. Plants* 37-1, *Rhus venenata. Poison Sumach.* . . Com. Names. Poison or swamp sumach . . Poison tree, Poison wood. **1908** Britton *N. Amer. Trees* 611, Other common names for this tree [= *Toxicodendron vernix*] are Swamp sumac, Thunderwood, and Poisonwood. **1960** Vines *Trees SW* 638, *Toxicodendron quercifolium* [=*T. pubescens*]. . . Also known locally as Poison-wood, Poison-weed [etc]. *Ibid* 641, *Toxicodendron vernix.* . . Vernacular names for the plant are Poison Elder, Poison Dogwood, Swamp Sumac, Poison-wood, and Poison-tree.

2 A small tree *(Metopium toxiferum)* native to Florida. [See quots 1731, 1908] Also called **bumwood, coral sumac, doctor gum, hog ~, hog plum 3, poison tree 2**

[**1731** Catesby *Nat. Hist. Carolina* 1.40 **Bahamas**, *The Poisson-Wood* [sic]. This is generally but a small Tree, has a light coloured smooth bark. . . From the trunc of this Tree distils a liquid black as Ink, which the Inhabitans say is Poison.] **1884** Sargent *Forests of N. Amer.* 54 **FL**, *Rhus Metopium.* . . *Poison Wood.* . . A tree . . reaching in the United States its greatest development on the shores of bay Biscayne, near Miami; one of the most common trees of the region. **1908** Rogers *Tree Book* 358, The *Poison Wood,* or *Hog Gum (Metopium Metopium* . .), a beautiful little West Indian sumach, breathes poison from its flowers and leaves not unlike that exhaled by Rhus toxicodendron, the poison ivy. . . In lower Florida the tree is abundant along the coast, and on the Keys. **1938** FWP *U.S. One* 292 **FL**, Pigeons are often seen flying over the road or feasting on the berries of the poison-wood tree. When bruised, the tree exudes a gum that blackens the trunk. **1961** Douglas *My Wilderness* 148 **Everglades FL**, Wild coffee . . was everywhere. So was the

poisonwood tree, whose slender trunk and grayish bark makes [sic] it most attractive. But it is poisonous to the touch, in the fashion of poison oak. **1966** *DARE* (Qu. S17, . . *Kinds of plants . . that . . cause itching and swelling*) Inf **FL**25, Poisonwood. **1967** Will *Dredgeman* 72 **swFL**, The poison wood, with its glossy green leaves and orange colored fruit. . . It looks something like a gumbo limbo, though the bark is greenish gray and doesn't peel. **1986** Pederson *LAGS Concordance*, 1 inf, **seFL**, Poison wood.

3 =**crabwood.**

1884 Sargent *Forests of N. Amer.* 121, *Sebastiania lucida.* . . Crab wood. Poison wood. . . Semi-tropical Florida, bay Biscayne to the southern keys. **1897** Sudworth *Arborescent Flora* 271 **FL**, *Gymnanthes lucida.* . . Common Names. . . Poisonwood. **1911** *Century Dict.* 4588, *Poisonwood.* . . A small euphorbiaceous tree, *Gymnanthes lucida,* of the same habitat [=the West Indies and southern Florida].

poisonwood tree See poisonwood 1

poisson bleu n

1 =**grayling.**

1896 U.S. Natl. Museum *Bulletin* 47.517 **AK**, *Thymallus signifer* . . Arctic Grayling; Poisson Bleu. **1949** Caine *N. Amer. Sport Fish* 92, Poisson Bleu. . . The back is purplish blue, gradually softening into a lighter purple on sides and lower margins.

2 =**blue catfish 1. LA**

1902 Jordan–Evermann *Amer. Fishes* 20 **LA**, In Louisiana this, the most valuable of all our catfishes, is known as the blue cat or poisson bleu. **1933** LA Dept. of Conserv. *Fishes* 420, The Blue Cat. . . Known also as the Great Fork-tail Cat, Poisson Bleu and the Mississippi Cat. **1976** Tryckare et al. *Lore of Sportfishing* 79, *Ictalurus furcatus* . . poisson bleu. . . The largest of the Mississippi catfishes and one of the most numerous species of the lower Mississippi Valley.

poisson (de) marais n

=**bowfin.**

1836 Richardson *Fauna Boreali-Amer.* 3.236 **Lake Huron**, *Amia ocellicauda.* . . *Poisson de marais.* . . Back and sides dark, belly and fins dark green. Head short, flattened at top and on the sides; eyes small; jaws even; mouth capacious; tongue obtuse. **1896** U.S. Natl. Museum *Bulletin* 47.113, *Amia calva* . . "John A. Grindle;" Lawyer; Poisson de Marais. **1933** LA Dept. of Conserv. *Fishes* 383, Throughout the rest of its range, the Grindle is known as the John A. Grindle, Poisson marais ("fish of the marshes") [etc]. **1949** Caine *N. Amer. Sport Fish* 133, Colloquial Names [for *Amia calva* are] . . Bowfin . . Poisson de Marais . . Speckled Cat.

po'jo n[1] See poor joe n[2] 2

pojo n[2] See poor joe n[1] 2

po'jo n[3] See poor boy

po-jo adj

1950 *PADS* 14.53 **SC**, *Po-jo.* . . Drab; dreary; poverty stricken. "Yuh look too po-jo."

pojo crane, po'joe See poor joe n[2] 2

pojo fly n

A **greenbottle fly 1**; see quots.

1978 *Prairie Drummer* (Colby KS) 18 Nov 2 **SC**, "Why, suh, those there flies is pojo flies," said the helper. . . "Boy, where do those blasted pojo flies usually hang out?" "Usually they hangs out around trash." "Boy, watch your tongue! Are you trying to say I'm trash?" "No suh, I ain't trying to say nothin'. But you can't fool a pojo fly." **1980** *DARE* File **SC**, Pojo flies. . . They're the big flies with the green backs that swarm around defication [sic], decaying animal bodies, etc.

poke n[1]

1a also redund *poke bag* (or *sack*) (cf Intro "Language Changes" I.4); rarely sp *polk:* A bag or sack, esp a small one; now usu a paper bag. [*OED2* a1276 →; "Now *dial.* exc. in *to buy a pig in a poke*"] **chiefly Midl, esp Appalachians** See Map on p. 240 Cf **pig in a poke, pocket n 1**

1806 (1970) Webster *Compendious Dict.* 229, *Poke* . . a small bag, pocket. [*DARE* Ed: This entry was carried over from Webster's English model.] **1862** *S. Lit. Messenger* 34.329 **VA**, A little poke of salt was borrowed and returned during the meeting. **1871** *Harper's New Mth. Mag.* 42.951 **IN,** If their wives or daughters start to town . . with a poke of feathers and a basket of eggs . . , the greedy toll-gate keeper will take one or the other for toll. **1895** *DN* 1.373 **seKY, eTN, wNC,** He had a poke of peanuts. **1901** Harben *Westerfelt* 171 **nGA,** Ef my ole woman knowed I'd tuck a poke uv 'er best goose feathers ter dab on a man she'd get a divorce. **1903** *DN* 2.325 **seMO,** *Poke.* . . A small bag. **1905** *DN* 3.65 **eNE,** *Poke.* *Ibid* 91 **nwAR,** *Poke.* **1911** *DN* 3.539 **eKY,** *Poke.* **1915** *DN* 4.228 **wTX,** *Poke.* **1923** *DN* 5.217 **swMO,** *Poke.* **1929** *AmSp* 4.303 **IA,** From some Southerner . . she may have learned "poke," the word she always used to designate a small bag. **1930** *DN* 6.89 **cWV,** *Poke.* **1931** *AmSp* 7.20 **swPA,** *Poke.* **1936** *AmSp* 11.373 **TN,** Many terms marked as archaic or dialectal in dictionaries are in current use here. Examples are *poke* for sack or bag. **1937** *Hall Coll.* **wNC, eTN,** *Poke.* . . A small bag; a sack—"a poke of tobacco" . . "a paper poke"—in former use, seems to have given way to 'paper bag' . . "a poke of flour." **1944** *PADS* 2.59 **cnMO, wNC, wVA, WV,** *Poke.* **1945** *Harder Coll.* **cwTN,** [Letter:] He gave me a polk ½ full of green beans late yesterday. **1949** Kurath *Word Geog.* 56, *Poke* is current, often by the side of *bag* or *sack,* in a large area extending from central Pennsylvania westward, and southward to the Carolinas. In Virginia the Blue Ridge forms the eastern boundary of the *poke* area, in North Carolina the Yadkin. **1950** *WELS* **WI** *(A cloth or paper container that you buy flour in)* 1 Inf, Poke—old-fashioned; many older Kentucky people still say poke instead of sack or bag [Inf's parents from Kentucky]; *(A smaller paper container for bringing groceries home from the store)* 1 Inf, Occasionally one hears poke. **1959** *VT Hist.* 27.153, *Poke.* . . A bag; a sack. Occasional. Caledonia. **1965–70** *DARE* (Qu. F22a, *A smaller paper container for bringing groceries home from the store)* 79 Infs, **scattered, but chiefly Midl, esp Appalachians,** (Paper) poke; **WV**11, Poke bag—a poke bag may also be made of cloth and have [a] handle; (Qu. F22b, *A smaller paper container for carrying a lunch: "He had his lunch in a _____."*) 28 Infs, **chiefly S Midl,** (Paper) poke; (Qu. F21, *A cloth or paper container that you buy flour in)* 18 Infs, **chiefly Midl,** Poke; **TX**91, Poke sack—old-fashioned; **VA**42, Paper poke—used occasionally; (Qu. F19, *A cloth container for grain)* Infs **CT**2, **IL**27, **IN**60, Poke; (Qu. F20, *A cloth container for feed)* Infs **IL**117, **IN**60, **NC**72, **PA**235, **WA**25, Poke; (Qu. F23, *A container made of rough, loosely-woven, brown cloth; commonly used for potatoes, etc)* Inf **TX**40, Poke; **WI**58, Gunny poke; (Qu. II3, *Expressions to say that people are very friendly toward each other: "They're _____."*) Inf **WA**3, Like two in a poke. **1968** *DARE* Tape **VA**9, I got a poke full of good ol' candy to give you now if you take it for the doctor. **1978** Massey *Bittersweet Country* 136 **Ozarks,** Flour, coffee, . . dried beans, and other staples were weighed and packaged in burlap sacks or paper pokes. **1984** Head *Brogans* 115 **eKY, eTN,** Although I never use the word "poke" now, I used it often as a child when referring to a paper bag. **1994** NC Lang. & Life Project *Dial. Vocab. Ocracoke* 14 **eNC,** Did you put the duck in the poke sack? **2000** *NADS Letters,* *Poke*—In Jack County, Texas, this means a sack, usually made of burlap. Some people also say "pokesack". If it's a paper sack, they say "paper poke".

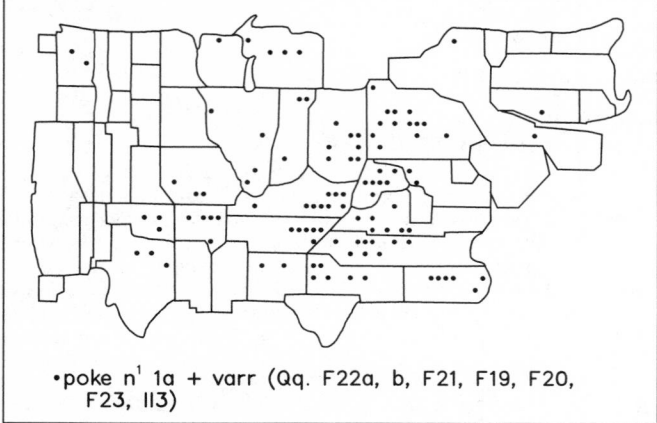

•poke n¹ 1a + varr (Qq. F22a, b, F21, F19, F20, F23, II3)

b Esp:

(1) A pouch or purse usu carried on one's person and used to hold money or personal possessions; by ext: a wallet or billfold; one's "roll" or stock of money. **scattered, but esp freq West**

[**1859** Matsell *Vocabulum* 68, *Poke* . . a purse.] **1914** Jackson *Crimi-*

nal Slang 66, *Poke.* . . General currency. A pocketbook. **1926** *AmSp* 1.652 [Hobo lingo], *Poke*—a wallet. **1939** *FWP Guide AK* xli, *Poke* . . a moosehide bag for gold dust, hence one's "roll" or wealth. **1944** Adams *Western Words* 117, *Poke*—Sack in which the cowboy carries his "plunder." The term is rarely used except in the Northwest. **1946** (1972) Mezzrow–Wolfe *Really Blues* 337, [Glossary:] *Poke:* pocket, wallet. **1958** Carrighar *Moonlight* 342 **AK,** Bush pilots fly supplies and machinery to the mines and bring the gold out—very informally. Sometimes it is carried in the standard brown leather "pokes," bags about a foot long and two inches wide, inconvenient to get the gold into and out of, it seems; but as often the gold is transported in bottles or coffee cans. **1965–70** *DARE* (Qu. U30, *What . . you keep money in when you carry it around with you)* Inf **CA**59, Poke—the leather sacks with a drawstring the old-timers carried; **CA**87, Poke—a buckskin sack, also used for raw gold dust; **CA**197, **WA**11, (A) poke; **IL**2, Poke—old-fashioned word, men's purse; **MN**42, Poke—billfold, used by poker players; **UT**3, Wallet—poke, unusual; **WI**48, Poke—men. **1966** *AmSp* 41.282 **West** [Carnie talk], *Poke.* . . A purse, billfold, or money bag. **1968** *DARE* Tape **AK**10, [Inf:] Fellow with a good, rich ground, he has a big poke. He goes into the town and says, "Everybody a drink!" Maybe he'll see that poke of gold again, maybe he won't. *Ibid,* [FW:] Did they actually carry it in little pouches? [Inf:] They have pokes. . . Pokes, you know . . it's got to be tight solid 'cause . . the gold will go through. . . [FW:] Did they use deerskin sometimes for that? . . [Inf:] Up here . . moose skin. **1970** Major *Dict. Afro-Amer. Slang* 92, *Poke:* roll of money.

(2) A bag made usu from the skin of a seal or the stomach of a small whale and used, inflated, as a float or buoy, or as a storage container, esp for oil; hence v *poke* to preserve in such a bag; vbl n *poking* preserving meat or fish in such a way. **N Atl, AK**

1884 U.S. Natl. Museum *Bulletin* 27.304, *Blackfish poke.* The stomach of the Blackfish (*Globiocephalus* [=pilot whale]) deprived of its inner membrane, inflated, and dried, painted white, wooden plug inserted and seized in neck. Provincetown, Massachusetts. . . The poke is bent on to the end of the line before it leaves the boat, and when the whale ceases its progressive motions the poke or buoy appears on the surface and the line is regained. **1887** Goode *Fisheries U.S.* 5.270, When several whales are killed . . the "floaters" are . . marked by attaching a small flag, . . the blackfish poke, or . . a "waif-drug." . . When the "pokes" are used, the officer gives the order to "Blow up! Blow up!" and a man with sound lungs grasps one of these membranous pouches and inflates it. **1889** Aldrich *Arctic AK* 56, Whole seal-skins are filled with air, making large air-bags called "pokes." These are fastened on seal-skin lines six or eight feet long, one or two being attached to each harpoon. **1926** Ashley *Yankee Whaler* 138 [Whaling terms], *Poke:* Blackfish or sealskin poke. A skin, bladder, or stomach which is inflated and used as a drug [=a block of wood fastened to a whale line and used to check the whale]. **1966** U.S. Dept. Interior *Indians AK* 12, [Caption:] These villagers are carrying a sealskin "poke" filled with seal oil which they will store for fuel. **1973** Oquilluk *People of Kauwerak* 239, Poke, a sack or pouch used for storage or carrying things, commonly used to describe a skin bag made of the entire body skin of the hair seal minus the head, and skillfully skinned so virtually no other holes or openings are made in the process. Empty inflated pokes are also used as floats in sea mammal hunting. **1978** *AK Mag.* July 88, Special preparations, such as drying or poking (marinating dry meat or fish in seal oil), elevates the iron content. **1981** *Fairbanks Daily News–Miner* (AK) 16 July 2 (Tabbert *Dict. Alaskan Engl.*), The women have been busy taking herring fish down, storing dry ones in big woven grass baskets and poking the fat ones in seal containers. **1991** Tabbert *Dict. Alaskan Engl.* 128, *Poke*—A whole, unsplit skin of a small seal removed by pulling it back over the carcass inside out beginning at the mouth. The resulting bag can either be inflated and used as a float, as for example in bowhead whaling, or used as a storage container for such things as seal oil, meat, and berries. Sealskin pokes are especially common in western and northwestern Alaska.

2 The stomach; hence adj *poke-hooked* of a fish: caught by the stomach; also fig. [*EDD poke* sb.¹ 8 "The belly; the stomach"; cf also *OED2 poke* sb.¹ 6 "The stomach of a fish. *colloq.* or *dial.*" and **1b(2)** above] **NEng**

1883 *Century Illustr. Mag.* 25.902 **MA,** Many . . fish . . are caught, not by the hook entering the jaws of the fish, but because it is fastened in their stomachs. In the Gloucester fisherman's language of to-day, a fish so captured is called "poke-hooked." **1905** Wasson *Green Shay* 130 **NEng,** I'll tell you the particular sort that turned my father's poke [Footnote: Disgusted him] for the rest-part of *his* life. **1907** Lincoln *Cape*

Cod 62 **MA,** And, would you b'lieve it, them two old critters, Beriah and Eben, gobbled the bait like sculpins. . . The first thing you know, she had 'em both poke-hooked. **1975** Gould *ME Lingo* 213, *Poke*—The stomach; no doubt deriving from the meaning of a bag or sack. Seldom used in an uplifting way, it usually has reference to unpleasant thoughts: "I got my poke full of him!" and, "Her food gives me a pain in the poke."

3 A cow's udder. [Cf *EDD* (at *poke* sb.[1] 1) "'Her milk-pokes' (of a cow)"]

    1968 *DARE* (Qu. K4, *The cow's udder*) Inf **VA**24, Bag; poke—old-fashioned, some say [this] [laughter].

poke v[1]

1 also with *up:* To urge, push, pressure. [Cf *OED2 poke* v.[1] 2 quot 1601]

    1913 Johnson *Highways St. Lawrence to VA* 56, Hurry down. You've got to go to the store. I've been pokin' you to go all the afternoon. **1950** *WELS (Humorous expressions meaning to urge somebody to do something. . . "He's a week late! I'm going to _____.")* 1 Inf, **seWI,** Poke him up. **1960** Wentworth–Flexner *Slang* 399, *Poke. . .* To attempt to influence; to attempt to create enthusiasm or promote action. **1968** *DARE* (Qu. Y6, . . *To put pressure on somebody to do something he ought to have done but hasn't: "He's a whole week late. I'm going to _____.")* Inf **CT**12, Poke him up on it; **DE**5, Poke him.

2 In marble play: see quots 1922, 1955.

    1890 *DN* 1.24 **KY,** To "fudge" is to *poke* or something similar. **1922** *DN* 5.187 **KY,** *Poke . .* =fudge. [*Ibid, Fudge. . .* In "keeps," to move the knuckles along the ground with the taw, and slip up. This is against the rules.] **1955** *PADS* 23.27 **cwTN,** *Poke. . .* Same as *fudge.*

3 also with *along:* To herd or prod (an animal). Cf **cowpoke** n[2] 1

    1942 Berrey–Van den Bark *Amer. Slang* 917.7 [Western terms], *[To]* herd cattle. . . poke cows, ride herd, run cattle. **1949** Guthrie *Way West* 37, Pa says I can herd the loose critters along, and him and you'll poke the teams. **1950** *WELS,* 1 Inf, **seWI,** I have heard the word *poke* used as "Poke along those cows." **1960** Wentworth–Flexner *Slang* 399, *Poke. . .* To herd, as cattle and sheep.

4 in phr *poke off on:* To put or push off on; see quot.

    1899 Woerner *Rebel's Daughter* 151 **Ozarks,** I must have Hettie off my hands too, or I can't make up with Emily. And if I poke her off on Bob, she'll get her back up and the trouble will be equally great in the other quarter. *Ibid,* Victor was about to object that he foresaw the same consequence in the case of Miss Shannon, if she were "poked off" on him. *Ibid* 152, He . . forgave his friend for "poking off" this lovely girl on him.

poke v[2]

1 To put in a **poke** n[1] 1a. [*OED2 poke* v.[2] 2 1596–a1758; "*Sc[ots]*"]

    1942 *Hench Coll.* **swVA,** Of course, I knew that in the mountains around here a bag is still called a poke, but could not help being amused when we were talking of decorating the Christmas tree and tying up packages for it, one woman said, "I speak to poke the candy." **1986** Pederson *LAGS Concordance,* 1 inf, **csTX,** Poked it—means to put in [a] sack [or] poke; heard in A[rkansas].

2 See **poke** n[1] 1b(2).

poke n[2]

1 also *poker:* A yoke or collar put around the neck of a cow, horse, or other animal to prevent it from jumping or breaking through a fence. **chiefly Nth** Cf **cow hook, goose poke, poke** v[3]

    1805 (1930) Hazard *Jrl.* 260 **RI,** Put Poker on one of my oxen. **1809** Kendall *Travels* 2.198, A hog . . by some mischance had turned his poke, so that his throat was squeezed into one of the acuter angles. **1828** Webster *Amer. Dict.* np **NEng,** *Poke. . .* In *New England,* a machine to prevent unruly beasts from leaping fences, consisting of a yoke with a pole inserted, pointing forward. **1876** Knight *Amer. Mech. Dict.* 3.1759, *Poke.* A device to be attached to a breechy animal to prevent its jumping over, crawling through, or breaking down fences. . . They vary with the kind of stock to which they are attached,—horses, cattle, hogs, or geese. **1910** *DN* 3.455 **seVT,** *Poke. . .* A wooden frame so constructed that it can be attached to the necks of animals to impede them and prevent them from jumping fences. **1927** (1970) Sears *Catalogue* 974, *Cow Poke. . .* Keeps Cattle From Wandering. . . Strong, light and

comfortable; long forks. . . Spur points stop animal from forcing way through fence. **1935** Sandoz *Jules* 125 **wNE** (as of 1880–1930), The next day the Freese cows came home with heavy pokes on their necks, put on by neighbors to prevent their fence crawling. **1950** *WELS Suppl.* **WI,** *Poke*—A yoke made of a crotched stick to keep cows from jumping fence. The stem of the crotch comes well down between the cow's front feet. **1952** *FWP Guide SD* 84, *Poke:* a wooden collar to restrain the fence-crawler. **1968–70** *DARE* (Qu. M11) Inf **NY**88, Poke—piece that goes around neck when a cow is in the field to keep her from going through a fence; **VA**70, Mean cows used to wear wooden yokes as punishment; a jumping cow wore a yoke to keep it in the pasture [FW: Later, showing me one, inf referred to these as "pokes."] **1980** *Greenfield Recorder* (MA) 8 Nov, The cattle and sheep sometimes were quite skilled in clambering over stone walls, so the leaders wore a devise [sic] that held a stick straight out in front at shoulder height or above and prevented them from climbing. It was called a "poke," I believe.

2 A slow or lazy creature; a stupid, boring, or plodding person. [*EDD poke* sb.[5] 18] Cf **poke-easy** Note: *Slowpoke* is widespread and std.

    1844 in 1965 *AmSp* 40.184, I have seen but two of his [=a racehorse's] get, and they were both unqualifiedly *worthless*—perfect pokes. **1856** Simms *Eutaw* 247 **SC,** "Did you pick up any fellows?" "A few pokes—not much; but they hev horses." **1872** *Galaxy* 14.736 **CT,** He pulls up this old poke of a horse. **1893** Shands *MS Speech* 50, *Poke. . .* This word is used by all classes to mean a slow person, and has its corresponding adjective *poky.* It is probably derived from the verb *to poke,* as meaning to feel or push one's way slowly. One who moves in this way is consequently called a *poke* or a *slow-poke.* **1895** *DN* 1.392, *Poke:* a slow person. O[ld-fashioned]. **1899** (1912) Green *VA Folk-Speech* 328, *Poke. . .* A lazy person; a dawdler. **1899** Woerner *Rebel's Daughter* 57 **Ozarks,** If you like it [=the study of grammar], you're a dryer poke than I took you for, from what Nellie told me about you. **1907** *DN* 3.215 **nwAR,** *Poke. . .* A lazy person. **1934** (1940) Weseen *Dict. Amer. Slang* 380, *Poke*—A bore; a poor companion; a stupid person; a lazy person. **1965–70** *DARE* (Qu. A18, . . *A very slow person: "What's keeping him? He certainly is _____!"*) Infs **CT**13, **IN**64, 75, **MI**17, 22, 50, **WI**69, A poke; (Qu. Y9, *Somebody who always follows along behind others: "His little brother is an awful _____."*) Infs **CA**138, **MA**74, Poke; (Qu. HH3, *A dull and stupid person*) Infs **IN**35, **MS**60, **PA**104, **VT**12, Poke.

3 A goad for prodding oxen. Cf **jill poke** n 5, **poke** v[1] 3

    1950 *WELS (The sharp pointed stick used to get oxen to move)* 2 Infs, **seWI,** Poke. **1967–69** *DARE* (Qu. K27) Infs **LA**18, **MN**40, **OH**30, Poke; **KY**58, Ox poke.

poke v[3], hence ppl adj *poked* Also rarely *poker* **esp NEast**

To put a **poke** n[2] 1 on an animal.

    1787 in 1889 *East Hampton NY Records* 4.256, To order the owners of all such cows or horsses, to yoke, poker or fetter them. **1828** Webster *Amer. Dict.* np **NEng,** *Poke. . .* To put a poke on; as, to *poke* an ox. **1850** *Knickerbocker* 35.24 **ceNY,** Upon two 'poked' colts, which we caught and bridled with beech withes, [we] descended to the shore of the Horicon. **1910** *DN* 3.454 **seVT,** *Poke. . .* To attach a "poke" to an animal.

poke n[3]

1 also attrib; also sp *polk:* =pokeweed 1a. [Algonquian; cf **pocan, puccoon**] **chiefly Midl** See Map on p. 242 Cf **pokeberry 1, pokeroot 1a, poke salad**

    1708 in 1921 *William & Mary Qrly.* 2d ser 1.190 **VA,** We call the plant here Poke, it bears a purple berry. **1731** Catesby *Nat. Hist. Carolina* 1.24, [The turtles [=turtledoves] of Carolina] feed much on the Berries of Poke, i.e. *Blitum Virginianum,* which are Poison. **1779** in 1789 Anburey *Travels* 2.375 **VA,** Vegetables not being over abundant in these back woods at any time . . we adopt the custom of the inhabitants who gather the leaves of the poke-plant, just as they shoot above ground and are tender and soft. **1792** Belknap *Hist. NH* 3.126, [Footnote:] *Poke* is the name by which the *garget* is known in the middle States. **1872** Schele de Vere *Americanisms* 405, The *Poke-weed* or *Poke* simply (Phytolacca decandra) is one of the most useful plants of the South, where all its parts are profitably employed: the root for medicinal purposes, the young shoots for the table after the manner of asparagus, and the berries as a favorite dye of rich purple with poor people. **1937** (1963) Hyatt *Riverlid* 79 **KY,** We picked wild mustard an' Shawnee an' Injun collards, polk, blue-thistle, Doctor Walker, wooly-breeches. **1938** Rawlings *Yearling* 12 **nFL,** There were poke-greens with bits of white bacon buried in them. **1942** Perry *Texas* 124, One of our springtime dishes is wild poke greens. By many it is considered a spring tonic. But unless well parboiled and re-cooked in different water, it is apt to be explosively cathartic. **1965–70** *DARE* (Qq. I28a, b, . . *Greens*) 71 Infs, **chiefly Midl,** Poke; **GA**13, **KY**69, 84, **MO**4, **TN**11, Poke green(s); **MO**20, Ozark poke greens; **AR**27, Pole [sic] **IN**39, Poke shoots; **KY**66, Poke tops; (Qu. H54, *Dishes made with greens: [. . kinds of 'greens' . . eaten];* total Infs questioned, 75) Infs **GA**1, **OK**1, 3, 19, 51, Poke; **MS**73, Polk [polk]; (Qu. I29, *Names or nicknames for asparagus*) Inf **MD**19, Poke—something like asparagus—some people eat it; (Qu. I35, . . *Kitchen herbs . . grown and used in cooking around here*) Inf **OK**17, Poke; (Qu. S17, . . *Kinds of plants . . that . . cause itching and swelling*) Inf **DE**4, Poke; (Qu. S21, . . *Weeds . . that are a trouble in gardens and fields*) Infs **AR**49, **DC**2, **IN**17, **NC**81, **VA**15, 59, Poke; **LA**28, Poke root or poke greens; (Qu. X37, . . *Words . . to describe people's legs if they're noticeably bent, or uneven, or not right*) Inf **NC**55, Legs as straight as a poke stalk; (Qu. X49, *Expressions . . about a person who is very thin*) Inf **TN**13, Looks like a poke stalk; (Qu. BB19, *Joking names for looseness of the bowels*) Inf **MD**30, If you ate poke that had not had water poured off while boiling at least twice, you were sure to get this ailment [=the skitters]. **1968** *DARE* FW Addit **VA**1, Poke—tops used for greens, berries are dried and given to children for croup; **VA**15, Poke, pokeweed. **1986** Pederson *LAGS Concordance* **Gulf Region,** 18 infs, Poke; 1 inf, Poke—made ink of; 1 inf, Poke—not poisonous, eat berries, leaves; 11 infs, Poke greens; 1 inf, The berries of the poke vine is poison; 1 inf, Poke wine—made from pokeberries. **1991** *Houston Chron.* (TX) 27 June np **MO**, [Headline:] *Proud dad, 91, still aglow over son, 2.* [Text:] He was born in Osceola, Ark., and credits his virility to a diet of home-grown, home-cooked food—especially wild "poke leaf" salads.

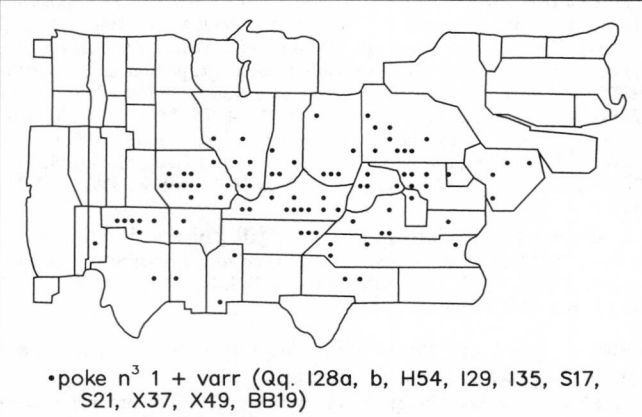

•poke n³ 1 + varr (Qq. I28a, b, H54, I29, I35, S17, S21, X37, X49, BB19)

2 also *stinking poke:* **=skunk cabbage 1a.**

1778 Carver *Travels N. Amer.* 518, Skunk Cabbage or Poke is an herb that grows in moist and swampy places. The leaves of it are about a foot long, and six inches broad, nearly oval, but rather pointed. The roots are composed of great numbers of fibres, a lotion of which is made use of by the people in the colonies for the cure of itch. There issues a strong musky smell from this herb. **1876** Hobbs *Bot. Hdbk.* 113, Stinking poke, Skunk cabbage, Symplocarpus (Ictodes) foetidus. **1896** *Garden and Forest* 9.292, Poke. . . The name as applied to Symplocarpus foetidus is English, and the application of it to Veratrum viride is due to the latter being confused with the former, owing to the fact that the two plants often grow in company, and to the unpracticed eye, bear a slight resemblance to each other in early spring when their leaves first appear. Hence both have received the same popular names. **1958** Jacobs–Burlage *Index Plants NC* 17, Symplocarpus foetidus. . . Ellebore; Irish cabbage; poke.

3 also *meadow poke:* An **Indian poke 1** (here: *Veratrum viride*). Cf **pokeroot 2**

1847 Wood *Class-Book* 557, V[eratrum] viride . . Poke. White Hellebore. . . Can. to Ga.—A large-leaved, coarse-looking plant, of our meadows and swamps. **1896** [see **2** above]. **1898** U.S. Dept. Ag. Div. Entomol. *Bulletin* 20.16, Veratrum viride. . . Meadow poke.

poke n⁴ [Abbr for **shitepoke**]

1 =green heron.

1791 Bartram *Travels* 293, A[rdea] viriscens, the green bitern or poke. **1844** DeKay *Zool. NY* 2.224, The *Poke, Chalk-line, Fly-up-the-creek,* or

Schyte Poke as he was called by our Dutch progenitors, is a southern species. . . It is common throughout the State, and, from some curious notions respecting its habits, is held in general contempt. **1874** Coues *Birds NW* 522, Ardea virescens . . Green Heron; Poke. **1925** (1928) Forbush *Birds MA* 1.334, Green Bittern; Poke; Fly-up-the-Creek. **1945** McAtee *Nomina Abitera* 27, Poke (this abbreviation [for *shitpoke* [sic]] . . is rather widely recorded, that is from Massachusetts to Florida and westward to North Dakota and Nebraska).

2 Either the **bittern** or the **least bittern.**

1883 *Amer. Naturalist* 17.4.432, From its common attitude of rest, with its bill pointing straight up, which, with its streaked plumage, makes it very difficult to distinguish from the stems of plants around it, it has gained the names "look-up," and "garde soleil [sic]." The name "poke" may refer to the same thing, but more probably to its slow, awkward movements. **1884** *Forest & Stream* 22.25, I was satisfied to be told that the queer bird *[Ardetta exilis]* . . was "a rail," "a mud hen," "a poke," or "a quak." **1945** McAtee *Nomina Abitera* 29, American Bittern *(Botaurus lentiginosus)*—Big shitpoke, . . Indian shitepoke, . . poke.

poke exclam Cf **poig, pooey**

Used as a call to pigs.

1914 *DN* 4.155 **NH**, [pok pok]. . . Call of pigs. **1973** Allen *LAUM* 1.266 (as of c1950), Calls to pigs at feeding time. . . poke [1 inf, **ceIA**].

poke n⁵ [Abbr for **pokey** n¹ 1]

A jail.

1950 *WELS Suppl.* **seWI**, Poke. . . A jail or prison. . . He was thrown in the poke. **1967–68** *DARE* (Qu. V11, . . *Joking names . . for a county or city jail*) Infs **IL**17, **MD**9, **NJ**9, **OR**4, **TX**9, Poke. **1986** Pederson *LAGS Concordance (Jail)* 1 inf, **cAL**, The poke.

poke n⁶ See **poke stalk**

poke along See **poke** v¹ 3

poke and plumb town n Also *poke and plum (town)* Cf **Plumb Nearly**

A very small town; see quots.

1954 *WELS Suppl.* **csWI**, [Radio:] *A poke and plumb town. . .* by the time you poke your head out of the window, you're plumb out of town. **1977** *DARE* File **cnNY**, *A poke and plum (town)*—A town so small that by the time you poke your head out the (train, bus, car) window, you're plumb out of town. **1985** Ladwig *How to Talk Dirty* 18 **Ozarks**, It's a poke and plumb town. You poke your head out the window and you're plumb out of town. **1989** *Country* June/July 18 **IL**, Every time I drive through a very small town, I remember my father-in-law's favorite description for such a place. "It's a poke 'n' plumb town," he'd say. "By the time you poke your head out the car window, you're plumb out of town!"

poke bag See **poke** n¹ 1a

pokeberry n

1 also attrib: The fruit of **pokeweed 1a;** the plant itself. [**poke** n³ 1] **chiefly Midl, esp S Midl** See Map

1774 (1900) Fithian *Jrl.* 1.269 **VA**, To Day Harry boil'd up a Compound of Poke-Berries, Vinegar, Sugar &c to make red Ink. **1821** Elliott *Sketch* 1.530, Phytolacca. . . Berry globular, juicy, dark purple. . . Poke berry. **1834** *Life Andrew Jackson* 70, Hit him in the pudding bag, make a pen of his neb, lush his muzzle with pokeberry juice. **1859** (1968) Bartlett *Americanisms* 329, Poke-Berry. The berry of the Phytolacca, from which a rich purple juice is extracted, and used as a dye. It is a favorite food for tame mocking birds. **1892** Torrey *Foot-Path Way* 79 **Cape Cod MA**, Across the road from the old house nearest the ocean stood a still more ancient-seeming barn . . but with . . tall, stout pokeberry weeds yet flourishing beside it. **1911** Porter *Harvester* 228 **IN**, In a sunny, open space arose tree-like specimens of thrifty magenta pokeberry. **1941** Percy *Lanterns* 50 **MS**, Quantities of little wiggly paths . . meandered everywhere and nowhere, bordered by . . bushes of pokeberry, indispensable for war-paint on our Indian days. **1965–70** *DARE* (Qu. I44, *What kinds of berries grow wild around here?*) 12 Infs, 8 **PA, TN, VA,** Pokeberries; (Qu. I28a, . . *Kinds of things . . you call 'greens' . . [Those that are eaten raw]*) Inf **OH**72, Pokeberry; **OK**10, Poke, pokeberry greens; (Qu. I28b, *Kinds of greens that are cooked*) Inf **OK**18, Pokeberry; **GA**85, Pokeberry greens; (Qu. I45, *If berries are not safe to eat . . "Don't eat those berries, they're _____";* total Infs questioned, 75) Inf **OK**3, Pokeberries; (Qu. I46, . . *Kinds of fruits that grow wild around here*) Inf **PA**150, Pokeberries; (Qu. S21, . . *Weeds . .*

that are a trouble in gardens and fields) Inf **TX3**, Pokeberries; **NC6**, Pokeberry; (Qu. S26b, *Wildflowers that grow in water or wet places*) Inf **NJ66**, Elderberry or pokeberry; (Qu. S26c, *Wildflowers that grow in woods*) Inf **MD29**, Pokeberry—near rocks and bushes—gets blue berry; (Qu. S26e, *Other wildflowers not yet mentioned; not asked in early QRs*) Inf **NJ45**, Pokeberry; (Qu. BB50d, *Favorite spring tonics*) Inf **AL39**, Pokeberries—red berries that grow on same plant as poke salad; **KY41**, Pokeberries in whiskey—a swig every day; **MS1**, Pokeberry root and poke salad; (Qu. DD28b, *. . Fermented drinks . . made at home*) Inf **KY16**, Pokeberry wine. **1966–68** *DARE* Tape **AL1**, She got pokeberry root for somethin'. . . You know poke salad . . you get the root from that; **IN30**, I have a piece of material that my great-great-grandmother . . prepared. . . The dyes were. . . made from a thing that we call here is pokeberries. **1986** Pederson *LAGS Concordance* **Gulf Region**, 46 infs, Pokeberry, pokeberries; 1 inf, Pokeberries—poisonous purple—like grapes; 1 inf, Pokeberries—used to make paint; 1 inf, Pokeberry—wine made of berry, salad of leaves; 1 inf, Pokeberry root—home remedy; 1 inf, Pokeberry roots—for rheumatism.

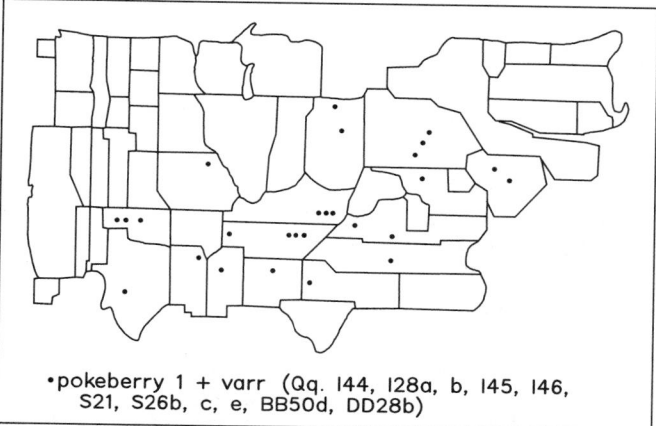

•pokeberry 1 + varr (Qq. 144, 128a, b, 145, 146, S21, S26b, c, e, BB50d, DD28b)

2 also *small pokeberry:* **=rouge plant 1.** Cf **pokeweed 3**
1936 Whitehouse *TX Flowers* 21, *Rouge Plant. Small Pokeberry (Rivina humilis). . .* The bright red berries often occur on the stems while flowers are still present. The low plants, a foot or more high, grow profusely in woods in Central Texas. [*Ibid, Ink-berry. Large Pokeberry (Phytolacca decandra)* is a leafy, stout, branched plant 3–9 ft. high, with . . purple berries.] **1960** Vines *Trees SW* 253, *Rivina humilis.* . . Vernacular names are Baby-pepper, Pokeberry, and Pigeon-berry. . . The fruit yields a red dye, or ink, and the leaves were once used in domestic medicine for catarrh and for treating wounds.

pokeberry corn n [From the red color of the kernels, resembling that of **pokeberry 1** or its juice] Cf **bloody butcher 1**
An **Indian corn 1** (here: *Zea mays* var *rugosa*) with red kernels.
1971 *Foxfire* Spring–Summer 98 **nGA**, Sometimes th'first one that got a red ear'ud get a ten-dollar prize. That's what they called pokeberry corn. Looked like poke come in it. And ever' once in a while you'd get a plumb red ear. And th'girl that got th'red ear, she chose her partner t'dance with later. **1983** Montell *Don't Go Up* 49 **csKY, cnTN**, Some farmers grew . . pokeberry corn, which grew especially large in the river bottoms.

poke bonnet n [*OED2* →] **formerly widespread, now more freq Sth, SW** See Map *old-fash*
A woman's bonnet with a broad, stiff brim that projects significantly beyond the face.
[**1798** *Thomas' MA Spy or Worcester Gaz.* (MA) 5 Sept [1]/1, Their pretty faces are either obscured by a black or white fly-flapper, or wholly hidden by their poking bonnets, unless you directly face them, and close by too.] **1840** *S. Lit. Messenger* 6.64 **AL**, "Good morning, Miss Priscilla," said Ketchum, penetrating the disguise of the poke bonnet and old cloak belonging to her mother. **1848** Burton *Waggeries* 74 **NYC**, The Queen of Palmyra ensconced her dignity in the close-fitting habit, poke bonnet, and green veil. **1848** Bartlett *Americanisms* 255, *Poke-bonnet.* A long, straight bonnet, much worn by Quakers and Methodists. **1870** (1871) Rae *Westward by Rail* 108 **UT**, The custom seems to prevail [among the Mormons] for one or two out of the several wives . . to wear 'poke bonnets,' resembling those which Quaker ladies wore in for-

mer days. **1875** *Appletons' Jrl.* 13.526 **MA**, Elizabeth Peabody, of Kindergarten and historical-chart fame, was a resident [of Concord MA], and the memory of her—a queer little lady in a black poke-bonnet—lingers yet. **1905** *DN* 3.16 **cCT**, *Poke-bonnet. . .* A long, straight bonnet. **1908** Fox *Lonesome Pine* 76 **KY**, She was looking sidewise, quite hidden by a scarlet poke-bonnet. **1950** *WELS* **WI** (*A cloth bonnet worn by women for protection from the sun*) 1 Inf, Sunbonnet—round, poke bonnet effect—long stays in the sides to hold stiff; 1 Inf, Poke bonnet—large bonnet, projecting front; 1 Inf, Sunbonnet—poke bonnet. **c1960** *Wilson Coll.* **csKY**, *Poke bonnet. . .* A type of home-made bonnet for women. **1965–70** *DARE* (Qu. W2, *. . A cloth bonnet worn by women for protection from the sun*) 21 Infs, **scattered, but more freq Sth, SW**, Poke bonnet; **CA65**, Poke bonnet—Inf's Missouri mother; **CA80**, Poke bonnet—at Santa Cruz or near it; **CT40**, Poke bonnet—old-fashioned; **MN2**, Poke bonnet—at one time, early 1920s; **NM9**, Poke bonnet—had slats on it to hold it around face; **VA69**, Poke bonnet—no longer used; Inf's grandmother wore; **WI18**, Poke bonnet—very little use. **1982** Slone *How We Talked* 28 **eKY** (as of c1950), A poke bonnet—an old-fashioned bonnet.

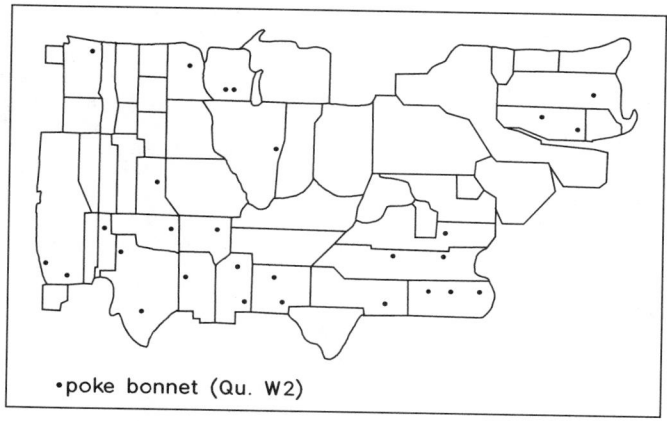

•poke bonnet (Qu. W2)

poked See **poke** v[3]

poke dinner n [**poke** n[1] **1a**] Cf **poke supper**
1954 *PADS* 21.34 **cnSC**, *Poke dinner. . .* A lunch carried to work in a paper bag.

poked out ppl adj phr [Cf *EDD* **poke** v.[2] 9 "To give offence. . . Hence *Poked, ppl. adj.* offended."]
Put out, upset.
1988 *DARE* File **nwMA**, She was poked out at the minister, so she voted no.

poke-easy n, adj **chiefly S Midl** Cf **poke** n[2] **2**
A slow or lazy person or animal; slow, easygoing.
1851 *S. Lit. Messenger* 17.758, She couldn't bear, she said, your psalm-singing, poke-easy, good for nothing, dumb-founded, sighing sort of beaux. **1888** Johnston *Mr. Absalom Billingslea* 3 **GA**, It's more'n prob'le that sech slow-goin' poke-easy creeters as what I am had ought to be left out thar. **1890** Johnston *Widow Guthrie* 288 **GA** (as of 1830s), Get along with you, and don't be so poke easy. **1909** *DN* 3.358 **eAL, wGA**, *Poke-easy. . .* A lazy or slow person or animal. **1912** *DN* 3.585 **wIN**, *Poke-easy. . .* A lazy, slow person. "Why, he's a regular poke-easy." **1915** *DN* 4.187 **swVA**, *Poke easy. . .* A lazy, slow person. **1916** *DN* 4.327 **KS**, *Pokeeasy. . .* An easy-going person. **1952** Brown *NC Folkl.* 1.578, *Poke-easy. . .* A slow, easy-going person.—General. **c1960** *Wilson Coll.* **csKY**, *Poke-easy. . .* A slow-poke. **1966–67** *DARE* (Qu. A18, *. . A very slow person: "What's keeping him? He certainly is _____!"*) Inf **AR32**, A poke-easy; **TX6**, Poke-easy—east Texas. **1982** *Smithsonian Letters* **cnKY** (as of 1930s), A man who was "poke-easy" might be essentially competent, but took so long to do his work that he was a thorn in the flesh to the more brisk workers. **1983** *MJLF* 9.1.51 **ceKY** (as of 1956), *Poke easy . .* a slow poke.

poke-hole n [Cf *EDD* **poke hole** "A small or wretched building."] Cf **chuckhole 2**, DS D7
A closet or cubbyhole.
1931–33 *LANE Worksheets* **cnRI**, Poke hole. . . closet. In the poke hole (where the broom is). **1950** *WELS Suppl.* **WI**, *Poke hole. . .* A small space in the house where you can hide things. **1951** Hough

Singing in Morning 91 **Martha's Vineyard MA,** That is one of the priceless advantages of old houses—if they do not have full-sized attics they have spaces under the eaves, and various poke-holes in which someone's forefathers stored broken spinning wheels, piles of tracts and magazines, trunks . . and all that sort of thing.

poke-hooked See **poke** n¹ **2**

poke-leaved milkweed See **poke milkweed**

pokelogan n Also *pokeloken;* for addit varr see quots [Algonquian] **NEng, Gt Lakes, NW** Cf **bogan, logan, pocosin**
An area of stagnant water or swamp connected to a lake or stream.
1848 *Union Mag.* (NY NY) 3.137 **ME,** Now and then we passed what McCauslin called a pokelogan, an Indian term for what the drivers might have reason to call a poke-logs-in, an inlet that leads nowhere. **1848** Bartlett *Americanisms* 255, *Poke-loken.* An Indian word, used by hunters and lumbermen in Maine, to denote a marshy place or stagnant pool, extending into the land from a stream or lake. **1872** Schele de Vere *Americanisms* 20, The term *pokeloken,* or *popelogan,* signifying, "marsh," has apparently more vitality in it, for it is still very largely used by lumbermen in Maine, and by their brethren in the Northwest . . when they speak of marshy ground extending inland from a lake or a stream. **1905** U.S. Forest Serv. *Bulletin* 61.43 **nNEng, nNY, MN, nWI, nMI** [Logging terms], *Pokelogan.* . . A bay or pocket into which logs may float off during a drive. **1969** Sorden *Lumberjack Lingo* 88 **NEng, Gt Lakes,** *Poke logan*—A bay or pocket into which logs may float during a drive. Same as logan. **1971** *DARE* File **sME coast,** In my fishing expeditions to the Maine Lakes I heard *logan* applied to little swampy places which would fit the definition of *bogan.* In some instances it was called a *pokelogan.*

poke milkweed n Also *poke-leaved milkweed* [From the resemblance of the leaves to those of **poke** n³ **1**]
A **milkweed 1** (here: *Asclepias exaltata*).
1843 Torrey *Flora NY* 2.120, *Poke-leaved Milkweed.* . . Stem 3–6 feet high, rather slender. **1891** Jesup *Plants Hanover NH* 28, A[sclepias] phytolaccoides. . . (Poke Milkweed). Common. **1910** Graves *Flowering Plants* 323 **CT,** Poke Milkweed. . . Moist woods and thickets. **1946** Tatnall *Flora DE* 210, *Poke Milkweed.* Frequent in moist thickets. . . Mid-June, July. **1968** Radford et al. *Manual Flora Carolinas* 850, *A[sclepias] exaltata.* . . Poke Milkweed. . . Corolla greenish white, outer surface often tinged with rose.

poke-nose(d) adj
Intrusively inquisitive, prying; hence n *poke-nose* a prying, snoopy person.
1862 *NY Daily Tribune* (NY) 7 June (*AmSp* 25.179), Among the articles which the [U.S.] Senate refused to tax are watches, plate, & dogs. The main reason for this [refusal] is the large expense of collecting & the poke-nose scrutiny involved in levying such taxes. **1866** *Old Guard* 4.737, Why, ever since it first transpired that negro slavery was profitable to us, and no longer profitable to them, haven't they been sending their puritanical poke-noses, to poison this element in our midst? **1915** *DN* 4.206, *Poke-nose,* unpleasantly inquisitive person. "That woman is such a poke-nose." **1942** Berrey–Van den Bark *Amer. Slang* 160.4, *Inquisitive; curious.* . . pokenosed. *Ibid* 399.1, *Meddler or inquisitive person.* . . pokenose. **1966–68** *DARE* (Qu. GG36a, *The kind of person who is always poking into other people's affairs: "She's an awful _____."*) Infs **NY42, WA11,** Poke-nose.

poke off on See **poke** v¹ **4**

poke of moonshine n [As a place-name in Maine and New York, *Poke of Moonshine* is a folk-etym from an unidentified Algonquian word (see Stewart *Amer. Place-Names* 379); how these two senses may relate to that is unclear.]
‡**1** See quot.
1931–33 *LANE Worksheets* **eCT,** Poke of moonshine. . . A jack o' lantern.
2 See quot.
1966 *DARE* (Qu. Y21, *To move about slowly and without energy*) Inf **SC19,** Moving like a poke of moonshine.

poker n¹
1 See **poke** n² **1.**

2 also *stove* (or *lid*) *poker:* A stove lifter. **scattered, but less freq Sth, S Midl** See Map Cf *cap lifter* (at **cap** n¹ **2a**)
1950 *WELS* (Round, flat pieces on a wood-burning stove that you take out when you put fuel in: What . . you use to remove these when the stove is hot) 11 Infs, **WI,** (Stove) poker. **1965–70** *DARE* (Qu. F11, *The thing you use to remove the lids . . from a wood-burning stove when it is hot*) 57 Infs, **scattered, but less freq Sth, S Midl,** (Stove) poker; **TN66,** Lid poker.

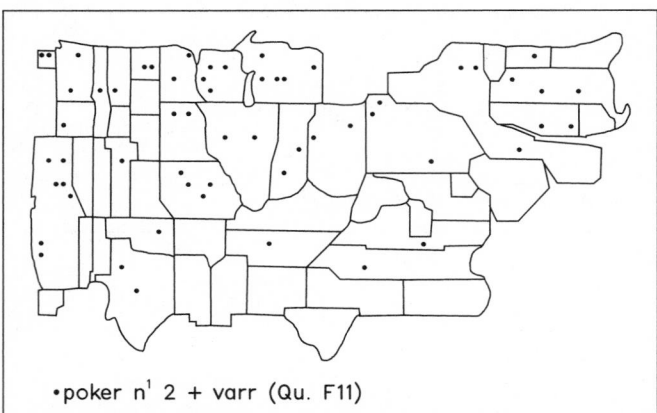

•poker n¹ 2 + varr (Qu. F11)

3 A type of woman's shoe; see quot.
1954 *Harder Coll.* **cwTN,** Pokers. . . Women's high-top shoes with notches around top.

poker v See **poke** v³

poker n²
1 also with *the:* Delirium tremens. **PA** Cf **pokerish**
1967–68 *DARE* (Qu. DD22, . . *Delirium tremens*) Infs **PA**142, 161, (The) poker; **PA**25, Whiskey poker. [**1991** Beam *Revised PA Ger. Dict.* 43, *Delirium tremens.* . . Poker.] **1997** *DARE* File **sePA,** Der Poker [for *delirium tremens*]. I certainly heard it frequently as a child. Mostly in Dutch, but also in English. . . Doesn't it come from English?
2 =**booger** n¹ **3.** [Cf obs *poker* demon, bugbear, and similar rel betw **booger** n¹ **1a** and **booger** n¹ **3**]
1892 *DN* 1.214 **cwMA,** Children in Belchertown . . used to call the thing in question [=a ball of mucus in the nose] a *poker* (rhyming with *joker, stoker*). **1969** *DARE* (Qu. X16, *Sticky mucus that forms in the nose—children's words for this*) Inf **VT**12, Poker.

poker face n
=**barn owl 1.**
1956 *AmSp* 31.185 **SC,** Poker face—Barn owl.

pokerish adj [From obs *poker* demon, bugbear (*OED2* 1601 →)] **esp NEng** *old-fash* Cf **poky** adj
Alarming, dreadful, spooky; affected by feelings of dread.
1827 *MA Spy & Worcester Co. Advt.* (Worcester MA) 21 Nov 1/4, A patriarchal ram who would fight any thing but a pokerish looking ducking gun. [**1828** Webster *Amer. Dict., Poker.* . . Any frightful object, especially in the dark; a bugbear; a word in common popular use in America.] **1833** Fergusson *Practical Notes* 228 **NY** (as of 1831), A grave and sententious gentleman in the hotel was detailing to me the desolation of the city during the last visitation of yellow fever. . . "I assure you, sir," he said, with a most portentous aspect, "it was monstrous *pokerish.*" **1835** Willis *Pencillings* 2.169 **NEng,** A pokerish-looking dwarf. **1837** *Daily Picayune* (New Orleans LA) 25 March 2/2, If you want to know how a feller feels when he is going to be hung, I'll tell you—he feels pretty pokerish. **1839** Hoffman *Wild Scenes* 2.67 **S Midl,** Yes—but we'd better yet have a light—my place here in front is cursed pokerish. **1895** *DN* 1.392 **NEng,** *Pokerish:* somewhat dangerous, alarming. **1905** *DN* 3.16 **cCT,** *Pokerish.* . . Frightful. 'The old church is a pokerish looking place.' **1937** Shepard *Pedlar's Progress* 4 **CT** (as of 1799), They spoke of "kickin' up a bobbery" and of "feelin' dreffle pokerish." **1943** *LANE* Map 534, 1 inf, **sME coast,** *Poky hole,* 'a dreary, pokerish spot.'

pokeroot n
1a The root of **pokeweed 1a;** the plant itself. [**poke** n³ **1**]
1687 in 1744 Royal Soc. London *Philos. Trans. for 1739* 41.150 **VA,**

Poake-root, i.e. *Solanum bacciferum,* a strong Purge, and by most deemed Poison. **1698** (1848) Thomas *Hist. & Geog. Acct.* 19 **PA,** There grows also in great plenty the *Black Snake-Root, . . Rattle-Snake-Root, Poke-Root,* called in *England Jallop.* **1876** Hobbs *Bot. Hdbk.* 91, Poke root, Garget root, Phytolacca decandra. **1883** (1971) Harris *Nights with Remus* 84 **GA** [Black], I aint tuck none er dat ar docter truck yit, ceppin' it's dish yer flas' er poke-root w'at ole Miss Favers fix up fer de stiffness in my j'ints. **1910** Graves *Flowering Plants* 171 **CT,** Common Pokeweed. . . Poke Root. . . The young leaves and shoots make an excellent pot-herb, but care must be taken to exclude any part of the root. **1964** Kingsbury *Poisonous Plants U.S.* 227, Pokeroot or decoctions of it was used by the American Indians and soon by the early settlers for a variety of illnesses. Occasionally, poisoning resulted from ill-advised treatments or accidental ingestion of pokeroot. **1968–70** *DARE* (Qu. S21, . . *Weeds . . that are a trouble in gardens and fields*) Inf **LA**28, Pokeroot or poke greens; **NC**49, Pokeroot; (Qu. BB50d, *Favorite spring tonics*) Inf **KY**90, Pokeroot juice. **1982** Slone *How We Talked* 118 **eKY** (as of c1950), Cows had the "murn"—Symptoms were like a cold; cough, runny nose, fever. Cure: poke root put inside an ear of corn.

b attrib: See **pokeweed 1b.**

2 The root of **Indian poke 1;** the plant itself. Note: Some of these quots may refer instead to **1** above.

1784 in 1785 *Amer. Acad. Arts & Sci. Memoirs* 1.492, *Veratrum. . .* White Helebore. Poke-root. Indian Poke. Common in wet meadows and swamps. June. **1814** Bigelow *Florula Bostoniensis* 374, Veratrum viride . . *Poke Root, American Hellebore.* . . Chiefly used in the country as an external application in cutaneous affections. **1894** *Jrl. Amer. Folkl.* 7.103 **NH,** *Veratrum viride* . . poke-root, Franconia, N.H. **1929** *Torreya* 29.149 **ME,** *Picea canadensis* was called "*Skunk Spruce*". . . *Veratrum viride,* "*Poke root.*" **1959** Roberts *Up Cutshin* 95 **seKY,** Now if one had the misfortune of catching something like the eetch, she would take this old pokeroot and make a ooze out of it and boil it and wash you with it and kill that eetch dead as a nit. **1967** *DARE* FW Addit **ceNY,** Indian poke, poke root, white (or) false hellebore—all are the root of *Veratrum viride.* **1986** Pederson *LAGS Concordance* **Gulf Region,** 7 infs, Pokeroot; 1 inf, Pokeroot—made tea for curing ground itch; 1 inf, Pokeroot—used to cure itch—poisonous.

3 =**rouge plant 1.** Cf **pokeberry 2, pokeweed 3**

1930 OK Univ. Biol. Surv. *Pub.* 2.60, *Rivina humilis* . . var. *glabra. . .* Smooth Dwarf Pokeroot.

poke sack See **poke** n¹ **1a**

poke salad n Also *poke sallet, polk salad;* for addit varr see quots [**poke** n³ **1** + **salad** B1] **chiefly Sth, S Midl** See Map The young shoots of **pokeweed 1a** cooked and eaten as greens; the plant itself.

1880 (1881) Harris *Uncle Remus Songs* 197 **GA,** I got mustard, en poke salid, en lam's garden in dat baskit. **1912** Green *VA Folk-Speech* 329, *Poke-sallet.* . . The young and tender leaves of the poke-weed are used for sallet, cooked with bacon. **1913** Kephart *Highlanders* 356 **sAppalachians,** This poke salat eats good. **1914** *DN* 4.160 **cVA,** *Poke-salad.* . . A kind of greens. **1922** *DN* 5.184 **GA,** *Poke salid.* . . An unidentified plant used for "greens." **1923** *DN* 5.217 **swMO,** *Poke salat.* . . A salad made from the poke weed. Greens. **1930** *AmSp* 5.207 **Ozarks,** A salad made of poke-weed leaves is always called *poke-sallet* in the Ozarks. **1939** *Hall Coll.* **eTN,** Poke sallit is made with poke weed. Poke weed has "great big old heavy red-looking stalks." **1952** Callahan *Smoky Mt.* 88, And bread was only one of the many uses of the fireplace for cooking, which included green beans . . "poke salet" made from the young shoots of pokeweed, and similar dishes cooked in kettles. **1965–70** *DARE* (Qq. I28a, b, . . *Greens*) 51 Infs, **chiefly Sth, S Midl,** Poke salad; **AR**47, **KY**5, 42, 44, 81, 90, **MO**8, **SC**32, 39, **TX**33, **VA**35, 42, Poke sallet; **GA**85, Pokeberry greens—when they are cooked, they are called poke salad [FW: People also often call the plant "poke salad."]; **MO**8, Wild mustard—you can get it canned; they call it poke sallet; (Qu. H54, *Dishes made with greens: [. . kinds of 'greens' . . eaten]; total Infs questioned,* 75) 13 Infs, Poke salad; (Qu. H56, *Names for . . pickles*) Inf **NC**48, Poke salad pickles; (Qu. S21, . . *Weeds . . that are a trouble in gardens and fields*) Infs **AR**49, **GA**84, **TX**51, Poke salad; (Qu. BB50d, *Favorite spring tonics*) Inf **GA**84, Poke salad—from pokeweed; [**MD**5, Cut poke (a plant like spinach that grows wild) when young, boil and eat with vinegar, salt, and pepper;] **MS**1, Pokeberry root and poke salad; **SC**39, A mess of poke salad; **NC**30, **TX**95, 104, Poke salad; **VA**42, Poke sallet; **TX**62, Pokeweed salad. **1968** *DARE* FW Addit **nwTN,** [Sign in grocery:] Polk Salid. **1970** Anderson *TX Folk*

Med. xvii, Not only did they eat poke salad and lamb's-quarters for greens, but they used them for medicines as well. *Ibid* 61, Rheumatism—Get poke salad roots, wash them, and place in some whiskey. Drink the whiskey off of the roots. **1986** Pederson *LAGS Concordance* **Gulf Region,** 83 infs, Poke salad; 1 inf, Poke salad—poisonous if not prepared properly; 1 inf, Poke salad—edible if eaten in early spring; 1 inf, Poke salad—poison if not cooked right; 1 inf, Poke salad—tastes like spinach—parboil it; 59 infs, Poke sallet; 1 inf, Mother cooked poke sallet with mustard; 1 inf, Poke sallet—wife boils 3 times; 1 inf, Poke sallet—grows around the outhouse—won't eat.

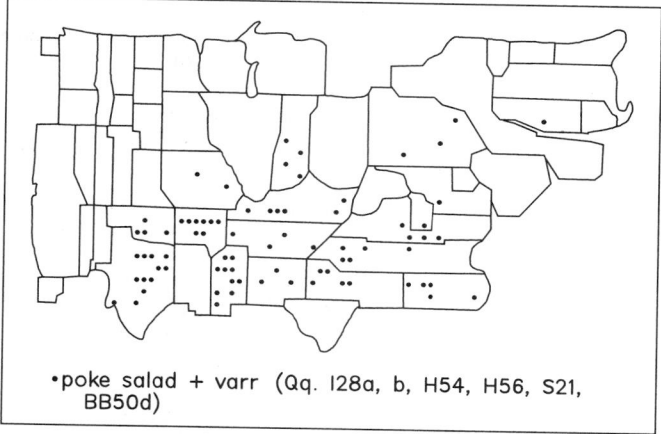

•poke salad + varr (Qq. I28a, b, H54, H56, S21, BB50d)

pokeshite n Also *pokeshike* [Metath for **shitepoke** or the var *shikepoke;* cf Intro "Language Changes" I.1]

1945 McAtee *Nomina Abitera* 29, Black-Crowned Night Heron . . pokeshike, South Shore, Massachusetts. **1966** *DARE* (Qu. Q8, *A water bird that makes a booming sound before rain and often stands with its beak pointed almost straight up*) Inf **FL**35, Pokeshite.

poke stalk n [**poke** n³ **1**] **S Midl**

1 also *poke, polk stalk:* A shotgun or rifle.

1936 *AmSp* 11.276 **eTN,** *Polk stalk.* Shot gun. 'He took his polk stalk to the woods.' **1945** Wallace *Barington* 19 **AR,** "He raised up that old long barrel and knocked the quail down as purty as I ever seen." "Papa's still got that damned old polk stalk." **1965–70** *DARE* (Qu. P37a, *Nicknames for a rifle*) Inf **AR**22, Poke stalk; (Qu. P37b, *Nicknames for a shotgun*) Infs **AR**51, **IN**18, **NC**30, (Old) poke stalk; **KY**84, Poke stalk [laughter]—for old single barrel; **SC**32, Poke stalk—long-barreled single shot; **VA**43, Old poke; [(Qu. X37, . . *Words . . to describe people's legs if they're noticeably bent, or uneven, or not right*) Inf **NC**55, Legs as straight as a poke stalk; (Qu. X49, *Expressions . . about a person who is very thin*) Inf **TN**13, Looks like a poke stalk].

2 attrib: See **pokeweed 1b.**

poke supper n [**poke** n¹ **1a**] **S Midl** Cf **box social**

A community fund-raising event at which bags containing homemade food are auctioned off.

1912 *Jrl. Amer. Folkl.* 25.139 **Appalachians,** *Poke-supper* (at which the food is served from pokes). **1913** Kephart *Highlanders* 264 **sAppalachians,** A substitute for the church fair is the "poke-supper," at which dainty pokes (bags) of cake and other home-made delicacies are auctioned off to the highest bidder. Whoever bids-in a poke is entitled to eat with the girl who prepared it, and escort her home. The rivalry excited among the mountain swains by such artful lures may be judged from the fact that, in a neighborhood where a man's work brings only a dollar a day, a pretty girl's poke may be bid up to ten, twenty, or even fifty dollars. **1932** Randolph *Ozark Mt. Folks* 236, Mostly they'd jest pass th' hat. . . Or else maybe they'd raise th' money with a poke supper or somethin'. **1968** Haun *Hawk's Done Gone* 60 **TN,** One time Eloyed asked to take her to the poke supper up there at the Cedar Grove schoolhouse and she wouldn't go. *Ibid* 61, Amy . . went to that . . poke supper with Enzor. Then he wouldn't even bid on her poke when it was put up for sale.

poke the puppy v phr [Euphem for **fuck the dog**]

To mark time, loaf, shirk work.

1989 *DARE* File **csWI,** *Poke the puppy*—When X returned from vacation to his job at the post office he was told that he was missed by his co-workers because his replacement, a man close to retirement, was just "pokin' the puppy," counting the days to retirement.

poke up See **poke** v[1] 1

pokeweed n   Cf **marsh poke**

1a also *polkweed:* A plant (*Phytolacca americana*) of the eastern US used for greens and in var remedies. [**poke** n[3] 1] For other names of this plant or its parts see **bogue-sang, cancerroot 3, coakum, cow poke** n[1], **foxglove 5, garget, haystack weed, Indian greens, Indian poke 2, inkberry 2, jalap, mockingbird berry, pigeonberry 1, pocan, poke** n[3] 1, **pokeberry 1, pokeroot 1, poke salad, poor man's asparagus, red-ink plant, redweed 1, scoke, wild spinach**

1750 in 1751 *Gentleman's Mag.* 21.306 **NY,** The Phytolacca . . [is] known to almost every one in America, by the name of pokeweed. **1822** Eaton *Botany* 390, *Phytolacca . . decandra* (poke weed). . . A good substitute for the Ipecac. **1840** MA Zool. & Bot. Surv. *Herb. Plants & Quadrupeds* 100, *Poke,* or *Virginia Poke,* or *Poke Weed.* This is a large, fleshy plant, often 6 feet high, . . rising from a very large root. **1859** (1880) Darlington *Amer. Weeds* 270, *P[hytolacca] decandra.* . . Poke. Poke-weed. . . The mature berries . . have been used by the pastry cook in making pies of equivocal merit. **1906** Johnson *Highways Missip. Valley* 120 **AR,** We had pokeweed and sour-dock greens with fat pork. **1940** Steyermark *Flora MO* 172, Pokeweed Family (Phytolaccaceae)—Pokeweed, Pokeberry (*Phytolacca americana*). . . The berries, root, and older leaves are considered poisonous, but the tender young leaves and shoots in the spring are edible and are commonly cooked for greens. A strong tea, made by boiling either the whole root or its bark, is sometimes used as a cure for the "seven-year itch." The root is the usual remedy for garget (swelling of the throat) in cattle. **1950** *WELS,* 1 Inf, **cWI,** Pokeweed. **1964** Batson *Wild Flowers SC* 42, Pokeberry, Polkweed, Indian Polk: *Phytolacca americana.* **1965–70** *DARE* (Qu. I28a, . . *Kinds of things . . you call 'greens' . . [Those that are eaten raw]*) Inf **IA**13, Pokeweed—not too common here; **PA**70, Pokeweeds; (Qu. I28b, *Kinds of greens that are cooked*) Inf **CT**24, Scoke—poisonous unless cooked and cured 2–3 years—might be pokeweed; **MA**15, Porkweed [sic]; (Qu. S21, . . *Weeds . . that are a trouble in gardens and fields*) Infs **FL**31, **NJ**39, **NC**12, **TN**6, Pokeweed; **IL**55, Pokeweed—has a purplish berry on it; (Qu. S26c, *Wildflowers that grow in woods*) Inf **VT**16, Pokeweed—grows in pastures. **1986** Pederson *LAGS Concordance,* 1 inf, **csAL,** Poke weed—purple berries—poisonous; 1 inf, **ceTX,** Pokeweed.

b also *pokeroot, poke-stalk;* attrib; Of religious conviction or activity: intense but short-lasting.   Cf **jimson-weed preacher**

1931 Goodrich *Mt. Homespun* 57 **sAppalachians,** "This poke-stalk religion ain't worth much, to my way of thinkin'," said Elvira, and seeing the puzzled look on Lois' face, she added, "Laws, child, ain't you seen pokeweed a growin' up so biggity in the summer time and then in the winter, nothin' left of it but a gray rag you couldn't kinnle a fire with?" Lois laughed as she realized the aptness of the simile. **1933** *AmSp* 8.1.51 **Ozarks,** *Poke-weed religion.* . . The sort that springs up quickly and looks impressive, but doesn't last well. **1939** *AmSp* 14.91 **eTN,** *Poke weed religion.* Conversion following hysterical revivals. 'My boy's got poke weed religion.' **1949** Webber *Backwoods Teacher* 113 **Ozarks,** Preachers from the "poke-root" and "lightnin'-bug" churches (brush arbors) were not likely to do anything to change that belief.

2 also *polkweed:* =**skunk cabbage 1a.**   Cf **poke** n[3] 2

1892 *Jrl. Amer. Folkl.* 5.104 **MA,** *Symplocarpus foetidus,* Polkweed. . . Brookline, Mass. **1959** Carleton *Index Herb. Plants* 93, *Pokeweed: Phytolacca americana . . ; Symplocarpus foetidus.*

3 as *small pokeweed:* =**rouge plant 1.**   Cf **pokeberry 2**

1961 Wills–Irwin *Flowers TX* 108, *Small Pokeweed—Rivina humilis.* . . *Great Pokeweed—Phytolacca americana.* . . Pokeweeds are probably better known for their attractive fruit clusters than for their modest pale flowers. . . The Pigeonberry or Small Pokeweed is found rather commonly . . in Central Texas, south to the Rio Grande, west to the Trans-Pecos. It is distinguished from the Scoke, or Great Pokeweed, by wavy-margined leaves, pale pink flowers, and red fruit. **1967** *DARE* Wildfl QR (Wills–Irwin) Pl.8D Inf **TX**44, Small pokeweed.

4 A **knotweed 1** (here: *Polygonum phytolaccifolium*).

1973 Hitchcock–Cronquist *Flora Pacific NW* 89, Alpine knotweed, pokeweed . . *P[olygonum] phytolaccaefolium.*

pokeweed salad See **poke salad**

pokey adj See **poky** adj

pokey n[1] Also sp *poky*

1 also *pogey;* also with *the:* A jail.   Cf **hokey-pokey** n[3], **poke** n[5]

1919 Darling *Jargon Book* 26, *Pokey*—a jail. **1950** *WELS* (*Joking or nicknames for a county or city jail*) 1 Inf, **cwWI,** Pokey. **1951** R.S. Prather *Bodies in Bedlam* 47 (*DAS* at *pokey*), Any excuse to toss me in the poky. **1961** Folk *Word Atlas N. LA* map 1511, *Jail* . . [less freq responses include] pokey. **1962** Atwood *Vocab. TX* 71, *Local prison.* . . [Among the responses] of less frequency . . *pokey.* **1962** in 1982 *Barrick Coll.* **csPA,** *Pokey*—jail. **1965–70** *DARE* (Qu. V11, . . *Joking names . . for a county or city jail*) 91 Infs, **scattered, but less freq Sth,** Pokey; **MD**31, **MI**27, **NY**214, Pogey; (Qu. N3, *The car or wagon that takes arrested people to the police station or to jail*) Infs **IN**22, **NJ**16, Pokey wagon; (QR, near Qu. N3) Inf **OH**67, Some people call a small jail the pokey, too. **1968** *DARE* Tape **NC**53, They're cutting down all the stills now around here because they're catching up with 'em, . . putting 'em in jail, in the pokey, they call it. **1976** Garber *Mountain-ese* 70 **sAppalachians,** Ranse got locked up in the pokey fer bein' drunk Sattiday. **1986** Pederson *LAGS Concordance* **Gulf Region,** 6 infs, Pokey; 2 infs, The pokey. **2001** *DARE* File **wNY,** Pokey—n., a jail.

‡2 See quot.

1968 *DARE* (Qu. F37, . . *An indoor toilet*) Inf **MD**24, The pokey—rustic-type people say [this].

pokey n[2] Also sp *poky* [Varr of *polka;* cf Intro "Language Changes" IV.1.b]

See quots.

1939 Shaw *Cowboy Dances* 90 **West,** Another old-time . . dance . . in the West is the polka . . which is often called the "pokey" in cowboy parlance. **1969** *DARE* (Qu. NN25b, *Weakened substitutes for 'damn' or 'damned': "Well, I'll be _____!"*) Inf **KY**47, A poky-dotted possum [laughter]—old-fashioned. **1984** Burns *Cold Sassy* 25 **nGA** (as of 1906), Loma . . bought . . what she called "a blue poky-dot foulard dress with an overskirt of Georgette crepe."

pokie n   Cf **china B1**

A kind of playing marble; see quot.

1957 *Sat. Eve. Post Letters* **cwWA** (as of c1905), I neglected to mention another type of marbles of the nature of vitreous ware sometimes referred to as 'pokies' (from porcelain) but most commonly called 'chinies'.

poking adv   Cf **poke** n[2] 2

In phr *poking slow:* Excessively or ploddingly slow.

1942 (1971) Campbell *Cloud-Walking* 6 **seKY,** Fess grumbled because his pap was so poking slow. *Ibid* 115, Lexie was so poking slow to come back home that Ishmael untied his nag and jogged off home.

poking vbl n See **poke** n[1] 1b(2)

poking slow See **poking** adv

poking stick n   **sAppalachians**

A fire poker.

1954 Roberts *I Bought Dog* 17 **seKY,** They was a big bunch of arn a-layin around there, like pokin sticks for his far. **c1960** *Wilson Coll.* **csKY,** *Poking stick.* . . An iron rod used to stir a fire; a poker. **1972** Hall *Sayings Old Smoky* 109 **swNC** (as of 1969), *Pokin' stick.* A poker for the fire. "[He's] stiffer than a pokin stick," said of a corpse.

poky adj Also sp *pokey*   **chiefly NH, ME**   Cf **pokerish**

Spooky, scary, eerie; see quots.

1858 *Harper's New Mth. Mag.* 17.368, These young officers were exceedingly anxious to see a ghost, and took a great deal of pains to plunge into all sorts of pokey places, in the hope of finding them tenanted by beings from the other world. **1871** *Scribner's Mth.* 3.31, I had a horror of that pokey old passage! **1913** *DN* 4.54 **seNH,** *Poky.* Spooky; suggestive of ghosts or something of the sort (though only in a slight degree). "That dark path through the woods is kind of a poky spot, aint it?" **1943** *LANE* Map 534 (*Haunted house*) **chiefly ME, NH,** 4 infs, Poky spot; 2 infs, Poky spot, 'a dark place'; 1 inf, Poky spot, 'a place where one is frightened'; 1 inf, Poky spot, 'a dark place where you don't know where you're going'; 1 inf, Poky spot, 'a boogerish place'; 1 inf, Poky spot, 'where you see a white light in the dark'; 1 inf, Poky spot, 'where ghosts live'; 1 inf, Poky spot, 'a spooky place'; 1 inf, Poky, 'dangerous, weird'; 1 inf, Poky, 'spooky'; 1 inf, Poky, 'scary'; 1 inf, Poky place, 'a scary place'; 1 inf, Poky hole, 'a dreary, pokerish spot.' **1973** Allen *LAUM* 1.385 **Upper MW** (as of c1950), What people might expect to see in a haunted house. . . Eastern *haunt* and *pokey spot* have nearly vanished, with only three instances of the former and one [*DARE* Ed: sugg by FW] of the latter.

poky n[1] See **pokey** n[1]

poky n[2] See **pokey** n[2]

poky pranto See **poco pronto**

poky weed n

A **cockleburr 1.**

  1967 *DARE* (Qu. S13, . . *A common wild bush with bunches of round, prickly seeds; when they get dry they stick to your clothing*) Inf **HI**11, "Poky weed" would be used about any such; (Qu. S15, . . *Weed seeds that cling to clothing*) Inf **HI**11, Poky weed.

Polack n, also attrib Usu |'po₁lɔk, -lɑk|; also |'po₁læk| Also *Polacker, Pollack, Pol(l)ock;* for addit pronc and sp varr see quots [Pol *Polak* a Pole, but perh immediately from Ger *Polack,* derog counterpart to neutral *Pole*] **widespread, but more freq Nth, N Midl** See Map *often derog* Cf **Hollacky, hunyak, Podunk** n 3, **Polander**

A Polish immigrant or person of Polish ancestry; broadly, a central European immigrant, a foreigner; hence adj *Polacky.*

  1855 *Putnam's Mag.* 5.620, *To my Poland Rooster.* . . But thou shall live, immortal Polack, thou,/ though Russia's eagle clips thy pinions now,/ To flap thy wings and crow with all thy soul,/ When freedom spreads her light from Pole to Pole. **1869** *Catholic World* 9.4, A few years later, Martinus Polaccus or Polonus, Martin the Polack, or the Pole, (Polack is now disused. Shakespeare makes Horatio say, *"He smote the sledded Polack on the ice,"*) who died in 1278 [etc]. **1879** Peck *Peck's Fun* 190 **seWI**, They got a veteran soldier and a Polack woman to allow the machine to experiment on them. **1883** (1958) Peck *Peck's Bad Boy & Pa* 202 **seWI**, You buy sour kraut of a wooden-shoed Polacker, who makes it of pieces of cabbage that he gets by gathering swill. **1898** Dunne *Mr. Dooley Peace & War* 234, Ye'er thoughts on this subject is inthrestin', but not conclusive, as Dorsey said to th' Pollack that thought he cud lick him. **1901** *DN* 2.145 **NY**, *Pollock* [polǝk]. . . A Pole. Cattaraugus Co., N.Y. In Tompkins Co. pron. [polɑrk]. **1913** *Industrial Worker* (Spokane WA) 12 June 4/2 **Philadelphia PA**, The Polock, the Jew, the Irish, the Negro, stood together like a stone wall. **1930** in 1944 *ADD* **cNY**, *Pollock.* . . ['po₁lɑk]. Common. **1937** Sandoz *Slogum* 232 **NE**, Where the white people, as they called themselves, let the Polaks gather. . . he could see that she didn't mind their Old Country ways. She did n't think them funny as some of the other Polish girls did. **1938** (1939) Holbrook *Holy Mackinaw* 11 **NEng**, "A skunk ain't no bottle of Floridy water, even if you calls him by one of them fancy Polark names," he said. (By "Polark," i.e., Polish, Jigger designated any foreign language, either dead or living.) **1950** *WELS* **WI** (*Names and nicknames for people of foreign background: Polish*) 25 Infs, Polack; 6 Infs, Polock; 2 Infs, Pollack; (*Common nicknames for people living in nearby settlements or places*) 3 Infs, Polacks. **1958** *Harper's Mag.* 216.64 **NJ**, He gets onto cursing all of them . . the wops and the polacks. **1964** *PADS* 42.47 **Chicago IL**, *Polack* is used frequently to designate people and characteristics of the central European peasantry, e.g., "He talks like a polack" means he makes such phonemic substitutions as alveolar (or dental) stops for tip-dental fricatives, or "He dresses like a polack" means he does not dress tastefully. This is extended to descriptive modifiers, e.g., *polacky* furniture. **1965–70** *DARE* (Qu. HH28, *Names and nicknames . . for people of foreign background*) 307 Infs, **widespread, but more freq Nth, N Midl**, Polack; **FL**7, ['polɔks]; (Qu. C25, . . *Kinds of stone . . about . . [. . size of a person's head], smooth and hard*) Inf **NY**183, Polack ['polæk] confetti; (Qu. C35, *Nicknames for the different parts of your town or city*) Infs **CT**17, **NY**130, Polack Town; **NY**130A, Polackville—derogatory; (Qu. X15, . . *Kinds of noses, according to shape or size*) Inf **NY**70, Polack ['poulɑk] nose—a big one; (Qu. CC4, . . *Nicknames . . for various religions or religious groups*) Inf **NY**87, Polack church; (Qu. DD35, . . *Card games*) Inf **NY**213A, Polack pitch; (Qu. FF4, *Names and joking names for different kinds of dancing parties*) Inf **CT**19, Polack hops; (Qu. HH18, *Very insignificant or low-grade people*) Inf **MA**28, Polack ['polɒk]—low-class Polish person; (Qu. HH30, *Things that are nick-*

named for different nationalities—for example, a 'Dutch treat') Inf **IN**32, Polack joke; (Qu. II25, *Names or nicknames for the part of a town where the poorer people, special groups, or foreign groups live*) Infs **CT**19, **MI**45, 68, 101, Polack Town. **1969** *DARE* Tape **MI**103, Unless the doctor was abnormally good as a Negro or a Polack ['polɑk], I'd go to a Dutch doctor because somehow I'd feel I could trust him better. *Ibid* **MA**58, Here's other names for immigrants: Polank ['polæŋk] or Podunk for Polish. **1970** *DARE* File **cMA** (as of c1915), Though *Polander* was the usual word in central Massachusetts in my childhood (and some *Polanders* were really Lithuanians) we said ['po₁lɒk] rhyming with *rock.* **1975** [see **Polack fiddle**]. **1989** Pederson *LAGS Tech. Index* 407 **Gulf Region**, 78 infs, Polacks; 2 infs, Dumb Polack; 2 infs, Polack [adj.]

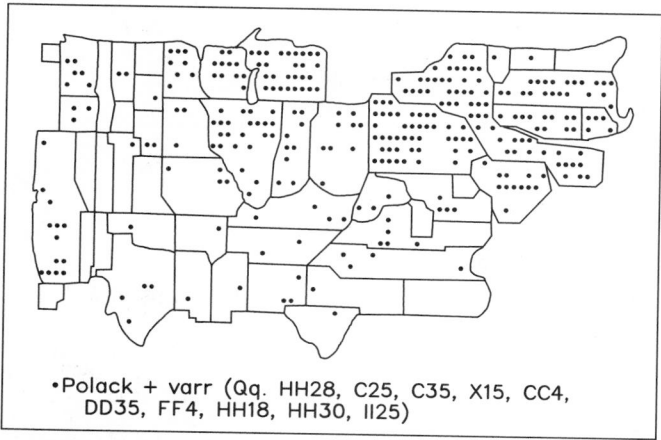

•Polack + varr (Qq. HH28, C25, C35, X15, CC4, DD35, FF4, HH18, HH30, II25)

Polack fiddle n [**Polack**]

  1975 Gould *ME Lingo* 213, *Polack fiddle*—The bucksaw. Before chainsaws, the crosscut saw was handled by two men and was mostly for felling trees. The bucksaw was a one-man tool, and preferred for *bucking* the down trees into four-foot lengths for pulpwood, or into saw-log lengths where the diameter wasn't too great. Polish woodsmen, who came to Maine in great numbers, were experts with these musical instruments. (In Maine woods lingo, *Polack* was pronounced Pole-lock.)

Polack mushroom n Also *Pole mushroom*

A bracket fungus; see quot.

  1967–68 *DARE* (Qu. S19, *Mushrooms that grow out like brackets from the sides of trees*) Inf **MI**64, Polack mushrooms I call them because the Polacks pick them; **MO**16, Pole mushrooms [sic].

Polacky See **Polack**

Polander n [Cf *OED2* polander (at *Poland* sb.[1] b) *"obs."*] **chiefly Nth, esp NEast** See Map on p. 248 *sometimes derog* Cf **Polack**

A person of Polish birth or descent; broadly, a central European.

  1624 in 1915 VA House of Burgesses *Jrls.* 28, The second supplie was a ship. . . [with] sixty persons, most gentlemen. . . except some *Polanders* to make Pitch, tarre, potashes, &c. **1779** (1827) Thacher *Military Jrl.* 179, This gentleman [=Count Pulaski] was a Polander, of distinguished rank and character. **1867** *Galaxy* 4.63 **NYC**, In a single block, there are . . 812 Irish, 218 Germans, 186 Italians, 189 Polanders, 12 French, [etc]. **1894** *Century Illustr. Mag.* 47.921 **CT**, Then there was another house, with some sort of poor immigrant in it—a "Polander," I believe they called him. **1909** in 1988 Palmer *Lang. W. Cent.* **MA** 37, I kept 2 men Alix and Ignus both Polanders but good men. **1931–33** *LANE Worksheets* **csMA**, Polanders . . Polish. The Polanders eat another kind of toadstools. **1934** *Hanley Disks* **cnMA**, We have some Polander families. **1935** Sandoz *Jules* 8 **wNE** (as of 1880–1930), A blond-bearded Polander climbed upon a barrel and pulled away at a red accordion. **1950** *WELS*, 1 Inf, **cWI**, Polander. **1965–70** *DARE* (Qu. HH28, *Names and nicknames . . for people of foreign background*) 12 Infs, **chiefly Nth, esp NEast**, Polander. **1970** Stewart *Amer. Place-Names* 380, *Polander Hollow* **NE**—From the settlement of Poles, who were often thus called. **1975** *DARE* File **cnMA**, Polander pink—Used in my family at least, in Athol, Mass. in WWI days to describe the bright purplish pink frequent in the cheap materials used in the "boughten" clothes worn by foreigners. They weren't necessarily Polish—in fact most of the people we called Polanders (derogatory) were Lithuanians. **1988** Palmer *Lang. W. Cent.* MA 37, ['pɔlændɚ]— 'Polander' referred to the Polish people. It was an awful name; they were wonderful, hardworking people.

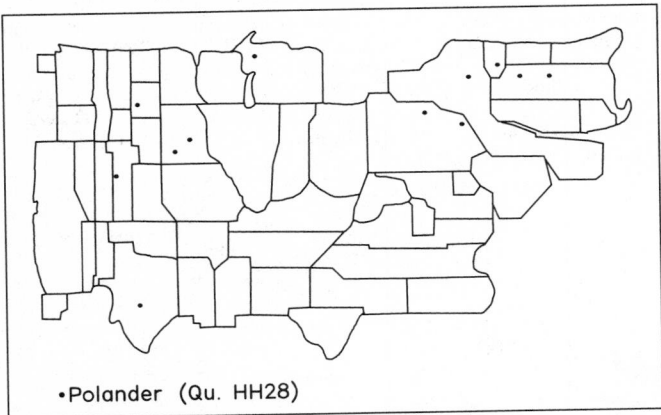

• Polander (Qu. HH28)

Polark See **Polack**

polar plant n [See quot 1914] Cf **compass plant 1**

A **rosinweed 1** (here: *Silphium laciniatum*).

1842 *Farmers' Cabinet* 15 Nov 111, At mid-day, the plane of the Polar plant passes through the sun, and thus it shuns the light. **1869** Porcher *Resources* 460, The rosin weed, which is sometimes called the polar or compass plant, because its leaves are said to point north and south, is said to be powerfully diuretic. **1901** Lounsberry *S. Wild Flowers* 517, Pilot, polar or compass-plant, resin or turpentine weed, is familiar from the prairies of Ohio southward to Alabama and Texas. **1914** Georgia *Manual Weeds* 447, *Compass plant.* . . Other English names: Pilotweed, Polar Plant [etc]. . . Many a traveler of the pioneer, roadless days of "going west" found this plant a very serviceable compass, for its large leaves are held nearly erect with their edges directed north and south.

pole n

1a also *tongue pole:* The tongue of an animal-drawn vehicle. [*OED2* pole sb.[1] 2.a [1390]–1813] **scattered, but chiefly Nth, N Midl, esp NEast** See Map

1699 in 1878 MA Hist. Soc. *Coll.* 5th ser 5.502, Pole of the Calash broken by the Horses frighted with a pistol. **1876** Knight *Amer. Mech. Dict.* 1761, *Pole.* . . The tongue of a vehicle. **1949** Kurath *Word Geog.* 57, *Tongue* (of a wagon). . . In New England and the Hudson Valley *pole* is in common use. In the remainder of New York State it is less common. *Pole* occurs also on the Atlantic coast from Sandy Hook in New Jersey to Cape Charles in Virginia, and especially in the Virginia Tidewater north of the James. Sporadic instances appear in the Philadelphia area and in Maryland west of the Bay. **1950** *WELS* WI (*The piece of wood that sticks out in front of a wagon [you put a horse on each side]*) 15 Infs, Pole; 5 Infs, Wagon pole. **1955** *PADS* 23.46 **Charleston SC**, *Wagon pole.* **1965–70** *DARE* (Qu. L45) 132 Infs, **scattered, but chiefly Nth, N Midl, esp NEast**, Pole; **OH**70, **PA**137, **TN**26, Buggy pole; **MI**23, The old people always called it the wagon pole; **NH**5,

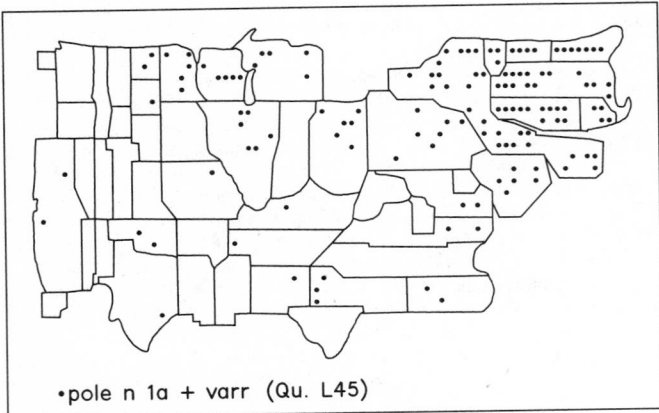

• pole n 1a + varr (Qu. L45)

Wagon pole; **TX**16, Tongue pole. [Of all Infs responding to the question, 74% were old; of those giving these responses, 86% were old.] **1969** Sorden *Lumberjack Lingo* 88 **NEng, Gt Lakes**, *Pole*—The tongue of a wagon or sleigh. **1973** Allen *LAUM* 1.213 **Upper MW** (as of c1950), For the shaft extending from a wagon . . the common term is *tongue,* ranging from 78% in Minnesota to 100% in Iowa and South Dakota. Competing with it is *pole,* which reveals its New England and Hudson Valley provenience by a strong Northern speech zone correlation. **1986** Pederson *LAGS Concordance* **Gulf Region** (*Tongue of a wagon*) 19 infs, (The) pole; 1 inf, Buggy pole—for a two-horse buggy.

b attrib; Of a work animal (or team of animals): harnessed alongside the tongue of a vehicle.

[**1760** (1925) Washington *Diaries* 1.136 **VA**, [I] put the Poll end Horses into the Plow in the Morn[in]g and the Postillion and hand Horse in, in the afternoon.] **1823** Cooper *Pioneers* 1.44 **cNY**, The leaders were of gray, and the pole-horses of a jet black. **1862** in 1903 Norton *Army Letters* 106, A driver riding the near pole mule and guiding his team with one line. **1889** *Harper's New Mth. Mag.* 79.160, The leaders sprang upward and onward . . , the pole-horses simultaneously crashing backward and downward. **1890** *Century Dict.* 4591, *Pole-horse.* . . A shaft-horse as distinguished from a leader; a wheeler. **1938** in Lib. of Congress *Amer. Memory: WPA Life Hist.* (Internet) **VT**, In those days when they wanted to move a building they'd hitch the three-four yoke oxen on each corner. . . The first yoke that come was the lead team, the ones between was the swing teams and the one on the pole was the pole team. **1944** Adams *Western Words* 117, *Pole team*—The horses nearest the vehicle when two or more teams are used. **1969** Sorden *Lumberjack Lingo* 89 **NEng, Gt Lakes**, *Pole team*—The team nearest to the load. [**1970** *DARE* (Qu. K32b, *The horse on the left side in plowing or hauling*) Inf **NJ**67, Pole horse.]

2 In tobacco curing: see quot 1967. Cf **poleburn, tier pole**

1890 [see **poleburn**]. **1905** Odlum *Culture of Tobacco* 77, The tobacco . . is hauled to the barn, placed astride the curing sticks . . and hung on the rafters or poles. **1967** Key *Tobacco Vocab.* 172 **CT**, *Pole*—16' length of wood over which laths of tob[acco] are hung in the shed. *Ibid* **PA**, In the old days . . they went to the woods and cut long poles and put them in instead of these square . . rectangular rails that we later had.

3 A slender tree; see quots; hence n *pole wood* wood from small or immature trees.

1894 in 1904 *DN* 2.400, We may distinguish three corresponding stages, namely, the 'thicket' or brushwood, the 'pole-wood' or sapling, and the 'timber' stage. **1900** Bruncken *N. Amer. Forests* 97, Today he goes over the same lands and takes what he left thirty years ago, this time down to the "pole" of eight inches and less in diameter. **1905** U.S. Forest Serv. *Bulletin* 61.17, *Pole.* . . A tree from 4 to 12 inches in diameter breasthigh. . . A *small pole* is a tree from 4 to 8 inches in diameter breasthigh. . . A *large pole* is a tree from 8 to 12 inches in diameter breasthigh. **1908** Day *King Spruce* 81 **ME**, He cut her [=the timber] three times. . . third time, even the poles. That's forestry as he practises it! He's robbin' the squirrels! **1947** Oakley *Restin'* 23 **eTN**, The old man was chopping up poles as I call them. The man had cut down trees out at the edge of yard or near by the woods and drag these poles into the house. **1958** McCulloch *Woods Words* 137 **Pacific NW**, *Poles*—Small merchantable timbers, peeled or unpeeled. **1984** *MJLF* 10.154 **cnWI**, *Pole wood.* Limbs and small trees cut for firewood. **1997** *DARE* File **NEng**, The partridge are all in the pole popple this time of year—those skinny, tall, parallel, young popples that don't have many lower branches, that grow up fast in a cut over area. Pole spruce are good for making canoe poles but not much else.

pole v

1 also with *it:* To move or travel, esp in a slow, leisurely, or aimless manner; to saunter, amble. [Cf *SND* powl v.[1] 2 "To propel oneself with the aid of a crutch . . ; hence, by extension, . . to walk at a good steady pace, to bowl along"] **chiefly S Midl**

1892 Harris *On Plantation* 111 **GA** [Black], I des put out, I did, an' I went a polin' home, an' it make me feel mighty good when I got dar. **1902** *DN* 2.242 **sIL**, *Pole.* . . To move. Especially in the phrases 'to *pole along,*' to travel leisurely or lazily; 'to *pole in,*' to arrive late, without haste, or regard to time. **1905** *DN* 3.90 **nwAR**, He come a-polin'. **1907** *DN* 3.225 **nwAR**, *Pole.* . . To move; to travel leisurely. **1924** (1946) Greer-Petrie *Angeline Gits an Eyeful* 22 **csKY**, Him and Bob come *a-pollin'* [sic] in when we-uns went to the big ball room. **1942** McAtee *Dial. Grant Co.* IN 49 (as of 1890s), *Pole* . . move or travel, especially slowly or dilatorily; "He poled in after dark". **1944** *PADS* 2.48 **eNC, VA,** *Pole along.* **1946** *PADS* 6.24 **eNC** (as of 1900–10), *Pole around.* . . To go around from place to place. Said of gangs of small boys prowling around and bent on mischief. Pamlico. **c1960** *Wilson Coll.* **csKY,** *Poling along.* . . slouching, going slowly or aimlessly. **1972** *Atlanta Letters* **cnGA,** My mother used to say of someone coming down the road: "Here comes somebody *poling* down the road." . . I believe the expression "poling" meant *slowly* but nothing to do with *water.* **a1975** Lunsford *It Used to Be* 176 **sAppalachians,** "To pole" means to walk. "I had to just pole it up through there."

2 To put **riders 1** on a fence.

1662 in 1901 Portsmouth RI *Early Rec.* 116, All out fences . . beinge sufishently Staked and pould. **1962** *Mt. Life* 38.1.18 **sAppalachians,** The mountain farmer . . "poles" his fences.

3 To carry (hay) on a pair of long poles; hence vbl n *poling.* [Attested earlier in US, but prob of Engl dial origin; cf *EDD pole* v. 7] Cf **hay pole 2**

1779 *Narragansett Hist. Reg.* I.92 *(DAE),* Made hay and poled. **1828** Webster *Amer. Dict., Pole.* . . To bear or convey on poles; as, to *pole* hay into a barn. **1940–41** Cassidy *WI Atlas,* 1 inf, **csWI,** Poling hay—method of carrying wild hay off the wet ground on which it grew: lay down 2 . . parallel poles, pile hay on these. Two men, one at each end. **1968** *DARE* (Qu. L11, *What do you do to hay in the field after it's cut?*) Inf **CT**14, Heap it up and pole it off—old-fashioned. [FW: used by Inf in conv] [Inf old]

poleax n Also *pole axe, poll axe* [Appar a reinterpretation of std *poleax* on the basis of *poll* the heavy striking face opposite the cutting edge of a std American-pattern single-bitted axhead] A single-bitted ax.

1800 in 1969 Herndon *Wm. Tatham Tobacco* 10 **VA,** Felling the timber with a poll-axe. [Footnote:] This is a short, thick, heavy-headed axe, of a somewhat oblong shape, with which the Americans make great dispatch. They treat the English poll-axe with great contempt, and always work it over again as old iron before they deem it fit for their use. **1939** *Hall Coll.* **wNC,** And my grandmother she grabbed the ax, . . pole-ax, and she went, hit it [a deer] one lick. **1953** Randolph–Wilson *Down in Holler* 53 **Ozarks,** City people often think that choppin' in choppin'-ax is redundant, not knowing that it distinguishes the ordinary double-bitted ax from the pole-ax and the broad-ax. **1956** Sorden–Ebert *Logger's Words* 26 **Gt Lakes,** *Pole-ax,* Used for chipping and driving wedges and for releasing a crosscut-saw from binding when trees were being felled. Used in felling trees in early logging. A single-bit-ax. **1964** Clarkson *Tumult* 368 **WV,** *Pole-ax*—An ax with a sharp blade on one side and square on the other side. . . Same as a single-bitted ax. **1966–70** *DARE* (Qu. L35, *Hand tools used for cutting underbrush and digging out roots*) Infs **KY**43, **TN**62, Poleax; **OK**18, Poleax—a regular ax sharpened on one side. **1966** *DARE* Tape **ME**19, [FW:] They use any different kinds of axes? [Inf:] Why, poleaxes. And some people call them double-bitted. The poleax and the double-bitted one. **1968** *Foxfire* 2.2.8 **nGA,** "Pole" Axe—A single bladed axe of the type the early farms had. **1975** Gould *ME Lingo* 213, *Pole-ax*—Maine for the single-bitted ax. **1997** *DARE* File **cnWI,** A poleax is a single-bitted axe. The blunt side is called the poll. It has a knob on it similar to de-horned cattle.

pole barn n Also *pole shed;* for addit varr see quots **chiefly Missip-Ohio Valleys, Gt Lakes, Upstate NY, CT, Mid Atl** See Map

A barn or shed constructed without a sill, having instead poles or studs sunk into the ground and sided with wood or corrugated metal.

1924 Croy *R.F.D.* 78 **MO,** [He] had gone to the pole barn with a rope around his waist played from the door by his wife. **1950** *AmSp* 25.85 **OR,** No longer heard is *old land,* though *pole barn* and *pole corral* still describe forms of construction. **1965–70** *DARE* (Qu. M1, *. . Kinds of barns . . according to their use or the way they are built*) 138 Infs, **chiefly Missip-Ohio Valleys, Gt Lakes, Upstate NY, CT, Mid Atl,** Pole barn; **CT**2, Pole barn—put poles in ground and build up; no foundation; **CT**14, Pole barn—more of a shelter than a barn; **IA**26, Pole barn—shelter for cattle, machinery, etc—most common type now; **IA**31, Pole barn—most common now; prefabricated; **IL**41, Pole barn—enclosed on three sides; made out of poles covered with sheet metal; **IL**73, Pole barn—open to the south; **KY**84, Pole barn—creosoted posts, metal sides and roofs, used for hay storage; **MI**47, Pole barn—sink poles in the ground, instead of having sills; poles covered with vertical boards on the outside; **MN**31, Pole barn—has a roof for sure; may not have sides;

MN40, Pole barn—a shelter, easy to get into; new barn; **MS**4, Pole barn—no foundation; made with creosote poles; **SC**19, Pole barn—also pole house; **SC**32, Pole barn—this is boarded up and the absence of any sills is especially significant in its construction—the poles are set into the ground; **SC**34, Pole barn—without sills; put posts in ground and put on siding; **SD**2, Pole barn—poles in ground 6 or 8 feet apart; 2 x 8's nailed on outside; [**SC**47, Log barn = pole barn; **WV**2, Pole barn same as log barn; small logs;] **AR**40, **MI**8, **MO**18, Pole-type barn; **CT**9, Pole-type barn—built today to save money; hayloft not needed for bales; more of a shed; **MO**11, **WI**24, 63, 66, Pole(-type) shed; **IN**17, Closed-face (*or* open-face) pole barn; **PA**141, Pole loafing barn; **WI**68, Pole buildings; (Qu. M22, *. . Kinds of buildings . . on farms*) Inf **MO**27, Pole shed. **1967** *WI Statist. Reporting Serv. Report* 8 Aug 2, Several farmers building new pole barns. **1970** *DARE* Tape **IL**114, [FW:] What is it made out of, metal or what? [Inf:] They just sat poles in the ground, you see, and then put hangers acrost each pole. They can soon build 'em, the pole barns. **1986** Pederson *LAGS Concordance,* 1 inf, **ceTX,** Pole barn—barn made of poles; 1 inf, **nwGA,** Pole shed. **1988** *DARE* File **cwWI,** A pole shed is a large building on a farm. It's made out of sheet metal, and is typically barn-sized, though not as tall. It houses farm machinery, miscellaneous farm equipment, etc. **1991** Heat Moon *PrairyErth* 378 **ceKS,** At the pole barn we get out, and I follow him in to see a peculiar-looking steel-wheeled tractor.

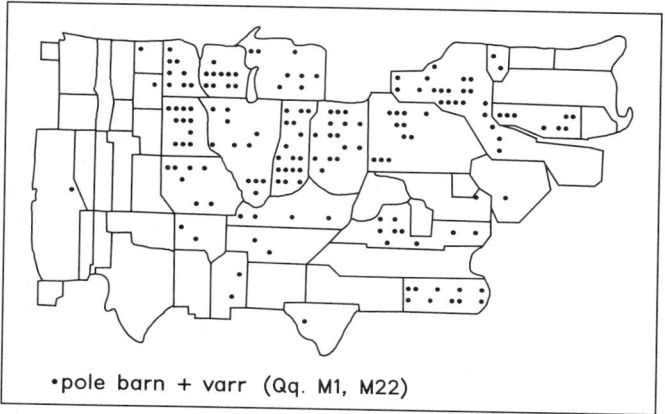

•pole barn + varr (Qq. M1, M22)

pole boat n

A shallow boat designed to be poled.

1827 in 1910 Commons *Doc. Hist. Amer. Industrial Soc.* 1.285, I saw three large pole boats loaded with bales of cotton. **1851** *De Bow's Rev.* 10.578 (as of 1820s), The town of Macon, in Georgia, had sprung up . . ; and the cotton received there from the rich and fertile country around, was seeking its way, but by the very slow process of pole-boats, to Darien. **1930** Shoemaker *1300 Words* 46 **cPA Mts** (as of c1900), *Poleboat*—A trim, graceful boat, of Indian design, propelled by a long pole, with metallic tip. **c1945** Hopkins *Okefenokee* 53 *(DA),* One Jesse Aldridge had made many poleboat loads of Okefenokee moonshine at this place. **1950** (1965) Richter *Town* 97 **OH,** Or you could go by boat clean to the grove's edge on the river bank, and that's how Chancey and his father and most of the boatmen went today, in rowboats and poleboats and flatboats. **1968** Adams *Western Words* 232, *Pole boat*—A river boat; so called because of the means by which it was propelled upstream. The boat, usually made of pine planks, was 20 to 30 feet long, 3 to 5 feet wide, 2 to 3 feet deep. It was pointed at both ends and had a flat bottom. Even when heavily loaded, it could be moved in water less than a foot deep. It was easily navigated downstream by means of ores [sic] or poles, but going upstream, especially against a rapid current, was a far different matter. The crew consisted of four, six, or eight men, depending on the size of the craft. Each man was armed with a long, stout pole made of ash or hickory, with a heavy, wrought-iron spike at one end. **1968** *DARE* (Qu. O1, *. . A small rowboat, not big enough to hold more than two people*) Inf **GA**30, Pole boat (one-man); **PA**155, Pole boat—even though they do use oars; (Qu. O10, *. . Kinds of boats*) Inf **GA**30, Pole boat.

poleburn n Also *pole sweat* [**pole** n 2] Cf **pole rot**

In tobacco curing: decay due to excessive moisture; hence v *poleburn.*

1868 *New Engl. Homestead* 22 Aug 116/4, Another thing to guard against, which occurs after the tobacco is hung for curing, is sweating, or 'pole burn.' **1890** *Century Dict.* 4591, *Pole-burn.* . . To discolor and lose flavor by overheating, as tobacco when hung too closely on poles in the first stage of the curing process. **1905** Odlum *Culture of Tobacco* 72, *Diseases of Tobacco while Curing (Pole Burn, Pole Sweat, or House Burn).*—Pole burn in the tobacco barn is due to excessive humidity, and is very likely to be present during prolonged warm wet weather. *Ibid* 77, If firing be delayed too long the tobacco may suffer from "pole burn." **1911** *Century Dict. Suppl., Pole-sweat.* . . Same as *pole-burn.* **1925** *Book of Rural Life* 9.5538, In very damp weather a rot may attack the leaves of tobacco and cause serious damage. This is known as *houseburn,* or *poleburn.* **1940** *AmSp* 15.134 [Tobacco market language], *Pole-sweat or house-burn.* Decomposition due to the fermentation of excessive sap or moisture in tobacco which is being cured in the grower's barn. **1967** *DARE* Tape PA6, In the shed. . . hang four-foot laths. . . They must dry, must have air. If it's damp, ugly weather, they get too damp and it starts to decay in there and that's called poleburn or pole rot. **1967** Key *Tobacco Vocab.* 33 **CT,** *Pole-burn* . . *pole-sweat* . . spoils the leaf for almost anything. *Ibid* **PA,** *Pole-burn.*

polecat n [*OED2* 1320 → for *Mustela putorius,* a strong-smelling European weasel]

1 =**skunk;** sometimes esp the small **spotted skunk.** Note: The 17th cent quots may refer instead to *Mustela* spp. **widespread, but more freq Sth, S Midl** See Map
  c1612 (1849) Strachey *Hist. VA Britannia* 193, A polecat, [in the "Indian" language:] *cuttenamvwhwa.* **1649** in 1838 Force *Tracts* 2.8.16 **VA,** *Martins, Poule Cats, Weesels, Minks:* but these Vermine hurt not Hens, Chickins or Eggs, at any time. **1688** in 1695 Royal Soc. London *Philos. Trans. for 1694* 18.124 **VA,** There are several sorts of *Wild Cats,* and *Poll-Cats.* **1709** (1967) Lawson *New Voyage* 124, Polcats or Skunks in *America,* are different from those in *Europe.* They are thicker, and of a great many Colours. . . They smell like a Fox, but ten times stronger. When a Dog encounters them, they piss upon him, and he will not be sweet again in a Fortnight or more. **1743** Catesby *Nat. Hist. Carolina* 2.62, *Putorius Americanus striatus—The Pol-Cat.* . . From some secret Duct, it emits such fetid Effluviums, that the Atmosphere for a large Space round shall be so infected with them, that Men and other Animals are impatient till they are quit of it. **1791** Bartram *Travels* 7 **GA,** Oppossoms are here in abundance, as also pole-cats, wild-cats [etc]. **1844** Thompson *Major Jones's Courtship* 55 **GA,** Thar it is—that black and white thing—on that log. . . P-e-u-g-h! oh, my lord; look out, fellers! its a pole-cat! **1902** *DN* 2.243 **sIL,** *Polecat.* . . The skunk, a term which is used. **1907** *DN* 3.225 **nwAR,** *Polecat.* . . The skunk. **1937** Grinnell et al. *Fur-Bearing Mammals CA* 322, The striped skunk is sometimes called "polecat," but this name is more generally applied to the smaller spotted species. **1949** Kurath *Word Geog.* 74, The regular Southern term for the skunk is *pole cat,* an expression that is common also in Pennsylvania west of the Susquehanna and in the South Midland. *Pole cat* doubtless was formerly more common in the Midland; the Northern *skunk* (of Indian origin), supported by literary usage, has made its way into the Midland and even into the Southern area. **1950** *WELS (Names and nicknames for the skunk)* 33 Infs, **WI,** Polecat. **1965–70** *DARE* (Qu. P26) 657 Infs, **widespread, but more freq Sth, S Midl,** Polecat; (Qu. P31) Infs **NY24, 231,** Polecat; **LA44,** Polecat—it will try to piss on you if it can; (Qu. P32) Inf **VA7,** Polecat; (Qu. V2c, *About a deceiving person, or somebody that you can't trust* . . *"I wouldn't trust him any further than I could* _____."; not asked in early QRs) Inf **NJ28,** Throw a polecat; (Qu. BB50b, *Remedies for chest colds*) Infs **IN10, OH65,** Polecat grease; (Qu. HH22b, *A very mean person* . . *"He's meaner than* _____.") Infs **IL116, LA37, NY241,** a polecat; (Qu. II11b, *If two people can't bear each other at all* . . *"Those two are* _____.") Inf **FL22,** Rattlesnake and polecat. **1966–69** *DARE* Tape **GA1,** Well, a polecat is smaller than a skunk. You got stripes more, you know, up and down. Sort of like stripes on a zebra or something like that, just white and black. They're close together. And a skunk, you got a black stripe down his back and on his sides is white. . . Both threw the scent the same way, but there's a difference in a polecat and a skunk. *Ibid* **GA74,** And until the skunk was aroused, which we called a polecat, you wouldn't know what it was. You might think it was a possum that he [=a dog] had treed in that. **1970** Tarpley *Blinky* 151 **neTX,** *Skunk* and *polecat* are used interchangeably as names for the black animal which has a white stripe and is notorious for its unpleasant odor. The frequency of *skunk* diminishes in ratio to the increase of the informant's age, while the reverse is true for *polecat. Skunk* is most popular among women, in the highest educational category, and in non-rural communities; the opposite trend may be noted for *polecat.* **1972** *PADS* 58.22 **cwAL,** Skunk. Northern *skunk* (17 [of 27 infs]) is more common than Southern and Midland *polecat* (9) as a primary response,

but a number of informants gave both terms. **1973** Allen *LAUM* 1.321 **Upper MW** (as of c1950), 27 infs, Polecat [8 of these infs indicated that they had heard this term from others.]; 1 inf, Polecat—spotted; 1 inf, Polecat—solid color; 1 inf, Polecat—It has wider stripes than a skunk; 1 inf, Polecat—It has stripes around its body; a skunk has stripes the length of its body; 1 inf, Polecat—Smaller and less vicious than a skunk. **1986** Pederson *LAGS Concordance* **Gulf Region,** 587 infs, Polecat(s); 8 infs, Polecat(s)—usual term; 1 inf, Polecat—more usual than skunk; 1 inf, Polecat—the right name; 1 inf, Polecat—its real name; 1 inf, We call them polecats; 1 inf, Polecat—older term; 1 inf, Polecat—old-fashioned country usage; 1 inf, Polecat—used formerly; 1 inf, Polecats—used when growing up; 1 inf, Polecats—older people use term more frequently; 1 inf, Polecat—not allowed to say—not "genteel"; 1 inf, Polecat—sprinkles you with water; 1 inf, Polecats—it took a long pole to kill them; 1 inf, Polecat—you know him when you done met him.

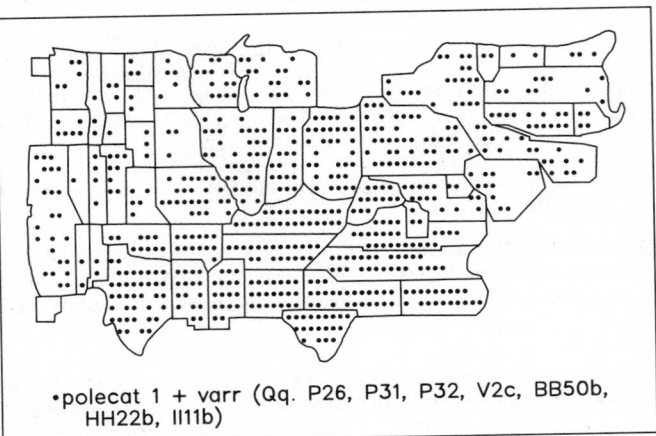

•polecat 1 + varr (Qq. P26, P31, P32, V2c, BB50b, HH22b, II11b)

2 Transf:
a A despicable or deceitful person. [Cf *OED2 polecat* sb. 2 1598–1790] **esp Sth, S Midl**
  1896 *Harper's New Mth. Mag.* 92.578 **VA,** Stand on your laigs, you polecat, and say you're a liar. [**1898** in 1917 Twain *What is Man* 170, He is . . a . . timid, sneaking, human polecat.] **1942** Berrey–Van den Bark *Amer. Slang* 397, *Contemptible person.* . . polecat. *Ibid* 435.1, *Disreputable person.* . . polecat. **1954** Harder *Coll.* **cwTN,** *Polecat.* . . A deceiving person. *Ibid,* Sneakin' 'round lak polecat. **1958** McCulloch *Woods Words* 137 **Pacific NW,** *Polecat.* . . A no-good man. [**1960** Carpenter *Tales Manchaca* 112 **cTX,** Indeed these human polecats added despicable refinements to their father's scurviness. They habitually got roaring drunk, beat their wives, and underfed, cursed, and abused their children.] **1966–70** *DARE* (Qu. V6, . . *Words* . . *for a thief*) Inf **IL126,** Polecat; (Qu. NN24, *Humorous substitutes for stronger exclamations: "Why the son of a* _____!") Inf **MO1,** Polecat. **1972** Shafer *Dict. Prison Slang* 29, *Pole cat*—an informer. **1981** Pederson *LAGS Basic Materials* **Gulf Region,** 1 inf, Polecat—[a] "sneaky" person; 1 inf, Polecat—referring to people; 1 inf, Polecat—of person you don't like; 1 inf, Polecats—could be used for people who "act ugly"; 1 inf, Polecat—not commonly used, more often of persons.
b A Black person. *derog*
  1981 Pederson *LAGS Basic Materials,* 1 inf, **cAR,** Polecats—derogatory term for Blacks; 1 inf, **seMS,** Black polecat—very dark [Black person]. [Both infs Black]

3 in phr *polecat under the table:* =**nigger in the woodpile 1a.**
  1932 Toone *Yankee Slang* 29, *Pole-cat under the table:* Crooked proposition; English: It has a nasty smell.

4 Among loggers:
a See quots.
  1931 *AmSp* 7.48 **Sth, SW** [Lumberjack lingo], "Tie men" who camp far out from the main camps are called "Ground Hogs" or "Pole Cats." These men often boast of living so far back in the woods that they use hoot owls for poultry and skunks for watch dogs.
b See quot. *joc* Cf **pole** n 3, **cat** n 1d
  1950 *Western Folkl.* 9.119 **nwOR** [Logger speech], *Pole cat* or *pole hack.* One who peels piling or telephone poles.

5 The foamy material that rises to the surface in boiling cane or sorghum syrup. [Appar from its strong odor] Cf **soo cat**

1968 *DARE* FW Addit **GA26,** Polecat—the foamy stuff that has to be dipped off when [cane sugar] syrup is being made. [FW: used by Inf and others; old-fashioned] **1998** *NADS Letters* **swAR,** Re: your inquiry about "polecat." As a young child (forty years ago) I heard the term applied to the syrup making process by a maternal great uncle (long ago deceased) who was the only grower of sorghum in our rural community in southwestern Arkansas. *Ibid* **seGA,** I asked a cousin of mine whose brother makes cane syrup in Waycross, Georgia [about the term *polecat* for cane-skimmings]. His answer was: ". . I have been able to find one person that has heard the skimmings called that, most of the people that I talked to has not heard of this, probably before our time." **2000** *Ibid* **cnFL,** In north central Florida . . [polecat] is *not* the stuff that is dipped off. It is the foamy stuff that cooks onto the side of the kettle. At a certain point, the syrup makers will announce "The polecat's ready," and everyone takes a piece of trimmed cane and scrapes it off the side. It's like taffy, and the longer it cooks, of course, the harder it gets. . . I don't think it smells all that strong, but you don't have to sniff real hard to get the full bouquet. **2000** *DARE* File—Internet **seGA,** You are very Wiregrass if . . you know what polecat is, the kind you eat that you scrape off the sides of a syrup kettle with a piece of cane stalk.

polecat bush n Also *polecat berry,* ~ *sumac*
Either of two **sumacs: fragrant sumac** or *Rhus trilobata.*
    1913 *Torreya* 13.232 **MO,** *Rhus canadensis* . . Polecat berries, Cedar Gap, Ozark Mts., Mo. **1937** U.S. Forest Serv. *Range Plant Hdbk.* B129, Skunkbush. . . other common names include lemita, lemonade sumac, polecat bush [etc]. **1940** Steyermark *Flora MO* 331, *Polecat Bush* . . *(Rhus aromatica)*. . . Throughout Mo. . . *Polecat Bush* . . *(Rhus trilobata* var. *serotina)*. . . Similar in habit and height. . . Southern, central, and eastern Mo. **1941** Writers' Program *Guide MO* 24, The sumach, which is locally called polecat bush. **1973** Stephens *Woody Plants* 330, *Rhus aromatica*. . . Aromatic sumac, fragrant sumac, polecat sumac.

polecat collard See **polecat weed**

polecat geranium n
A naturalized **lantana** (here: *Lantana montevidensis*).
    1933 Small *Manual SE Flora* 1142 **FL,** *L[antana] Selloviana* [=*L. montevidensis*]. . . Polecat-geranium. Weeping-lantana . . Roadsides, waste-places, pinelands, and woods. **1953** Greene–Blomquist *Flowers South* 109 **FL,** The weeping-lantana or "polecat-geranium" . . is a shrub with hairy leaves and magenta or lilac corollas. Naturalized. . . Coastal Plain, pinelands, roadside, and waste places. **1970** Correll *Plants TX* 1328, *Lantana montevidensis* . . Polecat-geranium. . . also established in Ga., Fla., Ala., Calif.

polecat pea n Cf **crowder**
A **black-eyed pea** (here: *Vigna unguiculata* subsp *unguiculata*).
    1988 Whealy *Garden Seed Inventory* (2d ed) 162, *Calico Crowder* (Herford Peas, Polecat Peas, Calico Cowpea). . . Mild flavor. . . Med-large white peas with maroon-red splotches. **1990** *Seed Savers Yearbook* 104 **TX,** *Pole Cat Peas*. . . [First source:] Calico crowder from TX, very heavy producer. . . [Second source:] calico crowder, been in my family 60+ yrs., came from my now deceased Grandfather . . from Mt. Calm TX.

polecat plant n
=**scarlet gilia.**
    1915 (1926) Armstrong–Thornber *Western Wild Flowers* 394, This [= *Ipomopsis aggregata*] grows on mountain sides and sometimes has a very disagreeable smell, hence the local name of Polecat Plant. **1967** Dodge *Roadside Wildflowers* 58 **SW,** The crushed leaves of skyrocket [=*Ipomopsis aggregata*] have a skunky odor, hence the name polecat plant.

polecat sumac See **polecat bush**

polecat tree n
1 also *polecat wood:* Usu **Carolina buckthorn 1,** but also **cascara 1.**
    1897 Sudworth *Arborescent Flora* 298, *Rhamnus caroliniana*. . . Polecat-tree (Tex.). Polecat-wood (Ark.) **1933** Small *Manual SE Flora* 832, *R[hamnus] caroliniana*. . . Indian-cherry. Yellow-wood. Polecat-tree. . . Fla. to Tex., Kans., and Va. **1960** Vines *Trees SW* 702, Other vernacular names [for *Rhamnus caroliniana*] are Yellow Buckthorn, Indian-cherry, Bog-birch, Alder-leaf Buckthorn, and Polecat-tree. **1974** (1977) Coon

Useful Plants 235, *Rhamnus purschiana* [sic]—Cascara sagrada, brittle wood, polecat tree.
2 A **false indigo 1** (here: *Amorpha fruticosa*).
    1940 Clute *Amer. Plant Names* 251, *Amorpha fruticosa*. Polecat-tree, sachet-bush, river locust. **1955** *S. Folkl. Qrly.* 19.235 **FL,** So far I have been unable to determine why False Indigo is called Polecat Tree *(Amorpha fruticosa)*.
3 A **hop tree** (here: *Ptelea trifoliata*). [See quot]
    1946 *Nat. Hist.* 55.143, The pretty little tree or shrub known scientifically as *Ptelea trifoliata* has many peculiarities and many names. . . some give it the epithet of Skunk Bush, or Polecat Tree, because of the unpleasant odor of its crushed leaves.
4 =**Florida anise-tree.**
    1960 Vines *Trees SW* 278, *Florida anise*. . . Other vernacular names are Polecat-tree [etc]. **1979** Little *Checklist U.S. Trees* 151, *Florida anise-tree*. . . Other common names—polecat-tree, purple anise-tree [etc].

polecat under the table See **polecat 3**

polecat weed n Also *polecat collard*
=**skunk cabbage 1a.**
    1739 (1946) Gronovius *Flora Virginica* 2.186, *Calla* aquatilis odore allii vehemente praedita, radice repente. vulgo *Pole Cadweed* [sic]. [= The water-dwelling *Calla*, which has a strong garlic odor and a creeping root. In common speech *Pole Cadweed*.] **1854** King *Amer. Eclectic Dispensatory* 922, The whole plant [=*Symplocarpus foetidus*], especially when bruised, emits a very disagreeable alliaceous odor, which has given rise to the several names, *Skunk-weed, Skunk-cabbage, Pole-cat-weed,* and *Meadow-cabbage*. **1949** Moldenke *Amer. Wild Flowers* 347, This plant [=skunk cabbage], also called midasears, parson-in-a-pillory, and polecatweed, is found in swamps and low meadows from Georgia (and possibly Florida) to Missouri, northward to Minnesota and Nova Scotia. **1958** Jacobs–Burlage *Index Plants NC* 17, *Symplocarpus foetidus*. . . Poke; cow collard, polecat-collard [etc]. **1970** *Living Museum* 31.180 **IL,** Known by such descriptive epithets as swamp cabbage, parson-in-a-pillory, polecatweed, and devil's tobacco, the skunk cabbage, a relative of jack-in-the-pulpit, ushers in the growing season.

polecat wood See **polecat tree 1**

pole drag n Cf **go-devil** n **2d**
A **travois.**
    1920 Hunter *Trail Drivers TX* 285 (as of 1880), While crossing the Washita we broke a wagon wheel, and had to use a pole drag for one hundred and fifty miles to Wolf Creek. **1975** Gould *ME Lingo* 110, The pole drag of the Indians—poles dragging like unattached thills behind a single horse—has been used for bringing game out of the woods.

pole dray n Cf **go-devil** n **2d**
    1950 *WELS Suppl.* **cwWI,** Pole dray—Like a stoneboat but without sideboards. Seen at the centennial exhibit. *Ibid,* Pole dray—another name for go-devil. (Lumbering term).

pole gate n Cf **pair of bars**
A simple gate consisting of loose poles that can be moved out of the way to allow passage.
    1940 U.S. Dept. Ag. *Farmers' Bulletin* No. 1832 46, In a timbered section pole gates . . may be economically used for fields entered infrequently. [*DARE* Ed: Photo shows gate of 6 loose poles that can be slid to one side.] **1949** Guthrie *Way West* 22 **MO,** He walked to the fence and let down the bars of the pole gate.

pole it See **pole** v **1**

polekitty n [By facetious analogy with **polecat 1**]
=**skunk.**
    2000 *NADS Letters* **cIN,** I live in central IN and of course we refer to skunks as polecats and polekittys.

Pole mushroom See **Polack mushroom**

polenta n [Ital; *OED2* c1000 →] **formerly esp CA, but now more widely recognized** See Map on p. 252
A type of cornmeal mush; see esp quot 1979.
    1895 (1900) Arnold *Century Cook Book* 227, *Polenta*. . . Make a cornmeal mush; boil it . . until it is firm. . . Pour [sauce] over it. **1950** *WELS (Dishes made with veal)* 1 Inf, **cnWI,** Polenta and veal. **1965–70** *DARE* (Qu. H24, . . *Names or nicknames . . for boiled cornmeal*) Infs

CA144, OR1, WA11, Polenta—Italian; CA24, Polenta—Italians use; put chicken, etc, in mush; CA126, Polenta—Italian dish, cornmeal with gravy and cheese; CA139, [pə'lɑntə]—cornmeal cooked with another kind of flour—cooked a long, long time; an Italian dish; NJ26, [pə'læntɪs]—Italian; (Qu. H25, . . *Names or nicknames . . for fried cornmeal*) Inf CA170, Polenta; (Qu. H45, *Dishes made with meat, fish, or poultry that everybody around here would know, but that people in other places might not*) Inf CA24, Polenta; CO27, Chicken polenta—cornmeal and chicken in a tomato paste; MA98, [po'lɛntə]—Italian; fine cornmeal; (Qu. H50, *Dishes made with beans, peas, or corn that everybody around here knows, but people in other places might not*) Inf CA126, Polenta; (Qu. H65, *Foreign foods favored by people around here*) Infs CA24, 105, 144, 170, MA98, Polenta; WA11, Polenta—Italian. **1971** Bright *Word Geog. CA & NV* 111, Polenta—1 response "a corn meal"; informant . . of Italian descent. . . polenta—1 response for 'scrapple'. **1979** Flagg *Cape Cod Cooking* 176, Although not like other pasta dishes, polenta is very popular. It is simply cornmeal mush, but served with cheese, gravy or sauce, as the Italians do. **1989** *Parade* 12 Nov 9, Versatile polenta, Italian-style cornmeal mush, turns up in chicken soup at Chez Panisse, a food mecca in Berkeley, Calif.

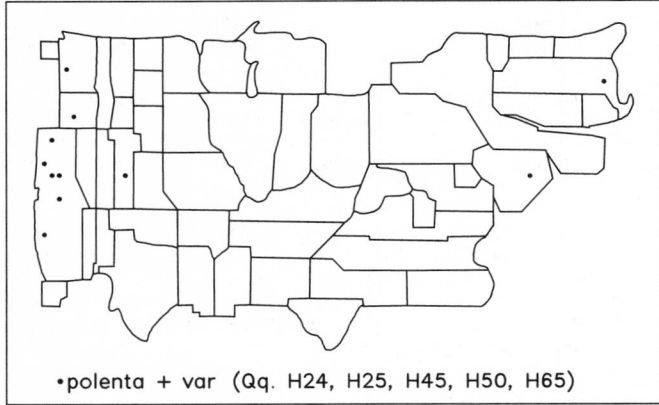

•polenta + var (Qq. H24, H25, H45, H50, H65)

pole railroad (or railway) See **pole road 2a**

pole road n

1 A road constructed with transverse poles or rails laid side by side; a corduroy road.

1864 in 1891 U.S. War Dept. *War of Rebellion* 1st ser 36.2.909, Wagon train took pole road in direction of Sycamore. **1903** *DN* 2.325 seMO, Pole-road. . . A causeway or crossway, made by laying down poles or logs close together and covering with earth. **1968–69** *DARE* (Qu. N27a, *Names . . for different kinds of unpaved roads*) Inf MD15, Pole road—poles laid over bad spots in muddy road, in old days; MO17, Pole roads; (Qu. N27b, *When unpaved roads get very rough, you call them _____*) Inf NJ56, Pole roads—rows of cedar rails. **1968** *DARE* Tape IN9, My great-grandmother told about coming up the knobs out north of us, that it was a pole road, an old mud pole road. **1986** Pederson *LAGS Concordance,* 1 inf, neTN, Pole roads; 1 inf, nwFL, Pole roads—use pine rails on muddy road. **1997** *DARE* File cnWI, The pole road refers to a corduroy road.

2 In logging:

a also *pole railroad,* ~ *railway:* A road with two parallel lines of poles laid along it to serve as rails for vehicles fitted with broad, flanged wheels.

1878 *Lumberman's Gaz.* 6 Apr 302 MI, [They] use on these pole railroad[s] trucks with iron wheels. *Ibid* 302, These pole roads can be laid in the "branch roads" direct to the skidways. *Ibid* 11 June 518 MI, Chas. Bowman has completed a 2½ mile pole railway on the north branch of the Cedar. **1893** *Scribner's Mag.* 13.708 MI, "Pole-roads" are built, where cars with wheels with concave faces run on poles instead of rails. **1913** Bryant *Logging* 242, Pole roads were formerly used by lumbermen because the material for construction could be secured on the operation at no expense except for labor and stumpage but they are primitive in character and are now seldom used except on an occasional small operation where sawed wooden rails or steel rails cannot be secured at reasonable cost. **1958** [see **2b** below]. **1961** Labbe–Goe *Railroads* 259 **Pacific NW,** [Glossary:] Pole Road: A railroad made of small poles in lieu of rails. **1969** Sorden *Lumberjack Lingo* 88 **NEng, Gt Lakes,** Pole road—A road like a railroad track built of ten-inch or larger logs, doweled together at the end and roughly dressed on top to fit iron

concave wheels on which logs were carried to the river or the landing on railroad-type cars. These roads were generally built over swamp areas. The logs were greased, particularly at the corners, for ease of hauling. A tram road. **1981** Howell *Surv. Folklife* 118 neTN, seKY, Pole roads were tracks of parallel peeled saplings, eight to ten inches in diameter, joined at the ends like sections or log pipe. Heavy flatbed wagons were pulled over these tracks by mules or horses. **1983** Montell *Don't Go Up* 93 **csKY, cnTN,** Some logging operations were large enough to merit construction of tram roads or pole roads from the river or railhead to the logging camps.

b A trough of longitudinal poles or logs along which logs are dragged or skidded; hence v phr *pole road* to drag logs using such a trough. **Pacific NW**

1919 *DN* 5.58 NW, Pole road. A trough-like path through the forest upon which logs are hauled by the donkey. ["]Connie Gilpin has changed jobs having gone chasing the pole-road when he was formerly blowing the whistles.["] Kalama Bulletin. **1958** McCulloch *Woods Words* 137 **Pacific NW,** Pole road. . . A V-shaped trough made of small logs used for hauling logs from the woods. . . A very crudely made trough of small poles intended to ease the skidding on poor ground. . . A railroad using small poles for rails, and horses or wheeled tractors for power. In this latter case the rolling stock all had cupped wheels. . . To haul logs by road donkey or otherwise, on a pole road or fore-and-aft road. **1967** *DARE* Tape WA20, Timber was felled and bucked, sawed into logs, in the woods and hauled out with these steam donkeys. . . And they were drug on the ground into a skid road or pole road or something and finally pushed down into water—the only transportation they had was water. . . [FW:] Could you explain for me the difference between a skid road and—I forget the other kind. [Inf:] A skid road is short logs, usually 10, 12 inches through, laying crossways of the direction you're going with to pull your logs. The skids were notched and they were greased with tallow and oxen pulled those. . . The pole road was where trees two and a half feet through and eighty to a hundred feet long were laid side by side with a smaller tree in between them—trimmed and placed and attached to one another in such a way they wouldn't spread apart. That was a pole road. **1967** *DARE* FW Addit cwWA, Pole road—replaced skid road—trough for cut logs to travel down from woods composed of two high logs with shorter log between, creating trough. Logs propelled along by steam donkey—old-fashioned.

pole road v phr See **pole road** n **2b**

pole rot n [**pole** n 2]
=poleburn.
1948 *AmSp* 23.310 csWI, Pole rot occurs when there is a great deal of damp weather between the harvest time and the first good frost. The tobacco is not yet brown, and the leaves begin to rot before the curing process can begin. **1965** *DARE* Tape WI1, This year has been a very bad year for tobacco because it's been so cold and damp . . so much of it has had pole rot. . . After you hang them on the pole, you know, they get rotten on the stems and the leaves fall off and fall to the ground. **1967** *DARE* [see **poleburn**].

pole shed See **pole barn**

pole sweat See **poleburn**

pole wagon n
1968 *DARE* (Qu. N41b, *Horse-drawn vehicles to carry heavy loads*) Inf CA86, Pole wagon—had two-by-fours bottom, shook by hand to spread dirt; OH42, Pole wagon—for gravel; you pull out one pole and the gravel came out the bottom. [Both Infs old]

poley n Cf *DS* X35
See quots.
1992 *DARE* File, Poley—rump, backside. **2000** *NADS Letters* CA, Poley—a cow's backside—farm term.

police n, v Usu |ˌpə'lis, ˌpo'lis|; also |plis|; also **chiefly Sth, S Midl** |'poˌlis, 'po'lis|; for addit varr see **A** below Pronc-sp *perlice* [*OED2* "In early use often pronounced ('pɒlɪs), as still often in Scotland and Ireland"]
A Forms.
1891 *DN* 1.160 cNY, The following words have the accent on the first syllable in most cases, though sometimes they are accented, as in educated speech . . *police*. **1916** Lowell *Men* 286 NEng, I told the perlice I hadn't nothin'. **1919** in 1993 Major *Calling the Wind* 20 [Black], I went to look fer 'im, en had the whole perlice station out all night huntin' 'im. **1928** *AmSp* 3.407 **Ozarks,** The hillman usually places a

strong emphasis upon the first syllable of . . *police.* **1936** *AmSp* 11.149 **eTX,** *Police* in careless or illiterate speech is sometimes [pliːs], sometimes [ˈpolis], with the accent shifted to the first syllable. **1941** *AmSp* 16.8 **eTX** [Black], *Police,* [ˈpoˌlis]. **1941** in 1944 *ADD* **eMA,** [Radio:] [plis]. **1942** Hall *Smoky Mt. Speech* 57 **wNC,** *Police* [pəˈlis] or [ˈpoˌlis]. **c1960** *Wilson Coll.* **csKY,** /ˈpoˌlis/—common. **1961** *Folk Word Atlas N. LA* 56, *Police,* the accent was generally shifted to the first syllable. **1965–70** *DARE* (Qu. N4, *A police vehicle*) 539 Infs, **widespread,** *Police* [in var combs]; **MD22, NJ67, SC4, 9, 21, 26, 42,** [ˈpolis]; **NY52, 70, PA72, 100, 167,** [plis]; **DC8, FL48, MD42,** [ˈpoˈlis]; (Qu. N3) Inf **MD13,** [ˈpoˈlis] car; (Qu. N33) Inf **LA15,** [ˈpoʊˌlis] jury member; (Qu. V9, . . *Nicknames . . for a policeman*) Inf **DC1,** [ˈpoʊˌlis] regularly; emphatic [ˈpoʊˈlis]; **MD9,** A police [ˈpoˈlis]; **MD21,** A police [ˈpolis]; **SC26,** [ˈpolis]; **TN27,** The real name is polices [ˈpoʊˌlisɪz]; **TX106,** [ˌpoˈlisɪz]—plural. **1966–68** *DARE* Tape **DC8,** And we have good bus service, nice fire department, and good police [ˈpoˌlis] department. *Ibid* **MD1,** [FW:] How did they finally get it stopped? [Inf:] Police [ˈpoˌlis]. And National Guard. *Ibid* **MS71,** The police [ˈpolis] walked up to question them. . . The boy hit the policeman [ˈpoˌlismən]. **1967** *DARE* FW Addit **nwLA,** *Police* [ˌpoʊˈlis]; "He's in the police jury room." **1968** [see **B1** below.] **1979** *NYT Article Letters* **Baltimore MD,** They stress the word *police* for police. **1994** Smitherman *Black Talk* 183, *PO-lice*—The police, A[frican] A[merican] E[nglish] pronunciation.

B As noun.

1 A police officer. [Scots; see *SND police* n. 3] **chiefly Sth, S Midl** Cf Intro "Language Changes" II.3, 7

1839 *Chicago American* 5 Sept. (*OED2*), There is a police in attendance . . in the theatre. **1856** (1928) Twain *Advent. Snodgrass* 8, He was a police. **1931** in 1970 Natl. Comm. Defense Political Prisoners *Harlan Miners* 202 **KY,** The Council hires the *Polices* and they knew if I got in I would be for another man. **1966–70** *DARE* (Qu. V9, . . *Nicknames . . for a policeman*) Infs **DC1, PA248, SC26,** Cop, police; **MD9, 21,** A police; **TN27,** The real name is polices; **TX106,** Polices; [**AR22,** Cops, police]. **1968** *DARE* FW Addit **Baltimore MD,** *Police* pronounced [ˈpoˈlis]. One policeman is *a police.* Common; not by highly educated. **1972** *Atlanta Jrl.–Constitution* (GA) 2 Jan mag sec 6 **neGA,** You couldn't get a police to work. **1986** Pederson *LAGS Concordance* **Gulf Region,** 9 infs, Polices; (Policeman; this question was asked chiefly in urban areas) 20 infs, Police. [16 of 29 total infs Black]

2 also in var phrr: Any of several children's games; see quots.

1950 *WELS* (*Games . . played during your childhood*) 1 Inf, **ceWI,** "Fire" or "police"—a rather sadistic game in which "it" chases the other players with a stick. When he catches a player he has the privilege of hitting him as hard as he pleases. **1966–67** *DARE* (Qu. EE3, *Games in which you hide an object and then look for it*) Inf **AL26,** Police and robber; (Qu. EE13a, *Games in which every player hides except one, and that one must try to find the others*) Inf **SC10,** Police find the robber— all of we goes in that thicket yonder.

police foot n

1963 Watkins–Watkins *Yesterday Hills* 131 **cnGA,** Athlete's foot, which for some reason the farmer called police foot, was treated with a poultice of cow manure.

police jury n **LA**

The governing body of a parish in Louisiana; hence n *police (jury) member.*

1840 *Picayune* 22 Aug. 2/1 (*DAE*) **New Orleans LA,** Will our friends. . . tell us what is meant in their city by the police jury. **1916** *DN* 4.270 **New Orleans LA,** *Police jury.* . . Board of Supervisors. (Official.) **1941** Writers' Program *Guide LA* 691, *Police jury*—The governing body of a parish. **1967** *Natchitoches Times* (LA) 19 Dec 1/8, Robert Lucky, Bobbie Cooper, and R.A. (Bob) Massey were elected to the Natchitoches Parish Police Jury from Ward 1 in the Democratic Second Primary Saturday. **1968** *DARE* (Qu. N33, *A man whose job is to take care of roads in a certain locality*) Inf **LA2,** Police member—in county roads [FW: that is, the delegate to the police jury from a certain ward]; **LA7,** Police member; **LA15,** Police jury member. **1968** *Leesville Leader* (LA) 15 Feb 1/7, A parish surplus of $50,000 was put to work "for as long as possible" by police jury members at the February 12 meeting of the parish governing body. **1984** Stall *Proud New Orleans* 171, *Police jury:* Same duties as county commissioner in other states. **1986** Pederson *LAGS Concordance,* 4 infs, **LA,** Police jury.

policeman n

Std sense, var forms.

Pl: usu *policemen;* also *policemans, policemens.* Cf Intro "Language Changes" II.3, **man B2**

1966 *DARE* (Qu. V10b, . . [*Joking names*] *for a marshal*) Inf **SC7,** Called policemans [ˈpolɪsmənz] now. **1970** *DARE* Tape **MS86,** We are paying these policemans . . the chief, five hundred dollars and the others, three. **1986** Pederson *LAGS Concordance* **Gulf Region,** 5 infs, Policemens; 2 infs, Policemans.

policeman's helmet n

A **jewelweed 1** (here: *Impatiens glandulifera*).

1973 Hitchcock–Cronquist *Flora Pacific NW* 289, Policeman's helmet . . I[mpatiens] glandulifera.

police member See **police jury**

policemens See **policeman**

policy man n

See quots.

1959 Lomax *Rainbow Sign* 109 **AL** [Black], When they walk up to your door, these old policy mens, these people tryin to sell you something, you can say any kind of impudent word to um. **1971** O'Connor *Complete Stories* 315, Scofield . . was an insurance salesman. . . but he sold the kind that only Negroes buy. He was what Negroes call a "policy man." *Ibid* 326, The Negro looked at her suddenly with a gleam of recognition. "Is you my policy man's mother?" he asked.

poling See **pole v 3**

polinky n Also sp *polinka, polinke, polinki* **esp PA**

See quots.

1888 *World* (NY NY) 14 Feb 6/6 **PA,** In all about two dozen people lived in the house, most of them men. Yesterday they all came to Hazleton and returned home drunk about 6 o'clock in the evening. They then indulged freely in "polinki," a mixture of bad beer and worse whiskey. **1889** (1971) Farmer *Americanisms* 429, Polinka or polinke.—A beverage made by mixing a gallon of cheap whiskey and a keg of beer together, with other foreign and nauseating ingredients. **1898** *Century Illustr. Mag.* 55.817 **PA,** After supper, following pay-day, a dozen boarders had formed a circle around a bucket containing a vile, poisonous liquor called *polinki.* **1938** (1964) Korson *Minstrels Mine Patch* 131 **nePA,** "Polinky" commemorates what once was the Slav's favorite refreshment and worst enemy. . . A recipe for making polinky: "Take an ordinary washtub or wash boiler, pour into it one keg of beer, one gallon of whiskey and half a pound of red pepper. Stir with a broom handle and drink from a tin cup at indiscretion."

polis See **poultice**

Polish n Cf **Dutch n 4, Indian n B2, Irish n¹ B1**

Dander, fighting spirit—in phr *get one's Polish up.*

1994 *DARE* File **cwMA,** Here in the Conn. River Valley another ethnic group can sometimes get its Polish [ˈpolɪš] up.

Polish dozen n

1995 *Daily Hampshire Gaz.* (Northampton MA) 6 Jan Suppl 6, The stuffed pastries come in four flavors . . and sell for $3.50 a Polish dozen, which is 14 pierogis.

Polish fire drill n
=**Chinese fire drill 1.**

1978 King *Stand* 486, I could make a bad decision and wind up killing both of you. I'm well on my way to killing Judge Farris and he's seconding my fucking nomination. What a Polish firedrill this turned out to be.

Polish flat n

1981 *DARE* File **Milwaukee WI,** A Polish flat is a two-story flat recognizable from the outside by three or four steps that go down to the ground floor about four feet below street level, and ten or twelve steps that lead up to the "first" floor.

Polish ham sausage See **Polish sausage**

‡polishing down vbl n [Var of *dressing down*]

1966 *DARE* (Qu. II27, *If somebody gives you a very sharp scolding . . "I certainly got a _____ for that."*) Inf **AR3,** Polishing down.

polishing rush n Cf **scouring rush**
A **horsetail 1.**

1900 Lyons *Plant Names* 147, *E[quisetum] hyemale*. . . The following names apply to this and other rough species: Dutch Rush . . Polishing Rush [etc].

Polish millet n Cf **millet**

A **crabgrass 1** (here: *Digitaria sanguinalis*).

1895 U.S. Dept. Ag. *Farmers' Bulletin* 28.25, Crab grass, finger grass, Polish millet. **1898** *Jrl. Amer. Folkl.* 11.283, *Panicum sanguinale* . . Polish millet. **1914** Georgia *Manual Weeds* 26, *Crab-grass*. . . *Other English names:* Finger Grass, Polish Millet [etc]. **1935** (1943) Muenscher *Weeds* 152, *Digitaria sanguinalis*. . . Finger-grass, Polish millet [etc].

Polish round steak See **round steak**

Polish sausage n Also *Polish ham sausage* **scattered, but esp Nth** See Map Cf **brat** n[2], **kielbasa**

A spicy, cased sausage usu made of pork.

1950 *WELS* **WI**, 11 Infs, Polish sausage; 1 Inf, Polish sausage—mostly pork, medium heavy spiced; 1 Inf, Polish ham sausage. **c1965** Randle *Cookbooks* (Ask Neighbor) 4.39, *Polish sausage and sauerkraut. Boil* Polish fresh sausage with garlic . . (or you can use Kielbasi) . . Remove sausage from kettle[;] do not puncture, if using Polish or Slovenian whole links of sausage. **1965–70** *DARE* (Qu. H40, *A small sausage that is put into a long roll or bun to make a sandwich*) Inf **IL29**, Polish sausage; (Qu. H41, *Kinds of roll or bun sandwiches . . in a round bun or roll*) Infs **MO**16, 29, Polish sausage; (Qu. H45, *Dishes made with meat, fish, or poultry that everybody around here would know, but that people in other places might not*) Infs **TX**13, **WI**47, Polish sausage; **NY**49, Kielbasy—Polish sausage; (Qu. H49) Inf **RI**3, Potatoes with [kɪˈbɑsə]—Polish sausage; (Qu. H65, *Foreign foods favored by people around here*) Infs **IL**117, **MN**11, **NY**105, 226, Polish sausage; **MD**8, Kielbasa—spicy Polish sausage; (Qu. HH30, *Things that are nicknamed for different nationalities—for example, a 'Dutch treat'*) Infs **CT**23, **MI**69, Polish sausage. **1967** *Watertown Daily Times* (NY) 14 June 23, [Advt:] Polish Sausage. **1969** *DARE* FW Addit **cwNY**, Broiled Polish sausage. **1973** Allen *LAUM* 1.289 (as of c1950) 2 infs, **ND**, Polish sausage. **1986** Pederson *LAGS Concordance* **esp csTX**, 10 infs, Polish sausage(s); 1 inf, Polish sausage—small, smoked sausage. [6 of 11 infs Black] **1988** *DARE* File **Milwaukee WI** (as of 1970s), Bunch of guys and I went looking for kielbasa . . it's kind of a spicy Polish sausage. **1997** *Ibid* **seWI** (as of c1915), My father remembers that his father, born near Milwaukee, Wisconsin, made Polish sausage in his meatmarket. It was a spiced pork sausage—similar to a brat, but spicier than a brat; **nwMA**, Kielbasa and *Polish sausage* are synonymous, but most people use the word *kielbasa*.

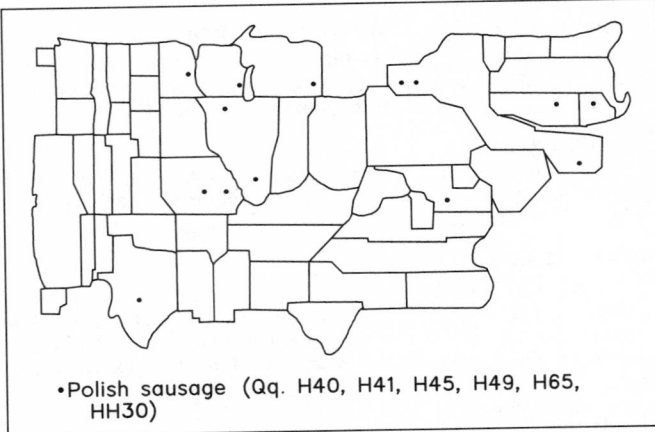

•Polish sausage (Qq. H40, H41, H45, H49, H65, HH30)

polish up v phr **scattered, but esp Inland Sth, W Midl; also NEast** See Map Cf **apple up**

To curry favor with (someone).

1965–70 *DARE* (Qu. II20b, *A person who tries too hard to gain somebody else's favor: "He's always trying to _____ the boss."*) 33 Infs, **scattered, but esp Inland Sth, W Midl, NEast**, Polish up; (Qu. JJ3a, *When a school child makes a special effort to 'get in good' with the teacher in hopes of getting a better grade: "He's trying to _____ again."*) Infs **KY**60, **NH**7, Polish up; **MO**13, Polish up the teacher; **WI**13, Polish her up.

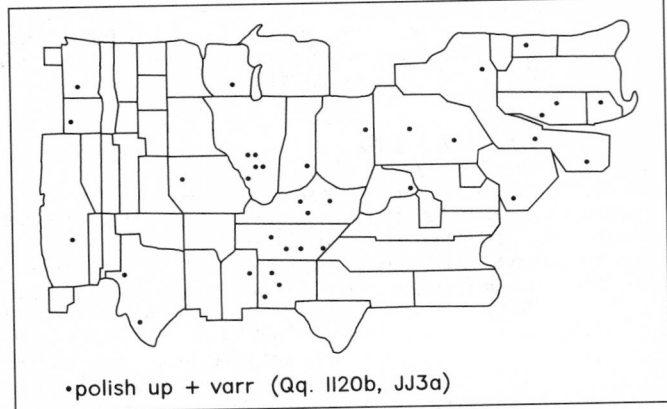

•polish up + varr (Qq. II20b, JJ3a)

polite adj, adv Pronc-spp **esp Sth, S Midl** *perlite, p'lite* Similarly adv *perlitely*, n *perliteness* Cf Intro "Language Changes" I.8

Std senses, var forms.

1844 Thompson *Major Jones's Courtship* 76 **GA**, Perliteness aint every thing. **1891** (1967) Freeman *New Engl. Nun* 94, He wore a beautiful coat an' a satin vest, an' he spoke jest as perlite. **1901** *DN* 2.183 **neKY** [Black], *Polite*—p'lite. **1923** (1946) Greer-Petrie *Angeline Doin' Society* 15 **csKY**, But he was perlite. **1938** in 1944 *ADD* **FL, GA**, Bow perlitely. **1954** *Harder Coll.* **cwTN**, He's jist as perlite's 'e kin be.

polite bird n

=**cedar waxwing**.

1914 Eaton *Birds NY* 2.357, They [=cedar waxwings] are called "polite birds" in many sections of the State because of the habit of bowing and "passing the word" along the line, and of passing a cherry. When the flock alights they ordinarily face all in the same direction. Occasionally before one will taste the fruit which has just been picked, he passes it to the next one on the limb and so it travels down the line, and on rare occasions has been seen to come back again along a limb full of birds, before any member of the company will deign to taste it.

politicianer n Also sp *polititioner* [*EDD*] **esp S Midl** arch Cf **-er** affix 1, **musicianer**

A politician.

1838 Neal *Charcoal Sketches* 137 **sePA**, It isn't saying much for your boss politicianer that he chose you. **1859** Taliaferro *Fisher's R.* 109 **nwNC** (as of 1820s), Speaking of politics reminds me of one more anecdote connected therewith. It was customary for "candidites" in olden times to treat with liquor; but after a while the temperance reformation reached Fisher's River . . and "polititioners" in treating had to change their "tacktucks" a little. **1872** Stearns *Black Man* 482 **KY**, A teacher of a white school . . gave as a reason for not being able to answer some political question, "that she was no politician*er*." **1889** *Century Illustr. Mag.* 37.409 **cnVA**, I ain't no politicianer, an' I allays votes the Whig ticket, like my daddy did afo' me. **1898** *Ibid* 55.831 **GA**, They [=duels] used to be ruther common, special' among big high-edicated people like lawyers and politicianers.

polk n[1] See **poke** n[1] **1a**

polk n[2] See **poke** n[3] **1**

polk n[3] See **pulka**

polka dot n

1 =**rock hind**. [See quot 1935]

1935 Caine *Game Fish* 93, Polka Dot. . . Head and lower part of body covered with orange spots that vary in size. **1946** LaMonte *N. Amer. Game Fishes* 56, *Rock Hind*. . . Names: Cabra Mora, Grouper, Hind, Speckled Hind, Polka Dot.

2 =**black trout 3**. [From its black and white coloring]

1978 *Wanigan Catalog* 6 **ME**, *Coach Dog*. . . Syn[onym]: Polka Dot. **1990** *Seed Savers Exchange* Summer 79, Polka Dot.

polka-dot turtle n

=**spotted turtle**.

1958 Conant *Reptiles & Amphibians* 42, Spotted turtle—*Clemmys guttata*. . . The "polka-dot turtle". . . Seldom in a hurry.

polk salad See **poke salad**

polk stalk See **poke stalk**

polkweed See **pokeweed 1, 2**

pollack n[1] Also *pollock*

1 Std: a North Atlantic food fish (*Pollachius virens*). [*OED2* 1502 →] Also called **Boston bluefish, coalfish 1, green cod 1, quoddy salmon**

2 also *Alaska pollack, Puget Sound* ~: =**walleye pollack.** esp AK

 1884 U.S. Natl. Museum *Bulletin* 27.407 **AK,** *Pollachius chalcogrammus. . . Pollack. . .* Very abundant around the Shumagin Islands, where it is one of the most important baits for cod. **1905** U.S. Bur. Fisheries *Rept. for 1904* 94 **AK,** The . . game fish in Alaska. . . whose capture affords more or less sport [include] . . Alaska pollack (*Theragra chalcogramma*). **1928** Pan-Pacific Research Inst. *Jrl.* 3.16 **WA, OR,** *Theragra chalcogrammus. . .* Puget Sound pollack. **1982** *Juneau Guide* 44 **AK** (Tabbert *Dict. Alaskan Engl.*), *Tomcod*—On a sunny summer day, you can usually find kids downtown catching these fish off the docks left and right. They are neither a cod nor a Tom. Ignored or worse by local fishermen, the tomcod is in fact a pollock—the same pollock discussed as a possible backbone for a new fishing industry in the region. **1989** Mickelson *Nat. Hist.* 69 **AK,** Pollock are seasonally the most abundant fish in P[rince] W[illiam] S[ound].

Pollack n[2] See **Polack**

poll axe See **poleax**

pollies, catching vbl n Cf **polly-boo** n[1] =**skitching.**

 1997 in 2001 *DARE* File—Internet **cnNY** (as of 1920s), "Catching pollies" was fun. That meant hitching your sled to a farmer's big empty bobsled and getting a free ride. Some parents forbade the practice, and some farmers wouldn't allow it, but it was quite common.

polliwog See **pollywog**

pollock n[1] See **pollack**

Pollock n[2] See **Polack**

polluted adj

1 See quot. [Cf *EDD pollute* v. 2 "Sc. Irel. . . *pass.* To be overrun, beset with."]

 1981 *High Coll.* **ceKY** (as of c1930), [*Polluted*] used in the Gorge with positive connotations, meaning to be thoroughly furnished with. . . "Them grapes used to be anywhere you went. The bushes were polluted with them and their vines just camouflaged the rocks."

‡**2** See quot.

 1967 *DARE* (Qu. KK30, *Feeling slowed up or without energy: "I certainly feel _____."*) Inf **OR**3, Polluted.

polly n

1 also *polly-wad:* See quots; hence comb *polly bag* a snood.

 1968–70 *DARE* (Qu. X3, *When a woman puts her hair up on her head in a bunch*) Inf **PA**142, Polly; **KY**75, Polly-wad [laughter]. **1998** *NADS Letters* **Ozarks,** Pollywad—I have heard older residents of the Ozarks use this term to describe a bun or ponytail, although not recently. This was probably 20 to 30 years ago that I heard it used. *Ibid* **swPA,** I'm originally from the Pittsburgh area and I've heard "Polly Wad" referred to as a hair bun. But. . . my assumption was always that it was not actually "Polly" but instead "Paulie". There seem to be thousands of women around Pittsburgh with the name/nickname Paulie. **2000** *Ibid* **KY,** In 1965 my roommate wore her hair this way and called it a polly. She was from Shelbyville, Kentucky and would have been born around 1946. A polly-bag to her was what I would call a snood, an open-work pouch to contain hair rolled and tied at the back of the neck. *Ibid* **IL,** Polly . . my grandmother (from Havana, Illinois) used this term to describe hair in a bun—she said it had to do with Pollyanna. *Ibid* **cPA,** I lived in central Pennsylvania during my high-school years. I distinctly remember that the mother of a girlfriend of mine suggested that she could do her hair in a "polly wad" for a school dance. I recall it because it struck me funny—I had never heard it.

‡**2** A chamber pot. Cf **peggy** n[2]

 1970 *DARE* (Qu. F38, *Utensil kept under the bed for use at night*) Inf **IL**113, Polly ['pɑli], commode, chamber pot.

‡**3** in phr *get a little polly on:* See quot.

 1966 *DARE* (Qu. DD13, *When a drinker is just beginning to show the effects of the liquor . . he's _____*) Inf **MI**10, Got a little polly on—sometimes said of a woman.

4 A female mule. Cf **jack** n[1] **20, jenny 1, Maud, molly** n[1] **1**

 1968 *DARE* (Qu. K50, *Joking nicknames for mules*) Inf **MN**12, Polly—a mare; jack—a male.

5 See **polly-boo** n[1].

6 See **pollywog 4.**

pollyanna n, often cap [After the character in Eleanor Hodgman Porter's children's novels *Pollyanna* (1913) and *Pollyanna Grows Up* (1915)] **chiefly N Midl, esp PA**

An arrangement by which each member of a group gives a gift to one other member chosen at random; a gift given according to such an arrangement; the person to whom one gives or from whom one receives such a gift.

 1985 *DARE* File **cMO,** We have just "had" our Pollyanna at our Christmas lunch, when all the members of my department exchanged gifts costing no more than a dollar. Each person had previously drawn the name of the person for whom he or she would buy a gift. After opening the present, the receiver tries to guess who has given it. Gifts are opened one by one as part of the fun. . . Our source is a woman who grew up on a farm near Kansas City, went to school in Kansas. . . She traces the custom back to her childhood. *Ibid* **DE** (as of c1935), One professor . . remembered his Aunt Martha speaking about a pollyanna exchange with her Bible class. This was about forty to fifty years ago in the state of Delaware. **1985** *NADS Letters* **cnNC,** It was the custom at Christmastime in this large family to hold a name-drawing, in which each person would draw the name of another family member to buy a relatively substantial gift for. My mother-in-law always referred to the giver as the recipient's *Pollyanna* (as in "Bob is Mary's Pollyanna."), a usage which she said she had known from her girlhood. **1986** *DARE* File **cOH,** A friend from Columbus, Ohio and I were talking about Christmas plans. I asked if she had bought all her Christmas presents yet. She said, "Oh, we're doing a pollyanna this year." She explained that this meant the family members had exchanged names and each would buy a present for that one person. *Ibid* **csPA,** Pollyanna—drawing names to exchange gifts at Christmas. **1991** *Ibid* **sNJ,** In this area, women's groups often draw names of people to whom they will give small gifts during the year, remembering birthdays, holidays, etc. If I draw your name, you are my pollyanna, but I am also considered your pollyanna. Both the giver and the receiver are considered the pollyanna. I remember this from the 1940s and '50s, and some groups continue the tradition today. **1997** *Ibid* **PA,** A number of locally educated friends and relatives—from Bucks, Montgomery and Chester counties— . . all knew "pollyanna" well: there seems to be some discrepancy about who was the actual pollyanna, the giver or the receiver or even the gift itself. . . The word was used very often for the concept in general, i.e. "to do a pollyanna." *Ibid* **Philadelphia PA,** I . . have used the term since I can remember. I am now 44 years old. I never met anyone who didn't know what it meant. Of course, the only time it is used is at Christmas. In work we would all pick a pollyanna for gift giving. [**1997** *NADS Letters* **nePA,** Pollyanna: this is like a secret santa in some uses—I've also heard it used to refer to "going in on a present together." I've also heard it used in reference to bridal showers—it's a little gift that you give to the bride-to-be that you don't put your name on because it is a little thing (like a box of Brillo pads or hand lotion or something) and you put it in the wishing well.]

polly bag See **polly 1**

pollybog See **pollywog 1**

polly-boo n[1] Also *polly (ride)* Cf **hooky bob** See quot 1895.

 1895 *DN* 1.398 **nNY,** *Polly-boo* . . when small boys in the streets attach their handsleds to cutters or other sleighs drawn by horses, it is called *polly-boo.* **1896** *DN* 1.422 **nNY,** *Polly:* for *polly boo.* **1966** *Good Old Days* 2.10.15 **cnNY** (as of c1910), In the winter you could hear the bells for blocks. Us kids would run to meet them and hitch a Polly ride. . . We would ride a ways and walk back.

polly-boo n[2] [Var of *OED2 parleyvoo* 2 (alter of Fr *parlez vous*) 1815 →]

A person of French background.

[**1891** Maitland *Amer. Slang Dict.* 199, *Parley-voo,* a Frenchman.] **1967** *DARE* (Qu. HH28, *Names and nicknames . . for people of foreign background: French*) Inf **OR**3, Polly-boo [ˌpaliˈbu].

polly-fox v chiefly Midl Cf ballyhack v

1 also with *around:* To equivocate, procrastinate, "beat about the bush"; to waste time; hence ppl adj, vbl n *polly-foxing,* pronc-sp *bolly-foxing.*

1873 OH Constitutional Convention *Official Rept.* 1.340, It is the avowed intention of this Convention to so shape that section that females may be appointed to offices. Now, if that is so, and if that is our desire, I do not want any "polly-foxing" about this thing. I want the words to designate what we want. **1914** *DN* 4.111 **cKS,** *Pollyfox. . .* To quibble or equivocate. "Judge Stewart calls the lawyers down when they pollyfox in a case." **1916** *DN* 4.345 **TN,** *Polly-fox . .* =dilly-dally, delay and discuss. "No use in polly-foxing about it, we have to do it." **1944** *PADS* 2.25 **cwNC, cwOH,** *Pollyfox. . .* To dilly-dally; to waste time. **1946** White *Autobiog.* 314 **ceKS,** The bank had for its President a shrewd old polly-foxing politician who had . . bought too many shares of stock in boom propositions, hotels that never paid, light and power companies set up in towns that waned and faded, and the assets of the bank were shot through with bad paper. **1970** *DARE* (Qu. A11, *When somebody takes too long about coming to a decision . . "I wish he'd quit ___."*) Inf **TN**47, Polly-foxing around. **1997** *DARE* File **cnMS,** I grew up in Mississippi. My mother used to say, "Quit your bollyfoxing." . . It means to quit wasting time or to quit acting silly.

2 See quot.

1936 *AmSp* 11.316 **Ozarks,** *Polly-fox. . .* To move quietly, to pussyfoot.

polly-fox around, polly-foxing See polly-fox 1

polly-in-a-bag n Also polly-in-the-bag PA Cf fagot n[1], hog maw

A dish of spiced ground meat and potatoes cooked in an animal's stomach or a pouch made from a piece of an animal's stomach.

1998 *DARE* File **sePA,** Do you have "Polly-in-the-bag?" Hog maul. Sausage and potatoes mixture cooked in the lining of a pig's stomach. York, Lancaster, PA . . I assume it's still current. . . I was born in 1932 and it was in common use. **1999** *NADS Letters* **PA,** This dish was prepared by my grandmother . . (b. 1883, d.1976). She grew up in Lancaster County, PA. The dish was a mixture of mashed or diced potatoes and pork (maybe some beef included) sausage. Salt, pepper, onion, a little celery, . . was stuffed into a pig's stomach, tied or sewed shut, then roasted in an oven. The finished product was sliced, sometimes spooned onto a platter. . . This information was from my mother . . , who has passed 80, and never served it to the next generation. *Ibid* **PA,** My husband's family was from the coal region of Pennsylvania. . . This branch of the family was from Wales. . . His grandmother (b. c1888) used the term Polly in a bag and "faggots" interchangeably. It is a meat dish: Ingredients: caul (thin transparent layer of tissue that lines the stomach) of a cow. Beef kidney / pork liver / lamb kidney / small, diced, fried potatoes and a lot of spices. Grind up the innards and add the spices and potatoes. Cut the caul into 2″ squares. Drop a spoonful of the mixture onto the caul and tie it up with string. They look like small bags. Boil them for about 30 minutes. The smell is vile and I have no idea of how it tastes.

‡pollymarbles n pl [Var of collywobbles] Cf colly marbles (at cholera morbus), gollywobbles, mollycoddle 2

1971 *DARE* File **ceMO,** *Pollymarbles*—collywobbles; usage of an elderly man in rural area south of St. Louis.

pollynose n Also pollywog; for addit varr see quots chiefly NYC Cf key n 2

See quots.

1978 *DARE* File **NYC** (as of 1920–40), *Pollynose*—A maple seed or samara as used by a child at play, who splits it and sticks it on his nose with the wing pointing forward [2 Infs]. **1987** *Ibid* **NYC, cCT** (as of c1970), *Pollynose*—A maple seed which children play with by splitting and sticking the bract on the bridge of the nose. **1994** Roth *Mercy* 64 **NYC,** There were certain trees . . which shed a small green seedpod that came twirling down. "Polly-noses," the kids named them; they could be split and were sticky and stuck to the bridge of one's nose. **1995** *DARE* File **NYC** (as of 1960s), I grew up in NYC in the 60's and we called

them pol(l)y noses. I've also heard them called pol(l)ywogs. *Ibid* **seNY,** *Polywogs* it is—for the maple seeds you stuck on your nose . . in the 40's but my sister (b. 1949) called them something else.

polly-pouts n pl

A fit of sulking; hence adj *polly-pouty* sulky.

1915 *DN* 4.222, *Polly-pouts, to have the,* to be sulky. "You must have the Polly-pouts. Was ist los?" Colloquial. **1942** Berrey–Van den Bark *Amer. Slang* 283.1, Polly-pouts, *the sulks. Ibid* 383.6, *Sullen; sulky. . .* polly-pouty.

polly ride See polly-boo n[1]

polly-wad See polly 1

‡Polly wants a corner n [Var of pussy wants a corner]

1970 *DARE* (Qu. EE2, *Games that have one extra player—when a signal is given, the players change places, and the extra one tries to get a place*) Inf **NC**88, Polly wants a corner.

pollywob, pollywod See pollywog 4

pollywog n Also polliwog

1 also *pollybog, pollywoggle, pollywoggy:* A **tadpole.** [*OED2* c1440 →] **scattered, but chiefly Nth, West** See Map

1838 (1843) Haliburton *Clockmaker* (2d ser) 269, Little ponds never hold big fish; there is nothing but pollywogs, tadpoles, and minims in them. **1867** Lowell *Biglow* 114 **'Upcountry' MA,** "Lord knows," protest the polliwogs,/ "We're anxious to be grown-up frogs." **1878** Beadle *Western Wilds* 262 **AZ,** The water . . was green, slimy, [and] full of vile pollywogs. **1899** (1912) Green *VA Folk-Speech* 329, *Pollywog. . .* A tadpole. **1906** (1907) Dickerson *Frog Book* 68, On . . the tenth day, we have veritable "pollywogs," as black as tiny coals, with tails that are in a continuous wiggle, and small round mouths that are in constant search for something to eat. . . The baby toad is not different from other babies in being very hungry when it first comes into the world. **1950** *WELS* (*Very young frogs—when they still have tails and no legs*) 36 Infs, **WI,** Pollywogs. **1965–70** *DARE* (Qu. P20) 254 Infs, **scattered, but chiefly Nth, West,** Pollywogs; **CA**101, **SC**69, Pollywoggies; **MA**80, Pollywoggles; **MO**10, Pollybogs. **1985** Clark *From Mailbox* 13 **ME,** The frogs will soon be serenading the season as they fill the waters with eggs for this year's pollywogs. **1986** Pederson *LAGS Concordance,* 2 infs, **GA,** Polliwogs; 1 inf, **ceTX,** Polliwogs—baby frogs.

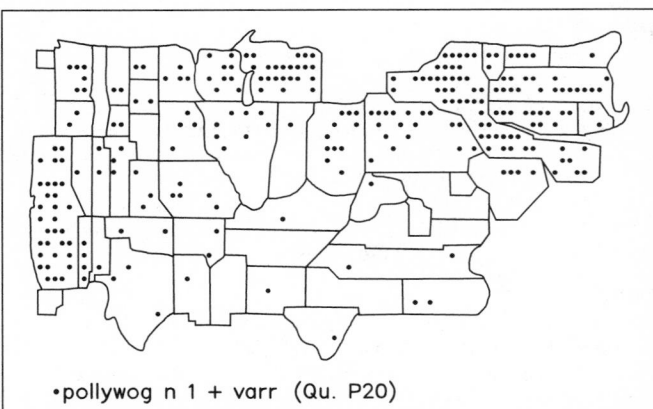

•pollywog n 1 + varr (Qu. P20)

2 =wiggler.

1887 Custer *Tenting* 76, Our rain-water was . . full of gallinippers and pollywogs. **1967–69** *DARE* (Qu. R14, *Small worm-like things [seen in rain barrels or standing water] that hatch into mosquitoes*) Infs **MN**29, 33, **MO**6, **NY**83, **OR**10, Pollywog(s).

3 A **horned rush** (here: *Rhynchospora corniculata*). [See quot]

1913 *Torreya* 13.228 **SC,** *Rhynchospora corniculata . .* Pollywog, Santee Club, S.C. An apt term taken from the beaked akenes.

4 also *polly, pollywob, pollywod:* A small catfish of the family Ictaluridae. **chiefly Gulf States, esp FL** Cf **mud cat 1, yellow cat**

c1940 Eliason *Word Lists FL* 11 **wFL,** *Polywog* [sic]. . . A small catfish having a brown color with spots. However, when catfish are spoken [sic] in general, *pollies* is used. **1966–70** *DARE* (Qu. P1, . . *Kinds* *of freshwater fish . . caught around here . . good to eat)* Inf **FL**27, A small cat called a pollywog—yellow-bellied cat; **KY**86, Pollywod— same as yellow cat; (Qu. P3, *Freshwater fish that are not good to eat)* Inf **FL**35, Pollywogs—small catfish. **1974** *DARE* File **cLA** (as of 1973), Small catfish are known as . . pollywobs in Jonesville, Louisiana. *Ibid* **cwFL**, Small catfish are known as pollywogs in Bartow, Florida. **1986** Pederson *LAGS Concordance*, 2 infs, **nwFL, seMS**, Polliwog; 1 inf, **nwTN**, Polliwog—small catfish; 1 inf, **ceTX**, Polliwog—mud cat.

5 A small fish used as bait; see quots.
1967–68 *DARE* (Qu. P7, *Small fish used as bait for bigger fish)* Infs **CA**1, 72, Pollywog(s). **1973** *DARE* File **Savannah GA**, Pollywog—A small killifish used as bait—Common. **1986** Pederson *LAGS Concordance*, 1 inf, **seGA**, Polliwog.

6 See **pollynose.**

‡**7** Perh a **Cajun** n¹ **1.** Cf **boogerlee, frog** n **B2**
1967 *DARE* Tape **AL**20, [Inf:] They're supposed to be French, you know, French descent. But we called them Pollywogs. I don't know why. . . They was a clan of people that lived on these bayous down there. And they'd fish, sell a few fish, and sit on the porch barefooted with their feet up on the banister some, and just live so easy. . . on the order of a Cajun. . . Supposed to be French, but they wasn't real French. . . [FW:] It's kind of a derogatory term, was it? [Inf:] Uh-huh.

pollywog v
See quot.
1985 Madson *Up River* 65 **Upper Missip Valley** (as of 1953), Polly-wogged for it. Waded around barefooted and felt for the clams and ducked down and got 'em and stuck 'em in a gunny sack.

pollywoggle, pollywoggy See **pollywog 1**

Polock See **Polack**

polonay n [Back-formation from *polonaise* a type of overdress, understood as a pl; cf **Chinee** n², **maltee**]
1880 *Scribner's Mth.* 19.921, I wish I hed the pattern o' that white polonay o'hern. **1897** Stuart *Simpkinsville* 159 **LA**, That black polonay she's got on, it was fo' dollars a yard. **1911** *DN* 3.549 **NE**, New folk-etymological singulars are, in addition to the common *Maltee, Chinee, Portugee, shay, polonay,* etc., the more recent *corp,* and *appendic,* which are not infrequently heard.

polpisy adj [*Polpis* Massachusetts, on Nantucket Island]
1916 Macy–Hussey *Nantucket Scrap Basket* 142 **MA**, "Polpisy"— Countrified, outlandish; a very old local term, dating back to a time when the people of that suburb were, perhaps, less in touch with the civilizing influences of the island's metropolis than at present. "Don't act Polpisy!" was said to a child who was awkward and ungainly.

polridge n
=**lesser scaup.**
1917 *Wilson Bulletin* 29.2.77 **WA**, *Marila affinis* . . polridge, Willapa Harbor, Wash.

Polski n Also *Poski* [Pol *Polski* Polish] Cf **Polander**
=**Polack.**
1950 *WELS* (Names and nicknames for people of foreign background: Polish) 1 Inf, **cWI**, Polski. **1964** *PADS* 42.40 **Chicago IL** [Terms of abuse], Terms [for Poles] . . from the language of the Polish immigrants themselves. . . *Poski* (from *Polski*) [one occurrence]. **1967–68** *DARE* (Qu. HH28, *Names and nicknames . . for people of foreign background)* Infs **MI**72, **NY**59, Polski.

poly See **poorly**

polyg n Pronc-sp *plyg* [Abbrs for *polygamist*] Cf **cohab**
1942 Stegner *Mormon Country* 125 **UT**, Orderville might have weathered its difficulties but for three things. . . The third was the polygamy prosecutions under the Edmunds-Tucker Act, and the coming of deputy marshals snooping for "polygs" and "cohabs." The men with plural wives . . fled to the underground. **1947** Morgan *Great Salt Lake* 324 **UT**, The appeal to the Supreme Court failed, and U.S. deputy marshals began "polyg hunts" the length and breadth of the territory. The polyga-mists were forced into hiding, some even going to Canada or Mexico in hope of finding a haven, but the raids kept a constant flow of polygamy and u.c. cases moving into the courts. **1997** *DARE* File **UT**, I still hear this term [=*polyg*]. Whether it has a negative or neutral connotation de-

pends quite entirely on the context. **2000** Launspach *ID Dial. Project* 6 **seID**, (Terms for Mormons) 2 infs, Plygs.

polypody n
Std: a fern of the genus *Polypodium.* For other names of var spp see **leather fern 1, licorice ~, little Polly, liverwort 2, moss fern, resurrection ~, rock brake b, ~ fern 2, sweet fern, tree ~**

‡**poly-woly** n [Hypocoristic var of *roly-poly*]
1966 *DARE* (Qu. X50, *Names or nicknames for a person who is very fat)* Inf **NM**7, Poly-woly [poliwoli]—for children. [Inf old]

pomace n
Std senses, var forms.

1 *pum(m)ice, pummace.* Note: These spp presumably repre-sent the std pronc ['pʌmɨs].
1786 (1925) Washington *Diaries* 3.137 **VA**, Beat about one Bushel of the Wild Crab into pumice. **1861** *ME Bd. Ag. Ag. ME for 1861* 44, The residuum left after expressing the oil [from menhaden], that is the cake, pumice, or as commonly called, the *chum,* . . contains nearly the whole fertilizing portions of the fish. **1899** (1912) Green *VA Folk-Speech* 67, *Apple-pummace.* . . The ground apples after the cider has been pressed out. **1916** *DN* 4.343 **MD**, Pummice. Variant of *pomace.* **1975** McDonough *Garden Sass* 162 **AR**, Pumice—This is the roughage of the sorghum stalk that comes out the back of the press after the juice has been extracted. **1985** Wilkinson *Moonshine* 113 **neNC**, In western North Carolina, apple brandy is distilled from a mash of pulverized ap-ples, called pumice.

2 *pommey, pummy.* [Perh the result of reinterpreting ['pʌmɨs] as a pl ['pʌmɨz], whence an analogical sg ['pʌmɨ]. The Engl dial evidence, however, is entirely for the sg use. Cf *OED2 pommey* 1842 →; *EDD pomace*] Cf **plummy**
a Used as a mass noun.
1884 *Bay State Mth.* 1.29 **MA**, A cousin of mine . . got his arm caught while cleaning the pummy out [of a cider press]. **1899** (1912) Green *VA Folk-Speech* 338, Pummy. . . Pummage; Pummies; Pomace. Ground apples in cider making; before and after the juice is pressed out. **1927** *AmSp* 3.139 **eME**, The older people. . . spoke of . . "pummy" (pomace). **1938** Matschat *Suwannee R.* 133 **neFL, seGA**, A small trough in the mill frame caught the juice and led it to a barrel. . . "Pummy"—cane pulp—fell from the other side of the mill. **1941** *LANE* Map 346 **swME**, The auxiliary informant defines [krɒᴰm] . . [as] æᵊpl pʌˇmɨˇɨ, the remains of apples after they have been squeezed in a cider press. **1941** Ward *Holding Hills* 111 **IA** (as of early 20th cent), Grinding cane is labor. . . [W]e must keep an eye on the barrel that it doesn't overflow, we must keep the stack of pommey mowed away where it wriggles out at the back of the mill. **1966** *DARE* Tape **ME**9, [FW:] Do they still have many starch factories here? [Inf:] Yes. There are quite a few starch factories. [FW:] Would you know how they operate with the potatoes? [Inf:] Well, they just grind them up and then wash out the pummy. [FW:] The what? [Inf:] The pummy—the pulp . . that's ground up, and it goes over a screen, and the starch part, and the water runs off. **1975** Gould *ME Lingo* 220, *Pummy*—Maine farmer's pronunciation of pom-ace, the residue from the press-cloths in squeezing cider. **1993** *DARE* File **sGA**, In typing an addition to my father's autobiography, I came upon his use of *pommey,* which he defines as 'mashed sugar cane' pro-duced in the process of making cane syrup. [Speaker's father is 82, rural.]

b Used as a count noun. **chiefly Midl, esp S Midl**
1877 in 1937 Ruede *Sod-House* 152 **KS**, He was very much amused to hear the folks [at the cane mill] talk about "them molasses" and being told to "take away them pummies" (pomace—crushed cane). **1899** [see **2a** above]. **1923** *DN* 5.218 **swMO**, Pummies. . . Pumice. Always used as if plural in form. "I've got to burn up them pummies." **1927** *AmSp* 2.362 **cwWV**, Pummies . . the pomace made in making cider. "I stepped on a bee in the pummies, and it stung me." **1929** *AmSp* 4.303 **IA**, "Pommeys" (really pomace) were the crushed stalks of the cane from which molasses was made in a neighbor's kiln, and the pommey pile was the cool, fragrant heap of bruised and shredded stems which made a play place more delightful than any haystack. **1953** Randolph–Wilson *Down in Holler* 275 **Ozarks**, Pummies. . . Pomace, sugar cane stalks that have been pressed in a mill. "Cane pomace is now used as a mulch for strawberries in Barry County, Mo.," according to the *Country Gen-tleman* (December, 1939, p. 9). People who live in Barry County gener-ally say, "Cane pummies *are* used," since they regard the word as a plu-

ral. **1958** *PADS* 29.14 **TN,** The crushed apples from the cider mill were referred to only as *pummies.* **1976** Garber *Mountain-ese* 72 **sAppalachians,** *Pummies.* . . Fruit pummies are left for slop after makin' cider or vinegar. **1982** *Barrick Coll.* **csPA,** The chickens use' to come an' eat the pummies, and they made them drunk. **1985** *NC Folkl. Jrl.* 33.40 **wNC** (as of c1920), Dad would gather enough apples to fill four or five wooden barrels, run them through the cider mill, and put the crushed fruit or "pummies" (pumice) away in some out-of-the-way place at the barn to ferment.

3 *pommels.*
a1883 (1911) Bagby *VA Gentleman* 10, How sick "us boys" used to get from drinking sweet cider and eating apple "pommels"!

4 *pummage.* [*OED2* pommage sb. 2 1789 →]
1899 [see **2a** above].

5 pl: *pummings.* Cf **plummy**
1973 *News & Courier* (Charleston SC) 25 Nov sec E 1/5, Pummings (squeezed cane stalks) are piled on a sled and dragged off to the woods for the hogs to root in. **1986** Pederson *LAGS Concordance*, 1 inf, **seGA,** (The) pummins—left over from ground cane.

pomarine jaeger n [*OED2* 1838 →]
Std: a **jaeger** n[1] (here: *Stercorarius pomarius*). Also called **jaeger gull, jiddy hawk, marlinspike 1, robber gull, sea hen 1, ~ robber**

pome See **poem**

pomegranate n Usu |ˈpɑm(ə)ˌgrænɨt, ˈpʌm-, ˌpɑm(ə)ˈgrænɨt, ˌpəm-|; also **chiefly S Midl** |ˈplʌmˌgrænɨt|; for addit varr see **A** below Pronc-spp *plumgranate, plumgranite, plumgranny, pumgranny*

A Forms.
1896 *Century Illustr. Mag.* 52.878 **AR,** Her two cheeks they hang out of her pink caliker sunbonnet thess like a pair o' ripe plumgranates. **1897** [see **B1** below]. **1926** [see **B2** below]. **1944** *PADS* 2.20 **sAppalachians,** *Plumgranny* [ˈplʌmgrænɨ]. . . Pomegranate. ((Also, reported from upper S.C., Tenn.)) **1953** [see **B2** below]. **c1960** [see **B2** below]. **1966–68** *DARE* (Qu. I53) Inf **GA3,** [ˈplʌmgrænəts]; **NC60,** [ˈpɑməgræmz]; **PA66,** [ˈpɑmɪˌgræmz]; **SC26,** [ˈplʌmˌgrænɨt]—Whites say [ˈpʌmgrænɨt]; (Qu. S26e) **HI6,** [ˈpoməˌgræm]. **1981** Pederson *LAGS Basic Materials,* [Proncs of *pomegranate* were recorded from 20 infs; of these, 7 were of the type [ˈplʌmˌgrænɨt], and there were single instances of [ˈplʌˤmˌgreˣnɨt], [ˈpləˣmˌgraˢˌɛnɨ], and [reˀdˈgræˌɛnɨts] (the last appar for *red pomegranates*).] **1982** [see **B2** below].

B Senses.

1 A **wild plum** such as **Canada plum** (*Prunus americana*).
1832 Williamson *Hist. ME* 1.109, The *wild Plum-tree* [Footnote: Prunus Sylvestris.] is of one species only, though of two or three varieties; it is of small size and scarce. [Footnote: Called also pomegranate, wild pear, and June-plum.] **1896** *Jrl. Amer. Folkl.* 9.187 **ME,** *Prunus nigra,* pomegranate, Orono, Me., West. **1897** Sudworth *Arborescent Flora* 237, *Prunus americana.* . . Wild Plum. . . Plum Granite. **1950** Gray–Fernald *Manual of Botany* 877, *P[runus] nigra* . . Canada Plum, "Pomegranate."

2 also *pomegranate melon*: Either **mango 3** or **smell melon;** see quots.
1926 *DN* 5.402 **Ozarks,** *Pum-granny,* or *plum-granny.* . . A small, yellow, gourd-like fruit, occasionally used as food. It is said that the name is somehow derived from pomegranate, which the hillman knows chiefly from the references in Scripture. **1939** Writers' Program *Guide KY* 439 **seKY,** Speech here is vivid and fresh. . . "Black as a wolf's mouth," "sweet-smellin' ez a plum-granite," "fine as fur in the North," are pioneer relics. **1953** (1977) Hubbard *Shantyboat* 310 **Missip-Ohio Valleys,** The vine peach, or as Tom called it, "plumgranate," was another wild fruit new to us. It ripened late in the sandy fields, about the size and color of a small yellow tomato, and could be made into a thick preserve. **1954** *Harder Coll.* **cwTN,** Plum granate melon . . a type of muskmelon . . smells better than it tastes, yellow and white stripes. *Ibid,* Plumgranny . . Pomegranate. **1956** McAtee *Some Dialect NC* 34, Pomegranate. . . A small striped melon, *Cucumis melo* var. *dudaim.* **c1960** *Wilson Coll.* **csKY,** Pomegranate. . . A small, sweet-smelling melon, eaten raw or preserved. *Ibid, Plum-granny.* . . Pomegranate. **1968** *DARE* (Qu. I4, . . *Vegetables . . less commonly grown around here*) Inf **VA2,** Sweet potatoes, pomegranates, mushmelons, watermelons; (Qu. I26, . . *Kinds of melons*) Inf **MO9,** Pomegranate melons. **1981**

Pederson *LAGS Basic Materials,* 1 inf, **cnGA,** Love melons, pomegranates—these two terms are equivalent. There are small melons given to girls by boys. They smell good; 1 inf, **nwGA,** Pomegranates; 1 inf, **cnMS,** Plumgrannies—small, yellowish, round. **1982** Slone *How We Talked* 26 **eKY** (as of c1950), Plum granny (pomegranate)—to us, a small melon, nice smell, edible but not tasty. **1998** *DARE* File **eKY,** I'd like to know the "real" term for something known as a plumgranny. It is/ was grown in eastern Kentucky and is (probably) a red colored fruit of some type. However, I never heard of anyone eating plumgrannies. . . Children carried them around because they gave off a gorgeous strong sweet smell. I've seen pomegranates in the grocery story and they're not the same thing.

pomer Christer See **palma Christi**

pomette bleue n [Fr *pommette bleue,* literally "little blue apple"]
A **hawthorn** (here: *Crataegus brachyacantha*).
1893 *Jrl. Amer. Folkl.* 6.141 **nwLA, eTX,** *Crataegus brachyacantha,* pomette bleue. [**1901** Lounsberry *S. Wild Flowers* 249, *Pomette Bleue.* . . This, the only blue fruited thorn in the south, is perhaps the largest and most beautiful of the genus. It is called Pomette Bleue by the French Acadians of Louisiana.] **1922** Sargent *Manual Trees* 533, *Crataegus brachyacantha* . . Pomette Bleue. [**1979** Ajilvsgi *Wild Flowers* 153 **eTX, wLA,** *Blueberry hawthorn.* . . A French name for this tree is *pomette bleu.*]

pomia n |poˈmiə| Cf **pão doce**
1965 *PADS* 43.16 **seMA,** Names for bread made with corn meal . . [põˈmiə] [3 of 9 infs]. *Ibid,* My Portuguese informants have informed me that [põˈmiə] is a form of *pão de milho,* or corn bread.

pomme blanche n [Fr, literally "white apple"; from the esculent root] **chiefly Upper MW, Plains States** Cf **pomme de prairie, ~ terre**
An **Indian breadroot,** usu *Psoralea esculenta*.
[**1823** James *Acct. of Exped.* 1.206 **NE,** They often bear a heavy staff of wood, sharpened to a broad edge at one end for the purpose of digging up the *Nu-ga-re,* or ground apple, called by the French *Pomme blanche.*] **1837** (1932) Chardon *Jrl.* 120 **cND,** All the Wives of the Village out after Pomme Blanche. **1841** Catlin *Letters Indians* 1.56, The "Pomme Blanche," or prairie turnip, . . is found in great quantities in these northern prairies, and furnishes the Indians with an abundant and nourishing food. **1886** Havard *Flora W. & S. TX for 1885* 501, *Psoralea esculenta* . . (Pomme Blanche.) Small herb, very common on the prairies of the Northwest, but very sparingly found in Western Texas. Its esculent tuberous roots are nutritive, wholesome, and pleasant to the taste. **1936** Winter *Plants NE* 98, Pomme Blanche. Prairie Apple. Indian Bread-root. Common in the prairie region. [**1937** U.S. Forest Serv. *Range Plant Hdbk.* W157, This plant is known under a variety of names as: the pomme blanche or pomme de prairie of the early French voyageurs, Indian turnip, prairie turnip, prairie potato or white apple of the American settlers, the aha or esharusha of the Crow Indian, and the pipsinnah of the Sioux Indians.] **1968** Barkley *Plants KS* 207, Pomme de Prairie, Pomme Blanche. Indian Breadroot. . . Prairies and plains.

pomme de prairie n [Fr, literally "prairie apple"; from the esculent root] **chiefly Upper MW, Plains States** Cf **pomme blanche, ~ de terre, prairie apple**
An **Indian breadroot,** usu *Psoralea esculenta*.
1844 Lapham *Geogr. Descr. WI* 78, [*Psoralia*] *esculenta* . . Pomme de Prairie. **1857** Gray *Manual of Botany* 94, *P[soralea] esculenta* . . the *Indian Turnip, Pomme Blanche,* or *Pomme de Prairie,* used as food by the aborigines,—may possibly occur on the Wisconsin side of the Mississippi. [**1891** Coulter *Botany W. TX* 75, *P[soralea] esculenta.* . . The "pomme blanche" or "pomme de prairie" of the voyageurs.] **1937** [see **pomme blanche**]. **1968** [see **pomme blanche**].

pomme de terre n [Fr, literally "ground apple" (in std Fr "white potato")]
1 An **Indian breadroot,** usu *Psoralea esculenta.* obs Cf **ground apple 1, pomme blanche, ~ de prairie**
1823 James *Acct. of Exped.* 1.218 **NE,** The squaws . . are often necessitated to dig the Pomme de terre . . and to scratch the ground-pea.

2 A **ground plum 1** (here: *Astragalus crassicarpus*).
1973 Hitchcock–Cronquist *Flora Pacific NW* 246, Ground or buffalo plum, pomme de terre . . *A[stragalus] crassicarpus.*

pommels See **pomace 3**

pommette bleue See **pomette bleue**

pommey See **pomace 2**

pomp v, hence ppl adj *pomped* [*OED2 pomp* v.[2] 1509 →; "Now dial."] Cf **pomper**

Usu with *up*: To pamper, flatter, spoil.

1886 *S. Bivouac* 4.349 ceTN, Pomped (pampered). **1887** *Amer. Philol. Assoc. Trans. for 1886* 17.41 eTN, wNC, Pomped, for pampered, I heard from a herder in the Great Smoky Mountains last summer, who spoke of a certain cow as "pomped up." **1937** (1977) Hurston *Their Eyes* 199 csFL, It was generally assumed that she thought herself too good to work like the rest of the women and that Tea Cake had "pomped her up tuh dat." **1948** Hurston *Seraph* 31 wFL, Here was the most wonderful man in all the world pomping her all up.

pomp n See **pump** n[1]

pompano n [Span *pámpano* for *Stromateus fiatola*] Cf **Irish pompano**

1 also *pampano, pompynose*: A saltwater fish of the genus *Trachinotus*, esp *T. carolinus*. **S Atl, Gulf States** For other names of var spp see **butterfish 1, cobbler** n[1] **4b, gaff-topsail pompano, oldwife 1c, palometa, permit, round pompano**

[**1778** Chappe d'Auteroche *Voyage CA* (transl. Anon.) 24, The pampano is very plenty in the southern part of the gulph of Mexico.] **1840** *Daily Picayune* (New Orleans LA) 1 Sept 2/1, There was a tall dinner party at the New Brighton Hotel, Pass Christian, on Sunday. Pompanos were plentiful, and sparkling hock flew about. **1873** in 1878 Smithsonian Inst. *Misc. Coll.* 14.2.25, *Trachynotus carolinus* . . Pompano (*Southern Coast*) . . pompynose (*New Orleans*). **1883** Twain *Life on Missip.* (Boston) 445 **New Orleans LA,** We had dinner . . the chief dish the renowned fish called pompano, delicious as the less criminal forms of sin. **1896** U.S. Natl. Museum *Bulletin* 47.943, Pompano; Palometa; Great Pámpano. **1902** Jordan–Evermann *Amer. Fishes* 204, *Pompano* means "grape leaf," and in Western Europe is appropriated by a very different fish. This name was applied to our fish by the Spanish colonists of America. **1926** Ferber *Show Boat* 176, Twenty-four hours—no more—must be the limit of his stay in the city whose pompano and crayfish and Creoles and roses and Ramos gin fizzes he loved. **1935** Caine *Game Fish* 107, *Permit—Trachinotus goodei*. . *Synonyms:* African Pompano[,] Big Pompano[,] Great Pompano . . Key West Pompano . . Mexican Pompano . . Pompano[,] Round Pompano. **1951** Taylor *Surv. Marine Fisheries NC* 274, At least four species of pompano occur off North Carolina. . *T[rachinotus] carolinus* . . is the most frequent of the species in this section. . All the pompanos are very popular game fishes farther south. **1965–70** *DARE* (Qu. P2, . . *Kinds of saltwater fish caught around here . . good to eat*) 18 Infs, 17 **S Atl, Gulf States,** Pompano; (Qu. P14, . . *Commercial fishing . . what do the fishermen go out after?*) Infs FL13, **LA**44, Pompano. **1986** Pederson *LAGS Concordance* **Gulf Region,** 12 infs, Pompano.

2 usu *California pompano*: A **butterfish 1** (here: *Peprilus simillimus*). **chiefly CA**

1882 U.S. Natl. Museum *Bulletin* 16.451, *S[tromateus] simillimus* . . *California Pompano*. . . Pacific coast of United States; abundant in summer; highly prized as a food-fish. **1884** Goode *Fisheries U.S.* 334, The California Pompano—*Stromateus simillimus*. . . This species, known here as the Pompano, reaches a length of eight inches and a weight of rather less than half a pound. **1911** U.S. Bur. Census *Fisheries 1908* 314, The poppy-fish (*Palometa simillima*) is miscalled the "California pompano." It is a delicate food fish. **1955** Zim–Shoemaker *Fishes* 92, Harvestfish [=*Peprilus* spp] live more to the south than Butterfish and are not as important as food fish. . . The California Pompano [= *Palometa simillima*] (not a true pompano) is a common Pacific harvestfish. **1968** *DARE* (Qu. P2, . . *Kinds of saltwater fish caught around here . . good to eat*) Infs CA36, 80, Pompano. **1991** *Amer. Fisheries Soc. Common Names Fishes* 66, *Peprilus simillimus* . . Pacific pompano.

pomped See **pomp**

pompeon See **pompion** n[1]

pomper v Also with *up* [Var of *pamper*; see *EDD pomper* v. "To feed up. A dial. form of 'pamper.'"] **chiefly S Midl** Cf **pomp** v

1815 in 1947 *AmSp* 22.281 [Americanisms noted by an Englishman],

Pamper—pomper (frequent). **1880** *Harper's New Mth. Mag.* 62.93 **CT,** Meat is reel costly, an' pomperin' the flesh is sinful. **1885** Murfree *Prophet of Smoky Mts.* 71 eTN, I never see a critter so pompered ez Jacob; he ain't got no medjure o' respec' fur nobody. **1902** *DN* 2.242 sIL, Pompered up. . . High fed. Rendered fastidious by extra care and attention to the person. **1903** *DN* 2.323 seMO, Pamper. . . Pronounced pomper. 'He pompers his horses.' **1907** *DN* 3.234 nwAR, Pomper. **1909** *DN* 3.358 eAL, wGA, Pompered up is frequently heard. **1913** Kephart *Highlanders* 278 sAppalachians, Pomper. **1915** *DN* 4.187 swVA, Pomper. **1930** Shoemaker *1300 Words* 45 cPA **Mts** (as of c1900), Pomper—To put in fine condition by artificial stimulants. **1936** *AmSp* 11.316 **Ozarks,** Pomper. . . To feed too much, to injure by overfeeding. 'Them chickens has been pompered on milk.' **1941** *AmSp* 16.24 sIN, Pomper. Spoil. 'That boy's been pompered to death.' **1942** Hall *Smoky Mt. Speech* 26 wNC, eTN, Substitution of [ɑ] or [ɒ] is usual in *jab, pamper, stab* [etc]. **1961** Seeman *In Arms of Mt.* 159 eTN, Brownie is the most "pompered up" ground hog in the county. He can always be sure of a supply of warm milk and cornbread. **1976** Garber *Mountain-ese* 70 sAppalachians, Don't pomper that child or you'll get him plumb spoilt.

pompey adj Cf **hickory bender, rubber ice**

See quots.

1904 *N.Y. World* Jan. 3 (*Century Dict. Suppl.* at *pompey* a[2]), The floor is *"pompey,"* as the firemen say, when it bulges and sags. It is then time to get out. That is all true. It was thought time and again that firemen had been lost in the building. **1911** *Century Dict. Suppl.*, Pompey. . . Bulging or sagging in a dangerous degree; said of a floor in a burning building; also, applied to ice when it is in a similar dangerous condition from thawing, etc. . . Local, U.S. **1968** *DARE* (Qu. B35, *Ice that will bend when you step on it, but not break*) Inf NY37, Pompey ice—particularly ice in swamp area.

pompey n

=**yellow-breasted chat.**

1919 Pearson et al. *Birds NC* 304, *Icteria virens virens*. . . The Chat, also locally called "Pompey," is an abundant summer visitor in central and western North Carolina, occurring almost everywhere in sunny thickets and among low second-growth trees.

pompeyed adj [Var of *pampered*; cf *OED2 pompey* v. 1860 →] Cf **pomper, pomp** v

1942 *AmSp* 17.70, Her mother, . . who is originally from West Virginia, often called her in her juvenile days a 'pompeyed child,' meaning a spoiled or overcoddled one. This expression seems to have come to America from England.

Pompey's head n Also *Pompey head* [From its appearance, in allusion either to *Pompey* as a typical male slave name or to *Pompey* the Great, who was murdered in 48 BC and whose head was sent to Julius Caesar.]

A type of meat dish; see quot 1940.

1890 McAllister *Society* 314 **Sth,** Some features of the everyday Southern dinner were *pilau* . . ; "Hoppin John," . . ; okra soup, . . ; shrimp and prawn pie; . . pompey head (a stuffed *filet* of veal); [etc]. **1940** Brown *Amer. Cooks* 135 **GA,** Mix meats well together . . form into a ball. . . During baking sprinkle . . with flour to make a fine crust that will eventually look like Pompey's woolly head. . . Pompey's Head varies greatly in different regions of the seaboard states, the name coming from the appearance of the dish rather than from its ingredients. **1941** Writers' Program *Guide SC* 153, The very names of certain dishes arouse curiosity and titillate the palate—Pompey's head, tipsy pudding, jambalaya [etc].

pompion n[1] Also *pompeon, pumpeon* [*OED2* a1545 →] =**pumpkin** n[1] **B1.**

1588 (1903) Hariot *Briefe Rept. VA* sig C2ᵛ, *Macócqwer,* according to their seuerall formes called by vs, *Pompions, Mellions,* and *Gourdes,* because they are of the like formes as those kindes in England. **1624** Smith *Genl. Hist. VA* 29, In May also amongst their corne they plant *Pumpeons.* **1670** Clarke *True 4 Plantations* 22, *Indian* Pompeons, the water Melon, and the Musk-Melon. **1788** (1925) Washington *Diaries* 3.407, The rest of the hands were about finishing . . pulling the large weeds from among the Pompions. **1840** *MA Zool. & Bot. Surv. Herb. Plants & Quadrupeds* 112, The Pompion or Pumpkin, for so it is written in England as well as in the United States, is more certain, and the varieties are more permanent. **1900** Lyons *Plant Names* 125, *C[ucurbita]*

Pepo. . . Pumpkin (of America), Pompion. The type is the common Field or Yellow Pumpkin. **1952** *NY Folkl. Qrly.* 8.187 **cwNY,** Other terms used out Canisteo-way were: "candlewood" for pine knots, and "pompions" for pumpkins.

pompion n[2] See **pompon 1**

pompion berry n

A **hackberry** (here: *Celtis occidentalis*); also the fruit of this plant.

1833 Eaton *Botany* 86, [*Celtis*] *occidentalis* . . nettle tree, pompion berry. **1859** (1968) Bartlett *Americanisms* 331, *Pompion Berry*. Another name for the fruit of *Celtis occidentalis*. **1872** Schele de Vere *Americanisms* 403, *Hack* berries or *Pompion* berries . . are obtained from a shrub, which at times reaches nearly the size of a tree (Celtis occidentalis), and are sweet and edible, not unlike so-called bird-cherries.

pom-pom n

A type of playing marble; see quot.

c1970 Wiersma *Marbles Terms, Pom-pom(s):* . . Marbles which have all kinds of designs and pretty colors.

pom-pom-pullaway n Also *pom-pom-Pete-away, pullaway, pump-pump-pullaway, pum-pum-pullaway;* for addit varr see quots **chiefly Gt Lakes, Upper MW, Plains States, Rocky Mts, sCA** See Map Cf **Dixie** n[1]**; king, king can I go; London loo**

A children's chasing game; see quots; also used as a phr in the game.

1889 Copeland *Hist. Clarendon* 369 **cwNY,** Pom-pom pull-away, leap-frog, crack-the-whip, ring-around, jump-the-rope and anty, anty over, are laid away in memory's play shop. **1895** *DN* 1.398, *King*. A common game among boys is known variously as . . *pom-pom-pealaway* (Ill., N.Y.), *pom-pom-pull-away* (Iowa, Minn., N.Y.), *Pom-pom-pull-away:* pron. [pʌm]. **1896** *DN* 1.422 **IA,** *Pom-pom, pump, pull away:* children's game after the fashion of "crack the whip." **1897** *KS Univ. Qrly.* (ser B) 6.91 **neKS,** *Pump, pump, pull away:* children's game after the fashion of "crack the whip." **1899** Garland *Boy Life* 25 **nwIA** (as of c1870s), The boys always went early, in order to have an hour at "dog and deer," or "dare-goal," or "pom-pom pullaway." **1901** *DN* 2.145 **cNY,** *Pullaway* . . the same as pom-pom-pull-away. **1906** *DN* 3.152 **nwAR,** *Pullaway*, a game, also known as "fox and goose," and played in the water. **1909** *DN* 3.402 **nwAR,** *Pull away*. . . A game. Ibid 414 **nME,** *Pullaway*. . . A children's game. One player begins as *stump* or catcher. When he calls *pull away* all the players have to run across a line. Those that he catches come over to his side and help him catch others when *pull away* is called again. **1910** *DN* 3.446 **wNY,** *Pom-pom-pull-away.* **1914** *DN* 4.111 **cKS,** *Pullaway*. . . A running game. **1916** *DN* 4.327 **KS,** *Pum pum pullaway*. . . Also, as in N.Y., W[estern] Res[erve], *pom pom pull a way*. A game of children or youths. The leader or *"it"* faces the rest, usually six or more. He shouts *"pum pum pull away."* At this they run toward the goal where he is. Each tagged one assists him to tag others. The sides change goals rapidly. When all are caught they start anew. Neb., Mich. **1917** *DN* 4.398 **neOH,** *Pom-pom-pullaway* [pʌm-pʌmˈpulə,we], the game. And—*peel-away*. . . [In Ia., [pum-pumˈpuləwe]. In Vt., "pump-pump pull away, anyway to get away."] Also Kan., Neb., N.Y. Ibid 404 **neOH,** *Pom-pom-pete-away.* = *pom-pom-pull-away.* W. Mass. **1919** *DN* 5.76 **wMA,** *Pom-pom-pullaway.* In 1898, in western Massachusetts, I knew this game as *pom-pom-pete-away. Pull-away* must have been the original form. **1929** Ellis *Ordinary Woman* 63 **CO** (as of early 20th cent), Then we played 'pum-pum-pull-away,' and how hard I would run, how hard I would try to get away from him, and how pleased when he would catch me, not caring how hard were the three slaps on the back! **1950** *WELS* **WI** (*Outdoor games that were played during your childhood*) 9 Infs, Pom-pom-pullaway; 8 Infs, Pump-pump-pullaway; 3 Infs, Pullaway; 1 Inf, Pum-pum-pullaway; 1 Inf, Pomp-pomp-pullaway; (*Games played on the ice in your neighborhood*) 2 Infs, Pump-pump-pullaway; 2 Infs, Pom(-pom)-pullaway; 2 Infs, Pom-pom(-poleaway); (*Hiding games that start with some special, elaborate way of sending the players out to hide*) 1 Inf, Pom-pom-pullaway. **1965–70** *DARE* (Qu. EE33, . . *Outdoor games . . that children play*) 113 Infs, **chiefly Gt Lakes, Upper MW, Plains States, Rocky Mts, sCA,** Pom-pom-pullaway; IA21, IL40, MN12, 23, 42, Pum-pum-pullaway; MI123, Pom-pom-Pete-away—one person in center of area; the rest on one side of room. All run to other side; center person tries to catch one, then another. Object [is] to get everybody in center; NH5, Pullaway—one player has to catch one of a group as they run across a line. Each player caught joins him—shout

"pom-pom-pullaway"; SD3, Pullaway—two goals, man in center says "pump-pump-pullaway," everyone runs toward the other goal. "It" tries to tag them and they become "it"; (Qu. EE27, *Games played on the ice*) Infs **IL**47, **IN**69, **MN**2, **UT**4, Pom-pom-pullaway; **WI**47, 50, Pom-pom-poleaway; IL97, Pom-pom—one guy gets in the middle; others have to get past him. He annexes players to his line by catching them; **MN**21, Pum-pum-pullaway; **WA**13, Poleaway—on skates; or pump-pump-pullaway; (Qu. EE12, *Games in which one captain hides his team and the other team tries to find it*) Infs **CO**7, **TX**18, Pom-pom-pullaway. **1971** *AmSp* 46.84 **Chicago IL,** *Pom-pom pull away, pom-pom Peter way.* **1986** Pederson *LAGS Concordance*, 1 inf, **swFL,** *Pom-pom-pull-away*—tackling game, rough. **1988** *WI State Jrl.* (Madison) 27 June sec D 1/1, Then he spoke of another we did play: Pump, Pump, Pull Away.

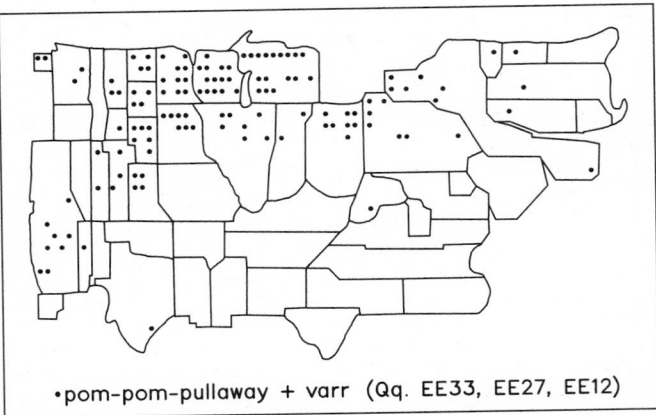

•pom-pom-pullaway + varr (Qq. EE33, EE27, EE12)

pompon n [AmSpan *pompón* in sense **1** below]

1 also *pompion, pompui:* A **grunt** n **1** (here: *Anisotremus surinamensis*). Also called **drum 3, margate fish c, marketfish, molly** n[1] **7c, sailor's choice 1d, saltwater bream 2**

1799 (1803) Ellicott *Jrl.* 255, A great abundance and variety of fish may be taken: such as . . pompui. **1849** Foster *NY in Slices* 42, From the plump and rosy Salmon of Portland, to the piquant Pompion of Pensacola and the Green Turtle of the Keys, every species of substantial and rare Fish can be found in the Markets of New York. **1902** Jordan-Evermann *Amer. Fishes* 431, The pompon is found from southern Florida and Mobile to Brazil. **1933** John G. Shedd Aquarium *Guide* 109, The Pompon is a large fish, reaching a length of two or three feet. It is fairly common on the south Atlantic coast. **1991** Amer. Fisheries Soc. *Common Names Fishes* 159, Pompon—see black margate.

2 =**margaret grunt.**

1935 Caine *Game Fish* 85, *Margaret grunt*—*Haemulon album*. . . Synonyms: Bream . . Pompon [etc]. **1946** LaMonte *N. Amer. Game Fishes* 64, *Margate Fish*. . . Names: Margaret Grunt . . Pompon [etc].

pompui See **pompon 1**

pomp up See **pomp**

pompynose See **pompano 1**

pon v [Pronc-sp for *pawn*]

1887 Amer. Philol. Assoc. *Trans. for 1886* 17.46 **Sth,** List of common Southern expressions—many of them vulgarisms—that have not, so far as I know, either old English or provincial English authority. . . To *pon'* (pledge). **1915** *DN* 4.187 **swVA,** *Pon*. Variant of *pawn*.

ponch See **paunch**

ponchka See **paczki**

pond n[1] [Var, prob by folk-etym, of **pound** n[2]]
=**pound** n[2] **2, 3;** hence n *pond net* =**pound net.**

1956 *Richmond Times–Dispatch* (VA) 6 July 6/5 (Hench Coll.) **ceVA,** Since crabs must shed before they can be packed, packers buy truckloads of them and put them in floats in the shedding ponds. Because of high mortality, the ponds must be located in a strong tide, but in order to weather storms they must be in fairly shallow water as well. **1962** Salisbury *Quoth the Raven* 156 **seAK,** When the Radio drew in on the other side of the pond, as the closed purse-seine is called, to brail out the herring, the net was opened to let out a portion of the excess of the haul.

Ibid 159, Bob has a "pond," an area inclosed between the two docks with the wire chicken fencing used in making the salmon traps, and his men have several times cast their seines and shunted the haul through a gap into the pond, to hold as live bait for the halibut fishing. **1966–69** *DARE* (Qu. P13, . . *Ways of fishing . . besides the ordinary hook and line*) Inf **MI**2, Pond net; **WI**78, Pond nets—have bigger mash [sic]. **1967–68** *DARE* Tape **MI**54, We had pond nets, pond nets up the shore here; **WI**75, [Inf:] And then when they have different, other kind of boats for fishing pond net. Those are open boats. . . [FW:] Now you just mentioned a pond net a moment ago. What's that? [Inf:] Well, a pond net is a trap net.

pond n² See **pond water 1**

pond apple n

A **custard apple 1** (here: *Annona glabra*). Also called **alligator apple, swamp ~**

1884 Sargent *Forests of N. Amer.* 23, *Anona laurifolia.* . . Pond Apple.—Semi-tropical Florida, cape Malabar to bay Biscayne, on the west coast, Pease creek to the Caloosa river, and through the West Indies. **1917** (1923) Rogers *Trees Worth Knowing* 170, The pond apple . . is our only representative of its genus that reaches tree form and size, and it is the second of our native custard-apples. **1939** FWP *Guide FL* 346 **ceFL,** In this jungle, and elsewhere on southern Merritt Island where the land has not been cleared, are found trees growing more than 200 miles north of their native habitat on the Florida Keys. . . [A]mong others, ironwood, gumbo limbo, soapberry, . . pond apple, and necklace bean. **1964** Will *Hist. Okeechobee* 35 **FL,** It's called Anona Glabra or Pond Apple. . . The custard apple trees loved wet, swampy ground. **1975** Natl. Audubon Soc. *Corkscrew* 11 **swFL,** The small, twisted trees growing here are custard or pond apples. They have dark green waxy leaves and during the late summer and early fall produce large greenish-yellow fruits much in favor among the raccoon population. **1997** *Audubon Mag.* July-Aug 80 **FL,** Wood stork nests . . are hidden in the moonflower vines covering the pond apple.

pondberry n

A **spicebush** (here: *Lindera melissifolia*).

1960 Vines *Trees SW* 295, *Lindera melissaefolia.* . . Vernacular names are . . Hairy Spice-bush, and Pond-berry. . . The plant is sometimes nibbled by marsh rabbit, and the fruit eaten by a number of species of birds.

pond bluet n [Appar from a similarity to **bluet 2**] Cf **ditch bluet**

A marsh plant (*Hydrolea ovata*).

1951 *PADS* 15.38 **TX,** *Nama ovatum* [=*Hydrolea o.*] . . Ditch, pond, or prickly, bluet.

pond brush n

A **forestiera** (here: *Forestiera acuminata*).

1921 Deam *Trees IN* 282, *Adelia acuminata* . . Pond Brush. Crooked Brush. . . Southwestern Indiana and southern Illinois south to northern Florida and Texas. . . It usually forms dense thickets on the bank that surrounds standing water and is usually associated with button-bush.

pondbush n

1 A **spicebush** (here: *Lindera benzoin*). *obs*

1810 Michaux *Histoire des Arbres* 1.86, *Pinus serotina.* The Pond Pine. *Ibid,* Le nom de *Pond pine,* Pin des mares, qui je lui donne, me paroît assez convenable, car on le trouve principalement autour des mares *Ponds* remplies de *Laurus estivalis, Pondbushes.* [=The name *Pond pine,* Pin des mares, which I give it, seems to me quite appropriate, for it is found principally around ponds (mares) full of *Laurus estivalis* [=*Lindera benzoin*], *Pondbushes.*]

2 =**pond spice 1.**

1860 Curtis *Cat. Plants NC* 92, Pond Bush. (*Tetranthera geniculata* [= *Litsea aestivalis*], Nees.)—Occupies small ponds in the Lower District, giving a gray smoky aspect to these localities. . . It is 10 or 15 feet high, with smooth, zigzag branches, and small oval leaves, ½ to 1 inch long, and red berries. **1933** Small *Manual SE Flora* 923, *G[labraria] geniculata.* . . Pond-spice. Pond-bush. **1960** Vines *Trees SW* 293, Pondspice—*Glabraria geniculata.* . . Common names include Pond-bush and Crooked Swamp-bush.

pond chicken n

1 Either the **Florida gallinule** or the **purple gallinule**; see quot. Cf **pond fowl**

1949 Sprunt–Chamberlain *SC Bird Life* 203, *Purple Gallinule.* . . *Local Names:* Bluepeter; Pondchicken; Marsh Hen. *Ibid* 205, "Pondchicken" is a name often applied to the Florida Gallinule, and the name is not inappropriate, for gallinules do remind one of barnyard chickens gone wild and aquatic. . . They twitch and jerk their tails frequently, and the astonishing medley of clucks, clacks, grunts, squawks, and shrieks sound like a barnyard gone crazy.

2 A **bullfrog 1.**

1954 *PADS* 21.34 **seSC,** Pond chicken . . Green frog, *rana catesbeiana.* Probably so called because of the edible hind legs, considered a delicacy. Williamsburg County and probably general along the coast. **1966** *DARE* (Qu. P22, *Names or nicknames for a very large frog that makes a deep, loud sound*) Inf **SC**9, Pond chicken—a frog sought for its legs. **1966** *DARE* FW Addit **SC**9, Pond chicken—not such a deep voice.

pond coot n

1 =**ruddy duck.** Cf **coot** n¹ **2b**

1927 Forbush *Birds MA* 1.280, *Ruddy Duck.* Other names . . Pond Coot. **1946** Hausman *Eastern Birds* 149, *Ruddy Duck.* . . Some seventy or so local names, among which are . . Pond Coot [etc]. . . These funny little ducks sail about like little toys. . . They splatter over the water for some distance before taking flight.

2 =**coot** n¹ **1.**

1955 MA Audubon Soc. *Bulletin* 39.444 **RI,** [The American Coot is called] Pond Coot. **1970** *DARE* (Qu. Q9, *The bird that looks like a small, dull-colored duck and is commonly found on ponds and lakes*) Inf **VA**79, Pond coot = coot.

pond crow n Cf **mud crow**

=**coot** n¹ **1.**

1917 (1923) *Birds Amer.* 1.214, American Coot . . Pond Crow. . . Prevailing color, slate, dark above and light below. **1955** Forbush–May *Birds* 168, *American Coot . . Other names:* Blue Peter . . Pond-hen; Pond-crow [etc].

pond cypress n

A **bald cypress** (here: *Taxodium ascendens*).

1901 Mohr *Plant Life AL* 325, *Taxodium distichum imbricaria* [=*T. ascendens*]. . . Pond Cypress, Upland Cypress. **1908** Britton *N. Amer. Trees* 91, The wood of the Pond cypress is said to be heavier and stronger than that of the Bald cypress. **1933** Small *Manual SE Flora* 31, *Taxodium imbricarium.* . . In lakes, pine-land ponds, creeks and small rivers in the coastal plain, apparently always over a clay subsoil, Virginia (Dismal Swamp) to Florida and Alabama. . . Pond-Cypress. **1946** West–Arnold *Native Trees FL* 11, The pond-cypress occurs in flatwoods ponds from Palm Beach County northward. While it never attains the great size of bald-cypress, the wood is equally valuable and is not differentiated by lumbermen. **1962** Kurz–Godfrey *Trees N. FL* 17, The pond-cypress is a small to medium-sized tree, commonly with buttressed bases, and with rounded or blunt-tipped "knees." **1980** Little *Audubon Guide N. Amer. Trees E. Region* 303, Pondcypress . . is found in shallow ponds and poorly drained areas from southeastern Virginia to southeastern Louisiana below 100′.

pond dogwood n Cf **dogwood**

=**buttonbush 1.**

1784 in 1785 Amer. Acad. Arts & Sci. *Memoirs* 1.409, *Cephalanthus.* . . Globe-Flower Shrub. Pond Dogwood. Button Bush. . . Common in watery swamps and pond-holes. **1828** Rafinesque *Med. Flora* 1.100, Button-wood Shrub. . . Vulgar Names—White Ball . . Pond Dogwood, Globe flower, in Louisiana *Bois de Marais.* **1837** Darlington *Flora Cestrica* 98 **sePA,** Western *Cephalanthus.* Vulgò—Button Bush. Pond Dog-wood. **1900** Lyons *Plant Names* 90, *C[ephalanthus] occidentalis.* . . Pond or Swamp Dogwood, River-bush, Swamp-wood. **1973** Stephens *Woody Plants* 458, Buttonbush, globe flower, honeyball, swamp sycamore, pond dogwood.

pond duck n

1 =**hooded merganser** or a similar duck. [*OED2* 1774 for a wild duck]

1926 (1949) McQueen–Mizell *Hist. Okefenokee* 136 **seGA,** Other migratory ducks include the pond duck. . . The pond duck is also a small duck, weighing from one to two pounds. He gets his name from the fact that he feeds almost exclusively in the ponds in the pine woods adjacent to the Swamp. **1955** *Oriole* 20.1.5 **GA,** Hooded Merganser . . Pond

Duck (as frequenting small bodies of water). **1969** *DARE* (Qu. Q5, . . *Kinds of wild ducks*) Inf **GA**89, Pond duck.
2 =**coot** n[1] **1.**
   c1960 *Wilson Coll.* **csKY**, *Coot.* . . Known locally as . . pond duck. It is usually classed as a duck with queer feet.

ponderosa pine n
1 Std: a common timber **pine 1** of the western US. Also called **big pine, black ~ 2c, blackjack ~ 2, bull ~ 1b, California white ~, foothills yellow ~, heavy-wooded ~, jack ~ 2d, longleaf ~ 2, Oregon white ~, pitch ~ c(1), red ~ 1c, rock ~ b, western yellow ~, white ~, yellow ~ 2** =**Jeffrey pine.**
   1979 Little *Checklist U.S. Trees* 194, *Jeffrey pine.* . . *Other common names* . . ponderosa pine.

pondey See **pondy**

pondfish See **pond perch**

pond fisher n
=**hooded merganser.**
   1923 *U.S. Dept. Ag. Misc. Circular* 13.7 **PA**, *Hooded Merganser.* . . *Vernacular Names.* . . *In local use.* . . pond fisher. **1940** Todd *Birds W. PA* 117, The Hooded Merganser differs from the other two species in shunning deep or running water; it prefers coves, ponds, overflowed meadows, and quiet water along the shore. On Presque Isle it was oftenest seen on the ponds, feeding in company with coots and pied-billed grebes—whence came the name "Pond Fisher" that was used by the local gunners.

pond fowl n Cf **pond chicken 1**
Either the **Florida gallinule** or the **purple gallinule.**
   1923 *U.S. Dept. Ag. Misc. Circular* 13.44, *Florida Gallinule.* . . *Vernacular Names.* . . *In local use.* . . pond-fowl (Ga., Fla.) *Ibid,* *Purple Gallinule.* . . pond-fowl (Ga., Fla.)

pond frog n
1 A **bullfrog 1,** usu *Rana clamitans.*
   1672 Josselyn *New-Englands Rarities* 38, The *Indians* will tell you, that up in the Country there are Pond *Frogs* as big as a Child of a year old. **1792** Belknap *Hist. NH* 3.174, Pond Frog, *Rana occellata* [sic]. **1832** Williamson *Hist. ME* 1.169, Of the *Frog kind* are six species:—1. the *Toad;* 2. the *pond Frog;* 3. the *speckled Frog;* 4. the *tree Toad;* 5. the *bull Frog;* and 6. the *green Frog.* **1884** *Century Illustr. Mag.* 28.47, I longed for the multitudinous chorus of my own bog; . . the rattling drums, kettle and bass, of our pond frogs. **1928** Pope–Dickinson *Amphibians* 37, *Green Frog—Rana clamitans.* . . Other common names include Spring Frog and Pond Frog. . . common along brooks and ponds. **1932** Wright *Life-Hist. Frogs* 2.352, *Rana clamitans.* . . Green Frog. Pond Frog. Spring Frog. Bullfrog. Bawling Frog. Yellow-throated Green Frog [etc].
2 A **tree frog** or similar frog; see quots.
   1922 Gonzales *Black Border* 302 **sSC, GA coasts** [Gullah glossary], *Fry-bakin* [sic] *frog*—the small pond frogs, whose constant cry is interpreted by the Negroes as "fry-bacon, tea-table; fry-bacon, tea-table." **1966** Dakin *Dial. Vocab. Ohio R. Valley* 2.388 **KY**, Kentucky has *sprat frog, swamp ~, pond ~, little ~, kitin' ~, squeaking ~, skracking ~, mud quackers,* and *peeper toad.* **1967–69** *DARE* (Qu. P21, *Small frogs that sing or chirp loudly in spring*) Infs **IL**14, **IN**31, **PA**128, Pond frogs; **KY**47, Too-tights, tree frogs, pond frogs [FW: none synonymous].

pond gannet n esp **FL, GA** Cf **gannet 2**
=**wood ibis.**
   c1940 Eliason *Word Lists FL* 10, [pɔnd gɑnɪt]: A wading bird having long legs and inhabiting ponds and small lakes. **1965–68** *DARE* (Qu. Q10, . . *Water birds and marsh birds*) Infs **FL**18, **GA**35, Pond gannet; **GA**7, Pond gannet—large; **GA**46, Pond gannets—long-legged, long-beaked. **2000** *DARE* File—Internet **seGA**, You are very Wiregrass if . . you know what a pond gannet (sp.) is.

pondgrass n
1 A **wheatgrass** such as *Pascopyrum smithii* or **quack grass 1.**
   1894 *Jrl. Amer. Folkl.* 7.103 **swNE**, *Agropyrum glaucum* [=*Pascopyrum smithii*] . . slough-grass, pond-grass, Colorado blue-grass, bluegrass. **1945** Wodehouse *Hayfever Plants* 44, Quackgrass (*A[gropyron] repens* Beauv.) is a wiry grass. . . known by many vernacular names . .

and locally by other names as stroil . . and pond grass [etc]. **1966** *DARE* (Qu. L9a, . . *Kinds of grass . . grown for hay*) Inf **FL**7, Pondgrass.
2 A **pondweed** (here: *Potamogeton pectinatus*).
   1900 Lyons *Plant Names* 303, *P[otamogeton] pectinatus* . . Fennel-leaved Pond-weed, Pond-grass. **1936** Winter *Plants NE* 18, *P[otamogeton] pectinatus* . . Fennel-leaved Pondweed. Very common pondweed of the sandhill lakes and rivers. Grows in fresh or alkaline water. Called also pond-grass. **1940** Clute *Amer. Plant Names* 153, *P[otamogeton] pectinatus* . . Fennel-leaved Pondweed. Pond-grass [etc].

pond guinea n Cf **marsh guinea**
1 Either the **Florida gallinule** or the **purple gallinule.** **FL**
   1923 *U.S. Dept. Ag. Misc. Circular* 13.44 **FL**, *Purple Gallinule.* . . *Vernacular Names.* . . *In local use.* . . pond-guinea. **1953** *AmSp* 28.277 **FL**, Pond guinea . . Purple gallinule. *Ibid,* Pond guinea . . Common gallinule. **1969** Longstreet *Birds FL* 56, *Purple Gallinule—Other names:* Blue Pete; Pond Guinea; Bonnet-walker. *Ibid* 57, *Common Gallinule—Other names:* Pond Guinea; Bonnet-walker.
2 A **bittern** (here: *Botaurus lentiginosus*).
   1953 *AmSp* 28.277 **MS**, Pond guinea . . American bittern.
3 =**white ibis.**
   1962 Imhof *AL Birds* 106, *White Ibis* . . *Other Names:* White Curlew, Spanish Curlew, Pond-guinea.
4 =**green heron.**
   1953 *AmSp* 28.277 **AL, MS**, Pond guinea . . Green heron.

pond hen n
1 =**coot** n[1] **1.**
   1888 Trumbull *Names of Birds* 117 **MA**, To some at Salem, Mass., and more commonly at Newport, R.I., [the American Coot is known as] *Meadow-hen* . . in Massachusetts at Provincetown, Buzzard's Bay, and West Barnstable, *Pond-hen.* **1955** Forbush–May *Birds* 168, *American Coot . . Other names* . . Pond-hen; Pond-crow; Meadow-hen; Water-hen; Mud-hen.
2 =**Florida gallinule.** Cf **gray pond-hen 2**
   1923 *U.S. Dept. Ag. Misc. Circular* 13.45, *Florida Gallinule.* . . Book Names. . . pond-hen [etc]. **1932** Bennitt *Check-list* 28 **MO**, *Florida gallinule.* . . Mud-hen . . gray pond-hen. **1955** Forbush–May *Birds* 166, *Florida Gallinule.* . . *Other names:* Gray Pond-hen [etc].

pond lily n Cf **Indian pond lily**
A **water lily** of the genus *Nuphar, Nymphaea,* or *Nelumbo,* but esp *Nuphar luteum.*
   1748 in 1934 Eliot *Field Husbandry* 11 **CT**, Not a natural Pond. . . over grown with Pond Lillies. **1825** (1910) Ayer *Diary* 250 **MA**, Mr. Vance's situation is the most romantic and delightful . . the shore on each side being lin'd with beautiful wild roses and pond-lillies. **1837** Darlington *Flora Cestrica* 318 **sePA**, *Strange nuphar. Vulgò*—Spatterdock. Yellow Pond-lily. **1849** Lyell *Second Visit* 2.245 **VA**, I saw floating the singular seed-vessel of the nuphar, or yellow pond lily (*Nelumbium*). **a1861** (1880) Eastman *Poems* 67 **VT**, But there is blue-eyed Willie,/ Who labors with the men,/ Who brings the sweet pond-lily / To Mary of the Glen! **1893** *Jrl. Amer. Folkl.* 6.136 **VT**, *Nuphar advena.* . . yellow pond lily. Ferrisburgh, Vt. **1901** Lounsberry *S. Wild Flowers* 163, *Nymphaea advena,* large yellow pond lily, or spatter dock, is common in the stagnant waters of ponds and the lower courses of streams. **1949** Moldenke *Amer. Wild Flowers* 17, Extremely abundant in the streams and sloughs of northeastern and peninsular Florida is the Florida pondlily, *N[ymphaea] macrophylla,* with erect or floating leaves often so dense as to hide completely the surface of the water. **1957** *Sat. Eve. Post Letters* **MO**, "Pond lily" rather than "water lily". **1965–70** *DARE* (Qu. S26b, *Wildflowers that grow in water or wet places*) 42 Infs, **scattered,** Pond lily (*or* lilies); **CT**15, **IA**18, **MI**2, **NJ**8, 19, **NY**87, Pond lily (*or* lilies)—same as water lily (*or* lilies); **MN**3, Pond lily—both yellow and white; grows right in small streams and still water; **NY**21, Pond lily or lily pads; **NY**52, White pond lilies, yellow pond lilies; **AK**1, **NY**165, Wild pond lily; (Qu. S22, . . *The bright yellow flowers that bloom in clusters in marshes in early springtime*) Inf **NC**12, Pond lilies? [Inf queries]; (Qu. S26a, . . *Wildflowers. . . Roadside flowers*) Inf **ME**7, Pond lily. **1966–67** *DARE* Wildfl QR Pl.56 Infs **WA**10, **NY**91, **OR**12, **MI**31, 57A, Yellow pond lily; **OH**37, **WA**15, Pond lily; pond lily is water lily. **1998** *DARE* File **MA**, White pond lilies were my grandmother's favorite flowers.

pond lizard n Cf **spring frog, ~ peeper**
See quot.

1968–69 *DARE* (Qu. P21, *Small frogs that sing or chirp loudly in spring*) Infs **IN**3, **KY**11, Pond lizards.

pond loon n

An adult **loon 1** (here: *Gavia immer*); see quot.

1917 *Wilson Bulletin* 29.2.75 **MA**, *Gavia immer.*—Adult is pond loon; young, sheep loon, Plymouth, Mass.

pond mullet n Cf **ama-ama**

=**striped mullet.**

[**1960** Gosline–Brock *Hawaiian Fishes* 154, *Mugil cephalus* does occur along open coasts, but it seems to prefer brackish-water areas. . . It is the form occurring in the mullet ponds.] **1967** *DARE* (Qu. P1, . . *Kinds of freshwater fish . . caught around here . . good to eat*) Inf **HI**14, Pond mullet.

pond net See **pond** n¹

pond nut n

=**water chinquapin.**

1832 (1919) Irving *Jrls.* 3.119 **NY**, Pond nuts like fresh almonds. **1950** Gray–Fernald *Manual of Botany* 641, *N[elumbo] lutea.* . . Yellow Nelumbo, Water-Chinquapin, Pond-nuts, Wonkapin. . . Tubers farinaceous and edible. Seeds also eatable. **1970** Correll *Plants TX* 633, *Nelumbo lutea* . . Yellow lotus, water-chinquapin, pond-nut. . . fruit nutlike, indehiscent.

pond oak n

Prob a **water oak** such as *Quercus nigra*.

1965–68 *DARE* (Qu. T10, . . *Kinds of oak trees*) Infs **FL**22, **TX**42, **WV**7, Pond oak.

pond perch n Also *pondfish*

Either the **red-breasted sunfish 1** or a **pumpkinseed 1** (here: *Lepomis gibbosus*).

1765 in 1903 Rowe *Letters* 82 **MA**, We caught at least ten dozn of Pond Perch. **1814** in 1815 Lit. & Philos. Soc. NY *Trans.* 403, *Freshwater Sunfish, or Pond Perch. (Labrus auritus.)* With speckled sides, yellow belly, and elongated gill-covers, marked with a black and red spot. **1818** *Amer. Monthly Mag. & Crit. Rev.* 2.247, Black-eared Pondfish—*Labrus appendix* [=*Lepomis auritus*]. **1838** MA *Zool. & Bot. Surv. Repts. Zool.* 38, The *Pomotis vulgaris*—*pond perch*—is seldom seen in the market, but is nevertheless a very good fish. **1886** Mather *Memoranda* 7 **neNY**, *Pomotis vulgaris.* . . Pumpkin seed, pond fish, etc. . . This little fish is quite handsome, but it is a voracious feeder. **1946** LaMonte *N. Amer. Game Fishes* 139, *Pumpkinseed* . . Names: Common Sunfish, Kiver, Kivvy, Pond Perch [etc]. **1983** Becker *Fishes WI* 828, *Pumpkinseed.* . . Other common names: pumpkinseed sunfish, yellow sunfish . . pond perch [etc].

pond pickerel n Also *pond pike*

Usu **chain pickerel,** but also a **redfin pickerel** (here: *Esox americanus americanus*).

1865 Norris *Amer. Angler's Book* 138, The Pond Pike, or Common Pike. The smaller species of Pikes are confined almost exclusively to the streams on the eastern slope of the Alleghanies. **1887** Goode *Amer. Fishes* 277, *Esox americanus,* the "Brook Pickerel," or "Banded Pickerel," sometimes also called the "Long Island Pickerel," "Trout Pickerel," and "Pond Pike," is comparatively small, rarely exceeding a foot in length, though occasionally reaching the weight of five to eight pounds. **1920** Packard *Old Plymouth* 330 **seMA**, Esox reticulatus . . [is] known sometimes as green pike or jack, but more often as pond pickerel. **1927** Weed *Pike* 42, *Esox americanus.* . . Pond Pickerel: occasional from Maine to southern New York. *Ibid* 45, *Esox niger.* . . Pond Pickerel; Lake Champlain region. Pond Pike; New Jersey. **1946** LaMonte *N. Amer. Game Fishes* 128, *Eastern Pickerel.* . . Names: Chain Pickerel . . Pond Pickerel [etc].

pond pine n

1 A **pine 1** (here: *Pinus serotina*) found in swamplands of the southern Atlantic plain. Also called **black pine 1d, bull ~ 1c, loblolly ~ 2, marsh ~, meadow ~ 1c, pitch ~ b(5), pocosin ~, spruce ~**

1810 [see **pondbush 1**]. **1822** Eaton *Botany* 392, [*Pinus*] *serotina* . . (pond pine). **1860** Curtis *Cat. Plants NC* 21, *Pond Pine.* . . This has considerable resemblance to the *Pitch Pine,* but is as remarkable for its scattered branches as that is for its crowded ones. . . In some localities it is called *Savanna Pine*. **1901** Lounsberry *S. Wild Flowers* 5, Pond pine,

an inhabitant of swamps near the coast, and which occurs from Florida to North Carolina, bears leaves which resemble somewhat those of Pinus heterophylla. **1950** Peattie *Nat. Hist. Trees* 24, *Pocosin Pine.* . . Other Names: Pond, Marsh, or Meadow Pine. **1962** Harrar–Harrar *Guide S. Trees* 62, Pond pine . . is a natural variety of the pitch pine and occurs along the coastal plain in swamps and low wet flats, known locally as "pocosins," from southern New Jersey to northern Florida and central Alabama. **1968** *State* (Columbia SC) 2 May sec B 14, Sealed bids will be accepted . . for the sale of approximately 609,567 board feet of pine sawtimber, Scribner scale, composed of approximately 80 pct. loblolly, 15 pct. longleaf, and 5 pct. pond pine.

2 A **slash pine** (here: *Pinus elliottii*). [Cf quot 1901 at **1** above]

1903 Small *Flora SE U.S.* 28, *Pinus heterophylla.* . . In swampy pine lands near the coast, South Carolina and Georgia. *Pond Pine. Slash Pine.*

pond sawbill n Cf **pond sheldrake, sawbill**

=**hooded merganser.**

1868 Cook *Geol. NJ* 795, *Lophodytes cucullatus.* Hooded Merganser. . . Is generally known inland as "Pond sawbill." **1923** U.S. Dept. Ag. *Misc. Circular* 13.7 **NJ**, *Hooded Merganser.* . . *Vernacular Names.* . . *In local use.* . . pond sawbill.

pond scoggin n [*pond* + **scoggin 2**] esp **GA**

Any of var birds of the family Ardeidae; rarely =**anhinga.**

1966–68 *DARE* (Qu. Q8, *A water bird that makes a booming sound before rain and often stands with its beak pointed almost straight up*) Inf **GA**20, Scoggins (nickname for any kind of water bird); pond scoggins; (Qu. Q10, . . *Water birds and marsh birds*) Inf **FL**35, Pond scoggin ['skɔlgən] [laughter] . . any kind of pond bird that stands on one leg; **GA**35, Pond scoggins, pond gannets—same—old-timers' names for all water birds. **1968** *DARE* Tape **GA**30, [FW:] What kind of birds are pond scoggins? [Inf:] I don't know as I ever saw one. [FW:] Johnny said just about any kind of swamp bird would be called that. [Inf:] Oh yeah, most all of them. You take the little blue heron, . . these white birds—the egrets. . . To the old-timers around here, it was all pond scoggins ['pɑˀənd ˌskɑˤgɪnz] with them. **1969** *DARE* FW Addit *Okefenokee* **GA**, Pond scoggin—the white egret of Okefenokee Swamp. So called formerly by grandmother (from this area). **1986** Pederson *LAGS Concordance,* 1 inf, **csGA**, Pond scoggin—long-legged crane. **2000** *NADS Letters* **seGA**, Here in southeast GA, a *pond scoggin* is a term for an Egret and sometimes an Anhinga. **2000** *DARE* File—Internet **seGA**, You are very Wiregrass if . . you know what a pond scoggin and a skeeter hawk is.

pond scoop See **scoop** n **1**

pond sheldrake n Also *pond shell-bird* [**sheldrake**] Cf **pond sawbill**

Either the common **merganser** (*Mergus merganser*) or the **hooded merganser.**

1888 Trumbull *Names of Birds* 64, At Ellsworth, Me., and in Massachusetts at North Plymouth, Buzzard's Bay, and West Barnstable, [the merganser is called] *pond sheldrake*. *Ibid* 73, [The hooded merganser is] known also at Bath [ME], to some of the gunners, and at Essex, Conn. as *pond sheldrake*. **1955** MA Audubon Soc. *Bulletin* 39.378, *American Merganser.* Big Pond Sheldrake (Mass. Sheldrake means pied drake.) *Ibid, Hooded Merganser.* . . Pond Sheldrake (Maine, Conn., R.I.) *Ibid* 379, Pond Shell-bird (Mass. Shell an error for sheld, which means pied.) **1982** Elman *Hunter's Field Guide* 226, *American Merganser* . . *Common & Regional Names:* freshwater sheldrake, pond sheldrake [etc]. *Ibid* 228, *Hooded Merganser.* . . *Common & Regional Names* . . sheldrake, pond sheldrake, pied sheldrake, summer sheldrake, swamp sheldrake [etc].

pond skater See **skater**

pond slider n Cf **pond terrapin, slider**

A **red-bellied turtle** (here: *Chrysemis scripta*).

1957 Blair et al. *Vertebrates U.S.* 292, *Pseudemys scripta* . . Pond slider. . . Atlantic Coast from Virginia south through north Florida and west along Gulf Coast to southern Tamaulipas [Mexico] and western Texas. North through Mississippi Valley to Wisconsin and Ohio. **1972** Ernst–Barbour *Turtles* 149, At night the pond slider sleeps while lying on the bottom, floating at the surface, or resting near the surface on brush piles on the limbs of overturned trees. **1979** Behler–King *Audubon Field Guide Reptiles* 452, *Pond Slider (Chrysemis scripta)*—Subspecies: Yellow-bellied, Red-eared, Cumberland, Big Bend.

pond spice n

1 A southern shrub (*Litsea aestivalis*) of swamps and ponds. [See quot 1966] Also called **crooked swamp-bush, pond-bush 2**

1821 Elliott *Sketch* 1.463 **GA, SC,** [*Laurus*] *geniculata* [=*Litsea aestivalis*]. . . A small tree, 10–15 feet high, very much branched. Grows around ponds, and in shallow water. Flowers February–March. *Pond-spice.* **1857** Gray *First Lessons* 380, T[*etranthera*] *geniculata* . . Pond Spice. . . Swamps, Virginia and southward. **1933** Small *Manual SE Flora* 923, G[*labraria*] *geniculata*. . . (Pond-spice, Pond-bush.) Swamps and ponds, Coastal Plain and rarely adj. provinces, Fla. to La., Tenn., and Va. **1960** Vines *Trees SW* 293, *Pond-spice.* . . Common names include Pond-bush and Crooked Swamp-bush. **1966** Grimm *Recognizing Native Shrubs* 112, *Pondspice.* . . A leaf-losing, aromatic shrub 6 to 10 feet high; growing in low wet woods and pond and swamp margins. *Branchlets* slender, zigzag frequently forked, spicy-aromatic when broken.

2 A **spicebush** (here: *Lindera* spp).

1901 Mohr *Plant Life AL* 519, *Benzoin* [*spp*] . . Pond Spice. . . Alleghenian to Louisianian area. Ontario; eastern Massachusetts west to Michigan and Missouri, south to Florida and central Texas.

pond sucker n

A **redhorse 1** (here: *Moxostoma* spp).

1967–69 *DARE* (Qu. P1, . . *Kinds of freshwater fish . . caught around here . . good to eat*) Inf **GA**89, Pond suckers, redhorse suckers; caught in creeks. The boys would say, "The suckers are running"; (Qu. P3, *Freshwater fish that are not good to eat*) Inf **SC**40, Pond sucker.

pond tern n

=**least tern.**

1925 (1928) Forbush *Birds MA* 1.122, *Sterna antillarum* . . Least Tern. *Other names:* Little Striker; Oyt; Pond Tern. **1946** Hausman *Eastern Birds* 325, *Least Tern—Sterna antillarum antillarum*. . . Other Names— Little Tern . . Pond Tern [etc].

pond terrapin n

A **red-bellied turtle** (here: *Chrysemys scripta*).

1921 U.S. Bur. Fisheries *Rept. for 1919* app 7.12, In the turtle pen on the lower Illinois (Grafton) *elegans* was about as common as *lesueurii*, and was known as the "pond terrapin," the other species being the "river terrapin." **1937** Cahn *Turtles IL* 160, *Pseudemys troostii* . . (Red-head; painted turtle; pond terrapin). **1953** Schmidt *N. Amer. Amphibians* 102, *Pseudemys scripta*. . . Southeastern North America. *Common name.*— Pond terrapin. *Ibid, Pseudemys scripta scripta*. . . Northern Florida to Princess Anne County, Virginia. *Common name.*—Yellow-bellied turtle, pond terrapin. **1967** *DARE* (Qu. P24, . . *Kinds of turtles*) Inf **SC**40, Pond tarrypin—same as pond turtle = yellow-belly cooter.

pond turtle n Cf **pond terrapin**

1 also *pond tortoise:* A **red-bellied turtle,** usu *Chrysemys picta.*

1884 Goode *Fisheries U.S.* 1.157, Three species of genus *Chrysemys,* the Pond Tortoises, inhabit the United States: *C. picta* . . *C. Belli* . . and *C. reticulata.* [*DARE* Ed: These species are now included in *Chrysemys picta.*] **1937** Cahn *Turtles IL* 129, *Chrysemys picta marginata* . . pond turtle. *Ibid* 138, *Chrysemys picta bellii* . . pond turtle. *Ibid* 145, *Chrysemys picta dorsalis* . . pond turtle. **1967–70** *DARE* (Qu. P24, . . *Kinds of turtles*) Infs **CT**17, **VA**79, 96, Pond turtle(s). **1969** *DARE* FW Addit **csKY,** Pond turtle—about 8 x 10 inches. **1986** Pederson *LAGS Concordance,* 1 inf, **seGA,** Pond turtle—lives in ponds; 1 inf, **seLA,** Pond turtle.

2 A turtle of the genus *Clemmys,* usu the western *C. marmorata.*

1860 U.S. War Dept. *Rept. Explor. Railroad* 3.292, *Actinemys marmorata,* Agass. The Western Pond Turtle. . . This, the only turtle yet known from the west of the Rocky mountains, is common in freshwater ponds and rivers west of the Cascade mountains. **1928** Pope–Dickinson *Amphibians* 76, Spotted Turtle—*Clemmys guttata.* . . Also called Pond Turtle and Speckled Tortoise in some localities. **1952** Carr *Turtles* 123, Pacific Pond Turtle—*Clemmys marmorata marmorata. Ibid* 127, Southern California Pond Turtle—*Clemmys marmorata pallida.* **1969** *DARE* (Qu. P24, . . *Kinds of turtles*) Inf **CA**117, Pond turtle. **1972** Ernst–Barbour *Turtles* 84, *Clemmys marmorata* . . Western Pond Turtle. **1979** Behler–King *Audubon Field Guide Reptiles* 455, *Western Pond Turtle.* . . Subspecies: Northwestern, Southwestern.

pond water n chiefly **Sth, S Midl**

1 also *pond:* Beer; illegally made liquor.

1950 *PADS* 14.76 **FL,** *Pond-water.* . . Moonshine liquor. **1966–70** *DARE* (Qu. DD25, . . *Nicknames . . for beer*) Inf **DC**12, Pond; **NC**31, **OK**52, Pond water.

2 in phr *weak as pond water;* Of coffee or liquor: very weak; hence n *pond water* very weak coffee. Cf **branch water 2**

c1960 Wilson *Coll.* **csKY,** *Weak as pond water*—said of weak coffee. **1966–70** *DARE* (Qu. H74b, . . *Coffee . . very weak*) Infs **AL**19, **FL**31, **KY**84, 85, **SC**22, 26, **TX**38, 99, Weak as pond water; **TN**5, Pond water. **1984** Wilder *You All Spoken Here* 164 **Sth,** *Weak as pond water:* Like some sermons and some booze.

3 in phrr (*as) slow as pond water;* Of persons: very slow.

1966–70 *DARE* (Qu. A18, . . *A very slow person: "What's keeping him? He certainly is _____!"*) Infs **GA**4, 11, **KY**84, (As) slow as pond water.

pondweed n

Std: an aquatic plant of the genus *Potamogeton.* For other names of var spp see **cane grass, cornstalk weed, duck grass 2, ~ moss, eelgrass 3, flag grass 2, foxtail 2, grass moss, ~ wrack 2, gray-duck grass, Indian ~ 2, maidenhair moss, muskie weed, nut grass 3, old-fashioned bay grass, pondgrass 2, potato moss, redhead grass 1, sago pondweed, turtle grass, widgeon ~**

pond worm n Also *pond wiggler* esp **GA** Cf **bonnet worm, Georgia wiggler, wiggler**

A worm used as bait in fishing.

1968 *DARE* (Qu. P5, . . *The common worm used as bait*) Inf **GA**41, Pon' worm. **1986** Pederson *LAGS Concordance,* 1 inf, **swGA,** Pond worms; 1 inf, **swGA,** Pond worms can be brownish, reddish or bluish; found near ponds; 1 inf, **swGA,** Pond worms—6–10 inches long; found in wet area of pond; 1 inf, **swGA,** Pond wigglers.

pondy adj Also sp *pondey* esp **Sth, S Midl**

Swampy; marshy.

1686 in 1899 Springfield MA *First Century* 2.266, The Revd. Mr. Pelatiah Glover desires . . thirty or forty acres of wet Pondy Land at poor brooke. **1770** (1925) Washington *Diaries* 1.427 **VA,** The Kanhawa . . in many places very rich; in others somewhat wet and pondy. **1805** (1905) Clark *Orig. Jrls. Lewis & Clark Exped.* 3.236, A low pondey Countrey. **1967–68** *DARE* (Qu. C7, . . *Land that usually has some standing water with trees or bushes growing in it*) Infs **GA**65, **SC**46, Pondy land. **1986** Pederson *LAGS Concordance* (*Swamp*) 1 inf, swGA, Pondy; 1 inf, **ceLA,** Pondy place; 1 inf, **cwTN,** Pondy place— always wet; 1 inf, **csMS,** Old pondy places.

pone n [Algonquian] Pronc-sp *poon*

1a also *pone cake, pony:* A cake or loaf, esp of corn bread, shaped with the hands and baked—often in phr *pone of bread.* chiefly **Sth, S Midl** Cf **bread n B1, potato pone**

[**c1612** (1849) Strachey *Hist. VA Britannia* 74, They . . receave the flower in a platter of wood, which blending with water, they make into flatt broad cakes . . they call appones.] **1796** (1905) Latrobe *Jrl. of Latrobe* 16 **VA,** A few biscuits, and pones of Indian and wheat bread. **1883** (1971) Harris *Nights with Remus* 204 **GA** [Black], She tuck'n fry 'im up a rasher er bacon, en bake 'im a pone er bread. **1890** *DN* 1.64 **KY,** *Dodger.* . . We have what we call "plain dodger," in which the meal is made up with cold water into *pones.* **1893** [see **1b** below]. **1894** *Outing* 24.201 **KY,** In a short time the pones were shaped and placed in the ashes. **1899** (1912) Green *VA Folk-Speech* 329, *Pone.* . . A loaf or cake of bread: as, "Holding a pone of corn-bread in her hand." **1903** *DN* 2.325 **seMO,** *Pone.* . . A loaf of corn-bread. **1905** *DN* 3.90 **nwAR,** 'Get three pones of baker's bread.' Not uncommon. **1910** *DN* 3.458 **FL, GA,** *Pone.* . . Loaf—a pone of bread. **1915** *DN* 4.228 **wTX,** *Pone.* . . A loaf. **1915** Hall *Claib Jones* 17 **KY,** We got the biggest pone of corn bread I ever saw. It would have weighed more than fifty pounds. **1933** Hurston in *Story* Aug 62 **FL** [Black], Ham hock atop a mound of string beans and new potatoes, and perched on the window-sill a pone of spicy potato pudding. **1939** *AmSp* 14.91 **eTN,** *Pony.* Pone of bread. **1946** *PADS* 5.32 **VA,** *Pone.* . . A hard, hand-shaped cake of corn bread; common everywhere. **1949** Kurath *Word Geog.* 67, Some Carolinians speak of a *pone of light-bread.* **1950** Stuart *Hie Hunters* 175 **eKY,** "I've put on a pone of corndodger fer the hounds," Arn said. "I'll soon have breakfast fer ye." **1966–70** *DARE* (Qu. H14, *Bread that's made with cornmeal*) Infs **GA**36, **KY**63, **MO**1, 17, Corn pones; **VA**69, Corn pones—look like corn pancakes, but lighter; flat cake, fried in grease; no milk or eggs; **OH**11, **VA**18, Pones; **KY**40, Pone of bread; **PA**18, Made [sic] a mush pone and eat with milk; (Qu. H19, *What do you mean by a biscuit? How are they made?*) Inf **NC**84, Pone—made into a pone; (Qu. H25, . . *Names or nicknames . . for fried cornmeal*) Inf **VA**88, Corn ponies; **TX**1, Pones. **1966** *DARE* Tape **FL**31, Well, you take your cornmeal and you have your greens boiling. And take some cold water and mix this cornmeal up. And I make mine up in little pones and lay 'em on top of this greens. **1975** *Appalachian Jrl.* 2.156 **wNC**, According to all those who recall eating gritted bread and corn dodgers fixed in this fashion, there is no food that surpasses either. . . Variations of the recipe are known as *hoe cakes, pone cakes, pone o' bread,* and *ash cakes.* **1986** Pederson *LAGS Concordance* **Gulf Region,** 65 infs, Pones; 38 infs, Pone(s) of bread; 28 infs, Pone(s) of corn bread; 1 inf, Pone of biscuit; 1 inf, A pone of light bread; 1 inf, Pone of wheat bread; 1 inf, Many a pone—of bread; 1 inf, In pones; 1 inf, Nice little pones; 1 inf, **seGA,** Grated potatoes made into a "poon." [*DARE* Ed: Most of these resps were in answer to questions about corn bread.] **1994** NC Lang. & Life Project *Dial. Dict. Lumbee Engl.* 9 **seNC,** Pone. . . Loaf, loaf of bread. [U]sed mostly by older speakers. *They bought a pone of bread.*

b also *pony:* Bread made with cornmeal, usu hand-shaped into a cake or loaf. **scattered, but chiefly Sth, S Midl**

[**1612** Smith *Map VA* 1.17, Eating the broth with the bread which they call *Ponap.*] **1634** (1865) *Relation MD* 17, Their ordinary diet is Poane and Omine, both made of Corne, to which they adde at times, Fish, Fowle, and Venison. **1743** Catesby *Nat. Hist. Carolina* 2.xvii, It [=Indian corn] is prepared various Ways, though but three principally; the first is baking it in little round Loaves, which is heavy, though very sweet and pleasant, while it is new. This is called *Pone.* **1893** Shands *MS Speech* 50, *Pone* [pon]. Used by all classes for a certain kind of corn-bread made with only water, meal, and salt. The word *pone* frequently has a more extended meaning than this, and is used for a loaf of any kind of bread. **1923** *DN* 5.217 **swMO,** *Pone.* . . Corn bread. **1939** *AmSp* 14.91 **eTN,** She's cooking pony for supper. **1943** Weslager *DE Forgotten Folk* 192, Corn bread (pone) is still occasionally made by the old folks, but many of the Moor children are as unfamiliar with the "corn foods" as today's city dweller. **1951** Johnson *Resp. to PADS 20* **DE** (*Names for bread made with corn meal*) Pone. **1954** *Harder Coll.* **cwTN,** Bread made with corn meal; often *pone.* **1957** Battaglia *Resp. to PADS 20* **eMD** (*Names for bread made with corn meal*) Pone. **1965– 70** *DARE* (Qu. H14, *Bread that's made with cornmeal*) Infs **CA**99, 174, **DE**2, **KY**62, **NY**206, **VA**26, Pone; **AL**58, Corn bread, pone—no difference; **KY**41, Pone—made with less ingredients and baked in a skillet; heavier than corn sticks or muffins; **MI**51, Pone; and then the other name for it is pone, of course; we don't use that much here, but in the South they talk of corn pone; **NJ**11, Pone—Southern expression; **NY**12, Pone—adopted from the South; **OR**3, Pone—the Southerners say; **PA**163, Pone, corn bread, spoon bread—all the same; **SC**32, Pone [pom]—like hoecake, but thicker; **LA**11, Corn bread pone—made in a skillet; **MA**48, Cornmeal pone; (Qu. H18, . . *Special kinds of bread*) Inf **NC**46, Pone—not corn, but a small round; **TX**1, Pone—made like biscuits but cooked in one big batch in skillets; (Qu. H25, . . *Names or nicknames . . for fried cornmeal*) Inf **NY**66, Pone. **1986** Pederson *LAGS Concordance* **Gulf Region,** 78 infs, Pone; 1 inf, Pone—cooked in a baker; 1 inf, Pone—cooked in a skillet on the fireplace; 1 inf, Pone—in a large pan; 1 inf, Pone—in a patty shape; 1 inf, Pone—old name for corn bread; 1 inf, Pone—made in loaves; 1 inf, Pone—shaped like two kidneys in a skillet; 1 inf, The pone—cooked in frying pan.

2 See quot. Cf **corn pone 2**

1968 *DARE* (Qu. H23, . . *Hot cooked breakfast cereal*) Inf **LA**43, Pone—old-fashioned; (Qu. H24, . . *Names or nicknames . . for boiled cornmeal*) Inf **LA**43, Corn pone or pone—old-fashioned.

3a A pathological lump or swelling on the body. **chiefly sAppalachians** Cf **pone v 2**

1895 *DN* 1.373 **seKY, eTN, wNC,** *Pone:* hard swelling. "He's got a pone in his side. I reckon ef it busts inside, he'll die right now." **1913** Kephart *Highlanders* 224 **sAppalachians,** Old Uncle Bobby Tuttle's got a pone come up on his side. **1929** in 1952 Mathes *Tall Tales* 98 **sAppalachians,** The "doctor" was putting the last touches of preparedness to his favorite and only surgical "instrument," with which he had lanced many a "bile, pone, or risin'." **1954** *Harder Coll.* **cwTN,** I got a pone on my lag's big's a apple. **1967** Williams *Greenbones* 130 **GA** (as of c1910), You got a pone over your ear like a goose-egg. What hit you? **1968–70** *DARE* (Qu. K47, . . *Diseases . . horses or mules commonly get*)

Inf **MS**87, [šabəz]—swells under stomach. A big pone hangs under the horse. If you stop it before it get to the horse's throat, it won't kill him; (Qu. X60, . . *A lump that comes up on your head when you get a sharp blow or knock;* not asked in early QRs) Inf **VA**13, Pone; (Qu. BB30, . . *A hard, painful swelling [often on a finger] that seems to come from deep under the skin*) Infs **KY**19, **WV**2, Pone. **1969** *DARE* FW Addit **TX**58, The wound on her abdomen from a month old operation had a "pone" under it. **1984** [see **3b** below]. **1990** Cavender *Folk Med. Lexicon* 29 **sAppalachians,** *Pone*—a painful lump on the body: "I've got a pone on my leg from when I accidentally hit myself with a hammer."

b Spec: a roll of body fat; hence n pl *the pones* the buttocks. **esp Sth**

1933 [see **pussle-gut**]. **1936** *AmSp* 11.316 **Ozarks,** *Pone.* . . A roll of fat. 'Paw eats too much lately—look at them pones all round his middle!' **1984** *Annals Internal Med.* 100.6.900 **cwAL,** A *pone* is a lump or swelling. . . Patients from the South are frequently concerned about pones. In my experience pones are usually harmless accumulations of fat, particularly in women, behind the knees or in the axillae. **1984** Wilder *You All Spoken Here* 54 **Sth,** She's got pones on her hips: Her buttocks are lumpy. **1986** Pederson *LAGS Concordance,* 1 inf, **nwFL,** The pones = the buttocks.

pone v

1 also with *up:* To shape into a **pone** n **1a.**

1986 Pederson *LAGS Concordance,* 1 inf, **neGA,** Pone it; 1 inf, **ceTN,** You just pone it up [*LAGS* Ed: =shape it] like you would.

2 also with *up:* To swell; hence ppl adj phrr *poned up* (or *out*) swollen.

1962 Krutch *More Lives* 7 **ceTN,** Well, Doc, I just hunkered down, it creeled, and then it poned up 'til I thought hit was agoin' to beal. **1981** Pederson *LAGS Basic Materials,* 1 inf, **neTN,** Puffed up, poned up, swelled; 1 inf, **neTN,** Swelled up; poned up; 1 inf, **neTN,** Puffed up; poned up; 1 inf, **neTN,** Poned up; swollen up. **1990** Cavender *Folk Med. Lexicon* 29 **sAppalachians,** *Pone.* . . Also used in the phrase "poned out" in reference to a swollen part of the body.

pone bread n

1 also *pon(e)y bread:* Corn bread, esp in the form of a **pone** n **1a.** **Sth, S Midl** See Map Cf **corn pone 1**

c1785 in 1907 *MD Hist. Mag.* 2.258, I procured some milk and excellent pone bread from a hut. **1833** Neal *Down-Easters* 1.47, I should like to know . . what . . he [=a Southerner] means by . . pone bread. **1879** *Scribner's Mth.* 18.233, "Pone" bread and beef stews had re-appeared in the *menu.* **1915** *DN* 4.228 **wTX,** 'Pone bread' is corn-bread cooked in individual pieces. **1934** Hurston *Jonah's Gourd Vine* 21 **AL** [Black], De rest uh y'all git yo' plates and come git some uh dese cow-peas and pone bread. **c1937** in 1970 Yetman *Voices* 67 **AL** [Black], Here come my mistis, and she say: "Now Cheney, I wants some pone bread for dinner." . . They wouldn't be no finger prints left on dat pone when Cheney got through pattin' it out, neither. **1937** *Hall Coll.* **wNC, eTN,** Pone-bread. . . Bread made of stiff dough shaped in the hands (corn). **1939** *AmSp* 14.90 **eTN,** I had to borrow a dust of meal to make pony bread for supper. **1940** *AmSp* 15.216 **FL,** Ponybread for *pone-bread* is sometimes used in Florida, but the user is trying to be smart or funny. It is always understood that *pone* is the word meant, not *pony.* **1946** *PADS* 5.33 **VA,** Pone bread. . . Corn bread; common everywhere. **1949** Kurath *Word Geog.* 67, Corn bread (in cakes). . . [I]n all the Atlan-

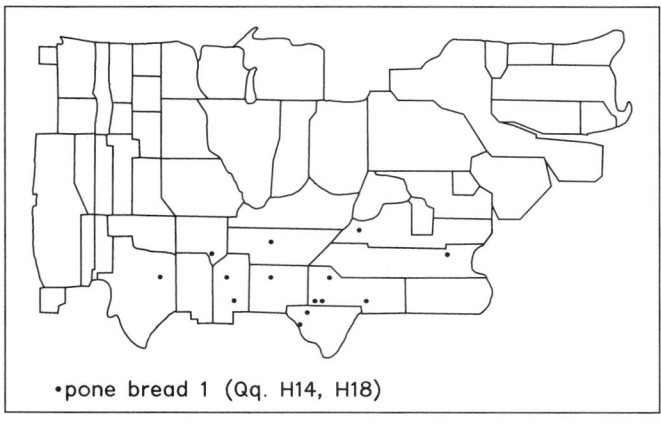

•pone bread 1 (Qq. H14, H18)

tic states south of Pennsylvania *pone, corn pone,* and *pone bread* are widely used, but *corn bread* is gaining ground. **1965–70** *DARE* (Qu. H14, *Bread that's made with cornmeal*) 12 Infs, **Sth, S Midl,** Pone bread; (Qu. H18, . . *Special kinds of bread*) Infs **FL18, GA70, MS1,** Pone bread. **1966** Dakin *Dial. Vocab. Ohio R. Valley* 2.313, *Corn bread. . . [C]orn pone, pone bread,* and *pone* for large cakes or "loaves" of corn bread are commonly remembered or used everywhere in the Valley. . . [I]n Kentucky *corn pone, pone,* and *pone bread* are about equally common. **1986** Pederson *LAGS Concordance* **Gulf Region,** 62 infs, Pone bread; 1 inf, Blacks called it poney bread.

2 also *pone light bread:* Wheat bread. Cf **loaf bread**

1969 *DARE* (Qu. H15, *Bread made with wheat flour*) Inf **KY28,** Pone bread—used wheat flour, not corn meal. **1986** Pederson *LAGS Concordance (Wheat bread)* 2 infs, **LA, MS,** Pone bread—(of) wheat flour; 1 inf, **cAL,** Pone bread may refer to light bread; 1 inf, **cGA,** Pone bread; 1 inf, **ceTN,** Pone bread or light bread; 1 inf, **nwFL,** Pone light bread.

pone cake See **pone** n **1a**

pone-crust coffee n Cf **crust coffee, essence** n **3**

1954 in 1957 *DE Folkl. Bulletin* 1.27, The way we used to get our coffee in the old days, we'd make up a batch of meal. . . We had a thing in the fire-place called pot-round. We'd hang it up on this pot-round and we'd bake that pone all day . . till it firmed [sic] a great big thick crust onto it. Then we'd take this-yere thick crust off, after the pone baked, an' lay it away, and then we'd take so much of dat crust, putt [sic] it in the coffee-pot, and boil it. And dat was where we got our coffee—ponecrust coffee.

poned out (or up) See **pone** v **2**

ponehead cat n [Prob from the broad, rather oval shape of the head; cf **pone** n **1a**]
=**eel catfish.**

1933 LA Dept. of Conserv. *Fishes* 421 **LA,** [Caption:] The eel cat (known also as the pone-head cat and willow cat).

pone light bread See **pone bread 2**

pone of bread See **pone** n **1a**

pones, the See **pone** n **3b**

pone up See **pone** v **1, 2**

poney bread See **pone bread 1**

pongal See **pungle**

pongee See **pungey**

pongy See **pungey**

ponhaws, ponhorse, ponhoss See **panhas**

poñil n [MexSpan] **SW**
=**Apache plume 1.**

[**1904** NM Ag. Exper. Station *Bulletin* 51.27, Associated with the desert willow is a rosaceous plant sometimes called Poñel by the Mexicans, (its botanical name is *Fallugia paradoxa*), which would be tolerably valuable in cultivation.] **1937** U.S. Forest Serv. *Range Plant Hdbk.* B77, Apache-plume, also known as fallugie and poñil, is a manybranched, often evergreen shrub, typically 2 to 3 feet tall. **1961** Wills-Irwin *Flowers TX* 124, Known also as the Ponil [sic], this, the only species of *Fallugia,* found considerable use among Indians in the Southwest and in nearby Mexico: small branches tied together served as brooms, straight older stems were used as arrow shafts, and it was believed that an infusion of the leaves washed into the scalp would promote hair growth.

ponki See **punkie** n[1] **1**

ponny n, v Cf **pung, punging, sliding pond**

1903 *DN* 2.352 **seNY,** Ponny. . . A sleigh-ride. 'Come on out and have a ponny.' Long Island. *Ponny.* . . To sleigh-ride. 'Come on out and ponny.' Long Island.

Pontiac fly n Also *Pontiac* Cf **gallinipper 1b**

A **warble fly** or similar fly; see quots.

1835 (1906) Bradley *Jrl.* 252 **NH,** They are called, improperly, gallinippers, that being the name of a fly which, in common with other species, oddly enough called *pontiacs,* from the old chief of that name, are

exceedingly troublesome to horses. **1967** *DARE* (Qu. R12) Inf **MI63,** Pontiac fly—lays the egg in the cow's back.

pontoon n

1 =**marsh rabbit 1.**

1935 Pratt *Manual Vertebrate Animals* 351, *S[ylvilagus] palustris* . . Marsh rabbit; pontoon. Body rather large and yellowish or reddish brown in color . . coastal portions of the southern States from Dismal Swamp to Mobile Bay; in swampy woods; habits aquatic, the animals taking very readily to water and swimming well. **1939** FWP *Guide FL* 25, An unusual type is the marsh rabbit, . . which is known locally as the 'pontoon.' It is somewhat smaller than the cottontail and may be distinguished by its smaller ears, shorter hind legs, and nearly unicolored tail. Except for the swamp rabbit, this is the only species of rabbit that will take to the water.

2 A large foot. *joc* Cf **barge 4, flatboat** n **3, gunboat 1**

1965–69 *DARE* (Qu. X38, *Joking names for unusually big or clumsy feet*) Infs **FL22, IL84, IN75, MN2, NY65, PA214, TN35, WI50,** Pontoons.

pontop prep Also sp *puntop* Also *pontopper* [See quot 1949] **SC, GA coasts** *Gullah*

On, onto.

1909 *S. Atl. Qrly.* 8.45 **sSC coast** [Gullah], Ol' Mis', 'im hab woice lak all dem Preston; ebry mo'nin' 'e gone 'pon topper piazza. **1922** Gonzales *Black Border* 41 **sSC, GA coasts** [Gullah], W'en da' t'ing come t'ru de bush en' look 'puntop me, me two eye' pop' out me head! *Ibid* 239, Scipio, you got a great load uh sin 'puntop yo' soul! **1939** Griswold *Sea Is. Lady* 5 **csSC** (as of 1861) [Gullah], De *Debble* mus' be 'pontop you' tail! **1949** Turner *Africanisms* 233 **SC, GA coasts** [Gullah], [pən tɒp] 'on,' i.e., 'upon the top,' used in such a sentence as, *He has five fingers upon the top of* (i.e., *on*) *his hand.* Cf. the Yoruba expression li₃ o₂ri₃ 'on,' lit. 'upon the top.' [*DARE* Ed: Subscript numerals indicate tone.] **1950** *PADS* 14.53 **SC** [Gullah], *Pontop* ['pʌn'tɑp]. . . On, on top of. "Pontop Edisto," on Edisto Island.

pony n[1] See **pone** n **1a, b**

pony n[2] Cf **horse B8**

In phrr *ride a* (or *the*) *cotton pony:* See quot.

1966–69 *DARE* (Qu. AA27, . . *A woman's menstruation*) Infs **IL45, MI10,** Riding a (*or* the) cotton pony.

ponyback ride See **pony ride**

pony bread See **pone bread 1**

ponyfoot n [Because the shape of the leaf resembles the print of a pony's foot]

A plant of the genus *Dichondra.* Also called **creeping Charlie 3, morning glory 1**

1970 Correll *Plants TX* 1242, *Dichondra* [spp] . . Pony-foot. *Ibid* 1243, *Dichondra argentea* . . Silver pony-foot. . . *Dichondra brachypoda* . . New Mexico pony-foot.

pony grass n [See quot 1911]

A **reedgrass a** (here: *Calamagrostis neglecta* or *C. inexpansa*).

1883 (1885) Allen *New Amer. Farm Book* 112 **neWI,** [Footnote:] The pony grass may perhaps be mentioned as one of the principal of the winter grasses in that region. **1911** *Century Dict. Suppl., Pony-grass.* . . One of the reedbents, *Calamagrostis neglecta,* native in northern Europe and North America, ranging along the northern borders of the United States, and most abundant in the Rocky Mountain region. It is liked by stock, especially horses, and has succeeded well under experimental cultivation. **1950** *WELS* (*Other kinds of grass that are hard to get rid of*) 1 Inf, **cWI,** Pony grass.

pony keg n [Transf from *pony keg* a small keg of beer] **Cincinnati OH**

A store selling beer, wine, ice, picnic and party supplies, and occas convenience items—freq used in names for such establishments.

1971 *DARE* File **Cincinnati OH,** [Advt:] M&M Pony Keg . . Beer . . Wines . . Party Supplies . . Champagnes . . Crushed Ice. [In the *Yellow Pages* from which the foregoing has been taken, there are, under "Beer," between the letters *F* through *M* alone, 41 establishments with "Pony Keg" as part of their name; e.g. *Glenway Pony Keg, Hardert's Cafe & Pony Keg, Kenwood Corner Delctsn & Pony Keg,* all advertising similar goods.] **1972** *Ibid* **swOH,** I'd really like to know whether this expression [=*pony keg*] is used outside the Cincinnati area—I've never heard it elsewhere. *Ibid* **swOH,** Pony keg—a liquor store (which supplies, among other things, pony kegs of beer). *Ibid* **Cincinnati OH,** If you pass a pony keg, get some cold meat. **1974** *Ibid* **OH,** It [=*pony keg*] came up in my language class in Cleveland, Ohio, and only students from the Cincinnati area knew it. **1997** *Ibid* **sOH,** A convenience store in Cincinnati is called a "Pony-keg." **2000** *Ibid* **Cincinnati OH** (as of c1960), "Pony keg" was a term used not so much for a small keg of beer, but for the carry-out or store which sold beer, soft drinks, snacks, deli items. Today we would call it a convenience store, but to us it was always pony keg. I don't know how many times my parents told me, "Run over to the pony keg and get a carton of Pepsi."

pony penning n **coastal VA, NC**
A drive or roundup of ponies; see quots.

1932 *Sun* (Baltimore MD) 27 July 4/3–4 (*Hench Coll.*), Chincoteague Island, one of Virginia's most interesting islands, will stage its annual rodeo, familiarly known as "pony-penning," on Thursday. . . The annual pony-pennings or roundups are not unlike those in the West. **1942** *Ibid* 31 July 2/2 (*Hench Coll.*), The land-connected Atlantic coast island of Chincoteague, which is famed for its trade in tough and semi-wild ponies from off nearby marshlands, held today a modified version of its annual "pony-penning day." **1946** *PADS* 6.24 **eNC,** *Pony penning.* . . The semiannual driving of "bank" ((wild)) ponies into a compound, where they are captured, to be branded or sold. On the banks of eastern N.C. Current. **1947** (1962) Henry *Misty* 43 **eVA,** "Pony Penning Day," he blurted out. "How did it start?" . . Grandpa Beebe liked the question. . . "In the yesterdays, when their corn was laid by, folks on Chincoteague got to yearnin' fer a big hollerday. So they sails over to Assateague and rounds up all the wild ponies. 'Twas big sport." . . "They swum the ponies acrost the channel to Chincoteague and put on a big show." **1958** *Washington Post* (DC) 30 July sec A 24/1, Approximately 225 wild ponies from the marshes and beaches of Assateague Island will be herded across the narrow channel to Chincoteague Wednesday for the fireman's carnival sales. . . The pony penning dates back to 1835. **1970** *DARE* (Qu. FF16, . . *Local contests or celebrations*) Inf **VA**50, Pony penning—Chincoteague—wild ponies on Assateague rounded [up] and forced to swim to Chincoteague, where some are sold at auction and others released to swim back to Assateague. **1994** *NC Lang. & Life Project Dial. Vocab. Ocracoke* 14 **eNC,** We had a pony penning once a year.

pony ride n Also *ponyback ride* Cf **horseback ride**
A piggyback ride.

1957 Battaglia *Resp. to PADS 20* **eMD** (*To carry someone, usually a child, on your back*) Give me a pony ride. **1967–70** *DARE* (Qu. Y31, *If a child asked his father to carry him on his back . . "Give me a _____."*) Infs **AZ**10, **CA**4, **MI**72, **MO**36, **OH**102, **SC**58, **WI**70, Pony ride; **IL**76, Ponyback ride.

poo See **po** exclam

pooch n[1] Also *poocher* [Cf **pooch** v] **chiefly Sth, S Midl**
A sack, pouch, protrusion; a swelling or bulge of the body; hence n *pooch-mouth;* adjs *pooch-jawed, pooch-mouthed.*

1904 Day *Kin o' Ktaadn* 199 **ME,** What do ye want to keep complainin' for, old pooch-mouth? **1908** Day *King Spruce* 216 **ME,** Take the combination of a candidate for governor, some fool women, crazy men . . and . . a pooch-mouthed blabber, and it's enough to trig any decent, honest, sensible woods fight ever yarded down. **1942** Warnick *Garrett Co. MD* 12 **nwMD** (as of 1900–18), Pooch-jawed . . jaws protruding at sides. **1969** *DARE* (Qu. X53a, . . *An oversize stomach*) Inf **MO**15, Pooch. **1971** Thompson *Coll.* **cnAL** (as of 1920s), She had pooches under her eyes. . . To a pregnant woman: you got a pretty good pooch already. . . Wonder what he keeps in them pooches in his jaws? [Thompson: Also known in Pike Co. GA 1971.] **1986** Pederson *LAGS Concordance,* 1 inf, **cnFL,** Old timers called a paper bag pooch or poocher; pooch = crocus sack. **1990** Cavender *Folk Med. Lexicon* 29 **sAppalachians,** Pooch—hernia. **1998** *DARE* File **cwCA,** I don't like to sew skirts with gathers, because it's hard to make them lie flat, and you often end up with a little pooch right where you don't need it.

pooch v Usu with *out* [Engl dial var of *pouch* v; cf *EDD pooch* sb.[1], v.] **chiefly Sth, S Midl**
To bulge, swell; to protrude; hence ppl adj *pooched,* ppl adj phrr *pooch(ed) out* swollen, distended, puckered.

1902 Day *Pine Tree Ballads* 136 **ME,** His mouth is pooched and sol-

emn and he'll never squeeze a smile. **1923** *DN* 5.217 **swMO,** Pooch. . . To distend or to swell, as an abscess. Generally followed with 'out.' **1942** Warnick *Garrett Co. MD* 12 **nwMD** (as of 1900–18), Pooched . . puffed out; humped. **1954** *Harder Coll.* **cwTN,** " 'At old usin's [*DARE* Ed: sic—for *rising's?*] 'bout pooch out now. She's a-comin' to head." " 'At nose's all pooched out, since 'e got 'er busted." **1958** Randolph *Sticks* 31 **Ozarks,** It looked like the fellow's wife was in the family way, but she pooched out faster than a natural baby ought to strut a woman. **1960** Criswell *Resp. to PADS 20* **Ozarks,** *Pooched out.* Of a swelling or sore on a person standing out from the arm, leg, skin; swollen. Very common once, not obsolete. **1966–67** *DARE* (Qu. BB32, *If somebody had a swelling—for example, in his whole face . . "Last week his face was all _____."*) Inf **NC**22, Pooch out; **WY**2, Pooched; **LA**18, Pooched out. **1976** Garber *Mountain-ese* 70 **sAppalachians,** *Pooch-out* . . protrude—Drinkin' beer makes your belly pooch out. **1983** *MJLF* 9.1.51 **ceKY** (as of 1956), *Pooched out* . . swollen. **1986** Pederson *LAGS Concordance* **Gulf Region** (*The pockets bulge*) 12 infs, Pooch out; 4 infs, Pooched out; 2 infs, Pooching (out). **1993** Mason *Feather Crowns* 5 **KY,** Hattie poked around, feeling Christie's abdomen. She examined the place between Christie's legs. "You're pooching out some," she said. "Now just lay back and wait real easy. We don't want to force it too soon." **1996** *People* 14 Oct 51 **NC,** When she [=Elizabeth Dole] realizes the [camera] shot calls for her to be seated, she balks. "My jacket will pooch out," objects Dole, 60, dressed in an elegant green suit. "And we all know what *that* looks like." **1996** *DARE* File **seTX,** I have known it [=*pooch out*] for decades, possibly all my life; **MS,** I thought all English speakers used *pooch out.* I've been using it all my life; **nKY,** Stuff which bulged or stuck out (especially if it was baggy or lumpy) definitely *pooched out* in Louisville in the 1950s; **NC,** If I slouch down in a chair, my stomach pooches out; **IA,** My mother . . used *pooch out* in Des Moines, Iowa, in the 1950s–70s; **GA,** I use the phrase *pooch out,* . . but . . only for things made of fabric or other soft material. . . [I]t seems to me also to be a rather feminine word; **sCA,** Have lived in southern California for all of my life, and *pooch out* has been around as long as I can remember; **nNJ,** The first time I ever heard [*pooch out*] was c1984 on Broadway at a play by Beth Henley . . , *Crimes of the Heart.* . . [A] crowd of us Northerners commented afterwards on what a funny phrase it was; **TX, OK,** She used to use [*pooch out*] years ago; **TN,** *Pooch out* doesn't seem odd to me at all; **TX** (as of 1940s); **cwCA** (as of 1950s).

pooch n[2] [Prob Span *puchera, puchero* stew] **West**
A dish consisting of canned tomatoes, sugar, and bread.

[**1885** *Outing* 5.412 **Mexico,** First there was vermicelli soup; then a palatable kind of a stew called *puchera,* heaped on a large platter, and composed of meat, maize, beans, carrots, gourds, and a variety of other vegetables.] **1936** Adams *Cowboy Lingo* 149, 'Pooch' was the name of a dish made of canned tomatoes, sugar, and bread. **1939** Rollins *Gone Haywire* 137 **MT,** The only feasible menu, in addition to gallons of coffee, seemed at the moment to be beans, "sow belly" (bacon), "pooch" (a stew of canned tomatoes, sugar and bread) [etc].

pooched ppl adj[1] [Var of *poached*]
1934 *AmSp* 9.94, The word *poached,* whether used in the sense of 'poached' or 'scrambled,' has several interesting phonetic variants. . . *Pooched* [putʃt] occurs in Marblehead (Essex County, Mass.)

pooched ppl adj[2], **pooched out** See **pooch** v

poocher See **pooch** n[1]

pooching vbl n[1] [Var of *poaching;* cf *EDD pooch* (at *poach* v. and sb.)]
1967 *DARE* (Qu. P35b, *Illegal methods of shooting deer;* not asked in early QRs) Inf **MA**45, Poochin' [pučɪn].

pooching vbl n[2] [**pooch** v] Cf *fudging* (at **fudge** v), *hudging* (at **hudge** v)
1967 *DARE* FW Addit **Brooklyn NYC,** Poochin'—hudging, fudging in marbles.

pooch-jawed, pooch-mouth(ed) See **pooch** n[1]

pooch out v phr, ppl adj phr See **pooch** v

poodle-doo n [Folk-etym var of **poule d'eau**]
=**coot** n[1] **1.**
1906 Johnson *Highways Missip. Valley* 32 **LA,** Several glossy wild ducks were afloat on the muddy water. They had been captured when wounded, and now their wings were clipped. Jake pointed out two of

them which he said were poodledoos, but he had no names for the others. **1938** FWP *Guide MS* 354 **nwMS,** About the lake are poules d'eau, called "poodle doos" by the Negroes. In southern Louisiana these birds are considered a delicacy, but Mississippians think their meat too fish-like. **1950** *PADS* 14.53 **SC,** *Poodle-doo.* . . A small bird of the rail family. French: *poule d'eau.* Cooper River region. **1983** *Reinecke Coll.* 9 **MS,** *Poule d'eau.* . . Moritz Jägendorf, folklorist, told me he got "poodledoo" in Mississippi.

poodle worm n

Perh a **woolly bear;** see quot.

    1966 *DARE* (Qu. R27, . . *Kinds of caterpillars or similar worms*) Inf **NC6,** Poodle worm—has lots of hair.

pooed (out) See pooh out

pooey exclam Also sp *pooie, poo-(w)ee, pooy;* for addit varr see quots **chiefly Missip-Ohio Valleys, Upper MW; also C Atl** See Map Cf **hoog, po** exclam, **poig, poo-gee, poy**

Used as a call to pigs.

    1902 *DN* 2.241 **sIL,** *Poo-we.* . . A call to hogs, prolonged and shrill. **1903** *DN* 2.325 **seMO,** *Pooy* or *poowee.* . . The common call for hogs. **1906** *DN* 3.122 **sIN,** *Poo-ee.* . . Pronounced *pyu-ee.* **1907** *DN* 3.225 **nwAR,** *Poo-wee. Ibid* 234 **nwAR,** *Pooy, poowee.* **1912** *DN* 3.586 **wIN,** *Pooey.* . . A call to hogs when they are a long distance away. **1932** *AmSp* 7.454, It is amusing to notice the different ways people call their pigs. . . A North Carolinian halloes, Pig-i, pig-i, prolonging the i's. But a Kentuckian, with his deep bass voice, cries, Poo-hee, poo-hee. **1942** McAtee *Dial. Grant Co. IN* 50 (as of 1890s), *Pooey* . . the basic term for calling distant swine, varied poo-ey, poo-ay, etc. . . "Pig" or "piggy", repeated, were used when the animals were near. **1944** *PADS* 2.59 **cMO,** *Poo-wee, powee* ['puwi, 'pʊwi]. . . A sound used to call hogs. Saline Co. Common. **1948** Davis *Word Atlas Gt. Lakes* app qu 70, 45 (of 233) infs, **OH, IN, IL, MI,** Poo-wee! **1949** Kurath *Word Geog.* 65, Other calls [which] occur in parts of the North Midland: *poo-ie!* in the Delaware Valley, especially on the Jersey side. . . also in common use in a well-defined area centering on Wheeling, West Virginia, presumably derived from the Delaware Valley. **1950** *WELS* **WI,** 5 Infs, Pooey (often repeated); 3 Infs, Pooie (often repeated); 1 Inf, Pooee; 1 Inf, ['pu-i]—common. **1960** *PADS* 34.57 **CO,** Poo-ee! (to pigs). . . more typical of [speech used by infs 60 years old or older who did not complete hs] . . than of other types, but . . not necessarily obsolete speech forms. **1965–70** *DARE* (Qu. K84, *The call used* . . *to get the pigs in at feeding time*) 27 Infs, **chiefly Missip-Ohio Valleys, Upper MW; also C Atl,** Pooey (sometimes repeated); **IN69,** [pu-i]; **VA70,** Pooey pig—repeated; **WI44,** Pig pig pooey—repeated; (Qu. NN22d, . . *Expressions used to drive away people or animals*) Inf **IA46,** Pooey—for a hog. **1966** Dakin *Dial. Vocab. Ohio R. Valley* 2.283, *Poo-(w)ie!* (rarely *pyooie!* or *pwooie!*). This expression . . is used in the Muskingum Valley and is common throughout Ohio from the Muskingum westward north and west of Zane's Trace . . and in Indiana east of the hilly triangle. *Pooie!* (also *pwooie!*) is used by scattered speakers in the Bluegrass (chiefly western) and the northeastern Pennyroyal. Some older speakers here also say *poog!* or *poogie!*. This variation, which may be a blend of *pooie!* and *pig(gie)!* or possible [sic] *pooie!* and the *choog!* of the Virginia Piedmont–Chesapeake Bay area, is also used occasionally along the Ohio in the southeastern hill section (in the Marietta area as *poo-ig!*). It is rare where *pooie!* is common. *Ibid* 285, Other variations and innovations are used by scattered individuals. . . *poa-ie!* . . *po-weeg!* . . *poyk!* . . *poor-gie!* **1967** *DARE* Tape **IA10,** Some of 'em calls . . ['pu:-i

'pu-i] pig pig. **1967** Faries *Word Geog. MO* 93, *Call to pigs.* . . [Among] the five in most common use . . *poo-ie!* (103 occurrences [among c700 infs]). **1973** Allen *LAUM* 1.266 (as of c1950), Calls to pigs at feeding time. . . pooie, pooie [25 infs, **chiefly NE, IA, MN**]. **1981** Pederson *LAGS Basic Materials,* 1 inf, **cGA,** Poo wee ['p'ʊʉ· ˌwi⁴] (falsetto).

poo-gee exclam Also sp *poogie;* for addit varr see quots Cf **po** exclam, **poig, pooey, poy**

Used as a call to pigs.

    1912 *DN* 3.586 **wIN,** *Poo-goo-gee.* . . A call to hogs when they are a long distance away. *Poo-gee* is used when they are nearer. **1950** *WELS,* 1 inf, **swWI,** ['pugə 'pugə 'pugə]. **1966** [see **pooey**].

poohed (out) See pooh out

poo-hee See pooey

pooh out v phr Also sp *poo out* **chiefly N Cent, Upper MW** See Map

To fail, grow weak or tired, come to nothing; hence adj (phr) *poo(h)ed (out).*

    1930 *AmSp* 5.282 **cnOH** [College slang], "To poo out" on someone is an expression common at Oberlin, the origin is supposed to be a corruption from "poop". . . It means to go back on, and also . . if a professor gives a bad lecture or reads old stuff, he "poos out." **1934** (1940) Weseen *Dict. Amer. Slang* 192 [College slang], *Poo out*—To back up or go back on. Also to make a poor showing. *Pooed out*—Fatigued. *Pooh out*—To fail. **1941** *AmSp* 16.320 **NE, SD,** *Poohed* or *poohed out,* exhausted, very tired, was used at Edgemont [SD] and at Yutan, Nebraska, 1938–39. **1942** Berrey–Van den Bark *Amer. Slang* 35.4, *Weaken.* . . Peg-, peter-, play-, pooh *or* poop out. *Ibid* 35.12, *Powerless.* . . pegged-, petered-, poohed *or* pooped out. *Ibid* 117.11, *Die.* . . play-, pooh *or* poop out. *Ibid* 129.6, *Decline in health.* . . pooh out. *Ibid* 213.7, *Abandon; desert; forsake.* . . poop *or* poo out on. **1950** *WELS* (*Words* . . *that people use about being very tired*) 4 Infs, **WI,** Poohed; 1 Inf, **csWI,** Poohed out. **1965–70** *DARE* (Qu. KK30, *Feeling slowed up or without energy:* "*I certainly feel* _____") 18 Infs, **chiefly N Cent, Upper MW,** (All) poohed out; **IL7, 82, IN73, NE10,** Poohed; (Qu. X47, . . "*I'm very tired, at the end of my strength*") Infs **CO22, IL26, IN30, IA34, MI67, NY224, OH80, WA9,** Poohed out; **HI1, IL28, IN73, OH19, 22, 49, WA9,** Poohed; (Qu. BB5, *A general feeling of discomfort or illness that isn't any one place in particular*) Inf **OH23,** All poohed out; **IN66, MI68,** Poohed (out); (Qu. BB39, *On a day when you don't feel just right, though not actually sick* . . "*I'll be all right tomorrow—I'm just feeling* _____ *today.*") Inf **IN66,** Poohed out. **1973** Allen *LAUM* 1.361 **Upper MW** (as of c1950), *Tired.* . . Some terms like . . *poohed* . . are more likely in very informal speech. *Poohed* is more recent. [14 infs, Poohed; 1 inf, All poohed; 1 inf, Just poohed; 13 infs, Poohed out; 6 infs, All poohed out.]

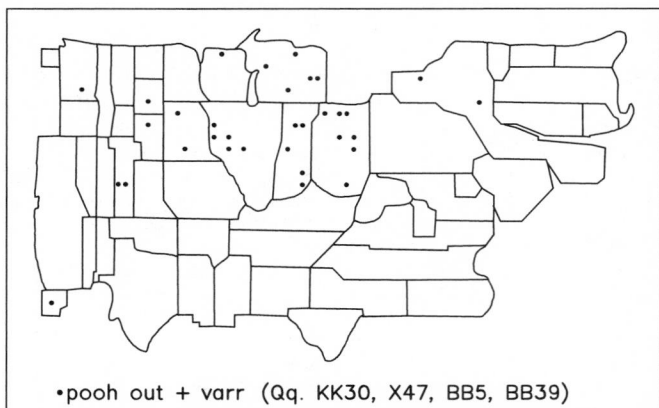

• pooh out + varr (Qq. KK30, X47, BB5, BB39)

pooie See pooey

pooig See poig

Pool n [See quot 1963] **nePA**

A person of racially mixed ancestry.

    1963 Berry *Almost White* 34, Near Tonawanda, Pennsylvania, the mixed-bloods are called Pools, inasmuch as Vanderpool is a common family name. [**1968** *DARE* Tape **PA117,** [FW:] Well, I was surprised that people down this far would know anything about Pools. [Inf:] Why?

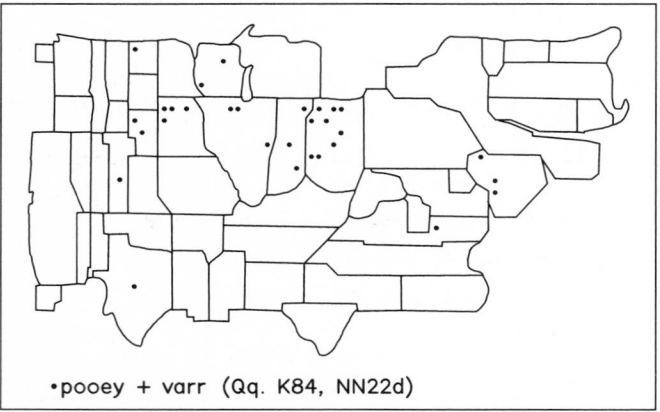

• pooey + varr (Qq. K84, NN22d)

[FW:] Well, I just thought that they were just. . . there's a place in Towanda [sic] they call Pool Town. [Inf:] Well, yes, that's down in South Towanda. That's where a lot of these people settled. And there's another place up there in Tarrytown. . . Where these people really originated from was. . . back in the early 1700s . . Sir William Johnson . . was the administrator of Indian affairs for the English government. . . He's supposed to have left over a hundred illegitimate children. . . When the French came in . . 1793, . . they brought in . . Negroes from Jamaica. . . So there's the French, the Indians, and the Negroes all combined in a sort of a relationship.]

pooldoo See **poule d'eau**

poon v, hence vbl n *pooning,* also *poon chasing* Cf **chase** n 1
In marble play: to shoot from a long distance at a marble from a standing position; see quot 1958.

1940 *Recreation* (NY) 34.110, *Games of marbles played throughout the country* . . Pooning. **1942** Berrey–Van den Bark *Amer. Slang* 665.1, *Pooning,* long distance marble playing. **1958** *Resp. to PADS 29* **nwCT,** Pooners [*DARE* Ed: no explanation of *pooners*]—To Poon—"Pooning" was a term used in a standing-up game. The player held the marble between the thumb and forefinger, squinted, took careful aim and tried the [sic] hit a marble on the ground. **1969** *DARE* (Qu. EE7, . . *Kinds of marble games*) Inf **RI**12, Poon chasing—throw at a marble; if you hit it, you win it.

poon n[1] See **poontang** 1

poon n[2] See **pone** n 1

poon chasing, pooning See **poon** v

poonchka, poonchkey See **paczki**

poontang n [Prob < Fr *putain* a prostitute]
1 also *poon:* Sexual intercourse; the female genitals; by ext: a woman, or women, as sexual object—freq used in ref to Black women. **orig Sth, now more widespread** *now esp freq among Black speakers*

1929 Wolfe *Look Homeward* 166 **NC,** "How many Dead Heads you got, son?" said Mr. Randall. . . "Do you ever try to collect from them?" . . "He takes it out in Poon-Tang," said Foxy. . . "Jazz em [= black women] all you like, . . but get the money." **1935** Caldwell *Journeyman* 10 **Sth,** A man feels the need of a little poontang to perk him up. [*DARE* Ed: Ref is to intercourse with Black women.] **1947** *AmSp* 22.55 [Pacific War language], *Poontang.* Intercourse. **1947** Willingham *End as Man* 78 **GA,** Poley looked out the window and saw a pretty Negro girl on the sidewalk. . . "Eye that poon tang there," he said. **1950** *AmSp* 25.234, The Southern term *poontang,* for sexual intercourse . . is. . . merely a heavily nasalized Creole pronunciation of the French word *putain,* whore, and undoubtedly spread through the South from French-speaking Louisiana. [The translator Keene] Wallis reports it as current in Missouri about 1915. **1963** Watkins–Watkins *Yesterday Hills* 28 **cnGA,** Let's go to Atlanter and git us some poontang. **1967–69** *DARE* FW Addit **LA**14, Poontang ['pun,tæŋ]—1) female sexual partner: "He's shacking up with some poontang." 2) sexual intercourse: "He gets a little poontang now and then." In Natchitoches this is general, applied regardless of the woman's race. In Red River Parish it refers to sex with a Negro, or to the Negro sexual partner; **cwNC,** Poontang ['pun,tɛɪn]— female genitals. **1970** Bullins *Electronic* 154 [Black], Maybe you'll go to Italy and git you some of that dago stuff. . . best damn poon tang in the world, boy. **1970** *Current Slang* 4.3–4.22 [NM State Univ slang], *Poon tang.* . . Vagina. **1972** Wambaugh *Blue Knight* 16, Watching all that young poon. **1982** Heat Moon *Blue Highways* 101 **AL** [Black], But whiteys that run things here don't mind a little black poontang now and then. **1988** Lincoln *Avenue* 17 **wNC** (as of c1940) [Black], I had a girl once with a poontang like a snappin' turtle. Wouldn't let go 'til it thundered. **1994** Smitherman *Black Talk* 183, *Poontang*—Euphemism for *Pussy.* **2001** *DARE* File **wNY,** Poon, poontang—n., the human female sexual apparatus.

2 See quot.

1986 Pederson *LAGS Concordance (Terms for cheap whiskey)* 1 inf, **ceGA,** Poontang; 1 inf, **seGA,** Poontang—not sure.

poo out See **pooh out**

poop v, n Also *poopie* **widespread, but more freq NEng, NY, Gt Lakes, S Atl, West** See Map Cf **poot** v[1], n 1
To break wind, fart; the act of breaking wind; a fart.

1899 (1912) Green *VA Folk-Speech* 329, *Poop.* . . To break wind. . .

The act of breaking wind. **1942** McAtee *Dial. Grant Co. IN Suppl. 1* 7 (as of 1890s), *Poop* . . to break wind; also to defecate. **1960** Criswell *Resp. to PADS 20* **Ozarks,** *Poop* (or . . *poot*) means to make or break wind. **1965–70** *DARE* (Qu. X55b, *Words for breaking wind from the bowels*) 146 Infs, **widespread, but more freq NEng, NY, Gt Lakes, S Atl, West,** Poop; **MN**33, Let a poop; **OH**12, Pooped; **MA**122, Poopie; **MA**59, Poops.

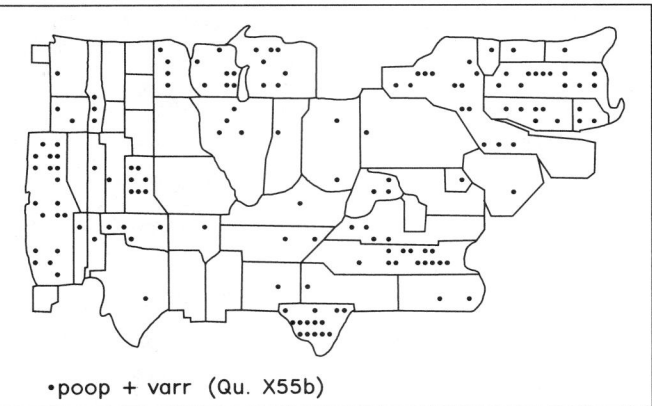

•poop + varr (Qu. X55b)

poopbird n [poop] Cf **pope** n[2], **pork-and-beans**
A **nighthawk** 1 (here: *Chordeiles minor*).

1945 McAtee *Nomina Abitera* 40, *Chordeiles minor.* . . [T]he sound accompanying the dive of the nighthawk. . . is perfectly imitated by a voluminous and lusty, dry, fart playing across a throbbing margin of anal membrane. That the more realistically inclined of our fellow citizens agree is evident from the following names: . . fontin' Jacob (i.e. farting Jacob), John's Island, Charleston County, South Carolina . . ; poopbird, South Carolina.

poopie See **poop**

poop-nose See **pope's nose**

pooquaw n Also *poquau* [From the same Algonquian source as **quahog;** see quot 1910] **MA, RI**
=**quahog** 1.

[1643 Williams *Key into Language* [107 *bis*], Poquaûhock, *Obs.* This the English call Hens, a little thick shel-fiish [sic] which the Indians wade deepe and dive for.] **1807** in 1846 MA Hist. Soc. *Coll.* 2d ser 3.58, The poquau is found in Old Town Harbour, at Cape Poge, and in Menemsha Pond: great quantities are exported. [Footnote to *poquau:*] Called the quahaug in the county of Barnstable. **1848** in 1935 *AmSp* 10.41 **Nantucket MA,** *Pooquaw.* Quahog or round clam. **1859** (1968) Bartlett *Americanisms* 332, *Pooquaw.* (Narraganset Ind., *poquawhock.*) The round clam, so called in Nantucket. In other parts of New England it is shortened to *Quahaug.* **1910** Hodge *Hdbk. Amer. Indians* 2.332, The last half of the word [=*poquaûhock*] has survived in English, while in Nantucket the first part has come down as *pooquaw.*

poor adj Pronc-spp *po', po-uh, pore* Cf **pour**
A Pronc varr.

1 |pu(r), puə, pʊ(r), pʊə|; **esp Nth (exc neNEng), N Midl, Gulf States**
1927 Shewmake *Engl. Pronc. VA* 43 **eVA,** *Poor.* The standard, or dictionary, pronunciation [*DARE* Ed: prob = [pʊɚ]], and two others, *po-uh* and *po',* are heard, according to the education or language pride of the particular speaker. **1944** Kenyon–Knott *Pronc. Dict.* 335, *Poor* [pur]; E[ast]S[outh] [pʊə(r, poə(r, pɔə(r]. **1961** Kurath–McDavid *Pronc. Engl.* 119, The vowels in *poor* . . /pur ~ puə ~ pur ~ pʊə . ./— In *poor* . . the high vowels /u ~ ʊ/ are in almost exclusive use in the North Midland and the North, except for northeastern New England. . . The high-back vowel current in the North and the North Midland ranges from a lowered [uˇ ~ uˇ·] to [ʊ ~ ʊ·], and its length varies. In Metropolitan New York the usual pronunciation of *poor* is [pu·ə], in Eastern New England [pʊə ~ puˇə], in Upstate New York and Pennsylvania [puˇɚ ~ puɚ]. . . South of Pennsylvania the high vowels /u ~ ʊ/ are rare. **1968** *DARE* (Qu. H42, . . *[A sandwich]* . . *in a much larger, longer bun, that's a meal in itself*) Infs **LA**23, 43, Poor [puə] boy. **c1970** Pederson *Dial. Surv. Rural GA* **seGA,** [Proncs of the type [puə], 17 infs [of a total of 64]; [puˇɚ], 12 infs; [po(ʊ), po(ʊ)], 16 infs; [poə, pɔə], 9 infs; [po(ʊ)ɚ, pɔɚ], 8 infs; [puuə], 3 infs; [puuɚ], 2 infs; [pɚ],

1 inf; [pʌɚ], 1 inf.] **1989** Pederson *LAGS Tech. Index* 177 **Gulf Region,** [*Poor*—433 infs gave proncs of the type [puɚ], 56 of the type [puɚ], 3 of the type [pʊ], 2 of the type [pu].]

2 |po(r), poə, pɔ(r)|; **chiefly neNEng, Sth, S Midl**

1843 in 1956 Eliason *Tarheel Talk* 316 **c,cnNC,** Pore. **1871** Eggleston *Hoosier Schoolmaster* 213 **sIN,** At the pore-house. **1883** Amer. Philol. Assoc. *Trans.* 14.52 **Sth,** *Poor* is pronounced *pore* almost universally in the South. **1890** *DN* 1.71 **LA,** *Pore:* poor. **1892** *DN* 1.231 **KY,** *Po'.* "To put up a po' mouth" = to plead poverty. **1893** Shands *MS Speech* 50, *Po'* [po]. Negro for *poor. Ibid,* *Pore* [poə]. Illiterate white for *poor.* This pronunciation, however, is used over almost the entire United States. **1895** *DN* 1.375 **seKY, eTN, wNC,** *Pore* (poor). **1903** *DN* 2.325 **seMO,** *Poor.* . . Pronounced pore. **1907** *DN* 3.235 **nwAR,** *Poor.* . . Pronounced [por]. **1909** *DN* 3.358 **eAL, wGA,** *Poor.* . . Pronounced [po] or [poə]. *Ibid* 359 **eAL, wGA,** *Pore.* . . Poor. [po] is perhaps the more common pronunciation. **1922** Gonzales *Black Border* 319 **sSC, GA coasts** [Gullah glossary], *Po'*—poor, also thin, lean, low in flesh. **1923** *DN* 5.217 **swMO,** *Pore.* . . Poor. **1927** [see **A1** above]. **1928** Peterkin *Scarlet Sister Mary* 162 **SC** [Gullah], Now look at em; po as a snake. **1933** Rawlings *South Moon* 141 **FL,** They're pore as snakes, and their tongues hangin' out for water. **1936** Reese *Worleys* 13 **MD** (as of 1865) [Black], She ain' glad on 'count ob dem po' daid boys. **1937** NE Univ. *Univ. Studies* 37.111 [Terms from play-party songs], *Pore.* . . (Often facetious.) Poor. "Whoop law, Lizzie pore gal."—"Liza Jane." **1954** *Harder Coll.* **cwTN,** Poor [por] folks. **1961** Kurath–McDavid *Pronc. Engl.* 119, In Virginia all the cultured informants . . use the mid vowel /o/ in *poor.* . . In the South and the South Midland the /o/ of *poor* . . /poə̯ ~ po ~ por . . / exhibits the same diaphones as in *four, door.* . . [T]he mid vowel /o/ occurs in *poor* . . with some frequency in northeastern New England, notably in coastal Maine and New Hampshire. **1965–70** *DARE* (Qu. H42, . . *[A sandwich] . . in a much larger, longer bun, that's a meal in itself*) 10 Infs, **chiefly Gulf States,** Poor [po(ʊ)] boy; **LA19, MS17, 54, 72, 73,** Poor [poə] boy; **MS1, 13,** Poor [poɚ] boy; **IL43,** [ˈpoʊˈjoʊ]; (Qu. K15, *A thin, bony, or poor-looking cow*) Infs **GA5,** 7, 9, 12, 16, (Old) po' cow; **GA46,** Old pore cow; **NM13,** Pore [poɚ]; (Qu. K44, *A bony or poor-looking horse*) Infs **GA7,** 9, 12, 16, (Old) po' horse; (Qu. P9, *When you're fishing but not catching any*) Inf **TN22,** Fishin's good, but catchin's pore [poɚ]; (Qu. Q22, *Joking names or nicknames for the common sparrow*) Infs **TN53,** Po'-house sparrows; (Qu. X52, . . *who had been sick was looking* _____) Inf **VA42,** Po' [poə]; **GA59,** Po' as a washing of soap; (Qu. CC7, . . *A person who goes to church very seldom or not at all*) Inf **VA42,** Po' Christian; (Qu. HH18, *Very insignificant or low-grade people*) Infs **DE1, KY30, SC40, VA25, 42,** Po' white trash; **VA21,** Po' whites. **1968** *DARE* FW Addit **ceTN,** [por] for "poor"—heard constantly in conversation with country Infs. c**1970** [see **A1** above]. **1989** Pederson *LAGS Tech. Index* 177 **Gulf Region,** [*Poor*—213 infs gave proncs of the type [por], 78 of the type [po], 17 of the type [pɔr], and 1 of the type [pɔ].]

3 |pʌr, pɝ|.

c**1970** [see **A1** above]. **1989** Pederson *LAGS Tech. Index* 177 **Gulf Region,** [*Poor*—20 infs gave proncs of the type [pʌɚ].]

B Sense.

Thin, scrawny; in poor health, run-down; used:

a Of an animal. **scattered, but chiefly Sth, S Midl, SW** See Map

1778 *MD Jrl. & Baltimore Advt.* (MD) 10 Feb 4/2, [The sheep] are very poor, and appear to have been out all winter. **1835** Crockett *Account* 90, Lean, lank, labber-sided pups, that are so poor they have to prop up agin a post-and-rail fence, 'fore they can raise a bark at my tin-cart. **1848** (1855) Ruxton *Life Far West* 152 **NM,** The rich buffalo or grama grass was exchanged for a coarser species, on which the hard-worked animals soon grew poor and weak. **1888** Jones *Negro Myths* 113 **GA coast,** De ting mose worry Buh Wolf life outer um. Eh fret so bout um tel eh biggin fuh tun rale po. **1899** (1912) Green *VA Folk-Speech* 329, *Poor.* . . Lean; meagre; emaciated: as, *poor* cattle. **1927** *AmSp* 2.360 **cwWV,** I told Mr. Jones that running for office was what made a greyhound poor. **1950** *WELS Suppl.,* His cows were so poor they could hardly stand up. **1965–70** *DARE* (Qu. K15, *A thin, bony, or poor-looking cow*) 111 Infs, **chiefly Sth, S Midl, SW,** Poor (cow); **AR33, CA193, NJ17, 58, TN35,** (Unhealthy,) poor-looking cow; **AR29, CA193, NC13, TX6,** (Awful *or* damn, old) poor cow; **MO37, TX78,** Poor as a snake; **MA72, NY66, RI2,** Poor-looking (creature); **FL32, MO18,** She's poor; **CA23,** Poor stock; **IL108,** Poor in flesh; **MS21,** Poor all over; **KY80,** Poor as a rail; **WI21,** Poor critter; **MS46,** Poor enough to count her ribs; **NE7,** Poor range cow; **WI40,** Poor rig; **GA46,**

Old pore cow; **NM13,** Pore; (Qu. K44, *A bony or poor-looking horse*) 86 Infs, **chiefly Sth, S Midl,** Poor (horse); **CA193, DC1, NC48, NJ58, TN62, WI54,** Poor-looking (horse); **MO4,** Poor and long-boned; **IL134,** Poor and shabby; **CT26, PA230,** Poor (as a) crow; **VA95,** Poor as hell; **MD15,** Poor colt; **MD34, MO2,** Poor old (bony) horse; **NY45,** Poor old nag; **WI40,** Poor rig; **MD42,** Poor skeleton horse; **GA52,** Real poor. **1985** Wilkinson *Moonshine* 84 **neNC,** The horse looked like a coat hanger. . . He was so poor he'd have to go twice through a place to make a shadow. **1986** Pederson *LAGS Concordance* **Gulf Region,** [12 infs used *poor* to describe a thin animal.]

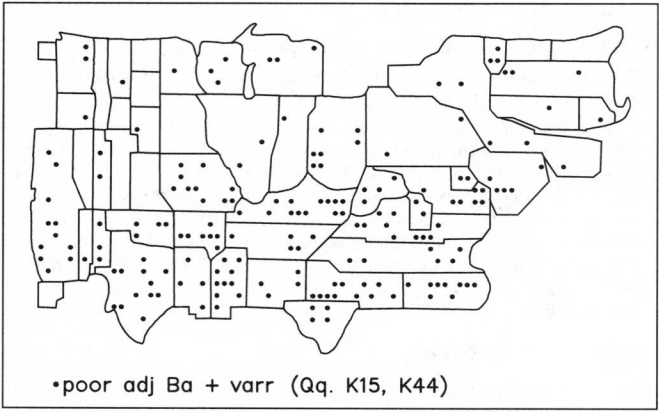

•poor adj Ba + varr (Qq. K15, K44)

b Of a person. **scattered, but esp Sth, S Midl** See Map Cf **poorly**

1758 (1855) Tomlinson *Military Jrls.* 15, Corperal Carpenter was taken poor. *Ibid* 25, This day at knight Leiut. Smith came back & very poor he was the rest of the guard returned well. **1823** in 1839 Mathews *Memoirs* 3.389 **sePA,** I said: 'You're a pleasant man; how's your wife?'—Landlord. 'Why, she's tolerable well, but *pretty poor* (very thin).' **1871** (1882) Stowe *Fireside Stories* 135 **MA,** Of all the racks o' bone I ever see, I never see a human critter so poor as he was. **1909** *DN* 3.414 **nME,** *Poor as a crow.* . . Poor in flesh. **1912** *DN* 3.586 **wIN,** *Poor* (or *thin*) *as gar broth.* . . Very poor or thin. **1930** Shoemaker *1300 Words* 47 **cPA Mts** (as of c1900), *Poor*—Thin, sickly looking. **1935** Hurston *Mules & Men* 47 **FL,** When a person is poor he look bright and de fatter you git de darker you look. **1941** *AmSp* 16.22 **sIN,** He eats so much it makes him poor (lean) to carry it. **1950** *WELS Suppl.* **csWI,** When I told Mrs. Duncan she could have my old coat for the missionary box she said, "Have you got too fat or too poor for it?" **1954** *Harder Coll.* **cwTN,** Poor as a fence rail . . of someone who is very thin. **1965–70** *DARE* (Qu. X49, *Expressions . . about a person who is very thin*) 33 Infs, **Sth, S Midl,** Poor; 23 Infs, **scattered,** Poor as a snake (*or* black snake, crow, cummer, jaybird, rail, snail, whippoorwill); **SC3, TX35,** Poor as Job's turkey; **ME4,** Awful poor; **CO20,** Eats so much it makes her poor to carry it; **GA43,** Poor thing; **GA7,** So poor you could read a newspaper through him; **MN12,** Very poor; (Qu. X52, . . *A person . . who had been sick was looking* _____) 18 Infs, **scattered,** Poor; **NY233, GA12, MO27,** Poor as a crow (*or* snake, whippoorwill); **LA37,** Very poor; **VA42,** Po'; **GA52,** Po' as a washing of soap; (Qu. BB38, *When a person doesn't look healthy*) 17 Infs, **scattered,** Poor;

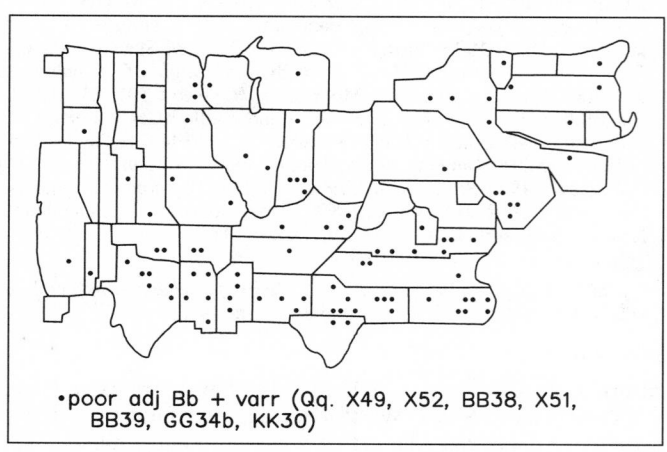

•poor adj Bb + varr (Qq. X49, X52, BB38, X51, BB39, GG34b, KK30)

(Qu. X51, *To lose weight because of sickness: "He was sick all winter and _____ [quite a bit]."*) 13 Infs, **scattered**, Got poor; NY233, Poor as a crow; (Qu. BB39, *On a day when you don't feel just right*) Infs **FL**15, **GA**12, **VA**42, Poor; (Qu. GG34b, *To feel depressed*) Inf **PA**35, Poor; (Qu. KK30, *Feeling . . without energy*) Inf NC30, Poor. **1968** Kellner *Aunt Serena* 146 **IN**, If he grew thin, he got poor, and if he grew excessively thin, he "went to nothing." **1986** Pederson *LAGS Concordance* **Gulf Region**, [13 infs used *poor* to describe a sick person.] **1995** *Signal Mag.* Dec np **cwTX**, Poor Ill. "Grandpa is poor."

poor v, n See **pour**

poor Annie n Also *poor Anne*

An **Indian poke 1** (here: *Veratrum viride*).

1900 Lyons *Plant Names* 389, *V[eratrum] viride.* . . British America . . to Georgia and Minnesota. . . Poor-Anne. **1910** Graves *Flowering Plants* 118 **CT**, *Veratrum viride* . . American White Hellebore. Indian Poke. Green Hellebore. Poor Annie. . . The rootstock is medicinal, is an active poison and is officinal. The early colonists used the plant as an insecticide.

poor as a dog See **dog** n B16b

poor as owl shit See **owl, poor as an**

poor-barker n [Var of *poor-buckra* (at **buckra 2b**)]
=**poor White 1**; hence n *poor barkery;* see quot 1952.

1890 *Catholic World* 52.251 **Sth** [Black], But den he warn't no po' barker. **1896** *DN* 1.412 **Sth**, "Poor Barkers," poor whites. **1952** Brown *NC Folkl.* 1.570, *Poor barkery.* . . "Poor white trash." Probably a corruption of Gullah *buckra*, "white man."

poor boy n Pronc-spp *po' boy, pore boy*

1 also *po' jo, poor boy('s) sandwich, poor man:* =**submarine sandwich. orig New Orleans LA; now widespread exc NEast, Mid Atl; esp freq Gulf States, TN, TX** See Map

1931 Soard's *New Orleans City Directory* 1139 *(Popik Coll.)*, Poor Boy Sandwich Shop (Mrs Amelia Weidenbacher). **1938** FWP *New Orleans Guide* 299, *Poor Boy Sandwiches*, foot-long, French bread sandwiches (10¢) crammed with a choice of cheese, meats, or seafood and garnished with lettuce, tomatoes, and dressing, which constitute New Orleans' own answer to the depression. **1947** Williams *Streetcar* 11 **New Orleans LA**, Tell Steve to get him a poor boy's sandwich 'cause nothing's left here. **1947** *True* 32.102 **New Orleans LA** [Black], A 'poor boy sandwich' is consisted of a half loaf of that long bread—real dry and a real thin slice of ham between it. . . You get it for five cents. **1950** *AmSp* 25.67 **New Orleans LA**, The *poor boy* [is] an oversize sandwich which made its initial appearance in the early 1920s in the waterfront cafés which catered to dock workers and truck farmers. . . Both the name and the sandwich appear to have been the invention of Clovis and Benjamin Martin, brothers, who established a small café in the French Market district of New Orleans in 1921. . . By 1931 a Po-Boy Sandwich Shoppe, Inc., and a Poor Boy Sandwich Shop appear in the telephone directory. **1954** Armstrong *Satchmo* 86 **New Orleans LA**, I would sit with them with my ten-cent mug of beer and my poor boy sandwich. **1960** (1966) Percy *Moviegoer* 156 **New Orleans LA**, Once in a while he would walk down to the Chinaman's at night and eat a po-boy. That was the only way he could eat. **1965–70** *DARE* (Qu. H42, . . *[A sandwich]* . . *in a much larger, longer bun, that's a meal in itself*) 106 Infs, **widely scattered exc NEast, Mid Atl; esp freq Gulf States, TN, TX**, Poor boy (sandwich); **LA**14, 31, **NY**144, **TX**81, Po' boy; **IL**43, Po' jo; **NE**7, Poor man. **1971** *Today Show* Letters **cIN**, I've chiefly heard your Poor Boy as *Pore Boy*; **seLA**, Down here what Dr. Cassidy called a "poor boy" is actually known as a "po' boy"; **seLA** (as of c1906), We moved to New Orleans in 1906, and our parents gave us 10¢ for lunch money when we went to school. At noon recess we would visit a nearby grocery store, and purchase a "Po-boy" made befor[e] your eyes, price 5¢. . . These sandwiches were made all over the City of New Orleans by small neighborhood grocery stores. What Martin Bros. did was to really commercialize them after the automobile became common. I went to the Gulf Coast Military Academy in 1917, and the "Po-Boy" was obtainable in Biloxie [sic] Miss., having spread from New Orl[e]ans. **1990** Burke *Morning for Flamingos* 22 **seLA**, I stopped at one of the bait and boat-rental shacks below the levee and bought two poor-boy shrimp sandwiches. **1992** *DARE* File, "Roastbeef Poorboy $2.75"—sign seen in the window of a sandwich shop in Madison, Wisconsin. **1997** *NY Times* (NY) 15 Mar 8/2 **New Orleans LA**, "Roast beef po boys, with gravy and mayonnaise," he said. "When you eat it, it

just runs down your arm." **2000** *DARE* File **TX**, In Waco, Texas, the division seemed to be: if it has cold cuts in it, it's a submarine, but if it has catfish or cajun chicken in it, it's a po boy.

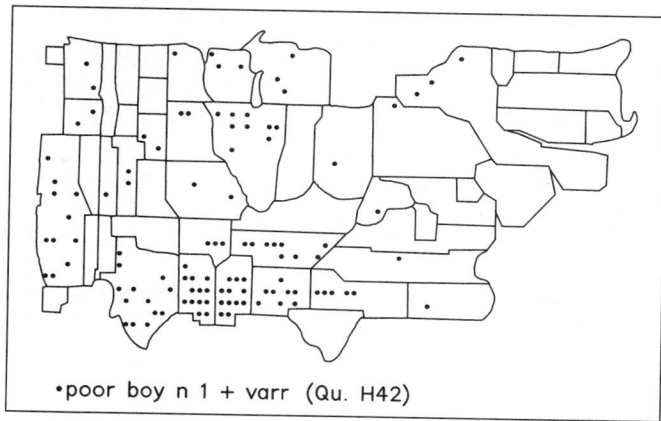

•poor boy n 1 + varr (Qu. H42)

2 Used of other inexpensive foods or drinks; see quots.

1942 Berrey–Van den Bark *Amer. Slang* 100.12, Poor boy, *a small whiskey.* **1949** *PADS* 11.9 **wTX** (as of 1911–29), *Poor boy:* . . Chili con carne.

3 attrib: Cheap, makeshift, improvised. **esp Gulf States** Cf **poor boy** v phr, **poor man's cake**, **~ pie**

1950 *AmSp* 25.233 **LA, TX**, *Poor boy* is used as an adjective to describe any cheap or makeshift mechanical device used in the oil fields. Thus a 'poor boy rig' is a piece of shoddy, stopgap equipment, and a 'poor boy core barrel' is a length of twisted pipe used for 'taking a core.' . . A 'poor boy outfit' is a company which is inadequately financed and equipped. . . Significantly, its use appears to be confined to the Louisiana oil fields, although one informant states that he heard the term in Texas about 1939. He assumes that it is known throughout the whole industry and estimates that it has been current for about twenty-five years. **1952** *AmSp* 27.232 **cnFL** [Argot of waiters], *Poor boy float.* Glass of water and a toothpick. **c1965** Randle *Cookbooks* (Ask Neighbor) 4.28 **OH**, *Poor Boy Meatloaf Stroganoff.* Leftover meatloaf . . mushroom pieces . . Au Jus Gravy Mix . . water . . sour cream. **1986** Pederson *LAGS Concordance*, 1 inf, **seAL**, Poor-boy cake—made with syrup and ginger; 1 inf, **nwMS**, Poor-boy corn bread—meal, water, salt, then bake it. **1999** *DARE* File **cOK**, During political campaigns, a common term is "poor boy signs." These are not yard signs. They are usually wooden signs, homemade. **1999** *NADS Letters* **cMI** (as of c1950), I grew up hearing this as an adjective. . . a poor boy shirt was one that had shrunk, faded, etc. and did not fit. . . A poor boy lunch at school was one you brought that was short on nearly everything. Perhaps a lard sandwich and an apple. **2000** *Ibid* **nwTN**, My grand mother sometimes cooks poor boy spaghetti in which she uses few ingredients. Usually limiting it to noodles, salt, pepper, and tomatoes, not tomato sauce. As far as I know she is from rural extreme north west Tennessee.

poor boy v phr **scattered, but chiefly SW, Gulf States** Cf **poor boy 3, poor hog** v phr

To make or repair in a hand-to-mouth or makeshift manner; with *it:* to make do, get by cheaply.

1939 in 1984 Lambert–Franks *Voices* 14 **OK**, In oil country, like around Ada or Seminole, if you have a hole goin' down and get broke, somebody will take pity on you and lend you enough to poor-boy it on down a little further. But not out around Hobart. **1979** *Today Show Letters* **TX** [Oil industry terms], To "po'-boy it" is to do anything, particularly to drill a well, in the least expensive fashion possible, using makeshift equipment and relatively unskilled labor. **1982** Caro *Yrs. Lyndon Johnson* 1.613 **TX** (as of 1930), The first success among the test wells being "poor-boyed" (drilled on credit, with frequent halts to raise money to go a few hundred feet deeper) by long-broke wildcatters in a poverty-stricken area of East Texas was eight miles east of Henderson. **1986** Pederson *LAGS Concordance*, 1 inf, **nwLA**, We poor-boyed it out—struggled to clean farm; [1 inf, **neTX**, Kind of poor-boy bached it—in camps]. **1998** *DARE* File **sLA**, "Well, I've been poor boyin' it for so long now, a few more years won't hurt me." "Are you takin' your girlfriend to some fancy restaurant, or will you have to poor boy it?" "Last year we poor boyed it, but this Christmas is going to be somethin'!" . . The folks that I've heard this from are around 50 years old or more and have never moved out of the Baton Rouge area—although they are very "rural" Baton Rouge. *Ibid* **wTX,** *Poor boy it*—Definitely used by my folks [aged 76 and 70] and I've heard the term used with a lot of the older West Texas people here [in Lubbock]. **1999** *Ibid* **cOK,** I have . . heard "poor boy it" back here. **1999** *NADS Letters* **seCA,** To "poor-boy-it" was common growing up in Ventura, CA 1950's. Of course there were a lot of immigrants from TX and OK and they may have brought it with them. *Ibid* **cAL,** This term is still used by my father. . . "Poor boy it" . . is to make do with what resources you had in regard to some specific project or endeavor—not, to my memory, ever speaking directly of money. **2000** *Ibid* **VA,** *Poor boy it*—People say that here when they don't have much money and are going to take a trip, staying in the car or with friends. *Ibid* **MS,** *Poor boy it*—Let's do something tonight. . . we'll have to poor boy it cause I didn't get paid. *Ibid* **c,cwIN,** Student: "Instead of having a mechanic, for example, fix something, you rig it up until you have the money—you poor boy it." *Ibid* **VA,** "Poor boy it" is in common use in piedmont Virginia. . . [I]t is generally applied to makeshift repairs. . . "When the radiator hose blew, I poor boyed it with some duct tape and nursed it to the garage." I have heard this all my life and I am in my mid-fifties. It is my impression that I have only heard this from white males of roughly my age or older.

poor boy('s) sandwich See poor boy

poor crab n Cf fat crab

A blue crab (*Callinectes sapidus*) that has just molted.

1942 *Chesapeake Biol. Lab. Pub.* 53.11, A "poor" crab is one which has recently shed its shell. As the crab, when it sheds, increases its original dimensions by about one-third, the "poor" crab tissues are watery and yield a comparatively small quantity of meat. Pickers in many cases throw such crabs into the refuse where they are a complete waste.

poor do n chiefly Sth, S Midl

1 Something inferior, unsuccessful, make-do; a shiftless, trifling person. [Cf *EDD poor do* (at *do* sb. 2) something that has turned out unsuccessfully, *make a poor do* (at *do* sb. 8.(4)) "to get on badly"]

1941 Justus *Cabin on Kettle Creek* 130 **KY, TN,** It's not much—ham shank, corn pone and shucky beans. Poor-do, but maybe you could stand it for one time. **1981** Pederson *LAGS Basic Materials,* 1 inf, **neTX,** Mush—used to call this "a poor do" because he didn't like it. **1994** *Montgomery Coll.* **eTN,** "He's entertaining a poor do." (=He's engaged in a project of little consequence.) "He married a poor do." (=a ne'er do well). **1998** *NADS Letters* **cSC,** Poor-do. . . I remember one of my grandmothers using this term as an apology for a skimpy meal. It was not used for any particular dish but as a generic term for a meal that didn't have much to it. Both of my grandmothers were from Saluda County, South Carolina. They were both in their nineties when they died in the 1980's. **2000** *Ibid,* Poor do—used generally for any meal made of scraps or leftovers. . . My mother . . (b. 1924) was raised on a farm in Kansas (near Abilene). As I grew up in California, I knew my mom and grandparents (who sometimes lived with us) used strange expressions that others had never heard of. *Ibid* **cnGA,** "Poor-do" was used mostly by women, and it was pronounced "*pore-do.*" The general usage was when a woman wished to speak disparagingly of a meal she had prepared (usually a very good one, indeed): "Well, it's a mighty poor do, but maybe we can get by on it." (Emphasis on the *do*. . . "*pore-do.*") I don't recall ever hearing the term applied to a specific dish. . . always to the meal itself. Less frequently heard was the application of the term to a dog or a rascally boy: "Hey, Poor-Do!" In this case the emphasis would be on the "*pore.*" ("Hey, *pore*-do!") Almost always, this was a term of affection for an ugly dog or a mischievous boy. I never heard it applied to a girl or any other animal.

2 also *poor doe,* ~ *doo;* also attrib: Any of var meager, make-do dishes or foodstuffs, often involving cornmeal or leftover corn bread; see quots.

1870 Duval *Advent. Big-Foot* 308 **cTX,** Our money gave out entirely, and we were compelled to live on watermelons, with now and then a dish of 'poor doe,' which, as you know, isn't much stronger diet than the watermelons. **1909** *Pioneer Days SW* 253, When we had hog meat we would fry a few pieces, take the grease and crumble corn bread in it, putting in water and salt, and we had a pot of soup called "poor doo." **1913** Kephart *Highlanders* 292 **sAppalachians,** The old Germans taught their Scotch and English neighbors the merits of scrapple, but here it is known as poor-do. **1953** Randolph–Wilson *Down in Holler* 273 **Ozarks,** *Poor-do.* . . Grease, shortening. "Fetch me a sack of flour, an' some poor-do for to make gravy." This used to be very common in northwestern Arkansas. **1954** *Harder Coll.* **cwTN,** *Poor-do.* . . Make it

out of meal, milk, and salt. **1956** Algren *Walk on the Wild Side* 167 **New Orleans LA** (as of 1930s), Ef'n I had money I'd buy flour 'n shortenin' for us to have a pan of poor-do gravy. **1958** *PADS* 29.14 **TN,** *Poor do* [poɔ- du]: A dumpling. "Of bread scraps, both corn and wheat, seasoned with salt and black pepper, and damped with water and baked a little." "Corn meal dumplings cooked on turnip greens." Obsolescent. Rep[orted] from Davidson, Humphreys, Perry, Warren, White [counties]. **1961** *McDavid Coll.* **csOK,** *Poor do*—call biscuit [made into] pudding. **1968–69** *DARE* (Qu. H37, . . *Words . . for gravy. Any joking ones?*) Inf **IN3,** Poor-do [por diu]; **KY40,** Poor-do [laughter]. **1971** Wood *Vocab. Change* 369 **Sth,** [*Bread:*] Additional volunteered words . . *poor do.* **1981** Pederson *LAGS Basic Materials,* 1 inf, **neTN,** Poor do = hush-puppy description; 1 inf, **neTN,** Poor do—like hushpuppies; [1 inf, **swAR,** Poor Joe = poor-do? scrapple/headcheese/meat]. **1982** Slone *How We Talked* 33 **eKY** (as of c1950), *Poor doe*—slang for water gravy (gravy made from water in place of milk, when no milk is available). *Ibid* 55, As it was thought that every meal must have gravy, sometimes water gravy was made, and nicknamed "poor do." **1984** Wilder *You All Spoken Here* 84 **Sth,** *Poor do:* Dumplin's of bread scraps dampened with water and baked; a concoction made by stirring corn meal and grease in a skillet, frying until it smokes, then adding water or milk. **1998** *NADS Letters* **eTN,** I grew up in Baltimore, but my parents were both from east Tennessee. . . "Poor-do" at our house was a very specific dish: leftover cornbread, crumbled up in a bowl, then covered with cold milk (regular or buttermilk) and eaten with a spoon like cereal. Usually it was a late-night snack. **1999** *Ibid* **neTX,** Poor-do. . . This is a dish the women in my family used to make during the Depression years. It is a cheap and makeshift dessert made from available supplies. . . This particular food was prepared by taking the leftover breakfast biscuits, breaking them into pieces, adding some home canned tomatoes, sugar and butter and baking. **2000** *Ibid* **cVA,** "Poor do" is gravy made from fat, flour, and water. I have heard it used perhaps twice in my life by white males of middle age in central Virginia.

3 also *pour-do:* See quot.

c1960 *Wilson Coll.* **csKY,** *Pour-do* (or *poor-do*). . . Sweet sauce to pour over puddings and cakes.

poor doe, poor doo See poor do 2

poor farm n

A farm where poor people are maintained at public expense.

1852 (1856) Gunnison *Mormons* 145, A Poor Farm of forty acres is in the centre, controlled by the bishops. **1895** *Atlantic Mth.* 75.31 **NH,** The latter had actually taken to her bed . . announcing that 'she'd rather go to the poor-farm and done with it than resk her life there another night.' **1902** Day *Pine Tree Ballads* 31 **ME,** Folks said that a man who was paralyzed required some special care,/ And allowed that the poor farm was the place; so they carried the old folks there. **1935** in 1986 Brewer *Easthampton Town Lodging House* 14 **MA,** The already large number of people being supported by the town—in or outside the Poor Farm . . convinced us that this problem of Welfare should no longer . . be handled by the Selectmen. **1951** West *Witch Diggers* 6 **IN,** "Getting off at The Junction, aren't you?" "If the train'll stop long enough." "It'll stop. Where next?" "The Poor Farm". . . "Permanent or visiting?" "Visiting." **1954** Forbes *Rainbow* 18 **NEng** (as of early 19th cent), [In] his Thanksgiving at the Poor Farm [=a painting] you could guess the turkey was a pauper. **1960** Carpenter *Tales Manchaca* 115 **cTX** (as of 1942), I was shocked the first time I saw my birth certificate and noted: "Place of Birth: Travis County Poor Farm." But I soon realized that it sounded almost as good as a log cabin in case I ever decided to run for a political office. **1967–69** *DARE* (Qu. II25, *Names or nicknames for the part of a town where the poorer people . . live*) Inf **MO37,** The poor farm—now it's called a nursing home; **TX36,** Poor farm. **1978** Whipple *Vintage Nantucket* 195 **MA,** Six years later there was a fire that was not so extensive but nonetheless tragic: on February 21, 1844, the Poor Farm at Quaise burned to the ground. **1978** *DARE* File **cnMA** (as of c1915), When I was a small child people with no means of support were taken to the *poor farm.* But a few years later the Massachusetts poor farms became town farms, by official decree, I presume.

poor fish See fish n B2

poor folks' plague n

A **louse B1.**

1966 *DARE* (Qu. R25, *Joking names for a head louse, or body louse*) Inf **FL7,** Poor folks' plague.

poor grub n

A **staggerbush** (here: *Lyonia ferruginea*).

1927 Boston Soc. Nat. Hist. *Proc.* 38.355 **Okefenokee GA,** One trail [made by cotton rats] extended over such ground and through a sparse growth of saw-palmetto, 'poor grub' (*Xolisma* [=*Lyonia*] *ferruginea*), and small oaks, and led down into some holes about the base of a burnt stump.

poor hog v phr Pronc-sp *pore-hawg* Cf **poor boy** v phr
To make do, get by.

1933 Williamson *Woods Colt* 6 **Ozarks,** "How are you fellers a-makin' it?" "Oh, jest a pore-hawgin' along." **1936** *AmSp* 11.316 **Ozarks,** *Pore-hawgin'.* . . Just getting along, not living in luxury. 'Weuns jest been a pore-hawgin' along.'

poor jo See **poor joe** n² 2

poor Job n [Prob folk-etym for **poor joe** n²] **GA**
Usu the **great blue heron,** but occas the **snowy egret** or a similar related bird.

1744 in 1840 GA Hist. Soc. *Coll.* 118 **GA,** [There are] numbers of the heron kind of different species and colors, some small ones of the most beautiful white, which are called poor Jobs, from their being generally very lean. **1791** Bartram *Travels* 293, A[rdea] violacca [sic; =*Nyctanassa violacea*], the crested blue bitern, (called poor Jobe.) **1850** Burke *Reminiscences of GA* 138, Many large birds lived in the marshes by digging worms and snails. The largest of these are the gannet and "poor job". . . The poor job is a good deal larger and as white as snow. **1913** *Auk* 30.491 **Okefenokee GA,** *Ardea herodias wardi* . . 'Po' Job'; 'Po' Jo'. . . The natives pronounced the 'Po' Job,' good eating; but when we tried a young one, all agreed that it was too bitter for our tastes. **1955** *Oriole* 20.1.2 **GA,** Great Blue Heron. . . Po Job, Po Joe. *Ibid* **GA,** Snowy Egret.—Poor Job, White Crane. **1969** *DARE* FW Addit **Okefenokee GA,** Poor Job = great blue heron. Said by East Okefenokee guide.

poor Joe n¹
1 =**Mexican clover.** Cf **poor toes**
1881 Phares *Farmer's Book of Grasses* 14, *Richardsonia scabra.* . . This is a native of Mexico and South America. It has become naturalized in Florida and the southern parts of other southern States. It is called Mexican Clover . . poor Joe, pigeonweed etc.
2 also *pojo:* A **buttonweed 1** (here: *Diodia teres*). **esp Sth, S Midl**
1901 *Torreya* 1.117 **GA,** *Diodia teres* . . Poverty-weed. Sumter [Co.] Poor-land weed. Coffee. Poor Joe. Spalding [Co.] **1959** Sanders *Echoes* 46 **swAR,** Our ball ground was an old abandoned field grown up in *pojo,* bitter weeds and bull nettles. The cows used it for their resting place at night. **c1967** GA Univ. *Weeds S. U.S.* 38, *Diodia teres*—poorjoe— Summer annual. . . Flowers small, tubular, pink, at leaf axils. . . Virginia buttonweed (*Diodia virginiana*) is similar to poorjoe, but perennial, coarser stems and leaves, larger seed pods. **1967–69** *DARE* (Qu. S9, . . *Kinds of grass that are hard to get rid of*) Inf **AR52,** Poor Joe; (Qu. S21, . . *Weeds* . . *that are a trouble in gardens and fields*) Inf **GA84,** Poor Joe. **1970** Correll *Plants TX* 1496, *Diodia teres* . . Poor joe, rough buttonweed. **1970** U.S. Ag. Research Serv. *Selected Weeds* 350, *Diodia teres* . . Poorjoe.

poor joe n² [Prob of West Afr origin (see quot 1949), affected in varying degrees by folk-etym; **poor Job,** though attested considerably earlier, prob represents a further folk-etym alteration] Cf *DBE*
1 =**green heron.**
1884 Henshall *Camping in FL* 36, Frank brought me one day a bird for identification, which he called a "fly-up-the-creek." "No," said I; "it is a small, green heron, called by the crackers a 'poor-Joe,' though why poor and why Joe, I can't tell you."
2 also *jo, po' jo(e), pojo crane, poor Joe bird, pore joe:* =**great blue heron. chiefly GA, SC** Cf **old joe, poor Job**
1909 S. Atl. Qrly. 8.48 **seSC,** The lank Blue Heron, from his emaciation, is the Po'jo, i.e., poor Joe. **1913** [see **poor Job**]. **1917** *Wilson Bulletin* 29.2.78 **LA,** *Ardea herodias.* . . jo, grand-jo, Marksville, La. **1940** (1941) Bell *Swamp Water* 33 **Okefenokee GA,** A poor-joe bird rose in agitation, squawking indignantly back at the boatman. **1941** *Sat. Eve. Post* 13 Sept 52 **Sth,** When I want a long-legged bird I'll shoot me down a pojo crane. **1941** Writers' Program *Guide SC* 389, The great blue heron is a dignified fisherman here, though among the natives his long lanky frame gives him the name of 'Po' Joe.' A perennial local question is: 'Did you ever see a fat "Po' Joe" sitting on a dead live oak

stump eating green blackberries and taking a fresh salt water bath?' **1943** Gabrielson *Wildlife Refuges* 117 **Okefenokee GA,** A "poor Joe," as goes the local designation for the angular, awkward, great blue heron, flaps away with dangling legs. **1949** Turner *Africanisms* 199 **sSC, GA coasts** [Gullah], [Words used in conversation:] ['poɹo] 'heron'—V[ai], po₃dʒo₃ 'heron.' Cf. Eng., *poor Joe.* [*DARE* Ed: Subscript numerals indicate tone.] **1955** [see **poor Job**]. **1966** *DARE* (Qu. Q10, . . *Water birds and marsh birds*) Inf **SC4,** Heron—called [pojo]. **1966** *DARE* FW Addit **SC10,** Old joe—water bird (heron), but everybody calls him po' jo. **1968** *Ibid* **seGA,** Pore joe—nickname for great blue heron. Common among swamp natives.
3 as *poor jo:* =**Louisiana heron.**
1917 *Wilson Bulletin* 29.2.78 **NC,** *Hydranassa tricolor ruficollis.*— Poor jo, Beaufort, N.C.

poor joe bird See **poor joe** n² 2

poor John n
1 The **hake 1a,** when preserved by drying. [Because it is considered mean fare; *OED2* c1585 →]
1833 Smith *Nat. Hist. Fishes MA* 202, The largest [hake] caught here seldom exceed two feet. They are denominated, when prepared for market, *poor-Johns.* The best hake are taken off Cape Cod, and sold under the name of *stock-fish.* **1890** *Century Dict.* 4620, *Poor-John.* . . The hake when salted and dried.
2 See quot. Cf **hopping John 1, poor do**
1941 Street *In Father's House* 44 **MS,** She [=a Black woman] cooks the best po'john of anybody around here.

poor-land daisy n
=**oxeye daisy 1.**
1900 Lyons *Plant Names* 99, C[hrysanthemum] Leucanthemum. . . Bull-, Bulls-eye-, . . Poor-land- or White Daisy. [**1906** Lounsberry *Wild Flower Book* 151 **Sth,** Most people . . love Daisies, but here it is a great disgrace to have them in the pastures. People like Uncle Hiram don't seem to know they are Daisies—he calls them "white weeds." When many of them are in a field . . , the farmers say, "Poor land, just covered with weeds."] **1988** Werner *Life & Lore* 88 **IL,** Daisy—*Chrysanthemum leucanthemum.* . . Along roadsides it provides considerable beauty, but in hayfields it can substantially diminish the quality of the hay. From this unfavorable characteristic comes [sic] several old common names: White Weed, Bull Daisy, Poorland daisy, Poverty weed [etc].

poor-land grass n Cf **sour grass**
1932 Hench Coll. **VA,** Poor-land grass, hen's nest grass = sour grass—tufted grass used to make hen's nests.

poor-land weed n Also *poor-weed* Cf **poor Joe** n¹ 2, **poverty-weed g**
A **buttonweed 1** (here: *Diodia teres*).
1898 *Jrl. Amer. Folkl.* 11.228, *Diodia teres.* . . button weed, poor weed. **1901** *Torreya* 1.117 **cGA,** *Diodia teres.* . . Poverty-weed. . . Poor-land weed. Spalding [Co.]

poorly adj Usu |'pʊrlɪ|; also **chiefly Sth, S Midl** |'po(r)lɪ| Pronc-spp *poly, porely* Cf **poor** adj **Bb**
Ill; weak; depressed.
1800 (1907) Columbia Hist. Soc. *Records* 10.92 **PA,** Paid Mrs. Ray a morning Visit.—found her & Mr. R. both very poorly with violent Colds. **1815** Humphreys *Yankey in England* 107, Poorly, miserably, ill. **1884** *Anglia* 7.270 **Sth, S Midl** [Black], To be po'ly = to be in poor health. **1890** *DN* 1.69 **KY,** Po'ly [poulɪ]: for *poorly.* "How d'you do?" "I am po'ly to-day." **1893** Shands *MS Speech* 50, *Poly* [polɪ]. Negro for *poorly,* used to mean in a bad state of health. **1903** *DN* 2.325 **seMO,** He is mighty porely and I'm afraid he won't live through the day. **1907** *DN* 3.234 **nwAR,** Poorly [porlɪ]. . . Sick, very ill. **1923** *DN* 5.217 **swMO,** Porely. . . In bad health. **1926** *AmSp* 2.80 **ME,** Persons who are ill but still able to be about regard themselves as "poorly." **1931** (1991) Hughes–Hurston *Mule Bone* 50 **cFL** [Black], My chillun is poly. **1946** *AmSp* 21.98 **sIL,** The rural or village dweller will tell you that he feels *poorly.* **1965–70** *DARE* (Qu. X52, . . *A person* . . *who had been sick was looking* _____) 174 Infs, **widespread,** Poorly; **FL27, HI1, MO21, WI66,** Very (or mighty) poorly; (Qu. BB38, *When a person doesn't look healthy, or looks as if he hadn't been well for some time* . . *"He looks* _____.") 82 Infs, **scattered,** Poorly; **CT23,** Real poorly; (Qu. BB39, *On a day when you don't feel just right, though not actually sick* . . *"I'll be all right tomorrow—I'm just feeling* _____ *today."*) 64 Infs, **scattered,** Poorly; (Qu. BB41, *Not seriously ill, but sick enough to*

be in bed: "*He's been* _____ *for a week.*") 18 Infs, **scattered,** Poorly; **AL**20, **MA**73, **NC**30, **NY**222, **OK**31, Feeling poorly; (Qu. BB5, *A general feeling of discomfort or illness that isn't any one place in particular*) Infs **IL**118, **MD**9, **MA**72, **NC**72, **SC**2, 64, **TX**79, **UT**3, Feeling (*or* feel) poorly; **FL**28, **KS**13, Poorly; (Qu. BB42, *If a person is very sick . . he's* _____) Infs **FL**51, **IL**126, **LA**6, (Pretty) poorly; **PA**188, Very poorly; (Qu. BB54, *When a sick person is past hope of recovery . . he's [a]* _____) Inf **FL**10, Poorly; (Qu. GG34b, *To feel depressed or in a gloomy mood:* "*She's feeling* _____ *today.*") Infs **CA**76, 197, **IL**86, **MA**58, **NY**92, **VA**24, Poorly. **1994** NC Lang. & Life Project *Harkers Is. Vocab.* 9 eNC, He looked mighty poorly at church today.

poor man See **poor boy**

poor man breeches n
A **dogtooth violet.**
  1968 *DARE* (Qu. S11, . . *Dog-tooth violet*) Inf **PA**152, Poor man breeches.

poor man patch See **poor man's patches**

poor man pudding See **poor man's pudding**

poor man's apple n Pronc-sp *porman's apple* Cf **apple melon**
Any of var fruits or vegetables; see quots.
  1914 *DN* 4.111 KS, *Poorman's apple.* . . A kind of melon. Also *Porman's apple.* **1962** McDavid *Coll.* cOK, Poor man's apple—a type of melon. **1998** *DARE* File eKS, A "poor man's apple" is a hedge-apple. . . The fruit is larger than an apple, inedible perhaps poisonous, green and very heavy. *Ibid* IN, KY, Poor man's apple—Indiana/Kentucky, rural, 1940s/50s; in widespread common use. Meaning: fruit of the pawpaw tree. . . "Poor man's" because pawpaws used to grow wild all over the place. **1999** *NADS Letters* swMO, My aunt . . used the term "poor-man's apple" along with "hedge-apple" interchangeably for as long as I can remember (that's forty years give or take). **1999** *DARE* File, Poor man's apple—a potato; eating poor man's apples; eating raw potatoes; heard this in the south, midwest, border states, Pennsylvania from whites, blacks and Native Americans. **2000** *NADS Letters* seOK, [I] remember hearing crabapples referred to as Poor Man's Apples when I was a kid (late 60's, early 70's). *Ibid* MS, Poor man's apple—grandmother used this to refer to little knotty crabapples off the tree in the back yard. *Ibid* KS, A poor-man's apple is a potato, sliced like an apple, and eaten raw. My mother often told me that she and her brothers and sisters were given these "poor man's apples" by my grandmother during the depression, as snacks to stave off hunger pangs. (My grandmother was born in the 1880's and raised from the age of 2 by her grandmother, in Iowa.) *Ibid* seKS, I remember my grandfather referring to Hedge Apples as "Poor Man's Apple." . . I have talked to several people that grew up on farms in the area and asked them if they had ever heard of it [=*poor man's apple*]. And every single one without skipping a beat, said "Hedgeapples"! *Ibid* OK, Poor man's apple, was usually the watermelon, easy to grow in the sandy soils which because of its porous quality, was ideal to grow in Oklahoma. *Ibid,* My father, . . born in Manhattan KS about 1905, used this term [=*poor man's apple*] to describe cantaloupe.

poor man's apple pie See **poor man's pie 3**

poor man's asparagus n
See quots.
  1953 Piercy *Shaker Cook Book* 247, *Poor Man's Asparagus*—2 pounds tender green onions . . butter . . flour . . cream . . salt . . pepper . . egg yolks. **1987** Childress *Out of the Ozarks* 31, Another treat found along creek banks was Poor Man's Asparagus—pale young shoots of "poke salad," a sort of wild spinach delicious with scrambled eggs.

poor man's bread n
Corn bread.
  1968 *DARE* (Qu. H14, *Bread that's made with cornmeal*) Inf **IN**48, Poor man's bread—same as corn pone. **1986** Pederson *LAGS Concordance,* 1 inf, neAL, Poor man's bread—hoecake.

poor man's cabbage n
A **winter cress.**
  1923 *Amer. Botanist* 29.150, *Barbarea vulgaris* is the "common winter cress," . . "Herb Barbarea" and "poor man's cabbage." **1973** *Foxfire 2*

78, Creases (*Barbarea verna*) . . (dry land cress . . bitter cress, poor man's cabbage).

poor man's cake n
See quots.
  1880 *Skandinavisk-Amerikansk Kogebog* 161, *Fattig Mands Kage* (Poor mans Cake). [Recipe starts with basic yeast dough and adds an egg, molasses, sugar, butter, raisins, and more flour.] **1948** Hutchison *PA Du. Cook Book* 137, *Poor Man's Cake.* . . Since this cake is made without eggs or butter, the flour should be sifted with the baking powder several times to ensure lightness. *c*1965 Randle *Cookbooks* (Ask Neighbor) 1.75, *Poor Man's Cake* . . raisins . . oleo . . vanilla . . soda . . baking powder . . flour . . sugar . . eggs . . apple pie spice . . walnuts. *c*1965 Randle *Cookbooks* (Plain Cookery) 3.17 OH, *Poor Man's Chocolate Cake* . . cocoa . . soda . . milk . . vanilla . . sugar . . flour . . shortening. **1970** *DARE* FW Addit eVA, Poor man's cake—made with fig preserves. Common. **1981** Hachten *Flavor WI* 279, *Poor Man's Cake.* . . This eggless, milkless, butterless recipe came from her husband's grandmother who baked the cake as a girl. In those days, walnuts [*DARE* Ed: The recipe calls for ¾ cup.] were comparatively cheap!

poor man's cheese n
Cottage cheese.
  1941 *LANE* Map 299 (*Cottage cheese*) 1 inf, seRI, Poor man's cheese, nickname. **1968** *DARE* (Qu. H60, *The lumpy white cheese that is made from sour milk*) Inf **CA**77, Poor man's cheese.

poor man's custard See **poor man's pudding**

poor man's daisy n
A **black-eyed Susan 2** (here: *Rudbeckia hirta*).
  1940 Clute *Amer. Plant Names* 86, *R[udbeckia] hirta.* Black-eyed Susan, . . poor-man's daisy [etc].

poor man's dish See **poor man's pie 2**

poor man's fertilizer n Also *poor man's manure* **chiefly NEast**
A snowfall, esp one occurring in late spring.
  [**1798** in 1977 Whiting *Early Amer. Proverbs* 404, A fall of snow . . supplies the place of manure.] **1959** *VT Hist.* 27.135, *Poor man's fertilizer.* . . A light fall of snow after the ground thaws. Common. *Ibid* 148, *Poor man's manure.* . . Common. Rural areas. **1967–70** *DARE* (Qu. B39, *A very light fall of snow*) Infs **NY**209, 233, Poor man's manure; **MA**5, Poor man's fertilizer. **1975** Gould *ME Lingo* 215, *Poor man's fertilizer.* **1979** *Harvard Post* (MA) 13 Apr 12/1 MA, A late snowfall like this is popularly known as "poor man's fertilizer," and certainly does the soil good. **1986** *DARE* File nwMA, A late spring snow is called poor man's fertilizer, and it really seems to make the grass green and the flowers grow. **2001** *Ibid* ceWI, You know what they call a late snow, don't you? Poor man's fertilizer.

poor man's grass n
Prob a **crabgrass 1.**
  1970 *DARE* (Qu. S9, . . *Kinds of grass that are hard to get rid of*) Inf **MA**78, Poor man's grass—another name for old-man's-beard or crabgrass.

poor man's gravy n Cf **poor do 2**
A meatless gravy of flour, milk or water, and fat, when available.
  1930 *DN* 6.88 cWV, *Poorman's gravy,* a food variously made, chiefly water and flour, plus bacon grease, possibly. **1954** Harder *Coll.* cwTN, *Poor man's gravy* . . made with fat, flour, and milk. **1967–68** *DARE* (Qu. H37, . . *Words . . for gravy. Any joking ones?*) Inf **AL**25, Poor man's gravy—take grease, flour, water—no meat; **LA**16, Poor man's gravy—this is made with flour and shortening when you don't have any meat; [**AR**47, Poor man's last chance]. **1984** Wilder *You All Spoken Here* 87 Sth, *Poor man's gravy:* Gravy made with most any grease and flour and water. **1986** Pederson *LAGS Concordance,* 1 inf, ceLA, Poor man's gravy—made from flour.

poor man's manure See **poor man's fertilizer**

poor man's orange n
1 The **tomato** (*Lycopersicon lycopersicum*).
  1950 *WELS* (*Other names or nicknames for tomatoes*) 1 Inf, ceWI, Poor man's orange.

2 Cabbage.

2000 *NADS Letters* **KS,** Poor man's orange (cabbage) was a familiar saying in my family. My grandmother said cabbage contains vitamin C and was a lot cheaper than oranges.

poor man's orchid n

1 An **iris B1.**

1966 *DARE* Wildfl QR Pl.26 Inf **WA**15, Poor man's orchids—iris is poor man's orchid. **1968** *DARE* (Qu. S24, *A wild flower that grows in swamps and marshes and looks like a small blue iris*) Inf **LA**17, Poor man's orchid.

2 A **dock** n[1] (here: *Rumex conglomeratus*).

1966 *DARE* Wildfl QR Inf **CO**7, Green dock . . on wastelands. The poor man's orchid.

poor man's oyster n Cf **mock oyster, oyster plant**
See quot.

1966 *DARE* (Qu. I4, . . *Vegetables . . less commonly grown around here*) Inf **GA**13, Poor man's oyster.

poor man's patches n Also *poor man patch* [See quot 1933] **FL** Cf **beggar patches, coat ~, patches**
A **stickleaf** (here: *Mentzelia floridana*).

1933 Small *Manual SE Flora* 897 **FL,** *Poor-man's patches. . .* Hammocks, sand-dunes, and shell-mounds, pen[insular] Fla. and the Keys. . . The barbed hairs on the leaves cause them to adhere very closely to clothing. **1955** *S. Folkl. Qrly.* 19.235 **FL,** *Poor-Man's Patches . .* is covered with barbed hairs which cling so tenaciously that one cannot gather the flowers without taking the entire plant. **1966** *DARE* (Qu. S15, . . *Weed seeds that cling to clothing*) Inf **FL**11, Poor man patch—little tiny green seeds.

poor man's pepper n

1 A **peppergrass 1:** usu *Lepidium virginicum,* but also *L. campestre* or *L. sativum.* [See quot 1979]

1890 *Century Dict.* 4383, *Poor man's pepper. . .* One of the pepperworts, *Lepidium campestre.* **1910** Graves *Flowering Plants* 201 **CT,** *Lepidium sativum. . .* Poor Man's Pepper. . . Sometimes cultivated as a salad plant. *Lepidium campestre. . .* Poor Man's Pepper. . . Cultivated fields, roadsides and waste places. **1968** Radford et al. *Manual Flora Carolinas* 494, *L[epidium] virginicum. . . Poor-mans Pepper. . .* Common weed of fields, gardens and other disturbed habitats. **1973** *Foxfire 2* 71 **sAppalachians,** Peppergrass (*Lepidium virginicum*) . . bird's pepper, poor man's pepper. **1979** Niering–Olmstead *Audubon Guide N. Amer. Wildflowers E. Region* 430, *Poor-man's Pepper (Lepidium virginicum). . .* Its seeds have a peppery taste and can be used to season soups and stews; the young leaves are used in salads or cooked as greens.

2 =**shepherd's purse.**

1973 *Foxfire 2* 73, Shepherd's purse (*Capsella bursa-pastoris*). . . St. James wort, poor man's pepper.

poor man's pie n

1 =**milk pie. esp PA**

1948 Hutchison *PA Du. Cook Book* 122, *Poor Man's Pie*—Butter . . flour . . sugar . . cream[,] Cinnamon[,] Nutmeg. Line a pie dish with pastry. Spread butter over the bottom. Dredge with flour. Sprinkle with sugar. Pour cream over all. Sprinkle with cinnamon and nutmeg. Bake. **1967** *DARE* (Qu. H63, *Kinds of desserts*) Inf **PA**40, Poor man's pie— same as milk pie. **1967** *DARE* Tape **PA**14, [FW:] Did you ever make a pie—I call it milk-flatcher. Usually they use the extra pie dough. . . They'd put it in a pie shell, and then they'd put in milk and flour and sugar and usually cinnamon. They'd make a paste out of the milk and flour and sugar, and they'd put cinnamon on top and little bits of butter. [Inf:] Oh, we call that the poor man's pie. . . Down at the church . . sometimes we make pies, and there's a little dough left, and one of them will say, "Well, now we'll make a poor man's pie."

2 also *poor man's dish:* A meat pie, often made with leftovers.

1950 *WELS* (*Names for a dish of several foods mixed together*) 1 Inf, **cWI,** Poor man's pie or poor man's dish—usually made from leftovers. **1967** *DARE* (Qu. H45, *Dishes made with meat, fish, or poultry that everybody around here would know, but that people in other places might not*) Inf **MI**68, Poor man's pie—leftover meats; a kind of stew; put a pie crust or a biscuit crust on top and bake it; **MO**38, Poor man's pie.

3 also *poor man's apple pie:* See quots.

1941 *LANE* Map 292 (*Apple dumpling*) 1 inf, **cnMA,** Poor man's apple pie. **1978** *Yankee* Nov 46 **NY,** Dear Oracle: My mother used to make poor man's pie. Do you know what the ingredients were? Answer: Crackers soaked in vinegar, and seasoned with sweetening and spice. There may be other varieties. **1986** Pederson *LAGS Concordance,* 1 inf, **cwGA,** Poor man's pie—layers of apple and dough—baked; 1 inf, **nwTN,** Poor man's pie—didn't have eggs.

poor man's pig See **poverty pig**

poor man's pudding n Also *poor man pudding, poor man's custard* Cf **cottage pudding**
Any of several desserts; see quots.

1787 *Daily Advt.* (NY NY) 16 May 2/4, As I have travelled thro' all the States, I will furnish the . . state bill of fare. . . Georgia, a poor-man's pudding with a glass of water. **1854** *Harper's New Mth. Mag.* 9.97, "It is only rice, milk, and salt boiled together." "Ah, what they call 'Poor Man's Pudding,' I suppose you mean." **1868** Channing *Recollections* 25 **RI,** I was fed entirely upon bread and milk, and whitepot, pronounced *whitpot.* This last was strictly a Rhode-Island dish, and sometimes called the "poor man's custard." **1879** (1965) Tyree *Housekeeping in Old VA* 400, *Poor Man's Pudding*—eggs. . . sour cream. . . melted butter. . . sugar. . . soda. . . nutmeg. Put the butter in after the flour. Make the consistency of pound cake batter. **1896** (c1973) Farmer *Orig. Cook Book* 328, *Poor Man's Pudding. . .* milk. . . rice. . . molasses. . . salt. . . cinnamon. . . butter. Wash rice, mix and bake same as Rice Pudding. At last stirring, add butter. **1906** *DN* 3.151 **nwAR,** *Poor man's pudding. . .* Cottage pudding. **1949** Brown *Amer. Cooks* 799 **TX,** *Poor Man's Pudding*—Cover mixed biscuit and light bread with sweet milk and let stand until soft. Add raisins and spice to taste, use 3 eggs and ¾ cup sugar to 1 quart milk. Dot with butter and bake slowly. **1967–69** *DARE* (Qu. H63, *Kinds of desserts*) Inf **CA**136, Poor man's pudding—plain vanilla pudding; **NC**76, Poor man's pudding—flour, raisins, (molasses) sugar, eggs, milk, butter, nutmeg; [**MA**5, Poor man's rice pudding—made with very little rice, sugar, milk, and a few raisins; creamy;] (Qu. H66a, *The sweet liquid that you pour over a pudding*) Inf **TN**27, Poor man pudding— made out of chocolate and sugar and water—cooked until it was thick.

poor man's rope n
=**Carolina jasmine.**

1970 Correll *Plants TX* 1201, *Gelsemium sempervirens. . .* Carolina-jessamine, poor man's rope. Smooth and twining shrubby perennial; stems high-climbing, wiry.

poor man's soap n
Any of var plants that lather like soap, as:

a A **brake** n[1] (here: *Pteridium aquilinum*).

1897 *Jrl. Amer. Folkl.* 10.147 **AL,** *Pteris aquilina . .* poor man's soap. [Footnote:] Because it will make a lather with water.

b A **spirea** (here: *Spirea tomentosa*).

1900 Lyons *Plant Names* 355, *S[piraea] tomentosa . .* Canada, south to Georgia and Kansas. . . Poor-man's-soap.

c =**sweet pepperbush.** Cf **latherbush, soapbush**

1968 *DARE* Tape **GA**31, [Inf **GA**30:] You have to—you know, take it and crumble it up in your hands. Rub it and dip it down in the water. . . Makes a lot of lather. And it cleans anything except grease. . . [Inf **GA**31:] But what do the old-timers call it, now? [Inf **GA**30:] Now, let me see. [Inf **GA**31:] Poor man's soap. [Inf **GA**30:] Poor man's soap. . . That's right. **1970** Correll *Plants TX* 1173, *Clethra alnifolia. . .* In swamps, about lakes and in wet woods and thickets in s.e. Tex. . . from Me. s. to Fla. and Tex. In some regions this species is known as "poor man's soap"—the flowers when crushed in water form a lather.

poor man's soup n
A soup made from odds and ends.

1942 McAtee *Dial. Grant Co. IN* 50 (as of 1890s), *Poor-man's soup . .* a "soup" extemporized from water, butter (or other fat), and salt. Frankly so-called by people who used it because they were poor. **1947** Bowles–Towle *New Engl. Cooking* 47, "Dried peas and bacon water," . . and "poor man's soup" made of odds and ends gathered together on short warning were old favorites.

poor man's turkey n
See quots.

1948 Hutchison *PA Du. Cook Book* 40, *Poor Man's Turkey. . .* Have the butcher cut a pocket in the [flank of] beef. Mix the potatoes, onions, and parsley with the beaten eggs, season, . . and stuff the pocket with the mixture. Roast. **1951** in 1986 *Barrick Coll.* **cePA,** *Poor man's turkey*—Pig's stomach, stuffed with pieces of pork, smoked sausage, onions and diced potatoes, parsley and seasoning, and baked in the oven.

poor mouth n [Scots, nIr dial]   **chiefly Midl, Sth**

In phrr *make a poor mouth, put up a poor mouth, talk poor mouth,* and varr: To complain (usu in an exaggerated way) of poverty or other misfortune.   Note: While *poormouth* v may once have been regional, it is now widespread.

1859 Duniway *Capt. Gray's* 174, He lives about six miles from here, an' makes a mighty poor mouth about me an' my old woman holdin' a square mile, when he can't git but half that for him an' seven children, bekase his wife's dead. **1884** *Anglia* 7.278 **Sth, S Midl** [Black], To put up mighty po' mouf = to make a sad tale of it. **1885** Howells *Rise Lapham* 461, You wanted to . . make a poor mouth to Mrs. Lapham. **1892** *DN* 1.231 **KY,** *Po'.* "To put up a po' mouth" = to plead poverty. **1905** *DN* 3.90 **nwAR,** 'He put up a po' mouth' (He pleaded poverty). Rare. **1909** *DN* 3.358 **eAL, wGA,** He's always puttin' up the po' mouth, when he's jest as well off as the rest of us. **1929** *AmSp* 5.127 **ME,** A person might be "a great hand to make a poor mouth" (an expression of discouragement). **1938** *AmSp* 13.74 **OH,** So and so is . . a great hand to make a poor mouth. **1939** FWP *ID Lore* 241, *Make a poor mouth*—plead poverty. **1952** Brown *NC Folkl.* 1.578, *Poor mouth, to talk.* . . To plead poverty. **1956** McAtee *Some Dialect NC* 34, *Poor mouth, put up a.* . . Plead poverty as a reason for not paying a debt. **1959** *VT Hist.* 27.149, *Cry poor mouth.* . . To plead poverty. . . Occasional. **1965** *NY Times* (NY) 29 July 16, It is hard to talk poor mouth just after the papers have written of your daughter's coming-out party for 2,000 guests. **1966** *DARE* (Qu. U42, *When somebody pretends to be poor but you know he's not . . he's _____;* total Infs questioned, 75) Infs **GA3, MS**50, 70, 72, Playing poor mouth; **MS**12, He has a poor mouth; **MS**39, Making a poor mouth, pulling a poor mouth; **FL**36, **GA**9, Putting up a (*or* the) poor mouth; **FL**5, Talking poor mouth. **1972** *Atlanta Letters* **cnGA,** He always talks po' mouth.

poor pine n

Either a **shortleaf pine 1** (here: *Pinus echinata*) or a **spruce pine** (here: *P. glabra*).

1896 Mohr–Roth *Timber Pines* 86 **FL,** The Shortleaf Pine. . . Common or Local Names. . . Poor Pine. *Ibid* 126, The Spruce Pine. . . Common or Local Names. . . Poor Pine. [*Ibid* 127, The timber [of *Pinus glabra*] is of inferior quality.] **1908** Britton *N. Amer. Trees* 34, [=*Pinus echinata*] . . is known under many common names, most of which have also been applied to other species of pine, as Yellow pine . . Pitch pine, Poor pine [etc]. *Ibid* 42, The wood [of *Pinus glabra*] is soft, weak, and brittle. . . It is not durable and but little used. . . The tree is also known as . . Poor pine.

poor pussy n Also *poor puss*

Any of var children's games, esp one in which one player tries to make another laugh by imitating a cat; see quots.

1905 *DN* 3.91 **nwAR,** *Poor pussy.* . . The name of a children's house-game. **1909** (1923) Bancroft *Games* 150, *Poor Pussy.* . . The players sit in a circle, except one who is chosen for Poor Pussy. Pussy kneels in front of any player and miaous. This person must stroke or pat Pussy's head and say, "Poor Pussy! . . " repeating the words three times, all without smiling. If the player who is petting Puss smiles, he must change places with Puss. The Puss may resort to any variations in the music of the miaou, or in attitude or expression, to induce the one who is petting to smile. **1931** in 1996 Horton *Island Out of Time* 115 **Chesapeake Bay MD,** There are only a few boys around, so they came and we played Blind Man's Bluff, Heavy, Heavy; Pleased or Displeased, Clap in Clap out, and Poor Puss. **1953** Brewster *Amer. Nonsinging Games* 26 **IN,** Poor Pussy. **1957** *Sat. Eve. Post Letters* **CA,** *Poor pussy*—Sit in a circle—one is IT who goes to different folks in circle & pats their head—saying poor pussy, poor pussy—the one receiving the petting answers like a cat—the funnier the better—the one who makes poor pussy or IT laugh becomes *it.* **1967–70** *DARE* (Qu. EE2, *Games that have one extra player—when a signal is given, the players change places, and the extra one tries to get a place*) Inf **IA**7, Poor pussy; **NY**199, Poor pussy—same as changing chairs, going to Jerusalem, and musical chairs; (Qu. EE4, *Games in which one player's eyes are bandaged and he has to catch the others and guess who they are*) Inf **NE**10, Poor pussy; (Qu. EE33, . . *Outdoor games . . that children play*) Inf **OH**98, Poor pussy—you squat before a person in a circle and say "meow" and make faces; he tries to pet you and say "poor pussy" without laughing. The first one to laugh is "it" and becomes "pussy."

poor Robin n

1 A **cleavers,** usu *Galium aparine.*

1900 Lyons *Plant Names* 167, *G[alium] Aparine.* . . Pig-tail, Pertimugget, Poor-Robin [etc]. **1971** Krochmal *Appalachia Med. Plants* 126, *Galium aparine.* . . milksweet, poor robin [etc]. **1974** (1977) Coon *Useful Plants* 237, *Galium verum*—Common cleavers, poor robin [etc].

2 See **poor Robin's plantain 2.**

poor Robin's plantain n

1 A **hawkweed** (here: *Hieracium venosum*).

1789 in 1793 *Amer. Philos. Soc. Trans.* 3.xx, The Hieracium *venosum* . . grows from the north to Virginia inclusively; is called *poor Robins plantain;* and said to frustrate the bite both of the rattle snake, and of his supposed precursor the *pilote-snake.* **1900** Lyons *Plant Names* 192, *H[ieracium] venosum.* . . Canada to Georgia, west to Nebraska and Manitoba. Rattlesnake-weed, Poor Robin's Plantain [etc]. **1953** Greene–Blomquist *Flowers South* 143, Perhaps the best known is the spring-blooming poor-Robin's plantain . . with a basal rosette of purplish-green leaves with light-green veins. **1971** Kieran *Nat. Hist. NYC* 165, In the woods you will find . . Rattlesnake Weed or Poor Robin's-plantain *(Hieracium venosum)* with a still looser cluster of yellow flowers aloft.

2 also *poor Robin:* A **robin's plantain 1** (here: *Erigeron pulchellus*).

1900 Lyons *Plant Names* 148, *E[rigeron] pulchellus.* . . Ontario to Florida and west to Minnesota. Robin's Plantain, Poor Robin's Plantain, Robert's Plantain [etc]. **1931** Harned *Wild Flowers Alleghanies* 559, *Robin's plantain.* . . A very common perennial known also under the familiar names, Blue Spring Daisy, Poor Robin, Rose-petty and Poor Robin's Plantain. **1948** Stevens *KS Wild Flowers* 407, *Erigeron pulchellus*—Poor-Robin's-Plantain.

poor Sam n Also *poss Sam*   *joc*

=**opossum.**

1927 Boston Soc. Nat. Hist. *Proc.* 38.263 **Okefenokee GA,** *Florida Opossum.* . . In the Okefinokee region this animal goes universally by the name of 'Possum.' On Chesser's Island, in addition, it is given, by way of pleasantry, the appellations of 'Po' Sam' and 'Sambo.' **1966–68** *DARE* (Qu. P31, . . *Names or nicknames . . for the . . opossum*) Infs **GA**3, **LA**29, Poor Sam; **MS**47, Poss Sam.

poor soul n Also sp *poor sole*   **TN**   Cf **corn dodger 2, poor do 2**

A cornmeal dumpling.

1932 (1946) Hibben *Amer. Regional Cookery* 59 **TN,** In middle Tennessee these corn dodgers, or dumplings, are called "poorsouls." **1958** *PADS* 29.14 **TN,** *Poor soles:* Another name for *poor do* [see quot 1958 at **poor do 2**]. **1986** Pederson *LAGS Concordance,* 1 inf, **neTN,** Poor soul—a cornmeal dumpling; small, round.

poor toes n Also *poor toe*

=**Mexican clover.**

1874 in 1889 Vasey *Ag. Grasses* 104 **AL,** The plant [=*Richardsonia scabra*] is known here by the name of "Mexican clover," "poor toes," or "pigeon-weed." Seventeen years ago it was but sparse; now it occurs in all our cultivated grounds, covering them with a luxuriant vegetation after the crops of the summer have been removed. **1889** *Ibid* 103, Mexican Clover . . Poor Toe; Pigeon-Weed, etc.

poor-weed See **poor-land weed**

poor White n

1 A low-class White person; with *the:* the class of such people.

1819 in 1823 Faux *Memorable Days* 118, The poor white, or white poor, in Maryland . . scarcely ever work. **1886** Ebbutt *Emigrant Life* 120, He was an emigrant from Tennessee, a "poor white," a man that the niggers looked down upon, almost too proud to work, but too poor to do without. **1903** *DN* 2.325 **seMO,** *Poor whites.* . . A term applied to a class of people in Northern Georgia and some other sections. **1907** *DN* 3.234 **nwAR,** *Poor whites.* . . The lowest class of southern whites. **1946** Nixon *Lower Piedmont* 19 **neAL,** Generally slaves and slave owners called them [=hillbillies] "po' whites" or "po' white trash." **1968–69** *DARE* (Qu. HH18, *Very insignificant or low-grade people*) Infs **NY**111, **PA**199, Poor Whites. **1986** Pederson *LAGS Concordance* **Gulf Region** (*The poor whites—white man's terms*) 39 infs, Poor white(s);

(The poor whites—black man's terms) 21 infs, Poor white(s); 1 inf, The poor white.

2 attrib:

a in comb *poor White trash;* hence adj *poor-White-trashy.* **scattered, but chiefly Sth, SW** See Map *derog*
1833 in 1835 Kemble *Jrl.* 2.112, The slaves themselves entertain the very highest contempt for white servants, whom they designate as "poor white trash." **1860** Hundley *Social Relations S. States* 257, Poor White Trash, a name said to have originated with the slaves, who look upon themselves as much better off than all "po' white folks" whatever. **1866** in 1966 Harris *Sut Lovingood's Yarns* 270 **TN,** Hit were a Georgia delicate in the poor white trash convenshun, whats a threatnin to spread a epidemic of lice in Quakerdelphia. **1893** Shands *MS Speech* 51, *Po' white trash.* The common name given by the negro to poor white people, whom he holds in utter scorn and detestation. **1934** Carmer *Stars Fell on AL* 6, He'd turn over in his grave if he knew what poor white trash are wearing the sheets now. **1936** Mitchell *Gone* 864 **GA,** And I can't forget how poor white trashy she's acted since she got a little money. **1939** Griswold *Sea Is. Lady* 653 **csSC** (as of 1908), "I hear she's going in for poor white trash now," Susan told Isabel. . . "Not satisfied uplifting the poor island darkies." **1946** [see **1** above.] **1951** Giles *Harbin's Ridge* 63 **KY,** Always content just to make out, which we considered poor-white-trashy in our parts. **1956** Ker *Vocab. W. TX* 379, Terms most generally current for "a poor white" are: *poor white trash* (19 responses [of 67 infs]. **1969** (1970) Angelou *Caged Bird* 27 **AR** [Black], Everyone I knew respected these customary laws, except for the powhitetrash children. Some families of powhitetrash lived on Momma's farm land behind the school. . . Since Momma told us that the less you say to whitefolks (or even powhitetrash) the better, Bailey and I would stand, solemn, quiet, in the displaced air. **1969–70** *DARE* (Qu. HH18, *Very insignificant or low-grade people*) 49 Infs, **scattered, but chiefly Sth, SW,** Poor White trash; (Qu. HH36, *A careless, slovenly woman: "She's just an old _____."*) Inf **OH**57, Poor White trash; (Qu. II21, *When somebody behaves unpleasantly or without manners: "The way he behaves, you'd think he was _____."*) Inf **SC**5, Poor White trash. **1970** Green *Ely* 537, Mr. George was known to the Negro as the cracker, sager or poor white trash. **1986** Pederson *LAGS Concordance* **Gulf Region** *(The poor whites—white man's terms)* 151 infs, Poor white trash; *(The poor whites—black man's terms)* 76 infs, Poor white trash; 1 inf, A poor white trash.

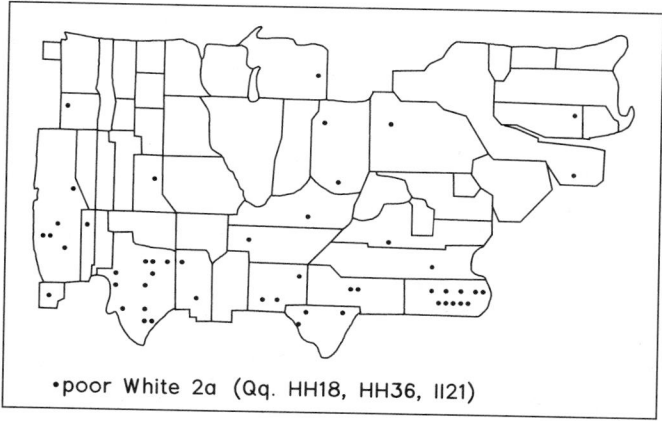

•poor White 2a (Qq. HH18, HH36, II21)

b rarely *poor Whitey;* in var other combs: See quots.
1853 Hammett *Stray Yankee in TX* 279, His overseer . . utterly unfitted for his situation, and far more of a companion than a master for negroes, was in consequence cordially despised by them, as coming within the list of "poor white folks," a class they think almost beneath contempt. **1871** Eggleston *Hoosier Schoolmaster* 71 **sIN,** These bands of desperadoes still found among the "poor whitey," "dirt-eater" class are the outcroppings of the bad blood. **1898** Dunbar *Folks from Dixie* 193 [Black], So's you would n't be eatin' off o' none o' these poor white people 'round here. **1963** Owens *Look to River* 94 **TX,** I'd druther be a nigger / Than a po' white man. **1970** *DARE* (Qu. HH18, *Very insignificant or low-grade people*) Inf **NC**84, Poor white folk. **1986** Pederson *LAGS Concordance* **Gulf Region,** 24 infs, (The) poor white people; 8 infs, Poor white folk(s); 6 infs, Poor white person; 5 infs, Poor white man; 2 infs, Poor white crackers; 1 inf, Poor white farmer; 1 inf, Poor white girl; 1 inf, Poor white peoples; 1 inf, Poor white section.

poor White trash(y) See **poor White 2a**

poor Whitey See **poor White 2b**

poorwill n

1 A nocturnal bird *(Phalaenoptilus nuttallii)* of the western US. [Echoic] Cf **whippoorwill**
1879 U.S. Natl. Museum *Proc. for 1878* 1.427 **cCA,** "Antrostomus" nuttalli.—Poor-will. **1888** *Century Illustr. Mag.* 35.664, At nightfall the poor-wills begin to utter their boding call from the wooded ravines back in the hills; not "whip-poor-will," as in the East, but with two syllables only. **1898** (1900) Davie *Nests N. Amer.* 284, Nuttall's Whip-poor-will, or Poor-will, as it is called, is found to be more or less abundant throughout various States and Territories of the West—in the interior valleys and foot-hills of California, Oregon and Washington, and in Arizona, New Mexico, Texas, Colorado, etc. **1917** (1923) *Birds Amer.* 2.171, I first heard the song of the Poor-will in a wild cañon in the mountains of New Mexico. . . It was a quiet summer night with the moon shining in great brilliancy. The surroundings were most impressive, and when the sudden cry of *poor-will, poor-will,* was borne on the air from across the cañon, it was as if a voice from the spirit-land had spoken. **1940** Gabrielson *Birds OR* 354, Nuttall's Poor-will. [*Ibid* 355, More people know it by its rapid, oft-repeated call, *poor-will, poor-will,* whistled endlessly from the vantage point of some hillside on a June evening.] **1966–68** *DARE* (Qu. Q3, . . *Birds that come out only after dark*) Inf **CA**78, Dusky poorwill; **CA**87, Whippoorwill or poorwill; (Qu. Q19, . . *Birds similar to the whippoorwill;* total Infs questioned, 75) Inf **NM**13, Poorwill. **1977** Udvardy *Audubon Field Guide Birds* 606, Poorwill. . . On warm nights in the breeding season this bird reveals its presence by uttering a melancholy call, the first note lower than the second; this sounds like its name, *poor-will.*

2 also *poor-will's-widow:* A **whippoorwill** (here: *Caprimulgus* spp).
1950 *WELS* (What other names do you have for the whip-poor-will?) 3 Infs, **WI,** Poorwill. **1960** Williams *Walk Egypt* 103 **GA,** "Whip. Whip!" a poorwill sighed. **1966** *DARE* (Qu. Q19, . . *Birds similar to the whippoorwill;* total Infs questioned, 75) Inf **FL**39, Poor-will's-widow, whippoorwill.

pooster about v phr Cf **pooter** v
1895 *DN* 1.398, *Pooster about* [pustɚ]: one who gets up in the night and walks around the house is said to pooster about.

poot v[1]

1 To break wind, fart. **chiefly Sth, S Midl** See Map Cf **poop**
1940 McCullers *Lonely Hunter* 234 **GA,** He broke wind. He stood in the room with eyes blindfolded and pooped. **1953** Randolph–Wilson *Down in Holler* 116 **Ozarks,** The refined hillman always says *break wind* or *poot* instead [of *fart*]. **1960** Criswell *Resp. to PADS 20* **Ozarks,** *Pooped out.* . . Used lately, but it is a doubtful term for these people because the word *poop* (or . . *poot*), means to make or break wind. **c1960** Wilson *Coll.* **csKY,** So lazy that he has to stop plowing to poot. **1965–70** *DARE* (Qu. X55b, *Words for breaking wind from the bowels*) 93 Infs, **chiefly Sth, S Midl,** Poot; **NC**55, Pooted a blue streak. **1979** *AR Times* Mar 37 [Arkansas talk], The humor of many expressions comes as much from the scatology as their incongruity, sayings like . . "He'd squeeze a nickel till the buffalo poots." **1991** Still *Wolfpen Notebooks* 71 **sAppalachians,** She was so deaf she couldn't hear herself poot. **1997** *W3* File **NC** (as of c1953), Beans, beans, a wonderful fruit,/ The more you eat, the more you poot.

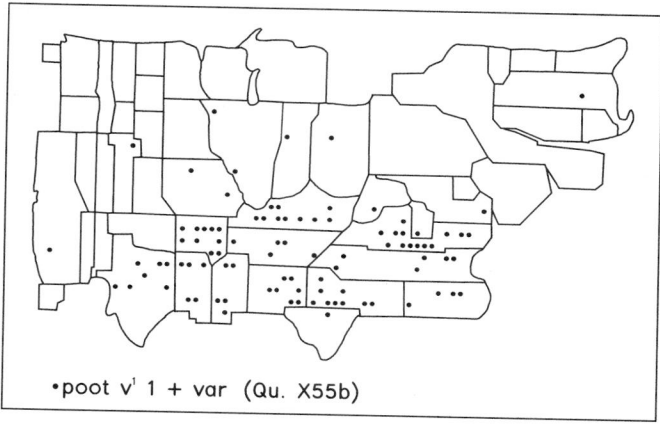

•poot v[1] 1 + var (Qu. X55b)

2 with *around:* To mess around, interfere.

1947 (1952) Ellison *Invisible Man* 163 [Black], The time when I was down with a touch of pneumonia and they put one of them so-called engineers to pooting around down here. Why, they started to having so much paint go bad they didn't know what to do.

3 in phr *poot the rug:* To die.

1936 *AmSp* 11.316 **Ozarks,** *Poot the rug. . .* To die. 'Pappy's jest about ready t' poot th' rug, I reckon.'

poot v² See **put** v

poot n **Sth, S Midl**

1 also *capoot:* A fart; the act of breaking wind; rarely, a belch; fig: the most insignificant or transitory thing. Cf **asspoots, fart in a whirlwind**

1899 (1912) Green *VA Folk-Speech* 329, *Poop. . .* The act of breaking wind. Also, *poot.* **1926** *DN* 5.402 **Ozarks,** *Poot. . .* Also used as a noun—"She ain't wuth a poot!" **1949** Hedgecock *Gone Are the Days* 18 **swMO** (as of 1902), He accidentally let a little "capoot," as we used to say. Or, as Benjamin Franklin might have phrased it, he broke a little wind, audibly. **1958** Randolph *Sticks* 30 **Ozarks,** We all knowed it didn't amount to a poot in a whirlwind. **1967** *DARE* (Qu. X55, *The sound that gas makes when it comes up from the stomach after a meal;* total Infs questioned, 75) Inf **AR47,** Poot. **1977** Morrison *Song of Solomon* 40 [Black], Your father . . he couldn't cook worth poot.

2 Used as a derog or sometimes affectionate term for a person; see quots. Cf **fart** n **a, b**

1941 Perry *Hold Autumn* 132 **TX,** His very own kids . . sayin Granpa's a goofy ole poot. **1944** *Infantry Journal* Sep 61 (*W3* File), Perhaps I'm an old poot by now, but some of today's company commanders might still be able to take a few lessons from the fuddy-duddies. **1976** *Playboy* Nov 210, "You son of a bitch, you just ate the Pointer Sisters' supper!" I said there hadn't been enough to sponsor a good burp, anyway, and why didn't he just send 'em some watermelon? "Oh, you reprehensible racist *poot*," he screeched. **1986** Conroy *Prince of Tides* 542 **SC,** They find this place, little brother, . . and there's no more time on the big clock. I didn't even think you two little poots [=his adult brother and sister] would remember this place.

poot exclam

See quots.

1918 (1920) Tarkington *Magnificent* 188, *"Poot!"* Aunt Amelia was evidently in a passion. **1924** *DN* 5.275 [Exclams], *Poot* (disg[ust]). **1926** *DN* 5.402 **Ozarks,** *Poot! . .* A common exclamation of disgust. **1940** McCullers *Lonely Hunter* 263 **GA,** 'You don't care a thing in the world about anybody but—' 'Aw, poot!' She slammed the door. **1992** *Newsweek* 31 Aug 32 **TX,** [Molly Ivins column:] The press was all atwitter about how Mrs. Bush was being "combative," "feisty" and even "nasty." Oh poot, she's always been tough as old boots. **1998** *DARE* File, I know two people from Tenn. (Knoxville area) that use the word "Poot." . . "Oh poot" or "Oh poot, they did it again." Meaning Oh well, so what.

poot- adv See **pretty** A2c

poot around See **poot** v¹ 2

pooter v [Cf *SND peut(e)r, pewt(e)r* (at *peuther* v.²) "To . . bustle around"] Cf **pooster about,** *DS* Y18, 20

1907 *DN* 3.196 **seNH,** *Pooter* ['putɚ]. . . To depart speedily. "I told him to git, and he just pooter, I can tell you."

pooter n Cf **poot root**

1954 Harder *Coll.* **cwTN,** *Pooters: . .* See *forty-fours.* [*Ibid, Forty-fours . .* white soup beans; so called because white beans are supposed to create an exorbitant amount of gas in the stomach.]

poot root n Cf **pooter** n

=sweet potato.

1967 *DARE* (Qu. I9, . . *Names [including nicknames] for potatoes*) Infs **AR55, TX37,** Poot roots—sweet potatoes. **1967** *DARE* FW Addit **seAR,** Poot roots = sweet potatoes (joking). **1981** Pederson *LAGS Basic Materials,* 1 inf, **neMS,** Yams, poot roots, or fart fruit.

pootschky See **puchki**

poot the rug See **poot** v¹ 3

pooty See **pretty** A1c

poo-wee See **pooey**

poo-week See **poig**

pooy See **pooey**

pop v¹

1 To cause to make a sudden sharp noise without otherwise affecting, as:

a To crack (a whip), make (a flexible object) snap; to make a cracking sound (with a whip). **chiefly Sth, S Midl, West** Cf **popper** n¹, **pop-the-whip**

1846 (1973) Porter *Quarter Race* 95 **MS,** Oh, the wagoner was a mighty man, a mighty man was he:/ He'd pop his whip, and stretch his chains, and holler "wo, gee!" **1897** (1952) McGill *Narrative* 79, Thus equipped . . the wagoner . . mounts the wheel saddle horse, seizes his long "gee" line, pops his whip, and punching his off wheel horse with his foot, we are soon on the road for Charleston. **1902** *DN* 2.242 **sIL,** *Pop. . .* To crack, as a whip; crack is never used. **1903** (1965) Adams *Log Cowboy* 132 **West,** Good, honest, truthful men as ever popped a whip, swore they saw that ox when they came in. **1903** *DN* 2.325 **seMO,** *Pop. . .* To snap. . . 'Pop the whip.' **1907** *DN* 3.225 **nwAR,** *Pop. . .* To crack (as a whip). **1909** *DN* 3.358 **eAL, wGA,** *Pop. . .* To crack (a whip). Common. **1941** Dobie *Longhorns* 250 **TX,** The young man took the long whip, not to lash the animals—for that was not the whip's function—but to pop it. He swung it lightly and tested the popper three or four times. **1966** *DARE* (Qu. K36a, *What do you say to make a horse go faster?*) Inf **NM13,** Pop with lines and whistle. **1967** Green *Horse Tradin'* 195 **TX,** A man up on top of a big load of something in that wagon was popping a line over those mules. *Ibid* 234, I . . let them run away from me—run up in the corners and snort and blow their noses and throw their heads up and pop their ears. **1967–69** *DARE* Tape **TX4,** All I had to do was just pop my whip and blow my horn; **CA160,** They [=mule skinners] always had a blacksnake and they'd pop it. I don't think they ever hit 'em very hard with it, but they scared 'em with it. . . It was a leather tube sort of a thing with a buckskin popper on it that tapered, you know, and it was loaded with shot in the main part. **1986** Pederson *LAGS Concordance,* 1 inf, **swLA,** Popping my cow whip; 2 infs, **cwMS, csTX,** Pop the whip; 1 inf, **csAL,** Belly buster will pop you like a whip.

b To gnash, snap (one's teeth); of one's teeth: to snap together; hence nouns *jaw-popping, teeth-popping.* **Sth, S Midl**

1913 Kephart *Highlanders* 81 **sAppalachians,** They'll run right in on the varmint [=a bear], snappin' and chawin' and worryin' him till he gits so mad you can hear his tushes pop half a mile. **1917** *DN* 4.415 **wNC,** *Pop. . .* To gnash. "I heard the old she poppin' her teeth." **1930** *Copeia* 4.153 **swGA,** One of the boys helping me said: 'If one of these ground puppies pops his teeth at you three times you'll die.' **1939** Hall *Coll.* **eTN,** Well, when they got there the bear went to makin' a noise—growlin' and poppin' its teeth. *Ibid* **eTN,** He could hear it poppin' its teeth. **1956** Gipson *Old Yeller* 95 **TX,** The squealing of the pig and the scent of his blood made the hogs beneath me go nearly wild with anger. You never heard such roaring and teeth-popping. **1957** TN Folk Lore Soc. *Bulletin* 23.74 **TN,** An' the bear wheeled on 'im an' he said it 'peared like he could feel it a-bitin' 'im nearly. He could hear it poppin' its teeth. **1969** *DARE* FW Addit **KY44,** Teeth-a-popping—teeth chattering [used in conversation]. **1970** *Foxfire* Spring–Summer 79 **nGA,** They had th'big boar bayed. . . He'uz standin' there chompin' his teeth—poppin' his teeth. **1982** Elman *Hunter's Field Guide* 580, Coughs, low woofs, grunts, and jaw-popping sounds are a final threat before an attack [by a grizzly bear].

c To snap (one's fingers); crack (one's knuckles); by ext, to go out to nightclubs or other places of amusement; hence vbl nouns *(finger-)popping;* n *finger-popper* a jazz enthusiast; a piece of music with a compelling rhythm.

1928 Peterkin *Scarlet Sister Mary* 257 **SC,** It was as easy for her as to pop her fingers. **1943** *New Yorker* 17 Apr 66 **Memphis TN** [Black], When coming in late at night don't. . . go to and fro in the hall singing, dancing or popping the fingers. **1955** *Metronome* July 22, Lord Buckley . . addresses this album of *classics* in *bop talk* to "Hipsters, Flipsters and Finger Poppin' Daddies." **1957** *NYT Mag.* 18 Aug 26, *Finger popper*—A cat (musician or hipster) who is swinging. **c1959** in 1964 Gold *Jazz Lexicon* 106, *Finger-popper:* a tune that lends itself to popping one's fingers. **1967** *DARE* (Qu. KK42b, *Expressions about a person who does something very easily: "He could do that _____."*)

Inf **AR**51, *Quicker than you could pop (or snap) your finger.* **1968** *Current Slang* 3.2.38 [Watts slang; Black], *Popping. . . Going to parties.—I think I should stop popping and do some work.* **1997** *DARE* File **cAL**, *Pop one's fingers. . .* The person I remember using the term most (and I don't remember her ever using "snap") was an African-American woman born in 1902 on a farm near Montgomery. . . And she was in fact the person who taught me how to "pop" my fingers! *Ibid* **ceAL**, I polled my undergraduate intro to linguistics class at Auburn (Alabama) but none had [heard] "pop" to mean "snap." About a third of them used "pop" with "knuckles" or "fingers" to mean 'to crack one's knuckles (fingers)'. . . However, I've found one native Alabamian woman in her 50s who says it's common. *Ibid* **cnAL**, "Pop one's fingers" is a phrase I heard in the 1950s and 1960s from some of my classmates in Birmingham, Alabama. . . I think it meant "snap one's fingers," though I wonder if it might have also meant "crack one's knuckles." *Ibid* **wGA**, I have heard "pop your fingers" to mean snap them, and I think it was from my grandfather, who has been dead for maybe 10 years. . . He was from rural West Georgia. *Ibid* **ceMO**, A friend of mine, African-American, reports that "finger popping" means that one is going out for the evening, as in "Are you going out finger-popping tonite?" No specific activity is referred to, though dancing is commonly meant. My friend was born in St. Louis, to parents from Alabama and Kentucky. She says she has used the expression most of her life.

2 also in phr *pop it to (one):* To crack a whip on (an animal); by ext, to sting.

1956 McAtee *Some Dialect NC* 34, *Pop . .* sting. "Every time I went near the hives a bee would pop me." **1968** *DARE* Tape **CA**100, We held the reins and popped the horse—we whipped to make 'em trot. **1986** Pederson *LAGS Concordance*, 1 inf, **cnAR**, Pop them [=animals] with a whip; *(Wasps)* 1 inf, **neLA**, Popped it to me = really stung me.

3 To break (something) with a snap; to break apart suddenly; with *off:* to break off suddenly. **Sth, S Midl**

1888 Jones *Negro Myths* 142 **GA coast**, Old Jack exclaimed: "Haw, Boy! when I graff [=grasp] my han on er teet [=tooth], eh bown fuh come, er de jaw pop,—one or tarruh." **1892** (1969) Christensen *Afro-Amer. Folk Lore* 90 **seSC**, So when Wolf tek hol' Rabbit le' go, an' de tail pop off in Wolf han', an' 'e ben pull so hard 'e fall down. **1903** *DN* 2.325 **seMO**, *Pop. . .* To . . break. . . 'Pop the stick in two.' **1909** *DN* 3.358 **eAL, wGA**, *Pop. . .* To snap or break. "Pop that watermelon open." **1916** *DN* 4.270 **New Orleans LA**, *Pop. . .* To snap. "I popped a string in my tennis racket." **1928** Peterkin *Scarlet Sister Mary* 84 **SC** [Gullah], You like to a popped you gizzard-string a-tryin to get July. **1930** *DN* 6.84 **SC**, Words used in other than their usual meanings. . . *pop,* snap, break. **1946** *PADS* 6.24 **NC**, *Pop. . .* To break. "He popped the stick in two." Pamlico. Common. **1970** *DARE* (Qu. OO8b, *If a man committed suicide by hanging, you'd say he _____ . . .*; not asked in early QRs) Inf **SC**68, Popped his neck.

4 To shell (peas or beans). Cf **pod** v 1

1953 *PADS* 19.13 **NC**, *Pop. . .* To shell (peas). Swansboro, N.C. **1986** Pederson *LAGS Concordance (To shell beans)* 2 infs, **ceGA, cwFL**, Pop them.

5 in phr *pop one's gums:* To argue. Cf **1b** above

1967–68 *DARE* (Qu. KK13, *. . Arguing: "They stood there for an hour _____ ."*) Inf **NC**52, Popping their gums; **SC**34, Chewing the rag, poppin' they gums.

pop n[1] Also rarely *pop beer, ~ juice, ~ water* **widespread, but less freq N Atl, ePA, Sth, eMO, sIL** See Map Note: The comb *soda pop* is not included here. Cf **coca-cola B, cola, dope** n 4, **soda, tonic**

A carbonated soft drink.

1840 Kennedy *Quodlibet* 139 **Sth**, [He] was not a man to be put down by the frothy, ginger-pop eloquence. **1882** Peck *Peck's Sunshine* 167 **seWI**, He would be justified in going into the hotel and ordering a bottle of pop, and then refusing to pay for it. **1899** (1912) Green *VA Folk-Speech* 330, *Pop. . .* An effervescent drink, like soda water, in bottles, flavoured. **1929** *AmSp* 5.71 **NE**, The milker . . fills the small bottle, perhaps a "pop," bottle. **1941** *LANE* Map 312 *(Soft drink),* [*Pop* is **scattered throughout NEng**]; 6 infs, 5 **ME, NH, VT**, Pop beer; 6 infs, **CT, MA**, Ginger pop [2 infs call it old-fashioned]; 1 inf, **seVT**, Pop water. **1948** Manfred *Chokecherry* 74 **nwIA**, Wilbur was sitting beside him holding a bottle of pop fizzing with alcohol spike. **1965–70** *DARE* (Qu. H78, *Ordinary soft drinks, usually carbonated*) 468 Infs, **widespread, but less freq N Atl, ePA, Sth, eMO, sIL**, Pop; **VA**26, Pop juice; **DC**12,

GA29, **MI**88, **MS**60, **MA**6, Pops. **1967** *Galena Gaz. & Advt.* (IL) 27 June 1/1, I guess Dennis doesn't go for orange pop. **1968** *Montevideo Amer.-News* (MN) 11 July 7/2, Danny Anderson . . suffered a fractured skull and other injuries when a pop cooler toppled over on him. **1982** *Barrick Coll.* **csPA**, *Pop*—soft drink. *Soda* in this area is only an ice-cream concoction. **1986** Pederson *LAGS Concordance (Soft drinks)* 28 infs, **scattered Gulf Region**, Pop; 1 inf, **cnGA**, Heard of pop, not a local term; 1 inf, **sMS**, Nobody says "soda" or "pop"; 1 inf, **cnTN**, Pop—used in the North. **1994** *DARE* File, I grew up in Michigan where it [= a carbonated beverage] was "pop." When I visited relatives in Georgia "pop" was a Popsicle or similar frozen treat. *Ibid* **OH**, My daughter used to refer to sparkling water as "coke water" and my son refers to it as "pop water." My daughter was born in N.C. while my son was born in Ohio. **1998** *DARE* File **MN**, Minneapolis . . used to be very definitely "pop" country. But now I see more and more signs which say "soda." *Ibid* **KS, wMO**, Kansas and western Missouri are pop areas too. I agree that 'soda' is taking over. **2000** *DARE* File **MS**, I . . asked one of the African American secretaries if she ever said "pop" for coke. She said, "Sometimes. It depends on my environment." When I asked her what kind of environment made her say "pop," she laughed and said "when I'm among my own kind." The two African American student workers who were listening to our conversation laughed and nodded. I told them why I was asking, and they all three said . . that "pop" was the common term among African Americans but that they often switched to "coke" in inter-racial conversations.

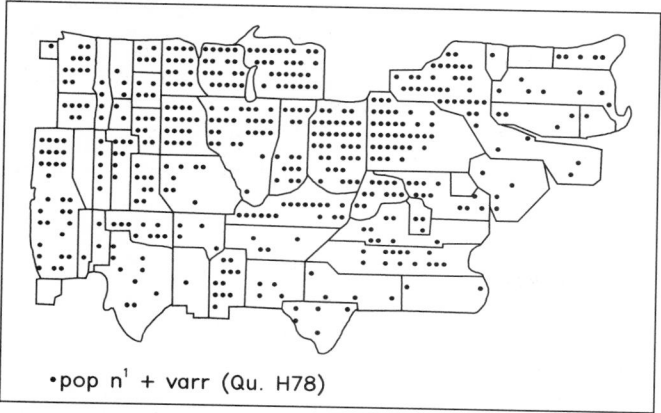

•pop n[1] + varr (Qu. H78)

pop n[2]

1 also *big-pop, gros-pop, old-pop:* A grandfather—often used as a quasi-personal name. **scattered, but esp Atlantic, Gulf States** See Map Cf **pop-pop** Note: *pop* in the sense "father" is widespread throughout the US.

1913 Johnson *Highways St. Lawrence to VA* 263 **MD**, I would have to go up to the barn and ask "Pop." I . . interviewed "Pop." **1961** *Folk Word Atlas N. LA* map 1206, Grandfather . . [less freq responses include] pop. **1965–70** *DARE* (Qu. Z3, *. . 'Grandfather'*) 19 Infs, **scattered, but esp Atlantic, Gulf States**, Pop; **NC**61, Old-pop. [*DARE* Ed: 6 of 20 Infs used *pop* to refer to both "father" and "grandfather."] **1986** Pederson *LAGS Concordance (Grandfather)* 4 infs, **GA, LA, MS, TX**, Pop; 1 inf, **cnGA**, Pop—because the family called him this; 1 inf, **ceAL**, His grandchildren call him Pop—familiar term; 1 inf, **cwTN**, His grandchild

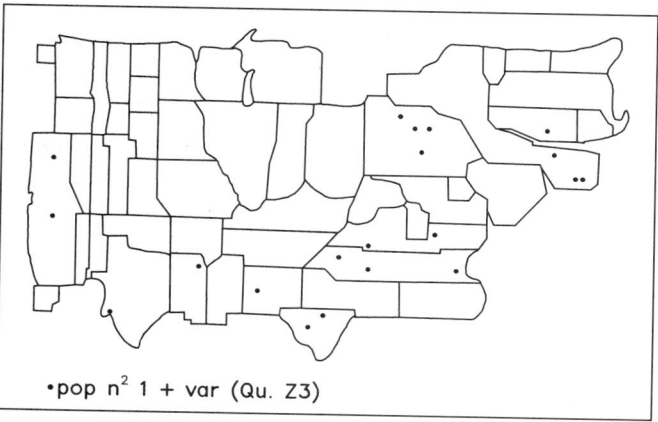

•pop n[2] 1 + var (Qu. Z3)

calls him Pop; 1 inf, **swAR,** Pop—paternal grandfather; familiar term; 1 inf, **csLA,** Big-Pop, Gros-Pop—familiar term.

2 attrib: =**papa 3.**

1969 *DARE* (Qu. K23, *Words used by women or in mixed company for a bull*) Inf **KY**16, Pop cow.

pop adv Also *a-pop*

Suddenly, abruptly; at once.

1966 *DARE* (Qu. KK53, *When one thing suddenly hits hard against something else: "He ran _____ into a car."*) Inf **NM**12, Pop, whack. **1986** Pederson *LAGS Concordance,* 1 inf, **cnTN,** They'd do it pop = straightaway, at once; I'd do it a-pop.

pop n³, v² See **pape**

pop-all See **pawpaw**

pop apple n Cf **apricot B**

=**maypop 1.**

1913 *Torreya* 13.232 **NC,** *Passiflora incarnata* . . Pop-apple, Church's Island, N.C.

pop ash n Also *poppy ash*

=**Carolina ash.**

1897 Sudworth *Arborescent Flora* 331, *Fraxinus caroliniana*. . . Poppy Ash (Ala.) **1933** Small *Manual SE Flora* 1039, Pop Ash.—Swamps, and low grounds, Coastal Plains and adj. provinces, Fla. to Tex., Mo., and S. Va. **1960** Vines *Trees SW* 864, Vernacular names are Poppy Ash, Pop Ash, and Water Ash. **1966** *DARE* (Qu. T15, . . *Kinds of swamp trees*) Infs **FL**39, **NC**24, Pop ash. **1971** Craighead *Trees S. FL* 64, Where water stands continuously, as in ponds and sloughs, cypress, water oak, pond apple, and pop ash predominate. *Ibid* 125, Included under the term "tree islands" are hammocks, bay heads, . . cypress strands and domes, . . custard apple swamps, and pop ash heads.

pop beer See **pop** n¹

pop beetle n

A **click beetle** (here: *Alaus oculatus*).

1967 *DARE* (Qu. R30, . . *Kinds of beetles;* not asked in early QRs) Inf **AR**52, Pop beetle—develops false eyes on its back.

pop call n Also *popcorn call, pop-in call* **chiefly Sth, S Midl** See Map

A short or unexpected visit; hence verbs *pop-call, popcorn-call* to pay such a visit.

1857 in 1972 Myers *Children of Pride* 290 **GA,** The 1st was . . a merry day in Savannah. The streets were filled with numbers on foot and in vehicles . . paying their New Year visits. . . I would not be found negligent . . accomplishing in the space of some five hours and a half forty or fifty "pop calls." **1922** in 1931 Davis *Hist. Blair Co. PA* 1.154 **cPA,** Instead of . . staying for a half-hour . . I make a pop call of a few minutes. **1942** Handy *Father of Blues* 27 **MO** (as of c1890) [Black], I shall never forget the pop-calls of policemen dropping in to catch vagrants. Their test for vagrancy was unique. If a man fell asleep in a poolroom chair, he was picked up. **1953** Randolph–Wilson *Down in Holler* 273 **Ozarks,** Pop-call. . . A very short visit. "Yes, he come here to see Sally once, but it warn't no more'n a pop-call." **1965–70** *DARE* (Qu. II14, *To pay a short visit: "Last night our new neighbors _____."*) 11 Infs,

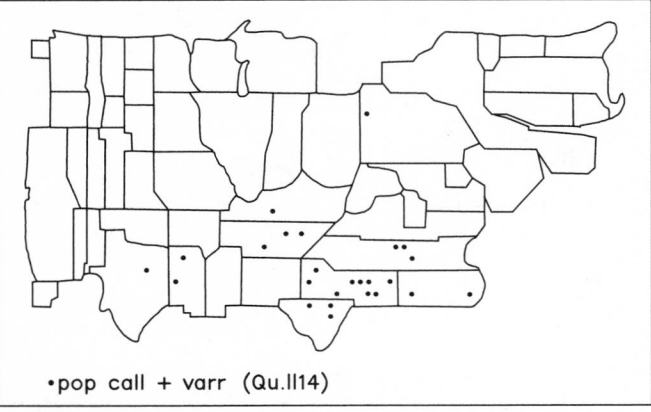

•pop call + varr (Qu.II14)

Sth, S Midl, Gave (*or* paid, give) us a pop call; 7 Infs, **esp Sth, S Midl,** Made (*or* paid) a pop call; **TX**43, Made a pop-in call; **FL**1, Dropped in; a pop call; **FL**8, **NC**88, **SC**69, Pop-called; **GA**19, Give us a popcorn call; **TN**53, Popcorn-called. [20 of 25 Infs old]

popcorn See **popcorn flower 1**

popcorn beauty n Cf **popcorn flower 2**

An **owl's clover** (here: *Orthocarpus erianthus* var *versicolor*).

1911 Jepson *Flora CA* 386, *O[rthocarpus] erianthus*. . . Var. *Versicolor* Jepson. Popcorn Beauty. **1915** (1926) Armstrong–Thornber *Western Wild Flowers* 498, The variety *versicolor,* Popcorn Beauty, has fragrant white flowers.

popcorn call n, v phr See **pop call**

popcorn cheese n Cf *DS* H60

A variety of cottage cheese.

1949 *Amer. Milk Rev.* May 10, Some localities . . distinguish . . textures of cottage cheese by such descriptive words as "baker's" . . "pot", "cup" . . "popcorn" . . etc., but the same terms mean different types . . in different communities. **1986** *WI Dairy Recipes* 42, Cottage cheese has had many names: Dutch cheese, pot cheese, . . popcorn cheese, and flake cheese.

popcorn fart n

1 in phrr *dry as* (or *drier than*) *a popcorn fart:* Very dry.

1970 *DARE* FW Addit **MI**112, A plant might be as dry as a popcorn fart. **1995** *DARE* File **seWI** (as of c1960), If a thing was very dry, my father would characterize it as "drier than a popcorn fart."

2 See quot. Cf *fart in a whirlwind*

1984 Wilder *You All Spoken Here* 110, *Like a popcorn fart in hell:* Unnoticed; like a fart in a whirlwind.

popcorn flower n **esp CA**

1 also *popcorn:* A plant of the genus *Plagiobothrys.* [See quot 1979] For other names of *P. nothofulvus* see **foothills snowdrops, forget-me-not 1d, nievitas**

1897 Parsons *Wild Flowers CA* 30, Pop-corn flower. White Forget-me-not. Nievitas. **1902** *Out West Mag.* May 512 **CA,** I love . . / . . / February's shower / Of "shooting-stars" minute;/ Flakes of the white and yellow "popcorn-flower." **1908** Johnson *Highways Pacific Coast* 143 **nCA,** There were multitudes of delicate bluebells, and there were "nigger toes" and "popcorn." **1934** Haskin *Wild Flowers Pacific Coast* 301, The white popcorn flower, or forget-me-not, grows in great abundance on dry open prairies from Oregon southward. **1951** Abrams *Flora Pacific States* 3.573, *Plagiobothrys hispidus* . . Bristly Popcorn Flower. *Ibid, Plagiobothrys nothofulvus* . . Rusty Popcorn Flower. **1967–69** *DARE* (Qu. S26a, . . *Wildflowers. . . Roadside flowers*) Inf **CA**4, Popcorn flower; **CA**140, Popcorn flower . . white, curled flowers look like popcorn; **CA**126, Popcorn; **CA**127, White popcorn, brown popcorn; (Qu. S26e, *Other wildflowers not yet mentioned;* not asked in early QRs) Inf **CA**41, Popcorn flower—like the fiddleneck, but yellow. [*DARE* Ed: Some of these Infs may refer instead to **2** below.] **1979** Spellenberg *Audubon Guide N. Amer. Wildflowers W. Region* 410, Popcorn Flower. . . Open flowers are clustered at the top of the coil, resembling pieces of popcorn.

2 An **owl's clover** (here: *Orthocarpus erianthus*). [See quot 1906] Cf **popcorn beauty**

1898 *Jrl. Amer. Folkl.* 11.276 **CA,** *Orthocarpus versicolor.* . . pop-corn flower, mossy pinks. **1906** (1918) Parsons *Wild Flowers CA* 54, Pelican-flower. Pop-corn flower. *Orthocarpus versicolor.* . . *Flowers.*—Pure white, fading pinkish; very fragrant. Lower lip of corolla with three very large sacs. **1915** (1926) Armstrong–Thornber *Western Wild Flowers* 498, Pink Johnny-Tuck, Pink Popcorn Flower—*Orthocarpus erianthus var. roseus.* **1961** Thomas *Flora Santa Cruz* 318 **cwCA,** *O[rthocarpus] erianthus* . . var *roseus.* . . Pelican or Popcorn Flower.

popcorn tree n [See quots]

A **tallow tree** (here: *Sapium sebiferum*).

1968 *DARE* (Qu. T16, . . *Kinds of trees . . 'special'*) Inf **LA**28, Popcorn trees (occas) or tallow trees—they have long flowers and white seeds that chickens eat. They are used when people want quick shade trees. **1972** *Names SC* 19.29, *Popcorn Tree* (Charleston and Horry Counties) . . *Sapium sebiferum.* . . The branches with the white fruits are very decorative and are sold by flower vendors in Charleston as *Pop-*

corn Tree. **1986** Pederson *LAGS Concordance,* 1 inf, **swAL,** Popcorn trees—white seed.

popcracker n **VA, NC** Cf **fire popper**
A firecracker.

    1884 Baldwin *Yankee School-Teacher* 32 **VA,** Even the sudden reports of the "pop-crackers," with which the little blacks always celebrate the holidays, failed to arouse an interest. **1887** Page *In Ole VA* 40, Hawg meat an' pop crackers don' meck Christmas. **1899** (1912) Green *VA Folk-Speech* 330, *Popcrackers.* . . Small Chinese fireworks. Firecrackers. **1914** *DN* 4.160 **cVA,** Pop-cracker. . . Firecracker. **1917** *DN* 4.415 **wNC,** Pop-crackers. . . Fire-crackers. **1966–70** *DARE* (Qu. FF14, . . Kinds of firecrackers) Infs **NC14, VA92,** Popcrackers.

pop-drop n Cf **eye-drop**
In marble play: see quot.

    c1970 Wiersma *Marbles Terms* **cnIL** (as of c1957), Pop drop . . over hand shot using marble pinched between thumb and index finger. Eg. I'll use a pop drop on that purie.

pope n[1]

1 =**painted bunting 1.** esp **LA** Cf **pape**
    [**1763** LePage du Pratz *Hist. LA* (transl. Anon.) 2.93, The Pope is a bird that has a red and black plumage.] **1890** *Century Dict.* 4620 **LA,** Pope. . . The painted finch, or nonpareil. **1917** (1923) *Birds Amer.* 3.73, *Painted bunting.* . . Other Names.—Painted Finch; Pope; Nonpareil [etc]. **1932** Bennitt *Check-list* 60 **MO,** Painted bunting. . . Nonpareil; painted finch; pope; butterfly finch; Paradise finch.

2 See **pope's nose.**

pope n[2] [Echoic; see quots] Cf **poop bird, pork-and-beans**
A **nighthawk 1.**

    1781 Peters *Genl. Hist. CT* 257, The Whipperwill [*DARE* Ed: appar misapplied to the nighthawk]. . . is also called the pope, by reason of its . . bawling out *Pope!* **1956** *MA Audubon Soc. Bulletin* 40.81 **CT,** Common Nighthawk. . . Pope (Conn. From the sound made by its wings while dropping through the air.)

pope's cap n Also *pope's crown* [Cf Fr *bonnet d'évêque* bishop's miter; fig, parson's nose (of fowl)] **LA** Cf **bishop's nose**
=**pope's nose 1.**

    1968 *DARE* (Qu. K73, . . Names . . for the rump of a cooked chicken) Inf **LA20,** Pope's cap—occasional; **LA39,** Pope's cap; **LA44,** Pope's crown—old-fashioned.

pope's nose n

1 also rarely *poop-nose, pope:* The rump of a cooked fowl. [*OED2* (at *pope* sb.[1] 8.b) 1796 →] **scattered, but esp Nth, N Midl, CA, TX** See Map

    1860 Morris *Tales Masonic Life* 289 **KY,** A rush was incontinently made to the hens, whose mighty skeletons were presently heard cracking with the dental apparatus of twenty-eight pair of jaws, until there wasn't a pope's nose left of the half dozen. **1899** (1912) Green *VA Folk-Speech* 330, *Pope's nose.* . . The fleshy part of the tail of a bird; the part on which the tail-feathers are borne. "The part that gets over the fence last." **1937** *AmSp* 12.104 **eNE** [Farm terms], The *wish bone* and *plow bone* of a fried chicken are well known; *pope's nose,* a name for the tail, is generally known. **1951** West *Witch Diggers* 72 **IN,** I've fobbed them paupers off tonight with nothing but necks and pope's-noses. **1954** Forbes *Rainbow* 329 **NEng,** Here was the pope's nose and the neck, and the first batch of gravy that came out too greasy. **1965–70** *DARE* (Qu. K73, . . Names . . for the rump of a cooked chicken) 83 Infs, **scattered, but esp Nth, N Midl, CA, TX,** Pope's nose; **MD34,** Pope; **IN32,** Poopnose. **1979** *UpCountry* Sept 38, Julia Child . . caused a tempest in a chicken pot . . when she referred to the tail of the bird as "the pope's nose." [**1982** *NADS Letters,* I have a query about an expression which puzzles me—'poke's nose'. This is what my late grandmother called the tail end of a cooked turkey or chicken. (I never heard it used in connection with a live bird, but then there weren't any around.) The 'nose' part seems to make sense because of the shape, but I wonder what a 'poke' is. (My grandmother was born in Missouri in 1887 and lived in Oklahoma, Kansas and Arkansas when she came to Michigan when she was around 50.)] **1989** *DARE* File **neWI,** The flopping tail of a (raw or cooked) plucked chicken or turkey is called the *Pope's nose* by members of my husband's large Dutch/Catholic family in DePere, Wisconsin. They claim the expression is fairly common within the large Dutch and Belgian Catholic population in the Fox River Valley area. **1999** *Ibid*

OR, Pope's nose—My grandfather used to say it rather often, much to the annoyance of my grandmother, so I guess you have at least one cite from Oregon. **1999** [see **2** below].

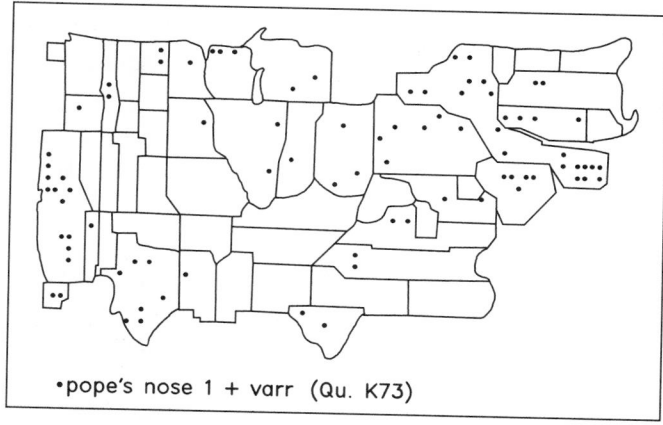

•pope's nose 1 + varr (Qu. K73)

2 The heel of a loaf of bread.

    1999 *DARE* File, When I was growing up, the "Pope's nose" was a term for the heel . . of a loaf of bread. . . When I started going with a gal I met in college . . I was delighted to discover that she understood what I mean[t] when I said "Pope's nose"—but she added "some people say that it means the part of the chicken that crosses the fence last." . . Peg's early years were spent in Minnesota; then her family spent three or four years in Tennessee; then they returned to the family home in Illinois. I was born in Chicago, with a native Chicago father and a mother born in the Ukraine. **2000** *Ibid* **csWI,** I was slicing bread the other day and my husband said to me, "Save me the Pope's Nose," meaning the end of the [Italian] bread which is pointed.

popeye n
=**cockeye.**

    1999 *DARE* File **swMI,** *Popeye* a car with only one headlight . . a game my mother taught me while traveling in a car.

popeye mullet n Cf **mullet** n[1]
=**striped mullet.**

    1984 *DARE* File **Chesapeake Bay** [Watermen's vocab], Striped mullet, black mullet, popeye mullet, jumping mullet. **1986** Pederson *LAGS Concordance,* 1 inf, **seMS,** Popeye mullet (sucker type).

popgun elder n Also *popgun wood* [See quot 1980] **esp SE** Cf **pipe elder**
An elder (here: *Sambucus nigra* subsp *canadensis*) whose hollowed stems are used to make popguns.

    1861 *Harper's New Mth. Mag.* Aug 363 **CT,** "Sambuca". . . was quite too learned a name, however, for the Bakertown boys. Their own plain elder or *pop-gun wood,* suited their tastes better. **1906** *Out West Mag.* Mar 176, The little shrubby popgun elder of the East is supplanted here by a tree twelve to twenty inches in diameter. **c1938** in 1970 Hyatt *Hoodoo* 1.685 **swMS** [Black], You get you some *popgun elder.* And you cut it five inches long, and then you cut in it five notches on that *popgun elder* a half an inch apart. **1966** *DARE* (Qu. T13, . . Names . . for . . box elder) Infs **FL7, GA5,** 9, Popgun elder. [**1980** *Little Audubon Guide N. Amer. Trees E. Region* 670, This common widespread shrub [=*Sambucus nigra* subsp *canadensis*] sprouts from roots. . . Whistles, popguns, and other toys can be made by removing the thick pith from the stems.] **1986** Pederson *LAGS Concordance,* 1 inf, **cnGA,** Popgun elder; 1 inf, **cMS,** Popgun elm [sic]—popguns made from hollow sticks.

pop-haw See **pawpaw**

popinac n Also sp *popinack* [Var of **opopanax**]

1 A **huisache** (here: *Acacia farnesiana*).

    1830 Rafinesque *Med. Flora* 2.243, *Mimosa,* L. or *Acacia* . . Popniac [sic], Goldbriar. **1900** Bailey *Cyclop. Horticult.* 1.8, *Acacia.* . . Farnesiàna. . . Popinac. Opopanax. Cassie. . . Grown in S. France for perfumery. **1936** Whitehouse *TX Flowers* 44, Huisache (*Acacia farnesiana*), also known as opoponax, popinac, cassie, and sweet acacia, is a tropical shrub or small tree. . . In Southern Texas it is highly valued as a honey crop. **1953** Greene–Blomquist *Flowers South* 53, Sweet-Acacia, Popinack, Yellow-Opopanax. . . Fla. to Tex.

2 also *white popinac:* A **lead tree** (here: *Leucaena leuco-cephala*).

1960 Vines *Trees SW* 505, White Popinac[s] Lead-tree—*Leucaena glauca.* **1970** Correll *Plants TX* 775, *Leucaena leucocephala.* . . Popinac. **1976** Bailey–Bailey *Hortus Third* 652, [*Leucaena*] *glauca* . . White Popinac. . . naturalized in s. Fla., Hawaii, and elsewhere.

pop-in call See **pop call**

pop it to (one) See **pop** v[1] **2**

pop juice See **pop** n[1]

popknot n
=**pumpknot.**

1966 *DARE* (Qu. X60, . . *A lump that comes up on your head when you get a sharp blow or knock;* not asked in early QRs) Inf **NC**37, Popknot.

poplar n Usu |ˈpɑplə(r)|; occas |ˈpɑpjələ˞| Pronc-spp *poppelor, popular*

A Forms.

1802 in 1956 Eliason *Tarheel Talk* 316 **c,cwNC,** *Poplar*—poppelor. **c1938** in 1970 Hyatt *Hoodoo* 2.1472 **seGA** [Black], Now yo' go to a *popular* [Hyatt: poplar] tree an' yo' take dat *popular* tree—take de head of it. **1949** in 1986 *DARE* File **seMI,** The poplar [ˈpɑpɪʊlɑ˞] gives more shade than you'd think. **1968–69** *DARE* (Qu. T12, *The kind of poplar tree that has sticky, sweet-smelling buds*) Inf **MO**10, [ˈpˈɑpjɪłə˞]; (Qu. T13, . . *Other names* . . *for* . . *poplar*) Inf **MO**37, [ˈpˈɑpjɪłə˞].

B Senses.

1 =**cottonwood 1.** [*OED2* 1382 →] **widespread, but less freq West** Cf **popple** n[1]

1671 in 1897 *SC Hist. Soc. Coll.* 5.333, This Land bears very good. . . Ash, Hickory, Poplar, Beach [etc]. **1755** Evans *Geogr. Essays* 28 **OH,** This has fine Land, wide extended Meadows, lofty Timber; . . Walnut, Chestnut and Poplar [fitted] for domestic Services. **1789** Morse *Amer. Geog.* 404 **KY,** The soil is deep and black, and the natural growth . . black locust, poplar, elm [etc]. **1830** Rafinesque *Med. Flora* 2.252, *Populus,* L. Poplar. All sp. useful. **1897** Sudworth *Arborescent Flora* 128, *Populus tremuloides.* . . Poplar (Vt., N.Y., Ill., Minn., Mont.) *Ibid* 129, *Populus grandidentata.* . . Poplar (Me., N.H., Vt., Mass., R.I., Conn., N.Y., N.H., Pa., W. Va., N.C., S.C., Ga., Ill., Wis., Ohio). *Ibid* 130, *Populus balsamifera.* . . Poplar (Wis., Minn.) **1965–70** *DARE* (Qu. T13, . . *Names* . . *for* . . *poplar*) 301 Infs, **widespread, but less freq West,** Poplar; **AR**16, Poplar tree; (Qu. T12, *The kind of poplar tree that has sticky, sweet-smelling buds*) 55 Infs, **scattered,** Poplar; **GA**65, **MI**71, 72, **MO**37, **OK**1, **VA**38, Poplar tree; (Qu. T15, . . *Kinds of swamp trees*) 18 Infs, **scattered,** Poplar; (Qu. T16, . . *Kinds of trees* . . *'special'*) 14 Infs, **scattered,** Poplar. [*DARE* Ed: Some of these Infs may refer instead to **2** below.] **1986** Pederson *LAGS Concordance* **Gulf Region,** 138 infs, Poplar.

2 =**tulip tree.** Cf **tulip poplar, yellow ~**

1709 (1967) Lawson *New Voyage* 100 **NC, SC,** The Tulip-Trees, which are, by the Planters, call'd Poplars, as nearest approaching that Wood in Grain, grow to a prodigious Bigness, some of them having been found One and twenty Foot in Circumference. **1837** Darlington *Flora Cestrica* 326 **sePA,** Tulip-bearing Liriodendron. *Vulgò*—Poplar. Tulip-Poplar. **1883** Hale *Woods NC* 128, Tulip Tree, or Poplar. . . In Europe, where it has been long and extensively introduced, it bears the name of *Tulip Tree.* . . This is much preferable to that of *Poplar* (which it bears in this and the Western States), because it has but little resemblance in any particular to the true Poplars. **1943** Peattie *Great Smokies* 277, In May the native magnolias display their large cream-colored blooms and the closely-related tulip tree ("poplar," as it is erroneously called) plays host to a myriad bees. **1953** Greene–Blomquist *Flowers South* 37, Tulip-Tree, Yellow-Poplar. . . It furnishes the valuable timber called "poplar" or "white-wood." **1961** Douglas *My Wilderness* 160 **wNC,** The king of the magnolias is the tulip tree that the mountain people call poplar. It reaches 175 feet high and is six to seven feet through in the Smokies. **1965–70** *DARE* (Qu. T13, . . *Other names* . . *for* . . *tulip tree*) Infs **GA**76, 80, **IL**143, **IN**49, 54, 79, 83, **MD**30, **NC**31, 36, 38, 47, **SC**41, Poplar; (Qu. T13, . . *Other names* . . *for* . . *poplar*) Infs **GA**18, 38, **KY**49, **NJ**58, **NC**16, **TN**14, 56, **VA**26, Poplar; tulip (tree *or* poplar); **KY**29, 39, **NC**55, Poplar, white poplar, yellow poplar; **PA**132, Poplar—"yellow" [*DARE* Ed: It is likely that some of the Infs who gave only "poplar" in response to this question also use it in reference to the

tulip tree.]; (Qu. T12, *The kind of poplar tree that has sticky, sweet-smelling buds*) Inf **NC**36, Tulip tree = poplar; **TN**14, Tulip poplar, poplar [FW: Later in conversation I discovered that the National Park people call it "tulip poplar," but the local people have always said just "poplar."]. **1970** Campbell et al. *Gt. Smoky Wildflowers* 28, Although frequently called *yellow poplar,* or just *poplar,* this big tree of the Smokies is related to the magnolia and is not a true poplar.

poplar balsam See **balsam poplar**

poplaree n [LaFr *pape fleuri,* literally "flowered pope"; cf **pape**]
=**Baltimore oriole** or a similar brightly-colored bird.

1983 Reinecke *Coll.* 9 **LA,** Poplaree, pape fleuri. . . a bright colored bird, esp. Baltimore Oriole. . . Rare. La. Fr. "Pope in bloom." [*DARE* Ed: or "Pope decorated with flowers"]

poplar-leaf snake n Also *poplar leaf, popple ~* [Because its triangular head resembles a poplar leaf] **esp NC**
=**copperhead snake 1.**

1966 *DARE* Tape **NC**21, Poplar leaf—I believe they call them copperheads. Now that's a poisonous snake, too. . . That's the old name for them here. **1966–70** *DARE* (Qu. P25, . . *Kinds of snakes*) Inf **NC**8, Poplar leaf; **NC**12, Poplar-leaf snake; **NC**21, Copperhead or poplar leaf; **NC**80, Poplar leaf—he's a pilot for the rattlesnake; **VA**46, Poplar-leaf snake—a type of moccasin; **NC**87, Popple leaf [ˈpɑpəlif]—spotted brown and gray, 3 or 4 feet long. Poisonous—found mostly by water, also in fields.

pop lash n Also *pop whip* [**pop** v[1] **1a**]
A whip with a **popper** n[1].

1946 *PADS* 6.24 **eNC** (as of 1900–10), Pop-lash. . . A rawhide whip used on oxen. . . Among timbermen around 1890. **1949** Kurath *Word Geog.* 56, Ox goad. . . *Pop lash* on Narragansett Bay (with scattered instances elsewhere in New England), in eastern New Jersey, and on the North Carolina coast. [*DARE* Ed: The attribution of *pop lash* to NEng appears to be an error; the relevant *LANE* map (179) shows no exx of *pop lash.*] **1967** Faries *Word Geog. MO* 128, A stout, pointed stick with a lash used in driving oxen. . . There are eleven instances of *(pop) lash.* **1970** *DARE* (Qu. K27, . . *The sharp-pointed stick used to get oxen to move*) Infs **NC**85, 87, Pop lash. **1986** Pederson *LAGS Concordance* (Whip) 1 inf, **seGA,** A pop whip—to urge horses with; 1 inf, **ceGA,** Pop whips—used on oxen.

po-po n Also *po* [Fr *pot (de chambre)*]
A chamber pot.

1950 *WELS* (Utensil kept under a bed for use at night) 1 Inf, **cWI,** Po—this is used by French. **1966** *DARE* (Qu. F38) Inf **GA**15, Po-po [ˈpopo]—by children only. **1967** Reinecke–Tsuzaki *Hawaiian Loan-words* 110, Popo. . . A chamberpot. (A children's term.)

pop off See **pop** v[1] **3**

popolo n Usu |poˈpolo|; also |ˈpopolo| [Haw] **HI**

1 A **nightshade 1** (here: *Solanum ptychanthum*).

[**1888** Hillebrand *Flora Hawaiian Is.* 307, *S[olanum] nodiflorum* [=*S. ptychanthum*]. . . Rather common in clearings of the woods and along their outskirts; the "Olohua" and "Popolo" of the natives, who eat the berries. The species is common in most tropical countries and cultivated in some as a potherb.] **1929** Pope *Plants HI* 213, Popolo—*Solanum nodiflorum* Von Jacquin. *Ibid* 214, Many people who are familiar with the common or Black Nightshade (*S. nigrum*) and know its poisonous properties, believe Popolo to be the same species of plant. This rumor no doubt has originated on account of the close resemblance of the two species. Investigation indicates that Popolo berries have no poisonous properties. **1948** Neal *In Gardens HI* 655, Black nightshade, popolo. . . The popolo has long played a valuable part in Hawaiian medicine. A cultivated form . . known as the garden huckleberry, has larger fruits, which are cooked for pies and preserves. **1967** *DARE* (Qu. S21, . . *Weeds . . that are a trouble in gardens and fields*) Inf **HI**2, [poˈpolo]—species of *Solanum*—eat it raw in fields, make into jam, pies.

2 A Black person.

1967 *DARE* (Qu. HH28, *Names and nicknames . . for people of foreign background*) Infs **HI**6, 13, [poˈpolo]—Negro. **1967** Reinecke–Tsuzaki *Hawaiian Loanwords* 110, Popolo [ˈpoːpolo]. . . Negro. (A derogatory slang expression.) **1969** *DARE* FW Addit **HI,** Popolo—

[ˌpou'poulou]—Derogatory slang for Negro, the equivalent of *nigger*. **1981** *Pidgin To Da Max* np **HI**, Popolo (poPOlo) Local boy—from Harlem.

pop one's gums See **pop** v[1] 5

popotillo n Also *popotilla* [MexSpan *popotillo*, ult from Nahuatl *popotl* broom]
=**Mormon tea 1.**
   1915 Wooton–Standley *Flora NM* 38, The shrubs are variously known as "popotillo," "cañatillo," "Mormon tea," and "Brigham Young weed." **1937** U.S. Forest Serv. *Range Plant Hdbk.* B73-1, Other local names [for the jointfir] include Brigham-tea, Mexican-tea, jointpine, popotillo [etc]. **1970** Correll *Plants TX* 82, *Ephedra aspera* . . Boundary Ephedra, popotillo. **1985** Dodge *Flowers SW Deserts* 70, Popotilla. . . The harsh, stringy stems . . , when dried, were used with the flowers in making a palatable brew.

popovers to catch meddlers n [Var of **layover(s) to catch meddlers**]
   1906 *DN* 3.151 **nwAR**, *Popovers to catch meddlers*. . . An evasive answer to inquisitive children. "What's that?" "Popovers to catch meddlers."

poppa See **papa**

pop-paw n[1] See **pawpaw** n[1]

pop-paw n[2] See **pa-paw**

poppee show See **poppy show**

poppelor See **poplar**

popper n[1] [**pop** v[1] 1a] **chiefly West** Cf **pop lash, whip-popper**
The thin, flexible section at the end of a whip that produces a sharp, cracking sound.
   1869 Atwell *Gt. Trans-Continental RR Guide* 34, How often the sharp ring of the "popper" aroused the timid hare or graceful antelope? **1877** in **1937** Ruede *Sod-House* 80 **KS**, The lash is about 1½ inches thick at the handle, and tapers to the popper, and a good hand will make them crack like a pistol. **1933** *AmSp* 8.4.51 **NE** [Pioneer vocabulary], *Ring his popper* was an expression meaning *crack his whip*—said of *bull whackers* in driving their teams. **1941** [see **pop** v[1] 1a]. **1959** Robertson *Ram* 103 **ID** (as of c1875), He had become an expert teamster who could make the buckskin popper of a fourteen-foot lash sound like a rifle shot. **1966** Dakin *Dial. Vocab. Ohio R. Valley* 2.134, Several informants commented that the flexible tip on the lash was "to crack" or spoke of it as "a/the cracker." None used "pop" in this sense, but "popper" was attested once. **1967–69** [see **pop** v[1] 1a]. **1976** Sublette Co. Artist Guild *More Tales* 161 **WY** (as of c1900), Drivers usually carried a short whip. This was a leather tapered tube about four feet long filled with shot. On toward the small end was about three feet of braided leather with a small loop at the end. Through this loop was doubled a semi-soft piece of leather called a "popper". **1991** Heat Moon *PrairyErth* 463 **KS** (as of 1864), A whip was given each driver of the outfit, the last being about sixteen feet in length with a "popper" (whip cracker) added and fastened to a whip stock eighteen inches in length by a buckskin thong.

popper n[2] See **papa**

poppers n [See quot]
A **ground-cherry** (here: *Physalis longifolia* var *subglabrata*).
   1963 Craighead *Rocky Mt. Wildflowers* 166, *Groundcherry—Physalis subglabrata*. . . *Other names*: Bladdercherry, Poppers. . . Calyx enlarges to a paperlike balloon or bladder. It may reach width of 1 in.

poppet n
1 A child, esp an attractive one. [*OED2* c1386 →]
   1859 *Atlantic Mth.* 4.319 **NEng**, But I used to think Mary was such a little poppet—that she'd do better for—Well, you know, I thought about some younger man. **1880** *Harper's New Mth. Mag.* 571 **NEng**, Janey [was] a round and rosy poppet, who adored Jack, and rebelled against her mother and Sarah hourly. . . Janey . . [was] round, fat, rosy, bewitching, as a child, and only a child, can be. **1930** Shoemaker *1300 Words* 46 **cPA Mts** (as of c1900), *Poppet*—A prematurely old, grave or over-dressed child. **1933** [see **2** below].

2 also *poppet-doll, poppy-doll, puppet*: A doll, esp a homemade one. [*OED2* 1413 →; "*Obs.*"] **chiefly S Midl**
   1911 *DN* 3.539 **eKY**, *Pŏppet-doll*. . . A homemade (rag) doll. **1933** *AmSp* 8.1.51 **Ozarks**, *Poppet*. . . A rag doll. The word is sometimes applied to a baby or a small child. **1939** Writers' Program *Guide KY* 117, Poppets (mountain dolls) . . are among the products of the "contemporary ancestors." **1940** (1978) Still *River of Earth* 44 **KY**, Euly came from behind the stove, leaving the corn cob poppets to ask a riddle Mother had whispered to her. **1942** (1971) Campbell *Cloud-Walking* 201 **seKY**, Shade's and Marthy's twin younguns, Critty and Cratty, wants a poppet awful bad, doll you ladies calls em. **1944** *PADS* 2.20 **sAppalachians**, *Poppy doll*. . . A home-made rag doll. Also *poppet doll*. *Ibid* 48 **NC**, *Puppet, poppet*. . . A doll. "She's as pretty as a poppet." Halifax and Surry cos., N.C. Also, reported from mountains of N.C. **1955** Ritchie *Singing Family* 174 **seKY**, Granny's voice sounded like she was talking to herself. 'I thought it was a purty poppy-doll—hush and don't cry.' **1972** *NYT Article Letters* **KY**, Puppet—doll. **1976** Garber *Mountain-ese* 70 **sAppalachians**, *Poppet* . . doll—Mother gave the baby a poppet to play with while she cooked dinner.

poppie See **poppy** n[2] 1

poppie cap n Cf **cap** n[1] 9
   1982 Slone *How We Talked* 33 **eKY** (as of c1950), Poppie caps—popcorn; also called "cap corn."

popping See **pop** v[1] 1c

popping-the (or -a)-whip See **pop-the-whip**

popple n[1] [*OED2* ?a1000 → for *Populus* spp] **chiefly NEast, Gt Lakes, IN** See Map on p. 284 Cf **poplar B1**
Often with modifier: Usu =**cottonwood 1**, but also **tulip tree** and occas used erron for **linden**.
   1670 in 1984 Rowley *MA Early Rec.* 1.214, The most northerlie angle is a poppell. **1724** in 1886 *Braintree MA Records* 151, So on to a pople, thence to another pople which we marked. **1818** in 1926 *DN* 5.384 **NEng**, [In a list of New England provincialisms:] *Popple* for poplar. **1830** (1892) McCall *Jrl.* 12.199 **NY**, The land . . is wet prairie or low land, with willow, alders, tamarack and some large aspen and popple. **1830** (1892) McCall *Jrl.* 12.199 **NY**, The land . . is wet prairie or low land, with willow, alders, tamarack and some large aspen and popple. **1894** *DN* 1.342 **CT**, *Popple*: for *poplar*. **1897** Sudworth *Arborescent Flora* 198 **RI**, *Liriodendron tulipfera*. . . Popple. **1910** *DN* 3.446 **cwNY**, *Poppel* [sic]. . . Poplar. **1948** *WELS Suppl.* **seWI**, I never heard the term "popple" until an old German farmer-neighbor here [=in Milwaukee] so named a tree on our street. We had many "popple" trees in Illinois. **1950** *WELS* **WI** (*Poplar*) 15 Infs, Popple; (*The kind of poplar that has sticky, sweet-smelling buds*) 1 Inf, Popple—general term for cottonwood; 1 Inf, Sweet popple; 1 Inf, Popple is the same as poplar locally—popple is the popular word; poplar is the bookish word; 1 Inf, Popple—white wood, light, soft, breaks easily; good for fire or paper; 1 Inf, Popple—same as poplar but [the word is] more common; (*Tulip tree*) 1 Inf, Yellow popple. **1959** *VT Hist.* 27.153, *Poplar* ['pɑpəl] . . pronc. Common. **1961** Douglas *My Wilderness* 183 **MD**, The tulip is called popple by the country people. It's a magnolia that rises in the Potomac region over a hundred feet in height and lives over two hundred years. **1965–70** *DARE* (Qu. T13, . . *Names* . . *for* . . *poplar*) 105 Infs, **chiefly NEast, Gt Lakes, IN**, Popple; **MA62**, Popple—what most people call 'em; **MI10**, You're beginning to hear "aspen," but everything but [bæm] is called "popple"; I call it "popple"; **MN28**, Popple—hear often; **NY219**, Popple tree; 19 Infs, 9 **IN**, Yellow popple; **MA78**, Yellow popple—expression comes from Connecticut Valley; **MN38, NY24, WI37**, Silver popple; **ME5, NH14**, Black popple; **PA29, 104**, Tulip popple; **ME5, NH14**, White popple; **MA4**, Blue popple; **MN38, NY206, OK52**, Yellow popple; **MI104, WI32**, Lombardy popple; **MN12, MA42**, Regular popple; **NY97**, Carolina popple; **NY209**, Balsam popple; **ME5**, Black popple; **MA42**, North Carolina popple; **MN12**, English popple; **MN23**, Norway popple; **ND1**, Silver popple; **PA29**, Tulip popple; **WI22**, Silver leaf popple; (Qu. T15, . . *Kinds of swamp trees*)
... continued: (Qu. T13, . . *Names* . . *for* . . *linden*) Inf **NY219**, Popple tree; **MA25**, Linden—form of popple; (Qu. T12, *The kind of poplar tree that has sticky, sweet-smelling buds*) 19 Infs, **Nth**, Popple (tree); **MA58**, Popple—same as quaking aspens in the West; **NH4**, Popple—just the regular popple (might be called aspen, too); **MA62**, Popple tree blossoms like a pussy willow; **AL11, MN2, NJ69, NY165, PA17, 216, VA73**, Sweet popple; **MI27, MN12, 29**, White popple; **MN29, NY206**,

Inf **MI**96, Popple; (Qu. T16, . . *Kinds of trees . . 'special'*) Infs **MN**12, **NY**92, Popple.   **1967–69** *DARE* Tape **MN**4, The bulk of it is a popple, poplar pulp, but there is a lot of jack pine being cut; **MN**12, This was a timbered country. Oak, popple—mostly grubbed out; **MN**15, Your natural standard reproducers back here will be the popple; **NY**183, On top you'd take willows and popple.   **1982** *DARE* File **WI**, My great uncle was telling me what kinds of trees to use for wooden shoes, and he told me to use basswood and popple wood.   **1996** *Ibid* **seMN**, Around here they call it [=poplar] popple. . . Generally popple is anything that's poplar or aspen.

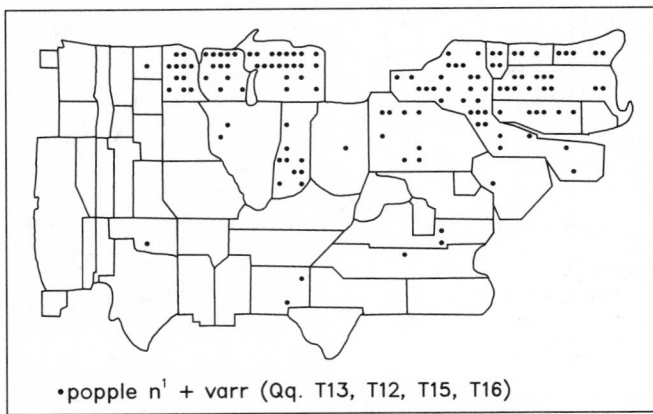

•popple n¹ + varr (Qq. T13, T12, T15, T16)

popple n² [See quot]
=lupine.
   1904 (1913) Johnson *Highways South* 41 **nFL, seGA** [Black], The boys picked . . some lupines which they called "popple," a name they explained by saying that the pods when crushed would go "pop-pop."

popple leaf See **poplar-leaf snake**

popple stone See **pumple stone**

poppo See **papa**

poppoos root See **papoose root**

pop-pop n Usu |'pɑ(p) 'pɑp| Also sp *pa-pop;* for addit pronc and sp varr see quot 1965–70 [Hypocoristic] **chiefly PA, NJ, DE, MD** See Map Cf **mom-mom, pap-pap**
   A grandfather—also used as a quasi-personal name.
   1951 Johnson *Resp. to PADS 20* **DE**, Grandfather: Pop-pop. **1965–70** *DARE* (Qu. Z3, . . *'Grandfather'*) 14 Infs, **chiefly NJ, PA**, Pop-pop; **DC**8, **MD**33, **NJ**23, **PA**11, Pop-pop [pɑp pɑp]; **DE**2, **PA**7, Pa-pop [pɑˌpɑp]; **PA**148, Pup-pup; **PA**90, Pa-pip ['pɑpɪp].   **1981** Pederson *LAGS Basic Materials,* 1 inf, **ceFL**, ['pʰɑˀ,pɑˀp]—his grandchildren say; 1 inf, **cLA**, ['pʰɑˀ,pʊp]—children's term; 1 inf, **swAL**, ['pʰɑˀp,pʰɑˀp].   **1998** Tyler *Patchwork Planet* 63 **eMD**, "Barnaby, hon," my grandma said, "it's me and Pop-Pop."   *Ibid* 195, I turned over my whole key ring, with that Chevy emblem my Pop-Pop gave me when he put the car in my name.   **2000** *DARE* File **nDE**, In the 1950s and 60s, in northern Delaware, one family of my relatives referred to the grandparents of their children as nana (nanna) and pop-pop, which I often heard

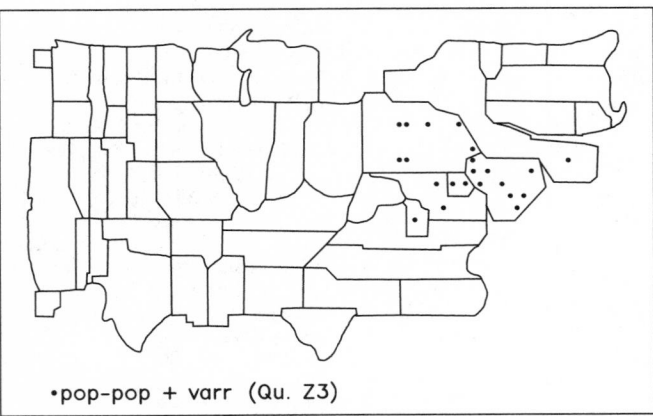

•pop-pop + varr (Qu. Z3)

as pup-up.   *Ibid* **MD,** That "Pup-up" is usually spelled "Pop Pop" here, and my in-laws in Baltimore used it too.   **2001** *Ibid* **NYC,** My grandfather . . was of Swedish ancestry but his wife . . was Irish; I don't know who initiated the Pop-pop name; both were born in Brooklyn in the 1880s or early 1890s.

poppose root See **papoose root**

poppy n¹
=tape grass.
   1913 *Torreya* 13.227 **NY,** *Vallisneria spiralis.* . . Poppy, Cayuga Lake, N.Y.

poppy n² Cf **pappy**
1 also *poppie:* A father—also used as a quasi-personal name. **scattered, but chiefly Sth, S Midl**
   1893 *DN* 1.332 **NJ,** *Pap, pop, poppy:* for papa.   **1902** *DN* 2.242 **sIL,** Poppy. . . Papa, used by children.   **1907** *DN* 3.225 **nwAR,** Poppy. . . Papa; used by children.   **1923** *DN* 5.217 **swMO,** Pap. . . Father. Also, *Pappy* and *Poppy.*   **1925** Dargan *Highland Annals* 55 **cwNC,** His poppie needed him in the field, an' he couldn't git the time right off.   **1932** Stribling *Store* 151 **AL,** No, Poppy, I didn't git none.   **1941** *LANE* Map 371 *(Dad, pa)* 1 inf, **csRI,** [pɒˈpɪ].   **1953** Randolph–Wilson *Down in Holler* 270 **Ozarks,** Pappy. . . Pap, paw, and *poppy* are also common.   **1965–70** *DARE* (Qu. Z1, . . *'Father'*) Infs **CA**134, **GA**72, **KY**40, 44, 52, **NY**83, **VA**31, Poppy; [(Qu. JJ1b, . . *A schoolteacher—a man*) Inf **NC**82, School poppy—not heard too much].   **1966** Dakin *Dial. Vocab. Ohio R. Valley* 2.422, *Father.* . . Rarely attested affectionate forms *poppy* and *popper.*   **1968** *DARE* Tape **VA**9, Poppy and Mommy waited a few days.   **1986** Pederson *LAGS Concordance (Father)* 4 infs, **AL, GA, TN, TX,** Poppy.
2 A grandfather.
   1965–70 *DARE* (Qu. Z3, . . *'Grandfather'*) 10 Infs, **scattered,** Poppy.   **1986** Pederson *LAGS Concordance (Grandfather)* 2 infs, **MS,** Poppy.

poppy adj
Of eyes: bulging; protuberant.
   1899 (1912) Green *VA Folk-Speech* 330, *Poppy.* . . Full or bulging. "His eyes are mighty poppy to-day."   **1907** *Westminster Gaz.* 11 Dec 12/1, An American exclaiming before a family picture: "My, what poppy eyes these Churchills have got!"   **1968–70** *DARE* (Qu. X21a, . . *Words . . used to describe people according to their eyes . . if they stick out*) Inf **PA**66, Poppy eyes; **VA**69, Poppy-eye; **CT**34, Poppy-eyed; (Qu. X21c, *If the eyes are very round*) Inf **VA**2, Poppy eyes.

poppy ash See **pop ash**

poppy-doll See **poppet 2**

poppy fish n
A **butterfish 1** (here: *Peprilus simillimus*).
   1911 U.S. Bur. Census *Fisheries 1908* 314, The poppyfish (*Palometa simillima*) is miscalled the "California pompano." It is a delicate food fish.

poppy mallow n
A **mallow B** of the genus *Callirhoe* whose flowers resemble those of the poppy (*Papaver* spp).   Also called **kingcup 2, meadow beauty 2, wild hollyhock, wine-cup**
   1861 Wood *Class-Book* 267, *M[alva] Papaver* . . Poppy Mallow. . . Ga., Fla. to La. A curious species, strongly reminding one of the poppy . . in the form and size of the bright red or purple fl[ower]s, and the very long . . upright peduncles.   **1870** *Amer. Naturalist* 3.162 **KS,** The Poppy-mallow *(Malva Papaver)* . . forms one of the most brilliant figures in the prairie carpet.   **1901** Lounsberry *S. Wild Flowers* 335, Clustered Poppy Mallow. *Callirhoe triangulata.* . . This one grows in dry soil, and appears very showy with its purple, poppy-like flowers.   **1940** Clute *Amer. Plant Names* 45, *Callirhoe.* Poppy Mallow. . . *C. digitata.* Fringed Poppy Mallow. *C. involucrata.* Purple Poppy Mallow. *C. triangulata.* Clustered Poppy Mallow.   **1967** *DARE* Wildfl QR (Wills–Irwin) Plates 25C.1–3 Inf **TX**44, Poppy mallow.   **1972** Brown *Wildflowers LA* 108, Poppy-mallow—*Callirhoe papaver.*

poppy show n Also sp *poppee show* [Scots, Engl dial; varr of *poppet show* (*OED2* [at *puppet show*] 1650 →; cf the parallel Scots dial *puppie show*). Fig uses occur in Brit slang and are widespread in Caribbean and W Afr creoles (see 1985 *AmSp* 60.189–92).] Cf **poppet**

A puppet show; a peep show; hence fig, a childish or ridiculous exhibition.

1860 Street *Woods & Waters* 337 **neNY,** Molly looked jeest as nice as a poppy-show, now I tell *you!* **1903** (1963) Newell *Games & Songs* 252, I possessed two pieces of glass, very nearly of a size, between which I used to place fallen poppy petals, in lovely kaleidoscopic patterns. . . When several little girls had gathered their poppy-shows together on a board we used to chant when any one passed: "Pinny, pinny, poppy show,/ Give me a pin and I'll let you know." . . We varied the show at other seasons with different flowers . . but we always called them poppy shows. **1939** (1962) Thompson *Body & Britches* 497 **NY,** Go on with your poppy-show! (puppet-show, nonsense). **1947** Ballowe *The Lawd* 49 **LA,** Mr. Effingham just stared. He had the most at stake. To him this was no poppee show. **1947** *Jrl. Amer. Folkl.* 60.37 **ceMO** (as of 1895–1900), A pin, a pin, a poppy show,/ Give me a pin, and I'll let you know. . . It is an old game common in England, where it was played just as we played it in St. Louis. Some of the children used a cardboard box containing colored pictures and a lighted candle. They charged a pin for the others to look in. **1968** *DARE* (Qu. W36, *What . . people say . . about a woman who uses a lot of cosmetics*) Inf **LA**40, Looks like a poppy show; [**FL**22, A poppy]. **1984** *AmSp* 59.99 St. **Louis MO** (as of 1920s), A pin, a pin, a poppy show;/ It's very nice inside, you know./ Give me a pin and I'll let you look in / To see my pretty poppy show. The central object of the rhyme . . was a shoe box with a small, square hole cut in one end and another small hole cut in the center of the lid. The inside of the box was decorated to look like a room—complete with miniature cardboard furniture and doll-like figurines . — after which a tiny candle was lit and set in the center of the box. . . Then the child who had constructed the show would walk slowly along the sidewalks of the local neighborhood, carrying the box and chanting in sing-song fashion the rhyme printed above. *Ibid* 115, And her dress'd go way up in the back, and you could see everything. That's when momma'd say, "Boy, look at Mrs. O! She's really putting on a poppy show, ain't she?"

pop-rind n Also *pop-skin*
See quots.

1953 Randolph–Wilson *Down in Holler* 273 **Ozarks,** *Pop-rind.* . . A meat-rind baked crisp. When a large family is eating pop-rinds, the stuff cracks like a bunch of little firecrackers. **1967** *DARE* Tape **TN**16, [FW:] What happens to the hide of the hog? [Inf:] Well, you eat it if you like. . . I like pop-skins myself. . . That's them skins. . . put 'em in the oven and bake 'em. They get right brittle.

pop-robin n
A sort of dumpling; see quots.

1957 Beadle *Reminiscences* 9 **CT** (as of c1845), Sometimes we had a supper of Indian hasty pudding, or of "Pop Robin," a dish we all liked. It consisted of boiled salted milk to which a little water was added if the milk was not abundant, and the whole thickened with a batter of wheat flour which was dropped into it gradually from a spoon, and these lumps of scalded flour formed the 'pop' of which we were very fond. **1981** *Des Moines Register* (IA) 26 Apr Picture 4/2, *Pop-robins?* You can make your own if you dough balls the size of plums in boiling maple syrup. Serve them with butter—and more maple syrup. The first pop-robins were cooked in the maple grove at sugaring-off when they were dropped into the syrup can and boiled in the snow. **1999** *NADS Letters* **NH** (as of c1980), "Pop-robins" were sweet dumplings that my grandmother would make in the springtime. I don't *think* they were boiled in maple syrup, but she would always serve them with maple syrup and vanilla ice cream. One of her friends always said that my grandmother made them "wrong"—that they should be deep-fried like a doughnut or "fried dough". We never figured out if this friend was confusing them with the Southern "hushpuppies".

popscull See **popskull**

pop-skin See **pop-rind**

popskull n Also *popscull, popskull whiskey* **chiefly sAppalachians** Cf **busthead 1, skull buster**
Liquor, esp illegal whiskey of inferior quality.

1865 *Republican Banner* (Nashville TN) 28 Sept 3/2, Under the divine aflatus [sic] of pop-skull there was such an awakening in that quarter as was never heard before. **1867** Harris *Sut Lovingood Yarns* 222 **TN,** Well, Maje cum blowin mad intu the doggery, an seein nobody, he jis' grabbed a bottil, an' tuck hisself a buckload ove popskull. **1913** Kephart *Highlanders* 137 **sAppalachians,** All of the moonshine whiskey

used to be pure, and much of it still is; but every blockader knows how to adulterate. . . Some add washing lye . . , then prime this abominable fluid with pepper, ginger, tobacco, or anything else that will make it sting. Even buckeyes, which are poisonous themselves, are sometimes used to give the drink a soapy bead. Such decoctions are known in the mountains by the expressive terms "pop-skull," "bust head," "bumblings" ("they make a bumbly noise in a feller's head"). **1929** *AmSp* 4.386 **KS** [Wet words], Such terms as . . *white lightning, pop-skull,* and *bust-head* are evidently references to the potency or the effect of the liquor designated. **1935** Sheppard *Cabins* 190 **NC Mts,** People come to expect certain qualities in the liquor from certain stills. "That's some of the ole popscull from Deer Mountain." **1939** Hall Coll. **wNC, eTN,** *Pop-skull.* . . Poor grade mountain whiskey. . . The expression is in general use here in the Smokies. **1940** *AmSp* 15.447 [TN mountain speech], *Popskull.* Low grade liquor. 'He's crazy on popskull.' **1941** *AmSp* 16.24 **sIN,** *Popskull.* Whiskey that is particularly powerful in its effect. **1943** *AmSp* 18.67 **SC,** *Popskull* (rotgut whiskey). **1965–70** *DARE* (Qu. DD21a, *General words . . for any kind of liquor*) Inf **NC**35, Popskull; (Qu. DD21b, *General words . . for bad liquor*) Infs **GA**7, 16, **NC**35, **SC**26, 40, 43, Popskull; (Qu. DD21c, *Nicknames for whiskey, especially illegally made whiskey*) Infs **GA**74, **OH**20, Popskull; (Qu. DD27, . . *Nicknames . . for wine*) Inf **GA**89, Popskull; (Qu. DD31, *Joking names for homemade hard liquor;* total Infs questioned, 75) Infs **GA**3, 7, Popskull. **1968** *Foxfire* 2.3.101 **nGA,** "Busthead" and "Popskull" are names applied to whiskey which produces violent headaches due to various elements which have not been removed during the stilling process. **1969** *DARE* Tape **GA**72, Popskull is another name for that very bad liquor. You can get a little high on it, and the next day your head feels like it's gonna split wide open and fall down on each shoulder. **1973** McCarthy *Child of God* 28 **TN,** He'd sit with the old man in the bloated sofa in the yard drinking with him from a halfgallon jar of popskull whiskey. **1986** Pederson *LAGS Concordance (Cheap whiskey)* 19 infs (12 **GA,** 4 **TN,** 2 **AL,** 1 **MS**), Popskull.

pop-the-whip n Also *popping-the* (or *-a)-whip, pop-the-rope* [**pop** v[1] **1a**] **chiefly Sth, Lower Missip Valley, West** See Map Cf **snap-the-whip, whip-popper**
The game of crack-the-whip.

1905 *DN* 3.90 **nwAR,** *Pop the whip.* . . Snap the whip (the name of a game). **1909** *DN* 3.359 **eAL, wGA,** *Pop the whip.* . . A boy's game, snap the whip. **1917** *DN* 4.420 **LA,** *Pop the whip.* =snap the whip. **1954** Harder Coll. **cwTN,** *Pop the whip.* . . A children's game. **1965–70** *DARE* (Qu. EE33, . . *Outdoor games . . that children play*) 18 Infs, **chiefly Sth, Lower Missip Valley, West,** Pop-the-whip; **LA**8, **TN**24, Popping-the-whip; (Qu. EE1, . . *Games . . children play . . in which they form a ring*) Infs **AL**15, **CA**102, **TX**3, Pop-the-whip; (Qu. EE27, *Games played on the ice*) Infs **CO**7, **MT**2, Pop-the-whip. **1966** *DARE* Tape **AL**3, [Aux Inf:] Did you all play pop-the-whip? **AL**6A, Whip-popper—that's . . when everybody makes a long line and then you run and the one in front kind of jerks it that way and tries to whip off the one on the end. . . Pop-the-whip is what we call it; crack-the-whip. **1968** *DARE* FW Addit **cLA,** *Pop-the-whip*—Hold hands in long line and try to break the hold of the people at the end—children's game. **1969** (1970) Angelou *Caged Bird* 23 **AR** [Black], And when he was on the tail of the pop the whip, he would twirl off the end like a top. **1986** Pederson *LAGS Concordance* **Gulf Region,** 12 infs, Pop-the-whip; 2 infs, Popping the whip; 1 inf, Popping a whip—childhood line game; 1 inf, Pop the rope—rough game.

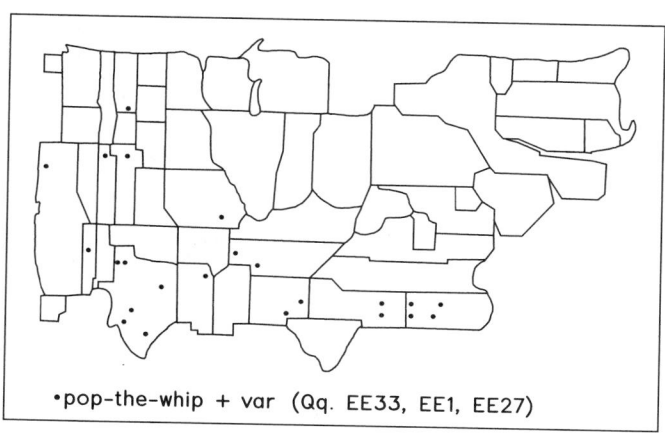

•pop-the-whip + var (Qq. EE33, EE1, EE27)

popular See **poplar**

populist bug n Cf **democrat bug**

A **box-elder bug** (here: *Boisea trivittata*).

1943 KS State Bd. Ag. *Report* 62.255.163, The "boxelder bug" . . is also known as "democrat bug" and "populist bug" in Kansas.

pop water See **pop** n¹

popweed n

=**bladderpod 1.**

1961 Wills–Irwin *Flowers TX* 120, Of the 50 species of Bladderpods known in North America, perhaps 15 grow in Texas. All are distinctive with their pea-sized bladderlike pods which pop when stepped on, hence another common name, Popweed.

pop whip See **pop lash**

poquau See **pooquaw**

poque n [See quot 1938] **AK**

A **ground cone** (here: *Boschniakia rossica*).

[**1938** (1958) Sharples *AK Wild Flowers* 24, B[oschniakia] glabra. A parasite on the roots of Alder. . . Eaten by the Indians, who call it "Poque." Southeastern Alaska and parts of the Interior.] **1974** Welsh *Anderson's Flora AK* 302, Ground-cone, Poque. . . Thickets, woodlands, and heath to tundra . . widely distributed in Alaska and Yukon. **1987** Hughes–Blackwell *Wildflowers SE AK* 50, Poque, Ground-cone. . . Woods, thickets (often among alders).

poquoson See **pocosin**

porch n

1 also *porch room*: A room added on to the main body of a house, often used as a kitchen; a kitchen. **chiefly NEng** Cf **ell** n¹ **1, 2, summer kitchen,** *DNE*

1892 *DN* 1.210 seMA, Porch: the "L" of a house. **1902** *DN* 2.242 sIL, Porch. . . Any kind of platform about a doorway, whether roofed or not. Sometimes an out-room for general purposes is called a porch. **1916** Macy–Hussey *Nantucket Scrap Basket* 163, "Porch"—Applied to an ell kitchen. A summer cottager who instructed the native man-of-all-work to sweep and clean the porch accused him of stupidity when she returned an hour or two later to find her kitchen nicely cleaned, while the veranda remained in the same disorder as when she went out. **1926** *DN* 5.388 ME, Porch. . . Shed or unfinished room in an "ell." Rare. **1926** *AmSp* 2.79 ME, Our summer kitchen in my grandfather's house where I was born has from its first occupancy been termed "the porch." Why, I cannot tell. I suspect it to be a relic of an earlier usage. **1929** *AmSp* 5.124 ME, The "porch" was a sort of extra shed-kitchen used as a laundry. **1941** *LANE* Map 352 *(Ell)*, Porch is variously defined as synonymous with *ell* . . [by 7 infs], as an older name for *ell* . . [by 5 infs], as 'a small ell' . . [by 1 inf] and as a partially open ell . . [by 1 inf]. It may be a finished room built on to the back of the house . . [by 9 infs], or a shed either attached in the same way . . [3 infs] or added at the back of the kitchen . . [5 infs]. Like the ell, the porch may be used as part of the living-quarters (thus frequently) or as a store room (thus . . [5 infs]). . . *Ell* and *porch* are frequently used in a special sense. Since in most New England farm houses the kitchen or cook room . . is situated in the rear of the house, and often represents a later addition to the original building, the terms denoting such an addition have come to be used by a number of informants as more or less interchangeable equivalents of *kitchen*. . . Thus . . *porch* is defined . . as an ordinary built-in kitchen . . [by 4 infs], an added 'kitchen ell' . . [by 2 infs] or a summer kitchen, an unfinished shed built on back of the kitchen proper . . [by 5 infs]. More often the *ell* or *porch* is said to be 'used as a kitchen' . . [by 12 infs] or as a kitchen and dining-room together . . [by 2 infs] or as either a kitchen or a shed . . [by 2 infs], or to 'include' or 'contain' the kitchen . . [by 10 infs]. . . 1 inf, Porch room, old-fashioned. **1973** Allen *LAUM* 1.169 **Upper MW** (as of c1950), When coal- or wood-burning stoves were used for cooking, summer heat made the kitchen so uncomfortable that, particularly on the farm, cooking was frequently done in temporary quarters elsewhere. Although many infs. are unfamiliar with such a place and have no word for it, most of those who do use *summer kitchen*. As is sometimes indicated, this may be only a porch, enclosed or screened or open. . . A number of equivalents also occur, mostly only once or twice. back porch . . [5 infs, **MN, NE, ND**]. porch . . [1 inf, **ND**].

2 See quots. Cf **back porch, front ~**

1942 Berrey–Van den Bark *Amer. Slang* 121.6, *Paunch; potbelly.* . . porch. **1967** *DARE* (Qu. X35, *Joking words for the part of the body that you sit on*) Inf **MN**10, Porch.

porch v See **poach** A1

porch child n Also *porch baby* Pronc-sp *po'ch chile* Cf **apron child, lap ~, yard ~**

See quot 1953.

1945 *PADS* 3.10 **cSC**, She's got one lap-chile, one po'ch chile, and three ya'd chillen. **1953** *PADS* 19.13 **sAppalachians**, *Porch baby.* . . A baby that is able to walk but is not allowed in the yard without someone to take care of him. A gate is often put up to keep the child from getting off the porch. **1984** Wilder *You All Spoken Here* 36 **Sth**, *Porch child:* One sufficiently advanced to play unattended on a porch with protective devices, such as railings.

porch room See **porch** n **1**

porch vine n

=**kudzu.**

1937 *Torreya* 37.98 **AL**, *Pueraria Thunbergiana.* . . Porch-vine.

porcupig See **porkepick**

porcupine n

Std: the North American quill-bearing mammal *Erethizon dorsatum.* Also called **bark-eater 2, hedgehog 1, pincushion 3, porkepick, porky** n², **prickly pear 2, ~ pig, quill pig, spear hog, spiketail, stinger**

porcupine egg n Cf **monkey ball 2**

A spiny seed or seedcase; see quots.

1931 Clute *Common Plants* 44, The prickly-looking fruits of the sycamore . . are called porcupine eggs. **1967** *DARE* (Qu. S13, . . A common wild bush with bunches of round, prickly seeds; when they get dry they stick to your clothing) Inf **AZ**9, Porcupine eggs. **1969** *DARE* File **AZ**, Porcupine egg—cocklebur. **1970** *DARE* FW Addit **MA**78, Porcupine eggs . . chestnuts with burrs.

porcupine fish n [*OED2* 1681 →]

A **puffer** n¹ **1** of the genus *Chilomycterus, Diodon,* or *Sphoeroides.* Also called **ball fish, burfish, balloonfish 1**

1873 in 1878 Smithsonian Inst. *Misc. Coll.* 14.2.15, *Chilichthys turgidus.* . . Rough puffer; porcupine-fish. . . Cape Cod to Florida. **1882** U.S. Natl. Museum *Bulletin* 16.862, Diodon [spp] . . *Porcupine-fishes.* . . Dermal spines strong, stiff, most of them two-rooted and erectile. **1898** *Ibid* 47.1745, *Diodon hystrix.* . . Porcupine-fish. . . Tropical seas; everywhere common; north to Lower California, Florida, and the Hawaiian Islands. **1939** Natl. Geogr. Soc. *Fishes* 150, The porcupinefish . . has the body everywhere covered with long, sharp spines which project in every direction like the quills of a hedgehog. *Ibid* 164, [Caption:] The porcupinefish . . can inflate itself into the form of a large ball. Its balloon shape and bristling spines then offer reassuring defenses against natural enemies. **1969** *DARE* File **ceNC**, Porcupine fish. **1983** *Audubon Field Guide N. Amer. Fishes* 763, *Porcupinefishes* (Family Diodontidae [*DARE* Ed: now included in Tetraodontidae])—These small to medium-sized puffers are quite robust and covered with spines.

porcupine grass n

=**needlegrass 1,** esp *Hesperostipa spartea.*

1857 Gray *First Lessons* 549, *S[tipa] spartea.* . . Porcupine Grass. . . Plains and prairies, from Illinois and N. Michigan northwestward. **1884** Vasey *Ag. Grasses* 42, *Stipa spartea* is called porcupine grass, arrow grass, and devil's knitting needles, from the long, stiff, twisted awns inclosing the seed. **1912** Wooton–Standley *Grasses NM* 57, The Porcupine Grasses belonging in the genus *Stipa* are an interesting and somewhat varied group. **1937** U.S. Forest Serv. *Range Plant Hdbk.* G114, The name porcupinegrass is sometimes applied to the whole genus [= *Stipa*] but is best restricted to those species (particularly *S. spartea*) which have very large, coarse, and quill-like awns. **1973** Hitchcock–Cronquist *Flora Pacific NW* 671, *Stipa* . . Needlegrass; Needle-and-thread; Porcupine-grass; Speargrass.

porcupine nest n Cf **hurrah's nest 4**

=**witches'-broom.**

1960 Teale *Journey into Summer* 100, Witch's-brooms, those still mysterious spurtings of tree growth that produce tangled masses of twigs—

known in the west as "porcupine nests"—appeared in many of the higher junipers.

porcupine palmetto n Also *porcupine palm*
=**blue palmetto 1.**

[**1869** Porcher *Resources* 605 **SC,** Our "Blue Palmetto" (*C. hystrix*) has thorns like porcupine quills.] **1942** Kennedy *Palmetto Country* 5 **FL,** Another low-lying palmetto—variously called the dwarf, needle, porcupine, blue, or creeping palmetto—has an even wider range than the saw palmetto. . . [I]ts recumbent trunk is surrounded by needle-sharp spikes. **1976** Bailey–Bailey *Hortus Third* 946, [*Rhapidophyllum*] *hystrix*. . . Needle palm, porcupine p[alm], blue palmetto.

porcupine plant n
See quot.

1931 *Jrl. Amer. Folkl.* 44.334 **LA,** You will write the names of your enemies and send it to house of your enemies, tightly sealed with the wax of the Porcupine Plant.

pore See **poor**

pore boy See **poor boy**

pore-hawg See **poor-hog**

pore joe See **poor joe** n[2]

porely See **poorly**

porgee, porgie n See **porgy** n[1]

porgie exclam See **pork** exclam

porgy n[1] Also sp *porgee, porgie* [Appar of multiple origins: in part < **pargo** and in part < **pogy;** perh also infl by other unknown elements] Cf Pronc Intro 3.I.2, 3.III.1, **black porgy, pogy**

1 A fish of the family Sparidae:
a Used generically or in contexts that do not allow firm identification.

1763 in 1952 *AmSp* 27.283 **SC,** In enumerating the Animal Part of our Food, I begin with the Fish;—Mullet, Whiting, Black-fish, Rock-fish, Sturgeon, Porgys, Trout, Bream, and many other Sorts of flat Fish. **1775** (1962) Romans *Nat. Hist. FL* xix, A little to the north hereof is a small reef with about 2 fathoms water on it, where vast quantities of groopers, snappers, amber-fish, porgys, margate-fish, rock-fish, yellowtails, Jew-fish, &c. may be taken. **1799** (1803) Ellicott *Jrl.* 255, Along the Florida Reef . . a great abundance and variety of fish may be taken: such as . . porgys, turbots, stingr[a]ys. **1896** U.S. Bur. Fisheries *Rept. for 1895* 388, *Sparidae.* The Porgies. **1933** LA Dept. of Conserv. *Fishes* 195, *The Sheepshead and Other Porgies* (Family *Sparidae*)—The Porgies are all sea fishes, most of which are deep bodied and oblong or oval in outline. . . The most important of the Louisiana Porgies is the Sheepshead. . . Smaller in size are several other Porgies which . . are good food fishes. The most common of these is the Pinfish [=*Lagodon rhomboides*]. **1955** Zim–Shoemaker *Fishes* 116, *Porgies* are small-mouthed fishes with strong jaw teeth, adapted to feeding on shellfish and crustaceans. Scup or Porgy . . is a sports and food fish. . . Sheepshead Porgy, common and large, affords sport to spear fishermen. *Ibid* 117, *Pinfish* [=*Lagodon rhomboides*] is a porgy. . . A fine-flavored fish. **1975** Evanoff *Catch More Fish* 209, Porgies [=*Stenotomus chrysops* and *Calamus* spp] like rocky bottoms or those covered with seaweed, mussels, oysters, clams or other shellfish. But smaller porgies will also be found over sandy bottoms. **1991** Amer. Fisheries Soc. *Common Names Fishes* 54, Sparidae—porgies.

b Spec:
(1) Std: a sparid food fish (*Pagrus pagrus*) of the Mediterranean and the Atlantic.
(2) A fish of the genus *Stenotomus*: usu =**scup 1,** but also **goatshead porgy.**

1735 Royal Soc. London *Philos. Trans. for 1734* 38.317, *Aurata Bahamensis* [=*Stenotomus chrysops*]. The *Porgy.* **1787** Gesellschaft Naturforschender Freunde *Schriften* 8.151, *Sparus chrysops.* . . *Aurata bahamensis.* . . *Porgee,* in Carolina. **1814** in 1815 Lit. & Philos. Soc. NY *Trans.* 1.404, *Big Porgee of New-York.* . . With changeable colors, forked tail, and large silvery eyes. **1848** Bartlett *Americanisms* 257, *Porgy,* or *Paugie.* . . (Indian, *scuppaug.*) A fish of the *sparus* family, common in the waters of New England and New York. . . It is singular

that one half the aboriginal name, *scup,* should be retained in Rhode Island and the other half, *paug,* changed into *paugie* or *porgy,* in New York. **1849** in 1857 Webster *Private Corresp.* 2.337, I . . caught some fish, namely, tautog and skippog, the same, I suppose, as are called "Porgee" in New York. **1878** [see **4** below]. **1884** Goode *Fisheries U.S.* 1.386, In New England it is generally called "Scup," while about New York the . . name . . [is] "Porgy." The latter name is particularly objectionable because. . . "poghaden," a . . name for the menhaden, . . has been changed into . . "porgy," thus leading to much confusion. . . The name "Porgy" [for *Stenotomus chrysops*] is in use about Charleston, South Carolina, but is usually applied to other members of the same family [=Sparidae]. **1896** U.S. Bur. Fisheries *Rept. for 1895* 388, *Otrynter* [=*Stenotomus*]. . . Deep-water Porgies. **1911** [see **5** below]. **1931–33** LANE Worksheets **CT,** The porgy and menhaden are entirely different fish. The porgy is a bottom feeder, and the menhaden is a top feeder. **1939** LANE Map 233 (*Porgy; pogy*), *Stenotomus argyrops* (a sparoid), a common food fish found from Cape Cod southward. . . is closely related to the sheepshead, flat and high-backed (sometimes described as shaped like a pumpkin seed), attaining a length of 1½ feet. This fish is called *porgy* [pɔrgɪ] or *poggy* [pɑgɪ] in Conn. **1965–70** DARE (Qu. P2, . . *Kinds of saltwater fish caught around here . . good to eat*) Infs **AL22, NJ22, NY63, RI15,** Porgy; **CT31,** Porgy ['prgɪ] = scup [skʌp]; **MD36,** Porgy ['pɑrgɪᵛ]; **NC1, 60, NY36, 47,** Porgy ['porgɪ]; **NJ60, 69, NY51, PA66,** Porgy ['pɔrgɪ]; **NJ67,** Porgy ['pargɪ]; **NY34, VA47,** Porgy ['pɒrgɪ]; **NY118,** Porgies ['porgɪz]; **NY236,** Porgies [pɔrgɪz]; (Qu. P14, . . *Commercial fishing . . what do the fishermen go out after?*) Infs **NC87, NJ60, NY36, SC66,** Porgies; **CT14,** Porgies ['porgɪz]; **NY235,** Porgies ['porgɪz]. [DARE Ed: Some of these Infs may refer instead to other senses.] **1974** McClane *McClane's New Std. Fishing Encycl.* 859, *Stenotomus chrysops.* . . Commonly known as "porgy" along the Northeastern United States coast. Apparently there are only two species in this genus, this and the common species of the Gulf of Mexico, the longspine porgy, *S. caprinus. S. chrysops*. . . lives on or near the bottom in the mid depths of the Continental Shelf. . . [and] readily takes bottom-fished baits. . . It is a good table fish. **1984** DARE File **Chesapeake Bay** [Watermen's vocab], Scup[₅] porgy[₅] maiden[₅] fairmaid.

(3) =**pinfish.** [See quot 1884]
1851 Herbert *Frank Forester's Fish & Fishing* 217, The Rhomboidal Porgee, *Sargus Rhomboides* [=*Lagodon rhomboides*], . . though very similar to the Big Porgee, . . [is] clearly distinct. **1884** Goode *Fisheries U.S.* 1.393, *Lagodon rhomboides.* . . bears considerable resemblance in its form to the scuppaug. . . [It] bears several other names, being known . . in the Saint John's River [FL] as the "Sailor's Choice" and "Porgy," . . and . . at Cedar Keys [FL] as the "Porgy." **1911** [see **5** below]. **1935** Caine *Game Fish* 55, *Lagodon rhomboides.* . . Porgy. **1983** Audubon *Field Guide N. Amer. Fishes* 616, This [=*Lagodon rhomboides*] is a very common porgy, but because of its small size it is seldom used as food.

(4) A fish of the genus *Calamus.* For other names of var spp see **grass porgy, saucereye ~, shad ~, whitebone ~**
1884 Goode *Fisheries U.S.* 1.394, *The Porgies of the Gulf.* . . A fish known as the "Sheepshead Porgy" is . . common about the Florida Reefs. . . There are other species, known by the name of "Porgy," which are found in this region, such as *Calamus bajonado,* common also at Charleston, . . *C. megacephalus, C. arctifrons,* and *C. macrops.* **1896** U.S. Bur. Fisheries *Rept. for 1895* 176, Porgy (*Calamus bajonado*). *Ibid* 389, *Calamus proridens.* . . Little-head Porgy. . . *Calamus penna.* . . Little-mouth Porgy. **1933** John G. Shedd Aquarium *Guide* 110, *Calamus proridens—Little-head Porgy. Calamus bajonado—Jolt-head Porgy.* This is the largest and most abundant of the genus. **1974** McClane *McClane's New Std. Fishing Encycl.* 504, *Calamus bajonado.* . . The flesh of this porgy is excellent to eat, being firm, moist, and white. **1991** Amer. Fisheries Soc. *Common Names Fishes* 54, *Calamus brachysomus* . . Pacific porgy.

(5) A fish of the genus *Diplodus.*
1884 U.S. Natl. Museum *Bulletin* 27.1198, *Black-tailed Porgy.—Diplodus holbrookii.* . . This species spawns in April on the coral banks off the Carolina and Georgia coasts, where it is more abundant than in any other locality. **1991** Amer. Fisheries Soc. *Common Names Fishes* 54, *Diplodus argenteus* . . silver porgy.

2 a **spot** (here: *Leiostomus xanthurus*).
1814 in 1815 Lit. & Philos. Soc. NY *Trans.* 1.405, *Little Porgee.* (*Labrus obliquus* [=*Leiostomus xanthurus*].) With raised back, oblique bars, and concave tail. **1903** NY State Museum & Sci. Serv. *Bulletin* 60.582 **NJ,** In Great Egg Harbor bay it [=*Leiostomus xanthurus*] is ex-

tremely common in summer and is sometimes known as porgee. **1905** NJ State Museum *Annual Rept. for 1904* 334, *Leiostomus xanthurus.* . . Spot. Cape May Goody. Goody. Porgy. . . Abundant on our coast, and on account of its small size is valued chiefly as a pan-fish of excellent flavor.

3 A **spadefish** (here: *Chaetodipterus faber*).

1842 DeKay *Zool. NY* 4.97, The popular names of *Three-tailed Sheepshead* and *Three-tailed Porgee*, were given them [=*Chaetodipterus faber*] by the fishermen in allusion to their prolonged dorsal and anal fin. **1878** U.S. Natl. Museum *Proc.* 1.380 **NC**, *Parephippus faber.* . . *Porgee; Pogy.* Common; used as a food fish. **1902** Jordan–Evermann *Amer. Fishes* 482, *C[haetodipterus] faber.* . . is the common spade-fish, angel-fish or porgee. **1911** [see **5** below].

4 A **menhaden 1,** usu *Brevoortia tyrannus.* **chiefly NEng**

1878 *Amer. Naturalist* 12.737, At the present day this name [= "poghagen" for *Brevoortia tyrannus*] is almost universally in use among the fishermen north of Cape Cod, though it is occasionally varied by . . "porgy." The use of the latter name should be carefully avoided: the same name . . being commonly applied to another fish, the . . "scup" (*Stenotomus argyrops*). **1880** *Harper's New Mth. Mag.* 61.504 **ME coast,** It quite depended upon their choice of position whether porgies should even make an appearance on the coast at all. **1884** [see **1b(2)** above]. **1905** Wasson *Green Shay* 134 **NEng,** He like to have squshed my hand into porgy-chum! [Footnote: Porgies ground into bait] **1914** Steele *Storm* 191 **Cape Cod MA,** For the first time that season the porgie fleet moved in around Long Point. **1932** Wasson *Sailing Days* 114 **cME coast,** Smaller schooners . . sometimes used seines, but with the sloops and double-ended "carryway" boats, once so numerous as "porgy catchers," they generally drew single fish over the side. **1939** *LANE* Map 233 (*Porgy; pogy*) 1 inf, **sCT**, *Porgy,* edible but rather oily. **1951** Taylor *Surv. Marine Fisheries NC* 93, Other names for the menhaden are: *porgie* [etc]. **1968–69** *DARE* (Qu. P4, *Saltwater fish that are not good to eat*) Infs **NY**63, **RI**15, Porgy. **1986** Pederson *LAGS Concordance* **Gulf Region,** 1 inf, Porgies—scrap fish, menhaden—not edible; 1 inf, Porgy; 1 inf, Porgy—a trashy fish, used for cat food.

5 Any of several **surfperches,** but esp *Rhacochilus vacca.* [See quot 1884] **Pacific**

1882 U.S. Natl. Museum *Bulletin* 16.597, *D[amalichthys] argyrosomus* [=*Rhacochilus vacca*]. . . *White Perch; Porgee.* . . Pacific coast of United States, north to Vancouver's Island; very abundant northward. **1884** Goode *Fisheries U.S.* 1.276, On the coast of Oregon the large species [of Embiotocidae] (especially *Damalichthys argyrosomus*) are called "Pogy" or "Porgee," in allusion to their undoubted resemblance to the scup or porgee of the East. *Ibid* 277, *Damalichthys argyrosomus.* . . On the coast of Washington and Oregon this species is known as "Porgee." **1911** U.S. Bur. Census *Fisheries 1908* 314, *Porgee,* or *Porgy.*—A name given to the surf-fish (*Damalichthys argyrosomus*) in Oregon and Washington; to the moonfish (*Chaetodipterus faber*) at Beaufort, N.C.; to the scup (*Stenotomus chrysops*) in New York and along the southern coast; to the sailor's choice (*Lagodon rhomboides*) in the St. Johns River and at Cedar Keys; and to several sparoids of the Gulf [of Mexico]. *Ibid* 317, *Surf-fish (Embiotocidae).* . . are also called "pogy" and "porgy" on the Oregon coast. **1953** Roedel *Common Fishes CA* 104, *Redtail Surfperch—Amphistichus rhodoterus.* . . Called "porgy" in the Pacific Northwest. *Ibid* 107, *Rubberlip Perch—Rhacochilus toxotes.* . . *Unauthorized Names:* Pile perch, porgy, niggerlip. *Ibid* 108, *Pile Perch—Rhacochilus vacca.* . . *Unauthorized Names:* Splittail perch, porgy, forktail perch. *Ibid* 109, *Black Perch—Embiotoca jacksoni.* . . *Unauthorized Names:* Bay perch, porgy, blue perch. **1991** Amer. Fisheries Soc. *Common Names Fishes* 159, Porgy—see redtail surfperch.

6 =**margaret grunt.** Cf **flannelmouth 1**

1884 Goode *Fisheries U.S.* 1.394, *The Margate-fish* [=*Haemulon album*]. . . is known only in the Gulf of Mexico. . . About Pensacola, where it is called the "Porgy," it is seldom eaten. . . At Key West it is brought to market in well-boats, and sells readily. The small ones there are called "Porgies" and the large ones "Margate-fish" and "Market-fish." **1911** U.S. Bur. Census *Fisheries 1908* 312, *Margate-fish (Haemulon album).*—A grunt found in southern Florida; known also as "porgy." . . They are caught mostly for bait, but in some places they are sold as food.

7 A **burfish** (here: *Chilomycterus schoepfi*).

1884 Goode *Fisheries U.S.* 1.170, *Chilomycterus geometricus* [=*C. schoepfi*]. . . In Southern Florida the names "Porgy," "Puffer," and "Puff Fish" are sometimes used.

8 =**black drum.**

1935 Caine *Game Fish* 65, *Pogonias cromis.* . . Big Porgy. . . Porgy.

Porgy n[2] Also *Porky* [By syncope and assim from **Portuguese** or one of its varr such as *Portagee*]

A Portuguese person.

1967–69 *DARE* (Qu. HH28, *Names and nicknames . . for people of foreign background: Portuguese*) Infs **CA**56, **OR**1, Porgies; **MI**101, Porky.

porgy sunfish n
=**bluegill 1.**

1938 Schrenkeisen *Field Book Fishes* 249, *Bluegill Sunfish.* . . Common names. . . Porgy Sunfish. . . A large, plain-colored sunfish without palatine teeth.

pork n

1 Used in var phrr to indicate that a woman's slip is showing; see quots.

1950 *WELS* (*Expressions or sly words of warning for a woman's slip showing*) 1 Inf, **ceWI,** You're slipping; pork is getting cheaper. **1968** *DARE* (Qu. W24a) Inf **AK**8, You're selling pork.

2 in phr *have the pork:* To be in trouble.

1979 Lewis *How to Talk Yankee* [26] **nNEng,** *Pork, had the.* In bad trouble. . . "Yessuh, when that warden found them twelve short lobsters under the life cushions, I knew I'd had the pork." **1982** *DARE* File **coastal ME,** Had the pork: caught red-handed.

3 in phr *haul pork:* See **haul ass 1.**

pork exclam Also *porgie, porky* Cf **poig, poke** exclam
Used as a call to pigs.

1967 Faries *Word Geog. MO* 93, Call to pigs. . . porgie! [1 of 700 infs] **1967** *DARE* (Qu. K84, *The call used . . to get the pigs in at feeding time*) Inf **IA**1, Porky; **PA**163, Pork—repeated.

pork and apple pie See **pork apple pie**

pork-and-beans n Also *beans bird* [See quot 1956] **NEng** Cf **poop bird, pope** n[2]
A **nighthawk 1** (here: *Chordeiles minor*).

1925 (1928) Forbush *Birds MA* 2.306, *Chordeiles virginianus virginianus.* . . *Other names:* Bull-bat; mosquito hawk; pork-and-beans [etc]. **1946** Hausman *Eastern Birds* 367, *Eastern Nighthawk.* . . *Other names*—Bull-Bat, Mosquito Hawk, Beans Bird [etc]. **1956** MA Audubon Soc. *Bulletin* 40.81, *Common Nighthawk.* . . Pope (Conn. From the sound made by its wings while dropping through the air.); Pork-and-beans (Maine. Allusion in a single name to the sound just mentioned and to the bird's common call note—often rendered as *peent.*) [**1967** *DARE* (Qu. Q4, . . *Kinds of hawks*) Inf **MA**5, Nighthawks say, "Beef, beef so high. Pork, pork so low."]

pork apple pie n Also *pork and apple pie, pork pie* **chiefly NEng**
A pie, usu a **deep-dish pie,** made with apples and pork.

1939 Wolcott *Yankee Cook Book* 219 **NEng,** *Pork apple pie.* . . Fill a deep dish with apples. Mix salt pork, sugar, spices and salt and sprinkle the mixture over the apples. Cover with pie crust. . . *Pork pie has a more succulent flavor than ordinary apple pie.* **1940** Brown *Amer. Cooks* 387 **MA,** *Pan Pie.* . . This classic dish was also called pork apple pie because, as one New Englander describes it, "there were layers of apple with little cubes of fat salt pork which cooked up and mingled with the apples when the pie was done." **1941** *LANE* Map 292 **ceME** (*Apple dumpling*) 2 infs, Pork pie, a deep-dish apple; 3 infs, Pork apple pie; 1 inf, Pork apple pie, baked in a shallow pie tin; 1 inf, Deep dish apple pie = pork apple pie, containing pork and molasses. **c1965** Randle *Cookbooks* (Plain Cookery) 1.51 **WI,** Pork n' apple pie—3 cup [sic] leftover roast pork, cut in 1" cubes[,] 2 tart apples . . [,] 4 T. brown sugar[,] ½ t. cinnamon[,] 1 cup pork gravy.

pork bird n [See quot]
=**Canada jay.**

1956 MA Audubon Soc. *Bulletin* 40.84 **ME,** [Canada jay. Camp Robber, Camp Thief (Maine. From its pilfering food about woodland camps.); Carrion Bird (Maine. From its feeding upon camp refuse.)] *Ibid,* Pork Bird (Maine. See first two notes.)

pork cake n Also *pork fruitcake*
A fruitcake made with salt pork for shortening.

1890 James *Mother James' Cooking* 309 **TX,** *Pork cake.* One pound fat salt pork (free of lean or rind) chopped very fine. Pour upon it one-half pint boiling water. One pound raisins seeded and chopped. One-fourth pound citron cut into shreds. Two cups sugar. One cup molasses. One teaspoon saleratus rubbed fine and put in molasses. **1939** Wolcott *Yankee Cook Book* 253 **MA,** *Pork Cake.* . . This cake conserves the more expensive shortenings and uses salt pork of which the supply was plentiful. It is a delicious cake and keeps fresh for months. **1940** Brown *Amer. Cooks* 86 **CT,** *Pork fruitcake.* . . Chop raw pork fat almost to mush, add boiling water, sugar, molasses that has been mixed with soda, fruits and spices, and sufficient flour to make a dough of fruitcake consistency. **1950** *WELS (Dishes made with pork in your neighborhood)* 1 Inf, **seWI,** Pork cake. **1957** Showalter *Mennonite Cookbook* 219 **VA,** *Pork Cake.* . . This is a good substitute for fruit cake and keeps for weeks. **c1970** *DARE* File **sIN,** Pork cake—a fruit cake made with lean pork as an ingredient; it was made by her grandmother and others in the community, and is still made. **1998** *DARE* File **nwMA,** The family has a recipe for a pork cake, which simply substitutes salt pork for the lard.

pork chop n Cf **borinki**
A Puerto Rican.

1976 *DARE* File **neIL,** My uncle, raised in Chicago, now living in Morton Grove and working in the Loop, told me that this was the phrase used to designate Puerto Ricans. "You know what they call them? Pork chops."

porkepick n Also *porcupig, porkpick, porky pig* [Fr *porc-épic;* cf *OED2* porcupine sb. 1.a.ε.]
=**porcupine.**

1665 in **1888** WI State Hist. Soc. *Coll.* 11.88, The speech being finished, they intreated us to be att the feast. We goe presently back againe to furnish us w[i]th woaden bowls. . . We had a role of porkepick about our heads, w[hi]ch was as a crowne. **1890** *AN&Q* 5.68, *Porcupig.*—This old name for a porcupine (Fr., *porc-épic*) is familiar to many from the old comic ballad of "More of More Hall." It is pleasant to find in one of John Burroughs' books, that the mountaineers about the head-waters of the Delaware still call the porcupine by this old name. **1967** *DARE* (Qu. P31, . . *Names or nicknames* . . *for the* . . *porcupine*) Infs **MI**47, **NY**6, Porky pig. **1975** Gould *ME Lingo* 215, *Porkpick*—Mainer's woodland condescension for the porcupine, from the French *porcpique*, but reserved mainly for *porkpick* stew. The porcupine is edible and can be made delicious by French-Canadian *choppers* who board themselves.

porkey See **porky** n[2]

porkfish n Also *porkie, porky* Cf **hogfish d, pigfish c**
A **grunt** n 1: usu *Anisotremus virginicus,* but also *Orthopristis chrysoptera.*

[**1734** Royal Soc. London *Philos. Trans.* 38.315, *Perca marina, Rhomboidalis fasciata.* The *Pork-Fish.* The *Bahamians* esteem this a good *Fish.*] **1887** Goode *Amer. Fishes* 81 **FL,** The Norfolk Hog-fish, *Pomodasys fulvomaculatus* [=*Orthopristis chrysoptera*], . . is the "Hog-fish," or "Grunt," of the Chesapeake . . and "Pork-fish" and "Whiting" at Key West. **1933** John G. Shedd Aquarium *Guide* 108, *Anisotremus virginicus*—Porkfish. This strikingly colored fish is abundant on the Florida coast, where it has considerable food value. **1946** LaMonte *N. Amer. Game Fishes* 68, Porkfish—*Anisotremus virginicus.* . . Names: Sisi, Porkie, Catalineta. **1986** Pederson *LAGS Concordance,* 1 inf, **seGA,** Porky—some kind of perch.

pork fruitcake See **pork cake**

porkie See **porkfish**

porkpick See **porkepick**

pork pie See **pork apple pie**

pork side n Also *pork siding* Cf **salt side, side meat, side pork**
Meat from the side of a hog, esp when preserved with salt.

1966 *DARE* (Qu. H38, . . *Words for bacon [including joking ones]*) Inf **MA**6, Pork side. **1967** *Mebane Enterprise & Hillsborough Jrl.* (NC) 13 Apr sec 1 6, [Advt:] Fresh Sliced Pork Side. **1971** *Today Show Letters* **KY,** In back-country Kentucky they fry "pork siding." **1986** Pederson *LAGS Concordance (A side [of bacon])* 3 infs, **GA, LA, MS,** Pork side(s).

pork squeak n Cf **bubble and squeak**
1969 *DARE* Tape **MA**58, Pork squeak is common fried salt pork.

porkwood n
A **blolly** (here: *Guapira discolor*) native to Florida; also its wood.

1884 Sargent *Forests of N. Amer.* 117 **FL,** *Pisonia obtusata* [=*Guapira discolor*]. . . Pigeon Wood. Beef Wood. Cork Wood. Pork Wood. Semitropical Florida, cape Canaveral to the southern keys; through the West Indies. **1979** Little *Checklist U.S. Trees* 141, *Guapira discolor.* . . *Other common names*—Brace blolly, roundleaf blolly, beeftree, beefwood, porkwood, pigeonwood.

porky n[1] See **porkfish**

porky n[2] Also sp *porkey* chiefly Nth, nCA See Map
=**porcupine.**

1902 Hulbert *Forest Neighbors* 146, We found the Porky asleep in the sunshine. **1916** Kephart *Camping & Woodcraft* 1.259, In northern woods the porcupine is a common nuisance. . . The "porky" has an insistent craving for salt and will gnaw anything that has the least saline flavor. **1930** Shoemaker *1300 Words* 44 **cPA Mts** (as of c1900), *Porkey*—A common name for the Canada porcupine in Northern Pennsylvania. **1950** *WELS (Other names used locally for* . . *Porcupine)* 12 Infs, **WI,** Porky. **1965–70** *DARE* (Qu. P31) 98 Infs, **chiefly Nth, nCA,** Porky. **1967** *DARE* Tape **MI**42, A porcupine walked out on a log that was sticking out and somehow or another he slid off of it. . . That poor porky. **1968** *PA Game News* Dec 35 **PA,** Several porcupine quills [were] sticking out. . . The snake eventually digested what must have been a small porky. [**1998** *DARE* File, The Porcupine Mountains, in the far westerly part of Michigan's Upper Peninsula, are known throughout Wisconsin as "the Porkies."]

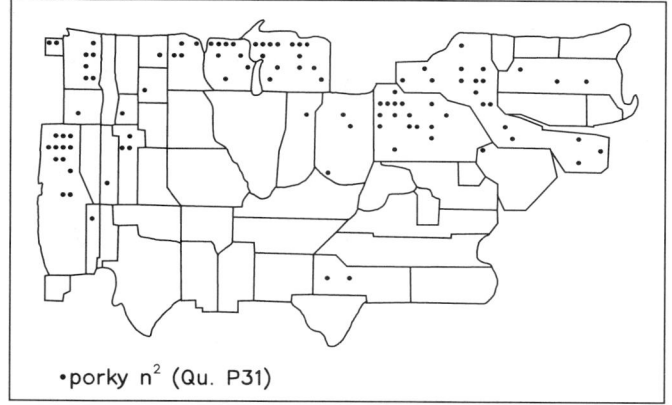

•porky n[2] (Qu. P31)

Porky n[3] See **Porgy** n[2]

porky exclam See **pork** exclam

porky adj
1968 *DARE* (Qu. GG19a, *When you can see from the way a person acts that he's feeling important or independent: "He surely is _____ these days."*) Infs **NY**100, 105, Porky.

porky pig See **porkepick**

porler See **parlor** A

porman's apple See **poor man's apple**

porpoise n [Malaprop for *pauper;* cf quot 1942]
1934 Hurston *Jonah's Gourd Vine* 184 **FL** [Black], Ah come heah from Wes' Foriduh uh porpoise, but look whut Ah got now. Ahm uh self-made man. *Ibid* 315, [Glossary:] *Porpoise,* pauper. [**1942** Hall *Smoky Mt. Speech* 95 **wNC, eTN,** Pauper ['pɔɚpɚ], ['pɒɚpɚ].] **1970** *DARE* (Qu. U41a, *Somebody who has lost everything and is very poor: "He's _____."*) Inf **NJ**67, A porpoise. [Inf Black]

porridge n
A **Gram** form.
Used as a count noun. [Perh connected with the fact that in Scots and Engl dial *porridge* is often construed as a collective plural]

1914 *DN* 4.68 **ME, nNH,** Able to set up an' eat a few porridges. . . Convalescent. Or, in good health. Usually the latter.

B Senses.

1 A food consisting chiefly of grains or legumes boiled to a soft consistency. **scattered, but esp Nth, N Midl** See Map

1684 (1977) Mather *Essay Providences* 147, Ashes were thrown into the porridge which they had made ready for their Supper, so as that they could not eat it. **1731** Seccombe *Father Abbey's Will,* Some Devil's Weed / And Burdock Seed,/ To season well your Porridge. **1827** in 1924 Kittredge *Old Farmer* 205 **NEng,** There came a most terrifying gust, and swoop it carried porridge pot, pork, pud'n and mother Drizzle all up chimney. **1896** Freeman *Madelon* 231 **NEng,** I've got to make some porridge for him. **1905** *DN* 3.16 **cCT,** *Porridge. . .* In the proverb, 'When it rains porridge my dish is always upside down.' **1939** Wolcott *Yankee Cook Book* 174 **NH,** If you are a New Hampshire Yankee, you have heard about and perhaps even eaten bean-porridge. . . The porridge was made by boiling beans in corned beef liquor and thickening the mixture with Indian meal. It was hardened in quart bowls. . . When eaten, slices were cut off and heated in a skillet. **1953** Piercy *Shaker Cook Book* 227, Shaker pease porridge. **1956** Ker *Vocab. W. TX* 289, *Mush, grits, gruel, porridge,* and *cereal* are all prepared by boiling [cornmeal] in water or milk. [*Porridge* was the resp of 1 of 67 infs.] **1965–70** *DARE* (Qu. H23, . . *Hot cooked breakfast cereal*) 78 Infs, **scattered, but esp Nth, N Midl,** Porridge; **NY21,** Cornmeal porridge; (Qu. H24, . . *Boiled cornmeal*) Infs **CT2, MA24, NY200, OR3, RI14, VA1, 13,** Porridge; **MA98,** Cornmeal porridge; (Qu. H25, . . *Fried cornmeal*) Infs **MI9, NY58,** (Fried) porridge; [(Qu. H50) Inf **MA5,** Pease porridge—Canadians make it;] (Qu. HH30, *Things that are nicknamed for different nationalities*) Inf **CA8,** Scotch porridge; (Qu. JJ15b, . . *"He doesn't know _____."*) Inf **MA14,** Beans from porridge; (Qu. KK42a, . . *A person who does something very easily: "For him that would be _____."*) Inf **RI13,** Porridge. [73 of 90 total Infs women] **1973** Allen *LAUM* 1.302 **Upper MW** (as of c1950), *Mush. . .* porridge [4 of 208 infs, **MN, NE, Canada**]. **1993** Thomas Co. Hist. Soc. (KS) *Prairie Winds* Mar 6 (as of c1890), Sunday morning breakfast was usually fresh rolls of bread and strawberry jam. The rest of the week we had porridge which had cooked all night on one of the stoves.

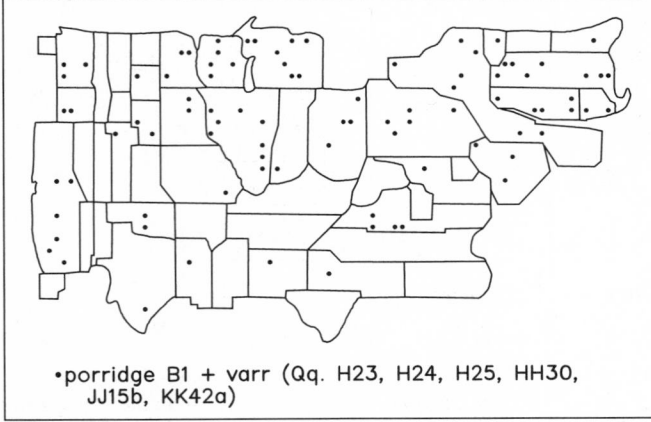

•porridge B1 + varr (Qq. H23, H24, H25, HH30, JJ15b, KK42a)

2 See **porridge ice.**

porridge ice n Also *porridge* **NEast, esp NEng** Cf **mush ice**
Floating ice with a granular texture: thin or weak ice.

1820 in 2000 Philbrick *In Heart Sea* 196 **Nantucket MA,** Porridge ice. **1880** *Scribner's Mth.* 19.331, The water was full of porridge-ice. **1892** *Auk* 9.335 **NEng,** It would appear that even these Ducks . . cannot endure the porridge ice which forms at times in these waters. . . They apparently must have considerable open water in order to exist. **1943** *LANE* Map 648 *(Froze)* 1 inf, **Long Is. NY,** Skum over, 'when it forms [paɹɻɪdʒ ɐˈɪs].' **1957** Rose *Block Is.* 47 **RI,** As a slight thaw gradually came, great floes of porridge ice, some a mile long, floated in the Sound. **1998** *NADS Letters* seNH (as of 1950s), When I was growing up in southeastern New Hampshire, 1950's, porridge ice described a soft, usually green-tinged ice that appeared early or late in the season. It could be up to several inches thick but its texture would vary from semi solid to that of oatmeal. . . Ice fishermen on lake Winnepesaukee would often stretch the use of the term to include ice on the lake that could not be trusted with the weight of a vehicle or a fishing shanty. *Ibid* **wMA** (as of 1940s-50s), Porridge ice: Ice formed in water that has been frothed up by the wind: filled with air bubbles and with a very rough surface. **1999** *Ibid* **NH** (as of c1980), "Porridge ice" was what my grandfather would

[use to] describe a kind of ice floating in water. . . It was a springtime condition when the sheet of ice on a pond started to melt and got brittle. It's hard to describe, but the solid sheet of ice would start to almost disintegrate, such that the sheet became formed of little cylinders of ice only lightly stuck together. The ice took on a cloudy appearance from the top. If you tossed a large stone on the ice . . the stone would break through and there would be [a] largr [sic] amount of little pebble-sized chunks of ice in the water, which had the rough consistency of oatmeal. Hence, "porridge ice". *Ibid* **Long Is. NY** (as of 1940s-50s), Porridge ice. . . The term describes mostly-frozen salt water. Seawater doesn't freeze the same as fresh at all. . . [T]he ice forms a thick, slushy layer. . . Porridge ice comes next. The water—or ice—is too stiff to move much. It sits there like oatmeal, too thick for boats, too thin for boots. **2000** *Ibid* **ME,** On the rivers, the ice flows would catch on narrow points or rock areas and cause ice jams. Most of the men would refuse to go out on them to set the dynamite need[ed] to clear the jam if they found porridge ice. *Ibid* **MA,** My Grandfather . . grew up in Massachusetts, out near Middlesex. . . A few times he showed me some floating ice that he called Porridge. Its a type of ice that is fairly slushy and generally breaks apart quickly and is swallowed up by the river or stream.

porson See **person**

Port n Also *Porto* [By apocope from **Portuguese**]
A Portuguese person.

1966–69 *DARE* (Qu. HH28, *Names and nicknames . . for people of foreign background: Portuguese*) Infs **CA17, 107,** Ports; **MA1,** Portos.

Portagee See **Portuguese**

portage road n Also *portage trail*
See quot.

1956 Sorden-Ebert *Logger's Words* 26 **Gt Lakes,** *Portage-road,* See tote-road. *Portage-trail,* A trail used to carry in supplies in a pack sack. [*Ibid* 38, *Tote-road,* A supply road to camp.]

Portagoose n Also sp *Portugoose* [From **Portuguese** construed as a plural, by facetious analogy with *goose/geese*]
A Portuguese person.

1967 *DARE* (Qu. HH28, *Names and nicknames . . for people of foreign background: Portuguese*) Inf **HI6,** Portagoose—jocular. **1983** Allen *Lang. Ethnic Conflict* 65, Portugoose.

portal n Also *portale* Usu |ˌporˈtɑl|; now also |ˈportəl| [Span] **SW**
A long, covered porch or portico.

1844 Gregg *Commerce* 1.144 **NM,** The only attempt at anything like architectural compactness and precision, consists in . . buildings, whose fronts are shaded with a fringe of *portales* or *corredores.* **1910** J. Hart *Vigilante Girl* 195 *(OED2)* **CA,** Arthur's chair was taken to the *portal,* where they found the major-domo and a group of *vaqueros* waiting. **1927** Cather *Death Comes* 2.51 **NM,** Under this *portale* the adobe wall was hung with bridles, saddles, [etc.] **1946** Waters *Colorado* 311, In each [town along the Colorado River], long portales like shadowy corridors of Spanish mission churches protected sidewalk travelers from the blazing sun. **1948** *SW Rev.* 33.245, What are now empty mule stalls there used to be the *portales* of a convent. **1972** Hamilton *Intriguers* 59 **AZ,** "I . . crawled to where I could watch the long porch outside the living room." . . I said, "Around these parts, that porch is known as a portal, ma'am. Accent on the last syllable." **1998** *DARE* File swNM, I talked with an Anglo carpenter about *portal.* He told me that most Anglos in this area say *portal* [with first-syllable stress]. . . He himself prefers *portal* [with second-syllable stress], but this is not the usual Anglo pronunciation around here. Another Anglo told me that the word *portal* for porch is originally from Northern New Mexico and has only recently entered this area . . with the popularity of Northern New Mexico architecture.

Portegee See **Portuguese**

portemonnaie n Also sp *portmonnaie, portmoney* [Fr *portemonnaie,* literally "carry money"] **chiefly NEng** *old-fash*
A change purse, pocketbook.

1850 Mitchell *Lorgnette* 173 **NYC,** Must give her the *porte monnaie* that Stiver gave me the other day. **1856** in 1862 Colt *Went to KS* 153 **NY,** I had better take the portmonnaie and pay him our fare. **1857** (1928) Twain *Advent. Snodgrass* 42, I've left my portmoney in the grocery. **1878** Harte *Man on Beach* 78 **CT** [Black], I left my port-money at home.   **1885** *Harper's New Mth. Mag.* 70.785, A battered porte-monnaie.   **1907** *DN* 3.196 **seNH**, Port-money... Port-monnaie... So pronounced.   **1941** *LANE* Map 368 *(Purse)* 1 inf, **nwCT**, Portemonnaie [puˠəɹt'mʌnɨ], formerly very common; 1 inf, **seCT**, ['pɔtmʌnɨ] [Inf indicates that this term is old or obsolete.]; 1 inf, **ceMA**, ['poˠətmʌnɨ]; 1 inf, **cVT**, [poət'mʌnɨ]; 1 inf, **seNH**, ['poətmʌ˅nɨ].   **1967** *DARE* (Qu. U30, *What... you keep money in when you carry it around with you)* Inf **MA5**, Portmoney—used by New England man Inf's age [=83]—change purse.

Portergee See **Portuguese**

portico n [By ext from *portico* a colonnade at the entrance to a building]   **chiefly Midl**   See Map
A porch on a house.

   1941 *LANE* Map 351 *(Porch)* **NEng**, *Portico* nearly always denotes a small covered doorway, sometimes including a small platform or the steps leading up to the door. It is so defined by 34 informants, about three quarters of those who use the term. The projecting cover... may be supported by side pillars.. or unsupported.   **1948** Davis *Word Atlas Gt. Lakes* app qu 11a *(Large porch with roof)* 4 (of 233) infs, **IL, MI, OH**, Portico; qu 11b *(Small porch with no roof)* 12 infs, 8 **OH**, Portico.   **c1960** Wilson *Coll.* **csKY**, Porches and their ilk [include].. portico.   **1965–70** *DARE* (Qu. D17, .. *The platform, sometimes with a roof, that's built on the front or the side of a house)* 31 Infs, **chiefly Midl**, Portico; (Qu. D11, *When you go into a house, the part just beyond the front door is the _____)* Inf **OH**80, Portico ['pɝdɪko]; **VA**13, Portico ['por,ticol]; (Qu. D12, *The part that's put on in winter around an outside door)* Inf **ME**15, Portico? [FW: Inf very uncertain]; **ME**23, Entry; some say portico; (Qu. D16, .. *Parts added on to the main part of a house)* [Inf **MD**7, Portico—local name for carport;] **OK**9, Portico. [28 of 34 total Infs old]   **1966** Dakin *Dial. Vocab. Ohio R. Valley* 2.55, Portico predominates in the greater Cincinnati area, in the interior hill counties of Indiana, in Kentucky west of the Bluegrass, and along the lower Ohio in Illinois... *Portico* seems most often to refer to a smaller porch, perhaps ornate and with a roof supported by pillars, at the formal entrance.   **1967** Faries *Word Geog. MO* 125, The general term *porch* (95 percent) is the usual word throughout Missouri. Three [of c700] informants list *portico,* and one lists *stoop.*   **1973** Allen *LAUM* 1.175 (as of c1950), Porch... portico [1 of 203 infs, **IA**].

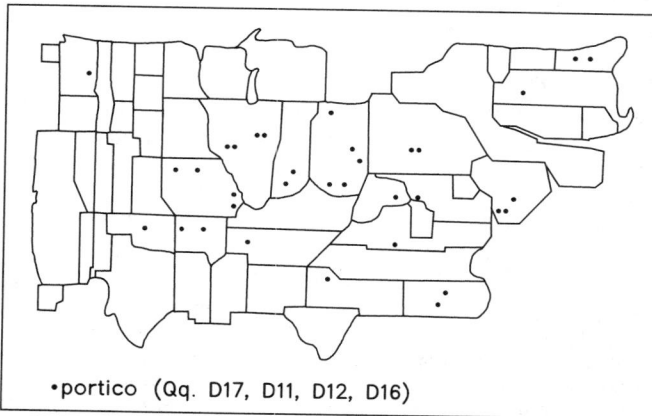

•portico (Qq. D17, D11, D12, D16)

Portland (cutter) See **Portland sleigh**

Portland fancy n **chiefly MA** *old-fash*
A type of country-dance; the music for this dance.

   1871 *Scribner's Mth.* 3.116 **seMA**, You should have beheld the graceful movements of the Portland Fancy and the Money Musk.   **1898** Wister *Lin McLean* 13 **WY** [Speaker from **MA**], Do yu' know the Portland Fancy?   **1904** Lovett *R. Gresham* 63 *(DA)*, Below, the couples.. were circling the hall in the rapidly weaving figures of the Portland Fancy.   **1939** Linscott *Folk Songs Old New Engl.* 108, *Portland Fancy*—Music: Portland Fancy... The melody is derived from an Irish reel... It is one of the favorites found on every country dance program. *The Dance*—Form as for "Sicilian Circle," except that two couples are abreast in sets of four around the circle, as in quadrille [sic] formation.   **1941** *LANE* Map 410 *(A dance)* 1 inf, **Boston MA**, German, cotillion, quadrille, schottische, Portland fancy—various old dances.   **1966–69** *DARE* (Qu. FF5a, .. *Different steps and figures in dancing—in past years)* Infs **MA**11, 40, 55, 73, Portland fancy. [All Infs old]   **1969**

DARE Tape **MA**29, Portland fancy, that was another old dance... In that one you change... partners.   **1998** *DARE* File **nwMA**, Portland Fancy is a familiar jig, in three parts which goes from the key of A to the key of D. We play it out of sheer stubbornness... But as for the dance, I've never seen it done... It was one of those contra dances that every New Englander knew at one time, and was done once at every dance.

Portland sleigh n Also *Portland (cutter)* [Prob from *Portland,* Maine]   **esp NEast**   Cf **Albany sleigh**
A type of light sleigh.

   1887 (1972) Walling *Recollections* 498 **NYC**, He noticed a Portland sleigh, in the shafts of which was a bob-tailed horse.   [**1893** *Outing* 21.369 **Canada**, Then I ran as if the fiend was on my track, for a four-minute bay roadster and a dainty Portland were behind.]   **1908** in 1971 Sears *1908 Vehicles* 66, We show on this page a Portland Cutter at $16.75.   **1922** (1926) Cady *Rhymes VT* 32, Our Portland sleigh will always stay / Inside my mind and body;/ There wasn't nothing in, or on,/ Or 'bout it, cheap or shoddy.   **1934** *Hanley Disks* **csCT**, Then there was the Portland sleigh, which was more trim, [with] a little bit higher back and straight sides and straight back.   **1967** *DARE* (Qu. N40b, .. *Sleighs for carrying people)* Inf **NJ**3, Portland cutter—made in Portland, Pennsylvania.   **1976** *WI Then & Now* Dec 2, The classic Albany (or Swell-body) and Portland (or Kimball) sleighs designed and built by craftsmen were latter-day city cousins of the homemade, utilitarian sledges that provided most of the winter overland transportation in Wisconsin before railroads and roads.

portly adj
1 Handsome, imposing.   [The original sense *(OED2* a1529 →), now largely replaced by the orig euphem sense "stout, corpulent"]
   1923 *DN* 5.217 **swMO**, Portly... Large, handsome. The word has no particular reference to corpulence or dignity.   **1956** McAtee *Some Dialect NC* 57, *Portly*.. in an older use, imposing: "The two of 'em look mighty portly driving around town in this new buggy" (Chapel Hill News Leader, Jan. 2, 1955).
2 See quots.
   1903 *DN* 2.325 **seMO**, Portly... Thrifty; lusty. 'He is a portly child.'   **1907** *DN* 3.235 **nwAR**, Portly... Thrifty, lusty.

portmoney, portmonnaie See **portemonnaie**

Porto n See **Port**

Portoreek adj, also used absol Also *Porty Reek, Po-t-rik* [Pronc-spp for *Porto Rica(n),* older form of *Puerto Rica(n)*]   **esp NEng**
   1924 *DN* 5.286 **Cape Cod MA**, Few grocers outside of Cape Cod would know what to produce when someone asked for a gallon of 'Porty Reek long lick'. But a real Cape Codder would know that a gallon of Porto Rico molasses was desired.   **1937** FWP *Guide MA* 331 **seMA**, Molasses was 'Porty Reek long-lick,' or 'long-tailed sugar.'   **1942** ME Univ. *Studies* 56.63, West Indian molasses was called *Portoreek* molasses from the sailors' pronunciation of Porto Rico.   **1989** (1990) Baden *Maryland's E. Shore* 109, An enterprising skipper... will serve a hearty breakfast of Ballard biscuits for sopping up "po-t-rik" the favorite molasses of watermen since 1893.

Port Orford cedar n [*Port Orford,* Oregon]
A **white cedar** (here: *Chamaecyparis lawsoniana*); also its wood.

   1884 Sargent *Forests of N. Amer.* 179, Port Orford Cedar... A large tree of the first economic value... Most common and reaching its greatest development along the Oregon coast.   **1898** *Jrl. Amer. Folkl.* 11.280 **CA**, *Cupressus Lawsoniana,* .. Port Orford cedar.   **1923** Abrams *Flora Pacific States* 1.74, *Chamaecyparis lawsoniana*.. As a lumber tree it is known as Port Orford Cedar, and as an ornamental, Lawson Cypress.   **1948** *Chicago Purchasor* Mar 23/2, Port Orford cedar is a white, or very pale, yellow wood, with a rather sour, cedar-like odor.   **1980** Little *Audubon Guide N. Amer. Trees W. Region* 304, Port-Orford-cedar is adapted to the humid climate of the Pacific Coast with its wet winters and frequent summer fog... Port Orford, Oregon.. [is] located in the center of the range.

portry See **poetry**

Portugee See **Portuguese**

Portugoose See **Portagoose**

Portuguese n, adj Also **esp sNEng, CA, HI** *Portagee, Porte(r)gee, Portug(u)ee, Portyg(h)ee* See Map at **A** below
Note: These forms illustrate two distinct phenomena: the use of [-t-] rather than std [-č-] (for which cf **creature, nature**) and the back-formation based on understanding the final [-z] as a plural marker (for which cf **Chinee** n[2], **maltee**). For the most part they seem to occur together, but see quot 1941 for some exceptions, and note that when a form like *Portugees* occurs as a plural noun, it is impossible to determine whether the final *-s* is intended as a plural marker or not. Cf **Porgy** n[2], **Port, Portagoose**

A Std sense, var forms.
1830 Cooper *Water-Witch* 2.197 **NY,** It being altogether unreasonable to suppose that a Portuguee should do what an Englishman had not yet thought of doing. **1860** *Atlantic Mth.* 6.735 **NEng,** Somehaow I caän't help mistrustin' them Portagee-lookin' fellahs. **1867** *Atlantic Mth.* Apr 434 **MA,** [A sailor boy:] Mother's a Portegee. . . [The mother:] I am a Portuguese, sir. **1899** Twain in *Century Illustr. Mag.* 59.78, Four sick sailors . . among them a "Portyghee." **1903** *DN* 2.300 **Cape Cod MA** (as of a1857), *Portergee. . .* Portuguese. **1910** Hart *Vigilante Girl* 327 **nCA,** They had driven out of the camp some "Portygees" who had dared to undertake working over the tailings as the Chinese were doing. **1911** *DN* 3.549 **NE,** New folk-etymological singulars are, in addition to the common *Maltee, Chinee, Portugee, shay, polonay,* etc., the more recent *corp,* and *appendic,* which are not infrequently heard. **1916** *DN* 4.267 **Cape Cod MA,** All the good pickers 've gone to west'ard 'n' the Portergees scalp so an' tear the vines so 't I guess I went astern on the Meadow Swamp. **1929** Wolfe *Look Homeward* 516, The gangs were of all races and conditions: Portugee niggers, ebony-black, faithful and childlike. **1930** *AmSp* 5.392 [Language of N Atl fishermen], *Portagee,* n. Portuguese. **1941** *LANE* Map 453, 1 inf, **seMA,** An Italian or Portuguese [pɔrrgiz]; 1 inf, **seMA,** *Dago,* Ital., Span. or [poˇətəgiz]; 1 inf, **ceMA,** A Portuguese [poˇətəgi]; 1 inf, **ceMA,** A Portuguese [pɔˇətʃəgɪi]. **1942** ME Univ. *Studies* 56.11 [Sea terms], Southern Europeans were Portygees or Dagos. **1946** Mora *Trail Dust* 161 **West,** He might be a Negro, or a "Portugee," or a Mexican, or a runaway sailor. **1965** *PADS* 43.17 **seMA,** Fish common in this area . . Portugee man-of-war [1 of 9 infs]. **1965–70** *DARE* (Qu. HH28, *Names and nicknames . . for people of foreign background: Portuguese*) 29 Infs, **chiefly sNEng, CA,** Portagee; **HI**1, [ˈpɑtɹgi]; **HI**6, [potəˈgi]; **HI**13, [ˈpɔtə.gi]; (Qu. H18, . . *Special kinds of bread*) Inf **CT**39, Portagee sweet bread; (Qu. DD27, . . *Nicknames . . for wine*) Inf **CA**168, Portagee red. **1968** McPhee *Pine Barrens* 64 **NJ,** I seen a Portugee scoop a half-barrel box in less than two minutes. **1969** *DARE* Tape **CA**168, We'd go to picnics. Like in Lafayette, Walnut Creek. . . Or these Portuguese [ˈpɔrtəgiz]— [Aux Inf:] Holy Ghost Sunday. [Inf:] Holy Ghost. **1969** *DARE* FW Addit **Honolulu HI,** They tell [ˈpourtə.gi] jokes here like they tell Polish jokes on the mainland. **1983** Beyle *How Talk Cape Cod* 10, When you refer to the Portuguese, who lend a nice flavor to the area's mix of folks, it is permissible to use the term "Portagees"—pronounced PORT-a-geese (singular = PORT-a-key).

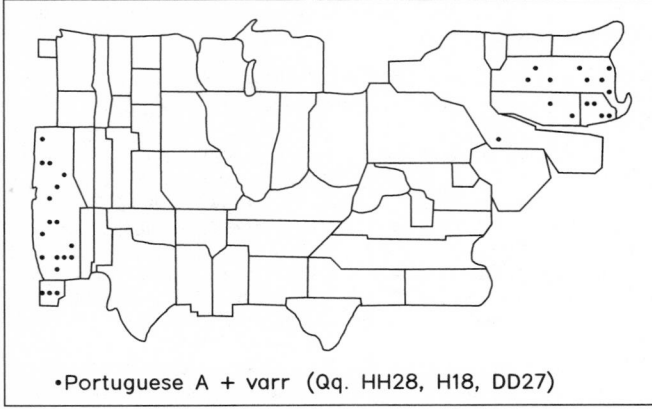

•Portuguese A + varr (Qq. HH28, H18, DD27)

B As noun.
A member of a mixed-race group living in Tennessee and North Carolina. Cf **Greek, Moor**

1945 Berry in *Amer. Jrl. Sociol.* 51.35, These outcastes [sic], whom I call "mestizos," are designated by a wide variety of names, none of them flattering. . . [T]hey are called "Greeks," "Portuguese," [etc]. **1963** Berry *Almost White* 27, North Carolina, besides its thousands of Lumbees, also has its "Portuguese," Smilings, the Laster Tribe, and Person County Indians. *Ibid* 36, Sometimes these outcasts are thought to be descendants of certain well known nationalities, and are named accordingly. For instance, we have . . the Greeks in South Carolina, and the Portuguese in Tennessee.

C As adj.
Used with derog force in var joc combs; see quots. Cf **Chinese fire drill 1, Mexican B1**
1924 *DN* 5.287 **Cape Cod MA,** A meeting where everyone is talking and no one is listening is commonly called a 'Portuguese Parliament'. **1938** Berger *Bowleg Bill* 156 **NEast,** It rose to a climax, it began dragging in personalities, parentage, ancestry, and finally threats of a fight. But they never do fight. From that point, the Portygee Parli'ment, if true to form, begins to subside, and finally gets down to yarning. **1960** *AmSp* 35.270 **cwCA,** A special type of depreciatory nomenclature has been applied to tools, mechanical devices, and work processes. . . Phrases in this category that I have heard in actual usage in San Francisco building construction and waterfront employment are: . . *Portugee lift, Portugee pump* [etc]. **1961** *AmSp* 36.272 **NW, West,** *Portagee chrome. . .* The aluminum paint used to cover spots on a truck's chrome when preparing it for resale. **1967** Stegner *Little Live Things* 249 **cwCA,** But Lucio had a Portygee gate in the fence above his pump house.

Portuguese bean n
A **broad bean 1** or similar bean; see quots.
1967 *DARE* (Qu. H36, *Kinds of soup*) Inf **HI**6, Portuguese bean soup—kidney beans, ham hocks; (Qu. I16, . . *Large flat beans*) Inf **CA**17, Portuguese beans—large flat ones eaten in the pod. **1981** *Pap Port.-Americans* 216, Favorite legumes include the broad beans which New Englanders sometimes call Portuguese beans. **1988** Whealy *Garden Seed Inventory* (2d ed) 71, *Portuguese* . . Lemstrom family heirloom . . excellent shell bean.

Portyg(h)ee See **Portuguese**

Porty Reek See **Portoreek**

pos See **post** n 1, 2b

posa See **pozo**

posada n [AmSpan < Span *posada* inn; cf quot 1978]
One of a series of pre-Christmas visits made to the homes of friends, in allusion to the Biblical story of Mary and Joseph's search for shelter in Bethlehem.
1967 *DARE* (Qu. FF9, *A Christmas gathering, at church or at someone's home, where there are songs and presents: "Are you going to the _____?"*) Inf **CA**4, Posada—Spanish custom; **TX**28, Posadas [pəˈsaðəs]. **1978** *Tucson Mag.* Dec. 105/1 *(OED2)* **AZ,** You may witness a real 'Las Posadas' celebration December 12 . . The candle-lighted procession of Carrillo School children will begin at the school . . and continue through one of the city's oldest neighborhoods, in emulation of the journey of Mary and Joseph seeking shelter. The 'inn' or posada for this evening's festivities will be the school itself, where refreshments will be served and a pinata will be broken.

poseetion See **position**

poses See **post** n 2b

posey See **posy**

posey-pot, posie-pot See **posy-pot**

posimon See **persimmon**

posina n [Pol *pierzyna*]
1973 Gawthrop *Dial. Calumet* 83 **nwIN,** The only foreign term which was written in by more than one informant was the Polish term, *posina,* which was listed by four [of 125] informants as their term for a bedcover filled with cotton. This term may be acquiring a loan-word status due to its use among several local church-affiliated women's groups who meet regularly and make quilts and comforters as money-raising projects. The Polish term would be associated with the hand-crafting of the article as well as with the ethnic church orientation.

position n Pronc-sp *poseetion* Cf Pronc Intro 3.I.5
Std sense, var form.

1936 *AmSp* 11.63 **seWV,** I have collected in a desultory way a few dialect peculiarities of south-eastern West Virginia. . . The pronunciation of
words like *condition, position, wish,* with the sound of *ee* in *feet*
(condeetion, poseetion, weesh).

Poski See **Polski**

poss v Also with *out* Pronc-sp *pawse* [Scots, nEngl, Ir dial
poss, pous] Cf **buck** v[3]
To agitate (clothes) in soapy water to clean them; hence n
pawser a device for agitating clothes in a washtub.

1898 (1899) Earle *Home Life* 234 **NEng,** In spite of all the bleaching
of the linen thread, it still was light brown in color, and it had to go
through at least twoscore other processes, of bucking, possing, rinsing,
drying, and bleaching on the grass. **1991** *DARE* File **MT,** I . . grew up
in Montana. My parents were second-generation Irish. . . A word that I
have been unable to trace is *pawser* with a sibilant s, referring to a device used to agitate laundry in a washtub. No one in this area [=IA] that
I know of ever heard of one. . . At the end of a short broomstick-like
handle, with about a seven inch short handle at an angle was a cone-
shaped galvanized metal *thing* with a fluted collar and interior shapings
that I suppose worked like a plunger. . . My mother also used pawse as a
verb, as in 'I'm going to pawse out a few things', without the device,
and perhaps in the bathroom sink.

possam See **possum** n **1**

posses See **post** n **2b**

possession v, hence n *possessioner* *?obs*
See quot.

1899 (1912) Green *VA Folk-Speech* 331, *Possession, v.* To chop line-
trees and renew landmarks. *Possessioner, n.* Possessioners are men appointed to go around and chop line-trees or otherwise mark between
people's landed property.

possession vine n
A **bindweed 1** (here: *Convolvulus arvensis*).

1942 *Torreya* 42.164 **TX,** *Convolvulus arvensis* . . Possession vine,
Texas Panhandle. **1970** Correll *Plants TX* 1246, *Convolvulus arvensis.* . . Bindweed, possession vine. Stems trailing or twining.

poss flower n [Du *paas-* Easter-] Cf **Easter flower 2, eating
poss, pass blummies**
A daffodil (*Narcissus* spp).

1957 *Sat. Eve. Post Letters* **neNJ,** Poss flowers, the old-fashioned,
early double daffodils with the fragrance. My mother . . , now 96 years
old . . , tells me that in her girlhood, these were always called Poss
flowers. They were very important as Easter flowers in those days since
there were few cultivated flowers.

possible n [Perh by ext from obs *possibles* equipment, personal
belongings (of a hunter or trapper)] *euphem*
See quots.

1985 *Amer. Jrl. Med.* Feb 183 **eTN,** *Possible* . . perineum—"I noticed
this cyst when I washed my possible." **1990** Cavender *Folk Med. Lexicon* 29 **sAppalachians,** *Possible*—the genitalia or perineum.

possimun See **persimmon**

possown(e) See **possum** n **1**

poss Sam See **poor Sam**

possum n

1 also *passonne, possam, possown(e):* =**opossum.**
1613 (1976) *Early Accts. Colonial VA* 41, The female Possown, which
will let forth her young out of her bellie. **1649** in 1838 Force *Tracts*
2.8.16, *Passonnes*—This beast hath a bagge under her belly into which
she takes her young ones, if at any time affrighted, and carries them
away. **1670** Clarke *True 4 Plantations* 14, Amongst the Beasts in *Virginia,* there are two kinds most strange. One of them is the Female
Possowne, which hath a bag under her belly, out of which she will let
forth her young ones, and take them in again at her pleasure. **1698**
(1848) Thomas *Hist. & Geog. Acct.* 14 **PA,** That strange Creature, the
Possam. **1709** (1967) Lawson *New Voyage* 125 **NC, SC,** The *Possum* is

found no where but in *America.* . . They are most like Rats of any thing.
I have, for Necessity in the Wilderness, eaten of them. Their Flesh is
very white, and well tasted, but their ugly Tails put me out of Conceit
with that Fare. **1893** Shands *MS Speech* 50, *'Possum* [pɑsm]. A common contraction of *opossum,* used by all classes. **1905** *DN* 3.16 **cCT,**
Possum. **1909** *DN* 3.359 **eAL, wGA,** *Possum.* . . Opossum. The full
form is never heard. **1960** Criswell *Resp. to PADS 20* **Ozarks,** Possum—only term for *opossum.* (In fact, who in H_____ ever called it
opossum, anyway.) **1965–70** *DARE* (Qu. P31, . . *Names or nicknames . . for . . opossum*) 756 Infs, widespread, Possum; [88 Infs,
scattered, Opossum]. **1967** *DARE* Tape **TX19,** Possum and other varmints—coyotes, they get a free ride there. **1986** Pederson *LAGS Concordance* **Gulf Region,** 399 infs, Possum(s); [24 infs, Opossum].

2 A **hognose snake** (here: *Heterodon platyrhinos*).
1938 Matschat *Suwannee R.* 28 **GA,** A harmless spreading adder, locally called the "possum," puts on such a ferocious appearance when
disturbed that the swampers firmly believe it to be poisonous. But call
possum's bluff, and it flops over and plays dead!

3 A Black person. Cf **coon** n[1] **2**
1900 *DN* 2.51 **New Orleans LA** [College words], *Possum.* . . A negro,
or negress. **1915** *DN* 4.235 **neOH,** *'Possum.* . . The negro errand boy in
the college office. **1966** *DARE* (Qu. HH28, *Names and nicknames . .
for people of foreign background: Negro*) Inf **GA3,** Possum.

4 in phr *possum in the woodpile:* =**nigger in the woodpile 1a.** Cf **DS** V1
1956 Moody *Home Ranch* 123 **CO** (as of 1911), "Wouldn't hurt none
to get the fences rode, but I reckon there's a possum in the woodpile."
Then he looked back at Hazel, and asked, "What you want a magpie
for?"

5 usu in combs, esp *Possum Hollow,* ~ *Trot:* Used as the
name or nickname for a remote or insignificant place, or a
poor or depressed part of a town. **chiefly Sth, S Midl** See
Map Cf **bend** n[1], **Dog Town, hollow** n[1] **B3, kingdom 1,
quarter** n **1**
1869 *Overland Mth.* 3.125 **TX,** We all have heard of some of our exquisite American names, such as Last Chance, . . Righteous Ridge . . , etc.;
but now read these from Texas: Lick Skillet, Buck Snort, . . Possum
Trot, Flat Heel, Frog Level. **1906** *DN* 3.151 **nwAR,** *Possum Flat, Possum Hollow . . , Possum Trot.* . . Facetious names of imaginary, or remote, insignificant places. **1935** *AmSp* 10.80, With its hills, hollows,
and swamps, southeast Missouri is well adapted to propagation of the
Podunk idea. The topography plays an important part in stimulating the
imagination. . . *'Possum Hollow* (pronounced 'holler,' [hɑlər]) enjoys
widespread use in the hill country. **1951** Johnson *Resp. to PADS 20* **DE**
(*Nicknames for nearby cities, villages, or districts*) Place: Possum Rd.
Its nickname: Possum Trot, Hog Wallow, Corner Ketch. **1954** Harder
Coll. **cwTN,** Place names: . . Possum Hollow, Swindle Creek. **1960**
Criswell *Resp. to PADS 20* **Ozarks,** *Possum trot.* . . I knew a town or
two called this locally. **1965–70** *DARE* (Qu. C34, *Nicknames for
nearby settlements, villages, or districts*) Inf **IL130,** Dog Town, Possum,
Bootjack—real names, not nick[names]; **KY88, NC32, NJ22, OH44,
PA205,** Possum Holler (*or* Hollow); **TN26,** Possum's Holler; **KY86,
NC34,** Possum Trot; **MS23,** Possum Bend; **KY37,** Possum Kingdom—
these are real names for real places, though very small; **IN30,** Possum
Ridge; **MS48,** Columbus was once Possum Town; **AR55,** Possum Val-
ley; (Qu. C35, *Nicknames for the different parts of your town or city*) Inf
NC83, Possum quarters; (Qu. II25, *Names or nicknames for the part of*

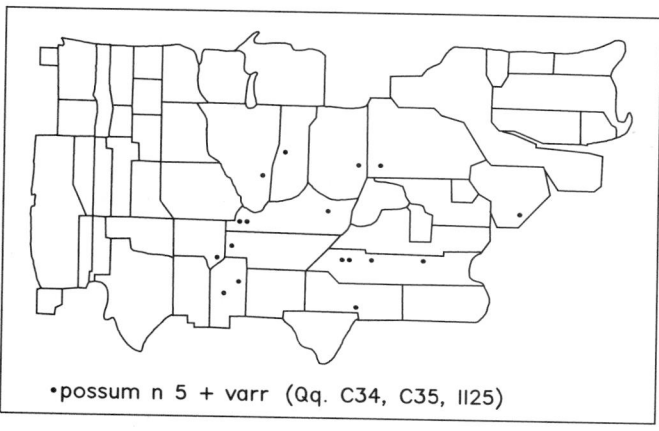

•possum n 5 + varr (Qq. C34, C35, II25)

a town where the poorer people, special groups, or foreign groups live) Inf **GA23**, Possum Hole; **NC36**, Possum Holler. **1970** Stewart *Amer. Place-Names* 384, The term 'trot' is here used in its chiefly southern sense of 'trail,' and the whole name indicates, or implies, a place so out-of-the-way that the opossums make established trails. *Possumtrot* is a common colloquial derogative for a small rural community, rarely occurring in 'official' use; but a *Possumtrot Branch* is an established name in GA. **1986** Pederson *LAGS Concordance*, 2 infs, **AR**, Possum Trot; 1 inf, **cnAR**, Possum Trot District; 2 infs, **ceTX**, Possum Walk; 1 inf, **cMS**, Possumneck—local community.

possum v

1 also with *it, out:* To feign death, illness, or sleep, act deceptively; to sulk; to feign (sleep). [From the opossum's habit of feigning death when threatened; cf std *play possum*] **Sth, S Midl**

1831 (1832) Flint *Hist. & Geog. Missip Valley* 1.67, In the common parlance of the country, any one, who counterfeits sickness . . is said to be 'possuming!' [*DARE* Ed: In the first ed of 1828 (titled *Condensed Geog.*) the word is spelled "oppossuming" (p. 102).] **1846** Levinge *Echoes from Backwoods* 2.32 **LA**, 'Possuming' is become an idiom; a term signifying any one who is humbugging or deceiving. **1853** (1854) Baldwin *Flush Times* 150 **AL**, All this time I was possuming sleep . . as innocent as a lamb. **1862** *Harper's New Mth. Mag.* 26.99 **TN**, So you see you must endure it to the end—fur thar's no possumin' thar. **1893** Shands *MS Speech* 50, 'Possum. . . This word is also used as a verb to signify *to feign* or *counterfeit.* **1899** (1912) Green *VA Folk-Speech* 331, *Possum. . .* To play possum; feign death; dissemble. **1909** *DN* 3.359 **eAL, wGA**, *Possum, v.i.* To deceive, pretend. "He's a-possumin." **1912** in 1965 TX Folkl. Soc. Pub. 4, Now when that nigger comes to, if she's been possumin', she sho' will be hungry. **1940** *Sat. Eve. Post* 6 Jan 32 **MS**, He closed his eyes and possumed sleep. **1942** Perry *Texas* 55, It may turn dark green and sick-looking but it'll just be possuming, because all the cotton that couldn't stand dry weather died a long time ago and left no seed. **1944** *PADS* 2.20 **sAppalachians**, *Possum. . .* To pout, sulk; from the sulking of the opossum. **1950** *PADS* 13.18 **cTX**, *Possum. . .* To sulk or play dead. Often also used as a noun: *playing 'possum.* **1966–70** *DARE* (Qu. BB27, *When somebody pretends to be sick . . he's* _____) Infs **LA28, TX103**, Possuming; **GA72**, Possum it; **NC40**, Possum out; (Qu. X43b, *If you sleep later than usual one day on purpose*) Inf **GA7**, Possuming. **1972** Hall *Sayings Old Smoky* 110 **eTN** (as of 1956), Ellis Ogle, Low Gap, Gatlinburg, said that when he was a young boy and was put to bed early, he could sometimes hear the older folks telling witch tales: "I lay there a-possumin' on 'em."

2 with *over:* See quot. Cf **coon** v **1, 2**

1949 *AmSp* 24.112 **seSC**, *Possum over. . .* To spring across (as over a fence) with the aid of a bent sapling.

possum apple n See **possum fruit**

possum baby n

See quot.

1991 Still *Wolfpen Notebooks* 62 **sAppalachians**, He had a bunch of children and the youngest was always his 'possum baby. *Ibid* 163, 'Possum baby: favorite.

possum belly n Also *possum box*

[In allusion to the abdominal pouch of the female opossum] Cf **cuna 2**

A compartment or sling under a vehicle; the position of a hobo riding underneath a railroad car; hence *possum belly (trailer)* a livestock trailer with an additional compartment below the main one.

1926 Maines & Grant *Wise-Crack Dict.* 12/1 (OED2), Possum belly—tent stake box carried under circus railroad cars. **1926** *AmSp* 1.652 [Hobo lingo], *Possum belly*—riding the deck of a passenger coach. [*Ibid* 651, *Deck*—underneath a passenger train.] **1929** Gordon *Born to Be* 114, In St. Louis I filled all my possum boxes with Red Lick-ker. **1931** *AmSp* 6.335 [Circus and carnival slang], *Possom-belly* [sic]. . . A compartment built underneath an animal-cage, slung between the front and rear axles, which is entered by a trap-door in the floor of the cage. **1932** *RR Mag.* Oct 369, *Possum belly*—Tool box under caboose. **1939** Rollins *Gone Haywire* 66 (DA), There was a sufficient supply of firewood in the 'cooney' or 'possum belly' (a baggy, dried cowhide fastened horizontally beneath the wagon box and used for carrying a reserve of fuel). **1940** Cottrell *Railroader* 134, *Possum belly*—A toolbox under the deck and accessible from the side of the caboose, also on some work cars such as bridge and building outfits and wrecking cars. **1947** Croy *Corn Country* 278, Sometimes he [=the pioneer] had to carry

his extra fuel . . by taking a cow hide and fastening it under his wagon to the running gears and to the hind axle. It sagged down into what he called his "possum belly." **1956** Ker *Vocab. W. TX* 194, Possum belly—cowhide for carrying firewood. [1 of 67 infs] **1969** *AmSp* 44.207 [Trucker jargon], *Possum belly*—Livestock trailer with a drop frame to haul small animals underneath heavy cattle. **1995** McCormack *Fields Pastures* 39 **cwAL** (as of 1960s), There was even a low-slung "possum belly" trailer, which had additional hauling space down between the front and rear tires.

possum berry n Cf **possum haw 1**

A **viburnum** (here: *Viburnum nudum*).

1894 *Jrl. Amer. Folkl.* 7.90 **MS**, *Viburnum nudum*, . . possum-berry, Ocean Springs, Miss.

possum box See **possum belly**

possum bush n Cf **tealeaf willow**

A **willow.**

1982 Slone *How We Talked* 106 **eKY** (as of c1950), Tea made from possum bush bark (pussy willow). **1984** Wilder *You All Spoken Here* 177 **Sth**, *Possum bush:* Pussy willow.

possum-ear n

A **hawkweed** (here: perh *Hieracium gronovii*).

1927 Boston Soc. Nat. Hist. *Proc.* 38.214 **Okefenokee GA**, [In a list of plants of the pine barrens:] *Hieracium (Gronovii?)* 'Possum-ear.'

possum-eyed adj

1968 *DARE* (Qu. X21b, *If the eyes are very sharp or piercing*) Inf **TN27**, Possum-eyed.

possum farmer n Cf **rock farm, rock rancher**

1995 Brophy *Coll.* 57 **swMO** (as of c1960), *Possum farmer.* [O]ne who lives on a farm but does no farming, only hunts and traps.

possum fruit n Also *possum apple, ~ persimmon, ~ plum*

[Because the fruit is eaten by opossums] Cf **possum wood 1**

=**persimmon B.**

1903 *DN* 2.325 **seMO**, *Possum-fruit. . .* Persimmons. A common wild fruit. (Facetious.) **1907** *DN* 3.235 **nwAR**, *Possum-fruit. . .* Persimmons. Also possum apples. "These frosts will ripen up the possum apples." **1936** Whitehouse *TX Flowers* 94, Mexican Persimmon (*Diospyros texana*) is also called 'possum plum, "chapote," and black persimmon. **1948** Hurston *Seraph* 16 **nwFL**, Possum persimmons spread their limbs among the rest. **1967** *DARE* FW Addit **cnLA**, Possum fruit—joking name for persimmons; **TX**, My father, from Gainesville, Texas, called them [=persimmons] "possum apples." **1968** *DARE* (Qu. I46, . . *Kinds of fruits that grow wild around here*) Inf **VA24**, Possum fruit—same as persimmons. **1981** Howell *Surv. Folklife* 64 **neTN, seKY**, *Diospyros virginiana*—Persimmon; possum apple—Fruit edible usually only after frost; Indians may have taught settlers to make persimmon bread. **1995** Brophy *Coll.* 57 **swMO** (as of c1960), *Possum apple.* [T]he persimmon.

possum grape n

1 Usu a **frost grape** (here: *Vitis vulpina*), but also other similar small wild **grapes** such as **catbird grape** or a **winter grape** (here: *Vitis cinerea* var *baileyana*). [See quot 1946] **chiefly S Midl** See Map

1926 *DN* 5.402 **Ozarks**, *Possum-grapes. . .* A small variety of wild grapes. **1946** *PADS* 6.24 **ceNC**, 'Possum grape. . . A bluish-purple berry about the size of a buckshot. It grows on vines in jungle-like areas and ripens after frost. Opossums are said to like it. (*Vitis cordifolia.*) Pamlico. Occasional. **1949** Webber *Backwoods Teacher* 103 **Ozarks**, Possum grapes which are mostly seed and hull and bitter to the taste but which give the finest juice when properly prepared. **1959** Lomax *Rainbow Sign* 89 **AL** [Black], I'd . . go up in a tree, get me a big, long bunch of grapes, those big ashy-lookin ones (call them "possum" grapes) that taste half sour and half sweet, and I'd eat um with salt. **1965–70** *DARE* (Qu. I46, . . *Kinds of fruits that grow wild around here*) 20 Infs, **chiefly S Midl**, Possum grape(s); **AR17**, Wild grapes, possum grapes—same; **KY37**, Two kinds of wild grapes—possum grapes—small blue ones; summer grapes—large sweet ones; **KY40**, Possum grape—little bitty ones, and sour; **OK27**, Possum grape—blue, small, sour; (Qu. I43) Inf **MO9**, Possum grapes; (Qu. I53, . . *Fruits grown around here . . special varieties*) Inf **GA72**, Fall grapes, possum grapes—same; good jam and jelly, grow wild. **1981** *High Coll.* **ceKY** (as of c1930), *Possum-grape. . .* (*Vitis cordifolia*) a type of small wild grape used in the Gorge for jelly (mixed with other fruit) and for wine. Informants distinguish between this grape and the *summer grape,* or *fall grape* as it is sometimes called, which is slightly larger and used in jellies and pies. Neither variety fully ripens or sweetens until after the first frost. *Ibid,* Now the *possum grape,* he's a rather small grape, but he's the juiciest thing you ever tasted nearly. Here's my mouth watering already! **1986** Pederson *LAGS Concordance* **inland Gulf Region,** 4 infs, Possum grape; 1 inf, Possum grape—grew wild here—small—ripens late; 1 inf, Possum grape—tiny wild berry used in wine; 1 inf, Mother made marmalade with possum grapes; 1 inf, Possum grapes—sour grapes. **1987** Childress *Out of the Ozarks* 30, The cedar tree is surrounded by black-walnut trees . . where possum-grape vines twist among the limbs like snakes. **2001** *DARE* File **ceOK,** The two Cherokee Indian informants from Tahlequah, Oklahoma, who told me about *possum grapes* also called them *winter grapes.* One of these informants—who was born in 1918—told me about *possum grape soup*—which is made with cornmeal and the juice of *possum grapes.*

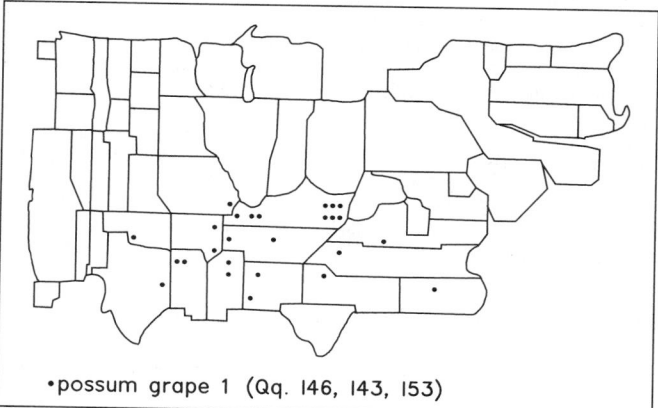

•possum grape 1 (Qq. I46, I43, I53)

2 A treebine of the genus *Cissus.* For other names of var spp see **elephant's trunk 3, ivy treebine, sorrel vine**

1933 Small *Manual SE Flora* 838, *Cissus* [spp] . . Possum-grape. **1942** Hylander *Plant Life* 370, Possum Grape or Marine Ivy *(Cissus)* has somewhat fleshy, simple or compound leaves; this vine is common on sandy shores from Florida to Texas and Kansas. The small black berries are not edible.

possum hair n Cf **frog hair 4**

1967 *DARE* (Qu. E20, *Soft rolls of dust that collect on the floor under beds or other furniture*) Inf **TX35,** Possum hair.

possum haw n

1 Either **dockmackie** or a similar **viburnum** (here: *Viburnum nudum*).

1860 Curtis *Cat. Plants NC* 90, Possum haw. . . The fruit is a deep blue. In the Mountains I have heard this called *Shawnee Haw.* **1927** Boston Soc. Nat. Hist. *Proc.* 38.377 **Okefenokee GA,** They [=deer] eat . . possum haws *[Viburnum nudum]*—nearly all the berries they can reach. **1960** Vines *Trees SW* 964, It [=*Viburnum acerifolium*] is also known under the vernacular names of Dockmackie, Arrowwood, Possum-haw [etc]. **1969** *DARE* FW Addit **GA51,** Possum haw—like a wild apple blossom—sweet.

2 A **holly** n[1] **1** (here: *Ilex decidua*). Also called **bearberry 6, meadow holly, swamp ~, turkeyberry, winterberry** Cf **possum holly**

1897 Sudworth *Arborescent Flora* 280 **FL,** *Ilex decidua.* . . Possum Haw. **1924** Deam *Shrubs IN* 177, *Ilex decidua* . . Possumhaw. . . This shrub is local, and found on the borders of sloughs, ponds, swamps and in low woods. **1942** Tehon *Fieldbook IL Shrubs* 162, Possumhaw—Swamp Holly. **1967** *DARE* (Qu. I44, *What kinds of berries grow wild around here?*) Inf **SC43,** Possum haws. [*DARE* Ed: This Inf may refer instead to **1** above.] **1986** Pederson *LAGS Concordance,* 2 infs, **swMS, ceGA,** Possum haw; 1 inf, **csMS,** Possum haws—little bushes. [*DARE* Ed: Some of these infs may refer instead to **1** above.]

Possum Hollow See **possum n 5**

possum holly n Cf **possum haw 2**

A **holly** n[1] **1** (here: *Ilex ambigua*).

1960 Vines *Trees SW* 654, *Ilex . . ambigua.* . . Vernacular names are Sand Holly and Possum Holly.

possum hunt v phr [Back-formation from vbl n phr *possum hunting;* cf Intro "Language Changes" III.3]

To hunt opossums.

1900 *Congressional Record* 11 Jan 33.1.784 **SC,** I used to 'possum hunt. **1905** *DN* 3.90 **nwAR,** Possum-hunt. . . To hunt opossums. 'We used to possum-hunt over yonder.' Common. **1938** Stuart *Dark Hills* 276 **eKY,** They had gathered the corn at home, got the wood, and possum-hunted at night.

possum in the woodpile See **possum n 4**

possum it See **possum v 1**

possum oak n

A **water oak** (here: *Quercus nigra*).

1884 Sargent *Forests of N. Amer.* 152, *Quercus aquatica.* . . Possum oak. . . Very common and reaching its greatest development along the large streams in the maritime pine belt of the eastern Gulf states. **1945** Wodehouse *Hayfever Plants* 79, 'Possum' oak . . is characteristic of high sandy borders of swamps and streams and rich bottom lands throughout the southeastern states from Delaware to Florida and westward to Missouri and eastern Texas. **1980** Little *Audubon Guide N. Amer. Trees E. Region* 401, "Possum Oak". . . A handsome, rapidly growing shade tree for moist soils in the Southeast.

possum out See **possum v 1**

possum over See **possum v 2**

possum persimmon See **possum fruit**

possum pie n S Midl

A **play-party** game; see quot 1936.

1906 *DN* 3.151 **nwAR,** Possum pie. . . A game. **1936** *Jrl. Amer. Folkl.* 49.205 [Ozark Mountain party games], In the old "Possum Pie" game the players all stand about in a circle and hold out their hands, while one boy or girl walks around singing: Possum pie is made of rye,/ The possum is the meat,/ It's rough enough an' tough enough,/ An' more than we can eat. At each word the singer touches a player's outstretched hand, then moves on to the next. The player whose fingers are tapped at the word "meat" must kiss the person whose fingers are touched at "eat," regardless of sex, age or inclination. **1939** FWP *Guide TN* 143, Related to the dance, and less subject to the disapproval of churchly folk, is the play-party. Though now less prevalent than in earlier times, when social diversions were fewer, it is still played to the singing of "Hog Drovers," "The Miller's Lot," "Slop the Hogs," and "Possum Pie," and like swinging games. **1998** *NADS Letters* **csMO** (as of 1947), Possum pie—I heard it mentioned as an "old-timey play party game" in Shannon County, Missouri. **2000** *Ibid* **cKS** (as of c1930), Possum pie—Mom remembers adults talking about this when she was very young. She doesn't know the exact game, but from the tone and conversation, she understood that it was rather risque for the time.

possum plum n

1 See **possum fruit.**

2 A **wild plum** (here: *Prunus minutiflora*).

1951 *PADS* 15.33 **TX,** *Prunus minutiflora* . . Dwarf, hog, or possum plum.

possum ray See **sea possum**

possum trot n

1 also *possum run:* =**dogtrot.**

1941 Johnston-Waterman *Early Architecture NC* 7, From Virginia came two log-house plans that seem to have originated there. These are called the Dog-Run (Breezeway, or Possum-Trot) and the Saddle-Bag houses. They are both based on the fact that logs cannot conveniently exceed twenty-four feet in length in house building. . . Therefore the structure of the house was divided into units not exceeding this size. **1975** McDonough *Garden Sass* 34 **AR,** More elaborate than these simple homes was the dog-trot style of house, which consisted of two separate log pens with a covered breezeway between them. This was also referred to as a possum trot, turkey run, wind-sweep, or But-and-Ben style. **1986** Pederson *LAGS Concordance,* 1 inf, **ceGA,** Possum trot—open area, entire length of house; 1 inf, **nwFL,** Possum run = dogtrot house.

2 See **possum n 5.**

possum wants a corner See **pussy wants a corner**

possum wood n

1 A **persimmon B** (here: *Diospyros virginiana*).   Cf **possum fruit**

1897 Sudworth *Arborescent Flora* 321 **FL,** Persimmon. . . Possumwood. **1950** Peattie *Nat. Hist. Trees* 535, Persimmon. . . Other Names: Possumwood. Date Plum. [*Ibid* 539, According to song and story, most 'possum hunts end at the foot of a 'simmon tree, and when Audubon came to paint his great picture of the opossums, he showed them devouring the strange, puckery-looking fruits, high in the branches of this grand old tree.] **1974** (1977) Coon *Useful Plants* 129, Persimmon . . possom [*sic*] wood.

2 A **silver bell 1** (here: *Halesia carolina*).   Cf **opossum wood**

1953 Greene–Blomquist *Flowers South* 95, Silver-Bell Trees, Bell-Trees (*Halesia*). . . The most common species is *H. carolina* which is variously called "Wild-Olive," "Possum-Wood," etc.

possy v

=**hosey.**

1956 *AmSp* 31.38 **MD,** Some of the many substitutes for *hosie* are in the dictionaries, but some are not. . . Of *aikies, evreese,* and *possy* (which I got from college students from New York City, Tennessee, and Maryland, respectively) . . I could find no trace.

post n

Std senses, var forms.   Cf **fist** n[1] **A, joist, nest A**

1 sg: usu |post|; also |pos|; pronc-sp *pos.*

1899 Chesnutt *Conjure Woman* 46 **csNC** [Black], Sent roun' fum [= from] pillar ter pos'. **1922** Gonzales *Black Border* 319 **sSC, GA coasts** [Gullah glossary], *Pos'—*(n. and v.) post, posts. **1991** Pederson *LAGS Social Matrix* 45 **Gulf Region,** [[pos] as the pronc of *post* (singular) was recorded from 140 infs. Of these, 49% were Black (as opposed to 22% of the whole sample). There is also a slight bias toward infs with less formal educ and toward those classified as belonging to the lower class.]

2 pl: usu |posts|; also:

a |'postəz, -ɪz|; pronc-spp *postes, postez, posties;* rarely double pl *postesses.* **chiefly Sth, S Midl** *old-fash* Cf **-es suff[1] 1a**

1867 Harris *Sut Lovingood Yarns* 129 **TN,** Lam'-postez tharfore am good things, when they keeps outen your way. **1903** *DN* 2.325 **seMO,** Posties. . . Pl. of post. **1906** *DN* 3.122 **sIN,** Postes. . . Regular pronunciation in two syllables of plural of *post.* **1909** *DN* 3.359 **eAL, wGA,** Postes. . . Plural of *post. Ibid* 402 **nwAR,** Postes ['postɪz]. . . A pronunciation of the plural for *post.* **1915** *DN* 4.187 **swVA,** Post. . . Dissyllabic *pl.,* postes, archaic. **1931** *AmSp* 7.94 **eKY,** Porch-postes, posts or pillars to support a porch. **c1937** in 1970 Yetman *Voices* 60 **GA** [Black], Our beds had big homemade posties. **1944** *PADS* 2.59 **cMO,** Postes ['postəz]: . . Posts. Saline Co. Fairly common. **1949** Webber *Backwoods Teacher* 217 **Ozarks,** We're makin' cedar posties. **c1960** [see **2c** below]. **1967** *DARE* FW Addit **ceTN,** Plural of *post* is ['postɪz]. Common among country people, Maryville TN; **wNC,** Pl. [poustɪz]. Common. **1986** [see **2c** below]. **1989** [see **2c** below]. **1991** Pederson *LAGS Social Matrix* 45 **Gulf Region,** [[postɪz] as the pl of *post* was recorded from 95 infs. Of these, 67% were Black (as opposed to 22% of the whole sample) and 95% were classified as belonging to the lower or lower-middle class (as opposed to 61% of the whole sample). There was also considerable bias toward older infs and those with less formal educ.] **2000** *DARE* File **seKY** (as of c1950), Postesses—(Posts) "Look at that line of fence postesses". Pronounced like Hostesses.

b |'posɪz, pos·|; pronc-spp *pos(s)es, pos.*

1912 Green *VA Folk-Speech* 331, Poses, n. pl. For *posts.* **1939** *LANE* Map 118 (*Posts*), The fieldworkers varied considerably in their transcription of the final consonant group in forms without [t]. On the map four types are distinguished: [-ss, -sˢ, -sᶻ, -s], of which the first represents three kinds of transcription found in the field records: [-ss, -s-s, -s·]. The type [-ss] may thus denote either a long fricative or a double fricative with two separate breath impulses; the latter is specifically indicated for . . [8 infs]. The types [-sˢ] and [-sᶻ, -sᶻ] probably both denote a long fricative with decreasing breath force. [The map shows that these forms without [t] are much commoner than the type [posts] throughout **NEng.** There are a few scattered instances of the type [post] in **sNEng.**] **c1960** [see **2c** below]. **1968** [see **2c** below]. **1976** Allen *LAUM* 3.313 **Upper MW** (as of c1950), Precisely one-third of the infs. retain the full cluster, 13% accept the step with the pronunciation [pos·t], and 60% offer the reduced plural [pos·]. **1986** [see **2c** below]. **1989** [see **2c** below].

1991 Pederson *LAGS Social Matrix* 45 **Gulf Region,** [[pos] as the plural of *post* was recorded from 245 infs. The social statistics of these infs do not appear to differ significantly from those of the whole sample.]

c |post|; pronc-sp *post.*

1939 [see **2b** above]. **c1960** *Wilson Coll.* **csKY,** Posts is still often /'postɪz/ or /posș/ or just /post/. **1968** *PADS* 50.33 **swTN** [Black], Informants who do not have a final /t/ in *post,* form the plural by lengthening the final /s/ of the base form, [pos·], /poss/ . . ; by adding /-ɪz/; or by adding the final /t/. . . [Two of 24 infs, types I and II] have the plural /poss/; . . [one type I inf] /posɪz/; [two type II infs] /post/. Five, four of whom are type I, add /-ɪz/ to the base form, /postɪz/. Two, . . [types I and III] who have the singular form /post/, have the plural form /poss/. For six, five type II and one type I, the plural form has the same shape as the singular, /post/. Five, four of whom are type III, have the plural /posts/. [*DARE* Ed: type I = infs with less than 8th-grade educ; type II = infs with hs educ; type III = infs with coll educ] **1976** [see **2b** above]. **1986** Montgomery–Bailey *Lang. Var. in South* 251 **neGA,** [A table shows the result of eliciting the plural of *post* from 29 infs of all classes. The results, in descending order of frequency, were: *post* (20 infs), *pos* (4 infs), *posses* (4 infs), *posts* (3 infs, 2 of whom used the unmarked *post* as well), and *postes* (1 inf). The two disyllabic forms were recorded only from Black infs.] **1989** Pederson *LAGS Tech. Index* 65 **Gulf Region,** [The most common plural forms of *post* are, in descending order of frequency, [post] (373 infs), [pos] (245 infs), ['postɪz] (95 infs), ['posts] (85 infs), and ['postɪz] (29 infs).] **1991** Pederson *LAGS Social Matrix* 45 **Gulf Region,** [[post] as the plural of *post* is recorded from 373 infs. The proportion of Black infs is about half that of the whole sample; in other respects the social statistics do not differ significantly from those of the whole sample.]

post v [A survival of *OED2* post v.[2] 5 "To make known, advertise . . by or as by posting a placard. . . *b. spec.* To expose to ignominy, obloquy, or ridicule by this means. Now *rare*"; 1642–1884] **chiefly ME**

Of a husband: to advertise that he will no longer accept responsibility for debts contracted by (his wife); hence nouns *post(ing) notice* an advertisement to this effect.

1749 in 1895 *Documents Colonial & Post-Revol. Hist. NJ* 12.518, Sarah . . eloped from her Husband's Bed and Board about ten Years ago, and thereon her said Husband posted her, forbidding all Persons to trust her on his Account. **1871** *Harper's New Mth. Mag.* 43.796 **RI,** My husband . . has thought proper to post me, and accuse me of having left his bed and board without cause. **1926** *DN* 5.388 **ME,** Post. . . Advertise. "Sam Jones has posted his wife," (meaning he has advertised that he will pay no more bills of her contracting because she has left his "bed and board.") Universal. **1929** *AmSp* 5.124 **ME,** A woman and man occasionally "parted" and she was "posted" by him, but in the old days, divorce was rare and it was said "he got a bill" or a "bill of divorce." **1966** *Ellsworth Amer.* (ME) 29 June 7/3, Post Notice—On and after this date June 15, I will pay no bills other than those contracted by myself. **1975** Gould *ME Lingo* 216, To *post* one's wife is to notify the public that you are no longer responsible for her debts, almost always a preliminary to a divorce. The *posting* notice in the weekly newspaper may not have too much legal standing, but at going rates Maine editors still print them.

post-and-bunk fence n

Prob =**bunk-and-toggle fence.**

1934 *Hanley Disks* **cME,** In the early days they used to have what they called a post-and-bunk fence.

post-and-rail fence n Also *post-and-railed fence, post-and-rail fencing, post and rail(s), post-and-railing (fence)* **chiefly NJ, Delmarva, WV, KY, OH, scattered NEng** See Map

A fence of horizontal rails mortised into, or otherwise fixed to, vertical posts.

[**1641** in 1857 New Haven (Colony) *Records* 54 **CT,** Fencing with . . strong and substantiall posts and rales . . nott above 18d.] **1684** in 1859 CT (Colony) *Pub. Rec.* 3.512, Great parte of my post and rayle fences being feched and burnt by the sowders. **1765** (1925) Washington *Diaries* 1.216 **VA,** Sowing . . 19 Bushls. in ye large cut within the Post and Rail fence. **1786** *Ibid* 3.30 **VA,** Post and rail fencing lately erected as yards for my stud horses. **1814** (1922) Tatum *Jrl.* 7.115 **NC,** The perpendicular Ditch is bordered with a post & railed fence. **1886** *Century Illustr. Mag.* 32.338 **NY,** It is impossible to come up at full speed and "fly" a high post-and-rails, in the way a hedge, brook, or low fence can be gone at. **1895** *DN* 1.373 **eTN**, *Post-an-railin'*: a kind of fence. "Won't you light an' hitch to the post-an-railin'?" **1912** Green *VA Folk-Speech* 331, *Post and railing*. . . A kind of fence made by setting posts in the ground and nailing six or eight planks to them; or fitting the planks in mortises. *Post* and *rail fence*. **1939** *LANE* Map 117 *(Rail fence)* 19 infs, **chiefly sNEng,** Post-and-rail [fence]. **c1960** *Wilson Coll.* **csKY,** *Post-and-rail fence*. . . A straight fence, with the rails laid or fastened to posts. **1965–70** *DARE* (Qu. L62, *A fence made of split logs*) 11 Infs, **esp NJ, MD, KY,** Post-and-rail (fence); **DE3,** Post-and-rail fence—had holes in the posts where the rails fitted; passing out of use; **MD32,** Post-and-rail fence—rails fit in holes in posts; straight instead of zigzag; **NJ20,** Post-and-rail—mortised; **PA169,** Post-and-rail—plant a post in ground with oval holes; split rails go in holes; **VA77,** Post-and-rail fence [same as] straight rail fence; **WV2,** Split-rail, post-and-rail fence—same thing; split-rail uses wire to fasten rail; **WV4,** Post-and-rail fence—two posts with rail held between them; **WV7,** Post-and-rail—post in ground, rails nailed to them; **[CO22,** Post rail—wired at top and bottom;] (Qu. L61, *Fences made of solid logs*) Inf **ME14,** Post-and-rail fence—drive posts in ground, bore holes through, set rails in holes; **NJ56,** Post-and-rail; (Qu. L64, *The kind of wooden fence that's built around a garden or near a house*) Infs **MA16, NJ20,** Post-and-rail (fence); (Qu. L65, . . *Kinds of fences*) Infs **CT29, NJ8,** 10, **OH31, VA68,** Post-and-rail (fence). **1983** *MJLF* 9.1.51 **ceKY** (as of 1956), *Post and railing fence* . . a wooden fence made by securing 2 or more rails horizontally between the posts. **1986** Pederson *LAGS Concordance (Rail fence)* 2 infs, **ceGA, csAL,** Post and rail; 1 inf, **swAL,** Post and rail—modern; 1 inf, **cnTN,** Post-and-railing fence.

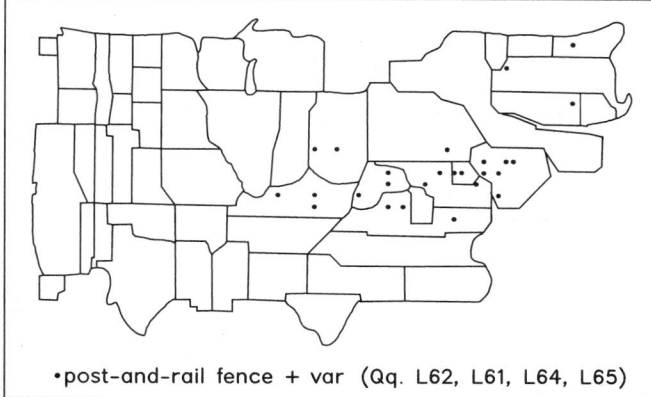

•post-and-rail fence + var (Qq. L62, L61, L64, L65)

post-and-rider (fence) n

Appar =**stake-and-rider fence.**

c1950 *Atlas Checklists* **WV,** *Post-and-rider*—fence made of wooden rails [1 inf, female, White, 26 years old, high school educ]. **1967–69** *DARE* (Qu. L61, *Fences made of solid logs, now or in the past*) Inf **PA13,** Post-and-rider fence; (Qu. L62, *A fence made of split logs*) Inf **KY58,** Double post-and-rider fence—a type of worm rail; post-and-rider fence.

post bar n Also *fence-post bar* Cf **posthole fence**

An iron bar used in digging postholes.

1969–70 *DARE* (Qu. L40, *A long iron bar used to move rocks and other heavy things*) Inf **NY216,** Fence-post bar; **NY233,** Post bar—large carrot-shaped end.

post cedar n [Because the wood is used for fence posts] Cf **post locust**

1 =**incense cedar.**

1884 Sargent *Forests of N. Amer.* 176, *Libocedrus decurrens*. . . Post Cedar. **1910** Jepson *Silva CA* 149, Incense Cedar . . shows exceeding durability in contact with soil and is, therefore, the favored timber for fence posts and rails in the Sierra settlements. . . By woodsmen it is variously called Red Cedar, White Cedar, Bastard Cedar, and Post Cedar.

2 A **white cedar** (here: *Chamaecyparis thyoides*).

1897 Sudworth *Arborescent Flora* 77 **DE,** *Chamaecyparis thyoides*. . . Post Cedar. **1950** Peattie *Nat. Hist. Trees* 71, Southern White Cedar. . . Other Names: Swamp or Post Cedar.

3 A **mountain cedar** (here: *Juniperus ashei*).

1970 Correll *Plants TX* 79, *Juniperus Ashei* . . Rock cedar, post cedar. . . In central and west Texas the wood of this species is the main

source of fence posts which are extremely durable when in contact with the soil. **1979** Little *Checklist U.S. Trees* 154, Mountain-cedar, rock-cedar, post-cedar.

post croaker n Cf **croaker** n[1] **1a(1)**

A **spot** (here: *Leiostomus xanthurus*).

1882 U.S. Natl. Museum *Proc.* 5.281 **TX,** *Liostomus* [sic] *xanthurus*. . . Chopa Blanca; Spot; Flat Croaker; Post Croaker. . . Very abundant along the coast. **1933** LA Dept. of Conserv. *Fishes* 180, The Spot or Post Croaker. . . A common fish of the Louisiana Gulf Coast.

post, deaf as a See **deaf** adj **B1b**

post driver n [See quot 1959]

A **bittern** (here: *Botaurus lentiginosus*).

1888 *Harper's New Mth. Mag.* 77.509, The call of the caribou . . is a hoarse, pumping sound, very much of the character emitted by that species of bittern called by some a "post driver" or "stake driver," only vastly louder. **1895** Ridgway *Ornith. IL* 2.138*, *American Bittern.* Popular synonyms. Stake-driver; Post-driver; Thunder-pump; Water-belcher [etc]. **1959** *Names* 7.119, Names suggested by the resemblance of the bittern "music" to resonant pounding include . . pile-driver (Ont., Fla.), post-driver (Mass., Ill.) **1969** *DARE* (Qu. Q8, *A water bird that makes a booming sound before rain and often stands with its beak pointed almost straight up*) Inf **MA68,** Bittern—also called post driver.

poster n

=**great northern bean.**

1954 *Harder Coll.* **cwTN,** Beans that are white when they dry; also known as *great northerners, navy beans, forty-fours, posters.*

postes(ses), postez See **post** n **2a**

post fence n Cf **posthole fence**

A fence built with posts set in the ground, usu a **post-and-rail fence.**

1961 Folk *Word Atlas N. LA* 126, *Fence made of wooden rails*. . . [rare responses include] post fence. **1967** LeCompte *Word Atlas* 164 **seLA,** *Fence made of wooden rails*. . . post fence [1 of 21 infs]. **1967–68** *DARE* (Qu. L62, *A fence made of split logs*) Inf **CA105,** Post fence; **MD29,** Post fence—same as rail fence—rails inserted in post; **PA13,** Post fence [FW illustr: posts with two rails or boards between them]; (Qu. L65, . . *Kinds of fences*) Inf **PA158,** Post fence [FW illustr: posts with two mortises for rails]. **1973** Allen *LAUM* 1.193 (as of c1950), Post fence . . [1 inf, **ND**]. three-~ fence . . [1 inf, **IA**]. **1986** Pederson *LAGS Concordance (Rail fence)* 2 infs, **cAR, cTX,** Post fence; 1 inf, **cnAL,** Post fences—wire between posts.

posthole n

Fig: nothing, empty space; hence used as the name of a nonexistent item used as the basis of a practical joke.

1919 Kyne *Capt. Scraggs* 67 **CA,** How goes it with the owner o' the fast an' commodious steamer *Maggie?* Git that consignment o' post-holes aboard yet? **1942** *AmSp* 17.104 [Truck driver lingo], *Load of post holes.* Empty trailer. **1953** *NY Times* (NY) 23 Sept 33/4 [Racing terms], *Sack of Post-Holes*—Another mythical object new employes are sent to find. **1965–70** *DARE* (Qu. HH14, *Ways of teasing a beginner or inexperienced person—for example, by sending him for a 'left-handed monkey wrench': "Go get me _____."*) Infs **MD2, MA53, NC72, NY32,** 187, **WV1, WI27,** Posthole(s); **WI2,** Dozen postholes from Sears; **VA31,** Posthole seeds; **LA16,** Stack of postholes; **[NC72,** Hole where a post had been]. **1969** *AmSp* 44.205 [Truck drivers' jargon], *Haul postholes*—Drive an empty truck, pull an empty trailer.

post-hole v, hence vbl n *post-holing* Also with *it*

To walk in snow sinking deeply with each step.

1999 *Trail & Timberline On-Line* Winter (Internet) **CO,** The first couple snowstorms of winter . . blanket your favorite trails, making for some miserable "post-holing." **2000** *AK Mag.* July 71, Snow is a better friend to the wolf, allowing the light, big-footed canids to run full-out. . . while the heavy moose post-holes and plows laboriously. **2000** *Outside Bozeman* Nov–Dec (Internet) **swMT,** Five miles and as many hours later, we slowed to a snail's pace, post-holing it through waist-deep snow. **2001** *DARE* File **nwMA,** He didn't have snowshoes and he was having a tough time. I just sank in a few inches with my snowshoes, but he was post-holing.

posthole fence n
=**post-and-rail fence.**

  1965 Needham–Mussey *Country Things* 18 **VT**, A posthole fence was something fancy, for the barnyard or in front of the house. . . You set up a row of posts, each one with two or three holes going right through, and you slipped the ends of the rails into these holes.

post-hole it See **post-hole** v

posthole owl n
=**burrowing owl.**

  1967 *DARE* (Qu. Q2, . . *Kinds of owls*) Inf **OR**13, Posthole owl—little owl, lives in ground.

post-holing See **post-hole** v

posties See **post** n **2a**

posting notice See **post** v

post locust n [Because the wood is used for fence posts] Cf **post cedar, ~ oak**
  A **black locust** (here: *Robinia pseudoacacia*).

  1897 Sudworth *Arborescent Flora* 258 **MD**, *Robinia pseudacacia*. . . Post Locust. **1908** Britton *N. Amer. Trees* 555, It [=*Robinia pseudacacia*] is also called Black locust, . . Post locust [etc]. [*Ibid*, The wood is very hard, strong, close-grained. . . It is very durable, being one of the most lasting of woods in contact with the soil, a favorite for fence posts.] **1960** Vines *Trees SW* 566, Other vernacular names [of *Robinia pseudo-acacia*] are White Locust, . . Post Locust [etc]. . . The wood is highly resistant to decay. **1973** Stephens *Woody Plants* 322, Post locust. . . is fast growing but short-lived.

post notice See **post** v

post oak n [Because the wood is used for fence posts]
  1a Usu an **oak** (here: *Quercus stellata*) native to much of the eastern US from southern New England to Kansas and central Texas; also the similar *Quercus margarettiae*, *Q. similis*, or **overcup oak 1. chiefly Sth, S Midl, OK, TX** See Map For other names of *Q. stellata* see **bottom oak 2, box ~, brash ~, cross ~, iron ~ a, overcup ~ 3, rough ~, sand burr ~, turkey ~, white ~**; for other names of *Q. margarettiae* see **runner oak**; for other names of *Q. similis* see **yellow oak** Cf **swamp post oak** Note: *Quercus margarettiae* and *Q. similis* were formerly considered to be varr of *Q. stellata*.

  [**1764** Reuter *Wachau* 559 (*DA*), Post Oak.] **1775** (1962) Romans *Nat. Hist. FL* 18, *Quercus alba pumilis* [=*Q. margarettiae*]. Dwarf white oak, or post oak. **1812** Michaux *Histoire des Arbres* 2.36, Mais dans le Maryland et dans une grande partie de la Virginie, où elle est très-multipliée . . elle est désignée sous celui de *Box white oak* . . , et quelquefois encore de *Iron oak* . . , et de *Post oak*. . . Cette dernière dénomination est . . la seule en usage dans les deux Carolines, la Géorgie et l'État de Ténessée. [=But in Maryland and a large part of Virginia, where it [=*Quercus stellata*] is very numerous . . it is called *Box white oak* . . , and at times also *Iron oak* . . , and *Post oak*. . . This last name is . . the only one in use in the two Carolinas, Georgia and the state of Tennessee.] **1837** Darlington *Flora Cestrica* 533 **sePA**, Barren White-Oak. Post-Oak. . . The wood is very durable; and is much valued for posts, &c. **1860** Curtis *Cat. Plants NC* 32, Post Oak. (Q. obtusiloba [=*Q. stellata*]). **1908** Britton *N. Amer. Trees* 336, It [=*Quercus lyrata*] is also called Swamp overcup oak, Post oak, Swamp post oak [etc]. **1946** West–Arnold *Native Trees FL* 50, *Quercus stellata*. . . Post Oak. *Ibid* 51, *Quercus stellata margaretta*. . . Dwarf Post Oak. **1965–70** *DARE* (Qu. T10, . . *Kinds of oak trees*) 123 Infs, **chiefly Sth, S Midl, OK, TX**, Post oak; **GA**1, Post oak—good for making posts; **IL**96, There [are] probably about forty different kinds. We group in the three groups—black, post, white [oaks]; **LA**3, Post oak—I think that's really a white oak; **OK**25, Post oak—also called blackjack; **SC**3, Post oak—not a special kind, just any that posts are made from. **1967–70** *DARE* Tape **TX**47, Split posts out of post oak; **TX**49, I could look out and see two post oak trees; **TX**89, They have oak. Various kinds of oak: red oak, post oak, live oak. **1973** Stephens *Woody Plants* 126, The post oak is a common tree in parts of eastern Kansas. . . It is not an important lumber tree, but may be used for railroad ties, fence posts, ornamental rail fences, and fuel. **1986** Pederson *LAGS Concordance* **Gulf Region**, 85

infs, Post oak(s); 6 infs, Post oak trees. [*DARE* Ed: Some of these infs may refer instead to **2** below.]

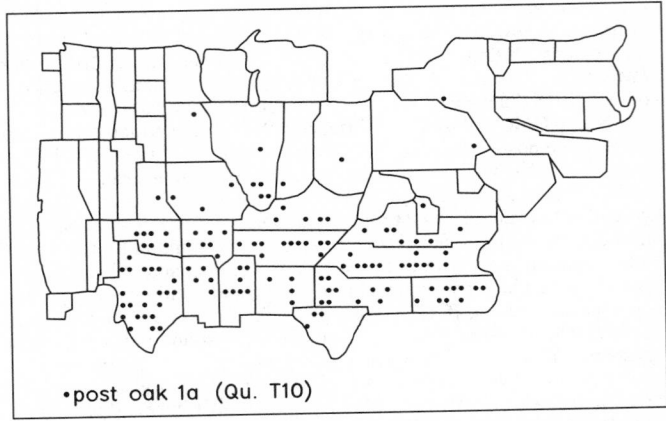

  •post oak 1a (Qu. T10)

  b attrib: Characterized by the growth of such oaks—used esp in reference to a particular type of usu heavy, whitish, infertile soil; hence adj *post-oaky*. Cf **crawfish clay, cross timbers**

  a1816 in 1848 GA Hist. Soc. *Coll.* 3.1.20, Between these rivers, there is some good post and black oak land. **1844** (1954) Gregg *Commerce* 356, Some of the uplands, however, known usually as 'post-oak flats,' like the marshy prairies, seem to be based upon quick-sand. The soil is of a dead unproductive character, and covered with small lumps or mounds of various sizes, and of irregular shapes. **1865** IL State Ag. Soc. *Trans. for 1861–64* 5.567, [Sugar cane] brought from the post-oak flats and red clay soil along the edge of the timber, has far excelled, in quality of sirup, that grown in the deep, black mold of the center of the prairie. **1882** *Econ. Geol. Illinois* 2.105 (*DAE*), We find some regular post-oak flats, with white soil and level surface. **1956** Ker *Vocab. W. TX* 81, *Land where scrubby oak grows*. . . post oak country [1 of 67 infs] . . post oak ground [1 inf] . . post oak land [2 infs] . . post oak thicket [1 inf]. **1970** *DARE* (Qu. C31, . . *Heavy, sticky soil*) Inf **TX**100, Post-oaky soil. **1975** McDonough *Garden Sass* 51 **AR**, "There's a mud they call 'post oak' mud. Now if you've got a field that's got that in it why that's the stickiest stuff—you go to plow through that and the mud'll just hang up on your plow like you're trying to plow through a bunch of toesacks. . ." (Mr. Simpson, who was from the same region, called this "crawfish clay" or "post oak flat," and said that this was a white clay.) **1986** Pederson *LAGS Concordance* **Gulf Region**, 1 inf, Post-oak mud; 1 inf, Post-oak flats—usually crawfishy land; 1 inf, Post-oak land—grows scrub oak—poor land; 1 inf, Post-oak land—red land; 1 inf, Post-oak land—in spots—white dirt—stands water; 1 inf, Post-oak land—cold-natured; stiff sand—packs down; 1 inf, Post-oak land—tight soil—sandy—post-oak trees; post-oak prairie—it's got white dirt in it.

  2 Esp **Oregon oak,** but also **blue oak 2** or a **live oak 2** (here: *Quercus wislizeni*). **Pacific**

  1897 Sudworth *Arborescent Flora* 153 **OR**, *Quercus garryana*. . . Pacific Post Oak. **1898** *Jrl. Amer. Folkl.* 11.279 **CA**, *Quercus Wislizeni* . . post oak, Monterey Co., Cal. **1910** Jepson *Silva CA* 213, In the North Coast Ranges it [=the Oregon Oak] is called Post Oak and is used in running barb-wire fences by the cattlemen, who find that it splits readily and is durable in contact with soil. *Ibid* 216, The wood [of the Blue Oak] has no value for constructive purposes, except for posts (whence "Post Oak"). **1961** Thomas *Flora Santa Cruz* 137 **cwCA**, Garry's, Oregon, or Post Oak. Rare in the Santa Cruz Mountains, usually occurring along the summits as individual trees. **1968** *DARE* (Qu. T10, . . *Kinds of oak trees*) Inf **CA**87, Post or white oak; **CA**97, Post.

post-oak flat(s) See **post oak 1b**

post-oak grape n [Because it grows on *post-oak land* (at **post oak 1b**)]
  Usu a **summer grape** (here: *Vitis aestivalis*), but also a **mustang grape.**

  1845 Page *Prairiedom* 83 **TX**, The post-oak grape . . grows abundantly on the high-lands bordering on the western rivers. **1891** Coulter *Botany W. TX* 62, *V*[*itis*] *aestivalis*. . . Abounding in the sandy post-oak woods of eastern Texas it is called "post-oak grape" or "sand-grape". **1938** Van Dersal *Native Woody Plants* 337, Post-oak [grape] (*Vitis lincecumii* [=*V. aestivalis* var *bicolor*]). **1961** McDavid *Coll.* **csOK**,

Post-oak grapes—mustangs. **1970** Correll *Plants TX* 1018, *Vitis Lincecumii* . . Post oak grape.

post-oak land, post-oaky See **post oak 1b**

post office n *joc, euphem* Cf **courthouse 2, federal building, office 2**

A toilet, esp one outdoors.

[**1942** Berrey–Van den Bark *Amer. Slang* 124.6, *Go to the toilet. . . mail a letter.*] **1950** *WELS* **WI** (*An outside toilet building; joking names*) 2 Infs, Post office; (*Names, joking or otherwise, for an indoor toilet*) 1 Inf, Post office. **1962** Atwood *Vocab. TX* 53, Outdoor toilet. . . a number of local, individualistic, and imaginative terms occur occasionally. [Footnote:] For example, . . *post office*. **1965–70** *DARE* (Qu. M21b, *Joking names for an outside toilet building*) 12 Infs, **scattered, but esp Missip-Ohio Valley**, Post office. **1986** Pederson *LAGS Concordance* **Gulf Region** (Outhouse) 1 inf, Post office—joking term children use; 1 inf, Post office—some people call it; 1 inf, Post office—joking name; catalogs there.

post office, there's a letter in the See **letter 2**

post rock n Also *stone-post rock* [Varr of *post-stone;* cf *OED2 post* sb.[1] 7.b, c]

A kind of limestone suitable for making fence posts.

1958 Muilenberg *Land of Post Rock* 3 **cnKS**, Whether you explore north-central Kansas by airway or by highway, you will know that you have reached "the land of the post rock"—or "Fencepost limestone country"—when you begin seeing miles and miles of stone fenceposts along roads and about the fields and pastures. **1967** *DARE* (Qu. C26, . . *Special kinds of stone or rock*) Inf **KS**4, They call Benton lime "stone-post rock," too. **1976** Wells *Barns U.S.A.* np **cKS**, The Barn is built of "post rock" which is the type of rock generally used as lintels above windows and doors.

post sled n Cf **frame sled, jumper 7c**

1943 *LANE* Map 573–74, A frame sled with post-supported seat and a device for steering: . . *post sled* [1 inf, **csVT**].

postur(e) See **pasture** n[1], v

posy n Also sp *posey*

1 A flower; a plant grown for its flowers; hence combs *posy-bed,* ~*-garden,* ~*-yard* a flower garden. **Nth, esp NEng** See also **posy-pot**

1842 Kirkland *Forest Life* 1.50 **MI**, He . . ploughed up every spring the rose-bushes and lilacs with which she had decorated her "posy-yard," saying that he could not tell one kind of *brush* from another. **1880** *Harper's New Mth. Mag.* 61.586 **NEng**, A "posy bed" by the south door made the yard gay and fragrant. **1882** *Century Illustr. Mag.* 23.766 **NEng**, I was weeding a flower bed. . . He . . called out sociably: "Good-mornin'! Working out in your posies, be ye?" **1887** *Harper's New Mth. Mag.* 75.306 **NEng**, I used to shet myself up here all day an' think I couldn't have no posy gard'n. **1887** (1895) Robinson *Uncle Lisha* 186 **wVT**, He went around to the front of the house, stepping carefully lest he should tread on Aunt Jerusha's posies, uncared for now and running wild. **1896** *DN* 1.437, *Posy* means a single flower in all American usage familiar to me. **1940–41** Cassidy *WI Atlas,* 1 inf, **cWI**, Posy-bed = flower bed. **1941** *LANE* Map 252 (*Pick flowers*) 8 infs, 5 **wMA**, Posies. [Commentary:] The term *posies* is regarded as older though still in use by [3 infs]. **1950** *WELS Suppl.* **ME**, Posy—used for flower. "That's a pretty posy." [Used by person] from Maine. **1982** *Barrick Coll.* **csPA**, *Posey*—flower.

2 in comb *posy-woman:* See quot.

1982 *Barrick Coll.* **csPA**, *Posey*-woman—Virgo, in the almanac.

3 See quot. [*OED2 posy* sb. I.1 "*Obs.* or *arch.*"]

1933 *AmSp* 8.1.51 **Ozarks**, *Posey.* . . This word means a flower, of course, but it also means the inscription, usually a couplet, engraved inside an old-fashioned wedding-ring.

posy bean n [See quot 1968]

See quots.

1887 (1895) Robinson *Uncle Lisha* 186 **wVT**, Posy beans and morning glories wandering away from the posts of the stoop to climb the tall pig-weeds. **1968** *DARE* (Qu. I20, . . *Kinds of beans*) Inf **NY**88, Posy beans—old-fashioned—called this because they have a pretty red blossom; broader than average, eaten as a string bean.

posy-bed (or -garden) See **posy 1**

posy-pot n Also sp *posie-pot, posey-*~ [**posy**]

1 also *posy-holder:* A vase.

1839 Kirkland *New Home* 135 **MI**, Our vase of flowers usually a broken-nosed pitcher, is a "posy-pot." **1891** *Scribner's Mag.* 10.347 **NEng**, Old blue and white "apothecary jars". . . form for us nowadays a fine "posy-holder." **1983** *MJLF* 9.1.51 **ceKY** (as of 1956), Posy pot . . a vase.

2 A flowerpot.

1913 Johnson *Highways St. Lawrence to VA* 33, It has a gay blossom that is quite attractive, and no doubt it escaped to the fields from some woman's posie pot. **1933** *AmSp* 8.1.51 **Ozarks**, Posey-pot. . . A flower pot, usually simply an old bucket or a discarded whiskey keg.

3 A bouquet. Cf **flowerpot 1**

1952 Brown *NC Folkl.* 1.578 **cnNC**, Posy-pot. . . A bouquet.—Guilford county.

posy-woman See **posy 2**

posy-yard See **posy 1**

pot n

1 A deep, metal container for boiling food or for other domestic purposes. **widespread, but more freq Sth, S Midl** See Map Cf **kettle B1**

1637 in 1850 CT (Colony) *Pub. Rec.* 1.12, If there be any . . kittles, pottes, tooles, or any thinges els that belonges to the commonwealth, . . they are to be delivered into the handes of the saide Constables. **c1738** (1929) Byrd *Histories* 190 **VA**, Several Deer came into our View as we marcht along, but none into the Pot. **1843** (1916) Hall *New Purchase* 145 **IN**, So she ons with the grate pot—that's old womin neighbour Ashford borrerd last year to bile sugar in—and she puts in her fat and begins a heatin it. **1889** Cooke *Steadfast* 13 **NEng**, On one side of the fire stood a bake-kettle and a four-legged pot. **1960** Criswell *Resp. to PADS 20* **Ozarks**, Pot, made of iron and usually placed next to the fire by taking off the stove cap. **1965–70** *DARE* (Qu. F4, . . *The deep metal container used to boil foods*) 440 Infs, **widespread, but more freq Sth, S Midl**, Pot; 32 Infs, **scattered**, Bean (*or* boiling, cook(ing), deep, dinner, etc) pot; (Qu. G14, *The rough metal pad that's used to scour pots and pans*) 58 Infs, **scattered, but more freq Sth, S Midl**, Pot cleaner (*or* scraper, scratcher, scrubber); **MN**34, Nylon mesh pot cleaner; **OR**4, Pot-scrub; **SC**70, Pot pad. **1966–67** *DARE* Tape **AL**1, We had . . these pots which she'd hang, sometimes two or three pots. . . They were black pots; **TN**16, We got a great big wash pot. Hold a big side of meat. **1971** Wood *Vocab. Change* 50 **Sth**, A large iron utensil used for boiling meat and potatoes is either a *pot* or *kettle,* the former having a preference that ranges from half to nearly all of the responses. **1973** Allen *LAUM* 1.200 (as of c1950), For a large metal vessel used outdoors for such purposes as rendering lard, cooking fodder, or making soap the common U[pper] M[idwest] term is *kettle.* . . Less frequent is *pot,* which does not occur at all in Nebraska. **1973** Gawthrop *Dial. Calumet* 70 **nwIN**, *Heavy iron vessel for boiling potatoes, etc.:* pot 75 [of 125 infs], kettle 47, pan 5, Dutch oven 2. **1989** Pederson *LAGS Tech. Index* 68 **Gulf Region,** *Kettle.* [265 infs gave the resp *pot,* 397 *washpot,* and 241 other compounds or collocations of *pot.* 355 infs gave the resp *kettle,* 57 *wash kettle,* and 108 other compounds or collocations of *kettle.*]

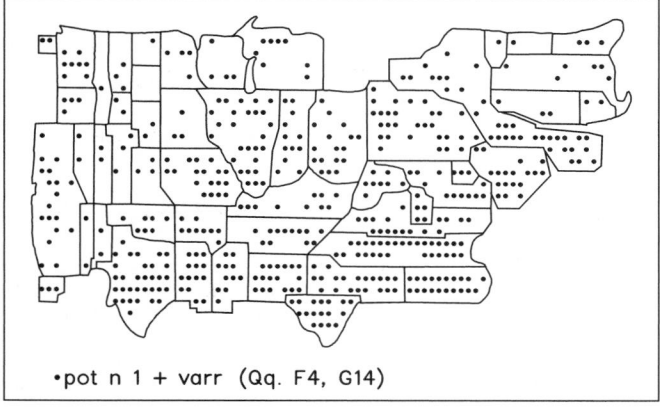

•**pot** n 1 + varr (Qq. F4, G14)

2 In distilling: a vessel of roughly cylindrical shape in which fermented mash is heated by direct action of fire; hence nouns *pot (still)* a distilling apparatus using such a vessel. **esp S Midl**   Cf **still-pot**

1935 *Sun* (Baltimore MD) 5 Feb 8/1 *(Hench Coll.)*, The production of corn whisky comes mainly from what is known as "pot stills," operated by small producers, . . and largely Southern states. **1942** Berrey–Van den Bark *Amer. Slang* 109.8, *Still. (The vessel or equipment used in distilling.)* Boiler, pot. **1947** Beebe *Mixed Train* 236, The Frankfort and Cincinnati is the whisky railroad of the world! Its lifeblood and being, its traffic and revenue, body and soul, are sour mash and potstill, bonded and blended, the wine of the grain, the spirit of the corn. **1950** *Sun* (Baltimore MD) 29 June 26/2 *(Hench Coll.)* **neMD,** Agents told of finding the 750 gallon still and a 500 gallon "pot" still on the farm of Dudley Everett. **1974** Dabney *Mountain Spirits* 126 **cnGA** (as of c1930), Now, on these copper pots, you can't help but scorch the whiskey ever once in a while. Don't make no difference how careful you are, because you've got to empty that mash in that hot pot. **1974** Maurer–Pearl *KY Moonshine* 30, A properly made pot still departs somewhat from the cylinder form in that it has its maximum diameter in the middle with a smaller diameter at each end. *Ibid* 121, *Pot*. . . (1) A pot still with all of its accessories. (2) Variant of *still-pot*. **1985** Wilkinson *Moonshine* 23 **neNC,** In North Carolina three kinds of stills are most often found: the pot, the submarine, and the steam plant. . . The pot is the simplest—an airtight kettle, with a cap on it, in which the mash is heated, and a coil running from the cap through a barrel of cool water as a condenser.

3 also *steam pot:* A steam engine or its boiler.   Cf **coffee-pot 1, kettle B3, teapot**

1932 *AmSp* 7.269 [Oil field language], *Pot*. . . A boiler. *Pot man*. . . The man who tends the boilers in which steam is generated for drilling. **1938** (1939) Holbrook *Holy Mackinaw* 263, *Pot*. A donkey engine. **1958** McCulloch *Woods Words* 138 **Pacific NW,** *Pot*—Usually said steam pot; any stationary steam engine, such as a loading donkey, a yarding donkey. Also applied at times to a locomotive. **1961** Labbe–Goe *Railroads* 259 **Pacific NW,** *Pot:* Or steam pot. A steam donkey. **1962** *AmSp* 37.134 **nwCA,** *Pot*. . . A locomotive. **1967** *DARE* Tape **TX19,** Some of the equipment used around a drilling rig—the boys all refer to the boilers as pots. . . They don't call them boilers. . . It furnishes steam power for a steam rig. Now nowadays you seldom . . ever see a steam rig anymore. **1969** Sorden *Lumberjack Lingo* 89 **NEng, Gt Lakes,** *Pot*—A donkey engine.

4 A toilet, esp an indoor one.   [Transf from *pot* chamber pot]

1942 Berrey–Van den Bark *Amer. Slang* 84.11, Toilet. . . pot. **1950** *WELS (An outside toilet building)* 1 Inf, **csWI,** Outhouse, john, biffy, can, privy, Chick Sales, shit house, used beverage department, outdoor plumbing, "the," Mrs. Jones, Mrs. Murphy, pot. **1966–69** *DARE* (Qu. F37, . . *An indoor toilet*) Infs **GA75, HI1, IN75, LA17,** Pot; (Qu. F37b, *Joking names; total Infs questioned, 75*) Inf **GA15,** Pot.

5 The last compartment in the diagram drawn for the game of hopscotch; pl: the game itself. [Scots, nEngl dial. It is unclear whether the game takes its name from the name of the compartment or from that of the marker used in the game; cf *EDD pot* sb.[1] 7 "The piece of broken crockery or flat stone used in the game of 'hop-scotch'," 8 "The last division or heading in the game of 'hop-scotch'"; *SND pot* n.[1] 4 "In the game of hopscotch . . : in pl., the names given to the seventh and eighth squares . . ; the game itself"] **NYC** *arch* Cf **potsy 1**

1883 Newell *Games & Songs* 188, Hop-Scotch. . . In Italy the three last divisions are the *Inferno, Purgatorio,* and *Paradiso.* In New York the last is called *Pot.* **1895** *Funk & Wagnalls Std. Dict.* 1390, *Pot*[1] n. . . pl. [*Funk & Wagnalls* Ed: Local, U.S.] (1) The game of hop-scotch. **1899** Champlin–Bostwick *Young Folks' Games* 414, *Hop scotch,* or *Pots.* . . Several forms of the figure are given below, B being the one commonly in use in New York, where the game is usually called Pots.

6 In marble play:

a A hole in the ground toward which marbles are thrown or rolled.   Cf **potty** n[2]

1950 *WELS Suppl.* **seWI,** Pot—small pit into which marbles must fall to win (no longer is a circle drawn). **1966** *DARE* Tape **MI19,** I think . . every grade has its own set of rules, because the little ones seem to make more pots than the big ones do. . . [FW:] How big would that hole be? [Inf:] I would say about an inch in diameter. . . just the depth of the marble. . . It wasn't a big pot. **c1970** Wiersma *Marbles Terms* **swMI** (as of

c1960), "*The pot*" . . a depression or hole dug by the turning of one's heel to make a round depression in sand or loose earth. Marbles were to be shot into this hole, the first player to do so winning all other marbles in play. *Ibid, Pot*—put a marble in the ground and try to roll the marble into the pot. *Ibid* **swMI** (as of 1960), *Pot* /pat/—The name of the hole which is dug in the ground to play a marble game similar to horseshoes. The players stand about 15 feet apart, facing each other, and take turns trying to throw a marble into the pot at the feet of his opponent. *Ibid, Pot*—a hole in the ground several inches deep and app. 4″ in diameter into which marbles are tossed in a game by the same name. **1973** Ferretti *Marble Book* 46, *Hole.* Also called pot. Holes in marbles games can vary in depth—from the size of a twelve-year-old's heel to something dug out with a garden spade. Shallow holes are called saucers.

b The ring in which marbles are placed or into which they are rolled; see also quot c1970.

1942 Berrey–Van den Bark *Amer. Slang* 665.1, Pot, ring, *the enclosed space . . in which marbles are placed at which the contestants shoot.* **1955** *PADS* 23.27 **cwTN,** *Pot:* . . The marble ring. **c1970** Wiersma *Marbles Terms* **neIL** (as of 1928), *Pot* /pat/. . . The pot is a large circle drawn on the pavement with a smaller square drawn in the middle. Everyone puts a small marble in the square and standing outside the circle tries to shoot the marbles out of the square but not out of the circle. In shooting, the large shooting marble must not remain within the boundaries of the square. *Ibid* **MN** (as of 1960), *Pot*—the circle into which the marbles are rolled. Noun. "Get it in the pot." *Ibid* **wMI** (as of 1924), *Pot*. . . One person sits down on the pavement and puts his legs in a V shape facing his opponents. . . This area formed by the legs is called the pot.

c also pl: Any of var marble games; see quots.   Cf **potty** n[2]

1895 *Funk & Wagnalls Std. Dict.* 1390, *Pot*[1], n. . . 13. pl. [*Funk & Wagnalls* Ed: Local, U.S.] . . A game played with marbles and three holes in the ground. **1934** *AmSp* 9.75 **csND,** *Pots.* A game, and the *baits* thereof, in which all the marbles are placed in a pot to which the contestants *lag*. **1950** *WELS* **WI** *(Different kinds of marble games)* 4 Infs, Pot; 1 Inf, Pot type, ring type; 1 Inf, Pot, peeny in the pot; 1 Inf, Pot—throw marbles at hole; nearest wins; 1 Inf, The pot—small hole in ground, shoot at one in it. The one who hits gets all marbles on ground; 1 Inf, Pot game—marbles are shot into holes dug at regular spaces; [1 Inf, **swWI,** Pot of gold—marbles in hole, try to put shooter in hole to claim whole group if accomplished]. **1961** Sackett–Koch *KS Folkl.* 222, *Pot.* A game played by several players. A hole is dug in the ground, and each player puts in from one to five marbles (the same number for each player). The players. . . shoot at the hole in turn until at least one of them has his shooter in the hole. If there is only one shooter in the hole, its owner wins all the marbles. **1965–70** *DARE* (Qu. EE7, . . *Kinds of marble games*) Inf **IA13,** Pot—dig a hole with heel and shoot them in; **IL9,** Pot—shooters have to try to get marbles in hole; first one to get in wins what's in the hole; **IL26,** Pot—whoever goes in the hole gets all the other marbles; **ME15,** Pot—shoot for a hole; **MN15,** Pot—a hole in the ground toward which you rolled the marbles; **MA1,** Pot—shoot/throw marble to decide who's first; **NY55,** Pot marbles—hit marbles out of pot, like pool; **CO42,** Pots—marbles in a hole, rolled or tossed marbles; if in, got all; [**OR10,** Five-pot poison; **ND3,** Jackpot—dig hole; whoever throws his marble in gets others; **PA22,** Shoot for pot]. **c1970** Wiersma *Marbles Terms, Pot.* . . Game in which players throw their marbles down and then try to shoot them in a hole which they've dug. If the second player shoots his in the hole after the first player, he wins the marbles. . . *Pots:* Game in which the objective is to shoot one's marble into the pot, or home base, and then capture the opponents' marbles by hitting them into the pot. *Ibid* **csCA,** *Pot.* . . A game in which the pot is used as the goal, the players starting from a throwing line. *Ibid* **swMI** (as of 1972), *Pot* . . a game in which the players shoot their marbles toward a hole or cavity in the ground. If they miss, they must put their marbles in the hole. Then the person who finally shoots his marble into the hole gets to keep all the marbles that were in it. **1975** Ferretti *Gt. Amer. Book Sidewalk Games* 154 **MN,** An intricate shooting-gambling game native to rural Minnesota utilizes the familiar heel-dug holes. It is called *Pots* and requires nine of them to be dug. Each player puts a number of marbles into the center pot. . . This becomes the Bank. Then, each shoots at the smaller holes, marked "win" or "lose." **1976** Knapp–Knapp *One Potato* 40, *Pots,* or the *Ring Game:* Each player puts the marbles he bets in the "pot," a circle drawn on the ground. The shooter keeps all the marbles he knocks from the circle.

d =**pottery** n[1]. [*EDD pot* sb.[1] 6 "A boy's marble composed of coarse clay"]   Cf **potty** n[1]

1966–69 *DARE* (Qu. EE6b, *Small marbles or marbles in general*) Inf

OH71, Pots; (Qu. EE6c, *Cheap marbles*) Infs **IN**23, **NE**11, **PA**11, Pots; **SC**54, Pots [FW sugg]; **NC**72, **NY**205, Pots [FW sugg; Inf doubtful]; **OK**42, Three or four chalkies equal one pot; two pots equal one flint.

7 in comb *great pot:* An important person. [Cf *OED2 pot* sb.¹ 9.d "A person of importance. (Usually *big pot*)"; 1880 →]

1912 *DN* 3.577 **wIN**, *Great pot.* . . A person of much importance. "He's in favor of it, and he's a great pot, too."

8 often in comb *old pot:* Used as a derog term for a person; see quots.

1937 (1959) Weidman *I Can Get It* 17 **NYC**, One of the pots that sat at the table on the platform was writing away with a pencil, her head bent down. **1942** Berrey–Van den Bark *Amer. Slang* 382.2, *A female, esp. a girl or young woman. (Many in disparagement.)* . . pot. *Ibid* 396, *Terms of disparagement.* . . pot. *Ibid* 439, *Woman of easy morals.* . . pot. **1950** WELS (*Uncomplimentary words and names with no definite meaning*) 1 Inf, **cwWI**, Old bag, pot, stinker, devil. **1951** Lewis *World So Wide* 152, Whatever the old pot may be, I'm sure he knows how to make it pay. **1968–70** DARE (Qu. AA6b, . . *A man who is fond of being with women and tries to attract their attention—if he's rude or not respectful*) Inf **PA**130, Pot; (Qu. GG38, *Somebody who is usually mean and bad tempered: "He's an awful _____."*) Inf **NY**223, Pot; **PA**234, Crab, old pot; (Qu. HH36, *A careless, slovenly woman: "She's just an old _____."*) Inf **WI**67, Pot—kids used to say; (Qu. HH40, *Uncomplimentary words for an old man*) Inf **MD**35, Old pot, fogy; **PA**234, Codger, old pot.

9 Used as the second element in var derog terms for a person. Note: The widespread and std term *crackpot* is not illustr here. [The earliest of these combs appears to be *stink-pot* (*OED2* 1854 →), transf from the earlier sense "earthen vessel filled with incendiary material for producing an offensive smoke." Similar metaphors are involved in combs like *piss-pot* and *smudge-pot*. The extension to combs like *fusspot* and *grouch-pot* was perh encouraged by the analogy of **box** n **5a** and the widespread *crackpot*.] Cf **box** n **5a, budget** n

1914 *DN* 4.150 [Navy slang], *Greasepot.* . . A cook. *Ibid* 164 **NW**, *Tallow pot.* . . The fireman of a locomotive. **1930** *Collier's* 1 Feb 12 **NYC**, All he sees . . is this rumpot ham [actor]. **1941** *AmSp* 16.70, *Drunken Person (or Habitual Drunkard)* . . rum-pot. **1944** *AmSp* 19.174 **MD**, In the Baltimore of my youth *pickaninny* was not used invidiously, but rather affectionately. So, indeed, was *tar-pot,* also signifying a Negro child. **1952** Mandel *Flee Angry* 30 **NYC**, Don't be an old fusspot or I'll pickle you. **1954** *Harder Coll.* **cwTN**, *Fusspot.* . . Someone who seems to be looking for reasons to be angry. **1957** *Holiday* March 156, How pitiful the American who cannot command the smile of a sexpot. **1965–70** DARE (Qu. GG14, . . *Someone who fusses or worries a lot*) 15 Infs, **esp CT, seNY, PA, scattered Midl**, Fusspot; **CT**3, **MA**58, Stewpot; **FL**14, Worry-pot; (Qu. HH11a, *Someone who is too particular or fussy—if it's a man*) 15 Infs, **chiefly CT, seNY, NJ**, (Old) fusspot; (Qu. HH11b, . . *If it's a woman*) 12 Infs, **chiefly CT, NY, NJ**, (Old) fusspot; **CA**136, Stewpot; (Qu. Y9, *Somebody who always follows along behind others: "His little brother is an awful _____."*) Inf **LA**25, Follow-pot; (Qu. AA7a, . . *A woman who is very fond of men and is always trying to know more—if she's nice about it*) Inf **NY**198, Sexpot; (Qu. AA7b, . . *If she's not respectable about it*) Infs **MN**34, **OH**44, Sexpot; (Qu. DD9a, . . *A person who smokes a great deal*) Inf **ID**5, Smoke-pot; **MN**8, Smudge-pot; (Qu. DD12, . . *A person who drinks steadily or a great deal*) Infs **NY**94, **TX**5, Rumpot; **MN**2, Sot-pot; **WY**42, Souse-pot; (Qu. GG38, *Somebody who is usually mean and bad tempered*) Inf **LA**17, Crank-pot; **PA**223, Piss-pot; (Qu. GG39, *Somebody who seems to be looking for reasons to be angry*) Inf **KY**40, Fusspot; **OH**45, Grouch-pot; (Qu. HH4, *Someone who has odd or peculiar ideas*) Inf **CA**202, Crank-pot; (Qu. HH5, *Someone . . queer but harmless*) Inf **MA**21, Crank-pot; (Qu. HH8, *A person who likes to brag*) Inf **GA**28, Brag-pot; **KY**75, Gas-pot; (Qu. HH9, *A very silly or light-headed person*) Inf **CA**158, Screw-pot; (Qu. HH12, *A person who is always finding fault about unimportant things*) Infs **CT**6, **KY**40, **NY**119, Fusspot; **CA**120, Pick-pot; (Qu. HH22a, *A mean or disagreeable person;* total Infs questioned, 75) Inf **OK**45, Crank-pot; (Qu. HH39, *A homosexual man*) Inf **OH**70, Sexpot; (Qu. HH40, *Uncomplimentary words for an old man*) Inf **MA**35, Stinkpot; (Qu. II36a, *Somebody who talks back or gives rude answers*) Infs **AK**5, **CA**169, **MN**15, Sass-pot.

10 in phr *put* (or *get*) *one's name in the (dinner) pot:* To expect someone to share a meal; to indicate that one expects to share a meal; *have one's name in the pot:* fig, to claim a share in some enterprise; *name in the pot:* a person expected to share a meal. **chiefly S Midl**

1883 (1971) Harris *Nights with Remus* 87 **GA** [Black], 'Ef you take'n rack off atter deze yer grapes, w'at Miss Meadows en de gals gwine do? I lay dey got yo' name in de pot. **1893** Owen *Voodoo Tales* 202 **SW** [Black], 'To put one's name in the dinner pot,' is a common form of the 'folk' for 'self-invited to a meal.' **1914** *DN* 4.111 **cKS**, *Put (one's) name in the pot.* . . To count on in planning a meal. **1923** *DN* 5.218 **swMO**, *Put one's name in the pot.* . . To provide a meal for an extra person. "Don't fergit t' put my name in the pot fer I'll shore be over fer dinner." **1927** *AmSp* 2.355 **cwWV**, *Get your name in the pot* (verb phrase), to come in before meal time. "You are just in time to get your name in the pot." **1939** *AmSp* 14.265 **IN**, To 'get one's name in the pot' means to let the hostess know in advance of his coming so that she may have plenty of food prepared. **1939** FWP *Guide NC* 95, Where the pattern of eating and sleeping is fairly elastic, no one bothers much over one more "name in the pot" or one more sleeper in a bedroom. The poorest backwoods housewife will offer the best she has. **1946** *Atlanta Jrnl. Mag.* 3 March 9/2 (DA), When one wants to be counted in on a deal he has his name in the pot. **1976** Garber *Mountain-ese* 72 **sAppalachians**, If you aim to eat wit us you've got to put your name in the pot early. **1977** DARE File, A friend of mine born in northern Kentucky uses the expression *Shall I put your name in the dinner pot?* It means *Would you like to share potluck with me?* It is said to someone who happens to be "on the premises" when dinner time approaches. **1998** DARE File **cnIN**, I hope you can come to supper, your name is in the pot.

11 in phr *put the big pot in the little one* and varr: To make emergency preparations to feed unexpected guests; to prepare a lavish meal, esp for guests; hence fig, to do something thoroughly; to enjoy oneself thoroughly. **chiefly Sth, S Midl**

1892 Smith *Farm & Fireside* 81 **GA**, Then the big pot ought to be put in the little pot, and everybody rejoice. **1892** *Jrl. Amer. Folkl.* 5.116 **NC**, "You'll find the latchstring on the outside," and "We'll put on the big pot and the little one," are forms of welcome or friendly invitation. **1893** *Outing* 23.473 [Black], She announced her intention of putting 'de big pot in de little one—dish-rag and all,' which means great things. **1909** *DN* 3.361 **eAL, wGA**, *Put the big pot in the little one (and make soup out of the legs).* . . To cook a big meal, prepare for visitors, try to surpass oneself in such preparation. **1927** *AmSp* 2.362 **WV**, *Put on the big pot and the little one* . . to prepare to cook for a large number of people. "We will have to put on the bit [sic] pot and the little one, for there will be a lot of raftsmen here to-night." **1941** Street *In Father's House* 26 **MS**, "Yes, sir, it's mighty good food," Woody said. "You sure put the big pot in the little pot, Mrs. Abernathy." **1942** *AmSp* 17.172 **sIL**, When company arrives, perhaps unexpectedly, the common remark is, 'We'll put the big pot in the little one!' **1942** Perry *Texas* 138 **eTX**, For an honored guest we "put the big pot in the little one, fry the skillet and throw the handle away." **1946** *PADS* 6.41 **swVA**, We'll put the little pot in the big pot and stew the dishrag. (We'll do our best to provide a meal for unexpected company). **1953** Randolph–Wilson *Down in Holler* 275 **Ozarks**, *Put the big pot in the little one.* . . To provide extraordinary hospitality, to feed a guest unusually well. "The preacher's a-comin', Maw! Kill the old rooster, an' put the big pot in the little-un!" **1959** *Hench Coll.* **DC**, Put the big pot in the little pot—Today Bob Kellogg was talking about this proverb. It means, to him, "to do things up brown," "really to do the best performance possible," etc. He grew up in Washington, D.C. *Ibid* **VA**, Clearly the luncheon was to be quite fancy, in keeping with the supposed high standing of the main guests. "Virginia is certainly putting the big pot in the little pot for this lunch." **1967** DARE (Qu. FF17, . . *A very good or enjoyable time: "We all had a _____ last night."*) Inf **TX**35, We put the big pot in the little one; (Qu. FF18, *Joking words . . about a noisy or boisterous celebration or party: "They certainly _____ last night."*) Inf **TX**18, Put the big pot in the little one. **1970** DARE FW Addit **sCA**, *Put on the big pot and the little*—meaning put on extra food for guests. **1985** DARE File **eTN**, Put on the big pot 'n the little 'un: . . go all out for an important guest. **1992** Mieder *Dict. Amer. Proverbs* 476, Put the big pot in the little one, kill a pumpkin, and churn. *Vars.:* (*a*) Put the big pot in the little one. (*b*) Put the big pot in the little one and make hash out of the skillet. (*c*) Put the big pot in the little one and make soup out of the legs. (*d*) Put the big pot in the little one and make soup out of the lid. (*e*) We'll put the big pot in the little one and fry the skillet. **1997** DARE File, In my family, to "put the big pot in the little one" means to cook an exceptionally good meal. I grew up in western Virginia, and this expression served as a compliment to someone whose dinner you thoroughly enjoyed.

12 in var phrr: Hell. *euphem*

1968–70 *DARE* (Qu. NN25a, *Weakened substitutes for 'damn'* . . : "_____ it all!") Inf **CT22**, To pot with; (Qu. NN26a, *Weakened substitutes for 'hell'*: "Oh _____!") Inf **CT22**, To pot with it; (Qu. NN26b, . . "*Go to _____!*") Infs **MO30, NY109, TX81, VT12, WI77**, Pot; **CT22**, Pot with it.

13 A person's head. [Cf std *crackpot*]

1967 *DARE* (Qu. X28, *Joking words . . for a person's head*) Inf **MI42**, Pot—occasionally.

14 A predicament, bad situation. Cf **jackpot 1**

1968 *DARE* Tape **CA100**, Two mills right above there—they're in the same pot—a couple years and they're closed.

15 See quot.

1966 *DARE* (Qu. V11, . . *Joking names . . for a county or city jail*) Inf **GA9**, Pot.

pot v See **put** v B2, 3

pot apple pie n Cf **apple pot-pie**

An apple **potpie 2**.

1941 *LANE* Map 292 *(Apple dumpling)* 3 infs, **CT**, Pot apple pie.

potash kettle n [In ref to the large kettles formerly used in concentrating potash]

See quots.

1859 (1968) Bartlett *Americanisms* 335, *Potash Kettles.* A term applied in the West to roundish elevations and depressions in the earth near the great lakes. They are attributed to the decay and washing away of the soft and easily decomposed limestone by which the ridges where they are found are probably underlaid. **1889** *Century Dict.* 3278, The district where the term [=*kettle-moraine*] was first used is southeastern Wisconsin. It was locally known as the *potash kettle country.* **1917** *DN* 4.398 neOH, *Potash kittle.* . . A depression in the earth with no outlet, resembling a kettle in shape. I have often heard my grandfather call these *potash kittles.* Is this known elsewhere? It is an interesting hint as to the importance of the potash industry in the early days of the W[estern] R[eserve].

potato n Usu |pə'teto|; for varr see **A** below

A Forms.

1 |pə'tetə(r), pɚ'tetɚ| and varr; pronc-spp *patata, patet(t)a, petator, petatur, pertater, pertetter, potater, puhtettuh.* Cf Pronc Intro 3.I.12.d

1800 in 1956 Eliason *Tarheel Talk* 316 cnNC, *Potato*—petators. **1839** [see **potato pone**]. **1843** (1916) Hall *New Purchase* 155 **IN**, We had "smashed petaturs!" **c1846** in 1981 *AmSp* 56.155 swIL, George made sweet *pertater* hills today. **1891** *DN* 1.164 cNY, [pɚ'tetɚz] < *potatoes.* **1891** (1967) Freeman *New Engl. Nun* 221, Then his hay crop had failed, an' his pertaters had all rotted. **1895** Brown *Meadow-Grass* 135 **NEng**, When you bile potaters, don't you let 'em run over onto the stove. **1922** Gonzales *Black Border* 320 sSC, GA coasts [Gullah glossary], *Puhtettuh*—potato, potatoes—usually sweet. **1928** *AmSp* 3.403 **Ozarks** (as of 1916–27), The final *o* in *potato* always becomes *er,* so that the word sounds like *potater,* and not infrequently the first *o* is modified in the same way, so that the form *pertater* is often heard. **1933** *AmSp* 8.2.44 neNY, [ə] often occurs in place of a clear vowel in such words as *potato* [pətetə]. *Ibid* 45, The [t] in . . *potatoes* may occasionally be heard as [d]. . . [pədedəz] (also popularly [tetrz]). **1936** *AmSp* 11.161 eTX, In addition to the usual sound of [ə] in the final syllable, some of the words listed above . . have [ɚ] in less literate speech. . . *potato.* **1938** Rawlings *Yearling* 190 nFL, Bear cracklin's and sweet pertaters rests so easy on her gums. **1941** *LANE* Map 266 *(Tomatoes, potatoes),* [The most common proncs of *potato* recorded belong to the std type [p(ə)teto, p(ə)teto]. Almost as common are those of the type [p(ə)tetə, p(ə)tetə]. Variants in which both *t*'s are voiced (or flapped) occur rarely, as do proncs with initial [b] (mostly of the type [bətetə], but also one instance of [bətejtow]); final [-ɚ] is recorded only once. Proncs in which the initial syllable is entirely lost are not common; most of these belong to the type [tetə, tetə], but there are single instances of [tetr, tetr, tɛtə, tɛta] and [tetɔ].] **1942** Hall *Smoky Mt. Speech* 80 wNC, eTN, *Potato* . . and *tomato* display little evidence of correction to [o], though they are heard fairly often with [ə] in the last syllable. They continue to flourish as [pə'teɪtə], ['teɪtə], etc. An informant of Waldens Creek (Sevier Co., Tenn.) reports that some of the less schooled families of his section say ['teɪtiz] and ['meɪtiz] . . , but these forms . . were unknown to the writer's informants in other areas. **c1960** *Wilson Coll.* csKY, *Potato*— /pə'tetɚ/ often; /'tetɚ/ is usually for fun. **1960** Criswell *Resp. to PADS*

20 Ozarks, The term is rapidly disappearing, but *pertaters* is still very common, and it is probably as old as *taters.* **1965–70** *DARE* (Qu. I9, *Other names . . for potatoes*) Infs **AR47, LA6**, Sweet potatoes ['swipə,teɪtəz]; **AR56**, Irish potatoes [ɔɚš pə'tetɚ]; **NY9**, [,pə'dedoz]; **SC39**, [azɚš pə'tetə]; **SC46**, [aɚš pə'teɪtə]; **SC57**, [aɚš pə'teɪtə]; **WV13**, [pəteɪdɚz]; (Qu. A21) Inf **KY28**, Hold your potater; (Qu. GG23b, . . "*Hold _____!*") Inf **VA15**, Your potaters; (Qu. LL22) Inf **VA15**, Small potaters. **1968** Moody *Horse* 166 nwKS (as of c1920), Suet renders out kind of yellowish, but if you only use one pound to three of hog fat, and simmer raw patata peelings in it a few minutes to clarify it, there can't scarcely anybody notice it. **1968** *DARE* Tape **GA25**, She rambled around until she found a kitchen and finally come back with a sweet potato [pə'tetə]; **MD28**, They'd make potato [pə'tetə] water; **NJ53**, I did send some in with tomatoes [tə'metəz] and sweet potatoes [pə'tetəz] and stuff like that. **1975** Gould *ME Lingo* 206, *Pertetter*—Potato, as nearly as type can approximate the Aroostook County pronunciation. **1979** Jordan *Yesterday in TX Hill Country* 46, Storing sweet potatoes, which we called *Patetas* because we had no German word for them, was a man's job. **1992** Martone *Townships* 170 cwIA, "Have you tried Edith's 'po-tay-toes' au gratin?" you may hear at an eastern Iowa church potluck, while western Iowans help themselves to more "po-tay-tuh" salad, or more often just grab a handful of " 'tater sheps."

2 |bə'teto, bə'tetə| and varr; pronc-spp *batado, batayda.*

1937 *AmSp* 12.107 eNE [Farm terms], Farmers . . commonly make use of such mispronunciations as . . *batadoes.* The potato is also called the *tater* or the *spud.* **1941** [see **A1** above]. **1982** *Barrick Coll.* csPA, *Potato*—pron. buh-tá-tuh. **1998** *DARE* File—Internet cePA [Language of the Hayna Valley], *Batayda*—potato.

3 |'tetə(r)|; also rarely |'teɪti| and varr; pronc-spp *tater, tato, tatur.* **widespread, but esp Sth, S Midl** See Map

1759 in 1882 Essex Inst. *Coll.* 19.65 **MA**, There we Dined upon codfish and taters. **1795** Dearborn *Columbian Grammar* 139, *List of Improprieties.* . . Taters for Potatoes. **1831** *Genesee Farmer* 1.50/3 **VA**, I once asked a Virginia skipper . . how they managed to keep them [= sweet potatoes] over the winter. "Why," said he, "I *reckon* it is the easiest thing in *natur,*—you must first dig a big hole in a bank, then *tote* your *taturs* in a cart and *dump* them in, [etc]." **1848** Lowell *Biglow* 146 'Upcountry' **MA**, Taters, *potatoes.* **1893** [see **A5** below]. **1899** (1912) Green *VA Folk-Speech* 439, *Tater.* . . A form of *potato.* **1902** *DN* 2.247 sIL, *Tater.* **1906** *DN* 3.123 sIN, *Tater.* . . Potato. The regular form. **1907** *DN* 3.227 nwAR, *Tater.* . . Potato. **1909** *DN* 3.380 eAL, wGA, *Tater.* . . Potato. . . *Tater* is a negroism used extensively among the illiterate whites. "Possum and taters is hard to beat." **1931** (1991) Hughes-Hurston *Mule Bone* 117 cFL [Black], You ain't had no taters for no pig to root up. **1933** [see **A1** above]. **1941** [see **A1** above]. **1942** [see **A1** above]. **1943** Writers' Program NC *Bundle of Troubles* 9, Each one of us picked out a row and started snaking along on our bellies, planting them tater eyes. **1950** *PADS* 14.66 SC, *Tater.* **c1960** [see **A1** above]. **1965–70** *DARE* (Qu. I9, . . *Names . . for potatoes*) 129 Infs, **widespread, but esp Sth, S Midl**, Taters [proncs of the types ['te(ɪ)tə(r)z], ['te(ɪ)də(r)z]]; 14 Infs, **chiefly Sth**, Taters [no proncs recorded]; **IL76, NY162**, ['tætərz]; **NH14**, ['teɪtoz]; **VA40**, Irish potatoes ['aəs 'tedəz]; (Qu. L34) Infs **KY34, NY62**, Taters; **NY230**, Tatoes; (Qu. S5) Inf **VA75**, Tato morning glory—leaf like a tato; [Further exx throughout

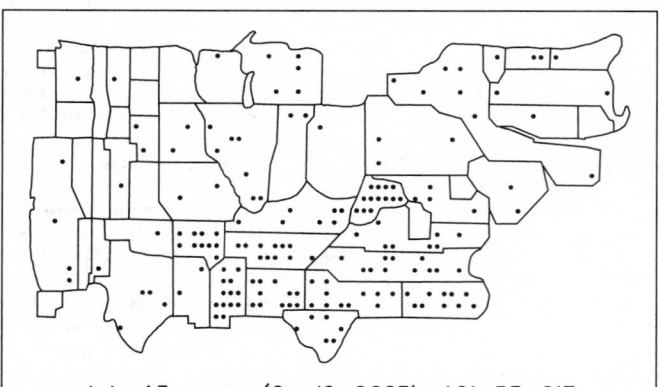

• *potato* A3 + varr (Qq. I9, GG23b, A21, B3, C17, C35, F23, H6, H17, H45, H47, I6, L34, M19, M22, N27b, R27, R30, S1, S5, V11, X9, X10b, X32, X55b, GG23c, JJ15b, KK42a)

DS; all exx are mapped.] **1981** *Smoky Mt. Traveler* Apr 13/2 **eTN**, There's also a full offering of specialty sandwiches, including tater chips and pickles.

4 |'tɛtə|; pronc-spp *tetter, tettuh.* **esp SC, GA** *esp Gullah*
1838 (1852) Gilman *S. Matron* 50 **SC**, Fayther says as how he wants Master Richard's horse to help tote some tetters to tother field. **1888** [see **B2** below]. **1922** Gonzales *Black Border* 333 **sSC, GA coasts** [Gullah glossary], *'Tettuh*—potato, potatoes—usually sweet. **1941** [see **A1** above]. **1950** *PADS* 14.67 **SC**, Tetter. . . Potato. Gullah.

5 pronc-sp *tate.*
1893 Shands *MS Speech* 62, *Taters* or *Tates.* . . The common names for *potatoes,* used by negroes and illiterate whites. **1967** *DARE* File **MI**, *'Tates,* meaning "potatoes."

B Senses.

1 Std: =**white potato.**

2 The edible tuberous root of the **sweet potato.** **chiefly Sth** *somewhat old-fash* Cf **Irish potato, white ~**
1610 in 1844 Force *Tracts* 3.1.13 **VA**, What should I speake of cucumbers, muske melons, pompions, potatoes . . which our gardens yeelded. **1753** Catesby *Nat. Hist. Carolina* 2.60, The *Virginian Potato.* . . The most Kinds, and best Potatoes, that I observed, were in *Virginia,* and because the Names, they are called by in different Colonies, are so various, I shall call them by those Names only by which they are known there. I have observed only five Kinds of Potatoes specifically different from one another, the *Common,* the *Bermudas,* the *Brimstone,* the *Carrot,* and the *Claret* Potatoes. **c1770** in 1833 Boucher *Glossary* l **MD**, The rogue escap'd, but all the *'moodies* I / For *Mollsey,* in my *'tatoe-hole,* put by. **1791** Bartram *Travels* 511 **SE**, Such a situation generally comprises a sufficient body of excellent land for planting Corn, Potatoes, Beans, Squash, Pumpkins, Citruls, Melons, &c. **1831** [see **A3** above]. **1859** Taliaferro *Fisher's R.* 257 **AL** (as of 1845), He . . handed me a plate of fried yam potatoes. "Take some 'taters, stranger." **1863** Porcher *Resources* 539 **Sth**, The Chinese yam *(Dioscorea batatas)* . . bears a large tuber, like the potato, and yields starch, sugar, etc. **1888** Jones *Negro Myths* 21 **GA coast**, One time de Bluefinch, . . de Pattridge, and de Sparruh all come inter cohoot ter plant tetter [Footnote: Sweet potatoes] and see who kin raise de bigges. **1909** *DN* 3.380 **eAL, wGA**, White potatoes are called *Irish potatoes;* sweet potatoes are usually called simply *potatoes.* **1922** [see **A1** above]. **c1960** *Wilson Coll.* **csKY**, *Potato pumpkin.* . . The kind that . . tastes, when cooked, very much like a sweet potato. *Ibid, Potato slip.* . . A sweet potato plant, drawn from a potato bed. **1965–70** *DARE* (Qu. H15, *Bread made with wheat flour*) Inf **SC26**, Potato bread—mash sweet potato in with the flour; (Qu. H18, . . *Special kinds of bread*) Inf **LA9**, Potato bread—[corn bread] with sweet potatoes; [22 Infs, **scattered**, Potato bread [type of potatoes not recorded];] (Qu. H19, . . *Biscuit*) Infs **NC8, 88, SC38, 56**, Potato biscuit(s)—[made with] sweet potato; **TN5**, Potato biscuits; **VA69**, Potato biscuit, sweet-potato biscuit—mash and add to dough; [**NC14, 84**, Sweet-potato biscuits;] (Qu. H48, *Baked dishes made of potatoes cut up with meat or cheese*) Inf **SC1**, Potato pudding if made with sweet potatoes; potato custard, made from any potatoes, [same as] potato pie except pie has a crust and custard doesn't; **GA10**, Potato pie; **FL31**, Candied potatoes—sweet potatoes; **SC46**, Possum and potatoes—sweet potatoes; (Qu. H63, *Kinds of desserts*) Infs **AL11, 60, FL1, LA9, MS79, 85, SC7, VA56**, Potato pie; [17 Infs, **chiefly Sth, Lower Missip Valley**, Sweet-potato pie; **VA39**, White-potato pie, sweet-potato pie;] (Qu. I9, *Other names . . for potatoes*) Inf **AL15**, Potatoes—really sweet potatoes, otherwise Irish potatoes; **AR55**, Taters—for sweet potatoes; **GA17**, Taters—sweet potato; **SC4**, Potato means yam here; the white kinds must be designated specifically; **SC9**, Yam = (sweet) potato. **c1965** *DARE* File, In Alabama and through most of the South there are potatoes and Irish potatoes; North there are potatoes and sweet potatoes. **1986** Pederson *LAGS Concordance* (Potatoes) 2 infs, **neAL, neGA**, (Po)tatoes—now means Irish potatoes, formerly sweet; 2 infs, **ceAR, neMS**, (Po)tatoes = sweet potatoes? 1 inf, **cnGA**, Potatoes—must be specified; 1 inf, **cwGA**, (Po)tatoes—to her, this means sweet potato; 1 inf, **csGA**, [O]possum and [po]tatoes; 1 inf, **cLA**, Potatoes—includes Irish and sweet; 1 inf, **cMS**, Bake potatoes of sweet potatoes; *(Sweet potatoes)* 7 infs, **AL, GA, MS, TN**, (Po)tatoes; 1 inf, **neTN**, They're all [po]tatoes—Irish, sweet, etc; [13 scattered infs gave var compounds of *potato* (e.g., *potato bank, potato bread*) in which *potato* is explicitly stated to refer to sweet potatoes]. **1996** *DARE* File, In the 1930's, of 39 speakers Guy Lowman interviewed for LAMSAS in GA, SC, and NC, only one used "potato" for what the majority (35) called "Irish (po)tatoes". Of the same speakers, 21 used "potatoes" or "taters" to refer presumably to sweet potatoes. . . My how quickly things

change. But there are still older speakers in rural areas who use the term "Irish potatoes" and who call the orange ones simply "potatoes", though if asked to clarify they specify them as "sweet potatoes". This is definitely the old-fashioned usage in the South.

3 in phr *hold one's potato* and varr: To be patient, wait, not be hasty. **chiefly Sth, S Midl** See Map Note: This phr was treated at **hold** v C1a (which see for further evidence), but part of the *DARE* QR evidence was inadvertently omitted; the full *DARE* quot is given below.
1965–70 *DARE* (Qu. GG23b, *If you speak sharply to somebody to make him be patient . . "Hold _____!"*) 10 Infs, **Sth, S Midl**, Your tater; **AL5, KY84, SC31, TX91**, Your potato; **GA89, TN26, TX5, VA15**, Your potatoes *(or* potaters); **AL58**, Your taters; [**LA17**, Your horses and fry your potatoes;] (Qu. GG23c, . . *Other expressions*) Infs **IL96, SC3**, Hold your tater; **NC41**, Hold your potato; **MS45**, Hold your potato till it gets cool; (Qu. A21, *When someone is in too much of a hurry*) Infs **KY28, NM11**, Hold your (po)tater.

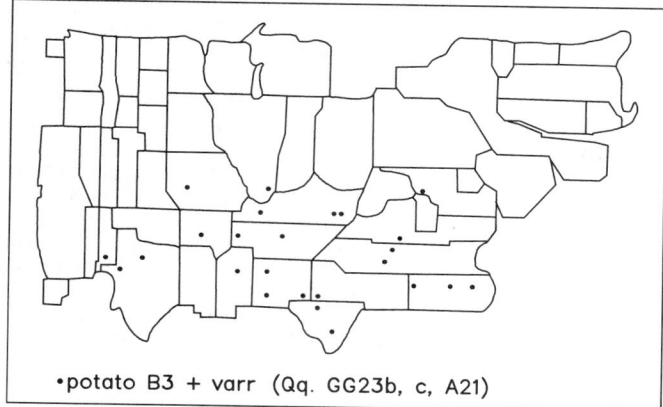

•potato B3 + varr (Qq. GG23b, c, A21)

4 A bump on the head. Cf **goose egg 1**
1969 *DARE* (Qu. X60, . . *A lump that comes up on your head when you get a sharp blow or knock;* not asked in early QRs) Inf **MA50**, Egg, potato.

potato bargain n eMA

An economical stew consisting chiefly of pork, onions, and potatoes.
1939 Wolcott *Yankee Cook Book* 110, "Necessity mess," "Potato bargain," or "Tilton's glory" [From a book of Vineyard recipes]. . . Slice the pork about ¼ inch thick. Peel and slice onions very thin. Place in the pot and fry briskly until very brown. Then put in the potatoes and fill the pot with water until it is about an inch above the potatoes. **1963** Haywood *Yankee Dict.* 124, *Potato bargain*—A dish well known to old Cape Codders. Fry out 3 slices of fat salt pork in an iron spider . . , add 7 potatoes . . , and 4 medium sized onions . . , salt and pepper to taste. Cover with water . . and cook until potatoes are done. **1978** *New Yorker* 6 Nov 129 **seMA**, Mrs. Coombs had testified about traditional Indian dishes such as Sheldrake stew, eel stifle, a stew called potato bargain, and cornmeal dumplings.

potato bean n Cf potato pea

A **groundnut B1** (here: *Apios americana*).
1940 Clute *Amer. Plant Names* 167, Potato-bean. *Apios tuberosa.* **1948** Stevens *KS Wild Flowers* 267, Potato Bean. . . The Indians, as well as the early settlers, found the cooked tubers palatable and nutritious. **1968** Barkley *Plants KS* 196, Groundnut. American Potato Bean. Thickets along streams. East half [of the state].

potato beer n Cf beer yeast

A fermenting mixture of boiled potatoes and other ingredients, used as leavening for bread.
1933 Sheffer *True Tales* 115 **nwPA** (as of 1898), A half gallon of "potato beer," which all of the old timers know is yeast for baking bread. **1983** *Barrick Coll.* **csPA**, Potato beer.

potato beetle n

1 A beetle of the genus *Leptinotarsa,* usu **Colorado potato beetle.** Cf **potato bug 2**
1868 *Amer. Naturalist* 3.129, The New Potato-beetle *(Doryphora* 10–

lineata), which is so destructive in the West, was long ago known at the base of the Rocky Mountains in Colorado. . . In 1864 it had crossed the Mississippi, and now it has covered half of the State of Illinois. **1874** U.S. Dept. Ag. *Rept. of Secy. for 1873* 153, The much-dreaded western potato-beetle . . made its appearance in the immediate neighborhood of Washington, D.C. **1882** (1903) Treat *Injurious Insects* 96, Prof. Riley was the first to make known the natural history and transformations of the Potato-beetle. **1954** Borror–DeLong *Intro. Insects* 407, The potato beetle, *Leptinotarsa decemlineata*. . . is a large yellow beetle striped with black . . , and is a very serious pest of potato plants over most of the country. **1965–70** *DARE* (Qu. R30, . . *Kinds of beetles;* not asked in early QRs) 25 Infs, **scattered,** Potato beetle; **ME12,** Potato beetle— striped; **ME20,** Potato beetle—like a ladybug; **MO2,** Two different kinds of potato beetles: one of them is hard-shelled; **PA79,** Potato beetle—yellow and black marks on his back, streaks; **NC67,** Tater beetle. [*DARE* Ed: Some of these Infs may refer instead to other senses below.]

2 A **blister bug** (here: *Epicauta* spp.).   Cf **old-fashioned potato beetle, potato bug 1, ~ fly**

1905 Kellogg *Amer. Insects* 293, The commonest Eastern species of blister-beetles belong to the genus Epicauta. They feed when adult on the leaves of potato—being therefore often called potato-beetles. **1967** *DARE* (Qu. R30, . . *Kinds of beetles;* not asked in early QRs) Inf **MO2,** Two different kinds of potato beetles . . they're called blister bugs, too.

3 The three-lined leaf beetle (*Lema trilineata*).   Also called **potato bug 3**

1911 *Century Dict. Suppl.,* Potato beetle. . . *Three-lined potato beetle,* an American chrysomelid beetle, *Lema trilineata,* yellow in color and with three black elytral stripes. It feeds on the leaves of the Irish potato. **1972** Swan–Papp *Insects* 459, *Three-lined Potato Beetle.* . . This is the familiar "old-fashioned potatobug." . . *Food:* Potato, other plants of the nightshade or potato family. **1980** Milne–Milne *Audubon Field Guide Insects* 609, *Three-lined Potato Beetle* . . (*Lema trilineata*). [*Ibid* 610, Voracious larvae gather in clusters on potato leaves, nibbling lacy holes and eventually consuming all but the midvein.]

potato bird n

1 =**lark sparrow.**

1889 Ridgway *Ornith. IL* 1.264, This [=the lark sparrow] is a rather rare summer resident. . . In St. Clair county I saw one pair; it is there called "potato bird"; people say that few survive the Paris green which they eat with the potato bugs.

2 See **potato-bug bird.**

potato bug n

1 =**blister bug.**   Cf **old-fashioned potato beetle, potato ~ 2, potato fly**

1799 in 1889 Drinker *Extracts Jrl.* 347 **sePA,** They call them [=a species of Cantharides] here . . the Potato-Bug, being numerous on the potato tops. Their backs are striped brown and yellow. **1838** *Hesperian* 1.42, This company, formed for the praiseworthy purpose of encouraging the growth of potato-bugs and manufacturing potato-bug oil. **1966– 69** *DARE* (Qu. R30, . . *Kinds of beetles;* not asked in early QRs) Inf **IL89,** Potato bugs—hard-shell and soft-shell; **MD3,** Potato bug—eats potato plants, smaller than Japanese [beetle] and larger than ladybug; grayish-green; **ME24,** Potato bug—has an odor; they fly; bright orange on parts of body; work on potatoes; **MI36,** Potato bugs—also a black potato bug, about an inch long; they fly; **MI47,** Potato bug—also a black bug that attaches to potatoes occasionally. **1983** *Barrick Coll.* **csPA,** *Potato bug*—small brown and yellow striped insect found on potato leaves.

2 also *Irish potato bug:* =**Colorado potato beetle;** also its larva.   Cf **potato beetle 1**

1869 MO State Entomol. *Annual Rept. for 1868* 110 **IA,** We found the little red and black spotted lady bug quite numerous and active, eating the eggs of the potato bug. . . The Colorado potato bugs nearly all disappeared here in June. **1909** Smith *Insect Friends* 249, The Colorado or 10-lined potato beetle, universally known as the "potato bug," . . was not always the pest that it is at present. **1940** Teale *Insects* 42, Potato bugs cause millions of dollars in damage every year by devouring the tender potato plants. **1965–70** *DARE* (Qu. R30, . . *Kinds of beetles;* not asked in early QRs) 70 Infs, **widespread exc Gulf States,** Potato bug; **NC49,** Irish potato bug; (Qu. R27, . . *Kinds of caterpillars or similar worms*) Infs **CO20, MD36, MO1, 10, OH70, PA242,** Potato bug. [*DARE* Ed: Some of these Infs may refer instead to other senses.] **1975** Gould *ME Lingo* 216, *Potato bug.* . . The Colorado beetle, which could lay waste a Maine potato field, long since controlled by insecticides.

3 also *old-fashioned potato bug:* =**potato beetle 3.**

1968 *DARE* (Qu. R30, . . *Kinds of beetles;* not asked in early QRs) Inf **VT4,** Potato bug—small, winged, sort of reddish. **1980** Milne–Milne *Audubon Field Guide Insects* 609, "Old-fashioned Potato Bug" (*Lema trilineata*). . . ¼" (6–7 mm). Reddish yellow.

4 =**Jerusalem cricket.   CA**   Cf **child of the earth 2**

1967–70 *DARE* (Qu. R30, . . *Kinds of beetles;* not asked in early QRs) Inf **CA22,** Potato bug—they pinch; I thought I was going to die sure; **CA173,** Potato bug or "child of the earth"—yellow-colored, hard-shelled; common in yards or new buildings. **1972** Swan–Papp *Insects* 79, *Jerusalem cricket.* . . A popular name in some places is "potato bug," possibly because they occasionally attack potato tubers. **1980** *NADS Letters* **CA,** In California, what is known as a potato bug is in actuality a "Jerusalem cricket". Back in Wisconsin, a "potato bug" lived and bred on a potato. Tinier than the J[erusalem] C[ricket] out here.

5 =**sow bug.**   [Perh because its shape when rolled into a ball resembles that of a potato]   Cf **ball bug, pill ~**

1979 *DARE* File **NC,** Potato bug—little things which live under stones and boards. When you lift the covers up the bugs roll up in a ball. **1996** *Ibid*—Internet, Potato bugs curl into a ball when threatened. **2000** *NADS Letters* **MD,** There are these little bugs that are common at least here on the east coast. If you touch them they roll into a little ball. . . I grew up in Maryland near Washington DC, and we always called them "potato bugs." I asked folks around where I live what they called them, and they all said potato bugs as well. **2001** *DARE* File **AZ,** Some people also call sow bugs "potato bugs". I've heard it used that way within my own family. Most of my mom's generation grew up in AZ around Phoenix and that's what they called 'em.

6 also *potato-bug mandolin:* A round-backed mandolin. [From its resemblance to **potato bug 2**]

1968 *DARE* FW Addit **nwAL,** *Tater bug*—mandolin. **1986** *Barrick Coll.* **csPA,** *Potato bug*—a round-bodied, striped mandolin. **1995** (1998) *Brophy Coll.* 57 **swMO** (as of c1960), Potato-bug mandolin. [A] lute, a mandolin with a rounded back, suggesting a potato-bug. **1998** *DARE* File **cwCA** (as of 1950s), When I was a child, my parents and grandfather used to call a mandolin a *potato bug.*

potato-bug bean n

See quot.

1968 *DARE* (Qu. I20, . . *Kinds of beans*) Inf **IN3,** [pətetə bəg binz].

potato-bug bird n Also *potato bird* [See quot 1936] =**rose-breasted grosbeak.**

1890 Warren *Birds PA* 247, Rose-breasted Grosbeak; Potato-bug bird. . . It is said that in some sections of Crawford county where this species resides in summer, many farmers protect them because they are great destroyers of "potato bugs." **1929** Forbush *Birds MA* 3.114, Mr. M.C. Howe, of Monson, Massachusetts, wrote to me . . "I had a chance to observe a pair of these birds [=rose-breasted grosbeaks] that were in my garden two years ago; they kept the potato patch entirely free from the Colorado potato beetle." This is now a well-recognized habit of the bird which has been known in some places as the "Potato-bug bird." **1936** Roberts *MN Birds* 2.337, Rose-breasted grosbeak . . *Other names:* "Potato-bug Bird," "Pea Bird," "Potato Bird." *Ibid* 340, It [=the rose-breasted grosbeak] is one of the few birds that eat in large quantity the potato-bug, taking both the soft larvae and the adult beetles, which are also fed to the young. . . It is this commendable trait that has earned for it, in many places, the name "Potato-bug Bird." **1941** Writers' Program *Guide CO* 397 **csCO,** During the 1870's the rose-breasted grosbeak . . developed a liking for the beetle [=**Colorado potato beetle**], devouring them in such great numbers that it became known as the "potato-bug bird," and its appearance in the fields was welcomed. **1963** Gromme *Birds WI* 217, Potato-bug Bird (Rose-breasted Grosbeak).

potato-bug mandolin See **potato bug 6**

potato bun n Also *potato roll*   **chiefly Nth, esp PA**   Cf **bun n¹ 1**

A dinner roll made variously, but including cooked potatoes, potato flour, or potato water.

1967–70 *DARE* (Qu. H18, . . *Special kinds of bread*) Inf **PA9,** Potato bun—bread flour with sugar and mashed potatoes; **PA242,** Potato buns, potato bread; (Qu. H32, . . *Fancy rolls and pastries*) Inf **PA9,** Potato buns; **PA41,** Potato buns—crumbs, potatoes; **PA150,** Potato buns— mashed potatoes; like hot cross, but not sweet. **1998** *NADS Letters* **ePA,** Potato buns . . are made with potatoes as well as wheat. *Ibid* **PA,**

Potato buns . . use mashed potatoes. . . They were usually heavily floured . . because . . the dough was extremely soft. *Ibid* **wPA,** Many people swear that potato rolls are the only acceptable receptacles for hot dogs and hamburgers. The buns/rolls/bread are made with . . potato water. *Ibid* **neWV,** You still find potato rolls sold in bakeries. *Ibid* **neIL,** Potato rolls . . are . . made with cooked potatoes (mashed or riced). *Ibid* **neIL,** Potato buns. . . The [cooked] potatoes were probably added to the dough for bulk because they were cheap and plentiful. *Ibid* **neIL, csMI, cWI, cWI, cwWA,** Potato buns [are made with] potato flour.

potato-chip tree n [From the thin, flat seed disks]

A **hop tree** (here: *Ptelea trifoliata*).

1946 *Nat. Hist.* 55.143, Known scientifically as *Ptelea trifoliata*. . . perhaps the common name of Potato Chip Tree is most appropriate, inasmuch as the ripe seeds look very similar to bits of potato chips. **1960** Vines *Trees SW* 593, Vernacular names [of *Ptelea trifoliata*] are . . Potatochip-tree [etc].

potato dandelion n

A **dwarf dandelion 1** (here: *Krigia dandelion*).

1970 Correll *Plants TX* 1723, *Krigia Dandelion* . . Potato-dandelion. . . Frequent in sandy soils, e. and s.e. Tex. **1972** Brown *Wildflowers LA* 209, Potato Dandelion—*Krigia dandelion*. . . Flower head yellow, about 1 inch in diameter, composed of all ray flowers.

potato drag n [EDD drag sb. 9 "A fork or rake for drawing out manure, &c., from a cart or cattle-lair; a fork for dragging turnips"] Cf potato hack

A potato hook.

1968 *DARE* Tape **NJ53,** You pull it [=sphagnum moss] with a drag, same as a potato drag. Pull it. . . You know what a potato drag is? What you dig potatoes with.

potato-famine Irish adj Cf Irish n[1] 2c, paper-shade Irish, lace-curtain 2

Being, or descended from, a person who emigrated from Ireland because of the Potato Famine of 1846–47.

1970 Lowell *Notebook* 106 **eMA,** We're burnt, black chips knocked from the blackest stock: Potato-famine Irish-Puritan, and Puritan—gold made them smile like pigs once. **1996** *DARE* File **csWI,** My Grandmother . . was *shanty Irish* by her own declaration, as opposed to cousin Grover Reynolds's wife Stella, who "put on airs" and acted like *lace-curtain Irish.* My great-grandmother Callahan was *potato-famine Irish*—born on a boat in Boston Harbor, July 1849.

potato fly n [See quot 1854]

A **blister bug** (here: *Epicauta* spp, esp *E. vittata*). Cf **old-fashioned potato beetle, potato beetle 2, ~ bug 1**

1806 in 1924 Kittredge *Old Farmer* 186, The potatoe fly, or bug, appears about the first of July. **1832** Williamson *Hist. ME* 1.172, *Lytta bittata; Potato fly,* (looks like a Spanish Fly.) **1854** King *Amer. Eclectic Dispensatory* 294, *Cantharis vittata.* Potato Fly. . . The Potato Fly is found principally in the middle and southern States; it makes its appearance in July and August, and feeds upon the potato plant. . . Its head is of a light-red color, with dark spots upon the top; the antennae are black; the elytra or wing covers are also black, with a central yellow longitudinal line, and yellow margins; the thorax is black, with three yellow lines; and the abdomen and legs are covered with an ash-colored down. **1911** *Century Dict. Suppl.,* Potato-fly. . . Any one of several species of blister-beetles which eat potato-leaves. *Epicauta vittata* is an example.

potato hack n[1] [OED2 hack sb.[1] 1.b "A two-pronged tool like a mattock, used for pulling up turnips, dragging dung, etc."; 1797 →] Cf potato drag

A potato hook.

1968 *DARE* Tape **NH14,** [FW:] Is there anything . . used for handling potatoes? [Inf:] Potato hack, we'd call them around here, and some call them a potato hook. . . [FW:] About seven, eight inches wide? [Inf:] Yes, the tines—oh, I'd say five inches long. . . They worked pretty good to cultivate . . in between the rows of a garden. You can dig the grass and weeds out with one of them.

potato hack n[2] [hack stack (as at hack n[6] a stack of tobacco leaves, and hack a stack of bricks piled up to dry)] Cf bank n[1] 1, hill n 2

1967 *DARE* (Qu. M19, *A place for keeping carrots, turnips, potatoes,*

and so on over the winter) Inf **SC30,** Tater hack—pile up spuds, cover with cornstalks, bank dirt; tap pile from bottom.

potato head n

A White person.

1968 *DARE* (Qu. HH28) Inf **CA81,** Whites are called potato head by Negroes. **1986** Pederson *LAGS Concordance* (Caucasian—neutral, jocular, and derogatory terms) 1 inf, **cwGA,** Potato head.

potato hill n

1 See **hill n 2.**

2 also *potato knob (hill):* A small, rounded hill. **esp S Midl** Cf **knob 1**

1819 (1821) Nuttall *Jrl.* 148 **seOK,** To the west continued a proximate chain of piney hills, with remarkable serrated summits, known by the familiar name of the Potatoe hills. **1934** (1970) Wilson *Backwoods Amer.* 170 **AR, MO,** We dropped by Sol Muster's place out among the tater-knob hills about Weddington Gap. **1967–70** *DARE* (Qu. C17, . . *A small, rounded hill*) Inf **AR47,** Potato hill—two or three miles across; **KY5,** Potato hill—small ones; **AR56,** Tater hill. **1986** Pederson *LAGS Concordance (Hill)* 1 inf, **cnAL,** Potato hill—very steep; 1 inf, **cMS,** [Po]tato knob—small rise, round like potato.

potato hole See hole n 3

potato jasmine n Cf wild potato

A **nightshade 1** (here: *Solanum triquetrum*).

1897 *Jrl. Amer. Folkl.* 10.52 **TX,** *Solanum triquetrum* . . potato jasmine, Waco, Tex.

potato knob (hill) See potato hill 2

potato lima n

A **lima bean;** see quot.

1941 *LANE* Map 259 (*Lima beans*) 1 inf, **swCT,** Potato limas, 'short and chubby', an early variety.

potato moss n

A **pondweed** (here: *Potamogeton pectinatus*).

1920 *Torreya* 20.18, *Potamogeton pectinatus* . . Potato moss.

potato onion n chiefly S Midl See Map on p. 306 Cf green onion 1

An **onion B** (here: *Allium cepa* Aggregatum Group).

1831 in 1832 *Genesee Farmer* 19 Feb 51 **wNY,** Potato-onions. . . each onion will produce from three to six large onions, and a cluster of small ones . . resembling the top-onion seed in appearance, excepting their location being at the bottom of the stocks, instead of the top. . . The stalk produces no seed of any kind on the top, the increase being from the bottom, from which peculiarly [sic] it derives its name. **1863** Burr *Field & Garden* 137, The Potato Onion produces no seeds, neither small bulbs upon its stalks, in the manner of many of the species of the Onion family; but, if a full-grown bulb be set in spring, a number of bulbs of various sizes will be formed, beneath the surface of the ground, about the parent bulb. **1884** Baldwin *Yankee School-Teacher* 179 **VA** [Black], 'Twus two poun' side meat I traded off p'tater ingens f'r. **1937** *Esquire* Feb 36 **KY,** I worked one day for Cy Shelton, pullin tater onions and carried them to the crib loft to dry. **1941** *LANE* Map 257 (*Onion*) 1 inf, **swCT,** *Potato onions,* also called *multipliers.* **1948** *Courier-Jrl.* (Louisville KY) 17 Feb sec 2 12/4 **seKY,** "Got any potato onions?" "Nary a one, Sam," she replied. Mr. Napier passed on down the road. Aunt Mary suddenly turned to her husband and exclaimed: "Lord have mercy, Matt, I bet Sam meant tater ingerns, an' her I set with plenty of 'em!" **1965–70** *DARE* (Qu. I5, . . *Kind of onions that keep coming up without replanting year after year*) Infs **IL142, IN7, 48, KY37, 69, NC36, 55, OH49, 52, 59, 75, VA2,** Potato onions; **CT4,** "Potato onion" down South; [same as] multiplier [or] Japanese onion; **OH41,** Potato onions—they're big like potatoes; (Qu. I6, *The kind of onions that come up fresh early in the year, and you eat them raw*) Infs **IL134, IN3, KY40, 44, 74, 85, TN13, VA7, 19, 35, 74,** Potato onions; **VA26,** Potato onions—don't go to seed, but are replanted year after year; **KY24,** Potato onions—planted in fall and eaten in spring; **KY42,** Tater onions—set them in the fall around first of November, go to eating them early in spring. **1966** Dakin *Dial. Vocab. Ohio R. Valley* 2.366, The names *potato onion* (apparently from the cluster of new bulbs which grow around the set—several informants say *hill onion*), *multiplier, multiplying onion,* and *winter onion* all clearly refer to the latter type [=multiplying onions planted in fall]. **1969** *DARE* FW Addit **KY,** Tater onions—early onions, with edible stems, often volunteer, growing around the garden. **1983** *MJLF* 9.1.59 **ceKY** (as of 1956), *Tater onions . . green onions.* **1986** Pederson *LAGS Concordance* **TN,** 3 infs, Potato onion(s); 1 inf, Potato onion—big, hot one; 1 inf, Potato onion—sets grow up to be potato onions; 1 inf, Potato onions—stay in ground all winter; 4 infs, (Po)tato onion(s); 1 inf, (Po)tato onion—the big ones have sets. **1990** *Seed Savers Yearbook* 145, *Potato Onion . . light-tan, form clusters of 2″ bulbs. Ibid, Potato Onion, Red . . Perennial. Ibid, Potato Onion, Yellow . . Perennial*—plant 1 bulb in fall; harvest either 1 large or clump of bulbs next August . . yields increase 5–10 times.

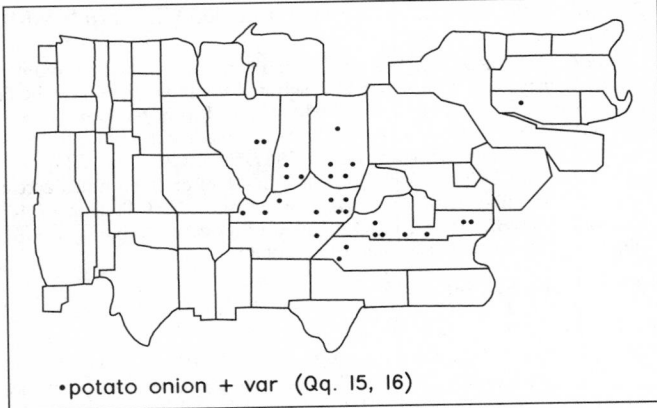

•potato onion + var (Qq. I5, I6)

potato patch v phr Cf *pea-patch(-farm)* v phr (at **pea patch** n) ?To compete in agricultural work or skills.

   1919 *DN* 5.35 **seKY,** *Tater-patch,* n., used as a verb. "He ain't got nothin' on me, I'll tater-patch with ary man in this county." Knott Co.

potato pea n [See quot 1922] Cf **potato bean**
A **groundnut B1** (here: *Apios americana*).

   1830 Rafinesque *Med. Flora* 2.193, *Apios tuberosa. . . Indian Potato, Potato Pea. Hopniss* of the Delaware tribes. . . Valuable plant, formerly cultivated by the Indians (yet by the Creeks) for the roots, which are like potatoes, or rather like *Helianthus tuberosus,* and the seeds like peas and as good. **1922** *Amer. Botanist* 28.75, *Apios tuberosa . .* is often called "wild wisteria". It is however, more frequently known as "ground-nut" in allusion to the rounded tubers. . . These tubers are edible and were, in fact, the first "potatoes" brought back from explorations in the New World. . . A considerable number of other names allude to these tubers among which are "potato pea", "Indian potato", "pig potato", and "white apples".

potato pie See **sweet-potato pie**

potato pone n Also *sweet-potato pone* [**pone** n 1a] **chiefly S Atl, Gulf States**
A sweet cake or pudding made chiefly of grated sweet potatoes and baked until thickened and browned.

   1839 *S. Lit. Messenger* 5.377 **NC,** Master Billy taking a piece of potato pone daintily between his fingers. . . [said] "This *patetta poon* is exceeding fine." **1847** (1979) Rutledge *Carolina Housewife* 130, *Sweet potato pone. . .* Peel and grate two moderate sized sweet potatoes; pour on it nearly a pint of cold water, four good spoonfuls of brown sugar, one good spoonful of butter; season with ginger to the taste. Bake in a moderate oven about three hours. **1932** Stieff *Eat in MD* 163, *Sweet potato pone. . .* Bake in a tin pan well buttered; when cold turn out. **1937** in 1977 *Amer. Slave Suppl. 1* 1.184 **AL,** Dey gib you extra syrup to make cakes wid an' sweet 'taters to make 'tater pone. **1938** Rawlings *Yearling* 11 **nFL,** That ain't sweet 'tater pone, is it, Ma? **1940** Brown *Amer. Cooks* 464 **MS,** *Sweet potato pone. . .* Select well cured sweet potatoes, wash, peel, and grate . . ; add sugar, spices, salt, and butter. . . Beat eggs, add milk, and stir into potato mixture. Pour into a generously buttered pudding dish and bake 1 hour in a moderate oven. Stir occasionally as the pudding browns on sides and top. **1942** Rawlings *Cross Creek Cookery* 183 **FL,** The most rudimentary sweet potato pone is a thick, gelatinous pudding. Small fry among poor blacks and whites consider it a treat of treats. **1950** *PADS* 14.53 **SC,** *Potato pone: . .* Grated sweet potato flavored with molasses, milk, spices, cloves, ginger, orange peel, according to taste, cooked and stirred often until thick. **1956** McAtee *Some Dialect NC* 34, *Potato pone . .* grated sweet potato pudding, baked. **1966** *DARE* Tape **FL41,** She makes a good potato pone. . . You make it out the sweet potatoes. You grated them. You grate the po-

tatoes raw. That's made with syrup. And you have a little brown sugar mix with it. And you just season it up good, and it cuts just like a cake, you know. **1967** *DARE* (Qu. H47, *Kinds of fried potatoes*) Inf **LA6,** Potato pone—you grate sweet potatoes and mix it with flour, spices, and sugar or syrup and then fry it; it can also be baked; (Qu. H63, *Kinds of desserts*) Inf **AL30,** Potato pone—sweet potatoes (peel and grate), syrup, sugar, eggs, butter; beat, bake in a pan. **1986** Pederson *LAGS Concordance,* 1 inf, **seMS,** Potato pones—from sweet potatoes; baked dessert; 1 inf, **seGA,** Potato pone—grated potatoes made into a "poon"; 1 inf, **ceLA,** Potato pone—like a pone of corn bread; 1 inf, **seAR,** Potato pone; 1 inf, **cLA,** Tato pone—various shapes; baked; 1 inf, **seMS,** A potato pone—made with sweet potatoes, syrup.

potato pudding See **sweet-potato pudding**

potato pump See **pump** n[1]

potato pumpkin See **potato squash**

potato riffle n esp NC
A bread or flat cake made with mashed potatoes; see quots.

   1952 Brown *NC Folkl.* 1.598 **wNC,** *Tater riffle* ['tetɚ]. . . Light bread. **1998** *NADS Letters* **wNC,** I was born in western North Carolina. . . Tater riffle is a batter bread made with a sliced, cooked, mashed potato and some of its cooking water, along with white flour, milk and/or butter, and yeast. Sugar may be added to encourage the yeast. It was used to provide a fast hot bread when there was no time for standard bread. . . A housewife would apologize for serving it to guests. **1999** *Ibid* **wNC,** Tater riffles in the mountains are made from left over mashed taters, mixed with onions (ramps), flour and egg, formed into small flat cookie size cakes. Dropped into hot grease they quickly brown. **2001** *Ibid* **csOR,** Tater riffle, ruffled potatoes, are re-mashed potatoes, sometimes mixed with a little flour and egg and a pinch of baking soda, then fried in the frying pan or baked until just barely golden on top. The riffle is the shape of the top which has ripples or ridges on it. They are also called potato fritters.

potato roll See **potato bun**

potato sausage n [Calque of Sw *potatiskorv*]
Sausage made with a mixture of ground potatoes, beef, pork, and onions.

   1951 Tufford *Scandinavian Recipes* 12, *Potatiskorv* (Swedish Potato Sausage). . . Grind potatoes and onion and mix with the ground meat [= pork and beef]. Add spices, salt and milk and mix thoroughly. **1966–67** *DARE* Tape **MI29,** One thing, though, that we do make among us a lot is potato sausage—that, of course, is a Swedish dish, too; **MN6,** But then of course we have potatiskorv, which we buy now, but it's potato [pə'teta] sausage. **1967–68** *DARE* (Qu. H45, *Dishes made with meat, fish, or poultry that everybody around here would know, but that people in other places might not*) Inf **MN11,** Potato sausage; (Qu. H65, *Foreign foods favored by people around here*) Infs **ID5, WY5,** Potato sausage; **KS7,** Potato sausage—2 lbs. ground potatoes . . , 2 lbs. ground beef, 1 lb. ground pork, ½ c. ground onion. Mix well and season. . . Fill casing. [3 of 4 Infs had Swedish-born parents.]

potato show n
   1970 *DARE* File **ceWI** (as of 1930s), And we used also to have movies in which the admission price was some kind of food, usually something canned. We called them "potato shows," and we all used to bring something and go. It was during the Depression and the food went to the really poor.

potato squash n Also *potato pumpkin* **esp S Midl** Cf **sweet-potato squash**
A **winter squash** (here: *Cucurbita mixta*).

   c1960 *Wilson Coll.* **csKY,** Potato pumpkin. . . The kind that has a neck and tastes, when cooked, very much like a sweet potato. **1965–67** *DARE* (Qu. I23, . . *Kinds of squash*) Infs **MS45, SC46,** Potato squash; **SC1,** Potato squash—big like a pumpkin, long; **SC34,** Potato squash—yellow on inside—shaped like crookneck squash, about as sweet as a sweet potato—use just like sweet potato; (Qu. I24, . . *Kinds of pumpkins;* total Infs questioned, 75) Inf **MS45,** Potato pumpkin; **MS60,** Potato pumpkin—about size of head, with a stripe in it. **1967** *Clarke Co. Democrat* (Grove Hill AL) 27 Apr 6/4 *(Mathews Coll.),* James T. Wilson, Jr. is shown holding the huge potato squash grown by his father.

potato thump n Also *mashed potato thump, potato tunk* **chiefly NEng** Cf **tunk, tunkup**

Mashed potatoes.

1914 *DN* 4.78 **ME, nNH,** *Potato thump. . .* Mashed potato. **1966** *DARE* (Qu. H49) Inf **NH6,** Potato thump—mashed potato beat up with salt, pepper, butter. **1966** *DARE* FW Addit **MA6,** Tater tunk—potatoes mashed and prepared on plate for individual serving. **2001** *NADS Letters,* Potato Thump was always a name for mashed potatoes when I was growing up. My mother came from Texas and my father from Massachusetts, so I am unsure where the origin. *Ibid* **VT,** My grandmother (born in 1934), who grew up in a poor home in central Vermont. . . has said that 'mashed potato thump' is what you call potatoes when you are too poor to have butter and milk to put in your potatoes, and you mash them with bacon grease. She said that it made them very thick, and when they cooled off even a little bit they went 'thump!' onto your plate from the spoon. She said that it was very appetizing, but they were poor, and it was the best they had when she was growing up. Someone of her generation would know the term in this area, but I doubt that anyone much younger would. It seems to have been used mostly during the depression.

potato time n
Dinner time.

1982 *Greenfield Recorder* (MA) 22 May sec A 6, All country people knew how important it was to get there before tater time, 12 o'clock, so dinner would be prepared. **1999** *DARE* File **ID** (as of 1980s), Potato time. . . The times I've heard it, it was the announcement/command to cease work for the mid-shift meal. User: A farmer born and bred in N. Idaho. . . User: A colleague on a construction job . . in S. Idaho. I don't know where he hailed from. I suspect Utah. The users of the phrase seemed to avoid it when that meal was not an indoor sit-down-to-a-plate-of-hot-food meal.

potato tree n Cf **potato jasmine**
A **nightshade 1** (here: *Solanum erianthum*).

1908 Britton *N. Amer. Trees* 828, Potato Tree. . . *Solanum verbascifolium.* . . a low-flat-headed tree in peninsular Florida and on Elliott's Key. . . It is most often a shrub and as such is frequent in the southern States. **1933** Small *Manual SE Flora* 1114, Potato-tree. . . Hammocks, pinelands, and roadsides, pen[insular] Fla. and Florida Keys. **1960** Vines *Trees SW* 917, It [=mullein nightshade] is also known under the vernacular name of Potato-tree. **1971** Craighead *Trees S. FL* 202, Potato tree, *Solanum verbascifolium.*

potato tunk See **potato thump**

potato vacation n Cf **cotton vacation**
1950 *WELS Suppl.* **cWI,** *Potato vacation*—Every fall at potato digging time school dismissed [sic] for a week or two while everyone picks up potatoes. Even the teacher. This time is made up at the end of the year along with the week for stone-picking.

potato wagon n Also *pumpkin wagon* Cf **Lord's bread-wagon**
See quots.

1936 *AmSp* 11.316 **Ozarks,** *Potato wagon.* . . This phrase is often mentioned in connection with thunder. Many hillmen dislike, for some superstitious reason, to speak of thunder directly. So they say 'th' 'tater wagon's a-rollin',' or something of the sort. **1956** Ker *Vocab. W. TX* 61, Storm with rain and thunder and lightning . . tater wagon's rollin' [1 of 67 infs]. **1982** *Smithsonian Letters,* Potato wagon going over the bridge: thunder. **1985** Ladwig *How to Talk Dirty* 14 **Ozarks,** That sounds like the tater (potato) wagons rolling around the heavens . . thunder. *Ibid* 15, Here comes the punkin' (pumpkin) wagon . . thunder.

potato worm n
A **hornworm:** usu *Manduca quinquemaculata,* but also *M. sexta.*

1848 in 1850 Cooper *Rural Hours* 202 **ceNY,** The common green potato, or tobacco-worm, is said to become a moth of this kind. **1869** MO State Entomol. *Annual Rept. for 1868* 95, The Potato or Tomato-Worm—Sphinx 5-maculata. . . This well known insect . . is usually called the Potato-worm. . . Many persons are afraid to handle this worm, from an absurd idea that it has the power of stinging with the horn on its tail. But this is a vulgar error and the worm is totally incapable of doing [sic] any direct harm to man, either with the conspicuous horn on its tail, or with any hidden weapon that it may have concealed about its person. **1882** (1903) Treat *Injurious Insects* 65, The most injurious insect to the Tomato, is the large green Caterpillar, of *Sphinx quinque maculata,*

which is called both "Tomato," and "Potato Worm." **1884** (1885) McCook *Tenants* 69 **PA,** This is the potato-worm, the tomato-worm, or the tobacco-worm, just as you choose to call it. You all know it—a large green caterpillar, with a kind of thorn on the tail, and oblique, whitish stripes on the side of the body. **1969** *DARE* (Qu. R27, . . *Kinds of caterpillars or similar worms*) Inf **IL52,** Potato worm—smaller than tomato worm, green.

potbelly n
1 =**lake trout 1,** usu **siscowet.**
1884 Goode *Fisheries U.S.* 1.488, About Grand Traverse Bay, Lake Michigan, two varieties [of lake trout] are also recognized, one being long, slim, and coarse-meated. . . [T]hose of the other form are called "Pot-bellies," being short and chubby, and invariably taken in deep water. **1911** *Century Dict.* 4649, Pot-belly. . . The lake-trout, *Cristivomer namaycush.* [*Century* Ed: Lake Huron.]

2 See **potgut 2.**
3 also *pottlebelly:* A **dace** (here: *Rhinichthys atratulus*).
1938 Schrenkeisen *Field Book Fishes* 144 **NH,** Black-nosed Dace. . . Potbelly or Pottlebelly. **1983** Becker *Fishes WI* 467, Blacknose Dace—*Rhinichthys atratulus.* . . Other common names: western blacknose dace, . . "potbelly" or "pottlebelly" because it is frequently distended with parasitic worms.

potch See **putch**

pot chamber n Also *potty chamber* [Prob for Fr *pot de chambre*]
A chamber pot.

1967–68 *DARE* (Qu. F38, *Utensil kept under the bed for use at night*) Inf **CA9,** Pot chamber; **MI94,** Potty chamber; [**LA31,** ['poʊˌčam]—the Frenchmen call it this; **NY199,** ['podəˌšæm]—French for chamber pot].

pot cheese n [Du *pot kaas*] **chiefly NY, NJ, nPA, CT** See Map on p. 308 Cf **cook cheese, Dutch ~, farmer's ~, smearcase, stink cheese**
Usu a dry form of cottage cheese; occas **cook cheese.**

1812 Paulding *Diverting Hist.* 111, Tell me thou heart of cork, . . and brain of pot-cheese. **1847** (1852) Crowen *Amer. Cookery* 206 **NY,** To Make Pot Cheese.—Put butter-milk and thick sour milk together . . , make it scalding hot, then take the curd from the whey with a skimmer, put it into a muslin or linen bag, tie it up and hang it to drain; after an hour or two, . . moisten it slightly with sweet cream, put a little salt to it, work the salt into it, and make it in balls the size of a teacup. . . Pot-cheese should be made fresh, once or twice a week. **1913** *DN* 4.54 ceNY, *Pot-cheese.* . . Cottage cheese. "Mrs. Henry will give pot-cheese for the church supper." **1936** *AmSp* 11.375, [A contributor says] that in northern New Jersey *pot cheese* and *cottage cheese* are interchangeable terms, but that in various other parts of the country may be found persons who do not know what is meant by *cottage cheese.* **1939** Wolcott *Yankee Cook Book* 215, Sour Milk Cheese [*Called also Dutch, Curd, Cottage Cheese and Connecticut Pot Cheese*]. . . Place the milk in a pan on the back of the stove or over hot water until curd has separated from whey. Spread a cheese cloth over a strainer, . . drain or squeeze quite dry. . . Add the butter, salt, pepper and cream. **1949** Kurath *Word Geog.* 71, The Hudson Valley expression [for cottage cheese] is *pot cheese,* which is modeled on Dutch *pot kees.* . . This term is now in general use in the Dutch settlement area and has spread eastward into Connecticut (the Housatonic Valley) and the New England settlements of Long Island, and westward to the Delaware and the head of the Mohawk. **1950** *WELS* (*The lumpy white cheese that is made from sour milk*) 1 Inf, **csWI,** Cottage cheese or pot cheese; (*Different kinds of home-made cheese*) [same Inf,] Cottage or pot cheese, Dutch cheese, smeerkaas— [these are all] same kind. **1950** *WELS Suppl.* **neWI,** Pot cheese—made with cooked casein. Calumet Co., around New Holstein (low German settlement). **1955** Taber *Stillmeadow Daybook* 269 **cwCT,** And from the big curds of pot cheese, so creamy and mild, to the sophisticated flavor of a Port Salut, it is all good. **1965–70** *DARE* (Qu. H60, *The lumpy white cheese that is made from sour milk*) 32 Infs, **chiefly NY, NJ, PA, CT,** Pot cheese; **CO27,** Pot cheese—common here; **MD27,** Pot cheese—made from cooked cottage cheese, also called stink cheese; **NJ29,** Cottage cheese; pot cheese—old-fashioned; **NY20,** Cottage cheese; pot cheese—old-fashioned; German lady; **NY72,** Pot cheese—old-fashioned; cottage cheese—high-toned; **NY92,** Pot cheese—made at home; cottage cheese—when the factory makes it; **NY94,** Cottage cheese—what we buy; pot cheese—when we make it ourselves—old-fashioned; **NY130,** Pot cheese—thick yellowish-white cheese; **NY220,**

Pot cheese—old-fashioned; cottage cheese—now; **PA**176, Pot cheese—drier than cottage cheese; **WI**20, Pot cheese—heard in Pennsylvania; **WI**47, Cottage cheese; pot cheese—different; dried. **1980** *NY Times* (NY) 5 Mar sec C 4, Cottage cheese is one of the first stages. . . Pot cheese is left to drain for a longer period. More whey drains away and it becomes a drier cheese. Farmer's cheese and pot cheese are practically identical, except that farmer's cheese is generally molded. **1986** Pederson *LAGS Concordance*, 1 inf, **ceTN**, Pot cheese—like cottage but cooked; 1 inf, **swGA**, Pot cheese—heard of; 1 inf, **swTN**, Pot cheese.

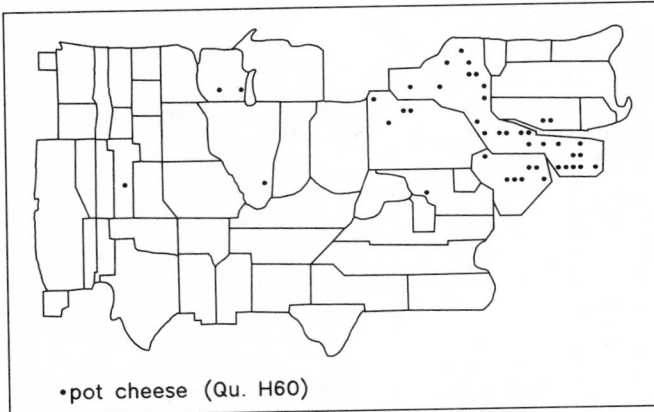

•pot cheese (Qu. H60)

pot closet See **closet 1**

pot-cotch n [Perh **pot** n **2** + var of **cooch** n]
1987 *DARE* File **nwMS** (as of 1960s), Here are words from autobiographical material that I collected in interviews with Black people in Marks, Mississippi, where I was a civil rights worker back in the sixties: pot-cotch—home-made liquor . . —from Black male from northwestern Mississippi born 1910, one year school.

pot dodger n
=**corn dodger 2.**
c1970 Pederson *Dial. Surv. Rural GA* **seGA** (*Other things made from corn meal*) 1 inf, Pot dodgers. **1986** Pederson *LAGS Concordance*, 1 inf, **cwGA**, "Corn balls" called pot dodgers when cooked; 1 inf, **csGA**, Pot dodgers or corn dodgers; 1 inf, **cwFL**, Pot dodgers—boiled in cheesecloth with greens; 1 inf, **cAL**, A pot dodger = corn dodger.

pot drunk adj [Not found elsewhere, but presumably belonging to the family of compounds like *pot-shaken* (*OED2* 1630) and *pot-valiant* in which *pot-* means "with drink," most of which appear to have been coined in the 17th cent]
Intoxicated.
1929 *WV Review* Oct 9, I once heard a man in our mountains speak of a fellow's being *pot drunk.*

poteridge See **partridge A3**

pot eten n Also *pot essen* [Du, Ger; literally "pot meal"] Cf **hutspot**
A dish of potatoes, other vegetables, and sometimes meat boiled together.
1940 *AmSp* 15.83 [Dutch in MI English], *Hutspot* ['hutspɔt] or *pot eten* ['pɔt-etən]. A combination of potatoes and cabbage; potatoes and carrots; potatoes and kale, or other vegetable boiled together and crushed. **1981** Hachten *Flavor WI* 213, *Pot Essen* (German)—2 pounds very lean pork, . . pearl barley, Diced sweet apples, cored but not peeled, 8 potatoes, peeled and sliced, Corn syrup. . . Simmer pork and barley . . for about 2½ hours. Add apples and potatoes. . . Serve warm with a little syrup and melted butter if desired.

potgut n
1 A **ground squirrel b** (here: *Spermophilus armatus*).
1957 Barnes *Nat. Hist. Wasatch Spring* 19 **UT**, We have seen these "pot guts", as the boys call them, climb over bushes but never up trees. **1959** Barnes *Nat. Hist. Wasatch Winter* 49 **UT**, Much confusion exists here concerning what is a "ground hog"; some think it to be the "pot gut" or ground squirrel (*Citellus armatus*) of the Wasatch hillsides.
2 also *potbelly, potguts:* =**mosquito fish.**
1963 Sigler–Miller *Fishes UT* 120, Western Mosquitofish. . . Common

Names . . potguts [etc]. **1966** *DARE* (Qu. P7, *Small fish used as bait for bigger fish*) Inf **FL**27, Potbellies; **FL**32, Potguts. **1968** *DARE* FW Addit **seLA**, *Potbelly*—small fish often caught along with cocahos and also used as bait. Up to two inches long.

pothead n [*OED2 pot-headed* 1533, *pothead* 1855]
A stupid person; hence adj *pot-headed* stupid.
1930 Shoemaker *1300 Words* 45 **cPA Mts** (as of c1900), *Pot-headed*—A heavy, stupid individual. **1975** Gould *ME Lingo* 217, Inland, a *pot head* is a citizen whose general intelligence suggests a chamber mug. A squash head.

pothead cow n
1968 *DARE* (Qu. K12, *A cow that has never had horns*) Inf **NC**81, Pothead cow.

potheaded See **pothead**

pothellion n
A kind of stew or **potpie 1.**
1890 *Century Dict.* 4652, *Pot-hellion*. . . A large pie made of beef, pork, potatoes, and onions baked in a pan. [*Century* Ed: Gloucester, Massachusetts.] **1975** Gould *ME Lingo* 217, *Pothellion*—An old coastal term for a kind of fish hash, sometimes called "dog-on-the-shore," but this coastal meaning has long been superseded by the woods meaning of an adjustable stew. Starting with scraps of salt pork to sauté brown-sugared venison cubes, the *pothellion* mulls along for a day or two as the cook improvises with whatever meat and vegetables are at hand. Rabbit, *pa'tridge,* squirrel, perhaps porcupine, and almost anything except fish may be considered. . . Traditionally, a *pothellion* is topped off with dumplings.

pothole n
1 A deep, round depression in rock, esp in the bed of a stream.
1827 McKenney *Sketches* 54 **NY**, The waters were once, in many places, some fifty feet above their present level; for their action upon the rocks is plainly seen in the *pot holes,* as the excavations are called. **1875** *Amer. Naturalist* 9.174 **West**, There are well-worn cavities in the sides of the mountains, showing how the running water . . formed the cavity much as a 'pot hole' is made in our streams at the present time. **1967** *DARE* Tape **MI**42, And that river where we used to swim—I don't know how we ever got out of that alive sometimes, because a lot of it is just clay and sand bottom but part of it there was rock bottom. And there was pot-holes . . where . . rocks was kept circling around I suppose for millions of years, and some of those things were—oh I'd say ten to fifteen, twenty feet in diameter. And a lot of 'em just about that deep. Almost perfectly around [sic]. **1999** *DARE* File **nwMI**, On the Upper Michigan Peninsula, where the Presque Isle River empties into Lake Superior, the river has a series of beautifully scoured potholes that look so round and polished they seem almost unnatural.
2 also *pothole lake:* A natural water-filled depression in the ground; a small lake or marshy area. **chiefly wGt Lakes, Upper MW, NW**
1902 White *Blazed Trail* 6 **eMI**, The pines stood on a country rolling with hills, deep with pot-holes. It became necessary to dodge in and out, here and there, between the knolls, around or through the swamps. **1944** Adams *Western Words* 118, *Pothole*—A bog hole. **1946** *Sun* (Baltimore MD) 5 July 11/3 (Hench Coll.), Madison, Wis.—Experimental planting of fish with airplanes gives promise for the "back in there" pot-hole lakes and spring holes. **1950** *WELS* (*A small pool of muddy water*) 1 Inf, **ceWI**, Pothole, pond. **1955** Johnson *50 Yrs.* 217 **ND**, In a small pot hole—not over ten rods at the widest—was the densest settling of ducks I had ever seen. We noticed that a long ravine led to this pot hole. **1958** McCulloch *Woods Words* 138 **Pacific NW**, *Pothole*—A small pond. **1960** *Washington Post & Times Herald* (DC) 29 Mar sec A 21, Maryland's Governor. . . declared he was greatly concerned with water conservation. . . noting a reported drop of four million in the number of duck-breeding potholes and lakes presently available to migratory waterfowl. **1964** O'Hare *Ling. Geog. E. MT* 104, Low land that holds water. . . pot hole [3 of 12 infs]. **1966** *Flathead Courier* (Polson MT) 13 Oct 4/5, He said the Birk car continued to travel southward for two-tenths of a mile before going off the left side of the road into a pothole where it was two-thirds submerged. **1968** *DARE* (Qu. C4b, *Is there any difference in the size [of a lake and a pond]?*) Inf **MN**29, Pothole—a small pond, can be very deep; **MN**42, Potholes—water that stands in a low place; (Qu. C7, . . *Land that usually has some standing water with*

trees or bushes growing in it) Inf **MN**42, Slough or pothole. **1973** Allen *LAUM* 1.233 (as of c1950) **ND, nwMN,** *Pot hole,* like *muskeg* not reported in New England, seems, in the sense of a small depression with standing water, to be limited to North Dakota and its eastern fringe. **1991** *Wausau Daily Herald* (WI) 28 July, [Headline:] Potholes: Tiny northern Wisconsin lakes hold big bass, lots of obstacles. *Ibid,* Today most of those lakes are less than 20 acres in size and the term "pothole" lake typically refers to any small northern Wisconsin lake that doesn't have a name.

3 A bowl-shaped depression in the surface of a road; hence adjs *potholed, potholey.* **scattered, but more freq Nth, esp NEast** See Map Cf **chuckhole 1, chughole**

1925 *Book of Rural Life* 8.4741, They [=waterbound macadam roads] depreciate mainly by raveling . . , and by the formation of "pot holes" caused by the dislodging of surface stone and accentuated by the subsequent pounding and grinding of the steel-tired wheels. **1940** *Sun* (Baltimore MD) 27 Feb 10/1 *(Hench Coll.),* The potholes, ruts, cracks and crevices that make motoring on so many of the city's streets unpleasant if not hazardous, particularly in the early spring, are much in the minds of Baltimoreans. **1965–70** *DARE* (Qu. N27b, *When unpaved roads get very rough, you call them* _____) 22 Infs, **scattered, but esp freq NEast,** (Full of) potholes; **NJ**12, **NY**127, **OR**1, **UT**3, Potholed; **NY**75, Potholes in them; **NY**63, **WV**3, Potholey (roads); (Qu. N30, *. . A sudden short dip in a road)* Infs **CT**42, **DC**11, **MI**97, **MA**30, **NJ**69, **NY**226, Pothole. **1968** *PADS* 49.24 **Upper MW,** [Table shows that *pothole* was given by 5.8% of Type I [=old, with little formal educ] *LAUM* infs, by 12% of Type II [=mid-aged, with approx hs educ] infs, but by 38% of college students recently surveyed from the same area.] **1973** Allen *LAUM* 1.400 (as of c1950), For a hole or depression in a street or road a frequent U[pper] M[idwest] term is *chuckhole,* used by a majority of the infs. in Midland speech areas—Iowa, South Dakota, and Nebraska. Minnesota was not investigated. *Chuckhole* competes with the simple generic *hole,* used by a majority in the two Dakotas. . . A minor variant, *pothole,* is strong in North Dakota but not elsewhere in the four states for which data are available. . . The 913 respondents [to the mail checklist] even more decidedly identify *chuckhole* or *chughole* as the dominant UM form. . . North Dakotans again are revealed as less likely to use anything but the generic *hole* . . but they also appear, along with Minnesotans, as users of *pothole,* which definitely is not Midland. **1986** Pederson *LAGS Concordance* (Channel cut by erosion in road or field) 5 infs, **Gulf Region,** Pothole(s). **1995** *DARE* File **OR,** They are commonly referred to as Potholes in Oregon, but I have heard, though infrequently, some refer to them as Chuckholes. I would tend to agree with the statement that Potholes is replacing Chuckholes in the NW. *Ibid* **OR,** For me it's a pothole. My wife, also an Oregonian, said that she's heard chuck hole, but from only her parents—no one her age would say chuck hole. *Ibid* **IN, MD.**

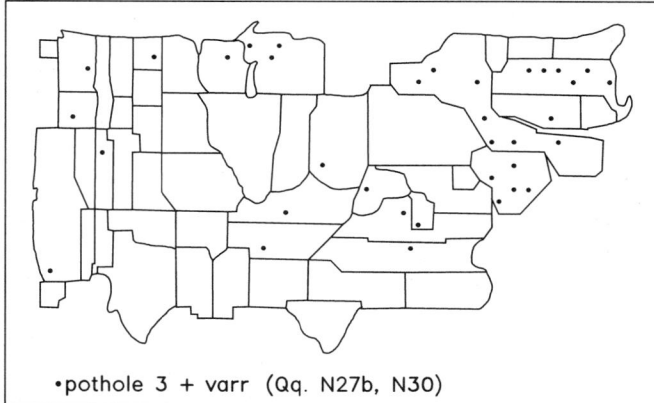

•pothole 3 + varr (Qq. N27b, N30)

pothole lake See **pothole 2**

potholey See **pothole 3**

pothook n

1 pl; also in combs *pothooks and hangers,* ~ *hen scratches:* Small hooked strokes in writing; illegible handwriting; hence adj *pothooky.* [*OED2* 1611 →] Cf **hen scratching**

1867 *Harper's New Mth. Mag.* 35.793, It was written in a cramped, pot-hooky hand. **1899** (1912) Green *VA Folk-Speech* 332, *Pothooks-and-hangers. . .* The first straight and crooked lines made by children

learning to write. **1951** *Sun* (Baltimore MD) 13 Sept 18/1, The left hand of the unlucky tyke was tied behind his back. Then, with a slate before him and a squeaky pencil in his right hand, he was bidden to write what were called "pot-hooks and hangers." A pothook was the letter S in reverse and the hanger was the letter J in reverse. **1952** Brown *NC Folkl.* 1.578, *Pot hooks and hen scratches:* . . Illegible writing. **1956** McAtee *Some Dialect NC* 34, *Pothooks and hen scratches. . .* Poor handwriting. **1968** *DARE* (Qu. JJ11, *Joking names for handwriting that's hard to read)* Inf **IN**38, Pothooks.

2 See quot.

1965–67 *DARE* (Qu. X37, *. . People's legs if they're noticeably bent, or uneven, or not right)* Infs **DC**6, **LA**8, **MS**45, Pothooks; **SC**26, He got regular pothooks; [**OK**13, Legs like pothooks].

3 One's hand. Cf **bread hooks, lunch hook**

1958 McCulloch *Woods Words* 138 **Pacific NW,** *Pothooks*—Hands. **1966** *DARE* (Qu. X32, *Joking or uncomplimentary words for the hands)* Inf **SC**19, Cotton pickers; hooks; pothooks.

pothooks and hangers (or hen scratches), pothooky See **pothook 1**

pot hound n **chiefly Sth, S Midl, SW** =**potlicker 2.**

1903 (1965) Adams *Log Cowboy* 238 **NM,** Common old pot hounds and everyday yellow dogs have gone out of style entirely. **1929** Dobie *Vaquero* 100 **SW,** We all had coughs and coughs till it was like a bunch of Texas pot hounds baying a 'possum when we tried to sleep. **1954** *PADS* 21.34 **SC,** *Pot hound:* . . A hound which hunts nothing but the pot, i.e., is good for nothing but to eat; a worthless hound. **1960** Criswell *Resp. to PADS 20* **Ozarks,** Pot hound—used of a dog that refuses to forage and hangs around the house for food; a generally useless animal. Common still. **1968–70** *DARE* (Qu. J2, *. . Joking or uncomplimentary words . . for dogs)* Infs **AL**61, **CA**171, **SC**66, **TX**51, **UT**4, Pot hound. **1976** Brown *Gloss. Faulkner* 154 **MS,** *Potlicker* . . a mongrel dog, one allowed to lick cooking pots and fed on table scraps (sometimes called a pot-hound).

pothouse n Also *pothouse grocery* Cf **grocery 1**

A disreputable tavern.

1809 Irving *Hist. NY* 1.254, [He was] distracted by petitions of "numerous and respectable meetings," consisting of some half a dozen scurvy pot-house politicians. **1837** Wetmore *Gaz. MO* 337, At a small pot-house grocery or dead-fall of the village . . there was a lingerer. **1873** Miller *Modocs* 105 **cnCA,** A pot-house politician should represent us at the court of St. James's, if such an Indian is to be taken as a representative of his race. **1970** *DARE* (Qu. DD30, *Joking names for a place where liquor is [or was] sold and consumed illegally)* Inf **TN**53, Pothouse.

potica n [Slovene; see quot 1991]

A yeast bread made by spreading a layer of dough with filling and rolling it up.

c1965 Randle *Cookbooks* (Ask Neighbor) 1.3 **OH,** *Crackling Potica. . .* Spread warm filling over dough which has been rolled to ½″ thickness. Roll like a jelly roll. Let rise until double in size. . . To make Mint Potica, substitute 1 c. chopped mint for 2 c. cracklings. **1967–68** *DARE* (Qu. H18, *. . Special kinds of bread)* Inf **KS**20, Potica [poˈtitsə]—a Yugoslavian bread; **MN**2, Potica [pəˈtitsə]—a kind of coffee cake, has ground nuts in it; (Qu. H32, *. . Fancy rolls and pastries)* Inf **CO**35, Potica [pətitsə]—Austrians—pastry slab covered with spices, rolled up, and cut up in loaves; (Qu. H65, *Foreign foods favored by people around here)* Inf **KS**20, Potica—Yugoslavian. **1981** Hachten *Flavor WI* 151, *Walnut Potica* (Yugoslavian). . . Make filling by adding honey and walnuts to melted butter. Stir in cream. Add sugar, salt, and dates. Cook until mixture starts bubbling. . . Roll out [yeasted] dough . . then pull with fingers until paper thin, being careful not to tear. . . Spread filling over entire area and roll up like a jelly roll. **1991** Kirlin–Kirlin *Smithsonian Folklife Cookbook* 114 **MD,** Potica is central to Slovenian cuisine. Literally it means 'something rolled in.' At social occasions it is served, unbuttered, either as a bread with the main course or as dessert with coffee.

potice See **poultice**

potlatch n [Chinook Jargon; see quot 1863 at **1** below] Also sp *potlach* **chiefly Pacific NW, AK**

1 A gift.

1844 (1845) Wilkes *Narr. U.S. Explor. Exped.* 4.310, After the bargain was completed, and the price agreed upon, under the form of "potlatch," or "gift," the equivalent was always to be again treated for, and thus the price . . was often very much enhanced. **1862** (1863) Winthrop *Canoe & Saddle* 57 **nwOR,** They [=Klickitat Indians] . . expressed the friendliest sentiments, perhaps with a view to a liberal "potlatch" of trinkets. [**1863** Gibbs *Chinook Jargon* 21, *Pot'-latch,* or *Paht'-latsh, n., v.* Nootka, *Pahchilt* (Jewitt); *Pachaetl,* or *Pachatl* (Cook). *A gift; to give.*] **1938** (1939) [see **potlatch** v 1]. **1942** *AmSp* 17.225 **Pacific NW** [Logger's talk], *Potlach,* to give or a gift.

2a A feast among Northwest-coast Indians at which the host makes a lavish distribution of gifts; a somewhat similar social event among Eskimos, usu held as a commemoration or expression of thanksgiving. *Note:* Only quots that appear to reflect first-hand experience are included here; no attempt has been made to illustrate the use of *potlatch* in anthropological literature or in other contexts that reflect book knowledge of these customs. Cf *DCan,* Tabbert *Dict. Alaskan Engl.*

1865 in 1884 Leighton *Life at Puget Sound* 25 **wWA,** There was going to be a great *potlach* at the coal-mines, where a large quantity of *iktas* would be given away,—tin pans, guns, blankets, canoes, and money. . . It seems that any one who aspires to be a chief must first give a *potlach* to his tribe. **1870** *Congressional Globe* 41st Cong. 2d Sess. 1647/2 **WA,** Let me say that I have been to distributions of annuities; they are called "potlashes" [sic] in my country, and I have seen blankets torn into quarters and distributed. I have seen bolts of red calico torn and a yard given to every grown squaw, and half a yard to every papoose. **1911** Clayson *Hist. Narr.* 56 **wWA** (as of c1880), The fact of the matter is a "Potlatch" is a great fair not where "everybody gives to everybody," but where *somebody gives to everybody.* **1962** Salisbury *Quoth the Raven* 42 **seAK,** The potlatch was an institution which was not merely a feast; it was more. If given at the completion of a house, or at the burial of the dead, or the carving of a totem pole and its erection, it afforded opportunity to pay those who had taken part in the work. **1963** Oswalt *Mission of Change in AK* 62, The ceremony termed "Sending a Messenger" has also come to be called a "potlatch" by both local Eskimos and whites. . . [A]long the Kuskokwim today it means any elaborate feast or ceremony, especially if gifts are exchanged or given. **1966** Loyens *Changing Culture* 173, The word "potlatch" made its appearance at Nulato around 1927. . . Prior to that time, all native communal food distributions were called "banquets." The word "potlatch," however, became firmly rooted in local usage. **1968** *DARE* Tape **AK11,** And they [=Taku Indians] did a dance, their regular potlatch dance. And then he [=the chief] would take a box of crackers and he would throw it to—every man got a box of crackers. . . And each woman got ten yards of calico. . . Each one got a blanket. **1975** *Fairbanks Daily News–Miner* (AK) 19 Aug 7 (Tabbert *Dict. Alaskan Engl.*) **cAK,** The talk was all of potlatch, which had been going on for several days. . . And on this day, Friday, the activity was beginning to intensify in preparation for Sunday when those making potlatch would climax the activities by giving away presents. **1988** *Anchorage Daily News* 25 June sec A 10 (Tabbert *Dict. Alaskan Engl.*), Gambell will have a potlatch Monday to celebrate the hunters' safe return.

b By ext: an extravagant party or bout of merrymaking.

1902 Wilson *Spenders* 357 **West,** This life of idleness you been leadin'—one continual potlatch the whole time—it wa'n't doin' you a bit of good. **1965** Bowen *Alaskan Dict.* 27, The potlatch spirit is still alive, and many old timers use the term to refer to an extravagant and pointless waste of goods. See *spree.* **1967** Stegner *Little Live Things* 203 **cwCA,** Lou LoPresti could not have picked a worse day for his potlatch [=a Fourth of July party] if he had consulted an astrologer.

3 also attrib: A communal festival or meal. Cf Tabbert *Dict. Alaskan Engl.*

1911 *Seattle Daily Times* (WA) 29 June 3, Appoint a committee . . for the sending of a large delegation . . to the Potlatch celebration, Seattle. **1934** *Sun* (Baltimore MD) 19 July 5/1 (Hench Coll.), The old pre-war potlatch spirit of Seattle will be revived with the annual "Seattle International Potlatch." . . Merry-making, dancing, sports and entertainment will feature the four-day celebration in keeping with the Indian name Potlatch, which means feasting. **1958** Carrighar *Moonlight* 328 **AK,** After the trapping season the Indians stage a potlatch, with dog races and games and dances. **1971** *Today Show Letters* **OR,** When the "hippies" here in the Northwest want a large gathering, they are using the Indian word "Potlatch," which means "a social gathering or celebration." **1981** *DARE* File **ID,** I went to school there [=Potlatch ID]. Church din-

ners on a Sunday afternoon were called "Potlatches." **1987** *Theata* 301 (Tabbert *Dict. Alaskan Engl.*), During the winter an annual carnival is held. . . Games, races, a basketball tournament, dances, raffles and a potlatch dinner are held.

potlatch v [Chinook Jargon; see quot 1863 at **potlatch** n 1] **Pacific NW, AK**

1 To give or loan; rarely, to borrow.

[**1847** Palmer *Jrl.* 150 **NW,** Words used in the Chinook Jargon. . . *Potlatch* Give.] **1938** (1939) Holbrook *Holy Mackinaw* 265, *Potlatch.* To give; a gift. **1942** [see **potlatch** n 1]. **1943** W.H. Chase *Sourdough Pot* xxiii 171 (*OED2*) **AK,** The deal was closed, the butter potlatched to her father. **1968** *DARE* (Qu. U16, . . *"I need five dollars before Saturday, will you* _____ *it to me?"*) Inf **AK1,** Stake me, potlatch me, can I potlatch five dollars from you? **1968** *DARE* Tape **AK11,** We used to say, "I potlatch you this." . . It's giving away is what it means. . . Kids at school used to say, "Potlatch me this."

2 To make a general distribution of, share out. *Note:* See note at **potlatch** n 2a. Cf Tabbert *Dict. Alaskan Engl.*

1898 *Land of Sunshine* Apr 219 **AK,** In case the sentence is carried out they will be compelled to "potlatch" a very large amount. **1933** Marshall *Arctic Village* 109 **AK,** Otherwise, everything which a man acquired he divided with his neighbors, or "potlatched" it as the local vernacular has it. **1989** *AK Fish & Game* Nov–Dec 37 (Tabbert *Dict. Alaskan Engl.*), Upon returning to Minto, Israel's moose was "potlatched" or shared with village elders.

3 as vbl n: Holding a **potlatch** n 2a.

1915 *Nature & Sci.* 195 **Pacific,** Potlatching has been bitterly opposed by missionaries and officials in charge of Indian affairs, who object to the practice as a sinful waste.

potlatcher n Cf **potlatch** n 2a, b, **potlatch** v 2

1958 McCulloch *Woods Words* 138 **Pacific NW,** *Potlatcher*—A generous man; from the Indian custom of Potlatch, or celebration at which they gave away their possessions.

potlicker n[1]

1 A contemptible person; a toady; similarly vbl n *potlicking* toadying. Cf **ass-licker 1, bootlick** n, v, *bootlicker*

1830 Royall *Mrs. Royall's S. Tour* 1.78, This was said like a man, and never came into the heads of pot-lickers and scrubs, picked out of the ashes. **1941** Writers' Program *Guide AR* 78, When dogs are used, shooting at anything except a deer while the hounds are in hearing becomes a high social offense; the unlucky gunner is branded a "potlicker" and finds invitations to deer hunts scarce the next year. **1966–68** *DARE* (Qu. II20a, *A person who tries too hard to gain somebody else's favor: "He's an awful* _____.") Infs **MI4, OH57,** Potlicker. **1968** *Current Slang* 3.2.38 [Watts slang; Black], *Pot-licking.* . . Oversolicitous behavior.—He made his way to the top only by *pot-licking.*

2 also attrib: A hound, usu one of mixed breed; a nondescript or worthless dog; hence adj *potlicking* of a dog: mongrel, worthless. **esp Gulf States** See Map

1929 (1951) Faulkner *Sartoris* 282 **MS,** Hole up here, you potlickin' fool [=a hunting dog]. **1940** Writers' Program *Guide TX* 383 **ceTX,** Pineland . . is a lumber-mill town in the piney woods. . . These people, who are highly individualistic, are largely of old English stock and speak a dialect that contains odd idioms. They . . call a hound a "pot-licker." **1947** *Clarke Co. Democrat* (Grove Hill AL) 30 Oct 4/3, A hound is a hound, regardless of whether he is July, Red Bone, Walker, potlicker, or just plain hush-puppy. **1948** Faulkner *Intruder* 5 **MS,** A true rabbit dog, some hound, a good deal of hound, maybe mostly hound, redbone and black-and-tan with maybe a little pointer somewhere once, a potlicker, a nigger dog which it took but one glance to see had an affinity with rabbits. **1949** Arnow *Hunter's Horn* 30 **eKY,** Them damned Tiller potlickers, they'll be th ones to git King Devil if he's ever got. **1953** Randolph–Wilson *Down in Holler* 273 **Ozarks,** *Potlicker.* . . A dog of mixed breed, often a mongrel foxhound. **1963** Owens *Look to River* 117 **TX,** "Looks like a pot-licking dog to me." Luster leaned toward the water. "He's pure bloodhound. You c'n tell by the droop-down ears. He may a looked like a pot licker, but he ain't when he gits on the trail of a convict." **1965–70** *DARE* (Qu. J1, . . *A dog of mixed breed*) Infs **KY16, 27,** Potlicker; (Qu. J2, . . *Joking or uncomplimentary words . . for dogs*) Infs **AR51, LA2, 20, 29, MS1, SC32, TX54,** Potlicker; **LA12,** Potlicker hound. [9 of 10 Infs male] **1967** LeCompte *Word Atlas* 194 **seLA,** *A worthless dog* . . pot-licker [4 of 21 infs]. **1982** Slone *How We Talked* **eKY** (as of c1950), *A pot-licker*—hound dog. **1986** Pederson *LAGS*

Concordance (Mongrel) 16 infs, **chiefly LA, MS**, Potlicker(s); 7 infs, 4 **MS**, Potlicker hound(s). [Typical comments are: "Just an old hound, not bred up"; "red hound"; "can be a bluetick"; "long ears"; "mixed breed"; "an old dog that ain't no-(ac)count"; "good for hunting"; "worthless."] **1996** *DARE* File **neTX** (as of 1920s–30s), That's a *pot-lickin' dog.*

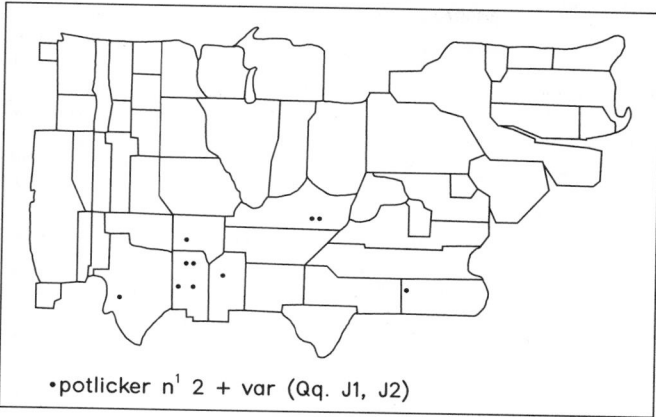

•potlicker n¹ 2 + var (Qq. J1, J2)

3 The index finger. Cf **lick-pot**
1972 Jones–Hawes *Step it Down* 12 **eGA** [Black], John Davis . . told us the finger names he had learned when he was a boy on St. Simons Island: thumb, potlicker, longman, lingman, littleman.

potlicker n² See **pot liquor**

potlicking vbl n See **potlicker** n¹ **1**

potlicking adj See **potlicker** n¹ **2**

pot liquor n Also sp *potlicker, potlikker* [*OED2* 1744 →] **scattered, but chiefly Sth**
The liquid in which meat or vegetables, esp greens, have been boiled; broadly, the liquid along with what has been boiled in it.
1819 *Amer. Farmer* 1.68, The common pot liquor, from the boiling of pork or bacon, . . [is] injurious to confined hogs. **a1883** (1911) Bagby *VA Gentleman* 47, A true Virginian. . . must . . begin on pot-liquor, and keep it up until he sheds his milk-teeth. **1895** Brown *Meadow-Grass* 269 **NEng**, "Such cold potatoes—" "B'iled in the pot-liquor!" she whispered, a knowing gleam in her blue eyes. **1899** (1912) Green *VA Folk-Speech* 332, Pot-liquor. . . The liquor in which bacon and cabbage have been boiled. **1909** *DN* 3.359 **eAL, wGA**, Pot-liquor. . . Liquor from boiled greens or field peas and fat meat. **1915** *DN* 4.240 **MA** [Colonial cookery terms], *Pot liquor.* Stock for soup. **1930** *Sun* (Baltimore) 17 May 1/3 (*OED2*), Pot liquor is the best way of preventing nearly all the diseases that we are heir to. **1945** FWP *Lay My Burden Down* 61 **NC** (as of 1850s) [Black], And sometime they would crumble bread in the potlicker and give us spoons, and we would stand round the pot and eat. **1950** *WELS* (*What words do you have for gravy*) 1 Inf, **cWI**, Pot liquor is an old-fashioned term. **1965–70** *DARE* (Qu. H24, . . *Names or nicknames . . for boiled cornmeal*) Inf **AL25**, Pot-liquor dumpling—boil turnip greens; the liquid is pot liquor; (Qu. H36, *Kinds of soup*) Inf **GA36**, Pot liquor—residue of turnips or other vegetables that have been boiled; (Qu. H37, . . *Words . . for gravy*) Infs **MO5, 6, NY226, SC67, WI29**, Pot liquor; **MA6**, Pot liquor—slop out of boiled dinner; (Qu. BB22, . . *Home remedies . . for constipation*) Inf **AL4**, Turnip-green pot liquor; [(Qu. II25, *Names or nicknames for the part of a town where the poorer people, special groups, or foreign groups live*) Inf **MD26**, Pot-liquor Flats]. **1966** *DARE* Tape **NC36**, What they make is pot liquor that's used from the vegetables and meat which is cooked. **1967** *DARE* FW Addit **GA21**, *Pot liquor*—the water turnip greens is cooked in. It's eaten by soaking corn bread in it. A real swamp dish. Country people around Okefenokee Swamp; **FL37**, *Pot liquor*—the juice in the pot after green beans have been cooked; lots of those old-timers liked the pot liquor better than the beans; **SC**, *Pot liquor*—liquid from cooked vegetable. **1982** Claiborne *Feast Made* 32 **MS**, The greens were. . . allowed to cook for hours. Once cooked, the liquid is much treasured by southern palates. It is called "pot likker" and you sip it like soup with corn bread. **1986** Pederson *LAGS Concordance*, 41 infs, 31 **AL, GA, MS**, Pot liquor. **1993** Delany–Delany *Having Our Say* 150 **Sth** [Black], When Mama and I were in Russia, after visiting London, we. . . were served cabbage soup at a hotel, and Mama and I laughed because in the South that is

known as "pot liquor." **1996** *DARE* File **seVA**, What's "pot liquor" for folks? For my immediate family, it's a big pot of snaps cooked with potatoes . . and a streak of lean, eaten with fried corn bread. . . I have a friend from western Kentucky whose family's pot liquor involves collards.

potluck meal n Also *potluck (dinner), potluck supper,* and var combs [By ext from *potluck* the luck of the draw, whatever food is being served] **widespread, but less freq Sth, C Atl, NY** See Map and Map Section Cf **covered-dish meal, pitch-in dinner, tureen ~**
A meal to which people bring food to share, usu without assignment of particular dishes; the food at such a gathering; also adj *potluck* in the form of such a meal.
[**1929** *AmSp* 4.420 [College English], *Pot luck*—Food contributed by the guest. *To take pot luck* is to bring food with one to a party. This is a Western usage, unknown in New York and New Jersey.] **1942** *AmSp* 17.129, General throughout the country is the custom among church organizations, neighborhood groups, assemblies of relatives and like gatherings of bringing food for a company dinner or supper. Usually the particular dish or dishes are assigned in advance. . . Another type is the *potluck dinner,* where presumably the menu is not arranged beforehand and each family brings what it pleases. **1948** *WELS Suppl.* **WI**, I grew up in central Wisconsin, and have always called such a meal a pot-luck, but his family in Oklahoma call it a "covered dish" meal. **1950** *WELS* **WI** (*When people bring hot dishes to a meeting place and share them together, you call that a _____ meal*) 46 Infs, Potluck; 1 Inf, Potluck supper; 1 Inf, Potluck generally known and occasionally used. **1960** Criswell *Resp. to PADS 20* **Ozarks**, Pot-luck suppers where everybody took a dish and nobody knew what anybody else was going to bring, except that women gossiped. **1965–70** *DARE* (Qu. H70, *When people bring baked dishes, salads, and so forth to a meeting-place and share them together, that's a _____ meal*) 429 Infs, **widespread exc Sth, C Atl, NY**, Potluck; 27 Infs, **chiefly NEast, S Midl**, Potluck supper (*or* dinner); (Qu. FF1, . . *A kind of group meeting called a 'social' or 'sociable'. . . [What goes on?]*) 21 Infs, **scattered exc Sth, Midl**, Potluck supper (*or* dinner); 18 Infs, **scattered, but esp CA**, Potluck; **CA154, IL25, NJ40**, Potluck social; **WI47**, Family potluck supper; **WA6**, Potluck deal; **WA3**, Potluck gathering; **IL126**, Potluck supper visit; (Qu. FF2, . . *Kinds of parties*) Infs **AR47, CA81, IL102, MI9, MO7, WI47**, Potluck suppers (*or* dinners); **CA107, 166**, Potlucks. **1965** *Rhinelander Daily News & New North* (WI) 12 Aug 4/7, The August meeting of Rhinelander Camera Club will be held . . at Diamond Lake picnic grounds. . . Lunch will be potluck in the form of a cookout. **1966** *Lynden Tribune* (WA) 8 Dec 6/4, Mrs. Frank Ruzicka, Jr., will be hostess . . for their 7:30 p.m. planned potluck Christmas dinner. **1966–70** *DARE* Tape **CA134**, Potlucks are more important than anything else; everybody brings his food to eat; **CA166**, We still went on picnics. . . Later on we started these potlucks; **CA182**, The volunteer fire hall is used for community functions such as . . a Valentine potluck and a Fourth of July parade; **MI28**, We all brought something for the meal. We had a potluck supper. **1968** *Post-Reg.* (Idaho Falls ID) 26 Jan 6/8, The local chapter will hold a "Washington's Birthday" party. . . Pot luck will be served. Cards and games will be played. **1980** *Sat. Review* Aug 77, A [church] notice announced a forthcoming "potluck dinner" with a number to call "for your food assignment." This new meaning for *potluck* crept in during the Fifties, I think. I don't know anyone under about 40 who knows the earlier and, to me, still official meaning of the term. **1999** *Isthmus* (Madison WI) 5 Nov 39 (as of c1970), Potluck

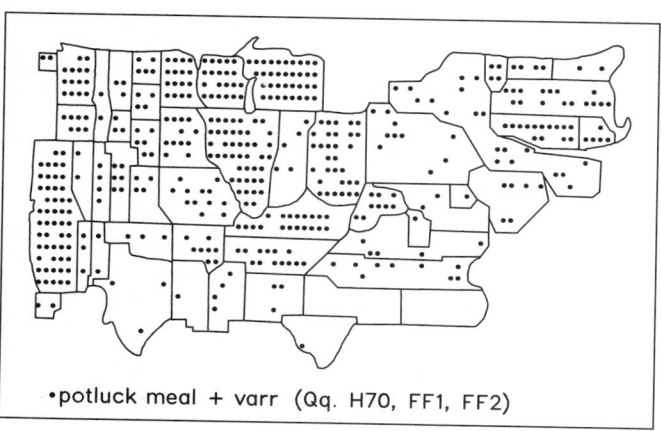

•potluck meal + varr (Qq. H70, FF1, FF2)

dinners, in particular, gave one gleeful license to sample a range of casseroles.

potpie n Cf **pan pie**

1 pronc-sp *pot poi:* A dish of meat and vegetables (or rarely vegetables or eggs alone) boiled or baked in a deep pot with one or more layers of piecrust, biscuit dough, dumplings, or noodles; by ext, a thin dumpling or noodle cut in squares and boiled in broth or stew; hence n *potpie bow* appar a noodle in the shape of a bow tie. **scattered, but chiefly N Midl, esp PA** See Map

1823 (1922) Anthony *New Bedford* 55 **MA**, Dined at father's—had a pot pie party at our house in the evening. **1843** (1916) Hall *New Purchase* 154 **IN**, An enormous pot-pie, and piping hot, graced our centre. . . The pie to-day was the doughy sepulchre of at least six hens, two chanticleers, and four pullets. . . What pot could have contained the pie is inconceivable. **1895** (1900) Arnold *Century Cook Book* 169, A Plain *Pot-Pie.* . . When the stew is ready, cook the dumplings, and place them on the same dish around the stew. **1899** (1912) Green *VA Folk-Speech* 332, *Pot-pie.* . . A pie made by lining the inner surface of a pot or pan with pastry, and filling it with meat, as, beef, mutton, fowl, etc., seasoning it and then baking. **1905** *DN* 3.16 **cCT**, *Pot-pie.* . . A meat pie. **1907** *DN* 3.216 **nwAR**, *Pot-pie.* . . A meat pie. **1939** Wolcott *Yankee Cook Book* 86, *Veal Pot Pie I.* . . Cover kettle and simmer until meat is tender. . . Make dumpling dough; carefully drop in dumplings. . . *Veal Pot Pie recipes of olden times call for a deep baking dish lined with baked pastry crust. . . The veal was then added and topped with pastry or cream of tartar biscuits, soda biscuits or dumplings.* **1940** Brown *Amer. Cooks* 36 **AR**, *Egg Potpie.* . . Put boiling water in baking dish and break 3 eggs into it. . . Cover with a layer of dumplings made from short biscuit dough, then a second layer of eggs, topped off with crust. **1948** Hutchison *PA Du. Cook Book* 57, *Berks County Chicken Potpie.* . . Line the bottom of the kettle with them [=potatoes]. Add a layer of noodles, then one of onions, sprinkle with salt, pepper, and parsley, and add a layer of chicken. Repeat this order. . . The top layer should be noodles. **c1965** Randle *Cookbooks* (Plain Cookery) 11 **OH**, *Pot Pie*—1 egg, beat well, add: ¼ t. salt, 1 c. cream or rich milk, enough flour to make stiff dough to roll. Roll out thin. Cut in 1½" squares. . . Drop in boiling beef or chicken broth. **1965–70** *DARE* (Qu. H45, *Dishes made with meat, fish, or poultry that everybody around here would know, but that people in other places might not*) 14 Infs, **scattered, but esp PA**, Chicken potpie; **NC88**, Chicken potpie—make a biscuit dough, roll very thin; add a layer of cooked chicken, a layer of pastry, more chicken, more pastry; **NJ40**, Chicken potpie—actually chicken and dumplings; **NY20**, Chicken potpie = chicken with dumplings; **PA13**, Chicken potpie, beef potpie—boiled, water and flour, roll out and cook in meat broth; **PA18**, Chicken potpie; boiled potpie—put dough into the beef stock; **PA9**, Boiled chicken potpie; **MI95**, **OH57**, **PA1, 26, 150, 163**, Potpie(s); **ME2**, Potpie—any kind of meat with potatoes, etc, and summer savory; **NY52**, Potpie—out of almost anything = stew with biscuits over the top; **NY94**, Meat pies or potpies—made in a deep dish with biscuits across the top; **OH84**, Potpie—roll out dough, cut into squares; boiled in chicken broth; not dropped like dumplings; **PA40, 52**, Potpie—chicken and beef; **PA119**, Potpies—dumplings, meat pies—crust; **PA22, 41, 128, 136**, Beef potpie; **PA110**, Ham potpie, potpie bows; **MD37**, Muskrat potpie; (Qu. H36, *Kinds of soup*) Inf **VA69**, Chicken noodle—if dumplings were added, it's called potpie; (Qu. H48, *Baked dishes made of potatoes cut up with meat or cheese*) Infs **IL113, NY43, PA196**, (Beef) potpie; **MD30**, Potpie—old word; casserole—new word; (Qu. H49, *Dishes made by boiling potatoes with other foods*) Infs **NY1, PA1**, (Chicken) potpie; **MD27**, Boiled potpie—boiled beef and potatoes, dough dumplings dropped in; **MD37**, Potpie—a stew with dumplings in it; (Qu. H50, *Dishes made with beans, peas, or corn that everybody around here knows, but people in other places might not*) Inf **MD27**, Baked corn potpie—corn and butter baked in pastry shell; (Qu. H68, *When food remains over from one meal and you heat it again for another meal. . . "She got out Sunday's roast and _____ [it]."*) Inf **IL131**, Made potpie of it; (Qu. FF1, *. . A kind of group meeting called a 'social' or 'sociable'. . . [What goes on?]*) Inf **NJ58**, Potpie supper. **1968** *Heirloom Cook Book* 28 **nIL**, *Pot Poi*—Put flour on a board and make a well in the middle. Add cooled broth from cooked meat and vegetables. Mix gently to a medium stiff dough. Roll or pat to twice the thickness of pie crust. Cut in approximately 2 inch squares and drop in *boiling* broth in pan with stew. . . Adding egg and butter make [sic] richer pot poi. **1968** *DARE* Tape **OH85**, [Inf:] To me, potpie is a dough that is cooked in broth. It is rolled out, cut in squares, and cooked in broth. . . [FW:] Do other people think of potpie as a kind of meat pie?

[Inf:] Not around here they don't. Now, some places they do. . . And my brother ran into that when he was in the Army when he was in the East. **1971** *Today Show Letters* **sePA**, Here in the Pennsylvania Dutch country potpie means a *boiled* meat pie. The crust is boiled too, producing a sort of square thin dumpling. Area noodle products include potpie bows. You just dump them into your seasoned meat broth and raw potatoes and simmer till done. . . A lot of frozen food manufacturers sell potpie that is not *pot* pie. It's *baked* meat pie. **1977** Anderson *Grass Roots Cookbook* 48 **sePA**, "Potpie" in Pennsylvania Dutch country means big squares of home-made egg noodles used to plump up chicken stew (Chicken Potpie). There are all kinds of potpie—fluffy ones leavened with baking powder, tender ones shortened with lard and "slippery" ones, which are plain egg noodles. **1986** Pederson *LAGS Concordance*, 1 inf, **nwFL**, Potpie—sold in stores, like chicken potpie? 1 inf, **neTX**, Potpie—made with chicken, etc.

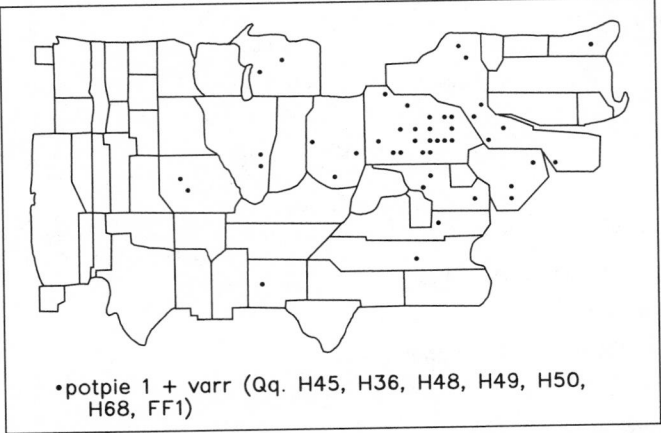

•potpie 1 + varr (Qq. H45, H36, H48, H49, H50, H68, FF1)

2 =**deep-dish pie.** See also **apple pot-pie** Cf **pot apple pie**

1848 Bartlett *Americanisms* 311, *Apple slump.* . . Called in other parts of the country an *apple pot-pie.* **1920** Kander *Settlement Cook Book* 285 **WI**, *Cherry Pot Pie.* . . Place cherries in pudding dish, lay biscuits on top, let steam 35 minutes. **1941** *LANE* Map 292 (*Apple dumpling*) 4 infs, **CT, RI, ME**, Apple pot pie; 1 inf, **cnCT**, Pot pie, with several layers [lɛ-ɪnz] of apples and crust; 1 inf, **seCT**, Pot pie = slump; 2 infs, **cnCT, seMA**, Pot pie [*DARE* Ed: heard but not used]; 1 inf, **seMA**, Pot pie = apple slump, ~ grunt; 1 inf, **csRI**, Apple slump, of apples and biscuit dough, steamed, 'like a pot pie.' **1950** *PADS* 14.54 **SC**, *Pot pie:* . . A fruit pie baked in a large, deep pan (formerly a pot) with wheat flour dumplings mixed in with the fruit; a cobbler. **1957** *NC Hist. Rev.* 34.524 **cnNC** (as of 1820s), How our mouths would water as he told us of the peach "pot pies." **c1960** Wilson *Coll.* **csKY**, *Pot pie:* . . A deep pie, a cobbler. **1965** *PADS* 43.16 **seMA**, Other names for a deep-dish apple pie . . apple pot pie [1 of 9 infs]. **1986** Pederson *LAGS Concordance* (*Cobbler*) 1 inf, **neTN**, Potpie = cobbler, family pie; 1 inf, **neTN**, Potpie—several layers of fruit; 1 inf, **neTN**, Potpie = family pie; 1 inf, **cnGA**, Potpie—deep-dish fruit pie; 1 inf, **nwFL**, Potpie—dumplings dropped in fruit, cooked in pot; 1 inf, **cwFL**, Potpie—has several layers.

potpie bow, pot poi See **potpie 1**

potra See **potro**

potrack n, v, hence vbl n *potracking* [Echoic] **Sth, S Midl**
The characteristic cry of the guinea fowl; to make this sound; by ext, a guinea fowl.

1840 *S. Lit. Messenger* 6.386, The guinea-fowls make a great racket, with their pot-rack. **1883** (1971) Harris *Nights with Remus* 193 **GA**, He heard a great commotion among the guinea-fowls. The squawking and pot-racking went on at such a rate that the geese awoke and began to scream. **1899** (1912) Green *VA Folk-Speech* 332, *Potrack.* . . The cry of the guinea fowl. **1906** Casey *Parson's Boys* 168 **sIL** (as of c1860), From its strident note of warning when anything strange happened about the place, the single Guinea-hen was called "Pot-rack!" **1909** *DN* 3.359 **eAL, wGA**, *Pot-rack.* . . A guinea-fowl. **1945** FWP *Lay My Burden Down* 112 **LA** (as of 1840s–50s) [Black], Come the daybreak you hear the guinea fowls start potracking down at the edge of the woods lot. **1949** Webber *Backwoods Teacher* 9 **Ozarks**, A dog barked not far away, drowning the distant potracking of guineas. **c1960** Wilson *Coll.* **csKY**, "Potrack"—What a guinea says and keeps on saying, ad nauseam. **1968** *DARE* FW Addit **GA22**, "Potrack" ['pɑt,ræk]—the sound a "guinea chicken" makes when it "hollers." **1979** *DARE* File **ceTX**, My guinea is laying, and she pot-racks all the time.

potrero n [Span "pasture"]

1 A pasture; a naturally enclosed meadow—freq used in place names. **chiefly CA**

1848 (1939) Sutter *New Helvetia Diary* 121 **CA**, 6 Men have been sent from the race, on acct. having no tools, employed them to get the small potrero repaired. **1854** *Calif. Chronicle* (S.F.) 16 May 4/5 (*DA*), Their claim . . covers the lands adjoining and beyond Mission creek, and known as the 'Potrero.' **1857** in 1941 *AmSp* 16.262 **CA** [Span words frequently used in English], *Potrero*, a colt pasture. **1886** Van Dyke *So. Calif.* 106 (*DA*), When, in the heat of day, one comes to some little *potrero* where pine-clad hills inclose a soft green meadow, . . then this bird makes a strange, sweet feeling in the wanderer's heart. **1892** *DN* 1.193 **TX**, *Potréro*: a pasture, generally for colts and young horses. Also a piece of land easily fenced in, situated in the bend of a stream or in a valley with a narrow pass for entrance. **1923** Saunders *S. Sierras* 105 **CA**, Ahead in the sun lay the Devil's *Potrero*—a verdant, wild-flowery bowl rimmed around with mountains. **1970** Stewart *Amer. Place-Names* 386, *Potrero*—Spanish 'pasture ground,' common in CA, sometimes as a specific, e.g. with creek, hill.

2 A steep-sided tongue of high land between two canyons. **SW**

1872 Bourke *Diary* 3 Dec **SW**, Hills break away in potreros. **1892** Bandelier *Final Rept.* 158 **SW**, These cliffs appear like pillars, or gigantic posts; hence their Spanish name "Potreros." The one forming the southern wall of the Cuesta Colorada gorge is an extensive plateau called Potrero Chato. **1933** *AmSp* 8.3.9 **SW**, Where high mesas are edged with sharp narrow points, these are called *potreros*, colt pastures, since they can be lightly fenced with sticks and stones across the broad end, and colts are afraid to venture down the steep sides. **1940** Fergusson *Our Southwest* 354, A potrero is a narrow ridge between canyons, and a saddle is a sag between peaks. **1953** Hewett–Dutton *Pajarito Plateau* 104 **NM**, The long, narrow potrero bounding the canyon on the north is entirely cut out for a distance of nearly a mile, thus throwing into one squarish open park the width of two small canyons and the formerly intervening mesa.

Po-t-rik See **Portoreek**

potro n Also fem *potra* [Span] **SW**

A young horse or mare, esp one not yet broken.

1857 in 1941 *AmSp* 16.265 **CA** [Span words frequently used in English], *Potro*, Colt. **1892** *DN* 1.193 **TX**, *Pótro, fem. pótra*: a young horse or mare not yet broken. **1929** Dobie *Vaquero* 8 **TX** (as of 1870s), Billie Colville, a rancher, told me that if I would break seven wild *potros* (young horses) he had, he would let me have my pick of the seven. **1962** Atwood *Vocab. TX* 56, A horse that has not been broken for riding may vary from the tame colt of the Eastern farm to the completely undomesticated animal of the Western prairies. . . Six informants in Southwest Texas give *potro* with this meaning. . **1967** *DARE* (Qu. K42, *A horse that is rough, wild, or dangerous*) Inf **TX**22, ['potrə]—just young and wild.

potry See **poetry**

pots See **pot** n[1] **5, 6c**

pots and kettles n [Prob folk-etym for **potash kettle**]

1969 *DARE* (Qu. C17, . . *A small, rounded hill*) Inf **MI**91, Pots and kettles—the size of a house.

Potsfield pickle(s) n esp **NEng**

A kind of relish of pickled chopped vegetables.

1939 Wolcott *Yankee Cook Book* 295 **MA**, *Potsfield Pickles*. . . "Old New England Recipe." . . chopped green tomatoes . . chopped red tomatoes . . chopped cabbage[?] 3 pints chopped onions . . red peppers . . celery[?] ½ cup horse-radish . . salt[?] 2 quarts vinegar . . sugar[?] ½ teaspoon cinnamon . . cloves . . mustard seed. **1966–67** *DARE* (Qu. H56, *Names for . . pickles*) Inf **MA**83, Potsfield pickles—like chili sauce; **NH**6, Potsfield pickles—a relish; (Qu. H57, *Tasty or spicy side-dishes served with meats*) Inf **NH**6, Potsfield pickle.

potsie See **potsy** 1

potstick n [*OED2* c1410 →; "Now only *dial.*"] esp **PA**

A stick or wooden spoon for stirring a pot.

1899 (1912) Green *VA Folk-Speech* 332, *Pot-stick*. . . A stick used for stirring a pot in soap-making; soapstick. **1930** Shoemaker *1300 Words* 45 **cPA Mts** (as of c1900), *Pot-stick*—A piece of wood used to stir a pot, also for beating children. **1968** *DARE* (QR, near Qu. F4) Inf **PA**150, Wooden spoon is a potstick. **1982** *Barrick Coll.* **csPA**, *Potstick*—spoon or stirrer used in cooking, and for punishing children.

pot still See **pot 2**

potsy n

1 also *patsy*; also sp *pot(t)sie, pottsy*; rarely pl: The game of hopscotch; the object used in this game. [Prob *pots* (at **pot** n **5**) + **-ie** suff[3] (also **-y**)] **chiefly NYC** See Map

1905 *Pedagogical Seminary* 12.503 **NYC**, Potsie—a primitive kind of hop scotch. **1928** *Amer. Mercury* 14.58 **NYC**, Potsies, as I learned long after, . . is the New York version of hopscotch. **1931** *Recreation* (NY) 24.672, *Potsy* is an adaptation of Hop Scotch. . . The "potsy" is a piece of tin, a rock or a puck. **1932** *Sun* (NY NY) 26 Mar 18/3, As any New Yorker will recognize, the potsy refers to the piece of tin can, doubled and redoubled and stamped flat with the heel, which is kicked from flagstone to flagstone . . by the hopping, juvenile player of the game potsy. **1957** *WELS Suppl.* **NYC** (as of c1930), Potsie (hop-scotch). **1965–70** *DARE* (Qu. EE19, *The game in which children mark a 'court' on the . . sidewalk, throw a flat stone in one section, then go on one foot and try to kick it or carry it out*) 11 Infs, 10 **NYC**, Potsy. **1967** *DARE* FW Addit **NYC** (as of 1950s), Potsie—object thrown into each box (successively) in hopscotch game. **1975** Ferretti *Gt. Amer. Book Sidewalk Games* 31, The most widely known and remembered sidewalk game is Pottsie. . . [Some people] call it *Hopscotch*. . . In parts of the Far West, it comes out *Potsie* (pronounced *Poh-tse*); but for most of the rest of us, it is *Pottsie*, or *Pottsy*, or *Potsy*. *Ibid* 37, The pottsie itself is important to the game. It is generally agreed that oblong pieces of slate chipped out of someone's patio or decorative sidewalk make the best pottsies. **1976** *Capital Times* (Madison WI) 1 Oct 38/2, *Totie Fields* told a friend she'll be fitted for an artificial leg this week "and by Halloween I'll be able to play you potsy." **1981** *AmSp* 56.21 **NYC**, Two persons I consulted reported *patsy* /'pætsi/ from the 1930s for Canarsie, Brooklyn, and for the northern Bronx . . , in both senses [=hopscotch, the object used in this game]. *Ibid* 22, My informants who knew *potsy* or *patsy* defined it in a number of ways: 1. For most New York City informants . . , it is the name of both the game and the object. This use was reported also for Middlebush, New Jersey (1930s). 2. For some New York City informants . . , it is the name of the game only, and there is no distinctive word for the object. This use was also reported for Muncie, New York (1950s). 3. For one New York City consultant . . , *hopscotch* is a boys' word and *potsy* is a girls' word for the game. . . Away from New York City, *hopscotch* and *potsy* are used in either of two ways: 4. *Potsy* is the object and *hopscotch* the game (New Rochelle, New York, 1920s). 5. The game is called either *hopscotch* or *potsy*, and there is no distinctive term for the object. **1983** *DARE* File **NYC** (as of 1950s), *Potsy*—The player uses an object—such as a key or key ring—and tosses it first into "1" [etc].

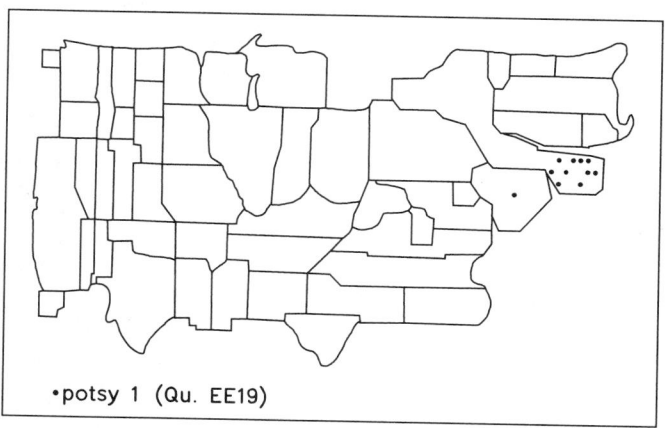

•potsy 1 (Qu. EE19)

2 also pl: A marble game in which players attempt to shoot marbles out of a ring. Cf **pot** n **6c**

1942 Berrey–Van den Bark *Amer. Slang* 665.1, Pots, potsies, ringer, *a game in which the players shoot marbles from a "pot" or ring.* **1950** *WELS* (*Different kinds of marble games*) 1 Inf, **ceWI**, Potsy. **1966** *DARE* (Qu. EE7, . . *Kinds of marble games*) Inf **MT**1, Potsies. **1985**

Runyan *Knuckles Down* 14, Potsies. . . Players alternate turns trying to knock the marbles out of the ring while keeping their shooters in the ring. If a shooter goes out, or the player misses, his turn is over. **3 =pottery** n[1].
1971 Bright *Word Geog. CA & NV* 117, [Marbles:] Potsies— "cheap"—1 [of 300 infs]—Sierra.

pot-tail n Also *pot-tails* [Appar by folk-etym or metanalysis from *pot ale* (*OED2* at *pot* sb.[1] 14); cf **pot** n **2** and *OED2 tail* sb.[1] 7] **sAppalachians** Cf **tailings**
The spent mash remaining in a still after distillation.
1917 *DN* 4.415 **wNC**, Pot-tails. . . The residue in a moonshine still after the backings are run off. **1959** *Hall Coll.* **wNC** *(Montgomery Coll.)*, [The liquor] wouldn't have any more strength, and then you had to pour up and clean your still, clean it all out, what they called the pot tails. **1968** *Foxfire* 2.3.91 **nGA**, At the end of each run, the plug stick . . is pushed in thus releasing the slop or "pot-tail" which flows through the tilted slop arm . . and trough into a bucket. **1974** Dabney *Mountain Spirits* xxiii **sAppalachians**, Pot-Tail: The mash left after a distillation. In copper pot stills, this leftover is dipped out and "slopped back" into the mash barrels and mixed with subsequent batches to be fermented. The result is sour mash whiskey.

potted (out) adj
Of a road: full of **potholes 3.**
1969–70 *DARE* (Qu. N27b, *When unpaved roads get very rough, you call them* _____) Infs **IL126, NY142,** Potted (out).

potter v, hence vbl n *pottering* **eMA** *old-fash* Cf **bandudelums**
See quots.
1791 (1905) Bentley *Diary* 1.254 **neMA**, After *pottering time* is over, which is running upon the broken ice without falling into the water & requires great activity, comes on *Marble time*. **a1870** Chipman *Notes on Bartlett* 335 *(DA)* **MA**, Potter. To tread upon ice floating, or to leap from one to another piece of it floating, or to walk upon loose spars floating upon water.—Eastern coast of Massachusetts. **1892** *DN* 1.211 **neMA**, Potterin. . . "Goin' potterin'" (a boy's sport). Salem.

potter n
=pottery n[1].
1971 Bright *Word Geog. CA & NV* 117, [Marbles:] Potters—"Porcelain"—1 [of 300 infs]—Sacramento Valley.

potteridge See **partridge A3**

pottering See **potter** v

pottersaw n [See quot 1931]
=sunfish (here: *Lepomis* spp).
[**1931** Read *LA French* 101, Patassa, a derivative of Choctaw *patàssa*, "flat," as used in the phrase *nàni patàssa*, "flat fish," is the generic name of the various species of sunfish that inhabit the fresh waters of Louisiana. . . Those persons who do not speak French refer to the sunfish by the erroneous term "perch."] **1947** Ballowe *The Lawd* 155 **LA**, The pottersaws [Footnote: Perch] in Cowpen is jess baiggin' to be ketched.

potter wasp n Also *potter's wasp* [See quot 1905]
A **wasp** of the family Vespidae, esp *Eumenes fraternus*. For other names of the latter see **jug-maker, mason wasp, vasemaker ~**
1852 Harris *Treatise Insects* 367, The potter-wasp (*Eumenes fraterna*) . . fills her clay cells with canker-worms. **1870** MO State Entomol. *Annual Rept. for 1869* 103, The Fraternal Potter-wasp (*Eumenes Fraterna*, Say). **1905** Kellogg *Amer. Insects* 498, Of mason- or potter-wasps, that is, solitary wasps that make a nest of clay or mud worked up with saliva, there are numerous species belonging to several different families. The daintiest mud-nests are the little vases of Eumenes. **1954** Borror–DeLong *Intro. Insects* 734, The Eumeninae, the mason or potter wasps, are a large and widespread group, and many species are very common. The species in the genus *Eumenes* construct juglike nests of mud which are attached to twigs and are provisioned with caterpillars. **1970** *DARE* (Qu. R20, *Wasps that build their nests of mud*) Inf **IL119,** Potter's wasp. **1972** Swan–Papp *Insects* 545, Potter wasp: *Eumenes fraterna*. . . It constructs a rounded vaselike nest of clay on twigs of trees and bushes.

pottery n[1] Also sp *pottry* **scattered, but chiefly West** Cf **china B1, clayie, pot** n **6d, potsy 3, potty** n[1]
A playing marble of fired clay.
1926 *AmSp* 2.66 **CO**, And the "migs," "agates," "glassies," "pureys," "commies" and "potteries" they talk about! Who'd know these strange-sounding things, unless he were fraternizing with school-ground company. **1950** *WELS* (Marbles: . . others) 1 Inf, **ceWI**, Glassies, agates, potteries, chinas. **1957** *Sat. Eve. Post Letters* **swMO** (as of c1914), The types of marbles used were Agates, Glassies, Pintos, Potties, Steelies and of course the lowest priced of all were called Scraggies. **a1960** Bailey *Resp. to PADS 20* **KS** (Marbles) Small ones: peewees, cheap ones: potterys [sic]. **1965–70** *DARE* (Qu. EE6c, *Cheap marbles*) Infs **ID2, 4, KS13, MT5, NJ69, OR15, SC54, WI60, WY1,** Potteries; (Qu. EE6d, *Special marbles*) Infs **CO3, OK42,** Potteries. **1971** Bright *Word Geog. CA & NV* 117, [Marbles:] Potteries—8 [of 300 infs]—San Joaquin Valley, Nevada.

pottery n[2] See **poetry**

pottery n[3] [Perh by analogy with *smithy* blacksmith, which is appar based on a misunderstanding of the second line of Longfellow's poem "The Village Blacksmith"]
A potter.
1973 *AmSp* 48.160, I interviewed a traditional potter in southern Alabama. During our conversation he asked me, "Are you a pottery?" . . Later, in eastern Kentucky, I was interviewing another traditional potter. . . In the course of the interview, he volunteered, "You have to work hard if you are going to be a pottery."

pottidge See **partridge A4**

pottie See **potty** n[1]

potties See **potty** n[2]

pottige See **partridge A4**

pottle-bellied adj [Engl dial; cf *OED2, EDD*]
Potbellied.
1941 *LANE* Map 458 *(Stout, paunchy)* 1 inf, **eME,** Pottle-bellied.

pottlebelly See **potbelly 3**

pottry See **pottery** n[1]

pottsie, pottsy See **potsy 1**

potty n[1] Also *pottie* [*EDD potty* sb.[1] "A boy's marble; a small round ball of clay used in the game of 'knur and spell'"] Cf **-ie** suff[3], **pot** n **6d**
=pottery n[1].
1958 *Resp. to PADS 29* **cnOK**, Pottie—a glazed pottery marble of larger diameter than 3/8 inch. **1967** *DARE* (Qu. EE6c, *Cheap marbles*) Infs **NE6, PA4,** Potties; **CO3,** Potties—made out of pottery.

potty n[2] Cf **jackpot 3, pot** n **6a, c**
A hole in the ground toward which marbles are thrown; also *potties*: a game involving such holes.
c1970 Wiersma *Marbles Terms*, Potties—from one line you throw your marble as close to the first pot as possible. The one who is closes [sic] shoots first, then you go all the way around into each pot (taking turns). When you have gone to all five you are poison and you can poison the pots you go into. You plaiy [sic] chasies with the additional rule that if you go into your opponents [sic] pot you loose [sic]. **1975** Ferretti *Gt. Amer. Book Sidewalk Games* 150, In *Potty*, a hole is dug into the dirt with the heel. All players throw their marbles in turn at the Pot from a throwing line about seven feet away. The player whose marble is closest to the hole . . goes first. He then shoots for the Pot and, once in, can use "spannies" to win other marbles; that is, he keeps any marble close enough to the Pot to fall within the distance created by stretching his thumb and forefinger. **1985** Runyan *Knuckles Down* 18, Potty. . . A small hole or pot is dug and a pitch line is marked 6–8 feet away. . . Players take turns pitching their marbles from the pitch line, trying to hit the target pot. *Ibid* 30, Potty—This is similar to a hole except that it is an essential part of "Pot" games.

potty adj
1 Potbellied, overweight. [*SND pottie* (at *pot* n.[1] 1) "pot-bellied, corpulent"]

1929 (1951) Faulkner *Sartoris* 170 **MS,** In the doorway Aunt Sally, a potty little woman in a lace cap, leaned on a gold-headed ebony walking-stick. **1970** *DARE* (Qu. X53a, . . *An oversize stomach*) Inf **VA**39, Kinda potty. **1986** Pederson *LAGS Concordance,* 1 inf, **swLA,** Potty—slightly overweight.

2 Dirty; hence adv *potty* very (dirty or black). [Cf *SND pot-black* (at *pot* n.[1] 2.(1))]

1954 *PADS* 21.34 **SC,** Potty. . . Dirty, especially of children and their clothes. *Potty black* is often heard. Probably from the iron pot which sat on the stove or over an open fire. **1983** *MJLF* 9.1.51 **ceKY** (as of 1956), Potty . . very dirty. *Ibid,* Potty dirty . . very dirty.

potty n[3] See **poddy** n

potty adv See **potty** adj **2**

potty chamber See **pot chamber**

potty mouth n [Prob from *potty* hypocoristic for **pot** n **4,** but cf **potty** adj **2**]
A person who habitually uses foul language; foul language.

1969 *Current Slang* 3.4.8 [Univ of KY slang], *Potty mouth.* . . A person who repeatedly uses foul language. **1976** *Time* 10 May 79, Potentially even more annoying is the widespread abuse of the [CB radio] channels—especially by so-called potty mouths using obscenities. **1995** Lesley *Sky Fisherman* 26 **OR,** Although capable of speaking without swearing, Seaweed seldom did, and his speech was peppered with what Gab called potty-mouth.

pouch See **poach A3**

pouched gopher n Also *pouch gopher*
=**pocket gopher 1.**

1879 U.S. Natl. Museum *Bulletin* 14.17, *Geomys bursarius* . . Pouched or Pocket Gopher.—Missouri to Minnesota and Nebraska. *Ibid, Geomys castanops* . . Texas Pouched Gopher.—Texas and New Mexico. . . *Thomomys clusius* . . Small-footed Pouched Gopher. **1961** Jackson *Mammals WI* 184, *Geomys bursarius bursarius.* . . In Wisconsin generally called pocket gopher. . . Other names include . . pouched gopher [etc]. **1967** *DARE* (Qu. P29, . . 'Gophers' . . other name . . or what other animal are they most like) Inf **LA**14, Very small pouch gophers—they are called salamanders.

pouched kangaroo rat See **pouched rat 2**

pouched rat n
1 A **pocket gopher 1,** usu *Geomys bursarius.*

1825 in 1974 *Fauna Americana* 153, *Geomys cinereus.* . . Vulgarly *Sand-rat, Goffer, Pouched-rat, Salamander,* &c. **1826** Godman *Amer. Nat. Hist.* 2.90, The Pouched-Rat. *Pseudostoma Bursarium.* . . [*Vulgarly called Salamander; Pouched-Rat; Sand-Rat; &c.*] *Ibid* 91, In Florida, Georgia, etc., and the plains adjacent to the Missouri, the pouched-rat is to be found in great numbers. **1864** (1873) Webster *Amer. Dict.* 580, *Gopher.* . . In Missouri, a common species is a pouched rat of a reddish or chestnut-brown color, with broad, mole-like fore feet, the *Geomys bursarius.* **1877** Dodge *Plains Great West* 36, The surface is undermined by a beautiful little animal called the gopher (on the high plains a small striped squirrel, on the southern plains a pouched rat). **1928** Baylor Univ. Museum *Contrib.* 16.3, The common name "gopher" always refers to a burrowing animal; but whereas a "gopher" is a land tortoise in Florida and a frog in some parts of Illinois, it is a bluish-black snake in Georgia, a pouched rat or pocket gopher in Kansas and Colorado, a striped ground squirrel in Indiana, and a gray ground squirrel in Wisconsin.

2 also *pouched kangaroo rat:* A **kangaroo rat 1;** see quots.

1856 U.S. Army Corps Topog. Engineers *Rept. RR* 1.90, New species of pouched rats, an owl, and magnificent antlers of a mountain sheep, had been secured. **1867** (1868) *Amer. Naturalist* 1.395, The Pouched Kangaroo Rat (*Dipodomys Ordii*). . . is one of the most abundant of the Rodents about Fort Whipple [in AZ], where it more nearly takes the place of the house rat.

pouch gopher See **pouched gopher**

po-uh See **poor**

pouig See **poig**

poule d' bois See **poule de bois**

poule d'eau n Usu |'pul,du|; also |'pul,do, 'pʊl,du|; for addit varr see quot 1965–70 Pronc-spp *pull-do(o), pooloo* [Fr, literally "water hen"] Cf **poodle-doo, puddle duck, puldoo grass**

1 =**coot** n[1] **1. chiefly LA** See Map

1853 Hammett *Stray Yankee in TX* 245, San Jacinto Bay is a beautiful sheet of water. . . covered in the winter months with an innumerable host of aquatic birds, from the poor, despised "poule d'eau" to the epicurean "Canvas-back." **1859** (1968) Bartlett *Americanisms* 347, Pull-doo. A small black duck found in the bays and inlets of the Gulf of Mexico. They seldom fly, but rely upon swimming and diving to evade pursuit. The word is probably a corruption of *poule d'eau,* i.e., water-hen. **1888** Trumbull *Names of Birds* 117, In Connecticut at East Haddam, and mouth of Connecticut River, and at Moriches, L.I., *pulldoo,* a corruption of the French *poule d'eau* (water-hen). **1931** Read *LA French* 61, *Poule d'Eau.* . . The Coot. . . Both the English and French natives of Louisiana use *poule d'eau* as the name of this bird, some of the former pronouncing it like English *pull doo.* **1946** Kopman *Wild Acres* 175 **LA,** He is communicative about . . coots, or *"poules d'eau,"* in a hidden lagoon. **1961** *PADS* 36.11 **sLA,** Poule d'eau or pooloo (coot or mudhen)—74.2 [percent of 70 infs]. . . [P]oule d'eau may be [pul'do] or ['pul,du]. **1965–70** *DARE* (Qu. Q9, *The bird that looks like a small, dull-colored duck and is commonly found on ponds and lakes*) Infs **FL**26, **LA**37, **TX**37, **UT**3, Pull-doo; **LA**3, 10, 15, 22, 29, 31, 44, ['pʊl,du]; **LA**18, 26, 35, **TX**12, ['pul,du]; **LA**14, ['pul,du]; —always spelt properly but never pronounced; **AL**31, ['pʌl,do]; **LA**33, ['pul,do]; (Qu. Q5, . . *Kinds of wild ducks*) Infs **LA**37, 44, Pull-doo; **LA**10, 15, 31, **MS**73, ['pʊl,du]; **AL**22, **LA**14, ['pul,du]. **1967** LeCompte *Word Atlas* 204 **seLA,** A ducklike bird that is often hunted in duck season . . *poule doo* [10 of 21 infs] . . *poule d'eau* [9 of 21 infs]. **1981** Pederson *LAGS Basic Materials,* 1 inf, **nwLA,** ['pʹʊʉˑˡ,dʊʉ] . . edible but smells bad. **1983** *Reinecke Coll.* 9 **LA,** Poule d'eau, pooloo ['pul,do, -du] . . coot, ducklike waterfowl, very common in winter, not much esteemed as food, but used in gumbo. Catholics were reportedly [sic] allowed to eat on Friday because of fishy taste and aquatic habitat. . . The general word.

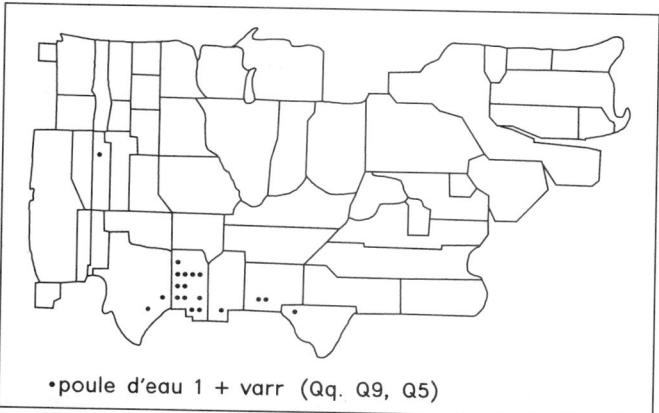

•poule d'eau 1 + varr (Qq. Q9, Q5)

2 usu as *rale poule d'eau:* =**Florida gallinule.**

1899 in 1900 LA Soc. Naturalists *Proc.* 94 **LA,** *Gallinula galleata.* . . *Florida Gallinule; Ralle* [sic] *Poule d'eau.* . . Common resident. **1916** *Times–Picayune* (New Orleans LA) 2 Apr mag sec 5/6, Florida Gallinule . . Ralle [sic] Poule d'Eau; Poule d'Eau de Marais. **1921** LA Dept. of Conserv. *Bulletin* 10.70 **LA,** The Florida gallinule . . or "rale poule d'eau" in local nomenclature, spends more time than the purple gallinule swimming in shallow, sheltered lagoons, and frequents in abundance the borders of fair sized marsh lakes. [**1931** Read *LA French* 65, *Râle.* . . The name bestowed on various species of rail and gallinule. . . *Râle Poule d'Eau* . . is the name of the Florida Gallinule. . . French *râle* is of uncertain origin.]

3 =**clapper rail.**

1950 *PADS* 14.54 **SC,** Pull-doo. . . The salt-marsh hen. Fr. *poule d'eau.*

poule de bois n Pronc-sp *poule d' bois* [See quot 1931] Cf **poule de marais**
=**ivory-billed woodpecker.**

1916 *Times–Picayune* (New Orleans LA) 16 Apr mag sec 1/2, Ivory-billed woodpecker . . Log God; Pique Bois; Poule d'Bois. . . It is not an uncommon bird in the heavy hardwood forest swamps of North Louisiana. [**1931** Read *LA French* 59, The large Ivory-billed Woodpecker . . is . . *La Poule de Bois,* "the wood hen."]

poule de marais n [LaFr, literally "marsh hen"]   Cf **poule de bois**
=pileated woodpecker B.
1917 *Wilson Bulletin* 29.2.81 **LA,** *Phloetomus pileatus.* . . Poule de marais, Indian hen, Marksville and Hamburg, La.

poultice n Pronc-spp *polis, potice*
Std sense, var forms.
1833 in 1956 Eliason *Tarheel Talk* 316 **cnNC,** Potice. **1954** *Harder Coll.* **cwTN,** Put a polis made out of beat up onions on the blisters.

poultice weed n [From its medicinal use]
A **mullein** (here: *Verbascum thapsus*).
1951 *PADS* 15.40 **TX,** *Verbascum thapsus* L.—Yellow-flowered mullein; poultice weed; flannel weed.

poultry wire n Also *poultry mesh,* ~ *netting*   **chiefly Sth, S Midl**   See Map   Cf **hen wire, hog** ~**, net** ~
Chicken wire.
1965–70 *DARE* (Qu. L63, *Kinds of fences made with wire*) 24 Infs, **chiefly Sth, S Midl,** Poultry-wire fence; **CT**10, Poultry netting or chicken wire; **GA**84, Poultry netting; **MI**20, Chicken fence—also poultry netting; **AR**51, Hog wire, poultry mesh—different kinds of net-wire fences; (Qu. L65, . . *Kinds of fences*) Inf **OK**1, Poultry-wire fence. [26 of 29 total Infs comm type 4 or 5, 25 old] **1986** Pederson *LAGS Concordance* **Gulf Region,** 9 infs, Poultry wire; 1 inf, Poultry-wire fence. **1998** *DARE* File **csWI,** I had never heard of poultry netting before I went to a local farmer's co-op store and tried to buy chicken wire. I finally located it among the rolls of fencing under a sign labeling it as "poultry netting."

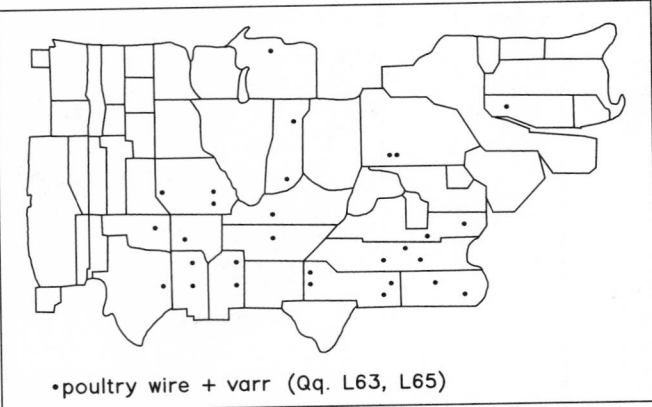

•poultry wire + varr (Qq. L63, L65)

pounce v [Appar *OED2 pounce* v.[1] 4 "To poke or thrust forcibly, esp with the foot or a stick. Now chiefly *Sc.*" Cf *EDD pounce* sb.[1] "A blow, esp one with a stick or the fist," *punce* v.[1] "To beat, strike, push by striking"]
To hit, assault; also fig.
1968 *DARE* (Qu. Y14a, *To hit somebody hard with the fist*) Inf **GA**44, He pounced [pæunst] him one. **1998** *NADS Letters* **cNY,** My grandmother, from the Finger Lake region . . [used to tell] my brother, "I'm agonna pounce your eyes boy." **1998** *DARE* File **cGA,** I remember my grandparents & great-aunt using this expression [=*pounce*]. . . I seem to recall getting a child's visual of someone attacking someone else, but not necessarily literally, like "the dog pounc'd the guinea hens" even though the dog was a dachshund and those birds could fly. *Ibid* **Queens NYC** (as of 1970s), My sister . . would threaten to 'pounce me one'. This meant to hit me with her fist. **1999** *NADS Letters* **IN,** "Pounce"—My mother used this as I was a child (I'm 31 years old) and I use this now. . . He pounced him a good one and then kicked him for good measure. He isn't worth pouncing. **2000** *Ibid* **AL, GA,** We still use that term in the same way in which the older GA woman used it, i.e. "Steve pounced Adam" to mean that Steve jumped on and hit Adam. . . In fact, my eight year old daughter . . said, unequivocally and without prompting, that "pounce" means to jump on someone and beat them up. We live in South Alabama. I have known this word used this way as long as

I can remember. I grew up in North Alabama and Georgia. My husband uses it too—he grew up in North Alabama. *Ibid* **swOH,** I'm 35 in Highland/Clinton Counties, Ohio and I have been pounced. I just figured it came from the way a cat pounced on a mouse. *Ibid* **cTX,** Pounced: I have in fact heard Texas kids use "pounce" this way. I always thought they were confusing "pounce on" with "trounce," but maybe not. If I recall, it doesn't always refer to hitting, at least not literally. If someone suffers a particularly humiliating defeat on the playground, whether it was a physical battle or not, it could be said that he or she "got pounced." **2001** *Ibid* **csVA,** Growing up in Lunenburg County, VA during the seventies and early eighties we (my cousins and I) also used pounced in a similar fashion. The phrase I remember best is "I'll pounce you if you don't stop."

pounce n
1952 Brown *NC Folkl.* 1.578, *Pounce.* . . An explosion. "There was a terrible pounce over in the south."—Central and east.

pound n[1] Usu |paʊnd|; also |pæʊnd, pæond, pɑʊnd| Pronc-sp *pahn*
A Forms.
1891 *PMLA* 6.166 **WV,** The sound (au, as in German Haus) is heard among a select few in *house, now,* etc., though the usual pronunciation is here (eu), never (ʌu). This latter diphthong (eu) is long (eeu) in *town, cow* and some other words, and short (eu) in most words: as *house, out, about, south, pound,* etc. **1941** in 1944 *ADD* 472 **Sth,** [Radio:] She weighs 300 [pæondz]. **1942** *AmSp* 17.150 **seNY,** Pound [pronounced with] [æu] [by] 6 [infs]—[ɑu] 2—[ɑu] 2. **1942** Hall *Smoky Mt. Speech* 45 **wNC, eTN,** The following words almost always have [æu] rather than [au]: . . pound. **1943** in 1944 *ADD* 472 **nWV,** ['pæond]. **1982** McCool *Sam McCool's Pittsburghese* 27 **PA,** *Pahn:* pound. "Give me a pahn of chippedchopped ham."
B Gram form.
Pl: usu *pounds;* also, chiefly when preceded by a number, *pound.* [*OED2 pound* sb.[1] 1 "Formerly used without change in the pl., a usage still sometimes retained after a numeral, esp. *dial.* and *colloq.*"] Cf *Intro* "Language Changes" II.7, **foot** n **B2b(1), mile B**
1623 in 1886 Neill *Virginia Carolorum* 69, [Footnote:] Mr. Bolton shall receive for his salary . . ten pound of tobacco. **1702** (1972) Mather *Magnalia* 1.17, The *Passage* of the *Persons* that peopled *New-England,* cost at least Ninety Five Thousand Pound. **1781** in 1884 Essex Inst. *Coll.* 21.282 **neMA,** Voted Sixty Pound hard Money to Defray Preching this year. **1867** Twain *Jumping Frog* 18, Why, blame my cats, if he don't weigh five pound! **1913** Kephart *Highlanders* 287 **sAppalachians,** I can make a hundred pound o' pork outen that hog. **1928** Peterkin *Scarlet Sister Mary* 261 **SC,** I can easy pick three hundred pound o cotton in a day. **1943** *LANE* Map 556 *(Two pounds),* [The plural form *pound* is **scattered throughout NEng.**] **1943** in 1944 *ADD* 472 **WV,** I'll get ennaway—2 pound o' that. **1949** *WELS Suppl.* **seWI,** The expression "buy 10 pound of nails . . " is very common here. **c1960** Wilson *Coll.* **csKY,** Pound is often used as a plural. **1967–68** *DARE* Tape **IN**36, Why, you can catch forty, fifty pound of bass; **MN**10, She was a large woman. 'Bout two hundred and twenty-five pound. **1970** *DARE* FW Addit **VA**47, Four pound, five year, etc—common. **1971** Bright *Word Geog. CA & NV* 178, *Two pounds* (of flour. . . Only 6% used *pound, foot, mile, ton,* etc. These instances were widely scattered in California; in Nevada only one was reported . .). **1975** Allen *LAUM* 2.51, The McDavids report *pound* as plural "distributed almost evenly throughout the three major dialect regions of the Atlantic Seaboard." In the North Central states it is most frequent in Indiana and Kentucky. In no states but West Virginia and Indiana is it favored by more than one of the cultivated infs. In the U[pper] M[idwest] the general frequency of *pound* as plural is lower than in the other investigated areas. **1991** Pederson *LAGS Social Matrix* 120 **Gulf Region,** [In contexts of the type "two pound(s) of flour," 592 infs used *pounds* and 215 *pound.* Men made up 53% of those responding *pounds,* and infs with less than 11 years of formal educ 40%; the corresponding figures for infs responding *pound* were 71% and 76% respectively.]

pound v **chiefly S Midl**
To hold a **pound party 1** for.
1921 *DN* 5.118 **KY,** Last night they pounded the new preacher. **1931** *Durant* (Okla.) *D. Democrat* 12 March 4/3 *(DA),* Caney Pastor Pounded. **1945** Street *Gauntlet* 76 **MO** (as of 1920s), The ladies are going to pound you soon. So you needn't buy much to begin with. **1946** *PADS*

6.24 **swVA**, *Pound*. . . To victual an (incoming) parson. Salem, 1940. Occasional. **1948** *Hench Coll.* **VA,** *Pound*—To give a pounding to. **1958** *PADS* 29.14 **TN,** *Pound:* To hold a party for, to bring presents to: To *"pound the preacher"* means that the members of the congregation bring a pound of food to the new preacher. . . Last year a young Methodist preacher's wife told me that they had been *pounded* the night before. **1968** *State* (Raleigh NC) 15 June 2/1 *(Mathews Coll.),* Here are some things my children have never seen or done. . . Never "pounded" their teachers. **1970** *DARE* (Qu. FF3, . . *'Showers' or 'gift parties')* Inf **TX**101, Pound the preacher—bringing food to church as gift for preacher. **1983** *MJLF* 9.1.51 **ceKY** (as of 1956), *Pound* . . to donate food, as an offering, to the preacher.

pound n²

1 also *pound yard:* A pen for domestic animals; esp a barnyard. [*EDD pound* sb.² 1 "A small enclosure; a sheepfold; a pig-sty"] **esp Delmarva**   See Map   Cf **cow pound**

   1899 (1912) Green *VA Folk-Speech* 333, *Pound*. . . (2) An enclosure in which animals are kept; a farm-pen. (3) A low pen made with planks for young turkeys when first hatched to keep them from straying. **1937** *Hench Coll.,* Eastern Shore of Virginia expressions. . . He is hauling shadows (=pine needles) in to the pound (=barn yard). **1938** *FWP Guide DE* 330, The barnyard of upper New Castle County becomes the "pound" of Kent County. **1939** *LANE* Map 110 *(Pig pen; hog house)* **seCT,** 1 inf, Hog pound; 1 inf, Pig pound. **1949** Kurath *Word Geog.* 55, *Cow pen*. . . In Delamarvia and on Albemarle Sound *(cow) pound* still predominates. **1951** Johnson *Resp. to PADS* 20 **DE** *(The fenced-in space near the barn where you keep the livestock)* Barnyard, cow lot; (old-fash) pound. **1957** Battaglia *Resp. to PADS* 20 **eMD,** Pound. **1957** *DE Folkl. Bulletin* 1.28, Pound, or pound-yard (barnyard). **1965–70** *DARE* (Qu. M13, *The space near the barn with a fence around it where you keep the livestock)* Infs **DE**1, 3, 5, **MD**38, 42, **NJ**16, **VA**49, Pound; **NJ**67, Pound, pound yard; (Qu. M14, *The open area around or next to the barn)* Inf **DE**5, Still the pound; (Qu. M15, *The place outdoors where pigs are kept)* Inf **NC**87, Hog pound. [All Infs old]

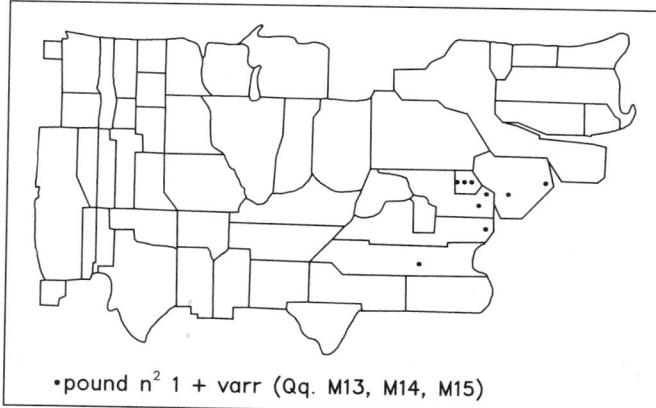

•pound n² 1 + varr (Qq. M13, M14, M15)

2 An enclosure or tank in which live fish or other aquatic creatures are kept; by ext, an establishment that deals in live lobsters; hence n *pound keeper* the manager of such an establishment.   **Atlantic coast**

   [**1867** Smyth *Sailor's Word Book* 510, *Pound*. A lagoon, or space of water, surrounded by reefs and shoals, wherein fish are kept, as at Bermuda.] **1905** U.S. Bur. Fisheries *Rept. for 1904* 420 **MD,** The floats are inclosed by a fence to prevent their being washed away by strong winds, and this inclosure [=for crabs] is commonly called a "pound." **1942** *Hench Coll.,* Terrapin pound—an underwater pen for the breeding of terrapin. **1950** *Sun* (Baltimore MD) 4 Feb 4/6 *(Hench Coll.),* Along the North Atlantic, the "pound" is where an informed gourmet goes when he has a lobster dinner in view. It's a tank of natural sea water, in store or restaurant, filled with swimming lobsters from which the buyer selects his own victim. **1975** Gould *ME Lingo* 217, As a well-known word with a precise meaning, it was the natural one for lobster dealers to assign to the enclosures they built for storing quantities of lobsters to await shipment and to hold for advantageous prices. The term "lobster pound" has been abused considerably by restaurants and wayside snack bars which use it as if any place or any thing containing lobsters is a *pound*. A true *pound* will be a sizeable cove closed off with a barrier that

holds the lobsters in captivity but permits free passage of sea water. **1978** Merriam *Illustr. Lobstering* 68 **ME,** *Pound*—A storage area for holding lobsters keeping them alive. It is usually made by closing off a small cove. . . Some lobster companies keep lobsters in tanks in buildings with constantly circulating water. These are also called pounds. *Ibid, Pound-Keeper*—A manager of a lobster pound, who often serves as a dealer as well. He may work for himself, a company, or a co-op.

3 also attrib; also *pound head, ~ pocket:* The inner enclosure of a fish trap; broadly, a **pound net.   chiefly Atlantic coast**   Cf **false pound, fish pound**

   1870 (1871) *Amer. Naturalist* 4.403, These fish being caught in gillnets and "pounds," are generally taken from the water [of Lake Michigan] some hours after being actually entrapped. **1884** U.S. Natl. Museum *Bulletin* 27.700, *Lake Erie pound boat*. . . These boats are used in the pound fisheries of the Great Lakes, and their peculiar construction enables them to carry large quantities of fish in shallow water and to lift the bowl of the pounds without upsetting. **1885** *NY Post* (NY) 28 Aug 3/1 **eNC,** We concluded the day by accompanying the fisherman and a neighbor as they went to "lift" their pounds. **1935** Lincoln *Cape Cod Yesterdays* 146 **eMA,** He is in the "pound," and the pound of a weir is, to a fish, the condemned cell. **1947** *Richmond Times–Dispatch* (VA) 3 Sept 6/1 *(Hench Coll.),* [A fisherman] continued, "We set in 60 feet of water, with 90-foot pound poles and 900 feet of leader. . . [A man will] need maybe 150 or 160-pound poles, $15 each at the water's edge with the bark on, and he'll have to put 'em up and down each year." **1947** [see **pound net**]. **1966–69** *DARE* Tape **NC**13, They have the pound nets, that's an old way of fishing in this area. . . It's a pound built and a leader to come to it; **NC**58, The old type fishing, the pound fishing, has passed away; **NC**65, They were all the way from thirty-two to thirty-five feet square—the pound pockets, they call 'em. And the lead leads right out from them pockets. . . Why, then they might have to go in your pound head. **1968–70** *DARE* (Qu. P13, . . *Ways of fishing . . besides the ordinary hook and line)* Infs **VA**46, 55, Pound; **NJ**22, Pounds—set way off shore. These are traps set on poles; fish follow the net into the narrow neck of the trap; **VA**47, Pound—used for kingfish, trout, and blowfish or swellfish; **VA**75, Pound trap; **NC**82, Pound fishing—big nets; had a lead, heart, and pound; the pound was like a pocket, had a trapdoor. **1976** Warner *Beautiful Swimmers* 126 **eMD,** A funnel at the apex of the turnbacks then leads the fish into a large circular "main pound" or holding area. **1984** *DARE* File **Chesapeake Bay** [Watermen's vocab], Pound trap. . . pound fyke.

4 in comb *crab pound:* See quot.

   1941 *Sun* (Baltimore MD) 15 Apr 26/2 *(Hench Coll.),* The [Maryland] Legislature banned the use of two types of devices which have come into use recently. . . [T]he other is a crab pound—a wire device built in zigzag style with traps at each of the corners which conservation officials said stopped everything and often caused crabs to kill each other before they could be taken.

pound barrel   See **pounding barrel**

pounder n   Cf **pounding barrel**

   1903 *DN* 2.301 **Cape Cod MA** (as of a1857), *Pounder*. . . A heavy crenellated clod of wood on a long handle used for pounding clothes in a *pound-barrel*.

pound hair   See **hair** n B9

pound head   See **pound** n² 3

pound (in) ppl adj [Var of *pounded;* cf *OED2 pound* v.² 2] Of cattle: confined, penned up.

   1969 *DARE* Tape **NC**60, When this law passed, you see, they had to take the cattle away. We didn't have them pen—pound in. . . They run at large out on the beach . . and in the woods. We didn't have to keep 'em pound.

pounding vbl n [See quot 1894]

In playing **morris:** capturing one of one's opponent's pieces by getting three of one's own in a line.

   [**1894** (1964) Gomme *Traditional Games* 1.416 **England,** As often as either of the players succeeds in accomplishing a row of three, he claims one of his antagonist's men, which is placed in the pound (the centre). . . The boys . . carved a "Marrel" pound on a block of stone.] **1899** Champlin–Bostwick *Young Folks' Games* 503, *Nine men's morris*. . . Each player's object . . is to form a row of three of his own pieces; and when this is done, he may take from the board any hostile piece (called "pounding"). **1938** (1941) Natl. Recreation Assoc. *Games* 26, *Mill.* . . When a player has formed a mill, he may take one of his opponent's men. This is called "pounding."

pounding n [**pound** v]

1 also *pounding party,* ~ *shower:* =**pound party 1. chiefly Sth, S Midl, TX** See Map
  1909 *DN* 3.359 **eAL, wGA,** *Pounding.* . . The custom of sending to the minister's home groceries, preserves, etc., each participant being supposed to give a pound. "We gave our new preacher a pounding last week." Sometimes called *pound-party,* but the latter is used in a specific sense. **1935** *Sun* (Baltimore MD) 16 Oct 7/5 *(Hench Coll.),* Plans for an old fashioned "pounding" for the benefit of the Home for Confederate Women, in Richmond, were announced. **1938** FWP *Guide MS* 14, The "to-do" will probably be a neighborhood party. . . It is purely social, with no labor, no "pounding presents" attached. **1940** Writers' Program *Guide TX* 115, Co-operation and neighborliness still motivate many customs, especially in east Texas—including . . poundings for the new preacher (when everyone brings a pound of food). **1945** Street *Gauntlet* 98 **MO** (as of 1920s), His congregation was planning to surprise them with a pounding party. **1956** McAtee *Some Dialect NC* 34, *Pounding.* . . Donation or pound party. . . originally from bringing a pound of something as a gift. "We gave the bride and groom a pounding." **1962** *Hall Coll.* **eTN,** You never hear of poundings any more. Usually had it for a minister when he first moved in a parsonage. **1965–70** *DARE* (Qu. FF3, . . *'Showers' or 'gift parties'*) Inf **AR**52, Pounding—gifts of food to the preacher or a new couple in the community. Called pounding because a pound was a good portion to bring; **MS**67, Pounding—for new preacher; **NC**76, There are poundings; **NC**88, Pounding—every[one] brings a pound of something to give the pastor . . , or if not him, some needy person; **SC**44, A pounding—a pound of some foodstuff to stock a preacher's larder—new; **SC**54, A pounding—stock the preacher's larder; **TX**39, Pounding—usually for the preacher and his family; **TX**98, A pounding—from pounds (of food); cans of food and supplies taken to a new preacher; **TX**104, Pounding—for new preacher; **VA**42, Pounding—for people about to be married or for a housewarming; old-fashioned; **CA**1, **NC**31, Pounding shower; **AL**10, 30, Pounding shower—(for a) new preacher; **MI**114, Pounding shower—families brought food for new preacher; **TX**91, Pounding shower—supplies . . to a new preacher; (Qu. FF1, . . *A kind of group meeting called a 'social' or 'sociable'. . . [What goes on?]*) Inf **NC**36, Poundings—for new pastor. **1969** *DARE* FW Addit **cNC,** *Pounding*—A surprise party when neighbors bring gifts or supplies (supposedly to the amount of a pound apiece). These occurred at various times, such as weddings, the coming of a new preacher, or some catastrophe. **1975** McDonough *Garden Sass* 140 **AR,** We have the pounding each time a new preacher arrives to preach at our church. We might even have the pounding for each new year he stays. **1991** *DARE* File **seNY,** Pounding = an unusual flood of gifts. **1998** *Ibid* **coastal NC,** All of them have been Members of the United Methodist Church for years. I asked them about pounding—all remembered them in the past but not recently—except one who said, "Oh yes, we just had a pounding for our new minister and his wife. It was a bit different however, for most of the people brought money instead of produce. That's the modern way."

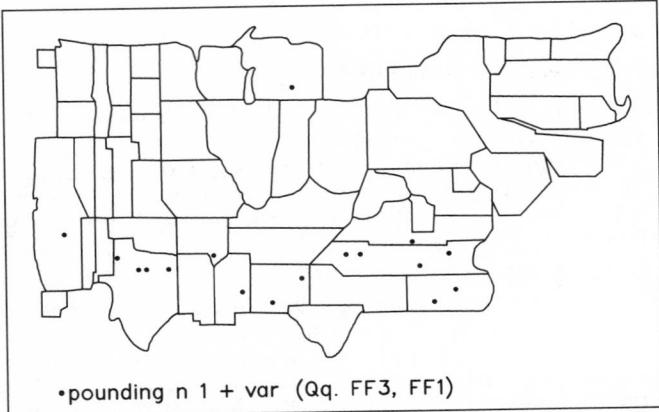

•pounding n 1 + var (Qq. FF3, FF1)

‡**2** =**pound party 2.**
  1966 *DARE* (Qu. H70, *When people bring baked dishes, salads, and so forth to a meeting-place and share them together*) Inf **AR**17, A pounding.

pounding barrel n Pronc-sp *paounding berrel* Also *pound barrel, pounding machine* **esp NEng** *old-fash* Cf **pounder**
A barrel in which clothes are washed by pounding them in soapy water with a wooden pestle.
  1853 MI State Ag. Soc. *Trans. for 1852* 4.87, One pounding barrel for clothes. **1855** Douglass *My Bondage* 346 **eMA,** Self-shutting gates, washing machines, pounding barrels, were all new things, and told me that I was among a thoughtful and sensible people. **1869** Stowe *Oldtown Folks* 340 **MA,** The thunder of the pounding-barrel . . announced that the washing was to be got out of the way before daylight. **1894** (1934) Robinson *Danvis Folks* 108 **VT,** I know where your boots be. In the paoundin' berrel in the back shed. **1903** *DN* 2.300 **Cape Cod MA** (as of a1857), *Pound-barrel.* . . A barrel in which clothes are pounded in washing. **1917** Baldwin *Making of a Township* 90 **ceIN** (as of 1851), When I was past seven years of age they got to using a pounding barrel. . . This barrel was about a third full of water. The clothes were soaped and put in. Then a wooden pestle was used to extract the dirt. **c1920** in 1993 Farwell–Nicholas *Smoky Mt. Voices* 127 **sAppalachians,** The men's working garments were beaten in a pounding-barrel; the other clothes were rubbed between the hands. **1931–33** *LANE Worksheets* **cCT,** *Pounding barrel*—used for washing clothes. Same as pounding machine.

pounding mill n
A machine for hulling or pulverizing grain by means of the vertical motion of a pestle in a mortar; spec:

a A rice-hulling mill. **SE**
  1846 *De Bow's Rev.* 1.337, The grain [=rice] is cleaned and prepared for market by means of the pounding-mill. **1874** *Scribner's Mth.* 8.141 **SC,** The flat-boats . . were poled up to the mill where the grain [=rice] was threshed, winnowed, and carried in baskets to the schooners which transport it to Charleston, and the "pounding mills." **1905** (1913) Pringle *Woman Rice Planter* 142 **SC,** The cows and pigs are fed on the flour, a gray substance that comes from the grain as the chaff is removed in the pounding mill. **1966** *DARE* (Qu. L32b, *In early days, how was the grain separated from the chaff?*) Inf **SC**9, Pounding mill; (Qu. L33, *How is the grain separated from the straw nowadays?*) Inf **SC**9, Pounding mill.

b A corn-hulling or grinding mill, esp a simple water-powered device of this type. **chiefly sAppalachians**
  1866 Bishop *Hist. Amer. Manufactures* 123, The first Water-mill erected in the Plymouth Colony was put up . . in January, 1633. . . But it is supposed to have been merely a pounding mill, by which the corn was cleared from the hull. *Ibid* 241 **NY** (as of c1800), They had two Glasshouses, a saw mill, pounding mill, and cross-cut mill. *Ibid* 603 **VA,** This expensive arrangement was made to secure a good site for a pounding-mill on the creek. **1917** *DN* 4.416 **wNC,** *Pounding-mill.* . . A mortar and pestle mill run by water from a spout that alternately fills, lowers, and spills out of a box fixed to the end of a walking beam opposite to the pestle. **1937** *Hall Coll.* **wNC,** At the pounding mill on Low Gap branch a dog stuck his head under the pestle [Hall:=pestle] trying to eat meal out of the box and was pounded to death. **1937** Thornburgh *Gt. Smoky Mts.* 144, Almost all known types of mills have been found, from a primitive pounding mill on Deep Creek, to "tub" mills, overshot mills, and steel turbine mills. **1939** FWP *Guide TN* 302, Near the spring is a rock with a depression in which early settlers ground corn into meal with the aid of a heavy pestle attached to a beam propelled by the current of the stream. The operation of this device, called a "pounding mill," was slow, but it could be carried on without attention.

pounding party (or shower) See **pounding** n 1

pound keeper See **pound** n[2] **2**

pound leather See **leather** 1b

pound net n **chiefly Gt Lakes, Mid Atl**
A fish trap consisting of a long fence of netting supported by poles that directs fish into a series of enclosures, from the last of which they are unable to escape; hence n *pound netting* the operation of catching fish with this device; n *pound netter* one who uses this device.
  1865 in 1882 MI Laws *Genl. Statutes* 1.577, The penalties of this section shall not apply or work injury to persons who are the present owners of pound or trap nets. **1884** U.S. Natl. Museum *Bulletin* 27.1023, *Pound-net of Lake Michigan.* . . Made of netting and held in position by

stakes driven into the bottom. **1899** (1912) Green *VA Folk-Speech* 333, *Pound-net.* . . In *fishing*, a kind of weir. **1911** U.S. Bur. Census *Fisheries 1908* 316, In California the Monterey Spanish mackerel . . is a most excellent food fish. They are caught on troll lines and in gill nets and pound nets. **1912** *Youth's Companion* 29 Feb 109/2 **eVA**, The pound-netters sailed early. **1931** *Sun* (Baltimore MD) 28 Mar 10/4 (*Hench Coll.*), As a fisherman who has spent nearly fifty years in the Chesapeake Bay section . . I will say . . that one pound net in a single season will destroy more fish than all the purse nets in the upper portion of the Chesapeake Bay would in fifty years. **1944** Nute *Lake Superior* 183 **MI, WI, MN**, The pound nets were set in sheltered positions in the shallow bays and at the mouths of rivers between Marquette and Grand Island. **1947** *Richmond Times–Dispatch* (VA) 3 Sept 6/1 (*Hench Coll.*), Schools dropped his needle and diagrammed a "pound net" on the ground, drawing with a small stick. "The leader is a big-mesh net running straight out in the water 900 feet. . . It runs right down to the bottom like a curtain." "The fish come near it and then turn and follow it along . . and they run into the first heart. . . They go out through a little opening at the point, into a smaller heart. . . The only opening they find out of that one goes into the pound, which has a bottom raised up off the bay bottom, and is just a big 50-foot cage. Then they go into the 30-foot pocket, and that's where the fisherman takes 'em out." **1949** *Fishing Gaz.* 15 Dec. 106/2 (*DA*), Several good catches of whitefish, however, were recently made by pound netters in this lake. **1966–70** *DARE* (Qu. P13, . . *Other ways of fishing*) Infs **DE4, NC18, 21, 27, VA47**, Pound net; **MD15**, Pound net—long leader runs out to crib—big square net that fish can get into but not out of; **MD45**, Pound net—net on poles, permanently placed in water; **MI109**, Pound net—on the bottom of the lake; **NJ22**, Pound nets—no pound nets here anymore; **NC13**, Pound nets—a leader goes out; fish follow it into net. **1966–70** *DARE* Tape **MD15**, Pound net is a big, long leader that runs off of the net onto it. And then they have what they call a crib. The fish will come up against this leader and then they'll follow that back and get caught in this crib. And then the fisherman goes there with a big net and he can dip them out; **NC13**, [see **pound** n² **3**]; **NC27**, I fish pound nets. First place I ever fish pound nets is Sea Garden, New Jersey; **NC58**, Now, the pound netting is, is not done much anymore; **NC59**, And of course they had pound nets at that time. It's called a pound net. . . Well, it gets its name because it's built round, like a pond. Completely round; **VA47**, You use gill nets, dragnets, and pound nets—fish traps, we call 'em. **1976** Warner *Beautiful Swimmers* 125 **eMD**, Each pound net requires no less than one hundred and thirty of them [=poles]. **1984** *DARE* File **Chesapeake Bay** [Watermen's vocab], Pound netters.

pound party n [From the convention that one brings a pound of some foodstuff; see quots]

1 also *pound shower, ~ social, ~ supper*: A party to which each guest brings a donation, usu of some staple foodstuff, for a minister, a needy family, or other charitable cause. **chiefly Midl, Cent** Cf **donation party, pound** v, **pounding** n

1877 Bartlett *Americanisms* 487, *Pound-Party.* An assemblage, usually the parishioners of a country clergyman whose salary is inadequate to his support, which on an evening agreed upon meets at his house, carrying tea, coffee, and other articles of necessity put up in pound packages, as contributions to him. **1909** [see **pounding**]. **1921** *DN* 5.118 **KY**, A pound party is a party in which the people voluntarily give the minister a surprise, by carrying in something like groceries, vegetables, etc. **1953** Brewer *Word Brazos* 17 **eTX** [Black], Dey hab poun' paa'ties whar evuhbody brung a poun' o' victuals to de pastuh evuh mont'. **1959** *Chicago Daily News* (IL) 4 Dec 4/3, The Guild of St. Joseph's Home for the Friendless will hold its 24th annual "pound" [sic] party at 3 p.m. Sunday. **1960** Criswell *Resp. to PADS* 20 **Ozarks**, Long ago there were pound suppers for newcomers in the neighborhood. . . Preachers were often the victims of these atrocities. **1961** Sackett–Koch *KS Folkl.* 194, Pound party, or pounding, the custom of taking foodstuffs to new people, especially ministers. Originally pounds of butter, lard, cakes, etc. Now canned food, etc. **1965–70** *DARE* (Qu. FF3, . . *'Showers' or 'gift parties'*) Inf **IA3**, Pound parties—usually for minister; everybody brought a pound of something; **IA9**, Pound party; **KS13**, Pound party—everyone takes a pound of something to a family in distress; **MA58**, Pound party—foodstuffs given to minister—old-fashioned; **OH93**, Pound party—to bring supplies for new preacher; **OH95**, Pound party—old-fashioned; a pound of food or supplies taken to minister; **OH98**, Pound party—old-fashioned; supplies to a new minister; **KS5**, Pound showers—for the new pastor; **KS15**, Pound shower—for the minister; everybody takes a pound of food; used to have these; **KY41**, Pound shower—take food or things that needy folks or sick folks need; (Qu.

FF1, . . *A 'social' or 'sociable'*) Inf **MI66**, Years ago they used to have pound parties for the minister. That's how he lived through the year, pretty near; **WV7**, Pound social—bringing food and stuff to someone.

2 also *pound supper*: A party to which each guest brings a contribution of food to be shared with the other guests. **chiefly Sth, S Midl**

1889 *Boston Jrl.* 22 Jan. 2/3 (*DAE*), The old-fashioned pound party has become this winter a fashionable city entertainment. **1904** (1913) Johnson *Highways South* 102 **nGA**, The parties at which these games [=dances] are played are quite apt to take the form of "Pound Suppers." To these the girls contributed cake, and each young man brought a pound of candy, or apples, or oranges, or crackers, or whatever he chose to furnish. **1909** *DN* 3.359 **eAL, wGA**, *Pound-party.* . . A party to which each guest brings a pound of eatables. **1938** in Lib. of Congress *Amer. Memory: WPA Life Hist.* (Internet) **cnSC** (as of c1860), Social amusements in the community consisted of pound parties at some neighbor's home during the winter nights, usually on Friday night. *Ibid* **cnSC**, What parties were the most popular? . . Well, pound parties. These were assemblies in private homes; each couple brought a package of something to eat for the table. *Ibid* **VT** (as of early 20th cent), At this time community life ranked high. Sociables, pound parties, quilting bees, barn-raisings, church attendance and cracker barrel politics were the recreational activities. **1942** Rawlings *Cross Creek* 41 **FL**, Mama says we're having a pound party tomorrow evening and she'd be proud did you come. **1966–70** *DARE* (Qu. FF1, . . *A 'social' or 'sociable'*) Infs **IN38, MO4**, Pound parties; **AR41**, Play parties, ice cream suppers, pound suppers; (Qu. FF2, . . *Kinds of parties*) Inf **IL113**, Pound parties—bring your own; **KY7**, Pound party; **KY75**, Pound parties—old-fashioned; everyone brought a pound of something such as food or candy and shared games and food; **MD20**, Pound party—every guest brought a pound of candy or cake; now obsolete; **SC39**, Pound party—everyone took a pound of something to eat—nuts, cake, etc. **1966–70** *DARE* Tape **GA1**, Well, when I was just a small kid, people around in the community would have what we call a pound supper, pound party. . . Our neighbors, they had one of the parties; **KY75**, The wintertime they had real nice what they call pound parties. You didn't necessarily have to take a pound, but everybody that went was supposed to take something. Candy apples, oranges, bananas, anything they wanted to. Cake. Then when everybody got there we had a pretty big feast. **1986** Pederson *LAGS Concordance*, 3 infs, **cnGA, csAR**, Pound suppers—everyone (or teenagers) brought a pound of food; 1 inf, **cnTN**, Pound supper—an old kind of party; 1 inf, **ceAR**, Pound supper—everybody brings pound of something; 1 inf, **ceGA**, Pound party—each brought a pound of something; 1 inf, **ceFL**, Pound party—everybody brought a pound of food.

pound pocket See **pound** n² **3**

pound sand down a rathole v phr Also *pour sand down* (or *in*) *a rathole, pound sand;* for addit varr see quots

1 Fig: to do the simplest thing—usu used in phrr *not to know* (or *have sense*) *enough to pound sand down a rathole* and varr. **chiefly west of Missip R, N Cent, Upstate NY**   See Map on p. 320   Cf **pour piss out of a boot**

1912 *DN* 3.581 **wIN**, He wouldn't know enough to pound sand in a rat-hole; so don't get him. **1914** *DN* 4.79 **ME, nNH**, *Sand in a rat-hole, don't know enough to pound.* . . Very stupid. **1923** *DN* 5.219 **swMO**, Don't know enough to pound sand in a rat hole. . . Stupid. Also, *Don't know enough to pound akerns in a woodpecker hole.* **1927** *AmSp* 2.364 **cwWV**, That man does not have sense enough to pound sand in a rat hole. **1937** Crane *Let Me Show You VT* 31, Ignorance, especially of the kind that lacks even common sense . . "Don't know enough to pound sand in a rat-hole." **1950** *WELS* **WI** ("He hasn't sense enough to _____.") 7 Infs, Pound sand in (or into, down) a rathole; ("He doesn't know _____.") 1 Inf, Enough to pound sand. **1965–70** *DARE* (Qu. JJ15a, . . "He hasn't sense enough to _____.") 62 Infs, **widespread exc C and N Atl, Sth, S Midl**, Pound sand down (or in, into) a rathole; 16 Infs, **scattered, but less freq Atl, Sth, S Midl**, Pour sand down (or in) a rathole; **IL26, MI68, 103, NY9, WI13**, Pound sand; **AK5, CA66**, Pound dirt in a rathole; **OK1**, Pound sand in rathole; **SD5**, Put sand in a rathole; **MO5**, Pour sand in the rathole; **OK1**, Pour sand in ratholes; [**TX104**, Pound sand in a boot;] **NY28**, Pound salt in a rathole; **AR56**, Pestle sand in a rathole; **IL15, OK6**, Drive sand in(to) a rathole; **MI51**, Pound salt; **CO27**, Pack sand in an anthole; (Qu. JJ15b, . . "He doesn't know _____.") Infs **CO47, KY70**, Enough to pour sand in a rathole; **MI68, 108**, Enough to pound sand; **MN30**, Enough to pound sand in a rathole. **1975** Gould *ME Lingo* 218, *Pound sand*—Another measurement of degree of intelligence: "He don't have brains enough to pound sand in a rat hole!" . . The term is also used for wasted time that might have been profitably engaged: "The lumber didn't come, so the carpenters pounded sand all afternoon." **1985** Ladwig *How to Talk Dirty* 14 **Ozarks,** He's so dumb he couldn't pound sand in a rathole. **1986** Pederson *LAGS Concordance,* 1 inf, **nwGA,** Easy as pounding sand in a rathole. **1992** *Houston Chron.* (TX) 5 Apr sec G 1, *Inept.* . . Didn't have sense enough to pound sand in a rat hole.

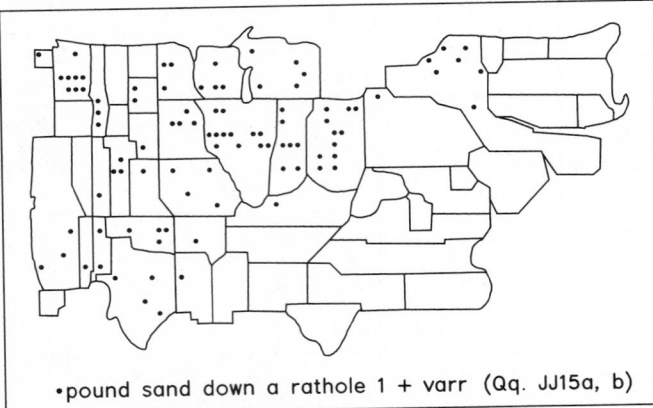

•pound sand down a rathole 1 + varr (Qq. JJ15a, b)

2 Fig: to do something pointless; to waste time; hence imper phr *go pound sand down a rathole* (and varr) go away, mind your own business.

1958 McCulloch *Woods Words* 138 **Pacific NW,** *Pound sand down a rat hole*—a. To do nothing. b. To work at some useless job. **1960** Criswell *Resp. to PADS 20* **Ozarks,** *Pound sand in a rat-hole.* . . To occupy oneself at a futile task. Used in comparisons, "like pounding sand in a rat-hole." Still very common. **1967–69** *DARE* (Qu. II22, *Expressions to tell somebody to keep to himself and mind his own business*) Inf **MA15,** Go pound sand in a rathole; **MA16,** Go pound sand; **NY7,** Go pound salt. **1975** [see **1** above].

pound shower (or social) See **pound party 1**

pound supper See **pound party 1, 2**

pound yard See **pound** n[2] **1**

pour v, n Usu |'po(ə)r, pɔ(ə)r, 'poə, 'pɔ(ə)|; also |pυə(r), pur, pυr| Pronc-sp *poor* Cf **poor** adj

A Forms.

1852 in 1927 Jones *FL Plantation Rec.* 73 **nwFL,** It . . Rained untill Night Just as Hard as it Could Poor. **1917** *DN* 4.398 **neOH,** Pour [pur], *v.t.* Pour. . . [*DN* Ed: In La., [pur].] Also Kan. **1927** *Ruppenthal Coll.,* Pour and *poor* are strangely transposed in pronunciation, esp. in southeastern Penna. and farther south. *Poor* is often pron. *pore* . . , while *pouring coffee* etc. is pron. . . like *pure,* except for omitting the *i* or *y* . . sound, before *u.* **1939** *LANE* Map 93 (*Shower*), [In *downpour,* a common response throughout NEng, 11 infs gave proncs of the type [-pυə, -pυ(ə)r] and 2 [-puə, -pur]. One inf gave the resp [purɨŋ reɪn].] **1970** *DARE* (Qu. B24) Inf **IL134,** ['purdaun]. **c1970** Pederson *Dial. Surv. Rural GA* **seGA,** [Of 16 exx of *downpour,* 13 were of the types [-p'o(ə), p'oɚ, p'ɔ(ə)]; 3 were of the types [-p'υə, -p'υɚ].] **1998** *DARE* File, My aunt once told me about a woman of her acquaintance who would "poor" water out of a pitcher.

B As verb.

1 in var phrr (see below): To rain hard. Note: The verb alone in this sense is std and not illustrated here.

a *pour down;* hence ppl adj *pouring-down.* **chiefly Sth, Midl, West** See Map

1931–33 *LANE Worksheets* **RI,** *Pour right down* . . rain very hard. **1960** Criswell *Resp. to PADS 20* **Ozarks,** It's really . . pouring down. **1965–70** *DARE* (Qu. B26, *When it's raining very heavily, you say, "It's raining _____."*) 11 Infs, **scattered Sth, Midl, West,** (It's) pouring down; **MO16,** It's just pouring down; **CA79,** It poured down—others say; **AR47,** Really pouring down; **ND3,** Poured down with buckets; (Qu. B24, *What do you call a sudden, very heavy rain?*) Infs **AR14, MS73, OH54,** (It's) pouring down; **MD21,** It poured down; **OR14, TX39,** Pouring-down rain; (Qu. B25, . . *Joking names . . for a very heavy rain*) Inf **OK18,** It really is pouring down. **c1970** Pederson *Dial. Surv. Rural GA* (*A very hard rain that doesn't last long*) 1 inf, **seGA,** Pouring-down

rain. **1986** Pederson *LAGS Concordance,* 3 infs, **AL, GA, TX,** Pour down; 1 inf, **ceTX,** It poured down; 1 inf, **cnTX,** Really pouring down; 1 inf, **swGA,** It look like it's going pour down; 1 inf, **cwAL,** It will really pour down; 4 infs, 3 **TN,** 1 **TX,** (A) pouring-down rain.

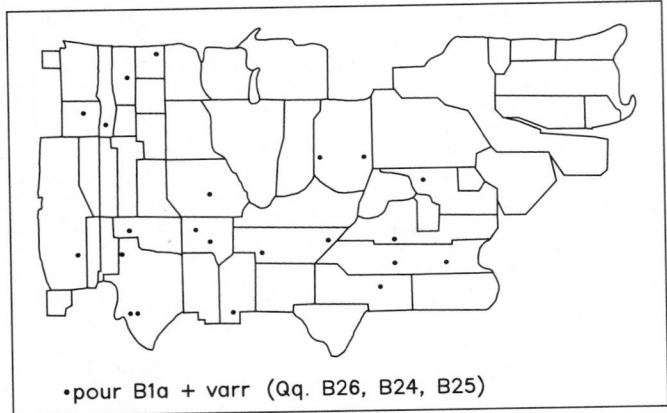

•pour B1a + varr (Qq. B26, B24, B25)

b *pour down rain.* **esp Sth, S Midl**

1939 *Hall Coll.* **wNC,** Looked like I could walk out on the clouds, and hit a pourin' down rain in the valley. **1966–68** *DARE* (Qu. B26, *When it's raining very heavily . . "It's raining _____."*) Infs **GA7, 27, TN11, VA1,** Pouring down rain; [**SC4,** Pouring down cats and dogs; **AL6,** Pouring down tadpoles]. **1967–68** *DARE* Tape **AR52,** It was pouring down rain as we went from San Francisco over into Oakland; **IN19,** It poured down rain the whole day. It was just the most miserable day you ever saw. **c1970** Pederson *Dial. Surv. Rural GA,* 1 inf, **seGA,** It poured down rain. **1986** Pederson *LAGS Concordance* (*Heavy rain*) 6 infs, **AL, AR, MS, TX,** (It was, etc) pouring down rain; 1 inf, **cMS,** It just poured down rain; 1 inf, **cGA,** It pours down rain; 1 inf, **csTX,** It was going to pour down rain, [it] poured down rain.

c *pour the rain (down).*

1941 in 1944 *ADD* 589 **nWV,** It's pouring the rain down. *Ibid* **sePA,** It poured the rain down. **1956** *Hall Coll.* **wNC,** If it poured the rain, she might shelter a little while, till the ground settled.

2 To apply a liquid insecticide to (an animal).

1981 *Des Moines Register* (IA) 15 Mar, [Advt:] 32 crossbred steers and heifers . . 5 way vaccinated, weaned, wormed and poured.

C As noun.

1 A shower of rain, downpour.

1939 *LANE* Map 93 (*Shower*) 1 inf, **ceNH,** A pour, heavier than *shower.* **1986** Pederson *LAGS Concordance* (*Heavy rain*) 5 infs, **AL, FL, TX,** (A) pour; 1 inf, **csLA,** Heavy pour.

2 See **pour-over 2.**

pour chamber lye out of a boot See **pour piss out of a boot**

pour cream n Also *pouring cream* Cf **pour-over 2**

Cream in liquid form (as opposed to whipped cream or ice cream).

1967 *DARE* FW Addit **cOR,** Pour cream—heavy (whipping) cream. Common. **1998** *DARE* File **cOR,** Pour cream is just cream that you pour out of a pitcher onto your pudding or other dessert, in contrast to whipped cream that you spoon onto the pudding. I associate it with the Southerners who came to work in the timber mill. **1999** *Ibid* **cOH,** In central Ohio thirty years ago pour-cream or pouring cream was lighter than whipping cream; it was half-and-half or coffee cream. Whipping cream was heavier and not synonymous with pour-cream. **1999** *NADS Letters,* I've also heard this term [=*pour cream*] used as a dessert topping for some kinds of puddings, i.e. bread pudding, apple pudding. The contrast is that the cream is not whipped, but is simply poured over the dessert. Though I currently live in southeast Idaho, I think my familiarity with the term may come from my central Oklahoma origins. **2000** *Ibid* **TX,** Pour Cream was heavy cream, like whipping cream, that was poured over pies, cakes, puddings or cobblers without being whipped. *Ibid,* Pour cream was the heavy cream that floated to the top of raw milk. You poured it off to use in making butter, or to pour over fruit or cereal (if you could afford to do so, otherwise it was sold to the creamery for household $$). . . I heard it as a southern term when I was a child. *Ibid* **nOR,** Pour-cream was the cream that had risen to the top of the bottle when the milk was brought into the house. It could be poured off from the bottles into a jar and used later for sauces or whipping. *Ibid* **cPA,** I was familiar with the term from my grandmother in central PA who would ask me if I wanted pour cream or ice cream on my cobbler.

pour-do See **poor do 3**

pour down v phr See **pour B1a**

pour-down n Also *pour-down rain, ~ shower, pouring-down* [Reversed cpd] Cf Intro "Language Changes" I.1, **pour-out** n
A torrential rain; a downpour.

1939 *AmSp* 14.43 SC, 'It's going to gust' in Pennsylvania is nothing but a Kentucky 'downpour' or a South Carolina 'pourdown' or even a Rhode Island 'tempest.' **1939** *LANE* Map 93 *(Shower)* 1 inf, **nwVT,** Regular pourdown; 1 inf, **seCT,** Real pourdown. **1941** Ward *Holding Hills* 181 IA (as of early 20th cent), "Better get home," he'd say. "Ye're sure to be caught in a pourdown!" **1953** Brewer *Word Brazos* 32 **eTX** [Black], Cain't in no wise hol' servuses in hit when hit comes a big pour-down, or a northuh. **1953** Randolph–Wilson *Down in Holler* 273 **Ozarks,** Pour-down. . . A cloudburst. **c1960** *Wilson Coll.* **csKY,** Pour-down: . . A cloudburst or sudden heavy rain. **1962** Atwood *Vocab. TX* 38, *Torrential rain. . . Other less common terms . . are flood, flash flood, pourdown,* and *waterspout.* **1965–70** *DARE* (Qu. B24, . . *A sudden, very heavy rain)* Infs **AL1, IL69,** 134, **LA37, MO21, NC37, TX12, VA69,** Pour-down; **NY61,** A pour-down rain; (Qu. B22, *Rain accompanied by thunder and lightning)* Inf **IL69,** Pour-down; (Qu. B25, . . *Joking names . . for a very heavy rain)* Infs **MD31, NC53, ND2, SD5, VA39, WA2,** Pour-down; (Qu. B27, *A sudden rush of water coming from heavy rain)* Inf **MO4,** Pour-down, downpour. **1966** Dakin *Dial. Vocab. Ohio R. Valley* 2.21 (as of 1950s), *Pour down, pouringdown* (three times, Kentucky, scattered). **1971** Bright *Word Geog. CA & NV* 140, *Heavy rain . . pour down* 3% [of 300 infs] P[attern] XIII [=chiefly central and northern CA]. **1989** Pederson *LAGS Tech. Index* 26 **Gulf Region,** *(Heavy rain)* 33 infs, Pourdown; 4 infs, Pourdown rain; 1 inf, Pourdown shower.

pour down rain v phr See **pour B1b**

pour-down rain (or shower) n See **pour-down** n

pouring ppl adj
Of a boil or wound: draining.

1966–68 *DARE* (Qu. BB36, *When there's an open sore and this yellowish stuff is coming out of it . . it's _____)* Infs **GA13, MD37,** Pouring.

pouring cream See **pour cream**

pouring-down ppl adj See **pour B1a**

pouring-down n See **pour-down** n

pour-off n Cf **pour-over 1**
A waterfall.

1953 Randolph–Wilson *Down in Holler* 273 **Ozarks,** Pour-off. . . A waterfall. **1986** Pederson *LAGS Concordance,* 1 inf, **cnAR,** Pour offs = waterfalls.

pour out v phr Cf **pour B1a**
To rain heavily.

1945 *Harder Coll.* **cwTN,** It began to rain yesterday evening rained all evening and most of the night it just poured out.

pour-out n Cf **pour-down** n
A torrential rain.

1966–69 *DARE* (Qu. B24, . . *A sudden, very heavy rain)* Inf **NC37,** Pour-out; (Qu. B25, . . *Joking names . . for a very heavy rain)* Inf **MO15,** Pour-out. **1986** Pederson *LAGS Concordance (Heavy rain)* 1 inf, **cnAR,** Pour out.

pour-over n

1 A waterfall. Cf **pour-off**
1902 *DN* 2.242 **sIL,** Pour-over. . . A waterfall. **1986** Pederson *LAGS Concordance (Waterfall)* 2 infs, **nwAL, nwFL,** Pourover; 1 inf, **neMS,** Pourover—he has heard.

2 also *pour:* See quots. Cf **pour cream**
1961 *McDavid Coll.* **csOK,** Pour over = sauce (Woman, 66 years old). **1968** *DARE* (Qu. H66a, *The sweet liquid that you pour over a pudding)* Inf **NY109,** Pour.

pour piss out of a boot v phr Also *pour chamber lye (or sand, water) out of a boot;* for addit varr see quots
Fig: to do the simplest thing—usu used in phrr *not to know* (or *have sense) enough to pour piss out of a boot* and varr. **scattered, but less freq Nth** See Map Cf **pound sand down a rathole 1**

1931 *PMLA* 46.1305 **sAppalachians,** He couldn't pour water outn a boot an' the directions on the heel. **1935** Davis *Honey* 322 OR, Plenty of men got big names by not doing anything except concealing the fact that they didn't know enough to pour chamber lye out of a boot. **1937** Crane *Let Me Show You VT* 31, Ignorance, especially of the kind that lacks even common sense . . "Don't know enough to . . pour water out of a boot." **1950** *WELS* ("He hasn't sense enough to _____.") 1 Inf, **swWI,** Pour water out of his shoes. **1958** Randolph *Sticks* 30 **Ozarks,** The mayor of Hatton Gap didn't know enough to pour chamber-lye out of a boot. **1960** Criswell *Resp. to PADS* 20 **Ozarks,** *Pour piss out of a boot. . . Always with a negative to designate an inept person. "Can't pour piss out of a boot." Still common.* **1965–70** *DARE* (Qu. JJ15a, . . *A person who seems to you very stupid: "He hasn't sense enough to _____.")* 39 Infs, **scattered, but more freq Sth, S Midl, SW,** Pour piss out of a boot; 21 Infs, **scattered, but more freq Sth, S Midl,** Pour water out of a boot; **CA96, CO47, IA31, MI72, MS37, NE11, NC76, VA39,** Pour pee out of a boot; **MO21, SC21,** Pour piss out a boot; **MS64, TX72,** Pour piss; **MD19,** Pour piss in a boot; **MO8,** Pour _____ out of a boot [FW: There is a blank she refused to fill in.]; **OR6,** Pour pee out of a pot; **MO27, OK27,** Pour piss out of a boot with (the) directions on the heel; **TX81,** Pour piss out of a boot if the directions were written on the heel and the toes cut out; **OK18,** Pour piss out of a boot, and if he did, he'd step in it; **AL10,** Pour water out of a boot with directions on the bottom; **AR51,** Pour water out of a boot by the directions; **VA69,** Pour water in his boots; **OH45,** Pour water in a boot with the directions on the heel; **HI6, VA25,** Pour water out of a boat (*or* barrel); **CA59, IL106, LA14,** Pour sand out of a boot (with the directions on the heel); (Qu. JJ15b, . . *A person who seems . . very stupid: "He doesn't know _____.")* Inf **CA39,** How to pour water out of a boot if the directions was on the heel; **GA23,** How to pour piss out of a boot with directions written on the heel; **KS6,** Enough to pour sand in a boot; **NE4,** Pour water out of a boot. [57 of 84 total Infs male] **1978** Gould *Greenleaf* 22 **ME,** You know, Ed's a real nice fellow, . . but he couldn't pour skim milk out of a rubber boot with the directions printed on the heel. **1984** Lesley *Winterkill* 27 **neOR,** Red Shirt laughed. "You don't know how to pour piss out of a boot yet." **1995** Karr *Liars' Club* 72 **eTX,** With every turn I make, Lecia's smile slides off of me as if she's saying, *You don't have the sense to pour piss from a boot*—then I wheel around the room one more time before coming back to that weary grin of hers—*with the instructions on the heel.*

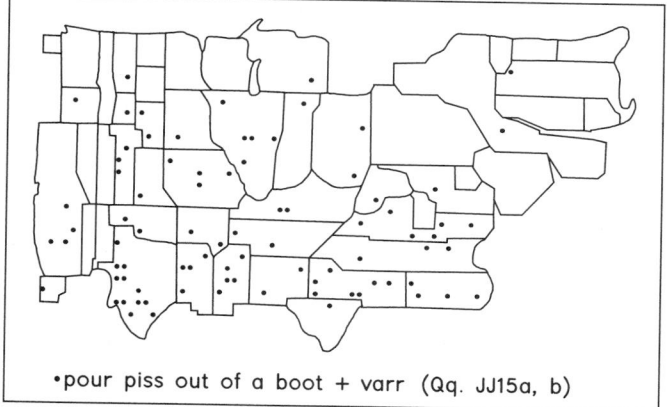

•pour piss out of a boot + varr (Qq. JJ15a, b)

pour sand down (or in) a rathole See **pound sand down a rathole**

pour the rain (down) See **pour B1c**

pour up v phr
To pour out, distribute by pouring.

1931 *AmSp* 6.216 IL, MN, WI [Influence of Swedish on English], She *poured up* the coffee. . . Hon *hällde upp* kaffet. **1944** *PADS* 2.48 **cwNC,** *Pour up:* . . To pour out. **1967** *DARE* Tape TX32, Your jelly is done. You turn the burner out and let it cool. Pour it up in glasses or jars.

1974 Maurer–Pearl *KY Moonshine* 121, *Pour up tr. v.* To distribute moonshine (after it has been temped to 100 proof) into containers for distribution.

pout n esp NEng Cf **bullpout, horned pout, mudpout**
Esp a **bullhead 1b** such as the **brown bullhead 1,** but also other freshwater catfishes of the family Ictaluridae such as the **white catfish 1.**

1707 Williams *Redeemed Captive* 20, There Seven of us Supped on the Fish, called *Bull-head* or *Pout,* and did not eat it up, the Fish was so very large. **1778** Carver *Travels N. Amer.* 171 **NY,** There is also [in Lake Ontario] a sort called the Cat-head or Pout, which are in general very large, some of them weighing eight or ten pounds. **1792** Belknap *Hist. NH* 3.178, Pout, *Silurus felis* [=*Ameiurus catus*]. **a1843** (1958) Barker *Recoll. First Settlement OH* 21, The Black Cat & the Pike were the leargest [sic] Fish . . the suckers & pouts, least. **a1862** (1864) Thoreau *ME Woods* 210, He would not touch a pout . . and said that neither Indians nor whites thereabouts ever ate them, which I thought was singular, since they are esteemed in Massachusetts. **1931–33** *LANE* Worksheets se**CT,** Pout—catfish. **1969** *DARE* (Qu. P1, . . *Kinds of freshwater fish . . caught around here . . good to eat*) Inf **MA**62, Pout.

pouting house n Also *pout-house* [*pout* to sulk]
See quots.

1968 *DARE* FW Addit sw**VA,** "When a man falls out with his wife, he'd go to his pout-house. He'd have just a bed in it so he could sleep by hisself." So-and-so "had one, a log cabin behind the house. Called it that too, his pout-house." **1969** *DARE* (Qu. M21b, *Joking names for an outside toilet building*) Inf **KY**43, Poutin' house.

poverty n [*OED2* 1523 →] Cf **poverty-poor**
Malnutrition, starvation.

1808 in 1956 Eliason *Tarheel Talk* 158 **NC,** The ride has not mended my apptite atoll. I am guitting verry weak with poverty. **1905** Biggers *From Cattle Range* 105 **TX,** Hundreds of mother cows had waded into bog holes, died of poverty or been drowned in the river. **1923** *DN* 5.217 sw**MO,** *Poverty.* . . Lack of feed. "That hog died f'm poverty."

poverty birch n [See quot 1950]
=**gray birch a.**

1897 Sudworth *Arborescent Flora* 139 **ME,** White Birch. . . Common names. . . Poverty Birch. **1938** Van Dersal *Native Woody Plants* 325, Birch. . . Poverty (*Betula populifolia*). **1950** Peattie *Nat. Hist. Trees* 168, Gray Birch . . Other Names: Poplar-leaved, Poverty, Wire or Small White Birch. [*Ibid* 269, This is no Aspen, or any of the Poplar sort, but a Birch and, though closely related to the princess Paper Birch, only a stunted sister of it, of no utility.]

poverty grass n [From their growing in poor soils or having little value as forage]
1 Any of var grasses, as:
a =**needlegrass 2,** esp *Aristida dichotoma.* [See quot 1912]
1833 Eaton *Botany* 27, [*Aristida*] *dichotoma* . . beard grass, poverty grass. **1837** Darlington *Flora Cestrica* 53 se**PA,** Forked Aristida. *Vulgò*—Poverty Grass. . . Dry sterile soils: Mica-slate hills: frequent. **1847** Wood *Class-Book* 595, A[ristida] *dichotoma* . . *Poverty Grass.* . . A slender grass, in sandy soil, U.S., common. *Ibid,* A. *tuberculosa* . . *Long-awned Poverty Grass.* . . A very singular species, in dry prairies, Ill. **1898** *Jrl. Amer. Folkl.* 11.283 **KS,** *Aristida purpurea* . . poverty grass. **1912** Wooton–Standley *Grasses NM* 53, Speaking generally of the whole genus [=*Aristida*] . . it is correct to say that they deserve the common name often given to them of "Poverty grass" because they are not valuable as forage and because their presence in abundance on any area indicates a dearth of good feed. **1937** U.S. Forest Serv. *Range Plant Hdbk.* G16, Three-awns, also commonly called needlegrasses, wiregrasses, and poverty grasses, constitute a large genus of the redtop tribe (Agrostideae) and are widely distributed throughout the Western States, being especially well represented in the Southwest. **1967–70** *DARE* (Qu. S9, . . *Kinds of grass that are hard to get rid of*) Infs **MA**100, **PA**169, Poverty grass [*DARE* Ed: Some of these Infs may refer instead to other senses below.]; (Qu. S15, . . *Weed seeds that cling to clothing*) Inf **OR**5, Poverty grass—gets between dog's toes.
b A **dropseed 3** (here: *Sporobolus vaginiflorus*).
1894 Coulter *Botany W. TX* 519, S[porobolus] vaginaeflorus . . Southern poverty grass. . . Dry sterile soil, northern Texas and eastward.

1912 Baker *Book of Grasses* 115, Sheathed Rush-grass. Southern Poverty-grass. *Sporobolus vaginaeflorus.* . . Dry and sandy soil. . . Vermont to Wyoming, south to Georgia and Texas. **1950** Gray–Fernald *Manual of Botany* 153, S[porobolus] vaginiflorus . . Poverty-Grass. . . Dry, open sterile soil.
c also *poverty oat grass:* An **oat grass c** (here: *Danthonia spicata*). [See quot 1914]
1895 Gray–Bailey *Field Botany* 472, Danthonia spicata . . Poverty Grass. **1914** Georgia *Manual Weeds* 50, This miserable little grass seems best contented when making some hard, worn-out meadow look shabby and miserable. Its name of "Poverty Grass" fits it well, for its presence seems to be a sure indication of poverty of soil. The grass itself is dry and tasteless, worth nothing either as hay or as pasture. **1937** U.S. Forest Serv. *Range Plant Hdbk.* G45, Poverty oatgrass. . . is well named, as it is an excellent indicator of poor soil and also is worthless as forage; no living thing, except perhaps meadow mice, will eat it unless forced to do so. **1940** Gates *Flora KS* 125 se**KS,** Danthonia spicata. . . Wildoatgrass, Poverty Grass. **1952** Strausbaugh–Core *Flora WV* 120, D[anthonia] spicata. . . Poverty grass. . . Common in dry, sterile soil throughout the State. **1968** *DARE* (Qu. S9, . . *Kinds of grass that are hard to get rid of*) Inf **WV**7, Poverty grass. **1974** Welsh *Anderson's Flora AK* 567, Poverty Oatgrass. . . Known in Alaska from extreme southern portion of the Panhandle and to be expected elsewhere.
d A **beardgrass:** either a **big bluestem** (here: *Andropogon gerardi*) or **little bluestem.**
1898 *Jrl. Amer. Folkl.* 11.282 **ME,** *Andropogon scoparius* [=*Schizachyrium scoparium*], . . and *Andropogon furcatus* [=*A. gerardii*], . . poverty grass, Southern Me. **1929** *Torreya* 29.149 **ME,** Andropogon scoparius, a grass growing in thin, sterile soil, was thought to "run out" and impoverish the soil, hence the name *"Wolf grass," "Poverty grass."* **1968** *DARE* (Qu. S9, . . *Kinds of grass that are hard to get rid of*) Inf **OH**41, Poverty grass—tall, three feet high.
e A **bromegrass** (here: either *Bromus hordeaceus* or *B. marginatus*).
1902 U.S. Natl. Museum *Contrib. Herbarium* 312 **CA,** Bromus marginatus. . . A rough, hairy grass . . known to the whites as "poverty grass." **1911** Jepson *Flora CA* 71, B[romus] hordeaceus. . . Sometimes called "Poverty-grass."
2 Any of var other plants, as:
a also *poverty plant:* =**beach heather.** NEng
1892 Torrey *Foot-Path Way* 81 **Cape Cod MA,** Equally new to me . . were the broom-crowberry and the greener kind of poverty grass (*Hudsonia ericoides*), inviting pillows or cushions of which, looking very much alike at a little distance, were scattered freely over the grayish hills. **1896** *Jrl. Amer. Folkl.* 9.182 **MA,** Hudsonia tomentosa . . poverty-grass, heath, dog's dinner. **1910** Graves *Flowering Plants* 283 **CT,** Hudsonia tomentosa. . . False Heather. Poverty Grass. **1948** Pearson *Sea Flavor* 46 se**NH,** Poverty grass, or *Hudsonia,* to call it by its scientific name, is the first flower to appear on the dunes. **1951** Hough *Singing in Morning* 39 **Martha's Vineyard MA,** Dried beach heather—also known popularly as . . poverty plant.
b A **spike rush** (here: *Eleocharis tenuis*).
1894 *Jrl. Amer. Folkl.* 7.103 **WV,** Eleocharis tenuis . . poverty-grass, kill-cow.
c =**broom crowberry.**
1894 *Jrl. Amer. Folkl.* 7.99 **MA,** Corema Conradii, Torr., poverty-grass, Provincetown, Mass. **1950** Gray–Fernald *Manual of Botany* 975, C[orema] Conradii. . . Poverty-grass.
d =**rabbit-foot clover.**
1900 Lyons *Plant Names* 377, T[rifolium] arvense. . . Rabbit-foot Clover . . Poverty-grass. **1922** *Amer. Botanist* 28.34, "Old field clover", "stone clover" and "poverty grass" allude to the habit this plant [=*Trifolium arvense*] has of growing in sterile soil.
e A **marsh elder 1** (here: *Iva axillaris*). Cf **povertyweed c**
1940 Clute *Amer. Plant Names* 262, Iva axillaris. Poverty-weed, poverty-grass, salt sage, bozzle-berry, bozzle-weed.
f A **Saint-John's-wort** (here: *Hypericum gentianoides*).
1940 Clute *Amer. Plant Names* 133, H[ypericum] gentianoides. . . Poverty-grass.
g A **rush n¹ B** (here: *Juncus tenuis*).
1940 Clute *Amer. Plant Names* 150, J[uncus] tenuis. . . Yard rush, wire-grass, poverty-grass.

poverty oat grass See **poverty grass 1c**

poverty pig n Also *poor man's pig* Cf *Hoover hog* (at **Hoover n 1c**)

The nine-banded armadillo (*Dasypus novemcinctus*).

1947 Cahalane *Mammals* 112, The meat is white and tender, and tastes like pork. In east Texas, the armadillo is often called "poverty pig" or "poor man's pig."

poverty pine n

1 =**Jersey pine.**

1880 Tourgée *Bricks* 94 **NC**, His rider's feet just . . [brushed] the low "poverty-pines" which grew by the roadside. **1903** Small *Flora SE U.S.* 28, *Pinus Virginiana*. . . In sandy soil or on stony ridges, Long Island to Indiana, Georgia and Alabama. Scrub or Jersey Pine. Poverty Pine. **1950** Gray–Fernald *Manual of Botany* 57, Poverty-[pine] or Scrub-P[overty pine]. . . Barrens and sterile soil.

2 =**Table Mountain pine.**

1908 Rogers *Tree Book* 48, The *Table-Mountain-Pine*. . . Its dingy colour, barren habitat and scraggly growth earn it the name, "poverty pine." **1950** Grimm *Trees PA* 62, The Table Mountain Pine is also known as the Bur Pine, Prickly Cone Pine or Poverty Pine. . . It is typically a tree of poor soil and of dry, barren, rocky mountain ridges.

poverty plant See **poverty grass 2a**

poverty-poor adj Cf **poverty**

Very poor, destitute.

1911 Porter *Harvester* 204 **IN**, A woman, even a poverty-poor woman . . cannot go to another woman on a man's whim. **1953** Randolph–Wilson *Down in Holler* 273 **Ozarks**, *Poverty-poor*. . . Destitute, near starvation. **1976** Garber *Mountain-ese* 71 **sAppalachians**, *Poverty-poor* . . destitute—We gave our used clothes to the poverty-poor families.

povertyweed n

Any of var often weedy plants that grow in poor soils, as:

a A **cudweed 1**: usu *Pseudognaphalium obtusifolium*, but also *P. macounii*.

1876 Hobbs *Bot. Hdbk.* 92, Poverty weed—Life everlasting—Gnaphalium polycephalum [=*Pseudognaphalium obtusifolium*]. **1896** *Jrl. Amer. Folkl.* 9.192 **ME**, *Gnaphalium polycephalum* . . poverty weed, Paris, Me. **1898** Ibid 11.229 **ME**, *Gnaphalium decurrens* [=*Pseudognaphalium macounii*] . . poverty weed, South Berwick, Me. **1979** Erichsen-Brown *Med. N. Amer. Plants* 403, *Gnaphalium obtusifolium*. . . Common names. Sweet or fragrant live everlasting, . . poverty weed.

b =**pearly everlasting 1.**

1894 *Jrl. Amer. Folkl.* 7.90 **ME**, *Anaphalis margaritacea* . . poverty-weed, Penobscot Co., Me. **1935** (1943) Muenscher *Weeds* 450, *Anaphalis margaritacea*. . . Silver button, Poverty-weed. **1974** (1977) Coon *Useful Plants* 102, Pearly everlasting, cotton-weed, live-long, poverty weed.

c A **marsh elder 1**, usu *Iva axillaris*. **West** Cf **poverty grass 2e**

1895 U.S. Dept. Ag. *Farmers' Bulletin* 28.27, Poverty weed . . Iva axillaris . . Montana to New Mexico. **1898** *Jrl. Amer. Folkl.* 11.230 **WY**, *Iva axillaris* . . poverty weed. **1941** Jaeger *Wildflowers* 278, Nevada poverty weed. *Iva nevadensis* (after *Ajuga iva*, one of the mints whose odor some of the species resemble). **1950** Stevens *ND Plants* 281, *Iva* [spp] Marsh Elder. Poverty Weed. **1973** Hitchcock–Cronquist *Flora Pacific NW* 532, *Iva* . . Poverty-weed; Marsh-elder.

d A **pussytoes** (here: *Antennaria plantaginifolia*).

1896 *Jrl. Amer. Folkl.* 9.191 **ME**, *Antennaria plantaginifolia* . . poverty weed, Paris, Me.

e =**oxeye daisy 1.** [*EDD* 1877 →] Cf **poor-land daisy**

1900 Lyons *Plant Names* 99, C[hrysanthemum] *Leucanthemum*. . . Pismire, Poverty-weed. **1914** Georgia *Manual Weeds* 493, Whiteweed, Midsummer Daisy, Poverty Weed [etc]. **1988** Werner *Life & Lore* 88 **IL**, *Chrysanthemum leucanthemum*. . . in hayfields . . can substantially diminish the quality of the hay. From this unfavorable characteristic comes [sic] several old common names . . Poverty Weed [etc].

f A **goldenrod 1** (here: *Euthamia graminifolia*).

1900 *Plant World* 3.133, Poverty weed, for *Solidago lanceolata* L. [=

Euthamia graminifolia], probably because of its frequent presence in poor or neglected ground.

g A **buttonweed 1** (here: *Diodia teres*). Cf **poor joe n[1] 2, poor-land weed**

1901 *Torreya* 1.117 **GA**, *Diodia teres*. . . Poverty-weed. . . Poor-land weed. . . Poor Joe.

h A plant of the genus *Monolepis*, usu *M. nuttalliana*. **West** For other names of this sp see **Indian spinach, patata n[1]**

1932 Rydberg *Flora Prairies* 297, *Monolepis* [spp] . . Poverty Weed. **1959** Anderson *Flora AK* 201, Nuttall Monolepis, Poverty Weed. . . Dry soil, central Alaska—N.W. Terr.—Minn.—Mo.—N. Mex.—Calif. **1967** Harrington *Edible Plants Rocky Mts.* 80, Nuttall Monolepis, Poverty Weed, Patata. . . Waste places, edges of lawns and gardens, often on alkaline or salty ground. **1974** (1977) Coon *Useful Plants* 96, Poverty weed, patata.

i A **cotton rose 3** (here: *Evax prolifera* or *E. verna*). [See quot 1936]

1933 Small *Manual SE Flora* 1404, *Filago nivea* [=*Evax verna*] . . Poverty-weed. . . Dry plains or stony soil, . . Ga. to Tex. **1936** Whitehouse *TX Flowers* 167, *Filago prolifera* [=*Evax p.*] . . [and] *Filago nivea*. . . Both of these plants are also known as poverty-weed. . . Poverty-weed is a suitable name for them in the sheep-grazing section of Central Texas which has been heavily over-grazed. In many pastures they take the place of grasses as a ground cover. **1946** Reeves–Bain *Flora TX* 259, E[vax] *multicaulis* [=*E. verna*]. . . Poverty Weed. . . Dry soil; often a weed.

j A **sagebrush 1** (here: *Artemisia ludoviciana*).

1933 *Torreya* 33.84 **ID**, *Artemisia gnaphalodes* [=*Artemisia ludoviciana*] . . Poverty weed, Boise, Idaho.

k An aster (*Aster* spp); see quot. Cf **heath aster, old-field ~**

1943 Peattie *Great Smokies* 168, In the first year after abandonment there is a one-year stage when horseweed and finger grass predominate; the next year ragweed and heather aster, appropriately called poverty-weed in some places, take over.

l A **ragweed 2.**

1966 *DARE* (Qu. S21, . . *Weeds* . . *that are a trouble in gardens and fields*) Inf **NM6**, Povertyweed—same as ragweed.

m A **beach heather** (here: *Hudsonia ericoides*). Cf **poverty grass 2a**

1971 GA Dept. Ag. *Farmers Market Bulletin* 25 Aug 8 **GA**, Hudsonia ericoides, commonly known as Poverty-weed, Beach-heather [etc].

powder n

A Gram form.

Used as a count noun. See also **baking powders**

1941 in 1944 *ADD* 472 **nWV** [Black], Washing powders. **1983** *MJLF* 9.1.51 **ceKY**, *Powders* . . face powder. **1986** Pederson *LAGS Concordance* (Quinine) 1 inf, **cTN**, Fever powders; (*Cake of yeast*) 1 inf, **nwFL**, Yeast powders.

B Sense.

A powdering, sprinkling. **chiefly NEast, N Cent, Appalachians** See Map

1965–70 *DARE* (Qu. B39, *A very light fall of snow*) 26 Infs, Powder of snow; **CA**177, **IN**82, **NJ**63, **PA**192, 215, **TN**35, Powder.

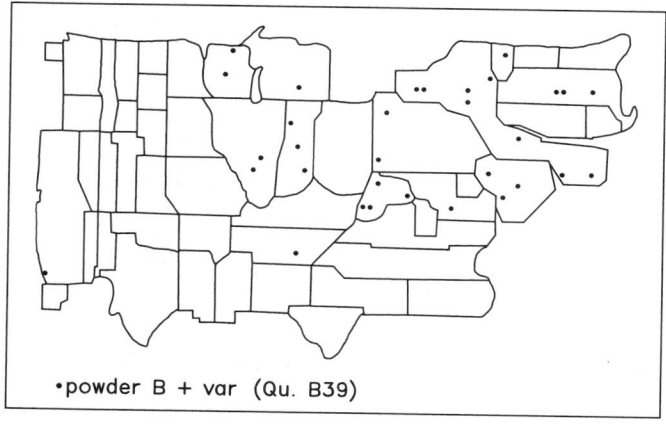

•powder B + var (Qu. B39)

powder horn n

A **chickweed 1b** (here: *Cerastium nutans*).

1903 Small *Flora SE U.S.* 424, *Cerastium nutans*. . . In woods, Nova Scotia to British Columbia, Florida and Mexico. Spring. Powder-horn. **1910** Graves *Flowering Plants* 177 **CT**, *Cerastium nutans*. . . Nodding chickweed. Powder-horn.

powdering n

Face powder.

1895 *DN* 1.373 **seKY, eTN, wNC**, *Powdering:* powder. "She has got powdering on her face." **1909** *DN* 3.402 **nwAR**, *Powderin'*. . . Face-powder. "She put powderin' on her face."

powder post n **chiefly NEng**

Wood reduced to powder, esp by insect action; the condition of being so affected; hence adj *powder-posted* damaged in this way.

1790 Deane *New Engl. Farmer* 151, The smaller kind [of timber worm] eats only the sappy parts of the wood, turning it to what is vulgarly called *powder-post*. **1845** Judd *Margaret* 313 **swME**, The grubs of the law have gnawed into us, and we are all powder-post. **1863** (1864) Mitchell *My Farm* 83 **NEng**, A wild, sweeping, gallant blaze, that wrapped old powder-post timbers in its roar, . . came crinkling through the roof in a hundred wilful jets. **1888** Jewett *King Folly* 125 **NEng**, The j'ints is all powder-posted. **1917** U.S. Dept. Ag. *Farmers' Bulletin* 778.[2], Inspect material in yards and storehouses annually . . and sort out and burn material showing evidence of powder post. *Ibid* 7, Powder-post causes a loss which falls alike on the dealer, the manufacturer . . , and the consumer of finished products. *Ibid* 16, The introduction into lumber yards and storehouses of material infested with powder post [should be] prevented. **1929** *AmSp* 5.123 **ME**, Fence posts were said to "rot between wind and water" and become "powder posted," a good description.

powder-post beetle n [**powder post**]

A beetle of the family Lyctidae or Bostrichidae. For other names of one of these see **short-circuit beetle**

1905 U.S. Dept. Ag. *Yearbook for 1904* 387, [Caption:] Work of powder post beetle, Sinoxylon basilare, in hickory poles. **1909** Smith *Insect Friends* 238, The species of *Lyctus* or powder post beetles . . occur[s] in the woodwork of houses or in furniture, and may create serious trouble. **1926** U.S. Dept. Ag. *Farmers' Bulletin* 1477.11, Powder-post beetles often ruin stored hardwoods . . by turning them into a flourlike powder. **1938** Brimley *Insects NC* 198, *Family Lyctidae, Powder-post Beetles[.]* These are very small elongate beetles that in all stages live in dry wood sometimes literally reducing it to powder. **1946** *Richmond News Leader* 16 Jan 10/3 (Hench Coll.), [In "Questions and Answers":] Can you tell me how to get rid of "flat heads"? They are in the first floor joists that go across the basement ceiling. I can hear them cutting. . . [Answer:] Whether they are powder-post beetles or termites or some other kind of pest, you can obtain instruction by taking or sending one of them to . . [the] State Entomologist. **1966** *News & Observer* (Raleigh NC) 22 Aug 24, One of the more common insects attacking the wooden understructure of a house are the powder post beetles. This name as used herein refers to several species of beetles which bore in wood and are so named because of the powder-like dust produced as a result of their working in wood. **1988** *Yankee* Jan 28 **NEng**, Each morning there is a pile of sawdust all around the base and on the shelves of the clock. There are numerous small holes in the veneer. Any idea how I can get rid of the pests? . . [Answer:] The insects are called powder-post beetles.

powder-posted See **powder post**

powder puff n

1 =**dandelion 1.** Cf **puffweed**

1966 *DARE* (Qu. S11, . . *Dandelion*) Inf **FL26**, Powder puff when it blows away.

2 A **cotton grass 1** (here: *Eriophorum callitrix*).

1967 *DARE* Wildfl QR Pl.2A Inf **OR9**, Powder puff.

3 =**Queen Anne's lace 1.**

1968 *DARE* (Qu. S6, . . *Queen Anne's lace: [Summertime roadside weed two feet high or so with a lacy white top]*) Inf **NY92**, Powder puff.

4 also *powder-puff bush:* A **mimosa 1** (here: *Mimosa strigillosa*).

1969 *SC Market Bulletin* 11 Sept 4/4, Seedlings of . . cork screw willows, powder puff bush and night blooming jessamine . . 25¢ each.

1970 Correll *Plants TX* 778, *Mimosa strigillosa* . . Powderpuff, vergonzosa. . . flowers in pink or purple globes. **1979** Ajilvsgi *Wild Flowers* 158 **eTX, wLA**, Powderpuff—*Mimosa strigillosa*.

5 A **star thistle** (here: *Centaurea americana*).

1936 Whitehouse *TX Flowers* 189, *Centaurea americana*. . . is also known as powder puffs. . . In one variety the fully-opened flower cluster has an outer border of numerous lavender flowers with cream-colored flowers in the center.

powder-puff tree n

A **silk tree** (here: *Albizia julibrissin*), naturalized chiefly in the southern US.

1979 Little *Checklist U.S. Trees* 47, *Albizia julibrissin* . . Silktree. . . Other common names—mimosa-tree, "mimosa," powderpuff tree.

powder room n **scattered, but more freq C Atl, Midl** See Map *somewhat more freq among women*

A bathroom in a private house, esp one with a toilet and lavatory, but no bathtub or shower, intended for the use of guests; a public restroom for women.

1941 Schulberg *What Makes* 272 **sCA**, She had just run into Laurette in the powder room [in a home where a party was being held]. **1945** Mencken *Amer. Lang. Suppl. 1* 640, During the days of Prohibition some learned speak-easy proprietor in New York hit upon the happy device of calling his retiring room for female boozers a *powder-room*. **1965–70** *DARE* (Qu. F37, *Names for an indoor toilet*) 24 Infs, **scattered, but more freq C Atl, Midl**, Powder room; **NC16, VA30**, Powder room [laughter]; **LA14**, Powder room—this is modern; **MD7**, Powder room—for public women's room; **MD14**, Powder room—in public places; **MD35**, Powder room—just toilet and washbasin, no tub. [25 of 30 Infs female] **1966** *York Co. Coast Star* (Kennebunk ME) 28 Apr 8/7, Large hall with powder room, living room with fireplace and den or TV room. Here is spacious living in quality not found in new homes. **1981** *New Yorker* 19 Jan 48 **swOH** (as of 1941), The ground-floor hall ran back through the house, with a "powder room" under the stairs. . . The powder room, chiefly for visitors, had a row of neatly monogrammed guest towels. **1986** Pederson *LAGS Concordance* (*Room with toilet and sink, no bath or shower;* this question was asked chiefly in urban areas) 11 infs, 5 **TX**, Powder room; 1 inf, **seFL**, Powder room—usually has mirror and bath; 1 inf, **cTX**, Powder room—to "ladies"; 1 inf, **ceTX**, Powder room—in house, no tub or shower; 1 inf, **csTX**, Powder room—half bath. [11 of 15 infs female]

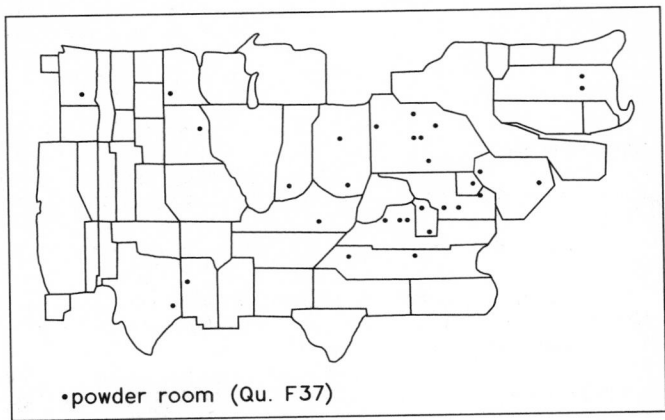

•powder room (Qu. F37)

powders See **powder A**

powder touch n

=**little blue heron.**

1956 *AmSp* 31.185 **NC**, Powder touch—Little blue heron—N.C.—A blue bird blotched with white.

powder wedge n

See quot.

1952 Brown *NC Folkl.* 1.578, *Powder wedge*. . . Same as *mauler, q.v. Ibid* 564, *Mauler:* . . An iron rod some twenty inches long and an inch and a half in diameter, part of it hollow and tapering to a point. The hollow portion is filled with powder and a fuse is inserted through a small lateral hole. The tapered end is driven into a log an inch or two; then the fuse is ignited. When the explosion takes place, the log is split. . . Called *powder wedge* in Guilford county.

pow'(e)ful See **powerful**

power n

1 A large number or quantity; a great deal, lot. [*OED2* a1661 →] **chiefly Sth, S Midl** *old-fash* Cf **nation** n[1]
1781 *PA Jrl. & Weekly Advt.* (Philadelphia) 20 June 3, *Power* is often used to supply the place of a noun of *multitude,* as "a power of folks," for a multitude of people. **1823** *Natl. Intelligencer* (DC) 1 May (*DN* 4.47) [Western dialect], *Power. . .* Quantity? "a power of hogs," "a power of corn." **1837** Sherwood *Gaz. GA* 71, *Power,* for much or many, *i.e.* he has read *a power*—he has a *power* of corn or negroes—he can lift a *power.* **1856** in 1862 Colt *Went to KS* 42, And we thought before morning that they [=rats] would take us bodily . . there came such "a power" of the "critters," as these southern people say. **1893** *KS Univ. Qrly.* 1.141 MO, KS, *Power:* a great deal. **1911** *DN* 3.539 eKY, *Power. . .* A large quantity. **1912** *DN* 3.586 wIN, *Power. . .* A vast quantity. "I understand he has a power of corn this year." **1914** *DN* 4.78 ME, nNH, *Power. . .* A great deal. "He's got a power o' money." **1915** *DN* 4.243 eTN, He raised a power and sold a heap and had a right smart left. **1923** *DN* 5.217 swMO, They's been a power o' rain lately. **1952** Brown *NC Folkl.* 1.578, *Power, a. . .* A great deal, very much; a great many, a crowd. "She's got a power of hair." . . General. Mainly old people. **1984** Wilder *You All Spoken Here* 141 **Sth**, A power of rain: When it rains pitchforks an' yearlin's.

2 An outstanding example.
1923 *DN* 5.217 swMO, He's a power of a talker.

3 A machine for converting the work of a horse or other animal into rotary motion for driving another machine—often in comb *horse power.*
1831 *Genesee Farmer* 1.132/1 NY, I have known many tolerably good [threshing] machines condemned, from having connected with it a weak, ill-contrived, and inaffective [sic] horse power. **1841** (1930) Sewall *Diary* 234 IL, *Thursday—29th* [July]. . . Received threshing machine and power from Winthrop and Monmouth agreeable to contract. *Ibid* 240, *Saturday—6th* [November]—Went to Beardstown, and brought home my thrashing machine and horse power. **1854** PA State Ag. Soc. *Report* 80, Martin H. Coryell, Bucks county, 1 horse power and threshing machine. **1872** (1876) Knight *Amer. Mech. Dict.* 2.1125, *Horse-power. . .* A machine in which the power of horses is exerted to drive other machinery. **1897** (1968) Sears *Catalogue* 143, *First Prize Dog Power. . .* This power can be operated by a dog, goat or sheep; yields 25 per cent. more power from a given weight of animal than any other. . . The power can be connected to any churn sold by us. **1899** Garland *Boy Life* 198 nwIA, The machine was a "J.I. Case" or a "Buffalo Pitts" separator, and was moved by five pairs of horses attached to a power staked to the ground, round which they travelled to the left, pulling at the ends of long levers or sweeps. **1902** (1969) Sears *Catalogue* 696, *Acme Two-Horse Sweep Power. . .* Each power is furnished complete with two sweeps, two sweep rods [etc]. *Ibid, Our Overhead One-Horse Power.* This style of horse power is very convenient. . . The power can be bolted to the timbers above the driveway and machines can be set on the floor either above or below the power. *Ibid, Acme Geared Tread Power. . .* One-Horse Double Geared Tread Power, with speed regulator. **1968** DARE (Qu. L32a, *In early days, how was the grain separated from the straw?*) Inf **PA**120, Horses on a tread power.

4 Religious inspiration or enthusiasm—often in phrr *have* (or *get*) *the power.* [Prob abbr for *the power of God;* see quot c1848]
[**1848** Burlend *True Picture* 57 IL, An individual started from his seat, exclaiming . . "I feel it," meaning what is commonly termed among them the power of God.] **1862** *Harper's New Mth. Mag.* 26.101 TN [Black], These exercizes had been prolonged nearly an hour when several of the seekers were taken with "the power." **1899** *Mth. S. Dakotan* 1.141, One sister got the power in right good Methodist fashion. **1901** *DN* 2.145 NY [College words], *Power. . .* In phrase, 'Have the power,' to go into an extraordinary state of religious excitement. Otsego, Seneca, Tompkins Co., N.Y. In Fulton Co., N.Y., to be under conviction, to be on the anxious seat, to go forward. **1910** *DN* 3.446 wNY, *Power. . .* In the expression "to get the power," to get into an extraordinary state of religious emotion or excitement. **1917** *DN* 4.416 wNC, *Power. . .* Religious ecstasy. "She had the power." Also Lake N.Y. **1923** Cook *50 Yrs.* 231, A great revivalist of the shouting Methodist school, who could soon have great numbers of blind followers under the influence of what he

styled "the power." **1927** *AmSp* 2.362 cwWV, *Power* . . religious enthusiasm. "I tell you that prayer had the power."

power doctor n [Perh folk-etym for *powwow doctor* (at **powwow** n 2), but cf **power 4**]
1949 Webber *Backwoods Teacher* 104 **Ozarks**, Gram Slocum—a queer old woman up Slocum Holler, who was sort of a "power doctor," i.e., one who could "do things," and who depended on charms rather than the "yarbs" we once saw her gathering in the woods.

powerful adj, adv Pronc-spp *pow'(e)ful*
A Forms.
1875 in 1884 Lanier *Poems* 178 [Black], I'se pow'ful skeered. **1885** Twain *Huck. Finn* 328 MO [Black], I lay he'd wait a pow'ful long time 'fo' I *ast* him. **1906** *DN* 3.151 nwAR, *Pow'ful.* . . Exceedingly, very. "He's pow'ful good to me." **1927** *AmSp* 2.362 cwWV, *Pow'eful* . . very strange. "Sis told a pow'eful story about the frummer [sic] when she came back from the store." **1953** Brewer *Word Brazos* 12 eTX [Black], De boss-mens don' git but pow'ful li'l' work outen 'em on a Monday. **1976** Ryland *Richmond Co. VA* 375, *Pow'ful*—very.
B As adj.

1 Very large, great, extraordinary. **chiefly Sth, Midl** Cf **nation** adj
a1822 in 1956 *AmSp* 31.270 SC, A *powerful* fire . . a *powerful* fish . . a powerful *snow.* **1822** Woods *2 Yrs. Residence* 294 IL, I also have got some beefs, and a *powerful* chance of corn. **1839** *S. Lit. Messenger* 5.377 NC, To be sure I did see a powerful sight of bear signs. **1843** (1916) Hall *New Purchase* 51 IN, If then we had, in a bad road, done by daylight about one and a half miles per hour, how were we likely to do three miles in the dark, and over what a native styled—"the most powerfullest road?" **1899** (1912) Green *VA Folk-Speech* 333, *Powerfull* [sic]. . . Great; numerous; numerically large. **1902** *DN* 2.242 sIL, *Powerful.* . . Extraordinary; immense; out of common. **1907** *DN* 3.225 nwAR. **1927** [see A above]. **1932** Stong *State Fair* 8 IA, They're going to have to raise some powerful hogs if they keep him out of the grand award this year. **1939** Hall Coll. wNC, Uncle Tobe said it was a powerful bear. **1952** Brown *NC Folkl.* 1.578, A powerful sight of folks came. **1966** *DARE* FW Addit MS, That's a powerful lot of money. **1968** *DARE* (Qu. LL5, *Something impressively big: "That cabbage is really a _____.")* Inf **MD**20, Powerful head of cabbage. **1970** *DARE* Tape VA96, I have a neighbor over here who's got a tremendous pond, powerful pond. He irrigates from it. **1985** in 1986 *Barrick Coll.* csPA, *Powerful*—intensifier, as in "a powerful mess of stuff" [i.e., a lot]. **1986** Pederson *LAGS Concordance,* 1 inf, nwTN, They're powerful hands to complain.

2 foll by infin: Strongly inclined, prone. Cf **awful 3, bad** adj **4**
1981 Harper-Presley *Okefinokee* 78 seGA (as of 1929), People was powerful to fight here in them days.

C As adv.

1 foll by adj or adv: Very. **scattered, but more freq Sth, S Midl** Cf **nation** adv
a1822 in 1956 *AmSp* 31.270 SC, *Powerful.* This word is much used by the middling and lower class of people in the interior of So: Carolina, in giving form to their ideas: instead of saying a person is very strong, they would say, *he is powerful;* or *powerful strong.* **1832** (1919) Irving *Jrls.* 3.171 NY, My gun is so powerful dirty. **1878** Hart *Sazerac Lying Club* 161 NV, He was seedy and battered, and he looked "powerful" dry. He entered a Main Street saloon. **1887** Amer. Philol. Assoc. *Trans. for 1886* 17.34 **Sth**, A gentleman from Ohio . . has attempted to indicate for me the words that were imported during or after the war from the South into Southern Ohio. He says the word *powerful* (very, exceedingly) was heard infrequently before the war in Ohio, but since then, among the laboring classes, especially among the descendants of refugees from Virginia, Kentucky, and Tennessee, it is used every day. **1892** *DN* 1.211 seMA, *Powerful:* very. . . "Powerful weak." **1893** Shands *MS Speech* 51, *Powerful.* . . The use of this word as an adverb meaning *very, exceedingly,* is pronounced vulgar by Webster; nevertheless it is used in Mississippi, with this sense, by a large number of well-educated people, I think, principally, by immigrants from South Carolina. **1899** (1912) Green *VA Folk-Speech* 333, *Powerfull* [sic]. . . Very. **1902** *DN* 2.242 sIL, *Powerful.* . . Very. **1903** *DN* 2.325 seMO, *Powerful.* . . In a high degree; extremely. 'He is a powerful bad man.' 'I'm powerful glad to see you!' **1905** *DN* 3.16 cCT, *Powerful.* . . Very. **1906** *DN* 3.122 sIN, *Powerful.* . . Extremely; in a great degree. **1906** [see A above]. **1909** *DN* 3.359 eAL, wGA, *Pow(e)rful.* . . Exceedingly, very. **1912** *DN*

3.587 **wIN,** *Powerful. . .* Exceedingly. **1940** Faulkner *Hamlet* 353 **MS,** A man would need to be powerful unlucky. **1953** [see **A** above]. **1965–70** DARE (Qu. LL35, . . *"This cake tastes _____ good."*) 19 Infs, **scattered exc West,** Powerful; (Qu. KK1a, . . *Very good* . . *"That pie was _____."*) Inf **VA42,** Powerful good; (Qu. LL37, . . *"I could have wrung her neck, I was so _____ mad."*) Inf **VA37,** Powerful. **1986** Pederson *LAGS Concordance,* 1 inf, **swAL,** Powerful good and powerful bad; 1 inf, **seAL,** I'm powerful religious. **1992** in 1993 Adero *Up South* 180 [Black], I've been cooking all morning and am powerful hungry now.

2 To a great extent, very much.

1882 *Century Illustr. Mag.* 23.884 **MS,** You mout move around here more'n a year an' never need a pistol, but ef you *should* happen to need one, you'd need it powerful. **1886** *S. Bivouac* 4.349 **sAppalachians,** She would be ninety-nine in August, she told me, . . and "her hair wuz a comin' out powerful."

powerfully adv

1 =**powerful C2.**

1870 in 1884 Lanier *Poems* 169 **GA,** Ellick he sat with his head bent down,/ A-studyin' and musin' powerfully. **1956** *Hall Coll.* **eTN,** My pappy is swelled powerfully ['pæfəlɪ].

2 =**powerful C1.**

1970 DARE (Qu. LL35, . . *"This cake tastes _____ good."*) Inf **NC82,** Very, mighty, powerfully.

power-hooking vbl n Cf **jig** v **1**

Jigging or snagging fish.

1967 DARE FW Addit **cAR,** *Power-hooking*—Saline County, Arkansas, term for fishing with a gig. [Term is used by] the folks who do this sort of thing.

powerhouse n Cf *DS* DD30

A tavern or speakeasy.

1939 (1962) Thompson *Body & Britches* 228 **NY** (as of c1820), The easiest and politest way to start a fight among the [Erie] canallers was to drop into any "power-house" or tavern on Saturday and mention with disrespect any of the counties of Ireland. **1950** *PADS* 14.54 **ceSC,** *Powerhouse:* . . A bootlegger's shop or place of business. Kingstree.

pow'ful See **powerful**

powvow See **powwow** v

powwow n [Of Algonquian origin; cf Massachuset *pauwau* priest, magician; he uses divination] **chiefly PA**

1 One who uses incantations or other magical rituals, esp in healing. Note: The obs or hist use in ref to an American Indian priest or shaman is not illustrated here.

c1770 [see **powwow** v **1**]. **1967** DARE Tape **PA4,** Suppose someone had an acne condition or a bad case of rheumatism or something in that order and they hadn't had much success with the doctors, they'll go to a man that's a powwow and he will ask them for an article that they carry with 'em. You might give him a pencil or a knife or something, and he makes mysterious movements and says mysterious words over the ailment. . . He daren't charge, that would be illegal, but he is allowed, he will accept a gift. **1967–70** *Ibid* **PA242** [see **2** below].

2 freq attrib: The art or practice of using incantations or other magical rituals, esp in healing. Cf **brauche**

1856 Kane *Arctic Explor.* 2.126, I [=a native of PA] have known several of them [=Eskimo shamans] personally, after my skill in pow-wow had given me a sort of correlative rank among them. **1895** in 1953 *PA Dutchman* 1 March 11/2 (*Mathews Coll.*), My father could powwow. So could his father. . . Powwow healing is by faith and prayers. We do it all in the German language. For each affliction there is a special prayer. **1901** *Scribner's Mag.* 30.525 **PA,** The "powwow-doctors" still repeat over many bedsides the mysterious formulas. **1929** *New Outlook* 23 Jan 134 **sePA,** To remove the spell a "powwow doctor" named Blymyer . . went to the home of the alleged sorcerer or "hexer" to get a tuft of his hair to bury in the earth as a cure of the family's ills. **1930** Shoemaker *1300 Words* 48 **cPA Mts** (as of c1900), *Pow-wow*—Orginally [sic] an Indian conference; now the muttering of cabalistic words by a hechs or would-be spell-binder. **1938** (1964) Korson *Minstrels Mine Patch* 147 **nePA,** The wise women were known among the Pennsylvania Germans [as] "hex-women," or "powwow women." **1945** *Sun* (Baltimore MD) 24 Oct 9–0/5 (*Hench Coll.*), The tragic failure of a mother's "Pow Wow" to save her baby's life brought charges of involun-

tary manslaughter. . . She relied . . on "pow wow" when the baby failed to gain weight. **1953** *AmSp* 28.252 **csPA,** *Pow-wow.* . . I have known only one practitioner, a 'pow-wow woman' whose particular virtue was a supposed ability to 'blow fire,' that is, to remove the pain and inflammation from burns and erysipelas by blowing on the affected parts. **1964** Smith *PA Germans* 153 **WV,** The pow-wow booklet was discovered in Pendleton County, West Virginia, in a neighborhood where the dialect is still spoken by many of the residents and in an area referred to as the "Dutchiest in West Virginia." **1967–70** DARE Tape **PA64** [see **powwow** v **2**]; **PA199,** When I had fallen into a fire when I was a kid, and I horribly burned this hand and arm, and they took me to a powwow doctor and he so-called took the fire out of the burn; **PA242,** [FW:] Have you ever heard of a powwow? [Inf:] Oh, yes, powwows. There are powwow doctors in the area, and I know that my parents and my grandparents powwowed. **1968** DARE (Qu. CC14, . . *Where one person supposedly casts a spell over another*) Inf **PA105,** Powwow.

powwow v [Cf **powwow** n] Pronc-sp *powvow* **chiefly PA**

1 To make use of incantations or other magical rituals, esp in healing; hence vbl n *powwowing* using such rituals; n *powwower* one who uses such practices. Note: The obs or hist use in ref to American Indian rituals is not illustrated here.

c1770 in 1833 Boucher *Glossary* xlix **MD, VA,** *Pow-wow* (as a verb); to use magic arts, to conjure; to foretell, or pretend to foretell. As a noun, it denotes a priest; or a person professionally devoted to, and engaged in, supernatural employments. **1812** *Beauties Brother Bull-Us* 55 **NEng,** There still remains a knot of *wizards* in one of the farms of Yankey land . . who are undoubtedly the genuine descendants of the witches and the *Pow-wowers.* **1882** (1971) Gibbons *PA Dutch* 402, In . . Lehigh, I remember a few years ago to have seen the names of two persons put down in the directory as *powvowers;* the word being spelled as pronounced in "Dutch." **1895** [see **powwow** n **2**]. **1908** *German Amer. Annals* 10.39 **sePA,** *Powwow.* To heal by conjuration. "She ought to get some one to powwow over her hand." **1935** [see **2** below]. **1938** Hark *Hex* 140 **PA,** Again the pow-wower walked back and forth across the strings, and for some time thereafter the rubbing and the walking alternated. **1938** (1964) Korson *Minstrels Mine Patch* 93 **nePA,** Jim Leh of Tower City had a wheal in his eye. . . 'Uncle Pete,' he says, 'I'm suffering with my eye. I want you to powwow for it.' **1943** Weslager *DE Forgotten Folk* 166, Old Mary Morgan . . was a doctor woman. . . She could make a boil go away by powwowing over it. She would take a table fork and wave it over the boil, all the time powwowing so no one could understand. **1952** *Reading Times* (PA) 3 July 7/3 (*Mathews Coll.*), This will be followed by pow-wowing by Aunt Sophia Bailer. . . She is believed to be the oldest powwower in the nation. **1965–70** DARE (Qu. BB51b, . . *'Magical' cures for corns or warts*) 9 Infs, **PA,** Powwowing; (Qu. BB51a, . . *Cures for corns or warts*) Inf **PA4,** Powwowing. **1967–70** DARE Tape **PA4,** He'll say, "At three o'clock this afternoon, you'll feel a sharp stab in that pain; don't get worried, that's part of the treatment. Now, you come back in three days and let me see how you've gone along, and if necessary we'll powwow some more"; **PA27,** [FW:] I was thinking it was a guy named Weaver . . who makes tonics and stuff and sells them to people. [Inf:] Well, now, he would be the old-time doctor. Does he powwow? [FW:] He doesn't powwow, but he makes these tonics; **PA64** [see **2** below]; **PA242** [see **powwow** n **2**].

2 To treat by means of incantations or other magical rituals.

1856 Kane *Arctic Explor.* 2.116, Among the rest was Awahtok [=an Eskimo], only now recovering from his severe frost-bite. . . I [=a native of PA] gave him a piece of red flannel and powwowed him. **1863** P.S. Davis *Young Parson* 154 (*DAE*), His father . . powwowed it [the child], and the doctor gave it some stuff, and now it's picking up agin. **1935** *AmSp* 10.170 **PA** [Engl of PA Germans], For the other thing, the use of white magic, of charms and spells to cure disease, to increase the yield of crops, or to facilitate childbirth—and there is a vast deal of it practiced through this region—the specialized word *pow-wowing* (of Algonquin origin) is used. There are *pow-wow* doctors, to whom one takes the baby sick with the *epizootic* to have it *pow-wowed.* **1967** DARE Tape **PA64,** Outside of Riegelsville, there was a powwow doctor. He was so wealthy, he didn't know what to do with his money. He never charged a cent, but people always donated wonderful money for powwowing. And I know my daughter had trouble with her speech and a woman begged me to have her powwowed. **1968–69** DARE (Qu. BB51b, . . *'Magical' cures for corns or warts*) Inf **PA68,** Powwow a wart off; **PA150,** Powwow them off; **PA175,** Powwow them off with some sort of group meeting; **PA202,** Powwowing them away. **1970** DARE File **PA,** *Powwow* v. "The child was powwowed for short growth." Used among whites, not Indians.

powwow doctor See **powwow** n 2

powwower, powwowing See **powwow** v 1

poy exclam Also *po-ee* Cf **po** exclam, **poig, pooey, poo-gee**
In var combs: Used as a call to pigs.

　1950 *WELS* (Call to pigs at feeding time) 1 Inf, **cwWI**, Poy poy.
1967 *DARE* (Qu. K84, *The call used . . to get the pigs in at feeding time*)
Inf **MO38**, Po-ee ['p'ɔ-,iˇi:] piggy piggy; **OH18**, Po-ee [po-i po-i po-i].

pozo n Also *posa; dimin pozuelo* [Span *pozo*] **SW**
A well, spring, water hole.

　[**1852** (1854) Bartlett *Personal Narr.* 2.466 **SW**, [Footnote:] *Noria* is
properly a wheel or engine for drawing water from a well; the term is
also applied to wells where wheels are so employed, to distinguish them
from *pozos,* or common wells.] **1856** (1928) Jaeger *Diary Fort Yuma*
121 **sCA**, Made 20 miles this drive in 8 hours & plenty of water at the
posa. **1892** *DN* 1.251 **TX**, *Pózo:* a spring, generally issuing from a hole
in the ground, not from a rock. . . The diminutive *pozuélo* is also frequently used. [**1912** Lumholtz *New Trails* 263 **Mexico**, Other pozos
were twenty feet in diameter, with a depression two feet deep. *Ibid*
262, A rim surrounded the depression about the hill where fresh water is
found. . . These curious springs numbered sixteen. . . The Mexicans had
the convenient word pozo (well, waterhole) for this peculiar formation.]
1932 Bentley *Spanish Terms* 185, *Pozo.* . . A water hole; a well; a cis-
tern; a spring. *Pozo* is restricted in written use to descriptive or other
writings dealing with the Spanish American territory in the Southwest
and elsewhere. In spoken English in the Southwest its use is not uncommon among those who know Spanish well. **1969** O'Connor *Horse &
Buggy West* 167 **AZ**, I have seen where deer and sheep have pawed to
make themselves *pozos,* or wells.

praakes See **prakes**

praar See **prayer**

practice v Usu |'præktɪs|; also |'præktaɪz| Pronc-spp *practize,
practyse* [*OED2* practise v. "The stress, originally, as still
dialectally, on *-ize* (prak'ti:z, prak'taɪz), was subseq. shifted to
the first syllable, whence also the change of z to s, perh. after
practice sb."]
Std sense, var forms.

　1841 (1952) Cooper *Deerslayer* 7 **NY** (as of c1740), I shall not frequent your society long, friend Natty, unless you look higher than four-
footed beasts to prac*tyse* your rifle on. **1851** Hooper *Widow Rugby's
Husband* 47 **AL**, She was tryin' to prac*tize* kissin on old 'Cherry.' **1902**
DN 2.242 **sIL**, Practize ['præktaɪz]. . . Practice. The noun is not. **1930**
in 1952 Mathes *Tall Tales* 180 **sAppalachians**, I'll prac-tize up
some new tunes an' I'll git off some new jokes fer 'em.

prada See **parada**

prairie n Usu |'prɛrɪ, 'prerɪ|; also |pə'rɛri, pə'rerɪ| Pronc-spp
pararie, perairie, praira, prare; for addit varr see **A** below
A Forms.

　1791 in 1935 Bradley *Jrl.* 17 **OH**, A prairia of two or three hundred
acres where the grass or wild oats is 8 or 10 feet high and very thick.
1794 in 1914 *Missip. Valley Hist. Rev.* 1.421, An open . . *Pararie* . .
handsomly intersperced with Small Copse of Trees. **1795** in 1907 *OH
Archeol. & Hist. Qrly.* 16.380, We saw several pararas, as they are
called. They are large tracts of fine, rich land, without trees and producing as fine grass as the best meadows. **1804** (1905) Lewis *Orig. Jrls.
Lewis & Clark Exped.* 7.38 **MO**, Got on our way at hard Scrable
Perarie. **1806** *Thomas' MA Spy or Worcester Gaz.* (MA) 16 July [1]/5,
A venerable Philosopher sitting in the middle of an immense Map,
marked with vast praires. **1812** in 1906 *IA Jrl. Hist. & Politics* 4.380,
The advanced g[u]ard having intirely skirted the praari . . Colo Cass and
Miller by Some means marched into the praary. **1816** in 1947 *AmSp*
22.209 **wIN**, *Pa-ra-rah* is a common pronunciation; but it is too great a
barbarism to be tolerated. By placing the letters in this manner, *prai-rie,*
the proper sounds cannot be mistaken. **1828** (1936) McCoy *Jrl. Exped.*
259 **PA**, To each home should be allowed 50 or 80 acres of wood-land,
and then as much prarie back as should be necessary. **1834** (1925) Evans *Jrl.* 3.183 **IN**, We met in our way with some high romantic Pararies.
1843 (1916) Hall *New Purchase* 135 **IN**, A powerful big pra*raree.
1858 Hammett *Piney Woods Tavern* 42, A feller that kin find his way . .
across the perara. **1893** Shands *MS Speech* 49, Perraries [pə'rerɪz]. Illiterate white for *prairies.* **1909** *DN* 3.359 **sAL**, Prare [prær]. . . Prai-

rie: a south Alabama pronunciation. **1916** *DN* 4.279 **NE**, *Praira*. . .
Prairie. **1917** *DN* 4.398 **neOH**, *Prairie* [pə'reri, 'preri]. . . Also Ill.,
Kan., Neb., Ky. **1921** Haswell *Daughter Ozarks* 18 (as of 1880s), [I]
hev seed the perarys of Elenoise. **1926** *AmSp* 1.412 **Okefenokee GA**,
They went on out ter the edge er the big perairie. **1934** *AmSp* 9.213
TX, Examples of substitution and addition of sounds are. . . *pararie* for
prairie. **1942** Hall *Smoky Mt. Speech* 106 **wNC, eTN**, *Prairie* in its
few occurrences was [pə'rærɪ]. **1965–70** *DARE* (Qu. C29) Infs **PA234**,
WA18, WI50, TX102, [,pəˑ'ɛrɪ]; **TN26, WV5**, [,pəˑ'rerɪ]; **MS1, 55**,
[,pəˑ'rerɪ]; **TN26, 34**, [prarə]; **TX52, 80**, [prerə]; **AL30**, [,pəˑ'rerɪ];
AL52, [pərəri]; **FL35A**, [pəˑ'rerɪ]; **GA19**, [prɑˑ'rerɪ]; **LA11**, [pəˑ'rerɪ];
MI101, ['pəræri]; **TX40**, [pəˑrɛ·rɪ]; **VA13**, [,pəˑ'rærɪ]; **WA19**, [pərerɪ];
WI47, ['pəˑɛəˑɪ]; (Qu. C6) Inf **GA31**, [pə'rerɪ]; (Qu. C19) Inf **AL30**,
[pə'rerɪ]; (Qu. L8) Inf **MS87**, [pə'rerɪ] hay; (Qu. L9a) Inf **TX89**, ['prerə]
grass; (Qu. Q4) Inf **GA25**, [pə'rerɪ] hawk. **1968–69** [see **B1** below].
1986 Pederson *LAGS Concordance,* 1 inf, **cnFL**, [pə'rɛˇrə]; 1 inf,
cnLA, [pəˑ'rɛˑ·əˑ]; 1 inf, **neTX**, [p'əˑ'rɛˑˑəˑrə].
B Senses.

1 A swamp or marsh. **chiefly GA, FL** Cf **floating prairie**

　1824 Wilson *Wanderer in Amer.* 111 **OH**, Those *prairies,* being
swampy, or in plain English, boggy land, exhale agues and fevers innumerable. **1916** *DN* 4.270 **New Orleans LA**, *Prairie*. . . Marsh. **1926**
(1949) McQueen–Mizell *Hist. Okefenokee* 62 **seGA**, Ii [sic] is rather
hard to determine how the so-called "prairies" of the Okefenokee came
by this name. These prairies are better described as marshes. . . One old
resident, who has visited our great West, advanced the theory that these
open spaces within the Swamp are called "prairies" for the reason that,
viewed from a distance, especially when the wind is blowing the saw-
grass, they resemble very much the real prairies of the western country.
1938 Rawlings *Yearling* 90 **nFL**, The lonely place of live oak islands
and saw-grass ponds and prairies. **1938** FWP *U.S. One* 306 **GA**, The
great expanse of swamp . . is broken by many acres of submerged trembling earth called "prairies". **1951** *Collier's* 24 Nov 16 **seGA**, The eastern half of the Okefenokee is open. There are "prairies" or great fields of
water from one to three feet deep, covered with white or yellow water
lilies. . . The boat trails through the prairies are kept open by the natural
flow of water. . . The prairies and open marshes are bordered by winding
bays of cypress . . and red maple. **1965** Will *Okeechobee Boats* 13 **FL**,
As fur as he could see thar weren't nothing but wet prairie. **1968** *DARE*
(Qu. C6, . . *A piece of land that's often wet, and has grass and weeds
growing on it*) Inf **GA31**, Prairie—in Okefenokee; (Qu. C29, *A good-
sized stretch of level land with practically no trees*) Inf **NY200**, Prairie—used to designate a swamp. **1968–69** *DARE* Tape **GA30**, [Inf:]
They'll bunch up out on these open prairies [pə'rɛ^ri·z] where there's
nothing but this old grass growing. . . [FW:] What are the prairies exactly? [Inf:] It's just a open swamp with not anything but just water and
grass and lily pads . . marsh. They have little clumps of bushes'll come
on in just little places; **GA51**, [Inf:] Now that pararie [,pu'rɛəˑɪ] business, that's the open water now, no thickets. . . [FW:] What kind of
plants grow on the pararie? . . [Inf:] Hundreds of different kinds. All
kind of water plants. . . So many I can't begin to name them all. **1970**
Detro *Generic Terms* 219 **LA**, The terms "prairie and/or marsh prairie"
referred to marsh surfaces rather firm under foot where the vegetation
was in closed formation and consisted mainly of grasses. **1986**
Pederson *LAGS Concordance,* 1 inf, **cnFL**, Prairie—low place; 1 inf,
cnFL, Prairie—woods, low and wet; 1 inf, **cFL**, Prairie—wet, standing
water, vegetation, no trees; 1 inf, **neFL**, Prairie—swamp and pond together; 1 inf, **neFL**, Prairie—mostly a wet place; 1 inf, **cnGA**, Prairie—
marsh; 1 inf, **seLA**, Prairie—marshland; *(Swamp)* 2 infs, **FL**, 1 inf, **TX**,
Prairie; *(Bottomland)* 3 infs, **FL, GA, MS**, Prairie.

2 A vacant lot or city block. **Chicago IL**

　1938 Farrell *No Star* 37 **Chicago IL**, He was afraid to go back to play
in the prairie because he might be laughed at. **1967** *DARE* FW Addit
Chicago IL, Prairie—any vacant lot, esp where children can play. Suburban, South Side—from male white college graduates. **1968** *DARE*
File **Chicago IL**, *Prairie football:* Kids' football played in a vacant lot.
1972 *Ibid* **Chicago IL**, *Prairie:* An empty lot, overgrown with weeds,
etc. **2000** *Ibid* **Chicago IL** (as of c1937), "Prairie," I think, applied
only to a fully empty block. An empty expanse on a block that also had
some completed buildings was called an "empty lot," or sometimes a
"vacant lot." . . We did some foraging on those "prairies"—that's where
we got our green onions, for example, and there were a couple of good
berry patches that I remember fondly. *Ibid* **Chicago IL** (as of c1942),
A prairie is an empty block.

prairie alligator n
A **walkingstick,** usu *Diapheromera femorata.*

1890 *Century Dict.* 4668, *Prairie-alligator*. . . An insect of the family *Phasmidæ;* one of the walking-sticks, usually the thick-thighed walking-stick, *Diapheromera femorata*. [*Century* Ed: Local, U.S.] **1894** *Harper's New Mth. Mag.* 88.456, The form [of walking stick] common over the greater part of the United States, . . [called in some states] "prairie alligators," our *Diapheromera femorata*. . . may be compared to an animated straw.

prairie apple n

1 An **Indian breadroot** (here: *Pediomelum esculentum*).

[**1820** in 1908 MO Hist. Soc. *Coll.* 3.21, The guide today gave me what he called *Pome De Prairie* (Prairie apple) which he found & which he says the Indians are very fond of—I ate of it; its taste resembling that of a *Buckeye nut;* its shape a Pear, & the color being whitish.] **1892** Gibson *Sharp Eyes* 57, The Indian turnip-root of the plains [was called] the prairie-apple. **1937** Stemen–Myers *OK Flora* 235, *Prairie Apple* or *Turnip*. Rather stout, from a large, turnip-shaped, starchy, edible root. . . Prairies. Oklahoma and Comanche counties. **1941** Writers' Program *Guide WI* 14, Among the remaining prairie plants, besides a wide variety of grasses, are the grass-like herbs called blue-eyed and yellow star grass and the herbs curiously named for fruit trees—ground plum, ground cherry, and prairie apple.

2 A **ground plum 1** (here: *Astragalus crassicarpus*).

1896 *Jrl. Amer. Folkl.* 9.185 swMO, *Astragalus Mexicanus* . . prairie-apple. . . Fruit eaten by children.

prairie ash n

=**green ash.**

1908 Britton *N. Amer. Trees* 799, Prairie Ash—*Fraxinus campestris*. This tree . . ranges from Montana to Manitoba, Wyoming and Kansas, preferably inhabiting valleys. **1940** Gates *Flora KS* 182, *Fraxinus pennsylvanica campestris* . . Prairie Ash. . . Along prairie streams, river banks, river bluffs along streams in prairies and plains.

prairie bass n

=**bowfin.**

1908 Forbes–Richardson *Fishes of IL* 39, The usual local name for this species [=*Amia calva*] is "dogfish" in the Great Lake region and upper Mississippi Valley. . . It has been found by our collectors offered for sale by hucksters as "prairie-bass" in southern Illinois.

prairie bean n

1 =**false lupine 1.**

1805 (1904) Lewis *Orig. Jrls. Lewis & Clark Exped.* 2.29, The Indians of the Missouri make great use of this cherry, . . mashing the seed boiling them with roots or meat, or with the prarie beans and white apple. **1932** Rydberg *Flora Prairies* 454, *Thermopsis*. . . Yellow Pea, Golden Pea, Prairie Bean. **1936** Thompson *High Trails* 85, Later in the season the prairie exhibits carpets of wild geranium, wild onion, lupine, prairie bean, wild rose, . . and many others.

2 A native bean *(Phaseolus maculatus)* of the southwestern US.

1886 Havard *Flora W. & S. TX for 1885* 501, *Phaseolus retusus* . . (Prairie Bean.) Common on prairies west of the Pecos, its creeping stems often 15 to 20 feet long.

prairie beardgrass n

=**little bluestem.**

1939 FWP *Guide KS* 11, Bluestem has the greatest forage value, and both species—big and little bluestem, also known as bluejoint turkeyfoot and prairie beardgrass—grow in almost all parts of the state. **1968** Barkley *Plants KS* 36, Andropogon scoparius . . Little Bluestem, Prairie Beardgrass.

prairie bird n

1 =**golden plover.**

1917 (1923) *Birds Amer.* 1.257, Golden Plover. . . *Other Names* . . Prairie-bird; Prairie Pigeon.

2 =**horned lark.**

1917 (1923) *Birds Amer.* 2.212, Horned Lark. . . *Other Names*. . . Prairie Bird [etc.]. **1946** Goodrich *Birds in KS* 313, Prairie [bird]—lark, horned.

3 =**lark bunting.**

1917 (1923) *Birds Amer.* 3.76, Lark Bunting. . . *Other Names*.— White-winged Blackbird; White-winged Prairiebird; Prairie Bobolink.

prairie bobolink n

=**lark bunting.**

1917 [see **prairie bird 3**].

prairie breaker (or breaking plow) See **prairie plow**

prairie burdock See **prairie dock**

prairie cane n

A cane of the genus *Arundinacea*.   Cf **brake** n^2 **b**, **mutton cane 1**

1906 Johnson *Highways Missip. Valley* 36 LA, We had before us the marshlands, spreading away like a green endless sea to the horizon, an unbroken level of saw-grass, flags, and prairie canes.

prairie chicken n

1 Std: a grouse of the genus *Tympanuchus,* esp *T. cupido pinnatus*.   For other names of these birds see **chicken B1, hen** n **B3, prairie grouse, ~ hen, ~ duck;** for other names of *T. c. pinnatus* see **barren hen, pheasant 1b, prairie cock, square-tail, wild hen, yellowlegs;** for other names of the extinct *T. c. cupido* see **barren hen, heath ~ 1, pheasant 1b, wild hen**

2 =**sharp-tailed grouse.**

1832 *Amer. Turf Reg.* Aug 589, The French Creoles call them [= grouse] "des phésants," the pheasants, or "poule de prairie," "prairie chicken," by which latter name, and "prairie hen," all the people of Illinois and Missouri still call them, and so little do they suppose there is another name for them, that a person would not be understood once in one hundred times, if he spoke of them under the name of grouse. **1888** Trumbull *Names of Birds* 139, *Sharp-tailed Grouse*. . . In portions of our Northwest where the pinnated grouse . . are not found, this bird is the *prairie chicken;* and Dr. Coues terms it *prairie chicken of the Northwest.* **1918** Grinnell *Game Birds CA* 561, The present species [=*Pediocetes phasianellus columbianus*] is often called "Prairie Chicken," but that name properly belongs to a bird *(Tympanuchus americanus)* which does not range west of the eastern border of the Rocky Mountains. **1936** Roberts *MN Birds* 1.396, When travelers into these parts, previous to the early part of the nineteenth century, made reference to Prairie Hens or Chickens it was the Sharp-tail that they saw, as there were no Pinnated here. **1953** Jewett *Birds WA* 212, *Columbian Sharp-tailed Grouse*. . . Other names: Prairie Chicken; Western Prairie Hen [etc.]. **1966** *DARE* (Qu. Q7, *Names and nicknames for . . game birds*) Inf **MI**36, Pintails—same as a partridge, half a pound heavier than a partridge, make a terrific noise when they take off. Red meat. Used to call them a "prairie chicken," but the right name for them is "pintail."

3 =**king rail 1** or **yellow rail.   FL, LA**

1932 Howell *FL Bird Life* 202, King Rail. . . Other Names: Marsh Hen; Prairie Chicken [etc.]. **1953** [see **4** below]. **1955** Lowery *LA Birds* 230, The Negroes who run these mowing machines are quite familiar with the birds [=yellow rails] and call them "little prairie chickens."

4 Any of var other water or marsh birds, as **green heron** or **coot** n^1 **1.**

1953 *AmSp* 28.278, The habitat called *prairie* in the designation *prairie chicken* for the green heron (N.C.), king rail (Fla.), and American coot (Md.) is wet savanna or marshland. And for the upland plover in Pennsylvania, it is perhaps only field, since the bird is called *feldhinkel* (field hen) by the Pennsylvania Germans. **1968** [see **prairie hen 5**].

5 An **upland plover** (here: *Bartramia longicauda*).

1953 [see **4** above].

6 =**sage grouse.**

1953 *AmSp* 28.278 **ID, WY,** The expression *prairie chicken* requires analysis because the local meaning of the attributive is so variable. . . For the sage grouse (Wyo., Idaho), the allusion is to the sagebrush plains.

prairie clover n Cf **indigo bush 2**

Any of var plants of the genus *Dalea,* usu those formerly included in the genus *Petalostemon*.   For other names of these see **monk's cap, pussyfoot 3, summer-farewell, tassel flower, thimbleweed**

1848 Gray *Manual of Botany* 105, *Petalostemon* [spp] . . Prairie Clover. **1901** Mohr *Plant Life AL* 565, *Kuhnistera purpurea*. . . Purple Prairie Clover . . Alleghenian area to Louisianian area. **1922** *Amer. Bot-*

anist 28.72, The "prairie clovers" are found in the genus *Petalostemum.* The common name is fairly appropiate [sic], for the species when in flower rather closely resemble clovers. **1948** Stevens *KS Wild Flowers* 284, *Petalostemum* [spp]—Prairie Clover. *Ibid* 285, *Petalostemum multiflorum*—Round-headed Prairie Clover. . . *Petalostemum candidum*—White Prairie Clover [etc]. **1979** Ajilvsgi *Wild Flowers* 165, Oklahoma prairie clover—*Petalostemum griseum.* . . endemic to East and Southeast Texas.

prairie coal n West Cf chip n[1] 1

Dried cow or buffalo droppings used as fuel.

1929 Dobie *Vaquero* 284 **West,** Our worst problem was getting fuel. The cow chips on the prairie were all covered up and even when found were too wet to burn readily. . . Among outfits dependent on this "prairie coal" it was customary for several men to scour out in different directions with gunny sacks, each bringing in what he could find. **1939** C.L. Douglas *Cattle Kings* 324 *(DA),* He could not bring himself to relish food cooked with 'prairie coal.' **1947** Croy *Corn Country* 278, He [= the pioneer] put the prairie into his speech. . . And dried buffalo droppings, used for fuel, became "prairie coal." **1947** Day *Big Country* 123 **TX,** Cow chips, which had been known quite flatly before as prairie coal, became Babcock coal in mixed company, or in the company of tenderfeet, whose squeamishness might thus be avoided. **1962** Atwood *Vocab. TX* 77, *Prairie coal.* . . "Cow-chips." **1977** Dunlop *Wheels West* 171, The [chuck wagon] cook used chips from the possum belly, or "prairie coal," and wood.

prairie cock n

1 A grouse such as a **prairie chicken 1. Cf sage cock**

1805 (1905) Clark *Orig. Jrls. Lewis & Clark Exped.* 3.123 seWA, Send out Hunters to shute the Prarie Cock a large fowl which I have only Seen on this river. **1846** W.G. Stewart *Altowan* 1.31 *(DAE),* The prairie cock (a large species of grouse, of a pepper-and-salt colour, and long, pointed tail) . . rose at their feet. **1900** Garland *Eagle's Heart* 107 **csND,** A belated prairie cock began to boom.

2 =roadrunner 1.

1917 *Wilson Bulletin* 29.2.81 **TX,** *Geococcyx californianus* . . local names . . prairie cock [etc].

prairie cocktail See prairie oyster 2

prairie colt n Cf brush colt, field ~

1 See quot.

1966–70 *DARE* (Qu. K43, *A horse that was not intentionally bred, or bred by accident*) Infs **AL**62, **AR**55, **IL**14, **ND**3, **OK**52, **TX**40, Prairie colt.

2 Transf: an illegitimate child.

1966–68 *DARE* (Qu. Z11b, . . *[A child whose parents were not married]*) Infs **LA**28, **OK**52, **TX**32, Prairie colt.

prairie coneflower n

1 A **coneflower 2,** esp *Ratibida columnifera.* For other names of the latter see **brush B2, gallito 2, Indian paint 8, Mexican hat, niggerhead 3l, niggertoe 5, thimbleflower**

1900 Lyons *Plant Names* 316, *R[atibida] columnaris* . . Long-headed or Prairie Cone-flower, is also called Brush. **1936** Whitehouse *TX Flowers* 173, Niggerhead. . . is also called Mexican hat, niggertoe, "gallitos," long-headed or prairie coneflower [etc]. **1970** Correll *Plants TX* 1644, *Ratibida Tagetes* . . Prairie cone-flower.

2 A **coneflower 1** (here: *Rudbeckia subtomentosa*).

1936 IL Nat. Hist. Surv. *Wildflowers* 363, The Sweet or Prairie Coneflower, *Rudbeckia subtomentosa* . . is an uncommon perennial of prairies and low ground in Illinois.

prairie cordgrass n

A **cordgrass** (here: *Spartina pectinata*).

1940 Gates *Flora KS* 137, Spartina pectinata . . Prairie Cordgrass, Sloughgrass. Marshes and along streams in both fresh and brackish water. **1952** Davis *Flora ID* 126, *Prairie Cordgrass.* . . Newf. to Wash., south to N.C., Texas and N.M. **1967** Braun *Monocotyledoneae* 134 **OH,** *Spartina pectinata* . . Prairie Cord Grass. . . Wet prairies, swamps, and coastal marshes.

prairie daisy n

=mountain daisy 2.

1961 Wills–Irwin *Flowers TX* 230, Mountain Daisy also has the common names Blackfoot Daisy, Prairie Daisy, and Rock Daisy, and is found throughout Texas west of Wilbarger, Bell, and Jim Wells counties.

prairie dock n Cf dock n[1]

1 also *prairie burdock:* A **rosinweed 1,** usu *Silphium compositum.*

1839 in 1856 MI State Ag. Soc. *Trans. for 1855* 419, *Silphium.* . . *terebinthinaceum.* . . Prairie dock. **1847** Wood *Class-Book* 336, S[ilphium] terebinthinaceum. *Prairie Burdock.* . . Prairies, Western and Southern States. **1897** IN Dept. Geol. & Nat. Resources *Rept. for 1896* 693, *S[ilphium] terebinthaceum* . . Prairie Dock. Rosin Plant. Prairies and roadsides; scarce. **1941** Walker *Lookout* 55 **TN,** A . . species of rosin-weeds . . that grows six feet tall. . . is sometimes called prairie dock. . . Each leaf is . . almost as stiff as a sheet of tin, somewhat resembling the large leaves of rhubarb.

2 A **feverfew 3** (here: *Parthenium integrifolium*).

1900 Lyons *Plant Names* 276, *P[arthenium] integrifolium.* . . American Feverfew, Prairie Dock [etc].

prairie dog n [From the resemblance of its cry to the barking of a dog] chiefly West See Map

A small burrowing rodent of the genus *Cynomys;* hence combs *prairie-dog town,* ~ *village* a colony of these animals. Also called **barking squirrel, dog** n[1] **B1a, gopher** n[1] **2b(2), ground squirrel c, marmot b, picket pin 2, prairie squirrel 2**

1774 in 1867 Peyton *Adventures* 121, One of the singular and interesting sights on my route [between Santa Fé and St. Louis] was the villages of the Prairie dogs. . . [H]is bark . . has given him his name. **1804** (1965) Lewis–Clark *Hist. Lewis–Clark Exped.* 1.111, We killed a dark rattlesnake, which had swallowed a small prairie-dog. **1825** in 1974 *Fauna Americana* 162, This interesting little animal is very sprightly, and has received the inappropriate name of *Prairie dog,* from a fancied resemblance of its warning cry to the hurried barking of a small dog. *Ibid,* As particular districts, of limited extent, are in general occupied by the burrows of these animals, such assemblages of dwellings are denominated *Prairie dog villages,* by hunters and others. **1872** Schele de Vere *Americanisms* 101, Another dweller on the prairie that bears a false name, is the *Prairie-Dog* (Cynomus ludovicianus), a genuine marmot, and called a dog only in acknowledgement of his short, sharp bark, by which he warns his companions against an approaching enemy. **1917** Anthony *Mammals Amer.* 204, One of the largest Prairie Dog towns yet reported begins in Trego County, Kansas, and extends along the divide north of the Smoky Hill River, practically without a break, to Colorado, a total distance of about 100 miles. **1965–70** *DARE* (Qu. P29, . . *'Gophers'. . . other name . . or what other animal are they most like*) 25 Infs, **chiefly West,** Prairie dog; **KS**10, Prairie dog—another name for gopher; **MN**33, Prairie dog—alternate name; **MS**6, Gophers, prairie dogs—same; (Qu. P27, . . *Kinds of squirrels*) Inf **CA**136, Prairie dogs—Oregon squirrels; **OK**32, Ground squirrel—same as prairie dog; (Qu. P31, . . *Names or nicknames . . for the groundhog*) Infs **CA**80, 120, **KS**6, 12, 20, **OK**11, **UT**9, Prairie dog; (Qu. P32, . . *Other kinds of wild animals*) Infs **AZ**11, **CO**20, **NM**3, 13, **OK**25, Prairie dog. **1988** *Sunset* June 83 **SD,** The *prairie dog* is fun to watch. . . Lookouts perch on mounds, ready to send up the alarm—a series of barks with tail flicking. **1993** Norris *Dakota* 156 **wSD,** Prairie dogs are more noticeable, as they denude the landscape with their villages.

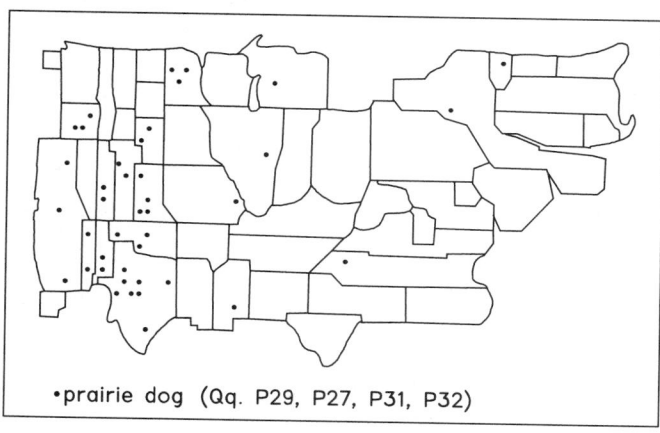

•prairie dog (Qq. P29, P27, P31, P32)

prairie-dog hunter n Also *prairie-dog ferret* [See quot 1917]
The black-footed ferret *(Mustela nigripes)*.

1885 *Amer. Naturalist* 19.922, The long-lost black-footed ferret, or prairie dog-hunter, of Western Kansas, whose rediscovery was recorded a few years since by Dr. Coues. **1917** Anthony *Mammals Amer.* 126, Locally it [=the black-footed ferret] is known as the Prairie Dog Hunter, or Prairie Dog Ferret, as it seems especially fond of that fat little beast— much, however, to the latter's distress. It is most often found in the holes of the defunct Dogs upon which it has feasted.

prairie-dog owl n Cf **prairie owl 1**
=**burrowing owl.**

1926 TX Folkl. Soc. *Pub.* 5.68, Out on the western plains, in the land of little rain and on its borders, lives, according to a fading popular belief, the most curiously assorted happy family in the world. There the prairie dog, the "prairie dog owl," and the rattlesnake all find home and companionship in the same burrow. Old time cow-punchers knew this to be a fact, but the prairie dogs and the scientists have always disagreed. **1935** Sandoz *Jules* 42 **wNE,** Somewhere a belated prairie-dog owl called a friendly "Who, who!" **1936** (1972) Ise *Sod & Stubble* 323 **KS** (as of c1900), From a lower corner of the pasture came the weird "ku ku" of the prairie dog owl. **1958** [see **prairie owl 1**]. **1966–67** DARE (Qu. Q2, . . *Kinds of owls*) Inf **KS6,** Prairie-dog owl; **MT5,** Ground owl—prairie-dog owl; **NM3,** Prairie-dog owls—small, have white heads, live in prairie-dog holes; **OK18,** Prairie-dog owl—lives in prairie-dog towns; **TX43,** Prairie-dog owl—lives in holes with prairie dogs.

prairie-dog town (or village) See **prairie dog**

prairie-dog weed n

1 A **fetid marigold 1** (here: *Dyssodia papposa*). Cf **dog-weed 2**

1896 *Jrl. Amer. Folkl.* 9.192 **SD,** *Dysodia chrysanthemoides* . . prairie-dog weed, Burnside, So. Dak. **1930** OK Univ. Biol. Surv. *Pub.* 84, *Dyssodia papposa.* . . Prairie-dog Weed.

2 A **marsh elder 1** (here: *Iva xanthifolia*).

1940 Clute *Amer. Plant Names* 262, *Iva xanthifolia.* . . prairiedog-weed, prairie ragweed.

prairie dove n Cf **prairie pigeon c**
=**Franklin's gull.**

1847 *Knickerbocker* 30.485 **WY,** And three eggs which he found in the nest of a prairie dove. **1891** Goss *Hist. Birds KS* 26, This beautiful bird [=Franklin's gull], called by the farmers the Prairie Dove, feeds largely upon the land, often great distances from the water. **1936** Roberts *MN Birds* 1.550, Its lovely Dove-like form and gentle, familiar ways appeal to the farmers of the west, with whom it keeps close company in its eager pursuit of the titbits turned up by the furrowing plowshare, and by them it is known as the "Prairie Dove" or "Prairie Pigeon." **1977** Bull–Farrand *Audubon Field Guide Birds* 412, They are much less numerous than formerly, but migrating flocks of "Prairie Doves" are still a familiar sight in spring on the southern plains.

prairie duck n [See quot]
A **prairie chicken 1** shot out of season.

1971 Lewis *Nothing Shadow* 86 **SD** (as of 1909), Our meal that evening was fried prairie chicken. . . All the settlers ate them, in season and out. Out of season we referred to them as "prairie ducks," a species not mentioned in the game laws, or any ornithology text.

prairie falcon n
A common large falcon *(Falco mexicanus)* of the western US. Also called **wavy**

1874 NY Acad. Sci. *Annals Lyceum Nat. Hist.* 10.9 **UT,** *Falco polyagrus.* . . Prairie Falcon. Somewhat common on the plains. Resident. **1923** Dawson *Birds CA* 4.1623, In spite of the fact that the Prairie Falcon is really one of the commonest Raptors in the West, its discovery within the United States was not reported till 1853, and it long remained a rare and little-known bird. **1937** Natl. Geogr. Soc. *Book of Birds* 1.170, The prairie falcon nests from southern British Columbia to Baja California, extending east to the eastern border of the Great Plains. **1966–69** DARE (Qu. Q4, . . *Kinds of hawks*) Infs **CA160, ND1,** Prairie falcon.

prairie feathers n pl **West** Cf **Missouri featherbed**
Hay used as a mattress or bed-covering.

1858 in 1941 Hafen *CO Gold Rush* 176, I have just completed a bedstead for Jim and me, and have filled the bed-tick with prairie feathers [grass]. **1901** Root–Connelley *Overland Stage* 338, They slept from year to year on ticks filled with hay—they called it "prairie feathers." **1937** (1943) Dick *Sod-House Frontier* 246, They made a mattress of "prairie feathers." This famous bed was made by spreading a thick layer of hay on the ground, placing two blankets over it and covering the blankets with another thick layer of hay. The traveler then took off his overcoat, for use as a pillow, and, fully clothed, wiggled down between the two blankets. **1944** Adams *Western Words* 119, *Prairie feathers*—What the cowboy calls beds stuffed with hay.

prairie fennel n
Either **biscuit root 1** or **wild parsley** (here: *Musineon* spp).

1901 U.S. Dept. Ag. Div. Botany *Bulletin* 26.125, Plants Suspected of Being Poisonous. Prairie fennels. (*Lomatium* and *Musineon* spp.) **1939** *Natl. Geogr. Mag.* Aug 219, First to peep forth are the tiny primroses and whitlows, followed soon . . by prairie fennel.

prairie fire n
An **Indian paintbrush 1** (here: *Castilleja coccinea*).

1892 *Garden and Forest* 614, Castilleja coccinea, with its scarlet-painted cup, is in the west called Prairie-fire. **1898** *Atlantic Mth.* 82.497, The scarlet painted cup, otherwise known as the Indian's paintbrush and prairie fire, splendid for color.

prairie fox n Cf **prairie swift**
=**kit fox.**

1839 Marryat *Diary* 74 **Gt Lakes,** [In list of fur obtained every year by American Fur Co.:] Prairie Fox. . . 5,000. **1842** *S. Lit. Messenger* 8.458 **Plains States,** Badgers were common; and prairie foxes of light and elegant proportions. **1846** Sage *Scenes Rocky Mts.* 241, For several nights I had a constant visitor in the shape of a prairie-fox,—a creature about twice the size of a large red squirrel. **1876** Burroughs *Winter Sunshine* 96, The prairie fox, the cross fox, and the black or silver-grey fox, seem only varieties of the red fox. **1928** Anthony *N. Amer. Mammals* 141, *Prairie Fox.* . . Found from southeastern British Columbia and southwestern Saskatchewan south to Wyoming; east into North Dakota.

prairie gayfeather n
A **blazing star 3** (here: *Liatris pycnostachia*).

1948 Wherry *Wild Flower Guide* 131, Prairie Gayfeather (*Liatris pycnostachya*). . . Midland states and adjacent regions. . . Well known as a garden plant. **1966** DARE FW Addit **WI79,** Blazing star . . also called prairie gayfeather. (It's the wild lavender bergamot.)

prairie gentian n

1 A **marsh pink 1** (here: *Sabatia campestris*).

1936 Whitehouse *TX Flowers* 98, Pink Texas Star. . . is also known as meadow pink, rose pink, pink prairie gentian [etc]. **1946** Reeves–Bain *Flora TX* 126, *S[abatia] campestris* . . Prairie Gentian.

2 A **catchfly gentian** (here: *Eustoma russellianum*).

1976 Bailey–Bailey *Hortus Third* 467, [*Eustoma*] *grandiflorum.* . . Prairie gentian. **1982** *Plants SW* (Catalog) 19, Gentian, Prairie— *Eustoma grandiflorum.* . . Colorado to Nebraska, south to New Mexico, Texas, and northern Mexico.

prairie goose n
=**Hutchins's goose.**

1888 Trumbull *Names of Birds* 4, On the coast of Texas [*Branta canadensis hutchinsii* is known as] *Prairie goose.*

prairie grass n
Any of var grasses such as **bull grass 1, cordgrass, dropseed 3, June grass 1b;** see quots.

1812 *CT Courant* (Hartford) 24 Nov 2/3, [They] were one night in danger, in consequence of the Indians setting the *prairie grass* on fire. **1848** (1932) Robinson *Jrl. Santa Fe* 10, The vegetables growing here . . are the common prairie grass, rosin weed, bull's eye, red root. **1890** FL Ag. Exper. Sta. Gainesville *Bulletin* 8.11, *Paspalum ciliatifolium* . . Prairie grass. **1894** Coulter *Botany W. TX* 519, *S[porobolus] asper* . . Prairie grass. . . Dry land, Texas, and northward. **1906** Rydberg *Flora CO* 38, *Koeleria* [spp] . . Prairie-grass, June-grass. **1920** *Torreya* 20.18 **MO,** *Spartina michauxiana* . . Prairie grass, ramrod grass, Peruque, Mo. **1965–70** DARE (Qu. L8, *Hay that grows naturally in damp places*) Infs **IL16, 24, MO3, 38, TX12,** Prairie grass; (Qu. L9a, . . *Kinds of grass . . grown for hay*) Infs **KS5, 7, MO8, OK10, 52, TX51, 89,** Prairie grass; (Qu. S9, . . *Kinds of grass that are hard to get rid of*) Infs **MO4, 18,** Prairie grass.

prairie ground squirrel See **prairie squirrel 2**

prairie grouse n

=**prairie chicken 1.**

[**1852** Tremenheere *Notes* 274 **Canada,** For common shooting, there is . . also prairie grouse in abundance.] **1861** Berkeley *Engl. Sportsman* 185 **Plains States,** Of these beautiful birds of game the prairie grouse is the largest. **1917** (1923) *Birds Amer.* 2.24, The Prairie Grouse weighs about two pounds and its flesh is tender, juicy, and delicious. **1982** Elman *Hunter's Field Guide* 26, *Common & regional names:* For pinnated grouse—*prairie chicken, prairie grouse* [etc.].

prairie grub n [*grub* a root or stump in the ground]

A **hop tree** (here: *Ptelea trifoliata*).

1876 Hobbs *Bot. Hdbk.* 92, Prairie grub [common name], Ptelea bark [English name], Ptelea trifoliata [botanical name]. **1930** Sievers *Amer. Med. Plants* 36, Hoptree. . . Other common names. . . ague bark, prairie-grub, quinine tree [etc.]. **1960** Vines *Trees SW* 593, Vernacular names are Three-leaf Hop-tree, . . prairie-grub [etc.].

prairie hare n Also *plains hare*

A **jackrabbit 1** (here: *Lepus townsendii*).

1840 MA Zool. & Bot. Surv. *Herb. Plants & Quadrupeds* 58, Lepus Virginianus . . Prairie Hare. . . This species is common throughout the New England States, and is known generally as the White Rabbit. **1879** U.S. Natl. Museum *Bulletin* 14.19, Lepus campestris . . Prairie Hare.—Central plains of North America. **1917** Anthony *Mammals Amer.* 280, Prairie Hare, Plains Hare. . . Although called the Prairie Hare, this species [=*Lepus campestris*] is found also on mountain slopes at altitudes of 10,000 to 12,000 feet on both the Sierra Nevada and the Rocky Mountains. Its range extends from middle Kansas northward to the plains of the Saskatchewan, Canada. **1961** Jackson *Mammals WI* 104, *Lepus townsendii campanius.* . . Vernacular names . . prairie hare [etc.].

prairie hawk n

Any of var hawks found on the prairies; see quots.

1817 (1906) Fordham *Personal Narr.* 143, Saw some prairie hawks, blue bodies, ash coloured belly and wings, tipped with black. **1844** in 1943 Carleton *Prairie Logbooks* 27, All this time the prairie-hawks and swallows, and various other birds, kept flying through the air as if half crazed. **1898** Canfield *Maid of Frontier* 201 *(DAE),* With a swoop like the swoop of the prairie hawk down swooping for the quail, the Paint Horse was away. **1965–70** *DARE* (Qu. Q4, . . *Kinds of hawks*) Infs **CO**22, **GA**25, **IL**27, 84, **OK**46, **TX**1, 11, **UT**9, Prairie hawk; **NM**3, Prairie hawk—large, white and brown.

prairie hay n

Hay made from var prairie grasses such as *Buchloe dactyloides.*

1845 *Cultivator* new ser 2.93 **IA,** There are tens of thousands . . without any kind of forethought of preparation for shelter or comfort, except what they may gather from a poor supply of prairie hay. **1870** in 1942 *Torreya* 42.158, *Bulbilis dactyloides* . . Prairie hay, northern Great Plains. **1923** *DN* 5.246 **KS,** Prairie hay. Hay from grass as it grows on the virgin prairie sod. **1965–70** *DARE* (Qu. L8, *Hay that grows naturally in damp places*) 19 Infs, **chiefly Missip Valley, Plains States, Cent,** Prairie hay; **LA**31, Prairie hay—on places less damp; (Qu. L9a, . . *Kinds of grass . . grown for hay*) Infs **KS**15, **OK**8, **TX**63, Prairie hay; **NM**6, Prairie hay—permanent pasture grass. **1986** Pederson *LAGS Concordance,* 2 infs, **ceAR,** 1 inf, **ceTX,** Prairie hay.

prairie hen n

1 Std: =**prairie chicken 1.**

2 =**sharp-tailed grouse. Cf prairie chicken 2**

1804 (1904) Lewis *Orig. Jrls. Lewis & Clark Exped.* 1.181 **SD,** Capt. Lewis . . Saw great numbers of Prarie hens. **1890** *Century Dict.* 4668, The sharp-tailed grouse, the prairie-hen or -chicken of the Northwest, locally called *whitebelly,* is a bird of more arid regions. **1936** [see **prairie chicken 2**]. **1953** *AmSp* 28.280 **WI, UT, WA,** *Prairie hen.* With the present-day normal meaning of the attributive, this name has been given to the prairie chicken rather generally, and to the sharp-tailed grouse less extensively (Wis., Utah, Wash., Saskatchewan).

3 A **king rail 1** or other **rail** n². **LA Cf prairie chicken 3**

1916 *Times–Picayune* (New Orleans LA) 2 Apr mag sec 5/6, Louisiana Clapper Hen . . Prairie Hen; Salt Water Marsh Hen. . . Its nesting habits and eggs resemble those of the king rail. **1921** LA Dept. of Conserv. *Bulletin* 10.88, By a strange misnomer, the large rails, or marsh hens, are also known as prairie hens in Louisiana, and reference to the prairie chicken as prairie hen has resulted often in much confusion. **1953** *AmSp* 28.280 **LA,** In *prairie hen* for the clapper rail, the allusion is to the open marshy tracts called "prairies" in Louisiana.

4 =**ring-necked pheasant.**

1968 *DARE* (Qu. Q7, *Names and nicknames for . . game birds*) Inf **WV**8, Prairie hen—same as ringneck pheasant.

5 A **coot** n¹ **1.**

1968 *DARE* (Qu. Q9, *The bird that looks like a small, dull-colored duck and is commonly found on ponds and lakes*) Inf **LA**20, Prairie chicken or prairie hen—it's dark gray [FW: =coot].

prairie horned lark See **prairie lark**

prairie June grass n

A **June grass 1b** (here: *Koeleria cristata*).

1913 (1979) Barnes *Western Grazing* 64, The principal grasses are the bunch grasses of the wheat-grass group . . , prairie June grass (*Koeleria cristata*) and blue joints. **1937** U.S. Forest Serv. *Range Plant Hdbk.* G76, Junegrass, also known as mountain junegrass, prairie junegrass, and koeleria, is a perennial bunchgrass and the only species of *Koeleria* native to western North America. **1973** Hitchcock–Cronquist *Flora Pacific NW* 647, Prairie Junegrass; Koeler's grass.

prairie lace n

A plant (*Bifora americana*) bearing small white flowers in umbels. Also called **dwarf Queen Anne's lace**

1936 Whitehouse *TX Flowers* 87, Prairie Lace. Dwarf Queen Anne's Lace (*Bifora americana*) is the pride of the North Texas prairie in late April and May. It is also found in Oklahoma and Arkansas. **1940** Writers' Program *Guide TX* 657 **nwTX,** In spring the blossoms of prairie flax, wild onions, hollyhocks, prairie lace and other wild flowers make pools of color.

prairie lark n Also *prairie horned lark*

=**horned lark.**

1805 (1905) Lewis *Orig. Jrls. Lewis & Clark Exped.* 6.187 **ND,** The Prarie lark, bald Eagle, & the large plover have returned. **1887** Ridgway *N. Amer. Birds* 348, Upper Mississippi Valley and region of the Great Lakes. . . O[tocoris] alpestris praticola . . Prairie Horned Lark. **1928** Aldrich *Lantern* 83 **NE,** And then on a morning, with the prairie-lark calling to him, he started. **1932** Bennitt *Check-list* 44 **MO,** Prairie horned lark . . Prairie lark; horned lark. **1945** Eifert *Birds* 108 **IL,** Prairie larks are flatland birds, the color of dust and dead grass. *Ibid,* There are birds out there, birds oblivious to cold wind and icy field—the prairie horned larks.

prairie lily n

1 A **wood lily** (here: *Lilium philadelphicum*).

1898 *Jrl. Amer. Folkl.* 11.281 **WI,** Lilium Philadelphicum . . prairie lily, Monroe, Wis. **1956** in 1969 *DARE* File **swMN** [Flora of Pipestone Natl. Monument], Lily, Prairie (Wild Lily). . . Lilium philadelphicum. **1967** Braun *Monocotyledoneae* 351, *Lilium philadelphicum.* . . The var. *andinum* . . , Western Red Lily or Prairie Lily, is interior in range, from Ohio westward and northwestward to Minnesota, British Columbia, Colorado, and New Mexico.

2 A **stickleaf** (here: *Mentzelia decapetala*). **West**

1900 Lyons *Plant Names* 245, M[entzelia] decapetala. . . Dakota and Montana to Texas. Gunebo Lily, Prairie Lily. **1949** Moldenke *Amer. Wild Flowers* 33, Perhaps handsomest of the group [=Loasaceae] is the prairielily, *Nuttallia decapetala,* also known as gumbolily.

3 =**rain lily 2** or **zephyr lily.**

1900 Lyons *Plant Names* 115, *Cooperia* [spp]. . . Prairie Lily. . . Two species, southern U.S. and Mexico. **1936** Whitehouse *TX Flowers* 10, Giant Rain Lily (*Cooperia pedunculata*). . . It is also called prairie lily [etc.]. **1968** Barkley *Plants KS* 100, Zephyranthes brazosensis. . . Prairie Lily, Eveningstar, Rain Lily. Prairies. Chautauqua and Montgomery Counties.

4 A **mariposa lily** (here: *Calochortus nuttallii*).

1933 *Torreya* 33.83 **MT,** Calochortus nuttalli . . Prairie lily, Forsyth, Mont.

5 A plant of the genus *Nemastylis.*

1951 *PADS* 15.29 **TX,** Nemastylis spp.—Celestials; prairie celestials; prairie lilies.

prairie mallard n

1 =**mallard 1.**

 1923 U.S. Dept. Ag. *Misc. Circular* 13.8 **MO,** Mallard. . . Vernacular Names. . . Prairie mallard.

2 =**gadwall.**

 1923 U.S. Dept. Ag. *Misc. Circular* 13.11 **MO,** Gadwall. . . Vernacular names. . . Prairie mallard. **1982** Elman *Hunter's Field Guide* 147, Gadwall. . . Common & Regional Names: gadwell . . prairie mallard [etc].

prairie mallow n

A **globe mallow 1** (here: *Sphaeralcea coccinea*).

 1924 *Amer. Botanist* 30.109, *M[alvastrum] coccineum*. . . is also called "prairie mallow" and "moss rose." **1949** Moldenke *Amer. Wild Flowers* 113, The red falsemallow, *M[alvastrum] coccineum,* is abundant on the prairies and plains from Manitoba to British Columbia and southward to Iowa, Texas, and New Mexico, and is frequently spoken of as the *prairiemallow.*

prairie marsh wren n

The long-billed **marsh wren** (*Cistothorus palustris*).

 1907 Anderson *Birds IA* 371, The Long-billed Marsh Wren, or rather its new subspecies, the Prairie Marsh Wren of Ridgway [sic], is a common summer resident in all parts of the state where suitable sloughs and marshes may be found. **1917** (1923) *Birds Amer.* 3.198, On the Great Plains and prairie districts, . . [the long-billed marsh wren] is known as the Prairie Marsh Wren. **1963** Gromme *Birds WI* 221, Wren, . . Prairie Marsh (Long-billed Marsh Wren).

prairie meadow mouse See **prairie mouse**

prairie mimosa n Also *mimosa*

A plant of the genus *Desmanthus.* For other names of var spp see **prickleweed**

 1906 Rydberg *Flora CO* 194, *Acuan* [spp] . . Prairie Mimosa. . . In rich bottom lands from Ind. and S.D. to Fla. and Tex. **1936** Winter *Plants NE* 63, *A[cuan] illinoensis* [=*Desmanthus i.*]. . . Mimosa. Throughout the state. **1937** Stemen–Myers *OK Flora* 211, *Acuan leptoloba*. . . Prairie Mimosa. **1979** Niering–Olmstead *Audubon Guide N. Amer. Wildflowers E. Region* 527, Prairie Mimosa; Prairie Desmanthus (*Desmanthus illinoensis*).

prairie morning glory n

=**man-of-the-earth 1.**

 1944 Wellman *Bowl* 56 **KS,** The frame was out of true, the result, as Simeon had said, of "tying into" one of the huge "dead-man" roots of the prairie morning glory, which sometimes reach the proportions of an actual corpse beneath the surface of the sod.

prairie mouse n Also *prairie meadow mouse,* ~ *short-tailed mouse*

A **meadow mouse** (here: *Microtus ochrogaster*).

 1857 U.S. Patent Office *Annual Rept. for 1856: Ag.* 99 **IL,** The prairie meadow-mouse is not a gregarious animal naturally. **1961** Jackson *Mammals WI* 236, *Microtus ochrogaster ochrogaster* . . Prairie Vole. . . Probably most frequently called prairie mouse or short-tailed prairie mouse in Wisconsin, when distinguished from the meadow vole. Other names include prairie meadow mouse, . . prairie short-tailed mouse [etc]. **1997** in 1999 *DARE* File—Internet **IN** [Commercial Tree Fruit Spray Guide], Determine species of mice (with snap traps). Three species may be found: Meadow Mouse . . , Prairie Mouse (Microtus ochrogaster), Pine Mouse.

prairie needle n Cf **needle** n **2**

See quot.

 1966 *DARE* (Qu. S15, . . *Weed seeds that cling to clothing*) Inf **ND9,** Devil's darning needle or prairie needles—seed of prairie grass.

prairie nigger n

 1993 *Houston Chron.* (TX) 23 July sec A 17, "Slavery was once a tradition. Killing Indians like animals was once a tradition. That doesn't make either of them right," said Sen. Ben Nighthorse Campbell, D-Colo., . . the only Indian in Congress. There are "still places in this country where American Indians are called 'prairie niggers,'" he said.

prairie oats n

A **grama grass 1** (here: *Bouteloua curtipendula*).

 1911 *Century Dict. Suppl.,* Side-oats. . . A grama-grass, *Atheropogon*

curtipendulus, ranging from New Jersey to the Rocky Mountains and southward into Mexico. . . Also called . . *prairie-oats.*

prairie onion n

A **wild onion.**

 1822 Woods *2 Yrs. Residence* 222 **seIL,** Prairie onions are common in moist situations. **1936** Whitehouse *TX Flowers* 8, Prairie Onion (*Allium nuttallii*) has short flower stalks 4–6 inches high growing from a very small bulb. . . The prairie onion is the same as Heller's onion (*Allium helleri*) and blooms in April. **1951** *PADS* 15.28 **TX,** *Allium* spp.—Cebolleta; prairie onion. **1961** Wills–Irwin *Flowers TX* 93, Showing a rather consistent preference for unshaded, frequently barren locations is Wild Onion, Prairie Onion, or Cebollita. **1987** Kindscher *Edible Wild Plants* 13, *Allium canadense* . . Wild onion, wild garlic, prairie onion [etc].

prairie owl n

1 =**burrowing owl.** Cf **prairie-dog owl**

 1846 Sage *Scenes Rocky Mts.* 110, The prairie-owl and rattlesnake maintain friendly relations with [prairie dogs]. **1872** Tice *Over Plains* 44, Defamers [of the prairie dog] even admit that he lives in amity and peace with the jackass-rabbit, the burrowing prairie owl, and even with the malicious rattlesnake. **1958** *PADS* 30.9 **wNE, wSD,** *Prairie owl* and *prairie dog owl,* equally frequent names for the burrowing owl (*Speotyto cunicularia hypugaea*), are expressions used by 23% of the Nebraska informants and by 16% of the South Dakotans, all in the western part of each state. **1966–68** *DARE* (Qu. Q2, . . *Kinds of owls*) Infs **MT3, WY5,** Prairie owl; **CO22,** Prairie owl—lives with prairie dogs in hole in ground; **KS15,** Prairie owls—live in prairie-dog towns.

2 =**short-eared owl.**

 1917 (1923) *Birds Amer.* 2.101, Short-eared Owl. . . Other Names.—Marsh Owl; Swamp Owl; Prairie Owl. **1967–68** *DARE* (Qu. Q2) Inf **IA29,** Prairie owl—medium-sized owl, looks like hoot owl; **IL7,** Prairie owl.

prairie oyster n

1 A bull's testicle prepared as food. Cf **mountain oyster**

 1941 *AmSp* 16.181 **SW,** Prairie oyster . . the testicles of a steer, a food morsel considered dainty. **1947** *PADS* 8.19, *Mountain oyster:* Heard in Kansas, 1944. More common term there appears to be *prairie oyster.* **1968** Adams *Western Words* 236, *Prairie oyster*—What the cowman calls the roasted or fried testicles of a bull, considered by some to be a delicacy. **1984** Wilder *You All Spoken Here* 89 **Sth,** *Prairie oysters, Oklahoma oysters:* Same as [mountain oysters]. **1986** Pederson *LAGS Concordance,* 1 inf, swAL, Prairie oysters—of cow. **1995** Brophy Coll. 57 swMO (as of c1960), *Prairie oyster.* A mountain oyster.

2 also *prairie cocktail:* A raw egg or egg yolk, seasoned, and drunk with vinegar or spirits.

 1890 *Century Dict.* 4668, *Prairie-cocktail.* . . A raw egg, peppered and salted, and drunk in vinegar or spirits. Also called *prairie-oyster.* [Century Ed: Western U.S.] **1940** Brown *Amer. Cooks* 240 **KS,** *Prairie Oyster* [Recipe includes 1 egg yolk, unbroken, Worcestershire, catsup, vinegar, lemon juice, red pepper, salt, Tabasco]. . . Serve in cocktail glass and swallow the yolk whole. **1945** *AN&Q* 5.88, Prairie oyster—whisky with raw egg. **1950** *CA Folkl. Qrly.* 9.382 **NM,** Take one or more prairie-oyster cocktails until the hangover is cured. **1954** (1962) Hunt *Cape Cod Cookbook* 111, *Prairie Oyster*—With a small glass in your shaking hand, pour into it about a teaspoon of good vinegar and knock a shell-less egg into it. Add a sprinkle of Worcestershire sauce, and salt and pepper over all. Upsadaisy. If one's good, two's better.

prairie phlox n

A **phlox,** usu *Phlox pilosa.*

 1919 (1923) House *Wild Flowers NY* 229, The Downy or Prairie Phlox (*Phlox pilosa* . .) occurs rather locally in New York. **1936** IL Nat. Hist. Surv. *Wildflowers* 252, No plant adds color to the patches of prairie along railroads and other waste places . . more effectively than does the Prairie Phlox. **1940** Clute *Amer. Plant Names* 266, *Phlox glaberrima.* Prairie phlox, meadow-phlox. **1951** *PADS* 15.38 **TX,** *Phlox drummondii* . . Pride-of-Texas; prairie wild phlox. **1968** *DARE* FW Addit **CO7A,** Prairie phlox. . . *Phlox audicola,* phlox order and family—prickly leaves, both lavender and white flowers, low and creeping. **1979** Ajilvsgi *Wild Flowers* 241, Prairie phlox—*Phlox pilosa.*

prairie pigeon n

Any of var migratory birds that pass through the prairie states in large flocks, as:

a An **upland plover** (here: *Bartramia longicauda*).

1874 Coues *Birds NW* 503, In most parts of the West, between the Mississippi and the Rocky Mountains, this Tattler, commonly known as the "Prairie Pigeon," is exceedingly abundant during the migrations. **1898** (1900) Davie *Nests N. Amer. Birds* 149, Bartram's Tattler. . . is known as Field "Plover," Upland "Plover," Grass "Plover," Prairie "Pigeon," and Prairie "Snipe." **1951** Kumlien–Hollister *Birds WI* 41, The "prairie pigeon" was but little molested until it became generally known that it was one of our best table birds, and consequently brought a good price in the city markets. From that time on it has been slaughtered . . in great numbers. **1961** Ligon *NM Birds* 117, It [=the upland plover] was formerly known, also, as Tattler, or Prairie Pigeon.

b =**golden plover.**

1881 *Forest & Stream* 17.225, The first bird we have named above [= the golden plover] was not known in the West where we were located as a plover at all, but as a "prairie pigeon." **1888** Trumbull *Names of Birds* 196 **IA** (as of a1881), It was common talk when I was in Iowa . . that the earlier settlers were annoyed by these birds [=golden plovers], which, in the absence of a better name, they called Prairie Pigeons. **1917** (1923) *Birds Amer.* 1.257, Golden Plover. . . Other Names. . . Prairie-bird; Prairie Pigeon.

c =**Franklin's gull. Cf prairie dove**

1902 *Everybody's Mag.* 6.496, Among all birds I do not know of a more beautiful species than the Franklin's Rosy Gull. . . They are found only in the West, and breed from Dakota northward to the Arctic Sea. . . The settlers call them "Prairie Pigeons." **1946** Hausman *Eastern Birds* 315, Franklin's Rosy Gull, Prairie Dove, Prairie Pigeon.

d =**pectoral sandpiper.**

1907 Anderson *Birds IA* 217, The Pectoral Sandpiper, Grass Snipe, or Jack-snipe, commonly known to Iowa hunters as the "Prairie Pigeon," is an abundant migrant in nearly all parts of the state.

e =**Eskimo curlew.**

1917 (1923) *Birds Amer.* 1.254, Eskimo Curlew. . . *Other Names . . Prairie Pigeon.* **1937** *Natl. Geogr. Mag.* Aug 200 **Missip Valley,** The Eskimo curlew, or "dough bird" or "prairie pigeon," as it was called by the gunners, apparently rivaled the passenger pigeon in numbers prior to 1885. **1949** *Amer. Photography* June 382, In the west the Eskimo curlew flights so resembled those of the passenger pigeon that they were called "prairie pigeons."

prairie pine n Also *prairie pines*

A **blazing star 3** (here: *Liatris spicata*).

1830 Rafinesque *Med. Flora* 2.237, *Liatris* [spp]. . . Many vulgar names, Backache root, Devilsbite . . Prairie Pines, Gayfeather [etc]. **1876** Hobbs *Bot. Hdbk.* 92, Prairie pine, Button snake root, Liatris spicata. **1900** Lyons *Plant Names* 212, *L[acinaria] spicata.* . . Rattlesnake's-master, Corn Snakeroot, Prairie-pine, Backache-root.

prairie pink n

1 A **marsh pink 1** (here: *Sabatia campestris*).

1886 *Century Illustr. Mag.* 32.787 **IA** (as of 1850s), In July and August it [=the Iowa prairie] is pink with the 'prairie pink,' dotted with scarlet lilies. [*DARE* Ed: This quot may apply instead to another sense below.] **1940** Gates *Flora KS* 183 **seKS,** *Sabatia campestris* . . Prairie Pink. Prairies, fields and ravines.

2 A **skeletonweed 3.**

1932 Rydberg *Flora Prairies* 890, *Lygodesmia* [spp] . . Skeletonweed, Prairie Pink.

3 A **phlox.**

1951 *PADS* 15.38 **TX,** *Phlox* spp.—Wild, prairie, or woods, pinks.

prairie plover n

1 =**mountain plover.**

1851 Kelly *Excursion* 1.83, A stand of prairie plover most opportunely made their appearances as we pulled up. . . They were in splendid condition—a size bigger than our plover, and a shade browner in plumage, but otherwise strictly alike. **1898** (1900) Davie *Nests N. Amer. Birds* 158, Mountain Plover. . . More properly called Prairie Plover, but it seems to have been badly named, for it certainly is a prairie bird, inhabiting the most barren prairies, as well as the watered regions of the United States, from the plains to the Pacific. **1918** Grinnell *Game Birds CA* 481, The Mountain Plover, or Prairie Plover as this species has more aptly been called elsewhere, is typically an inland bird.

2 An **upland plover** (here: *Bartramia longicauda*).

1888 Trumbull *Names of Birds* 173, In Southern Wisconsin, Mr. Kumlien informs me, in 1851 this bird, then very common there, was

known as the *prairie plover*, and also as the *prairie snipe*. **1923** U.S. Dept. Ag. *Misc. Circular* 13.64 **MO, WI,** Upland Plover. . . prairie-plover.

3 =**golden plover.**

1890 *Century Dict.* 4668, The American golden plover, *Charadrius dominicus*. Also called *prairie-plover* and *prairie-snipe.*

prairie plow n Also *prairie breaker, ~ breaking plow* Cf breaking plow

A plow adapted for breaking sod; see quot 1872.

1831 (1930) Sewall *Diary* 136 **IL,** Sat off with team, and a prairie plow which came in late last night with instructions, to commence breaking prairie. **1839** in 1840 *Cultivator* 7.33 **IA,** It may be amusing to eastern readers, to hear a description of a "prairie plow." Fancy, then, a plow share weighing 125lbs., the beam fourteen feet long, attached to a pair of cart wheels, to the tongue of which are hitched from three to seven yoke of oxen. **c1860** in 1950 *AmSp* 25.311 **KS,** Behind the oxen they could see the great prairie plow of steel; its progress was unbelievably slow. Four times before it reached the end of the field the operator was forced to stop. . . One time the lay refused to scour and the soil adhered to it in a gummy mass so that it had to be scraped off with wooden paddles. **1867** Dixon *New Amer.* 38, When the ground is . . cut by the prairie breaker, the rosin-weed disappears. **1872** (1876) Knight *Amer. Mech. Dict.* 1782, *Prairie-plow.* A large plow supported in front on wheels, and adapted to pare and overturn a very broad but shallow furrow-slice. **1884** Knight *New Mech. Dict.* 130, *Breaker.* . . The . . prairie breaker. . . is light and strong, and, like plows of its class, turns a flat furrow. **1902** (1969) Sears *Catalogue* 678, *Acme Prairie Breaking Plows.* . . Our Prairie Breaker combines many desirable qualities. **1967** *DARE* (Qu. L18, *Kinds of plows*) Inf **CO**22, Prairie plow.

prairie plum n

A **wild plum** (here: either *Prunus umbellata* or **chickasaw plum**).

1814 Brackenridge *Views of LA* 62, Amongst the species of plums in Louisiana . . there is none more interesting than the prairie plum, *(prunus chickasa)* which literally covers tracts of ground. **1827** *Western Mth. Rev.* 1.323, Prairie plums are abundant in the prairies of Illinois and Missouri. **1851** *S. Lit. Messenger* 17.569, Having pretty thoroughly exhausted the prairie plumb crop, . . they were now prone to the land of pork and beans. **1908** Britton *N. Amer. Trees* 487, Black Sloe—*Prunus umbellata.* . . Also called . . Prairie, Oldfield, Chicasaw, or Bullace plum, this is a small tree, frequent in river swamps and in hammocks of the coastal region, from South Carolina to Louisiana, north to Arkansas. **1949** *World–Herald Mag.* (Omaha NE) 3 July 2/1 *(DA),* Fuel was one of the toughest problems. The Poole family tried prairie plum bush, seldom thicker than a man's thumb. **1966** *DARE* (Qu. I46, . . *Kinds of fruits that grow wild around here*) Inf **MS**54, Wild plums, prairie plums.

prairie pointers n

A **shooting star** (here: *Dodecatheon meadia*).

1897 Parsons *Wild Flowers CA* 206, Among the children the various forms are known by a number of names, such as "mad violets," "prairiepointers," "mosquito-bills," and "roosters'-heads." **1948** Wherry *Wild Flower Guide* 99, Midland Shootingstar (*Dodecatheon meadia*). . . Called by the early settlers of the Midlands *Prairie-Pointers,* being far more abundant then it is now.

prairie potato n

An **Indian breadroot** (here: *Pediomelum esculentum*).

1823 in 1828 Beltrami *Pilgrimage* 2.321 **MN,** We devoured whatever they gave us, and everything appeared to me delicious, even some roots which they call *prairie-potatoes,* and which I had before thought detestable. **1828** *Western Mth. Rev.* 2.139, [The Shoshoni] lived indolently on dried venison and salmon, and prairie potatoes. **1871** U.S. Dept. Ag. *Rept. of Secy. for 1870* 408, *Prairie potato* or *bread food.* . . It is also called Indian turnip. **1917** Kephart *Camping* II.379 *(DA),* Potato, Prairie. Prairie turnip. Indian or Missouri breadroot. The *pomme blanche* of the voyageurs. *Psoralea esculenta.* . . Often sliced and dried by the Indians for winter use. Palatable in any form. **1931** (1960) Dobie *Open Range* 307, Indian bread root. . . called also prairie potato. **1974** (1977) Coon *Useful Plants* 169, *Psoralea esculenta* . . prairie potato. A plant of the western mountains, it is a . . plant with an edible root which was considered as a special luxury to the Indians of that area.

prairie racer n Also *prairie runner* **TX** =**coachwhip snake.**

1908 Biol. Soc. DC *Proc.* 21.74 **cnTX,** *Zamenis flagellum* . . Coachwhip Snake; Prairie Runner. A common species in the prairie districts. **1928** Baylor Univ. Museum *Contrib.* 16.15 **TX,** *Masticophis flagellum flavigularis.* . . On account of its physical appearance it is called *Whip-snake* and of its rapid movements, *Prairie Racer, Prairie Runner,* and *Race-runner.* **1958** Conant *Reptiles & Amphibians* 150, *Western Coachwhip.* . . Called "prairie runner" in some parts of its range. **1967–70** *DARE* (Qu. P25, *. . Kinds of snakes*) Infs **TX**78, 101, Prairie racer; **TX**13, Prairie runner; **TX**19, Prairie runner—same as coachwhip. **1986** Pederson *LAGS Concordance,* 1 inf, **csTX,** Prairie runner—snake.

prairie ragweed n
A **marsh elder 1** (here: *Iva xanthifolia*).
  1940 [see **prairie-dog weed 2**].

prairie rattlesnake n Also *prairie rattler*
1 A **rattlesnake 1** of the western US: usu *Crotalus viridis,* but also the **speckled rattlesnake.** For other names of the former see **black rattlesnake, faded midget, mountain rattler, rattler 1, rock rattlesnake c, timber ~**
  1817 Brown *Western Gaz.* 31 **IL,** The only venomous serpents, are the common and *prairie* rattlesnake, and copper-heads. [*DARE* Ed: This quot may refer instead to **2** below.] **1835** Parker *Trip to TX* 52, Then, there is the prairie rattlesnake, about a foot long. Their bite is not considered very dangerous. **1890** *Century Dict.* 4668, *Prairie-rattlesnake.* . . One of several different rattlesnakes inhabiting the prairies, as the massasauga, *Sistrurus catenatus,* and especially *Crotalus confluentus.* **1914** *Copeia* 12.2 **AZ,** In the summer of 1913 the writer saw only three species of snakes on the Painted Desert, Arizona. These were the prairie rattlesnake *(Crotalus confluentus),* bull snake . . , Arizona ribbon snake. **1947** Pickwell *Amphibians* 59, *Crotalus viridis,* the Prairie Rattlesnake, is very widely distributed, occurring throughout central United States, and subspecies range west to the Pacific. **1966** Wheeler–Wheeler *Amphibians & Reptiles ND* 82, The prairie rattler avails itself of prairie dog burrows for three purposes: a refuge in emergencies; winter quarters; and a source of food, namely young prairie dogs. **1966–68** *DARE* (Qu. P25, *. . Kinds of snakes*) Infs **KS**20, **OH**33, **OK**18, Prairie rattler; **TX**11, Ground rattler, pygmy rattler, diamondback rattler, prairie rattler. **1986** Pederson *LAGS Concordance,* 1 inf, **cTX,** Prairie rattlers—snakes—poisonous.
2 =**massasauga.**
  1883 *Amer. Naturalist* 17.1186 **cIL,** Since September last I have had a prairie rattlesnake *(Caudisona tergemina)* in confinement. **1890** [see **1** above]. **1918** *Copeia* 58.67 **NY,** On June 2, 1917, while taking a botanical trip to the southeastern end of Bergen Swamp just beyond Bergen, N.Y., I had the opportunity to see two specimens of the prairie rattler. **1967–68** WI Acad. *Trans.* 56.30 **WI,** The massasauga was also known as the prairie, and spotted rattlesnake. **1969** *DARE* (Qu. P25, *. . Kinds of snakes*) Inf **IL**32, Only prairie rattler found around here.

prairie reed-bird n
=**lark bunting.**
  1855 Acad. Nat. Sci. Philadelphia *Proc. for 1851* 5.218 **wTX,** *C[alamospiza] bicolor.* . . Prairie Reedbird. I first met with this bird on the Rio Grande, between Santa Fé and Cañada. **1932** Bennitt *Check-list* 62 **MO,** Lark bunting. . . White-winged blackbird; prairie reed-bird.

prairie rocket n
A **wallflower,** usu *Erysimum capitatum.*
  1900 Lyons *Plant Names* 150, *E[rysimum] asperum.* . . Western Wallflower . . Prairie Rocket. **1932** Rydberg *Flora Prairies* 370, *Cheirinia* [spp] . . Wall-flower, Prairie-rocket, Yellow Phlox. **1968** Barkley *Plants KS* 165, Erysimum asperum . . Prairie Rocket. . . High plains coming east on prairies. *Ibid,* Erysimum inconspicuum . . Prairie Rocket. **1973** Hitchcock–Cronquist *Flora Pacific NW* 168, Prairie rocket. . . *E[rysimum] asperum.*

prairie rooter n
1 See **rooter 1.**
2 =**hognose snake.**
  1966 *DARE* (Qu. P25, *. . Kinds of snakes*) Inf **OK**18, Hog snake or prairie rooter.

prairie rose n
Any of var roses found on the prairie, but esp the climbing *Rosa setigera.*
  1822 Woods *2 Yrs. Residence* 218 **seIL,** The prairie-roses, balm . . and

sassafras-wood . . have all powerful scents. **1849** Howitt *Our Cousins in OH* 110, The prairie-rose also began to blossom, and its long pendent branches, drooping for yards from the portico, were adorned with clusters of deep rose-colored flowers. **1888** *Century Illustr. Mag.* 13.662 **nwND,** The carpet of prairie roses, whose short stalks lift the beautiful blossoms but a few inches from the ground. **1935** Sandoz *Jules* 78 **wNE,** Sometimes he stopped to pick a handful of prickly prairie roses growing along the sandy slope of a gully, pink-striped with scarlet, great splotches of pale light in the dusk, and heavy with fragrance. **1966–68** *DARE* (Qu. S26a, *. . Wildflowers. . . Roadside flowers*) Inf **WI**12, Wild rose—prairie rose; (Qu. S26e, *Other wildflowers not yet mentioned;* not asked in early QRs) Inf **OK**32, Prairie rose—grows anywhere. **1968** *DARE* Wildfl QR Pl.102 *(Rosa virginiana)* Inf **MN**37, Wild rose or prairie rose.

prairie runner See prairie racer

prairie rushgrass n
A **muhly (grass)** (here: *Muhlenbergia cuspidata*).
  1930 OK Univ. Biol. Surv. *Pub.* 2.51, *Muhlenbergia cuspidata* . . Prairie Rush-grass. **1973** Hitchcock–Cronquist *Flora Pacific NW* 650, Prairie rush-grass. . . *M[uhlenbergia] cuspidata.*

prairie schooner n Cf canal boat
  1970 *DARE* (Qu. X38, *Joking names for unusually big or clumsy feet*) Inf **CA**208, Prairie schooners.

prairie senna n [See quot 1922] Cf senna n[1] B
A **partridge pea** (here: *Chamaecrista fasciculata*).
  1876 Hobbs *Bot. Hdbk.* 92, Prairie senna, Cassia chamaecrista [= *Chamaecrista fasciculata*]. **1922** *Amer. Botanist* 28.30, *Cassia chamaecrista.* . . is "partridge pea" though it is not likely that partridges feed on it. It is distantly related to the medicinal senna and in consequence is sometimes called "prairie senna." **1950** Gray–Fernald *Manual of Botany* 886, *C. fasciculata.* . . Partridge-Pea, Prairie-Senna. . . Sandy open soil.

prairie shoestring See shoestring 1a

prairie short-tailed mouse See prairie mouse

prairie smoke n
1 An avens (here: *Geum triflorum*). [See quot 1949] Also called **Apache plume 3, grandfather's beard 4, johnny smokers, maidenhair 2, old-maid's-hair, old-man's-whiskers 1, pink plumes 1, tassels, torch flower**
  1896 *Jrl. Amer. Folkl.* 9.187 **ME,** *Geum triflorum* . . prairie smoke. **1938** FWP *Guide IA* 15, The prairie meadows abound with pink and white shootingstars, golden ragwort, and long-plumed purple avens (prairie smoke). **1949** Moldenke *Amer. Wild Flowers* 122, *S[ieversia] triflora,* the *oldmanswhiskers,* has purple calyxes and yellowish or flesh-colored corollas. Its fruits are surmounted by long plumelike styles whose fluffy grayish aspect have earned the plant the name of *prairie-smoke.* **1967** *DARE* Wildfl QR Pl.100 Inf **OR**12, Prairie smoke. **1968** Pochmann *Triple Ridge* 227 **cWI,** I saw the wood lily today. . . High on a hill near the pasques and prairie smoke *(Geum triflorum)* . . , it is off to one side of the crest. **1992** *Nature Conserv. Mag.* May/June 30 **NY,** The scientist's survey . . uncovered a small population of rare prairie smoke, *Geum triflorum,* previously believed to be extinct in the state.
2 A **pasqueflower** (here: *Pulsatilla patens*). [See quot 1949]
  1893 *Jrl. Amer. Folkl.* 6.136 **MN,** *Anemone patens,* var. *Nuttalliana.* . . prairie smoke, crocus. **1949** Moldenke *Amer. Wild Flowers* 5, After the plant [=*Pulsatilla patens*] has flowered, a head of long-tailed silky fruitlets surmounts the stem and imparts to large colonies of these plants a distinctive smoky appearance similar to that of the smoketree, for which reason the plant is frequently called *prairiesmoke.* **1952** *Sun* (Baltimore MD) 26 Feb 10/7 **SD,** The Pasqueflower . . is a bluish open bell shaped wild flower of the prairies. . . Patches of the flower at a distance give the impression of a bluish haze. This gives rise to its more familiar name "prairie smoke."

prairie snake n Cf prairie racer
A **bull snake** or similar snake.
  1845 Frémont *Rept. Rocky Mts.* 12, A large prairie snake . . was occupied in eating the young birds. **1965–68** *DARE* (Qu. P25, *. . Kinds of snakes*) Infs **MT**5, **OK**1, **TX**54, Prairie snake; **MO**18, Bull snake or the prairie snake.

prairie squirrel n

1 Any of several **ground squirrels b,** often *Spermophilus tridecemlineatus.*

1857 U.S. Patent Office *Annual Rept. for 1856: Ag.* 74, Striped and Spotted Prairie-squirrel. . . This little animal, so well known on our prairies, resembles the common chipmuck [sic], . . and is of about the same size, or a little longer. **1872** Schele de Vere *Americanisms* 101, A gray burrowing squirrel (Spermophilus franklinii), known also as the prairie squirrel. **1917** Anthony *Mammals Amer.* 218, Thirteen-striped Ground Squirrel. . . Other Names.—Striped Gopher, Striped Prairie Squirrel. **1966** *DARE* (Qu. P27, . . *Kinds of squirrels*) Inf **MT3,** Prairie squirrels—also called gopher.

2 also *prairie ground squirrel:* **=prairie dog.**

1810 Pike *Expeditions* 155, We . . killed some prairie squirrels, or wishtonwishes. **1844** Gregg *Commerce* 2.228, It was denominated the 'barking squirrel,' the 'prairie ground-squirrel,' etc., by early explorers. **1858** in 1966 Boller *MO Fur Trader* 57, Sometimes, I go to a village of prairie squirrels . . , about 2½ miles from the Fort. **1941** Vestal *Short Grass Country* 61 **Plains States, eSW,** In the '90's some enterprising ranchers killed and dressed prairie dogs which they shipped east to market as "prairie squirrels." They were so much in demand for a while, that buyers were sent west to contract for shipments.

prairie starblossom n

A **marsh pink 1** (here: *Sabatia campestris*).

1951 *PADS* 15.37 **TX,** *Sabatia campestris* . . Prairie star-blossom; Texas pink; Texas prairie-star.

prairie strawberry See strawberry

prairie swift n Cf prairie fox

=kit fox.

1967–68 *DARE* (Qu. P32, . . *Other kinds of wild animals*) Inf **KS15,** Prairie swifts; **TX5,** Prairie swift—small red fox.

prairie tea n Cf Mexican tea 4, nettle cure

A croton (here: *Croton monanthogynus*).

1894 *Jrl. Amer. Folkl.* 7.98, *Croton monanthogynus* . . prairie tea [Footnote: Used as tea], common from the Gila to the Rio Grande. **1976** Bailey–Bailey *Hortus Third* 338, [*Croton*] *monanthogynus* . . Prairie tea. . . Va. to Kans., s. to Ga., Tex.

prairie trout n

A **channel catfish** (here: *Ictalurus punctatus*).

1969 *WI Conserv. Bulletin* 34.1.17 **WI,** Some people are unimaginative enough to call the prairie trout by its approved hand-book name, channel catfish.

prairie turnip n

An **Indian breadroot** (here: *Psoralea esculenta*).

1814 Brackenridge *Views of LA* 249 **SD,** The prairie turnip, is a root very common in the prairies, with something of the taste of the turnip, but more dry; this they eat dried and pounded, made into gruel. **1841** Catlin *Letters Indians* 1.56, The "Pomme Blanche," or prairie turnip, . . is found in great quantities in these northern prairies, and furnishes the Indians with an abundant and nourishing food. **1876** Hobbs *Bot. Hdbk.* 93, Prairie turnip, Bread root, Psoralea esculenta. **1930** OK Univ. Biol. Surv. *Pub.* 2.68, *Psoralea esculenta.* . . Indian or Prairie Turnip. **1942** Hylander *Plant Life* 180, The Prairie Turnip . . is unusual in having a thickened tuberous root, rich in starchy substances.

prairie violet n

1 A **violet** (here: either *Viola pedatifida* or *V. nuttallii*).

1930 OK Univ. Biol. Surv. *Pub.* 2.72, *Viola pedatifida* . . Prairie or Larkspur Violet. **1936** Winter *Plants NE* 93, *V[iola] nuttallii.* . . Yellow Prairie Violet. **1950** *WELS* (*A flower like the violet; has ragged leaves, appears early in spring on stony open hilltops*) 1 Inf, **csWI,** Bird's-foot violet, prairie violet, cutleaf violet. **1968** Barkley *Plants KS* 242, Viola nuttallii Pursh. Yellow Prairie Violet.

2 A **wallflower** (here: *Erysimum inconspicuum*).

1974 Welsh *Anderson's Flora AK* 208, Erysimum inconspicuum . . *Prairie Violet.* . . Open woods, dry slopes, stream gravels, and roadsides; in the eastern half of Alaska and most of the Yukon.

prairie vulture n

=turkey vulture.

1899 Garland *Boy Life* 71 **nwIA** (as of c1870s), One day . . he scared a great black bird from the spot where the colt was buried. It was the prairie vulture or "turkey-buzzard."

prairieweed n

A **cinquefoil** (here: *Pentaphylloides floribunda*).

1900 Lyons *Plant Names* 304, P[otentilla] fruticosa. . . Shrubby Cinquefoil, Hardhack, Prairie-weed. **1935** (1943) Muenscher *Weeds* 291, Shrubby cinquefoil, Black brush, Prairie weed. **1960** Vines *Trees SW* 422, Some of the vernacular names of the plant [=*Potentilla fruticosa*] are Golden Hardhack, Prairie-weed, and Shrubby Cinquefoil.

prairie willow n

A **willow** (here: *Salix humilis*).   Also called **gray willow, mountain ~, pussy ~, sage ~ a, upland ~**

1892 IN Dept. Geol. & Nat. Resources *Rept. for 1891* 153, S[alix] humilis . . Prairie Willow. **1901** Lounsberry *S. Wild Flowers* 111, S[alix] humilis, prairie willow, grows southward as far as North Carolina and Tennessee. **1942** Tehon *Fieldbook IL Shrubs* 52, The Prairie Willow is a shrub of very wide range extending from Newfoundland westward into North Dakota, and southward in the East to Florida and in the west to Texas. **1973** Wharton–Barbour *Trees KY* 503, Salix tristis . . Dwarf Prairie Willow. . . It is frequent especially in the Cumberland Plateau, Knobs, and Mississippian Plateau.

prairie wolf n [See quot 1947]

=coyote B1.

1804 (1904) Lewis *Orig. Jrls. Lewis & Clark Exped.* 1.108, A *Prairie Wolf* come near the bank and Barked at us this evening. **1823** James *Acct. of Exped.* 1.168 **IA,** The prairie wolves roam over the plains in considerable numbers. **1846** in 1956 Sage *Letters & Papers* 1.193, Of these there are five distinct classifications, viz: The big white or buffalo wolf; the shaggy brown, the black; the gray, or prairie wolf; and the cayeute, (wa-chunka-monet,) or medicine-wolf of the Indians. **1857** in 1924 *Jrl. Amer. Hist.* [New Haven] 18.47, Saw something like a shaggy yellowish dog stealing across the prairie, but which the driver said was a prairie wolf. **1899** Garland *Boy Life* 127 **nwIA,** The prairies were populous with a sort of wolf, half-way between the coyote of the plains and the gray wolf of the timber land. They were called simply "prairie wolves." **1947** Cahalane *Mammals* 252, Sometimes, particularly in forested regions, the name "brush wolf" is used to indicate that the coyote can be found frequently in the cutover country close to man's habitations, while the more intolerant true wolf keeps to the heavy timber. Similarly, the term "prairie wolf" has been applied on the plains. **1968–70** *DARE* (Qu. P32, . . *Other kinds of wild animals*) Inf **IL115,** A few prairie wolves [FW: Inf thinks it's a dog.]; **WI22,** Coyote or prairie wolf. **1982** Elman *Hunter's Field Guide* 344, Coyote. . . Common & Regional Names: prairie wolf, brush wolf.

praise house n SC, GA Gullah

A small building used for religious meetings.

1862 in 1906 Pearson *Letters from Port Royal* 20 **SC,** I went with him to the praise-house, where he has his school. **1867** Allen *Slave Songs* xiv **seSC** [Gullah], Song and dance are alike extremely energetic, and often, when the shout lasts into the middle of the night, the monotonous thud, thud of the feet prevents sleep within half a mile of the praise-house. **1869** (1870) Higginson *Army Life* 20 **csSC,** The desk is a bequest of the slaveholders, and the settee of the slaves, being ecclesiastical in its origin, and appertaining to the little old church or "praise house," now used for commissary purposes. **1888** Jones *Negro Myths* 159 **GA coast** [Gullah], At the "Praise-House" his seat was never vacant. **1930** Woofter *Black Yeomanry* 236 **seSC,** Masters allowed their people to worship in plantation groups, usually at the house of one of the older people, sometimes in a special praise house. . . With the breakdown of ante-bellum plantations and the shifting of the freed population, praise houses disappeared from most sections to be supplanted by churches. . . On St. Helena the praise house remains the local, face-to-face unit of worship. Here services are held on three nights in the week, while churches hold services only on Sunday. **1934** *Natl. Geogr. Mag.* Feb 253 **seGA coast,** The negroes are all good Baptists now. . . [P]ractically every home in all the settlements is also within a few steps of a "praise house." **1939** Griswold *Sea Is. Lady* 139 **csSC** (as of 1865), Harriet's school, a remodeled cotton barn, was the largest of the five on the island. Emily's was the decrepit plantation praise-house. *Ibid* 140, The grown-ups of the plantation assembled at the praise-house. **1998** *Washington Post* (DC) 20 Sept sec E 10/5 **seSC,** Down the road was a "praise house," a one-room building used as a Gullah meeting house as far back as the early 1800s. It's a white clapboard structure, almost hauntingly simplistic. Local African Americans still use it for occasional meetings.   **1998** Kingsolver *Poisonwood Bible* 530 **GA coast,** Late in the evening we will sometimes pull into the dirt parking lot of a clapboard praise house and listen to old, dark Gullah hymns rising out the windows.

praise meeting n

1 A prayer meeting.   *Gullah*

1862 *N. Amer. & U.S. Gaz.* 14 July 1/8 **seSC** [Gullah], When dey come to de praise meeting dat night dey sing about it.   **1862** in 1906 Pearson *Letters from Port Royal* 36 **SC** [Gullah], He had been up to the praise-meeting by Uncle Peter's invitation.   **1863** *Continental Mth.* 4.195 **SC coast** [Gullah], The present opportunities for religious worship which the freedmen enjoy consist of their 'praise meetings'—similar in most respects to our prayer meetings.   **1892** (1893) Botume *First Days* 222 **seSC,** They had a praise-meeting before the house, as they believe the spirit remains with the body until daylight, when it takes leave and goes home to the heavenly Father as the morning stars go out.   **1922** Gonzales *Black Border* 319 **sSC, GA coasts** [Gullah glossary], *Praise-meetin'*—prayer-meeting.   **1984** Joyner *Down by Riverside* 171 **SC coast** (as of a1866) [Gullah], Through their active participation in praise meetings . . the slaves of All Saints Parish voiced their deepest values and proclaimed—and partly shaped—their sense of community.

2 Fig: see quot.   Cf **blessing**

1969 *DARE* (Qu. Y12a, *A fight between two people, mostly with words*) Inf **VT**12, Praise meeting.

praise up v phr   Cf *please up* (at **please** v **B1**)

To talk (something or someone) up; to compliment, flatter.

1841 *N. Amer. Rev.* 52.141, He went on for some minutes, praising up the party and the "venerable president."   **1856** (1857) Parker *MN Hdbk.* 103, You think, perhaps, that Western people are extravagant in praising up the many attractions of life in the West.   **1860** *Ladies' Repository* Apr 239, She had been ambitious to . . be an equal companion for him; and now to hear him coolly praise up a girl who had just moved into the place.   **1873** Bear *Life & Travels* 212 **OH,** They told me to praise up Douglas, for he had many friends.   **1884** Smith *Bill Arp's Scrap Book* 80 **GA,** They got up and gave us a first class breakfast, and I praised 'em up lots.   **1884** *Anglia* 7.269 **Sth, S Midl** [Black], *To praise up* = to flatter.   **1908** Johnson *Highways Pacific Coast* 104 **sCA,** But new people were coming in on every train looking for property to invest in; and the papers were praising it up all the time, so that hearing of prices constantly on the rise they'd get in a hurry to buy.

praitie See **pratie**

prakes n pl |ˈprɑkəs| Also sp *praakes* [Yiddish]

=holishkes.

1949 (1986) Leonard *Jewish Cookery* 199, *Holishkes* (Meat filled cabbage leaves, also called *Praakes* and *Galuptzi,* depending on locale).   **1968** *DARE* (Qu. H52, *Dishes made with fresh cabbage*) Inf **PA**171, Prakes [ˈprɑkəs]—stuffed cabbage.   **1970** Feinsilver *Yiddish* 197, *Prakes*—Rolled cabbage leaves stuffed with chopmeat (often with added rice) and cooked in tomato sauce, seasoned sour or sweet-and-sour. Rumanian and Hungarian Jews call them *halishkes.*

praline n Usu |ˈprɑˌlin, ˈprɔ-, ˌprɑˈlin, ˌprɔ-|; also |ˈpreˌlin|; by metath LA |ˌplɑˈrin|; for addit varr see **A** below   Pronc-spp *plarine, prawleen, pyrine*

A Forms.

1893 Owen *Voodoo Tales* 39 **MO** [Black], It was the fragrance of prawleens, that compound of New Orleans molasses, brown sugar, chocolate, and butter.   **1916** *DN* 4.346 **LA,** *Plarine* [ˈplɑrin]. . . Praline. New Orleans.   **1945** Saxon *Gumbo Ya-Ya* 361 **LA,** Negro women hawk pecan and coconut pralines, calling, 'Pyrines! Pyrine candy!'   **1965–70** *DARE* (Qu. H80) Infs **SC**4, 22, **TN**11, **TX**29, 43, 52, [ˈpreˌlin(z)]; **LA**14, 16, 33, **TX**3, 73, [ˈprɑˌlin(z)]; **AL**19, **LA**3, **TN**11, [ˈprɔˌlin(z)]; **KY**8, **LA**40, **TX**4, [ˌprɔˈlinz]; **LA**19, 23, **PA**131, [ˈprɔˌlinz]; **GA**29, [prəˈlinz]; **LA**28, 40, [ˌprɑˈlinz]; **TX**15, [ˌpreˈlinz]; **TX**33, [ˈpreɪˌlinz]; **TX**42, [ˈpreiˌlinz]; **LA**20, [ˌplɑˈrinz]; (Qu. H32) Inf **SC**11, [ˈpreˌlinz].   **1967** LeCompte *Word Atlas* 323 **seLA,** *Praline* is the standard French word for nuts cooked in a burnt sugar. In English and French, the tendency is to pronounce the word "plarine"—an excellent example of metathesis.   **1970** [see **B** below].   **1981** Pederson *LAGS Basic Materials,* 1 inf, **cnLA,** [prɔˠɔˣlĭʧ¹nz].   **1983** Reinecke *Coll.* 9 **LA,** *Plarine* [plɑˈrin]. . *Praline.*   **2000** *NADS Letters,* The locally interesting thing about pralines in Texas is that they are pronounced [ˈprelinz] in Central Texas, but [ˈprɔlinz] in East Texas. . I was in New Orleans once, and

decided to pursue the pronunciation to its source, so I located a store in the French Quarter which specialized in pralines, in all colors and flavors. I found a young woman behind the counter, who from appearances looked as though she might be a local Cajun . . , and asked her what she called them. Her response was a delightful [ˈprɑrinz]. . . In South Texas . . there was no regular name for them at the time, except perhaps "pecan candy".

B Sense.

A patty of candy made usu with brown sugar and pecans, or, less freq, with other nuts, sesame seeds, or coconut.   **formerly esp LA, TX, but now widely recognized**   See Map   Cf **benne**

1861 *Atlantic Mth.* 8.286 **sLA,** The complexion of Miss Mellasys announced a diet of alternate pickles and *pralines* during her adolescent years.   **1894** *Harper's New Mth. Mag.* 89.918 **New Orleans LA,** Munching a praline of pecans—she was always munching them, had a passion . . for them—she soared in imagination up to the plane where dwelt in immortality the Spenserian stanzas of "Childe Harold."   **1916** *DN* 4.270 **New Orleans LA,** *Praline* [ˈprɔlin]. . . A cream candy of brown sugar with raisins and nuts.   **1949** *Times–Picayune* (New Orleans LA) 6 Nov mag sec 6/3, This "praline woman" was to Loyola what the hot tamale, oyster, and ice cream men were to LSU.   **1961** *PADS* 36.14 **LA, TX,** Two terms that are clearly of Louisiana origin have spread into all major portions of Texas. One of these is *praline,* which is replacing the older *pecan patty* as the name for a flat candy made with pecans. Another is *gumbo* for a kind of soup containing okra.   **1965–70** *DARE* (Qu. H80, *Kinds of candy . . made at home*) 31 Infs, **chiefly TX, LA,** Praline(s); **SC**4, **TX**11, 43, Pecan praline(s); **LA**20, Plarine; (Qu. H32) Inf **SC**11, Pralines.   **1967** *DARE* FW Addit **TX,** *Praline* [ˈpreɪˌlin]—candy made of pecan fudge and pecan halves. When cooked, they are poured on a flat pan and allowed to cool. They make flat, round paddies [sic].   **1970** *DARE* File **LA,** *Praline* = the candy made with pecans, sugar and corn syrup, and cream. In southeast and central Texas, where I grew up, I knew this candy as [ˈpˈreɪlin] . . ; later, I came to know it as a [ˈprɑlin]. In this area [=Baton Rouge and New Orleans], the word is almost universally (among Blacks, that is) metathesized to either [ˈplɑrin] or (with a shift in accent) to [plɑˈrin].   **1983** Reinecke *Coll.* 9 **LA,** *Praline* [ˈprɑlin] . . a flat crisp candy patty made of brown sugar and pecans, of white sugar and grated coconut, or (among Cajuns) of brown sugar and sesame seed. . . General, as in La. Fr.   **1984** Stall *Proud New Orleans* 171, *Praline:* A bon bon made of pecans browned in sugar. . . The pecan praline became the most poular [sic] confection of our city.   **1986** Pederson *LAGS Concordance,* 8 infs, 5 **LA,** Praline(s).   **1997** *NY Times* (NY) 15 Mar 8/3 **New Orleans LA,** A recent health study ranked New Orleans as the most obese city in the United States. . . [N]o other city could hold a spatula to New Orleans (bread pudding, pralines, beignets, cream sauces).

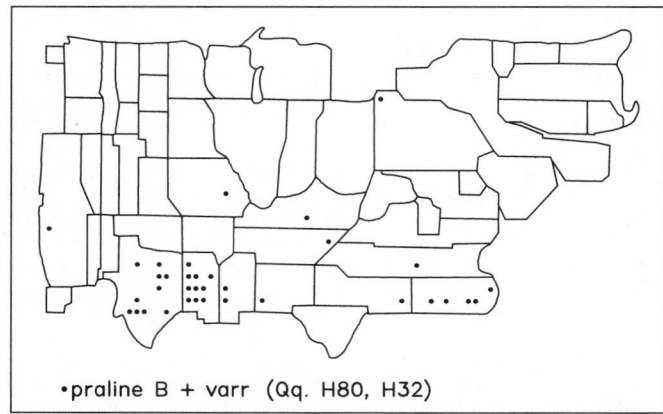

•praline B + varr (Qq. H80, H32)

pram n chiefly Nth   See Map   Cf **dinky** n[2], **dory** n[2], **johnboat 1**

A small, usu square-bowed boat, designed to be used with oars, sails, or motor.

1937 *Sun* (Baltimore MD) 31 July 10/4, In the pram class, Bucky Wilson . . scored a surprise victory.   **1965** *PADS* 43.19 **seMA,** Small rowboat large enough for two . . pram [1 of 9 infs].   **1965** *Rhinelander Daily News & New North* (WI) 12 Aug 3/5, [Advt with photo of boat:] Limited Supply! 10 And 12 Ft. Appleby Prams.   **1965–70** *DARE* (Qu. O1, . . *A small rowboat, not big enough to hold more than two people*)

17 Infs, **chiefly Nth,** Pram; **AK**1, Pram—small, square-ended boat; **CA**4, Pram—V-shaped or flat bottom, a square bow; **MI**123, Pram—square front; **MN**21, Pram—square-bowed; (Qu. O9, *. . Kinds of sailboats*) Inf **RI**6, Prams—square-fronted boat; (Qu. O10, *. . Kinds of boats*) Inf **RI**4, Prams—like a rowboat only square on each end. [22 of 23 Infs male] **1966** *AmSp* 41.237, Size and hull characteristics form the basis for classifying all small sailboats. The smallest are called *Prams,* and they measure up to about 10 feet long. **1968** *DE Coast Press* (Rehoboth Beach & Lewes) 23 May 4/3, For Sale—10-ft. sailing pram, mahogany trim, new, dacron sail, fiberglass mast and boom, two oars, $200. **1986** Pederson *LAGS Concordance (Rowboat)* 1 inf, **swFL,** Pram.

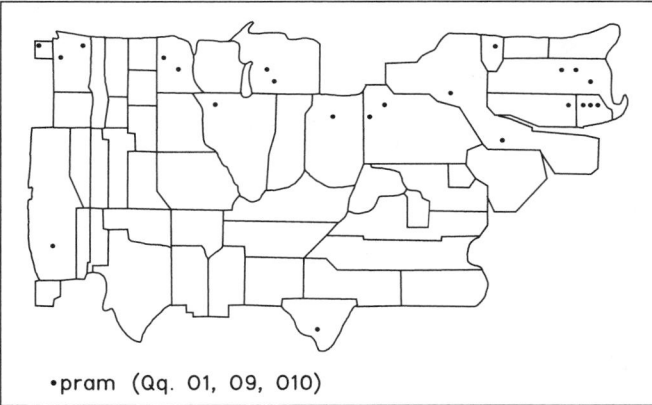

•pram (Qq. O1, O9, O10)

prank v[1] [*OED2 prank* v.[2] 1530 →; *"Obs.* or *dial."*]

1 with *with:* To play with; to fool, meddle with; to tease. **chiefly S Midl**

1845 (1997) Horton *Poet. Works* xiii (Internet) **NC** [Black], Having got in the way of carrying fruit to the college at Chapel Hill on the Sabbath, the collegians who, for their diversion, were fond of pranking with the country servants . . began also to prank with me. **1890** *Overland Mth.* 16.502, He began pranking with the engine. He tried several things about it that would not move, and got hold of some that did, but made no apparent change in the situation. **1897** *Outing* 30.456, A little wind . . was pranking with the quaking asp leaves. **1924** Raine *Land of Saddle-Bags* 100 **sAppalachians,** The children love to prank with the dog. **1927** *DN* 5.476 **Ozarks,** Thet fool boy'll ruinate hisse'f, a-prankin' with thet 'ar choppin'-axe. **1930** *VA Qrly. Rev.* 6.244 **AR,** An up-country Arkansawyer . . may . . prank with the young'uns while the crops go to naught. **1942** (1971) Campbell *Cloud-Walking* 238 **seKY,** Uncle Blessing let the doctor men prank with his own eyes for a spell, measuring him for specs to see better through. **1947** Ballowe *The Lawd* 102 **LA,** "That's ma sign," Patsy cried, throwing herself into Sol's arms. "Efn the Lawd was to prank with me He w'u'dn't do hit with no mawkin'bird." **1949** Perry *Granny Van* 77 **TX** [Black], Ain't tetched that fire, Mrs. Van. You know I don't prank with no *gas* stove. **c1960** *Wilson Coll.* **csKY,** *Prank:* . . To fool or tinker with. **1966** *DARE* Tape **MS**61, [FW:] How did you happen to get kicked this one time? [Inf:] This was an old . . gentle mule, . . but I think it had been pranked with a right smart. **1977** Norman *Kinfolks* 114 **eKY,** Taxes are awful and the heat and when you call the water company it takes it a month to come, and you can't see television because of this sarcastic neighbor Mr. Ortiz who pranks with the electricity. **1982** Slone *How We Talked* 30 **eKY** (as of c1950), *"Prank"* with someone—bother or tease. **1986** Pederson *LAGS Concordance,* 1 inf, **cwTN,** Pranking with him—fooling with him; 1 inf, **ceAR,** Just fooling with him, pranking with him.

2 also with *around:* To play, fool around; to play tricks. **chiefly Sth, S Midl** See Map

1884 *Anglia* 7.271 **Sth, S Midl** [Black], *To prank en' pester 'roun'* = to be troublesome. **1938** Matschat *Suwannee R.* 210 **neFL, seGA,** "Chicken snake," Pompano said with a delighted grin. . . "They're partial to droppin' on folks an' twistin' round their shoulders an' lookin' in their faces. Ain't no harm, but they like to prank a bit." **1946** *AmSp* 21.190 **seKY,** *Prank* . . to play. 'The doctor pranked around in my eye.' **1965–70** *DARE* (Qu. GG32a, *To habitually play tricks or jokes on people: "He's always _____."*) 21 Infs, **chiefly Sth, S Midl,** Pranking; **KY**40, **MS**1, **NC**2, **TX**43, **WV**18, A-pranking; **AR**52, **IN**82, **NY**123, Pranking around; **KY**6, Pranking on someone; [**MO**23, Pranking some

of his tricks]. **1986** Pederson *LAGS Concordance,* 1 inf, **cTN,** Pranking around = fooling around, doing pranks; 1 inf, **cnAR,** Pranking = playing pranks.

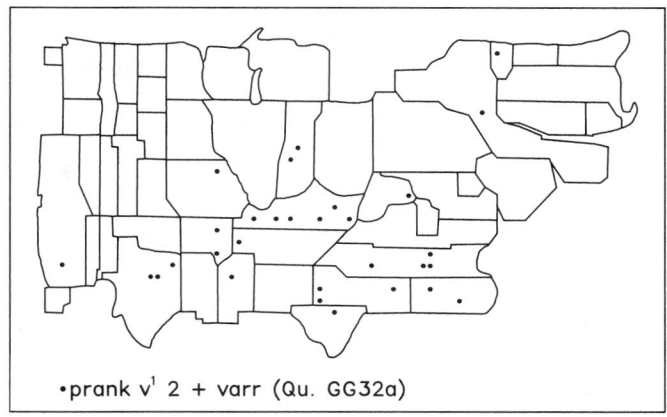

•prank v[1] 2 + varr (Qu. GG32a)

prank v[2] [*OED2 prank* v.[3] *"Obs.* or *dial."*]

To prance, caper.

1927 Jones *FL Plantation Rec.* 54 **nwFL,** John Evans discovered him in the stable one day, striking a horse with a switch, "to see him prank", as Demps put it with a twinkle in his eye. **1934** Carmer *Stars Fell on AL* 23 [Black], "I belongs to the Babtists and we don't dance." . . "I just pranks a bit," said Lula pridefully, "I don't do no real dancin'." **1955** Ritchie *Singing Family* 141 **seKY,** We'd prank around and sing and make jokes and carry on, and hoe maybe four rows while they over there hoed sixteen.

prank around See **prank** v[1] 2

prank with See **prank** v[1] 1

p'raps See **perhaps**

prar See **prayer**

prararee, prare See **prairie**

Prasbattery See **Presbytery**

prat n Also sp *pratt* [*OED2* 1567 →] **esp Inland Nth, N Midl, West** See Map Cf **hinder** n

The buttocks.

1914 Jackson *Criminal Slang* 66, *Pratt.* . . General usage. The human rear; the buttocks. **1920** in 1944 *ADD* **cNY,** *Pratt.* . . The buttocks. Current. **1930** Shoemaker *1300 Words* 45 **cPA Mts** (as of c1900), *Prat*—A "jab in the prat", a blow in the vicinity of the buttocks. **1950** *WELS (Joking words for the part of the body that you sit on)* 9 Infs, **WI,** Prat. **1960** Criswell *Resp. to PADS* 20 **Ozarks,** *Fanny* very recent and *pratt* almost unknown. **1965–70** *DARE* (Qu. X35) 24 Infs, **esp Inland Nth, N Midl, West,** Prat; (Qu. Y1, *. . Expressions . . for a person suddenly falling down: "He slipped on the steps and took quite a _____."*) Inf **MI**103, Slipped on his prat.

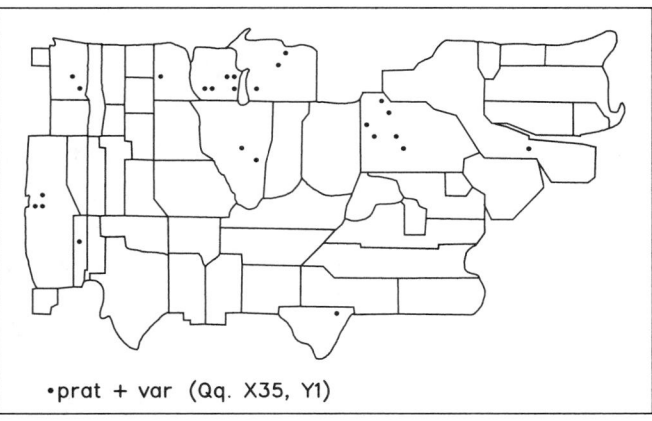

•prat + var (Qq. X35, Y1)

prate v [*prate* to chatter]

1 with *for:* To imitate the call of (a passenger pigeon) in order to lure it; hence vbl n *prating* luring a passenger pigeon in this way; n *prating* the call of the passenger pigeon. *hist*

1853 (1949) Thoreau *Jrl.* 5.71 **MA,** He. . . *Prated* for them; they came near and then flew away. **1854** *Ibid* 7.35, Their *prating* . . is like a sharp creak. **1899** (1909) Earle *Child Life* 317 (as of 18th cent), Boys learned "to prate" for pigeons, that is, to imitate their call. This was useful in luring them within gun-shot. **1945** *Auk* Jan 136 **cnMA,** Many and many a time . . have I heard my father *prate* for pigeons. . . Wild pigeon prating consisted of voice delivered through *tightly* approximated lips, with a buzz or vibration of those lips, in two somewhat prolonged, high-pitched monotones.

2 See quot. [*EDD prate* v. 2 "Of a hen: to make the peculiar noise indicating she is about to lay"]

1927 *AmSp* 3.137 **eME,** A loudly singing hen was said to "prate." "The pullets are prating and will lay soon."

prate for See **prate 1**

pratie n |'preti| Also *praitie, prittie* [Ir dial var of *potato*]

A **white potato.**

1837 in 1874 Hawthorne *Passages Amer. Note-Books* 43 **ME,** Nobody . . shall drive me out of this house, till my praties are out of the ground. **1921** *DN* 5.113 **CA,** *Praties.* . . Potatoes. Irish. Current. **1962** Wyld *Low Bridge* 21 **cNY** (as of early 19th cent), Food in general was called *prog* [by Erie Canal workers], boiled or baked potatoes were *pritties* (cf. the Irish *praties*), and buttermilk was *skimmagig.* **1966–68** *DARE* (Qu. I9, . . Names *[including nicknames] for potatoes*) Infs **MD17, MI1,** Praties ['pretiz]. **1995** Brophy *Coll.* 57 **swMO** (as of c1960), *Praities.* [P]otatoes (Irish-American term; Old Stock Americans said tators, taters, pertaters, or spuds).

prating n, vbl n See **prate 1**

pratt See **prat**

prawleen See **praline**

prayer n Usu |prɛr, 'prɛə(r), prær, 'præə(r)|; also **Sth, S Midl** *old-fash* |'prɑə| Pronc-spp *pra(a)r*

Std sense, var forms.

1875 in 1884 Lanier *Poems* 179 **GA** [Black], I know'd he couldn't stand dat pra'r. **1890** *DN* 1.69 **KY,** Pra'r ['prɑə]: for *prayer,* by old people. **1893** Shands *MS Speech* 51, Prar ['prɑə]. Illiterate white and negro pronunciation of *prayer.* **1913** Kephart *Highlanders* 202 **sAppalachians,** Lyin' John (whose "mouth ain't no praar-book, if it *does* open and shet"). **1960** Carpenter *Tales Manchaca* 13 **cTX** (as of 1872), I went to a prar meeting last Sunday night.

prayer bead n [See quot 1892]

=**crab's eye.**

1890 *Century Dict.* 4672, Prayer-bead. . . A seed of the plant Indian licorice, *Abrus precatorius.* **1892** (1974) Millspaugh *Amer. Med. Plants* 46–6, The Prayer Bead, the seed of the Indian Liquorice (*Abrus precatorius,* Linn.) is a beautiful little scarlet oval with a black spot. These seeds . . are also used in the manufacture of rosaries. **1976** Bailey-Bailey *Hortus Third* 3, [*Abrus*] *precatorius* L. Rosary pea, . . prayer-beads, coral-bead plant [etc].

prayer beetle See **prayer bug**

prayer bones n pl Also *prayer handles*

The knees.

1878 Pinkerton *Molly Maguires* 142, "The neophyte will kneel!" said Lawler. "Now get down on your prayer-bones," whispered Monaghan; and McKenna knelt upon the carpet. **1914** *DN* 4.78 **ME, nNH,** *Prayer-handles.* . . Knees. **1916** *DN* 4.327 **KS,** *Prayer bones.* . . Knees or shins; as to get down on one's *prayer bones,* to plead, to ask mercy. **1927** *AmSp* 2.362 **cwWV,** *Prayer bones* . . knees. "Every one get down on his prayer bones." **1942** Whipple *Joshua* 445 **UT** (as of c1860), With Isabella on her prayer-bones begging, 'Oh, forgive me!' **1944** Botkin *Treas. Amer. Folkl.* 531, If you kneel down to save your poor old back, the little grains of sand eat into your prayerbones. **1950** *WELS* (*Joking names for the knees*) 17 Infs, **WI,** Prayer bones; 1 inf, **csWI,** Prayer handles. **c1955** Reed-Person *Ling. Atlas Pacific NW,* 1 inf, Prayer bones. **1965–66** *DARE* (Qu. X36, *Joking names for the knees;* total Infs questioned, 75) Infs **AR40, FL39, NM7, 9, OK13, 31, 47,**

Prayer bones. **1979** *NYT Article Letters* **nMN,** My little nephew from Northern Minnesota used this term to describe his knees. We were going under a fence, and he told me to "get down on my prayer bones" to go under the fence. **1992** *Houston Chron.* (TX) 5 Apr sec G 4, *Knees:* Prayer bones.

prayer book n Cf **California prayer book**

A packet of cigarette papers.

1941 Writers' Program *Guide WY* 464, *Prayer book*—The book of cigarette papers. **1942** Berrey–Van den Bark *Amer. Slang* 111.8, *Prayer book,* a book of cigarette papers. **1944** Adams *Western Words* 119, *Prayer book*—What the cowboy calls his book of cigaret papers. **1984** Wilder *You All Spoken Here* 195 **Sth,** *Prayer book:* A book, or pack, of cigarette papers for building or rolling your own.

prayer bug n Also *prayer beetle, praying ~, praying bug*

=**praying mantis B.**

1966–69 *DARE* (Qu. R9b, *An insect that holds up its front feet as if saying a prayer;* not asked in early QRs) Infs **NY1, SC32, WA15,** Prayer bug; **KS12,** Prayer beetle; **KY5,** Praying bug; **MO2,** Praying beetle.

prayer ground See **praying ground**

prayer handles See **prayer bones**

prayer mantis See **praying mantis**

prayer stick n

A stick of wood whittled so that thin shavings curl outward from the core; see quots.

[**1916** Seton *Woodcraft Manual Girls* 190, If you have no birch bark, it is a good plan to shave a dry soft-wood stick, leaving all the shavings sticking on the end in a fuzz, like a Hopi prayer stick.] **1959** Martin *Gunbarrel* 60 **WY,** Standing a small piece of firewood on end, he whittled shavings down from the top with his pocket knife, leaving them anchored to the wood at the bottom. When finished, the whittled end looked like a coarse broom. "My mother used to call these prayer sticks," he remarked, "but she didn't know where the name came from. I guess because you stick 'em in the stove and pray the fire will go."

praying anthis See **praying mantis**

praying beetle (or bug) See **prayer bug**

praying grompus n Cf **grampus 2, 3**

=**praying mantis B.**

1968 *DARE* (Qu. R9b, *An insect that holds up its front feet as if saying a prayer;* not asked in early QRs) Inf **VA2,** Praying ['grɔmpəs].

praying ground n Also *prayer ground* [Appar a literal application of the metaphorical phr *on praying ground* in a state of being able to pray] **chiefly among Black speakers**

A secluded piece of ground suitable for prayer.

1933 in 1983 Taft *Blues Lyric Poetry* 189, I even went to my praying ground : dropped down on bended knees / I ain't crying for no religion : Lordy give me back my good gal please. **c1937** in 1970 Yetman *Voices* 53 **TX** [Black], Us niggers used to have a prayin' ground down in the hollow and sometime we come out of the field . . scorchin' and burnin' up with nothin to eat, and we wants to ask the good Lord to have mercy. *Ibid* 231 **GA** [Black], One thing dat's all wrong with dis world today is dat dey ain't no "prayer grounds." Down in Georgia where I was born—dat way back in 1852—us colored folks had prayer grounds. My mammy's was a old twisted thick-rooted muscadine bush. She'd go in dere and pray for deliverance of de slaves. Some colored folks cleaned out kneespots in de canebrakes. Cane, you know, grows high and thick, and colored folks could hide demselves dere and nobody could see and pester dem. **1942** Hurston *Dust Tracks* 278 **FL** [Black], People, solemn of face, crept off to the woods to "praying ground" to seek religion.

praying horse n

=**praying mantis B.**

1968 *DARE* (Qu. R9b, *An insect that holds up its front feet as if saying a prayer;* not asked in early QRs) Inf **IN17,** Praying horse.

praying mantis n Also *prayer mantis, praying (m)anthis, praying mantle, preying mantis*

A Forms.

1965–70 *DARE* (Qu. R9b, *An insect that holds up its front feet as if* *saying a prayer;* not asked in early QRs) 622 Infs, **widespread,** Praying mantis; **WA**1, Praying anthis; **DE**1, Praying manthis; **IL**62, 89, **NY**109, Praying mantle(s); **MA**42, Prayer mantis; (Qu. R9a, *An insect from two to four inches long that lives in bushes and looks like a dead twig*) 25 Infs, **scattered,** Praying mantis. **1968** *AmSp* 43.52, [Results of a Kansas State University survey on names for *dragonfly:*] Of the 1,518 informants . . 1,370 had only *praying mantis.* . . Other names for 'praying mantis' . . included *preying mantis,* 1; *prayer mantis,* 1.

B Sense.

Std: an insect of the family Mantidae. Also called **broomstick, daddy longlegs 2, devil's horse 1, ~ mantis, ~ darning needle 3, ear sewer 2, granddaddy 3, haymaker 3, hobbyhorse 5, horse racer 2, johnny cockhorse, mosquito hawk 2c, mule killer 2, old granddad, piss mare, prayer bug, praying grompus, ~ horse, ~ sexton, preacher bug, racehorse 1, rearhorse, snake doctor, ~ feeder, soothsayer, stick bug, walkingstick**

praying sexton n
=praying mantis B.
1969 *DARE* (Qu. R9b, *An insect that holds up its front feet as if saying a prayer;* not asked in early QRs) Inf **IN**58, Praying sexton.

pray through v phr **esp Sth, S Midl**
To experience spiritual ecstasy or salvation through intensive prayer; to assist (one) to this experience through prayer.
1903 (1997) Compton *Life* 37 (Internet) **wNC,** Precious souls knelt upon the street, and prayed through to victory. **1926** (2000) Ray–Ray *Twice Sold* 33 (Internet) **MO,** I had heard older ones say, "pray through," and I had often heard others tell about how the Lord shook their dungeon and the chains fell off, and how they had seen the devil go. . . I had heard and seen them as they were taken into the church. The elders were called to the front and they were asked to give in their experience, and, if their testimony did not ring clear they were told to go back and pray through until they were sure, without the least shadow of a doubt, that the work was done. **1938** Stuart *Dark Hills* 242 **eKY,** If you'd been there when I prayed through,/ I would not be denied;/ You'd been a-praying and a-shouting too,/ I would not be denied. **1949** Webber *Backwoods Teacher* 16 **Ozarks,** Once you get the meetin' to goin' good. . . then I can he'p pray the others through when we get them to the altar. *Ibid* 174, She feared she was damned. Her one hope was to get "prayed through." She was convinced that when the Lord saved her, she would feel some inward lightning bolt. **1968** *DARE* FW Addit **LA,** *To pray (somebody) through*—To pray for and/or with someone until he receives the gift of the Holy Ghost—that is, begins to shout praises aloud. *Ibid* **OK,** The expression "to pray through" was used by Pentecostal and Holiness sects around Atoka, Oklahoma, in 1949–50 (and no doubt still is), but it meant to pray until one felt he had gotten through to the Holy Ghost. It was not transitive. **2001** *DARE* File—Internet **ceTX,** Praying through refers to the act or [sic] one praying continually for the Holy Spirit to give saving faith. When the Holy Spirit supposedly does this, the person is said to have "prayed through."

p'razza See **piazza**

pre- pref[1] In unstressed position, usu |pri-, prɪ-, prə-|; also freq |pə(r)-| Pronc-spp *p'-, per-, puh-, pur-* Cf **prezactly, pro-** Std sense, var forms.
1830 in 1944 *ADD* **VA,** Purtend. **1835** (1927) Evans *Exped. Rocky Mts.* 14.212 **IN,** I visited this Indian encampment and found them in a dreadful perdicament. **1837** Sherwood *Gaz. GA* 71, *Provincialisms.* . . *Perserves,* for preserves. **1858** Hammett *Piney Woods Tavern* 128, When he see what a perdickement he was in. **1891** *DN* 1.163 **cNY,** [pəˈpæɚd], 'prepared.' **1894** Riley *Armazindy* 55 **IN,** Them baby's eyes / Is my Henry's, jes' p'cise! **1896** Harris *Sister Jane* 311 **GA,** "Percizely!" responded Uncle Jimmy Cosby. **1905** *DN* 3.58 **eNE,** *Metathesis,* especially of *r,* is very frequent: . . perscription. **1909** *DN* 3.356 **eAL, wGA,** *Per-*. . Constantly confused with *pro* and *pre. Perfound, percession, perpose,* etc., *persent, pertend, parpare, perserve,* etc. **1923** (1946) Greer-Petrie *Angeline Doin' Society* 20 **csKY,** She flounced off and pertended she didn't hear him. **1927** Kennedy *Gritny* 137 **sLA,** [Black], A callin' noise like dat noise . . sho do puhdick somh'n. **1936** *AmSp* 11.148 **eTX,** Words whose first syllable is spelled *pre* show a good deal of variety. In the speech of the better educated, the first syllable in such words is pronounced [prɪ], [prɛ], [prə]. . . In less literate speech, this syllable is often [pə], [pɚ]: [pəˈfɝ]; [pɚˈfɝ], for *pre-*

fer. Other examples: *prepare, prescribe, prescription, present* (verb), *presume, pretend, prevent.* **1937** *AmSp* 12.126 **Upstate NY,** Metathesis . . is common, especially when [r] is one of the affected sounds; thus: . . presume [prɪˈzum]. **1941** *AmSp* 16.8 **eTX** [Black], *Prefer, prescribe, pretend,* [pəˈfʌ:], [pəˈpæə], etc. **1963** *Julian Apple Day* 9 **csCA,** Wal, then they was kinda in a perdicament. **1968–70** *DARE* (Qu. B21, *When fine drops of moisture are falling*) Inf **PA**205, Percipitating; (Qu. H75, *When a housewife is going to preserve fruit in jars, she says she's going to _____ some fruit*) Infs **PA**119, **VA**45, Perserve. **1973** Walker *In Love* 62 [Black], My husband pervailed on me for us to go. **1976** Garber *Mountain-ese* 67 **sAppalachians,** I've gotta get my perscription refilled at the drugstore.

pre- pref[2] See **per-** pref[1]

preach v **widely scattered, but less freq NEast, West** See Map
Used in var often interrog phrr to imply that a man is wearing his best clothes; see quots.
1965–70 *DARE* (Qu. W38, *When a man dresses himself up in his best clothes . . he's _____*) 20 Infs, **chiefly Sth, Missip-Ohio Valleys,** Going (out) to preach; **MI**78, **WI**27, Where you going to preach? **MO**37, Are you gonna preach somewhere today? **MO**2, Ask him where he's going to preach; **CA**59, Going to preach tonight; **MS**1, Gone out to preach; **IA**3, **MO**3, (Must be) gonna preach; **MO**20, Ready to preach; **MO**5, 27, **SC**34, Where you gonna preach (today)? **OK**42, Where are you going to preach at this evening? **OK**18, Where are you going to preach today? **VT**8, Going preaching; **OH**97, Where are you preaching?(Qu. W39, *Joking ways of referring to a person's best clothes*) Inf **IN**15, Where you going to preach tonight? **IL**80, Where're you gonna preach? [**NE**11, Preaching clothes;] **PA**42, Where are you preaching? **1975** Gould *ME Lingo* 218, *Preachin'*—The question, "Where're you preachin'?" expresses astonishment at seeing somebody all dressed up. Something of the same Maine sartorial deference toward the church is found in *stiff as a church,* which see.

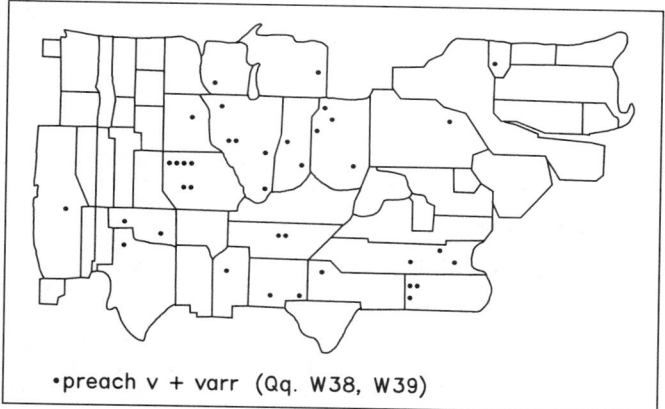

•preach v + varr (Qq. W38, W39)

preach n [*OED2* c1500 →] Cf **preachment**
A sermon, exhortation; preaching.
1832 Kennedy *Swallow Barn* (Schele de Vere *Americanisms*) **VA,** He told us, if we wanted to hear a regular preach, to stand fast. **1858** Green *Reformed Gambler* 119 **Missip R,** Wonder if we can't get some old hoss to give us a preach? That coon over there . . looks like one o' them gospel-shop men. Suppose you ask him to give us a sermon? **1867** Harris *Sut Lovingood Yarns* 59 **TN,** He never said Hell-sarpints onst in the hole preach. **1888** Whitney *Leslie Goldthwaite* 85 **NEng,** A word of his is as much as a whole preach of anybody's else. He says a word now and then, and it hits. **1942** Whipple *Joshua* 78 **UT** (as of c1860), Once more a timid contentment, food for our bellies, good preach for our hearts. **1972** Cooper *NC Mt. Folkl.* 94, *Made a preach*—preached a sermon.

preacher n
1 also *preacher bird:* **=red-eyed vireo.**
1875 Flagg *Birds Seasons New Engl.* 45, The Preacher is more generally known by his note, because he is incessant in his song, and particularly vocal during the heat of our long summer days, when only a few birds are singing. . . Though constantly talking, he takes the part of a deliberative orator, who explains his subject in a few words and then makes a pause for his hearers to reflect upon it. **1903** Dawson *Birds*

OH 1.295, "The Preacher" not infrequently enforces his homilies by hopping down slowly from the tree-tops and bringing the truth home to his hearers. **1914** Eaton *Birds NY* 2.367, It [=the red-eyed vireo] has frequently been called the "preacher bird" from his habit of keeping up his little refrain with almost singsong monotony throughout the day, almost throughout every day of the summer. **1941** *Vermonter* June 137, The preacher-bird—the red-eyed vireo—perched in a tall maple. **1969** Longstreet *Birds FL* 128, At other times, the red-eyed vireo's chattering is so deliberate and argumentative in tone, that the bird has been called "preacher."

2 =**wood ibis.**
   1932 Howell *FL Bird Life* 113, Wood Ibis. . . Other Names: . . Preacher [etc]. **1969** Longstreet *Birds FL* 28, Wood Stork (Ibis)— *Other names:* Preacher; Spanish Buzzard [etc]. *Ibid* 29, Because of their solemn and reproachful expression, they are often referred to as "preachers".

3 also *old preacher*: =**great blue heron. GA**
   1926 *AmSp* 1.417 **Okefenokee GA**, The birds, Preachers [Footnote: Ward's Herons], they're a powerful shy bird. **1955** *Oriole* 20.1.2 **GA**, Great Blue Heron. . . *Preacher* (from its dignified appearance). **1968** *DARE* (Qu. Q10, . . *Water birds and marsh birds*) Inf **GA**20, Old preacher—nickname for great blue heron.

4 =**firefly 1.**
   1947 McDavid *Coll.* **neFL**, Preacher = lightning bug.

5 See **preacher Jack.**

6 Used as a term of address for a Black man; see quots.
   1950 *AmSp* 25.230 **ceMS**, *Preacher.* A male Negro tenant; a term frequently used by plantation owners in address. **1986** Pederson *LAGS Concordance,* 1 inf, **swTN**, Preacher—used by whites to blacks; 1 inf, **swMS**, Preacher—black man called if name not known.

7 See **preacher's seat.**

preacher bird *n*

1 A **phoebe** (here: *Sayornis phoebe*).
   1917 *Wilson Bulletin* 29.2.82 **KY**, *Sayornis phoebe* . . bridge, moss, preacher, or spider bird, Hickman, Ky.

2 See **preacher 1.**

preacher bug *n*
=**praying mantis B.**
   1967 *DARE* (Qu. R9b, *An insect that holds up its front feet as if saying a prayer; not asked in early QRs*) Inf **TX**33, Preacher bug.

preacher flower   See **preacher Jack**

preacher-in-the-pulpit *n*   Also *priest-in-the-pulpit*

1 The showy orchis (*Galearis spectabilis*).
   1837 Darlington *Flora Cestrica* 504 **sePA**, *O[rchis] spectabilis.* . . Showy Orchis. *Vulgo*—Priest in the Pulpit. **1884** Miller *Dict. Engl. Names of Plants* 112, Preacher-in-the-pulpit. *Orchis spectabilis.* **1900** Lyons *Plant Names* 267, [*Orchis*] *spectabilis.* . . Showy Orchis; Gay, Purple or Spring Orchis, Preacher-in-the-pulpit. **1959** Carleton *Index Herb. Plants* 94, *Preacher-in-the-pulpit:* Arum maculatum; Orchis spectabilis; Rhoea discolor.

2 See **preacher Jack.**

preacher Jack *n*   Also *preacher,* ~ *flower,* ~-*in-the-pulpit,* ~-*of-the-flowers,* ~ *plant,* preacher's box, ~ plant   **scattered, but more freq NY, PA, wGt Lakes**   Cf **Jack-the-preacher, minister-of-the-woods**

A jack-in-the-pulpit 1.
   1950 *WELS* (*Jack-in-the-pulpit*) 1 Inf, **ceWI**, Preacher plant, Johnny-the-preacher; 1 Inf, **ceWI**, Preacher plant; 1 inf, **seWI**, Preacher-in-the-pulpit. **1965–70** *DARE* (Qu. S1, . . *Jack-in-the-pulpit*) 20 Infs, **chiefly NY, PA, WI, IA**, Preacher Jack; **WI**37, Preacher Jack [FW: His grandfather used to call it this.]; **NJ**2, **NY**107, 142, **PA**1, 53, Preacher; **MI**9, Preacher flower; **PA**235, Preacher-of-the-flowers; **MI**104, **NC**47, **PA**70, 176, Preacher plant; **AR**42, Preacher's plant; **MN**38, Preacher's box.

preacher lice   See **preacher's lice**

preacher-man *n*   **chiefly Sth, S Midl**

A preacher.
   1863 Burnett *Incidents* 193 [Black], Massa sold me, fore I was old 'nuff to know my mudder, to a preacher man in Florida. **1897** *Overland*

Mth. (2d ser) 29.640 **West**, As soon as we got word of it we were right after 'em, and we put up a job to get this preacher man to go along. **1899** (1912) Green *VA Folk-Speech* 334, *Preacher-man.* . . A preacher. **1913** Kephart *Highlanders* 286 **sAppalachians**, Everywhere in the mountains we hear of biscuit-bread, ham meat . . women-folks, preacher-man. **1930** *VA Qrly. Rev.* 6.248 **S Midl**, There are the analogous compounds . . preacher-man [etc]. **c1960** *Wilson Coll.* **csKY**, *Preacher man.* . . Preacher. **1969** *DARE* (Qu. NN24, *Humorous substitutes for stronger exclamations: "Why the son of a _____!"*) Inf **MO**20, Preacher-man. **1972** Cooper *NC Mt. Folkl.* 95, *Preacher-man*—preacher. **2000** *DARE* File, I recall that one of the big pop hits of 1969 was Dusty Springfield's recording of *Son of a Preacher Man.*

preacher meat *n*   Cf **gospel bird, preacher's gravy**
   1978 *Our Smokies Heritage* Oct 302 **eTN**, Chickens played an important part in the diet of mountain people. . . [S]ome people referred to chickens as "preacher meat", as a chicken was almost always killed when the preacher came to dinner.

preacher nose   See **preacher's nose**

preacher-of-the-flowers   See **preacher Jack**

preacher, pay the *v phr*   **esp Sth, S Midl**
Used to suggest that someone's good fortune has been bought; see quot.
   1965–70 *DARE* (Qu. CC11, *When somebody has had a lot of good luck . . he* _____) Infs **TX**3, **WV**2, Has been paying the preacher; **VA**11, Must be livin' right or paying the preacher; **GA**89, Must have been paying the preacher; **VA**101, Paid his preacher; **IN**69, Paid the preacher; **NC**37, Has paid the preacher good; **TN**66, Pays the preacher; **TX**101, Pays the right preacher; [**VA**41, Must a been paying the salary at church].

preacher plant, preacher's box   See **preacher Jack**

preacher seat   See **preacher's seat**

preacher's gravy *n*   Cf **preacher meat**
   c1970 *DARE* File **sIN**, *Preacher's gravy*—milk gravy; a gravy made with meat drippings, flour and milk—so called because if the preacher drops in you can add more milk and stretch it enough to ask him to remain for the meal.

preacher's lice *n*   Also *preacher lice, priest's* ~*, priester louse* [Cf Dan *præstelus,* Sw *prästlus,* literally "priest-louse, minister-louse," applied to var clinging seeds]
=**beggar ticks 1.**
   1967–68 *DARE* (Qu. S14, . . *Prickly seeds, small and flat, with two prongs at one end, that cling to clothing*) Inf **IA**12, Preacher's lice; **MN**19, Priest's lice; **MN**42, Preacher lice; **WI**58, Priester louses.

preacher's nose *n*   Also *preacher nose, preacher's piece*   **chiefly Sth, S Midl**   See Map
=**pope's nose 1.**
   1965–70 *DARE* (Qu. K73, . . *Names . . for the rump of a cooked chicken*) 13 Infs, **chiefly Sth, S Midl**, Preacher's nose; **AR**52, **FL**2, Preacher's piece; **MS**81, Preacher nose. **1999** *DARE* File, Growing up in Mississippi and Arkansas with Methodist and Baptist kinfolk, I always heard it called the preacher's nose.

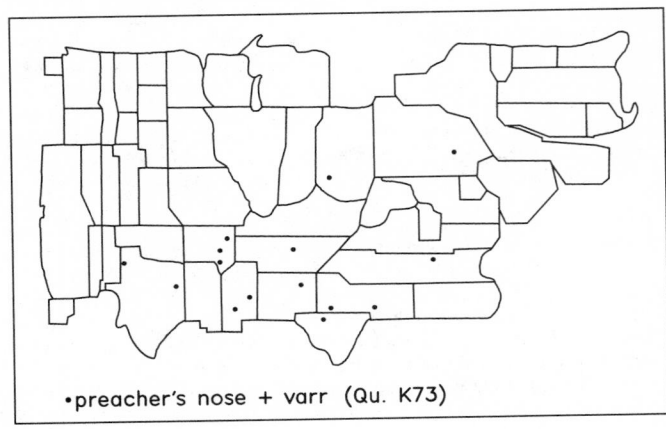

•preacher's nose + varr (Qu. K73)

preacher's plant See **preacher Jack**

preacher's seat n Also *preacher (seat)*
See quots.

1953 Randolph–Wilson *Down in Holler* 273 **Ozarks,** *Preacher's seat. . .* A peculiar semirecumbent position. When boys in swimming "do the preacher's seat," they leap into the water buttocks down, with the head and feet up. **1984** *DARE* File **csPA** (as of 1978), Preacher—(swimming) a dive off the board with both hands together in prayer position. **1986** Pederson *LAGS Concordance,* 1 inf, **cGA,** Preacher seat—hitting flat on your bottom.

preaching n [Scots, nIr dial] **chiefly Sth, S Midl**
A religious service.

1826 Flint *Recollections* 62 **KY,** The bell of the court-house . . would, on a half hour's previous notice, generally assemble a full audience, to what is here technically called "a preaching." **1836** (1937) Poole *Yankee School Teacher* 20.657 **LA,** The Sabbath. Attended a "preaching" in the courthouse. Heard a discourse from Mat. 5th by Dr. Baker. **1860** (1937) Lewis *Diary Pike's Peak* 14.219 **PA,** Attended Campbellite preaching . . this morn. **1895** *DN* 1.392 **KY,** Preachin': church service. **1903** *DN* 2.325 **seMO,** Preaching. . . Meeting; service. 'We all went to preaching last Sunday.' **1906** *DN* 3.122 **sIN,** Preachin. . . Religious service of any kind. "Ther's preachin' to-night." *Ibid* 151 **nwAR,** Preaching. . . Church; divine service. "They attended preaching here last Sunday." **1909** *DN* 3.359 **eAL, wGA,** Preachin(g). . . Church services. **1923** in 1952 Mathes *Tall Tales* 6 **sAppalachians,** The Lord willin', I aim to do it. I reckon some of you-uns 'll be out to the preachin'. **1967** Fetterman *Stinking Creek* 47 **seKY,** He won't let them go in that store during preachin'. People go into preachin' and don't leave until it breaks. **1986** Pederson *LAGS Concordance,* 1 inf, **ceMS,** Preaching—church service; 1 inf, **seAL,** Let's go to preaching—to church; 1 inf, **cMS,** When preaching's over—the church service.

preaching funeral See **funeral B1**

preachment n [*OED2* c1330 →] Cf **preach** n
A sermon; a tiresome discourse.

1774 (1961) Adams *Diary* 2.132 **MA,** [W]e heard . . a dutchified english Prayer and Preachment. **1840** *S. Lit. Messenger* Mar 162, But what the devil have you got such a congregation [=a mob] here for? Is it a street preachment? Oh I remember; Dad is a bit of a politician, and means to harangue you. **1913** Morley *Carolina Mts.* 14, She began going to church and profiting according to her light on the "preachment." **1931** Randolph *Ozarks* 75, The hillman still calls a sermon a *preachment,* just as Shakespeare did. **1942** (1971) Campbell *Cloud-Walking* 135 **seKY,** That's too pretty and calm-like to make a loud preachment about.

preach one's funeral See **funeral B2**

preambulator See **perambulator**

'preciate See **appreciate**

precipitate n Pronc-spp *pacifity, percipity*
Std sense, var forms.

1966 Welsch *Treas. NE Folkl.* 154 (as of 1880s), Red percipity . . was . . rubbed into our scalps. **1967** *DARE* FW Addit **AR**51, Red pacifity [pəˈsɪfɨtɪ]—salve for getting rid of head lice.

prehaps See **perhaps**

presackly See **prezactly**

presarve See **preserve**

Presbytery n, hence adj, n *Presbyterian* Pronc-spp *Prasbattery, Presbattery, Presbyterium, Presmuterian, Prisbeterun*
Std senses, var forms.

1827 (1939) Sherwood *Gaz. GA* 139, Provincialisms. . . Presbattery, for Presbytery. **1837** Sherwood *Gaz. GA* 71, Provincialisms. . . Prasbattery, for Presbytery. **1843** (1916) Hall *New Purchase* 372 **IN,** Prisbeteruns and tother baby sprinklurs. **1929** *WV Review* Oct 30, Presbyterian with a long *by* strongly accented. **1937** (1972) *Amer. Slave* 2.94 **SC,** You know he's a good 'Presmuterian' (Presbyterian). **1942** Hall *Smoky Mt. Speech* 66 **eTN, wNC,** Presbyterian [ˌprɛzbəˈtæərən]. **1954** in 1958 Brewer *Dog Ghosts* 83 **eTX** [Black], De bigges' white Presbyterium chu'ch.

presentation quilt n Also *presentation album*
=**album quilt.**

1949 Ickis *Quilt Making* 207, The Album or Presentation Quilts are made up of elaborately designed blocks, each created and carefully stitched by a different woman. As the name indicated, they expressed friendship or admiration for a particular person. **1974** Newman *Quilting* 87, There are album, presentation, or friendship quilts made up of fanciful blocks, each created by a different person. **1991** *Quilting Today* June/July 10, Twentieth-century quilt scholars have enjoyed both recounting and speculating upon Album Quilt themes. "Legacy quilts," . . "Presentation Albums," "Friendship quilts," . . and "Quotation quilts" abound.

preserve n Pronc-spp *perserve, presarve,* aphet *sarve* Cf **pre-pref**[1], **serve** v
A Forms.

1837 Sherwood *Gaz. GA* 71, *Provincialisms. . . Perserves,* for preserves. **1843** (1916) Hall *New Purchase* 155 **IN,** Preserved apples, preserved water melon-rinds, and preserved red peppers and tomatoes—all termed, for brevity's sake, (like words in Webster's dictionary,) "'sarves." **1976** Garber *Mountain-ese* 71 **sAppalachians,** Ma put up two dozen jars uv grape presarves last week. **1985** *DARE* File **WV,** Sarves: In West Virginia, canned preserves.

B Senses.

1 usu pl: Canned fruit. **chiefly Sth, S Midl** See Map Note: *Preserves* in the sense of "jam" is widespread and not included here.

1843 [see **A** above]. **1899** (1912) Green *VA Folk-Speech* 334, *Preserves. . .* Fruits preserved in sugar. [*DARE* Ed: This quot may instead refer to a different food item.] **1926** *AmSp* 2.78 **ME,** Of course pie will be in evidence, as well as cookies and preserves. Preserves will very likely be home-canned fruit, rather than the more concentrated confections that you would find in the other states. **1965–70** *DARE* (Qu. H75, *When a housewife is going to preserve fruit in jars, she says she's going to _____ some fruit*) 12 Infs, **chiefly Sth, S Midl,** Make (some) preserves; **FL**17, Make preserves or can fruit; **DC**1, Make preserves; today I did my peaches, etc; **KY**79, Make preserve; (Qu. H63, *Kinds of desserts*) Inf **NM**12, Preserves; **SC**3, Peach preserves; apples and peaches grow here; **MO**38, Watermelon preserves; (Qu. H66b, *The sweet liquid that you pour over ice cream*) Infs **KY**79, **MS**73, Preserves; **NC**44, **LA**33, Strawberry preserve(s). **1969** *DARE* Tape **CT**21, [FW:] What's the difference between jams and preserves? [Inf:] Preserves, well that would be the fruit itself, to me, like you put up halves of peaches in syrup. **1985** [see **A** above]. [**1986** Pederson *LAGS Concordance (Cling peach)* 1 inf, **ceTX,** Preserving peach.]

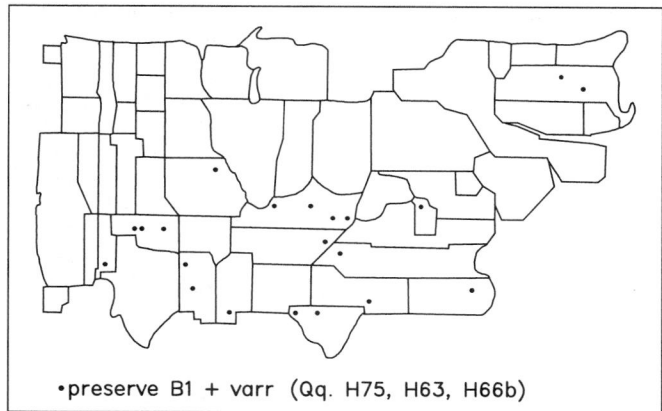

•preserve B1 + varr (Qq. H75, H63, H66b)

2 A piece of dried apple. Cf *snit* (at **schnitz** n[1])
1986 Pederson *LAGS Concordance (Dried pieces of apple)* 1 inf, **seFL,** Apple preserves; 1 inf, **seMS,** Preserves; 1 inf, **cnGA,** Preserves—dried apples; 1 inf, **swMS,** Dry preserve.

pres-eye-dent See **president**

'preshate See **appreciate**

president n Usu |ˈprɛzəˌdənt, -ɨˌdɛnt|; also |ˈprɛzəˌdɪnt| Pronc-spp *pres-eye-dent, prezzydent, prisidint* Cf **-ment A**
Std sense, var forms.

1893 Shands *MS Speech* 28, *-ent*. . . It is a characteristic of the illiterate white inhabitants of the pine district of Mississippi to give special emphasis to the pronunciation of this syllable when final; as, président. **1907** *DN* 3.197 **seNH,** *Prisidint*. . . President. "Any news from the prisidint?" Unusual. **1909** *DN* 3.349 **eAL, wGA,** *-ment, suffix.* Commonly with strongly accented pronunciation in *president, settlement, compliment,* etc. **1922** Gonzales *Black Border* 320 **sSC, GA coasts** [Gullah glossary], *Prezzydent*—president. **1933** Rawlings *South Moon* 262 **nFL,** Take hit to Washin'ton to the pres-eye-dent. **1936** *AmSp* 11.162 **eTX,** *President* . . in East Texas usually [carries] secondary stress on the final syllable, which is pronounced with nasalized [ĭ] . . ['prɛzə,dĭnt]. **1968** *DARE* (Qu. GG19b) Inf **MO9,** ['prɛzɪ,dɨnt].

Presmuterian See **Presbytery**

prespirate See **perspirate**

prespiration See **perspiration**

prespire See **perspire**

press n[1]

1 also in combs: Any of var kinds of furniture for the storage of clothes and other household items; a wardrobe, cabinet, buffet, or chest of drawers. **scattered, but chiefly Sth, S Midl** See Map Cf **clothespress 1, Jackson press**

1806 (1970) Webster *Compendious Dict.* 235, *Press,* . . a case for clothes. [*DARE* Ed: This entry was carried over from Webster's English model.] **1899** (1912) Green *VA Folk-Speech* 334, *Press*. . . An upright case or cupboard in which clothes, books, china, or other articles are kept. Book-press. **1936** *Esquire* Nov 56 **KY,** I take one of Finn's white shirts out of the press for him. **1939** *AmSp* 14.29 **SC** [Citadel argot], *Press*. . . A large piece of furniture, comprising a series of shelves and a hanging space, used for storing a cadet's authorized possessions (unauthorized possessions are usually kept in the laundry bag). **1941** *LANE* Map 338 *(Clothes closet)* **NEng,** *Clothes press* and *wardrobe* denoting a piece of furniture (not a built-in recess) are given in the commentary. . . 12 infs, Clothes press; 2 infs, Press. **c1960** *Wilson Coll.* **csKY,** *Press:* . . A movable or separate place to hang clothes; . . a wardrobe. **1965–70** *DARE* (Qu. E1, *A piece of furniture that stands against the wall, and you hang clothes in/on it)* Infs **IN30, KY61, OH61, SC4, 22, 46, 51, TN1, VA63,** Press; (Qu. E3, *A piece of furniture in which you lay clothes flat)* Infs **AR38, NJ38, TX65,** Press; **NJ38,** Linen press; (Qu. E5, *A piece of furniture with a flat top for keeping tablecloths, dishes, and such)* Infs **KY61, TN1, 5, TX91,** Press; **NC17,** China press; **CA36,** Linen press. [14 of 16 Infs old] **1967–68** *DARE* FW Addit **CO,** *Press*—corner, solid wood, also called *cupboard* and *armoire;* **VA28,** *Press*—a cabinet for storing dishes or food in drawers and/or on shelves—a general term. Three types: *pie press*—not too tall; had tin doors with holes punched in them in a certain pattern, *three-cornered press, corner cupboard.* **1971** Wood *Vocab. Change* 49, The piece of furniture in which clothes can be hung is ordinarily called a *wardrobe.* It synonyms, *clothes press* and *press* occur in Tennessee, Georgia, Alabama, Florida, and Oklahoma. **1976** Ryland *Richmond Co. VA* 375, *Press*—a tall "wardrobe," clothespress, used in bedrooms before closets were built-in; also, china-press, for china. **1986** Pederson *LAGS Concordance,* 1 inf, **cLA,** *Press*—two doors, shelves, hanging space, heavy, tall; 1 inf, **cnMS,** China press—made of cheaper wood; like a closet.

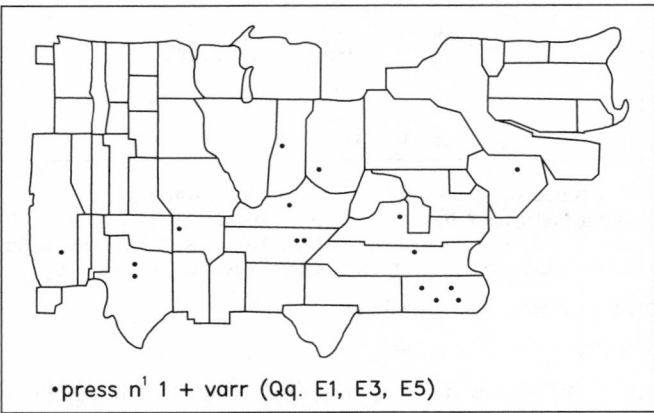

•press n[1] 1 + varr (Qq. E1, E3, E5)

2 Transf: a closet. Cf **clothespress 2**

1941 *LANE* Map 338 *(Clothes closet)* **NEng,** The map shows the terms . . denoting a small room or built-in recess in the wall with a door or a curtain. . . [*Clothes press* is widespread;] 5 infs, Press. **1965–70** *DARE* (Qu. D7, *A small space anywhere in a house where you can hide things or get them out of the way)* Infs **CT26, IL129, KY52, PA134, VA104,** Press; (Qu. D8, *The small room next to the kitchen [in older houses] where dishes and sometimes foods are kept)* Inf **KY55,** Press; (Qu. E2, *A built-in space in a room for hanging clothes)* Infs **AL43, IN82, KY52, OH59, 61, PA134,** Press. **1966** Dakin *Dial. Vocab. Ohio R. Valley* 2.45, *Clothes closet.* . . Along the Ohio River from the Big Sandy to the Pennsylvania border and in the Muskingum Valley south of the National Road *(clothes) press* is the usual term. . . In Ohio west of the Scioto and in Indiana *(clothes) press* is used, usually in addition to *closet,* by scattered informants. . . In Kentucky scattered informants know *(clothes) press* or have heard others use it, but it apparently has had little currency other than in the northeastern Mountain region settled by expansion from the Big Sandy and more closely related to adjoining West Virginia (where *clothes press* is fairly common along the Ohio). **1969** *DARE* Tape **KY56,** Press—a closet-type place to put sticks of tobacco in. **1971** Wood *Vocab. Change* 49 **Sth,** When a storage room is a part of the floor plan, it is ordinarily called a *closet* or a *clothes closet.* . . *Press* and *clothes press* have scattered occurrences. **1973** Allen *LAUM* 1.168 **Upper MW** (as of c1950), *Clothes closet* (built in). . . 1 inf, **swIA,** Press; [2 infs, **sMN,** Clothes press]. **1976** Lynn–Vecsey *Loretta Lynn* 1 **eKY,** In eastern Kentucky we say the word "press" instead of "closet."

3 A pressing situation. [*OED2 press* sb.[1] 3 "*Obs.* or *arch.*"]

1932 Stribling *Store* 455 **AL,** "Toussaint was in a press," she called back in her soft voice. "I thought I would help him out." **1967** Fetterman *Stinking Creek* 51 **seKY,** So much one season, so much another season; it keeps me in a press.

4 Fig: see quot Cf **oven 2**

1952 Brown *NC Folkl.* 1.579, *Press, in the*. . . *Foetus in utero.* "He has eight children and another one in the press."

press n[2] See **press peach**

press v, hence ppl adj *pressed* *among Black speakers*
To remove the natural tight curls from hair; to straighten (the hair); hence n *presser* an iron used to do this.

1970 *DARE* Tape **TN46,** Let me tell you how the natural came about: Girl, everybody came on that march with their hair all pressed and curled and looking good, honey. And this rain came. . . This girl, she wasn't getting her hair fixed, but she had it all slicked back, you know, as best as she could. . . She said, "Lord, my hair is a mess." . . Stokely Carmichael said, "Why don't y'all let it go like that; just wear it. . . be natural." **1970** *DARE* FW Addit **KY** [Black], To straighten the hair with a hot iron. **1986** Pederson *LAGS Concordance (Hairstyles)* 1 inf, **cAR,** Pressed = straightened; 1 inf, **neMS,** Pressed; 1 inf, **seMS,** Presser—for straightening hair; of iron; heated. [All infs Black] **1994** Smitherman *Black Talk* 184, *Press*—To *straighten* the hair by using a hot comb.

press board n Also *pressing board*
An ironing board, esp a small one designed spec for sleeves or trouser legs.

1849 Foster *NY in Slices* 14 **NYC,** The press-board has been placed across the back corner of the shop. **1862** (1882) Stowe *Pearl of Orr's Is.* 29 **ME,** That dignitary sits . . looking majestically over the press-board on her knee, where she is pressing the next year's Sunday vest of Zephaniah Pennel. **1876** Knight *Amer. Mech. Dict.* 3.1785, *Pressing-board.* . . An ironing-board upon which seams are pressed. **1890** Holley *Samantha among Brethren* 78 **NY,** She had her press-board in her hand and a coat over her arm—. **1896** Harris *Sister Jane* 17 **GA,** Make that nigger fetch you a chair—I've got this pressboard on my lap, or I'd fetch it myself. **1912** Green *VA Folk-Speech* 335, *Pressing board.* . . A board about three feet long, six inches wide at one end and eight at the other, to slip into the legs of trowsers to press the seams on. **1939** M.B. Picken *Lang. Fashion* 116 *(OED2)*, *Pressboard,* padded board, a small ironing board, used for pressing fabrics when sewing.

pressed adj *among Black speakers*
1 See **press** v.
2 Well dressed.
1971 Roberts *Third Ear* np [Black], *Pressed* . . to be very well dressed. **1972** Claerbaut *Black Jargon* 76, *Pressed*. . . neatly dressed; fashionably

attired: *The cat is pressed, man!* **1972** Kochman *Rappin'* 165 [Black], Being well dressed is . . expressed kinetically ("pressed"), and . . the term refers to a favored norm.

pressed meat (or souse) See **press meat**

presser See **press** v

pressing board See **press board**

pressing club Also *pressing parlor,* ~ *shop* **esp Sth** *old-fash*
A clothes cleaning and pressing establishment.

1967 Green *Horse Tradin'* 281 **TX**, I had been keeping a special ordered blue serge suit in the pressing parlor in town, and I would ride in horseback, put my horse in a corral next to the feed mill, then go to the pressing parlor and the barbershop and get smoothed off and dressed up. **1969** Green *Wild Cow Tales* 92 **West**, It wasn't much of a hotel—just an old frame buildin' with eight or ten rooms upstairs and the dining room and lobby and a small pressin' parlor at the back of the buildin' on the ground floor. **1970** *Thompson Coll.* **cnAL** (as of 1920s), *Pressing club* . . establishment where clothes are pressed (and usually cleaned too). **1971** *DARE* File **GA**, Pressing club—a cooperative dry-cleaning and clothes-pressing establishment. In Georgia, etc. Now black usage; was also white c1892. **1984** Wilder *You All Spoken Here* 170 **Sth**, *Pressing club:* Predecessor of dry cleaning plants. **1986** Pederson *LAGS Concordance,* 1 inf, **csGA**, Pressing club—for cleaning unwashable material; 1 inf, **ceTX**, Pressing shop—in old days; 1 inf, **ceMS**, Pressing shops. [All infs old]

press meat n Also *pressed meat,* ~ *souse* **Sth, S Midl** See Map
=**headcheese 1.** Note: *Pressed meat* as a generic term for processed meat products appears to be widespread; only the specific application to headcheese is illustrated here.

1956 Ker *Vocab. W. TX* 274, *Processed meat loaf made of hogs' jowls. . .* press meat. [3 of 67 infs] **c1960** *Wilson Coll.* **csKY**, *Pressmeat: . .* A fairly common name, formerly, for souse. **1965–70** *DARE* (Qu. H43, *Foods made from parts of the head and inner organs of an animal*) 12 Infs, **scattered Sth, S Midl**, Press meat; **GA**8, 75, 79, 88, **KY**22, 71, Pressed meat; **AL**52, Pressed souse; (Qu. H45, *Dishes made with meat, fish, or poultry that everybody around here would know, but that people in other places might not*) Inf **TN**95, Pressed meat. **1966** Dakin *Dial. Vocab. Ohio R. Valley* 2.339, *Press(ed) meat* (usually uninflected) is common west of the Bluegrass. This term, which seems to be a synonym for *souse,* is rare in the Bluegrass and unknown in the Mountains. It does not appear north of the Ohio. **1967** *Good Old Days* 4.5.33 **nwAR**, She did take the ears, feet and head of the hog and convert them into pressmeat or souse. This can still be bought in some supermarkets today, but it is expensive, is considered a delicacy. **1967** *DARE* Tape **SC**46, [FW:] Did you ever have anything you call press meat? [Inf:] That's the same thing as souse meat. When they fix this souse meat, put it in a container. I've seen old time people put it in a flat, big flat pan, put a lid over it, maybe a wooden lid and set heavy irons on top of it, to press it. Press it down tight . . and have vinegar poured over it. . . The feet and head cooked together would stick together without pressing. I don't know why they wanted to press it. **1971** Wood *Vocab. Change* 350 **Sth**, [*A Pork Loaf*—The response *pressed meat* is found almost entirely in northern Georgia.] **1972** *PADS* 58.20 **cwAL**, *Pressed meat . .* occurs as a primary response (1 [of 27 infs]) and as an alternate

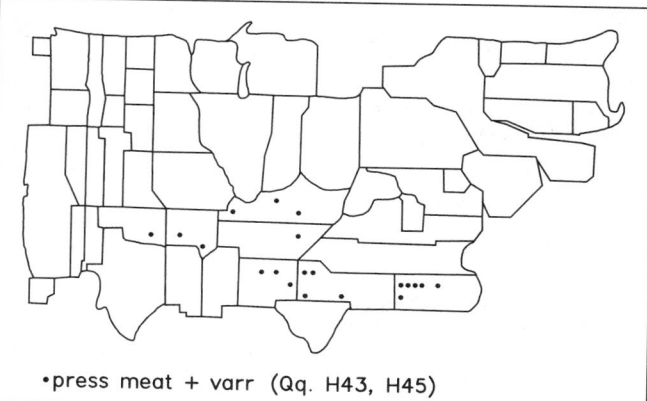

•press meat + varr (Qq. H43, H45)

to *souse meat* (4). **1972** *Atlanta Letters* **nwGA**, I have "Souther-isms" [sic] and use them often in my conversation—much to the dismay of my modern children. . . Press meat. **1973** Gawthrop *Dial. Calumet* 72 **nwIN**, *Pressed meat loaf made of hogs' jowls, head, etc.* . . pressed meat 4 [of 125 infs]. **1986** Pederson *LAGS Concordance* **Gulf Region** *(Headcheese)* 81 infs, 53 **GA**, Press meat; 15 infs, Pressed meat; *(Liver sausage)* 4 infs, Press meat; *(Scrapple)* 4 infs, Press meat.

press peach n Also *hard-press peach, press, press-seed peach, press-stone* ~ **chiefly Sth** See Map Cf **clingstone, plum peach**
A peach in which the flesh adheres to the seed.

1912 Green *VA Folk-Speech* 335, *Presses. . . Press-peaches;* peaches the flesh of which clings to the seed. **1939** Harris *Purslane* 74 **cNC**, Up the hill to the right was the peach orchard with its luscious yellow clearseeds and big red presses flavoring the air. **1949** Kurath *Word Geog.* 72, *Cling-stone peach. . .* The old Southern terms are *press peach* and *plum peach. Press peach* is used in a widening belt that runs from lower Delaware to Georgia. The greater part of South Carolina and the eastern half of North Carolina have this expression, but in Virginia it is now confined to the points of land on Chesapeake Bay. **1955** *PADS* 23.42 **e,cSC, eNC, seGA**, *Press peach* 'clingstone' (not in the cities of Charleston or Beaufort). **1961** Folk *Word Atlas N. LA* map 1004, Peach whose meat sticks to seed . . cling peach 62% [of 275 infs] . . press peach 26%. **1962** Atwood *Vocab. TX* 60, *Clingstone peach. . .* Neither the Virginia *plum peach . .* nor the Carolina *press peach . .* can be said to have established itself; both usages are confined to informants over sixty. **1965–70** *DARE* (Qu. I52, *The kind of a peach where the hard center is tight to the flesh*) 40 Infs, **chiefly Sth**, Press peach; **AL**8, **FL**18, 19, 26, 28, **NC**5, 18, 25, Press; **NC**15, Press peaches; **LA**28, Press-stone peach; [(Qu. I51, *The kind of a peach where the hard center is loose*) Inf **MS**13, Pressed peach]. **1968** *DARE* Tape **GA**69, [FW:] I notice you refer to clingstone and freestone. . . Because I've heard people around here say press peaches, now, what are those? [Inf:] A press peach is a clingstone. **c1970** Pederson *Dial. Surv. Rural GA* **seGA** (*What do you call a peach whose meat sticks to the seed?*) 36 [of 64 infs], Press (peach); 4 infs, Press-stone (peach); 1 inf, Press-seed; 1 inf, Hard-press peach. **1971** Wood *Vocab. Change* 42, *Peaches. . . Press peach* is the second choice [to *cling, cling peach,* or *clingstone*] in Georgia and close to that position in Mississippi, Florida, and Louisiana. **1990** Pederson *LAGS Regional Matrix* 400, [156 infs, **chiefly Sth**, Press (peach).]

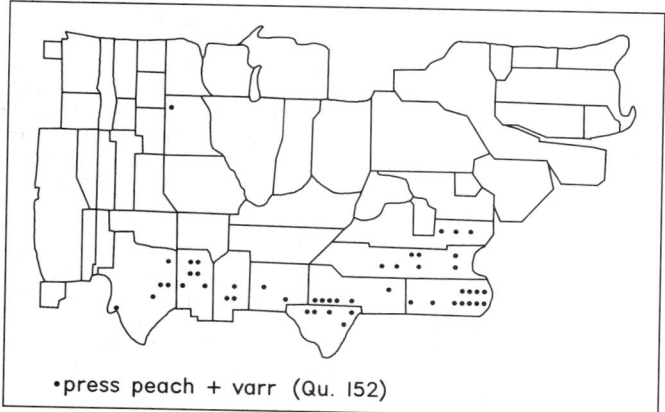

•press peach + varr (Qu. I52)

press pine n
See quot.

1970 *DARE* (Qu. T17, . . *Kinds of pine trees;* not asked in early QRs) Inf **KY**80, Press pine—flat, almost leaf-like needle.

press-seed (or -stone) peach See **press peach**

pret- See **pretty A2a**

pretickelar, preticklar See **particular**

pretty adj, adv, n Usu |ˈprɪti, -ɪ, ˈprɪdi, -ɪ|; freq |ˈpɜˈti, ˈpɜˈdi|; for addit varr see **A** below
A Forms.
1 Full forms.
a eye-dial sp *pritty.*
1815 Humphreys *Yankey in England* 107, *Pritty,* pretty. **1898** Lloyd

Country Life 21 **AL,** Now, Miss Elvira want [=wasn't] to say pritty, but she was good and sweet. **1912** Green *VA Folk-Speech* 335, *Pritty. . .* For *pretty.*

b |'pɜ(r)ti, -ɪ, 'pɜ(r)di, -ɪ|; pronc-spp *purty, purdy.*   For addit pronc and sp varr see quots

1830 in 1944 *ADD* **VA,** Purty. **1843** (1916) Hall *New Purchase* 412 **IN,** Perttee powerful smart feller! **1851** [see **C1b** below]. **1871** Eggleston *Hoosier Schoolmaster* 63 **sIN,** You're a purty gal, a'n't you? **1891** *DN* 1.163 **cNY,** [pɜˈti] < pretty. **1895** *DN* 1.375 **seKY, eTN, wNC,** Purty. **1905** *DN* 3.103 **nwAR,** ['pɜˈti]. **1915** *DN* 4.188 **swVA,** *Purt, purty.* Variants of *pretty.* **1923** *DN* 5.218 **swMO,** *Purty lookin'.* **1932** Randolph *Ozark Mt. Folks* 130, Purty a critter as ever was saw in these parts. **1932** Stong *State Fair* 96 **IA,** The madder he [=a hog] gets the purtier he is. **1933** *AmSp* 8.45 **neNY,** [pɜˈti]. **1936** [see **A1c** below]. **1938** Rawlings *Yearling* 23 **nFL,** There ain't been a purty Baxter since the name begun. **1941** *LANE* Map 457, [The adj *pretty* was elicited, usu in the context *pretty dress.* After proncs of the type ['prɪti] the commonest type was ['puti], but this was also regarded as obsolete by 24 infs, old-fashioned by 21, and "older but natural" by another 8. Next most freq were those of the type ['pɜti, pɚti]. Other significant types recorded, in descending order of frequency were: ['pɪti, 'pɤti, 'preti, 'puɪti, 'pruti, 'prʏti, 'pruti, 'pʌti].] **1942** Hall *Smoky Mt. Speech* 17 **wNC, eTN,** *Pretty,* usually ['pɜˈti], sometimes ['puɚti], rarely ['prɪti], ['prɜti]. **1943** *LANE* Map 497, [The adv *pretty* was elicited in the context *pretty well* & similar responses to "How are you?" In general the distribution of pronc types is similar to that for the adj on Map 457, but proncs of the type ['pɜti, 'pɚti] are proportionally more freq both in relation to the std type ['prɪti] and to ['puti].] *Ibid* Map 714 *(Almost),* [The adverb *pretty* was recorded in the contexts *pretty near* or *pretty nigh.* The main full proncs recorded were, in descending order of frequency, ['puti], ['prɪti], and ['pɚti], with a few instances of ['pɪti] and ['pɤti]. The main types of reduced forms were [pɚt] and [prɪt], with a few instances of ['prɪtn̩], [prut], [prʏt] and [put]. In addition, the commentary records an instance of [put nais] for *pretty nice.*] **1950** Bissell *Stretch on River* 89 **eMO,** I grant you, it's purdy in a way. **c1960** Wilson *Coll.* **csKY,** Pretty is usually ['puɚti], rarely ['pɜˈti/]. **1965–70** *DARE* (Qu. LL30) [Note: All proncs of *pretty* in resp to this question were in the combs *pretty near(ly), pretty nigh.* In these combs the first syllable of *pretty* may have primary or secondary stress; when it is reduced to a single syllable it may also be unstressed.] 60 Infs, **scattered,** [proncs of the types [prɪti, -ɪ, prɪdi, -ɪ, prɪdi, -ɪ]]; **AL6, OH92, PA175, TX19,** [prɪtə]; **WI48,** 51, [prʌti]; **MA16,** [prɪʔə]; **IA31,** [pretɪ]; **WI27,** [pruti]; 16 Infs, **scattered,** [proncs of the types [pɚti, -ɪ, pɚdi]]; 8 Infs, **scattered,** [proncs of the types [pɚtə, pɚdə]]; **SC2,** 3, [proncs of the type [pʌɚti]]; **SC59,** [puɚti]; **NY83,** [pudɪ]; 25 Infs, **scattered,** [proncs of the type [pɚt, pɚd, pʌɚt]]; **NY68,** 94, **TN12,** 23, **TX29,** [proncs of the type [pɚti]]; **CA10,** [pɚʔ]; **IL126,** [pɛɚt]; 19 Infs, **scattered,** [proncs of the types [prɪt, prɪt]]; **CA107,** [prɪtn̩]; **IA31,** [pret]; **WI21,** [prɪd]; **KY72,** [pɛd]; **SC9,** [put]; (Qu. KK27) [Note: Proncs of *pretty* in resp to this question were recorded sporadically in combs such as *pretty spry, pretty chipper.*] 18 Infs, **scattered,** [proncs of the types [prɪti, -ɪ, prɪdi, -ɪ, prɪdɪ, -ɪ]]; **TX95** [prɪdə]; 12 Infs, **scattered,** [proncs of the types [pɚti, -ɪ, pɚdi, -ɪ]]; **WI51,** [prəti]; **KS20,** [preˆti]; (Qu. B1, . . *It's a _____ day*) Inf **TX90,** Purdy; (Qu. W30) Inf **IA22,** Purty; **MO35,** Purdy it up; (Qu. W36) Inf **TX89,** Painted up purdy good; (Qu. W37) Inf **TX89,** Purtied up; (Qu. EE34, . . *A child's toy*) Inf **TN59,** Purty; (Qu. GG11) Inf **NY219,** Purty anxious; (Qu. GG26) Inf **CA192,** Purty near folded; (Qu. KK45) Inf **TN23,** Purty near got hurt; (Qu. MM5) Inf **IL39,** Prit nigh; (Qu. MM6) Inf **TN20,** Purty nigh. **1989** Pederson *LAGS Tech. Index* 95, [Proncs of the adj *pretty* were elicited, esp in the context "pretty dress"; the main pronc types and the numbers of infs using them were: ['prɪti] 380, ['preti] 12, ['pɜˈti] 170, ['puɚti] 24, ['pruti] 48, ['prʌti] 17, [puti] 17, ['pʌti] 7, ['pɜˈti] 8.] **1990** Smith *Understanding Speaking S. Lang.* 6, *Perty.* **1991** Heat Moon *PrairyErth* 73 **ceKS,** He was purta near all crippled up and couldn't ride.

c |'puti, 'pudi, 'pʌti, 'pʌdi|; pronc-spp *pooty, putty.*   For addit pronc and sp varr see quots   **esp NEast, Sth** *old-fash*

1825 Neal *Brother Jonathan* 1.5 **CT,** A military personage, of "pootty considerable" authority, in the province of Connecticut. **1834** Davis *Letters Downing* 62 **NY,** I've all along tho't Jack a pooty smartish sort of a chap. **1843** (1916) Hall *New Purchase* 151 **IN,** I starts off puttee considerable peert and brisk. **1848** Lowell *Biglow* 6 **'Upcountry' MA,** I dunno but wut it 's pooty / Trainin' round in bobtail coats,—/ But it 's curus Christian dooty / This ere cuttin' folks's throats. **1848** in 1956 Eliason *Tarheel Talk* 316 **cnNC,** Putta. **1849** *Ibid* **cnNC,** Puty.

1869 Stowe *Oldtown Folks* 196 **MA,** Had a putty good time in the old house, I reckon. **1884** Smith *Bill Arp's Scrap Book* 72 **nwGA,** Its as putty as a rainbow. **1884** *Anglia* 7.273 **Sth, S Midl** [Black], To be putty tollerbul sartin = to be pretty certain. **1888** Jones *Negro Myths* 63 **GA coast,** Eh hab een eh pocket er pooty, smoode rock, bout de size ob er tukrey agg. **1893** Shands *MS Speech* 50, *Pooty* [puti]—Negro and illiterate white for *pretty.* **1894** *DN* 1.333 **NJ,** Pretty: pron. [pɜˈti, puti]. **1906** *DN* 3.152 **nwAR,** Everybody rag as pooty ['puti] as you can. **1908** *DN* 3.284 **eAL, wGA,** Double comparatives . . are frequent, as in . . mô puttier. **1909** *DN* 3.398 **nwAR,** He got putty het up by the argument. **1919** [see **A2c** below]. **1927** Ruppenthal *Coll.* **KS,** *Pooty . .* pron. to rime with foot . . pretty. **1930** in 1944 *ADD* **eVA** [Black], |pʌdi|. Ah meets 'm puddy neah ev'y meetin night. **1936** *AmSp* 11.245 **eTX,** Pretty—*[Plantation-Type]* ['pʌti]—*[Hill-Type]* ['pɜˈti]—*[Negro]* ['puti]. [Footnote: In ['pɜˈti] the first syllable is extremely short.] **1941** [see **A1b** above]. **1943** [see **A1b** above]. **1965–70** [see **A1b** above]. **1970** *DARE* Tape **CA193,** Come out putty [p'uɹi] near even with the depot. **1989** [see **A1b** above].

d |'pruti, -di; 'prɪti; 'preti, -di|; pronc-sp *prooty.*   For addit pronc and sp varr see quots

1850 in 1956 Eliason *Tarheel Talk* 316 **cnNC,** Pruty. **1916** *DN* 4.279 **NE,** *Pratty. . .* Pretty: infrequent. **1926** *AmSp* 1.409 **Okefenokee GA,** The island . . looked prooty an' green. **1937** in 1944 *ADD* **swVA,** |pruˈdi|. A pretty girl. **1937** *AmSp* 12.287 **Shenandoah Valley VA,** *Pretty* sometimes becomes ['predi] or [preti]. **1938** *AmSp* 8.51 **Boston MA,** [ðə 'pruti gɜl]. **1941** [see **A1b** above]. **1943** [see **A1b** above]. **1965–70** [see **A1b** above]. **1989** [see **A1b** above].

2 Reduced forms, usu in combs *pretty near(ly), pretty nigh.*

a |prɪt(n̩)-, prut-, pret-|; pronc-spp *pret-, prit-, prid-, prin-.* For addit pronc and sp varr see quots

1943 [see **A1b** above]. **1965–70** [see **A1b** above]. **1969** *AmSp* 44.238 **s,cIN,** Her dress was so short you could pret' near see her hieronymus. **1969–70** *DARE* Tape **CA160,** While we were gone the armistice [of WWI] was signed, and time we got back they'd discharged [prɪdnɪɚ] everybody, so they kept me; **CA196,** If they wanted to go anywhere, they ['prɪtnɪɚ] had to go on snowshoes or they didn't get there; **CA200,** There are very few of us left. They [prɪtnɪɚ] all passed away. **1975** Gainer *Witches* 15 **sAppalachians,** Prin nearly . . almost. "He choked her prin nearly to death." **1978** Kalibabky *Hawdaw* **neMN,** Well, we're pretnear there. Only five miles to go. **1982** Slone *How We Talked* 42 **eKY** (as of c1950), We got to eat, pret nigh all tatters. **2000** *DARE* File **eLong Is. NY,** Prit near: almost.

b |pɚt(n̩)|; pronc-spp *pert-, purt-.*   Cf **pretty near it**

1915 *DN* 4.188 **swVA,** *Purt, purty.* Variants of *pretty.* **1916** *DN* 4.278 **KS, NE,** *Pert nigh. . .* Pretty nearly, almost. **1931** *AmSp* 7.94 **eKY,** The hill . . is purt nigh straight-up-and-down. **1943** [see **A1b** above]. **1946** *AmSp* 21.98 **sIL,** *Purt nigh,* nearly. **1965–70** [see **A1b** above]. **1966–69** *DARE* FW Addit **DE4,** [,pɚt'nɪɚ-]; **MS,** Purt nigh; **ceNC,** ['pɜˈt,nɪɚ-]; **neTN,** [,pɚtn̩'na·] = almost. **1967** *DARE* Tape **AZ4,** A horse has got to run from here to that house over there [pɚtnɪɚ], before he ever can catch that calf. **1975** Gainer *Witches* 15 **sAppalachians,** It's purt nigh to midnight. **1976** in 1982 Powers *Cataloochee* 380 **cwNC,** I pert-near got my eyes beat out last night. **1985** *DARE* File **OK,** Purt nigh, but not plumb: in Oklahoma, close, but no cigar.

c |put, pʌt|; pronc-spp *pet-, poot-, put-.*   For addit pronc and sp varr see quots

1916 *DN* 4.278 **NE,** I didn't have typhoid fever, but I came pet nare it. **1919** *DN* 5.38 **OK** [English of Cherokee Indians], *Poot'. . .* Pretty (preceding some other word, such as: *poot' near, poot' fast,* etc.). *Pooty* good is also heard. **1942** McAtee *Dial. Grant Co. IN* 49 (as of 1890s), *P'near,* contraction of pretty near. *Ibid* 51, *Put-nigh . .* almost. **1943** [see **A1b** above]. **1965–70** [see **A1b** above]. **1967–68** *DARE* Tape **IA11,** I . . looked at it to see what the matter was and the little pin in there . . [p'utnɪɚ] ready to fall out; **IN51,** That's [putnɪɚ] a sixty-four dollar question; **MI42,** I [p'udn nɪɚ] lost my life in that one, too. **1971** *AmSp* 46.304 **WV, KY,** In the basin of the Big Sandy River in West Virginia and Kentucky, one encounters the word [,paʔ'na:] ~ [,pat'ʔna:] ~ [,patʔn'a:], with the meaning 'almost.' The canonical form is evidently /'pait'nai/.

B As adj.

Usu of a child: pleasant, well-behaved.   Cf **D** below

1878 *Appletons' Jrl.* 5.415 **NEng,** Young ladies, however plain or uncomely of feature, if yet they are pleasant in their manners, and entertaining in their conversation, will be called in New England "very pretty girls." **1931** *PMLA* 46.1310 **sAppalachians,** "Pretty" means "nice," "obedient," as in "You're a 'pretty' child if you let me comb your hair"; used ironically it also means "disobedient," as in "You're a 'pretty' thing, to treat your mother that-a-way!"

C As noun.

1a A small object valued because it is pretty or amusing; a trinket, toy. **chiefly Sth, S Midl, esp sAppalachians** Cf **play-pretty**

1736 *Boston News–Letter* (Earle) *(DAE)*, Children's Silver Peaks & Flowers, Dutch Prettys. **1762–66** in 1956 Eliason *Tarheel Talk* 269 NC, 2 Doz. Dutch prettys. **1895** *DN* 1.392 wFL, Pretty . . a toy. **1899** (1912) Green *VA Folk-Speech* 335, . . Pretty toys or things. "Pretties for the children." **1902** *DN* 2.242 sIL, *Pritty*. . . A flower or boquet [sic]; a toy; a jewel, or any small object of pleasing appearance. **1904** *DN* 2.420 nwAR, *Pretty*. . . Toy. "Baby, are these your pretties?" **1907** *DN* 3.225 nwAR, *Pretty*. . . Any small object of pleasing appearance, such as a flower, a toy, or a jewel. **1924** Raine *Land of Saddle-Bags* 105 sAppalachians, I want to buy a *pretty* for my baby-child. **1927** *AmSp* 2.362 cwWV, *Purties* . . playthings. **1931** Hannum *Thursday April* 42 wNC, She would spend the rest of her days seeing that these last least ones got the life she had always wanted—the loving and pretties. **1932** (1974) Caldwell *Tobacco Road* 171 GA, The last pretty I got for Pearl was some green beads on a long string. **1940** (1978) Still *River of Earth* 64 KY, "He's fretted with being alone," Mother said. "Find him a pretty to play with." **1954** Tolbert *Bigamy Jones* 168 wTX (as of 1870s), Tell Mistress Delores I'm coming back to get her. I'm not coming back as plain old Elmer Jones, who brought her pretties and loved her. **1967–69** *DARE* (Qu. EE34, . . *A child's toy*) Infs GA75, 76, KY34, LA32, MO18, TN14, 16, Pretty; KY34, Baby's pretties; TN59, Purty. **1968** Haun *Hawk's Done Gone* 272 TN, Claude talked about the pretty he would have for Annie when she come back. **1968** *DARE* FW Addit VA1, "You made some pretties ['pɝtiz] today"—paper chain, paper hat, and drawing made by kindergarten child. **1969** *DARE* Tape IL39, Hobby and craft and all the pretties that you make. **1994** NC Lang. & Life Project *Dial. Dict. Lumbee Engl.* 10 seNC, Purty. . . A knickknack, brick-a-brack. *Momma keeps lots of purties on her shelf.* Also used in the expression *I wouldn't take a purty for you,* which means 'I wouldn't trade you for anything'.

b Used without definite reference in phrr *bet a pretty, give* (or *take*) *a pretty* and varr. **chiefly Sth, S Midl**

1851 in 1956 Eliason *Tarheel Talk* 138 cn,cNC, I would not send her an ugly *pirty* for a pirty. **1883** (1971) Harris *Nights with Remus* 172 GA [Black], He got sump'n' in dar wat he won't take a purty fer. **1909** *DN* 3.359 eAL, wGA, *Pretty*. . . A toy, something pretty. "I wouldn't take a pretty for that knife." Common. Also *purty.* **1909** Porter *Girl Limberlost* 387 cnIN, I'd give a pretty to know that secret thing you say you don't. **1915** *DN* 4.187 swVA, *Pretty*. . . "I wouldn't take a pretty for that." Also *pritty* and *purty.* **1927** *AmSp* 2.277 TX, *I'll bet you a pretty*—I'll bet you a good deal. **1933** Rawlings *South Moon* 37 nFL, Ab's got him one thing I'd give a pretty for. **1952** Brown *NC Folkl.* 1.579, *Pretty, bet (give) a*. . . A form of light verbal wager. "I bet a pretty he never told her where he'd been.["]—General. **1954** Tolbert *Bigamy Jones* 16 wTX (as of 1870s), I'd give a pretty to marry up with that one. **1968** *DARE* Tape AL48, She bet a pretty it happened when somebody knocked on their door. **1986** Pederson *LAGS Concordance,* 1 inf, swMS, I wouldn't have taken a pretty for it; 1 inf, nwGA, Wouldn't take a pretty for it; 1 inf, cMS, Wouldn't have took pretty [sic] for her. **1994** [see C1a above].

2 pl: Fine or delicate clothes.

1913 London *Valley of Moon* 103 CA, Almost, it seemed, she could visualize the women who had kept their pretties and their family homespun in its drawers. **1970** *DARE* (Qu. W39, *Joking ways of referring to a person's best clothes*) Inf VA45, Pretties.

D As adv.

In a pleasant, well-behaved way. Cf **B** above.

1878 *Scribner's Mth.* 16.812, Now hush! Don't you dare be crying! Just as sure as you live, if you do / I'll call up my big dog to bite you, and I'll make my papa kill you too!/ And then where'll you be? So play pretty. **1995** Brophy Coll. swMO (as of c1960), Play pretty. [T]o "play nice," as an exhortation to playing children.

pretty boy n
A **zinnia.**

1931 Goodrich *Mt. Homespun* 40 sAppalachians, We compared our nomenclature: . . the "pretty boys" that flourished in the fence corners, were, in my dictionary, zinnias.

pretty-by-night n Also *pretty-ma-night, ~-my-night, ~-per-night* [From the flower's opening in the evening] **chiefly S Midl, esp KY, sOH**

A **four-o'clock 1** (here: *Mirabilis jalapa*).

1872 Eggleston *End of the World* 169 **Ohio Valley,** She planted some pretty-by-nights in an old cracked blue-and-white tea-pot. **1897** *Jrl. Amer. Folkl.* 10.53 swOH, *Mirabilis Jalapa* . . pretty-per-night, Sulphur Grove, Ohio. [Footnote: Not pretty by night, although it means the same.] **1936** Morehouse *Rain on Just* 41 NC, Dolly . . could just see the garden posies. Prettymanights were standing thick and green. Before another full moon, they'd be opening wide in the late evening. **1940** (1978) Still *River of Earth* 173 KY, Father came just before dark, and the pretty-by-nights were open and peart by the doorsill. **1947** (1962) Henry *Misty* 92 eVA, You kin cut a few of them purty-by-nights and some bouncin' Bess fer a centerpiece. **1951** *PADS* 15.11 sAppalachians, Mirabilis jalapa. . . Pretty-by-night. **1952** Giles *40 Acres* 157 csKY, We have had to teach Honey to leave the hummingbirds alone. She thinks they are giant insects darting into the cup of the morning-glories or the four-o'clocks, or "pretty-by-nights." **1982** Slone *How We Talked* 48 eKY (as of c1950), Pretty My Nights—4 o'Clocks.

prettyface n
A **brodiaea** (here: *Triteleia ixioides*).

1949 Moldenke *Amer. Wild Flowers* 355, The *golden brodiea* or *prettyface, Calliprora ixioides,* has salmon-yellow flowers veined with dark purple. **1961** Thomas *Flora Santa Cruz* 125 cwCA, *B[rodiaea] lutea* . . Common Calliprora, Pretty Face [etc].

pretty girls' station n Also *pretty girls' house* **esp sAppalachians**
= **lemonade.**

1939 Harris *Purslane* 90 cNC, The sugar maple would soon be leafless now, and the green grass where the cousins had played "pretty girls' house" and "red statue" all summer would soon be as brown as the thistle birds. **1940** Harbin *Fun Encycl.* 765, Pretty girls' station. . . This old game is variously named, "Lemonade," . . "Georgia Town." **1952** Brown *NC Folkl.* 1.62, Pretty Girls' Station. . . In Indiana and, I believe, in neighboring states, the game is known as 'Lemonade.' **1966–68** *DARE* (Qu. EE33, . . *Outdoor games . . that children play*) Inf NC36, Pretty girls' station—Pantomime your supposed occupation; TN8, Pretty girls' station—A type of charade; WV1, Pretty girl [sic] station—Teams several yards apart; one team advanced doing things; other has to guess what you're going: 1—Here I come; 2—Where are you from? 3—Pretty girls' station; 4—What's your occupation; 5—Work; 6—Get to it. After they guess, they chase you to your base. If they catch you, you have to change sides; WV5, Pretty girls' station—Recite rhymes while advancing to other base; you perform an action; they have to guess what you're doing.

pretty grass n
= **mariposa lily.**

1890 *Century Dict.* 4715, *Pretty-grass*. . . A plant of the genus *Calochortus*. These plants are grass-like below, but have large and beautiful flowers. Also called *butterfly-weed, mariposa-lily,* and *wild tulip.* **1959** Carleton *Index Herb. Plants* 94, Pretty grass: Calochortus [spp].

pretty-ma(or -my)-night See **pretty-by-night**

pretty Nancy n
= **garden catchfly.**

[**1892** *Jrl. Amer. Folkl.* 5.93, Silene Armeria, . . pretty Nancy. Franklin Center P[rovince of] Q[uebec].] **1931** Clute *Common Plants* 135, The garden catchfly . . was anciently called pretty Nancy. This term, entirely meaningless as it stands, when turned about and straightened up a bit, is none other than none-so-pretty.

pretty near it adv Also *pert night, purt night, ~ nite* Also sp *prettyneart* Cf **pretty A2b**
Nearly, almost.

1911 *DN* 3.539 eKY, *Prettynēart* (=pretty near it). . . Almost; e.g., "He was prettyneart sick." **1931** *AmSp* 7.92 eKY, The reddishes are purt night big enough to have a mess. **1942** Whipple *Joshua* 51 UT (as of c1860), Got to celebrate! This pert night calls for a toot! **1968–69** *DARE* (Qu. LL30, . . *"He fell off the ladder and _____ [broke his neck]."*) Inf GA77, Pretty near [pɝt niˇr] it; IA31, Pretty near it ['pə˞t‚nə˞t]—hear from a little south of here. **1982** Slone *How We Talked* 26 **eKY** (as of c1950), Purt nite (also, purt near)—almost.

pretty-per-night See **pretty-by-night**

pretty-quick n
A **thrasher** (here: *Toxostoma curvirostre*).
 1917 *Wilson Bulletin* 29.2.84 **AZ**, *Toxostoma curvirostre palmeri.*—Pretty-quick, Wickenburg, Ariz.

preying mantis See **praying mantis**

prezactly adv Also *persacitly, persackly, perzackly, perzactly, presackly, prezackly, puhzac'ly* [Blend of *precisely* and **exactly**] Cf **edzact**
Exactly.
 1851 Burke *Polly Peablossom* 53 **MO**, 'Mister Bar,' sez I, 'the place whar you's er standin' ain't prezackly healthy.' **1858** Hammett *Piney Woods Tavern* 60, It jest fixed my frizen perzackly. **1901** *Century Illustr. Mag.* 62.904 **Sth** [Black], So perzackly lak Ole Marse's. **1905** *DN* 3.63 **eNE**, *Perzackly, prezackly.* . . Intensive of *exactly.* **1909** *DN* 3.356 **eAL, wGA**, *Perzackly, prezackly, zackly.* . . Variants of *exactly.* **1922** Gonzales *Black Border* 321 **sSC, GA coasts** [Gullah glossary], *Puhzac'ly*—exactly, precisely. **1953** Randolph–Wilson *Down in Holler* 273 **Ozarks**, *Prezactly.* . . I have heard it . . , but not often. Apparently it is a combination of *precisely* and *exactly.* **1972** Cooper *NC Mt. Folkl.* 94, *Perzactly*—exactly. **1974** Fink *Mountain Speech* 19 **wNC, eTN**, *Persackly* . . exactly. "She done persackly right." **1982** Slone *How We Talked* 26 **eKY** (as of c1950), Persacitly—exact.

prezzydent See **president**

pricker n **NEast, N Cent** Cf **picker, sticker**
A thorn or burr.
 1907 *DN* 3.196 **seNH**, *Pricker.* . . Brier, bramble. "Boys get prickers in their feet when they go barefoot." **1950** *WELS* **WI** (*Sharp points on the stems of rose bushes, berry bushes, etc. . . small*) 16 Infs, Prickers; 1 Inf, Prickle, pricker, picker; 1 Inf, Prickers or stickers. **1967–69** *DARE* (Qu. S13, . . *A common wild bush with bunches of round, prickly seeds; when they get dry they stick to your clothing*) Inf **MN2**, Burrs—just the piece that sticks to you—also called prickers; (Qu. S14, . . *Prickly seeds, small and flat, with two prongs at one end, that cling to clothing*) Infs **MI80, MN2, NY6**, Pricker(s); **NY83**, Pricker bushes; (Qu. S15) Inf **IL45**, Sandburrs—little round ball full of prickers. **1982** *Barrick Coll.* **sePA**, *Pricker*—briar, thorn—Philadelphia. **1983** *Greenfield Recorder* (MA) 21 May [Hemenway column], A double yellow rose with so many 'prickers' it was of no use in a bouquet but was a lovely shrub. **1996** [see **picker 1**]. **2001** *DARE* File **cMA**, Prickers—thorn bushes, called so because they prick you. (This is a word that is active in my vocabulary and that has confused some in nearby towns but all of my childhood pals know and use this.)

prickleaf n
A **pricklyleaf** (here: *Thymophylla acerosa*).
 1931 U.S. Dept. Ag. *Misc. Pub.* 101.166, *Prickleaf (D[ysodia] acerosa* . . *)* a small, bushy, rather agreeably scented plant 4 to 12 inches high with very fine, glandular, pricklelike leaves . . occurs on low dry hills from western Texas to southern Nevada.

prickleback n
Std: a fish of the family Stichaeidae. For other names of var spp see **monkeyface eel**

pricklecone pine n Also *prickly-cone(d) pine*
Any of var western **pines**: usu **bishop pine**, but also **bristlecone, digger**, and **knobcone pine**.
 1858 Warder *Hedges* 250, *Pinus Sabiniana*, or Prickly-coned Pine, has long leaves. **1897** Sudworth *Arborescent Flora* 25 **ID**, *Pinus attenuata.* . . Common Names. . . Prickly-cone Pine. Ibid 28 **CA**, *Pinus muricata.* . . Prickle-cone Pine. **1908** Rogers *Tree Book* 47, *Prickle-Cone Pine (P. muricata* . . *).* . . . The oblique cones, whose thickened scales are armed with sharp, strong beaks, are conspicuous by their persistence for years unopened on the branch. **1980** Little *Audubon Guide N. Amer. Trees W. Region* 284, Bishop Pine—"Santa Cruz Island Pine"—"Prickle-cone Pine."

prickle poppy See **prickly poppy**

prickler ash See **prickly ash 2**

prickler weed n [By metath and perh folk-etym] =**pickerelweed**.
 1969 *DARE* FW Addit **Okefenokee GA**, Prickler weed = pickerel weed. Said by Okefenokee guide.

prickleweed n
A **prairie mimosa** (here: *Desmanthus illinoensis*).
 1933 Small *Manual SE Flora* 656, *A[cuan] illinoense.* . . Prickleweed. . . Rich soil and river banks. **1960** Vines *Trees SW* 503, Illinois Bundle-flower. . . Common names are Prairie Mimosa and Prickle Weed.

prickly ash n
1 Std: a shrub or small tree of the genus *Zanthoxylum.* For other names of var spp see **angelica tree 2, colima, correosa, doctor's club, Hercules'-~ 2, Indian catch-blanket, monkey-fooler, pellitory, pepperbark, pepperwood 2, rabbit gum 1, satinwood, sea ash 1, spitberry, sting-tongue, suterberry, tear-blanket, tickle-tongue, tongue-bush, toothache tree, uña de gato, wait-a-bit, wild lime, ~ orange, yellowheart, yellowwood**
2 also *prickler ash;* =**Hercules'-club 1.** **chiefly Sth** Note: Some of these quots may apply instead to **1** above.
 1709 (1967) Lawson *New Voyage* 101 **NC, SC**, Prickly-Ash grows up like a Pole; of which the *Indians* and *English* make Poles to set their Canoes along in Shoal-Water. **1743** (1946) Gronovius *Flora Virginica* 150, [Angelica baccifera, sive Aralia arborescens spinosa] *Gumbriar & Prikly-ash.* **1830** Rafinesque *Med. Flora* 116, Many ignorant herbalists . . call likewise Prickly Ash, the *Aralia Spinosa*, whose true name is Prickly Elder or Angelica tree. **1898** *Jrl. Amer. Folkl.* 11.228 **KY**, *Aralia spinosa* . . prickly ash, Bowling Green. **c1937** in 1977 *Amer. Slave Suppl. 1* 1.414 **AL**, Prickler ash was er nodder that was taken in der spring; hit was 'spose ter clean their blood uv all impurities. **1945** Saxon *Gumbo Ya-Ya* 535 **LA**, Toothache. . . Rub the gums with the bark or seed of a Prickly Ash (known on Pecan Island as the Toothache Tree), or insert some in the cavity. **1966** *DARE* (Qu. S26e, *Other wildflowers not yet mentioned;* not asked in early QRs) Inf **SC27**, Prickly ash—*Aralia spinosa*—used in folk medicine. **1967** *DARE* Tape **TX1**, [Aux Inf:] What was that wild plant he used for medicine? [TX1A:] Well, . . he used prickly ash and he used cramp bark and he used black alder and he used witch hazel. **1986** Pederson *LAGS Concordance*, 1 inf, **swLA**, Prickly ash = devil's-walking-stick.

prickly-coned pine See **pricklecone pine**

prickly-cone pine n
1 See **pricklecone pine.**
2 See **prickly pine 1.**

prickly elder n
=**Hercules'-club 1.**
 1830 [see **prickly ash 2**]. **1876** Hobbs *Bot. Hdbk.* 110, Spikenard tree, Prickly elder, Aralia spinosa. **1950** Peattie *Nat. Hist. Trees* 493, *Hercules'-club.* . . Other Names: Angelica-tree. Spikenardtree. Prickly Ash. Prickly Elder. **1974** Morton *Folk Remedies* 29 **SC**, Devil's-Walking Stick . . Prickly Elder.

prickly grass n Also *prickly weed*
A **glasswort** (here: *Salicornia europaea*).
 1940 Clute *Amer. Plant Names* 141, *S[alicornia] Europaea* . . prickly grass, pickle-plant. **1974** (1977) Coon *Useful Plants* 96, Samphire, prickly-weed.

prickly lettuce n Also *prickly wild lettuce*
A **wild lettuce** (here: *Lactuca serriola*). Also called **compass plant 4, horse thistle 2, horseweed 5, milk thistle 1, milkweed 4, wild opium**
 1890 *Century Dict.* 3422, Prickly lettuce, *Lactuca Scariola.* **1914** *Georgia Manual Weeds* 540, *Prickly lettuce.* . . Habitat: All soils; invades all crops. **1939** Medsger *Edible Wild Plants* 161, Prickly Lettuce. . . The young leaves are very tender, and for that reason it makes a very good salad plant. **1968** Barkley *Plants KS* 379, Lactuca serriola L. (L. scariola) Prickly Wild Lettuce.

prickly pear n See also **bull cactus, bull-tongue ~, cactus rose, comal cactus**

1 Std: a **cactus B1** of the genus *Opuntia*; the flesh or pear-shaped fruit of this cactus. For other names of these see **buckhorn cholla, cane ~, chain cactus, ~-fruit cholla, cholla, cigarette cactus, clockface, cow's tongue 1, cow-tongue prickly pear, coyote cactus, darning-needle ~, dead ~, deerhorn ~ 1, desert Christmas ~, devil's pincushion 2, devil's-tongue, diamond cactus, dollar ~, dollar-joint prickly pear, elkhorn cactus, flapjack ~, golden cholla, goldplush, grizzly bear cactus, hedgehog ~ 2, holycross cholla, hunger cactus, Indian pear 2, ~ fig 1, jo-jumper, jumping cholla, niggertoe 4, nopal, old man 1d, old-man's-hand, pancake pear, panini, pear n, pear pad, pencil cholla, ~ cactus b, rabbit-ear 2, rattail cactus, silver cholla, staghorn ~, tasajillo, teddybear cholla, tesajo, tree cactus, tuna, turkey cactus, walkingstick cholla**

2 =**porcupine.** Cf **prickly pig**

[1878 Hart *Sazerac Lying Club* 43 **NV,** A ground-hog is a animal which some people calls a porkypine . . ; they're stickier than them prickly pears what grows in the deserts around this section of country.] 1967 *DARE* (Qu. P31, . . *Names or nicknames . . for . . porcupine*) Inf **KS**5, Prickly pear.

prickly phlox n esp **CA**

A **gilia:** usu *Leptodactylon californicum,* but also *L. pungens.*

1897 Parsons *Wild Flowers CA* 206, Prickly Phlox. . . At a little distance the plant-stems have almost the look of a cactus, so densely are they clothed with the small, rigid leaves. 1942 Hylander *Plant Life* 443, Prickly Phlox . . is an erect widely branched shrub with prickly palmately lobed leaves and dense clusters of pink flowers, growing in chaparral of southern California. 1973 Hitchcock–Cronquist *Flora Pacific NW* 371, [*Leptodactylon] pungens* . . Prickly phlox. . . widespread cordilleran sp. of dry places from des[ert] to mid elev. in drier mts. E Cas[cades].

prickly pig n Cf **quill pig**

=**porcupine.**

1966 *DARE* (Qu. P31, . . *Names or nicknames . . for . . porcupine*) Inf **MT**4, Quill pig, prickly pig.

prickly pine n

1 also *prickly-cone pine* =**Table Mountain pine.**

1860 Curtis *Cat. Plants NC* 20, Prickly Pine. . . The cones give the chief peculiarity and interest to this Pine. . . The scales [are] armed with very broad strong sharp spines, which are one sixth of an inch long and bent toward the top of the cone. 1897 Sudworth *Arborescent Flora* 28 **NC,** Table-mountain Pine. . . Prickly Pine. 1950 Grimm *Trees PA* 62, *Table Mountain Pine.* . . The cones are quite distinctive. . . The thick scales are terminated by large, stout, and strongly hooked spines. . . The Table Mountain Pine is also known as . . Prickly Cone Pine. 1950 Peattie *Nat. Hist. Trees* 29, *Bur Pine.* . . Other Names: Table Mountain, Southern Mountain, Prickly, or Hickory Pine.

2 =**lodgepole pine.**

1897 Sudworth *Arborescent Flora* 23 **UT,** Lodgepole Pine. . . Common Names. . Prickly Pine. 1908 Britton *N. Amer. Trees* 29, Lodge Pole Pine. . . It is also called Prickly pine, White pine, Black pine [etc].

prickly poppy n Also *prickle poppy* [*OED2* 1724 →]

A thistle-leaved poppy of the genus *Argemone,* esp *A. mexicana.* For other names of var spp see **bird-in-the-bush, chicalote, devil's-fig, flowering thistle, fried egg 1, Indian paint 7, Mexican poppy, milk thistle 2, thistle poppy, thorn apple, ~ poppy, wild poppy, ~ hollyhock, yellow thistle**

1833 Beck *Botany N. & Middle States* 21, A[rgemone] mexicana. . . Penn. to Flor. W. to Miss. . . Prickly Poppy. 1863 Porcher *Resources* 28 **NC,** Devil's Fig; Prickly Poppy; Mexican Poppy [etc]. . . Charleston District, grows around buildings in rich spots; vicinity of Charleston; Newbern, N.C. 1910 Graves *Flowering Plants* 197 **CT,** *Argemone mexicana.* . . Mexican or Prickly Poppy. . . Rare. Roadside in New Haven. 1936 Whitehouse *TX Flowers* 33, Texas Prickly Poppy (*Argemone delicatula*). . . grows in dry soil in Central Texas. The prickly poppies bloom most profusely in April. 1966 *DARE* Wildfl QR

(Wills–Irwin) Pl.12b Inf **TX**34, Prickly poppy. 1967 Dodge *Roadside Wildflowers* 11, *Pricklepoppy*—One of the common and distinctive drouth resistant perennials of the Southwest is the thistle poppy, prickly poppy, or chicalote. 1968 *DARE* (Qu. S26a, . . *Wildflowers. . . Roadside flowers*) Inf **CA**60, Prickly poppy—A big white flower also called thistle poppy.

prickly sage n

A **gilia** (here: *Leptodactylon pungens*).

1931 U.S. Dept. Ag. *Misc. Pub.* 101.139 **West,** Prickly gilia . . , locally known as false phlox and prickly sage, is low and sprawling, largely in sagebrush and juniper types, from Montana to Washington, California and Colorado.

prickly tight n Cf **sticktight**

A **cockleburr 1.**

1970 *DARE* (Qu. S13, . . *A common wild bush with bunches of round, prickly seeds; when they get dry they stick to your clothing*) Inf **MA**124, Prickly tights.

prickly weed See **prickly grass**

prickly wild lettuce See **prickly lettuce**

prick on v phr

Of wind: to increase.

1905 Wasson *Green Shay* 183 **sME coast,** I cal'late this breeze will prick on [Footnote: Increase] heftier right along till then, anyways. 1939 *LANE* Map 91 (*The wind is getting stronger*) 1 inf, **seMA,** Breezing up, usually; *pricking on,* at sea.

prickwood n

=**burning bush 1.**

1950 FWP *Guide ID* 62, The burning bush (wahoo, prickwood, spindletree), a close relative of the climbing false bittersweet, is a curious little tree that looks much like the wild plum except for its bark.

prid- See **pretty A2a**

pride n [Cf *EDD* pride sb. 4 "The uterus of a sow"; perh also related are *SND* pride n.[2] "The spleen of an animal" and *OED2* pride sb.[3] "*Obs. Rare.* . . .? The spleen of a deer."] Cf **proud adj 2, 3**

A sexual organ, as:

a pl: The male genitals.

[c1738 (1929) Byrd *Histories* 292 **VA,** Take the large Pride of the Beaver, Squeeze all the Juice out of it, then take the small Pride, and Squeeze out about 5 or 6 drops. Take the inside of Sassafrass Bark, Powder it, and mix it with the Liquor, and place this Bait conveniently for your Steel Trap. [*DARE* Ed: The reference is to the musk glands of the beaver, frequently confused with the testicles; cf *DCan beaver pride, DNE pride.*]] 1923 *DN* 5.217 **swMO,** Prides. . . The privates, the reproductive organs. 1953 Randolph–Wilson *Down in Holler* 104 **Ozarks,** The male organs are frequently known as the *prides,* and the word pride has thus acquired a certain obscene significance. 1995 Brophy *Coll.* 57 **swMO** (as of c1960), *Prides.* [T]he male sex organs.

b The ovary of an animal.

1899 (1912) Green *VA Folk-Speech* 335, *Pride.* . . The ovary of female animals, particularly the sow. 1944 *PADS* 2.48 **sVA,** *Pride.* . . The ovary of an animal. . . Obsolescent. Also, reported from S.C.

pride ash tree n

See quot.

1970 Anderson *TX Folk Med.* 14, Colds[.] Chew the leaves from a pride ash tree. *Anderson* [County].

pride of Barbados n Also *Barbados pride*

A **poinciana** (here: *Caesalpinia pulcherrima*) noted for its showy flower. Also called **flame tree, flower fence**

[1756 Browne *Civil & Nat. Hist. Jamaica* 225, Barbadoes Pride. . . It now grows wild in many places about *Liguanea,* and makes a beautiful shew when in bloom.] 1908 Britton *N. Amer. Trees* 548, Barbados flower. . . is also known as Barbados pride, Flower fence, and Bird of paradise flower. 1929 Pope *Plants HI* 107, This plant [=*Caesalpinia crista*] is closely related to our well known "Pride of Barbadoes." 1982 Perry–Hay *Field Guide Plants* 46, *Caesalpinia pulcherrima.* . . Barbados pride; pride of Barbados; flower fence; dwarf poinciana; peacock flower; paradise flower.

pride of China n
=Chinaberry 1.
1785 (1925) Washington *Diaries* 2.383 **VA,** Next 3 rows of the Seed of the Pride of China. **1831** Royall *Mrs. Royall's S. Tour* 2.83 **GA,** The pride of China (*alias* China-tree) in full bloom, . . the genial sunshine, and the pleasant shade [in Savannah]. **1884** (1885) McCook *Tenants* 261 **TX,** [Caption:] Pride-of-China tree stripped of leaves on one side by cutting-ant. **1901** Mohr *Plant Life AL* 588, Pride of China. Bead Tree. . . Introduced and extensively cultivated for ornament throughout the Louisianian area. South Carolina to Florida, west to Texas. **1952** Taylor *Plants Colonial Days* 24, The chinaberry has other common names, among them China tree, pride of China, pride of India, and bead tree.

pride of India n
1 =Chinaberry 1. esp SC
1803 Davis *Travels* 79 **SC,** The mocking-bird . . was warbling, close to my window, from a tree called by some the Pride of *India,* and by others the Poison-berry Tree. **1893** *Harper's New Mth. Mag.* 86.756 **neFL,** This causeway broadened into a sandy street under huge pride-of-India trees, whose branches met overhead. **1936** Smith–Sass *Carolina Rice* 61 **SC,** A pathway just north of the vegetable garden led through a short avenue of Pride-of-India trees into a pasture. **1949** Sprunt–Chamberlain *SC Bird Life* 487, The Redstart . . may be often found feeding about the abundant Pride of India or "umbrella" trees near Negro cabins and settlements. **1966–67** *DARE* (Qu. 144, *What kinds of berries grow wild around here?*) Inf **SC4,** Pride of India—has poison berries; (Qu. T16, . . *Kinds of trees . . 'special'*) Inf **SC43,** Pride of India—same as chinaberry.
2 A goldenrain tree (here: *Koelreuteria paniculata*).
1931 Otis *MI Trees* 278, China-tree. . . Also, but incorrectly, called the *Varnish-tree* and *Pride of India.* **1971** Kieran *Nat. Hist. NYC* 198, There are many other introduced species doing so well in our area that it's quite possible they may "go native" in the long run. This would include the Golden-rain Tree or Pride-of-India [etc].

pride of the meadow n
A **meadowsweet 2** (here: *Filipendula vulgaris*).
1847 Wood *Class-Book* 257, *S[piraea] filipendula.* Pride of the Meadow. . . A very delicate herb, often cultivated. **1910** Graves *Flowering Plants* 235 **CT,** *Filipendula hexapetala.* . . Pride of the Meadow. Dropwort.

pride of the mountain(s) See **mountain pride**

pride of the peak n
A **fringed orchid** (here: *Platanthera peramoena*).
1933 Small *Manual SE Flora* 371, *B[lephariglottis] peramoena.* . . Pride-of-the-peak. Pink-fringe-orchid. **1950** Correll *Native Orchids* 95, *Habenaria peramoena.* . . Common names: Purple Fringeless-orchid, Purple-spire Orchid, Purple Fretlip, Pride-of-the-peak.

prideweed n
A **horseweed 1** (here: *Conyza canadensis*).
1822 Eaton *Botany* 273, *[Erigeron] canadense* . . fleabane, prideweed. . . Powdered leaves useful in stopping blood. **1892** (1974) Millspaugh *Amer. Med. Plants* 80-1, Canada fleabane, Horse-weed, Butter-weed, Colt's tail, Pride-weed [etc]. **1904** Henkel *Weeds Used in Med.* 36, Canada Fleabane. . . Other common names.—Horseweed, colt's tail, scabious, prideweed [etc]. **1931** Harned *Wild Flowers Alleghanies* 562, Horseweed. . . A very coarse, unattractive weed familiarly known to the farmer under the names Horseweed, Bitterweed, Prideweed, Mare's tail, Butterweed and Hogweed. **1965** Teale *Wandering Through Winter* 244 **KY,** Here in the rich soil the horseweed or Canada fleabane or prideweed or butterweed or colt's-tail—*Leptilon canadense*— . . had attained its maximum growth.

pridy adj Also sp *pridey* [Corn dial; cf *EDD pridy* adj. 1, 2] Proud; handsome.
1961 *Mt. Life* 37.3.30 **sAppalachians,** To ridge folks, he was a drunk. A big, handsome, no 'count drunk. . . She sighed and shook her head. . . "I wish you could have knowed him before he got like this. La, he was a pridey man!" That word pridey was a favorite of Mama's. . . If a thing is pridey, you can take great pride in it. *Ibid* 31, La, black walnut's a

pridey wood! That dado will be a grand sight. **1995** *Brophy Coll.* 57 **swMO** (as of c1960), *Pridy.* [P]rideful, proud.

priest n [*OED2 priest* sb. 7 1851 →; "Chiefly in Ireland."]
1971 *DARE* File **DE,** *Priest* = weapon used to kill an exhausted fish— "performer of the last rites." Used by deep-sea fishermen in Delaware ports—Sussex Co., etc.

priester louse See **preacher's lice**

priestfish n
A **black rockfish 1** (here: *Sebastes mystinus*).
1898 U.S. Natl. Museum *Bulletin* 47.1784, *Sebastodes mystinus.* . . (Pêche Prêtre; Priest Fish; Black Rockfish.) **1933** John G. Shedd Aquarium *Guide* 129, *Sebastosomus mystinus*—Priestfish; Black Rockfish. This is the member of the family most abundant around San Francisco in shallow water. It reaches a length of fourteen inches and receives the name Priestfish from the dark color of its skin.

priest-in-the-pulpit See **preacher-in-the-pulpit 1**

priest's lice See **preacher's lice**

prim See **primost**

prime v [*OED2 prime* v.³ "To prune or trim (trees)" 1565 →]
To pluck the lower leaves off a growing tobacco plant; hence n *primer* one who plucks the leaves; vbl n *priming* the act of plucking leaves; n *priming* the leaf (or leaves) so plucked.
1792 Pope *Tour U.S.* 63, [The Creek Indians] scarcely ever weed, hill, prime, top or succour their Tobacco. **1899** Floyd *Cultivation Tobacco FL* 14, The first priming, which means the first four leaves taken from the stalk, also the last priming . . are kept separate. **1904** Glasgow *Deliverance* 166 **VA,** The very primings ought to be as good as some top leaves. **1938** *Daily Progress* (Charlottesville VA) 21 Oct 5/1 (*OED2*), Following the change from 'stalk cutting' to 'priming' (cutting of separate leaves for curing in bundles), less heat was required. **1940** *AmSp* 15.134 [Tobacco market language], *Priming.* Taking the lower, worthless leaves off a plant. **1944** *PADS* 2.69, *Prime.* . . To pluck the lower dead or worthless leaves. ((In Va., N.C.: also to pluck the good leaves for curing. Same as to *pull.* Current.)) *Primer.* . . One who primes tobacco. *Primings.* . . The lower leaves, formerly waste, now one of the grades on the market. **1966–70** *DARE* Tape **DC5,** [Inf:] For a man to have a good crop of tobacco he should start to prime the tobacco when he grows his tobacco plants. [FW:] He should start priming? . . What does that mean? [Inf:] That means get all the plants in there the same size; **FL26A,** They have what you call a primer who would go in the field and pick off so many leaves to prime it. Took so many leaves to the stalk; **NC8,** They try to use the same day if possible, every week. . . to prime it, as they call it . . and we say priming because we take off the leaves that are ready. In other words, prime the ones that are ready and leave the ones that are not ready to be harvested. *Ibid,* They try to have people who know tobacco, that are accustomed to it and know when the tobacco is ripe and ready and to know which leaves to pick and which to refuse. . . And the ones who have to work around the barn . . they will know whether they've got good primers in the field or not, because the tobacco will be laying, laid straight in the trucks; **OH57,** Prime is taking off the lower leaves and then it'll be cut; **VA40,** We didn't prime it then. We cut, straight, the whole stalk and threw it on a stick and put nine and ten stalks to the stick. *Ibid,* You start at the bottom, that's what you call the priming and then after your priming . . they pick out some of the burnt leaves, but now they don't care whether they pick out it or not. **1967** Key *Tobacco Vocab.* 119 **CT,** Priming—older term; picking— more recent. **1969** *NC Folkl.* 17.34 **wNC,** There was a further grade called *ground lugs* which might be got by *priming* the patch before cutting time.

prime-blank See **point-blank A4**

primer See **prime**

primary n [Scots, Engl dial var of *OED2 praemunire* sb. 3 "*Obs.* . . A difficulty . . predicament."] *obs*
A predicament.
1837 Sherwood *Gaz. GA* 71, *Provincialisms.* . . *Primary,* for predicament. **1975** McDonough *Garden Sass* 112 **AR** (as of 1832), It weren't long, though, before he . . got into a priminary.

priming See **prime**

Primitive Baptist n Also *Primitive* Cf **foot-washing Baptist,**
hard-shell adj 2 **chiefly Sth, S Midl** See Map

An extremely conservative Baptist religious group; see quot
1980; a member of such a group.

1851 Burke *Polly Peablossom* 143 **AL,** Brethren Crump and Noel
were both members of the Primitive Baptist Church. **1856** in 1956
Eliason *Tarheel Talk* 288 **nw,cwNC,** Was recived by examinytion on the
primitive baptis faith. **1908** *DN* 3.319 **eAL, wGA,** Hardshell. . . A
Primitive Baptist. **1934** Carmer *Stars Fell on AL* 58, All I know is the
hardshells call 'emselves Primitives. They pay their debts, they vote Republican, and they take their whiskey straight, as the feller says. *Ibid*
61, Us that believe ever' word in the Bible . . us Primitive Babtists, will
stand an' see judgment pronounced on the dancin', card-playin', carnal-
minded sinners, on them that read the unscriptural works of men on religion. **1943** *Natl. Geogr. Mag.* 84.768 **sAppalachians,** One of the most
interesting services is the "foot washin'" of the Primitive Baptists. **1954**
Harder Coll. **cwTN,** *Hard shells*. . . Nickname for members of the Primitive Baptist Church. **c1960** *Wilson Coll.* **csKY,** *Foot-washing*. . . A religious rite among certain faiths, as the Primitive Baptists. **1965–70**
DARE (Qu. CC2, . . *Predominant religious denominations*) Infs **GA**31,
42, **NC**87, **TN**6, 15, **VA**42, Primitive Baptist; (Qu. CC3, . . *Religions
that have come in recently . . or are a bit different from the common
ones*) Infs **AL**16, **GA**82, 89, **PA**202, Primitive Baptist; (Qu. CC4, . .
Nicknames . . for various religions or religious groups) Infs **GA**13, 44,
NC1, Primitive Baptists; **GA**31, **LA**3, Primitive Baptists [are the same
as] Hardshell Baptists; **MS**33, Primitive Baptist—footwashing Baptists.
1980 Mead *Hdbk. Denominations U.S.* 54, The Primitive Baptists have
the reputation of being the most strictly orthodox and exclusive of all
Baptists. Unique in that they have never been organized as a denomination and have no administrative bodies . . , they represent a protest
against "money-based" missions and benevolent societies and against
"assessing" the churches to support missions, missionaries, and Sunday
Schools. *Ibid* 55, The result was confusion; there was no chance under
such conditions for growth as a denomination and little chance even for
a fellowship or quasi unity. This is apparent in the variety of names,
some friendly and some derisive, that have been applied to them, such as
"Primitive," "Old School," "Regular," "Anti-mission," and "Hard Shell."
In general, the term "Primitive" has been widely accepted and used.
1983 *MJLF* 9.1.42 **ceKY,** *Hardshells*. . . Primitive Baptists. **1986**
Pederson *LAGS Concordance (Baptist),* [Of 24 infs who responded with
Primitive Baptist and combs, 15 were from **GA,** and the rest scattered in
AL, FL, TN.]

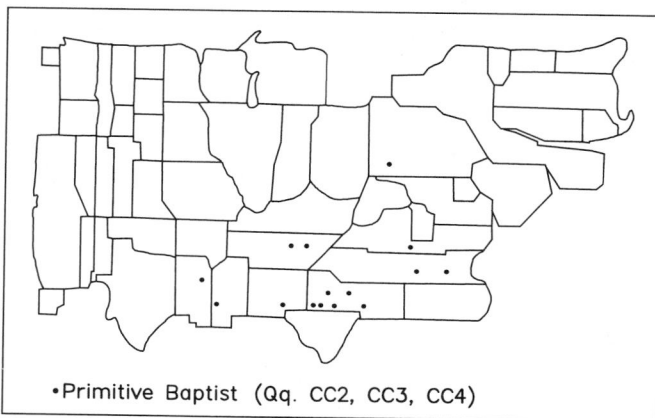

•Primitive Baptist (Qq. CC2, CC3, CC4)

primost n Also *prim* [Norw *prim(ost)*] **esp WI, MN**
A type of cheese usu made by boiling whey or undrained
curds.

1902 *DN* 2.258 **csWI,** [Footnote:] In Stoughton, . . the words *flat-
bread* (Norse Flatbröd), a thin bread, *lefse* and *kling* (Norse lefsa, kling)
the same sugared and layered, and *prim-ost,* a brown sweet cheese, are
everywhere used like native English words. Stoughton is a town of about
3500 inhabitants, two-thirds of which are Norwegians. **1950** *WELS* **WI**
(*Home-made cheese*) 1 Inf, Primost—whey cheese; 1 Inf, Primost—
Norw—a whey cheese; 1 Inf, Prim—Scandinavians make "prim" from
milk. **1951** Tufford *Scandinavian Recipes* 67, *Brøm*. . . Cook buttermilk until it begins to curdle, add flour slowly to thicken. . . Add sugar
and cook until thick and brown. . . This is a brown cheese like "pri-

most." **1966** *Badgerland* (Stoughton WI) 15 Oct 8/2, A variety of open
sandwiches such as "Gaffel' bit" (bit of fish on sliced egg), "Primost",
and "Gjeit Ost" (cheese sandwiches). **1968** *DARE* (Qu. H60, *The
lumpy white cheese that is made from sour milk*) Inf **MN**13, Primost—
['primost]—a soft, spreading white cheese made of milk of newly fresh
cow. **1973** Allen *LAUM* 1.294 (as of c1950), Primost—The whey
boiled down [1 inf, ceMN]. **2000** *DARE* File **csWI,** I first met *primost*
when I came to Wisconsin in 1975.

primpy adj
Fastidious, finicky; affected.

1859 (1968) Bartlett *Americanisms* 342, *Primpy*. Fastidious in the duties of the toilet, finical. A woman's word. **1899** *Century Illustr. Mag.*
58.804, Aunt Melissy was always a spry woman . . very stirring and
primpy, too. . . She dressed him all up neat and proper in his very best
things. **1915** *DN* 4.215, *Primpy,* finical. "If she wasn't so primpy, she'd
be a better student." **1967–69** *DARE* (Qu. W37, *When a woman puts
on her good clothes and tries to look her best . . she's* _____) Inf
HI6, Primpy; (Qu. W40, . . *A woman who overdresses*) Inf **NY**83, Too
primpy woman; (Qu. HH35, *A woman who puts on a lot of airs: "She's
too* _____ *for me."*) Infs **KY**6, 40, Primpy; (Qu. HH38, *A womanish
man*) Inf **TN**6, Primpy.

primrose n

1 =**evening primrose a.**

1784 in 1785 Amer. Acad. Arts & Sci. *Memoirs* 1.438 **PA,** Oeno-
thera. . . Primrose. . . Common in old fields. July. This plant is very
generally known by the name of *Scabious,* and seems to have been mistaken for the *Scabiosa arvensis* of Linnæus. **1830** Rafinesque *Med.
Flora* 2.247, *Oenothera biennis* . . Sundrop, Primrose tree, Scabish.
1897 IN Dept. Geol. & Nat. Resources *Rept. for 1896* 660, *O[enothera]
sinuata*. . . Sinuate-leaved Primrose. Sandy cultivated fields. **1956**
McAtee *Some Dialect NC* 57, *Primrose*. . . the *Hartmania* or *Oenothera
speciosa*. Chapel Hill. **1961** Thomas *Flora Santa Cruz* 251 **cwCA,**
O[enothera] micrantha. . . Small Primrose. **1967** *DARE* Wildfl QR
Pl.145A Inf **CA**24, Primrose.

2 =**evening primrose b.**

1941 Jaeger *Wildflowers* 173, Narrow-leaved primrose. *Oenothera
refracta*. . . Especially plentiful from Baker northward on the Mohave
D[esert]. *Ibid,* Purple primrose. *Oenothera heterochroma*. . . A Nevada
species which enters the mountains of the Death Valley Nat[ional]
Mon[ument]. **1944** Abrams *Flora Pacific States* 2.200, *Oenothera
chamaenerioides* . . , Willow-herb Primrose. *Ibid, Oenothera nevadensis*. . . Nevada Primrose. **1967** *DARE* Tape **CA**4, [FW:] What are your
favorite desert flowers? [Inf:] I think the combination of verbena, primrose and coreopsis is most impressive.

3 =**evening primrose c.**

1936 Whitehouse *TX Flowers* 83, Square-bud primrose. Day Primrose.
Creamcups (*Meriolix spinulosa*) has yellow cup-shaped flowers which
last only twenty-four hours but which are open during the day. **1961**
Wills–Irwin *Flowers TX* 165, Day-primrose—*Oenothera serrulata*. . .
Distribution: Manitoba and Minnesota to Texas, New Mexico, and Mex-
ico.

4 A wild rose.

2000 *DARE* File **seWI** (as of c1950), My parents (natives of Wisconsin), neighbors of their generation, and many people in farming communities always referred to the wild, usually few-petaled, roses as "primroses." This seems to have been the common usage, and I still hear
occasional references to the "primroses" growing along rural roads and
pasture fences.

primrose willow n
A **false loosestrife,** esp *Ludwigia decurrens*.

1890 *Century Dict.* 3257, *Jussiaea*. . . The genus is sometimes very
properly called *primrose-willow*. **1910** Shreve *MD Plant Life* 460,
Jussiaea decurrens. . . Upright Primrose-willow. **1949** Moldenke *Amer.
Wild Flowers* 92, The primrosewillows (*Jussiaea*) are found mostly in
the southeastern part of our area [=North America north of the Rio
Grande]. **1970** Correll *Plants TX* 1133, *Ludwigia decurrens*. . . Primrose-willow.

prin- See **pretty A2a**

prince feather See **prince's-feather 2**

Prince of Paris n Also *Prince of Paris lost his hat, Prince of
Pilsen*

A children's game; see quots 1909, 1957.

1909 (1923) Bancroft *Games* 232, *Prince of Paris. . .* A player is chosen as leader; the others are numbered consecutively . . and all are seated. The leader . . says, "The Prince of Paris has lost his hat. Did you find it, Number Four, sir?" whereupon Number Four jumps to his feet and says:—"What, sir! I, sir?" . . "Yes, sir! You, sir!" . . "Not I, sir!" . . "Who, then, sir?" . . "Number Seven, sir." Number Seven . . must jump at once to his feet. . . "Not I, sir! . . Number Three, sir!" Number Three immediately jumps to his feet, and the same dialogue is repeated. The object of the game is for the leader to try to repeat the statement . . before the last player named can jump to his feet and say, "What, sir! I, sir?" If he succeeds . . he changes places with the player who failed in promptness, that player becoming leader. **1945** Boyd *Hdbk. Games* 95, *The Prince of Paris.* **1953** Brewster *Amer. Nonsinging Games* 26, *The Priest Has Lost His Cap. . .* Other names by which this game is known include . . The Prince of Paris. **1957** *Sat. Eve. Post Letters* **KS**, The "Prince of Pilsen" was an indoor game, played at parties, etc. It had to be played Fast and Furiously. Players sat in chairs around the room. Each one was given a number. Then the one "it" stood in the middle and announced at the start of the game, "The Prince of Pilsen lost his hat. Number _____ took it!" The one who had that number . . must quickly jump to his feet, and say, "Who, Sir, I, Sir?" "Yes, Sir, you, Sir!" "No, Sir, not I Sir, Number _____ took it," etc. Anyone caught "napping" was the next one "it." *Ibid* **neWI** (as of c1890s), Old games . . Prince of Paris Lost His Hat. *Ibid* **MI**, Games . . played in Allegan County Michigan during the first twenty years of this century . . Prince of Paris lost his hat.

prince's-feather n Also *princess feather*

1 A **knotweed 1** (here: *Polygonum orientale*). Also called **gentleman's cane, kiss-me-over-the-fence, ladyfinger 4, love-lies-bleeding 3, prince's-plume 1, ragged sailor 1**

1822 Eaton *Botany* 401, *[Polygonum] orientale* (prince's feather). **1840** MA Zool. & Bot. Surv. *Herb. Plants & Quadrupeds* 103, *P[olygonum] orientale. . .* Princess' Feather. . . is a large and tall exotic, with large broad leaves, and flowers in long and flexuous and pendulous spikes of a bright-reddish color. **1931** Harned *Wild Flowers Alleghanies* 151, Prince's Feather. . . Flower clusters dense, large, slightly fragrant and of a beautiful bright rose color. Easily cultivated and very showy. **1968** *DARE* FW Addit **NY**91, Kiss-me-over-the-garden-wall or princess feather.

2 also *prince-feather:* An **amaranth.**

1847 Wood *Class-Book* 471, A[maranthus] hypochondriacus. *Prince's Feather. . .* This species is native in the Middle States, and cultivated often as a garden annual. **1893** Owen *Voodoo Tales* 6 **MO**, The prince's-feather and the broom-corn nodded their tall heads together. **1912** Mathews *Amer. Wild Flowers* 112, *Amarantus hybridus* Forma *hypochondriacus.* . . In cultivation called Prince's Feather. **1935** Glasgow *Vein of Iron* 83 **wVA**, She had never failed in summer to flaunt a few gaudy blossoms, usually prince's-feather or cockscomb, before the door of her hovel. **1956** Rayford *Whistlin' Woman* 34 **AL**, In the front yards of houses were beds of princess feathers. **1968** *DARE* (Qu. S11, . . *Bachelor's button*) Inf **MO**4, The bachelor's button, the cornflower, prince-feathers, and cockscombs belong to the same family.

3 Any of var other plants; see quots.

1919 *DN* 5.58 **NW**, *Prince's feather.* Laburnum. **1968** *DARE* (Qu. S6, . . *Queen Anne's lace:* [*Summertime roadside weed two feet high or so with a lacy white top*]) Inf **CA**105, Princess feathers. **1997** in 2002 (acc) TX A&M Univ. *Plantanswer Machine* (Internet), Prince's feather is an old common name for plumed celosia, an easy to grow annual flower. Colorful red and yellow plumes can be dried for winter arrangements, as well as being long-lasting cut flowers.

prince's pine n Also *princess pine*

1 =**pipsissewa.** esp **CA, NW** Cf **noble pine**

1807 (1969) Pursh *Jrl. Bot. Excursion* 12 **seNY**, The Pyrola umbellata, called here Princess Pine. **1822** Eaton *Botany* 236, *[Chimaphila] umbellata* . . prince's pine, bitter wintergreen. **1897** Parsons *Wild Flowers CA* 104, The prince's pine is a charming little plant, and may be found beneath the undergrowth in the great coniferous woods of the Sierras, where it sits demurely with bowed head, like some cloistered nun engaged with her own meditations. **1939** (1973) FWP *Guide MT* 14, In the moister parts of the lower montaine forest are Moneses and prince's pine. **1949** Peattie *Cascades* 235, That pretty little shrub . . is pipsissewa or prince's pine, Chimaphila umbellata. It has narrow, toothed, leathery leaves and four to eight nodding pink flowers in a loose termi-

nal cluster. **1967** *DARE* Wildfl QR Pl.152A Infs **MI**31, 57, **WA**30, Princess pine. **1969** *DARE* Tape **CA**136, Princess-pine tea. . . it was suppose to been kind of a . . kidney medicine. . . a little low plant that grew up high in the mountain.

2 =**jack pine 1.**

1884 Sargent *Forests of N. Amer.* 201, *Pinus Banksiana. . .* Gray pine. Scrub pine. Prince's pine. . . A small tree, 9 to 22 meters in height . . barren, sandy soil, or, less commonly, in rich loam. **1950** Peattie *Nat. Hist. Trees* 17, Jack Pine. . . Other Names: Gray, Black, Black Jack, Scrub, Princess, or Banksian Pine. **1966–68** *DARE* (Qu. T5, . . *Kinds of evergreens, other than pine*) Inf **MI**2, Princess pine—like a tree, but about five feet high, no needles, soft cedar-like branches; (Qu. T17, . . *Kinds of pine trees;* not asked in early QRs) Inf **WI**52, Princess pine.

3 A **club moss** (here: *Lycopodium obscurum*).

1898 *Plant World* 2.14 **sPA**, Prince's Pine, for *Lycopodium obscurum.* **1969** *DARE* (Qu. T5, . . *Kinds of evergreens, other than pine*) Inf **CT**28, Princess pine—just a root up from the ground. **1995** Brako et al. *Scientific & Common Names Plants* 47, [*Lycopodium*] *obscurum* . . princess-pine, tree club-moss.

prince's-plume n

1 =**prince's-feather 1.**

1923 Amer. Joint Comm. Horticult. Nomenclature *Std. Plant Names* 378, [*Polygonum] orientale. . .* Princesplume. **1933** Small *Manual SE Flora* 457, *P[olygonum] orientalis.* . . Prince's-plume.

2 also *princess plume:* A western plant of the genus *Stanleya,* esp *S. pinnata.* For other names of the latter see **desert plume, Indian cabbage 2, Paiute ~, wild ~, yellow poker**

1943 Elmore *Ethnobotany Navaho* 50, *Cleome pinnata* Pursh. Prince's Plume. . . This plant is used as a medicine for glandular swellings. **1966–67** *DARE* (Qu. S26e, *Other wildflowers . . ;* not asked in early QRs) Inf **CA**2, Prince's-plume; **CA**4, Golden prince's-plume. **1968** Abbey *Desert Solitaire* 28 **seUT**, I can see the princess plume with its tall golden racemes. **1975** Zwinger *Run River* 246 **UT**, Among them are prince's plume, several milkvetches, and rice grass. **1987** Kindscher *Edible Wild Plants* 215, Prince's plume has been referred to as the "sentinel of the Plains" because of its conspicuous, plumelike spikes of yellow flowers, which especially stand out against a darkened skyline.

princess feather See **prince's-feather**

princess pine See **prince's pine**

princess plume See **prince's plume 2**

princeton n esp **Nth, N Midl** See Map

A man's short hairstyle; see quot.

1965–70 *DARE* (Qu. X5, . . *Different kinds of men's haircuts*) Infs **CA**162, **IL**97, 98, **MI**42, 75, **OH**46, **PA**76, 94, 131, 167, Princeton; **AK**8, Princeton—flat (crew-type) on top, combed back at the sides—modern, young men; **CT**34, Princeton—short but with a pompadour; **MI**123, Princeton—medium-length front, rest in "butch" cut; **MO**14, Princeton—fairly short, medium short, parted. In front brushed to one side up a little bit; **MO**26, Princeton—a butch haircut (same as a crew cut); **PA**93, Princeton—same as joe college. [10 of 16 Infs young; 13 coll educ]

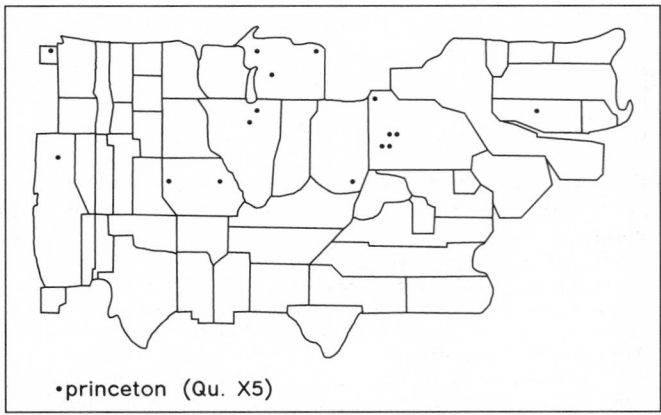

•princeton (Qu. X5)

prink v, hence vbl n *prinking* Also with *up* [*OED2 prink* v.[2] 2 1576 →]

To dress or groom oneself with care, primp; to arrange or adorn; hence adj *prinky* overly concerned with one's appearance; ppl adjs *prinked out,* ~ *up* dressed up.

1775 in 1856 Moore *Songs & Ballads* 100, All prinked up in *full bag-wig.* **1806** (1970) Webster *Compendious Dict.* 236, *Prink. . .* to dress for show. [*DARE* Ed: This entry does not appear in Webster's English model.] **1858** O.W. Holmes *Aut. Breakf.—t* ii. (1865) 15 *(OED2)*, Ironing out crumpled paragraphs, starching limp ones, and crimping and plaiting a little; it is as natural as prinking at the looking-glass. **1899** (1912) Green *VA Folk-Speech* 335, *Prink. . .* To deck; adorn; dress ostentatiously or fantastically. **1899** (1977) Norris *McTeague* 188 **San Francisco CA**, Was there time to make herself look otherwise, and who was there to be pleased when she was all prinked out? **1905** *DN* 3.16 **cCT**, *Prink. . .* To dress in a finical manner. **1934** *WV Review* Dec 77, A couple of years ago I heard a man in southern West Virginia . . mention something about women *prinking up* so much. **1940** *Sun* (Baltimore MD) 31 Jan 6/4 *(Hench Coll.)*, While at home she should not keep you waiting while she prinks in her room. **1941** *LANE* Map 358, *Dress up. . .* Terms referring primarily to 'making up' the face and hair [include] *. . prink,* ~ *up. . .* The following terms are thus restricted by various informants: Used only of men: *prink* [by 3 infs, **se,ceCT**]. . . 1 inf, **nwCT**, "We might say She persists in being prinky." **1946** *PADS* 5.33 **VA**, *Prink. . .* Get dressed; not common. **1968** *DARE* (Qu. W37, *When a woman puts on her good clothes and tries to look her best . . she's* _____) Inf **NY53**, Prinking. **1995** Tyler *Ladder of Yrs.* 279 **eMD**, She prinked her skirt out around her.

printcloth sack n Also *printcloth bag, print(ed) sack* **Sth, S Midl**

A cloth container made of printed cloth.

1965–67 *DARE* (Qu. F21, *A cloth or paper container that you buy flour in*) Inf **AL14**, Print sack—from older days when the sacks were printed material; **AR54**, Print sack; **AL15**, Printcloth bag—made dresses of it; **AL1**, Printcloth sack. **1986** Pederson *LAGS Concordance (Sack)* 2 infs, **AR, LA**, Print sack(s); [1 inf, **swTN**, Printcloth—for flour sacks; made clothes;] 1 inf, **neAR**, Printed sacks.

Prisbeterum See **Presbytery**

priscimmon See **persimmon**

prise See **prize** v²

prisidint See **president**

prisoner's base n Also *prison bar,* ~ *base, prison(er's) goal,* ~ *gool, prisoners, prisoner's race* **chiefly Nth, N Midl, West** See Map Cf **dare-base**

A game of tag with many variations, in which one team tags and imprisons members of the other team; see quots.

1781 in 1971 Denny *Military Jrl.* 41, This business reminds me of a play among the boys, called Prison-base. **1806** (1905) Clark *Orig. Jrls. Lewis & Clark Exped.* 5.118, Our party devided and played at prisoners base untill night. **1865** [see **poison B1b(1)**]. **1883** Newell *Games & Songs* 164, *Prisoner's Base. . .* The two parties stand on the same line, and the bases are placed diagonally opposite . . so that each base is nearer to the enemy's forces than to those of the side to which it belongs. The game is opened by a challenge given by one leader to the other; each player can tag any one of the opponents who has quitted his line before he has left his own. Any player tagged must go to his base. Any player who can reach his base in safety may release a prisoner. **1891** *Jrl. Amer. Folkl.* 4.224 **Brooklyn NY**, *Prisoner's Base*—Two even sides are chosen, and go upon opposite sides of the street. . . One of the players starts the game by running into the middle of the street, and another from the opposite side will try to capture him. While the first is running back, one from his side will endeavor to capture his pursuer, and this is continued, any player having the right to take those who ran out before him, and being protected from their attack. The prisoners solicit the players on their own side to rescue them, which they may do by touching them, although the rescuers themselves run great chance of being caught. The side wins that makes captives of their opponents. **1895** *DN* 1.398 **cNY**, *Prison goal, prison gool, prison base, prisoner's base:* all these names of the game are more or less common in central N.Y. **1899** (1912) Green *VA Folk-Speech* 335, *Prisoner's-base. . .* A children's game in which one player strives to touch others as they run from one base or goal to another. **1901** *DN* 2.145, *Prisoner's goal. . .* Another name for prisoner's base. **1952** Brown *NC Folkl.* 1.72, *Prisoner's Base.* **1953** Brewster *Amer. Nonsinging Games* 56, *Prison Base. . .* The game

ends either with the exhausting of the enemy's forces or by a count of heads after a certain time has elapsed, the side having the more players being the winner. **1957** *Sat. Eve. Post Letters* **neIL**, On the ice with skates we played . . prisoner's goal. **1963** *North Rascal* 27 **WI** (as of 1918), Girls had to wear swimming suits and come in earlier from our evening games of prisoner's base and run-sheep-run. **1965–70** *DARE* (Qu. EE33, . . *Outdoor games . . that children play*) 16 Infs, **scattered, esp Nth, N Midl**, Prisoner's base; **IL16**, Prisoner's base—two teams, two bases. One team has to approach a line near other base and run home to their own base before tagged by opponents—if tagged they join opponents' team; **NJ39**, Prisoner's base—choose up sides—"it side" has to catch the others. When a man is caught, he is a prisoner and must stay so until freed by a man on his side who must touch him; the prisoner is guarded; **NH5**, King's land—similar to prison bar, but players simply changed sides when tagged; **VA13**, Prison base; **OH42**, Prisoners—like red rover; **IL107**, Prisoner's race; (Qu. EE1, . . *Games . . children play*) Inf **VT12**, Prisoner's base; (Qu. EE13a, *Games in which every player hides except one, and that one must try to find the others*) Inf **TX33**, Prisoner's base; (Qu. EE14, . . *The place where the player who is 'it' has to wait and count while the others hide*) Inf **IL11**, Prison base; (Qu. EE27, *Games played on the ice*) Inf **WI77**, Prisoner's gool. **1984** *DARE* File **seNY**, Our very best game . . was Prisoner's Base or Prisoners' Base. I don't know which. There had to be at least four on a side. We drew a line across the street and a circle for the bases about fifteen or twenty feet back from the line, on each side. Each base had four or five small stones in it. Object of the game was to steal the other side's stones.

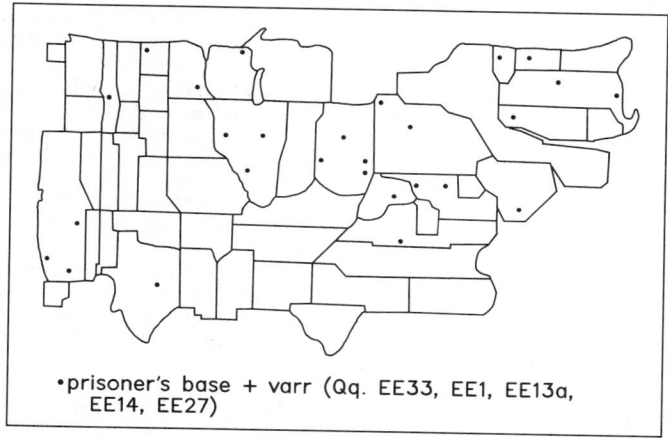

•prisoner's base + varr (Qq. EE33, EE1, EE13a, EE14, EE27)

priss v

1 also with *around;* rarely *prissy;* Esp of a woman: to walk or go about in an ostentatious or affected manner. **chiefly Sth, S Midl, TX** See Map

1946 McCullers *Member* 67 **AL**, He prisses around with a pink satin blouse and one arm akimbo. **1954** Welty *Ponder Heart* 71 **MS**, I just prissed across the yard and up the steps to the porch and around the washing machine to the front door and called for Narciss. **1965–70** *DARE* (Qu. Y22, *To move around in a way to make people take notice of you: "Look at him* _____.") 17 Infs, **chiefly Sth, S Midl, TX**, Priss; **FL51, GA63**, Priss [used of women]; **TX27, 28,**

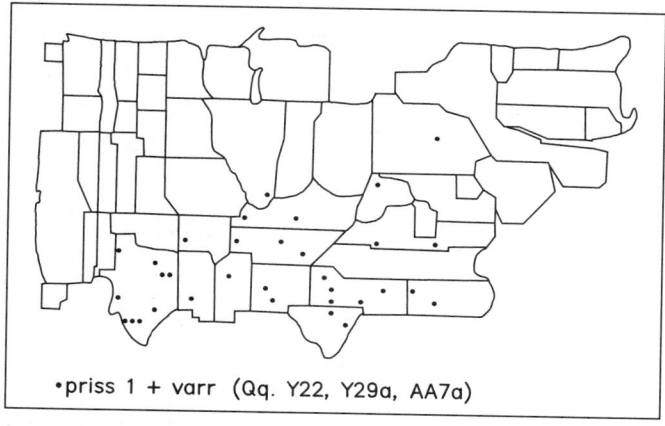

•priss 1 + varr (Qq. Y22, Y29a, AA7a)

Priss—girls, show off—boys; **TX**39, 52, Priss—if (it's) a girl; **GA**23, **VA**39, Prissing; **GA**6, Look at her prissing; **AR**31, **KY**11, Priss(ing) around; **LA**23, Priss around—said of a lady; **TX**40, Priss around—little girls; show off—if it's a little boy; **VA**2, Prissy; (Qu. Y29a, *To 'go out' a great deal, not to stay at home much:* "*She's always _____.*") Inf **GA**73, Prissing around; (Qu. AA7a, . . *A woman who is very fond of men and is always trying to know more—if she's nice about it*) Inf **KY**85, Prissing around. [23 of 33 Infs young or mid-aged] **1984** Burns *Cold Sassy* 201 **nGA** (as of 1906), 'I don't need your permission,' I told her, and I just prissed over and got them [=a string of beads]. **1986** Pederson *LAGS Concordance,* 1 inf, **ceAR,** Priss around—of a woman; 1 inf, **cGA,** She prissing around like she sixteen. **1988** Kingsolver *Bean Trees* 4 **KY,** Candy Stripers, town girls with money for the pink-and-white uniforms and prissing around the bedpans on Saturdays like it was the holiest substance on God's green earth they'd been trusted to carry.

2 with *up:* To adorn; to decorate.

1967 *DARE* (Qu. W30, *When a woman adds decorations to make something more attractive . . "It's too plain—I think I'll put on a few flowers to _____ it up."*) Inf **SC**34, Priss.

priss around See **priss 1**

priss up See **priss 2**

prissy adj, also used absol

1 rarely *prissy-prim, ~-rissy:* Prim; priggish; sissified. **widespread exc NEng** See Map

1895 Harris *Mr. Rabbit* 40 **GA,** Once, when I was courting, I spoke of a sitting hen, but the young lady said I was too prissy for anything. **1905** *DN* 3.91 **nwAR,** Prissy. . . Precise, nice, over-particular. 'She's awful prissy.' Rare. **1909** *DN* 3.359 **eAL, wGA,** Prissy. . . Very particular, over-nice, precise, squeamish. . . Universal. **1915** *DN* 4.215, Prissy, a cross in meaning between *precise* and *sissy.* "She is a prissy girl." Colloquial. **1918** *DN* 5.19 **NC,** Prissy, prudish, overly modest or scrupulous. **1927** *AmSp* 2.362 **cwWV,** Prissey [sic] . . a boy who acts like a girl. "Don't be such a prissey, Jim." **c1950** *Halpert Coll.* 50 **wKY, nwTN,** Prissy . . =impudent, audacious in an annoying manner. [Halpert: Comment was added that the term is sometimes applied to effeminate boys; but, if so, this would seem nearer to the usual meaning: "prim, precise or over-precise." The explanation given when *prissy* is applied to boys is *prim* + *sissy.*] **1965–70** *DARE* (Qu. HH11b, *Someone who is too particular or fussy—if it's a woman*) 132 Infs, **widespread exc NEng,** Prissy; **TN**53, Prissy-rissy; (Qu. HH35, *A woman who puts on a lot of airs:* "*She's too _____ for me.*") 41 Infs, **scattered, but esp Sth, S Midl,** Prissy; **GA**44, Miss Prissy-prim; (Qu. HH11a, *Someone who is too particular or fussy—if it's a man*) 36 Infs, **scattered,** Prissy; [**VA**46, Prissly;] **FL**35, **NC**47, Too prissy; **MO**15, Awful prissy; (Qu. HH38, *A womanish man*) 14 Infs, **scattered,** Prissy; (Qu. GG14, . . *Someone who fusses or worries a lot, especially about little things*) Inf **PA**165, Prissy; (Qu. HH2, . . *A citified person*) Inf **NC**82, Prissy; (Qu. HH34, *General words . . for a woman, not necessarily uncomplimentary*) Inf **FL**7, Prissy heifer. **1967** *DARE* FW Addit **LA**14, *Prissy*—affected, over-precise. **1985** *DARE* File **cwIN,** Little girls, ladies, too easily shocked are "prissy-butts." **1986** Pederson *LAGS Concordance,* 3 infs, **AR, LA, MS,** Prissy.

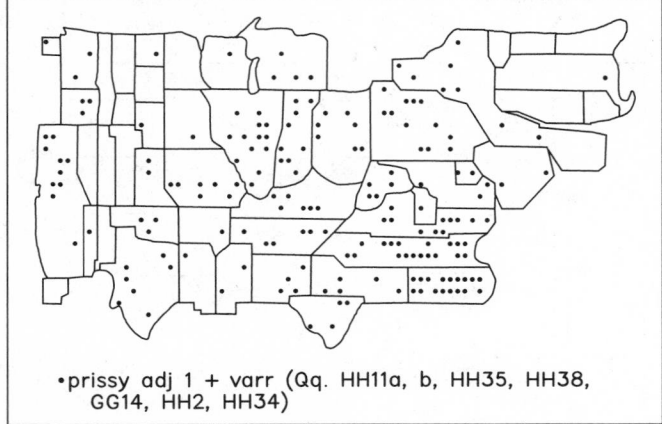

• prissy adj 1 + varr (Qq. HH11a, b, HH35, HH38, GG14, HH2, HH34)

2 Lively, sprightly.

1968 *DARE* (Qu. KK27, *A very lively, active old person:* "*For his age,*

he's _____.") Inf **GA**45, Prissy. **1986** Pederson *LAGS Concordance* (*She's quite lively*) 1 inf, **cMS,** Prissy—they "spruce up" and feel good; 1 inf, **cnAR,** Prissy—old, active woman.

prissy v See **priss 1**

prissy-prim (or -rissy) See **prissy** adj **1**

prit- See **pretty A2a**

prittie See **pratie**

pritty See **pretty A1a**

private adv

In a private home; see quot.

1978 *DARE* File **Milwaukee WI,** To "live private," among Milwaukeeans of Polish background, is said commonly, meaning that one lives in a home or private house, not in an apartment building or other group housing.

privateer n

Any of var small hawks, as **Cooper's hawk, pigeon hawk 1, sharp-shinned hawk.**

1917 *Wilson Bulletin* 29.2.81 **VA,** *Accipiter velox.*—Privateer, Wallops I[slan]d, Va. *Ibid, Falco columbarius.*—Privateer, Wallops I[slan]d, Va. **1955** MA Audubon Soc. *Bulletin* 40.441 **CT,** *Cooper's Hawk.* . . Privateer (Conn. From its speed and piratical actions).

private house n **NYC**

A house usu owned and occupied by a single family.

1938 in Lib. of Congress *Amer. Memory: WPA Life Hist.* (Internet) **NYC,** That was a big private house on Lexington Avenue. *Ibid* **Bronx NYC,** Thirty years ago, Tinton Avenue was a tree-lined, suburban street. Now it is bleak and stony. Apartment houses . . blot out the sun. The little private house is ever in shadow, gripped in the vise of two dirty, brick tenements. *Ibid* **Bronx NYC,** A large converted private house on a rather quiet street. *Ibid* **Brooklyn NYC,** Private house remodelled into apartments. **1939** *Ibid* **NYC,** Got two rooms in a private house with a private bath. **2001** *Forward* (NY NY) 27 Apr 14/5 **NYC** (as of 1930s), The Greenbergs lived in a "private" house, as we who lived in tenements referred to the few single-family homes around us. We spoke of the families in them as "rich." **2001** *DARE* File **NYC** (as of 1950s), For those of us of working-class background who grew up in apartment houses or the projects or tenements, a "private house," that is, a detached one- or two-family home, represented wealth and comfort, and visiting one was always a treat for me who never knew anything other than cramped apartment-dwelling.

privy n

1 also *privy bush:* The privet (*Ligustrum sempervirens*) or other dense, hedge-forming shrub; hence nouns *privy (hedge), privy wall* a hedge designed to provide privacy. [*OED2* 1573 →; prob by folk-etym from *privet*] **esp Midl**

1786 (1925) Washington *Diaries* 3.37 **VA,** Took the covering off the Plants in my Botanical garden, and found none living . . except some of the Acasce or Acacia, flower fence, and privy. **1876** Hobbs *Bot. Hdbk.* 93, Privy, Privet, Ligustrum vulgare. **1917** in 1944 *ADD* 476 **sWV,** Sweep your yard with a privy broom. **c1960** *Wilson Coll.* **csKY,** Privet (or privet bush). . . A hedge shrub, often called privy-bush. **1982** Slone *How We Talked* 29 **eKY** (as of c1950), Privy bush—a hedge bush. **1999** *NADS Letters* **GA,** Within the last 12 months or so I heard a native Georgian use the term 'privy hedge' to describe *Ligustrum sinense,* or the common privet. The speaker is about 65 years of age. **2000** *NADS Letters* **ME,** My sense of it is that any type of shrub that is placed in a row to hide the house from the street is called a privy hedge. *Ibid* **eVA,** [A] privy bush or hedge is planted for privacy, to keep the neighbors from seeing into the back yard. *Ibid* **NC, VA,** My maternal grandmother's family is from North Carolina and Virginia. They come from "old money", and when visiting family members I remember hearing about people's hedge walls around their grounds or gardens being called privies. They said it was to keep homelife privy or private. . . I still use the term, but I say "privy hedge" or "privy wall", so people know what I am referring to. *Ibid* **WV,** I grew up in southern West Virginia (Charleston) and we always referred to any hedge (that was thorny) as a "privy hedge". I am aware of the word "privet" but always thought of that as referring to a specific type of well trimmed hedge in a nice landscape. *Ibid* **cIN,** About privy hedges—Growing up in Central IN, I thought that was exactly the correct term for a hedge used to separate, or make private, a yard or property line. . . It's not a term often encountered, but I know I've heard it used recently in a garden tour here in Central IN (Johnson County) by someone (most likely an older person).

2 =**matrimony vine.**

1892 *Jrl. Amer. Folkl.* 5.101 **OH,** *Lycium vulgare,* privy; Jackson vine; jasmine. Mansfield, O.

privy spider n [See quot]

A black widow spider (*Latrodectus mactans*).

1938 Brimley *Insects NC* 473, *L[atrodectus] mactans.* . . Black widow: hour-glass spider; privy spider; black spider with-a-red-spot. Statewide, occurring throughout the year under loose planks, rubbish, in outhouses and similar shady places.

privy vine n

=**coral vine 3.**

1970 Correll *Plants TX* 526, *Antigonon* [spp]. . . Privy-vine. A tropical American genus of about 8 species.

privy wall See **privy 1**

prize v[1] [*OED2 prize* v.[1] 2 c1440 →; "*Obs.* in literary use."]

1 To set or estimate the value of; to price.

1713 in 1879 MA Hist. Soc. *Coll.* 5th ser 6.387, Owen [=a constable] took [in a tax dispute] a Cow of Veisy pris'd at £4.0-0. **1787** in 1915 *New Engl. Hist. & Geneal. Reg.* 69.304 **MA,** I went to Groton to Prize of some Cattle. **1856** in 1862 Colt *Went to KS* 138 **NY,** Father says he shall have the damage done to the cornfield prized, go and present it and get pay. **1901** *DN* 2.145 **NY,** *Prize.* . . To ask the price of goods in a store. **1944** *PADS* 2.69 **S Midl** [Tobacco words], *Prize.* . . To estimate the value of.

2 See quot.

1944 *PADS* 2.69 **S Midl** [Tobacco words], *Prize.* . . To raise the price of by bidding higher.

prize n

1a A lever. [*OED2 prize* sb.[4] 1 13 . . →; "Now *dial.*"]

1807 (1919) Bedford *Tour to New Orleans* 55 **VA,** Was grounded on shore—made exertions with the poles—these ineffectual, leaped into the water and with prizes forced her [=a boat] off. **1899** (1912) Green *VA Folk-Speech* 336, *Prize.* . . A lever. **1902** *DN* 2.242 **sIL,** *Prize.* . . A lever. **1907** *DN* 3.225 **nwAR,** *Prize.* . . A lever. **1909** *DN* 3.361 **eAL, wGA,** *Prize.* . . A lever. Universal both as verb and noun. **1967** *DARE* (Qu. L40, *A long iron bar used to move rocks and other heavy things*) Inf **MN2,** Prize.

b attrib in combs *prize bar, ~ beam, ~ log, ~ pole.* **chiefly Sth, S Midl** See Map

1800 in 1969 Herndon *Wm. Tatham Tobacco* 44 **VA,** The ordinary apparatus for prizing consists of the prize beam, the platform, the blocks, and the cover. **1923** *DN* 5.217 **swMO,** *Prize-pole.* . . A lever. **1956** *Hall Coll.* **eTN,** Aunt Becky Cable was the strongest woman in this cove. . . She'd be out with a prize pole and an axe pullin' them stumps out. **1965–70** *DARE* (Qu. L40, *A long iron bar used to move rocks and other heavy things*) 13 Infs, **esp Sth, S Midl,** Prize bar; 9 Infs, **esp SC,** Prize pole; **SC40,** Prize pole—if it's made of wood; **SC47,** Prize pole—for the heaviest job; crowbar made of a sapling or tree; [**MS81,** Prizing bar;] (Qu. L39, *An iron bar with a bent end, used for pulling nails, opening boxes, and so on*) Inf **IL27,** Prize bar. **1967** Key *Tobacco Vocab.* 168 **TN,** Davis spoke of "prize-pole" when describing how they packed

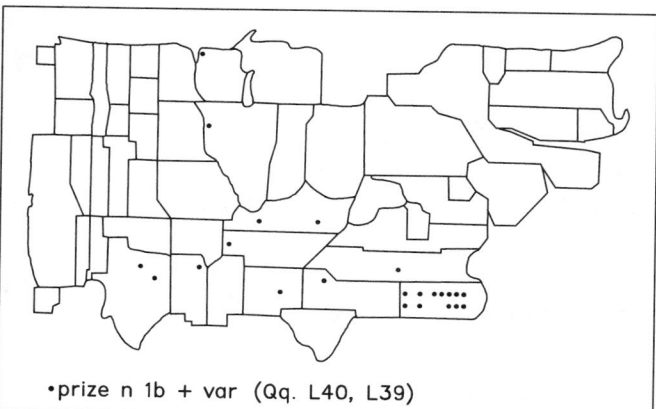

• prize n 1b + var (Qq. L40, L39)

the tob[acco] into bales. **1973** in 1996 *Montgomery Coll.* **eTN,** These men down here was on that big dam with a big crowbar, raising them splash boards like that, you know, over a prize log. **1983** *MJLF* 9.1.52 **ceKY** (as of 1956), *Prize bar* . . a straight iron bar used as a lever. **1986** Pederson *LAGS Concordance,* 1 inf, **csGA,** Prize pole—used instead of x-frame; 1 inf, **ceFL,** Prize pole—to jack up a car; 1 inf, **neAR,** Prize pole—used to move logs with; 1 inf, **cnLA,** Prizing up with a prize pole; 1 inf, **ceTX,** Prize pole—pine; to pry car out of mud if stuck.

2 An act of prying.

1979 Lewis *How to Talk Yankee* [26] **nNEng,** Put that crowbar under it and give her a good prize.

prize v[2] Also sp *prise*

1 To move, raise, or press with a lever; to pry. [*OED2 prize* v.[3] 1 1686 →; this remains the std Brit form but has been generally replaced in the US (and occas in Brit dial) by *pry.*] **chiefly S Midl; also Sth**

1818 in 1824 Knight *Letters* 107 **KY,** Some words are used, even by genteel people, from their imperfect educations, in a new sense . . to prize for to raise by lever. **1840** *S. Lit. Messenger* 6.225 **VA,** It was in vain we remonstrated, and offered to help him "prize" his stage out again. **1899** (1912) Green *VA Folk-Speech* 336, *Prize.* . . To force or press, especially force open by means of a leaver [sic]. To pry. **1901** *DN* 1.376 **seKY, eTN, wNC,** *Prize* = pry. **1902** *DN* 2.242 **sIL,** *Prize.* . . To press down, as with a lever. *Prize.* . . To pry, as with a lever. **1906** *DN* 3.151 **nwAR,** *Prize.* . . To pry. "These boys would prize open the door and remove the brass knobs and other pieces of machinery."—Fayetteville Daily. **1916** *DN* 4.302 **LA, NC, VA,** *Prise.* . . To pry. . . "He prised the door open." c**1920** in 1993 Farwell–Nicholas *Smoky Mt. Voices* 128 **sAppalachians,** Le's prise this rock up. **1923** *DN* 5.217 **swMO,** *Prize.* . . Pry, meaning to lift with a lever. **1932** Randolph *Ozark Mt. Folks* 153, An' when Bud tuck an' prized th' led off, thar was a heap o' gold-money! **1937** *AmSp* 12.287 **wVA,** *Prise* (to pry up). **1942** Faulkner *Go Down* 51 **MS,** He prised the brick up with his knife blade. **1958** McCulloch *Woods Words* 139 **Pacific NW,** *Prize up*—To lift with a lever of some kind. **1966** *DARE* (QR at Qu. N24, *To prize up.* **1967–69** *DARE* FW Addit **KY**47, Prize open a jar = pry open a jar; **KY**65, The burglar tried to prize open a window; **LA**10, Sometimes we'd have to prize his jaws apart; **LA**28, [praız] = pry. **1976** Ryland *Richmond Co. VA* 375, *Prize*—pry; "Prize open those oysters." **1986** Pederson *LAGS Concordance (Hoist)* 1 inf, **cnLA,** Prize down on it; 1 inf, **csAL,** Prize it; 1 inf, **cnLA,** Prizing up with a prize pole.

2 To compress (tobacco) into hogsheads, originally in a press operated by a huge lever; hence vbl n *prizing;* n *prizery* a place for compressing tobacco. **chiefly S Midl**

1724 (1865) Jones *Present State VA* 40, [They] by Degrees *prize* or press it with proper Engines into great Hogsheads. **1800** in 1969 Herndon *Wm. Tatham Tobacco* 43 **VA,** *Prizing,* in the sense in which it is to be taken here, is, perhaps, a local word . . and must be defined to be the act of pressing or squeezing the article which is to be packed into any package . . so that the size of the article may be reduced in stowage. [**1827** (1935) Bolling *Diary* 43.330 **VA,** Finished hanging up all the tobo. in the Prize House.] **1829** in 1956 Eliason *Tarheel Talk* 288 **cn,cNC,** I have prized to hogsheads of tobacco and got tow more under prise. **1863** in 1865 IL Dept. Ag. *Trans. for 1861–64,* 5.669, Tobacco of this description should be . . prized lightly in the casks so as to admit of a free and open leaf. **1938** *Richmond News Leader* (VA) 28 Sept 24/1 *(Hench Coll.),* Every warehouse that I visited . . looked like a mad house. Leaf flowed in much faster than the shippers were able to get it to their prizeries. **1940** *AmSp* 15.134 [Tobacco market language], *Prizing.* Packing tobacco under pressure. **1944** *PADS* 2.69 **S Midl** [Tobacco words], *Prize.* . . To put in hogsheads for aging and press down hard with machinery. **1967** Key *Tobacco Vocab.* 169 **MD.**

3 See quots.

1953 Randolph–Wilson *Down in Holler* 273 **Ozarks,** *Prize: v.t.* and *v.i.* To pry, to snoop. "*Prizin'* round me" means "prying into my affairs," according to Clay Fulks of Mena, Ark. Some hillfolk use *prizin'* to mean objecting or complaining. **1995** *Brophy Coll.* 57 **swMO** (as of c1960), *Prize.* [T]o pry, to snoop.

prize bar (or beam) See **prize n 1b**

prize log n[1] Cf **scrabble log**

In logging: a log without a mark of ownership, which can be claimed by anyone who finds it.

1905 U.S. Forest Serv. *Bulletin* 61.44 [Logging terms], *Prize logs.*

Logs which come to the sorting jack without marks denoting ownership. (N[orthern] F[orest]) **1958** McCulloch *Woods Words* 139 **Pacific NW,** *Prize log*—A log floating free of any boom, unbranded, and hence the prize of the first man to claim it. **1969** Sorden *Lumberjack Lingo* 90 **NEng, Gt Lakes,** *Prize logs*—Logs which came to the sorting jack without marks denoting ownership.

prize log n[2], **prize pole** See **prize** n **1b**

prizery, prizing See **prize** v[2] **2**

pro- pref When unaccented: usu |pro-, prə-|; also freq |pə(r)-| Pronc-spp *per-, pur-;* for addit pronc and sp varr see quots Cf **pre-** pref[1], **promenade**
Std sense, var forms.
   1815 Humphreys *Yankey in England* 107, *Pertest,* protest. **1837** Sherwood *Gaz. GA* 71, *Provincialisms. . . Perdigious,* for prodigious. *Ibid, Pervision,* provision. **1851** Hooper *Widow Rugby's Husband* 24 **AL,** Well the Lord'll purvide. **1867** Lowell *Biglow* xxxii 'Upcountry' **MA,** *Purtend. . . purvide. . .* are universal vulgarisms, and not peculiar to the Yankee. **1891** *DN* 1.163 **cNY,** [pɚ'dus], 'produce'; [pɚ'tɛkšn], 'protection'; [pɚ'vaɪdn̩], 'providing'; [pɚ'vɪẓn̩z], 'provisions'. **1893** Shands *MS Speech* 49, *Per.* The syllable *pro,* when the first in a word, is generally pronounced by negroes and illiterate whites as *per* [pɜ]; e.g. *perfess, perfessor, perduce, perpose, pernounce.* **1909** *DN* 3.356 **eAL, wGA,** *Perfesser. . .* Professor. **1909** [see **pre-** pref[1]]. **1910** Hart *Vigilante Girl* 144 **nCA,** The . . express messengers gets paid for purtectin' it. **1914** *DN* 4.78 **ME, nNH,** *Purvider, a good. . .* A generous husband. **1914** *DN* 4.160 **cVA,** Ceceh, yo' don't p'onounce yo' 'ahs' at aw! **1922** Gonzales *Black Border* 320 **sSC, GA coasts** [Gullah glossary], *Puhtek*—protect, protects. **1927** Kennedy *Gritny* 40 **sLA** [Black], Goin' suppoat you . . an' puvvide you wid shoes an' vittuls an' things. **1932** Randolph *Ozark Mt. Folks* 50, We jest tackled it one syllable at a time, a-pernouncin' as we went 'long. **1936** *AmSp* 11.150 **eTX,** *Procession, procure, produce, production, profession, prohibit, promote, pronounce, propose, protect, protest, protracted, provoke,* are: . . [prə'djus], [prə'dʌkʃən], etc., and in less literate speech, [pə'djus], [pə'dʌkʃən], etc. **1937** *AmSp* 12.126 **Upstate NY,** Metathesis . . is common, especially when [r] is one of the affected sounds; thus: . . *produce* [pr̩'dus]. **1941** *AmSp* 16.8 **eTX** [Black], *Proceed, produce, prohibit, protect, protest, protracted, provoke,* [pə'si:d], [pə'dju:s], etc. **c1960** *Wilson Coll.* **csKY,** *Protect* /pɚ'tɛkt/ common. **1965–70** *DARE* (Qu. JJ1b, *. . A schoolteacher—a man*) 83 Infs, **widespread,** Professor [Of Infs for whom proncs were recorded, 55 gave [prə-] for the first syllable and 11 [pro-].]; 186 Infs, **widespread,** Perfesser; (Qu. X12, *. . Large front teeth*) Inf **VA69,** Pertruding teeth; (Qu. BB2, *If a person is careful not to put much weight on his injured leg, you might say he was _____ that leg*) Infs **MO**19, 32, 36, Pertecting. **1966** *DARE* Tape **FL**19, As long as they burn the woods every year, why that would keep down the snakes . . it protects [p''tɛks] them. **1982** Slone *How We Talked* 21 **eKY** (as of c1950), I will go, pervidin' it don't rain.

proach See **poach** A2

proag See **prog** v

probably adv Usu |'prɑbəblɪ, -i|; also |'prɑb(ə)lɪ, -i| Pronc-spp *probly, prolly*
Std sense, var forms.
   1909 *DN* 3.360 **eAL, wGA,** *Probly. . .* Probably. **1926** Ferber *Show Boat* 138, Prolly won't be able to open there, neither. **1927** Shewmake *Engl. Pronc. VA* 42, *Probably.* In rapid, careless, or illiterate speech *prob'ly* is used. **1934** *AmSp* 9.160, We Americans have a habit of omitting the second syllable in *probably, government, Saturday* [særdɪ], *interest,* etc. **1942** *AmSp* 17.156 **seNY,** *Probably* . . [prɑbəlɪ] . . [prɑblɪ]. **1955** Faulkner *Big Woods* 192 **MS,** Shucking corn prob'ly. **c1960** *Wilson Coll.* **csKY,** *Probably* is most often |'prɑblɪ|. **1966** *DARE* (Qu. GG27b) Inf **ME**5, Probly it isn't so black as you think. **1976** Garber *Mountain-ese* 71 **sAppalachians,** *Probly* . . probably—We'uns will probly be over to see you'ens next Sunday. **1996** *WI State Jrl.* (Madison) 6 Oct sec G 1/6, He'd always marvel, with mock jealousy, that our old M [=a tractor] could "prolly" outpull his WD-9.

probiscis, probiscus See **proboscis**

probly See **probably**

proboscis n Usu |pro'bɑsəs, prə-; pro'bɑskəs, prə-|; for addit varr see quot 1965–70 Pronc-spp *probiscis, probiscus, proboses* **chiefly Nth, N Midl, West** See Map *joc*
The nose.
   1942 Berrey–Van den Bark *Amer. Slang* 121.69, *Nose. . .* proboscis. **1965–70** *DARE* (Qu. X14, *Joking words for the nose*) 18 Infs, **chiefly Nth, N Midl, West,** Proboscis; **IL**7, 17, 30, **MI**96, **WI**64, Proboscis [prə'bɑskəs]; **AR**40, [prə'bɑsəs]; **CA**178, [prə'bɑskəs]; **CT**15, [prə'bɑsɪs]; **IL**5, [prə'bɑ:ˌskɪs]; **IL**35, [prə'bouˌsɪs]; **IN**30, ['proˌbɑsɚs]; **KS**2, [pro'bɑskɪz]; **MN**18, [prəboskəs]; **NY**93, [pro'bɑskəs]; **NY**205, [pro'bɑsɪs]; **OH**6, [pro'bɑsɪs]; **PA**216, [prɑ'bɔsɪs]; **WI**43, [pro'bɑsəs]; **NC**48, **PA**234, Probiscis; **PA**188, [prob'ɪskəs]; **MS**23, Proboses; (Qu. X15, *. . Kinds of noses, according to shape or size*) Inf **NY**209, Probiscus; **MA**30, [pro'bɑsəs]. **1998** Myers *Eat Drink* 43 **sePA,** Just as I reached the kitchen door, it flew open, narrowly missing my prominent proboscis.

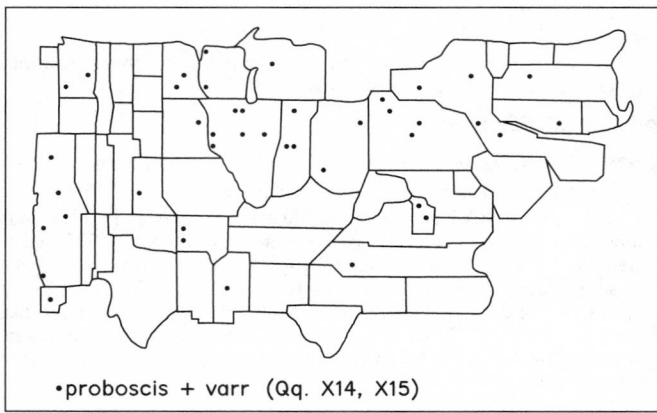

•proboscis + varr (Qq. X14, X15)

proboscis worm n
=**bloodworm 1** (here: *Glycera* spp).
   1974 McClane *McClane's New Std. Fishing Encycl.* 558, Another name for the bloodworm is the "proboscis worm" because its snout is extended or retracted at will and acts as a burrowing organ. The bloodworm's mouth is armed . . [and] may fasten onto a finger.

proboses See **proboscis**

process n *among Black speakers* Cf **conk** n[3], **do** n[1] **3, process** v
A chemical method for straightening and styling the hair; transf: the hair so straightened and styled; the chemicals used in the procedure.
   1964 in 1971 Clarke *Harlem* 319, Sonny rubbed the process in so thick with his rubber gloves, it started stingin' a little t'rough the heavy layer of grease he packed in my scalp. *Ibid* 324, By Friday my process'd need retouchin'. **1965** Little *Autobiog. Malcolm X* 261, They had just banished from their lives forever that phoney, lye-conked, metallic-looking hair, or "the process," as some call it these days. **1968** *Current Slang* 3.2.38 [Watts slang; Black], *Process. . .* Hair that has been straightened or waved with the use of harsh chemicals. A permanent wave. **1969** *DARE* (Qu. X5, *. . Different kinds of men's haircuts*) Inf **IN**75, Process—for Blacks. **1972** Claerbaut *Black Jargon* 76, *Process* . . a hairstyle for a black male which results from straightening the normally bushy or kinky hair. **1974** Matthews–Amdur *My Race* 23 **NYC,** A poor man's process—the kind you got at the barber shop every six months instead of once a month—might leave part of the hair with its natural kinkiness and the rest with the color of the chemicals. **1986** Pederson *LAGS Concordance (Hairstyles)* 1 inf, **swAL,** Process—in 1950s, using hot comb; 1 inf, **seFL,** Process (male); 1 inf, **seFL,** Permanent process—to straighten black's hair. [All infs Black] **1994** Smitherman *Black Talk* 184, *Process* See *Conk.* [*Ibid* 83, *Conk*—A male hairstyle, popular before the 1970s, in which the hair is straightened using a mixture of lye, white potatoes, and eggs.]

process v *among Black speakers* Cf **process** n
To straighten and style the hair by chemical means; hence ppl adj *processed;* also fig.
   1970 *DARE* (Qu. KK38, *To put preparations on the hair to hold it close to the head and make it shiny: "I wish he wouldn't _____ his hair down so!"*) Inf **PA**247, Process. **1972** Claerbaut *Black Jargon* 76, *Processed mind . .* a mentality which is alienated from black culture and tends to take on white attitudes: *He may have a natural, but he's still got a processed mind.* **1974** Matthews–Amdur *My Race* 23 **NYC,** He was

dark-skinned, and had processed hair. **1986** Pederson *LAGS Concordance (Hairstyles)* 1 inf, **cnAL**, Processed. [Inf Black]

procession flower n [*OED2* 1633 →]

A **milkwort** (here: *Polygala incarnata*).

1876 Hobbs *Bot. Hdbk.* 93, Procession flower, Milkwort, Polygala incarnata. **1900** Lyons *Plant Names* 299, [*Polygala*] *incarnata* . . eastern U.S. to Mexico. . . Procession-flower. **1949** Moldenke *Amer. Wild Flowers* 52, In the same general region grows a dainty little pink- or rose-flowered species, *P. incarnata*. . . It is often called processionflower or rogationflower, and blooms continuously throughout the year in the southern part of its range.

proddy adj esp West Cf prod, on the

Irritable; bad-tempered; aggressive.

1932 Tooné *Yankee Slang* 29, Proddy—aggressive. **1958** Latham *Meskin Hound* 62 **cTX**, Hell, I've got more sense'n to jump into a bunch of proddy hogs thataway. **1966–67** *DARE* (Qu. K16, *A cow with a bad temper*) Inf **KS6**, She's kinda proddy ['prɑdi]; **NM6**, Proddy. **1966** *DARE* Tape **OK30**, One big, old, proddy cow was in there. She was on the prod when they cut her horns off. I was out in the middle of the corral, getting her horn, and she come at me and hit me right in the middle of the back and knocked me halfway across the corral. **1995** Brophy *Coll.* 58 **swMO** (as of c1960), Proddy, on the prod. [T]ouchy, easily angered, looking for a fight.

prodject See project v

prod, on the adj phr Rarely *on a prod* chiefly West

1 Irritable, angry, on the offensive—freq in phr *go on the prod;* by analogy, adj phr *off the prod* calm, docile. Cf **proddy**

1903 (1965) Adams *Log Cowboy* 80 **West**, The family was on the prod bigger than a wolf, and there was no use reasoning with them. **1907** White *AZ Nights* 119, "Why, kid," said he, "you can't do nothin' with a cow that gets on the prod that away 'thout you ropes her; and what could you do with her out there if you did rope her?" **1910** Bronson *Reminiscences Ranchman* 56 **WY**, Kid, it is shore up to yu t' go on th' prod. Horn him wi' th' meanest cuss words you knows, 'specially 'bout his closest kin folk. *Ibid* 66, Th' main trick, Kid, 's t' keep her off th' prod 'n' sweet tempered. Ef yu crowds her too hard 'n' gits her on th' fight, it's 'Katy bar th' door' wi' yu, 'n' adios t' her 'n' her calf. **1929** *AmSp* 5.75 **NE** [Cattle country talk], A cook (or a cow) out of temper is "on a prod." **1929** Dobie *Vaquero* 14, Finally if he [=a steer] did get up, he would be so "on the prod" that nothing could come close enough to touch him with a forty-foot pole. **1929** Ellis *Ordinary Woman* 180 **CO** (as of early 20th cent), One morning George is peeved (only we didn't have this word then—we would have said, 'on the prod') at our little stove, which refuses to draw, and he kicks the door off. **1937** Sandoz *Slogum* 85 **NE**, He could see that she was really on the prod this time, like a cow smelling blood. **1958** [see **2** below]. **1966–69** *DARE* (Qu. K16, *A cow with a bad temper*) Infs **IA8, NM13**, On the prod; **TX66**, That cow's on the prod; (Qu. GG4, *Stirred up, angry: "When he saw them coming he got _____."*) Inf **TX80**, On the prod; (Qu. GG39, *Somebody who seems to be looking for reasons to be angry: "He's . . _____."*) Infs **IL11, TX29**, On the prod; (Qu. GG40, *Words or expressions meaning violently angry*) Infs **CO21, TX80**, On the prod; (Qu. HH26, *A person who is always ready to stir up trouble*) Inf **IL11**, On the prod. **1966** [see **proddy**]. **1970** *DARE* FW Addit **KY76**, Western usage for a mean cow: "She's on the prod." Kansas-Colorado border 1904–05. **1975** Newell *If Nothin' Don't Happen* 8 **nwFL**, From the very first, Tarley were tough. I don't mean bad nor always on the prod nor nothin' like that. **1995** [see **proddy**].

2 Active, on the go.

1958 McCulloch *Woods Words* 126 **Pacific NW**, *On the prod*—a. Mad. b. An eager beaver, anxious to get the work done. **1969** *DARE* (Qu. Y29a, *To 'go out' a great deal, not to stay at home much: "She's always _____."*) Inf **CT27**, On the go, on the prod.

prod pole n Also *prod rod*, *~ stick* [Redund] chiefly Rocky Mts, SW See Map

A goad; a pike.

1936 Adams *Cowboy Lingo* 22 **West**, The 'prod pole'. . . was a pole about six feet long, with a steel spike on the end and a heavy handle. It was used to prod cattle into cattle cars. **1941** Writers' Program *Guide WY* 464, Prod pole—A short sharp stick used in handling cattle. **1950** *Western Folkl.* 9.122 **nwOR** [Sawmill workers' speech], Prod pole. See Pike pole. **1965–70** *DARE* (Qu. K27, . . *The sharp-pointed stick used to*

get oxen to move) 12 Infs, **chiefly Rocky Mts, SW**, Prod pole; **CO33**, Prod pole—a sharp brad on the end; **CO47**, Prod rod; **MO19**, Prod stick.

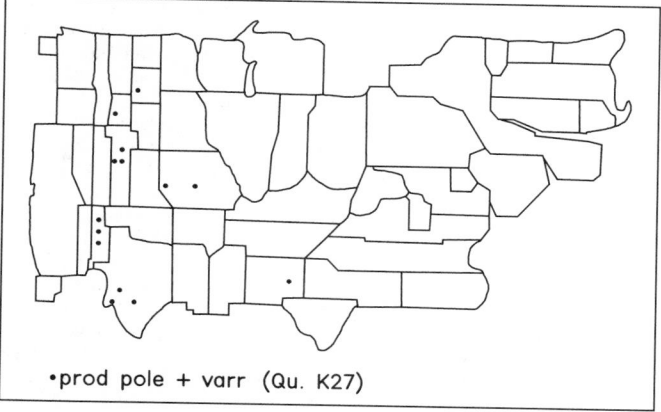

•prod pole + varr (Qu. K27)

proffer v [*OED2* proffer v. 2 "Obs. or arch."] esp sAppalachians

With infin: To offer.

c1920 in 1993 Farwell–Nicholas *Smoky Mt. Voices* 129 **sAppalachians**, He proffered to fix the gun for me. **1931** *PMLA* 46.1304 **sAppalachians**, He proffered to go to mill fer me. **1952** Brown *NC Folkl.* 1.579, *Proffer.* . . To offer as a gift: to tender one's assistance. "He proffered to help me build the boat."

prog n¹ |prɑg, prog| Also *progue* Cf prog v

1 A stick or pole intended for poking, probing, or snagging. [*OED2* 1615 →]

1894 *DN* 1.337 **sNJ**, *Progueing iron* or *progue*: iron rod 4½ to 7 feet long used to progue . . for cedar logs. **1968–69** *DARE* (Qu. K27, . . *The sharp-pointed stick used to get oxen to move*) Inf **IL73**, Progue [prog]; **MD22**, Prog [prɑg]; (Qu. P13, . . *Ways of fishing . . besides the ordinary hook and line*) Inf **NJ17**, Progue [progə]—a long (8 to 10 feet) wooden pole with an iron point on one end and a hook on the other; you poke in the mud for snapping turtles with it during cold weather; **NJ31**, Progue [prog]—a long pole with an iron point on one end and a small hook on the other; you use this in cold weather; poke in the mud with the point and then hook out the turtle with the other end.

2 A poke, thrust. [Scots, nEngl dial]

1950 Moore *Candlemas Bay* 291 **ME**, "Gi' me one progue at him [=a shark]," he said. "Just one progue, Lord God, that's all I ask. You put me over him, Russ, I'll do the rest."

3 An act of prowling or exploring. Cf **prog v 2**

1981 Harper–Presley *Okefinokee* 143 **seGA**, *Progue*—To prowl or explore, according to Jack Mizell and Tom Chesser, who spoke of a "progue about in the swamp."

prog v |prɑg, prog, pro(ʊ)g| Also *proag*, *progue* [Scots, Engl dial; cf *OED2* prog v.¹, v.², *EDD* prog]

1 tr: To poke, stab; to probe; with *up:* to stir up.

1938 Matschat *Suwannee R.* 288 **neFL, seGA**, *Progue:* to goad. **1941** O'Donnell *Great Big Doorstep* 72 **LA**, Take the cover of a coffeecan. Prog it fulla holes for grating the stale bread good. **1950** Moore *Candlemas Bay* 292 **ME**, "Well, Warren," Russ said, "you're over him. Progue him, why don't you?" *Ibid*, "Ayeh," Warren grunted. "Progue up a man-eater, I guess not." **1996** Horton *Island Out of Time* 5 **Chesapeake Bay MD**, Between the channel edge and my front yard, egrets, herons, and gulls progged the shallow, submerged grass beds for soft crabs and minnows and grass shrimp.

2 also with *about, around, on;* intr: To probe; to poke or prowl about in search of something; broadly, to wander, idle about; hence vbl nouns *prog(g)ing;* combs *progueing iron*, *~ stick*. **chiefly Sth, S Midl, esp Chesapeake Bay** Cf **peruse, prog n¹ 1, progger**

1856 *Knickerbocker* 48.433, Nex mornin' airly I goes down to the mash, an' while proguein' round I got a shot at some black ducks. **1894** *DN* 1.337 **NJ**, *Progue:* pron. [prog]. To search for anything imbedded in the mud, as clams, terrapins, or cedar logs, by means of a sounding rod. **1894** [see **prog n¹ 1**]. **1899** (1912) Green *VA Folk-Speech* 336, *Prog.* . . To go prowling about, as for pickings, forage. **1931** (1991) Hughes–

Hurston *Mule Bone* 139 **cFL** [Black], Me and him done progue'd 'round together goin' in swimmin' an' playin' ball an' serenadin' de girls an' de white folks. **1935** Hurston *Mules & Men* 128 **FL**, We proaged on thru the woods. **1944** [see **progger**]. **1946** *PADS* 6.24 **ceNC** (as of 1900–10), *Progue* [prog]. . . To probe, as in a wound. Pamlico. Common. *Progue around* [prog]. . . To go around somewhat at random, as if in some way bent on mischief and creating a little suspicion. Said of gangs of small boys. Pamlico. Occasional. **1949** Webber *Backwoods Teacher* 63 **Ozarks**, "He took a stick and progued around in the hole." That is—probed. **1951** *DE Folkl. Bulletin* 1.7/2, *Prog* (pronounce "o" as in "hot"; to poke about in the mud for clams, etc., to make a living this way). **1952** Brown *NC Folkl.* 1.579, *Prog* [prɑg]. . . To work aimlessly, piddle; to roam around idly. **1968** *DARE* FW Addit **DE**8, *Progueing* ['proʊgɪn] *stick*—a broom handle used for killing muskrats. **1969** *DARE* Tape **GA**50, I have been proguin' ['proʊgɪn] for 'em [=alligators], you know, playing with him when he's in the cave. And he'd stick his nose up through the ground. [FW:] You'd be . . going after him with a long stick or something? [Inf:] With a hook on the end of the stick. **1976** Warner *Beautiful Swimmers* 285 **eMD**, Progging is a lower Eastern Shore term for poking around marsh creeks or potholes and capturing whatever is handy. It could be . . terrapin or snapping turtle. . . Progging can also be the occasional trapping of muskrat and mink. **1981** [see **prog** n¹ 3]. **1995** *DARE* File **NC** (as of 1925), Only one person did I ever hear say "prog"—a Back Mountain beautiful old lady. She asked me what I had come upon progging around, and used it about my wanderings whenever we met. **1996** Horton *Island Out of Time* 67 **Chesapeake Bay MD**, The islanders just call it "progging about." "Progging" is spoken with a long "o." . . Here, "progging" remains a rich and active word, as: "My teenager don't love to progue around in the refrigerator none"; or, "What I wouldn't give to progue around in a big library." **1997** *AmSp* 72.18, The following are some selective lexical items found in Smith Island: . . *proging* [progɪn] 'collecting arrowheads'.

prog n² [*OED2* 1655 →; cf **prog** v 2]
Food, provisions; also fig: spoils, ill-gotten gains.

1834 *Life Andrew Jackson* 249, The Bank wards off your blows, and shows the *public* that it does *four fold* more for 'em then your *pets*, tu which you sent the prog. **1837** Smith *Col. Crockett's Exploits* 128 **NY**, I've let myself out for fourteen dollars a month, and find my own prog and lodging. **1899** (1912) Green *VA Folk-Speech* 336, *Prog*. . . Victuals gotten by begging; hence, victuals in general; food. **1952** Brown *NC Folkl.* 1.579, *Prog* [prɑg]. . . A lunch given to a traveler (member of the family or departing guest), to be eaten during his trip. **1962** Wyld *Low Bridge* 21 **cNY** (as of 1800s), Food in general was called *prog*, boiled or baked potatoes were *pritties* (cf. the Irish *praties*), and buttermilk was *skimmagig*.

prog about (or around) See **prog** v 2

progger n [**prog** v 2]   **esp Chesapeake Bay**
One who forages about marshes and beaches in search of clams, turtles, frogs, or other small prey.

1887 Goode *Fisheries U.S.* 5.2.604 **CT**, The class of men who get them [=quahaugs] and the soft clams mainly, are a miserable set who help the oystermen in winter and "go clamming" in summer. They are locally known as "proggers." **1944** *Sun* (Baltimore MD) 9 June 4/3 **MD** (Hench Coll.), A progger, in fact, is a fellow that goes progging for frogs and is generally a habitue of the marsh regions of both Delaware and Maryland. **1976** Warner *Beautiful Swimmers* 284 **eMD**, Dewey Landon . . sometime blacksmith, rubber-faced comic . . and marsh progger extraordinary. **1996** Horton *Island Out of Time* 68 **Chesapeake Bay MD**, And among them, a transcendent few are proggers, existences webbed wonderfully into this waterland. Their gleanings and discoveries continually enhance and reforge the bonds between human and natural communities here. . . A true progger loves, above all, to roam the edges where land and water merge. *Ibid* 70, Proggers just go out to see what we can see, find what we can find.

progging See **prog** v 2

proggy adj
See quot.

1985 *DARE* File, I heard *proggy* used in conversation . . in Wanville, Kentucky. [It was used] to describe neighbors who were very frugal, possibly a little stingy.

proging, prog on See **prog** v 2

progue See **prog** n¹, v

progueing iron (or stick) See **prog** v 2

prog up See **prog** v 1

pro-hi n ['proˌhaɪ]   [Abbr for *prohibitionist*]

1 also *prohide:* A teetotaler; a prohibitionist.   **scattered, but esp CA**

1942 McAtee *Dial. Grant Co. IN* 50 (as of 1890s), *Prohi* . . nickname for an advocate of prohibition of the liquor traffic. **1967–70** *DARE* (Qu. DD33a, *A person who drinks no liquor at all*) Infs **CA**145, 158, 197, Pro-hi; **CA**136, Pro-hi ['prohaɪ]; **CA**147, Pro-hi ['proˌhaɪ]; (Qu. DD33b, *A person who is actively against drinking*) Infs **CA**145, 163, 171, Pro-hi; **AR**55, **CA**15, Pro-hi ['proʊˈhaɪ]; **CA**168, Prohide; **IL**135, Pro-his ['proˈhaɪz]. **1967** *DARE* FW Addit **AR**55, Pro-hi ['proʊˌhaɪ]—one who is against drinking. "She's a real pro-hi if there ever was one. She's pizen against liquor."

2 also attrib: Prohibition; a federal government agent who enforces the tax laws on alcohol.   Cf **revenuer**

1930 *AmSp* 6.119, *Prohi*. . . Prohibition: Prohi Force To Be Culled. **1931** *AmSp* 7.112 [Underworld argot], *Prohi*. . . A prohibition agent. **1949** *AmSp* 24.11, *Prohi* [pronounced prohai]. . . Federal or law enforcement. "Them goddam, low-down, sonuvabitch prohi bastards."

prohide See **pro-hi** 1

projec(k) See **project** v

projecky adj [From *projeck* var of **project** v 1]
See quot 1906.

1883 (1971) Harris *Nights with Remus* 102 **GA** [Black], Brer Rabbit 'gun ter feel his fat, he did, en dis make 'im git projecky terreckly. **1906** *DN* 3.151 **nwAR**, *Projecky*. . . Inquisitive and venturesome. "That child's always getting hurt; she's so projecky."

project v, hence vbl n *projecting* In these senses freq |'prɑʤɪk, 'prɑʤɛk| Also with *around* Pronc-spp *prodject, projec(k), projic(k)* [Appar survival and extension of *OED2* project 2 "To form a plan, design, scheme, or project; to scheme. *Obs.*"]   **chiefly Sth, S Midl**   Cf **projecky**

1 To scheme; to experiment, engage in speculative ventures; broadly, to tinker, meddle, fool (with); hence ppl adj *projecting* inventive, enterprising.

1828 Hall *Letters West* 290 **KY**, A man who goes into the woods, as one of these veterans observed to me, "has *a heap* of little *fixens* to *study out*, and a great deal of *projecking* to do, as well as hard work." **1845** Thompson *Pineville* 28 **GA**, As he sprang from his seat and found his arms firmly pinioned behind, and the shouting increased, he was at once convinced that the boys had been "projectin'" with him. **c1873** De Vere *MS. Notes* 171 (Mathews Coll.), *Projeckin'* vice [=in place of] projecting vice prospect[in]g, [is] frequent in K[entuck]y and farther W[est] vice planning. **1884** *Anglia* 7.262 **Sth, S Midl** [Black], *To projick wid* = to experiment with. *Ibid* 273, *To be projickin' longer* = to undertake. **1890** Johnston *Widow Guthrie* 37 **GA** (as of 1830s), I shouldn't want no man . . to be projeckin in that kind o' style with a girl that was anything to me. *Ibid* 201, Among 'em they got to projecking and fooling with the case, and the fact they knew, they killed her. **1892** Smith *Farm & Fireside* 318 **GA**, Who has been here projecting with my pens and letter pads, and turned over my inkstand and messed up my papers? **1893** Shands *MS Speech* 51, *Projicking* ['prɑʤɪkɪn]. A word used by negroes and illiterate whites to mean *fooling, trifling;* as, "If you don't stop your projickin' with me, I'll lick you." **1899** (1912) Green *VA Folk-Speech* 336, *Projecking*. . . Trying experiments; inventive; enterprising. . . In one sense, as playing pranks. "Don't be projecking with that clock." **1902** *DN* 2.242 **sIL**, *Projectin* ['prɑʤɪkɪn]. . . 1. Pottering; doing little chores. 2. Prospecting. 3. Scheming or planning to do work in a different manner from the ordinary. **1902** Day *Pine Tree Ballads* 143 **ME**, He got to projickin' 'bout what 'twould prob'ly cost. **1903** *DN* 2.326 **seMO**, *Project* or *projeck* (accent on first syl.) . . To experiment. **1906** *DN* 3.122 **sIN**, He's always projeckin' with something new. **1907** *DN* 3.225 **nwAR**, *Projectin'*. . . 1. Pottering; doing little chores. 2. Prospecting. 3. Scheming to do work in an unusual manner. **1909** *DN* 3.361 **eAL, wGA**, He is always a projeckin' with some new contraption. *Ibid* 402 **nwAR**, He was projec'in' around with some powder an' got his eye-winkers singed off. **1922** Gonzales *Black Border* 320 **sSC, GA coasts** [Gullah glossary], *Projic'*—to "monkey with," to hazard. **1933** *Hench Coll.* **VA**, *Projeckin*, often with *around*—heard ever since I came to Virginia in 1922. E.g. "What are you doing, John?"

"Oh, projeckin around with this tricycle to see if I can fix it." "What are you doing, Mrs. Michie?" "Projeckin to see if I can change these plants around . . to make the garden look better." **1946** *PADS* 6.24 **ceNC** (as of 1900–10), *Projeck* ['prɑdʒɛk]. . . To meddle with. **c1960** *Wilson Coll.* **csKY,** *Project* (or *projeck*) *around:* . . Tinker or even meddle. The present participle is most common, *projecking.* /'prɑdʒɪk/.

2 To go prospecting or prying about, prowl, forage; to go about in search of amusement; to loaf, fool around. Cf **prog** v **2**

1845 Thompson *Pineville* 107 **GA,** You see what comes of your projectin' about town. **1902** *DN* [see **1** above]. **1906** *DN* 3.151 **nwAR,** *Projec' around.* . . To make visits, make calls. "They can't work for you Sunday; that's when they go projeckin' around." **1907** [see **1** above]. **1907** White *AZ Nights* 226, One old terrapin, with grey chin whiskers, projected over, with his wife, and took a peek through the slats of my coop. *Ibid* 229, So we stayed on, and kept a raisin' these tan-laigs [= chickens] for the fun of it. I used to like to watch 'em projectin' around, and I fed 'em twict a day about as usual. **1913** Kephart *Highlanders* 171 **sAppalachians,** Hell's banjer! they don't go prodjectin' around looking for stills. They set at home on their hunkers till some feller comes and informs. *Ibid* 203, In every settlement there is somebody who makes a pleasure of gathering and spreading news. Such a one we had. . . It is amusing to record the many ways he had of announcing his mission by indirection. . . "Oh, I'm jes' prodjectin' around." **c1937** in 1977 *Amer. Slave Suppl. 1* 1.387 **AL,** When he got sort of ole for woodchoppin' he jes project 'roun' at de stores downtown cleanin' up some and fotchin' and carryin' for the boss men. **1952** Brown *NC Folkl.* 1.579, *Projeck* ['prɑdʒɛk]. . . To play, show lack of seriousness, cut up.—General. . . To wander about, walk about aimlessly; to pry.—General. **1969–70** *DARE* (Qu. Y27, *To go about aimlessly, with nothing to do: "He's always _____ around the drugstore."*) Infs **AL56,** Projecking ['prɑjɪkɪn]; **TN42,** Projecking ['prɑjɪkɪn]—has heard old folks say. **1976** Garber *Mountain-ese* 71 **sAppalachians,** Joe spends the whole day jest projectin' around the town.

project n
1 See quot.
1902 *DN* 2.242 **sIL,** *Project* ['prɑdʒɪk]. . . 2. A construction or contrivance for any purpose. 3. A toy. 4. A puzzle.

2 A magic charm. See also **heave a project**
1884 *Bay State Mth.* 1.32 **MA,** Did you ever try any projects? . . O! there's ever so many! One is, you pick two of them big thistles 'fore they are bloomed out, then you name 'em and put 'em under your piller; the one that blooms out fust will be the one you will marry. **1896** *Amer. Folkl. Soc. Memoirs* 4.38 **NEng,** Love divinations or love charms, I have found, are popularly known as "projects" in parts of New England and on Mt. Desert. **1908** Wasson *Home from Sea* 287 **sME coast,** The cal'lation was to have them projects work a good deal same 's a love-potion done.

project around, projecting vbl n See **project** v

projecting ppl adj See **project** v **1**

projic(k) See **project** v

prolly See **probably**

promenade v Pronc-spp *permanate, perminade* Cf **pro-** Std sense, var forms.
1844 Thompson *Major Jones's Courtship* 75 **GA,** He was . . ridin out with this young lady and walkin out and perminadin, as he called it, with that one. **1922** in 1981 Harper–Presley *Okefinokee* 169, She permanates so nicely.

prompt v, hence vbl n *prompting* **chiefly NEast**
To call the figures of (a dance); hence n *prompter.*
1846 *Amer. Whig Rev.* 3.249 **MA,** And low the silvery laugh went round,/ And loud the prompter's call,/ And gaily gleamed the twining dance,—/ It was the Pilgrim Ball. **1873** Twain–Warner *Gilded Age* 147, They heard the scream of the jiggered and tortured violin, . . and saw the moving shapes of men and women in quick transition, and heard the prompter's drawl. **1882** Carpenter *J.W. Pepper's Universal Dancing Master* 1 **sePA,** [Title continued:] Prompter's Call Book and Violinist's Guide. By . . Philadelphia's Leading Dancing Master. . . Containing . . the music of all the principal dances arranged for the violin, with the prompter's calls printed on each dance just where they occur in dancing. **1893** French *Prompter's Hdbk.* 74 **NEng,** Quadrille. *As prompted by*

H.A. Martin, Nashua, N.H. **1938** in Lib. of Congress *Amer. Memory: WPA Life Hist.* (Internet) **CT,** I see one hundred and twenty couples on the Opr'y House floor. Dancin' the California reel. . . Gus Blakeslee was prompter. **c1938** *Ibid* **TX,** Dan Wheeler, the celebrated cowboy caller, who was known all over the West for his ability was on hand as prompter for the dance. **1966** *DARE* FW Addit **cMA,** Prompter— stands on stage and gives the orders at a square dance or contra-dance. "We didn't like his prompting."

prone into v phr, hence adj phr *proned into* **chiefly Sth** *esp freq among Black speakers*
To implant, instill, inculcate in.
1880 (1881) Harris *Uncle Remus Songs* 231 **GA** [Black], Tu'n a Mobile nigger loose in dis town, fote [=fourth] er July or no fote er July, an', me er him, one is got ter lan' in jail. Hit's proned inter me. **1883** (1971) Harris *Nights with Remus* 226 **GA** [Black], Ef dey wuz any jealousness proned inter me, I'd des lay yer en pout. **1884** *Anglia* 7.263 **Sth, S Midl** [Black], *To be proned inter* = to be well established in. *Ibid* 275, *'Taint bin proned inter* = it has not been given. **1888** *Overland Mth.* 12.141 **Sth** [Black], En its bein' proned inter me, right heah, how't I'se seen chil'en w'at got dem same kin' ov tu'key manners. **1896** Harris *Sister Jane* 116 **GA,** "That poor little boy will never be found in the round world!" she cried. "It's proned into me." **1909** *DN* 3.360 **eAL, wGA,** *Prone.* . . To impress deeply or vigorously, put in at birth. "It just warn't proned into that dog to ketch that rabbit."

prong n
1 A tributary stream. **chiefly Sth, S Midl**
1725 in 1940 *AmSp* 15.300 **VA,** To a Gum on the south side of the north prong of the Spring Swamp. **1796** in 1916 Hawkins *Letters* 27 **S Atl,** [Cross] a branch and take up one prong, the lands rich tho' broken, the timber large. **1859** (1968) Bartlett *Americanisms* 344, *Prong.* A branch or arm of a stream or inlet. Southern. **1899** (1912) Green *VA Folk-Speech* 336, *Prong.* . . A branch of a river. **1906** *Forest & Stream* 29 Dec 1021 **Chesapeake Bay,** The fishermen did not think we could get through to Golden Hill on the Honga River, because the way was long, and "prongs" that lead into pockets numerous. **1909** *DN* 3.360 **eAL, wGA,** *Prong.* . . Twig or branch of a tree, fork of a stream. Used rarely in the second sense. *Ibid* 402 **nwAR,** *Prong.* . . Branch. Interchangeable with fork. "The west prong of White River runs down the road." **1915** [see **3** below]. **1933** *AmSp* 8.1.51 **Ozarks,** *Prong.* . . One branch of a road or stream which has divided. *When you-all git t' th' place whar th' creek forks, be shore an' foller th' left-hand prong.* **1935** *AmSp* 10.154 **MD,** Waters of Maryland. . . *Prong.* Rare. **1942** [see **3** below]. **1956** (1964) Fink *That's Why* 4 **wNC, eTN,** The Smoky [Mountain] words are *creek, branch, fork* or *prong. Fork* and *prong* generally have added the name of the larger stream of which it is tributary, as *West Prong of the Little Pigeon River.* **1969** *DARE* (Qu. C14, *A stretch of still water going off to the side from a river or lake)* Inf **GA73,** Prong of water. **1976** Garber *Mountain-ese* 71 **sAppalachians,** *Prong.* . branch of a stream—We found better fishin' up the left prong uv the river. **1991** Weals *Last Train* 17 **eTN,** Thunderhead Prong, the stream that drains the northeast slope of Thunderhead Mountain and is one of the main feeders of Middle Prong.

2 A branch of a road.
1863 in 1888 U.S. War Dept. *War of Rebellion* 1 ser 22.1.504, Cornfields on both sides for the distance of nearly a mile, where it [=a road] again forks, the right prong turning across the Fourche and what is called the levee. **1889** *Catholic World* 50.371, Our advance continued until we reached the point where the "Telegraph" road forked, the right prong going to Orange Court-House, the left to Richmond. **1933** [see **1** above].

3 A twig, branch, or fork of a tree. **Sth, S Midl**
1905 *DN* 3.91 **nwAR,** *Prong.* . . Twig, branch. 'If they [i.e., farmers driving wagons] were loaded with apples, there would be four or five of the nicest apples sticking on top of the prongs of a limb.' Common. **1909** [see **1** above]. **1914** *DN* 4.160 **cVA,** *Prong.* . . Crutch (of a slingshot). "Ovah neah thuh branch yo' kin find a prong foah my gravehshootah" (gravel-shooter). **1915** *DN* 4.188 **swVA,** *Prong.* . . A branch of either a tree or a river. **1942** Hall *Smoky Mt. Speech* 32 **wNC, eTN,** *Prong,* much used in the sense of 'a tributary stream,' or 'a large branch of a tree.'

4 A branch of a canyon.
1929 Dobie *Vaquero* 273 **West,** It is cut through by many canyons, or prongs. The country I wanted was along one of the middle prongs.

1932 *DN* 6.232 **West,** *Prong.* Sometimes heard in Western Texas for the fork of a river or the branch of a canyon. I have met with it but rarely.

prong at v phr [By ext from *prong* to stab or pierce]
To annoy; to poke fun at.

1900 Day *Up in ME* 67, He pronged at Foster the evening through / While the folks were having a merry laugh. **1914** *DN* 4.78 **ME, nNH,** *Prong at. . .* To urge, annoy, importune.

prong of Christian See **palma Christi**

pronto pup n
=**corn dog.**

1947 *Compact* Jan 105 *(Popik Coll.), "Dun in the bun"* is the passing-word for the Pronto Pup, the latest thing in the hot dog department. By using a special flour-mix a batter can be made in which the frankfurter can be dunked before immersion in a deep fryer. Three minutes later, out comes the weenie cooked in its own jacket. **1965** *Rockport Democrat* (IN) 13 Aug 16/1, *Annual Homecoming*—Jenkins Post 254 American Legion. . . Free Entertainment—Beer Garden—Pronto Pups. **1968** *DARE* (Qu. H40, *A small sausage that is put into a long roll or bun to make a sandwich*) Inf **MN28,** Pronto pup—a hot dog inside a cornmeal and flour dough and deep-fat fried. **1986** Pederson *LAGS Concordance* **cwFL,** 1 inf, Pronto pups—dipped in batter; browned; on sticks; 1 inf, Pronto pups = corn dogs. **1997** *DARE* File **KS,** Here in Kansas we have "pronto pups" by the way, which are known as corn dogs elsewhere.

prooen See **prune**

proof n Usu |pruf|; also |prʊf| Cf **roof**
Std senses, var form.

1903 *DN* 2.352 **nKY,** *Proof,* n. Pronounced [prʊf], riming with roof [rʊf].

proof v chiefly **NY**
To require (a person) to provide evidence of being of legal drinking age.

1988 in 2001 (acc) Lexis–Nexis—Legal Research *State Case Law: NY* (Internet), The record in this proceeding establishes . . that these sales could have been prevented if the minors had been proofed either at the door or at the bar when ordering drinks. **1998** in 2001 (acc) Lexis–Nexis—Legal Research *State Case Law: NJ* (Internet), Defendant's counsel argued the plaintiff had the burden to establish that it was apparent that each was a minor at the time, and whether or not they had been proofed. **1998** *Cornell Mag. Online* Nov–Dec (Internet) **cNY,** Another positive [about turning 40]: I am never proofed in a bar. **2001** *DARE* File **wNY,** When I worked in a supermarket in high school, I had to wear a button that said *"Proof We Must".* I had it in my collection of buttons in my dorm room at UMass, and it bewildered and amused all the New England kids, who said 'carded' (and only 'carded'). . . (I worked for Wegmans, the western NY chain.) *Ibid* **NYC,** As far as I can determine after much inquiry, "proof" is limited strictly to the New York metropolitan area, including suburban Long Island and Westchester and New Jersey but not including exurban Connecticut and NJ. **2001** *DARE* File—Internet **cwNY,** Anyone wishing to purchase alcoholic beverages will be proofed at the bar.

proof vial n esp **sAppalachians**
In moonshining: a small glass bottle used to determine the alcohol content of newly made whiskey.

1952 Brown *NC Folkl.* 1.579, *Proof vial. . .* A small vial used to proof newly made whisky.—West. **1968** *Foxfire* 2.3.49 **nGA,** *Proof Vial*—a glass tube used to check the bead of the whiskey. A Bateman Drop bottle was the most popular as it held exactly one ounce, and was just the right shape. Others used now are bottles that rye flavoring comes in, or a government gauge. **1969** *DARE* Tape **GA72,** Most people uses an old-fashioned Bateman drop bottle for a proof vial. They hold exactly a ounce, which is one-sixteenth of a pint, and you fill it about three-fourths full of this alcoholic liquid and dip your hand in water and turn your thumb up like that. . . and let the water drip off of the tip of their little finger into this vial, and if it takes twenty-five or thirty drops to kill it, it's too high. They usually proof it on down till it takes anywhere from eight to twelve drops to kill two-thirds of a proof-vial full. Then you've got whiskey that'll check out by a government gauge, anywhere from a hundred to a hundred and twelve or fifteen proof. **1974** Dabney *Mountain Spirits* xxiv **sAppalachians,** *Proof Vial:* A small glass tube

used to test the whiskey bead. The operator would shake the vial of whiskey and hold it horizontally to check the bead. Some distillers added drops of water to determine the proof and the volume of water needed for the "blending tub."

proon over v phr
1952 Brown *NC Folkl.* 1.579, *Proon over: . .* To brood over.—Central and east.

prooty See **pretty A1d**

property n
Livestock.

1914 Furman *Sight* 34 **KY,** I would come down the branch of a morning and beg her to let me milk the cow and feed the property. *Ibid* 45, I am sot down here in the midst of rack and ruin, with . . the fence rotten and the hogs in the corn, the property eatin' their heads off. **1952** Giles *40 Acres* 4 **csKY,** Here there is a pocket of pure Appalachianism and our older people still speak the tongue. . . Livestock is called "property".

prossy adj [*SND* prossie, prowsie (at *pross* v.) "Stuck-up, conceited. Obs. exc. *arch.*"]
c**1960** *Wilson Coll.* **KY,** *Feisty. . .* Showing off, prossy.

prostrate n, also attrib [Folk-etym for *prostate*]
The prostate gland.

1976 Garber *Mountain-ese* 71 **sAppalachians,** *Prostrate . .* prostate—Lige had an operation on his prostrate glands. **1982** *Barrick Coll.* **csPA,** *Prostate*—pron. prostrate. **1984** *Annals Internal Med.* 100.900 **cwAL,** Having *prostrate* trouble is certainly more descriptive than having prostate trouble. **1986** Pederson *LAGS Concordance,* 1 inf, **cwFL,** Prostrate [=prostate] trouble. **1994** NC Lang. & Life Project *Ocracoke Brogue* 165 **seNC,** "We had a lot of cancer around here." . . "What kind?" . . "Mostly lung cancer." . . "Prostrate cancer too." **1996** *Chicago Tribune* (IL) 21 Feb sec 1 13/5, Consider the following diseases: hypertension, prostrate cancer and breast cancer. . . Prostrate cancer and breast cancer certainly occurred. **1999** *WI State Jrl.* (Madison) 13 Oct sec A 3/4, [From a notice seeking participants for a research study:] Enlarged Prostrate? . . Do you have a diagnosis of Benign Prostatic Hyperplasia . . sometimes referred to as an enlarged prostrate? **2000** *DARE* File—Internet, Is the kanda the prostrate or prolapsis uteri?

prothonotary warbler n
Std: a warbler *(Protonotaria citrea)* of swamps and bottomlands in the eastern US. Also called **gold bird, golden warbler b, swamp canary, ~ warbler, ~ yellowbird, willow warbler**

protracted meeting n Also *protractive meeting* chiefly **Sth, S Midl** Cf **distracted 1**
=**big meeting.**

1832 *Princeton Rev.* 4.486, Protracted meetings, when properly conducted, (a people being properly prepared for them) are often highly useful. **1834** *Biblical Repertory* 6.337 **KY,** This circumstance suggested the idea of *protracted* meetings; that the ministers might have the opportunity of meeting people at one time and one place. **1848** Bartlett *Americanisms* 264, *Protracted meeting.* A name given in New England to a religious meeting, protracted or continued for several days, chiefly among the Presbyterians, Congregationalists, Methodists, and Baptists. **1899** (1912) Green *VA Folk-Speech* 337, *Protracted-meeting. . .* A meeting held in the country churches and preaching continued several days, usually among the Baptists and Methodists. **1906** Johnson *Highways Missip. Valley* 141 **Ozarks,** "I've seen it [=the schoolhouse] packed fullest when we was havin' protracted meetin's." It seemed that these meetings were revivals of religion, and there had been three series the previous winter, each under a different minister, and each continued from evening to evening for about two weeks. **1916** *DN* 4.341 **seOH,** *Protracted meetings.* Evangelistic services. General. **1923** in 1952 Mathes *Tall Tales* 3 **sAppalachians,** Preacher Ike, as an ever-watchful laborer in the Lord's vineyard, discerned the signs of the time as auspicious for a "protracted meetin'." **1942** (1960) Robertson *Red Hills* 204 **SC,** At a protracted meeting at New Olive Grove Church she suddenly announced that she had backslid. **1945** *AmSp* 20.306 **SC,** This prized interim, called by all classes and colors *lay-by time,* is the period which, for over a hundred years, has been devoted by the whites to *protracted meetings* and by the Negroes to *big meetings.* A few of the white people, especially the better educated, sometimes say *revival,* although there seems to be no feeling that the more common term, *protracted meeting,* is 'low class.' They almost never use the expression *big meeting,* which is the one most often used by Negroes. The Negroes, on the other hand, sometimes say *protracted meeting* but never *revival.* The word *protracted* is seldom used in any other connection. (White [pəˈtræktɪd ˈmitn̩]; Negro [ˈtræktɪd ˈmitn̩]; humorous [ˈdɪsˌtræktɪd ˈmitn̩].) **1946** Driscoll *Country Jake* 176 **KS,** Farmers from far and near came to the Big Meetings, sometimes called Protracted Meetings, and, by the unsaved, Distracted Meetings, to see Mrs. Leonard glorify God with her circus stunt and hear her yell. **1948** Hurston *Seraph* 3, During "protracted meeting," another name for the two weeks of revival that came around every summer-time, most anybody was liable to get full of the spirit and shout in church and sing and pray. **1960** Hall *Smoky Mt. Folks* 61, *Protractive meetin':* a series of revival services continued for a week or two. **1967** *DARE* Tape **AL**15, They had protracted meetings in the summer. . . That's where they had preachin' at night and day. . . Weekdays, too, for a week at the time, in the summer. It would be protracted from one . . Sunday to the next. **1986** Pederson *LAGS Concordance,* 1 inf, **neMS,** Revival was formerly called protracted meeting; 1 inf, **nwLA,** Protracted meeting—camp meeting, revival in youth; 1 inf, **nwLA,** Protracted meeting—old-time social activity; 1 inf, **cwAL,** Protracted meetings—used to call revivals; 1 inf, **nwMS,** [Pro]tracted meetings.

‡prottle n [Cf *EDD protlins* "The refuse left after lard has been refined"]

See quot.

1937 Gardner *Folkl. Schoharie* 53 **ceNY,** It was with this finger smeared with prottle that the doctor would describe a magic circle over the afflicted part of a patient. [Footnote to *prottle:*] The informant described prottle as a salve compounded of lard and the extract produced from steeping the bark of an elder tree.

proud adj

1a Pleased, happy, glad. [Engl dial] **chiefly Sth, S Midl** See Map

1827 (1939) Sherwood *Gaz. GA* 139, *Provincialisms. . . Proud,* for glad, as I should be proud to see you. **1887** (1967) Harris *Free Joe* 92 **cGA** [Black], Mistiss and Miss Lady, dee wuz mighty proud 'bout Marster. **1895** *DN* 1.373 **eTN, wNC,** *Proud:* for happy. "She will be proud to have her tooth stop aching." **1903** *DN* 2.326 **seMO,** *Proud. . .* Glad. 'I am mighty proud to meet you.' **1904** *DN* 2.420 **nwAR,** *Proud. . .* Glad. 'She was the proudest woman you ever saw when I told her that her husband had left life insurance.' **1905** *DN* 3.16 **cCT,** *Proud. . .* Glad. 'I should be proud to see you.' **1909** *DN* 3.360 **eAL, wGA,** *Proud. . .* Glad, happy. **1917** *DN* 4.416 **wNC,** *Proud. . .* Pleased. "I was proud to hear from you." **1927** *AmSp* 2.362 **cwWV,** *Proud . .* pleased. "I am proud to meet you." **1933** Rawlings *South Moon* 187 **FL,** She said, "Aunt Py-tee, I reckon you're proud Lant ain't brought hisself home a wife yit." . . "No," she said, "I'll be proud to see him marry. I gits lonesome, Kezzy." **1936** *AmSp* 11.369 **nLA,** *Proud. . .* Glad; happy; as, 'I'm proud you've come.' **1944** *PADS* 2.11 **AL,** *Proud. . .* Glad, pleased. **1946** *PADS* 5.33 **VA,** *Proud (to see someone):* Pleased (to see someone); common everywhere. **1952** Brown *NC Folkl.* 1.579, *Proud. . .* Pleased, happy. **1965–70** *DARE* (Qu. GG28, *To be very pleased or happy about something: "She managed to come home for Christmas, and everybody was ______ to see her."*) 31 Infs, **chiefly Sth, S Midl,** Proud; **MS**71, So proud; (Qu. GG17, *Other words for longing . . "She had been so lonely—she was really ______ [to see him]."*) Infs **GA**23, **KY**65, Proud; (Qu. GG29, *To be in a good or pleasant mood: "This morning he seems to be feeling ______."*) Inf **CA**81, Proud; (Qu. NN10a, *Expressions [such as 'hello'] used when you meet somebody you know quite well*) Inf **KY**21, Proud to see you. **1973** McCarthy *Child of God* 112 **TN,** Be proud you wasn't like old man Parton up here got burned down in his bed that time. **1989** Pederson *LAGS Tech. Index* 296 **Gulf Region,** *(Glad [to see you])* 96 infs, Proud. *Ibid* 338, *(Mighty glad)* 1 inf, Awful proud; 7 infs, Mighty proud; 103 infs, Proud; 8 infs, So proud; 3 infs, Sure (am) proud. **1997** *DARE* File **AR,** Here's a local expression—the word 'proud' used to mean 'glad'—as in "I'm so proud for those folks for winning the lottery," or as on an answering machine I encountered once, "I'd be proud to return your call."

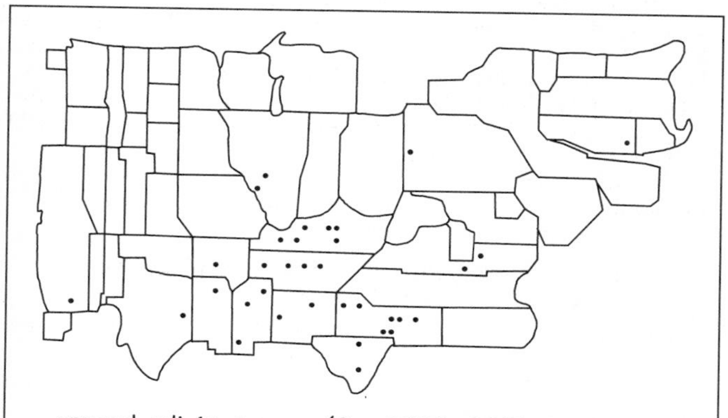

•proud adj 1a + varr (Qq. GG28, GG17, GG29, NN10a)

b with *of:* Grateful for; pleased with.

1986 Pederson *LAGS Concordance,* 1 inf, **csAR,** He'd be proud of it—her father—of a needed rain; 1 inf, **neFL,** I'm proud of it—grateful for the growth of FL. **1994** NC Lang. & Life Project *Dial. Dict. Lumbee Engl.* 9 **seNC,** *Proud of. . .* Thankful for, grateful. *Be proud of all the good things you've got.*

2 Usu of a female animal: sexually excited; in heat; hence v *proud* to be in heat. [*OED2 proud* a. 8.b 1575 →] **Sth, S Midl**

1899 (1912) Green *VA Folk-Speech* 337, *Proud. . .* To be excited by sexual desire: as, a *proud* bitch. **1909** *DN* 3.360 **eAL, wGA,** *Proud. . .* To be in heat: said of a female dog. **1919** *DN* 5.34 **seKY,** *Proud. . .* Applied to a "hot" female dog, "bitch," or "slut." **c1938** in 1970 Hyatt *Hoodoo* 3.2414 **GA** [Black], Dey claim dat yo' kin git a dog livah whilst a dog is *proudin',* . . an' if yo' kin git dat dog livah an' give it to dem to eat, dat dey would git hung. **1952** Brown *NC Folkl.* 1.580, *Proud. . .* Of female animals: *maris appetens* [*DARE* Ed: "in heat"; literally "eager for the male"]. **1984** Wilder *You All Spoken Here* 97 **Sth,** *Proud:* In heat.

3 Of a castrated horse: retaining some of the characteristics of a stallion—usu used in combs *cut proud, proud cut;* see quots. Cf **ridgeling**

1923 *DN* 5.217 **swMO,** *To cut proud* = to castrate improperly so that passion is not eliminated. **c1960** *Wilson Coll.* **csKY,** *Proud-cut:* adj. Castrated animal still is "cagey." **1965–66** *DARE* (Qu. K31, *A horse that's only partly castrated;* total Infs questioned, 75) Inf **NM**3, Proud cut—kind of a stag (a bull that's castrated after it's 3–4 years old); **OK**43, Proud cut—they'll cover a mare; **OK**49, Proud cut; **OK**10, Cut proud; **UT**3, Proud (adjective). **1967** *DARE* FW Addit **seOR,** *Proud cut*—a horse that's been half cut, one ball is inaccessible. **1995** *Brophy Coll.* 58 **swMO** (as of c1960), *Proudcut.* [D]escriptive of a horse gelded too late, so that he stays highspirited and stallionlike.

proud v See **proud** adj **2**

proud cut See **proud** adj **3**

proud flesh n Also *plowed flesh, ~ fresh, proud fresh;* for addit varr see quots

Std sense, var forms.

1943 *LANE* Map 515 *(Proud flesh),* [There are 11 instances of *plowed flesh,* 9 of *proud fresh,* and 6 of *plowed fresh.* Several infs used more than one form, including one who used the std form and all three non-std forms in the course of one conversation. One corrected *plowed fresh* to *plowed flesh,* and another *plowed flesh* to *proud fresh.* One inf commented, "It's spelled [flɛʃ] but always called [frɛʃ]. The doctor pronounces it that way too."] **1965–70** *DARE* (Qu. BB29, . . *The red flesh that sometimes grows in a wound and keeps it from healing right*) [787 Infs, **widespread,** Proud flesh;] 12 Infs, **esp Midl,** Plowed flesh. **1973** Allen *LAUM* 1.365 **Upper MW** (as of c1950), *Proud flesh. . . Plowed flesh* [offered by 4 infs] is another phonetic variant . . sufficiently different so as to yield a new lexical item that semantically might be held to be not too inappropriate. . . *Prod flesh* [offered by 19 infs], also a phonetic variant, has a different origin. Weakening of the glide in the diphthong of *proud* produced a form which, since *proud* semantically does not seem to accord with *flesh,* apparently gained its own lexical independence although *prod* is even less semantically congruous. It is found only in Midland speech territory. **1989** Pederson *LAGS Tech. Index* 285 **Gulf Region,** *(Proud flesh)* 28 infs, Plowed flesh; 2 infs, Plowed flush; 15 infs, Plowed fresh; 493 infs, Proud flesh; 2 infs, Proud flush; 23 infs, Proud fresh.

proudful adj [Scots, Engl dial]

Full of pride; very proud.

1928 Peterkin *Scarlet Sister Mary* 247 **SC** [Black], Andrew was a fine-looking fellow. Such a proudful fellow too. She would like to see him humble just once. **c1937** in 1977 *Amer. Slave Suppl. 1* 1.323 **AL**, We is proudful niggers, though. **1941** Justus *Cabin on Kettle Creek* 61 **KY, TN**, She had never felt more proudful over anything.

proud of See **proud** adj **1b**

prune n Pronc-spp *prooen, pru-en, pru-in* [Cf *OED2 prune* sb. A with forms *pruin, pruen, pruan(t)*]
Std senses, var forms.

1921 Thorp *Songs Cowboys* 60 **SW**, We had figs an' fudge an' whipped-up pru-in / An' angel-cake all dipped in goo-in,/ "My Gawd," said Tex, "my stomick's ruin'." **1934** *Language* 10.2 **cPA**, *Prune* is . . pronounced in two syllables, *prooen*. **1953** *AmSp* 28.252 **csPA**, *Prune*. . . In popular speech often pronounced ['pruən]. **1958** *DE Folkl. Bulletin* 1.32, *Pru-ens* (local pronunciation of "prunes"). **1973** *DARE* File **swPA** (as of 1920s), Prunes were "pruins." . . Pronunc. early 1920's, Monongahela PA.

prune picker n
1 A Californian.

1918 Ruggles *Navy Explained* 112, *Prune picker*—A native of California. So called because of the abundant prune crops. **1929** *AmSp* 4.343 [Vagabond lingo], *Prune picker*—A native son of California. **1932** *AmSp* 7.269 [Oil field language], *Prune-picker*. . . A Californian. **1969** *DARE* FW Addit **cCA**, *Prune picker*—A Californian. **1976** *Harper's Weekly* 26 Jan 18 **AZ**, "Prune picker" (one who generally wears fruit boots): a term Arizonans use for Californians. **1986** *DARE* File **csOK**, A junior high teacher told all of us in her class to remember if Californians make fun of us [=Okies] that they are called *prune pickers*.

2 See quots.

1942 Berrey–Van den Bark *Amer. Slang* 456.2, *Inexperienced or inferior workman*. . . prune picker. *Ibid* 913.5, *Tenderfoot*. . . prune picker. **1958** McCulloch *Woods Words* 45 **Pacific NW**, A man wearing bib overalls in the western Oregon woods was known as a prune-picker, that is, more a farmer than a logger. *Ibid* 140, *Prune picker*. . . A part time logger, part time farm worker.

psalm n Usu |sam|; also freq |sæm|; for addit varr see quots Pronc-spp *persalm, psa'm, sam* Cf **calm, palm**
Std sense, var forms.

1836 (1955) *Crockett Almanacks* 55 **wTN**, They found the preachers all very earnestly engaged, some a praying, and some a preaching, and some a singing sams. **1851** Burke *Polly Peablossom* 69 **MS**, She . . screamed, an' prayed, an' tried to sing er sam. **1890** *PMLA* 5.195 **neVA**, Words like . . *psalm* . . have two equally authorized standard pronunciations, each of which appear to be traditional. . . [sæm] . . [sɑm]. **1891** *Ibid* 6.163 **WV**, Here . . we find the clearer, lighter sound of *a* as in . . *psalm*. . . The other sound . . [sæm] . . is heard, though less frequently than in Fredericksburg, Va., or in Charleston, S.C. **1891** *DN* 1.121 **cNY**, [sæm]. . . 'psalm'. **1892** *DN* 1.240 **cwMO**, *Psalm*. Generally [sæm]. **1893** Shands *MS Speech* 74, *Psalm* [sæm]. This pronunciation is very common in Mississippi, even among educated people. **1905** *DN* 3.56 **eNE**, The . . vowel [æ] . . sometimes prevails in *calm* . . *psalm*. *Ibid* 103 **nwAR**, [sæm] (psalm). **1909** *DN* 3.365 **eAL, wGA**, *Sam* [sæm]. . . Psalm. This pronunciation is sometimes heard in the pulpit. **1923** *DN* 5.216 **swMO**, *Psa'm*. . . Psalm. **1933** *AmSp* 8.2.45 **neNY**, There is a general tendency to sound the [l] in . . *psalms*. **1939** in 1970 Hyatt *Hoodoo* 2.1179 **seGA**, Yo' . . take de Bible—dat is if yo' don't know it by heart—it's de seven *persalm*. **1943** *LANE* Map 528 (*Psalm*) **NEng**, [Proncs of the type [sam, sɑm] predominate, whereas proncs of the type [sæm] are found scattered throughout the region. Fourteen infs characterize the latter type as older. One inf, **neMA**, reports having heard the pronc [pə'sɑzəm], and another, **seME**, reports that [pəsɑˁm] was an old pronc.] **1965** *DARE* FW Addit **ME**, *Psalm* pron[ounced] [sæm]. **c1980** *DARE* File **NC, SC**, I can testify that /æ/ was still an educated pronunciation of *psalm* in a part of central North Carolina and South Carolina around 1919.

pshew See **shew**

ptarmigan n
Std: a bird of the genus *Lagopus*. Also called **snow grouse, white ~**. For other names of *L. lagopus* see **willow grouse, ~ partridge, ~ ptarmigan, white partridge**; for other names of *L. leucurus* see **mountain grouse 3, ~ quail 2, par-**

tridge **B4, snowbird, snow partridge, white quail, white-tailed grouse, ~ ptarmigan**; for other names of *L. mutus* see **rock ptarmigan**

p'tickler See **particular**

pu See **pieu**

pua-hilahila See **hilahila** n **2**

puber lice See **bube lice**

public work n, often pl Also *public job* chiefly sAppalachians
A public or private enterprise employing significant numbers of laborers; employment by such an enterprise.

1921 (1973) Campbell *Southern Highlander* 211 **sAppalachians**, Men, too, are accustomed to walk many miles under all sorts of conditions, to and fro from the "public works," as railroad, logging, and similar operations are called. **1924** Raine *Land of Saddle-Bags* 9 **sAppalachians**, Men take out logs, go to the monthly Court at the county seat, drive cattle, and occasionally go to earn some "cash money" at "public works" (by which is meant any enterprise employing a number of men, such as building a courthouse or a bit of railway, work at a sawmill or at a coal mine). **1927** *DN* 5.469 **Appalachians**, *Public works*, at. In the employ of a public corporation. **1956** *Hall Coll.* **eTN**, I didn't work at farmin' so awfully much. I worked at public works for twenty five years. . . I worked on loggin' jobs, in loggin' camps, road camps. . . I did about ten mile of railroad up there. **1958** *PADS* 29.14 **TN**, *Public works*: Day labor, especially urban day labor. "I'm going on public works," i.e., becoming a day laborer. Rep[orted] from Robertson, Perry [Counties]. May be limited to older rural use. **1964** *Chicago Daily News* (IL) 23 Sept 37/1 **MS**, Like many of the farmers, Allen does what they call in Leake County "public work." That is, he has an outside job. **1970** *Thompson Coll.* **AL, GA**, Public work—work at any kind of job except farming. "He has to keep on trying to make a living farming on account of he just ain't got enough sense for public work." Birmingham '20's, Pike and Spalding Cos., GA '71. **1981** *High Coll.* **ceKY** (as of c1930), *Public job* or *public work*: . . any job done off the home place, and for which a person gets paid. I've heard both of these expressions used in the Gorge, and they seem to be a generalization of *public works* or official work done for public use. . . "My first public work was teaming over at the oil fields." **1986** Pederson *LAGS Concordance*, 1 inf, **neGA**, Public job—any job other than on your own farm.

publish v [Appar transf from phr *publish the banns* (*OED2* 1488 →)] chiefly NEast
To announce formally the intention of (a person) to marry.

1651 in 1903 *Essex Antiq.* 7.45 **MA**, Mr. Phillips of Rowley, having been published, writes to the General Court saying that there is no one to marry him. **1712** (1901) Hempstead *Diary* 20 July 13 **seCT**, Samll & Hannah Fox Published. **1751** (1899) MacSparran *Letter Book* 65 **RI**, Read Prayers at Home, and published Tom Weeks & Ruth Browne ye 2d time. **1783** (1915) *New Engl. Hist. & Geneal. Reg.* 69.296 **MA**, Rebecah Little was Published. **1838** Kettell *Yankee Notions* 135, To make a long story short, Josh and Hannah were published the next Sunday. **1885** (1886) Stapleton *Major's Christmas* 124 **NEast**, Then say you will marry me, and we will be published to-day. **1940** Yoder *Rosanna* 149 **PA**, They decided that Thursday, January the twenty-first, was to be the wedding day, and as they had to be published (marriage announced at the close of preaching service) two Sundays before, they would be published on Sunday, January tenth. **1963** Hostetler *Amish Soc.* 174, The deacon reports his findings to the bishop who announces or "publishes" the intent of the couple at the next preaching service. . . After being "published" the bridegroom lives at the bride's home until the wedding day. **1968** *Budget* (Sugarcreek OH) 25 July 12/3 **nwMD**, Published at Paradise yesterday morning were Shelley Graybill and Alice Martin. **1975** *Ibid* 20 Mar 8/3 (*OED2*), Published today in above district were Sam, son of Joe J. Yoders and Mary, daughter of Eli H. Weavers. Their wedding to be Saturday, April 5.

puccoon n Pronc-sp *percoon*; for arch spp see quots [Algonquian; see quot 1910 at **1** below]
1 also *puccoon root*: A **gromwell**, esp *Lithospermum canescens, L. carolinense,* or *L. incisum,* or its root; a red dye prepared from the root. Note: Some of these quots may refer instead to other senses below.

1612 Smith *Map VA* 13, *Pocones*, is a small roote that groweth in the mountaines, which being dryed & beate in powder turneth red. **c1612**

(1849) Strachey *Hist. VA Britannia* 64, Their heads and shoulders they paint oftennest, and those red, with the roote pochone. *Ibid* 192, *Poughkone, the red paint or dye.* **1696** (1769) Plukenet *Almagestum* 30, Anchusa minor lutea *Virginiana, Puccoon* Indigenis dicta, quà se pingunt *Americani.* [=The small yellow anchusa of Virginia, called *puccoon* by the natives, with which the Americans paint themselves.] **1714** (1860) Lawson *Hist. Carolina* 281, They sometimes use pecoon root, which is of a crimson color, but it is apt to die the hair of an ugly hue. **c1738** (1929) Byrd *Histories* 122, Our Chaplain observ'd with concern, that the Ruffles of Some of our Fellow Travellers were a little discolour'd with pochoon, wherewith the good Man had been told those Ladies us'd to improve their invisible charms. **1822** Eaton *Botany* 203, *[Batschia] canescens* (puccoon, false bugloss). . . A red substance covering the root is the puccoon of the Indians. **1910** Hodge *Hdbk. Amer. Indians* 2.315, *Lithospermum vulgare,* the puccoon of the Virginia Indians. . . The word *puccoon,* spelled earlier puccon, poccon, pocon, pocoan, pocones, etc., is derived, as the "poccons, a red dye," in Strachey's and Smith's vocabularies indicates, from one of the Virginian dialects of Algonquian. In s.w. Virginia puccoon is locally abbreviated 'coon.' According to Trumbull and Gerard the word is from, or from the same root as, the name for blood. **1951** *PADS* 15.39 **TX**, *Lithospermum gmelinii.* . . Orange, musky, piney-wood, or dye-root, puccoon. **1964** Batson *Wild Flowers SC* 99, Puccoon: *Lithospermum caroliniense.* **1966–67** *DARE* (Qu. S22, . . *The bright yellow flowers that bloom in clusters in marshes in early springtime*) Inf **IL**50, Puccoon—tiny yellow flower with fuzzy leaf and stem; (Qu. S26a, . . *Wildflowers.* . . *Roadside flowers*) Inf **IA**3, Puccoon ['pʌkun]. **1968** *DARE* FW Addit **CO**7A, Puccoon [,pə'kun]—gromwell.

2 also *puccoon root:* =**bloodroot 1.**   Cf **coon root**

1775 (1924) Cresswell *Jrl.* 72, Clark . . showed me a root that the Indians call pocoon, good for the bite of a Rattle Snake. . . The roots are exceeding red. **1795** Winterbotham *Amer. U.S.* 3.398, Among the native and uncultivated plants of New-England, the following have been employed for medicinal purposes. . . Blood root, or puccoon, *Sanguinario* [sic] *Canadensis.* **1872** Schele de Vere *Americanisms* 61, The *puccoon,* also, mentioned by Kercheval . . , and long known under that name to early settlers, is now more generally called *Bloodroot,* and continues to be a favorite remedy with all who deal in simples. **1893** *Jrl. Amer. Folkl.* 6.137, *Sanguinaria Canadensis,* puccoon. Banner Elk, N.C. puccoon root. Anderson, Ind. coon-root. West Va. white puccoon, N.Y. **1902** [see **3** below]. **1937** (1963) Hyatt *Kiverlid* 99 **KY**, Sometimes they'd use puccoon root—blood tree they called hit. **1945** Pickard–Buley *Midwest Pioneer* 66 (as of 1825), As the spasms became more infrequent, calomel and alloes were administered, followed by castor oil, powdered birch bark, fennel seed, and pechoon roots in hard cider. **1946** Stuart *Tales Plum Grove* 13 seKY, Above his eyes were long white eyebrows almost as white as percoon petals and very much longer. **1966** *DARE* Wildfl QR Pl.77 Inf **AR**44, Bloodroot . . puccoon. **1969** *DARE* (Qu. S26c, *Wildflowers that grow in woods*) Inf **KY**40, Puccoon—bluish flower; bloodroot. **1979** Erichsen-Brown *Med. N. Amer. Plants* 318, Bloodroot. . . Common names. Puccoon root, red-puccoon, red Indian paint [etc].

3 =**goldenseal 1.**

1902 *Jrl. Amer. Folkl.* 15.255, The principal plants now called *puccoon* by speakers of English in the United States and Canada are: 1. the "blood-root" (*Sanguinaria Canadensis*); 2, the "yellow *puccoon,*" or the "yellow-root" (*Hydrastis Canadensis*). **1968** *DARE* (Qu. S3, *A flower like a large violet with a yellow center and small ragged leaves—it comes up early in spring on open, stony hilltops*) Inf **IN**30, Yellow puccoon.

puccoon root See **puccoon 1, 2**

puchki n Also sp *pootschky, pushky, putchski, puuchkii* [See quot 1991] **AK** For addit exx see Tabbert *Dict. Alaskan Engl.*
Either of two similar plants eaten raw as a celery-like food: an **angelica 1a** (here: *Angelica lucida*) or a **cow parsnip 1** (here: *Heracleum lanatum*).

1945 Collins et al. *Aleutian Is.* 69, Another important food was the pith of the stem or leaf stalk of the cow-parsnip (*Heracleum lanatum*). . . In May or June the tender stems were skillfully torn open and the delicate pith extracted and eaten raw. It is sometimes known by the adopted Russian name of "pootschky." **1951** Winchell *Home Bering Sea* 60 **AK**, There was also a weed called *putchski,* somewhat resembling celery, whose crisp stalk was very good. **1982** *AK Geographic* 9.3.26 **Pribilof Is. AK**, Almost everywhere, it seems, we find the seacoast angelica (*Angelica lucida*), locally called *puuchkii.* Adults and children

consume the plant's celerylike stalks. **1985** AK Dept. Fish Game *AK Habitat Management Guide SW* 2.490, Beach celery, commonly call [sic] pushky, is a commonly used green. **1991** Tabbert *Dict. Alaskan Engl.* 173, In the Aleutian and Alaska Peninsula/Kodiak areas the two plants [=*Heracleum lanatum* and *Angelica lucida*] are regularly referred to as *wild celery* and as *puchki* (spelled variously). The latter is from *puchka,* an infrequent Russian name for the cow parsnip.

puck n [*Puck* a mischievous or malevolent sprite]
1 A mischievous or difficult child.
1942 Berrey–Van den Bark *Amer. Slang* 398.4, *Mischievous child.* . . Puck. **1979** *NYT Article Letters* **Ocracoke Is. NC**, *Puck*—they call little kids that are crying puck.
2 A sweetheart.
1993 *Coast Watch* Sept/Oct 14 **Outer Banks NC**, [Caption:] Puck—a sweetheart. **1994** NC Lang. & Life Project *Dial. Vocab. Ocracoke* 14 **eNC**, *Puck.* . . A sweetheart. Generally used by middle-aged and younger people. Also generally used by women or to refer to women. *Melinda is his puck.*

pucker n [*OED2* 1741 →]   Cf **puckersnatch**
A state of agitation, confusion, haste, or anger; a commotion, fuss—also in phr *get a pucker on* to get angry.
1825 Neal *Brother Jonathan* 1.202 **CT**, Edith was in tears; Jotham, powerless with amazement;—Miriam, in a 'plaguy pucker'. **1834** *Life Andrew Jackson* 186, Gosh! what a pucker the Adams men were in when they discovered that the gineral had more than doubled his rival. **1897** *KS Univ. Qrly.* (ser B) 6.56 seKS, Pucker: "Works like a charm and no pucker." **1899** (1912) Green *VA Folk-Speech* 337, *Pucker.* . . A state of flutter, agitation, or confusion; a fuss; with a touch of ill-temper. **1901** *DN* 2.145 **NY**, *Pucker.* . . In phrase, 'Don't get a pucker on'—don't get angry. **1903** *DN* 2.300 **Cape Cod MA** (as of a1857), *Pucker.* . . Hurry. 'Don't be in such a great pucker.' **1959** *DARE* File **NH** (as of 1920s), In [the] White Mountains section you were asked, "What's your pucker?" (hurry). **1977** *Yankee* Jan 113 **cME coast**, Pucker means hurry.

pucker v
1 See quot.
1914 *DN* 4.111 cKS, *Pucker.* . . In the phrases *prepare* or *proceed to pucker,* make ready to do or act.
2 usu with *up*; Of the sky or weather: to cloud up, become threatening; hence ppl adj *puckered* clouded up.
1939 *LANE* Map 90 (*Clouding up*) 1 inf, **eME coast**, Puckering up for a storm. **1954** Tolbert *Bigamy Jones* 32 **wTX**, The skies puckered up and it rained for weeks. **1967** *DARE* (Qu. B6, *When clouds begin to increase . . it's* _____) Inf **KY**31, Puckering up to rain. **1984** Wilder *You All Spoken Here* 142 **Sth**, "The sky's been puckered all day," the Outer Banks native said, "but it ain't commenced to rain yit."

puckerbrush n **Nth, esp nNEng**
A tangled growth of bushes and small trees; an area covered with such growth.
1901 *Rhodora* June 159 **ME**, We found after struggling through the "pucker-brush" which formed an almost impassible barrier before it, . . that it was a most interesting place. **1950** Moore *Candlemas Bay* 262 **ME**, I recall the time he tried to fertilize Cow Island, little dump of rocks he owned, nothing ever growed there but puckerbrush. **1964** Gould *Parables of Peter* 46 **ME**, He found a rhubarb thrusting itself into prominence through the puckerbrush. **1966–67** *DARE* (Qu. C28, *A place where underbrush, weeds, vines and small trees grow together so that it's nearly impossible to get through*) Inf **ME**20, Puckerbrush—low stuff and thorny—like blackberries; **ME**22, Puckerbrush [laughter]; (Qu. C33, . . *Joking names . . for an out-of-the-way place*) Inf **OH**29, Puckerbrush. **1967** *DARE* Tape **IL**12, I was down at Carbondale, here, three years ago, or in around that section, and they seem to have an awful lot of what we call puckerbrush or wasteland. They don't have the good land there that we have here in the northern part of the state. **1970** *Torrington Reg.* (CT) 30 Dec 6, Puckerbrush is a Down East term for the miserable mess of tree sprouts that follows a logging operation, that invades a farmer's pastures, and surges up on the millions of acres under electric power transmission lines. **1970** *DARE* FW Addit **MI**, Puckerbrush—where teenagers go to make out. Inf: 35-year-old man . . near Howell, Michigan. **1975** Gould *ME Lingo* 219, *Puckerbrush*—Small, thick undergrowth difficult to pass through; bushes. Also the Mainer's general term for the wilderness and back country: "Nellie's been in

the puckerbrush all summer cooking at a boy's camp." **1984** Lesley *Winterkill* 158 **neOR,** I'm not in any hurry to go goosing steers around in the pucker brush. **1989** Mosher *Stranger* 67 **nVT** (as of 1952), I was certain that I heard low chuckling near us in the puckerbrush. **1996** *DARE* File **ceNY** (as of 1960s), You'll get all scratched up in those pickers. There are lots of pickers in the puckerbrush. **1999** *Ibid* **ME,** Puckerbrush (pronounced puck-a-brush) meaning scrubby underbrush. **2001** *DARE* File—Internet **NV,** There is *nothing* on earth compared to an old Jeep for getting 'round in the hills and puckerbrush. *Ibid* **VT,** Uncle Carl lived on a farm out in the puckerbrush of Vermont in a house that had no electricity and no indoor plumbing.

puckered See **pucker** v 2

puckered out adj phr [Var of *tuckered out*]
Tired out, exhausted.
   1966–68 *DARE* (Qu. X47, . . *"I'm very tired, at the end of my strength"*) Infs **SC21, VA9,** Puckered out. **1986** Pederson *LAGS Concordance (Tired; exhausted)* 1 inf, **seMS,** Puckered out; *(He is worn-out)* 2 infs, **cAL, cnTX,** Puckered out.

‡puckergee v
   1983 *DARE* File **ceWI,** Puckergeed along—hurried.

puckering string n Also *puckerstring*
Usu a drawstring; also fig: see quots.
   1910 *DN* 3.454 **seVT,** *Puckering-string.* . . To "break one's puckering string" means to lose control of one's self and burst into hysterical giggling. **1941** Dobie *Longhorns* 244 **TX,** The wagon sheet at the front was open, though closed with the puckering string at the rear. **1942** Warnick *Garrett Co. MD* 12 **nwMD** (as of 1900–18), *Puckering-string* . . a cord for closing the mouth of a bag. **1942** McAtee *Dial. Grant Co. IN* 50 (as of 1890s), *Puckering string* . . a cord or strip of cloth for drawing together the mouth of a bag, or for making a constriction in clothing. **1942** McAtee *Dial. Grant Co. IN Suppl. 1* 7 (as of 1890s), *Puckering string* . . anal sphincter; "Hold onto the _____" was an urge to make every effort to postpone defecation until reaching a suitable place. **1947** Stegner *Second Growth* 1 **NH,** When Helen came downstairs in her raincape her mother was standing in the open front door, bending to peer up past the porch roof at the sky. 'Looks if the world was in a bag with the puckerstring pulled,' she said. **1986** Pederson *LAGS Concordance (Purse)* 1 inf, **ceTN,** With a puckering string.

puckersnatch n [*EDD pucker-snatch* a difficulty] **Nth, esp NEast** Cf **pucker** n
A difficult or muddled situation; an agitated state; something tangled, bungled, or confused.
   1930 Shoemaker *1300 Words* 48 **cPA Mts** (as of c1900), *Puckersnatch*—A hopelessly tangled spool of thread or skein. **1959** *VT Hist.* 27.153 **cs,seVT,** *Puckersnatch.* . . A difficulty; a complicated situation. Rare. **1963** Haywood *Yankee Dict.* 126 **NEng,** *Puckersnatch*—This term the old timers used to describe a hasty and unskillful job of sewing. **1970** *DARE* File **VT** (as of c1920), Puckersnatch—a tizzy. "I'm in a puckersnatch." "What a puckersnatch!" **1980** in 1983 Beyle *How Talk Cape Cod* 26, *Puckersnatch*—A job done hastily and without skill and, it goes without saying, sure to be brought to your attention by the fastidious Cape native. **1988** Mieder *As Sweet* 17 **VT,** He got into a puckersnatch. [He got into a tight corner.] **1998** *DARE* File **nwPA,** A friend was in the hospital, . . and he said that his momentary discomfiture was "just another puckersnatch . ." meaning a bad little thing happening, a snag, an interruption. *Ibid* **NE, NW** (as of c1900), "Puckersnatch" is a hand-seamstress' descriptive word for a tangle in her sewing thread in which a loop of thread (the pucker) is caught by a smaller loop which draws tight about it (the snatch). . . [A] puckersnatch is easily released if the sewer is smart enough to go against all instinct and gently tug on the pucker.

puckerstring See **puckering string**

pucker tree n
=**persimmon B.**
   1986 *WI Alumnus Letters* **NC,** "The pucker tree" . . is the persimmon tree, and I guess (I'm from North Carolina) it is called a pucker tree over quite a bit of the south. . . If you eat a green persimmon, it gives you the best possible pucker—turns your mouth inside out and backwards.

pucker up See **pucker** v 2

Puckey-Huddle n
Used as a joking name for an out-of-the-way place.
   1930 *AmSp* 10.80 **MO,** With its hills, hollows, and swamps, southeast Missouri is well adapted to propagation of the *Podunk* idea. . . *Puckey-Huddle* stands in a class by itself, apparently a freak of fancy. The expression came to have a humorous connotation through the influence of a small town newspaper, the Bismark *Sun,* which once ran a series of 'rube' sketches entitled 'The Boy from Puckey-Huddle.' I recently inquired about the location of the place and received the reply: 'Oh, it's out on *Huzzah.*' **1968** *DARE* (Qu. C34, *Nicknames for nearby settlements, villages, or districts*) Inf **NY69,** Puckey-Huddle [laughter].

puckleback See **buckleback**

pudding n Pronc-sp *pudd'n*
1 often in combs: A sausage; sausage meat; esp a mixture of head meat, viscera, and meat scraps boiled and ground together; hence n *pudding meat* this mixture or its components. **scattered, but chiefly Midl, Mid and S Atl** See Map Cf **hog-head pudding, head ~, liver ~**
   1869 *Overland Mth.* 3.129, In most of the Atlantic Southern States there is a dish to be found about hog-slaughtering time, named "puddings." It consists of swine's flesh, bread, sage, and other matters of nourishment and seasoning, chopped fine and then squirted out into links from the end of a sausage-gun. **1933** *Baltimore Sun* 16 Dec 1/6 (Hench Coll.) **Harrisburg PA,** The free lunch of bologna, "pudding meat," cheese, onions and what not may not come back in a big way to stimulate thirst, but Pennsylvania grog shops already are advertising free clam chowder, sauer kraut and snapper soup. **1935** *AmSp* 10.171 **PA** [Engl of PA Germans], *Pudding.* Not a dessert, but a meat dish, *ponhows.* **1940** Writers' Program *Guide MD* 477 **swMD,** That the inn has no plumbing is accepted without a murmur for the sake of breakfasts beginning with fruit and cooked cereal, and working through fried chicken, ham and eggs, and hot breads to that mysterious but delicious black meat concoction called 'pudding.' **1946** *PADS* 5.33 **VA,** *Pudding.* . . A sausage of pig's entrails, cereal, etc.; fairly common. **1965–70** *DARE* (Qu. H43, *Foods made from parts of the head and inner organs of an animal*) 39 Infs, **chiefly Mid and S Atl,** Liver pudding; 17 Infs, **scattered, but esp PA, S Atl,** Blood pudding; 16 Infs, **chiefly Mid Atl,** Pudding(s); **KY71, 84, MO8, VA1,** Hog('s) head pudding; **IL29, PA146, 176,** Pudding meat; **OH81,** Head pudding; **SC19,** Hog pudding; **SC26,** Kidney pudding; **PA18,** Meat pudding; **SC22,** Tripe pudding; (Qu. H45, *Dishes made with meat, fish, or poultry that everybody around here would know, but that people in other places might not*) Inf **MN11,** Fish pudding; **OK53,** Blood pudding; **PA150,** Fried mush and pudding; **PA66,** Goose pudding; **PA41,** Liver pudding; **PA242,** Pudding, pudding broth; (Qu. H63) **NJ67,** Blood pudding; (Qu. H65, *Foreign foods*) Inf **MA40,** Blood puddings. **1967** *DARE* Tape **PA14,** In the winter time we killed hogs and then it was mush and pudding. . . You ground different things—the liver, heart, and such things—and cooked them and made puddings. Then we made big kettles of mush, you made it out of cornmeal and then you eat these puddings over the mush. **1968** *Ibid* **MD26,** [Inf:] If you put a little ground puddin' in with it, why they call it scrapple. [FW:] What's puddin'? [Inf:] That there's the head of the hog and the liver and the hearts and the rinds, like that. Make puddin' out of that. . . You'd cook it and then grind it up, you see. Then fry it; **MD28,** I don't know if that's spelled that way but that's the way people pronounce it—puddin'. And they use all the head meat: the tongues, the

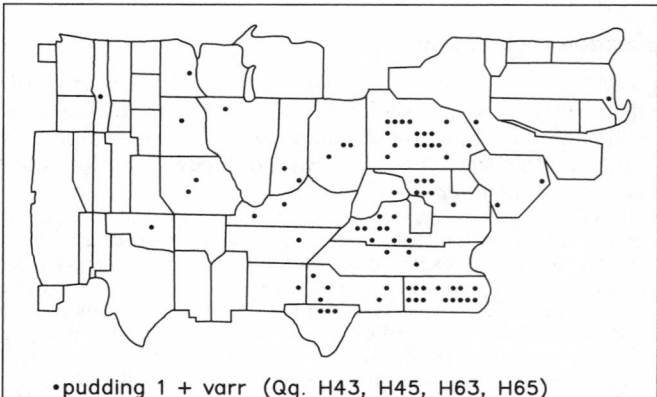

•pudding 1 + varr (Qq. H43, H45, H63, H65)

kidneys, the liver, and I guess just like any scraps that they have lie. And they boil that. And then they grind it up. And then they put it back into the kettle and they cook it some more. . . And then they pour it out in pans and mold it in square pans like that. **1976** *PA Folklife* Spring 30, *Pudding,* a concoction prepared at butchering, consisting of hog jowls, liver, heart, kidneys, and other hog parts, cooked and ground together. **1982** *Barrick Coll.* **csPA,** *Puddin'*—liver pudding; a mixture of hog meat, trimmings, liver, and skin cooked together when butchering. Usu. served fried and ladled over bread. *Puddin' meat*—At butchering, trimmings intended for puddin'. **1986** Pederson *LAGS Concordance (Liver sausage)* 143 infs, **chiefly eTN, GA, FL,** Liver pudding; 8 infs, Pudding; 3 infs, Hog pudding (*or* blood pudding); (*Blood sausage*) 10 infs, Pudding; (*Headcheese*) 1 inf, **GA,** Pudding.

2 Cornmeal mush. **NEast** Cf **hasty pudding 1, Indian ~, poor man's ~ 3**

1622 Mourt's *Relation Iournall Plimoth* 32 **eMA,** We gave him strong water, and bisket, and butter, and cheese, & pudding, and a peece of a mallerd. **1949** Kurath *Word Geog.* 17, *Hasty-pudding . .* is the well known New England term for mush made of corn meal. West of the Hudson *hasty-pudding* is very rare. We find instead *Indian pudding, corn meal pudding,* or simply *pudding* (especially in the phrase *milk and pudding*). **1965–70** *DARE* (Qu. H24, . . *Names or nicknames . . for boiled cornmeal*) Infs **NY**72, 88, 96, Pudd'n (and milk); **RI**9, Meal pudding.

pudding bag n Also *pudding-bag plant* NEng
An **orpine** (here: *Sedum telephium*).

1892 *Jrl. Amer. Folkl.* 5.96 **MA,** *Sedum Telephium . .* pudding-bag plant. Mass. . . Because of a children's custom of blowing up a leaf. **1899** (1909) Earle *Child Life* 389 **NEng,** From the live-for-ever, or orpine [leaves] . . we made . . a bladder which, when blown up, would burst with a delightful pop. The New England folk-names by which this plant is called, such as frog-plant, blow-leaf, pudding-bag-plant, show the wide-spread prevalence of this custom. **1914** Georgia *Manual Weeds* 202, Common Opine [sic] or Live-Forever. . . *Other English names:* Live-long, Aaron's Rod, Purse Plant, Pudding-bags. . . By careful lateral pressure with the finger-tips the two surfaces of a leaf may be separated, making a "purse," or "pudding-bag." **1967** *DARE* (Qu. S26e, *Other wildflowers not yet mentioned; not asked in early QRs*) Inf **MA**5, Pudding bags—fleshy part can be made to yield inflatable sac—some kind of sedum. [**1980** *Greenfield Recorder* (MA) 21 June Sec B 3/2, There was one plant, quite common, that we children used to make "pudding bags." We did it by picking off the thick fleshy leaves, rubbing them very gently between finger and thumb until the thin outer skin separated. Then we would put the stem end in our mouths and blow them up into little "pudding bags."] **1983** *DARE* File **cwMA,** *Pudding bags* heard [for **bag leaves**] 1980 and after.

puddingberry n
=bunchberry 1.

1840 (1969) Torrey–Gray *Flora N. Amer.* 1.653, *C[ornus] Canadensis. .* In the northern portions of the New-England States, the fruit is employed as an ingredient in plum-pudding, and is called Pudding-berry. **1844** Lapham *Geogr. Descr. WI* 80, [In a list of "the more useful or interesting plants of Wisconsin":] Cornus Canadensis . . pudding berry. **1892** *Jrl. Amer. Folkl.* 5.97 **NH,** Cornus Canadensis, bunch plums; pudding-berry. . . Probably from its insipid character. **1973** Hitchcock–Cronquist *Flora Pacific NW* 339, Puddingberry . . an excellent garden subject.

pudding cow n [From its fitness only for **pudding 1**]
1968 *DARE* (Qu. K15, *A thin, bony, or poor-looking cow*) Infs **MD**20, 30, Pudding cow; **VA**24, Pudding cow—on the market a poor cow or an old cow is called a puddin' cow.

pudding-footed adj
Having large awkward feet; hence n *pudding foot* a horse with such feet.

1944 Adams *Western Words* 120, *Puddin' foot*—A big-footed or awkward horse. **1944** Wellman *Bowl* 263 **KS,** A pudding-footed black horse. **1951** West *Witch Diggers* 145 **IN,** Dandie was coming down the hall, pudding-footed in his arctics.

pudding meat See **pudding 1**

puddingstone n Also *pudding rock* [*OED2* 1753 →] chiefly Nth, esp NEast

Conglomerate; a piece of conglomerate.

1805 (1876) Bigelow *Jrl.* 36 **eMA,** The stones here are a kind of composition or pudding stone. **1847** in 1941 Writers' Program *Guide UT* 356, We have been shut up in a narrow valley from 800 to 1200 feet, and the most of the distance we have been walled in by vertical and overhanging precipices of red pudding-stone, and also red sand-stone. **1937** [see **puddlestone**]. **1951** Hough *Singing in Morning* 238 **Martha's Vineyard MA,** The footscraper is gone, and we see few conch shells or puddingstones such as formerly ornamented the entrances of so many Island homes. **1967–68** *DARE* (Qu. C26, . . *Special kinds of stone or rock*) Inf **MA**5, Puddingstone—conglomerate rock; **MA**72, Puddingstone—some sort of a boulder; if you hit it with a hammer it would break—it's rotten; that's called conglomerate; **NJ**4, Puddingstone—purple with white blotches, up in the hills; Victorian Inn at Boonton was known as Puddingstone Inn (because of stones in fireplace); **OH**15, Pudding rock—rock embedded in shale; **PA**146, Conglomerate rock or puddingstone. **1980** *DARE* File **RI,** Puddingstone: Conglomerate rock reported as common R.I. by students at URI class. **1998** *Ibid* **WI,** I'd never heard the term until I came to Wisconsin. People seem to use puddingstone for that smooth-textured, reddish, jaspery stone that has chunks of other rocks in it.

pudding time n [Engl dial; cf *EDD*] old-fash
Time for dinner; fig: the nick of time.

1834 in 1839 Townsend *Narr. Rocky Mts.* 131, As it was pudding time with us, our visitor was of course invited to sit and eat. **1854** Simms *Woodcraft* 429, Get out, my dear fellow, and let us hurry in to dinner. You are just in pudding time. **1898** (1899) Earle *Home Life* 104, At one period, when pudding was part of the dinner, it was served first. Thus an old-time saying is explained, which always seemed rather meaningless, "I came early—in pudding-time." **1899** (1912) Green *VA Folk-Speech* 337, *Pudding-time. . .* The time for pudding, that is, dinner-time. The nick of time; critical time. **1926** *AmSp* 1.616, A lady recently wrote me from Putnam County, New York, saying that "Half an hour pudding-time is mighty soon gone" was often used by her grandfather when a child was late for dinner. The grandfather was born in Cleveland, Ohio, about 1814, and was of English and Scotch ancestry. **1947** Bowles–Towle *New Engl. Cooking* 175, A century and a half ago the invitation, "Come at pudding time," was a way of saying, "Come in time for dinner."

puddle around v phr Cf **piddle v 1**
To putter around, idle about.

1949 in 1986 *DARE* File **Sth** [Black], [Overheard conversation:] When it storms I get into a dark corner. . . I stay in my corner and don't puddle around no more. **1966–70** *DARE* (Qu. A10, . . *Doing little unimportant things: . . "What are you doing?" . . "Nothing in particular—I'm just _____."*) Infs **IL**5, **NY**233, Puddling around; (Qu. KK31, *To go about aimlessly looking for distraction: "He doesn't have anything to do, so he's just _____ around."*) Inf **FL**31, Puddling.

puddle duck n
1 A domestic duck. **Sth, S Midl**

c1870 in 1904 AL Hist. Soc. *Trans.* 4.484, Why a hog has no more chance to live among these thieving negro farmers than a juney bug in a gang of puddle ducks. **1877** *Scribner's Mth.* 15.6 **MD,** Presently we heard a shrilly feeble whistle, precisely such as the young puddle-duck of the barn-yard makes in his earliest vocal efforts. **1883** (1971) Harris *Nights with Remus* 135 **GA** [Black], I bin a-knowin' dat gal now gwine on sence she 'uz knee-high ter one er deze yer puddle-ducks. **1899** (1912) Green *VA Folk-Speech* 338, *Puddle-duck. . .* The common domestic duck; so called from its characteristic habit of puddling water. **1927** Kennedy *Gritny* 147 **sLA** [Black], Dey sho is a fine flock o' ducks, for being nothin' but plain puddle ducks. **1967–68** *DARE* (Qu. Q5, . . *Kinds of wild ducks*) Inf **LA**12, Puddle duck—that used to be the only kind we knew; a little brown duck raised domestically; **MD**3, Puddle duck—domestic animal, much like a goose, usually black and white, larger than a muscovy.

2 also *puddler duck, puddling ~:* Any of var wild dabbling ducks; see quots. **esp Sth, S Midl**

1932 Howell *FL Bird Life* 139, *Mud Teal. . .* Resorts chiefly to fresh-water ponds and marshes, feeding in shallow water with Mallards, Widgeons, and other "puddle ducks." **1932** Randolph *Ozark Mt. Folks* 114, If you set it with copperas it gives a kinder greenish-lookin' brown, like a puddle-duck's neck. **1965–70** *DARE* (Qu. Q5, . . *Kinds of wild ducks*) Infs **FL**17, **MS**63, **NC**54, **ND**3, **TX**5, 40, **VA**79, Puddle duck; **GA**72, Puddle duck—same as mud duck; **LA**7, Puddle duck—they're blue; the drakes is blue, the hens is not blue—a little white around the neck; **IA3**, Puddling or paddle ducks—ducks that stay in shallow water; (Qu. Q10, . . *Water birds and marsh birds*) Inf **CA95**, Puddler duck—hops and skips up the river—small duck. **1975** Gores *Hammett* 132 **cwCA**, Puddle ducks . . and mud hens . . skittered away over the draining tidal flat at the train's approach. **1982** Elman *Hunter's Field Guide* 127, The pond and river species, the dabbling ducks, belong to the tribe *Anatini* of the subfamily *Anatinae*. Also called dippers or puddle ducks, they include the black duck, gadwall, mallard, pintail, shoveler, the continent's three kinds of teal, and the widgeon. *Ibid* 168, The only North American puddle duck whose distribution is restricted to the western third of the continent, the cinnamon teal has a migratory pattern that is hardly more than a shift to the warmer part of the range.

puddler n [Cf **puddle around**]

1988 *Spinner* 4.134 **seMA** (as of c1938) [Fishing industry jargon], *Puddler:* A captain who fishes on grounds where there are no fish.

puddler (or puddling) duck See **puddle duck 2**

puddlestone n Also *puddle rock* **esp NEng**

=**puddingstone.**

1869 *Manufacturer & Builder* 1.73, To imitate a conglomerate marble or puddle-stone, several groundwork colors may be used in small quantities. **1937** FWP *Guide ME* 305 **cME**, *Clifton*. . . is in a town where hills are composed of 'puddle rocks' or pudding stone, in which stones of many colors and shapes are held together by a conglomerate mass. **1996** in 2001 *DARE* File—Internet **seMA**, Continue 60 feet along the river bank across some puddlestone boulders (an unusual geologic formation in Walpole). **2001** *Ibid* **Boston MA**, What a great way to see the town . . stone walls made of flat slate, so different from our puddlestone walls around here.

pudd'n See **pudding**

pudge v

1 also *podge:* To move slowly, plod. [Scots, Engl dial; cf *SND pudge; EDD, OED2 podge*]

1904 Day *Kin o' Ktaadn* 193 **ME**, Old Tag . . pudges along to the tin box on the mantel. **1914** *DN* 4.78 **ME, nNH**, *Podge*. . . To go slowly. . . "Thar he was, podgin' along."

2 with *up:* See below.

a See quot.

1892 *DN* 1.211 **seMA**, *Pudge up* [pʌǰ]: to rouse and stimulate; to "prod."

b To concoct, throw together; see quot.

1914 *DN* 4.78 **ME, nNH**, *Pudge*. . . I'll pudge up suthin' fer supper.

3 also with *around:* To poke around; see quot 1932. [Cf *EDD podge* v.2 "To poke about"] Cf **prog** v **2**

1932 *Natl. Geogr. Mag.* July 120 **seVA**, [Caption:] Overtaken by darkness on starless nights, the swamp man crawls into a log for safety or to sleep. "We always 'pudge' around first to rout out any copperheads." **c1932** Hench Coll. **seVA**, Dalton . . whose home is in that part of Virginia [=Dismal Swamp], says he knows the word [=pudge] well. He supposed it a form of "punch."

4 also *podge:* In marble play: see quot 1899; hence vbl n *podging*. Cf **fudge** v, **hunch** v **2a**

1899 (1912) Green *VA Folk-Speech* 338, *Pudge*. . . In playing marbles to gain in distance by moving the hand suddenly forward just before shooting the marble. **1968** *DARE* Tape **DE3**, If you wanted to what we called pluck. . . You held your hand off the ground. . . If you were plucking. . . You didn't dare move your hand forward, if you did we'd call that podging ['pɑjɪŋ].

pudge around See **pudge 3**

pudgetty See **pudjicky**

pudge up See **pudge 2**

pudjicky adj Also *pudgetty, putchity, putchy, puxy;* for addit varr see quots [Etym unknown, but cf Engl dial *patchy* cross, testy] **chiefly Nth, esp NEng**

Sensitive; sullen; grouchy.

1866 (1881) Whitney *Leslie Goldthwaite* 37 **MA**, She's dreadful *pudjicky*, Emma Jane is; she won't have anything without it's exactly right. **1890** Jewett *Strangers* 13 **NEng**, Women folks is dreadful

pudjicky about their cookin'. **1891** *Jrl. Amer. Folk.* 4.71 **eMA**, *Pudgicky.*—similar to preceding [=pernickety], but with a notion of being cross and fretful. **1895** in 1944 *ADD* **swIN**, *Putchiky.* **1905** *DN* 3.64 **eNE**, *Putchiky, putchyʉ* [sic; cf quot 1911]. Sullen, pettish. "Johnny is a little putchiky to-day." **1909** *DN* 3.414 **nME**, *Pudgicky*. . . Disgruntled. **1911** *DN* 3.546 **NE**, *Pudjiky, putchy* [ʌ] [*DARE* Ed: prob indicates ['pʌǰi]]. . . Sullen, or pettish. "Mary's acting a little pudjiky today." **1916** *DN* 4.279 **NE**, *Putchity*. . . Variant of *pudgiky, putchy.* **1917** *DN* 4.437 **NY**, The following entries in Miss Pound's list of terms from Nebraska represent usage also common in New York State: *can't most always* . . *putchity* . . *tagtail.* **1921** *Harper's Mth. Mag.* May 801, "Susanna's feeling mighty puxy today; better walk wide". . . There was no going in the kitchen on Susanna's puxy days. We could hear her banging and clattering her pots and pans. The meals would be served with the air of a martyr. **1927** *AmSp* 3.141 **ME**, "Pudgetty" . . peevish or grouchy. **1959** *VT Hist.* 27.153, *Pudjicky*. . . Fussy; sensitive. **1984** *DARE* File **seMA** (as of c1905), ['pʌčɪki]—said of a child who is restless or unhappy. **1993** *DARE* File **csVT** (as of 1856), Lyddy ain't been over to see us all winter. Your mother's gettin' pudjicked.

pueblo n [Span *pueblo* people, village] **SW**

A village, esp an American Indian community made up of contiguous flat-roofed, many-storied, adobe or stone buildings built in terraces and serving as a communal dwelling; such a building itself.

1808 *Amer. Reg.* 3.1.154 **CA**, Santa Cruz . . and a *pueblo* of the same name in its neighborhood, form the northern frontier of . . Monterrey [sic]. **1836** Edward *Hist. TX* 162, When the Alcaldes or the citizens of the *pueblo* are plaintiffs or defendants, the conciliation shall be had . . before the first Corregidor. **1844** Gregg *Commerce* 1.273 **NM**, The cacique . . collects together the principal chiefs of the Pueblo in an *estufa*. **1848** *Santa Fe Republican* 31 Aug. 2/3 (*DAE*), Our colors were streaming from the top of one of the [Taos] Pueblos, (a house some five stories high). **1878** Beadle *Western Wilds* 190, The white cross of the chapel, without which no Mexican town can be called a *pueblo*. **1892** *DN* 1.194 **TX**, *Puéblo*: a village. **1903** *NY Post* (NY) 19 Dec 7/1, An Indian "pueblo" perched high on barren cliffs in desert Arizona. **1967** *DARE* (Qu. C34, *Nicknames for nearby settlements, villages, or districts*) Inf **CO26**, Pueblos. **1979** *New Yorker* 5 Mar 98 **NM**, Teen-age girl says pueblo closed except for chapel. **1985** Fierman *Guts & Ruts* 61 **SW**, The government concluded in its case that the lease with Solomon Bibo was drawn up with the common consent of the Acoma Pueblo [=an Indian community].

pueo n [Haw] **HI**

=**short-eared owl.**

1902 Henshaw *Birds Haw. Is.* 78, Pueo. Short-eared Owl. *Ibid* 80, Its native name, pueo, is a good rendering of its cry which it commonly utters as it hunts in the early morning. **1944** Munro *Birds HI* 66, The pueo, originally worshipped as a god by the Hawaiians, is spread over all the islands. **1994** Stone-Pratt *Hawai'i's Plants* 264, Pueo feed mostly on rats and mice but also take small birds.

puff n **chiefly NEng** See Map

A quilt or **comforter 1.**

1898 (1899) Earle *Home Life* 250 **NEng**, "Girls won't take the trouble to make pressed quilts nowadays, it's as much as they'll do to tack a puff," that is, make a light quilt with thick wadding only tacked together

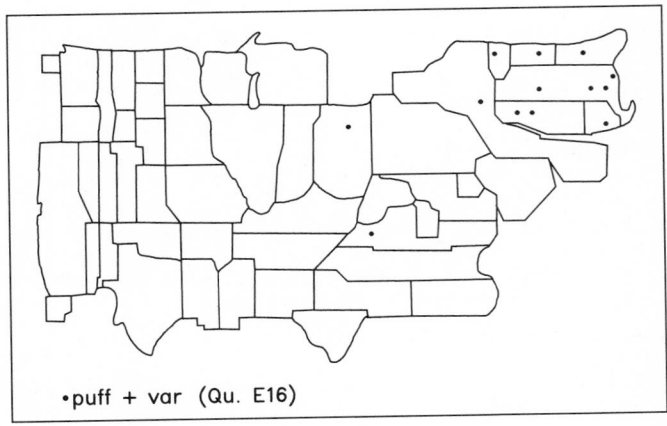

•puff + var (Qu. E16)

from front to back, at regular intervals. **1907** *DN* 3.248 **eME,** *Puff.* . . A bed covering filled with cotton. Recent. **1941** *LANE* Map 342 *(Quilt; comforter)* 26 infs, **scattered NEng,** Puff; 1 inf, **MA,** Down puff. **1965** *PADS* 43.21 **seMA,** A thick quilt . . puff [1 of 9 infs] . . down puff [1 of 9 infs]. **1965–70** *DARE* (Qu. E16, *A padded covering used on a bed, mostly for warmth)* 12 Infs, **chiefly NEng,** Puff; **OH**11, Down puff. **1973** Allen *LAUM* 1.229, *Quilt* or *comforter.* . . 1 inf, **IA,** Puff; 1 inf, **MN,** Down puff. **2000** *DARE* File **nwMA** (as of 1960–present), The puff I had on my bed as a child was covered with a slippery fabric. I would end up lying there shivering, too afraid of unknown horrors lurking under the high bed to reach down and pull it back over me when it slid off. The thick fiberfill puff my husband and I have now is covered with cotton sheeting and doesn't slide off.

puff adder n Also *puffing adder, ~ viper*
=hognose snake.

  1882 *Amer. Naturalist* 16.566, Twice afterward I noticed this strange habit of the puff adders. **1928** Baylor Univ. Museum *Contrib.* 16.14 **TX,** Hog-nosed Snake. . . Its common names, *Blowing Adder, Blowing Viper, Puffing Viper, and Puff Adder,* are applied to it on account of its ability to hiss long and continuously. **1965–70** *DARE* (Qu. P25, . . *Kinds of snakes)* 21 Infs, **scattered,** Puff adder; **CT**36, Puff adder—bluffer, **NJ**41, **TX**11, 72, Puffing adder. **1974** Shaw-Campbell *Snakes West* 69, Flattening its head and neck to further add to its ominous appearance, it will hiss or blow loudly and strike out savagely toward the attacker. Again and again it will repeat this action in an altogether convincing performance that has earned it the names "puff adder," "death adder," "sand viper"—all more dramatic surely than the unflattering name "hognose snake." **1986** Pederson *LAGS Concordance,* 1 inf, **ceAL,** Puff adder.

puffball n

1 also *puff mushroom:* A usu stalkless, globose **mushroom B1** that often discharges its spores in a cloud when touched, usu of the family Lycoperdaceae. [*OED2* 1649 →] **chiefly Nth, N Cent** For other names of var of these see **devil's puffball, ~ snuff, devil's-snuffbox 1, fluffball, fuzzball 2, Indian snuffbox, mare's egg, old-man's-snuffbox, pasture mushroom 2, smokeball, smutball, snuffball, snuffbox, tuckahoe** Cf **bolita, deer head, devil's dust, ~ footstool, nigger's pipe**

  1822 Eaton *Botany* 454, *Sclerotium* . . *semen* (barked puff-ball) . . globular or pear-form, blackish, becoming rugged. **1869** Porcher *Resources* 699, Giant Puff Ball, *(Lycoperdon giganteum).* . . It is the largest of all the puff balls and is really a delicious thing. . . It has been mentioned by medical writers that the spores of the Puff balls have narcotic properties, and it is an anasthetic [sic] agent, acting somewhat like chloroform when inhaled, but I have never experienced any effects of the kind from its use as a vegetable. **1908** Hard *Mushroom Edible* 533 **nwOH,** A friend of mine . . saw in a wood-pasture twenty-five of these giant puffballs. Being impressed with the sight and having some grain sacks in his wagon he filled them and brought them home. . . That evening we supplied twenty-five families with slices of these puffballs. **1924** *Torreya* 24.48 **NY,** We also found a "fairy ring" thirty feet in diameter containing scores of gemmed puffballs of unusual size. In the Middle West, the giant puffball sometimes grows in giant "fairy rings"! **1944** Wellman *Bowl* 152 **KS,** There's one good thing here on the plains—puff-balls. They grow right out on top of the grass. . . When they're dry they got a real soft brown powder in 'em—the best thing you ever see for stoppin' nose bleed, or any other bleedin'. **1950** *WELS (A large round mushroom, often bright colored)* 17 Infs, **WI,** Puffball; *(Small plants, shaped like an umbrella, that grow in woods and fields: Those safe to eat)* 2 Infs, **seWI,** Puffballs; *(What are some of the favorite remedies in your locality and what sicknesses are treated with them)* 1 Inf, **cwWI,** Soot or puffball smoke for bleeding. **1965–70** *DARE* (Qu. S18, *A kind of mushroom that grows like a globe . . sometimes gets as big as a man's head)* 412 Infs, **chiefly Nth, N Cent,** Puffball(s); **MI**49, Puff mushroom; **MO**2, Puff mushroom; (Qu. I37, *Small plants shaped like an umbrella that grow in woods and fields—which are safe to eat)* Infs **MN**36, **MA**16, **NC**55, **NJ**58, **OH**95, Puffballs; (Qu. I38, *Small plants shaped like an umbrella that grow in woods and fields—which are not safe to eat)* Infs **IN**41, 69, **MI**34, **WI**5, Puffballs. **1980** Marteka *Mushrooms* 116, You should look for a puffball that is entirely white inside when cut in half vertically and which has the consistency of cream cheese. *Ibid* 124, The gemmed puffball *(Lycoperdon perlatum)* is so beautiful close up that it reminds me of the delicate eggs fashioned

by Carl Fabergé. **1994** Guterson *Snow Falling* 153 **nwWA,** She knew where lady fern grew and phantom orchids and warted giant puffballs.

2 **=dandelion 1** or similar plant with a round, fluffy seed head. Cf **puffweed**

  1830 Rafinesque *Med. Flora* 2.18, Common Dandelion. . . *Vulgar.* Pissabed, Puff-ball, &c. **1900** Lyons *Plant Names* 365, Dandelion . . Puff-ball [etc]. **1939** *Hand Coll.* **OH,** Puffballs are the seed of a particular type of weed in Ohio. They float through the air and are easily caught. A wish is then made. The puffball is then blown into the air, if it sails, the wish will come true.

3 **=balloon vine.** Cf **love-in-a-puff**

  1896 *Jrl. Amer. Folk.* 9.185 **OH,** *Cardiospermum Halicacabum,* L., puffball, balloon-vine, Sulphur Grove, Ohio.

4 pl: **=Barbara's buttons.**

  1946 Reeves-Bain *Flora TX* 266, M[arshallia] *caespitosa* Nutt. (Puffballs). . . Open grounds. Spring, summer.

‡5 **=A cocklebur 1.**

  1968 *DARE* (Qu. S13, . . *A common wild bush with bunches of round, prickly seeds; when they get dry they stick to your clothing)* Inf **PA**165, Sticktights; puffball.

6 A kind of cloud; see quots.

  1950 *WELS (Names you have for particular kinds of clouds)* 1 Inf, **cnWI,** Puffballs (denoting severe winds due soon). **1967–68** *DARE* (Qu. B11, . . *Other kinds of clouds that come often)* Inf **IN**41, Puffballs—small clouds that come and go in summer; **PA**49, Puffballs [FW illustr shows clouds that make up **mackerel sky**].

‡7 An unidentified duck.

  1969 *DARE* (Qu. Q5, . . *Kinds of wild ducks)* Inf **MI**108, Puffball.

puff clover n

A **sour clover** (here: *Trifolium fucatum).*

  1979 Spellenberg *Audubon Guide N. Amer. Wildflowers W. Region* 512, *Puff Clover (Trifolium fucatum).* . . The enlargement of the corolla into a papery bladder is unusual.

puffer n[1]

1 also *puffer belly, puff fish;* A fish of the family Tetraodontidae, esp of the genus *Sphoeroides,* but also including the genera *Lagocephalus, Diodon, Canthigaster,* and *Chilomycterus.* [From its ability to inflate its body] For other names of var spp see **balloonfish 2, bellows fish 2, blowfish 1, blow-toad, chicken of the sea 2, chicken squab, globefish 1, gourdfish, jugfish, porcupine fish, puff toad, rabbitfish a, sea squab, sucking toad, sugar ~, swellfish, swelltoad, toadfish**

  1807 in 1846 MA Hist. Soc. *Coll.* 2d ser 3.55, The puff fish, or swell fish, or bellows fish, is a cartilaginous fish. **1814** in 1815 Lit. & Philos. Soc. NY *Trans.* 1.473, *Puffer. (Tetrodon turgidus).* . . The belly is loose and flabby; and it may be distended to a large size, apparently at the will of the fish. This happens frequently after he is taken from the water. The air is inhaled with a sucking or swilling noise. **1842** DeKay *Zool. NY* 4.328, This curious fish [=*Tetradon turgidus*] receives its popular names of *Puffer* and *Blower,* from its being enabled to inflate itself when taken from the water. **1884** Goode *Fisheries U.S.* 1.170 **sFL,** Swell Fishes and Puffers. . . These fishes are commonly known by such names as "Burr Fish," "Ball Fish," "Swell Fish," and "Toad Fish"; while in Southern Florida the names "Porgy," "Puffer," and "Puff Fish" are sometimes used. **1903** NY State Museum & Sci. Serv. *Bulletin* 60.619, The smooth puffer is a common resident of tropical seas, on our coast ranging from Cape Cod to Brazil. It reaches a length of 2 feet. According to Parra its flesh is poisonous. **1965** *PADS* 43.17 **seMA,** Fish common in this area . . puffer bellies [1 of 9 infs]. **1969** *DARE* (Qu. P4, *Saltwater fish that are not good to eat)* Inf **CT**23, Puffers. **1998** (acc) U.S. Dept. Ag. *Integrated Taxonomic Info. System* (Internet), *Canthigaster* [spp]—Vernacular Name: *sharpnosed puffers.*

2 See **puffing pig.**

puffer n[2] [Ger *Kartoffel-puffer* potato fritter]
A potato pancake.

  1967 Schilla *Prairies* 67 **ND,** Nothing would do but that they should have potato pancakes—a German dish called "puffers" by his family. **1969** *DARE* (Qu. H20b, . . *Names . . for pancakes)* Inf **MI**93, Puffers—potato pancakes.

puffer belly, puff fish See **puffer** n[1] **1**

puffick See **perfect**

puffin n [*OED2* 1337 →]
Std: a bird of the family Alcidae: in northern Atlantic North America, *Fratercula arctica;* on the Pacific coast, either the horned puffin *(Fratercula corniculata)* or the tufted puffin *(Lunda cirrhata).* Also called **sea parrot.** For other names of *F. arctica* see **jew duck 1, noddy 4, parakeet 2, tinker, water hen;** for other names of *L. cirrhata* see **Ikey 3, jew duck 1**

puffing adder See **puff adder**

puffing pig n Also *puffer* [See quot 1946]
=**harbor porpoise.**
  1884 Goode *Fisheries U.S.* 1.14, On the Atlantic coast occurs most abundantly the little Harbor Porpoise, Phocaena brachycion . . , known to the fishermen as "Puffer." **1905** Townsend *Birds Essex Co. MA* 13, Two other mammals are also not infrequently seen in this coast region: the harbor porpoise or "puffing pig" *(Phocaena phocaena)* and the bottle-nosed dolphin. **1946** Dufresne *AK's Animals* 199, The Harbor Porpoise . . is often seen swimming just below the surface, strings of bubbles in its wake. The sighing sound it makes as it rises for air has given it the local name of "puffing pig." **1983** *Audubon Field Guide N. Amer. Fishes* 811, The Harbor Porpoise is also known as the Common Porpoise, Herring Hog, and, because of its loud blow, Puffing Pig.

puffing viper See **puff adder**

puff mushroom See **puffball**

puff toad n
A **puffer** n[1] **1.**
  1968 *DARE* Tape **DE3**, We have . . balloonfish—we call 'em puff toads. They swell up like a balloon when you catch 'em.

puffweed n
=**dandelion 1.** Cf **puffball 2**
  1968 *DARE* (Qu. S11, . . *Dandelion*) Inf **IL27**, Puffweed.

pufitly See **perfect**

pug n Also *patty pug*   **chiefly NEng, wGt Lakes, CA**   See Map
A bun or knot of hair.
  1965–70 *DARE* (Qu. X3, *When a woman puts her hair up on her head in a bunch*) 53 Infs, **chiefly NEng, wGt Lakes, CA,** Pug; **MA5,** Patty pug. **1967** *Boston Globe* 21 May 17/1 *(OED2),* The old fashioned idea of a dark, gloomy building . . with an old fashioned old lady with glasses and a pug hair-do for a librarian are out these days. **1969** *DARE* Tape **CA138,** Usually they [=women] pulled the hair back, you know, pretty straight and put a pug on their head, a pug in the back of their neck. . . And the oil was used to keep it smooth.

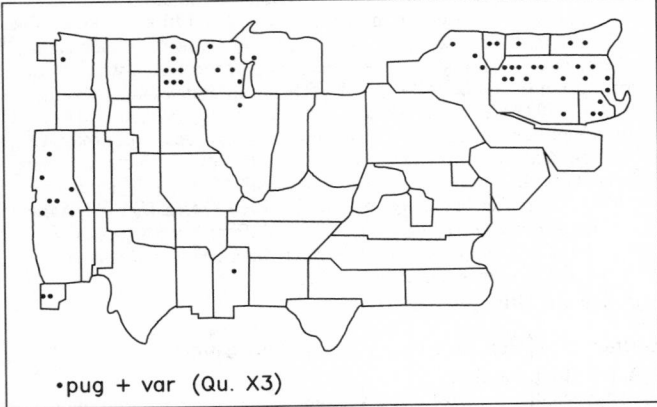
•pug + var (Qu. X3)

pugamoo n
=**hog sucker.**

  1983 Becker *Fishes WI* 678, *Northern Hog Sucker.* . . Other common names: hogmolly . . pugamoo.

Puget Sound pine n **Pacific NW**
=**Douglas fir.**
  1897 Sudworth *Arborescent Flora* 47 **WA,** *Pseudotsuga taxifolia.* . . Puget Sound Pine. **1958** McCulloch *Woods Words* 140 **Pacific NW,** *Puget Sound pine*—Douglas fir.

Puget Sound pollack See **pollack 2**

puggle v Also *poggle* [Frequentative of *pug;* cf *EDD pug* v.[3] 1 "To thrash; to poke; to punch; to thrust" and *puggle* v. 1 "To poke"]
To poke; to grope.
  1909 in 1944 *ADD* **cCT,** I poggled in the bag for a vest button. **1984** Wilder *You All Spoken Here* 45 **Sth,** Puggle: Punch; annoy, as one pokes at varmints in hollow gum logs.

pugnose buffalo n
=**bigmouth buffalo.**
  1933 LA Dept. of Conserv. *Fishes* 441, The Common Buffalofish or Redmouth Buffalo . . has come to be known under many popular names [including] Stub Nose Buffalo, Chub Nose Buffalo, Pug Nose Buffalo [etc]. **1983** Becker *Fishes WI* 615, *Bigmouth Buffalo.* . . Other common names: redmouth buffalo . . pugnose buffalo.

pug-nosed shiner n
1 A **moonfish 2** (here: *Selene setipinnis*).
  1884 Goode *Fisheries U.S.* 1.322 **NY, RI,** The Blunt-nosed Shiner. . . This fish . . was called by DeKay "Blunt-nosed Shiner" . . varied to "Pug-nosed Shiner" . . in the New York market and in Narragansett Bay. **1903** NY State Museum & Sci. Serv. *Bulletin* 60.434, The horsefish has several additional common names: sunfish, . . blunt-nosed shiner, pug-nosed shiner [etc].
2 also *pugnose shiner:* A **shiner 1** (here: *Notropis anogenus*).
  1943 Eddy–Surber *N. Fishes* 145, *Pugnose Shiner.* . . This minnow. . . occurs in the glacial lake regions from eastern North Dakota through Minnesota, Wisconsin, Michigan, northern Illinois, Indiana, and Ohio, and into the St. Lawrence drainage of New York. **1983** Becker *Fishes WI* 559, *Pugnose Shiner* . . Other common names: pug-nosed shiner, shiner. **1991** Amer. Fisheries Soc. *Common Names Fishes* 22, *Notropis anogenus* . . pugnose shiner.

pugnose rattler n
=**hognose snake.**
  1967 *DARE* (Qu. P25, . . *Kinds of snakes*) Inf **SC63,** Pugnose rattler.

pugnose shiner See **pug-nosed shiner 2**

pugnuckle n Cf **pugnuckle** v
A dancing party.
  1966 *DARE* (Qu. FF4, *Names and joking names for different kinds of dancing parties*) Inf **MS8,** Pugnuckle (boys and girls break).

pugnuckle v Cf **pugnuckle** n
To fornicate.
  1962 Faulkner *Reivers* 154 **MS,** It aint fair that it's just women can make money pugnuckling while all a man can do is just try to snatch onto a little of it while it's passing by. [**1976** Brown *Gloss. Faulkner* 156, *Pugnuckling* . . : fornicating, screwing. Apparently a nonce-word invented by Faulkner for this novel.]

pug-ugly adj, n [Prob infl by *plug-ugly* a coarse person, roughneck]
Very unattractive; a very unattractive person.
  1909 *DN* 3.360 **eAL, wGA,** Pug-ugly. . . A very ugly person: often used as a term of familiar address. "Hello, old pug-ugly!" **1967** *DARE* File **WI,** *Pug-ugly*—meaning homely.

puh- See **pre-** pref[1]

puhhaps See **perhaps**

puhtettuh See **potato A1**

puhtickluh See **particular**

puhzac'ly See **prezactly**

puig See **poig**

puka n [Haw] **HI**

An opening or anything resembling one, such as a hole, door, the number zero, etc.; also used fig and attrib; see quots.

1938 Reinecke *Hawaiian Loanwords* 30, *Puka*. . . 1. A doorway, a gateway; any place of entrance or egress. 2. Any sort of hole, from the least to the greatest, in any material or thing. . . V[ery] F[requent]. **1951** *AmSp* 26.21 **HI,** Common localisms in Hawaii, used for convenience or more colorful expression, are . . *puka* (any sort of hole or cavity; it is also used for 'zero' . .). **1960** Wentworth–Flexner *Slang* 410, *Puka*. . . Any small, private place, such as a pigeonhole in a desk, a safe, a purse, a small suitcase, or the like. . . [taboo] The female genitals. *Both meanings W.W.II USN use in Pacific.* **1966** Morimoto *Hawaiian Dial. Engl.* 106, One puka puka. This term seems to have had its origins *circa* June 12, 1942, at Oakland, California. It originated among the members of the 100th Battalion [=a battalion of Japanese-American soldiers]. "Puka," the Hawaiian word for "hole," had been used humorously for "zero" as in telephone numbers at that time. Thus the term "one puka puka" meant "one zero zero" or "one-hundred." **1967** *DARE* (Qu. W24b, *Sayings to warn a man that his pants are torn or split*) Inf **HI**9, Puka pants; (Qu. LL15, *To write ten . . what figure do you put after '1'?*) Inf **HI**13, Puka. **1967** *DARE* Tape **HI**2, This iron is jabbed in vertically, pulled towards the planter, which makes a puka. **1972** Carr *Da Kine Talk* 117 **HI,** Puka head (Hawaiian + English). 'Head injury', such as a cut scalp. *Puka* means 'hole' or 'perforation'. **1981** *Pidgin To Da Max* np **HI,** Puka. . . Swiss cheese get plenny dese. "Ey, you get pukas eenside yo' head o' wot?" **1984** Sunset *HI Guide* 85, Puka—hole, door. **1997** *NY Times* (NY) 2 Mar sec F14/4 **HI,** For many who grow up in Hawaii, standard English may be a second or even a third language. Their common tongue is pidgin. . . Visitors may even get a pidgin primer on the plane from the mainland. They arrive ready for leis, knowing that aloha also means goodbye and that mahalo means thank you. But to many Hawaiians, big pukas remain in their akamai. . . In other words. . . you can plug these holes (pukas) in your expertise (akamai) quickly (wikiwiki).

puke v esp **S Midl**

Of a still or its contents: to boil over; to cause to boil over.

1967 *DARE* Tape **TN**9, Sometimes when you're boiling a still . . it pukes over, you know, through the worm and it makes strings in the whiskey. Well, if you use a thumper it goes down in the bottom of your thumper and it don't go up in your coil and go through your still. **1968** *DARE* FW Addit **LA,** Puke = to boil up mash into the distilling tube—results from boiling too fast when distilling homemade whiskey. "You got to boil it slow or the still will start puking." **1972** *Foxfire Book* 325 **nGA,** Beer which bubbles over or "pukes" into the relay barrel is returned to the still via the relay arm. **1974** Dabney *Mountain Spirits* 126 **nGA** Did you ever strain your whiskey? "No, because it bein' made with steam thataway, it never did puke. That's what you called it when it got that white [solid matter, meal, etc.] in it. That way you had to strain it." **1974** Maurer–Pearl *KY Moonshine* 122, Puke. . . To allow the still to boil over into the connections. This often necessitates dismantling the still and cleaning out the connections, the thump-keg, and the condenser. "Don't throw no more wood on that fire, you'll puke the still." **1982** Slone *How We Talked* 70 **eKY** (as of c1950), Sometimes, if the fire got too hot under the still, it caused the mash to get mixed with the whiskey, ruining it. Then it was said that the still had "puked."

puke n

1 A despicable person, or rarely, animal. [From *puke* an emetic]

1847 (1962) Robb *Squatter Life* 152, Captain and all hands are a set of cowardly *pukes!* **1859** Taliaferro *Fisher's R.* 36 **nwNC** (as of 1820s), You're a purty set uv ill-begotten, turkey-trottin' pukes, to raise a quarrel with a peaceubble man. **1899** (1912) Green *VA Folk-Speech* 338, *Puke*. . . A disgusting person. **1909** *DN* 3.360 eAL, wGA, *Puke*. . . A low or contemptible fellow. **1912** *DN* 3.586 wIN, *Puke*. . . A mean, contemptible fellow, especially one who is morally unclean. **1930** Shoemaker *1300 Words* 44 **cPA Mts** (as of c1900), Puke—An affected, conceited person. **1944** *PADS* 2.48 **VA,** Puke: n. A low, disgusting person. **1966** *AmSp* 41.282 **Pacific,** Puke. . . A despised person. Synonymous with *jerk* or *creep*. **1986** Strickland *Vermonters* 61, That little chestnut [horse] was a rotten little puke to hitch. **2000** in 2001 *DARE* File—Internet, Get it through your heads, you . . pathetic pukes, this

country is never going to fully bow down to you Right-Wing, Bible and Gun-Toting, . . fascist pigs.

2 A Missourian.

[**1831** *New Engl. Mag.* 1.224 **nwIL, swWI,** About one fourth of the settlers were foreigners, principally Irish. The rest, as classified by themselves, were Missourians, Suckers, and Pukes;—the latter name implying natives of Kentucky.] **1835** Parker *Trip to TX* 87 **Missip Valley,** The inhabitants. . . of Michigan are called *wolverines;* . . of Missouri, *pukes.* **1843** (1916) Hall *New Purchase* 294 **IN,** This Protestant assembly was a gathering of delegates principally from the land of Hoosiers and Suckers; but with a smart sprinkling of corn-crackers, and a small chance of Pukes from beyond the father of floods. **1885** *N. Amer. Rev.* 141.433, Among the rank and file, both armies, it was very general to speak of the different states they came from by their slang names. Those from . . Missouri, Pukes. **1953** Randolph–Wilson *Down in Holler* 274 **Ozarks,** *Puke: n.* A native of Missouri. **1967** *Good Old Days* May 11, I am a Missourian and I am very proud to be a Missouri puke.

3 In distilling: mash that has boiled over.

1972 *Foxfire Book* 315 **nGA,** *Relay Barrel* or *Dry Barrel*—a fifty gallon barrel with connections for the cap arm, relay arm, and long thump rod. Catches "puke" from the still during boiling and conveys it back into the still.

puke hawk n
=**parasitic jaeger.**

1945 McAtee *Nomina Abitera* 37 **WA,** Parasitic Jaeger. . . puke-hawk, Grays Harbor, Washington.

puker n [**puke** v]
=**relay barrel.**

1974 Maurer–Pearl *KY Moonshine* 122, Puker. . . A primitive dephlegmator between the still and the thump-keg that returns any boiled-over mash to the still, thereby preventing it from contaminating the distillate.

puke up one's heels See **heels, throw up one's**

pukeweed n [From its use as an emetic]
=**Indian tobacco 1.**

1830 Rafinesque *Med. Flora* 2.22, *Lobelia inflata. Names. . . Vulgar.* Indian Tobacco, Wild Tobacco, Emetic Weed, Puke Weed. **1914** Georgia *Manual Weeds* 411, Bladder-pod, Gag-root, Pukeweed, Emetic Root. . . The writer knows, from the foolhardy experiments of childhood, that the chewing of a single green "bladder-pod" will constrict the muscles of the throat and bring on most unpleasant throes of nausea. **1945** Pickard–Buley *Midwest Pioneer* 171 (as of c1805), To cleanse the stomach and to aid in raising heat and promoting perspiration Dr. Thomson found *Lobelia inflata,* the "Puke Weed," most useful. **1971** Krochmal *Appalachia Med. Plants* 164, Lobelia Inflata. . . Common Names: gagroot, . . pukeweed [etc.].

pulaski n, often attrib [Edward C. *Pulaski* (1866–1931) Amer. forest ranger] esp **NW**

See quot 1956.

1924 *Frontier* Nov 20, I saw Paul [Bunyan], his back bowed, his Pulaski swingin' like a flail. *Ibid* 19, Paul carried a Pulaski tool, which is a combination mattock an' axe. **1946** *Trail & Timberline* June 91 (DA), Planting hoes, grub hoes, and Pulaski hoes have been provided by the rangers. **1956** Sorden–Ebert *Logger's Words* 26 **Gt Lakes,** *Pulaski,* A tool used in fire fighting. A combination tool equivalent to an ax and hoe. **1956** *AmSp* 31.151 **nwCA** [Logger lingo], *Pulaski*. . . A light single-bit ax with a straight handle, having a narrow adzlike trenching blade attached to its head. **1958** McCulloch *Woods Words* 140 **Pacific NW,** *Pulaski*—At first this was a fire fighting tool, named after Ranger Pulaski, U.S. Forest Service, famed for his life saving work in the big 1910 fire in Idaho. The tool he developed has an ax on one side and a light grub hoe blade on the other. Now it is used for pulling out the blocks of wood made in forming the undercut with a power saw, when falling timber. **1986** Klinkenborg *Making Hay* 88 **wMT** (as of early 20th cent), Then they went in with pulaskis and ripped out the stumps by hand. **1989** Lesley *River Song* 5 **cnOR,** Too many [fires] to douse with the five-gallon, hand-pump extinguishers and too many to turn under with Pulaskis, the half hoes–half axes they carried.

puldoo grass n Cf **poule d'eau 1**
=**ditch grass 2.**

1913 *Torreya* 13.226 **FL,** *Ruppia maritima* . . puldoo grass, St. Vincent

I[slan]d, Fla. The adjectival portion of this term is a modification of Poule d'eau, a name applied by the French citizens of the Southern States to the coot (*Fulica americana*).

pulka n Also *polk, pulk(ha)* [Lapp *pulkke,* Finnish *pulkka*] **AK**   Cf **ahkio**

A small, boat-shaped sled.

[**1793** Morse *Amer. Universal Geog.* 2.32 **Lapland,** Cofined [sic] in one of those carriages or pulkhas.] **1897** in 1981 Tabbert *Alaskan Engl.* 218 **AK,** Polks, or pulkhas, are used, and found to be superior to other sledding implements, as they float almost on top of the snow, never break the legs of the deer ahead or abaft of them, and very seldom catch in driving through the thickest forest. **a1922** (1953) Brooks *Blazing* 410 **AK,** The small "pulka" or Lapland sled, fashioned out of half a log and rounded at the bottom, while making a good passenger vehicle, was not adapted to hauling freight. **1951** Schwalbe *Dayspring* 131 (Tabbert *Dict. Alaskan Engl.*), The coming of the Lapps added an attractive touch to the Alaskan landscape. . . It was a most interesting sight to see caravans of from ten to fifty [reindeer] each in bright trappings hitched to sled or pulka. **1973** *AK Mag.* Mar sec A 4, At the Willow Winter Carnival in 1972, a small but significant race was run. . . it was the first pulka race in North America. Each racer was on cross-country skis and accompanied one dog which pulled a small, covered, canoe-shaped sleigh called a pulka. . . The Lapp-originated pulka has been used in Scandinavia for years. . . The pulka, actually a small toboggan with sides and a canvas cover, is usually about four feet long. **2000** *DARE* File— Internet **AK,** Skijoring and pulka racing with members of the Alaska Skijoring and Pulk Association.

pull v

1a To pick, gather (flowers, fruits, or leaves) from a tree or plant; hence vbl n *pulling;* n *puller.* [*OED2* pull v. 1.c 1340–70 →; "Now chiefly *Sc.*"] **chiefly Sth, S Midl**   Cf **break v B7, fodder-pulling**

1805 Parkinson *Tour* 384, To pulling the corn. **1842** in 1843 *S. Cultivator* 15 Mar 9 **SC,** The fodder was pulled on the 3d of August. **1856** in 1956 Eliason *Tarheel Talk* 258 **csNC,** The Army woms are destroying our corn. . . they have stript of the blades to the year like the fodder was puld. **1882** *Century Illustr. Mag.* 24.873 **GA,** The first work toward gathering the corn crop in Georgia is to strip the stalks of their blades, *i.e.,* "pull the fodder," which is done in August or September. **1902** *DN* 2.242 **sIL,** Pull. . . To pick or pluck, as 'to pull a flower.' The words pick or pluck are not used. **1906** *DN* 3.122 **sIN,** Pull. . . To pick, as a flower. *Ibid* 152 **nwAR,** Pulling time. . . Time to gather vegetables, etc. *Ibid* 153, *Pull.* . . To pick, pluck. "Pull all the flowers you want." One pulls corn, grapes, fodder, etc. **1909** *DN* 3.360 **eAL, wGA,** Pull. . . To pick or pluck. "The baby pulled the flowers." Universal. **1912** *DN* 3.586 **wIN,** We are going to pull melons to-day. **1939** (1962) Thompson *Body & Britches* 162 **NY,** One day he came tearing out of his house to rebuke a neighbor who had stopped his "rig" on the road to pull a few cherries. **1941** *LANE* Map 252 (*Pick flowers*) 2 infs, **MA,** Pull flowers; 1 inf, **neMA,** Pull, of pond lillies. **1944** *PADS* 2.69 **S Midl** [Tobacco words], *Pull.* . . To strip leaves from the stalk. *Puller.* . . one who pulls leaves. **1946** *PADS* 5.33 **VA,** *Pull flowers:* Pick flowers; common everywhere. **1946** *PADS* 6.24 **ceNC,** Pull (strip) fodder. . . To pull corn leaves from the stalk, tie them in bundles, and hang them on the stalk to dry. Pamlico. Common. **1966–67** *DARE* Tape **AR55,** They pull it [= the green tomato] before it gets turning at all, and they wrap it in paper; **GA1,** Back in them days, we pulled fodder—that's the blades off the corn for feed. And then later on, after a frost, we'd go back there then and we called it . . pulling corn. A heap of folks called it breaking corn. We called it pulling corn and picking cotton. **1973** *DARE* File **Ozarks** (as of c1910), When one picked cotton he was. . . pullin' pods. **1986** Pederson *LAGS Concordance* **Gulf Region,** 23 infs, Pull(ed) (*or* pulling) fodder; 1 inf, Pull hands (of fodder); 1 inf, Pull the fodder; 1 inf, Go to pulling your fodder; 1 inf, Pulled pussley (*Pick flowers*) 13 infs, Pull(ed) (some flowers, the flowers, etc); 5 infs, Pull (some *or* the) corn; 1 inf, And you pulled corn; 1 inf, Pulling corn; 1 inf, Pull cotton; 1 inf, Pulling bolls; 1 inf, Pulling cotton = picking; 1 inf, Pulling cotton—boll and all; 1 inf, Pull those pears—steal by pulling off the trees; 1 inf, Pulled peaches. **1998** *DARE* File **OK, TX,** In Oklahoma a white informant born in 1907 calls a cotton picker a *puller.* (He is from Garvin County.) He and two other white informants—one from Hollis, Oklahoma born 1940—one from Childress, Texas born 1925—all talk about *pulling* cotton not *picking* it—or as the Texas informant put it "pullin' bolls." I heard *pulling* cotton also from an older white woman in Oklahoma.

b in fig phr *pull corn:* To snore.   *joc*

1965–70 *DARE* (Qu. X45, . . *Joking expressions . . about snoring*) Infs **FL**18, **VA**69, Pulling corn.

2 Of a team or vehicle: to ascend (a hill) successfully or effectively; to labor up (a hill).

1939 in Lib. of Congress *Amer. Memory: WPA Life Hist.* (Internet) **SC,** Rounding the curves, pulling the hills, and crossing through woods and creeks, between Monticello and the home of T.J. Oliver . . , brought to mind the old couplet, "Over the river and through the woods / To Grandfather's house we go." **1946** McAtee *Dial. Grant Co. IN Suppl. 3* 8 (as of 1890s), *Pull a hill* . . succeed in ascending; "Do you think the team can pull Conner's Hill with that load?" **1959** Sanders *Echoes* 48 **swAR,** He would just wait until they got them perfected and able to pull the hill out East Main Street in high gear. **1998** *DARE* File, One day on Car Talk, the popular National Public Radio show hosted by Tom and Ray Magliozzi, . . a caller from the South mentioned going on a trip from Georgia to Ohio during which his car was good for a while, but then after a few hours got so that it wouldn't pull a hill (i.e. would not go up a hill effectively—it lost lots of speed and barely made it to the top). Tom and Ray were surprised by the expression, which they had never heard. . . I was familiar with it myself, having grown up in Iowa . . and Missouri thereafter. I heard it used by my father, who had grown up in Missouri but worked in Arkansas for a while in the 1930's. **1999** *DARE* File **sCA,** One of the vans was burning up both an engine and a transmission. Black smoke was just blowing all around the thing as we pulled the Sepulveda grade.

3 in phrr *pull (the) tits* and varr: To milk a cow.   **widespread, but chiefly Nth, Midl**   See Map   Cf **pump v 1**

1957 Battaglia *Resp. to PADS 20* **eMD** (*Joking terms for milking a cow*) Pull tits. **c1960** Wilson Coll. **csKY,** Pull tits. . . Joking name for milking a cow. **1965–70** *DARE* (Qu. K8, *Joking terms for milking a cow: A farmer might say, "Well, it's time to go out and _____."*) 143 Infs, **chiefly Nth, Midl,** Pull (the) tits; 30 Infs, **scattered,** Pull the cow (*or* the faucet *or* the juice *or* the milk *or* the teats, etc).

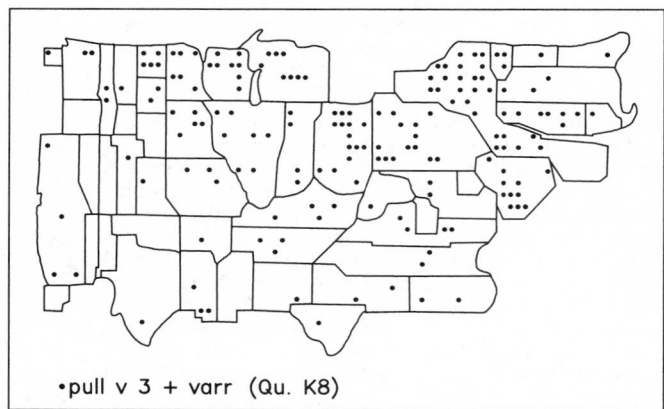

•pull v 3 + varr (Qu. K8)

4 To cut with a **puller** n 2a.   Cf **hack v¹ 1, puller n 2b**

1966 *DARE* Tape **GA7,** You'll take . . what we call a puller. . . Usually they pull 'em [=the trees] about three years and then they quit. . . We hardly ever put over one cup to the tree . . , one face at a time. **1986** Pederson *LAGS Concordance,* 1 inf, **ceGA,** Pulling boxes—from pine trees; turpentine work.

5 =**pump v 2.**   Cf **double-head 2**

1973 *DARE* FW Addit **cSC,** Pull—To ride someone on a bicycle (i.e., a second person). Current. **2001** Carter *Hour Before Daylight* 91 **cwGA** (as of 1930s), Except for the times when I "pulled" one of the boys in front of me on the bar of my bicycle, I parked it and walked or ran with the others.

6 in phr *pull one for (a sum of money):* To cost or charge one (a sum of money); see quot.

1966 *DARE* (Qu. U8a, . . *"It cost me ten dollars."*) Inf **NC3,** Pulled me for; **SC3,** Pulled me for; an insurance man pulled her for twenty-eight dollars to join Medicare; **SC11,** Pulled me for ten.

pull n

1 A quantity (of corn leaves gathered for fodder).   [**pull v 1a**]

1944 Buckmaster *Deep River* 339 **GA** (as of 1859), Got a year's pull

of fodder, got cotton all baled and ready, got corn and 'taters, and livestock.
2 See **puller 2a.**

pull-and-hold-back n
=**devil's-claw 4.**
    1933 Small *Manual SE Flora* 489, *P[isonia] aculeata.* . . Cock-spur.
Devil's-claws. Pull-and-hold-back. Old-hook. **1938** Baker *FL Wild
Flowers* 73, Pull-and-Hold-Back. . . Vinelike shrub armed with stout recurved spines. **1960** Vines *Trees SW* 252, Devil's-claw Pisonia. . Vernacular names are Garabato Prieto, Garabato Blanco . . and Pull-and-
hold-back.

pullaway See **pom-pom-pullaway**

pull back n Also *pull-back cable,* ~ *line* Cf **back line 1,**
haulback
    A cable that hauls a piece of equipment back to a starting
point; a ski tow.
    1905 U.S. Forest Serv. *Bulletin* 61.39 **Pacific,** *Haul back.* A small wire
rope, travelling between the donkey engine and a pulley set, used to return the cable. . . [Also called] back line, pull back, trip line. **1937** *Wrn.
Hotel Reporter* Jan 33/2 (Popik Coll.) **ceCA,** The owners of the Soda
Springs Hotel on the Auburn road to Reno are gladdening the hearts of
skiers by installing a very-up-to-date ski pullback . . , reports the Sacramento office of the National Automobile Club. **1958** McCulloch *Woods
Words* 140 **Pacific NW,** *Pull back cable*—An old name for a haulback;
and in this case the drum on which it was wound was called the pull
back drum. *Pull back line*—A haulback on a skyline carriage. Also used
as a brake on a gravity swing, lowering logs from a height to the landing. **1966** *DARE* Tape **SD4,** [Inf:] With the two pull-backs you can pull
from any part of that stope. [FW:] You'd call the, the one pulling it away
from you the pull-back cable. [Inf:] Yeah. That'd be the pull-back cable.

pullboat n
    A barge equipped with a donkey engine for skidding logs in a
swamp.
    1903 *Scientific Amer.* 17 Oct 276 **LA,** In the cypress swamps of Loui-
siana there are employed what are known as pull-boats, an evolution
from the plan of placing a hoisting engine upon a scow and snaking
the logs out of the swamp. . . The endless-rope pull-boat engines have
44-inch winding drums. **1905** U.S. Forest Serv. *Bulletin* 61.44 **Sth**
[Logging terms], *Pull boat.* A flatboat, carrying a steam skidder or a
donkey, used in logging cypress. **1913** Bryant *Logging* 208, In the cypress forests the slack-rope skidder is mounted on a large scow, and the
machine complete, consisting of an upright boiler . . with two engines
operating two main drums and usually a third small drum, is called a
pullboat. **1933** Rawlings *South Moon* 63 **nFL,** The drum on the pullboat chattered, the gears ground and creaked. **1968** Adams *Western
Words* 239, *Pullboat logging*—In logging, a system of moving logs by
means of a hauling engine mounted on a boat.

pull bone See **pully bone**

pull candy See **pulled candy**

pull-corn n
    1967 *DARE* FW Addit **LA7,** *Pull-corn* ['pʊl₁kɔn]—molasses made by
adding raw cane juice to syrup that has almost finished cooking, and
then cooking the mixture down.

pull-do(o) See **poule d'eau**

pulled candy n Also *pull candy, pull(ed) taffy, pulling candy,
pully candy* **chiefly Atlantic, Sth, S Midl** See Map
    Taffy or taffy-like candy.
    1965 *Colonial Kitchens* 156 **neGA,** *Pulled candy*—2 cups sugar, 2 ta-
blespoons vinegar (apple). . . Boil until when dropped in ice water is
brittle. . . Pour on marble slab and pull with tips of fingers. **1965–70**
DARE (Qu. H80, *Kinds of candy . . made at home*) 14 Infs, **esp Atlantic, Sth, S Midl,** Pull candy; **KY25, 63, OH57, WI49,** Pulled candy;
CT5, TX81, Pulled molasses candy; **TN24,** Pull molasses candy;
MA83, PA40, 126, 203, Pull taffy; **MS2, PA2, WI52,** Molasses pull
candy; **ME11,** Molasses pully candy; **LA20,** Pulling candy; **TX35,**
Pully candy; (Qu. H82b, *Kinds of cheap candy that used to be sold years
ago*) Inf **PA18,** Pull taffy; **MD30, NV7,** Pulled taffy; **PA235,** Pulled
candy. **1969** *DARE* FW Addit **KY,** *Pulled cream candy*—old-fashioned
homemade candy.

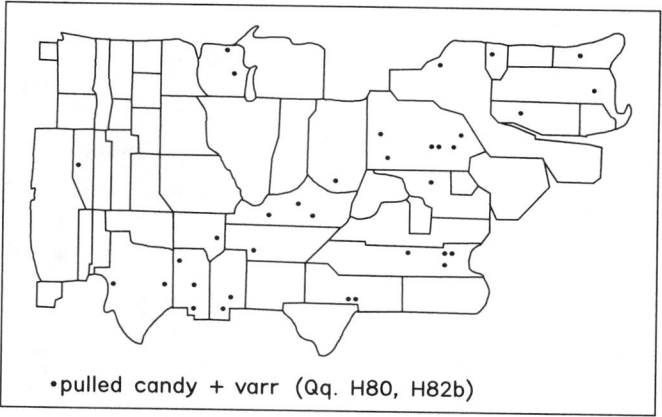

•pulled candy + varr (Qq. H80, H82b)

puller n
1 See **pull** v **1a.**
2 In turpentine production:
a also *pull:* A long-handled tool with a curved cutting edge
designed to cut on the pull-stroke, used to extend the **chip**
n¹ **2a.** Cf **hack** n¹ **2a, hacker b, pull** v **4**
    1896 *Pop. Sci. Mth.* 48.470, [Caption:] Chipper. Pusher. Open Hacker.
Closed Hacker. Scraper. Puller. *Tools used in the Turpentine Industry.*
1941 *AmSp* 16.237 **csGA** [Turpentine industry terms], When the trees
grow in height, the chipper discards the hack and uses what is known as
a *puller,* with which he pulls off a small portion of wood from each tree.
1966–68 *DARE* Tape **GA7,** [Inf:] Then you get a long piece of wood
that don't have any weight on the end of it and you put your puller in it.
It's similar to the hack, but it's a little different. [FW:] What's the difference? [Inf:] Well, there wasn't . . too much difference, nothing but the
handle on it at the end; **GA23,** After you've chipped it as high as you
can go, you have what's called a puller. **2000** Humphreys *Nowhere* 83
csNC (as of c1865), It was a three-sided file for honing hacks and pulls
and scrapers.
b One who uses this tool.
    2000 Humphreys *Nowhere* 3 **seNC,** His daughter . . learned turpentin-
ing at his side, watching and helping as he moved from chopper up to
dipper and puller, then teamster, woods-rider, and at last stiller.

pullet bone n Also *pullit bone* [Prob a play on the homophony
of *pullet* a young hen and *pull it* v phr] **esp AL, GA**
=**pully bone.**
    1967–70 *DARE* (Qu. K74, *A bone from the breast of a chicken, shaped
like a horseshoe*) Infs **AL14, GA52,** Pullet bone. **1971** Wood *Vocab.
Change* 369 **Sth,** Additional volunteered words [for a bone shaped like a
Y and found in chicken breasts] . . breast bone . . pullit bone. **1986**
Pederson *LAGS Concordance* (Wishbone), 2 infs, **GA,** Pullet bone; 1 inf,
cAL, Pullet bone—biggest end will marry first.

pulley bat n [Perh folk-etym for *bullbat;* cf **bullbat 3**]
    A **leather-winged bat.**
    1981 Pederson *LAGS Basic Materials,* 1 inf, **cnGA,** Pulley bats,
leather-winged bat—bats, same variety.

pulley bone See **pully bone**

pull foot v phr [*OED2* (at *foot* sb. 29a) 1818] **chiefly NEng**
Cf **pull one's foot**
    To walk or run rapidly; to leave in a hurry.
    1843 *Brother Jonathan* (NY NY) 495 **NEng,** "I pulls foot *for dear
life.*" I *pulls foot*—is capital Yankee; *for dear life,* capital English, but un-
heard of in Yankee land. **1848** Bartlett *Americanisms* 265, *To pull foot.*
To walk fast; to run. **1858** Hammett *Piney Woods Tavern* 126 **CT,** Spry
as he pulled foot, the Major was right behind. **1887** (1895) Robinson
Uncle Lisha 43 **wVT,** Mr. Schoolmarster, 'f you get to Uncle Chase's
'fore I du, you'll hafter pull foot for it lively. **1932** Tooné *Yankee Slang*
29, *Pull foot:* Run away, pull up your feet and "make tracks." **1960** *VT
Hist.* 28.133, *Foot.* To pull foot lively. (To get started quickly.)

pull freight See **pull one's freight 1**

pull-haul v phr, hence vbl n *pull(y)-hauling* [Cf *EDD pully-
hauly* (at *pully-haul*) a struggle] **esp ME**

To argue, contend.

1909 *DN* 3.414 **nME,** *Pull-haul.* . . To bicker, contend. **1914** *DN* 4.152 **ME,** *Pullhaul.* . . "Whenever a new person comes to town there is a lot of pullhauling among the churches." **1942** ME Univ. *Studies* 56.41, They [=ship's officers] also disliked a person who was given to *pull-hauling* . . or *pully-hauling* . . that is, arguing vainly, or at cross purposes.

pullikins n pl Also *pullicans, pullikens, pullykins* **chiefly Sth, S Midl**

Any of var instruments used for gripping small objects, esp a dentist's forceps; see quots.

1843 (1973) Porter *Big Bear AR* 171 **MS,** He sings out for the pinchers—swore they were his favorite insterments—always used 'em—beat pullicans to h—! **1850** Lewis *La. Swamp Doctor* 23 *(DAE),* The swamp doctor. . . practices dentistry with a gum lancet and a pair of pullikins. **1892** *DN* 1.231 **KY,** *Pullikins:* a dentist's forceps. **1909** *DN* 3.360 **eAL, wGA,** *Pullikins.* . . A dentist's forceps. This is an interesting example of folk etymology. *Pelican* is the name of a dentist's forceps, so-called because shaped like the pelican's beak. Naturally *pull-ikin* resulted, and the final *-s* was added on the analogy of *tongs, pincers,* etc. **1912** *DN* 3.586 **wIN,** *Pullikins.* . . A dentist's forceps. In fairly general use. **1945** Pickard–Buley *Midwest Pioneer* 161 (as of a1850), Difficult cases were taken to the country doctor, who, with a torturous crank-like lever known as a "pullikin" or a turnkey, sometimes achieved the desired result. This instrument worked on the leverage principle, the grip increasing with the amount of resistance offered. It could not easily break the jaw, for its main arm pressed down while the loose end, placed under the tooth, lifted. **1946** *PADS* 6.24 **ceNC,** *Pullikins.* . . Forceps. Pamlico. Occasional. **1949** *AmSp* 24.112 **cGA,** *Pullikins.* . . Tweezers for pulling teeth. **1952** Brown *NC Folkl.* 1.580, *Pullykins.* . . Forceps, pincers.— Central and east. **c1960** Wilson *Coll.* **csKY,** *Pullikins.* . . Instrument used by a dentist to pull teeth. **1966** *DARE* (Qu. F33, *A small tool that you hold in one hand, with 'jaws' for gripping things*) Inf **FL37,** Pullikins—with hooks for pulling; **NC8,** Pullikins. [FW: Corrected to pliers] **2000** Humphreys *Nowhere* 104 **csNC** (as of c1865), In the other pocket was a pair of pullikens, for extracting teeth.

pulling See **pull** v **1a**

pulling bog vbl n

Pulling cattle out of bog holes.

1941 Cleaveland *No Life* 106 **cwNM,** Another invaluable report would be that of finding a cow 'bogged down.' Rain puddles sometimes became death traps of sticky mire unless the victims were rescued in time. So 'pulling bog' was a routine of the rainy season. **1945** Thorp *Pardner* 246 **SW,** On account of the overflow from the tanks, many of these waterings had bog holes, and the cattle that . . were weak, sometimes got stuck in them. If not pulled out soon, they would die. "Pulling bog" was a regular part of a puncher's job. The boys would rope the bogged critters, then hitch the ropes around their saddle horns and haul them out.

pulling bone See **pully bone**

pulling candy See **pulled candy**

pulling corn vbl n [Cf **pull** v **1a**] *joc*

Snoring.

1965–70 *DARE* (Qu. X45, . . *Joking expressions . . about snoring*) Infs **FL18, VA69,** Pulling corn.

pulling the badger See **pull the badger**

pulling the chicken See **chicken pulling**

pull in one's horses See **horse** B13

pullit bone See **pullet bone**

pull leather See **leather** **1a**

pullnut See **bullnut**

pull one's chain See **chain, rattle one's**

pull one's foot v phr **seSC** *Gullah* Cf *make one's manners* (at **manner** n **1**), **pull foot**

To move the leg as in making a bow or curtsey.

1930 Stoney–Shelby *Black Genesis* 190 **seSC,** Br' Rabbit pull he foot good to him, but he feel dat please' wid heself he jis' grinnin' all ober he

face. **1930** Woofter *Black Yeomanry* 212 **seSC,** To be unclean is "no-manners," likewise to fail to "pull de foot" and curtsey to one's elders. **1939** Griswold *Sea Is. Lady* 131 **csSC** (as of 1865) [Gullah], You blin', 'oman?—make you' mannuh! An' you chillun—pull you' foot!

pull one's freight v phr

1 also *pull freight, pull out one's freight:* To depart, esp hurriedly. **chiefly West** Cf **haul ass 1**

1894 *Harper's New Mth. Mag.* 88.887, I concluded I'd rather drink myself to death on good whiskey at Del's than on the stuff we got on the range [in TX], so I pulled my freight and came East again. **1895** Remington *Pony Tracks* 252 **NM,** [The] wily old fellow . . concluded that we were not a cow outfit, whereat he had discreetly "pulled his freight." **1897** *KS Univ. Qrly.* (ser B) 6.91 **neKS,** *Pull your freight:* get out. **1905** *Everybody's Mag.* 13.814 **TX,** The Kid . . considered it not incompatible with his indisputable gameness to perform that judicious tractional act known as "pulling his freight." **1913** London *Valley of Moon* 277 **cwCA,** I guess we got a celebration comin', seein' as we're going to pull up stakes an' pull our freight from the old burg. **1937** NE Univ. *Univ. Studies* 37.112 [Terms from play-party songs], *Pulled his freight.* . . Departed. "Rabbit skipped de garden gate, Picked a pea and pulled his freight."— ' Tain't Goin' to Rain No More." **1938** Beebe *High Iron* 223 [Railroad terms], *Pull freight, to:* To depart or to give up a job. **1939** (1973) FWP *Guide MT* 415, *Pull freight*—To go away; move on. **1950** *WELS* ("I guess it's about time for me to _____.") 2 Infs, **WI,** Pull (out) my freight. **1958** McCulloch *Woods Words* 140 **Pacific NW,** *Pull freight*—To get out of camp. **1966–67** *DARE* (Qu. Y18, *To leave in a hurry: "Before they find this out, we'd better _____!"*) Inf **SD8,** Pull our freight; (Qu. Y19, *To begin to go away from a place: "It's about time for me to _____."*) Infs **FL15, IL12,** Pull my freight. **1984** Wilder *You All Spoken Here* 68 **Sth,** *Pull freight for the tules:* Run for cover; head for tall timber; take to the bushes; take to the brush; make tracks; go to the le'ward; hit the grit. "Tules" are bullrushes growing on over flowed land. **1995** Brophy *Coll.* 58 **swMO** (as of c1960), *Pull freight.* [T]o leave, to depart. [P]ull freight for the tules. [T]o decamp, abscond, hide out (West).

‡2 See quot. [Perh by confusion with *pull one's weight*]

1967 *DARE* (Qu. JJ26, *If somebody has been doing poor work or not enough, the boss might say, "If he wants to keep his job he'd better _____."*) Inf **OR10,** Pull his freight.

pull onion n

An **onion B;** see quot.

1966 Dakin *Dial. Vocab. Ohio R. Valley* 2.367, *Green onion, spring onion,* and *young onion* seem most often to mean the onions which are planted in the spring and grow singly. . . Numerous miscellaneous terms are used by scattered speakers: *pull onions, fresh onions* [etc] . . appear once or twice.

pull out one's freight See **pull one's freight 1**

pull-stick n

See quots.

1938 FWP *Guide DE* 368, The only cable ferry in Delaware. . . until 1930 the power was supplied by the ferryman and his passengers using notched pull-sticks on the steel cable. **1940** Writers' Program *Guide MD* 410 **ce,cs,seMD,** *Upper Ferry* . . by the Wicomico, one of two places on the river where a small scow takes passengers and vehicles from shore to shore. . . Pull sticks are available to persons willing to help the ferryman haul the scow across by the wire cable. **1942** Footner *MD Main* 197, For the huskier sort of passengers there are "pull-sticks" to help haul the scow across by its wire cable.

pull taffy See **pulled candy**

pull the badger v phr, hence vbl n *pulling the badger* **SW**

To play the practical joke known as a **badger fight.**

1898 in 1921 Thorp *Songs Cowboys* 36 **NM,** Where Frank Smith "pulls the badger" on knowin' tenderfeet. **1915** *DN* 4.228 **wTX,** *Pullin' the badger.* . . A universal game in which many unfortunate newcomers are humiliated. **1961** [see **badger fight**].

pull-the-peg n

=**mumblety-peg.**

1932 Farrell *Young Lonigan* 272 **Chicago IL** (as of 1916), They played pull-the-peg, and told dirty jokes while the knife was passed from left to right. **1957** *Sat. Eve. Post Letters* **Chicago IL,** "Pull the pig" or "knife" was played with a jack knife. The one who lost the game must pull a wooden peg out of the ground with his teeth; **nwWA,** A two bladed jacknife was sufficient equipment with which to play 'Mumblty [sic] Peg' or otherwise known as 'Pull the Peg.' **1968** *DARE* (Qu. EE5, *Games where you try to make a jackknife stick in the ground*) Inf **PA94,** Pull-the-peg—pull knife out with teeth.

pull the pin v phr Cf bunch v[2]

To quit, leave; rarely in phr *pull the pin on* to dismiss.

1926 *AmSp* 1.250 **PA** [Railroading terms], To leave the service, "pull the pin." **1927** *AmSp* 2.391 [Vagabond argot], To *bunch,* or to *drag it,* means to quit. To *pull the pin* has the same meaning. This is a railroad term and means to uncouple. **1938** Beebe *High Iron* 223, *Pull the pin, to:* To knock off work or go home for the day. **1940** Cottrell *Railroader* 134, *Pull the pin*—To leave a town. Derives from the link-and-pin coupler days. **1960** Korson *Black Rock* 354 **PA,** When a railroad boomer "pulled the pin" (quit his job). **1962** *AmSp* 37.134 **nwCA,** *Pull the pin. . .* To quit: 'He pulled the pin yesterday.' On the railroad this meant to pull the pin to release a car. **1968** *AmSp* 43.289 [Vocab of Railroading], *Pull the pin. . .* be fired from a job: "They pulled the pin on him." **1969** *AmSp* 44.22 **Pacific NW** [Painter jargon], *Pull the pin. . .* To leave the *job,* to get away from the job, to quit for the night.

pull-the-rope n

=**pom-pom-pullaway.**

1901 *DN* 2.145 **nNY,** *Pull-the-rope. . .* Name of a game; the same as pom-pom-pull-away but played chiefly on ice.

pull the tits See pull v 3

pull-tie n

1906 *DN* 3.152 **nwAR,** *Pull-tie. . .* String-tie. "Let's see if that's a pull-tie."

pull tits See pull v 3

pull-up muhly n

A **muhly grass** (here: *Muhlenbergia filiformis*).

1950 Hitchcock–Chase *Manual Grasses* 381, *Muhlenbergia filiformis. . .* Pull-up muhly. . . Open woods and mountain meadows, South Dakota and Kansas to British Columbia, south to New Mexico and California. **1973** Hitchcock–Cronquist *Flora Pacific NW* 650.

pull wool See wool

pully bone n Also *pull(ey) bone, pulling bone* [EDD *pull bone, pulling bone*] chiefly Sth, S Midl, TX, OK, IL, IN See Map Also called boy 2, breakbone, breastbone, chicken bone 1, crossbone 2, funnybone 3, good-luck bone, hook ~, hug-me-tight 3, love bone, lucky ~ 1, marriage ~, pullet ~, merrythought

The wishbone.

1877 Bartlett *Americanisms* 502, *Pulling-Bone.* The common name in Maryland, Virginia, &c., for the yoke-like breast-bone of chickens, by pulling which till it breaks children and young ladies settle which will be the first married. **1905** *New Engl. Cook Book* 274, You will dislodge the V-shaped bone, corresponding to the "merrythought" or "pull-bone" of chickens. **1906** *DN* 3.152 **nwAR,** *Pully-bone. . .* Wishbone. **1909** *DN* 3.360 **eAL, wGA,** *Pull(y)-bone. . .* Wishbone. Very common. **1912** *DN* 3.586 **wIN,** *Pully-bone. . .* Wishbone, which is rarely heard. **1915** *DN* 4.188 **swVA,** *Pully-bone. . .* Wishbone. **1923** *DN* 5.218 **swMO,** *Pulley bone. . .* The wish bone of a fowl. **1933** *AmSp* 8.1.51 **Ozarks,** *Pulley bone.* **1939** *LANE* Map 215 *(Wishbone)* 1 inf, **neMA,** Pulling-bone. **1946** *PADS* 5.34 **VA,** *Pull bone, pulling bone. . .* Wishbone; east of the Blue Ridge. . . *Pully bone. . .* Wishbone; west of the Blue Ridge and in the southern Piedmont. *Ibid* 6.24 **eNC,** *Pullybone. . .* The wishbone. **1949** Kurath *Word Geog.* 63, *Wishbone. . .* The V-shaped clavicles of a fowl are variously known as *wishbone, pully-bone, pull-bone (pulling bone),* and *lucky-bone. . .* The usual Southern and South Midland expression is *pully-bone, pull-bone.* This term is also current among the older folk in the North Midland, notably in southern New Jersey and southwestern Pennsylvania. . . *Pull-bone* is characteristic of southern New Jersey, Chesapeake Bay, the Potomac Valley, and the Charleston area of South Carolina. **1952** Brown *NC Folkl.* 1.580, *Pulley-bone.* **1965–70** *DARE* (Qu. K74, *A bone from the breast of a chicken, shaped like a horseshoe*) 251 Infs, **chiefly Sth, S Midl, TX, OK, IL, IN,** Pully bone; 12 Infs, **scattered,** Pull bone; **MD38, VA14,** 26, Pulling bone. **c1970** Pederson *Dial. Surv. Rural GA* **seGA** *(What do you call a chicken bone . . that children like to have?)* 26 [of 64] infs, Pully bone; 5 infs, Pull

bone; 1 inf, Pullin' bone. **1984** Burns *Cold Sassy* 64 **nGA** (as of 1906), Papa . . reached for the pully-bone, my favorite piece of fried chicken except for the head. **1985** *DARE* File **TN,** Pulley bone.

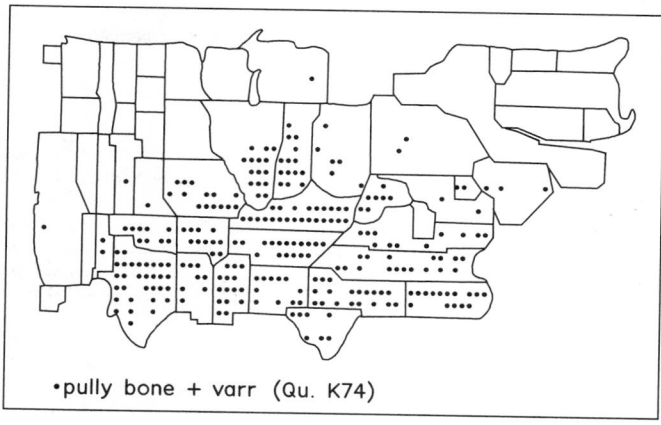

•pully bone + varr (Qu. K74)

pully candy See pulled candy

pully-hauling See pull-haul

pullykins See pullikins

pulpit n Usu |'pʊlˌpɪt|; also |'pʌlˌpɪt, -ət|; esp Sth, S Midl |pʊl'pɪt, 'pʊl'pɪt, 'pʌl-|; for addit varr see quots

Std sense, var forms.

1906 *DN* 3.152 **nwAR,** *Pulpit. . .* Pronounced [pʊl'pɪt]. An exception to the rule that recessive accent is well nigh universal. **1916** *DN* 4.347 **cTX** (as of 1896), *Pulpit. . .* Accented on the second syllable. Common among southern negroes. **1942** Hall *Smoky Mt. Speech* 75 **wNC, eTN,** Words which . . showed an unweakened [ɪ] were: *minute, pulpit* (with secondary stress) ['pʊlˌpɪt]. **1965–70** *DARE* (Qu. CC6, *The place where the preacher stands to give the sermon*) 381 Infs, **widespread,** ['pʊlˌpɪt]; 226 Infs, **widespread,** ['pʌlˌpɪt]; 162 Infs, **widespread,** ['pʊlpɪt, -ət]; 95 Infs, **scattered,** ['pʌlpɪt, -ət]; 29 Infs, **scattered,** ['pʊlˌpɪt]; **LA14,** ['pʊlˌpɪt]—less educated usage; 15 Infs, **scattered,** ['pɔlˌpɪt, pol-]; 11 Infs, **esp Sth, S Midl,** ['pʊˌpɪt, pu-, pʌ-, pa-]; **FL36, SC32, VA69,** ['pʊl'pɪt]; **MS59, TN37, TN59,** ['pʌl'pɪt]; **IL140, MS6,** 20, 30, 63, 71, ['pʊl'pit]; **AL30, MO23,** [ˌpʊl'pɪt]; **MS30,** ['pʊl'pɪt]; **NY131,** ['pʊlpɪt]; **TX86,** ['puəlbɪt]; **MO19,** ['fʊlˌpɪt]. **1967** *DARE* Tape **AL14,** He would have the Bible layin' up there on the ['pʊˇəlˌpɪt]. **c1970** *DARE* File **sIN, wKY,** ['pʌːpɪt]. Common. **1981** Pederson *LAGS Basic Materials,* 3 infs, **GA, MS, TX,** [pˈʊ<əlˌpɪˇt]. **1982** Barrick *Coll.* **csPA,** *Pulpit*—pron. púll-pit.

pulpit pounder n Cf Bible banger, table tapper

A vociferous preacher.

1906 Casey *Parson's Boys* 323 **sIL** (as of c1860), That snortin' pulpit pounder hez been at large too long. He's had warnin's enough; more'n we generally give his stripe, and all he's done is to blow an' make fun of 'em. Hangin' 's too good fer him. **1937** *AmSp* 12.281, Among the more apt slang epithets [used by O. Henry in his stories] is *pulpit-pounder* for *preacher.* **1942** Berrey–Van den Bark *Amer. Slang* 327.7, *Preacher. . .* pulpit . . pounder.

pulque n [MexSpan] SW Cf mescal 1, 2

A fermented drink made from the juice of any of var large **agaves,** esp *A. atrovirens.*

1796 Morse *Amer. Universal Geog.* 1.729, Pulque is the usual wine or beer of the Mexicans, made of the fermented juice of the Maguei. **1859** (1968) Bartlett *Americanisms* 260, The different species [of maguey] furnish pulque, sisal hemp, aguardiente, bagging, etc. **1888** Sheridan *Personal Memoirs* 1.28 **SW,** To prevent scurvy we used the juice of the maguey plant, called pulque. **1892** *DN* 1.194 **TX,** *Púlque:* the fermented juice of *Agave Americana* or *maguey.* **1930** Dos Passos *42nd Parallel* 317, They drank pulque and they had a bottle of whisky with them. **1932** Bentley *Spanish Terms* 187, Of the four Mexican beverages, *sotol, mescal, tequila,* and *pulque,* the latter is the most generally used and the best known to Americans. **1951** Corle *Gila* 348, From the agave are made pulque, mescal, and tequila, all three intoxicating beverages. **1985** Dodge *Flowers SW Deserts* 97, Many species of agave are found in various parts of the desert. . . If the young stalk is cut off, the sweet sap may be collected and fermented to form highly intoxicating beverages. . . mescal, pulque. . . and tequila.

pulse n [Var of **pus** n¹]

1984 Annals Internal Med. 100.900 **wAL,** Some words have become misspelled and mispronounced. . . pus, pulse. **1985** Amer. Jrl. Med. Feb 183 **eTN,** Pulse . . purulent material.

pulse warmer n

A wristlet.

1876 Bourke Diary 1 Mar **WY,** "Pulse warmers" about 6 inches long will preserve the wrists. **1896** E. Higginson Land of Snow Pearls 223 (DAE), Mother, where's my Sund'y pulse-warmers at? **1940** Mencken Happy Days 304 **MD,** Simultaneously, my mother began assembling a large stock of extra-heavy stockings and underclothes, and a great battery of mufflers, mittens and pulse-warmers, and to it was added a pair of massive goloshes. **1942** Warnick Garrett Co. MD 12 **nwMD** (as of 1900–18), Pulse-warmer. . . knitted covering for the wrist. **c1960** Wilson Coll. **csKY,** Pulse-warmer. . . A knitted wristband. **1983** Hansen Fox & Geese 19 **ME,** The cuff [of a mitten] was separate, a Wrister, and stayed on even when a man had to take off his mittens in the woods to do a fine adjustment on a bit of harness or a tool. Wristers have also been called "pulse warmers."

pulu n [Haw] **HI**

Fiber from a tree fern of the genus Cibotium, formerly used to stuff mattresses and pillows.

1833 in 1963 Tolmie Jrls. 144 **HI,** Met Madame Boki & retinue, her brows encircled with garlands of pulu. **1836** Sandwich Is. Gaz. & Jrl. of Commerce (Honolulu HI) 22 Oct [4]/1, A species of moss, called pulu is found here, and is used for stuffing beds. **1873** in 1966 Bishop Sandwich Is. 71 **HI,** I notice that the foreigners never use the English or botanical names of trees or plants, but speak of ohias, ohelos . . pulu (tree fern) [etc]. Ibid 89, He . . put down a shake-down of pulu (the silky covering of the fronds of one species of tree-fern), with a sheet over it, and a gay quilt of orange and red cotton. **1888** Hillebrand Flora Hawaiian Is. 546, On Hawaii this tree [Cibotium menziesii], intermixed with the two following species, formed extensive thickets in former times which have been nearly cleared away by the pulu gatherers, who ruthlessly sacrifice the whole tree in order to get easily at the wool. **1924** Amer. Botanist 30.20 **HI,** The finest of them [=tree ferns] is the pulu fern (Cibotum Chamissoi), whose uncoiling young fronds are clothed with a glistening silky capillary chaff of an old gold color, fine and soft as the finest wool; formerly collected under the vernacular name of pulu for filling pillows and mattresses. **1967** Reinecke-Tsuzaki Hawaiian Loanwords 110, Pulu, /pulu/. . . The yellow fuzz from the stem of the hapu fern (Cibotium splendens), formerly gathered in large quantities and exported for styptic purposes and for stuffing cushions. (The industry is now dead.)

puma n [Span < Quechua]

=mountain lion.

[**1774** Goldsmith Hist. Earth 3.232, The Puma, which has received the name of the American Lion.] **1840** MA Zool. & Bot. Surv. Herb. Plants & Quadrupeds 35, Felis concolor. . . The Puma, or American Lion. **1937** Grinnell et al. Fur-Bearing Mammals CA 541, As used in California, the names mountain lion, cougar . . , puma, and panther all refer to the same animal. **1965–70** DARE (Qu. P31, . . Names or nicknames . . for . . panther) Infs **CA3, 23, 87, 114, 153, CO41, IN62, LA34, MT4, NM6, NY74, 81, 105, TX26, 54, WV5,** Puma; (Qu. P32, . . Other kinds of wild animals) Inf **MA74,** Puma—got loose from the animal farm. **1968** DARE Tape NC53, A panther or a cougar, they've got a real long tail like a puma or a mountain lion.

‡pumble v [Var of pummel; cf Intro "Language Changes" I.8, chimney, family]

1966–70 DARE (Qu. Y14a, To hit somebody hard with the fist) Inf **AR40,** Pumble; (Qu. Y15, To beat somebody thoroughly: "John really _____ that fellow!") Inf **IL114,** Pumbled ['pʌmbɫd].

pumgranny See **pomegranate**

pumice n¹ See **pomace 1**

pumice n² Pronc-spp pumie, pummy, purmy [By reduction of the compound pumice stone from ['pʌmɪs'stoun] to ['pʌmɪ'stoun] (cf OED2 pumice A.γ 1565 →; pumice-stone A.δ 1578 →)]

Std sense, var forms.

1907 DN 3.197 **seNH,** Pummy-stone. . . Pumice-stone. **1913** DN 4.27 **NW,** Pummy. . . A volcanic ash, extremely light in weight. The dust is very hard on the lungs, etc. As it is very white, the glare of the sun on it is nearly blinding. With rain it packs well and makes fine roads, but when dry it is very dusty. The term is also applied to a light, porous, volcanic rock that is found floating in several of the Oregon rivers that rise in volcanic regions, as the Rogue River, Des Chutes, etc. **1917** DN 4.398 **neOH,** Pummy-stone ['pʌmɪstən]. . . Pumice stone. M. Also N.H., Mass., Ill., Ia. **1923** DN 5.244 **LA,** Purmy stone. Pumice stone. **1950** WELS Suppl. **cWI,** In reference to pummy stone. In our family this was a stone we used to thoroly clean and polish the big cast iron pancake griddle. Ibid **csWI,** We always called it [=a whetstone] "pummy-stone." **1958** McCulloch Woods Words 141 **Pacific NW,** Pumie—Pumice soil, the light stuff which flies up in great clouds of dust on many logging roads in the pine country. **1967** DARE FW Addit **cOR,** Pummy ['pʌmi] rock—pumice.

pummace See **pomace 1**

pumma Crissul See **palma Christi**

pummage See **pomace 4**

pummice See **pomace 1**

pummies See **pomace 2a, b**

pummings See **pomace 5**

pummy n¹ See **pomace 2**

pummy n² See **pumice** n²

pump v

1 Fig: to milk (a cow); to do the milking. Cf **pull** v **3**

1967–69 DARE (Qu. K8, Joking terms for milking a cow: A farmer might say, "Well, it's time to go out and _____.") Infs **CO4, KS5, MN40, NV8,** Pump the cow(s); **CA152, LA15, WV3,** Pump; **IN3, NY148,** Pump 'em (out).

2 To pedal a bicycle with a second rider on the handlebars or crossbar; to give (someone) a ride in this fashion; hence vbl n pumping. Cf **pull** v **5, pump** n³

1986 DARE File **cn,csTX** (as of 1940s), Pump. As a youth this was a common term for giving someone a ride on a bicycle. . . One could pump someone on the handlebars or on the bar between the seat and handlebars. **2000** Ibid **ceTX,** Last night a friend and I saw a man riding a bicycle with his girlfriend riding on the front crossbar. I said, "Oh look—that guy's pumping his girlfriend," to which my friend, who is the same age as I am but is from upstate New York, responded with a puzzled look. I explained that growing up in Houston we called giving someone a ride on your bicycle (which had no 2nd seat) "pumping". You could ride on the crossbar or on the fender, or sometimes even on the handlebars (if there wasn't a basket to get in the way). **2001** Ibid **cwCA** (as of c1955), If there were two kids but only one bicycle, we could say, "Hop on; I'll pump." Or we could say, "Do you want me to pump you?"

pump n¹ Also pomp [Etym uncert; cf Fr pampe blade, leaf (of corn), EDD tump "A store heap of potatoes, turnips, &c., covered with straw and enclosed with earth."] **MS, LA** Cf **bank** n¹ **1**

A heap of sweet potatoes or other vegetables covered with cornstalks, mulch, earth, and sometimes bark, sheet metal, or the like for winter storage; freq in comb potato pump; hence v pump to store in this way.

1953 (1977) Hubbard Shantyboat 331 **Lower Missip Valley,** In their gardens we saw peas already climbing the sticks, and small ventilated mounds of earth where sweet potatoes were stored. Tom had called these mounds, as near as we could make out, "pomps." **1966–67** DARE (Qu. M19, A place for keeping carrots, turnips, potatoes, and so on over the winter) Inf **MS21,** Potato pump; **LA8,** Potato pump—built of dirt and corn stalks and grass, sharp at the top with a vent on top and a door on the sloping side [drawing in text]; **LA10,** Pump—constructed of cornstalks with dirt thrown over them. **1986** Pederson LAGS Concordance (A place for storing produce in winter) 1 inf, **cLA,** Pump; 2 infs, **nwMS, neLA,** Pump—for potatoes; 1 inf, **cwMS,** Pump—of potatoes; 1 inf, **cwMS,** Pump—storage for potatoes; 1 inf, **swMS,** Pump—potatoes; store in pile; 1 inf, **swMS,** Pump—for potatoes; dirt piled on; 1 inf,

swMS, Pump—storing potatoes, dry, made of hay; 1 inf, **neLA,** Pump the potatoes to keep them fresh; 1 inf, **neLA,** Pump—for potatoes; 1 inf, **cLA,** Pump—for potatoes, kept underground; 1 inf, **nwMS,** Sweet potatoes put in a pump; 1 inf, **cLA,** A pump—of cypress bark; scuttle hole for potatoes; 1 inf, **nwMS,** Potato pump—sweet potatoes put in; 1 inf, **swMS,** Potato pump—for storing potatoes, dug in ground; 1 inf, **swMS,** Potato pump—in winter for potatoes and turnips; 1 inf, **csMS,** Potato pump—heard of; 1 inf, **neLA,** Potato pump—cover with stalks, dirt, hay; a shed; 1 inf, **cLA,** Potato pump—cornstalks over potatoes, dirt, tin; 1 inf, **swMS,** Pump the potatoes—dig a hole, cover with tin tub. [10 of 16 total infs Black]

pump n[2] [Ger *auf Pump*] **NE**

In phr *on pump:* On credit.

    1928 *AmSp* 4.132 **cnNE,** "On pump" is the "sandhiller's" term for buying necessities at the inland store on credit. **1930** *N. Amer. Rev.* 229.425 **nwNE,** Usually the settler had only a portion of that sum or none of it, so he got his home "on tick" or "on pump," meaning, in sandhill parlance, he charged it. **1939** FWP *Guide NE* 111, Eloquent of the life of the sandhiller are: . . on pump (buying necessities at the store on credit).

pump n[3]

    1986 *DARE* File **nwWI,** Pump meaning a lift on a bicycle. I remember hearing and using the word in this sense in Brule, Wisconsin in the early to mid 1940's.

pump bird See **pumper**

pumpeon See **pompion** n[1]

pumper n Also *pumper-gor, pump handle, pump(ing) bird, pump sucker* Cf **thunder pumper**

A **bittern** (here: *Botaurus lentiginosus*).

    1917 *Wilson Bulletin* 29.2.78 **MN,** *Botaurus lentiginosus.* . . [P]umper. **1944** Hausman *Amer. Birds* 10, The bird [=the American Bittern] is often called the Stake Driver or Pumper from its call notes, which are among the most curious notes uttered by any native bird. They sound like the syllables *punk-a-dunk,* as though the bird were driving a stout stake into a resonant mud bank. Some listeners liken them to the sounds made by a musically gurgling pump. It has been averred that while uttering these notes the bird's bill is driven deep into the mud. This, however, is not the case, the bird's bill being thrust forward into the air with each utterance. **1950** *WELS* (A small heron that makes a booming sound before rain, and often stands with its head pointed up) 1 Inf, **swWI,** Bittern, pumper. **1959** *Names* 7.117, Various herons "freeze" or stand still in a nearly erect position, but the bitterns seem to have this habit most strongly developed. . . This habit has not escaped folk attention and it is the basis for a number of interesting names. Among them are, pumphandle (N.J.) [etc.] *Ibid* 119, Likening the bittern's vocalization to the sounds made by the operation of an old-fashioned suction-pump has also been a fruitful source of folk-names. Among these allusions are . . pumper (Mass., Minn., N. Dak. . .), pump-sucker (Ind., Ill., Wis.) [etc.]. *Ibid* 120, Onomats that have been applied to the bittern as names . . pumper-gor (Mass.) [etc.]. **1967** *DARE* (Qu. Q8, *A water bird that makes a booming sound before rain and often stands with its beak pointed almost straight up*) Inf **MA5,** Pump bird (it's a bittern); (Qu. Q10, . . *Water birds and marsh birds*) Inf **NY6,** Pump handle—crane-like marsh bird—looks like a guy working a water pump. **1968** *DARE* Tape **GA30,** They was called a pump bird. Well, he makes a pumping sound when he hollers. . . he pumps, you know . . he's called a pumping bird.

pumping See **pump** v 2

pumping bird See **pumper**

pumpkin n[1] Pronc-spp *pungkin, punkin(g), punkun*

A Std sense, var forms.

    1843 (1916) Hall *New Purchase* 155 **IN,** And "punkun-butter!"—and "punkun-jelle!"—and corn bread in all its glory! **1852** in 1956 Eliason *Tarheel Talk* 316 **cs,seNC,** Punkings. **1853** Simms *Sword & Distaff* 451 **SC** [Black], He eyes shut, and he face wid no more 'spression in 'em, dan a greasy punkin. **1899** (1912) Green *VA Folk-Speech* 339, *Punkin.* . . Pronounced pung'kin. **1904** Day *Kin o' Ktaadn* 21 **ME,** The squashes are snoutin' the punkins. **1907** *DN* 3.235 **nwAR,** *Punkin-custard.* **1915** *DN* 4.228 **wTX,** *Punkin.* Pumpkin is never used. **1926** *AmSp* 2.81 **ME,** Strangely enough the word [=*bumpkin*] is pronounced as it is spelled, whereas *pumpkin* is uniformly spoken "punkin'." **1929** Sale *Tree Named John* 62 **MS** [Black], Peter, Peter,

Punkin eater/ . . put her in a punkin-shell / En den he kep' 'er ve'y well. **1937** NE Univ. *Univ. Studies* 37.112 [Terms from play-party songs], Little piece of puddin' An' a punkin pie. **1942** McAtee *Dial. Grant Co. IN* 50 (as of 1890s), *Punkin.* . . This pronunciation is so universal that one never hears "pumpkin" without its seeming forced. **1965–70** *DARE* (Qu. C34, *Nicknames for nearby settlements, villages, or districts*) 18 Infs, **scattered,** Punkin center (or town, college, hollow, hook, run); (Qu. GG19b, *When you can see from the way a person acts that he's feeling important or independent: "He seems to think he's _____."*) 16 Infs, **scattered,** Some punkins; (Qu. P1, . . *Kinds of freshwater fish . . caught around here . . good to eat*) 13 Infs, **scattered,** Punkinseed(s); **OK11,** Punkinseed perch; (Qu. X28, *Joking words . . for a person's head*) 10 Infs, **scattered,** (Regular) punkin head; **CA184, PA142, WV3,** Punkin; (Qu. C35, *Nicknames for the different parts of your town or city*) Inf **OK46,** Punkin center; (Qu. H18, . . *Special kinds of bread*) Infs **CA157, PA163,** Punkin bread; (Qu. H63, *Kinds of desserts*) Infs **AR52, KY62, 84, NY75, 206, OH44, WA14,** Punkin pie; **NC76,** Punkin pudding; (Qu. H82a, *Cheap candies sold especially for schoolchildren*) Inf **IL99,** Punkin seeds; (Qu. I4, . . *Vegetables . . less commonly grown around here*) Inf **KY34,** Punkins; (Qu. I23, . . *Kinds of squash*) Infs **CA113, 170, KY17, 37,** Punkin squash; **MD30,** Cow punkin; (Qu. I24, . . *Kinds of pumpkins;* total Infs questioned, 75) Inf **AR27,** Pie punkins; yellow punkins; (Qu. I26, . . *Kinds of melons*) Infs **NC44, 45,** Punkins; (Qu. N37, *Joking names for a branch railroad that is not very important or gives poor service*) Infs **IN30, 58, MN36, OH45, 47, VA8,** Punkin vine; (Qu. P3, *Freshwater fish that are not good to eat*) 8 Infs, **NEng,** Punkinseeds; (Qu. P37a, *Nicknames for a rifle*) Infs **CA145, WA1,** Punkin slinger; (Qu. P38, *What . . you put into a rifle to shoot*) Infs **PA10, 168,** Punkin ball; (Qu. R30, . . *Kinds of beetles;* not asked in early QRs) Infs **AL2, 38, GA46, 65, 77, 84, TX59,** Punkin bug; **KY88,** Punkin beetle; (Qu. T16, . . *Kinds of trees . . 'special'*) Inf **LA15,** Punkin ash; (Qu. U41b, *Somebody who has lost everything and is very poor: "He's poor as _____."*) Inf **NJ53,** Piss and punkin'; (Qu. W42a, . . *Nicknames . . for men's sharp-pointed shoes*) Inf **CA208,** Punkin-slitters; (Qu. X12, . . *Large front teeth that stick out of the mouth*) Inf **TX98,** He could bite a punkin through a rail fence; (Qu. X13a, . . *Joking names . . for teeth*) Inf **TN23,** Punkin-snappers; (Qu. X50, *Names or nicknames for a person who is very fat*) Inf **NY24,** Eat like a punking; (Qu. Z12, *Nicknames and joking words meaning 'a small child': "He's a healthy little _____."*) Inf **UT3,** Punkin; (Qu. AA3, *Nicknames or affectionate names for a sweetheart*) Inf **MA42,** Punkins; (Qu. AA28, . . *Joking or sly expressions . . women use to say that another is going to have a baby . . "She['s] _____."*) Infs **KY33, TX104,** Swallowed a punkin seed; **MI47,** She musta been eating some punkin seeds; (Qu. FF14, . . *Kinds of firecrackers*) Inf **PA167,** Punkin balls; (Qu. FF16, . . *Local contests or celebrations*) Inf **OH31,** Punkin show; (Qu. GG19a, *When you can see from the way a person acts that he's feeling important or independent: "He surely is _____ these days."*) Inf **FL26,** Some punkins; (Qu. HH1, *Names and nicknames for a rustic or countrified person*) Infs **NJ1, NY149,** Country punkin; (Qu. HH3, *A dull and stupid person*) Inf **MD17,** Punkin head; (Qu. II23, *Joking names for the people who are, or think they are, the best society of a community: The _____*) Inf **CA20,** Some punkins; (Qu. JJ15b, *Sayings about a person who seems to you very stupid: "He doesn't know _____."*) Inf **TN13,** He doesn't know beans from punkins. **1982** Slone *How We Talked* 26 **eKY** (as of c1950), Punkin.

B Senses.

1 Std: the large globular fruit of a vine (*Cucurbita pepo*). Also called **pompion** n[1] For other names of varieties of *C. pepo* see **cheese pumpkin, cow ~, pie ~, sugar ~**

2 usu pl; used predicatively: Someone or something important, superior, or remarkable usu in phr *some pumpkins.*

    1846 (1973) Porter *Quarter Race* 118 **OH,** As Old T. is *known,* and Dick [=a horse] has been heard of, the boys are rather shy—but one of them thinks he's got a scrub that's "some pumpkins!" **1858** Hammett *Piney Woods Tavern* 63, Sime and the thief war fastened on to another; and the thief—he war some punkins that feller—hollerd out that Sime were the villain, and *thar* he war. **1862** (1864) Browne *Artemus Ward Book* 228, "Alexander the Grate was punkins," I continered, but Napoleon was punkinser! **1872** Schele de Vere *Americanisms* 525, The Hubbites, as Bostonians are apt to be called now . . are said to have derived, from their attachment to this vegetable, and the esteem in which it is universally held among them, the phrase *some pumpkins,* expressive of high appreciation. . . It is stated, however, by one high in authority among New Englanders, that this explanation of the term is not the true one, although the latter cannot well be stated, because it would offend ears polite. (J.H. Trumbull.) **1884** *Anglia* 7.261 **Sth, S Midl** [Black], *To be 'some punkins'* =to be of some value. **1890** *DN* 1.70, Note . . the New England phrase, 'some punkins,' to express a high degree of ability. "He's some punkins." **1892** *DN* 1.210 **seMA**, He thinks he's some punkins. **1905** *DN* 3.20 **cCT**, *Some pumpkins*. . . Any body or thing large or important. *Ibid* 64 **eNE**, *Some punkins*. . . Said of those who are pretentious or prominent. "He thinks he's some punkins." **1906** *DN* 3.157 **nwAR**, *Some punkin*. . . Of some consequence. "He thinks he's some punkin." **1909** *DN* 3.373 **eAL, wGA**, *Some punkin*. . . A person of importance. "He thinks he's some punkin." *Some punkins* is not used as far as I know. *Ibid* 416 **nME**, *Some pumpkins*. . . Of considerable account. **1910** *DN* 3.449 **cwNY**, "He thinks he's some punkins"; said of those who are pretentious or prominent. **1912** *DN* 3.591 **wIN**, He is some punkins, just the same. **1959** *VT Hist.* 27.153, *No great pumpkins* ['pʌnkɪnz] [sic]. . . Of little worth. Common. **1965–70** *DARE* (Qu. GG19b, *When you can see from the way a person acts that he's feeling important or independent: "He seems to think he's _____."*) 16 Infs, **scattered**, Some punkins; **MI**26, Some pumpkins; (Qu. GG19a, *When you can see from the way a person acts that he's feeling important or independent: "He surely is _____ these days."*) Inf **FL**26, Some punkins; (Qu. II23, *Joking names for the people who are, or think they are, the best society of a community: The _____*) Inf **CA**200, Some punkins. [16 of 18 Infs old] **1978** *UpCountry* Oct 5 **wMA**, General Electric is very big pumpkins in Pittsfield Mass., and Jenifer House is some pumpkins in Great Barrington. **1991** *Macoupin Co. Enquirer* (Carlinville IL) 6 **cwIL**, [From a 1961 issue quoting "oldsters":] A boy or possession was sometimes rated as some punkin.

pumpkin n[2] [Prob var of *bumpkin*, but cf *country squash* (at **country** n B2f)]
In phr *country pumpkin*: a rustic; a **hillbilly** n **1**.
1958 *AmSp* 33.265 **Upper MW**, *Pejorative Designations of Rural Dwellers*. . . country 'punkin.' **1967** *DARE* (Qu. HH1, *Names and nicknames for a rustic or countrified person*) Infs **CT**2, **NC**61, Country pumpkin; **NJ**1, **NY**149, Country punkin.

pumpkin ash n [See quot 1908]
An ash *(Fraxinus profunda)* of the southeastern and central US. Also called **red ash, swell-butt ~**
1903 Small *Flora SE U.S.* 918, *Fraxinus profunda*. . . In swamps or on river banks, Pennsylvania to Missouri, south to Georgia. Pumpkin Ash. **1908** Rogers *Tree Book* 439, The common name, pumpkin ash, refers to the bulging and ridged or buttressed base of the tree from which the straight trunk rises. **1939** FWP *Guide FL* 300, Among the trees are maple, gum, the bald cypress with fluted base, and the slender-trunked pumpkin ash. **1968** *DARE* (Qu. T16, . . *Kinds of trees . . 'special'*) Inf **LA**15, Punkin ash—a spongy kind. **1987** *Nature Conserv. News* 37.2.15 **IN**, Extensive southern wetland system with swamp cottonwood/pumpkin ash plant community.

pumpkin-blossom coot n [See quot 1955] **MA**
The American **scoter** *(Melanitta nigra)*.
1888 Trumbull *Names of Birds* 107 **MA**, At North Plymouth, Fairhaven, and New Bedford, [the American Scoter is called] *copper-nose* and *copper-bill*, and at Edgartown, *pumpkin-blossom coot*. **1925** (1928) Forbush *Birds MA* 1.271, *Scoter*. . . Black coot butterbill; butternose; copperbill; copper-nose; yellow-nose; yellow-bill; pumpkin-blossom coot. **1955** *AmSp* 30.185 **MA**, The large, partly yellow bill of the otherwise black American scoter has caused it to be called *pumpkin-blossom coot*.

pumpkin chaser See **pumpkin roller**

pumpkin custard n
Pumpkin-pie filling baked either in a dish or a crust.
1903 *DN* 2.326 **seMO**, *Pumpkin custard*. . . Pumpkin pie. **1907** *DN* 3.235 **nwAR**, *Punkin-custard*. . . Pumpkin pie. **1935** Frederick *PA Dutch* 145, *Pumpkin Custard*—½ pint pumpkin[,] 2 egg[,] 1 tablespoonful flour[,] 1 cup brown sugar[,] ¼ teaspoonful ginger[,] ¼ teaspoonful of nutmeg[,] 1 lump of melted butter[.] Mix all with a pint of milk and sprinkle cinnamon on top. **1939** Wolcott *Yankee Cook Book* 205, *Pumpkin custard*. . . Pour into baking dish or individual molds and set in pan of hot water. Bake in moderate oven. . . Serve warm or chilled. **1939–43** in 1944 *ADD* **nWV**, [*Punkin-custard*]. . . applied to a small oblong portion; whereas a larger wedge-shaped portion is punkin pie.

‡**pumpkin-eater** n Cf **eat a pumpkin through a knothole, be able to**
1968 *DARE* (Qu. X12, . . *Large front teeth that stick out of the mouth*) Inf **GA**59, Pumpkin-eater.

pumpkin head n
A foolish or stupid person.
[**1848** (1849) Irving *Hist. NY* 247, Beside each pumpkin-head peered the end of a rusty musket.] **1884** Twain *Huck. Finn* 151, Ef we hadn' . . ben sich punkin-heads . . we'd seed de raf'. **1898** Frederic *Deserter* 143 **OH**, You can't raise a plug [of tobacco] in a whole regiment of 'em. Regular pumpkin-heads! **1899** (1912) Green *VA Folk-Speech* 339, *Punkin-head*. . . A stupid fellow; a dolt. **1918** Lincoln *Shavings* 232 **eMA**, Can't make a man out of a punkinhead. **1919** *DN* 5.62 **CA**, *Pumpkin-head*, a dull, stupid fellow. **1929** *AmSp* 5.119 **ME**, A stupid individual was a "mutton head," "punkin head," "lunk head," or "dumber than a stump." **1938** *AmSp* 13.74 **OH**, So and so is . . a mutton head, a punkin head, a lunk head. **1941** *LANE* Map 465 *(Fool)* 2 infs, **NH**, Pumpkinhead. **1986** Pederson *LAGS Concordance (That fool!)* 1 inf, **nwLA**, Pumpkin heads—people without much intelligence.

pumpkin husker See **pumpkin roller**

pumpkin pine n [See quot 1850] **chiefly ME**
The fine-grained, yellowish wood of old-growth **white pine** (here: *Pinus strobus*); an old-growth **white pine** tree.
1807 in 1809 Kendall *Travels* 3.145 **ME**, Of the white pine, the lumberers distinguish two varieties, one of which they call punkin pine. . . The name punkin (pompion) they employ on account of the softness and fine grain of the wood. **1850** Emerson *Rept. Trees & Shrubs* 63 **MA**, The white pines receive different names, according to their mode of growth and the appearance of the wood. When growing densely in deep and damp old forests, with only a few branches near the top, the slowly-grown wood is perfectly clear and soft, destitute of resin, and almost without sap-wood, and has a yellowish color, like the flesh of the pumpkin. It is then called pumpkin pine. **1907** *Springfield W. Repub.* 29 Aug. 15 *(DAE)*, The virgin white pine has practically disappeared from New England and huge 'pumpkin pines' four and five feet in diameter are now a matter of tradition. **1932** Wasson *Sailing Days* 54 **cME coast**, That wood of original native growth known as "pumpkin pine." **1937** FWP *Guide ME* 110, Southworth carved more than five hundred figureheads, spending about eighteen days to a figure. . . The material used was pumpkin pine, common on the Maine coast at that time. **1966** *DARE* Tape **ME**19, I've seen pine trees four feet. . . Pumpkin pine, we call 'em. **1975** Gould *ME Lingo* 221, *Punkin pine*—A term now used indifferently for the eastern white pine *(pinus Strobus)*, but originally it meant the clear lumber from the old-growth pines of Maine whose age had mellowed the resinous content until the grain suggested the meat of a pumpkin. Pine varies greatly in texture and heft, depending on the soil and exposure where it grows, and not all pine boards have the quality that *punkin pine* conveys. Very little true *punkin pine* is available today, but all cabinet makers and home-workshop buffs try to find some. **1988** *DARE* File **ME**, *Punkin' pine*—A term used in Maine for old-growth white pine that is almost free of grain, and knots. Very suitable for carving figureheads and other objects in the round. **2000** *Ibid* **nwMA**, I've never heard of a pine on the stump referred to as a pumpkin pine. That term is used for the boards and the color they eventually turn, and it's used by retailers. The woodsmen I've known never use it.

pumpkin roller n Rarely *pumpkin chaser, ~ husker, ~ thrasher* derog
A rustic; a greenhorn.
1905 *DN* 3.91 **nwAR**, *Punkin-roller*. . . Uncouth countryman. 'He's a punkin-roller—a regular hill-billy.' Common. **1934** (1970) Wilson *Backwoods Amer.* 160 **AR, MO**, Moonshinin' a man's game. Can't jest any punkin-roller stick it. **1936** *AmSp* 11.276 **eTN**, *Pumpkin roller*. A farmer. 'He is a poor pumpkin roller.' **1940** Writers' Program *Guide NV* 75, A *flat-heeled peeler* or *pumpkin roller* is an amateur cowboy, or a farmer who has turned cowboy. **1941** *LANE* Map 450 *(A rustic)* 1 inf, **sME coast**, Pumpkin chaser; 1 inf, **seMA**, Pumpkin thrasher, usually. **1943** Korson *Coal Dust* 5, Full-time miners naturally resented them [= farmer-miners] and expressed their distrust by calling them "winter diggers," "wheats," "corncrackers," "hay johns," "pumpkin rollers," "clodhoppers," "greenies," "scissorbills," and "sagers." **1949** Emrich *Wild West Custom* 164 **MT, ID**, Many of these greenhorns actually were farmers, cowboys or lumberjacks who worked in the fields and on ranches during the summer and supplemented their wages by work in the mines in winter. . . In Montana and Idaho, they are more frequently referred to as . . *punkin rollers*. **1971** Green *Village Horse Doctor* 264 **cwTX** (as of 1940s), Pumpkin rollers came from various parts of the world to drill wells, cut down good mesquite trees, and plow up grass to raise something that the goverment already had too much of and the

market was bad. **2000** Launspach *ID Dial. Project* 5 **seID,** (*If a person from the country came to the city what might city people call them behind their back*) 1 inf, Pumpkin husker.

pumpkinseed n

1 also *pumpkinseed perch:* A sunfish of the genus *Lepomis,* esp *L. gibbosus,* but also **bluegill 1, longear sunfish,** and **orangespotted sunfish. chiefly NEng** See Map For other names of *L. gibbosus* see **bream B3, flatfish 3a, Indianfish, kivver, moccasin 2a, peacock sunfish 2, pond perch, punkie** n², **redbelly 1, red-eared sunfish 2, robin 2, round sunfish, sun bass, ~ perch, sunny, tobacco box, yellowbelly** Cf **black bream, gourdseed sucker**

1815 (1846) MA Hist. Soc. *Coll.* 2d ser 3.102 **NH,** There are, however, various kinds of smaller fish, viz. . . bill fish, pumpkin seed, or flat fish, &c. **1842** DeKay *Zool. NY* 4.32, The numerous spots on its body has occasioned it to be called by the whimsical name of *Pumpkin-seed,* in some districts of the State. **1865** Norris *Amer. Angler's Book* 116, This beautiful little fish, associated in the minds of all anglers with the first rudiments of a piscatorial education, is known in the Middle and Southern States as the Sunfish or "Sunny." Yankee boys call them "Punkin Seeds." **1906** *DN* 3.152 **nwAR,** Pumpkin seed. . . A diminutive kind of fresh-water fish. "Looks mighty tough on a fellow to stay on the creek bank all night and catch nothing but a measly little pumpkin seed." **1911** [see **2** below]. **1965–70** *DARE* (Qu. P1, . . *Kinds of freshwater fish . . caught around here . . good to eat*) Infs **CT**2, 6, 31, 36, **MN**12, **MA**58, **NY**1, 74, **RI**4, 6, Punkinseed; **MI**103, Punkinseed—like a bluegill; **VA**8, Bluegill = sunfish = punkinseed; **VT**12, Punkinseed = rock bass; **OK**11, Punkinseed perch; (Qu. P3, *Freshwater fish that are not good to eat*) Infs **MA**1, 6, 16, 68, **NH**4, **VT**4, Punkinseed, **VT**16, Punkinseed—rock bass; **RI**12, Pumpkinseed; (Qu. P7, *Small fish used as bait for bigger fish*) Inf **IL**115, Punkinseed. [22 of 23 Infs male] **1994** NC Lang. & Life Project *Dial. Dict. Lumbee Engl.* 10 **seNC,** *Pumpkin seed.* . . A fish in the bream family.

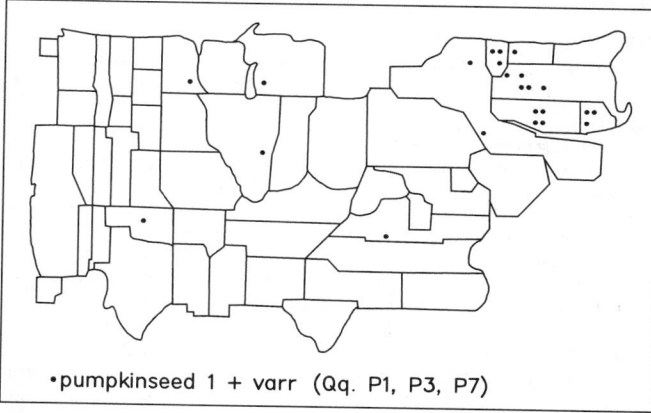

•pumpkinseed 1 + varr (Qq. P1, P3, P7)

2 A **butterfish 1** (here: *Peprilus triacanthus*). **CT**
1903 NY State Museum & Sci. Serv. *Bulletin* 60.458 **CT,** In Connecticut it [=the butterfish] is called pumpkin seed and at Norfolk starfish. **1911** U.S. Bur. Census *Fisheries 1908* 314, Pumpkin-seed.—A name applied to the sunfish (*Eupomotis gibbosus*) of the brooks of New York and New England, and to the butterfish (*Poronotus triacanthus*) in Connecticut. **1939** Natl. Geogr. Soc. *Fishes* 68, *Poronotus triacanthus* has several names, being known as dollarfish in Maine, as butterfish in Massachusetts and Norfolk . . and pumpkinseed in Connecticut. **1968** *DARE* (Qu. P2, . . *Kinds of saltwater fish caught around here . . good to eat*) Inf **CT**14, Pumpkinseeds.

3 also attrib: Any of var broad, shallow boats.
1884 Henshall *Camping in FL* 15, The boats are necessarily of light draught, and center-boarders. There are the "skimming-dish," the "pumpkin seed," and the "flat-iron" models, all half-round yacht-built boats, broad and beamy, cat-rigged or sloop-rigged. **1890** *Century Dict.* 4845, *Pumpkin-seed.* . . 3. A type of yacht-built boat, broad and cat- or sloop-rigged. It is a very wet sailer. *Henshall.* [*Century Dict.:* Florida.]—4. A very flat, wide row-boat, of the shape of a pumpkin-seed, used in water that is shallow or encumbered with weeds or grass. [*Century Dict:* U.S.] **1965** *PADS* 43.19 **seMA,** Small rowboat large enough for two . . punkin-seed [1 of 9 infs]. **1985** Rattray *Advent. Dimon* 17 **Long Island NY,** All of us had grown up with boats, from little pumpkinseed gunning skiffs to whaleboats.

4 A type of snowshoe.
1921 *Outing* 79.105, By far the most popular snowshoe is the pumpkin-seed type. . . The shape is that of a pumpkin seed with a tail attached. **1922** Ibid 80.331 **MA,** I used "Indian Runner," "Canadian," "Pumpkin Seed" and on trails the "Bear paw," but never for all purposes or any purpose have I ever used a shoe that compares with the Alaskan.

5 also *pumpkin skin:* A light-skinned Black person. Cf **high yellow**
1922 Gonzales *Black Border* 321 **sSC, GA coasts** [Gullah glossary], *Punkin-skin*—pumpkin colored or mulatto Negro. **1926** Van Vechten *Nigger Heaven* 286 [Black], *Punkin-seed:* see high yellow. [*Ibid* 285, *High yellow:* mulatto or lighter.]

pumpkinseed perch See **pumpkinseed 1**

pumpkin skin See **pumpkin seed 5**

pumpkin thrasher See **pumpkin roller**

pumpkin tree n

=**alpine fir.**
1897 Sudworth *Arborescent Flora* 53 **CA,** *Abies lasiocarpa.* . . Common Names. . . Pumpkin Tree. **1908** Britton *N. Amer. Trees* 77, White Fir. . . This Fir, variously called White balsam fir, Oregon balsam fir, Alpine fir, Downy cone fir, Mountain balsam, and Pumpkin tree, has probably a greater range than any other American fir.

pumpkin vine n

A small or branch railroad.
1946 in 1953 Botkin–Harlow *Treas. Rail. Folkl.* 287, Here is one of the chief joys of knocking about on those little Southern punkin-vines; no studied, from-the-teeth-out courtesy for policy's sake, but old-time, homespun friendliness that comes from the heart. **1968** *DARE* (Qu. N37, *Joking names for a branch railroad that is not very important or gives poor service*) Infs **IN**30, 58, **MN**36, **OH**45, 47, **VA**8, Punkin vine; **IN**39, 69, Pumpkin vine.

pumpkin wagon See **potato wagon**

pumpknot n Also *pumpknock, punkknot* [Etym uncert; cf arch *pumple* pimple and **knot** n¹ **2a**] **chiefly S Midl** See Map Cf **popknot**

A bump or swelling, esp one on the head caused by a blow.
1933 *AmSp* 8.1.51 **Ozarks,** Pump-knot. . . A lump, a swelling. *Did you see that 'ar big pump-knot on Rafe's head? Looks like somebody must of difted him with a axe handle, or somethin'.* **1944** *PADS* 2.11 **nwGA,** Pump-knot. . . A swelling, such as that produced—"pumped up"—by a bump or blow, or the sting of a bee or wasp. **1952** Brown *NC Folkl.* 1.580 **wNC,** Pump-knot. . . A knot on the head produced by a blow. **1955** Ritchie *Singing Family* 189 **seKY,** Look out, biggety-britches, you going to fall and make a pump-knot on your noggin. **1965–70** *DARE* (Qu. X60, . . *A lump that comes up on your head when you get a sharp blow or knock;* not asked in early QRs) 18 Infs, **chiefly S Midl,** Pumpknot; **AR**52, **IN**32, **TN**3, **TX**51, **WV**2, 3, Punkknot; **VA**2, Pumpknock; (Qu. X59, . . *The small infected pimples that form usually on the face*) Inf **TN**12, Pumpknots. **1973** McCarthy *Child of God* 9 **TN,** He was layin flat on the ground lookin up at everbody with his eyes crossed and a pumpknot on his head. **1974** *DARE* File, *Punkknot* (pumpknot)—A word much used by Mother, born in Tell City, Indiana, c1885; she moved to White Co., Illinois, as a young girl. **1983** *MJLF* 9.1.52

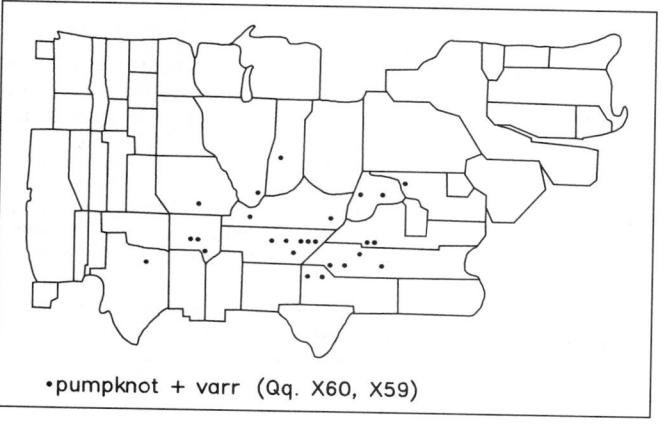

•pumpknot + varr (Qq. X60, X59)

ceKY (as of 1956), *Pump knot*. . . a lump on the head from a blow. **1990** Cavender *Folk Med. Lexicon* 29 **sAppalachians,** *Pump knot*—a swelling produced by a blow to the body or sting from an insect: "I got this pump knot on my head from where he hit me." **1999** *DARE* File **KY,** *Pump knot*—results from being hit or bumped by something that raises a knot, generally in the area of, or around, the head, rising so rapidly that you can almost see it grow. I first heard this in London Kentucky when a person I was talking to told me about her daughter running into the door and banging her forehead and she "got a pumpknot".

pumplefoot n [Engl dial; cf *EDD*] **esp ME** Cf **pudding-footed**

A clubfoot; hence *pumple-footed* club-footed.

1908 Day *King Spruce* 166 **ME,** Don't you think a man with pumple-feet is an infernal fool to try to learn to skate? **1913** *DN* 4.5 **ME,** *Pumplefoot*. . . Clubfoot. **1914** *DN* 4.78 **ME, nNH,** *Pumple-footed*. . . Club-footed.

pumple stone n Also *popple stone* [*EDD* pumple-stone 'a pebble-stone' < *pumple* pimple; cf **pumplefoot**]

1975 Gould *ME Lingo* 220, *Pumple stones*—Rounded beach stones used to anchor rockweed *banking* (winter insulation about the foundation of a house). *Pumple stones* are also used to border front walks and driveways and flower beds. There was a time a front walk of crushed clam shells and *pumple stones* was much admired, particularly if the *pumple stones* were neatly whitewashed. Often *pumple* gets the sound of *popple*.

pump log n

A hollowed-out log used as a water pipe.

1816 *N. Amer. Rev.* 3.429 **NH,** He declared also, that the mill for grinding apples, which is an overshot, and is fed by a pump log . . would often stop during the day. **1844** *Knickerbocker* 23.443 **NY,** The cool spring water . . was conveyed the whole distance in 'pump-logs.' **1855** (1858) Bennett *Chronology of NC* 108, He had some men repairing pump-logs, through which water was carried from the mountain side to his hotel. **1937** Lincoln *Wilmington DE* 207, The committee reported that it would require eight hundred and thirty-five feet of pump-logs. **1950** *WELS Suppl.* **ceWI,** *Pump logs*—Vertical log with hole in it. Spring water flows out of the hole into a trough. Had *pump logs* in summer kitchen or shed, in cheese house, and in barn. *Ibid*, *Pump logs:* Logs approximately four feet long and eight inches in diameter, having a longitudinal bore. Used in place of metal pipes to conduct water from its source (a spring) to the desired outlets. Logs are buried end to end below the frost level. **1965** Needham–Mussey *Country Things* 91 **VT,** The one place he always used pine was for pump-logs. After they got tired of bringing water from the well a bucket at a time, they figured they'd pipe it from the spring.

pump-pump-pullaway See **pom-pom-pullaway**

pump sucker See **pumper**

pum-pum-pullaway See **pom-pom-pullaway**

punch v

1 To drive or herd (cattle); to work as a cattle driver or herder; hence vbl n *punching*. **West** Cf **bullpuncher 1, cowpuncher, dog punch, puncher 1, 2**

1875 *Overland Mth.* 14.449 **West,** I'll teach yer how to punch bulls, an' you kin convert me an' the Injin. **1890** *Stock Grower & Farmer* (Las Vegas NM) 21 June 4/1, J.O. Phillips . . will be initiated into the business of punching cattle. **1902** Wister *Virginian* 167, I was goin' back to punch cattle or fight Indians. **1914** *DN* 4.164 **AZ,** *Punch*. . . To drive or round up,—used of cattle and tourists. *Ibid* 165 **AZ,** *Punch*. . . To work as a cowboy. **1923** Sinclair *Parowan Bonanza* 276, You'd still be punchin' cows for your dad. **1929** *AmSp* 5.57 **NE** [Cattle country talk], "Cowboy" is the commonly known term for one who "punches" or "herds" cattle. **1933** *AmSp* 8.1.30 **nwTX** [Ranch diction], *Punch*. To handle cattle professionally. **1995** Brophy Coll. 58 **swMO** (as of c1960), *Punch cows*. [T]o herd cows; more correctly, to tend cows in transit in railroad cars, to prod the cows to keep them on their feet.

2 also with *out*: To bulge, protrude; hence ppl adjs *punched out, punching up* bulging, protruding. Cf **pooch** v

1986 Pederson *LAGS Concordance* (Bulge) 1 inf, ceTN, Punch out; 2 infs, **csGA, cwAL,** Punch out = bulge; 1 inf, **cnGA,** Punched out; 1 inf, **cnTN,** Proud flesh is raw, angry, and punching up.

punch n[1]

1 See **puncher 1.**

2 See **punching stick.**

3 See **punch stick 1.**

punch n[2] See **paunch**

punchball n esp NYC

A game similar to baseball played with a rubber ball that is hit with the fist.

1935 Ware *Greenwich Village* 144 **NYC,** The district abounded in block teams . . who played the ubiquitous game of punchball. **1957** *Sat. Eve. Post Letters* **Springfield MA** (as of 1917–26), *Punchball*—A baseball type game, any number of players on a side! The batter would throw a soft rubber ball into the air himself and punch it with his fist. . . A variation . . allowed the fielder to get a batter out by hitting him with the ball as he ran the bases. **1968–70** *DARE* (Qu. EE11, *Bat-and-ball games for just a few players [when there aren't enough for a regular game]*) Inf **NY250,** Punchball; (Qu. EE33, *Other outdoor games*) Inf **NY119,** Punchball—like baseball except players would punch the ball; played in the gutter or backyard. **1977** *NY Times* (NY) 6 July 29, And stick-ball and punchball haven't changed. **1995** *DARE* File **Brooklyn NY** (as of 1950s), Punch ball was also scored like baseball except there was no pitcher. The person who was "up" tossed the (ever-present) spaldeen in the air and punched it. *Ibid* **NYC** (as of c1925), *Punch ball* . . in which the rubber ball was bounced on the pavement, then struck with the fist; a baseball-like game . . usually played at the intersection of two streets, with the corners forming the three bases and home plate; sometimes a pitcher was used, who tossed the ball underhand to the batter so that it reached him on one bounce. **2000** *Ibid* **Brooklyn NYC** (as of c1950), Punchball . . a baseball-style team game played with a Spaldeen on an asphalt baseball court, wherein the batter threw the ball up in the air, like a tennis serve, and had to punch it. *Ibid* **NYC,** We had . . punchball in Manhattan (Washington Heights) too.

punched out See **punch** v 2

puncher n

1 rarely *punch:* One who drives draft animals—usu in combs *bullpuncher, dog puncher, mule* ~. Cf **bullpuncher 1, dog punch**

1870 *Territorial Enterprise* (VA City NV) 21 Apr 3/1, Even a boss driver [of a mule team] is liable to suffer the indignity of being called a "mule puncher." *Ibid* 17 Sept [3]/1, All this time the punchers are flying actively from ox to ox, plying their sticks right and left. **1893** *Scribner's Mag.* 13.711, A young "bull-puncher" in a Wisconsin logging camp became in middle life Congressman, then United States Senator. **1901** *Everybody's Mag.* June 582, Hickock was the only officer who was able to maintain order among the mule punchers, bull whackers, and tough soldiers at Hays City. **1926** Willoughby *The Trail Eater* 61 (Tabbert *Dict. Alaskan Engl.*) **AK,** Slim will take out the champion team, and I've already sent up the Yukon for Jake Minto and Harry Dunn, both A-1 dog-punchers. **1954** McDavid Coll. **seKY,** Mule punch = mule driver. **1958** McCulloch *Woods Words* 141 **Pacific NW,** *Puncher*. . . An ox team driver, known also as bull puncher. **1966** *PADS* 46.24 **cnAR** (as of 1952), *Bull puncher*. . . A driver of oxen. **1967** *DARE* FW Addit **LA2,** Bullpuncher—a man that drives oxen.

2 =**cowpuncher 1. West** Cf **bullpuncher 1, mutton puncher, punch v 1, sheep puncher**

1890 *Stock Grower & Farmer* 15 Mar 5/3 (*DAE* at *necked calf*), If some passing puncher should hear the peculiar bawl that a necked calf makes, he is dead sure to investigate. **1893** in 1932 *AmSp* 7.259 **NE** [Cowboy terms], *Puncher*—a cattle-driver. **1903** (1965) Adams *Log Cowboy* 268 **West,** Just a couple of punchers, who had been drinking a little. **1913** in 1914 Stewart *Letters* 269 **WY,** So when a couple of "punchers," otherwise cowboys, took the room next to ours, we could hear every word they said. **1929** *AmSp* 5.57 **NE** [Cattle country talk], "Cowboy" is the commonly known term for one who "punches" or "herds" cattle (or "herds" horses, never "punches" them). More commonly, a cowboy is a "puncher," "cow puncher," "cow hand," "cow poke," "waddie," or "ranchman." **1929** Dobie *Vaquero* 1, As for "cowpuncher" and "puncher," I do not recall having heard the terms in the old days, and the use of them, however common in the Northwest, is still limited, among men of the older generation at least, on the ranges of South and West Texas. **1933** *AmSp* 8.1.30 **nwTX** [Ranch diction], *Puncher, cow-puncher*. A professional handler of cattle. **1936** McCarthy *Lang. Mosshorn* np **West** [Range terms], *Puncher*. . . A common term applied to a cowboy. **1949** *Pacific Discovery* July–

Aug 1, Two biologists, sent to the Pribilofs to study fur seals, unexpectedly found themselves 'punchers in a "Reindeer Roundup" on St. Paul. **1968** Adams *Western Words* 239, *Puncher* . . a man who works cattle.

3 In logging: one who operates a skidding or hauling engine—usu in combs, esp *donkey puncher.* [Transf from **1** above] **Pacific NW**

    1919 *DN* 5.81 **nwWA**, *Donkey puncher.* Engineer on donkey engine. **1940** Writers' Program *Oregon* 369, The donkey-puncher, or engine operator, "opens her up" and the log rises above stumps and brush as he yards it to the landing. **1941** *AmSp* 16.233 [Lumberjack jargon], *Donkey puncher.* One who operates a donkey engine. **1949** Peattie *Cascades* 159 **Pacific NW**, The tractor-puncher—heir of the bullpuncher and donkeypuncher—could yard timber down any old mountainside. **1950** *Western Folkl.* 9.118 **nwOR** [Logger speech], *Loci puncher.* Locomotive engineer. **1956** *AmSp* 31.151 **nwCA** [Logger lingo], *Puncher.* . . The operator of a logging engine known as a donkey. **1958** McCulloch *Woods Words* 50 **Pacific NW**, *Donkey Puncher*—The best known woods term for donkey engineer, one of the key men in an old time steam camp. **1961** Labbe–Goe *Railroads* 257 **Pacific NW**, *Donkey Puncher:* The engineer who operated the donkey. *Ibid* 259, *Puncher:* See donkey puncher. **1967** *DARE* FW Addit **cwWA**, Donkey puncher—someone who runs a steam donkey. **1982** *Smithsonian Letters* **Pacific NW** (as of early 20th cent), I was raised in the lower Columbia river logging country. . . The whistle punk . . signaled the donkey puncher (operator) when to go and when to stop by means of a wire which reached from the logging area to the whistle on the donkey.

4 also *air puncher, coal ~, puncher machine:* See quots.

    1918 Peele *Mining Engineers' Hdbk.* 1116, *"New Ingersoll" coal puncher* or pick is for undercutting in flat, or in pitching seams, the angle of which does not exceed 10° to 15°. While cutting in coal no rotation of the bit is necessary, as for drills. **1973** *PADS* 59.47 **sIL, WV, VA** [Bituminous coal mining vocab], *Puncher* . . an air-driven undercutting machine which makes a four feet wide *undercut* in the *face* of the coal by driving a spiked bar back and forth. . . air puncher [in **eKY**] . . puncher machine [in **wKY**].

5 See **punch stick 1.**

puncher grass See **puncture vine**

puncher machine See **puncher 4**

puncher vine See **puncture vine**

punching See **punch** v 1

punching stick n Also *punch (stick)*   **Sth, S Midl**   Cf **battling stick**

A stick used to stir clothes in a washpot.

    1966 *DARE* FW Addit **SC**, Punch stick—what you stir clothes in a washpot with. **1975** McDonough *Garden Sass* 92 **AR**, Annie Campbell called this [=a battling stick] the "punchin' stick." **1986** Pederson *LAGS Concordance*, 1 inf, **cMS**, Punching stick—to punch clothes in boiling water; 1 inf, **cnTX**, Women washed with a punching stick; 1 inf, **cnTX**, Punching stick—for washing clothes; 1 inf, **neTN**, Big old punching stick—stir clothes in hot water; 1 inf, **swTN**, Punch—used to agitate clothes when washing.

punching up, punch out See **punch** v 2

punchkey See **paczki**

punch stick n

1 also *punch, puncher:* A goad.

    1966 Dakin *Dial. Vocab. Ohio R. Valley* 2.132, *Whip.* . . Other names, all mentioned only once or twice . . *punch stick.* **1966–70** *DARE* (Qu. K27, . . *The sharp-pointed stick used to get oxen to move*) Inf **AR**21, Cow puncher; **IN**13, Puncher; **GA**3, **LA**12, Punch (stick).

2 See **punching stick.**

punch the icebox See **tap the icebox**

punchy See **paunch**

puncture vine n Also *puncture weed;* pronc-spp *puncher grass, ~ vine* [See quots]   **West, esp CA**   See Map

A prostrate vine *(Tribulus terrestris)* of the caltrop family noted for its spiny carpels. Also called **automobile weed, bullhead 4, goathead, Mexican sandburr, sandburr 2e, tackweed**

    1925 Jepson *Manual Plants CA* 603, *T[ribulus] terrestris* L. Puncture Weed. . . Native of Eur[ope], becoming naturalized near railway stations, thence spreading as a serious pest. **1931** Clute *Common Plants* 55, Our caltrop is fond of growing along desert roadsides and other waste places where the fruits may come in contact with the tires of automobiles, greatly to their detriment. It has now become puncture-vine and automobile-weed with every indication that these manufactured names, like the fruits, will stick. **1946** Reeves–Bain *Flora TX* 77, *Tribulus* [spp]. . . Puncture Plant. **1950** Stevens *ND Plants* 195, Puncture Vine. . . The spines of the fruits stick into auto tires but do not actually puncture them. **1965–70** *DARE* (Qu. S13) Inf **AZ**15, Puncture weed—because it punctures tires; (Qu. S14, . . *Prickly seeds, small and flat, with two prongs at one end, that cling to clothing*) Inf **CA**7, Puncture vine; **CA**140, Puncture vine—grows flat on the ground—will puncture a tire; (Qu. S15, . . *Weed seeds that cling to clothing*) Infs **CA**4, 9, 87, 208, Puncture vine; **CA**12, **UT**13, Puncture weed; **CA**99, Puncher grass—needlelike, will puncture tire—against the law to have; **CA**200, Puncher vine; (Qu. S21, . . *Weeds . . that are a trouble in gardens and fields*) Inf **CA**97, Puncture weed. **1979** Spellenberg *Audubon Guide N. Amer. Wildflowers W. Region* 805, This is one of the West's most unloved weeds. . . The spines easily pierce bicycle tires, hence the common name Puncture Vine. **1982** *NADS Letters* **neOK**, The plant whose seed pod is . . known as *bullhead* . . is *Tribulus terrestris,* Calthrop family. The common name given for it in the *Audubon Society Field Guide to North American Wildflowers* is punctureweed. This term . . seemed to be in frequent use here while I was growing up, during the 50's, it now seems to be used much less often.

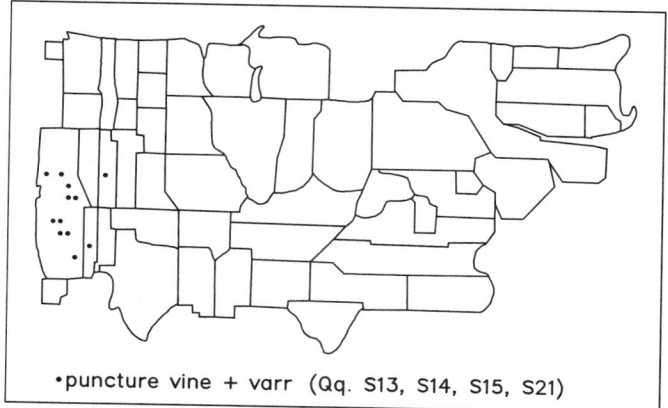

•puncture vine + varr (Qq. S13, S14, S15, S21)

puncture weed n

1 See **puncture vine.**

2 =**nohu 1.**

    1938 Baker *FL Wild Flowers* 118, *Tribulus cistoides.* Caltrop. Puncture-weed. . . Waste places. All the year. Fla. to Ga. and Tex. **1953** Greene–Blomquist *Flowers South* 63, Puncture-Weed, Bur-Nut *(Tribulus cistoides).* . . *Tribulus* means trouble, for the fruits of punctureweed attach themselves by means of barbed spines to clothing and even to the skin.

punee n Usu |'puneʔe, 'pune:|; for addit varr see quots [Haw *pūne'e*] **HI**

A couch or sofa.

    1938 Reinecke *Hawaiian Loanwords* 31, Pune'e ['puneʔe] ['pune:]. . couch. . F[requent]. **1951** *AmSp* 26.23 **HI**, Other common Hawaiian words are . . *punee* (a couch or day bed). **1954** *Ellery Queen's Mystery Mag.* 4.31 **HI**, Anne and I sitting on the *punee* with the two visiting women discussing the smartest places to dine. **1954–60** Hance et al. *Hawaiian Sugar* 6, Punee . . ['pune-e]. Sofa. **1967** Clark *All the Best HI* 55, Punee—a studio couch. Hotelkeepers renting rooms and apartments use the word freely, even to malihinis. **1967** *DARE* (Qu. E7, *The piece of upholstered furniture that you can stretch out on to rest*) Inf **HI**8, [pu'ne-e]; **HI**9, ['pune-e]; (Qu. E9, *A piece of upholstered furniture that seats three people*) Inf **HI**1, [pu'ne:]. **1972** Carr *Da Kine Talk* 88 **HI**, *Hawaiian Words Commonly Heard In Hawaii's English.* . . *Pūne'e.* Couch.

pung n Also *pung sleigh;* rarely *bung* [Abbr for earlier *tom pung,* of Algonquian origin, and ult akin to *toboggan*] **chiefly NEng, NY**   See Map on p. 378

A simple utility sleigh with a box body and usu a single set of low runners—also in combs *bob pung, double (runner)* ~, *traverse* ~ a similar sleigh supported by a pair of bobsleds.

1824 Cooper *Lionel Lincoln* 2.134, He was in the act of seating himself in the pung. **1832** Cooper *Pioneers* 3, [Footnote:] The latter [= Americans] draw a distinction between a sled, or sledge, and a sleigh; the sleigh being shod with metal. Sleighs are also subdivided into two-horse and one-horse sleighs. Of the latter, there are . . the "pung," or "tow [sic]-pung," which is driven with a pole [etc]. **1845** Judd *Margaret* 173 **NEng** (as of 18th cent), Below were seen two large sleds, each drawn by five or six boys, coming up the lot. . . These were sledges or pungs, coarsely framed of split saplings, and surmounted with a large crockery crate. **a1861** (1880) Eastman *Poems* 15 **VT**, His head hangs down, and his bones stick out,/ And he scarcely can turn the old pung about. **1895** Coffin *Daughters Revol.* 87 **NEng**, We pile into a double pung, ride in the moonlight. **1907** *DN* 3.248 **eME**, *Pung.* . . A sleigh with long, low body for carrying produce, groceries, merchandise, etc. **1917** Eaton *Green Trails* 195 **MA**, Tom knows from long experience exactly where . . the snow will suddenly pack into diagonal ridges across the road, . . so that his "pung" rides them like a boat on a choppy sea. **1926** *AmSp* 2.80 **ME**, A farmer may be seen coming into town in a "pung," which is a variety of sleigh having a box extension to hold produce. **1939** (1962) Thompson *Body & Britches* 307 **NY**, He was comin' home with his old horse and a pung—a Canadian *jumper.* Tell the Professor that's a single sleigh without seats, used to draw wood; the driver walks behind or stands up on the load. **1943** *LANE* Map 573–74, The following terms for 'double sled' are given on the map: . . *double runner pung* [1 inf, **ceMA**] . . *bob pung* [1 inf, **RI**] . . *traverse pung* [3 infs, **ME**]. . . The chief types of 'single sleds' and the names given to them are: . . B. Work sleds . . (a) with short runners: *pung . . pung sleigh* . . (b) with long runners: *pung.* [*Pung* was recorded from more than 160 infs **throughout NEng**.] **1946** Gould *Yankee Storekeeper* 143 **ME**, I got out our old pung, pulled it over to the hill, and invited everyone to ride. I sat on the sled between the shafts and steered the pung down the hill. **1953** *NY Times* (NY) 24 July 15/7 *(Hench Coll.)*, The New York State Education Department revealed today that . . the state still had fifty horse-drawn vehicles [in use as school buses]. . . Carriages, buckboards and wagons were employed, and pungs, sleds with box-like bodies, were popular. **1956** Sorden–Ebert *Logger's Words* 26 **Gt Lakes**, *Pung,* A rude oblong box on poles. The poles served both as the shafts and the sled runners. Used by Indians and pioneers in hauling. **1965–70** *DARE* (Qu. N40a, . . *Sleighs . . for hauling loads*) 45 Infs, **chiefly NEng,** Pung; (Qu. N40b, . . *Sleighs for carrying people*) 12 Infs, **NEng,** Pung; **NH**14, Bung; (Qu. N40c, *Other kinds of sleighs*) Inf **MA**58, Pung; (Qu. N41a, . . *Horse-drawn vehicles . . to carry people*) Infs **MA**23, **NH**16, Pung; (Qu. N41c, *Horse-drawn vehicles to carry light loads*) Inf **MA**6, Pung sleigh. [44 of 52 total Infs old] **1967–69** *DARE* Tape **MA**37, Well, in the wintertime there was the sleighs, and then there was one that'd take the place of a Democrat wagon, it's called a pung . . runners on it and quite a good-sized body with one seat and pants [sic] for another seat to put on it; **NY**27, I'll tell you again about your pung that you wanted to know about. That's just one sled with a box on it. . . . There were two seats you had, depending on how big it was. . . They used them drawing ore and drawing wood. That's why they were quite popular. **1973** Allen *LAUM* 1.219 **Upper MW** (as of c1950), *Sled.* . . pung [3 infs, **IA, NE**]. **1980** *Greenfield Recorder* (MA) 15 Mar sec A 4/1, A farmer had to have a sled, one or two-horse,

and also a "pung," which these days is replaced by a "pick up truck," to do errands, carry small loads and do such work. They had long one-piece runners not like the traverse sleds. They often were fitted with a removable seat that could be fastened down to the floor with cleats so it wouldn't tip up. By putting it as far back as possible, it made a two-seated sleigh so all the family could ride to church. **1988** Palmer *Lang. W. Cent. MA* 60, [pəŋ]—They weren't fancy at all. They were kind of square, and had wider runners [than the sleigh], lower down—as if you took the wheels off the wagon, had the seats in there, and put runners on it.

pungale See **pungle**

pungey n |ˈpʌŋgi, -ɪ| Also *pongee, pongy, pungie, pungy* **Delmarva**
A small keel schooner once used extensively for oyster dredging and local trading.

1852 MacKinnon *Atlantic & Transatlantic* 1.89 **MD**, The Pongees, or oyster boats . . are the most elegant and yacht-like merchant-craft in the world. They are from sixty tons downward. **1854** Simms *Southward Ho* 28 **VA**, Their most innocent name is 'pungo' [sic]—a sort of schooner, hailing mostly from Manhattan and Massachusetts. They prey upon the Virginia oyster banks, ostensibly under the forms of law. . . For the better oysters . . the 'pungos' pay three shillings. **1867** *De Bow's Rev.* 3.44 (as of 1860), The oyster business of Baltimore employed several hundred vessels. . . A large number of these were boats called "pungies," carrying from 200 to 500 bushels each. **1873** Watkins *Pine & Palm* 52 **eMD**, On this part of the bay . . we met hundreds of steam and sailing vessels . . , from the lithe dancing pongy and sturdy tug to the regular merchant ship. **1884** *Forest & Stream* 14 Feb 57, We have another style of boat in the Chesapeake, the American rival of the English deep boats. It is here styled a pungey. The pungey is regularly built, that is, timbered and planked and is narrow and deep, with no waist to obstruct the seas that may sweep over her. This is a remarkably fast and able sea boat, much used for oyster dredging in winter. **1899** (1912) Green *VA Folk-Speech* 338, *Pungy.* . . A small schooner with a low log-gunnel instead of a waist around the deck. **1939** *Sun* (Baltimore MD) 4 Apr 12/7 *(Hench Coll.)*, The pungy was a keel boat with no centerboard. . . Usually she had no rail but rather high water ways with ample scupper holes. The beam was rather wide, bows bluff above water but a clean run fore and aft under the water line. . . When I was a youngster the pungy was used in the bay for dredging oysters during the season and for carrying miscellaneous cargo at other times. She usually made a trip to the West Indies for pineapples during the spring. **1942** Footner *MD Main* 207, The largest Chesapeake Bay vessel is the "pungie," a broad-beamed schooner of shallow draft. **1963** Brewington *Chesapeake Bay Canoes* 39 (as of c1870), The pungys were too deep in draft to work successfully in the shallow rivers during the closed oyster season when all vessels turned to transporting farm produce and lumber. **1968** *DARE* (Qu. O9, . . *Kinds of sailboats*) Inf **DE**4, Pungey [ˈpʌŋgi]—a sailboat with no centerboard, two masts; **MD**36, Pungey [ˈpʌŋgiˑ]—boat—like schooner, but has keel instead of centerboard; **MD**45, Pungey [ˈpʌŋgi]—no centerboard, two masts, square stern; **NJ**16, Pungey [ˈpʌŋgi]. **1996** Horton *Island Out of Time* 43 **Chesapeake Bay MD**, More than a thousand sailcraft—four-masted schooners, sloops, pungies, and bugeyes—dragged heavy iron dredges ceaselessly across the "rocks," as the reeflike agglomerations of oysters were called, catching them by the hundreds of bushels a day.

pungie See **punkie** n[1] **1**

punging vbl n **NEng, NY** *old-fash* Cf **bum-riding**
The act or sport of catching a ride on a passing **pung**.

1892 Howells *Quality of Mercy* 101 **NY**, A gait which . . exposed him to the ridicule of such small boys as observed his haste, in their intervals of punging. One, who dropped from the runner of a sleigh . . , jeered him for the awkwardness with which he floundered out of its way in the deep snow. **1913** *Outing* 61.538 **NEng**, All other winter sports might fail us or grow stale, but pungin', real pungin', on the heel of the runner of a real pung, remained till the February thaw, at least, and often long into March. **1957** *Sat. Eve. Post Letters* **NH**, "Punging" was a sport in winter. Running after "pungs" to catch a ride; if the driver was good natured, O.K., if not, out we went. **1962** Morison *One Boy's Boston* 32 **eMA** (as of c1900), Pungs as well as sleighs were the vehicles of the small-boy sport of punging. . . You ran after the sleigh, placed your feet on a runner and held on.

pungkin See **pumpkin** n[1]

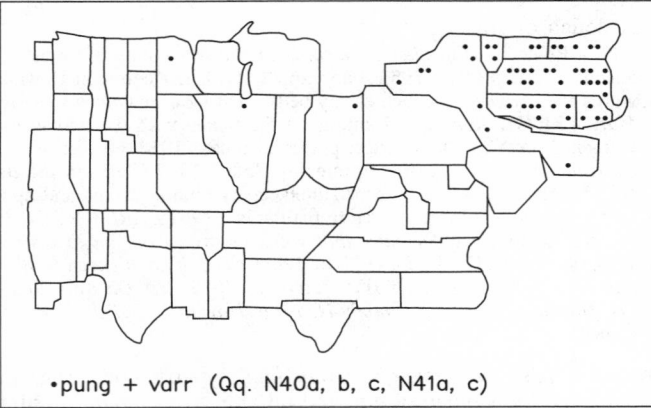

•pung + varr (Qq. N40a, b, c, N41a, c)

pungle v Also *pongal, pungale* Also with *down, up* [Span *póngale* put it down] **chiefly West**

To shell out; to plunk down (money); to pay up; also fig.

1851 *Alta Californian* 19 July *(DA)*, A singular genius . . was 'pongal-ing down' huge piles of gold at a monte table. **1857** *San Francisco Call* (CA) 6 Jan. 2/2 *(OED2)*, 'Pungale down, gentlemen; come, pungale', as the vingt-et-un lady used to say. **1867** *Terr. Enterprise* (Virginia, Nev.) 23 Feb. 3/3 *(DA)*, All night the clouds pungled their fleecy treasure. **1877** Wright *Big Bonanza* 339, They have kicked the bully Miner; they have ducked him in the ditch, but they can't make him pungle. **1884** Twain *Huck. Finn* 41, "I hain't got no money, I tell you. You ask Judge Thatcher; he'll tell you the same." "All right. I'll ask him; and I'll make him pungle, too, or I'll know the reason why." **1910** E.S. Field *Sapphire Bracelet* xii.141 *(OED2)*, I'll have him arrested, and then make him pungle up something handsome before I'll agree not to appear against him. **1967–68** *DARE* (Qu. U8b, . . *"I paid ten dollars for it."*) Infs **CA36, OR4,** Pungled up; (Qu. U18, *If you force somebody to pay money that he owes you, but that he did not want to pay . . "I finally made him _____."*) Infs **CA15, 36, 87, OR4,** Pungle up. **1968** *DARE* FW Addit **CA62,** *Pungle*—"Oh, boy, look at that stuff pungle"—of soil crumbling to reveal rich ore. **1975** Gores *Hammett* 130 **San Francisco CA,** Hammett had coffee and pungled up the required fifty cents. **1989** *DARE* File **OR,** I'll contact Belknap Press about a review copy of Volume II, but of course if they can't provide one, I'll pungle up the funds to acquire it.

pung sleigh See **pung**

pungy See **pungey**

punied up adj

=**puny** adj **1.**

1989 *Country* June/July 18 **ceMO,** Our neighbors have brought smiles to our faces time after time with their country expressions. If you're feeling out of sorts or not up to par, you're "feeling puny" or "all punied up".

punish v **chiefly S Midl**

To suffer.

1892 (1893) Botume *First Days* 125 **seSC** (as of c1864), "Her gone to bed an' have a fine gal; but I tell you, ma'am, her bad off. Her punish too much," meaning she suffered too much. **1892** *DN* 1.231 **KY,** *Punish:* to suffer. "I punished so in my new shoes." **1896** *DN* 1.422 **PA,** *Punish*. . . Used in the sense of suffering for lack of something; e.g. "I couldn't get any water, and my! how I did punish." **1902** *DN* 2.242 **sIL,** *Punish*. . . To suffer from pain, heat, or cold. **1924** (1946) Greer-Petrie *Angeline Gits an Eyeful* 11 **csKY,** Whut if the pore old thing's done tuck the colic, and is a-punishin' (suffering)? **1931** Goodrich *Mt. Homespun* 42 **sAppalachians,** I'm right sharply decayed since you saw me . . I can't do much work and that frets me, but I ain't a punishing any; a body ought to be thankful for that. **1940** (1978) Still *River of Earth* 128 **KY,** "Why, child," she said, "he's bound to walk in time, bounden to rise up and find his own way. Gee-o, I'm punishing to try walking agin myself." **1944** Howard *Walkin' Preacher* 250 **Ozarks,** Hit come on her yesterday. She's been punishin' turrible since. **1949** Turner *Africanisms* 275 **seSC** [Gullah], Me own sin what I had in this world, that weigh me down before I commence to see goodness. I had to punish through the valley before I could see light. **1982** Ginns *Snowbird Gravy* 98 **nwNC,** Do wrong before I thought, unthoughted, then punish for it.

punk n[1] See **whistle punk**

punk n[2]

1 Decayed or rotten wood, esp when used as tinder; hence adj *punk* decayed, rotten. Cf **punky** adj

1705 Beverley *Hist. VA* 3.49, Or else they take Punck, (which is a Sort of a Soft Touchwood, cut out of the knots of Oak or Hiccory Trees . .). **1827** *Western Mth. Rev.* 1.443 **nwIN,** In digging into this mound, there were found two pieces of rotten wood, vulgarly called punk. **1848** (1855) Ruxton *Life Far West* 53 **Rocky Mts,** Fire-making is a simple process with the mountaineers. Their bullet-pouches always contain a flint, and steel, and sundry pieces of "punk" or tinder. [Footnote to *punk:*] A pithy substance found in dead pine-trees. **1899** (1912) Green *VA Folk-Speech* 339, *Punk*. . . Wood decayed through the influence of a fungus or otherwise, and used like tinder. **1950** *WELS Suppl.* **nWI,** *Punk*—Decayed dry wood. A dry log with a large rotted center emits a sound very close to "punk" when it is struck. **1966–69** *DARE* (Qu. KK7, *When wood . . is starting to decay inside . . "It's _____ inside."*) Infs **GA15, IL15, MA48, OR3,** Punk; **PA74,** Turning to punk.

1966 *DARE* Tape **NH6,** You can use poor wood, all kinds, limbs and heavy and punk—wood that you wouldn't use so much in the house for wood. **1976** Ryland *Richmond Co. VA* 375, *Punk*—wood decayed by fungi, will not burn.

2 also *punk mushroom*: A bracket fungus sometimes used as tinder. **formerly chiefly N and C Atl; now esp PA** See Map

1687 in 1744 Royal Soc. London *Philos. Trans.* 41.1.149 **VA,** As the *East-Indians* use *Moxa*, so these burn with *Punk*, which is the inward Part of the Excrescence or Exuberance of an *Oak*. **1762** Gronovius *Flora Virginica* 175, *Agaricus* coriaceus juglandicus. . . *Punck hic vulgo dictus*. [=The leathery walnut tree agaric. . . here commonly called *punck*.] **1830** Rafinesque *Med. Flora* 2.186, Punk is the Indian name for all perennial fungi growing on trees and of a spongy nature: useful to make spunk or touch wood to light easily fire with [sic]. Those growing on pines and hickories are commonly deemed best. **1896** Robinson *In New Engl. Fields* 248, Punk, the tinder of the Indians and our forefathers, now gone out of use except for some conservative Canuck to light his pipe or for boys to touch off their small ordnance. **1905** *DN* 3.16 **cCT,** *Punk*. . . A kind of fungus used for tinder. **1941** *LANE* Map 280 *(Toadstool)* 1 inf, **csCT,** Punk, touchwood, fungi eaten by the Italians. **1941** Hench *Coll.* **cVA,** *Punk*—A dry mushroom that grows on a tree. Though hard to light, it won't go out when finally lighted. . . "Let's get a piece of punk." **1965–70** *DARE* (Qu. S19, *Mushrooms that grow out like brackets from the sides of trees*) 9 Infs, 8 **PA, MD, VA,** Punk; **OK1,** Punk—if you light it, it burns; you could put it in your pocket lit when traveling and blow on it to start a fire; **PA204,** Punk—very seldom use this term; **WA20,** Punk; conk; **PA180,** Punk mushrooms; **NC48, PA191,** Punks.

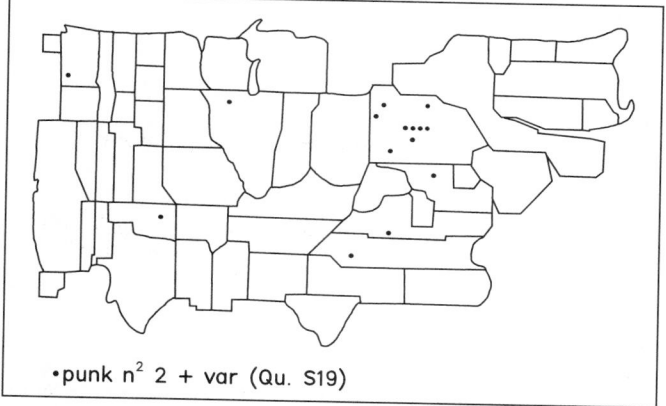

•punk n[2] 2 + var (Qu. S19)

3 =**bally** n[1].

1976 Warner *Beautiful Swimmers* 143 **Chesapeake Bay,** In addition to sponges, the egg-heavy females [=blue crabs] are variously known as "lemon bellies," "ballies," "busted sooks" and "punks." **1984** *DARE* File **Chesapeake Bay** [Watermen's vocab], Sponge crab[s] brood crab[s] cushion crab . . punk.

punk n[3], **punkey** See **punkie** n[1] **1**

punkie n[1]

1 also *ponki, pungie, punk(ey), punkie fly, ~ gnat, punky*: A biting dipterous insect of the family Ceratopogonidae, usu of the genera *Culicoides* or *Leptoconops*. [See quot 1910] **chiefly Upstate NY, PA** See Map on p. 380 Also called **all-jaw, barn fly 2, black gnat, burning fly 2, cow ~ 2, dominicker 6, midge 2, midget 1, minge, moose fly 2, no-see-um 1, sand flea 2, ~ fly 1, ~ gnat** Cf **black mosquito, buck fly 2**

1769 (1906) Smith *Tour Great Rivers* 42 **nwNY,** We begin to be teazed with Muscetoes and little Gnats called here Punkies. **1840** *Knickerbocker* Sept 270 **MI,** Of all the tortures of this nature, that inflicted by the *gnat*, (sand-flies, punkies, brulos, for they bear all these appellations,) is the least endurable. **1858** in 1896 Mitchell *Coll. Poems* 291, Sweet, ever, to think of the forests,/. . . / To think of the camp-fires we builded / To baffle those terrible pungies. **1895** *Sun* (NY NY) 30 July 9/1, Punkey, punky, the sand fly, a minute insect well known to sportsmen and camping parties. **1910** Hodge *Hdbk. Amer. Indians* 2.328, *Punkie*. . . A minute gnat called also sand-fly or midge . . the bite of which produces an intolerable itching and smarting sensation as if a spark of fire had dropped upon the naked skin. These winged atoms are, says Loskiel, "called by the [Lenape] Indians *ponk,* or 'living ashes,' from their being so small that they are hardly visible, and their bite as painful as the burning of red-hot ashes." . . *Punky,* or *punkie,* is from the Dutch of New York and New Jersey *pûnki,* pl. *pûnkin,* from (by vocalic addition) Lenape *pûnk* or *ponk.* **1930** Shoemaker *1300 Words* 48 **cPA Mts** (as of c1900), *Ponkis*—small almost invisible insects, hard biters; said to be sparks from the pyre of an Indian murderer, burned alive, near Old Town, Pa. **1950** *WELS Suppl.* **cWI,** The little biting insect here is called by some no-see-ems and by some punks and I assure you they really hurt. **1965–70** *DARE* (Qu. R11, *A very tiny fly that you can hardly see, but that stings*) 12 Infs, 9 **NY,** Punkie, **NY22,** No-see-ums, midgets, midges, punkies—all the same; they *do* sting; **NY155,** Punkie fly; **WV2,** Punkie gnat—Williams River is full of them—drive you off the river about 4 p.m.; (Qu. R10, *Very small flies that don't sting, often seen hovering in large groups or bunches outdoors in summer*) Inf **NY75,** Punkies—but they bite; (Qu. R15a) Infs **NY1, PA182, 218,** Punkies; (Qu. R22) Infs **NY155, 183,** Punkies. [17 of 19 total Infs male] **1967** *DARE* File **NY,** Punkies—black flies, very small, bad biters.

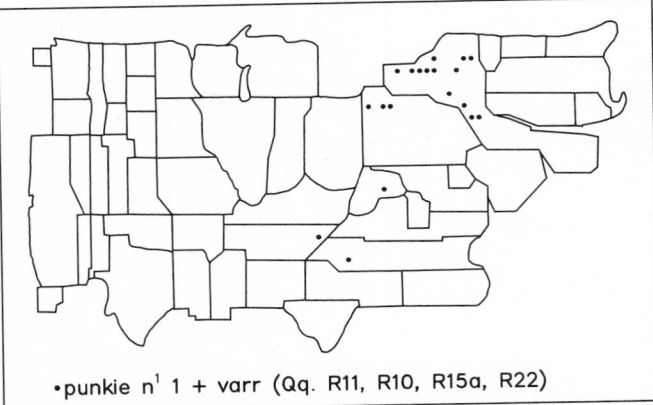

•punkie n¹ 1 + varr (Qq. R11, R10, R15a, R22)

2 A **midge 1** (here: family Chironomidae).
    1968–69 *DARE* (Qu. R10, *Very small flies that don't sting, often seen hovering in large groups or bunches outdoors in summer*) Inf **NY191,** Punkies; **PA68,** Gnats—also called punkies; **PA73,** Punkies—same as gnats.

punkie n² Also *punky*
=**pumpkinseed 1.**
    1957 Trautman *Fishes* 520 **OH,** As a small boy, between 1906–10, I well remember the many "Punkies" which my father and I caught "pole fishing." **1983** Becker *Fishes WI* 828, Pumpkinseed. . . Other common names . . punky [etc].

punkie fly (or gnat) See **punkie** n¹ **1**

punkin(g) See **pumpkin** n¹

punkknot See **pumpknot**

punk mushroom See **punk** n² **2**

punkun See **pumpkin** n¹

punky adj [**punk** n² **1**]   **chiefly Nth, N Midl**   See Map   Cf **doty 1**
Of wood: decayed; hence fig: soft, unsound, easily broken.
    1803 *Balance* (Hudson NY) 8 Mar 75/3, Even in New England, there is some timber so *punky* that the French *saw* might easily pass through it, particularly the little state of Rhode Island. **1872** Huntington *Road-Master's Asst.* 117, A bridge may . . have a small knot partially decayed, or "punky," as it is termed. **1886** *Harper's New Mth. Mag.* 74.105 **ME,** George's mother's folks did have a kind of a punky spot somewhere in their heads. **1926** Rickaby *Ballads Shanty-Boy* 63 **WI,** Were you punky, were you hollow,/ You had been a lucky fellow. **1950** *WELS* (*That tree is beginning to decay: It's all _____ inside*) 5 Infs, **WI,** Punky. **1955** *Sun* (Baltimore MD) 9 Aug 16/8 (*Hench Coll.*), All of the punky and weak wood was removed and a glass and resin putty applied to smooth out the sleek lines. **1965–70** *DARE* (Qu. KK7, *When wood . . is starting to decay inside . . "It's _____ inside."*) 33 Infs,

chiefly Nth, N Midl, Punky; (Qu. KK24, *Something that breaks easily: "She broke her arm again: Her bones must be _____."*) Inf **CT4,** Punky. **1990** *Yankee* Mar 84 **nwVT,** The fuelwood he collected seemed too punky, though, to bring his outsized kettle to a rolling boil.

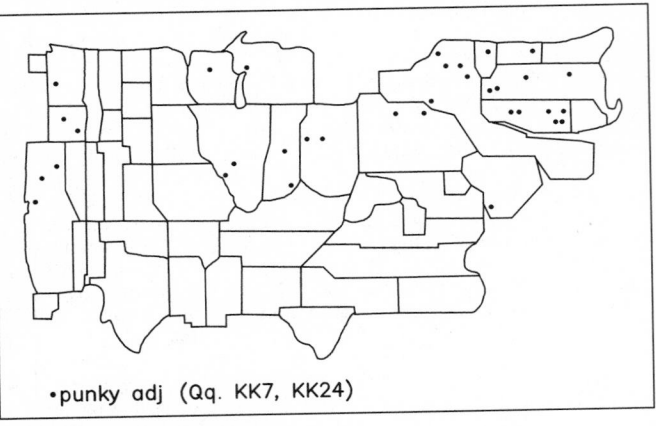

•punky adj (Qq. KK7, KK24)

punky n¹ See **punkie** n¹ **1**

punky n² See **punkie** n²

punt n [*OED2* c1000 →]   **scattered, but esp Nth, N Midl, CA** See Map   See also *duck punt* (at **duckboat**)
Any of var small non-sailing boats, esp one that is flat-bottomed and square-ended, or propelled by poling.
    1746 *London Mag. & Mth. Chronologer* 15.573, We ourselves step'd into a small *Punt,* and put off to the *Shallop.* **1835** Ingraham *South-West* 1.142 **New Orleans LA,** A hundred skiffs, wherries, punts . . were darting about in all directions. **1859** (1968) Bartlett *Americanisms* 349, *Punt.* In Maryland and Virginia, a small boat made with the body of a large tree. In England, a *punt* is a flat-bottomed boat. **1883** *Century Illustr. Mag.* 26.731 **RI,** One may see anchored in the little cove behind Castle Hill . . a trim sloop or two, and various dories and punts. **1899** (1912) Green *VA Folk-Speech* 339, *Punt.* . . A flat-bottomed, square ended, mastless boat of varying size and use, made of a large tree. **1948** Camp *Hunter's Encycl.* 921, The punt shown in Plate IX also is common to this area [=the West and Midwest]. While higher and wider of beam than the boats normally used on the rivers and sloughs, they can be poled with ease except through thickly grassed areas. **1950** Moore *Candlemas Bay* 17 **ME,** He came up blowing, headed for Russ's punt, tied up alongside his dragger. **1965–70** *DARE* (Qu. O1, . . *A small rowboat, not big enough to hold more than two people*) 15 Infs, **scattered Nth, N Midl, CA,** Punt; **AK1,** Punt—square-ended, one-man boat, mostly to go ashore from anchored boat; **ME10, 22,** Punt—(generally) flat-bottomed; **MN36,** Punt—reading term; **VT12,** Punt [FW sugg]—a bobbed-off rowboat; (Qu. O2, *Nicknames . . for an old, clumsy boat*) Infs **MA5, MD36, NY54, WA17,** (Old) punt; (Qu. O10, . . *Kinds of boats*) Inf **CA36,** Punt—a little boat, holds one man who poles himself a short distance. **1966** *DARE* Tape **ME24,** [FW:] What do you call that little boat you use to get out to your lobster boat in? [Inf:] We call it skiff. Some people call it tender. Some call it a punt; **ME25,** We use what they call a skiff or punt. . . Looks more like a flatiron than any-

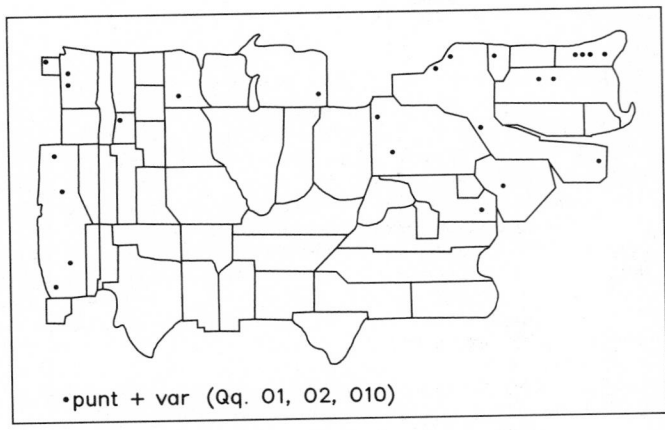

•punt + var (Qq. O1, O2, O10)

thing. **1974** McClane *McClane's New Std. Fishing Encycl.* 503, *John-boat*—This common-type rowboat is known by several names dependent upon the locale. . . New Englanders call the design a punt or sometimes simply skiff, which, technically, is a name applied to any small rowboat.

puntop See **pontop**

puny adj

1 Sickly, weak, "under the weather"—occas in phr *on the puny list.* **widespread, but esp Sth, S Midl** See Map

1838 in 1956 Eliason *Tarheel Talk* 137 **NC,** I found your dear Aunt Catherine in a very puny state, not entirely confined, but obliged to rest herself on a bed more or less every day. **1841** *Spirit of Times* 27 Mar 42 **AR,** Bill Spence is got to be well on to no account—he is mighty puny—ailing in his breast—sorter consumpty. **1884** *Anglia* 7.263 **Sth, S Midl** [Black], *To look mighty spin'lin' en' puny* = to look delicate. **1887** (1967) Harris *Free Joe* 54 **GA,** That gal looks mighty puny. She's from the North, and I reckon she's homesick. **1903** *DN* 2.326 **seMO,** *Puny.* . . Ill; sick. **1905** *DN* 3.91 **nwAR,** *Puny.* . . In poor health. **1906** *DN* 3.122 **sIN,** *Puny.* . . Ill, sick. "He's feelin' puny agin." **1909** *DN* 3.360 **eAL, wGA,** *Puny.* . . In poor health. Universal. **1915** *DN* 4.188 **swVA,** *Puny.* . . Not in good health. **1931** *AmSp* 7.91 **eKY,** *Puny,* sickly. **1946** *AmSp* 21.98 **sIL,** *Puny,* ailing. **1952** Brown *NC Folkl.* 1.580, *Puny list, on the.* . . Sick, indisposed. "He's on the puny list today and can't work." **1965–70** *DARE* (Qu. BB38, *When a person doesn't look healthy, or looks as if he hadn't been well for some time . .* "He looks _____.") 264 Infs, **widespread, but esp Sth, S Midl,** Puny; **DC**8, **FL**51, **SC**34, Kinda puny; **AZ**2, **IN**32, Right puny; **NY**92, Mighty puny; (Qu. X52, *. . A person . . who had been sick was looking _____*) 161 Infs, **widespread, but esp Sth, S Midl,** Puny; (Qu. BB39, *On a day when you don't feel just right, though not actually sick . .* "I'll be all right tomorrow—I'm just feeling _____ today.") 66 Infs, **chiefly Sth, S Midl,** Puny; (Qu. KK30, *Feeling slowed up or without energy:* "I certainly feel _____.") 19 Infs, **chiefly Sth, S Midl,** Puny; (Qu. BB41, *Not seriously ill, but sick enough to be in bed:* "He's been _____ for a week.") 18 Infs, **chiefly Sth, S Midl,** Puny; **SC**19, **VA**105, Feeling puny; **FL**26, **OK**11, Kind of puny; **KY**41, On the puny list; (Qu. BB5, *A general feeling of discomfort or illness that isn't any one place in particular*) Infs **TN**3, **TX**5, 32, Feeling puny; **AL**26, **KY**60, Puny; **IN**15, **TX**33, Puny feeling; **KY**19, Puny-looking; (Qu. BB16b, *If something a person ate didn't agree with him, he might just feel a bit _____*) Infs **AL**26, **IL**126, **TN**59, Puny; (Qu. BB42, *If a person is very sick . . he's _____*) Inf **GA**72, Pretty doggone puny. **1966** *Pike Co. Courier* (Murfreesboro AR) 23 Sept np, Mrs. E.T. Williamson is on the puny list. We hope she is better soon. **1991** *DARE* File **NC,** In addition to feeling "puny, dauncy" . . you can add "rode hard and hung up wet".

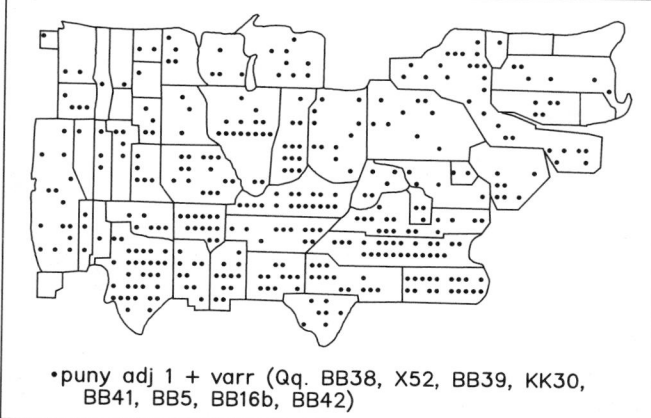

•puny adj 1 + varr (Qq. BB38, X52, BB39, KK30, BB41, BB5, BB16b, BB42)

2 Of weather: see quot.

1975 *Appalachian Jrl.* 2.159 **wNC,** *Puny* weather means it is unpleasant, perhaps overcast and drizzling rain.

puny v

1 To be ill; also with *around:* to go about in a listless, languid fashion. **chiefly S Midl**

1893 (1958) Wister *Out West* 159, Texas Vocabulary. . . To puny—to be ill. **1923** *DN* 5.218 **swMO,** *To puny around* = to go about in a dull, lifeless, languid way. **1949** Arnow *Hunter's Horn* 378 **KY,** What's a

troublen you? You've been a punyen around an a pinen away, sour and sullen as a ole woman. **1974** Fink *Mountain Speech* 20 **wNC, eTN,** *Punying, punying around* . . not well, languid, etc. "I've been punying around quite a spell." **1976** Garber *Mountain-ese* 72 **sAppalachians,** *Punyin'-around* . . not well—Jake ain't well, he's still jist punyin' around the house. **1982** Slone *How We Talked* 103 **eKY** (as of c1950), *Puning* [sic] *around*—not real sick, yet not quite well. **1984** Wilder *You All Spoken Here* 201 **Sth,** *Puny aroun':* To be ailing; indisposed; off one's feed.

2 with *away:* To waste away.

1941 Street *In Father's House* 73 **MS,** Two other Martin children are buried there. Odell and Baby Bee. . . Baby Bee's real name was Ben, Jr. and he just sort of dried up and punied away when he was a baby.

puny around See **puny** v **1**

puny away See **puny** v **2**

puny list, on the See **puny** adj **1**

puore(ly) See **pure**

pup n [Prob from the size] **AK**

1 A small branch creek or ravine; also used in place names.

1898 U.S. Geol. Surv. *Annual Rept. for 1896–97* 3.231 **AK,** Müller kept his pups a short distance up the ravine, a little way from his camp. Miners seeking for some term to designate this ravine used to call it "the place where Müller keeps his pups;" but this long circumlocution became naturally shortened in course of time, so that the phrase was simply "Müller's pups;" and eventually the plural was omitted, and the ravine became "Müller's pup." The term seemed to fill a gap in the nomenclature of the miners. . . being restricted to the short, usually dry ravines of very steep gradient which furrow the hills and run into larger and well-marked valleys. [**1898** Haskell *2 Yrs.* 253, Once I heard the word "pup" mentioned. In Yukon parlance that means "gulch." Every creek has its pups, and if any of them become of considerable importance they may have pups also.] [**1902** *Pop. Sci. Mth.* 61.232, The principal streams [in the Klondike region] are known as creeks; the short steep tributaries which flow into these as 'gulches'; and the streamlets which feed these as 'pups.'] **1939** *AK Sportsman* April 26 (Tabbert *Dict. Alaskan Engl.*), [We] followed him a mile or so down the river through the brushy flats until we came to a small ravine, or "pup" as it was called by the sourdoughs. **1968** *DARE* (Qu. C1, *. . A small stream of water not big enough to be a river*) Inf **AK**2, Pup [pʌp]—very small side stream running into a not necessarily main stream. **1976** Hobbs–Specht *Tisha* 118 **AK,** They'd built themselves a sturdy little cabin on Forty-five Pup. A pup was just a little creek that branched off a bigger one, and Forty-Five was so named because it branched off of Chicken Creek at a forty-five degree angle.

2 See **pup-hook.**

3 See **puppy** n **3.**

pu-pap See **pap-pap**

pupfish n

Any of several **killifishes 1** native to the Southwest.

1957 Blair et al. *Vertebrates U.S.* 156 **seCA,** *Cyprinodon salinis.* . . Death Valley pupfish. **1965** Teale *Wandering Through Winter* 48 **Death Valley CA,** Why pupfish? When we watched one of these plump, dark, inch-long desert minnows swimming about . . Nellie noticed the way its pectoral fins moved alternately like the forepaws of a swimming dog. That seemed as good an explanation as any for the name. **1983** Becker *Fishes WI* 753, The family [=Cyprinodontidae] includes the Devils Hole pupfish, Owens River pupfish, Comanche Springs pupfish, and Pahrump killifish of the southwest, all of which are endangered.

pup-hook n Also *pup* Cf **dog** n¹ **B2**

In logging: see quots.

1956 Sorden–Ebert *Logger's Words* 26 **Gt Lakes,** *Pup-hook,* A small hook at the end of a loading line or chain. **1958** McCulloch *Woods Words* 141 **Pacific NW,** *Pup*—A loading line hook.

pupmobile n **AK**

A small railroad flatcar pulled by dogs.

1935 *AK Sportsman* Jan 8, The journey presented no particular difficulty for the reason that "pupmobile" transportation was available. . . [The abandoned narrow-gauge railroad bed] hung stubbornly together . . to permit a well-trained dog team to haul an iron wheeled car over it with a fair degree of safety. **1939** FWP *Guide AK* 380, Residents furnish their own means of transportation, whether flange-wheeled automobiles, handcars, or "pupmobiles" (a small push car to which are harnessed a dozen dogs). **1943** *AK Sportsman* July 14 (Tabbert *Dict. Alaskan Engl.*), The "Pupmobile Railroad," built in 1900, runs from Nome to Shelton. . . Prospectors also use the line, with little flanged-wheel cars, six or eight feet long, pulled by four to nine dogs. **1970** *AK Sportsman* May 17, [Caption:] A "pupmobile" on the Seward Peninsula Railroad. . . [Vehicles] like this one were pulled by dog teams and became known as "pupmobiles."

puppa(h) See **papa**

puppet See **poppet 2**

puppet root n
An **Indian poke 1** (here: *Veratrum viride*).
1830 Rafinesque *Med. Flora* 2.273, Veratrum viride. . . *Wolf bane, Dackretter, Puppet root.* . . Used once to poison arrows. Lately to tan leather very quick. It contains *Veratrine*, a narcotic alkali. **1898** U.S. Dept. Ag. Div. Botany *Bulletin* 20.16, American False Hellebore. *Veratrum viride. Other names.* . . Indian poke; meadow poke . . puppet root . . bugbane.

puppy n
1 also *puppy-dog*: =**mud puppy b.**
1899 Bergen *Animal Lore* 62 **MD**, Ground-dog or ground-puppy or puppy, salamander, *Necturus maculatus. Chestertown, Md.* **1935** Hyatt *Folkl. Adams Co. IL* 468, I was out sweeping the sidewalk when I saw something on the walk. I went over to see what it was and it happen to be a little puppy dog *(salamander).* I started to killing it and a colored man that was walking up the street holler over at me and said, 'Don't kill it. . . I could dry it up and make a powder out of it and put it in a little paper bag and carry it, and if anyone was across the street I could drop it on the sidewalk, and if the wind was in the right way to carry it across the street, it would go up their nostril and poison them and they would be full of puppy dogs.' **c1938** in 1970 Hyatt *Hoodoo* 1.189 **seNC**, He told her dat some [Hyatt: ground] *puppies* would be [Hyatt: in her], an' told her if de puppies came out an' didn't look back an' bark at her, dat he could cure 'er; but if dey came out an' looked back an' bark at her, he wouldn't cure 'er. **1967** *DARE* FW Addit **swAR**, Puppy-dog = mud puppy, salamander. Hardly any other term than "puppy-dog" is ever used here for the lizard-like amphibian.
2 See quot. Cf **dog** n[1] **B3**
1947 McDavid *Coll.* **ceSC**, Puppies—guards on 'firedogs' to keep log from rolling.
3 also *pup*: A foot. Cf **dog** n[1] **B6**
1934 (1940) Weseen *Dict. Amer. Slang* 150, Puppies—The feet. **1935** *AmSp* 10.9, The American imagination is fertile in creating humorous names, usually metaphorical, for human feet and the shoes that protect them. . . Animal nomenclature gives us *hoofs* and *pads*, as well as *dogs* and *puppies*. **1942** Berrey–Van den Bark *Amer. Slang* 121.29, Feet. . . pups. **1995** Brophy *Coll.* 58 **swMO** (as of c1960), Pups, puppies. [F]eet, "dogs."

puppy drum n esp Mid Atl Cf **rat red**
A small or young **red drum**; see quots.
1893 *Outing* 22.94 **eNC**, Small drum from eight to twelve inches in length are caught in set nets in the shoal waters of Pamlico Sound about Hatteras. . . They are called "puppy-drum" by the natives. **1944** *Richmond Times–Dispatch* (VA) 20 Oct 18 (Hench Coll.), There is nothing the matter with the gray and salmon trout, the rockfish and the puppy drum, all of which feed at times close to shore lines and jetties. **1951** Taylor *Surv. Marine Fisheries NC* 266, *Sciaenops ocellatus.* . . Anglers fish for both adult and young (puppy drum), which are abundant on the beaches. **1966** *DARE* Tape **NC27**, Me and this feller Gilbert from Texas caught two hundred and seventy small ones, from two to five pounds. . . [FW:] What kind were they? [Inf:] Puppy drum. **1974** McClane *McClane's New Std. Fishing Encycl.* 787, The larger drum are usually caught . . along the Carolina coast to New Jersey. Young "redfish" or "puppy drum", generally weighing less than 10 pounds, are also taken in southern Florida and along the Gulf Coast.

puppyfoot n
The ace of clubs in a deck of playing cards; similarly n *puppy paws* the suit of clubs.
1907 *Hoyle's Games* 410 (OED2), Puppy foot, the ace of clubs. **1932** *Daily Progress* (Charlottesville VA) 26 Feb 6/6 (Hench Coll.), The ace

of clubs is often called the puppyfoot. **1942** Berrey–Van den Bark *Amer. Slang* 744.3, Puppy-foot, *the ace of clubs.* [**1965** *AmSp* 40.251 [Canine terms], Puppy-dog feet. Clubs (Warrack–Grant [=Alexander Warrack and William Grant, *A Scots Dialect Dictionary*]). [*DARE* Ed: Entry not found.]] **1968** *DARE* FW Addit **seGA**, Puppy paws—children's term for the club suit in cards. "Who's got the jack of puppy paws?"

puppytail n
A **sweet pepperbush** (here: *Clethra alnifolia*).
1974 Morton *Folk Remedies* 49 **SC**, Puppytail. . . *Clethra alnifolia* var. *tomentosa.* . . Flowers . . borne in erect, cylindrical, terminal spikes 4 to 7 in. long. Seed capsule downy, round, . . containing many seeds. . . Common in coastal plain of South Carolina.

puppy toes n Cf **cat's-paw 4**
A **burning bush 1** (here: *Euonymus americanus*).
1972 GA Dept. Ag. *Farmers Market Bulletin* 11 Oct 8, Hearts-a-bustin is only one of many common names for Euonymus americanus. Others include "Puppy Toes," . . "Spindle Bush" [etc].

pupu n Also sp *puu-puu* [Haw *pūpū*] **chiefly HI**
An hors d'oeuvre; hence comb *pupu pup* a cocktail frankfurter.
1967 Reinecke–Tsuzaki *Hawaiian Loanwords* 111, Pupu. . . A relish, esp. when served with alcoholic beverages. **1968** *Liberty News* (NY) 13 June 2, Lantern Restaurant—Chinese-American Menus—Specializing in *puu-puu* platters. **1969** *DARE* File **HI**, Pupu ['pupu]: hors d'oeuvres. *Pupu pups*—tiny hot dogs known elsewhere as cocktail franks. **1974** Ibid **HI**, Pupu. . . Originally: sea or land shells; now almost exclusively for hors d'oeuvres and cocktail snacks. **1984** Sunset *HI Guide* 85, Pupu—shell, hors d'oeuvre. **2001** *DARE* File **HI**, I found *pupus* on menus on Kauai last week. . . There seemed to be no special meaning setting it apart as something different from *appetizer*.

pupule adj, n |ˈpuˈpule| [Haw] **HI**
Crazy, insane; an insane person.
1938 Reinecke *Hawaiian Loanwords* 31, Pupule ['puˈpuːle]. . . Crazy; insane. . . A crazy person. **1951** *AmSp* 26.21 **HI**, Some localisms are handy euphemisms: . . *pupule* (crazy). **1967** Clark *All the Best HI* 55, Pupule—crazy, "nuts." **1967** *DARE* (Qu. HH6, *Someone who is out of his mind*) Inf **HI13**, Pupule [pu'pule]. **1972** Carr *Da Kine Talk* 117 **HI**, *Pupule head* (Hawaiian + English). 'Addled head', a crazy person. *Pupule* is the Hawaiian term for insane. **1997** *NY Times* (NY) 2 Mar sec F 14/5 **HI**, For many who grow up in Hawaii, standard English may be a second or even a third language. Their common tongue is pidgin. . . [P]eople from bankers to busboys grew up speaking it. As adults, they gather pau hana (after work) over drinks and complain that the hui (company) they work for is making them pupule (crazy). . . Editors at The Honolulu Star-Bulletin chuckled one day. . . "My Hawaiian bus driver said I was filled with the spirit of Pupule," the woman wrote. "What a nice way to put it. The spirit of Pupule will stay with me forever." Or until she learned some pidgin.

pupu pup See **pupu**

pur- pref[1] See **pre-** pref[1]

pur- pref[2] See **pro-**

purdy See **pretty A1b**

pure adj, adv Usu |pjʊr, pjuə(r)|; also **chiefly S Midl** |pjor|; **Sth** |pjo|; for addit varr see quot 1941 Pronc-spp *puore, pyo, pyore;* similarly *puorely* Cf **poor** adj
A Forms.
1894 Riley *Armazindy* 31 **IN**, As puore and ca'm a sleep fer me / And sweet a sleep as his! **1922** Gonzales *Black Border* 321 **sSC, GA coasts** [Gullah glossary], *Pyo'*—pure, also fully, absolutely; as: "de pyo' nutt'n'!" absolutely nothing. **1923** (1946) Greer-Petrie *Angeline Doin' Society* 21 **csKY**, Her chinywar' was puore gold. **1924** Raine *Land of Saddle-Bags* 211 **sAppalachians**, Hit bubbles right out'n the ground, hit's bound to be puore. **1927** *DN* 5.470 **Appalachians**, Pure . . pyore. **1928** *AmSp* 3.404 **Ozarks** (as of 1916–27), The *u* in *pure* is always turned into long *o*, and preceded by a *y* sound, so that the word must be spelled *pyore* or *puore*. **1929** *Sat. Eve. Post* 17 Aug 11 **Lower Missip Valley** [Black], He too hard to fool, dat Cap'm Sam! He a pyore case! **1929** Sale *Tree Named John* 49 **MS** [Black], Nobody goes but de pyo' in heart. **1931** [see **purely**]. **1931** *PMLA* 46.1304 **sAppalachians**, That room's a pyore hurrah's nest. **1941** *LANE* Map 308 (Genuine) **NEng**, [Of 47 resps, 19 were of the types [pɪʊ(ə)r, pju(ə)r]; 10 [pjʊə]; 8 [pjuə]

5 [pɪu(ə)r]; 3 [pçʋə(r)]; 1 [pɪ˞ʋə]; 1 [pjᴜur].] **1949** Webber *Backwoods Teacher* 88 **Ozarks**, She comes around actin' so pyore an' holy. **1955** Ritchie *Singing Family* 81 **seKY**, That man's a pyore fool. **1967** *DARE* FW Addit **cwNC**, *Pure* . . [pjor].

B As adj.

Real, veritable, regular.   **Sth, S Midl**

1919 *DN* 5.34 **seKY**, My boy's a pyore scholar, and reads after Shakespeare. **1928** Peterkin *Scarlet Sister Mary* 31 **SC** [Gullah], I told you to kneel down an' thank God an' here you is singin a reel song an' crossin you feets. Dat's a sin, gal, a pure sin. **1929** [see **A** above]. **1931** *PMLA* [see **A** above]. **1938** Rawlings *Yearling* 19 **nFL**, I cain't raise young uns in a pure thicket. *Ibid* 55, I'm in a pure fix. **1941** Faulkner *Men Working* 24 **MS**, Ifen you don't say something to him soon, he'll have a pure fit. **1941** *Sat. Eve. Post* 10 May 36 **eKY**, A pure bee swarm o' chaps. **1955** [see **A** above]. **1956** McAtee *Some Dialect NC* 35, *Pure death.* . . Severe pain. "I suffered pure death." **c1960** *Wilson Coll.* **csKY**, It's a pure sin to do that. **1986** Pederson *LAGS Concordance*, 1 inf, **cLA**, A pure fool.

C As adv.

Also *pure-out:* =**purely.** [*OED2 pure* adv. C.1 1297 →; "now dial. (esp *U.S.*)"] **Sth, S Midl**

1928 Peterkin *Scarlet Sister Mary* 36 **SC** [Gullah], Lawd, gal, I'm dat sorry, I could pure cry like a baby. **1930** Stoney–Shelby *Black Genesis* 101 **seSC**, De longer he wait, de mo' Br' Wolf han's pure itch for lick Br' Rabbit. **1932** Faulkner *Light in August* 332 **MS**, He was pure crazy by now, standing on the corner and yelling at whoever would pass. **1939** Griswold *Sea Is. Lady* 509 **csSC** (as of c1893) [Gullah], But ef you got one good green of sanse, bes' keep you' eye pure cyas' down vhen you pass' um in fiel' an' road. **1940** (1941) Bell *Swamp Water* 18 **Okefenokee GA**, "You cain't just pure-out miss the sing," Mabel said. **1940** (1978) Still *River of Earth* 206 **KY**, "I hear Coonie Todd's a good woman, and sets honor by her dead husband," she said. "Got a homeseat her pure own. That's more'n most folks can brag about." **1960** Williams *Walk Egypt* 10 **GA**, But he's pure got to be to the mill today to grind. **1986** Pederson *LAGS Concordance*, 1 inf, **cTN**, [A] moon-eyed horse is pure blind at night; 1 inf, **swGA**, Pure hard-down mean; 1 inf, **csGA**, Pure ornery—of a mule; 1 inf, **cTX**, Pure ugly; (*He* _____ *dreaded* . . *the place*) 1 inf, **seFL**, Pure dreaded; (*The poor whites*) 1 inf, **nwGA**, Pure lazy; 1 inf, **csAL**, Pure sorry; (*I didn't know he'd get* _____) 1 inf, **cMS**, Pure mad. **1994** *NC Lang. & Life Project Dial. Dict. Lumbee Engl.* 10 **seNC**, *Pure.* . . Certainly, definitely, undoubtedly. This adverb can only be used to intensify the meaning of verb phrases which indicate something negative. *You pure made a mess in here.*

pure n See **purie**

puredee adj, adv Also *pure-d, pure dee old, pure o.d., pure oldee, pure-t* [Prob orig euphem for *pure damn(ed)*] **chiefly Sth, S Midl**

Genuine, real, just plain; very, really, completely.

1938 FWP *Guide MS* 15, It's the pure D truth. **1941** Perry *Hold Autumn* 203 **TX**, "Them folks are mean out there," Mrs. Clampett said. "Just pure dee mean." **1952** Harwin *Home is Upriver* 8 (*Hench Coll.*), Kip's lip curled at this slovenly practice, one which he had always called puredee shif'less. *Ibid* 187, You're a puredee heller. **1953** Randolph–Wilson *Down in Holler* 275 **Ozarks**, *Pure dee.* . . Genuine, indubitable. "No, them ain't no chigger-bites. That's the pure dee seven-year itch!" **1958** Latham *Meskin Hound* 53 **cTX**, It's pure-dee hog-hunting weather. **1964** Tyler *If Morning Ever Comes* 44 **NC**, He loafed about his office playing patience in a white uniform and pure-T bare feet, which scared all his patients away. **1968** *DARE* (Qu. HH3, *A dull and stupid person*) Inf **LA**35, Pure-d dumb. **1970** Tarpley *Blinky* 144 **TX**, *Waste food fed to swine* . . pure dee old slop [rare]. **1970** *Harper's Mag.* Apr 80 **TX**, Elliott . . found a pair of nearly new overalls. . . dry socks and one of his father's gray work shirts. "Lordy, lordy. You wouldn't know me from a pure-dee old scissorbill," Grady said wryly, with satisfaction. **1970** *Thompson Coll.* **cnAL** (as of 1920s), The pure-dee, stomp-down real old-time religion. **1972** in 1993 Major *Calling the Wind* 348 **NYC** [Black], So this one day Miss Moore rounds us all up at the mailbox and it's puredee hot and she's knockin herself out about arithmetic. **1981** *DARE* File **MS**, To my mind that is pure O.D. nonsense. **1982** *NADS Letters* **IN**, I have heard *pure D.* in Southern Indiana used as what seemed to be a negative intensifier—it most often precedes a negative word, *nonsense, mean, ornery,* etc; **MS**, During my youth, I often heard the usage in question, always, or nearly always—as "pure oldee"; **MO**, As a teenager in Pulaski and Phelps Counties in Missouri, I learned that . . "O.D." refers to "Olive Drab" "Army issue." . . So, in "pure O.D.

nonsense," the "O.D." is merely a superlative; I have never heard it used in the full form, or in a positive sense; **LA**, Around 1950, I heard and used the phrase "pure D" ['pjou 'di] or ['pjouɚ 'di] (note the two primary stresses). It was used pejoratively (e.g., in response to a tall story, "That's a load of pure D horse shit!"); **ceTX**, In this part of Texas, as well as the Houston area where I grew up, we said, not "pure O.D. _____," but "pure dee old (something)." **1986** Pederson *LAGS Concordance*, 1 inf, **cwFL**, Pure D hell—unqualified hell; they give you pure D hell; 1 inf, **cwAR**, Pure D plumb nasty—extremely nasty; 1 inf, Pure D old belly—just plain belly. **1995** *Signal Mag.* Dec np **cwTX**, Puredee—"That catfish was puredee good." Pure D(amn) good.

puree See **purie**

purely adv [*OED2 purely* adv. 2.b 1297 →; "Now *U.S. dial.*"] **Sth, S Midl**

Simply, completely, certainly, very.

1931 *AmSp* 7.91 **eKY**, *Puorely,* purely, absolutely. "That Irick [sic] man is jist puorely low-down mean." **1938** Rawlings *Yearling* 168 **nFL**, He's purely ailin'. **1942** (1971) Campbell *Cloud-Walking* 20 **seKY**, Ishmael knowed pine-blank the racket would purely kill Marthy. **1952** Harwin *Home is Upriver* 198 (*Hench Coll.*), I'd purely like to see that old woman. **1956** McAtee *Some Dialect NC* 35, *Purely.* . . Very. "It is purely warm today." *Obs. exc. Dial.* **1969** *DARE* (Qu. LL35, *Words used to make a statement stronger:* "This cake tastes _____ good.") Inf **KY**25, Purely. **1972** Cooper *NC Mt. Folkl.* 95, *Purely likes to eat*—really likes to eat. **1979** Carpenter *Walton War* 146 **sAppalachians**, I am purely afraid to risk some things. **1986** Pederson *LAGS Concordance* **Gulf Region** (*He really dreaded the place*) [15 infs responded with *purely dreaded* (or *hated*), and in response to other questions, 11 infs gave such resps as "Just *purely* run over us," "Adversity is bitter, but it's *purely* sweet," etc.] **1987** Kytle *Voices* 161 **NC** [Black], He was little and sometimes he did spill things, and I do purely hate to walk on sugar.

pure o.d., pure oldee See **puredee**

pure-out See **pure C**

pure quill See **quill** n 5

pure-t See **puredee**

purey See **purie**

purgatory n Also *pegatory, purg, purgie (in the hole), purgy* A marble game that involves a series of holes into which a marble must be rolled or tossed; also *purgie-hole:* one of the holes used in this game, generally the last in the series.

1892 *DN* 1.220 **DC**, *Purgy:* the hole in the dirt which was the first goal into which to get your marble. **1893** Shands *MS Speech* 74, *Purgatory.* A name given to a game of marbles, which is played by rolling a marble in a series of holes, the last one in the series being called *purgatory,* or *purg.* **1957** *Sat. Eve. Post Letters* **swCA**, My brother and I played "purgatory" with marbles. [*DARE* Ed: Diagram shows four holes, of which the fourth is named "purgatory." Players must work through the series and back again.] **1965–70** *DARE* (Qu. EE7, . . *Kinds of marble games*) Infs **OK**18, Pegatory—dig a round hole; **CA**65, Purgatory—a little hole marble game; three big holes and one small to get in; **CA**102, Purgatory—make holes, try to get the marbles in the holes; **CA**165, Purgatory—dig three holes, shoot from base to get into holes, kind of patterned after baseball; **CA**209, Purgatory—dig three holes in the ground, shoot your marbles from one to the other till circle is completed and then in reverse, and then you're out of purgatory; **IL**96, Purgatory—same as *over;* seven holes in the ground; taw has to be rolled in each hole; **TX**18, Purgatory; **AZ**8, Purg; **NM**9, Purg—have three holes, make one after the other; **DC**12, Purgie; **DC**8, Purgie in the hole—like golf. **1966–70** *DARE* Tape **AZ**8, The game purg is a marble game. The players, any number of players, begin by scooping out three round holes in the ground; **KY**75, We'd start out with three holes in the ground . . four–five feet . . apart. We'd start to shooting at these holes and make it, and then we would have a what we called a purgatory, which would be ten or twelve feet away from the other holes. The first fella that made it to this purgie-hole, he'd win the game; **NM**9, We just played a game of purg, and that can be a gambling game also. All the marbles can be yours if you can win, but usually it's just a gentle little game for the beginners to play; **WY**1, Purgatory was made with a series of holes, just like a golf game. We played a diamond-shaped game. And then, way off, sometimes a hundred feet, was another hole. That was purgatory. **1974** *DARE* File **KS** (as of 1890), Purgatory—a marble game.

purge v

1 To vomit; to cause to vomit. [Cf *OED2* purge v. 4.b]

1902 *DN* 2.242 **sIL**, Purge. . . To vomit. **1907** *DN* 3.225 **nwAR**, Purge. . . To vomit. **1969–70** *DARE* (Qu. BB17, *Other words or expressions . . for vomiting*) Inf **NY232**, Purge; (Qu. BB18, *To vomit a great deal at once*) Inf **IN82**, Purge. **1986** Pederson *LAGS Concordance*, 1 inf, **ceGA**, Take purging medicine—to induce vomiting.

2 Of a corpse: to foam at the mouth.

1945 Saxon *Gumbo Ya-Ya* 559 **LA**, He won't purge (foam at the mouth) when he dies. (Means he speaks his mind.) [**1969** *DARE* Tape **KY6**, What they call lay him out—they washed him clean and dressed him. . . They'd cork him, all openings, to keep him from purging.] **1993** Gibbons *Charms* 80 **NC** (as of c1937), She said to her mother, "I heard you ask if he purged. Did he?" My grandmother stopped . . and said, "Yes, he did." The fact that he had foamed at the mouth immediately upon dying indicated that he had had a great backjam of wishes and desires and truths that were never spoken.

purgie (in the hole), purgy See **purgatory**

purie n Also *pairie, peerie, peery, perrie, perry, pirie, pure(e), pur(e)y* [Prob from *SND* peerie n.[1] 6 "A small stone marble," infl by assoc with *pure*] Cf **clearie, glassie**

A transparent clear or colored glass marble without inclusions.

1901 *DN* 2.145 **OH**, Pury. . . Agate, higher-priced marble. Cleveland, O. **1926** *AmSp* 2.66 [Playground argot], Hear the chatter that comes out of a marble-shooting ring. . . [T]he "migs," "agates," "glassies," "pureys," "commies" and "potties" they talk about! Who'd know these strange-sounding things, unless he were fraternizing with school-ground company. **1950** *WELS Suppl.* **seWI**, Purey—a clear glass of a single color. **1958** *PADS* 29.39 **WI**, Purey, pirie. . . A clear glass marble. **1961** Salinger *Franny* 75 **NYC**, An unclouded blue marble (known to marble shooters, at least in the twenties, as a "purey"). **1965–70** *DARE* (Qu. EE6d, *Special marbles*) Infs **CT37, IL68, NY89, 119, OH65, TX54**, Puries; **CA1**, Puries—colored clear glass; **CA166**, Puries—clear glass without air bubble; **MN28**, Puries—the clear ones you can see through; **NY40**, Puries—one pure color; **CA118**, Perries ['pɛriz]—think it's one that [is] just perfectly clear; **MI89**, Perries ['pɛriz]; **MI117**, Perries ['pɛriz]—clear marbles; **MI118**, Piries [piriz]; **MI123**, Piries [pɪɚiz]; **MN1**, Peerries [piriz]—clear ones; **LA34**, Pure—a clear marble; (Qu. EE6a, . . *Different kinds of marbles—the big one*) Inf **WA22**, Perrie; (Qu. EE6b, *Small marbles or marbles in general*) Inf **HI9**, Piries ['piriz]—translucent; (Qu. EE6c, *Cheap marbles*) Inf **AK5**, Puries [pjuriz]—clear glass; **NJ27**, Puries. **1968** *DARE* Tape **NY40**, You had your puries ['pju,riz]. They was worth more; sometimes maybe it might be worth four or five of different sort of colored marbles. . . A purey—a pure colored one—would cost more than an ordinary multicolored one. **c1970** Wiersma *Marbles Terms* **swMI** (as of c1940), Puries . . interchangeable for clearies—a solid clear glass marble. *Ibid* **NY, MI, UT,** Purie . . clear, uncolored marble. *Ibid* **swMI** (as of 1960), Puries [pjuriz]—Clear marble. *Ibid* **swMI**, Purie(s), peerie(s): ['pɪuriz, 'piriz]. . . A small, transparent, clear marble which is made usually of glass and can be different colors. *Ibid* **swMI** (as of c1960), Peery [piri] . . a clear glass marble of any size. *Ibid* **swMI**, Peerie [piri] . . a translucent marble of most any color with no design. . . When I asked the girl why she called it a "peerie" she said, "Because you can peer through it." *Ibid* **swMI** (as of c1960), Perry (purey)—see "Clearsy". *Ibid*, Pairies—transparent solid color marbles. *Ibid*, Perrys—type of marble (small)[;] Peeries—a clear marble (origin prob fr. Perry) **1973** Ferretti *Marble Book* 50, Purey. Small clear glass marbles. **2001** *DARE* File **Chicago IL** (as of 1940s), Marbles were called Mibs. Some were Bowlers and other were Purees.

‡purification n

The afterbirth.

1935 Hyatt *Folkl. Adams Co. IL* 100, When a cow calves, bury the purification under an apple tree and next time she will bear a female calf.

purify n [By apocope from *purifier*] Cf **fertilize, flyswat**

1945 Saxon *Gumbo Ya-Ya* 526 **LA**, Jack Vine tea is the best blood purify you can get.

purloo See **pilau** n[1]

purmy See **pumice** n[2]

purp n [Pronc-sp for *pup*]

1887 (1892) Hinman *Corporal Si Klegg* 580, "Looks . . more like a . . dog-kennel 'n . . a house fer two men ter live in." . . [T]hat . . little tent. . . was immediately christened the "pup" tent, and till the end of the war it was known only by that name, through all the armies, from the Potomac to the Rio Grande. Often the ridicule . . was intensified by . . making it "purp." **1911** *DN* 3.546 **NE**, Purp (ɒ). . . Frequent for *pup, puppy.* **1916** *DN* 4.341 **MA, NY, seOH**, Purp. . . A dog. Common in S. & W. dialect stories. **1921** *DN* 5.110 **CA**, Purp. . . Pup, dog. Doubtless by the introduction of "the dog's letter." **1927** *AmSp* 2.362 **cwWV**, Purp . . a young dog. "Will you sell me that purp?" **1948** Manfred *Chokecherry* 257 **nwIA**, The dog hopped up, but not quite in time. . . "Keep that damned purp to home then."

purple alexanders n Also *purple alexander*

A **meadow parsnip 1** (here: *Thaspium trifoliatum*).

1843 Torrey *Flora NY* 1.272, Thaspium atropurpureum. . . *Purple Alexanders.* **1900** Lyons *Plant Names* 368, T[haspium] trifoliatum. . . Purple Meadow-parsnip, Purple Alexanders. **1959** Carleton *Index Herb. Plants* 95, *Purple Alexander:* Thaspium aureum.

purple anise n

=**Florida anise-tree.**

1933 Small *Manual SE Flora* 534, I[llicium] floridanum. . . Purple-anise. Stink-bush. . . Swamps and low hammocks, Coastal Plain, N. Fla. to La. and N. Ala. . . The flowers have the odor of decaying fish. **1960** Vines *Trees SW* 278, Other vernacular names are Polecat-tree, Poison Bay, . . Purple-anise tree [etc]. **1979** Little *Checklist U.S. Trees* 151, Polecat-tree, purple anise-tree [etc].

purple black-eyed Susan n Cf **black-eyed Susan**

Perh = **purple coneflower.**

1968 *DARE* (Qu. S26a, . . *Wildflowers. . . Roadside flowers*) Inf **LA17**, Purple black-eyed Susans.

purple bonnet n

A **water shield 1** (here: *Brasenia schreberi*).

1920 *Torreya* 20.21 **TN**, Brasenia schreberi. . . Egg bonnet, purple bonnet, Reelfoot Lake, Tenn. **1942** Hylander *Plant Life* 600, Purple Bonnet *(Brasenia),* found in still waters from Florida to Texas and northwards . . the flowers have a dull purple perianth of linear sepals and petals. **1959** Carleton *Index Herb. Plants* 95, *Purple bonnet:* Brasenia peltata.

purple coneflower n Cf **purple black-eyed Susan**

A plant of the genus *Echinacea,* esp *E. purpurea.* For other names of var spp see **black sampson, comb** n **B5, combflower 1, coneflower 3, hedgehog coneflower, niggerhead 3k, nigger heel 4, Indianhead root, rattlesnake weed 1c, red sunflower, Sampson root 2, snakeroot**

1848 Gray *Manual of Botany* 223, Echinacea [spp]. . . Purple Coneflower. . . Rays rose-purple, rather persistent; disk purplish. **1910** Graves *Flowering Plants* 393 **CT**, Brauneria [spp]. . . Purple Coneflower. *Ibid,* Echinacea angustifolia. . . Purple Cone-flower. . . Adventive from the West. **1930** OK Univ. Biol. Surv. *Pub.* 2.83, Brauneria purpurea. . . Red Sunflower. Purple cone-flower. Black Sampson. **1949** Moldenke *Amer. Wild Flowers* 206, In the tall purple coneflower, *E. purpurea . . ,* the 12 to 20 rays are purple, crimson, or rarely pale. . . The disk is purple. **1961** Wills–Irwin *Flowers TX* 234, Purple Cone-flower, or Black sampson as it is sometimes called, is found east from Randall, Garza, Kerr, and De Witt counties to the Louisiana border, most commonly in fields and open woods in limestone or gravelly soils. **1967** *Ozark Visitor* (Point Lookout MO) Feb 6, Beyond the horsemint stood the purple cone flower with its long petals drooping like ears of an old hound dog. This is a plant that had more uses among Indians than any other. Its flowers were used as an antidote for snake bite; burned as a smoke treatment for headache, chewed for toothache and brewed into an externally applied mild anaesthetic.

purple dewdrop n

A **lobelia B1** (here: *Lobelia puberula*).

1970 Correll *Plants TX* 1521, Lobelia puberula Michx. Downy lobelia, purple dewdrop. . . In swamps, wet woods, bogs, prairies and open fields, usually in wet places. . . in s.e. U.S., w. to Okla. and Tex.

purple dogwood n

A **dogwood 1** (here: *Cornus alternifolia*).

1897 Sudworth *Arborescent Flora* 310 **PA**, *Cornus alternifolia.* . . Purple Dogwood. **1908** Britton *N. Amer. Trees* 741, Blue Cornel. . . This small tree, or more often tall shrub, is also known as the Purple dogwood, Umbrella tree, Pigeonberry, and Green osier. **1940** Clute *Amer. Plant Names* 97, Purple dogwood, umbrella-tree, pigeon-berry.

purple finch n

Std: a **grosbeak** (here: *Carpodacus purpureus*). Also called **English robin 7, gray linnet 2, linnet 2, purple grosbeak, red linnet 2, ~ sparrow 2, strawberry bird**

purple-fingered grass n

A **big-bluestem** (here: *Andropogon gerardii*).

1862 *Atlantic Mth.* 10.388 **eMA**, Purple-Fingered Grass. . . is a very tall and slender-culmed grass, three to seven feet high, with four or five purple finger-like spikes raying upward from the top. **1941** *Torreya* 41.45, *Andropogon furcatus* Muhlenberg—Purple-fingered grass.

purple gallinule n Cf Florida gallinule

Std: a **gallinule** (here: *Porphyrula martinica*) of the southern US. Also called **blue Peter, ~ rail, bonnet walker, bumpybutt, English rail 2, Indian hen 4, ~ pullet 6, mammy coot 1, marsh guinea, ~ hen 1c, moonshine 3, mud hen 1c, pond chicken 1, ~ fowl, ~ guinea 1, water hen, target-arse bird**

purple grackle n

Std: a **grackle B** (here: *Quiscalus quiscula*). Also called **chock n[1], crow blackbird, jackdaw 1, long-tailed blackbird, maize thief, ricebird 3** Cf **Florida grackle**

purple grosbeak n

=purple finch.

[**1730** Royal Soc. London *Philos. Trans.* 36.430, *Cocothraustes purpurea*, the purple Gross-Beak.] **1898** (1900) Davie *Nests N. Amer. Birds* 355, Purple Finch. . . Called Purple Grosbeak, Crimson Finch or Linnet. It is found breeding regularly in the northern tier of States. **1917** (1923) *Birds Amer.* 3.5, Purple Finch. . . Other Names.—Purple Linnet; Purple Grosbeak [etc]. **1944** Hausman *Amer. Birds* 515, Grosbeak, Purple—See Finch, Purple.

purple haw n

=bluewood.

1884 Sargent *Forests of N. Amer.* 4, *Condalia obovata,* . . Blue Wood, Log Wood, Purple Haw. **1931** U.S. Dept. Ag. *Misc. Pub.* 101.112, Bluewood, known locally as brasil, capulin, logwood, and purple haw . . is limitedly browsed. **1939** Tharp *Vegetation TX* 61, Bluewood; Purple Haw *(Condalia).* **1960** Vines *Trees SW* 697, Bluewood Condalia. . . Other vernacular names are Brazil, Logwood, Bluewood, Purple Haw [etc].

purple-leaf maple See purple maple

purple loco n

A **locoweed**: either a **milk vetch** (here: usu *Astragalus mollissimus*) or a plant of the genus *Oxytropis,* esp *Oxytropis lambertii.*

1901 U.S. Dept. Ag. Div. Botany *Bulletin* 26.100, In addition to the white loco weed . . in Montana . . the most important are . . the purple loco weeds (*A. blankinshipii* Rydberg, *A. besseyi* Rydberg, and *A. lagopus* (Nutt.) Greene). **1913** (1979) Barnes *Western Grazing* 257, [Caption:] Woolly or Purple Loco (*Astragalus mollissimus*). **1937** U.S. Forest Serv. *Range Plant Hdbk.* W41, Woolly loco, sometimes called purple, stemmed, Texas, and true loco, is a low, tufted, perennial herb poisonous to livestock. **1950** Stevens *ND Plants* 186, *Oxytropis lambertii.* . . Purple Loco. . . This species is regarded as poisonous, but less so than some others. **1979** Spellenberg *Audubon Guide N. Amer. Wildflowers W. Region* 507, Purple Loco; Lambert's Loco; Colorado Loco (*Oxytropis lambertii*). . . One of the most dangerously poisonous plants on western ranges, it is lethally toxic to all kinds of livestock.

purple loosestrife n [*OED2* 1548 →]

A **loosestrife 2** (here: *Lythrum salicaria*). Also called **dogtongue blossom, milk willow herb, rainbowweed**

1836 Lincoln *Famil. Lectures* 2.114, [*Lythrum*] *salicaria,* (purple loose-strife). . . Wet meadows. **1909** Doubleday *Amer. Flower Garden* 93, Loosestrife, Purple. . . Bright purple. June to August; 2 to 8 feet. Best bright-coloured flowers for late summer, for swamps, and wet meadows. Flowers in lax terminal spikes. **1946** Tatnall *Flora DE* 184, Purple Loosestrife. Infrequent, in marshes and borders of ponds and streams. . . Piedmont and Coastal Plain. **1972** Courtenay–Zimmerman *Wild Flowers* 26, Purple Loosestrife, *Lythrum salicaria.* **1994** *USA Today* (Arlington VA) 23 Aug 6A **RI**, Roger Williams Park Zoo has imported more than 1,000 beetles from Europe in hopes they'll devour purple loosestrife, a weed that grows up to seven feet tall and is choking the other plants in the wetlands exhibit.

purple maple n Also *purple-leaf maple*

A purple-leaved variety of Norway **maple** *(Acer platanoides).*

1967–70 *DARE* (Qu. T14, . . *Kinds of maples*) Infs **GA**70, **PA**242, Purple maple; **OR**1, Purple-leaf maple.

purple marshlocks n

A **cinquefoil** (here: *Comarum palustre*).

1927 *Torreya* 27.32 **NJ**, Purple marshlocks. *Comarum palustre.* A bog herb with compound leaves and purple flowers. . . recorded only from Budd's Lake, Morris County, New Jersey. **1934** Haskin *Wild Flowers Pacific Coast* 185, Purple Marsh-locks (*Comarum palustre).* . . The distinguishing feature of this species is its large, dark purple flowers, nearly an inch in diameter, quite different from the usual yellow cinquefoils.

purple martin n Cf bee swallow, black ~, blue martin

Std: a **martin** *(Progne subis).* Also called **bee martin 3, black ~, blue swallow 2, box bird, brown martin, bull swallow, gourd martin, house ~, martin-house swallow, rainbird 1b**

purple milkweed n

A **milkweed 1** (here: usu *Asclepias purpurascens*).

1848 Gray *Manual of Botany* 367, *A[sclepias] purpurascens.* . . Purple Milkweed. . . N. England to Michigan, not common eastward. **1897** IN Dept. Geol. & Nat. Resources *Rept. for 1896* 666, *A. purpurascens.* . . Purple Milkweed. Borders of dry, sandy fields; scarce. **1948** Stevens *KS Wild Flowers* 180, *Asclepias purpurascens—*Purple Milkweed. . . Flowers somewhat variable in color—those of our photograph had purplish-red petals. . . Handsome, and desirable for the wild-flower garden.

purple milkwort n

A **milkwort** (here: *Polygala sanguinea*).

1843 Torrey *Flora NY* 1.149, Polygala sanguinea. . . *Purple Milkwort.* . . Moist meadows and sandy fields; rather common. **1897** IN Dept. Geol. & Nat. Resources *Rept. for 1896* 650, *P[olygala] viridescens.* . . Purple Milkwort. . . Low, sandy soil; scarce. **1949** Moldenke *Amer. Wild Flowers* 52, Purple milkwort, *P[olygala] sanguinea,* common in fields and meadows from Nova Scotia to Minnesota and south to North Carolina and Louisiana. **1979** Niering–Olmstead *Audubon Guide N. Amer. Wildflowers E. Region* 702, Field Milkwort; Purple Milkwort.

purple mouse-ears n [From the two upright petals of the purple flower] Cf mouse-ear

A **monkey flower 1** (here: *Mimulus douglasii*).

1951 Abrams *Flora Pacific States* 3.730, *Mimulus Douglasii.* . . Purple Mouse-ears. **1961** Thomas *Flora Santa Cruz* 313 **cwCA**, *M[imulus] douglasii.* . . Purple Mouse-Ears. Occasional on bare sand, serpentine, grassy slopes, and in clearings on brush-covered slopes.

purple nightshade n

A **nightshade 1**: *Solanum dulcamara, S. elaeagnifolium,* or *S. xanti.*

1911 NJ State Museum *Annual Rept. for 1910* 675, The introduced *S[olanum] dulcamara* (Purple Nightshade or Bitter Sweet) is perfectly naturalized along the coastal islands, where it is as characteristic as some of the native species. **1915** (1926) Armstrong–Thornber *Western Wild Flowers* 462, Purple Nightshade *Solanum Xanti.* . . This is much handsomer than most of the eastern Nightshades. **1936** Whitehouse *TX Flowers* 128, Purple Nightshade (*Solanum eleagnifolium*) is sometimes called silver-leaved nightshade or "trompillo." **1951** *PADS* 15.39, *Solanum eleagnifolium.* . . Purple, prickly, or Mexican, nightshade; poison weed. **1961** Thomas *Flora Santa Cruz* 303 **cwCA**, *S[olanum] xantii* Gray var. *intermedium* Parish. Purple Nightshade.

purple pimpleback See **purple wartyback**

purple rocket n

A cruciferous herb (*Iodanthus pinnatifidus*). Also called **false rocket**

> **1900** Lyons *Plant Names* 202, *Iodanthus*. . . Purple or False Rocket. . . Herb with violet or white flowers in panicled racemes. **1940** Gates *Flora KS* 159, Iodanthus pinnatifidus. . . Purple Rocket. River banks. **1972** Courtenay–Zimmerman *Wild Flowers* 21, Purple Rocket, *Iodanthus pinnatifidus:* without hairs; leaves stalked; riverbanks.

purple sage n

1 A **sage 1**, usu *Salvia leucophylla*.

> **1911** CA Ag. Exper. Sta. Berkeley *Bulletin* 217.1020, *Salvia leucophylla*. Purple, White Leaved and Silver Sage. **1923** *Natl. Geogr. Mag.* 43.205 **AZ,** The purple sage . . found in the crevices of these "bald-heads." **1967–68** DARE (Qu. S26c, *Wildflowers that grow in woods*) Inf **CA65,** Sage or purple sage; (Qu. S26e, *Other wildflowers not yet mentioned;* not asked in early QRs) Inf **CA4,** Blue or purple sage (in desert). **1982** *Plants SW* (Catalog) 49, Beautiful flowering shrubs requiring only the simplest of care, the salvias are the "purple sage" of the old west.

2 also *purple sagebrush:* A **silverleaf 8** (here: *Leucophyllum frutescens*).

> **1951** PADS 15.40 **TX,** *Leucophyllum texanum*. . . Purple sage-brush. **1960** Vines *Trees SW* 921, The Spanish vernacular name, Cenizo, is much used in the Southwest. . . Other vernacular names are Ash-bush, Wild Lilac, Purple Sage [etc]. **c1979** TX Dept. Highways *Flowers* 51, Cenizo is also called Purple Sage in Texas. . . After rains the ashy gray leaves of Cenizo almost disappear under a mass of purplish blossoms.

purple sandpiper n

Std: a small eastern sandpiper with purple winter plumage (*Calidris maritima*). Also called **rockbird 1, rock plover 1, ~ snipe 1, rockweed bird, winter goose, ~ peep, ~ rockbird, ~ snipe**

purple strawberry bush n

A **burning bush 1** (here: *Euonymus atropurpureus*).

> **1971** Krochmal *Appalachia Med. Plants* 116, *Euonymus atropurpureus*. . . Common Names: Eastern wahoo . . purple strawberry bush [etc].

purple thistle n

A **button snakeroot 2** (here: *Eryngium leavenworthii*).

> **1936** Whitehouse *TX Flowers* 89, False Purple Thistle. Eryngo (*Eryngium leavenworthii*) is not a true thistle, but it is popularly known as one. **1951** PADS 15.37 **TX,** *Eryngium leavenworthii*. . . Purple thistle; false thistle.

purpletop n [From the purple panicles]

A tall grass (*Tridens flavus*) of the eastern US. Also called **false redtop 2**

> **1941** Justus *Cabin on Kettle Creek* 29 **KY, TN,** The same old signs appeared to prove that fall had come again; goldenrod plumes in the fence rows, purple tops in the hollow, and sumac bushes along the creek blazing like brushwood flames. **1946** Tatnall *Flora DE* 25, T[riodia] flava. . . Purpletop. **1950** Hitchcock–Chase *Manual Grasses* 213, Tridens flavus. . . Purpletop. . . Old fields and open woods, New Hampshire to Nebraska, south to Florida and Texas. **1967** Braun *Monocotyledoneae* 92, Triodia flava. . . Tall Redtop. Purpletop. Grease Grass. . . A tall to moderately tall grass common along roadsides and in old fields, with handsome panicle of purple or rarely yellow spikelets.

purple torch n

A **hedgehog cactus 3** (here: *Echinocereus engelmannii*).

> **1973** *AZ Highways* Mar 39, Whether you call them Strawberry Hedgehog, Calico Hedgehog, or Purple Torch (Echinocereus engelmannii), everyone finds the blossoms most attractive and delicate.

purple veil n

The egg mass of the **goosefish.**

> **1905** *Natl. Geogr. Mag.* July 337, Off the New England coast a curious object is often found floating on the water, somewhat resembling a lady's veil . . of a violet or purple color. The fishermen allude to it generally as the "purple veil". . . On examining the substance with a magnify-

ing glass . . it was obvious that the purple veil, as a whole, was the egg-mass of a fish.

purple wartyback n Also *purple pimpleback*

A **freshwater clam** (here: *Cyclonaias tuberculata*).

> **1941** *AmSp* 16.156 **Missip Valley,** There is a pink, a white, and a fat mucket; a purple and a three horned warty-back. **1982** U.S. Fish & Wildlife Serv. *Fresh-Water Mussels* [Wall chart], *Purple Pimpleback*. Preferred habitat: rocky areas, riffles. Historically widespread. . . Nearly extirpated. **1991** IL Nat. Hist. Surv. *Biol. Notes* 137.16, The purple wartyback has historically occurred in the Illinois River. **1992** *Nature Conserv. Mag.* Nov/Dec 17, Richard Neves . . rises up on his knees, spits out his snorkel and presents a beanbag-sized clamshell. "*Cyclonaias tuberculata*," he declares. "Purple wartyback."

purplewort n

A **cinquefoil** (here: *Comarum palustre*).

> **1910** Graves *Flowering Plants* 233 **CT,** *Potentilla palustris*. . . Purplewort. New Haven. . . June-July. **1919** (1923) House *Wild Flowers NY* 132, Purple or Marsh Cinquefoil; Purplewort. . . In swamps and peat bogs. **1940** Clute *Amer. Plant Names* 7, P[otentilla] palustris. Marsh Cinquefoil. Purple cinquefoil . . purplewort, purple marsh-locks.

purs See **pus** n[1]

purse n[1] Usu |pɜ(r)s|; also *arch* |pʌs|; for addit varr see quots Pronc-sp *puss*

Std sense, var forms.

> **1843** (1916) Hall *New Purchase* 270 **IN,** [They] all from that moment united in determined and active hostility towards . . "every puss proud aristocrat big-bug, and darn'd blasted Yankee in the New Purchase." **1851** Hooper *Widow Rugby's Husband* 49 **AL,** Less make up a puss for him. **1883** (1971) Harris *Nights with Remus* 172 **GA** [Black], Ef I aint done come traipsin' off en lef' my ole man money-pus. **1899** (1912) Green *VA Folk-Speech* 339, Puss. . . Purse. Money-puss. **1915** *DN* 4.188 **swVA,** *Purse* [pɔs]. **1941** *LANE* Map 368 *(Purse)* [About 50 proncs of the type [pʌs] are recorded, mostly from **ME, NH,** and **neMA.** In only 10 cases is this the only pronc recorded; usually this form was given (often at the FW's suggestion) as an alternative to another (usu of the types [pɚs] or [pɜs]); 9 infs indicated that it was obsolete and 19 that it was "older, but still in use." One auxiliary inf offered the pronc [pɑˆs].]

purse n[2] See **pus** n[1]

pursimond See **persimmon**

purslane n [*OED2* a1387 →]

1 Std: a plant of the genus *Portulaca*. For other names of var spp see **carpet pussley, cooter grass 2, duckweed 2, Fourth of July 3, French pusley, hog parsley, milk purslane 2, moss rose 2, pigweed 4, pussley 1a**

2 An **amaranth** (here: *Amaranthus blitoides*).

> **1898** *Jrl. Amer. Folkl.* 11.277 **KS,** *Amarantus* [sic] *blitoides* . . pigweed, purslane, matweed.

3 =**Mexican clover.**

> **1925** *Book of Rural Life* 6.3512, This plant [=Mexican clover] is also known as *purslane* or *pusley,* but is entirely different from the northern weed known by that name. . . It is a native of Mexico, but has spread as a weed through the southern part of the Gulf states.

pursley n See **pussley 1a**

pursley adj, **pursley-gut(ted)** See **pussly**

pursly See **pussley 1a**

pursy minnow n

A **killifish 1** (here: *Cyprinodon* spp).

> **1896** U.S. Natl. Museum *Bulletin* 47.670, *Cyprinodon* [spp]. . . Pursy Minnows. . . Body very short and stout, the back elevated. *Ibid* 671, *Cyprinodon variegatus*. . . Pursy Minnow. **1906** NJ State Museum *Annual Rept. for 1905* 198, Genus *Cyprinodon*. . . The Pursy Minnows. *Cyprinodon variegatus*. . . Killi Fish. Pursy Minnow. **1911** *Century Dict. Suppl.*, Minnow. . . Pursy minnows, species of the genus *Cyprinodon,* small fishes found in brackish waters of America.

purt- See **pretty A2b**

purt night (or nite) See **pretty near it**

purty See **pretty A1b**

pury See **purie**

pus n[1] Usu |pʌs|; also |pɛrs, pɝs| Pronc-spp *purs(e);* cf Intro "Language Changes" I.8 Cf **pulse, purse** n[1]
Std sense, var forms.
    1966 *DARE* (Qu. BB35, *The yellowish stuff that comes out of a boil when the head breaks*) Inf **SC**27, Pus, also purse [pɛɝs]—Negro. **1981** Pederson *LAGS Basic Materials,* 1 inf, **swAL,** [p'ɝs] corrected to [p'ʌs]. **1983** *MJLF* 9.1.52 **ceKY,** *Purs* . . pus.

pus v, hence vbl n *pus(s)ing* Cf **matterate**
Of a wound or abcess: to discharge pus.
    1948 Manfred *Chokecherry* 53 **nwIA,** Instantly the wound popped open, and yellow and purple and bloody pus geysered out and ran over Elof's foot. . . Pa nodded sagely, "There. See? Now me, I call that pusin'." **1950** *WELS Suppl. (Yellow stuff coming out of a sore; "Its _____")* 1 Inf **ceWI,** Pussing. **1967–69** *DARE* (Qu. BB36, *When there's an open sore and this yellowish stuff is coming out of it . . it's _____*) Infs **CA**140, **IL**9, **MO**6, **NY**7, **RI**6, **WI**30, Pussing.

pus n[2] See **pus-gut**

pus-gut n Also *pus(s), pus-guts* [Appar varr of *pussy-gut* (at **pussy** adj[1]), perh by assoc with [pʌs] pronc var of **purse** n[1]] =**pussle-gut;** hence adj *pus-gutted.*
    1941 *LANE* Map 458 *(Stout, paunchy)* 3 infs, **CT, VT, ME,** He (i)s a pus-gut; 1 inf, **CT,** He has a big [pʌs] (belly); 1 inf, **eMA,** He's getting quite a pus on him. **1957** *Sat. Eve. Post Letters* **nAL,** *Pussle-gut*—not very elegant but often shortened to Puss and used as a nick-name for fat people (especially around the middle). **1965–70** *DARE* (Qu. X50, . . *A person who is very fat*) Infs **CA**15, **MD**9, **OH**72, Pus-gut; **KY**19, Pus-gutted; (Qu. X53a, . . *An oversize stomach*) Infs **CA**36, **MD**9, **MO**19, **NY**197, **OH**72, **PA**148, Pus-gut; **IL**36, Pus-guts; (Qu. X53b, *An oversize stomach that results from drinking*) Inf **VT**16, Pus-gut. **1995** Brophy *Coll.* 58 **swMO** (as of c1960), *Pus-gut.* [A] fat stomach; a fat-stomached person.

push n

1 A crowd; a group of persons of a particular sort, esp a criminal gang; rarely, a collection of things. [*OED2* 1718 →]
    1896 *DN* 1.422 **NY,** *Push:* the best society. "He's in de push." **1897** *KS Univ. Qrly.* (ser B) 6.91, *Push:* the "procession;" as, "He is in the push."—General. **1900** *DN* 2.53 [College slang], *Push.* . . A crowd. **1900** Willard *Tramping* 396, *Push:* a gang. **1913** in 1914 Stewart *Letters* 247 **WY,** A water company had met there . . the sheep-men were holding a convention . . and supper was ordered for the whole push. **1916** *DN* 4.279 **NE,** *Push.* . . = caboodle, group of persons. "He ejected the whole push." [Also Mass., Pa., Mich., Kan.] **1921** *DN* 5.117 **eKY,** *Push,* a crowd, the "whole lay-out." Old cant term. **1927** *DN* 5.460 [Underworld jargon], *Push.* . . A gang of criminal tramps or yeggs. **1927** *AmSp* 2.385 [Vagabond argot], Any kind of a gang was known as a *push,* a word credited to Australia, but I think it is a sister of the *mob* of the city underworld. **1934** Vines *Green Thicket* 13 **cnAL,** I love to foller a whole push of black suckers or red horses waverin' along. **1941** *AmSp* 16.24 **sIN,** *Push.* Group. 'I met the whole push as I was going to town.' **1942** McAtee *Dial. Grant Co. IN* 71 (as of 1890s), *Whole push* . . a whole collection of persons or things. **1986** Pederson *LAGS Concordance (The whole crowd)* 3 infs, **AL, GA, LA,** (The) whole push; 1 inf, **ceTX,** The whole push and caboodle; *(Passel)* 1 inf, **cnLA,** Push = whole bunch.

2 See **pusher.**

push broom n Also *push brush, pushing broom* **widespread, but chiefly Nth, N Midl, West** See Map
A long-handled broom that is pushed.
    1926 in 2001 *W3* File, Push Broom—Made to get the dust that is too heavy for the dry mop and a little too fine for the broom. **1954** Carson *Old Country Store* 3 **Nth,** The proprietor . . pushed the push broom. **1965–70** *DARE* (Qu. F36, . . *Kinds of brooms*) 235 Infs, **widespread, but chiefly Nth, N Midl, West;** **CA**139, **KS**19, Push brush; **MO**27, **TX**5, Push-type broom; **FL**15, Floor push broom; **OR**1, Pushing broom. **1968** Kellner *Aunt Serena* 172 **IN,** He swept out the store . . scattering Floor Compound over the boards and shoving it along with a push-broom.

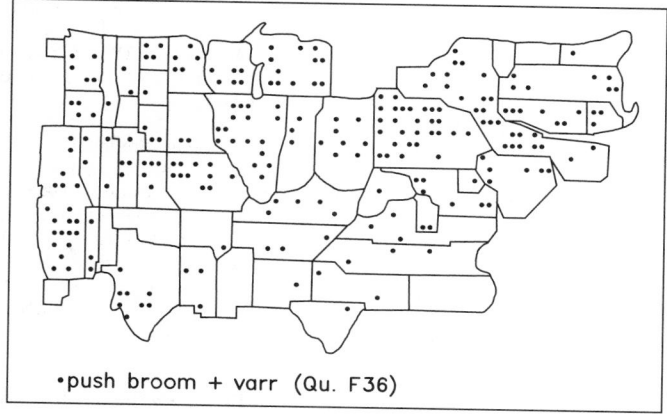

•push broom + varr (Qu. F36)

push buggy n Also *push carriage*
A **baby carriage 1** or **2.**
    c1902 Clapin *New Dict. Amer.* 324, *Push-buggy.* Baby-carriage. **1908** *German Amer. Annals* 10.40 **sePA,** *Push-buggy.* (Rare.) Baby carriage. "Put the baby in the push-buggy." . . fr. Ger. *schieb-wagen.* **1966** Dakin *Dial. Vocab. Ohio R. Valley* 2.430, *Baby carriage.* . . The name indicates the method of propulsion of a *pushcart,* but this term (and the *push buggy* attested by one speaker) suggest transition names used to differentiate between the vehicles which were pulled and those designed to be pushed. **1966–67** *DARE* (Qu. N43, *Vehicles for a small child—the kind it has to sit up in*) Inf **FL**33, Push buggy; **NY**5, Push carriage. **1986** Pederson *LAGS Concordance (Baby carriage)* 3 infs, **AL, GA, MS,** Push buggy (or buggies).

pushcart n
A **baby carriage 1** or **2.**
    [**1921** *Daily Colonist* (Victoria, B.C.) 12 Oct. 16/3 *(OED2),* (Advt.), Child's wicker push-cart, price $5.] **1950** *WELS (Vehicles for babies and small children . . that they have to sit up in)* 2 Infs, **WI,** Pushcart. **1961** Folk *Word Atlas N. LA* map 504, *Vehicle to push the baby* . . baby buggy [46% of 275 infs] . . Others [3%] push cart, go-cart, baby cart. **1965–70** *DARE* (Qu. N43, *Vehicles for a small child—the kind it has to sit up in*) 44 Infs, **scattered,** Pushcart; (Qu. N42, *Vehicles for a baby or small child—the kind it can lie down in*) Infs **TX**64, **WA**28, Pushcart. **1966** Dakin *Dial. Vocab. Ohio R. Valley* 2.430, *Baby carriage.* . . Several related terms—gocart (the most common), (baby) pushcart . . have scattered use in all the Valley states. **1986** Pederson *LAGS Concordance Gulf Region (Baby carriage)* 5 infs, Pushcart.

pushency n Also *duepushency, pushincy* [Prob blend of *push* + *urgency* or *emergency*] **chiefly Sth, S Midl**
Urgent necessity, emergency.
    1896 *DN* 1.422 **cTX,** *Pushincy:* emergency. **1898** Lloyd *Country Life* 146 **AL,** I reckon she could do that in case of a pushency. **1905** *DN* 3.64 **eNE,** *Pushency.* . . Urgency. "In case of pushency." **1909** *DN* 3.360 **eAL, wGA,** *Pushency.* . . Emergency. "In case of pushency, you can call on me." Facetious. *Ibid* 402 **nwAR,** *Pushincy.* . . Emergency. Slang. "In such a pushincy I would do what I could." **1939** Hench *Coll.* **NC,** *Pushency,* Negro portmanteau word from *push* v. and *urgency.* Told me Jan. 13, 1939. **1942** *AmSp* 17.170 **sIL,** *Duepushency.* A homemade word invented by a farmer in these parts who is described as a 'character,' and whose talk is in his self-made vocabulary.

pusher n

1 also *push, pusher boss, push-up:* A boss, foreman, or supervisor. **scattered, but esp freq West**
    1905 U.S. Forest Serv. *Bulletin* 61.50 [Logging terms], *Straw boss.* . . A subforeman in a logging camp. . . Syn.: head push. **1924** Holliday *Mining-Camp Melodies* 113 **MT,** The "Big Push". . . He has to make her pay. He's Supe, you see. **1926** *AmSp* 1.652 [Hobo lingo], *Pusher*—contractor's foreman. **1927** *DN* 5.460 [Underworld jargon], *Pusher.* . . A foreman. **1930** Williams *Logger-Talk* 18 **Pacific NW,** *Push:* A foreman. **1932** *AmSp* 7.269 [Oil field language], *Pusher.* . . A foreman. **1938** (1939) Holbrook *Holy Mackinaw* 263, *Push.* Camp foreman. *Ibid, Side push.* A minor foreman. **1939** FWP *ID Lore* 244, A bundlestiff (itinerant worker) wheeled in over the road and hit the push-up (foreman) for a job. He put him to work sky-hooking (top-loading). **1940** *AmSp* 15.220 **cwTX,** If this 'wrangler' is playful but not vicious,

the 'pusher' (foreman) may claim that 'he'll do to ride the river with.' **1941** *AmSp* 16.233 [Lumberjack jargon], *Push or Pusher.* The foreman in the field who directs the actual logging operations. **1946** *CA Folkl. Qrly.* 5.163 **MT,** The superintendent [of the mine] . . is the "push" or "big push." **1950** *Western Folkl.* 9.116 **OR** [Logger speech], *Big push, the.* The superintendent. **1958** McCulloch *Woods Words* 115 **Pacific NW,** *Main push*—The superintendent or head man around an outfit. **1959** *AmSp* 34.79 **nwCA** [Logger lingo], *Push.* . . A camp boss, assistant superintendent, or man in charge of a side in the woods. **1965–70** *DARE* (Qu. HH43a, *The top person in charge of a group of workmen*) 18 Infs, **scattered,** Pusher; (Qu. HH43b, *The assistant to the top person in charge of a group of workmen*) 14 Infs, **scattered,** Pusher; **CA**197, **MI**120, Little (*or* straw) push; **TX**95, Gang pusher; **PA**149, Pusher boss; (Qu. GG19b, *When you can see from the way a person acts that he's feeling important or independent: "He seems to think he's _____."*) Inf **PA**234, Big push; (Qu. HH17, *A person who tries to appear important, or who tries to lay down the law in his community: "He'd like to be the _____ around here."*) Infs **PA**75, **NY**195, **CT**10, Head (*or* hold, main) push. **1966** *DARE* Tape **MI**10, The camp foreman in the area, according to whatever status he happened to have, was either the straw boss or the bull of the woods or the push. **1969** *AmSp* 44.22 **Pacific NW,** *Pusher.* . . A foreman at a painting job.
2 also *push bread:* A piece of bread used to push food onto a fork or spoon.

1942 McAtee *Dial. Grant Co. IN* 51 (as of 1890s), *Pusher* . . a piece of bread used by a child to push food onto a spoon or fork. **1987** Kytle *Voices* 162 **NC** [Black], One time he got a lot of this stuff all at once, and at supper he was still so excited he kept dropping his piece of push bread. **2000** *DARE* File **AL** (as of c1970), My roommate talked about needing a pusher (a piece of bread) to get the last few pieces of food onto her fork without being so rude as to use her fingers.

pushincy See **pushency**

pushing broom See **push broom**

pushion-berry n [Scots, nEngl var of *poison;* cf *SND, EDD*]
A **bittersweet** (here: *Solanum dulcamara*).

1900 Lyons *Plant Names* 349, *S[olanum] Dulcamara.* . . Poison-berry, Pushion-berry. **1930** Sievers *Amer. Med. Plants* 11, Poisonberry, poisonflower, pushion-berry, morel.

push juice See **push water**

pushky See **puchki**

push little ducks in the water, mean enough to adj phr
Also *mean enough to push (baby) chickens in the creek;* for addit varr see quots   **chiefly Sth, S Midl, West**   See Map
Very mean.

1946 *PADS* 6.40 **eNC** (as of 1900–10), He is *mean* enough to push blind bitties (biddies) in the creek. . . Occasional. **1965–70** *DARE* (Qu. HH22c, . . *A very mean person* . . *"He's mean enough to _____."*) 13 Infs, **esp Sth, S Midl, West,** Push little ducks in the water (*or* branch); **NE**11, **TX**80, Push (baby) chickens in the creek; **NC**38, Push little biddies in the creek; **WI**34, Push little chickens in the water; **TN**24, Push up little chickens off in the water. [**1984** Wilder *You All Spoken Here* 107 **Sth,** *Push:* One pushes stalled automobiles, grocery carts, little old ladies off sidewalks, and biddies in the creek.]

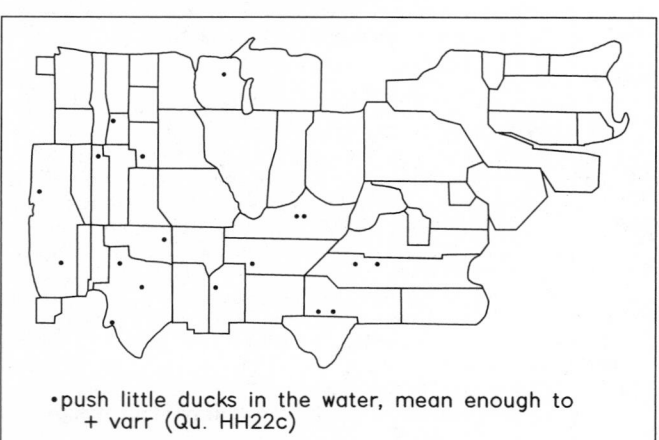

•push little ducks in the water, mean enough to
+ varr (Qu. HH22c)

push-me-cart n Cf **push plow**
1966 *DARE* FW Addit **WA**15, *Push-me-cart,* a garden cultivator.

push plow n
A garden cultivator that is pushed by the operator rather than pulled by an animal or tractor.

1969 *SC Market Bulletin* 24 July 3/4, Old garden push plow, $5. **1984** *DARE* File **csPA,** Push-plow—garden cultivator. **1986** Pederson *LAGS Concordance (Harrow)* 1 inf, **nwFL,** Push plow; *(Plow)* 2 Infs, **LA, AR,** Push plow; 1 inf, **cnAR,** Push plow—garden plow; made like any other plow; *(Tiller)* 1 inf, **cTX,** Push plows.

push pole n [Cf *DA pushing pole*]   **esp FL**
A pole for propelling a boat.

1890 *Scribner's Mag.* 7.309 **FL,** While he [=a Seminole Indian] makes or repairs his sails, nets, push-poles, or cleans his rifle, she prepares his meals. **1926** (1949) McQueen–Mizell *Hist. Okefenokee* 38, The hunters using long, forked poles known as "push poles" and standing in the stern of the boat would push it rapidly over the prairie with this forked pole. Much more speed can be made by this method than by rowing or paddling, and oars and paddles cannot be used in the Swamp. **1938** Matschat *Suwannee R.* 52 **neFL, seGA,** "Ye an' me hain't lost," Freeman Carter told the push-pole in his hand. **1965** Will *Okeechobee Boats* 77 **FL,** Charley, in his dugout canoe with a push pole but no paddle.

push row v phr, hence vbl n *push rowing*
To row facing forward.

1957 Beck *Folkl. ME* 85, 'Bout forty year ago I and my brother was tew the nothe side o' Eagle Island in a fourteen foot double ender. I was standin' on the for'r'd thwart an' Brother was aft, push-rowin'. **1975** Gould *ME Lingo* 222, *Push rowin'*—Rowing facing forward. Maine lobstermen prefer this and often call it rowin' "Maltese fashion." It violates more stylish rules of handling oars, and they say in the British and U.S. Navies it is positively forbidden. The Maine fishermen who are looking for pot buoys and trawl buoys excuse their lack of conformity by explaining that it's easier to see out of the front of your head. **1999** in 2000 *DARE* File—Internet **swCA,** It can be a challenge to handle both oars and tiller at once (especially if you want to push row, to see where you're headed). **2001** *DARE* File **ME,** There's a paragraph to describe the picture [of a wooden boat]. One sentence says "You can push row if you want to see where you're going, or pull on the oars to see where you've been." [*Ibid* **eCanada,** My father came from Gaspé, Québec, of Irish descent. He mentioned a few times, that I can remember, that he credited his health and strength to both rowing and push rowing between Plateau Island (his father's lighthouse) and the mainland at Point St. Peter's.]

push-up n[1] See **pusher**

push-up n[2] Cf **move-up, work-up**
A baseball game played with few players; see quots.

1957 *Sat. Eve. Post Letters* **GA** (as of c1905), Whenever several boys—not enough for two teams—were together, one was sure to yell "push-up one". Others would take it up, "push-up two", "three", "four", etc. The game, known as "push-up", was played with a home plate and one base. The player calling "one" was the first batter; "two" was the catcher; "three" the pitcher; the balance in the field, the lower numbers in the infield; the others in the outfield. A played [sic] kept his batting turn until put out. [If] the batter hit a fly which was caught, the catching player immediately came to bat, regardless of his previous position, thus changing the batting order as far as those two players were concerned. The other players remained in status quo. But, if the batter was put out by other methods, he took the last place in the outfield, the catcher became the batter, the pitcher became the catcher and all the other players moved up one notch nearer the coveted batting position. **1966** *DARE* Tape **AL**4, Town ball is . . referred to as "push-up" sometimes. . . You'd start in the field. Now if you caught a fly . . [you'd] immediately go to bat. . . If you caught a ball and threw it to the first baseman. . . If he failed to catch the ball you moved to first. . . The man who's on first would go to second, and on to third. Then you became pitcher, then you was catcher. . . Then he got to be . . at bat. . . This was called—I've heard it called town ball, then I've heard it called a push-up. . . Every time you'd get one out, then you'd just push up to the next station, you see, the next base.

push water n Also *push juice*   **esp S Midl**
Gasoline.

1940 *AmSp* 15.447 **eTN,** *Push water.* Gasoline. 'I want five gallons of push water.' **1968–70** *DARE* (Qu. N15a, . . *Gasoline . . cheaper kind*) Infs **GA**72, **TX**98, Push water; (Qu. N15b, . . *Gasoline . . expensive kind*) Inf **SC**57, Push juice.

pusing See **pus** v

pusley See **pussley 1a, 2**

puss n[1] See **purse** n[1]

puss n[2] See **pus-gut**

puss clover See **pussy clover**

pussel-gut See **pussle-gut**

pussey See **pussy** adj[1]

puss give me your corner See **pussy wants a corner**

pussified adj Also *pussyfied*
Effete; sissified.
  1967 *DARE* (Qu. HH2, *Names and nicknames for a citified person*) Inf **OH**7, Pussified. **1992** Martone *Townships* 175, It was months after I moved to western MA before I could really sleep in the pussified whisper of New England's windsound. **1995** Karr *Liars' Club* 74 **eTX,** She had a recipe for a black and garlicky roux that a Cajun neighbor lady had taught her. . . Yankee gumbos are full of tomatoes and okra and all manner of pussyfied spices, but that game gumbo Lecia fixed. . . was a thin, black, elemental soup that opened your sinuses . . and left you tasting garlic and sassafras root for days.

pussing See **pus** v

puss in the corner See **pussy wants a corner**

‡**pussle** v
See quot.
  1933 Rawlings *South Moon* 73 **nFL,** "The pore feller's as heavy totin' as a buck in the scrub." Another said, "It'll pussle us to git him home."

pussle-gut n Also sp *pussel-gut;* also *puzzle-gut* [Appar varr of *pussy-gut* (at **pussy** adj[1])] **chiefly Sth, S Midl** Cf **pus-gut, pussly**
A potbelly; a potbellied person; hence adj *pussle-gut(ted).*
  1909 *DN* 3.361 **eAL, wGA,** Pussle-gutted. . . Same as *pussy-gutted.* **1931** (1991) Hughes–Hurston *Mule Bone* 101 **cFL** [Black], De puzzle-gut rascal. . . we oughter have him up in conference an' put him out de Methdis' faith. **1933** Hurston in *Story* Aug 63 **FL** [Black], "He got a puzzlegut on 'im and he so chuckle-headed, he got a pone behind his neck." . . "He ain't puzzle-gutted, honey. He jes' got a corperation." **1933** Rawlings *South Moon* 133 **nFL,** "I hears folks call him and his old lady, 'Bull-bat and Whip-poor-will.' Jest somethin' about them." Lant laughed. "Sort o' pussle-gutted, eh?" **1940** Faulkner *Hamlet* 266 **MS,** Before that pussel-gutted Hampton come prowling around here. **1957** [see **pus-gut**]. **1965–68** *DARE* (Qu. X53a, . . *An oversize stomach*) Infs **GA**3, 77, **OH**32, **VA**1, 9, Pussle-gut; **AL**3, **MS**1, Pussle-gutted. **1974** Betts–Walser *NC Folkl.* 7 **cnNC,** Pusslegut: a fat person. **1974** Dabney *Mountain Spirits* 129 **cnGA,** You know they always send up the holler two revenue men. . . great big fat, pussle-gutted. You know, fellers that can't run. **1976** *NYT Mag.* 10 Oct 111 **Sth,** All watched over by a savage God, by the dead and by pussle-gutted deputies, who always went around calling black men "boy."

pussley n
1a also *pursl(e)y, pusley, pusslet, pussle(y)-weed, pussly, pussweed:* A **purslane 1,** usu *Portulaca oleracea.* **scattered, but esp freq NEast, NCent, Atlantic** See Map *somewhat oldfash*
  1805 (1904) White *Jrl.* 28 **MA,** I filled my little tin kettle with pusley for greens, which grew in a corn field there. **1833** Greene *Life Dr. Dodimus* 2.71 **eMA,** All their writin is like pussly and witch-grass—you never can know where to find it. **1892** *DN* 1.240 **MO,** Purslain or pursly [?] ['pʌslɪ]. [*DN* Ed: ['pʌslɪ] is all but universal in Michigan . . and New England.] **1893** Shands *MS Speech* 51, Pursly or Pussly ['pɜˈslɪ] or ['pʌslɪ]. The common names for *purslane.* **1899** (1912) Green *VA Folk-Speech* 339, Pussly. . . A plant. one of *purslane.* **1907** *DN* 3.197 **NH,** Pusley. . . Purslane. "Pusley makes good greens." **1909** *DN* 3.360 **eAL, wGA,** Pu(r)sley. . . Purslane. Universal. By confusion with *parsley.* "Go pull up some pussley for the pigs." **1930** Shoe-

maker *1300 Words* 48 **cPA Mts** (as of c1900), *Pursley*—Purslane. **1950** *WELS* (*What do you include under the word "greens" in your neighborhood?*) 1 Inf, **cwWI,** Pussley. **1960** Criswell *Resp. to PADS 20* **Ozarks,** Purslane (pursley, once in a while pusley). . . pig weed. **1965–70** *DARE* (Qu. S21, . . *Weeds . . that are a trouble in gardens and fields*) 80 Infs, **scattered, but esp freq NEast, N Cent, Atlantic,** Pussley; 24 Infs, **scattered,** Pursley; **IN**67, Wild pursley; **NC**49, Pusslet, Pussleweed; **OK**18, Red pursley; **SC**40, Pussley-weed; **WI**17, Puss weed; **MN**7, ['pjuzli]; (Qu. I28a, . . *Kinds of things . . you call 'greens'. . [Those that are eaten raw]*) 11 Infs, **scattered,** Pussley; **IN**67, Wild pursley; **WV**16, Pursley; (Qu. I28b, *Kinds of greens that are cooked*) Infs **CA**36, **CT**6, **MD**30, **MA**37, 58, **RI**16, Pussley; **TX**40, **VA**26, Pursley; (Qu. I35, . . *Kitchen herbs . . grown and used in cooking around here*) Inf **MA**98, Pussley; (Qu. S9, . . *Kinds of grass that are hard to get rid of*) Infs **CT**26, **NJ**58, Pussley; **OH**2, Pursley; **SC**17, . . *Kinds of plants . . that . . cause itching and swelling*) Inf **OH**98, Pussley; (Qu. BB51a, . . *Cures for corns or warts*) Inf **VA**46, Pussley. [104 of 122 total Infs old] **1986** Pederson *LAGS Concordance,* 16 infs, 5 **AL,** 6 **nwFL,** Pussley. **1991** *DARE* File **seNY,** Pussley = purslane.

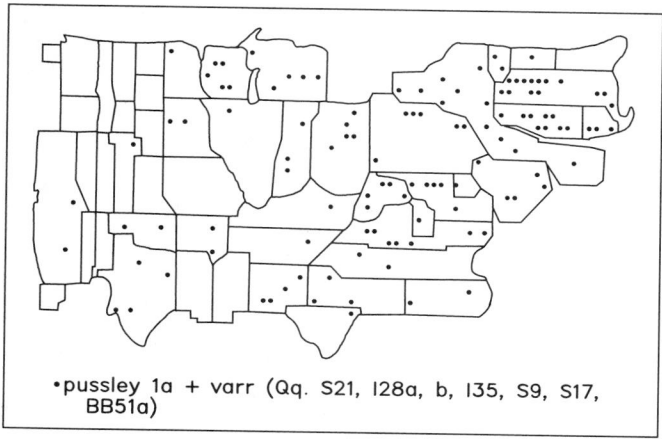

•pussley 1a + varr (Qq. S21, I28a, b, I35, S9, S17, BB51a)

b in phr *meaner than pussley* (and varr): Extremely mean or ill-tempered.
  1853 *Yankee Notions* 2.111 **NEng,** Aunt Betsey tells a story of one of her neighbors, when she lived in the country, who was "meaner than pusley." **1939** (1962) Thompson *Body & Britches* 495 **NY,** Meaner than pusley (purslane). [Proverbs] **1950** *WELS* (*A mean or disagreeable person [is] meaner than _____.*) 3 Infs, **WI,** Pussley. **1965–70** *DARE* (Qu. HH22b, . . *A very mean person . . "He's meaner than _____."*) 9 Infs, **esp NEast,** Pussley; **OH**2, Pursley; **PA**118, Pursley—the worst weed you can get in your garden; (Qu. GG38, *Somebody who is usually mean and bad tempered: "He's an awful _____."*) Inf **OH**2, Meaner than pursley.

2 also *pusley:* =**Mexican clover.**
  1925 [see **purslane 3**]. **c1967** GA Univ. *Weeds S. U.S.* 39, *Richardia scabra*—Florida purslane (pusley). . . Occasionally grazed, a honey plant.

3 =**sea lettuce 1.**
  1976 Warner *Beautiful Swimmers* 53 **Chesapeake Bay,** In some places it [=the Chesapeake] produces too much plant life. Not eelgrass, but rather the less attractive sea lettuce. "Too much pussley," Ben called it. "Clogs up your bag; spend too much time picking it out."

pussley-weed, pussly n See **pussley 1a**

pussly adj Also sp *pursley* Cf **pussle-gut**
=**pussy** adj[1]; hence n *pursley gut;* adj *pursley-gutted.*
  1950 *PADS* 14.55 **SC,** Pursley gut ['pʌslɪ], pussle gut: . . A large, flabby stomach; one having such a stomach. Sometimes abbreviated to *p.g.* by way of euphemism. Pursley-gutted, adj. **1965** *DARE* (Qu. X50, . . *A person who is very fat*) Inf **MS**59, Pussly ['pʌslɪ]. **1986** Pederson *LAGS Concordance,* 1 inf, **cwGA,** Pussly—obese.

puss'n(ully), pusson(ully), pussun(ully) See **person**

puss-weed See **pussley 1a**

pussy n
1 usu pl; also *pussycats:* =**rabbit-foot clover.** Cf **pussy clover**

1896 *Jrl. Amer. Folkl.* 9.186 **MA, Long Is. NY,** *Trifolium arvense* . . pussies, pussy-cats. **1898** [see **pussy clover**]. **1900** [see **pussy clover**]. **1922** *Amer. Botanist* 28.33, The soft furry covering of *Trifolium arvense* seems to have caught the fancy of nature-lovers to judge of such names as "rabbit's-foot clover", "hare's-foot clover", "pussy clover", "pussies," ["]pussy-cats," and "dogs and cats." **1959** Carleton *Index Herb. Plants* 96, *Pussies:* Trifolium arvense.

2 also *pussycat;* usu with modifier: **=skunk.** Cf **civet cat 2, kitty** n **1, polecat 1, woods pussy**

1916 Kephart *Camping & Woodcraft* 1.260, "Boys," I warned in a stage whisper, "for the love of God, don't breathe: there's a skunk at the foot of my bed!" . . It came straight over to the fireplace and sniffed my toes. The other boys offered all sorts of advice, and I talked brimstone back at them—we had found that pussy didn't care a hang for human speech so long as it was gently modulated. **1921** *DN* 5.113 **CA,** *Sachet kitten, sachet pussy.* . . Pole cat. Sierra Nevada. **1950** *WELS* **WI** *(Names and nicknames for the skunk)* 1 Inf, Poison pussy; 1 Inf, Sachet pussy; 1 Inf, Striped pussycat. **1961** Jackson *Mammals WI* 374, Northern Plains Skunk. . . In Wisconsin, commonly called skunk. Other names include . . striped pussy cat. **1965–70** *DARE* (Qu. P26, *Names and nicknames . . for a skunk*) 14 Infs, **scattered,** Pussycat; **MD25, NY101, 105, 233, TX54, WV14,** Stink-pussy; **CA45, NH10, NJ21, PA234,** Perfume(d) pussy; **CA168, RI4,** Striped pussycat; **GA77, TX37,** Streamlined pussy with a fluid drive; **NY74, TX9,** Stinking pussy; **OH79, VT4,** Pussy; **WV12, 13,** Mountain pussycat; **IL54,** Black pussycat, an old Polish fellow used to call them because he didn't know what they were; **MA32,** Black pussy; **MA47,** Wild pussy; **MI44,** Pole-pussy; **MI120,** Puttycat; **MN35,** Puddycat; **NH10,** Scented pussycat; **NY93,** Pussy with a stripe down its back; **NY207,** Scented pussy; **ND9,** Stripe-pussy; **VT16,** Black and white pussy. **1986** Pederson *LAGS Concordance* (Skunk, polecat) 1 inf, **nwLA,** Pussycat; 1 inf, **ceTX,** A pussy with a fluid drive; 1 inf, **csTX,** Pussycat—[the term] is quite common around here.

3 **=catbird 1.**

1956 MA Audubon Soc. *Bulletin* 40.128 **ME,** *Catbird.* . . Pussy. . . Familiar form of the ordinary name.

4 also *dust pussy, pussycat, pussy willow:* A roll of dust found under the furniture. **chiefly Nth, esp NEast** See Map Cf **kitten 1**

a1932 in 1944 *ADD* **nOH,** *Pussy.* . . A roll of dust that comes under rugs, beds, & bureaus or in the corners of the room. . . So called perh. because of the resemblance to pussy willows. **1949** *Ladies' Home Jrl.* July 141, She still dominated her sisters: while she neglected her own clothing and the dust pussies piled up under her bed and into the shoes she kept there, she stood over the girls while they . . swept around and under their beds. **1949** *WELS Suppl.* **csWI,** A friend of mine always says she can sit and read a good book and let the pussies gather under the bed and sometimes they get big enough to have kittens. **1954** *Ibid* **csWI,** Concerning the fuzz or dust formed under furniture and beds, we always called it "pussy willows." **1965–70** *DARE* (Qu. E20, *Soft rolls of dust that collect on the floor under beds or other furniture*) 16 Infs, **chiefly Nth, esp NEast,** Pussies; 11 Infs, **chiefly Nth,** Pussycats; **IL5,** Dust pussies; **IN66,** Little pussies; **IL113,** Pussy; **NY107, 128, PA60, 200, WA8,** Pussy willows. **1980** *Hand Coll.* **ID** (as of c1920), The puffs of dust and lint that collect in corners and under furniture are called "Pussies." **1982** *Greenfield Recorder* (MA) 27 Nov 6, What do you call the dust fluff that collects under the bed? I had always heard "pussycats," but a friend from Laconia, N.H., always said "house moss."

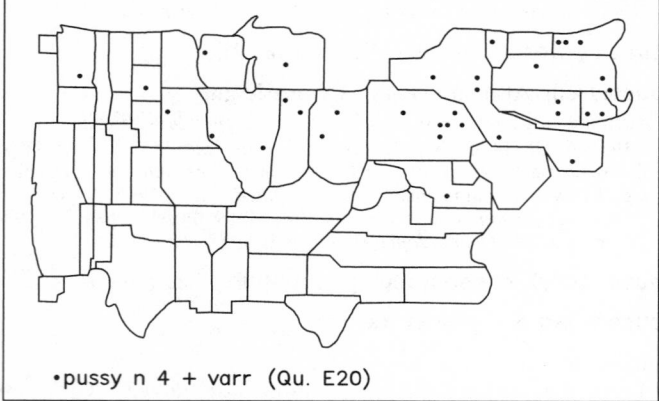

•pussy n 4 + varr (Qu. E20)

5 also *pussycat:* **=cat** n **3a, b.**

1896 *DN* 1.422 **cNY,** *Pussy:* a game played with a small bat (usually part of a broomstick) and a small block 1″ by 4″, which is also termed a *pussy.* *Ibid* 422 **seNY,** *Pussy cat:* same as *pussy* above. **1968** *DARE* (Qu. EE10, *A game in which a short stick lying on the ground is flipped into the air and then hit with a longer stick*) Infs **NJ18, 33,** Pussy.

pussy adj[1] |ˈpʌsɪ, -ɪ| Also sp *pussey* [Engl dial var of *pursy* short-winded, fat] Cf **pus-gut, pussle-gut, pussly**

Fat, bloated, potbellied; rarely, short-winded; hence n *pussy-gut(s)* a potbelly, a potbellied person; adj *pussy-gutted* potbellied.

1844 Stephens *High Life in NY* 2.92 **CT,** And then he strutted right in the door-way, as pussy and pompous as a prize pig jest afore killing time. *Ibid* 103, I thought we'd all made a purty good Thanksgiving dinner, . . and I can't tell when I've felt so big and pussy. **1894** *DN* 1.342 **wCT,** *Pussy* [pʌsɪ]: fat, corpulent, pot-bellied. **1899** (1912) Green *VA Folk-Speech* 339, *Pussy.* . . Fat; corpulent; inclined to puff and pant with slight exertion. **1906** *DN* 3.152 **nwAR,** *Pussy-gutted.* . . Corpulent. "He's terrible pussy-gutted." **1909** *DN* 3.361 **eAL, wGA,** *Pussy-gutted.* . . Corpulent, having a large abdomen. Often used as a term of contempt. "You low-lifed, pussy-gutted scounderl [sic]." *Ibid* 402 **nwAR,** *Pussy guts.* . . A corpulent man. *Ibid, Pussy-gutted.* . . "He's getting so pussy-gutted, he'll have to go through a door sideways.["] *Ibid* 414 **nME,** *Pussy.* . . Pursy. **1914** *DN* 4.78 **ME, nNH,** *Pussy.* . . Stout, fat. *Ibid* 111 **cKS,** *Pussy* [pʌsɪ]. . . Purly. **1930** Shoemaker *1300 Words* 46 **cPA Mts** (as of c1900), *Pussey*—Fat, plump-looking. **1941** *LANE* Map 458 *(Stout, paunchy),* [*Pussy* is common throughout **NEng,** although some infs characterize it as "not polite," 3 infs as rare, and 2 as old-fashioned. 6 infs specified that *pussy* was used only of men. Typical comments are: "A pussy man 'has a big belly or lots of loose fat'."; "A pussy man is fatter than a stout man."; "*Pussy,* flabby all over."] **1946** *PADS* 6.25 **ceNC** (as of 1900–10), *Pussy* [ˈpʌsɪ]. . . Pursy; fattish, bay-windowed. Said of middle-aged men who have gained weight. . . Common. **1947** *PADS* 8.20 **ceIA** (as of 1915–40), Pussy. *Ibid* 28 **neMO** (as of 1890–1922), Pussy. **1949** Webber *Backwoods Teacher* 88 **Ozarks,** A lantern-jawed ol' varmint with a big golden watch chain acrost his ol' pussy-gut an' a Bible under his arm. **1952** Brown *NC Folkl.* 1.580, *Pussy-gutted* [ˈpʌsɪ-]. . . Fat-bellied. **1958** *Sat. Eve. Post Letters* **sIN** (as of 1910–20), *Pussey.* . . Rhymes with "hussy". Used to describe a mountainous soft, fat person. Never applied to a young child or baby, but rather to depict an unhealthy, diabetic type fat in an older person. **1965–70** *DARE* (Qu. X50, *Names or nicknames for a person who is very fat*) 12 Infs, **scattered,** Pussy [proncs [ˈpʌsɪ] or [ˈpʌsɪ] recorded from three Infs]; (Qu. X53a, . . *An oversize stomach*) Inf **OK1,** He's awful pussy [ˈpʌsɪ]; **TX42,** Pussy [ˈpʌsɪ]; (Qu. X53b, *An oversize stomach that results from drinking*) Inf **AZ10,** Pussy [ˈpʌsɪ].

‡**pussy** adj[2]

1927 *DN* 5.476 **Ozarks,** *Pussy.* . . Countrified, awkard [sic]. "She's th' pussiest ol' woman in th' hull settlement."

pussyball n Cf **kittenball**

1993 *NADS Letters* **WV** (as of 1940s), When I was growing up, softball was a game for girls and for boys too young or too "soft" to play "hardball," or baseball. . . Softball was contemptuously known as "pussyball" among boys, because of the sexual slang term *pussy* for girls and women.

‡**pussy bump** n Cf **bump** n **1, fuck bump**

1970 *DARE* (Qu. X59, . . *The small infected pimples that form usually on the face*) Inf **TX86A,** Pussy bumps—if you get some pussy they'll go away. [Inf is Black]

pussycat See **pussy** n **2, 4, 5**

pussycats See **pussy** n **1**

pussy clover n Also *puss clover, pussyfoot* ~, *pussy's* ~ Cf **pussy** n **1**
=rabbit-foot clover.

1898 *Jrl. Amer. Folkl.* 11.226 **MA,** *Trifolium arvense* . . puss clover, pussy, Newton, Mass. **1900** Lyons *Plant Names* 377, Rabbit-foot Clover. . . Pussy Clover, Pussy-cats, Pussies. **1914** Georgia *Manual Weeds* 229, Rabbit-foot clover. . . Other English names. . . Pussy Clover [etc]. **1922** [see **pussy** n **1**]. **1929** *Torreya* 29.150 **ME,** Trifolium arvense, *Pussy-foot Clover.* **1959** Carleton *Index Herb. Plants* 96, *Pussy's clover:* Trifolium arvense.

pussyfied See **pussified**

pussyfoot n

1 A **saxifrage** n[2].

1879 (1888) Brush *Col.'s Opera Cloak* 72, The little saxifrage was thick along the road—"pussy-foot" Leslie called it. **1950** *WELS Suppl.* csWI, Pussy foots—Saxifrage? Same thing Mrs. Eaton calls "cat's paws" at any rate. Sometimes pron[ounced] |pusi futs|—just for fun.

2 =**cat's-breeches**.

1963 Craighead *Rocky Mt. Wildflowers* 153, Waterleaf—*Hydrophyllum capitatum*. . . Other names: Woolen-breeches, Cats-breeches, Pussyfoot. . . Waterleaf has broad, fleshy, pinnately divided leaves and globular heads of white to purplish-blue flowers closely resembling a cat's paw. Stamens are longer than rest of flower and form talons of the cat's paw.

3 A **prairie clover** (here: *Dalea obovata*).

1970 Correll *Plants TX* 830, *Petalostemum obovatum*. . . Pussyfoot. . . Sandy prairies of s. Tex., n. to Travis and Colorado cos.

pussyfoot clover See **pussy clover**

pussy give me your corner See **pussy wants a corner**

pussy-gut(s), pussy-gutted See **pussy** adj[1]

pussy in the corner See **pussy wants a corner**

pussy on the pole See **pussy wants a corner**

pussypaws n Also *pussy's paws* [See quot 1897]
A low western herb of the genus *Cistanthe*.

1897 Parsons *Wild Flowers CA* 70, Pussy's-paws is a very plentiful plant in the Sierras. . . The flower-clusters grow in a bunch, much like the pink cushions on pussy's feet, whence the pretty common name. **1949** Moldenke *Amer. Wild Flowers* 72, Common in fine gravelly or sandy soil of open places . . is the pussypaws, *Spraguea umbellata*. **1967** *DARE* FW Addit **OR**12, Mountain Buckwheat or Mount Hood Pussy Paws (among Garden Club people, *not* widespread beyond).

pussy plant n
A **lady's slipper 1**.

1968 *DARE* FW Addit **VA**15, Pussy plant—occasional name for lady slipper. Not used in polite company.

pussy's clover See **pussy clover**

pussy's ear n Cf **cat's ear 1**
A **mariposa lily** (here: either *Calochortus monophyllus* or *C. tolmiei*).

1897 Parsons *Wild Flowers CA* 278, Cat's-ears. Pussy's ears. . . Pure-white or purplish-blue flowers, which are also covered with hairs and delicately fringed with hairs on the margin. . . The children are specially fond of them, and know them as "cat's-ears" and "pussy's-ears." **1915** (1926) Armstrong–Thornber *Western Wild Flowers* 60, White Pussy's Ears—*Calochortus Maweanus*. . . Cal., Oreg. *Ibid*, Yellow Pussy's Ears. . . *Calochortus Benthami*. . . California hills. **1959** Munz–Keck *CA Flora* 1347, *C. Tolmiei*. . . Pussy Ears.

pussy's paws See **pussypaws**

pussy's tobacco n [Blend of **pussytoes** + **ladies'-tobacco**]
A **pussytoes** (here: *Antennaria plantaginifolia*).

1968 Barkley *Plants KS* 350, *Antennaria plantaginifolia*. . . Plantain-leaf Pussytoes, Ladies' Tobacco. Pussy's Tobacco.

pussytoes n Also *pussy's toes*
A woolly herb of the genus *Antennaria*. Also called **cat's-ear 3, ~-foot 3, ~-paw 2, cottonweed 1a, cudweed 2, ever-lasting n 1, Indiana tobacco, ladies'-~ a.** For other names of the common *Antennaria plantaginifolia* see **dog-toes, four-~, Indian tobacco 4, love's test, mouse-ear 2, pearly ever-lasting 2, povertyweed, pussy's tobacco, rattlesnake plantain 2, white ~.**

1892 *Jrl. Amer. Folkl.* 5.98 **MA**, *Antennaria plantaginifolia* . . pussy's toes. Worcester, Mass. **1914** Georgia *Manual Weeds* 441, Plantain-leaved everlasting—*Antennaria plantaginifolia*. . . Ladies-Tobacco, Pussy-toes. . . Labrador to Nebraska, southward to Georgia and Texas. **1937** U.S. Forest Serv. *Range Plant Hdbk.* W16, Pussytoes, often known as catsfoot, catspaws, and everlasting, is a genus of woolly, perennial

herbs well represented in the West. **1961** Douglas *My Wilderness* 20 **CO**, Pearly everlasting and pussytoes seem to march with yarrow all the way, even as they do out of Yakima, Washington. **1967** *DARE* FW Addit **OR**12, Pussytoes (related to and like pearly everlasting but a bit pink). **1968** *DARE* (Qu. S20) Inf **PA**89, Ladies' toes, pussytoes; (Qu. S26a, . . *Wildflowers*. . . *Roadside flowers*) Inf **NJ**45, Pussytoes—grow in moist acid soil, in early spring, very fragile, low to ground, whitish color. Three little petals like pussy toes hang down. **1990** *Plants SW* (Catalog) 17, *Antennaria parviflora*—Pussytoes. . . In spring little white flowers on 3 in. stalks resemble cats' paws.

pussy wants a corner n Also *possum wants a corner; puss(y) in the corner; puss(y), give me your corner;* for addit varr see quots [*OED2 puss in the corner* (at *puss* sb.[1] 5) 1709 →] Cf **corners, kitty wants a corner**
A game in which all the players but one are stationed at the corners of a room or at other specified goals, and attempt to exchange places without allowing the remaining player to occupy one of the goals.

1855 *Harper's New Mth. Mag.* 10.419 **NY**, They [=Adam and Eve] never played "blind-man's buff," or "Pussy wants a corner." **1896** *DN* 1.422 **nOH, wNY**, *Pussy-wants-a-corner*: same as *puss-in-the-corner*. **1897** *Century Illustr. Mag.* 53.349, The manœuvers . . now became more like the play of pussy-wants-a-corner. **1899** Champlin–Bostwick *Young Folks' Games* 562, *Puss in the corner*, a game played by several persons, each of whom stands in the corner of a room. One player, chosen as Puss, stands in the middle. As the others change corners . . which they try to do when the Puss is not looking, he attempts to slip into one of the corners, and if he succeed, the player thus left out must be Puss in his turn. The game may be played out of doors, when trees, posts, or stones may be used as corners. **1905** *DN* 3.91 **nwAR**, *Pussy, I want your corner*. . . The name of a game. Also called 'Pussy wants a corner.' **1909** *DN* 3.361 **eAL, wGA**, *Puss(y), gi(ve) me your corner*. . . Name of a children's game. **1909** (1923) Bancroft *Games* 163, *Puss in a corner*. **1910** *DN* 3.447 **wNY**, *Pussy wants a corner*. . . The name of a game. **1937** in 1977 *Amer. Slave Suppl. 1* 1.246 **AL**, The children of the plantation played ring games, "puss, puss in the corner," "next door neighbor." **1953** Brewster *Amer. Nonsinging Games* 96, *Pussy Wants a Corner*. . . is sometimes called also Puss, I Want Your Corner. **1957** *Sat. Eve. Post Letters* **NYC** (as of 1945–51), *Pussy in the corner*—Where you arranged yourself on a square on the sidewalk and joined hands with someone on an opposite or diagonal corner. The "Pussy" stood in the middle and tried to step on a vacant corner before you did. If there was a free corner it was declared *poison* and no one used it. [*DARE* Ed: In addition, there were other respondents who simply offered the name of the game without a description, six of whom (4 **IL**, 1 **IA**, 1 **NV**) know the game as *pussy wants a corner*, two (1 **NJ**, 1 **PA**) as *pussy in a corner*, and one (**VA**) as *puss in a corner*.] *Ibid* Philadelphia **PA** (as of 1908), *Pussy on the pole*—This was a game, played at the corner of the intersection. . . [M]any stores had awnings from their building line to the curb-line. . . [A]n average awning would have about six poles. . . Six players would get on the poles . . and try and run from one pole to the other, before the "IT" player, could grab the pole. **1965–70** *DARE* (Qu. EE2, *Games that have one extra player—when a signal is given, the players change places, and the extra one tries to get a place*) 110 Infs, **scattered exc NEng**, Pussy wants a corner; 9 Infs, **scattered**, Puss in the corner; **CA**87, **MI**34, **PA**112, Pussy in the corner; **KY**5, Puss, I want your corner; **KY**40, Pussy wants your corner; **IA**7, **NY**199, Poor pussy; **AK**5, Pussy in a corner; **CO**3, Pussy, pussy in the corner; (Qu. EE33, . . *Outdoor games* . . *that children play*) Infs **CA**136, **IL**130, **KY**11, **MI**103, 108, **PA**216, Pussy wants a corner; **CT**5, **KY**34, Puss in the corner. **1970** *DARE* Tape **MI**122, We'd play pussy wants a corner. One guy, you know, would say, "I want a corner." And then we'd all have to change and . . try to get one of the corners that we had. **2000** *NADS Letters* **MO**, I'm originally from Union, Missouri, and my grandfather taught his grandkids the game, "possum-wants-a-corner." . . The game: one person is designated the possum and must make his/her way to the other players' "houses" (meaning wherever that person stood—we usually played outside and used trees as houses) to ask for a corner. While the possum is asking for a home, the other players are switching homes behind his/her back.

pussy willow n[1] [See quot 1869]
Any of var **willows**, but esp *Salix discolor*. For other names of *S. discolor* see **bog willow, mouse bush, silver willow, swamp ~**

1869 Fuller *Uncle John* 52 **NY**, The *aments* appear before the leaves, and are covered with hairs so soft and silken, that children often call them 'Pussy-Willows.' **1900** Lyons *Plant Names* 330, *S. discolor. . . Glaucous Willow, Pussy Willow, Bog, Swamp or Silver Willow. Catkins of this and some other species called Pussy-cats.* **1942** Tehon *Fieldbook IL Shrubs* 49, The Pussy Willow is a common shrub in wet and swampy situations throughout northeastern North America. [*Ibid* 48, The staminate catkins, known as "pussies," are ¾ to 2 inches long.] **1953** Strausbaugh–Core *Flora WV* 282, *S[alix] caprea . .* goat willow, and *S. cinerea . .* gray willow, are widely planted for their large showy catkins ("pussies") developed in early spring; in West Virginia these plants are known as pussy willows. **1965–70** *DARE* (Qu. T15, *. . Kinds of swamp trees*) 22 Infs, **scattered,** Pussy willow; **MA**15, Pussy-willow bush; (Qu. S26a, *. . Wildflowers. . . Roadside flowers*) Infs **KS**8, **RI**12, Pussy willow; (Qu. S26b, *Wildflowers that grow in water or wet places*) Infs **IL**14, 26, 40, **MI**69, **MO**12, **OH**44, **PA**152, Pussy willow(s); (Qu. S26d, *Wildflowers that grow in meadows;* not asked in early QRs) Infs **MN**2, 3, Pussy willow(s); (Qu. S26e, *Other wildflowers not yet mentioned;* not asked in early QRs) Infs **MI**120, **NC**83, Pussy willow(s); (Qu. T16, *. . Kinds of trees . . 'special'*) Infs **IL**41, **RI**15, Pussy willow.

pussy willow n² See **pussy** n **4**

put v Usu |pʊt|; also |pʌt|; chiefly *Gullah* |pɪt| Pronc-spp *pit, poot, pute, putt* [All of these forms have antecedents in Scots and Engl dial; *pit* is the common form in Scots and nEngl dial, and *putt* is attested in various parts of England and in Scotland as a differentiated form along with *pit.*]

A Pronc varr.

1809 in 1956 Eliason *Tarheel Talk* 316 **cnNC,** Pute. **a1824** (1937) Guild *Jrl.* 3.272 **VT,** I see him poot it in. **1847** Hurd *Grammatical Corrector* 87, *Put* ["incorrect" pronc = [pʌt]; "correct" pronc = [pʊt]]. **1874** (1895) Eggleston *Circuit Rider* 145 **sOH** (as of early 19th cent), Jist putt! The young man pronounced the vowel in "put" very flat, as it is sounded in the first syllable of "putty." **1888** Jones *Negro Myths* 1 **GA coast,** Buh Rabbit . . mek plan to pit trouble on Buh Alligatur. **1892** *DN* 1.240 **cwMO,** *Put* [pʌt]. In Kansas City very often made a perfect rhyme for *but, cut.* [*DN* Ed: So in New England often.] **1902** *DN* 2.242 **sIL,** *Put. . .* Pronounced [pʌt] not [pʊt]. **1905** *DN* 3.103 **nwAR,** [pʌt] and [pɪt] (< *put*). **1907** *DN* 3.225 **nwAR,** *Put. . .* Pronounced [pʌt] and [pʊt]. **1909** *DN* 3.361 **eAL, wGA,** *Put. . .* Often pronounced [pʌt]. **1917** *DN* 4.398 **neOH,** *Put* [pʌt]. **1922** Gonzales *Black Border* 273 **sSC, GA coasts,** 'E binnuh cook supper, en' 'e gone to de shelf fuh git salt fuh pit een de hom'ny. **1936** *AmSp* 11.29 **eTX,** *Put . .* frequently [pʌt]. **1937** *AmSp* 12.288 **wVA,** [pʌt]. **1939** Griswold *Sea Is. Lady* 121 **csSC** (as of 1865) [Gullah], Dem Rebel buckra gwine study fuh pit we back in slabery quick as dey lan'. **1942** Hall *Smoky Mt. Speech* 37 **wNC, eTN,** One hears a distinct [ʌ] in *put.* **1961** Kurath–McDavid *Pronc. Engl.* 147, In the North and the North Midland, *put* has the vowel /ʊ/ of *book* on all social levels. From the Potomac southward and on the Delmarva Peninsula, only cultured speakers use this pronunciation consistently. In these areas *put* has the vowel /ʌ/ of *cut* rather generally in folk speech and not infrequently in the speech of the middle group. This usage prevails also in the upcountry of the Carolinas and to some extent in the valley of the Kanawha in West Virginia. Relics of /ʌ/ survive in the southern counties of Pennsylvania, in northern West Virginia, and in northeastern New England. **1967–68** *DARE* FW Addit **AR,** Put [pʌt]— heard from a "poor White" in Monticello, Ark. Overheard from old woman in grocery, Clarksville, Ark; **TN,** *Put* consistently pronounced [pʌt]. Common among country people, Maryville, Tenn; **GA,** *Put* (all tenses) pronounced [pʌt] by nearly everybody, Folkston, Georgia; **LA**27, *Put* [pʌt]—old-fashioned, and not universal among older residents. **1989** Pederson *LAGS Tech. Index* 362 **Gulf Region,** [The pronunciation of *put* was recorded in the phr *put it on.* The prevailing vowel was [ʊ], with over 600 instances, and there were 60 instances of [ʌ]; there were 4 instances each of [ə] and [ɨ], all in cases where *put* was unaccented.]

B Gram forms.

1 pres exc 3rd pers sg: usu *put;* rarely *puts.*

1960 Williams *Walk Egypt* 28 **GA,** Now I gon tell you. You gon puts in a garden, corn and sass and cow-chop. **1966** *DARE* Tape **NC**9, Some people puts salt, some don't, some people just puts a little water.

2 past: usu *put;* rarely *pot, putten(ed).* [These forms reflect the Scots, nEngl dial inflection of *pit:* past *pat* (nEngl also *pot*), past pple *putten, pitten* (also *pat, pot*).]

1919 *DN* 5.39 **eTN,** *Pot,* v., pret. and p.p. of *put.* **1938** Rawlings *Yearling* 228 **nFL,** I puttened my head back under the bearskin and I was as warm as a squirrel in a holler tree. **1946** *Word Study* Dec 8 **MO**

(as of c1900), Johnny putten 'putten' where he should have putten 'put'. **1950** *PADS* 14.55 **GA,** *Putten* [pʊtn]. . . "He putten 'putten,' where he oughta putten 'put'."

3 past pple: usu *put;* rarely *pot, putten.* [See **B**2 above]

1872 Schele de Vere *Americanisms* 445, The term [=*boughten*] is evidently due to Scotch settlers, who also say, "I have *putten* on my coat." **1919** [see **B**2 above].

C Sense.

To set out rapidly; to depart in a hurry, "clear out." **chiefly NEast, S Midl**

1834 (1925) Evans *Jrl.* 3.208 **IN,** He coragiously [sic] puts her to full flight and with whip & spur puts after her away over the plains for miles. **1839** Marryat *Diary* 1.198, Clear out, quit, and put—all mean "be off". **1851** Burke *Polly Peablossom* 51 **MO,** As soon as day crack he hollered up his puppies, an' put! **1859** Taliaferro *Fisher's R.* 138 **nwNC** (as of 1820s), I seized holt [of a bear's tail], and shouted at the top uv my voice, . . 'Charge, Chester! charge!/ On, Stanley! on!' And the bar he put, and I knowed tail holt were better than no holt, and on we went, bar'l and all, the bar at full speed. **1874** [see **A** above]. **1884** Baldwin *Yankee School-Teacher* 17 **NY,** That's what made me pull up stakes and come. Folks said I wouldn't live till spring, and I up an' put. That was two year ago come March, and I'm alive an' kickin' yit. **1902** (1904) Rowe *Maid of Bar Harbor* 55 **ME,** *Put,*—you sauce box! **1906** *DN* 3.152 **nwAR,** *Put. . .* To leave on the run. "Now you just put, and don't you show up here again." **1924** (1926) Vollmer *Sun-Up* 45 **wNC,** I reckon he wuz a puttin' fer the woods back yonder. **1929** *AmSp* 5.128 **ME,** "He put for the house" meant to hurry in. **1959** *VT Hist.* 27.153, *Put. . .* Go home; leave. . . Occasional. **1968** *DARE* FW Addit **cwNY,** *Put for home*—"get along home." **1983** *DARE* File **swME,** One of the Board members said there was no fee, "but you had better *put* before we vote to charge one." . . It reminded me of a phrase that was current in my youth: "He *put* for dear life", meaning he left in a hurry.

put n |pʊt|

An invitation.

1908 *German Amer. Annals* 10.40 **sePA, MD,** *Put. . .* Invitation. "I did not go to the party because I didn't get a put." **1968** *DARE* (Qu. FF6, *Expressions . . meaning 'to be asked to go to a party': "Did you get a _____ to the party?"*) Inf **MD**20, Put [pʊt]—old word; **MD**23, 25, Put [pʊt].

put- adv See **pretty** A2c

put a fire out See **fire** B6

put a hex on See **hex** n 2

put a hurting on See **hurting** 2

put a spider in one's biscuit v phr Also *put a spider in one's dumpling;* for addit varr see quots

To communicate bad news; to injure a person, esp by use of **conjure** n **1;** see quots.

1909 *DN* 3.361 **eAL, wGA,** *Put a spider in one's biscuit (dumpling, bread, etc.) . .* To tell one a piece of bad news, do one an injury. A facetious way of saying 'poison one.' **c1938** in 1970 Hyatt *Hoodoo* 1.256 **neVA** [Black], They say, "I'm going to put a spider in your grub." *Ibid* **NYC** [Black], If a person is going to put a spider in your head, they say, "I'm gon'a put a spider in your dumplin'." *Ibid* **seNC** [Black], "Put a spider in your dumplin'" mean [sic] they gon'a *root work* you.

put at v phr [Scots dial] **esp S Midl**

To importune, press.

1910 Johnson *Highways Rocky Mts.* 40 **ceKS,** I lived over by the crick then, and I'd be livin' there now, only the man who owned this farm put at me for a trade—half of my place for his eighty here. **1926** Roberts *Time of Man* 170 **cKY,** Next year they all put at Preacher Wilder to teach a school and he gave in. **1942** *Sat. Eve. Post* 16 May 21 **eTN,** I thought of . . how he'd put at Pap to wed me. **1968** *DARE* (Qu. OO43a, *About pleading with somebody: "She said she was afraid to be alone and _____ [with me to stay]."*) Inf **VA**15, Put at me.

put away v phr **esp Sth, S Midl** Cf **lay away** v phr **1**

To bury.

1890 *Harper's New Mth. Mag.* 80.713 **cwNH,** Don't make me tell all that—how I dug that little grave an' all! how I put her away. **1896** *Ibid* 93.777 **TN,** Betty, poor soul! came from Virginia; and even Smith

Stover can hardly be so heartless as to put her away in the land he is certain to lose. **1950** *WELS Suppl.* **cwWI,** Put away = bury. "We put ma away just a year ago today." Rare. **1952** Brown *NC Folkl.* 1.580, *Put away.* . . To bury.—Central and east. **1956** *Hall Coll.* **eTN,** I came over . . to see if you could give me a suit of clothes to put him away. *Ibid* **wNC,** Years ago when they died they made their own caskets and put 'em away. **1960** Carpenter *Tales Manchaca* 173 **cTX** (as of 1916), Tommie was undecided whether . . to "put her away" in the Negro cemetery. **1975** Gainer *Witches* 15 **sAppalachians,** *Put away* . . to bury the dead. "They tuk Pa through that door when they put him away." **1986** Pederson *LAGS Concordance,* 2 infs, seAL, cwTN, Put away = buried.

put bad mouth on See **bad mouth** n 1

putch n Also *potch* [Swiss dial *putsch* a blow, Ger *Patsch* a slap]
See quots.

1996 *DARE* File **WI,** I have learned to use . . words like . . *putch* [pʌč] (punishment), *schlucky* (messy), *tinge* (a small amount) . . at home, but I do not use them with strangers. *Ibid* **WI,** The woman I babysit for says to her children, "Be careful or I'll give you a potch [pɑč]," meaning a spanking. *Ibid* **ceWI,** Putch [pʌč] means a spanking.

putchity See **pudjicky**

putchski See **puchki**

putchy See **pudjicky**

put down v phr

1 To preserve (food), esp in a large container; hence vbl n *putting down.* [Engl dial]

1843 *Knickerbocker* 21.436 **VT,** Daniel Gilbert's property. . . *cut up* very handsomely (to borrow the common figure upon such occasions, derived from the putting down of pork for the winter). **1889** Cooke *Steadfast* 229 **NEng,** Who'll put down my pork and beef as Almiry did? **1925** *Book of Rural Life* 3.1712, The U.S. Department of Agriculture gives the following directions for putting down eggs in water glass. **1931–33** *LANE Worksheets* **seMA,** Flagroot grows in fresh water; spindle is two inches long; you eat the spindle. You take it up when young and put it down in sugar. **1940** Brown *Amer. Cooks* 634 **NC,** *Krauted Beans*—Put down green string beans with salt, like sauerkraut. **1960** Criswell *Resp. to PADS 20* **Ozarks,** *Kraut,* used only for cabbage cut up and put down in salt brine. **1965** Guthrie *Blue Hen's Chick* 7 **MT,** Putting down sauerkraut. Putting up mincemeat. **1968** *DARE* Tape **NY123,** I think of the amount of canning and preserving and pickling and putting down of foodstuffs that used to be done in our home. **1969** *DARE* (Qu. H75, *When a housewife is going to preserve fruit in jars, she says she's going to _____ some fruit*) Inf **IL37,** Put down. **1993** *DARE* File **OH,** Grandma and grandpa in Ohio . . used this phrase, but not just for canned food. . . "I put down 14 quarts of watermelon pickles yesterday." **1997** *Ibid* **nwMA,** We put up fruits and vegetables in canning jars. We put down sauerkraut in a crock with a plate on it, with a weight on top of the plate to keep it down in the brine. We put down eggs in waterglass in crocks, and we put pickles down in crocks.

2 To give up the use or practice of. [*OED2* (at *put* v.[1] 42.h) 1807 →] **esp S Midl**

c1885 in 1981 Woodward *Mary Chesnut's Civil War* 587 **SC,** Money, paper money, has depreciated so in value, they cannot live within their income, so they are going to put down their carriage and horses. **1966–70** *DARE* (Qu. DD10, . . *"He isn't smoking any more—a month ago he _____."*) Inf **MS6,** Put them down; **VA69,** Gave it up; quit [FW: "Put it down" is what Inf actually said to a friend about quitting smoking.]

3 intr: To rain. **esp S Midl** Cf **make down** v phr 3

1946 *PADS* 6.25 **swVA,** *Putting down.* . . Raining hard. . . Salem. Reported, 1940. **1952** Brown *NC Folkl.* 1.580 **cnNC,** *Put down:* . . To snow or rain a great deal.—Granville county. **1958** *PADS* 29.15 **TN,** *Putting down:* Raining. "It's just a-puttin' down out there." Rep. from Clay, Perry [Counties].

4 in phr *put (something) down for* and varr; In **conjure** n 1: to hide (something with magical power) with the purpose of doing harm to.

1935 Hurston *Mules & Men* 343 **LA** [Black], He [=a conjure doctor] names that something has been put down for the patient. **c1938** in 1970 Hyatt *Hoodoo* 1.172 **seNC** [Black], I had a aunt, she got *hurt.* . . And so she went to a *doctor* and found out that somebody had put somepin down for her. It somepin wrahpped up in a little bundle and they had it

over the door. It was some kinda powder and some sharp instruments in there, look kinda like pins. *Ibid* 193 **seSC** [Black], And den jes' like if anybody's tryin' to do anything to you or *putting down* anything for yuh—well, dat lodestone, it would move, you know. *Ibid* 198 **seNC** [Black], A *root doctor* fixed him some medicine. An it holp him, too; but you see, jis' like they put somepin down for yah, all the medicine you take it won't cure you.

pute See **put** v

puthery adj [Engl dial]
1938 Matschat *Suwannee R.* 289 **neFL, seGA,** *Puthery:* sultry or close.

put in v phr

1 To intervene, involve oneself (usu uninvited) in a discussion or affair; to butt in.

1845 (1968) Simms *Wigwam & Cabin* (1st ser) 43 **NC** (as of a1817), I thought how soon . . I might see, without being able to put in, the long yellow hair of Betsy and the babies twirling on the thumbs of some painted devil of the tribe. **1855** *Harper's New Mth. Mag.* 11.602 **LA,** The unfortunate victim hollowed out, 'Oh, Moses, if you have any love for your brother, *put in,* and divide this fight!' **1901** W.N. Harben *Westerfelt* 290 (*OED2*), You wus tellin' me . . 'at the lan' an' house wus in yore name an' her'n, an' 'at I had no right to put in. **1967** *DARE* Tape **NV2,** [Inf:] The passengers . . they only rode with you in the winter. [Aux Inf:] Could I put in? [Inf:] Yeah. [Aux Inf:] In the summertime.

2 To set in, fall to; to begin (to do something); with *to:* to start (doing something). **chiefly Sth, S Midl**

1857 in 1924 *Jrl. Amer. Hist.* [New Haven] 18.43 **RI,** Supper was announced, and we put in heartily. **1884** *Anglia* 7.268 **Sth, S Midl** [Black], *To put in w'en do* [sic] *time come* = to begin at the right time. **1926** *AmSp* 1.410 **Okefenokee GA,** An' then 'e [=a bear] put in ter gnaw on it. **1939** in 1944 *ADD* **seAL,** He put in to tell me how to drive. **1940** (1941) Bell *Swamp Water* 65 **Okefenokee GA,** "Howdy, Mr. Tulle. Hit's fixing to put in to raining, ain't it?" "Yes, sir, fixing to go at it," Tulle said. **1941** *Sat. Eve. Post* 10 May 112 **eKY,** After I'd shingled the roof, . . I put in to dig. **1986** Pederson *LAGS Concordance,* 1 inf, seAL, When I'd put in to jump from the tower; 1 inf, cwLA, Me and this little-old girl put in to make a garden; ([We] intend [to go soon]) 1 inf, cAR, Fixing to put in.

put-in n [**put in** v phr 1]
An appropriate time to speak; a matter that calls for one's involvement; uninvited comment, interference.

1853 'Mark Twain' *Hannibal Jrnl.* 25 May (*DAE*), Never speak when it's not your 'put-in.' **1883** Eggleston *Hoosier Schoolboy* 26 **IN,** It's your put-in now, Riley. **1891** Garland *Main-Travelled Roads* 61, Oh, you shet up. Who wants your put-in? **1902** Harben *A. Daniel* 301 (*DAE*), This ain't no put-in o' mine, gracious knows! **1937** (1963) Hyatt *Kiverlid* 15 **KY,** They ain't no body axin' fer your put in. **1968** Kellner *Aunt Serena* 113 **cIN** (as of c1920), "I wouldn't be s'prised she done it herself," remarked Mary Rose. "She's got guilt wrote all over her." "We don't need any of your put-in!" I began angrily, but Virginia soothed me. **1984** Wilder *You All Spoken Here* 190 **Sth,** *Put in:* Unsolicited comment, as in "Nobody ast for nary bit of her put in."

put in one's (best) licks See **lick** n 4b

put in to See **put in** v phr 2

put mouth on See **mouth** B3

put-on n **chiefly Sth, S Midl** See Map on p. 394 Cf **put-on** adj
An affected, pretentious, or insincere person; hence adj *put-on-ish* affected, pretentious.

1909 *DN* 3.361 **eAL, wGA,** *Put on.* . . To act consciously, show off. *Put-on.* . . A person who puts on. . . "He's a regular *put-on.*" **1948** Cather *Old Beauty* 135 **NE,** Folks in middle age make a mistake when they think they can better themselves. They can't, not if they have any heart. And the other kind don't matter—they aren't real people—just poor put-ons that try to be like the advertisements. **1966–70** *DARE* (Qu. HH2, *Names and nicknames for a citified person*) Inf **TN65,** Put-on; (Qu. HH8, *A person who likes to brag*) Inf **GA13,** Put-on; (Qu. HH35, *A woman who puts on a lot of airs: "She's too _____ for me."*) Inf **GA83,** Much of a put-on; **AL4, IN49, MS64, 80, NC63, NY217, SC69,** Put-on-ish; (Qu. II20a, *A person who tries too hard to gain somebody else's favor: "He's an awful _____."*) Infs **AL30,**

KY36, Put-on; (Qu. II23, *Joking names for the people who are, or think they are, the best society of a community: The _____*) Inf **KY**36, Put-ons; (Qu. II35, *A person who is disliked because he seems to think he knows everything*) Inf **GA**13, Put-on. **1986** Pederson *LAGS Concordance,* 1 inf, **nwTN,** No put-on—of "common-type person."

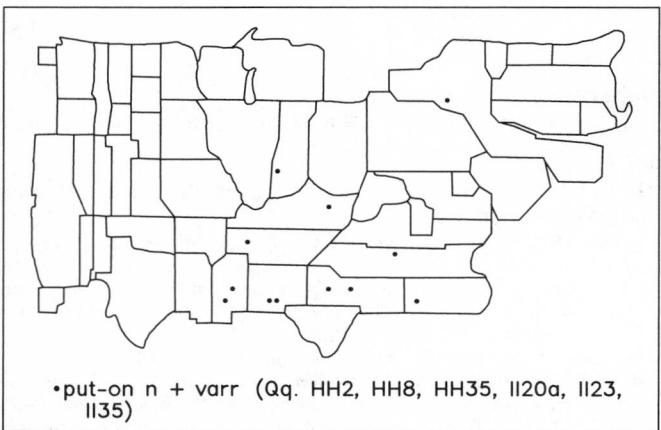

•put-on n + varr (Qq. HH2, HH8, HH35, II20a, II23, II35)

put-on adj [Appar transf from *put-on* assumed, feigned] Cf **put-on** n

Of a person: pretentious, affected.

1965–70 *DARE* (Qu. HH35, *A woman who puts on a lot of airs: "She's too _____ for me."*) 11 Infs, **scattered,** Put-on.

put on a nose bag See **nose bag**

put one in the dozen(s) See **dozen** n **B1**

put one's feet under the table See **foot** n **C5c**

put one's foot on (something) See **foot** n **C5h**

put one's foot up See **foot** n **C5e**

put one's mouth on v phr For addit varr see quots **Sth** Cf **bad mouth** n

Fig: to put a curse on.

1937 in 1977 *Amer. Slave Suppl. 1* 1.327 **AL** [Black], The Elder indignantly "put his mouth on him, and he will have bad luck from now on." **1938** Rawlings *Yearling* 20 **nFL,** Ora Baxter was plainly built for childbearing. But it had seemed as though his seed were as puny as himself. "Or Lem put a mouth on me," he thought. The babies were frail, and . . they sickened and died. **c1938** in 1970 Hyatt *Hoodoo* 1.256 **seVA** [Black], They claim that older people *put their mouth on you.* They predict something that is going to happen to you. They say to you, "That's all right, seven years will never rot." That means you will have tough luck. While saying that they point the forefinger of their right hand at you. That is sure tough luck for you. **1950** *PADS* 14.47 **SC,** Mouth, *mouf.* . . Bad luck; only in the phrase *to put mouf on,* to conjure, and cause to have bad luck. **1952** Brown *NC Folkl.* 1.567, Mouth, to put *(one's) _____ on (a person):* . . To curse one.—Chapel Hill.

put one's name in the dinner pot See **pot 10**

put-on-ish See **put-on** n

put on the dog(s) See **dog** n[1] **B5a**

put on the fan See **fan, turn on the**

put on the high-hat See **high-hat** n **2**

put on the morral See **morral**

put on the nose bag See **nose bag**

put out v phr

1 intr: To leaf out; of leaves, grass, etc: to come out, sprout. [Cf *OED2 put out* (at *put* v.[1] 48.1) 1626 →, the corresponding tr sense]

1806 (1808) Gass *Jrl.* 328 **MD, WV,** The grass and plants here are just putting out. **1941** in 1944 *ADD* **KY,** The part of Kentucky I'm from, the trees don't start puttin' out till the last of May. **1941** Stuart *Men of*

Mts. 184 **KY,** The Doctor said if he could pull him through the spring till the leaves quit putting out, then he would be all right till the leaves started to fall again. **1967** Green *Horse Tradin'* 281 **TX,** It was spring of the year and grass had put out. The mesquites were leafing out.

2 intr: To work hard. **esp Sth** See Map

1938 Rawlings *Yearling* 397 **nFL,** Pity hit take a thing like this to make you put out. **1965–70** *DARE* (Qu. JJ26, *If somebody has been doing poor work or not enough, the boss might say, "If he wants to keep his job he'd better _____."*) Infs **DE**1, 3, **GA**9, 73, **MA**58, **MS**52, **NC**17, Put out; (Qu. KK29, *To start working very hard: "He was slow at first but now he's really _____."*) Infs **FL**6, **GA**5, 11, **MT**1, **NC**38, **SC**19, 24, **TX**95, Putting out; (Qu. LL32, *Expressions meaning that one man's ability is not nearly as great as another man's: "John can't [or doesn't, or isn't] _____ Bill."*) Inf **PA**108, Can't put out like; **VA**26, Put out like Bill does. **1968** *Current Slang* 3.1.11 **MN,** Put out. . . To study diligently.—College students, both sexes.

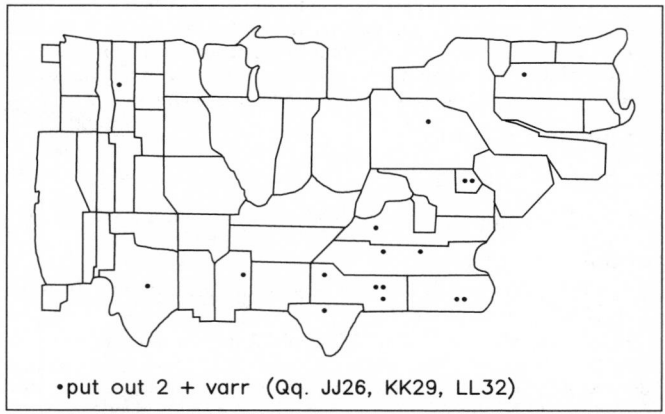

•put out 2 + varr (Qq. JJ26, KK29, LL32)

put over v phr [*OED2 put* v. 50.c 1593 →; "Now *dial.*"]

To pass, while away (time).

1925 Dargan *Highland Annals* 59 (*Montgomery Coll.*) **wNC,** I finds ol' Jim so out o' heart about her, I stays to help him put over a couple o' hours.

put over one's head See **head** n **D5**

puts See **put** v **B1**

put (a slave) in one's pocket See **pocket** n **9**

put (something) down for See **put down 4**

putt See **put** v

putten See **put** v **B2, 3**

puttened See **put** v **B2**

put the bad mouth on See **bad mouth** n **1**

put the bag on See **bag** n **B**

put the ding on See **ding** v[1] **4**

put the fixment(s) on See **fixment** n **3**

put the flookan on one See **flookan 2**

put the hex on See **hex** n **2**

put through a course of sprouts See **sprouts**

putting down See **put down 1**

put-together(s) n

In phr *in all one's put-togethers* and var: In one's whole life; in one's experience.

[**1862** in 1883 U.S. War Dept. *War of Rebellion* 1st ser 8.169, In all my life put together of wine and ardent spirits I never drank so much as one gallon.] **1955** *AmSp* 30.154 **WV,** I never saw anything like that in all my *put-togethers.* **c1955** in 1965 *DARE* File, [In all my] born days. Common. Not quite so common is "in all my put-togethers." **1986** Pederson *LAGS Concordance,* 1 inf, **nwMS,** In your whole put together [Pederson: =in your whole life?]

putty adj See **pretty** A1c

putty v Also with *around* [Var of *putter*] **esp ME**
To occupy oneself with trifles; to idle.
1943 *LANE* Map 568 *(Loafing)* 4 infs, **ME**, Puttying around. **1966** *DARE* (Qu. KK31, *To go about aimlessly looking for distraction: "He doesn't have anything to do, so he's just _____ around."*) Inf **MS**45, Puttying. **1975** Gould *ME Lingo* 222, *Putty*—For putter: "Rainy day, so I puttied with the catches on the kitchen cupboards." . . To *putty* around is to dawdle, and to be busy with unimportant things.

puttylegs n
A **black duck** 1 (here: *Anas rubripes*).
1955 MA Audubon Soc. *Bulletin* 39.314 **MA**, Black Duck. . . Puddle Duck, Puttylegs [etc.].

putty, not to know v phr Also *not to know shit from putty*
To be stupid or ignorant.
1896 *DN* 1.422 **NY, nOH**, *Putty:* "He don't know putty," he doesn't know anything. **1968–69** *DARE* (Qu. JJ15b, *Sayings about a person who seems to you very stupid: "He doesn't know _____."*) Infs **NY**88, 165, Putty; **IA**31, Shit from putty. **1983** *DARE* File **ceWI**, Someone doesn't know putty—ignorant.

puttyroot n Also *puttyroot orchid* [See quot 1837]
An orchid (*Aplectrum hyemale*). Also called **Adam-and-Eve** 1, **Adam-and-Eve-and-their-son**
1822 Eaton *Botany* 250, *[Corallorhiza] hyemalis* . . adam and eve, putty root. . . A cement resembling putty may be made of the root. **1837** Darlington *Flora Cestrica* 511 **sePA**, Winter Aplectrum. *Vulgò* Adam & Eve. Putty-root. . . The *tubers* contain a viscid gum, which, according to *Pursh*, affords a strong cement for broken china, or glass. **1910** Graves *Flowering Plants* 136 **CT**, Putty-root. Adam-and-Eve. . . The root is medicinal. **1940** Steyermark *Flora MO* 100, Adam-and-Eve, Putty Root (*Aplectrum hyemale*). **1948** Wherry *Wild Flower Guide* 44, Putty-root Orchid. **1968** *DARE* (Qu. S26c, *Wildflowers that grow in woods*) Inf **PA**99, Puttyroot. **1985** Wilkinson *Moonshine* 91 **neNC**, Conjure doctors are also called root doctors because they sell Adam and Eve roots, which they collect from ditch banks and bottle up in little vials. Putty root is what they are.

put up v phr
1 To put away, stow away; to save for future use. **chiefly Sth, S Midl** See Map
1932 Stong *State Fair* 255 **IA**, Would you mind putting up the truck? **1965–70** *DARE* (Qu. Y47, *To hide something away for future use: "I know he's got it _____ somewhere."*) 21 Infs, **esp Sth, S Midl, TX**, Put up; **MD**20, Put up for safekeeping; (Qu. E21, . . *About a room that needs to be put in order* . . "*I'm just going to _____ this room.*") Inf **NC**16, Put up my trash. **1967** *DARE* Tape **TX**33, He was always real neat when he was little, and he kept all of his things picked up and put up. . . I found the dog put up very carefully in Stephen's toy box along with the rest of his toys! **1969** *DARE* FW Addit **KY**, Put up—to store, put away, or put in storage as in a closet; **NY**, I've put up the groceries, i.e., put them away; **cwNC**, Put it up—put it away. **1973** Patrick *Coll.* **cAL**, Put up—save (money). He put up more than a hundred dollars. **1979** Gillespie–Fraser *To Be Or Not To Bop* 384 [Black], "Is this an arrest?" I asked. "No, they'd just like to speak to you." "Well, do you

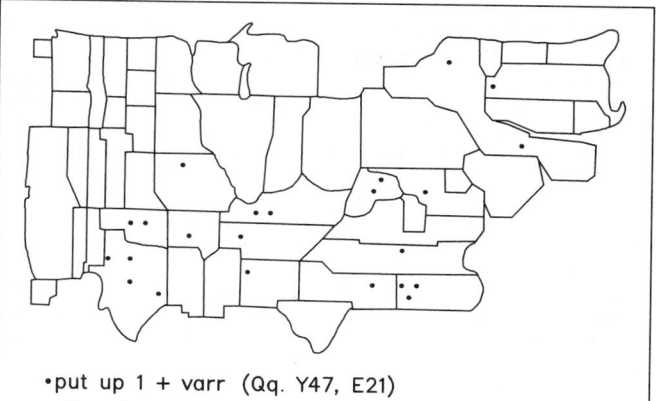

•put up 1 + varr (Qq. Y47, E21)

mind if I go upstairs and put up my camera?" . . I went upstairs and put up my camera and came back and went with him. **1986** *DARE* File **cnGA**, *Put Up* (Coffee). . . In Atlanta put up meant put away in the cupboard. **2000** *DARE* File **TX**, Also, we seem to use "put up" differently around here. In TX it means "to put away," as in "put up your toys."

2 To flush (game) from cover. **esp Nth**
1926 in **1931** McCorrison *Letters Fraternity* 105 **NEng**, But if he is not gun shy . . time and patience I believe will give us a dog to be proud of. I wish you were here tomorrow morning—to shoot the birds *I think* I could put up with Mac. **1950** *WELS* (When a hunter or dog comes up on a game animal or bird and makes it run or fly) 2 Infs, **WI**, Put up. **1966–69** *DARE* (Qu. P39b, *If a hunter or a dog makes a bird or a covey fly*) Infs **IL**41, **NM**13, **NY**191, **NY**219, Put them (*or* it, him) up; **NY**1, Puts it up; **RI**15, Put up the bird. **1985** Wilkinson *Moonshine* 128 **NEast**, In about a mile we turned onto a dirt road and travelled across a plowed field, putting up birds and dust, and when we reached a secluded corner, by some tall woods, Garland parked. **1985** Rattray *Advent. Dimon* 127 **Long Is. NY**, "Helloooo," I shouted, and the echoes helloooed up the creek, putting up some ducks. **1999** Proulx *Close Range* 25 **WY**, They rode along the creek and put up a pair of mallards who flew downstream.

3 To set to cooking; to prepare (food or drink, esp coffee). **chiefly NYC, seNY**
1958 Humphrey *Home from the Hill* 99 **neTX**, I jumped out of bed and run in and lit the stove and put the coffee up. . . I went back to the kitchen and laid the table. The coffee was perking by that time. **1968–69** *DARE* (Qu. H73, . . *Preparing coffee: the housewife says, "I think I'll go and _____ some coffee."*) Inf **NY**67, Put up; **CA**132, Put up—old-fashioned. **1972** *NYT Article Letters* **NY**, "To put up" meaning to cook or prepare, as in "I'm going to put up the chicken now." **1982** *NADS Letters*, I grew up in New York City (born in 1948). . . There are two expressions which always seem curious to my Oregon-born husband and also, to friends in various parts of the country. The first is very much in use today: "put up the water" for "heat up the water." **1986** *DARE* File **NJ, NY**, *Put Up* (Coffee)—I grew up hearing this term used to mean *prepare* coffee, tea, etc. This seems to be the New York, New Jersey meaning. **1993** Isaacs *After All* 25 **Long Is. NY**, Gevinski returned to the library, loudly sipping what smelled like overboiled convenience-store coffee from a cardboard cup. . . "I'd have been glad to put up a pot of coffee or make some tea." **1995** *DARE* File **NY**, Thanks to Alison . . , who puts up coffee overnight as she puts out cats. *Ibid* **NYC**, I remember hearing about putting up coffee. . . This was Brooklyn in the 50's. *Ibid* **NYC**, *Put up*—When requesting someone to make or prepare coffee, "Put up the coffee" was the usual expression, and even though I have not lived in New York for 25 years, that is the idiom which naturally comes to me and which I still use. **1996** Isaacs *Lily White* 339 **Long Is. NY**, Nice as nice can be. She put up a pot of coffee and defrosted a Mrs. Smith apple pie for the crime scene crew.

4 To pay court, show affection (to). Cf **set up** v phr **2**, DS AA1
1941 *LANE* Map 404 *(Courting her)* 1 inf, **sME**, Puttin' up to her; making eyes at her.

5 To lay (a baby) down.
1969 *DARE* FW Addit **cnCT**, Put her up—put the baby to sleep.

6 Of the wind or tide: to increase.
1905 Wasson *Green Shay* 186 **NEng**, Yes, I know well the tide is puttin' up [Footnote: Increasing] all this week on the full o' the moon. **1932** Wasson *Sailing Days* 49 **cME coast**, Seem's though they cal'lated to haul her [=a boat] a dite further ahead afore strippin' of her, and as the tides was puttin' up for a high run, they was in hopes of layin' her in exactly the right place maybe the very next day. **1971** Green *Village Horse Doctor* 7 **cwTX** (as of 1940s), During this early-morning session that I was stretchin' an ear out for, I heard the argument that the wind was puttin' up as it blew down the main street, which ran north and south, so I decided I would hole up here for a few days until the weather broke.

put up a holler See **holler** n[1] C4

put up a poor mouth See **poor mouth**

putz n |puts| [Ger *putz* a decoration] **chiefly PaGer area**
A Nativity scene, esp one placed beneath a Christmas tree; hence vbl n *putzing* visiting neighbors to look at their Nativity scenes.

1902 *NYT Mag.* 14 Dec 15 **cePA,** Only the chosen few can afford to have a really impressive "putz" which fills half a room, and represents a landscape in miniature. . . This more elaborate "putz" requires not only money for its erection, but artistic handiwork. **1926** *Ladies' Home Jrnl.* Dec. 82/2 *(DA),* The putz is simply the pictured story of the Nativity, built near or at the base of the Christmas tree. **1938** Hark *Hex* 186 **cePA,** Everybody's curious to know what kind of putz everybody else has this year, so they go around visiting. **1950** Klees *PA Dutch* 422, Over Bethlehem and Nazareth way the Moravians baked white and brown Christmas cookies, which they served with wine to callers who came between Christmas and Twelfth Night to see the putz. **1964** *This Week Mag.* 28 Nov 16 *(Mathews Coll.)* **cePA,** Throughout Christmas neighbors "go putzing" to admire each other's handiwork. Every door is open to visitors. Coffee or tea is served and plates of cookies are passed. **1968** *DARE* (Qu. FF9, *A Christmas gathering, at church or at someone's home, where there are songs and presents:* "*Are you going to the* _____?") Inf **NJ29,** Pennsylvania Dutch call a Christmas display a putz. **1980** *Americana* 8.78 **cePA,** Visitors may view the elaborate Christmas putz, or crèche, at the Christian Education Building. *Ibid* 29 **cnNC,** The Christmas putz or nativity scene may also be viewed. **1987** *Jrl. Engl. Ling.* 20.173 **ePA,** [B]oth informants who used the term [= *putz*] had lived in Allentown for a number of years. Seven other informants [out of 100 total] indicated that they have heard it, but four of them know it only in reference to particular church exhibits of the Moravians. Lancaster County residents have an opportunity to learn the word *putz* because of the publicity surrounding the annual *putz* of the Lititz Moravian Church. . . Such publicity, however, has not made *putz* a common term. **1995** *DARE* File **csWI** (as of 1940s), The Christmas Putz [pʊtz] was used in Dane Co. Wis. for what is now usually called a *creche* or just a plain *manger scene* in New England.

putz v |pʌts| Usu with *around;* rarely *putzy* [Etym uncert; perh var of **futz;** cf also Yiddish *putz* penis, contemptible person; Ger *putzen* to clean, decorate]   **esp wGt Lakes**   See Map
=**futz 1.**

   1950 *WELS (When somebody goes around looking for something to do to amuse himself:* "*He doesn't have much to do today, so he's just* _____.") 2 Infs, **WI,** Putzing around. **1965–70** *DARE* (Qu. A10, . . *Doing little unimportant things:* . . "*What are you doing?*" . . "*Nothing in particular—I'm just* _____.") Infs **MI**122, **MN**33, 34, **NY**76, **PA**134, Putzing around; **MI**108, Putzing ['pʌtsɪn] around; **MN**22, Putzing; **CA**4, Putzying; (Qu. Y27, *To go about aimlessly, with nothing to do:* "*He's always* _____ *around the drugstore.*") Inf **WI**48, Putzing ['pʌt,sɪn]; (Qu. KK31, *To go about aimlessly looking for distraction:* "*He doesn't have anything to do, so he's just* _____ *around.*") Inf **MI**46, Putzing ['pʌtsɪn]. [9 of 10 Infs female] **1982** Rosten *Hooray for Yiddish* 263, *Putz*—Rhymes with "cuts." . . *As a verb.* . . To waste time (as the English "futz"). **1983** *DARE* File **MN,** *(About little unimportant things: somebody asks,* "*What are you doing?*" *and you answer,* "*Nothing in particular—I'm just* _____.") Putzing around. **1993** *Capital Times* (Madison WI) 29 Nov sec A 7/3, I'm just useless, I sort of putz around all day. **1994** *Ibid* 8 Dec sec B 1/2, [She] has always been an artist. First paint-by-number, then creating her own little designs. . . always "putzing" with art. **1997** *DARE* File **sePA,** When you spend a lot of time not doing much: "I was just putzing around at the flea market all day." **2000** *NADS Letters* **MN,** Rutz around = putz around = putter. **2000** *DARE* File **seWI** (as of 1960), When I was a kid my mother would say she was just putzing ['pʌtsɪn] around if she was filling time with minor tasks. She still uses this expression.

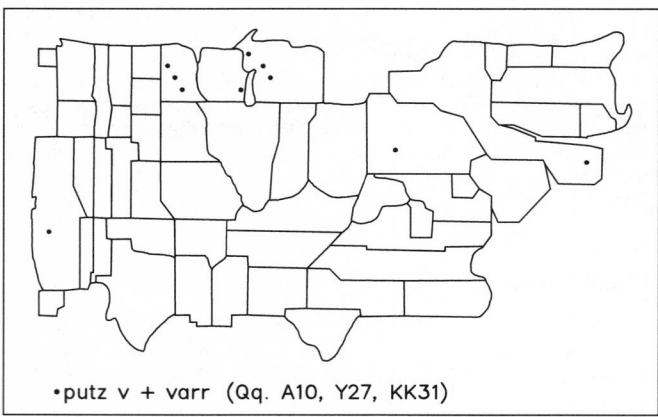

• putz v + varr (Qq. A10, Y27, KK31)

putzy See **putz** v

puuchkii See **puchki**

puu-puu See **pupu**

puxy See **pudjicky**

puzzle-gut See **pussle-gut**

puzzle-love See **love-in-a-puzzle**

pwig See **poig**

pya See **pia**

pyanna See **piano**

pyazzuh See **piazza**

pyeerten See **pearten**

pyert See **peart** adj

pye weed n
=**Joe-Pye weed 1.**

   1961 Douglas *My Wilderness* 184 **MD,** More conspicuous was the common pye weed with its pink flowers and serrated leaves which have a vanilla-like scent when crushed. This flower was named for the old Indian medicine man, Joe Pye, who practiced his art in Massachusetts in the late eighteenth century.

pygmy See **pygmy owl**

pygmy cedar n   Also *pigmy cedar*
An evergreen desert shrub (*Peucephyllum schottii*). Also called **desert fir**

   1925 Jepson *Manual Plants CA* 1158, *P[eucephyllum] schottii.* . . Pigmy Cedar. Glabrous very much branched shrub 3 to 9 ft. high. . . Washes of the foothills and gravelly sides of cañons . . Mohave Desert; Colorado Desert; e. to Ariz., s. to L. Cal. **1957** Jaeger *N. Amer. Deserts* 270, Desert Fir or Pigmy Cedar. . . A rounded, dark-green evergreen shrub of medium height with abundant fir-like leaves and light-yellow, bell-shaped flower heads.

pygmy owl n   Also *pigmy owl, pygmy*
A small western owl of the genus *Glaucidium* (here: usu *G. gnoma,* but also *G. brasilianum*).

   1858 Baird *Birds* 62, *Glaucidium gnoma.* . . The Pigmy Owl. . . The smallest owl known to inhabit North America. **1898** (1900) Davie *Nests N. Amer. Birds* 247, The Pigmy Owl feeds upon insects and the smaller rodents, which it hunts by day as well as by night. **1923** Dawson *Birds CA* 3.1128, In spite of his insignificant size, the Pigmy is a dashing little brigand, and no bird up to the size of a Robin is safe from its clutches. **1961** Ligon *NM Birds* 144, In the Sacramento Mountains one sunshiny morning, the author timed the whistling of a Pygmy perched near the top of a pine. **1977** Udvardy *Audubon Field Guide Birds* 693, Pygmy Owl. . . Sparrow-sized.

pygmy pocket rat See **pocket rat 3**

pygmy rattlesnake n   Also *pigmy rattler,* ~ *rattlesnake, pygmy rattler*
A small **rattlesnake 1** (*Sistrurus miliarius*) of the southeastern US. Also called **ground rattlesnake 1**

   1921 *Outing* Aug 217, The pigmy rattlesnake (known also as the hognosed rattler) is found in the Southeastern States. **1928** Baylor Univ. Museum *Contrib.* 16.19 **eTX,** Pigmy Rattlesnake. . . This is the Ground Rattlesnake of eastern Texas from Texarkana south to Houston. **1952** Ditmars *N. Amer. Snakes* 245, The range of the Pygmy Rattlesnake [extends] through the entire southeastern region (except in the higher mountains) from the Carolinas to Florida and westward to Oklahoma and Texas. **1966–70** *DARE* (Qu. P25, . . *Kinds of snakes*) Infs **GA**19, 25, 76, **LA**34, **MI**112, **TX**11, Pygmy rattler; **FL**16, Pygmy rattlesnake. **1967** *Dothan Eagle* (AL) 24 Feb 5/2, Jones said $15 will be given for the largest number of coral snakes entered and $15 for the largest number of Pigmy or Ground Rattlers. **1972** GA Dept. Ag. *Farmers Market Bulletin* 24 May 1/3, Species of rattlesnakes found in Georgia are the eastern diamond back, the timber rattler, the pigmy rattler, and the canebrake rattler.

pykle See **pightle**

pyo(re) See **pure**

pyramid flower n Also *pyramid (plant)* Cf **monument plant**
A **columbo** (here: *Frasera caroliniensis*).

1822 Eaton *Botany* 282, *Frasera* . . *caroliniensis* . . pyramid flower, columbo root. **1876** Hobbs *Bot. Hdbk.* 94, Pyramid flower, Pyramid plant, American columbo, Frasera Carolinensis. **1890** *Century Dict.* 4873, Pyramid. . . The American columbo, or Indian lettuce, *Frasera Carolinensis.* **1949** Moldenke *Amer. Wild Flowers* 230, The yellow gentian or pyramidflower *F. carolinensis,* growing up to 7 feet tall, is the only eastern representative of the group.

pyrine See **praline**

pyrrhuloxia n
Std: a **grosbeak** (here: *Cardinalis sinuatus*). Also called **gray cardinal, ~ grosbeak, Mexican cardinal**

pytel See **pightle**

pyxie moss n Also *pixie moss, pyxie*
A mosslike trailing evergreen (*Pyxidanthera barbulata*). Also called **flowering moss 1, pine-barren beauty 1**

1882 *Harper's New Mth. Mag.* 65.65, The delicate pyxie *(Pyxidanthera barbulata),* a little prostrate trailing evergreen, forming dense tufts or masses. . . is strictly a pine-barren plant, and its locality is confined to New Jersey and the Carolinas. . . When we find its haunts, it is often in such profusion that the ground is thickly carpeted with its delicate sprays. **1892** *Jrl. Amer. Folkl.* 5.100 **NJ,** *Pyxidanthera barbulata,* pyxie moss. **1941** Writers' Program *Guide SC* 15, Spring flowers are abundant and beautiful, and here and there is found one of the loveliest little plants in the State—the pyxie, also known as flowering moss and pine barren beauty. **1956** [see **sand myrtle 1**]. **c1991** SC Forestry Comm. *Sand Hills* [5] **neSC,** Pixie Moss. . . has a delicate pink bloom and a fern-like appearance. *Ibid* [6], Vegetation on the mountain. . . includes . . the diminutive pixie moss. **1997** *NADS Letters, Pixie moss* is a type of plant that grows in North and South Carolina. It's called "Well's (sandhill) Pixie-Moss" there, and its Latin name is *Pyxidanthera barbulata.* It is, I believe, now on the endangered species list.

q-ter n Also *cue, cute, cutor, k(y)uter, q, q.t., quetor;* for addit varr see quots [Varr of *quarter*]

A twenty-five-cent piece, quarter; a tip, esp of twenty-five cents; one who tips this amount.

1927 *AmSp* 2.390 [Vagabond argot], A dime is a *deemer;* a quarter, a *kyuter.* **1929** *AmSp* 4.342 [Vagabond lingo], *Kuter*—A quarter dollar. **1931** *AmSp* 7.106 [Underworld argot], *Cutor. . .* A twenty-five-cent piece. *Ibid* 113, *Quetor. . .* A twenty-five cent piece. **1937** *AmSp* 12.155 [Caddy terms], A *fish* and a *Q* is equivalent to a dollar and a quarter, the nominal caddy fee. **1939** *AmSp* 14.240 **Los Angeles CA** [Hotel slang], *Quetor.* Twenty-five cent tip; one who tips a quarter. **1942** Berrey–Van den Bark *Amer. Slang* 559.13, *Quarter.* Cute, cutor, . . kuter, kyuter, q.t., quetor, qutor. **1968–70** *DARE* (Qu. U23, *. . A 25-cent piece)* Inf **PA**94, Q-ter [kjutɚ]; **VA**73, Cue [kju]. [Both Infs young] **1970** Abrahams *Deep Down* 265 **PA** [Black], *Cue*—Used here to mean *tip* in the sense of money given for services. **1970** Major *Dict. Afro-Amer. Slang* 43, *Cue:* a tip, money given to a waitress or waiter as a token of gratitude.

quabird n Also *quawbird* [From its cry] Cf **quack 1, quawk** n[2] **1**

A **night heron,** usu *Nycticorax nycticorax.*

1791 Bartram *Travels* 293 **S Atl,** A[rdea] clamator, corpore subceruleo [=the crying heron with bluish body], the quaw bird, or frogcatcher. **1813** (1824) Wilson *Amer. Ornith.* 7.110, The food of the Night Heron, or Qua-bird, is chiefly composed of small fish, which it takes by night. **1834** Nuttall *Manual Ornith.* 2.54, *Qua Bird,* or *American Night Heron.* [*Ibid* 55, They utter a sort of recognition call, like the guttural sound of the syllable '*kwah,* uttered in so hollow and sepulchral a tone, as almost to resemble the retchings of a vomiting person.] **1835** Audubon *Ornith. Biog.* 3.275, The Night Heron. . . in South Carolina. . . is named "the Indian Pullet," in Lower Louisiana the Creoles call it *"Gros-bec,"* the inhabitants of East Florida know it under the name of "Indian Hen," and in our Eastern States its usual appellation is "Qua Bird." **1874** NY Acad. Sci. *Annals Lyceum Nat. Hist.* 10.386, *N[yctiardea] grisea. . .* Black-crowned Night Heron; "Qua Bird." Summer sojourner. **1903** Dawson *Birds OH* 2.477, *Black-crowned Night Heron. . .* Qua-bird; Quawk; Night Squawk. **1917** *DN* 4.426 **LA,** *Gros-bec. . .* The yellow-crowned night heron . . also called *qua-bird.* **1968** *DARE* (Qu. Q3, *. . Birds that come out only after dark)* Inf **GA**28, [kwo] bird.

quack n Cf **quawk** n[2]

1 also *quag, quak:* =**night heron.** Cf **quabird**

1844 Giraud *Birds Long Is.* 280 **seNY,** When roaming about at night, it [=the black-crowned night heron] is heard uttering at intervals a loud guttural sound,—from which it has by gunners received the appellation of "Quack" or "Quawk." **1955** MA Audubon Soc. *Bulletin* 39.312, *Black-crowned Night Heron. . .* Quag (New England); Quak . . (Mass.). **1962** Imhof *AL Birds* 98, *Yellow-crowned Night Heron. . . Other names:* Gros-bec, Quak. . . The call of this bird is pitched higher than that of the other night heron.

2 A **bittern** (here: *Botaurus lentiginosus*).

1959 *Names* 7.117, Names usually applied to the black-crowned night-heron occasionally are offered as for the bittern, examples being: couac (French, Que., La.), quack (Ill.), quawk (Pa., N.J.), quock (Va.) [etc].

3 See **quack grass 1.**

4 See **quack grass 2.**

quack digger n Also *quacker*

A harrow intended especially for eradicating **quack grass.**

1950 *WELS (What is generally used to break up lumps in a field?)* 1 Inf, **seWI,** A drag—quack digger. **1965** *Bee* (Phillips WI) 19 Aug 15/1, [Advt:] John Deere Side Rake . . Quack Digger; International 1-Bottom Plow. **1966** *DARE* Tape **MI**12, [Inf:] You had the plows and we got a drag with it—a quacker for it—what they called a field cultivator. [FW:] How'd the quacker work? [Inf:] Well, that tears up your ground. [FW:] It is rotating? [Inf:] No, it just got spring teeth on it. **1968** *DARE* (Qu. L18, *Kinds of plows)* Inf **MN**40, Quack digger or spike-tooth harrow; (Qu. L20, *The implement used in a field after it's been plowed to break up the lumps)* Inf **MN**40, Quack digger.

quack grass n [Var of **quick grass**]

1 also *crack grass, quack, quack-root grass:* A weedy naturalized grass (*Elytrigia repens*). **chiefly Inland Nth, N Midl, Appalachians** See Map Also called **couch grass 1, devil's-grass 1, dog grass 1, durfee ~, Dutch ~, knotgrass 2, quake grass 1, quick ~, quitch ~, squitch ~, twitch ~, wheatgrass, wire grass, witchgrass**

1822 Eaton *Botany* 494, *Triticum . . repens,* (wheat-grass, couch-grass, quack-grass . .) . . Very troublesome in fertile soil, and useful in barren sand. **1833** Beck *Botany N. & Middle States* 416, *T[riticum] repens. . .* A troublesome weed. *Couch Grass. Quack.* **1839** Buel *Farmer's Companion* 144, To clean the ground of the roots of foul plants, as dock, quack, etc. *Ibid* 151, One of our neighbors has been enabled completely to eradicate quack-grass in his Indian corn. **1868** U.S. Dept. Ag. *Rept. of Secy. for 1867* 347 **NY,** Quack produces better hay than timothy for cattle. **1906** Johnson *Highways Missip. Valley* 226 **MN,** He lost his hat-band one summer day and he picked some quack grass and tied it around his hat. When he come in at night his wife took off the quack grass and put it in the fire, and not long afterward she emptied out the ashes from the stove, and within a few days there come up a lot of quack grass where she throwed them ashes. **1914** Georgia *Manual Weeds* 61, If it were put to a vote, perhaps most farmers would name Quack-grass as the most obnoxious of its tribe; yet it makes good hay and two crops a year of it, is sweet pasture grazing which cattle eat greedily, and its matted "couch" of interlacing rootstocks make [sic] it an unsurpassed soil-binder. **1950** *WELS* **WI** (*The kind of wild grass that throws out strong underground roots and is hard to get rid of)* 43 Infs, Quack grass; 2 Infs, Quack (grass) or witchgrass; 2 Infs, Quack (grass) or quitch grass; 1 Inf, Quack or quitch grass—said to be "the root of all evil"; 1 Inf, Twitch grass or quack grass. **1965–70** *DARE* (Qu. S8, *A common kind of wild grass that grows in fields: it spreads by sending out long underground*

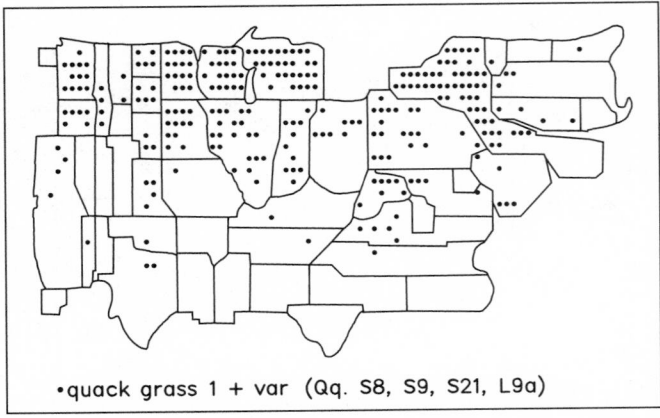

•quack grass 1 + var (Qq. S8, S9, S21, L9a)

roots) 257 Infs, **chiefly Inland Nth, N Midl, Appalachians,** Quack grass; **CT**2, **MI**34, Crack grass; (Qu. S9) 10 Infs, **scattered,** Quack grass; (Qu. S21) 10 Infs, **chiefly Inland Nth,** Quack grass; (Qu. L9a, *. . Kinds of grass . . grown for hay*) 8 Infs, **Inland Nth,** Quack grass. **1966** *DARE* Tape **MI**23, He had invented this, as a roller harrow, for the purpose of eradicating quack grass. **1969** *DARE* File **WI,** Quack-root grass = quack grass. **1995** Brako et al. *Scientific & Common Names Plants* 214, Quackgrass—*Elytrigia repens.*

2 also *(sweet) quack:* A **holy grass** (here: *Hierochloe odorata*).

1914 Georgia *Manual Weeds* 37, Vanilla-Grass—*Hierochloe odorata.* . . Quack-grass. . . The name of "Quack" or "Sweet Quack," which western farmers have given this grass is confusing, for the true Quack-grass flowers in June and its matted "couch" of rootstocks is near the surface, while Vanilla-grass flowers in early spring and its rootstocks are deep in the soil.

3 A **panic grass** (here: *Panicum repens*).

1965 Neal *Gardens HI* 73, Among 30 panicums in Hawaii is quack grass (*P. repens* L.), from the Eastern Hemisphere, a weedy, creeping perennial.

quacking asp(en) See **quaking aspen**

quack-root grass See **quack grass 1**

quadrille n Usu |k(w)ə'drɪl|; for addit varr see quot 1965–70
Pronc-sp *cadrill*   **chiefly Nth, N Midl, West**   See Map
A type of square dance performed by four couples.

1826 (1831) Woodworth *Melodies* 108, The gay belles of fashion may boast of excelling / In walz or cotillion—at whist or quadrille. **1839** *Chicago American* 2 Nov. (*DAE*), Mrs. Ingersoll . . employs the winter here in giving dancing lessons and quadrille and cotillion parties. **1857** Gunn *Physiology Boarding-Houses* 169 **NYC,** A young wife is not in the best of health or temper on the morning subsequent to six hours' active performance of polkas, cotillions, quadrilles, schottisches, etc. **1860** *De Bow's Rev.* 29.321 **LA,** Never . . is absent from the festive gatherings of our people, young or old, the measures of the quadrille, or the dizzy whirlings of the waltz. **1903** Fox *Little Shepherd* 230 **KY,** The dance was a quadrille and the figure was "Grand right and left." **1912** (1914) Sinclair *Flying U Ranch* 181 **MT,** The Happy Family knew those ways as they knew the most complicated figures of the quadrilles they danced so lightfootedly. **1950** *WELS Suppl.* **csWI,** [kə'drɪl] frequent in Cottage Grove, esp in "waltz quadrille." **1965–70** *DARE* (Qu. FF5a, *. . Different steps and figures in dancing—in past years*) 18 Infs, **chiefly Nth, N Midl, CA,** Quadrille(s); **NM**12, **OH**11, Quadrille—square dance; **MT**3, Quadrille—long time ago; **CA**137, Cadrill—takes eight [sic] couples; **CA**197, Cadrill—a square dance; **CA**209, Cadrill; **ID**2, **MA**6, 29, [kə'drɪl], **IL**29, [kə'drɪlz]—now called square dancing; **MA**55, 69, [kwo'drɪl(z)]; **AZ**11, [kwæ'drɪl]; **MO**13, [kwɑ·'drɪɫ]; **MA**11, [kwɒ'drɪl]; **MA**40, ['kwɒdrɪl]; **MA**48, [kə'drɪl, kwæ'drɪl]; **MA**6, Ten-pin [kədrɪl]; nine-pin quadrille—extra man supposed to step out and steal a partner; **MA**73, Nine-pin quadrille—an odd man put in the middle.

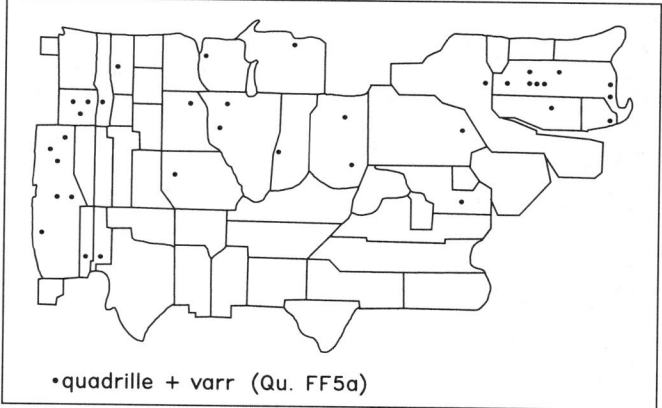

•quadrille + varr (Qu. FF5a)

quag See **quack 1**

quahaug n See **quahog** n

quahaug v See **quahog** v

quahog n **chiefly eMA** |'kohɒg, -hɑg| (repr in *DARE* quots by sp *cohog*); **chiefly RI** |'kwɔhɒg| (repr by *quahog*); less freq **esp**

seMA |'kwohɒg| (repr by *quohog*)   For addit pronc and sp varr see **1** below   [Algonquian; see quots 1902, 1981 at **1**]

1 A marine bivalve mollusk of the genus *Mercenaria,* usu *M. mercenaria,* native to the Atlantic and Gulf coasts.   **chiefly N Atl coast, esp MA, RI**   See Map   For other names of *M. mercenaria* see **blunt** n¹, **bullnose, cherrystone, hard-shell clam 1, littleneck 1, pooquaw, round clam**

[**1643** Williams *Key into Language* 107, *Poquaúhock.* . . This the English call Hens, a little thick shel-fish, which the Indians wade deepe and dive for.] **1781** Peters *Genl. Hist. CT* 262, The oysters, clams, quauhogs, lobsters, crabs, and fish, are innumerable. **1788** (1888) Cutler *Life* 1.416 **NEng,** Went into the water; found a great number of clam cohog shells. **1799** (1907) Bentley *Diary* 2.312 **neMA,** They are not the long large Clams of our Beaches, nor the Quahoag. **1815** in 1816 MA Hist. Soc. *Coll.* 2d ser 4.289, The quahaug clam is common. **1826** Morton *New Engl. Mem.* 388, The characters of the shell, here described, and which is denominated a *clam-shell,* are applicable to the *quahawg.* **1851** (1976) Melville *Moby-Dick* 63 **MA,** They first caught crabs and quohogs in the sand. **1867** Lowell *Biglow* xli 'Upcountry' **MA,** We have a few words, such as *cache, cohog,* . . but how many can we be said to have fairly brought into the language? **1902** *Jrl. Amer. Folkl.* 15.255, Quahog (quahaug). A New England name of the round or hard clam (*Venus mercenaria*). Probably a "reduction" of the Indian word seen in the Narragansett *poquaúhock.* It is worth noting that the first part of this word has survived in Nantucket as *pooquaw . . ,* while elsewhere the last part seems to be retained as *quahog.* **1903** *N.Y. Ev. Telegram* 20 Oct. 4 (*DAE*), Shall we eventually get down to nothing but quohogs and chowder? **1903** *DN* 2.291 **Cape Cod MA** (as of a1857), The *w*-sound frequently assimilated or disappeared after a consonant: . . *cōhaug* = *quahaug.* **1904** *DN* 2.424 **Cape Cod MA** (as of a1857), *Clam.* . . Applied commonly to the long thin-shelled bivalve, sometimes to a fresh water variety, but never to the round, hard-shelled bivalve, which is called *quahaug.* **1939** *LANE* Map 235 *(Round clam),* The spelling *quahog* is here used to refer indifferently to pronunciations of the types of [kwɔ(h)ɒg, kwɑ-, kwo-, ko-, kwe-, kwi-, kwɒg, kwæg]. . *Quahog* always has initial stress, except for the two cases of [kwə'hɒg] recorded in . . [sRI] (as the only response) and in . . [ceRI] (beside ['kwɔ^hɒg, 'kwŏhɒg]). **1949** Kurath *Word Geog.* 22, The large clam, known as the *round clam* in most of Connecticut, has generally retained its Indian name from New London to Nantucket and from Cape Cod to Maine. From eastern Connecticut to Nantucket, including Narragansett Bay, *quahog . .* —beginning like *quarter*—is the usual form of this word; on Massachusetts Bay and in Maine the form is *cohog,* beginning like *coat.* Between these two sections, notably in the Plymouth area, both these pronunciations are current as well as *quohog,* starting like *quote,* which looks like a blend of the two. **1965–70** *DARE* (Qu. P18, *. . Kinds of shellfish*) Infs **MA**3, 7, 9, 13, 27, 50, 55, 72, 97, **VA**47, Cohogs [proncs of the type ['kohɒgz, -hɒgz]]; **NH**18, **RI**6, 15, Cohogs [proncs of the type ['kohɑgz, -hɑgz]]; **ME**16, **MA**45, **GA**11, Cohogs; **RI**1, 8, 17, Quahogs ['kwɔhɒgz]; **RI**4, Quahogs ['kwɔhɒ·gz]; **RI**12, Quahog ['kwoɑg]; **NY**34, Quahogs [kwɑgz]; **DE**4, **MA**40, Quohogs ['kwɔhɒgz]; **MA**34, Quohog ['kwohɒg]; **MA**55, Quohogs [kwowɒgz]; (Qu. H36, *Kinds of soup*) Inf **MA**73, Clam chowder, Quahog chowder; (Qu. H45) Inf **RI**9, Quahog ['kwɔhɒg]—used for chowder instead [of] clams, but you call it clam chowder. **1966** *DARE* Tape **ME**17, [FW:] Are there any different kinds of clams and scallops that they get, or just one kind? [Inf:] Yes, sir. There's cohogs [,ko'hɑgz], and there's hinge clams, and there's river clams here. **1968** *DARE* FW Addit **DE**4, Quohog ['kwoʊ,hɒg]—clams. **1981** Meinkoth *Audubon Field Guide Seashore*

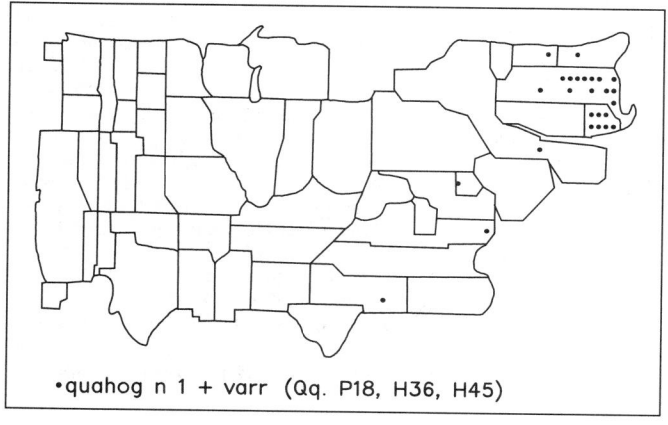

•quahog n 1 + varr (Qq. P18, H36, H45)

559, The name "Quahog" (pronounced Kwo-hog or Co-hog) is derived from two Narragansett Indian words meaning "dark" or "closed", and "shell." *Ibid* 560, *Southern Quahog—(Mercenaria campechiensis)*. . . This species is heavier and broader than its close relative, the Northern Quahog. Although their ranges overlap, the Southern Quahog has not been exploited for food nearly so much as its northern relative. **1983** Beyle *How Talk Cape Cod* 20, When you get to talking about the hardshell clam known as a "quahog" or "quahaug"—also spelled "quohog" or "cohog"—*do* try to pronounce it correctly ("co-hog" or "ko-hog" is proper Cape Coddese). **1988** Nickerson *Days to Remember* 162 **Cape Cod MA** (as of c1925), Opening quohogs (hard-shell clams) can be easy.

2 as *false quahog, ocean ~:* A similar bivalve mollusk *(Arctica islandica).* Also called **mahogany clam**

1884 U.S. Natl. Museum *Bulletin* 27.232, *Cyprina islandica*. . . This clam is the "sea-clam" or "false quahaug." . . It is easily distinguished from the true quahaug *(Venus mercenaria)* by its brown epidermis. **1974** Abbott *Seashells* 381, *Arctica islandica* . . Ocean Quahog. . . A common, commercially dredged species found in sandy mud from 5 to 80 fathoms. **1981** Rehder *Audubon Field Guide Seashells* 792, *Ocean Quahog*. . . This is a highly esteemed food source and the basis of an extensive commercial fishery from Rhode Island south to Virginia. It somewhat resembles the common Northern Quahog.

quahog v, hence vbl n *quahogging* Also *cohog, quahaug* **NEng, esp MA**

To dig for or gather **quahogs;** hence n *quahogger* one who does this; a boat used in doing this.

1905 Lincoln *Partners* 76 **Cape Cod MA**, How's the quahaugin' nowadays? **1913** *DN* 4.56 **Cape Cod MA**, *Quahog*. . . To rake for quahogs. "Been cohoggin' every day since Tuesday." *Ibid, Quahogger*. . . (1) Any boat, usually a small power boat, used in raking for quahogs. (2) A man who rakes for quahogs. **1915** (1916) Johnson *Highways New Engl.* 209 **Nantucket MA,** Just now quahauging is the great thing. The whole bottom in the harbor and for miles and miles outside is covered with quahaugs. **1935** Lincoln *Cape Cod Yesterdays* 53, If you are a professional—if you "go quahauging" regularly, to earn a living—you do work hard. Indeed you do. *Ibid* 55, The Bay is seldom very rough, land is not far distant, and the deep quahauger knows how to handle a boat. **1939** *LANE* Map 235 *(Round clam)* 1 inf, **seCT,** [kwohɒɡɪn], 'digging for quahogs.' **1949** Knight *Bass Derby Murder* 122 **NEng,** I was down to the pond quahoggin' all afternoon.

quaik See **quoit A3**

quail n Cf **partridge**

1 =**bob-white. formerly chiefly NEng; now widespread east of Rocky Mts** Also called **bird B1**

1625 Morrell *New Engl.* 15, All along the Maine: The Turtle, Eagle, Partridge, and the Quaile. **1637** (1972) Morton *New English Canaan* 70, There are quailes also, but bigger then the quailes in England. **1701** Wolley *2 Yrs. Jrl.* 40 **NY,** They have great store of wild-fowl, as Turkys, Heath-hens, Quails, Partridges, Pigeons. **1792** Belknap *Hist. NH* 3.171, In the southern and middle States, the quail is called a partridge, and the partridge a pheasant. **1812** [see **partridge B1**]. **1818** in 1822 Cobbett *Year's Residence U.S.A.* 43, Chickens . . as big as American Partridges (misnamed quails). **1872** [see **partridge B1**]. **1923** U.S. Dept. Ag. *Farmers' Bulletin* 1375.17 **IL,** *Open seasons:* . . Quail (bob-white). . . Nov. 10–Dec. 10. **1958** Humphrey *Home from the Hill* 48 **neTX,** Real game, men's game: gray and fox squirrels, a few, occasionally a coon hungry enough to come marauding that close to town, coveys of quail out of season that he could watch. **1965–70** *DARE* (Qu. Q7, *Names and nicknames for . . game birds*) 571 Infs, **widespread east of Rocky Mts,** Quail [*DARE* Ed: Some of these Infs may refer instead to **2** below.]; (Qu. K76, . . *Kinds of poultry . . raised around here*) 33 Infs, **chiefly SE, Gulf States,** Quail(s); (Qu. Q14) 22 Infs, **scattered,** Quail; (Qu. P32, . . *Other kinds of wild animals)* Infs **AL22, GA1, NY63, TN46,** Quail; (Qu. Q9) Inf **NH14,** Quail. **1968–70** *DARE* Tape **GA71,** We have quail, a lot of, several quail here, and we hunt for them. *Ibid* **IN36,** I got some quail hunting around here. I bought fifty quail and turned 'em loose on the place when I first moved here. *Ibid* **IN51,** I never hunted quail much. Not enough to fool with. I just didn't like the sport. *Ibid* **TX96,** There's quite a few of quail. . Quail season is closed with the exception of a month and a half in the fall of the year. **1986** Pederson *LAGS Concordance* **Gulf Region,** 49 infs, Quail(s); 1 inf, Quail = partridge; 1 inf, Quails = bobwhites, partridges; 1 inf, Quail's like a small turkey.

2 Any of several related game birds native to the western US:

esp **California quail 1,** but also **Gambel's quail, harlequin ~, mountain ~ 1,** or **scaled ~.**

1853 *San Diego Herald* 22 Oct 2/4 *(AmSp* 26.224), A party of gentlemen . . returned Thursday evening, laden with spoil. To say nothing of quail, grouse, chapparal cock, and rabbits. **1869** Browne *Adventures* 76 **AZ,** Quail were very abundant as we drew near our first camping-place on the Gila. **1872** McClellan *Golden State* 211 **CA,** There is abundance of trout in the adjacent streams, and of bear, deer, and quail in the hills. **1874** Coues *Birds NW* 434, Along the Gila and Colorado. . . these scrubby trees [=mesquite and mimosa] form dense interlacing copses, only to be penetrated with the utmost difficulty, but beneath their spreading scrawny branches are open intersecting ways, along which the Quail [=*Callipepla gambelii*] roams at will, enjoying the slight shade. **1903** (1950) Austin *Land of Little Rain* 23 **neCA,** The inhabitants have the faculty of quail for making themselves scarce in the underbrush at the approach of strangers. *Ibid* 101 **sCA,** At this time when . . the young quail cry "cuidado." **1918** Grinnell *Game Birds CA* 516, The Valley Quail [=*Lophortyx californicus*] . . because of its great popularity as a game bird . . has been referred to under a variety of names, . . but to the great majority of the residents of California this and the closely similar California and Catalina Island quails are known simply as "quail." **1923** Dawson *Birds CA* 4.1580, The Quail's year begins some time in March or early April, when the coveys [of *Lophortyx californicus*] begin to break up. *Ibid* 1588, That the Quail [=*Callipepla gambelii*] should trust the Rat is rather surprising, but I recall having startled a covey of very young quails which took instant refuge in a rat's nest. **1965–70** *DARE* (Qu. Q7, *Names and nicknames for . . game birds*) 49 Infs, **Pacific, esp CA; also SW,** Quail; **CA87,** Quail—the mountain quail; **CA96,** Quail—the desert quail here, mountain quail higher; **CA97,** Quail—valley quail, mountain quail; **CA105,** Quail—California, valley, mountain quail; **CA150,** Quail—mountain quail, valley quail; **CA207,** Quail—mountain, valley; **HI14,** Quail—California quail and Chinese quail; **NM3,** Quail has topknot; **NM13,** Quail (fool hen, Gamble's quail, white-tip quail); **NV6,** Quail—the white-breasted, the tinged quail, the dove-colored quail—varieties; **TX5,** Quail—valley and Mexican blues or scale quail; **WA6,** Quail—California, valley; (Qu. Q14) Infs **CA2, 140, WA24,** Quail; (Qu. K76) Inf **OK27,** Quail just a bobwhite that's scaled; feathers look like fish scales; (Qu. P32, . . *Other kinds of wild animals)* Inf **CA203,** Quail. **1968** *DARE* Tape **CA103,** They're killing off all the quail. **1977** Udvardy *Audubon Field Guide Birds* 594, *Oreortyx pictus*. . . This quail migrates on foot from high territory where it breeds to protected valleys, where it winters in coveys of 6–12 birds.

3 The eastern **meadowlark 1.** Cf **marsh quail, meadow ~, nigger ~**

1956 MA Audubon Soc. *Bulletin* 40.130 **ME,** *Meadowlark* . . Quail. [**1969** *DARE* (Qu. Q15, . . *Kinds of larks)* Inf **RI4,** Padlocks [laughter]—it's classified by government as quail. It's migratory.]

quailberry n

A **wolfberry** (here: *Symphoricarpos occidentalis).*

1924 *Amer. Botanist* 30.32, *Symphoricarpos occidentalis* is known . . as . . "quail-berry."

quail brush n

1 also *quail bush:* A **saltbush 1** (here: *Atriplex lentiformis).*

1918 Grinnell *Game Birds CA* 540, Throughout its range the Desert Quail is a close associate of the mesquite and "quail brush," the latter being a species of *Atriplex.* **1931** U.S. Dept. Ag. *Misc. Pub.* 101.31, Big saltbush *(A[triplex] lentiformis),* sometimes called quailbrush, is perhaps the largest of our native saltbushes. **1933** Harrington *Gypsum Cave NV* 196, *Atriplex lentiformis* . . Quail bush. **1960** Vines *Trees SW* 239, Big Saltbush—*Atriplex lentiformis*. . . Also known under the names of Lens-scale Saltbush and Quail-bush. . . Growing in dense stands it affords excellent cover for wildlife. **1967** *DARE* (Qu. S26e, *Other wildflowers not yet mentioned;* not asked in early QRs) Inf **AZ2,** Quail bush. [*DARE* Ed: This Inf may refer instead to **2** below]. **1982** *Plants SW* (Catalog) 48, *Quailbrush—Atriplex lentiformis*. . . Birds and rodents . . relish the seed.

2 =**mountain mahogany 2.**

1920 *Torreya* 20.21 **sAZ,** *Cercocarpus* spp. . . quail brush, Apache plume.

quail bush n

1 See **quail brush 1.**

2 =**fragrant sumac.**

1960 Vines *Trees SW* 630, Skunk-bush Sumac—*Rhus aromatica*. . .

Squaw-bush, Quail-bush, Agrillo, and Lemita. . . The fruit is known to be eaten by 25 species of birds, especially the gallinaceous birds such as various species of quail [etc].

quail hawk n [See quot 1961]   Cf **partridge hawk**
Usu **Cooper's hawk,** but also **sharp-shinned hawk.**

1874 NY Acad. Sci. *Annals Lyceum Nat. Hist.* 10.380, *N[isus] Cooperi.* . . Cooper's Hawk; "Swift Hawk;" "Quail Hawk." **1917** (1923) *Birds Amer.* 2.67, Cooper's Hawk—*Accipiter cooperi.* . . Pigeon Hawk . . Quail Hawk . . Striker. **1925** Bailey *Birds FL* 68, Sharp-shinned hawk. . . *Accipter velox* (Blue darter, Quail hawk). **1961** Ligon *NM Birds* 62, Cooper's Hawk—*Accipiter cooperii.* . . The Cooper's Hawk, or Blue Darter, is in bad repute with sportsmen and bird lovers alike. It aptly may be called the Quail Hawk since, in the Southwest at least, it seeks out and preys on Quail whenever and wherever they are available. **1965–70** *DARE* (Qu. Q4, . . *Kinds of hawks*) Infs **AL**25, **CA**24, 136, 199, **KS**12, **MO**38, **OK**1, Quail hawk.

quailhead n
Any of three sparrows with quail-like markings on the head: **sharp-tailed sparrow, lark ~, white-crowned ~.**

1844 DeKay *Zool. NY* 2.164, The Quail-Head.—*Ammodramus caudacutus.* . . The name of *Quail-head,* by which this species is distinguished among our gunners, is derived from its distant resemblance to the head of the common Quail. Like the preceding, it is found only in salt marshes, where it breeds. **1898** (1900) Davie *Nests N. Amer. Birds* 376, Lark Sparrow. *Chondestes grammacus.* . . Several birds may be seen running in the grass with lowered heads like quails, from which manner, in some places they receive the name of "Quail-heads." **1923** Dawson *Birds CA* 1.234, *Chondestes grammacus strigatus* . . Quail-head. *Ibid* 238, A finger-ring slipped over the Quail-head's head will pass twenty-three patches of pure color,—black, white, chestnut and buffy, before it encounters a streaky admixture of flaxen, black and rufous-tawny on the hindhead. [**1923** WV State Ornith. *Birds WV* 52, White Crowned Sparrow. . . I will never forget the first one I ever saw. It was when I was a boy living in Canada. . . We called him "quail-head," as we knew no name for him.] **1953** Jewett *Birds WA* 635, Western Lark Sparrow. *Chondestes grammacus strigatus.* . . Other names: Quail-head; Western Lark Finch. **1955** *AmSp* 30.180, *Quailhead* suggests the conspicuous striping of the head of the sharp-tailed sparrow (N.Y., Pa., N.J.), lark sparrow (Ohio, Texas), and white-crowned sparrow (W.Va.) **1970** *DARE* (Qu. Q21, . . *Kinds of sparrows*) Inf **NY**233, Crown sparrow or quailhead—white streak on either side of head.

quailhead bean n
See quot.

1944 *Jrl. Amer. Folkl.* 57.281 **NY,** The beans were "pole beans" (they were colored like calico beans, "quail-head beans" some people call them).

quail's delight n
A **bristlegrass 1** (here: *Setaria italica*).

1937 *Torreya* 37.95 **csSC,** *Setaria italica.* . . Quail's-delight, Hilton Head Id., S. Car.

quail snipe n esp Long Is. NY
=**dowitcher.**

1844 DeKay *Zool. NY* 2.255, The *Dowitchee, Red-breasted Snipe, Quail Snipe,* or *Brown-back,* arrives on the coast of New-York towards the latter part of April. **1844** Giraud *Birds Long Is.* 264 **seNY,** *Scolopax noveboracensis.* . . Red-breasted Snipe. . . The whistling note of the Red-breasted, or "Quail Snipe," as it is termed in some sections of the Island, is well known to the practical bay-gunner. **1910** Eaton *Birds NY* 1.305, The Dowitcher . . , also called Red-breasted snipe, Robin snipe, Brown-back, Gray-back, and Quail snipe, is fully as gregarious as the Yellow-legs and often occurs in dense bunches over the bars and mud flats of Long Island. **1955** *AmSp* 30.180 **NY, NJ,** *Quail snipe* definitely refers to the plump body and ruddy breast of the dowitcher.

quail sparrow n
=**grasshopper sparrow.**

1917 (1923) *Birds Amer.* 3.26, Grasshopper Sparrow—*Ammodramus savannarum australis.* . . Quail Sparrow; Yellow-winged Sparrow. **1946** Hausman *Eastern Birds* 591, Eastern Grasshopper Sparrow—*Ammodramus savannarum australis* . . Quail Sparrow. **1969** *DARE* (Qu. Q21, . . *Kinds of sparrows*) Inf **GA**76, Quail sparrow—a sparrow a dog will point.

quaintun See **acquaintun**

quair(e) See **queer**

quairy See **quarry**

quait See **quoit A1**

quak See **quack 1**

quake v Cf Intro "Language Changes" II.10
Std sense, var form.
Past: usu *quaked;* also *quoke.*

1899 (1912) Green *VA Folk-Speech* 341, *Quoke.* . . Strong past tense of *quake.*

quake n See **quoit A3**

quake grass n

1 =**quack grass 1.**

1840 MA Zool. & Bot. Surv. *Herb. Plants & Quadrupeds* 250, *T[riticum] repens.* . . Quake, or Quack, or Couch Grass. . . This is a troublesome grass of gardens and fields. **1887** Beal *Grasses N. Amer.* 1.167, *A[gropyron] repens.* . . Quake . . Grass or Creeping Wheat. . . This grass is well known in most of the older portions of our country. **1930** Sievers *Amer. Med. Plants* 49, *Quack Grass.* . . Other common names. . . Quake grass. **1950** *WELS* (The kind of wild grass that throws out strong underground roots and is hard to get rid of) 1 Inf, **cwWI,** Quake grass.

2 A **bromegrass** (here: *Bromus briziformis*).

1950 Gray–Fernald *Manual of Botany* 103, *B[romus] brizaeformis.* . . Quake-Grass. . . Roadsides and waste places, local. **1967** Braun *Monocotyledoneae* 72 **OH,** *Bromus brizaeformis.* . . Quake Grass. . . Recorded from Erie County.

3 See **quaking grass.**

quakenasp See **quaking aspen**

quaker n

1 See **quaking aspen.**

2 The female **summer tanager.**   [Because it is less brightly colored than the male]

1899 in 1900 LA Soc. Naturalists *Proc.* 108, *Piranga rubra.* . . Summer Redbird; Quaker. **1916** *Times–Picayune* (New Orleans LA) 23 Apr 5, *Summer Tanager.* . . Female . . Quaker.

3 See **Quaker ladies 1.**

4 See **Quaker stew.**

quaker ash See **quaking aspen**

Quaker beauty See **Quaker ladies 1**

Quaker bird n
=**cedar waxwing.**

1890 Warren *Birds PA* 258, *Ampelis cedrorum.* . . Cedar Waxwing . . Quaker-bird.

Quaker bonnet n, usu pl

1 A **bluet 2,** usu *Houstonia caerulea.*   Cf **lady bonnet, Quaker ladies 1**

1898 Britton–Brown *Illustr. Flora* 3.212, *Houstonia coerulea.* . . Bluets. . . Called also Quaker Ladies, Quaker bonnets, Venus' Pride. **1900** Lyons *Plant Names* 194, *H[oustonia] coerulea.* . . Nuns, Quaker-bonnets, Quaker-ladies [etc]. **1931** Harned *Wild Flowers Alleghanies* 460, Bluets . . *Houstonia caerulea.* . . Familiarly known also under the names of Innocence, Quaker Ladies, Venus' Pride and Quaker Bonnets. **1949** Moldenke *Amer. Wild Flowers* 171, The common bluets, *Houstonia caerulea.* . . Among the plant's many popular names are wildforgetmenot, angeleyes, quakerladies, and quakerbonnets. **1959** Carleton *Index Herb. Plants* 96, *Quaker bonnet:* Houstonia purpurea. **1966** *DARE* (Qu. S11, . . *Bluets*) Inf **PA**1, Quaker bonnet.

2 also *Quaker's bonnet(s):* =**lupine.**   Cf **grandma's cap**

1900 Lyons *Plant Names* 231, *Lupinus* [spp]. . . The names Sun-dial, Old-maid's-bonnets, Quaker's-bonnets and Wild Lupine or Lupin are almost indiscriminately applied to the various species. **1915** (1926) Armstrong–Thornber *Western Wild Flowers* 252, *Quaker Bonnets—Lupinus laxiflorus.* . . The younger leaves and calyxes are silvery with down, the flower buds form long, pretty, silvery clusters. **1937** U.S.

Forest Serv. *Range Plant Hdbk.* W112, Lupines. . . These plants have many common names, including blue-bean . . quakerbonnts [sic] [etc]. **1949** Moldenke *Amer. Wild Flowers* 132, One of the most popular plants in the eastern part of our area is the quakerbonnets, *L. perennis.* **1995** Brako et al. *Scientific & Common Names Plants* 214, Quaker's-bonnet—*Lupinus perennis.*

Quaker courtship n Also *the Quaker's wooing*

A musical game; see quots.

1883 Newell *Games & Songs* 94 **CT,** *Quaker Courtship.* In this piece, two children (in costume or otherwise) impersonate a Quaker paying his addresses to a young lady of the world. [Music and verses follow.] **c1927** in 1952 Brown *NC Folkl.* 1.123, [Game title:] *Quaker Courtship.* [Lyrics:] Madam, I come here a-courting,/ Oh, oh, oh;/ I'm in earnest, I'm not sporting,/ Oh, oh, oh. . . Here's a ring worth twenty shilling;/ It's yours if you are willing./ What care I for rings or money?/ I want a man to call me honey. [*Ibid* 124, [Footnote:] Contributor's note: "A middle-aged man told me it was a 'ring game' when he was a boy. . . He played this rollicking tune on his violin, and said he would not play the game now because he had 'learnt better.' From this I inferred that the game had been a sort of dance."] **1939** Linscott *Folk Songs Old New Engl.* 276, *The Quaker's Wooing.* . . The game is a variation of "The Keys to Heaven." . . The ballad is a dramatic representation and probably was a mummers' dance. [Lyrics:] "Madam, I have come a courtin'. . . " "I want none of your Quaker action. . . " "Love, I'll be a Presbyterian. . . Then we'll be of one persuasion. . . " "I want none of your turncoat religion. . . I want a man that's a real good Christian. . . Take thy cheer, my loving brother. . . Since you can't catch me—go catch another."

Quaker fip n Also *Quaker nickel* Cf **fip, Yankee dime**

A kiss.

1846 *Quincy* (Ill.) *Whig* 28 Feb. 2/2 *(DA),* However happy he might have been to pay the *Quaker fip,* . . he was mortified at her seeming want of modesty in demanding it in the presence of so many witnesses. **1897** *KS Univ. Qrly.* (ser B) 6.56 **OH,** *Quaker-fip:* a kiss. **1957** *Sat. Eve. Post Letters,* [Two expressions meaning "a kiss":] The first I remember my old German grandmother using to me as a small child—she usually offered it as payment for a favor I'd do for her. It was "Quaker nickel." The other means the same, but I haven't any idea where it came from. It is a "Yankee dime."

Quaker girls See **Quaker ladies 1**

Quaker, how is thee? n Cf **Queen Dido is dead, Quaker meeting, ~ courtship**

See quot.

1883 Newell *Games & Songs* 130, [Title:] *Quaker, How is Thee?* [Lyrics:] "Quaker, Quaker, how is thee?"/ "Very well, I thank thee."/ "How's thy neighbor, next to thee?"/ "I don't know, but I'll go see." The question is accompanied by a rapid movement of the right hand. The second child in the ring inquires in the same manner of the third; and so all round. Then the same question is asked with a like gesture of the left hand, and, after this has gone round, with both hands, left foot, right foot, both feet, and finally by uniting all the motions at once. "A nice long game," as our little informant said. *New York, Philadelphia, etc.*

Quaker ladies n

1 also *Quaker, Quaker beauty, ~ girls, ~ lady:* A **bluet 2** (here: *Houstonia caerulea*). **chiefly NEast, esp PA** See Map Cf **little washerwomen**

1871 *Scribner's Mth.* 2.102, Tenderest of all in yonder woods, where hepatica and May-blossom, and Quaker-ladies twinkle into life. **1872** Schele de Vere *Americanisms* 405, The pretty little *Bluets* (Oldenlandia caerulea) [is] a delicate little herb, which in early spring fills the wood with its tufts of pale-blue flowers, each having a small yellow eye in the centre, known also as *Quakers.* **1892** *Jrl. Amer. Folkl.* 5.97 **MA,** *Houstonia coerulea,* blue-eyed babies . . Quaker ladies. Concord Mass.; Boston . . Quaker beauty. **1901** Lounsberry *S. Wild Flowers* 475, *H[oustonia] coerulea,* bluets, innocence, Quaker ladies, or bonnets, is much more generally distributed than the mountain species—therefore better known and of more widely acknowledged charm. **1902** *New Engl. Mag.* new ser 26.260 **ceMA,** In open, moist, grassy places you will find the Houstonia that delicate little flower with so many pretty local names, bluets, innocence, Quaker-ladies, and sky-bloom. **1931** [see **Quaker bonnet 1**]. **1949** [see **Quaker bonnet 1**]. **1951** *PADS* 15.19 **NJ,** *Houstonia coerulea* . . Quaker-girls. **1965–70** *DARE* (Qu. S11, . . *Bluets*) 25 Infs, 12 **PA,** Quaker ladies; **NJ**58, Quaker ladies—in Penn-

sylvania. [23 of 26 Infs old, 21 female] **1967–68** *DARE* Wildfl QR Pl.209b **AR**44, **NY**91, Quaker ladies; **OH**14, Quaker lady. **1967** Borland *Hill Country* 120 **nwCT,** In the meadow that sloped down to the bog were a few patches of bluets . . which some call Quaker Ladies and some call Innocence.

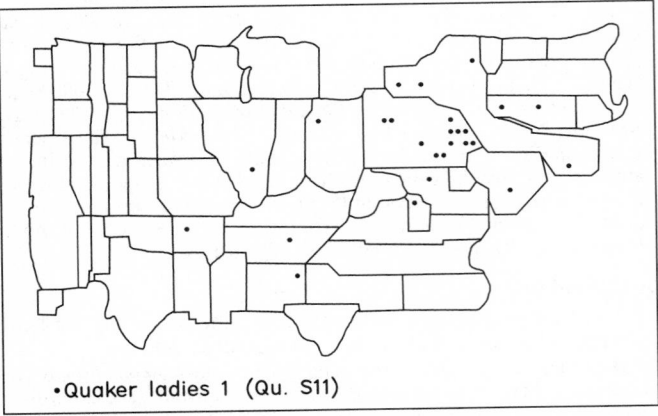
•Quaker ladies 1 (Qu. S11)

2 A **lupine** (here: *Lupinus perennis*). Cf **Quaker bonnet 2**

1967 *DARE* Wildfl QR Pl.106 Inf **MI**57, Quaker ladies.

Quaker lady n

1 See **Quaker ladies 1.**

2 A **spirea** (here: *Spiraea alba*).

1900 Lyons *Plant Names* 355, *S[piraea] salicifolia* [=*S. alba*]. . . Bride-wort, Quaker-lady. **1919** (1923) House *Wild Flowers NY* 1.129, *Meadowsweet; Quaker Lady—Spiraea latifolia* [=*S. alba* var *latifolia*]. . . Flowers white or pinkish. . . Spiraea alba . . has . . white flowers. It is much less abundant than Spiraea latifolia. **1940** Clute *Amer. Plant Names* 231, *Spiraea salicifolia.* Mock willow, quaker lady.

Quaker loon n

=red-throated loon.

1917 *Wilson Bulletin* 29.2.75 **WA,** *Gavia stellata.* . . Quaker loon, Willapa Harbor, Wash.

Quaker meeting n Cf **Quaker prayer meeting**

A children's game; see quots 1967–69, 1993.

1967–69 *DARE* (Qu. EE33, . . *Outdoor games . . that children play*) Inf **PA**22, Quaker meeting—all sit quietly, and one would give directions. The others must follow directions without laughing; [**VT**16, Quaker's meeting [*DARE* Ed: no description provided]]. [**1976** Knapp-Knapp *One Potato* 53, The game of Chinese School comes right out and encourages disorder. The rhyme that starts it was once a sectarian taunt: Quaker meeting has begun,/ No more laughing, no more talking,/ No more chewing chewing gum.] **1993** *DARE* File **Boston MA** (as of c1940), My father would say "Quaker meeting has begun. No more talking, no more fun." It was a way to get kids to calm down and be quiet. The game was, how long could you sit there without talking! The silence during the game Quaker Meeting never lasted long. No one got pursued if they talked. Everyone just laughed and said something like "Ooh! You talked first!" *Ibid* **Columbus OH,** "Quaker meeting has begun / No more laughing, no more fun / If you dare to crack a smile / You will have to run a mile"—as a game among grade-school children. If you were the first to laugh or talk you would lose, as in a stare-down, if you're the first to blink.

Quaker nickel See **Quaker fip**

Quaker prayer meeting n Cf **Quaker meeting**

See quot 1957.

[**1894** (1964) Gomme *Traditional Games* 2.90 **Engl,** *Quaker's Wedding*—[Chant:] Hast thou ever been to a Quaker's wedding?/ Nay, friend, nay./ Do as I do; twiddle thy thumbs and follow me.—The leader walks round chanting these lines, with her eyes fixed on the ground. Each new comer goes behind till a long train is formed, then they kneel side by side as close together as possible. The leader then gives a vigorous push to the one at the end of the line [next herself, and that one to the next], and the whole line tumble over.] **1957** *Sat. Eve. Post Letters* **neWI** (as of 1890s), Quaker prayer meeting: Parlor Game. The Leader kneels on the floor at one end of the room. The others kneel beside him, shoulder to shoulder, all down the line. The Leader begins by saying, "Verily, verily must I this day," and each person repeats the statement in turn; the Leader continues, "Visit my brother Abner," and this is repeated clear down the line; the Leader says, "who is very sick." As this is being repeated down the line he sways heavily against the one [next] to him and the result is the whole line goes down like a row of dominoes.

Quaker's bonnet(s) See **Quaker bonnet 2**

Quaker stew n Also *Quaker;* formerly *stewed Quaker* Cf **stew**

A nonalcoholic cough syrup consisting principally of a sweetener heated with vinegar.

1857 *Putnam's Mag.* 9.486 **CT,** While I stirred the "stewed Quaker" that I was cooking for Uncle Payne's cold, we arranged a plan for the confusion of Joe. **1888** *Century Illustr. Mag.* 35.674, Frank's cold was being most considerately treated: . . a little saucepan of "stewed Quaker" . . was bubbling on the stove. **1890** *Century Dict.* 4890, *Stewed Quaker,* a posset of molasses or honey, stewed with butter and vinegar, and taken hot as a remedy for colds. [Colloq.] **1906** *Pocumtuc Housewife* 41 **nwMA,** A Quaker stew is good for an inflamed throat and itching cough. Take a piece of butter the size of a shagbark, a pint of molasses, a little vinegar and a dash of red pepper. Boil until it strings. Take hot or cold. **1966** *DARE* (Qu. BB50a, . . *Favorite remedies . . for a cough*) Inf **ME5,** Quaker stew—half cup of molasses, dash of cayenne pepper, 2 tbsp of vinegar, heat. [Inf old] **1968** Harris *S. Home Remedies* 59 **NC,** A preparation [for sore throat and hoarseness] called Quaker; 1 cup of vinegar with a tablespoon of honey. *Ibid* 78, For croup and colds: Take a concoction called Quaker. This is a combination of sugar, butter and vinegar.

Quaker's wooing, the See **Quaker courtship**

quaking aspen n Also *quacking asp(en), quakenasp, quaker, ~ ash, ~ tree, quakie pole, ~ tree, quaking ash, ~ asp, quaky*

A **cottonwood 1** (here: *Populus tremuloides*), native chiefly to the Rocky Mts., North Central, and Northeastern US. Also called **aspen poplar, quiverleaf, trembling aspen, ~ poplar**

1822 (1898) Fowler *Jrl.* 143 **NM,** The timber on the mountains Heare is Pitch Pine Spruce Pine Hemlock and quakenasp. **1825** in 1918 Dale *Ashley–Smith Explor.* 152 **UT,** This range of mountains is . . closely timbered with pine, cedar, quaking-asp. **1859** in 1942 Hafen *Overland Routes* 11.171 **VA,** We . . halted at a small quaking aspen grove. **1878** Hart *Sazerac Lying Club* 121 **NV,** It was situated in a beautiful, grassy cañon, through which ran a pretty little stream, its banks fringed with willows and quaking aspens. **1882** U.S. Natl. Museum *Proc.* 5.87, *Populus tremuloides.* Aspen; "Quaking Asp." **1894** *Jrl. Amer. Folkl.* 7.99, *Populus tremuloides* . . quaking asp, Mansfield, O., N.E., Iowa. **1905** *Eve. Post* (NY NY) 2 Sept sec 3 1/6 **UT,** I have seen quakenasp groves on the summer range, where you could wade miles and miles through these bluebells. **1930** Shoemaker *1300 Words* 49 **cPA Mts** (as of c1900), *Quaking-ash*—The aspen, or quaking asp. **1948** *UT Humanities Rev.* 2.191, For purifying the blood after a long winter. . . "quakie-pole" tea," [sic] made from the bark of quaking asps. *Ibid* 192, An infusion of this bark was boiled down until it became a poisonous blackish green, and a spoonful of that was administered . . every day for about a month in the spring. "Quakie trees" are coated in the spring with a whitish powder which the Indians used to lick off for "what ailed them." **1960** Vines *Trees SW* 92, Quaking Aspen—*Populus tremuloides.* . . Some of the vernacular names in use are . . Popple . . Quiver Leaf . . and Woman's Tongue. **1963** Burroughs *Head-First* 58 **CO,** We might picnic at the reservoir, venture to Pond Lily Lake—a place of mystery hidden deep among the quakers a couple of miles north of town. **1965–70** *DARE* (Qu. T16, . . *Kinds of trees . . 'special'*) Infs **MI112, 123, NV5, TN6,** Quaking aspen; **CO31,** Quaking aspens or quakies or quakers; **CO37,** Quaking aspen—leaves always tremble—myth that the aspen made the cross on which Christ [was] crucified so now the leaves always tremble; **ID3, WY4, 5,** Quaking asp; **NV8,** Aspen or quaking asp; **UT10,** Quaking asp, but most people call them the aspen; **CO39,** Quaker tree—quaking aspen; (Qu. T13, . . *Poplar*) Infs **MI108, MN14, NY103, OR1, 13,** Quaking aspen; **IA8, OH12, SD8,** Quaking asp; **AR52,** Quaking ash; **CA120,** Cottonwood—like quackin' aspen—also grow in mountains; (Qu. T12, *The kind of poplar tree that has sticky, sweet-smelling buds*) Inf **WA20,** Quaking asp—not a poplar; **MA58,** Popple—same as quaking aspens in the West; (Qu. T15, . . *Kinds of swamp trees*) Infs **CA163, WY1,** Quaking asp; **WA15,** Quaking aspen;

CA120, Quackin' aspen; **IN69,** Quackin' asp. **1967** *DARE* FW Addit **IA,** Aspen—a native here, like a poplar; also "quaking aspen." **1968** Adams *Western Words* 241, *Quaker*—What the cowman calls a quaking aspen tree. **1977** in 1982 *Barrick Coll.* **csPA,** *Quaker ash*—poplar. **1981** *KS Qrly.* 13.2.69, *Quakies* . . trees of the quaking aspen variety that grow in higher elevations along water courses, used in construction of early buildings; also "quaking asp."

quaking grass n Also *quake grass* [*OED2* 1597→ for *Briza* spp]

=**rattlesnake grass 1.**

1821 Schoolcraft *Narr. Jrl.* 93, The margin of the lake [=Lake Huron] is skirted with bull-rushes, quake grass, (*briza canadensis* [=*Glyceria canadensis*],) and other aquatic plants. **1889** Vasey *Ag. Grasses* 69, *Glyceria canadensis* (Rattlesnake Grass; Tall Quaking Grass). . . It is quite an ornamental grass, resembling the quaking grass (*Briza*). *Ibid* 109, Tall Quaking Grass. . . Cattle are fond of it, both green and when made into hay. **1910** Graves *Flowering Plants* 74 **CT,** *Glyceria canadensis.* . . Tall Quaking Grass. . . Frequent. Bogs, open swamps and ditches. June-July.

quaky See **quaking aspen**

qualify v

1 To put (one) to an oath, cause (one) to testify; to swear, testify; hence ppl adj *qualified* absolutely certain. [Prob by ext from *qualify* to administer or to take an oath of office]

1800 in 1956 Eliason *Tarheel Talk* 289 **nwNC,** Betsey when exammend sed she wod be quilified that there was no such talk there that day. **1827** Cooper *Red Rover* 1.216, A seafaring man, by your dress? and one in search of a ship, as I am ready to qualify to. **1840** *S. Lit. Messenger* 6.507, Why, it is cousin Liddy he's sparking—but it's no use, I can qualify. **1845** Thompson *Pineville* 65 **cGA,** Any one who had observed the severe scrutiny with which the crowd regarded those veiled women . . would have been qualified that but one sentiment prevailed in that company, and that was, that all was not right in that buggy. **1848** Bartlett *Americanisms* 267, *To qualify.* To swear to discharge the duties of an office; and hence to make oath of any fact; as, 'I am ready to qualify to what I have asserted!' **1858** Hammett *Piney Woods Tavern* 123, He never raised that crop [of hair, on his head], and I'll be qualified to that on a stack of bibles. **1903** *DN* 2.326 **seMO,** *Qualify to.* . . To cause to make affidavit. 'He signed the statement and was qualified to it before a justice of the peace,' that is, swore to it. **1950** *PADS* 14.55 **SC,** Qualified. . . certain, sure. "I's qualified it's so." Negro usage.

2 See quot 1899; hence adj *unqualified.* [*OED2* 1591→]

1816 in 1824 Knight *Letters* 72 **VA,** They [=Virginians] have no cider, perry, or common beverage for table-drink; but, instead, for the ladies, water unqualified. **1877** Hallock *Sportsman's Gaz.* 649 **eFL,** A drink of raw unadulterated water is not always acceptable. Some people "qualify" it—indeed the majority of settlers "qualify" it so much that the original taste of the *aqua* is lost in that of the qualifier. **1897** *KS Univ. Qrly.* (ser B) 6.56 **KS,** *Qualifying*—[Putting] sugar and cream in coffee. **1899** (1912) Green *VA Folk-Speech* 340, *Qualify.* . . To modify the quality or strength of; make stronger, dilute, or otherwise fit for taste: as, to *qualify* liquors. **2000** *NADS Letters* **MI,** My mother always uses the word qualify when she talks about making gravy mixing the milk and the flower [sic] and water, she also uses it talking about adding butter that is melted to a batter. She is now 62, born in Detroit Michigan and raised by a family with Swedish roots. *Ibid,* Qualify. This term to show off the literacy of a person. . . When I heard it used, it was used as "modification", i.e. to qualify tea with milk, was to modify the tea with milk to dilute the caffeine. I haven't heard this word in common usage.

quality n, also attrib [*OED2* "Now *dial.* or rather *arch.*"] chiefly **Sth, S Midl**

The social or economic elite of a community; one of its members.

1859 Taliaferro *Fisher's R.* 105 **nwNC** (as of 1820s), The best of company, even the "quality," visited his house. *Ibid* 217, A few families (called the "quality") could afford coffee once a week. **1886** *S. Bivouac* 4.343 **sAppalachians,** Quality (people of —). **1899** (1912) Green *VA Folk-Speech* 340, *Quality.* . . The better class of people. **1902** *DN* 2.242 **sIL,** *Quality.* . . Person of *quality.* 'You think you're quality'; 'the Smiths are quality.' **1907** *DN* 3.225 **nwAR,** *Quality.* . . Person of quality. **1924** (1946) Greer-Petrie *Angeline Gits an Eyeful* 1 **csKY,** Gittin' 'quainted with all that *quality,* who wuz a-visitin' Betty Bowles. **1930** Shoemaker *1300 Words* 49 **cPA Mts** (as of c1900), *Quality*—The older and more prosperous families of a community. **1934** Hurston *Jonah's Gourd Vine* 11 **AL** [Black], Who can't look at ole Beasley? He ain't no quality nohow. **1951** Johnson *Resp. to PADS 20* **DE** (*Names and nick-names for the part of a town where the well-off people live*) Quality Hill. **1957** Faulkner *Town* 245 **MS**, You talk about change to quality, what you gets back is a quarter or a half a dollar or sometimes even a whole dollar. It's just trash that cant think no higher than a nickel or ten cents. **1967–68** *DARE* (Qu. C35, *Nicknames for the different parts of your town or city*) Inf IL3, Quality Hill; (Qu. II24, *Names or nicknames for the part of a town where the well-off people live*) Infs **MD**30, 33, **PA**114, Quality Hill; **IL**7, Quality Knob; **IN**38, Quality Row. **1984** Wilder *You All Spoken Here* 105 **Sth**, *Quality:* Quality folk; people with class and pedigree.

qualm n Usu |kwɑm|; also |kwæm| Cf **calm, palm**

A Form.

1893 Shands *MS Speech* 6, Among the educated classes *palm, calm, psalm, qualm,* and similar words are correctly pronounced, but the illiterate of both colors pronounce the *a* as [æ].

B Sense.

Pl: Feelings of nausea. Cf **quim-quams**

1943 *LANE* Map 503 (*Sick at his stomach*) 1 inf, **Nantucket MA**, He had the qualms [kwɔˆ·mz].

qualm v

To make sick or uneasy.

1884 *Harper's New Mth. Mag.* 69.701, If one is . . qualmed by the show of . . confectionery. **1963** *AmSp* 38.159 **cwNY**, Since last year University of Buffalo undergraduates have used *qualm* as a verb, synonymous with *bother* or *worry,* as in: "It doesn't qualm me a bit."

qualmish adj, hence n *qualmishness* Also sp *quamish* [*OED2* 1548→] esp **NEng, Sth** Cf **squamish**

Affected by nausea, queasy.

1787 (1936) Dewees *Jrl.* 12 **PA**, The boat tossing about a good deal occasioned one to feel a little quamish. **1843** (1847) Field *Drama Pokerville* 64 **MO**, "Don't you feel a qualmishness at your stomach, now?" . . "Yes, yes, sick!" **1899** (1912) Green *VA Folk-Speech* 340, *Qualmish.* . . Sick at the stomach; inclined to vomit; affected with nausea. **1932** *DN* 6.284 **cwCT**, *Quamish.* Feeling uneasy in the stomach; "when you aren't really sick at your stomach, but by-and-by you're going to be." **1943** *LANE* Map 503 (*Sick at his stomach*) 2 infs, **CT, RI**, ['kwɒmɪʃ]. **1968–70** *DARE* (Qu. BB16b, *If something a person ate didn't agree with him, he might just feel a bit _____*) Infs **NC**77, **RI**1, Qualmish ['kwɑmɪʃ]; **NY**75, ['kwɒmɪʃ]; **VA**52, Qualmish—like he might got to vomick. **1994** NC Lang. & Life Project *Dial. Vocab.* Ocracoke 14 **eNC**, Quamish. . . Sick to the stomach. . . *I felt quamished* [sic] *on the ferry.*

qualmy adj Pronc-sp *qua'my* [*OED2* 1562→]

=**qualmish.**

1852 *S. Lit. Messenger* 18.21, We have known it not infrequently to happen, that young gentlemen who were desperately smitten would feel qualmy at the very sight of provisions. **1859** Taliaferro *Fisher's R.* 126 **nwNC** (as of 1820s), I toddled down to the seaboard to git a bait ov oysters, feelin' considible qualmy 'bout my gizzard. **1923** *DN* 5.218 **swMO**, *Qua'my.* . . Qualmy. **1967** *DARE* (Qu. BB16b, *If something a person ate didn't agree with him, he might just feel a bit*) Inf **MI**65, Qualmy ['kwɑwmɪ]. [FW: the merest glide where the [-l-] maybe used to be]

quamash See **camas**

quamish adj See **qualmish**

quamish n See **camas**

quamquidle See **conquedle**

qua'my See **qualmy**

quandy n

1 also *quandie, quondy:* =**old-squaw. NEng**

1852 in 1876 *Forest & Stream* 7.212 **eMA**, *Harelda glacialis.* Quandie. **1870** *Fur Fin & Feather* 119, Along the coast of New England it [=the long-tailed duck] is generally called the quondy. **1876** *Forest & Stream* 7.245 **MA**, The "quaudie," [sic] (long-tailed duck) is also called the "old squaw," (never "old wife" hereabout) from its constant chattering. **1888** Trumbull *Names of Birds* 89 **eMA**, Two other

odd names met with among old New England gunners are *scoldenore,* at Portsmouth, N.H., and *quandy,* at North Scituate and Plymouth, Mass. **1892** *Auk* 9.330, This sprightly little salt water Duck frequents the New England coast . . where it is well known under the cognomens of Oldsquaw, Oldwife, and Quandy. **1955** MA Audubon Soc. *Bulletin* 39.375 **MA**, Old Squaw. . . Quandy.

2 The female **goldeneye 1.**

1925 (1928) Forbush *Birds MA* 1.246, *Glaucionetta clangula americana* . . Golden-eye. . . Quandy (Female). **1932** Bennitt *Check-list* 20 **MO**, American goldeneye. *Glaucionetta islandica* . . quandy (female). **1955** MA Audubon Soc. *Bulletin* 39.316, American Golden-eye . . Quandy (All [of New England]. The female.)

quar(e) See **queer**

quark See **quawk** n[2] **1, 3**

quarl See **coil** v

quarrel n, v Usu |'kwɔrəl|; also esp **NEast** |'kwɑrəl|; for addit varr see quots Cf Pronc Intro 3.I.2.b Pronc-spp *quarril, quawl, querrel, quoil, quo(r)l;* similarly n *quarrelment* pronc-spp *quarrilment, quawlment* Cf **forest, orange**

A Std senses, var forms.

1877 *Harper's New Mth. Mag.* 54.293 **CT**, His folks querreled. **1883** [see **B** below]. **1884** *Anglia* 7.278 **Sth, S Midl** [Black], *To keep on quollin'* = to continue quarrelling. **1890** *DN* 1.39 **ME**, Quarrel. . . [kwʌrɪl] (and perhaps also -əl), *not* [kwɔrəl]; *it requires a conscious effort for me to give* [ɔ] *in the first syllable.* **1891** [see **B** below]. **1892** *DN* 1.212 **ceMA**, *Quarrel:* [kwɔrɪl]. **c1920** in 1944 *ADD* **cNY**, [kwɔrəl]. **1922** Gonzales *Black Border* 321 **sSC, GA coasts** [Gullah glossary], *Quarril, quawl*—quarrel, quarrels. *Ibid, Quarrilment, quawlment.* **1923** (1946) Greer-Petrie *Angeline Steppin'* 41 **csKY**, When a married couple can't find something bigger to quorl about than a pocket handkercher. **1927** Kennedy *Gritny* 45 **sLA** [Black], For Gawd sake, stop y'all quoilin' an' set down. **1929** [see **B** below]. **1933** *AmSp* 8.2.44 **neNY**, Quarrel [kwɔrəl]. **1936** *AmSp* 11.73 **Upstate NY**, *Low Back Vowels Before 'R' Plus A Vowel* . . quarrel . . 72 [exx of [ɑ]] 5 [of [ɒ]] 59 [of [ɔ]]. *Ibid* **NYC**, 5 [exx of [ɑ]]. *Ibid* 74 **NY**, In addition to those instances . . in which the [r] of *quarrel* is followed by a vowel, the word shows 76 instances of [ɑrl], 41 [of [ɔrl], and one instance of [ɒrl]. *Ibid, Low Back Vowels After* [w] . . quarrel . . 148 [exx of [ɑ]] 6 [of [ɒ]] 100 [of [ɔ]]. **1942** *AmSp* 17.38 **seNY**, *Quarrel* has [kwarəl] 10, [kwarl] 17, [kwɑ:l] 4, [kwɔrl] 1. **1953** Kenyon–Knott *Pronc. Dict.* 349, *Quarrel* ['kwɔrəl, 'kwɑr-, 'kwɒr-, -rl]. **1965–70** *DARE* (Qu. Y7) Inf **VA**73, ['kwɒəlɪn]; (Qu. Y12a) Inf **IL**34, ['kourəl]; **NJ**6, [kwɔrl]; (Qu. KK13, . . *Arguing: "They stood there for an hour _____."*) Inf **FL**19, ['kwɔrlɪn]; **MO**1, ['kwɔɑr·lɪn]; **MO**9, ['kwɔrɫ]; **ND**2, ['kwɔrlɪn]; **NJ**10, ['kwɔrlɪn]; **NY**149, ['kwarrɛlɪn]; **NY**190, ['kwarrɛllɪn]; **VA**72, ['kwɑrəlɪn]; (Qu. KK14) Inf **MO**11, ['kwɔrɫ]; (Qu. KK15) Inf **PA**240, [kwɑ·rl].

B As verb.

To use abusive language, find fault; with *at* or *with:* to scold, nag, find fault with. **Sth, S Midl** *esp freq among Black speakers*

1883 (1971) Harris *Nights with Remus* 97 **GA** [Black], Brer Wolf, he tuck'n 'buse Brer Fox . . en den Brer Fox, he tuck'n quol back at Brer Wolf. **1891** Page *Elsket* 131 **VA** [Black], Soon as ole Mis' Twine see me she began to quoil. **1929** (1951) Faulkner *Sartoris* 87 **MS** [Black], Here you quoilin' too . . Miss Jenny yellin' at me twell I wuz plum out de gate, and now you already started at dis en'. **1970** *DARE* (Qu. Y7, *When one person never misses a chance to be mean to another or to annoy another: "I don't know why she keeps _____ me all the time!"*) Inf **VA**73, Quarreling with. [Inf Black] **1973** Gt. Smoky Mt. Natl. Park Recordings 80:5 (*Montgomery Coll.*) **eTN**, I remember Etter quarreling at you and Ray, you know, for running through the house and making such a fuss. **1983** Abbott *Womenfolks* 164 **AR**, People never scolded anybody, they "quarreled at" a person, and anyone in a bad temper was "a-quarrelin'." **1994** in 1996 *Montgomery Coll.* **eTN**, She quarreled at her husband so much that she left him.

quarry n, v Usu |'kwɔrɪ, 'kwɑrɪ|; also |'kwɛrɪ, 'kwɜ-, 'kwɪr-|; for addit varr see quots Pronc-spp *korry, quairy, quayry, queery, querry*

Std senses, var forms.

1849 in 1956 Eliason *Tarheel Talk* 316 **cNC**, Querry. **1873** in 1955 Lee *Mormon Chron.* 2.231 **UT**, Others hauling, some querrying Rock &c. **1887** *Atlantic Mth.* 60.331 **cVA** [Black], "'Pears like dem folks been diggin' a grave up dar," says Newton. "Korryin' o' limestone," replies Jim. **1889** *Harper's New Mth. Mag.* 80.120 **West,** That thar rock house o' his'n, which he have quayried the rock an' put up hisse'f. *Ibid,* He 'ain't tetched the ole quayry, hez he? **1891** *DN* 1.156 **cNY,** Diphthongization sometimes occurs, as in . . [kwaɪrɪ] < *quarry.* [**1901** *DN* 2.146 **cNY,** *Quarry.* . . Name of a street in Ithaca sometime [sic] pron. [ˈkɔrɪ], even by those who live upon it. The frequency of this pron. is shown by the remark of a student: "I haven't lived in Ithaca long enough to say [ˈkɔrɪ] street."] **1909** *DN* 3.414 **nME,** *Querry.* **1923** *DN* 5.218 **swMO,** *Quairy.* **1941** Nixon *Possum Trot* 11 **neAL,** It [=Possum Trot] is three miles from the discontinued railway station of Tredegar, where a small lime quarry and a limekiln were operated for several years around the turn of the century. **1942** Hall *Smoky Mt. Speech* 33 **wNC, eTN,** *Quarry* is always either [ˈkwɛrɪ] or [ˈkwɜrɪ]. **1960** Criswell *Resp. to PADS* 20 **Ozarks,** *Quarry* [kwɛri]. No other pron[unciation] ever heard here. Still so. **1965–70** *DARE* (Qu. C27, *A hillside or deep hole where stone is taken out;* total Infs questioned, 75) Infs **AR1, OK4,** 18, 42, 51, (Rock) querry; **AR25, MS1,** (Rock) [ˈkwɛrɪ]; **FL11, OK21,** [ˈkwɛrɪ]; **OK1,** [ˈkwɪrɪ]; **UT3,** [ˈkwori], rock [ˈkwɛrɪ]; **DC1,** [kwɒrɪ]; **DC3,** [kwaˌɪrɪ]; (Qu. C4a) Inf **IN68,** [ˈkwæriɪ]; (Qu. C4b) Inf **MD8,** [ˈkwori]; (Qu. C26, . . *Special kinds of stone or rock*) Inf **KY84,** [ˈkwɛˌʌi]; **IN48,** [ˈkwɛri] stone; (Qu. C34) Inf **AL11,** [kwɛrˌ]; (QR, near Qu. M20) Inf **IL31,** [ˈkwɛri] stone. **1967** *AmSp* 42.295 **csIN,** *Quarry.* . . All the workers of this area seem to pronounce it [ˈkweri], not [ˈkwori]. **1967–69** *DARE* Tape **AZ7,** [FW:] Where does the sandstone come from? [Inf:] Well, our [ˈkweri] is about five miles this side of Holbrook; **KY13,** It all come out of the same [ˈkweri]; **KY14,** [ˈkwɛrɪd]. **1967** *DARE* FW Addit **NC,** Quarry [ˈkwɜˌi]. **1975** Gould *ME Lingo* 223, *Querry*—Approximate sound of quarry when spoken by a Mainer. **1976** Garber *Mountain-ese* 73 **sAppalachians,** *Queery* . . quarry. **1976** Allen *LAUM* 3.35 (as of c1950), A footnote to the pronunciation of /æ/ and /ɛ/ before intersyllabic /r/ is provided by the deviant form /kwɛri/ observed in the speech of . . [2 infs, **IA**] for the word *quarry.* **1979** *Greenfield Recorder* (MA) 15 Sept sec A 4/1, A man named Nash . . querried and sold dinosaur footprints. **1981** Pederson *LAGS Basic Materials* **Gulf Region,** [Of the eight pronunciations of *quarry* recorded, three were of the type [ˈkwɛˌi]; there were two examples of [æ] in the first syllable and one each of [ɑ], [ɔ], and [ɪ].] **1983** *MJLF* 9.1.52 **ceKY** (as of 1956), *Querry.*

quartee n [Abbr for *quartillo* < Span *cuartillo*] **chiefly LA old-fash** Cf **picayune**

Orig one-fourth of the Spanish real or bit; later one-fourth of a dime, or two-and-one-half cents' worth of (some commodity); rarely one-fourth of a dollar.

1839 *Daily Picayune* (New Orleans LA) 6 Feb 2/2, He vas vell known in all the quartee shops and cabarets round the market. **1886** *Boston Herald* 18 July *(DA)* **LA,** If the purchaser demands quartee (2½ cents' worth) rice, and quartee beans, two lagniappes are given. **1909** *DN* 3.402 **AR, LA,** *Quartel* [sic]. . Two and one half cents. **1916** *DN* 4.270 **New Orleans LA** [Idiom of non-French White speakers], *Quartee.* . . Two and a half cents. **1923** *DN* 5.244 **LA,** *Quartee.* . . 1. One fourth of a 'bit' (12½ c.), later, one fourth of ten cents. 2. One fourth of a dollar; a quarter. **1949** *Times–Picayune* (New Orleans LA) 11 Sept mag sec 12/3, [Cartoon:] Quartee red beans, quartee rice,/ Little piece of salt meat to make it taste nice. **1968** *DARE* FW Addit **New Orleans LA,** *Quartee* [ˌkwɔəˈti]—The value of a quarter of a dime. In the old days you could get for a nickel a quartee of rice and a quartee of red beans. If change for a quartee was needed, it was made with a ticket. Old-fashioned—many younger people have never heard of this. It was reported by an old man, native to the Irish channel. **1983** Reinecke *Coll.* 9 **LA,** *Quartee* . . [kwɔˈti]. . The value of 2½ cents, or a token arbitrarily assigned that value by merchants who gave them in change. "When daddy went to school, he gave the groceryman a nickel, and got a ham sandwich and a quartee change." "You could buy a quartee's worth of sugar." Obsolescent. . . Once general in N[ew] O[rleans].

quarter n

1 pl; often with *the;* often in combs: A neighborhood or district in a town or city, esp a poor one where Black people live. [By ext from *quarters* a group of cabins on a plantation housing slaves, and later, farmhands; prob also infl by *quarter* section of a city, as in *French Quarter, student quarter*] **chiefly Sth, Lower Missip Valley** See Map

1889 (1971) Farmer *Americanisms* 445, *Quarters.*—The negro huts on a plantation in slavery times; the term still survives to designate the houses of black people. **1903** *DN* 2.326 **seMO,** *Quarters.* . . Houses occupied by negro farm hands. In the days of slavery these houses were

generally grouped near the planter's house. 'It was late and the men had all gone to quarters.' **1907** *DN* 3.235 **nwAR,** *Quarters.* . . Houses occupied by negro farm-hands (or other farm hands). **1965–70** *DARE* (Qu. C35, *Nicknames for the different parts of your town or city*) Infs **MS2,** 23, 65, 72, Negro (*or* nigger) quarters; **AL6,** Reilly's Quarters—slum; **AR52,** Niggertown, or the quarters; Grayson Quarters, Calhoun Heights—it's owing to who they work for; **FL48,** Butler's Quarters—Butler used to own all the land around; **GA22,** Nigger quarters—old-fashioned; **LA7,** Toler Quarters; **LA11,** The quarters—where colored people live; **LA14,** The square, the hill, the quarters—all Negro sections; **LA40,** The quarters—the place where Negroes live; **NC83,** Possum quarters; **TX33,** The quarters—colored people; **TX35,** Nigger quarters; cheap-rent quarters; **TX100,** Neill Quarters—Negro area; (Qu. II25, *Names or nicknames for the part of a town where the poorer people, special groups, or foreign groups live*) Infs **AR6, LA28,** 14, 21, **MO9, TX35,** Negro (*or* nigger) quarters; **MO9, LA6, TX33,** (The) quarters; **AR52,** Grayson Quarters; **FL19,** Colored quarters; **FL48,** Skipper Quarters; **GA23,** Bud Griffis Quarters—colored section; White quarters—White houses; **LA2,** The quarters [FW: used in conv for where Negroes live]; **SC40,** In the quarters—the low-rent Negro section; **TX95,** Stokes Quarters; [**TX32,** Nigger quarter; **TX98,** The quarter; **CT30,** Foreign quarter;] (Qu. C34, *Nicknames for nearby settlements, villages, or districts*) Inf **LA7,** Hatcher's Quarters—group of houses where there used to be a plantation house; **MS2,** Robert's Quarters. **1968** *DARE* FW Addit **seGA,** A company-owned logging town gone to seed. The population is constantly diminishing, is currently less than 400; most of these are contained in the "quarters" (the colored section). **1981** Palmer *Deep Blues* 55 **nwMS,** A lot of the blues singers lived in what they called the quarters, . . and that's not a name we gave it. They called it 'quarters' after the term 'slave quarters.' **1986** Pederson *LAGS Concordance,* 1 inf, **swAR,** The quarters—blacks lived; 1 inf, **cnGA,** Down in the French quarters; 1 inf, **ceTX,** The Negro quarters = neighborhood they lived in; (*Urban neighborhoods*; this question was asked chiefly in urban areas) 1 inf, **seAL,** Nigger quarters—where most black people live; 1 inf, **seFL,** The Quarters—a black area in Ojus; 1 inf, **swGA,** The quarters; 1 inf, **seMS,** The Quarters—mostly black, not all low income; 1 inf, **seMS,** Red Quarters—black section of Wiggins.

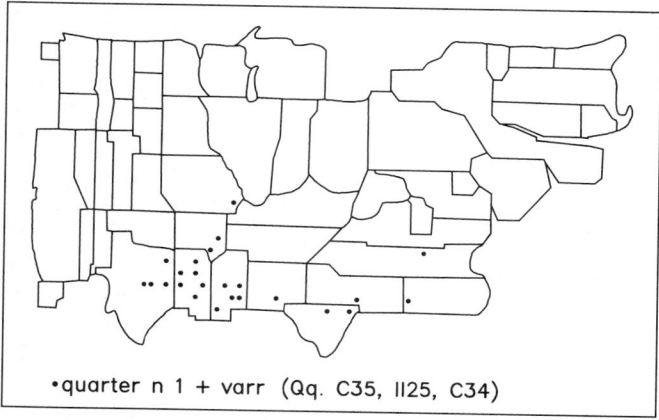

•quarter n 1 + varr (Qq. C35, II25, C34)

2 A fourth of a mile. **chiefly Sth, S Midl**

1784 Smyth *Tour U.S.A.* 1.22 **VA,** In the southern part of the colony, and in North Carolina, they are much attached to *quarter-racing.* **1828** Cooper *Prairie* 1.56, I can make myself heard a mile in these open fields, and his camp is but a short quarter from us. **1884** *Century Illustr. Mag.* 29.118 **GA,** There was a quarter-track . . if he chose to enjoy the pleasures of horse-racing. **1893** Shands *MS Speech* 51, *Quarter.* . . The illiterate whites of Mississippi . . use it to mean a quarter of a mile. They very rarely, indeed, say a quarter of a mile, but nearly always simply a quarter. They seem to think it necessary to say half of a mile, eighth of a mile, etc., but rarely ever quarter of a mile. **1896** *DN* 1.422, *Quarter:* specifically, a quarter of a mile. "I walked a quarter." **1907** Wright *Shepherd* 18 **swMO,** Jim Lane lives up the trail 'bout half a quarter. **1923** (1946) Greer-Petrie *Angeline Doin' Society* 15 **csKY,** We driv thoo [=through] two rows of big maple trees fur about a *quarter* afore we come in sight of the house. **1938** Rawlings *Yearling* 348 **nFL,** The dug-out's less'n a quarter up the run. **1939** Hall *Coll.* **wNC, eTN,** *Quarter*—Frequently used for 'a quarter of a mile'. "Off he come down, down the hill about a quarter." "So the dogs took after him and he went out I judge about a quarter." **1947** Lomax *Advent. Ballad Hunter* 263 **TX,** Keep straight ahead fur about a quarter, . . then turn to the left fur a mile and a half. **1951** *PADS* 16.53, *Quarter.* . . A quarter of a mile, usually referring to the first quarter of a race.   **1986** Pederson *LAGS Concordance,* 1 inf, **swAR,** I had to tote the thing a quarter.

3 A break taken at midmorning or midafternoon; hence comb *quarter lunch* a snack taken at this time.   Cf **lunch 1, quarter v 2**

1966 *PADS* 46.28 **cnAR** (as of 1952), *Quarter lunch.* . . A snack for eating between quarters of the working day, either at mid-morning or mid-afternoon.   **1997** [see **quarter v 2**].

quarter v

1 To move diagonally; hence vbl n *quartering.*   **scattered, but esp Sth, S Midl**   Cf **cater v, kitter, quartering adv**

1846 Sage *Scenes Rocky Mts.* 291, Three buffalo bulls . . rushed down a steep hill-side, quartering towards me.   **1894** *Outing* 24.387, Just as the dogs were sent on, a laggard sprang from under my feet. I was so surprised that I missed, and the bird quartered past the Judge.   **1895** *Ibid* 26.401 **WY,** We . . changed our direction so as to "quarter" by them, intending if we succeeded in that to circle gradually hear [sic] them.   **1938** Rawlings *Yearling* 260 **nFL,** His bear was quartering from him, but he was able to draw a bead on the left cheek from the rear.   **1948** Camp *Hunter's Encycl.* 644, For example, the 2-o'clock shot may involve a target traveling at exactly right angles across your front, or it may be the right-quartering quail serving as the example above.   **1958** McCulloch *Woods Words* 143 **Pacific NW,** *Quartering to the tree—* Yarding slantwise across a hill to the landing.   **1965** Davis *Summer Land* 28 **cnNC,** It was all I could do to keep up with Tree . . quartering down the slope with briars and limbs whipping at me in the dark.   **1976** Garber *Mountain-ese* 73 **sAppalachians,** *Quartering* . . diagonaling. This hoss ain't so fast but he is shore good at quartering.   **1981** Pederson *LAGS Basic Materials (Kitty-cornered)* 1 inf, **seGA,** Quartered (pret. = cut across a field) . . quartered across (pret., of the line from corner to corner [in tick-tack-toe, e.g., upper left to lower right]) . . quartered (=relationship) (pret.)

2 To take a midmorning or midafternoon break; hence comb *quartering time* break time.   Note: The definition in quot 1905 is prob erroneous.

1902 *DN* 2.243 **sIL,** *Quarterin-time.* . . The middle of the morning or evening. The hour completing a quarter of a day.   **1905** *DN* 3.402 **nwAR,** *Quarterin' time.* . . Time to cease work. Time to stop work and go to *quarters.*   **1948** White *Farmer's Hdbk.* 416, Quartering time: during the long days at harvest time or other emergency work, fifteen minutes are taken out at mid-morning, and mid-afternoon to grease and check machines and for the men to rest and refresh themselves; this brief period of rest is known as quartering time.   **1952** Brown *NC Folkl.* 1.581 **w,nNC,** *Quartering time.* . . Resting time for workers between forenoon and afternoon.   **1965** *DARE* (Qu. A3, *The time between the middle of the day and supper time*) Inf **OK1,** Quartering time—3:00 p.m.   **1966** *PADS* 46.28 **cnAR** (as of 1952), *Quartering time.* . . The time when a quarter lunch is eaten.—"Quarterin' time was about 9:30 to 10:00 in the morning and 2:30 to 3:00 in the evenin'."   **1997** *DARE* File **cAR,** *Quarter lunch* is the first break of the day. During The Reconstruction, workers would work sunup to sundown. In the course of 12 to 14 hours of hard labor, you can't work half a day and have lunch; you'll get hungry before that. Usually the first quarter was 3–4 hours after sunup and 2nd quarter was 3–4 before sundown. Quarters are about 20–30 min, with lunch being an hour, usually. In the South, many fields have a large tree in the middle for breaks when field workers would quarter or lunch.

quarter boss See **quarters boss**

quarterdeck n   Cf **boat shell, half deck**

A **slipper shell** (here: *Crepidula fornicata*).

1949 Palmer *Nat. Hist.* 362, *Quarter-deck, Boat Shell—Crepidula fornicata.*   **1981** Rehder *Audubon Field Guide Seashells* 464, *Crepidula fornicata.* . . *Flat shelf covering* ⅓–½ *of rear has a sinuous edge with a slight central indentation.* . . This common shell is sometimes known as the Boat Shell or Quarterdeck.

quarter hand n

1 A person who does, or is allotted, one-fourth the amount of work expected of an able-bodied adult.   *hist*   Cf **half hand 1**

1856 Olmsted *Journey Slave States* 433 **SC, GA,** The children beginning as 'quarter-hands,' advancing to 'half-hands,' and then to 'three-quarter hands;' and finally, when mature, and able-bodied, . . to 'full hands.'   **1936** Smith-Sass *Carolina Rice* 70 (as of 1850s), The young

negroes were called 'half-hands' and were allotted a half-task; those still younger, and yet too old to be kept as nurses to the babies were 'quarter-hands.'

2 =**fourth hand.**   Cf **half hand 2**

1967 *DARE* (Qu. L3, *A man who lives on the farm and does the work, but divides the expenses and profits with the owner*) Inf **LA14,** Half hand, quarter hand—different types of tenants.

quartering adv   Pronc-sp *quatering*   Cf **catering, kittering, quarter v 1**

Diagonally, at an angle.

1852 Beardsley *Reminiscences* 236 **NY,** He [=a buck] stopped about sixteen rods from me, presenting his side, though standing rather quartering.   **1883** Twain *Life on Missip.* (Boston) 51 **MO,** I see a black something floating on the water away off to stabboard and quartering behind us.   **1894** *Century Illustr. Mag.* 47.854 **NY,** Our people, in sawing or nailing anything at an angle other than a right angle, do not place it or cut it "quartering,"—which is the recognized technical term,—but "catering."   **1909** *DN* 3.361 **eAL, wGA,** *Quaterin(g).* . . Diagonally.   **1912** Green *VA Folk-Speech* 340, *Quartering.* . . Not directly, but obliquely. "He crossed the field quartering."   **1938** in Lib. of Congress *Amer. Memory: WPA Life Hist.* (Internet), After the place had been selected for the camp, the leading teams stopped at the place designated, and the next immediately to the rear and quartering, with the forward wheels nearly even with the hind wheels of the first wagon.   *Ibid* **TX,** On this same stampede, one of the fellows was riding full speed and his horse hit a fence sort of quartering and threw that boy over the fence.   *Ibid* **TX** (as of 1872), We went quartering up the mountain.   **1940** in 1944 *ADD* **swPA, nWV,** *Quartering.* . . 'I walked quarterin' across the street.' Old illit. speaker.   **1974** Fink *Mountain Speech* 21 **wNC, eTN,** *Quartering* . . diagonally. *"He walked quartering across the field."*

quartering vbl n   See **quarter v 1**

quartering n   Cf **beef club**

The practice of distributing freshly slaughtered meat to one's neighbors.

1975 McDonough *Garden Sass* 72 **AR,** Newman said that on Chickalah Mountain, "Most of the time when they'd kill a beef in the summertime, why they'd just dress it and they'd cut off what they wanted and they'd start peddling it out among the neighbors, you know. And maybe a week or two from then some other guy would kill one. By doing that in the community—somebody killing one ever week or ten days—they'd have fresh meat all summer." Another man said, "When we killed a beef we divided it out; everybody got some." This practice, called "quartering," was used all over the state and was apparently an old British custom.

quartering time See **quarter v 2**

quarter lunch See **quarter n 3**

quarters boss n   Also *quarter boss*   [*quarters* living accommodations]   Cf **bull of the woods 1**

One who maintains law and order in a logging camp.

1935 Hurston *Mules & Men* 92 **FL,** I spoke to the quarters boss and the swamp boss [of the lumber company] and both agreed that it was all right, so I strowed it all over the quarters that I was going out to the swamp with the boys next day.   **1942** Hurston *Dust Tracks* 191 **cFL** [Black], It is a sad, parting song. Each verse ends up with: Quarters Boss! High Sheriff? Lemme git gone from here!   *Ibid* 195, Dat Cracker Quarters Boss wears two pistols round his waist and goes for bad.   **1968** *DARE* Tape **GA30,** The [logging] company had their own law, what we called a quarter boss. He didn't do anything, only just keep order among the niggers, and the whites, too. And if a man done a crime in there [=in the Okefenokee Swamp], why, he taken him and brought him out.

quarter-sizer n   Cf **half-sizer**

c1970 Wiersma *Marbles Terms* **swMI,** *Quarter-sizers*—between the size of a half-sizer and a normal marble.

quarter to nine, (as close as) a adj phr   [From the position of the hands on a clock at that time]   Cf *DS* II2b, II3

Of a relationship between people: very close.

1980 De Vries *Consenting Adults* 162 **IL,** This was to be explained later on when we had become "a quarter to nine"—his term for a relationship as close as the two hands of a clock are at that hour. He held out two fingers to illustrate.   *Ibid* 166, We remained a quarter-to-nine, though he sometimes called us three-fifteen, which, of course, comes to the same thing. **1997** *DARE* File **AR** (as of c1970), We were watching TV and there were people on there kissing and [my grandmother] said they were "closer than a quarter to nine." On another time when she almost . . [got] hit by another car she said "that was almost as close as a quarter to nine." My grandmother was raised in Missouri but married and has lived in Arkansas for the past 50-odd years. **2000** *DARE* File [Heard on National Public Radio], Fred Mertz on *I Love Lucy* said of a couple of lovebirds, "They're closer than a quarter to nine."

quartervine n [See quot 1890]
=cross vine 1.

 1890 *Century Dict.* 4899, *Quarter-vine.* . . An American vine, *Bignonia capreolata*. It is so called because, owing to the projection of medullary tissue in four wing-like layers from the middle to near the surface, a short section of the stem, when gently twisted in the hand, will divide into quarters. **1960** Vines *Trees SW* 924, *Bignonia capreolata.* . . Vernacular names are Tendriled Trumpet-creeper and Quarter-vine. **1970** Correll *Plants TX* 1443, *Quarter-vine.* . . Climbing in trees in moist woods in the e. Tex. pinelands. **1976** Bailey–Bailey *Hortus Third* 162, *Quarter v[ine].* . . Woods and swamps, Va. and Fla., w. to Ill., La., e. Tex.

quasky See **oquassa**

quate See **quoit A1**

quatering See **quartering** adv

quauhog See **quahog** n

quawbird See **quabird**

quawk v, n[1] Pronc-sp *quouk* [nEngl dial]
Of a bird: to caw, squawk; a caw, squawk.

 1884 Jewett *Country Dr.* 62 **ME**, One of the young turkeys had come hoppin' and quawkin' round the doorsteps with its leg broke. **1899** (1912) Green *VA Folk-Speech* 340, *Quawk.* . . To croak; caw. *Ibid*, *Quawk*, n. Imitative of the sound made by the cry of fowls. **1937** (1963) Hyatt *Kiverlid* 27 **KY**, I seed two of the hens makin' fer the big woods a-quoukin' purt nigh ever' mornin' about day-break.

quawk n[2] [Imit]
1 also *couac, qu(w)ark, quawker, quo(c)k, quowk*: **=night heron.** **scattered, but chiefly NEast** Cf **huac, quabird, quack 1**

 1844 DeKay *Zool. NY* 2.227, The *Black-crowned Night Heron*, or *Quawk.* . . derives its popular name from the deep guttural cry, resembling that word in sound. **1844** [see **quack 1**]. **1890** *DN* 1.75 **Cape Cod MA**, *Quawk* [kwɔk]: the night-heron. Elsewhere . . called *squawk*. **1890** *Century Dict.* 4902, *Quawk.* . . The qua-bird or night-heron, *Nyctiardea grisea nævia*. Also *quark, squawk*. [*Century* Ed: Local, U.S.] **1899** Howe–Sturtevant *Birds RI* 44, *Nycticorax nyticorax* [sic] *naevius* . . Black-crowned Night Heron . . Quwark. **c1902** Clapin *New Dict. Amer.* 139, *Couac*, koo-ak. A species of heron (Nyctiardea grisea), frequenting the Gulf of St-Lawrence region, and so called from its peculiar cry. . . **1917** *Wilson Bulletin* 29.78 **NY**, *Nycticorax nycticorax naevius* . . Quawker, Montauk, Long Island. **1930** Shoemaker *1300 Words* 48 **cPA Mts** (as of c1900), *Quawk*—A night heron. **1939** FWP *Guide IL* 528 **cnIL**, A grove of larches that serves as the summer home of a colony of black-crowned night herons. Known as "quawks" because of their bickering nature, they have migrated to the grove for at least forty years, usually coming about the first of April. **1947** Kieran *Footnotes on Nature* 8 **seNY**, The young farmer . . said the . . birds were "Quowks," but it was some years later . . that I first laid eyes on Black-crowned Night Herons and recognized them as the owners . . of those weird voices heard under cover of darkness in Dutchess County. **1950** *WELS (Birds that come out only after dark)* 1 Inf, **WI**, Quawk. **1954** Sprunt *FL Bird Life* 35, Black-crowned Night Heron: . . Local Names: Quock. *Ibid* 37, Yellow-crowned Night Heron: . . Local Names: Quock. **1955** MA Audubon Soc. *Bulletin* 39.312, *Black-Crowned Night Heron*. . . Quark, . . (Mass.); Quawk, Quok (General). **1955** *Oriole* 20.2 **GA**, *Black-crowned Night Heron*. . . *Quok* . . from a common call. **1962** Imhof *AL Birds* 95, *Black-crowned Night Heron*. . . *Other name*: Quok. . . Once the adult is well known, identifying the immature night heron is simpler than it sounds, for this bird utters a flat call, the "quok" which gives it its common name. **1968** *DARE* (Qu. Q3, . . *Birds that come out only after dark*) Inf **CT5**, Quawk [kwɔk]—local name; (Qu. Q10, . . *Water birds and marsh birds*) Inf **NY53**, Night-feeding heron—

quawks. **1968** *DARE* Tape **NY53**, This tree used to harbor about fifty birds that were called quawks [kwɔks], but their real name was night-feeding heron. . . And just about when the sun was setting, they'd fly off to feed in the marshes, and as they went overhead, you'd hear them saying quawk, quawk, quawk.
2 also *couac, quock*: A **bittern** (here: *Botaurus lentiginosus*). Cf **quack 2**

 1917 *Wilson Bulletin* 29.2.77 **VA**, *Botaurus lentiginosus*. . . Quock, Wallops I[slan]d, Va. **1959** *Names* 7.117, Names usually applied to the black-crowned night-heron occasionally are offered as for the bittern, examples being: couac (French, Que., La.), quack (Ill.), quawk (Pa., N.J.), quock (Va.) [etc]. **1966** *DARE* (Qu. Q8, *A water bird that makes a booming sound before rain and often stands with its beak pointed almost straight up*) Inf **NC27**, Quawk [kwɔ˞k].
3 as *quark*: A **coot** n[1] **1** (here: *Fulica americana*).

 1955 MA Audubon Soc. *Bulletin* 39.444 **MA**, American Coot . . Quark. . . Probably from a note.
4 as *kwawk*: **=great blue heron.**

 1991 *DARE* File **seNY**, Kwawk = great blue heron (after the cry).

quawker See **quawk** n[2] 1

quawl(ment) See **quarrel A**

quayry See **quarry**

quebrada n [Span < *quebrar* to break] **SW** *obs* Cf **barranca**
=break n[1] **3.**

 1849 Wise *Los Gringos* 28, A little way back in the *quebiadas* [sic], or broken ground, is like stepping over angular Flemish roofs. **1862** Winthrop *John Brent* 211 **West**, We took breakneck leaps across dry quebradas in the clay. **1890** *Century Dict.* 4903, *Quebrada.* . . A gorge; a ravine; a defile: a word occasionally used by writers in English on Mexican and South American physical geography, and by the Spanish Americans themselves, with about the same meaning as *barranca*. **1894** *DN* 1.325 **TX**, *Quebráda*: a strip of broken country, cut up by arroyos . . or barrancas. . . From *quebrar*, to break.

quee n Cf **tobaccoroot**
A **valerian** (here: *Valeriana edulis*).

 1939 FWP *Guide MT* 18, Quee or *racine de tabac*, used as tobacco by the Indians, grows abundantly in Madison County. The Tobacco Root Mountains were named after it.

queek-queek n [Echoic]
A **nuthatch.**

 1970 *DARE* (Qu. Q23, *The insect-eating bird that goes headfirst down a tree trunk*) Inf **KY88**, Queek-queek ['kwik kwik].

queen n
1 often with *the*: A **milkweed butterfly** (here: *Danaus gilippus*) with mahogany-brown wings speckled with white towards the margins, native chiefly to the Gulf States and southwestern US.

 1902 Holland *Butterfly Book* 84, *Anosia berenice* . . (The Queen). *B[asliarchia] bulstii* . . is found in Arizona, and there flies with the Queen. **1938** Brimley *Insects NC* 257, *D[anaus] berenice*. . . The Queen. Southern Pines, May. **1949** Swain *Insect Guide* 108, The queen . . occurs in the southwestern United States. **1981** Pyle *Audubon Field Guide Butterflies* 714, Male Queens possess brushes, or hair pencils, within the tips of their abdomens. **1985** Sedman–Hess *Butterflies W. Cent. IL* 83, Queens observed in Illinois result from rare immigrations and the species does not withstand our cold winter tempataures [sic]. The larval stages feed on milkweeds not located in our area.
2 also attrib: The female of a **map turtle** (here: *Graptemys pseudogeographica*). Cf **queen turtle**

 1921 U.S. Bur. Fisheries *Rept. for 1919* app 7.13, A turtle buyer from Philadelphia. . . stated that the terrapin were used as a substitute, or partial substitute, for diamond-back, and that for this purpose the males were not desired. What was wanted was the egg-bearing or "queen" terrapin. . . The river fishermen were unable to distinguish the sexes; but the Philadelphia buyer . . readily picked out the "queens" from a lot of terrapin at hand.
3 also *queenie*: A marble that is smaller than a shooter. Cf **king** n **2**

1968 *DARE* Tape **IA**27, This one's called a queen, because it's the second biggest. . . It's made out of steel. . . It's a steelie. **c1970** Wiersma *Marbles Terms* sw**MI**, *Queenies*—multi-colored marble, smaller than peeries. [**1993** *DARE* File **Alberta Canada** (as of c1955), We did have an entire hierarchy of marbles: No. 1 = "Shooter"; No. 2 = "Queen"; No. 3 = "Cat's Eye"; Ultimate weapon = "Steely". This was immediately post-war so ball-bearings were still in short supply.]

4 See **king** n **1**.

Queen Ann See **quinine**

Queen Anne's lace n

1 also *Anne's lace, Queen Anne ~, Queen Annie's ~ (handkerchief), queen's lace*: A **wild carrot** (here: *Daucus carota*). Also called **chiggerweed 4** Cf **lace flower 1, lady's lace, powder puff 3**

1873 in 1976 Miller *Shaker Herbs* 148, *Daucus carota*. Bee's Nest Seed. Queen Anne's Lace. **1895** U.S. Dept. Ag. *Farmers' Bulletin* 28.29, Wild carrot, bird's nest, devil's plague, Queen Anne's lace . . *Daucus carota*. **1902** (1909) Mathews *Field Book Amer. Wild Flowers* 306, Wild Carrot or Queen Anne's Lace or Bird's Nest—*Daucus carota*. . . The dull white flowers . . are gracefully disposed in a radiating pattern as fine as lace. **1907** Freeman *By the Light* 52 se**MA**, She walked slowly between the fields, which were white and gold with queen's-lace and golden-rod. **1928** Aldrich *Lantern* 168 **NE**, Along the grassy roadway, one's skirts touched Queen Anne's lace, field mustard and yarrow. **1947** Beebe *Mixed Train* 88, Wading pleasantly through springtime Arkansas meadows brave with daisies and queen's lace. **1964** Batson *Wild Flowers SC* 80, Queen Anne's Lace, Wild Carrot: *Daucus carota*. **1965–70** *DARE* (Qu. S6, *Other names . . for Queen Anne's lace: [Summertime roadside weed two feet high or so with a lacy white top]*) 87 Infs, **widespread, but more freq Sth, S Midl**, Queen Anne's lace; 43 Infs, **widespread**, Queen Annie's lace; **FL**31, **NJ**8, **RI**5, **WI**78, Queen Anne lace; **SC**67, Anne's lace; **GA**80, Queen Annie's lace handkerchief; **MO**25, Queen's lace [*DARE* Ed: 429 Infs are listed as having given no response. It is impossible to determine whether the FWs meant that they had no name at all for this plant or merely none besides *Queen Anne's lace*.]; (Qu. S21, . . *Weeds . . that are a trouble in gardens and fields*) Inf **OH**68, Queen Anne's lace; (Qu. S26a, . . *Roadside flowers*) Infs **KY**35, **NJ**30, **NC**52, **PA**74, **TN**24, Queen Anne's lace; **TX**64, Wild queen's lace; (Qu. S26d, *Wildflowers that grow in meadows;* not asked in early QRs) Inf **VA**64, Queen Anne's lace; (Qu. S26e, *Other wildflowers not yet mentioned;* not asked in early QRs) Inf **IL**67, Queen Anne's lace; **MI**53, When the dust bowl blew out the South in 1933, we got Queen Anne's lace and hawkweed for the first time; **DC**2, Orange flowers—head similar to Queen Anne's lace; **FL**20, Granddaddy's beard—like Queen Anne's lace—hangs in clusters. [*DARE* Ed: Some of these Infs may refer instead to other senses below.] **1969** *DARE* FW Addit **NC**, Queen Anne's lace—wild carrot, which doesn't grow much right in this area. Story: "Wild carrot is called Queen Anne's lace because Queen Anne of England used to wash her own lace handkerchiefs, and when she laid them out to dry, you couldn't tell them from the wild carrot." **1979** Spellenberg *Audubon Guide N. Amer. Wildflowers W. Region* 327, *Wild Carrot; Queen Anne's Lace*. . . The flowering heads served 18th-century English courtiers as "living lace," hence the common name. **1982** Barrick *Coll.* cs**PA**, *Queen Anne's lace*—Daucus carota. Also *wild carrot*.

2 =**yampah**.

1937 U.S. Forest Serv. *Range Plant Hdbk.* W48, Yampa, a smooth, slender, erect perennial plant of the carrot or parsnip family (Umbelliferae), is also known as squawroot, wildcaraway, breadroot, Queen-Annes-lace, and Indian-potato. **1949** Moldenke *Amer. Wild Flowers* 147, In the Far West another group of plants (*Eulophus* [=*Perideridia*]) is known as *queen-annes-lace*. These carrotlike herbs grow up to 5 feet in height. **1995** *DARE* File s**CA**, I know the yampa plant (*Carum gairdneri*) only as Queen Anne's lace. It was a surprise for me living in Wisconsin to hear the *Daucus carota* referred to as Queen Anne's lace, although I did see a resemblance to the plant I knew in California.

3 also *Queen Annie's lace*: A **bishop's weed 1** (here: *Ammi majus*).

1946 Reeves–Bain *Flora TX* 227, *A[mmi] majus*. . . Cultivated for ornament. Known locally as "Queen Ann's [sic] Lace." **1967–68** *DARE* (Qu. S6) Inf **AL**30, Queen Annie's lace—knew this as a garden flower; **LA**40, We cultivate and call it Queen Anne's lace. **1982** *Plants SW* (Catalog) 27, *Queen Anne's Lace see Bishop's Weed*.

4 also *queen's lace*: Any of var plants of the family Apiaceae, such as a **cow parsnip 1** (here: *Heracleum lanatum*); see

quots. Cf **dwarf Queen Anne's lace, queen weed, wild parsnip**

1961 Wills–Irwin *Flowers TX* 168, Queen-Anne's-lace, *D[aucus] carota* . . can be readily told . . by the central flower of each umbel, usually a deep purple. . . Several other plants of the Carrot Family [= Apiaceae], most of them smaller and native to the state, are also known as Queen-Anne's-lace. **1967–68** *DARE* (Qu. S6, . . *Queen Anne's lace: [Summertime roadside weed two feet high or so with a lacy white top]*) Inf **CA**20, Queen Anne's lace—not right here—wild carrot—wild parsnip; **CA**60, Queen Anne's lace—grows up in the mountains—wild parsnip; **CA**140, Queen's lace—very ornate, leaf pinnately divided—is actually anise or wild licorice; (Qu. S17, . . *Kinds of plants . . that . . cause itching and swelling*) Inf **AK**1, Queen Anne's lace poisons some people.

Queen Annie's lace See **Queen Anne's lace 1, 3**

Queen Annie's lace handkerchief See **Queen Anne's lace 1**

queen bee n Cf **king bee**

A person, usu a woman, in a position of authority or dominance.

1930 Shoemaker *1300 Words* 49 c**PA Mts** (as of c1900), *Queen-bee*—A domineering woman, gifted with leadership. **1965–70** *DARE* (Qu. AA21, . . *Joking expressions . . about a wife who gives the orders and a husband who takes them from her*) Inf **KY**11, She's the queen bee; (Qu. AA22, *Joking names that a man may use to refer to his wife*) Inf **NY**80, Queen bee; (Qu. GG19b, *When you can see from the way a person acts that he's feeling important or independent: "He seems to think he's _____."*) Inf **MN**6, Queen bee; (Qu. HH17, *A person who tries to appear important, or who tries to lay down the law in his community: "He'd like to be the _____ around here."*) Infs **IL**46, **OH**37, (The) queen bee—if it's a woman; **MS**8, **OR**1, **TX**5, Queen bee; **NC**51, Queen bee—for a woman; (Qu. II23, *Joking names for the people who are, or think they are, the best society of a community: The _____*) Inf **RI**13, To a girl—do you think you're the Queen of Sheba (*or queen bee*)? **WA**13, She's the queen bee.

queen blackbird n
=**red-winged blackbird**.

1967 *DARE* (Qu. Q11, . . *Kinds of blackbirds*) Inf **CA**31, Queen blackbird—tuft of red feathers on each side.

queen-cup n Also *queen's cup*

A **bead lily** (here: *Clintonia uniflora*) native chiefly to the Pacific Northwest and Alaska.

1915 (1926) Armstrong–Thornber *Western Wild Flowers* 50, Queen-cup . . *Clintonia uniflora*. . . In rich moist soil, in shady woods, we find this lovely flower, with a white chalice and heart of pale gold, surrounded by two or three, beautiful, large, glossy leaves. **1937** FWP *Guide ID* 110, Spring beauties (queencups). **1938** (1958) Sharples *AK Wild Flowers* 37, *C[lintonia] uniflora*. "Queen's Cup," "Blue Bead." . . white, 6-petaled flowers; rarely two on a stem; followed by blue berries. . . Occurs only in southern part of the Territory. **1949** Peattie *Cascades* 236 **Pacific NW**, The beautiful white star that mixes with the Canadian dogwood and the pipsissewa is alpine beauty, Clintonia uniflora. Between the two or three tulip-like leaves it bears a single, pure white star which is truly an alpine beauty. On occasion I have heard it called Queen's cup. **1966** *DARE* Wildfl QR Pl.17 Inf **WA**10, If white—then queen-cup.

queen delight See **queen's delight**

Queen Dido is dead n Also *Queen Dido* Cf **Quaker, how is thee?**

A type of follow-the-leader game.

1923 Acker *400 Games* 286, *Queen Dido*—The players are seated in a circle. The leader turns to his right-hand neighbor, and the following conversation takes place: "Queen Dido is dead!"/ "What did she die of?"/ "Doing this." As the leader says "Doing this," he clinches his right fist and taps it up and down on his knee. The neighbor immediately imitates the movement and turns to his neighbor, starting the same conversation and movement as that already described. This continues until every one is tapping his knee. The leader then turns to his neighbor with the same information, but this time adding to the first movement the action of tapping the left knee with the left fist. The conversation and movement proceed around the circle as before. The third time the leader taps the floor with the right foot, at the same time continuing movement of the hands; the fourth time both feet are tapped, the fifth time the head is bobbed backwards and forwards. The game may be repeated from the beginning. **1945** Boyd *Hdbk. Games* 121, *Queen Dido Is Dead*—The players sit in a circle, and one of them says to his neighbor, "Queen Dido is dead." His neighbor asks, "How did she die?" The first player answers, "She died doing this," making a movement such as tapping his foot, which all the other players copy and repeat continuously. **1957** *Sat. Eve. Post Letters* **WI,** Queen Dido—The players are all seated. One starts the game by telling his neighbor "Queen Dido is dead." The neighbor asks "How did she die?" He answers "Doing so and so" as he keeps one hand waving. The neighbor then tells his neighbor the same thing and does the same thing all down through the line until all are waving one hand. The starter then tells the same thing and waves both hands and all are waving both hands all down through the line. The third round, keep one foot tapping along with both hands waving. Fourth round, both feet tapping; fifth round, nod the heads; sixth round, jump up and down with head, feet and hands all going [at] the same time.

Queen Elizabeth root n   Cf **queen weed root**
Perh a **horse balm.**

c**1938** in 1970 Hyatt *Hoodoo* 1.596 se**VA,** They use *John de Conker* and they uses *King of the World* too—they have that in a powder too, and then they use dragon's blood and *Queen Elizabeth root.* They have all that in powder and they say if you sprinkle round their door, ain't no law coming there. **1942** Kennedy *Palmetto Country* 167 ne**FL,** [From the catalog of a conjure shop:] Queen Elizabeth Root—A very special root. To answer questions, tie a piece of white thread, 13 inches long, to the root with the opposite end of the thread held between the thumb and forefinger. Medium addresses root: 'Will the person standing before me have his wish fulfilled?' If the answer is 'yes,' the root will circle to the right. If not, the root remains motionless. Full form roots, $3.50; half female form, $2 each.

queenfish n

1 A small marine fish *(Seriphus politus)* of California waters. Also called **croaker** n[1] **1a(2), herring** n[1] **3a, kingfish 3, sea trout c(3), shiner 2g, tomcod**

1882 U.S. Natl. Museum *Bulletin* 16.582, *S[eriphus] politus.* . . Queen-fish. . . Coast of California; very abundant southward; north to San Francisco. **1883** (1886) Lalor *Cyclop. Political Sci.* 2.217, The queen-fish, the bagre and the roncador are . . well known in California. **1915** *Nature & Sci.* 122 **CA,** Along the wharves, . . queen-fish *(Seriphus politus)* . . and a variety of surf-fishes, are also taken. **1953** Roedel *Common Fishes CA* 94, *Queenfish.* . . Of minor significance as a market fish. . . Regarded with contempt by most sportsmen. **1975** Evanoff *Catch More Fish* 108, Other fish caught by Pacific bottom anglers include the queenfish, . . and Pacific tomcod. **1991** *Amer. Fisheries Soc. Common Names Fishes* 55, *Seriphus politus* . . queenfish.

2 A **wahoo** (here: *Acanthocybium solandri*).

1935 Caine *Game Fish* 142, Wahoo—*Acanthocybium solandri* . . Queenfish. **1946** LaMonte *N. Amer. Game Fishes* 25, Wahoo—*Acanthocybium solandri* . . Queenfish. **1976** Tryckare et al. *Lore of Sportfishing* 123, Wahoo . . Other common names: . . queenfish, . . jack mackerel. . . An elongate, semifusiform, mackerel-like body.

queen flower n
=**crape myrtle.**

1965 Neal *Gardens HI* 618, Crape myrtle, queen flower. . . Panicles of pink, white, or purple, scentless flowers develop at branch tips.

queenie See **queen 3**

queen in the meadow See **queen of the meadow 3**

queen of meadow See **queen of the meadow 3, 4**

queen of the forest n   Cf **queen of the meadow 1, ~ prairie 1**
A **meadowsweet 2** (here: *Filipendula occidentalis*).

1961 Peck *Manual OR* 433, *F[ilipendula] occidentalis.* . . Queen-of-the-Forest. . . Banks of Trask and Tillamook Rivers. **1973** Hitchcock–Cronquist *Flora Pacific NW* 211, *F[ilipendula] occidentalis.* . . Queen-of-the-forest. . . Rock crevices near high water line.

queen of the lights See **queen's delight**

queen of the meadow n

1 also *meadow queen, queen of the meadows:* A **meadowsweet 2** (here: *Filipendula ulmaria*). [*OED2* 1597]   Cf **queen of the prairie 1**

1784 in 1785 *Amer. Acad. Arts & Sci. Memoirs* 1.451, *Spiræa foliis lanceolatis inæqualiter serratis subtus tomentosis floribus duplicato-*

racemosis. Syst. Nat. *Queen of the Meadows.* Blossoms red or purple. In moist pastures. [*DARE* Ed: This quot may refer instead to **2** below.] **1822** Eaton *Botany* 478, *Spiraea ulmaria* . . queen of the meadow. **1836** (1840) Phelps *Lectures on Botany* 141, *Spiraea ulmaria* . . queen of the meadow. **1876** Hobbs *Bot. Hdbk.* 69, Meadow queen . . Spiraea ulmaria. **1910** Graves *Flowering Plants* 235 **CT,** *Filipendula Ulmaria.* . . Queen of the Meadow. Meadow Queen. **1940** Clute *Amer. Plant Names* 6, *F[ilipendula] ulmaria.* . . Queen-of-the-meadow. . . meadow-queen. **1959** Carleton *Index Herb. Plants* 80, *Meadow queen:* Filipendula ulmaria. *Ibid* 96, *Queen-of-the-meadow:* Filipendula hexapetala (Spiraea filipendula).

2 also *meadow queen, queen of the meadows:* A **spirea:** usu *Spiraea alba* or *S. a.* var *latifolia,* but also *S. tomentosa.*

1843 Torrey *Flora NY* 1.198, *Spiraea salicifolia* [=*S. alba*]. . . Queen-of-the-meadow . . Shrubby or suffruticose, 3–5 feet high. . . Wet bushy meadows. **1847** Wood *Class-Book* 256, *S[piraea] salicifolia.* . . *Queen of the Meadow.* . . A small shrub in meadows, thickets, U.S. and Brit. Am. . . Flowers white, often tinged with red. **1890** *Century Dict.* 3672, *Meadow-queen.* . . *meadow-sweet.* . . Any plant of the genus *Spiræa,* and primarily *S. Ulmaria* . . in the United States more especially *S. salicifolia.* **1893** *Jrl. Amer. Folkl.* 6.140 **NY,** *Spiraea salicifolia,* queen of the meadows. **1900** Lyons *Plant Names* 355, *S[piraea] tomentosa.* . . Meadow-queen. **1903** Small *Flora SE U.S.* 514, *Spiraea salicifolia.* . . Meadow-sweet. Meadow queen. **1933** Small *Manual SE Flora* 608, *S[piraea] latifolia* [=*S. alba* var *latifolia*]. . . Meadow-queen. **1940** Clute *Amer. Plant Names* 9, *S[piraea] salicifolia.* . . Queen-of-the-meadow.

3 also *queen in the meadow, ~ of meadow:* A **boneset 1:** usu *Eupatoriadelphus purpureus,* but also *E. fistulosus* or *E. maculatus.*   Cf **king-of-the-meadow 1**

1840 MA Zool. & Bot. Surv. *Herb. Plants & Quadrupeds* 124, *E[upatorium] purpureum,* . . and *E. verticillatum* . . , often called Queen of the Meadow, and Joe Pye Weed. . . A decoction of the roots is often used in the western part of the State as a remedy for the painful disease, the gravel. **1854** King *Amer. Eclectic Dispensatory* 457, *Eupatorium purpureum.* . . Queen of the Meadow. . . likewise known by the names of *Gravel root, Joe-pye, Trumpet-weed.* *Ibid* 458, Queen of the Meadow grows in swamps and low grounds from Canada to Virginia. **1864** *Catalogue of Herbs* np sw**ME,** *Queen of the meadow*—Eupatorium purpureum. **1892** *Jrl. Amer. Folkl.* 5.98 **MA,** *Eupatorium purpureum* . . Queen-of-the-meadow. Worcester Co., Mass. **1894** *Ibid* 7.92 **IN,** *Eupatorium purpureum* . . queen-of-the-meadow. **1896** *Ibid* 9.192 **ME,** *Eupatorium purpureum* . . queen of the meadow, Oxford County, Me. **1937** Thornburgh *Gt. Smoky Mts.* 23, In late summer or early fall one sees . . the purple iron-weed and lavender Joe-pye-weed or Queen-of-the-meadow. **1965–70** *DARE* (Qu. S26a, . . *Wildflowers.* . . *Roadside flowers*) Infs **KY**40, **NC**36, **OH**37, **VA**26, Queen of the meadow; **KY**34, Queen in the meadow; (Qu. S25) Inf **NY**232, Queen of the meadow—late in fall, pinkish blossom, quite tall. **1966–68** *DARE Wildfl QR* Pl.228 (*Eupatorium purpureum* = [*Eupatoriadelphis purpureus*]) Infs **NC**36, **OH**37, 82, Queen of the meadow. **1968** Radford et al. *Manual Flora Carolinas* 1056, *E[upatorium] maculatum* . . , Queen-of-the-meadow, Joe-pye-weed. . . *E. fistulosum,* . . Queen-of-the-meadow, Joe-pye-weed. . . Stems hollow. **1968** *DARE* FW Addit **NY,** Queen of the meadow—leaves grow the same as boneset, but the flowers are pink or lilac-colored—used as stomach remedy and for asthma; **VA,** Queen of the meadow . . *Eupatorium purpureum.* **1970** *NC Folkl.* 8.24, The juice of the queen of the meadow is good for the kidneys. **1972** *Foxfire Book* 242 n**GA,** *Kidney Trouble.* . . Take one root from a queen-of-the-meadow plant. Boil it in one pint of water until it makes a dark tea. Strain and drink a cup a day until you are well. **1981** *High Coll.* ce**KY** (as of c1930), *Queen-of-meadow:* . . name used in the Gorge for *Eupatorioum* [sic] *fistulosum,* a plant more commonly known as Hollow Joe-Pye Weed. This purple flower grows to a height of seven feet. Its hollow stem, according to one informant, was used to raid and sip whiskey hidden in the fields during the time moonshining flourished in the area earlier this century.

4 as *queen of meadow:* A **cardinal flower** (here: *Lobelia cardinalis*).

1897 *Jrl. Amer. Folkl.* 10.49 **Long Is. NY,** *Lobelia cardinalis* . . queen-of-meadow, Southold, L.I.

5 A **meadow rue** (here: *Thalictrum pubescens*).   Cf **king-of-the-meadow 1**

1899 *Plant World* 2.199, Queen of the Meadow for *Thalictrum polygamum.* . . Possibly suggested by the delicate grace of the plumes of blossom.

queen of the meadows See **queen of the meadow 1, 2**

queen of the mountain See **king of the mountain 1**

queen of the prairie n

1 A **meadowsweet 2** (here: *Filipendula rubra*). Cf **queen of the meadow 1, ~ forest**

1848 Gray *Manual of Botany* 116, *S[piraea] lobata* [=*Filipendula rubra*]. . . *Queen of the Prairie*. . . Meadows and prairies, Penn. to Ohio and Michigan. . . Flowers deep peach-blossom color. **1852** Noll *Bot. Class-Book* 2.100 **PA,** *S[piraea] lobata*. . . *Queen of the Prairie.* **1897** Creevey *Flowers* 146, *Queen of the prairie*. . . A stately, beautiful plant adorning the meadows and prairies south and west of Pennsylvania. **1933** *Small Manual SE Flora* 610, *Queen-of-the-prairie*. . . Swamps and low grounds. . . Spr.–sum. **1951** Voss–Eifert *IL Wild Flowers* 204, Queen-of-the-prairie . . blossoms in July in certain chosen spots in northern Illinois. It is a plant not of the western prairies but of those extending west of the Alleghenies from Pennsylvania across to Iowa and into Michigan, and down even into Georgia where the true prairie does not exist. **1969** *DARE* Wildfl QR Pl.93A Inf **WI**80, Queen of the prairie. **1972** Courtenay–Zimmerman *Wild Flowers* 38 **Gt Lakes,** *Queen of the prairie*. . . Wet meadows and prairies.

2 A **boneset 1** (here: *Eupatoriadelphus purpureus*). Cf **queen of the meadow 3**

1940 Clute *Amer. Plant Names* 82, *E[upatorium] purpureum* . . queen-of-the-prairie. **1959** Carleton *Index Herb. Plants* 96, Queen-of-the-Prairie: *Eupatorium purpureum*; *Filipendula rubra* (*Spiraea filipendula*).

3 as *queen of the prairies*: =**grama grass 1.**

1982 *Plants SW* (Catalog) 35, *Grama Grass—Bouteloua*. . . Sometimes called the "Queen of the prairies" these are more of the grasses that built the cattle industry of the Old West.

queen palm n

An introduced palm (*Syagrus romanzoffianum*). For names of the seed see **monkey-nut 4**

1948 Neal *In Gardens HI* 106, The queen palm . . is grown ornamentally in parks and along streets, as it is in southern California, southern Florida, and Hawaii. . . The queen palm is closely related to the coco palm. **1960** McGeachy *Hdbk. FL Palms* 16, *Arecastrum romanzoffianum*—Also called Feather Palm and Queen Palm. [*Ibid* 17, This Palm. . . in many respects, is similar to the Royal Palm. . . Its fronds are softer and more graceful. . . It lacks, however, the smooth green leaf of the Royal; for near its own top the bases of old leaf stalks remain.] **1976** Bailey–Bailey *Hortus Third* 102, Queen Palm. . . Older plants tolerate temperatures to 20° F. Considered the best substitute for royal palms where these cannot be grown. Commonest exotic palm in cent. Fla.

queenroot See **queen's root**

queens See **quince**

queen's button n

A **buttercup 1** (here: *Ranunculus acris*).

1896 *Jrl. Amer. Folkl.* 9.180 **OH,** *Ranunculus acris* . . queens-button, Sulphur Grove, Ohio.

queen's crown n

1 See **queen's wreath.**

2 A **stonecrop:** usu *Sedum rhodanthum*, but also **roseroot.** Cf **king's crown, rose ~**

1961 Douglas *My Wilderness* 19 **CO,** Queen's (or rose) crown (*Sedum rhodanthum*) has a rounded head of pink flowers. **1967** Harrington *Edible Plants Rocky Mts.* 146, *S[edum] rhodanthum*, commonly called "queen's crown" . . has rose-colored flowers clustered in a terminal head. We have eaten the leaves both raw and boiled for 15 minutes, finding them very acceptable when taken young. **1974** (1977) Coon *Useful Plants* 121, *Sedum roseum*—Stonecrop, roseroot, Queen or King's crown. An "alpine" plant found in many mountainous places both east and west in which the rose-scented roots as well as the young leaves are rated as being good for salad use.

queen's cup See **queen-cup**

queen's delight n Also *queen delight,* by folk etym *queen of the lights*

A plant of the genus *Stillingia,* usu *S. sylvatica.* Also called **queen's root.** For other names of var spp see **corkwood 3, silverleaf 3, yawroot**

1830 Rafinesque *Med. Flora* 2.266, *Stillingia sylvatica*. . . *Queens delight*. . . Very active, specific in . . chiefly syphilitic and all venereal diseases, also lepra and elephantiasis. **1894** *Jrl. Amer. Folkl.* 7.98 **GA,** *Stillingia Sylvatica,* . . queen's delight (corrupted into "queen of the lights"). **1903** Small *Flora SE U.S.* 704, *Stillingia*. . . The plants flower in the spring and summer or throughout the year in the extreme South. *Queen's Delight.* **1928** Benét *John Brown* 247, The red is pokeberry-juice, the grey is green myrtle,/ The deep black is queen's delight. **1938** Baker *FL Wild Flowers* 125, *Queen's Delight*. . . Genus *Stillingia*—The common names of these plants can scarcely be due to aesthetic delight, for the plants are not attractive. Certain species, however, have been used in household medicine, and as a black dye. **c1938** in 1970 Hyatt *Hoodoo* 1.630 **csNC,** Dat's de best herb dey is in de woods, de *Queen Delight*—dat's fo' yo' blood. Dat will purify yo' blood. **1954** McAtee *Suppl. to Nomina Abitera* [4], Queen's Delight, Queen's Root (*Stillingia spp.*) . . Philip F. Allan informs me that the root is said to resemble male genitalia. **1958** Jacobs–Burlage *Index Plants NC* 91, Queen's delight; queen's root. . . The dried root of this perennial herb. . . has been reported to be of value in scrofula, syphilis, liver and cutaneous diseases, bronchitis, laryngitis, and lung complications. **1960** Vines *Trees SW* 624, *Stillingia*. . . *aquatica*. . . Vernacular names are Queen's Delight and Queen's Root. The plant is rather short-lived. [*Ibid, Range.* Swamps and wet pinelands. Southeastern Louisiana; eastward to Florida and northward to South Carolina.] **1964** Kingsbury *Poisonous Plants U.S.* 197, *Stillingia treculeana*. . . Queen's delight. . . is a perennial herb of western and central Texas. . . As little as 0.5 per cent or less of an animal's weight of leaves and stems was quickly lethal to sheep. **1967–68** *DARE* Tape **GA**25, We had to go out every spring and dig up what was known as queen's delight and make a tonic out of the roots. . . My mother would split them up and boil them and make a tea. . . They said it was a blood cleanser; **TX**1A, He used balmony, he used prickly ash, he used scrap bark. . . Queen's delight was a blood purifier. **1970** *NC Folkl.* 8.26, Queen's delight tea, made from its roots and whiskey, was best for neuralgia.

queen's jewels See **queen's wreath**

queen's lace See **Queen Anne's lace 1, 4**

queen snake n Also *queen water snake*

A **water snake** (here: *Regina septemvittata*). Also called **leather snake, moon ~, willow ~, yellow-bellied ~**

1902 Smithsonian Inst. *Annual Rept. for 1900* 2.104 **MD,** Specimen of Queen snake, *Natrix leberis,* from Great Falls, Md. **1930** OK Univ. Biol. Surv. *Pub.* 2.224, *Natrix septemvittata*. . . Queen Snake. . . (Eastern Oklahoma). **1953** Schmidt *N. Amer. Amphibians* 158, *Natrix septemvittata*. . . Queen snake, moon snake, queen water snake. **1968** *PA Game News* July 45 **PA,** Water snakes. Not the relatively rare (in Pennsylvania) little Kirtland's water snake; not the crayfish-eating queen water snake; but rather try for the big, nasty-tempered, fish-eating northern banded water snake. **1979** Behler–King *Audubon Field Guide Reptiles* 648, Queen Snake. . . Range: S. Great Lakes region and se. Pennsylvania south to Gulf Coast. Isolated populations in n. Michigan and sw. Missouri and nw. Arkansas. . . Feeds almost entirely on crayfish, particularly those recently shed and soft-bodied. **1981** Vogt *Nat. Hist. WI* 162, Queen snakes. . . rather than lying on rocks in the sun . . usually float on the surface of the water or hide under rocks in the water or along its edge.

queen sora n Cf **king sora**

=**Virginia rail.**

1925 Bailey *Birds FL* 42, Virginia Rail. . . *Rallus virginianus* (Queen sora).

queen's root n Also *queenroot* Cf **queen weed root**

=**queen's delight,** usu *Stillingia sylvatica.*

1854 King *Amer. Eclectic Dispensatory* 910, *Stillingia sylvatica.* Queen's Root. . . This plant is also known by the name of *Queen's Delight, Yaw-root,* and *Silver-leaf*. . . This plant is found growing in pine-barrens and sandy soils from Virginia to Florida, and in Mississippi and Louisiana. **1873** in 1976 Miller *Shaker Herbs* 221, Queen's Root. . . *Stillingia sylvatica*. . . Invaluable in scrofula, syphilis, liver and cutaneous diseases, bronchitis, laryngitis, and lung complaints. **1876** Hobbs *Bot. Hdbk.* 94, Queens' root, Stillingia, Stillingia sylvatica. **1901**

Lounsberry *S. Wild Flowers* 303, *Stillingia sylvatica*. . . Perhaps the queen's delight is more generally known by its practical name of queen's root, for very early in the spring many people sally forth quite oblivious to any other sensation than that of collecting its roots to later use in medicinal ways. **1903** Small *Flora SE U.S.* 704, *Stillingia*. . . Queen's Delight. Queen-root. **1942** Kennedy *Palmetto Country* 167 neFL, [From the catalog of a conjure shop:] Queen's Root. There is a legend of a queen who wished to become a mother, and she made a tea from this root and drank it; 50¢. **1960** [see **queen's delight**]. **1974** Morton *Folk Remedies* 149 SC, Queen's root . . *Stillingia sylvatica*. . . (Current use): Root in 2 qts. water boiled down to 1 qt. and the decoction taken to cure boils, also for stomachache. . . Charleston and through the South.

queen's taste, to the *adv phr* Also *to a queen's taste, to a* (or *the*) *king's taste*   *somewhat old-fashioned*

Perfectly, to perfection; exactly as would be desired.

[**1886** *Catholic World* 42.470 **NYC**, It's rale Lent with *her*. It an't . . fish, done up to the queen's taste, at two dollars a pound.] [**1889** *N. Amer. Rev.* 148.24, The British Minister . . played his hand "to the queen's taste," and before you [=T.F.Bayard, Secretary of State 1885–89] knew it, you had become disastrously involved.] **1891** *NY Sporting Times* (NY) 19 Sept 4/3, A number of young blood Leaguers are playing ball to the queen's taste. **1902** Harben *Abner Daniel* 279, You worked 'im to a queen's taste—as fine as split silk. **1905** *DN* 3.91 **nwAR**, *Queen's taste*. . . Perfection. 'He did it to a queen's taste.' Rare. **1911** Saunders *Col. Todhunter* 126, They've got you finished off to the queen's taste. **1950** *WELS* WI (*Something very well done:* . . "It's done *to _____.*") 4 Infs, A (or a) queen's taste; 2 Infs, A (or the) king's taste. **1965–70** *DARE* (Qu. KK3a, . . *The perfect condition—for example, in cooking:* "It's done to _____.") 31 Infs, **scattered**, A (or the) queen's taste; **SC5**, **TX12**, The queen's taste [FW sugg]; **NJ4**, **VA31**, Queen's taste; **CT6**, The queen's taste—his mother (English) used it; **MD30**, The queen's taste, [corr to] the king's taste; **OH75**, The queen's taste, the king's taste; **TX42**, The queen's taste—old-fashioned; **IA15**, **KY11**, The (or a) king's taste; (Qu. KK3b, *Something done perfectly—for example, a piece of work:* "It's done to _____.") Infs **CA24**, **164**, **MA71**, (The) queen's taste; **CA20**, The queen's taste [FW: Inf unsure if food or furniture]; **CA107**, A queen's taste, a king's taste; **PA39**, **VA21**, The king's taste; (Qu. W37, *When a woman puts on her good clothes and tries to look her best . . she's _____*) Inf **NY43**, Dressed to a queen's taste. [46 of 49 Infs old]

queen's wreath *n* Also *queen's crown, ~ jewels* =coral vine 3.

1936 Whitehouse *TX Flowers* 17, Queen's crown or wreath (*Antigonon leptopus*), a lovely pink-flowered vine widely cultivated in Texas, is a member of the buckwheat family. **1967** *DARE* (Qu. S6) Inf **TX3**, Queen's wreath. **1970** Correll *Plants TX* 526, *Queen's wreath*. . . Commonly planted in s. and e. halves of Tex., in the s. part occasionally volunteering (especially about old homesteads), summer–fall. **1982** Perry-Hay *Field Guide Plants* 80, *Antigonon leptopus* . . queen's jewels; queen's wreath [etc]. . . *Flowers*: small and globular in tangled masses on long racemes which terminate in tendrils . . bright pink.

queen triggerfish *n* [*OED2* 1924 →]

A **triggerfish** (here: *Balistes vetula*).

1933 John G. Shedd Aquarium *Guide* 156 **RI**, Queen Triggerfish. . . This prettily marked species. . . once . . was captured in a pound net at Narraganset Bay. **1939** *FWP Guide FL* 30, There are queen triggerfish, commonly called 'old wenches' because of shrewish wrinkles etched in blue on the background of their yellow faces. **1976** Tryckare et al. *Lore of Sportfishing* 129, Queen Triggerfish. . . Massachusetts south to West Indies and Brazil. **1983** Audubon *Field Guide N. Amer. Fishes* 754, The Queen Triggerfish can change color in response to changes in its background and in light intensity; however, the bright blue stripes on the head persist. It is common and used as food throughout much of its range. **1991** Amer. Fisheries Soc. *Common Names Fishes* 69, *Balistes vetula* . . A[tlantic] . . queen triggerfish.

queen turtle *n* Cf **queen 2**

A **soft-shell turtle** (here: *Trionyx muticus*).

1937 Cahn *Turtles IL* 176, *Amyda mutica* . . Spineless soft-shell; queen turtle; leatherback; soft-shell. *Ibid* 182, *Amyda mutica* is much less vicious than is *Amyda spinifera*, but its disposition is by no means docile. . . It is this fact of relative tempers of the two species which has won for the milder *mutica* the local name of "queen" turtle, while its more voracious relative is known as the "king" turtle.

queen water snake   See **queen snake**

queen weed *n* Cf **Queen Anne's lace 4**

The parsnip (*Pastinaca sativa*).

1894 *Jrl. Amer. Folkl.* 7.89 **WV**, *Pastinaca sativa*, . . queen-weed.

queen weed root *n* Cf **knob grass 1, Queen Elizabeth root, queen weed**

Prob **horse balm** (here: *Collinsonia canadensis*); see quot.

c**1938** in 1970 Hyatt *Hoodoo* 1.631 **wNC**, But if yo's makin' whiskey an' yo' scared de law runnin' on yo', yo' git *queen weed root* an' yo' git it near—on de low end of de mountain. Yo' cain't git it on flat country . . Yo' git one dem *queen weed roots* . . an' boil it. It got a elbow on it ovah five j'ints an' de j'ints is ovah a inch jes' lak dat—knots, all lak a rattlesnake's tail, yo' know, got dat bell on de rattlesnake tail. Well, it got lil knots on it an' yo' kin tell where dose j'ints is yo' know.

queer *adj* Usu |kwɪr, kwɪə, kwir, kwiə|; also **chiefly S Midl, Sth** |kwer, kwɛr, kwær, kwɑr|; for addit varr see quots   Pronc-spp *quair(e), quar(e)*

A Forms.

1845 Thompson *Pineville* 65 **cGA**, Well, they's monstrous quare lookin' wimin flesh, that's a fact. **1893** Shands *MS Speech* 51, *Quare* [kwær]. Illiterate white for *queer*. This is exactly the same pronunciation as is used by the Irish. **1899** Chesnutt *Conjure Woman* 23 **csNC** [Black], But dat wa'n't de quares' thing 'bout de goopher. **1903** *DN* 2.326 **seMO**, *Queer*. . . Pronounced quare. **1906** *DN* 3.123 **sIN**, *Queer*. . . [kwer]. **1907** *DN* 3.235 **nwAR**, *Queer*. . . Pronounced quare [kwær]. **1909** *DN* 3.361 **eAL, wGA**, *Quare*. **1915** *DN* 4.188 **swVA**, *Quair* [kwɛə]. **1923** *DN* 5.218 **swMO**, *Quair*. **1927** *DN* 5.470 **sAppalachians**, *Quar*. **1928** *AmSp* 3.404 **Ozarks**, *Ai* becomes *ee* in *chair*, but the reverse exchange occurs in *queer*, which is nearly always turned into *quair* or *quar*. **1931** *AmSp* 7.91 **eKY**, *Cora* had a quar look in her eye when he busted in without knockin'! **1933** *AmSp* 8.1.23 **Appalachians**, *Quare* for *queer* seems to be pretty well confined to the Kentucky and Tennessee mountain sections. **1937** Hall *Coll.* **eTN**, He was very contrary and queer-turned [kwær tɜ‧nd]. **1939** *Ibid*, The children's all a little queer ['kwær]. *Ibid*, He was [kwær], contrary and mean. *Ibid*, She's queer [kwɑɚ] now and don't have good recollection. **1950** Stuart *Hie Hunters* 27 **eKY**, That proper talk is quaire to us. **1952** Brown *NC Folkl*. 1.581, *Quare* [kwæə, -r]. **1955** Ritchie *Singing Family* 164 **seKY**, It was a kind of a quare Christmas tree. c**1960** *Wilson Coll*. **csKY**, *Queer* is sometimes, even yet, [kwær]. **1961** Kurath-McDavid *Pronc. Engl*. 117, The Vowels in *ear*, . . *beard*, *queer*. . . Mid-front /e/ is the usual vowel in *ear*, *beard*, etc., in South Carolina and Georgia. It is usually articulated as a longish [eˑ ~ ɛˑ] sound and contrasts sharply with the /æ/ phoneme of *care, stairs*, etc. *Ibid* 118, The word *queer* is exceptional in that /e/ is rather widely used in the Upper South and the South Midland [as well as the Lower South]. **1965–70** *DARE* (Qu. HH4, *Someone who has odd or peculiar ideas or notions*) Infs **AL33, IN10, 19, 45, KY19, 40, TN14, 15, 30,** Quare; **NC33, TX11, VA26,** [kwɛə]; **GA72,** [kwæˑɚ]; **MS64,** Quare [kwæəɹ]; **RI4,** [kweə]; **SC3, 40,** [kweə]; **SC19, VA15,** [kwɛə]; (Qu. BB7) Inf **KY19,** [kwɜˑɚ]; (Qu. HH5) Inf **KY19,** Quare; **RI4,** [kweə]; **SC11,** [kweə]; (Qu. HH39) Infs **GA28, 30,** [kwɛə]; **SC7,** [kwiɚ], [kwɛɚ]; **SC44,** [kwɛə]; **VA2,** [kwɑɚ]; (Qu. II7) Inf **SC32,** [kwæˑɚ]. **1967** *DARE* FW Addit **KY34**, [She] thought I had a "quare" job, but she said she was quite willing to answer my questions if she was sure that it was helping ['hɛpɪn] somebody. [**1976** Allen *LAUM* 3.30 (as of c1950), The Vowels in *ear*, . . *queer—*/ir - ɪr/. . . In *ear* and the other key words [including *queer*] historic /i/ appears only along the range from [i] to [ɪ] in the U[pper] M[idwest]. South Atlantic [e] and [ɜ] do not occur.] **1989** Pederson *LAGS Tech. Index* 275 **Gulf Region**, [479 infs had pronunciations of the type [kwiɚ, kwiɜ]; 40 infs [kweɚ, kwɛɜ]; 37 infs [kwæɚ, kwæɜ, kwæ]; 37 infs [kwiɚ, kwiɜ]; 6 infs [kwɑɚ]; 5 infs [kwuɚ].] **1990** Cavender *Folk Med. Lexicon* 30 **sAppalachians**, *Queer* . . sometimes pronounced "quar." **1999** *DARE* File—Internet **eMA** [Boston Online *The Wicked Good Guide to Boston English*], "The New Kids on the Block ah wicked quayuh." Carrie-Anne Dedeo reports that when she was in middle school, the long-A sound was so pronounced that "I saw most people spelling it (in notes and graffiti on desks) as 'quare' instead of 'queer'.[?]]

B Sense.

See quot. [Cf *SND* *queer* adj. 3 "As an intensive: considerable, very great . . freq. in phr. *a queer lot* a large amount"]

1931 *PMLA* 46.1304 **sAppalachians**, That's a quare (queer) knife. (A very good one.) *Ibid* 1310, As in slang, many words have taken on new meanings, several of which are the exact antitheses to each other. . . "Quair" (queer) means both "demented," or "unbalanced," as in "Here lately she acts 'quair,'" and "large," or "unusual," as in "My feller! that's a 'quair' piece of horseflesh!"

queerisome See **queersome**

queerous n [Prob blend of *queer* + *curious;* cf *SND queerious*]
1903 *DN* 2.311 **seMO,** Curious. . . Pronounced queerous [ˈkwɪrəs].

queer proper adj phr
Of language: formal or standard (as opposed to colloquial or dialectal).
[**1950** Stuart *Hie Hunters* 27 **eKY,** City folks talk proper! They don't talk like us. That proper talk is quaire to us.] **1963** Edwards *Gravel* 181 **eTN** (as of 1920s), Any use of language not commonly heard in Speedwell environs is called "quare proper," and of course anyone who uses "quare proper" language is listened to with silence, but when he is gone his "quare proper" language is parroted with considerable laughing and derision.

queersome adj Also *queerisome* Cf **-some**
Odd, strange; fey.
1848 (1855) Ruxton *Life Far West* 29 **Rocky Mts,** Is the top-knot gone, boy . . for my head feels queersome, I tell you. **1900** Day *Up in ME* 133, He said that he seed the Old Gal when she twitched / A fistful o' hair out the gray hosses' tail / For a-makin' witch tattin'. She'd hung on a nail / The queerisome web. **1914** *DN* 4.78 **ME, nNH,** Queerisome. . . Queer, strange. **1960** Williams *Walk Egypt* 241 **GA,** It feels—queersome.

queery adj, n[1]
Strange, different; one who is strange or odd; a homosexual.
1860 *Vanity Fair* 20.99, A woman full of cheery, queery, roly-poly, drolly notions. **1940–41** Cassidy *WI Atlas,* 1 inf, **swWI,** [ˈkwɪˑrɪ æktɪn]—different acting than other people; 1 inf, **csWI,** [vɛrɪ kwɪrɪ]—if he was "a little different to other people." **1968–70** *DARE* (Qu. HH11a, *Someone who is too particular or fussy—if it's a man*) Inf **NJ64,** Queery, oddball, fusspot; (Qu. HH39, *A homosexual man*) Inf **CT8,** Homosexual, pansy, queer; also queery. **1981** Pederson *LAGS Basic Materials,* 1 inf, **cnTN,** [ˈkreˑɪzɪ ~ ˈkwɪˑɚˑ]; 1 inf, **seAL,** [ˈkwɪˑɚ ˈkjɚjəs]—*curious* more natural to her.

queery n[2], v See **quarry**

quee-wee See **cui-ui**

quelite n |kɛˈliˌte| [MexSpan < Nahuatl *quilitl*] **SW** Cf **kelly weed**
Any of var plants used as greens, such as an **amaranth** or a **lamb's quarter(s) 1;** see quots.
1912 Smithsonian Inst. *Annual Rept. for 1911* 458 **NM,** Besides the seeds of the lamb's quarters the plants themselves, the leaves and young shoots, were cooked as "greens," just as they frequently are in other parts of North America. Additional succulent plants such as the purslane, the Rocky Mountain bee weed *(Peritoma serrulatum),* a small composite *(Pectis angustifolia),* and many others were treated in the same way. All plants used thus are known by the Spanish name of quelite. **1912** Lumholtz *New Trails* 130 *(DA),* Quelite, inexpensive and easy to cultivate, should be accepted by civilized households. **1920** Saunders *Useful Wild Plants* 128, Along our southwestern border from Texas to California and southward into Mexico a species of Amaranth grows *(Amaranthus Palmeri* . .), known as . . *quelite* (a general name . . , I believe, for greens). . . *Quelite* is highly regarded when young and tender as a vegetable for men, and when cut and stacked, as a winter feed for cattle. . In the judgement of white people who know it, [it] is a dish resembling asparagus in flavor, and rather superior to spinach. **1943** Elmore *Ethnobotany Navajo* 43, *Chenopodium album.* . . Quelite. . . The young tender plants are . . boiled as herbs alone or with other foods. Large quantities are eaten in the raw state. *Ibid* 45, *Amaranthus blitoides.* . . Quelite. *Ibid* 46, *Amaranthus retroflexus.* . . Quelite. . . The plants are eaten after being boiled. . . Sometimes they are boiled and fried in lard, or just boiled and canned. **1949** Curtin *By the Prophet* 47 **AZ,** *Amaranthus palmeri.* . . Quelite. . . When young and tender, the leaves are cooked for greens. *Ibid* 70, *Chenopodium* spp. . . Quelite. . . In spring the leaves are boiled in water, salt added, and when cooked the liquid is strained off; then the greens are fried in grease and

eaten. **1966** *DARE* (Qu. I28a, . . *Kinds of things . . you call 'greens'*) Inf **NM5,** Quelites [kəˈlitəs] (also called lamb's quarter). **1970** Correll *Plants TX* 543, *Atriplex arenaria.* . . Quelite. *Ibid* 559, *Amaranthus retroflexus.* . . Quelite. [**1981** Pederson *LAGS Basic Materials,* 1 inf, **csTX,** [ˈkɛlɨ wid] (Eng.) Same as [kˈɛˈliˌte] (Span.)]

quelten (down or up) See **quilt** v **1**

quercitron n [Appar coined by Bancroft (see quot 1794) from *quercus* oak + *citron* yellow]
The bark of a **black oak** (here: *Quercus velutina*), or the dye produced from it; hence nouns *quercitron (oak)* the tree itself.
1794 Bancroft *Exper. Researches* 319, The *Quercitron* bark is produced by the Quercus nigra of Linnæus . . and is one of the objects of a discovery, of which the use and application for dying, calico-printing, &c. are exclusively vested in me, for a term of years, by an act of parliament passed in the 25th year of his present Majesty's reign. *Ibid* 321, The *Quercitron* colouring matter may be readily extracted by water, even when it is only blood warm. **1810** Michaux *Histoire des Arbres* 1.25, Q[uercus] tinctoria. . . *Black oak* (Chêne noir), seule dénomination dans tous les Etats du milieu, de l'ouest et du midi. *Quercitron oak,* nom du commerce. [=Q[uercus] tinctoria. . . *Black oak* (Chêne noir), the only name in all the middle, western, and southern states. *Quercitron oak,* name in commerce.] **1812** *Ibid* 2.113, C'est la partie cellulaire de l'écorce de cette espèce de Chêne [=*Quercus tinctoria*] qui fournit le Quercitron, dont on fait actuellement un très-grand usage pour teindre en jaune la laine, la soie et les papiers à tenture. [=It is the cellular part of the bark of this species of oak [=*Quercus tinctoria*] that furnishes the quercitron which is in great use at present for dyeing wool, silk, and colored papers yellow.] **1837** Darlington *Flora Cestrica* 531 **sePA,** Q[uercus] tinctoria. . . Black Oak. Quercitron. *Stem* 60 to 80 to 90 feet high, and 2 to 3 to 4 feet in diameter, with large spreading branches above,—the bark rough and blackish. . . The *bark* is an article of commerce . . and is exported in large quantities, under the name of *Quercitron.* **1894** Coulter *Botany W. TX* 416, Quercitron. Yellow-barked or Black Oak . . occurs in east Texas and in rocky ravines and mountains near the mouth of the Pecos. **1897** Sudworth *Arborescent Flora* 169, *Quercus velutina.* . . Common Names. . . Quercitron Oak (Del., S.C., La., Kans., Minn.) **1950** Grimm *Trees PA* 167, The Black Oak is also known as the Yellow Oak or Quercitron. . . The bark is rich in tannic acid and used for tanning leather. The yellow inner bark . . is sometimes used medicinally as an astringent. **1980** Little *Audubon Guide N. Amer. Trees E. Region* 410, Black Oak—"Yellow Oak"—"Quercitron Oak." **1995** Brako et al. *Scientific & Common Names Plants* 214, Quercitron—*Quercus velutina.*

querl See **coil** v

querly See **quirley**

querrel See **quarrel**

querry See **quarry**

question n, v Usu |ˈkwɛsčən|; also |ˈkweščən, ˈkwɛssən, ˈkwɛstən|; for addit varr see quots Pronc-spp *queshton, queshtun;* also *Gullah squeschun, squestion*
Std senses, var forms.
1837 Sherwood *Gaz. GA* 71, Queshton, for question. **1905** Chesnutt *Col.'s Dream* 150 **Sth** [Black], Why didn' he wan' ter talk ter de black cat? Whoever heared er sich a queshtun! **1922** Gonzales *Black Border* 322 **sSC, GA coasts** [Gullah glossary], Queschun[,] squeschun—(n. and v.) question, questions, questioned, questioning. **1930** Woofter *Black Yeomanry* 50 **seSC,** Squestion for *question.* **1930** Stoney-Shelby *Black Genesis* 67 **seSC,** Nobody wid de right senses goin' ax you any squestion 'bout 'em! *Ibid* 75, Dem mock at him when he ax dem squestion, an' mek answer. **1981** Pederson *LAGS Basic Materials* **Gulf Region,** 39 infs, [Proncs of the type [ˈkwɛstʃən];] 1 inf, [ˈkwɛˑʃtʃən]; 1 inf, [ˈkwɛˑʃtʃɪ̩z]; 1 inf, [ˈkwɛʃtʃɪ̩z]; 1 inf, [ˈkwɛˑʃtʃən]; 1 inf, [kˈwɛˑʃtʃɪn]; 1 inf, [kwɛ^əʃtɪ̩z]; 1 inf, [kwɛˀʃtɪ̩]; 1 inf, [kwsʃɪ̩]; 1 inf, [ˈkwɪˀsʃnz]; 1 inf, [ˈkwɛˀəstʔɪ̩].

question mark n
1 also *question-mark butterfly, question sign:* A brush-footed butterfly *(Polygonia interrogationis)* native to the US east of the Rocky Mountains. [See quot 1985] Also called **violet tip.** For other names of the chrysalis see **hop master**
1902 Holland *Butterfly Book* 164, *Grapta interrogationis* . . The Ques-

tion-sign. . . is one of our commonest butterflies. . . It ranges all over the United States, except the Pacific coast. **c1930** Brown *Amer. Folkl. Insect Lore* 4, The chrysalis of the question-mark butterfly . . had large golden spots on its back. **1972** Harris *Butterflies GA* 254, Question Sign; Question Mark. . . Found throughout the state. **1985** Sedman–Hess *Butterflies W. Cent. IL* 72, Question Mark. . . The silvery marking on the undersurface of the hindwing is broken resulting in a slender, curved line and small dot, which approximates a question mark.

2 See quot. [From the shape]
1983 *MJLF* 9.1.52 **ceKY** (as of 1956), *Question mark . . a sickle.*

question-mark butterfly, question sign See **question mark 1**

quetor See **q-ter**

quich grass See **quitch grass**

quick adj
Of the ground: soft and moist; shifting. Note: In comb *quicksand* this sense is std and widespread.
1966 *DARE* Tape **ME26**, There was a little quick place there that they had to come through; the road was just grubbed out, and they had one horse and . . a wooden-shod sled, . . and when he come up over this, he lost off a bag of beans. **1969** *DARE* (Qu. C11, *Soft, wet sand in streams or wet places, that draws people and things down into it*) [932 Infs, **widespread**, Quicksand;] **IN62**, Quick muck.

quick adv
1 in phrr *(as) quick as:* As soon as. Cf **2** below
1958 Latham *Meskin Hound* 36 **cTX**, Git the dogs and be ready to hit the brush quick as they deliver me some saddle horses down at their pens. **1969** *DARE* Tape **KY17**, Just as quick as dark come, you could look out there at her grave and see a light. **1982** Cazden et al. *Folk Songs Catskills* 17, I first became interested in music pretty young. I played the jew's-harp as quick as I got my teeth. **1986** Pederson *LAGS Concordance*, 1 inf, **cAL**, Quick as one sting you, swallow you one of those—capsules.

2 in compar constrs: More likely; more willingly, sooner.
1968 *DARE* FW Addit **PA142**, "Sooner" in idiomatic expressions of the type "sooner X than Y." "It'd quicker cost you more than ten dollars than less." **1993** *DARE* File **KS**, *Quicker* was used in place of *sooner.* "I'd quicker die than go out with you" or "It'd quicker cause more trouble than not."

3 in phr *fit too quick:* See quots. Cf *fit too soon* (at **soon**)
1967 *DARE* (Qu. OO37a, *Talking about clothes shrinking: "The first time my wool socks were washed they _____";* not asked in early QRs) Inf **IA3**, Fit too quick—an expression used about fitting too tightly. **1982** *Barrick Coll.* **csPA**, *Quick*—easy? "This lid fits too quick." (i.e., too large for the pot.)

quick n[1]
An instant; a moment.
1986 Pederson *LAGS Concordance*, 1 inf, **cwFL**, I'll be there in a pair of quicks.

quick n[2] [Prob var of *crick* a pain spasm, but cf *EDD quick* adj.[1] 9 "Sharp, piercing"] Cf **quickie, quirk** n[2]
A sudden, sharp pain.
1965–68 *DARE* (Qu. BB3a, *. . A pain that strikes you suddenly in the neck*) Infs **MS63, TN27**, Quick; [**MI44**, Quick pain in the neck]. **1983** *MJLF* 9.1.52 **ceKY** (as of 1956), *Quick . . a crick (in the neck).*

quick v Also *quicken* **chiefly S Midl**
To prick the quick of the hoof of (a horse); hence ppl adj *quicked.*
1915 *DN* 4.188 **swVA**, *Quick*, v.t. Horse shoeing. To drive a nail into the *quick.* **1937** *Hall Coll.* **eTN**, The nails in his feet quicked him (the horse). **1939** *Ibid* **wNC**, You quicken the heel when you stick a tack in it. **1957** Faulkner *Town* 37 **MS**, Snopes quicked it with the first nail; whereupon Houston picked Snopes up and threw him hammer and all into the cooling tub. **1961** McDavid Coll. **csOK**, *Quicken*—to drive a nail into the quick of a hoof. [Inf a farmer, old, gs educ] **1967** *DARE* Tape **TX26**, If you fit the shoe too close, and get in too close on the inner wall, you got what we call a quicked horse. You prick him, you quick him, and he's lame. **1986** Pederson *LAGS Concordance*, 1 inf, **neAR**, To quicken that horse—drive a nail in hoof's quick; nail in quick of horse's hoof—it'll quicken.

quick-and-dirty n Also *quick-and-filthy, ~-greasy* **Nth** =**greasy spoon.**
1942 Berrey–Van den Bark *Amer. Slang* 814.4, *Cheap restaurant. . . quick* and *filthy.* **1950** *WELS* (Nicknames . . *for a small eating place*) 1 Inf, **WI**, Quick-and-dirty. **1967–68** *DARE* (Qu. D39, . . *Nicknames . . for a small eating place where the food is not especially good*) Inf **CT9**, Quick-and-greasy; **OH15**, Quick-and-dirty. **1968** *Harper's Mag.* Jan 14 **MA**, The office of the Massachusetts Electric Company was temporarily converted into a mock-up of a quick-and-dirty and its sign replaced with one that read *Al's Bean Pot.* **1970** *New Yorker* 17 Jan 23 **NYC**, It was after one when he finished, and we stopped for lunch at a quick-and-dirty on East Ninety-sixth and talked shop.

quick as See **quick** adv

quick as scat See **scat** n **1**

quick cheese n Cf **cook cheese**, *DS* H60
Cottage cheese.
1941 *LANE* Map 299 (*Cottage cheese*) 1 inf, **CT**, Quick ch[eese], old people's term.

quick consumption n Also *quick con, ~ fever* **esp Nth** old-fash
=**galloping consumption.**
1844 *Ladies' Repository* 4.263, Her disease at first yielded to medicine, but soon after a relapse brought on an inflammatory fever, which was followed by quick consumption. **1868** *Catholic World* 6.826, Anne Atherton's case was a peculiar one. They called it quick consumption, for want of a better name. **1897** *New Engl. Mag.* 21.665, We fall back on the very reasonable supposition that one of the other Pilgrims had the disease in an incipient form and that exposure and "catching cold" changed this incipient disease into an acute tubercular broncho-pneumonia (quick consumption). **1943** *LANE* Map 510 (*Tuberculosis*) 1 inf, **cCT**, Quick consumption, long consumption; 1 inf, **nwCT**, Quick consumption, slow consumption, galloping consumption; 1 inf, **ceMA**, Quick consumption is pretty bad; 1 inf, **swMA**, Quick consumption; 1 inf, **seVT**, Quick consumption = galloping tuberculosis; 1 inf, **ceVT**, There's quick consumption and there's old-fashion or lingering consumption. **1950** *WELS* **WI** (*Tuberculosis*) 1 Inf, Quick con or galloping con if progress of disease is very rapid; 1 Inf, Consumption, quick consumption, galloping consumption—old-fashioned. **1950** *WELS Suppl.* **cWI**, *Quick fever*—T.B. **1960** Bailey *Resp. to PADS 20* **KS**, Tuberculosis—Quick consumption. **1965–70** *DARE* (Qu. BB10, . . *Names or nicknames . . for tuberculosis*) Infs **CA101, CT6, MI68, 110, NY8, 126, 191**, Quick consumption; **CA87**, Quick consumption—old-fashioned; **IA11**, Quick consumption—went in less than a year; **MI2**, Quick consumption [FW sugg]—I've heard; **MA5**, Consumption, galloping consumption; quick consumption—another kind; **MA48**, Galloping consumption—same, seemed to affect the younger people; **PA104**, Quick consumption—didn't last very long, quick death; **TN27**, Quick consumption—occasionally, for when it killed you fast; [**CA53**, Quick pneumonia—old-fashioned]. [13 of 14 Infs old] **1967** *DARE* Tape **MI68**, Her own parents died from what she called quick consumption. Probably, I guess, pneumonia, as we diagnose it today.

quicked See **quick** v

quicked-up adj phr
Hurriedly arranged.
1893 Shands *MS Speech* 51, *Quicked up.* . . I once heard an illiterate white inhabitant of Lafayette County use this expression for *sudden, hastened.* He said, "You know his leaving was a quicked-up thing." **1993** *DARE* File **KS**, *Quicked-up* was used a lot in reference to "shotgun" weddings. Come to think of it, I don't think I *ever* heard it used in any other context.

quicken See **quick** v

quicken tree n [*OED2* 1548→ for other spp of *Sorbus*]
A **mountain ash 1.**
1930 Shoemaker *1300 Words* 49 **cPA Mts** (as of c1900), *Quicken-tree*—The mountain ash.

quicker than hell beating tanbark See **hell 5**

quicker than scat See **scat** n **1**

quick fever See **quick consumption**

quick grass n [*OED2* 1617→]
=**quack grass 1.**
   1851 (1854) *Amer. Farmer's Hand-Book* 69, This crop is recommended as an effectual destroyer of that frequent pest of the field, called couch-grass, quick-grass, &c. **1895** U.S. Dept. Ag. *Farmers' Bulletin* 28.25, Quick grass. . . New England to Minnesota. **1932** Rydberg *Flora Prairies* 131, Quick-grass, Quack-grass. **1968–70** DARE (Qu. S8, *A common kind of wild grass that grows in fields: it spreads by sending out long underground roots, and it's hard to get rid of*) Infs **IL**138, **KS**15, **MA**25, **NY**45, Quick grass. **1976** Bailey–Bailey *Hortus Third* 41, Quick g[rass]. . . A troublesome weed in the n[orthern] states.

quickie adj [Cf *EDD quick* adj.[1] 9 "Sharp, piercing"] Cf **quick n**[2]
Of a part of the body: experiencing sharp pain or extreme sensitivity.
   1984 *Annals Internal Med.* 100.899 **cwAL**, My knee is quickie means that the knee is sensitive and has sudden sharp pains. **1990** Cavender *Folk Med. Lexicon* 30 **sAppalachians**, Quickie—[used of] a sore area on the body that has a normal appearance but is sensitive to the touch.

quick-in-the-hand n [*OED2* (at *quick* adj. D) 1785→; see quot 1931]
=**jewelweed 1.**
   1830 Rafinesque *Med. Flora* 2.231, Impatiens. . . Touchmenot, . . Quickinthehand. . . Two sp. *I. fulva* and *pallida*, both in common use for jaundice and asthma, as a tea. . . Leaves used for piles and wash for wounds: they dye wool saffron color and yellow. **1876** Hobbs *Bot. Hdbk.* 94, Quick in the hand. . Impatiens pallida. **1900** Lyons *Plant Names* 200, I[mpatiens] aurea. . . Quick in-the-hand [sic]. **1931** Clute *Common Plants* 137, The seed-pods of the garden balsam (*Impatiens balsamina*) burst open impatiently at the slightest touch, a fact which the generic name indicates. The plant has long been known as touch-me-not from the Latin *Noli-me-tangere*, but a more expressive name is the backwoodsman's quick-in-the-hand. Apparently this does not refer so much to the rapidity with which the seedpods explode as it does to the fact that it seems alive ("quick") in the hand that tries to grasp it. Our two common species of jewel-weed are well known for the same habit. **1974** (1977) Coon *Useful Plants* 72, Impatiens biflora—Jewelweed . . quick-in-the-hand. . . This plant will also be found in botanies under *I. pallida* or *I. capensis*.

quick on the draw See **draw n 7**

quicksilver weed n Also *quicksilver* [See quot 1961 Douglas] Cf **silverweed 4**
A **meadow rue**: usu *Thalictrum dioicum*, but also *T. pubescens*.
   1893 *Jrl. Amer. Folkl.* 6.136 **ME**, Thalictrum dioicum, quicksilver weed. Penobscot Co., Me. **1910** Graves *Flowering Plants* 188 **CT**, Thalictrum dioicum. . . Quicksilver Weed. Rocky hillsides in rich soil. **1940** Clute *Amer. Plant Names* 5, T[halictrum] Polygamum [=*T. pubescens*]. . . Quicksilver-weed, . . rattlesnake-bite. **1961** Douglas *My Wilderness* 230 **NH**, The lower woods are filled with meadow rue that in places grows nearly knee-high. It is known locally as quicksilver, by reason of its silvery sheen when submerged in water. It has tiny purple flowers, some upright, some drooping, depending on the sex. **1961** Smith *MI Wildflowers* 127, Quicksilver-weed—Thalictrum dioicum. . . This and other species of Meadow-rue are often cultivated for the attractive light-green foliage and the feathery flower clusters. **1969** *DARE* Wildfl QR Pl.71 (*Thalictrum dioicum*) Inf **WI**79, Quicksilver. **1976** Bailey–Bailey *Hortus Third* 1104, [Thalictrum] dioicum. . . Quicksilver weed. . . Que. to N. Dak., s. to Ga. and Mo.

quick start n Cf **easy walker**
A rubber-soled canvas shoe; a sneaker.
   1982 *DARE* File **wMT** (as of 1971), "Oh, you got a new pair of quick-starts, eh?!" My friend was referring to a new pair of sneakers. **1997** *NADS Letters* **OH**, I first heard the word from my ex-husband, who explained that quickstarts were sneakers and were called such because their soles were rubber, thereby giving the wearer good traction and a "quick start" off the pavement. **1998** *Ibid* **MS**, During my mid-sixties college days in Mississippi, my friends used "quickstarts" and "pointed

toe quickstarts" as slang for sneakers. **2000** *Ibid*, Quickstarts—"a type of sneakers"—report from Indianapolis by a student who heard it running track in high school. = tennis or running shoes.

quickstep n Also with *the;* also pl; often in combs Cf **green-apple quickstep, two-step**
Diarrhea.
   1776 in 1935 *PA Mag. Hist. & Biog.* 59.330, Yesterday & today I have been much unwell, troubled with the quick step, attended with Severe gripings. **1778** in 1889 CT Hist. Soc. *Coll.* 7.350 **CT**, I am not well for I have got the Quik [sic] Step. **1900** *DN* 2.53 [College slang], Quickstep. . . Diarrhœa. . . In compounds 'Pennsylvania quickstep,' . . Seminary quickstep . . ; Tennessee quickstep. **1950** WELS **WI** (*Diarrhea or looseness of the bowels*) 2 Infs, Quickstep; 1 Inf, Green-apple quickstep; 1 Inf, Virginia quickstep; 1 Inf, Tennessee quickstep. **1958** McCulloch *Woods Words* 143 **Pacific NW**, Quick step—A dose of dysentery. **1965–70** DARE (Qu. BB19, *Joking names for looseness of the bowels*) Infs **CA**49, **IN**28, **MI**55, **PA**202, **VA**30, **VT**12, **WV**12, Green-apple quickstep; **NY**107, **PA**223, Pennsylvania quickstep; **UT**10, **WY**4, Rocky Mountain quickstep; **LA**14, Confederate quickstep; **MI**44, **UT**4, (The) quickstep; **OK**11, The Oklahoma quickstep; **PA**63, Quicksteps; **PA**162, Backdoor quicksteps.

quickwater n chiefly **Nth**, esp **ME** Cf **swift water**
Rapidly flowing water in a stream or river; white water.
   a1843 (1958) Barker *Recoll. First Settlement OH* 41, Devol . . built the first floating Mill to be opperating upon & put in action by the naturel Current of the Ohio, in the Quick waters between the Island and the Main. **a1862** (1864) Thoreau *ME Woods* 276, The Indian navigator naturally distinguishes by a name those parts of a stream where he has encountered quick water and forks. **1905** U.S. Forest Serv. *Bulletin* 61.44 [Logging terms], Quickwater. . . That part of a stream which has fall enough to create a decided current. (Gen.) **1908** Johnson *Highways Pacific Coast* 258 **OR**, The current ain't strong enough. The [fish] wheels does best in quick water. **1932** Wasson *Sailing Days* 3 **cME coast**, Light canoes of birch bark so valiant in running the frequent rapids or "quick-water." **1941** Williams *Strange Woman* 207 **ME**, They was coming down-river in a canoe with two Indians paddling, and they hit a little quick water, and young Poster let on to be scared. **1956** Sorden–Ebert *Logger's Words* 26 **Gt Lakes**, Quick-water, See white-water. *Ibid* 41, White-water, That part of a stream which has fall enough to create a decided current, making white foam. Same as quick-water, rapid-water. **1966** DARE (Qu. C3, *A place in a swift stream where the surface of the water is broken*) Inf **ME**10, Quickwater; (Qu. O18, *Different currents or actions of the water that are important when you're in a boat*) Inf **ME**9, Quickwater—fast water—in river. **1966** DARE Tape **ME**26, If you're in quickwater or something, see, you might want to let go quick.

quickweed n
=**galinsoga.**
   1950 Stevens *ND Plants* 287, Galinsoga ciliata. . . Quickweed. **1954** Harrington *Manual Plants CO* 597, Galinsoga. . . Quickweed. . . The 2 species are very similar and intergrade somewhat in our material. **1967** Harrington *Edible Plants Rocky Mts.* 76, Quickweed is often very abundant, as any weed is apt to be, and certainly is worth a trial as food. It would be especially good in a mixture with some other plant of more pronounced flavor, because of the bland taste of the plant. **1970** Kirk *Wild Edible Plants W. U.S.* 138, Quickweed. . . may be found growing in moist, open ground throughout the West, except, apparently, for Washington and Oregon. **1974** *WI Acad. Rev.* Summer 22, Quickweed (*Galinsoga ciliata*).

quiddle v[1]
1 also with *about, around:* To trifle, fuss over unimportant matters; to fiddle about; hence n *quiddle(r)* one who fusses over small matters; vbl n and ppl adj *quiddling* fussing, trifling, mincing. [*EDD quiddle* v.[1] and sb.[2] "To make a fuss about trifles; to fuss, fiddle about; to fret. . . A fussy, over-particular person."] chiefly **NEng** Cf **piddle**
   1828 *Johnson's Engl. Dict.* (ed. Worcester) 1048 **NEng**, To Quiddle. . . To busy one's self about trifles. Common in New England. The word is also used as a substantive. **1835** *New Engl. Mag.* 9.280, It [=fresco] is a style entirely interdicted to the quiddlers—who rely upon diligent imitation, who combine from memory, rather than draw from imagination. **1841** Webster *Amer. Dict.* 2.407, Quiddle. . . To spend or waste time in

trifling employments, or to attend to useful subjects in a trifling super-ficial manner. *Quiddler*. . . One who spends time in trifling niceties. *Quiddling*. . . Spending time in trifling employments. *Quiddling*. . . The spending of time in trifling employments. **1856** Emerson *English Traits* 108 **eMA,** The Englishman is very petulant and precise about his ac-commodation at inns, . . a quiddle about his toast and his chop. **1860** Emerson *Conduct* 133 **eMA,** Neither will we be driven into a quiddling abstemiousness. **1869** Stowe *Oldtown Folks* 240 **NEng,** Lose an hour in the morning, and you may chase it till ye drop down, you never'll catch it! That's the way things goes, and I should like to know who's a going to stop to quiddle with young uns? **1869** Bowles *New West* 157 **MA,** Stop the treaty-making humbug. . . Neither party keeps the bargain. The Indian is cheated; the Senate changes the provisions; a quiddling Secretary of the Interior or Indian Commissioner refuses to carry it out. **1877** Bartlett *Americanisms* 509, *Quiddling.* Unsteady; uncertain; minc-ing, as a "quiddling gait." **1880** *Scribner's Mth.* 20.227, Bold, strong, free from quiddling lines, they [=engravings] hold with a firm grasp the conceptions of the artist. **1881** in 1987 Alcott *Selected Letters* 255 **NEng,** Fortunately punctuation is a free institution & all can pepper to suit the taste. I dont care much, & always leave proof readers to quiddle if they like. **1891** (1967) Freeman *New Engl. Nun* 428 **NEng,** You've been quiddlin' out there all the mornin'. . . Don't, for the land's sake, putter so long. **1997** *NADS Letters,* My grandmother . . is from Mis-souri, but when I was growing up in northeastern Oklahoma, [she] used to yell at us to "quit quiddlin' about." **[1999** *Ibid* **NH** (as of c1980), My grandfather used to "quibble around" or "quibble about" the garage or his woodshop in the cellar. (At least, I always thought he said "quib-ble.") "Quibbling" would be things like sorting a jar full of mixed-size screws by size, or sorting through the scrap wood pile looking for insect damage, etc. . . We would also use the word "putter" to mean the same thing as "quibble."] **2000** *Ibid,* Quiddle—"to busy oneself with unim-portant things". A student heard it from an aunt in Connecticut and an-other heard it she thinks from friends in Maine 'just quiddling around.'

‡**2** See quot.
1969 *DARE* (Qu. JJ43, *To give away a secret or tell a piece of news too soon: "He wasn't supposed to know. Somebody must have _____."*) Inf **CT25,** Quiddled.

quiddle n See **quiddle** v¹ **1**

quiddle v² [Cf *EDD whiddle* v. "Sc. . . To move in a short, quick flight; to go lightly and rapidly" and *EDG* 209 "Initial *kw* . . has often become *hw* . . especially in . . Sc."]
1909 *DN* 3.421 **Cape Cod MA** (as of a1857), *Quiddle.* . . To crawl on the flesh. "I felt a flea quiddle, quiddle round me all night."

quiddler See **quiddle** v¹ **1**

quiddling See **quiddle** v¹ **1**

quidow See **cuidado**

quien sabe phr Pronc-sp *keen sabe, quien savvy* [Span *quién sabe*] **SW**
Who knows?—also used attrib: questionable, enigmatic.
1836 in 1921 Lamar *Papers* 1.436 **TX,** Austin I doubt not will be elected and will do well provided he selects a *good* Cabinet—and an honest one—quen [*sic*] Sabe. **1847** Reid *TX Rangers* 53, The govern-ment was charitably bound to suppose . . they had recklessly laid *violent hands upon their own lives!* "Quien sabe?" **1858** Stone *Put's Golden* 38, But really it is a *quien sabe* case. **1910** Bronson *Reminiscences Ranchman* 67 **WY,** Ef yu b'ars too far west hit'll be lay out unde' yu saddle blanket, fo' yu an' *keen sabe* case whar yu brings up. **1916** Ben-edict–Lomax *Book of TX* 199, But the decline in the production of honey . . may have robbed Uvalde of her world's championship. Quien sabe? **1932** Bentley *Spanish Terms* 189 **SW,** *Quien sabe* English modifications, *quien savvy* . . [ki:en 'sæbi:, kɪn 'sæbi:, kɪen 'sævi:, kɪn 'sævi:] Who knows? . . In spoken conversation the use of *"quien sabe?"* is often accompanied by a non-committal shrug of the shoulders. *Ibid* 238 **SW** [Exx of bilingualism among Americans], [Letter:] I am trying to close an agreement which will permit me to do research work for them this summer, *pero Quien sabe?* **1933** *AmSp* 8.1.32 **nwTX** [Ranch diction], *Quien sabe* (pronounced something like *kin savvy*). The name of one of the many secret brands used for branding mavericks. The *quien sabe* brand consisted of interlocking half circles. Literally *who knows?* **1949** *Southwestern Rev.* Summer 235/1 (*OED2*), One yarn thrown in as a sort of *quien sabe?* item suggests an even more unpalat-able morsel.

quiet adj, v Pronc-sp *quient* Cf Intro "Language Changes" I.8, *mighnt* (at **may** v **Ab**)
Std senses, var form.
1905 *DN* 3.58 **eNE,** Intrusive *n,* the "nasal infix," occurs in . . quie(n)t . . ; but it is rare except in *[Uni(n)ted States, migh(n)t].*

quieten v Often with *down* [*OED2* 1828→] **chiefly Sth, S Midl** Cf **-en** suff⁵
To make or become quiet.
1882 *Century Illustr. Mag.* 23.529 **NC,** Old Man [Rogers]. Mother, kinder quieten down. *Mrs. Rogers.* A nice time to quiet down! **1890** *Catholic World* 52.260 **Sth** [Black], Pres'n'y mist'ess quietened down. **1930s** in 1944 *ADD* **eWV,** Quieten down. **1936** *AmSp* 11.317 **Ozarks,** *Quieten down.* . . To become quiet. 'We-all better wait till things kind of quieten down an' blow over.' **1937** Hall *Coll.* **eTN,** Ye cain't come nigh a bear jest atter he's . . ben caught in a trap. Ye have to let him quieten down fust. **1939** Harris *Purslane* 279 **cNC,** Now le's find a empty bench on Capitol Square and quieten our stomachs. **c1960** *Wil-son Coll.* **csKY,** *Quieten*—To make quiet. **1965–70** *DARE* (Qu. B13, *When the wind begins to decrease . . it's _____*) Infs **AR1, MI108, TX43,** Quietening (down); (Qu. X10b, *To tell a person to stop talking—not very politely*) Infs **IL114, OK42, TN33, 34,** Quieten down; (Qu. GG23c, . . *Expressions [to tell someone to be patient]*) Infs **GA77, MO10,** Quieten down; (Qu. GG27a, *To get somebody out of an unhappy mood . . "Everything's going to be all right, so _____."*) Inf **MO10,** Let's quieten down; (Qu. JJ25) Inf **AK8,** That quietened him; (Qu. NN19, *When you want people to stop talking for a moment so that you can listen for something*) Infs **TN1, TX76,** Quieten down. **1967–70** *DARE* FW Addit **GA19,** They'll quieten it off; **AL,** Quieten those children! **1968–69** *DARE* Tape **GA74,** He'd quieten down and go back to sleep; **VA112,** Now, in shallow water, if you have a thunderstorm . . you'll see him [=a crab] going wild, streaking for deep waters. . . He'll get off of that shallow water, whack, and he won't come back there no more till it quietens down in maybe a day or two. **1973** Allen *LAUM* 1.361 (as of c1950), *Keep calm.* . . quieten down [2 infs, **SD, NE**]. **1976** Garber *Mountain-ese* 73 **sAppalachians,** Jed, go outside and see iffen you can quieten them dogs from barkin'. **1986** Pederson *LAGS Concordance* **Gulf Region** (Keep calm!) 14 infs, Quieten down; 2 infs, (Got it) quieten [past pple] down; (*Wind's letting up*) 3 infs, Quietening down; 2 infs, Quieten down; (*Call to a dog*) 1 inf, Quieten down.

quiet root n Cf **white root**
See quot.
1923 Parsons *Folk-lore Sea Islands* 198 **csSC,** There is a white root called "quiet root" good for a crying child. You scrape off the outer skin, "scrape off de firs' bark, get de nex' bark," boil it, and in it boil the child's food.

quile v¹ See **coil** v

quile v² Usu with *down, up* [Var of *quail,* prob infl by *quile* var of **coil** v; cf *EDD quail* v.¹ 3 "To quiet down" and v.¹ 8 "To quell; to subdue through fear"; cf also *SND quall* v. "Of wind, etc.: to lull, abate"] **chiefly S Midl**
To make or become quiet; to settle down.
1818 in 1824 Knight *Letters* 107 **KY,** Some words are used, even by genteel people . . in a new sense; and . . pronounced very uncouthly, as . . to quile for to quiet. **1845** *Amer. Whig Rev.* 2.603 **SW,** "Let's quile up." And with that word he spread his buffalo-robe on the floor. **1887** (1967) Harris *Free Joe* 172 **cGA** [Black], Mars Peyt he try ter quile 'im, but dat nigger man done gone! **1894** *Scribner's Mag.* 16.49 **sAppa-lachians,** An' I'd jess quile down at home in my sock feet an' never git up, lessen it wus to eat aw to go to bed. **1915** *DN* 4.188 **swVA,** *Quile up,* become quiet. **1923** *DN* 5.218 **swMO,** *Quile.* . . to quiet down or submit, as a querulous child. "You young-uns quile down now an' be-have y'r se'ves." **1930s** in 1944 *ADD* **nWV,** Get her quiled down. [kwaɪld]. **1944** *PADS* 2.59 **swMO,** My least 'un coughed till he couldn't sleep; then I put a greasy rag 'round his neck, and he jist quiled down and slept till mornin'. **1968** Haun *Hawk's Done Gone* 335 **TN,** Lom told Hubert he would just have to quile down a bit, that they had to have the money. **1997** *DARE* File **AL,** My grandmother, who was raised in South Alabama . . near Montgomery, sometimes said "quilte" (. . /kwaɪlt/ . .) for "quiet." "Give that baby some milk so he'll quilte down. The baby quilted down some after his bottle."

quiler n [sEngl dial (*EDD coilers,* also *quilers, quoilers* "The breeching; the chain attached to the breeching of a harness")]

One of the straps that connects the breeching of a horse harness to the shaft or pole; a breeching strap or holdback.

1889 *AN&Q* 3.255 **sNJ,** More remarkable is the fact that the leather bands which hold the traces to the shafts are 'hold backs' in rocky North Jersey, and 'quilers' in sandy South Jersey. **1894** *DN* 1.333 **NJ,** *Quiler:* holdback strap. **1911** *Century Dict. Suppl., Quilers.* . . The breeching-strap of a harness. . . [*Century* Ed: Prov. Eng. and U.S. (Pennsylvania).] **1969** *DARE* FW Addit, [kwalɚ]—the thing that goes around the shaft—separate strap that hooks to the britchin on the harness, so when horse backs he can push wagon.

quile up See **quile** v²

quill n

1 usu pl: A set of panpipes. [Cf *OED2 quill* sb.¹ 1.c "A musical pipe, made of a hollow stem"; 1567→] **Sth, S Midl**

1879 *Harper's New Mth. Mag.* 59.515 **GA,** We glanced corroboratively at a gaping dozen or two of tow-heads, ranging in size from five feet downward, like the quills in a darky's pipe of Pan. **1883** Harris *Nights with Remus* 69 **GA,** Uncle Remus declared that Brother Rabbit could perform upon the quills, an accomplishment to which none of the other animals could lay claim. [Footnote to *quills:* The veritable Pan's pipes. A simple but very effective musical instrument made of reeds, and in great favor on the plantations.] **1886** *Century Illustr. Mag.* 31.521, But to show how far the art of playing the "quills" could be carried . . see this "quill tune" . . from a gentleman who heard it in Alabama. **1922** Talley *Negro Folk Rhymes* 303 **TN** [Black], In my early childhood I saw many sets of "Quills." They were short reed pipes, closed at one end, made from cane found in our Southern canebrakes. **1942** (1965) Parrish *Slave Songs* 16 **GA coast,** If you live in the neighborhood of a cane-brake, there may be an old Negro who can demonstrate the kind of music to be obtained from a set of reed-pipes, called "quills," made from graduated lengths of cane tightly wedged into a frame. **1950** *PADS* 14.55 **SC,** *Quills.* . . Pipes of Pan, made by boys from joints of green cane. **1975** McDonough *Garden Sass* 230 **AR,** Another old and unusual instrument is the set of quills. . . made by the workers out in the canefields, and to make them . . "You just take an old fishing cane, you see, and you just cut 'em." **1986** Pederson *LAGS Concordance,* 1 inf, **ceMS,** Quill—homemade musical instrument.

2 A steam-locomotive whistle. [From its resemblance to a **quill** n 1; see quot 1945] **chiefly Sth** Cf **quill** v 4

1940 *RR Mag.* Apr 50, *Quill*—Southern word for whistle. **1945** in 1953 Botkin–Harlow *Treas. Railroad Folkl.* 340, To my thinking, the most popular quills were the three- four- and five-cell chimes, bored from blocks twelve to eighteen inches in length. *Ibid* 342, What a whistle! . . yours is the prettiest quill I've ever heard! **1961** *Listener* (London BBC) 24 Aug 270, The fabled Casey Jones . . was a "quill artist" of note, who always carried with him his own quill (that is what they used to call a chime in the deep South). **1967** Williams *Greenbones* 138 **GA** (as of c1910), "Like the sweetest quill I ever heard," one said. He meant train whistles.

3 A small tube, as: see below. [*OED2 quill* sb.¹ 2.a "A small pipe or tube. . . *Obs.*" c1433–1712]

a A spile for tapping a **sugar maple** tree. [Cf *OED2 quill* sb.¹ 2.b "A tap or faucet. *Obs.*" 1611–1727]

1938 FWP *Guide CT* 370 **seCT,** Arched maples . . are sometimes tapped for the sap by country children who make their quills of elder and sumach. In early spring these trees are bright with shiny tin buckets hung in soldier rows just below the quills. **1968** *DARE* Tape **CT3,** We tap our trees right here on the place using a regular quill and brace and bit.

b A drinking straw. **esp S Midl**

1913 Johnson *Highways St. Lawrence to VA* 66 **seNY,** They drank the water, and they all had sore lips and a sore mouth. Then they got quills for to suck through, but it still made 'em have sore tongues and sore throats. **1949** *AmSp* 24.11 **KY** [Argot of the moonshiner], *Quill.* . . A straw used to sample beer in the vats. . . 'Hand me that quill. I'm fixing to drink some beer out of this barrel.' **1974** Betts–Walser *NC Folkl.* 7, *Quill:* a drinking straw. **1974** Dabney *Mountain Spirits* xxiv **sAppalachians,** *Quill:* A straw used to sample still beer. **1995** *DARE* File **TN,** My mother was just here for a visit. While we were out at a fast food restaurant, she asked me to get her a "quill." I looked blank, and then asked, "Do you mean a straw?" She looked startled and said yes. . . She is from Tennessee, . . and is 88 years old. **1997** *Ibid* **seTN,** I asked my mother-in-law, "What is a quill?" She replied without any hesitation, "That's a straw."

c in phrr *drink from* (or *piss through*) *the same quill* and var: To be very friendly.   Cf **quill** v 5

1805 Sewall *Parody* 9 **MA,** Betwixt us jointly claiming but *one* will,/ And always meekly oozing thro' *one* quill. **1965** *S. Folkl. Qrly.* 29.158 **eKY,** Several field informants added the companion saying to suggest extreme congeniality: *They pissed through the same quill.* **1967–70** *DARE* (Qu. II3, *Expressions to say that people are very friendly toward each other: "They're _____."*) Inf **IL96,** Both pissing through the same quill; **TN15,** They drink from the same quill; **VA41,** They piss through the same quill [laughter]; (Qu. II11a, *If two people don't get along well together . . "They don't _____."*) Inf **TN15,** Drink from the same quill. **1984** Wilder *You All Spoken Here* 18 **Sth,** *They piss through the same quill:* They are like two peas in a pod—not a dime's difference between them.

4 also *coon's quill, goose ~, tooth ~:* A toothpick, usu one made from a goose quill. [*OED2 quill* sb.¹ 3.e 1784] *old-fash*

[**1888** Cable *Bonaventure* 154 **LA,** I never use a quill toothpick.] **1950** *WELS* **WI** (*Names and nicknames for a toothpick*) 5 Infs, Quill; [1 Inf, Years ago men carried quills in their vest pockets for toothpicks; some had gold ends fastened to a small chain;] 1 Inf, Tooth quill—old-fashioned. **1965–70** *DARE* (Qu. G11, *Other names or nicknames for a toothpick*) 17 Infs, **scattered,** Quill(s); **IL50, IN28, MD19, NY205, OR1, SC29,** Quill [FW sugg]; **IN7, SC34,** Quill [FW sugg]—old-fashioned; **MA40, OH38,** Quill—old-fashioned; **AL27,** Quill [FW sugg]—remembered in older times actually used a goose quill cut down and sharpened; **DC12,** Quill [FW sugg; Inf has heard, doesn't use]; **IA33,** Quill—in the old days; [**IA41,** Quill [FW sugg]—not a toothpick, but used for the same purpose;] **LA31,** Quill—old-fashioned; old-timers used a goose quill and kept it in their pocket; **MD28,** Quill [FW sugg]—once people used to carry a toothpick made of quill around with them; it was used over and over; **NY41,** Quill—heard used; **NY233,** Quill—whittled feather; **NC34,** Quill—older; **OH75,** Quill—my grandfather said that; **OK1,** Some old-timers made toothpicks out of turkey or goose feathers, called "quills"; **PA142,** Quill—heard, not used; **SC43,** Quill [FW sugg]—out of use now; **SC56,** Quill—a permanent one, everybody had his own, made from a feather; **NJ21,** Coon's quill—this is a coon's penis, dried and shaved down, used as a joke, but they were used; **AR2, SC19,** Goose quill; **KY25,** Goose quill—old-fashioned type of toothpick; [**MA122,** Goose [kwilɜ];] **MD30,** Tooth quill [FW sugg]—usually made of celluloid; **NC36,** Tooth quill—goose and turkey quill; [**CT39,** Quill—not actual name, made of quill; **ME11,** Used to have quill toothpicks, not now; **MS38,** Goose-quill toothpick;] **TN57,** Quill [FW: Inf not familiar with any other name, but in the old days real quills or feathers were used this way]. [47 of 52 Infs old]

5 in phr *the pure quill* and var: Something that is pure, genuine, of the highest quality; hence adjs *pure-quill* (rarely *real-quill*) genuine; adv *pure-quill* genuinely. [Prob transf from earlier application to cinnamon or cinchona bark, which are least subject to adulteration when formed into *quills* or rolls of dried bark]

1884 Lewis *Sawed-Off Sketches* 23, There's hairs of six different colors sticking in the splinters, and these blood-stains are the pure quill. **1888** in 1971 Farmer *Americanisms* 443, When religun is religun, an' it's the pure quill an' no water in it, there's never one of us but kin take it in large doses. **1916** *DN* 4.327 **KS,** *Quill.* . . Anything of a high degree of excellence. *The pure quill with a bead on it.* . . "That tobacco is the pure quill." **1935** Davis *Honey* 330 **OR,** Bottles of rattlesnake oil, which he offered as a specific for rheumatism. To prove that his product was the pure quill, he also exhibited as a side-attraction a row of half-gallon fruit-jars, each containing one large live rattler. **1936** *AmSp* 11.317 **Ozarks,** *Pure quill.* . . The genuine product, unadulterated and undiluted. **1949** Peattie *Cascades* 142 **Pacific NW,** Real-quill logging began on the bottoms of the Cascades' foothills with the California gold rush. **1956** Algren *Walk on the Wild Side* 127 **Sth,** Don't mean to appear ongrateful, miss, for you've been pure-quill kind. *Ibid* 152, It's the pure quill, . . you can smell the feet of the boys who plowed the corn. **1958** *Julian Apple Day* [3] **csCA,** That's what I'm a-telling you, the pure quill truth about my old pal, Pegleg Smith. **1959** *VT Hist.* 27.153, *Pure quill.* . . The best of anything. Rare.

6 in phr *of the same quill:* Of the same sort.

1927 Ruppenthal *Coll.* **KS,** *Same quill*—alike. . . Both men are braggarts of the same quill.

7 See **quill** v 3.

‡**8** in comb *pine-quill:* =**needle 1;** hence adj *quilless* having no needles.

1871 Miller *Songs of Sierras* 147, Black, quilless pines . . / Stand dark and sullen in the silent courts. **1873** Miller *Modocs* 180, On that side, where only grass has grown and pine-quills fallen . . , the ground is often broken.

9 See quot.

1968 *Foxfire* 2.73 **nGA,** The conservative sanger [=ginseng cultivator] only dug roots in the fall of the year and carefully replanted the seeds, or the rhizome extension called a "quill", or "bud".

quill v

1 To move quickly.   Cf **quill-wheel** v 1

1869 *Overland Mth.* 3.127 **TX,** A trig, smirk little horse . . often has to "june," or "quill," or "get up and quill." **1889** (1971) Farmer *Americanisms* 446 **TX,** *To get up and quill.*—To depart in haste; to move quickly. **1942** Warnick *Garrett Co. MD* 12 **nwMD** (as of 1900–18), *Quillin'* . . going at a rapid pace.

2 To apply a medicinal powder to (someone or something) by blowing it out of a **quill** n 3; esp, to hasten labor in (a woman) by provoking sneezing by use of a **quill** n 3; hence ppl adj *quilled* born following such a procedure.

1945 Pickard–Buley *Midwest Pioneer* 32 (as of 1824), For instance, when the baby proved too reluctant to enter the world "on its own," a bit of dried snuff blown into the mother's nose by way of a goose quill would bring on sneezing paroxysms and probably the desired results. (Persons so introduced were spoken of in later life as having been quilled babies.) **1953** Randolph–Wilson *Down in Holler* 275 **Ozarks,** J.H. Young, of Galena, Mo., told me of a backwoods healer who *quills* a woman in labor by filling a turkey quill with snuff and blowing it in the patient's face; the theory is that the snuff makes the woman sneeze, and the babe will be born instanter! Farmers used to *quill* a sore on an animal by blowing some medicinal powder on it through a quill. **1983** *MJLF* 9.1.52 **ceKY** (as of 1956), *Quill* . . to stick a straw up the nose of a woman in labor in order to make her sneeze. This hastens delivery in a stubborn labor case. [Inf is a midwife.]

3 To toady, **brownnose;** to curry favor with; hence n *quill* the attempt to win favor; n *quiller* one who makes such an attempt.

1918 *DN* 5.27 **NW,** To quill. . . To secure, or attempt to secure, marks by a "quill." Often as in "to quill the prof." *Ibid, Quill.* . . An effort to secure a high mark by any method of cajolery, bluff, etc. Embalmed for an era in the sentence, "The quill is mightier than the pen." Washington State College. *Ibid, Quiller.* . . One who quills. **1942** Berrey–Van den Bark *Amer. Slang* 291.4, *Curry favor; toady.* . . quill. *Ibid* 848.4, *Curry favor with instructors.* . . quill. **1968** *DARE* (Qu. JJ3a, *When a school child makes a special effort to 'get in good' with the teacher in hopes of getting a better grade: "He's trying to _____ again."*) Inf **MO34,** Quill. **1970** *Thompson Coll.* **cnAL** (as of 1930s), *Quill* . . to be extra polite to, to do things for, one's superior(s) at work.

4 To blow (a steam-locomotive whistle), esp in a personal and characteristic way; hence vbl n *quilling* the practice or technique of doing this.   [**quill** n 2]

1939 *Reader's Digest* Dec 55, There never was a man who could quill a whistle like old Casey Jones. **1945** Hubbard *Railroad Ave.* 356, *Quilling*—Personalized technique of blowing a locomotive whistle, applicable only in the days before the whistles became standardized. **1947** *Richmond* (Va.) *News Leader* 13 May 13/5 *(OED2)*, But the art of *'quilling',* or 'making her talk', went out with electric and diesel locomotives, with their shrill horns and pneumatic whistles.

5 See quot.   Cf **quill** n 3c

1969 *DARE* FW Addit **KY44,** They're a-quilling too much—women who are too friendly and spend all their time gossiping.

quillaree n Also *killorill*   [Echoic]

A **wood thrush** (here: *Hylocichla muestelina*).

1919 Pearson et al. *Birds NC* 330, The Wood Thrush, . . or "Quillaree," arrives in North Carolina in the forepart of April. . . This bird is a very melodious singer, the loud and liquid notes sounding particularly sweet in the early morning, and doubtless the mountain name "Quillaree" is a supposed imitation of its song. **1970** *DARE* (Qu. Q14) Inf **NY233,** Woods thrush—woods robin or killorill.

quillback n Also *quillback carp(sucker), quillback sucker*   [See quot 1896]   **chiefly Missip-Ohio Valleys**

A carpsucker of the genus *Carpiodes*.

1882 *U.S. Natl. Museum Bulletin* 16.119, *C[arpiodes] cyprinus.* . . Quillback. . . Body much arched above. **1884** Goode *Fisheries U.S.* 1.615, The different species . . known as . . "Carpsuckers," . . "Quillback," etc., abound in all the larger bodies of water south and west of New York as far as the Rio Grande. The species are probably but two in number, very similar. They reach a weight of four or five pounds, and form an abundant but not excellent food. **1896** *U.S. Natl. Museum Bulletin* 47.167, *Carpiodes velifer.* . . *Quillback.* . . Anterior rays of dorsal [fin] always elevated or filamentous, sometimes as long as base of fin. **1933** John G. Shedd Aquarium *Guide* 45, *Carpiodes velifer*—Quillback. **1956** Harlan–Speaker *IA Fish* 74, *Quillback Carpsucker—Carpiodes cyprinus.* . . More quillback are taken by anglers than any other carpsucker. *Ibid* 75, *River Carpsucker—Carpiodes carpio* . . *Other names* . . quillback. . . *Highfin Carpsucker—Carpiodes velifer* . . *Other Names* . . quillback. **1968–69** *DARE* (Qu. P1, . . *Kinds of freshwater fish . . caught around here . . good to eat*) Inf **KY43,** Quillback—size of croppie, flat, with large back fin turning to tail; (Qu. P3, *Freshwater fish that are not good to eat*) Inf **IA22,** Quillback—resembles a buffalo; **OH58,** Quillback. **1968** *DARE* Tape **OH58,** There's suckers, lot of people eat them, but I don't on account of they're too bony. . . A quillback is a little better than the sucker, but not much; it's full of bones, too. **1983** Becker *Fishes WI* 630, *Quillback—Cyprinus cyprinus.* . . Other common names: quillback carpsucker, . . quillback sucker. *Ibid* 633, The quillback flesh is white, flaky, sweet, and very tasty, particularly in the spring. Its suitability as a food fish is marred by the large number of bones. *Ibid* 637, Commercial fishing reports for the Wisconsin waters of the Mississippi River include river carpsuckers in the catch with the quillback and the highfin carpsucker under the heading "quillback." *Ibid* 638, *Carpiodes velifer.* . . Other common names . . quillback carp. **1991** Amer. Fisheries Soc. *Common Names Fishes* 24, *Carpiodes cyprinus* . . quillback.

quillback buffalo n
=**smallmouth buffalo.**

1908 Forbes–Richardson *Fishes of IL* 72, *Ictiobus bubalus* . . *Quillback Buffalo.* . . Dorsal [fin] rays 27 to 30, the longest a little less than half base of fin. **1933** LA Dept. of Conserv. *Fishes* 442, The Smallmouth Buffalo has . . received a confusion of popular names. Included are Razorback Buffalo . . Quillback Buffalo . . and Baitnet Buffalo. **1983** Becker *Fishes WI* 625, *Smallmouth Buffalo—Ictiobus bubalus.* . . Other common names: razorback buffalo, . . quillback buffalo.

quillback carp(sucker), quillback sucker See **quillback**

quill cane n

A **cordgrass** such as *Spartina cynosuroides*.

1933 *Torreya* 33.82 **LA,** *Spartina* sp.—Quill cane, Cameron Parish, La. **1942** *Ibid* 42.158 **LA,** *Spartina cynosuroides.* . . Quill cane, coastal Louisiana.

quill cat See **quill pig**

quilled See **quill** v 2

quiller See **quill** v 3

quill fern n
=**marsh fern.**

1900 Lyons *Plant Names* 141, *D[ryopteris] Thelypteris.* . . Quill Fern.

quill hog See **quill pig**

quilling wheel See **quill wheel** 1

quill melon n esp Gulf Region

A **banana melon** or similar melon; see quots.

1966–67 *DARE* (Qu. I26, . . *Kinds of melons*) Infs **LA2, 9, MS1, 23, SC1, 46,** Quill melons; **MS60,** ['kweəl ˌmɛlən] [sic]—long. **1986** Pederson *LAGS Concordance* **Gulf Region** *(Muskmelon)* 5 infs, Quill melon(s); 3 infs, Quill melon—kind of cantaloupe (*or* the first cousin to a cantaloupe); 2 infs, Quill melon—long; 2 infs, Quill melon—(oblong,) yellow meat; 1 inf, Quill—the long yellow one; 1 inf, Quill—melon, long rather than round; 1 inf, Quill melon—large variety of cantaloupe; 1 inf, Quill melon = banana melon, grows long; 1 inf, Quill melons—long muskmelons, 2 to 3 feet long; 1 inf, Quill melon—long, white, fried in slices; 1 inf, Quill melon—yellow, two feet long or larger; 1 inf, Quill melon—long, like okra, sweet taste; 1 inf, Quill melon—yellow and long; 1 inf, Quill melon—long, sweet; 1 inf, Quill melon—longer

than a cucumber, yellow meat; 1 inf, Quill melon = mushmelon, cantaloupe.

quill pig n Also *quill cat*, ~ *hog*, *quilly* **chiefly Nth, esp
NEast** See Map
=porcupine.
   1856 *Putnam's Mag.* 8.254 **ME,** One or two halts among the cranberry bushes, on which his hedgehogship (quill-pig is the vernacular)
was browsing, and . . we stepped over the edge of Katahdin. **1885**
Harper's New Mth. Mag. 71.225 **nNY,** The cabin was . . tenanted only
by an interesting family of what the guides quaintly call "quill pigs."
1905 *N.Y. Ev. Post* 30 Jan. 6 (*DAE*), Two years ago the 'quill pig,' as it is
familiarly known in the Maine woods, was convicted of girdling and
killing valuable forest trees. **1909** *DN* 3.414 **nME,** *Quill pig.* . . Hedgehog [=**hedgehog 1**]. **1917** Anthony *Mammals Amer.* 217, Anyone who
has traveled in the woods of the northern United States is familiar with
the Porcupine, or Quill Pig. . . In the Adirondacks when deer were formerly hunted with hounds. . . hunters . . shot every Quill Pig they saw.
1928 in 1931 McCorrison *Letters Fraternity* 172 **NEng,** One dead quill
pig must be near by, for Buster and Mac have both come in several times
with their noses decorated with quills. **1947** Cahalane *Mammals* 575,
The porcupine has its quota of natural foes. . . Of course some of these
predators, young or inexperienced, suffer . . as a result of blundering encounters and leave the quill pig strictly alone thereafter. **1965–70**
DARE (Qu. P31, . . *Names or nicknames . . for the . . porcupine*) Infs
CO41, ME8, MA58, MT4, NH4, 14, NY23, 148, PA166, Quill pig;
MI14, Indians called them a "quill pig," but I've never heard it around
here; **NY71,** Quill pig—old-fashioned; **NY183,** Quill cat, quill pig;
NY20, 198, PA28, 128, TX88, WI62, Quill cat; **NY37, 44,** Quill cat
[FW: Inf has heard]; **NY207, TX104,** Quill cat [FW sugg]; **KY76,** Quill
hog; **MI2,** Quillies. [19 of 24 Infs old]

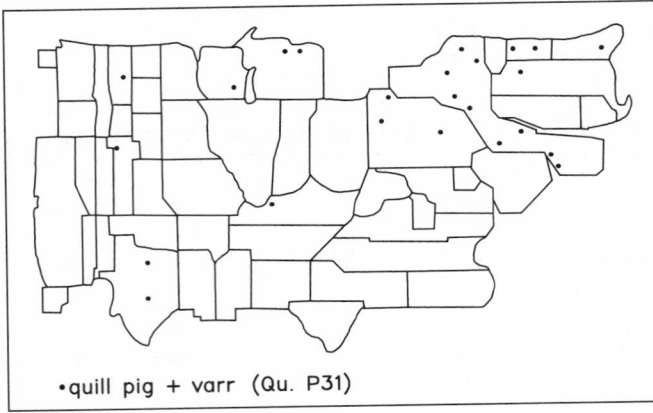

•quill pig + varr (Qu. P31)

quilltail n Also *quilltail(ed) coot* [See quot 1923]
=ruddy duck.
   1888 Trumbull *Names of Birds* 112 **NJ,** [Ruddy Duck:] At Tuckerton,
N.J., Quill-tail Coot. **1890** *Century Dict.* 4913 **NJ,** Quilltail. . . The
ruddy duck, *Erismatura rubida*. Also called *quilltail coot.* **1917** (1923)
Birds Amer. 1.152, Ruddy Duck—*Erismatura jamaicensis* . . Quill-tailed
Coot. . . Both sexes have . . the tail composed of 18 stiff feathers, often
spiny-pointed. **1923** Dawson *Birds CA* 4.1481, These saucy tails [of
Oxyura jamaicensis] are composed of stiff, spiny feathers, having shafts
denuded towards the tips, more or less, according to season, so that the
birds are popularly known as . . Quill-tails. **1953** Jewett *Birds WA* 151,
Oxyura jamaicensis rubida. . . Other names: Wire-tail; Quill-tail.

quill-toot n [Prob < **quill** n 1]
=piping plover.
   1924 Howell *Birds AL* 114, *Piping Plover.* . . On Long Island [AL] the
species is sometimes called by the suggestive name of "quill-toot."

quill wheel n
   1 also *quilling wheel*: A device resembling a spinning wheel,
used for winding thread on shuttle quills. *old-fash*
   1845 *Amer. Whig Rev.* 2.347, And if a water-power of capacity
sufficient to turn an old-fashioned Connecticut quill-wheel was found, it
was "booked" with astonishing avidity. **1878** *Scribner's Mth.* 17.47
NY, The quill-wheel, and the spinning-wheel, and the loom, are heard
no more among us. **1887** Alcott *New CT* 113, The "rolls" were spun

into threads, then run upon spools by the "quill wheel and blades," and
thus made ready for the shuttle. **1895** (1969) Montgomery Ward *Catalogue* 346, The Eureka Warp Measuring Machine, measures the warp as
it runs from the skein on to the spool; it can be used on any kind of a
quill wheel. **1917** Baldwin *Making of a Township* 87 **ceIN,** For weaving, there was the spool-holder, warping-bars, loom, quill-wheel, wind-
ing-blades, shuttle-quills, spools and yard-string. To try to describe all
the attachments pertaining to a loom would be a task. **1932** Randolph
Ozark Mt. Folks 105, Windin' th' thread on these hyar quills is mighty
tedious. . . I've saw reg'lar leetle quillin'-wheels for windin' 'em. 'Bout
th' size of a flax-wheel they was, an' they shore did make it a heap easier. **1937** (1963) Hyatt *Kiverlid* 114 **KY,** Git yer quill-wheel out an'
fetch out the windin' blades an' be a windin' some of yer quills.
   2 Fig: see quots. Cf **quill-wheel** v
   1892 *KS Univ. Qrly.* 1.98 **KS,** Quill-wheel: a 'rattle-trap' wagon.
1959 *VT Hist.* 27.166 **c,cnVT,** Quill wheel . . a disagreeable person.
Rare.

quill-wheel v Also sp *quilwheel* [**quill wheel** n]
   1 To roam about.
   1953 Randolph–Wilson *Down in Holler* 275 **Ozarks,** Quill-wheel. . .
To move about, to cover or patrol a large area. One of Rose O'Neill's
neighbors in Taney County, Mo., said of a restless old woman: "She's always quill-wheelin' around."
   2 To yield, give up; to collapse.
   1851 Hall *College Words* 251, At the Wesleyan University, "when a
student . . 'knocks under,' or yields a point, he says he *quillwheels*, that
is, he acknowledges he is wrong." **1905** *DN* 3.17 **cCT,** Quilwheel. . . To
collapse physically. 'I thought I should quilwheel,' i.e. give up from ex-
haustion. **1951** *Chr. Sci. Monitor* (Boston MA) 20 Oct 8/1 **wCT,**
Grandmother's word was "quill-wheel." . . When she said, recalling
some moment of extreme embarrassment, surprise, or consternation: "I
thought I'd 'quill-wheel'," she meant exactly what her great-granddaughter means today when she says: "I thought I'd flop!"

quillwort n
   1 Std: a plant of the genus *Isoetes*.
   2 A **boneset 1** (here: *Eupatoriadelphus purpureus*). **esp Appalachians**
   1894 *Jrl. Amer. Folkl.* 7.92 **WV,** *Eupatorium purpureum* . . quill-wort,
Indian gravel root. **1958** Jacobs–Burlage *Index Plants NC* 52, *Eupatorium purpureum.* . . Quillwort. . . This species. . . causes . . crampy
pains in the stomach and bowels, increased heart action, and a run-down
feeling. **1971** Krochmal *Appalachia Med. Plants* 156, *Eupatorium
purpureum* . . quillwort. . . Leaves . . are coarsely toothed. **1974** (1977)
Coon *Useful Plants* 108, Quillwort. . . A plant with as many common
names as this is surely one known to people all over the East and South
where it grows in generally moist situations.

quilly See **quill pig**

quilt v
   1 also *quelten (down, up)*: To beat, thrash; hence vbl n *quilting.* [*EDD* quilt v.[1] "In gen. dial. use in Eng. and Amer. Also
in form *quelt*"] *old-fash*
   1834 *Life Andrew Jackson* 161, The gineral had visited him onct afore;
arter whippin and takin all from him, the governor becom'd all at onct
his rale friend. The gineral alwase made friends of those he quilted.
1836 (1838) Haliburton *Clockmaker* (1st ser) 171, He [=a horse] helped
me once to ginn a blue-nose a proper handsum quiltin. *Ibid* 175, If I
didn't quilt him in no time you may depend; I went right slap into him,
like a flash of lightning into a gooseberry bush. *Ibid* 176, [This horse
is] none of your Cumberland critters, that the more you quilt them, the
more they won't go. **1858** Hammett *Piney Woods Tavern* 118, If ye
come back with a pesky long face, and a dirty look, I'll give you a rale,
fust rate, A number one quiltin. **1930** Shoemaker *1300 Words* 48 **cPA
Mts** (as of c1900), Quilt—To thrash, or beat. **1942** *AmSp* 17.171 **swIL,**
To *quelten down*. A variation of the verb *to quilt*, used with 'up' and
'down,' or also singly, meaning 'to beat or thrash thoroughly.'
   2 See quot. [Prob pun on **1** above and nautical term *beat* to
sail against the wind]
   1905 Wasson *Green Shay* 181 **NEng,** Let her quilt in [Footnote: Go] a
piece furder on that western shore afore you try to club [Footnote: An-
chor] her, ef you know when you're well off!

quilting See **quilt 1**

quilting frame n Also *quilting horse*
Fig: a thin, bony cow or horse.
   1969 *DARE* (Qu. K15, *A thin, bony, or poor-looking cow*) Infs **GA**72, 77, Quilting frame; (Qu. K44, *A bony or poor-looking horse*) Inf **KY**43, Quilting horse—he was going to a quilting, 'cause he was riding the frames; **SC**39, Quilting frame [laughter].

quilt with v phr
To use as a blanket or covering.
   1933 Rawlings *South Moon* 56 **FL**, You're took, Py-tee. It were that-a-way with your Ma. . . You best lay down and git you warm. . . You kin quilt with the counterpane 'til time to git you undressed.

quilwheel See **quill-wheel** v

quim-quams n pl Cf **jimjams, qualm, whimwham**
   1967 *DARE* (Qu. BB16b) Inf **CO**14, Quim-quams—mild emotional upset.

quince n Pronc-spp *queens, quinch*
Std senses, var forms.
   1899 (1912) Green *VA Folk-Speech* 341, Quinch. . . A form of quince. **1990** Kingsolver *Animal Dreams* 44 **nAZ**, I couldn't identify a quince tree to save my life. I only remembered the word because of the way people [=English speakers] here pronounced it—"queens"—with their Spanish-influenced vowels. *Ibid* 64, The man with his back to me said, "It's in Ray Pilar's apples and quince." He pronounced it "queens."

quinceanera n [AmSpan *quinceañero, -a* fifteen-year-old] **Span settlement areas**
A young woman's fifteenth birthday celebration; a coming-out party.
   [**1975** Galvan–Teschner *Diccionario* 70 **TX**, Quinceañera or Quinciañira—girl who is just turning fifteen and in whose honor a "coming-out" part [sic for *party*] is traditionally given.] **1989** *DARE* File **Tucson AZ**, [Newspaper advt:] Drachman's Bridal & Tuxedo—Clearance Sale On select bridal gowns, quinceanera dresses, party and evening dresses. **1993** *San Antonio Express–News* (TX) 25 July sec K 10/6, [Headline:] Quinceanera. [Text:] Patricia Angelica Vega celebrated her 15th birthday Saturday with a Mass at St. Bonaventure Catholic Church. A reception in her honor followed. **1993** *WI State Jrl.* (Madison) 18 July sec C 1/2, [Headline:] Quinceanera—It's when Hispanic girls eagerly enter womanhood. *Ibid,* Continuing a tradition begun by their Aztec ancestors in Mexico generations ago, the two girls celebrated their 15th birthday, or quinceanera, a combination coming-out party and renewal of faith, family and community. **1993** *DARE* File **csWI**, When my sister had her quinceanera, her picture was in the paper. **1995** *Ibid* **TX**, The quinceanera is . . an almost weekly occurrence here in San Antonio. **2000** *Pacific Sun* 8 Mar 36/1 **NYC**, [Movie review:] In "Home," Francisco, just arrived from Mexico, meets Maria at a "Sweet 15" party and discovers that they're both from the same village. . . [Photo caption:] *New arrivals . . meet at a quinciñera* [sic] *party in The City.*

quinch n[1] See **quince**

quinch v, n[2] [Cf *OED2* quinch "To start, flinch"; →1627] Cf **squinch, winch**
To wince; a twinge.
   1946 McCullers *Member* 76 **AL**, It leaves you too lonesome afterward. When you walk home in the evening on the way from work, it makes a little lonesome quinch come in you. **1995** Brophy *Coll.* **swMO** (as of c1960), Quinch. [T]o wince.

quinch grass n [Var of **quitch grass**]
=**quack grass 1.**
   1969–70 *DARE* (Qu. S8, *A common kind of wild grass that grows in fields: it spreads by sending out long underground roots, and it's hard to get rid of*) Infs **FL**51, **MO**32, Quinch grass.

quinch owl See **squinch owl**

quindar n Also *quinder* [Cf *OED2* whinder, obs var of *winder* widgeon]
A **scaup** (here: *Aythya affinis, A. americana,* or *A. marila*); formerly also a **goldeneye 1** (here: *Bucephala clangula*).
   1792 Belknap *Hist. NH* 3.168, Quindar, *Anas bucephala?* **1832** Williamson *Hist. ME* 1.142, There [are] . . in all no less than nineteen species [of ducks]. . . 14. *Quindar* [Footnote: Anas Bucephala]; 15. *red*

head *Quindar* [Footnote: Anas Ferina]. **1955** MA Audubon Soc. *Bulletin* 39.315, Redhead. . . Red-head Quindar (Maine. N.H. Meaning of quindar unknown). . . *Greater Scaup Duck.* . . Quinder (N.H.) *Ibid* 316, *Lesser Scaup Duck.* . . Quinder (N.H.)

quinine n Usu |ˈkwaɪˌnaɪn|; also **esp eNEng, Sth** |ˈkwɪnaɪn, kwɪnˈaɪn|; for addit varr see quots Pronc-sp *kuinine* Also, by folk-etym, *Queen Ann* [Orig Quechua, via Span *quinina* or Fr *quinine*]
Std sense, var forms.
   1845 Kirkland *Western Clearings* 66 **MI**, Every body knows if you've got to have the ague, why you've got to, and all the high land and dry land, and *Queen Ann* [Footnote: Quinine] in the world wouldn't make no odds. **1887** (1888) Harte *Phyllis* 74, Bradley sez you're loading yerself up with so much o' that bitter bark—kuinine they call it over there—that you'll lift the ruff off your head next. **1890** *Century Dict.* 4915, Quinine (|ˈkwɪnɪn| or |kɪˈnɪn| or |ˈkwaɪnaɪn|). **1913** (1919) *WNID,* Quinine. . . The pron. [ˈkwaɪnaɪn] apparently decidedly prevails in America, although [kwɪˈnɪn], which is preferred in British usage, is also common; [kɪˈnɪn], [ˈkwɪnaɪn], and [ˈkwɪnɪn] are also heard. **1925** *Book of Rural Life* 8.4586, Quinine, [ˈkwaɪnaɪn]. **1961** Kurath–McDavid *Pronc. Engl.* 166, *(Quinine).* . . /ˈkwainain/ . . is in nearly universal use in the Midland (from New Jersey and Pennsylvania to western North Carolina) as well as in Maryland and in Upstate New York; it predominates decisively in the Hudson Valley and in southwestern New England. In the South it is fairly evenly matched with other pronunciations, except for the Low Country of South Carolina and Georgia and parts of eastern Virginia. /ˈkwainai/ is uncommon to rare only in parts of the Lower South and of Eastern New England. The type of /ˈkwɪnain ~ kwɪˈnain/ is largely confined to two areas on the Atlantic coast: New England and the South. In New England it predominates decisively in Maine, New Hampshire, and most of Vermont, and only less so in eastern Massachusetts and adjoining parts of Rhode Island. In western New England and New York State it is of rare occurrence except for the St. Lawrence Valley. In the South this type is fully established in the Low Country of South Carolina and adjoining parts of Georgia. It is only less common in eastern North Carolina and in the Upcountry of South Carolina. . . [In eastern Virginia] /ˈkwɪnain ~ kwɪˈnain/ predominate between the lower James River and the Rappahannock, especially in Richmond and vicinity, but not elsewhere. As a prestige pronunciation, usually with end stress, this type has been adopted by cultured speakers as far north as Annapolis and Baltimore, Md. Some cultured Philadelphians also use this pronunciation. . . An occasional /ˈkwinain/ . . occurs along the coast of the Carolinas. The type of /kwɪˈnin ~ kɪnˈin/ . . is used by a minority in southwestern New England and the Hudson Valley, including Metropolitan New York. . . The most widespread American type, /ˈkwainain/, with shifted stress, is an out-and-out spelling pronunciation. **1965–70** *DARE* (QR, near Qu. BB15) Inf **SC**24, [ˈkwɪnain]; (Qu. BB50b) Inf **TX**35, [ˈkwɪnain]; (Qu. BB50d) Inf **GA**59, [ˈkwɪnan]; **SC**44, [ˈkwɪnain]. **1967** [see **quinine water**]. **1973** *PADS* 60.54 **seNC**, Quinine. . . our informants predominantly said /kwɪnain/; only two [of 12 infs] used . . /kwainain/. **1992** [see **quinine water**].

quinine brush n
A **bitterbrush 1** (here: *Purshia tridentata*).
   1931 U.S. Dept. Ag. *Misc. Pub.* 101.53, Bitterbrush (*Purshia tridentata*). . . is frequently called buckbrush; other English names often applied to it are antelope-brush, black sage, deer brush, and quinine brush. **1937** U.S. Forest Serv. *Range Plant Hdbk.* B116, Bitterbrush. . . Other common names often applied to this plant [=*Purshia tridentata*] are antelope-brush, quinine-brush, black sage and deer-brush. . . Bitterbrush is a very appropriate common name because of the extremely bitter taste of the herbage.

quinine bush n **West**
1 Any of var **silk tassels**; see quots.
   1897 Parsons *Wild Flowers CA* 370, Quinine-bush. *Garrya elliptica.* . . The bark and leaves have an intensely bitter principle, similar to quinine and equally efficacious. . . *G. Fremonti* . . is the shrub usually spoken of as "quinine-bush," . . and whose leaves were used as a substitute for quinine in the early days among the miners. **1920** Saunders *Useful Wild Plants* 206 **West**, *Garrya elliptica.* . . is known locally as Quinine-bush and Fever-bush. **1937** U.S. Forest Serv. *Range Plant Hdbk.* B81, As a rule, all parts of the silktassels are permeated with an intensely bitter, quininelike substance, which doubtless accounts for the general low palatability of the genus. . . Tasseltree [=*Garrya elliptica*], known also as . .

quinine-bush, . . ranges from Oregon to California. . . The "Forty-niners" used a tea made from a mixture of this species and Frémont silktassel as a substitute for quinine. . . Wright silktassel, known . . [as] quinine-bush, is. . . sometimes grazed to some extent by cattle during the winter. **1960** Vines *Trees SW* 116, *Garrya wrightii*. . . is also known under the vernacular name of Quinine-bush. . . Some species [of *Garrya*] contain an alkaloid, garryin, which is used medicinally. **1980** Little *Audubon Guide N. Amer. Trees W. Region* 575, "Quininebush" *Garrya elliptica*. . . Although various parts have a bitter taste, as the name "Quininebush" suggests, goats browse the foliage.

2 A **cliffrose** (here: *Cowania mexicana*).

1915 (1926) Armstrong-Thornber *Western Wild Flowers* 226, *Cowania Stansburiana*. . . For some occult reason this shrub is called Quinine Bush at the Grand Canyon. **1937** U.S. Forest Serv. *Range Plant Hdbk.* B68, Cliffrose—*Cowania stansburiana*. . . is often called quinine-bush because its twigs are very bitter. **1960** Vines *Trees SW* 425, *Cowania stansburiana*. . . is known locally under the vernacular name of Quinine-bush. The Hopi Indians are reported to have used it as an emetic and as a wash for wounds and sores. . . It is an important browse plant for cattle and sheep, and is the staple food for mule deer in some areas. **1968** Abbey *Desert Solitaire* 24 **seUT,** The cliffrose is practical as well as pretty. . . Concealed by the flowers at this time are the leaves, small, tough, wax-coated, bitter on the tongue—thus the name quinine bush—but popular just the same among the deer as browse when nothing better is available—buckbrush. **1981** Benson-Darrow *Trees SW Deserts* 272, *Cowania mexicana* var. *Stansburiana* . . Cliffrose, Quinine Bush. . . Despite the bitter taste of the foliage, the cliffrose is an important browse plant for deer and livestock. The plant is particularly abundant about the Grand Canyon.

quinine cherry n [See quot 1934] Cf **Peruvian**

The bitter cherry (*Prunus emarginata*).

1931 U.S. Dept. Ag. *Misc. Pub.* 101.69, *Bitter cherry (P[runus] emarginata),* known also as . . quinine cherry, is perhaps the commonest and best known of the native western tree cherries. **1934** Haskin *Wild Flowers Pacific Coast* 155, *Prunus emarginata*. . . The fruit is small—about the size of a pea—and is red, and exceedingly bitter. The local names of bitter cherry, and quinine cherry refer to this quality of the fruit. **1960** Vines *Trees SW* 394, *Prunus emarginata*. . . Vernacular names are Quinine Cherry . . and Plum-leaf Cherry. **1976** Elmore *Shrubs & Trees SW* 143, Quinine . . cherry. . . Indians ate the bitter fruits and made a tonic from the bark. **1980** Little *Audubon Guide N. Amer. Trees W. Region* 466, "Quinine Cherry". . . As the common name indicates, the fruit is not edible; like the bark and leaves, it is intensely bitter.

quinine flower n Also *quinine herb,* ~ *plant*

=**marsh pink 1** (here: *Sabatia brevifolia*).

1900 Lyons *Plant Names* 328, *S[abatia] Elliottii*. . . Quinine-flower, Quinine-plant, Quinine-herb. **1958** Jacobs-Burlage *Index Plants NC* 99, *Sabatia elliottii*. . . Quinine flower; quinine plant; quinine herb. . . This herb grows in eastern and central North Carolina. It has been used in medicine.

quinine fungus n

A **mushroom B1** (here: *Fomitopsis officinalis*).

1975 Smith *Field Guide W. Mushrooms* 51, *Fomes officinalis* (Quinine fungus). . . The taste is very bitter. [*Ibid* 52, It has been harvested for use in making bitters, and as a substitute for quinine.]

quinine herb (or plant) See **quinine flower**

quinine tree n

A **hop tree** (here: *Ptelea trifoliata*).

1897 Sudworth *Arborescent Flora* 267 **MI,** *Ptelea trifoliata*. . . Quinine-tree. **1931** Otis *MI Trees* 273, *Ptelea trifoliata*. . . More abundant near the shores of the Great Lakes. . . Also known as the *Quinine-tree*. **1931** Clute *Common Plants* 121, Among other plants reputed to be a cure for malaria were . . the ague-bark or quinine tree (*Ptelea trifoliata*). The latter, however, is not the species from which true quinine is obtained. **1960** Vines *Trees SW* 593, *Ptelea trifoliata*. . . Vernacular names are . . Quinine-tree . . and Wingseed. . . The fruit was once used as a substitute for hops in beer brewing.

quinine water n esp **Gulf Region**

A carbonated beverage containing quinine.

1967 *DARE* FW Addit **sLA,** Quinine ['kwɪnaɪn] water. Also ['kwaɪnaɪn] water. **1986** Pederson *LAGS Concordance,* 8 infs, **Gulf Region,** Quinine water. **1992** *DARE* File **seGA** (as of c1970), A friend

from Savannah used to talk about buying [kwɨ'na:n] water. I was struck by the phrase not only because I (from California) would have said ['kwaɪ,naɪn], but also because I didn't know what the drink was.

quinine weed n

1 A **centaury** (here: *Centaurium beyrichii*).

c1979 TX Dept. Highways *Flowers* 16, *Mountain-pink* thrives on gravelly limestone hills of Central Texas, and westward. . . Also known as . . Quinine Weed, pioneers used dried plants to reduce fever. . . *Centaurium beyrichii*.

2 A **guayule** (here: *Parthenium hysterophorus*).

1995 Brako et al. *Scientific & Common Names Plants* 214, Quinine-weed—*Parthenium hysterophorus*.

quink n Also *quink goose* [Echoic]

A **brant 1** (here: *Branta bernicla*).

1890 *Century Dict.* 4915, Quink-goose. . . The brent-goose, *Bernicla brenta.* **1917** (1923) *Birds Amer.* 1.161, Brant—*Branta bernicla glaucogastra*. . . Quink . . Burnt Goose. **1946** Hausman *Eastern Birds* 127, American Brant—*Branta bernicla hrota*. . . Quink.

quinnat (salmon) n [See quot 1910]

=**chinook salmon.**

[**1836** Richardson *Fauna Boreali-Amer.* 3.219 **Canada,** This salmon . . is known by the name of *quinnat*.] **1879** U.S. Natl. Museum *Bulletin* 14.58, *Oncorhynchus quinnat*. . . Quinnat or Sacramento Salmon. Northwest Coast of America; south to California. **1884** Goode *Fisheries U.S.* 1.480, The first scientific name by which the fish was commonly known was *Salmo quinnat*. . . The common name of the Salmon, at least among the Columbia River Indians that lived near the mouth of the Willamette, was "Quinnault," of which *Quinnat* is a corruption, and the scientific name was undoubtedly taken from the Indian name of the fish. **1904** *Salmon & Trout* 154, The quinnat salmon (*Oncorhynchus tschawytscha*) bears a number of other names in different regions. . . The euphonious Indian names, quinnat and chinook, are those in most general use. **1910** Hodge *Hdbk. Amer. Indians* 2.343, *Quinnat.* An economically important species of salmon. . . From *t'kwinnat,* the name of this fish in Salishan dialects current in the Columbia r. region. **1948** *Pacific Discovery* July-Aug 26, When referring to "salmon" we will mean the true salmon (also known as quinnat, chinook or king) which invariably dies after spawning. **1968** *DARE* (Qu. P1, . . *Kinds of freshwater fish . . caught around here . . good to eat*) Inf **AK**1, Quinnat [kwɪ'nɑt]—in Canadian area. **1983** Becker *Fishes WI* 312, *Chinook Salmon—Oncorhynchus tshawytscha* . . Other common names: chinook, . . quinnat. . . The chinook salmon, a Pacific Ocean salmon, was recently introduced into the Lake Michigan and Lake Superior drainage basins.

quinsyberry n [*OED2* 1866 for *Ribes nigrum*]

A **currant B1** (here: *Ribes americanum, R. hudsonianum,* or *R. nigrum*).

1876 Hobbs *Bot. Hdbk.* 95, Quinsy berry, Black currant, Ribes nigrum. **1940** Clute *Amer. Plant Names* 60, *R[ibes] Hudsonianum*. . . Quinsyberry. *Ibid* 229, *Ribes nigrum*. Black-berry. Quinsy-berry. **1960** Vines *Trees SW* 317, *Ribes americanum*. . . is also known under the vernacular names of Wild Black Currant and Quinsyberry.

quint n, hence adj *quinty*

1916 Macy-Hussey *Nantucket Scrap Basket* 142, "*Quint*"—An abbreviation of quintessence; applied to a "pernickety" old maid; from a local saying describing such a person, "she's the quintessence of old maid stewed down to a half pint." The corresponding adjective is "quinty."

quintal n Also *kental, kentle, kintal;* for addit varr see quots [*OED2* c1470 →; spp with both *qu-* and *k-* are attested from all periods] **coastal NEng** Cf *DNE*

Esp in fishing: a hundredweight; loosely, a large amount.

1645 in 1880 Suffolk Co. MA *Deeds* 1.65, One thousand Kintalls of dry Cod fish. **1651** in 1883 *Ibid* 2.126, Thirty two quintals of merchantable Codd. **1689** in 1886 MA Hist. Soc. *Coll.* 6th ser 1.92, I have Shipt on board the ship. . . one Hundred kentals of Marchandable Cod fish. **1724** in 1909 Essex Inst. *Coll.* 45.92 **MA,** Having about fifteen hundred Kentalls on board. **1779** in 1884 *Ibid* 21.279, Voted the Parish Rate to be 80 Quintals of scale fish for the Present year. **1806** (1970) Webster *Compendious Dict.* 169, *Kentle* . . in trade a hundred weight. [*DARE* Ed: This entry does not appear in Webster's English model.] **1884** *NY Herald* (NY) 27 Oct 6/2, Havana Markets. . . Butter—Superior American, $59 @ $61, currency, per quintal. **1890** Jewett *Strangers* 168 **coastal ME,** I would n't give a kentle o' sp'iled fish for the whole on 'em. **1890** *Century Dict.* 4916, *Quintal.* . . [Also *kintal,* and formerly *kental, kintle.* . .] A weight of 100 pounds. **1903** *DN* 2.291 **Cape Cod MA** (as of a1857), Short vowels frequently differed in quality . . *e* for *i* . . *kentle.* **1969** *DARE* Tape **MA**57, A q-u-i-n-t-a-l is 200 pounds. They called it a kentle ['kɛntl]. The fishermen said ['kwɛntl]. And it's 200 pounds of fish. [*DARE* Ed: Inf may have confused the fishermen's quintal with the metric quintal of 100 kg or approx 220 lbs.] **1975** Gould *ME Lingo* 152, *Kental*—Maine pronunciation and often spelling of *quintal.* *Ibid* 223, *Quintal*—See *cantel* and *kental.* . . [T]he word is generally written *quintal* and pronounced kant'l and kent'l. . . Although still used for a hundredweight in the fisheries, *quintal* is given a highlander meaning of a considerable amount, quite a good deal, without reference to a precise amount. **1988** Nickerson *Days to Remember* 74 **Cape Cod MA** (as of c1915), The size of the catch was always referred to as so many "kentles" (quintals), not boxes as today.

quinty See quint

quiration n Cf miration
An inquiry.

1886 *Century Illustr. Mag.* 32.201 **VA,** An' he so p'inted in he quiration I ain' had time to study ef I ever see him befo'. **1955** *DE Folkl. Bulletin* 1.20, *Quiration* (inquiry—as in "to make quiration about things").

quirk n¹ See quirt

quirk n² Cf quick n²
A sudden, sharp pain.

1966–67 *DARE* (Qu. BB3a, . . *A pain that strikes you suddenly in the neck*) Inf **NY**14, Quirk; (Qu. BB3b, *A sudden pain that strikes you in the back*) Inf **SC**4, Quirk [kwɛrk]—has heard it.

quirl See curl

quirley n Also *spill-quirley* Also sp *curly, querly, quirlie, quirly* [Cf *kwirl, quirl* (at **curl**)]
A cigarette, esp a hand-rolled one.

1932 Tooné *Yankee Slang* 30, *Quirly, quirley, querly:* Cigarette. **1939** FWP *ID Lore* 244, The following is reported as the talk of a southwest Idaho cowboy: In the mornun the night-herder rolls out of his soogan (bed-roll) and rolls a quirlie (cigarette). **1940** *AmSp* 15.335 **wNE** [Smokers' slang], A cigarette is a *cig,* . . a *lung-duster,* or a *quirley* (or *spill-quirley*). [Footnote to *quirley:*] Dr. R.D. Scott reports the use of *quirley* for *cigarette* among the cowpunchers of Arizona and New Mexico. 'Whip off a quirley.' **1944** Adams *Western Words* 122, *Quirly*—The cowboy's name for his cigarette. **1946** *NYT Mag.* 20 Oct 35 [Rodeo lingo], *Quirley:* hand-rolled cigarette. **1967–70** *DARE* (Qu. DD6b, *Nicknames for cigarettes*) Inf **KY**84, ['kwɜ·li]; **PA**35, Used to call them curlies ['kɑrliz]. [Both Infs male]

quirt n Also rarely *quirk* [MexSpan *cuarta*] **chiefly West, esp SW**
A riding whip usu consisting of a short, heavy handle and a tapering lash; hence v *quirt* to strike with this instrument; n *quirting* a whipping.

1845 *Amer. Whig Rev.* 1.127 **TX,** The "quirt," with its long heavy lash of knotted raw-hide [was] in his hand. **1888** Roosevelt in *Century Illustr. Mag.* 35.854 **West,** A first-class rider will sit throughout it all without moving from the saddle, quirting his horse all the time. [Footnote to *quirting:*] Quirt is the name of the short flexible riding-whip used throughout cowboy land. The term is a Spanish one. **1892** *DN* 1.247 [Spanish and Mexican words used in Texas], *Cuárta:* whip of cowhide or horsehide. The form used all over Texas is *quirt.* **1907** White *AZ Nights* 114, At the slap of my quirt against the stirrup, all the cows immediately about me shrank suspiciously aside. **1910** Mulford *Hopalong* 52 **SW,** He says you did—an' somebody quirted him. **1929** *AmSp* 5.62 **NE** [Cattle country talk], When the "rider" is "saddled" on the "pony," he may hold in one hand a "quirk" ("quirt") or "lasher," a short whip, having a small lead-filled handle and rawhide lashes two feet or more long. Sometimes the quirt is used to kill rattlesnakes and snap at weeds, as well as to "push" an animal. **1932** Bentley *Spanish Terms* 130, The *quirt* is held on the hand of the rider by means of a leather strap loop. The cowboy uses it to insure proper action of his mount, to urge or to punish his cattle, or as a defense. . . The word is almost universally used by riders in the West and Southwest. *Ibid* 131, From the noun has come the verb to *quirt* and the Anglicized *quirting* used in such a phrase as "He gave the animal a sound quirting." **1945** FWP *Lay My Burden Down* 176 **LA** (as of c1865) [Black], He rid in the fields with a quirt and rope

and chair on his saddle. **1957** in 1958 Brewer *Dog Ghosts* 7 **TX** [Black], Unkuh Jonas . . comed to be tiahed of bein' 'buked an' scorned an' beat neahly 'bout to deaf wid a raw-hide quirt by his ole massa. **1965–68** *DARE* (Qu. K36a, *What do you say to make a horse go faster?*) Inf **OK**8, Hit him with quirt; [(Qu. L53a, *The band that goes under a horse's middle to hold a saddle on*) Inf **TX**54, Quirt [*DARE* Ed: perh by confusion with *girt*]]. **1970** *DARE* Tape **CA**192, Quirt . . it's just a short rope with a lash on it, it's about twelve inches, to hit the horse. **1986** Pederson *LAGS Concordance,* 13 infs, **chiefly TX, also AR, LA,** Quirt.

quishion See cushion

quisutsch n Also *kisutch, quisutch*
=coho salmon.

1882 U.S. Natl. Museum *Bulletin* 16.307, *O[ncorhynchus] kisutch.* . . *Silver Salmon; Kisutch;* . . *Coho Salmon.* . . Head shorter than in a young Quinnat of the same size. **1896** U.S. Bur. Fisheries *Rept. for 1895* 290, *Oncorhynchus kisutch.* . . *Kisutch;* . . *Quisutsch.* From San Francisco northward, especially in Puget Sound and the Alaskan fjords. **1896** U.S. Natl. Museum *Bulletin* 47.480, *Oncorhynchus kisutch.* . . Kisutch; . . Quisutsch. *Ibid* 481, *Kisutch,* the vernacular name in Alaska and Kamchatka. **1904** *Salmon & Trout* 164, The silver salmon . . is also known as . . kisutch, hoopid, and coho salmon. . . Its average weight in the United States is only eight pounds, but in Alaska it is nearly twice as large. **1946** LaMonte *N. Amer. Game Fishes* 107, Quisutch. . . Goes into fresh water to spawn in the lower tributaries and dies after spawning. **1976** Tryckare et al. *Lore of Sportfishing* 75, *Coho Salmon.* . . Other common names: kisutch, silver salmon [etc]. . . The coho is very abundant in Alaskan waters.

quit v
1 To leave, abandon (a person). **widespread, but less freq NEast, West**

1833 *New Engl. Mag.* 5.412, A number of years ago a hardy, enterprizing young man, son of the famous old Mr. John Bull, and known by the familiar name of Brother Jonathon, becoming dissatisfied with the treatment he received from the old man, resolved to quit him. **1891** *Catholic World* 54.332, He was thirty years old when . . he resolved on quitting his wife and only child. **1925** *AmSp* 1.153 **West,** To "quit" means that you are through, you know enough to know that you are through, and there will be no resumption. A woman will say, "My husband got mad at me for bobbing my hair and quit me." **1926** *AmSp* 1.350, My observation is that of one who was born in New York State sixty-odd years ago, and who has lived nearly all his life in that state and the District of Columbia. . . Your contributor writes: "A woman will say, 'My husband got mad at me for bobbing my hair and quit me.' It is a hard word for the dyed-in-the-wool Easterner to assimilate." I am a dyed-in-the-wool Easterner, but I should use the same word if I had occasion to express the same idea. **1928** *Ruppenthal Coll.* **KS,** When he found she was dating several other students he quit this co-ed cold. **1934** Hurston *Jonah's Gourd Vine* 74 **AL** [Black], How come you don't quit 'im? Come on, and fetch de chillun wid you! **1939** *Hall Coll.* **wNC,** Well, he quit me there. Said he was goin' to camps. **1960** Criswell *Resp. to PADS 20* **Ozarks,** He quit her, she quit him. **1965–70** *DARE* (Qu. AA12, *If a man loses interest in a girl and stops seeing her . . he* _____) 93 Infs, **widespread, but less freq NEast, West,** Quit her; **AL**42, **MI**24, 27, **MS**84, **TN**43, **WA**11, Quit her [FW sugg]; **PA**237, **TX**12, Quit her cold; (Qu. AA11, *If a man asks a girl to marry him and she refuses, . . she* _____) Infs **AL**61, **KY**44, Quit him; (Qu. AA13, *When two people who have been 'going steady' or were engaged, stop going together . . "I guess they* _____.") Inf **SC**64, Quit each other. **1966** *DARE* Tape **AL**13, He got married and got two children, and he done quit his wife and he's goin' wild; **OK**37, He got married again. He lost his wife. His second wife quit him. She's in California now. **1973** Allen *LAUM* 1.373, Scattered respondents voluntarily wrote in the following equivalents [of "to turn him down"]: . . *quit him* [5 of 1064 infs]. It would appear now that *quit him* is a Midland expression. **1986** Pederson *LAGS Concordance* **Gulf Region** *(She turned him down)* 70 infs, Quit him (*or* her); 4 infs, She has (*or* she's) quit him; 3 infs, (She) done quit him; 2 infs, Wife quit him = left him; 1 inf, I can quit you = leave you; 1 inf, She had quit that boy; 1 inf, She quit the boy—stopped seeing him; 1 inf, She's quitting him; 1 inf, Keep her from quitting you; *(When are you coming again)* 1 inf, I'm quitting you; *(Widow)* 1 inf, A man is "grass widow" if his wife quits him.

2 with *off:* To stop doing something; to cease from.

1861 *S. Lit. Messenger* 32.51, So they gist quit off old fashioned work. **1894** *Advance* (Chicago IL) 1 Mar 140/1, I don't see how you ever made up your mind to quit off [=to drop out of college]. **1914** *DN* 4.111 **KS,**

Quit off. . . To quit. **1916** *DN* 4.327 **NE,** *Quit off.* . . To quit; stop. **1927** *AmSp* 2.362 **cwWV,** *Quit off* . . to stop. "I have quit off chewing tobacco." **1970** *DARE* Tape **FL50,** I used to, now I quit it off. I used to smoke. I used to chew tobacco.

3 with *out:* To leave abruptly or suddenly; to stop; with *out of:* to leave (a place) abruptly; to stop (some activity).

1941 Skidmore *Hawk's Nest* 11 **Sth,** All four my young'uns was goin' to school the same time. . . Then the de-pression come along and they clear quit out. **1974–75** in 1996 *Montgomery Coll.* **wNC, eTN,** I had to quit out and go to school. **1986** Pederson *LAGS Concordance,* 1 inf, **cnGA,** The reason I had to quit out—quit school; 1 inf, **neMS,** Quit out of business. **1993** *DARE* File **cIA** (as of 1970s), *Quit out of there* was very common for my friends and me back in high school in Iowa City. If we needed to leave a building in a hurry: "We quit out of there right away." . . I think I'd never use it in any form but the whole phrase "quit out of there," and that it implies you had to leave unexpectedly and with alacrity.

quitch grass n Also sp *quich grass* [*OED2* c700→] Cf **quinch grass**
=**quack grass 1.**

1790 Deane *New Engl. Farmer* 230, *Quitch-Grass,* called also *Witch-Grass, Twitch-Grass, Couch-Grass, Dutch-Grass,* and *Dogs-Grass,* a most obstinate and troublesome weed, which fills the soil with white stringy roots and is harder to subdue than any other weed. . . Land that is much infested with this weed should be laid down to grass; and . . burn beating should be applied, which will go near to conquer it. **1843** (1844) Johnson *Farmer's Encycl.* 360, Couch or quitch grass . . is a trou-blesome perennial, fortunately but little known in the United States. **1859** (1880) Darlington *Amer. Weeds* 390, Quitch-grass. . . in some lo-calities . . may afford an acceptable pasturage—where other grasses will not thrive—but in the northern States it is considered desirable to keep our farms as clear of it as possible. **1861** Wood *Class-Book* 802, *Couch-grass. Quich Grass.* Culm trailing at the lower joints, *from creep-ing rhizomes.* **1881** Phares *Farmer's Book of Grasses* 70, *T[riticum] repens,* Couch, Quitch, . . Dog Grass and many other names. **1892** IN Dept. Geol. & Nat. Resources *Rept. for 1891* 158, *Agropyron repens.* . . Couch, Quich, or Quock-grass [*sic*]. **1897** IN Dept. Geol. & Nat. Re-sources *Rept. for 1896* 601, Quitch-grass. Old fields and cultivated grounds; common. . . A vile weed which is yearly becoming more trou-blesome. **1912** Baker *Book of Grasses* 238, Quitch-grass. . . New-foundland to the Northwest Territory, south to Virginia, Ohio, and Iowa. **1950** *WELS (The kind of wild grass that throws out strong underground roots and is hard to get rid of)* 2 Infs, **WI,** Quitch grass.

quite adj
1917 *DN* 4.398 **neOH, NEng, IL,** Quite. . . Of considerable size or importance. "Why, those are quite fish." No doubt an extension of the adverbial use as in "He is quite a lad."

quite n See **quoit A5**

quit off See **quit 2**

quit out (of) See **quit 3**

quits exclam [From the phr *call it quits;* cf **-s** suff[2]] **scattered, but less freq Sth, S Midl, SW, Cent** See Map Cf **calf rope, holler**

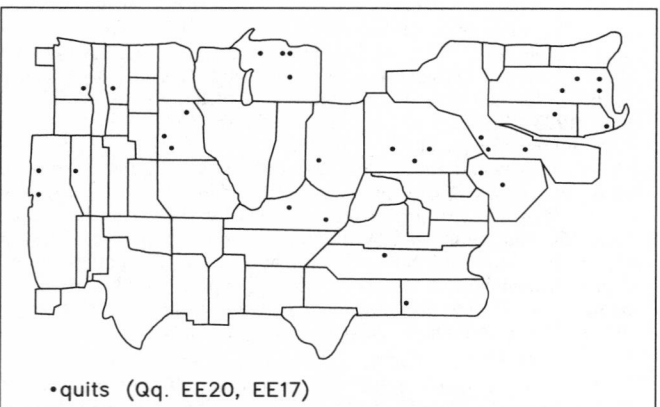

•quits (Qq. EE20, EE17)

Used to request a truce or respite in a fight or active game.
1950 *WELS (When two boys are fighting and the one who is losing wants to stop, he calls out)* 6 Infs, **WI,** Quits. **1965–70** *DARE* (Qu. EE20) 28 Infs, **scattered, but less freq Sth, S Midl, SW,** Quits; **CT23,** He calls "quits"; **IA13,** Quits [FW: Inf unsure]; [**PA90,** Play quits; I quit;] (Qu. EE17, *In a game of tag, if a player wants to rest, what does he call out so that he can't be tagged?*) Inf **NC47,** Quits—children say this.

quit stick See **quitting stick**

quit stone n
=**freestone 2.**
1967 LeCompte *Word Atlas* 313 **seLA,** Peach whose meat doesn't stick to the stone. . . *quitte noyau* [6 of 21 infs]. . . *pêche à quitte noyau* [3 infs]. . . quit stone [2 infs]. . . *Quitte* is from the standard French *quit-ter* (to be free of); *noyau* is standard French for "fruit stone."

quitting stick n Also *quit stick* **esp S Midl** See Map Cf **finishing stick**
A toothpick.
1965–70 *DARE* (Qu. G11, *Other names or nicknames for a toothpick*) 10 Infs, **chiefly wS Midl,** Quitting stick; **LA2,** Quit stick. [9 of 11 Infs old, 8 gs educ, 11 comm type 4 or 5]

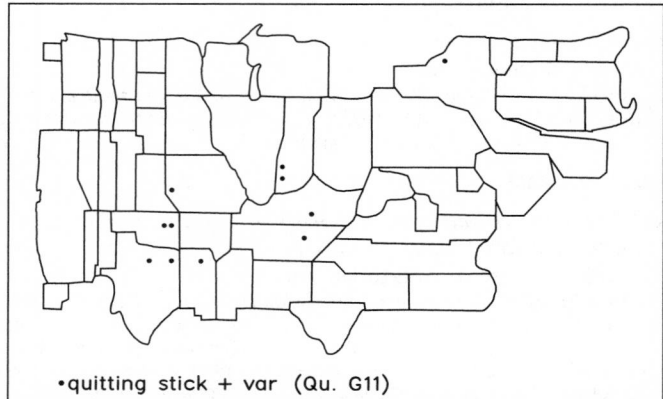

•quitting stick + var (Qu. G11)

quituate v [By facetious analogy with *graduate*] **scattered, but chiefly S Midl**
To drop out of school, quit (school); hence n *quituation* with-drawal from school.
1889 *Harper's New Mth. Mag.* 79.242, What good does that do those hundred and thirty-five thousand who, if they do not formally graduate from the New York schools, do, as they say out West, "quituate"? **1906** *DN* 3.152 **nwAR,** Quituate. . . To leave school or college before the end of the course. Facetious. **1909** *DN* 3.361 **eAL, wGA,** Quituate. . . To leave college or school before graduation. Facetious. **1911** *DN* 3.547 **NE,** Quituate. . . A blend of *graduate* and *quit.* Facetious. "Is he still in school?" "No, he quituated." **1927** Ruppenthal *Coll.* **KS,** Quituate—to quit or stop or cease to attend school. In analogy to graduate (humor-ous). **1937** in 1952 Mathes *Tall Tales* 218 **sAppalachians,** Shortly after Ike's "quituation" from Noah Dilrod's school, he was left an orphan with the farm and the bunch of yearlings on the pasturage. **1949** Webber *Backwoods Teacher* 80 **Ozarks,** "She jist went one week, though. Then she stopped an' got married. She never graduated—she quituated." He paused for me to smile at this chestnut. **c1960** Wilson *Coll.* **csKY,** Quituate—Contemptuous reference to someone's leaving school without graduating. **1976** Garber *Mountain-ese* 73 **sAppala-chians,** Johnnie couldn't pass his grades so he decided to quituate school. **1982** *Barrick Coll.* **csPA,** Quituate . . humorous formation to describe quiting [*sic*] school. **1995** in 1996 *Montgomery Coll.* **eTN,** Quituate.

quiver See **kivver**

quivering owl n Also *quivery owl* Cf **shivering owl**
A **screech owl 1** (here: *Otus asio*).
c1940 *LAMSAS Materials (Screech owl)* 2 infs, **swNJ,** Quivering owl. **1944** Howard *Walkin' Preacher* 207 **Ozarks,** Only the quivery owl was out to greet me as I walked into Cross Timbers. **1986** Pederson *LAGS Concordance (Screech owl)* 1 inf, **seAL,** Quivering owl—cry signals

death in the family; 1 inf, **cLA,** Quivering owl—gives chills, fever, in 24 hours; *(Hoot owl)* 1 inf, **swMS,** Quivering owl. [All infs Black]

quiverleaf n
=**quaking aspen.**
    1876 Hobbs *Bot. Hdbk.* 95, Quiver leaf, American poplar, *Populus tremuloides.* **1910** Graves *Flowering Plants* 141 **CT,** Quiver-leaf. . . One of the first trees to take possession of clearings. The bark is medicinal. **1933** Small *Manual SE Flora* 411, *P[opulus] tremuloides.* . . *Quiver-leaf.* . . Woods and thickets. **1960** Vines *Trees SW* 93, *Populus tremuloides.* . . Some of the vernacular names in use are . . Quiver Leaf [etc.] **1995** Brako et al. *Scientific & Common Names Plants* 214, Quiver-leaf—*Populus tremuloides.*

quivery owl See **quivering owl**

quizzit v Also *quizzet, squizzit* [*EDD quiset* "To question; to ask prying questions. A shortened form of *obs.* Eng. *v.* 'inquisite,' to inquire into."]
To question; to inquire into, examine.
    1922 Gonzales *Black Border* 322 **sSC, GA coasts** [Gullah glossary], *Quizzit*—(quiz) ask, asks, asked, asking; to question, questions, questioned, questioning. *Ibid* 328 [Gullah glossary], *Squizzit*—a rarely used variant of "quizzit." *Ibid* 230, Dey [=rabbits] does climb high 'puntop de tussock. So we paddle 'long en' quizzit all de tussock. *Ibid* 257, B'Cudjo so hongry fuh ketch de rokkoon, dat 'e nebbuh quizzit de limb w'at him bunnuh seddown 'puntop. **1930** Woofter *Black Yeomanry* 54 **seSC,** *Quizzet* = to question closely.

quobsque weed n
A **goldenrod 1** (here: *Solidago tenuifolia*).
    1919 (1923) House *Wild Flowers NY* 2.296, Slender Fragrant Goldenrod; Quobsque Weed—*Euthamia tenuifolia.*

quoby See **cope** v[2]

quock See **quawk** n[2] **1, 2**

quoddy salmon n [Abbr for *Passamaquoddy* Bay, in eastern Maine]
=**pollack** n[1] **1.**
    1884 Goode *Fisheries U.S.* 1.230 **ME,** Along the coast of Maine. . . at Eastport these fish [=*Pollachius virens*] are often called "Quoddy Salmon."

quohaug, quohog See **quahog** n

quoil v[1] See **coil** v

quoil v[2] See **quarrel**

quoit n Usu |kwɔɪt|; for pronc and sp varr see **A** below
A Forms.
    1 |kwe(ɪ)t|; pronc-spp *quait, quate.* [*OED2 quoit* sb.1.a.γ 1560→] **formerly widespread, now esp NJ, PA, Upstate NY, wMA** See Map
    1806 (1970) Webster *Compendious Dict.* 244, Quate. . . a quoit. [*DARE* Ed: This entry does not appear in Webster's English model.] **a1824** (1937) Guild *Jrl.* 3.294 **VT,** If a man would not drink gamble pitch quates and play ball & he was not considered one of the first. **1872** Schele de Vere *Americanisms* 527, *Quates* is a common name of the game of quoits in Pennsylvania. **1890** *DN* 1.50 **Ontario Canada,** [*Quoits.* A very common pronunciation is [kwets].] *Ibid* 56 **NEng,** The pronunciations noted [in Ontario] for *deaf* . . and *quoits* are also known in New England. *Ibid* 75, *Quate* [kweɪt]: a quoit. New England and Philadelphia. "To pitch quates." **1892** *DN* 1.212 **ceME,** [kwets] was the only pronunciation I knew till I saw the word *quoits* in print. *Ibid* 234 **KY,** *Quate.* *Ibid* 240 **Kansas City MO,** *Quoit.* Generally [kwet] in Kansas City. I am not sure I ever heard any other pronunciation. **1894** *Century Illustr. Mag.* 48.874, "Quoit" is pronounced "quait" in most rural districts in America, I believe. **1895** *DN* 1.399 **cNY,** She quoit [ši kwet]: a quoit that is pitched with the concave side up. **1899** (1912) Green *VA Folk-Speech* 340, *Quait.* . . A form of *quoit.* **1907** *DN* 3.197 **seNH,** *Quait* [kwet]. . . "We always said *quaits* till the high school teacher taught us to say quoits [kɔɪts]." **1912** *DN* 3.568 **cNY,** *Quaits.* **1915** *DN* 4.188 **swVA,** *Quates,* n. pl. Quoits. Also *quakes.* **1917** *DN* 4.398 **neOH,** *Quaits* [kwets]. . . Quoits, which is virtually nonexistent on W[estern] R[eserve]. **1919** [see **B** below]. **1936** *AmSp* 11.308 **Upstate NY,** [kwets] for *quoits.* **1939** *LANE* Map 199 *(Horseshoes,*

quoits), Quoits (quaits, quaiks, craits, etc.) [Proncs of the type [kwe(ɪ)ts] (with a few instances of the minor var [kre(ɪ)ts]) predominate **throughout NEng,** followed by [kwɔɪts, kwɔɪts]. Approx 40 infs, **chiefly eNEng,** gave proncs of the type [kwe(ɪ)ks], and about 15 scattered infs [kɔɪts, kɔɪts].] **1946** *PADS* 6.25 **eNC,** *Quates* [kwets]. . . *Quoits;* a game similar to "horseshoes." . . Rare. **1948** Davis *Word Atlas Gt. Lakes* app qu 83, 13 (of 233) infs, **chiefly MI,** Quoits; 15 infs, **chiefly MI,** Quates; 1 inf, **MI,** Quates; 1 inf, **MI,** Quakes. **1950** *WELS* **WI,** 9 Infs, Quoits; 1 Inf, Quates; 1 Inf, [kwets] [FW sugg]—commoner than [kwɔɪts] but older. **1965–70** *DARE* (Qu. EE37, *The game where you try to throw metal rings or something similar over a stake in the ground*) 65 Infs, **chiefly NJ, PA, Upstate NY, wMA,** Quaits [proncs of the type [kwe(ɪ)ts]]; **NJ**35, [kwets], [kwɔɪts]; **OH**15, We call it [kwets], but I suppose it should be [kwɔɪts]; **NY**68, Pitching [kweɪts]; (Qu. X38, *Joking names for unusually big or clumsy feet)* Inf **VA**13, [kweɪts]; (Qu. FF16, . . *Local contests or celebrations)* Inf **NJ**9, Contests with quaits. **1966** [see **B** below]. **1973** [see **B** below].

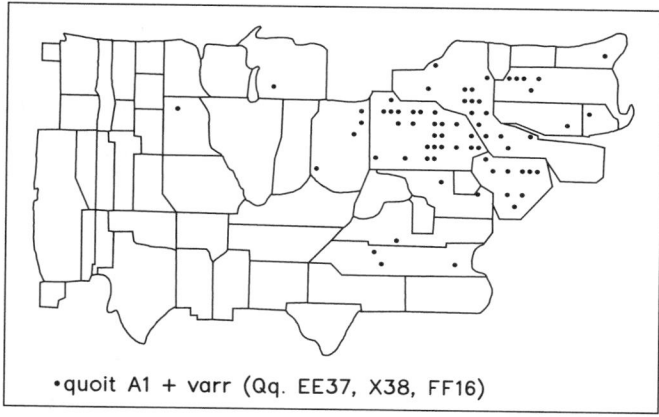

•quoit A1 + varr (Qq. EE37, X38, FF16)

    2 |kɔɪt, koɪt|. [This is the earliest form of the word (*OED2* 1388→) and is still common in Brit Engl.] *old-fash*
    1907 [see **A1** above]. **1939** [see **A1** above]. **1967–69** *DARE* (Qu. EE37, *The game where you try to throw metal rings or something similar over a stake in the ground)* 18 Infs, **scattered, but esp Nth, N Midl,** [kɔɪts]; **MO**11, **OH**37, 38, **PA**190, 200, 206, [koɪts]. [20 of 24 Infs old]

    3 |kwek|; pronc-spp *quaik, quake.* **esp NEng**
    1915 [see **A1** above]. **1939** [see **A1** above]. **1948** [see **A1** above]. **1967** *DARE* (Qu. EE37, *The game where you try to throw metal rings or something similar over a stake in the ground)* Inf **MA**45, [kweks]. [Inf old]

    4 |kre(ɪ)t|; pronc-sp *crait.*
    1939 [see **A1** above].

    5 |kwɑ(ɪ)t|; pronc-sp *quite.*
    c1955 Reed–Person *Ling. Atlas Pacific NW,* 1 inf [of c50], Quites. **1969** *DARE* (Qu. EE37) Infs **MI**101, 106, [kwɑɪts]; **TN**37, [kwɑts].
B Sense.
A ring, disk, or other object used for pitching in a game; pl but sg in constr: A game in which such an object is pitched at a target; the game of horseshoes. **widespread, but more freq Nth, N Midl, Plains States, Pacific, esp NEast** See Map on p. 424 *old-fash*
    1775 (1934) Fithian *Jrl.* 114, The Men, for Exercise, play at Quoits, hunt Deer, Turkeys, Pheasants, &c. **a1824** [see **A1** above]. **1832** Williamson *Hist. ME* 1.507, The principal amusements of the natives are dancing; footraces; wrestling; quoits; chequers. **1894** (1977) Montgomery Ward *Catalogue* 56.232, *Parlor Quoits.* Another popular and interesting game for either parlor or lawn; consists of two turned posts, firmly set in nicely finished brass, 8 inches in diameter, and four quoits five inches in diameter, made of wood and firmly wound with heavy, fancy colored webbing. **1919** *DN* 5.58 **NW,** *Quates.* . . Quoits. That stone is flat and round enough to play quates with. **1939** *LANE* Map 199 **NEng,** The terms *quoits* (quaits, quaiks, etc.) and *horseshoes* are not always equivalent. Several informants state that the game of quoits is played with horseshoes . . ; but others state that *quoits* and *horseshoes* refer to different games. . . Twenty-three informants use *quoits* of a game played with metal rings, or of the rings themselves . . ; two use it of rope rings. . . Thirteen informants use *quoits* of a somewhat different

game, in which stones or flat rocks are pitched at a target, or of the stones themselves. **1946** [see **A1** above]. **1965–70** *DARE* (Qu. EE37, *The game where you try to throw metal rings or something similar over a stake in the ground*) 216 Infs, **widespread, but more freq Nth, N Midl, Plains States, Pacific, esp NEast,** Quoits [and varr; see **A1, 2, 3** above]; **NY68,** Pitching quaits [Of all Infs responding to the question, 12% were young; of those giving these responses, 3% were young.]; (Qu. FF16, . . *Local contests or celebrations*) Inf **NJ9,** Contests with quaits; **PA126,** Quoit contest. **1966** Dakin *Dial. Vocab. Ohio R. Valley* 2.236, Everywhere in the Ohio Valley people speak of *playing* or *pitching horseshoes* or *horseshoe pitching* and those who live west of Ohio have no other name for this game. In the southern Knobs region and in the southern Mountains of Kentucky some speakers say only *quates* and others who usually say *horseshoes* know and sometimes use this older name. A pronunciation of the type [kweɪts] is regular. *Quoits* is even more commonly used and remembered in Ohio—where a pronunciation of the type [kwɔˈɪts] is usual. . . In Kentucky *quates* appears almost always to be the equivalent of *horseshoes,* but Ohioans frequently make a distinction. *Quoits* often means a game played with flat iron rings pitched or tossed to encircle a peg. **1973** Allen *LAUM* 1.248 **Upper MW** (as of c1950), Although a few older infs. still apply the term *quoits* and its variant *quates* to the game using a metal ring, a larger number have retained the term but shifted the referent to the game with horseshoes. This term clearly has a Northern orientation. . . The *quates* form, however, . . is found only in the first settled areas of Minnesota. Except perhaps in Canada, both forms are probably obsolescent as designations for the horseshoe game.

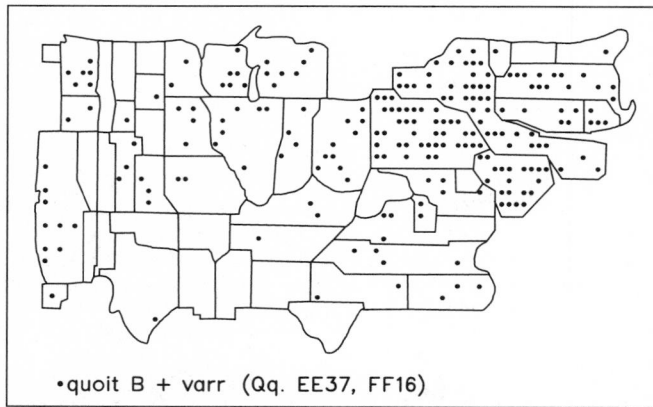

•quoit B + varr (Qq. EE37, FF16)

quok See **quawk** n[2] **1**

quoke See **quake**

quol See **quarrel**

quondy See **quandy 1**

quongqueedle See **conquedle**

quonk-a-ree n [Echoic] Cf **quillaree** =**red-winged blackbird.**

　1899 Howe–Sturtevant *Birds RI* 67, *Agelaius phoeniceus.* . . *Quonk-a-ree.* . . An abundant summer resident.

quop(e), quopy See **cope** v[2]

quorl n, v[1] See **quarrel**

quorl v[2] See **coil** v

quota n Usu |ˈkwotə|; also |ˈkwoto, ˈkotə| Pronc-sp *quoto*
Std sense, var form.

　1776 in 1914 Filson Club *Pub.* 27.38 **KY,** [We are] willing . . to support the . . cause, by raising our Quoto of men.　**1818** Fessenden *Ladies Monitor* 172 **NEng,** Provincial words. . . to be avoided. . . *Quoto* for quota.　**1912** *DN* 3.587 **wIN,** Quota. . . Usually pronounced *quoto.*　**1923** *DN* 5.218 **swMO,** Quoto. . . Quota.　**1967** *DARE* Tape **TX5,** The government would guarantee us a price, provided we stayed within our quota [ˈkotə] of acres.

quote v, n Usu |kwot|; also *old-fash* |kot| Pronc-spp *cote, kote*
Similarly n *kotation* [Spp with *c* are the earliest attested and remained common into the 17th cent; the pronc with [k-] competed with [kw-] as the std pronc at least through the end of the 18th cent.]

A Forms.

　1833 Neal *Down-Easters* 1.108, And then ye koted some varses.　**1862** (1864) Browne *Artemus Ward Book* 189 **ME,** If you'll alow me to kote from your troothful advertisement.　**1899** (1912) Green *VA Folk-Speech* 129, *Cote.* . . To quote.　**1903** *DN* 2.352, *Quote.* Quotation. Pronounced kote, kotation. It would be interesting to determine how many words show this change.　**1911** *DN* 3.506 **Sth, S Midl,** *Quote*—*kw* 199 [infs]—*k* 35. While the spelling-pronounciation [sic] with *kw* has gained the upper hand, the evidence shows that the simple *k-* sound . . has perpetuated itself in the speech of some educated Southerners.　**1928** *Ruppenthal Coll.* **KS,** *Quote,* pronounced like "coat." "He can kote Scripture."

B As verb.

To echo, sound.

　1941 Writers' Program *Guide OK* 121, Hill folk are apt to say "et" for "ate." . . The Elizabethan "quote" is often a substitute for "echo." [*DARE* Ed: There does not appear to be any relevant "Elizabethan" sense of *quote.*]　**1952** Brown *NC Folkl.* 1.581, *Quote.* . . To sound, to make a noise. "I heard a gun quote over in the woods."

quoto See **quota**

quouk See **quawk** v, n[1]

quowa See **cope** v[2]

quowk See **quawk** n[2] **1**

quup See **cope** v[2]

quwark See **quawk** n[2] **1**

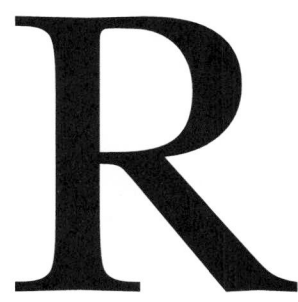

raal See **real** adj, adv

raar See **rare** v

rabais shop n |ræ'be, 'rɑ,be| [Fr *rabais* discount, reduced price] **New Orleans LA**
A small shop selling cheap or secondhand goods; hence n *rabais* inexpensive articles, secondhand goods.

[**1886** *Harper's New Mth. Mag.* 73.304 **sLA,** The "blanchisseuse en fin," the "coiffeuse," the "garde malade," the little hunchback who kept the "rabais," the passers-by to and from mass, the market-woman with her basket, the paper-boy with his papers—all came.] **1917** *DN* 4.420 **New Orleans LA,** *Rabais shop* [ræ'be]. . . A retail shop, or notion store. **1945** Saxon *Gumbo Ya-Ya* 46 **New Orleans LA,** The cry '*Au rabais!*' might best be translated as 'Off price!' Today, Orleanians are likely to refer to any small notions or drygoods store as a '*rabais* shop.' **1983** *Reinecke Coll.* 9 **LA,** *Rabais shop* . . ['rɑ,be·]—a small neighborhood shop commonly kept by widows, old maids, selling notions, thread, toys. Often in front room of double house or shotgun. N[ew] O[rleans] Fr. with same meaning, from word for cut-rate or discount. . . Obsolete as institution, obsolescent as word. **1987** Rose *I Remember Jazz* 155 **New Orleans LA,** For several years, in the 1960s, Raymond owned and operated a rabais shop on Bourbon Street. . . [R]abais is not quite junk. It's not necessarily antiques, because the things are not necessarily old. It's just stuff the owner collected because he wanted to. Raymond hadn't especially wanted to run a rabais shop. But Catherine, in the interests of sanitation, had demanded that he clean out his private room.

rabbit n Usu |'ræbɪt|; rarely |'rægɪt|; pronc-sp *raggit, ribbit.*
A Forms.
1935 *AmSp* 10.79, *Raggit* ['rægɪt] for *rabbit* is reported from Idaho, Missouri, Oklahoma, and Nebraska. Occasionally it is used facetiously, but mostly it is spoken seriously by the uneducated. **1939** in 1944 *ADD* 491 **eWV,** Ribbit.
B Senses.
1 Used as a lucky word; see quots. [*OED2* 1920 →]
1952 *Badger Folkl.* 1.12, Another correspondent . . says that in her family it is a tradition to court Lady Luck by saying "Rabbit! Rabbit!" as first words on the first day of every month. Then you climb out of bed over the foot and are bound to prosper. **1978** Gould *Greenleaf* 6 **ME,** He looked at the luminescent wrist watch he had gotten while in the Army; "Rabbit-rabbit," he muttered, recognizing the month change, obedient to his father's superstition. *Ibid* 51, When he awoke at six thirty, he recalled that this was the first day of March and sat up in bed: "Rabbit-rabbit." **1982** *DARE* File **MA** (as of 1910s), I believe I put some material in the files on *rabbit* which I knew in my childhood as a lucky word. You said it when you first woke in the morning on the first day of the month. You said nothing before you said *rabbit* or the lucky spell was broken. . . I found it the other day . . in an English novel by Miss Reade. . . It's *white rabbits* here, plural. **2000** *DARE* File **SC,** A friend of mine (80ish native of South Carolina) phoned me last Wednesday [= 1 March] and said "rabbit, rabbit" when I answered. She then explained that all her life she had heard this expression, which is used on the first of the month to wish someone good luck, but had never understood where it might have come from or whether it was only a South Carolina usage.

2 In railroading: see quot 1945. Cf **hoptoad 2**
1932 *Santa Fe Employes' Mag.* Jan 34, A derail is a *hop toad* or a *rabbit.* **1938** Beebe *High Iron* 223 [Railroad terms], *Rabbit:* Derail iron. **1945** Hubbard *Railroad Ave.* 356, *Rabbit*—A derail; an arrangement for

preventing serious wrecks by sidetracking runaway trains, cars, or locomotives on a downgrade. Unlike regular sidetracks, the derail ends relatively abruptly on flat trackless land instead of curving back onto the main line. The term *rabbit* is applied to this device because of the timidity involved. **1976** Gould *Blackie's RR Hdbk.* 17, Rabbit: Derail iron.

3 pl; also *bunny rabbit(s):* A **snapdragon** (here: *Antirrhinum majus*). [*EDD* (at *rabbit* sb. 2)] Cf **rabbit's-mouth**
1900 Lyons *Plant Names* 39, *A[ntirrhinum] majus*. . . Bunny-rabbit, Rabbits. **1923** *Amer. Botanist* 29.61, Other names for the plant [=*Antirrhinum majus*] are . . "calf's-" "rabbit's-" and "dragon's-" mouth. "Bunny rabbits" and "bull dogs" are but other names of similar reference. **1940** Clute *Amer. Plant Names* 29, *A[ntirrhinum] majus*. . . Bunny rabbits.

rabbit bells n
A **rattlebox 1a:** usu *Crotalaria rotundifolia,* but also *C. incana.*
1931 Clute *Common Plants* 99, Soft and delicate species are often named for animals whose fur is equally soft or who possess other attributes of daintiness. Of this nature are rabbit-bells (*Crotalaria rotundifolia*) [etc]. **1933** Small *Manual SE Flora* 679, *C[rotalaria] rotundifolia*. . . *Rabbit-bells*. . . Pinelands, dry woods, and sandy places. **1955** *S. Folkl. Qrly.* 234 **cFL,** The distinguishing feature of *Rabbit Bells* (*Crotalaria incana*) . . is the oblong inflated seed pod in which the ripe seeds rattle. **1975** Duncan–Foote *Wildflowers SE* 72, *Rabbit-bells—Crotalaria rotundifolia*. . . Fla into se La, c Ala, c Ga, and se Va; also ne Ga and c NC.

rabbitberry n
1 =**buffalo berry.**
[**1804** (1808) Gass *Jrl.* 41, Small red berries, the Indian name for which in English means rabbit berries.] **1804** (1905) Lewis *Orig. Jrls. Lewis & Clark Exped.* 7.52, We found Some red berreys which they call Rabbit berrys. **1846** Browne *Trees* 429, *Shepherdia argentea*. . . Rabbit Berry . . , in its natural habitat [=the West], is a small, rather narrow-topped shrub. . . The berries. . . are devoured with avidity by all frugivorous birds. **1892** Apgar *Trees Nth. U.S.* 132, *Shepherdia argentea*. . . *Rabbit-berry*. . . A small handsome tree, 5 to 20 ft. high, wild in the Rocky Mountains, and sometimes cultivated east. **1931** U.S. Dept. Ag. *Misc. Pub.* 101.119, Silver buffaloberry (*L[epargyrea] argentea*) . . locally known as buffaloberry . . and rabbit berry. **1950** Stevens *ND Plants* 212, *Shepherdia canadensis*. . . *Rabbitberry.* Bushy plant, not over 1 m. high.

2 =**partridgeberry 1.**
1898 *Plant World* 2.14 **sPA,** During a recent visit to the mountains of Southern Pennsylvania, the following local names of plants were noted as in use: . . Rabbit berry, for *Mitchella repens.*

rabbit bread n Cf **fox frost 2, jack ~ 3, rabbit ice**
The ice that forms on the ground at the base of plants; see quots.
1960 Williams *Walk Egypt* 269 **GA,** Rabbit bread dotted the pasture, little white lumps of ice forced up by the cold. **1966** *PADS* 46.28 **cnAR** (as of 1952), *Rabbit bread*. . . Small curls of ice that form on the ground around the base of a plant.—"Did you ever see any rabbit bread?"

rabbit brush n **West** Cf **rabbit bush, rabbitweed**
1 Any of numerous, often similar composite plants with usu yellow flower heads, as:

a A shrub of the genus *Chrysothamnus,* native to the western US. Also called **chamise 2, false goldenrod 2, rabbit bush 1, ~ sage, rabbitweed 3, rayless goldenrod, yellowbrush;** for other names of var spp see **goldenbush 2, yellow sage**

1871 in 1923 Pellett *Amer. Honey Plants* 284, Rabbit brush abounds here on the desert heather, vales and hillsides. . . It has the fragrance of honey and is now fed upon largely by the bees. **1903** (1950) Austin *Land of Little Rain* 51 neCA, In September young linnets grow out of the rabbit-brush in the night. **1909** in 1914 Stewart *Letters* 18 **WY,** Our horse was midside deep in rabbit-brush, a shrub just covered with flowers that look and smell like goldenrod. **1941** Cleaveland *No Life* 293, Today we old-timers argue the question of whether rabbit brush is 'taking the country.' Those who rise to its defense say that it affords shelter for the cattle against the strong spring winds and tends to deter soil erosion. Moreover, the miles upon miles of woody-stalked, gray-green-leaved bushes that often grow shoulder-high blossom out in the fall into a mass of bloom that even to prejudiced eyes is a glorious riot of yellow and gold. **1966** *DARE* (Qu. T16, . . *Kinds of trees* . . *'special'*) Inf **ID1,** Rabbit brush. **1967** *DARE* Tape **OR1,** Rabbit brush—a lot of people mistake that with sagebrush; it grows right into the sagebrush. . . The rabbit brush is slimmer, the stalks are slimmer and straight. . . The bark on rabbit brush is kind of a light green, and it isn't shaggy-looking. **1967** *DARE* FW Addit **OR12,** Rabbit brush—Composite. **1980** *Blair & Ketchum's Country Jrl.* Oct 46, The first mule I ever owned was rescued from a prairie dog town in southern Colorado, where she had lived for who knows how long on fresh air and rabbit-brush.

b A plant of the genus *Ericameria,* esp *E. nauseosa.* [See quot 1890] For other names of var spp see **chamise 2, false goldenrod 2, goldenbush, golden fleece, goldenweed 1, greasewood 1, mock heather 1, pine bush, rabbit ~ 1, rabbitweed 3, rayless goldenrod, rubber brush, ~ rabbit-brush, rubberweed 2, turpentine bush, white sage, yellowbrush** Note: Many of these species were formerly included in the genus *Haplopappus.*

1890 *Century Dict.* 4924, Rabbit-brush. . . A tall shrubby composite plant, *Bigelovia graveolens* [=*Ericameria nauseosa*], growing abundantly in alkaline soils of western North America. . . It furnishes a safe retreat for the large jack-rabbits of the plains. **1931** U.S. Dept. Ag. *Misc. Pub.* 101.156, Bloomer rabbit brush [=*Ericameria bloomeri*] . . is an anomalous species, distinctly of the rabbit brush (Chrysothamnus) habit save for its rayed flower heads. **1967** *DARE* Wildfl QR (Craighead) Pl.22.7 Inf **CO29,** Rabbit brush; Pl.49A Inf **OR8,** Like rabbitweed/brush—a little. **1973** Hitchcock–Cronquist *Flora Pacific NW* 524, Rabbitbrush g[oldenweed] . . H[aplopappus] *bloomeri* [= *Ericameria b.*]

c =**rayless goldenrod** (here: *Bigelowia* spp).

1898 *Jrl. Amer. Folkl.* 11.229 **CO,** *Bigelovia* (sp.), rabbit brush. **1940** Clute *Amer. Plant Names* 253, *Bigelovia hirsuta* [=*Bigelowia nuttallii*]. Rabbit-brush.

d also *spring rabbit-brush:* A **horsebrush 1,** usu *Tetradymia glabrata.*

1931 U.S. Dept. Ag. *Misc. Pub.* 101.176, Littleleaf horsebrush (*Tetradymia glabrata*) is . . known also as greasewood and spring rabbit brush. **1964** Kingsbury *Poisonous Plants U.S.* 437, *Tetradymia glabrata.* . . Littleleaf horsebrush, spring rabbitbrush, coal oil brush. **1967** *Merck Vet. Manual* I.2, Photosensitization has also been reported . . in poisoning by . . *Tetradymia* (horsebrush or rabbit-brush) species.

e A **jimmyweed** (here: *Isocoma pluriflora*).

1931 U.S. Dept. Ag. *Misc. Circular* 101.156, Jimmyweed (. . *Isocoma wrightii* [=*I. pluriflora*]), often called rabbit brush and rayless goldenrod, is a half shrub. . . Its taste is bitter-resinous and under normal conditions livestock do not relish it. **1937** U.S. Forest Serv. *Range Plant Hdbk.* B13, Jimmyweed [=*Isocoma pluriflora*] . . sometimes is called rabbitbrush, apparently because of its similarity to some species of rabbitbrush (*Chrysothamnus* spp.) . . Bloomer rabbitbrush . . , whitestem goldenweed . . , and singlehead goldenweed . . are common, and occasionally abundant, western shrubs.

f A **snakeweed** (here: either *Gutierrezia sarothrae* or *G. texana*).

1936 Winter *Plants NE* 143, G[utierrezia] *sarothrae.* . . Broom Weed. . . Also called Rabbit-brush. . . Occasional in the western counties

of the state. **1936** Whitehouse *TX Flowers* 157, The Texas rabbit-brush (*Gutierrezia texana*) of West Texas is so much like the broom-weed [= *G. sarothrae*] that only a close observer can distinguish them.

g A **burr sage** (here: *Ambrosia deltoidea*).

1966 *DARE* (Qu. T16) Inf **NM13,** Burrobrush or rabbit brush . . looks like a willow.

2 =**mountain mahogany 2.**

1920 *Torreya* 20.21 s**AZ,** *Cercocarpus* spp.—Rabbit brush.

rabbit bush n West

1 =**rabbit brush 1a** or **b.** [See quot 1973]

1852 U.S. Army Corps Topog. Engineers *Exped. Gt. Salt Lake* 235 **UT,** The only vegetation, to-day, has been a little dwarf artemisia, grease-bush, rabbit-bush . . and an occasional dwarf cedar on the bluffs. **1861** Burton *City Saints* 591 **NV,** An expanse of white sage and large rabbit-bush. **1924** *Amer. Botanist* 30.33, "Rabbit-brush" or bush refers in common parlance of the west to the various species of *Bigelovia* [here: =*Chrysothamnus* or *Ericameria*]. **1973** Stephens *Woody Plants* 494, *Chrysothamnus nauseosus* [=*Ericameria n.*] . . Rabbitbush. . . Jack rabbits, deer and antelope browse on the foliage, which at certain seasons forms a large part of their diet. Smaller mammals, especially the ground squirrel, feed on the fruits and use the shrub as a cover for their dens. [*Ibid* 496, *Chrysothamnus.* . . Important browse plants for larger mammals as well as jack rabbits.] *Ibid* 498, *Chrysothamnus pulchellus.* . . As the name "rabbitbush" might imply, rabbits eat the foliage and the young fruiting heads and use the plant as protection from the sun.

2 A **false indigo 1** (here: either *Amorpha canescens* or *A. fruticosa*).

1940 Clute *Amer. Plant Names* 168, Rabbit bush. *Amorpha fruticosa. Ibid* 250, *Amorpha canescens* . . false indigo, rabbit bush.

3 A **burr sage** (here: *Ambrosia deltoidea*). Cf **rabbit brush 1g**

1945 Benson–Darrow *Manual SW Trees* 363, *Franseria deltoidea* [= *Ambrosia d.*]. . . Bur sage or rabbit bush, as some call it, is one of the worst hayfever plants of the early spring. **1979** *Tucson Citizen* (AZ) 28 Apr sec A 3/9, *Pollen count* (yesterday) . . Rabbit Bush 4.

rabbit-choker See rabbit-twister 1

rabbit deer n

=**mule deer.**

1969 *DARE* (Qu. P32, . . *Other kinds of wild animals*) Inf **CA168,** Coast range deer (about 90 pounds), also called rabbit deer.

rabbit dew n

See quots; also fig.

1987 *McDavid Coll.* se**GA,** Rabbit dew: "mist." [From the "ridge," McIntosh Co., GA; Inf male, 72, some hs educ, farmer] **1998** *DARE* File **TX,** Rabbit Dew. . . My grandfather used to use this phrase in reference to someone who is a suspect. . . usually in reference to the grandchildren when they are guilty of some mischief. . . "He's got a bit of the rabbit dew about him." I guess the inference is that he's been in the garden early (or somewhere like the cookie jar) when he wasn't supposed to be and therefore has a guilty "air" about him. . . like a rabbit would collecting dew on his paws. **1999** *NADS Letters* sw**MO,** "Rabbit dew" . . refers to the fact that rabbits usually feed in the early morning or late evening when the dew is on the grass. . . You can watch them shaking the excess off as they move from higher grasses into the short, mown grass. **2000** *Ibid* ce**GA,** Rabbit dew is specifically the low mist which arises after a quick cool rain shower during very hot weather (July, August, say). That's when the rabbits are a'cookin' their dinner, or so my Mother told me in Emanuel Co., GA, early 1950's. Also called rabbit smoke. *Ibid* I've heard both my grandmother (aged 75 from Mississippi) and some older men my husband works with (ages 50–65 from Alabama) use this term [=*rabbit dew*]. It refers to a light mist like what's found in the wee hours of the morning (before dawn truly breaks) when the rabbits are out.

rabbit dog n Also rabbit hound

A mongrel, cur.

1966 *DARE* (Qu. J2, . . *Joking or uncomplimentary words* . . *for dogs*) Inf **AR17,** Rabbit dog. **1986** Pederson *LAGS Concordance* (*Mongrel* . . *worthless dogs*) 8 infs, 5 **LA,** Rabbit dog; 1 inf, cw**AR,** Rabbit hound—worthless dog.

rabbit drive n Also *jackrabbit drive* **West**
A roundup of rabbits for slaughter.

1887 *Lisbon* (N. Dakota) *Star* 23 Dec. 7/1 *(OED2)*, Several hundred people . . assembled to engage in the rabbit drive. **1931** *Durant* (Okla.) *D. Democrat* 26 Jan. 1/6 *(DA)*, Huntsmen gathered here today for a jack rabbit drive near Cambridge. **1963** Symons *Many Trails* 119, A hunt in the manner of the California rabbit drives. **1967** *DARE* Tape **ID**7, We'd pull rabbit drives. Where . . we'd make a fence with hog netting, hog wire fence. And then we'd make it in the shape of a V out in the desert. Then we'd all get scattered out with clubs and rocks. You wouldn't dare take any guns of any kind because you'd shoot one another, so you just used clubs and rocks and kept the . . rabbits ahead of you. And they'd run into this fence and then . . we'd had a big, long wire, then we'd pull up, like a gate, and then you'd have 'em inside this deal and you'd get in and kill 'em. *Ibid* **ID**13, In some areas, the jackrabbits were bad. In fact, across the river they used to build up some kind of fence corners and have what they call . . rabbit drives and drive them in there and just slaughter 'em with clubs because they had to get rid of 'em. **1970** *DARE* (Qu. FF16, *. . Local contests or celebrations*) Inf **TX**80, Rabbit drives—rabbits shot, not eaten. **1977** *New Yorker* 11 July 43 **AK,** We have rabbit drives there. Drive the rabbits from one end of the island to the other and kill them. **1996** *DARE* File **csID** (as of c1915–35), When I lived in a small southern Idaho community made possible by an irrigation project, we were plagued by the thousands of jackrabbits that lived in the surrounding desert. Especially after a dry summer, they would come to our irrigated fields and simply mow down the alfalfa. To protect our crops we had rabbit drives, in which we used gangs of men and boys on foot, plus a couple on horseback, to drive the rabbits to a corner made by the intersection of two right-angle fences where they were clubbed to death.

rabbit-ear n

1 An **oyster B1** (here: *Crassostrea virginica*).
1881 Ingersoll *Oyster-Industry* 247, Rabbit-ear—A long, slender oyster. See *Coon-heel.*

2 also *rabbit-ears:* A **prickly pear 1** such as *Opuntia microdasys.*
1946 (1948) Free *All about House Plants* 202, Rabbit Ears (O[puntia] *microdasys*) has small "pads" with no spines, but plenty of golden glochids (barbed bristles) in dense tufts arranged in diagonal lines. **1969** *DARE* (Qu. S26e, *Other wildflowers not yet mentioned;* not asked in early QRs) Inf **NJ**58, Rabbit-ear, a cactus—grows in sandy area and toward pine barrens. **1976** Bailey–Bailey *Hortus Third* 793 **TX,** [Opuntia] *microdasys. . . Rabbit-ears. . .* Joints orbicular to oblong, . . velvety-pubescent.

rabbit-eared chair n
See quot 1997.
1979 *Greenfield Recorder* (MA) 25 Aug, The chair rails in the old houses were put there for a practical purpose to keep the wood chair backs from gouging the plaster, the old rabbit-eared chairs were the worst offenders. **1997** *DARE* File **nwMA,** "Rabbit-eared" is the term auctioneers around here use when selling armless, plank-seated chairs whose back posts extend above the splat and are cut an an angle so that the top of the post actually does resemble a rabbit's ear. They were made here by local craftsmen in the early 19th century. We had one in the dining room of our old house.

rabbit-ears n

1 The hare's-ear mustard (*Conringia orientalis*). [See quot 1914]
1914 Georgia *Manual Weeds* 189, *Conringia orientalis. . .* Rabbit-ears. [*Ibid* 190, Stem leaves oblong, rather thick, also smooth and glaucous, shaped like a rabbit's ears and clasping the stem by two rounded auricles at the base.] **1935** (1943) Muenscher *Weeds* 260, *Conringia orientalis. . .* Rabbit-ears. . . Common in grain fields in . . the northwestern states; infrequent elsewhere.

2 See **rabbit-ear 2.**

rabbiteye n

1 also *rabbiteye blueberry, rabbit's-eye ~:* A **blueberry 1** (here: *Vaccinium ashei*) native to the southeastern US. [See quot 1989]
1923 Amer. Joint Comm. Horticult. Nomenclature *Std. Plant Names*

520, *Vaccinium. . . virgatum* [here: =*V. ashei*] . . Rabbiteye B[lueberry]. **1937** U.S. Forest Serv. *Range Plant Hdbk.* B154, Some attempt has also been made . . to test rabbiteye blueberry . ., also called southern blueberry, now cultivated commercially in the Southeastern States where it is native. **1968** *DARE* (Qu. I44, *What kinds of berries grow wild around here?*) Inf **LA**40, The low huckleberries that grow about a foot high are called rabbiteyes. **1971** GA Dept. Ag. *Farmers Market Bulletin* 10 Mar 1/2, Dr. Brightwell . . has taken native Rabbiteye blueberry plants and . . developed five varieties that meet all tests. **1986** Pederson *LAGS Concordance (Names of local berries)* 1 inf, **nwFL,** Rabbit eyes—blueberries. **1989** Whealy *Fruit Inventory* 207, Vaccinium ashei; rabbiteye blueberry, so called for the pink color of its ripening berries. **1995** Brako et al. *Scientific & Common Names Plants* 214, Rabbit's-eye blueberry—*Vaccinium ashei.*

2 See quot. Cf **goose eye**
1939 FWP *Guide TN* 416 [Moonshiner terms], When aged, the deep red liquor was clear of verdigris (fusel oil) and held a bead the size of number five shot. There were no 'rabbit eyes on it to pop off' (big bubbles that foam and burst as soon as the bottle is shaken).

rabbiteye blueberry See **rabbiteye 1**

rabbitface n

A **delphinium** (here: *Delphinium virescens*).
[**1936** Whitehouse *TX Flowers* 26, *Delphinium albescens* [=*D. virescens*]. . . The white flowers resemble rabbit faces and are tinged with green and purple.] **1961** Wills–Irwin *Flowers TX* 111, *Delphinium virescens. . .* Prairie Larkspur, or Rabbit-face, is a slender perennial seen most commonly on flat grassy prairies and plains but occurring throughout most of the state.

rabbit fence n Cf **galloping fence**
See quots.
1959 *Hench Coll.* **wVA,** [Legend on postcard:] The variety of rail fences in this area are Snake, Post and Rail, and Galloping or Rabbit. **1966** Dakin *Dial. Vocab. Ohio R. Valley* 2.104 **KY,** The use of the split rail fence designated Type G seems quite limited regionally. [*DARE* Ed: Illustration shows a fence consisting of a single line of rails, confined at their ends by a pair of vertical posts and supported by an additional pair of crossed poles.] References to this type and its distinctive names are common only in the Kentucky Mountains and adjoining Knobs from the headwaters of the Kentucky River southward. . . The usual name for such a fence is *galloping fence,* but an Estill County informant also calls it a *rabbit fence.*

rabbit fire n
=**Easter fire.**
1940 Writers' Program *Guide TX* 637 **cTX,** Another observance is that of the "Easter fires" on the surrounding hills. For years beacons of blazing brush, lighted by local high school students, have thrown their flames skyward every Easter Eve. The children of the town view the conflagrations as "rabbit fires," their legend being that the rabbits use them to cook and color the eggs which are found in the Easter nests the next morning.

rabbitfish n
Either of two fishes of the family Tetraodontidae:
a A **puffer** n[1] **1** (here: *Lagocephalus laevigatus*).
1787 Gesellschaft Naturforschender Freunde *Schriften* 8.189, *Tetrodon laevigatus* [=*Lagocephalus laevigatus*]. . . *Rabbit Fish.* . . Rabbit- oder Kaninchen-Fisch soll er in Carolina wegen seines sehr weissen Fleisches genannt werden, welches von einigen gespeißt wird. Er wurde im Hafen zu Rhode-Eyland gefangen. [=*Tetrodon laevigatus* [=*Lagocephalus laevigatus*]. . . *Rabbit Fish.* . . It is supposed to be called Rabbitfish in Carolina on account of its very white flesh, which is eaten by some. It was caught in the harbor at Rhode Island.] **1879** U.S. Natl. Museum *Bulletin* 14.24, *Tetrodon laevigatus. . . Rabbit-fish.*—Cape Cod to Florida. **1897** NY Forest Fish & Game Comm. *Annual Rept. for 1896* 244, *Lagocephalus lævigatus. . .* Rabbit-fish; Smooth Puffer.—Occasionally taken in the fall in Gravesend Bay. **1905** NJ State Museum *Annual Rept. for 1904* 362, *Lagocephalus laevigatus. . .* Puffer. Rabbit Fish. . . Teeth large. Lips very thick, fleshy and papillose. **1921** *Copeia* 99.73 **Long Is. NY,** *Lagocephalus laevigatus.* Rabbit-fish. One [caught] November 5th, 8 inches in total length. **1941** Faherty *Big Old Sun* 255 **FL Keys,** "I'm a blow-puffing rabbitfish," he sputtered. **1991** Amer. Fish-

eries Soc. *Common Names Fishes* 161, Rabbitfish—see smooth puffer . . striped burrfish.

b A **burfish** (here: *Chilomycterus schoepfi*).

1873 in 1878 Smithsonian Inst. *Misc. Coll.* 14.2.15, *Chilomycterus geometricus* [=*C. schoepfi*]. . . Spiny box-fish; rabbit-fish *(Vineyard Sound)*. . . Cape Cod to Florida. **1898** U.S. Natl. Museum *Bulletin* 47.1748, *Chylomycterus* [sic] *schoepfi*. . . *Rabbit-fish*. . . The body is capable of considerable inflation. **1933** John G. Shedd Aquarium *Guide* 161, *Cyclichthys* [=*Chilomycterus*] *schoepfi—Spiney* [sic] *Boxfish; Burrfish; Rabbitfish.* This is the common Burrfish of the Atlantic coast. Its spines are short with broad bases forming an almost complete coat of armor. **1991** [see **a** above].

rabbit flower n [*EDD* (at *rabbit* sb. 1.(1)) 1882]
=**butter-and-eggs 1.**

1949 Moldenke *Amer. Wild Flowers* 272, *Linaria vulgaris*. . . The common name of *butter-and-eggs* for this plant seems appropriate because of the colors of the corolla, but the names *eggs-and-bacon* . . and *rabbitflower* are a bit more obscure in their application.

rabbit-foot n

1 also *rabbitsfoot:* A **freshwater clam** (here: *Quadrula cylindrica*).

1941 *AmSp* 16.155 **Missip Valley,** [There are many varieties of freshwater mussels, but the button-cutter is ignorant of any technical terminology for them. His names are mostly descriptive and frequently picturesque. . . Arkansas . . Elephant Ear.] *Ibid* 156, Rabbit Foot. **1992** Cummings–Mayer *Field Guide Freshwater Mussels MW* 32, *Rabbitsfoot—Quadrula cylindrica*. . . Medium to large rivers in mixed sand and gravel. . . Rare throughout its range. Endangered in Illinois, Indiana, Missouri, and Ohio.

2 also *rabbit's foot:* A **hareleaf** (here: *Lagophylla congesta*).

1960 Abrams *Flora Pacific States* 4.156 **CA,** *Lagophylla congesta*. . . Rabbit-foot. . . Hot, dry, open slopes. **1961** Thomas *Flora Santa Cruz* 360 **cwCA,** *L[agophylla] congesta*. . . Rabbit's Foot. Occasional on dry chaparral slopes on the eastern side of the Santa Cruz Mountains.

3 See **rabbit-foot clover.**

4 See **rabbit-foot grass.**

rabbit-foot clover n Also *rabbit-foot, rabbit's-foot (clover)*
A naturalized clover (*Trifolium arvense*). Also called **oldfield clover 1, poverty grass 2d, pussy** n **1, pussy clover, stone ~**

1817 Eaton *Botany* 84, [*Trifolium*] *arvense* (field clover, or rabbit-foot). **1848** Gray *Manual of Botany* 106, *T[rifolium] arvense*. . . Rabbit-foot Clover. . . The corolla whitish with a purple spot; the heads becoming grayish and very softly woolly. **1848** in 1850 Cooper *Rural Hours* 125 **cNY,** The downy "rabbit-foot," or "stone-clover," the common red variety . . [is] introduced. **1892** IN Dept. Geol. & Nat. Resources *Rept. for 1891* 140, *Trifolium arvense*. . . Rabbit-foot or Stone Clover. **1916** Keeler *Early Wildflowers* 131, A little later come . . the Rabbit's-Foot with soft and silky grayish heads, and the Buffalo Clover, red and white. **1954** *AmSp* 29.15, *Trifolium arvense*, a cosmopolitan, woolly-headed clover, . . is known in America both as the rabbitfoot (clover) and hare's-foot (clover). . . Rabbitfoot clover is the commonest designation in the United States, whereas hare's-foot is the usual British term. **1969** *DARE* (Qu. S26d, *Wildflowers that grow in meadows;* not asked in early QRs) Inf **RI**15, Rabbit's-foot clover. **1971** Kieran *Nat. Hist. NYC* 140, Then there is the Rabbit-foot or Old Field Clover *(Trifolium arvense)* that grows in poor ground or waste places and hangs out grayish-pink woolly heads of flowers that resemble miniature powder puffs.

rabbit-foot grass n Also *rabbit-foot, rabbit's-foot (grass)*
A beardgrass (here: *Polypogon monspeliensis*).

1923 Abrams *Flora Pacific States* 1.147, *Polypogon monspeliensis*. . . Rabbit's Foot. . . Common in waste places and along irrigating ditches at moderate altitudes. Alaska to Mexico; occasional in the Atlantic States. **1940** Gates *Flora KS* 136, Polypogon monspeliensis. . . Rabbit-foot Grass. Sandy soil along the Arkansas river. **1946** Tatnall *Flora DE* 31, *P. monspeliensis*. . . *Rabbit's-foot Grass.* Frequent in saline soil, from Cape Charles northward to Worcester and Wicomico Counties. **1961** Thomas *Flora Santa Cruz* 94 **cwCA,** *P. monspeliensis*. . . Rabbit's Foot Grass. A common weed of wet areas, drainage ditches, creek bottoms, and along the edges of puddles and ponds. **1974** Welsh *Anderson's*

Flora AK 597, *Polypogon monspeliensis* . . *Rabbitfoot*. . . Panicle dense, spikelike, . . puberulent.

rabbit grass n

1 See quots. Cf **cotton grass 1**

1940 Faulkner *Hamlet* 90 **MS,** Here he come all the way down to Mississippi . . and bought him up two thousand acres of as fine a hill-gully and rabbit-grass land as ever stood on one edge about fifteen miles west of Jefferson. **1967** *DARE* (Qu. S9, . . *Kinds of grass that are hard to get rid of*) Inf **TN**6, Rabbit grass. **1969** *DARE* FW Addit **GA**51, Rabbit grass—a really low-to-the-ground plant having very limber stems, pale green, fuzzy, 10 inches or so long, branching, with no other leaves. **1976** Brown *Gloss. Faulkner* 158, *Rabbit-grass* . . apparently used as another name for *sedge* because rabbits frequently take cover in it.

2 A **chickweed 1a** (here: *Stellaria media*).

1951 *PADS* 15.31 **TX,** *Alsine media*. . . Rabbit-grass.

rabbit gum n

1 A **prickly ash 1** (here: *Zanthoxylum clava-herculis*).

1960 Vines *Trees SW* 595, *Zanthoxylum clava-herculis*. . . Vernacular names are Toothache, . . Rabbit Gum, . . and Wait-a-bit. A number of species of birds eat the fruit.

2 See **gum** n[2] **3c.**

rabbit hawk n chiefly **Sth, S Midl** See Map

Usu the **marsh hawk 1** or the **red-tailed hawk;** occas another hawk, such as the **red-shouldered hawk.**

1851 *De Bow's Rev.* 11.54 **LA,** *Hawks* of five kinds, and all numerous. 1st, *Rabbit Hawk;* 2d, *Hen Hawk;* 3d, Blue-tail Hawk, or *Blue Darter;* 4th, Swallow-tailed Hawk, dove-colored back, white belly; 5th, *Sparrow Hawk.* **1880** Cable *Grandissimes* 43 **LA,** A great rabbit-hawk sat alone in the top of a lofty pecan-tree. **1891** *Leighton News* (AL) 1 June np, *Marsh Hawk*. . . This is the species known here as "Rabbit Hawk," and may be easily recognized by the conspicuous white spot on the lower part of the back. . . It is often seen flying low over the fields, searching every patch of sedge grass very carefully for its favorite food. Possibly it *sometimes* catches a rabbit. **1913** *Auk* 30.495 **Okefenokee GA,** *Buteo borealis borealis.* Red-tailed Hawk; 'Rabbit Hawk.' **1949** Sprunt–Chamberlain *SC Bird Life* 159, Eastern Red-tailed Hawk. . . *Local Names:* Hen-hawk; Rabbit-hawk. . . It is a highly valuable species as a control on swarming numbers of rodents, mainly rats and mice. *Ibid* 175, *Marsh Hawk*. . . Local Names: Rabbit Hawk. [*Ibid* 176, While it preys on birds at times, . . its main dependence is upon rodents, rats, mice, and rabbits.] **1955** *Oriole* 20.1.5 **GA,** Red-tailed Hawk. . . *Rabbit Hawk* (remains of rabbits were found in 64 of 754 stomachs). **1964** *PADS* 42.22 **cKY,** Rabbit hawk. The marsh hawk (*Circus cyanea*), so called because of its flying low over the pastures in search of rodents. **1965–70** *DARE* (Qu. Q4, . . *Kinds of hawks*) 37 Infs, **chiefly Sth, S Midl,** Rabbit hawk; **AL**35, **GA**89, **KY**21, 68, 86, 88, **SC**34, **TN**26, Rabbit hawk—big (*or* large) (hawk); **MS**47, **SC**32, 46, 57, Rabbit hawk, chicken hawk—same; **CA**160, **NC**67, Rabbit hawk—red-tail(ed) hawk; **GA**1, Rabbit hawk—larger [than chicken hawk]; **GA**7, Rabbit hawk—big, white-breasted; **MS**6, Rabbit hawk, blue darter—same; **OK**11, Rabbit hawk—chases anything running on ground; **OK**42, Rabbit hawk—larger than blue darter and chicken hawk; **PA**121, Rabbit hawk—sassy ones; **TN**24, Rabbit hawk—big hawk with white spot on the tail, flies right low on the ground.

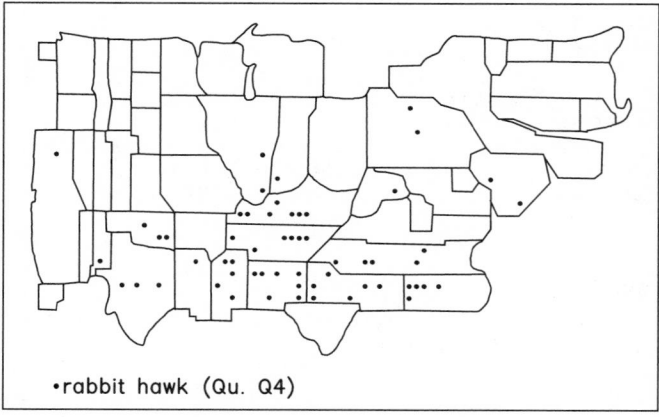

•rabbit hawk (Qu. Q4)

rabbit heart n
Tachycardia.

1970 *DARE* (Qu. BB7, *A feeling that lasts for a short while, with difficult breathing and heart beating fast*) Inf **PA**237, Rabbit heart—he scares quick in the heart; probably [heard] from [people in] Cincinnati or Connecticut.

rabbit hedge n
=Osage orange.

1941 Writers' Program *Guide AR* 314 **nwAR**, Small stacks of logs . . may be piles of hard *bois d'arc*, going through a four-year period of seasoning. *Bois d'arc*, known variously as ironwood, Osage orange, mock orange, bowwood, yellowwood, hedge, applewood, or rabbit hedge, is highly prized by makers of archery equipment.

rabbit hole n Cf **bunny-in-the-hole**
A marble game; see quots.

1955 *PADS* 23.28, *Rabbit-hole* . . variant of bun-hole. **1966–70** *DARE* (Qu. EE7, . . *Kinds of marble games*) 8 Infs, **scattered**, Rabbit hole; **AL**54, Rabbit hole—kids would dig four or five holes in the yard, try then to shoot to knock other marbles in them; **CT**6, Rabbit hole— sounds familiar; you used to roll them, now you throw them; **IL**85, Rabbit hole—first one to shoot their marble into a small hole dug in the dirt wins; **NY**154, Rabbit hole—agate dropped in center of ring, then used to hit others out of the ring; **NY**205, Rabbit hole—try to throw marble into little depression in ground; **PA**130, Rabbit hole—make a four-foot diameter ring, put a mark in middle, see who can get closest.

rabbit hound See **rabbit dog**

rabbit ice n Cf **rabbit bread**
See quots.

1953 Randolph–Wilson *Down in Holler* 276 **Ozarks**, *Rabbit-ice*. . The flower-like ice formations sometimes seen on the stems of dittany weed; evidently a fine spray of liquid comes out of these stems near the ground and is frozen. Some Ozarkers believe that rabbit-ice has medicinal value. **2000** *NADS Letters* **seMO**, "Rabbit ice" . . is hoar-frost found at the base of small woody stems early in the morning after a rain when the temperature has dropped to below freezing. Heard in the Bootheel of Missouri in 1965. Used by adults that had been reared in the local vicinity.

rabbit jump n Cf **frog-hop**
A short distance.

1968 *DARE* (Qu. MM4, . . *A short distance past* . . "*The mail box is just _____ the pine tree.*") Inf **PA**138, Rabbit jump past; (Qu. MM24, . . '*A short distance*': "*The river is just a _____ from the house.*") Infs **MD**26, **NH**14, Rabbit jump.

rabbit lettuce n
1 An umbelliferous plant *(Bowlesia incana)* found from Florida to California, often growing in lawns.

1946 Reeves–Bain *Flora TX* 224, *B[owlesia] incana*. . . Rabbit Lettuce. . . Annual, trailing herb. . . Early spring.

2 A wild green; see quot. Cf **wild lettuce**

1949 Arnow *Hunter's Horn* 157 **KY**, Her good sense told her she wouldn't find wild greens, not on a dry March day, but she took a milk bucket and the butcher knife and went hunting, the pups . . stepping on the few thin-leaved bunches of rabbit lettuce she did find.

rabbit-meat n [*EDD* (at *rabbit* sb. 1.(7)) 1879]
A **dead nettle 1** (here: *Lamium purpureum*).

1900 Lyons *Plant Names* 214, *L[amium] purpureum*. . . Red Dead-nettle, . . Rabbit-meat. **1901** Lounsberry *S. Wild Flowers* 448, *Lamium purpureum*, sweet archangel, rabbit-meat, or red dead nettle also from Europe and Asia, has perhaps secured its strong foothold in this country through the transportation of its seeds in ballast.

rabbitmouth sucker n Also *rabbitmouth*
=harelip sucker.

1882 U.S. Natl. Museum *Bulletin* 16.144, *Q[uassilabia] lacera*. . . Hare-lip Sucker; . . Rabbit-mouth Sucker. **1890** *Century Dict.* 4901, *Quassilabia*. . . A genus of catostomoid fishes of the United States; the hare-lip suckers. *Q. lacera* is the cutlips, or May, splitmouth, or rabbit-mouth sucker, a singular fish of the Ohio valley and southward[;] . . a peculiar formation of the mouth . . has suggested both the technical and

the vernacular names. *Ibid* 4924, *Rabbit-mouth* . . the *rabbit-mouth sucker*, a catostomoid fish. **1908** in 1911 U.S. Bur. Fisheries *Report* 317, *Sucker*. . . The different species are known as . . "rabbit-mouth," . . "red horse" [etc].

rabbit owl n [From its preying upon rabbits] Cf **coo-coo owl, hoot ~ 1**
Either the barred owl *(Strix varia)* or the **great horned owl**.

1966–70 *DARE* (Qu. Q2, . . *Kinds of owls*) Infs **FL**51, **GA**91, **ME**22, Rabbit owl; **AL**35, Rabbit owl (same as hoot owl); **OK**52, Rabbit owl— a big owl that goes "coo." **1986** Pederson *LAGS Concordance* (Hoot owl) 1 inf, **swTN**, Rabbit owl.

rabbit pea n Also *rabbit's pea* [Perh from the pubescence, but see quot 1922]
=goat's rue.

1900 Lyons *Plant Names* 120, *C[racca] Virginiana* [=*Tephrosia v.*] . . Goat's Rue, . . Rabbit Pea. **1922** *Amer. Botanist* 28.73, *T[ephrosia] Virginica* [sic]. . . "Rabbit pea" and "turkey pea" are names probably of fanciful origin. **1933** Small *Manual SE Flora* 706, *Rabbit's-pea*. . . Dry, usually acid sandy soil, various provinces, Fla. to La., Man[itoba], and Me. **1938** Rawlings *Yearling* 199 **FL**, A rabbit-pea vine was in blossom beside the road. **1967** *DARE* (Qu. S11) Inf **SC**46, Rabbit peas. **1976** Bailey–Bailey *Hortus Third* 1101, *[Tephrosia] virginiana*. . . *Rabbit's pea*. Per[ennial] to 2 ft., young growth white-silky-pubescent.

rabbit plantain n
A **plantain** (here: *Plantago major*).

1973 *Foxfire 2* 85 **KY, TN**, *Plantago major*. . . Rabbit plantain. . . A very common dooryard weed. . . [T]he leaves are edible when young, rich in calcium, and make excellent greens, especially when added to mustard. . . *Plantago lanceolata*. . . can also be eaten, but leaves of rabbit plantain are preferred.

rabbit root See **rabbit's-root**

rabbit sage n [Prob from a resemblance to **sage 1**]
=rabbit brush 1a.

1931 U.S. Dept. Ag. *Misc. Pub. 101* 160, Rabbit brush is the name probably most commonly applied to this genus [=*Chrysothamnus*] in the West. . . Rabbit sage, rayless-goldenrod, and yellowbrush are also in frequent use. *Ibid* 161, *Douglas rabbit brush* [=*C. viscidiflorus*] . ., known also as Douglas (or tall) rabbitsage . . is a species varying greatly both in form and stature. **1937** U.S. Forest Serv. *Range Plant Hdbk.* B54, *Chrysothamnus spp.* . . These plants . . are frequently called rabbitsage.

rabbit's ear n
A **sheep sorrel** (here: *Rumex acetosella*).

1973 Kluger *Wild Flavor* 72 **IN**, While hunting greens . . I learned to know . . sheep sorrel as "rabbit's-ear."

rabbit's-eye blueberry See **rabbiteye 1**

rabbit's foot n
1 A **wild sarsaparilla** (here: *Aralia nudicaulis*). Cf **rabbit's-root**

1940 Clute *Amer. Plant Names* 96, *A[ralia] nudicaulis*. . . Rabbit's-foot. **1971** Krochmal *Appalachia Med. Plants* 54, *Aralia nudicaulis*. . . Rabbit's foot. . . The roots and rhizomes have been used as a diuretic, diaphoretic, and cough remedy.

2 See **rabbit-foot 1**.

3 See **rabbit-foot 2**.

4 See **rabbit-foot clover**.

5 See **rabbit-foot grass**.

rabbit's-foot clover See **rabbit-foot clover**

rabbit's-foot grass See **rabbit-foot grass**

rabbit's milkweed n Also *rabbit's milk*
A **milkweed 1** (here: either *Asclepias amplexicaulis* or *A. humistrata*).

1901 Mohr *Plant Life AL* 675, *Asclepias humistrata*. . . *Rabbit's milkweed*. . . North Carolina to Florida, west to Mississippi. **1958** Jacobs–Burlage *Index Plants NC* 20, *Asclepias amplexicaulis*. . . Rabbit's milk. . . This milkweed grows throughout North Carolina. . . It is said to be poisonous and has been used to heal wounds and sores. It kills warts, is used in tattooing, as a food, and for cordage.

rabbit's-mouth n Also *bunny-mouth* Cf **rabbit B3**

A **snapdragon** (here: *Antirrhinum majus*).

1876 Hobbs *Bot. Hdbk.* 95, Rabbits' mouth, Snap dragon, Antirrhinum majus. **1900** Lyons *Plant Names* 39, *A[ntirrhinum] majus.* . . Rabbit's-mouth, Bunny-mouth. **1923** [see **rabbit B3**].

rabbit's pea See **rabbit pea**

rabbit's-root n Also *rabbit root* Cf **rabbit's foot 1**

A **wild sarsaparilla** (here: *Aralia nudicaulis*).

[**1840** Hooker *Flora Boreali-Amer.* 1.274, "The crees use the root of this plant . . under the name of *wawpoos-ootchepeh,* (Rabbit-root,) and also apply the bruised bark of its root to recent wounds." *(Richardson)*] **1876** Hobbs *Bot. Hdbk.* 95, Rabbits' root, American sarsaparilla, Aralia nudicaulis. **1900** Lyons *Plant Names* 42, *A[ralia] nudicaulis.* . . Rabbit's-root. . . *Rhizome* of this . . alterative, stimulant, diuretic. **1930** Sievers *Amer. Med. Plants* 62, *Aralia nudicaulis.* . . Rabbitroot. [*Ibid* 63, The rootstock is rather long, creeping, somewhat twisted, and possesses a very fragrant, aromatic odor and a warm, aromatic taste.]

rabbit-tail grass n

=**hare's tail 2.**

1959 Carleton *Index Herb. Plants* 97, Rabbit-tail-grass: Lagurus ovatus. **1976** Bailey–Bailey *Hortus Third* 634, *[Lagurus] ovatus.* . . Rabbit-tail g[rass]. . . Panicle to 1¼ in. long, nearly as thick, pale and downy.

rabbit tea n

A medicinal tea made from **rabbit tobacco 1.**

1966 *DARE* (Qu. BB50a, . . *Favorite remedies . . for a cough*) Inf **GA6**, Rabbit tea; (Qu. BB50d, *Favorite spring tonics*) Inf **GA6**, Rabbit tea—made from rabbit tobacco. [**1974** Morton *Folk Remedies* 65 **SC**, *Life everlasting,* . . *Rabbit tobacco.* . . *Gnaphalium obtusifolium.* . . Life everlasting "tea" is the most popular native cold remedy in South Carolina. It is bitter and sugar is added when it is given to babies or lemon juice or extract to make it more acceptable to older children. It may be taken in combination with "moonshine."] [**1986** Pederson *LAGS Concordance,* 1 inf, **cAL**, Rabbit-tobacco tea—good for fever; 1 inf, **nwFL**, Rabbit-tobacco tea—would help break a fever.]

rabbit thorn n

=**wolfberry,** usu *Lycium pallidum.*

1925 Jepson *Manual Plants CA* 890, *L[ycium] pallidum.* . . Rabbit Thorn. . . Densely branched excessively thorny shrub, 1½ to 3 ft. high and as broad. **1947** (1976) Curtin *Healing Herbs* 59, Lycium pallidum . . *Rabbit thorn.* . . This homely, spiny shrub, with stubby leaves and small red berries, was one of Frémont's discoveries in 1844, although the Spanish residents in our Southwest had already known it. **1957** Jaeger *N. Amer. Deserts* 292, Mexican Rabbit Thorn. . . Lycium brevipes. Rigid spiny shrub, with lavender flowers and small green, several-seeded, tomato-like fruits. Colorado Desert south into Mexico. **1960** Vines *Trees SW* 916, The plant [=*Lycium torreyi*] is also known by the vernacular names of . . Rabbit-thorn [etc]. **1989** Mayes–Lacy *Nanise* 136, *Rabbit thorn* . . *Lycium pallidum.* . . *Navajo Uses—Medicinal:* The ground root is used for toothache. The bark and dried berries are part of Navajo life medicine.

rabbit tobacco n

1 Any of several similarly woolly composite plants; see below. Cf **Indian tobacco, ladies'-tobacco**

a A **cudweed 1,** usu *Pseudognaphalium obtusifolium.* **chiefly SE, VA** See Map

1880 (1881) Harris *Uncle Remus Songs* 66 **GA**, "Den Brer Rabbit . . tuck a big chaw terbarker." "Tobacco, Uncle Remus?" asked the little boy, incredulously. "Rabbit terbarker, honey. You know dis yer life ev'lastin' w'at Miss Sally puts 'mong de cloze in de trunk; well, dat's rabbit terbarker." **1894** *Jrl. Amer. Folkl.* 7.92 **NC**, Gnaphalium polycephalum . . rabbit-tobacco. **1901** *Torreya* 1.117 **GA**, Gnaphalium obtusifolium. . . Rabbit-tobacco. . . Known universally by this name in Georgia. The dried leaves are smoked by boys. **1909** *DN* 3.361 **eAL, wGA**, Rabbit-tobacco. . . Life-everlasting, cudweed. It is a common practice among the young boys to smoke or chew the dried leaves of this herb. **1937** *AmSp* 12.235 **Ozarks**, On all the poor land in the middle

and far West there is a weed known as rabbit weed and as rabbit tobacco. This is sometimes, I believe, used to adulterate tobacco and is certainly used by boys. **1965–70** *DARE* (Qu. S20) 10 Infs, **chiefly SE**, Rabbit tobacco; **AL46**, Rabbit tobacco. . . As kids we smoked it, but never till the leaves turned gray and velvety—it is good for congestion; **NC72**, Rabbit tobacco—same as Indian tobacco—smokable; **VA2**, Rabbit tobacco—smoke or chew the bitter leaves; (Qu. S6) Inf **NC41**, Rabbit tobacco; (Qu. S21, . . *Weeds . . that are a trouble in gardens and fields*) Infs **AR52, NC49, SC2, 21**, Rabbit tobacco; **NC76**, Rabbit tobacco—leaves, when they dry out, you can smoke; (Qu. S26a, . . *Wildflowers. . . Roadside flowers*) Inf **GA38**, Boneset (similar to rabbit tobacco); **VA26**, Life-everlasting = tobacco plant = rabbit tobacco; (Qu. S26d, *Wildflowers that grow in meadows;* not asked in early QRs) Inf **VA57**, Rabbit tobacco; (Qu. S26e, *Other wildflowers not yet mentioned;* not asked in early QRs) Inf **SC27**, Life-everlasting—same as rabbit tobacco; medicinal—smoked it to cure sinus trouble; made tea from it; (Qu. T16) Inf **GA84**, Rabbit tobacco—ivory bloom, narrow whitish leaves, smoked in pipes by children; (Qu. BB50d, *Favorite spring tonics*) Inf **GA6**, Rabbit tea—made from rabbit tobacco; (Qu. DD3b) Inf **GA17**, Kids smoke rabbit tobacco. **1975** Thomas *Hear the Lambs* 159 **nwAL**, I knew it when I tasted it. My ma used to make rabbit-tobacco-and-hog's-foot tea. **1976** Lynn–Vecsey *Loretta Lynn* 31 **eKY**, Sometimes we both smoked rabbit tobacco, which grows wild in the hollers. That's the plant Mommy calls "Life Everlasting" and uses for tea. **1986** Pederson *LAGS Concordance* **Gulf Region** (*Cigars and cigarettes*) 25 infs, Rabbit tobacco; (*Roots: medicinal use*) 6 infs, Rabbit tobacco (tea); (*Cigarettes*) 1 inf, Rabbit tobacco, weed smoked as a child; (*Undesirable grass in cotton field*) 1 inf, Rabbit tobacco. **1995** White *Sleeping* 198 **GA**, In the backyard of the Harrises' little cabin we planted a butterfly garden—buddleia, pentas, and lantana for their nectar; and rabbit tobacco and passionflower, the food plants for the larvae of the gulf fritillary and painted lady.

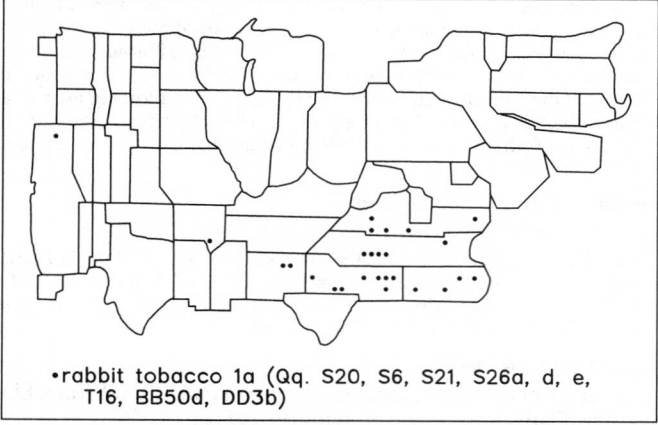

•rabbit tobacco 1a (Qq. S20, S6, S21, S26a, d, e, T16, BB50d, DD3b)

b A **cotton rose 3** (here: *Evax verna*).

1930 OK Univ. Biol. Surv. *Pub.* 2.84, Evax prolifera. . . Rabbit tobacco. **1936** Whitehouse *TX Flowers* 167, Large Rabbit Tobacco (*Filago prolifera* [=*Evax p.*]) is a low plant less than six inches high. . . The flowers . . are borne in woolly, rather flattened heads which are about half an inch broad. **1970** Correll *Plants TX* 1613, Evax. . . Rabbit-tobacco. Cotton-rose.

c A **cotton rose 2** (here: *Filago verna*).

1930 OK Univ. Biol. Surv. *Pub.* 2.84, Filago nivea [=*F. verna*]. . . Rabbit-tobacco. **1936** Whitehouse *TX Flowers* 167, Small Rabbit Tobacco (*Filago nivea*) is a smaller plant [than *Evax prolifera*] but is more densely clothed with woolly hairs. . . In many pastures they [=the above-named plants] take the place of grasses as a ground cover. The leaves may be chewed for gum. The rabbit tobacco is closely related to the cudweeds and everlastings. **1937** Stemen–Myers *OK Flora* 568, *Filago nivea.* . . *Rabbit Tobacco.* . . Flowers . . all cottony at the apex.

d A **blackroot 2** (here: *Pterocaulon virgatum*).

1934 *Torreya* 34.134 **FL**, Rabbit-tobacco, Pterocaulon undulatum [=*P. virgatum*], a composite with nearly cylindrical long heads of small white blossoms; . . and a blueberry, *Vaccinium nitidans,* are a few of the many other plants which add beauty and interest. **1938** Baker *FL Wild Flowers* 226, Pterocaulon undulatum. Rabbit-tobacco. Blackroot. Heads tiny, whitish, in woolly spikes. . . Leaves . . densely woolly and pale beneath. **1974** Morton *Folk Remedies* 121 **SC**, *Blackroot; rabbit to-*

bacco . . *Pterocaulon pycnostachyum* [=*P. virgatum*]. . . *South Carolina (Current use)*: Decoction of root is taken for cold and menstrual cramps[,] . . to relieve asthma[,] . . and . . as a cold remedy. [*Ibid* 122, *Other utility*: Leaves have been chewed as a tobacco substitute.]

e =pearly everlasting 1.
1966–67 *DARE* Wildfl QR Pl.211A Inf **AR**44, Rabbit tobacco—kids smoke this; I have—it tastes terrible; **NC**36, Rabbit tobacco.

2 See quot.
1936 *AmSp* 11.317 **Ozarks**, *Rabbit tobacco.* . . Dried rabbit dung, sometimes mixed with cut smoking tobacco.

rabbit tooth n Also *Peter Rabbit tooth*
An upper incisor, esp a bucktooth.
1950 *WELS (Large front teeth that stick out of the mouth)* 1 Inf, **cWI**, Rabbit teeth; 1 Inf, **csWI**, Rabbit teeth if they make a V. **1965–70** *DARE* (Qu. X12, . . *Large front teeth that stick out of the mouth*) 32 Infs, **scattered**, Rabbit teeth; **PA**175, Peter Rabbit teeth; (Qu. X13a, . . *Joking names . . for teeth*) Inf **IL**45, Rabbit teeth. **1969** *DARE* Tape **NY**159, [FW:] What would you call teeth that stick right out like— [Inf **NY**158:] They call 'em protruding, don't they? There's a name for it, too. What is it? What do they call the teeth when they— [Inf **NY**159:] Rabbit teeth. **1991** *DARE* File **seWI**, The trouble started when my rabbit tooth [pointing to his upper front tooth] got cavitated.

rabbit tracks n pl Cf **chicken tracks**
=hen scratching.
1970 *DARE* (Qu. JJ11, *Joking names for handwriting that's hard to read: "I can't make anything out of his _____."*) Inf **KY**90, Rabbit tracks.

rabbit-twister n
1 also *rabbit-choker*: A country person, hillbilly.
1905 Biggers *From Cattle Range* 127 **cTX**, I reckon a lot of these land boomers and wood haulers and rabbit twisters will want to mob me in broad open daylight. **1933** *AmSp* 8.1.51 **Ozarks**, *Rabbit-twister.* . . Derisively applied to hillmen, some of whom are said to live largely upon rabbits, which they twist out of hollow logs with a forked stick. Comparable to *hillbilly, ridge-runner,* etc. **1954** *Harder Coll.* **cwTN**, *Rabbit-twister*—a rustic, a backwoodsman. **1973** Allen *LAUM* 1.350 (as of c1950), A rustic. . . rabbit choker [1 inf, **ceMN**].

2 A country-dancer; similarly n *rabbit-twisting*.
1915 *DN* 4.228 **wTX**, *Rabbit-twisting.* . . The usual name for country dancing, the dancers being called *rabbit-twisters*.

rabbit vine n
A **groundnut B1** (here: *Apios americana*).
1916 *Torreya* 16.238 **SC**, *Apios tuberosa* [=*A. americana*]. . . Rabbit vine, Cat I[slan]d.

rabbit violet n
=bird's-foot violet 1.
1966 *DARE* (Qu. S26c, *Wildflowers that grow in woods*) Inf **GA**5, Velvet violet—rabbit violet.

rabbitweed n
1 A **snakeweed** (here: *Gutierrezia sarothrae*).
1884 *Harper's New Mth. Mag.* 69.502 **WA**, The wide level benches that lay between the foot-hills and the prairies—middle lands, . . covered with sorry bunch-grass and rabbit-weed—were neglected. **1940** Clute *Amer. Plant Names* 168, Rabbit-weed. *Gutierrezia sarothrae.*

2 =pingue.
1911 *Century Dict. Suppl., Picradenia.* . . A variety of *P. floribunda* [= *Hymenoxys richardsonii*] is widely distributed in the southwestern United States and is locally known as *rabbit-weed* or *pingue*.

3 =rabbit brush 1a or **b.**
1902 *Everybody's Mag.* 6.36 **nwNM**, There is a yellow-green dye that is used occasionally; it is made from the flowering tops of the rabbit-weed (*Bigelovia graveolens*). **1924** *Amer. Botanist* 30.33 **West**, "Rabbit-brush" or bush refers in common parlance of the west to the various species of *Bigelovia* [here: =*Chrysothamnus* or *Ericameria*]. "Rabbit-weed["] and "rayless or false goldenrod" are less frequently used. **1967** *DARE* Wildfl QR Pl.49A Inf **OR**8, Like rabbitweed/brush—a little.

4 A **cudweed 1** (here: *Pseudognaphalium obtusifolium*).
1937 [see **rabbit tobacco 1a**].

5 =velvetleaf 1.

1940 Clute *Amer. Plant Names* 249, *Abutilon Theophrasti.* Rabbit weed, wild cotton, cheese-plant.

rabbit wire n Cf **hen wire, hog ~**
A type of wire mesh; see quot 1992.
1968–69 *DARE* (Qu. L63, *Kinds of fences made with wire*) Inf **KY**39, Slick wire (woven wire fence); rabbit wire—a type of slick wire; **OH**78, Rabbit-wire fence. **1970** GA Dept. Ag. *Farmers Market Bulletin* 30 Dec 8/1 **GA**, Mourning Doves will nest on wire cone forms in hardwood or pine trees. Place wire forms six to 16 feet above the ground. "Rabbit" wire will do nicely. **1986** Pederson *LAGS Concordance*, 1 inf, **seMS**, Poultry and rabbit wire—wire fences. **1992** *DARE* File, *Rabbit wire.* Heard on a TV program by a gardener from Oklahoma. It appeared to be wire cloth or wire mesh about ¼″ mesh. Perhaps the term is more widespread than I have heard.

rabbitwood n [See quot]
=oil nut 2.
1901 Lounsberry *S. Wild Flowers* 148, By the mountaineers the plant [=*Pyrularia pubera*] seems to be wholly known as the "rabbitwood," for these animals gnaw its bark to such an extent that it is quite unusual to find one which has not been more or less peeled.

rabbity adj
Timid, cowering.
1937 Sandoz *Slogum* 363 **NE**, Cash would be enough for those rabbity, slack-pants farmers. **1940** (1942) Clark *Ox-Bow* 79 **NV**, Joyce gave me a rabbity look and ran after me a few steps. **1948** Young *Light* 29 **OH**, I don't believe he knows what goes on around him half the time. Rabbity. But a good Secretary-Treasurer, nevertheless. Completely under the weight of John Fenno's thumb, and pliable. **1952** Brown *NC Folkl.* 1.582, *Rabbity.* . . Hiding in a field (like a rabbit). **1998** *DARE* File (as of 1940s), She was a pretty girl, in a rabbity sort of way. Never mixed much with the other young people; too shy to speak even when she was spoken to.

racacha n Usu |ˈrɑkə͵čɑ|; also |͵rɑ͵čɑˈčɑ|; for addit varr see quots Also *raquecha, rockachaw* [LaFr < AmSpan (*ar*)*racacha* for *Arracacia* spp < Quechua *rakkácha*] **LA**
1 A **burr grass**; also the spiny burr of such a plant.
1917 *DN* 4.420 **LA**, *Raquecha* [ˈrɑkə͵šɑɔ]. . . A sort of cockle-burr. **1931** Read *LA French* 146, *Racacha* is used along the Gulf Coast and in the city of New Orleans as the name of the Bur-Grass or Hedgehog Grass. *Ibid* 147, *Racacha* has found its way into English, and is used in the sense of "sand-spur" as far west as Texas. . . In Alabama it distinguishes the burgrass from the Small Burgrass (*Cenchrus carolinianus* Walt.), the latter being usually known as the *sand-spur*. *Ibid*, *Racacha* is pronounced as a French word [by the Louisiana-French], except that the *ch* has the value of Spanish *ch*. In English the stress falls on the first syllable; otherwise the English pronunciation . . is like the Louisiana-French. **1967–68** *DARE* (Qu. S13, . . *A common wild bush with bunches of round, prickly seeds; when they get dry they stick to your clothing*) Inf **LA**14, Racacha [͵rɑ͵čɑˈčɑ]—local name for sandbur; (Qu. S15, . . *Weed seeds that cling to clothing*) Inf **LA**14, Sandburs or racacha; **LA**37, Racacha—has stickers all around [FW: This is the sandbur.] **1981** Pederson *LAGS Basic Materials*, 1 inf, **seLA**, [ˈrɑˀkə͵tʃɑˀʔ]—on the beach; sting the feet; 1 inf, **seLA**, [ˈrɑˀkɪ͵tʃɑˀʔd]—goat grass (grows on the ground by the sea, like a vine). **1983** Reinecke *Coll.* 10 **LA**, Racacha, Rockachaw [ˈrɑkə͵tʃɑ, -tʃɔ] . . a painful cockleburr growing by gulf shore.
2 See quots.
1923 *DN* 5.244 **LA**, *Raquecha.* . . A Creole who is conservative in temperament: used in a derogatory sense. [**1931** Read *LA French* 147, Some Acadians apply the term *racacha* to an old horse or an old man.] **1983** Reinecke *Coll.* 10 **LA**, Racacha, rockachaw. . . Also, with first pron. [=[ˈrɑkə͵tʃɑ]], an uncouth or culturally conservative La. French person (rare.)

raccoon n
Std: a stout-bodied nocturnal mammal (*Procyon lotor*) native to most of the US and distinguished by its black facial mask outlined in white and its bushy black-ringed tail. Also called **bandit, chaoui, fisher raccoon, ringtail 1, sand coon, wash bear**

raccoonberry n
=mayapple 1.

1830 Rafinesque *Med. Flora* 2.59, *Podophyllum montanum* [=*P. peltatum*]. . . Names. . . Raccoon Berry, . . Ground Lemons, &c. **1867** De Voe *Market Asst.* 379 **NYC,** *Mandrake, May-apple, raccoon-berry,* or *wild lemon.*—This fruit is a stranger in our markets, and only occasionally found among our citizens; and, no doubt, if it was esteemed at all, it would be cultivated and become more plentiful. **1910** Graves *Flowering Plants* 194 **CT,** *Podophyllum peltatum.* . . Raccoon-berry. . . The fruit is edible and harmless but disagreeable to many persons. **1958** Jacobs–Burlage *Index Plants NC* 24, *Podophyllum peltatum.* . . Raccoonberry. . . Commercial supplies [of this plant] come chiefly from Virginia, North Carolina, Kentucky, Indiana, and Tennessee. **1976** Bailey–Bailey *Hortus Third* 891, *Mayapple,* . . *raccoon berry.* . . fr[uit] yellowish or rarely red, 2 in. long, pulp edible.

raccoon fox n Also *coon fox*
=ring-tailed cat.

1859 Cooper–Suckley *Nat. Hist. WA Terr.* 3.114, The ring-tailed bassaris, often called raccoon fox, is common in California, where the people came it. **1873** *Amer. Naturalist* 7.115 **nCA, swOR,** The "Raccoon Fox," as the miners called it, had occasionally been tamed. **1937** Grinnell et al. *Fur-Bearing Mammals CA* 1.172, The term, "coon-fox," although little used, expresses the relationship of this animal rather more accurately than any of the rest [of various names].

raccoon grape n

1 A grape such as **fox grape 1,** a **frost grape** (here: *Vitis vulpina*), or a **winter grape** (here: *Vitis cinerea*). [See quot 1830] Cf **coon grape 1**

1830 Rafinesque *Med. Flora* 2.124, *V*[*itis*] *ursina* [=*V. cinerea*]. . . Raccoon Grape. . . From Ohio to Louisiana and Texas, near streams, called Bear and Raccoon Grape, because greedily eaten by these animals. Grapes of middlesize, commonly purplish, ripe in September and October. **1834** Audubon *Ornith. Biog.* 2.80, The Racoon Grape. *Vitis æstivalis, Mich.* . . The Racoon Grape is characterized by . . the small size of the bluish-black fruit. **1920** *Torreya* 20.23 **PA,** *Vitis labrusca.* . . Raccoon grape, Coatsville, Pa. **1960** Vines *Trees SW* 731, *Vitis vulpina.* . . Vernacular names are . . Raccoon Grape, Riverbank Grape, and August Grape. The fruit can be made into preserves and wine. A number of birds and mammals also eat the fruit.

2 See **coon grape 2.**

raccoon oyster See **coon oyster**

raccoon perch n [From the dark stripes that appear to encircle its body] Also *coon perch*
A **yellow perch** (here: *Perca flavescens*).

1878 U.S. Natl. Museum *Bulletin* 12.72 **TN,** *List of Fishes of Nashville, as given by a Fisherman.* . . Coon Perch. **1896** *Ibid* 47.1023, *Perca flavescens.* . . Raccoon Perch. . . Sides with 6 or 8 broad, dark bars, which extend from the back to below the axis of the body. **1939** Natl. Geogr. Soc. *Fishes* 132, *Perca flavescens.* . . Like other fishes of extended range, it has several names in different localities, such as ringed perch, raccoon perch, red perch, or striped perch. **1966** *DARE* (Qu. P1, . . *Kinds of freshwater fish . . caught around here . . good to eat*) Infs **NC**10, 15, Raccoon perch. **1967** *State* (Raleigh, N.C.) 15 June 60/3 *(Mathews Coll.),* Two poles started bending at once and I landed two raccoon perch that would probably weigh about a pound each. **1997** *DARE* File **csWI,** A few years ago cousins of mine from Dubuque, Iowa, returned from a day of fishing in Lake Mendota to tell me they had caught a number of "raccoon perch." I was charmed by the obvious reference to the fishes' stripes, but I have always known the same fish as "lake perch" or simply "perch."

race n[1] **S Midl**
A pursuit of a game animal by dogs; hence v *race* to pursue with dogs; also fig.

1894 *Forest & Stream* 43.400 **TN,** But they had not gone 200 yds on the fox race. **1929** (1951) Faulkner *Sartoris* 331 **MS,** While the scent lay well on the wet earth, old General started the red fox that had baffled him so many times. All through the night the ringing, bell-like tones quavered and swelled and echoed among the hills, and all of them save Henry followed on horseback, guided by the cries of the hounds but mostly by the old man's and Buddy's uncanny and seemingly clairvoyant skill in anticipating the course of the race. *Ibid* 332, "Too bad Johnny ain't here. . . He'd enjoy this race." "He was a feller fer huntin', now." **1952** Brown *NC Folkl.* 1.567, That young dog o' mine's jest nat-

urally got the best mouth I ever heard in a race. **1965** *Hench Coll.* **cnVA,** A bear went up Weakley Hollow. . . Somebody called a friend who had two bear dogs. When they were put off the truck and put on the bear's track, they set off up the hollow, barking in their excitement. When Mr. Weakley told me of the episode, he said, "Those dogs track a great time. I love to hear a race." **1966–67** *DARE* Tape **AR**15, I got one [=a hunting dog] out yonder—when he goes to barking, well, we're fixing to have a race. *Ibid,* Unless you have a dog that won't run a deer, it's hard to have a fox race. *Ibid,* A fox hunter, he doesn't want to kill his fox. . . You go for the sport . . for the race. *Ibid* **NC**36, We do not ride the hounds here because of the rough terrain. . . We usually go on to some high point where the dogs will run around you and you will be able to hear the complete race from . . the point that you're sitting. **1974** Maurer–Pearl *KY Moonshine* 123, *Race.* . . The chase to escape law enforcement officers. It may be either by car or on foot. Such a chase is quite common, since federal officers seldom shoot first at violators of the liquor law. "Me and the law had a race." "I shore give the law a race yesterday." **1982** Powers *Cataloochee* 165 **cwNC** (as of a1940), When Mark Hanah and Eldridge Caldwell related that Thanksgiving was the time for the traditional bear hunt and also the wild hog race, . . a 'race' was the same as a hunt. They would race the small hogs or 'ridgerooters', four or five year olds, each weighing two or three hundred pounds, way back in the mountains. **1986** Wear *Sugarlands* 61 **ceTN** (as of early 20th cent), A handsome blue eyed boy came to the door, and said they had heard about us having a bear visit us, so they wanted to have a race, I told him we saw it back at the barn near the old sawdust pile.

race n[2] [*OED2* 1547 →] **now chiefly S Midl**
Usu in comb *race of ginger:* A gingerroot; by ext, a small piece; hence comb *race ginger* ginger in the root.

1781 in 1915 MA Hist. Soc. *Coll.* 7 ser 10.157, Race Ginger 22d. **1877** *Atlantic Mth.* 40.558, The ginger cleaner . . is a sort of rough grater to remove the bark from the root to make *race*-ginger, the merchantable form when dried. **1879** (1965) Tyree *Housekeeping in Old VA* 351, *Lightened Gingerbread.*—1½ pound of flour. ½ pound butter. ½ pound sugar. 6 eggs. 6 races of white ginger. **1899** (1912) Green *VA Folk-Speech* 342, *Race.* . . Root: as, a *race* of ginger; ginger in the root. **1905** (1975) Miles *Spirit of Mts.* 174 **eTN,** When Gran'ma sends over to borrow a "race o' brimstone" it recalls a passage in Twelfth Night [sic for *The Winter's Tale*] about "a race or two of ginger." **1913** Kephart *Highlanders* 291 **sAppalachians,** "Can I borry a race of ginger?" means the unground root. **1931** Randolph *Ozarks* 76, Shakespeare uses the word *race* in its original meaning of root—"nutmegs seven, and a race or two of ginger"; very few Americans use the word in this sense today, but a *race o' ginger* is still perfectly intelligible to the Ozark housewife. **1937** (1963) Hyatt *Kiverlid* 37 **KY,** Drinkin' a brew o' bone-set tea with a little dab o' race ginger in it fer sich ailments. **1944** *PADS* 2.20 **sAppalachians,** Race . . (From O. Fr. *rais,* "root.") A small quantity, or root (of ginger). . . It is heard now only in race-ginger, that is, ginger in the root, not ground. **1982** Slone *How We Talked* 61 **eKY** (as of c1950), Boil a few "races" (the unground roots of the ginger plant) in water.

race bird n
A **crested flycatcher** (here: *Myiarchus crinitus*).

1910 Wayne *Birds SC* 101, *Myiarchus crinitus.* . . Crested Flycatcher. . . This bird has many local names and among them "Freight" and "Race Bird."

race ginger See **race** n[2]

racehorse n

1 A mantid. Cf **rearhorse**

1890 *Century Dict.* 4926, *Race-horse.* . . A rear-horse; any mantis.

2 Perh a tiger beetle (*Cicindela* spp); see quot.

1968 *DARE* (Qu. R30, . . *Kinds of beetles;* not asked in early QRs) Inf **LA**40, Racehorse—they have long legs, are black with red around the belly. Kids hitch them to matchboxes and have races.

3 also *racehorse smear:* A card game; see quots. Cf **smear**

1967–68 *DARE* (Qu. DD35, . . *Card games*) Inf **MN**16, Racehorse—a variation of smear, using two people. Smear—each person gets six cards: a high card, low card, jack; **MN**5, Racehorse [šmiɚ]. **1974** Gibson *Hoyle* 13, *Airplane:* A form of *Partnership Pinochle . . ,* in which four cards are exchanged by partners winning the bid. Also termed *Racehorse.*

racehorse chub n

A **stone roller** (here: *Campostoma anomalum*).

1983 Becker *Fishes WI* 476, *Campostoma anomalum*. . . Racehorse chub. . . Body generally slender, nearly round.

racehorse smear See **racehorse 3**

race man n Also *race woman*

A Black person—usu used by Black speakers to express a strong sense of racial solidarity.

1902 *Cleveland Gaz.* (OH) 30 Aug 2/2, A "Great Race Man" Says He Won't. . . His secretary announced that Mr. [Booker T.] Washington would have nothing to do with the movement to contest the validity of Virginia's new constitution. **1918** *Cleveland Advocate* (OH) 22 June 1/5, Race Women Take Machinists' Jobs. . . The United States Pipe and Foundry Company . . has set the pace for other employers of labor by putting two Colored women to work as helpers in the machine shop. **1928** Fisher *Walls Jericho* 304 **NYC** [Black], Race-man (woman)—See boogy. [*Ibid* 297, Boogy—Negro. A contraction of *Booker T.,* used only of and by members of the race.] **1936** *Chicago Defender* (Natl. ed.) (IL) 13 June 16/5, One Race man, finding out this outrage, fired on the officers. *Ibid,* An aged Race man stoned and beaten almost to death by a bunch of young white men. **1942** Hurston *Dust Tracks* 225 **FL** [Black], A "Race Man" was somebody who always kept the glory and honor of his race before him. *Ibid* 226, It was a mark of shame if somebody accused: "Why, you are not a Race Man (or woman)." People made whole careers of being "Race" men and women. They were champions of the race. **1969** *PADS* 51.29 **IL** [Vocab of race relations in prison], Names *Used in common by both Negroes and Whites.* . . civil rights man, mau mau, race man. **1994** Smitherman *Black Talk* 188, *Race Man.* . . A person devoted to, *down for* the race, promotes African American Culture, and staunchly defends Blacks.

race nag n Cf **race runner 1**

A **whiptail** (here: *Cnemidophorus sexlineatus*).

1934 *Natl. Geogr. Mag.* 65.609 **Okefenokee GA,** Other species are the ground lizard . . and the six-lined lizard, the last well deserving the local name of "race nag." **1938** Matschat *Suwannee R.* 67 **Okefenokee GA,** The race nag (six-lined lizard), the ground lizard, and the orange-tailed skink are all found in the swamp in numbers.

race of ginger See **race** n²

racer n

1 Any of var snakes; see below. See Map Section Cf **speckled racer**

a also *racer snake:* A large, slender, fast-moving snake (*Coluber constrictor* and subspp) native to much of the US. Also called **black snake 1, climber, cowsucker 1, gray runner, hoop snake, milk ~ 2, pilot ~ 3, runner 4.** For other names of var subspp see **black racer 1, blue ~ 1, buttermilk snake, moccasin 1c**

1818 *Amer. Monthly Mag. & Crit. Rev.* 3.446, *Coluber velox.* . . (Racer Snake.) Black, belly white, tail blue underneath, 8 feet long, slender, very swift. **1823** James *Acct. of Exped.* 1.375 **swIA,** *Coluber constrictor*—Racer. **1842** DeKay *Zool. NY* 3.36, The Black Snake [=*Coluber constrictor*] is a bold, active, wild and untameable animal. . . In various parts of the State they have the popular names of *Racer, Pilot* and *Black Snake.* **1882** *Amer. Naturalist* 16.566 **KS,** It is not an unusual occurrence to find . . racers (*Bascanium constrictor*) . . with the entire contents of quail . . nests within their capacious stomachs. **1909** *DN* 3.291 **eAL, wGA,** Black-runner. . . Also called *black racer* or simply *racer.* **1919** *Copeia* 67.11 **NY,** *Coluber constrictor.* . . "Black Snake," "Racer." This species is becoming rare where it was once common. **1946** Stuart *Plum Grove Hill* 85 (*DA*) **KY,** They slid to the foot of the mountain like racer snakes before a new-ground fire. **1965–70** *DARE* (Qu. P25, . . *Kinds of snakes*) Infs **FL**20, **MA**80, **NC**37, **PA**126, **TX**42, 72, **WA**12, Racer(s); **MA**5, Racer, runner—black snake; **MA**68, Black snake—sometimes called racers; **IN**68, **MS**63, Racer(s). **1979** Behler–King *Audubon Field Guide Reptiles* 596, *Racer*—(*Coluber constrictor*). . . 34–77″. [*Ibid* 598, Often observed streaking across roads. . . When hunting, it holds its head high and moves swiftly through cover.] **1986** Pederson *LAGS Concordance* **Gulf Region,** 6 infs, Racer; 1 inf, Runner.

b =**pilot black snake.**

1842 DeKay *Zool. NY* 3.37, It [=the pilot black snake] is manifestly

the snake which has been frequently described to me, of great length and prodigious velocity, and to which they gave the name of *Racer* and *Pilot.* As these names are also frequently applied to the Black Snake [= *Coluber constrictor*], I had supposed that species to have been intended by their descriptions. **1890** *Century Dict.* 4927, *Racer.* . . A snake . . also called *pilot black-snake* or *pilot-snake.* [**1892** IN Dept. Geol. & Nat. Resources *Rept. for 1891* 502, Our indistinctly spotted and almost jet black form [=*Elaphe obsoleta obsoleta*] is not distinguished by most people from the Black-racer, although it is a very different snake. The latter is a slenderer snake and has very smooth scales in only seventeen rows.] **1967** *DARE* (Qu. P25, . . *Kinds of snakes*) Inf **AR**52, Racer or chicken snake.

c =**corn snake.**

1911 *Century Dict. Suppl., Racer.* . . In the Southern States, applied to the corn-snake, *Callopeltis getulus* [*DARE* Ed: appar erron for *guttatus*], a large harmless snake of a reddish-brown color with redder markings.

d also *racer snake:* =**whip snake.** [See quot 1947] **SW**

1912 CA Univ. *Univ. CA Pub. Zoology* 7.353 **NV,** *Bascanion taeniatum* (Hallowell) Striped Racer. . . The racer was taken on a hot dry mesa. **1925** TX Folkl. Soc. *Pub.* 4.50, On account of an ancient folk story, the slender racer snake . . is considered a very dangerous animal by the generality of poor whites and negroes. **1941** Writers' Program *Guide UT* 28, There are . . . three types of whiptail or racer snakes. **1947** Pickwell *Amphibians* 43 **SW,** This Snake [=*Masticophis flagellum piceus*] lives up fully to its name of "racer," for it travels over the ground with great rapidity. **1966–69** *DARE* (Qu. P25, . . *Kinds of snakes*) Infs **CA**114, 199, **NM**13, **OK**52, Racer (snake); **NM**3, Racer snake—whitish-red.

e =**ring-necked snake.** Cf **horse racer 1**

[**1958** Conant *Reptiles & Amphibians* 140, Many people believe Ringnecks are young Racers.] **1967–69** *DARE* (Qu. P25, . . *Kinds of snakes*) Inf **MA**15, Racer—have rings around them; **PA**12, Racer—stripe around its neck. **1974** Cohen *Ramapo Mt. People* 149 **nNJ, seNY,** Finally, there is the racing snake or the blue racer, as it is known elsewhere. . . "I stepped on this snake. He was about six foot long. . . This snake raised up on its tail, it's [sic] whole body extended into the air, and that snake chased me all the way from the spring back to the house. . . [I]t was a black snake—long, skinny—and it had a ring around its neck."

2 A thin or emaciated specimen of:

a The **lake trout 1. Gt Lakes**

1884 Goode *Fisheries U.S.* 488, About Grand Traverse Bay, Lake Michigan, two varieties [of *Salvelinus namaycush*] are also recognized, one being long, slim, and coarse-meated, taken in shallow water, and are known as "Reef Trout," or when very large are called "Racers"; they are supposed to follow the schools of whitefish; those of the other form are called "Pot-bellies." **1902** Jordan–Evermann *Amer. Fishes* 204, Lake trout. . . Occasionally individuals, very thin in flesh and sickly-looking, known as "racers" by fishermen are found swimming near the surface; no sufficient cause has been discovered for this condition, as they are no more afflicted with parasites than healthy fish. **1976** *DARE* File Isle Royale **MI,** A racer was a skinny trout with a big head and a skinny body. There was probably a food supply problem. We couldn't find it in later years, but it was frequent in the 1890s [*DARE* Ed: when Inf's father fished], however.

b An Atlantic **salmon B1a** (here: *Salmo salar*). **ME**

1832 Williamson *Hist. ME* 1.159, The *Salmon.* . . stay till the next May, when they return with their young to the sea; these are "the racers" so called. **1950** Everhart *Fishes ME* 20, The majority of the adult fish [=*Salmo salar*] migrate back to the ocean after . . spawning. . . Occasionally one may linger in the river until spring and migrate then at which time they are commonly called "racers" because they are very thin from lack of nourishment during the winter months after spawning. **1975** Gould *ME Lingo* 225, *Racer*—A fresh-water term for a female salmon whose spawning cycle has gone awry. She thins out, and takes on the appearance of going hungry, as if she spent all her time racing about.

3 also *sandhill racer:* A **whiptail** (here: *Cnemidophorus sexlineatus*). Cf **race runner 1**

1909 *DN* 3.365 **eAL, wGA,** *Racer.* . . A small fleet-footed lizard. See *sand-sifter.* **1986** Pederson *LAGS Concordance,* 1 inf, **csMS,** Sandhill racer.

4 =**roadrunner 2.**

1917 *Wilson Bulletin* 29.2.81, *Geococcyx californianus*. . . Local names. . . Racer, rattlesnake-killer, road-runner [etc].

racer snake See **racer 1a, d**

race runner n

1 =**whiptail**, esp *Cnemidophorus sexlineatus*. Cf **race nag, racer 3, roadrunner 2**

1928 Baylor Univ. Museum *Contrib.* 16.13 **TX**, I have heard [*Cnemidophorus*] *gularis* called . . *Black-throated Race-runner* and *Spotted Race-runner* because of its coloration and disposition to "race" with any one pursuing it. **1930** *Copeia* 2.28 **neOK**, *Cnemidophorus gularis gularis* . . Spotted race-runner. . . *Cnemidophorus sexlineatus* . . Race-runner. . . In captivity race-runners feed readily on insects. **1935** Hurston *Mules & Men* 130 **FL** [Black], And de race runner was running so fast to git away from dat coach whip dat his tail got so hot. **1948** *Pacific Discovery* Mar–Apr 10, The big tessellated race runners . . (*Cnemidophorus tessellatus*). . . rushed through the brush, like racing stallions. **1955** Carr–Goin *Guide Reptiles* 261 **FL**, *Cnemidophorus sexlineatus* . . Six-lined Racerunner. . . *General Appearance.*—A slim, fast, athletic, ground-dwelling lizard with a bright eye and stripes. **1979** Behler–King *Audubon Field Guide Reptiles* 561, The Racerunner is most active in the morning, when it can be seen basking or hunting for insects.

2 =**coachwhip snake**. Cf **racer 1d**

1928 Baylor Univ. Museum *Contrib.* 16.15 **TX**, Western Coach-whip Snake—*Masticophis flagellum glavigularis*. . . On account of its . . rapid movements [it is called] . . *Race-runner.*

racetrack n Cf **racehorse 3**

A table game; see quot.

1970 *DARE* (Qu. EE40, . . *Table games* . . *using dice*) Inf **PA245**, Racetrack.

raceweed n Cf **quickweed**

A **galinsoga** (here: *Galinsoga ciliata*).

1959 Gillespie *Compilation Edible Wild Plants WV* 115, Raceweed (*Galinsoga ciliata* . .) Very common in all parts of West Virginia. June to November. . . The young plants are used as potherbs.

race woman See **race man**

rachacha See **racacha**

Rachel and Jacob See **Jacob and Rachel**

racing adj

1907 *DN* 3.248 **eME**, *Racing, adj.* In heat, of a cow.

rack n[1]

1 A cloud, esp a small, dark one that presages rain. [Transf from *rack* a mass of blowing clouds] **chiefly Sth, S Midl, esp Mid Atl**

1939 Hench *Coll.* **NC, TN, VA**, This summer he tested people as to whether they knew the word "rack" with the meaning of small cloud. People from Virginia, Tennessee, and North Carolina did. People from South Carolina did not. **1943** *Ibid* **seVA**, [He] pointed to some big thunder-clouds and said: "Thunder-racks in the north. Rain tomorrow." **1952** *Ibid* **cVA** (as of 1940s), Johnson . . used to live on a farm north of Ivy, Va. The farmer who ran his farm used the word *rack* for *small cloud.* . . "It's going to rain tomorrow. Lots of black racks in the west." **1952** Brown *NC Folkl.* 1.582, *Rack.* . . A small cloud. "Racks are forming in the west; I think we're going to have rain." . . Central and east.

2 also *reck, rock;* in phrr *by (the) rack of (one's) eye* and varr: Using sight and judgment alone, without further rule or guide. [Engl dial *by (the) rack of (the) eye*] **esp Mid Atl coast**

1899 (1912) Green *VA Folk-Speech* 342, *Rack.* . . To be guided in working by the eye, without line or rule. To work by *rack of eye.* **1956** *DE Folkl. Bulletin* 1.24, Reck of eye (eye-reckoning—as in "Jes' did it by reck of eye!") **1963** Brewington *Chesapeake Bay Canoes* 14 **MD**, In the more poorly-built canoes of these regions, the eye alone is used in attaining the form; this is known colloquially as the "winchumsquinchum" method, or "built by rack of eye." **1968** *DARE* (Qu. KK48, *When you work something out as you go, without having a plan or pattern to follow:* "I didn't have anything to go by, so I just did it _____.") Inf **MD36**, From the rack of my mind; **NC76**, By the rock of my eye; **NC79, 82**, (By) the rock of my eye—especially for leveling things; **NC79, 82**, (By) the rock of my eye. **1984** Wilder *You All Spoken Here* 194 **Chesapeake Bay**, Rack

of eye: Chesapeake boat builders' term for building a boat without blueprints; the plans are in one's head. **1997** *DARE* File **eNC**, "By rack of the eye" definitely does occur in Ocracoke and other Outer Banks areas. It was described to me by a 45-year-old carpenter as "normal"—it wasn't even viewed as "dialect." He also said that it could be used to refer to accuracy in terms of time.

rack n[2]

1 also in var combs: A frame placed on a vehicle to hold a large load, as of hay, grain, or short lengths of wood; rarely, a vehicle provided with such a rack. See also **hayrack 1**

1867 *Scientific Amer.* 16.284, Comstock's Lumber Wagon Rack. . . In the rack represented in the engraving the body of the wagon is inclined by means of bolsters of differing heights. **1876** Knight *Amer. Mech. Dict.* 3.1850, Rack. . . A frame to carry hay or grain, placed on a wagongears instead of a box-bed, for hauling in the harvest. . . The device is also placed on a wagon-frame for hauling wood and other materials. **1877** *Harper's New Mth. Mag.* 55.348 **cME coast**, Those were the blessed days when . . the creaking of an infrequent hay cart or wood rack was sufficiently startling to send a whole family to the windows. **1902** (1969) Sears *Catalogue* 715, The Acme Combination Grain, Hay and Stock Rack is the only practical combination rack built. . . A rear end stock gate and a rear hay standard are furnished with each rack. **1925** *Book of Rural Life* 4.2536, The hayrack is usually made on the farm, and the form varies widely with the use and locality. In some places the rack consists simply in a floor with a standard at the front and rear, while in others, sides as well as ends are provided. . . The average rack is about seven feet wide and fourteen feet long, with sides three feet high. **1942** ME Univ. *Studies* 57.133, *Rack.* A sled body for hauling short bolts, as *pulpwood.* **1948** Manfred *Chokecherry* 96 **nwIA**, He stood on one leg, holding the lump of the other above the vibrating, throbbing floor boards of the wooden rack. **1958** McCulloch *Woods Words* 145 **Pacific NW**, *Rack car*—A railroad car specially equipped with stakes or racks to handle pulpwood. **1961** Hall *String Too Short* 50 **NH**, Fifteen of the piles filled the old rack. **1965–70** *DARE* (Qu. L13, *The kind of wagon used for carrying hay:* [. . *special wagon, or frame put on ordinary wagon*]) 15 Infs, **scattered**, Rack; **IL59**, Rack—the rack is made to fit a special wagon; **MD42**, Rack—sides flaring out; both [*DARE* Ed: i.e., this and "flat bottom"] were special frame put on farm wagon; 9 Infs, **chiefly IL**, Rack wagon; **DE5**, Rack wagon—a regular wagon with the box set off and they put this rack on there; **IL65**, Rack wagon—frame put on running gears of wagon; **IA1**, Bale rack; **IA14**, Basket rack—a frame put on a wagon; **CT17, IN53, MI116**, Flat rack; **IA6**, Flat rack—now, all baled, no sides; **KS9**, Flat rack—for bales; hay rack for loose hay; **MN16**, Rack and wagon—years ago; **WY1**, Rack put on wagon or bobsleigh; **MD34**, Farm wagon—some had hay rack, also called straw rack, on it; **IL134**, Wagon rack; **DE1**, Wagon with a flam rack—the rack flammed out—put on regular wagon; **OK14**, Just an ordinary wagon with a rack on it; (Qu. N40b, . . *Sleighs for carrying people*) Inf **MI56**, Rack; (Qu. N41b, *Horse-drawn vehicles to carry heavy loads*) Inf **OH61**, Flatbed wagons with racks; **NY37**, Rack trucks (vehicle had sides with slats on it); **MA42**, Rack wagon. **1966** *DARE* Tape **ME26**, [Inf:] I lumbered. . . I've seen teams come in . . seven cords on once. [FW:] What kind [of] sleds they use? [Inf:] Bobsleds and rack. **1967** *DARE* FW Addit **seOR**, California rack—a horse-drawn freight wagon. **1986** Pederson *LAGS Concordance* (*Hayrack*) 1 inf, **csAL**, A big rack on the wagon—hayrack; 1 inf, **swAL**, Rack—on hay wagon; 1 inf, **nwAR**, Rack—frame on wagon; 1 inf, **cwFL**, Racks—built on wagons to carry wood.

2 also *saw rack, wood* ~; for addit varr see quots 1965–70, 1989: An X- or occas A-shaped frame to hold wood for sawing. **chiefly Sth, S Midl** See Map Cf **jack** n[1] **6**

1948 Davis *Word Atlas Gt. Lakes* app qu 59b, 5 [of 233] infs, **eOH**, Rack. **1949** Kurath *Word Geog.* 59, In the Alleghenies the saw horse is sometimes called a (*wood*) *jack.* In southern Ohio we find *rack, wood rack* in this sense. **1965–70** *DARE* (Qu. L59, *An implement with an X-frame . . to hold firewood for sawing*) 44 Infs, **chiefly Sth, S Midl**, Rack; **MS58**, Racks; 34 Infs, **chiefly Sth, S Midl**, Saw rack; **KY29, OK14, TN16**, Sawing rack; 23 Infs, **chiefly Sth, S Midl**, Wood rack; **NC15**, Wood saw rack; (Qu. L58, *An implement with an A-shaped frame . . that you put boards on to saw them*) 9 Infs, **Sth, S Midl**, Rack; **AL26, GA77, KY86, SC19**, Saw rack; **VA105**, Wood rack. **1966** Dakin *Dial. Vocab. Ohio R. Valley* 2.169, Throughout Kentucky generally, the most common name for the *sawbuck* . . is *wood rack, saw rack*, or simple *rack.* . . [These terms] predominate everywhere except in the north-central section of the state bounded by the lower Kentucky and Green Rivers. . . A few speakers in this area use *rack* or *wood rack* for the rack of Type B [=the A-shaped frame] also. . . North of the river, *rack, wood rack,* and *saw rack* are scattered in the counties along the Ohio from the Big Sandy to Pennsylvania, and in the interior counties of Illinois. **1967** Faries *Word Geog. MO* 85, Several other terms are in scattered use: the North Midland expressions *wood rack* (38 occurrences [among 700 infs]), used predominantly south of the Missouri River and especially in the Southeast Lowland, *rack* (14 occurrences), and *wood jack* (6 occurrences). **1983** *MJLF* 9.1.54 ceKY (as of 1956), *Saw rack* . . a rack for sawing wood. The legs are in the shape of two "X's" with the joining piece attached where the legs cross. *Ibid* 61, *Wood rack* . . a saw rack. **1989** Pederson *LAGS Tech. Index* 83 **Gulf Region,** 81 infs, Rack; 77 infs, Woodrack; 39 infs, Saw rack; 2 infs, Bucksaw rack; 2 infs, Rack for wood; 2 infs, Sawing rack; 1 inf, Cotton [sic, for *cutting*?] rack; 1 inf, Log rack; 1 inf, Rack to saw wood on; 1 inf, Yard rack. [*DARE* Ed: Most of these infs specified that they were referring to the device with X-shaped supports.]

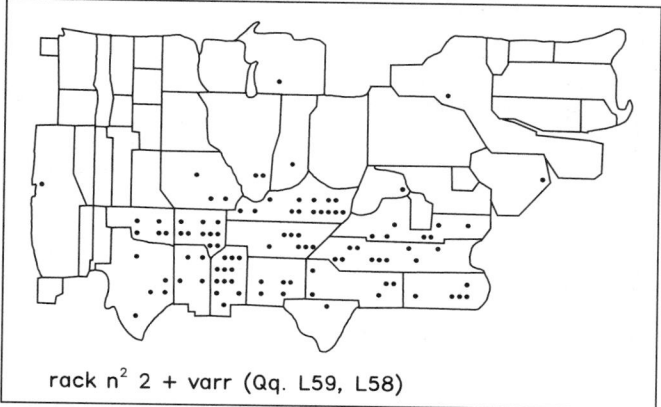

rack n² 2 + varr (Qq. L59, L58)

3 A very thin, bony animal; hence adj *racky.* [*OED2 rack* sb.⁴ 3.b, but here perh conceived as extension of *rack* framework] Cf **hat rack 1, hayrack 5, rack of bones**
  1967–68 *DARE* (Qu. K15, *A thin, bony, or poor-looking cow*) Infs **NJ**10, **SC**43, Rack; (Qu. K44, *A bony or poor-looking horse*) Inf **NJ**29, Rack; **MD**24, Racky.

4 A set of teeth; see quots.
  1968–69 *DARE* (Qu. X13b, *Joking names for false teeth*) Inf **LA**18, Rack—niggers use this; (Qu. DD2, *The portion or quantity of tobacco chewed at one time: "He's always got a big _____ in his cheek."*) Inf **GA**77, He's got a bundle in the rack—always meant chewing tobacco; [(Qu. DD3b, *How . . people take snuff*) Inf **GA**72, Rackin'—put snuff in one's jaw]. **1977** Dillard *Lexicon* 109, Dentists report, for example, that their poor Black patients speak of upper and lower *racks*.

5 A woman's breasts.
  1968–69 *DARE* (Qu. X31, . . *A woman's breasts*) Infs **IN**75, **PA**76, 165, (A) rack. [**1970** *Current Slang* 4.3–4.22 [NM State Univ slang], *Rack.* . . A woman with a large bust.]

rack v¹ Often with *up* scattered exc NEast See Map Cf **rank** v 1, **rick** v
To stack.

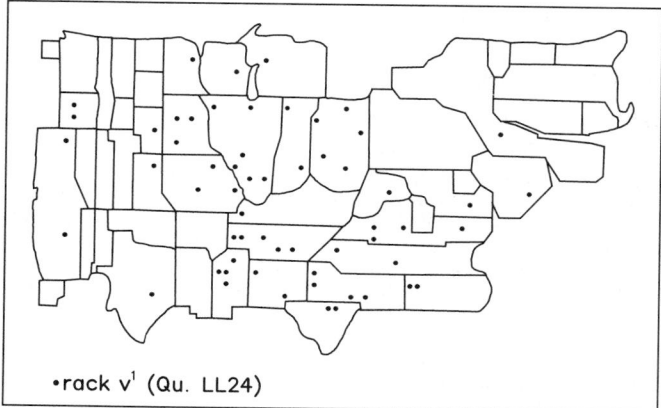

•rack v¹ (Qu. LL24)

1839 (1930) Sewall *Diary* 208 **IL,** Harris and myself racked up about 1500 brick. **1938** Faulkner *Unvanquished* 13 **MS,** Father was everywhere, with a sapling under each arm . . racking the [fence] rails into place while Joby and Loosh were still arguing. **1965–70** *DARE* (Qu. LL24, *To keep firewood neat you have to cut it, split it, and _____ it up*) 59 Infs, **scattered exc NEast,** Rack. **1966** *DARE* Tape **NM**14, Every man is supposed to clean out his plate . . and take it and put it over in the tub. That's what we call rackin' 'em—rack the dishes. **1981** Pederson *LAGS Basic Materials,* 1 inf, **cwTN,** Racked it up—of wood; 1 inf, **cTX,** Stackin' it; rackin' it [=wood].

rack n³ See **hayrack 4**

rack n⁴, v² See **wrack**

rack v³ [From *rack* a gait of a horse] **chiefly S Midl**
Often with adv: To move rapidly, bustle around; to depart, set out.
  1884 *Anglia* 7.268 Sth, S Midl [Black], *To rack off* = to run off. **1903** *DN* 2.326 seMO, *Rack out.* . . To start out. (Humorous.) 'Let's rack out for home.' **1930** [see **Rackensack**]. **1932** Randolph *Ozark Mt. Folks* 269, That's all for t'night, folks—soon as Brother Hamrick says a word o' prayer we'll jest let music rest an' go rackin' 'long home. **1939** Hall Coll. wNC, And we'd rack out next mornin' after them bear. **1953** Randolph–Wilson *Down in Holler* 276 **Ozarks,** *Rack.* . . To move rapidly, to make haste. "I seen Jimmy a-rackin' down the road like the Devil was after him." **1967** *DARE* (Qu. Y29a, *To 'go out' a great deal, not to stay at home much: "She's always _____."*) Inf **LA**2, Racking around; (Qu. Y29b, . . *About a man [who doesn't stay home much]: "He's always _____."*) Inf **LA**2, Racking around. **1967** Williams *Greenbones* 29 **GA** (as of c1910), "You get you some rest while I rack around. In three or four hours I'll send you up some dinner." . . She had told him what she had to do when they reached town: find the local preachers . . , have some handbills printed and hire a couple of small boys to tack them up.

rackabone (horse), rackabones See **rack of bones**

Rackansacker See **Rackensack**

rack barn n
  1966 *PADS* 45.20 cnKY, *Rack barn.* . . A barn in which the rails run the width of the building rather than the length.

Rackensack n Also *Rackensac, Rack-in-sack, Rackin Sack, Rackinsaw* [By metath, redup; cf Intro "Language Changes" I.1, 3] joc
Arkansas; hence n *Rackensack(er)* an Arkansan.
  1841 *Picayune* 10 Jan 2/2 (*Mathews Coll.*), The 'Rackinsaw' man had a 'pint companion' or 'tickler' with him which he wanted filled with whiskey. **1845** in 1912 Thornton *Amer. Gloss.* 2.974, The balance [of the inhabitants of IL] are John Bulls, Paddies, Pukes, Wolverines, . . Hawk Eyes, Rackensacks [etc]. **1845** in 1974 Masterson *AR Folkl.* 182, There's a beautiful land, 'tis a western track,/ And they call it by name "The Rack-in-sack!" **1851** Burke *Polly Peablossom* 192 **AR,** Below Little Rock, our captain . . took on board a tall lathy gentleman. . . I imagine that he held some public office in the "Rackensac" capital. **1906** *DN* 3.152 nwAR, *Rackensack.* . . Arkansas. Facetious metathesis. ["]We're in Rackensack now." *Ibid, Rackensacker.* . . Arkansan. "She and I are both Rackensackers." Facetious. **1930** Holden *Alkali Trails* 65 **wTX** (as of 1886), The roads were full of covered wagons going east. Many of the wagons were conspicuous for the inscriptions crudely written upon the wagon sheets. One said, "In God we trusted; went west and got busted." Another, with more sentiment, had, "Last fall came from Rackin Sack, got sorry and now go rackin back"—a rather dry and cynical thrust at Fate. **1931** Allsopp *Folkl. Romantic AR* 2.87, Some people have referred to Arkansas in a slighting or derisive way as "Rackensack." This sportive nick-name originated through a chance epithet applied in a spirit of anger by a Mississippian many years ago. **1953** Randolph–Wilson *Down in Holler* 276 **Ozarks,** *Rackensack.* . . A derisive name for Arkansas. **1958** Foote *Civil War* 1.279 (as of 1862), McCulloch, the dead-shot former Ranger . . rode among his Texans and Arkansans; "Texicans" and "Rackansackers," they were called—hard-bitten men accustomed to life in the open.

rackerbone See **rack of bones**

rackergaited adj
  1914 *DN* 4.78 **ME, nNH,** *Rackergaited.* . . Loose-jointed.

racket n[1] Also *rackett, racquet(te)* **NEast** Cf **mal de raquette**

A snowshoe or similar device for traversing snow or soft ground.

[**1626** Purchas *Pilgrimes* 5.827, Their Dogs . . haue rackets tyed vnder their feet, the better to runne on the snow.] **1677** Hubbard *Narrative* 2.27 **NEng,** It was not possible for any to have travelled that way, unless they carried *Rackets under their feet,* wherewith to walk upon the *top of the Snow.* **1704** in 1868 NH *Prov. & State Papers* 2.419, They have upwards of 30 pr of Snow Shoes and Racketts already made. **1780** (1899) Parkman *Diary* 199 **MA,** I was drawn by a number of Rackettmen, in a very handsome Sleigh. *Ibid* 207, Another snowstorm . . covers ye Rackett Tracks and fills ye Roads again. **1829** *VA Lit. Museum* 1.460, Rackets. "Snow shoes." *New England.* **1843** (1940) Ferris *Rocky Mts.* 244 **NY,** The snow was now reduced to the depth of a foot, but very soft and saturated with water, so that we sank through almost to the ground at every step, even with our rackets on. **1866** Copeland *Country Life* (5th ed) 740 **MA,** If it is soft the horses should have meadow-shoes, called rackets, to keep them from sinking in. **1890** *Scribner's Mag.* 8.348 **NEng,** When luncheon was over he went off to the stable-yard, where Hampton shod him with the great rackets, four feet in length. [**1897** *Outing* 29.362 **Canada,** When the racquette is fastened the heel and toe are free.] **1942** Peattie *Friendly Mts.* 292, French Canadians in the United States have nearly a hundred local "racquette" clubs scattered throughout New England and New York. **1949** *Boston Globe* (MA) 14 Aug (Fiction Mag.) 2/2, This mysterious stranger . . put on racquets like any bushman and disappeared.

racket n[2] **chiefly Sth, S Midl**

A quarrel, fight, altercation.

1834 *Life Andrew Jackson* 27, The numerous scrapes and rackets it was his honer now tu take a share in got him intu a grate practice . . for the dangers which was comin. **1902** *DN* 2.243 **sIL,** *Racket* . . A violent altercation or personal encounter. **1903** *DN* 2.326 **seMO,** *Racket* . . Disturbance; fight. 'They had a racket at the saloon.' **1906** *DN* 3.122 **sIN,** *Racket* . . Fight; altercation. "They raised a racket nigh the meetin'." **1907** *DN* 3.225 **nwAR,** *Racket* . . A violent altercation or personal encounter. **1909** *DN* 3.361 **eAL, wGA,** *Racket* . . A personal encounter, fight. **1942** McAtee *Dial. Grant Co. IN* 51 (as of 1890s), *Racket* . . quarrel. **1942** Warnick *Garrett Co. MD* 12 **nwMD** (as of 1900–18), *Racket* . . a quarrel. **1956** McAtee *Some Dialect NC* 35, *Racket* . . quarrel. **c1960** *Wilson Coll.* **csKY,** *Racket* . . A noise, a quarrel. **1962** *Mt. Life* 38.4.11 **sAppalachians,** If the "flouter" responds to the thrust of the jaw with a flood of invective that leads to threats of violence frustrated by bystanders who "hold 'em apart," the affair is characterized as a "racket." **1966–70** *DARE* (Qu. Y12a, *A fight between two people, mostly with words*) Inf **KY**51, Racket; (Qu. Y12b, *A real fight in which blows are struck*) Inf **VA**2, A racket; (Qu. KK15, *A disagreement or quarrel: "They had _____ about where the fence was to be."*) Infs **AR**31, **KY**91, **NC**55, **SD**8, **VA**29, A racket. **1967** *DARE* FW Addit **TN**13, Inf used *racket* with the meaning of "argument" in conversation; she said it's very common. **1983** *MJLF* 9.1.52 **ceKY** (as of 1956), *Racket* . . a noisy fight.

racket n[3] [Var of *rocket*]

1624 Smith *Genl. Hist. VA* 60, In the evening we fired a few rackets, which flying in the ayre so terrified the poore Salvages, they supposed nothing vnpossible we attempted. **1845** Thompson *Pineville* 52 **cGA,** "D—n your sky-rackets," said Boss, "who's them?" **1848** Bartlett *Americanisms* 305, Sky-racket. The vulgar pronunciation of *sky-rocket.* **1858** Hammett *Piney Woods Tavern* 114, He shot over across like a sky-racket. **1967** *DARE* FW Addit **nwLA,** Skyracket—arrangement of five cardboard tubes on a block, connected by a fuse. It sends its five exploding charges into the air in turn. This is not the trade name of the particular brand I saw. The boys selling them said, "Some people call 'em skyrackets."

racket store n Also *racket, rackit store* **formerly more widespread; now esp TX** See Map *old-fash*

A variety store.

1832 in c1923 Lamar *Papers* 3.292 **TX,** He gave the necessary order and we rushed on knocking down and running over fences palings other obstructions untill we took possession of Callahans (now Sims) Town the stone House Thorns establishment and Roberts' now raquits store. **1892** *Hist. Rev. York Co.* 47 **PA,** Michael L. Reily, Racket Store. One of the most extensive stores of merchandise in McSherrystown is that of the above. **1894** *Dly. Ardmoreite* (Ardmore, Okla.) 30 April 1 (*advt.*)

(*DA*), The Racket Store. **1905** *DN* 3.91 **nwAR,** Racket (store) . . Bazar [sic]. 'There are two rackets in Springdale.' 'I bought it at the big racket store.' Universal. **1916** *DN* 4.341 **OH, KS, LA,** Racket store . . A five and ten cent store. **1921** (1923) Greer-Petrie *Angeline Seelbach* 22 **eKY,** I'd always thought the Rackit Store up at the county seat was a powerful high building, but I wish you might see some of them thar Chicago houses! **1929** Wolfe *Look Homeward* 316 **NC,** I bought him a cheap pair [of pants] at the Racket Store for every-day wear. **1933** *Hench Coll.* **cVA,** There is in town [=Charlottesville] a store that sells many kinds of goods—shoes, clothing, cloth, curtain material, etc. It is called "The Racket Store." **1939** in Lib. of Congress *Amer. Memory: WPA Life Hist.* (Internet) **SC,** In 1885 I got my first job as clerk in R.C. Davis' Racket Store. The racket store, you know, was the predecessor of the modern five-and-ten-cent store. One could buy anything from a tin cup to a paper of pins, and get it cheap. **1941** Ward *Holding Hills* 188 **IA** (as of early 20th cent), Long ago we had a store of cheap odds and ends; we called this The Racket. **1943** *AN&Q* 3.71, Jefferson Davis Purcell, originator of the early "racket stores," forerunners of the five-and-ten-cent stores, died in Lexington, Kentucky, on June 27. He was associated at one time with a New York City establishment. To avoid the East's high rents, he moved into the South and opened what is said to be the original racket store in Lynchburg, Virginia, in 1883. **1949** *PADS* 11.9 **wTX,** Racket store . . A notion store; a five-and-ten-cent store. **c1955** Reed–Person *Ling. Atlas Pacific NW,* 5 [of c50 infs], Racket store. **1962** Atwood *Vocab. TX* 69, General or variety store. A store that sells various kinds of cheap merchandise goes by a number of names, the most frequent of which is *racket store* . ., although this is steadily losing ground. **1965–70** *DARE* (Qu. U43, . . *The kind of store where most articles cost . . only five or ten cents;* not asked in early QRs) 15 Infs, 13 **TX,** Racket store; **GA**89, Racket store—[they] sell all sorts of things; **PA**234, Racket store—'cause they have everything makes a racket. [14 of 17 Infs old; 9 Infs indicated that this is old-fashioned or obsolete.] **1987** *DARE* File **csTX** (as of c1910), My maternal grandfather J.K. Elkins and his son E.R. Elkins built up a chain of 5–10–25¢ stores in the small towns surrounding Yoakum. In the beginning their first store was called "Elkins Racket Store." **1996** *Ibid* **TX,** In Brownsville, we had an old store, closed by 1950, which was labeled "Racket Store," but we had both a Kress's and a Woolworth's, oddly side by side on the main street, which I and everyone I can recall called "ten-cent stores". *Ibid* **swKS** (as of c1950), As a child, I regularly heard my grandmother use the term "racket store" for *variety store* or *ten-cent store.* My grandmother was born (1884) in central Illinois but grew up and lived her young life on a farm in southwestern Kansas.

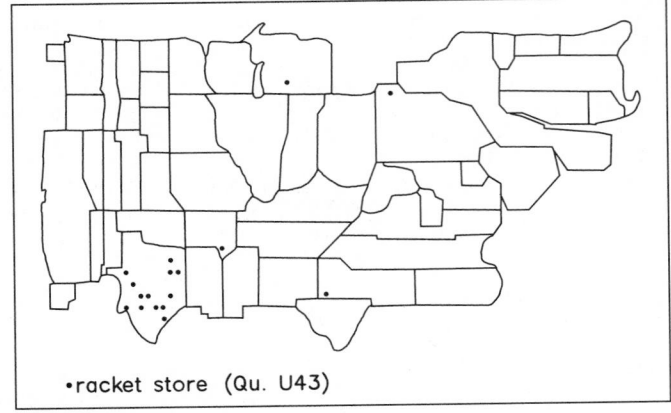

•racket store (Qu. U43)

rackett See **racket** n[1]

rackety adj [Prob var of *rickety*]

Unstable, falling to pieces.

1824 Irving *Tales of a Traveller* 1.55, An old rackety inn, that looked ready to fall to pieces. **1843** *Ladies' Repository* 3.90, Two chairs immediately set, one with the back broken off, the other rackety and unstable. **1878** *Harper's New Mth. Mag.* 57.579 **CT,** Granny Culver's rackety belongings were hustled into the second story. **1945** FWP *Lay My Burden Down* 115 **LA** (as of c1865) [Black], Fort Scott was all run down. . . Just old rackety walls and leaky roofs, and a big pole fence made outen poles sot in the ground all tied together, but it was falling down too. **1968–69** *DARE* (Qu. KK20a, *Something that looks as if it might collapse any minute: "That old shed is certainly _____."*) Infs **IN**68, **MO**37, Rackety; (Qu. KK25, *Something that bends or yields*

easily: "That willow branch is very _____.") Inf **NY**70, Rackety.
1975 Gould *ME Lingo* 225, *Rackety*—Noisy, and also used interchangeably with "rickety" for wobbly, unstable.

rackily See **racklety**

Rack-in-sack, Rackin Sack, Rackinsaw See **Rackensack**

rackit store See **racket store**

racklety adj Also *rackily* Cf Intro "Language Changes" I.8,
raggly, ramshacklety, ricklety
=**rackety.**

  1967–69 *DARE* (Qu. KK20a, *Something that looks as if it might collapse any minute: "That old shed is certainly _____."*) Inf **AR**47, Rackily ['rækəli]; (Qu. KK23, *Weak or unsteady: "I think the footbridge will hold but it is a bit _____."*) Inf **AR**47, Rackily; **MO**37, Racklety.

rack of bones n Also *rackabone (horse), rackabones, rackerbone, rag-a-bones* [Cf *EDD ragabanes, rackle of bones, rickle ~, ruckle ~, ruggle ~*]
A very thin, emaciated person or animal; hence attrib: emaciated; ramshackle.

  [**1804** (1965) Ordway *Jrls.* 128, We Saw the rack of Bones of a verry large fish.] **1854** (1923) Holmes *Tempest & Sunshine* 37 **KY**, Turn that old rackerbone of your'n straight round and turn down that ar street. **1871** (1882) Stowe *Fireside Stories* 135 **MA**, Of all the racks o' bone I ever see, I never see a human critter so poor as he was. **1872** *Galaxy* 13.480, "Who said you didn't?" answered Nan, still speaking with icy deliberation, and still eyeing her rack-o'-bones dwelling. **1884** Baldwin *Yankee School-Teacher* 10 **VA** [Black], An' I'll start up dat pore creetur arter ye. He's nothin' b't a rack o' bones. **1900** *Congressional Record* 33 app 6 Mar 117/2 **NY**, A Western farmer had a college-bred son who went off preaching. . . He came back with an old rackabone. **1903** *DN* 2.300 **Cape Cod MA** (as of a1857), *Rack-o'-bones.* . . A lean horse. **1911** (1912) Lincoln *Cap'n Warren* 140 **MA**, If she fell on that poor rack-o'-bones . . 'twould be the final smash. **1937** Gardner *Folkl. Schoharie* 83 **ceNY**, As he was about to drive on, he saw approaching a black rackabone horse driven by a woman. **1949** *Sat. Eve. Post* 2 Apr 97 **ceMA**, Mount that rack o' bones you call a horse and ride in front o' me. **1950** *WELS* **WI** (*A thin, bony, or poor-looking cow*) 2 Infs, Rack of (*or* a) bones; (*Joking or uncomplimentary names for horses*) 2 Infs, Rack o(f) bones; [2 Infs, Bone rack;] (*A person who is very thin*) 2 Infs, Rack of bones. **1965–70** *DARE* (Qu. K15, *A thin, bony, or poor-looking cow*) 23 Infs, **scattered, but esp N Cent**, Rack of bones; **IL**83, Rag-a-bones; [**NY**84, **VA**24, Bone rack;] (Qu. K44, *A bony or poor-looking horse*) 23 Infs, **scattered, but esp Nth**, Rack of bones; **IL**83, Rag-a-bones; [**IL**11, 69, **PA**23, Bone rack;] (Qu. X49, *. . A person who is very thin*) Infs **SC**24, **TN**67, **WI**27, A rack of bones. [29 of 41 total Infs male]

racktify v Also *ractify, rectify* [Prob varr of **wreck** + **-ify**] **esp SC**
To damage, break down; hence ppl adj *ractified* (pronc-spp *racktify, raptify, rectified*) rickety; mentally disturbed.

  1909 *S. Atl. Qrly.* 8.44 **seSC**, *Rectify* is used to mean *break, to destroy; rectified* to signify *distracted in mind, broken in strength*. **1922** Gonzales *Black Border* 322 **sSC, GA coasts** [Gullah glossary], *Racktify*—to break, breaks, broke, broken, breaking. Confuse in mind: "Da' buggy racktify"—that buggy is dilapidated. "Da' 'ooman racktify een 'e min'"—that woman's mind is distracted. **1950** *PADS* 14.55 **SC**, *Ractify, rectify.* . . To break, damage or destroy; to overthrow the reason, render insane or *ractified*. Probably an extension of *wreck* or *wrack*. **1966** *DARE* (Qu. KK23, *Weak or unsteady: "I think the footbridge will hold but it is a bit _____."*) Inf **SC**10, Raptify ['ræptɪfaɪ].

rack up See **rack** v[1]

rack wagon n **chiefly N Midl, esp cIL** See Map
A wagon with a **rack** n[2] 1.

  1965–70 *DARE* (Qu. L13, *The kind of wagon used for carrying hay: [. . special wagon, or frame put on ordinary wagon]*) Infs **IL**70, 104, 142, **IN**53, **NJ**50, **PA**51, Rack wagon; **DE**5, Rack wagon—a regular wagon with the box set off, and they put this rack on there; **IL**19, Rack wagon—a special wagon; **IL**65, Rack wagon—frame put on running gears of wagon; **IL**80, Rack wagon—one wagon; then there were box wagons used for hauling grain; **IL**108, Rack wagon—frame on ordinary wagon.

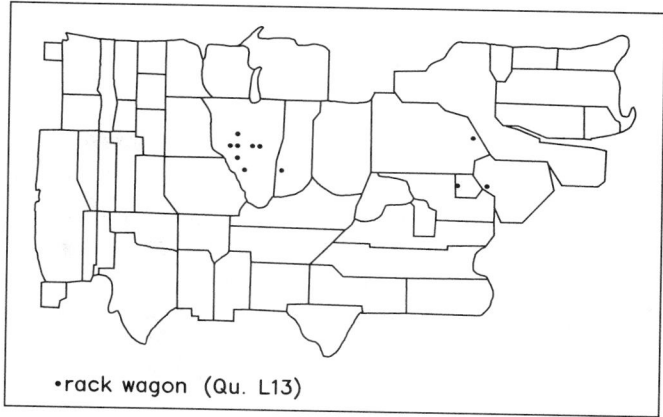

• rack wagon (Qu. L13)

racky See **rack** n[2] 3

racquet(te) See **racket** n[1]

ractified, ractify See **racktify**

raddio See **radio**

raddy See **ready** adj 2

radiator n Usu |'redi,etə(r)|; also **esp PA** |'rædietə(r)|
Std sense, var pronc.

  1943 in 1944 *ADD* **WV**, [Radio:] Flush ['rædietr] several times. **1943** *Ibid* **nWV**, ['ræd]-. **1950** [see **radio**]. **1958** Resp. to *PADS* 29 **csPA**, A few words and expressions which we've heard here in Harrisburg that are new and interesting to us (we are from Massachusetts). . . *rădiator*—this seems to be the usual pronunciation here, rather than the long-a sound which is familiar to me. . . We have heard all these used by both poorly-educated and well-educated people. **1968** *DARE* FW Addit **DE**3, Radiator ['rædi,eɪtə]. **1971** *Today Show Letters* **sePA**, I have found a very reliable indicator of someone from the Philadelphia area is how a person pronounces the word "radiator". Almost without exception, native Philadelphians pronounce the first "a" in radiator as though it were the first "a" in radical. **1982** *Barrick Coll.* **csPA**, Radiator—pron. ['rædietə] . . (as in *rad*ical). **1996** *DARE* File **sePA**, My mother says ['redi,etə]; my father says that Philadelphians say both ['redi,etə] and ['rædi,etə]. **2001** *DARE* File, Radiator—In NYC & environs, the 1st *a* is pronounced as in *fat*.

radical (weed) n
A **horse nettle 1:** usu *Solanum carolinense*, but also *S. dulcamara*.

  1894 *Jrl. Amer. Folkl.* 7.95 **WV**, *Solanum Carolinense,* . . sand-brier, radical. **1930** Sievers *Amer. Med. Plants* 36, *Solanum carolinense.* . . Other common names. . . Radical-weed. [*Ibid* 37, *Part used.*—The ripe berries, carefully dried.] **1959** Carleton *Index Herb. Plants* 97, *Radical-weed:* Solanum dulcamara.

radio n Usu |'redɪ,o|; also |'rædi,o| Pronc-spp *raddio, reddio*
Std sense, var forms.

  1941 Faulkner *Men Working* 84 **MS**, "Well now. Ain't that just dandy. About that raise, I mean," said maw. "And about that raddio too. I've allus wanted one." **1944** *ADD* 491 **cNY** (as of c1928–43), Freq. ['rædio] raddio. **1950** Hubbell *Pronc. NYC* 60, For *radio*, ['rædɪ,ou] may be heard on the uncultivated level although it is not, I think, so common as it was a few years ago. *Radiator*, however, is still often pronounced with [æ] by uncultivated speakers. **1987** Childress *Out of the Ozarks* 39, [A television is] a reddio that gives off pitchers.

‡radio-see-um n
=**dowser 1.**

  1965 *DARE* (Qu. CC13b, *. . The person who knows how to use a forked stick to find water*) Inf **FL**22, Radio-see-um. [FW: The Inf could offer no more on this but insisted on this response.]

radish n Usu |'rædɪš|; also *somewhat old-fash* |'rɛdɪš|; for addit varr see quots Pronc-spp *red(d)ish* [Varr of this type are old in Brit Engl and remain common in dialect speech north of the Thames.]
Std sense, var forms.

1845 in 1952 Green *Samuel Maverick* 291 **SC,** I am yet taking . . horse redish root Parsley root tea, slippery Elm Tea & water mellion seed Tea for the cholick. **1890** *DN* 1.6 c**NY,** The sound [ɛ] instead of [æ] (written *a*) in *catch, radish,* eks (=*axle*). **1893** Shands *MS Speech* 53, *Reddish* [rɛdɪš]. This pronunciation of *radish* is practically universal among the uneducated classes, and is frequently heard in the conversation of the more cultivated. **1899** (1912) Green *VA Folk-Speech* 349, *Reddish.* **1905** *DN* 3.56 e**NE,** Cases where [æ] is likely to become very close, passing into [ɛ], are:—*catch* (*ketch* is very widespread), *radish, rather* and *gather*. **1907** *DN* 3.191 se**NH,** *Horse-reddish.* **1909** *DN* 3.363 e**AL,** w**GA,** *Redish.* **1910** *DN* 3.443 w**NY,** *Horse-reddish.* **1911** *DN* 3.539 e**KY,** *Rădish.* Pronounced rĕddish. **1912** *DN* 3.587 w**IN,** *Reddish.* **1916** *DN* 4.340 e**OH, PA,** *Radish* [rɛdɪš]. **1931** *AmSp* 7.92 e**KY,** The reddishes are purt night big enough to have a mess. **1933** *AmSp* 8.2.44 ne**NY,** In some cases [æ] may be replaced by [ɛ], as in *catch* [kɛtʃ], *radish* [rɛdɪʃ]. **1935** *AmSp* 10.294 **Upstate NY,** Miscellaneous variations between [ɛ] and [æ]. . . *radish* . . 2 [ɛ] . . 33 [æ]. **1936** *AmSp* 11.19 e**TX,** *Catch* and *radish* are often pronounced [kjɛtʃ], ['rɛdɪʃ] in East Texas by the less well educated. **1937** *AmSp* 12.107 e**NE,** Farmers. . . commonly make use of such mispronunciations as *redishes,* . . *punkins,* and *batadoes.* **1950** *WELS Suppl.* ce**WI,** *Radish*—reddish, used occasionally. **1961** Kurath–McDavid *Pronc. Engl.* 140, In cultivated speech *radish* has the vowel /æ/ . . , except for a few scattered instances. . . The vowel /ɛ/ . . predominates decisively in the folk speech of the Eastern States, except in parts of New England, being in nearly universal use in the South and South Midland. . . Only a few elderly cultured speakers have retained it. Several informants along the South Carolina coast say [radɪš]. The social dissemination of the variants clearly shows a trend toward /æ/ in common speech, except perhaps in some rural sections. **1968** *DARE* FW Addit **NY70,** Radishes ['rɛdɪšəs]. **1973** *PADS* 60.42 se**NC,** *Radish.* . . Among our informants, seven said /æ/, two said /æ/ slightly raised, while three still said /ɛ/. **1976** Allen *LAUM* 3.277 (as of c1950), Three-fourths of the U[pper] M[idwest] infs. have /æ/ as the stressed vowel in *radish.* . . /rɛdɪš/ appears as a strong minority pronunciation in southern Minnesota and in the Midland speech territory of Iowa and Nebraska, where it is more common among the less educated than with Type II [=mid-aged, with approx hs educ] speakers. As is true in the East, the trend seems to be toward /æ/. **1991** Pederson *LAGS Social Matrix* 141, [Statistics for the responses ['rɛdɪš(ɪz), given by 170 infs, show a strong bias towards older, less educated, and lower class infs.]

rael See **real** adj, adv

raft n [Prob after assim of final [t], the pl form was remodeled by analogy with *calf/calves* and *half/halves.*] Cf **shaft**
Std sense, var forms. Pl: usu *rafts;* also *raves* [rævz].
  1903 *DN* 2.352 **MN,** *Raft* . . pl. raves [rævz]. The plural so pronounced by lumbermen in the northwest.

raft duck n [*raft* a large congregation of floating wildfowl] Cf **drift fowl**
Any of var ducks that typically congregate on the water in large numbers, as:
a One or more of the **scaups,** esp the **greater scaup, lesser scaup, redhead 1a(1),** or **ring-necked duck.**
[**1709** (1967) Lawson *New Voyage* 153, Raft-Fowl includes all the sorts of small Ducks and Teal, that go in Rafts along the Shoar, and are of several sorts, that we know no Name for.] **1824** Latham *Genl. Hist. Birds* 10.302, Scaup Duck [=*Anas Marila*] . . is known in Georgia, and called by some the Raft Duck. [Footnote:] But the Raft Duck, truly so called is another species. *Ibid* 352, Raft Duck. *Anas fuligula* [*DARE* Ed: here =*Aythya collaris*]. . . round the middle of the neck a deep chestnut collar about an inch in breadth. **1856** *Porter's Spirit of Times* 13 Dec 242/2, Of ducks, the most numerous, at this season, are the scaups, *Fuligula Marila,* known . . in Virginia as the "raft duck." **1872** Coues *Key to N. Amer. Birds* 289, *Greater Scaup Duck. Big Black-head. Blue-bill. Raft Duck* [etc]. . . *Lesser Scaup Duck. Little Black-head* (with other names of the foregoing). Extremely similar; smaller. **1888** Trumbull *Names of Birds* 51, [*Aythya americana*]. From Pamlico Sound [NC] to South Carolina commonly known as the *Red-Headed Raft-Duck.* **1897** *Auk* 14.286 **LA,** *Ring-necked Duck.—*Known as *Canard noir* and Raft-duck. **1898** Elliot *Wild Fowl* 156, The Red Head . . is a deep-water Duck and keeps out in the center of rivers or lakes, congregating at times in such numbers as to form immense rafts; hence it is sometimes called "Raft Duck." **1903** Dawson *Birds OH* 604, *Aythya marila.* . . *Raft Duck.* . . The larger bodies of water inland . . are resorted to in

much greater numbers than are the smaller waters. A large duck loves large water. **1919** Pearson et al. *Birds NC* 54, Currituck Sound supports during the winter months more wildfowl, perhaps, than any other equal area in eastern North America. . . [S]uch raft-ducks as Lesser Scaup, and Redhead pass the winter there in incredible numbers. . . On Pamlico and Core sounds. . . [t]he raft-ducks . . are mostly Redhead and Scaup, with large numbers of Scoters, Mergansers, Buffleheads, Old Squaws, Lesser Scaup, and a few of the fresh-water ducks. **1955** *Oriole* 20.1.4 **GA,** *Ring-necked Duck.* . . *Raft Duck* (from its assembling on the water in dense flocks, suggesting rafts). . . *Greater Scaup.* . . *Raft Duck.* . . *Lesser Scaup.* . . *Raft Duck, Little Raft Duck.* . . *Ruddy Duck.* . . *Raft Duck* (see note on that term under Ring-necked Duck). **1975** Johnsgard *Waterfowl N. Amer.* 347, The "rafting" behaviour of migrant and wintering scaup is well known and is indicated by their vernacular names—"raft duck," "flock duck," and "troop duck." **2001** *WI Nat. Resources* Feb 14, Scaup go by a number of different monikers in addition to "bluebill." Other common names include the mussel duck, black head . . and raft duck.
b =**ruddy duck.**
  1955 [see **1a** above].
c =**eider duck.**
  1955 MA Audubon Soc. *Bulletin* 39.376 **MA,** *American Eider.* . . Raft Duck. . . From its assembling in dense flocks on the water.

raft tide n [**tide**]
A period of high water that allows rafts of logs to be floated downstream.
  1915 *DN* 4.188 sw**VA,** *Raft tide.* . . Tide sufficient to float rafts. **1976** Garber *Mountain-ese* 73 s**Appalachians,** The loggers are waitin' fer raft-tide to market their logs.

rag n[1]
1 in phrr *take the rag off(en) the bush, take the rag off,* and varr: See below. [Perh in ref to a feat of rifle-shooting (cf quot 1843 at **1a** below), but cf *EDD take the rag off the edge* (at *rag sb.*[1] 1.(6)) "to surpass, arouse admiration."]
a To surpass all others, be outstanding; to be astonishing or outrageous, be the last straw.
  1810 in 1924 Austin *Papers* 1.176, Dr. J.W. takes the rag off the bush a door below your old place of residence. **1810** Norfolk (Va.) *Gazette* 19 Sept. 2/3 (1939 Thornton *Amer. Gloss.*), This "takes the rag off the bush" so completely, that we suppose we shall hear no more . . about the Chesapeake business. **1837** *Davy Crockett's Almanack Wild Sports of West* 1.iii.40 (*OED*2), I can take the rag off—frighten the old folks—astonish the natives—and beat the Dutch all to smash. [**1843** (1916) Hall *New Purchase* 108 **IN,** And without question, then and there [=at a rifle-shooting match] was present every chap in the settlements that could split a bullet on his knife blade or take the rag off the bush.] **1844** Stephens *High Life in NY* 1.56, Wal, . . if this don't take the rag off the bush!—cousin Mary's got to gadding about so much, that she has to send round word when she is a going to stay at hum one evening. **1859** Taliaferro *Fisher's R.* 86 nw**NC** (as of 1820s), That takes the rag off uv the bush. **1923** (1946) Greer-Petrie *Angeline Steppin'* 34 cs**KY,** We could have a dance that would *simply take the rag offen the bush.* **1929** *AmSp* 5.20 **Ozarks,** *Take th' rag off 'n th' bush.* . . A jocular expression denoting profound astonishment. One of my neighbors greeted his first airplane with: "Gawd dam'! Don't thet 'ar take th' rag off'n the bush?" **1930** *DN* 6.84 c**SC,** *To take the rag off the bush.* . . To pass the limit of what is acceptable, morally, socially, etc. "He took the rag off the bush when he went to preaching drunk." Common. **1933** Williamson *Woods Colt* 107 **Ozarks,** They've walked on towards the church-house, leavin' the woods colt behind, a-starin' and a-shakin' like a fool. By Gawd, that shore takes the rag off the bush! **1942** Perry *Texas* 134, If you were visiting in a Texas home and a transient jackass entered the living room, ate all the flowers out of the vases, and then quietly departed, your host, after a moment of utter bewilderment, might remark, "Well, that *does* take the rag off the bush." **1954** *AmSp* 29.228 cw**NJ,** [He] described a series of grievances, and introduced the last, the final, one with, 'But what *really* swiped the rag off the bush. . . ' **1965–70** *DARE* (Qu. GG22b, *When you have come to the end of your patience . . "Well, that certainly _____."*) Infs **GA36, MN2, MO4, NJ8, OH18,** 61, **TX81,** Takes the rag off the bush; **NH17,** Takes a rag off the bush; [**KY50,** Puts the rag on the bush;] (Qu. GG20, . . *'Very much surprised': "When those two got married, I was certainly _____."*) Inf **VA31,** That certainly takes the rag off the bush; (Qu. GG22a, *When you have come to the end of your patience . . "Well that's the _____."*) Inf **TX5,** Takes the rag off the bush; (Qu. NN7, *Exclamations of surprise: "They're getting married*

next week? Well, _____.") Inf **TX**81, Wouldn't that take the rag off the bush. **1991** *DARE* File e**VA**, "Well, if that don't *take the rag off the bush*" means something contrary to the expected has happened.

b To behave in a loud and unrestrained fashion, "carry on."

1953 Randolph–Wilson *Down in Holler* 291 **Ozarks**, *Take the rag off the bush.* . . Dean E.H. Criswell tells me that in Dade County, Mo., it means "to rant, rave or carry on in an exaggerated manner." When a farmer's daughter got into trouble with a drummer, her father "sure did take the rag off'n the bush." **1967** *DARE* (Qu. FF18, *Joking words . . about a noisy or boisterous celebration or party: "They certainly _____ last night."*) Inf **TN**13, Took the rag off.

2 in phrr *take the rag off* (or *off of, offen, over*) and varr: To beat, surpass.

1833 *New Engl. Mag.* 5.81, Then we 'll go without him, says the General, for I don't allow no man to take the rag off of you nor me. **1855** Haliburton *Nature* 1.37 **CT**, How often have I laughed over the fun of the forecastle . . and . . I would back that place for wit against any barroom in New York or New Orleans, and I believe they take the rag off of all creation. **1858** Hammett *Piney Woods Tavern* 115 **CT**, I swan to man ef it didn't take the rag off of any picter in creation I ever see. **1858** *Harper's New Mth. Mag.* 16.281, A number of farmers were . . telling stories about their work, . . when one of them took the rag off the whole of them by relating his experience. **1865** Sedley *Marian Rooke* 103 **CA**, I guess Sacramenty and Frisky'll have to take the rag off the Bar [=a settlement]. **1870** *Punchinello* 1.396, I've clumb some pretty tall hills in my day, . . but that 'ere gettin' up them stairs jest switches the rag off of all on 'em. **1898** Lloyd *Country Life* 183 **AL**, As a quitter I reckon maybe Lige Runnels would take the rag and pull up the bush over any man in the Rocky creek settlement. **1903** *DN* 2.333 se**MO**, *Take the rag off.* . . To excel; to outshine. 'She takes the rag offen anything in our settlement.'

3 Used in var phrr referring to menstruation; hence v (phr) *rag (it)* to menstruate; vbl n *ragging*. [*rag* a sanitary napkin]

1948 *Word* 4.183, The most consistent term used by . . men . . is *the rag*, or *she's got the rag on.* This men's term, interestingly, reflects the material culture of over twenty-five years ago. **1948** *AmSp* 23.249, *Riding the rag*, menstruating. **1965–70** *DARE* (Qu. AA27, . . *A woman's menstruation*) 15 Infs, **scattered**, (She's) got the rag on; 12 Infs, **scattered**, (She's) on the rag; 9 Infs, **scattered**, Wearing (*or* riding) the rag; **CT**29, **NJ**8, **NY**80, 87, **PA**245, (She) has the rag on; **CT**31, **MA**6, **NY**2, 102, (Putting the) rag on; **CA**36, **GA**84, **PA**76, Rag time; **LA**20, 25, Rags; **IL**21, Ragging; **KY**10, Ragging time; **MI**118, Ragging it; **NH**18, She got the rag on; **NY**241, Got a rag on; **PA**216, Rag's on; **SC**69, Her rag; **VA**54, On a rag. [**1967** *Current Slang* 2.1.5, *On the rag.* . . In a bad mood. . . College males, Arizona—I had a lousy time last night because she was *on the rag*.] **1970** *DARE* FW Addit **OH**97, *On the rag*, meaning a woman's menstruation. **1971** *AmSp* 46.82 **Chicago IL**, Menstrual period: . . *wearing the rag . . rag time . . ragging. . .* sanitary napkin: . . *rag*. **1978** *MJLF* 4.1.38 c**TX**, Euphemisms for menstruation—They also used terms suggestive of feminine hygiene products: "on the rag."

4 By ext; in phr *get the rag out* and varr: to hurry; to start working. *somewhat old-fash*

1927 *AmSp* 2.366 cw**WV**, *Take the rag out* . . stop loafing. "Take the rag out and do a day's work, boys." **1965–70** *DARE* (Qu. A20, *Joking ways of telling somebody to hurry*) 9 Infs, **scattered**, Get the rag out; **GA**30, Get the rag out and let's go; **MI**109, **PA**29, 233, **SC**32, Get the rag out of your ass; **MI**105, Get the rag out; (Qu. A19, *Other ways of saying "I'll have to hurry": "I'm late, I'll have to _____."*) Infs **FL**35, **WA**17, Get the rag out; (Qu. JJ26, *If somebody has been doing poor work or not enough, the boss might say, "If he wants to keep his job he'd better _____."*) Infs **NC**30, **NJ**1, **WA**30, Get the rag out; (Qu. KK29, *To start working very hard: "He was slow at first but now he's really _____."*) Inf **TN**1, Got the rag out. [14 of 17 total Infs old] **1997** *DARE* File cn**OH** (as of 1920s), *Get the rag out*, as I know it from workmen (factory or other manual jobs) is a *men's* phrase, usually imperative, said by a foreman or boss, and refers to a menstrual "rag." The whole phrase . . is *Get the rag out of your ass!*—which means "Don't pretend to be in no condition to work. Don't shirk. Be a man!"

5 See **rag house.**

6 in phr *have a rag to pick*: =**crow to pick, have a.**

1968 *DARE* (Qu. KK14, *Something that people disagree about: "I have a _____ to pick with you."*) Inf **PA**108, Rag.

7 See quot.

1942 McAtee *Dial. Grant Co. IN* 51 (as of 1890s), *Rag* . . scum that forms on boiled milk.

8 A paper dollar. [Perh from the earlier use of *rag(s)* as derogatory terms for paper money in general]

1929 *AmSp* 4.358, Other terms for money . . *rag*, a dollar. **1935** *AmSp* 10.19 (as of c1900) [Criminal argot], *Rag*. A paper dollar. Modern *ace* or *buck*. *Rags*. Paper money. (Obs.) **1939** *AmSp* 14.240 [Hotel slang], *Rag*. Dollar tip; one who tips a dollar. **1967** *DARE* (Qu. U26, *Names or nicknames . . for a paper dollar*) Inf **IA**8, A rag.

9 See quot.

1970 *DARE* (Qu. J5, *A cat with fur of mixed colors*) Inf **VA**105, Rag.

rag v[1] Also with *on* [*OED2 rag* v.[2] "*dial.* and *slang*"; 1.b 1808 →]

To tease, harass, annoy; to engage in teasing.

1900 *DN* 2.54 **NJ** [College slang], *Rag*. . . To tease, banter. **1905** *DN* 3.91 nw**AR**, *Rag*. . . To tease. 'The boys ragged him and he got mad at 'em.' Universal. **1952** *New Yorker* 8 Mar 34 **NC**, Sometimes we'd rag one another in the rough, gloves-off manner that is safe only for friends. **1966–69** *DARE* (Qu. Y7, *When one person never misses a chance to be mean to another or to annoy another: "I don't know why she keeps _____ me all the time!"*) Inf **AL**3, Ragging; (Qu. GG3, *To tease: "See those big boys trying to _____ [that little one]."*) Infs **GA**44, 74, **MS**1, **NY**202, **VA**33, Rag. **1972** *Atlanta Letters* **AL**, I, an Alabaman and true Southerner, married a yankee and I have always been kidded about my "Southern expressions." Some pet ones are: . . Being "ragged"—means being kidded about something. **1985** *Los Angeles Times* (CA) 26 Aug, "Ballarag," she notes, "has been shortened to *rag*, as in, 'Mother, don't *rag* on me—I've had a bad day.'"

rag v[2] See **rag** n[1] 3

rag n[2] [*EDD rag* sb.[4] 4 "A disturbance, . . a dispute, quarrel"; *SND* n.[2] I.1 "A disturbance, a noisy dispute"]

A fight.

1968 *DARE* (Qu. Y12b, *A real fight in which blows are struck*) Inf **PA**94, Rag.

rag-a-bones See **rack of bones**

Rag Alley See **Rag Town**

rag baby n

A rag doll.

1809 in 1853 U.S. Congress *Debates & Proc.* 19.1165 **MA**, If they insist upon dressing up, in their own way, their rag-babies, and will shake and beat them about for their own amusement, it is not for me to interfere. **1848** *Ladies' Repository* 8.75 **NEng**, Susy . . made them a rag-baby's head [for a scarecrow], and Jim put his old hat on it. **1859** (1931) DeLong *Jrls.* 10.49 **NY**, Was in the House after waking up and finding a big rag baby in bed with me. **1887** (1967) Harris *Free Joe* 103 **GA**, She'll be a-yerkin' me aroun' thereckly like I wuz a rag-baby. **1894** in 1941 Warfel–Orians *Local-Color Stories* 741 s**AR**, With elaborate apologies for the state of her cabin, which was indeed strewn with trash, improvised rag babies, and pallets, she proceeded to wipe off a chair with her apron. **1899** (1912) Green *VA Folk-Speech* 343, *Rag-baby*. . . A doll made entirely of rags or scraps of cloth, usually in a very artless manner. **1900** *New Engl. Mag.* 22.19, Girls who crave the luxuries of a doll's wardrobe, would not care for the rag babies . . which these children value. **c1960** *Wilson Coll.* cs**KY**, *Rag-baby*. . . Rag-doll.

rag bee n

A work party in which the participants make new articles from old pieces of cloth.

1942 Whipple *Joshua* 504 **UT** (as of c1860), He . . went about with his head above such things as ladies' rag-bees. **1968** *DARE* (Qu. H70, *When people bring baked dishes, salads, and so forth to a meeting-place and share them together, that's a _____ meal*) Inf **NY**69, A bee might be any kind of bee—a rag bee, where ladies sewed carpet rags.

rag bread n Cf **rag muffin, ~ toast**

A confection made from small pieces or scraps of pie dough; see quots.

1996 *DARE* File **PA**, A coworker from Pennsylvania mentioned some kind of "rag bread" which is basically pie dough rolled flat, cut into strips, buttered and cooked on top of a Franklin stove, and at some point rolled into little cylinders. *Ibid* cs**PA**, I still make rag bread—although in my family's version (Adams County, PA) it's what you do with the trimmings of pie crust . . , and they're not only buttered, but we sprinkle cinnamon sugar on them and bake them alongside the pies.

rag building (or bungalow) See **rag house**

rag-chewing vbl n, n Pronc-sp *rag-chawing* Also *rag-chewing contest, ~ match* [Cf *chew the rag*] Cf **chewing match**
Arguing; a protracted discussion, conversation, or argument.
1885 *Santa Fe Weekly New Mexican & Live Stock Jrl.* (NM) 1 Oct 1/3, After a few minutes rag-chawing a verdict of "came to his death from unknown causes," is promptly rendered. **1904** Hobart *I'm from MO* 66, The news of the proposed joint debate spread like wildfire, and it soon became patent that whoever won the rag-chewing contest would also win the election. **1919** Kyne *Capt. Scraggs* 226 **CA,** It's agin the rules to have rag-chewin' and backbitin' on the *Maggie II*. **1950** WELS **WI** (*Joking words for a meeting where there is a lot of talking*) 2 Infs, Rag-chewing contest; 1 Inf, Rag-chewing match; 1 Inf, Rag-chewing. **1966** Barnes–Jensen *Dict. UT Slang* 35, Rag chewing . . long argumentative talk. **1966–67** DARE (Qu. KK12, *A meeting where there's a lot of talking:* "They got together yesterday and had a real _____.") Infs **NC41, SC32,** Rag-chewing; **CA33,** Rag-chewing—gossip; **SC21,** Rag-chewing contest.

Rag City See **Rag Town**

rag damp adj phr Cf **high** adj **B1**
Of tobacco that is curing: so moist as to be limp.
1967 Key *Tobacco Vocab.* 54 **CT,** Tobacco will not dampen unless the thermometer is over 40 . . we figure 60 . . and then it'll come down. If it goes too high, if it goes up higher than that, it gets rag damp, then we can't take it down.

rageous adv [Cf *EDD rageous* adj. "Outrageous; angry, furious"]
Furiously, extremely.
1969 DARE (Qu. GG40, *Words or expressions meaning violently angry*) Inf **GA77,** Rageous mad.

ragesome See **-some**

ragfish n [See quots 1881, 1911]
A marine fish (*Icosteus aenigmaticus*) of the Pacific coast.
[**1881** *U.S. Natl. Museum Proc. for 1880* 3.65, Entire body characterized by a lack of firmness, as it [=*Icosteus ænigmaticus*] can be doubled up as readily as a piece of soft, thick rag.] **1911** *Century Dict. Suppl.,* *Rag-fish.* . . A fish of the genus *Icosteus,* found on the shores of California, remarkable for its flat, flabby body. **1932** *Copeia* 32.65, The ragfish is a frequent visitor in Puget Sound. **1991** Amer. Fisheries Soc. *Common Names Fishes* 63, *Icosteus aenigmaticus* . . P[acific] . . ragfish.

ragged-ass(ed) See **raggedy-ass(ed)**

ragged breeches n
=**cat's-breeches.**
1937 U.S. Forest Serv. *Range Plant Hdbk.* W98, Ballhead waterleaf is also known as . . ragged breeches. It is a low, perennial herb with . . deeply-lobed, long-stalked, hairy leaves.

ragged cup n [See quot 1914] Cf **Indian cup 1**
Either of two **rosinweeds:** usu **cup plant 1,** rarely *Silphium laciniatum.*
1817 Eaton *Botany* 96, [*Silphium*] *perfoliatum,* (ragged cup). **1854** King *Amer. Eclectic Dispensatory* 873, *Silphium Perfoliatum.* Indian Cup-plant. . . also known by the name of *Ragged Cup*. **1914** Georgia *Manual Weeds* 449, *Silphium perfoliatum.* . . Ragged Cup. . . Leaves opposite, . . coarsely toothed, . . and forming rather deep cups which retain dew and rain. **1931** Harned *Wild Flowers Alleghanies* 568, *Silphium perfoliatum.* . . This rough, coarse plant is. . . called, also, Ragged Cup. **1959** Carleton *Index Herb. Plants* 97, *Ragged cup:* Silphium laciniatum.

ragged fringed orchid (or orchis) See **ragged orchid**

ragged gut n
Appar a wild green; see quot.
1982 Slone *How We Talked* 47 **eKY** (as of c1950), Ragged gut. [DARE Ed: in a list of "salet" plants]

ragged lady n
1 =**fennel-flower.** Cf **lady-in-a-chaise 2, lady-in-the-green, ragged sailor 3**
1847 Wood *Class-Book* 149, N[igella] damascena. . . A hardy annual . . to which have been applied the gentle names of "ragged lady," "devil in a bush," &c. **1892** *Jrl. Amer. Folkl.* 5.91 **WI,** *Nigella Damascena.* . . Ragged lady. **1900** Lyons *Plant Names* 261, *Nigella.* . . *Damascena.* . . Ragged Lady.
2 A **cornflower 1** (here: *Centaurea cyanus*).
1855 *Ladies' Repository* 15.555 **CT,** Violets and bluebells nestled lovingly at the feet of the aristocracy. Soldiers in green flirted with ragged ladies. **1898** (1899) Earle *Home Life* 442 **MA,** Our bachelor's-buttons are ragged sailors in a neighboring state; they are corn-pinks in Plymouth, ragged ladies in another town, blue bottles in England, but cyanus everywhere.

ragged orchid n Also *ragged (fringed) orchis, ~ fringed orchid, ~-lip'd orchis* [See quots]
A **fringed orchid** (here: *Platanthera lacera*).
1814 Bigelow *Florula Bostoniensis* 206, *Ragged Orchis.* . . *Orchis lacera.* . . This is our most common species. . . Lip of the nectary reflexed, divided into three narrow, wedge shaped segments, fringed at the end. **1832** MA Hist. Soc. *Coll.* 2d ser 9.153 **cwVT,** [Orchis] lacera, Ragged-lip'd orchis. **1901** Lounsberry *S. Wild Flowers* 78, Ragged orchid . . grows at times as high as two feet. . . The flowers measure about an inch long and when young are of a vivid, intense green. **1912** Mathews *Amer. Wild Flowers* 90, *Ragged Fringed Orchis.* . . *This* orchis is a thing of "shreds and tatters." **1948** Wherry *Wild Flower Guide* 34, *Habenaria lacera.* . . Also known as the *Ragged Orchid* in reference to the strikingly fringed lip divisions. **1966** DARE Wildfl QR Pl.39B Inf **MI7,** Ragged fringed orchid. **1979** Niering–Olmstead *Audubon Guide N. Amer. Wildflowers E. Region* 658, Ragged Fringed Orchid. . . Whitish-green or creamy-yellow flowers with *highly-lacerated, 3-parted lip petals* are in spike-like clusters. [*Ibid* 659, At least 10 other greenish-flowered species occur in our range [=the eastern half of the US], but none with the lip so fringed.]

ragged out See **rag out**

ragged robin n
1 A campion, usu *Lychnis flos-cuculi.* [OED2 1741 →; see quot 1902] For other names of this sp see **Indian paintbrush 5, ~ pink 7**
1822 Eaton *Botany* 343, [*Lychnis*] *flos-cuculi* (ragged robin . .) petals torn: capsule 1-celled, roundish. **1857** Gray *Manual of Botany* 60, *Lychnis.* . . Cockle. Ragged Robin. . . The cottony covering of such species as the L. coronaria of our gardens . . [has] been used for wicks. **1902** (1909) Mathews *Field Book Amer. Wild Flowers* 122, Ragged Robin. . . The pink, or crimson, or light violet petals of the ragged-looking flowers are deeply cut into four lobes each. . . Common in wet and waste ground, from Me., south to N.J., and southwest to Penn. **1935** (1943) Muenscher *Weeds* 229, Ragged Robin. . . Locally common in the middle Atlantic states. . . Petals 5, red. **1968** DARE (Qu. S11) Inf **WI50,** Ragged robin—not wild, not the same as cornflower. **1976** Bailey–Bailey *Hortus Third* 688, [*Lychnis*] *Flos-cuculi.* . . Raggedrobin. . . Petals deep rose-red or white. . . Naturalized from Que. to Penn.
2 also *raggedy robin, raggety ~:* A **cornflower 1,** usu *Centaurea cyanus.* **chiefly Sth, Midl** Cf **ragged lady 2, ~ sailor 4, raggedy Ann 2**
1849 Howitt *Our Cousins in OH* 94, Florence had in her garden . . larkspurs and ragged-robins. **1896** *Jrl. Amer. Folkl.* 9.191 **OH, MD,** *Centaurea Cyanus,* . . ragged robin, Ohio, Baltimore, Md. **1911** Porter *Harvester* 302 **IN,** For the living room, she used wild ragged robins in the blue bowl. **1929** Bell *Some Contrib. KS Vocab.* 170, *Cornflower.* . . A blue flower, sometimes called *ragged robin,* cultivated in Kansas. . . Sometimes erroneously called *bachelor's buttons.* **1949** WELS Suppl. **WI,** The term "bachelor's buttons" is used for the compact yellow or white little flower, as well as for the "ragged robin" hereabouts. **1960** Williams *Walk Egypt* 128 **GA,** The world was full of small winds. . . Ragged-robin stirred indigo and mauve and white, and dusty miller bloomed in white patches. **1965–70** DARE (Qu. S11, . . *Bachelor's button*) 67 Infs, **chiefly Sth, Midl,** Ragged robin(s) [DARE Ed: Some of these Infs may refer instead to other senses.]; **CA40,** Ragged robin or blue cornflower—Missouri; **DC2,** Cornflower or ragged robin . . grows wild, looks like cultivated bachelor's button, summer; some call it bach-

elor's button; **MD**17, Cornflower, ragged robin—same thing, deep blue; **OH**78, Bachelor's button, cornflower, ragged robin—we use all three equally; **IN**14, 30, **KY**56, Raggedy robin; (Qu. S3, *A flower like a large violet with a yellow center and small ragged leaves—it comes up early in spring on open, stony hilltops*) Infs **KS**1, **MI**92, **NC**14, **OH**56, **PA**162, Ragged robin; (Qu. S26e, *Other wildflowers not yet mentioned; not asked in early QRs*) Inf **SC**67, Ragged robin—not the same thing [as bachelor's button]—a *wild* flower; **VA**25, Raggety robin; (Qu. S23, *Pale blue flowers with downy leaves and cups that come up on open, stony hillsides in March or early April*) Inf **PA**26, Ragged robin; (Qu. S26a, . . *Wildflowers. . . Roadside flowers*) Inf **IN**32, Ragged robin. **1968** *DARE* Tape **IN**14, Then I have a bed of ragged robins . . or some of the older people call them chimney corner pinks, of all colors.

3 A **farewell-to-spring** (here: *Clarkia pulchella*).   **NW** Cf **raggedy Ann 3**

1937 St. John *Flora SE WA & ID* 272, *Clarkia pulchella*. . . *Deer Horn; Ragged Robin*. . . Petals . . lavender to purple with lighter veins. . . Open or rocky places, abundant. **1963** Craighead *Rocky Mt. Wildflowers* 120, *Clarkia pulchella*. . . Ragged-robin. . . During a favorable season it will flower so profusely that entire hillsides are given a pinkish cast. **1966–67** *DARE* (Qu. S3, *A flower like a large violet with a yellow center and small ragged leaves—it comes up early in spring on open, stony hilltops*) Inf **WA**12, Ragged robin; (Qu. S11) Inf **WA**8, Ragged robin; **WA**24, Ragged robin—different from bachelor's button—cerise-colored flower, like carnation. **1966** *DARE* FW Addit **WA**10, *Clarkia pulchella*—deerhorn; ragged robin. Clarkia—named by discoverer Lewis for Clark. **1979** Spellenberg *Audubon Guide N. Amer. Wildflowers W. Region* 627, In the . . Beautiful Clarkia (*C[larkia] pulchella*), sometimes called Deerhorn Clarkia or Ragged-robin Clarkia, from southern British Columbia to southeastern Oregon and east to western Montana, the middle lobe of each petal is twice as wide as the side ones.

4 A **wild carrot** (here: *Daucus carota*).

1950 *WELS* (*Other names in your locality for Queen Anne's lace*) 1 Inf, **WI**, Wild carrot, ragged robin.

5 =**chicory 1**. Cf **ragged sailor 2**

1968 *DARE* (Qu. S11, . . *Bachelor's button*) Inf **MD**23, Ragged robin—different plant [from bachelor's button]—tall with blue flowers.

ragged sailor n

1 =**prince's-feather 1**.

1859 (**1880**) Darlington *Amer. Weeds* 279, Oriental Polygonum. Ragged Sailor. Prince's Feather. . . This showy species . . has become sparingly naturalized. **1897** *Jrl. Amer. Folkl.* 10.54 **ME**, *Polygonum orientale*. . . Ragged sailor, Paris, Me. **1910** Graves *Flowering Plants* 162 **CT**, *Polygonum orientale*. . . Ragged Sailor. . . An old-fashioned plant still frequent in cultivation. **1959** Carleton *Index Herb. Plants* 97, *Ragged sailor:* Centaurea cyanus; Polygonum orientale.

2 =**chicory 1**. Cf **blue sailors 1, ragged robin 5**

1896 *Jrl. Amer. Folkl.* 9.191 **NY**, *Cichorium Intybus*. . . Ragged sailors, blue daisies, Southold, L[ong] I[sland]. **1906** (**1918**) Parsons *Wild Flowers CA* 306, A certain tall, fine plant . . bearing beautiful ragged blue flowers. . . has become quite plentiful . . in the last few years, and whole fields may often be seen covered with its [=*Cichorium intybus*'s] lovely . . blossoms, which are known as "ragged sailors," and "wild bachelor's buttons." **1966–68** *DARE* (Qu. S11) Inf **NY**60, Bachelor buttons, ragged sailor [same as] chicory; (Qu. S25, . . *The small wild chrysanthemum-like flowers . . that bloom in fields late in the fall*) Inf **MS**72, Ragged sailors.

3 =**fennel-flower**. Cf **ragged lady 1**

1896 *Jrl. Amer. Folkl.* 9.180 **MA**, *Nigella Damascena*. . . Ragged sailor, Jack-in-the-pulpit, Rutland, Mass.

4 A **cornflower 1** (here: *Centaurea cyanus*). Cf **blue sailors 2, ragged robin 2, raggedy Ann 2**

1888 *Scribner's Mag.* 4.203 **NH**, The flowers that she had planted herself had bloomed all summer in the garden; there were still some ragged sailors and the snowberries and phlox and her favorite mallows. **1898** (**1899**) [see **ragged lady 2**]. **1909** Doubleday *Amer. Flower Garden* 58, Cornflower, Ragged Sailor, Bachelors' Buttons (Centaurea cyanus). Pure blue, singularly fringed trumpets, borne in thistle-like heads. . . Also white, pink, wine-coloured, lilac, and purple. **1942** Hylander *Plant Life* 496, The commonly cultivated Bachelor's Button—also known as Ragged Sailor— . . has long-stemmed flower heads with blue, pink or white flowers. **1959** [see **1** above]. **1967–68** *DARE* (Qu. S11, . . *Bachelor's button*) Infs **CT**15, **NJ**2, **NY**49, Ragged sailor.

5 =**bouncing Bet 1**.

1898 *Jrl. Amer. Folkl.* 11.223 **WI**, *Saponaria officinalis*, . . ragged sailor, Monroe, Wis.

raggedy Ann n

1 A **spider lily** (here: *Hymenocallis narcissiflora*).

1959 Carleton *Index Herb. Plants* 97, *Raggedy Ann:* Hymenocallis calathina [=*H. narcissiflora*].

2 A **cornflower 1** (here: *Centaurea cyanus*). Cf **ragged lady 2, ~ robin 2, ~ sailor 4**

1966 *DARE* (Qu. S11, . . *Bachelor's button*) Inf **NC**3, Cornflower, raggedy Anns.

3 Prob a **farewell-to-spring**. Cf **ragged robin 3**

1966 *DARE* (Qu. S3, *A flower like a large violet with a yellow center and small ragged leaves—it comes up early in spring on open, stony hilltops*) Inf **WA**8, Raggedy Anns.

raggedy-ass(ed) adj Also *ragged-ass(ed)* Cf **half-assed** adj
Raw, inexperienced; unkempt, ragged.

[**1928** Nason *Sergeant Eadie* 134, What kind of a raggedy-seat, cadet outfit is this that don't know where their own kitchen is?] **1929** Niles et al. *Songs My Mother* 182, The raggedy assed cadets are on parade. **1954** McAtee *Suppl. to Nomina Abitera* [3] **CA**, *Ragged-ass Gulch*, Klamath National Forest, California. **1956** (**1973**) Holiday–Dufty *Lady Sings* 56, I'd have to travel five hundred to six hundred miles on a hot or cold raggedy-ass Blue Goose bus. **1968** *DARE* [(Qu. FF22b, . . *Clubs and societies*) Inf **MI**76, R.A.L. Club—Royal American Loyalists, polite name]; (Qu. FF23, . . *Joking names . . for . . clubs or lodges*) Inf **MI**76, Ragged-Ass Loafers—R.A.L. Club, real name for it. **1969** *DARE* Tape **MA**58, Some expressions. . . Ragged-ass Jews [laughter]. I don't know why they was any more ragged than any other. **1969** McPherson *Hue & Cry* 58, Who taught you the moves when you were just a raggedy-ass waiter? **1971** R. Flanagan *Maggot* 252 (*OED2*), Respect what man, you raggedy-assed little fuck? **1972** Kochman *Rappin'* 406 [Black], A nice woman does not dress in "raggedy-ass clothes". **1984** Wilder *You All Spoken Here* 52 **Sth**, *Ragged-assed:* Unkempt.

raggedy robin See **ragged robin 2**

raggety robin See **ragged robin 2**

Raggie See **Raggy**

raggify v [*rag* + **-ify**]
To reduce to rags.

1930 Stoney–Shelby *Black Genesis* 32 **seSC**, De fig bush shake like it been in a hebby wind, an' de leaf raggify deyself 'ginst de branches.

ragging See **rag** n[1] **3**

raggly adj Also *raggly-ass* [Cf *EDD* raggily (at *raggil* sb.) "shabby, untidy"] Cf **racklety**
Run-down, dilapidated.

1966 *DARE* (Qu. D21, *A small, poorly-built house, or one in rundown condition*) Inf **GA**4, Old raggly house. [Inf Black] **1968** Moody *Coming of Age MS* 53 [Black], Automatically my eyes were drawn from the tombstones to that little raggly school building. *Ibid* 177, "Hollywood bedroom set! In that little raggly-ass house," I thought to myself.

rag gourd n Cf **dishrag gourd**
=**vegetable sponge**.

1895 Gray–Bailey *Field Botany* 192, *Luffa, Rag Gourd*. . . The interior portion [of the fruit] becoming detached when dry and useful as a sponge. **1976** Bailey–Bailey *Hortus Third* 684, *Luffa*. . . *Rag g[ourd]*. . . Grown in the U.S. mostly as ornamentals or for the "vegetable sponge" provided by the dried, reticulate, fibrous interior of the fruit.

Raggy n Also *Raggie*
A member of a culturally distinct group of people living in the vicinity of Mt. Riga, Connecticut; broadly, any longtime resident of this area.

[**1839** *S. Lit. Messenger* 5.39 **CT**, After passing the furnaces of Mount Rhiga, (called Mount *Raggy* by the natives,) we came upon a lake, four miles in extent, with the Katskills for a background.] **1938** FWP *Guide CT* 421 **nwCT**, Along the lower slopes of Mt. Riga, tucked away in shallow mountain coves, are the cabins of 'The Raggies,' a 'lost' people about whom little is known. **1965** (**1975**) Sloane *Wood* 61 **CT** (as of

1865), Perhaps the name Raggy started from the charcoal men who lived around Mt. Riga; one seldom knew their names and when one asked, it was often an unpronounceable European name, so they were just called "Rigys" in those days. But when wood became scarce and coal was introduced into iron-making, the Rigys became very poor and ragged. Then the name Raggie seemed to fit even better. **1968** *DARE* Tape **CT9**, Mount Riga ['rɑɪgə] is sometimes called . . more like Mount Raga ['ræ·gə]. . . It's called Mount Raga ['ræ·ɪgə], and these people who live in the shade of it or on the slopes of it, I think, are called Raggies ['ræ·gɪz], basically because of that . . , then they become sort of a term for a local character.

raghead n

One who wears a turban or **head rag**, esp used as a derog term for a person from India or the Middle East.

1921 *DN* 5.111 **sCA**, *Raghead*. . . A Hindu; any Asiatic. From the turbanned Asiatics who are common on the campus. **1967** *DARE* (Qu. HH28, *Names and nicknames . . for people of foreign background*) Inf **CA15**, Raghead for Hindus. **1977** *Jrl.–Courier* (Jacksonville IL) 6 Nov 3/2, Around his head he twisted a turban made of strips cut out of a burlap sack [for a Halloween costume]—he was a raghead for sure—with a goose feather stuck in front. **1990** Burke *Morning for Flamingos* 94 **seLA**, [Fifteen minutes later came in the form of a Latin man with a black bandanna tied down on his head.] *Ibid* 96, The raghead who brought your kilos. **1997** *DARE* File, I've heard . . *raghead* for both Arabs and Iranians in military slang.

rag house n Also *rag (bungalow);* for addit varr see quots chiefly West

A tent or tentlike shelter.

1851 in 1922 Clappe *Shirley Letters* 94 **CA**, The first artificial elegance which attracts your vision is a large rag shanty, roofed, however, with a rude kind of shingles. *Ibid* 123 **CA**, No one remained to protect the calico shanties, the rag huts, and the log cabins. **1890** Custer *Following* 220 **cKS**, Even that [=a dugout] I envied, for the wind could not toy with its habitation . . as it did our "rag houses." **1919** *DN* 5.58 **NW**, *Rag bungalow.* Tent. Mrs. Billy Letterman and small daughter Dorothy moved in last Saturday and are now occupying their *rag bungalow* on Thistle Hill. Kalama Bulletin. (and frequently) *rag mansion.* Billy Letterman built a new porch on his *rag mansion* Sunday. Kalama Bulletin. **1927** *DN* 5.460 [Underworld jargon], *Rag-house*. . . A tent. **c1930** Swann *Lang. Circus Lot* 14, *Rag:* Tent. **1941** Writers' Program *Guide WY* 266, 'Raghouses' of canvas and wood were hurriedly built, but soon the railroad decided to move division headquarters to Wasatch, Utah, 12 miles west; 24 hours later only two persons remained in Evanston. **1968** Adams *Western Words* 243, *Rag bungalow*—A logger's term for a tent used as living quarters; also called *rag house.* **1968** *DARE* (Qu. D21, *A small, poorly-built house, or one in rundown condition*) Inf **NC50**, Rag building.

rag it See **rag** n[1] 3

rag-jag n [Var of *EDD* rag-jack (at *rag* sb.[1] 3.(I)(a))]

A **goosefoot** (here: *Chenopodium album*).

1900 Lyons *Plant Names* 95, *C[henopodium] album*. . . Rag-jag. . . Used as a pot-herb.

rag, light a See **light a shuck**

rag mansion See **rag house**

rag mouth n [In ref to the use of cloth patching in a muzzle-loading rifle]

1969 *DARE* (Qu. P37a, *Nicknames for a rifle*) Inf **KY6**, Rag mouth—muzzle-loading.

rag muffin n Cf **rag bread, ~ toast**

See quots.

1905 in 1940 Brown *Amer. Cooks* 322 **cME**, *Rag muffins*—Take as much raised dough as required, roll it thin, spread with butter, and sprinkle well with sugar and a little cassia. Roll up as for jelly roll and cut in slices. Let rise and bake. **1940** Brown *Amer. Cooks* 477 **MO**, *Rag muffins*—Roll good biscuit dough almost as thin as pie crust. Beat sugar and butter to a cream, spread over the dough. . . Roll up like jelly roll, slice 1½ inches thick. Bake in hot oven.

rag on See **rag** v[1]

rag out v phr, hence ppl adj phr *ragged out* Rarely *rag up* Cf DS W37, W38

To dress up; to dress, provide clothing to.

1865 Browne *Artemus Ward Travels* 50 **MO**, Don't make fun of our clothes. . . We ain't goin' to *rag out* till we git to Nevady! **1893** *KS Univ. Qrly.* 1.141 **KS**, *Ragged out:* well dressed. **1894** in 1925 Moses *Repr. Amer. Dramas* 20, Speaking of clothes, don't you think me and ma are ragged out pretty well for folks right off a ranch? **1894** Riley *Armazindy* 5 **IN**, Purtier girl you never seen—/ 'Ceptin' she lacked schoolin', ner / Couldn't rag out stylisher. **1929** Gordon *Born to Be* 133 [Black], I bought a new suit, patent leather shoes—I ragged myself up the best I knew how. **1941** *LANE* Map 358 *(Dress up)* 5 infs, **CT, MA, VT**, Rag out; 1 inf, **csMA**, Rag out, 'vulgar'; 1 inf, **seME**, Rag up, modern expression. **1968** Adams *Western Words* 243, *Rag-out*—A cowboy's expression meaning *to dress in one's best.* **1975** Gould *ME Lingo* 226, *Rag out*. . . A sailor joining a ship's crew without necessary clothing beyond what he was wearing would be *ragged out* from the vessel's *slop chest.* . . A man who buys a new suit accordingly *rags* himself *out,* and a lady who passes outgrown children's clothing along to a neighbor is "ragging the poor little ones out."

ragshag n esp NEng

A ragtag; a ragged person, esp a fantastically dressed masquerader.

1887 *Conn. Courant* 7 July (1890 *Century Dict.* 4939), While the *Ragshags* were marching, . . [he] caught his foot in his ragged garment and fell. **1890** *Century Dict.* 4939, *Ragshag*. . . A very ragged person; especially one who purposely dresses in grotesque rags for exhibition. [*Century* Ed: *Colloq.*] **1903** *DN* 2.300 **Cape Cod MA** (as of a1857), *Rag-shag, n.* Rag-tag. **1907** *DN* 3.197 **NH**, *Rag-shags*. . . Antiques and horribles. Strafford, N.H.

rag shag and bobtail(s) n

A motley group.

1887 *N. Amer. Rev.* 145.166 (as of 1827), Well, here you all are, rag, shag, and bobtail. **1928** Aldrich *Lantern* 24 **NE**, It's bad enough to have the whole kit 'n' bilin' in the country comin' 'n' trackin' up,—all the rag-shag 'n' bob-tails bringin' their stuff.

rag shanty See **rag house**

ragtag v

With *with:* ?To become involved with, get mixed up with.

1940 (1978) Still *River of Earth* 34 **KY**, "Wonder she hain't gone crazy, the way you carry on, rag-tagging with the Law." "I've been in jail just ten days this solid year."

rag toast n Cf **rag bread**

1906 *Pocumtuc Housewife* 36 **nwMA**, *Rag Toast.* Brown all the broken bits of bread in the oven and put them in the bottom of a large dish. Make an ordinary milk porridge and pour over it.

Rag Town n Also *Rag Alley, ~ City*

Used as a nickname for a settlement composed of **rag houses**, or a poor or run-down part of town.

1859 (1965) Marcy *Prairie Traveler* 276 **West**, From thence to "Ragtown," on Carson River, is three miles. **1917** Webster *Gold Seekers* 123 **CA** (as of 1849), Sacramento City at this time was built principally of cloth houses and tents. . . It was generally known as the "Rag City." **1932** *AmSp* 7.269 [Oil field language], *Rag town*. . . The tent part of a boom town. **1966–70** *DARE* (Qu. C34, *Nicknames for nearby settlements, villages, or districts*) Inf **TX39**, Rag Town—cowboy name for Amarillo in old days; (Qu. C35, *Nicknames for the different parts of your town or city*) Inf **CA111**, Rag Alley—used to throw rags and cans out in alley; western part of city; **KY76**, Rag Town—along the river town, low class of people; **NM11**, Years ago: Rag Town and Rawhide Flat; (Qu. W41, . . *Expressions . . for someone whose clothes never look right*) Inf **KY77**, From Rag Town; (Qu. II25, . . *The part of a town where the poorer people . . live*) Inf **KY11**, Rag Town—where the poor lived, because the people wore rags for clothing; **KY77**, Rag Town; **VA31**, Rag Town—people stuffed the broken windows with rags.

rag up See **rag out**

ragweed n Cf **false ragweed, iron ~, prairie ~**

1 Std: =**ragwort**. [*OED2* 1658 →]

2 A plant of the genus *Ambrosia*, esp such spp as *A.*

artemisifolia, A. psilostachya, and *A. trifida.* Also called **hogweed 2a.** For other names of var spp see **bitterweed, burr sage, carrot weed 2, giant ragweed, hot-weed, povertyweed 1, Roman wormwood, sandburr 2b, stammerwort, stickweed, tassel weed, whiteweed, wild tansy** Note: Those western spp listed at **burr sage** and formerly included in the genus *Franseria* are now included in *Ambrosia.*

1790 Deane *New Engl. Farmer* 176, The milk of cows in summer is sometimes made very bitter by their feeding on rag-weed. **1840** MA Zool. & Bot. Surv. *Herb. Plants & Quadrupeds* 142, A[mbrosia] elatior. . . Rag Weed. . . The bruised leaves were formerly in popular use as an application to wounds and bruises. . . *A. trifida.* . . Under the same common names as the last. **1870** *Amer. Naturalist* 4.582, Prominent among [the flora of the prairies are] . . the rag-weeds (*Ambrosia*), the wormwoods (*Artemisia*), . . and the psoraleas. **1912** Blatchley *IN Weed Book* 151, *Ambrosia artemisiæfolia.* . . Ragweed. . . Probably the most common and widely distributed weed in the State, occurring everywhere in both cultivated and pasture land. . . A prairie form, the lance-leaved ragweed (*A. bidentata* . .) occurs frequently in the western counties of the State. **1931** U.S. Dept. Ag. *Misc. Pub.* 101.153, *Franseria* spp. . . Members of this genus are frequently called . . ragweed, and, if so, are apt to be confused with the ragweed genus (*Ambrosia* spp). **1950** WELS (*Names for kinds of liquor*) 1 Inf, **WI,** Ragweed bitters. **1965–70** DARE (Qu. S21, . . *Weeds . . that are a trouble in gardens and fields*) 447 Infs, **widespread,** Ragweed(s); **MO**13, Dwarf ragweed; **PA**89, Giant ragweed; (Qu. S9, . . *Kinds of grass that are hard to get rid of*) Inf **MS**23, Ragweed; (Qu. S17, . . *Kinds of plants . . that . . cause itching and swelling*) Infs **IA**22, 47, **MO**18, **TN**30, **WA**33, Ragweed(s); (Qu. S26a, . . *Wildflowers. . . Roadside flowers*) Inf **MO**21, Ragweeds; (Qu. S26d, *Wildflowers that grow in meadows; not asked in early QRs*) Inf **IL**95, Ragweed; (Qu. S26e, *Other wildflowers not yet mentioned; not asked in early QRs*) Inf **VT**4, Ragweed. [DARE Ed: Some of these Infs may refer instead to other senses.] **1979** Niering–Olmstead *Audubon Guide N. Amer. Wildflowers E. Region* 356, The pollen of this species [= *Ambrosia trifida*], like that of other Ragweeds, is spread by the wind and is a principal cause of hay fever.

3 A **guayule** (here: *Parthenium hysterophorus*). Cf **false ragweed 2**

1933 Small *Manual SE Flora* 1416, P[arthenium] hysterophorus. . . Ragweed. . . Fla. to Tex., Mo., and Pa. **1936** Whitehouse *TX Flowers* 176, Ragweed. . . *Parthenium hysterophorus.* . . is a widely branched plant two to three feet high and grows in dense masses.

4 Prob a **cornflower 1** (here: *Centaurea cyanus*). Cf **ragged lady 2, ~ robin 2, ~ sailor 4, raggedy Ann 2**

1968 DARE (Qu. S3, *A flower like a large violet with a yellow center and small ragged leaves—it comes up early in spring on open, stony hilltops*) Inf **KS**15, Ragweed.

ragweed worm n
Appar the larva of a longhorn beetle; see quots.

[**1912** Blatchley *IN Weed Book* 150, Both it [=*Ambrosia trifida*] and the common ragweed [=*A. artemisifolia*] harbor a small ash-gray, long-horned beetle (*Dectes spinosus* . .), the larvae of which hibernate in their stems.] **1968** DARE (Qu. P6, . . *Kinds of worms . . used for bait*) Inf **OH**82, Ragweed worm, in a knob in a ragweed.

ragwort n
Std: a plant of the genus *Senecio.* Also called **butterweed 2, ragweed 1, squaw-weed;** for other names of var spp see **cat's-paw 3, chickenweed 1, dusty miller 4, felonweed, field yarrow, fireweed d, German ivy, golden ragwort, lambstongue groundsel, marsh fleabane 2, mastodon flower, mountain marigold 2, mourning ragwort, old man 1f, old-man-in-the-spring, stammerwort, stinking willie, tansy ragwort, yellowtop, yerba cana**

raig'n See **reckon**

rail n[1]

1 also *railing:* The rung of a ladder.

1966–70 DARE (Qu. F34, *The wooden cross-pieces that you put your feet on when you go up a ladder*) Infs **GA**17, **IL**97, **KY**81, **MI**1, **NY**30, Rails; **DC**12, Railings.

2 A timber or pole from which tobacco is hung for curing. Cf **comb rail, rack barn**

1966 PADS 45.20 **KY,** Rails. . . Lengths of two-by-four stock running in pairs the length of the barn. . . Rails are four feet apart vertically and horizontally, and support sticks of tobacco during the curing process. . . "I leave the bottom rails vacant." **1967** Key *Tobacco Vocab.* **PA,** Rail—used mostly: "the pole or the rail"; "In the old days . . they went to the woods and cut long poles and put them in instead of these square . . rectangular rails that we later had." *Ibid* **MO,** Rail. *Ibid* **KY,** Tier, tier pole; "rails" is used in the "Blue Grass." *Ibid* **TN,** Pole, tier pole, rail.

rail n[2]
Std: a bird of the family Rallidae. Also called **marsh hen 1, mud ~ 1, meadow ~ 1, railbird;** for other names of var of these birds see **clapper rail, coot** n[1] **1, Florida gallinule, kicker** n[3]**, king rail 1, mouse ~, purple gallinule, sedge hen 1, sora, Virginia rail, yellow ~**

rail n[3] See **ral**

rail adj, adv See **real** adj, adv

railbird n chiefly N and C Atl
A **rail** n[2], usu the **sora;** also vbl n *railbirding* hunting such a bird.

1808 Ashe *Travels America* 160, [Among the birds described by Catesby] Soree. Rail-bird—*Rallus Virginicus.* **1859** PA Laws *Laws Genl. Assembly* 640, It shall be unlawful for any person or persons to shoot, kill, trap or destroy rail birds or reed birds. **1865** *Atlantic Mth.* 15.95 **PA,** Gunners congregated in numbers dangerous to themselves, shooting rail and reed-birds. **1925** Parrish *Perennial Bachelor* 21 **MD,** So Victor went "down state" with his brother Willie and Sam Blow to shoot reedbirds, and railbirds, and ducks in the marshes. **1937** (1965) Stone *Bird Studies* 1.343 **NJ,** The Sora is *the* rail of the marshes of the Delaware and is usually designated by sportsmen simply as "Rail" or "Rail-bird." **1938** FWP *Guide DE* 339, Until recent years this and similar marshes were famous for the September sport of "railbirdin'". **1955** MA Audubon Soc. *Bulletin* 39.443 **NEng,** Sora. . . Rail Bird. **1968** DARE (Qu. Q7, *Names and nicknames for . . game birds*) Inf **DE**4, Railbird; (Qu. Q10, . . *Water birds and marsh birds*) Infs **CT**13, **NJ**15, 21, 22, Railbird(s). **1975** Newell *If Nothin' Don't Happen* 43 nw**FL,** Along with the ducks there was a heap of coots and marsh hens, tender little good-eatin' birds that Yankees call rail birds. There's two or three kinds of 'em in the saltwater marsh and a littler one in the freshwater marshes.

rail herring See **real herring**

railing See **rail** n[1] **1**

railly See **really** adv, adj

rail pasture n
1933 AmSp 8.4.51 **NE** [Pioneer vocabulary], *Rail pasture* was used rather than pasture or corral.

rail pen See **pen** n[1] **B3**

railrider n
A vagrant who hitches rides on railroads.
1967–70 DARE (Qu. HH19, *Other words or nicknames for a tramp*) Infs **KY**94, **NJ**1, **NY**190, **PA**94, Railrider.

railroad n See **railroader**

railroad v
1 To hurry; to deal with (something) quickly.
1938 Stuart *Dark Hills* 55 ne**KY,** "You will have to miss school long enough to cut that knob piece of corn." "I'll cut it all on Saturday," I said. That Saturday. . . I "railroaded" the corn from daylight until four o'clock that afternoon. . . My father would not believe that I had cut fifty-four shocks until he counted them. **1942** Berrey–Van den Bark *Amer. Slang* 53.8, Go fast; hurry. . . railroad. *Ibid* 156.3, Do carelessly or hastily. . . railroad (through). *Ibid* 245.11, Work energetically: "hustle." . . railroad. **1966–67** DARE (Qu. W28, *When a woman is in a hurry and has to sew up a torn place quickly . . "I'll just _____."*) Inf **SC**26, Railroad it—means you're taking long stitches; [(Qu. Y50, *To undertake or carry out a job: "That's a big job for just one person to _____."*) Inf **MO**5, Railroad].

2 To malinger.

1967 *DARE* (Qu. BB27, *When somebody pretends to be sick . . he's
————*) Inf **NY**8, Railroading.

railroad Annie n Cf **railroad daisy**

An **orange milkweed.**

1968 *DARE* (Qu. S7, *A kind of daisy, bright yellow with a dark center,
that grows along roadsides in late summer*) Inf **NJ**24, Railroad Annie—
orange milkweed.

railroad apartment See **railroad flat**

railroad daisy n Cf **railroad flower**

=**black-eyed susan 2.**

1967 LeCompte *Word Atlas* 235 se**LA**, Railroad daisy [1 of 21 infs].
1968 *DARE* (Qu. S21, *. . Weeds . . that are a trouble in gardens and
fields*) Inf **LA**43, Railroad daisies (yellow flowers); (Qu. S26a, *. .
Wildflowers. . . Roadside flowers*) Inf **LA**43, Railroad daisies. **1997**
DARE File **LA**, Railroad daisies are yellow wildflowers with brown centers. . . My mother's family is from a small town called Plaquemine,
near Baton Rouge, and people in her family often use [the term]. **1998**
NADS Letters e**MT**, **ND**, I've heard what I call a brown-eyed Susan referred to as a "railroad daisy" in North Dakota and Eastern Montana.
They're able to grow beside the road and beside railroad tracks where
it's relatively gravelly but also sunny. *Ibid* **MI**, I would pick them [=
black-eyed Susans] for my Mother and he [=an uncle] called them "railroad daisy." **1998** *DARE* File c**GA**, Railroad daisy! black-eyed susan!
[I] recall my great-aunt using this expression. I believe I've also heard it
mentioned as an affectionate term by my Godmother, who's lived in
New Orleans for the past 30-odd years. **1998** *NADS Letters* **KY**, Railroad daisy: I remember my mom, who was from McRoberts, KY (deep
in Appalachia) using this term—it refers to a Black-Eyed Susan.

railroader n Also *railroad*

1968 *DARE* (Qu. H41, *. . Kinds of roll or bun sandwiches*) Inf **NY**80,
Railroader—Italian bread with cold cuts, etc, down the center; (Qu.
H42, *. . [A sandwich] . . in a much larger, longer bun, that's a meal in it-
self*) Inf **NY**80, Railroad.

railroad flat n Also *railroad apartment* [From the resemblance
to a series of railway cars] **chiefly NYC**

An apartment consisting of a series of narrow rooms arranged
in line.

1956 *New Yorker* 22 Sept 149 **NYC**, A five-room railroad flat above a
butcher store. **1960** Rockwell *Adventures* 30 **NYC** (as of c1900), When
I was six or seven . . we moved in with my grandfather, who lived in a
railroad apartment at 152nd Street and St. Nicholas Avenue. **1968**
DARE Tape **NY**49, In another type of house, an apartment that stretches
from front to back is usually known as a railroad apartment. But it isn't
true of a brownstone house, because it doesn't go directly back. It goes
to one side, you know, so it's not known as a railroad apartment. *Ibid*
NY50, A railroad flat is when all the rooms go straight through in a row,
like a railroad train is. . . You had the parlor in the front of the house and
the kitchen in the back of the house and all the bedrooms were strung
out in a row in the middle in a straight line. **1986** Pederson *LAGS Concordance,* 1 inf, cn**TN**, Railroad—apartments; 1 inf, se**FL**, Railroad
flat—term for it in the North. **1991** *DARE* File **NYC** (as of c1920),
New York City tenements were never more than six stories high. . . the
lots were 25 feet wide and this accomodated [sic] two apartments p[l]us
a long hall leading to the front room without having callers . . walk
through two bedrooms. These were called "railroad flats" for the rooms
were arranged like a string of cars. **1993** Delany–Delany *Having Our
Say* 133 **NYC** [Black], These were long, narrow apartments, like railroad flats. **1998** *NYT Mag.* 23 Aug 64 **NYC**, The building was one of
those narrow tenements that line the streets of New York, with a Chinese
laundry on the ground level and three railroad flats on each floor above.

railroad flower n Cf **railroad daisy**

A **tiger lily.**

1998 *NADS Letters,* Some 15 years ago I picked up the term "railroad
flower" in WV for the common tiger lily. . . Tiger lilies grow wild along
the railroads, where there is open space and therefore sun.

railroad hyacinth n

A **camas 1** (here: *Camassia scilloides*).

1951 *PADS* 15.38 **TX**, *Quamasia hyacinthina* [=*Camassia scilloides*]. . . Railroad hyacinth. This plant likes to grow at the damp feet of

embankments and was so named when favorable situations were furnished mainly by railroad banks.

railroad lily n

A **day lily 1** (here: *Hemerocallis fulva*).

1954 Welty *Ponder Heart* 29 **MS**, The Peacocks are the kind of people
keep the mirror outside on the front porch, and go out and pick railroad
lilies to bring inside the house, and wave at trains till the day they die.
1982 *DARE* File, In Hadley, MA and Madison, WI the Hemerocallis is
called "railroad lily" because escapes from gardens grow alongside railroad tracks.

railroad puccoon n

A **gromwell** (here: *Lithospermum incisum*).

1951 *PADS* 15.39 **TX**, *Batchia linearifolia* [=*Lithospermum
incisum*]. . . Yellow, prairie, or railroad, puccoon (it loves railroad embankments and right-of-ways).

railroad time n

1 Rapid progress.

1864 (1938) Cate *Two Soldiers* 41, I obtained another horse and we
made railroad time until we reached Big Creek. **1926** *AmSp* 1.410
Okefenokee GA, So yer better know I 'uz makin' all the railroad time I
could.

2 Time as kept by a railroad line; hence precise clock time or
(after the early 1880s) standard time (as opposed to local or
sun time).

1865 *Atlantic Mth.* 15.230 **NEng**, She is . . so punctual that railroad
time might be kept by her instead of a chronometer. **1880** *N. Amer. Rev.*
131.529, On the other hand, the disadvantage of having the factory operatives begin work on railroad time and stop on local time, [etc] . . all
indicate the need of the adoption of such a common time as already exists in the European countries. **1883** *Century Illustr. Mag.* 26.796, The
system proposed is based . . upon readily understood principles. *First
that the same standard should be used by all lines within sections as
largely extended as may be possible, without entailing such a difference
between local and railroad time as to cause inconvenience to the public.*
1946 Wilson *Fidelity Folks* 42 sw**KY**, He said that Fidelity kept sun time
rather than railroad time because it was nearer the sun. **1952** Brown *NC
Folkl.* 1.582, Railroad time. . . Correct time.—Central and east. **1956**
McAtee *Some Dialect NC* 36, Railroad time. . . Correct time. c**1960**
Wilson Coll. cs**KY**, Railroad time . . standard time as opposed to "sun
time". **1969** *DARE* Tape **GA**84, Everybody would be in the field by
sunup. At eleven-thirty, which was sun time, and the sun timin' was
twenty minutes ahead of railroad time. Railroad time is now, was then, is
what standard time is now. **1976** *DARE* File **MA**, *Railroad time* is
probably old-fashioned. I have heard old people in the Ohio-Erie, Pennsylvania area tell of having to make the distinction between this and *sun
time*. This was before time zones were created. **1984** Wilder *You All
Spoken Here* 63 **Sth**, *Railroad time:* Correct time. You can't set your
watch by television times.

3 The time of day expressed as two cardinal numbers, the first
representing the hour and the second the number of minutes
after the hour. [Cf *railway time* in this sense, which is not entered in *OED* or *OED2*, but which appears in the def of *and*
I.1.b, first published in 1884]

1967 *DARE* (Qu. A6, *What time is this? [. . clock face at 10:45]*) Inf
MA72, Quarter of eleven—railroad time, ten forty-five; (Qu. A7, *. .
What time is this? [. . clock face at 10:30]*) Inf **MA**72, Ten-thirty rail-
road time.

railroad vine n

1 A **morning glory 1**: usu *Ipomoea pes-caprae,* but also *I.
violacea.* For other names of *I. pes-caprae* see **beach morning glory 1, pohuehue, wild morning glory**

1913 *Torreya* 13.233 **FL**, *Ipomoea pes-caprae.* . . Railroad vine, St.
Vincent I[slan]d, Fla. **1933** Small *Manual SE Flora* 1085, *I[pomoea]
Pes-Caprae.* . . *Railroad-vine.* . . Coastal sand-dunes, Fla. to Tex. and
Ga. **1953** Greene–Blomquist *Flowers South* 103, *Railroad-Vine
(Ipomoea Pes-Caprae)* . . seems to prefer growing in the most inhospita-
ble situations, creeping along railroad tracks, roadsides, and ocean
beaches. **1970** Correll *Plants TX* 1250, *Ipomoea Pes-Caprae.* . . *Ipomoea Tuba
[=I. violacea].* . . Sandy beaches. *Ibid* 1252, *Ipomoea Pes-caprae.* . .
Railroad vine. . . Beaches and dunes along Gulf Coast. **1971** Gantz
Naturalist in S. FL 80, Railroad vine sprawls over the sand, bearing an

occasional morning glorylike flower. . . Its botanical name is *Ipomaea pes-caprae*. **1979** Niering–Olmstead *Audubon Guide N. Amer. Wildflowers E. Region* 475, Railroad Vine (Ipomoea pes-caprae). . . [T]his showy vine sometimes grows across beaches almost to water's edge.

2 =kudzu. Cf **Arkansas traveler 2**

1956 McAtee *Some Dialect NC* 57, Railroad vine. . . The kudzu (Pueraria thunbergiana). Chapel Hill.

railroad worm n chiefly NEast

The apple maggot (*Rhagoletis pomonella*); hence adj *railroady* of an apple: tunneled by this maggot.

1890 *Century Dict.* 4942 NEng, Railroad-worm. . . The apple-maggot (larva of *Trypeta pomonella*): so called because it has spread along the lines of the railroads. **1914** (1919) Slingerland–Crosby *Manual Fruit Insects* 33, Sometimes the burrows run for some distance just beneath the skin [of an apple], showing through as darkened trails, from which the insect [=*Rhagoletis pomonella*] has received, in some localities, the name of railroad worm. **1953** U.S. Dept. Ag. *Yearbook for 1952* Pl. XI, The apple maggot, or railroad worm, causes brown tunnels or burrows inside the apple. . . It appears in the largest numbers in July in orchards throughout the Northeastern States and northern part of the Midwest. **1966–67** *DARE* FW Addit NH5, Railroady apples—wormy (have tracks all through them); sePA, An apple, when it is full of worms, is full of "railroad worms" because of the tracks they make. **1972** Swan–Papp *Insects* 625, Apple Maggot. . . Sometimes called the "railroadworm" for its extensive tunneling of the pulp [of apples]. **c1978** *DARE* File cnMA (as of c1915), Railroady—said by my mother of apples which had brown "tracks" in them made by worms. If we picked up an apple from the ground to eat, she might say, "If it's railroady, don't eat it—throw it away."

rail runner n

A **fence lizard 1** (here: *Sceloporus undulatus*).

1941 Writers' Program *Guide AL* 24, The gray-brown fence lizard, or rail-runner, is general over the State.

rail-splitter n

1 A rustic. **esp Sth, S Midl**

1867 *Galaxy* 3.700, We have chosen our rulers from among tailors and rail-splitters long enough. **1895** *Harper's New Mth. Mag.* 91.608, The adventurous sons of Kentucky and Tennessee . . came into a new country full of grass and cattle. Here they found Mexicans by the hundred, all on horses. . . This sight must have stirred memories in the rail-splitter's blood, for he joined the sport upon the instant. [**1955** Shankle *Nicknames* 259, Abraham Lincoln came to be known as the *Rail Splitter* because as a young man, he split rails to earn his living.] **1965–70** *DARE* (Qu. HH1, *Names and nicknames for a rustic or countrified person*) Infs GA3, NC40, WV5, 7, 10, WI49, Rail-splitter. **1971** Wood *Vocab. Change* 298 OK, 3 [infs] Railsplitter. *Ibid* 385, Rail splitter: a rustic.

2 A sharp-pointed shoe.

1969 *DARE* (Qu. W42a, . . *Nicknames . . for men's sharp-pointed shoes*) Inf CT27, Rail-splitters.

rail-splitting n Cf logrolling 1, maul rails

A cooperative gathering for the purpose of making fence rails.

1966 *DARE* (Qu. FF4, *Names and joking names for different kinds of dancing parties*) Inf FL29, Rail-splittings—split rails in the day, danced at night—obsolete.

raily See really adv, adj

raimy See ramie

rain n

Christmas-tree tinsel.

1979 *Oregonian Article Letters* nwOR, As a boy growing up in Portland, I called the silvery stuff you hang on Christmas trees "rain". **1980** *DARE* File NJ, The silvery stuff on a Christmas tree is what I grew up calling icicles, learned to call tinsel. . . Joel, from Short Hills, calls it rain and insists that he's not alone in this. **1998** *NADS Letters* NYC, [I knew] rain for single-strand tinsel, in New York City in the 1930s–1950s. *Ibid*, Rain . . is presently common in Gloucester County, (southwestern) New Jersey, . . and was known to me in Bergen County, (northeastern) New Jersey, where I . . lived . . 1931–1950. *Ibid*, I can confirm that as a child growing up in 1950s New Jersey, we put rain on our Christmas tree. My parents, also raised in NJ in the 30s, used the term. *Ibid* swPA, nWV, "Rain" or perhaps "tinsel rain" was the manufac-

turer's term used on the box of this material used for Christmas decorations in the 1960s, 1970s, and probably still. . . The stuff was known to us as "icicles." *Ibid*, My wife Nora, born 1953 in Colorado Springs and raised primarily in West Texas by a West Texas father and a Montana mother (who spent considerable time after WWII in New Jersey), always used this meaning [=tinsel] of rain.

rainbar n

A divining rod.

1969 *DARE* (Qu. CC13a, . . *A forked stick that's used to show where there's water underground. . . [What kind of wood?]*) Inf NC61, Witch's stick; rainbars; ['kʌnjəz] [=conjurer's] stick.

rain-barrel mosquito n Cf rainworm 2

A **mosquito** n[1] **B1;** see quots.

1904 NY State Museum & Sci. Serv. *Bulletin* 79.328, Culex Pipiens Linn. House or rain barrel mosquito—This mosquito appears to love human habitations and may be found breeding throughout the warmer months in any open receptacle containing fresh water. One or two rain barrels are sufficient to produce millions of the pests. **1926** Essig *Insects N. Amer.* 535, The rainbarrel mosquito, *Theobaldia incidens* [=*Culiseta i.*] . . , is a large dark mosquito with spotted wings. . . The larvae . . are often found in rainbarrels, hence the common name. . . It is one of the commonest species in California and a ready biter.

rainbells n

A **toothwort** (here: *Cardamine integrifolia*).

1961 Thomas *Flora Santa Cruz* 182 cwCA, D[entaria] californica . . var. *integrifolia* [=*Cardamine integrifolia*]. . . Rainbells. . . Fields, open slopes, and occasionally in shade.

rainberella n [Joc blend of *rain* + *umbrella*] Cf sunberella

1966–67 *DARE* (Qu. W1c, . . *Joking names . . for an umbrella*) Infs IA8, MS45, Rainberella.

rainbird n Cf rain crow 1, ~ dove

1 Any of var birds that show increased activity or call more frequently before rain, or are thought to presage rain, as:

a Either the **golden plover** or an **upland plover** (here: *Bartramia longicauda*).

1819 Thomas *Travels W. Country* 161, The *meadow lark*, the *kildee*, and the *land plover* inhabit the prairies. The last has been called the *rain bird*, from its notes being more frequently heard in the calm that precedes changes of the atmosphere. **1951** *AmSp* 26.268, Birds, other than swallows, whose increased activity seems to have won them the title of 'rain bird' include golden plover (N.J.); upland plover (Ind.); common redpoll (N.Y.); slate-colored junco (Maine, N.Y., Ky.)

b also *rain swallow:* =**swallow. chiefly LA**

1916 *Times–Picayune* (New Orleans LA) 23 Apr mag sec 5 LA, Rainbird applied to all swallows [=Hirundinidae]. **1917** *Wilson Bulletin* 29.2.83 KY, LA, VA, Swallows in general—Rain-birds. **1951** *AmSp* 26.268, Rain bird. . . has been given to species more active, and especially to those more vociferous, immediately preceding rain. Apparently all the swallows are known as rain birds, somewhere or other, in the United States, and the French equivalent *oiseau de pluie* applies to all occurring in lower Louisiana. . . One reason why these birds hawk about near the ground before rain is that their insect prey is doing that very thing. **1968** *DARE* (Qu. Q14) Inf LA26, They have rainbirds, but they are not cuckoos—small birds that fly around before a rain; (Qu. Q20, . . *Kinds of swallows and birds like them*) Inf LA22, Rain swallows—them little old blue-looking like; fly way up in the air. **1986** Pederson *LAGS Concordance*, 1 inf, cLA, Rainbirds = thunderbirds, live in chimney.

c Esp the **yellow-billed cuckoo**, but also the **black-billed cuckoo** or the **mangrove cuckoo. chiefly Midl, esp Appalachians** See Map on p. 446

1932 Howell *FL Bird Life* 286, *Coccyzus minor*. . . Rain Bird. . . Florida Keys, and southwest coast of Florida. **1946** Hausman *Eastern Birds* 346, Yellow-billed Cuckoo. . . Other Names . . Rainbird. *Ibid* 347, Maynard's Cuckoo. . . Other Names—Mangrove Cuckoo, . . Rainbird. **1951** *AmSp* 26.269, Yellow-billed Cuckoo. . . Rain bird—Pa., Md., Fla. . . [For] *Black-billed Cuckoo.* . . Vt., Md. **1965–70** *DARE* (Qu. Q14, . . *Names . . cuckoo*) 14 Infs, **chiefly Midl**, Rainbird; DC2, A cuckoo or rainbird; MD26, Cuckoo—rainbird, also called rain dove; MD30, Rainbird, rain crow.

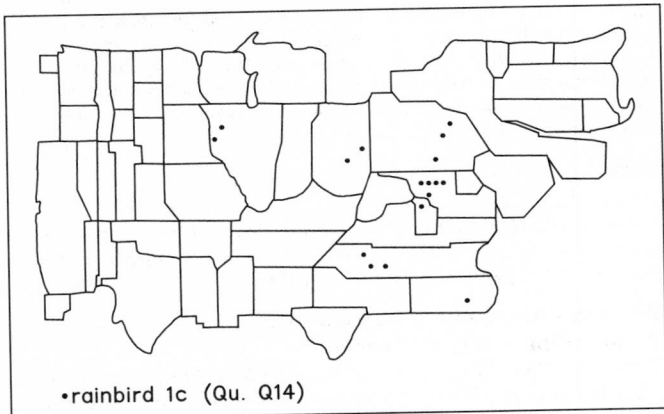

•rainbird 1c (Qu. Q14)

d =**junco** n[1].
1917 *Wilson Bulletin* 29.2.83 **KY,** *Junco hyemalis.*—Rain-bird, Hickman, Ky. **1951** [see **1a** above]. **1966** *DARE* (Qu. Q14) Inf **WA2,** Rainbird—whistles when it's going to rain.

e =**whippoorwill.**
1945 *AN&Q* 5.11 **IL,** Despite the dominance of *whippoorwill,* there are a number of local names for the bird: . . "rainbird" (Illinois, from calling before a rain).

f =**yellowthroat.**
1951 *AmSp* 26.269, Because of their calling or singing more noticeably than usual before rain, the following species, too, have been dubbed 'rain birds': mourning dove (Wis.); . . masked yellowthroat (Ga.); and cardinal (Pa.)

g A **redpoll 1** (here: *Carduelis flammea*).
1951 [see **1a** above]. **1956** MA Audubon Soc. *Bulletin* 40.254, Common Redpoll. Rain Bird (N.H. Its coming supposed to presage rain.)

h =**mourning dove 1.**
1951 [see **1f** above]. **1967** *DARE* (Qu. Q14) Inf **PA18,** Mourning dove or rainbird; **PA29,** Doves are rainbirds.

i =**cardinal 1.**
1951 [see **1f** above].

2 =**tree frog.** Cf **rainfrog 1**
1931–33 *LANE Worksheets* **seCT,** A ground toad is distinct from the rainbird or tree toad.

rainbo See **rainbow 3**

rainbow n
1 See **rainbow trout.**
2 Something curved; hence attrib: bent, crescent-shaped.
1938 in 1970 Hyatt *Hoodoo* 2.1085 **New Orleans LA,** She also had a *rainbow* arm, this perky, this zippy little woman. *Ibid* 1094, She said she also had a *rainbow arm.* . . "My arm [is] shaped like a rainbow." . . "What does that mean?" "That means that nobody can do me no harm." **1952** *Badger Folkl.* 1.19 [Logging language], *"She's a rainbow."*—A crooked log. **1985** Madson *Up River* 175 **Upper Missip Valley,** There are strange effects out there on the River in a small boat. Deep holes, shallows, wing dams, rainbow reefs, and channel crossings all affect the surface.

3 also sp *rainbo:* A playing marble with a colored band or bands around or inside it.
c1970 Wiersma *Marbles Terms* **swMI,** Rainbo . . a solid colored marble with a different colored streak running through it. This streak is in the same pattern as the color found in cateyes. It was probably coined a "rainbo" because of its similarity in color and design to a rainbow. *Ibid* **neOH,** Rainbow. . . A playing marble with variegated bands of color. *Ibid* **swMI,** *Different types of marbles.* . . Rainbow. *Ibid* **MS,** *Rainbow* . . a transparent marble with several different lines of color on top of each other within it.

4 A **red-bellied dace** (here: *Phoxinus erythrogaster*). Cf **rainbow chub**
1982 Sternberg *Fishing* 21, Southern redbelly dace, or *rainbows,* have a reddish belly and two dark bands on the side. They are found in the Midwest and South in small streams.

5 A **freshwater clam** (here: *Villosa iris*).
1991 IL Nat. Hist. Surv. *Biol. Notes* 137.17, *Villosa iris* . . rainbow. . . A species that is apparently declining statewide, the rainbow was re-

cently listed as endangered in Illinois. **1992** *Nature Conserv. Mag.* 42.6.22 **VA,** A mussel sampler from the remarkable Clinch Valley fauna [includes] . . *rainbow, Iris villosa* [etc.].

rainbow cactus n [See quot 1973]
A **hedgehog cactus 3** (here: *Echinocereus pectinatus* varr or *E. rigidissimus*).
1893 *Garden and Forest* 6.429, One [booth] sells the "Rainbow Cactus," which is a good species of Echinocactus. **1896** *Jrl. Amer. Folkl.* 9.188 **AZ,** *Cereus pectinatus,* . . rainbow cactus. **1897** *Garden and Forest* 10.98 **CO,** Echinocereus vividiflorus. . . It is usually known as Rainbow Cactus, on account of the bright-colored spines. **1900** (1903) James *In & Around Grand Canyon* 325, Rainbow cactus, with brightcolored zones. **1949** Moldenke *Amer. Wild Flowers* 103, The *rainbow cactus, Echinocereus rigidissimus,* of Arizona, has red or pink spines and purple flowers. **1973** *AZ Highways* Mar 12, A most attractive Arizona native is the Rainbow Cactus. . . It derives its name from the effect of the alternately colored spines which lie compressed flat around the stem. **1976** *Express–News* (San Antonio, Texas) 27 Nov. 10-c/I *(OED2),* We . . saw a spiny little cactus growing upright out of the ground like a fat ear of corn. Its bands of colors were the colors of the rainbow—and that's its name—the rainbow cactus. **1987** Bowers *100 Roadside Wildflowers* 83, Rainbow cactus grows on rocky slopes in desert grassland and oak woodland. Several varieties occur from Arizona to Texas.

rainbow chub n Cf **rainbow 4**
The finescale **dace** (*Phoxinus neogaeus*).
1983 Becker *Fishes WI* 451, *Finescale Dace.* . . Other common names . . rainbow chub. . . Body dark brown. . . Between the back and the lateral stripe, a light olive stripe. . . Lower half of body lightly pigmented above to silvery white on midventral surface. Sides in mature male often with a yellow, orange, or reddish wash.

rainbow conk n
A bracket fungus (here: *Polyporus versicolor*). Also called **turkeytail**
1948 Boyce *Forest Pathology* 402, *Polystictus* [=*Polyporus*] *versicolor* . ., the rainbow conk, causes a soft white spongy rot. . . The thin tough leathery annual conks, up to 2 inches or more in width, have . . more or less conspicuous multicolored zones [on the upper surface].

rainbow darter n Also *rainbow fish*
A **darter 1** (here: *Etheostoma caeruleum*). Also called **johnny 2, soldierfish**
1882 U.S. Natl. Museum *Bulletin* 16.517, *P[oecilichthys] caeruleus.* . . *Rainbow Darter.* . . Males olivaceous . . ; sides with 12 indigo-blue bars . . separated by bright orange interspaces; caudal fin orange, edged with bright blue; . . cheeks blue; throat and breast orange. . . One of the most gorgeously-colored darters, but less graceful than most of them. **1890** *Century Dict.* 4943, *Rainbow-fish.* . . The blue darter, *Pœcilichthys cæruleus.* **1903** NY State Museum & Sci. Serv. *Bulletin* 60.518, The . . rainbow darter . . is found in the Ohio valley and in some parts of the Mississippi valley. **1943** Eddy–Surber *N. Fishes* 201, The body of the rainbow darter is stout. . . This fish reaches a length of 2½ inches. **1983** Becker *Fishes WI* 932, *Rainbow Darter.* . . Other common names: rainbow fish.

rainbow herring See **rainbow smelt**

rainbow perch n Also *rainbow seaperch*
Either of two **surfperches** of the Pacific coast: usu *Hypsurus caryi,* but also *Embiotoca lateralis.*
1933 John G. Shedd Aquarium *Guide* 137, *Taeniotoca lateralis* [= *Embiotica l.*] . . *Rainbow Perch.* This is the handsomest fish of the family, being heavily spotted and streaked with bright blue. **1946** LaMonte *N. Amer. Game Fishes* 91, Rainbow Perch—*Hypsurus caryi.* . . California coast. . . Horizontal stripes of red, orange, and light blue on body. . . *Striped Perch—Taeniotoca lateralis* . . *Names* . . Rainbow Perch. . . San Diego, California, to Vancouver Island. **1953** Roedel *Common Fishes CA* 105, Rainbow Perch—*Hypsurus caryi.* . . Brightly colored, chiefly shades of orange. . . The vivid colors fade soon after death. **1983** *Audubon Field Guide N. Amer. Fishes* 642, Anglers catch 10,000 to 20,000 Rainbow Seaperches [=*Hypsurus caryi*] annually along the California coast.

rainbow runner n [See quot 1960]
A widely distributed carangid fish (*Elagatis bipinnulata*).

Also called **runner 5, shoemaker** n[1] **3, skipjack 1f, Spanish jack, yellowtail**

1946 LaMonte *N. Amer. Game Fishes* 37, Rainbow Runner. . . A Southern fish. . . Straggles north to New York. Out of range in the Pacific. **1960** Gosline–Brock *Hawaiian Fishes* 169, The rainbow runner derives its name from its color, which is bluish on the upper half of the body and paler below with a yellowish tinge. **1983** *Audubon Field Guide N. Amer. Fishes* 597, The Rainbow Runner resembles the Cobia, but is readily distinguished by its bright colors and finlets. . . It is highly esteemed as a food and game fish.

rainbow seaperch See **rainbow perch**

rainbow smelt n Also *rainbow herring* [See quot 1974]

The American **smelt** *(Osmerus mordax)*.

1896 *U.S. Natl. Museum Bulletin* 47.524, *Osmerus dentex* [=*O. mordax*]. . . *Rainbow Herring.* . . Coast of Alaska and south on the Pacific Coast . . ; a brilliantly colored fish, the flesh of firmer texture than in the rest of the genus. **1911** *Century Dict. Suppl.,* Rainbow smelt. . . The brilliantly colored smelt, *Osmerus dentex,* found on the coast of Alaska. It forms an important part of the food of the natives. Also called *Alaska smelt.* **1955** *U.S. Arctic Info. Center Gloss.* 65, *Rainbow herring.* The northwest smelt. **1974** *WI Univ. Fish Lake MI* 22, *Rainbow Smelt* . . coloring: silvery with pale green back; purple, blue and pink iridescent reflections on side. . . During spring spawning runs. . . rainbow smelt display the distinctive characteristics that account for their name. In the streams they shimmer colorfully, though once out of water they fade quickly to a lifeless silvery white. **1991** *Amer. Fisheries Soc. Common Names Fishes* 27, *Osmerus mordax* . . A[tlantic]-F[reshwater]-P[acific] . . rainbow smelt.

rainbow snake n

A glossy blue-black snake *(Farancia erythrogramma)* with longitudinal red and yellow stripes and a sharp spine at the tip of the tail, native to the southeastern US. Also called **hoop snake, mud ~, stinging ~, thunderbolt**

1908 Ditmars *Reptile Book* 366, The Rainbow Snake lives in swampy, timbered areas and along the borders of streams, where it burrows into the damp soil. **1935** Pratt *Manual Vertebrate Animals* 203, *A[bastor] erythrogrammus.* . . Rainbow snake. . . Virginia to the Gulf. **1949** *N.O. Times–Picayune Mag.* 23 Oct. 2/2 *(DA),* Mrs. Rainbow Snake laid herself a passel of nice white eggs, top, and 15 of them hatched, below. **1979** Behler–King *Audubon Field Guide Reptiles* 611, The Rainbow Snake is usually docile and the spine is harmless.

rainbow sucker n

A **white sucker** (here: *Catostomus commersoni*); see quot.

1949 Caine *N. Amer. Sport Fish* 160, In some states because of a lack of fishing variety the [white] sucker is the most popular species. . . During the spawning season the male turns nearly black on top and a pronounced lateral line is bordered below by a broad pinkish stripe; during this period it is commonly called black sucker or rainbow sucker.

rainbow trout n Also *rainbow* Cf **black mountain trout**

A **trout** (here: *Oncorhynchus mykiss*) native to lakes and streams of the western US, now widely introduced elsewhere. Also called **blueback trout, California ~, channel ~, coaster** n[3] **2, half pounder, hardhead 2b, kamloops trout, mountain ~ 1, redside 1, salmon B1b, salmon trout 1c, silver ~ 2, speckled ~, square-tailed ~, steelhead ~, summer salmon, winter ~**

1882 *U.S. Natl. Museum Bulletin* 16.312, *S[almo] irideus* [= *Oncorhynchus mykiss*]. . . *Rainbow Trout.* [*Ibid* 313, Streams west of the Sierra Nevada, . . to Oregon; very abundant, and subject to many variations in size, form, and color.] **1904** *Salmon & Trout* 252, The rainbow is the hardiest of the salmon-trouts, for it will thrive in water of a higher temperature than is suitable for other species. **1909** Holder–Jordan *Fish Stories* 139, The trout par excellence of California, found in almost every permanent brook, is the one to which I gave, in 1878, the name of rainbow trout, this name being a translation of *Salmo iridia,* given it in 1854 by Dr. W.P. Gibbons, of Alameda. **1920** *Outing* 76.197, I said that I caught trout in a tin pan, and here's the proof. This old lunker of a rainbow gave me a bath. **1933** *NY Times* (NY) Apr 3/5 *(Hench Coll.),* This special planting of 20,000 includes brown, rainbow and native trout. **1965–70** *DARE* (Qu. P1, . . *Kinds of freshwater fish . . caught around here . . good to eat)* 84 Infs, **widespread, but esp Nth, West,** Rainbow trout; 17 Infs, **chiefly Nth, West,** Rainbow(s); (Qu.

P2, . . *Kinds of saltwater fish caught around here . . good to eat)* Inf **OR5,** Rainbow trout. **1966** *DARE* Tape **MI32,** Besides pike, we got a spring and fall run of rainbow. They run while the snow's still on the ground. **1978** *AK Fishing Guide* 63, Some rainbows are found on the north side of the Alaska Peninsula north of the Aleutians. . . This chunky trout in fresh water has a liberal sprinkling of black spots on a dark background above, light to almost white below, and a rosy strip from gill cover to tail on the middle of each side. **1986** Pederson *LAGS Concordance* **Gulf Region,** 17 infs, Rainbow trout; 1 inf, Rainbows.

rainbowweed n
=**purple loosestrife.**

1900 Lyons *Plant Names* 235, *L[ythrum] Salicaria.* . . Rainbow-weed. **1940** Clute *Amer. Plant Names* 94, Purple Loosestrife. . . Rainbow-weed. **1959** Carleton *Index Herb. Plants* 97, *Rainbow-weed:* Lythrum salicaria.

rainbow yellowtail See **yellowtail**

rain bullfrogs See **bullfrogs, rain**

rainch See **rinse 5**

rain crow n

1 Any of var birds whose calls are thought to presage rain, as: see below. **chiefly Sth, Midl** See Map on p. 448 Cf **rainbird 1, rain dove**

a Esp the **yellow-billed** or **black-billed cuckoo,** but also the **mangrove cuckoo.** Cf **cowbird 2, mockingbird 6**

1806 (1905) Lewis *Orig. Jrls. Lewis & Clark Exped.* 5.205, I saw both yesterday and today the Cookkoo or as it is sometimes called the *rain craw* [sic]. **1831** Audubon *Ornith. Biog.* 1.19, The Dutch farmers of Pennsylvania know it [=the yellow-billed cuckoo] better by the name of *Rain Crow.* **1872** Coues *Key to N. Amer. Birds* 190, They [=American cuckoos] are . . noted for their loud jerky cries, which they are supposed to utter most frequently in falling weather, whence their popular name, "rain crow." **1885** Thompson *By-Ways* 48, For instance, the well-known guttural croaking of the yellow-billed cuckoo is, in the West and South generally believed to presage rain; hence the bird is known amongst the rural people by the name of rain-crow. **1906** Johnson *Highways Missip. Valley* 100 **TN** [Black], Dar's lots er birds hyar—peckerwoods an' sapsuckers an' yallerhammers an' robins; an' dar's de rain crows what set up in de trees an' holler when it's fixin' for to rain. **1937** FWP *Guide ID* 95, The yellow-billed cuckoo (rain crow, rain dove, storm crow, chowchow) has a black bill. . . His song is a succession of spasmodic gurgles. **1953** Randolph–Wilson *Down in Holler* 276 **Ozarks,** *Rain crow.* . . A bird whose cry is supposed to indicate rain. In most sections of the Ozarks, *rain crow* means the yellow-billed cuckoo *(Coccyzus americanus).* **1954** Sprunt *FL Bird Life* 242, *Coccyzus minor maynardi.* . . *Local Names:* Black-eared cuckoo; Rain Crow. *Ibid* 243, The Mangrove, or Black-eared Cuckoo, occurs regularly in suitable habitat. . . The notes are similar to those of the yellow-billed Cuckoo, having the peculiar guttural quality and rolling cadence of this family. . . *Coccyzus americanus americanus.* . . *Local Names:* Rain Crow. *Ibid* 244, The rolling, guttural call notes, so long associated by many with weather prediction, are far oftener heard than the bird is seen. . . *Coccyzus erythropthalmus.* . . *Local Names:* Rain Crow. **1965–70** *DARE* (Qu. Q14, . . *Names . . cuckoo)* 162 Infs, **chiefly Sth, Midl,** Rain crow; **GA25, IL81, NC36,** Rain crow—yellow-billed cuckoo; **CT29,** Yellow-billed rain crow, black-billed rain crow; **FL16,** Rain crow—catbird, mockingbird; **GA65,** Rain crow—cowbird; **MA68,** Rain crow—always means a heat wave when you hear them—a sure sign; **TN65,** Rain crow—scavenger—lays eggs in nests of other birds; **TX84,** Yellow-billed rain crow; **TX91,** Rain crow, cuckoo—different; **VA15,** Rain crow—mockingbird—this one eats the tent caterpillars; (Qu. Q8) Inf **AL2,** Rain crow—makes a noise like a dove, before rain; **FL9,** Rain crow—in tree; **GA18,** Rain crow—same as yellow-billed cuckoo; **NC72,** Rain crow—a very shy bird—the cuckoo; **OK1,** There's a small brown rain crow that performs this service, hollering before it rains; **OK11,** Rain crow—hollers after a rain; **OK25,** Rain crow—in trees; **TN1,** Rain crow—land bird; (Qu. Q11) Inf **MO5,** Rain crow—about size of a bluejay, kind of a grayish [color], cackling sound; (Qu. Q12, . . *Kinds of crows;* total Infs questioned, 75) Inf **FL27,** Rain crows—not cuckoo; **OK1,** Rain crow—not a real crow; (Qu. Q23, *The insect-eating bird that goes headfirst down a tree trunk)* Inf **VA43,** Rain crow. **1967** *Ozark Visitor* (Point Lookout MO) Feb 6, High in the arboreal world a yellow-billed cuckoo clucked out the call that has earned him the title of rain crow. **1986** Pederson *LAGS Concordance,* 2 infs, **nwAR, ceTN,** Rain crow; 1 inf, **swTN,** Rain crow—forecasts rain.

b A bird of the family Ardeidae, such as the **green heron.**

1923 Dawson *Birds CA* 4.1907, *Anthony's Green Heron.* . . *Butorides virescens anthonyi* [=*B. striatus*]. . . Synonyms.—*Fly-up-the-Creek. Rain Crow.* **1951** *AmSp* 26.269, Two other rain crows, the reason for this naming of which is obscure, are the green heron (Calif.) and the brown-backed oyster catcher (Va.) **1965–70** *DARE* (Qu. Q8, *A water bird that makes a booming sound before rain and often stands with its beak pointed almost straight up*) 59 Infs, **chiefly Sth, Midl,** Rain crow [*DARE* Ed: Some of these Infs probably refer instead to **1a** above; 24 Infs gave this resp to both Qu. Q8 and Qu. Q14.]; **LA**40, Rain crow—a little shorter-legged than a crane, not a cuckoo; (Qu. Q10) Inf **KY**88, Rain crow; (Qu. Q14) Inf **IN**3, Rain crow—shypoke; **VA**38, When you see a rain crow go down[stream], going to be a fresh up[stream] [FW: from description, =little blue heron].

c =**mourning dove 1.**

1940 Todd *Birds W. PA* 706, Crow . . Rain-, *see* Cuckoo, Black-billed and Yellow-billed; Dove, Eastern Mourning. **1951** *AmSp* 26.269, The mourning dove, known also as . . *rain crow* (D.C., Va., Mo.), may have got part of its reputation as a rain bird through confusion on account of its somewhat similar size and color, and perhaps even notes, with the cuckoos, our most generally known rain fowl. **1968–70** *DARE* (Qu. Q14) Inf **KY**65, Rain crow . . this is a turtledove [FW: =mourning dove]; **KY**72, Rain crow—mourning dove; **MD**36, Rain crow or turtledove—same thing. **1981** *High Coll.* ceKY (as of c1930), *Rain crow* . . mourning dove, whose call is supposed to indicate approaching rain. . . "When the rain crows start to holler, it's going to rain." **1993** Mason *Feather Crowns* 173 **KY,** Christie fell in and out of sleep, reaching for the babies, confusing their cries with rain crows calling out for rain. **2001** *DARE* File **WV,** When I was about 4 years old, I asked what bird was making a particularly haunting call, and she told me it was a "rain crow." That haunting call, I learned later, was that of the mourning dove. My mother was born and raised in New Cumberland, W. Va.

d A **woodpecker** such as the **flicker** n[2] **1** or the **pileated woodpecker B.** [Cf *OED2* *rainbird* sb. 1 1555 → for the green woodpecker (*Picus viridis*)]

1951 *AmSp* 26.269, Because of their calling or singing more noticeably than usual before rain, . . we have as *rain crow* the pileated woodpecker (Quebec, Maine) and Clark's nutcracker (Oreg.) **1968** *DARE* (Qu. Q14) Inf **NY**71, Rain crow [FW: This apparently refers to the flicker]; (Qu. Q17, . . *Kinds of woodpeckers*) Inf **NY**71, High-holer or rain crow.

e An **oyster-catcher** (here: *Haematopus palliatus*).

1951 [see **1b** above].

f Clark's **nutcracker a** (*Nucifraga columbiana*).

1951 [see **1d** above].

g A **whippoorwill** or similar bird. Cf **rainbird 1e**

1966–69 *DARE* (Qu. Q3, . . *Birds that come out only after dark*) Infs **FL**34, **TX**3, Rain crow; **GA**77, Rain crow—between sundown and dark; **OK**18, Whippoorwill—some call them rain crow.

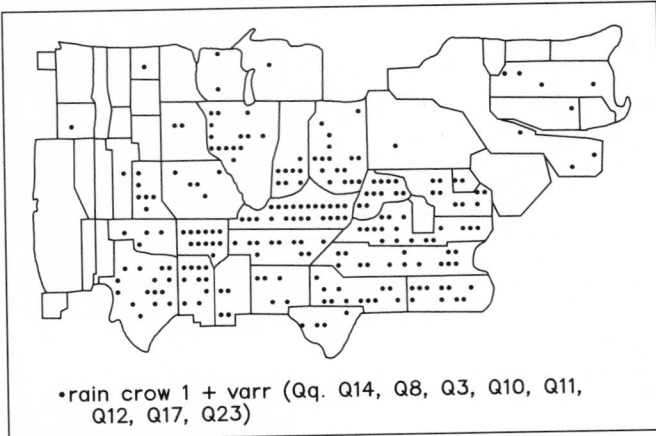

•rain crow 1 + varr (Qq. Q14, Q8, Q3, Q10, Q11, Q12, Q17, Q23)

2 See quot.

1939 *AmSp* 14.91 eTN, *Raincrow.* A court house loafer. 'The raincrow hangs out around the square.'

rain dog n [Prob by analogy with **sun dog**] Cf **rain seed, water dog**

An atmospheric phenomenon supposed to presage rain; see quots.

1866 Clemens in *Sacramento Daily Union* (CA) 24 Aug 3/2, What the sailors call "raindogs"—little patches of rainbow—are often seen drifting about the heavens in these latitudes. **1958** *Hand Coll.* swOH, A rain dog in the evening means rain that night, or the next morning.

rain dove n Cf **rainbird 1, rain crow 1**

1 Either the **black-billed** or the **yellow-billed cuckoo.**

[**1832** Nuttall *Manual Ornith.* 1.551, *Yellow-billed Cuckoo.* . . frequently betrays his snug retreat by his monotonous and guttural *ków ków ków ków* or *koo koo koo koo,* . . uttered rather low and plaintively, like the call of the Dove. . . This note [is] supposed to be most clamorous at the approach of rain.] **1898** (1900) Davie *Nests N. Amer. Birds* 256, This bird [=the yellow-billed cuckoo] is known by several names, such as . . *Rain Dove* . . , which are likewise applied to the Black-billed species. **1903** Dawson *Birds OH* 367, The bird [=the black-billed cuckoo] is fond of wet weather, and especially appreciates the sultry mugginess which often precedes a rain. It is at this time that its notes are most likely to be heard, this habit having won for him in connection with the Yellow-billed species, the title of Rain-Crow or Rain-Dove. **1937** [see **rain crow 1a**]. **1956** MA Audubon Soc. *Bulletin* 40.80 ME, *Yellow-billed Cuckoo.* . . The bird is most clamorous before a rain. . . Rain Dove. . . The species is much like the Mourning Dove in general appearance. . . *Black-billed Cuckoo.* . . This bird is scarcely distinguished from the Yellow-billed species by the general public. . . Rain Dove. **1968–70** *DARE* (Qu. Q8) Inf **OH**72, Rain dove; **PA**138, Rain doves—before a rain; (Qu. Q14, . . *Names* . . *cuckoo*) Inf **MD**26, Rainbird—also called rain dove; **SC**67, There is a rain dove and a mourning dove.

2 =**mourning dove 1.**

1854 in 1885 Taylor *Life & Letters* 1.278 **PA,** The birds know me already, and I have learned to imitate the partridge and the rain-dove, so that I can lure them to me. **1951** *AmSp* 26.269, The mourning dove, known also as *rain dove* (Wis., Oreg.), . . may have got part of its reputation as a rain bird through confusion on account of its somewhat similar size and color, and perhaps even notes, with the cuckoos, our most generally known rain fowl. **1968** *DARE* FW Addit **PA**169, Rain dove —mourning dove. **1970** *DARE* (Qu. Q14) Inf **PA**242, Rain dove— mourning dove.

3 Perh a **whippoorwill.** Cf **rain crow 1g**

1967 *DARE* (Qu. Q3, . . *Birds that come out only after dark*) Inf **IL**26, Rain dove.

rain-fish See **rainwater fish 2**

rainfrog n

1 also *rain toad:* =**tree frog.** **chiefly Sth** See Map Cf **rainbird 2**

1827 McKenney *Sketches* 158 **MI,** We found the few people who live near its mouth . . [with] rain frogs on the logs of their huts to sing them to repose. **1928** Baylor Univ. Museum *Contrib.* 16.9 TX, *Hyla versicolor versicolor* . . *Hyla versicolor chrysoscelis.* . . Tree Frogs of this type. . . are known either as *Raintoads* on account of their noisy piping during or after rains, or *Chameleon Frogs* on account of their frequent changes of color. **1932** Wright *Life-Hist. Frogs* 310, *Hyla squirella.* . . *Common Names*—Southern Tree Frog. . . "Rain Frog." *Ibid* 316 **Okefenokee GA,** Scraper Frog called 'Rain Frog' by natives here about. **1943** Weslager *DE Forgotten Folk* 173, When the rain frog climbs up a tree and hollers, it will soon muddy up and start to rain. The tree frog turns the color of the tree he climbs, so you can't see him. But you sure can hear him. **1950** *WELS* **WI** (*Names for the tree frog*) 2 Infs, Rainfrog; 1 Inf, Rain toad—childhood belief that tree toads (or rain toads) fell with the rain; (*Small frogs that sing or chirp loudly in spring*) 1 Inf, Rainfrog. **1958** Conant *Reptiles & Amphibians* 279, *Hyla cinerea.* . . This is a "rain frog," a vernacular name shared by other members of the group, especially the Squirrel Treefrog. Some country people believe these amphibians are weather prophets, but although they tend to sing mostly in damp weather, they may call as lustily before fair weather as before foul. *Ibid* 281, [*Hyla squirella:*] Called a "rain frog" in many parts of the South. . . The so-called "rain call," usually voiced away from water, is a scolding rasp, quite squirrel-like. **1965–70** *DARE* (Qu. P21, *Small frogs that sing or chirp loudly in spring*) 76 Infs, **chiefly Sth,** Rainfrogs; (Qu. R8, . . *Kinds of creatures that make a clicking or shrilling or chirping kind of sound*) Inf **SC**63, Rainfrogs. **1968** Lester *To Be A Slave* 151, The rain fell in torrents and kept falling till it was about a flood. The rain frogs begin to holler and calling more rain and it rained and rained. Then the rain crow got up in a high tree and he hollered and asked the Lord for rain. **1986** Pederson *LAGS Concordance*, 149 infs, **Gulf Region**, Rainfrog(s); 1 inf, **nwMS**, Rain toad, a different variety, signals rain.

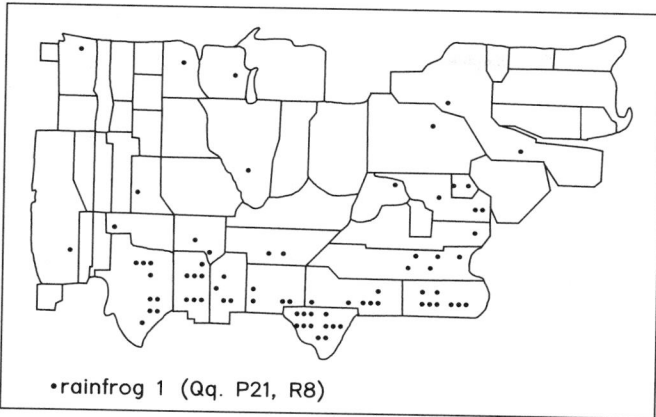

•rainfrog 1 (Qq. P21, R8)

2 also *rain toad:* A spadefoot **toad** such as *Scaphiopus couchi.*

1928 Baylor Univ. Museum *Contrib.* 16.9, *Scaphiopus couchi.* . . This yellow-green, smooth-skinned, burrowing toad is widely distributed in Texas. . . *Rain Toad.* Couch's Spadefoot is very noisy after rains, therefore it is the Rain Toad of middle Texas. **1966** *DARE* (Qu. P22, *Names or nicknames for a very large frog that makes a deep, loud sound*) Inf **NM13**, Rainfrog—comes out where water collects after a flood—they bury themselves in mud until rain.

3 also *rainy day frog:* A narrowmouth **toad** (here: *Gastrophryne carolinensis*).

1932 Wright *Life-Hist. Frogs* 452, *Gastrophryne carolinensis.* . . Common Names . . "Rainy Day Frog." "Rain Frog." *Ibid* 460 **Okefenokee GA,** In 1912 we made the following notes: This species. . . to some sounded like the bleat of a young lamb. . . As one approached the frogs the shrillness of the note became very marked. On the following afternoon the frogs began again during a rain. The natives associate it with such weather and term it the "Rainy Day Frog." *Ibid* 462, Humidity is the important factor in this species in particular. They are truly a "Rainy Day Frog."

rain frogs See **frogs, rain**

rain go-devils See **go-devil n 5**

rain gutter n **scattered, but esp West** See Map Cf **gutter n[1] 1, rainspout**

An **eaves trough** or downspout.

1861 *Scientific Amer.* 4.397, William H. Henderson, of Franklin, Ind., for an Improvement in Beading Rain Gutters. **1965–70** *DARE* (Qu. D28, *What hangs below the edge of the roof to carry off rain-water?*) 13 Infs, **scattered, but esp West,** Rain gutter(s); (Qu. D29, *The pipe that takes the collected rainy-water down to the ground or to a storage tank*) Inf **CA182,** Rain gutter. **1973** Allen *LAUM* 1.178 (as of c1950) 1 inf, **NE,** Rain gutters: Suspended. **1984** *DARE* File **UT,** (*The pipe that takes the water from these to the ground or to a storage tank*) Rain gut-

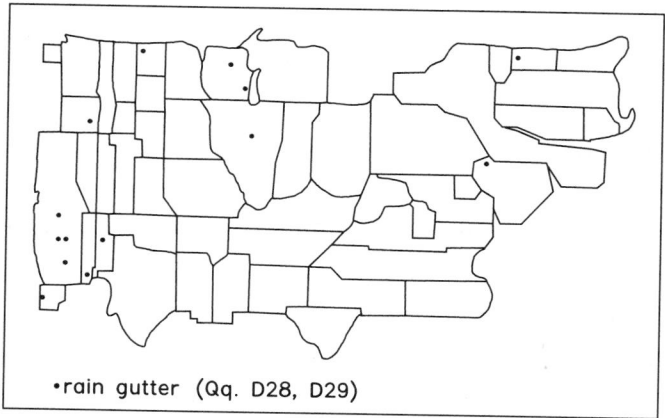

•rain gutter (Qq. D28, D29)

ter. *Ibid* **UT, nCA,** (*What hangs below the edge of the roof to carry off rain-water*) Rain gutter. **1997** *DARE* File **cwCA** (as of c1955), When I was growing up, we talked about the *rain gutters* on the house, perhaps to distinguish them from the *gutters* in the street. Sometimes, though, the *rain gutters* were referred to as *gutters.*

rain-hat trumpet n [From the shape of the leaf]
A **pitcher plant 1** (here: *Sarracenia minor*).

1976 Bailey–Bailey *Hortus Third* 1007, [*Sarracenia*] *minor.* . . Hooded p[itcher] p[lant], rainhat-trumpet. . . N.C. to Fla.

rain hawk n Cf **rainbird 1, rain crow 1, ~ dove**
See quots.

1951 *AmSp* 26.269 **OH,** Rain hawk . . *Yellow-billed cuckoo . . black-billed cuckoo.* **1970** *DARE* (Qu. Q8, *A water bird that makes a booming sound before rain and often stands with its beak pointed almost straight up*) Inf **VA70,** Rain hawk.

rain hen n Cf **rainbird 1c, rain crow 1a, ~ dove 1**
Either the **black-billed** or the **yellow-billed cuckoo.**

1951 *AmSp* 26.269 **OH,** Rain hawk . . *Yellow-billed cuckoo . . black-billed cuckoo.*

rainified adj [*EDD* "Inclined to rain, like rain"] Cf **-ified**
Likely to rain.

1918 *DN* 5.15 **Martha's Vineyard MA,** *Rainified.* Rainy appearance of sky. "It's looked kind o' rainified all the morning." So far as I know, limited to one individual, who is rather given to coinages. **1953** Randolph–Wilson *Down in Holler* 45 **Ozarks,** Speaking of the prospects of rain, a woman said to me, "It sure don't look very rainified this evenin'."

rain lily n [From its blooming after rain] **chiefly Gulf States, esp TX**

1 =**zephyr lily** (here: *Zephyranthes* spp, esp *Z. brazosensis*).
1897 *Jrl. Amer. Folkl.* 10.145 **TX,** Cooperia Drummondii [=*Zephyranthes brazosensis*], . . rain lilies, . . Waco, Tex. **1933** Small *Manual SE Flora* 320, *Zephyranthes.* . . Rain-lilies.—An infusion made from the bulbs is used by the Seminoles to cure toothache. **1948** Stevens *KS Wild Flowers* 48, *Cooperia drummondii*—Rain-lily. . . Flowers and leaves borne concurrently. . . On the Prairies. **1961** Wills–Irwin *Flowers TX* 98, Two kinds of Rain-lily grow in Texas. The Giant Rain-lily [=*Cooperia pedunculata*] . . is found in fields and open woods over much of the central region. . . The other species, . . *Zephyranthes brazosensis* . . is smaller in almost every respect . . [and] more widespread. **1967** *DARE* (Qu. S26b) Inf **LA4,** Rain lilies—come up after a rain. **1972** Brown *Wildflowers LA* 27, White Rain-lily—*Zephyranthes candida.* . . Also Texas and Mississippi. . . Pink rain-lily, *Z. grandiflora* . . , with flowers from pink to rose is widely cultivated in Louisiana. **1979** Spellenberg *Audubon Guide N. Amer. Wildflowers W. Region* 324, *Rain Lily (Zephyranthes longifolia).* . . Resembling a Daffodil, but much smaller and more delicate. **1999** *S. Living* Sept 90, Rain lily (*Zephyranthes candida*) usually begins to bloom in late July. . . Its common name refers to the blooms that magically appear after rains.

2 A plant of the genus *Cooperia*, usu *C. pedunculata.* Also called **cebolleta, evening star 2, fairy lily 2, prairie ~ 3, star ~, zephyr ~**
1936 Whitehouse *TX Flowers* 10, *Giant Rain Lily (Cooperia pedunculata)* has lovely fragrant white flowers which last only a day or two. **1939** Tharp *Vegetation TX* 49, Rain Lily (*Cooperia* spp.) **1951** *PADS* 15.29 **TX,** *Cooperia* spp.—Rain lilies; prairie-lilies. **1961** [see **1** above]. **c1979** TX Dept. Highways *Flowers* 29, *Rain lily* blooms seem to appear almost miraculously a few days after heavy rains from spring to fall. . . *Cooperia pedunculata.*

3 as *yellow rain lily:* =**copper lily.**
1946 Reeves–Bain *Flora TX* 56, *H[abranthus] texanus.* . . Yellow Rain Lily. . . On prairies following rain. **1951** *PADS* 15.29 **TX,** *Atamasco texana* [=*Habranthus texanus*]. . . Copper-lily; . . yellow rain-lily.

rainmaker n

1 A **tree frog.** Cf **rainfrog 1**
1950 *WELS* (Names for the tree frog) 1 Inf, **WI,** Rainmaker.
2 Perh =**green heron.** Cf **rain crow 1b**
1950 *WELS* (A small heron that makes a booming sound before rain, and often stands with its head pointed up) 1 Inf, **csWI,** Rainmaker.

rain mother n
1954 *WELS Suppl.* **csWI,** Another cloud formation—"Rain mother"—not "horse tails"—fleecy and delicate. Usually precedes rain. . . I heard the term "rain mother" in the villages of Schneyville and Clarno . . , and I do not know its origination. . . However I know one lady who used the expression was an English woman. I also know that my son-in-law who is half English and half Irish knows both the "horse tail" and the "rain mother."

rain nigger babies See **nigger baby 3**

rain owl n [See quot 1917]
The barred owl *(Strix varia)*.
1890 Warren *Birds PA* 150, *Syrnium nebulosum* [=*Strix varia*]. . . Barred Owl; Rain Owl. **1917** (1923) *Birds Amer.* 2.103, *Strix varia varia.* . . Rain Owl. [*Ibid* 104, During the day they [=barred owls] seldom call except in rainy or cloudy weather.] **1919** Burns *Ornith. Chester Co. PA* 57, *Strix varia varia* Barred Owl, . . "rain owl." **1938** Oberholser *Bird Life LA* 339, It [=the barred owl] is sometimes called . . 'rain owl', . . or simply 'owl'. **1946** Goodrich *Birds in KS* 317, Owl, rain . . owl, northern barred.

rain pigeon n Cf **rainbird 1c, rain crow 1a, ~ dove 1**
=**yellow-billed cuckoo.**
1951 *AmSp* 26.269 **OH,** Rain pigeon . . *Yellow-billed cuckoo.*

rain pitchforks (and hammer handles, hammerheads, etc)
See **pitchfork 3b**

rain poison v phr
1950 *WELS* (*What people say when rain and sunshine come together*) 1 Inf, **ceWI,** [It's] raining poison.

rainpour n
A downpour.
1970 *DARE* (Qu. B24, . . *A sudden, very heavy rain*) Inf **VA69,** Rainpour ['rɛnpɔə]. [Inf Black] **1986** Pederson *LAGS Concordance* (*Heavy rain*) 1 inf, **nwFL,** Rain pour. [Inf Black]

rain seed n Also *seed cloud* **chiefly S Midl** Cf **mackerel sky,** *DJE*
One of a group of usu small clouds thought to presage rain; as mass noun: such a cloud formation.
1869 *Overland Mth.* 2.373 **TX,** Presently the sky was harrowed into a white and ruddy clod-land, sowed with rain-seeds; but in half an hour the harvest was ripe, and gathered into great crisp-looking shocks, bulging up above the green world. **1892** *DN* 1.231 **KY,** Rain seeds: the clouds that make the mackerel sky. **1939** Harris *Purslane* 6 **cNC,** There was going to be some weather. Rain-seed in the east, a queer look about the sun all day. **1952** Brown *NC Folkl.* 1.582, *Rain-seed.* . . Mottled clouds (supposedly indicative of rain).—Central and east. **1960** Williams *Walk Egypt* 106 **GA,** "Looks like rain seeds." It was midmorning, and the sky was stippled with cloud flakes. **c1960** *Wilson Coll.* **csKY,** *Rain seeds* . . small clouds in a 'mackerel sky'. **1965** *Dict. Queen's English* 10 **NC,** *Rainseed:* Brownish, mottled clouds. The rainseed passed over and 'fore long it was raining. **1966–69** *DARE* (Qu. B10, . . *Long trailing clouds high in the sky*) Inf **AR52,** Rain seed; **GA22,** Rain seeds; **AL30,** Seed clouds; (Qu. B11, . . *Other kinds of clouds that come often*) Inf **AR38,** Rain seed; **MO37,** Rain-seed clouds; **TN14,** Seed clouds.

rain-shaker n *joc* Cf *DS* W1c
An umbrella.
1950 *WELS* (*What do you open up and hold over your head when it rains? . . joking names*) 1 Inf, **cwWI,** Rain-shaker.

rain shelter See **range shelter**

rain sparrow n
See quot.
1966–70 *DARE* (Qu. Q21, . . *Kinds of sparrows*) Infs **ME6, TN53,** Rain sparrow(s).

rainspout n **scattered, but esp PA, MD, NJ** See Map Cf **spout**
A spout or downspout for rainwater; an **eaves trough.**
1870 *Overland Mth.* 5.80, At the proper season a pair of them [=swallows] took possession of a rain-spout across the street from my win-

dow. . . But they were subject, like the city itself, to inundations, which would boom down the spout, and carry out the whole structure pell-mell. **1877** *Manufacturer & Builder* 9.236 **PA,** Austin's patent corrugated expanding rain-spout has stood the test of years. . . The manufacturers, Messrs. Austin, Obdyke & Co., of Philadelphia, have always received the first premium wherever their pipe has been exhibited. **1890** *Century Illustr. Mag.* 41.227 **MD,** It contains . . a honeysuckle . . which later on, frightened at the surroundings, had with one great spring cleared the slippery wall between, reached the rain spout above, and by its helping arm thus escaped to the roof and the sunlight. **1940** Writers' Program *Guide PA* 381, Rainspouts extend from roofs over sidewalks to spill water into the gutters. **1949** Kurath *Word Geog.* fig 54, [The terms *spouts, water spouts,* and *rain spouts* (undifferentiated) are shown to occur chiefly in PA, MD, and WV.] **1956** Ker *Vocab. W. TX* 99, The Midland *spouts* is recorded for Lubbock and . . Scurry counties. *Rain spouts* is also reported by one informant of Scurry county. **1962** *PADS* 38.38 **IL,** In the rest of the territory under study the Northern term [=*eaves troughs*] is dominant almost nowhere but in the Peoria and Moline–Rock Island urban areas. Otherwise, *gutters, rain spouts* and *water spouting* predominate in Midland territory. **1965–70** *DARE* (Qu. D29, *The pipe that takes the collected rain-water down to the ground or to a storage tank*) 34 Infs, **scattered, but esp PA, MD, NJ,** Rainspout; (Qu. D28, *What hangs below the edge of the roof to carry off rain-water?*) 19 Infs, 13 **PA, MD,** Rainspout(s). **1967** Faries *Word Geog. MO* 74, Occurrences of *spouts, spouting, water spouts,* and *rain spouts,* all common in the North Midland and in West Virginia, are sparsely scattered throughout Missouri, but appear five times in St. Louis County. **1973** Allen *LAUM* 1.177 **Upper MW** (as of c1950), *Spouting* and *rainspouts,* common in Pennsylvania, Maryland, and upper West Virginia, consistently turned up in the Midland speech area, southern Iowa, with a few isolated instances elsewhere. **1977–78** Foster *Lexical Variation* 55 **NJ,** Rain-gutters. . . Vertical. . . Rainspout 15 [of 166 infs]. **1978** Michener *Chesapeake* 488 **MD,** The two Steeds [=people], tumbling from their widow's walk, had caught momentarily on rainspouts edging the roof, and then fallen heavily into flower beds. **1985** *DARE* File **MD, PA, VA,** (*The pipe that takes the water from these to the ground or to a storage tank*) Rainspout [4 infs]. *Ibid* **MD,** (*What hangs below the edge of the roof to carry off rain-water?*) Rainspout [1 inf].

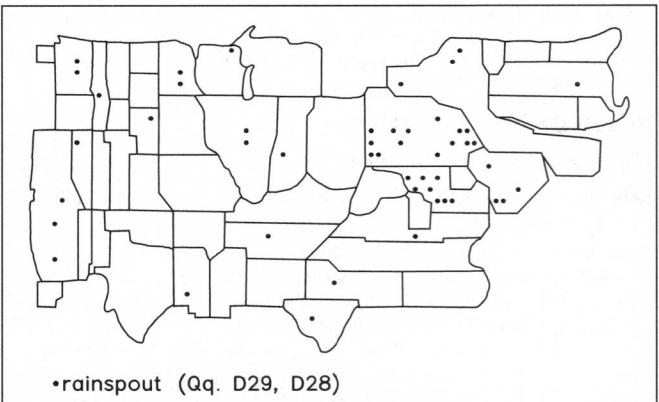

•rainspout (Qq. D29, D28)

rainspouting n **esp MD, PA** Cf **spouting**
An **eaves trough** or downspout.
1968 *DARE* (Qu. D28, *What hangs below the edge of the roof to carry off rain-water?*) Infs **MD21, 41, PA110, 203,** Rainspouting; (Qu. D29, *The pipe that takes the collected rain-water down to the ground or to a storage tank*) Infs **MD14, 41, 50,** Rainspouting. **1973** Allen *LAUM* 1.178 (as of c1950) 1 inf, **NE,** Rain spouting.

rainstick n
An umbrella.
1950 *WELS* (*What do you open up and hold over your head when it rains? . . joking names*) 3 Infs, **ce,seWI,** Rainstick. **c1960** *Wilson Coll.* **csKY,** *Rainstick* . . pert name for umbrella; no German influence here, directly. **1965–70** *DARE* (Qu. W1c, . . *Joking names . . for an umbrella*) 26 Infs, **scattered east of Missip R exc NEng,** Rainstick. **1973** Allen *LAUM* 1.227 (as of c1950) 1 inf, **MN,** Rain stick.

rain swallow See **rainbird 1b**

rain toad See **rainfrog 1, 2**

rain tree n

1 =**monkeypod.** **HI**

1928 Pan-Pacific Research Inst. *Jrl.* 3.2.6 **HI,** Samanea [=*Albizia*], monkey-pod or rain tree. **1948** Neal *In Gardens HI* 352, The name "rain tree" is due to a . . legend that rain constantly falls from its branches, a phenomenon explained as "the ejections of juice by cicadas." **1967** *Malamalama* 9.1.7 **HI,** Along the Mall [at the University of Hawaii] an avenue of rain trees, sometimes inaccurately called monkeypod trees (*Samanea saman*), provides ample shade. **1976** Bailey–Bailey *Hortus Third* 1001, *Rain tree.* . . A fast-growing, ornamental shade tree.

2 A **goldenrain tree** (here: *Koelreuteria paniculata*).

1955 *S. Folkl. Qrly.* 19.234 **FL,** The *Golden Rain Tree* . . [is] locally shortened to *Rain Tree.* . . According to the garden editor of the Florida *Times–Union,* the folk name is derived from the terminal panicles of many small flowers, which fall in a breeze like "golden rain." **1967–70** *DARE* (Qu. T16, . . *Kinds of trees* . . '*special'*) Inf **KS**8, Rain tree—very small, silvery-green cast to them. **1986** Pederson *LAGS Concordance,* 2 infs, **cFL,** Raintrees.

rainwater fish n

1 also *rainwater killifish:* A **killifish 1** (here: *Lucania parva*).

1896 U.S. Natl. Museum *Bulletin* 47.665, *Lucania parva.* . . *Rainwater Fish.* . . Very common at Key West, in shallow waters and tide pools close to the shore, especially where fresh waters soak in the sea; . . equally abundant about the mouth of the Potomac in brackish ponds and tide ditches. **1938** Schrenkeisen *Field Book Fishes* 178, *Rainwaterfish.* . . A small killifish with a small mouth. . . On Long Island [NY] it is sometimes locally abundant in the weed in quite fresh water of creeks tributary to the salt bays, and may not occur in salt water. In Florida it is abundant in quite salt water, apparently scarce in fresh. . . Atlantic coast from Connecticut to the Gulf of Mexico. **1955** Carr–Goin *Guide Reptiles* 66 **FL,** Rainwater Killifish. . . A small, insipid-looking fish one to two inches long. **1966** WI Acad. *Trans.* 55.126 **LA,** *Lucania parva* . . rainwater killifish. **1991** Amer. Fisheries Soc. *Common Names Fishes* 35, *Lucania parva* . . A[tlantic]-F[reshwater]-P[acific] . . rainwater killifish.

2 also *rain-fish:* A related freshwater **killifish 1** (here: *Leptolucania ommata*) native to Florida and Georgia.

1934 *Natl. Geogr. Mag.* 65.605 **seGA,** The Okefinokee shelters one of the tiniest fishes in the world—the rain-water fish, *Leptolucania ommata.* . . It was formerly known only in Florida and was considered rare there; but it exists in untold thousands in the coffee-colored waters of the Okefinokee. **1938** Matschat *Suwannee R.* 34 **seGA,** In the swamp alone over thirty species of fish are found. The rain-fish, supposed to be one of the rarest in the world, breeds there in millions.

rainwater killifish See **rainwater fish 1**

rainworm n

1 =**earthworm.** [*OED2* c1000 →, but in much of its US distribution prob calque of Ger *Regenwurm*]

[**1841** Rauch *Psychology* 61 **PA** [German-born author], When the rainy season commences, they, as do the rain-worms when the sun shines, disappear in caves.] **1855** *Harper's New Mth. Mag.* 11.200, The common rain-worm is carefully gathered in China, and, raw or roasted, considered most palatable food. **1929** *KY Folkl. & Poetry Mag.* 4.1.9 **Chicago IL,** Among a number of prep school boys in Chicago, I found that they were known as "rain worms" and that there was a very general belief that they came down in rain. This, because they were usually seen on the pavements in the city after a rain. **1939** *LANE* Map 236 (*Earthworm*) 3 infs, **sME coast, seMA,** Rainworm. **1941** *Nature Mag.* 34.137, Other names [for the earthworm] and localities provide: dewworm (southern Vermont), eel-worm (western Connecticut), and rainworm (Pennsylvania). **1941** *Language* 17.330 **WI** [*LANCS* fieldwork], *Rainworm*—2 [of 50 infs]. . Both German-derived . . [1 inf] gave the German word too. . . *Rainworm* probably re-introduced, and not spread. **1948** Davis *Word Atlas Gt. Lakes* app qu 75, 2 (of 233) infs, **MI, OH,** Rainworm. **1949** Kurath *Word Geog.* 75, Scattered instances of *rain worm* are found in the Pennsylvania German area (cf *Regenwurm*), in the German settlements on the Yadkin in North Carolina, in Nobleboro, Maine (a Palatine town), and on Buzzards Bay in Massachusetts, where it must be of English origin (cf Old English *regenwyrm*). **1962** Atwood *Vocab. TX* 58, *Rainworm,* which was recorded occasionally in German-speaking areas of the East, also occurs in Texas, but rarely. Nine of the ten users are of German-speaking background. **1965** *PADS* 43.20 **seMA,** Names for an earthworm: rainworm [5 of 9 infs]. **1967** Faries

Word Geog. MO 111, There are ten instances of *rain worm* . . , known especially in the Pennsylvania German area and in other German settlements. **1967–70** *DARE* (Qu. P5, . . *The common worm used as bait*) Infs **MI**67, **NY**240, **RI**15, Rainworm; (Qu. P6, . . *Kinds of worms* . . *used for bait*) Inf **MO**12, Little rainworms; **TX**54, Rainworm; (Qu. R27, . . *Kinds of caterpillars or similar worms*) Inf **MI**67, Then we have the big nightcrawlers, too, and I've heard them called "rainworms," sometimes just "worms." **1982** Sternberg *Fishing* 56, Sometimes called the *dew* or *rain worm,* the native nightcrawler appears on roads and sidewalks after spring rains. Average length is 6 to 7 inches, but some are 10 inches or longer. Its color varies from brownish-pink to purplish-red.

2 The larva of a **mosquito n[1] B1;** a **wiggler.**

1969 *DARE* (Qu. R14, *Small worm-like things [seen in rain barrels or standing water] that hatch into mosquitoes*) Inf **MI**93, Rainworm.

rainy day frog See **rainfrog 3**

rair See **rare** v

raise v

A Forms.

Past, past pple: usu *raised;* also:

1 *raise.*

1899 Chesnutt *Conjure Woman* 32 **csNC** [Black], W'en de wah broke out, Mars Dugal' raise' a comp'ny. **1986** Pederson *LAGS Concordance Gulf Region,* [48 infs used *raise* as preterite of *raise;* 38 infs used *raise* as past participle of *raise.*]

2 *riz, rose, ruz.* Note: Historically, these forms belong to *rise.*

1890 Holley *Samantha among Brethren* 175 **NY,** I have seen them that this mind cure religion had fairly riz right up, and made 'em nigher to heaven every way. **1909** *DN* 3.415 **nME,** *Riz,* v. pret. and *pp.* Rose or raised. **1916** *DN* 4.301 **MA,** *Rose.* . . Raised: of animals. "He rose that calf. He knows she ain't pure alderney 'cause he rose her." Becket, Mass. **1923** *DN* 5.219 **swMO,** He . . shore rose hell when Doc set 'is arm. **1957** *Sat. Eve. Post Letters* **seMA,** Bread was *riz* overnight, cut down and riz again in the morning. **1966** *DARE* (Qu. P39b, *If a hunter or a dog makes a bird or a covey fly*) Inf **MI**26, Raised 'em; or "My dog 'rose' some birds, or 'ruz' [rʌz] even." **1968** *DARE* Tape **NJ**50, They pumped there pretty near all day. . . and they riz that little brook. His water out of that well was the brook. **1976** Garber *Mountain-ese* 75 **sAppalachians,** The carpenters riz the frame for the house in jist one day. **1984** *DARE* File **csPA,** Rose—past tense [of] *raise:* "God rose him up from the dead" (radio preacher).

B Transitive senses.

1 To rouse (usu a game animal) into moving; to start, flush.

1858 in 1966 Boller *MO Fur Trader* 155 **MO,** The "Four-Bears[n]" [=a group of Indians] having sent word not to let any of the Whites come for fear that they would "raise" the buffalo. *Ibid* 165, A band of elk had been seen raised, without any apparent cause, and it was supposed that a Santee or Cut-Head war party were hovering around. **1874** J.W. Long *Amer. Wild-Fowl Shooting* 9.157 (*OED2*), Watch this old fool of a duck coming, and see me 'raise her'. **1949** *PADS* 11.25 **CO,** *Raise.* . . To scare out of hiding. **1965–70** *DARE* (Qu. P39a, *When a hunter or a dog finds a game animal and makes it start running* . . *he* _____ *it*) Infs **IN**42, **NJ**8, **PA**126, Raised; **IL**26, **KS**7, Raise; **MI**26, Raises; (Qu. P39b, *If a hunter or a dog makes a bird or a covey fly*) Infs **CA**87, **CT**9, **MT**4, **NJ**3, 8, Raised it; **CA**45, Raised the birds; **OH**36, Raised them; **NY**88, Raises it; **TX**26, Raises 'em.

2 To cause to show oneself, rouse; to find (someone or, rarely, something).

1875 Twain *Sketches New & Old* (Hartford) 90, But I can't raise anybody with this bell. **1891** (1967) Freeman *New Engl. Nun* 254, Guess I'll go round to the back door an' see if I can raise anybody. **1902** *DN* 2.243 **sIL,** *Raise.* . . 1. To cause to appear, especially in such an expression as 'I hollered him but failed to raise him.' 2. To find, especially after protracted search, as 'I finally raised it.' **1903** *DN* 2.326 **seMO,** *Raise.* . . Find. 'I've hunted all day, but can't raise him.' **1907** *DN* 3.235 **nwAR,** *Raise.* . . To find. **1910** *DN* 3.447 **wNY,** *Raise.* . . To find. "I've looked for him, but I can't raise him." **1912** *DN* 3.587 **wIN,** *Raise.* . . To arouse or wake. "I whistled and yelled for fifteen minutes, but I couldn't raise anybody." **1915** *DN* 4.188 **swVA,** *Raise.* . . To arouse so as to hold communication with. "I called loud at the house but I couldn't raise anybody." **1938** Hertzler *Horse & Buggy Dr.* 66 **KS** (as of early 20th cent), Those same dogs prevented an approach to the house and it was sometimes difficult to raise the occupant. **1942** McAtee *Dial.*

Grant Co. IN 51 (as of 1890s), *Raise* . . find; "I looked all over the place before I raised him". (Southern Ill.) **1998** *DARE* File **NEng,** I walked all the way around the house calling their names, but I couldn't raise anyone; **csWI,** I kept trying to call them all morning, but I couldn't raise anybody. I wonder if something's wrong with their phone; **cwCA, nwKS** (as of c1960), I couldn't raise anyone—they must be out of town.

3a To bring up, form the manners of (a child). [*OED2* 1744 →; this sense appears to be obs or dial in Brit Engl] Note: Despite a long history of usage-book disapproval, this sense is used throughout the US by speakers of all social groups and levels. The comb *raise up* in this sense is more restricted in distribution and is treated separately at **3b** below. Cf **raised in a barn, raising 1, rear** v[1] **1**

1762 (1961) Adams *Diary* 1.233, The story of Prats Death was told. His Honor said it would be a Loss to his family. He was in a fair Way to have raised it. **1817** Paulding *Letters from South* 1.85, You know I was raised, as they say in Virginia, among the mountains of the north. **1827** (1939) Sherwood *Gaz. GA* 139, *Raised,* for brought up, educated. **1836** (1838) Haliburton *Clockmaker* (1st ser) xi [sic for ix] **NEng,** I don't know as ever I felt so ugly afore since I was raised. **1899** (1912) Green *VA Folk-Speech* 344, *Raise.* . . To promote the growth and development of; bring up; rear; grow; breed; as, to raise a family of children; to raise crops, plants, or cattle. **1904** *DN* 2.420 **nwAR,** *Raise.* . . To bring up. 'I was raised in Pike County.' The biblical expression 'bring up' is never used, though 'rear' is often used consciously instead of *raise.* **1931** (1991) Hughes–Hurston *Mule Bone* 106 **cFL** [Black], Shet up you nasty lil heifer, sassin' me! You ain't half raised. . . I'm goin' on down to de church an' tell yo' mammy. But she ain't been half raised herself. **1932** Stong *State Fair* 238 **IA,** I was raised to run a farm—and you weren't. **1934** Carmer *Stars Fell on AL* 41, He was raised polite and didn't think he ought to interrupt. **1956** McAtee *Some Dialect NC* 36, *Raise* . . train. "I was raised to tell the truth." **1958** McCulloch *Woods Words* 145 **Pacific NW,** *Raised on the river*—Said of a man good at handling logs. **1962** Atwood *Vocab. TX* 65, If a woman has brought children to maturity, most Texas informants would say that she *raised* them. . . This usage predominates in all age and educational groups. *Reared* is clearly an educated form. **1965–70** *DARE* (Qu. Z17, *To take care of or bring up a child:* "All her children were _____ [on the farm].") 657 Infs, **widespread,** Raised; **SC26,** Raise [*DARE* Ed: The social statistics of the Infs giving these responses are virtually identical to those of all Infs responding to this question.]; (Qu. II21, . . "*The way he behaves, you'd think he was _____.*") 312 Infs, **scattered, but somewhat more freq Sth, S Midl, TX,** Raised in a barn [and other resps with *raised* or *raise*]; (Qu. AA15b, . . *Joking ways . . of saying that a man is getting married.* . . "*He _____.*") Infs **NC40, OK1, OR3, SC24,** Has taken a girl (*or* baby) to raise; (Qu. AA15c, . . *A woman*) Inf **CA36,** Took a boy to raise; (Qu. II36a, *Somebody who talks back or gives rude answers*) Inf **TX31,** Ill-raised person. **1968** *DARE* Tape **CA87,** He didn't raise a boy of his own. **1973** Allen *LAUM* 1.343 (as of c1950), Most [U]pper [M]idwest infs. "raise children," about one in five "brings up" children, and a very few, with a high school education, "rear" them. **1976** Garber *Mountain-ese* 73 **sAppalachians,** Mr. Jones shore is industrious to raise sich a big family.

b with *up:* See quots. **chiefly Sth, S Midl** See Map *esp freq among speakers with little formal educ* Cf **C2b** below

1797 J. Pettigrew *Let.* 22 March (Univ. N.C. MS.) *(DAE),* The thoughts of ingratitude or disobedience to a parent who has rased one up from the cradle. **1929** *Hearst's International* Oct 63 **NYC,** She slips this baby off to her sister in a little town in Spain to raise up. **1934** (1970) Wilson *Backwoods Amer.* 153 **Ozarks,** Noah and Sody . . were born and raised up on . . Drake's Creek. **1941** *LANE* Map 395 *(She has brought up),* [*Raised* occurs with freq throughout **NEng;** *raised up* is fairly common in **ME, NH, VT,** but infreq in **sNEng.**] **1944** *PADS* 2.35 **Sth,** *Raised up with, to be.* . . To grow up with. Buncombe Co., N.C. (Also Va., S.C., Tenn. Rather common.) **1952** Giles *40 Acres* 5 **csKY,** To my chagrin I learned that allowances were made for me because I was "from off," I had not been properly "raised up" and I therefore could not be expected to know much. **1965–70** *DARE* (Qu. Z17, *To take care of or bring up a child:* "All her children were _____ [on the farm].") 21 Infs, **chiefly Sth, S Midl,** Raised up; **SC10, 26,** Raise up; (Qu. II21, . . "*The way he behaves, you'd think he was _____.*") Infs **GA6, IN68, NY14,** Raised up in a barn; **OK58,** Raised up alone; **GA13,** Raised up with the hogs. [13 of 29 total Infs comm type 5, 16 gs educ or less] **1966** Dakin *Dial. Vocab. Ohio R. Valley* 436, In the context "She has *reared* three children" the usual verb everywhere in the Ohio Valley is *raised.* . . A relatively small number of older, less educated speakers say *raised up.* **1967** *Advance-Monticellonian*

(Monticello AR) 5 Oct 1/1, "I was raised up in the saw and lumber business," John Porter Price, owner and operator of the mill, said. **1967–68** *DARE* Tape **AL33,** [FW:] About how many people lived around the area then? . . [Inf:] Very few settled when I was raised up. *Ibid* **GA30,** I was raised up to call 'em a whooping crane. *Ibid* **MD9,** We raised 'em up as animals. We didn't try to help 'em when we should have. *Ibid* **NY113,** I raised up five children, four boys and a girl. **1967** *DARE* FW Addit **LA,** He was raised up with 'em and his daddy was raised up with 'em and *his* daddy was raised up with 'em; **TN,** When you and me was raised up. **1986** Pederson *LAGS Concordance* **Gulf Region,** [There are 116 exx of *raise up* 'to rear (a child)' used in var phrr.]

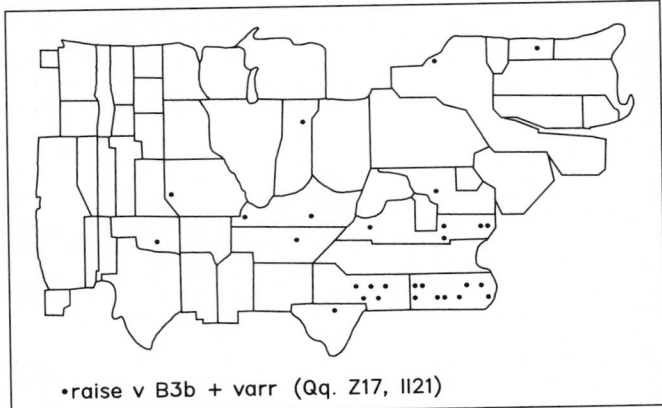

•*raise* v B3b + varr (Qq. Z17, II21)

4 To restore (one confined to bed) to health.

1821 Howison *Upper Canada* 306 **NY,** I've been sick on this road this fortnight. Dr. S_____ raised me last week; he's a dreadful clever man, and said, if I didn't begin taking on wine, I would never get smart, and this is my bottle of wine. **1943** *AmSp* 18.237 **LA** [Black], *Raise* . . restore to health. 'Mama said, "Kin you raise her?" and de doctor said, "I think I can." '

5 To begin or lead (a song). Cf **hoist** v **C1i(1)** [Chiefly Scots dial; cf *EDD*] **esp Sth**

1847 Hurd *Grammatical Corrector* 117, In some parts of the south and west, it [=*raise*] is also used improperly in another sense, thus: I was obliged to *raise* the hymn; that is, to *commence the singing* of the hymn. **1856** Olmsted *Journey Slave States* 26, An old negro . . raised a hymn, which soon became a confused chant. **1898** Westcott *Harum* 275 **NY,** I like music ever so much, an' so does David, though I guess it would floor him to try an' raise a tune. **1905** in 1913 Pringle *Woman Rice Planter* 274 **SC,** I knew I would have to "raise" the hymn—that means stand up in your pew and sing it without accompaniment. **1928** Peterkin *Scarlet Sister Mary* 341 **SC,** He began lining out the hymn to be sung, two lines at a time. . . Brer Dee raised it, all the people joined in singing it. **1984** Wilder *You All Spoken Here* 180 **Sth,** H'ist the tune; *raise the tune:* The song leader pitches the tune of the song to be sung.

6 To reach the top of (a hill or rise). Cf **rise** v **B2**

1804 (1965) Ordway *Jrls.* 168, We raised a Steep bank back of this bottom. **1861** *Vanity Fair* 4.59 **ME,** All of a suden we riz a hill, and then we stoped. **1869** Twain *Innocents* 494, Just before we came to Joseph's Pit, we "raised" a hill, and there, a few miles before us, . . lay . . the sacred Sea of Galillee [sic]. **1914** *DN* 4.111 **cKS,** *Raise.* . . To mount; climb. "I saw the team raise a hill." **1927** *AmSp* 2.362 **cwWV,** *Raise* . . to go up the hill. "We saw the team raise the hill more than an hour ago." **1934** (1936) Barrows *Ubet* 280 **MT,** Every time I would raise a ridge, I expected to see him, for the signs were fresh.

C Intransitive senses.

1a Used in var senses where *rise* would be std. [*OED2 raise* v.[1] 37 1470–85 →; "*Obs. exc. U.S.*"; cf *Webster's Dict. Engl. Usage*] Cf **lay** v

1770 in 1918 *MD Hist. Mag.* 13.61, I am quite indifferent whether Stephenson takes or Refuses the tob[acc]o, as I think the Price will raise again. **1794** (1914) Clark *Jrl.* 438 **VA,** I omitted to mention that a considerable rain fell on the 18th & 19th & that the waters of the Miamis River [were] raising fast. **1835** (1961) Strang *Diary* 58 **NY,** Yesterday the creek raised very high. **1884** *Anglia* 7.275 **Sth, S Midl** [Black], To *raise up* = to rise. **1902** *DN* 2.243 **sIL,** *Raise.* . . To rise, as the sun. . . The verb rise is not used. **1904** *DN* 2.420 **nwAR,** The moon had just raised a little above the hills. **1906** *DN* 3.122 **sIN,** The crick, or the sun, is raisin'. **c1938** in 1970 Hyatt *Hoodoo* 2.1478 **seGA** [Black], Well, during at de time dat they [=a pair of stars] raises, yo' get de inside part. **1942** Faulkner *Go Down* 354 **MS** [Black], Raise up and get yo foa clock coffy. **1943** *LANE* Map 657 *(Rose)* 8 infs, **NH, VT, wMA,** Raised; 1 inf, **nwRI,** Why don't the heat raise? **1965–70** *DARE* (Qu. B19, *When fog begins to go up into the air . . it's _____*) 54 Infs, **scattered exc Sth, NEng,** Raising; **KY31, MD26, TN14,** A-raising(g); (Qu. B20, *When the wind begins to increase . . it's _____*) Infs **CO17, IL39, IN76, IA36, MI22, MO1, OH79, PA164,** Raising; (Qu. B20, *If fog goes up very fast: "It's _____."*; total Infs questioned, 75) Inf **OK9,** Raising; (Qu. C2, *. . When you see the water in a stream getting higher;* total Infs questioned, 75) Inf **FL37,** Raising; (Qu. P39b, *If a hunter or a dog makes a bird or a covey fly*) Inf **GA72,** Made him raise. [54 of 63 total Infs comm type 4 or 5, 50 old] **1969** *DARE* Tape **CA145,** I got there and the fog raised just right; **IL69,** When you get in that tough land sometimes those plows would raise out of the ground. **1973** Allen *LAUM* 1.151 (as of c1950), The sun rose at six. . . *Raised* . . with two occurrences each in Minnesota, Iowa, and eastern South Dakota, is a relic form reported by Type I [=old, with little educ] speakers only. **1986** Pederson *LAGS Concordance* **Gulf Region** *(The wind is)* 6 infs, Raising; 1 inf, Raising up; 1 inf, The wind's raised = has gotten stronger; *(Rise)* 3 infs, (Begins to) raise; 1 inf, I saw the sun raise; 1 inf, Raised up—of a fish in water; 1 inf, Raised up = rose; 1 inf, The cream would raise on it; 1 inf, Raise up = rise, of a person who couldn't arise; [At other questions:] 1 inf, You'd raise up and see who's running (a)round the church; 1 inf, It don't raise up as high; 1 inf, Bristles raise up; 1 inf, Fixing to raise up—i.e., about to get up; 1 inf, Raised up—of a sunken vault.

b Spec; rarely with *up;* of bread dough: to increase in volume by the action of yeast. **widespread exc Sth, TX**   See Map

c1965 Randle *Cookbooks* (Ask Neighbor) 1.90 **OH,** Grease top and let raise 1 hour. **1965–70** *DARE* (Qu. OO6a, *. . "The room was warm, so the dough _____ [quickly]."*) 390 Infs, **widespread exc Sth, TX,** Raised; **AZ1, CA139, KY52, 71, OH75, PA128, WI76,** Would (*or* could) raise; **AL15, IL57,** Raise; **CA167,** Did not raise; **NY45,** Raised good; **KY69,** Raised up; **CA24,** Raises; (Qu. OO6b, *. . "She put the dough in the oven . . before it had _____ enough."*) 340 Infs, **widespread exc Sth, TX,** Raised; **CO47, NY24, OH55, 65, TN1, 23,** Time (*or* chance) to raise; **WY1,** Raise; **VA9,** Raised good; **KY69,** Raised up. **1966–68** *DARE* Tape **IN3,** It usually took overnight for that kind of east to raise; **MI22,** You knead it real good, 'til it doesn't even stick to your hands. And, you let it raise. Twice. And then you put it in pans and let that raise. **1986** Pederson *LAGS Concordance,* 1 inf, **csTX,** To make the bread raise.

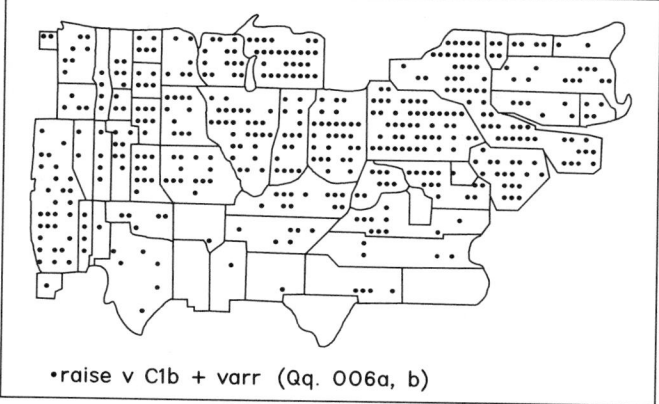

•raise v C1b + varr (Qq. OO6a, b)

2 Used in var senses that do not correspond to std senses of *rise,* as:

a Of animals: to live and reproduce, breed.   **SE**

1938 Rawlings *Yearling* 19 **nFL,** The scrub's a fitten place for the game to raise, and all wild things. . . I cain't raise young uns in a pure thicket. **1968** *DARE* FW Addit **GA22,** "Skeeters is not bad to raise there"—meaning there aren't many mosquitoes there; **GA25,** "They raise in the water"—describing the life cycle of certain insects. **c1970** Pederson *Dial. Surv. Rural GA,* 1 inf, **seGA,** We have one [kind of worm] that grows and raises around woodpiles; 1 inf, **seGA,** Caterpillar grow on the plum trees—I mean, raise on the plum trees; 1 inf, **seGA,** They [=mosquitoes] raise in the flowers. **1971** GA Dept. Ag. *Farmers Market Bulletin* 3 Feb 8/2, These are fungus gnats and raise in moist soil and decaying food. **1986** Pederson *LAGS Concordance,* 1 inf, **cwTN,** They raise

here = breed and grow here; 1 inf, **cnTN,** Won't raise—of fish that won't reproduce; 1 inf, **seMS,** They raised in a rotten hole in the tree.

b usu with *up;* Of a person: to grow up, be reared.   **esp SE** Cf **B3b** above

1924 Raine *Land of Saddle-Bags* 103 **sAppalachians,** We didn't have no fotch-on clothes when I was a-raisin'. **1956** Hall *Coll.* **eTN** *(Montgomery Coll.),* Mr. Barnes lived in North Carolina and raised up there. **1966** *DARE* Tape **SC10,** That's the one [=the church] I raise up in. *Ibid* **SC26,** I raise up in that church. **1968** *DARE* FW Addit **GA26,** All my forebears raised up in the Okefenoke [ˌokɪfɪ'nok]. **1986** Pederson *LAGS Concordance,* 1 inf, **neFL,** When I was raising up = growing up; 1 inf, **nwTN,** Back when I was a kid, raising up; 1 inf, **cnAR,** Where us childrens raised up = were reared.

c Of plants: to grow, flourish.

1967–69 *DARE* (Qu. OO35b, *. . "That land is poor—nothing has ever _____ there."*) Inf **MO6,** Raised; **NY2,** Raised on it.

raise n

1 in phr *make a raise:* To acquire means, accumulate a reserve of money; to come into possession (of).

1830 Ames *Mariner's Sketches* 240 **MA,** Many a time I have seen a group of English and American seamen whose money was spent, before their 'liberty' was out, disencumbering themselves of jackets, shoes and silk handkerchiefs, to 'make a raise' for the mutual accommodation of the party. **1838** Neal *Charcoal Sketches* 96 **PA,** I made a raise of a horse and saw, after being a wood-piler's prentice for a while. **1878** Beadle *Western Wilds* 41, At last I made a little raise . . an' concluded to come home. **1887** Francis *Saddle & Mocassin* 103 **West,** Once a miner always a miner. Found in any other walk in life, the old prospector is only "lying by" to tide over evil times, or "making a raise" to enable him to return to his favourite pursuit. **1899** (1912) Green *VA Folk-Speech* 344, *Raise.* . . An acquisition; a getting or procuring by special effort, as of money or chattels; as, to make a raise of a hundred dollars. **1928** *Ruppenthal Coll.* **KS,** You must have made a raise somewhere the way you are blowing in money. **1942** McAtee *Dial. Grant Co. IN* 42 (as of 1890s), *Make a raise* . . improve in material welfare; "If we can [make a raise] we'll soon leave the old place." **1966** Barnes–Jensen *Dict. UT Slang* 29, *Make a raise, to* . . to get money or another thing of value. "I was broke but I made a raise, and got back home."

2 A rise in the level of a stream; a flood.

1927 *AmSp* 2.358 **cwWV,** Did your johnboat get away the last raise? **1967** *DARE* Tape **LA5,** [FW:] What currents are important in the river? . . [Inf:] The low stage of water like this, . . about two, three miles an hour, I'd imagine. And then when it gets on up, oh, fifteen, twenty foot raise in the river, you got about . . five, six mile current.

3 A small hill; a rise.

1969 *DARE* (Qu. C17, *. . A small, rounded hill*) Inf **PA184,** Raise. **1986** Pederson *LAGS Concordance* *(A hill)* 1 inf, **csTX,** A raise. **1998** *DARE* File **OK,** *Raise*—a small hill.

raised ppl adj

1 also rarely *raise;* Of baked goods: leavened with yeast. **scattered, but chiefly Nth, N Midl**   See Map on p. 454   Cf **rise** v **B3**

1837 Coraham *Treatise on Bread* 29 (Ernst) *(DAE),* Loaf or raised bread. **1887** Parloa *Miss Parloa's Kitchen Companion* 751, *Raised Loaf Cake.* . . When it has risen to a sponge, add the raisins, and pour the batter into three buttered pans. Let it rise in the pans for one hour. Bake for an hour and a half. **1889** Cooke *Steadfast* 189 **NEng,** Her "election cake" . . wore only the style of "raised cake." **1890** *Harper's New Mth. Mag.* 81.707 **NEng,** I've got raised biscuit for supper. **1896** (c1973) Farmer *Orig. Cook Book* 80 **eMA,** Raised Waffles. . . By using a whole yeast cake, the mixture will rise in one and one-half hours. *Ibid* 82, *Raised Doughnuts.* . . Scald and cool milk; when lukewarm, add yeast cake dissolved in water, salt, and flour enough to make a stiff batter; let rise over night. **1906** *Pocumtuc Housewife* 20 **nwMA,** Raised Biscuit. Are made much like bread except that a little shortening is used and they are allowed to get lighter. *Ibid* 30, *Raised Cake.* One and a half cups of bread dough, one cup of sugar, one half cup of butter, one egg, a little soda, nutmeg and cinnamon to taste, a cup full of chopped raisins. Bake as soon as made. **1914** Atherton *Perch of the Devil* 28 **MT,** I've got fried chicken . . and raised biscuit. **1949** Kurath *Word Geog.* 21, For the homemade wheat bread baked in loaves Eastern New England has *white bread, yeast bread,* and *raised-bread* or *riz-bread.* . . In the same area doughnuts made of raised dough are called *raised doughnuts* or *riz doughnuts.* **1963** Adamson *Household Hints* 215 **NEng** (as of late 1800s), *New Orleans,* or other good brown sugar, is best for raised, fruit, and wedding cake. **1965–70** *DARE* (Qu. H28, *Different shapes or types of doughnuts*) 62 Infs, **scattered, but chiefly Nth, N Midl,** Raised doughnut; **MA69,** Raised cruller; **VT13,** Raised sweet doughnut; (Qu. H19, *What do you mean by a biscuit? How are they made?*) 19 Infs, **chiefly NEast, Gt Lakes,** Raised biscuit(s); **PA235, WI13,** Raised dough; **CA167, NY92,** Raised rolls; **IL49,** Corn raised biscuits; (Qu. H15, . . *Made with wheat flour*) Infs **CA174, ME7, MA18,** Raised bread; **SC26,** Raise bread; (Qu. H18, . . *Special kinds of bread*) Inf **NC34,** Raised corn bread; **PA126,** Raise breads; (Qu. H20b, . . *Names . . for pancakes*) Inf **IA12,** Raised pancakes; (Qu. H26, *A round cake of dough, cooked in deep fat, with a hole in the center*) Infs **ME16, PA40,** Raised doughnut; (Qu. H29, *A round cake, cooked in deep fat, with jelly inside*) Infs **IA12, ME19, OH49, WI62,** Raised doughnut; (Qu. H30, *An oblong cake, cooked in deep fat*) Inf **PA128,** Raised cake; (Qu. H32, . . *Fancy rolls and pastries*) Inf **VT13,** Raised rolls. **1967** Faries *Word Geog.* MO 99, To describe bread made of white flour and baked in loaves, the Missouri informants rarely employ any term other than . . *light-bread* (652 occurrences [among 700 infs]). Thirty-nine use *wheat bread* . . , with nine and two respectively using the Northern *raised bread* and *riz-bread.* **1972** *PADS* 58.19 cwAL, Wheat bread. Southern and South Midland *light bread* (12 [of 27 infs]) and Coastal Southern *loaf bread* (7) are most frequent. . . North and North Midland *(wheat) bread* (3) and Eastern New England *white/raised bread* (3) occur also. **1986** Pederson *LAGS Concordance (Doughnut)* 1 inf, cLA, Raise doughnut—allowed to rise before frying; 1 inf, csTN, Raised doughnuts (with yeast); 1 inf, cwFL, Raised doughnuts (made with yeast); 1 inf, **seFL,** Raised doughnuts.

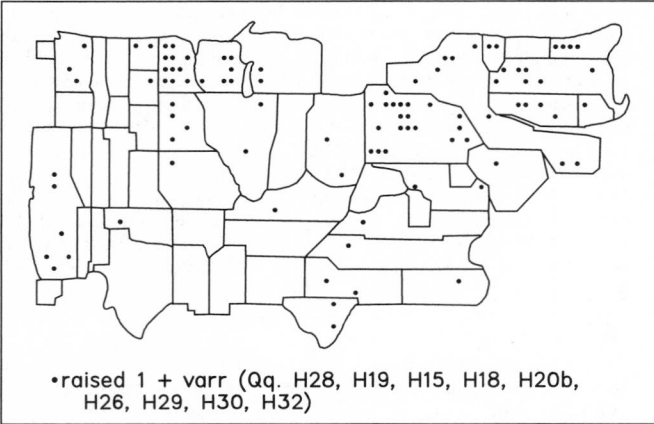

•raised 1 + varr (Qq. H28, H19, H15, H18, H20b, H26, H29, H30, H32)

2 Of a dwelling: having the main floor higher than ground level, either on piles or on an above-ground basement.

1968 *DARE* (Qu. D23, *A house that is divided in two through the middle*) Inf **LA23,** Raised double—basement with shotgun double. **1968** *DARE* FW Addit **New Orleans LA,** *Raised cottage,* also *raised single:* a house with a basement—common. **1986** Pederson *LAGS Concordance,* 1 inf, csAL, Raised cottage—front steps to second-floor porch. **1991** *DARE* File **NJ,** Along the East Coast and on the banks of streams subject to flooding, at least in New Jersey, there are "raised ranch houses". These are single floor houses raised on piles usually about 8 feet above the ground level. The open ground beneath the house is used as a garage and for rough storage. I have not heard the term used out here in the West.

raise day n

The day on which a fishnet is raised.

1953 (1977) Hubbard *Shantyboat* 302 **Missip-Ohio Valleys,** Every other day, ordinarily, is "raise day," and it might seem an easy method of fishing. The nets, however, always need attention: they must be moved in or out, set in a new place, the holes made by snags and gar fish mended.

raised gravy n Also *raising gravy* Sth, S Midl Cf red-eye gravy

A gravy usu made from the drippings and scraps left in the pan after frying meat.

1965–69 *DARE* (Qu. H37, . . *Words . . for gravy. Any joking ones?*) Inf **AL1,** Raised gravy [same as] red-eye gravy; **GA79,** Raised gravy—juice out of ham, no water added, same as red-eye gravy; **MS60,** Raised gravy; **AL11,** Raisin' gravy. **1986** Pederson *LAGS Concordance,* 1 inf,

nwGA, Raised gravy—with flour and milk, raised ham gravy = raised gravy; 1 inf, **cwGA,** Raised gravy = thickened; [1 inf, **nwGA,** Red-eye gravy—raised with coffee, meat gravy]. **1998** *NADS Letters* MS, I have heard "Raised Gravy" used . . to describe the process of making gravy from drippings left from frying chicken, ham, or sausage. Flour is gradually added into the grease to produce a thick gravy which is then liberally applied to biscuits, or the meat itself, or potatoes. *Ibid* sKY, "Raised gravy" . . was used to denote the gravy made after frying cured ham. The skillet was then left on the stove to get very hot, then cold water was poured into it and the cold against the hot skillet made the "stickeys" that were stuck to the skillet turn loose or raise from the bottom. When this was poured into a bowl the grease would raise to the top. . . In some areas this is called "red eye gravy." *Ibid* swTN, Peggy remembers this from . . Oak Ridge and Memphis, Tennessee. I first ate it during visits to . . the South during the 40s. . . I immediately associate this with "biscuits and raised gravy." **2000** *Ibid* MS, I have friends, natives of Tippah County, who say that in the 30's and 40's "Raised Gravy" was a synonym for "Red Eye" gravy. That is gravy made with grease and water, but not thickened with flour. *Ibid* sWV, People . . in southern West Virginia make "raised Gravy"[*] this way: First, they fry slices of country cured ham in a skillet. . . Then the slices are removed from the pan, and boiling water is added immediately. This "raises" all the delicious brown bits of ham left in the pan. Add a little salt and black pepper, and boil for about five minutes. This is served over hot biscuits. It differs from other gravies in that it is not thickened with flour or cornstarch. *Ibid* KY, Raised gravy—My father and aunts, from Bow, Kentucky, used this term to refer to a gravy that was *not* pot gravy and *not* red-eye. It was "raised" from saved grease and flour, plus milk or water.

raised in a barn adj phr Also *raised in a pigpen;* for addit varr see quot 1965–70 **widespread, but somewhat more freq Sth, S Midl, TX** See Map Cf **born in a barn; brought up in a barn; sawmill, born in a**

Fig: unmannered, uncouth—used esp of one who neglects to shut the door.

1908 *DN* 3.402 nwAR, Raised in a barn. . . 1. Ill-mannered, boorish, or uncouth. 2. Applied to a person who never closes a door. **1941** *AmSp* 16.25 sIN, MO, *Was you raised in a barn?* Said to one who fails to close a door. **1942** McAtee *Dial. Grant Co. IN* 52 (as of 1890s), *Raised in a barn* . . untutored. "He must have been [raised in a barn] as he don't know enough to shut the door." **1948** *WELS Suppl.* seWI, 30 yrs. ago non-door-closing children "must have been raised in a barn." **1956** McAtee *Some Dialect NC* 36, *Raised in a barn* . . unmannered. **1965–70** *DARE* (Qu. II21, *When somebody behaves unpleasantly or without manners: "The way he behaves, you'd think he was _____."*) 222 Infs, **widespread, but somewhat more freq Sth, S Midl, TX,** Raised in a barn; 41 Infs, **scattered,** Raised in a pigpen (*or* hogpen, pigsty); 55 Infs, **scattered,** Raised in a backwoods (*or* barnyard, bunkhouse, cave, etc); **GA6, 13, IN68, NY14,** Raised up in a barn (*or* shit house); **SC26,** Raise in a stable. **1986** Pederson *LAGS Concordance,* 1 inf, swAL, He must have been raised in a barn; 1 inf, ceMS, Was you raised in a barn?—If you don't shut door; 1 inf, swAR, Was you raised in a barn?

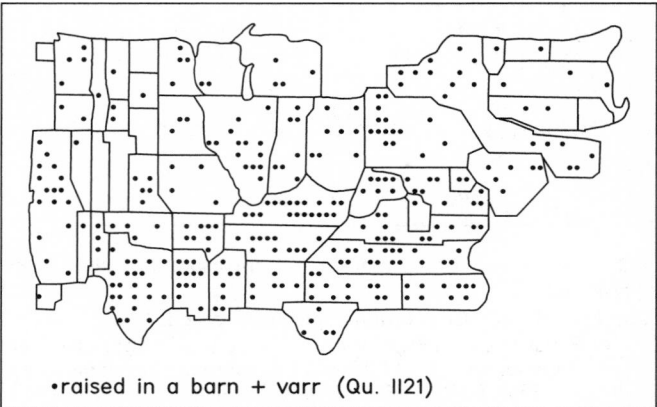

•raised in a barn + varr (Qu. II21)

raise down v phr

To lower.

1970 *Thompson Coll.* AL, Raise it down real slow an easy-like. **1973** *Ibid* MI, Raise it down = to lower something in some [automotive] shops in Detroit. **1978** *AP Letters,* A Clarksville [GA] woman who lived in Ohio for years was visiting her parents—it started to rain and she told her son to raise the window down.

raise gravy v phr [Punning allusion to **raised gravy**]
=**raise sand.**

1998 *NADS Letters* **MS,** Two ladies in the midst of a spat were described as having been ' . . raising gravy outside the fellowship hall.'

raise hail Columbia See **hail Columbia**

raise jack See **jack** n¹ 14

raise Ned See **Old Ned 3b**

raise Neddy-jingo See **Neddy-jingo**

raise Old Ned See **Old Ned 3b**

raise rim v phr
=**raise sand.**

1917 *DN* 4.398 **neOH,** Raise rim. . . To raise Cain, a rumpus, etc. "He raised rim when he heard of it."

raise Sam See **Sam** n³ 1

raise sand v phr Also *kick up sand* **chiefly Sth, S Midl**
To make a disturbance.

1892 *DN* 1.231 **KY,** *Sand.* "To raise sand" is slang for to get furiously angry, the same as "to raise Cain." **1893** Shands *MS Speech* 74, *Raise sand.* This expression is very common, meaning *to create a disturbance, to raise a row.* **1905** *DN* 3.92 **nwAR,** *Raise sand.* . . To make a great disturbance; to go into a rage and stir up confusion. 'He just raised sand when they told him about it.' Common. **1909** *DN* 3.362 **eAL, wGA,** *Raise sand.* . . To make a great disturbance, get angry and stir up confusion. **1915** *DN* 4.188 **swVA,** *Raise sand.* . . To make a great disturbance. **1916** *DN* 4.345 **FL,** When I tries to put him [baby] to sleep, then he sure do raise some sand. **c1938** in 1970 Hyatt *Hoodoo* 1.482 **ceNC,** Well, when yo' have a whole lotta trouble in de house—raisin' Sam, dey cain't git along—yo' kin take ole shoes wit sulphur an' cayenne peppah, yo' got fiah, jes' throw 'em in dere. **1947** Ballowe *The Lawd* 80 **LA,** Aun' Polly raised baldy sand because he was late for supper, even set cold grub before him, but it didn't do a bit of good. **1953** Randolph–Wilson *Down in Holler* 276 **Ozarks,** *Raise sand.* . . To create a scene or disturbance. "Paw sure will raise sand when he hears 'bout Lizzie a-sleepin' with the sheriff." The phrase *kick up sand* carries the same meaning. **1966–70** *DARE* (Qu. FF18, *Joking words . . about a noisy or boisterous celebration or party:* "They certainly _____ last night.") Infs **MS15, NC84, SC11,** 58, **VA71,** Raised sand; (Qu. KK11, *To make great objections or a big fuss about something:* "When we asked him to do that, he _____.") Infs **FL52, LA12, OK31, VA38,** Raised sand; (Qu. KK13, . . *Arguing:* "They stood there for an hour _____.") Inf **DC11,** Raising [seɪŋ] [sic]. **1971** Mitchell *Blow My Blues Away* 83 **nwMS** [Black], I don't like fighting. I like to marry and have something and live together for something. Have a happy home, not no home that you got to raise sand all the time. **1986** Pederson *LAGS Concordance,* 1 inf, **swGA,** They was supposed to raise sand (= make noise); 1 inf, **cwFL,** He's been raising sand (=a fuss); 1 inf, **cwFL,** Sometimes they call it raising sand; 1 inf, **cTN,** Raising sand (getting upset); 1 inf, **csAL,** Raise sand (=cause trouble); police coming raising sand (=police coming); 1 inf, **csLA,** My children always raise sand with me; 1 inf, **ceAR,** Raising sand (of dogs, noisy, excited by bobcats); 1 inf, **cwAR,** Fixing to raise sand with him; 1 inf, **cwLA,** The dogs were raising sand; 1 inf, **swLA,** Raising sand (=angry); 1 inf, **ceTX,** Raise sand (of calves bawling); 1 inf, **cwLA,** I wouldn't go out there and raise no sand; 1 inf, **nwLA,** Raise more sand (a)bout that = show displeasure. **1998** *DARE* File **MS,** *To raise sand*—meaning to make a fuss—I have heard this usually from Blacks around Marks, Mississippi, but I have also heard it from a young white man there.

raise up See **raise** v B3b, C1b, 2b

raise up fuss v phr
To gather strength.

1968 *DARE* FW Addit **swVA,** I was so tired I couldn't raise up fuss to dry a leaf.

raisin n Usu |'rezɨn|; also **Sth, S Midl** *old-fash* |'rizɨn| Pronc-spp *reason, reesin, reezin* [The pronc ['rizɨn] competed with ['rezɨn] for std status at least through the end of the 18th cent in England.]

Std sense, var forms.

1789 Webster *Dissertations Engl. Lang.* 116, *Reesin* for *raisin* is very prevalent in two or three principal towns in America. One of the standard authors gives us this pronunciation; and another gives us both *raisin* and *reesin.* But all the others pronounce the word *raisin* . . ; and derivation, analogy and general custom, all decide in favor of the practice. **1893** Shands *MS Speech* 8, The [i] sound is heard in [rizɪnz] for *raisins.* **1899** (1912) Green *VA Folk-Speech* 348, *Reason.* . . A form of *raisin.* **1899** *Harper's New Mth. Mag.* 98.498 **Sth** [Black], Ef you'll stick one of 'em on a piece o' scalloped reesin-box paper, an' indite some po'try verses to suit hit, . . when Minervy gits it she'll . . start out an' hunt a reader. **1909** *DN* 3.363 **eAL, wGA,** *Reesin.* . . Raisin. Cf. Falstaff's pun, 1 *Henry IV,* ii.4. **1919** *DN* 5.34 **seKY,** *Reezins.* . . Raisins. Knott Co. **1923** *DN* 5.242 **KY,** *Reezins.* Pronunciation of *raisins.* **c1960** Wilson *Coll.* **csKY,** Raisin is rarely |'rizn̩|.

raising n

1 also *raising up;* rarely *raisings:* Early training in appropriate social behavior, upbringing; manners, breeding. [**raise** v B3] **chiefly S Midl** *chiefly rural* See Map

1842 *Ladies' Repository* 2.285, Selfishness and humorsomeness had devoured her sensibilities, and she was a petulant, spoiled grown baby. . . She had been unlucky in her "raising." **1884** Johnston *Old Mark* 263 **GA,** If that child don't show raisin', *I* don't know what you mean *by* raisin'. **1903** *DN* 2.326 **seMO,** The child was spoiled in raisin. **1907** *DN* 3.235 **nwAR,** *Raisin(g).* . . Bringing up. **1909** *DN* 3.363 **eAL, wGA,** *Raisin(g).* . . Bringing up, manners. "You ain't got no raisin.'" **1912** *DN* 3.587 **wIN,** People in that township don't show much raisin'. **1915** *DN* 4.188 **swVA,** *Raisin'.* . . Rearing; 'bringing up.' **1916** *DN* 4.347 **cTX** (as of 1896), *Raising.* . . Breeding; manners. "Don't forget your raisin." So in W[estern] Res[erve] and among southern negroes. **1927** *AmSp* 2.362 **cwWV,** Have you children forgotten your raising? **1939** Hall *Coll.* **eNC,** In my raisin' up two or three besides yer own would go with sick people. **1940** Stuart *Trees of Heaven* 297 **neKY,** "God Almighty, Tarvin," says Anse, "have you lost all your raisin?" **1955** Ritchie *Singing Family* 31 **seKY,** If you should start to talk about the other things—the things inside you—folks might think you were getting above your raising. **c1960** Wilson *Coll.* **csKY,** *Raising:* . . One's native culture, manners, general attitude: "Show your raisin'." **1965–70** *DARE* (Qu. II21, *When somebody behaves unpleasantly or without manners:* "The way he behaves, you'd think he was _____.") Infs **KY6,** 50, 85, **VA26,** Didn't have any raising; **TN65,** Didn't have any raisings; **KY40,** Didn't have no raising; **VA2,** 25, Had no raising (at all); **KY85, TN15,** Hadn't had any raising; **IL76, TN1,** He had no raising; **AR41, KY74, OK18,** (He) never had any raising; **TN12,** He's got no raising; **GA72,** Way above his raising; **MS69,** You didn't have any raising; (Qu. II36b, *Of somebody who talks back or gives rude answers . . "She certainly is _____!")* Inf **TN15,** Has bad raising. [15 of 17 total Infs comm type 4 or 5] **1967** *DARE* Tape **AL33,** We had hard time. But I tell 'em that I'm proud of my raisin'. And I ain't forgot it. And I hope to God I never do. **1986** Pederson *LAGS Concordance,* 1 inf, **cnGA,** He'll finally come back to his raising; 1 inf, **seGA,** Owing to how lots of your folks had a little better raising; 1 inf, **ceTN,** Awful hard to get the raising out of you—habits.

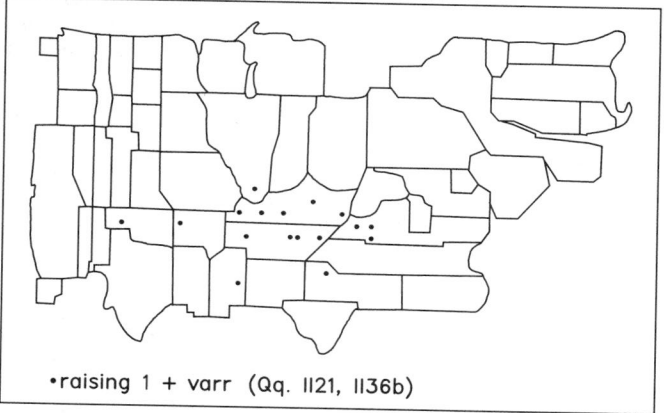

•raising 1 + varr (Qq. II21, II36b)

2 A cooperative social gathering for the purpose of raising the frame of a building. **NEast, esp NEng** Cf **barn raising 1, house ~**

1772 (1888) Cutler *Life* 1.38 **MA,** At Robert Dodge's, at a raising. **1807** (1904) Roe *Diary* 55 **NY,** We have been to the Raising of Nathanel Smiths Barn. **1818** (1920) Clark *Diary* 2313 **CT,** I got to Canfields store—Talk about having raisin to morrow. **1825** Neal *Brother Jonathan* 1.54 **CT,** The Raising. . . The people of New England live in framehouses. The frame of any building . . being ready, the publick pour in from all sides; and, for a mouthful of bread and cheese, or a bit of mince-pie, and a "twig o' cider" a piece, put up the frame for the owner, in a frolick. **1859** (1922) Jackson *Col.'s Diary* 12 **PA,** One of the brother Catholics had a "raising" today . . and, as a natural consequence, a dance in the evening. **1898** (1899) Earle *Home Life* 408 **NEng,** A "raising" might be of a church or a schoolhouse, or of a house or barn for a neighbor. **1907** *DN* 3.197 **seNH,** Raising. . . A gathering of persons for the purpose of erecting the frame of a building. "There was plenty of hard cider at the raising." **1910** *DN* 3.447 **cwNY,** Raising. . . An assemblage of persons who meet to set up the frame of a building, especially a barn. **1952** Hostetler *Amish Life* iv **PA,** These "raisin's" attract several hundred persons. . . Operations begin before sunrise and by evening the barn is completely set up. **1965–70** *DARE* (Qu. FF2, . . *Kinds of parties*) Inf **MA58,** Raisings; **MA69,** Raisings of barns; **MA69,** Raisings of houses. **1969** *DARE* Tape **MA58,** One term, an old term is a raising—putting up a building. Raising the frame, you know, when everybody got together and had a big time; **MA68,** One thing they had years ago they never had for years is what they call a raising. They used to have those. When they was puttin' up a new barn or house or anything, why, they put the frame of it up, they'd have all our men push it—push the frame up there. What they'd call a raising.

3 rarely pl: Yeast or other leavening agent. Cf **rising** n 2

1872 Schele de Vere *Americanisms* 529, *Raising,* for yeast, a favorite term in New England. **1935** Sandoz *Jules* 356 **wNE** (as of 1880–1930), Nothing to eat but two old pancakes without raisin' or syrup, an' not a smidgin of flour left. **1941** *LANE* Map 290 *(Yeast)* 1 inf, **RI,** Hop raising, an old name for yeast, made from potatoes, a handful of hops and yeast in a yeast jug. **1966** *DARE* (Qu. H17, . . *Kinds [of yeast])* Inf **NC37,** Raisin's. **c1970** Pederson *Dial. Surv. Rural GA,* 1 inf, **seGA,** You ain't got put no raising (baking powder) in it.

4 A boil, abscess, or other swelling. Cf **rising** n 1

1966–69 *DARE* (Qu. BB33a, . . *A swelling under the skin, bigger than a pimple, that comes to a head*) Infs **AR3, GA6, KY44,** Raising; (Qu. BB37, *When yellowish stuff comes out of a person's ear, he has a _____*) Inf **KY44,** Raising in his ear. **1975** *Appalachian Jrl.* 2.158 **wNC,** An inflammation is a *risin'* or *raisin'.*

raising gravy See **raised gravy**

raisings, raising up See **raising 1**

raisin jack See **jack** n 13b

rake v[1]

A Forms.

1 pres: usu *rake;* also *roke.* Cf **break** v **A1**

1930 Stoney-Shelby *Black Genesis* 28 **seSC** [Black], God . . tell him for 'struct she in all de t'ing she is fittin' for do, like roke (rake) path, an' burn leaf, an' sich-like.

2 past, past pple: usu *raked;* also **chiefly S Midl** *rok(e), ruck, ruk(e).* [*roke* and *ruck* appear to be recent formations by analogy with *broke* (std past and non-std past pple of *break*) and *tuck* (non-std past and past pple of *take*); cf **break** v **A2, 3, take**]

1913 Kephart *Highlanders* 284 **sAppalachians,** Examples of a strong preterite with dialectical change of the vowel are bruk, brung, . . friz, roke or ruck (raked). **1923** *DN* 5.219 **swMO,** Ruk. . . Raked. **1930** *VA Qrly. Rev.* 6.246, There are sundry preterites with dialect changes: . . rok or ruck for raked. **1940** *AmSp* 15.447 **eTN,** Ruck. Raked. 'Cut the grass and ruck it.' **1944** *PADS* 2.48 **cnNC, nwSC,** Roke (rok). . . Preterite and past participle of *rake.* "Do you want this yard roke up?" Guilford Co., N.C.; Spartanburg, S.C. Illiterate. Rare. **1950** *PADS* 14.57 **SC,** Roke: pret. and *past part.* of *rake.* "I done roke up de leaves": also *ruck.* **1975** Chalmers *Better* 65, He drug the ground and ruke the leaves, while his woman-person shuk the rug. **1976** Garber *Mountain-ese* 76 **sAppalachians,** Charles came over and raked the hay for us yesterday. **1982** Ginns *Snowbird Gravy* 204 **nwNC,** And in ten or fifteen minutes, he ruck her out a 'tater. **1986** Pederson *LAGS Concordance,* 1 inf, **neAR,** You roke it up = raked.

B Senses.

1 also with var advs (see below): To scold severely, attack verbally. Cf **raking-out**

a without adv; hence in phr *raking* a severe scolding—also in phr *rake (one) up one side and down the other.* **chiefly S Midl**

1907 *Black Cat* June 7 **NYC,** I'll bet somebody has got a raking for losing it. **1927** *AmSp* 2.362 **cwWV,** Rake him up one side and down the other . . to reprimand severely. "The teacher raked the boys up one side and down the other for throwing snowballs." **1942** [see **B1b** below]. **1943** McAtee *Dial. Grant Co. IN Suppl. 2* 11 (as of 1890s), Rake . . scold. **c1950** Halpert *Coll.* 52 **wKY, nwTN,** Raking them up one side and down the other = scolding severely. **c1960** Wilson *Coll.* **csKY,** Rake (or rake over the coals). . . scold very severely. **1963** Edwards *Gravel* 19 **eTN** (as of 1920s), While Uncle Jeems was raking my pa I was going through his pockets to find the candy which I knew he had somewhere. **1966–70** *DARE* (Qu. II27, *If somebody gives you a very sharp scolding . . "I certainly got a _____ for that."*) Infs **GA6, IN32, 42, KY10, 74, MO15, NY22, OR13,** Raking.

b with *down;* hence nouns *rake-down, raking-down.*

1854 *La Crosse Democrat* (WI) 17 Jan 2/4, Mr. Wright . . gave Smith a small raking down. **1859** (1968) Bartlett *Americanisms* 354, Rake down. A taking down, a scolding. . . I would submit with a good grace to a "rake down," if I could only succeed in starting again his "gray goose quill."—*N. Y. Spirit of the Times.* **1883** (1971) Harris *Nights with Remus* 181 **GA** [Black], I see yo' daddy gwine 'long down de road des now, en he gimme a rakin' down 'kaze I make 'way wid de sparrer-grass. **1883** (1971) Shields *Life S. Prentiss* 125, The "raking down" which Prentiss had given his prosecutor was worth that. **1942** Berrey-Van den Bark *Amer. Slang* 295.2, Scold; reprimand. . . rake down, rake up one side and down the other. **1967–68** *DARE* (Qu. Y3, *To say uncomplimentary things about somebody*) Infs **MN33, 34,** Rake (or raking) them down; (Qu. Y7, . . *To be mean to another or to annoy another*) Inf **MN33,** Raking me down; (Qu. II27, . . *A very sharp scolding . . "I certainly got a _____ for that."*) Inf **OH57,** Raking-down; **SC32,** Rake-down. **1975** Gould *ME Lingo* 227, Rakin' down—A term for a bawling out; a reprimand intended to improve a person's looks, manners, dispostition [sic], etc. . . "You should-da heard the rakin' down she gave me when my dog chased her cat!"

c with *over;* hence n *raking-over.* Cf **coals, rake (one) over the**

1965–70 *DARE* (Qu. II27, . . *A very sharp scolding . . "I certainly got a _____ for that."*) 18 Infs, **scattered,** Raking-over; (Qu. Y3, *To say uncomplimentary things about somebody*) Inf **MT5,** Rake him over.

2 with *after* or in phrr *rake after (a) cart:* To follow a haying crew, raking up hay that is left behind by the loaders. [*EDD rake* v.[1] 3; see also *OED2 raker-after* 1641 (at *raker* sb.[1] 1)] **chiefly Nth**

1853 Stephens *Farmer's Guide* 2. app 55, It is especially efficient in raking after a cart while loading, and also in cleaning up the scatterings among haycocks. **1878** *Scribner's Mth.* 16.526 **NEng,** Now the wagon comes surrounded by its rattling "hay riggin'," with the legs of the pitcher and the unfortunate who "mows away" and "rakes after," dangling over its side. **1879** Taylor *Summer-Savory* 68 **cNY,** Yonder in the meadow is a man "raking after," and he is eighty. **1884** *Century Illustr. Mag.* 28.457, Through the long summer days he followed his father, dropping corn or hoeing potatoes, and later carrying the men their dinners in the hay-field, or "raking after." **1899** Garland *Boy Life* 107 **nwIA,** Lincoln began work in the field by "raking after." Every middle aged man in the West will know what that subtends. It brings to mind a gloomy urchin, with a long handled rake, following a huge, half-loaded wagon. **1900** *New Engl. Mag.* 22.522 **CT,** Besides his other duties of spreading hay and raking after cart, he must turn grindstone before breakfast to sharpen all the scythes. **1917** *DN* 4.398 **neOH,** Rake after. . . To follow a group of haymakers, wagon, or the like, with a hand-rake, and gather the hay left behind. "You may rake after while we load." Also N. Eng., Ill., N.Y.

3 See quot.

1923 Parsons *Folk-lore Sea Islands* 208 **csSC,** The few baskets I saw on Hilton Head and Defuskie were shallow baskets, used "fo' rakin' grits;" i.e., washing corn.

4 To scratch the sides of a horse with the rowels of one's spurs to provoke it to buck; to scratch (a horse) in such a way.

1928 *AmSp* 4.131 **cnNE,** If the horse is sullen and refuses to "pitch," the rider may "rowl," "scratch," or "rake" him, making threads of scratches from "end to end" on the sides of the horse with his spurs. **1941** Writers' Program *Guide WY* 122, The tales 'traded' give life and currency to such expressions as 'cow sense,' 'chew it finer,' 'maverick,' 'raking a horse,' 'rustler,' 'hog tie,' and 'running iron.' *Ibid* 464, *Rake*—to scratch a horse with spurs, or drag the spurs along his neck, to make him buck. **1944** Adams *Western Words* 122, *Raking*—Synonymous with *scratching*. It generally applies when the rider gives his legs a free swing, rolling the rowels of his spurs along the horse's sides from shoulder to rump, and is one of the highest accomplishments aspired to by bronc riders.

rake v[2] [*OED2 rake* v.[2] 1.a a1023 →; "Now only *dial.*"]
1914 *DN* 4.79 **ME, nNH**, *Rake*. . To gad about.

rake after, rake after (a) cart See **rake** v[1] **B2**

rake down v, n See **rake** v[1] **B1b**

rake one over the coals See **coals, rake (one) over the**

rake one up one side and down the other See **rake** v[1] **B1a**

rake over See **rake** v[1] **B1c**

rake over the coals See **coals, rake (one) over the**

rake up one side and down the other; raking See **rake** v[1] **B1a**

raking after See **rake** v[1] **B2**

raking-down See **rake** v[1] **B1b**

raking-out n Cf **rake** v[1] **B1**
1966–68 *DARE* (Qu. II27, . . *A very sharp scolding* . . *"I certainly got a _____ for that."*) Infs **GA1, 61, SC34**, Raking-out.

raking-over See **rake** v[1] **B1c**

raking over the coals See **coals, rake (one) over the**

ral n Also *rail, rale;* also with *the,* and in comb *the old ral* Cf **Old Arthur, rover**
Syphilis.
1899 Harrell *Hot Springs Dr.* 77 **AR**, He was the man who coined the word which became a part of the daily nomenclature of the place. There was the "ral-hole," the "ral-can," which was a tin can, like a coffee-pot with a bail. . Everyone used the name, in its compounds and singly, "ral," which had come to signify a certain social disease. . It was a word invented . . when a trim, meek little man, who wore a clerical garb, and sanctimonious expression of face, assured him that "he had come to try the water for a bad case of neuralgia." "New what!" said the outspoken landlord. "Don't call it new; it's the 'old ral' you've got, my boy, and these baths will cure you." **1925** *AmSp* 1.24, For "syphilis," "pox" was used widely many years ago, but has given place more recently to the simple abbreviation "syph," to "ral" in the South, and to "blood disease" in the press. Venereal diseases are commonly called "social diseases." **1942** *Collier's* 12 Sept 15 **Sth**, Floyd had spent the winter in Shreveport and had brought back what everybody thought was the Old Ral. **1956** Longstreet *Real Jazz* 73, It was a tough row, and it got you. The old rale, the sauce, the reefers, or you froze to death in doorways, too stewed to move. **1960** Wentworth-Flexner *Slang* 418, *Ral*—*ral, the*—*rail*—*rail, the.* . . Syphilis; a case of syphilis. *Orig. Southern use. Orig. "ral"; "rail" is a variant.*

rale adj, adv See **real** adj, adv

rale n See **ral**

rale poule d'eau See **poule d'eau 2**

raley See **really** adv, adj

rallack v [nEngl dial var of *rollick;* cf *EDD rallack* v. 1] Cf **rollix**
1899 (1912) Green *VA Folk-Speech* 344, *Rallack*. . To run about after pleasure instead of attending to business. "He goes rallacking about from one place to another."

rally v [Cf *OED2 rally* v.[1] 4.d "*Sporting*: To harry"] Cf *DS* P39a, b

1956 McAtee *Some Dialect NC* 57, *Rally* . . start waterfowl flying so as to improve shooting. Upper Currituck Sound.

rally dog n [Cf **rally** v] Cf **catch dog, find dog**
A dog trained to herd cattle.
1954 *True* June 66 **TX**, I usually get one or two 'find' dogs out of a litter, maybe a good 'catch' dog, and the rest I use for 'lead' and 'rally' dogs.

ralph v, n Also personified as *Ralph* [Echoic] Cf **earl** v
To vomit; vomit.
1968 *Current Slang* 2.3.7 [Air Force Academy slang], *Ralph*. . To vomit. **1968** *DARE* (Qu. BB17, . . *Vomiting*) Inf **PA162**, Ralph; also a noun. **1975** *AmSp* 50.64 **AR** (as of c1970), *Ralph*. . Vomit—"There's ralph on your shirt." **1986** Pederson *LAGS Concordance* (Vomit—crude term) 1 inf, **cAR**, Calling Ralph; 1 inf, **swGA**, Ralph—crude term; 1 inf, **nwLA**, Ralph—that's when you throw up; calling Ralph; 1 inf, **nwLA**, Holler for Ralph; 1 inf, **csTX**, Ralph—joking. **1986** *DARE* File **nIN**, Native of South Bend recalls first hearing the word *ralph* used in the middle 1970s and as recently as 1982 at Notre Dame. Of someone who's vomiting or appears as if they're about to vomit, someone may say: "Sounds like Tom's ralphing," or "I think Ralph's coming round again." The word is pronounced in the back of the throat as if retching. **1998** Mitchard *Most Wanted* 119 **TX** [Speaker from **NYC**], Now, I love tequila. It's the only liquor that doesn't make me feel, before or during, as though I'm one step from phoning ralph.

raly See **really** adv, adj

ram n

1 A male goat. [Perh abbr for **ram goat**] Cf **buck** n[1] **1b**
1950 *WELS* **WI** (*A male goat*) 3 Infs, Ram; [(*A female goat*) 1 Inf, Ram [sic];] (*A goat that habitually strikes people with its horns*) 2 Infs, Ram; [1 Inf, Battering ram]. **1965–70** *DARE* (Qu. K68) 13 Infs, **scattered**, Ram; **CA63**, Ram [Inf doubtful]; **MI98**, Ram—he's always bunting; **MA6**, He's a buck, ram—he bunts you; **MI23**, Bucking ram; **VT16**, Butting ram; **ME5**, An old ram [Inf doubtful]; (Qu. K67a, . . *A male goat;* total Infs questioned, 75) Infs **GA5, MS66**, Ram. **1986** Pederson *LAGS Concordance* (Male sheep) 3 infs, **nw,cLA, csTX**, Ram—male goat; 2 infs, **cwAL, neTX**, Ram—goat; 1 inf, **seAL**, Ram—[inf] "thought it was a male goat"; 1 inf, **cLA**, Ram—male goat? also male sheep; 1 inf, **cTN**, Ram—sheep or goat; 1 inf, **csLA**, A ram or a buck—[inf] uses for "goat."

2 A type of three-masted schooner; see quot 1953. **Chesapeake Bay**
1904 *Nautical Gaz.* 14 Apr. 211 (*Mathews Coll.*), Geo. K. Phillips & Co., Bethel, Del., have on the stocks a three-masted ram schooner 140 ft. long. **1909** *Sun* (Baltimore MD) 1 Aug 14/2 (*OED2*), Capt Andrew Hubbard . . saw the queer craft coming down stream. He shouted at Captain Insley 'That's certainly a Nanticoke ram.' **1936** *Ibid* 8 Dec 11/1 (*Hench Coll.*), Oyster Business Expanding—The sloops, rams, schooners and power boats that ply the Chesapeake Bay and tributaries in the Maryland, Virginia and North Carolina trade are busier than they have been in many years. **1938** FWP *Guide DE* 363, A type of vessel developed at Lewisville and known as a "ram," had a flat bottom, straight deadrises, and carried three masts but no topmasts. **1953** *Sun* (Baltimore MD) 18 Oct mag sec 19/2, The "ram," developed in the upper waters of the Nanticoke River, was an awkward looking vessel. It was a three-masted, bald-headed, schooner-rigged vessel. Designed primarily to negotiate the then narrow Chesapeake and Delaware Canal, it was a flat-bottomed, wall-sided, centerboard craft. **1955** *Ibid* 25 Aug 34/8 (*Hench Coll.*), The Coast Guard major board of investigation into the foundering of the schooner Levin J. Marvel . . ended yesterday with a board member accusing the ram's skipper of violating three specific marine laws.

ram v

1 usu with *around:* To run around boisterously; to gad about, go out in search of pleasure. **chiefly NEast, Gt Lakes** See Map on p. 458
1939 Aurand *Quaint Idioms* 29 [PaGer], It's a nice day to go *ramming around*. **1940** White *Wild Geese* 263 **AK** (as of 1890s), They had had a grand time. Just no, nothing special. Just ramming around. **1946** *AmSp* 21.209 **CT**, In Lyme, Connecticut, where I live, there is a word, used by young and old alike, but chiefly by the young, that interests me. . . It is *ram* as a verb, meaning 'to run slightly wild, to dash here and there play-

fully.' It is usually heard followed by *around*. **1950** *WELS Suppl.*
cwWI, *Ramming around*—for "tearing around". "Now don't be ramming around all night. Get home by 12:00." **1965–70** *DARE* (Qu.
Y29b, . . *About a man [who doesn't stay home much]:* "He's always _____.") Infs **GA**7, **NY**2, Ramming; **IL**12, **IA**47, **MI**116,
NJ15, **NY**221, **PA**7, 18, 63, 231, Ramming around; **NY**20, Ramming
around—gadding around; **NY**7, Ramming around—tomcatting around;
NY96, Ramming around—conversational for young fellows out in cars
riding around; **VT**12, Ramming round; (Qu. Y29a, *To 'go out' a great
deal, not to stay at home much:* "She's always _____.") Inf **GA**7,
Ramming; **NJ**15, Ramming around; **NY**96, Ramming around—conversational for granddaughters going noisily from back to front of the house
and back through the house again; **PA**231, Ramming around—on the
go; (Qu. KK31, *To go about aimlessly looking for distraction:* "He
doesn't have anything to do, so he's just _____ around.") Inf **NJ**16,
Ramming. **1979** Lewis *How to Talk Yankee* [27] **nNEng**, *Ramming*. On
the town. "Al's not coming to work today?" "No, called in sick. He was
ramming around all last night and won't be worth nawthin' this morning." **1982** *Barrick Coll.* **csPA**, *Ram around*—to run around, usu. in a
boisterous manner. **1982** *DARE* File **ME coast**, *Rammin'*: raising hell.
1998 *DARE* File **csWI** (as of c1968), If I was running or playing too
boisterously indoors, my grandmother would tell me to quit ramming
around.

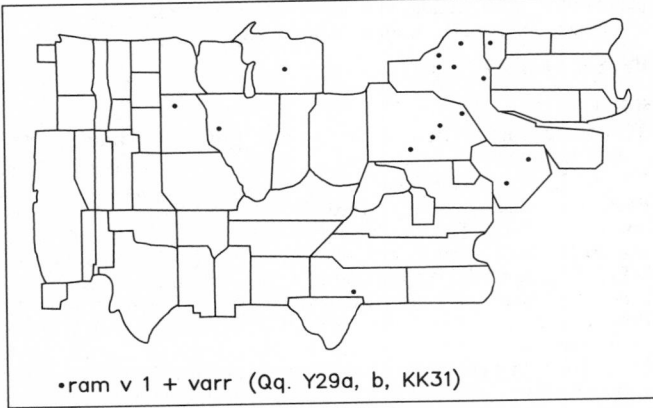

•**ram v 1 + varr** (Qq. Y29a, b, KK31)

2 See quots.
  1996 *DARE* File **nwMS** [Black], To ram—to take food without one's
parents' permission from the refrigerator, e.g., Who's been rammin'?
1998 *Ibid*, While in Mississippi I consulted with the black woman I
heard *ram* from for "take food without parental permission." She was
born in 1927 and did not finish grade school. She uses *ram* meaning "to
take unauthorized food" as an extension of a wider meaning "to insert
the hand into something" as in "I rammed in the envelope"—i.e., I put
my hand inside the envelope.

ramack v [*EDD* rammack v. 1 "To . . rush about riotously," 2
"To turn things topsy-turvy"]
See quot 1953.
  [**c1920** in 1993 Farwell–Nicholas *Smoky Mt. Voices* 132 **sAppalachians**, Rammick.] **1953** Randolph–Wilson *Down in Holler* 276
Ozarks, Ramack ['ræmæk]. . . To search, to ransack. "I been a-ra-
mackin' the whole country for sang-root, but I cain't find none
nowheres."

ramada n [Span] **chiefly SW**
An open-sided, usu freestanding shelter, orig roofed with
brush or branches.
  1869 in 1929 Hayes *Pioneer Notes* 289 **sCA**, I paid them a dollar for
my bath, at the rustic bathing establishment they have constructed, consisting of two goods' boxes sunk in the ground, sheltered by a *ramada*.
1875 Bourke *Diary* 2 Apr **swCA**, Slept this night under the "ramada".
1919 Chase *CA Desert* 316, The family was already breakfasting . .
under the *ramada*, or brush-roofed shed, which is the general livingroom during the hot months. **1968** Abbey *Desert Solitaire* 129 **seUT**,
Through the storm of sunlight over the baking sandstone of the 33,000-
acre terrace to the shade and relative coolness of the ramada. **1969**
O'Connor *Horse & Buggy West* 60 **AZ**, A Mexican institution adopted
by a good many Americans was the ramada, a brush shelter open on
four sides. **1976** *AZ Republic* (Phoenix) 27 May sec B 15/3, Desert
Foothills Scenic Drive . . a 17-mile desert drive, with ramadas and rest

rooms. **1998** *AZ Daily Star* (Tucson) 17 May sec H 1/4, [Caption:] At
left, mesquite posts and ocotillo ribs form free-standing ramada. [Text:]
"Ramadas have always been an integral part of desert living." . . Eleven
ramadas are scattered throughout the Tucson Botanical Gardens. . .
[T]hey range from the most traditional Native American version (mesquite beams and saguaro ribs) to stucco and lattice to the most contemporary welded steel designs. **1998** *NADS Letters* **cnNM**, The word [=
ramada] is commonly used now, here in Santa Fe, NM, to describe
shade structures about 8 feet high, on poles, with either slats of wood or
small branches laid or attached horizontally on top. The slats alternate
with open areas, giving a nice semi-shade. They can be attached to
houses as part of a porch, or freestanding. *Ibid* **SW**, Ramadas are seen
throughout the Southwest as brush-covered shelters from the sun. Especially on the Navaho Reservation nearly every hogan grouping has at
least one Ramada. . . These are usually open on all four sides but sometimes are more lean-to type. *Ibid* **cnCA**, We recently bought a mobile
home which we placed on property in the mountains. The roof was not
strong enough for the snow load so we were required to have a ramada
built. It is a regular roof placed on supports that covers . . the mobile
[home]. More like a carport.

ramadero n
A thicket.
  1929 Dobie *Vaquero* 206 **SW**, Down in a *ramadero* of spined bushes
and trees that seem to cover all space except that occupied by prickly
pear, a man . . is sitting on a horse. **1932** *DN* 6.232 **West**, *Ramadero*.
This word is sometimes heard in the Southwest for *thicket*. **1967** *DARE*
(Qu. C28, *A place where underbrush, weeds, vines and small trees
grow together so that it's nearly impossible to get through*) Inf **TX**28,
Ramadero.

ram around See **ram v 1**

ram beer n Cf **buck** n[4]
=cane beer.
  1955 *AmSp* 30.158 **AL**, M.M. Mathews informs me [=F.W. Bradley]
that sugar-cane beer was made from the skimmings of the juice as it was
boiled into sirup. It was the custom in Alabama during his boyhood, he
writes, to put the skimmings into a clean flour barrel and allow them to
ferment, which they would do in a day or two. Then there was drawn off
from the bottom of the barrel a fine beer which was very much enjoyed. . . Other names resulting from the present investigation are: . .
ram beer [Bradley: allied to *buck*, or from its strength?].

rambler n
A ranch-style house.
  1958 *Washington Post & Times Herald* (DC) 16 Aug sec B 1/4, These
3-bedroom, full-basement ramblers and split-foyer ramblers will be sold
on terms of no money down to qualifying GI buyers. **1967** *Times-
Crescent–Charles Co. Leaf* (La Plata MD) 27 July sec A 6/4, Bryans
Road—Jenkins Lane. Lovely 5 bedroom brick Rambler, 3 baths, rec.
room, many more nice features. 1¼ Acre. Mid $30's. **1968** *Winona
Daily News* (MN) 17 May sec 7 B/2, Three-bedroom rambler in scenic
Gilmore Valley, large lot, carpeting and drapes like new, built-ins and
many closets. **1968** *McDavid Coll.* **WA**, Rambler, a type of house, low,
spreading. **1970** *Smithfield Times* (VA) 20 May 15/3, [Advt:] *Smithfield*—air conditioned attractive six room (3 bedroom, 2 baths) rambler
with attached garage, on large lot. **1983** *Daily Herald* (Provo UT) 27
May 33/8, [Advt:] ½ acre lot, . . barn + elegant 1635 sq ft rambler.
Ibid, Rambler, bi-level or split entry w/kitchen, living, dining, 2 bdrm,
bath. **1998** *DARE* File **cwMN**, [Real estate advt:] Cute & Cozy Rambler . . w/Nice Back Yard. Open, Large Rooms And Some Hardwood
Floors. Eat In Kitchen & Formal Dining Area. **1999** *DARE* File **MN**,
When I spoke of a house as a "rambler," nobody knew what I meant.
They said, "It's not a car."

rambuctious See **rambunctious**

rambump See **rambutt**

rambunctious adj Also *rambuctious, rambumptious, rambunkshus, rambunksious, rumbunctious*
Std sense, var forms.
  1830 *Boston Eve. Transcript* (MA) 1 Sept 3/1, If they are
"rumbunctious" at the prospect, they will be "riprorious" when they get
a taste, for a "copious acquaintance" with Vinegar. **1866** Smith *Bill Arp*
54 **GA**, A plan was set on foot to procure a fierce and rambunkshus animal from the mountains of Hepsidam. **1904** (1969) Robins *Magnetic*

North 80 **AK**, [It] hasn't thought of sleetin' yet or anything else rambunksious. **1909** *DN* 3.62 **eAL, wGA**, *Rambu(n)ctious.* . . Noisy and unruly, unconventional, boisterous. **1911** *DN* 3.547 **NE**, *Rambumptious.* . . Obstreperous, forward.

rambutt v Also *rambump, rampooch* Cf **buck** v[1] **B6c, bump** v 1

See quots.

1923 *DN* 5.218 **swMO**, *Rambutt.* . . To seize a person by his arms and legs and to ram his buttock [sic] forcibly against a tree or post. *Rampooch.* . . Same as above. **1953** Randolph–Wilson *Down in Holler* 277 **Ozarks**, *Rampooch.* . . To engage in a kind of horseplay in which a boy is seized by his arms and legs, and his buttocks swung violently against a tree trunk. . . *Rambutt, rambump, bump,* and *buck* . . are used with the same meaning.

ramby See rammy

ram cat n Cf **ram goat**

A male cat; also fig in comb *ram-cat stew* a makeshift stew.

1672 Josselyn *New-Englands Rarities* 16, The *Ounce* or *Wild Cat,* is about the bigness of two lusty Ram Cats. **1819** (1820) Irving *Hist. NY* 2.150, Like two furious ram cats on the very point of a clapper-clawing. **1870** *Putnam's Mag.* 15.296, A physician, prescribing syrup of buckthorn, wrote his prescription according to the usual abbreviation . . *"Syr. Rham. Cat."* The lady patient . . declared that she would not take a syrup of ram cats for any body under heaven. **1912** Green *VA Folk-Speech* 344, *Ram-cat.* . . A male cat. **1966** *DARE* (Qu. H36, *Kinds of soup*) Inf **ME**19, Ram-cat stew, anything you can get goes in it.

ramdown n

See quot 1911.

1908 Day *King Spruce* 5 **ME**, You ain't goin' to sluice the rest of us, are you, just because you've gone to work and got your own load busted on the ramdown? *Ibid* 197, They traversed wastes of splintered devastation, blocked ram-downs, choked twitch-roads, and hideous snarls of cross-piled timber. **1911** *Century Dict. Suppl., Ramdown.* . . A steep declivity in a logging-road, upon which boughs (or hay) are placed, in winter, to check the movements of the loaded sleds. [*Century* Ed: Maine.]

ram-down (stove) n

1975 Gould *ME Lingo* 227, *Ram-down*—A wood-burning stove meant for heating rather than cooking, and originally turned out by Wood & Bishop foundry in Bangor. Although Wood & Bishop long since went out of business, their *ram-down* stoves are still doing splendid service in Maine woods camps. The entire top of the stove lifts, so long *junks* of firewood may be rammed down inside. The front of the *ram-down* had a hearth.

ram goat n [*OED2* 1575–1634] Cf **ram** n 1, **ram cat**

A male goat.

1634 in 1881 Boston Registry Dept. *Records* 2, A rate [shall be assessed] for the goates keeping and other charges in rambe goats. **1796** Barton *Disappointment* 73 **PA**, He's got a beard like a ram-goat, and a nose like a bald-eagle! **1897** (1952) McGill *Narrative* 162 **SC**, They saw the old ram goat of the flock suspended by his horns. **c1938** in 1970 Hyatt *Hoodoo* 2.1482 **seGA**, Black cow's milk and den a *ram goat.* **1968** *DARE* (Qu. K68, . . *A goat that habitually strikes people with its horns*) Inf **GA**39, Ram goat, billy goat.

ramie n Also sp *raimy* Cf **ranny** n 1

A calf, esp a small or sickly one.

1936 *AmSp* 11.276 **eTN**, *Ramie.* Young calf. 'The ramie is in the pasture.' **1998** *NADS Letters*, Ramie—I recognize this as a word for a calf, particularly a young calf. Trouble is I don't know when or where it became part of my vocabulary. The possibilities would be Arizona, 1948–49; Missouri Ozarks, summer 1947; eastern Kentucky, summer 1946. **2000** *Ibid* **OH**, I have a friend from Ohio, in his early 70's who said that "Raimy" was a term in wide use in the 30's and 40's in rural Ohio. He said his father used the term for calves. *Ibid* **CA**, Ramie—the runt or a sickly calf. *Ibid* **eTN**, My grandparents (both deceased), my still living great aunts and uncles . . , my aunts, uncles, and cousins . . still use this term [=*ramie*] in eastern Tennessee (Knox, Sevier, and Jefferson counties). They use it to mean a small, usually scrawny or runty, calf.

rammy adj Also sp *ramby* [Cf *OED2* rammish a.[1] 2, a.[2] 2]

Wild, furious, lecherous.

1908 *S. Atl. Qrly.* 7.345 **seSC** [Gullah], They still . . curb a spiritedly violent horse with "Whoa, suh! Don't get ramby!" **1973** Allen *LAUM* 1.360 *(Angry)* 1 inf, **nwNE**, Rammy. **1999** Proulx *Close Range* 168 **WY**, He's just as rammy as he can be. . . I got a hard enough life I don't need a put up with a sex maniac neighbor comin at me.

ramole See **romal**

ramp n[1] Also *ramp door*

A sloping outside cellar door. Cf **bulkhead 1, hatchway**

1966–70 *DARE* (Qu. D20, *Names for a sloping outside cellar door*) Infs **MA**10, **TX**102, Ramp; **IN**79, Ramp [FW: Inf seemed to question this response.]; **VA**30, Ramp door.

ramp n[2] Also *ramps, rampscallion* [*OED2* ramp sb.[2] 3.a 1826 →, *ramps* 1538 → "north. dial. and Sc."; both terms refer to the European *Allium ursinum*]

A **wild onion:** usu *Allium tricoccum,* but occas another such as *A. cernuum* or *A. vineale.*

1828 *Daily Natl. Intelligencer* (DC) 15 Nov 2/5 **swMI**, The Common wild leek is also abundant, . . which the southern immigrants call *ramps.* **1894** *Jrl. Amer. Folkl.* 7.101 **NC, WV**, *Allium,* sp[ecies], Banner Elk, N.C. . . *Allium tricoccum,* . . ramps, West Va. **1917** *DN* 4.406 **wNC**, *Bait.* . . I et me a bait o' ramps, and tasted them for a week afterwards. **1927** *AmSp* 2.363 **cwWV**, *Ramps* . . wild onions. "The cows have eaten ramps, and we cannot use their milk." **1933** *Small Manual SE Flora* 288, *A[llium]* *alleghiense* [=*A. cernuum*]. . . *Mountain-ramp.* . . Cliffs and rocky soil, Blue Ridge to Appalachian Plateau, Ga. to Tenn. and Va. . . *A. vineale.* . . *Ramp.* . . Ga. to Ark., Mo., and N.H. *Ibid* 289, *V[alidallium] tricoccum* [=*Allium t.*] . . *Wild-leeks.* *Ramp. Rampscallions.* . . The bulbs, being pleasantly flavored, are much sought after by the natives of the mountains. **1933** *AmSp* 8.1.51 **Ozarks**, *Ramp.* . . A kind of wild onion or garlic. **1939** *TN Acad. Sci. Jrl.* 14.280, One kind [of wild onion] is much sought after by the mountain folk, who call it "ramps," and gather and eat its bulb with great relish. **1940** Brown *Amer. Cooks* 876 **WV**, A ramp is a species of wild garlic and whenever ramp feasts are held the feasters become social pariahs. Yet the cooking of ramps is an honored ceremonial in one section of our state. **1955** *Seattle Daily Times* (WA) 5 Apr 7/1 **eTN**, The gift was a basket of ramps, described by the donors as a supergarlic, ten times as powerful as onions. . . a group from Cocke Co., Tenn., where the ramps, which look like slender green onions, are grown. **1960** Williams *Walk Egypt* 149 **GA**, Tuck Tate is fixing to set up front with the quartet, and he's been eating ramp. **1966–68** *DARE* (Qu. 16, *The kind of onions that come up fresh early in the year, and you eat them raw*) Inf **NC**33, Ramp; **VA**24, Ramp—wild, tops are eaten; (Qu. I7, *The small plants like onions with hollow green leaves that are cut up in a salad*) Inf **VA**7, Ramps; (Qu. I28b, *Kinds of greens that are cooked*) Inf **WV**12, Ramps; (Qu. BB50d, *Favorite spring tonics*) Inf **NC**30, Ramps—wild onion. **1981** *Smoky Mt. Traveler* Apr 14 **Pigeon Forge TN**, With . . the fragrant smell of bar-be-que chicken and ramps, local mountain residents and tourists alike will spend a delightful Sunday . . at the annual Ramp Festival. **1983** *Gourmet* Apr 44, West Virginians . . make the biggest fuss over ramps, this distinctly North American species of wild onion (known botanically as *Allium tricoccum*). **1995** Williams *Gt. Smoky Mts. Folklife* 174 **wNC, eTN**, Most of the lore about ramps, however, deals not with their procurement but with their odor, or rather the odor they produce in humans who consume them.

Ramp n[3] [Etym uncert; cf quot 1963]

A **Melungeon.**

1946 *Social Forces* 24.443 **VA**, In southwest Virginia they [=Melungeons] are known also as Ramps and occur in the counties of Giles, Lee, Russell, Scott, Washington, and Wise. **1963** Berry *Almost White* 35 **VA**, In Wise County, Virginia, a common name for its hybrid population is "Ramps." Its origin is debatable, but the local explanation is that it comes from "rampion," a wild, onionlike plant which these people habitually gather and eat.

ram pasture n

A bunkhouse or dormitory for men.

1934 *Superior Telegram* (WI) 13 Dec 3/5 (as of 1853), The upper half story [of a hotel] was the "ram pasture" and often as many as 200 male guests would unroll their blankets and bunk anywhere. **1956** Sorden-Ebert *Logger's Words* 27 **Gt Lakes**, *Ram-pasture,* A hotel room larger than the barroom of a saloon in which lumber-jacks slept on cots or on the floor. **1968** Adams *Western Words* 243, *Ram pasture*—What the cowboy sometimes calls the bunkhouse. **1975** Gould *ME Lingo* 227, *Ram pasture*—The *barroom* or bedroom in a lumber camp, and now used for anything in the dormitory category. **1976** *Northeast Folkl.* 17.89 **ME** [Logging terms], The attic was simply one big room. "They used to call that the ram-pasture," Ernest Kennedy said, "and that was full of beds. . . there was probably a dozen or fifteen people sleep up there. It had windows in each end, that's all." . . The ram-pasture seems to have been a kind of overflow area where transients and troublemakers could be accomodated [sic].

ramp door See **ramp** n[1]

rampike n Also *ranpike* [Engl dial word of unknown origin and variable form, first attested (*OED2* at *rampick*) as an adj in combs *ranpike tree* (1593), *rampicke bough* (1594), *ranpick tree* (1627)] **Nth** Cf *DCan*
An upright, dead tree trunk.
1868 *Harper's New Mth. Mag.* 36.437, An old rampike kept in sight until its form grew hideous. **1888** (1971) Hubbard *Woods ME* 94, The land is mostly low and flat, and was overflowed to a great extent at the time Chase Dam was in use. As a consequence, a forest of dead trees, or "rampikes," bristles on that side, and makes a picture of dreariness. **1905** U.S. Forest Serv. *Bulletin* 61.44 [Logging terms], *Ram pike.* A tree broken off by wind and with a splintered end on the portion left standing. (N[orthern] F[orest]) **1950** *WELS Suppl.* **cwWI**, *Rampike*— Dead stub of a tree found after fire or flooding usually. **1956** Sorden-Ebert *Logger's Words* 27 **Gt Lakes**, *Ram-pike*, A standing dead tree from which the limbs and top have been broken or burned off. **1958** McCulloch *Woods Words* 145 **Pacific NW**, *Rampike*—A tall dead tree. **1969** DARE FW Addit **MI**, *Ranpike* ['ræn,paɪk]—lumberjacks here also called this tree the "widow-maker"; it falls silently. . . "Ranpike" was taller than what would here be termed a stub; almost full-length, even; denuded. It was a dead hemlock or spruce, but not a maple or birch. **1984** *MJLF* 10.154 **cnWI**, *Rampike.* A standing, dead tree trunk.

rampooch See **rambutt**

ramps n[1] See **ramp** n[2]

ramps n[2] [Var of *rams* < Ger *Rams, Ramsch;* cf *rounce,* prob < Fr *rams* in same sense]
A trick-taking game played with cards or dominoes.
1850 in 1929 Saxon *Old LA* 178 **cwLA**, After supper we played at the game of Ramps till very late, and we were very much amused at Bag Dad. *Ibid* 179, We found mother and father alone in the sitting room playing Ramps; and although it was late they played several games after that. **1909** *DN* 3.362 **eAL, wGA**, *Ramps.* . . A game at dominoes. Probably corrupted from *rounce.*

rampscallion See **ramp** n[2]

rampse v [Var of *ramp*]
To rush or roam about, esp in search of sexual encounters; to gad about, gallivant.
1929 Ellis *Ordinary Woman* 149 **CO** (as of early 1900s), If you think you can rampse around all night, why, you're off your base, that's all! **1953** Randolph-Wilson *Down in Holler* 277 **Ozarks**, *Ramp, rampse.* . . To rush wildly about. The term is most often applied to bulls or other male animals, but sometimes to men. "A fresh-married feller ain't got no business a-rampin' round them tourist-camps." **1954** *Harder Coll.* **cwTN**, *Ramp, rampse* . . rush wildly about.

ramptious adj
=**ramstugious.**
1953 Randolph-Wilson *Down in Holler* 277 **Ozarks**, *Ramptious.* . . Wild, active, dangerous, like a mad bull. **1954** *Harder Coll.* **cwTN**, *Ramptious.*

ramrod n Also abbr *rod* **chiefly S Midl, West** See Map
A boss, foreman, or person in charge, esp one who is a rigid disciplinarian.
1880 (1881) Nye *Bill Nye & Boomerang* 60, John Humpfner, the ramrod of the New York House, feared that the explosion might break the large French plate glass windows of his palatial hotel. **1905** *DN* 3.92 **nwAR**, *Ramrod.* . . Mainstay, manager, superintendent. 'He's the ramrod of the concern.' 'Where's the ramrod?' Common. **1934** (1940) Weseen

Dict. Amer. Slang 83 [Logging and mining terms], *Ramrod*—A superintendent; a manager. **1936** Adams *Cowboy Lingo* 21, To begin with, the owner himself had divers titles, such as 'presidente,' 'ramrod' or 'rod,' 'big auger,' [etc.]. **1936** *AmSp* 11.276 **eTN**, *Ramrod.* School teacher. 'The ramrod lives here.' **1938** in Lib. of Congress *Amer. Memory: WPA Life Hist.* (Internet) **TX** (as of 1884), I located the ramrod and hit him for a job. **1942** *AmSp* 17.75 **wNE**, The man in charge of a herd on the trail is the *trail boss* or *ramrod.* **1942** Berrey-Van den Bark *Amer. Slang* 459.3, *Task master.* . . *ramrod. Ibid* 913.6, *Rancher; cattleman.* . . *Spec.* . . *ramrod* . . , *the owner.* **1953** Randolph-Wilson *Down in Holler* 277 **Ozarks**, *Ramrod.* . . A leader, a boss, a person of great influence. "There's five fellers on the school board, but old man Burns is the ramrod. The rest of 'em does whatever he says." **1958** McCulloch *Woods Words* 145 **Pacific NW**, *Ramrod*—A foreman. **1959** *AmSp* 34.80 **nCA** [Logging terms], *Straw boss, ramrod.* . . The foreman under the general foreman or super. **1965–70** DARE (Qu. HH43a, *The top person in charge of a group of workmen*) Infs **AL50, CA158, OK6, TN1, 30, TX26, 81, VT12, 16,** *Ramrod;* **UT3,** Foreman, pusher, ramrod; (Qu. HH43b, *The assistant to the top person in charge of a group of workmen*) Inf **TX26,** Assistant ramrod; **CA93, KY91,** Ramrod; (Qu. HH17, *A person who tries to appear important, or who tries to lay down the law in his community: "He'd like to be the _____ around here."*) Infs **AR52, IL143,** Ramrod; (Qu. II23, *Joking names for the people who are, or think they are, the best society of a community: The _____*) Inf **AR52,** Ramrods. [12 of 16 total Infs male] **1968–69** DARE FW Addit **CA**, *Ramrod*—boss—mining terms—California; **IA31,** Chief ramrod—top foreman, "foreman of all the foremans." **1969** *AmSp* 44.22 **Pacific NW** [Painter jargon], *Ramrod.* . . The foreman or *leadman* of a paint crew . . a bad foreman . . a leadman that often overdoes it; a poor foreman, one who keeps riding you. **1986** Pederson *LAGS Concordance,* 1 inf, **seLA**, The ramrod = the boss.

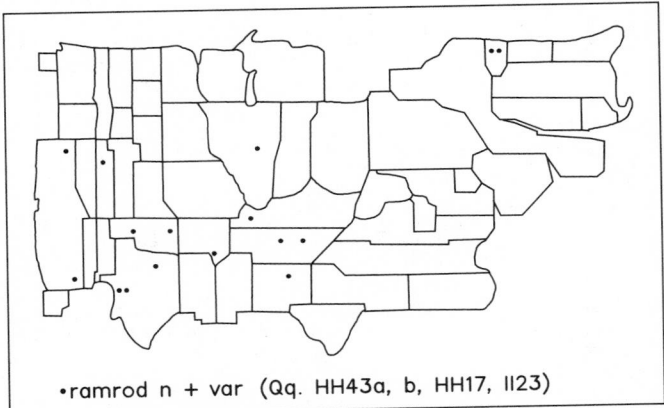

•ramrod n + var (Qq. HH43a, b, HH17, II23)

ramrod v
1 also abbr *rod:* To boss, manage, esp in a strictly disciplined way; to sponsor, be the force behind; hence n *ramrodder* a **ramrod** n.
1942 Berrey-Van den Bark *Amer. Slang* 220.5, *Manage; direct.* . . *Spec.* . . *ramrod* . . , *to be a strict disciplinarian or taskmaster. Ibid* 940, *Miscellaneous western terms.* . . *ramrod, to boss.* **1942** Perry *Texas* 60, The Panhandle is ramrodded by the city of Amarillo. **1944** Adams *Western Words* 129, *Roddin' the spread*—Bossing the outfit. **1950** *Horse Lover Mag.* Aug-Sept 21 *(Mathews Coll.),* The June Polso, Montana, Rodeo was ramrodded by a salty oldtimer named Buck Winter. **1956** McAtee *Some Dialect NC* 36, *Ramrod.* . . Manage, boss. "If I was ramroddin' this thing. . ." **1970** DARE (Qu. HH43a, *The top person in charge of a group of workmen*) Inf **IL143,** Ramrodder. **1973** Symons *Where Wagon Led* 1.118, I ramrodded the Circle Diamond for quite a few years after that—back and forth 'tween Montany and Canady. **1979** *Tucson* (Arizona) *Citizen* 20 Sept. 11A/3 *(OED2),* Scores of volunteers rallied around this charitable event which was ramrodded by the city of Tucson.
2 To force, drive through against opposition or difficulty.
1952 Brown *NC Folkl.* 1.582 **wNC**, *Ramrod.* . . To force, deceive, or overpersuade one into doing something. "The politicians have ramrodded the people into voting for this measure." **1958** McCulloch *Woods Words* 146 **Pacific NW**, *Ramrod the job*—To ram a piece of work through to a finish. **c1960** Wilson *Coll.* **csKY**, *Ramrod.* . . Force some-

thing or someone. **1976** *Publishers' Weekly* 1 Mar 84 **West,** The skittish livestock Kingman must ramrod to a distant army post. *Ibid* 8 Mar 57, Railroad builders par excellence who ramrod tracks across the virgin countryside.

ramrodder See **ramrod** v 1

ramrod grass n

A **cordgrass** (here: *Spartina pectinata*); hence n *ramrod hay.*

1920 *Torreya* 20.18 **MO,** *Spartina michauxiana* [=*S. pectinata*]. . . Prairie grass, ramrod grass, Peruque, Mo. **1968** *DARE* (Qu. L8, *Hay that grows naturally in damp places*) Inf **IA**22, Ramrod hay or slough hay. **1995** *Brophy Coll.* 61 swMO (as of c1960), *Ramrod grass.* [S]lough-grass, which is tall and straight.

rams n Usu with *the* **chiefly C Atl** See Map Cf **maniportia**

Delirium tremens.

1967–70 *DARE* (Qu. DD22, . . *Delirium tremens*) Infs **DE**1, **NJ**33, Rams; **DE**3, He's got the rams; **MD**31, The rams [ræmz]—modern word; **PA**27, D.T.'s, heard but never used *rams;* **PA**36, D.T.'s, also called the rams; **PA**245, The rams.

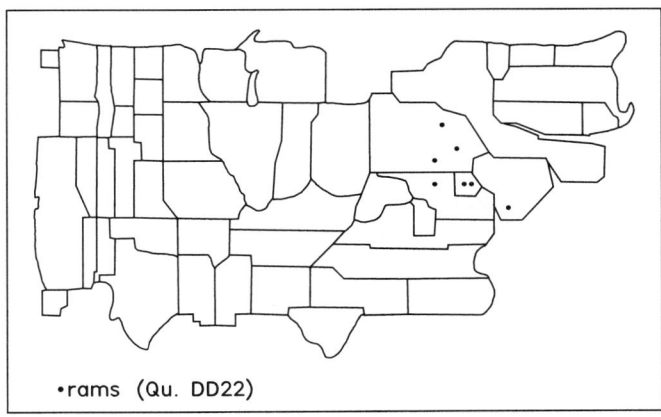

•rams (Qu. DD22)

ramsack v Also *ramshack, ramshag* [Varr of *ransack;* cf *EDD ramsack*] **scattered, but esp Sth, Midl**

1 To search through in an exhaustive, messy, or destructive way; ransack; to rummage, search.

1837 Sherwood *Gaz. GA* 71, *Ramsack,* for ransack. **1858** *De Bow's Rev.* 24.237, Mercantile enterprise seems to have ramsacked the "uttermost parts of the earth," to procure supplies of this article. **1899** (1912) Green *VA Folk-Speech* 344, *Ramsack.* . . To search thoroughly; seek carefully in all parts; overhaul in detail. Ransack. **1901** Churchill *Crisis* 413 ceMO, Supper, Miss Jinny. Lawsy, if I ain't ramshacked de premises fo' you bof. **1935** Hurston *Mules & Men* 133 FL, [Part of a tall tale:] Me and my buddy Joe Wiley was ramshackin' Georgy [=Georgia] over when we come to a loggin' camp. *Ibid* 323 **FL,** Me and my buddy and two three more,/ Going to ramshack Georgy everywhere we go. **1959** Faulkner *Mansion* 272 **MS,** That door leads back into the house and he dont aim to have none of us master-carpenter candidates maybe ramshagging the joint as a farewell gesture on the way out. **1962** Faulkner *Reivers* 13 **MS,** Now you got to ramshack the country to locate another back window you can crawl in. **1965** Brewer *Worser Days* 132 **NC** [Black], I got a li'l eight-year-ol' girl at home, an' she lack to ramshack thu my pocketbook all de time. **1965–70** *DARE* (Qu. Y48, *To look in every possible place for something you've mislaid . . "I've _____ [the house looking for them].")* 21 Infs, **scattered, but somewhat more freq Sth, Midl,** Ramsacked; (Qu. V5a, *To take something of small value that doesn't belong to you—for example, a child taking cookies: "Who's been _____ the cookies?")* Inf **MD**31, Ramsacking. **1983** *MJLF* 9.1.52 ceKY (as of 1956), *Ramsack* . . to look through other people's possessions, ransack. **1997** *DARE* File GA, In describing the damage done to her church building . . she [=a 65-year-old woman, born in rural nGA] exclaimed, "First they broke in the door to the pastor's office, and ramsacked that; then they got into the secretary's office, and ramsacked that." **1998** *DARE* File cnIN, Yes, we have used the word ramsack. It was used in Indiana quite a lot. . . I always thought when you ramsacked anything you looked through it thoroughly but also left it in a mess (like opening all the drawers and leaving the contents scattered on the floor) that kind of thing.

2 To wreck; to put out of shape or order; hence ppl adj *ramshacked.*

1964 Will *Hist. Okeechobee* xi c,ceFL, *Ramshack*—to wreck. **1966–68** *DARE* (Qu. KK70, *Something that has got out of proper shape: "That house is all _____.")* Infs **AL**3, **GA**3, **MO**9, Ramshacked. **1975** *Appalachian Jrl.* 2.151 wNC, If one has *ramshacked* a place, he has left it in a complete mess. **1984** *Annals Internal Med.* 100.899 wAL, Ramshack (my blood pressure runs up and ramshacks my nerves and my brain).

‡ramsasspatorious adj

1916 *DN* 4.279 NE, *Ramsasspatorious.* . . Excited, anxious, impatient. "Don't get ramsasspatorious."

ram's claws n Cf **devil's-claw 3**

A **buttercup 1** (here: *Ranunculus repens*).

1900 Lyons *Plant Names* 316, *R[anunculus] repens.* . . Ram's-claws. **1959** Carleton *Index Herb. Plants* 97, *Ram's claws:* Ranunculus repens.

ramshack v See **ramsack**

ramshack adj [Prob abbr for *ramshackle*]

Run-down, in disrepair.

1941 *Sat. Eve. Post* 10 May 113, Ramshack house, a-setting on a rock. **1966–70** *DARE* (Qu. KK70, *Something that has got out of proper shape: "That house is all _____.")* Infs **SC**26, **VA**39, Ramshack.

ramshack n¹ See **ramshackle** n

ramshack n² [Echoic]

=**red-bellied woodpecker.**

1913 *Auk* 30.497 Okefenokee GA, *Centurus carolinus.* . . 'Shamshack'; 'Ram-shack'; 'Chad-cherries'. . . The 'Sham-shack' has a variety of call-notes, which. . . has doubtless given rise to the local names. **1955** *Oriole* 20.10 GA, Red-bellied Woodpecker. . . (in reference to common utterances of this polyphonic bird) . . *Ram-shack.*

ramshacked See **ramsack 2**

ramshackeldy, ramshackelty See **ramshacklety**

ramshackle v [*OED2 ransackle* (and varr) 1621 →; "*Obs.* exc. *north. dial.*"; *EDD ramshackle* v.²] Cf **ramshackled**

To ransack, plunder.

1983 *Lutz Coll.* NJ, Yesterday a woman in Ramsey said that a certain house had been ramshackled. . . [The informant] is a descendant of several of the very early Bergen County settlers. . . She meant *ransacked.* That is, people had gone through the house searching for antiques and other valuables.

ramshackle n Also *ramshack* [*ramshackle* adj, **ramshack** adj; prob infl by *shack*]

A run-down or makeshift house.

1909 *DN* 3.362 eAL, wGA, I wouldn't live in such a ramshackle. **1920** (1921) Sandburg *Smoke & Steel* 41 **Chicago IL,** People clean as the prayers of Jesus here in the / faded ramshackle at Congress and Green. **1928** *AmSp* 4.128 NE, Sometimes the homes of the settlers were "dumps" or "ramshackles," part sod, part frame and tar paper. **1930** Shoemaker *1300 Words* 49 cPA Mts (as of c1900), *Ramshackle*—A tumble down house or shanty. **1966–70** *DARE* (Qu. D21, *A small, poorly-built house, or one in rundown condition*) Infs **MI**28, **PA**203, Ramshackle; **ND**9, Ramshackle, dump; [**CT**13, **LA**40, Ramshackle—adjective;] **IL**141, Ramshack.

ramshackled ppl adj

1 also obs spp *ranshackld, ranshacled:* Dilapidated, ramshackle. [Engl dial; ppl adj < *ransackle,* **ramshackle** v, varr of *ransack,* perh infl by Scots dial *camshacle* to distort, disorder]

1675 in 1878 MA Hist. Soc. *Coll.* 5th ser 1.10, A window which was all ranshacled. **1703** in 1886 *Ibid* 6th ser 1.276, Barn and Outhousing Ranshackld. **1883** *Amer. Missionary* Dec 367, [The Chinese Wall is] a barbaric, ramshackled old thing of a great many centuries. **1909** *DN* 3.362 eAL, wGA, *Ramshackle(d).* . . In bad state of repair, run down, unkept, unstable. **1965–70** *DARE* (Qu. KK20a, *Something that looks as if it might collapse any minute: "That old shed is certainly _____.")* Infs **CO**29, **GA**73, **MN**42, **NC**51, **TX**32, Ramshackled; (Qu. KK70,

Something that has got out of proper shape: "*That house is all _____.*") Infs **CA213, GA84,** Ramshackled; **NE8,** Ramshackled— this means more run-down; **VA99,** Ramshackled; (Qu. D21, *A small, poorly-built house, or one in rundown condition*) Inf **CA91,** Ramshackled.

2 Used as a euphem for "damned."

    1924 *DN* 5.275 [Exclams], I'll be ramshackled.

ramshacklety adj Also *ramshackeldy, ramshackelty, ramshackledy* [Cf Intro "Language Changes" III.1] **chiefly Sth, S Midl** See Map Cf **racklety, ramshackly, shacklety** Dilapidated.

    1905 *DN* 3.92 **nwAR,** Ram-shackelty. . . Shaky; about to go to pieces from age and neglect. 'He drove by in a ram-shackelty wagon.' Common. **1909** *DN* 3.362 **eAL, wGA,** Ramschacklety [sic]. . . Same as ramshackle. **1911** *DN* 3.546 **NE,** Ramshackeldy. . . Extension of *ramshackle, ramshackled.* **c1960** *Wilson Coll.* **csKY,** Ramshackelty: . . Shaky, in bad repair. **1965–70** *DARE* (Qu. KK20a, *Something that looks as if it might collapse any minute: "That old shed is certainly _____.*") 15 Infs, **Sth, S Midl,** Ramshackledy; (Qu. KK23, *Weak or unsteady: "I think the footbridge will hold but it is a bit _____.*") Infs **DE1, MS64, TX95,** Ramshackledy. [15 of 17 total Infs old or mid-aged]

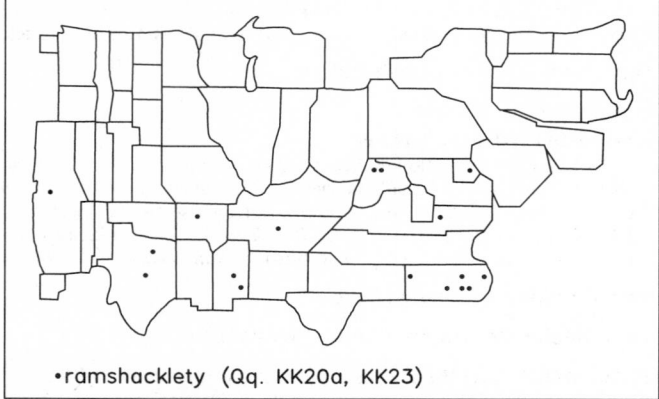

•ramshacklety (Qq. KK20a, KK23)

ramshackly adj [Cf Intro "Language Changes" III.1] **formerly more widespread, now esp Sth, S Midl** Cf **shackly** Dilapidated, ramshackle.

    [**1840** *S. Lit. Messenger* 6.386, Used to go down there with the girls, by the school-house, a 'ramshackling' old house.] **1861** *Vanity Fair* 30.98 **NYC,** At this instant the ramshackly door of the apartment flew open on its single surviving hinge. **1872** *Scribner's Mth.* 5.189, The two gentlemen kindly invited me to take a seat in the ramshackly *einspänner* which they had engaged. **1883** Twain *Life on Missip.* (Boston) 475, Strung along below the city, were a number of decayed, ram-shackly, superannuated old steamboats, not one of which had I ever seen before. **1899** (1912) Green *VA Folk-Speech* 344, Ramshackly. . . Out of gear or repair; crazy; tumbledown. Ramshackle. **1901** *Harper's Mth. Mag.* 102.233 **NM,** A drug-store, an "opera-house," and a ramshackly "Palace Hotel," all of frame. **1941** Percy *Lanterns* 272 **nwMS,** Already the slave quarters looked ramshackly. **1967–68** *DARE* (Qu. KK20a, *Something that looks as if it might collapse any minute: "That old shed is certainly _____.*") Inf **LA6,** Ramshackly; (Qu. KK64, *Speaking of the part of a city that was once very fine, but isn't any more: "The neighborhood is sort of _____.*") Inf **GA18,** Ramshackly ['ræmšækɪlɪ]; **GA31,** Ramshackly. **1986** Pederson *LAGS Concordance,* 1 inf, **csTN,** Run-down ramshackly old shack.

ramshag See **ramsack**

ram's-head n Also *ram's-head lady's slipper* [From the shape of the flower]

A **lady's slipper 1** (here: *Cypripedium arietinum*).

    1824 Bigelow *Florula Bostoniensis* 328, Cypripedium arietinum. . . Ram's Head. . . Flower. . . Petals greenish brown, the upper one much broadest, Lip small, inflated, acute, reticulated with red and white. It has been compared in shape to a sheep's head, the lateral petals representing the horns. **1869** Fuller *Uncle John* 125 **NY,** One species [of lady's slipper] is called the 'Ram's Head,' from the very singular form

of the flower. **1891** Jesup *Plants Hanover NH* 44, C[ypripedium] arietinum. . . Ram's-Head. **1907** *St. Nicholas* Aug 939, Only by rare good fortune will the ram's-head . . reward our search. **1936** Eaton *Wild Gardens New Engl.* 70, The most curious of our native lady's slippers is the ram's head . . but you will have to search long and far to find that. **1966–67** *DARE* Wildfl QR Pl.32B Infs **MI7, MI57A,** Ram's-head. **1987** Case *Orchids* 73, *Ram's-head Lady's-slipper.* . . This smallest native *Cypripedium.* . . has long been considered rare, especially in some areas where it occurs; yet, in the heart of its range, it is sometimes common.

ram's horn n

1 A **cat's-claw** (here: *Acacia greggii*).

    1897 Sudworth *Arborescent Flora* 250, Acacia greggii. . . Common Names. . . Ramshorn. **1908** Britton *N. Amer. Trees* 523, Acacia Greggii. . . This small tree is also called Catsclaw, . . and Ramshorn. [*Ibid* 524, The fruit is . . much curved and contorted, and constricted between the seeds.]

2 A **unicorn plant,** usu *Proboscidea louisianica.* **esp TX**

    1903 Small *Flora SE U.S.* 1097, Martynia Louisiana [=Proboscidea louisianica]. . . Capsule 8–15 cm. long, strongly curved. . . Ram's Horn. **1951** *PADS* 15.41 **TX,** Martynia spp. . . Ram's horns. **1961** Wills–Irwin *Flowers TX* 210, Devil's-claws [=Proboscidea louisianica], also known as Ram's-horns or the Unicorn-plant, occurs in scattered localities over much of Texas, but most commonly in the southern and western portions. **1970** Correll *Plants TX* 1449, Proboscidea louisianica. . . Ram's horn. . . Nat. to s. U.S. but spontaneous northw.; sometimes cult. for its young pods which are made into pickles.

3 A variety of hot pepper *(Capsicum annuum);* see quots.

    1967 *DARE* (Qu. I22b, . . *Peppers—large hot*) Inf **SC43,** Ram's horn—has a crook in it often. **1990** *Seed Savers Yearbook* 171, Ram's Horn . . 6–9″ long x 1–1.5″ wide fruit, often curled into loose "ramshorn" shape, surface with peculiar contorted convoluted texture, med-hot, very prolific, good for picante sauces or fresh on sandwiches.

ramsquaddle v

To beat, thrash.

    1830 *Vt. Statesman* (Castleton) 1 Sep. 1/2 *(DA),* The persecutors of Henry Clay: They ought to be ramsquaddled and chewed up by a ring-tailed roarer. **1830** *NY Constellation* (NY) 11 Sept 2/5 **SE,** May I be tetotally twisted if I cant ram-squaddle two like you. **1963** Carson *Social Hist. Bourbon* 51, The Kentuckian was the half-horse, half-alligator man, full of fun and fight, with a gargantuan capacity for punishing his jug without getting ramsquaddled. **1979** *AR Times* Mar 37 [Arkansas talk], There are the euphemisms, "tallywacker," "pizzle" and "prong"; the hyperbolical tongue-twisters, "bodaciously" (completely), "ram-squaddled[″]" (badly beaten), and "obflisticated," meaning thoroughly confused.

ramste(a)d See **ranstead weed**

ramstugious adj Also *ramstudious, ramstugenous, ramstuginous, ramstujous* [*SND* ramstageous, ramstugious "Rough, coarse, uncouth"] **esp Midl** Cf **ramptious**

Violent and reckless in behavior; outrageous, quarrelsome, passionate.

    1847 in 1912 Thornton *Amer. Gloss.* 721 **PA,** [An old he-bear] is as ramstugenous an animal as a log-cabin loafer in the dog-days. **1848** *Oquawka* (Ill.) *Spectator* 12 Feb. 6 *(DAE)* **cwIL,** Can you make a ramstugious speech and abuse all the har off a man's head? **1851** Byrn *Ark. Doctor* 81 *(DAE),* The old lady bawled out, 'There comes our ramstuginous little doctor.' **1909** *DN* 3.362 **eAL, wGA,** Ramstudious, ramstugious. . . Rambunctious, rough and ready; also full of animal passion. **1912** *DN* 3.587 **wIN,** Ramstugious. . . Rampageous. **1937** *Hall Coll.* **eTN,** Ramstujous [ræmstudʒəs] (Probably a nonce word, apparently unknown to others)—Quarrelsome; having a chip on the shoulder. Having a superabundance of energy? **1985** Madson *Up River* 52 **Upper Missip. Valley,** They [=raftsmen] were universally regarded as ramstugenous alligators who played about the same role in the river towns that the wildest of the Texas drovers filled at Kansas railheads.

‡ramzy adj

    1970 *DARE* (Qu. X17, . . *A damp cellar that had been shut up for some time would smell _____*) Inf **TX86,** Ramzy.

ran See **run** v **A2a**

ranahan n [Perh **ranny** n 1 + **hand** n B1]   **West**   Cf **ranny** n 2

An experienced cowhand.

1936 Adams *Cowboy Lingo* 22, The cowboy was known, too, by such slang names as 'ranahan' (which really referred to a top hand). **1936** McCarthy *Lang. Mosshorn* np **West** [Range terms], *Ranahan*. . . An experienced "hand" or cowboy.

ranai See **lanai**

ranch n [AmSpan *rancho* a rude farmhouse, makeshift village] **chiefly West**   See Map

An establishment for raising cattle, horses, or sheep on rangeland; a farm of any sort; the buildings associated with such an establishment—often in combs specifying the main product of the establishment.

1826 (1933) Sibley *Santa Fe Diary* 169 **NM,** Sen. Romaro called & requested me to ride to the Ranch tomorrow morning. **1831** (1973) Pattie *Personal Narr.* 221, I . . proceeded to a *ranch,* where I procured a horse for three dollars. **1857** (1859) Olmsted *Journey TX* 160, Some live upon the produce of farms and cattle-ranches. **1860** (1936) Hawley *Diary* 339 **CO,** Saw a few fine ranches, which are called farms in the states. **1869** *Terr. Enterprise* (Virginia, Nev.) 30 March 3/4 *(DA),* A gentleman named Zivits, owning a wood ranch south of Empire, several times brought in rock for assay. **1869** Browne *Adventures* 396 **ceCA,** Several fine valleys, now used as hay and cattle ranches, lie between Aurora and Bodie. **1875** *Congressional Record* 20 Feb 3.2.1537 **CA,** This is not the sheep-ranch proposition. **1878** Taylor *Between the Gates* 266 **CA,** To call a place where bees are harbored and robbed, a ranch, is about as bad as to name the grazing range of lowing herds a cattle academy. **1888** Lindley *Calif. of South* 240 *(DA),* There are a few great grain-ranches in the valley. **1899** *South Dakotan* 1.194, One . . man from Missouri brought in a herd of cows and established a milk ranch on Slate creek. **1910** *Out West Mag.* Feb 155 **sCA,** "Look at these orange ranches!" orated the other comfortably. **1927** *AmSp* 2.277 **CA,** *Ranch*—a large farm [used on the Pacific Coast and in the Middle West]. **1929** *AmSp* 5.53 **NE** [Cattle country talk], A "ranch," . . may vary from about fifteen hundred to thirty thousand acres of "grazing" and "hay" land. "Ranch" may denote the entire ranching establishment, the principal buildings, or the collective persons who operate the establishment. *Ibid* 54, The ranch owner's or the foreman's house is called the "ranch house." **1929** *San Antonio Express* (Advertising Section), June 2 (Bentley *Spanish Terms*), Bargain of bargains, Goat, Sheep, and Cattle Ranch; Chicken Ranch Supreme, Finest in South Texas, 15 acres. **1932** *DN* 6.232 **West,** *Ranch*. Originally *rancho* and limited to the Southwest, the word has become current all over the West generally, for any sort of farm. The real ranch, as we may say, is the cattle ranch; but there are many other kinds, especially, of late, dude ranches[.] The word is used not only for the buildings, but sometimes for the whole range of country round about. **1937** *AmSp* 12.105 **eNE** [Farm terms], The word *ranch* usually means a large livestock farm with hundreds or thousands of acres of pasture but no cultivated crops. **1943** *CA Folkl. Qrly.* 2.41, Where I came from a *ranch* means cowboys, the open range, and Texas longhorns. Hereabouts [=CA] a ranch may be a chicken farm, an artichoke patch, or a house in the suburbs. **1949** *Prairie Schooner* 23.48, He applied for a job managing a big stock ranch in Montana. **1965–70** *DARE* (Qu. L1, *A man who is employed to help with work on a farm*) 13 Infs, **West,** Ranch hand; **MT3,** Ranch help; **NV9,** Ranch worker; (Qu. L6b, *A piece of land under cultivation—if it's several acres*) 13 Infs, **chiefly West,** Ranch; (Qu. C29, *A good-sized stretch of level land with practically no trees*) Inf **CA90,** Farm, ranch; **LA7,** Ranch [Inf doubtful]; **FL9,** Ranch land; (Qu. L2, *The extra house on a large farm where a hired man and his family live*) Infs **CA131, MO34, WA20,** Ranch house; **CA97,** Ranch house—peculiar to this district; **NE5,** Ranch hand's house; (Qu. L6a, . . *A piece of land under cultivation—less than an acre*) Inf **NM6,** Some would say ranch—half-acre to ten thousand; (Qu. L7, *A piece of land with a hay crop planted on it*) Infs **CA138, 141, 181, OR13,** Ranch; **CA117,** Alfalfa ranch; **WA12,** Hay ranch; (Qu. M22, . . *Kinds of buildings . . on farms*) Infs **CA17, TX1, WA27,** Ranch house; **TX4,** Ranch house—main house; **TX22,** Headquarters ranch house; (QR, near Qu. M22) Inf **HI2,** Ranch—cattle always—may be small or large; (Qu. AA22, *Joking names that a man may use to refer to his wife: "I have to go down and pick up my _____."*) Inf **WA6,** Boss of the ranch. **1967–69** *DARE* Tape **AK6,** It was horses, to start with, kind of a horse ranch; **AZ4,** We bought a ranch; **CA10,** We lived on a ranch . . and it was a 25-acre ranch; **CA161,** Some of the grain farmers

and those like that live on the ranches; **NE1,** [FW:] That's fairly good-sized ranch around here, isn't it? [Inf:] No. Ours is not so big. I say ranch because he does keep a lot of cattle there on what he has. But we only have five hundred and twenty acres out there. **1973** Allen *LAUM* 1.190 **Upper MW** (as of c1950), *Farm.* This item was added late in the fieldwork in order to ascertain the eastern limits of *ranch.* An original distinction between *farm* and *ranch* became blurred when *ranch* came to be applied to a huge fenceless tract for wheat-growing. . . In general, *ranch* is limited to cattle-raising areas west of the Missouri river. **1976** Maclean *River Runs Through* 184 **wMT** (as of 1919), You will note that Mr. Smith and I both said "ranch hands" and not "cowboys"—in the Forest Service we called cowboys ranch hands to show what we thought of them. **1986** Pederson *LAGS Concordance,* 33 infs, **Gulf Region,** Ranch; 1 inf, **cAL,** Like a man having about ten acres, then calling it a ranch; 1 inf, **swMS,** Ranch (or "range"?; large pasture); 1 inf, **neLA,** Ranch—raise cows for milk; *(Pasture; range)* 1 inf, **cTN,** Ranch—heard in another part of the country; 1 inf, **csTX,** Ranch—more than 500 acres; "farm" if smaller.

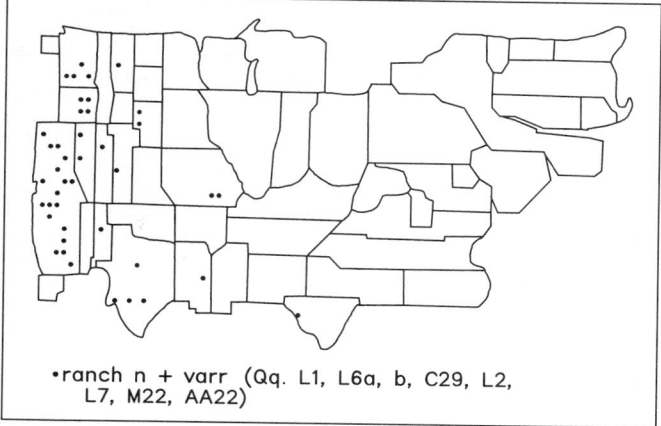

•ranch n + varr (Qq. L1, L6a, b, C29, L2, L7, M22, AA22)

ranch v[1], hence vbl n *ranching*

Also with *it:* To raise livestock on, or grow the main product of, a **ranch** n; to raise animals or crops on (a **ranch** n).

1863 in 1937 *Frontier & Midland* 17.288 **ID,** A ranch is properly a grazing farm and the term "ranching" sometimes means farming but is generally applied in this country to taking care of stock. **1866** Bret Harte in *Californian* 26 May 1/1 **CA,** Ranchin' out this way? **1872** Twain *Roughing It* 242 **NV,** He had been farming (or ranching as the more customary term is) in Washoe District. **1873** Beadle *Undeveloped West* 267 **ceCA,** "Ranching" came next, and all this industry is not lost. **1890** *Internatl. Annual Anthony's Photographic Bulletin* 3.32 **sCA,** Any enterprising young tourist . . "can find plenty of work and fun among the jolly fellows who ranch it" in the West. **1890** *Stock Grower & Farmer* (Las Vegas NM) 29 Mar 6/3, Stockmen. . . have ranched there from ten to twenty years. **1897** Hough *Story Cowboy* 79 **TX,** This ended what was probably one of the very first of the attempts at horse ranching east of the Rockies on the cow range. **1929** *Provo Herald* (Provo, Utah), Aug. 16 (Bentley *Spanish Terms*), Russ Mangleby, halfback, is ranching near his home town. . . Pearl Pollard . . is ranching at Winnifred, Montana. **1940** (1942) Clark *Ox-Bow* 150 **NV,** Someone had lived there once, though, and tried to ranch the place. **1966** *Roswell Daily Rec.* (NM) 11 Mar 2/3, She . . ranched on the Hondo for many years. **1998** *DARE* File **cOR,** [Plaque at John Day Fossil Beds Natl Monument:] The Cant Ranch is one of the best-preserved examples of early 20th century ranching operations in the John Day River Valley.

ranch v[2]   See **rinse** 5

ranch egg n **West**

A fresh egg.

1886 *Overland Mth.* 7 advt sec 7, Daily Fresh Supplies of the Best Table Butter and Fresh Ranch Eggs. **1908** *Sunset* Dec 792, If you were working with ranch eggs, store eggs or yard eggs, it might be different. **1943** Howard *Montana* 144, Ranch eggs at this time cost a dollar a dozen. **1943** *CA Folkl. Qrly.* 2.41, Many California localisms have to do with food. I have noted, among them, *ranch egg* for fresh egg. **1966** Wibberley *Out of Depths* 149 **CA,** Two ranch eggs with ham. **1967** *DARE* File **NV,** Ranch eggs—apparently fresh eggs right from the farmer. **1998** *DARE* File, On restaurant menus in the West it's common to find "ranch eggs" on the menu. The implication is that the eggs have come straight to the restaurant from the poultry farm—they haven't sat on a grocery store shelf.

rancheman See **ranchman**

rancher n **chiefly West** Cf **rock rancher, stump ranch**

One who operates and usu owns a **ranch** n—often in combs specifying the main product of the ranch.

1836 in 1921 Lamar *Papers* 1.337 **TX**, Capt King went . . for the purpose of chastising some ranchers who were said to be those who had been also plundering in refusio [sic]. **1836** (1935) Field *3 Yrs. TX* 29, At his approach he was . . met by two hundred Mexican Ranchiers and Indians. **1869** *Harper's New Mth. Mag.* 39.470 **Rocky Mts**, The little valley that satisfies the "hay rancher." **1876** *Gold Hill* (Nev.) *News* 5 Oct. 3/5 (*DA*), 'Old Kentuck,' the well known chicken rancher of the Sutro road, will leave shortly for Sacramento. **1878** Beadle *Western Wilds* 106 **NV**, The needs of miners and stock-ranchers in the adjacent mountains have built up a few trading towns. **1884** Shepherd *Prairie Exper.* 125 **nCA**, If stock-owners are in power, they say to the small rancher, 'Fence your fields.' **1904** *Country Life* July 287, The Montana sheep-rancher figures that the wool will pay all expenses. **1929** *AmSp* 5.53 **NE** [Cattle country talk], A "rancher" is a member of the proprietary class. . . In Nebraska the word "rancher" generally refers to one who also has land under cultivation. **1949** *Los Angeles Times* (CA) 7 May sec 1 11/3 **seCA**, Grain ranchers . . have completed an extensive war against ground squirrels. **1966** *DARE* (Qu. HH1, *Names and nicknames for a rustic or countrified person*) Inf **WA**33, Rancher. **1968** *DARE* Tape **CA**87, There was the ranchers that kept the bees, kept a few cattle, and also had the hay farms. **1986** Pederson *LAGS Concordance* (*A rustic*) 1 inf, **seTX**, Ranchers—local term; not abusive; (*The poor whites*) 1 inf, **seTX**, Rancher.

rancheria clover n

Macrae's clover (*Trifolium macraei*), native to the Pacific states. Also called **Indian clover**

1925 Jepson *Manual Plants CA* 546, T[*rifolium*] *atropurpureum* [=T. *macraei*]. . . *Rancheria clover*. . . Valleys and hillsides, 20 to 3000 ft. **1944** Abrams *Flora Pacific States* 2.531, Common Indian or Rancheria Clover. . . Western British Columbia to southern California. **1961** Thomas *Flora Santa Cruz* 216 **cwCA**, Rancheria Clover. Grassy slopes, . . April–June. **1973** Hitchcock–Cronquist *Flora Pacific NW* 276, Rancheria c[lover] . . T[*rifolium*] *macraei*.

rancheria grass n **esp CA**

A **wild rye** (here: *Leymus mollis* subsp *mollis*).

1857 U.S. War Dept. *Rept. Explor. RR* 6.3.92 **CA**, *Elymus arenarius*. . . It grows in all parts of California where there are deserted Indian lodges, and is, therefore, called by the inhabitants "rancheria grass." **1880** (1883) U.S. Census Office *Rept. Ag.* 961 **Pacific NW**, *E*[*lymus*] *arenarius*, in northern California and northward, where it is called rancheria-grass; its seeds are gathered by the Digger Indians for food; it ranges to Asia and northern Europe, but not to the eastern states. **1894** *Jrl. Amer. Folkl.* 7.104 **CA**, *Elymus arenarius* [=*Leymus mollis* subsp *mollis*], . . rancenria [sic] grass. **1911** Jepson *Flora CA* 77, *Rancheria-grass*. . . Common on maritime sand dunes, sandy beaches, and coast bluffs.

ranchero n [AmSpan] **SW** *old-fash* Cf **rancho**

=**rancher**, usu one who is a Mexican or Mexican-American.

1826 in 1924 Austin *Papers* 31 Oct 1482 **TX**, The old Ranchero was much surprised, but overjoyed to see me. **1827** in 1858 Dewees *Letters TX* 66, A few wealthy rancheros dwell in the country [=Mexico], who own vast herds of stock, of all kinds. **1857** in 1941 *AmSp* 16.265 **CA** [Span words used in English], *Ranchero*, Farmer. **1860** in 1948 *Western Folkl.* 7.16 **swCA**, Rancheros and others must now pay debts. . . and sell on a lifeless market. **1892** *DN* 1.194 **TX**, *Ranchéro*: a man who keeps a *rancho* . . or lives in one. Seldom used. *Ibid* 251 **TX**, *Ranchéro*. . . Add: According to Captain Hardie this word is used very extensively. **1897** Lummis *King of Broncos* 27 **NM**, King he was, not only of the broncos, but among the thoroughbreds of the few wealthy rancheros. **1903** (1965) Adams *Log Cowboy* 12 **West**, A number of different rancheros [=Mexican ranch owners] had turned in cattle in making up the herd. **1929** Dobie *Vaquero* 123 **West**, My took me among various Mexican rancheros, and I want to say here that I found

them strictly honest. **1932** Bentley *Spanish Terms* 191, *Ranchero*. . . Rancher is used more commonly today. A *ranchero* is always a Mexican; a "rancher" may be either Mexican or American. [**1968–70** *DARE* (Qu. FF16, . . *Local contests or celebrations*) Inf **CA**176, Ranchero Days—parade and beard-growing; (Qu. FF22b, . . *Clubs and societies . . for men*) Inf **CA**65, Ranchero Visitadores—visit ranches; limited membership for well-to-do; rough it.]

ranchers fireweed See **fireweed j**

ranch fence n Also *ranch-style fence, ranch-type* ~

A wooden-rail fence; see quots.

1961 Folk *Word Atlas N. LA* map 602, Fence made of wooden rails . . [other responses include] ranch fence. **1965–69** *DARE* (Qu. L65, . . *Kinds of fences*) Inf **FL**22, Ranch fence—2 rails on bottom with rails crossing all around; **RI**7, Ranch fence; **PA**72, Ranch-style fence; **CO**19, Ranch-type fence. **1986** Pederson *LAGS Concordance*, 1 inf, **cnAR**, A ranch fence; 1 inf, **seMS**, Ranch fence—boards across top and bottom; x-shaped.

ranch fried potatoes n pl Also *ranch(-style) fries,* ~ *potatoes* **scattered, but esp West** Cf **cottage fried potatoes, sheepherder 2**

See quots.

1967 *DARE* (Qu. H47, *Kinds of fried potatoes*) Inf **CA**11, Ranch fried—bacon and onions first, then potatoes; put lid on. **1972** *Nation's Restaurant News* 22 May 56 (*Popik Coll.*), Our Regular, Crinkle, . . Steak, Home, Ranch Style, and Cosmo Fries from Idaho. **1998** *NADS Letters* **MT**, The "ranch-fried potatoes" I've had in Montana are leftover baked or boiled potatoes that have been fried with onions for sure and green peppers maybe. Bacon I didn't see. *Ibid* **UT**, The term Ranch Potatoes was used for fried potatoes—cooked crispy, not steamed, and didn't contain bacon though they sometimes had onions. *Ibid* **eMD**, I have heard the term "ranch fries" used in reference to potatoes cut in lengthwise wedges, then coated with seasonings and fried. *Ibid*, I have had "Ranch-fried potatoes" served to me as anything from french-fries topped with chili to what I would imagine is a more accurate representation: Diced potatoes, fried with onions, bacon, peppers, some sort of chili spice and cheese. *Ibid*, "Ranch fries" refers to the way the potatoes are cut, not the way they're cooked. . . "Ranch fries" are wedge-shaped pieces. *Ibid*, This [=*ranch fried potatoes*] was a term used in my Arkansas/Oklahoma Ozark family for potatoes fried as you describe, with onions and bacon. You do them until they're brown. *Ibid* **nwOR**, I've seen Ranch Fried Potatoes to be just about anything added to cubed potatoes which are then fried. I believe they're just the "cowboy" version of Farm Potatoes. *Ibid* **sCA**, In addition to bacon and onions, I believe they [=*ranch fried potatoes*] also typically contain green bell pepper slices. The idea is to take cubed potatoes and "spice them up" in some way that is reminiscent of what one might eat for breakfast on a ranch.

ranching See **ranch** v[1]

ranch in Texas n

=**farm** n 3.

1967 *DARE* (Qu. KK62, *When you want to make it clear that you will not do something: "I wouldn't do that for _____."*) Inf **IL**20, Ranch in Texas.

ranch it See **ranch** v[1]

ranchman n Also *rancheman* **West** Cf **rancher, ranchero**

One who owns or is employed in operating a **ranch** n.

1856 *Porter's Spirit of Times* 4 Oct 75 **CA**, The dusty, rusty, rough-clad, huge-pawed creatures, known as ranch-men. **1866** *OR State Jrl.* 30 June 1/3, A number of ranchmen are selling out and moving before the approaching railroad whistle. **1872** Twain *Roughing It* 242 **NV**, The witnesses were called—legislators, high government officers, ranchmen, miners, Indians. **1872** Tice *Over Plains* 158 **CO**, Many of these ranchmen have realized comfortable fortunes by their business. **1890** Langford *Vigilante Days* 2.112 **nwID**, Near Lewiston they fell in with a rancheman. **1929** *AmSp* 5.54 **NE** [Cattle country talk], "Ranchmen" are employees as well as employers, though employees are for the most part named after their special work or functions. **1967–70** *DARE* Tape **CA**87, There was the cattlemen, ranchmen, and of course then there was the ranchers that kept the bees, kept a few cattle, and also had the hay farms; **TX**24, [He] was one of the biggest ranchmen in that part of the country; **TX**82, My father was a ranchman, my brothers were all ranchmen. My son is a ranchman. Also in the bank and also a lawyer. I have only the one son.

ranchman's twine n
  1956 Almirall *From College* 216, [It] was fastened in front to one of the logs with stout baling wire (often called "ranchman's twine").

rancho n [AmSpan] **West** *old-fash*
  =**ranch** n.
  1840 (1841) Dana *2 Yrs.* 119 **swCA**, The nearest house, they told us, was a Rancho, or cattle-farm, about three miles off. **1841** McCalla *Advent. TX* 38, I . . encamped with the . . party, on the Sevilla Creek, on which Patton's rancho was soon after attacked by Indians. [*DARE* Ed: This quot may illustrate the obs sense "rude farmhouse" instead.] **1857** in 1941 *AmSp* 16.261 **CA** [Span words used in English], *Rancho*, a large tract of land owned by one party. **1892** *DN* 1.194 **TX**, *Ráncho*: a ranch. **1897** Lummis *King of Broncos* 7 **NM**, He was youngest of the dozen vaqueros of the big rancho. **1936** McCarthy *Lang. Mosshorn* np **West** [Range terms], *Rancho*. . . The buildings and surrounding lands of a ranch owner. **1968** *DARE* (Qu. L6b, *A piece of land under cultivation—if it's several acres*) Inf **CA**57, Rancho.

ranch potatoes See **ranch fried potatoes**

ranch road n esp **TX** Cf **farm-to-market road**
  A road running on or to a **ranch** n—used in western Texas as an official designation for a class of secondary highways.
  [**1863** in 1889 U.S. War Dept. *War of Rebellion* 1st ser 26.1.413 **sTX**, I also expect a couple of lots [of cotton] in from a point 70 miles from here on the King's ranch road.] **1923** Herrick *Lilla* 262 **WY**, Lilla walked a little way down the ranch road. **1967–69** *DARE* (Qu. N27a, *Names . . for different kinds of unpaved roads*) Infs **TX**43, 67, Ranch road(s); (Qu. N29, . . *Names . . for a less important road running back from a main road*) Inf **TX**1, Ranch roads; **TX**68, Ranch road—a kind of highway. **1969** *Today's Health* Sept 44, We planned to jounce over ranch roads in search of pioneer camp sites, springs, and ruins of frontier forts. **1986** Pederson *LAGS Concordance* (*Lane, from public road to house*) 1 inf, **ceAL**, Ranch road; 1 inf, **swMS**, Ranch road—large, tree-lined. **1998** *NADS Letters* **wTX**, Ranch Road: Texas has several grades of rural roads, excluding US highways and interstates. *State Highways* are funded/maintained by the State DoT. *Farm-to-Market* roads are funded/maintained by counties. *Ranch Roads* are funded/maintained by counties but are unpaved; there really aren't very many of these anymore. I must confess that this latter category may be an unofficial designation, but rather common here. *Ibid* **swTX**, Ranch road . . has always denoted a road from the main highway or county road to the ranch house, even though that road may be miles long, as they often are on large ranches in Texas. *Ibid* **TX**, Ranch roads are characteristically known to be dirt or gravel. No rancher is going to pave the long "driveway" through his land. When we see any other road resembling this, be it a country road or a street off a highway, we call it a ranch road. *Ibid* **TX**, In Texas, the term "ranch road" is a state highway department designation for a secondary road used to connect outlying ranches with a main highway. . Ranch road is also used to refer to a poor quality track on a ranch but there is no requirement that the track connect any ranch building to a public road. In Central Texas, any track on a ranch is called a ranch road. . such ranch roads are largely internal to the ranch and may refer to a track connecting a well or stock tank to a pasture, a barn to a cattle pen, or similar use. *Ibid* **nCA**, Ranch road—we used this phrase to describe the unpaved road out by our house when I attended school at California State University Chico. *Ibid* **TX**, In Texas, there are roads named "Farm road" (in the East) or "Ranch road" (in the West) followed by a number. . These are not quite highways, typically 2 lanes, but usually fully paved and well maintained. . They give farmers and ranchers access to haul their crops or livestock to the main highways.

ranch-style fence See **ranch fence**

ranch-style fries See **ranch fried potatoes**

ranch-type fence See **ranch fence**

rancid See **ranstead weed**

Randall grass n Also sp *Rannel grass* esp **VA**
  A **ryegrass 1**: usu *Lolium pratense*, occas also *L. perenne*.

1881 Phares *Farmer's Book of Grasses* 63, F[estuca] pratense [= *Lolium pratense*], known generally as meadow fescue, locally in Virginia as Randall grass, is a perennial, with round smooth stems two to three feet high, in mountain lands in Virginia six feet high. **1889** Vasey *Ag. Grasses* 71, [*Lolium pratense*] ripens its seeds long before any other grass, and consequently affords a very early nip to cattle. It has been raised under various names in Virginia, as "Randall grass," and in North Carolina as "evergreen grass." **1915** *DN* 4.188 **swVA**, *Rannel grass*. **1922** U.S. Dept. Ag. *Farmers' Bulletin* 1254.20, Meadow fescue . . , also called . . in the South, Randall grass, is a hardy perennial grass. *Ibid* 32, Perennial rye-grass (*Lolium perenne* . .) is also known as . . darnel and Randall grass, but the last two names properly belong to other grasses. **1945** Wodehouse *Hayfever Plants* 39, Meadow fescue . . , also called . . Randall or evergreen grass, is. . . cultivated for hay and pasture. . . It flowers in June and July and is known to cause hayfever.

random scoot See **rantum scoot**

rang v See **ring** v B2a

rang n[1] See **ring** n[1]

rang n[2] See **ring** n[2]

range coop See **range shelter**

ranged See **ring** v B1b, 2b

range, go over the v phr Also *cross over the range* **West** Cf *DS* BB56
  To die.
  1879 *Missouri Republican* (St. Louis) 22 Oct 3/7 (*AmSp* 16.269), If you wish to express the demise of a friend you would say in Southern Colorado that 'he'd gone over the range'. **1887** *Scribner's Mag.* 2.508 **West**, "To go over the range" is to die, as any reader of Bret Harte's frontier stories knows; but once it was limited to cattle. **1933** *AmSp* 8.4.51 **NE** [Pioneer vocabulary], *Going over the range* meant to die. **1936** *AmSp* 11.197 [Euphemisms for dying], Crossed/gone over the range. **1941** Writers' Program *Guide WY* 462, Go over the range—To die. **1942** *AmSp* 17.72 **Rocky Mts**, Cross over the range—the old-timer's euphemism for dying.

range house, range roost See **range shelter**

ranger's button n
  The woolly-head **parsnip B** (*Sphenosciadium capitellatum*).
  1959 Munz–Keck *CA Flora* 1029, S[phenosciadium] capitellatum. . . *Ranger's Button*. . . Swampy places, 300–10,400 ft. . . e. Ore., Ida., w. Nev., . . Calif. **1979** Spellenberg *Audubon Guide N. Amer. Wildflowers W. Region* 330, Ranger's Button. . . A stout, tall plant with numerous tiny white *flowers in compact, separate white "buttons"* at the ends of hairy branches.

range shelter n Also *chicken range, range (shelter) coop, range house, ~ roost;* also, perh by folk-etym, *rain shelter* esp **NEast** See Map Cf **hover**
  A portable shelter for poultry.
  1936 in 2001 *DARE* File—Internet **cnPA**, [Diary entry:] Went to Mansfield after Rocks chickens. Work at Range Shelter. **1967–69** *DARE* (Qu. M16, *The small shelter for a hen that can be moved about*

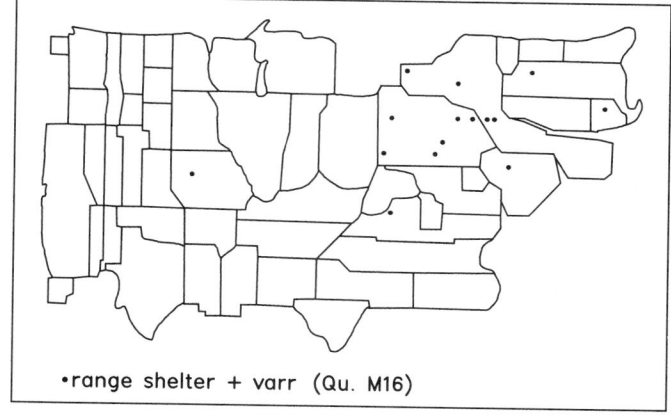

•range shelter + varr (Qu. M16)

from place to place) Infs **NY**75, 122, 164, **PA**21, 43, 166, 212, 230, Rain shelter; **VA**32, Rain shelter—50 to 200, moved by horse or tractor; **MO**11, **MA**58, **PA**23, Range shelter; **NY**93, Range house or range shelter or chicken range—they move these about on skids; **RI**4, Range coop; **NJ**45, Range roost—roof, wired-in sides; 2 or 4 rows of roosts; set in field; [(Qu. M15, *The place outdoors where pigs are kept*) Inf **VA**77, Rain shelter.] **1975** Gould *ME Lingo* 228, *Range.* . . Maine farmers do not use *range* for pasturage, as in the West, but the term is applied to poultry runs; *range* shelters are open-sided protection for birds put out to *range.* **2001** *DARE* File—Internet **sAL**, I went out about an hour after dark and saw only one cockerel in the range shelter coop. *Ibid* **cwWA**, [Caption:] This is a modified range shelter. The top lifts off.

range sire See **sire 1**

rango See **wrango**

rangy adj

Walleyed.

1966 *DARE* (Qu. X26b, *If a person's eyes look in different directions, looking outward, he's* _____) Inf **WA**18, Rangy.

ranikaboo n, also attrib Also *ranicky, rani-cum-boogerie, rannikaboo, rannygazoo, reinikaboo, renicky(-boo)*

A deceptive story or scheme; a prank, racket, or scam.

[**1893** *KS Univ. Qrly.* 1.141 **KS**, *Rally-kaboo:* irregular, not according to the standard.] **1901** *DN* 2.146, *Reinikaboo.* . . "A newspaper story which is midway between a fake and a statement of fact; a statement of news out of all proportion and almost out of relation to the facts, yet having a certain origin and shadowy foundation." Washington corr. St. Louis *Globe–Democrat.* **1907** White *AZ Nights* 255, "You _____ _____ bluffer!" shouted a voice, "don't you think you can run any such ranikaboo here!" **1916** *DN* 4.328 **KS**, *Renicky.* . . Also *ranicky,* or *renicky-boo.* "He wants to run some sort of bluff or renicky on us." **1935** Davis *Honey* 164 **OR**, Damned if I don't believe this is a rannikaboo them Forty-Gallon church people down the valley has got up to rob pickers away from me, anyhow. **1940** *Time* 14 Oct 28, Wilkie went to New York City to tour Democratic Brooklyn. . . Still he refused to make a . . speech, still turned down . . pleas . . to let loose with a ring-tailed, rabble-rousing rannygazoo. **1944** Wellman *Bowl* 106 **KS**, An' I don't want that ranikaboo state government of Topeka nosing around out here. **1945** Thorp *Pardner* 125 **SW**, We were raised with horses, and we felt that if any of the other riders thought they could run any rani-cum-boogeroo on us, they were welcome to try. **1947** *Sun* (Baltimore MD) 20 Jan 1/2 **AZ**, A ranikaboo in Arizona would be known as a prank in other states.

rank adj

1 Vigorous, fast. [*OED2 rank* a. 2.a "Stout and strong. *Obs.* exc. *dial.*"; 3.a "Having great speed or force; swift"; 3.b "So *rank-runner. Obs.*"]

1883 (1971) Harris *Nights with Remus* 237 **GA** [Black], We aint got many swimps en crabs up yer in Putmon county, but w'en it come ter settin' up wid comp'ny en hangin' 'roun' atter dark fer ter make de time pass away, we er mighty rank. **1887** (1967) Harris *Free Joe* 216 **GA** [Black], Hit 'u'd take a mighty rank runner fer ter ketch one nigger man w'at I'm got some 'quaintance wid. **1975** *Appalachian Jrl.* 2.159 **wNC**, To say a horse is *rimptious* or *foolish* means he is spirited; whereas, a *rank* horse is fast-gaited or spirited.

2 Wild, uncontrollable, mischievous; very eager; hence adv *rank* brashly. [*OED2 rank* a. 3.a "impetuous, violent"; a1225 →]

1899 (1912) Green *VA Folk-Speech* 345, *Rank.* . . Eager; anxious; impatient: as, he was rank to do it. **1926** in 1931 McCorrison *Letters Fraternity* 110 **NEng**, Mac had gone crazy; had all I could do to hold him. And no shot fired. He was so rank I gave up all thought of shooting and took shells from gun. **1939** (1962) Thompson *Body & Britches* 199 **NY**, A [whaling] man who is wild to go, not afraid of anything, is *rank*. **1943** *LANE* Map 551 (*The Civil War*) 1 inf, **nwCT**, In the South they call it the Surrender. The men are placid about it, but the women are rank as the Old Harry . . about it. **1951** *PADS* 16.54 [Racetrack argot], *Rank:* adj. Of a horse: to be unruly at the starting post. **1951** *Sun* (Baltimore MD) 23 May 20/2 (*Hench Coll.*), Alarmed [=a racehorse] was rank and seems likely to improve. **1958** Blasingame *Dakota Cowboy* 164 **SD**, They turned out to be the rankest buckers I ever saw, among

them being . . Danger, Widow Maker, . . and others that were . . ready to paw a man apart at the least excuse. **1965** Davis *Summer Land* 116 **cnNC**, "Old folks," Papa said. "They'll be the ruin of us yet." "I wonder if you'd speak up so rank if your pap was here." **1966** *DARE* (Qu. HH26, *A person who is always ready to stir up trouble*) Inf **FL**4, Troublemaker; he's rank. **1967** Green *Horse Tradin'* 256 **TX**, They were the rankest, big draft-type horses that I had ever had any experience with. When you roped them, they choked and pawed and fought. **1969** Green *Wild Cow Tales* 222, These cattle were so rank and on the prod that I didn't dare walk around in the pasture afoot. **1975** [see **1** above]. **1985** Rattray *Advent. Dimon* 167 **Long Is. NY**, John and Elias woke me before dawn, rank to get down to the beach.

3 Crowded together; numerous. [*OED2 rank* a. 8 a1400–50 →; "*Obs.* exc. *north. dial.*"]

1887 Amer. Philol. Assoc. *Trans. for 1886* 17.46 **Sth**, List of common Southern expressions. . . *Rank* (as "Haunts was mighty rank 'bout dar"). **1899** (1912) Green *VA Folk-Speech* 345, *Rank.* . . Standing in close order; thick on the ground: as, a rank crop of wheat or corn.

4 Of a blue crab: about to begin shedding. Cf **green** adj 1, **peeler crab, shedder**

1968 *DARE* Tape **MD**43, [Inf:] And then we have what we call the rank peeler. . . [FW:] But what's a rank peeler? [Inf:] That's the last stage before it's a soft crab. . . Well, in other words, a rank peeler would probably shed into a soft crab tomorrow. **1976** Warner *Beautiful Swimmers* 27, We are getting a few more peeler crabs approaching their last moult. . . If they are truly "rank," or already weak and with only hours to go before busting, he will put them in the pails. **1996** Horton *Island Out of Time* 23 **Chesapeake Bay**, It is, of course, the "wives" that the crabbers seek, because at this time of year each one is guaranteed to be what is called a "rank peeler." "Rank" here means the sook-to-be is showing a bright reddish tinge, no larger than a fingernail clipping, along the edge of her rear swim fins. It signifies that she is within a day or hours of shedding, or peeling off her shell, and need only be held briefly in wooden trays through which seawater is pumped before her market value is transformed from a few cents as a hard crab to as much as a dollar and a half commanded by big spring softies.

rank n

1 A long, narrow stack, esp a **rick** n 2. **chiefly S Midl**

1902 *DN* 2.243 **sIL**, *Rank.* . . A pile of anything regularly and evenly laid up, as 'a rank of wood, brick, etc.'[*] **1906** *DN* 3.152 **nwAR**, *Rank.* . . Half a cord. "I want a rank of wood." Clay Co. **1912** Green *VA Folk-Speech* 345, *Rank.* . . Line; row: "The wood was piled in long ranks."[*] To rank. . . To pile in lines. **1923** *DN* 5.218 **swMO**, *Rank*, n. or v. See *Rick*. *Ibid, Rick*, n. or v. Wood, cut any length, arranged uniformly in a pile eight feet long and four feet high. "I ricked up two ranks o' wood." **1952** Hench *Coll.* **cnVA**, Mr . . Seale called a stack of wood a rank: "That's a nice rank of wood." **1954** *Harder Coll.* **cwTN**, *Rank.* . . A stack of wood, either a rick or a cord. **1978** Massey *Bittersweet Country* 85 **Ozarks**, I made the wagon bed out of pine but the rest of it's made out of white oak. It's just the right size for a rank of wood. A rank, it don't make no load at all. **1986** Pederson *LAGS Concordance*, 1 inf, **neAL**, Ranks of hay prepared—readied for the baler; 1 inf, **ceAR**, Rank of wood; 1 inf, **neAR**, Rank or cord of wood; [1 inf, **neAR**, Rank = a wagonload;] 1 inf, **cLA**, Rank—4 to a cord; 1 inf, **nwTN**, Rank of wood—4′ x 8′, 4′ long. **1986** *Barrick Coll.* [see **rank** v 1].

2 See **rank** v 3.

rank v, hence vbl n *ranking*

1 also with *up*: To stack up, esp in long rows. **chiefly Inland Nth, Midl** See Map Cf **rack** v[1], **rank** n 1, **rick** v

1859 T.D. Price *Diary* (MS.) 25 Dec. (*DAE*), Drew some firewood on sled to rank in shed. **1888** Kirkland *McVeys* 335 (*DAE*) **IL**, All this time they were busy ranking up the wood the teamsters were throwing off. **1902** *DN* 2.243 **sIL**, *Rank.* . . To lay up in even and regular tiers or courses. **1903** *DN* 2.326 **seMO**, *Rank.* . . To lay side by side, as cordwood. 'I will give one dollar a cord for cutting, splitting and ranking.' **1905** U.S. Forest Serv. *Bulletin* 61.44 [Logging terms], *Rank.* . . To haul and pile regularly, as, to *rank* bark or cord wood. (Gen.) **1907** *DN* 3.225 **nwAR**, *Rank.* . . To lay up in regular tiers or courses. **1912** [see **rank** n 1]. **1923** [see **rank** n 1]. **1950** *WELS* **WI** (*To keep firewood neat, you cut it, split it, then* _____ *it up*) 3 Infs, Rank; 1 Inf, If cordwood or pulpwood you cord it up or rank it up, but you pile telephone poles. **1954** *Harder Coll.* **cwTN**, *Rank up.* . . To stack wood. **1965–70** *DARE* (Qu. LL24, *To keep firewood neat you have to cut it,*

split it, and _____ it up) 36 Infs, **chiefly Inland Nth, Midl,** Rank.
1968 *DARE* Tape IL29, Then he cut his own wood and haul it home in
the wintertime. Rank it up alongside the house and get it all ready;
NJ52, I've cut wood. . . Trim it and heap it up. Rank it up in cords.
1986 *Barrick Coll.* **csPA,** *Rank*—v. and n. stack in rows, as "to rank
firewood," and "a rank of wood for the stove." Also *rank up,* as in "Rank
up that wood for me." **1986** Pederson *LAGS Concordance,* 1 inf,
neAR, Rank it up—of firewood; 1 inf, **ceLA,** Rank it [=hay] up—not
done locally; 1 inf, **swTN,** Stack it or rank it—referring to firewood; 1
inf, **nwTN,** Rank up that stovewood; 1 inf, **nwTN,** Ranked it up—piled
wood in cords; 1 inf, **swTN,** Ranked it up—referring to firewood; 1 inf,
cwTN, (Wood) was ranked = was stacked; **ceLA,** Ranking wood—
stacking cut wood for storage. **1999** *DARE* File **TN,** In rural West
Tennessee when you stack fire wood, you "rank" it.

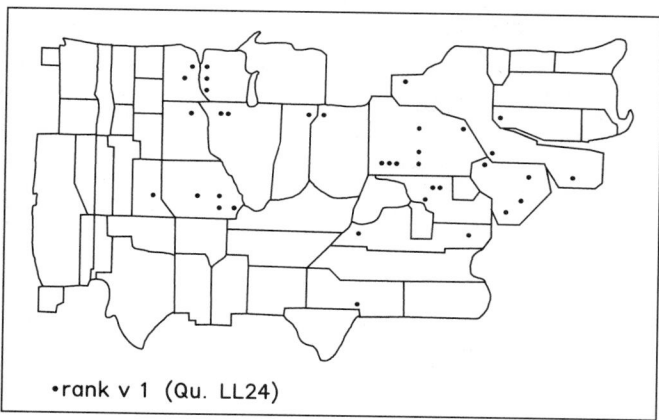

•rank v 1 (Qu. LL24)

2 To park (a car).
1958 *Think* Jan 10 **NJ,** Where most people *park* cars, residents of
Trenton *rank* them and those in southern Delaware *file* them. **1972**
DARE File **NJ** (as of c1920), *Rank,* to park (cars)—the common word in
Trenton, NJ.

3 also with *out;* also in phr *rank on (someone):* To tease, insult; hence n *rank* a subject of ridicule.   *esp freq among Black
speakers*   Cf **jive** v[1] **1, signify 1**
1934 *AmSp* 9.290 **PA** [Black student slang], *Rank. To kid* a person; to
make light of; to harass. **1958** *Jrl. Social Issues* 14.3.16, The term
"ranking," used to refer to the pattern of intra-group aggressive repartee,
indicates awareness of the fact that this is one device for establishing the
intra-group status hierarchy. **1966–68** *DARE* (Qu. Y3, *To say uncomplimentary things about somebody*) Inf NY81, Rank out. **1973** Dundes
Mother Wit 316 (as of 1971) [Black], "Barbara was trying to *rank*
Mary," to put her down by typing her. **1978** *Engl. Jrl.* Dec 56, "We're
ranking people out." . . "What does that mean?" I asked. . . "We're saying things about other people to put them down," answered one helpful
student. **1986** Pederson *LAGS Concordance (Playing the dozens)* 1 inf,
swAL, Ranking—has heard of; apparently has heard of game; 1 inf,
neFL, Ranking—exchanging insults; 1 inf, **seFL,** Ranking—has heard;
1 inf, **cnGA,** Ranking—heard of; chide each other; 1 inf, **ceTN,** Ranking—like a duel; insulting one's mother; 1 inf, **cTX,** Ranking—heard;
ranking on me; 1 inf, **ceTX,** Ranking—heard. [4 of 7 infs Black] **1996**
DARE File **sCA** (as of c1956), As a teenager I knew the verb *rank (out)*
to insult, to ridicule, as in, "You're rankin' me, man; don't rank me out,
man"; hence also as a noun meaning to be a ridiculous or socially unacceptable person. Both words were very common.

rank *adv* See **rank** *adj* 2

ranking bar n [*ranking* prob from its use in stacking wood or
bark (cf **rank** v 1) + *bar* pronc-sp for *barrow* (cf **wheelbarrow**)]
1905 U.S. Forest Serv. *Bulletin* 61.44 [Logging terms], *Ranking bar.*
See Handbarrow. [*Ibid* 39, *Handbarrow.* Two strong, light poles held in
position by rungs, upon which bark or wood is carried by two men.]

ranking jumper n [Cf **ranking bar** and **jumper 7a**]
1905 U.S. Forest Serv. *Bulletin* 61.44 [Logging terms], *Ranking
jumper.* A wood-shod sled upon which tanbark is hauled (N[orthern]
F[orest]).

rank on (someone), rank out See **rank** v 3

rank up See **rank** v 1

ranned See **run** v A1c

Rannel grass See **Randall grass**

rannikaboo See **ranikaboo**

ranny n [Cf Ir dial *ranny* a thin or stunted person or animal]
1 See quots.   Cf **ramie**
1935 *AmSp* 10.271 [Stockyard language], *Rannies.* Common-bred
southern calves of poor quality. **1950** *WELS* (*A sheep that is kept as a
pet*) 1 Inf, **cnWI,** Ranny—common. **1998** *NADS Letters,* My wife,
from Louisville, KY, recalls hearing this term [=*ranny*] when she was
young, around 1947 or so, in reference to both calves and horses. Her
family owned farms, so she was around farmers. **1999** *Ibid* **cTX,** [I]
am in cattle partnership with Joe Reynolds. . . He uses it [=*ranny*] . . but
[I] do not hear it used by anyone else. Our families' lands are next to
each other, we grew up in same environment and we're near the same
age. Don't know where he got it, although he does attend more livestock
auctions than I do. The ones he calls rannies are always out of poor
quality or very old cows that usually are incapable either because of age
or genetics or both of raising a quality calf. He typically uses the word
as a plural noun. "I'll buy some rannies" " . . got some rannies." Sometimes as an adjective " . . little ranny kind of whiteface." **2000** *DARE*
File—Internet **ceTX,** Tri-County Livestock Market, Inc. in New Sum-
merfield, Texas will meet all your livestock marketing needs. . . The following is a current sale order for Saturday Sales: Sale Order 1. Stock
and Feeder Calves 2. Rannies / Dogies 3. Horses / Mules [etc].
2 also *rannycavoo:* A cowboy.   *sometimes derog*   Cf **ranahan**
1907 Sinclair *Lure Dim Trails* 159 **NW,** There's going to be roundups
like these old Panhandle rannies tell about, when the green grass comes.
1924 James *Cowboys N. & S.* 25, Then it was about time for the
"rannies" to pull up their ponies and figger where to go next. They remembered how they left Texas and how every State from there north
was feeling the pinch of the fences. **1934** (1940) Weseen *Dict. Amer.
Slang* 104, *Ranny*—A cowboy on the open range. **1942** Henry *High
Border* 165 **nRocky Mts,** Catfish Joe, Hell-roaring Jones, Theodore
Roosevelt, et al., were in the vernacular of the High Border "cowpokes,"
"rannies," "rannycavoos," "hombres," or in a more refined manner, simply "cowboys." **1999** L'Amour *Beyond Gt. Snow Mts.* 50 **TX,** "Nobody
ever checks that herd of mixed brands. After we're finished here, they'll
just be left to drift back on the range from that long valley where you're
holdin' 'em." "And then these rannies could move in an' brand the
unbranded stock for themselves." **1999** *DARE* File **TX,** Ranny. . .
Texas, 1940's & '50's. Referring to a no 'count hand.

rannygazoo See **ranikaboo**

ranpike See **rampike**

ranshackld, ranshacled See **ramshackled 1**

ransom tansom (tee) n Also *ransom-tansom-tee-i-oh, ransy
tansy tee*
=here comes a duke.
[**1883** Newell *Games & Songs* 48 **NEng,** A little girl from the middle
of the room goes dancing up to the first one in the row, singing, "Here
comes a duke a-roving,/ Roving, roving,/ Here comes a duke a-roving,/
With the ransy, tansy, tea!/ With the ransy, tansy, tario!/ [etc]." *Ibid* 49,
A vulgarized form of the same game is common through the Middle
States: *Boys.* "We are three *ducks* a-roving, (thrice)/ With a ransom
dansom dee."/ [etc.].] **1957** *Sat. Eve. Post Letters* **sIN** (as of c1905), The
girls had a singing game called "Ransom-Tansom-Tee". . . The girls divided in equal numbers formed two lines, one line skipped forward singing "Here comes five dukes a-riding a-riding a-riding, Here comes five
dukes a-riding. Ransom tansom tee." . . Anyway it turned out that the
dukes were looking for a bride and after several verses they would
choose one—and the game kept on till all the dukes had brides. *Ibid*
MI (as of c1900), We played a game which we called "Ransy Tansy
Tee." It began by choosing a leader who was the "Duke" and started by
singing "Here comes a duke a ro-o-oaming." . . It was quite a long
drawn out affair, lasting until all the contestants had been chosen as
the "Duke's" bride. **1975** Ferretti *Gt. Amer. Book Sidewalk Games*
107, *Ransom-Tansom*—Another sidewalk game that is characterized by

chanting and choosing and that includes the popularity of selection and the stigma of rejection is Ransom-Tansom-Tee-I-Oh. It was popular up in Michigan in the 1930s and 1940s.

ranstead weed n Also *ramste(a)d, ranstead, ransted (weed),* and, by folk-etym, *rancid* [See quot 1830]
=**butter-and-eggs 1.**
1791 in 1793 *Amer. Philos. Soc. Trans.* 3.173, Linaria, Ransted. **1830** Watson *Annals Philadelphia* 642, The "Ranstead weed". . . came first from Wales, being sent as a garden flower for Mr. Ranstead of Philadelphia, an upholsterer and a Welshman. **1837** Darlington *Flora Cestrica* 368 sePA, *Common Linaria.* . . Toad-flax, Ransted weed. Butter and eggs. . . This foreigner is extensively naturalized. **1895** U.S. Dept. Ag. *Farmers' Bulletin* 28.29, Ramstead . . Linaria vulgaris . . New England to Wisconsin. **1900** Lyons *Plant Names* 226, L[*inaria*] *vulgaris.* . . Ramsted, Ranstead, Rancid. **1912** Blatchley *IN Weed Book* 131, Toad-flax. Ranstead. . . Frequent in dense tufts or patches along banks, roadsides and railways. **1930** OK Univ. Biol. Surv. *Pub.* 2.80, Butter-and-eggs. Ramsted. [**1967** *DARE* Wildfl QR Pl.196 *(Linaria vulgaris)* Inf SC41, Ram's head [*sic*].]

ransy tansy tee See **ransom tansom (tee)**

rantankerous adj Also sp *rantanckerous* [Varr of *cantankerous,* perh infl by *rant* v] **chiefly Sth, S Midl**
Bad-tempered, unruly; fierce; hence rarely adv *rantankerous* fiercely, furiously.
1832 Paulding *Westward Ho* 1.180 KY, Not he, the rantanckerous squatter. **1845** Thompson *Pineville* 178 GA, She better not come a cavortin' 'bout me with any of her rantankerous carryin's on this mornin'. **1851** Burke *Polly Peablossom* 147 MS, He was the durndest, rantankerous hoss-fly that ever clum a tree! **1859** Taliaferro *Fisher's R.* 89 nwNC (as of 1820s), It makes me rantankerous mad to hear sich little stuff, it does. *Ibid* 134, This scrape had made a rantankerous impression on me. **1897** *KS Univ. Qrly.* (ser B) 6.56 KS, *Rantankerous:* noisy, lawless. **1898** Lloyd *Country Life* 176 AL, She is red-headed and rantankerous and come from fightin stock. **1898** Harris *Tales Home Folks* 48 GA, They never had such a rantankerous nigger to deal with. **1905** *NY Tribune* (NY) 19 Dec 1/2, NY Senator Depew has had one [Christmas gift] coming to him. His "rantankerous" friend . . has been getting it ready for him.

rantum scoot n Also *random scoot, rantum scooting* [From *rantum scootum,* var of *rantum scantum* harum scarum, disorderly]
An outing with no definite destination.
1878 *Atlantic Mth.* 41.645 neNY, Starting out for a day's tramp in the woods, he would ask whether we wanted to take a "reg'lar walk, or a random scoot," the latter being a plunge into the pathless forest. . . And when the way became altogether inscrutable, "Waal, this is a reg'lar random scoot of a rigmarole." [**1885** *Harper's New Mth. Mag.* 70.614 **FL,** He's a deal sight more serious-minded than most of the rantum scootum boys one has to put up with in a wanderin' life like this.] **1896** *DN* 1.423 Nantucket MA, *Rantum scoot:* pleasure drive. **1916** Macy-Hussey *Nantucket Scrap Basket* 142, "*Rantum Scoot*"—A term, we believe, peculiar to Nantucket, and very old. It means a day's "cruise" or picnic about the island, usually a drive, but it might be on foot. The distinctive feature of such an excursion is that the party has no definite destination, but rather a roving commission, in which respect such a trip differs from a "squantum". . . "Rantum" is probably a corruption of random. **1997** *DARE* File **Nantucket MA,** "Rantum scooting"—random scouting: picnics, trips with no destination.

rap full adj phr
Fig, of a person: full of food.
1975 Gould *ME Lingo* 228, *Rap full*—Filled sails, drawing well, were *rap full*. Hence, wherever in Maine you hear *rap full* it means complete, loaded, satiated: "Can't touch another morsel—I'm rap full!"

rapid adj [Cf *EDD* rapid "Violent; severe; esp used of pain."]
Prone to violent anger.
c1937 in 1972 *Amer. Slave* 2.170 SC [Black], Marse Gillam sho was rapid. I saw him whip my mammy till you couldn't put a hand on her shoulder and back widout touching a whelp. Marse Gillam killed a man and dey put him in jail in Newberry, but he died befo' de trial come off. **1952** Brown *NC Folkl.* 1.582, *Rapid, to get.* . . To become very angry,

bellicose. "Don't get too rapid, big boy; I might have to take you down."—Central and east. Mainly Negroes.

rap jacket n Also *rap jack* Also sp *wrap jack(et)* **Sth, S Midl**
A contest of endurance in which people beat one another with switches; hence v phr *play rap-jacket* to administer a beating; v phr *rap jack* to beat with a stick.
1880 (1881) Harris *Uncle Remus Songs* 125 **GA** [Black], He let inter Brer Fox wid de hick'ries, en de way he play rap-jacket wuz a caution ter de naberhood. **1884** *Anglia* 7.275 **Sth, S Midl** [Black], *To play rap-jacket* = to thrash soundly. **1893** Shands *MS Speech* 52, *Rap-jacket.* . . A term used by all classes to mean a game of whipping, in which two boys are given switches, and whip each other with all of their might until one says "enough." They both thus have their jackets thoroughly rapped, if they happen to have on those garments. Two boys who have been fighting at school are very frequently punished by the teacher's making them play *rap-jacket* until he tells them to stop. **1909** *DN* 3.362 **eAL, wGA,** *Rap-jacket.* . . A game in which the contestants stand up and whip each other with keen limber switches until one yields or runs away. Also *wrap-jacket.* **1972** Jones-Hawes *Step it Down* 186 eGA [Black], Mama and them would take those long switches . . and they would play Rap Jack, just hit one another with the switches. . . Mama used to play it, too . . and they'd stand out there, used to rap jack one another. **c1974** Jones *Ozark Hill Boy* 6 AR (as of c1910), The favorite games were— "Double Cat", "Fox and Hounds", "Anti-over", "Wrap Jack", "Follow the Leader", "Head in the Hat", . . and many other games requiring little or no equipment.

rapper dandies n [*EDD* 1853]
The fruit of a **bearberry 2** (here: *Arctostaphylos uva-ursi*).
1900 Lyons *Plant Names* 44, A[*rctostaphylos*] *Uva Ursi.* . . Rapper dandies (the fruit). [*DARE* Ed: Perh based on Brit source.]

rap the can n Cf **kick the can**
1966 *DARE* (Qu. EE33, . . *Outdoor games . . that children play*) Inf AR13, Rap the can (hit the tin can with a stick).

raptify See **racktify**

raquecha See **racacha**

raquettes n
See quot.
1983 Reinecke Coll. 12 **LA,** Raquettes. . . [rɑˈkɛt]. . . Indian stick-ball, as played by area Choctaws still. Popular with N[ew] O[rleans] white and Black creole population into 1920's. Also the two "raquettes" or spoons used by each player. My grandfather, J.A. Reinecke Sr., was a captain of the "LaVille" team at the turn of the century.

rare v Also sp *ra(a)r, rair* [Orig merely pronc varr of *rear,* but now often perceived as a separate word. The relation of the two forms is complex, but it would appear that for some speakers *rare* is the form used for all senses of *rear* that are current in colloquial US English (but only rarely for senses that are primarily literary), while for others *rare* is used only for some or all of the extended senses (esp the widely known phr *raring to*) that do not correspond to std senses of *rear.*] Note: Exx of the sp *rear* are included here when proncs of the *rare* type are clearly indicated.
1 with *up* or *back;* Transf: to lift or tip up or back.
1850 Garrard *Wah-to-yah* 252, The old coon . . rared his head back. **1917** in 1944 *ADD* sWV, He rared the hog trough up & sot it on its end. **1981** Pederson *LAGS Basic Materials,* 1 inf, swMS, Rear [ræˀɛɚ] back—tilt it back.
2 also with *up:* To bring up (a child). Cf **rear** v¹ **1**
1837 Sherwood *Gaz.* GA 71, *Rared,* for reared;—he was *rared,* or he rared; *Reared* is the proper word—to educate, or elevate, is the meaning. **1939** Hall Coll. eTN, "I was reared up there." The pronunciation [ræɚd] is noteworthy. The common expression in the Smokies seems to be 'raise'. **1941** *LANE* Map 395 *(She has brought up)* 1 inf, cME coast, [ræˀ·əd] [response characterized by inf as old or obsolete]. **1967** *DARE* FW Addit GA19, "When I was rarin' [ˈrɛrɪn] up. . . " "When I was rared up. . . " "That young 'un was hell to rare. . . " **1968** *DARE* (Qu. Z17, . . "All her children were _____ [*on the farm*].") Inf GA19, Rared up. **1970** Tarpley *Blinky* 206 neTX, She (raised, reared, brought up, etc.) three children . . 61.5% [of 200 infs] raised—28.0%

reared—8.0% brought up—1.0% other responses—brung up[ɹ] raised up[ɹ] rared (reared). **1981** Pederson *LAGS Basic Materials* **Gulf Region,** [Of the approximately 200 infs who offered forms of the verb *rear* in the sense "to bring up (a child)," most used proncs of the types [rɪə(r)] or [riə(r)]. 13 infs, 5 **GA,** used proncs of the types [rɛə(r), reɪ] or [ræə(r)].]

3 often with *up:* To stand up, rise; esp, of a quadruped: to stand up on the hind legs, rear; hence n **rare** an instance of so standing.

1833 *Sketches D. Crockett* 92 **eTN,** He just *rared* up upon his hind legs. **1869** *Overland Mth.* 3.128 **TX,** He [=a mustang] will . . stop so "suddent," and "rare up" behind, that the rider continues his travels a little distance on his own account, and alights upon his pate. **1872** Schele de Vere *Americanisms* 530, In the South the verb to *rear,* used of horses, is pronounced *rare.* **1891** *DN* 1.124 **cNY,** [ræɚ] (to rise) < rǽran, 'rear.' **1892** *DN* 1.233 **KY,** *Rear up* [rɛə ʌp]. "The colt reared up." [*DN* Ed: In New England also *rear* in this sense is often [rɛə] or [ræə], but before [ʌp] an *r* is heard: [ræ(ə)r ʌp].] **1899** (1912) Green *VA Folk-Speech* 346, *Rare. . . Rear.* To rise up; assume an elevated posture: as, a horse or other annimal [sic] in standing on its hind legs alone. **1909** *DN* 3.421 **Cape Cod MA** (as of a1857), *Rare up. . .* To rear from the hind legs, of a horse, etc. **1914** *DN* 4.78 **ME, nNH,** *R'ar up. . .* Rear up, rise. **1923** *DN* 5.218 **swMO,** *Rare. . .* To rear on the hind legs, to indulge in loud, angry words. **1939** *Hall Coll.* **wNC,** It kept a-rarin' up like it was comin' towards him. *Ibid* **wNC,** I rared [rɛəd] up with my 32 Winchester, took him behind the shoulder with a bullet. **1942** Warnick *Garrett Co. MD* 12 **nwMD** (as of 1900–18), *Rare . .* rise on the hind legs (Obs. exc. Dial.) **1949** *PADS* 11.9 **wTX** (as of 1911–29), *Rare* [rær]: . . To rear. A horse *rares* up even with the educated in the saddle, but children are *reared.* **1953** *Hall Coll.* **wNC,** This oldest dog he /rɛrd/ on his feet. **1962** Fox *Southern Fried* 41 **SC,** Gene stood in the very center of the gallery and rared up as tall as he could. **1965** *DARE* FW Addit **NM10,** Rare up . . —speaking of goats—"They rare up and bunt." **1968** *DARE* (Qu. OO32b, *If a person can't sleep steadily but keeps on waking . . "Every night this week I've _____ [several times]."*) Inf **NY68,** Rared [rɛrd] up. **1979** Carpenter *Walton War* 147 **sAppalachians,** "Hit's jist a rare (rear) and a pitch from one day-end to another and no pity took on anybody." Said of a man and his family who quarreled all the time. **1982** *Barrick Coll.* **csPA,** The horse rared and throwed him.

4 with *back;* Of an animal or person: to draw oneself up and back, esp in an imposing or threatening manner; to lean back in a posture of defiance or relaxation; also fig; hence ppl adj *rared back.* **Sth, S Midl** Cf **rear** v[1] **3, rearback** n, **rearback** adj

1899 (1912) Green *VA Folk-Speech* 346, *Rare back. . .* To sit up straight with the head thrown back. "There she sat in the carriage, rared back, who but her." **c1920** in 1993 Farwell-Nicholas *Smoky Mt. Voices* 132 **sAppalachians,** I do love, of a winter night, to build a good log fire, and jest rar' back and eat big apples. **1933** Rawlings *South Moon* 81 **nFL,** She had never tried to rule the boy, but she felt a new and frightening responsibility. Her small voice rose shrilly. "Don't you go to rarin' back on your dew-claws!" **1936** *Esquire* Nov 57 **eKY,** I like to ride a train . . just to rare back and puff a cigar. **1941** Percy *Lanterns* 46 **MS,** When these rared back and held their claws wide apart. **1942** McAtee *Dial. Grant Co. IN* 52 (as of 1890s), *Rare. . .* Also used with respect to persons as in the phrase, "rared back", meaning sitting or standing very erectly. **1944** *PADS* 2.18 **sAppalachians,** Jud rared [reared] back on his dew claws and struck at Lonzo. **1954** Tolbert *Bigamy Jones* 182 **wTX** (as of 1870s) [Black], He just rared back against the cotton-wood and with his last breaths made that speech about coming back from death as a wolf. **1965** Wolfe *Kandy-Kolored Baby* 224, All the old people drive down to the railroad station and park alongside the tracks and rare back and socialize on the car fenders. **1967** *DARE* Tape **TX26,** He'll rare back this-a-way, and that's a nice stop for a rider, to rare back this way. **1976** Ryland *Richmond Co. VA* 375, *Rare back*—draw one's self up, as for "giving him a piece of my mind." *Ibid, Rared back*—leaning back, usually meaning full of pride. **1981** Pederson *LAGS Basic Materials,* 1 inf, **nwFL,** Rear [rɛ·ə] back in = lean back in; 1 inf, **cwGA,** Reared [ræ^ɛəd] back—sat up very straight; 1 inf, **seAL,** Reared [ræ^·əd] back—of a person; 1 inf, **cnAR,** Is just setting there all reared [ræ^·əd] back.

5a occas with *around, up;* rarely in phr *rare the roof up:* To become violently angry or excited; to rage, storm, rush wildly; hence ppl adjs *rared up, raring* very angry or excited; adj phr

raring mad very angry. [Cf *EDD rear* v.[2] 6 "To behave violently or excitedly" and 11 "To mock, gibe; to scold" and *rearing* ppl. adj. 7 "Excited; talking loudly and boastingly; mocking."] **chiefly Sth, S Midl** Cf **rear** v[1] **2**

1871 (1892) Johnston *Dukesborough Tales* 135 **GA,** Ef you ever see a person rip an' rar, it war Cousin Malviny. **1902** *DN* 2.243 **sIL,** *Rare. . .* To get in a passion; to find fault, or criticise. **1903** *DN* 2.326 **seMO,** *Rare* (rear). . . To rant; to talk abusively. **1906** *DN* 3.123 **sIN,** *Rare. . .* To become violent; get into a rage. *Ibid* 152 **nwAR,** *Rar'. . .* To be in a state of excitement. *Ibid* 153 **nwAR,** *Rear* [ræə]. . . To show great anger. "They would just rear, they were so mad." **1907** *DN* 3.235 **nwAR,** *Rare* (rear). . . To rant; to talk abusively. **1913** Kephart *Highlanders* 138 **sAppalachians,** When I protested that raw whiskey would ruin the infant's stomach, the mother replied, with widened eyes: "Why, if there's liquor about, and she don't git none, *she jist raars!"* **c1920** in 1993 Farwell-Nicholas *Smoky Mt. Voices* 132 **sAppalachians,** He r'ard around on one leg. **1923** [see **3** above]. **1927** *AmSp* 3.138 **eME,** If rushing he was "in an awful whacket" or . . "r'aring and tearing." **1930** Shoemaker *1300 Words* 51 **cPA Mts** (as of c1900), *Rair up*—To become suddenly angry. **1938** Rawlings *Yearling* 26 **nFL,** "I'm daresome to break the news to your Ma." "She'll rare for certain," Jody agreed. **1945** FWP *Lay My Burden Down* 70 **GA** (as of c1865) [Black], Old Miss, she cuss and rare worse'n a man. 'Way 'fore day she be up hollering loud enough for to be heard two miles. **1946** McCullers *Member* 77 **AL** [Black], 'Well, T.T. is a fine upstanding colored gentleman,' said Berenice. 'You never hear of T.T. raring around like a lot of other mens.' **1952** Brown *NC Folkl.* 1.583, *Rare and pitch (charge): phr.* To quarrel violently; to create a disturbance.—General. **1954** *Harder Coll.* **cwTN,** *Rared the roof up. . .* had conniption fits. **1956** Moody *Home Ranch* 99 **CO** (as of 1911), I started to hate him, and then I remembered that sometimes I rare into things just the same way he does. **1965–70** *DARE* (Qu. GG40, *. . Violently angry*) Infs **AL48, IA17, KY10, NC69, TN30,** Raring; **MI63,** Raring mad; (Qu. KK11, *To make great objections or a big fuss about something: "When we asked him to do that, he _____."*) Inf **FL19,** Just raring; **NJ39,** Rared, flew up in the air; (Qu. KK28, *Feeling ambitious and eager to work*) Inf **NC61,** Rared up and ready to go; **NY68,** Raring; (Qu. LL37, *. . "I could have wrung her neck, I was so _____ mad."*) Inf **OH38,** Raring. **1966** *PADS* 46.28 **cnAR** (as of 1952), *Rare. . .* Rave, rage—"She jist rared about it."

b esp as ppl adj *raring,* prec infin: Very eager, wild (to do something).

1927 Hart *Bellamy Trial* 10 **NY,** Both sides are rarin' to go, and they're not liable to touch their peremptory challenges. **1950** *PADS* 14.56 **SC,** *Rearing* ['ræriŋ]. . . Eager, keen, anxious, "Rearing to go." A horse often rears in his eagerness to begin a race. **1956** Moody *Home Ranch* 123 **CO** (as of 1911), What you rarin' to ride fence for, gal? Didn't you kids get enough ridin' this past week? **1965–70** *DARE* (Qu. KK28, *Feeling ambitious and eager to work*) 173 Infs, **widespread, but less freq Pacific,** Raring to go; **WA30,** A-raring to go; **NC30,** Raring and ready to go; **WI47,** Ready and raring to go; [**NJ4,** Rearing to go;] (Qu. AA4a, *. . A man who is very eager to get married*) Infs **CA79, 154, LA3, 11, MO29,** Raring to get married; **CA164, LA11,** Raring to go; **LA2,** Raring to marry; (Qu. AA4b, *. . A woman who is very eager to get married*) Infs **LA3, MO29,** Raring to get married; (Qu. BB47, *Feeling in the best of health and spirits*) Infs **NY70, 234, PA175,** Raring to go; (Qu. GG7, *. . "Though we were only ten minutes late, she was all _____."*) Inf **PA118,** Raring to go; (Qu. GG10, *. . "He certainly seems _____ to marry that girl.";* total Infs questioned, 75) Inf **AR39,** Raring; (Qu. GG29, *To be in a good or pleasant mood*) Inf **PA69,** Raring to go; (Qu. KK29, *. . "He was slow at first but now he's really _____."*) Infs **CA80, NM4, NY163, VA86,** Raring to go; (Qu. LL38, *. . "He wasn't _____ willing to come.";* total Infs questioned, 75) Inf **AR39,** Raring to come. **1969** *DARE* Tape **CA117,** I'm tired and frustrated and rarin' to rip these things off my eyes. My eyes itch. **1986** Pederson *LAGS Concordance* **Gulf Region,** 16 infs, Raring to go; 1 inf, Raring and ready to go; 1 inf, Raring to do it; 1 inf, Just raring to get aholt of it; 1 inf, I'm a-raring to go; 1 inf, Raring to roam.

6 in phrr *rare on (one), rare (one) out:* To attack verbally, berate.

1909 *DN* 3.362 **eAL, wGA,** *Rare* ([rær] or [rɑr]). . . To rant, fuss and fume. "Don't come rarin on me about it." **1954** *Harder Coll.* **cwTN,** *Rare on. . .* To scold; occasionally to curse someone. . . "Paul rard on me." **1954** *PADS* 21.35 **SC,** *Rare out: . .* Same as *bless out.* Dutch Fork.

7 with *down:* See quots. [Appar formed by analogy with *rare up*]

1967 *DARE* FW Addit **WA**24, *Rare* ['rɛər] *down*—stamp down. **1981** Pederson *LAGS Basic Materials,* 1 inf, **neAR**, *Rear* [ræ^·ɚ] down = press down.

8 with *off;* Of a horse: to throw off by rearing. [Cf **3** above]

1969 *DARE* (Qu. OO30a, . . *"John got a bad horse and was _____ [off]."*) Inf **IN**67, Rared, threw.

rare n See **rare** v **3**

rare around See **rare** v **5a**

rare back See **rare** v **1, 4**

rared back See **rare** v **4**

rare down See **rare** v **7**

rared up See **rare** v **5a**

rare off See **rare** v **8**

rare (one) out, rare on (one) See **rare** v **6**

rareripe n [From adj *rareripe* early ripe]

1 also *rareripe peach:* A variety of **freestone** peach (*Prunus persica* cv). **chiefly NEast**

1722 *New-Engl. Courant* (Boston MA) 3 Sept 2/1, Having in his Garden a plentiful Crop of *Rare-Ripes,* he agreed with an *Ethiopian* Market-Man . . to bring him a Horse-load of them to Town. **1819** *KY Almanac for 1820* 26, I was presented with a fine rare ripe peach. **1845** (1847) Downing *Fruits Amer.* v **NY**, The classical antiquarian must pardon one for doubting if, amid all the wonderful beauty of the golden age, there was anything to equal our delicious modern fruits—our honied Seckels, . . our melting Rareripes. **1857** *U.S. Patent Office Annual Rept. for 1856: Ag.* 336 **NY**, *Red Rareripe.*—We have a number of varieties of the peach under this name—some, no doubt, propagated from seedlings grown in Western New York, and others from something else. **1884** *N.Y. Wkly. Tribune* 20 Feb. 11/1 *(DA),* Rare-ripes [are] red-fleshed, and yellow-fleshed, but red at the stone. **1922** Hedrick *Cyclop. Hardy Fruits* 189, A century ago Yellow Rareripe was at the head of the list of yellow-fleshed, freestone peaches—fruits largest, handsomest, and best-flavored of all. . . Yellow Rareripe originated near Flushing, New York, over a hundred years ago. **1931–33** *LANE Worksheets* **csCT**, Rareripe—a kind of peach. **1932** *DN* 6.284 **swCT**, *Rareripes.* A kind of peaches.

2 An **onion** n B; see quots. **chiefly sNEng** See Map Cf **green onion 1, spring ~**

1790 Deane *New Engl. Farmer* 196, Even an onion which is partly rotten will produce two, three, or four good ones, if the seed stems be taken off as soon as they appear. They ripen earlier than young ones, have the name of rare-ripes, and will sell at a higher price. **1791** Freeman *Town Officer* 93 **MA**, Bunches of Onions . . to be shipped . . weigh as follows, viz. Rare-Ripes *two and a half pounds.* **1949** Kurath *Word Geog.* 23, *Rare-ripe* . . for the spring onion is common on Narragansett Bay, Martha's Vineyard, and Nantucket, but it occurs also in Essex County, Massachusetts, and in the Connecticut Valley towns from Middletown to Windsor. **1950** *WELS (The kind of onions that last from year to year)* 1

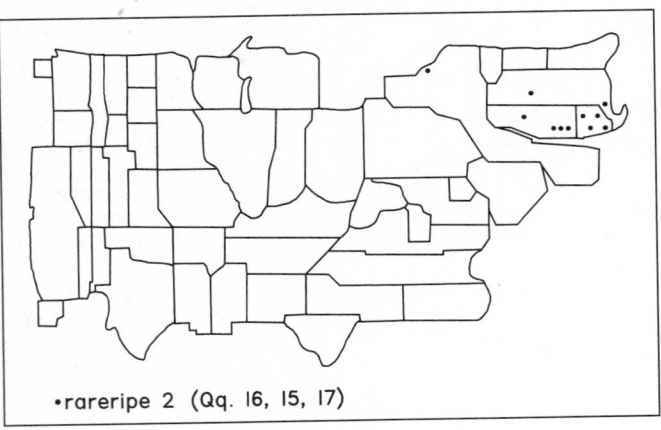

•rareripe 2 (Qq. 16, 15, 17)

Inf, **cwWI**, Winter onions, rare ripes, multipliers. **1965–70** *DARE* (Qu. I6, *The kind of onions that come up fresh early in the year, and you eat them raw*) 10 Infs, **chiefly sNEng**, Rareripes; (Qu. I5, *The kind of onions that keep coming up without replanting year after year*) Infs **CT**12, **RI**16, Rareripes; (Qu. I7, *The small plants like onions with hollow green leaves that are cut up in a salad*) Inf **CT**17, Rareripes. [10 of 11 total Infs old] **1971** Wood *Vocab. Change* 299 **Sth**, 3 [of c1000 infs] rare ripes. **1982** *Smithsonian Letters* **RI**, Rareripe—a long green onion.

rareripe peach See **rareripe 1**

rare the roof up See **rare** v **5a**

rare up See **rare** v **1, 2, 3, 5a**

raring See **rare** v **5a, b**

raring mad See **rare** v **5a**

rasberry See **raspberry**

rasher n[1]

A slice of some foodstuff. Note: The limited sense "a thin slice of bacon or ham" is std and is not illustrated here.

1890 Johnston *Widow Guthrie* 164 **GA** (as of 1830s), You look as comfortable as a bee on a rasher of watermelon. **1965** in 1983 Johnson *I Declare* 52 **nwFL**, I went over to get me a rasher of light bread.

rasher n[2] [*DA* "App. f. local P[ortu]g[uese] *rasciera,* a kind of fish"]

The vermilion **rockfish 3** (*Sebastes miniatus*).

1882 *U.S. Natl. Museum Bulletin* 16.663, *S[ebastodes] miniatus.* . . *Rasciera; Rasher.* Color above deep vermillion, mottled with flesh-color on the sides, the belly light red. **1887** Goode *Amer. Fishes* 267, *Sebastichthys miniatus* is known to the Portuguese fishermen at Monterey [CA] as the "Rasher," a name of uncertain origin and othography [sic]. **1902** Jordan–Evermann *Amer. Fishes* 497, The rasher, *S[ebastes] miniatus,* is another important species reaching a length of 2 feet and abundant from San Francisco to San Diego. **1953** Roedel *Common Fishes CA* 127, *Vermilion Rockfish.* . . One of the more important commercial species. . . *Unauthorized Names* . . borracho, rasher. **1991** *Amer. Fisheries Soc. Common Names Fishes* 162, Rasher—see vermilion rockfish.

raspberry n Usu |'ræz,bɛri, 'ræz,bɝi|; also |'ræs-|; *old-fash* |'rɒz-, 'rɑz-| Pronc-spp *rasberry, rawsberry, rawzberry, rosb(er)ry;* for addit pronc and sp varr see quots

A Forms.

1828 in 1918 Dale *Ashley–Smith Explor.* 270 **OR**, Those Inds. bring Pacific rasberrys and other berries. **1899** (1912) Green *VA Folk-Speech* 346, *Rasberry.* . . A form of *raspberry. Raasb'r'y.* **1904** *DN* 2.427 **Cape Cod MA** (as of a1857), *Rosberry.* . . Raspberry. **1907** *DN* 3.249 **eME**, *Rosb'ry.* . . Raspberry. Common pronunciation. **1911** *DN* 3.512 **Sth, S Midl**, *Raspberry* [with [s]:] 89 [with [z]:] 152. [*DARE* Ed: based on a survey of 241 college students] **1913** *DN* 4.54 **seNH**, *Raspberries* ['rɑz-bɛr-rɪz]. . . The usual meaning. **1917** *DN* 4.399 **neOH, PA**, *Rosberry* ['rɒzbɛrɪ]. . . Raspberry. ['ræzbɛrɪ] is also known. ['ræzbɛrɪ] is an acquired pronunciation. General. [*DN* Ed: In Pa., [ɔ], [ɑ], and [æ].] **1922** (1926) Cady *Rhymes VT* 16, By George! that rozberry pie is good. **1927** *AmSp* 3.139 **eME**, The older people. . . spoke of . . "rosbry" (raspberry), "punkin," [etc]. **1937** *AmSp* 12.107 **eNE** [Farm terms], Farmers. . . commonly make use of such mispronunciations as . . *rawsberries, punkins,* and *batadoes.* **1950** *WELS Suppl.* **csWI**, Raspberries [rɒsbɛriz]. [Used by an elderly woman born in Germany.] **1959** *VT Hist.* 27.154, *Raspberry* ['rɒzbɛrɪ] and ['rɒzbri]. Occasional. **1961** Kurath–McDavid *Pronc. Engl.* 137, *Raspberry* has the vowel /æ/ of *bat* in all of the Eastern States. But in New England and the New England settlements to the west, rarely elsewhere, several other pronunciations are also current, although /æ/ predominates decidedly in cultivated speech . . and has extensive currency among the middle group. In northeastern New England the /ɒ/ of *law* . . is rather common . . , in Upstate New York the corresponding /ɔ/, which is also still heard to some extent in the folk speech of Western New England. /ɔ/ also has some currency along the Ohio River in West Virginia. . . A third vowel, the /a ~ ɑ/ of *car,* occurs with some frequency in southern New England and northwestern Vermont, and in scattered instances along the Great Lakes. . . Outside the New England settlements only a few instances of an unrounded low vowel, either /ɑ/ or /ɑ/, have been observed. **1965–70**

DARE (Qu. I44, *What kinds of berries grow wild around here?*) 489 Infs, **widespread, but less freq Sth, West,** Raspberries [alone or in var combs]. [Proncs were recorded from nearly all these Infs. By far the commonest proncs were of the types ['ræz₁bɛriz, 'ræzbɚiz]. 31 Infs, **scattered,** offered proncs with [s] rather than [z] in the first syllable (usu ['ræs₁bɛriz]); other proncs of note were: **ME1,** ['razbɚiz]; **MA6,** ['ræzbriz]; **MN12,** [razbɛri]; **NJ8,** [reˇzbɛriz]; **NJ64,** [razbɚiz]; **NY2,** ['rɔz₁bɚiz]; **NY9,** ['razbɛri]; **WI10,** [roˁzbɛriz].] **1966** *DARE* File **cwWI,** *Raspberry* pronounced *rawzberry* was common usage in our community at least until 1915 or so. **1975** Gould *ME Lingo* 229, *Rawzbree*—The exact way older Mainers say raspberry. Younger folks seem to have flattened it to razzbree. **1978** *Greenfield Recorder* (MA) 26 Aug, Do you know any old people who still use some of the old New England ways of pronouncing words? They may tell you "rosbries" are ripe now. **1982** Slone *How We Talked* 90 eKY (as of c1950), We had a lot of blackberries, "raseberries" (raspberries), huckleberries, wild strawberries and "hozzies" (haws). **1989** Pederson *LAGS Tech. Index* 222 **Gulf Region,** [c600 proncs of *raspberry* were recorded. The first syllable appears as [ræz-] in over 500 of them, and the devoiced variants [ræz̦-] or [ræs-] in a further 62. There are 22 instances of the raised variants [rɛz-] or, rarely, [rɛs-]; and 3 with low vowels ([raz-, rɔz-]).]

B Sense.

Std: any of var plants of the genus *Rubus;* also the usu red or black fruit that separates from the receptacle when mature. For other names of var of these see **blackcap 1, cloudberry, fingerberry, flowering raspberry, Hitchcock-berry, mountain raspberry, mulberry, pigeonberry 5, scotch cap, thimbleberry, wineberry** Cf **dewberry 1, salmonberry**

raspberry bug n

A **negro bug** (here: *Corimelaena pulicaria*).
1911 *Century Dict. Suppl.,* Raspberry-bug. . . The flea-like negro-bug. **1966** *DARE* (Qu. R30, . . *Kinds of beetles;* not asked in early QRs) Inf **MI17,** Raspberry bug—smells bad.

raspberry pieplant See **pieplant**

raspberry rose n

=**flowering raspberry.**
1933 Small *Manual SE Flora* 619, R[ubacer] odoratum. . . Raspberry-rose. . . Rocky banks and woods. **1953** Greene–Blomquist *Flowers South* 47, Flowering Raspberry, Raspberry Rose. . . The rose-purple blossoms . . attract attention even at some distance from the trails and highways of the s. Appalachian Mountains during the summer months. . . The fruits . . are very fragrant as if dipped in perfume.

raspberry shrub See **shrub** n²

raspilla n [MexSpan "prickle"]

A **mimosa 1** (here: *Mimosa malacophylla*).
1960 Vines *Trees SW* 514, Vernacular names [of *Mimosa malacophylla*] are Raspa-huevos and Raspilla. **1970** Correll *Plants TX* 778, *Raspilla.* Liane climbing in trees or forming a tangle, . . the stems armed with recurved prickles.

rass See **rice**

rassle up See **wrastle**

rassling jack (or root) See **wrestling jack**

rastas See **rastus** n²

raster n Also pl rastra SW hist

=**arrastra.**
1851 *San Francisco Herald* (CA) 28 July 2/3 **SW,** Rastra, or track mills, (a simple construction for amalgamating,) are now being made, each of which will pulverize and amalgamate forty-five hundred pounds of the quartz per day. **1857** Borthwick *3 Yrs. CA* 245, The quartz vein was several hundred yards above the rasters. **1885** *Wkly. New Mexican Rev.* 2 April 3/4 (*DA*), Messrs. Probst and Gonzales will construct an old style Mexican 'raster,' crushing the ore with heavy boulders and horse power.

rastle See **wrastle**

rastra See **raster**

Rastus n¹ [Aphet form of *Erastus*]

1 also attrib: Used as a nickname for a Black man; a supposedly typical Black person.
1888 *Amer. Missionary* 49.95, Meanwhile, we think we hear Uncle Rastus quoting the prophecy, "The morning cometh and also the night." **1896** Mills–Marion *Rastus on Parade* 3, [Song lyrics:] Rastus my soldier boy he leads the band today. **1909** *Lippincott's* May 636, Rastus's Baby [title]. *Ibid,* Ain' he de spit o' Ras?/ Po' li'l lammie! **1932** F. DuBose *Episodes in Black & White* 1 (*OED2*), Two little pickaninnies were sitting by the fire when in came Uncle Rastus with a pumpkin pie. **1944** *AmSp* 19.172, In my boyhood *Cuffy* was being supplanted by *Rastus.* **1965** Little *Autobiog. Malcolm X* 30 **MI,** Wherever I showed my face, the audiences . . "niggered" and "cooned" me to death. Or called me "Rastus." **1965–70** [see **rastus** n²]. **1967** *DARE* (Qu. HH28, *Names and nicknames . . for people of foreign background*) Inf **IA5,** Negro—Rastus ['ræstəs]. **1986** Pederson *LAGS Concordance,* 1 inf, **csGA,** Rastus row—back seat of bus; where blacks sat.

2 See quot. Cf **black man 1**
1966 *DARE* (Qu. CC8, . . *The devil*) Inf **ME9,** Rastus.

rastus n² Also rastas, rastus plow, restus (plow) [Trademark *Rastus* 1934 →] esp KY See Map

A shovel cultivator with three (or rarely more) shovels.
1965–70 *DARE* (Qu. L18, *Kinds of plows*) Inf **IN45,** Rastus; **IN13,** Rastus plow—three-shovel plows for one horse (corn, tobacco); **KY18,** Restus plow—a three-footed plow for cultivating; (Qu. L25, *The implement used to clean out weeds and loosen the earth between rows of corn*) Inf **KY6,** Rastus ['ræstɪs]—has three shovels instead of two; **KY75,** Rastus or rastus plow—old-fashioned; three shovels, used mainly for tobacco; etymology unknown; **KY76,** Rastus—colored people worked tobacco; colored people called Rastus: transferred to plow; **KY80,** Rastus—three shovels—tobacco; **KY84,** Rastus—occasionally for corn, but usually for tobacco [FW: Inf thought it was called "rastus" because it was used for tobacco, which was worked by slaves and later Negro tenant farmers]; **KY16, 27,** Restus (plow). **1966** *Cynthiana Democrat* (KY) 28 Apr 6/7, *Public Auction* . . 2–3 shovel plows; rastas; -A- harrow. [**1968** *DARE* FW Addit **TN26,** Rastus ['ræstəs]: As best I could understand from Inf's description, a rastus is a wooden beam that fits diagonally across the main beam of a plow about where the plow-handles join. It has three holes bored in it so that three plows may be fitted, not two as with the double shovel.] **1968** *KY Folkl. Rec.* 14.39 **KY,** *Plowing,* as was the case with corn, was done with a *bull-tongue, double-shovel,* or eventually with a *Rastus* plow. **1970** *DARE* Tape **KY75,** The main plow in this section of the country was a rastus plow, which was a three-point plow, and it would really loosen up the soil and tear it up. **1983** *MJLF* 9.1.52 ceKY (as of 1956), Rastus plow . . a three-shoveled cultivating plow. **1986** Pederson *LAGS Concordance,* 1 inf, **cnTN,** Rastus—3 or 4 shovels; is a go-devil; 1 inf, **ceTN,** Rastus.

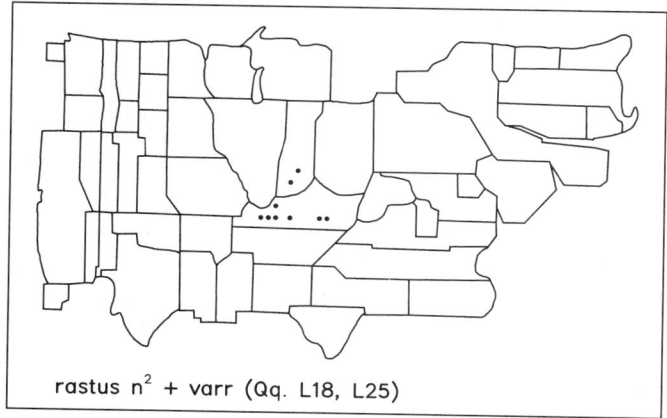

rastus n² + varr (Qq. L18, L25)

rat n

1 =**muskrat 1;** hence v *rat* to trap **muskrats;** vbl n *ratting.* [*DCan* 1584 →] **chiefly Nth, Midl** See Map on p. 472 Cf **marsh rabbit 2**
1832 Kennedy *Swallow Barn* 1.307 **VA,** I have got no more than two rats. **1841** (1952) Cooper *Deerslayer* 39 **NY,** A shallow bay . . had got

the name of "Rat's Cove," from . . its being a favorite haunt of the muskrat. **1874** Long *Amer. Wild-Fowl* 49, To build a Blind in a rat-house, a large one like a small hay-stack should be selected. **1906** *Forest & Stream* 29 Dec 1020 **Chesapeake Bay,** Prolific as the muskrat is, one-half mile section on Slaughter Creek yielded but half a hundred rats last winter. **1923** *Anchorage Daily Times* (AK) Jan 9 *(Tabbert Coll.),* A very peculiar trait of the muskrat, noted by many trappers, is when the rat has to come up for air and none is available, the muskrat will come up against the ice and blow an air-bubble, then take it back in again. **1936** *Sun* (Baltimore MD) 16 Mar 7/4 **MD,** The cold weather . . didn't prevent the lower Shore farmers from enjoying their unique dish of "rats and greens." . . The "winter cress" is a native uncultivated weed. The women and children gather it from the fields while the farmer father visits his muskrat traps on the marshes and returns with the second important ingredient of the dish. **1950** *WELS (Names used locally for . . muskrat)* 8 Infs, **WI,** Rat(s). **1965–70** *DARE* (Qu. P31, . . *Names or nicknames . . for the . . muskrat)* 39 Infs, **chiefly Nth, Midl,** Rat(s). [37 of 39 Infs male] **1968** *DARE* Tape **DE**7, [FW:] You mentioned, too, that you . . used to trap muskrats. [Inf:] Yeah. . . When I first started trappin' they had made a trap and the rat would cut off—cut his foot off. **1986** Pederson *LAGS Concordance,* 1 inf, **swLA,** Rat—a muskrat; 1 inf, **nwMS,** Rat country—where muskrats flourish. **1991** *DARE* File **NEast, WI,** Everyplace I've ever talked with anyone about muskrat trapping, they've called 'em rats. **1991** Kirlin–Kirlin *Smithsonian Folklife Cookbook* 175 **MI,** In Monroe muskrat dinners are not only community fund raisers, they also serve as important family events. In fact, the "rat" is so integrated into this community that it. . . is trapped from November to February. **1996** Horton *Island Out of Time* 73 **Chesapeake Bay MD,** I always loved to rat. Rattin' takes you everywhere in the island. . . There isn't the market for muskrat or other fur as there once was.

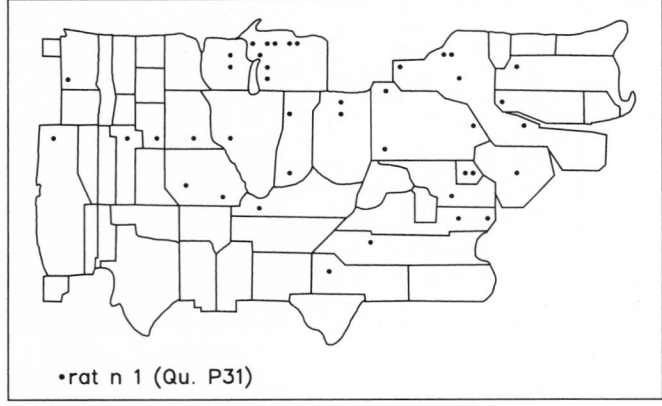

•rat n 1 (Qu. P31)

2 One who sells bootleg whiskey; hence n *rat house* a small building where such whiskey is sold anonymously. Cf **blind tiger**

1911 *DN* 3.539 **eKY,** Rat. . . One who peddles, or otherwise retails, "moonshine" whiskey "on the sly." **1974** Dabney *Mountain Spirits* 149 **sAppalachians,** Before and after the turn of the century, "rat houses" had been part of the Appalachian frontier scenery—small log cabins seven or eight feet square with tiny openings next to the road. The buyer [of illegal whiskey] would pass his jug into the hole, along with his money. From the inner darkness would emerge the filled jug, with only the hand of the seller to be seen. **1982** Slone *How We Talked* 69 **eKY** (as of c1950), *A rat house*—a small house with a little window that had a small wooden shutter with a hole through it, through which the transaction of selling whiskey was done without the buyer seeing or hearing anyone.

rat v

1 also with *around:* To idle about; to shirk work or school; to malinger. **esp Gulf States, Missip Valley** See Map

1857 (1930) DeLong *Jrls.* 9.154 **NY,** Put up at the Haun House, ratted around some and went to bed. **1929** *Sat. Eve. Post* 17 Aug 11, Arguing wages with the mate is only one phase of the ritual of roustabouting. It is all a game, the general objective of which is to make Captain Sam think they are working hard when in reality they are loafing, or "ratting." **1939** in Lib. of Congress *Amer. Memory:* WPA *Life Hist.* (Internet),

Once, an antiquated porter at the old Holliday House, fronting the river at Cairo, Ill., sang this one [=coonjine song] for me: "Where wuz you las' night?/O tell me whar you wuz las' night?/ Rattin' on de job / In Saint Chawles Hotel." Which requires some explanation. "Ratting" is rouster lingo for "loafing." The St. Charles Hotel referred . . to a warm cleared space beneath the steamboat boilers. **c1960** *Wilson Coll.* **csKY,** Ratting. . . Loafing on the job. **1965–70** *DARE* (Qu. A9, . . *Wasting time by not working on the job)* Infs **LA**31, **MS**2, 60, 85, Ratting; **LA**40, Ratting around; **TX**104, Ratting on the job; (Qu. BB27, *When somebody pretends to be sick . . he's* _____) Inf **MS**60, Ratting; **AL**34, Ratting on one; (Qu. JJ26, *If somebody has been doing poor work or not enough, the boss might say)* Inf **IN**41, Quit ratting. **1973** Allen *LAUM* 1.378, *Ratting,* known from other sources to have been used in St. Paul schools more than a generation ago [to mean "playing hooky"], did not turn up during the fieldwork. **1983** Abbott *Womenfolks* 167 **AR,** Sometimes the four of us would dress and get in the car and drive around Hot Springs, buying thread and snaps at the dry-goods store, visiting some spring or other and drinking from tin cups, or "ratting up and down," as my aunt called it, on Central Avenue.

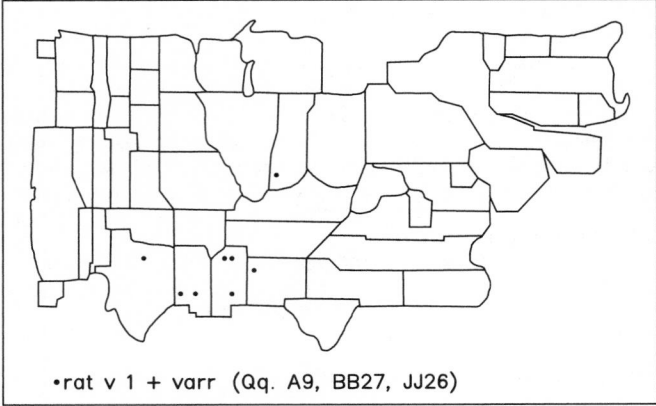

•rat v 1 + varr (Qq. A9, BB27, JJ26)

2 See **rat** n **1.**

rat adv See **right**

rat and cat See **cat and mouse 1**

ratany n

Std: a plant of the genus *Krameria.* For other names of var spp see **crimson beak, heart-nut, sandburr 2d, white ratany**

rat around See **rat** v **1**

ratban See **ratsbane 1**

ratbane See **ratsbane**

rat burner n Also *rat match*

1967–70 *DARE* (Qu. F46, . . *Matches you can strike anywhere;* not asked in early QRs) Inf **SC**70, Rat burners—rats would strike them; **NY**23, Rat matches—rats gnaw them and start fire.

rat cat n Also *mouse and rat cat* **chiefly Sth, S Midl** See Map Cf **mouse cat**

1965–70 *DARE* (Qu. J6, *A cat that catches lots of rats and mice . . "She's a good _____."*) 13 Infs, **chiefly Sth, S Midl,** Rat cat; **AR**55, Rat catcher or rat cat—new fangled; **IL**93, Mouse and rat cat.

ratch v¹ See **reach** v¹ **A1**

ratch v²

1 To search, root about. [Scots, nEngl dial; *EDD ratch* v.² 2 "To ransack, ferret about"]

1968 *DARE* FW Addit **ID,** To ratch in drawers or closets for something—dig about in an untidy manner. Associated with a rat-like activity. **2000** *NADS Letters* **TN,** I have lived in Tennessee, both in Middle Tennessee (Murfreesboro) and on the edge of the Cumberland Plateau (McMinnville) since I was 10, and I've grown up using the word *ratch* as a verb, with it meaning to "root around or search for something." "I'll just have to ratch around for those recipes, now. . . " I haven't heard it used in the sense of restless movement, though. It's always, in my expe-

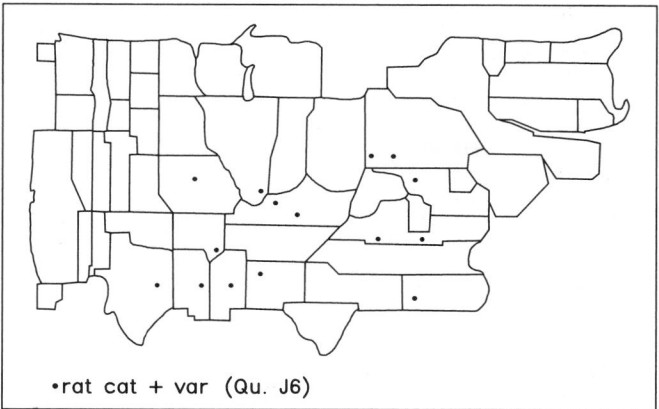

•rat cat + var (Qu. J6)

rience, referred to searching for something. Friends of mine from West Tennessee (near Shiloh) also use the term to mean looking for something.

2 also *ratchet:* To move about restlessly.   [Cf *EDD ratch* v.² 2 "To . . ramble"]

1985 *WI Alumnus Letters* **UT,** "Ratch" . . means to be restless, to twist and turn, move around a great deal as to "ratch" around in bed at night. . . [I]t was an everyday word for us living in Utah, and easily understood anywhere in Salt Lake City or Ogden. . . The origin of this word is probably from the tool, the ratchet. **1999** *NADS Letters* **TX,** Never used these [=*ratch* or *ratched*] but I have always used rachet around or ratcheted around in the same sense of moving restlessly or aimlessly. I'm sixty and have lived in Texas most of my life. **2000** *Ibid* **cnPA,** I have heard "ratch" use[d] in north central PA in refering to your second example [="He ratched around in bed last night."] It comes from hill usage around Trout Run and the area I grew up in.

rat cheese n Also *rat-trap (cheese)*

Cheddar cheese, esp that with a strong odor.

1910 Rinehart *Window at the White Cat* 97 **PA,** "It's rat trap cheese, that stuff," he growled. "The other ran out an hour ago and didn't come back. . . You can kill that with mustard, if it's too lively". **1927** *Amer. Mercury* 10.28 **DC,** Every afternoon, just before the four o'clock rush, a small plate of rat-trap cheese and a bowl of crackers and gingersnaps were put out. **1939** *Sun* (Baltimore MD) 4 May 8/5 *(Hench Coll.),* I was astonished at the . . editorial writer who . . was guilty of saying, in regard to macaroni, that "it is merely associated with a dish whose other component part is rat cheese." **1944** Mencken *Christmas Story* 27 **MD,** The waiters spread a substantial lunch of rye bread, rat-trap cheese, ham, bologna [etc]. **1953** *Sun* (Baltimore MD) 1 May 16/1 *(Hench Coll.),* [Headline:] A Big Boom In Rat-Cheese Production. **1956** McAtee *Some Dialect NC* 36, *Rat cheese.* . . Cheddar cheese, from being used to bait rat traps. **c1960** *Wilson Coll.* **csKY,** *Rat cheese:* . . Facetious reference to common hoop cheese. **1960** Williams *Walk Egypt* 206 **GA,** The men . . took over the store. . . They bought a dime's worth of rat cheese or a box of soda crackers. **1963** Adamson *Household Hints* 196 **NEng** (as of late 19th cent), *Boiled Rattrap Cheese.* . . add ¼ lb. of finely grated strong store cheese—the kind called "rattrap". **1966** *DARE* Tape **MA6,** [Inf:] Rat cheese. [FW:] Rat cheese. What would that be? [Inf:] That's a real strong one. **1971** *Today Show Letters* **sw,csMS,** Rat . . cheese—Cheddar cheese in round wooden boxes. **1986** Pederson *LAGS Concordance,* 1 inf, **csGA,** Rat cheese (with a hole in it); 1 inf, **cLA,** Rat cheese—we called it; 1 inf, **neTX,** Rat cheese—but says it is yellow & smooth. **1989** *DARE* File **cwAL** (as of c1940), I don't remember the term 'hoop cheese' but it is an expected way of describing the block cheese that we called 'rat-trap cheese' (the cheapest kind in the store).

ratchet n

1 See quot.

1976 Brown *Gloss. Faulkner* 122 **MS,** The hames have a series of holes (illogically called a ratchet), and the loggerhead's two hook-ends are fitted into two of these. The choice of holes permits variation of the line of draft and hence of the depth of plowing.

2 in combs *Georgia ratchet, ratchet stock:* Appar =**Georgia stock.**

1986 Pederson *LAGS Concordance,* 1 inf, **cwGA,** A Georgia ratchet = single plow stock; 1 inf, **cwFL,** Ratchet stock = scooter stock.

ratchet v See **ratch** v² 2

rat dog n

1 A rat guard; see quot.

1968 *DARE* FW Addit **New Orleans LA,** *Rat dog*—a metal disk that goes around a wire to keep rats and squirrels from following wires into houses.

2a also *rattail:* A **rat terrier** or other small dog; see quots.

1986 Pederson *LAGS Concordance,* 1 inf, **cwLA,** Rat dog; 1 inf, **cTN,** Rat dog or rattail—like fox feist, but bigger. **1998** *NADS Letters,* Rat dog: That is what we call our newly acquired terrier mix. It came naturally, so I expect that too arises from the Louisville [KY] area at about the same time [=c1947]. My wife says that her grandfather called small terrier type dogs rat dogs. *Ibid* **OR,** "Rat Dog" . . is a derogatory statement pertaining to small dogs, usually when they are about the size of a medium to large rat. It is also implied to state a worthless nature to the animal. *Ibid, Rat dog* . . was used in the mid-50's in the Piedmont area of South Carolina as a term for small terriers, or even small dogs in general, which were also referred to as feists. *Ibid,* I always understood *rat dog* to be any small breed of dog.

b Spec: see quot.

1998 *NADS Letters* **swCA,** In our old neighborhood in San Fernando our Latino neighbors all called their Chihuahua-looking dogs "rat dogs." . . [T]hese rat dogs are smaller and sleeker than what I would call a Chihuahua. When I asked the neighbors, they said that the two breeds were different from each other. *Ibid* **sCA,** A rat dog . . is a chihuahua (the tiny Mexican dog) because of their small, nearly hairless, big-eared, squirmy bodies.

rate See **right**

ratfish n

1 A chimaera *(Hydrologus colliei)* of the Pacific coast.   Also called **rattail 2**

1882 U.S. Natl. Museum *Bulletin* 16.55, *C[himæra] colliæi.* . . *Ratfish.* . . Color grayish, with numerous round white spots. **1896** U.S. Bur. Fisheries *Rept. for 1895* 226, *Hydrologus colliei.* . . *Rat-fish.* . . Pacific coast from Monterey northward to Alaska. **1926** Pan-Pacific Research Inst. *Jrl.* 3.3.11 **OR, WA,** *Hydrolagus colliei.* . . Ratfish. **1967** *DARE* (Qu. P4, *Saltwater fish that are not good to eat*) Inf **WA22,** Ratfish. **1974** McClane *McClane's New Std. Fishing Encycl.* 785, *Ratfish.* . . Its head is relatively large, with a pointed snout, and a clublike projection is located between the eyes of the male. **1983** *Audubon Field Guide N. Amer. Fishes* 362, Care should be taken in handling a Ratfish, as the venomous spines can cause a painful wound, and the clasping organs are quite sharp.

2 A **bonefish 1** (here: *Albula vulpes*).

1972 Sparano *Outdoors Encycl.* 379, *Common names:* Bonefish, ratfish, banana. . . *Albula vulpes.* . . The bonefish's upper jaw—a snout, really—is far longer than the lower, giving the fish a suckerlike look.

ratgut n [Var of *rotgut*]   esp PA, NY, NJ   See Map

1965–70 *DARE* (Qu. DD21b, *General words . . for bad liquor*) Infs **NJ35, NY64, PA**29, 36, 55, 142, 245, Ratgut; **KS20,** Ratgut, [corr to]

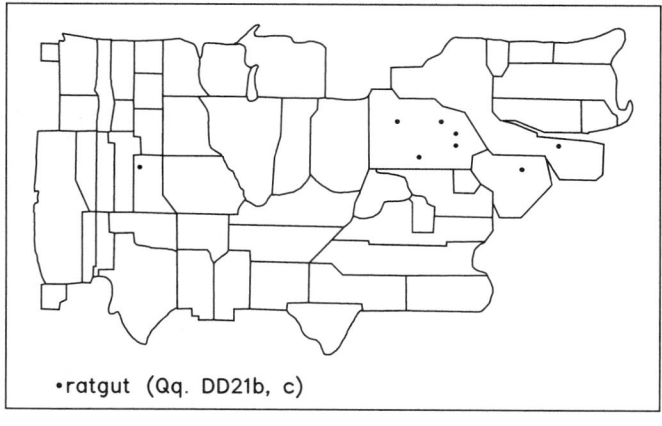

•ratgut (Qq. DD21b, c)

rotgut; (Qu. DD21c, *Nicknames for whiskey, especially illegally made whiskey*) Inf **PA**29, Ratgut. [7 of 8 Infs old] **1998** *NADS Letters* **NJ,** *Ratgut* was given by two informants. A pre-1940 woman from Elizabeth, NJ, who said that during Prohibition it's what they called wood alcohol. Another from Bridgeton, Cumberland Co., born between 1940 and 1970 had heard of it. **2000** *Ibid* **seNY** (as of 1950s, 60s), Ratgut. . . I heard this term from . . my father and two uncles. *Ibid* **nwOH,** I'm originally from Ohio—Lima. I'm 50 years old. When I was a teen, we used to call booze "ratgut." *Ibid* **nDE,** I am familiar with the term ratgut in connection with strong or nasty tasting liquor and especially whiskey. I have lived in Delaware all my life, in New Castle County. . . I heard the term as a child in the 1960's. *Ibid* **NJ,** I am familiar with the term ratgut as you have described it. **2001** *Ibid* **NYC.**

rat hawk n
=**marsh hawk 1.**
    1955 *Oriole* 20.5 **GA,** Marsh Hawk. . . Rat Hawk. **1967** *DARE* (Qu. Q4, . . *Kinds of hawks*) Inf **TX**3, Rat hawk.

rather adv Usu |'ræðə(r)|; also |'rʌðə(r), 'rɛðə(r), 'rɑðə(r)| Pronc-sp *ruther;* also *rayther, raythur, redder, redduh, reether, re(i)ther, rudder, rudduh*
    A Forms.
    1815 Humphreys *Yankey in England* 108, Rather (pronounced narrow on the first syllable) frequently used to diminish or qualify the term to which it is applied—sometimes pronounced *ruth-er.* **1819** in 1956 Eliason *Tarheel Talk* 316 **c,cwNC,** Reither. **1843** (1916) Hall *New Purchase* 216, I raythur allow as maybe perhaps. **1847** Hurd *Grammatical Corrector* 88, Rather ["incorrect" pronc = ['rʌðɚ]; "correct" pronc = ['ræðɚ]]. **1851** Hooper *Widow Rugby's Husband* 22 **AL,** You are reether hard down on your Union friends. **1853** Simms *Sword & Distaff* 581 **SC** [Black], I much rudder (rather) b'long to good maussa. **1858** Hammett *Piney Woods Tavern* 43 **TX,** I rayther reckon your anxious mother don't know ye'r out. **1871** Eggleston *Hoosier Schoolmaster* 40 **sIN,** I tuck a sheet off the bed to splice out the table-cloth, which was ruther short. *Ibid* 225, Marthy would ruther vacate. **1884** *Anglia* 7.262 **Sth, S Midl** [Black], To rudder have = to prefer. **1891** *PMLA* 6.172 **TN,** D'ruther for *had rather* is a common contraction and mispronunciation. **1891** *DN* 1.145 **cNY,** [rʌðr]. **1893** Shands *MS Speech* 7, [æ] is changed . . to [ʌ] in *ruther* for *rather.* **1894** Riley *Armazindy* 69 **IN,** A ruther *stylish* feller. **1902** *DN* 2.228 **sIL, As.** . . I'd ruther do this as that. **1903** *DN* 2.326 **seMO,** Rather. . . Pronounced ruther. **1904** Day *Kin o' Ktaadn* 95 **ME,** I'd ruther live here on this hill. **1905** *DN* 3.56 **eNE,** Rether. **1907** *DN* 3.235 **nwAR,** Rather. . . Pronounced [rʌðɚ]. **1909** *DN* 3.365 **eAL, wGA,** Ruther. **1912** *DN* 3.588 **wIN,** Ruther. **1914** *DN* 4.79 **ME, nNH,** Ruther. **1917** *DN* 4.399 **neOH,** Ruther, druther [rʌðr, drʌðr]. **1922** Gonzales *Black Border* 323 **sSC, GA coasts** [Gullah glossary], Redduh—rather. *Ibid,* Rudduh—rather. **1923** *DN* 5.219 **swMO,** Ruther. **1929** in 1952 Mathes *Tall Tales* 145 **sAppalachians,** I'd ruther ye'd make me a offer. **1935** *AmSp* 10.296 **Upstate NY,** Of the other words of this type in my records, *rather* is the most variable; it appears 215 times with [æ], 28 times with [a], 36 times with [ɑ], and 18 times with [ʌ], and the distribution shows a somewhat greater preference for [a] and [ɑ] in the southern and Eastern sections than in other parts of the state. **1937** *AmSp* 12.289 **wVA,** ['ræðr]. **1938** *AmSp* 13.50 **eMO,** ['rɛðɚ]. **1939** *AmSp* 14.124 **seSC,** ['rɑðə]. **1942** *AmSp* 17.34 **seNY,** Rather . . 42 [instances of] [æ] . . 45 [a] . . 80 [ɑ]. **1949** Turner *Africanisms* 260 **seSC** [Gullah], [rʌr]. **1961** Kurath–McDavid *Pronc. Engl.* 138, *Rather* with the vowel /æ/ of *gather* is the usual pronunciation among the middle class in the North and the North Midland. In southern New England, in Metropolitan New York, and in parts of Pennsylvania it is also fairly frequent in folk speech. . . South of Pennsylvania, /æ/ is the usual pronunciation . . among the cultured, except in coastal South Carolina, Georgia, and Florida. . . *Rather* riming with *father* is strictly a cultivated pronunciation. . . In folk speech, *rather* has the vowel /ʌ/ of *brother* fairly generally throughout the South and the South Midland, in Delmarva, in New Jersey, and in northeastern New England. . . *Rather* with the /ɛ/ of *feather* occurs to some extent in all of the major speech areas. . . [T]he /ɛ/ of *feather* and the /ʌ/ of *brother* are sharply recessive among cultured speakers, except along the coast of the Lower South. **1965–70** *DARE* (Qu. JJ32, . . "I'd _____ [have a dog].") 700 Infs, **widespread,** Rather [proncs of the type ['ræðə(r)]]; 75 Infs, **scattered, but esp Upstate NY, wNEng, Sth, Missip Valley,** Ruther [proncs of the type ['rʌðə(r)]]; 34 Infs, **scattered, but less freq Nth, West,** Rether [proncs of the type ['rɛðə(r)]]; 26 Infs, **scattered, but esp Atlantic,** Rather [proncs of the type [rɑðə(r),

rɑðə(r)]]; **CT**5, ['rɛðə]—her old aunt says ['rʌðə]; **LA**2, ['ræðə], but most everybody here would say ['rʌðə]; **LA**14, ['rɑðə]—cultured, ['ræðə]—common; **MO**8, ['rɪðɪ]; **NC**36, ['rɒðɚ]; **SC**10, ['rɛdɚ]. [Of all Infs responding to Qu. JJ32, 12% were comm type 1 or 2, 25% gs educ or less; of those giving the response *ruther,* 5% were comm type 1 or 2, 42% gs educ or less; of those giving the response *rether,* 3% were comm type 1 or 2, 32% gs educ or less; of those giving proncs of the type [rɑðə(r), 'rɑðə(r)], 36% were comm type 1 or 2, 18% gs educ or less.] **1968** *DARE* FW Addit **neMD,** Rather ['rɛðə]. **1969** *DARE* Tape **TX**75, I'm gonna spank you and send you in the other room, which I'd rather ['rɑðə] not do. **1983** *MJLF* 9.1.54 **ceKY,** Ruther. **1989** Pederson *LAGS Tech. Index* 338 **Gulf Region,** [Of 704 proncs of *rather* tabulated, 302 had the vowel [æ], 206 [ɛ], 134 [ʌ], and 58 [ɑ].]
    B Gram forms.
    1 Used quasi-verbally without expressed auxiliary where *(woul)d rather* (rarely *had rather*) would be expected. Note: That this is primarily a matter of ellipsis rather than reinterpretation as a modal auxiliary (or full verb) is suggested by the interrogative order "You rather . . ?" (instead of "Rather you . . ?" or "Do you rather . . ?"). The only examples we have of full-verb morphology (past tense *rathered,* in student essays) may not reflect natural usage.
    1856 in 1862 Colt *Went to KS* 83 **NY,** Willie. . . said "Willie *rather* have white bread," and the little fellow will eat it clear, and relish it much better than children with pampered appetites do their rounds of goodies. **1884** Baldwin *Yankee School-Teacher* 21 **NY,** She's a dabster at piecin' quilts though! I do b'lieve she ruther do that than t'eat when hungry. **1926** *AmSp* 1.292 **NE,** An interesting instance of an adverbial form, in the comparative degree, made into a verb appears in: "When my brother finished high school he wanted to travel but my parents *rathered* he would stay at home." This I found in a freshman theme. **1937** (1977) Hurston *Their Eyes* 159 **csFL** [Black], Ah ruther be shot wid tacks than fuh you tuh act wid me lak you is right now. **1939** *Hench Coll.,* [From a student exam:] The monk in the Canterbury Tales cared nothing for the order to which he belonged. He rathered good horses and good food. **1942** [see **B2b** below]. **1943** *LANE* Map 717 (*I'd rather*) 8 Infs, **scattered NEng,** I rather. **1950** Moore *Candlemas Bay* 13 **ME,** Which you rather have, Pa? A hundred hosspower engine or an ash breeze? **1966** *DARE* Tape **SC**7, I bankfish. I have fished from a boat but I rather be on the dirt. **1986** Pederson *LAGS Concordance* **Gulf Region,** [24 infs offered examples of quasi-verbal *rather;* typical examples are: "I rather stay home," "I rather not," and "You rather have this one?"]
    2 Used with *(woul)d,* or quasi-verbally, with a direct object in the form of:
    a A noun or noun phrase (hence equivalent to *would rather have*).
    1923 *DN* 5.244 **LA,** Rather. . . To prefer. "I rather that one." **1939** [see **B1** above]. **1966–68** *DARE* (Qu. JJ32, . . "I'd _____ [have a dog].") Inf **LA**37, Rather the cat [FW: this syntax common here]; **SC**10, Redder the dog. **1968** *DARE* FW Addit **NEast,** Do you want the white ones or would you rather the gray? **LA**41, Maybe you'd just rather coffee [FW: This probably comes from Baton Rouge, where Inf grew up. . . It seems to be characteristic of areas of French influence; I heard *rather* + noun in St. Martinville, Franklin, and Grand Isle.]; **csLA,** I also heard "I'd rather the green one" in town [=Franklin]. **1986** Pederson *LAGS Concordance,* 1 inf, **seMS,** I'd rather that than bricks.
    b A *to-* infinitive clause (hence equivalent to *would prefer*). *esp freq among Black speakers*
    1942 Faulkner *Go Down* 59 **MS** [Black], I ruther never to know than to find out later I have been fooled. **1986** Pederson *LAGS Concordance,* 5 infs, 3 **MS,** (I'd) rather not to go; 1 inf, **swMS,** (I)'d rather not to do it; 1 inf, **cMS,** I'd rather for you to ask me; 1 inf, **cMS,** [I] rather for you to call their name. [All infs Black]

rather n Also *ruther* **chiefly Sth, W Midl** See Map Cf **druthers**
Usu pl: A preference, choice, desire.
    1891 Johnston *Primes & Neighbors* 71 **GA,** If I had my ruthers, I don't know that I'd o' ruther somebody have run a knife into my heart! **1892** *KS Univ. Qrly.* 1.98 **KS,** Ruther: choice, as, If I had my ruther; also, druther. **1903** *DN* 2.326 **seMO,** 'I would stay at home if I had my rather.' Also pronounced ruther. **1909** *DN* 3.362 **eAL, wGA,** Rathers. . . Preference, choice. Often pronounced *ruthers.* **1912** Green

VA Folk-Speech 362, If I had my ruthers I would take this one. **1913** Kephart *Highlanders* 283 **sAppalachians,** A person has a rather about where he'd be put. **1914** *DN* 4.111 **cKS,** *Rathers. . .* Wishes; preference. Also *ruthers.* **1915** *DN* 4.188 **swVA,** *Rathers. . .* Choice; preference. "State your rathers." **1930** Faulkner *As I Lay Dying* 106 **MS,** And if I had my ruthers, you wouldn't be here a-tall. **1935** Hurston *Mules & Men* 162 **FL,** You was . . beggin' me to choose my ruthers. **1942** McAtee *Dial. Grant Co.* IN 54 (as of 1890s), *Ruthers* . . choice; "If I had my _____, I'd take this one". **1947** Ballowe *The Lawd* 3 **LA,** "Efn Ah had ma ruthers," he said, "Ah'd take his Katy." **1947** (1962) Henry *Misty* 150 **eVA,** If ye won't state yer rathers, I got a fine idea. **1952** Brown *NC Folkl.* 1.587, *Ruthers and desires. . .* Wishes *(rathers)* and desires; usually: "to let one have his ruthers and desires."—General. Illiterate. **1965–70** *DARE* (Qu. JJ33, . . *"I'll take a cat, but if I had my _____ I'd take a dog."*) 48 Infs, **chiefly Sth, W Midl,** Rathers; 22 Infs, **chiefly Sth, S Midl,** Ruthers; **MO10, NC9,** Rather. **1974** (1975) Shaw *All God's Dangers* 71 **AL** [Black], Well, everybody's got a rather, but some folks carries their rathers too far.

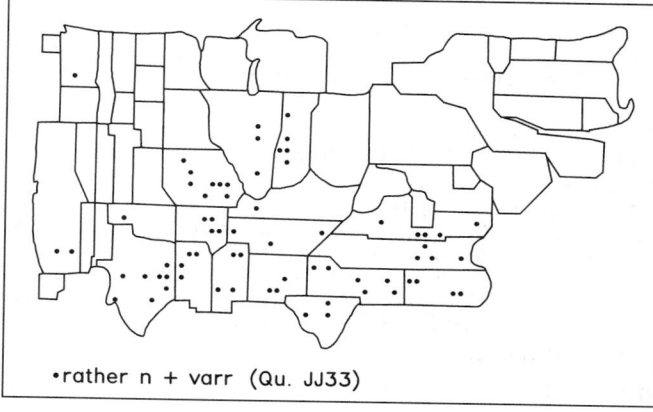

•rather n + varr (Qu. JJ33)

rathered See **rather** adv **B1**

rathole, pour sand down (or in) a See **pound sand down a rathole**

rat house See **rat** n **2**

rat-killing n **scattered, but more freq Sth, S Midl**

Fig: whatever one is occupied with at the moment; miscellaneous tasks—freq used in phr *go on with one's rat-killing* (and varr) to carry on with what one is doing.

1905 *DN* 3.81 **nwAR,** *Go on with one's ratkillin'. . .* To proceed. 'Go on with your ratkillin'.' **1908** *DN* 3.316 **eAL, wGA,** *Go on with one's rat-killin'. . .* To proceed. **1927** *AmSp* 2.355 **cwWV,** *Go on with your rat-killing* (verb phrase), to make the best of a bad business. "The council will go on with its rat-killing in the bond issue." **1942** McAtee *Dial. Grant Co.* IN 30 (as of 1890s), *Go on with the procession* . . said by one dropping out of an activity, meaning "Don't stop on my account." *Go on with the rat-killin'* . . same as preceding. **1967** *DARE* File **csOK,** I've got a lot of rat-killing to do. **1968** *DARE* FW Addit **nwLA,** *Go ahead about your rat-killing*—go ahead about your affairs, business, etc. **c1970** *DARE* File **seNE,** Get on with my rat-killing; get along with my rat-killing—get on with what I've been doing. **1979** *Ibid,* Rat-killing: Present business, occupation, or work-at-hand; usually incidental or trivial. "I'll get to that when I finish this rat-killing." "When you finish your rat-killing, come on over for coffee." My mother (born in 1919) commonly uses this phrase and has since I can remember (from the mid 1940s, sCA). My wife (born in 1942, Madison, WI) says she uses it and has always known it. **1996** *Ibid* **neTX** (as of 1920s–30s), *Get on with your rat killing*—meant to get back to the job you'd started. Ex.: I'll leave so you can get on with your rat killing. **1998** *Ibid* **cnIN,** In regards to Get on with my or your rat killing, [the phrase] was used frequently back in Indiana. It always meant to me—to get on with the work at hand and stop fiddling around. I guess I still use it especially on cottage cleaning day when horsing around has taken over. **1999** *Ibid* **WV** (as of c1940s), If she happened to interrupt you in something and then changed her mind, she would tell you to "go on about your rat killing" or, in other words, just go on about your business and ignore the interruption.

rat match See **rat burner**

rat owl n

1 A **screech owl 1** (here: *Otus asio*).

1917 *Wilson Bulletin* 29.2.81 **KY,** *Otus asio.* . . Field, . . rat, or red owl, Hickman, Ky.

2 =**barn owl 1.**

1925 Bailey *Birds FL* 75, *Barn owl. . . Tyto alba pratincola (Monkey faced owl, Snake owl, Rat owl)* . . this owl . . feeds principally upon rats. **1966** *DARE* (Qu. Q2, . . *Kinds of owls*) Inf **FL7,** Rat owl.

rat red n Cf **bull redfish, puppy drum**

A small **red drum.**

1933 LA Dept. of Conserv. *Fishes* 174, The term "Rat Red" is used to describe young Redfish [=*Sciaenops ocellatus*] due to the popular but erroneous idea that the "Rat Red" is a separate species. **1968** *DARE* (Qu. P2, . . *Kinds of saltwater fish caught around here . . good to eat*) Inf **LA37,** Redfish: rat red—not more than a foot and a half long; bull red—any large redfish. **1983** *Audubon Field Guide N. Amer. Fishes* 623, *Red Drum.* . . Large specimens, usually much smaller than 5′ (1.5m), are called "bullreds," small ones "ratreds."

rat-root n

A **snowberry** (here: *Chiococca alba*).

1953 Greene-Blomquist *Flowers South* 121, *Snow-Berry (Chiococca alba).* . . The natives of the Florida Keys, not knowing much about snow, call it "rat-root" from the ratty odor of its roots.

ratsbane n Also *ratbane* **chiefly S Midl**

1 also *ratban, wild ratsbane,* and, by folk-etym, *ratsvane, rat's vein:* A **pipsissewa:** usu **spotted wintergreen,** occas also *Chimaphila umbellata.*

1892 *Jrl. Amer. Folkl.* 5.100 **VA,** *Chimaphila maculata,* ratsbane; wild arsenic. Blue Ridge, Va. **1901** *Torreya* 1.117 **GA,** *Chimaphila maculata.* . . Rat's-bane. **1937** in 1976 *Weevils in the Wheat* 73 **VA** [Black], Cough: Rats vein herb and heart leaf or crowfoot leaf. **1940** Clute *Amer. Plant Names* 39, *C[himaphila] maculata.* . . Rat's-bane. . . *C. umbellata.* . . Rat's-bane. **1949** Arnow *Hunter's Horn* (May ed., 2d printing) 373 **KY,** She wanted to give all the others [=children] a round of molasses and wormseed and sulphur now, and then . . some good strong tea made with life everlasting, sweet fennel, ratbane, and feverweed, for every last one of them was wormy as could be. **1967** *DARE* FW Addit **SC41,** Ratbane—cooked and fed to sick cows—*Chimaphila umbellata.* **1968–69** *DARE* (Qu. S26c, *Wildflowers that grow in woods*) Inf **GA70,** Ratsbane—four white flowers, look like balls, veiny leaves; (Qu. S26e, *Other wildflowers not yet mentioned;* not asked in early QRs) Inf **NC49,** Rat's vein—used to mix in meal to help bring a horse's appetite back. **1968** *DARE* FW Addit **VA2,** Rat's vein—small mountain flower used as an herb—white with tiny red center, ½ foot high. **1970** *NC Folkl.* 18.24, Ratsbane (ratsvane) is used in treating kidney trouble. **1970** Hyatt *Hoodoo* 1.468 **VA,** She goes and git some ratban [Hyatt: ratsbane] roots, an' git a he ratban root . . an' a she ratban root. A he is got streaks up it, white streaks on de leaf; an' de she is jis' a solid small green leaf. She boils a tea out of it separate, an' take de she ratban-root tea, give all of dat, an' jis' a half of de he. An' dat cured it [=a liver ailment]. [*DARE* Ed: The terms *he* and *she ratban* prob refer to different spp of *Chimaphila.*] **1975** Hamel–Chiltoskey *Cherokee Plants* 62, Wintergreen, spotted; wild rats bane. . . Stew in hogs lard to cure tetter and ringworm; . . tea of leaves for colds and fever; tea for milksick; tea to make baby vomit; use to kill rats.

2 A **rattlesnake plantain 1** (here: *Goodyera pubescens*).

1894 *Jrl. Amer. Folkl.* 7.100 **NC,** *Goodyera pubescens,* . . ratsbane, Banner Elk, N.C. **1924** *Amer. Botanist* 30.151, "Scrophula [sic] weed [=*Goodyera pubescens*] alludes to reputed medicinal properties but "rat's-bane" seems to be a manufactured name if not, perhaps, a careless rendering of "rattlesnake plantain." **1979** Erichsen-Brown *Med. N. Amer. Plants* 297, *Goodyera pubescens.* . . Ratsbane. **1986** Pederson *LAGS Concordance,* 1 inf, **cnGA,** Ratbane—green with little white veins.

rat snake n

1 A snake of the genus *Elaphe;* also a snake formerly included in this genus, as *Bogertophis rosaliae* or *Senticolis triapsis.* **chiefly Gulf States, S Atl** See Map Also called **chicken snake 1.** For other names of var snakes of the genus *Elaphe* see **black snake 2, corn ~, fox ~, house ~ 2, magno-**

lia ~, mouse ~ 1, oak ~, pilot black ~, pilot ~ 2, timber ~, tree ~, white oak ~, witch ~; for other names of *Bogertophis rosaliae* see **H snake**   Cf **hammock snake**

1907 *Country Life* July 328 **Sth,** The yellow rat snake or chicken snake is one of the most useful and is entirely harmless. **1909** Biol. Soc. DC *Proc.* 22.134 **NC,** *Coluber guttatus. Rat Snake.* One killed . . in May, 1906. **1930** OK Univ. Biol. Surv. *Pub.* 2.223, Gray rat snake [=*Elaphe obsoleta spiloides*]. **1955** Carr–Goin *Guide Reptiles* 276, *Elaphe obsoleta rossalleni.* . . Restricted to Florida . . and perhaps occurring . . in the rat snake populations of Sarasota and Martin counties. . . Somewhat arboreal. **1965–70** *DARE* (Qu. P25, . . *Kinds of snakes*) 35 Infs, 34 **Gulf States, S Atl,** Rat snake. **1966** *DARE* Tape **FL**19, This rat snake . . or house snake, that they say if you have one, don't get rid of it because it . . catches the rats and things. **1971** GA Dept. Ag. *Farmers Market Bulletin* 6 Oct 8 **GA,** A rat snake. . . [w]hen caught or disturbed, . . may excreet [sic] a fowl [sic] smelling fluid from glands at the base of the tail. They are all fast active snakes and are nonpoisonous. Members of this family are beneficial to man since they prey on rodents that harm crops, grains, and vegetables. **1974** Shaw–Campbell *Snakes West* 100, The rat snakes eat rodents and are therefore drawn toward agricultural areas where rodent populations, with bountiful repasts available, have sleek coats and large litters. *Ibid* 101, Slender, green or olive in back color, the green rat snake (*Elaphe triapsis* [= *Senticolis triapsis*]) is occasionally confused with the smooth green snake. *Ibid* 102, Another . . snake that . . extends its range into the American West is the Trans-Pecos rat snake (*Elaphe subocularis* [= *Bogertophis rosaliae*]). **1986** Pederson *LAGS Concordance* **Gulf Region,** 23 infs, Rat snake(s); 3 infs, Rat snake(s)—[same as] chicken snake(s); 2 infs, Rat snakes—nonpoisonous.

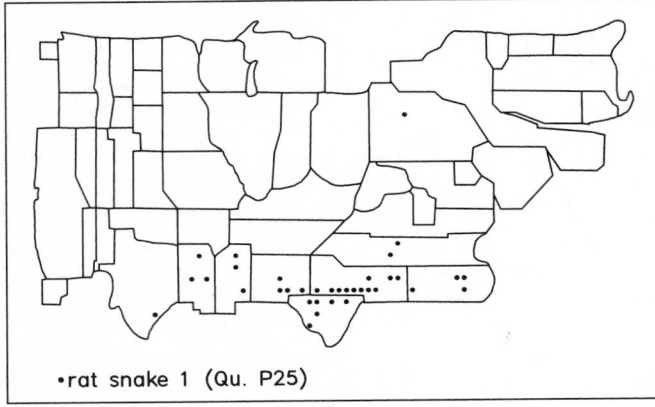

•rat snake 1 (Qu. P25)

2 =indigo snake.

1928 Baylor Univ. Museum *Contrib.* 16.16 **TX,** *Drymarchon couperi melanurus* [=*D. corais*]. . . Small, brightly colored examples are sometimes called *Indigo Snakes* and a few persons know the reptile as the *Rat Snake*. **1952** Ditmars *N. Amer. Snakes* 100, [It is not a rare sight in the South to see one or more of these big snakes [=*Drymarchon corais*] in immediate proximity to houses in the outlying districts. They are tolerated by the Negroes as ratters, and specimens have been known to remain for years about a plantation, even being picked up by children, who regard them as pets.] *Ibid* 186, *Blue Bull Snake, Mexican Rat Snake, Drymarchon corais melanurus.* . . The western form, occurring in southern and southwestern Texas, has considerable olive or dull brown on the upper portion.

rat stripper n
=mountain lover.

1892 *Jrl. Amer. Folkl.* 5.94 **NJ,** *Pachystima Canbyi,* rat-stripper. **1933** Small *Manual SE Flora* 818, *P[achystima] Canbyi.* . . *Rat-stripper.* . . Limestone cliffs and shaded banks.

ratsvane, rat's vein See ratsbane 1

rattail n

1 also *rattail fish:* A grenadier of the family Macrouridae: usu *Macrourus berglax,* but also **marlinspike 2** or other related fishes.

1882 U.S. Natl. Museum *Bulletin* 16.811, *M[acrourus] fabricii* [=*M.*

berglax]. . . *Rat-tail; Grenadier.* . . Massachusetts to Greenland and Norway, in deep water; not rare. **1884** Goode *Fisheries U.S.* 1.244, The Grenadiers. . . are particularly abundant in the Western Atlantic. . . The largest species, and the one best known to the fishermen, is *Macrurus rupestris* [=*Macrourus berglax*], called "Rat-tail Fish" as well as "Onion-fish". It is exceedingly abundant on all of our off-shore banks, attaining a length of three feet and a weight of four or five pounds. **1898** U.S. Natl. Museum *Bulletin* 47.2583, *Macrourus bairdii* [=*Nezumia b.*] . . Common Rat-tail. **1929** Pan-Pacific Research Inst. *Jrl.* 4.4.5 **CA,** *Coryphænoididae* [=Macrouridae]. The Grenadiers; Rat-tails. **1960** Amer. Fisheries Soc. *List Fishes* 22, Most grenadiers, or rat-tails, live in deep water, but one species is found in Atlantic shore waters.

2 =ratfish 1.

1884 Goode *Fisheries U.S.* 1.663, *Chimæra Colliei* [=*Hydrolagus c.*] . . This fish . . is known as the 'Rat-fish' or 'Rat-tail.' . . It is very abundant everywhere from Monterey Bay northward along the coast, especially in deep bays.

3 A knotweed 1 (here: *Polygonum virginianum*).   Cf **rattail grass 2**

1953 Strausbaugh–Core *Flora WV* 330, *T[ovara] virginiana.* . . *Virginia Knotweed. Rattail.* . . Stem terete, . . sheaths hairy and fringed; . . flowers in loose, naked, long and slender spikes. . . Common throughout the state.

4 =pickerelweed.

1966 *DARE* Wildfl QR Pl.8 Inf **NC**38, Rattails—used to be white.

5 A type of cigar; see quots.

1940 *AmSp* 15.335 **NE** [Smokers' slang], A cigar is *rope, a stogie, hemp, a havana, a rat-tail,* or *elropo*. **1968–70** *DARE* (Qu. DD6a, *Other names or nicknames for cigars*) Inf **KY**24, Pittsburgh stogies—made of inferior tobacco and called rattails; **PA**237, Rattails—Italian cigar; (Qu. DD7, *Different names for cigars . . according to size, shape, or the way they're made*) Infs **KY**24, **PA**167, Rattail.

6 See **rat dog 2a.**

rattail cactus n Also *rattail opuntia*
A **prickly pear 1** (here: *Opuntia leptocaulis*).

1893 *Garden and Forest* 6.429, Tasajo . . and the Rat-tail Opuntia . . are represented [in a display of cacti at the Columbian Exposition] by large plants. **1896** *Jrl. Amer. Folkl.* 9.189 **AZ,** *Opuntia frutescens* [=*O. leptocaulis*], rat-tail cactus. **1929** Dobie *Vaquero* 203 **SW,** *Tasajillo* (rat-tail cactus), which, excepting the *cholla*, has more thorns per square inch than any other growth known to vaqueros, which in winter is bizarre and beautiful with a studding of red berries that are fancied by blue topknot Mexican quail and wild turkeys. **1940** Writers' Program *Guide TX* 450 **csTX,** Here also grows every type of thorny vegetation known to the Southwest; the catclaw, huajillo, agarita, *vara dulce,* amargosa, rat tail cactus, Spanish dagger, and the shunned *junco*. **1961** Wills–Irwin *Flowers TX* 160, The Tasajillo, Rat-tail Cactus, or Pencil Cactus, is one of the slenderest cacti known, often forming thickets with its curving spiny stems.

rat-tailed maggot n Also *rattail maggot* [*OED2* 1768 →; see quot 1905]
The larva of a syrphid fly (*Eristalis* spp) used as bait in ice fishing.   Also called **ice mouse, mousie 1, spike**

1901 Howard *Insect Book* 152, The most famous of all the syrphus flies is . . *Eristalis tenax* and its larva is one of the rat-tailed maggots. **1905** Kellogg *Amer. Insects* 339, Those syrphid larvae most often written about are the curious "rat-tailed maggots" . . , larvae . . have the posterior extremity of the body greatly elongate and projecting to serve as a breathing-tube. There is a spiracle (breathing-pore) at the tip of this "tail," and the body projects upward so that its tip reaches the air, while the rest of the larva's body remains underneath the water. **1969** *WI Conserv. Bulletin* 34.3.31 **WI,** Another group of syrphus-flies, called drone flies, has larvae that . . have a telescoping tube at the rear of their bodies which they can extend several inches to the surface of the water for air. These long-tailed fellows are called rat-tailed maggots and they are well known to ice fishermen who use them for panfish bait. **1980** Milne–Milne *Audubon Field Guide Insects* 669, Larvae, called rat-tailed maggots, are usually found on wet carrion and in open latrines. **1987** *DARE* File **Madison WI,** A mousie is the larva of a syrphid fly, *Eristalis* spp, and is also called rattail maggot. It's widely distributed, but only called "mousie" in ice-fishing areas around here, probably in the Midwest.

rattail fish See **rattail 1**

rattail grass n

1 =**joint tail.**

1903 Small *Flora SE U.S.* 56, *Manisurus*. . . Perennial, often tall grasses, sometimes with rootstocks, narrow flat leaf-blades, and cylindric articulated terminal and axillary spikes. . . Rat-tail Grass.

2 A **lady's thumb** (here: *Polygonum persicaria*). Cf **rattail 3**

1966 *DARE* Wildfl QR Pl.47B Inf **CO**11, Rattail grass.

rattail maggot See **rat-tailed maggot**

rattail opuntia See **rattail cactus**

rattail pink n

An **ice plant 1.**

1892 *Jrl. Amer. Folkl.* 5.97 **MA**, *Mesembryanthemum*, sp. . . Rat-tail pink. Dorchester, Mass.

rattan (vine) n [Because it is used for some of the same purposes as the *rattan* palm]

=**supplejack** (here: *Berchemia scandens*).

1860 Curtis *Cat. Plants NC* 117, Rattan. Supplejack. . . A very tough flexible vine running up trees. . . The berry is dark purple . . with a thin coat and a hard smooth nut. **1901** *Torreya* 1.117 **GA**, *Berchemia scandens*. . . Rattan-vine. **1913** *Ibid* 13.232 **LA**, *Berchemia scandens*. . . Black-jack, rattan vine, Abbeville, La. **1933** Rawlings *South Moon* 41 **nFL**, Scrub met swamp in a twisting moil of briers and rattan and moccasins. Only cypresses reared their feathery heads from gigantic bases. **1941** Writers' Program *Guide AR* 301, Back in the shade are clumps of rattan, whose long, snake-like withes are used as whips by country boys to play "burn-out". The boys select five- or six-foot lengths of limber rattan, lock their left hands, and lay on until one or the other has had enough. **1960** Vines *Trees SW* 688, Another vernacular name [for *Berchemia scandens*] is Rattan-vine in allusion to the strong, pliant stems, which are much used in making wickerware. **1979** Ajilvsgi *Wild Flowers* 14 **wLA, eTX**, Muscadine *(Vitis rotundifolia)* and rattan-vine *(Berchemia scandens)*. . loop and twist about the smaller trees in their search for the sun. **1986** Pederson *LAGS Concordance,* 4 infs, **Gulf Region,** Rattan; 1 inf, **nwGA**, Rattan vines.

rat terrier n Pronc-sp *rat tarrier*

A small dog of a type sometimes used for hunting rats.

1855 Thomson *Doesticks* 284 **NY**, The chief . . pawned his uniform and star to get money to bet on a rat-terrier. **1867** Twain *Jumping Frog* 14 **MO**, Smiley had rat-tarriers, and chicken cocks, and tom-cats, and all them kind of things. **1892** M.A. Jackson *Gen. Jackson* 393 *(DAE)*, [His] walls were decorated with pictures of race-horses, fine stock, game-cocks, and a *famous rat-terrier!* **1892** *DN* 1.233 **KY**, Rat terrier [ræt tɛərɪə]. [In New England the second word is pronounced [tɛrɪə].] **1917** *DN* 4.398 **neOH**, Rat tarrier . . [ræt ˈtærɪɚ]. Rat terrier. Also Ill., Ia., Kan. **1946** McAtee *Dial. Grant Co. IN Suppl. 3* 8 (as of 1890s), *Rat terrier* . . the only terrier known to me in youth was so-called; it was used to kill rats routed from their harborage or released from a trap. I have seen the breed referred to in print as the black and tan terrier. **1959** Lahey–Hogan *As I Remember It* 14 **swKS** (as of 1890), Aunt Mary was so kind and joyful, and she brought home as a bride a little black rat-terrier dog which we dearly loved. **1986** Pederson *LAGS Concordance* **Gulf Region,** 7 infs, Rat terrier; 3 infs, Rat terrier—small, noisy (dog); 1 inf, Rat terrier—very mean; 1 inf, Rat terrier—very small. **1998** *NADS Letters* **MS**, I used to have a dog that was called a 'Rat Terrier'. The history I was given was that these dogs were once used expressly to root out rats and other vermin and are now used widely for possum hunting. They are seriously ugly dogs which definitely deserve the name. *Ibid* **MI**, I called . . to find out what a rat terrier was. Apparently they are small (16″ tall), short haired terriers, good for hunting rodents.

ratting See **rat** n **1**

rattle n [Abbr for **rattlesnake**] **chiefly S Atl, Gulf States** Cf **water rattle**

1949 *Scientific Mth.* 68.57, The dreaded water moccasin . . all too often turns out to be the banded water snake *(Natrix sipedon)*, erroneously called the "water rattle" and "water pilot" in certain localities. **1952** Ditmars *N. Amer. Snakes* 113, "Water Rattle" . . *Natrix taxispilota*. . .

Maryland to central Florida and westward to Louisiana. Particularly common in swampy waterways of South Carolina, Georgia and Florida. *Ibid* 114, These snakes . . [are] equally feared. . . One reason for respect with which they are held comes from a trait of lying in a circular coil, half hidden in matted swamp grass, and striking like a flash. . . In such places there is always the thought of the dangerous Canebrake Rattler, which coils in similar fashion and in color of dark individuals is not much different; hence a common name, among the Negroes, of this water snake—the "Water Rattle". **1967–70** *DARE* (Qu. P25, . . *Kinds of snakes*) Inf **GA**34, Grand [sic] rattle; **TX**37, Timber rattle; **NC**85, Water rattle—brown, speckled, not a rattlesnake. **1968** *DARE* Tape **CA**89, They had all these rattlesnakes there to watch 'em. Well, 'course we know that that'd be a good place for rattles. **1986** Pederson *LAGS Concordance (Snakes)* 1 inf, **csAL**, Ground rattle, water rattle—in water, has lost its rattle; 1 inf, **swAL**, Timber rattle; 1 inf, **ceMS**, Ground rattle [= rattler].

rattlebags n [*EDD* 1837] Cf **bull rattle, rattlebox 1d** =**bladder campion.**

1900 Lyons *Plant Names* 345, *S[ilene] vulgaris*. . . Rattle-bags. **1910** Graves *Flowering Plants* 180 **CT**, *Silene latifolia*. . . Rattle Bags. . . Grassland, roadsides and waste places. **1933** Small *Manual SE Flora* 507, *Silene latifolia*. . . Bladder-campion. Cow-bells. Rattle-bags.

rattlebag weed n Cf **rattlebox 1b, rattlepod 2, rattle vetch, rattleweed b**

A **milk vetch** (here: *Astragalus mollissimus*).

1940 Clute *Amer. Plant Names* 16, *A[stragalus] mollissimus*. . . Rattle-bag weed.

rattle band n Also *rattle banding* Cf **bull band,** *DS* AA18 =**shivaree** n **B1.**

1993 *AmSp* 68.220 **PA**, An item whose regional variants have been recognized and described for many years is the term for a 'noisy celebration given to a newly married couple by the neighbors where the couple is supposed to give a treat'. . . My own research into the dialect of south east-central Pennsylvania has led me to the discovery of still another living variant—*rattle band(ing)*.

rattle bean n

A **rattlebox 1h** (here: *Sesbania drummondii*).

1960 Vines *Trees SW* 545, Other common names for Drummond Rattlebox are . . Rattle Bean, Coffee Bean, and Senna.

rattle bells n Cf **rabbit bells** =**rattlebox 1a** (here: *Crotalaria* spp).

1953 Greene–Blomquist *Flowers South* 57, *Rattle-boxes, Rattle-bells (Crotalaria)*. . . When the seeds are mature, they come loose and rattle within the dry, inflated pod before it splits open.

rattlebox n

1 Any of var plants whose seed vessels rattle when dry; see below. Cf **rattlepod, rattleweed**

a A plant of the genus *Crotalaria*, esp *C. sagittalis*. Also called **rattle bells, rattlepod 1, rattleweed c;** for other names of var spp see **crazyweed, locoweed, rabbit bells, rattlesnake weed 1e, wild pea**

1817 Eaton *Botany* 80, *[Crotalaria] sagittalis*, (rattle-box). **1848** Gray *Manual of Botany* 108, *Crotalaria*. . . Rattle-box. . . Name from . . the loose seeds rattling in the coriaceous inflated pods. **1884** *Amer. Naturalist* 18.1148, Experiments . . prove that *Crotalaria sagittalis*, the Rattle-box, is a "loco-plant." **1898** *Jrl. Amer. Folkl.* 11.225 **IA**, *Crotalaria sagittalis*, . . rattle-box, Council Bluffs, Iowa. **1938** Baker *FL Wild Flowers* 103, Rattle-Box. . . These common peas of sandy ground bloom more or less all the year. **1943** Holt *G.W. Carver* 199, He would caution stockmen against the rattlebox *(Crotalaria)*. **1953** Greene–Blomquist *Flowers South* 57, Rattle-boxes. . . An infusion from the pods is used by the Seminoles as a cure for sore throat. **1979** Niering–Olmstead *Audubon Guide N. Amer. Wildflowers E. Region* 526, Rattlebox. . . The rattling of the dry seeds in the pod accounts for both the common and the genus names.

b also *rattlebox weed*: A **milk vetch** such as *Astragalus mollissimus.*

1871 U.S. Dept. Ag. *Rept. of Secy. for 1870* 419, *Milk vetch, (Astragalus.)*—A genus of leguminous plants, several species of which . . are commonly called Indian pea, pop-pea, ground plum, or rattle-box weed. **1896** *Jrl. Amer. Folkl.* 9.185 **CA,** *Astragalus mollissimus,* . . rattle-box weed, loco-weed. **1942** Hylander *Plant Life* 282, The Eastern Loco-weed or Rattlebox grows in the Atlantic coast region.

c A **silver bell 1** (here: *Halesia carolina*).

1884 Sargent *Forests of N. Amer.* 106, *Rattlebox.* . . *Silver-bell Tree.* . . Mountains of West Virginia to . . eastern Texas. **1903** Small *Flora SE U.S.* 915, *Mohrodendron Carolinum.* . . Rattlebox. **1927** Mason *Lure Great Smokies* 28, Plumed peawood—termed 'rattlebox' by the mountaineer. **1953** Greene–Blomquist *Flowers South* 95, The most common species of *H[alesia] carolina* which is . . called . . "Rattle-Box." . . It has a 4-winged fruit and is widely distributed in woods and on stream banks from the mountains to the lower Piedmont.

d =**bladder campion.** Cf **bull rattle, devil's-rattlebox, rattlebags**

1893 *Jrl. Amer. Folkl.* 6.138 **MA,** *Silene cucubalus,* rattle-box. Berkshire Co., Mass.

e A **false loosestrife** (here: *Ludwigia alternifolia*).

1900 Lyons *Plant Names* 230, *L[udwigia] alternifolia* . . , eastern U.S., is called . . Rattle-box. **1919** (1923) House *Wild Flowers NY* 187, *Rattlebox.* . . Fruiting capsule . . opening by an apical pore but finally also dehiscent; many seeded. **1930** OK Univ. Biol. Surv. *Pub.* 2.73, *Ludvigia alternifolia.* . . Rattle-box. **1966** DARE Wildfl QR Pl.145B Inf **SC**41, Rattlebox. **1967** DARE FW Addit Inf **AR**44, Rattlebox—*Ludwigia alternifolia.*

f A **partridge pea** (here: *Chamaecrista fasciculata*).

1909 DN 3.356 **eAL, wGA,** *Pepper-box.* . . The name of a small leguminous plant and its fruit. When the seeds are dry the pod makes a tiny rattle if shaken. Also called *partridge (pottige)-pea,* and *rattle-box.*

g A **wild yam** (here: *Dioscorea villosa*); also its seed vessel. Cf **devil's-bones**

1911 (1916) Porter *Harvester* 387 **IN,** I just noticed *discorea* [sic] *villosa* has the finest rattle boxes formed. *Ibid* 418, Sketch this sarsaparilla plant and this yam vine. It grows on your veranda, too—the rattle box, you remember.

h A plant of the genus *Sesbania,* usu *S. drummondii* or *S. punicea.* Also called **rattlebush 2, siene bean;** for other names of var species see **coffee bean 2, coffeeweed 1a, Colorado River hemp, indigo 2c, locust B2, macaw plant, poison bean, rattle bean, rattlepod 3, red locust 2**

1933 Small *Manual SE Flora* 704, *D[aubentonia] Drummondii* [= *Sesbania d.*] . . *Rattle-box.* . . Sandy waste-places and cult. grounds, Coastal Plain, Fla. to Tex. **1964** Kingsbury *Poisonous Plants U.S.* 353, *Sesbania spp.* . . Rattlebox. . . Three species of closely related legumes of the Gulf Coastal Plain have been found toxic to livestock. **1972** Brown *Wildflowers LA* 77, *Red Rattlebox—Daubentonia punicea.* . . Widespread but not abundant in southern Louisiana marshes. *Ibid* 78, *Rattlebox—Daubentonia texana.* . . Widely distributed in southern Louisiana from the Pearl River to the Sabine River margin of fresh-water marsh, often in standing water, on elevations in brackish and saline marshes. . . Seed reported as poisonous. **1979** Hallowell *People Bayou* 16 **sLA,** Woven into its [=the marsh's] fabric are over one hundred plant species, bearing such curious names as sensitive jointvetch, rattlebox, floating-heart, and stinking fleabane.

i A **bugbane 1** (here: *Cimicifuga americana*).

1949 Moldenke *Amer. Wild Flowers* 9, The *American-bugbane.* . . inhabits the mountains of central New York and Pennsylvania south to Tennessee and Georgia and is sometimes called *mountain-rattlebox* in allusion to the rattling noise produced by the seeds in the many dry follicles.

j A **senna** n[1] **B1** (here: *Senna covesii*).

1971 Dodge *100 Desert Wildflowers* 30 **SW,** Senna [=*Senna covesii*] is sometimes called "rattlebox" because the nearly ripe seeds rattle in their woody pods when the plant is stirred, startling the hiker who immediately thinks "rattlesnake!"

2 A talkative person. Cf **box** n **5a**

[**1860** *Harper's New Mth. Mag.* 20.192 **NEng,** Tom retorted on these cutting gifts with a present of a spelling-book (for Nelly never did spell quite right), and crushed the dearest friend into silence by the irony of a rattlebox!] **1869** *Ibid* 40.129, If you will but let me edge in one word, rattle-box, I will instruct you. **1919** DN 5.65 **NM** [Among hs students], *Rattle-box,* a talkative fellow; a flighty person. "She is such a rattle-box one cannot depend on her." **c1950** Halpert Coll. 52 **wKY, nwTN,**

Rattlebox = a chatterer. **1967–68** DARE (Qu. HH7a, *Someone who talks too much, or too loud: "He's an awful _____."*) Inf **ID**5, Jabberbox, chatterbox, loudmouth, blabbermouth, rattlebox; **WI**70, Gabber, rattlebox.

rattlebox weed See **rattlebox 1b**

rattlebrush See **rattlebush 2**

rattlebush n

1 A **wild indigo** (here: *Baptisia tinctoria*). [See quot 1922]

1828 Rafinesque *Med. Flora* 1.79, *Baptisia tinctoria.* . . Rattle-bush. [*Ibid* 80, Pistil . . succeeded by a swelled oblong pod of a bluish black color, with a row of small rattling seeds.] **1854** King *Amer. Eclectic Dispensatory* 272, *Baptisia tinctoria.* . . Rattle bush. **1892** (1974) Millspaugh *Amer. Med. Plants* 52-1, *Baptisia tinctoria.* . . *Com[mon] Names.*—Wild Indigo, . . rattle bush [etc]. **1922** *Amer. Botanist* 28.31, *B[aptisia] tinctoria.* . . is usually called "wild indigo." . . "Rattle-bush" refers to the ripe pods in which the seeds rattle, but the term is better deserved by allied species. **1971** Krochmal *Appalachia Med. Plants* 72, *Baptisia tinctoria.* . . Rattlebush. . . Most authors agree that the herb has value as a febrifuge, tonic, purgative, and antiseptic.

2 also *rattlebrush:* =**rattlebox 1h,** usu *Sesbania drummondii.* [See quot 1970]

1933 Small *Manual SE Flora* 704, *D[aubentonia] Drummondii* [= *Sesbania d.*] . . *Rattle-bush.* . . Sandy waste-places and cult. grounds, Coastal Plain, Fla. to Tex. **1949** Moldenke *Amer. Wild Flowers* 131, A great many of these [=members of the family Fabaceae], . . such as . . rattlebushes (*Daubentonia* [=*Sesbania*]). **1964** Kingsbury *Poisonous Plants U.S.* 353, *Sesbania spp.* . . Rattlebrush. . . Three species of closely related legumes of the Gulf Coastal Plain have been found toxic to livestock. **1970** Correll *Plants TX* 836, *Sesbania Drummondii.* . . *Rattlebush.* . . The seeds are loose in the mature pods which rattle when the bush is in motion, hence the common name. **1979** Ajilvsgi *Wild Flowers* 168, Rattlebush—*Sesbania drummondii.* . . Seeds reportedly poisonous to cattle.

rattle cohosh n Cf **rattletop 1**

A **bugbane 1** (here: *Cimicifuga racemosa*).

1910 Graves *Flowering Plants* 192 **CT,** *Cimicifuga racemosa.* . . Rattle Cohosh. . . Rich, often rocky woods. Norfolk, plentiful at one locality.

rattled snake See **rattlesnake 1**

rattle grass n Cf **rattlesnake grass 4**

A **bromegrass** (here: *Bromus briziformis*).

1973 Hitchcock–Cronquist *Flora Pacific NW* 625, Estab[lished] in waste areas, along roadsides, and on overgrazed land . . rattle grass. . . *B[romus] brizaeformis* [sic].

rattlehead, rattlemouth See **rattletongue**

rattlepod n [From the seed vessel, which rattles when dry] Cf **rattlebox, rattleweed**

1 =**rattlebox 1a.**

1824 Bigelow *Florula Bostoniensis* 267, *Crotalaria sagittalis.* . . *Rattle Pod.* . . A small hairy plant with turgid pods. **1861** Wood *Class-Book* 310, *Crotalaria.* . . Rattle Pod. . . From the rattling of the loose seeds in the horny pod. **1890** FL Ag. Exper. Sta. Gainesville *Bulletin* 8.12, *Occasional Weeds.* . . Crotalaria incana. . . Rattle Pod. **1970** Correll *Plants TX* 800, *Crotalaria.* . . *Rattlepod.* . . Legume greatly inflated, typically several to many-seeded.

2 =**milk vetch.**

1898 Davidson *CA Plants* 133, There are the "rattle-pods," so common in sandy soil; this plant is called loco weed by the stockmen, and is believed to loco horses. **1932** Rydberg *Flora Prairies* 476, *Phaca* [= *Astragalus*]. . . *Rattle-pod.* . . Pod membranous or papery, inflated. . . Seeds numerous. **1940** Gates *Flora KS* 204, Astragalus longifolius [= *A. ceramicus*]. . . Rattlepod. . . **1950** Stevens *ND Plants* 182, *Astragalus canadensis.* . . *Little Rattlepod.* . . The pod clusters remain stiffly upright all winter. Indian children used them for rattles. **1973** Hitchcock–Cronquist *Flora Pacific NW* 230, *Astragalus.* . . Locoweed; Milk-vetch; . . Rattle-pod.

3 A **rattlebox 1h.** Cf **rattlepod bean, siene bean**

1929 Dobie *Vaquero* 9 **TX,** To make sure that the firecrackers exploded in a strategic spot we cut siene (rattle pod) switches, split the ends, and inserted the firecrackers in the split.

4 A **false loosestrife** (here: *Ludwigia alternifolia*).

1931 Clute *Common Plants* 110, Among others that rattle without reference to serpents is the rattle-pod (*Ludwigia alternifolia*).

5 A **bugbane 1** (here: *Cimicifuga racemosa*).

1940 Clute *Amer. Plant Names* 256, *Cimicifuga racemosa.* Cohosh-bugbane, rattle-pod.

rattlepod bean n

See quot.

1951 *PADS* 15.34 **TX,** *Cassiaceae.* . . Mostly called coffee beans and rattle-pod beans.

rattler n

1 =**rattlesnake 1. widespread, but less freq NEng, Delmarva** See Map

1828 Cooper *Prairie* 2.257 **Plains States,** It would be no easy matter to judge of the temper of the rattler by considering the fashions of the moose. **1880** *Scribner's Mth.* 20.223 **Rocky Mts,** Out from the hole crawled a huge rattler. **1903** *DN* 2.326 **seMO,** *Rattler.* . . Rattlesnake. **1907** *DN* 3.205 **nwAR,** He killed a *rattler* that had ten rattles and a button. **1938** Matschat *Suwannee R.* 29 **neFL, seGA,** The black one a-tolls people in to whar the rattler can nip 'em. **1950** *WELS* **WI** (*Kinds of snakes found in your neighborhood*) 3 Infs, Rattler; 1 Inf, Swamp rattler. **1965–70** *DARE* (Qu. P25, . . *Kinds of snakes*) 370 Infs, **widespread, but less freq NEng, N Midl,** (Black, brown, field, marsh, mountain, sand, water, etc) rattler; **FL13,** King snake—kills rattlers. **1986** Pederson *LAGS Concordance,* 50 infs, **Gulf Region,** Rattler(s).

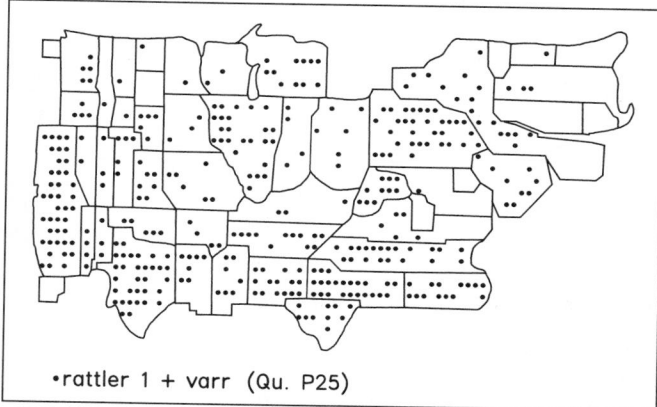

•rattler 1 + varr (Qu. P25)

2 An **oyster B1;** see quot. Cf **clucker 1**

1894 *DN* 1.333 **NJ,** *Rattlers:* oysters in poorest condition. So called because they rattle in their shells.

3 A **cricket frog** (here: *Acris gryllus*).

1882 *Amer. Naturalist* 16.707, Ditches in a low meadow were being repaired. . . The one striking feature of the locality, at this time, was the wonderful abundance of little "rattlers" (*Acris crepitans*), as I prefer to call them. **1932** Wright *Life-Hist. Frogs* 156, *Acris gryllus.* . . *Common Names.* . . Peeper. Rattler. . . Savannah Cricket Frog. [*Ibid* 169, If one can imagine a rattling of pebbles mingled with the screech of a violin string in a high note, he may have a suggestion of the cricket-frog's note.]

4 =**kingfisher.**

1919 Burns *Ornith. Chester Co. PA* 60, *Ceryle alcyon*—Belted Kingfisher, "kingfisher," "rattler."

5 An **earthworm;** see quot. Cf **ground rattler 2**

1966 *DARE* (Qu. P6, . . *Kinds of worms* . . *used for bait*) Inf **GA5,** Rattlers—up to 12 inches long, just like earthworms, caught by putting a stick in ground which they will crawl up on.

6 A **toy rattle.** [*OED2* "obs."] **esp Sth, S Midl** Cf **-er affix 1**

1934 (1943) W2, *Rattler.* . . *Obs.* . . A rattle. **1942** in 1944 *ADD* **Sth,** Baby's rattler. Radio, K. Kyser. **1968** *DARE* (Qu. EE34, . . *A child's toy*) Inf **NC82,** Rattler, teething ring, stuffed animals. **1986** Pederson *LAGS Concordance* (A toy) 2 infs, **neTN, swTN,** Rattler; 1 inf, **cAL,** Rattler—baby toy; 1 inf, **ceTX,** A rattler is a play-pretty.

rattleran(d) n [*rattle* (of uncertain sense) + *OED2 rand* sb.[1] 2.a "A strip or long piece . . of meat. . . Now only *dial.*" Cf Engl dial *plate-rand* (at *OED2 plate* sb. 12)] **MA** *arch*

The plate or rear under-portion of a forequarter of beef.

1859 in 1957 *Western Folkl.* 16.105 **MA,** What have you got to-day? Sirloin, good beefsteak, rattleran? **1867** De Voe *Market Asst.* 57 **ceMA,** The plate-piece (in Boston called *rattle-ran*) is commonly used for corned or salted beef, and the best for pressing. **1896** (c1973) Farmer *Orig. Cook Book* 183 **ceMA,** The best pieces of corned beef are the rattle rand and fancy brisket. . . The rattle rand contains a thick lean end; the second cut contains three distinct layers of meat and fat. . . The rattle rand has a thin end, which contains but one layer of lean meat and much fat. **1947** Bowles–Towle *New Engl. Cooking* 9 (as of c1850), *Century-Old Plymouth Succotash—*"One quart of large white beans . . ; six quarts of hulled corn; six to eight pounds of corned beef from the second cut of the rattle rand, which should be corned for only three or four days [etc]."

rattleroot n Cf **rattle cohosh, rattlepod 5, rattletop 1, rattleweed a**

A **bugbane 1** (here: *Cimicifuga racemosa*).

1876 Hobbs *Bot. Hdbk.* 95, Rattle-root, Black cohosh, Cimicifuga racemosa. **1892** (1974) Millspaugh *Amer. Med. Plants* 11-1, *Cimicifuga racemosa.* . . *Com[mon] names.* . . Rattle-root. **1949** Arnow *Hunter's Horn* 242 **KY,** Bill Dan vomited some more, his vomit smelling of pumpkin seed, walink, and rattleroot. **1966** *State* (Raleigh NC) 15 Aug 10/1 (*Mathews Coll.*), They'd climb the hills and search for rattleroot, stone root, jellicoe. **1971** Krochmal *Appalachia Med. Plants* 96, Rattle root. . . The roots and rhizomes are considered valuable in treating chronic rheumatism.

rattlesnake n

1 also rarely *rattled snake, rattletail* ~: A pit viper of the genus *Crotalus* or *Sistrurus.* **widespread, but less freq Inland Nth, N Midl, C Atl** See Map Also called **belltail, bush eel, buzz tail, rattle, rattler 1.** For other names of var snakes of the genus *Crotalus* see **black rattlesnake, brush rattler, diamondback rattlesnake, dog-headed ~, faded midget, green rattlesnake, mountain sidewinder, prairie rattlesnake, rock ~, sidewinder 1, speckled rattlesnake, tiger ~, timber ~;** for other names of var snakes of the genus *Sistrurus* see **black rattlesnake, ground ~ 1, highland rattler, massasauga, pygmy rattlesnake** Cf **dumb rattlesnake, water rattle** See also **coil snake, kitchen rattlesnake**

1630 Higginson *Nevv Englands Plantation* sig C3[r], There are some Serpents called Rattle Snakes, that haue Rattles in their Tayles. **1748** in 1889 Washington *Writings* 1.6 **VA,** This day see a Rattled snake, ye first we had seen in all our journey. **1792** Belknap *Hist. NH* 3.174, The rattle snake of New-Hampshire is of a darker colour, and less variegated than that which is found about the blue hills, in Suffolk county, Massachusetts. **1867** Cozzens *Sayings Dr. Bushwhacker* 106 **NY,** A Enormous Rattletail Snake—a regular whopper. **1894** *Jrl. Amer. Folkl.* 7.112 **Allegheny Mts,** Rattlesnake venom cures cramp-colic. **1950** *WELS* **WI** (*Kinds of snakes found in your neighborhood*) 11 Infs, Rattlesnake; 1 Inf, Diamondback rattlesnake. **1965–70** *DARE* (Qu. P25, . . *Kinds of snakes*) 294 Infs, **widespread, but less freq Inland Nth, N**

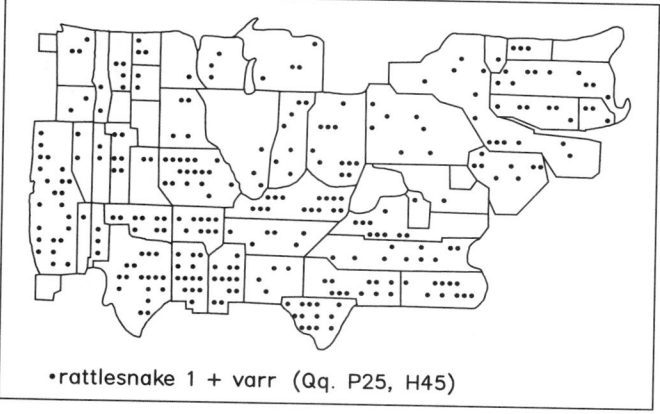

•rattlesnake 1 + varr (Qq. P25, H45)

Midl, C Atl, (Black, diamond, green, etc) rattlesnake; **CA**111, King snakes—devour the rattlesnakes [Of all Infs responding to the question, 54% were male; of those giving these responses, 67% were male.]; (Qu. H45, *Dishes made with meat, fish, or poultry that everybody around here would know, but that people in other places might not*) Inf **TX**33, Rattlesnake steak. **1986** Pederson *LAGS Concordance* **Gulf Region,** 149 infs, Rattlesnake(s); 1 inf, Rattlesnake meat edible.

2 See **rattlesnake melon.**

rattlesnake bite n Cf **rattlesnake-bite cure**

A **meadow rue** (here: *Thalictrum pubescens*).

    1892 *Jrl. Amer. Folkl.* 5.91 **NH,** *Thalictrum polygamum* [=*T. pubescens*], rattlesnake-bite. **1959** Carleton *Index Herb. Plants* 97, *Rattlesnake bite:* Thalictrum polygamum.

rattlesnake-bite cure n Cf **rattlesnake weed 1g**

A **wild carrot** (here: *Daucus pusillus*).

    1896 *Jrl. Amer. Folkl.* 9.189 **CA,** *Daucus pusillus,* . . rattlesnake-bite cure, *yerba del vibora* (Span.)

rattlesnake brome (or chess) See **rattlesnake grass 4**

rattlesnake fern n

Usu a grape fern of the genus *Botrychium,* esp *B. virginianum,* but also a **flowering fern.** [See quot 1968 *Foxfire*] Note: Many species of *Botrychium* were formerly included in *Osmunda.*

    1814 Pursh *Flora Americae* 2.656, *Botrychium.* . . *virginicum* [sic]. . . it is known by the name of *Rattle Snake Fern.* **1830** Rafinesque *Med. Flora* 2.201, *Botrychium.* . . *Rattlesnake Ferns.* Several species, mild astringents. *Ibid* 249, *Osmunda.* . . *Rattlesnake Fern.* Many Sp[ecies]. . . Roots demulcent, . . esculent. . . *O. virginica* [=*Botrychium virginianum*] deemed efficient for bites of Rattlesnakes. **1876** Hobbs *Bot. Hdbk.* 95, Rattlesnake fern, Botrychium fumarioides [=*B. biternatum*] and other species. **1911** Waters *Ferns* 327, Rattlesnake-fern. . . *Botrychium obliquum* [=*B. dissectum*]. **1931** Clute *Common Plants* 109, It will be recalled that the spore-cases of one of our ferns are borne in spikes that so strongly suggest the rattles of the rattlesnake that it is commonly known as the rattlesnake fern. **1968** McPhee *Pine Barrens* 131 **cNJ,** Wherry pointed out rattlesnake ferns. **1968** *Foxfire* June 51 **GA,** The rattlesnake fern (Botrychium virginianum) is. . . a lacy leaved fern with spikes of yellow-brown spore cases. . . [which] supposedly resemble the rattles of a rattlesnake. The bright yellow spore powder is applied to insect bites or snake bites. **1988** Werner *Life & Lore* 162 **IL,** There are several other native species with names that would also indicate value in treating rattlesnake bites. Yet none of them have been proven valuable for this purpose. The list includes Rattlesnake Fern, *Botrichium virginianum.*

rattlesnake flag n Cf **rattlesnake master d, ~ weed 1a**

A **button snakeroot 2,** usu *Eryngium aquaticum* or *E. yuccifolium.*

    1828 Rafinesque *Med. Flora* 1.88, This [=*Cimicifuga racemosa*] is one of the numerous Indian cures for the bites of snakes . . [9] but they consider the *Eryngium aquaticum* & *E. yuccifolium* (corn Snakeroot, or Rattle-snake flag) as by far more powerful and efficient. **1876** Hobbs *Bot. Hdbk.* 95, Rattlesnake flag, Corn snake root, Eryngium yuccefolium [sic]. **1900** Lyons *Plant Names* 150, *E[ryngium] aquaticum.* . . Rattlesnake Flag. . . *Root* acrid-aromatic, . . emetic. [Lyons: Other species are credited with similar properties.] **1949** Moldenke *Amer. Wild Flowers* 148, *E[ryngium] synchaetum* [=*E. yuccifolium*]. . . *Rattlesnakeflag* . . [is] applied to this and related species because of their reputed value in cases of snake bite. **1971** Krochmal *Appalachia Med. Plants* 114, *Eryngium aquaticum.* . . Rattlesnake flag.

rattlesnake grass n

1 also *rattlesnake manna grass:* A **manna grass** (here: *Glyceria canadensis*) native chiefly to the northeastern and north central US. Also called **pearl grass, quaking ~, Tuscarora rice**

    1814 Bigelow *Florula Bostoniensis* 25, *Briza Canadensis* [=*Glyceria canadensis*]. . . *Rattlesnake grass.* . . A large grass found in meadows and readily recognized by its swelling spikelets. **1843** Torrey *Flora NY* 2.466, *Glyceria Canadensis.* . . *Rattlesnake-grass.* . . Margins of swamps: rather frequent. **1889** Vasey *Ag. Grasses* 69, *Glyceria canadensis* (Rattlesnake Grass; Tall Quaking Grass). . . It is quite an orna-

mental grass, resembling the quaking grass *(Briza).* **1925** *Book of Rural Life* 6.3344, *G[lyceria] canadensis,* a pretty plant found in wet places in the North, is called *rattlesnake grass* for no particular reason; certainly the large pyramidal, purplish panicles do not rattle. **1952** Strausbaugh–Core *Flora WV* 138, Rattlesnake Mannagrass. . . Blades rough on both sides. **1966** *Good Old Days* 2.11.27 **cIL** (as of 1907), Part of the road I traveled ran through the Sangamon River bottom. Sometimes in the fall of the year, I would stop by the roadside and gather some rattle snake grass for decorative purposes. **1988** Werner *Life & Lore* 162 **IL,** There are several other native species with names that would also indicate value in treating rattlesnake bites. Yet none of them have been proven valuable for this purpose. The list includes . . Rattlesnake Grass, *Glyceria canadensis.*

2 A grass of the genus *Briza.* [See quot 1925]

    1822 Eaton *Botany* 211, *[Briza] maxima* (rattlesnake grass . .) spike cordate, about 7-flowered. Flowers very large. **1836** (1840) Phelps *Lectures on Botany* 82, *Briza.* . . *media,* (quaking grass, rattlesnake grass . .) panicle erect. **1895** Gray–Bailey *Field Botany* 474, *Briza maxima.* . . *Large Quaking Grass* or *Rattlesnake Grass.* . . Spikelets . . becoming dry and papery, rattling in the wind,—whence the common name. **1925** *Book of Rural Life* 8.4656, Rattlesnake Grass—(Briza media and B. minor). . . is so-called because the dried flower clusters rattle when shaken, the sound resembling that made by a rattlesnake.

3 =**slough grass.**

    1911 *Century Dict. Suppl., Slough-grass.* . . A stout subaquatic perennial grass, *Beckmannia erucæformis.* . . It bears narrow one-sided spikes suggesting the rattle of a rattlesnake, whence sometimes called *rattlesnake-grass.*

4 also *rattlesnake brome,* ~ *chess:* A **bromegrass** (here: *Bromus briziformis*). [See quot 1941] **esp NW, Pacific** Cf **rattle grass**

    1923 Abrams *Flora Pacific States* 1.233, *Bromus brizaeformis.* . . Rattlesnake Grass. . . Washington to California, rare in the eastern States. **1937** St. John *Flora SE WA & ID* 34, *Rattlesnake Brome.* . . Spikelets . . elliptical, compressed. **1941** Writers' Program *Guide CO* 306 **seCO,** In spring and early summer, stretches of prairie land here are carpeted with . . brome grasses. One variety . . , known as rattlesnake grass, grows close to the ground and dies before the dry season. When walked upon, it gives forth a rustling sound. **1952** Davis *Flora ID* 94, *Rattlesnake Chess.* . . This is fair forage for stock. **1973** Hitchcock–Cronquist *Flora Pacific NW* 625, Rattlesnake g[rass]. . . B[romus] brizaeformis.

rattlesnake juice See **rattlesnake oil**

rattlesnake killer n
=**roadrunner 1.**

    1877 Hodge *Arizona* 224, There is also a small bird, no larger than the wren, which is called the rattlesnake-killer. **1917** *Wilson Bulletin* 29.2.81, *Geococcyx californianus.* . . Local names. . . Racer, rattlesnake-killer, road-runner [etc]. **1955** *AmSp* 30.183 **TX,** The road runner has won . . other names denoting its prowess in snake-dispatching: . . *rattlesnake killer.*

rattlesnake leaf n

A **rattlesnake plantain 1** (here: *Goodyera pubescens*).

    1822 Eaton *Botany* 294, *[Goodyera] pubescens* (rattle-snake leaf). . . This plant is confounded with the Hieracium venosum by our root doctors, as the leaves of both are reticulate, radical and depressed. **1830** Rafinesque *Med. Flora* 2.224, *Goodyera pubescens.* . . *Rattle snake leaf.* . . Deemed by some empirics a specific for the scrofula, the fresh leaves are applied . . and the warm infusion used as tea freely. **1876** Hobbs *Bot. Hdbk.* 95, Rattlesnake leaf, Net leaf plantain, Goodyera pubescens. **1924** *Amer. Botanist* 30.151, *Epipactis pubescens* . . is still another witness to the association of harmless plants with poisonous serpents. In this case there is slightly more reason for the name for the leaves are finely reticulated with white which might be held to simulate scales. . . The plant is known as . . "rattlesnake leaf."

rattlesnake manna grass See **rattlesnake grass 1**

rattlesnake master n Also *rattlesnake's master* Cf **rattlesnake-bite cure, rattlesnake root, ~ weed**

Any of var plants that have been used to treat snakebite, as:
a A **rattlesnake root 2b** (here: *Prenanthes alba*). *obs*

    1806 Beers *Farmer's Calendar* (Utica NY) sig D4[r], Notwithstanding a free use of sweet oil, plantane, hoarhound, *prenanthet* [sic] *alba,* called here rattlesnake's master, &c. the swelling and pain progressed.

b =blazing star 3, esp *Liatris scariosa* or *L. squarrosa.*

1814 Pursh *Flora Americae* 2.509, L[*iatris*] *scariosa.* . . In mountain meadows: Virginia to Carolina. . . L[*iatris*] *squarrosa.* . . In sandy woods and fields: Virginia, Kentucky, and Carolina. . . This [=*L. squarrosa*] and the preceding [=*L. scariosa*] are known among the inhabitants of those countries by the name of *Rattle-snake's Master.* **1830** Rafinesque *Med. Flora* 2.237, *Liatris.* . . Many vulgar names, . . *Rattlesnake master,* . . *Rough root,* &c. All have a tuberous medical root . . smelling like turpentine or juniper. . . Very useful in dropsy, . . pains in the breast, after pains of women and bites of snakes, both internally and topically. **1836** Latrobe *Rambler in N. Amer.* 1.126 **MO,** Every where among the long grass, the *Liatris,* or rattlesnakes'-master shoots up, and displays its spike of red flowers. **1840** MA *Zool. & Bot. Surv. Herb. Plants & Quadrupeds* 121, *Liatris.* . . The species are considered an antidote for the bite of the rattlesnake, and *L. scariosa* is often called *Rattlesnake's Master.* **1876** Hobbs *Bot. Hdbk.* 96, Rattlesnakes' master, Water eryngo, Eryngium aquaticum. . . Button snake root, Liatris spicata. . . Blazing star, *[Liatris]* squarrosa. . . False aloe, Agave Virginica. [**1901** Lounsberry *S. Wild Flowers* 501, Through the South they [=plants of the genus *Liatris*] are rather generally looked upon as rattlesnake-masters. . . *L. squarrosa.* . . is . . , perhaps more than any other, . . sought as a rattlesnake-master. From the globular tubers a decoction is made, "powerful good" to cure snake-bites. . . *L. spicata.* . . When the rattlesnakes are less vicious than their wont, it seems that the decoction made from this plant is held in reserve to cure backache.] **1931** Harned *Wild Flowers Alleghanies* 505, [*Liatris squarrosa* is] also called Colic-root and Rattlesnake-master. The tuberous root has been used for sore throat and the bruised pulp for snake bites.

c An **agave** (here: *Manfreda virginica*).

1830 Rafinesque *Med. Flora* 2.187, *Agave virginica* [=*Manfreda v.*] . . *Rattlesnake master.* . . Chewed in obstinate diarrhoea by the Cherokees, violent, but efficient. **1894** *Jrl. Amer. Folkl.* 7.101 **SC,** *Agave Virginica,* . . rattlesnake's master. **1930** OK *Univ. Biol. Surv. Pub.* 2.56, False Aloe. Rattlesnake Master. **1970** Correll *Plants TX* 423, *False aloe, rattlesnake-master.* Leaves all from the base. **1975** Duncan–Foote *Wildflowers SE* 264, *Rattlesnake-master.* . . Common. Dry, rocky, sandy places, thin woods. **1988** Werner *Life & Lore* 163 **IL,** Rattlesnake Master, *Agave virginica.* . . The Meskwakis used the root of Rattlesnake Master for the bites of rattlesnakes and several other kinds of venomous animals.

d =button snakeroot 2, usu *Eryngium aquaticum* or *E. yuccifolium.* Cf **rattlesnake flag**

1857 Gray *First Lessons* 151, E[*ryngium*] *yuccæfolium.* . . *Rattlesnake-Master.* . . New Jersey to Wisconsin, and southward. **1870** (**1871**) *Amer. Naturalist* 4.581, Other remarkable forms are the Indian plantain . . and the yucca-leaved rattlesnake master *(Eryngium yuccæfolium),* with its linear grass-like, bristly fringed leaves. **1911** NJ *State Museum Annual Rept. for 1910* 594, *Eryngium aquaticum.* . . *Rattlesnake Master.* . . Common on the salt marshes of the coast. . . A peculiar plant. . . *Eryngium yuccifolium.* . . *Tall Rattlesnake Master.* **1936** Whitehouse *TX Flowers* 89, Other common names of this group [= plants of the genus *Eryngium*] include . . rattlesnake master, and button snake-root, the two latter from their accredited property of curing snake-bites. **c1938** in 1970 Hyatt *Hoodoo* 1.244 [Black], Yo' kin take, now, if yo' want a good *gamblin' hand*—now, yo' kin go out an' dere's somepin out in de woods grows dat called rattlesnake master [Hyatt: or button snakeroot *(Eryngium aquaticum)* southern U.S.A.] . . One's a she an' one's de man—one grows a white flower, dat's de she; an' de one dat grows de red flower, dat de man. **1953** Greene–Blomquist *Flowers South* 84, *Rattlesnake-Masters (Eryngium).* . . The odd shape and color of their leaves and button-like heads . . make them useful. **1979** Niering–Olmstead *Audubon Guide N. Amer. Wildflowers E. Region* 330, *Rattlesnake Master (Eryngium yuccifolium).* . . They [=leaves] were once credited with a variety of curative powers.

e =starry campion.

1898 U.S. *Bur. Amer. Ethnology Annual Rept. for 1897* 1.426, The campion *(Silene stellata),* locally known as "rattlesnake's master". . . Among the white mountaineers, the juice is held to be a sovereign remedy for snake bites, and it is even believed that the deadliest snake will flee from one who carries a small portion of the root in his mouth. **1970** *NC Folkl.* 8.29, According to Cherokee Indians, you will die [if bitten by a rattlesnake] unless you use great plant campion or "rattlesnake's master" *(Silene stella)* to counteract the bite.

f A **speedwell** (here: *Veronica officinalis*).

1898 *Plant World* 2.198 **sPA,** Rattlesnake Master for *Veronica officinalis* . . , the . . [name] derived from the use of the plant as a remedy for snake bites.

g A **fringed orchid** (here: *Platanthera ciliaris*).

[**1901** Lounsberry *S. Wild Flowers* 76, *Rattlesnake's Master.* . . *Habenaria ciliaris* [=*Platanthera c.*] . . The yellow fringed orchid is one of the plants that appeals strongly to the native mountaineers who respect it as a rattlesnake's master. In its deeply fringed lip they claim a resemblance to the forked tongue of the snake, while the anther sacs represent to them his fangs. But although staunchly asserting the efficacy of various plants in this cause the conscientious native, when asked if he would rely on one for his own cure, usually answers: "Wall no, I'd take whiskey."] **c1938** in 1970 Hyatt *Hoodoo* 1.634 **swAL** [Black inf], "What does rattlesnake master look like?" "It's a lily—looks kinda like a lily. It grows in de woods." "Has a flower on it?" "Yes, suh, it has a yellah flow'r and when yo' see one it looks jes' like a snake's mouth." *Ibid* **seGA,** It's a thing look like a lily, name of rattlesnake master. Dat's one of de luckiest roots dey is out for business. Take dis heah rattlesnake master an' set it out in a bucket like yo' would a lily—or pot—an' take some water an' spit on it ever' mornin'. Business will come to yo'. **1950** Correll *Native Orchids* 64, *Habenaria ciliaris.* . . Rattlesnake's Master.

h A **rattlesnake plantain 1** (here: *Goodyera pubescens*). Cf **rattlesnake leaf, ~ tongue**

1938 Matschat *Suwannee R.* 87 **neFL, seGA,** Thar be the rattlesnake master [Matschat: rattlesnake plantain], an' all he need to do was to chaw the leaves. [**1943** Peattie *Great Smokies* 189, A little orchid, the rattlesnake plantain, with net-veined leaves, looks enough like a snakeskin to suggest that it may be a "rattlesnake master" or cure for snake bites.]

i An asterlike plant (here: *Sericocarpus linifolius*).

1959 Carleton *Index Herb. Plants* 98, Rattlesnake master: . . Sericocarpus bifoliatus [=*S. linifolius*].

rattlesnake melon n Also *rattlesnake (watermelon), Georgia rattlesnake (melon);* for addit varr see quots **chiefly Sth, S Midl**

A cultivar of the **watermelon** that has a rind with prominent markings resembling those of a **rattlesnake 1.**

1855 Davis *Farm Bk.* 152 *(DA)* **AL,** This day has been spent in planting small patch crops—Watermelons—Muskmelons—Squashes cucumbers—Rows 1 to 8 Rattlesnake . . 9 to 13 Ice Rind. **1883** GA *Dept. Ag. Pub. Circular No. 35* 8.47, Water-melons. "Rattle-snake". . . Commenced to ripen July 16th. An excellent variety. **1909** *DN* 3.362 **eAL, wGA,** Rattlesnake(-melon). . . A favorite variety of watermelons, having a light gray rind with dark green stripes, somewhat like the coloration of the rattlesnake. **1954** *Harder Coll.* **cwTN,** Rattlesnake watermelon—long, green with white stripes. **1965–70** *DARE* (Qu. I26, . . *Kinds of melons)* Infs **FL6, 37, KY28, LA28, NC50,** Georgia rattlesnake melons; **CO20, GA72, IL117, MS35, MO9, TX42,** Rattlesnake melons; **NC55, OH22, TX54,** Rattlesnake watermelons. **1986** Pederson *LAGS Concordance* **Gulf Region,** 64 infs, Rattlesnake(s); 25 infs, Georgia rattlesnake(s); 13 infs, Rattlesnake melon(s); 4 infs, Rattlesnake watermelon(s); 1 inf, Colorado rattlesnake; 1 inf, Dixie rattlesnake; 1 inf, Florida rattlesnake; 1 inf, Rattlesnake color—with stripes, red meat; 1 inf, Rattlesnake stripe. **1988** Whealy *Garden Seed Inventory* (2d ed) 399, Watermelons. . . *Georgia Rattlesnake* . . Old Southern favorite . . , thin very tough rind, light-green with irregularly mottled dark-green Rattlesnake-like stripes, firm sweet bright-rose flesh. **1990** *Seed Savers Yearbook* 258, Georgia Rattlesnake . . pale-green with dark-green stripes, very long shape, 30 lbs. and up. *Ibid* 260, *Rattlesnake* . . 10–50 lbs., long light green rind covered with rattlesnake markings of darker green, very sweet and good.

rattlesnake oil n Also *rattlesnake juice, ~ whisky* Cf **snake oil**

Poor-quality or illicit whiskey.

1867 Baker *Hist. U.S. Secret Serv.* 246, It is hardly worth the while to present to the Government a bill for a few decanters and rattlesnake whisky. **1965–70** *DARE* (Qu. DD21a, *General words . . for any kind of liquor)* Inf **GA72,** Rattlesnake juice; (Qu. DD21b, *General words . . for bad liquor)* Infs **AZ13, 15, CA105, KS18, MS59, NY89,** Rattlesnake oil; **OH76,** Rattlesnake juice; (Qu. DD21c, *Nicknames for whiskey, espe-*

cially illegally made whiskey) Inf **GA**72, Rattlesnake juice. **1969** *DARE* Tape **GA**72, We have a variety of names for this homemade whiskey in this county. . . rattlesnake juice.

rattlesnake pike n

A **sauger** n[1] (here: *Stizostedion canadense*).

1947 Dalrymple *Panfish* 220, Colloquially, the Sauger is also your old friend the Sand Pike, or Gray Pike, or Ground Pike, or Rattlesnake Pike, or Pickerel, or Pickering, or—of all things—Horse-fish!

rattlesnake pilot n chiefly Sth Cf pilot snake

1 also *pilot rattlesnake, rattlesnake's pilot:* =**copperhead snake 1.** [See quot 1928]

1851 *De Bow's Rev.* 11.53 **LA**, *Rattlesnake Pilot*—Small, short, having a button on the end of the tail; said to be poisonous. **1928** Baylor Univ. Museum *Contrib.* 16.19 **TX**, *Rattlesnake's Pilot* is the commonest vernacular name for the Copperhead and is based on the old bottomland myth that this snake leads the rattlesnake to its prey. **c1940** Newman–Murphy *Conserv. Notes* 5 **LA**, Among the poisonous snakes may be mentioned . . copper head (rattlesnake pilot). **1950** *PADS* 14.56 **SC**, *Rattlesnake pilot.* . . The copperhead. There seems to be no factual basis for the name. **c1960** *Wilson Coll.* **csKY**, Rattlesnake pilot. . . A snake that is supposed to accompany a rattlesnake. **1965–70** *DARE* (Qu. P25, . . *Kinds of snakes*) Infs **AR**52, **LA**2, 7, 15, 20, **SC**7, 43, Rattlesnake pilot(s); **IL**4, Rattlesnake pilots are the nonpoisonous, non-rattling variety of rattlers; **LA**8, Rattlesnake pilot—poison; **SC**40, Rattlesnake pilot—reputedly signal the nearness of a rattler; **SC**63, Rattlesnake pilot—marked like a rattler, no rattles—reportedly poisonous; **GA**16, Pilot rattlesnake. [*DARE* Ed: Some of these Infs may refer instead to **2** below.] **1986** Pederson *LAGS Concordance*, 7 infs, 4 **MS**, 2 **AL**, 1 **csLA**, Rattlesnake pilot(s); 1 inf, **cAL**, Rattlesnake pilot—he's got three or four names; 1 inf, **seAL**, Rattlesnake pilot—female snake; 1 inf, **swAL**, Rattlesnake pilot = copperhead; 1 inf, **cwAL**, Rattlesnake pilot—local term for copperhead; 1 inf, **cwAR**, Rattlesnake pilot—small snake 15–18″ long. [*DARE* Ed: Some of these infs may refer instead to **2** below.]

2 a **king snake 1** (here: *Lampropeltis getulus*). [See quot 1894]

1894 U.S. Natl. Museum *Proc.* 17.324 **FL**, *Lampropeltis getulus.* . . Rather common in south Florida, where it is sometimes known under the name of "king snake," and is then said to kill and devour the rattlesnake. Sometimes it is called "rattlesnake pilot," and is then regarded as the guide of that snake! **1967** *DARE* (Qu. P25, . . *Kinds of snakes*) Inf **TX**1, King snake (rattlesnake pilot).

rattlesnake plantain n

1 An orchid of the genus *Goodyera*. [See quots 1778, 1987] Also called **lattice leaf, rattlesnake violet 2;** for other names of var spp see **adder's tongue 2, ~ violet 1, ratsbane 2, rattlesnake leaf, ~ master h, ~ root 2h, ~ tongue, ~ weed 1d, scrofulaweed, squirrel ear, white plantain**

1778 Carver *Travels N. Amer.* 482, Remedies . . Providence has bounteously supplied, by causing the Rattle Snake Plantain, an approved antidote to the poison of this creature, to grow in great profusion where-ever they are to be met with. **1843** Torrey *Flora NY* 2.284, *Goodyera pubescens.* . . Rattlesnake Plantain. . . Rhizoma somewhat branching, throwing off thick fleshy fibrous roots. **1897** Robinson *Uncle Lisha's Outing* 32 **wVT**, Tangles of hobble bush sprawled over the russet carpet of hemlock leaves, gayly flecked with variegated rattlesnake plantain. **1906** (1918) Parsons *Wild Flowers CA* 100, The rattlesnake plantain is frequently met with under the coniferous trees of our northern woods. Its common name comes from the mottling of its leaves, which is similar to that of the rattlesnake's skin. **1966–67** *DARE* Wildfl QR Pl.41A Infs **CO**7, **WA**10, Rattlesnake plantain; Pl.41B Infs **MI**57, **NY**91, Rattlesnake plantain; **MI**7, Rattlesnake plantain—checked and white-ribbed leaves; [**MI**31, Rattlesnake something]. **1968** *DARE* (Qu. S26c, *Wildflowers that grow in woods*) Inf **PA**89, Rattlesnake plantain. **1987** Case *Orchids* 190, The snakelike patterns of the leaves, the plantainlike leaf rosette, and the long, slender flower spike combine to give the group [= *Goodyera* spp] their common name—rattlesnake plantains.

2 also *rattlesnakes' plantain:* A **pussytoes** (here: either *Antennaria dioica* or *A. plantaginifolia*).

1830 Rafinesque *Med. Flora* 2.224, The *Gn[aphalium] plantagineum* and *dioicum* [=*Antennaria plantaginifolia* and *A. dioica*] . . have many names, . . *Rattle snake plantain* [etc]. . . Both . . used . . against the negro poison and rattle snake bites: Indians will for a trifle allow them-

selves to be bitten and cure themselves at once. **1876** Hobbs *Bot. Hdbk.* 96, Rattlesnakes' plantain, . . *Antennaria plantagineum.* . . *Goodyera repens.*

rattlesnake root n Cf rattlesnake master, ~ weed, snakebite, snakeroot

1 Any of var plants that have been used to treat snakebite.

1687 in 1964 *Ethnohistory* 11.12 **VA**, Among their herbs I have had 40 several sorts or near that number showed me as great secrets, for the *Rattle-snake root,* or that kind of *snake root* which is good for curing the bite of the *rattlesnake.* But I have no reason to beleive that any of them are able to effect the cure. **1698** (1848) Thomas *Hist. & Geog. Acct.* 19 **PA**, There grows also in great plenty the *Black Snake-Root,* . . *Rattle-Snake-Root, Poke-Root,* called in *England Jallop.* **1759** in 1775 Burnaby *Travels* 7 **VA**, Tobacco and Indian corn are the original produce of the country; likewise the pigeon-berry and rattle-snake-root. **1792** Pope *Tour* 98, *Rattle-snake* Root . . from its strong aromatic Smell, the *Rattle-Snake* will never approach, and [it] is accordingly used by the *Indians* to banish *that* and other Serpents from their Lodgments. **1945** Saxon *Gumbo Ya-Ya* 543 **LA**, *Other conjure paraphernalia.* . . Rattlesnake Root. **1967** *DARE* Tape **TX**1A, Well, he used pecan bark, and he used balmony, and he used prickly ash, and he used scrap bark, and he used . . rattlesnake root. . . Queen's delight was a blood purifier.

2 Spec:

a An **Indian poke 1** (here: *Veratrum viride*). *obs* Cf **rattlesnake weed 1k**

1743 (1946) Gronovius *Flora Virginica* 195, *Veratrum caule simplicissimo.* . . floribus albis spicatum dense stipatis, caule singulari, foliis plantagineis humi stratis, . . radice magna tuberosa. *Rattle-Snake-root.* . . Radix masticata nauseum movet. [=*Veratrum with a very simple stalk.* . . [and] a spike of crowded white flowers, a single stalk, plantain-like leaves lying on the ground, a large twisted tuberous rootstock. *Rattle-Snake-root.* . . The chewed root causes nausea.]

b also *rattlesnakes' root:* A plant of the genus *Prenanthes.* Also called **cankerweed, drop flower, gall of the earth 2, lion's foot, white lettuce;** for other names of var spp see **cancerweed 1, cankerroot 3, joy-leaf, milkweed 5, rattlesnake master a, snake gentian, wild lettuce**

1682 (1836) Ash *Carolina* 11, They have three sorts of the *Rattle-Snake Root* which I have seen; the *Comous* or *Hairy,* the *Smooth,* the *Nodous* or *Knotted* Root: All which are lactiferous, or yielding a *Milkie Juice.* **1760** Lee *Intro. Botany* 314, Rattlesnake Root, Dr. Witts, *Prenanthes.* **1837** Darlington *Flora Cestrica* 444 **sePA**, *P[renanthes] alba.* . . Rattle-snake root. . . The *root* of the *P. serpentaria* . . is one of the many frontier remedies for the bite of snakes. **1876** Hobbs *Bot. Hdbk.* 96, Rattlesnakes' root, . . *Nabalus albus.* . . *Trillium pendulum.* . . *Cimicifuga racemosa.* **1910** Graves *Flowering Plants* 413 **CT**, *Prenanthes.* . . Rattlesnake-root. [*Ibid* 414, All species of *Prenanthes* have been used as a remedy for the bites of venomous snakes.] **1936** IL Nat. Hist. Surv. *Wildflowers* 391, The Rattlesnake Root . . , *Prenanthes racemosa* . . , grows in marshes and other open wet places. . . The . . Tall Rattlesnake Root, *Prenanthes trifoliata* [sic]. . . grows in thickets and woods. **1941** Walker *Lookout* 49 **TN**, The old man reached his bony fingers into his trouser pocket and drew out a small rattlesnake-root about an inch long, with the request that it be eaten. **1973** Hitchcock–Cronquist *Flora Pacific NW* 542, Arrow-l[eaf] r[attlesnake-root]. . . *P[renanthes] sagittata.* . . Western r[attlesnake-root]. . . *P. alata.* **1988** Werner *Life & Lore* 162 **IL**, There are several other native species with names that would also indicate value in treating rattlesnake bites. Yet none of them have been proven valuable for this purpose. The list includes . . Rattlesnake Root, *Chamaelirium luteum* . . [and] *Pre[n]anthes* (several species).

c also *rattlesnake snakeroot:* =**Seneca snakeroot.**

1738 *Va. Gazette* 30 June 4/2 *(DA)*, The Seneca Rattle-Snake Root must be more extensive use than any Medicine in the *Materia Medica.* **1806** *Thomas' MA Spy or Worcester Gaz.* (MA) 30 Apr, Seneca, or rattle snake root . . has been celebrated as a specific in the cure of croup. **1840** Pereira *Elem. Mat. Med.* II.1257 *(OED2)*, Senega or seneka root . . sometimes called the seneka-snake-root, or the rattlesnake-root, is imported from the United States in bales. **1900** Lyons *Plant Names* 298, *P[olygala] Senega.* . . Canada to N. Carolina, west to Minnesota. . . Rattlesnake root. **1940** Clute *Amer. Plant Names* 125, *P[olygala] Senega.* . . Rattlesnake snake-root. **1979** Erichsen-Brown

Med. N. Amer. Plants 360, *Common names* [of *Polygala senega*]: Senega root, rattlesnake root, mountain flax.

d A **colicroot 2** (here: prob *Aletris farinosa*).   *obs*   Cf **bitter grass**

1744 (1841) Byrd *Westover MSS* 40 **VA,** I found near our camp some plants of that kind of rattlesnake root, called star-grass. The leaves shoot out circularly, and grow horizontally and near the ground. The root is in shape not unlike the rattle of that serpent, and is a strong antidote against the bite of it. It is very bitter, and where it meets with any poison, works by violent sweats, but where it meets with none, has no sensible operation but that of putting the spirits into a great hurry, and so of promoting perspiration.

e also *rattlesnakes' root:* A **bugbane 1** (here: *Cimicifuga racemosa*).

1828 Rafinesque *Med. Flora* 1.85, *Botrophis serpentaria* [=*Cimicifuga racemosa*]. . . Rattle-Snake-root. [*Ibid* 88, This is one of the numerous Indian cures for the bites of snakes: they use the root chewed and applied to the wound.] **1876** [see **2b** above]. **1892** (1974) Millspaugh *Amer. Med. Plants* 11-1, *Cimicifuga racemosa*. . . *Rattlesnake root.* [*Ibid* 11-2, It was also used as a remedy against the bites of venomous snakes, with what success history does not relate, but we can easily judge.] **1930** Sievers *Amer. Med. Plants* 23, Rattlesnake-root. . . is a conspicuous woodland plant on account of its tall flowering spikes. **1971** Krochmal *Appalachia Med. Plants* 96, Rattlesnake root. . . In Appalachia, a tea made from the root is used to treat sore throat.

f also *rattlesnakes' root:* A **trillium**, usu either **nodding trillium** or *Trillium erectum*.

1830 Rafinesque *Med. Flora* 2.96, *Trillium latifolium* [=*T. erectum*]. . . Rattlesnake Root. [*Ibid* 103, They say . . that the roots [of *Trillium* spp] chewed, will cure instantly the bite of rattle-snakes, both in men and cattle. Mr. Hawkins saw an Indian make the experiment for a gill of rum: how it acts was not stated.] **1876** [see **2b** above]. **1892** (1974) Millspaugh *Amer. Med. Plants* 175-1, Trillium erectum. . . Purple trillium, . . Rattlesnake root. **1971** Krochmal *Appalachia Med. Plants* 256, *Trillium erectum*. . . Rattlesnake root. . . The Indians of Appalachia cooked pieces of the root in food as an aphrodisiac.

g =**blazing star 2.**

1830 Rafinesque *Med. Flora* 2.182, *Abalon . . albiflorum* [= *Chamaelirium luteum*] . . *Rattle-snake Root.* . . Used by empirics and Indians for cholics, fevers, worms, &c. **1950** Gray–Fernald *Manual of Botany* 425, *Rattlesnake-root.* . . Meadows, thickets and rich woods. **1976** Bruce *How to Grow Wildflowers* 172, *Chamaelirium luteum* . . hardly lives up to some of the dramatic common names applied to it— Devil's Bit, Blazing Star, Fairy Wand, Rattlesnake Root. **1988** [see **2b** above].

h A **rattlesnake plantain 1** (here: *Goodyera pubescens*). Cf **rattlesnake leaf, ~ tongue**

1873 in 1976 Miller *Shaker Herbs* 217, *Goodyera pubescens* . . Rattlesnake Root.

i A **horse balm** (here: *Collinsonia canadensis*).

1937 *Torreya* 37.100, *Collinsonia canadensis*. . . Rattlesnakeroot, Charleston, W. Va. ([Dr. Benjamin Smith] Barton [1766–1815]).

rattlesnake's master   See **rattlesnake master**

rattlesnake snakeroot   See **rattlesnake root 2c**

rattlesnake's pilot   See **rattlesnake pilot 1**

rattlesnakes' plantain   See **rattlesnake plantain 2**

rattlesnakes' root   See **rattlesnake root 2b, e, f**

rattlesnakes' violet   See **rattlesnake violet**

rattlesnakes' weed   See **rattlesnake weed 1a, b, d**

rattlesnake tongue n   Cf **adder's tongue 2**

A **rattlesnake plantain 1** (here: *Goodyera pubescens*).
1898 *Jrl. Amer. Folkl.* 11.273 **NJ,** Goodyera pubescens, . . rattlesnake tongue, Moorestown, N.J.

rattlesnake tree n

A **hop tree** (here: *Ptelea trifoliata*).
1946 *Nat. Hist.* 55.143, In some regions it is known as the Rattlesnake

Tree, because of the rattling noise of the dried paper-like seed coverings when stirred by a fall breeze.

rattlesnake vine   See **rattlesnake weed 2**

rattlesnake violet n Also *rattlesnakes' violet*   Cf **adder's violet**

1 A **violet** such as *Viola hirsutula, V.* x *primulifolia*, or *V. sagittata.* [See quot 1854]

1818 *Amer. Jrl. Science* 1.368 **MA,** Rattlesnake violet *(Viola primulifolia)* in full flower. **1854** King *Amer. Eclectic Dispensatory* 961, The *Viola Ovata,* or rattlesnake violet, has been highly recommended in the bites of rattlesnakes. **1876** Hobbs *Bot. Hdbk.* 96, Rattlesnakes' violet, Adders' tongue, Erythronium Americanum. . . Viola ovata [=*Viola hirsutula*]. **1940** Clute *Amer. Plant Names* 134, *V[iola] fimbriatula* [= *V. sagittata*]. . . Rattlesnake violet.

2 =**rattlesnake plantain 1.**

1840 MA Zool. & Bot. Surv. *Herb. Plants & Quadrupeds* 201, *G[oodyera] pubescens*. . . Rattlesnake Violet. . . This plant has great reputation among root and Indian doctors, as a remedy for scrophulous affections. In the only case I ever knew it applied, no perceptible effect followed. **1898** *Jrl. Amer. Folkl.* 11.280 **NY,** *Goodyera* (sp.), rattlesnake's violet, Alcove, N.Y. . . Leaves sometimes used for making salve.

3 =**dogtooth violet.**

1876 [see **1** above]. **1900** Lyons *Plant Names* 151, *E[rythronium] Americanum*. . . Rattlesnake's Violet. . . *Plant* reputed alterative, emetic. **1949** Moldenke *Amer. Wild Flowers* 328, *Erythronium* . . [is] commonly known under the . . ever inaccurate names of *adderstongue* and *dogtoothviolets*, as well as . . *rattlesnakeviolets*.

rattlesnake watermelon   See **rattlesnake melon**

rattlesnake weed n   Cf **rattlesnake master, ~ root**

1 Any of var plants that have been used to treat snakebite, as:

a also *rattlesnakes' weed:* A **button snakeroot 2,** usu *Eryngium aquaticum* or *E. yuccifolium.*   Cf **rattlesnake flag**

1668 (1671) Skinner *Etymologicon* sig Gggg2ᵛ, *Rattle* Snake-Weed, Polyrrhizos Virginiana, sic dicta, quia ad morsum Serpentis κροταλίζοντος Virginiani, & fortasse ad quosvis alios Venenatos, & alia quavis Venena, eximia est Antidotus. [=*Rattle* Snake-Weed, Polyrrhizos Virginiana, so called because it is an outstanding antidote to the bite of the Virginia rattlesnake, and perhaps to any poisonous snake or any poison whatever.] [*DARE* Ed: This quot may refer instead to another sense below.] **1760** Lee *Intro. Botany* App 314, Rattlesnake Weed, *Eryngium.* **1876** Hobbs *Bot. Hdbk.* 96, Rattlesnakes' weed, . . Hieracium venosum. . . Goodyera pubescens. . . Eryngium aquaticum. **1900** Lyons *Plant Names* 150, *E[ryngium] aquaticum*. . . Rattlesnake weed. *Root* acrid-aromatic, diaphoretic, expectorant, emetic. [Lyons: Other species are credited with similar properties.] **1949** Moldenke *Amer. Wild Flowers* 148, The names . . *rattlesnakeweed . .* and *snakeroot* are applied to . . species [of *Eryngium*] because of their reputed value in cases of snakebite. **1971** Krochmal *Appalachia Med. Plants* 114, *Eryngium aquaticum*. . . Rattlesnake weed. . . In large doses, infusions have been used as emetics.

b also *rattlesnakes' weed:* A **hawkweed** (here: *Hieracium venosum*).

1843 Torrey *Flora NY* 1.414, *Hieracium venosum*. . . *Rattlesnake-weed*. . . This is one of the numerous plants supposed to be antidotes to the bite of the Rattlesnake, but its virtues are probably overrated, if not altogether imaginary. **1876** [see **1a** above]. **1891** Jesup *Plants Hanover NH* 24, H[ieracium] venosum. . . (Rattlesnake-weed.) **1910** Shreve *MD Plant Life* 488, Rattlesnake Weed. Throughout the state; in dry forests; common. **1931** Harned *Wild Flowers Alleghanies* 492, *Rattlesnake-weed*. . . The veinings [of the leaves] undoubtedly gave rise to their supposed efficacy as a remedy for snake bites. **1985** Clark *From Mailbox* 161 **ME,** This month [=May], yellow rattlesnake weeds bloom here, looking like prim, refined dandelions on firm and slender stems. **1988** Werner *Life & Lore* 162 **IL,** There are several other native species with names that would also indicate value in treating rattlesnake bites. Yet none of them have been proven valuable for this purpose. The list includes . . Rattlesnake Weed, *Hieracium venosum.*

c A **purple coneflower** (here: either *Echinacea angustifolia* or *E. purpurea*).

1846 in 1848 Emory *Notes Reconnoissance* 387 **KS,** The prairies were covered with tall stalks of the rattlesnake weed, (rudebeckia purpurea

[=*Echinacea purpurea*]). **1940** Clute *Amer. Plant Names* 253, *Brauneria* [=*Echinacea*] *angustifolia*. Rattle-snake weed.

d also *rattlesnakes' weed:* A **rattlesnake plantain 1** (here: *Goodyera pubescens*). Cf **rattlesnake leaf, ~ tongue, ~ violet 2**

1876 [see **1a** above]. **1900** Lyons *Plant Names* 280, *P[eramium] pubescens* [=*Goodyera p.*]. . . Rattlesnake-weed. . . *Plant* reputed alterative. **1924** *Amer. Botanist* 30.151, *Epipactis pubescens* [=*Goodyera p.*]. . is still another witness to the association of harmless plants with poisonous serpents. In this case there is slightly more reason for the name for the leaves are finely reticulated with white which might be held to simulate scales. . . The plant is known as "rattlesnake weed." **1940** Clute *Amer. Plant Names* 47, *E[pipactis] pubescens*. . . Rattlesnake-weed.

e A **rattlebox 1a**; see quot.

1892 *Jrl. Amer. Folkl.* 5.94 **OH**, *Crotalaria (ovalis?)*, rattlesnake-weed, Mansfield, O[hio].

f A **water horehound** (here: *Lycopus americanus*).

1897 *Jrl. Amer. Folkl.* 10.53 **MO**, *Lycopus sinuatus* [=*L. americanus*], . . rattlesnake weed, Southwestern Mo. . . Herb said to be an antidote for the bite of rattlesnakes.

g A **wild carrot** (here: *Daucus pusillus*). **West**

1898 *Jrl. Amer. Folkl.* 11.227 **CA**, *Daucus pusillus*, . . rattlesnake weed. **1911** Jepson *Flora CA* 293, *D[aucus] pusillus*. . . *Rattlesnake Weed*. . . The herbage is in rural repute as an antidote for the bite of the rattlesnake. **1973** Hitchcock–Cronquist *Flora Pacific NW* 324, Chiefly w Cas[cades] with us; . . Rattlesnake weed. **1979** Ajilvsgi *Wild Flowers* 214 **TX**, *Rattlesnake-weed*. . . Easily identified by the bracts which extend beyond flower umbels.

h A **spurge** (here: *Euphorbia albomarginata*). **esp CA**

1898 Davidson *CA Plants* 177, One of . . [the California Euphorbias], rattlesnake weed, is common in the south. **1925** Jepson *Manual Plants CA* 600, *E[uphorbia] albomarginata*. . . *Rattlesnake Weed*. . . Plains and mesas. **1951** Abrams *Flora Pacific States* 3.38, Rattlesnake Weed. . . Southern California . . to Utah and Texas. **1974** Munz *Flora S. CA* 411, *Rattlesnake Weed*. . . Common on dry slopes below 4000 ft.

i A **rayless goldenrod** (here: *Bigelowia* spp.).

1936 Reichard *Navajo Shepherd* 45 **NM**, A yellow-green commonly seen is made by brewing the leaves and stems of one of the goldenrods (Bigelovia) called by some whites "tall rattlesnake weed", by others "sneezeweed". **1998** *DARE* File neAZ, When I visited a Navajo friend in Monument Valley three years ago, he pointed out a composite plant used in dyeing and said that whites often called it "rattlesnake weed."

j A **bugbane 1** (here: *Cimicifuga racemosa*).

1940 Clute *Amer. Plant Names* 2, *C[imicifuga] racemosa*. . . Rattlesnake-weed.

k An **Indian poke 1** (here: *Veratrum viride*). Cf **rattlesnake root 2a**

1940 Clute *Amer. Plant Names* 16, *V[eratrum] viride*. . . Rattlesnake-weed [sic].

l =**Seneca snakeroot.**

1970 *NC Folkl.* 8.15, Seneca root, called rattlesnake weed, when boiled into tea, was a popular remedy for chills, fever, and any ague.

2 also *rattlesnake vine:* See quot.

1951 *PADS* 15.34 **TX**, *Fabaceae*—Numerous members of the pea family, both vine and upright weed, are lumped together as rattlesnake vines or weeds, because the sound of their shaken dry seed pods suggest [sic] the warning whirr of our most famous reptile.

rattlesnake whisky See **rattlesnake oil**

rattletail snake See **rattlesnake 1**

rattletongue n Also *rattlehead, rattlemouth* Cf **rattlebox 2**

A garrulous or gossiping person; hence adj *rattle-tongued*.

1876 Larned *Talks Labor* 32 **NY**, I am ashamed of myself; but you threw me on a subject which runs away with me. I hope, ladies, you will not think that I am always such a rattle-tongued egotist as I have been tonight. **1916** *DN* 4.341 seOH, Rattle tongue. A gossiping person. **1949** Arnow *Hunter's Horn* 177 **KY**, But before God he wouldn't show it, no more than he would show he was afraid; not before Sue Annie, and have the old rattle-tongue tell . . that he'd been scared. **1966–69**

DARE (Qu. HH7a, *Someone who talks too much, or too loud: "He's an awful ___."*) Inf **GA**19, Rattlemouth, blabbermouth; **MA**35, Rattlehead, gossip, rattletrap, blabberbust; **NC**4, Rattletongue.

rattletop n

1 A **bugbane 1**: usu *Cimicifuga racemosa*, but also *C. americana*. Cf **rattle cohosh, rattlepod 5, rattleroot, rattleweed a**

1900 Lyons *Plant Names* 101, *C[imicifuga] racemosa*. . . Rattle-top. **1933** Small *Manual SE Flora* 513, *C. racemosa*. . . *Rattle-top*. . . Woods, various provinces. **1953** Strausbaugh–Core *Flora WV* 398, *C. racemosa*. . . Rattletop. . . Common in every county throughout the State. **1964** Campbell et al. *Gt. Smoky Wildflowers* 62, *Cimicifuga americana*. . . Common names include . . *rattletop*. **1971** Krochmal *Appalachia Med. Plants* 96, *Cimicifuga racemosa*. . . Rattle-top. . . In Appalachia, a tea made from the root is used to treat sore throat.

2 =**velvetleaf** (here: *Abutilon theophrasti*).

1982 Barrick Coll. csPA, *Rattle-top*—common weed whose dry seed pods rattle. [DARE Ed: A photograph supplied by Prof. Barrick established the identity of this plant.]

rattletrap n

1 A noisemaker with a wooden tongue that is vibrated by the rotation of a toothed wheel.

1917 Baldwin *Making of a Township* 406 **ceIN**, It was my lot to protect the corn from them [=squirrels] and the birds by going around the field before breakfast sounding the alarm, "Hooppee, shoe ye, yo, show show shoe, ye yo!" with the rattletrap in hand. That was made with a big notched wheel fixed in a frame, a board a foot and a half long so placed that as I turned the wheel with a crank it made all the noise to my desire. **1939** Hall Coll. (Montgomery Coll.) eTN, I guess you people would like to know about serenades and how young folks got along back seventy years ago and longer. We had serenades. They'd make old big rattle traps they'd call 'em. . . My, My! How they'd rattle and bang around. **1963** *Chr. Sci. Monitor* (Boston MA) 26 Apr 6/6 nwNC, The carvers' line of folk toys also includes . . the rattletrap (Mountaineer version of the Halloween noisemaker). **1972** Cooper *NC Mt. Folkl.* 34, For many decades and until stores became plentiful, the children's Christmas toys and gifts were mainly homemade. There were dolls, yarn balls, whistles, geehaw whimmydiddles or ziggerboos, rattle traps, noisemakers or bull roars and flipperdingers. **1972** in 1982 Powers *Cataloochee* 174 cwNC (as of a1940), "I was thinking about toys we had back in the hills. . . We had a thing, I'm not sure what it was called, I'll call it a ratchet. It was made of wood about so long, and at one end was a kind of sprocket arrangement with a handle. And you could make that thing go around and make a lot of noise." . . *Mark Hannah:* "I've seen this one, too. I could also make one. I called it a Rattle Trap." **1979** *PA Folklife* 29.29, The device that served the colonial watchman as a billyclub and an alarm is now only a rattletrap used on New Year's Eve or occasionally at a callithumpian serenade. **1983** *MJLF* 9.1.52 ceKY (as of 1956), *Rattletrap* . . a noisemaker for a chivaree. **1986** Pederson *LAGS Concordance*, 1 inf, ceTN, Rattletraps—noisemakers. **1996** *Midwest. Folkl.* 22.1.8 cwIN, [They] had a rattle trap Dunning's grandfather-in-law built sometime in the latter half of the 19th century. Within its wooden frame, it had three cross pieces; slats were attached to the bottom piece and were tucked under the middle one. The third piece attached to a cranking handle outside the frame. This piece had notches or gears that slapped the slats when turning.

2 The belted **kingfisher** (*Megaceryle alcyon*).

1925 Bailey *Birds FL* 80, *Belted Kingfisher*. . . *Streptoceryle alcyon alcyon* (*Rattletrap*). . . The fresh water fishermen do not like these birds, owing to their habit of taking small edible fish.

rattle vetch n

A **milk vetch** (here: *Astragalus canadensis*).

1933 Small *Manual SE Flora* 709, *A[stragalus] carolinianus* [=*A. canadensis*]. . . Rattle-vetch—Dry woods and riverbanks. **1950** Gray–Fernald *Manual of Botany* 911, Rattle-vetch. . . Md. and W. Va. to Ga. and Tenn.

rattleweed n Cf **rattlebox, rattlepod**

Any of var plants with seed vessels that rattle when dry, as:

a also, perh erron, *rattlewood:* A **bugbane 1** (here: *Cimicifuga racemosa*).

1791 in 1793 *Amer. Philos. Soc. Trans.* 3.114, *Actæa racemosa* [=

Cimicifuga r.] (American Bane-berry, Black Snake-root, Rattle-weed.) **1838** Huntington (Penna.) *Courier* 15 Sep. 4/5 (*DA* at *black* 1.c), American Remedies Wanted . . Rattle Weed or Black Cahash [sic]. **1893** *Jrl. Amer. Folkl.* 6.136 **NC**, *Cimicifuga racemosa*, rattle-weed. Banner Elk, N.C. **1903** Small *Flora SE U.S.* 431, *Cimicifuga racemosa*. . . Black Snakeroot. . . Rattle-wood. **1930** Sievers *Amer. Med. Plants* 23, Rattle-weed. . . is a conspicuous woodland plant on account of its tall flowering spikes. **1975** Hamel–Chiltoskey *Cherokee Plants* 30, Rattleweed. . . Roots in alcoholic spirits for rheumatism. **1983** *MJLF* 9.1.52 **ceKY** (as of 1956), *Rattle Weed* . . a medicinal herb.

b =**milk vetch. West** Cf **rattle vetch**
1851 (1874) Glisan *Jrl. Army Life* 70 **KS**, The rattle-weed . . derives its name from the fact that its pod is full of loose seed, and makes a rattling noise when dry, if touched by the passer-by. **1883** *Harper's New Mth. Mag.* 66.503 **AZ**, The loco, or rattle-weed, met with also in California, drives them [=horses] raving crazy. **1898** *Jrl. Amer. Folkl.* 11.225 **CA**, *Astragalus* (sp.), rattle weed, loco weed. **1936** Winter *Plants NE* 102, *Phaca* [=*Astragalus*]. . . Rattle-weed. **1954** CA Div. Beaches & Parks *Pt. Lobos Wild Flowers* 11, As the common name implies, the Rattle-weed produces brown pods one to two inches long enclosing loose seeds that rattle when disturbed. **1966** *DARE* (Qu. S20) Inf **OK**52, Rattleweeds—they have peas or beans in 'em—jackrabbits hide under them. **1966** *DARE* FW Addit **NM**12, Rattleweed—a form of locoweed; pea comes loose and rattles in dry husk—sounds like a rattler and will scare a man. **1985** Dodge *Flowers SW Deserts* 118, Rattleweed. . . ranges from the driest, hottest parts of the desert to high mountain peaks and the far north.

c A **rattlebox 1a,** esp *Crotalaria sagittalis.*
1898 U.S. Dept. Ag. Div. Botany *Bulletin* 20.31, *Crotalaria sagittalis*. . . Rattleweed; wild pea. . . The seed pods. . . are much inflated, and as the walls are stiff and thin and very resonant, they make excellent miniature rattles when the seeds have become detached. **1922** *Amer. Botanist* 28.32, *Crotalaria sagittalis*, . . the inflated pods of this species in which the seeds rattle at the slightest jar make the name of . . "rattleweed" . . appropriate. **1968** Schmutz et al. *Livestock-Poisoning Plants AZ* 137, *Rattleweed—Crotalaria* sp. These sandy-land forbs . . may cause death in all classes of livestock.

d A **locoweed:** usu *Oxytropis lambertii*, but also *O. sericea.* **West**
1901 U.S. Dept. Ag. Div. Botany *Bulletin* 26.86 **MT**, *Aragallus spicatus* [=*Oxytropis sericea*]. . . The pod is one-celled and when ripe the seed produces a rattling sound which gives the plant the name rattleweed. **1913** (1979) Barnes *Western Grazing* 257, White Loco or Rattle Weed in flower (*Aragallus lamberti*). **1937** U.S. Forest Serv. *Range Plant Hdbk.* W139, Crazyweed [=*Oxytropis lambertii*] is also called stemless loco and, less frequently, rattleweed. **1968** Schmutz et al. *Livestock-Poisoning Plants AZ* 26, Rattleweed. . . *Oxytropis lambertii* grows on sandy soils in open areas of eastern Arizona.

e A **wild indigo 1** (here: *Baptisia tinctoria*). Cf **rattlebush 1**
1933 Small *Manual SE Flora* 676, B[aptisia] *tinctoria*. . . Rattleweed. . . Southern mountain folk use the plant both for dye and as a flybrush. **1945** Pickard–Buley *Midwest Pioneer* 41 (as of c1820), Strong tea of pokeberry leaves or rattleweed was recommended for smallpox victims. **1961** Smith *MI Wildflowers* 194, Rattleweed. . . Indian children used the dried stalks with the inflated seed pods as rattles.

f See quot.
c1940 *Hall Coll.* **wNC, eTN**, Rattleweed—plant name—popular name for goat's beard.

g A **senna** n[1] **B1**; see quot.
1985 Dodge *Flowers SW Deserts* 93, Desert Senna, Rattleweed. . . *Cassia* [=*Senna*] *bauhinioides*. . . *Cassia armata*. . . *Cassia lindheimeriana*. . . Brown, woody seed pods.

rattlewood See **rattleweed a**

rat-trap (cheese) See **rat cheese**

raunch v, hence ppl adj *raunching* (pronc-sp *ronchen*)
To swagger; to bully, intimidate.
c1939 in 1984 Lambert–Franks *Voices* 254 **OK**, Used to be pipe pullers were just about the ronchenest bunch you ever saw. . . They were plenty tough, I'm telling you. I got drunk and did my share of hell-raising right along with 'em, but after I married I kinda settled down. **1967** *DARE* File **ceWI**, *Raunching*—the swagger of a cocky or inebriated man, most commonly on horseback (shades of Cat Ballou!); "He came

raunching down the street, pistols bobbing awkwardly up and down his bent frame."

rauncher n [Etym uncert; cf **raunch**] esp **NEng**
An extraordinarily large example of its kind; hence adj phr *raunching big* very large.
[**1848** in 1935 *DN* 6.454 **RI**, *Rauncher*. [*DN* Ed: No explanation given; no doubt too early for the sense 'ranchman.']] **1950** Moore *Candlemas Bay* 39 **ME**, He had hit the south spur, drowned under by one old rauncher of a high-run tide. **1957** *Sat. Eve. Post Letters* **cIN**, My community has yielded up such pleasantly memorable expressions as these: . . "raunchin' big," or something is a "rauncher," being big. **1975** Gould *ME Lingo* 228, *Rauncher*—A large male deer, and in proper usage the word is reserved for that. But by extension it means anything extra-sized, and at sea it can be a big wave that bumps head on. To "take on a *rauncher*" is to tackle a situation you may not be able to handle. **1979** Lewis *How to Talk Yankee* [7] **nNEng**, *Cruncher* . . large deer. Also rauncher, baister.

raunching See **raunch**

raunching big See **rauncher**

raunchy adj Cf **faunchy, raunch**
Wild; frantic; distraught.
1954 Tolbert *Bigamy Jones* 11 **wTX** (as of 1870s), Then she sort of came unstrung. . . "It's the twins. They got me so raunchy I'm like a horse that has been beat over the head with the bridle. . . Those boys are wilder than two coyote pups." **1966–70** *DARE* (Qu. K16, *A cow with a bad temper*) Inf **CA**211, Raunchy; (Qu. K42, *A horse that is rough, wild, or dangerous*) Inf **ND**5, Such a horse is said to be snaky or raunchy.

raus mit ('em) See **heraus mit 'em**

ravage v
1931 Randolph *Ozarks* 81, *Ravish* and *ravage* always mean rape in the hill country, and are not mentioned in polite conversation.

raves See **raft**

raw bar n chiefly **Atlantic,** esp **Mid Atl**
An oyster bar.
1943 *Sun* (Baltimore MD) 5 Oct 16/6 (*Hench Coll.*), The boys at the raw bar in the end of Bill's place last night said the way oysters are this season a feller'll have to eat shells and all to get a mess. **1967** *DARE* FW Addit **DC**, *Raw bar*—seafood counter. **1973** *Washington D.C. Yellow Pages* 1314 (*OED*2), Chuck O'Brien's Riverboat. . . Informal raw bar. **1998** *DARE* File, A search of the internet for advertisements for raw bars found them located chiefly along the Atlantic coast, especially in the Mid Atlantic states.

raw beef, chaw See **chaw raw beef**

rawbone adj Also *rawboned* [*OED*2 *rawbone* 1593 →; "*Obs.*"; *rawboned* 1591 →] **widespread, but somewhat less freq Nth** See Map Cf **rawny**
Having the bones prominently visible beneath the skin; thin, bony, gangling.

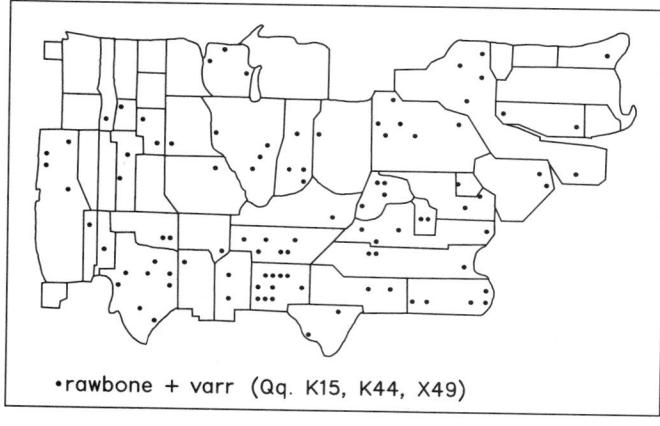

•rawbone + varr (Qq. K15, K44, X49)

1834 *New Engl. Mag.* 7.152, Well, Gentlemen ; as there was no remedy, our Notary mounted this raw-boned steed. **1834** *S. Lit. Messenger* 1.181 **VA,** Simon found it impossible to keep up with me, mounted as he was on a high trotting, rawboned devil. **1844** *Lexington Observer* 27 Nov. 1/3 (*DA* at *Cape Cod*), A raw boned yankee made his appearance. **1899** (1912) Green *VA Folk-Speech* 347, *Rawboned.* . . Having little flesh on the bone; lean and large-boned; gaunt. **1904** Clay-Clopton *Belle* 256 **AL** (as of c1860), They were a guard, flanking on each side an old "jimber-jawed, wobble-sided" barouche, drawn by two raw-boned horses. **1925** (1926) James *Drifting Cowboy* 210 **West,** He was a big powerful 'gruller' horse, tall and rawboned and all muscle. **1965–70** *DARE* (Qu. K15, *A thin, bony, or poor-looking cow*) 53 Infs, **scattered, but less freq Nth, West,** Rawbone; **OK20, VA1,** (Old) rawbone cow; **AL38, CA105, CT9, GA3, NY219, WY1,** Rawboned; (Qu. K44, *A bony or poor-looking horse*) 41 Infs, **scattered, but less freq NEast, West,** Rawbone; **TX71, VA1, WV13,** Rawbone horse; 10 Infs, **scattered,** Rawboned; (Qu. X49, *Expressions . . about a person who is very thin*) Infs **TX18, VA24,** Rawbone. **1974** (1975) Shaw *All God's Dangers* 5 **AL** [Black], He was a kind of rawboned, slender man like I am.

rawbones n

A **rawbone** person or animal.

1966–69 *DARE* (Qu. K15, *A thin, bony, or poor-looking cow*) Infs **GA1, MD3,** Rawbones; (Qu. K44, *A bony or poor-looking horse*) Infs **CA105, IL66,** Rawbones; (Qu. X49, *Expressions . . about a person who is very thin*) Inf **GA7,** Rawbones.

rawbony adj **chiefly Sth** See Map
=rawbone.

a1930 in 1991 Hughes–Hurston *Mule Bone* 30 **cFL** [Black], Jus' take yo' rawbony cow an' gwan tuh de woods, fuh all I keer. **1965–70** *DARE* (Qu. K15, *A thin, bony, or poor-looking cow*) 29 Infs, **chiefly Sth,** Rawbony; (Qu. K44, *A bony or poor-looking horse*) 28 Infs, **chiefly Sth,** Rawbony; **GA14,** Rawbony horse; (Qu. X49, *Expressions . . about a person who is very thin*) Infs **GA1, MS37, NJ67, OK13, SC46, TX35,** Rawbony; (Qu. X52, . . *A person . . who had been sick was looking* _____) Inf **OK13,** Rawbony. **1986** Pederson *LAGS Concordance,* 1 inf, **ceTX,** Rawbony = gangling.

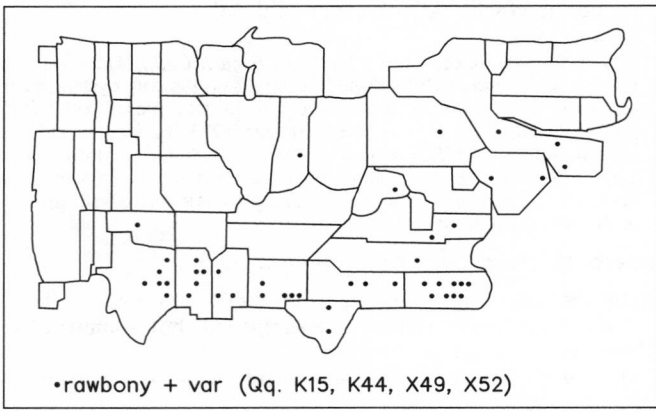

•rawbony + var (Qq. K15, K44, X49, X52)

raw-fried potatoes n pl Also *raw fries* **chiefly Nth, N Midl** See Map Cf **American fried potatoes 2, American raw fry** =fresh fried potatoes; hence v *raw-fry*.

1948 Hutchison *PA Du. Cook Book* 90, Raw fried potatoes. **1950** Klees *PA Dutch* 428, Serve [sausage] with raw-fried potatoes, an admirable way of cooking potatoes that seems to be known only to the Pennsylvania Dutch. **1950** *WELS Suppl.* **cwWI,** Raw-fry—To fry foods not previously cooked. Particularly potatoes—cottage fry. "There were no potatoes to warm up, so we raw-fried some." **1954** Jordan *Hell's Canyon* 73 **ID,** But it is permissible to put on the table veal, pork, turkey, chicken, sturgeon, fresh vegetables from the store, cream, pie if at supper, cake any time, and raw-fried potatoes constantly. **1965–70** *DARE* (Qu. H47, *Kinds of fried potatoes*) 85 Infs, **chiefly Nth, N Midl,** Rawfried; **DE3, ME16, MN42, NJ21, 23, NY94, OH98,** Raw fries; **PA41,** Old-fashion raw-fried. **1977** Anderson *Grass Roots Cookbook* 50 **sePA,** Raw-Fried Potatoes. . . [A]re similar to hashed browns, except that raw instead of cooked potatoes are fried, which gives them a crisper texture. **1984** *MJLF* 10.154 **cnWI,** Raw Fries. Potatoes peeled and fried, especially when there are no cold boiled potatoes for hash. Maine: Fried potatoes.

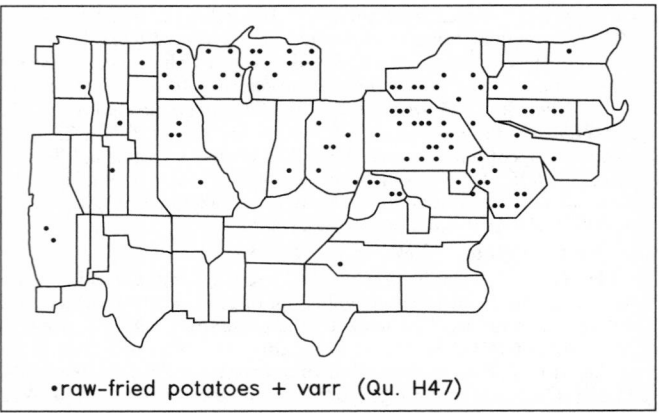

•raw-fried potatoes + varr (Qu. H47)

‡rawgut n Cf **catgut, hoggut**

1968 *DARE* (Qu. DD21b, *General words . . for bad liquor*) Inf **PA167,** Rawgut.

rawhead and bloodybones n For varr see quot 1966–70 [*OED2* c1550 →] **chiefly Sth, S Midl** Cf **bloodybones, redeye 6**

A specter, hobgoblin.

1637 (1972) Morton *New English Canaan* 320, Hee made Fairecloaths Innocent back like the picture of Rawhead and blowdy bones. **1775** in 1859 Moore *Diary Amer. Revol.* 1.8 **PA,** In vain are their scare-crows, raw-head and bloody bones, held up to deter us from taking the most effectual means for our security. **1853** Simms *Sword & Distaff* 349 **SC,** Lord! that I should live to be squeezed to death by a nigger, and sufficated in the arms of a raw-head and bloody bones like this! **1899** (1912) Green *VA Folk-Speech* 347, *Rawhead.* . . A nursery bugbear of frightfull aspect; usually coupled with *bloody bones.* **1934** Hurston *Jonah's Gourd Vine* 122 **AL** [Black], " 'Bye. Doan let de booger man ketch yuh." "Don't let ole Raw-Head-and-Bloody-Bones waylay yuh neither." **c1937** in 1977 *Amer. Slave Suppl. 1* 1.171 **AL** [Black], Some er de folks used to sceer us niggers ter death wid the tale 'bout "Raw Head and Bloody Bones", ef us didn't mind dem but since I been grown I ain't never seed no haints. **1945** *SW Rev.* 31.32 **TN,** I never got over the day my Sister came charging out at me screaming, "Raw-head and Bloody Bones!" **1955** Ritchie *Singing Family* 13 **seKY,** We'd . . raise such a ruckus that Mom would send in to tell us we better settle or Old Rawhead-and-Bloodybones would get us. **1966–70** *DARE* (Qu. EE41, *A hobgoblin that is used to threaten children and make them behave*) Infs **AL15, 37, NC30, TX104,** Rawhead and bloodybones; **TN16,** Rawhead and bloodybones—he's a mean bugger; **KY29,** Raw-heels and bloodybones; **MS6,** Redhead–bloodybones. **1984** Burns *Cold Sassy* 89 **nGA** (as of 1906), For a moment I swelled with importance, getting talked about like that. Then for no good reason I saw myself as Raw Head and Bloody Bones, spinning into nothing under giant [train] wheels and thunder. **1986** Pederson *LAGS Concordance,* 1 inf, **nwLA,** Rawhead and bloodybones—parents told children of.

rawhide n

1 attrib:

a Of a person: tough, experienced.

1883 Sweet–Knox *Mexican Mustang* 18, I'm just pining away for a fight. I'm a raw-hide Texan, *I* am. **1957** Kerouac *On the Road* 21, Here came this rawhide old-timer Nebraska farmer.

b Characterized by the use of rawhide for makeshift repairs; employing makeshift methods. Cf **haywire adj 1**

1936 McKenna *Black Range* 159 **NM** (as of 1880s), Rawhide outfits were usually made up of ten or fifteen wagons strung out for miles. **1950** in 1953 Botkin–Harlow *Treas. Railroad Folkl.* 274, A rawhide railroad was a road that depended on cheap substitutes or extreme economies.

c Exacting hard work. Cf **rawhide v 3**

1950 in 1953 Botkin–Harlow *Treas. Railroad Folkl.* 274, As the Walla Walla railroad kept its crews busy, it was a rawhide line.

2 A cowboy, esp an experienced one. *sometimes derog*

1936 Adams *Cowboy Lingo* 27, A man old in the ways of the West was sometimes called a 'rawhide.' **1937** in Lib. of Congress *Amer. Memory: WPA Life Hist.* (Internet) **cTX,** I was in good hands, because practically all of the waddies were old rawhides, and top hands. *Ibid* **cTX,** Goodnight had the top rawhides working for him and a square bunch. **1937** *DN* 6.620 **swTX,** He [=the cowboy] is indifferently called *cow-hand, ranch-hand, cowpuncher, rawhide* [etc]. **1939** Abbott–Smith *We Pointed Them* 161 **MT,** Rawhides. [Footnote:] Derisive Northern name for Texas cowhands. It referred to the Texans' habit of mending whatever broke down or fell apart on the trail, from a bridle to a wagon tongue, by tying it up with strips of rawhide. **1941** Dobie *Longhorns* 226, When they got up into the Northwest, the trail men were dubbed "rawhides."

3 An emaciated animal or person.   Cf **rawbones**

1940 Writers' Program *Guide NV* 77, *Dogs* are poor, weak calves, while *rawhides* are weak cows. **1967–69** *DARE* (Qu. K15, *A thin, bony, or poor-looking cow*) Inf **AR55,** Rawhide; (Qu. K50, *Joking nicknames for mules*) Inf **NC68,** Rawhide; (Qu. X49, *Expressions . . about a person who is very thin*) Inf **AR55,** Rawhide.

rawhide v, hence vbl n *rawhiding*

1 To drive or beat with a rawhide whip; hence n *rawhiding* a whipping.

1848 *Knickerbocker* 18.519, The editor, it was predicted, would catch a raw-hiding before sun-set. **1858** *Porter's Spirit of Times* 6 Feb 356/3 **cwNY,** One of our citizens was rawhided in the street, and in the presence of numerous spectators, by a Mr. Huntington. **1883** Twain *Life on Missip.* (Boston) 61, Some raftsmen would rawhide you till you were black and blue. **1949** *Sat. Eve. Post* 7 May 103/1 *(DA)* **NW,** Joe went along as packer, rawhiding a string of bony horses up into the brownie country and cooking for the party. **1954** *Harder Coll.* **cwTN,** Rawhidin(g). . . A whipping. *Raw-hide* v.

2 To tease, rib, haze.   **chiefly West**

1899 *Century Illustr. Mag.* 57.656, With the progress of civilization, hazing in the colleges is on the wane, and so is "rawhiding" on the railroads. **1933** *AmSp* 8.1.32 **nwTX** [Ranch diction], *Rawhide.* To tease. **1938** in *Lib. of Congress Amer. Memory: WPA Life Hist.* (Internet) **cwTX,** The youngest fellow on the works always had to take the "rawhiding," but I soon learned to hold my own. I was hired to work on "macaroni" farms, sent to buy "striped paint," but was not as bad as the fellow who looked all day in a mud puddle for a frog, because they needed it on the railroad. **1941** Dobie *Longhorns* 237 **TX,** The ultimate in "guying," "ragging," deviling a human being was appropriately termed "rawhiding." **1942** Perry *Texas* 135, Ranching terms that have come into the language are legion. . . Ribbing, or a series of embarrassing jokes at a person's expense, is called "rawhiding" from the old days when a newcomer in a cow camp was sometimes hazed with a pair of rawhide chaps. **1969** *DARE* (Qu. Y7, *When one person never misses a chance to be mean to another or to annoy another: "I don't know why she keeps _____ me all the time!"*) Inf **GA77,** Rawhiding.

3 To overwork or mistreat (workers or machinery).   Cf **rawhider 2**

1930 Williams *Logger-Talk* 27 **Pacific NW,** *Raw-hide:* Drive a crew. **1940** Cottrell *Railroader* 135, A foreman who is overbearing—"rawhides" his men. **1950** in 1953 Botkin–Harlow *Treas. Railroad Folkl.* 274, But rawhide had some other meanings. As a verb, it meant to treat harshly, to oppress, to overwork. **1956** Sorden–Ebert *Logger's Words* 27 **Gt. Lakes,** *Raw-hide,* To hurry. Same as bull-em-through. **1958** McCulloch *Woods Words* 146 **Pacific NW,** *Rawhide.* . . To "ride" men, trying to force more work out of them.

4 To chastise verbally, "chew out"; hence n *rawhiding* a scolding.

1948 *Time* 2 Feb 10, Truman stormed into Congress and gave Alexander Fell Whitney, co-leader of the strike, one of the savagest verbal rawhidings ever dealt a private citizen by a President of the U.S. **1969** *DARE* (Qu. II27, *If somebody gives you a very sharp scolding . . "I certainly got a _____ for that."*) Inf **MT4,** Rawhiding.

5 To drag in a rawhide sack.   *hist*

1941 Writers' Program *Guide UT* 132, About 1869, ore produced by the Emma Mine at Alta was "rawhided" to the mouth of Little Cottonwood Canyon. The process of "rawhiding" consisted of loading ore into green skins and using horses to drag it down to the nearest road, where it could be transferred to ox-drawn wagons and hauled to the railroad terminal at Ogden. **1947** Bailey *River of No Return* 179 *(DA)* **ID** (as of late 19th cent), In the winter it [*DA* Ed: mail] was transported by sled, on horses wearing snowshoes, or raw-hided—wrapped in a buffalo hide and pulled by horse or man power.

6 To carry, esp on one's back.   **sAppalachians**

1917 *DN* 4.416 **wNC,** *Rawhide.* . . To carry on one's back. "I rawhided

that sack acrost the mountain." **c1940** *Hall Coll.* **wNC,** "We was rawhidin' the casket across the river." "Can I he'p you rawhide them suitcases over to the car?" This expression is said to be used by old-timers. **1952** Brown *NC Folkl.* 1.583, *Rawhide.* . . To bear an object on one's back.—West. **1961** Seeman *In Arms of Mt.* 15 **eTN,** It was no drawback to Edwin that . . the boards would have to be "raw-hided" up the steep bank, plank by plank. **1974** Dabney *Mountain Spirits* 16 **sAppalachians,** Many older mountain men with crooked backs can attest to their younger days of "rawhiding" sugar and meal into tough mountain terrain and then barrels of whiskey on the opposite trip out. **1979** *Our Smokies Heritage* Sept 277 **wNC, eTN,** After the bark was peeled it was allowed to dry. It was then loaded in sacks and *rawhided* from the woods to the nearest wagon road. It was . . called "rawhiding" for a simple reason. A heavy load of tanbark in a sack was guaranteed to wear all the hide off your shoulders and back in the coarse [sic] of a day.

7 Of a cowboy: to camp out alone in search of stray cattle.

1936 McCarthy *Lang. Mosshorn* np **West** [Range terms], *Rawhidin'. .* a cowboy gathering cattle alone on the range with an individual camp outfit. **1961** Adams *Old-Time Cowhand* 251, If a man was sent out to prowl alone and stayed for some time, he took an individual camp outfit, and was said to be "rawhidin'." **1973** Allen *LAUM* 1.408 (as of c1950), *Rawhide, vb.* To send out several cowpunchers on their own, to eat with sheepherders or by themselves, in order to discover the mavericks. Hence: rawhiding, *sb.* This practice developed after the fencing-in of the range and the obsolescence of the roundup [1 inf, **SD**].

8 See quot.

1927 *AmSp* 2.363 **cwWV,** *Rawhiding . .* to slip logs over steep places. "The men have raw-hided all that side of the hill." [*DARE* Ed: The example suggests that the meaning is "To scar (a hillside) by sliding logs down it."]

rawhider n

1 An early settler in the Southwest.   *hist*   Cf **rawhide** n **1b**

1908 *Pacific Mth.* Feb 155 **SW,** I was first, as old rawhiders all confessed;/ I'm the last of all rough riders and the best. **1936** McKenna *Black Range* 159 **NM** (as of 1880s), The rawhiders got their name from the many uses they had for cowhide. . . All rawhiders came from West Texas years before farming and drilling for oil became common there. They were on the move nearly all the time, driving their horses and cattle with them, also numerous large cur, or mongrel dogs. The families traveled in covered wagons, which overflowed with women and children. **1937** in *Lib. of Congress Amer. Memory: WPA Life Hist.* (Internet) **TX,** I once heard a speech at Hamilton about that, and the speaker said that the rawhiders held this country back 50 years by cutting them fences down. I went to him and told him that if it hadn't of been for the rawhiders running the Indians out, people still couldn't live here.

2 One who overworks or mistreats workers or machinery.

1931 *Writer's Digest* 11.42 [Railroad terms], *Rawhider*—A conductor or engineer who is especially hard on men and equipment. This term is chiefly applied to engineers who punish locomotives to the limit without getting satisfactory results. **1945** Hubbard *Railroad Ave.* 357, *Rawhider*—Official, or any employee, who is especially hard on men or equipment, or both, with which he works. A *rawhider,* or *slave driver,* delights in causing someone to do more than his share of work. Running too fast when picking up a man on the footboard, or making a quick stop just short of him when he is expecting to step on, so that he has to walk back, are two ways it is done; but there are almost as many ways of *rawhiding* as there are different situations. **1958** McCulloch *Woods Words* 146 **Pacific NW,** *Rawhider*—a. A man who drives himself and his men to get the job done. b. An unfair boss.

3 See quot.

1981 *KS Qrly.* 13.2.69, *Rawhider . .* skilled craftsman who makes riatas, hondus [sic], and other Hispanic-California horsegear from scratch.

rawhiding vbl n See **rawhide** v

rawhiding n See **rawhide** v **1, 4**

rawny adj Also *rawny-boned* [*EDD* rawny adj.¹ "Big and awkward," *rawny* adj.² "Tall, thin, and bony"]   **NEng, esp ME, NH** Cf **rawbony**

=**rawbone.**

1868 Brackett *Farm Talk* 63 **ME,** "How much do you make their girth?" " 'Bout seven foot; rawny-boned too." **1891** *New Engl. Mag.* 3.780, At quarter before nine, our hostess, who was a stolid, rawny, elderly woman, gave us an ill-smelling oil-lamp. **1941** *LANE* Map 459

(Emaciated, peaked) 4 infs, **ME, NH,** Rawny; 1 inf, **seNH,** Cf. [rɒ^·nɪ^] = 'big-boned, loose-jointed'; 1 inf, **seNH,** Cf. [rɒ^·nɪ] = 'bony, large of frame'; 1 inf, **sME,** *Rawny,* of persons and cows, = 'bony.' **1966** *DARE* Tape **ME26,** He was a big, rawny-boned man.

rawsberry See **raspberry**

rawsum See **rosin A2a**

rawzberry See **raspberry**

rayless goldenrod n Cf **false goldenrod 2, goldenrod 1, 2**
Std: any of var composite plants of the genera *Bigelowia, Chrysothamnus, Ericameria, Haplopappus,* and *Isocoma.* For other names of plants of the genus *Bigelowia* see **rabbit brush 1c, rattlesnake weed 1i**

Raymond n Cf **Hughie, Lawrence, Old Betsy, ~ Hannah, ~ Huldy**
Rain personified.
2000 *DARE* File **MS,** Yesterday morning I was sitting here in my office listening to the pounding hammers or whatevers of the construction workers outside my window, when I heard one of them yell, "Come onnn, Raymond!" The black clouds were gathering, with rain imminent. That took me back many years to when my brother spent a couple of summers in college working on a city surveying crew in Jackson. I remember his imitating what some of the regular crew members would start saying if rain looked likely (meaning they'd get to quit work): "Come on down here, Raymond!"

rayshure See **razor**

rayther, raythur See **rather adv**

razor n Pronc-spp *rayshure, razoo, razzer*
A Forms.
1867 Harris *Sut Lovingood Yarns* 60 **TN,** P'raps sumbody hes been a-cuttin shoe-strings outen a sandy deer-skin wif yur rayshure; yu wants hit ground, don't yu? **1893** Shands *MS Speech* 52, By many negroes a razor is called a *razoo.* **1922** Talley *Negro Folk Rhymes* 147, If I ever ketches dat city Coon,/ He railly mought see my razzer soon. *Ibid* 211, He's been drinkin' razzer soup.
B Sense.
See **razor clam.**

razorback n
1 See **razorback hog.**
2 The black **crappie** (*Pomoxis nigromaculatus*).
1887 Goode *Amer. Fishes* 69, It [=*Pomoxis nigromaculatus*] is also called "Razor Back." **1947** Dalrymple *Panfish* 84, Here, my friend, are the various names by which you would address . . the Crappie . . : Razorback [etc.].
3 =**Missouri sucker.**
1951 Harlan–Speaker *IA Fish* 58, *Cycleptus elongatus.* . . Razor-back. [*Ibid* 59, There are . . from 31 to 32 soft rays in the long dorsal fin.] **1983** Becker *Fishes WI* 611, Missouri sucker, razorback, . . "muskellunge" in the lower Wabash River in Indiana.
4 A **heelsplitter** (here: *Lasmigona complanata*). Cf **razor clam**
1992 Cummings–Mayer *Field Guide Freshwater Mussels MW* 92, *Lasmigona complanata.* . . Razorback. . . Large, rounded, compressed, relatively thin shell, bluntly pointed at the posterior end.
5 See quot. Cf **camelback 3**
1967–69 *DARE* (Qu. K44, *A bony or poor-looking horse*) Infs **IN63,** 80, **MO37, TX43,** Razorback.

razorback boar See **razorback hog**

razorback buffalo (fish) n Also *razor-backed buffalo* **chiefly Missip Valley**
=**smallmouth buffalo.**
1886 U.S. Natl. Museum *Proc. for 1885* 8.13 **MO,** *Ictiobus urus* [=*I. bubalus*]. . . Razor-back Buffalo. **1908** Forbes–Richardson *Fishes of IL* 72, *Ictiobus bubalus.* . . Razor-backed buffalo. . . Body compressed, back much elevated. **1943** Eddy–Surber *N. Fishes* 103, Razorback Buffalofish. . . The head is small and more compressed and pointed than that of the largemouth buffalofish. **1956** Harlan–Speaker *IA Fish* 73, Razorback buffalo fish. . . The food consists largely of crustaceans, insect lar-

vae, small mollusks and plant material. **1967** *DARE* Tape **LA5,** You got two different kinds of buffalo. . . What they call a razorback buffalo is the humpback. **1983** Becker *Fishes WI* 625, *Ictiobus bubalus.* . . Other common names: razorback buffalo. . . humpback buffalo. . . Back highly arched and ridgelike. **1986** Pederson *LAGS Concordance,* 1 inf, **cwTN,** Razorback buffalo.

razorback clam See **razor clam**

razor-backed buffalo See **razorback buffalo (fish)**

razor-backed musk turtle n [See quot 1958]
A **musk turtle 1** (here: *Sternotherus carinatus*).
1958 Conant *Reptiles & Amphibians* 37, Razor-backed Musk Turtle. . . The upper shell reminds one of the legendary razor-backed hog. A keel is present in *all* turtles of this species, from newest hatchling to oldest adult, and sides of the carapace slope down like a tent. . . A turtle of the streams and great river swamps of the mid-South. **1979** Behler–King *Audubon Field Guide Reptiles* 443, Razor-backed Musk Turtle. . . Quite shy, unlike other musk turtles; it rarely bites or expels musk.

razorback hog n Also *razorback, ~ boar, ~ pig, ~ rooter* **chiefly Sth, Sth Midl**
A swine of a lean, long-legged variety often occurring in a wild or semi-wild state; broadly, any inferior swine. Also called **Carolina racehorse, devil's right bower, elm peeler 1, hazel splitter 1, hickory grubber, land pike, Mexican hog 2, mountain hog, piney-woods rooter, ridgeback 1, rooter 1, swamper, wind splitter, woods hog**
1849 Barrow *Facts NE TX* 57, Hogs are a very numerous family, but they are of very indifferent breed, and receive the appellation of "razor backs," which is significant enough of their appearance. **1861** *Atlantic Mth.* 8.153 **NEng,** Well, the poorer they was, the quicker they'd eat him up, I guess,—ef they could eat such a razor-back. **1879** U.S. Dept. Ag. *Special Rept.* 12.189 **FL,** I have not learned of a single person having an improved breed of pigs. All depend on the "razorback" or "land pike." **1882** Sweet–Knox *Sketches TX Siftings* 17, To the traveler through Texas one of the strangest and most peculiar features of the landscape is the razor-back hog. **1899** (1912) Green *VA Folk-Speech* 347, *Razorback.* . . A hog whose back was somewhat the shape of a sharp ridge. The formation accompanied by long legs, is characteristic of breeds of hogs that have long been allowed to run wild in the woods and waste places. **1906** *DN* 3.153 **nwAR,** *Razor-back.* . . A half-wild hog. **1909** *DN* 3.362 **eAL, wGA,** *Razor-back.* . . A lean hog that runs wild in the swamps. Hence any poor grade of hog. **1923** *DN* 5.218 **swMO,** *Razor back.* . . A thin, scrawny, under size hog. **1926** (1949) McQueen–Mizell *Hist. Okefenokee* 163 **seGA,** The typical, long tusk, vicious razorback hog is fast becoming extinct. **c1960** Wilson *Coll.* **csKY,** Razorback—a lean, wood-living hog, all snout and bones. **1967–70** *DARE* (Qu. P32, . . *Other kinds of wild animals*) Infs **NV8, TN65,** Razorback; (Qu. K55, *A pig that doesn't grow well and is not worth keeping*) Inf **CA31,** Razorback. **1967–68** *DARE* FW Addit **CA101,** Razorback = thin pig; **LA,** Razorback—feral hog supposed to have descended from hogs brought to Louisiana by the Spanish. It is distinguished from the woods hog by fiercer disposition and *wattles*—loose strips of hide under the jaws. **1986** Pederson *LAGS Concordance* **Gulf Region,** 93 infs, Razorback(s); 15 infs, Razorback hog(s); 3 infs, Razorback(s) = piney-wood(s) rooter(s); 1 inf, Razorback—breed associated with Arkansas, not wild hog; 1 inf, Razorback—just an unhealthy hog, not wild; 1 inf, Razorback—particular breed of wild hogs; 1 inf, Razorbacks—skinny, poor, just an old poor hog; 1 inf, Razorbacks—they wasn't very beautiful; 1 inf, Razorbacks—poor hogs, skinny, bony; 1 inf, Razorbacks—local ones—skinny, high backbones; 1 inf, Razorback—poor hog, not breed; 1 inf, Razorback—old range hog; 1 inf, Razorbacks or scrub hogs; 1 inf, Razorbacks—wild pigs in woods, thin; 1 inf, Razorbacks = piney-woods hogs, flatwood hogs; 1 inf, Razorback—thin, lives on acorns, good bacon; 1 inf, Razorbacks—with long snouts; 1 inf, Razorbacks—in the woods; 1 inf, Razorbacks—tamed, used for eating; 1 inf, Razorbacks—edible, good meat, can hunt; 1 inf, Razorback—skinny, long snout; 1 inf, Razorbacks—wild skinny ones; 1 inf, Razorback—wild hogs; 1 inf, Razorback—hog that "got too poor," i.e. skinny; 1 inf, Razorback—not always wild; 1 inf, Razorbacks—with balls on them big as your fist; 1 inf, Razorbacks—in the woods; 1 inf, Razorback—good bacon, may not be long-legged; 1 inf, Razorback—mixed breed; 1 inf, Razorback—wild hogs; 1 inf, Razorback—domestic hog variety, black, large tusks; 1 inf, Razorback—skinny, stunted; 1 inf, Razorback boar; 1 inf, Razorback hog—thin, long legs; 1 inf, Razorback hogs—wild; 1 inf, Razorback pig; 1 inf, Razorback rooter.

razorback sucker n
=humpback sucker.

1896 U.S. Natl. Museum *Bulletin* 47.184, *Xyrauchen cypho. . . Razor-back Sucker. . .* Body stout, compressed, the head low, the profile ascending to the prominent hump. . . Basin of the Colorado and Gila rivers; very abundant where the water is not too cold. **1963** Sigler–Miller *Fishes UT* 105, Razorback sucker. . . may be taken on hook and line but apparently it does not accept bait readily. . . This large sucker is easily identified, except when young, by the sharp-edged hump on its back. **1991** Amer. Fisheries Soc. *Common Names Fishes* 25, Razorback sucker.

razorbill n

The black **skimmer 1** *(Rynchops nigra)*.

1791 Bartram *Travels* 295, Rynchops niger, the shearwater or razor bill. **1844** DeKay *Zool. NY* 2.297, *Rhynchops nigra. . .* The *Shearwater, Razor-bill, Cutwater, Skimmer, Flood Gull,* and *Skippang,* for it is known under all these names, reaches our coast from tropical America in May. **1924** Howell *Birds AL* 34, Black Skimmer . . Razor-bill. **1969** Long-street *Birds FL* 70, Razorbill. . . The long thin bill, which is black with a red base, has a short upper mandible. The slender lower jaw is longer, very sharp, and when the bird fishes close to the water it brushes the surface lightly and tiny sea creatures are easily picked up by the knifelike projection.

razor-billed auk n Also *razorbill*

Std: an auk *(Alca torda)* of the North Atlantic. Also called **ice bird, murre 1, noddy 4, parrotbill, sea crow e, tinker, turre**

razor blade n Cf **coonheel**

An **oyster B1** (here: *Crassostrea virginica*).

1881 Ingersoll *Oyster-Industry* 247 **CT**, Razor-blade. A long, slim oyster. **1968** *DARE* (Qu. P18, . . *Kinds of shellfish*) Inf **MD**36, Long oyster or razor blade—narrow, shaped like handle of straight razor, not caught commercially.

razorboiler See **reservoir**

razor clam n Also *razor, razorback clam, razor fish, ~ shell (clam)* [*OED2 razor* 1610 →, *razor fish* 1602 →, *razor shell* 1752 →; from the resemblance of the shell to a straight razor] Any of various bivalve mollusks of the families Solenidae and Solecurtidae, esp of the genera *Ensis, Siliqua, Solen,* and *Tagelus,* which usu have elongate and laterally compressed shells. Also called **jackknife clam, long clam 2;** for other names of *Siliqua* spp see **sea clam c**

1637 (1972) Morton *New English Canaan* 227, Raser fishes there are. *Ibid,* [Footnote:] We, in this country, have not retained the European taste for mussels and for razor-shells (*Solen*). **1792** Belknap *Hist. NH* 3.183, Razor Shell Clam, *Solen ensis.* **1843** DeKay *Zool. NY* 5.242, *Solen ensis. . .* is the common *Razor-shell* of our shores, and. . . is esteemed . . as a good article of food. **1873** Murphy *OR Business Directory* 152, The clam is found in all the salt waters of the State; the razor-fish is less abundant and more local; mussels are very common. **1892** *Auk* 9.333 **NEng**, Oldsquaws do not seem to be at all particular in regard to their food, eating. . . short razor shells (*Siliqua costata*). **1901** Arnold *Sea-Beach* 457, Solenidae—In this family are included the long slender bivalves commonly known as "razor-shells." . . It is no easy matter to capture a "razor" when once he has taken warning, for he will dig down into the sand about as fast as one can follow with a spade. **1920** CA Fish & Game Comm. *Fish Bulletin* 4.48, *Tagelus californicus. . .* Incorrectly called razor clam. *Ibid* 50, It [=*Solen sicarius*] and the preceding species [=*Tagelus californicus*] are sometimes confused with the true razor clam; when razor clams are reported from sheltered bays which they never inhabit it is safe to assume that *Solen* or *Tagelus* were the forms dug. *Ibid,* Razor Clams—*Siliqua lucida . . Siliqua patula. . . Other names*—Razor shell. **1948** *Trailways Mag.* Fall 27/1 *(DA),* Any and all fall frequent victim to a variety of baits ranging from spile worms to razorback clams to live smelt and bone jigs. **1954** Abbott *Amer. Seashells* 444, *Solecurtus cumingianus . .* Corrugated Razor Clam. *Ibid* 445, *Solecurtus sanctaemarthae . .* St. Martha's Razor Clam. **1965** *PADS* 43.17 **seMA**, Shellfish common in this area . . razor clams [1 of 9 infs]. **1965–70** *DARE* (Qu. P18, . . *Kinds of shellfish*) Infs **AK**1, 9, **CA**25, **CT**14, **OR**5, **RI**4, **VA**47, **WA**11, 20, Razor clam(s); **CT**17, Razors. **1986** Pederson *LAGS Concordance,* 1 inf, neFL, The lungeroni [sic] knife or razor clam. **1989** Mickelson *Nat. Hist.* 44 **AK**, Although razor clams often occur on surf swept sandy beaches where they are common

subtidally, they are most abundant on sandy channel edges and bars in shallow estuaries. *Ibid* 186, Razor—*Siliqua patula*.

razor fish n

1 A **wrasse** of the genus *Hemipteronotus*. [*OED2* 1753 for *Hemipteronotus novacula* in the Mediterranean; cf quot 1933]

1882 U.S. Natl. Museum *Bulletin* 16.605, *Xyrichthys* [=*Hemipteronotus*]. . . *Razor-fishes. . .* Body oblong, compressed. . . Cheeks and opercules naked, or with only a few very small scales below the eye. . . *X. lineatus* [=*Hemipteronotus novacula*]. . . *Razor-fish.* Occasional on our Southern coasts. **1933** John G. Shedd Aquarium *Guide* 143, *Xyrichthys psittacus*—Razorfish. . . The body is greatly compressed, its shape resembling that of the blade of an old fashioned razor. **1973** Knight *Cook's Fish Guide* 387, Razorfish (. . g[oo]d). **1986** Pederson *LAGS Concordance,* 1 inf, **csGA**, Razor fish—like mackerel, but leatherlike skin. **1991** Amer. Fisheries Soc. *Common Names Fishes* 58, *Hemipteronotus martinicensis . .* A[tlantic] . . rosy razorfish[·] *Hemipteronotus novacula . .* pearly razorfish[·] *Hemipteronotus splendens . .* green razorfish[·]

2 See **razor clam.**

razor-legged adj Cf *DS* X37, *hatchet-legged* (at **hatchet B3b**) See quot.

1942 Hurston *Dust Tracks* 143 **FL** [Black], It is an everyday affair to hear somebody called a . . razor-legged . . so-and-so!

razor shell (clam) See **razor clam**

razzer See **razor**

razzled adj

Confused, rattled.

1969 *DARE* (Qu. GG2, . . 'Confused, mixed up': "So many things were going on at the same time that he got completely _____.") Infs **IN**75, **MA**58, Razzled.

re- pref [Prob in most cases representing a conscious attempt to "correct" a habitual aphet form] *esp freq among Black speakers* Used in place of var other prefixes of Latin origin; see quots.

1891 Page *Elsket* 136 **ceVA** [Black], I still reposed, in co'se, 'twuz 'bout de ring. **1922** Gonzales *Black Border* 80 **sSC, GA coasts** [Gullah], I repeah een dis tribunul fuh rupezunt dis defenseless female. *Ibid,* I am sattisfy', yo' onnuh, dat I kin repeal to yo' onnuh' sense ub jestuss. *Ibid,* De wil'cat t'row 'eself 'pun 'e back onduhneet' de harricane tree fuh refen' 'eself 'genst de pack ub houn'. **1926** Van Vechten *Nigger Heaven* 282 **Harlem NYC** [Black], Pacify yo'self. Doan git recited. **1929** (1951) Faulkner *Sartoris* 114 **MS** [Black], You jes' got ter lay down de law. . . You jes' got ter resert yo'self, Marse John. **1937** in 1977 *Amer. Slave Suppl. 1* 1.251 **AL** [Black], All dis here repression comes on an' dere war'nt no work fo' de people tuh do. **c1937** in 1976 *Weevils in the Wheat* 79 **VA** [Black], You see you would git a "remit" to go to dese places. You would have to show your "remit." **c1938** in 1970 Hyatt *Hoodoo* 1.425 **cSC** [Black], An' yo' make dat up as a powder an' let it resolve [Hyatt: dissolve] an' yo' kin use dat. **1979** *AmSp* 54.99 **ME** (as of 1899–1910), Resurrection. . . Insurrection.

reach v[1]

A Forms. [Cf *EDD reach* v.[1] and *OED2 reach* v.[1], *retch* v.[1]]

1 pres: usu *reach*; also **chiefly Sth, S Midl** *re(t)ch*; rarely *ratch*.

1837 Sherwood *Gaz. GA* 71, *Provincialisms. . . Rech,* for reach. **1883** (1971) Harris *Nights with Remus* 95 **GA** [Black], Brer Rabbit, he'll retch up en take down de trivet. **1899** (1912) Green *VA Folk-Speech* 351, *Retch. . .* To reach. "Retch me that plate." **1903** *DN* 2.327 **seMO**, *Retch. . .* Reach. 'Retch now and help yourself' is an old-fashioned invitation, at table. **1909** *DN* 3.363 **eAL, wGA**, *Retch. . .* To reach. Somewhat rare. **1915** [see **reach n A**]. **1922** Gonzales *Black Border* 323 **sSC, GA coasts** [Gullah glossary], *Retch*—reach, reaches, reached, reaching. **1928** *AmSp* 4.132 **cnNE**, Retch up and hang the "glim" (the lantern). **c1940** Eliason *Word Lists* 14, *Retch* [retʃ]: Reach. Used by old persons. **1966** *DARE* FW Addit **cwNC**, *Reach* v. [retʃ]—among older folks. **a1975** Lunsford *It Used to Be* 167 **sAppalachians**, "Retch" is used for "reach." "Say, Tom, retch me that pitchfork." **1982** Slone *How We Talked* 27 **eKY** (as of c1950), *Retch . .* pass something. **1999** *NADS Letters* **cwWV**, Both of my grandparents always used the word 'ratch' to mean 'reach for or reach into.' . . "She ratched in the drawer." . . "Ratch me the salt shaker." . . They were both born around 1905 in Huntington WV, and lived there all their lives.

2 past: usu *reached;* also **chiefly Sth, S Midl:**

a *re(t)ch.*

1888 Jones *Negro Myths* 43 **GA coast,** Eh bin dark wen eh retch de man house. **1899** Chesnutt *Conjure Woman* 157 **csNC** [Black], W'en she retch' de ole plantation en seed her baby. **1912** *DN* 3.587 **wIN,** *Retch,* pret. of *reach.* **1914** Furman *Sight* 63 **KY,** He retch over and lifted my glasses. **1923** [see **A3a** below]. **1928** Ruppenthal *Coll.* **KS,** *Rech*—past of reach, as He rech round a tree. **1932** Randolph *Ozark Mt. Folks* 137, He retch up an' onhooked his powder-horn. **1939** *Hall Coll.* **wNC,** The bear rech around and snapped the drawin' chain in two. **1939** *AmSp* 14.91 **eTN,** *Retch.* Reached. 'He retch for the gun.' **1944** [see **A3a** below]. **1946** *AmSp* 21.190 **seKY,** *Retch,* v. pret., reached. 'He retch his hands up to heaven.' **1953** Brewer *Word Brazos* 9 **eTX** [Black], He done put on de armuh of de Lawd when he rech fo'teen. **1959** Lomax *Rainbow Sign* 72 **AL** [Black], Mister Sands retch over and got a hammer. **1962** [see **A3a** below]. **1966** *DARE* FW Addit **MS,** Heard a Negro say, "When I retch that age." **1967** *Ibid* **LA**8, Rech [rĕč], preterit of reach. **1987** Jones–Wheeler *Laughter* 150 **Appalachians,** Damned if that big black hog of mine didn't bite both of 'em before I retch 'em up through there again.

b *ratched, retched.*

1845 Hooper *Advent. Simon Suggs* 194 **AL,** Jess . . retched out and cotcht the line and tried to pull it in. **1894** in 1941 Warfel–Orians *Local-Color Stories* 739 **nAR** [Black], I retched up an' stricken a match. **1916** [see **A3b** below]. **1960** Hall *Smoky Mt. Folks* 10 **wNC, eTN,** Ramsey jumped astride its back, "retched" around and killed him with his hunting knife. **1996** *DARE* File **AR,** A friend was visiting some distant relatives in rural Arkansas. As they drove up to the house, the [relative] came out waving in greeting. As she did so, she said, "I seed I knowed ya when ya driv up, so I retched out and wove at ya." **1999** [see **A1** above]. **2000** *NADS Letters* **cMS,** Ratch—only heard as slang for reached . . ratched in the cabinet for something.

c *rutch.*

2000 *DARE* File **AR,** A worker in the local ice house said he'd been under fire standing next to a house near the end of the war, "and this German gal rutch down and grub me by the shirt and drug me up inside."

3 past pple: usu *reached;* also **chiefly Sth, S Midl:**

a *re(t)ch.*

1923 *DN* 5.218 **swMO,** *Retch.* . . Reached. **1944** *PADS* 2.12 **Sth,** *Retch* [rɛtʃ]: pret. and p.p. of *reach.* Deep South. Vulgar. **1962** *Mt. Life* 38.1.16 **sAppalachians,** Verbs which retain either the strong preterites of Middle English or variant preterites of the English dialects . . *Present*—reach—*Past*—rech—*Past Participle*—rech.

b *retched.*

1896 Harris *Sister Jane* 251 **GA,** You could 'a' retched out and tetched him with the end of your fingers. **1916** *DN* 4.340 **seOH,** Reached [rĕčt]. **1972** *Atlanta Letters* **cnGA,** Here are a few "Southern-ism" or colloquial expressions. . . Have you ever etched and retched round and scratched where it etched.

c *reach.*

1968 *DARE* Tape **GA**61, I attended a college out East; at that time, it had reach the philosophy in that section, it had reach its peak known as progressive education. [Inf Black] **1986** Pederson *LAGS Concordance,* 1 inf, **cnLA,** When the gospel have reach all over the world. [Inf Black]

B Senses.

1 To hand over, pass. **chiefly Sth, S Midl**

1885 Twain *Huck. Finn* 217, So he writes on a little scrap of paper, *"obsequies,* you old fool," and folds it up and goes to . . reaching it over people's heads to him. **1899** (1912) Green *VA Folk-Speech* 351, Retch me that plate. **1902** *DN* 2.243 **sIL,** *Reach.* . . To hand, as 'reach me the book.' **1907** *DN* 3.225 **nwAR,** *Reach.* . . To hand. **1909** *DN* 3.362 **eAL, wGA,** *Reach.* . . To hand. "Reach me that saw." **1954** Tolbert *Bigamy Jones* 81 **wTX** (as of 1870s), That fellow there wouldn't pass the lightbread. So I just reached me some is all. **1986** Pederson *LAGS Concordance (Go bring)* 1 inf, **neTN,** Reach it here; 1 inf, **neLA,** Reach me (my coat); 1 inf, **swFL,** Reach me a hammer; 1 inf, **nwTN,** Reach me so-and-so, would you; 1 inf, **nwGA,** Reach me the hammer; 1 inf, **csTX,** Reach me the broom; 1 inf, **swMS,** Reach me the hammer. **1987** [see **A2a** above].

2 To strike (someone). [Cf *EDD reach* v.[1] 6 "To strike, give (a blow)"]

1950 *Western Folkl.* 9.119 **nwOR** [Logger speech], *Reach him one.* To

strike. "He was talking when he should have been listening, so I reached him one; after that he did his talking by hand."

3 To be sufficient. [Prob calque of PaGer *reeche,* Ger *reichen,* but cf *OED2 reach* v.[1] 14.d] **esp PaGer area**

1935 *AmSp* 10.168 **PA** [Engl of PA Germans], The sugar won't reach (there isn't enough). **1941** *AmSp* 16.24 **sIN,** *Reach.* To suffice. 'The coffee won't reach.' **1964** *Ferhoodled Engl.* [4] [PaGer], The jelly is all and I'm afraid the apple butter won't reach. **1968** *Helen Adolf Festschrift* 38 **cePA,** *Reach* (Pennsylvania German *reeche*) for 'to be enough'; for example, "The apples won't reach." **1999** Millersville Univ. Center for PA Ger. Studies *Jrl.* Fall 23, *To reach.* Run to the neighbors and borrow a cup of sugar. I don't know if what I have _____. 17.5% [of 40 infs], *will reach;* 82.5%, *will be enough.*

4 To stretch, overextend. [Cf *OED2 reach* v.[1] 11 "To stretch; to draw or pull *out.* . . *Obs.* exc. *dial.*"]

1964 *Ferhoodled Engl.* [16] [PaGer], When I was in town today, I bought myself poor—Buying new shoes for the kinner (children) reaches me so in the pocketbook.

5 See quot.

1937 *Frontier & Midland* 18.14, He stood thar a long time, never movin or retchin his eyes down.

reach n Also *retch*

A Form.

1899 (1912) Green *VA Folk-Speech* 351, *Retch.* . . Reach. "In my retch." **1915** *DN* 4.188 **swVA,** *Retch.* Variant of *reach, n.* and *v.*

B Senses.

1 A shaft or pair of shafts connecting the front and rear axles of a wheeled vehicle, the front and rear bobs of a bobsled, or a sled or trailer to a truck or tractor. **chiefly Nth** See Map

1876 Knight *Amer. Mech. Dict.* 3.1887, *Reach.* . . A pole connecting the rear axle to the *bolster* of a road-wagon. A *coupling-pole.* **1895** (1969) Montgomery Ward *Catalogue* 593, Buggy gearing in the rough, made of carefully selected stock. . . Reaches, str'ig't 1 x 1 in. 6 ft. *Ibid,* Wagon Reaches, select white oak in the rough. *Ibid* 594, Bob Reaches, 1 to a set, 2 x 4 x 48. **1897** Lewis *Wolfville* 173 **AZ,** At last I ups an' make a hammock outen a Navajo blanket . . an' swings the Colonel to the reach of the trail wagon. **1903** (1965) Adams *Log Cowboy* 330 **SW,** He ordered the wagon unloaded and the reach lengthened. **1913** Bryant *Logging* 186, *Four-wheeled Wagons.*—These are strongly constructed, with . . extension reach for handling logs of various lengths. **1925** *Book of Rural Life* 2.932, *The Buggy* is made up of the *gear,* comprising wheels, axles, reaches (braces between front and rear axles) and other necessary parts to connect these [etc]. . . The reach may be made either single or double. **1942** ME Univ. *Studies* 57.133, *Reach.* A steel shod wooden pole for fastening tractor sleds together. *Ibid* 167, All reaches are made out of small hardwood trees, aprox. [sic] 4″ in diam. . . Reach lengths for 28′-0″ racks, Front sled to tractor 6′ feet. Between sleds 14′ feet. Between loads 10′ feet. **1958** McCulloch *Woods Words* 146 **Pacific NW,** *Reach.* . . A wood or metal beam connecting a logging truck and its trailer. **1961** *AmSp* 36.273 **NW** [Log-truck driver's language], *Reach.* . . The steel shaft connecting a tractor and a trailer. **1965–70** *DARE* (Qu. L48, *The part of a wagon that goes crosswise underneath and has a wheel at each end*) Infs **IA**19, **IL**33, **MA**15, **NV**2, **PA**193, Reach; **CT**17, The reach runs between the axles; **NY**27, The reach connects the two exes; **NY**233, Reach—hold[s] hind wheels and front wheels together; **OH**68, Reach—goes from the front axle to the

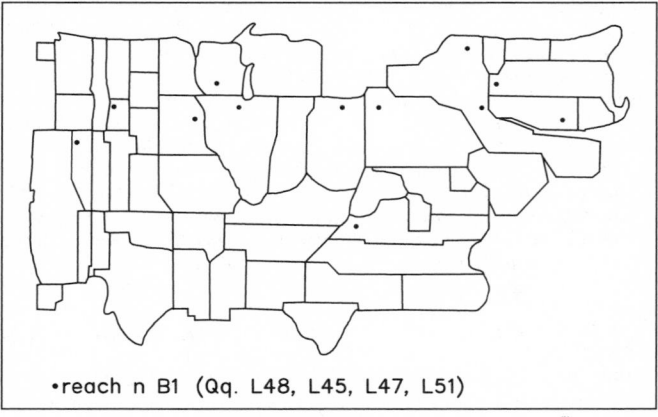

•reach n B1 (Qq. L48, L45, L47, L51)

rear axle; (Qu. L45, *The long piece of wood that sticks out in front of a wagon, and you put a horse on each side*) Inf **VA**24, Tongue; reach— some call; (Qu. L47) Inf **WI**21, Reach—connects back to wheels [Inf doubtful]; (Qu. L51) Inf **WY**1, Wagon hounds, reach—parts of a wagon. [11 of 12 Infs old]

2 =double-runner a.

[1912 *DN* 3.566 **cNY**, Two sets of runners attached, for example, with reach and box; or merely two sleds joined together by a board in coast- ing . . *double ripper.*] **1969** *DARE* FW Addit **RI** (as of c1920), *Reach*—two sleds in tandem with a board across the top.

reach v² [Older form of *retch*. While the sp *reach* is obs, the corresponding pronc [rič] still occurs as an alternative to [rěč] in std Brit Engl.]

[1943 *LANE* Map 504 *(Vomit)* 1 inf, **NB**, [rijtʃ].] **1984** *Annals Inter- nal Med.* 100.6.900 **cwAL**, Retch [has become] *reach.*

read v¹ *esp freq among Black speakers* Cf **read off, read out** To express blunt criticism of; hence n *reading* a dressing down.

1942 Hurston *Dust Tracks* 194 **FL** [Black], She was giving a "read- ing," a word borrowed from the fortune-tellers. She was giving her op- ponent lurid data and bringing him up to date on his ancestry, his looks, smell, gait, clothes, and his route through Hell in the hereafter. **1986** Pederson *LAGS Concordance (Playing the dozens)* 1 inf, **seFL**, Reading you—used now; 1 inf, **cnTN**, They were reading each other—like the dozens. [Both infs Black] **1994** Smitherman *Black Talk* 192, *Read*—To tell someone off in no uncertain terms and in a verbally elaborate man- ner. **1999** *DARE* File **LA**, I heard read used by itself to mean, more or less, to put someone in their place. This was in Baton Rouge, LA in ~1990. I got the idea that it was current in the gay community at the time and that it had come from Black English. *Ibid* **cwCA**, "Read" is used extensively in the gay community, especially by gay men and drag queens. . . A: "Did you see Richard call William a 'bitch'?" B: "Yeah, he read him good." A: "You gonna read her?" B: "Not really. She al- ready knows she's ugly."

read v² See **redd 4**

read after See **after B2**

read around v phr To read (something) aloud by turns.

1944 Wellman *Bowl* 50 **KS**, He read the psalm through. When he finished they "read a chapter round," taking turns, verse and verse, the worn Bible passing from hand to work-roughened hand, until the nightly stint was completed.

reading n¹ Also *reading-writing* Cf **writing** Reading material that is printed, typed, or written in separate characters rather than in joined script.

1935 *AmSp* 10.237, One of the colored inmates, but little removed from illiteracy, was asked if he could read. His answer was, 'I can read reading but I can't read writing.' The obvious explanation was that he could read printed matter, but was unable to read script. **1937** *Hench Coll.*, This [=a comic strip] refers to the comic distinction between read- ing writing (i.e. writing that is written in capitals or with separate let- ters . .) as opposed to writing writing which is cursive script. **1959** Faulkner *Mansion* 154 **MS**, Evidently there was a Snopes somewhere now and then that could read reading, whether he could read writing or not. **1976** Brown *Gloss. Faulkner* 160, *Reading* . . printed or typed ma- terial, as opposed to "writing," which is handwritten material. This dis- tinction between "reading" and "writing" is a common one.

reading n² See **read** v¹

reading-candy n **1907** *DN* 3.197 **seNH**, *Readin'-candy.* . . Lozenge bearing a sentimen- tal motto in red. "We had lots of fun with readin'-candy."

reading-off See **read off**

reading room n Also *back reading room* Cf **library B2** A toilet room or privy.

1950 *WELS* (An outside toilet building; joking names) 1 Inf, **seWI**, Reading room; (Names, joking or otherwise, for an indoor toilet) 2 Infs, **sw,cwWI**, Reading room. **1965–70** *DARE* (Qu. M21b, *Joking names*

for an outside toilet building) 11 Infs, **scattered, but esp Nth, N Midl,** Reading room; **CT**14, Back reading room; (Qu. F37, . . *An indoor toilet*) Infs **CT**12, **WA**30, Reading room; (Qu. F37b, *Joking names for an in- door toilet;* total Infs questioned, 75) Inf **FL**6, Reading room. **1986** Pederson *LAGS Concordance (Outhouse)* 3 infs, **AL, LA,** Reading room—joking term; 1 inf, **AL,** The reading room.

reading-writing See **reading** n¹

read off v phr Cf **read** v¹, **read out** To reprimand, express blunt criticism of; hence nouns *read(ing)-off* a reprimand.

1947 Berrey–Van den Bark *Amer. Slang Suppl.* 21.1 [Military slang], Read-off, *a disciplinary order announced at a formation, hence a repri- mand.* *Ibid* 21.2, Read off, *to announce a disciplinary measure, hence to reprimand.* **c1950** Halpert Coll. 52 **wKY, nwTN,** Read off = to give someone a piece of your mind. "She sure read him off about that." "I read her off pretty roundly." "He really gave me a thorough reading off." **1954** Dodson *Away Boats* 210, You heard 'em read me off, Sir? **1966– 70** *DARE* (Qu. II27, *If somebody gives you a very sharp scolding . .* "I certainly got a _____ for that.") Infs **TX**74, **VA**41, Read-off; (Qu. JJ22, *To express your opinion . .* "I went to the meeting, and _____.") Inf **NM**4, Read 'em off; (Qu. JJ35b, . . *Expressions [. . when you have just about reached the point of telling somebody what you think of him]* Inf **CA**59, Read him off. **1998** *DARE* File **SC**, Read off/out—we used that as kids in neSC. I later learned to read someone's beads as a synonym, read the riot act, etc. **1999** *NADS Letters* **swMO,** I have heard my father [from **cIL**] use the term "read off" quite a number of times. In fact he's done it to me . . especially when he gets angry. I have been read off by many people, and I have read off a few myself.

read one one's titles clear See **read one's title clear**

read one's pedigree, to See **pedigree**

read one's plate v phr For addit varr see quots Cf **talk to one's plate** To say grace before a meal.

1858 *Ladies' Repository* May 317, When Charlie went home next day, his pa and ma were surprised to hear him at the dinner-table demand them to "be quiet till I read on the plate, like grandpa and the preacher does." **1940** *AmSp* 15.447 **eTN,** Read your plate. An expression used to indicate the returning of thanks at the table. 'Will you read your plate, Miss Mary?' **c1950** Halpert Coll. **sOH,** The custom referred to was no doubt the same as that in Southern Ohio, seventy years ago; plates were placed on the table upside down and left that way until time for the meal to begin. Then a blessing was called for: "Please read the bottom of your plate." **1966** *DARE* FW Addit **OK**42, Read off the plate—to say grace.

read one's title(s) clear v phr Also *read one one's titles clear* [Joc adaptation of the first words of a hymn by Isaac Watts (1674–1748), "When I can read my title clear to mansions in the skies," on the analogy of such phrr as *read one a lesson, read one the riot act, read one's pedigree* (at **pedigree**)] To reprimand someone, express one's frank opinion of some- one.

1942 McAtee *Dial. Grant Co. IN* 52 (as of 1890s), *Read one's title clear* . . tell a person just what one thinks of him, i.e., how rotten he is; "She read his title clear". This phrase doubtless adopted from one of Watts' hymns, but with a very altered meaning. **1942** Warnick *Garrett Co. MD* 12 **nwMD** (as of 1900–18), *Read one's title clear* . . give a rep- rimand. **1956** McAtee *Some Dialect NC* 36, *Read one's title clear* . . tell a person just what one thinks of him, always in a derogatory sense. **1984** Wilder *You All Spoken Here* 78 **Sth,** *I read his titles clear:* Gave him what for; gave him down the country (hell). **1998** *DARE* File **seNC,** A usage in my grandmother's family [she was born 1900 . .] is connected with "read" meaning to reprimand. It has a vaguely literary or archaic legal sound, but I heard it all my life . . "She really read him his titles clear."

read out v phr Cf **read** v¹, **read off** To reprimand, express blunt criticism of.

1958 *PADS* 29.15 **TN,** Read out: Rebuke strongly. "Read him out" rep[orted] from Bedford [County]. **1967–68** *DARE* (Qu. Y3, *To say un- complimentary things about somebody*) Inf **IA**4, Read him out but good; (Qu. II27, *If somebody gives you a very sharp scolding, you might say*) Inf **MI**108, [I] was read out; (Qu. JJ35b, . . *Expressions [. . when you* *have just about reached the point of telling somebody what you think of him])* Inf **NJ47**, Read him out. **1998** [see **read off**]. **1998** *NADS Letters* **swTN**, My paternal grandmother (born Tipton County, TN 1861) and maternal grandfather (Tipton County, 1870) regularly used *read out* for 'criticize sharply.' *Ibid* **nePA**, *Read one out . .* sounds familiar to me . . from northeastern Pennsylvania, where I lived in the early 1970s. *Ibid,* When I was in the U.S. Navy in the '60s, a commonly used expression for being verbally scolded was, "He read him out."

read the dog-law v phr
To scold; to read the riot act.
1903 Wasson *Cap'n Simeon's Store* 213 **ME,** You'd ought to heerd that woman o'his'n take and say over to him! Ef she did n't jest everlastin'ly read the dog-law right out loud about that time.

ready adj
1 Intoxicated.
1938 *AmSp* 13.317 **NE** [Black], *High, ready, sent, right, lushed* refer to various stages of intoxication. **1940** *Hench Coll.* **cVA,** Geo. Walker . . this evening was speaking of a woman whom he sees often as she passes his shop. One time recently she went by "drunk as a coot. Boy, she was dead ready." **1968** *DARE* (Qu. DD13, *When a drinker is just beginning to show the effects of the liquor . . he's _____*) Inf **IN13**, Getting ready.
2 Aware, in tune with advanced taste, "hip"; hence used as a vague term of commendation; also adv (pronc-sp *raddy*) in a "hip" way. *chiefly among Black speakers*
c1938 N.E. Williams *His Hi De Highness of Ho De Ho* 35/2 *(OED2)* [Black], When an individual or a piece of music is high class or greatly admired, we indicate it by saying, "He's ready!" or "That's ready." **1945** Saxon *Gumbo Ya-Ya* 9 **LA** [Black], We used to sing, clap our hands, and you know what "raddy" is? Well, that's the way we used to walk down the street. *Ibid* 11, And she was off through the crowd around the floats, walking 'raddy' to attract attention. **1968** *Current Slang* 3.2.36 [Watts slang; Black], *Not ready. . .* Not hip; old-fashioned.—He's *not ready;* he's a square. **1970** *Ibid* 5.2.8 [Black univ student slang], *He ain't ready. . .* Unaware of what is happening. **1970** Major *Dict. Afro-Amer. Slang* 96, *Ready:* (1930's–40's, revived in 60's) hip; receptive. **1971** Roberts *Third Ear* np [Black], *Ready . .* acceptable; OK.

ready n
In phrr *good* (or *big*) *ready:* A thorough state of preparation, a good start.
1866 Greeley *Amer. Conflict* 2.136 (as of 1862), The President therefore suggested that he [=Gen. McDowell] might get a "good ready," and start on Monday, which was agreed on. **1867** Twain in 1872 *Buyers' Manual* 76, I could have ketched them cats if I had on a good ready. **1878** Taylor *Between the Gates* 71 **CA,** A time hardly long enough for a century-plant to get a good ready for blossoming. **1883** Twain *Life on Missip.* (Boston) 500, We backed out and "straightened up" for the start—the boat pausing for a "good ready," in the old-fashioned way. **1887** Kirkland *Zury* 538 **IL,** *Ready. . .* preparedness, as "to get a good ready." **1897** Lewis *Wolfville* 2 **AZ,** So we begins to draw in our belts an' get a big ready. **1940** White *Wild Geese* 177 **AK,** This voyage ain't going to be no picnic, and you might as well make up your minds to it and get a good ready.

ready v Usu with *up* Also sp *reddy* [Folk-etym for **redd** based on its semantic overlap with *ready* to make ready, prepare; cf *OED2 ready* v. 3.a, *EDD ready* v. 1] Cf *reddying comb* (at **redding comb**)
=**redd 3a;** hence n *ready-up* one who tidies up.
1864 *Harper's New Mth. Mag.* 28.616 **NEng,** The pot ought to be a-bilin' for dinner, and the Kitchen to be readied up. **1872** [see **redd 3a**]. **1938** *FWP Guide MS* 14, She readies-up the house, cooks the family meals, and gathers the eggs. **1941** *Time* 1 Sept 50, The Captain ordered Marie to ready up his country place . . for weekend guests. **1941** Ward *Holding Hills* 145 **IA** (as of early 20th cent), Our older sister was big enough to help with the house work, and had something of a reputation as a "ready-up." **1950** (1965) Richter *Town* 136 **OH,** They reddied up the house pretty well the next few days. **1967–69** *DARE* (Qu. E21, . . *About a room that needs to be put in order . . "I'm just going to _____ this room."*) Inf **PA221**, Ready; **NV2**, Ready up. **1973** Allen *LAUM* 1.173 (as of c1950), She *cleans up* (the room) every morning. . . readies up [1 inf, **IA**]. **1976** Garber *Mountain-ese* 74 **sAppalachians,**

Reddy-up (v) tidy up, make neat—Let's all get busy and reddy-up the kitchen dishes.

ready-all-over intj
Used as a call in the game **Antony-over A.**
1966 *DARE* (Qu. EE23a, *In the game of andy-over . . what . . you call out when you throw the ball*) Inf **NC14**, Ready-all-over.

ready bread n
=**baker's bread.**
1967 *DARE* (Qu. H13, *Bread that is not made at home*) Inf **IL9**, Ready bread.

ready-come-down n
1952 Brown *NC Folkl.* 1.583, *Ready-come-down. . .* Plenty of money. "They say he has the ready-come-down."—General.

ready-heater See **red-heater**

ready-made money n [Var of *ready money*]
1931 (1991) Hughes–Hurston *Mule Bone* 147 **cFL** [Black], If you was a thousand miles from home and you didn't have no ready-made money.

ready-roll n esp **Sth, S Midl**
A factory-made cigarette.
1949 *PADS* 11.10 **wTX** (as of 1911–29), *Ready-rolls:* . . Factory-made cigarettes. **1952** Callahan *Smoky Mt.* 170, [Footnote:] Its [=cheap tobacco's] quality was not the highest but it was the best a lot of the boys could afford, and they rolled their cigarettes from it whereas formerly they had reveled in "ready rolls." **1954** Harder *Coll.* **cwTN,** *Ready roll. . .* Factory-made cigarettes. **1968** *DARE* (Qu. DD6b, *Nicknames for cigarettes*) Inf **LA18**, Ready-roll. **1972** Shafer *Dict. Prison Slang* 32, *Ready roll . .* factory-rolled cigarettes. **1982** Slone *How We Talked* 26 **eKY** (as of c1950), *Ready roll*—cigarette. **1986** Pederson *LAGS Concordance (Cigarettes)* 2 infs, **nwLA, seMS,** Ready-roll cigarette(s); 1 inf, **seMS,** Ready rolls = cigarettes other than handmade; *(Are cigarettes ever called anything else?)* 2 infs, **neMS, csGA,** Ready roll(s).

ready to ride out, look See **ride out** v phr **1**

ready up v, **ready-up** n See **ready** v

reaf hook See **reap hook**

real adj, adv Usu |ri(ə)l, rɪ(ə)l|; also **chiefly NEng, Sth, S Midl** |re(ə)l| Pronc-spp *raal, rael, rail, rale, reel, rele, rill* Cf Pronc Intro 3.I.3.c
Std senses, var forms.
1834 *Life Andrew Jackson* 16 **ME,** At a cokfite he was a rale screamer. **1843** (1916) Hall *New Purchase* 54 **IN,** Tisn't nun of your spice-wood or yarb stuff, but the rele gineine *store* tea. *Ibid* 147, But most when they find a rale sincerity-hearted white, would a blame sight sooner scalp themselves than him. *Ibid* 221, Carltin's a reel 'ristekrat. **1844** Stephens *High Life in NY* 1.201 **CT,** It was the rale critter, I can tell you. **1848** in 1935 *DN* 6.454 **RI,** *Raal* for *Real.* **1851** Hooper *Widow Rugby's Husband* 123 **AL,** "Is it a *rail* woman in thar?" asked a skeptical dirteater. **1853** Simms *Sword & Distaff* 97 **SC,** Now, this widow and her son are of the true grit—people of *raal* blood. **1871** (1882) Stowe *Fireside Stories* 7 **wMA,** Lois was a rael sensible woman. **1894** Riley *Armazindy* 47 **IN,** Wouldn't swop it fer a' old Gin-u-wine raal crown o' gold! **1906** Johnson *Highways Missip. Valley* 29 **LA,** He may be honest for ninety-nine years and then steal if he gets a raal good chance. **1908** (1911) Gale *Friendship Village* 30 **WI,** I don't know of a soul rill sick. . . They wasn't a soul rill flat down sick. **1909** *DN* 3.361 **eAL, wGA,** *Rail. . . Real.* **1923** *DN* 5.218 **swMO,** *Rale. . . Real.* **1933** *AmSp* 8.1.50 **Ozarks,** A boy aint a rale hunterman till he's kilt him a Injun hen. **1942** Hall *Smoky Mt. Speech* 14 **wNC, eTN,** In the language of older people, *real* and *really* are often [reəl] and ['relɪ]. **c1960** Wilson *Coll.* **csKY,** *Real* is sometimes, among older people /rel/.

real n Also *realer, realie, really* **chiefly Nth, esp NY, NJ**
In marble play: =**agate 1.**
1896 *DN* 1.423 **seNY,** *Realer:* for *real agate.* A term in marbles. **1918** *DN* 5.27 **NW,** *Really. . .* An agate marble. Children. **1949** *NY Herald Tribune* (NY) 1 Aug 13/1 **NYC,** Now a shooter, or "real," as the aficionados call it, looks a lot like an ordinary marble, but any kid who knows a heist-shot from a knuckle-down can tell you the difference. **1957** *Sat. Eve. Post Letters* **Boston MA,** In the scheme of things, six miggles (clay marbles) equaled one glassy and ten or so glassies equaled

one "real" or aggie (agate). Oh to be the owner of a "real." **1958** *Resp. to PADS 29* **NJ** (as of early 20th cent), In N.J., also, a reel [sic] was a real agate. . . i.e. a carnelian (you spell it cornelian). **1968–70** *DARE* (Qu. EE6a, . . *Different kinds of marbles—the big one that's used to knock others out of the ring*) Inf **NY36**, Realie—different from the others, but used for the same purpose—more prestige attached to it; **NY37**, Realies—expensive ones; (Qu. EE6d, *Special marbles*) Inf **NJ19**, Reals—had special design; regular marbles a penny, 5¢ for reals; **NJ64**, Real—the marble you shoot for; **NY36**, Realies; **NY60**, Real. **1971** Bright *Word Geog. CA & NV* 117 **cwCA**, Realies—"Real high-class glass, the best." 1 [inf] East Bay.

real down See **down** adv **B2**

realer See **real** n

real herring n Pronc-sp *rail herring*
=**glut herring.**
    1907 NJ State Museum *Annual Rept. for 1906* 137, *Pomolobus aestivalis.* . . Rail Herrin. Real Herring. . . A herring, with a distinctly black peritoneum, ascends the Delaware tide-water as far as Trenton. . . They appear later than the alewife and spawn nearer shore. . . More slender and differing in color from the alewife.

realie See **real** n

realize v
    1952 Brown *NC Folkl.* 1.583, *Realize.* . . To recognize. "I didn't realize you with that new hat."—Central and east.

really adv, adj Pronc-spp *ral(e)y, rail(l)y, reely, rilly* Cf **real** adj, adv
A Forms.
    1795 Dearborn *Columbian Grammar* 137, *List of Improprieties.* . . Raley for Really. **1815** Humphreys *Yankey in England* 108, *Railly,* really. **1834** *Life Andrew Jackson* 242 **ME,** You raley wished to be *above* 'em in the administration of government. **1843** (1916) Hall *New Purchase* 225 **IN,** If you reely wants to hear about them two young fellers, I don't kere to tell about that Blue Fire scrape. **1871** (1882) Stowe *Fireside Stories* 21 **MA,** He seemed railly quite penitent. *Ibid* 169, The day before she reely hed forgot all about that there was any Indians in the country. **1871** Eggleston *Hoosier Schoolmaster* 45 **sIN,** Raley I'm obleeged to Mr. Means fer this honor. **1901** Harben *Westerfelt* 9 **nGA,** I railly would try to have a little more pride. **1909** *DN* 3.361 **eAL, wGA,** *Rail(l)y.* . . Really. **1931** Faulkner *Sanctuary* 303 **TN,** "Reely, I'm right ashamed," Miss Myrtle said. **1933** Rawlings *South Moon* 12 **nFL,** A body'd figger you r'aly seed somethin'. **1942** [see **real** adj, adv]. **1942** Perry *Texas* 87, The jack rabbit. . . hauls in those wind-resisting ears, straightens out, and, as a colored friend of mine says, "raley zizzes." **1982** McCool *Sam McCool's Pittsburghese* 29 **PA,** Rilly: really—"Pittsburghers think Klondikes are rilly good." **1993** *Capital Times* (Madison WI) 24 July sec D 5/1, Couldn't they merely be the product of a vocal minority of women who are rilly, rilly, rilly PO'd?
B As adj.
Real, genuine. Cf **really truly**
    1916 *DN* 4.343 **NE,** *Really.* . . Real. "That is no really baby." . . General in "*really* truly." **1943** in 1944 *ADD* 496 **nWV,** 'That's a really hound.' Boy age 10. **1991** Still *Wolfpen Notebooks* 69 **sAppalachians,** That's his really wife, the one he's married to. He's got two or three others he don't talk about.

really n See **real** n

really truly adj phr Cf **really** adj **B**
Real, genuine.
    1899 *Overland Mth.* 34. 547 **CA,** Here was an example . . which showed to the embryo tars the perfection to be expected of them should they ever become really, truly man-o'-war's men. [**1908** L.M. Montgomery *Anne of Green Gables* xi.114 (*OED2*), They all had puffed sleeves . . it was awfully hard there among the others who had really truly puffs.] **1911** (1916) Porter *Harvester* 324 **IN,** There are fairies! Really truly ones! They have found the remainder of the willow dishes. **1911** Dreiser *Jennie* 249 **IN,** She thinks you are her really truly uncle. **1942** *Morgantown Post* (WV) 2 May 5/7 (*ADD*), The [family] have one of the prize sites with a really, truly beach. **c1960** Wilson *Coll.* **csKY,** *Really-truly:* adj or adv. Real, really. The standard form is really and truly.

realm n Usu |rɛlm|; also |reləm| Pronc-sp *rellum* Cf Intro "Language Changes" I.8, **elm, film**
Std sense, var form.
    1905 *DN* 3.103 **nwAR,** Svarabhakti . . [reləmz]. **1919** *DN* 5.36 **AR, KY,** Rellum. . . Dissyllabic pronunciation of *realm.*

ream n, v
    1899 (1912) Green *VA Folk-Speech* 348, *Ream.* . . A ring of grass twisted and put around the ends of an oxbow under the "key" to adjust the bow to the size of the steer's neck. The "key" went through a hole in the bow above the "ream." *Ream.* . . To put the ream on the bow. *Ream up,* to tighten the bow.

reamy adj [Cf *EDD ream* v.² 2 "to be elastic," 3 "To tear, split open"]
    1913 *DN* 4.5 **ME,** Reamy. . . Not firm, of cloth.

reap v
Std sense, var forms.
Past, past pple: usu *reaped;* also *rep(t).*
    1847 Hurd *Grammatical Corrector* 88, *Reaped* ["incorrect" pronc = [rep]; "correct" pronc = [ript]]. **1891** *DN* 1.165 **cNY,** *Rep* < *rept* for *reaped.* **1896** *DN* 1.423 **cNY,** *Reap:* pret. *rep* common in N.Y.c. < ME. *rep.* **1902** *DN* 2.243 **sIL,** *Rept.* Preterit and *pp.* of reap. **1941** McDavid *Coll.* **nNY,** [rɛp], preterit of *reap.*

reap hook n Also *reaping hook,* occas *reaf hook, reaper* ~, *reathing* ~ [*OED2 reap-hook* 1591 →, *reaping hook* (at *reaping* vbl. sb.²) a1700 →; cf also *EDD reap* v. II.1.(2)] **chiefly Sth, S Midl** See Map
A curved blade, usu fitted with a short handle, used esp for cutting grass or harvesting grains; a sickle. Note: For the distinction sometimes made between a reap hook and a sickle see quot 1899.
    1638 in 1885 *Archives of MD* 3.76, I have seised . . a reaping hooke [and] 5. dozen of truck-knives. **1714** *Boston News–Letter* (MA) 18 Oct [2]/2, To be sold by Mr. *Jonathan Belcher* . . Sickles and Reap Hoops [sic]. **1786** (1925) Washington *Diaries* 3.83 **VA,** Immediately set to cutting the heads with reap hooks. **1870** U.S. Dept. Ag. *Rept. of Secy. for 1869* 451 **cFL,** Those who don't mow with the hoe do so with the reaping hook. **1899** (1912) Green *VA Folk-Speech* 348, *Reap-hook.* . . A reaping hook for cutting grain that requires to be sharpened, as distinguished from a "toothed hook" or sickle; the difference is always made in old inventories, the two being always mentioned. **1903** in 1961 Pringle *Woman Rice Planter* 36 **SC,** Thursday the field was cut down by the hands with small reap-hooks. **1926** *DN* 5.402 **Ozarks,** *Reapin'-hook.* . . Sickle. **1931** Hannum *Thursday April* 63 **wNC,** Thursday April stood . . , still gazing at the path in the grass which Joe's reaping-hook had left. **1938** FWP *Guide MS* 95, At maturity indigo stood three feet in height. Before going to seed, it was cut with a reap hook. **1947** McDavid *Coll.* **SC, GA,** Reap hook—sickle. Common in SC and GA. Sometimes pronounced /rif/. **1965–70** *DARE* (Qu. L28, *Tools used in the past for cutting grain*) Infs **KY27, 49, NC21, TN1, 16, VA3, 14,** Reap hook; **GA22,** Reap hook—for rice and rye; **GA28,** Reap hook—for cutting rice; **KY39,** Reap hook—six-inch handle, toothed blade; for oats; **SC57,** Reap hook—for millet; **TX13,** Reap hook—short handle; **GA16,** Reaf hook; **OH78,** Reaping hook; **LA22,** Reaper hook; **OK14,** Reathing [ri·ðɪŋ] hook—this is smaller than a cradle; (Qu. L35, *Hand*

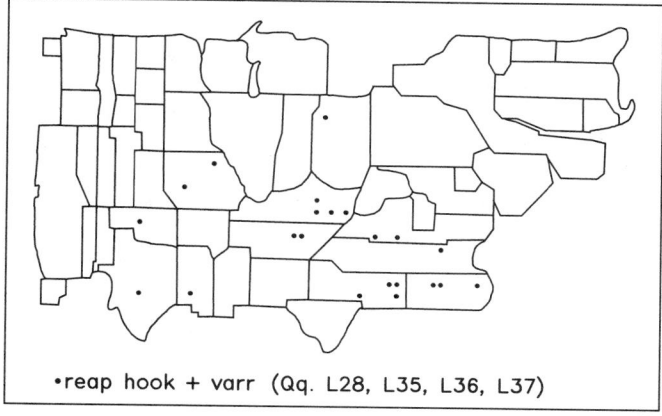

•reap hook + varr (Qq. L28, L35, L36, L37)

tools used for cutting underbrush and digging out roots) Inf **GA**3, Reaf [rif] hook; (Qu. L36) Inf **MO**38, Reap hooks; (Qu. L37, *A hand tool used for cutting weeds and grass*) Infs **MO**20, **SC**1, 39, 57, Reap hook; **KY**29, Reap hook—short handle [or] long handle; **VA**3, Reap hook— one-foot handle; **GA**3, Reaf hook; **OK**14, Reathing hook. [19 of 22 total Infs old] **1966** *DARE* Tape **SC**19, A regular reap hook. . . Just a steel blade and put on a wooden handle. And that thing is hooked around. . . Grab that bunch of rice and take that reap hook and just cut it right open. **1986** Pederson *LAGS Concordance,* 1 inf, **neTN,** Harvested wheat with a reap hook; 1 inf, **cnGA,** Reap hook—one-handed implement; 1 inf, **csMS,** Reap hook—for cutting oats; 1 inf, **seMS,** A reap hook—used in cutting hay; 1 inf, **neFL,** Reap hooks—scythes, used with rice.

reap up v phr [*OED2 reap* v.² 1580 →; "Now only *dial.*"]
1946 *PADS* 6.25 **ceNC,** Reap up. . . To bring up an old topic for rediscussion, usually a rankling topic. Pamlico. Common.

rear v¹
1 also with *up:* To bring up (a child).   Cf **raise** v **B3, rare** v **2**
[**1847** Hurd *Grammatical Corrector* 117, [Optional Words and Phrases:] *Raised,* for *reared,* or (according to many respectable writers), *brought up.*] [**1872** Schele de Vere *Americanisms* 529, *Raise,* too, has in America almost superseded the two words employed in England, to *grow* crops on a farm, and to *rear* children in a family. No one here says that he was "reared," but that he was *raised* in Pennsylvania.] **1941** *LANE* Map 395 (*She has brought up*) **NEng,** *Reared* is described as the usual term by [2 infs] . . ; as rare by [3 infs] . . ; as modern by [5 infs] . . ; and as older or old-fashioned by [19 infs]. [The map shows *brought up* and *raised* to be the std terms throughout NEng; *reared* (rarely *reared up*) was given by 49 infs, and in 15 of these cases it was suggested to the inf.] **1955** Potter *Dial. NW OH* 144, The literary *reared* was given at a ratio of only 1 in 10 by the middle-aged, 1 in 5 by the old, and 1 in 6 by the young. **1961** Folk *Word Atlas N. LA* 209, Although people of all ages used both *reared* and *raised,* there is a slight variation according to age. Older adults were more likely to say *reared* than were the young people. *Ibid* map 1204, Raised 72% [of 275 infs] . . reared 26% . . brought up 2%. **1962** Atwood *Vocab. TX* 65, If a woman has brought children to maturity, most Texas informants would say she *raised* them (75[% of 273 infs]). This usage predominates in all age and educational groups. *Reared* (23[%]) is clearly an educated form. **1965–70** *DARE* (Qu. Z17, *To take care of or bring up a child: "All her children were* _____ *[on the farm]."*) 241 Infs, **widespread, but somewhat more freq Sth, S Midl,** Reared; **KY**36, **SC**7, Reared up [Of all Infs responding to the question, 32% were coll educ, 57% female; of those giving these responses, 42% were coll educ, 64% female.]; (Qu. II21, . . *"The way he behaves, you'd think he was* _____ *."*) 11 Infs, **scattered,** Reared in a barn (*or* hogpen, etc); **KS**5, Poorly reared); **VA**91, Raised and not reared. **1966** Dakin *Dial. Vocab. Ohio R. Valley* 2.436, In the context "She has *reared* three children" the usual verb everywhere in the Ohio Valley is *raised.* Informant 155.1 reports that she said *raised* "as a child" but says *reared* "now." Her reason for claiming this usage is probably much the same as that of several other informants who insist that *reared* is "correct"—for all that they use *raised* conversationally. It seems quite clear that the older "correct" *rear* has been largely supplanted by *raise.* **1967** *DARE* Tape **LA**14, She assailed him. . . "You know better than to say, 'I was . . born and done raised.'" Uncle Bill . . answered her, "Sister . . you know a man couldn't be elected and reelected . . if he were 'reared.'" **1967** *DARE* FW Addit **swAR,** Reared = brought up—this is used by [two Infs] . . , both college educated. . . [Another Inf] whose English is closer to common Magnolia usage, always says "raised"; **TN**21, "You hear so many country people say 'reared up' or 'reared' instead of 'raised.'" (She considers "reared" substandard.) **1973** Allen *LAUM* 1.343 **Upper MW** (as of c1950), Most U[pper] M[idwest] infs. "raise" children, about one in five "brings up" children, and a very few, with a high school education, "rear" them. **1989** Pederson *LAGS Tech. Index* 233 **Gulf Region,** 162 infs, Rear(ed); 12 infs, Born and rear(ed); 5 infs, Rear(ed) up; 5 infs, Borned and rear(ed).

2 with *up;* also *rear up on one's hind legs;* Fig: to become irritated or angry.
1842 Hawes *Sporting Scenes* 1.74, Pardon, pardon, boys, for rearing up [=speaking snappishly] and caracoling, in this irregular fashion. **1886** James *Bostonians* (Amer. ed.) 102, Mrs. Farrinder was liable to rear up, as they used to say down in Pennsylvania. **1972** Shafer *Dict. Prison Slang* 32, *Rear up*—to get angry. **1987** *DARE* File **ceNY** (as of

1932), If the victim retaliates, he may "rear up on his hind legs" and get "as mad as a wet hen."

3 with *back:* =**rare** v **4.**
1899 *Century Illustr. Mag.* 58.358 [Black], An' den I say, seein' 'im straighten up an' rear back as 'e walk, steppin' high: "No; dat mus' be Marse George Dunc'n!" **1927** Kennedy *Gritny* 215 **sLA** [Black], Sho will make you rear back an' smack yo' lips manful, after you done sopped some o' dese light biscuits in dis good ole-time Creyall gravy.

4 =**rare** v **5b.**
1948 Hurston *Seraph* 292 **FL,** Copasetty! I'm rearing to go.

rear n¹
1 The upstream end of a log drive; logs that have become lodged or stranded; hence combs *dry rear, high rear* logs stranded on the banks; *floating rear* logs in the water but unable to move downstream.   Cf **pick** v **3c, sack** v **1a**
1878 *Lumberman's Gaz.* 20 Apr 352/4 **MI,** The head of the Pine river drive is at the foot of Van Etten Lake, and the rear at the middle forks. **1893** *Scribner's Mag.* 13.715 **MI,** Whether the drive is being moved on floods from dams, or on natural water, there are great fluctuations in depth of water; and, as a consequence, as the rear passes along, large numbers of logs which have been thrown out beyond the limit of the present flow of water, lodging on the bank, on the flats, and in false channels, must be got into the moving drive. **1905** U.S. Forest Serv. *Bulletin* 61.44 [Logging terms], *Rear.* . . The upstream end of a drive; the logs may be either stranded or floating. "Floating rear" comprises those logs which may be floated back into the current; "dry rear," those which must be dragged or rolled back. **1908** Day *King Spruce* 347 **ME,** There were now one hundred and sixty herders of the wild flock, with Barnum Withee . . to take command of the rear. **1913** Bryant *Logging* 377, The drive on small streams continues until all of the logs have left the banking ground. A crew then starts to "pick rear," which consists in collecting all the stranded logs along the stream and in the sloughs and putting them into the water so that they will go out with the drive. **1942** ME Univ. *Studies* 57.88, During the waiting period, the drivers throw piled wood into the stream or take down high rear. *Ibid* 100, Because of deeper and swifter water, a crew is necessary on each side of the stream, in taking the rear down the larger streams. Sometimes all the crew moves to one side if there is a bad stretch of rear on that side, with the other clear of wood. **1956** Sorden-Ebert *Logger's Words* 27 **Gt Lakes,** *Rear,* The upstream end of a drive; the logs either in the water or on the bank. **1966** *DARE* Tape **ME**26, [Inf:] There's one fellow there, put him sacking rear . . 'cause he couldn't ride the lumber. [FW:] He was sacking what? [Inf:] Rear. [FW:] What's that? [Inf:] Well, that's the stuff that's left behind the main glut, the stuff that you kick out. . . Strays, see, in the bushes and like that.

2 attrib in var combs (as *rear boat,* ~ *crew,* ~ *foreman*) referring to the operation of following a log drive and returning lodged or stranded logs to the main channel.
1893 *Scribner's Mag.* 13.715 **MI,** Behind them follows the "rear crew," the name indicating the work they do. **1958** McCulloch *Woods Words* 146 **Pacific NW,** *Rear boat*—A heavy river boat used in rearing a drive. Where there were no roads the camp gear followed down behind the crew in a rear boat. *Rear foreman*—The head man of the clean-up crew at the back end of the drive.

rear v², hence vbl n *rearing* Also with *it*
To follow (a log drive) and return lodged or stranded logs to the main channel.
1958 McCulloch *Woods Words* 146 **Pacific NW,** *Rear.* . . To roll stranded logs into the river behind a drive. The progress of the drive was measured by the advance of the rear, because the drive was not done till all the logs possible were brought in. In figuring how long it would take to drive a certain distance, river men would say they could "rear it" so many miles a day. **1958** [see **rear** n¹ **2**].

rear n²
An amount of snuff taken at one time.
1925 *AmSp* 1.137 **Pacific NW,** When he leaves the cookhouse he "fogs-up" on his pipe, or takes a "rear of snoose." "Snoose" is a certain brand of Swedish snuff; it is moist and hot with pepper, and the man who is not used to it will find his gums burning and his head swimming when he tries his first "rear."

rear back v See **rear** v[1] **3**

rearback n [Cf *rare back* at **rare** v **4**, **rear** v[1] **3**]
See quots.
1922 Rollins *Cowboy* 285, In the "rear back," or "back fall," according as one termed it, the horse, attempting to stand on its hind legs, quivered, unintentionally lost its balance, and fell. **1929** *AmSp* 5.65 **NE** [Cattle country talk], During a "rearback," "back fall," "back throw," or "side throw," the "bronc" rears up and attempts to stand erect on his hind legs.

rear-back adj Also *rear-backted* [Appar varr of *reared back*; cf *rared back* at **rare** v **4**, **rear** v[1] **3**]
Standing up stiffly.
1934 Hurston *Jonah's Gourd Vine* 70 **AL** [Black], Boys with "rear-back" hair held down by a thick coating of soap. **1949** Faulkner *Knight's Gambit* 11 **MS**, A widower of sixty or more, portly, white-headed, with an erect and dignified carriage which the Negroes call 'rear-backted.'

rear boat (or crew, foreman) See **rear** n[1] **2**

rearhorse n [See quot 1901] Cf **devil's horse 1**
=**praying mantis B.**
1859 (1968) Bartlett *Americanisms* 356, *Rear Horse.* The vulgar name, at the South, for the orthopterous insect called the Mantis. **1869** U.S. Dept. Ag. *Rept. of Secy. for 1868* 308, The *Mantes* or "rear-horses" prey upon other insects. **1899** (1912) Green *VA Folk-Speech* 348, *Rear-horse.* . . Pronounced *rare*. The mantis. **1901** Howard *Insect Book* 327, They [=mantids] are more commonly known, however, in the south, as "rearhorses," from the rearing attitude assumed when about to grasp another insect. **1948** Wolfe *Farm Gloss.* 203, *Mantis.* . . Often called Rear-horses.

rearing, rear it See **rear** v[2]

rear jockey See **jockey 3**

rearovers to catch meddlers n pl [Var of **layover(s) to catch meddlers**; cf *EDD rare overs for meddlers* (at *rare overs*)]
1906 *DN* 3.153 **nwAR**, *Rearovers* ['rærovəz]. . . Used as an evasive answer to children. "What's that?" "Rearovers to catch meddlers."

rear up See **rear** v[1] **1, 2**

rear up on one's hind legs See **rear** v[1] **2**

reason See **raisin**

reata n Also sp *riata, riato, riatta* [Span *reata*] **chiefly SW**
A rawhide rope; a **lariat.**
1846 *Californian* (Monterey CA) 12 Sept 1/1, A riata (rope) was made fast to the broken bone and the jaw dragged out. **1853** *Harper's New Mth. Mag.* 7.308 **West**, Each mule being secured by a long *réata* . . was permitted to graze until sunset. **1892** *DN* 1.194 **TX**, *Reáta:* a lariat. **1897** Lummis *King of Broncos* 9 **NM**, Juan had the reata unknotted from his saddle-horn and held it ready to run out the noose. **1914** *DN* 4.165 **AZ**, *Riata.* . . A lasso. **1920** Hunter *Trail Drivers TX* 336 (as of c1880), Lots of them have laid down their saddles, spurs and hobbles, coiled the riatta, and crossed the River Styx. **1929** Dobie *Vaquero* 25 **West**, The rawhide reata, which the vaqueros of Texas and Spanish America had used for generations, was coming into use on ships. **1932** Bentley *Spanish Terms* 194, In America reata signifies a cord or rope made of woven or braided leather or rawhide strands; a hard-twisted rope of any kind used for lassoing purposes. *Reata,* the Spanish form of the word, is used about as often by English-speaking cowboys and others along the border as *lariat.* **1936** McCarthy *Lang. Mosshorn* np **West** [Range terms], *Riato,* An occasional term for rope. **1937** *DN* 6.621 **swTX**, It may be added that along the border *riata* is as common for "lariat," as is *lazo* for "lasso." **1962** Atwood *Vocab. TX* 50, *Rope used with cattle.* Aside from the universal *rope,* the old ranching term *reata* . . is still current, presumably for a rawhide rope rather than one made of hemp. It is distinctly concentrated in Southwest Texas, although there are a few occurrences in the West. **1966** *DARE* FW Addit **NM**13, Riata—a lariat or "lasso," often made of leather.

reathing hook See **reap hook**

reback v Cf **bob** n[3] **1**, **bob** v[1], **hooky ~**
1901 *DN* 2.146 **wNY**, *Reback* ['ribæk]. . . To catch on bobs.

rebby adj [From *reb* abbr for *rebel*]
See quot.
1993 Delany–Delany *Having Our Say* 10 **cNC** [Black], The rebby boys tend to stand out, make themselves known. Rebby is what we used to call racist white men. I guess it's short for rebel.

Rebellion n Also *Great Rebellion, War of (the)* ~ **Nth, N Midl**, esp **NEng** *old-fash* Cf **Rebel War, Revolution** ~
The American Civil War.
1862 in 1863 Headley *Gt. Rebellion* 1.7, Unexampled success . . has attended our Agents in canvasssing [sic] for the *"Great Rebellion."* **1864** in 1935 *IA Jrl. Hist. & Politics* 33.146 **NYC**, Seemed dissatisfied with the Rebellion, but reticent. **1873** *Newton Kansan* 6 March 2/2 *(DA)*, The Committee did not underrate the great services of the soldiers and sailors of the war of the rebellion in preserving our free-institutions. **1890** Langford *Vigilante Days* 2.412 **TN**, Just before the great rebellion I was married to one I dearly loved. **1948** *Chicago Daily Tribune* (IL) 29 Feb sec 1 6/3, The library has the 127 volumes of the War of the Rebellion Official Records. **1966** Dakin *Dial. Vocab. Ohio R. Valley* 2.516, The Civil War is still quite commonly called *The War of the Rebellion* by older speakers above the river. Significantly, this expression is rarely heard outside the Mountains in Kentucky. **1966** FWP *Guide VT* 85, After the Great Rebellion Vermonters were "too tuckered out" by the war and the thirty preceding years of intense emotionalism to get excited about anything. **1969** McDavid *Unpleasantness* 197, The Rebellion (*Great Rebellion, War of the Rebellion*) was used by northern politicians from the beginning. It was the term consistently used by the federal government, as in Andrew Johnson's presidential proclamation of amnesty in 1865. *Ibid* 198, In New England *Rebellion* is nearly as common [in Linguistic Atlas records] as *Civil War,* especially in Maine, New Hampshire, and Vermont. It is not limited to the oldest New England informants; many of the younger ones also use the term. Most informants, of course, also say *Civil War.* In the Atlantic states the area in which *Rebellion* is widespread includes New England, New York state, and roughly the northern third of New Jersey and Pennsylvania. From New England westward, even in the area of Yankee settlement, its incidence falls off . . it is very rare in metropolitan New York and the lower Hudson Valley. Outside the area of New England settlement *Rebellion* is much less common and is normally confined to the oldest informants. *Ibid* 199, As we go farther west, *Rebellion* becomes less common. . . Since everywhere in the North Central region *Rebellion* is commonest in the speech of the oldest informants, it is plainly a dying term. **1970** *DARE* (Qu. FF21b, . . *About old jokes people say: "The first time I heard that one _____."*) Inf **TX**104, Was in the War of Rebellion. **1973** Allen *LAUM* 1.383 (as of c1950), In the U[pper] M[idwest] nearly all speakers use simply *Civil War.* A few, largely in Type I [=old, with little educ] and in Iowa and Nebraska, offer *The Rebellion, War of the Rebellion,* . . [etc], but only four of these do not also use *Civil War.* **1986** Pederson *LAGS Concordance (Civil War)* 3 infs, **nwAR, seAL, cwMS**, (The) War of the Rebellion; 1 inf, **cnTN**, War of the Rebellion—Northern name; 1 inf, **swMS**, War of the Rebellion—heard, Southerners object; 1 inf, **cwAL**, War of Rebellion; 1 inf, **nwGA**, War of Rebellion—another name, she doesn't use; 1 inf, **neFL**, The Rebellion—only in the North; 1 inf, **csGA**, Rebellion—some say; 1 inf, **swGA**, Rebellion; [2 infs, (The) Civil War was a) rebellion].

rebelsome See **-some**

rebel violet n Cf **Confederate violet**
A **violet** (here: *Viola sororia*).
1967 *DARE* (Qu. S26e, *Other wildflowers not yet mentioned;* not asked in early QRs) Inf **TN**22, Rebel violet—gray, cross between white and blue.

Rebel War n Cf **Rebellion, Revolution War**
The American Civil War.
1943 *LANE* Map 551 *(The Civil War)* 1 inf, **sRI**, Rebel War. **1956** Algren *Walk on the Wild Side* 96 **wTX**, Dove . . squinted up in perplexity at a heroic sculpture. "Must be somebody from the Rebel War," he finally decided. **1969** McDavid *Unpleasantness* 200, [In the Linguistic Atlas records] *Rebel War* is found once in New York, twice in North Carolina, once in South Caroliina [sic], and once in Georgia. Apparently to southerners being a *rebel* is ideologically less offensive than participating in a *Rebellion.*

reb'm See **reverend**

rebozo n Also *reboso, reboza;* for addit varr see quots [Span *reboza*] **SW**

A large shawl worn chiefly by Spanish-American women as a covering for the head and shoulders.

[**1807** J. Pinkerton *Mod. Geogr.* (rev. ed.) III.185 *(OED2),* The Mexican ladies . . when they are at home, or go out in a carriage, . . wear what is called the *rebozo,* or muffler, like the shawls now used at Madrid.] **1831** (1973) Pattie *Personal Narr.* 286 **NM,** The Indian women were all clad in blue petticoats, a cotton *camisas,* with bosom and sleeves ruffled; then thrown gracefully over a blue and white striped *revoza* or scarf, all of their own manufacture. **1853** in *Wkly. New Mexican* 9 Dec. (1864) 2/2 *(DAE),* Some blanketed, with sombreros and cigarritoes, . . some with rebosos. **1892** *DN* 1.194 **TX,** *Rebóso:* the headgear of Mexican women, corresponding somewhat to the *mantilla* of the mother country. **1895** (1969) Graham *Stories of Foot-hills* 134 **CA,** The lake itself was not more placid than the señora's face under her black rebozo. **1909** Austin *Lost Borders* 167 **SW,** Marguerita leaned her fat arms on the table, wrapped in her blue reboza. **1910** Hart *Vigilante Girl* 77 **nCA,** Over the body he draped the *serape,* and then . . he covered the swollen and disfigured face with her *rebozo,* and set forth.

reb'ren' See **reverend**

reccolation See **recollect**

receipt n Pronc-spp *resate, reseet* [*OED2* c1386 →] *old-fash*

A recipe.

1847 (1852) Crowen *Amer. Cookery* [iii] **NY,** The writer of these receipts has been for the last eight years collecting information and practising every variety of plain and fancy cookery. **1847** (1979) Rutledge *Carolina Housewife* v, This volume . . contains upwards of five hundred and fifty receipts. **1851** Hooper *Widow Rugby's Husband* 96 **AL,** He sold the reseet to old Mrs. Spraggins. **1858** Hammett *Piney Woods Tavern* 102, He worked the old docter's resate till it was equil to a Californy gold mine. **1909** *DN* 3.362 **eAL, wGA,** Receipt. . . Recipe. **1913** (1919) *WNID* (at *receipt*), Receipt (in the sense of a formula of ingredients or of directions regarding their mixture) applies esp. to cookery, *recipe,* in strict usage, to medicine. . . But *recipe* is often used in the sense of *receipt.* **1926** *DN* 5.388 **ME,** Receipt. . . Recipe. . . Common. **1931** *AmSp* 6.218, I write *recipe* but say *receipt.* My mother has always used *receipt;* she came to Boston from the Middle West at the age of seven, and Boston . . is the basis of my dialect. Of late I have found myself using my wife's form, *recipe,* in speech as well as in writing. She grew up in Caldwell, N.J.; her mother uses *recipe,* but her mother's mother (Homer, N.Y.) still says *receipt.* *Ibid* 390, My mother says *recipe* but writes *receipt.* She was born in North Carolina and did not come to the Middle West until after her marriage. Her Pennsylvania Dutch mother . . used *receipt.* **c1938** in 1970 Hyatt *Hoodoo* 2.1793 **wTN** [Black], Yes, dese ole receipts. **1950** *WELS* **WI** (*Written directions for cooking a dish, baking a cake, etc*) 17 Infs, Receipt [Of these Infs, 6 gave *receipt* as their only response; of the rest, 6 indicated that it was an old-fashioned alternative to *recipe* and 4 that it was less common or used by other people.]; 1 Inf, Recipe; [ri'sit]—said this till they went to school. **1960** Criswell *Resp. to PADS 20* **Ozarks,** Receipt—Universal term for *recipe* until lately. Now not common. **1965–70** *DARE* (Qu. H79, . . *The exact directions for cooking a certain dish, making a cake, and so on*) 136 Infs, **widespread, but more freq Midl, NEast, Mid Atl,** Receipt [Of all Infs responding to the question, 70% were old; of those giving the response *receipt,* 80% were old; of these 136 Infs, *receipt* was the only response of 23 (nearly all the others gave *recipe* as well); 4 are recorded as having used it in conversation, and 3 as having explicitly indicated that it was the current or most common term. On the other hand, 75 indicated that it was older, old-fashioned, or obsolete, and another 8 said that they had heard it from other people but did not use it themselves.]; **AR55,** Receipt—Negro usage; **IA22,** Receipt; recipe—really the correct one; **MD37,** Receipt—only illiterates say this; **MD39,** Receipt [FW: Inf remembers this from years back; FW heard her use it spontaneously in conv.]; **MA48,** Recipe, receipt—spelled the same, pronounced different; **MI61,** I never did know whether it was "receipt" or "recipe"; I guess I use one as much as the other; **SC4,** Recipe—spelled this way, but pronounced as "receipt"; (Qu. FF3, . . *'Showers' or 'gift parties'*) Inf **WI5,** Receipt showers—bring receipt, one ingredient, and the pan you make it in. **1977** Anderson *Grass Roots Cookbook* 115 **sSC,** Miz Smith would go to parties and get receipts and come back and tell me how something looked and tasted. **1982** Barrick *Coll.* **csPA,** Receipt—recipe—Common before 1960.

rech See **reach** v **A1, 2a, 3a**

recitation bench n Also *recitation seat, reciting bench*

1 A bench, esp at the front of a one-room schoolhouse, for students being examined orally.

1841 *Ladies' Repository* 1.108, He selects the best University . . ; relies much upon the aid of his superior classmates, and places his head upon the recitation bench in the vain hope that the intellects of others operating on his passive soul, will mold him into a genius. **1850** Mayhew *Pop. Educ.* 387 **MI,** *Plan of a School-house for fifty-six Scholars.* . . II, recitation seats. **1864** *Harper's New Mth. Mag.* 29.456 **Sth,** I saw my little sister with a timid, half-frightened manner moving to the recitation-bench. **1887** *Lippincott's* 40.293, [A student at Yale] never tires of inscribing his class numerals on recitation-benches. **1932** Randolph *Ozark Mt. Folks* 43, Th' teacher he had a leetle table an' a stool all t' hisse'f, with a big long recitin' bench in front whar he could keep his eye on th' young-uns. **1946** Driscoll *Country Jake* 120 **KS** (as of c1900), A history recitation was in progress, with a dozen pupils sitting on the recitation bench, each rising to recite when called upon. **1949** Arnow *Hunter's Horn* 139 **KY,** Lee Roy, you an Ruby git up to this here recitation bench; bring your arithmetic an tablets an pencils. Now, Ruby, soon's th door opens you stand up an start sayen th fives. **1949** Webber *Backwoods Teacher* 48 **Ozarks,** Likely-looking ones [= books] I placed on the table . . beside the four, long, recitation benches. **1968** *DARE* Tape **MI96,** And this courtroom [being used as a combined classroom for 9th–12th grades] was a big place . . it had eight rows of seats and four large recitation seats. **1971** *Today Show Letters* **sTN** (as of c1925), Recently in speaking with a friend who had taught in the rural area of southern Tennessee, she said . . that a bench in the front of the classroom was called a recitation bench. The students occupied this bench when they were called on to recite.

2 By ext: see quot.   Cf **anxious bench 1**

1969 *DARE* (Qu. CC5, *Names for seats in a church, especially near the front*) Inf **NY219,** Recitation seat.

reckanize See **recognize**

recken See **reckon**

reckerlection See **recollect**

reckermember, reckomember See **recomember**

reckommend See **recommend**

reckon v Usu |'rɛk(ə)n|; also |'rɛkŋ, 'rɛgŋ, 'rɪkŋ|; for addit varr see **A** below   Pronc-spp *raig'n, recken, reckin, reck'n, reckun*

A Forms.

1907 Wright *Shepherd* 90 **Ozarks,** I reckin as how Wash can back his jedgment there. **c1920** in 1944 *ADD* **cNC,** [ɑɪ rɛgən]. **1936** *AmSp* 11.162 **eTX,** *Reckon* is always ['rɛkŋ] or ['rɛkʰŋ], never ['rɛkən]. **1937** *AmSp* 12.288 **wVA,** A survey of the speech of a group of young women college students in the Valley elicited the following pronunciations: . . ['rɛgɪn]. **1940–41** in 1944 *ADD* 498 **AR,** [Radio:] [aɪ 'rɪkn . . 'rɛkɪn]. **1941** *AmSp* 16.157 **NYC** [New York dialect], *Reckun*—reckon. **1944** [see **B1c(2)** below]. **1944** *PADS* 2.35 **NC,** *Reckon* ['rɛkŋ, 'rɛgŋ, 'rɛkɪn, 'rɛkən]. . . To suppose (so). "I reckon you are right." **1965** *Dict. Queen's English* 4 **NC,** *Recken* (for believe): I recken we'll go to town on Saturday. **1967** *DARE* FW Addit **nwLA,** [rɛkŋ]. **1984** Burns *Cold Sassy* 104 **nGA** (as of 1906), You need to understand that in *Cold Sassy* . . [w]e . . say . . *raig'n* for reckon.

B Senses.

1a To believe, think, suppose—often used parenthetically. [*OED2* 1513 →] **scattered, but more freq Sth, S Midl** See Map

1707 in 1879 *MA Hist. Soc. Coll.* 5th ser 6.186, Reckon'd we were not to enquire any further. [*DARE* Ed: The author freq omits *I,* so this is prob not an ex of the phenomenon illustrated at **B1c(1)** below.] **1790** Tyler *Contrast* 5.i, Something dang'd cute I reckon. **1810** (1912) Bell *Journey to OH* 37, The people here talk curiously, they all reckon instead of expect. **1823** *Natl. Intelligencer* (DC) 1 May *(DN 4.47),* Western dialect. . . reckon. . . To suppose, to affirm. **1825** Neal *Brother Jonathan* 1.46 **CT,** [Addressing a speaker from **VA:**] "Break yourself, will you, of these execrable Virginia-isms . . *I reckon—jest*—mighty bad—leave me *be.*" "You say *jest,* yourself, sir," "I know it. . . We all *say* that, which none of us would *write.*" **1827** (1939) Sherwood *Gaz.* **GA** 139, *Reckon,* for presume, or suppose. **1887** (1967) Harris *Free Joe* 7 **GA,** Evans owns this place, I reckon. **1893** Shands *MS Speech* 53, *Reckon* ['rɛkn]. This word is almost always used in the ordinary conversation of our best educated people for *think* or *suppose,* and corresponds to a like use of *guess* in the Northern States. **1899** Edwards *Defense* 30 **GA,** I reck'n deir pa can take care of 'em. **1899** (1912) Green *VA Folk-Speech* 348, *Reckon.* . . To hold a supposition or impression; have a notion; think; suppose: as, "I reckon a storm is coming." **1902** *DN* 2.243 **sIL,** *Reckon.* . . To suppose; to guess. Used also in assenting or dissenting, affirming or denying. **1903** [see **B1b** below]. **1904** *DN* 2.420 **nwAR,** *Reckon.* . . To think. For a negative of 'reckon' see 'don't guess', above. 'Guess' also occurs affirmatively, but not so often as 'reckon.' 'I reckon it will rain to-day.' **1905** *DN* 3.17 **cCT,** *Reckon.* . . To think, believe. 'Well, I reckon so.' **1907** *DN* 3.216 **nwAR,** *Reckon.* . . To think, believe. **1909** *DN* 3.362 **eAL, wGA,** *Reckon.* . . To suppose, think, 'guess.' Very common. **1910** *DN* 3.457 **seKY,** I reckon I know my lesson this morning. **1912** *DN* 3.587 **wIN,** *Reckon.* . . I reckon he will do as well as any. **1939** *Hall Coll.* **wNC,** "I reckon I'll be at home next week end." "I ain't hit nary un, I don't reckon." **1946** [see **B1b** below]. **1950** *PADS* 14.56 **SC,** *Reckon.* . . To have or hold an impression, thought, supposition or opinion; hence, to suppose, guess. **1965–70** *DARE* (Qu. JJ34, *When you decide it would be to your advantage to do something* . . *"Yes, I _____ I'll be better off that way."*) 219 Infs, **chiefly Sth, S Midl, TX,** Reckon; (Qu. P9) Inf **TN**14, Bad day, I reckon; (Qu. GG12, *To have an inner feeling that something is about to happen: "There she comes now, I _____ she would."*) Inf **VA**15, Reckoned; (Qu. JJ37, *When you have reason to believe that someone is not honest: "I'm not sure, but I _____ that man is a thief.";* total Infs questioned, 75) Inf **OK**48, Reckon; (Qu. KK55c, . . *Expressions of strong denial*) Inf **IL**126, I reckon not; (Qu. NN1, . . *Words like 'yes': "Are you coming along too?"*) Infs **GA**7, **LA**29, **NC**37, I reckon (so); (Qu. NN3, . . *'Don't you agree?': "She's a nice-looking woman, _____?" or "We ought to come back here again, _____?"*) Inf **NC**33, Do you reckon; **GA**18, 19, 31, 36, **TX**81, Don't you reckon; **SC**32, Reckon so; **GA**23, You reckon; (Qu. NN4, . . *Ways of answering 'no': "Would you lend him ten dollars?" "_____."*) Inf **MD**13, I reckon not; **IL**126, I'd reckon not. **1965–69** *DARE* FW Addit **MA,** *Reckon*—I think or suppose. Usually used after a moment's mental hesitation and thought; **swNC,** *Reckon*—think, guess; e.g., I reckon I'll do that; **nwLA,** *Reckon* [rekŋ]—think or suppose: "Maybe I shouldn't have said anything, you reckon?"; **seMD,** *Reckon*—used in the sense of "think," "suppose"—much more common here than in Baltimore, where it occurred only sporadically; **neNC,** I reckon I can. **1984** Burns *Cold Sassy* 220 **nGA** (as of 1906), Her face was more freckledy than usual, I reckon from being out with the horse. **1987** Jones–Wheeler *Laughter* 136 **Appalachians,** He'd no sooner hit the water, I don't reckon, until I heard a racket behind me and felt something nudge me.

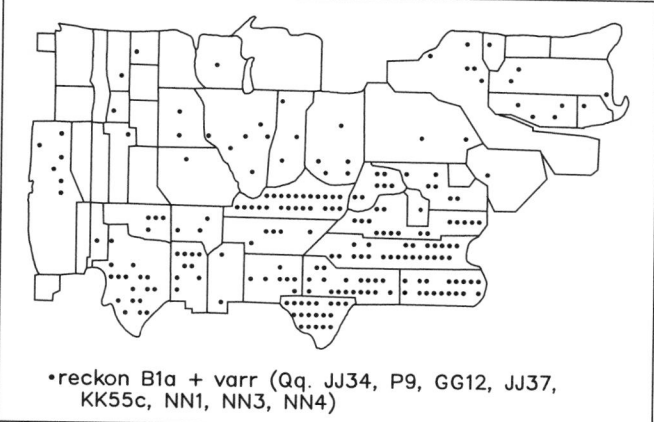

•reckon B1a + varr (Qq. JJ34, P9, GG12, JJ37,
KK55c, NN1, NN3, NN4)

b in phr *I reckon:* I believe so, yes; I agree—usu in resp to a question. **Sth, S Midl**

1903 *DN* 2.326 **seMO,** *Reckon.* . . Suppose. 'I reckon you had give out expecting me.' Also used as a word of assent: 'Can you cash this check for me?' 'I reckon.' This word is very common, but is never used in the sense of 'calculate' as many dialect writers seem to think. **1904** *DN* 2.420 **nwAR,** *I reckon.* . . Equivalent to 'yes.' 'When he asked her if she would care for him in sickness and cook for him in health, and be his wife the remainder of his life, she stopped picking wool, studied for a minute, took the snuff-stick out of her mouth, turned around, spit a stream of tobacco juice into the fire and said, 'I reckon.' [?] **1938** Rawlings *Yearling* 43 **nFL,** "You cold, son?" "I reckon." **1946** *PADS* 5.34 **VA,** *Reckon:* Suppose; common everywhere among all classes. . . I

reckon, used parenthetically or as an affirmative reply. **1966** *DARE* (Qu. NN1, . . *Words like 'yes': "Are you coming along too?"*) Infs **GA**7, **NC**37, I reckon; (Qu. NN2, *Exclamations of very strong agreement*) Inf **FL**26, I reckon. **1984** Head *Brogans* 115 **eKY, eTN,** If someone asks me if I'm feeling all right, I'll reply, "I reckon". **1986** Pederson *LAGS Concordance,* 1 inf, **cnMS,** I reckon—used as answer = I reckon so.

c Used elliptically at the beginning of a sentence:

(1) for *I reckon.*

1891 (1967) Freeman *New Engl. Nun* 220, He ain't dangerous. Reckon he won't hurt nobody but himself. **1917** Mathewson *Sec. Base Sloan* 47 *(DAE),* Reckon you paid a heap of money. **1938** Matschat *Suwannee R.* 53 **neFL, seGA,** Recken as how they-uns was plumb keerless. **1938** Rawlings *Yearling* 3 **nFL,** Reckon it's because they can't move none. **1956** Moody *Home Ranch* 20 **CO** (as of 1911), "Didn't get lost, did you?" he called. "Reckoned you'd come in about sundown last night." **1976** Ryland *Richmond Co. VA* 375, *Reckon so*—I guess so.

(2) for *do you reckon*—used to introduce yes-or-no questions. **Sth, S Midl**

1923 *DN* 5.218 **swMO,** Reckon he'll come? **1932** (1974) Caldwell *Tobacco Road* 9 **GA,** Reckon you could make her stop doing that, Jeeter? **1944** *PADS* 2.11 **Sth,** *Reckon* [rekŋ], (([ˈrɛkŋ])). . . An equivalent of *think* in its loosest sense. "Reckon so?" = "Do you think so?" Over wide areas of the South. Generally colloquial. **1981** Pederson *LAGS Basic Materials,* 3 infs, **cnAL, neAR, cTX,** Reckon = do you suppose; 1 inf, **cwGA,** Reckon = do you reckon. . . [*DARE* Ed: ellipsis in orig]

(3) by ext: used to introduce other questions where *do you reckon* inserted after the interrogative word(s) would be expected. **Sth, S Midl**

1918 *DN* 5.20 **NC,** *Reckon when,* when do you think? **1923** *DN* 5.218 **swMO,** *Reckon.* . . To assume or suppose. Cf. *'Low.* Also used in an idiomatic form of query. . . "Reckon who he is?" "Reckon how old he is?" **1929** *AmSp* 5.19 **Ozarks,** *Reckon.* . . The word is used in many peculiar sentences, as: "Reckon whut time it is?", "Reckon whar Paw is at?", "Reckon whar has he got thet 'ar corn hid out at?" **1939** in 1944 *ADD* 498 **seAL,** Reckon how he does that? [**1940** (1941) Bell *Swamp Water* 23 **sGA,** You reckon whar that rascal went at?] **1946** *PADS* 6.25 **ceNC,** *Reckon when:* . . "When do you reckon?" Among children asking older persons details about a report or a story. Pamlico. **1954** *Harder Coll.* **cwTN,** "Reckon where he's a going?" "Reckon when will he come?" or "Reckon when he'll come?" **1986** Pederson *LAGS Concordance,* 1 inf, **seMS,** Reckon what that was? = What do you reckon . . ?

2 To wonder. Note: This has appar developed from the idiom illustrated at **B1c(3)** above through the loss of interrogative force.

1941–42 in 1944 *ADD* 499 **wAR,** [I] reckon how he [could know]. . . Reckon what that ol' skinflint wants. . . Now [I] reckon what he ever did that fer? . . I reckon how they got back home. . . I reckon why she never brung it herself. . . I reckon how many that schoolhouse will hold. Radio, Lum & Ab. [*DARE* Ed: Bracketed pronouns were inserted—perhaps erroneously—by *ADD* Ed. First-person pronouns in last three exx may be misinterpretation on the part of radio personalities.] **c1960** *Wilson Coll.* **csKY,** *Reckon:* . . Wonder: "Reckon how long he'll be gone."

recluse spider n Cf **brown recluse spider**

A **violin spider** (here: *Loxosceles reclusa*).

1968–69 *DARE* (Qu. R28, . . *Kinds of spiders*) Infs **IN**45, 58, Recluse spider. **1986** Pederson *LAGS Concordance,* 1 inf, **ceAL,** Recluse spider.

recognizate v

To recognize.

1891 Page *Elsket* 120 **VA,** He boldly declared that he "would 'a' recognizated me for one of de rail quality."

recognization n Pronc-sp *reconization* [From *recognize* by analogy with the usu relation of verbs ending in *-ize* to nouns ending in *-ization*]

Recognition.

1934 (1943) *W2, Recognization* . . Recognition. . . Obs. **1941** in 1944 *ADD* 499 **Sth,** *Recognization* . . [ˈrɛkənaɪzˈeʃn̩]. The miners want reconization.

recognize v Usu |'rɛkəg,naɪz, -ɪg-|; also |'rɛkənaɪz, -kədnaɪz, -kəknaɪz|; for addit varr see quots Pronc-spp *reckanize, reco'nize, ruckuhnize*
Std sense, var forms.
1847 Hurd *Grammatical Corrector* 88, *Recognise* ["incorrect" pronc = [rɛ'kɑgnaɪz]; "correct" pronc = ['rɛkɑgnaɪz]]. **1905** *DN* 3.58 **eNE,** *Recognize* often loses its *g.* **c1920** in 1944 *ADD* 499 **cNY,** ['rɛkənaɪz]. Usual. **c1920** in 1993 Farwell–Nicholas *Smoky Mt. Voices* 133 **sAppalachians,** I didn't reco'nize you. **1922** Gonzales *Black Border* 323 **sSC, GA coasts** [Gullah glossary], *Ruckuhnize*—recognize, recognizes, recognized, recognizing. **1941** *LANE* Map 423, [After proncs of the type ['rɛkəg₍ɪ₎naɪz, 'rɛkɪg₍ɪ₎naɪz], the most common, found **throughout NEng,** are ['rɛkə₍ɪ₎naɪz] and ['rɛkəd₍ɪ₎naɪz]. Other significant varr, found occas, are ['rɛkəʔnaɪz] and ['rɛkŋnaɪz]. Three infs reported a var accented on the second syllable: "[rɪ'koˇgnaɪz], heard from old people"; "[rɪ'kaˀgnaez], jocular mispronunciation"; "[rɪˇ'kɒgnaˀɪz], heard from others."] **1942** *AmSp* 17.156 **seNY,** In *recognize* [the records show], [gn] 61 [instances], [kn] 3, [dn] 2, [n] 18. **1984** Burns *Cold Sassy* 155 **nGA** (as of 1906), Papa, I bet y'all didn't reck-anize Grandpa when he came in without his beard and all.

recollect v Usu |,rɛkə'lɛkt|; also |rɛk'lɛkt|, |'rɪkəlɛkt|, |,rɪkə'lɛkt| Pronc-spp *'lect, re(e)-collect, ricolleck, ricollect, ricollick;* for addit pronc and sp varr see quots Similarly nouns *reccolation, reckerlection, rickolliction*
1854 in 1983 *PADS* 70.48 **ce,sePA,** Pa talked very quer about things . . we were frightened he had overexerted himself . . lost his reccolations nearly we sent Larry for the Doctor. **1891** *DN* 1.127 **cNY,** [rɛk'lɛkt] . . 'recollect.' **1893** Shands *MS Speech* 53, *Rickollection* [rɪkəlɪkšn̩] Illiterate white for *recollection.* **1901** *DN* 2.183 **neKY** [Black], *Recollect*—ricolec. **1902** *DN* 2.243 **sIL,** *Recollect.* . . Pronounced ['rɪklɪk], or ['rɪkəlɛkt], with accent on first syllable. **1904** Day *Kin o' Ktaadn* 72 **ME,** The boys, I ricollick, they all clubbed in / An' bought a brindle bull. **1917** in 1944 *ADD* 499 **sWV,** Ricollect. **1923** *DN* 5.219 **swMO,** *Ricollect.* . . Recollect. **1931** *PMLA* 46.1315 **sAppalachians,** *E,* short. . . Like short *i,* as in "chist" . . and "ricollect." Like *i* in *machine,* as in "ree-collect" (recollect). **1934** Hurston *Jonah's Gourd Vine* 40 **AL** [Black], Ah knowed, Ah seed reckerlection in yo' face. **1936** Reese *Worleys* 38 **MD** (as of 1865) [Black], I ain' ricolleck dat word anywheres in de Bible. **1940–42** in 1944 *ADD* 499 **AR,** [Radio:] ['ri,klɛkt], -[kə]-. Don't you re-c'lect? . . D' y' re-collect? . . I don't ree-collect. **1942** Hall *Smoky Mt. Speech* 53 **wNC, eTN,** *Recollect,* which has secondary stress on the first syllable, is often [,rɪkə'lɛkt] in the speech of elderly people; otherwise, [rɛk-] and [rɪk-]. **1945** FWP *Lay My Burden Down* 127 **LA** (as of 1850s) [Black], I 'lect how Marse say, "Don't go into the field dirty Monday morning." **1972** *Atlanta Letters* **seGA,** A word my father used often was "Re-collect" instead of "remember". . . We were all born & raised in Georgia.

recollectment n Cf **-ment B**
The power of remembering.
1936 in 1977 *Amer. Slave Suppl. 1* 1.132 **AL** [Black], He kep' him 'roun his office jes' fer his recollectment.

recomember v Also *reckermember, reckomember, recommember* [Blend of *recollect* + *remember*] **chiefly Sth, S Midl**
To remember; hence n *recommemb'ance* memory.
1887 (1967) Harris *Free Joe* 91 **GA** [Black], Dis de fus' time w'at he reckermember anybody come. **1899** Chesnutt *Conjure Woman* 202 **csNC** [Black], It des flash' 'cross my recommemb'ance. **1911** *DN* 3.546 **NE,** *Recommember.* . . Occasional for *remember.* A contamination of *remember* and *recollect.* **1912** *DN* 3.587 **wIN,** *Recommember.* . . Sometimes used for *remember.* Used facetiously. **1915** *DN* 4.188 **swVA,** *Recommember.* **1928** Ruppenthal Coll. **KS,** To recomember—to recollect. I just can't recomember when it was. Illit. and humorous. **1934** Vines *Green Thicket* 25 **cnAL,** Howsomever that was ever got up, I don't reckomember. **1947** (1962) Henry *Misty* 32 **eVA,** Recommember how Uncle Jed said his horse broke a leg trying to follow the Phantom at the roundup? **c1960** *Wilson Coll.* **csKY,** *Recomember:* . . To remember—usually humorous. **1967–68** *DARE* (Qu. JJ29, . . Something that may have happened in the past: "Have you met him before?" "Not that I _____") Inf **SC45,** Recomember [rɛkəmɪmbɚ]; **VA15,** Recomember [rɛkəmɛmbɚ]. **1976** Garber *Mountain-ese* 74 **sAppalachians,** *Recomember* . . recall to mind—I kaint recomember whether I shet the barn door or not. **1991** *DARE* File (as of 1938), Another close friend had a word which he used frequently (ca. 1938 and later): "Recomember".

recommend v, n Usu |,rɛkə'mɛnd|; also |'rɪkəmɛnd, ,rɪkə'mɛnd| Also sp *reckommend;* pronc-sp *ricommend*
A Forms.
1841 [see **B** below]. **1891** [see **B** below]. **1941** in 1944 *ADD* **AR,** [Radio:] ['rɪkəmɛnd]. **1942** Hall *Smoky Mt. Speech* 21 **wNC, eTN,** Other miscellaneous developments are . . *recollect, recommend* (both of these often with [rɪk-] in older speakers). **1967** *DARE* FW Addit **TN13,** "Recommend" pronounced [,rɪkə'mɛnd].
B As noun.
A recommendation. Cf **invite**
1804 Dow *Life & Travels* 141 **CT,** This morning I went on shore, having no proper recommends with me. **1817** in 1920 *WI Mag. Hist.* 3.355 **VT,** The Indian agent, Mr. Johnson, gives him a written recommend to us for friendship and protection. **1832** (1961) Strang *Diary* 15 **NY,** There is no complaint against me and they offer me a good recommend. **1841** (1952) Cooper *Deerslayer* 246, And as for f'erceness, it's no great ricommend to a soldier. **1884** *Anglia* 7.264 **Sth, S Midl** [Black], *To put yo' hand ter reckommends* = to write a recommendation. **1891** Johnston *Primes & Neighbors* 129 **GA,** My ricommends to both you boys is, to keep on standin' squar' up to the rack tell the fodder fall. **1898** Westcott *Harum* 216 **nNY,** I took the tickits on the feller's recommend. **1909** *DN* 3.362 **eAL, wGA,** *Recommend.* . . Recommendation. **1928** Ruppenthal Coll. **KS,** If you want a job you'll have to have a recommend from the last place you worked. **1936** *AmSp* 11.376, *Recommend,* not recommendation, is the noun form in official use among the Mormons, e.g., 'A person married in the Temple must first have a recommend from the Bishop.' **1942** Stegner *Mormon Country* 177 **UT,** If August Dehn can satisfy the conditions he can get from his Bishop or from the Stake President a slip called a "recommend," which will insure his admission.

reconization See **recognization**

reco'nize See **recognize**

recrop n Also *recropping*
A second cutting of hay.
1968 *DARE* (Qu. L10, *After hay has been cut, then it grows back and you cut it again, you'd call that _____*) Inf **NJ31,** Recrop, second crop; (Qu. L24, *A crop or part of a crop that springs up and grows by itself from old seed*) Inf **NH14,** A recrop ['rikrɔp]. **1986** Pederson *LAGS Concordance* (Second cutting of clover, grass) 1 inf, **ceTX,** Recropping.

rectified, rectify See **racktify**

rectly See **directly**

red adj, n
A As adj.
In combs and phrr:
a Used in allusive ref to a woman's menstruation, as:
(1) *red flag:* see **flag** n² **2.**
(2) *red river.* **chiefly S Midl, Lower Missip Valley** See Map
1954 *AmSp* 29.298 **TX, OK,** Red River is up (M[en] and W[omen] Texas and Oklahoma). **1965–70** *DARE* (Qu. AA27, . . Names or ex-

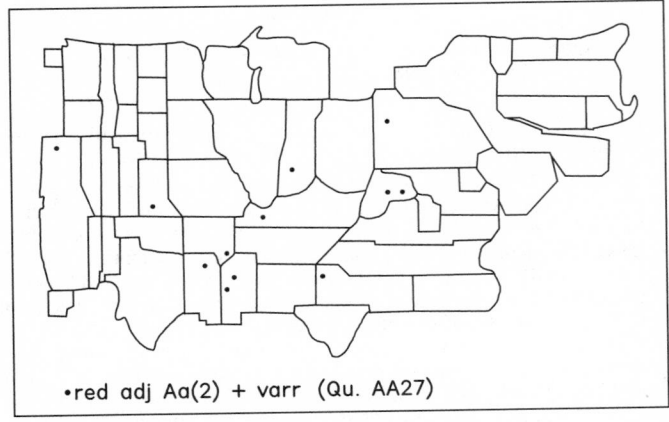

•red adj Aa(2) + varr (Qu. AA27)

pressions . . for a woman's menstruation) 10 Infs, **chiefly S Midl, Lower Missip Valley,** Red river is up (*or* flowing, rising, running); **WV**8, 13, Red river. [10 of 12 total Infs male, 8 gs educ or less]

(3) in var other combs and phrr: see quots.

1948 *Word* 4.183, Female anthropomorphisms . . are numerous. . . Some of these combine with allusions to red: *My red-headed aunt from Red Bank, aunt Emma from Reading, Grandma's here from Red Creek.* . . The use of red or blood in speaking of menstruation is more often found in male speech than in female: *the Red Sea's out, she's got the bloody monthlies,* and *blood and sand,* are or were common euphemisms in the speech of men. **1965–70** *DARE* (Qu. AA27, . . *Names or expressions . . for a woman's menstruation*) Inf **MI**55, Little old lady with the red shawl; **CA**87, Paint the barn red; **NY**109, Red creek; **NY**105, Red king; **OK**12, Red-letter days; **DC**11, Red sails in the sunset; **MS**29, Red wagon is down; **CO**33, When the board's red; **TX**95, Her redheaded aunt is visiting; [**MN**2, In the red]. [6 of 10 total Infs female, 5 gs educ or less]

b Used in allusive ref to a person's desire for marriage or sexual activity: see **red in the comb.**

B As noun.

1 See **redfish a.**

2 See **red salmon.**

3 See **red leaf.**

4 The yolk of an egg. **esp GA** *among Black speakers* Cf **yellow**

1970 McDavid *Coll.* **nGA,** The red [=yolk]. [Inf Black] **c1970** Pederson *Dial. Surv. Rural GA* **seGA** (*What do you call the center part of an egg?*) 1 inf, Red. [Inf Black] **1986** Pederson *LAGS Concordance* (*Yolk*) 2 infs, **eGA,** The red of the egg; 1 inf, **nwFL,** Red. [All infs Black]

red v See **redd**

red adder n Cf **adder 1**

1 =**copperhead snake 1.**

1818 *Amer. Jrl. Science* 1.84, *Scytalus Cupreus,* or Copper-head Snake, . . [is known] in New-England, by the names of *rattlesnake's mate* and *red adder.* **1838** Geol. Surv. OH *Second Annual Rept.* 188, *T[rigonocephalus] contortrix.* . . Red adder and copper-head of common language. **1859** (1968) Bartlett *Americanisms* 99, *Copperhead.* . . It has various other popular names, as . . Red Adder. **1968** *DARE* (Qu. P25, . . *Kinds of snakes*) Inf **CT**2, Red adders.

2 A young **milk snake 1** (here: *Lampropeltis triangulum*).

1958 Conant *Reptiles & Amphibians* 171, *Young* [of *Lampropeltis triangulum*]: Blotches bright red and forming basis for the name "red adder." A frequent victim of the ridiculous belief that it milks cows. Also killed because of its superficial resemblance to the Copperhead—and the vernacular name "adder" doesn't help matters.

red alder n

Either of two alders:

a A **hazel alder** (here: *Alnus serrulata*) native to much of the eastern US.

1876 Hobbs *Bot. Hdbk.* 96, Red alder, Tag alder, Alnus rubra [here: = *Alnus serrulata*]. **1930** Sievers *Amer. Med. Plants* 33, Red alder. . . is found in swamps and along the marshy banks of streams from New England south to Florida and Texas and westward to Ohio and Minnesota. **1960** Vines *Trees SW* 141, *Alnus serrulata.* . . Vernacular names are . . Red alder. . . It was formerly used in the treatment of intermittent fever. **1981** Pederson *LAGS Basic Materials,* 1 inf, **cnGA,** [reˑd ɔˑvˑlda p'ɛˑvˑaˑz] [*LAGS* Ed indicates that the last word is uncertain.]

b An alder (*Alnus rubra*) native chiefly to the Pacific NW. [See quot 1980] Also called **Oregon alder**

1897 Sudworth *Arborescent Flora* 144, *Alnus oregona* [=*A. rubra*]. . . *Common Names.* . . Red Alder (Cal., Oreg.) **1910** Jepson *Silva CA* 199, The Red . . Alder . . is distributed from the Santa Inez Mountains northward to southeastern Alaska. . . The bark is thin, red when cut. **1972** Viereck–Little *AK Trees* 144, Red alder is common throughout southeast Alaska on stream bottoms. **1980** Little *Audubon Guide N. Amer. Trees W. Region* 378, The leading hardwood in the Pacific Northwest, Red Alder is used for pulpwood, furniture, cabinetwork, and tool handles. . . The common name describes the reddish-brown inner bark and heartwood.

red American larch See **red larch**

red-and-yellow pea n

A **deervetch** (here: *Lotus wrightii*).

1937 U.S. Forest Serv. *Range Plant Hdbk.* W111, When plentiful, red-and-yellow pea is often a range plant of considerable importance—at least in the Southwest, where its palatability averages high for all classes of livestock, but especially for sheep. **1967** Dodge *Roadside Wildflowers* 29 **SW,** Red-and-yellow pea . . is grazed by deer and cattle. . . *Lotus wrightii.*

red ash n

Usu either of two similar ashes, **green ash** or **pumpkin ash;** rarely **Carolina ash.**

1784 in 1785 Amer. Acad. Arts & Sci. *Memoirs* 1.492, *Fraxinus.* . . The White Ash. The Red Ash. The Black Ash. The Prickley Ash. **1785** Marshall *Arbustrum* 50, *Fraxinus* americana. . . *Carolinian or Red Ash.* **1813** Michaux *Histoire des Arbres* 3.112, *Fraxinus tomentosa.* The red ash. . . Des diverses espèces de Frênes . . , celle-ci est plus multipliée dans la Pensylvanie, le Maryland et la Virginie. Elle est le plus habituellement désignée par le nom de *Red ash* . . , et très-souvent aussi par celui de *Frêne,* sans aucune autre distinction specifique. [=*Fraxinus tomentosa.* The red ash. . . Of the various species of ash . . , this one is the commonest in Pennsylvania, Maryland and Virginia. It is most commonly known by the name of *Red ash* . . , and very often also simply as *ash,* without any other specific distinction.] [*Ibid* 113, Lorsque les arbres sont isolés, et aux approches de l'automne, le duvet dont elles [= les feuilles] sont couvertes endessous, est de couleur rousse. C'est delà qu'est venu probablement à cette espèce, la distinction particulière de *Frêne rouge.* [=When the trees are solitary, and at the approach of autumn, the down with which they [=the leaves] are covered underneath is of a reddish-brown color. It is probably from this that the species has acquired the specific name red ash.]] **1822** Eaton *Botany* 283, [*Fraxinus*] pubescens [=*F. pennsylvanica*], . . red-ash. **1860** Curtis *Cat. Plants NC* 54, *Red Ash.* . . The young shoots [are] clothed with a thick whitish down, which changes, in the Fall, to a reddish tint, from whence it probably derived its common name. **1884** Sargent *Forests of N. Amer.* 109, *Red Ash.* . . Common and reaching its greatest development in the north Atlantic states. . . Somewhat used as a substitute for the more valuable white ash. **1908** Rogers *Tree Book* 435, Red ash. . . The common name of this species probably refers to the red inner layer of the outer bark of the branches. **1936** Winter *Plants NE* 179, *F. pennsylvanica.* . . Green, Red or Black Ash. Found throughout Nebr. especially along streams. **1950** Gray–Fernald *Manual of Botany* 1148, *Red* or *Pumpkin-A[sh]. . . F[raxinus] profunda.* . . Inundated swamps and bottoms. . . Small to very tall (up to 40 m.) tree. **1950** Grimm *Trees PA* 328, The Red Ash. . . is not a common tree in Pennsylvania (in spite of its scientific name), occurring locally in the eastern and southern portions of the state. **1966–69** *DARE* (Qu. T13) Inf **ME**3, Red ash; (Qu. T16, . . *Kinds of trees . . 'special'*) Inf **NY**199, Red ash. **1968** Radford et al. *Manual Flora Carolinas* 830, *Red* or *Pumpkin A[sh].* Large tree. . . Low woods. **1980** Little *Audubon Guide N. Amer. Trees E. Region* 652, A northeastern variation [of *Fraxinus pennsylvanica*] with twigs, leafstalks, and underleaf surfaces all densely covered with hairs has been called red ash. *Ibid,* "Red Ash"—*Fraxinus profunda.* . . Large tree with enlarged and buttressed base and narrow crown of spreading branches. [*Ibid* 653, This uncommon species is similar to Green Ash but has very large leaves and fruit.]

redback n

1 See **red-backed salamander.**

2 See **red-backed sandpiper.**

red-backed salamander n Also *redback*

A **salamander 1** of the genus *Plethodon:* in the eastern US usu *Plethodon cinereus,* but also *P. dorsalis* and *P. serratus;* in the Pacific NW *P. vehiculum.*

1839 MA Zool. & Bot. Surv. *Fishes Reptiles* 245, *S[alamandra] erythronota* [=*Plethodon cinereus*]. . . The red-backed Salamander. . . The motions of this species are very agile. **1879** Smith *Catalogue Reptilia MI* 8, *Plethodon erythronotus.* . . Red-backed Salamander. **1928** Pope–Dickinson *Amphibians* 23, *Red-backed Salamander—Plethodon cinereus.* . . Found under stones, rotting logs and in other damp places. **1947** Pickwell *Amphibians* 9, *P[lethodon] vehiculum,* the Western Red-backed Salamander . . , has, as the common name implies, a broad reddish band extending from the snout to the base of the tail; it occurs from British Columbia to western Oregon. **1953** Schmidt *N. Amer. Amphibians* 33, *Plethodon cinereus.* . . Red-backed Salamander. . .

Plethodon cinereus angusticlavus [=*P. dorsalis*]. . . Narrow-striped red-backed salamander. . . *Plethodon cinereus serratus* [=*P. serratus*]. . . Ouchita red-backed salamander. *Ibid* 39, *Plethodon vehiculum*. . . Western red-backed salamander. **1981** Vogt *Nat. Hist. WI* 55, From April through October, red-backed salamanders are active at night. . . Like the four-toed salamander, redbacks will lose their tails easily.

red-backed sandpiper n Also *redback*

A small **sandpiper** *(Calidris alpina)* widely distributed esp in coastal areas. Also called **black-bellied sandpiper, black-breast 1, blackheart 1, brant-bird 2, driver 11, dunlin, fall snipe, frostbird 3, frost snipe 1b, grass-bird 2e, gray-back 1g, leadback 1, longbill 2, oxbird, oxheart, sand snipe, stib, ti, winter snipe**

1813 (1824) Wilson *Amer. Ornith.* 7.25, Red-backed Sandpiper. *Tringa alpina*. . . inhabits both the old and new continents, being known . . in the United States, along the shores of New Jersey, by that of the Red-back. **1839** MA *Zool. & Bot. Surv. Fishes Reptiles* 367, The *Red backed Sandpiper, Tringa alpina,* is called . . in this country the Red-back, or the Ox-bird. **1880** *Forest & Stream* 15.4, Red-backed sandpiper . . red-back. Known on the coast from Maine to Florida. **1904** Wheelock *Birds CA* 66, *Red-backed Sandpiper*. . . This species may be known in any plumage by its curved bill. **1938** Oberholser *Bird Life LA* 261, *Red-backed Sandpiper*. . . This bird, frequently called . . simply 'red back', is in spring plumage one of the most easily distinguished of the smaller shorebirds. **1956** MA *Audubon Soc. Bulletin* 40.19, *Red-backed Sandpiper*. . . Redback (Maine, Mass. The feathers of the upper parts of adults are largely bright cinnamon.) **1977** Bull–Farrand *Audubon Field Guide Birds* 365, These handsome birds, . . known as Red-backed Sandpipers, are very tame and thus easy to approach and study.

red bamboo n Cf **bamboo, red-berried ~**

A **greenbrier** (here: either *Smilax pumila* or *S. walteri*).

1927 *Boston Soc. Nat. Hist. Proc.* 38.220 **Okefenokee GA,** *Smilax pumila*—'Red bamboo'. *Ibid* 230, *Smilax Walteri*—'Red bamboo'. *Ibid* 377, They [=deer] eat huckleberries, red bamboo [*Smilax*] berries, palmetto [*Serenoa*] berries [etc]. **1986** Pederson *LAGS Concordance,* 1 inf, **seGA,** Red bamboos.

redband See **redside 1**

red baneberry n

A **baneberry 1** (here: *Actaea rubra*). Also called **black cohosh 2, chinaberry 3, China plant, cohosh 1a, coral-and-pearl, coralberry 2, herb Christopher, honeysuckle 5a, poisonberry 2, redberry f, red cohosh, snakeberry, snakeroot, toadroot**

1814 Bigelow *Florula Bostoniensis* 129, *Actaea rubra,* Red Bane berries. . . grows in swamps and dark woods.—May, June. **1891** Jesup *Plants Hanover NH* 2, Red Baneberry. . . Rich woods; common. **1936** IL Nat. Hist. Surv. *Wildflowers* 111, The Red Baneberry . . is also found in Illinois woods but is less common. **1966–68** DARE Wildfl QR Plates 62A–62B Infs **MI**7, 31, **MN**14, Red baneberry. **1968** *DARE* (Qu. S26e, *Other wildflowers not yet mentioned;* not asked in early QRs) Inf **MN**14, Red baneberry. **1979** Niering–Olmstead *Audubon Guide N. Amer. Wildflowers E. Region* 726, *Red Baneberry*. . . When in flower the clustered stamens give this plant a feathery appearance. The showy red fruits are poisonous.

redbark pine n

=**Jeffrey pine.**

1897 Sudworth *Arborescent Flora* 22, *Pinus jeffreyi*. . . Redbark Pine.

red bass n **chiefly S Atl**

=**red drum.**

1842 DeKay *Zool. NY* 4.75, *Corvina ocellata* [=*Sciaenops ocellatus*]. . . At Charleston [SC], it is called *Bass*, . . and *Red Bass*. It is a highly esteemed fish. **1884** Goode *Fisheries U.S.* 1.372, In the Carolinas, Florida, and the Gulf, we meet with the names . . 'Red Bass,' . . and 'Channel Bass.' **1935** Caine *Game Fish* 39, *Sciaenops ocellatus*. . . Grayish, iridescent silver sides which shade to a copperish red towards the back. . . Red bass. **1986** Pederson *LAGS Concordance,* 5 infs, **neFL,** Red bass.

red bay n

1 An evergreen tree *(Persea borbonia)* native from southern Delaware to southern Florida and southern Texas. Also called **baygalls, Florida mahogany, isabella-wood, laurel tree 4, sweet bay, tisswood, white bay**

1731 Catesby *Nat. Hist. Carolina* 1.63, The Red Bay. . . These Trees are not common in *Virginia,* except in some Places near the Sea. In *Carolina* they are every where seen, particularly in low swampy Lands. **1765** (1942) Bartram *Diary of a Journey* 14 **SC,** Trees which naturaly grows there is ye Pignut[,] . . hop hornbeam . . red bay. **1802** Drayton *View of SC* 68, Red bay tree. . . Grows in the lower country. **1894** *Jrl. Amer. Folkl.* 7.97, *Persea Carolinensis,* . . red bay, Ala., N.C. **1917** (1923) Rogers *Trees Worth Knowing* 129, The Red Bay. . . [furnishes] the cabinet-maker and carpenter with a beautiful, bright red, close-grained wood for fine interior finish and furniture. **c1938** in 1970 Hyatt *Hoodoo* 1.470 **seGA** [Black], He [Hyatt: a *root doctor*] fixed me some raid bay. It grows jis' like a—jis' like that [Hyatt: demonstrates] an' all de stems on it is raid. . . You kin take that [Hyatt: stems] an' boil it an' bathe in it nine time, but don't po' de watah out. **1938** Rawlings *Yearling* 182 **nFL,** The red bay and the loblolly were in full blossom. **1966–70** *DARE* (Qu. T15, . . *Kinds of swamp trees*) Inf **FL**49, Red bay—wood like iron; **NC**1, Red bay; (Qu. T16, . . *Kinds of trees* . . 'special') Inf **GA**25, Red bay. **1971** in 1983 Johnson *I Declare* 118 **nwFL,** Neither our sweetbay nor our red bay is the laurel from which we get food-seasoning bay leaves, but the red bay leaves resemble it and have a flavor of their own. **1986** Pederson *LAGS Concordance,* 1 inf, **neFL,** Red bay trees.

2 =**loblolly bay 1.** Cf **tan bay**

1765 (1942) Bartram *Diary of a Journey* 36 **FL,** We . . staid at Mr. Davis's, who walked with us about his land, on which grew . . red bay 2 foot in diameter and 100 high. **1927** *Boston Soc. Nat. Hist. Proc.* 38.287 **Okefenokee GA,** Along a Bear trail near the south end of Floyd's Island certain trees, including a 'red bay' *(Gordonia Lasianthus)* and a magnolia *(Magnolia foetida),* were much gnawed and scratched. **1933** Small *Manual SE Flora* 877, *G[ordonia] Lasianthus*. . . Large trees with firm furrowed gray bark. . . *Red-bay*. . . The bark is sometimes used for tanning. **1969** *DARE* Tape **GA**48, [FW:] How was the tan ooze made, what kind of bark did you use? [Inf:] We used red bay. . . We didn't ever use no white bay. **1976** Bruce *How to Grow Wildflowers* 144, *Gordonia lasianthus,* the Loblolly-bay (also called Tan-bay, Black-laurel, and, erroneously, Red-bay) has much the same range as *Stewartia malacodendron.*

3 A **sweet bay** (here: *Magnolia virginiana*).

1900 Lyons *Plant Names* 236, *M[agnolia] Virginiana*. . . Red Bay. **1933** *Torreya* 33.83, *Magnolia virginiana*. . . Red bay, Okefinokee Swamp, Ga.

4 A **cardinal flower** (here: *Lobelia cardinalis*). [Perh folk-etym for **red betty**]

1940 Clute *Amer. Plant Names* 106, *L[obelia] cardinalis*. . . Red bay.

red bean n **scattered, but more freq Gulf States, West, Missip-Ohio Valleys** See Map Cf **Mexican bean 1, red kidney ~**

A **red kidney bean** *(Phaseolus vulgaris* var) or **pinto bean.**

[**1846** *De Bow's Rev.* 2.31, Beans are cultivated pretty extensively [in Mexico] . . ; the best is the most common, a red bean resembling very much in form, taste and flavor, our southern red or cow pea.] **1903** *Ev-*

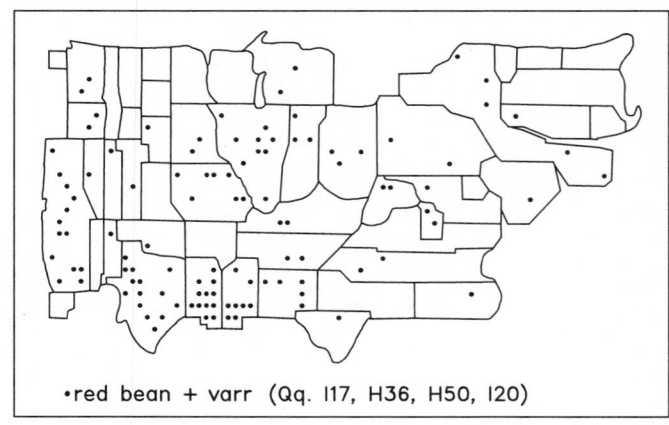

•red bean + varr (Qq. 117, H36, H50, I20)

erybody's *Mag.* 9.8 **cCA,** Here we met Blake, a husky young fellow with a world of good cheer in his make-up, who gave us excellent bread, some well-cooked red beans, and an apple pie. **c1938** in 1970 Hyatt *Hoodoo* 1.570 **LA,** You kin git a pound of red beans and put it up under the steps. **1940** Brown *Amer. Cooks* 277, Red beans are preferred above all other varieties in Louisiana. **1956** Ker *Vocab. W. TX* 249, The Mexican brown bean is commonly called *pinto, red bean,* and *frijole. . . Red bean. . .* is reported by thirteen older informants and by eight younger informants of all types. **1965–70** *DARE* (Qu. I17, *Beans . . that are dark red when they are dry*) 110 Infs, **scattered, but more freq Gulf States, West, Missip-Ohio Valleys,** Red beans; (Qu. H36, *Kinds of soup*) Inf **LA23,** Red bean soup; (Qu. H50, *Dishes made with beans, peas, or corn that everybody around here knows, but people in other places might not*) Inf **LA38,** Red bean soup; **CA91, TX81,** Red beans; **LA23,** Red beans and rice; (Qu. I20, *. . Kinds of beans*) Inf **CA126,** Red beans. **1967** *Refugio Co. Press* (TX) 12 Apr 4/1, [School menu:] Frito pie, red beans, lettuce and tomato salad, hot bread and butter, chocolate pudding. **1983** *Reinecke Coll.* 10 **LA,** *Red beans. . .* A dish of kidney beans boiled for hours with a bit of "salt-meat" or ham and served with boiled rice. **1986** Pederson *LAGS Concordance* **Gulf Region,** 30 infs, Red bean(s); 1 inf, Red beans—eaten dried; 1 inf, Red beans—turn red when cooked; 2 infs, Red beans and rice; 1 inf, Louisiana red beans.

red-bean vine n [From the red seeds]
=crab's eye.
    1900 Lyons *Plant Names* 8, *A*[*brus*] *precatorius. . .* Red-bean vine.

redbeard n [See quot 1890]
A **sponge** (here: *Microciona prolifera*).
    1890 *Century Dict.* 5018, *Redbeard. . .* The red sponge, *Microciona prolifera,* which commonly grows on oysters, forming a beard on the shell. [*Century* Ed: Local, U.S.] **1981** Meinkoth *Audubon Field Guide Seashore* 327, *Redbeard Sponge. . .* On rocks, pilings, oysters and other shells . . below low-tide line. . . Nova Scotia to Florida and Texas; Washington to c. California. . . The Red Beard Sponge was the first animal shown to reorganize its form from experimentally separated cells.

red bee bird See **bee bird 2**

red beech n
The American beech *(Fagus grandifolia)* or its wood—used esp (in contrast to **white beech**) to distinguish specimens in which the reddish heartwood predominates. Cf **red fir a**
    1637 (1972) Morton *New English Canaan* 183, Beech there is of two sorts, redd and white. **1792** Belknap *Hist. NH* 102, *Beech. . .* Of this there are three varieties. The white and the red are used as fewel. **1812** Michaux *Histoire des Arbres* 2.170, Ils [=les habitans des Etats les plus septentrionaux] donnent à l'espèce que je décris le nom de *White Beech,* Hêtre blanc, et à l'autre, celui de *Red Beech,* Hêtre rouge, distinction faite d'après la couleur du bois et non d'après celle du feuillage. [=They [=the inhabitants of the northernmost states] give to the species which I describe the name of *White Beech,* and to the other, that of *Red Beech,* a distinction made according to the color of the wood and not according to that of the foliage.] **1850** Emerson *Rept. Trees & Shrubs* 162 **MA,** I have been unable to find more than one kind of beech in Massachusetts. The workers in the wood speak commonly of the white and the red. . . I . . believe the appearance in the wood . . has given rise to these names. . . The heartwood is of a reddish hue. Where it predominates, the log is called red beech. Timber, in which the white sap wood is most conspicuous, is called white beech. **1890** Newhall *Trees NE Amer.* 70, Lumber-men make the distinction of "Red Beech" and "White Beech," claiming that the former is harder, with a redder and thicker heart-wood. **1894** *Jrl. Amer. Folkl.* 7.99 **NY,** *Fagus sylvatica* [here: =*F. grandifolia*] . . , white beech, red beech. **1897** *Ibid* 10.144 **West,** *Fagus ferruginea* [=*F. grandifolia*], . . white beech, red beech. **1964** Stupka *Trees* 43 **Smoky Mts,** At lowest elevations . . the 'white' beech, of primarily southern distribution, may be recognized. . . 'Red' beeches appear in the upper cove forests (3500–4500 ft.). The third beech type, the 'gray,' appears . . above 4500 ft.

red beet egg n esp **PA**
A hard-boiled egg that has been pickled together with beets.
    [**1916** *DN* 4.279 **NE,** *Red beets. . .* Cf. German "rote Ruebe." Beets, no distinction from white beets being intended. "Please pass the red beets." Reported from a German community. [*DN* Ed: Also Kan.]] **1951** *Reading Times* (PA) 17 Sept 11/1 (*Mathews Coll.*), Oh Yeh!

Fassnachts, Baked Ham, Red Beet Eggs, Potato Salad [etc]. [**1968** *DARE* (Qu. H57, *. . Spicy side-dishes*) Inf **PA136,** Red beets and eggs.] **1977** Anderson *Grass Roots Cookbook* 50 **sePA,** Mrs. Rohrer, in making Red Beet Eggs, would use her home-grown, home-pickled beets. **1998** Millersville Univ. Center for PA Ger. Studies *Jrl.* Autumn 17, So, you ask if my children are aware of their PG heritage? Yes, mostly because of the food—I certainly couldn't give up boiled chicken pot pie, chicken corn soup, shoo fly pie, pickled beets and red beet eggs and *Schmierkaes* and apple butter and you don't serve food without the stories that go with it. **2000** *DARE* File **WI** (as of c1950), As a child I always looked forward to eating red beet eggs at the homes of my father's extended family. These were delicious, beautifully-colored, hard-cooked eggs pickled in the same mix as the cooked red beets, sometimes together with the beets and their juice, but more often after the beets were removed from the mix. **2002** *DARE* File—Internet **PA,** Is your M[other] I[n] L[aw] Pennsylvania Dutch? Believe it or not, pink pickled eggs (or, as we call them here, Red Beet Eggs) are standard fare in this neck of the woods.

red bell n
1 A **fritillary** (here: *Fritillaria recurva*).
    1942 Whipple *Joshua* 190 **UT** (as of c1860), It seemed natural for Free to load this girl with sego lilies and red bells and tell her about his world. **1966** *Good Old Days* Apr 4 **CA** (as of c1890), There would be the old-fashioned Indian pink or paint brush, red bell, buttercup, johnny-jump-up and many others. **1969** *DARE* (Qu. S26e, *Other wildflowers not yet mentioned;* not asked in early QRs) Inf **CA144,** Red bell.
2 pl: A **wild columbine** (here: *Aquilegia canadensis*).
    1933 Small *Manual SE Flora* 514, *A*[*quilegia*] *canadensis. . .* Redbells. **1940** Clute *Amer. Plant Names* 218, *Aquilegia Canadensis.* Red bells.

red-bellied bream n Also *redbelly bream* Cf **bream B3, redbelly 1, red-bellied perch**
Either the **red-breasted sunfish 1** or a **longear sunfish** (here: *Lepomis megalotis*).
    1865 Norris *Amer. Angler's Book* 118, I have been told that the Red-bellied Bream is taken of a pound weight in the still waters of North and South Carolina. **1903** NY State Museum & Sci. Serv. *Bulletin* 60.479, The long-eared sunfish [=*Lepomis auritus*] . . is known under many common names, among which are . . red-bellied bream . . and redbreast. **1933** LA Dept. of Conserv. *Fishes* 349, The Longear has now many common names [as] . . Long-eared Sunfish, . . Blackears, . . Red-bellied Bream. . . Many of these . . it shares in common with other species. **1949** Caine *N. Amer. Sport Fish* 43, Redbelly Bream. **1967** *DARE* File **AR,** Redbelly, or red-bellied bream—name for a large variety of sunfish with a small mouth.

red-bellied dace n Also *redbelly, ~ chub, ~ dace, ~ shiner*
A **dace:** usu either *Phoxinus eos* or *P. erythrogaster,* but also *P. oreas.* For other names of *P. eos* see **leatherback 4, yellowbelly dace;** for other names of *P. erythrogaster* see **rainbow 4**
    1820 *Western Rev.* 2.237, Redbelly Shiner. *Luxilus erythrogaster. . .* It . . might be called . . Kentucky Red belly. I saw it in the Kentucky river. . . It is called Red belly Chub. **1882** U.S. Natl. Museum *Bulletin* 16.153, *C*[*hrosomus*] *erythrogaster. . .* Red-bellied Dace. . . Males in spring with the belly . . bright scarlet. **1886** Mather *Memoranda* 29 **Adirondacks NY,** Red Bellied Dace. . . A beautiful little fish much like the black-nosed dace. **1929** OK Univ. Biol. Surv. *Pub.* 1.2.89, *Chrosomus erythrogaster. . .* Red-belly Dace. . . The nuptial tubercles, as shown by the breeding male . . , are very characteristic. **1943** Eddy-Surber *N. Fishes* 135, The southern redbelly dace is a small, brownish-olive minnow with black spots on the back. *Ibid* 136, Northern Redbelly Dace. . . Similar to the southern redbelly dace except that the jaws and snout are shorter. **1957** Blair et al. *Vertebrates U.S.* 105, *Chrosomus oreas. . .* Mountain redbelly dace. . . Appalachian mountain region of West Virginia, Virginia, and North Carolina. . . *Chrosomus eos. . .* Northern redbelly dace. *Ibid* 106, *Chrosomus erythrogaster. . .* Southern redbelly dace. **1983** *Audubon Field Guide N. Amer. Fishes* 448, [The] Northern Redbelly Dace . . grows to 2″. . . The Southern Redbelly Dace spawns during the spring and early summer in swift riffles over the gravel nests of other minnows. *Ibid* 449, Mountain Redbelly Dace. . . Breeding males of this species are among the most colorful fishes in North America.

red-bellied garter snake See **red-bellied snake**

red-bellied hawk n CA
=red-shouldered hawk.

1898 Grinnell *Birds Pacific Slope* 21 **CA,** *Buteo lineatus elegans. . . Red-bellied Hawk.* Tolerably common in the lower parts of the county [=Los Angeles County], especially in the oak and willow regions. **1904** Wheelock *Birds CA* 150, The Red-bellied Hawk is exceptionally fond of bathing, and in California it usually builds within a hundred yards of water. **1923** Dawson *Birds CA* 1687, All authorities are agreed in giving the Red-bellied Hawk a clean bill of health poultry-wise. . . The Red-bellied Hawk is an exceedingly useful species. **1957** Pough *Audubon W. Bird Guide* 53, *Red-shouldered Hawk* (Red-bellied Hawk). . . Resident along the Pacific coast from s. British Columbia to n. Lower California and n.w. Mexico.

red-bellied moccasin See moccasin 1b

red-bellied nuthatch n
=red-breasted nuthatch.

[**1808** Wilson *Amer. Ornith.* 1.43, Red-bellied Black-capped Nuthatch.] **1832** Nuttall *Manual Ornith.* 1.583, *Red-bellied Nuthatch. . . Sitta canadensis. . .* Beneath rust-color. **1870** (1871) *Amer. Naturalist* 4.546 **NJ,** [The] Red-bellied Nuthatch. . . has as unmusical a note as ever fell upon one's ear. **1903** Dawson *Birds OH* 240, *Red-bellied Nuthatch. . . General Range.*—North America at large. **1936** Roberts *MN Birds* 2.83, *Red-bellied Nuthatch. . .* As a few birds remain throughout the winter there is some uncertainty in the earliest spring and latest fall dates. **1963** Gromme *Birds WI* 216, Nuthatch, . . Red-bellied (Red-breasted Nuthatch).

red-bellied perch n Also *redbelly perch* chiefly Sth Cf perch n¹, redbelly 1

Usu the **red-breasted sunfish 1,** but also a **longear sunfish** (here: *Lepomis megalotis*).

1855 Simms *Forayers* 276 **SC,** The red-belly perch of the Edisto is not one of its aldermen, but it is nevertheless a good citizen—well to do in the waters—armed to make himself respected where he goes. **1887** Goode *Amer. Fishes* 66, *Lepomis auritus. . .* in Pennsylvania . . is called "Sun Perch." . . Elsewhere it is the . . "Red Bellied Perch." **1897** Johnston *Old Times GA* 144 (as of 1830s), If it was fish, all the invalid had to do, was to specify the kind, say sucker, cat-fish, eel, or perch, and if the latter, whether bream, silver, or red-belly. **1903** NY State Museum & Sci. Serv. *Bulletin* 60.479, The long-eared sunfish [=*Lepomis auritus*] . . is known under many common names, among which are the following . . red-bellied perch and redbreast. **1949** Caine *N. Amer. Sport Fish* 43, Redbelly Perch. **1965–70** *DARE* (Qu. P1, . . *Kinds of freshwater fish . . caught around here . . good to eat)* Inf **MS**72, Redbelly perch. **1986** Pederson *LAGS Concordance,* 2 infs, **LA,** 1 inf, **csGA,** 1 inf, **csMS,** Redbelly perch.

red-bellied sapsucker See red-bellied woodpecker

red-bellied snake n Also *red-bellied garter snake, redbelly (snake)*

A small snake (*Storeria occipitomaculata*) native to much of the eastern half of the US. Also called **copperhead snake 3, fire ~, grass ~ 4, ground ~ b, spot-necked ~**

[**1709** (1967) Lawson *New Voyage* 126, Red-bellied Land-Snakes [are found in Carolina].] **1883** WI Chief Geologist *Geol. WI* 1.424, *Storeria occipitomaculata. . .* Red-bellied Snake. Abundant. **1922** *Copeia* 111.80 **NY,** Both the red-bellied and the milk snakes are very common in this section of the Catskill Mountains. **1951** Conant *Reptiles OH* 92, *Red-bellied Snake. . .* A small snake attaining a length of about a foot. . . The color above is light grey brown or chestnut brown to black. . . The belly is uniformly red or pink. **1968** *DARE* (Qu. P25, . . *Kinds of snakes)* Inf **NC**80, Redbelly snake. **1974** Shaw–Campbell *Snakes West* 132, The red-bellied snake . . is also called . . red-bellied garter snake. **1981** Vogt *Nat. Hist. WI* 160, Jordan . . has found redbellies stiffening and playing dead when attacked, displaying the bright red belly. . . In May 1973 . . I found a young red-bellied snake coiled under a bit of bark.

red-bellied snapper n Also *redbelly* Cf red snapper 3

A **red grouper 1** (here: *Epinephelus morio*).

1879 U.S. Natl. Museum *Bulletin* 14.49, *Epinephelus morio. . . Red-bellied Snapper. . .* Southern Atlantic States. **1891** *Century Dict.* 5018, *Redbelly. . .* The red grouper, *Epinephelus morio.* **1911** U.S. Bur. Census *Fisheries 1908* 316 **FL,** The red grouper (*Epinephelus morio*) is

called . . "red-bellied snapper" in Florida. **1946** LaMonte *N. Amer. Game Fishes* 53, *Epinephelus morio. . .* Red-bellied Snapper.

red-bellied snipe n
The long-billed **dowitcher.**

1884 U.S. Natl. Museum *Bulletin* 27.184, *Macrorhamphus griseus scolopaceus. . . Red-bellied Snipe. . .* Western North America, including Mississippi Valley, north to Alaska . . ; occasional on Atlantic coast. **1917** (1923) *Birds Amer.* 1.230, The Long-billed Dowitcher is known locally as . . the Red-bellied Snipe.

red-bellied sunfish n Also *redbelly sunfish* Cf redbelly 1, red-bellied bream, ~ perch, sunfish
=red-breasted sunfish 1.

1906 NJ State Museum *Annual Rept. for 1905* 292, *Lepomis auritus. . .* Red Bellied Sun Fish. [*Ibid* 293, Belly and breast bright orange.] **1968** *DARE* (Qu. P1, . . *Kinds of freshwater fish . . caught around here . . good to eat)* Inf **IN**35, Redbelly sunfish.

red-bellied terrapin See red-bellied turtle

red-bellied trout See redbelly 8

red-bellied turtle n Also *red-bellied terrapin, redbelly*

Usu a turtle of the genus *Pseudemys,* esp *P. rubriventris,* but also any of var other turtles of the genera *Chrysemys* or *Trachemys.* Also called **cooter n 1, mud turtle 2c(2), slider, terrapin.** For other names of *Chrysemys picta* see **lady turtle, painted ~, pond ~ 1, red-legged ~, skillpot, snake turtle;** for other names of *Pseudemys concinna* see **Methodist, river cooter, soft-shell ~, Suwannee chicken, ~ turtle;** for other names of *P. rubriventris* see **golden stripe, red fender;** for other names of *Trachemys scripta* see **Baptist B, hard-backed cooter, hard-shell turtle, lady terrapin, painted turtle, pond slider, ~ terrapin, red-eared turtle, redhead 3, yellow-bellied turtle**

1829 NY Acad. Sci. *Annals Lyceum Nat. Hist.* 3.101, Red-bellied Tarapin, vulg. . . Inhabit in rivers from New-Jersey to Virginia, chiefly, I believe, in such as are rocky. . . This species has been described by Mr. Say as the Emys serrata, to which it has no resemblance, none of the marginal plates being serrate, and the back being destitute of a keel. **1884** Goode *Fisheries U.S.* 1.154, Of these [turtles] the most important is the "Red-bellied Terrapin," *Pseudemys rugosa* [=*P. rubriventris*]. **1916** *Copeia* 38.95 **MA,** The Red-bellied Terrapin [=*Pseudemys rubriventris*] has been known for some years to inhabit certain ponds in Plymouth County, where it seems to remain localized. **1952** Carr *Turtles* 272, Although never attaining the high position of the diamondback in public esteem, the red-belly [=*Pseudemys rubriventris*] formerly supported regular fisheries. . . Today . . this turtle still may be seen in the markets of Washington, Baltimore, and Philadelphia. *Ibid* 278, The Florida red-bellied turtle [=*P. nelsoni*] is usually not recognized as distinct from *P. . . peninsularis* by the local people, who eat both. **1968–69** *DARE* (Qu. P24, . . *Kinds of turtles)* Inf **DE**3, Redbelly; **IL**32, Redbelly—about 8 inches in diameter, red belly, most common turtle around here; **NJ**21, Redbelly. **1979** Behler–King *Audubon Field Guide Reptiles* 446, *Alabama Red-bellied Turtle* (*Chrysemys alabamensis* [=*Pseudemys a.*]) *Ibid* 447, Alabama Red-bellies. *Ibid* 449, *Florida Red-bellied Turtle* (*Chrysemys nelsoni* [=*Pseudemys n.*]) . . [T]he Florida Red-belly is often seen basking . . on logs. *Ibid* 451, *Red-bellied Turtle* (*Chrysemys rubriventris* [=*Pseudemys r.*]) . . Red-bellies prefer basking sites near deep water. **1984** Wilder *You All Spoken Here* 173 **Sth,** Cooter, slider, red belly, yellow belly: Terrapin; Pseudemys scripta. **1998** *Natl. Wildlife* 36.6.26, In Florida's Big Cypress Swamp. . . the red-bellied turtle. . . spends much of the day basking on logs or vegetation, and even has been seen sunning itself on alligator nest mounds.

red-bellied water snake n Also *redbelly*

A **water snake:** usu *Nerodia erythrogaster,* rarely *N. fasciata.*

1879 Smith *Catalogue Reptilia MI* 6, *Tropidonotus erythrogaster, . .* Red-bellied Water Snake. **1908** Biol. Soc. DC *Proc.* 21.76 **cnTX,** *Tropidonotus sipedon fasciatus* [=*Nerodia fasciata*]. . . *Red-bellied Water Snake. . .* Living specimens are brilliantly colored, deep shades of red and yellow prevailing. **1937** Pope *Snakes Alive* 202, *Red-bellied Water Snake. . .* Widely distributed in south-central and eastern United States. **1951** Conant *Reptiles OH* 70, Red-bellied Water Snake; Red-Belly. **1966** *DARE* Tape **NC**21, Never had so many snakes around my house . . since I been here, and where they came from I don't know, and they were poisonous snakes, too: cottonmouth, moccasins, redbellies, and I don't know, all kinds. **1979** Behler–King *Audubon Field Guide Reptiles* 633, Red-bellied [water snake] *(N[erodia] e[rythrogaster] erythrogaster),* belly red, orange, or pink.

red-bellied woodpecker n Also *redbelly, red-bellied sapsucker* [See quot 1731]

A **woodpecker** (here: *Centurus carolinus*) native to much of the eastern half of the US. Also called **calico woodpecker, chad** n[1]**, chad-cherries, cham-chack, chaw-chaw, checkered woodpecker, chowchow 2, guinea woodpecker 2, ladder-backed woodpecker 3, orange borer, ramshack** n[2]**, red-headed woodpecker 2, sapsucker 1, woodchuck, zebra woodpecker**

1731 Catesby *Nat. Hist. Carolina* 1.19, *The Red-bellied Woodpecker.* . . The Belly, near the Vent, . . is stained with red. **1808** Wilson *Amer. Ornith.* 1.113, [The] Red-bellied Woodpecker. . . prefers the largest, high-timbered woods, and the tallest decayed trees of the forest. **1844** DeKay *Zool. NY* 2.189, *The Red-bellied Woodpecker.* . . comes to us from the South in the spring. **1891** *Leighton News* (AL) 15 June np, *Red-bellied Woodpecker.* Commonest of all our speckled Woodpeckers except Downy. . . It seldom comes about houses . . , but is found chiefly in the woods. **1913** *Auk* 30.497 **Okefenokee GA**, *Red-bellied Woodpecker.* . . Abundant throughout the wooded portions of the swamp, in both the pines and the cypresses. **1932** Howell *FL Bird Life* 308, In Florida, Red-bellied Woodpeckers are found chiefly in hammocks, groves, and wet bottomland timber. **1965–70** *DARE* (Qu. Q17, . . *Kinds of woodpeckers*) Infs **CT5**, Red-bellied sapsucker; **GA25, IA25, IL41, MI120, WI8,** 58, Red-bellied woodpecker; **GA38, IA3,** Redbelly. **1973** Allen *LAUM* 1.324, The red-bellied woodpecker . . is known to only two Iowa infs., one of whom calls it *redbelly.*

red bells See **red bell 2**

redbelly n

1 Usu the **red-breasted sunfish 1** or a **longear sunfish** (here: *Lepomis megalotis*), but also a **pumpkinseed 1** (here: *Lepomis gibbosus*) or related fish. **chiefly Sth** Cf **red-bellied bream, ~ perch**

1791 Bartram *Travels* 12 **GA,** We presently took some fish, one kind of which is very beautiful; they call it the red-belly. It is as large as a man's hand . . ; the belly is of a bright scarlet red, or vermilion . . ; the ultimate angle of the branchiostege extends backwards with a long spatula, ending with a round, or oval particoloured spot, . . verged round with a thin flame-coloured membrane. **1820** *Western Rev.* 2.49, *Icthelis megalotis.* . . A fine species, called Red-belly, Black-ears, Black-tail Sunfish, &c. It lives in the Kentucky, Licking, and Sandy rivers, &c. **1894** Johnston *Little Ike* 80 **GA,** [He went] angling for horny heads and pretty little red-bellies in the creek near by. **1938** Schrenkeisen *Field Book Fishes* 244, *Lepomis auritus.* . . Redbelly. *Ibid* 246, *Lepomis gibbosus.* . . Redbelly. *Ibid* 248, *Lepomis megalotis.* . . Redbelly. **1946** LaMonte *N. Amer. Game Fishes* 139, *Pumpkinseed.* . . *Names* . . Red Belly. **1965–70** *DARE* (Qu. P1, . . *Kinds of freshwater fish . . caught around here . . good to eat)* Infs **FL16, NC3,** Redbellies. **1967** [see **red-bellied bream**]. **1986** Pederson *LAGS Concordance* **Gulf Region,** 2 infs, Redbelly; 2 infs, Redbellies; 1 inf, Redbellies = breams; 1 inf, Redbellies = small perch; 1 inf, Redbelly = sun perch.

2 See **red-bellied snake.**

3 See **red-bellied snapper.**

4 See **red-bellied turtle.**

5 See **red-bellied woodpecker.**

6 See **red-bellied dace.**

7 See **red-bellied water snake.**

8 also *red-bellied trout:* =**cutthroat trout.** Cf **redside 2**

1999 *DARE* File **swID,** The sides and bellies of cutthroat trout often turn a dramatic dark red. Sometimes they are referred to as "redbellied [trout]." . . I expect I would say . . "I caught my limit of redbellies."

9 See quots. Cf **pink belly**

1968 *DARE* (Qu. EE33, . . *Outdoor games . . that children play)* Inf **LA43,** Redbelly—get a guy down on the grass and rub his belly on the ground till it was red. **1986** Pederson *LAGS Concordance (Rough games)* 1 inf, **seFL,** Redbelly (paddled guy's belly until red). **2000** *NADS Letters* **nwGA** (as of c1965), Giving someone the "red-belly." . . [A]s kids, we would get another kid, pull his shirt up, then slap on his

belly until it turned red. . . "We gave Joe a redbelly today because he had told on us for missing school yesterday."

redbelly bream See **red-bellied bream**

redbelly chub (or dace) See **red-bellied dace**

redbelly perch See **red-bellied perch**

redbelly racer n Cf **racer 1b**

Prob a **pilot black snake.**

1968 *DARE* (Qu. P25, . . *Kinds of snakes)* Inf **PA166,** Redbelly racer.

redbelly shiner See **red-bellied dace**

redbelly snake See **red-bellied snake**

redbelly sunfish See **red-bellied sunfish**

red belt n Also *red belt fungus*

A **conk** n[2] **1** (here: *Fomitopsis pinicola*).

1938 Boyce *Forest Pathology* 473, The red belt fungus, *Fomes* [= *Fomitopsis*] *pinicola* . . causes a brown cubical rot. [*Ibid* 474, The hard woody perennial shelf- to hoof-shaped conks may attain a width of 2 feet. . . The upper surface is rather smooth, zoned, gray to black in color, and commonly has a wide red margin.] **1972** Miller *Mushrooms* 181, "Red Belt Fungus". . . On logs and stumps of hardwoods and conifers but rarely on living trees except in A[laska] and the Yukon. **1987** McKnight–McKnight *Mushrooms* 126, Redbelt. . . Solitary or in groups of several. . . Inedible. . . Fresh specimens are readily recognized by the red band near the margin.

red-berried bamboo n Also *redberry bamboo* Cf **red bamboo**

A **greenbrier** (here: *Smilax walteri*).

1938 Van Dersal *Native Woody Plants* 324, Bamboo, . . Red-berry *(Smilax walteri).* **1953** Greene–Blomquist *Flowers South* 13, *Red-berried Bamboo.* . . is the most ornamental of our native bamboos. One of the delightful sights of the autumn vegetation is the bunches of pointed, coral-red berries hanging from the trees of stream margins and swamps. **1960** Vines *Trees SW* 71, The plant is also known under the vernacular names of Red-berry Bamboo . . and Sarsaparilla. The fruit is known to be eaten by at least two species of birds, and is nibbled by marsh rabbit. **1976** Bailey–Bailey *Hortus Third* 1050, *[Smilax] Walteri.* . . *Red-berried bamboo.* . . N.J. to Fla. and e. Tex.

red-berried buckthorn See **redberry g**

red-berried moonseed See **moonseed 2**

redberry n

Any of var red-fruited plants or the fruit itself; see below.

a also *swamp redberry:* A **cranberry** (here: *Vaccinium macrocarpon*). Cf **redberry k**

1785 (1925) Washington *Diaries* 2.338 **VA,** I discovered . . the red berry of the Swamp. **1830** Rafinesque *Med. Flora* 2.48, *Oxycoca macrocarpa.* . . Common Cranberry, . . Swamp Redberry. **1876** Hobbs *Bot. Hdbk.* 115, Swamp redberry, Common cranberry, Vaccinium oxycoccos.

b A **buffalo berry** (here: *Shepherdia argentea*). *obs*

1805 (1904) Clark *Orig. Jrls. Lewis & Clark Exped.* 1.299, The underbrush [along the Little Missouri River] is willow . . the red burry and Choke cherry. **1806** (1905) Lewis *Orig. Jrls. Lewis & Clark Exped.* 5.302, The bottoms [of a creek off the Big Horn River] on the Star[boar]d Side . . covered with timber . . together with the red berry or Buffalow Grees bushes. **1819** Warden *Statist. Political Hist. U.S.* 3.136, The undergrowth [along the Missouri River] consists of hazel, arrow-wood, red-berry, crab-apple, wild pea vine, and rushes.

c A **bearberry 2** (here: *Arctostaphylos uva-ursi*).

1828 Rafinesque *Med. Flora* 1.57, *English Name—Bear-berry.* . . *Vulgar Names*—Mountain Box, Redberry, Upland Cranberry. **1892** (1974) Millspaugh *Amer. Med. Plants* 390–1, Bearberry, mountain box, red berry.

d also *redberry tea:* A **wintergreen** (here: *Gaultheria procumbens*).

1828 Rafinesque *Med. Flora* 1.202, *Gaultheria repens* [=*G. procumbens*]. . . *Vulgar Names* . . Redberry, . . Redberry-tea. [*Ibid* 204, The whole plant has long been known and used as a pleasant common drink in the country. . . The berries have a peculiar grateful flavor, and are eaten by children, although rather dry.] **1876** Hobbs *Bot. Hdbk.* 96, Redberry tea, Checkerberry, Gaultheria procumbens. **1930** Sievers *Amer. Med. Plants* 63, Redberry tea. [*Ibid* 64, These [=flowers] are followed by . . berries, which, after they ripen in autumn, are bright red, mealy, and spicy.] **1971** Krochmal *Appalachia Med. Plants* 128, Red-berry tea. . . Primarily a source of true wintergreen oil.

e A **ginseng B1** (here: *Panax quinquefolius*).

1830 Rafinesque *Med. Flora* 2.52, Panax quinquefolium [sic]. . . Ginseng. . . Redberry. **1876** Hobbs *Bot. Hdbk.* 96, Redberry, Ginseng, Panax quinquefolium. **1974** (1977) Coon *Useful Plants* 69, Red-berry. . . has been hunted and dug as a medicinal plant for many years.

f =**red baneberry.**

1900 Lyons *Plant Names* 14, A[ctaea] rubra. . . Red-berry. **1979** Erichsen-Brown *Med. N. Amer. Plants* 348, *Red baneberry.* . . *Common names* . . Redberry.

g also *red-berried buckthorn, redberry ~:* A **buckthorn** (here: *Rhamnus crocea*) native to California.

1911 Jepson *Flora CA* 252, R[hamnus] crocea. . . Red-berry. Low densely branched . . shrub. . . Berry bright red. **1951** Abrams *Flora Pacific States* 3.63, Rhamnus crocea. . . Red-berried Buckthorn or Redberry. . . Low much-branched shrub. . . Berry red, sweet, obovoid. **1979** Little *Checklist U.S. Trees* 247, Rhamnus crocea. . . Redberry, redberry buckthorn. . . Generally a shrub but sometimes a small tree.

h The fruit of the **toyon.**

1921 *DN* 5.114 **CA,** Red-berries. . . Toyon berries.

i =**possum haw 2.**

1940 Clute *Amer. Plant Names* 168, Red-berry. Ilex decidua.

j A **juniper 1** (here: *Juniperus pinchotii*). Cf **redberry juniper**

1970 *DARE* (Qu. T5, . . *Kinds of evergreens, other than pine*) Inf **CA**181, Redberry. **1975** Lamb *Woody Plants SW* 100, The cone of redberry is yellow-red to reddish-brown. . . The growth form is shrubby, rarely forming a tree in New Mexico but becoming treelike in Texas.

k A **mountain cranberry 1** (here: *Vaccinium vitis-idaea*). [*DCan* 1933, 1953] **wAK** Cf **redberry a**

1983 in 1991 Tabbert *Dict. Alaskan Engl.* 175, Redberry = lowbush cranberry. **1988** *Fairbanks Daily News–Miner* (AK) 5 Oct 13 (Tabbert *Dict. Alaskan Engl.*), There were plenty of blueberries this year which was surprising to all. Also there were plenty of cranberries or red berries. **1991** Tabbert *Dict. Alaskan Engl.* 175, In western Alaska v[accinium] vitis-idaea is also called *redberry,* a name which is reported also for it from Newfoundland and Labrador.

redberry bamboo See **red-berried bamboo**

redberry buckthorn See **redberry g**

redberry eugenia See **redberry stopper**

redberry juniper n Cf **redberry j**

A **juniper 1** of the southwestern US: usu *Juniperus pinchotii,* but also **cherrystone juniper** or *J. erythrocarpa.*

1938 Van Dersal *Native Woody Plants* 149, Juniperus pinchotii. . . Red-berry juniper. . . Wood durable but soft; very local. **1960** Vines *Trees SW* 32, Juniperus pinchotii. . . Red-berry Juniper seems to be rather hardy, especially as to fire damage, and will sprout from the stump. *Ibid* 34, Juniperus monosperma. . . Vernacular names are Cherrystone Juniper, Red-berry Juniper [etc]. **1969** *DARE* (Qu. T5, . . *Kinds of evergreens, other than pine*) Inf **TX**68, Redberry juniper. **1976** Elmore *Shrubs & Trees SW* 17, Cherry-stone or redberry juniper. . . [is] the characteristic juniper of northern Arizona and New Mexico. . . The berries are copper color (rarely bluish), succulent and unappetizing, but can be eaten if need be. **1980** Little *Audubon Guide N. Amer. Trees W. Region* 313, *Redberry Juniper—Juniperus erythrocarpa.* . . Evergreen shrub or small tree with . . bright red "berries." [*Ibid* 314, Though named in 1936, this juniper [=*J. erythrocarpa*]. . . previously was not separated from Pinchot Juniper, which has cones of similar reddish color.] *Ibid* 317, Pinchot Juniper—"Redberry Juniper". . . Cones . . berrylike, *reddish,* hard and *dry,* mealy.

red-berry moonseed See **moonseed 2**

redberry stopper n Also *redberry eugenia* Cf **red stopper**

A **stopper** (here: *Eugenia confusa*).

1946 West–Arnold *Native Trees FL* 155, Eugenia confusa . ., redberry

eugenia, is . . characterized by bright-scarlet fruits and long-pointed leaves. **1962** Harrar–Harrar *Guide S. Trees* 544, *Redberry Eugenia.* . . The largest of the native eugenias. . . This tree extends southward from Biscayne Bay over the Keys. **1982** *Miami Herald* (FL) 24 Oct sec H 11, *E. confusa.* . . is commonly called redberry stopper.

redberry tea See **redberry d**

red betty n

A **cardinal flower** (here: *Lobelia cardinalis*).

1894 *Jrl. Amer. Folkl.* 7.93 **VT,** Lobelia cardinalis. . . Red Betty, Ferrisburgh, Vt. **1940** Clute *Amer. Plant Names* 226, *Lobelia cardinalis.* Red Betty, red cardinal.

redbill n

1 also *red-billed gull:* Either of two similar **terns:** the Caspian **tern** (*Sterna caspia*) or the **royal tern.**

1921 LA Dept. of Conserv. *Bulletin* 10.137 **LA,** The Caspian tern. . . is known sometimes, like the next species [=*Sterna maxima*], as . . "red-billed gull." **1924** Howell *Birds AL* 28, The Caspian tern. . . may be distinguished from the gulls by its deep-red, straight-pointed bill. . . Both this species and the royal tern are known to the baymen as "redbills." **1925** Bailey *Birds FL* 7, Caspian tern. . . *Hydroprogne caspia imperator* (Red bill, Gannet stricker [sic])—This handsome large tern is common in our waters during the spring and fall months. *Ibid* 7, Royal tern. . . *Thalasseus maximus* (Gannet striker, Big striker, Big red bill) . . a few breed in suitable places along our East Coast. **1962** Imhof *AL Birds* 282, *Royal Tern.* . . *Other name:* Redbill. . . It is white except for light gray wings, a black cap, an orange-red bill, and black feet. *Ibid* 284, *Caspian Tern.* . . *Other name:* Redbill. . . Although it resembles the Royal Tern, this species . . has a *heavier, blood-red bill.* **1969** Long-street *Birds FL* 69, *Royal Tern.* . . *Redbill.* . . The royal tern . . is the commonest tern that stays in the state during winter.

2 The black **oyster-catcher** (*Haematopus bachmani*). Cf **redbill snipe**

1923 U.S. Dept. Ag. *Misc. Circular* 13.73, Black Oyster-catcher. . . *Vernacular names.* . . Redbill.

redbill buzzard n Cf **black-bill buzzard**

=**turkey vulture.**

1967 *DARE* (Qu. Q13, *Names . . for the vulture*) Inf **SC**43, Redbill buzzard.

red-billed coot n Cf **pumpkin-blossom coot**

The American **scoter** (*Melanitta nigra*).

1955 MA Audubon Soc. *Bulletin* 55.377 **RI,** American Scoter. . . Red-billed Coot. . . A misnomer, yellow [=color at the base of the bill] being called red.

red-billed gull See **redbill 1**

red-billed mud hen n Cf **white-billed mud hen**

=**Florida gallinule.**

1874 NY Acad. Sci. *Annals Lyceum Nat. Hist.* 10.387 **IL,** G[allinula] chloropus. . . Florida Gallinule; "Red-billed Mud-Hen." **1895** (1907) Wright *Birdcraft* 248 **CT,** Red-billed Mud Hen. . . Summer resident of the Housatonic River. **1913** *Pacific Coast Avifauna* 23, The local name "red-billed mud-hen" would seem to be an appropriate one for this bird, as the red bill is a distinguishing mark as far as the bird can be seen. **1925** (1928) Forbush *Birds MA* 366, Gallinula chloropus. . . Red-billed Mud-hen. **1955** MA Audubon Soc. *Bulletin* 39.443, Red-billed Mud Hen . . (Mass. Most of the bill and the contiguous frontal plaque are sealing-wax red . .).

redbill snipe n esp Gulf States Cf **redbill 2, snipe**

An **oyster-catcher** (here: *Haematopus palliatus*).

1923 U.S. Dept. Ag. *Misc. Circular* 13.72 **MS,** Haematopus palliatus. . . *Vernacular Names.* . . Redbill snipe. **1932** Howell *FL Bird Life* 214, *Redbill Snipe.* . . Formerly a common resident, breeding on all coasts. **1962** Imhof *AL Birds* 219, American Oystercatcher. . . Redbill Snipe. . . It has a *black head* and *neck* and a large, *bright red bill* adapted to opening the shells of mollusks.

red birch n

1 A **sweet birch** (here: *Betula lenta*). obs

1785 Marshall *Arbustrum* 19, Betula lenta. Red Birch. This grows to a pretty large size, spreading into many slender pliable branches. The leaves are smooth, heart-shaped, oblong, sharp-pointed, and finely and slightly sawed on their edges. **1792** Belknap *Hist. NH* 3.99, *Birch.* Of this we have four species. . . *Red* or *Yellow (betula lenta.)* This is chiefly used for fewel, and is much esteemed.

2 A **river birch** (here: *Betula nigra*).

1816 Warden *Chorographical Statist. Descr. DC* 167, [Birch] (red). . . *[Betula] rubra* [=*B. nigra*]. **1848** in 1850 Cooper *Rural Hours* 385 ceNY, The *red birch*, also a tree of the largest size, is the kind used for brooms. **1882** U.S. Natl. Museum *Proc.* 5.85 IL, IN, *Betula nigra.* Red Birch. . . Commoner than the last [=*B. lenta*] in similar situations [= along banks of streams]. **1900** (1927) Keeler *Our Native Trees* 308, The Red Birch is a beautiful tree; the bark of a full grown trunk is dark, but small stems and branchlets are really red and in the sunlight are positively brilliant. This red bark easily sloughs loose and shows the paler bark beneath. **1921** Deam *Trees IN* 90, The fact that other species of birch are so rare in Indiana, is the reason that this species [=*Betula nigra*] is simply called "Birch." Outside of Indiana it is known as red birch and river birch. **1947** Collingwood–Brush *Knowing Trees* 172, Stream and river banks, the shores of ponds, and swampy forest land in the eastern third of the United States are the natural habitat of the river or red birch. **1980** Little *Audubon Guide N. Amer. Trees E. Region* 366, "Red Birch"—"Black Birch"—*Betula nigra.*

3 =**western birch.**

1900 Lyons *Plant Names* 62, B[etula] occidentalis . . , Western Red Birch. **1931** U.S. Dept. Ag. *Misc. Pub.* 101.18, *Red birch* (*B. fontinalis* [=*B. occidentalis*]), . . is an important browse species on many sheep and goat ranges, its palatability ranging from fair to very good. **1936** McDougall–Baggley *Plants of Yellowstone* 47, *Red birch* . . is a large shrub or small tree with smooth, dark bark and ovate, toothed leaves. **1965** DARE (Qu. T15, . . *Kinds of swamp trees*) Inf UT3, Red birch. **1980** Little *Audubon Guide N. Amer. Trees W. Region* 382, "Red Birch" . . *Betula occidentalis.* . . This uncommon but widespread species is the only native birch in the Southwest and the southern Rocky Mountains. Sheep and goats browse the foliage.

4 A **paper birch** (here: *Betula papyrifera* var *kenaica*) native to Alaska.

1908 Sudworth *Forest Trees Pacific* 256, The Kenai birch is a . . little known Alaskan birch, called "red birch" and "black birch," names long used for the eastern birch (*Betula nigra*). **1922** Sargent *Manual Trees* 216, *Betula papyrifera* var. *kenaica.* . . *Red Birch.* . . *Leaves* . . dark dull green above, pale yellow-green below. **1972** Viereck–Little *AK Trees* 138, Red birch. . . Small to medium-sized tree 20–80 ft. **1979** Little *Checklist U.S. Trees* 62, Red birch. *Range*—S. interior Alaska n. of Kenai Pen[insula] w. to Kodiak Is[land] and base of Alaska Pen.

redbird n Cf **summer redbird, winter ~**

Any of var birds with mostly red, orange, or reddish plumage, as:

a =**Baltimore oriole.**

1669 Shrigley *True Rel. VA MD* 3, Fowle naturally to the Land are . . Red-birds, the Baltenore [sic] bird, being black and yellow [etc]. **1825** Bryant in *U.S. Lit. Gaz.* 286, The red-bird warbled, as he wrought / His hanging nest o'erhead. **1890** Warren *Birds PA* 216, *Icterus galbula.* . . The terms . . Fire-bird and Red-bird, are in allusion to the orange coloration, brightest on the breast, but varying in amount as well as brilliancy with age and season. He is also called Hang-nest and Hanging-bird.

b also *reddy bird:* =**cardinal 1.** chiefly Sth, S Midl See Map

[**1670** (1937) Denton *Brief Descr.* 6 seNY, There is also the red Bird, with divers sorts of singing birds.] **1709** (1967) Lawson *New Voyage* 148 NC, SC, The Red-Birds (whose Cock is all over of a rich Scarlet Feather, with a tufted Crown on his Head, of the same Colour) are the Bigness of a Bunting-Lark, and very hardy, having a strong thick Bill. **1759** (1775) Burnaby *Travels* 10 VA, In the woods there are . . the mocking-bird, the red-bird or nightingale, [and] the blue-bird. **1810** Wilson *Amer. Ornith.* 2.38, The sprightly figure, and gaudy plumage of the Red-bird . . will always make him a favorite. **1867** Latham *Black & White* 186 sLA, The green peas . . are devoured before the gardener can pick them, by the 'red birds,' the bright red cardinals. **1885** Thompson *By-Ways* 159 neGA, In the region of Tallulah Falls I met with an old man whose chief business was snaring red-birds (cardinals) for the sake of their skins. **1906** DN 3.153 nwAR, Red-bird. . . Cardinal bird. Well-nigh universal. **1929** (1951) Faulkner *Sartoris* 337 MS, They saw red-birds darting like arrows of scarlet flame. **1942** Rawlings *Cross Creek* 80 nFL, A red bird sang from the pecan tree by the kitchen door. "Is

that ol' reddy-bird good to eat?" she asked me. **1965–70** DARE (Qu. Q14) 31 Infs, **chiefly Sth, S Midl**, Redbird(s); LA2, Cardinal—that's the right name for them old redbirds, ain't it? (Qu. Q16) Inf NC49, Red-bird; (Qu. Q23) Infs MO39, OH98, TX40, 84, 85, Redbird(s) = cardinal(s). **1966** DARE Tape FL26, They don't come as much as the blue jays and redbirds do; FL39, Recently I had a redbird, a cardinal, build a nest in one of my orchid pots. **1982** Barrick *Coll.* csPA, Red-bird—cardinal. **1986** Pederson *LAGS Concordance* **Gulf Region,** 28 infs, Red-bird(s). **2000** NADS Letters AL, Redbird—In Alabama, a cardinal.

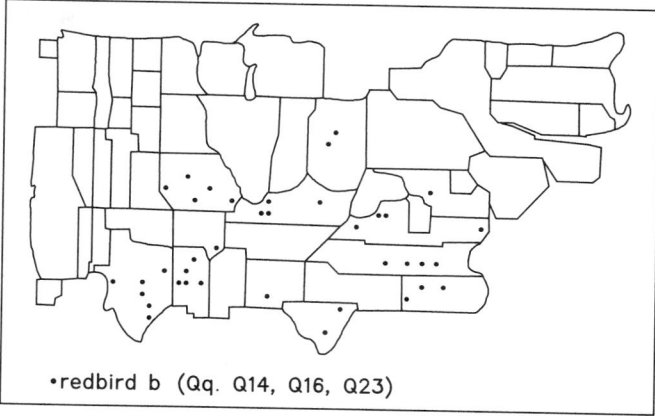

•redbird b (Qq. Q14, Q16, Q23)

c freq *black-winged redbird,* rarely *sandhill ~:* =**scarlet tanager.**

1791 Bartram *Travels* [290 *bis*] NC, SC, Merula flammula [=*Piranga olivacea*], sand-hill redbird of Carolina. **1844** Giraud *Birds Long Is.* 135 NY, Scarlet Tanager. . . This splendid species is better known to many persons by the name of . . "Black-winged Red Bird." **1917** *Wilson Bulletin* 29.2.83 swKY, *Piranga erythromelas* [=*P. olivacea*]. . . Black-winged redbird, redbird. **1929** Forbush *Birds MA* 3.129, *Scarlet Tanager.* Other names: *Black-winged red bird.* **1936** Roberts *MN Birds* 2.329, *Piranga erythromelas.* . . Black-winged Redbird. **1956** MA Audubon Soc. *Bulletin* 40.253, *Scarlet Tanager.* Black-winged Redbird (Rather general.) . . Red Bird (Rather general.)

d =**summer tanager.**

1844 DeKay *Zool. NY* 2.175, *Pyranga æstiva* [=*Piranga rubra*]. . . The *Red-bird* . . comes to us from the South, but not in great numbers, and only during the hottest part of the summer. **1913** *Auk* 30.499 Okefenokee GA, *Cardinal;* 'Redbird (with black chin).' . . *Summer Tanager;* 'Redbird (without black chin).' **1944** Hausman *Amer. Birds* 566, *Piranga rubra rubra.* . . Redbird. . . Male: our only completely red bird. The Cardinal . . has a black face. The red of the Summer Tanager is a duller red than that of the Scarlet Tanager. **1955** *Oriole* 20.1.13 GA, Summer Tanager.—Redbird (rather general) . . the plumage of the male is chiefly dull red to vermillion.

e =**marbled godwit.**

1956 MA Audubon Soc. *Bulletin* 40.20, *Marbled Godwit.* . . Red Bird . . (Mass. General ground color pale cinnamon.)

redbird cactus n Also *bird cactus, redbird flower* [See quots 1953, 1982] =**jewbush.**

1933 Small *Manual SE Flora* 804, P[edilanthus] tithymaloides. . . *Red-bird flower.* . . Hammocks and pinelands, Everglade Keys, pen[insular] Fla. and Florida Keys. **1953** Greene–Blomquist *Flowers South* 112, *Pedilanthus tithymaloides.* . . Its fleshy, zigzag stems bear . . small lopsided flowers like miniature red birds which have given it the erroneous name "bird-cactus." **1959** Carleton *Index Herb. Plants* 98, *Red bird cactus:* Pedilanthus tithymaloides. **1982** Perry–Hay *Field Guide Plants* 70, Redbird flower. . . *Flowers* . . individually like tiny red birds. . . Flowers mainly in summer.

red bluebell n

A **virgin's bower** (here: *Clematis texensis*).

1951 PADS 15.31 TX, *Clematis texensis.* . . Red bluebell; bell flower.

red blue jay n [From its resemblance to the **blue jay 1**] Cf **red jay** =**cardinal 1.**

1936 Roberts *MN Birds* 2.334, *Eastern Cardinal. . . Other names. . .* "Red Blue Jay."

red bone n

1 also attrib; freq cap: A person of mixed race, esp one believed to be partly American Indian and belonging to a distinct social group in parts of South Carolina, Louisiana, and eastern Texas. **now chiefly LA, TX** See Map Cf **bone n 5, brass ankle, Croatan, redleg, sabine**

1891 *Amer. Hist. Assoc. Papers* 5.466 **NC, SC,** At one time the Croatans were known as "Redbones," and there is a street in Fayetteville so called. **1907** Hodge *Hdbk. Amer. Indians* 1.365, Across the line [from NC] in South Carolina are found a people, evidently of similar origin [to the Croatans], designated "Redbones." . . All of these are local designations for people of mixed race with an Indian nucleus. **1940** Brown *Amer. Cooks* 269 **LA,** The Cajuns. . . live close to the earth and the "redbones" who subsist in the bayous on crawfish. **1953** *Newsweek* 30 Mar 28 **LA,** Whenever a shotgun blasts or dynamite explodes . . in strike-ridden Elizabeth, La., somebody always blames the "redbones." This is a purely local term applied rather loosely to the native sons of Allen and Rapides Parishes. . . Legend has it that the ancestors of the "redbones" were Spaniards and Mexicans . . , American fugitives from justice . . , adventurers who found refuge in the pine forests of central Louisiana, mingling with each other and the five tribes that ranged the woodlands before them. **1956** *Mathews Coll.* **New Orleans LA,** I have seen and known quite a few of the type designated as "red bone negro." Their color is unmistakable—a sort of copperish yellow, with features quite unlike the average pure African. **1963** Berry *Almost White* 27, South Carolina abounds in groups who are "neither fish nor fowl." There are the Croatans in Marlboro, Marion and Dillon counties, the Red Bones of Richland, the Red Legs of Orangeburg, the Buckheads of Bamberg, the Goins of Williamsburg and the Turks of Sumter. . . In western Louisiana are a numerous people known as Red Bones. **1965–70** *DARE* (Qu. HH28, *Names and nicknames . . for people of foreign background*) Infs **TX**35, 37, Red bone(s); (Qu. HH29a, . . *People of mixed blood—part Indian*) Inf **LA**2, Red bones—part Indian and part French, some say part nigger; **LA**14, Red bone—Indian and White and Negro mixed; low-class people; **LA**16, Red bone—mixed Indian, Negro, Mexican; **LA**28, 32, Red bone; **TX**35, Red bone; (Qu. HH29b, . . *People of mixed blood—part Negro*) Inf **TX**16, Red bone. **1967** *DARE* Tape **LA**14, The red bone (at least around here) is always an admixture of the White (usually a French or Spanish, I think, from the age that they have been here—the length of time) and French, French and Spanish. And some Indian. The Indian streak is definitely needed for the word to be used correctly around here. . . The Indian cheeks and the piercing eyes and lank black hair often characterizes these people. You definitely can see the Indian in 'em. And they seldom know anything else about their background. **1983** [see **pink** n[2] **3c**]. **1986** Pederson *LAGS Concordance,* 1 inf, **nwLA,** Red Bones—Cajuns; 1 inf, **nwLA,** Red Bone—Indian/Spanish mixture; 1 inf, **cLA,** Red Bone—swamp person; 1 inf, **sLA,** Red Bone Georgians—violent people from South Georgia; 1 inf, **cLA,** Red Bone—White, Black, Indian; 1 inf, **ceLA,** Red Bone—in West Louisiana; 1 inf, **cnLA,** Red Bone—Indian or Negro; 1 inf, **cwLA,** Red Bones—mixed blood—Spanish and White? 1 inf, **swLA,** Red Bones; **ceTX,** Red Bones—mixed Mexican/Indian/French/Black; 1 inf, **ceTX,** Red Bones. **1990** Burke *Morning for Flamingos* 25 **seLA,** He was a strange-looking man who had moved about in that nether society of people of color in southern Louisiana—blacks, quadroons, octoroons,

and redbones. . . Like all redbones, people who are a mixture of Negro, white, and Indian blood, he had skin the color of burnt brick, and his eyes were turquoise.

2 freq attrib: A type or strain of American hound with a solid or predominantly red coat, often used to hunt raccoons. **chiefly Sth, S Midl** Cf **black-and-tan, bluetick**

1893 *Scribner's Mag.* 14.420 **GA** (as of 1840s), Mr. John Respess, of Putnam County . . had given up "Old Spot" and his kind, and was cultivating the Redbone dog. The Redbones had speed and bottom, but they lacked body and bone. They were too light. **1916** *Field & Stream* 21.177, Good Redbone, Pennsylvania or Portsmouth hound stock is what we want up North. **1937** *Hall Coll.* **eTN,** He's half red bone-hound and half cur an' can kill a coon in a minute. **1943** Writers' Program NC *Bundle of Troubles* 135, Grandpap'd got him one of them Redbones and crossed her with a Beagle expecting to raise something extra. **1945** FWP *Lay My Burden Down* 177 **KY** (as of c1865) [Black], The leader of that pack of hounds . . wa'n't no blood hound. She was a plain old red-bone possum [sic] and coon dog. **1948** Camp *Hunter's Encycl.* 812, The Redbone was a strain of Southern hound which was used in fox hunting for a number of years. . . He has become a specialist after coon and possum, and there is no section of the South where he cannot be found—or, rather, some hound or pack whose owner boasts of their Redbone lineage. Almost any solid red hound of the smallish order, or red with black saddle, is generally called "Redbone" by those who are not intimately acquainted with his immediate ancestry. **1948** Faulkner *Intruder* 5 **MS,** A true rabbit dog, some hound, a good deal of hound, maybe mostly hound, redbone and black-and-tan. **1958** Humphrey *Home from the Hill* 48 **neTX,** He kept a pack of about fifteen foxhounds, and he liked to have one or two of all breeds on a chase for the harmony of their differently pitched voices. He had Black and Tans, Redbones, Goodmans, Blueticks and Redticks, Walkers, Triggs, a pair of Plott hounds. **1962** *Clarke Co. Democrat* (Grove Hill AL) 4 Jan 8/7 (*Mathews Coll.*), Lost—A Red Bone female hound on Mt. Seller's hunting club. **1967** *DARE* Tape **LA**3, The black-and-tan and bluetick and red bone, they're slower. They're more used for coon dogs. **1975** *Foxfire* 3.38 **nGA,** I had a *good* stock a'dogs—blue tick and redbone mix, and black and tan. **1982** Mason *Shiloh* 234 **wKY,** He recommended the Georgia redbone hound for intelligence and patience.

redbread n

See quot.

1975 Gould *ME Lingo* 229, *Redbread*—The crimson-orange roe in a cooked lobster: more often called coral.

red bream n

=**red-breasted sunfish 1.**

1935 Caine *Game Fish* 26 **Sth,** *Lepomis auritus*. . . Red Bream. **1986** Pederson *LAGS Concordance (Common freshwater fish)* 1 inf, **ceAR,** Red bream.

redbreast n

1 Any of several birds, as:

a A **robin 1.** [*OED2* c1401 → for *Erithacus rubecola*] Cf **red-breasted robin 1, robin redbreast 1**

1775 Clayton in *Phil. Trans.* LXVI.105 (*OED2*), Of small birds there are several sorts; the red breast, speckled on the back like a partridge [etc.]. **1796** *Bickerstaff Alm. 1796* (Norwich, Conn.) B[v] *(DA),* Yet the red breast chirrups cheary, While the mittened lass attends. **1919** Burns *Ornith. Chester Co. PA* 112, *Planesticus migratorius migratorius.* . . "Redbreast." . . Abundant summer resident. **1925** *Book of Rural Life* 4668, *Redbreast,* . . a name properly applied to the little *English robin,* . . but also commonly used in speaking of the larger American robin. **1926** Roberts *Time of Man* 273 **KY,** You could see. . . birds in the trees in the spring of the year. Springbirds and redbreasts. **1969** *DARE* (Qu. Q14) Inf **CA**111, Robin—redbreast.

b =**knot** n[2]. Cf **red-breasted plover, ~ robin 2, ~ sandpiper, ~ snipe 3**

1852 in 1876 *Forest & Stream* 7.212 **eMA,** *Tringa canutus.* Adult, red-breast; young, gray-back. **1889** Ridgway *Ornith. IL* 2.42, *Tringa canutus.* . . Popular Synonyms. . . Red-breast (adult). **1892** *Auk* 9.146 **Cape Cod MA,** Here in former years large numbers . . frequented the Dennis marshes . . with the Knots or Redbreasts (*Tringa canutus*). **1956** MA Audubon Soc. *Bulletin* 40.18 **MA, ME,** American Knot. . . Red-breast. **1970** *DARE* (Qu. Q10, . . *Water birds and marsh birds*) Inf **VA**47, Redbreast—knot.

c See **red-breasted nuthatch.**

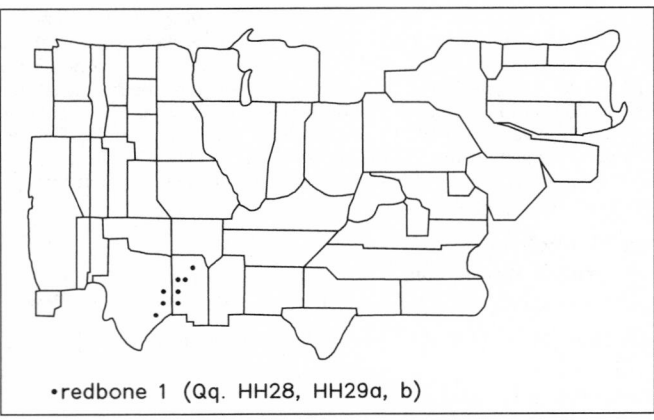

•redbone 1 (Qq. HH28, HH29a, b)

d See **red-breasted snipe 1**.

e The passenger pigeon (*Ectopistes migratorius*).

1930 Shoemaker *1300 Words* 51 **cPA Mts** (as of c1900), *Red breast*—The male wild pigeon (ectopistes migratorius).

f =**rose-breasted grosbeak**. Cf **robin redbreast 2**

1932 Bennitt *Check-list* 59 **MO**, *Rose-breasted grosbeak*. . . Redbreast.

g See **red-breasted blackbird**.

2 =**red-breasted sunfish 1**. **S Atl** See Map Cf **red-breasted bream**

1887 Goode *Amer. Fishes* 66, *Lepomis auritus*. . . is called . . "Red Breast." **1903** NY State Museum & Sci. Serv. *Bulletin* 60.479, The long-eared sunfish [=*Lepomis auritus*] has a very extensive range and is known under many common names, among which . . [is] redbreast. **1926** (1949) McQueen–Mizell *Hist. Okefenokee* 53 **seGA**, No fishing is allowed during the bedding season of bream and red-breast. **1955** Carr–Goin *Guide Reptiles* 91 **FL**, *Lepomis auritus* . . Redbreast. . . Breast region from bright orange to red. **1965–70** *DARE* (Qu. P1, . . *Kinds of freshwater fish* . . *caught around here* . . *good to eat*) Infs **GA7, 28, SC7, 11, 19, 21, 26, NC43**, Redbreast; **GA3**, Redbreast—a perch; **GA5**, Brim = redbreast = redbreast perch; **GA16**, Redbreast, warmouth—perch; **NC24**, Redbreast—panfish; **NC49**, Redbreast—a lot of people call it a robin; **SC34**, Redbreast—a bream with a red belly; **NC40**, Redbreast—a bream with a red breast. **1972** *DARE* File **FL**, Redbreast—type of panfish similar to bream . . common, Holmes County, Florida. **1986** Pederson *LAGS Concordance* (*Common freshwater fish*) 3 infs, **GA**, 1 inf, **nwFL**, Redbreast.

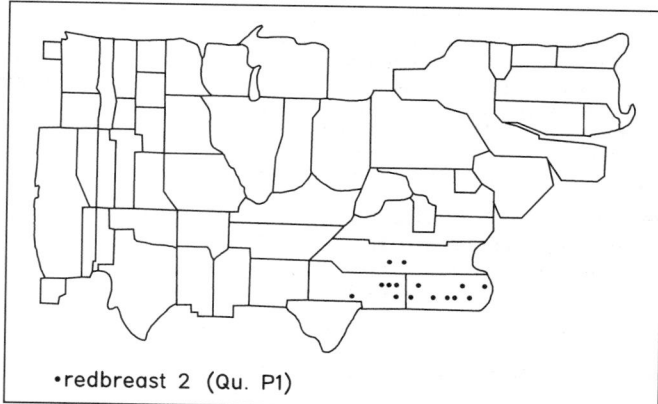

•redbreast 2 (Qu. P1)

redbreast blackbird See **red-breasted blackbird**

redbreast bream (or brim) See **red-breasted bream**

red-breasted blackbird n Also *redbreast (blackbird)* Cf **red-winged blackbird**

See quot.

1967–70 *DARE* (Qu. Q11, . . *Kinds of blackbirds*) Infs **CA62, IL14, KS15**, Red-breasted blackbird; **VA38**, Red-breasted blackbird—along creeks; **CO46**, Redbreast blackbird; **CA210**, Redbreast, yellowbreast.

red-breasted bream n Also *redbreast bream, ~ brim* Cf **bream B3, red bream, redbreast 2**

Usu the **red-breasted sunfish 1**, but also a **longear sunfish** (here: *Lepomis megalotis*) or a **bluegill 1**.

1896 U.S. Natl. Museum *Bulletin* 47.1001, *Lepomis auritus*. . . *Redbreast Bream*. . . Belly largely orange red. **1902** Jordan–Evermann *Amer. Fishes* 346, *Lepomis auritus*. . . The red-breasted bream. . . can be taken readily on the hook baited with angleworm. **1969** *DARE* (Qu. P1, . . *Kinds of freshwater fish* . . *caught around here* . . *good to eat*) Inf **GA89**, Brim—most common: bluegill brim, redbreast brim. **1974** McClane *McClane's New Std. Fishing Encycl.* 786, *Lepomis auritus*—Regionally known as the . . redbreast bream, it is one of the brightest colored and gamiest of the medium-sized sunfish. **1986** Pederson *LAGS Concordance* (*Common freshwater fish*) 1 inf, **cwGA**, Redbreast bream.

red-breasted hawk n Cf **red-bellied hawk**
=**red-shouldered hawk**.

1923 Dawson *Birds CA* 4.1683, *Buteo lineatus elegans*. . . *Red-breasted Hawk*. . . Underparts usually rich red—more uniform than in the reddest [*Buteo*] *swainsoni*. **1967** *DARE* (Qu. Q4, . . *Kinds of hawks*) Inf **TX32**, Red-breasted hawk.

red-breasted merganser n

Std: a **merganser** (here: *Mergus serrator*). Also called **becscie, bracket, brownbird 3, Chicago mallard, diver, fish duck 1, fisherman 1, French drake, fuzzy-head, ganser, garbill, hairy crown, ~ head, Indian** n **B5, ~ sheldrake, Irish canvasback, jack** n[1] **23c, Mississippi buck, pheasant duck 2, pied sheldrake, robin 4, sawbill, scale duck, sea robin 2, sheldrake 1, shelduck 1, shell-bird, Spanish drake, spring buck, ~ sheldrake, water witch, wood sheldrake, stud, whistler**

red-breasted nuthatch n Also *redbreast*

A **nuthatch** (here: *Sitta canadensis*). Also called **ass-up, brown-breasted nuthatch, Canada ~, chestnut-sided ~, creeper 2, devil-downhead 2, flycatcher 1c, nuthatcher, red-bellied nuthatch, rose-breasted ~, sapsucker 2, topsy-turvy bird, tree mouse, upside-down bird**

1890 Warren *Birds PA* 316, The Red-breasted Nuthatch breeds sparingly in the higher mountainous and northern parts of the state. **1914** Eaton *Birds NY* 2.499, *Red-breasted Nuthatch*. . . *Under parts rusty or reddish brown*. **1918** (1927) Chapman *Our Winter Birds* 35, *Red-breasted Nuthatch*. . . About September first, if you think you hear some one blowing a penny trumpet from a nearby pine or spruce tree, you will probably find that it is a Redbreast announcing his arrival from the north. **1946** Hausman *Eastern Birds* 435, *Sitta canadensis*. . . Redbreast. **1956** MA Audubon Soc. *Bulletin* 40.127, Winter feeding stations furnish meals to some unusual visitors like the Red-breasted Nuthatch. **1966–68** *DARE* (Qu. Q23, *The insect-eating bird that goes headfirst down a tree trunk*) Infs **CO7, IA3, MI36, PA155**, Red-breasted nuthatch. **1977** Bull–Farrand *Audubon Field Guide Birds* 685, *Red-breasted Nuthatch*. . . Often creeps downward headfirst on tree trunks.

red-breasted plover n Also *redbreast plover* Cf **plover, redbreast 1b**
=**knot** n[2].

1888 Trumbull *Names of Birds* 179, At Pine Point, Me. and in Massachusetts at Boston markets, North Scituate, Provincetown, Plymouth, and West Barnstable, [the knot is called] *red-breast plover*. **1925** (1928) Forbush *Birds MA* 1.402, *Calidrus canutus*. . . Gray red-breasted plover.

red-breasted rail n Cf **red rail**
1 =**king rail 1**.

1835 Audubon *Ornith. Biog.* 3.27 **SC**, The Great Red-Breasted Rail, or Fresh-Water Marsh-Hen, *Rallus Elegans*, . . is abundant in South Carolina. **1874** NY Acad. Sci. *Annals Lyceum Nat. Hist.* 10.387, *R[allus] elegans*. . . Red-breasted Rail. . . Summer sojourner; sometimes resident in southern portions [of Illinois]. **1898** (1900) Davie *Nests N. Amer. Birds* 123, The King Rail, . . or Red-breasted Rail, is distributed in summer from New York southward, breeding throughout the inland marshes. **1932** Bennitt *Check-list* 27 **MO**, *King rail*. . . Red-breasted rail. . . Throughout the state. **1955** *Oriole* 20.1.6 **GA**, *Red-breasted Rail* (the front of neck and the breast are from tan to reddish-cinnamon). **1963** Gromme *Birds WI* 217, Rail, . . Little Red-breasted (Virginia Rail), . . Red-breasted (King Rail).

2 usu *little red-breasted rail*: =**Virginia rail**.

1874 NY Acad. Sci. *Annals Lyceum Nat. Hist.* 10.387, *R[allus] Virginianus*. . . Little Red-breasted Rail. Resident [in Illinois], except in northern portions. **1899** Howe–Sturtevant *Birds RI* 45, *Rallus virginianus* [=*R. limicola*]. . . *Red-breasted Rail*. **1936** Roberts *MN Birds* 1.443, *Rallus limicola limicola*. . . *Little Red-breasted Rail*. . . Most of underparts cinnamon or reddish-brown. . . A miniature of the big King Rail. **1963** [see **1** above].

red-breasted robin n Cf **robin, robin redbreast**
1 A **robin 1**. Cf **redbreast 1a**

a1862 (1864) Thoreau *ME Woods* 321, I saw in Maine between July 24 and August 3, (1857) . . *Turdus migratorius* (red-breasted robin), some everywhere. **1956** MA Audubon Soc. *Bulletin* 40.128, *American Robin*. . . Red-breasted Robin (Maine. The underparts of the breeding male are chiefly cinnamon-rufous to reddish tawny.) **1968** *DARE* (Qu. Q14) Inf **VT10**, Red-breasted robin.

2 also *redbreast robin*: =**knot** n[2]. Cf **redbreast 1b**

1955 *AmSp* 30.181 **NC,** The knot. . . is also known simply as . . *red-breasted robin.* **1966** *DARE* (Qu. Q7, *Names and nicknames for . . game birds*) Inf **MS**72, Redbreast robin.

red-breasted sandpiper n Cf **redbreast 1b, red-breasted plover, ~ snipe 3**
=**knot** n².

1813 (1824) Wilson *Amer. Ornith.* 7.47, *Red-breasted Sandpiper.* . . [is a] prettily marked species. **1844** DeKay *Zool. NY* 2.243, *The Red-breasted Sandpiper.* . . presents such varieties in its plumage, dependant [sic] upon age and season, as to have received several different names. **1881** *Forest & Stream* 17.226, By May 20th we shall begin to hear the dual whistling note of the red-breasted sandpiper (*Tringa canutus,* Linn.) **1917** (1923) *Birds Amer.* 1.231, *Knot.* . . *Other Names.* . . Red-breasted Sandpiper. **1946** Hausman *Eastern Birds* 276, *Knot.* . . Some twenty-five or more local names, among which . . Red-breasted Sandpiper. . . A short-billed, rather large chunky sandpiper with short legs and a light, reddish-brown breast.

red-breasted sapsucker See **red-breasted woodpecker**

red-breasted snipe n Cf **snipe**

1 also *redbreast:* =**dowitcher.** [See quot 1954]

1813 (1824) Wilson *Amer. Ornith.* 7.45, The Red-breasted Snipe [= *Limnodromeus griseus*] arrives on the sea coast of New Jersey early in April. **1874** *NY Acad. Sci. Annals Lyceum Nat. Hist.* 10.383 **IL,** *M[acrorhamphus] griseus.* . . Red-breasted Snipe; Gray Snipe. **1895** Elliot *N. Amer. Shore Birds* 52, *Dowitcher.* On the Atlantic seaboard, where it is called in various localities, the Red-breasted Snipe, . . this species is one of the most common and well known of the "Bay-birds." **1921** LA Dept. of Conserv. *Bulletin* 10.75, *Dowitcher, or Red-breasted Snipe.* . . Its superficial resemblance to the jacksnipe attracts the attention of hunters to the dowitcher [=*Limnodromus scolopaceus*]. . . In every particular except size, shape, and general coloring, however, the dowitcher is entirely different from the snipe. **1923** U.S. Dept. Ag. *Misc. Circular* 13.51 **MA, MS,** The vernacular names for the . . [short-billed and long-billed] dowitcher[s] are hardly separable. . . *In local use.* . . Redbreast. **1936** Roberts *MN Birds* 1.512, *Limnodromus griseus scolopaceus.* . . "Red-breast." **1954** Sprunt *FL Bird Life* 186, *Limnodromus griseus griseus.* . . The spring plumage is bright and handsome, and the red of the underparts is responsible for the local name of "Red-breasted Snipe." **1963** Gromme *Birds WI* 217, Snipe, . . Red-breasted (Dowitcher).

2 A **woodcock** (here: *Philohela minor*). *obs*

1830 *Cabinet Nat. Hist.* 1.97, This bird is known throughout the United States, under different names, as the snipe, big snipe, red-breasted snipe, and mud snipe, and, in some parts of the country, through ignorance, is not considered fit to eat, although they are generally held in the highest estimation as an article of luxury.

3 =**knot** n². Cf **redbreast 1b, red-breasted plover, ~ sandpiper**

1890 *Century Dict.* 5018, *Red-breasted sandpiper, Tringa canutus.— Red-breasted snipe.* . . same as *redbreast.* **1918** Grinnell *Game Birds CA* 365, The Knot, Red-breasted Snipe, or Robin Snipe, as this species has been variously called, is not abundant when compared with most other shore birds found in California. **1923** U.S. Dept. Ag. *Misc. Circular* 13.53 **WA, WI,** *Knot.* . . *Vernacular Names.* . . *In local use.* . . Red-breasted snipe. **1954** Sprunt *FL Bird Life* 179, *American Knot.* . . *Local Names* . . Red-breasted Snipe. . . Underparts *solid cinnamon.* **1969** Longstreet *Birds FL* 64, *Red-breasted Snipe.* . . When these birds reach Florida in the fall they have donned their winter feathers and people scarcely notice. . . When they go north in spring, however, they attract attention for at this time the throat and breast flaunt reddish feathers.

red-breasted sunfish n

1 also *redbreast sunfish;* Std: a freshwater **sunfish** (here: *Lepomis auritus*) common from New England to Florida. Also called **black-eared bream 2, bream B3, flatfish 3a, horn-eared sunfish, hound-eared ~, kivver, leather-ear 1, longear sunfish, perch** n¹ **2, pond perch, redbelly 1, red-bellied bream, ~ perch, ~ sunfish, red bream, redbreast 2, red-breasted bream, redbreast perch, red perch 3, ~ robin 3, ~-tailed bream, roach** n¹ **2, robin 2, sun perch, tobacco box, yellowbelly, yellowbreast sunfish, yellow perch**
2 =**bluegill 1.**

1946 LaMonte *N. Amer. Game Fishes* 138, *Bluegill Sunfish.* . . *Names* . . Red-breasted Sunfish.

red-breasted teal n [See quot 1918]   **chiefly West**
=**cinnamon teal.**

1852 U.S. Army Corps Topog. Engineers *Exped. Gt. Salt Lake* 323, *Pterocyanea Rafflesii* [=*Anas cyanoptera*]. . . The Red-breasted Teal appears to be a common bird in Utah. **1874** Coues *Birds NW* 567, *Querquedula cyanoptera.* . . Cinnamon Teal; Red-breasted Teal. . . In North America, from the Rocky Mountains to the Pacific, north to the Columbia [River]. **1918** Grinnell *Game Birds CA* 124, The bright coloration of this duck . . has been the basis for its several vernacular names. The chestnut or cinnamon color of the under surface has given rise to its accepted vernacular name, Cinnamon Teal, also a common hunter's name, Red-breasted Teal. **1928** Bailey *Birds NM* 126, Red-breasted Teal. . . Usually found among the sedge that borders sloughs near a watercourse. **1953** Jewett *Birds WA* 123, *Anas cyanoptera.* . . Red-breasted Teal. **1982** Elman *Hunter's Field Guide* 167, *Cinnamon Teal* . . *Common & regional names* . . red-breasted teal.

red-breasted woodpecker n Also *red-breasted sapsucker*
A **sapsucker 1** (here: *Sphyrapicus ruber*) native chiefly to the western US.

1839 Audubon *Ornith. Biog.* 5.179 **NW,** Red-breasted woodpecker, *Picus Ruber* [=*Sphyrapicus ruber*], . . has most of the habits of the common Red-headed species. **1887** Ridgway *N. Amer. Birds* 289, Pacific coast district, south to Fort Tejon, California, north to southern Alaska. . . *Red-breasted Sapsucker.* **1923** Dawson *Birds CA* 2.1012, *Sphyrapicus ruber ruber.* . . *Red-breasted Woodpecker.* *Ibid* 1013, The Red-breasted Sapsucker does puncture trees and drink sap both in summer and in winter. **1968** *DARE* (Qu. Q17, . . *Kinds of woodpeckers*) Infs **KS**7, **MN**38, **UT**9, Red-breasted woodpecker. **1977** Udvardy *Audubon Field Guide Birds* 645, Northwest coast and Sierra Nevada birds ("Red-breasted Sapsucker") have *entire head, throat, and breast bright red* with *deep yellow belly.* **1986** Pederson *LAGS Concordance* (*Woodpecker*) 1 inf, **cwAR,** Red-breasted woodpecker; 1 inf, **neFL,** Redbreasted sapsucker—black-and-white checked.

redbreast perch n Cf **perch** n¹ **2, red-bellied perch**
=**red-breasted sunfish 1.**
1966 *DARE* (Qu. P1, . . *Kinds of freshwater fish . . caught around here . . good to eat*) Inf **GA**5, Redbreast perch—same as redbreast.

redbreast plover See **red-breasted plover**

redbreast robin See **red-breasted robin 2**

redbreast sunfish See **red-breasted sunfish 1**

redbrush n

1 A **dogwood 1:** usu *Cornus stolonifera,* but also *C. amomum.*

1892 *Jrl. Amer. Folkl.* 5.97, *Cornus stolonifera,* red-brush. Central States. **1896** *Ibid* 9.189 **MO,** *Cornus sericea* [=*C. stolonifera*], . . red brush, Morgan County, Mo. **1935** *Yale Rev.* 25.177 **KY,** The sawbriars and the shoemakers and the redbrush are mighty fine markers [=grave markers] for a lot of the Hollow folks. **1940** Clute *Amer. Plant Names* 97, *C[ornus] amomum.* . . Red-brush. *Ibid* 98, *C. stolonifera.* . . Redbrush.

2 A **bear oak** (here: *Quercus ilicifolia*). [See quot 1953]

1938 Van Dersal *Native Woody Plants* 350, Red brush (*Lippia berlandieri* [=*L. graveolens*], *Quercus ilicifolia*). **1953** Strausbaugh-Core *Flora WV* 308, *Q[uercus] ilicifolia.* . . The red-brown, dry leaves often persist through the winter, giving rise to the local name, "Redbrush." The acorns are eaten by black bears and wild turkeys.

3 A **bee brush** (here: *Lippia graveolens*).

1938 [see **2** above]. **1960** Vines *Trees SW* 888, *Red-brush—Lippia graveolens.* . . Western, aromatic, pubescent shrub, more rarely a small tree. **1970** Correll *Plants TX* 1331, *Lippia graveolens.* . . *Redbrush Lippia.* . . Slender aromatic shrub.

red buckeye n [From the red flowers]
A **buckeye 1** (here: *Aesculus pavia*). Also called **firecracker plant 2, fish poison 1, horse chestnut 2, woolly buckeye**

1857 Gray *First Lessons* 83, *Æ[sculus] Pavia.* . . Red Buckeye. . . Fertile valleys, Virginia, Kentucky, and southward. **1901** Lounsberry *S. Wild Flowers* 325, Red buckeye. . . By its bruised branches and roots a most disagreeable odour is emitted while the latter contain a mucilaginous substance which many natives utilise as soap. **1936** IL Nat. Hist. Surv. *Wildflowers* 190, The Red Buckeye . . is a highly ornamental shrub or small tree of southern Illinois. . . The flowers, having a bright red corolla and tubular calyx, bloom in May. **1962** Harrar–Harrar *Guide S. Trees* 482, *Red Buckeye.* . . occurs sparsely along the coastal plain from southeastern Virginia to western Florida, thence, west through the Gulf states to western Louisiana. **1979** Ajilvsgi *Wild Flowers* 188, *Red buckeye.* . . Large shrub or small tree, often clumped.

redbud n

A tree of the genus *Cercis*, esp *C. canadensis.* Also called **Judas tree.** For other names of *C. canadensis* see **bleeding heart 4, fish blossom, Junebud, pinkbud, salad tree**

1705 Beverley *Hist. VA* 4.56, [The people of VA] dish up [roots, herbs, etc] various ways, and find them very delicious Sauce to their Meats . . ; such are the Red-Buds, Sassafras-Flowers, Cymnels, Melons, and Potatoes. **1709** (1967) Lawson *New Voyage* 106, The Red-Bud-Tree bears a purple Lark-Heel, and is the best Sallad of any Flower I ever saw. **1770** in 1918 *MD Hist. Mag.* 13.72, He is an obliging man, desier young to Collect Locust & Red Bud seeds, Hickory & Walnuts Pine Cones. **1819** (1821) Nuttall *Jrl.* 92 AR, The Red-bud . . was commonly in flower. **1849** Howitt *Our Cousins in OH* 12, There grew . . the red-bud, or Judas tree, by the budding of which, in old time, the Indian regulated the sowing of his corn. **1872** *Harper's New Mth. Mag.* 44.372, The redbud and dogwood blossoms had again appeared and vanished on the Kentucky hills. **1901** Lounsberry *S. Wild Flowers* 258, On gray, dull days when the spring is approaching, it is fairly startling to look up . . and find the red bud in bloom; for like the reddest burst of sunset it lightens up the tree's bare branches and all the landscape. **1938** Rawlings *Yearling* 48 nFL, The flowers of red-bud and jessamine . . had come and gone. **1965–70** *DARE* (Qu. T16, . . *Kinds of trees . . 'special'*) 50 Infs, **chiefly Sth, Midl,** Redbud tree; (Qu. S17, . . *Kinds of plants . . that . . cause itching and swelling*) Inf **VA**30, Redbud; (Qu. S26a, . . *Wildflowers. . . Roadside flowers*) Infs **CA**126, **MO**39, Redbud; (Qu. S26c, *Wildflowers that grow in woods*) Infs **CA**150, **IN**49, **KY**82, **NC**21, Redbud; **OK**9, Redbud tree; **CA**137, Redbuds; (Qu. S26d, *Wildflowers that grow in meadows;* not asked in early QRs) Inf **MS**47, Redbud; (Qu. S26e, *Other wildflowers not yet mentioned;* not asked in early QRs) Infs **CA**140, **KY**35, 49, **MS**47, **TX**84, Redbud; (Qu. T9) Infs **GA**18, **IN**40, **OH**37, 85, **TN**14, Redbud; (Qu. T12) Inf **MO**25, Redbud; **TX**106, Redbud bushes; **OH**97, Redbud tree; (Qu. T13) Inf **DC**2, Redbud; (Qu. T14) Inf **NC**8, Redbud; (Qu. T15, . . *Kinds of swamp trees*) Infs **FL**20, **NC**72, **VA**7, Redbud. **1986** Pederson *LAGS Concordance* **Gulf Region,** 54 infs, Redbud(s); 6 infs, Redbud tree(s); 3 infs, Redbud land.

redbud winter n Also *redwood winter* Cf **blackberry winter, linen britches ~, oak ~**

See quots.

1940 (1978) Still *River of Earth* 127 **KY,** "Even come spring," Grandma said, "we've got a passel of chills to endure: dogwood winter, redbud, service, foxgrape, blackberry. . . There must be seven winters, by count. A chilly snap for every time of bloom." **1982** Slone *How We Talked* 98 eKY (as of c1950), *Redwood winter*—A few cold days in April when the redbuds bloom.

redbug n Also *redbug chigger* **chiefly Sth** See Map Cf **chigger 1, jigger** n[2] **2**

=harvest mite, usu *Trombicula irritans.*

1827 Williams *View W. FL* 29, Red bugs are numerous, especially in mossy woods; they are nearly imperceptible to the naked eye; but . . could scarcely be a greater torment. **1872** Morrell *Flowers & Fruits* 381, The red bugs . . used to annoy me greatly when a boy, after playing over mossy logs. **1905** *DN* 3.68 nwAR, *Red-bug.* . . Chigoe. 'You know the chigger is the red-bug. It burrows under the skin.' 'Chigger' is more common in N.W. Arkansas. **1906** Johnson *Highways Missip. Valley* 44 **LA,** The numerous wood-ticks and red-bugs I had encountered had left their marks. **1932** *Natl. Geogr. Mag.* July 128 **NC, VA,** Man's master in Dismal Swamp is a tiny insect almost invisible to the naked eye—the ferocious little demon known in the South as the red bug. "After you've been here a while and acquire the 'swamp odor,' red bugs don't bother you much," the swamp man explained. **1965–70** *DARE* (Qu. R22, *Very small red insects, almost too small to see, that get under your skin and cause itching*) 180 Infs, **chiefly Sth,** Redbugs; **GA**77, Redbug chiggers; (Qu. R24) Inf **NC**33, Redbugs. **1972** *PADS* 58.22 cwAL, *Red bug.* Red bug (19 [of 27 infs]) is most common, but *chigger* (7) occurs as a primary response among older informants. A number of

informants gave both terms. **1985** Wilkinson *Moonshine* 132 neNC, Garland said they were chiggers, also called red-bugs. I had the heaviest concentration around my ankles and shins and knees. **1986** Pederson *LAGS Concordance* (Small insects that burrow in your skin and raise welts) 524 infs, **Gulf Region,** Red bug(s).

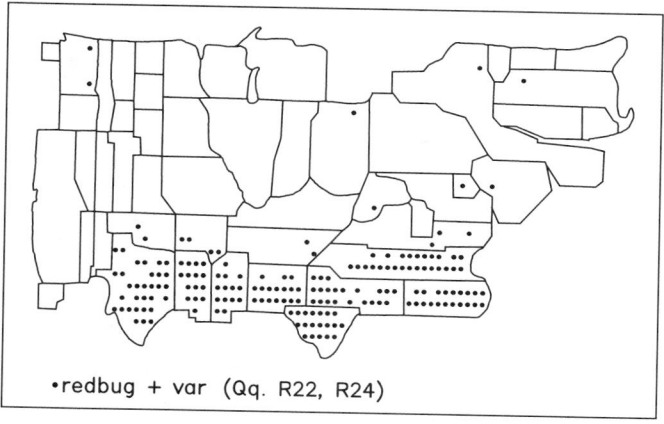

•redbug + var (Qq. R22, R24)

redbug plant n Cf **chiggerweed**
=orange milkwort.

[**1901** Lounsberry *S. Wild Flowers* 296, *Orange Milkwort.* . . At least they [=natives of FL] knew better than I that these blossoms especially the haunts of chiggers or red bugs, which would soon make my life a burden to me.] **1966** *DARE* Wildfl QR Pl.123A Inf **NC**28, Redbug plant.

red caille n **LA** Cf **half caille, little ~, speckled ~, yellow ~**
The male **summer tanager.**

1911 *Forest & Stream* 77.174 **LA,** *Piranga rubra.* . . Male, Red Caille, Chef Menteur, La. **1916** *Times–Picayune* (New Orleans LA) 23 Apr mag sec 5, *Summer Tanager.* . . Male. . . Red Caille.

red campion n

Std: a **catchfly 1** (here: *Silene dioica*). Also called **adder's flower, devil's-flower**

redcap n

A **red-headed woodpecker 1** (here: *Melanerpes erythrocephalus*).

1969 *DARE* (Qu. Q17, . . *Kinds of woodpeckers*) Inf **MI**93, Redheaded woodpecker—redcap.

red cardinal n Also *red cardinal flower*

1 also *red cardinal plant:* A **cardinal flower** (here: *Lobelia cardinalis*).

1830 Rafinesque *Med. Flora* 2.25, *Lobelia siphilitica, L. cardinalis.* . . are called blue and red Cardinal Flowers. **1869** *Amer. Naturalist* 3.211, Many of the fern-like mosses . . do perfectly well if planted in a very small quantity of soil upon this top stone. . . The red cardinal plant (*Lobelia cardinalis*), seem[s] especially adapted for this purpose. **1900** Lyons *Plant Names* 228, *L[obelia] cardinalis.* . . Red Cardinal. **1967** *DARE* Wildfl QR Pl.220 Inf **SC**41, Red cardinal flower.

2 A **coral tree** (here: *Erythrina herbacea*). Cf **cardinal-spear**

1938 Van Dersal *Native Woody Plants* 124, *Erythrina arborea* [=E. *herbacea*]. . . *Red-cardinal.* . . A large shrub to small or large tree, or vine. **1953** Greene–Blomquist *Flowers South* 59, *Red-cardinal.* . . Racemes [of flowers] . . red, scarlet, or crimson. . . The bright-red seeds . . are often gathered and used for beads. **1960** Vines *Trees SW* 560, *Erythrina herbacea.* . . Also known under the vernacular English . . names of Cardinal Spear, . . Red Cardinal-flower. **1974** Morton *Folk Remedies* 57 **SC,** *Red Cardinal.* . . Root steeped (like tea) and the infusion applied to hives or other skin irritation. **1980** Little *Audubon Guide N. Amer. Trees E. Region* 521, "Red-cardinal". . . SE. North Carolina to S. Florida, including Florida Keys and west to E. and S. Texas. . . This unusual tropical tree extends its range northward as a shrub or perennial herb, but is killed back to the ground each winter.

red cardinal plant See **red cardinal 1**

red cedar n

1 Any of several **junipers 1,** but esp *Juniperus virginiana;* also the wood of such a tree.   Cf **cedar 1, cedar brake 2**

1666 in 1836 Carroll *Hist. Coll. SC* 12, In the barren sandy ground grow most stately *Pines,* white and red *Cedars, Ash, Birch, Holly,* . . etc. **1737** (1911) Brickell *Nat. Hist. NC* 63, The *Red Cedar* is encompassed with a vast number of Branches, which grow gradually less and shorter, as they approach the top of the Tree, so that it grows exactly in the Form of a Pyramid.   **1792** Belknap *Hist. NH* 3.111, *Juniperus virginiana.* . . The wood of the red cedar, is more durable, when set in the earth, than any other wood growing in this country.   **1817** *N. Amer. Rev.* 5.316 **seMA,** The stump of a red cedar stood near the shore.   **1851** *Knicker-bocker* 37.377 **NY,** The country-bred traveller . . inhales the odor of the red-cedar buckets.   **1901** Lounsberry *S. Wild Flowers* 18, *J[uniperus] Virginia,* red cedar, . . occurs in various forms from a low shrub to a tree, often one hundred feet high. . . The fragrant, bright red wood of the tree is valuable, as it does not decay.   **1938** Van Dersal *Native Woody Plants* 330, Cedar. . . Red *(Juniperus scopulorum, Juniperus virginiana, Thuja plicata).*   **1961** Douglas *My Wilderness* 187 **MD,** The red cedars that stud them—the cedar whose berries are loved by the birds and who gave its name to the cedar waxwing—had been sprayed white.   **1965–70** *DARE* (Qu. T5, . . *Kinds of evergreens, other than pine*) 30 Infs, **scattered, but esp C Atl, N Cent,** Red cedar; **VA8,** Virginia red cedar; **CO9,** Western red cedar; (Qu. T15, . . *Kinds of swamp trees*) Infs **NJ17, 22, WI58,** Red cedar; (Qu. T16, . . *Kinds of trees* . . *'special'*) Infs **KY35, NY211, WI78,** Red cedar; (Qu. S17, . . *Kinds of plants* . . *that* . . *cause itching and swelling*) Inf **NC80,** Red cedars; (Qu. T17, . . *Kinds of pine trees; not asked in early QRs*) Inf **NY52,** Red cedar.   **1986** Pederson *LAGS Concordance,* 3 infs, **TN,** Red cedar.

2 often with modifier: An arborvitae (here: *Thuja plicata*) native chiefly to the Pacific NW and Alaska.   Also called **cedar 2, giant cedar**

1884 Sargent *Forests of N. Amer.* 7, The red fir, the hemlock, and the red cedar *(Thuya* [sic]) are still important elements of the forests.   *Ibid* 177, *Red Cedar. Canoe Cedar.* . . Wood . . dull brown tinged with red, the thin sap-wood nearly white; . . used . . exclusively by the Indians of the northwest coast in the manufacture of their canoes.   **1897** Sudworth *Arborescent Flora* 71 **ID, OR, WA,** *Thuja plicata.* . . Red Cedar.   **1900** Lyons *Plant Names* 370, *T[huja] gigantea.* . . Pacific Red Cedar, Oregon Red Cedar [etc].   **1917** (1923) Rogers *Trees Worth Knowing* 269, The red cedar . . is the giant arbor-vitae of the coast region from British Columbia to northern California and east over the mountain ranges into Idaho and northern Montana.   **1938** [see **1** above].   **1968** *DARE* (Qu. T5, . . *Kinds of evergreens, other than pine*) Inf **AK1,** Western red cedar.   **1980** Little *Audubon Guide N. Amer. Trees W. Region* 321, Particularly resistant to rot, Western Redcedar is the chief wood for shingles and one of the most important for siding, utility poles, fenceposts, paneling, outdoor-patio construction, and boatbuilding.

3 =**incense cedar.**

1897 Sudworth *Arborescent Flora* 64 **ID,** *Libocedrus decurrens.* . . Red Cedar.   **1910** Jepson *Silva CA* 149, Incense Cedar. . . by woodsmen . . is variously called Red Cedar, White Cedar, Bastard Cedar, and Post Cedar.

red cherry n

1 also *wild red cherry:* A **wild cherry,** usu **pin cherry 1;** also its fruit.

1716 Petiver *Petiveriana* 12, Red-*Cherry.* A large Tree in the *Woods,* not much unlike the *Cornel berry.*   **1737** (1911) Brickell *Nat. Hist. NC* 77, The *Red Cherry* Tree, is very scarce, and rarely to be met with, it's [sic] Virtues and Uses are much the same of those with us.   **1813** Michaux *Histoire des Arbres* 3.159, *Cerasus borealis* [=*Prunus pensyl-vanica*]. . . Cet arbre est désigné par les noms de *Small Cherry* . . et de *Red Cherry.* [=The tree is designated by the names of *Small Cherry* . . and of *Red Cherry.*]   **1848** (1932) Robinson *Jrl. Santa Fe* 8 **MO,** On the banks of the creek we found an abundance of red cherries growing on small bushes.   a**1862** (1864) Thoreau *ME Woods* 313, *Prunus Pennsyl-vanica* (wild red cherry), very common at camps, carries, &c., along rivers; fruit ripe August 1, 1857.   **1931** Harned *Wild Flowers Alle-ghanies* 248, *Wild Red Cherry (Prunus pennsylvanica).* . . Fruit cherry red without bloom, . . with sour flesh, its stone round.   **1950** Peattie *Nat. Hist. Trees* 381, *Prunus pennsylvanica.* . . Bird, Pin, Pigeon, Red or Wild Red, Cherry.   **1969–70** *DARE* (Qu. T16, . . *Kinds of trees* . . *'special'*) Infs **KY43, 76,** Red cherry.

2 =**sour cherry.**   Cf **pie cherry**

1837 Darlington *Flora Cestrica* 288 **sePA,** *Prunus Cerasus.* . . Red or Sour Cherry. . . The fruit . . is extensively used by the pastry cook.   **1868** (1870) Gray *Field Botany* 119, *P[runus] Cerasus, Garden Red Cherry.* . . An acid red globose fruit.   **1910** Graves *Flowering Plants* 245 **CT,** *Prunus Cerasus.* . . Sour, Pie, Red, Morello or Old-fashioned Cherry. . . Cultivated for its fruit.   **1970** *DARE* (Qu. I53, . . *Fruits grown around here* . . *special varieties*) Infs **IA12, OH4,** Red cherries.

red chickweed n   Cf **chickweed**

=**scarlet pimpernel.**

1818 Eaton *Botany* 134, *Anagallis.* . . *arvensis* (red chickweed, scarlet pimpernell . .).   **1832** Williamson *Hist. ME* 1.122, *Red chickweed* is a beautiful low plant procumbent on the ground.   **1897** *Jrl. Amer. Folkl.* 10.49 **West,** *Anagallis arvensis.* . . Red chickweed.   **1995** Brako et al. *Scientific & Common Names Plants* 7, *Anagallis* . . *arvensis* . . red-chickweed.

red clover n

Std: a perennial clover *(Trifolium pratense)* widely planted as a hay and pasture crop.   Also called **bee bread, cow clover 1, honeysuckle 1, German clover, mammoth ~, meadow ~, peavine ~, redtop ~, suckles, sweet clover**

redcoat n

1 The bedbug *(Cimex lectularius).*

1911 *Century Dict. Suppl., Redcoat.* . . The bedbug. [*Century* Ed: Local, U.S.]   **1916** U.S. Dept. Ag. *Farmers' Bulletin* 754.2, In New York they are styled "red coats," and in the west "crimson ramblers".

2 Perh =**Maltese cross.**

1968 Coatsworth *ME Memories* 155, The honesty by the door is still called "silver shillings," as the bright scarlet flower is called "redcoats."

3 also *redcoat moss:* See **red-cup moss.**

red-cockaded woodpecker n   Cf **black-headed woodpecker**

Std: a **woodpecker** (here: *Picoides borealis*) native to pine woods in the southeastern US.   Also called **sapsucker 1**

red cod   See **red rock cod**

red cohosh n

=**red baneberry.**

1828 Rafinesque *Med. Flora* 1.89, The *A[ctaea] rubra.* . . [is] called . . Red Cohosh by the Indians.   **1907** Hodge *Hdbk. Amer. Indians* 1.321, Red cohosh is red baneberry.   **1979** Erichsen-Brown *Med. N. Amer. Plants* 348, *Actaea rubra.* . . Common names. Red cohosh [etc].

red coon-root n

1 A **hepatica** (here: *Hepatica nobilis obtusa*).

1926 Puckett *Folk Beliefs S. Negro* 375, For cramps, a brass ring; tea from red coon-root *(Hepatica triloba);* or a dime about the ankle are all equally effective.

2 =**bloodroot 1.**   Cf **coon root, red puccoon**

1968 *Foxfire* Summer 50 **sAppalachians,** Bloodroot. . . is the "red-coonroot" of the mountains.

red crab n

A crab *(Cancer productus)* native to the Pacific coast.

1884 Goode *Fisheries U.S.* 1.771, *The Red Crab—Cancer productus.* . . is a very common species in the Bay of San Francisco. . . *Cancer productus.* . . is found along the entire Pacific coast of the United States.   **1901** Arnold *Sea-Beach* 278, The red crab. . . is of large size. . . In color the animal is dark red above and yellowish beneath in the adults. . . This is an edible crab, but is not taken for the markets.   **1981** Meinkoth *Audubon Field Guide Seashore* 644, Although adults are uniformly brick-red, young Red Crabs are strikingly varied: white, brown, blue, red, or orange—either solid or patterned.

red crossbill n

The common crossbill *(Loxia curvirostra).*   Also called **salt-bird, screw bill**

1867 (1868) *Amer. Naturalist* 1.44 **NEast,** The Common or Red Crossbill . . is of desultory habits.   **1895** Minot *Land-Birds New Engl.* 174, Red Crossbills may be seen near Boston every month in the year.   **1919** Gilmore *Birds of Field* 293, When in late November, the first real stress of winter came with the deeper snows, a flock of Red Crossbills took up their temporary abode in the evergreen trees near the camp. **1949** Kitchin *Birds Olympic Peninsula* 238 **wWA**, Red Cross-bill. . . Small flocks of these strange little birds may be encountered at any time of the year in any section of the wooded areas of our mountains. **1964** Phillips *Birds AZ* 183, The Red Crossbill epitomizes cardueline traits, for it breeds in winter, with snow draped around the nest—when and where abundant cone crops permit. **1977** Bull–Farrand *Audubon Field Guide Birds* 698, Like the Red Crossbill, these birds [= *Loxia leucoptera*] use their cross mandibles to extract seeds from the cones of pines and spruces.

redcrown n

A **redpoll 1** (here: *Carduelis flammea*).

1956 MA Audubon Soc. *Bulletin* 40.254, *Common Redpoll. . .* Redcrown (Mass. The forehead is poppy red to crimson.)

red-cup moss n Also *redcoat (moss)* Cf **British soldier 2**

A **reindeer moss** (here: *Cladonia bellidiflora*).

1892 *Jrl. Amer. Folkl.* 5.105 **NEast**, *Cladonia bellidiflora* (a common lichen), red-cup moss. **2002** *DARE* File **NEng** (as of 1960s–70s), I remember, as a kid, calling reindeer moss "redcoat moss." *Ibid*, I did hear the term "redcoats" or "red soldiers" at Camp Takodah while walking in the woods with someone . . and we saw some of this [reindeer] moss.

red curlew n Cf **redbird e**

=**marbled godwit.**

1813 (1824) Wilson *Amer. Ornith.* 7.30, Our gunners call it [=the marbled godwit] the *Straight-billed Curlew*, and sometimes the *Red Curlew*. **1844** DeKay *Zool. NY* 2.253, It is described in the books as the *Great Marbled Godwit*, a name entirely unknown to the people of the country. With us it is generally called the *Marlin*, and less frequently *Red Curlew*. **1917** (1923) *Birds Amer.* 1.241, *Limosa fedoa. . .* Red Curlew. **1956** MA Audubon Soc. *Bulletin* 40.20, *Marbled Godwit. . .* Red Curlew (Mass. General ground color pale cinnamon.)

red cypress n

=**bald cypress.**

1854 Wailes *Rept. on Ag. & Geol. MS* 349, The Red Cypress, the most valuable variety, not floating, in consequence of its greater specific gravity, can only be brought out by pinning or securing the log between others of a more buoyant kind. **1860** Curtis *Cat. Plants NC* 29, Taxodium distichum. . . The *Red Cypress* has its heart of a reddish tint, is preferable . . for timber, and cannot be split. This variety is easily recognized by its straight trunk, (not always having a swollen base,) generally with a small top, and by the wounded bark having a reddish tinge. **1884** Sargent *Forests of N. Amer.* 184, Red Cypress. . . A large tree of great economic value . . ; common and forming extensive forests in the south Atlantic and Gulf states. **1979** Little *Checklist U.S. Trees* 282, *Taxodium distichum . . var. distichum. . .* Red-cypress.

redd v Also sp *red* [The origins and development of the forms and senses treated here are complex and undoubtedly reflect the complete or partial fusion of several originally unrelated words. Cf *OED2 redd* v.¹, v.², *rid* v., and the etym notes at the individual senses below.] Cf **ready** v, **redden up**

1 Used in var senses where *rid* is standard, esp as past pple *red* in phr *get red of*; also vbl n *redding*. [*OED2 redd* v.¹ 2 14 . . →; *EDD redd* v.³] *old-fash*

1848 Lowell *Biglow* 67 **'Upcountry' MA**, 'T would be better to hang 'em,/ An' so git red on 'em soon. **1891** *DN* 1.128 **cNY**, This [ɛ] replaces [ɪ] . . also in [rɛd] (Eng. 'rid' < *hreddan*). **1891** *PMLA* 6.165 **WV**, The sounds [ɪ] and [ɛ] are often interchangeable, as [lɛd] for *lid*, [rɛd] for *rid* [etc]. **1905** *DN* 3.56 **eNE**, The change of [ɪ] to [ɛ], is seen in. . . *red*. **1917** *DN* 4.398 **neOH**, *Red. . .* Rid, in the phrase, *git red of*, = "get rid of." It is my impression that in the vernacular of the '80's *red* was used for *rid* in all current senses. **1935** *AmSp* 10.293 **Upstate NY**, Single instances appear of [rɛd] for *rid*, [ə'gɪn] for *again* [etc]. **1942** Hall *Smoky Mt. Speech* 15 **wNC, eTN**, Laxer and lowered varieties of [ɪ], often reaching [ɛ], may frequently be heard in *different*, *lid*, *rid* . . [rɛd]. **1943** *LANE* Map 569 *(Get rid of him)*, [Red for *rid* in this expression occurs **throughout NEng** and is the dominant form in **nNEng**. While it was the first or only resp of many infs, a number regarded it as an older variant of *rid*.] **c1960** *Wilson Coll.* **csKY**, Rid in *get rid of* is often /rɛd/. **1968** Kellner *Aunt Serena* 65 **cIN** (as of c1920), A child's first household duty was redding things of dust.

2 also *rid*: To clear off (land) for planting; to clear (some-thing) off of land. [*OED2 rid* v. 1.a "*esp.* to clear land of trees, undergrowth, etc."; *EDD rid* v.² 1; *SND redd* v.¹ 4.(2)]

1895 *DN* 1.392 **cwPA**, "Red the ground (for planting)," . . looks like *rid* (of stumps, etc). **1941** *Sat. Eve. Post* 10 May 112 **KY**, It would take Adam's grands and greats to rid that ground in time for planting. **1986** Pederson *LAGS Concordance*, 1 inf, **csGA**, We ridded the trees off of it.

3 also with *up*: To put in order, tidy; spec: see below. [*OED2 redd* v.² 3.a, b, 6.a, b, *rid* v. 1.c; *EDD red(d* v.¹ 1, 2, *rid* v.¹ 5, 6; *SND redd* v.¹ 6.(3), 7.(1), *rid* v. 5.(2), 6]

a also *ret, rid(d);* also with *out*: To tidy up, clean up or out (a room, house, cupboard, etc); to clean house, tidy up; hence vbl n *redding up* housecleaning, tidying up. **scattered, but chiefly N Midl, esp PA** See Map on p. 512

1842 *Spirit of the Times*, Aug. 12 (1912 Thornton *Amer. Gloss.*) **sePA**, I never used to red up their chamber without thinking of it.—Phila[delphia]. **1867** *Galaxy* 3.658, She went in and out as usual, 'redding up' the room for the night. **1869** *Atlantic Mth.* 24.477 **sePA**, When a death occurs, our Dutch neighbors enter the house. . . Some "redd up" the house. **1872** Schele de Vere *Americanisms* 531, *Ready*, to, in the sense of setting to rights, is an old English term surviving in our speech. . . The word is often heard in America, but more generally assumes the equally old form, to *redd*. **1876** in 1969 *PADS* 52.54 **seIL**, I stayed in the house all day and red up my trunk and box. **1887** *Amer. Philol. Assoc. Trans. for 1886* 17.41 **Sth**, To *red* or *red up*, as "red up a room," i.e. 'to make ready,' is still common in East Tennessee, and I have found one example in a New England Sunday-school book. It is not unknown in Ohio. **1892** *KS Univ. Qrly.* 1.98 **KS**, *Red up:* to make tidy. **1895** [see **3c** below]. **1897** Higginson *From Land* 132 **wWA**, "You got your front room red up . . ?" "No; I ain't had time to red up anything." **1902** *DN* 2.243 **sIL**, Rid [rɛd] or rid up [rɛd əp]. . . To tidy up; to clean up an apartment or house. **1904** *DN* 2.400 **cNY**, Red up. . . To tidy up, slick up a room. **1905** *DN* 3.64 **eNE**, Red up the room. **1907** *DN* 3.225 **nwAR**, Rid [rɛd] *(up). . .* To tidy up. **1914** *DN* 4.78 **ME, nNH**, Red up, rid up. . . Tidy, sweep, put in order. **1919** T.K. Holmes *Man from Tall Timber* xii.144 (*OED2*), I'll rid up the place and get our dinner. **1923** *DN* 5.218 **swMO**, To red up a room. **1930** in 1952 Mathes *Tall Tales* 168 **sAppalachians**, This bit of social and domestic philosophy brought no audible response from the busy wife, who was briskly "ridding up" the bed. **1933** *AmSp* 8.1.25 **c,nWV**, One hears *We'd better rid up the house, Let's rid things up while we have a chance*, and similar expressions. South of West Virginia the word is *red*. **1940** Richter *Trees* 104 **OH** (as of early 19th cent), Then she went in and redd out the cabin. **1941** *LANE* Map 336 *(She cleans up every morning)* 4 infs, Redd(s) up [heard]; 3 infs, Redds up; 1 inf, Redd up [old or obs]; 1 inf, Red up—an old New England word, oftener used by womenfolks; 1 inf, Redds up—heard formerly, esp from the Dutch; 1 inf, Redd up—grandmother's expression; 1 inf, Redds up—the usual expression, regarded as Scotch; 3 infs, Rids up [old or obs]; 2 infs, Rid(s) up [heard]; 1 inf, Rids up [first resp]; 1 inf, Rids up—regarded as a Canadian expression; 1 inf, Rids the house—old-fashioned expression. **1950** *PADS* 14.56 **SC**, Redd up the parlor before company comes. **1952** Brown *NC Folkl.* 1.583, *Redd (up). . .* To set a house in order; to clear a table. . . General. **1953** Randolph–Wilson *Down in Holler* 277 **Ozarks**, *Red up. . .* To clean, to put in order. "I got to red up this here house if we're goin' to have company." Isabel Spradley, of Van Buren, Ark., thinks that the cabin should be *retted* up, but it sounds like a *d* rather than a *t*, to my ear. **1965–70** *DARE* (Qu. E21, . . *About a room that needs to be put in order . . "I'm just going to _____ this room."*) 85 Infs, **scattered, but esp freq PA**, Redd up; CA36, LA14, MA98, NJ2, PA52, Redd; PA131, 206, Redd it up; IL3, Redd out; OH38, 65, 72, PA184, 189, 203, Rid (it) up; (Qu. A10, . . *Doing little unimportant things*) Inf NY34, Redding up—old-fashioned; (Qu. E22, *If a house is untidy*) Inf PA203, Needs redding up; (Qu. KK1b, . . *'In the very best condition': "His farm is _____."*) Inf PA161, Redded up; (Qu. KK34, . . *Very neat and clean: "Her house always looks _____."*) Infs NC38, PA161, (All) redd up. **1966** Dakin *Dial. Vocab. Ohio R. Valley* 2.50, *Cleans up. . . Redd up* is common throughout Ohio except in the lower Miami Valley, but is fairly rare outside of this state. . . The word is occasionally given as *ridd*. Three of the four Illinois informants who might use it say this. **1973** Allen *LAUM* 1.172 **Upper MW** (as of c1950), *Red up . .* is usually described as an old term now disused. Its variant *rid up . .* is equally obsolescent. **1977** Miles *Ozark Dict.* 8, Ret-up the house before the preacher gets here. **1982** Barrick Coll. **csPA**, *Redd out*—clean out—"I got to redd out my cupboards." *Redd up—straighten up*—Common. **1982** Slone *How We Talked* 20 **eKY** (as of c1950), "Ridden up the house"—Making it ready for company. The daily chores; sweeping, dusting, making the beds. **1986** Pederson *LAGS Concordance,* 1 inf, **cnAL,** Redd up—has heard, not her term; 1 inf, **nwAR,** Redding the house—"pioneer expression", not used; 1 inf, **cnGA,** Redd up—I heard people call it; 1 inf, **cGA,** Redd up—others' term, seldom heard or used; 1 inf, **cwGA,** Redd up—used only by blacks; 1 inf, **swGA,** Redd up—heard, never used; 1 inf, **neTN,** Redd up = get house ready, mother always said; 1 inf, **csTN,** Redd up—Sister-in-law in PA says; 1 inf, **csTN,** Redding—comes from "readying"; 1 inf, **neTN,** Redding up—natural response; 1 inf, **neTN,** Redds the house—not very common. **1993** [see **3b** below].

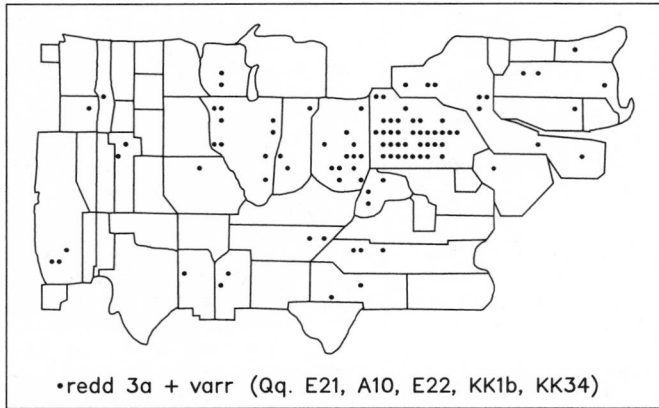

•redd 3a + varr (Qq. E21, A10, E22, KK1b, KK34)

b also *ret, rid;* also with *off:* To clear off (a table), esp after a meal; occas, to clear (dishes) off a table. **scattered, but chiefly N Midl, esp PA** See Map

1940 Richter *Trees* 284 **OH** (as of early 19th cent), She went on redding off her table and making a long ado of washing his knife. **1942** (1971) Campbell *Cloud-Walking* 10 **seKY,** Then Sary stopped the talk to red up the table and set away things. **1942** Whipple *Joshua* 153 **UT** (as of c1860), All she asked of that trashy Willie was to redd up the table and take care of the victuals. **1950** *WELS Suppl.* **csWI,** I'll red the table, but you girls will have to do the dishes. **1952** [see **3a** above]. **1965–70** DARE (Qu. G10, *When the meal is all over, what do you have to do to the table?*) 19 Infs, **chiefly MD, OH, PA, WV,** Redd it up; 15 Infs, **chiefly PA,** Redd it (*or* the table) off; 13 Infs, **chiefly PA, Appalachians,** Redd the table (*or* it); CA85, OH44, PA22, 203, Redd off (the table); IL63, VA28, Redd up the dishes; PA235, Redd up; NM12, Ret the table; CO11, IA12, MD17, MI9, 77, WI3, Rid it (*or* the table); PA72, 165, 186, Rid it (*or* the table) off; OH65, Rid it up; IL113, Rid up; NC84, Rid the dishes; (Qu. G9, *When you have to get the table ready for a meal, you say "It's time to _____."*) Inf VA31, Redd the table. **1968** Kellner *Aunt Serena* 82 **IN,** Only hicks . . said things like, "I'll redd up the table." **1973** DARE File **cwPA** (as of c1960), Ret up = red up (the table, after a meal). **1982** *Smithsonian Letters* **OH,** Here are a couple of expressions my mother-in-law, from Wood County, Ohio, used to use. . . "I'll red the table," meaning to clear it and put away the food. **1986** Pederson *LAGS Concordance,* 1 inf, **swTN,** Redd the table = clear the table. **1993** DARE File **NC,** *Everybody* in my family used the verb *to redd.* "Somebody please redd off the table." "I have to redd up in here before company comes."

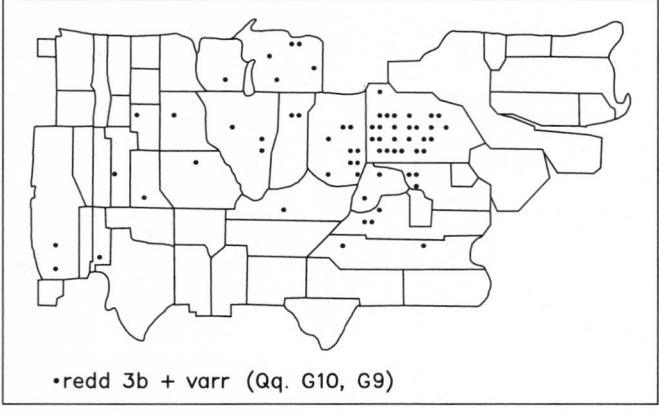

•redd 3b + varr (Qq. G10, G9)

c also with *out:* To comb (one's hair); to groom oneself; hence vbl n *redding.* **esp Appalachians** Cf **redding comb**

1878 *Johnson's New Universal Cyclop.* 4.151, In the U.S. we may trace a Scotch ancestry by expressions like . . *red* ("comb out") the hair, a *redding* comb. **1887** *Amer. Philol. Assoc. Trans. for 1886* 17.41 **eTN,** A woman in East Tennessee to-day speaks of *redding* up her hair of a morning, when it needs combing. **1895** DN 1.392, *Red, rid:* to arrange, prepare, put in order. . . [I]n other examples received the meaning given is prominent; *e.g.* ["]to red up a room," "to red out one's hair" (reddin' comb, from Ohio, as a coarse comb). **1924** Raine *Land of Saddle-Bags* 207 **sAppalachians,** I hain't had time to redd my hair. **1927** DN 5.471 **Appalachians,** *Redd.* . . To make tidy;—used only of the hair. **1928** Chapman *Happy Mt.* 300 **eTN,** And such was his haste to be at Allardene's home that Waits got there in a manner before himself, and came upon a house where was a great stirring, for all were redding for the day. **1931** *AmSp* 7.94 **eKY,** *Red-up,* to tidy. "Come right in, Fields, though I hain't had a minit to red-up the house or my hair neither." **1941** *LANE* Map 358 (*Dress up*) 1 inf, **ME,** *Red up,* older expression. **1952** Brown *NC Folkl.* 1.583, *Redd the hair.* . . To comb the hair. . . General. Rare. **1975** King *S. Ladies & Gentlemen* 146, She takes care to "red up" so that she and Sonny will look as much like a couple as possible.

4 also *read, rid, ride:* To clean (hog intestines); hence vbl n *ridding* cleaning out (intestines). [*OED2 rede* v.2 2; *EDD read* v.1 4; *SND rede* v.2 3, *redd* v.1 4.(6) "To clean the intestines of a slaughtered animal of their fat."] **esp Sth, S Midl**

1895 DN 1.392, "To rid guts," *i.e.* to remove the "gut lard." **1899** (1912) Green *VA Folk-Speech* 351, *Rid.* . . To separate or free from anything superfluous or objectionable; disencumber; clear. . . To *rid* hog-guts of the fat for making lard. **1936** *AmSp* 11.317 **Ozarks,** *Red the guts.* . . To clean the intestines of hogs. At hog-killing time the entrails are split open, emptied, wound on sticks and hung up to dry. Later on they are used in making soap and the like. **1972** *Atlanta Letters* **neGA,** How you like Chittlens? They are good if they are rid good. Ridding Chittlens is an art. **1986** Pederson *LAGS Concordance,* 1 inf, **ceAL,** Riding them = washing intestine of hog—chitlins; 1 inf, **seGA,** Reading them—chitlins; examining and removing fat.

red dace n Cf **dace**
A **shiner 1** (here: *Notropis cornutus*).
1842 DeKay *Zool. NY* 3.207, *Leuciscus cornutus* [=*Notropis c.*] . . This very beautiful little fish. . . has the various popular names of . . *Red Dace* [etc]. **1884** Goode *Fisheries U.S.* 1.617, The . . "Red Dace" abounds in all streams from New England to Kansas and Alabama, being in most waters more numerous than any other species.

red daisy n
=**orange hawkweed.**
1895 U.S. Dept. Ag. *Farmers' Bulletin* 28.27, Orange hawkweed, . . red daisy. . . Hieracium aurantiacum. [Where injurious:] New York. **1914** Georgia *Manual Weeds* 554, Red Daisy. . . Fields, meadows, pastures, roadsides, waste places. [*Ibid* 555, The heads are about an inch broad when fully opened, flaming orange-red.] **1959** Carleton *Index Herb. Plants* 98, Red daisy: Hieracium aurantiacum.

redd comb See **redding comb**

red deer n
=**whitetail deer.**
1625 in 1910 Smith *Travels & Wks.* lxix **VA** (as of 1607), There is also great store of Deere both Red and Fallow. **1698** (1848) Thomas *Hist. & Geog. Acct.* 15 **PA,** There are in the Woods abundance of *Red Deer* (vulgarly called *Stags*). **a1782** (1788) Jefferson *Notes VA* 55, There remains then the buffalo, red deer, fallow deer, wolf, roe, glutton, . . and water rat. **1814** *Sporting Mag.* 44.62, The method of approaching . . the red deer . . by means of *fire-hunting them,* (which is a well-known custom in the Southern Provinces of America, and in constant practice) is invaluable. **1885** *Wkly. New Mexican Rev.* 18 June 4/6 (DAE), [Near Santa Fe] wild turkeys are common; also the black-tailed and red deer. **1967–69** DARE (Qu. P32, . . *Other kinds of wild animals*) Infs **AZ**11, **KY**11, **MN**15, **OH**16, Red deer.

reddening See **redding** n

reddening comb See **redding comb**

redden up v phr [redd 3a + -en suff5] Cf *reddening comb* (at **redding comb**)

1926 *DN* 5.388 **ME**, *Red up* (redden up). . . To make tidy a house. "Wait until I redden up a bit." Common.

redder See **rather** *adv*

red devil *n*

1 also *red devil pepper*: A hot pepper (*Capsicum* spp).
1950 *WELS* (*Any kinds of small, hot peppers grown in your neighborhood*) 2 Infs, **ceWI**, (Little) red devils. **1965–70** *DARE* (Qu. I22a, . . *Peppers—small hot*) Infs **AL**1, 20, **AZ**8, **GA**92, **IL**98, **NC**72, **VA**71, Red devils; (Qu. I22b, . . *Peppers—large hot*) Infs **TX**37, Red devil peppers; **NY**210, Red devils.

2 See quot. Cf **redworm 1**
1968 *DARE* (Qu. P6, . . *Kinds of worms . . used for bait*) Inf **WI**48, Red devil.

3 See quot.
1954 *AmSp* 29.298, The following are additional terms [for menstruation] which have been reported. . . [T]he *red devil* (*W*[omen], collegiate).

red devil pepper See **red devil 1**

redding *n* Also *reddening* Pronc-sp *red'nin* [*OED2 redding* sb. 1 1292–3 →; "Now only *dial.*" *EDD* ruddnin (at *rud* v.¹ 5) "a piece of red haematite used for reddening"]
Red ocher or similar material used esp to color brickwork.
1866 (1881) Whitney *Leslie Goldthwaite* 115 **NH**, The brick hearth and jambs [were] aglow with fresh "redding." **1899** (1912) Green *VA Folk-Speech* 349, Redding. . . A compound used to redden the jambs and hearth of an open wood-fireplace. Red ochre. **c1938** in 1970 Hyatt *Hoodoo* 1.711 **New Orleans LA**, You get some red'nin' [Hyatt: reddening] and you get you some *lucky perfume* and you get some *van-van* and scrub your house Wednesdays and Mondays and Fridays. *Ibid* **seLA**, Take cinnamon, brown sugah, reddenin'—it's jis' lak a powder but it's red, an' yo' scrubs with that. *Ibid* 470, Red-brick powder is an ordinary red brick . . ground to a powder. Redding is sometimes used as a substiute. Both could be bought at a hoodoo drug store.

redding *vbl n* See **redd 1, 3c**

redding comb *n* Also *redd comb, reddening ~, reddying ~, ridding ~* Pronc-spp *red'n comb, red'nin ~* [Scots, nIr, nEngl dial; cf *EDD* at *ready* v. 3.(2), *red(d* v.¹ 2.(4), *rid* v.¹ 6.(2)] esp **S Midl** Cf **ready** *v*, **redd 3c, redden up, tucking comb**
A comb for ordering or cleaning the hair.
1870 Duval *Advent. Big-Foot* 188 **TX**, I met with a serious misfortune in the loss of my "fine-tooth comb" . . which was my only "ark of safety" against the swarms of vermin. . . [N]othing will answer in place of a "ridding comb," under such circumstances. **1878** [see **redd 3c**]. **1886** *S. Bivouac* 4.349 **sAppalachians**, Redding-comb. **1887** Amer. Philol. Assoc. *Trans. for 1886* 17.42 **eTN**, *Redding*-comb, or *reddying*-comb, that is, the comb used to clear out the hair when tangled and long, as "Where's the reddin'-comb? I want to do up my hair." It is the opposite of *tuck*-comb. It is used in East Tennessee. **1893** *KS Univ. Qrly.* 1.141 **OH**, Redding-comb: a coarse comb. **1902** *DN* 2.243 **sIL**, Reddingcomb ['rɛdŋkŏm]. . . A fine-toothed comb. **1903** *DN* 2.327 **seMO**, Ridding-comb. . . A fine-toothed comb. **1916** *DN* 4.328 **KS, TX**, Redding comb. . . A comb with very fine teeth, used to clean hair and scalp thoroughly. **1923** (1946) Greer-Petrie *Angeline Steppin'* 33 **csKY**, He wanted me to git out my *red'n comb* and see if I couldn't fix my ha'r like them city wimmen was a-wearin theirn. **1933** *AmSp* 8.4.51 **NE** [Pioneer vocab], A coarse comb used to rid one's hair of snarls, lice, etc., was a *riddin' comb*. **1944** *PADS* 2.21 **sAppalachians**, Red'nin'-comb, redd-comb. . . The ordinary long comb for combing women's hair. *Red'nin'* for *redding*, or *ridding* (of lice), originally, for which the fine-comb or "gray-back" chaser is now used. **1950** *PADS* 14.56 **SC**, Redding comb. . . A straight comb for untangling, straightening and smoothing the hair, as contrasted with a *back comb, roach comb,* or *side comb,* all of which are worn in the hair, and are more or less ornamental. **1953** Randolph–Wilson *Down in Holler* 277 **Ozarks**, Redding comb, reddening comb. . . An ordinary heavy comb, with which the mountain woman "reds out" snarls in her hair. . . A fine-toothed comb is called a *finin' comb* or a *booger comb*. **1982** Slone *How We Talked* 21 **eKY** (as of c1950), A "reddin' comb"—A large comb, in comparison to a fine comb. . . A "reddin' comb" was of larger teeth or prongs. It was used to get the tangles from the hair, while the fine comb was used to get bugs from the hair.

redding up See **redd 3a**

reddio See **radio**

reddish See **radish**

redd off See **redd 3b**

red dog *n* chiefly **wPA, WV, OH** See Map
The reddish cinders resulting from the burning of coal-mining refuse, often used as a road surface; hence v *reddog* to surface (a road) with this material; freq in comb *red-dog road*.
1931 *AmSp* 7.20 **swPA**, *Red-dog*. A variety of red shale, impervious to water, used for laying road-beds. **1940** Writers' Program *Guide PA* 566 **cwPA**, Between Harmarville and Blawnox are piles of 'red dog,' a reddish-brown earth stripped off the surface in order to expose underlying bituminous coal deposits. Chunks of soft coal in these piles frequently become ignited, producing blue and yellow flames that at night cast an eerie glow over the landscape. **1942** *Morgantown Post* (WV) 7 Oct 10/5, He also said that unpaved streets in all sections of the city are being reddogged in preparation for cold weather. **1948** Rosskam–Rosskam *Towboat River* 243 **Ohio R**, It was a red-dog road, kinda rough to walk on, you know. **1965–70** *DARE* (Qu. N27a, . . *Different kinds of unpaved roads*) Infs **PA**70, 134, 197, 199, 209, **WV**16, Red-dog road; **OH**47, Red-dog road—the ash from coal slag; **OH**78, Red-dog road— the slag from the coal mines was put on the road; **PA**191, Red-dog road—refuse from the mines used as materials; (Qu. N23, *Other kinds of paved roads*) Inf **PA**70, Red-dog road. **1976** Lynn–Vecsey *Loretta Lynn* 3 **eKY**, The road was paved up to the mines, then it was topped with just coal slag—"red dog," we called it. **1979** *DARE* File **nWV, wPA**, You'd drive up the hill on the Pinchot, then turn off on the red dog. **1980** McDavid Coll. **nWV** (as of 1940), ['rɛd ˌdɒˆ·g]—the burnt "fallings" from a coal mine: soapstone, slate, etc. It was spread to form the surface of rural roads. **1980** *NADS Letters* **PA**, Coal mining generates . . debris—dirt, rocks, etc. which may contain some coal but in insufficient quantities to justify the process required for separation. Large piles of this scrap grew and in many cases ignited by spontaneous combustion and smoldered for long periods. The final product . . was a material, red in color and the consistency of something between stones and cinders. The area name for it was "red dog." The physical properties and the low price (free?) made it an excellent choice for improving the surface of a dirt road, hence the term "red dog road." *Ibid* **swPA**, I grew up in Pittsburgh and have always identified a common (in Pittsburgh) substance as 'red dog'. It was stone, a red-orange color veined with white and it had a cleaving pattern like shale. It almost always appeared in quantity—as drainage stone, road surface, etc.

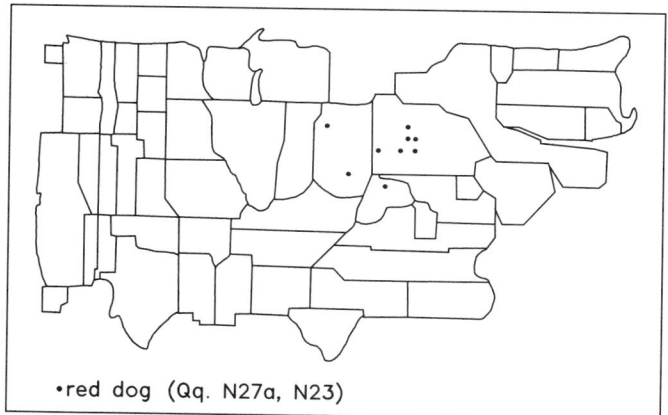

•red dog (Qq. N27a, N23)

red dogwood *n*
A **dogwood 1:** usu *Cornus seriacea*, but also *C. amomum*.
1856 *Harper's New Mth. Mag.* 12.654, I gently caressed . . that portion of my countenance where whiskers were rapidly sprouting, though as yet undiscernible upon the surface, as smooth as a leaf of the red dogwood. **1940** Clute *Amer. Plant Names* 98, C[ornus] stolonifera [=C. seriacea]. . . Red dogwood. **1942** Tehon *Fieldbook IL Shrubs* 217, *Cornus stolonifera* . . Red-Dogwood. . . Its smooth branches are purplish to bright red. **1966–69** *DARE* (Qu. T16, . . *Kinds of trees . . 'special'*) Infs **MI**36, **MO**15, **PA**111, Red dogwood tree. **1973** Stephens *Woody Plants* 414, *Cornus amomum*. . . Red dogwood. . . Our plants are most quickly recognized in the winter when the clustered growth habit and the

red limbs can be seen. *Ibid* 422, *Cornus stolonifera.* . . Red dogwood, red osier. . . Bark usually red, occasionally greenish. **1986** Pederson *LAGS Concordance,* 1 inf, **ceTN,** Red dogwood.

redd out See **redd 3a, c**

red drum n **chiefly Atl**

A **drum 1** (here: *Sciaenops ocellatus*) of the Atlantic and Gulf coasts. Also called **bar bass, bull redfish, channel bass, croaker** n[1] **1a(1), old drum, puppy ~, rat red, red bass, redfish a, redhorse 2, reef bass, saltwater ~, school ~, sea ~ 1b, spot, spotted bass, spottail, spud**

1709 (1967) Lawson *New Voyage* 159 **NC, SC,** The Red Drum is a large Fish much bigger than the Bluefish. The Body of this is good firm Meat, but the Head is beyond all the Fish I ever met withal for an excellent Dish. . . People go down and catch as many Barrels full as they please, . . especially every young Flood, when they bite. **1772** in 1924 Phillips *Notes B. Romans* 123 **FL,** The sea . . Abounds here in fish of all kinds, that are Usually found in those Latitudes, Principally . . Spanish Mackerel, Grunts[s], Black and Red Drum [etc]. **1875** Scott *Fishing Amer. Waters* 458, Both the red and black drums afford the angler great sport; but for the table the red drum is infinitely the superior of the two fishes, which are the most numerous in the estuaries and bayous of Florida; also very plenty along the coast of Virginia during the month of May. *Ibid* 459, The red drum is red on back, fins, head, tail. **1905** NJ State Museum *Annual Rept. for 1904* 333, Red Drum. . . A very common fish on our southern coast, especially about Cape May and in Delaware Bay. As a food-fish it is important, reaching a length of 5 feet and a weight of 75 pounds. **1965–70** DARE (Qu. P2, . . *Kinds of saltwater fish caught around here . . good to eat*) Inf **MD**36, Red drum—long, red, black spot on tail; **NC**12, Red drum or channel bass; **NC**80, **SC**63, Red drum. **1966–67** DARE Tape **NC**27, Fall here, that's the main fishing, is the channel bass. We call 'em red drum, *Field and Stream* calls 'em channel bass. I turned one loose last year, weighed fifty pounds; **TX**18, In the fall I like to wade these shallow back bays and catch big redfish. Some people call 'em red drum or drum. . . Up on the east coast, Virginia, up in there, they call 'em channel bass, but we call 'em redfish. **1984** DARE File **Chesapeake Bay** [Watermen's vocab], Drum (red and black). **1994** [see **redfish a**].

redduh n See **rather** adv

redd up See **redd 3**

reddy See **ready** v

reddy bird See **redbird b**

reddy gravy See **red-eye gravy**

reddying comb See **redding comb**

rede n [Scots dial; see *EDD rede* sb.[2]]

1930 Shoemaker *1300 Words* 51 **cPA Mts** (as of c1900), Rede—The ghost or "double" of a living person.

redear n

1 See **red-eared sunfish 1.**
2 See **red-eared turtle.**

red-eared pond slider See **red-eared turtle**

red-eared sunfish Also *redear sunfish*

1 also *redear:* A freshwater **sunfish** (here: *Lepomis microlophus*). Also called **chinquapin 6, redgill, shell-cracker, stumpknocker, yellow bream**

1902 Jordan-Evermann *Amer. Fishes* 354, *Red-eared Sunfish— Eupomotis heros* [=*Lepomis microlophus*]. . . Found from northern Indiana to Florida and the Rio Grande. **1937** TN Acad. Sci. *Jrl.* 12.45, [Caption:] The Red-Eared Sunfish. Only the males have the red tip on the opercular flap. **1957** Trautman *Fishes* 516, Redear Sunfish. . . Males with a conspicuous red spot on the posterior border of [opercular] flap; in females this spot is orange. *Ibid* 518, At Buckeye Lake the Redear seemed to require less vegetation than did the Pumpkinseed, and as much as, or more, than did the Bluegill. **1966–70** DARE (Qu. P1, . . *Kinds of freshwater fish . . caught around here . . good to eat*) Inf **IL**135, Redear; **OK**25, Redear—a perch. **1968** DARE FW Addit **LA**15, [The Inf] identified the *chinquapin bream* or *chinquapin* as being the same fish as the one called *shellcracker* in Florida. This fish is called

red-eared sunfish (occasionally) or *red-gill* in central Arkansas. **1972** Sparano *Outdoors Encycl.* 361, *Redear Sunfish.* . . A large and very popular sunfish in the South, the redear has a small mouth. **1986** Pederson *LAGS Concordance* (Common freshwater fish) 1 inf, **ceAL,** Redear sunfish—[term] elsewhere used for shellcracker. **1991** Amer. Fisheries Soc. *Common Names Fishes* 47, *Lepomis microlophus* . . redear sunfish.

2 A **pumpkinseed 1** (here: *Lepomis gibbosus*).

1933 LA Dept. of Conserv. *Fishes* 350, *The Pumpkinseed or Red-Eared Sunfish.* . . This pretty fish is to be found from the Great Lakes to the Gulf Coast. **1949** Caine *N. Amer. Sport Fish* 43, Pumpkinseed. . . [Also called] Red-ear Sunfish. . .

red-eared turtle n Also *redear, red-eared pond slider, ~ terrapin* [See quot 1979]

A **red-bellied turtle** (here: *Trachemys scripta elegans*).

1915 *Copeia* 19.15, I may add that a red-eared terrapin (*Pseudemys elegans* [=*Trachemys scripta e.*]) was captured in Oldmans Creek, N.J. . . It is doubtless an introduction or escaped individual, as the species is a native of the Gulf States. **1952** Carr *Turtles* 251, The red-eared turtle can usually be recognized . . by its low, nearly or quite unkeeled and smooth shell. *Ibid* 254, Young red-eared turtles are the universal pet-shop turtle. **1958** Conant *Reptiles & Amphibians* 58, Baby Red-ears, commonest of all pet turtles, are sold in enormous numbers. **1972** Ernst-Barbour *Turtles* 148, *C[hrysemys] s[cripta] elegans* . . , the red-eared turtle, occupies the Mississippi valley from Illinois to the Gulf. **1979** Behler-King *Audubon Field Guide Reptiles* 452, *Pond Slider.* . . Red-eared (*C[hrysemys] s[cripta] elegans*), with wide red stripe behind eye, dark smudge on each plastron scute.

redear sunfish See **red-eared sunfish**

red elephant n Also *little red elephant*

An **elephant's head** (here: *Pedicularis groenlandica*).

1906 Rydberg *Flora CO* 318, Little Red Elephant. . . *Pedicularis groenlandica.* . . In swamps and wet meadows. **1923** *Amer. Botanist* 29.65, From the shape of the flowers, also, *Pedicularis Groenlandica* is known as "red elephant." **1937** U.S. Forest Serv. *Range Plant Hdbk.* W143, Little (or little red) elephant. . . Most of the common names applied to this plant allude to the resemblance of the reddish or purplish flowers to the head of an elephant. **1957** Roberts-Nelson *Wildflowers CO* 44, One of the ways to interest children in flowers is a hunt for the little red elephant. The bold forehead, flapping ears and upturned trunk never fail to please them. **1979** Spellenberg *Audubon Guide N. Amer. Wildflowers W. Region* 766, Little Red Elephants. . . Dense racemes of flowers that are perfect little . . elephant heads. . . Throughout the western mountains.

red elm n

1 A **slippery elm** (here: *Ulmus rubra*) native to much of the eastern two-thirds of the US. [See quot 1973]

1789 in 1798 *Amer. Museum* 7.6/1 [sic *DA*—quot not found], In many parts of the state of New-York, grows a tree called by the inhabitants 'red-elm.' **1805** (1904) Clark *Orig. Jrls. Lewis & Clark Exped.* 1.299 **SD,** There is some timber . . which consists of Cottonwood red Elm [etc]. **1832** MA Hist. Soc. *Coll.* 2d ser 9.157 **cwVT,** [Ulmus] fulva [= *Ulmus rubra*], Red elm. **1848** in 1870 Drake *Pioneer Life* 73 **KY,** Of the whole forest the red or slippery elm was the best [for livestock fodder]. . . It was then that I first observed that the buds of these and other trees grow and swell during the winter. **1891** Jesup *Plants Hanover NH* 37, U[lmus] fulva. . . Red Elm. Slippery Elm. **1950** Grimm *Trees PA* 195, The Slippery Elm is also known as the Red, Gray, or Moose Elm. . . The mucilaginous inner bark is sometimes chewed—a favorite of country urchins. **1965–70** DARE (Qu. T11, . . *Kinds of elm trees*) 82 Infs, **chiefly Missip–Ohio Valleys, NEast,** Red elm [DARE Ed: Some of these Infs may refer instead to **2** below.]; **AR**42, **IN**83, **MI**116, **MA**58, **OH**4, Red elm—same as slippery elm; **VT**10, Red elm—same tree as swamp elm and slippery elm. **1970** DARE Tape **MI**125, One was just a common gray elm, and the other one was a red elm. **1973** Wharton-Barbour *Trees KY* 519, *Ulmus rubra.* . . The tree is occasionally called red elm because of the reddish heartwood. **1986** Pederson *LAGS Concordance* (Names of local trees) 2 infs, **cwAR, cTN,** Red elm (tree). [DARE Ed: These infs may refer instead to **2** below.]

2 Any of var other elms native chiefly to the South and South Midland areas, as **winged elm, a white elm** (here: *Ulmus americana*), **cedar elm,** or **September elm;** see quots.

1897 Sudworth *Arborescent Flora* 180, *Ulmus crassifolia.* . . Red Elm (Tex.) *Ibid* 182, *Ulmus alata.* . . Red Elm (Fla., Ark.) **1897** *Jrl. Amer.*

Folkl. 10.143 **swMO**, *Ulmus Americanus* [sic], . . red elm, white elm. **1908** Rogers *Tree Book* 236, One [elm], found in Georgia and Tennessee, . . was named from its red-brown wood, the *Red Elm.* **1938** Van Dersal *Native Woody Plants* 334, Elm, Red *(Ulmus alata, Ulmus fulva, Ulmus serotina).* **1960** Vines *Trees SW* 210, *Cedar Elm.* . . Vernacular names are . . Red Elm [etc.]. . . The wood is considered inferior to other elms because of its brittle and knotty character. *Ibid* 211, *Winged Elm.* . . Vernacular names are . . Red Elm [etc.]. *Ibid* 212, *Ulmus serotina.* . . Also known as the Red Elm. It resembles the American Elm somewhat in shape of the tree, but is not as large. **1980** Little *Audubon Guide N. Amer. Trees E. Region* 424, "Red Elm"—*Ulmus serotina.*

redeye n

1 Any of several fishes of the family Centrarchidae, as: see below. [*OED2* c1672 → for *Leuciscus erythrophthalmus*]

a also *redeyes:* A **rock bass 1** (here: *Ambloplites rupestris*).

1820 *Western Rev.* 2.54, *Ohio Red-eye, Aplocentrus calliops.* . . lives in the lower parts of the Ohio, in Green river, &c. Vulgar names Red-eyes, Bride pearch, Batchelor's pearch, Green bass, &c. [*DARE* Ed: This scientific name appar described a conflation of var fishes; see quot 1877 below.] **1857** *Spirit of Times* 21 Mar 38 **KY**, The *craw-fish* . . is found to be sometimes an excellent bait . . for the angler who is pursuing . . the rock-bass, or the "*red-eye*," to use the nomenclature of Kentucky. **1877** U.S. Natl. Museum *Bulletin* 9.22, *Aplocentrus calliops.* . . A myth, described from a drawing by Mr. Audubon. . . The name "Red-Eye" in the region which this fish is supposed to inhabit is chiefly applied to the Rock-Bass *(Ambloplites rupestris).* **1897** *Outing* 30.438 **N Cent**, The rock-bass. . . also termed . . "red-eye"—frequently turned up as black as one's boots. **1939** Natl. Geogr. Soc. *Fishes* 115, The rock bass, red eye, or goggle eye, is one of our commonest game fishes in streams and lakes throughout the Mississippi Valley . . [and] Great Lakes [regions]. **1951** Harlan–Speaker *IA Fish* 137, Redeye. . . The mouth is large and the eye red like the warmouth, but the warmouth has but 3 spines in the anal fin. **1965–70** *DARE* (Qu. P1, . . *Kinds of freshwater fish . . caught around here . . good to eat)* Infs **AL**38, **IL**54, **IN**58, **KY**28, **TN**1, 7, Redeye(s); **IL**54, Redeye—that's a sunfish; **VA**8, Rock bass = redeye; (Qu. P7, *Small fish used as bait for bigger fish)* Infs **GA**7, 34, **NC**49, Redeye. [*DARE* Ed: Some of these Infs may refer instead to other senses below.] **1986** Pederson *LAGS Concordance (Common freshwater fish)* 8 infs, **GA, TN**, 1 inf, **cnFL**, Redeye(s); 1 inf, **ceGA**, Redeye—fish used for bait; 1 inf, **csGA**, Redeye—type of sun perch; 1 inf, **neTN**, Redeye—like a bass but shorter; 1 inf, **ceTN**, Redeyes—ten-inch long flat fish. [*DARE* Ed: Some of these infs may refer instead to other senses below.]

b A **warmouth** (here: *Chaenobryttus gulosus*).

1877 NY Acad. Sci. *Annals Lyceum Nat. Hist.* 10.361 **GA**, Taken in the South Fork of the Ocmulgee River, where the species [=*Chaenobryttus gulosus*] is known as "Bream" and "Red Eye." **1884** Goode *Fisheries U.S.* 1.405, *Chænobryttus gulosus.* . . This species is known throughout the South by the name of "Warmouth." The names . . "Goggle-eye," and "Red-eye" it shares with others of its relatives. **1933** LA Dept. of Conserv. *Fishes* 342, The Warmouth Bass has come to bear many confusing popular names. These are . . Redeye [etc.]. **1968** *DARE* (Qu. P3, *Freshwater fish that are not good to eat)* Inf **VA**1, Redeyes. **1976** Tryckare et al. *Lore of Sportfishing* 102, *Warmouth Bass.* . . Other common names . . redeye [etc.]. . . Has a large mouth, a protruding jaw, and a red eye. . . Not a game fish of the first rank, but edible.

c = **green sunfish 1.**

1882 U.S. Natl. Museum *Bulletin* 16.473, *L[epomis] cyanellus.* . . Red-eye; Blue-spotted Sun-fish. . . Color variable, the prevailing shade green. **1903** NY State Museum & Sci. Serv. *Bulletin* 477, The blue-spotted sunfish, also known as the green sunfish and redeye, occurs from the Great Lakes region, throughout the Ohio and Mississippi valleys south to Mexico. **1909** [see **1d** below]. **1933** LA Dept. of Conserv. *Fishes* 347, The Green Sunfish, like so many of its relatives, rejoice [sic] in a wide variety of popular names, [as] . . Little Redeye, . . Redeye. **1983** Becker *Fishes WI* 822, *Lepomis cyanellus.* . . Little redeye.

d Any of var other fish of the genus *Lepomis,* such as a **longear sunfish** (here: *Lepomis megalotis*).

1909 Holder–Jordan *Fish Stories* 240, Some of these [=sunfish] are called blue-gills, dollardee, red-eye, rock-bass, grass-bass. **1949** Caine *N. Amer. Sport Fish* 43, This plethora of nicknames covers the pumpkinseed and its six closely related cousins listed in the text that follows [=*Lepomis cyanellus, L. megalotis, L. auritus, L. microlophus, L. punctatus, Chaenobryttus gulosus*]. . . Redeye [etc.].

e = **black bass 1.** Cf **red-eyed bass 1**

1935 Caine *Game Fish* 3, *Large-mouthed Black Bass.* . . Redeye. *Ibid*

7, *Small-mouthed Black Bass.* . . Redeye. *Ibid* 10, *Spotted Small-mouthed Black Bass* [=*Micropterus punctulatus*]. . . Redeye. **1946** LaMonte *N. Amer. Game Fishes* 134, *Micropterus dolomieui.* . . *Names* . . Redeye. . . Not present in the Gulf States. **1972** Sparano *Outdoors Encycl.* 360, *Micropterus coosae.* . . An inhabitant of the southeastern states. . . A large portion of the redeye's diet is insects, but it also feeds on worms, crickets, and various baitfish. **1976** Tryckare et al. *Lore of Sportfishing* 101, *Micropterus coosae.* . . Fins and eyes are red. . . Occasionally reaches 4½ lb (2 kg), but the majority of redeyes are smaller. **1983** Becker *Fishes WI* 801, *Smallmouth Bass.* . . Other common names . . redeye.

2 Any of var birds, as:

a = **red-eyed vireo.**

a1862 (1864) Thoreau *ME Woods* 172, The birds sang quite as in our woods,—the red-eye, red-start, veery, wood-pewee, etc. but we saw no blue birds in all our journey. **1892** Torrey *Foot-Path Way* 12 **NH**, The song of the Philadelphia vireo comes nearest to the red-eye's. **1911** Howell *Birds AR* 73, It [=*Vireo flavifrons*] lives in upland timber tracts in company with the red-eye. **1929** Forbush *Birds MA* 3.181, Throughout the long hot summer days. . . he begins with the Robin at early dawn, but in time the Robin tires. Not so the Red-eye. **1954** Sprunt *FL Bird Life* 372, The Red-eye ranges rather high and is a tree dweller in summer.

b = **semipalmated plover.**

1917 (1923) *Birds Amer.* 1.261, *Semipalmated Plover.* . . *Other Names* . . Red-eye. . . Eye-ring bright orange; iris, hazel. **1946** Hausman *Eastern Birds* 254, *Semipalmated Plover.* . . Redeye.

c = **black-crowned night heron.**

1913 *Auk* 30.503 **Okefenokee GA**, *Black-crowned Night Heron;* 'Redeye.' . . The local name is certainly appropriate. **1955** *Oriole* 20.1.2 **GA**, *Black-crowned Night Heron.* . . Red-eye.

3 = **copperhead snake 1.**

a1870 Chipman *Notes on Bartlett (DAE),* Red-eye, . . a copperhead. **1968** *DARE* (Qu. P25, . . *Kinds of snakes)* Inf **CT**17, Copperheads = "redeyes."

4 See quot. Cf **cranberry bean, pinkeye, red bean**

1950 *WELS (Flat beans that are striped or speckled with red)* 1 Inf, **WI**, Redeyes.

5 also *red-eye juice,* ~ *whiskey:* Low-quality liquor; sometimes spec whiskey adulterated to give it a reddish color. [Generally held to refer to its effect on the eyes of those who drink it, but perh orig simply in ref to its color; cf **red liquor, white-eye**] **formerly chiefly Sth, S Midl; now more widespread**

1819 in 1860 Claiborne *Life Quitman* 1.42 **KY**, Whiting and I had to treat to 'red-eye' or 'rot-gut,' as whisky is here called. **1851** Burke *Polly Peablossom* 50 **MO**, I've hearn o' mean folks in my time, . . but ever sense that feller, Bonnel, sold me a pint of red-eye whiskey—an' half ov it backer juice—for a coon-skin, an' then guv me a brass picayune fur change, I've stopped talkin'. **1856** Brewerton *War in KS* 75 **MO**, Nigger Jim, who has a bottle of Red-eye whisky, "warranted to kill forty rods round the corner," in his pocket, thaws out under its influence and becomes gradually enthusiastic. **1860** Hundley *Social Relations S. States* 227, Log-wood, juniper berries, dog-leg tobacco . . are all said to be used; and, owing to their different effects, have originated the expressive names of "bust-head," "rifle-whisky," "tangle-foot," "red-eye." **1899** (1912) Green *VA Folk-Speech* 349, Redeye. . . A strong, fiery whiskey; so called from its effect on the eyes of drinkers. **1906** *DN* 3.153 **cwAR**, *Red-eye.* . . Whiskey. Logan Co. **1907** *DN* 3.249 **eME**, *Red eye.* . . Whiskey. **1909** *DN* 3.363 **eAL, wGA**, *Red-eye.* . . Whisky. **1912** *DN* 3.587 **wIN**, *Red-eye.* . . Whisky. **1919** *DN* 5.42 [Hobo cant], *Red eye.* Whiskey. **1927** *DN* 5.460 [Underworld jargon], *Red eye.* . . Cheap whisky. **1931** *AmSp* 7.50 **Sth, SW** [Lumberjack lingo], There are plenty of native liquors "on tap" for the refreshment of the men. The "drinks" are "pine-top," "white mule," "mountain dew," "honey dip," and "red eye." **1949** *PADS* 11.10 **wTX** (as of 1911–29), *Red-eye whiskey, red-eye:* . . Bad whiskey. **1952** Brown *NC Folk.* 1.583, *Red-eye.* . . Very strong inferior whisky. **1954** *Julian Apple Day* [4] **csCA**, A group of city slickers from San Diego arrived in Julian the night before election day with either a wagonload of red-eye, or money enough to freely purchase the local snake-remedy. **c1960** *Wilson Coll.* **csKY**, *Red-eye.* . . Bad whiskey. **1960** Criswell *Resp. to PADS* 20 **Ozarks**, Red-eye—A very old term for whiskey, probably rare now. **1965–70** *DARE* (Qu. DD21b, . . *Bad liquor)* 23 Infs, **scattered**, Redeye; **FL**28, Redeye—from reading, not heard here; **IL**135, Old redeye; (Qu. DD21a, *General* *words . . for any kind of liquor)* Infs **CA**105, **CO**9, **IN**45, **NM**11, Redeye; **NM**3, Red-eye juice; (Qu. DD21c, . . *Whiskey, especially illegally made)* Infs **IA**8, **ME**9, **NY**92, **SC**64, Redeye. **1981** Mebane *Mary* 37 **cnNC,** Uncle Josh would bring a bottle of red-eye with him and Daddy would laugh. . . It was a dark, clear red, like red Kool-Aid, only the liquid looked heavier than Kool-Aid. . . Sometimes when Uncle Josh didn't have any red-eye, he'd bring white lightning, but red-eye was the most highly prized.

6 also *redeye and bloodybones, redeyes:* **=boogerman 1, 2.** Cf **plat-eye, rawhead and bloodybones, red man**

[c1938 in 1970 Hyatt *Hoodoo* 1.54 **NC,** Grandfather looked back. He saw a big black man with red eyes. Grandfather said a prayer and the thing jumped in the water, made a terrible noise and disappeared. *Ibid* 295 **TN,** People said that if a man's eyes is red or somepin like that, then he could do diff'rent things to you. *Ibid* **VA,** When you see these old people and their eyes is red, they're conjures.] **1966** *DARE* (Qu. CC17, *Imaginary animals or monsters)* Inf **SC**26, Redeye—a person may have it; if he gets behind you you'll run till you kill yourself; (Qu. EE41, *A hobgoblin that is used to threaten children and make them behave)* Inf **GA**1, Redeye and bloodybones. **1968** *DARE* File **cSC,** Redeye—the devil, the Bad Man, an avenging demon. Reported by an educated woman of 50 as having been used by her grandmother. **1986** Pederson *LAGS Concordance (Devil, boogerman)* 1 inf, **swAL,** Red eyes. [**1998** *DARE* File **cnOH** (as of 1929), *Redeye and bloody bones,* a "game" intended to frighten others by suddenly shouting the words and gesturing as if with horror.]

7 See quot.

1994 Smitherman *Black Talk* 192, Red eye—A long, hard stare, usually directed at a person.

8 A clear marble with a red center. Cf **cat's-eye 1**

c1970 Wiersma *Marbles Terms* **seMI,** Red-eye—marble with a red center. . . Got any red-eyes? *Ibid* **NJ** (as of 1955), Red eye—a red cat's eye marble.

9 See **red-eye gravy.**

redeye and bloodybones See **redeye 6**

redeye bass See **red-eyed bass**

redeye bream See **red-eyed bream**

red-eyed adj

1 Crazy, furious.

1935 Davis *Honey* 38 **OR,** Her pa was red-eyed on Bible-bangin'. I remember well. He heerd heavenly voices, or claimed to. **1941** Writers' Program *Guide WY* 464, Red-eyed—Mad. **1944** Adams *Western Words* 125, Red-eyed—Angry.

2 See quot.

1953 Randolph–Wilson *Down in Holler* 277 **Ozarks,** Red-eyed. . . Obviously guilty, red handed. "The sheriff ketched Bill red-eyed this time, an' they got him in the jail-house right now."

red-eyed bass n Also *redeye bass* Cf **redeye 1**

1 A **black bass 1,** esp *Micropterus coosae.* For other names of the latter see **redeye 1e**

1951 Harlan–Speaker *IA Fish* 108, *Northern Smallmouth Bass. . . Other Names . .* redeyed bass. . . The smallmouth is frequently confused with the largemouth as they are quite similar in appearance. **1957** Blair et al. *Vertebrates U.S.* 168, *Micropterus coosae.* . . Redeye bass. . . In southeastern streams, from the Alabama to the Savannah Rivers in Alabama and Georgia. **1969** *DARE* (Qu. P1, . . *Kinds of freshwater fish . . caught around here . . good to eat)* Inf **GA**76, Redeye bass. **1976** Tryckare et al. *Lore of Sportfishing* 101, *Micropterus punctatulus . .* redeye bass. *Ibid, Redeye Bass . . Micropterus coosae. . .* A member of the black bass family that is often confused with the smallmouth bass, *M. dolomieui,* and the spotted bass, *M. punctatum. . .* The most distinctive identification is the red color of the eyes and fins. . . Young redeye bass have a distinctive pattern of dark-colored vertical bars. **1991** Amer. Fisheries Soc. *Common Names Fishes* 47, *Micropterus coosae . .* F[reshwater] . . redeye bass.

2 A **rock bass 1** (here: *Ambloplites rupestris*).

1951 Harlan–Speaker *IA Fish* 121, *Northern Rock Bass. . . Other Names—*Redeye, redeye bass. . . Common in many of the smallmouth bass streams of northeast Iowa and in a few lakes in northern Iowa. **1976** Tryckare et al. *Lore of Sportfishing* 102, *Rock Bass. . .* Other com-

mon names . . redeye bass [etc]. **1991** Amer. Fisheries Soc. *Common Names Fishes* 116, Bass, redeye . . see also rock bass.

red-eyed bream n Also *redeye bream* Cf **bream B3, redeye 1a, b**

Usu a **rock bass 1** (here: *Ambloplites rupestris*), but also a **warmouth** (here: *Chaenobryttus gulosus*).

1882 U.S. Natl. Museum *Bulletin* 16.468, *C[haenobryttus] gulosus. . . *War-mouth; Red-eyed Bream. . . Virginia to Texas; abundant only southward. **1935** Caine *Game Fish* 24, Rock Bass. . . Red-eye Bream. **1976** Tryckare et al. *Lore of Sportfishing* 102, Rock Bass. . . Other common names . . red-eyed bream [etc].

red-eyed devil n Cf **devil-diver 1**
=red-necked grebe.

1917 *Wilson Bulletin* 29.2.74 **WA,** *Columbus holboelli* [=*Podiceps grisegena*]. . . Red-eyed devil, . . Willapa Harbor, Wash.

red-eyed gravy See **red-eye gravy**

red-eyed sunfish n

1 also *redeye sunfish:* A **rock bass 1** (here: *Ambloplites rupestris*).

1935 Caine *Game Fish* 24, Rock Bass. . . Red-eye Sunfish. **1938** Schrenkeisen *Field Book Fishes* 248, *Lepomis megalotis. . .* Red-eyed Sunfish. *Ibid* 253, *Ambloplites rupestris. . .* Red-eyed Sunfish. **1976** Tryckare et al. *Lore of Sportfishing* 102, Rock Bass. . . Other common names . . redeye sunfish [etc].

2 A **longear sunfish** (here: *Lepomis megalotis*).

1933 LA Dept. of Conserv. *Fishes* 349, The Long-ear has now many common names [such as] . . Red-eyed Sunfish. **1938** [see **1** above]. **1946** LaMonte *N. Amer. Game Fishes* 139, *Lepomis megalotis. . .* Red-eyed Sunfish.

red-eyed towhee n Cf **white-eyed towhee**
=rufous-sided towhee.

1898 (1900) Davie *Nests N. Amer. Birds* 395, The Red-eyed Towhee. . . is a spirited bird and spends a great deal of its time on the ground. **1939** *Natl. Geogr. Mag.* 353, The one species found east of the Mississippi River is the well-known red-eyed towhee. **1984** Wilder *You All Spoken Here* 59, Joree: A red-eyed towhee.

red-eyed vireo n

Std: a **vireo** (here: *Vireo erythrophthalmus*). Also called **grasset 3, greenlet, hanging bird 2, hangnest bird, little hangbird, ~ hangnest, magnolia bird, preacher 1, redeye 2a**

red-eye gravy n Also *red-eye, red-eyed gravy, red-eye ham gravy* Pronc-sp *reddy gravy* chiefly **Sth, S Midl** See Map Cf **black-eye gravy, brindle ~, brown-eye ~, frog-eye ~, hog-eye ~, red ~**

A reddish, usu unthickened, gravy made from the drippings of ham or other cured meat.

1945 *SW Rev.* 30.143 **TN,** Pinky brown slices of cured ham that almost floated in red-eye gravy. **1957** *Hall Coll.* **wNC,** Red-eye gravy, when you fry ham, let it burn on the skillet a little; use a little water or coffee. c1960 *Wilson Coll.* **csKY,** Red-eye gravy: . . Ham gravy with red globules of fat on top. **1962** *Natl. Geogr. Mag.* July 84 **eTN,** "Red-eye gravy" was ham or sausage juice and water. **1965–70** *DARE* (Qu. H37, . . *Words . . for gravy)* 52 Infs, **chiefly Sth, S Midl,** Red-eye gravy; 11 Infs, **chiefly Sth, S Midl,** Red-eye; **GA**88, **TN**57, Red-eyed gravy; **KY**5, Reddy gravy—ham; red-eyed gravy—ham, old-fashioned; **IL**91, Red-eye ham gravy. **1971** *Today Show Letters* **Sth,** Red-eyed gravy—Made by adding strong coffee to ham grease. **1973** *DARE* File **Ozarks** (as of c1910), Redeye. . . Gravy made of ham drippings and milk. **1975** McDonough *Garden Sass* 73 **AR,** All Arkansans, both yesterday and today, have used the meat from the hogs to make two of their favorite kinds of gravy. With the ham goes "redeye gravy" . . delicious as a sop for hot biscuits or cornbread. **1977** Anderson *Grass Roots Cookbook* 103 **cnNC,** The Red-Eye Gravy isn't ladled over the ham but over hot biscuits, split in half, or over boiled rice or hominy grits. . . Put the ham slices on a warm platter, pour the drippings into a small heatproof bowl and add the coffee to the skillet. Bring quickly to a simmer, scraping up from the bottom all browned bits (these are the "red eyes"). **1986**

Pederson *LAGS Concordance* **Gulf Region,** 24 infs, Red-eye gravy [10 infs specified that it is made from ham, 2 that it is thinned with coffee].

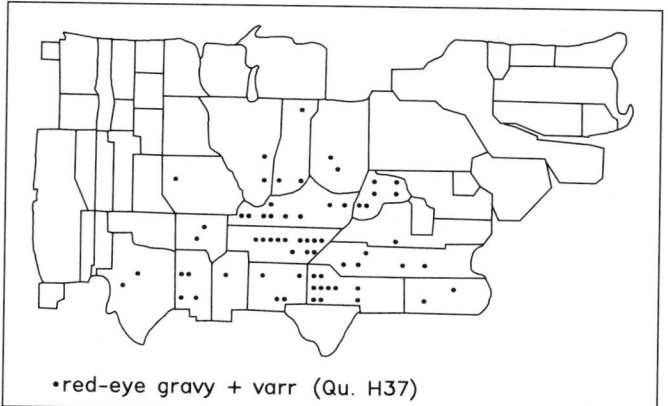

•red-eye gravy + varr (Qu. H37)

red-eye juice See **redeye 5**

redeye perch n Cf **perch** n[1] **2, redeye 1a**
A **rock bass 1** (here: *Ambloplites rupestris*).

1935 Caine *Game Fish* 24, *Rock Bass.* . . Red-eye Perch. **1976** Tryckare et al. *Lore of Sportfishing* 102, *Rock Bass.* . . Other common names . . redeye perch [etc].

redeyes See **redeye 1a, 6**

redeye sunfish See **red-eyed sunfish 1**

red-eye whiskey See **redeye 5**

red fallfish n Cf **fallfish**
A **shiner 1** (here: *Notropis rubricroceus*).

1882 U.S. Natl. Museum *Bulletin* 16.189, *M[innilus] rubricroceus.* . . *Red Fall-fish.* . . In high coloration the whole body is more or less red. **1887** (1888) Jordan *Sci. Sketches* 122, The little red "fallfish," found only in the mountain tributaries of the Savannah and the Tennessee. **1935** Pratt *Manual Vertebrate Animals* 77, Red fallfish. . . Headwaters of the Tennessee and Savannah Rivers.

red feather n
=Indian paintbrush 1.

1915 (1926) Armstrong–Thornber *Western Wild Flowers* 470, These gaudy plants [=*Castilleja* spp] are well named Indian Paint Brush, for the flower-cluster and leaf-tips look as if they had been dipped in color. Red Feather is also good but Painted Cup is rather poor, as there is nothing cup-like about the flower.

red-feathered hawk See **red-shafted hawk**

red fender n
A **red-bellied turtle** (here: *Pseudemys rubriventris*).

1884 Goode *Fisheries U.S.* 1.154, The animal [=*Pseudemys rubriventris*] is also known under the names "Potter," "Red-fender," and "Slider."

redfin n
1 also *redfin dace, red-fin(ned) minnow, redfin shiner:* Any of several cyprinids, esp either of two **shiners 1:** *Notropis cornutus* or *Lythrurus umbratilis.* **chiefly NEast, Missip Valley**

1817 *Amer. Monthly Mag. & Crit. Rev.* 1.289 **NY,** The Red-fin, or *C[yprinus] cornutus,* having elegant scarlet fins and knobs, or long protuberances over the head. **1820** Rafinesque *Ohio R. Fishes* 50, *Semotilus diplemia* [=*S. atromaculatus*]. . . Length from three to four inches, often called Minny or Red-fin. Observed in the Kentucky river near Estill. **1826** in 1910 Buffalo Hist. Soc. *Pub.* 290 **NY,** New fish caught in the canal within the few days past, are the chub, the red fin, and some small Otsego bass. **1882** U.S. Natl. Museum *Bulletin* 16.186, *M[innilus] cornutus.* . . *Red-fin.* . . Entire region east of the Rocky Mountains excepting the South Atlantic States and Texas. *Ibid* 197, *M. diplæmius* [=*Lythrurus umbratilis*]. . . *Red-fin.* . . Ohio and Upper Mississippi Valley and lake region. *Ibid* 198, *M. ardens* [=*Lythrurus a.*] . . *Southern Red-fin.* . . Males in spring tuberculate, the entire body and fins

brilliant red; crimson in spring, becoming more scarlet later. . . Cumberland, Upper Tennessee, and Roanoke Rivers. **1886** Mather *Memoranda* 24 **NY,** In the outlet of Canachagala are the red-fin shiners. *Ibid* 28, *Luxilus cornutus* [=*Notropis c.*] . . Red fin. Males in spring, or breeding, dress. . . It was only by opening many specimens that I convinced a dozen or more of the [Adirondack] guides that they were male and female, showing them that while eggs were always present in their "shiners," the "red-fins" were always filled with milt. **1891** Jesup *Plants Hanover NH* 59, N[otropis] megalops [=*N. cornutus*]. . . Red-Fin. R[hinichthys] atronasus [=*R. atratulus*]. . . "Red-fin." **1908** Forbes–Richardson *Fishes of IL* 143, *Notropis lutrensis.* . . *Redfin.* . . This little fish is especially distinguished . . by the brilliancy of its color. **1939** *LANE* Map 234 *(Minnow),* Names of common bait fish, recorded incidentally: . . *Redfin* [3 infs, **CT, NH**]. **1965–70** *DARE* (Qu. P3, *Freshwater fish that are not good to eat)* Inf **NH**14, Redfin shiners; **NY**23, Redfins—four or five inches; **NY**71, Redfins—something like a chub, have horns on their nose part of the time, sometimes eaten; (Qu. P7, *Small fish used as bait for bigger fish)* Inf **ME**6, Redfins—shiners; **MN**42, Redfins—a walleye bait; **MS**60, Redfins; **MS**89, Redfin minnow; **IA**29, Red-finned minnow—a flat minny 2½" long at biggest. **1983** Becker *Fishes WI* 467, *Rhinichthys atratulus.* . . Redfin dace. *Ibid* 517, *Notropis umbratilis* [=*Lythrurus u.*] . . Redfin. . . In Wisconsin, the redfin shiner occurs in the Mississippi River and Lake Michigan drainage basins. *Ibid* 518, *Notropis cornutus.* . . Redfin shiner. *Ibid* 523, *Notropis chrysocephalus.* . . Redfin shiner. *Ibid* 554, *Notropis lutrensis.* . . Redfin shiner. **1986** Pederson *LAGS Concordance (Small fish used for bait)* 1 inf, **cnMS,** Redfins; 1 inf, **ceLA,** Redfin minnow.

2 also *redfin redhorse, ~ sucker:* A **redhorse 1:** esp *Moxostoma macrolepidotum,* but also *M. breviceps* or *M. carinatum.*

1902 Jordan–Evermann *Amer. Fishes* 63, *Moxostoma aureolum* [=*M. breviceps*]. . . This sucker has received many common names, among which [is] . . redfin sucker. . . *Moxostoma crassilabre* [=*M. macrolepidotum*]. . . Among the vernacular names applied to it are . . redfin, and mullet. **1943** Eddy–Surber *N. Fishes* 117, Redfin . . *Moxostoma aureolum.* . . The tail as well as the lower fins are always red. **1956** Harlan–Speaker *IA Fish* 77, *Moxostoma aureolum.* . . Redfin, redfin sucker. . . The fins, especially the tail fin, are bright orange or sometimes blood red. *Ibid* 78, *Moxostoma carinatum.* . . Redfin redhorse. . . The lower fins are often tipped with red, especially the males in the breeding season. **1983** Becker *Fishes WI* 665, *Moxostoma macrolepidotum.* . . Redfin, redfin sucker. . . Caudal and dorsal fins pale to bright red in life . . ; paired fins salmon to reddish orange; anal fin orange or red with whitish edge. *Ibid* 674, *Moxostoma carinatum.* . . Redfin redhorse. . . Caudal and dorsal fins red in life, lower fins orange to reddish orange.

3 A **yellow perch** (here: *Perca flavescens*).

1890 *Century Dict.* 5020, *Redfin.* . . The common yellow perch of the United States, *Perca flavescens.* Also *yellowfin* [*Century* Ed: Southern U.S.] **1976** Tryckare et al. *Lore of Sportfishing* 100, *Perca flavescens* . . redfin. . . Anal and pelvic fins bright orange; pectoral fins light.

4 See **redfin pickerel.**

redfin croaker See **croaker** n[1] **1a(1)**

redfin dace, red-fin(ned) minnow See **redfin 1**

red-finned pike See **redfin pickerel**

red-finned trout n Also *redfin trout*
Either a **Dolly Varden 1** or a **brook trout.**

1935 *AK Sportsman* Jan 29, The ubiquitous Dolly Varden. . . has . . such confusing names as . . red-finned trout [etc]. **1976** *DARE* File **Isle Royale MI,** Redfin trout are brook trout.

redfin pickerel n Also *redfin, red-fin(ned) pike* **chiefly S Atl**
A **pickerel 1:** esp *Esox americanus americanus* or a **grass pickerel 1** (here: *Esox americanus vermiculatus*), but also the **chain pickerel.** For other names of *E. a. a.* see **branch pike, ditch ~, grass pickerel 1, ~ pike 1b, hammerhandle, jack** n[1] **24a(1), mountain trout 3, mud pike, pike** n[1] **1b, pond pickerel, trout ~**

1927 Weed *Pike* 42 **NC,** *Esox americanus.* . . Red-finned Pike. *Ibid* 45, *Esox niger.* . . Red-finned Pike. **1933** John G. Shedd Aquarium *Guide* 56, *Esox americanus*—Red-fin Pickerel; Mud Pike; Banded Pickerel. **1955** Carr–Goin *Guide Reptiles* 47 **FL,** *Esox americanus* . . Redfin Pickerel. . . Fins usually reddish or pinkish. **1957** Trautman *Fishes* 208, *Central Redfin Pickerel* . . *Esox americanus vermiculatus.* . .

Ohio. . . prime habitat for the Redfin Pickerel. **1966–68** *DARE* (Qu. P1, . . *Kinds of freshwater fish . . caught around here . . good to eat*) Infs **GA**34, **NC**15, Redfin or grass pickerel; **NC**49, Redfin pike; **SC**40, (Redfin) pike; (Qu. P7, *Small fish used as bait for bigger fish*) Inf **SC**40, (Redfin) pike. **1976** Tryckare et al. *Lore of Sportfishing* 78, *Redfin Pickerel—Esox americanus americanus*. . . The redfin has an elongate body, long head, and jaws of the northern pike. *Ibid, Esox americanus vermiculatus*—Other common names: Redfin pickerel. **1986** Pederson *LAGS Concordance (Common freshwater fish)* 1 inf, **ceGA**, Redfin pike.

redfin redhorse See **redfin 2**

redfin shiner See **redfin 1**

redfin sucker See **redfin 2**

redfin trout See **red-finned trout**

red fir n

A western fir, as:

a =**Douglas fir**—used esp (in contrast to **yellow fir**) to distinguish specimens in which the reddish heartwood predominates. Cf **red beech**

1844 Lee–Frost *10 Yrs. OR* 81, The red fir constitutes the greater part of the timber in the country, which is a very inferior quality of timber, being of no more value than our hemlock. **1898** *Jrl. Amer. Folkl.* 11.280 **WA**, *Pseudotsuga Douglasii*, . . red fir, . . Pierce Co., Wash. **1910** Jepson *Silva CA* 115, The sapwood [of *Pseudotsuga menziesii*] is nearly white, the heartwood reddish-brown ("Red Fir") or yellow ("Yellow Fir"). The young rapid growth in the open woods produces "Red Fir," the older slower growth in denser woods is "Yellow Fir." **1937** St. John *Flora SE WA & ID* 15, Douglas Fir, or Red Fir. . . A very common tree, foothills and mountains. **1967–68** *DARE* (Qu. T5, . . *Kinds of evergreens, other than pine*) Infs **OR**13, **WY**1, Red fir; (Qu. T16, . . *Kinds of trees . . 'special'*) Infs **OR**13, Red fir; (Qu. T17, . . *Kinds of pine trees;* not asked in early QRs) Inf **CA**105, Douglas fir or red fir. **1977** Churchill *Don't Call* 45 **nwOR** (as of c1918), A bastard fir was nothing more than a young Douglas fir in the transition period from young mature, or red, fir into old mature, or yellow, fir. **1979** Little *Checklist U.S. Trees* 218, *Pseudotsuga menziesii*. . . Red-fir.

b A fir *(Abies magnifica)* native chiefly to California and southwestern Oregon. Also called **silvertip 2, white fir**

1884 Sargent *Forests of N. Amer.* 214, *Abies magnifica*. . . Red Fir. . . Wood . . light red, the sap-wood somewhat darker. **1897** Sudworth *Arborescent Flora* 58 **CA**, *Abies magnifica*. . . Red Fir. **1916** Sudworth *Spruce & Balsam Fir* 38, "Red fir" [for *Abies magnifica*]. . . refers appropriately to the deep red-brown bark. **1969** *DARE* (Qu. T5, . . *Kinds of evergreens, other than pine*) Inf **CA**130, Douglas fir, white fir, red fir; **CA**155, Red fir. **1980** Little *Audubon Guide N. Amer. Trees W. Region* 254, "Red Fir" . . *Abies magnifica*. . . Named for its characteristic bark, this magnificent conifer forms almost pure forests at high altitudes.

c =**noble fir.**

1884 Sargent *Forests of N. Amer.* 214, *Abies nobilis*. . . Red Fir. . . Wood. . . light brown streaked with red, the sap-wood a little darker. **1908** Sudworth *Forest Trees Pacific* 128, *Abies nobilis*. . . The woodman's and lumberman's name for this tree is . . sometimes "red fir." . . There is . . little about the tree to deserve the name "red fir." **1953** Peattie *Nat. Hist. W. Trees* 198, *Abies procera*. . . Red Fir. . . Bark on old trunks bright red-brown under the thickly appressed scales. **1980** Little *Audubon Guide N. Amer. Trees W. Region* 255, Noble Fir—"Red Fir" "White Fir". . . A handsome tree with large, showy cones.

d A **silver fir 2a** (here: *Abies amabilis*).

1897 Sudworth *Arborescent Flora* 57 **MT**, *Abies amabilis*. . . Red Fir. **1908** Britton *N. Amer. Trees* 81, *Abies amabilis*. . . This magnificent tree . . is also called . . Red fir, and by lumbermen erroneously Larch. . . Its greatest size is attained in the Olympic Mountains of Washington. **1953** Peattie *Nat. Hist. W. Trees* 196, Red, Amabilis, or Lovely Fir. . . *Twigs* . . light orange-brown, becoming dark purple and at last reddish brown. **1979** Little *Checklist U.S. Trees* 33, *Abies amabilis*. . . Red fir.

redfish n

Any of var fishes, as:

a also *red:* =**red drum. Gulf States** See Map

[**1758** LePage du Pratz *Histoire Louisiane* 1.36 **Gulf coast**, Le Poisson rouge est ainsi nommé à cause de son écaille qui est rouge & large comme un écu de six livres sur les gros.] [**1763** LePage du Pratz *Hist. LA* (transl. Anon.) 1.26, The redfish is so called, from its red scales, of

the size of a crown piece.] **1834** *S. Lit. Messenger* 1.121 **TX**, The waters too, furnish their finny . . treasures,—the red fish, buffalo [etc]. **1851** Hooper *Widow Rugby's Husband* 166 **AL**, He added with ineffable disdain, "d—n Redfish." **1884** Henshall *Camping in FL* 28, The red-fish or channel bass *(Sciæna ocellata)* is exceedingly common on the coast of Florida. **1931** *Copeia* 2.49 **TX**, Many fishermen may be seen in pursuit of 'redfish' about the north end of Laguna Madre. They generally stand in several feet of water, using rod and line. **1946** Stilwell *Hunting in TX* 96, To catch redfish in the surf you fish in close. **1965–70** *DARE* (Qu. P2, . . *Kinds of saltwater fish caught around here . . good to eat*) 18 Infs, **Gulf States,** Redfish; **TX**12, Reds; (Qu. P14, . . *Commercial fishing . . what do the fishermen go out after?*) Infs **FL**17, **LA**37, 44, **TX**19, 101, Redfish; (Qu. FF16, . . *Local contests or celebrations*) Inf **LA**37, Redfish rodeo. **1965–67** *DARE* Tape **FL**14, We cook grouper and mullet and redfish and snapper; **FL**22, You get mullet, flounder, trout, croaker, redfish. All kinds of fish; **FL**46, There's plenty good fish to be caught. . . You can get . . snoop, snapper, sheephead, . . red, and . . mullet; **TX**18, Up on the east coast, Virginia, up in there, they call 'em channel bass, but we call 'em redfish. **1975** Evanoff *Catch More Fish* 191, Even the smaller channel bass called "reds" will feed at night. **1986** Pederson *LAGS Concordance* **Gulf Region** *(Saltwater fish)* 80 infs, Redfish; 1 inf, **nwFL**, Red = redfish, channelfish. **1994** *NY Times* (NY) 27 July sec B 5/1, When asked about the availability of the celebrated Louisiana redfish, which was nearly depleted during the Cajun cooking craze in the mid-1980's, Ms. Spicer explained that the redfish has made a comeback.

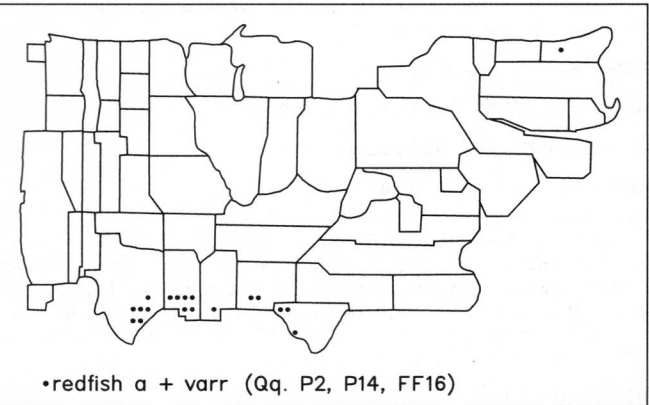

•redfish a + varr (Qq. P2, P14, FF16)

b A **rockfish 3:** usu the **rosefish** or a **black rockfish 1** (here: *Sebastes melanops*). **chiefly AK, ME**

1873 in 1878 Smithsonian Inst. *Misc. Coll.* 14.2.23 **ME**, *Sebastes viviparus* [here: =*S. marinus*] . . Red-fish; bream. **1888** Kingsley *Riverside Nat. Hist.* 3.249 **MA**, The *S[ebastes] marinus* is variously known as the rose-fish, red-fish, red-perch, Norway haddock, John Dory, etc. **1907** U.S. Dept. Commerce Bur. Fisheries *Document* 618.64 **AK**, The redfish or "black bass" of Sitka *(Sebastodes melanops)*, an excellent food fish and quite abundant. **1955** U.S. Arctic Info. Center *Gloss.* 68, Rosefish. . . An important food fish, *Sebastes marinus,* of the North Atlantic and adjacent northern seas, . . colored bright orange-red when adult, mottled red-brown when young. Also called . . 'redfish.' **1957** *ME Coast Fisherman* July 22, Redfish ("rosefish" to the professor), once considered a trash fish, now rates second only to haddock in N.E. landings. **1959** *Wall St. Jrl.* (NY NY) 13 May 14, New England accounts for more than 80% of U.S. production of ground fish fillets. . . Ground fish, or "bottomfish," . . include ocean perch (also called redfish or rosefish) . . and many other kinds. **1966** *DARE* (Qu. P2, . . *Kinds of saltwater fish caught around here . . good to eat*) Inf **ME**16, Redfish—often sold as ocean perch; **ME**22, Rosefish—old-fashioned [term]; "redfish" common now—"ocean perch" when sold in stores. **1966** *DARE* Tape **ME**24, We use herring, redfish trimming, bream we call it. **1991** Amer. Fisheries Soc. *Common Names Fishes* 85, The . . names redfish and ocean perch apply to all Atlantic species including the three [= *Sebastes fasciatus, S. marinus,* and *S. mentella*] in our region [=the US and Canada].

c =**sockeye salmon.** Cf **little redfish**

1881 *Amer. Naturalist* 15.181 **Pacific NW**, Only the quinnat and blueback (then called red-fish) have been found in the fall at any great distance from the sea. **1904** *Salmon & Trout* 161, The blue-back salmon . . is known under the name [sic] redfish . . and sockeye. . . The fish when fresh from the sea has a bright blue back and silvery sides and underparts. . . At the spawning period the back and sides become red. **1925** *Book of Rural Life* 4868, Sockeye salmon, also called . . *redfish*. . . The flesh is deep red, finely grained and rich in red oil. **1955** U.S. Arctic Info. Center *Gloss.* 66, Red salmon. A relatively small fish, *Oncorhynchus nerka,* weighing about 7 pounds but second in commercial importance only to the king salmon. Also called 'sockeye,' 'redfish.' **1976** Tryckare et al. *Lore of Sportfishing* 76, Sockeye Salmon. . . Other common names . . redfish [etc].

d also *California redfish:* =**sheepshead 4.**

    1882 U.S. Natl. Museum *Bulletin* 16.602, *H[arpe] pulchra* [=*Pimelometopon pulchrum*]. . . *Red-fish; Fat-head.* . . Coast of California, . . very abundant. **1911** U.S. Bur. Census *Fisheries 1908* 314, The redfish of California. . . reaches a weight of 12 to 15 pounds, but is not a valuable food fish. **1953** Roedel *Common Fishes CA* 117, *Pimelometopon pulchrum.* . . Redfish, fathead, humpy. **1976** Tryckare et al. *Lore of Sportfishing* 119, California redfish. . . Young fish are orange red overall with seven round, black blotches on fin areas.

e =**cutthroat trout.**

    1943 Eddy–Surber *N. Fishes* 89, (Silver Trout, Tahoe Trout, Redfish) *Salmo clarkii henshawi.* . . has a green back and coppery silver sides.

red flag See flag n² 2

red-flannel berry n

A **thimbleberry;** see quot.

    1967 *DARE* Wildfl QR Pl.101 Inf **MI**57, Red-flannel berries—thimbleberry—doesn't grow down here [= Upper Peninsula]. In Oregon we called 'em red-flannel berries.

red flannel hash n Also *flannel hash, red ~* chiefly NEng

A hash, esp corned-beef hash, containing red beets.

    1907 *DN* 3.248 **eME,** Red flannel hash. . . Beet hash. *Red hash.* . . Beet hash. "There'll be a red-hash supper at the vestry to-night." **1923** *Nation* 26 Dec 732 **ME,** Salt codfish. . . boiled with beets and served with pork scraps (cubes of salt pork fried brown), it is considered delectable. If any is left over, it can be chopped fine and "het up" for breakfast as "red flannel hash." **1926** *AmSp* 2.78 **ME,** She will probably serve you a concoction known as "red flannel hash." That is, it will be red, if there are enough beets left over. **1939** Berolzheimer *U.S. Cookbook* 88 **NEng,** *Red flannel hash* (A Typical Green Mountain Dish). . . Traditionally this is the second appearance of the New England boiled dinner. Any leftover meat and vegetables may be used. Chop beets and potatoes, mix with the chopped beef, and season with salt and pepper. **1939** Wolcott *Yankee Cook Book* 73, *Red flannel hash*—1 tablespoon butter—1 cup chopped cooked corned beef—3 cups chopped boiled potatoes—1 cup chopped cooked beets—½ chopped onion. **1959** *VT Hist.* 27.140, *Red flannel hash.* . . One of the recipes for red flannel hash calls for equal parts of onion, ground beef, and beets. Common. **1966–68** *DARE* (Qu. H45, *Dishes . . that everybody around here would know, but that people in other places might not*) Inf **MA**10, Red flannel hash—meat (corned beef, leftover roast beef), potato, beets (enough to color it nice and red); **MA**73, Red flannel hash—hash with red beets; **OH**65, Flannel hash—the leftover boiled dinner; (Qu. H47, *Kinds of fried potatoes favored around here*) Inf **NH**15, Red flannel hash—made with beets—colors potatoes. **1967–69** *DARE* FW Addit **cOR,** Red flannel hash—chopped-up remains of New England boiled dinner when beets have been used; **cVT,** Red flannel hash—beets and potatoes and cooked meat ground up. **1986** *DARE* File **Block Is. RI,** Aunt Ivah says that this is a Block Island dish, and it is customary hash, with added beets. **1991** *Ibid* **seNY,** Red flannel hash = another beef dish I have the receipt for.

red flicker See red-shafted flicker

red-flowering locust See red locust 1

red fox n

1 Std: a North American fox *(Vulpes vulpes).* Also called **cross fox, colored ~, Sampson ~, silver ~**

2 also *Virginia red fox:* =**gray fox.** Cf **southern fox, Virginia ~**

    1859 Taliaferro *Fisher's R.* 150 **nwNC** (as of 1820s), We started a rale old Virginny red fox. **1937** Grinnell et al. *Fur-Bearing Mammals CA* 2.437, The gray fox is sometimes called "red fox" by the uninitiated, because of the reddish color on its under parts; but this is an unfortunate name, for it invites confusion with the totally distinct red fox of another genus.

red fox squirrel See red squirrel 2

redgill n Cf bluegill 1

=**red-eared sunfish 1.**

    1968 *DARE* FW Addit **cAR,** This fish [=shellcracker] is called red-eared sunfish (occasionally) or redgill in central Arkansas.

red grape n

=**catbird grape.**

    1933 Small *Manual SE Flora* 837, *V[itis] palmata.* . . Berry . . black, destitute of any bloom. . . *Red-grape. Cat-grape.* **1940** Steyermark *Flora MO* 352, Red Grape (Vitis palmata). . . Blooming later than any of the other Mo. grapes. **1970** Correll *Plants TX* 1019, *Vitis palmata.* . . *Red grape.* . . On margins of ponds or sloughs, or in low woods . . from La. and Tex., n. to Ind., Ill. and Ia.

red grass-bird n Cf grass-bird 1

=**song sparrow.**

    1844 DeKay *Zool. NY* 2.165, *Ammodramus palustris* [=*Melospiza melodia*]. . . *Female,* scarcely different from the male, except in the absence of the black frontlet and black streaks on the crown. . . This species . . is often called the *Red Grass-bird* in this State. . . Its nest is on the ground. **1917** (1923) *Birds Amer.* 3.50, *Song Sparrow. . . Other Names.* . . Red Grass-bird. **1944** Hausman *Amer. Birds* 514, Grass-bird, Red—see Sparrow, Song.

red gravy n

1 also *red ham gravy, red sop:* =**red-eye gravy.** chiefly Sth, S Midl See Map

    1939 Harris *Purslane* 302 **eNC,** We like them for breakfast with red ham gravy. **1940** Brown *Amer. Cooks* 770 **TN,** *Red ham gravy*—Add a small amount of boiling water to the hot grease in which ham has been fried. **1942** (1960) Robertson *Red Hills* 66 **SC,** Hominy was such a good food, eaten with butter or with sliced tomatoes or with red gravy, and it was so cheap. **1949** *Sat. Eve. Post* 2 July 68 **KY,** The ladies were in the kitchen, cooking up some of that fine Kentucky country ham and red gravy. **1954** *Harder Coll.* **cwTN,** *Red gravy,* made from bacon fat. **1959** *IN Mag. Hist.* 55.233 (as of c1920), Many a person might be tired of fried chicken and flour gravy yet be able to make a satisfying meal on fried ham and red sop, plus the rest of the table's load. **1965–70** *DARE* (Qu. H37, . . *Words . . for gravy*) 15 Infs, **Sth, S Midl,** Red gravy [Of these Infs, 10 mentioned that it was made with ham or equated it with red-eye (gravy).]; **NY**92, Red gravy—a Southern boy used to make this—from North Carolina; **TX**40, Red gravy—same as brindle gravy; **VA**4, Red gravy—few call it that; Inf just called it ham gravy. [11 of 18 Infs comm type 5, 9 gs educ] **1986** Pederson *LAGS Concordance* **GA,** 1 inf, Red gravy; 1 inf, Red gravy—no milk; 1 inf, Red gravy = ham gravy; 1 inf, Red gravy—unthickened; 1 inf, Ham meat and red gravy.

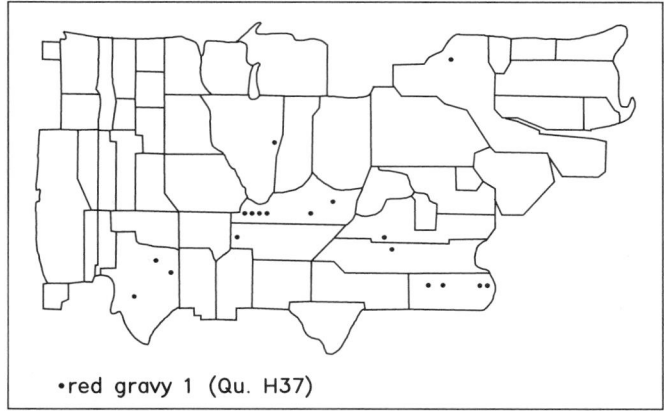

•red gravy 1 (Qu. H37)

2 See quots.

    1968 *DARE* (Qu. H37, . . *Words . . for gravy*) Inf **LA**23, Red gravy—with tomato. **1999** *DARE* File **sLA,** I was raised in New Orleans, where we have our own group of unusual words and phrases, and I have enough to do trying to remember not to say red gravy for tomato sauce.

red grouper n

1 A **grouper 1a** (here: *Epinephelus morio*) native chiefly to the South Atlantic and Gulf coasts. Also called **brown snapper, red-bellied ~, red ~ 3, spotted grouper**

1842 DeKay *Zool. NY* 4.23, This beautiful fish, which is not unusual in our markets in June and July, . . is called by the fishermen, *Groper* and *Red Groper*. It is a southern species, and is brought hither from the reefs of Florida. **1905** NJ State Museum *Annual Rept. for 1904* 308, Red Grouper. . . On our coast it is a straggler, most likely in the Gulf Stream. **1939** Natl. Geogr. Soc. *Fishes* 188, The red grouper. . . is a good food fish and its color of reddish brown gives it a striking appearance. **1975** Evanoff *Catch More Fish* 106, The groupers are a large family, such as the red, black, yellow, and Nassau groupers. **1983** *Audubon Field Guide N. Amer. Fishes* 542, The Red Grouper is one of the most common and commercially important groupers, especially in Florida.

2 A **grouper 1b** (here: *Mycteroperca venenosa*).

1935 Caine *Game Fish* 77, *Mycteroperca venenosa*. . . Red Grouper. **1946** LaMonte *N. Amer. Game Fishes* 53, *Mycteroperca venenosa*. . . Red Grouper. . . The fish changes color rapidly and confusingly.

red gum n

1 =**sweet gum** or its wood—used esp (in contrast to **white gum**) to distinguish specimens in which the reddish heartwood predominates. **chiefly Sth, S Midl** See Map

1839 *S. Lit. Messenger* 5.113 **Sth**, Dislodge the rackoon from its lofty hole in the red-gum tree. **1884** Sargent *Forests of N. Amer.* 86, *Liquidambar Styraciflua*. . . Red Gum. . . A large tree, often 30 to 36 or, exceptionally, 48 meters in height. **1916** Seton *Woodcraft Manual Girls* 288, *Sweet Gum, Star-leaved*, or *Red Gum*. . . [R]emarkable for . . the unsplitable nature of its weak, warping, perishable timber. **1950** Peattie *Nat. Hist. Trees* 307, Red or Star-leaved Gum. . . Pink or ruddy heartwood. *Ibid* 310, To the lumberman the heartwood of this tree is Red Gum, and the sapwood . . is marketed separately as if it were a different wood. **1965–70** *DARE* (Qu. T15, . . *Kinds of swamp trees*) 17 Infs, **esp Sth, S Midl**, Red gum; (Qu. T13) Inf **GA3**, Sweet gum—same as red gum; **GA89**, Sweet gum—sap gum—same as red gum; **LA3**, Red gum—has little balls on it, same as sweet gum; **LA7**, Red gum grows bigger than white gum; **LA15**, Red gum has red heart, five-pointed leaves, sometimes sold for mahogany; (Qu. T16, . . *Kinds of trees . . 'special'*) Inf **DC2**, Red gum—dark, rich red in fall. [20 of 23 Infs male] **1986** Pederson *LAGS Concordance*, 8 infs, **Gulf Region**, Red gum (tree).

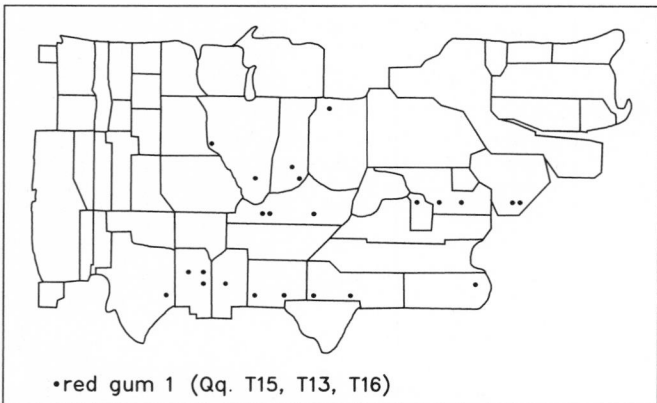

•red gum 1 (Qq. T15, T13, T16)

2 A eucalyptus (here: *Eucalyptus camaldulensis* or *E. tereticornis*). [*AND* 1788 →] **CA** Cf **gum tree 3**

1888 Lindley–Widney *CA of South* 326, Red-gum *(Eucalyptus)* trees pay twenty per cent per annum on the investment as fuel-producers. **1908** CA Ag. Exper. Sta. Berkeley *Bulletin* 196.31, *Eucalyptus rostrata* [=*E. camaldulensis*], the Red Gum, is now finding considerable use for interior finish and furniture. **1911** *Ibid* 217.1011, *Eucalyptus rostrata* [=*E. camaldulensis*]. . . Red Gum. . . Under cultivation in many parts of California. . . Considerable honey from the flowers. **1942** Hylander *Plant Life* 394, Introduced into California some forty years ago, and . . now commonly seen throughout the southern and central parts of the state. . . Red Gum [=*Eucalyptus camaldulensis*] has smaller leaves and fruits [than *E. globulus*], the latter with beaked or conical pointed caps. **1968** *DARE* (Qu. T16, . . *Kinds of trees . . 'special'*) Inf **CA36**, Eucalyptus—especially the red gum, blue gum, flowering eucalyptus, [and] dwarf eucalyptus—a bush eucalyptus.

red hake n

A **squirrel hake** (here: *Urophycis chuss*).

1955 Zim–Shoemaker *Fishes* 75, The Squirrel or Red Hake . . is

smaller than the others, averaging 1 to 3 lb. **1983** *Audubon Field Guide N. Amer. Fishes* 498, Red Hake (*Urophycis chuss*). . . Their flesh is soft and their fighting qualities are too poor to make them attractive to anglers.

red ham gravy See **red gravy 1**

redhammer n Cf **hammerhead 6, nail-pounder, yellowhammer**

A **woodpecker;** see quot.

1968–69 *DARE* (Qu. Q17, . . *Kinds of woodpeckers*) Inf **IN83**, Redhammer—same as redhead; **NC54**, Redhammers—some call 'em woodchucks.

red-handy adj [Var, perh by folk-etym, of *red-handed*]

1940 (1941) Bell *Swamp Water* 158 **Okefenoke GA**, When I got there, I heered her crying sort of loud, not yelling, and I knowed I'd caught him red-handy, and I kicked open the door.

red hash See **red flannel hash**

red haw n

1 =**hawthorn** or its fruit. **esp Missip-Ohio Valleys** See Map

1716 Petiver *Petiveriana* 12, Red *Haw*. Of an agreeable Taste, and four times as big as ours in *Europe*. **1787** Amer. Acad. Arts & Sci. *Memoirs* 2.1.159 **Ohio Valley**, Black Haw, four inches diameter, and producing good fruit. Red Haw. **1824** Doddridge *Notes Indian Wars* 86 **PA, VA**, Red haws grew on the white thorn bushes. **1860** Curtis *Cat. Plants NC* 82, *Red Haws*. Thorny shrubs, sometimes tree-shaped, with white flowers, . . and colored (generally red) fruit containing 1 to 5 bony seeds. **1893** *Jrl. Amer. Folkl.* 6.141, *Cratægus coccinea*, var. *mollis*, red haw. Gen[eral] in Central States. **1896** *Ibid* 9.187 **IL, OH**, *Cratægus tomentosa* [=*C. calpodendron*], . . red haw, Sulphur Grove, Ohio, Central Ill. **1921** Deam *Trees IN* 212, *Crataegus mollis*. . . Red Haw. . . Fruit ripens in September, . . scarlet. . . This thorn is well distributed over Indiana. **1944** Duncan *Mentor Graham* 237 **IL**, He talked of red haws, wood violets, May apples, lady-slippers, and dogwood—in a land that had no shade. **1965–70** *DARE* (Qu. I46, . . *Kinds of fruits that grow wild around here*) 13 Infs, **esp Missip-Ohio Valleys**, Red haw(s); **TX85**, Black and red haws; (Qu. I43, *What kinds of nuts grow wild around here?*) Inf **MO9**, Red haws; (Qu. I44, *What kinds of berries grow wild around here?*) Infs **KY5, MO22, TX67**, Red haws; (Qu. T16, . . *Kinds of trees . . 'special'*) Infs **AR56, IA38, IL14, 56, MD36**, Red haw; **TX106**, Red haw bushes. **1986** Pederson *LAGS Concordance*, 6 infs, **AR**, 3 infs, **LA**, 4 infs, **MS**, 3 infs, **TX**, Red haw(s); 3 infs, **swLA, ceTN, ceTX**, Red haw tree; 1 inf, **cLA**, Red haw bush.

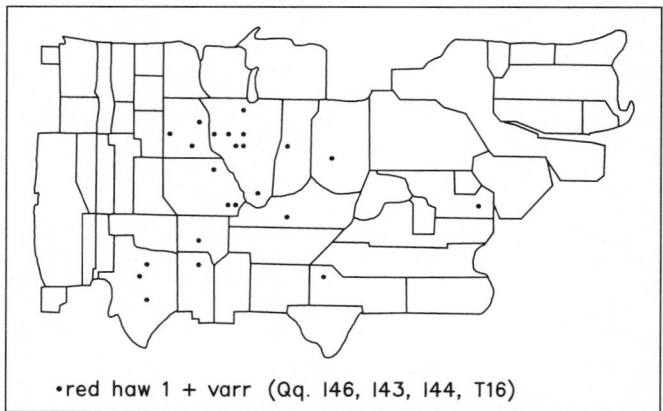

•red haw 1 + varr (Qq. I46, I43, I44, T16)

2 A **holly** n[1] **1** (here: either *Ilex decidua* or *I. vomitoria*).

1913 TX Acad. Sci. *Trans. for 1910–12* 12.80 **ceTX**, *Ilex decidua* Walt. Called a "Red Haw" here; also Yaupon. **1913** *Torreya* 13.232 **LA**, *Ilex vomitoria*. . . Red haw or hoy, Chef Menteur, La.

red hawk n

=**red-tailed hawk.**

1895 (1907) Wright *Birdcraft* 218, *Buteo borealis*. Red Hawk. . . It is often difficult to identify the larger Hawks on the wing; but the *red tail* is a distinctive mark of the adults of this species at all seasons. **1917** (1923) *Birds Amer.* 2.71, *Red-tailed Hawk*. . . Other Names.—Red Hawk [etc]. . . *Tail, bright rust-red* or rufous above. **1944** Hausman *Amer.*

Birds 517, Hawk, Red—see Hawk, Red-tailed. **1965–70** *DARE* (Qu. Q4, . . *Kinds of hawks*) Infs **FL**29, **IN**27, 80, **LA**14, **OH**72, **PA**184, **TX**1, 33, 43, 84, Red hawk.

redhead n

1 Any of several birds, as:

a A duck, as: see below. Cf **creek redhead, little ~**

(1) also *red-headed broadbill, red-head(ed) duck:* A **scaup** (here: *Aythya americana*). [*OED2 red-headed duck* (at *red-headed* a. 2.a) 1678 (for *Netta rufina*)] Also called **broadbill 1, dos gris, fall duck, fiddler ~ 2, fool ~ 2, good god 2, mule duck 2, pochard, quindar, raft duck a, Washington canvasback**

1709 (1967) Lawson *New Voyage* 154 **NC, SC,** Red-Heads, a lesser fowl than Bull-Necks, are very sweet Food, and plentiful in our Rivers and Creeks. **1814** Wilson *Amer. Ornith.* 8.110 **NY, NJ, Mid Atl,** Red-Headed Duck. *Anas Ferina* [here: =*Aythya americana*]. . . The Redhead is twenty inches in length. **1838** Geol. Surv. OH *Second Annual Rept.* 166, Fuligula ferina . . *Red-headed Duck. Ibid* 187, The pochard, or red-head, is so nearly allied in color to the canvass-back that they are often mistaken, one for the other. It is a more frequent visitor of our borders, and is highly valued for the table. **1879** Rathbun *Revised List Birds* 38 **cNY,** Red-head Duck. Not uncommon as a Spring and Autumn migrant. **1888** Trumbull *Names of Birds* 50, *Red-head* or *Red-headed duck:* very generally known as such . . by gunners. . . At Seaford (Hempstead), L[ong] I[sland] [NY], it is the *Red-headed broadbill.* **1950** *WELS (Kinds of wild ducks in your general neighborhood)* 10 Infs, **WI,** Redhead(s). **1965–70** *DARE* (Qu. Q5, . . *Kinds of wild ducks*) 88 Infs, **chiefly C Atl, Gt Lakes, West,** Red-head(ed) (duck) [*DARE* Ed: Some of these Infs may refer instead to other senses below.] **1966–69** *DARE* Tape **NC**25, You can name a redhead duck; **NC**76, I use stilt blinds; you kill blackheads, redheads, and Canadian geese. **1982** Elman *Hunter's Field Guide* 199, Men who have lived their lives on Puget Sound or the Chesapeake may still mistake distant redheads stitched over a gray morning for canvasbacks, but redheads are darker and a trifle shorter. *Ibid* 200, A redhead of either sex has a blue-gray bill with a whitish ring behind the black nail, but the drake's. . . head and neck are chestnut red.

(2) =**canvasback duck.**

1888 Trumbull *Names of Birds* 47 **sePA,** Canvas-back. . . In the neighborhood of Philadelphia hunters were in the habit of supplying the market with this duck, under the name of "Red-head." **1925** (1986) Phillips *Nat. Hist. Ducks* 3.121, *Vernacular Names.* . . Canvas-back, . . Can, Redhead [etc].

(3) =**European widgeon.** Cf *bastard redhead* (at **bastard 2**), **red-headed widgeon**

1923 U.S. Dept. Ag. *Misc. Circular* 13.11 **GA,** *European Widgeon. . . Vernacular Names. . . In local use . .* redhead. **1955** *Oriole* 20.1.4 **GA,** *European Widgeon. . . Redhead* (the head of the male is chiefly reddish-brown).

b A **red-headed woodpecker 1,** usu *Melanerpes erythrocephalus.*

[**1764** in 1925 Fries *Rec. Moravians* 579, Red Heads . . do much harm to the corn.] **1831** Audubon *Ornith. Biog.* 1.145 **Sth,** As soon as the Red-heads have begun to visit a Cherry or Apple tree, a pole is placed along the trunk of the tree. **1874** Coues *Birds NW* 291, I do not think that any Red-heads [=*Melanerpes erythrocephalus*] endure the severer winters of the Upper Missouri. **1897** Fox in *Harper's New Mth. Mag.* 95.359 **KY,** Stallards air as thick down thar as redheads in a deadenin'. **1928** Skinner *Guide Winter Birds NC* 134, Finally the Red-head [= *Melanerpes erythrocephalus*] got a mate and between the two of them they managed to occupy the nest hole and keep the intruding Starlings out. **1947** IA Acad. Sci. *Proc.* 54.377 **Upper Missip Valley,** This honey must support a large number of bees throughout the winter, which may in turn account for the winter colony of Redheads, numbering as high as twenty in some winter seasons. **1965–70** *DARE* (Qu. Q17, . . *Kinds of woodpeckers*) 83 Infs, **widespread exc NEng, Pacific,** Redhead(s). **1986** Pederson *LAGS Concordance (Woodpecker)* 107 infs, **Gulf Region,** Redhead(s).

c also *red-headed linnet:* =**house finch.** [*OED2 red-headed linnet* (at *red-headed* a. 2.a) 1674 (for *Carduelis cannabina* and *C. cabaret*)] Cf **red linnet**

1898 (1900) Davie *Nests N. Amer. Birds* 356, *House Finch.* . . This bird is known as the Red-headed Linnet. . . It is a very common bird in the interior region of the United States, from Nevada, Utah and Colorado

southward, and is also abundant on the Pacific coast. **1917** (1923) *Birds Amer.* 3.7, *House Finch.* . . Red-headed Linnet; . . Red-head. . . The House Finch or Red-headed Linnet through many parts of the West is the commonest bird about the dooryard. . . The bird is so familiar and abundant through parts of California and it has such a strong taste for the fruits planted by man, that Red-head and his wife are often regarded as a nuisance. **1946** Goodrich *Birds in KS* 317, [Colloquial name:] Linnet, red-headed . . [Common name:] finch, common house.

d also *redhead tanager:* The western tanager *(Piranga ludoviciana).*

1946 Hausman *Eastern Birds* 564, *Western Tanager.* . . *Other Names* . . Black-and-yellow Redhead, Redhead Tanager. . . Male . . Head and throat bright red. **1953** Jewett *Birds WA* 594, *Western Tanager.* . . Other names: Red-head. . . Head and neck bright orange or red.

2 also *red-headed lizard, red-head(ed) skink:* A **skink** (here: *Eumeces fasciatus*). Cf **red-headed scorpion**

1854 Wailes *Rept. on Ag. & Geol. MS* 328, Ligosoma quinquelineatus [=*Eumeces fasciatus*]. Redheaded lizard. **1908** Biol. Soc. DC *Proc.* 21.73 **cnTX,** *Red Head.* . . This lizard . . in the post-oak country . . is as common as *Sceloporus spinosus* [=*S. olivaceus*]. **1925** TX Folkl. Soc. *Pub.* 4.51 **nwLA,** The most dangerous animal . . is the large red-head, . . which is supposed to chase persons who invade its haunts. **1926** TX Folkl. Soc. *Pub.* 5.61 **Sth,** The red-headed skink . . is common in the timbered regions of the South. . . The bottomland negroes believe that either its bite or sting will produce death. **1928** Baylor Univ. Museum *Contrib.* 16.13 **TX,** Red-head Skink. . . There are any number of color patterns and variations, dependant [sic] on age and locality.

3 also *red-headed turtle:* A **red-bellied turtle** (here: *Trachemys scripta*). Cf **red-eared turtle**

1937 Cahn *Turtles IL* 160, *Pseudemys troostii* [=*Trachemys scripta* subsp *troosti*]. . . Red-head. [*Ibid* 162, The head shows many stripes of yellow or orange, fine dorsally and coarser ventrally and laterally. A very conspicuous blood red or orange red stripe starts at the posterior margin of the eye and extends backward upon the neck, . . and affords an excellent field mark for the identification of the species.] **1986** Pederson *LAGS Concordance,* 1 inf, **csTX,** Red-headed turtle.

4 A **milkweed 1** (here: *Asclepias curassavica*).

1876 Hobbs *Bot. Hdbk.* 96, Red head, Bastard ipecac, Asclepias curassavica. **1959** Carleton *Index Herb. Plants* 98, *Red head:* Asclepias curassavica.

5 A **dewberry 1.**

1969 *DARE* FW Addit **KY**5, Redhead, redheads = dewberries; old-fashioned.

redhead-and-whitewing peckerwood See **red-headed wood-pecker 1**

redhead buzzard See **red-headed vulture**

redhead duck, red-headed broadbill (or duck) See **redhead 1a(1)**

red-headed adj Cf **red-eyed 1**
Fig: angry.

1967 *DARE* (Qu. GG40, *Words or expressions meaning violently angry*) Inf **TX**5, Get red-headed. **1973** Allen *LAUM* 1.360 **Upper MW** (as of c1950), *Angry.* . . red-headed [1 inf **IA**].

red-headed buzzard See **red-headed vulture**

red-headed knocker See **red-headed woodpecker 1**

red-headed linnet See **redhead 1c**

red-headed lizard See **redhead 2**

red-headed Louisa n Also *redhead Louisa* [By folk-etym from genus *Lewisia*]

A **bitterroot 2** (here: *Lewisia rediviva*).

1937 U.S. Forest Serv. *Range Plant Hdbk.* W105, Bitterroot is occasionally known as redhead Louisa. **1947** *Nature Conserv. Mag.* 40.444 **MT,** Other common names [of *Lewisia rediviva*] are . . redheaded Louisa [etc]. **1963** Craighead *Rocky Mt. Wildflowers* 46, Redhead Louisa. . . The only conspicuous white to pinkish flower that appears to be leafless. **1967** *DARE* FW Addit **OR**12, Bitterroot *(Lewisia rediviva)* (rock rose, or red-headed Louisa) locally—sand lily.

red-headed merganser n
=**hooded merganser.**
   1969 *DARE* (Qu. Q5, . . *Kinds of wild ducks*) Inf **CA**140, Red-headed merganser.

red-headed pecker See **red-headed woodpecker 1**

red-headed peckerwood (or sapsucker) See **red-headed woodpecker**

red-headed scorpion n Also *redhead scorpion*   **chiefly Sth**
Cf **redhead 2, scorpion B2**
A **skink** (here: *Eumeces fasciatus*).
   1891 in 1896 IL State Lab. Nat. Hist. Urbana *Bulletin* 3.257, [*Red-headed Lizard. . .* Total length about eight inches.] *Ibid* 258, This form is commonly known as the red-headed scorpion in southern Illinois. **1926** TX Folkl. Soc. *Pub.* 5.61, *"Ole Red-head Scarpion". . .* Common in the timbered regions of the South. . . In the negro vernacular, scorpion, or "scarpion," means a poisonous animal. . . "Chillun, yo bettah keep way from ole red-head scarpion; yo go neah whah he is, he sho chase en sting yo. Ef he sting yo, yo sho gwine ter die." **1928** Baylor Univ. Museum *Contrib.* 16.13 **TX,** *Eumeces fasciatus. . . Red-head Scorpion.* The large adult male which has a broad red head and uniform dorsal coloration. **1938** Matschat *Suwannee R.* 67 **Okefenokee GA,** According to many of the swamp folk the red-headed scorpion, one of the seven species of lizards found in Okefenokee, barks like a dog and is deadly poisonous. Neither statement is true. **1970** *DARE* (Qu. R21, . . *Other kinds of stinging insects*) Inf **VA**46, Red-headed scorpion [FW: used in conv]. **1970** *DARE* Tape **VA**46, There are a few redhead scorpions in there. **1986** Pederson *LAGS Concordance,* 1 inf, **cwAR,** Red-headed scorpion = slick-headed scorpion; 1 inf, **cwTN,** Redheaded scorpion—6–8″ long, "vig'rous-looking."

red-headed skink See **redhead 2**

red-headed sparrow n
Either of two sparrows with rufous caps: the **field sparrow a** in the eastern US or the rufous-crowned sparrow (*Aimophila ruficeps*) in the western US.
   1955 *Oriole* 20.1.14 **GA,** *Field Sparrow.—Red-headed Sparrow* (the crown is rusty-brown). **1968** *DARE* (Qu. Q21, . . *Kinds of sparrows*) Inf **UT**5, Red-headed sparrow.

red-headed stepchild n
Fig: someone or something that is unwanted or badly treated—freq in phr *beat like a red-headed stepchild* to beat severely; to best definitively (in a game or contest).
   1941 *AmSp* 16.23 **sIN, MO,** *Like a red-headed stepchild.* Unjustly, unkindly. 'They treat him like a red-headed stepchild.' **1943** *AmSp* 18.67 **SC,** [**IN** sayings used elsewhere:] *Like a red-headed stepchild.* **1999** in 2001 *DARE* File—Internet **OK,** "My mother would beat me like a red-headed stepchild if I did that."—spoken by one of my coworkers when she was asked if she had a tattoo. **2000** Columbia College *Columbia Chron. Online* 22 May (Internet) **neIL,** There's no coverage anymore. Racing is the red-headed stepchild of the sports pages. **2000** in 2001 *DARE* File—Internet **Boston MA,** Am I the only one who thought Al Gore beat Dubya like a red-headed stepchild last night? **2001** *Ibid* **seMI,** And thus concludes my tale of the funny runner from Ann Arbor Huron who beat me like a red-headed stepchild for the better part of my sophmore [sic] season. **2001** *Cumberland Times–News* (MD) 18 May (Internet), Red-headed step child, that is what I felt like at the meeting of the North Garrett County Rescue Squad. **2001** *WI State Jrl.* (Madison) 11 Sept sec B 3, [Ann Landers column:] Just because my parents couldn't get their lives straight didn't mean mine should be torn to pieces. . . [Signed] *Red-Headed Stepchild in Kentucky.*

red-headed teal n Also *redhead teal, ~ widgeon*
=**green-winged teal.**
   1888 Trumbull *Names of Birds* 28 **NC,** *Green-winged Teal. . .* At Morehead, N.C., *red-headed teal.* **1917** (1923) *Birds Amer.* 1.122, Red-headed Teal. . . Adult Male. . . *Head and upper neck, rich chestnut with a glossy green patch behind eye.* **1921** *LA Conserv. Rev.* 10.54, *Green-winged Teal. . .* Other local names are "cognotte", or "congo" and "read-head [sic] teal". **1955** MA Audubon Soc. *Bulletin* 39.314, *Green-winged Teal. . .* Red-head Wigeon [sic] (Mass. The head of the male, except for a large green mask, is chestnut; "widgeon" is applied to many of the smaller ducks.) **1982** Elman *Hunter's Field Guide* 178, *Anas crecca carolinensis. . .* Redhead teal, . . breakfast duck.

red-headed turtle See **redhead 3**

red-headed vulture n Also *red-head(ed) buzzard*
=**turkey vulture.**
   1843 Marryat *Travels Snake Indians* 334, The most common birds of prey are . . the black and red-headed vulture. **1932** Bennitt *Check-list* 21 **MO,** *Cathartes aura septentrionalis. . .* Red-headed vulture. [**c1938** in 1970 Hyatt *Hoodoo* 1.423 **seGA,** De buzzard, yo' use him fo' his grease, fo' a chile dat is born an' nevah walks—yo' grease with it. An' a person dat is stiff-limbed an' a person dat has rheumatism uses his grease—de *red-head one,* de buzzard.] **1966–70** *DARE* (Qu. Q13, *Names . . for the vulture*) Infs **DC**4, **FL**51, Red-headed buzzard. **1973** Flach *Yankee German-America* 13 **csTX,** A salve for chest pains was made by rendering rattlesnake fat and applying it with a feather from a red-headed buzzard.

red-headed widgeon n Also *redhead widgeon* [*OED2* (at *red-headed* a. 2.a) 1678 (for *Aythya ferina*)] Cf **redhead 1a(3)**
=**European widgeon.**
   1911 *Forest & Stream* 77.173 **NC,** *European Widgeon. . .* Redhead Widgeon at Currituck Sound, N.C. The writer also can vouch for the use of the last name, as he heard the chief guide at the Currituck Club remark when handling one of these birds: "That is what we call a redhead widgeon." **1918** Grinnell *Game Birds CA* 112, All the California records [for *Anas penelope*] are from near the coast. Mr. F.J. Smith of Eureka writes us that three Red-headed Widgeons have been taken on Humboldt Bay. **1932** Howell *FL Bird Life* 135, *European Widgeon. . .* Other Name: *Red-headed Widgeon.* **1953** Jewett *Birds WA* 125, Redheaded Widgeon. . . *Adult male . .* head and neck rich russet brown. **1955** MA Audubon Soc. *Bulletin* 39.314, *European Widgeon. . .* Redheaded Widgeon (Mass. The head and upper neck of the male are chiefly cinnamon red).

red-headed woodcock n Also *redhead woodcock, red-headed wood hen* Cf **woodcock, wood hen**
=**pileated woodpecker B.**
   1845 Thompson *Pineville* 90 **GA,** Out flew a large red-headed woodcock. **1864** in 1996 Owen *Letters to Laura* 142 **TN,** We also had two large black red-head wood-cocks. **1953** *AmSp* 28.284, Pileated woodpeckers. . . *Red-headed woodcock* has been heard in Quebec, Maine, Virginia, North Carolina, and Florida. **1955** *Oriole* 20.1.9 **GA,** *Pileated Woodpecker. . . Red-headed Woodcock* ("woodcock" as a striking bird of the woodland). **1986** Pederson *LAGS Concordance (Woodpecker)* 1 inf, **ceTX,** Redheaded wood hen.

red-headed wooden pecker See **red-headed woodpecker 1**

red-headed wood hen n See **red-headed woodcock**

red-headed woodpecker n Also *red-head(ed) peckerwood, ~ sapsucker, redhead woodpecker*
1 also *redhead-and-whitewing peckerwood, red-headed knocker, ~ (wooden) pecker:* A **woodpecker** (here: *Melanerpes erythrocephalus*) with an entirely red head and large white wing patches, native to much of the eastern two-thirds of the US.   Also called **flag bird, German woodpecker, half-a-shirt, hammerhead 6, jellycoat, jerry coat, lobster B3, peckerwood 1, pique bois, redcap, redhead 1b, redtop woodpecker, sapsucker 1, shirttail n 2, summer woodpecker, white shirt, whitewing, woodcock, woodchuck**
   1730 Royal Soc. London *Philos. Trans.* 36.427 **NC, SC,** *Picus capite toto rubro,* the Red-headed Woodpecker. **1792** Belknap *Hist. NH* 3.166, Red Head Woodpecker—*Picus erythrocephalus.* **1805** (1905) Lewis *Orig. Jrls. Lewis & Clark Exped.* 3.57 **MT,** One of them brought . . a redheaded woodpecker of the large kind common to the U States. **1838** Geol. Surv. OH *Second Annual Rept.* 179, The yellow-bellied and the red-headed woodpeckers are the only species . . that forsake us in winter—all the others are permanent residents. **1860** in 1869 *Amer. Naturalist* 2.599, I saw a Red-head Woodpecker high on the eastern slope of the Rocky Mountains, but none on the west side. **1884** *Century Illustr. Mag.* 29.222 **ME,** A red-headed woodpecker . . drums upon a lightning-rod on his neighbor's house. **1919** Burns *Ornith. Chester Co. PA* 61, Red-headed Woodpecker, "red-head woodpecker." Tolerable common summer resident. **c1960** *Wilson Coll.* **csKY,** Redheaded peckerwood—the common red-headed woodpecker which everyone knows at sight. **1965–70** *DARE* (Qu. Q17, . . *Kinds of woodpeckers*) 533 Infs, **widespread,** Red-headed woodpecker; 69 Infs, **widespread,** Redhead woodpecker; **KY**65, 76, 88, **MS**21, **SC**41, **TN**24,

TX52, Red-headed peckerwood; **KY**82, **LA**7, Redhead peckerwood; **AL**17, Red-headed sapsucker; **MS**81, Redhead sapsucker; **IN**19, Red-headed knocker; **TX**1, Red-headed pecker; **MA**58, Small red-headed woodpecker; (Qu. Q18, *Joking names and nicknames for woodpeckers*) Infs **DC**2, **GA**18, **SC**32, Red-headed woodpecker. [*DARE* Ed: Some of these Infs may refer instead to other senses below.] **1986** Pederson *LAGS Concordance* **Gulf Region** *(Woodpeckers)* 55 infs, Redheaded woodpecker(s); 35 infs, Redheaded peckerwood(s); 16 infs, Redhead peckerwood(s); 13 infs, Redhead woodpecker(s); 3 infs, Redhead(ed) sapsucker(s); 1 inf, Redheaded wooden peckers; 1 inf, Redhead-and-whitewing peckerwood. [*DARE* Ed: Some of these infs may refer instead to other senses below.]

2 =**red-bellied woodpecker.**
1930 OK Univ. Biol. Surv. *Pub.* 2.146, Red-bellied Woodpecker. . . *Local Names* . . red-headed "sapsucker," . . orange borer. **1955** *Oriole* 20.1.10 **GA**, Red-bellied woodpecker. . . Red-headed Sapsucker (the crown and nape are red; "sapsucker" a term applied to practically all of our woodpeckers, is nevertheless a misnomer . .). **1962** Imhof *AL Birds* 332, Red-bellied Woodpecker. . . Red-headed Woodpecker. . . The *male* has a bright *red crown* and *nape,* while only the *nape* of the *female* is *red.* Young birds are brown-headed but still readily recognizable. **1969** Longstreet *Birds FL* 89, The red-bellied woodpecker is often called the red-headed woodpecker, which is quite a different bird.

3 =**California woodpecker.**
1967–69 *DARE* (Qu. Q17, . . *Kinds of woodpeckers*) Inf **CA**31, Black and white—the red-headed [woodpecker]; **CA**78, California acorn or red-headed woodpecker; **CA**140, Red-headed woodpecker—not one with topknot; an indigenous species to California.

4 Any of var other **woodpeckers** with a red patch on the head, as **flicker** n² **1, pileated woodpecker B,** or a **sapsucker 1** (here: *Sphyrapicus ruber*). Note: Some of these quots may refer instead to other senses above.
1857 U.S. Patent Office *Annual Rept. for 1856: Ag.* 134, The red-headed or golden-winged wood-pecker, having the temerity to approach this vicinity, is repelled and discomfitted with great promptness. **1927** Forbush *Birds MA* 2.289, To-day throughout Massachusetts its [= *Melanerpes erythrocephalus*] presence is mostly traditional, and many people still apply the name Red-headed Woodpecker to any woodpecker with red on its head. [**1953** Jewett *Birds WA* 404, *Sphyrapicus varius ruber.* . . Crimson-headed Woodpecker.] **1956** MA Audubon Soc. *Bulletin* 40.83 **VT**, *Yellow-bellied Sapsucker.* Red-headed Woodpecker (Vt. The forehead and crown are crimson.) *Ibid* **ME**, *Pileated Woodpecker.* . . Red-headed Woodpecker (Maine. The crown and crest of the male are poppy red.) **1965–70** *DARE* (Qu. Q17, . . *Kinds of woodpeckers*) 32 Infs, **CA, WA, OR,** Red-headed woodpecker; **CA**87, 130, Redhead woodpecker; **CA**137, Large red-headed woodpecker. **1986** Pederson *LAGS Concordance (Woodpeckers)* 1 inf, **cnLA,** Redhead sapsucker—large, about size of chicken.

redhead grass n
1 also *redhead pondweed:* A **pondweed** (here: *Potamogeton perfoliatus*).
1913 *Torreya* 13.226 **FL, NC,** *Potamogeton perfoliatus.* . . Redhead grass, Currituck Sound, N.C., St. Vincent I[slan]d, Fla. **1950** Gray-Fernald *Manual of Botany* 79, Red-head P[ondweed]. . . Calcareous or brackish waters.

2 A **ditch grass 2** (here: *Ruppia maritima*).
1920 *Torreya* 20.18 **VA**, *Ruppia maritima.* . . Redhead grass, Horn Point, Va.

redhead Louisa See **red-headed Louisa**

redhead peckerwood See **red-headed woodpecker**

redhead pondweed See **redhead grass 1**

redhead sapsucker See **red-headed woodpecker**

redhead scorpion See **red-headed scorpion**

redhead skink See **redhead 2**

redhead tanager See **redhead 1d**

redhead teal See **red-headed teal**

redhead widgeon n
1 See **red-headed widgeon.**
2 See **red-headed teal.**

redhead woodcock See **red-headed woodcock**

redhead woodpecker See **red-headed woodpecker**

redheart n
1 A **ceanothus** (here: *Ceanothus spinosus*) native to southwestern California. [See quot 1980]
1925 Jepson *Manual Plants CA* 620, C[eanothus] *spinosus.* . . *Red-heart.* . . Mountains near the south coast. **1959** Munz-Keck *CA Flora* 978, Red-heart. . . Large or arborescent, 2–6 m. tall, with smooth olive-green bark; . . fl[ower]s pale blue to almost white. **1980** Little *Audubon Guide N. Amer. Trees W. Region* 546, "Redheart"—*Ceanothus spinosus. Ibid* 547, It [=*C. spinosus*] is called "Redheart" because of the dark red wood, which makes good fuel.

2 also *red (ring) rot:* A stem decay in conifers caused by a fungus *(Fomes pini).*
1913 Bryant *Logging* 124, Punk knots which are an indication of red heart or rot often render a log practically worthless. **1938** Boyce *Forest Pathology* 417, Red ring rot, . . [or] red heart, . . is caused by the ring scale fungus . ., which is now commonly called *Fomes pini.* . . It is particularly severe on Douglas fir, larches, pines, and spruces. . . The incipient stage appears as a discoloration of the heartwood. *Ibid* 418, The incipient stage is often termed red heart. **1950** Moore *Candlemas Bay* 107 **ME,** The house was starting in to go right now, the way all the fine old houses went, as surely as if red rot had got into its solid beams and were eating it hourly down. **1968** *DARE* FW Addit **GA**51, Redheart—a rot or disease of yellow pines when old: it occurs at the top of the tree, and can be seen from the ground. The word probably refers to an effect seen in the timber when cut.

redheart hickory n Cf **red hickory, whiteheart ~**
Usu a **shagbark hickory** (here: *Carya ovata*); occas also **bitternut 1.**
1897 Sudworth *Arborescent Flora* 113 **MS,** *Hicoria ovata.* . . Redheart Hickory. **1940** Clute *Amer. Plant Names* 160, C[arya] *ovata.* . . Red-heart hickory. *Ibid* 254, *Carya cordiformis.* . . Red heart hickory. **1960** Vines *Trees SW* 130, *Carya ovata.* . . Vernacular names are . . Red Heart Hickory [etc]. . . This nut . . is the common hickory nut of commerce. **1979** Erichsen-Brown *Med. N. Amer. Plants* 70, *Carya ovata.* . . A tall, slender, straight tree. . . Red-heart hickory.

redheart pine n [From its distinctive red-orange heartwood] Cf **heart pine**
=**longleaf pine 1.**
1967–70 *DARE* (Qu. T17, . . *Kinds of pine trees;* not asked in early QRs) Inf **AL**17, Longleaf pine—redheart pine; **VA**70, Redheart pine—tall—a few branches at the top—when you cut the tree the wood in the center is red.

red-heater n Also *ready-heater* [Folk-etyms for *radiator*]
1896 *DN* 1.423 **cNY**, Red-heater: pop. etym. for *radiator.* **1939** Hench Coll. **cVA**, The Negroes in Charlottesville often say red-heater for radiator. **1943** in **1944** *ADD* (at *radiator*), Ready-heater. Reported.

red heather n
A **mountain heather 2** (here: either *Phyllodoce breweri* or *P. empetriformis*).
1915 (**1926**) Armstrong-Thornber *Western Wild Flowers* 352, Red Heather—*Phyllodoce Breweri.* . . A charming little shrub. . . This makes heathery patches on high mountain slopes. . . Red Heather—*Phyllodoce empetriformis.* . . Much like the last, but the nodding flowers are smaller and not quite so pretty. . . It forms beautiful patches of bright purplish-pink color on mountainsides. **1925** Jepson *Manual Plants CA* 742, P[hyllodoce] *breweri.* . . Red Heather. . . Alpine, 7000 to 12,000 ft. **1938** (**1958**) Sharples *AK Wild Flowers* 101, *P. empetriformis.* The Red Heather. The flowers are. . in clusters shaded from old rose to dark red. Interior [of Alaska]. **1953** Jewett *Birds WA* 212, The food of the ptarmigan is largely vegetable in nature, including the . . leaves and flowers of red . . heather *(Phyllodoce empetriformis).* **1972** Viereck-Little *AK Trees* 215, *Phyllodoce empetriformis.* . . Red heather. . . Low matted evergreen shrub . . with pink to red flowers.

red hickory n Cf **redheart hickory**
A **hickory B1,** as:
a A **pignut 1:** usu *Carya glabra* or *C. ovalis,* but also **bitternut 1.**
1709 (**1967**) Lawson *New Voyage* 105 **NC, SC,** There is another sort, which we call red Hiccory, the Heart thereof being very red, firm and

durable; of which Walking-Sticks, Mortars, Pestils, and several other fine Turnery-wares are made. **1813** Muhlenberg *Catalogus Plantarum* 88, Juglans . . glabra (porcina)—smooth hickory, red hic'ry, pignut. **1897** Sudworth *Arborescent Flora* 115 **DE**, *Hicoria glabra*. . . Red Hickory. **1950** Peattie *Nat. Hist. Trees* 141, *Red Hickory—Carya ovalis*. . . *Wood* very heavy, . . with light or dark brown heartwood and a thick paler sapwood. *Ibid* 142, Most people and certainly most lumbermen do not remark the Red Hickory in any way different from several of the other kinds of Hickory. **1953** Strausbaugh–Core *Flora WV* 290, *C[arya] cordiformis* . . *bitternut hickory. Red hickory*. . . Wood less valuable than that of other hickories. **1962** Harrar–Harrar *Guide S. Trees* 138, Red Hickory—*Carya ovalis*. *Ibid* 141, The red hickory has numerous varieties. . . Pearnut red hickory. . . is widely distributed through the Deep South. Carolina red hickory. . . is restricted to the mountains of North Carolina. Northern red hickory. . . also occurs widely through the South from North Carolina south through the Gulf states. **1969** *DARE* (Qu. T16, . . *Kinds of trees* . . *'special'*) Inf **KY**39, Red hickory. **1980** Little *Audubon Guide N. Amer. Trees E. Region* 348, Red Hickory (*[Carya glabra]* var. *odorata* [=*C. ovalis*]), a variety with nearly the same range, has the fruit husk splitting to base, usually 7 leaflets, and often shaggy bark.

b =**mockernut hickory.**

1897 Sudworth *Arborescent Flora* 114 **FL**, Mockernut (Hickory). . . Red Hickory. **1908** Britton *N. Amer. Trees* 230, *Mocker Nut*. . . is also known as . . Red hickory, . . Common hickory, and Bull nut. [*Ibid* 231, The wood is very hard, . . close-grained, and dark brown.] **1933** Small *Manual SE Flora* 406, *Carya tomentosa*. . . Mockernut. . . Red-hickory. **1950** Moore *Trees AR* 34, *Mockernut Hickory*. . . Local Names . . Red Hickory. **1960** Vines *Trees SW* 132, *Carya tomentosa*. . . Vernacular names are . . Red Hickory [etc].

red hind n

1 A **grouper 1a** (here: *Epinephelus guttatus*). Also called **calico hind, coney** n[2] **b**

1896 U.S. Natl. Museum *Bulletin* 47.1158, *Epinephelus maculosus* [= *E. guttatus*]. . . *Red Hind*. . . Spots on body vivid scarlet red. . . West Indies; Carolina to Brazil. **1946** LaMonte *N. Amer. Game Fishes* 56, *Red Hind*. . . North to the Florida Keys and occasionally as far as Charleston, South Carolina (summer). . . Small red dots all over the body. **1976** Tryckare et al. *Lore of Sportfishing* 97, *Red Hind*. . . An excellent table fish.

2 =**graysby.**

1896 U.S. Natl. Museum *Bulletin* 47.1141, *Petrometopon cruentatus*. . . Red Hind. [*Ibid* 1142, In the typical form . . , from rather deep water and among rocks, the ground hue in life is a livid reddish gray, . . and the spots are vermilion. . . Brazil to Florida Keys; a beautiful fish.] **1946** LaMonte *N. Amer. Game Fishes* 57, *Coney*. . . *Petrometopon cruentatus*. . . Red Hind, Graysby.

redhorse n

1 also *redhorse sucker*: A **sucker,** usu of the genus *Moxostoma*, but also of the genus *Scartomyzon*. **chiefly N Cent, Sth, S Midl, TX** See Map Also called **mullet** n[1] **3**; for other names of var spp see **Des Moines plunger, golden mullet, green ~, horsefish 2, jumping mullet 2, jump-rock, lake shad 2, muley carp, pond sucker, redfin 2, red mullet 2, ~ sucker 1, white mullet, white-nosed sucker, white ~**

1796 in 1916 Hawkins *Letters* 38 **SE**, This is the most valuable creek known here for. . . trout, perch, rock, red horse. **1819** Thomas *Travels W. Country* 212 **IN**, The *red horse* is also of the *sucker* kind. It is large and bony, weighing from five to fifteen pounds. **1849** Lanman *Letters Alleghany Mts.* 65 **NC**, On inquiring of a homespun angler what fish the river did produce, he replied: "Salmon, black trout, red horse, hog-fish, suckers and cat-fish." **1881** Tourgée *Royal Gentleman & Zouri* 488 **Sth**, I tole Mars Ben I was gwine to send over a piece ob red-hoss baked in der ash-heap for de missus. . . He knows what a good fish is like when Uncle Peter's cooked it. **1933** Williamson *Woods Colt* 222 **Ozarks**, One of 'em bent his gig a-jabbin' down agin the rocks, aimin' to git him a big redhorse with it. **1939** Hall Coll. **eTN**, The creek was full of fish . . bass, white suckers, silversides, red-horses, hog mollies. **1950** WELS **WI** (*Kinds of fish that are good to eat*) 1 Inf, Redhorse; (*Kinds of fish not commonly eaten*) 4 Infs, Redhorse; 1 Inf, Redhorse sucker. **1955** Johnson *50 Yrs.* 181 **nMN** (as of early 20th cent), With these long-handled spears, and a gunny sack for carrying the fish, we would set out along the jungle-like growth of the Mississippi River banks in early spring at the time of the Red Horse and Sucker spawnings. **1965–70** *DARE* (Qu. P1, . . *Kinds of freshwater fish* . . *caught around here* . .

good to eat) 23 Infs, **chiefly N Cent, S Midl**, Redhorse; **GA**84, 89, **MI**32, **VA**43, Redhorse sucker(s); (Qu. P3, *Freshwater fish that are not good to eat*) 20 Infs, **chiefly N Cent**, Redhorse; **SC**40, Redhorse sucker; (Qu. P7, *Small fish used as bait for bigger fish*) Infs **FL**32, **TX**72, Redhorse; **SC**32, Redhorses—used to seine for them; **TX**19, 74, Redhorse minnows [*DARE* Ed: attrib use of *redhorse*]; **PA**168, Redhorse sucker; (Qu. P14, . . *Commercial fishing* . . *what do the fishermen go out after?*) Infs **MO**38, **TN**22, Redhorse. **1966** *DARE* Tape **AR**36, [FW:] What kind of fish did you catch around here? [Inf:] All kinds, mostly. Caught cat . . and bass, croppie, redhorse. **1986** Pederson *LAGS Concordance,* 11 infs, **Gulf Region,** Redhorse(s); 1 inf, **ceGA**, Redhorse suckers.

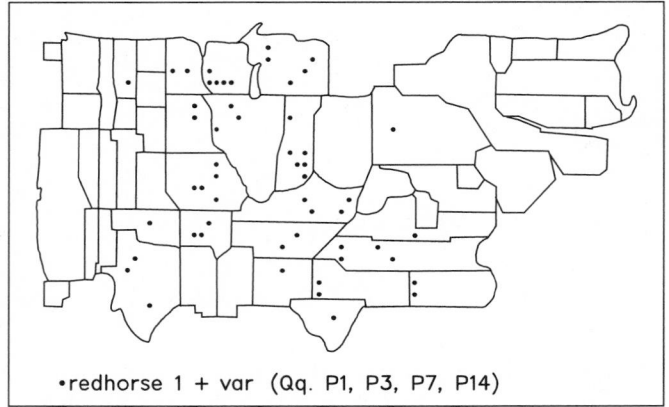

•redhorse 1 + var (Qq. P1, P3, P7, P14)

2 =**red drum.**

1882 U.S. Natl. Museum *Bulletin* 16.571, *S[ciaenops] ocellata* [sic]. . . Red Horse. **1911** U.S. Bur. Census *Fisheries 1908* 314, *Sciaenops ocellatus*. . . is called . . in Florida and the Gulf states, "redfish" and "red horse." **1966** *DARE* (Qu. P2, . . *Kinds of saltwater fish caught around here* . . *good to eat*) Inf **SC**9, Redhorse.

3 Corned beef. Cf **salt horse**

1864 in 1960 Jackson *Some Boys* 184, Supper . . is coffee & Red Hoss. **1900** *DN* 2.54 [College slang], *Red-horse*. . . Corned beef; also called horse. [Northwestern University, Evanston, Ill.] **1905** Bowe *With 13th MN* 24, Of bean-soup, hard-tack, and red-horse / . . we have had our fill. **1941** Smiley *Hash House Lingo* 46, *Red horse*—corned beef. **1956** Sorden-Ebert *Logger's Words* 27 **Gt Lakes**, *Red-horse*, Corned-beef.

4 See quot 1982.

[**1968** Thrush *Dict. of Mining* 904, *Red horse*. . . York[shire, England]. A red clay body in the Upper Magnesian Limestone.] **1982** *McDavid Coll.* **cwNY** (as of 1949), *Red horse*—hard pan subsoil (red clay). (From a cultivated speaker, 74 years old.)

redhorse bread n SC

=**hush puppy 1.**

1941 Writers' Program *Guide SC* 154 **neSC**, In the northeastern section of the State, fish fried in cornmeal and served with red horse bread (made of cornmeal and named for a variety of fish called red horse) finds especial favor. **1950** *PADS* 14.56 **SC**, *Red-horse bread:* . . Thick corn meal cakes fried in deep fat in which fish have been fried. Same as *hush puppies*. . . Probably named from the *red-horse* fish, with which it was cooked or eaten. **1962** Fox *Southern Fried* 140 **SC**, Coley lighted a fire in the wood stove and warmed up some red-horse bread. **1966–68** *DARE* (Qu. H14, *Bread that's made with cornmeal*) Inf **SC**19, Redhorse bread—put onions, pepper, cornmeal in balls, fry, eat with fish; (Qu. H25, . . *Fried cornmeal*) Inf **SC**19, Redhorse bread; **SC**43, Redhorse bread—pancake-sized, cooked at fish fries; **SC**51, Redhorse bread—about the same as hush puppies.

redhorse mosquito n Cf **horse mosquito**

A **mosquito** n[1] **B1** (here: *Psorosphora ciliata*).

1924 (1925) Stansbury *Lake of Gt. Dismal* 95 **VA**, The yellow fly raises a burning blister with every bite; and, helped by the "red-horse mosquito," gnats and gallinippers, can, it is said, kill a mule.

redhorse shiner n Cf **redfin 1**

A **shiner 1** (here: *Notropis lutrensis*).

1983 Becker *Fishes WI* 554, *Notropis lutrensis*. . . Redhorse shiner. . . In Wisconsin . . occurs only in the Mississippi River drainage basin.

redhorse sucker n

1 See **redhorse 1**.

2 A **sucker** (here: *Catostomus ardens*).

1963 Sigler–Miller *Fishes UT* 94, *Catostomus ardens* . . redhorse sucker. . . This species has been credited with considerable importance as food but it is little utilized where excellent food fishes such as trout are readily available.

red-hot n

1 also *red-hot ball*: A small, red, cinnamon-flavored candy. [Trade name *Red Hots*] Cf **hot ball 1**

1942 McAtee *Dial. Grant Co. IN* 52 (as of 1890s), *Redhots* . . small lentil-shaped candies, red in color, and cinnamon in flavor. 1949 *PADS* 11.10 wTX (as of 1911–29), *Red-hot*. . . A red-colored cinnamon candy. 1965–70 *DARE* (Qu. H82a, *Cheap candies sold especially for school-children*) Infs FL51, GA4, LA9, MN1, MO5, NY130, OK9, Red-hots; (Qu. H82b, *Kinds of cheap candy that used to be sold years ago*) Infs AR56, CA39, 87, CO11, IL23, LA40, Red-hots; RI3, Red-hot balls; (Qu. BB50a, . . *Remedies . . for a cough*) Inf KS10, Red-hots—little red cinnamon candies. 1968 Kellner *Aunt Serena* 175 cIN (as of c1920), I hastened to the candy case . . trying to decide between paper-wrapped kisses, cinnamon-flavored red-hots, licorice whips, . . and stick candy in assorted flavors. 1988 *Isthmus* (Madison WI) 26 Aug 23, She picked all her favorites of Red Hots, Jolly Rogers, Jaw Breakers, and M+Ms.

2 A bat-and-ball game for a small number of players; see quots. **LA**

1968 *DARE* (Qu. EE11, *Bat-and-ball games for just a few players*) Inf LA25, Red-hot—you just had two bases; hit the ball and run to the base, sometimes back home (rules varied a lot); LA32, Red-hot—the batter goes out and goes to the field, catcher bats, pitcher catches, etc. 1968 *DARE* Tape LA37, Play it with a softball, usually. . . It's also called red-hot, you know, we play it—first base, or red-hot, we call it. If you red-hot, you won't get out, you know, you'll be safe and never be put out.

red-hot ball See **red-hot 1**

red hot pepper See **hot pepper**

red-hot poker n

1 Std: a plant of the genus *Kniphofia*, esp *K. uvaria*.

2 A **summer cypress** (here: *Kochia scoparia*). **WI** Cf **Chicago fire, fireball 4, firebush 2**

1950 *WELS Suppl.,* 1 Inf, ceWI, There is also a rather long-stemmed blossom which is called "red-hot poker." On the bush "Chicago fire" or "firebush." 1975 Logan *Land Remembers* 165 swWI (as of c1920), We argued half the summer about whether the red flowers should be called Indian paintbrush, red-hot poker, fireball, or scarlet cup.

redick(i)lous See **ridiculous**

redicule See **ridicule**

red Indian paint See **Indian paint 1**

red Indians n

An **Indian paintbrush 1** (here: *Castilleja coccinea*).

1892 *Jrl. Amer. Folkl.* 5.101 MA, *Castilleia* [sic] *coccinea*. . . Red Indians.

red-ink plant n

=**pokeweed 1a**.

1866 Lindley–Moore *Treas. Botany* 885, Its dark-purple berries . . contain a purplish-red juice somewhat resembling red ink, and hence it is sometimes called the Red-ink Plant. 1893 Parsons *How Know Wild Flowers* 92, Pokeweed. Garget. . . The berries serve as food for the birds. . From their dark juice arose the name of "red-ink plant," which is common in some places. 1899 (1909) Earle *Child Life* 398, The country child could also dye a vivid red with the juice of the pokeberry, the "red-ink" plant, or with the stems of the bloodroot. 1935 (1943) Muenscher *Weeds* 218, *Phytolacca americana*. . . Red-ink plant. 1971 Krochmal *Appalachia Med. Plants* 190, Red-ink plant. . . produces spikes or racemes of dark purple berries.

red in the comb adj phr **chiefly S Midl** See Map

Eager to get married; occas, sexually excited; hence phr *one's comb is getting red* and varr: one is eager to get married.

1906 *DN* 3.153 nwAR, *Red in the comb*. . . Anxious to marry. "That old widower's getting red in the comb." 1929 *AmSp* 5.19 **Ozarks,**

When a mountaineer says of a woman that "her comb shore was red" he means that she was in a state of sexual excitement. 1941 Stuart *Men of Mts.* 293 eKY, W'y Lottie lost her man about two years ago. Her comb has been red ever since. 1960 Criswell *Resp. to PADS 20* **Ozarks,** *Red in the comb,* as well as *comb getting red,* used of young girls reaching the nubile period. 1965–70 *DARE* (Qu. AA4a, . . *A man who is very eager to get married*) 14 Infs, **chiefly S Midl,** Red in the comb; **AR18, KY44, OK27, TN1, VA11,** Comb (i)s (a-)getting red; **IL96,** Comb turning red; (Qu. AA4b, . . *A woman who is very eager to get married*) Infs **KY5, 44, 77, MO10,** Her comb's (a-)gettin(g) red; **AR3, GA57, WA30,** Her comb (i)s red; **CA99,** Her comb's getting awful red; **KY70,** Her comb's turning red; **TN57,** Red in the comb; [**KY44,** Her comb's sprouting out]. [26 of 28 total Infs comm type 4 or 5, 23 old, 17 male] 1983 *MJLF* 9.43 ceKY (as of 1956), *Her comb is getting red again . . :* When a widow or divorcee acts like she is again ready for male attention, "her comb is getting red again." This usage might stem from the fact that a hen's comb becomes pale when she is setting and after when she is raising her chicks. When she starts laying, her comb becomes red again.

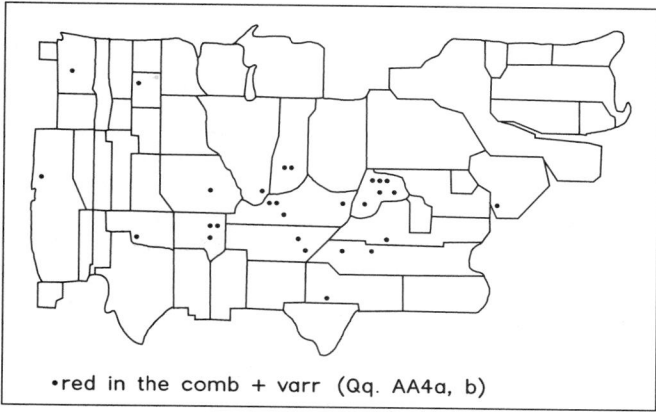

•red in the comb + varr (Qq. AA4a, b)

red ironwood n Cf **ironwood**

An evergreen tree (*Reynosia septentrionalis*) native to southern Florida.

1884 Sargent *Forests of N. Amer.* 39, *Red Iron Wood. Darling Plum*. . . Wood heavy, exceedingly hard, strong, close-grained . . ; color, rich dark brown, the sap-wood light brown. 1933 Small *Manual SE Flora* 831, *Red-ironwood*. . . The fruit is edible.—The dark-brown heartwood . . is used locally for cabinet-work.—The fruits are pleasantly flavored. 1971 Craighead *Trees S. FL* 200, Darling plum (red ironwood), *Reynosia septentrionalis*.

redish See **radish**

red jasmine n Also *red jessamine* Cf **jasmine 2c**

A **cypress vine 1** (here: *Ipomoea quamoclit*).

1830 Rafinesque *Med. Flora* 2.232, *Ipomoea quamoclit*. . . *Red Jessamine,* &c. From Florida to Mexico, beautiful vine. 1876 Hobbs *Bot. Hdbk.* 29, Cypress vine, Red jessamine, Ipomea [sic] quamoclit. *Ibid* 59, Jasmine, Red, Cypress vine, Ipomoea quamoclit. 1949 Moldenke *Amer. Wild Flowers* 266, The former [=*Ipomoea quamoclit*]—also called . . redjasmine—has its leaves dissected into many threadlike divisions arranged like the parallel teeth of a comb.

red jay n Cf **red blue jay**

=**cardinal 1**.

1968–69 *DARE* (Qu. Q16, . . *Kinds of jays*) Inf IN31, Red jay; IN62, Cardinal called a red jay.

red jessamine See **red jasmine**

red juniper n

A **juniper 1** (here: *Juniper virginiana*).

1897 Sudworth *Arborescent Flora* 92, *Juniperus virginiana*. . . Red Juniper. 1908 Britton *N. Amer. Trees* 118, It [=*Juniperus virginiana*] is variously known as . . Red juniper, . . and Juniper bush. . . The wood is soft, close-grained, weak, red with a whitish sapwood. 1931 Otis *MI Trees* 65, *Red Juniper*. . . Prefers loamy soil on sunny slopes; dry, rocky hills; also borders of lakes and streams and peaty swamps. 1979 Little *Checklist U.S. Trees* 157, *Juniperus virginiana*. . . Red juniper.

red kidney bean n **chiefly NEast** See Map Cf **navy bean, red ~, white kidney ~**

A reddish kidney-shaped bean (*Phaseolus vulgaris* cv).

1949 *Natl. Geogr. Mag.* Aug 159, "Common bean" . . *Phaseolus vulgaris*. . . includes our dry, field varieties, such as . . Red Kidney. **1965–70** *DARE* (Qu. I17, *Beans . . that are dark red when they are dry*) 26 Infs, **chiefly NEast,** Red kidney beans.

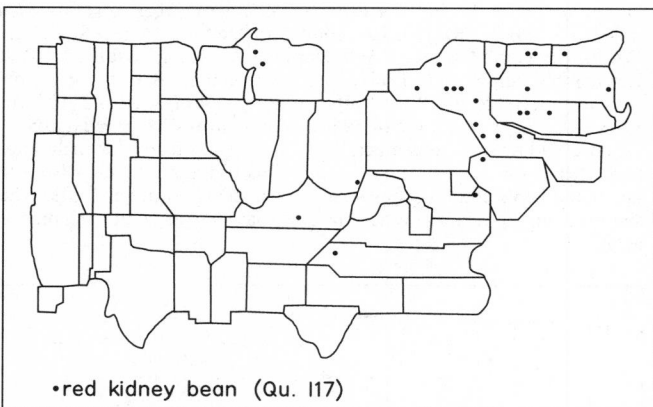

•red kidney bean (Qu. I17)

red lane n Also *red road* [Brit dial; cf *EDD red lane* (at *red* adj. 1.(25))]

The gullet.

1843 (1846) Haliburton *Attaché* (1st ser) 2.89 **NEng,** I was . . ridin' in my shirt-sleeves, and a thinkin' how slick a mint-julep would travel down red-lane, if I had it. **1848** Bartlett *Americanisms* 272, *Red lane.* A vulgar name for the throat, chiefly used by tipplers. **1899** (1912) Green *VA Folk-Speech* 349, *Red lane.* . . The throat; what one swallows is said to go down the *red lane.* **1904** *DN* 2.400 **cNY,** *Red-lane.* . . The alimentary canal. "Where's that candy gone?" "Down the red-lane." A boy's word. **1930** Shoemaker *1300 Words* 49 **cPA Mts** (as of c1900), *Red lane*—The throat. **1933** Hench Coll. **VA,** An often and jocularly used phrase for the gullet of a human is "red lane." . . "What happened to that apple pie?" . . "It went down the red lane." **1950** *PADS* 14.56 **SC,** *Red lane.* . . The throat. Children's usage. "Down the little red lane." **1954** *Harder Coll.* **nFL,** *Red lane.* . . The throat. Children's usage. . . Heard in N. Florida. **1968** *DARE* FW Addit **PA**142, Put too much of his money down the red lane = drank too much. **1969** *DARE* (Qu. X7, *Other names for the throat*) Inf **IL**37, Red lane—a children's term. [**1986** Pederson *LAGS Concordance,* 1 inf, **ceTN,** Red vein—for throat, usual term.] **1995** Brophy Coll. 62 **swMO** (as of c1960), *Red road.* [T]he throat, gullet, mouth. [D]own the red road = swallowed, eaten, devoured.

red lantern oil See **red oil**

red larch n Also *red American larch*

A **tamarack** (here: *Larix laricina*).

1785 Marshall *Arbustrum* 103, *Pinus-Larix rubra.* Red American Larch-Tree. [*Ibid* 104, The leaves are pretty long . . coming out in . . small bundles spreading like a painter's brush.] **1803** Lambert *Descr. Pinus.* 58, The cones of both [trees] are sent from America annually to Mr. Loddige, one under the name of black, and the other of the red Larch. **1832** MA Hist. Soc. *Coll.* 2d ser 9.153 **cwVT,** [Pinus] microcarpa, Red larch. **1897** Sudworth *Arborescent Flora* 32 **MI,** *Larix laricina.* . . Red Larch. **1908** Britton *N. Amer. Trees* 50, The American Larch, also called . . Red larch, . . grows mainly in swamps and on banks of lakes and streams. **1950** Peattie *Nat. Hist. Trees* 33, Red Larch. . . goes further north than any other tree in North America.

red lark n [*OED2* 1776 →]

A **pipit** (here: *Anthus spinoletta*).

1832 Nuttall *Manual Ornith.* 1.450, *Red Lark.* . . This is a winter bird of passage in most parts of the United States, arriving in loose, scattered flocks. **1883** Nuttall Ornith. Club *Bulletin* 8.78, In my long list of local American names for this species [=*Anthus spinoletta*] occur the following: *Titlark,* . . *Red Lark.* **1946** Hausman *Eastern Birds* 470, *American Pipit.* . . Other Names—American Titlark, . . Red Lark. . . Upper parts warm olive-brown.

red larkspur n Cf **lady's eardrop 4, larkspur**

A **delphinium** (here: *Delphinium nudicaule*) native to California and Oregon.

1902 U.S. Natl. Museum *Contrib. Herbarium* 7.347 **nwCA,** *Delphinium nudicaule.* . . The common red larkspur of the region. **1911** Jepson *Flora CA* 167, *Red Larkspur.* . . Banks of rivulets and rocky summits of the Coast Ranges. **1944** Abrams *Flora Pacific States* 2.182, Red Larkspur. . . Upper petals yellow, tipped with red. **1961** Peck *Manual OR* 340, *Red Larkspur.* . . Sepals scarlet, . . petals reddish-yellow. . . Southern Curry, Josephine and Jackson Co[untie]s [OR] to Calif.

red laurel n Cf **laurel 3**

A **rhododendron** (here: *Rhododendron catawbiense*).

1937 *Hall Coll.* **eTN,** We have red laurels and white laurels here in these mountains. **1944** *PADS* 2.35 **wNC,** *Red laurel* (when purple). . . Rhododendron. **1986** Pederson *LAGS Concordance,* 1 inf, **neTN,** Red laurel = rhododendron.

red leaf n Also *red* **S Midl** Cf **long red**

A grade of tobacco made up of leaves from near the top of the plant.

1941 Writers' Program *Guide MO* 493, The first man removes the "flyings" . . ; the next takes off the "trash" . . ; a third man removes the "lugs," still another takes off the "bright leaf"; then the "red leaf" at the top comes off. **1966** *PADS* 45.21 **cnKY,** *Red* . . = tips. . . "Red has been bringing better prices since the filter cigarette." *Ibid* 26, *Tips.* . . A grade made up of the top leaves on the plant. (Also *red, tail end*). . . "The tips are used for pipe and chewing tobacco." **1967** *Key Tobacco Vocab.* 135 **KY,** Burley: 1. flyings 2. lugs 3. white leaf 4. red leaf 5. tips. *Ibid* **TN,** Farmers say: 1. lugs 2. smokers 3. reds 4. tips. *Ibid* **MO,** 1. flyings 2. trash/lugs 3. red leaf; 1. flyings 2. trash/lugs 3. (bright) leaf 4. red: long red, short red; tips. **1968–69** *DARE* Tape **IN**45, Grade it as we go. Start pulling the leaves from the bottom . . for trash. And above that we have what we call lugs. These are the better grades. And then, the higher you go, the thicker the leaf becomes, and the redder. And that's what we call red leaf. And right in the top we might have short tips. Those are your cheaper grades; **KY**9, They used to, way back yonder, make five grades of it. But now they only make about three. And those grades—one next to the bottom, to the ground, is called a trash. And another one is called a lug. And they put the rest of it in what they call a red leaf; **KY**21, Three to four grades. . . I call them trash, lugs, red, and tips; **KY**56, [FW:] What are the old grades they used to use? . . [Inf:] The next was bright. And then, in the top, was red. And then, some called it short red or tips. That come off in the very top, tip of it; **OH**57, Well, a tobacco plant has different grades on it: the top is the tip, of course; and down next . . would be the bright leaf; then the next would be the lugs; then it would be the red leaf, then the flyings. **1969** *NC Folkl.* 17.34 **wNC,** Commonly used grades in the Cumberland Valley . . were dog-trash, trash, lugs, bright leaf, red leaf, and tips.

redleg n

1 See **red-legged black duck.**
2 See **red-legged partridge.**
3 See **red-legged turtle.**
4 as *Red Leg:* A member of a racially mixed group of people living in Orangeburg County, South Carolina. Cf **red bone 1**

1945 *Amer. Jrl. Sociol.* 51.34 **cSC,** People . . who do not fit into the biracial caste system. . . These outcastes, whom I call "mestizos," are designated by a wide variety of names, none of them flattering. . . In one section of Orangeburg County they are "Red Legs." **1963** Berry *Almost White* 95, I received several of those Red Leg families into the church while I was there. They have their own church at Black Creek, but they thought they were too good for that church, and that's why they wanted to join mine. **1966** *DARE* FW Addit **cSC,** *Red Legs*—interracial mixture of white and negro, belonging to neither society. From western part of Orangeburg County.

red-legged black duck n Also *redleg, red-legged duck* =**black duck 1.** Cf **October duck, red paddle**

1909 Field Museum Nat. Hist. *Zool. Ser.* 9.321, The Red-legged Black Duck is not uncommon in Illinois and Wisconsin during migrations. **1917** (1923) *Birds Amer.* 1.116, *Anas rubripes.* . . Red-legged Duck. Feet, orange-red with dusky webs. **1923** U.S. Dept. Ag. *Misc. Circular* 13.9 **DE,** Names locally applied to the subspecies of the black duck, the red-legged black duck (*Anas rubripes rubripes*) . . redleg; red-legged duck. **1943** Musgrove–Musgrove *Waterfowl IA* 19, *Anas rubripes rubripes* . . redleg. . . . The red-legged black duck is lighter-colored throughout the head [than the common black duck]. **1955** MA Audubon Soc. *Bulletin* 39.314 **MA,** *Black Duck.* . . Redleg. **1982** Elman *Hunter's Field Guide* 143, *(Anas rubripes)* Common & regional names . . *redleg.*

red-legged mallard n Also *redlegs*
=**mallard 1.**

1923 U.S. Dept. Ag. *Misc. Circular* 13.8 **MO,** *Mallard.* . . *Vernacular Names.* . . *In local use.* . . Red-legged mallard, redlegs (birds of the fall flight so known.) **1932** Bennett *Check-list* 18 **MO,** *Common mallard.* . . Red-legged mallard; . . redlegs. **1943** Musgrove–Musgrove *Waterfowl IA* 19, Sportsmen commonly believe that there are several species of mallards in our state, calling them the big northern mallards, . . cornfield mallards, and red-legged mallards. Actually they are all one species. **1982** Elman *Hunter's Field Guide* 150, *Mallard.* . . Common & regional names . . *redlegs.*

red-legged partridge n Also *redleg*
The chukar *(Alectoris chukar).*

1953 Jewett *Birds WA* 227, *Rock Partridge.* . . Other Names: Chukar Partridge; Red-legged Partridge. . . Bill and feet red. **1982** Elman *Hunter's Field Guide* 37, *Chukar Partridge.* . . Common & regional names: *red-legged partridge, redleg.*

red-legged plover n Also *redlegs*
=**ruddy turnstone.**

1888 Trumbull *Names of Birds* 186 **seMA,** Names applied to the species [=*Arenaria interpres*] . . in Massachusetts at New Bedford, *Redlegs,* and . . *red-legged plover* in . . eastern Massachusetts. **1918** Grinnell *Game Birds CA* 489, *Ruddy Turnstone.* . . *Other names* . . Red-legged Plover. **1925** (1928) Forbush *Birds MA* 1.478, *Red-legged Plover.* . . Legs and feet more orange than red. **1953** Jewett *Birds WA* 250, Red-legged Plover. . . More common on coast in spring. **1955** MA Audubon Soc. *Bulletin* 39.446, *Ruddy Turnstone.* . . Red-legged Plover (Mass., R.I.); Redlegs (Mass. The legs and feet are more orange than red.)

red-legged turtle n Also *redleg(s), red-legged terrapin, redleg turtle* esp PA, NJ
A **red-bellied turtle** (here: *Chrysemys picta).*

1937 Cahn *Turtles IL* 129, *Chrysemys picta.* . . Red-legged turtle. [*Ibid* 132, Two bright red stripes on the anterior surface of the fore limbs, and three on the under surface of the hind limbs. Tail with yellow or orange stripes. Other soft parts mottled with red and yellow.] **1967–69** *DARE* (Qu. P24, . . *Kinds of turtles*) Infs **PA**17, 35, 205, Redleg turtle(s); **NJ**1, **PA**28, Redleg(s); **PA**155, Red-legged terrapin; **NJ**3, Red-legged turtle. **1982** *Barrick Coll.* **csPA,** *Red-leg*—Eastern painted turtle. Chrysemys picta.

redlegs n
1 See **red-legged mallard.**
2 See **red-legged plover.**
3 See **red-legged turtle.**
4 =**wood turtle.**

1979 Behler–King *Audubon Field Guide Reptiles* 454, *Wood Turtle (Clemmys insculpta).* . . Skin of neck and forelegs often reddish orange. . . "Ole redlegs" is reputedly an intelligent turtle.

redleg turtle See **red-legged turtle**

red light n
1 also *red light, green light; one-two-three red light;* for addit varr see quots: A children's game with many variations, but in which typically all the players (except the one who is "it") may advance toward some goal until "it" says "red light," at which point anyone whom "it" detects still moving is penalized.

1945 Boyd *Hdbk. Games* 115, Red Light, or Cheese It. . . All face in the same direction and move forward while *It* counts any number up to ten and adds, "cheese it." . . Immediately after saying, "cheese it," *It* turns about and sends back to the starting line any players whom he sees moving even slightly. **1949** *Hoosier Folkl. Bulletin* 8.19 **IN, NY,** *Red Light*—Players run from the goal while the person who is "It" counts to ten. When "It" says "Red light," all the players must stop. Anyone caught moving is assessed a penalty of so many backward steps. If "It"

says "Green light," the players may advance until he says "Stop." The object is to reach the leader. **1950** *WELS* **WI** *(Hiding games that start with some special, elaborate way of sending the players out to hide)* 4 Infs, Red light; 1 Inf, Red light—"1, 2, 3, 4, 5, red light." Call this; they all run; one caught not stopping at the words "red light" is "it"; 2 Infs, Red light, green light; 1 Inf, Red light, green light—players can run to hide when "it" says "green light"; must stand still when "red light" is called; 1 Inf, Red, yellow, and green light. **1957** *Sat. Eve. Post Letters* **cwKY** (as of c1930), We played "red-light" and its variants "steal-steps" and "Chinese school." *Ibid* **sNJ** (as of c1930), Good fun it was, too, as were "red light" and "giant steps" all of which would be played by all comers on long spring and summer evenings. *Ibid* **seMI** (as of c1930), Red Light, Green Light (a variation of Hide and Seek). **1965–70** *DARE* (Qu. EE16, *Hiding games that start with a special, elaborate method of sending the players out to hide*) 110 Infs, **widespread,** Red light; **CA**82, Red light—not a hiding game; you drink milk until "red light" is called out; **IA**34, Red light—we used to call it "cut the cheese"; **NE**9, Red light [FW sugg]—we always called this run sheep run, and our children call it red light; **NY**234, Red light [FW sugg]—same as hide-and-seek; **PA**133, Red light; mother, may I—neither of these are actually hiding games; red light more like elaborate tag game. One who is "it" hides eyes, must count and then yell "red light" or "green light" and count again; no one can keep moving on "red light"; **IL**97, **IN**61, **NY**119, **OH**46, 90, **PA**163, Red light, green light; **IL**100, Red light, green light—no hiding; **IN**75, Red light, green light; mother, may I—neither are actually hiding games; **MI**72, Red light, green light is a hiding game, but I can't remember it; **PA**22, Green light, red light; **PA**74, Red light stop; (Qu. EE33, *Other outdoor games*) 24 Infs, **scattered, but esp Atl,** Red light [10 of these Infs described variations of the basic type described in the definition above.]; **FL**28, Red light—sneak up to base without being seen; **IL**26, Run sheep run—like red light; **NC**63, Red light or may I—where permission is granted to go a certain distance; you have to say "red light" or go back; **SC**5, Red light, I spy—hiding games; **VA**71, Red light—one child is "it"; the others stand before "it" and receive commands: "Take ten giant steps" or "two baby steps." . . "It" then covers his eyes . . and counts the number of steps he has asked a child to take. Then "it" turns around and shouts "red light." If kid is still moving, he's out; **CO**14, **GA**58, **IA**32, **NY**28, **WI**47, Red light, green light; **FL**30, Green light, red light; **AL**46, One-two-three red light; (Qu. EE2, *Games that have one extra player—when a signal is given, the players change places, and the extra one tries to get a place*) Infs **LA**34, **NC**63, Red light; **VA**50, 78A, Red light and green light; (Qu. EE3, *Games in which you hide an object and then look for it*) Inf **MD**2, Red light; (Qu. EE4, *Games in which one player's eyes are bandaged and he has to catch the others and guess who they are*) Inf **NY**130, Red light; (Qu. EE12, *Games in which one captain hides his team and the other team tries to find it*) Inf **MD**2, Red line; red light—older name? (Qu. EE13a, *Games in which every player hides except one, and that one must try to find the others*) Infs **NY**211, **WI**18, Red light. **1967–68** *DARE* Tape **IL**2, Well, of course everyone played hide-and-go-seek, and red light was quite a common game; **WI**18, [Inf:] When we played red light, there'd be one person blinding, who was "it." And . . he would count "one, two, . . ten, red light." And then he could open his eyes. If he'd say "green light," "yellow light," or any other light, you could keep on running to where your hiding place was. But the minute he said "red light," you had to stop. And then he could see which direction you were heading in, and would have some inclination of where you were going to hide. . . And of course if he opened his eyes [and] you thought he was going to say "green light" and he said "red light," then he'd catch you and you were out of the game or something. . . [FW:] And he could do this as many times until everyone was out of sight? [Inf:] Yes. . . Then you would just keep on going and hide where you want. . . Then he starts out . . to find you. Then the first one he finds is the next one to be "it." And he hollers "all-ee, all-ee oxen free." And everybody else comes back in. **1977–78** Foster *Lexical Variation* 77 **NJ,** *Red Light* or *1-2-3 Red Light* is the traditional name for a game in which the players can advance toward the leader while his back is turned. The leader signals his intention to face the other players with a call that usually is identical to the name of the game; anyone seen moving is sent back to the start line. *Ibid* 78, The name *Red Light Green Light* or *Red Light Green Light 1-2-3* is a recent innovation in New Jersey, although it may be older in New York City and Philadelphia. . . It was adopted rapidly in heavily suburbanized areas by middle-class children but diffused more slowly into distant suburbs and working-class or ethnic neighborhoods. *Ibid* 79, The sole *Red Light Yellow Light Green Light* response was given by a 20-year-old non-college black male from Passaic County. **1986** Pederson *LAGS Concordance* **Gulf Region** *(Line and running games;*

this question was asked chiefly in urban areas) 5 infs, Red light; 1 inf, Red light—all run until one says "stop"; 2 infs, Red light green light; 1 inf, Red light, one, two, three—line game, eyes shut; (*Hiding games;* this question was asked chiefly in urban areas) 1 inf, Red light—running and hiding; 1 inf, Red light green light; (*Ring games;* this question was asked chiefly in urban areas) 1 inf, Red light. **1994** Bolton *Gal* 60 **seSC** [Black], We used to play a game called Devil Devil Come and Get Me, and a game called Red Light Stop.

2 A traffic signal. **scattered, but chiefly Sth, S Midl, PA** See Map   Cf **stop-and-go light**

   1957 Battaglia *Resp. to PADS* 20 **eMD** (*The lights that direct traffic at busy crossings*) Red lights. **c1960** *Wilson Coll.* **csKY**, Red light: . . Traffic light of any color. Very modern. **1965–70** *DARE* (Qu. N9, *The colored lights that control the cars at busy road crossings*) 90 Infs, **scattered, but chiefly Sth, S Midl, PA**, Red light(s). **1967** *DARE* FW Addit **neTN**, *Red light* = traffic light, in giving directions: "Go to the second red light and take a left." (But when asked "What do you call that?" answer is "Traffic light.") Common among less educated speakers. **1998** *DARE* File **TN**, And *never never* say "traffic light" or "traffic signal" or even "green light." It's always "red light," preferably with the stress on *red.* **2000** *NADS Letters*, Redlight—In Alabama, no one calls it a traffic light. The pronunciation is spoken quickly and peculiarly accented, i.e., *Red*light. (

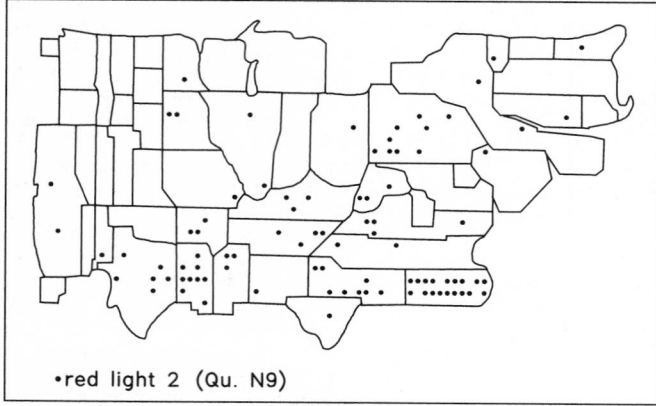

•red light 2 (Qu. N9)

red light, green light See **red light 1**

red lily n

A **lily 1** such as:

a also *(wild) orange-red lily, wild red ~:* A **wood lily** (here: *Lilium philadelphicum*).

   1672 Josselyn *New-Englands Rarities* 42, Red Lillies grow all over the Country innumerably, amongst the small Bushes. **1784** in 1785 Amer. Acad. Arts & Sci. *Memoirs* 1.434, *Red Lily.* Blossoms red, spotted with black. Common on borders of meadows. July. **1814** Bigelow *Florula Bostoniensis* 82, *Lilium Philadelphicum . . Common red lily. . .* is a less shewy, but equally beautiful species. **1872** Tice *Over Plains* 96 **CO**, I here found a splendid red lily, as large as a cup, (*Lillium Philadelphicum*). **1901** [see **b** below]. **1911** NJ State Museum *Annual Rept. for 1910* 345, *Lilium philadelphicum. . . Red Lily. . .* Frequent in open ground in the northern counties. **1936** IL Nat. Hist. Surv. *Wildflowers* 53, The bud of the Wild Orange-red Lily is greenish, but when the always erect flower opens, the perianth is shown to consist of 6 reddish orange parts with purple spots. . In western states a deep red variety [= *Lilium philadelphicum* var *andinum*] is more frequently found. **1967–70** *DARE* (Qu. S26d, *Wildflowers that grow in meadows;* not asked in early QRs) Inf **MA78**, Orange-red lilies; (Qu. S26e, *Other wildflowers not yet mentioned;* not asked in early QRs) Inf **MA5**, Wild red lily. **1979** Spellenberg *Audubon Guide N. Amer. Wildflowers W. Region* 585, *Red Lily. . .* Once much more common than now. It is too often picked by visitors.

b usu as *southern red lily:* A **lily 1** (here: *Lilium catesbaei*) native to Central Atlantic and southeastern regions of the US. Also called **leopard lily 2, pine ~ 2, tiger ~**

   1848 Gray *Manual of Botany* 494, *L[ilium] Catesbaei. . . Southern Red Lily. . .* Flower solitary, open-bell-shaped, . . *scarlet,* spotted with dark purple and yellow inside. **1901** Lounsberry *S. Wild Flowers* 51, *L[ilium] Philadelphicum,* wild red or wood lily, has the same peculiarity as the southern red lily of having its petals narrowed into long claws at

their bases, and which are spotted with purple. . . This is a lily, however, subject to many variations. **1950** Gray–Fernald *Manual of Botany* 435, *L. Catesbaei. . .* Southern Red L[ily]. . . Var. *Longii. . .* Long's Red L[ily]. **1964** Batson *Wild Flowers SC* 30, *Southern Red Lily. . .* Native to low pinelands and blooms in summer. North Carolina to Louisiana. **1979** Niering–Olmstead *Audubon Guide N. Amer. Wildflowers E. Region* 602, The Southern Red Lily . . has alternate, lanceolate leaves pressed against the stem.

c as *wild red lily:* The Canada **lily 1** (*Lilium canadense*).

   1940 Clute *Amer. Plant Names* 12, *L[ilium] Canadense.* Wild Red Lily.

red line n

1 Any of var active games for children.

   1888 *Amer. Anthropologist* 1.279 **DC**, *Games of chase. Tag, cross-tag, hand chase,* and *red line* are the most rudimentary. . . [T]he fourth is the running of the gauntlet, the one caught taking the place of him who has lain in wait. **1957** *Sat. Eve. Post Letters* **cwCA** (as of c1920), *Red line.* A line was drawn in the middle of the street . . ; the curb behind each team was called a goal. The object was to try to reach the goal of the opposing side and return without being caught. The zone behind each goal being a 'safety.' The side that kept the most trapped behind its goal and unable to return across the 'red-line' was the winner. **1968** *DARE* (Qu. EE12, *Games in which one captain hides his team and the other team tries to find it*) Inf **MD2**, Red line, red light (older name?)—same thing; **MD8**, Red line—very similar if not identical to cat and mouse; (Qu. EE33, *Other outdoor games*) Inf **IN30**, Red line; **WI24**, Steal the sticks or red line—two teams trying to get a stick from the other's pile without getting caught. **1968** *DARE* Tape **MD8**, We had a game that we called red line. One person would hide . . and you would be in teams . . and you would each have a different color, and you'd hide like within the area of a block, and you would call out your colors and then the person would try to guess where you were, and they'd have to bring you all in, but you'd try to run in free . . yourself.

2 See **red sign (crab).**

red linnet n Cf **linnet**

1 =**scarlet tanager.**

   1792 Belknap *Hist. NH* 3.173, Red Linnet, *Tanagra rubra.* **1956** MA Audubon Soc. *Bulletin* 40.253 **NH**, *Scarlet Tanager. . .* Red Linnet (N.H. "Linnet" is usually applied to birds of singing ability; this one is a fair songster.)

2 =**purple finch.**

   1899 Howe–Sturtevant *Birds RI* 69, *Carpodacus purpureus. . . Red Linnet.*—A common summer resident, and frequently seen during the winter months. **1929** Forbush *Birds MA* 3.10, *Red Linnet.* [*Ibid* 11, *Adult male:* Suffused largely with rosy-red, usually brightest on top of head and conspicuous on rump, throat and upper breast; a wide stripe of red over eye.] **1956** MA Audubon Soc. *Bulletin* 40.254, *Purple Finch. . .* Red Linnet (Mass., Conn., R.I. The fully-plumaged male has much pinkish red to crimson in its coloration.)

red lion n esp **NEast**

An elaborate version of a game of tag; see quots.

   1853 (1860) Taylor *January & June* 154 **Chicago IL**, Here [on the ice] a game of goal is going on, and here, a game of 'red lion'. **1891** *Jrl. Amer. Folkl.* 4.225 **Brooklyn NYC**, *Red Lion.* The players "count out" to see who shall be "Red Lion," who must retreat to his den. Then the others sing:—Red Lion, Red Lion,/ Come out of your den,/ Whoever you catch / Will be one of your men. Then the Red Lion catches whom he can, and takes him back to his den. The others repeat the call, and the two come out together and catch another player, and this is continued until all are caught. The first one caught is Red Lion for the next game. Another way: One boy is chosen "Red Lion" as before, and the others select one of their number as "chief," who gives certain orders. The chief first cries "Loose!" to the Red Lion, who then runs out and catches any boy he can. When he catches a boy, he must repeat "Red Lion" three times, and both he and the boy whom he has caught hurry back to the den to escape the blows which the other players shower upon them. The chief may then call out "Cow catcher," when the Red Lion and the boys he has caught run out of the den with their hands interlocked, and endeavor to catch one of the others by putting their arms over his head. . . The chief may call out these [*DARE* Ed: and other] commands in any order he likes after the first, and repeat them until all the boys are caught. **1906** Lovett *Old Boston Boys* 10, The games played by the boys of Chestnut and the adjacent streets are most pleasantly recalled; among which "I Spy," "The Red Lion," and "Punk" stand out prominently. **1911** Shute *Plupy* 201 **NH,** Evenins when we wuz playin' "Red Lion," 'n "Run Sheep Run," 'n "How Many Miles to Barbaree," 'n "Tit-Tat-two" on peoples winders with a brick. **1932** (1953) Smith *Games* 242, *Lion Hunt* (Red Lion). . . When the Lion thinks the moment is opportune he chases the Hunters. . . To capture a Hunter he must hold him long enough to call "Caught" three times. Then the Chief Lion and his prey, now called a "Little Lion," rush separately for the den to avoid a beating from the rest of the Hunters. . . The next time the Lions leave their den they must do so with joined hands. To capture a player they must encircle and hold him until they yell "Caught" three times. **1957** *Sat. Eve. Post Letters* **ceMA,** Red Lion.

red liquor n Also *red whiskey* [From its color, in contrast to the "white" (i.e., colorless) appearance of un-aged moonshine; cf **white lightning, ~ liquor, ~ mule, ~ whiskey**] **chiefly Sth, S Midl** Cf **redeye 5**
A distilled liquor, usu whiskey, with a reddish color that is legitimately achieved by aging, though sometimes achieved with additives; legally produced liquor.
1891 Maitland *Amer. Slang Dict.* 220, Red liquor (Am.), whisky. **1893** James *Cow-Boy Life in TX* 54, After tanking him up on red liquor they started him out to paint the town red. **1894** *Banner of Gold* 21 April 243/3 (*Mathews Coll.*), When I come out I found I didn't like red licker any more. **1903** *DN* 2.327 **seMO,** Red-liquor. . . Whiskey. [*Ibid* 336, *White-liquor.* . . The raw product of distillation. Moonshine whiskey.] **1907** *DN* 3.235 **nwAR,** Red-liquor. . . Whiskey. **1913** Kephart *Highlanders* 137 **sAppalachians,** A slick-faced dude from Knoxville . . told me once that all good red-liquor was aged, and that if I'd aged my blockade it would bring a fancy price. Well sir, I tried it; I kept some for three months—and, by godlings, *it ain't so.* **1914** *DN* 4.111 **cKS,** Red liquor. . . Applied to low grades of spirituous liquor. **1929** *AmSp* 4.385 **KS** [Wet words], The common *red liquor* or *barrel goods* is said to be produced by aging ordinary *hooch* in a charred keg, or more often by the addition of a little iodine, burnt sugar or other artificial coloring matter. **1929** Gordon *Born to Be* 107 **cwFL,** How'as the trip up north? Didja bring any red lick-ker back widjah? **1967** Fetterman *Stinking Creek* 152 **seKY,** Red whiskey costs $2 a half pint. **1977** *AmSp* 52.116, Terms for either taxed or untaxed liquor: . . Red (essentially, corn) whiskey: *buckeye . . , redeye . .* [applied to that of poor quality in **TN**], *red liquor . .* [applied to that of poor quality in **GA**]. **1985** Wilkinson *Moonshine* 18 **neNC,** Garland pursues violations concerning two kinds of liquor—white and red. Red liquor is a catch-all term for legal spirits. Usually it means whiskey. (The amber color of whiskey derives from the charred oak barrels in which it is aged.) . . White liquor is privately made whiskey, and occasionally brandy, on which no taxes have been . . paid. **1986** Pederson *LAGS Concordance,* 1 inf, **ceFL,** Red whiskey—commercial; 1 inf, **nwGA,** Red whiskey = inspected; 1 inf, **cwTN,** Pretty red whiskey—government-taxed whiskey. **1995** McCormack *Fields Pastures* 131 **cwAL** (as of 1960s), In the dim lantern light, I noticed the liquid in the labeled bottle appeared dark-colored, so I assumed it was "red" whiskey, so called because it had been legally made and store bought.

red locust n

1 also *red-flowering locust:* Usu a **black locust** (here: *Robinia pseudoacacia*), but also clammy **locust B1** (*R. viscosa*) or bristly **locust B1** (*R. hispida*).
1810 Michaux *Histoire des Arbres* 1.39, Robinia pseudoacacia . . *Red locust* (Acacia rouge) [etc]. . . Noms donnés à cet arbre sur les bords de la rivière Susquehannah, eu égard à la couleur de son bois. [=Robinia pseudoacacia . . *Red locust* [etc]. . . Names given to this tree on the banks of the Susquehanna river, referring to the color of the wood.] **1897** Sudworth *Arborescent Flora* 258 **TN,** Robinia pseudoacacia. . . Red Locust. *Ibid* 262 **AL,** Robinia viscosa. . . Red-flowering Locust. **1922** *Amer. Botanist* 28.28, R[obinia] viscosa is known occasionally as "red locust." **1950** Moore *Trees AR* 85, Robinia pseudoacacia. . . Red . . Locust. . . *Wood* . . brown or rarely light greenish brown with pale yellow sapwood. **1960** Vines *Trees SW* 566, Robinia pseudoacacia. . . Vernacular names are . . Red Locust, Red-flowering Locust. **1968** *DARE* (Qu. T16, . . *Kinds of trees . . 'special'*) Inf **LA15,** Red locust—has big, scary-looking thorns. **1969** *DARE* FW Addit **seKY,** Red locust—has red flowers—bristly locust.

2 A **rattlebox 1h** (here: *Sesbania punicea*). Cf **locust B2**
1953 Greene-Blomquist *Flowers South* 162, Red-locust, Purple-Sesban (Daubentonia punicea)—Drooping flower clusters of brilliant or-

ange-scarlet (rarely rose-purple) make this . . shrub a striking color note. . . Its resemblance to the locust gives one common name, but purple does not seem descriptive of its color.

red louse n
=**harvest mite.**
1864 OH State Bd. Ag. *Annual Rept. for 1863* 143, Late oats were injured by a red insect, called by farmers "red lice." **1889** *Century Dict.* 3526, *Louse.* . . Certain mites or acarids are sometimes called *lice,* as the harvest-ticks, known as *red-lice,* the itch-mite or itch-louse, etc.

red maids n
A plant (*Calandrinia ciliata*) of the far western and southwestern US. Also called **kisses 2, wild portulaca**
1901 Jepson *Flora CA* 185, C[alandrinia] caulescens . . var. *menziesii.* . . *Red Maids.* . . 2 or 3 to 18 in. high; . . petals . . crimson or rose-red. **1939** *Natl. Geogr. Mag.* Aug 232, *Purslane Family.* . . *Portulacaceae.* . . Their thick and juicy leaves are of value in salads. . . One, which has beautiful blossoms as well as edible herbage, is red maids of grassy meadows on the Pacific coast. . . The flowers remain open only a few hours, but during this period offer a glimpse of brilliant rose-purple, satiny petals. **1967** Gilkey-Dennis *Hdbk. NW Plants* 108, *Red maids.* . . Occasional in cultivated fields. **1979** Spellenberg *Audubon Guide N. Amer. Wildflowers W. Region* 680, *Red Maids (Calandrinia ciliata).* . . Small, *brilliant, bright reddish-pink, shallowly bowl-shaped flowers.* . . California to Washington; east to southwestern New Mexico.

red man n Cf **black man 1, redeye 6**
=**boogerman 1, 2.**
1966 *DARE* (Qu. EE41, *A hobgoblin that is used to threaten children and make them behave*) Inf **AL6,** Red man. **1973** Allen *LAUM* 1.385 (as of c1950), *Devil.* . . red man [1 inf, **MN**]. **1986** Pederson *LAGS Concordance* (Devil, boogerman) 1 inf, **cwAL,** Red man.

red-man v [See quot 1892]
To punish by mob action; fig, to treat unfairly.
[**1892** (1893) Cushing *Story of Post Office* 354 **WV,** There was . . an organization in West Virginia called 'Red Men,' who were banded together for certain purposes known only to themselves.] **1975** Gainer *Witches* 15 **sAppalachians,** *Red-man* (v.), to punish without legal process, by vigilante organization. "They red-manned Si Tenner because he was allus beatin' his wife." **2000** *NADS Letters* **eVA,** I heard an old man say that the government "red manned" his son when he was discharged from the Army. *Ibid* **NJ,** I have . . heard the term red-manned as you describe it, and if I am remembering correctly, was told it referred to the treatment, or more properly lack of just treatment, imposed upon the Native Americans.

red mangrove n
A **mangrove 1** (here: *Rhizophora mangle*).
1900 Lyons *Plant Names* 319, R[hizophora] mangle. . . Red Mangrove. **1908** Rogers *Tree Book* 401, Red Mangrove. . . Florida from Mosquito Inlet to Cedar Keys, rounding the southern end of the peninsula, and outlying islands. . . Wood for wharf piles and fuel. **1925** *Book of Rural Life* 3327, The *red mangrove* . . , which is probably the best known, sometimes reaches a height of seventy-five feet. **1967** Will *Dredgeman* 17 **FL,** Now we plunged into a dense forest of a most remarkable tree. Ed said it was the red mangrove. Far different from the sprangly and bush-like variety which grows on tidal flats along the sea, this mangrove, tall and straight as any pine, and with bark smooth and gray, reared upward thirty or forty feet, but balanced on buttressing, sprangly roots arching down from many feet above the ground. **1982** Perry-Hay *Field Guide Plants* 104, Red mangrove. . . The wood is very durable, is able to withstand water and is also used as a source of charcoal.

red maple n
An American **maple,** usu *Acer rubrum.* For other names of the latter see **burning maple, hard ~, mast ~, piss ~, plane tree 2, scarlet maple, soft ~, swamp ~, water ~, whistlewood, white maple, yellow ~**
[**1772** Kalm *Travels N. Amer.* (transl. Forster) 1.157, It was therefore easy to determine the genus to which such trees belonged. Such were the red maple, or *Acer rubrum,* and the *Laurus æstivalis,* a species of bay.] **1792** Belknap *Hist. NH* 3.112, Of the *Maple* we have three species. . . 2. The *Red (acer rubrum)* grows in swamps, and is fit only for fewel. **1883** Zeigler-Grosscup *Heart of Alleghanies* 307 **wNC, eTN,** My

brother . . was leaning partly out the front window there, where now glows the red maple. **a1887** (1919) Sturtevant *Edible Plants* 21, *A[cer] rubrum* . . Red Maple. Swamp Maple. . . In Maine, sugar is often made from the sap. **1913** *Auk* 30.485 **Okefenokee GA,** The red maple *(Acer rubrum)* is less common. **1947** Kieran *Footnotes on Nature* 174 **seNY,** I heard a Warbling Vireo in a Red Maple on the far side of the swamp. **1965–70** *DARE* (Qu. T14, . . *Kinds of maples*) 321 Infs, **widespread,** Red maple; **NC30,** Hard red maple; (Qu. T16, . . *Kinds of trees . . 'special'*) 12 Infs, **esp Nth, Cent,** Red maple; (Qu. T3, *The tree that produces syrup and sugar*) Infs **MD22, MA25,** Red maple; (Qu. T13) **NC49,** Red maple; (Qu. T15, . . *Kinds of swamp trees*) Infs **NY142, PA89, 99, SC3, 43, VA47,** Red maple. **1986** Pederson *LAGS Concordance* **Gulf Region,** 6 infs, Red maple(s); 1 inf, Red maple tree.

red marlin n Cf **marlin** n[1] **1a**
=**marbled godwit.**

1876 *Forest & Stream* 7.149 **NY,** About of the same size [as the jack curlew] is the red marlin, which has a reddish brown color and a long, straight bill. *Ibid* 11.193 **NJ,** Last Saturday morning we came to anchor off Barnegat Light. . . The birds flew thick for about three hours, red marlins, ring-tail marlins and beach snipe. **1888** Trumbull *Names of Birds* 206 **Long Is. NY,** *Marbled Godwit.* . . At Shinnecock Bay, L[ong] I[sland], *red marlin.* **1944** Hausman *Amer. Birds* 519, Marlin, Red— see Godwit, Marbled.

red mavis n [*OED2 mavis* a1366 → for the European song thrush *(Turdus musicus)*]
1 =**brown thrasher.** Cf **red mockingbird**

1854 (1969) Thoreau *Walden* 171 **eMA,** Near at hand, upon the topmost spray of a birch, sings the brown-thrasher—or red mavis, as some love to call him—all the morning. **1877** *Forest & Stream* 8.145, The brown thrush—also called . . red mavis . . —inhabits the Eastern United States. **1956** MA Audubon Soc. *Bulletin* 40.128 **MA,** *Brown Thrasher.* . . Red Mavis (Mass. Plumage above reddish brown to cinnamon-rufous . .).

2 A **wood thrush** (here: *Hylocichla mustelina*).

1956 MA Audubon Soc. *Bulletin* 40.128 **MA,** *Wood Thrush.* . . Red Mavis (Mass. The general color above is tawny to cinnamon brown . .).

red milkweed n
A **milkweed 1:** usu *Asclepias rubra*, but also *A. lanceolata*.

1946 Tatnall *Flora DE* 210, *A[sclepias] rubra.* . . Red Milkweed. Infrequent, in all three counties of Delaware. **1972** Brown *Wildflowers LA* 143, *Red Milkweed—Asclepias lanceolata.* . . Corolla reflexed, dull red. . . Fresh to brackish marshes, wet sites in pinelands. . . *Red Milkweed—Asclepias rubra.* . . Corolla reflexed, red with tinges of yellow-orange. . . Bogs, marshes, and wet pineland sites. **1979** Ajilvsgi *Wild Flowers* 234, *Red milkweed* . . *Asclepias rubra.* . . *Flower:* pale pink to dull red or lavender. . . May-August.

red milkweed beetle n Cf **milkweed beetle**
A beetle of the genus *Tetraopes*, usu *T. tetraophthalmus*.

1895 Comstock-Comstock *Manual Insects* 574, The Red Milkweed-beetles, *Tetraopes.* . . are several species of bright-red beetles that are common on milkweeds *(Asclepias).* Our most common species . . is *T. tetraophthalmus.* . . The larva bores in the roots and the lower parts of the stems of milkweed. **1954** Borror-DeLong *Intro. Insects* 398, The species of *Tetraopes* . . are red with black spots. . . *T. tetraophthalmus* is a common species feeding on milkweed, and is often called the red milkweed beetle. **1989** Entomol. Soc. Amer. *Common Names Insects* 121, *Tetraopes tetraophthalmus*—red milkweed beetle.

red minnow n Cf **minnow B1**
Any of var cyprinids, such as a **shiner 1** of the genus *Lythrurus* or *Notropis.*

1820 Rafinesque *Ohio R. Fishes* 52, *Red Minny. Rutilus? ruber.* . . It is a slender fish, only two inches long, compressed and of a fine purple red. It may belong to this genus, or to any other of this tribe. It is commonly called Red Minny. **1877** NY Acad. Sci. *Annals Lyceum Nat. Hist.* 10.375 **GA,** We heard several peculiar vernacular names for fishes on the Rock Castle and Cumberland [rivers], some of which may be worth recording . . Red Minnow. Lythrurus ardens [etc]. **1882** U.S. Natl. Museum *Bulletin* 16.153, *Chrosomus* [=*Phoxinus*]. . . *Red Minnows.* . . Size small. Colors in spring brilliant. **1955** Carr–Goin *Guide Reptiles* 59 **FL,** *Notropis maculatus* . . Red Minnow. . . A graceful, often reddish, little minnow with a spot on the base of the tail. **1965** *DARE* (Qu. P7, *Small fish used as bait for bigger fish*) Inf **MS58,** Red and plain minnows.

red mockingbird n Cf **mockingbird 2, red mavis 1**
=**brown thrasher.**

1688 in 1693 Royal Soc. London *Philos. Trans.* 17.995 **VA,** The Red Mocking . . sings very well, but has not so soft a Note as the gray Mocking Bird. **1916** *Times–Picayune* (New Orleans LA) 30 Apr 1, *Brown Thrasher* . . Red Mockingbird.

red molly n Cf **green molly, molly** n[1] **8**
A **summer cypress** (here: *Kochia americana*).

1941 Jaeger *Wildflowers* 48 **Desert SW,** Red Molly. Kochia americana. . . Red molly is a perennial herb with many erect branches . . arising from a woody crown.

red moonseed See **moonseed 2**

red morning-glory n
A **cypress vine 1** (here: *Ipomoea coccinea*).

1900 Lyons *Plant Names* 313, *Q[uamoclit] coccinea* . . Small Red Morning-glory. **1903** Small *Flora SE U.S.* 961, On banks and in thickets. . . *Red Morning-glory.* **1940** Gates *Flora KS* 177, Red Morning-glory. Thickets. East half [of Kansas]. **1975** Duncan-Foote *Wildflowers SE* 138, *Red Morning-glory.* . . Fla into Ariz, cw Ill, s Mich, s Pa, and se Mass. May-Oct.

red moss n
A **saxifrage** n[2] (here: *Saxifraga oppositifolia*).

1938 (1958) Sharples *AK Wild Flowers* 132, *S[axifraga] oppositifolia.* "Red Moss." . . Flowers showy, bright magenta, borne singly on very short stems. Southwestern and Southeastern Alaska.

redmouth n
1 also *red-mouth(ed) grunt:* Any of var **grunts 1,** usu of the genus *Haemulon*, esp *H. aurolineatum.* [See quot 1884] For other names of *H. aurolineatum* see **flannelmouth 1, margate fish b, tomtate**

1842 DeKay *Zool. NY* 4.84, The Speckled Redmouth. *Hemulon fulvomaculatum* [=*Orthopristis chrysoptera*]. *Ibid* 85, The Yellow-finned *Redmouth. Hemulon chrysopteron* [=*Haemulon aurolineatum*]. . . Base of the lower jaw within and without of a beautiful vermilion. Tongue and fauces bright red. **1879** U.S. Natl. Museum *Bulletin* 14.47, *Hæmylum arcuatum* [=*H. aurolineatum*]. . . Blue-cheeked Redmouth. . . *Hæmylum elegans* [=*H. sciurus*]. . . Blue-striped Red-mouth. . . *Hæmylum arara* [=*H. plumieri*]. . . Arara Redmouth. **1882** U.S. Natl. Museum *Proc.* 5.276 **FL,** *Red-mouth Grunt.* *Hæmulon arcuatum.* . . A single large specimen obtained at Pensacola. *Ibid* 602 **eNC,** *Red-mouthed Grunt.* . . *Hæmulon aurolineatum.* . . Mouth, within, bright brick-red, becoming yellowish red on lining of opercles. **1884** Goode *Fisheries U.S.* 1.397, The Grunts or Pigfishes. . . They, without exception, are distinguished by the brilliant red color of the inside of the mouth and throat, from which they have sometimes been called Red Mouths, or Flannel Mouths. *Ibid* 398, The Redmouth Grunt, *Diabasis aurolineatus*, is . . familiar to Florida fishermen, and often taken on the Saint John's Bar. It has also been recently found to be common in Charleston on the Saint John's Bar. **1905** NJ State Museum *Annual Rept. for 1904* 319, *Orthopristis chrysopterus.* . . Speckled Red Mouth. **1935** Caine *Game Fish* 81 **Sth,** *Haemulon flavolineatum.* . . Red-mouth Grunt. *Ibid* 83, *Haemulon macrostomum.* . . Redmouth. **1991** Amer. Fisheries Soc. *Common Names Fishes* 139, Grunt, red-mouth—see tomtate.

2 See **red-mouthed buffalo.**

redmouth adj See **red-mouthed**

redmouth buffalo(fish) See **red-mouthed buffalo**

red-mouthed adj Also *redmouth* [Prob implying "having the mouth wide open," hence "ranting, verbose"]
Used as a derog epithet for a politician or lawyer.

1851 Hooper *Widow Rugby's Husband* 23 **AL,** The red-mouthed nullifiers swore that you was feedin' us *soup-tails* on bull-beef. **1967– 68** *DARE* (Qu. HH44, *Joking or uncomplimentary names for lawyers*) Inf **IN42,** Red-mouthed lawyer; **PA35,** Redmouth lawyer.

red-mouthed buffalo n Also *redmouth (buffalo),* ~ *buffalofish*
=**bigmouth buffalo.**

1878 U.S. Natl. Museum *Bulletin* 12.214, *Ictiobus bubalus* . . Agassiz [=*I. cyprinellus*]. . . Red-mouth Buffalo Fish. *Ibid* 216, The young . . are sold in the Illinois markets under the name of Red-mouth Buffalo, the adult being called simply Buffalo. **1902** Jordan–Evermann *Amer. Fishes* 40, This species [=*Ictiobus cyprinellus*] is also known as the red-mouthed buffalo, and big-mouthed buffalo. **1908** Forbes–Richardson *Fishes of IL* 67, In the red-mouth buffalo . . the . . teeth have a smaller grinding surface. *Ibid* 71, The mongrel buffalo appears. . . distributed throughout the Mississippi Valley practically as the red-mouth is, but less abundantly. **1933** LA Dept. of Conserv. *Fishes* 441, Like the other two species of Buffalo, the Redmouth has a mouth well suited for collecting food from the soft mud of river bottoms. **1943** Eddy–Surber *N. Fishes* 100, Redmouth Buffalofish. . . The head is large, with a blunt and broadly rounded snout. **1983** Becker *Fishes WI* 615, Bigmouth Buffalo. . . Other common names: redmouth buffalo [etc]. **1991** Amer. Fisheries Soc. *Common Names Fishes* 120, Buffalo, redmouth—see bigmouth buffalo.

red-mouth(ed) grunt See **redmouth** n 1

red mullet n Cf **mullet** n[1]

1 A **goatfish** 1 (here: *Mullus auratus*).

   1902 Jordan–Evermann *Amer. Fishes* 268, The single species of this genus in our waters is the red mullet . . (*M[ullus] auratus*) which is found on our Atlantic coast from Cape Cod to Pensacola. **1905** NJ State Museum *Annual Rept. for 1904* 327, *Mullus auratus*. . . Goat Fish. Red Mullet. . . Along the side an irregular dull and rather dark red band. . . Above and below this several blotches of a similar red color. **1933** John G. Shedd Aquarium *Guide* 113, *Mullus auratus*. . . The Red Mullet is occasionally taken in quantities along the Atlantic coast from Cape Cod southward but is not always plentiful.

2 A **redhorse** 1 (here: *Moxostoma macrolepidotum*).

   1935 Pratt *Manual Vertebrate Animals* 59, *M[oxostoma] macrolepidotum*. . . Red mullet. . . Color silvery, lower fins orange-red. **1938** Schrenkeisen *Field Book Fishes* 93, In coastal streams of Delaware Bay to North Carolina . . is . . the Eastern Redhorse, also called Red Mullet.

red'n comb See **redding comb**

red-neck n

1 See quot. Note: The relation of this sense to the later ones is not clear; it is possible that it represents merely a special application of sense **2** below.

   1830 Royall *Mrs. Royall's S. Tour* 1.148 **csNC,** It must astonish every one, after what I have said . . that I received but one dollar in Fayetteville! This may be ascribed to the *Red Necks,* a name bestowed upon the Presbyterians in Fayetteville. How many names these people have, matters not, they still gather money; you cannot shame them!

2 A poor, White, rural Southerner—used with a very wide range of connotations, but now esp applied as a derog term for a White person perceived as ignorant, narrow-minded, boorish, or racist; hence adjs *red-neck(ed)*, *red-necky* belonging to or typical of such people. **chiefly Sth, S Midl, esp Gulf States** See Map Cf **poor White**

   1891 in 2001 *AmSp* 76.435 **MS,** Primary on the 25th. And the "rednecks" will be there. And the "Yaller-heels" will be there also. And the "hayseeds" and "gray dillers," they'll be there, too. **1893** Shands *MS Speech* 53, Red-neck. . . A name applied by the better class of people to the poorer inhabitants of the rural districts. The word explains itself: men who work in the field, as a matter of course, generally have their skin burned red by the sun, and especially is this true of the back of their necks. **1904** *DN* 2.420 **nwAR,** Redneck. . . An uncouth countryman. "The hill-billies come from the hills, and the rednecks from the swamps." The expression "rednecked hillbilly" also occurs. **1913** Davis *Life Speeches* 42 **AR,** If you red-necks or hill-billies ever come to Little Rock be sure and come to see me—come to my house. **1924** *World's Work* 48.83 **Sth** [Black], And if he does get them how can he be sure but that some night some poor cracker will get his gang together and come around to drive him out without any particular reason other than that the red-necks think he is getting along too well? **1938** Daniels *Southerner* 183 **swMS,** As we rode over the exquisitely tended earth I was interested in uncovering the opinion that a good unit manager must have in him the stout, earthy qualities of the redneck, but such a redneck is by no means to be confused with po' whites. . . Poor white men in the South are by no means all po' white even in the hills. **1941** Percy *Lanterns* 20 **MS,** The poor whites—"hill-billies," "red-necks," "peckerwoods," they are often derisively called—did not remain outside the Delta. **1942** *Amer. Mercury* 55.223.96 **Harlem NYC** [Black], *Red neck*—poor Southern white man. **1942** Faulkner *Go Down* 43 **MS,** To Lucas the sheriff was a redneck without any reason for pride in his for-

bears nor hope for it in his descendants. **1948** *Life* 13 Sept 52 **LA,** Russell's mannerisms were so much like those of his father, the late Senator Huey ("Kingfish") Long, that many a Redneck thought he was seeing a ghost. **1960** *Washington Post* (DC) 30 Apr sec A 6 **LA,** While an audience of New Orleans' proudest citizens looked on in embarrassed suspense, "Uncle Earl" [=Earl K. Long] cavorted in typical "red-necked" style at a fashionable luncheon honoring de Gaulle. **1964** *PADS* 42.31 **Chicago IL,** The most characteristic feature of Negro terms for Caucasian is the tendency to expand particularized designations for Caucasians to include all members of the race, e.g., terms for poor Southerners: *peckerwood*, . . and *redneck*. **1965–70** DARE (Qu. HH1, *Names and nicknames for a rustic or countrified person*) 16 Infs, **chiefly Sth, S Midl, esp MS,** Red-neck; **FL52,** Red-neck—ref to White cops; **LA2,** Red-neck—people up around Ruston are red-necks; **MS88,** Red-neck—referring to country Whites; **TN30,** Red-neck, cracker—these names are applied to people from Georgia, Alabama, Mississippi, West Tennessee, etc; **TN66,** Red-neck—political term; (Qu. HH18, *Very insignificant or low-grade people*) Inf **MO29,** Red-necks; **PA236,** Red-necks—if White; **TX72,** Red-necks—[used for] Arkies and Okies. **1975** *AmSp* 50.64 **AR** (as of c1970), *Redneck*. . . Person regarded as socially unacceptable because of unsophisticated manners—"That redneck jumped up and down like an idiot." **1986** Pederson *LAGS Concordance (Rustic)* 88 infs, **Gulf Region, esp MS, seLA, AL, FL, cTN,** Red-neck(s); 1 inf, **cnGA,** Red-neck—following local politician; 1 inf, **cwGA,** Red-neck—used more in recent years; 1 inf, **swGA,** Red-neck—narrow-minded, bigoted and poor, white; 1 inf, **seFL** [Black], Red-neck—general pejorative for non-black; 1 inf, **swTN** [Black], Red-neck—racial prejudice, not necessarily rural; 1 inf, **neMS,** The red-necks—from the hills, = hillbillies; 1 inf, **ceMS,** Red-neck—could be friendly or derogatory; 1 inf, **nwMS,** Red-neck = country man, pejorative; 1 inf, **seMS,** Red-necks—in Louisiana, not derogatory; 1 inf, **cMS,** Red-necks—refers to farmers, not an insult; 1 inf, **seLA,** Bayou red-necks—of Cajuns; 1 inf, **ceAR,** Red-neck—is Arkansas Hoosier, playfully bad; 1 inf, **nwLA,** Red-neck—of attitude; belligerent, loud; 1 inf, **nwAR,** Real red-neck; (*Poor whites—white man's terms*) 52 infs, **Gulf Region,** Red-neck(s); 1 inf, **neTN,** Red-necks—newer word; 1 inf, **cwGA,** Red-necks = South Georgians; 1 inf, **ceGA,** In Georgia we call them red-necks; 1 inf, **swGA,** Red-neck—Alabamian; 1 inf, **csGA,** Red-neck—pejorative, used by non-southerners; 1 inf, **swTN,** Red-neck—a Mississippi term; 1 inf, **cnMS,** Red-neck—if black uses is considered cursing; 1 inf, **cwMS** [Black], Red-neck—used by white men, not an unsult; 1 inf, **csLA,** Red-neck = Mississippian; 1 inf, **cAR,** Red-neck—used for policemen; rough; 1 inf, **cAR** [Black], Red-necks—used by whites to other whites; 1 inf, **cwMS,** Mississippi red-neck = Georgia cracker; 1 inf, **cnMS** [Black], Old red-neck—more recently; (*Poor whites—black man's terms*) 46 infs, **Gulf Region,** Red-neck(s); 1 inf, **cnGA,** Red-necks—in the papers; 1 inf, **seGA** [Black], Red-necks—also white usage; 1 inf, **cnFL,** Red-neck—Georgia term; 1 inf, **ceAL** [Black], Red-neck—Southern white, now used; 1 inf, **swTN,** Red-neck—a Mississippian; 1 inf, **cwTN,** Red-neck—"a square"; dresses neatly, children use; 1 inf, **swMS,** Red-neck—Mississippian called by others; 1 inf, **cLA,** Red-neck—Mississippi; 1 inf, **seFL** [Black], Red-neck cracker; 1 inf, **cwFL** [Black], Purely red-neck—students in rural school; (*Caucasian—neutral, jocular, and derogatory terms*) 38 infs, **Gulf Region,** Red-neck(s); 1 inf, **swGA,** Red-necks—come out of the piney woods, uneducated; 1 inf, **neAL** [Black], Red-neck, esp illiterate, prejudiced white; 1 inf, **cTN,** Red-necks—don't work or bathe, really "country"; 1 inf, **cMS,** Red-necks—blacks' term, derogatory, slang, in jest; 1 inf, **seMS,** Red-neck—what people in MS

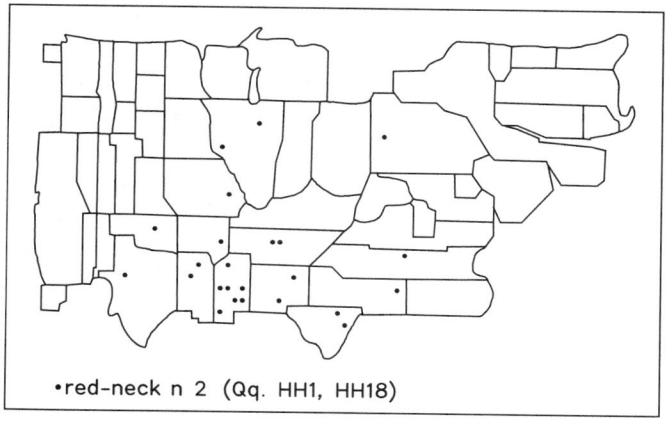

•red-neck n 2 (Qq. HH1, HH18)

call person in LA; 1 inf, **ceLA,** Red-neck—man from MS; 1 inf, **ceAR,** Red-neck—someone from Alabama; 1 inf, **neLA,** Red-necks—they call Mississippians; 1 inf, **seFL** [Black], Red-neck cracker; 1 inf, **cnGA** [Black], Georgia red-neck; 1 inf, **cnGA** [Black], Sandhill red-neck—not specifically poor; 1 inf, **swAL** [Black], Red-neck white people—prejudiced, use racial terms; 1 inf, **seFL** [Black], You nasty-ass red-neck. **1989** *Encycl. S. Culture* 1140, In modern usage the term *redneck,* which did not come into common usage until the 1930s, is usually a negative expression describing a benighted white southerner. **1998** *DARE* File **OK,** Another white male from Purcell, Oklahoma, also born in 1958 . . uses *rednecky* meaning "rustic, countrified."

3 Anger, hostility; hence adjs *red-neck(ed)* angry, hostile, ill-tempered; v *red-neck* to become angry.

1911 *Sharon Springs Times* 12 Jan 3/4 (1916 *DN* 4.328) **wKS,** It is disagreeable to have men before the county board, displaying their temper and red neck. **1914** *DN* 4.111 **cKS,** Red neck, *n. phr.* Ill temper; anger. **1942** Berrey–Van den Bark *Amer. Slang* 284.6, *Ill-tempered. . .* red-necked. *Ibid* 284.8, *Angry. . .* red-necked. **1960** Wentworth–Flexner *Slang* 424, *Red-necked. . . Angry. Rural use.* **1998** *DARE* File **OK,** There is the use of the word *redneck* to mean "easily offended", "bad tempered." A white male from Purcell, Oklahoma . . born in 1958, mentions "a redneck colored person," meaning a black man he knew who frequently got into fights. Another white male from Purcell, Oklahoma, also born in 1958 . . , said "Next time he *rednecks on* me." He was referring to someone (white) who had threatened to attack him. *Ibid* **NM,** An Anglo man born in 1949 who grew up on a ranch near Tularosa in eastern New Mexico uses the expression *to get redneck*—meaning to become hostile; to act as if ready to attack.

4 A Roman Catholic; an Irish person. [*EDD* (at *red* adj. 1.(31))] **chiefly N Midl, West** See Map

1929 Ellis *Ordinary Woman* 202 **CO** (as of early 20th cent), But soon George starts to complain that it was run by a bunch of 'red necks,' 'chaws,' 'flannel mouths,' 'Micks'—all names for Irishmen. **1965–70** *DARE* (Qu. CC4, . . *Nicknames . . for various religions or religious groups*) 10 Infs, **OH, West,** Red-necks—Catholics; **NM5,** Red-necks—Catholic, perh because many Irish have red necks and are Catholics; **OH27,** Red-necks; **OR1,** Catholics are red-necks or Micks; (Qu. HH28, *Names and nicknames . . for people of foreign background*) Inf **PA247,** Red-neck—Irish; [**NY239,** Red-noses—Irish]. [12 of 14 Infs hs or coll educ, 10 female] **c1971** Hall *Snake River Valley* (Terms for Catholics) 1 inf, **csID,** Red-necks.

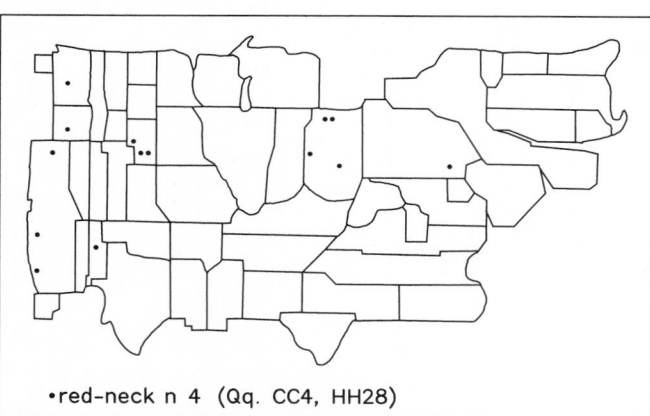

•red-neck n 4 (Qq. CC4, HH28)

5 A Communist, revolutionary; a union sympathizer—orig applied abusively to, and then adopted by, members and supporters of the National Miners' Union. **Appalachians**

1931 in 1970 Natl. Comm. Defense Political Prisoners *Harlan Miners* 108 **KY,** They asked me what I was doing with those high powered rifles, but I never had any, and the I.W.W. literature. They called me a red neck. . . Is that a communist? . . Yes. **1932** (1970) *Ibid* 75 **KY,** You have been here to [sic] long already and remember to [sic] other red neck reporters got what was coming to them so don't let the sun go down on you here. *Ibid* 293 **KY,** In Wallins Creek as in Evarts the small store-keepers and the townspeople generally seemed to be in sympathy with the rednecks, as they call the members of the N.M.U. **1932** *New Republic* 70.70 **KY,** They shot one of those Bolsheviks up in Knox County this morning. . . That deputy knew his business. He didn't give the red neck a chance to talk, he just plugged him in the stomach. **1935** *AmSp* 10.19 (as of c1900) [Criminal argot], *Red-neck.* 1. A variant of *roughneck;* any honest working man. (Obs.) 2. One who belongs to a la-

bor union or sympathizes with union men in a strike. **1943** Korson *Coal Dust* 430 **wPA** (as of late 1920s), Red Necks, keep them scabs away,/ Red Necks, fight them every day. **1997** *DARE* File, The word "redneck" is found in the Appalachian Coal Field literature for the 1920–30s. It is reported to have arisen in reference to the red handkerchiefs striking miners wore around their necks as an emblem of their pro-union stance. . . I've . . been told by a few West Virginia students that "redneck" was used in the coal camps with . . [this] meaning.

6 Appar =**red bone 1.**

1963 Berry *Almost White* 185, In western Louisiana there are thousands of "Red Bones" and "Red Necks" who, early in the nineteenth century, were classified as "free colored," but now enjoy a sort of qualified status as white people. **1986** Pederson *LAGS Concordance,* 1 inf, **ceTX,** Red-neck—part black and part French.

7 =**canvasback duck.**

1847 *Sangamo Jrnl.* (Springfield, Ill.) 22 April 1/4 *(DA),* The 'Canvass back' and 'Red neck,' started up in fields on all sides. **1872** WI Laws *Private & Local in the Year 1872* 186, No person shall catch, kill or otherwise destroy . . any "mallard or red neck" duck. **1888** Trumbull *Names of Birds* 47 **sePA,** *Canvas-back. . .* In the neighborhood of Philadelphia hunters were in the habit of supplying the market with this duck, under the name of . . "Red-neck". **1925** (1986) Phillips *Nat. Hist. Ducks* 3.121, *Aythya valisineria. . . Red-neck. . . Adult Male. . .* Top of head, fore part of face and chin nearly black, but remainder of head and the neck bright rufous chestnut.

red-neck adj See **red-neck** n **2, 3**

red-neck v See **red-neck** n **3**

redneck buzzard See **red-necked buzzard**

red-necked adj See **red-neck** n **2, 3**

red-necked buzzard n Also *red-neck buzzard* Cf **red-headed vulture**

=**turkey vulture.**

1955 Forbush–May *Birds* 94, *Cathartes aura septentrionalis. . .* Red-necked Buzzard. **1970** *DARE* (Qu. Q13, *Names . . for the vulture*) Inf **MS81,** Red-necked buzzard.

red-necked grebe n

Std: a **grebe** (here: *Podiceps grisegena*). Also called *bastard loon* (at **bastard 2**), **bobtail 3, britten, devil-diver 1, dipper 3c, diver, hell-diver 1, henbill 2, loon 2, peggy loon, pinquin(t), red-eyed devil, redthroat 2, sheldrake loon, sinker 5, ting-tang, water witch, wear-hen**

red-necked phalarope n [*OED2* 1817 →]

=**northern phalarope.**

1895 Elliot *N. Amer. Shore Birds* 25, The Northern or Red-necked Phalarope is perhaps not so abundant in the extreme north as the Red Phalarope. **1925** (1928) Forbush *Birds MA* 1.375, *Red-necked phalarope. . .* sides of neck and fore neck "rich rust red." **1951** Pough *Audubon Water Bird* 256, Red-necked Phalarope. . . The color pattern of the breeding plumage is distinctive, although in the male it is duller and less bold. **1977** Bull–Farrand *Audubon Field Guide Birds* 327, The Northern or "red-necked Phalarope" belongs to a group in which the female is brighter than the male and the male incubates the eggs.

red-necky See **red-neck** n **2**

red nigger n

A light-skinned Black person; a member of a mixed-race group believed to be partly American Indian in origin.

1963 Berry *Almost White* 33, Worst of all, as these folk see it, are those names which explicitly identify them with Negroes. . . In Colleton County, South Carolina, the label "Red Niggers" is occasionally heard, when none are around. **1968** *DARE* FW Addit **LA32,** Red nigger—a light-colored Negro. **1986** Pederson *LAGS Concordance* (Child of racially mixed marriage) 1 inf, **swGA,** Old red nigger [inf Black].

red'nin See **redding** n

red'nin comb See **redding comb**

red-nose n, v Cf **red-neck** n **3, reds**

1911 *DN* 3.539 **eKY,** *Red-nose, n.* Discouragement, "the blues." . . *v. int.* To be downcast or discouraged.

red oak n

1 Any of several **oaks,** usually with bristle-tipped leaves and acorns maturing in the second year, native chiefly to the eastern half of the US. Note: *Red oak* in reference to any oak wood with a reddish color is std and is not illustrated here. Cf **black oak, white ~**

1633 in 1889 *Plymouth MA Records* 1.64, Lott lyeth on the easterly side of the fourth lott and att the south end bounded with a Rid oake stake. **1634** Wood *New Engl. Prospect* 1.16, Of Oakes there be three kindes, the red Oake, white and black. **1754** *SC Gaz.* (Charleston) 5 Feb 3/2, Choice land at *Beech Hill,* for rice indico and corn, well timber'd with pine and cypress, red and white oak. **1804** in 1930 Dunbar *Life* 229 MS, The soil is not rich, bearing great numbers of pines, interspersed with red oak, hickory and dog-wood. **1842** Harris *Treatise Insects* 397 NEng, The largest galls found in this country are commonly called oak-apples. They grow on the leaves of the red oak. **1850** [see **2f** below]. **1899** Garland *Boy Life* 382 nwIA (as of c1870s), The stove was a big square box into which some public-spirited soul rolled huge red oak "grubs." **1906** *DN* 3.124 nwAR, Black oak, red oak, scrub oak, white oak—Various kinds of oak. **1960** [see **2a** below]. **1965–70** *DARE* (Qu. T10, . . *Kinds of oak trees*) 496 Infs, **widespread eastern half US,** Red oak; **not** native(ly); **WA6,** Cultivated red oak; (Qu. T16, . . *Kinds of trees . . 'special'*) Infs **GA18, MS60, MA58, NC72, NY103, OK11, PA223, TX75,** red oak. **1980** Little *Audubon Guide N. Amer. Trees E. Region* 376, The leaves and lobes of red (or black) oaks are bristle-tipped; bark is usually blackish and furrowed; the bitter-seeded acorns mature in autumn of the second year, with two sizes usually present.

2 Spec:

a also *northern red oak:* An **oak** (here: *Quercus rubra*) native to much of the eastern half of the US exc for Florida and Texas. Also called **black oak, gray ~ 1, leopard ~, mountain ~ d, Spanish ~, turkey ~, yellow ~**

1635 (1976) *Relation MD* 22, The Timber of these parts is very good . . ; the white Oake is good for Pipe-staves, the red Oake for wainescot. **1792** Belknap *Hist. NH* 3.99, *Oak.* Of this we have four species in New-Hampshire. . . 2. Red, (quercus rubra.) Of this species there are three varieties. (I.) The *red,* which grows sometimes on high and dry land, but delights in a moist soil, and is generally found on the declivities of hills and borders of swamps. **1812** Michaux *Histoire des Arbres* 2.126, *Quercus rubra.* Red Oak. . . Partout où il se trouve, il est connu des habitans sous la seule dénomination de Chêne rouge, bien que quelquefois, dans la Pensylvanie . . il soit confondu avec le *Quercus falcata* dont on lui donne le nom. [=*Quercus rubra.* Red Oak. . . Everywhere it occurs, it is known to the inhabitants exclusively as "red oak," though in Pennsylvania it is sometimes confused with *Q. falcata,* whose name is applied to it.] **1860** Curtis *Cat. Plants NC* 41, Red Oak. (Q. rubra . .). The acorns in particular furnish a character which at once discriminates this from all the *Red Oaks,* they being of larger size (1 inch long) and having very *flat shallow cups.* . . This tree extends farther north than any other of our Oaks, reaching into Canada. **1903** Small *Flora SE U.S.* 351, *Quercus rubra.* . . The trunk clothed with a rough, close, often mottled bark. . . In woods, Nova Scotia and Ontario to Minnesota and Kansas, Florida and Texas. *Red Oak.* **1944** Hyland–Steinmetz *Woody Plants ME* 15, Northern Red or Red Oak. . . Common and locally abundant. . . Dry or moist woods, often in rocky places. **1960** Vines *Trees SW* 186, *Quercus rubra.* . . The wood is considered to be better than that of other Red Oaks. **1967–70** *DARE* (Qu. T10, . . *Kinds of oak trees*) Inf **MA68,** Black and red [oak] probably the same; **IL45, 119, NC48,** Northern red oak. **1986** Pederson *LAGS Concordance,* 1 inf, **neGA,** Northern red oak.

b also *southern red oak:* An **oak** (here: *Quercus falcata*) native to much of the eastern half of the US exc for the western Great Lakes and New England areas. Also called **black oak, bottom ~ 2, finger ~, Spanish ~, swamp red ~**

1775 (1962) Romans *Nat. Hist. FL* 19, *Quercus rubra Carolinensis, virens muricata.* Carolina red oak, prickly when young. **1785** Marshall *Arbustrum* 123, *Upland Red Oak.* . . The timber is generally worm eaten, or rotten at heart, therefore of little esteem. It is likewise commonly known by the name of Spanish Oak; and, I think, has some varieties differing in the size of their fruit and leaves. **1812** Michaux *Histoire des Arbres* 2.104, *Quercus falcata.* . . Dans les deux Carolines et la Géorgie, elle est désignée . . *Red oak.* [=*Quercus falcata.* . . In the two Carolinas and Georgia it is called . . *Red Oak.*] **1882** *Bot. Gaz.* 7.48 cTX, The sides and part of the top of this great bluff are covered with a thick growth of mountain cedar (*Juniperus occidentalis,* var.

conjungens), red oak (*Quercus rubra* [here: =*Q. falcata*]) [etc]. **1897** Sudworth *Arborescent Flora* 171, *Quercus falcata.* . . Red Oak (Va., Ga., Ala., Fla., Miss., La., Ind., N.C.) **1938** Van Dersal *Native Woody Plants* 220, *Southern red oak.* . . A large tree . . ; much attacked by heart rot. **1950** Moore *Trees AR* 50, *Southern Red Oak.* . . Local Names . . Red . . Oak. . . *Leaves* vary extremely in size and shape, many types occurring on the same tree; . . always bristle-tipped. . . Wood sold with northern red oak and used for same purposes. **1967–70** *DARE* (Qu. T10, . . *Kinds of oak trees*) Infs **IL119, NC48,** Southern red [oak].

c A **black oak** (here: *Quercus velutina*).

1731 Catesby *Nat. Hist. Carolina* 1.23, *The Red Oak.* . . The Bark is dark colour'd, very thick and strong, and for tanning preferable to any other kind of Oak; the grain is coarse; the Wood spongy, and not durable. **1822** Eaton *Botany* 419, [*Quercus*] *discolor* [=*Q. velutina*] . . false red oak. . . leaves oblong, . . pubescent beneath and on both sides when young; . . acorn ovate. **1938** Van Dersal *Native Woody Plants* 346, Oak . . Red (*Quercus coccinea, Quercus rubra, Quercus velutina*). **1974** (1977) Coon *Useful Plants* 142, *Quercus velutina* . . red oak. . . This species of oak has bark . . used in dyeing wool and silk. **1986** Pederson *LAGS Concordance,* 2 infs, neGA, nwTN, Red-oak bark—used in tanning leather; 1 inf, nwLA, Red-oak ooze—used for coloring leather.

d also *water red oak:* =**pin oak 1a.**

1785 Marshall *Arbustrum* 122, *Water Red Oak.* This grows most naturally by creek sides, or in low wet places, rising to the height of a pretty large tree; generally thick set with slender lateral branches. **1940** Clute *Amer. Plant Names* 269, *Quercus palustris.* . . Red oak. **1950** Moore *Trees AR* 52, *Quercus palustris.* . . Local Names . . Water Red Oak. **1968–69** *DARE* (Qu. T10, . . *Kinds of oak trees*) Infs **MA25,** red oak—same; **MA47,** Piss oak—about impossible to burn the stuff—might be the red oak; **NY68,** Piss oak—that's red oak; **PA136,** Red oak—watery. **1986** Pederson *LAGS Concordance,* 1 inf, **neAR,** Pin oak = red oak.

e =**scarlet oak 1.**

1812 Michaux *Histoire des Arbres* 2.116, *Quercus coccinea.* . . Dans les Etats du Nord, il n'est connu . . sous le nom de Chêne rouge. [= *Quercus coccinea.* . . In the northern states it is known . . under the name of red oak.] **1837** Darlington *Flora Cestrica* 532 sePA, *Q*[*uercus*] *coccinea.* . . Red Oak. Scarlet Oak. . . This is a fine tree. **1850** Emerson *Rept. Trees & Shrubs* 144, *Quercus coccinea.* . . This handsome tree is almost every where known by the name of the red oak, and is thence confounded with a tree which is inferior to it in every valuable property. **1908** Britton *N. Amer. Trees* 293, *Scarlet Oak.* . . is also called Red oak, Black oak, and Spanish oak. **1945** Wodehouse *Hayfever Plants* 77, The scarlet oak . . , also known as . . red oak, . . [has] a distribution from Maine to North Carolina and westward to Ontario and Missouri. **1980** Little *Audubon Guide N. Amer. Trees E. Region* 385, "Red Oak" . . *Quercus coccinea.* . . Large tree with a rounded, open crown of glossy foliage, best known for its brilliant autumn color.

f also *dwarf red oak:* A **bear oak** (here: *Quercus ilicifolia*). Cf **redbrush 2**

1812 Michaux *Histoire des Arbres* 2.96, Cette petite espèce de Chêne est connue dans les Etats du Nord et du milieu, sous les . . noms de *Bear oak,* . . de *Black scrub oak,* . . et de *Dwarf red oak.* [=This little species of Oak is known in the northern and middle states under the . . names of *Bear oak,* . . of *Black scrub oak,* . . and of *Dwarf red oak.*] **1850** Emerson *Rept. Trees & Shrubs* 150, *Quercus ilicifolia.* . . is commonly known by the name of . . dwarf red oak, and sometimes bear oak, from the fondness of bears for its fruit. *Ibid* 152, The fourth group [of oaks found in New England] . . includes the black, the scarlet, the red and the bear oak, so nearly allied as to be generally considered the "red oaks;" and in many places this single name includes them all. **1966–70** *DARE* (Qu. I43, *What kinds of nuts grow wild around here?*) Inf **NY233,** Red oak acorns—bitter; (Qu. T10, . . *Kinds of oak trees*) Inf **ME8,** Red oak—little.

g =**Texas oak** (here: *Quercus texana*).

1884 Sargent *Forests of N. Amer.* 148, [*Quercus rubra:*] Var. *Texana* [=*Q. texana*] . . Red Oak. . . A tree 21 to 24 meters in height. **1908** Britton *N. Amer. Trees* 292, *Quercus texana.* . . A small tree with spreading branches, in dry, rocky soil of southern and western Texas, where it is called Red oak. **1960** Vines *Trees SW* 193, *Quercus texana.* . . Also known under the names of Texas Red Oak, . . Red Oak. **1980** Little *Audubon Guide N. Amer. Trees E. Region* 402, "Red Oak" . . *Quercus nuttallii* [=*Q. texana*]. . . The foliage resembles Pin Oak.

h =**cherrybark oak.**

1901 Robertson *Inlander* 310, I des gwine down to de branch to git me some red-oak bark. **c1938** in 1970 Hyatt *Hoodoo* 2.1400 **seVA**, They only uses the red oak bark, cherry bark and the daniel-line [Hyatt: dandelion] flowers. **1966–68** *DARE* (Qu. T10, . . *Kinds of oak trees*) Inf **NC49**, Red oak—bark used for medicine; (Qu. BB50c, *Remedies for infections*) Infs **MD17, NC55**, Red-oak bark; **AL4**, Red-oak police [= poultice]—bark ooze, they call it. **1967** *DARE* FW Addit **AR47**, Red-oak-bark tea used for poultice for rheumatism. **1974** Morton *Folk Remedies* 125 **SC**, "*Red Oak*" . . *Quercus pagoda*. . . *South Carolina*. . . The inner bark is used fresh, or, for future use, is dried and powdered. It is boiled and the "tea" taken for head congestion, colds, fever, rheumatism and diarrhea. . . An extract has been commonly applied to cancers and indolent ulcers. **1979** Little *Checklist U.S. Trees* 231, *Quercus falcata* var. *pagodifolia* [=*Q. pagoda*]. . . *Other common names* . . red oak. **1981** *High Coll.* **ceKY** (as of c1930), *Ooze* . . medicine made from red oak bark which has been chipped and boiled, and is used in the Gorge to cure sores, cuts, and snake bite. **1986** Pederson *LAGS Concordance,* 1 inf, **cwLA**, Inside bark of a red oak good for diarrhea; 1 inf, **csTN**, Red-oak bark—boiled for horse's swollen legs; 1 inf, **neAL**, Red-oak bark—toothache remedy, applied to cheek; 1 inf, **cwLA**, Red-oak poultice from bark to draw out infection; 1 inf, **cnLA**, Red-oak roots to cure sores; 1 inf, **swGA**, Bark from the red oak tree for stomach trouble; 1 inf, **ceLA**, Red oaks—bark used in curing ground itch; 1 inf, **csMS**, Red oak bark put in chickens' water for cholera; 1 inf, **nwMS**, Red oak for stomach ailments; 1 inf, **csAL**, Red oak—chicken medicine made from its bark.

i Any of var other specific **oaks**; see quots.

1913 *Torreya* 13.229 **LA**, *Quercus laurifolia*. . . Red, pin or water oak, Abbeville, La. **1960** Vines *Trees SW* 177, *Quercus phellos*. . . Other local names are Water Oak, . . Red Oak [etc]. **1968** *DARE* (Qu. T5, . . *Kinds of evergreens, other than pine*) Inf **CA87**, Live oak or pin oak or red oak—all the same; (Qu. T10, . . *Kinds of oak trees*) Inf **CA87**, Red oak [*DARE* Ed: prob refers to **canyon oak 1**]; **NY52**, Rock—similar leaves to red oak.

3 =**chinquapin 3.**

1910 Jepson *Silva CA* 241, It was with a lively sense of protest that I learned that the hide of this tree [=*Castanopsis chrysophylla* var *minor*], called by the woodsmen "Red Oak," went into the tanbark cords indifferently with Tan Oak bark. **1911** Jepson *Flora CA* 125, *Castanopsis chrysophylla*. . . Often called Chestnut, Red Oak, and Bur Oak.

red oak snake n

=**corn snake.**

1968 *DARE* (Qu. P25, . . *Kinds of snakes*) Inf **GA47**, Red oak [snake].

red of, get See redd 1

red oil n Also *red lantern oil,* ~ *sperm* ~, ~ *taillight* ~

A nonexistent substance used as the basis of a practical joke; see quots.

1921 *DN* 5.95 **swOH**, *Red oil,* or red sperm oil. Employee told to get some for the red lantern. **1965–69** *DARE* (Qu. HH14, *Ways of teasing a beginner or inexperienced person* . . "*Go get me* _____.") Inf **PA223**, Red lantern oil; **MS1**, Red oil; **PA202**, Red oil for the red light; **IL80**, Red taillight oil.

red onion n

See quots.

1930 *New Outlook* 26 Mar 488 **swVA**, The Eighteenth Amendment and good roads have produced endless rows of speakeasies, known variously as half-way houses, moonlight inns, "red onions," barbecues, and So-and-So's Place. **1931** *Writer's Digest* 11.42 [Railroad terms], *Red Onion*—Railroad eating house. **1932** *Santa Fe Mag.* Jan 35, Railroad sleeping quarters are referred to as *red onion, broken knuckles* or the *struggle for life*—the first man up gets the best pair of pants. [**1967–68** *DARE* (Qu. D39, . . *A small eating place where the food is not especially good*) Inf **NY105**, White onion; (Qu. DD30, *Joking names for a place where liquor is [or was] sold and consumed illegally*) Inf **OR1**, Blind onion.]

red osier n Also *red osier dogwood* scattered, but esp NEng Cf **green osier, red dogwood**

Any of several **dogwoods 1**, but usu *Cornus sericea*. For other names of *C. sericea* see **dogberry a, kinnikinnick 2b, poison dogwood 2, redbrush 1, red dogwood,** ~ **willow 2, squawbush, waxberry cornel**

1807 (1923) Pursh *Jrl. Bot. Excursion* 48 **neNY**, Cornus several sorts, among which is the Osier rouge or Red osier. **1822** Eaton *Botany* 252,

[*Cornus*] *sericea* . . red osier. . . About 7 feet high. Berries bright blue. **1832** *MA Hist. Soc. Coll.* 2d ser 9.148 **cwVT**, [Cornus] sanguinea, Red osier. **a1862** (1864) Thoreau *ME Woods* 174, There grew . . *Cornus stolonifera* [=*C. sericea*], or red osier, whose bark, the Indian said, was good to smoke. **1917** Eaton *Green Trails* 99 **MA**, A pair of catbirds . . nest each year in a red-osier dogwood. **1924** Deam *Shrubs IN* 239, *Cornus stolonifera*. . . *Red-osier Dogwood.* . . Branches purplish-red to bright-red, smooth; . . branchlets green or reddish and pubescent at first, becoming purplish-red or bright-red and smooth by the end of the season. **1940** Clute *Amer. Plant Names* 97, C[ornus] *amomum*. . . Red osier. *Ibid* 98, *C. stolonifera*. Red Osier. **1960** Vines *Trees SW* 796, *Cornus stolonifera*. . . Called Redosier Dogwood because the bark resembles that of the Osier Willow. *Ibid* 799, *Cornus alternifolia*. . . is also known under the vernacular names of . . Red-osier Dogwood [etc]. **1966–68** *DARE* (Qu. T15, . . *Kinds of swamp trees*) Inf **WI32**, Red osier; (Qu. T16, . . *Kinds of trees* . . '*special*') Inf **MA6**, Red osier; **WI8**, Red osier dogwood. **1966** *DARE* FW Addit **cMA**, Red osier—same family as dogwood. **1979** Little *Checklist U.S. Trees* 99, *Red-osier dogwood*. . . Very widely distributed. . . *Cornus sericea.* **1999** *DARE* File **nwMA**, In late February and early March we'd make it a point to look for the red osier in the marshy areas. When the stems of the bushes turned a brilliant red we knew spring was coming. I didn't know it was a dogwood until I came to Wisconsin.

red out See redd 3c

red owl n Also *red screech owl*

A **screech owl 1** (here: *Otus asio*) in the rufous color phase.

1785 Pennant *Arctic Zool.* 231, Red. O[wl]. With yellow irides: horns, head, back, and wings, of a pleasant tawny red, streaked with black: the scapulars marked with large white spots. **1812** Wilson *Amer. Ornith.* 5.83, [The] *Red Owl*. . . [is] well known by its common name, the *Little Screech Owl.* **1883** *Century Illustr. Mag.* 26.681, The nests were probably plundered at night, and doubtless by the little red screech-owl. **1919** Burns *Ornith. Chester Co. PA* 58, *Otus asio asio* . . "red owl." . . Common resident. **1923** *WV State Ornith. Birds WV* 22, *Adult in Red Phase:* Prevailing color bright rust-red. . . The screech owl is sometimes called . . red owl. **1956** *MA Audubon Soc. Bulletin* 40.81 **CT**, *Screech Owl*. . . Red Owl (Conn. There are color variants, perhaps phases, one of which is rufous.) **1962** Imhof *AL Birds* 306, Red Owl. . . The Screech Owl . . normally has two color phases. One phase is gray, and the other a bright reddish-brown, the latter being by far the more common in Alabama. **1967** *DARE* (Qu. Q2, . . *Kinds of owls*) Inf **MO13**, Red owl. **1986** Pederson *LAGS Concordance,* 1 inf, **csTX**, Red owl's an owl—small, same as screech owl.

red paddle n Cf **red-legged black duck**

=**black duck 1.**

1917 *Wilson Bulletin* 29.2.77, *Anas rubripes*. . . The black-legged form is known as nigger black duck, and the other [=the red-legged form] as red paddle. **1982** Elman *Hunter's Field Guide* 143, (*Anas rubripes*) Common & regional names . . red-paddle.

red paintroot See Indian paint 1

red pape See red pop

red pea n [*DJE* 1727 →]

A reddish variety of the **black-eyed pea** (here: *Vigna unguiculata*).

1805 Parkinson *Tour* 352 **nNJ**, He showed me some of the red peas so much famed in America. **1819** *Plough Boy* 1.130 **SC**, Permit me to recommend to the notice of the farmers of your vicinity, the culture of the common red pea, (cow peas) for the purpose of making a most substantial rich winter fodder. **1864** in 1866 Jones *Rebel Diary* 2.272 **VA**, Bought a bushel of red peas to-day for $30.00—the last for sale—the rest being taken for *horses*. Such is the food that my family is forced to subsist on. **1986** Pederson *LAGS Concordance,* 1 inf, **cwGA**, Big red pea, little lady pea [etc]. **1999** *DARE* File—Internet [Mt. Sunshine Farms *Quality Dried Beans*], Red Iron Clay Peas—Also referred to as the Cow Pea, Field Pea, Red Pea, Zipper Pea, the Clay Pea is a fast cooking pea, and another southern favorite. **2000** *NADS Letters* **GA**, Red peas, moore peas and crowder peas. . . All different kinds of peas similar to in taste but not black eyed peas or jumping jack. All would do for the new years day ritual of eating black eyed peas.

red perch n

1 A **yellow perch** (here: *Perca flavescens*).

1792 Belknap *Hist. NH* 3.178, Red Perch, *Perca fluviatalis.* **1819** Warden *Statist. Political Hist. U.S.* 1.431 **VT,** The following fishes are found in the Lakes Champlain [etc] . . red-perch, white-perch [etc]. **1902** Jordan–Evermann *Amer. Fishes* 366, Among other names by which it [=*Perca flavescens*] is known are American perch, raccoon perch, red perch, and striped perch. **1939** Natl. Geogr. Soc. *Fishes* 132, Like other fishes of extended range, it [=*Perca flavescens*] has several names in different localities, such as . . red perch. **1975** Evanoff *Catch More Fish* 89, The yellow perch *(Perca flavescens)* is also called the red perch. **1983** Becker *Fishes WI* 886, *Yellow Perch.* . . Other common names . . red perch, striped perch.

2 also *red sea perch:* **=rosefish.** Cf **redfish b**

1842 DeKay *Zool. NY* 4.61, It [=*Sebastes marinus*] is called, by our fishermen, *Red Sea Perch,* and they say it is found only in deep water. **1871** *Amer. Naturalist* 5.400 **ME,** The common *Sebastes,* or "Red Perch" at Eastport, feeds upon the same species [=*Thysanopoda* and *Mysis*] when they come around the wharves, but probably does not pursue them to the same extent as the herring and pollock. **1905** NJ State Museum *Annual Rept. for 1904* 370, *Sebastes marinus.* . . Red Sea Perch. . . A bright red fish . . which is occasionally taken off our north shore in deep water. **1911** U.S. Bur. Census *Fisheries 1908* 314, *Rosefish.* . . A brilliantly colored fish found off the north Atlantic coast as far south as New York. It is also called "red perch."

3 A fish of the family Centrarchidae such as the **red-breasted sunfish 1** or a red-spotted **sunfish** *(Lepomis miniatus).* **chiefly Sth, S Midl** Cf **goggle-eye 1a(2), perch** n[1] **2, red-bellied perch**

1878 U.S. Natl. Museum *Bulletin* 12.72 **TN,** *List of Fishes of Nashville, as given by a Fisherman.* . . Sun Perch. Coon Perch. . . Red Perch. **1933** LA Dept. of Conserv. *Fishes* 347, *Sclerotis miniatus* [=*Lepomis m.*] . . The Red Perch is very small, the average length being only about four inches, but its coloration creates a decidedly beautiful appearance. **1933** *AmSp* 8.1.51 **Ozarks,** Red perch. . . A broad, varicolored sun perch, common in the Ozark streams. **1938** Schrenkeisen *Field Book Fishes* 244, *Lepomis auritus.* . . Red Perch. *Ibid* 245, *Lepomis miniatus.* . . Red Perch. **1967–70** *DARE* (Qu. P1, . . *Kinds of freshwater fish . . caught around here . . good to eat)* Infs **AL31, NC87, NY212, TN37, TX9,** Red perch; **LA2, 12,** Red perch has a small mouth. [*DARE* Ed: Some of these Infs may refer instead to **1** or **2** above]. **1986** Pederson *LAGS Concordance* **Gulf Region,** 5 infs, Red perch; 1 inf, Red perch = goggle-eye perch.

4 **=garibaldi.**

1884 Goode *Fisheries U.S.* 1.276, On the California coast occurs. . the 'Garibaldi'. . . The names 'Gold-fish' and 'Red Perch' are also used, . . referring to its brilliant orange colorations.

red phalarope n

Std: a **phalarope** (here: *Phalaropus fulicarius*). Also called **bullbird, gulf bird, harbor goose, hen snipe, herring bird, Jersey goose, mackerel ~, sea ~ 1, sea plover, ~ snipe 1c, squealer, web-footed peep, whalebird**

red pie n

A vinegar pie.

1987 *DARE* File **cNE,** My mother used to make vinegar pie, only we called it red pie. I think it was because the caramelized sugar took on a reddish color.

red pine n

1 A **pine 1,** as:

a **=Norway pine.** [*DCan* 1767 →]

1809 Kendall *Travels* 3.145 **ME,** I have referred the *sapling* of the lumberers to the yellow, red or Norway pine; but this is a mistake. [**1810** Michaux *Histoire des Arbres* 1.45, *Pinus rubra.* . . Cet arbre est connu par tous les François du Canada sous le nom de *Pin rouge,* nom que lui ont conservé les Anglois qui sont venus habiter cette colonie. Dan la partie la plus septentrionale des Etats-Unis . . il est designé sous celui de *Norway pine.* [=*Pinus rubra.*] . . This tree is known to all the French in Canada as the *red pine,* a name which has been kept for it by the English who have come to settle in that colony. In the northernmost part of the United States . . it is known as the Norway pine.]] **1832** Browne *Sylva* 239, *Red or Norway Pine.* . . The bark upon the body of the tree is of a clearer red than upon that of any other species in the United States; hence is derived its popular name, *Red Pine.* **1844** Lapham *Geogr. Descr. WI* 82, Pinus resinosa, . . red pine. **a1862** (1864) Thoreau *ME Woods* 249, We landed on a rocky point . . to look at some

Red Pines *(Pinus resinosa)* . . and get some cones. **1898** *Jrl. Amer. Folkl.* 11.280 **WI,** *Pinus resinosa,* . . red pine. **1945** MI Ag. Exper. Sta. Technical *Bulletin* 201.13, Scattered throughout the region are also white pine *(Pinus Strobus)* and red pine *(Pinus resinosa).* **1965–70** *DARE* (Qu. T17, . . *Kinds of pine trees;* not asked in early QRs) 84 Infs, **chiefly NEast, N Cent,** Red pine; (Qu. T5, . . *Kinds of evergreens, other than pine)* Inf **AR24,** Red pine; (Qu. T16, . . *Kinds of trees* . . *'special')* Inf **MN14,** Red pine. **1996** *Capital Times* (Madison WI) 29 Nov sec B 8 **nWI,** Those areas . . contain white spruce, red pine and balsam fir in the upland areas.

b **=longleaf pine 1.** *obs* Cf **redheart pine**

1810 Michaux *Histoire des Arbres* 1.64, *P[inus] palustris.* . . Dans les Etats du Nord, . . [il est connu] quelquefois . . [sous le nom de] *Red pine.* [=*P[inus] palustris.* . . In the northern states . . [it is known] sometimes . . [by the name of] *Red pine.*] **1842** Buckingham *Slave States* 1.177, The Georgia pitch pine is abundant, and it is a highly valuable tree. This is called by a great variety of names, such as the southern, the red, the brown, the yellow, and the long-leaved pine; but they all indicate the same kind of tree. **1869** Porcher *Resources* 578 **Sth,** That variety of long-leaved pine which . . is known by the name of red pine, is most esteemed, and in the opinion of some shipwrights is as solid and durable on the sides of vessels as the white oak.

c **=ponderosa pine 1.**

1845 Frémont *Rept. Rocky Mts.* 233, The white spruce is frequent; and the red pine, *(pinus colorado* of the Mexicans,) which constitutes the beautiful forest along the flanks of the Sierra Nevada to the northward, is here the principal tree, not attaining a greater height than 140 feet, though with sometimes a diameter of 10. **1897** Sudworth *Arborescent Flora* 20, *Pinus ponderosa.* . . Red Pine. **1953** Peattie *Nat. Hist. W. Trees* 79, Pinus ponderosa . . Western Red . . Pine. **1968** *DARE* (Qu. T17, . . *Kinds of pine trees;* not asked in early QRs) Inf **CA42,** Red pine.

d **=lodgepole pine.**

1910 Jepson *Silva CA* 83, It [=*Pinus contorta*] is also called . . in the Uinta Mountains of Utah, Red Pine. **1967–68** *DARE* (Qu. T17, . . *Kinds of pine trees;* not asked in early QRs) Infs **OR4, UT7,** Red pine.

2 **=Douglas fir.**

1897 Sudworth *Arborescent Flora* 47 **UT, ID, CO,** *Pseudotsuga taxifolia.* . . Red Pine. **1966** Barnes–Jensen *Dict. UT Slang* 35, *Red Pine* . . a name sometimes given to the Douglas fir *(Pseudotsuga mucronata)* which grows in the higher mountains of the Wasatch range.

red pine squirrel n Also *red piney squirrel* Cf **pine squirrel**

A **red squirrel 1** (here: *Tamiasciurus hudsonicus*).

1940 Richter *Trees* 4 **OH** (as of early 19th cent), Red piney squirrels tearing at the bucks to geld them. **1961** Douglas *My Wilderness* 250 **ME,** After a burn or after clear cutting. . . the frisky, talkative red-pine squirrel arrives.

red plum n Also *wild red plum*

Either **Canada plum** or another **wild plum** (here: *Prunus americana*).

1772 in 1899 McClure *Diary* 59 **PA,** Red plums grow in great abundance in this country. **1819** Schoolcraft *Lead Mines MO* 28, Of these [=wild fruits], the following is a catalogue: Grape, Red plumb, Percimmon [etc]. **1843** Torrey *Flora NY* 1.194, *Prunus Americana.* . . *Red Plum.* . . Fruit . . mostly reddish-orange when ripe, with a juicy yellow pulp and a thick tough skin. It is palatable when cultivated, but rather acerb in a wild state. **1897** Sudworth *Arborescent Flora* 236, *Prunus nigra.* . . Red Plum (Me., Vt., Ont., Mich.) *Ibid* 237, *Prunus americana.* . . Red Plum (Del., Pa., N.C., Miss., La., Nebr.) **1913** Otis *MI Trees* 161, *Canada Plum. Red Plum.* . . Fruit . . a fleshy drupe, . . with a tough, thick, orange-red skin nearly free from bloom, and yellow flesh adherent to the flat stone. Eaten raw or cooked. **1943** Fernald–Kinsey *Edible Wild Plants E. N. Amer.* 239, Such species as . . the *Wild Red* or *Yellow Plums,* P[runus] americana and P. nigra, . . are usually well known where they are used and are used for sauces, pies, preserves, jams and jellies. **1970** *DARE* (Qu. I46, . . *Kinds of fruits that grow wild around here)* Inf **KY84,** Red plums. **1987** Kindscher *Edible Wild Plants* 174, *Prunus Americana* . . and *P. nigra* . . , our two species of Wild Yellow or Red Plum. . . The native orchard was seldom regularly planted, but [was] oftener the accidental result of seeds dropped in the vicinity of camping grounds and villages.

redpoll n

1 also *redpoll sparrow:* Either of two similar small red-capped birds: *Carduelis flammea* or *C. hornemanni.* [*OED2*

1738 → for *Carduelis cannabina*] For other names of these birds see **linnet 3;** for other names of *C. flammea* see **little meadowlark 3, rainbird 1g, redcrown, snowbird**

[**1785** Pennant *Arctic Zool.* 379, Lesser Redpoll. F[inch]. With a red spot on the forehead.] **1811** Wilson *Amer. Ornith.* 4.42, Lesser Red-Poll—*Fringilla Linaria.* **1877** Burroughs *Birds & Poets* 97 **NY,** Other Northern visitors that tarried with me the same winter were the tree or Canada sparrow and the red-poll. **1884** *Century Illustr. Mag.* 29.220, They sweep by me and around me in flocks,—the Canada sparrow, the snow-bunting . . the red-poll, the cedar-bird. **1898** (1900) Davie *Nests N. Amer. Birds* 360, Hoary Redpoll [=*Carduelis hornemanni*]. . . is found in abundance from Alaska to the Atlantic coast, . . only along the northern tier of States in winter. *Ibid, Redpoll* [=*C. flammea*]. . . Breeds occasionally in northern New England. . . This form of the Redpoll seems to be the common breeding bird on the mainland of Kamchatka. **1951** Kumlien–Hollister *Birds WI* 79, Hoary Redpoll. . . An irregular winter visitor. *Ibid* 80, *Redpoll.* . . In the southern part of the state the redpoll, like others of the northern birds which appear only in winter, is . . usually found in good numbers at different times of the season. **1968** *Cook Co. News–Herald* (Grand Marais MN) 9 May 2/6, Every bare patch of ground was covered with hundreds of juncos, redpolls, siskins, tree and fox sparrows. **1968–69** *DARE* (Qu. Q21, . . *Kinds of sparrows*) Infs **NY**97, 171, Redpoll sparrow. **1977** Bull–Farrand *Audubon Field Guide Birds* 578, Common Redpoll (*Carduelis flammea*). . . Smaller than a sparrow. Pale, brown-streaked, with *bright red cap* and black chin. Male has a pink breast. *Ibid* 579, Hoary Redpoll (*Carduelis hornemanni*). . . Smaller than a sparrow. Brown-streaked, with a *red cap.* Male has a pale pink breast. Similar to the Common Redpoll but slightly paler.

2 also *redpoll warbler:* The palm **warbler** (*Dendroica palmarum*). Cf **yellow redpoll**

1844 DeKay *Zool. NY* 2.89, The Red-poll Warbler. . . although very abundant in the Southern States from November to April, . . has seldom been noticed in this State, where it appears to be shy and solitary. **1874** Coues *Birds NW* 68, I am entirely ignorant of the nidification, which is described by Dr. Brewer as follows: "The Red-Poll usually selects for the site of its nest the edge of a swampy thicket." **1895** Minot *Land-Birds New Engl.* 123, Except in the summer season, they [=pine warblers] are often more or less gregarious, and associate with the "Redpolls" (*D[endroica] palmarum hypochrysea*). **1910** KY Hist. Soc. *Register* 8.18, Red-poll Warbler. . . Quite common. . . Exclusively a terrestrial bird; generally associating in flocks with the smaller sparrows. **1929** Forbush *Birds MA* 3.270, *Red-poll Warbler.* . . Top of head chestnut, sometimes blackish near base of bill. **1969** Longstreet *Birds FL* 136, *Red-poll Warbler.* . . Resides in Florida from early fall until late spring. . . A sociable family bird, flocks of 50 or more can be seen in flatwoods, hammocks, prairies, marshes, old fields, cultivated lands, towns, yards, and along the Gulf beaches.

red pollom n Cf **little pollom**

A **wintergreen 2** (here: *Gaultheria procumbens*).

[**1828** Rafinesque *Med. Flora* 1.205, All the plants which have more or less the smell and taste of *Gauteria* [sic], contain the same Oil and principle, and may probably be available equivalents. They are *Gautiera hispidula* and *Spirea ulmaria*, roots of *Polygala paucifolia* and *Spirea lobata*, bark of *Betula lenta* or Sweet Birch tree &c. They are called Pollom by the Indians.] **1876** Hobbs *Bot. Hdbk.* 97, Red pollom, Checkerberry, Gaultheria procumbens. **1924** *Amer. Botanist* 30.14, If "proclam," . . and "red pollom" are anything more than children's names for the plant [=*Gaultheria procumbens*], I am at a loss to account for them. **1971** Krochmal *Appalachia Med. Plants* 128, *Gaultheria procumbens.* . . Red pollom.

redpoll sparrow See **redpoll 1**

redpoll warbler See **redpoll 2**

red pop n Also *red pape* **LA** Cf **green pop, pape**

The male **painted bunting 1.**

1911 *Forest & Stream* 77.174 **LA,** *Passerina ciris.* . . female, Green Pop; male, Red Pop; Chef Menteur, La. . . Pop is merely the English fonetic spelling of the French name "pape" (pope) by which these birds are known to irreverent Louisianians. **1938** Oberholser *Bird Life LA* 629, *Painted Bunting.* . . The male. . . is called commonly . . in Louisiana 'pape rouge' or 'red pop'. **1955** Lowery *LA Birds* 551, Pape, red. See Bunting, Painted. **1983** Reinecke *Coll.* 8 **LA,** *Pape, Pop . .* a small very colorful song-bird, esp. painted bunting. . . Also "red-pop" La. Fr. "pape," pope.

red poplar n

=**balsam poplar.**

1970 *DARE* (Qu. T12, *The kind of poplar tree that has sticky, sweet-smelling buds*) Inf **MS**82, Red poplar; (Qu. T13) Inf **MS**82, Red poplar.

red puccoon n Cf **orange puccoon, puccoon 2, white ~, yellow ~**

=**bloodroot 1.**

1830 Rafinesque *Med. Flora* 2.78, *Sanguinea canadensis.* . . Red Puccoon. . . Root perennial, . . emitting a bright orange juice. **1896** *Jrl. Amer. Folkl.* 9.181 **OH,** *Sanguinaria Canadensis.* . . Red puccoon, Sulphur Grove, Ohio. **1932** *Country Life* 62.67 **Appalachians,** One of the loveliest . . of the mountain wildings is Bloodroot, or Red Indian Paint. . . The Indians were accustomed to call it Red Puccoon, and used its highly colored juice to stain the canes and the white-oak laths for their baskets in times of peace, and in more troublous days it served as their war paint. **1953** Greene–Blomquist *Flowers South* 39, *Red-Puccoon.* . . The juice is red and is especially abundant in its short rootstocks. **1966** *DARE* Wildfl QR Pl.77 **AR,** Red puccoon. **1979** Erichsen-Brown *Med. N. Amer. Plants* 318, *Bloodroot.* . . Common names. Puccoon root, red-puccoon, red Indian paint [etc].

red racer n esp **CA** Cf **racer 1d**

A **coachwhip snake:** usu *Masticophis flagellum piceus*, but also *M. f. testaceus* or *M. f. cingulum.*

1886 Van Dyke *Southern CA* 155, The "red racer" is a long, lithe snake of bright-red color, with a black head, and of wonderful speed. **1915** *Copeia* 15.4 **CA,** The following snakes were observed within one-half day's walk of the city of Los Angeles during the years 1913 and 1914 . . Red Racer, *Zamenis flagelliformis frenatus* [etc]. **1928** Baylor Univ. Museum *Contrib.* 16.15, Western Coach-whip Snake. . . In Trans-Pecos Texas, the names *Pink Racer* and *Red Racer* are applied to specimens in nuptial coloration whose upper and under surfaces have either a pinkish or deep reddish suffusion. **1949** *Los Angeles Times* (CA) 22 June sec 3 16/4, Found locally are blue racers, gopher snakes, red racers, California boa, California king, and garter snakes. **1965–70** *DARE* (Qu. P25, . . *Kinds of snakes*) 13 Infs, 11 **CA,** Red racer. **1968** *DARE* Tape **CA**81, [FW:] You said that red racers are mean all the time, though. [**CA**89:] They kinda got a mean disposition, don't they? [**CA**87:] . . Some of them . . are as much as five feet long or better. They're red. . . Big, long snake. **1974** Shaw–Campbell *Snakes West* 88, The wide variety of color patterns in the coachwhip is dramatically illustrated by the differences within and between three of the principal subspecies. One of these is called the red racer (*M[asticophis] f[lagellum] piceus*), found over much of southern California, southern Nevada, the extreme southwest corner of Utah, and southern Arizona. . . The western coachwhip (*M. f. testaceus*). . . is usually tan, although occasionally it is red or pink in Colorado, New Mexico, and Trans-Pecos Texas. . . The banded red racer (*M. f. cingulum*). . . may be reddish-brown with widely separated pairs of pink crossbands along the rear portion of the body.

red rail n Cf **red-breasted rail**

1 also *little red rail:* =**Virginia rail.**

1874 *Forest & Stream* 1.325 **PA,** Where fifty soras are killed but one or two red rails are boated. **1890** Warren *Birds PA* 69, *Virginia Rail; Little Red Rail.* . . Notwithstanding the fact that the plumage of the Virginia and King Rails is similar, the species can readily be distinguished by the great difference in size. **1923** U.S. Dept. Ag. *Misc. Circular* 13.42, *Virginia Rail.* . . Little red rail (Va.); . . red rail (N.J., Pa., Del.)

2 as *big red rail:* =**king rail 1.**

1890 Warren *Birds PA* 67, *King Rail; Big Red Rail.* . . Sides and front of neck and breast bright rufous.

red rat snake n

=**corn snake.**

1952 Ditmars *N. Amer. Snakes* 79, *Corn Snake, Red Rat Snake, House Snake, Elaphe guttata.* . . Southern New Jersey to Florida; westward to Missouri and Louisiana. **1958** Conant *Reptiles & Amphibians* 156, This [=*Elaphe guttata*] is the "red rat snake," a species much in demand as a pet for small boy, camp, or classroom.

red rattle n [*OED2* 1578 → for *Pedicularis sylvatica* or *P. palustris*]

A **lousewort 1** (here: *Pedicularis flammea*).

1949 Moldenke *Amer. Wild Flowers* 281, The *redrattle, P[edicularis] flammea*, with its . . upper lip crimson or purple, also extends from Greenland and Labrador to Alaska.

red ribbons n

A **farewell-to-spring** (here: *Clarkia concinna*).

1925 Jepson *Manual Plants CA* 673, *C[larkia] concinna. . . Red Ribbons. . .* Calyx-lobes crimson, linear-lanceolate. **1949** Moldenke *Amer. Wild Flowers* 93, *Redribbons. . .* blooms in May and June . . in the California Coast Ranges.

red rim See **red sign (crab)**

red ring rot See **redheart 2**

red river See **red** adj, n **Aa(2)**

Red River maple n [*DCan* 1887 → for *Acer negundo*]   Cf **river maple**

Usu **box elder**, but also **silver maple**.

1897 Sudworth *Arborescent Flora* 291 **ND**, *Acer negundo. . .* Red River Maple. **1911** *Century Dict. Suppl., Maple. . . Red River maple. (a)* The silver maple. *(b)* The box-elder. **1960** Vines *Trees SW* 677, *A[cer] negundo. . .* Vernacular names are Maple-ash, . . Red River Maple.

Red River oak n

=**Texas oak**.

1960 Vines *Trees SW* 198, *Quercus nuttallii* [=*Q. texana*]. . . Other names for it are . . Red River Oak, and Pin Oak. **1979** Little *Checklist U.S. Trees* 238, *Nuttall oak. . . Other common names—red oak, Red River oak, pin oak*.

Red River weed n

A **marsh elder 1** (here: *Iva xanthifolia*).

1935 (1943) Muenscher *Weeds* 506, *Iva xanthifolia. . .* Red-river-weed.

red road See **red lane**

red robin n

1 An **Indian paintbrush 1** (here: *Castilleja coccinea*).   *obs*

1837 Darlington *Flora Cestrica* 375 **sePA**, *Crimson Euchroma* . . Painted cup. Red Robin.

2 =**herb Robert**.   [*EDD* 1866 →]

1900 Lyons *Plant Names* 172, *G[eranium] Robertianum. . .* Red-Robin. **1910** Graves *Flowering Plants* 261 **CT**, Herb Robert. Red Robin. Rocky ledges, usually in shade. **1961** Smith *MI Wildflowers* 215, *Red Robin. . .* Flowers rose to reddish-purple, sometimes white. **1967** *DARE* FW Addit **AR44**, *Red robin—Robertiella robertiana*.

3 =**red-breasted sunfish 1**.   Cf **robin 2**

1916 *Copeia* 36.80 **NC**, *Lepomis auritus*. Red Robin. Common. **1969** *DARE* (Qu. P3, *Freshwater fish that are not good to eat*) Inf **NC60**, Red robin.

4 =**purple martin**.

1970 *DARE* (Qu. Q14, . . *Names . . martin*) Inf **TN53**, Red robin.

red robin snow n [Perh **red robin 4**]   Cf **martin storm, robin snow**

1954 *WELS Suppl.* **swWI**, Have you heard the late spring snows referred to as "red robin snow"? My father used this term many years ago.

red rock cod n Also *red cod*

1 Any of several **rockfish 3**; see quots.   Cf **red rockfish**

1884 Goode *Fisheries U.S.* 1.265, This species [=*Sebastes pinniger*] is usually called simply "Red Rock-cod" or "Red Rock-fish" and not distinguished from the two preceding [=*S. miniatus* and *S. ruberrimus*]. **1909** U.S. Dept. Commerce Bur. Fisheries *Document* 645.75 **AK**, *Red rock cod (Sebastodes* [=*Sebastes*] *ruberrimus*) is known from southeast Alaska, where it attains a length of more than two feet and a weight of many pounds. It is a good food fish, its flesh fairly firm and of good flavor, and numbers are marketed each season. **1911** U.S. Bur. Census *Fisheries 1908* 314, *Sebastodes melanops. . .* A food fish found from southeastern Alaska to California. It is also known as "red cod." **1928** Pan-Pacific Research Inst. *Jrl.* 3.13 **OR, WA**, *Sebastodes ruberrimus. . .* Red rock-cod. **1943** *AK Sportsman* Jan 20, Large quantities of red cod or "red snapper" are treated in a like manner. **1953** Roedel *Common Fishes CA* 126, *Sebastodes pinniger. . .* Chiefly orange in color. . . Red rock cod. *Ibid* 127, *Sebastodes miniatus. . .* Chiefly vermilion or brick red in color. . . Red rock cod. *Ibid* 130, *Sebastodes chlorostictus. . .* Flesh pink vaguely mottled with rose above. . . Red rock cod. *Ibid* 131, *Sebastodes constellatus. . .* Orange to vermilion. . . Red rock cod.

2 A **thornyhead** (here: *Sebastolobus alascanus*).

1936 *AK Sportsman* Aug 17, Then there are such undesirable varieties as mud sharks, dog-fish, devil fish, turbot and a variety of red cod they call "idiots." **1953** Roedel *Common Fishes CA* 136, *Sebastolobus alascanus. . .* Bright red, a dark blotch or blotches on the spiny portion of the dorsal fin. . . Deep sea red rock cod.

red rockfish n Cf **red rock cod 1**

Any of several **rockfish 3**, but esp *Sebastes ruberrimus*.

1882 U.S. Natl. Museum *Bulletin* 16.665, *Sebastodes ruber* [= *Sebastes ruberrimus*]. . . Red Rock-fish. . . The adults . . are nearly plain brick red. . . Pacific coast, from Santa Barbara northward; abundant. **1884** Goode *Fisheries U.S.* 265, *Sebastichthys ruber* [=*Sebastes ruberrimus*]. . . This species is usually the "Red Rockfish" *par excellence. Ibid*, [see **red rock cod 1**]. **1911** U.S. Bur. Census *Fisheries 1908* 314, *Sebastodes melanops. . .* A food fish found from southeastern Alaska to California. It is also known as . . "red rockfish." **1939** Natl. Geogr. Soc. *Fishes* 235, *Red Rockfish (Sebastodes rosaceus). . .* The red rockfish is distinguished . . by four or five bright rose-pink spots along the back on each side of the fins. . . The rest of the body is orange red, and the fins are rosy, mottled with orange. This species is found . . in considerable abundance off southern California but less commonly off the coasts of Washington and Oregon. **1978** *AK Fishing Guide* 87, The red rockfish of Alaska, as well as the black rockfish . . , are excellent eating. **1991** Amer. Fisheries Soc. *Common Names Fishes* 163, Rockfish, Alaskan red—see rougheye rockfish. *Ibid* 164, Rockfish, red—see yelloweye rockfish.

red rock trout n

A **greenling** (here: *Hexagrammos decagrammus* or *H. superciliosus*).

1896 U.S. Bur. Fisheries *Rept. for 1895* 434, *Hexagrammos decagrammus* (Pallas). Red Rock-trout; Boregat. **1898** U.S. Natl. Museum *Bulletin* 47.1872, *Hexagrammos superciliosus. . . Red Rock Trout. . .* Colors usually bright, but varying through green, brown, and bright red, usually dark green with large round red spots. . . A very showy species. **1902** Jordan–Evermann *Amer. Fishes* 502, *H[exagrammos] superciliosus*, the red rock-trout, occurs from Bering Island to Monterey Bay. **1955** Zim–Shoemaker *Fishes* 142, Rock Greenlings, or Red Rock Trout, are usually brown (some are green); they are northern fishes.

red roncador n

1 A **croaker** n[1] **1a(2)** (here: *Cheilotrema saturnum*) of the Pacific coast.   Also called **black bass 4, ~ perch 2c, ~ croaker, ~ roncador, Chinese croaker 1**

1882 U.S. Natl. Museum *Bulletin* 16.572, *S[ciaena] saturna. . .* Red Roncador. . . Black, with coppery lustre. **1884** Goode *Fisheries U.S.* 1.379, *Corvina saturna. . .* is known where found as the "Red Roncador." . . It feeds largely on crustaceans and spawns in July. **1946** LaMonte *N. Amer. Game Fishes* 82, *Sciaena saturna. . .* Red Roncador. . . North to Point Conception, California. . . Reaches about 15″.

2 =**roncador 1**.

1946 LaMonte *N. Amer. Game Fishes* 82, *Roncador stearnsi. . .* Red Roncador. . . North to San Francisco, California. . . Reaches 5 or 6 pounds.

redroot n

Any of various plants, as:

a A **ceanothus**, usu **New Jersey tea**.   **chiefly eastern half US** Cf **redheart 1, redshank 2**

1709 (1967) Lawson *New Voyage* 84 **NC, SC**, The Red-Root whose Leaf is like Spear-Mint, is good for Thrushes and sore Mouths. **1762** Gronovius *Flora Virginica* 33, *Ceanothus foliis trinerviis. . . Red-rod* [sic] for dying. **1796** in 1916 Hawkins *Letters* 46 **Atlantic**, In the month of May on the small bushes, particularly the red root, there is to be seen . . a white froth, and in every lump of it there is one or two flies. **1830** Rafinesque *Med. Flora* 2.205, *Ceanothus officinalis* [=*C. americanus*]. . . *Jersey Tea, Red root.* Small shrub, with a red root. . . The root is better than the leaves. . . The roots die [sic] red, and make a red ointment with lard. . . The powder, infusion and tincture are used. **1870** MO State Entomol. *Annual Rept. for 1869* 35, The Red-root or New Jersey Tea-plant (*Ceanothus Americanus*). **1910** Graves *Flowering Plants* 275 **CT**, *Ceanothus. . .* Red-root. . . The root and leaves were formerly used for dying wool red. Medicinal. **1960** Carpenter *Tales Manchaca* 162 **cTX**, I must have consumed gallons of senna tea, our standby for purgative purposes. For the reverse effect we drank red root tea. [Footnote to *red root tea*:] *Ceanothus evatus*, also known in Texas as Indian tea. **1973** Stephens *Woody Plants* 368 **Plains States, Upper MW,** *Ceanothus americanus* . . var. *pitcheri* . . New Jersey tea, redroot. *Ibid* 372, *Ceanothus herbaceus*. . . New Jersey tea, redroot. **1993** Grimm–Kartesz *Illustr. Book Wildflowers* 502, *Redroot—Ceanothus herbaceus*. . . Western Maine to Quebec and Manitoba, south to western Georgia and Texas. . . *Small-leaf Redroot—Ceanothus microphyllus*. . . Coastal plain; southern Georgia and Alabama south into Florida.

b =bloodroot 1.

1830 Rafinesque *Med. Flora* 2.78, *Sanguinaria canadensis*. . . Redroot. . . Root . . brownish red outside, pale within, emitting a bright orange juice. **1843** Torrey *Flora NY* 1.43, *Blood-root. Red-root. Red Puccoon*. . . The root or rhizoma has long been an officinal article. **1896** *Jrl. Amer. Folkl.* 9.181 **ME,** *Sanguinaria Canadensis* . . red root. **1937** Eaton *Handicrafts* 145 **sAppalachians,** Redroot, called coonroot sometimes, shocks the bowels, good for kidney trouble too. **1979** Erichsen-Brown *Med. N. Amer. Plants* 318, *Sanguinaria canadensis*. . . The root is thick and covered with fine rootlets, from it grows the leafstalk. . . Redroot.

c A plant *(Lachnanthes caroliniana)* with bright red roots and a terminal cluster of woolly yellowish flowers. Also called **bloodroot 2, dyeroot, Indian paintroot, ~ redroot, ~ root 2, paint-root, pinkroot 2, spirit weed**

1822 Eaton *Botany* 267, *Dilatris*. . . *tinctoria* [=*Lachnanthes caroliniana*] . . red root. . . Leaves long, naked, linear. **1848** Gray *Manual of Botany* 481, *Red-root*. . . *L. tinctoria*. . . Sandy swamps, Rhode Island and N. Jersey, thence southward near the coast. **1901** Mohr *Plant Life AL* 446, *Red Root*. . . Carolinian and Louisianian areas. **1933** Small *Manual SE Flora* 358, *Red-root*. . . Bogs and wet pinelands, often acid. **1976** Fleming *Wild Flowers FL* 31, *Redroot*. . . The root has a red sap, and the older species name *tinctoria* indicates it may have been used as a dye. **1993** Grimm–Kartesz *Illustr. Book Wildflowers* 63, *Redroot*. . . gets its name from its bright red roots. . . The narrow and grass-like leaves are in a basal cluster, with only a few small ones along the stem.

d A **bittersweet** (here: *Celastrus scandens*).

1833 Eaton *Botany* 85, *Celastrus*. . . *scandens* . . red root. . . Retains its scarlet berries through the winter. **1940** Clute *Amer. Plant Names* 127, *C[elastrus] scandens*. . . Red-root.

e A **gromwell:** usu the corn gromwell *(Buglossoides arvense),* occas also *Lithospermum canescens* or *L. incisum.*

1860 Emerson *Conduct of Life* 100, He . . wakes up from his idiot dream of chickweed and red-root. **1892** IN Dept. Geol. & Nat. Resources *Rept. for 1891* 148, *Lithospermum arvense* [=*Buglossoides a.*] . . Redroot. A great pest in wheat-fields. **1912** Blatchley *IN Weed Book* 114, *Lithospermum arvense*. . . Redroot. . . Common in the northern half of the State along railways, roadsides and in cultivated fields; less common but rapidly spreading southward. . . It is . . very difficult to remove from grain fields. **1951** *PADS* 15.39 **TX,** *Batchia linearifolia* [=*Lithospermum incisum*]. . . Red root.

f also *redroot amaranth, ~ pigweed, ~ weed:* =**amaranth,** esp *Amaranthus retroflexus.*

1872 VT State Bd. Ag. *Report* 1.268, The green amaranth or red root, when it springs up after cultivation is over, . . will, in the few weeks that remain before frost, fully perfect its seeds. **1897** *Jrl. Amer. Folkl.* 10.53 **OH,** *Amaranthus retroflexus,* . . red root, Sulphur Grove, Ohio. **1898** *Ibid* 11.277 **KS,** *Acnida tuberculata* [=*Amaranthus rudis*] . . red-root. . . *Amaranthus retroflexus* . . red-root. **1899** MacMillan *MN Plant Life* 259, The amaranths [are] known also as . . redroots. *Ibid* 261, The redroot pigweed, a familiar barn-yard plant, is another . . form. **1949** Curtin *By the Prophet* 47 **AZ,** *Amaranthus palmeri*. . . Redroot. . . When young and tender, the leaves are cooked for greens. **1950** *WELS* (Other weeds common in your locality) 2 Infs, **WI,** Pigweed [same as] redroot (pigweed). **1953** Nelson *Plants Rocky Mt. Park* 64, *Redroot amaranth, Amaranthus retroflexus*. . . A stout weed . . growing along roadsides and on waste ground. **1965–70** *DARE* (Qu. S21, . . *Weeds . . that are a trouble in gardens and fields*) 24 Infs, **esp NEast, OH, UT, CA,** Redroot(s); **CO4, NY160, PA165, VA82,** Pigweed—same as redroot; **GA70, WV8,** Redroot—same as hogweed; **MD23,** Redroot—long narrow red root; **PA11,** Redroot—long red root to it; **MD26, NY71, VA46,** Redroot weed; (Qu. I28b, *Kinds of greens that are cooked*) Infs **MA58, NY106, PA221,** Redroot; **CT24,** Redroot—type of pigweed; **NH12,** Hogweed—right name is redroot; (Qu. S17, . . *Kinds of plants . . that . . cause itching and swelling*) Inf **WI17,** Redroot; (Qu. S20) Inf **NM9,** Redroot. [*DARE* Ed: Some of these Infs may refer instead to other senses.] **1967** *DARE* Tape **CO1,** [FW:] What kind of weeds are those? . . [Inf:] Lamb's quarter or redroot. **1973** *Foxfire 2* 65, *Amaranthus hybridus*. . . Red-root pigweed. . . Opposite, oval leaves are

often tinged with red, and stems and roots are bright red. . . Young leaves . . are delicious cooked alone, or mixed with stronger mustardy greens. **1987** Kindscher *Edible Wild Plants* 19, Redroot. . . *Amaranthus graecizans*. . . Young plants (spring best)—cooked; seeds (fall)—eaten raw, cooked as cereal or mush, or used as flour.

g A vinelike shrub *(Morinda roioc)* native to Florida. Cf **yellowroot**

1896 *Jrl. Amer. Folkl.* 9.190 **FL,** *Morinda Roioc,* . . red root, Florida Keys.

h An avens (here: *Geum canadense* or *G. virginianum*).

1900 Lyons *Plant Names* 172, *G[eum] Virginianum*. . . Red-root. **1933** Small *Manual SE Flora* 617, *G[eum] canadense*. . . Redroot. **1940** Steyermark *Flora MO* 263, *Red-root (Geum canadense* . . var. *Camporum* . .). Throughout Mo. Begins to bloom the last of May.

i A **swamp loosestrife** (here: *Decodon verticillatus*).

1913 *Torreya* 13.233 **MI,** *Decodon verticillata*. . . Red-root, New Richmond, Mich.

j also *redroot buckwheat:* A **wild buckwheat:** usu *Eriogonum racemosum,* but also *E. jamesii.*

1937 U.S. Forest Serv. *Range Plant Hdbk.* W70, Redroot eriogonum (*E[riogonum] racemosum*) is a white-woolly herb . . arising from a thick, red-colored, woody taproot. . . James eriogonum (*E. jamesii*), known locally as . . redroot, ranges from Kansas and Colorado to Arizona, Texas, and south into northern Mexico. **1941** Jaeger *Wildflowers* 30 **Desert SW,** *Red-root buckwheat. Eriogonum racemosum*. . . The one or more erect stems of this perennial species rise . . from a reddish taproot.

redroot amaranth See **redroot f**

redroot buckwheat See **redroot j**

redroot (pig)weed See **redroot f**

red rot See **redheart 2**

red rover n For varr see quots

1 A children's game with many variations, in which individual players are typically challenged by name to cross from one side to the other of an open area while attempting to elude capture or break through the linked arms of an opposing team; the person who is "it" in some versions of this game—also used as a call in this game. [Brit dial; cf 1898 Gomme *Traditional Games* 2.107, 1969 Opie–Opie *Children's Games* 239–41]

1891 *Jrl. Amer. Folkl.* 4.224 **Brooklyn NYC,** *Red Rover.* The boy who is "it" is called the "Red Rover," and stands in the middle of the street, while the others form a line on the pavement on one side. The Red Rover calls any boy he wants by name, and that boy must then run to the opposite sidewalk. If he is caught as he runs across, he must help the Red Rover to catch the others. When the Red Rover catches a prisoner, he must cry, "Red Rover" three times, or he cannot hold his captive. **1932** (1953) Smith *Games* 247, *Red Rover*. . . City boys play this variation of Pull Away by running across the street from curb to curb. They call, "Red Rover, come over, or I'll pull you over." **1957** *Sat. Eve. Post Letters* (as of early 1920s), Then there was that rough classic, "Red Rover, Red Rover, send so-and-so over!" in which a child from one line attempts to break thru the connected hands of the opposite line. . . This game was played in the East as well as in Ohio and in Indiana in the early twenties. *Ibid* **cnTN** (as of c1900), "Red Rover, Red Rover, let Mary come over". . . Mary would run from her side to the other side and try not to get caught. If she did get caught, she was then on the other side and when the game was over, the side who had the most, won. *Ibid* **neIL** (as of c1930), I guess everyone played "Red Rover" and called a player to run thru the line of children. *Ibid* **neIL** (as of c1940), A school playground favorite was called "Red Rover." Two lines of children, equal in number, joined hands very firmly as a sort of chain and the two lines stood facing each other at a distance of about ten to fifteen feet and one line would call to one child in the other line, "Red rover, red rover, let Johnny (or Mary, etc.) come over." And Johnny would run as fast as he could and try to break through the clasped hands of the line that called him. If he failed, he joined the opposition line, if he succeeded, he chose one child from that line and then both rejoined his original line. **1965–70** *DARE* (Qu. EE33, *Other outdoor games*) 184 Infs, **widespread, but less freq NW, Plains States, Mid Atl,** Red rover; **CT9, NY24, 66,** Red rover, come over; **VT5,** Come on over, rover; rover, come over; **AK5,** Red rover, red rover; **NY68,** Red, red rover; **MN11,** Rover, red rover; **MD8,** Rover, rover, I dare you over; (Qu. EE1, . . *Games . . in which they form a ring, and either sing or recite a* *rhyme*) Inf **CO**14, Circle red rover—one kid in the center had to break out; **OH**97, **TN**66, Red rover; (Qu. EE2, *Games that have one extra player—when a signal is given, the players change places, and the extra one tries to get a place*) Inf **CT**23, Red rover, tag, cat in a corner; (Qu. EE12, *Games in which one captain hides his team and the other team tries to find it*) Inf **CT**19, Red rover [Inf doubtful]; **CT**39, Red rover, run sheep run; (Qu. EE27, *Games played on the ice*) Infs **MT**1, **WI**47, Red rover; (Qu. EE28, *Games played in the water*) Inf **VA**109, Red rover. **1966–67** *DARE* Tape **AL**3, Everybody plays red rover, don't they? **AL**6, Red rover, red rover, send So-and-so over; **IN**1, Sort of a singing-type thing is red rover. . . Two even teams are lined up parallel to each other and there's a captain on each team and the captain yells. . . "Red rover, red rover, send someone right over." **1975** Ferretti *Gt. Amer. Book Sidewalk Games* 201, In the simplest version of Red Rover, the man in the middle . . is "It." He stands in the middle of the street and, beginning with one team, points to one member and chants, "Red Rover, Red Rover, let Chrissie come over!" Chrissie then has to dash across the street . . without being tagged. If Chrissie is tagged, he remains in the center as an assistant to "It." . . Another version has the two teams but no middleman. The captain of each team does the chanting: "Red Rover, Red Rover, let Johnny come over!" . . In this version, all members of the defending team link arms, and it is Johnny's business to try and break through any link that he can. If he succeeds, he is free to return to his own team. If he fails, he becomes part of the team he runs into. **1977** *NY Times* (NY) 6 July 29, It was a game as valid to him and his friends as stoop-ball, kick the can, ring-a-lievio, red rover and salugi were to an earlier generation.

2 =**Antony-over A, B1.**
 1957 *Sat. Eve. Post Letters* **cwNY** (as of c1900), We played Red Rover Come Over—which sounds like your Andy-Come Over. **1966–69** *DARE* (Qu. EE22, . . *The game in which they throw a ball over a building . . to a player on the other side*) Infs **AL**54, **FL**31, **WA**30, Red rover; **FL**10, Red rover [FW: Her daughter suggested this response.]; (Qu. EE23a, *What do you call out when you throw the ball*) Inf **AL**54, Red rover, it's coming over; **FL**10, Red rover, red rover, here it comes over; **FL**31, Red rover, red rover, will you come over.

reds n pl Also *mean reds* Cf **mean** adj 3, **red-nose**
With *the:* A state of depression; the blues.
 1967 *DARE* (Qu. GG34a, *To feel depressed or in a gloomy mood: "He has the _____ today."*) Inf **AL**19, Mean reds; **TX**37, Reds.

red sage n

1 A **summer cypress** (here: *Kochia americana*). **chiefly CA**
 1923 in 1925 Jepson *Manual Plants CA* 330, *K[ochia] americana*. . . Red Sage. . . Herbage grayish or rusty. **1944** Abrams *Flora Pacific States* 2.89, *Kochia americana*. . . Red Sage. . . Perennial, with a stout woody root and a branched woody crown. **1959** Munz-Keck *CA Flora* 381, *Red-Sage*. . . Occasional and local on alkaline flats. **1973** Hitchcock–Cronquist *Flora Pacific NW* 100, Red sage. . . *K. americana*.

2 A **sage 1** such as *Salvia coccinea*. **chiefly TX**
 1936 Whitehouse *TX Flowers* 126, *Red Sage*. . . *Salvia coccinea*. . . is native to the Gulf States, in Texas growing in woods near the coast. The red flowers are nearly an inch long. **1953** Greene–Blomquist *Flowers South* 111, Red . . sage (*S. coccinea*) is the only red-flowered native sage which is both conspicuous and easily recognized. **1961** Wills–Irwin *Flowers TX* 196, *Shrubby Red Sage—Salvia greggii*. . . South Central and West Texas. **1967** *DARE* Wildfl QR (Wills–Irwin) Pl.42B Inf **TX**44, Shrubby red sage—pinkish. **1970** Correll *Plants TX* 1368, *Salvia penstemonoides*. . . Big red sage. . . Edwards Plateau, June–Oct.; endemic. **1993** Grimm–Kartesz *Illustr. Book Wildflowers* 232, *Red Sage (Salvia coccinea)*—This, our only native sage with red or scarlet flowers[,] . . grows in sandy hammocks, waste places, and along roadsides in the coastal plain from S.C. south to Fla. and west to Tex.

red salamander n

1 A mud **salamander 1** of the genus *Pseudotriton*, usu *P. ruber.*
 1891 in 1895 IL State Lab. Nat. Hist. Urbana *Bulletin* 3.361, *Spelerpes ruber* [=*Pseudotriton r.*]. . . Red Salamander. . . Color above red or reddish brown, with numerous dusky specks or spots. **1953** Schmidt *N. Amer. Amphibians* 48, *Pseudotriton ruber*. . . New York to the Gulf coastal plain; not in Atlantic coastal plain. . . Red salamander. **1958** Conant *Reptiles & Amphibians* 241, Both the Red and Mud Salamanders (*Pseudotriton*) are red or reddish, and details must be checked carefully to tell them apart. *Ibid* 244, Mud and Red Salamanders [=*Pseudotriton montanus* and *P. ruber*] are easily confused—even experienced herpetologists have trouble with them. **1979** Behler–King *Audubon Field Guide*

Reptiles 353, *Red Salamander (Pseudotriton ruber)*. . . Robust red salamander with short legs and tail. Young coral-red to reddish-orange above, adults orange-brown to purple-brown.

2 A **salamander 1** (*Ensatina eschscholtzi*) native to Pacific coastal areas.
 1947 Pickwell *Amphibians* 10 **Pacific,** *Ensatina eschscholtzi eschscholtzi*, the . . Red Salamander . . , a strikingly reddish animal, . . has been found under wet paper left by picnickers and in other localities in the Santa Clara County area. **1953** Schmidt *N. Amer. Amphibians* 43, *Ensatina eschscholtzi oregonensis*. . . Northern Pacific red salamander.

red salmon n Also *red* [*DCan* 1859 →] **chiefly AK**
=**sockeye salmon.**
 1881 Greene *Cape Cod Folks* 137, He . . related anecdotes redolent of 'red salmon' and . . 'strawberries as big as teacups' . . in places where he had sailed. **1891** U.S. Fish Comm. *Bulletin for 1889* 195 **AK,** The Red Salmon (*Oncorhynchus nerka*). This is the blue-back of the lower Columbia River. . . It does not seem to exist south of the Columbia River. Northward it is found as far as the Yukon. **1909** Holder–Jordan *Fish Stories* 149, In the sea, and in the early runs, its body is bright metallic blue in color. . . Later, the body turns crimson-red, while the head takes on a shade of olive-green. The names blueback and red salmon are both appropriate, according to the season. **1936** *AK Sportsman* Sept 16, The Columbia River blueback, alias sockeye on Puget Sound, [is] . . most commonly known as red salmon in Alaska. **1968** *DARE* (Qu. P1, . . *Kinds of freshwater fish . . caught around here . . good to eat*) Inf **AK**1, Sockeye—a "red"—spawn only in lakes; (Qu. P2, . . *Kinds of saltwater fish caught around here . . good to eat*) Inf **AK**9, Red salmon. **1978** *AK Fishing Guide* 55, Red Salmon. . . of great commercial value because of their rich, oily, ruby-red flesh. *Ibid* 59, Most red salmon fishermen work their flies too much. . . Flies that work on reds can be purchased in Alaskan tackle shops. **1991** Tabbert *Dict. Alaskan Engl.* 132, However, in Alaska, although *sockeye* is used, the more frequent name is *red salmon*, often shortened to *red*, especially in the plural.

red salt n Also *red salt grass* Cf **salt grass a(1), white salt**
A **cordgrass** (here: *Spartina patens*).
 1937 Chapman *New Engl. Village Life* 72 **CT,** The meadow itself as it was freed from overflow [of sea tide] tended to produce a better grade of grass; sedge gave place to red-salt and red-salt to blackgrass. *Ibid* 129, In March wind and sunshine . . the red-salt grass began to show golden browns again.

red sandpiper n
=**knot** n[2].
 1888 Trumbull *Names of Birds* 178, *Knot* . . red sandpiper. **1917** (1923) *Birds Amer.* 1.231, *Tringa canutus*. . . Red Sandpiper. . . In summer, color of upper parts grayish-brown and the breast rufous-brown; in winter, plain gray above and white below. **1953** Jewett *Birds WA* 267, Red Sandpiper. . . on occasion, very abundant along the coast of Washington, particularly in spring.

red scale n Cf **shad scale**
An **orach** (here: *Atriplex rosea*).
 1935 (1943) Muenscher *Weeds* 204, *Atriplex rosea*. . . Red scale. . . Common in waste places about the irrigated sections from the northern Rocky Mountain states to California. **1941** Jaeger *Wildflowers* 51 **Desert SW,** Redscale. . . *Atriplex rosea*. . . When dried it is one of our common tumbleweeds. **1961** Thomas *Flora Santa Cruz* 150 **cwCA,** Redscale. . . A weed in disturbed areas and along the edges of cultivated fields. **1974** Munz *Flora S. CA* 357, Redscale. . . Widespread in Calif.; to L. Calif., Wash., Atlantic Coast.

red screech owl See **red owl**

red sculpin n Cf **sculpin**
An **Irish lord** (here: *Hemilepidotus hemilepidotus*).
 1898 U.S. Natl. Museum *Bulletin* 47.1935, *Hemilepidotus hemilepidotus*. . . Red Sculpin.

red sea perch See **red perch 2**

red-seed n
=**blazing star 2.**
 1900 Lyons *Plant Names* 93, *C[hamaelirium] luteum*. . . Red-seed.

red-shafted flicker n Also *red flicker, red-shafted woodpecker* Cf **yellow-shafted flicker**
A western color form of the **flicker** n[2] **1** with a red "mous-

tache" in the male and salmon pink coloring under the wings and tail.

1831 Wilson *Amer. Ornith.* 4.245 *(DA)*, Red-shafted Woodpecker. *Colaptes Mexicanus.* **1848** (1962) U.S. Army Corps Topog. Engineers *Abert's NM Rept.* 42, The groves on each side of the road were full of stellar jays, (garrulus stelleri,) red shafted flickers. **1860** in 1869 *Amer. Naturalist* 2.599, [The] Red-shafted Flicker . . is common throughout the Rocky Mountains. **1913** *Pacific Coast Avifauna* 9.55, *Red-shafted Flicker.* . . Ants seem to be the favorite food of these birds. **1959** Barnes *Nat. Hist. Wasatch Winter* 11 **UT,** As we enter the home yard, . . a red-shafted flicker is interested in a Boston ivy. **1966–69** *DARE* (Qu. Q17, . . *Kinds of woodpeckers*) Inf **CA3,** Red flicker; **CA78, 140, CO7,** Red-shafted flicker; **WA15,** Red-shafted woodpecker. **1977** Udvardy *Audubon Field Guide Birds* 642, *"Red-shafted Flicker".* . . A large woodpecker. . . Salmon pink wing and tail linings of western flickers are conspicuous in flight.

red-shafted hawk n Also *red-feathered hawk*
Perh =**red-shouldered hawk.**
   1968–69 *DARE* (Qu. Q4, . . *Kinds of hawks*) Inf **AZ15,** Red-shafted hawk; **CT15,** Red-feathered hawk.

red-shafted woodpecker See **red-shafted flicker**

redshank n

1 The common **tern** *(Sterna hirundo).*
   1898 (1900) Davie *Nests N. Amer. Birds* 41, *Common Tern. Sterna hirundo.* . . Red-shank. . . It is an abundant bird throughout its North American range. **1956** MA Audubon Soc. *Bulletin* 40.22, *Common Tern.* . . Redshank (Mass. The feet are orange vermilion.)

2 also *redshanks:* A **ceanothus,** usu a **New Jersey tea** (here: *Ceanothus americanus*). Cf **redroot a**
   1797 Smith *Nat. Hist. GA* 1.29, The caterpillar . . also eats the red root or red shank, but is rarely to be met with, though the butterfly is often seen both in Georgia and Virginia. [**1869** Porcher *Resources* 132 **Sth,** *Ceanothus americanus.* . . This plant possesses a considerable degree of astringency, and has been used in gonorrhoeal discharges. . . The Indians employed it in lues venerea.] **1926** Puckett *Folk Beliefs S. Negro* 385 **MS,** Bluestone is often used along with an ointment, of which lard is the base, in connection with "red shanks" tea, and it may be that the astringent action does actually stop the discharge [of gonorrhea] and work an apparent cure. **1938** Baker *FL Wild Flowers* 133, *Redshank. New Jersey Tea*—Genus *Ceanothus*—Our plants of this genus show a low bushy growth, and bloom profusely in many clusters of tiny flowers. c**1938** in 1970 Hyatt *Hoodoo* 2.1525 [Black], Yo' git chew [=you] a piece of *red shank,* . . a piece of queen's delight [Hyatt: or queenroot]. . . [and other miscellaneous ingredients]. . . It will [Hyatt: cure] 'em of any case of vener'al disease dere is. **1986** Pederson *LAGS Concordance (Roots)* 1 inf, **nwFL,** Redshank—make a tea for bowel trouble.

3 also *redshanks:* =**yerba del pasmo** (here: *Adenostoma sparsifolium*).
   1902 *Out West Mag.* May 515 **SW,** [Footnote:] [This is] doubtless the small tree known in this region as "red-shank." **1931** U.S. Dept. Ag. *Misc. Pub.* 101.53, It [=*Adenostoma fasciculatum*] and its congener, redshanks, . . *(A. sparsifolium),* may have medicinal properties. **1974** Munz *Flora S. CA* 741, *Red-shank.* . . Arborescent, . . the trunks red-brown and freely exfoliating.

4 =**barnyard grass.** Cf **redshank grass**
   1920 *Torreya* 20.18 **SC,** *Echinochloa crus-galli.* . . Red-shank, Brunswick Co., S.C. **1966** *DARE* (Qu. L8, *Hay that grows naturally in damp places*) Inf **GA16,** Redshank.

redshank grass n Cf **redshank 4**
A **bullgrass 1** (here: *Paspalum boscianum*).
   1916 *Torreya* 16.236 **SC,** *Paspalum boscianum.* . . Red-shank grass, Kinloch Club, S.C.

redshanks See **redshank 2, 3**

red shiner n Cf **redfin 1**
A **shiner 1:** usu *Cyprinella lutrensis,* occas also *Notropis atherinoides.*
   1929 OK Univ. Biol. Surv. *Pub.* 1.83, *Notropis percobromus* [=*N. atherinoides*]. . . Red shiner. . . Arkansas River system in Oklahoma. **1951** Harlan–Speaker *IA Fish* 97, *Notropis lutrensis lutrensis* [= *Cyprinella l.*] . . The plains red shiner is found largely in the streams. . . It is a deep-bodied fish with dark back, silvery-blue sides, and red fins.

1964 Lowe *Vertebrates* 142, *Notropis lutrensis.* . . Red Shiner. . . This eastern bait and forage fish. . . is now widely distributed in warm-water streams, lakes and ponds in Arizona. **1967** Cross *Hdbk. Fishes KS* 126, The red shiner [=*Cyprinella lutrensis*] is one of the most abundant fishes of Kansas, and is almost ubiquitous in its distribution. **1970** WI Acad. *Trans.* 293, *Notropis lutrensis.* . . Red shiner. **1983** *Audubon Field Guide N. Amer. Fishes* 439, *Notropis lutrensis.* . . The most common shiner in the turbid, silty streams of the midwestern Plains Region, the Red Shiner is an important forage and bait fish.

red-shinned hawk n Also *redshin hawk*
Perh a **red-shouldered hawk.**
   1967–68 *DARE* (Qu. Q4, . . *Kinds of hawks*) Infs **PA49, 89,** Redshin hawk; **VA8,** Red-shinned hawk.

red shitepoke n Cf **shitepoke B1**
A **sandhill crane 1** (here: *Grus canadensis*).
   1949 Leopold *Sand Co. Almanac* 99 **WI,** The cranes whinnied . . and retreated to the far fastnesses. 'Red shitepokes' the haymakers called them, from the rusty hue which at that season often stains the battleship-gray of crane plumage.

red shoemake See **red sumac**

red-shoulder See **red-shouldered hawk**

red-shouldered blackbird n
=**red-winged blackbird.**
   1858 Baird *Birds* 529, *Red-shouldered Blackbird.* . . The shoulders and lesser coverts rich crimson. **1890** Warren *Birds PA* 212, *Theo. S. Wilkinson, Myrtlegrove plantation, lower coast, Louisiana,* writes as follows in . . 1886 . . : "The rice crop in Louisiana . . is much damaged by birds, principally the Red-shouldered Blackbird." **1953** Jewett *Birds WA* 586, Red-shouldered Blackbird. . . inhabits the willows and cottonwoods along rivers, lagoons, and lakes, and has even been seen feeding on pine seeds on the ground under the yellow pines. **1967** *DARE* (Qu. Q11, . . *Kinds of blackbirds*) Inf **TX5,** Red-shouldered blackbird.

red-shouldered hawk n Also *red-shoulder (hawk), red-shouldered buzzard,* ~ *chicken* (or *hen*) *hawk;* rarely ~ *falcon*
A large hawk *(Buteo lineatus)* native chiefly to the eastern half of the US and the Pacific coast. Also called **chicken hawk 1, dominecker 4, frog hawk 2, hen** ~**, rabbit** ~**, red-bellied** ~**, red-breasted** ~**, winter** ~
   1785 Pennant *Arctic Zool.* 206 **Long Is. NY,** Red Shouldered. Falcon. . . back of a deep brown, edged with rust-color. **1812** Wilson *Amer. Ornith.* 6.86, [The] Red-Shouldered Hawk. . . preys on Larks, Sandpipers and the small Ringed Plover, and frequently on Ducks. **1844** DeKay *Zool. NY* 2.10, The *Red-shouldered Buzzard,* or *Winter Hawk,* breeds in the Southern States. **1880** *Cimarron News & Press* 23 Dec. 1/5 *(DAE)* **NM,** Their representatives here are the red-tailed, red-shouldered, . . and ferruginous buzzards. **1884** *Harper's New Mth. Mag.* 68.622 **NEng,** The red-shouldered hawk is a handsome bird. **1899** in 1900 LA Soc. Naturalists *Proc.* 99, *Red-shouldered Hawk.* A winter resident only. **1945** MA Audubon Soc. *Bulletin* Mar 39, There are some pairs of nesting Red-shoulders, Sharp-shins or Broad-wings. **1950** *WELS (Kinds of hawks in your neighborhood)* 4 Infs, **WI,** Red-shouldered hawk. **1965–70** *DARE* (Qu. Q4, . . *Kinds of hawks*) 23 Infs, **chiefly NEast, Gt Lakes,** Red-shouldered hawk; **GA18, IA45, NJ21, OH16, PA155, SC4,** Red-shoulder hawk; **GA20,** Red-shouldered chicken hawk; **NH5,** Red-shouldered hen hawk. **1977** Udvardy *Audubon Field Guide Birds* 637, *Red-shouldered Hawk.* . . Large, long-winged hawk with rust-barred underparts, *reddish shoulders,* [and] a *narrowly banded tail.*

red-shouldered heron n
=**great blue heron.**
   1785 Latham *Genl. Synopsis Birds* 3.85 **NEast,** Red-shouldered h[eron]. . . *Ardea Hudsonias.* . . By some supposed to be the *female* of the last [=Great Heron]. **1917** (1923) *Birds Amer.* 1.184, *Great Blue Heron.* . . Other Names.—Red-shouldered Heron. **1946** Hausman *Eastern Birds* 100, *Ardea herodias herodias.* . . Red-shouldered Heron. . . Neck brownish.

red-shoulder hawk See **red-shouldered hawk**

redside n

1 also *redband, redsides, red-sided trout:* =**rainbow trout. Pacific NW**

1901 *Sunset* June/July 74 **sOR,** I got a good wetting in landing a three-and-a-half-pound red-side. **1904** *Salmon & Trout* 250, I caught the rainbow on similar flies. . . The eddies below outjutting rocks, or the swift and narrow waters between them, all yielded "the redsides," as they are often called on the Pacific slope. *Ibid* 252, The differentiation between the rainbow and steelhead lies apparently and solely in the scales; those on the latter being always smaller than in the typical "redsides." **1949** Peattie *Cascades* 318 **OR,** This is the habitat of the famous McKenzie River "redside," a compact and active rainbow particular in his feeding habits, difficult to fool, and marvelous to eat. **1956** Harlan–Speaker *IA Fish* 57, *Rainbow Trout.* . . Red-sided trout. . . The rainbow trout . . [has] a prominent horizontal red band on the side. **1967** *DARE* (Qu. P2, . . *Kinds of saltwater fish caught around here . . good to eat*) Inf **OR5,** Rainbow trout or redsides. **1979** *NYT Article Letters* **Pacific NW** [Fishing terms], Redside: rainbow trout. **1999** *DARE* File **sID,** A term for the rainbow trout—redband.

2 also *red-sided trout:* **=cutthroat trout.** Cf **redbelly 8**

1948 Baumann *Old Man Crow's Boy* 49 **ID,** Frenchy thought they were very close kin to our black-speckled trout, though these cutthroats, called "red-sides," had the vivid red markings on their lower jaws from which they get their name. **1999** *DARE* File **swID,** A common term for the cutthroat trout—redside. . . "I caught my limit of redsides today." (Don't I wish.) . . Some folks call them redsides, especially during their spawn. I'll call them 'red-sided trout' to indicate these cutthroat were spawners.

3 See **redside dace.**

4 See **redside shiner.**

redside dace n Also *redside, red-sided minnow, ~ shiner* [See quot 1943] Cf **red dace**

A **dace** (here: *Clinostomus elongatus*). Also called **shiner 1**

1873 in 1882 MI Laws *Genl. Statutes* 1.581, Nothing in this act shall be construed as prohibiting . . any person from catching mullet, suckers, red-sides, wall-eyed pike, or sturgeon. **1882** U.S. Natl. Museum *Bulletin* 16.232, *S[qualius] elongatus.* . . Red-sided Shiner. . . Great Lakes and Upper Mississippi Valley, chiefly from Pennsylvania to Minnesota. **1884** *Ibid* 27.487, *Squalius elongatus.* . . Red-sided Minnow. . . Western Pennsylvania; Ohio Valley; Great Lakes; Upper Mississippi Valley. **1896** *Ibid* 47.240, *Leuciscus elongatus.* . . Red-sided Shiner. . . Sides with a broad black band; . . the front half of the lateral band bright crimson in spring males. **1943** Eddy–Surber *N. Fishes* 136, The redside dace is a medium-sized minnow with a broad, black lateral band, the front half of which is bright crimson in spring males. **1957** Trautman *Fishes* 330 **OH,** The Redside Dace frequented brooks and small streams whose waters were normally very clear. . . Many pools contained brush or roots which the Redsides used as emergency cover. **1983** Becker *Fishes WI* 446, Redside Dace—*Clinostomus elongatus.* . . red-sided shiner. *Ibid* 449, The redside dace occurs in schools, and. . . will jump several inches into the air to catch a hovering insect.

red-sided bream See **redside shiner 1**

red-sided minnow, red-sided shiner See **redside dace**

red-sided sucker See **red sucker 2**

red-sided trout See **redside 1, 2**

redsides See **redside 1**

redside shiner n Also *redside, red-sided bream*

A **shiner 1** of the genus *Richardsonius* native to the western US.

1884 U.S. Natl. Museum *Bulletin* 27.489, *Richardsonius balteatus.* . . Red-sided Bream. Columbia River region. **1963** Sigler–Miller *Fishes UT* 76, *Richardsonius balteatus* . . Redside shiner, . . red-sided bream. . . One of the commonest and most widely distributed minnows in Utah. *Ibid* 77, The adults have a prominent orange to red or pink stripe on each side. . . The red stripe . . is especially bright in breeding males—hence the name redside—and . . is also present in a more somber shade in the females, particularly during the breeding season. **1983** *Audubon Field Guide N. Amer. Fishes* 455, Redside Shiner (*Richardsonius balteatus*). . . Slow-flowing creeks, rivers, and ditches; also ponds and lakes. *Ibid* 456, Lahotan Redside (*R. egregius*) . . inhabits streams and lakes of . . N. Nevada and NE. California. . . Increasing populations of Redside Shiners have overcrowded some lakes, reducing the trout population.

redside sucker See **red sucker 2**

red sign (crab) n Also *red line, ~ rim* Cf **pink sign**

A blue crab (*Callinectes sapidus*) close to shedding.

1970 *DARE* Tape **VA112,** The one that's real ripe will shed on the coming tide. . . He's got a blood-red rim on him just like a rainbow. . . If they put the white sign in with the pink rim, or the red rim, . . the white sign will go to that . . pink rim and red rim and eat him. **1976** Warner *Beautiful Swimmers* 27 **Chesapeake Bay,** We are getting a few more peeler crabs approaching their last moult of the season. . . Invariably the females will be "red sign," which means they will moult very soon, if not "busters" that have already started. . . The red-sign crabs moult within less than two days. **1984** *DARE* File **Chesapeake Bay** [Watermen's vocab], Red rim. Red line. Red sign.

red snapper n

1 Any of several **snappers** of the genus *Lutjanus*, but usu *L. campechanus.* **chiefly S Atl, Gulf States**

1775 (1962) Romans *Nat. Hist. FL* lii, The fish . . most commonly caught are such as seamen know by the following names, viz . . red, gray and black snappers, dog snappers, . . mangrove snappers. **1802** (1803) Ellicott *Jrl.* 255, Along the Florida Reef, and among the Keys, a great abundance and variety of fish may be taken: such as . . black, red, and gray snappers. **1879** *Harper's New Mth. Mag.* 60.26 **NYC,** The next dish was baked red snapper. **1911** U.S. Bur. Census *Fisheries 1908* 316, The red snapper (*Lutjanus aya* [=*L. campechanus*]). . . is a large fish, bright red in color, and is found from Long Island southward, but is most abundant on the coasts of Georgia, Florida, and the Gulf states. **1935** Caine *Game Fish* 105, *Muttonfish—Lutjanus analis.* . . Red or pinkish in hue but olive-green above. . . Red Snapper. *Ibid* 106, One of the principal members of the snapper family, it [=*Lutjanus analis*] is sometimes confused with the red snapper [=*L. campechanus*]. *Ibid* 130, *Mangrove Snapper—Lutjanus griseus.* . . Bronze-green above, shading into a brassy red on side and light gray on belly. . . Red Snapper. . . Those from the deep water are usually redder than those from the shallow water. **1965–70** *DARE* (Qu. P2, . . *Kinds of saltwater fish caught around here . . good to eat*) 19 Infs, **S Atl, Gulf States,** Red snapper(s); (Qu. P14, . . *Commercial fishing . . what do the fishermen go out after?*) Infs **FL21, GA3, 16, SC63, TX17,** Red snapper. **1983** *Audubon Field Guide N. Amer. Fishes* 605, *Lutjanus campechanus.* . . Red Snappers account for a substantial part of the food fishery on the Gulf Coast. **1986** Pederson *LAGS Concordance,* 67 infs, **Gulf Region,** Red snapper(s).

2 A **rockfish 3,** usu *Sebastes ruberrimus, S. melanops,* or *S. miniatus.* [See quot 1978] **AK, Pacific**

1909 U.S. Dept. Commerce Bur. Fisheries *Document* 645.74 **AK,** This species [=*Sebastes melanops*] is found scattered along the Pacific side of the district, being, so far as known, most abundant in southeast Alaska, especially around Sitka, where it is sometimes called redfish and red snapper. **1944** *AK Sportsman* July 19, Even our Alaska red snapper is not a red snapper, nor is it a red cod. It is a variety of rock fish, sometimes marketed as "pink fish." **1946** Dufresne *AK's Animals* 286, Rarely will you hear the Red . . Rockfish (*S[ebastes] ruberrimus*) called anything but "red snapper." **1953** Roedel *Common Fishes CA* 127, *Sebastodes miniatus.* . . Chiefly vermilion or brick red in color. . . Red snapper. **1966–70** *DARE* (Qu. P2, . . *Kinds of saltwater fish caught around here . . good to eat*) Infs **AK9, CA25, 211, WA1, 17,** Red snapper; (Qu. P14, . . *Commercial fishing . . what do the fishermen go out after?*) Infs **CA168, WA11,** Red snapper(s). **1978** *AK Fishing Guide* 87, The red or scarlet rockfish is commonly called the red snapper in Alaska because of its superficial resemblance to the true red snapper in the Atlantic.

3 **=red grouper 1.** Cf **red-bellied snapper**

1935 Caine *Game Fish* 74, *Red Grouper—Epinephelus morio.* . . [No] clear shades of red except on jaws and lower side of head, and these markings are more of a salmon color. . . Red Snapper. **1946** LaMonte *N. Amer. Game Fishes* 53, *Epinephelus morio.* . . Red Snapper. . . Many color phases, ranging from solid black to almost solid light red.

red sop See **red gravy 1**

red sorrel n Cf **redtop 2, redweed 2**

A **dock** n¹: usu a **sheep sorrel** (here: *Rumex acetosella*), but occas the similar *Rumex hastatulus.*

1894 *Jrl. Amer. Folkl.* 7.97 **WV,** *Rumex acetosella,* . . red sorrel. **1912** Blatchley *IN Weed Book* 63, *Rumex acetosella.* . . Red Sorrel. . . Leaves very sour, often picked and eaten. **1964** Batson *Wild Flowers SC* 41, *Sorrel, red sorrel, sheep sorrel: Rumex hastatulus.* . . This plant and the closely related species [=*R. acetosella*] mentioned below . . are pleasantly sour and sometimes used as a salad-plant. **c1967** GA Univ. *Weeds S. U.S.* 36, *Rumex acetosella—red sorrel.* . . Flowers yellowish to red on raceme. . . Found in lawns, pastures, abandoned fields. **1969** *DARE* (Qu. S15, . . *Weed seeds that cling to clothing*) Inf **IL**104, Red sorrel will stick to damp clothing; it's found in strawberry plots. **1973** Hitchcock–Cronquist *Flora Pacific NW* 91, Red . . s[orrel] . . *R[umex] acetosella.*

red sparrow n

1 =**fox sparrow.**

[**1791** Bartram *Travels* 291, F[ringilla] rufa [=*Passerella iliaca*], the red, or fox-coloured ground or hedge sparrow.] **1955** *Oriole* 20.1.14 **GA**, Fox sparrow.—Red Sparrow (from its rufescent coloration). **1969** *DARE* (Qu. Q21, . . *Kinds of sparrows*) Inf **IL**46, Red sparrow. [*DARE* Ed: This Inf may refer instead to **2** below.]

2 =**purple finch.**

1932 Bennitt *Check-list* 60 **MO**, *Carpodacus purpureus purpureus.* . . Red sparrow. . . C[ommon] W[inter] R[esident] throughout the state.

red sperm oil See red oil

red-spotted chub n

=**hornyhead c.**

1884 U.S. Natl. Museum *Bulletin* 27.485, *Ceratichthys biguttatus.* . . Red-spotted Chub; . . Horny Head. . . It reaches a length of 9 inches and is used for food.

red-spotted lizard n

=**leopard lizard.**

1928 Baylor Univ. Museum *Contrib.* 16.11 **TX**, Leopard Lizard. . . In the Trans-Pecos country, this species [=*Gambelia wislizenii*] is, when in nuptial coloration, called the *Red-spotted Lizard.*

red-spotted sunfish n

=**orangespotted sunfish.**

1882 U.S. Natl. Museum *Bulletin* 16.479, *Red-spotted Sunfish.* . . Sides with many conspicuous round salmon-red spots. **1938** Schrenkeisen *Field Book Fishes* 248, *Red-spotted Sunfish.* . . A small, highly colored sunfish. . . Especially abundant in sandy streams. **1956** Harlan–Speaker *IA Fish* 136, Redspotted sunfish. . . Many are taken [by fishermen] . . since they are everywhere in shallow water and have ravenous appetites. **1983** Becker *Fishes WI* 840, *Lepomis humilis.* . . Redspotted sunfish. . . In Wisconsin . . known only from the Mississippi River drainage basin.

red-spotted trout n

1 =**brook trout.**

1830 *Cabinet Nat. Hist.* 1.147 **PA**, In other lakes, . . where there are none of the lake trout, the red-spotted trout of the streams, or salmo fontinalis, is the common and only one. **1842** DeKay *Zool. NY* 4.235, *Salmo fontinalis.* . . *Red-spotted Trout.* . . *Characteristics.* With vermilion dots, and larger yellow spots in the vicinity of the lateral line. **1904** *Salmon & Trout* 215, The habits of the cut-throat trout are similar to those of his Eastern brother, the red-spotted trout ([*Salvelinus*] *fontinalis*). **1983** Becker *Fishes WI* 316, *Brook Trout.* . . Other common names . . redspotted trout . . Red spots, sometimes surrounded by bluish halos, on sides.

2 =**Dolly Varden 1.**

1882 U.S. Natl. Museum *Bulletin* 16.319, *S[alvelinus] malma.* . . *Red-spotted Trout.* . . The sides with round red spots near the size of the eye, the back commonly with smaller paler ones, a feature of coloration which distinguishes this species at once from the others. **1884** Goode *Fisheries U.S.* 1.504, This species [=*Salvelinus malma*] is known in the mountains [of the western US] as "Lake Trout," "Bull Trout," "Speckled Trout," and "Red-spotted Trout." **1938** Schrenkeisen *Field Book Fishes* 57, Red-spotted Trout. . . A large trout with a slender little compressed body. . . Color . . much as in a brook trout. **1976** Tryckare et al. *Lore of Sportfishing* 74, Red-spotted trout. . . in rapid, cold water streams . . rises rapidly to a fly and . . has a reputation of being a very game species.

red sprangletop n

A **sprangletop** (here: *Leptochloa mucronata*). Also called **feather grass 3, salt grass a(6)**

1940 Gates *Flora KS* 130, Leptochloa filiformis [=*L. mucronata*]. . . Red Sprangletop. . . Open or shady ground, fields and sandy river banks. **1968** Barkley *Plants KS* 49, Red Sprangletop. . . Scattered in east two-

thirds [of Kansas]. **1970** Correll *Plants TX* 235, *Red sprangletop.* . . Moist soil and mud, . . late spring-fall.

red spruce n [*OED2* 1777 →]

A **spruce** (here: *Picea rubens*). Also called **he-balsam, double spruce 1, single ~ 1, snake ~, tamarack, white spruce, yellow ~, yew pine**

1810 Michaux *Histoire des Arbres* 1.123, On désigne encore quelquefois l'*Abies nigra* sous le nom de *Red spruce,* Sapin rouge, par suite de l'influence que certaines localités exercent sur la qualité de son bois. [=The *Abies nigra* is also sometimes called by the name of Red spruce because of the effect which certain localities have on the quality of its wood.] **1897** Sudworth *Arborescent Flora* 35, *Picea rubra.* . . Red Spruce. **1939** Medsger *Edible Wild Plants* 220, Red Spruce, *Picea rubra.* . . Young twigs and leaves are used in making the famous beverage, "spruce beer." **1952** Strausbaugh–Core *Flora WV* 46, *Red Spruce.* . . Originally one of our principal timber trees, covering an estimated 469,000 acres, now largely removed. **1966–68** *DARE* (Qu. T5, . . *Kinds of evergreens, other than pine*) Infs **CO**37, **ME**8, **NC**48, Red spruce; (Qu. T17, . . *Kinds of pine trees; not asked in early QRs*) Inf **MI**96, Red spruce. **1980** Little *Audubon Guide N. Amer. Trees E. Region* 285, Where the ranges overlap, Black Spruce [=*P. mariana*] is distinguishable from Red by its smaller dull gray cones curved downward on short stalks and remaining attached.

red squirrel n

1 A squirrel of the genus *Tamiasciurus,* esp *T. hudsonicus.* Also called **boomer** n[1] **1, chickaree, ferrididdle 1, pine squirrel 1.** For other names of *T. douglasii* see **redwood squirrel;** for other names of *T. hudsonicus* see **gopher** n[1] **2b(5), mountain boomer 1, ~ squirrel 1, ~ tacky, red pine squirrel, spruce ~**

[**1637** (1967) Morton *New English Canaan* 212, There are Squirils of three sorts, very different in shape and condition; one. . . is red, and hee haunts our howses and will rob us of our Corne.] **1682** (1836) Ash *Carolina* 73, There are . . the Red, the Grey, the Fox and Black Squirrels. **a1782** (1788) Jefferson *Notes VA* 51, Lesser gray squirrel, Black squirrel, Red squirrel. **1846** [see **prairie fox**]. **1849** (1911) Thoreau *Week on Concord* 242 **NEng**, The larger red squirrel or chickaree, sometimes called the Hudson Bay squirrel. **1886** Burroughs *Signs & Seasons* 61 **NEng**, The red squirrel does not lay by a store of food for winter use, . . yet in the fall he sometimes hoards in a tentative, temporary way. **1915** *Nature & Sci.* 107 **CA**, Mammals are likewise plentiful [in the San Joaquin valley] and include . . red squirrels or chickarees. **1947** Cahalane *Mammals* 389, *Red Squirrel—Tamiasciurus hudsonicus, T. douglasii.* . . Like an angry alarm clock, going off at 5 A.M., the red squirrel explodes into staccato sound. **1965–70** *DARE* (Qu. P27, . . *Kinds of squirrels*) 359 Infs, **chiefly Nth, Appalachians,** Red squirrel [*DARE* Ed: Some of these Infs may refer instead to **2** below.]; 20 Infs, **chiefly NEast, N Cent,** Red squirrel—small(er) (*or* smaller than fox squirrel); **IL**29, **WI**70, 72, Gray squirrel . . bigger than the red squirrel; **KY**35, **MI**27, Red squirrel—not same as (*or* different from) fox [squirrel]; **MI**65, Red squirrel a lot smaller, very competitive, will chase a fox squirrel; **MN**21, Red squirrel—fox [squirrel] is a bigger squirrel; **MN**29, Fox [squirrel] larger than a red squirrel; **MN**33, Red squirrel—smaller and reddish; **NC**30, 35, 37, **VA**8, Red squirrel—(same as) mountain boomer; **NJ**31, 39, 53, Red squirrel—chickaree(s); **NY**231, Red squirrel—fox [squirrel] is much bigger; **PA**168, Red squirrel—also [called] pine squirrel, little bigger than a chipmunk. **1967** *PA Game News* Dec 53 **PA**, Some people detest the cheeky red squirrel, but to me he is the most comical and entertaining critter in the woods. **1981** Pederson *LAGS Basic Materials,* 1 inf, **ceTN**, Red squirrel . . mountain boomers; 1 inf, **swTN**, Red squirrel, fox squirrel [are] different kinds.

2 also *red fox squirrel:* =**fox squirrel.**

1923 U.S. Dept. Ag. *Farmers' Bulletin* 1375.18 **KS**, *No open season:* . . red, gray, and black squirrels. **1932** Randolph *Ozark Mt. Folks* 180, We took our way toward the high hardwood ridges, because it is here that the fox-squirrels play—big tawny fellows which the natives call red squirrels. **1961** Jackson *Mammals WI* 164, *Sciurus niger rufiventer* . . Western Fox Squirrel. . . Other names include big red squirrel [etc]. **1965–70** *DARE* (Qu. P27, . . *Kinds of squirrels*) 43 Infs, **chiefly Sth, Midl,** Red squirrel [*DARE* Ed: Some of these Infs may refer instead to **1** above.]; 17 Infs, **esp Sth, S Midl, N Cent,** Red fox squirrel; **AR**16, 22, 42, 48, 52, **IA**29, **IL**115, **IN**80, **KS**20, **KY**24, **MI**105, **MS**6, 11, 53, 66, **MO**16, **OH**45, **TX**43, **WV**3, Red squirrel—(same as) fox squirrel; **OK**46, Gray squirrel is smaller than red [squirrel]; (Qu. P29

Inf **KS**17, Red fox squirrel. **1982** Elman *Hunter's Field Guide* 399, [The] fox squirrel. . . was probably named for the suffusion of red in its fur. (In some areas it is also known as the red squirrel, a name more properly applied to the little pine squirrels.) **1986** Pederson *LAGS Concordance* **Gulf Region,** 147 infs, Red squirrel(s) [*DARE* Ed: Some of these infs may refer instead to **1** above.]; 25 infs, Red fox (squirrel *or* squirrels); 22 infs, Red squirrel(s) = fox squirrel(s); 11 infs, Red squirrel(s)—larger (than gray squirrel); 1 inf, Red squirrel = cat squirrel.

redstart n [*OED2* 1570 → for a bird of the genus *Phoenicurus*]
A North American bird of the genus *Setophaga:* usu *S. ruticilla,* but also *S. pictus.* For other names of the former see **firetail, yellow-tailed warbler**

1731 Catesby *Nat. Hist. Carolina* 1.67, *Ruticilla Americana. The Redstart.* . . These Birds frequent the Shady Woods of *Virginia;* and are seen only in Summer. **1812** Wilson *Amer. Ornith.* 5.120, The Redstart extends very generally over the United States. **1860** in 1870 *Amer. Naturalist* 3.33, The Redstart (Setophaga ruticilla) was one of the commonest birds in the Missouri bottom-lands. **1917** (1923) *Birds Amer.* 3.167, The Redstart is not only one of the most conspicuously colored of the Warblers, but is perhaps the most restless and active of this essentially nervous and fidgety family. **1950** Bissell *Stretch on River* 89 **eMO,** The big broad stream [=the Mississippi] would roll very wide and slick, on down between islands and towheads . . with snakes and lumpy toads in the sandy scrub, redstarts and blackburnians fluttering in the pale cottonwoods. **1965** Bailey–Niedrach *Birds CO* 710, We watched the redstart [=*Setophaga pictus*] for about fifteen minutes. . . This warbler was not as "flitty" as redstarts usually are. **1975** Logan *Land Remembers* 81 **swWI** (as of c1920), They were redstarts, a bird all wings and motion. **1977** Udvardy *Audubon Field Guide Birds* 658, *American Redstart.* . . Its flashy color and constant movement while frequently drooping its wings and fanning its tail to expose its bright signal patches make this flycatcher warbler unmistakable.

red stem ivy n
See quot.

1982 Slone *How We Talked* 104 **eKY** (as of c1950), *Seven year etch* (itch)—caused by a parasite being under the skin. . . Another cure is to bathe in water in which red stem ivy has been boiled.

red-stemmed peavine n Cf **peaweed 1**
A **milkvetch** (here: *Astragalus emoryanus*).

1940 *Amer. Vet. Med. Assoc. Jrl.* 97.125 **TX,** The status of the red-stemmed peavine as a forage plant is subject to two widely divergent opinions among ranchers.

red stopper n Cf **redberry stopper, white ~**
A **stopper:** usu *Eugenia rhombea,* but also *E. confusa.*

1884 Sargent *Forests of N. Amer.* 89, *Eugenia procera* [=*E. rhombea*]. . . *Red Stopper.* Semi-tropical Florida. **1922** Sargent *Manual Trees* 774, *Eugenia confusa.* . . *Red Stopper.* . . A tree . . with a straight trunk. . . *Wood* . . bright red-brown. **1962** Harrar–Harrar *Guide S. Trees* 544, *Red Stopper—Eugenia rhombea.* . . The fruits are orange, tinged with red or black. . . *Red Stopper—Eugenia confusa.* . . The fruits are scarlet.

red sturgeon n
=**lake sturgeon.**

1884 U.S. Natl. Museum *Bulletin* 27.493, *Acipenser rubicundus.* . . *Red Sturgeon.* Mississippi Valley; Great Lakes and northward. **1903** NY State Museum & Sci. Serv. *Bulletin* 60.66, Red sturgeon. . . in Lake Erie . . spawns in June, for which purpose it ascends the rivers in large schools till stopped by obstructions or insufficient depth of water. **1933** LA Dept. of Conserv. *Fishes* 412, Known also as the . . Red Sturgeon . . , the Lake Sturgeon has been recorded as reaching a length of nine feet and a weight of over 100 pounds. **1943** Eddy–Surber *N. Fishes* 57, Red Sturgeon. . . is the largest of the native fishes of Minnesota and neighboring states. **1983** Becker *Fishes WI* 221, *Acipenser fulvescens.* . . Red sturgeon.

red sucker n

1 A **redhorse 1** (here: *Moxostoma macrolepidotum*). Cf **redfin 2**

1983 Becker *Fishes WI* 665, *Moxostoma macrolepidotum.* . . Red sucker. . . Paired fins salmon to reddish orange; anal fin orange or red with whitish edge. **1986** Pederson *LAGS Concordance (Common freshwater fish)* 1 inf, **csTN,** Red sucker.

2 also *red-side(d) sucker:* =**longnose sucker.**

1836 Richardson *Fauna Boreali-Amer.* 3.116, *Cyprinus (Catostomus) Forsterianus* [=*Catostomus catostomus*]. . . Red Sucker [so called by] Fur Traders. . . [W]e found it in Lake Huron and Great Slave Lake. **1878** U.S. Natl. Museum *Bulletin* 12.175, *Catostomus longirostris* [=*C. catostomus*]. . . Long-nosed Sucker. . . Red-sided Sucker. **1886** Mather *Memoranda* 32 **NY,** *Long-nosed Sucker.* . . Red sucker, in breeding season. . . Common in most Adirondack waters and . . readily distinguished by its long nose. **1908** Forbes–Richardson *Fishes of IL* 84, *Catostomus catostomus.* . . *Red Sucker.* . . Found in lower Lake Michigan. **1943** Eddy–Surber *N. Fishes* 111, Red Sucker. . . is variable in coloration. The spring males . . have a broad, rosy lateral band, which persists until late in summer. **1983** Becker *Fishes WI* 688, *Catostomus catostomus.* . . red sucker, redside sucker.

3 A related **sucker** (here: *Catostomus tahoensis*).

1935 Pratt *Manual Vertebrate Animals* 56 **neCA,** *C[atostomus] tahoensis.* . . Red sucker. . . Region of Lake Tahoe; very abundant.

red sumac n Also *red shoemake*
Usu **smooth sumac,** but also **dwarf sumac.**

1813 Muhlenberg *Catalogus Plantarum* 32, Rhus glabrum, red, smooth Sumach. **1847** in 1914 Williams et al. *Readings IN Hist.* 351, For Yellow Jaundice. Take a double handful of wild cherry tree bark . . ; the same quantity . . of the bark of the red sumach roots [etc]. **1896** Freeman *Madelon* 197 **NEng,** Every white alder-bush in the spring raised you up anew before me to madden me with vain longing, and every red sumach in the fall. **c1902** Clapin *New Dict. Amer.* 333, *Red sumac.* A tree, the leaves of which are largely used, by Indians and trappers, as a substitute for tobacco. **1944** AL Geol. Surv. *Bulletin* 53.147, *R[hus] glabra.* . . White (or red) sumac. Grows naturally in dry but fairly rich soils, especially near rivers. *Ibid* 148, *R. copallina.* . . Black (or red) sumac. Prefers dry to sandy soils, but not as sensitive to fire as the preceding. **1965–69** *DARE* (Qu. T13, . . *Names . . for . . sumac*) Infs **CT**6, 30, **GA**70, **NY**1, 2, **OK**1, Red sumac; **ME**5, Red shoemake. **1976** Elmore *Shrubs & Trees SW* 28, Red . . sumac. . . *Rhus glabra.* . . Dark red trusses of glandular fruits easily identify this shrub far into the winter after its leaves have dropped. In the autumn, . . the leaves . . turn a bright red, scarlet or red violet, adding a brilliant touch of color to the countryside. **1986** Pederson *LAGS Concordance (Sumac)* 2 infs, **MS,** 1 inf, **cnGA,** Red sumac.

red sunflower n
A **purple coneflower** (here: *Echinacea purpurea*).

1900 Lyons *Plant Names* 69, *B[rauneria] purpurea* [=*Echinacea p.*] . . Red Sun-flower. **1901** Lounsberry *S. Wild Flowers* 520, *Red Sunflower.* . . *Brauneria purpurea.* . . More gorgeous than any Rudbeckia and infinitely more charming are these great, heavy heads of crimson blossoms. **1930** OK Univ. Biol. Surv. *Pub.* 2.83, *Brauneria purpurea.* . . Red Sunflower. Purple cone-flower. Black Sampson. **1974** (1977) Coon *Useful Plants* 107, *Echinacea purpurea* . . red sunflower. This is a tallish growing perennial widely found in the Midwest.

redtail n

1 See **red-tailed hawk.**

2 See **redtail chub.**

3 See **red-tailed skink.**

4 See **red-tailed snapper.**

5 also *redtail (cat) squirrel:* =**fox squirrel.** Cf **cat squirrel 3, red ~ 2**

[**1961** Jackson *Mammals WI* 165, The under side of the tail in all . . specimens [of *Sciurus niger*] I have examined has been clearly of orange fulvous tone.] **1968–69** *DARE* (Qu. P27, . . *Kinds of squirrels*) Inf **LA**44, Redtail = fox squirrel; **NJ**54, Redtail—has red tail. **1986** Pederson *LAGS Concordance (Squirrels)* 1 inf, **cnMS,** Redtail squirrels; 1 inf, **ceTX,** Redtail cat squirrel.

redtail chub n Also *redtail (minnow)*
=**hornyhead c.**

1820 Rafinesque *Ohio R. Fishes* 48, *Luxilus Kentuckiensis* [=*Nocomis biguttatus*]. . . Vulgar names, Indian Chub, Red-tail, Shiner, &c. Length about four inches. It is reckoned an excellent bait for anglers, because it will swim a long while with the hook in its body. **1982** Sternberg *Fishing* 20, Hornyhead chubs, or *redtail chubs,* have a lateral band that extends to a tail spot. They prefer gravelly streams from Wyoming to New York, south to Arkansas. **1983** Becker *Fishes WI* 485, *Nocomis* *biguttatus*. . . Redtail chub. . . Young with a reddish caudal fin. **1986** Pederson *LAGS Concordance (Bait)* 1 inf, **seAL**, Redtail minnow.

red-tailed bream n
=**red-breasted sunfish 1.**

1865 Norris *Amer. Angler's Book* 118, "*Ichthylis rubricunda* [sic]," is the Red-Bellied Perch, or Red-Tailed Bream. **1867** Storer *Hist. Fishes MA* 14, *Pomotis appendix*. . . The Red-tailed Bream. **1903** NY State Museum & Sci. Serv. *Bulletin* 60.479, The long-eared sunfish has a very extensive range and is known under many common names, among which are . . red-tailed bream [etc]. . . The species is common in streams east of the Alleghanies from Maine to Florida, and in tributaries of the Gulf of Mexico to Louisiana. **1938** Schrenkeisen *Field Book Fishes* 244, *Lepomis auritus*. . . Red-tailed Bream. **1976** Tryckare et al. *Lore of Sportfishing* 102, Red-tailed bream. . . Very similar to the pumpkin-seed and other sunfishes.

red-tailed buzzard (or chicken hawk) See **red-tailed hawk**

red-tailed coot n
=**Florida gallinule.**

1968 *DARE* (Qu. Q9, *The bird that looks like a small, dull-colored duck and is commonly found on ponds and lakes*) Inf **CA**78, Florida gallinule—the red-tailed coot.

red-tailed hawk n Also *red-tailed buzzard*, ~ *chicken hawk, redtail (hawk), red-tail(ed) hen hawk*

A large hawk (*Buteo jamaicensis*) with a rust-colored tail, found throughout most of the US. Also called **black hawk 2, chicken ~ 1, fantail 1, Harlan's hawk, hen ~, pi-ank, rabbit hawk, red ~**

1805 (1905) Clark *Orig. Jrls. Lewis & Clark Exped.* 3.257 **nwOR**, Large red tailed Hawks, ravens & crows in abundance. **1812** Wilson *Amer. Ornith.* 6.76, Red-tailed Hawk. *Falco borealis*. . . Early the next morning the unfortunate Red-tail was found a prisoner. **1839** Audubon *Synopsis Birds* 6, *Buteo borealis*. . . Red-tailed Buzzard. **1869** *Atlantic Mth.* 23.582 **DC**, [The turkey-buzzards'] movements when in air are . . identical with those of our common hen or red-tailed hawk. **1917** (1923) *Birds Amer.* 2.71, Red-tailed Hawk. . . Other Names. . . Red-tail; . . Red-tailed Buzzard. . . The Red-tailed Hawk's shrill *kee-er-r-r* attracts . . attention to its circling flight. . . Although known throughout the country as "Hen Hawk," the Red-tailed very seldom raids the chicken-yard. **1945** Mathews *Talking Moon* 4 **nOK**, I had come back to the very spot where I had lain as a boy, watching the circling of the red-tailed hawks. **1950** *WELS* **WI** (*Kinds of hawks in your neighborhood*) 4 Infs, Redtail hawk; 4 Infs, Redtail hawk; 1 Inf, Red-tailed hen hawk. **1965–70** *DARE* (Qu. Q4, . . *Kinds of hawks*) 50 Infs, **widespread**, Redtail hawk; 47 Infs, **widespread**, Red-tailed hawk; **MO**39, Little redtail hawk; **MO**18, Old redtail hawk; **VT**13, Redtail hen hawk; **GA**20, Red-tailed chicken hawk; **NH**5, Red-tailed hen hawk; **CA**78, Western red-tailed hawk. **1967** *PA Game News* Nov 50 **PA**, A number of red-tailed hawks and about fifty loons . . had already passed. . . An immature goshawk . . made two spectacular swoops at a redtail, missing by inches! **1977** Bull–Farrand *Audubon Field Guide Birds* 639, The Red-tail rarely takes poultry, feeding mainly on small rodents. Certain western birds, with dark brown, faintly banded tails were formerly considered a separate species that was called "Harlan's Hawk."

red-tailed skink n Also *redtail* Cf **blue-tailed skink**
A **skink** (here: *Eumeces egregius*).

1953 Schmidt *N. Amer. Amphibians* 153, *Eumeces egregius*. . . Southern Alabama and Georgia through Florida. . . Florida red-tailed skink. **1955** Carr–Goin *Guide Reptiles* 262, *Eumeces egregius* . . Striped Red-tailed Skink. . . A small, shiny lizard with a reddish tail. . . The reddish (pink to orange) tail distinguishes this form from all other eastern lizards. *Ibid* 263, *Eumeces onocrepis* [=*E. egregius* subsp *onocrepis*] . . Brown Red-tailed Skink. . . A small, shiny, red-tailed lizard. . . Distinguished by the red tail. **1958** Conant *Reptiles & Amphibians* 104, The Redtails are so slender and their legs so short that they seem almost snakelike in appearance and actions. . . They are most often found in open areas of dry sand.

red-tailed snapper n Also *redtail (snapper)* Cf **red snapper 1**
A **snapper** (here: *Lutjanus synagris*).

1898 U.S. Natl. Museum *Bulletin* 47.1270, *Neomaenis synagris*. . . Lane Snapper; . . Red-tail Snapper. . . Caudal [fin] deep blood-red. . .

Very common almost everywhere from Tampa to Brazil. **1946** LaMonte *N. Amer. Game Fishes* 59, *Lutjanus synagris*. . . Red-tail Snapper. . . Rosy above, shading to olive-silvery below. . . Dorsal [fin] and tail red. **1976** Tryckare et al. *Lore of Sportfishing* 110, Red-tailed snapper. . . A sport fish usually taken by bait rather than lure. A good table fish. **1986** Pederson *LAGS Concordance (Fish)* 1 inf, **seFL**, Redtail—saltwater.

redtail (hen) hawk See **red-tailed hawk**

red taillight oil See **red oil**

redtail minnow See **redtail chub**

redtail snapper See **red-tailed snapper**

redtail sparrow n Cf **red sparrow 1**
=**fox sparrow.**

1969 *DARE* (Qu. Q21, . . *Kinds of sparrows*) Inf **RI**17, Redtail sparrow—called in books rufous or fox sparrow.

redtail squirrel See **redtail 5**

redthroat n
1 =**red-throated loon.**

1955 MA Audubon Soc. *Bulletin* 39.309 **MA**, Red-throated Loon. . . Red-throat. . . Adults in breeding plumage have a long-triangular chestnut patch on the foreneck.

2 =**red-necked grebe.**

1955 MA Audubon Soc. *Bulletin* 39.309 **ME**, Holboell's Grebe. . . Redthroat. . . Adults of both sexes have the lower throat and front and sides of the neck deep brownish red.

red-throated loon n
Std: a **loon 1** (here: *Gavia stellata*). Also called **buckalew bird, cape-race, cobble n[3], diver, eel tricker, gray loon, gun greaser, little loon, pegging awl, pegmonk, pepper-shinned loon, Quaker ~, redthroat 1, spikebill, sprat loon, teal, touchmonk**

red-throated sapsucker See **red-throated woodpecker**

red-throated trout n Also *redthroat trout*
=**cutthroat trout.**

1897 NY Forest Fish & Game Comm. *Annual Rept. for 1896* 223 neCA, *Salmo mykiss* [=*Oncorhynchus clarkii*]. . . Black-spotted Trout; Red-throat Trout. **1903** NY State Museum & Sci. Serv. *Bulletin* 60.250, Red-throat Trout (Introduced [in New York]). **1949** Caine *N. Amer. Sport Fish* 79, *Salmo clarkii*. . . Redthroat Trout. **1976** Tryckare et al. *Lore of Sportfishing* 73, Red-throated trout. . . characterized by two very distinct red or pink streaks on underside of jaws.

red-throated woodpecker n Also *red-throated sapsucker*
A **sapsucker 1** (here: *Sphyrapicus ruber* or *S. varius*).

1874 NY Acad. Sci. *Annals Lyceum Nat. Hist.* 10.377 **IL**, Yellow-bellied Woodpecker. Red-throated Woodpecker. Winter sojourner in southern portion. **1889** Ridgway *Ornith. IL* 1.380, *Sphyrapicus varius*. . . Red-throated Sapsucker. **1895** Minot *Land-Birds New Engl.* 331, *Sphyrapicus varius nuchalis*, . . the . . Red-throated Woodpecker, . . differs from true *varius* in having a red patch on the hind-head or nape, and more or less red on the throat of the female. **1930** OK Univ. Biol. Surv. *Pub.* 2.134, The yellow-belly is a fairly common winter resident in Oklahoma. . . Local Names . . red-throated woodpecker, . . red-throated sapsucker. **1946** Goodrich *Birds in KS* 318, Sapsucker, red-throated—sapsucker, yellow-bellied.

redthroat trout See **red-throated trout**

red thrush n
=**brown thrasher.**

1789 Morse *Amer. Geog.* 60, American Birds [which] have been enumerated [include the]. . . Red Thrush. **1865** *Atlantic Mth.* 15.523, The Mavis, or Red Thrush, sneaks and skulks like a culprit. **1883** Nuttall Ornith. Club *Bulletin* 8.75, *Harporhynchus rufus*. . . Its strong color and mimicking voice gives us . . Red Thrush. **1956** MA Audubon Soc. *Bulletin* 40.128, Brown Thrasher. . . Red Thrush. **1962** Imhof *AL Birds* 397, Red Thrush. . . This bird is rich reddish-brown above. . . Its song is similar to that of the Mockingbird but is less varied.

redtick n Also *red-ticked hound* Cf **bluetick**
An American hound marked with red spots.

1958 Humphrey *Home from the Hill* 48 **neTX,** He kept a pack of about fifteen foxhounds, and he liked to have one or two of all breeds on a chase for the harmony of their differently pitched voices. He had Black and Tans, Redbones, Goodmans, Blueticks and Redticks, Walkers, Triggs, a pair of Plott hounds. **1962** *Clarke Co. Democrat* (Grove Hill AL) 4 Jan 8/6 *(Mathews Coll.),* Lost—Red ticked hound, 2 years old. **1966** *DARE* Tape **AR**15, [FW:] What kind of dogs do you have for fox dogs? [Inf:] There are different breeds all right. . . You have the redtick, and you have the bluetick.

red-tipped blackbird n
=**red-winged blackbird.**

1968 *DARE* (Qu. Q11, . . *Kinds of blackbirds*) Inf **VA**8, Red-tipped blackbird.

red titi n Cf **black titi 2, titi, white titi**
=**he-huckleberry 1.**

1897 Sudworth *Arborescent Flora* 277 **FL,** *Cyrilla racemiflora.* . . Red Titi. **1923** Pellett *Amer. Honey Plants* 343, *Cyrilla racemiflora.* . . occurs . . in the edges of swamps and along streams. It is . . known as . . red ti-ti. **1939** Tharp *Vegetation TX* 61, Red or White Titi. **1979** Little *Checklist U.S. Trees* 122, Red titi. . . Coastal Plain from se. Va. to c. Fla. and w. to se. Tx.

redtop n

1 Any of several grasses; see below. Cf **wild redtop**

a also *redtop grass:* Any of var **bentgrasses 1,** but esp *Agrostis stolonifera,* which is often used for hay or pasturage.

1790 Deane *New Engl. Farmer* 172, The *Herd-grass* of the southern States, is called also . . *Red-top.* . . The red-top is particularly valuable, as it will grow and sod the first year on banks, when no other grass will thrive. *Ibid* 188, The Rhode-Island bent, as it is called, or red-top grass, will do with less drying than some other grasses. **1818** Taylor *Arator* 204, A large meadow in bottom land, of a grass called red top or herd's grass, was cut in dry weather. **1843** Torrey *Flora NY* 2.441, *Agrostis vulgaris.* . . *Red-top. Herd's-grass.* . . Pastures and moist meadows. **1881** Phares *Farmer's Book of Grasses* 40 **Sth,** *A[grostis] vulgaris,* Red Top Grass. . . It and timothy being adapted to the same soils and maturing at the same time do well together and produce an excellent hay. But the red top will finally root out the timothy—if pastured much it will do so sooner. **1912** Wooton-Standley *Grasses NM* 86, *Agrostis.* . . Redtop. *Ibid* 88, *Agrostis alba.* . . *Red-top.* This grass grows well in the higher mountains at elevations of more than 7000 feet in wet soils. **1935** Davis *Honey* 1 **OR,** A ten-mile stretch of cree-meadow with wild vetch and redtop and velvet-grass reaching clear to the black-green fir timber of the mountains. **1937** U.S. Forest Serv. *Range Plant Hdbk.* G8, The characteristic reddish or purplish hue of the flower heads of many species [of *Agrostis*] . . gives rise to the name, redtop. . . It seems preferable to use redtop, as a generic name for most of the native range species of *Agrostis*. **1965–70** *DARE* (Qu. L9a, . . *Kinds of grass . . grown for hay*) 78 Infs, **chiefly NEast, S Midl, Rocky Mts,** Redtop; **MO**21, Redtop grass; **TN**62, **VA**14, Redtop = herd's grass; (Qu. L8, *Hay that grows naturally in damp places*) Infs **NH**5, **NY**209, **OR**13, **VA**68, Redtop; (Qu. L9b, *Hay from other kinds of plants [not grass];* not asked in early QRs) Infs **NC**54, **PA**230, **RI**16, **VA**24, Redtop; (Qu. L22, *When talking about a crop he intends to plant . . a farmer might say, "This year, I'm going to ——— a crop of oats/corn/cotton, etc."*) Inf **IL**142, Seed redtop; (Qu. L34, . . *Most important crops grown around here*) Inf **NV**2, Redtop; (Qu. S8, *A common kind of wild grass that grows in fields: it spreads by sending out long underground roots, and it's hard to get rid of*) Inf **IL**83, Redtop; (Qu. S9, . . *Kinds of grass that are hard to get rid of*) Infs **MI**2, **MO**8, **VA**30, Redtop; (Qu. S26a, . . *Wildflowers. . . Roadside flowers*) Inf **FL**27, Redtop; (Qu. S26e, *Other wildflowers not yet mentioned;* not asked in early QRs) Inf **FL**27, Redtop. [*DARE* Ed: Some of these Infs may refer instead to other senses below.] **1979** Niering-Olmstead *Audubon Guide N. Amer. Wildflowers E. Region* 684, *Redtop (Agrostis alba).* . . The fine, pinkish-tinged, cone-shaped flowering panicles are especially beautiful in open fields. **1986** Pederson *LAGS Concordance,* 1 inf, **cwAR,** Redtop grass; 1 inf, **neAR,** Redtop hay.

b =**purpletop.** Cf **false redtop 2**

1829 Eaton *Botany* 447, *Windsoria.* . . *seslerioides* [=*Tridens flavus*] . . red-top . . about 6-flowered. **1912** Baker *Book of Grasses* 170, Tall Red-top, often shoulder-high and bearing long, tapering leaves,

rises in striking contrast to the lower growth. This grass . . is found from southern New England to the Gulf. **1950** Gray-Fernald *Manual of Botany* 130, *Tall Red-top.* . . Dry fields, roadsides, openings and borders of woods. **1967** Braun *Monocotyledoneae* 92 **OH,** *Tall Redtop.* . . A tall to moderately tall grass common along roadsides and in old fields. . . Eastern half of the United States.

c A **bluegrass 1** (here: *Poa palustris*). Cf **false redtop 1**

1843 Torrey *Flora NY* 2.458, *Poa serotina* [=*P. palustris*]. . . *Redtop.* . . Wet meadows, valley of the Hudson and western parts of the State. **1861** Wood *Class-Book* 798, *P[oa] serotina.* . . *Meadow Redtop.* . . Wet meadows and woods, common in the N. States and Can. . . Makes excellent hay.

d as *redtop millet,* ~ *panic grass* (or *panicum*): A **panic grass:** usu *Panicum rigidulum,* but also *P. adspersum.*

1889 Vasey *Ag. Grasses* 28, *Panicum agrostoides* [=*P. rigidulum*]. (Redtop Panicum.) This is a perennial grass, commonly growing in large clumps in wet meadows or on the muddy margins of lakes and rivers. It grows 4 to 6 feet high . . and developes [sic] . . reddish panicles. . . This grass . . makes fair hay if cut before flowering time. . . It may be utilized as a hay crop in low grounds, but it is doubtful if it can be made productive on dry, tillable land. **1933** *Torreya* 33.82, *Panicum adspersum.* . . Red-top millet, Leon County, Fla. **1940** Gates *Flora KS* 132, Panicum agrostoides. . . Redtop Panicgrass. Wet meadows, ditches and borders of ponds.

2 also *redtop sorrel,* ~ *weed:* A **sheep sorrel** (here: *Rumex acetosella*).

1873 in 1976 Miller *Shaker Herbs* 236, *Rumex acetosella.* Red Top Sorrel. Field Sorrel. . . A common weed in pastures and waste grounds. **1935** (1943) Muenscher *Weeds* 198, Red-top sorrel. . . Frequently considered as an indicator of acid soil. **1966–70** *DARE* (Qu. S21, . . *Weeds . . that are a trouble in gardens and fields*) Infs **FL**51, **MD**29, **MS**38, Redtop; **VA**77, Redtop weed. **1973** *Foxfire 2* 63, *Rumex acetosella* . . redtop. . . A common weed of fields and roadsides, with reddish stems from six inches to two feet tall, and creeping roots. The leaves are arrow-shaped and often red-tinged. Flowers and seeds appear in reddish spikes. . . Leaves are edible and rich in vitamin C.

3 also *redtop grass:* A **sedge B1:** either a **saw grass 1** (here: *Cladium mariscus*) or a **galingale 1** (here: *Cyperus odoratus*).

1913 *Torreya* 13.228 **AR,** *Cyperus engelmannii* [=*C. odoratus*]. . . Red-top grass, Lake Wapanoc, Ark. **1926** *Ibid* 26.4 **SC,** *Mariscus jamaicensis* [=*Cladium mariscus*]. . . Redtop grass, McClellanville, S.C. **1942** *Ibid* 42.158 **LA,** *Cladium jamaicense* [=*C. mariscus*]. . . Redtop.

4 =**green-tailed towhee.**

1928 Bailey *Birds NM* 709, The Green-tailed Towhee, or Red Top, as he is sometimes called, finds his food largely by scratching over the ground in Towhee fashion under sagebrush, oak brush, or chaparral.

5 See **redtop woodpecker.**

6 See **redtop clover.**

7 See quot.

1958 McCulloch *Woods Words* 147 **Pacific NW,** Red top—A tree infested with beetles, or a tree whose top has been girdled by porcupines. In both cases the dying crown turns reddish-brown.

redtop cane n Also *redtop sorghum* **TX**
A **sorghum** (here: *Sorghum bicolor* Saccharatum group).

1938 in Lib. of Congress *Amer. Memory: WPA Life Hist.* (Internet) **nwTX,** The main crops grown are Kaffir, Milo, Hegari, Red-top Sorghum and oats. . . Trench Silos, in which the Red-top Sorghum mainly is stored as a reserve food supply, are being used extensively. **1968–70** *DARE* (Qu. L9a, . . *Kinds of grass . . grown for hay*) Inf **TX**102, Redtop cane; (Qu. L9b, *Hay from other kinds of plants [not grass];* not asked in early QRs) Inf **TX**54, Redtop cane. **1999** *Cattle Today* Mar (Internet) **sTX,** I started out on the kid jobs. My Grandfather grew red top cane for winter forage. This was cut and bundled by a rowbinder and then shocked. Cattle were then allowed to graze the cut-over cane, but somebody had to keep the cattle out of the shocks. **2000** *DARE* File—Internet **nwTX,** Spring Forage Seeds available at Gayland Ward Seed Company. . . Open Pollinated Seed—Early Sumac (Red Top Cane). **2001** *NADS Letters* **sTX,** My dad (80 years old) remembered red-top cane from South Texas (the Rio Grande Valley) where it was grown for hay in 1950's. He said it made a sweet hay.

redtop clover n Also *redtop*
=**red clover.**

1879 *Scribner's Mth.* 19.248 **NY,** If the cultivator can wait for the . .

red-top clover he will find it far better, both to enrich and to lighten up his heavy soil. **1885** *South Fla. Sentinel* (Orlando) 29 July 4/2 *(DAE)*, Red top clover will grow and do well in our Sumter Co. soil. **1966–70** *DARE* (Qu. L9a, . . *Kinds of grass . . grown for hay*) Infs **AR**18, 56, Redtop clover; (Qu. L9b, *Hay from other kinds of plants [not grass]; not asked in early QRs*) Infs **AR**18, **MA**47, **VA**38, Redtop clover; **IN**63, Alsike, redtop—clovers for horse hay; **VA**75, Redtop—old-fashioned clover.

redtop grass See **redtop 1a, 3**

red topknot woodpecker See **redtop woodpecker**

redtop millet (or panic grass, panicum) See **redtop 1d**

redtop sorghum See **redtop cane**

redtop sorrel (or weed) See **redtop 2**

redtop woodpecker n Also *redtop, red topknot woodpecker*
=red-headed woodpecker 1.
   1967–69 *DARE* (Qu. Q17, . . *Kinds of woodpeckers*) Infs **CT**2, **TX**26, Redtop; **NJ**52, Redtop = downy woodpecker; **IN**55, Redtop woodpecker; **KY**56, Red topknot woodpecker. **1973** Allen *LAUM* 324 **cnND,** *Woodpecker. . . Red-shafted woodpecker* and *redtop* turn up as singletons. **1986** Pederson *LAGS Concordance*, 1 inf, **cGA,** Redtop—another name for peckerwood.

red trout n
=lake trout 1.
   1766 in 1903 Rowe *Letters* 94 **eMA,** [I] caught a fine Red Trout. **1879** *Forest & Stream* 12.409 **NEng,** I landed several trout in Lake Winnipiscogee, weighing from three to six pounds each. . . These trout are classified under lake trout, red trout or lake salmon. **1903** NY State Museum & Sci. Serv. *Bulletin* 60.267, The lake trout has received many names, among which are the following: . . red trout [etc].

reduct v [Engl dial; *OED2* 1599–1738]
To deduct.
   1896 *DN* 1.423 **wFL,** *Reduct:* subtract. "Reduct my time from what I owe."

red up See **redd 3a**

red viper n Cf **viper**
=copperhead snake 1.
   1842 DeKay *Zool. NY* 3.54, It [=*Agkistrodon contortrix*] has various popular names in different districts; the most common of these are, in this State, *Copper-head, . . Red Viper* [etc]. **1859** (1968) Bartlett *Americanisms* 99, Copperhead. . . has various other popular names, as . . Red Viper, Red Adder.

red wagon n **chiefly SE** See Map Cf *fix one's wagon* (at **fix v B4b)**
In phrr *one's (little) red wagon* and varr: One's business or problem.
   1966–70 *DARE* (Qu. GG21a, *If you don't care what a person does . . "You can go ahead and do it _____."*) Inf **NC**84, It'll be your red wagon; **NC**52, It's your little red wagon; (Qu. II22, *Expressions to tell somebody to keep to himself and mind his own business*) Infs **AL**60,

MS49, Run your own little red wagon; **SC**11, 45, Tend (to) your little red wagon; **SC**34, Pull your own little red wagon; [**FL**35, Peddle your own wagon]. **1968** *Current Slang* 3.2.33 [Watts slang; Black], *Little red wagon. . .* Social problem, bag.—Living in Watts is your *little red wagon*. **1984** Burns *Cold Sassy* 10 **nGA** (as of 1906), Well, this time next year Grandpa would be married, and if he didn't like what was put before him it would be Miss Love's little red wagon, not Mama's or Aunt Loma's. **1986** Pederson *LAGS Concordance*, 1 inf, **swLA,** That'll be my little red wagon—i.e., my affair.

red wasp n **chiefly Sth, S Midl, TX** See Map
A **paper wasp** of the genus *Polistes*.
   1965–70 *DARE* (Qu. R21, . . *Other kinds of stinging insects*) 84 Infs, **chiefly Sth, S Midl, TX,** Red wasp; **FL**9, Red wasp—guinea wasp smaller than red; **LA**8, Yellow jacket smaller than red wasp, but makes a nest like it; **LA**10, Guinea wasp—yellow, smaller than red wasp and meaner—same kind of nest; **OK**52, Red wasp—also called paper-makers; (Qu. R20) Inf **MO**3, Red wasp makes a paper nest. [**1980** Milne–Milne *Audubon Field Guide Insects* 834, Paper Wasps (*Polistes* spp.) . . Head and body *mostly reddish brown . . with yellow rings and reddish areas on abdomen. . .* Female has brown face. Wings amber to reddish brown.] **1986** Pederson *LAGS Concordance* **Gulf Region,** 84 infs, Red wasp(s); 5 infs, Red waspes; 1 inf, Red wasp—larger than guinea wasp; 1 inf, Red wasp all red; 1 inf, Red wasp—reddish-colored.

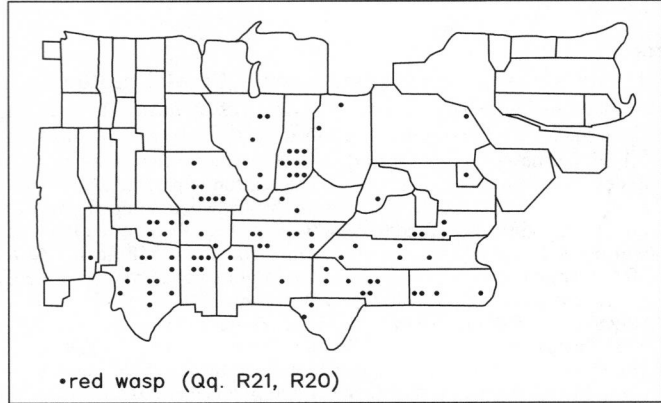

•red wasp (Qq. R21, R20)

redweed n
1 =pokeweed 1a.
   [**1624** Smith *Genl. Hist. VA* 170, [In the Bermudas] is also frequently growing a certaine tall Plant, whose stalke being all ouer couered with a red rinde, is thereupon termed the red weed.] **1900** Lyons *Plant Names* 287, *P[hytolacca] decandra. . .* Redweed. **1936** Winter *Plants NE* 196, *P[hytolacca] americana. . .* Pokeberry. . . Found in Nebr. only in the southeastern portion of the state. . . Called also Ink-berry or Redweed.

2 A **sheep sorrel:** usu *Rumex acetosella*, but also *R. hastatulus*. Cf **redtop 2**
   1890 FL Ag. Exper. Sta. Gainesville *Bulletin* 8.9, Rumex Engelmanni [=*R. hastatulus*]. . . Red weed, Sorrel. **1894** *Jrl. Amer. Folkl.* 7.97 **WV,** *Rumex acetosella, . .* red sorrel, red weed. **1935** (1943) Muenscher *Weeds* 198, *Rumex Acetosella. . .* Red-weed. . . Panicles appearing reddish when mature. . . Frequently considered as an indicator of acid soil. **1965–70** *DARE* (Qu. S21, . . *Weeds . . that are a trouble in gardens and fields*) Infs **AL**38, **IL**69, **MI**96, **ND**9, **NJ**31, **SC**53, 63, **VA**105, Redweed. [*DARE* Ed: Some of these Infs may refer instead to **4** below.]

3 =orange hawkweed.
   1898 *Jrl. Amer. Folkl.* 11.230 **ME,** *Hieracium aurantiacum, . .* red weed, . . Dover, Me.

4 A **goosefoot** (here: *Chenopodium rubrum*).
   1940 Clute *Amer. Plant Names* 255, *Chenopodium rubrum.* Red-weed.

red whiskey See **red liquor**

red wiggler n **chiefly SE** See Map Cf **Georgia wiggler, redworm 1**
An **earthworm,** esp *Eisenia foetida* or *Lumbricus rubellus*.
   1965–70 *DARE* (Qu. P6, . . *Kinds of worms . . used for bait*) 12 Infs, **chiefly SE,** Red wiggler(s); **FL**34, Georgia red wiggler; (Qu. P5, . . *The common worm used as bait*) Infs **GA**54, 65, 72, 89, **IA**29, **MS**63,

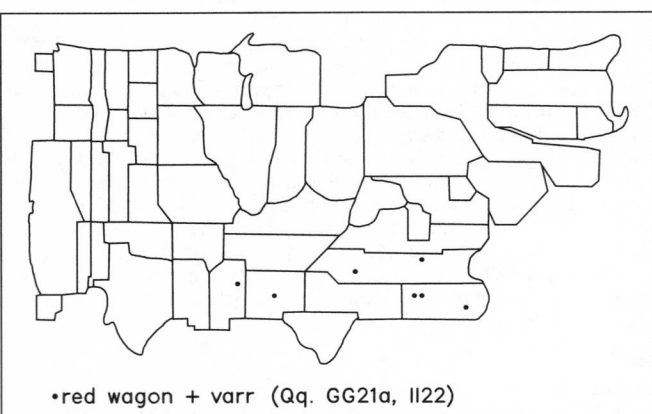

•red wagon + varr (Qq. GG21a, II22)

NC15, **TX**74, Red wiggler(s). **1967** *DARE* FW Addit **NY**, Red wiggler—red, transparent worm—grows in dung. **1969** *SC Market Bulletin* 11 Sept 3, Hybrid red worms and red wigglers for organic gardening, $4.50–1000. **1969** *DARE* Tape IL68, [Inf:] We raise our own worms, and we always have bait. [FW:] Do you have any special names? . . [Inf:] Red wiggler. . . red wiggler worms. **c1970** Pederson *Dial. Surv. Rural GA* **seGA** (*What do you call ordinary worms used for bait in fishing?*) 2 infs, Red wigglers; (*What do you call large worms used for bait?*) 1 inf, Red wigglers. **1982** Sternberg *Fishing* 56, The manure worm is red with whitish bands along its 3- to 4-inch body. It is raised by bait suppliers in the South and sold as the *red worm*. Another commercially grown type is the *red wiggler*, which grows to about 2 inches in length. **1986** Pederson *LAGS Concordance*, 32 infs, **Gulf Region**, Red wiggler(s); 1 inf, **nwAL**, Red wiggler—small; 1 inf, **ceGA**, Red wiggler—raised commercially; 1 inf, **cnGA**, Red wiggler—bigger than earthworm; 1 inf, **cGA**, Red wigglers—little; 1 inf, **swGA**, Slop worms are called red wigglers; 1 inf, **swGA**, Red wigglers—short worms; 1 inf, **swGA**, Red wiggler worms; 1 inf, **cwLA**, Red wigglers = redworms; 1 inf, **neMS**, Red wiggler—the kind he grows for fishing.

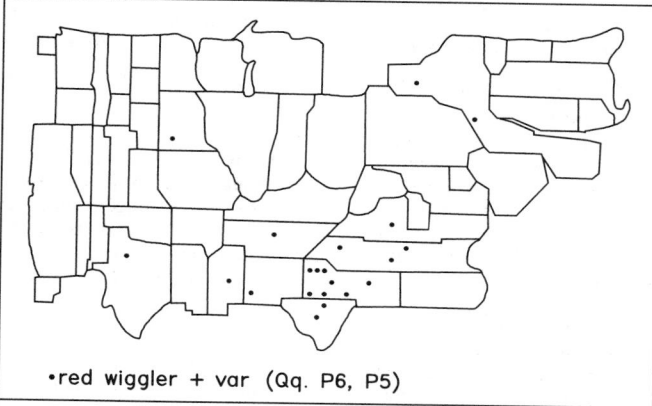

•red wiggler + var (Qq. P6, P5)

red willow n [*DCan* 1743 →]

1 Any of several **willows,** esp the western *Salix laevigata.*
1784 in 1785 Amer. Acad. Arts & Sci. *Memoirs* 1.491, *Salix.* . . The White Willow. The Red Willow. The Rose Willow. The Dogwood. The Osier. **1814** Brackenridge *Views of LA* 231 **Upper Missouri R,** These skin canoes are stretched over the red willow. **1897** Sudworth *Arborescent Flora* 122 **MT,** *Salix fluviatilis* [=*S. melanopsis*]. . . Red Willow. **1910** Jepson *Silva CA* 176, *Salix laevigata.* . . Branchlets one-winter-old reddish brown. . . The Red Willow grows along living streams. **1923** Abrams *Flora Pacific States* 1.489, *Salix lasiandra* [=*S. lucida* subsp *lasiandra*]. . . Red Willow. . . Twigs deep red, lustrous. *Ibid* 490, *Salix laevigata.* . . Red or Polished Willow. . . Branchlets yellowish to reddish-brown. **1960** Vines *Trees SW* 97, *Salix interior* [=*S. exigua*]. . . Known under the vernacular names of Riverbank Willow, . . Red Willow, and White Willow. *Ibid* 111, *Salix lasiandra.* . . Also known under the vernacular names of Black Willow, Red Willow [etc]. **1966–68** *DARE* (Qu. T15, . . *Kinds of swamp trees*) Infs **ID**5, **MI**27, **MN**16, **SD**8, **TX**5, Red willow. [*DARE* Ed: Some of these Infs may refer instead to **2** below.] **1980** Little *Audubon Guide N. Amer. Trees W. Region* 352, "Red Willow" . . *Salix bonplandiana.* . . Tree with broad, rounded crown of spreading branches.

2 A **dogwood 1;** see quots.
1876 Hobbs *Bot. Hdbk.* 97, Red willow, Swamp dogwood, Cornus sericea. **1896** *Jrl. Amer. Folkl.* 9.189 **MO,** *Cornus sericea,* . . red willow. **1920** *Torreya* 20.24 **MI,** *Cornus stolonifera* [=*C. sericea*]. . . Red willow, Traverse City, Mich. **1940** Clute *Amer. Plant Names* 97, *C[ornus] amomum.* . . Red willow. **1955** U.S. Arctic Info. Center *Gloss.* 66, Red willow. . . Red osier dogwood. **1964** Batson *Wild Flowers SC* 80, *Swamp dogwood, red willow: C[ornus] stricta* [=*C. foemina*]. . . A medium-sized shrub with red twigs and stems. . . Fruit blue. **1974** (1977) Coon *Useful Plants* 120, *Cornus stolonifera* . . red willow. . . It is reliably reported that the Indians of the West and the early pioneers used to gather the inner bark of the stems, dry and smoke it, and that such smoking gives a narcotic effect, which if overdone, may cause stupefaction. **1979** Erichsen-Brown *Med. N. Amer. Plants* 142, *Red Willow—Cornus amomum.* . . A shrub 1–3 m tall, the pith of the young twigs dark brown. . . New England and Que. to Ont., s. Ind., and s. Ill., s. to S.C. and Ala.

redwing n

1 See **red-winged blackbird.**

2 also *red-wing(ed) teal:* =**gadwall.**
1911 Howell *Birds AR* 18, The gadwall, known frequently as . . "red wing," is a common winter visitant in the State. **1943** Musgrove-Musgrove *Waterfowl IA* 24, Gadwall. . . Other names . . redwing. . . Adult male. . . Shoulders of the wing rich reddish-brown. **1966–70** *DARE* (Qu. Q5, . . *Kinds of wild ducks*) Infs **FL**29, **TX**84, Redwing; **MN**34, Redwing teal; **RI**4, Red-winged teal. **1982** Elman *Hunter's Field Guide* 147, *Anas strepera.* . . Redwing. . . She [=the female gadwall], too, has a white speculum, but her black and chestnut wing patches are smaller and duller.

redwing blackbird See **red-winged blackbird**

redwing bobolink n Cf **bobolink, reedbird, ricebird, white-wing blackbird**
=**red-winged blackbird.**
1967 *DARE* (Qu. Q11, . . *Kinds of blackbirds*) Inf **SC**43, Redwing bobolink.

red-winged blackbird n Also *redwing (blackbird)*

Std: a bird (*Agelaius phoeniceus*), the male of which is black with red shoulder epaulets, widely distributed in the US; also the similar tricolor blackbird (*A. tricolor*) of the Pacific coast. Also called **marsh blackbird, queen ~, red-tipped ~.** For other names of *A. phoeniceus* see **British lady, corn thief 1, maize bird, ~ thief, maybird 4, officer, one-one 3, quonk-a-ree, red-shouldered blackbird, red-tipped ~, redwing bobolink, red-winged starling, reedbird 2, ricebird 4, starling, swamp blackbird**

red-winged hawk n Also *redwing hawk*

Prob =**red-shouldered hawk.**
1968–70 *DARE* (Qu. Q4, . . *Kinds of hawks*) Infs **CA**117, **PA**126, Red-winged hawk; **VA**84, Redwing hawk.

red-winged starling n Also *redwing starling*

=**red-winged blackbird.**
1731 Catesby *Nat. Hist. Carolina* 1.13, The red-wing'd Starling. . . The whole Bird (except the upper part of the Wings) is black, and would have little beauty, were it not for the Shoulders of the wings, which are bright scarlet. **1791** Bartram *Travels* 291, the red winged sterling, or corn thief. **1854** Wailes *Rept. on Ag. & Geol. MS* 319, *Sturnus prædatorius.* Red-winged starling. **1881** *Amer. Naturalist* 15.393 **IA,** The Red-winged Starlings generally leave this region before we have any severely cold weather. **1923** WV State Ornith. *Birds WV* 44, *Agelaius phoeniceus.* . . *Redwinged Starling.* . . Breeds commonly in West Virginia. **1956** MA Audubon Soc. *Bulletin* 40.130, *Red-winged Blackbird.* . . Red-wing Starling (Mass., Conn. Various birds of this family are miscalled starlings.)

red-winged teal See **redwing 2**

red-winged woodpecker n Also *redwing woodpecker* Cf **red-shafted flicker**
=**flicker** n² **1.**
1953 Jewett *Birds WA* 397, *Colaptes cafer collaris* [=*C. auratus*]. . . Red-winged Woodpecker. . . *Under side of wings and tail red.* **1966–70** *DARE* (Qu. Q17, . . *Kinds of woodpeckers*) Inf **MS**87, Redwing woodpecker; **MT**4, Red-winged woodpecker.

redwing hawk See **red-winged hawk**

redwing starling See **red-winged starling**

redwing teal See **redwing 2**

redwing woodpecker See **red-winged woodpecker**

red wolf n

A wolf (*Canis rufus*) native to Louisiana and Texas.
1845 *Amer. Whig Rev.* 2.517 **TX,** The red wolf says, whoo!—ooh! whoo!—ah! / The Injine says, whoo!—ooh! whoo!—oo! **1865** (1869) Tenney *Nat. Hist.* 39, The Red Wolf, *C. occidentalis,* var. *rufus,* Aud. & Bach., of Texas, is mixed red and black above, lighter beneath. **1942** Allen *Extinct & Vanishing Mammals* 229, The typical form of red wolf was slightly the smallest of the three races and the most southwestern,

with a range extending from central Texas southwestward to the Mexican tableland. **1952** Burt *Field Guide Mammals* 53, *Red Wolf.* . . Small individuals in the light color phase are difficult to distinguish from the Coyote. **1980** Whitaker *Audubon Field Guide Mammals* 538, *Red Wolf.* . . *Reddish fur*, with interspersed blackish hairs; also black, brown, yellowish, or gray. . . Feeds primarily on hares and rabbits, small rodents, and birds. **1986** Pederson *LAGS Concordance*, 1 inf, **ceTX**, Red wolf.

redwood n

1 Any of several shrubs or smaller trees, as a **dogwood 1**, the **redbud**, a **red willow 1**, or a **swamp loosestrife** (here: *Decodon verticillatus*); see quots. **eastern half US** Cf **redbrush 1, red osier, redshank 2, swamp willow**

1778 Carver *Travels N. Amer.* 31 **Gt Lakes**, About all the great lakes, is found a kind of willow, termed by the French, bois rouge, in English, red wood [DCan: =*Cornus stolonifera*]. **1785** (1925) Washington *Diaries* 2.368 **VA**, The Dogwood buttons were just beginning to open as the Redwood (or bud) blossom. **1805** (1904) Lewis *Orig. Jrls. Lewis & Clark Exped.* 1.299, The under brush is willow, red wood, (sometimes called red or swamp willow). *Ibid* 2.179, The undergrowth consists of . . honeysuckle small, and the red wood, the inner bark of which the engages are fond of smoking mixed with tobacco. **1819** Warden *Statist. Political Hist. U.S.* 3.97 **WI**, In the lower parts are found oak, elm, . . red-wood, sumach. **1965–70** *DARE* (Qu. T16, . . *Kinds of trees . . 'special'*) Infs **AL**19, 37, **DC**13, **GA**91, **IA**22, **LA**14, **MA**122, **WV**17, Redwood; **NY**71, Redwood—limber stock, bark has a reddish cast, grows in damp places—sometimes the top grows over and roots into the ground [*DARE* Ed: =*Decodon verticillatus*]; (Qu. S26c, *Wildflowers that grow in woods*) Inf **KY**21, Redwood [FW: =redbud]; **LA**15, Redwood—in woods. **1970** *DARE* File **VA**, Redwood—[same as] Judas tree. **1982** [see **redbud winter**]. **1986** Pederson *LAGS Concordance* (Local tree) 3 infs, **TX**, 2 infs, **AL**, 1 inf, **neTN**, Redwood; 1 inf, **csTN**, 1 inf, **cnTX**, Redwood tree; (*Local shrub*) 1 inf, **cwFL**, Redwood. **2000** Bly *My Lord* 192 **MN**, The wood came from an eighty just north of Carolyn's animal hospital. . . The following January they stood in the snow, brushing against the spiny redwood bushes, and swede-sawed up all the trunks.

2 Usu a large evergreen tree (*Sequoia sempervirens*) native to California and Oregon, but also the related giant **sequoia** (here: *Sequoiadendron giganteum*); also the wood of such a tree. For other names of *S. sempervirens* see **coast redwood, sequoia orig CA, now widespread**

1839 Leonard *Narr. Advent.* 44, In the last two days travelling we have found some trees of the Red-wood species, incredibly large—some of which would measure from 16 to 18 fathom round the trunk at the height of a man's head from the ground. **1853** (1928) Knight *Diary* 52 **OR**, These mountains are a dense forest of pines, fir, white cedar or red-wood. **1857** Gray *First Lessons* 152, Over twelve hundred layers have actually been counted on the stump of an aged tree, such as the Giant Cedar or Redwood of California. **1908** Sudworth *Forest Trees Pacific* 140, The wood [of *Sequoiadendron giganteum*] is widely useful for commercial purposes, passing in the market as "redwood;" though lighter and more brittle than the coast redwood, it is said to be not less valuable for lumber. **1950** *L.A. Times* Midwinter 3 Jan. 63/1 *(DA)*, The monumental redwoods, thousands of years old, stand with silent splendor in the snow. **1965–70** *DARE* (Qu. L65, . . *Kinds of fences*) 10 Infs, **scattered**, Redwood fence; (Qu. T5, . . *Kinds of evergreens, other than pine*) 8 Infs, **CA**, Redwood; **CA**42, Redwood—coast and gigantica [sic]; **CT**37, Redwoods—gone now; **RI**10, California redwood; (Qu. T16, . . *Kinds of trees . . 'special'*) 10 Infs, **CA**, Redwood; (Qu. L64, *The kind of wooden fence that's built around a garden or near a house*) Infs **CA**117, **TX**105, Redwood fence; **CA**91, Redwood board fence—expensive; redwood stake fence. **1967** *DARE* Tape **CA**69, That's in northern California, near the Oregon border on the coast. That's the coastal redwood as opposed to the Sequoia redwood. **1980** *Little Audubon Guide N. Amer. Trees W. Region* 299, Redwood . . "California Redwood"—*Sequoia sempervirens*. . . The world's tallest tree. *Ibid* 301, Giant Sequoia—"Sierra Redwood" . . *Sequoiadendron giganteum*. **1986** Pederson *LAGS Concordance* **Gulf Region**, 18 infs, Redwood (fence *or* fences); 1 inf, Redwood fencing.

redwood chipmunk See **redwood squirrel**

redwood ivy n

An **inside-out flower** (here: *Vancouveria planipetala*).
1959 Munz–Keck *CA Flora* 112, *V[ancouveria] planipetala.* . . Redwood-ivy. . . Shade of woods, . . Monterey Co. to sw. Ore.

redwood lily n

=**chapparal lily.**
1897 Parsons *Wild Flowers CA* 72, Redwood Lily. *Lilium rubescens.* [*Ibid* 74, The favorite haunts of this lily are high and inaccessible ridges, among the chapparal, or under the live-oak or redwood.] **1911** Jepson *Flora CA* 95, *L[ilium] rubescens.* . . Near the coast [of CA] called Redwood Lily; towards the interior Chaparral or Chamise Lily. **1949** Moldenke *Amer. Wild Flowers* 324, The . . *chaparral lily*, . . of California, has nearly white flowers, . . [and] is known as the *redwood lily.* **1968** *DARE* (Qu. S26e, *Other wildflowers not yet mentioned*; not asked in early QRs) Inf **CA**105, Redwood lily. **1979** Spellenberg *Audubon Guide N. Amer. Wildflowers W. Region* 586, Redwood Lily, . . which grows in brush or woods in the Coast Ranges of central and northern California, has . . flowers . . that are at first white with purple spots but age to a rich wine color.

redwood pea n

A **vetchling** (here: *Lathyrus torreyi*).
1944 Abrams *Flora Pacific States* 2.619, *Lathyrus Torreyi.* . . Redwood Pea. . . Open woods, . . western Washington to the Coast Ranges of central California. **1961** Thomas *Flora Santa Cruz* 220 **cwCA**, Redwood Pea. Coniferous forests in Santa Cruz County. . . May–June.

redwood rose n

=**wood rose.**
1915 (1926) Armstrong–Thornber *Western Wild Flowers* 222, Redwood Rose—*Rosa gymnocarpa.* . . A charming kind, . . usually growing in shady mountain woods. . . The flowers are an inch or less across, usually single, with light yellow centers and bright pink petals. **1934** Haskin *Wild Flowers Pacific Coast* 177, The redwood rose is the smallest and dainties [sic] of its kind. . . As the name indicates, this species extends its range southward into the redwood region of California.

redwood sorrel n

A **wood sorrel** (here: *Oxalis oregana*).
1897 Parsons *Wild Flowers CA* 196, Redwood-Sorrel. *Oxalis Oregana.* . . In deep woods . . the beautiful leaves and delicate flowers of the redwood-sorrel cover the ground with an exquisite tapestry. **1946** Peattie *Pacific Coast* 64, Perhaps the commonest of all the flowering plants is the redwood sorrel, the Oregon oxalis, that often carpets every foot of ground, far as eye can see, with its bright green shamrock leaves. **1979** Spellenberg *Audubon Guide N. Amer. Wildflowers W. Region* 650, Redwood Sorrel. . . forms lush, solid, inviting carpets on the cool floor of coastal redwood forests.

redwood squirrel n Also *redwood chipmunk*

A **red squirrel 1** (here: *Tamiasciurus douglasii*).
1906 Stephens *CA Mammals* 91, The Redwood Chipmunk is . . tame and unsuspicious. **1935** Pratt *Manual Vertebrate Animals* 329, *S[ciurus] douglasii.* . . Pine squirrel; redwood squirrel. . . In coniferous forests. **1968** *DARE* (Qu. P27, . . *Kinds of squirrels*) Inf **CA**101, Redwood squirrel; **CA**105, Redwood or brown squirrel.

redwood violet n Also *redwoods violet*

A **violet** (here: *Viola sempervirens*).
1920 Rice–Rice *Pop. Studies CA Wild Flowers* 58, I have found the little Redwood Violet growing in the depths of those mighty forest areas. **1951** Abrams *Flora Pacific States* 3.126, Redwood Violet. . . Western British Columbia southward mainly west of the Cascade Mountains, to the California Coast Ranges. **1973** Hitchcock–Cronquist *Flora Pacific NW* 299, Mostly in moist woods . . redwoods v[iolet].

redwood winter See **redbud winter**

redworm n Cf **bloodworm 1**

1 An **earthworm**, esp *Eisenia foetida* or *Lumbricus rubellus*. [*OED2* a1450 →] **scattered, but chiefly Sth, S Midl** See Map Cf **Louisiana pink worm, manure ~, pink ~, red wiggler, shitworm**
1840 *Spirit of Times* 29 Aug 306/3 **Sth** (Weingarten *Suppl. Notes*), Goggle-eye lights upon a red worm. **1905** *DN* 3.68 **nwAR**, Redworm. . . Angle-worm, earthworm. 'It isn't moist enough here for redworms.' Common. **1923** *DN* 5.218 **swMO**, Red worm. . . Fish worm, angle worm, earth worm. **1938** Stuart *Dark Hills* 60 **KY**, When the red worms came to the top of the ground around the hog pen it was time to go fishing. **1946** *PADS* 5.34 **VA**, Red-worm. . . Earthworm; only west of the New River. **1949** Kurath *Word Geog.* 74, Red-worm is the usual expression in the mountains of North Carolina and adjoining

parts of Virginia, West Virginia and Kentucky, and relics of it occur in Pennsylvania. **1953** *AmSp* 28.253 **csPA,** *Red-worm.* . . A common, small earthworm (not a nightcrawler) used as bait in fishing. In general use. **1958** *PADS* 29.15 **TN,** *Redworm.* . . A fishing worm. Rep[orted] from Coffee, Hamilton, Perry, Robertson [Counties]. **1965–70** *DARE* (Qu. P5, . . *The common worm used as bait*) 138 Infs, **scattered, but chiefly Sth, S Midl,** Redworm; (Qu. P6, . . *Kinds of worms . . used for bait*) 35 Infs, **scattered,** Redworm. **1966** Dakin *Dial. Vocab. Ohio R. Valley* 393, *Red-worm* is common in all of Kentucky except the Bluegrass and is regular in the Mountains. This name is not common north of the Ohio, but is used in southeastern Illinois along the Ohio and the Wabash and appears to predominate locally in Marion County, Indiana. **1970** *NC Folkl.* 8.28, Aching joints; if stiff, they were massaged with redworm oil. **1971** *AmSp* 46.182 **Chicago IL,** Words with Midland and Southern designations brought to Chicago by recent immigrants, especially blacks: . . *red worm.* **1982** Sternberg *Fishing* 56, The manure worm is red with whitish bands along its 3- to 4-inch body. It is raised by bait suppliers in the South and sold as the *red worm.* **1986** Pederson *LAGS Concordance,* 273 infs, **Gulf Region,** Red worm(s).

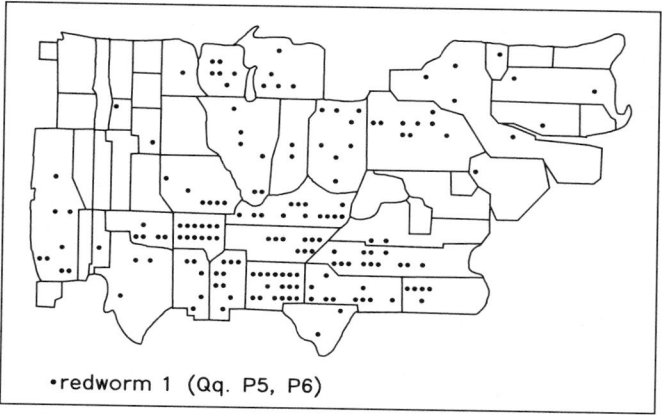

•redworm 1 (Qq. P5, P6)

2 A clam worm (here: *Nereis virens*).

1939 *LANE* Map 236, 1 inf, **swME,** Redworm = clam worm, long and flat.

ree v [Cf *OED2 read* v. 2.a "To make out or discover the meaning or significance of (a dream, riddle, etc.)"]
See quot.

1955 *AmSp* 30.234 **ceIN,** *Ree. Ree me this riddle* meant to read, guess, or solve this riddle, meanings differing from the 'sift' of dictionaries.

ree adj Also *rhea* [*EDD ree* adj.[2] 1 "of a horse: restive, frolicsome"]

1891 *Jrl. Amer. Folkl.* 4.71 **ePA,** *Ree Horse,* or *Rhea Horse.*—A frisky or unmanageable horse.

ree-collect See **recollect**

ree corn n [*Ree* var of *Arikara* an Amer Ind tribe noted for growing this variety of corn]
A variety of **Indian corn 1;** see quots.

1881 U.S. Bur. Indian Affairs *Report* 36 **ND,** Yield of crops raised by Indians from 580 acres, . . estimated: Ree corn (a small early variety), 345 acres, 3,500 bushels. **1917** Will–Hyde *Corn among Indians* 24 **SD,** Ree corn, talked of by all the tribes, had been officially distributed on many of the reservations.

reed n

1 Std: a tall perennial grass of the genus *Arundo* or *Phragmites.* For other names of *Arundo donax* see **giant reed a;** for other names of *Phragmites australis* see **bentgrass 2, cane grass, foxtail 3, giant reed b, reed grass b, wild broom corn**

2 A **wild rice** (here: *Zizania aquatica* or *Z. palustris*).

1837 Darlington *Flora Cestrica* 93 **sePA,** *Z[izania] aquatica.* . . Indian Rice. Reed. . . 4 to 6 or 7 feet high. . . Swampy rivulets. **1903** Small *Flora SE U.S.* 112, *Zizania aquatica.* . . In swamps and along creeks and rivers. . . Wild Rice. Reeds. **1912** Baker *Book of Grasses* 89, *Indian Rice. Wild Rice. Reeds. Zizania palustris.* . . New Brunswick to Manitoba, south to Florida and Texas. **1920** *Torreya* 20.18, *Zizania aquatica.* . . Reed is the name that has long been, and still is in use in the vicinity of Philadelphia, Pa., and Wilmington, Del. **1955** *Oriole* 20.1.12

GA, *Reed Bird* (as frequenting "reeds" or wild rice, upon the grain of which it feeds).

3 See **reed cane.**

reedbird n Cf **prairie reed-bird**

1 also *reedy:* =**bobolink B.** esp **C Atl** See Map

1795 in 1802 Priest *Travels U.S.A.* 90 **sePA,** [Among a] wonderful variety of small birds . . , the *reed-bird,* or american ortolan, justly holds the first place. [Footnote to *reed-bird:* so called from their note resembling the word *reed.*] **1815** *Lit. & Philos. Soc. NY Trans.* 1.126, Considerable doubts have also been suggested with respect to that interesting bird called the rice bird, reed bird, or bob lincoln (emberiza oryzivora). **1856** *Porter's Spirit of Times* 11 Oct 90/3 **sePA,** Niggers ain't fit to shoot reedies. *Ibid,* The small boy . . volunteers some information regarding a "ree-ee-dy" that he just saw. **1872** Schele de Vere *Americanisms* 372, The *bobolink* . . is the same bird as the *Reed-bird* on the banks of the Delaware, and the *Rice-bird* still farther South. **1895** (1907) Wright *Birdcraft* 165, Bobolink . . *After moult* Reed-bird. **1897** *Oölogist* 14.48 **OH,** By the Fourth of July the Bobolink's wild bubbling song shows sign of waning. . . He is degenerating into a grating, metallic voiced seed eating, russet-yellow "reed bird." . . He soon loses his suit of black already worn, and becomes the plain brown "Reed-bird." **1925** Parrish *Perennial Bachelor* 21 **MD,** So Victor went "down state" with his brother Willie and Sam Blow to shoot reedbirds, and railbirds, and ducks in the marshes. **1950** *PADS* 14.56 **SC,** *Reedbird.* . . Bobolink. **1950** *WELS* **WI** (*Other names for bobolink*) 2 Infs, Reedbird—[so called] in the South; 2 Infs, Reedbird. **1956** *DE Folkl. Bulletin* 1.22, Reedbirds—the local name for the bird that on northward migrations, in spring, has bright black and gray plumage and is called bobolink. In the Carolinas and Georgia . . they were called rice-birds. **1965–70** *DARE* (Qu. Q14, . . *Names . . for these birds: bobolink*) Infs **DE**3, 4, **GA**91, **MD**15, 20, 34, 40, 48, **MS**73, **NY**100, **PA**26, 34, Reedbird; **MA**21, **NY**53, Reedbird [FW sugg]; (Qu. Q10, . . *Water birds and marsh birds*) Infs **MD**34, **NJ**21, Reedbird; **MD**3, Reedbirds—small, dark birds that nest in reeds; marsh birds—another name for reedbirds; **MD**15, Reedbirds—small, dark.

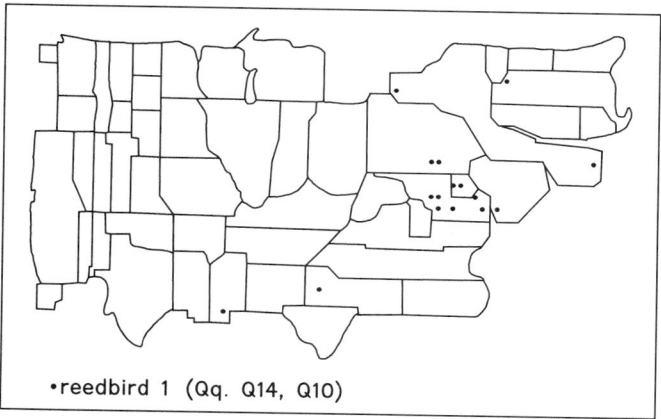

•reedbird 1 (Qq. Q14, Q10)

2 =**red-winged blackbird.**

1925 Bailey *Birds FL* 96, Red-Winged Blackbird. . . *Agelaius phoeniceus predatorius* (Reed bird, Rice bird, Marsh blackbird). **1950** *WELS,* 1 Inf, **cwWI,** Red-winged blackbird—the ricebird and reedbird of the South. **1955** *Oriole* 20.1.12 **GA,** *Reed Bird* (as frequenting "reeds" or wild rice, upon the grain of which it feeds). . . *Red-winged Blackbird.*

3 =**sora.**

1925 Bailey *Birds FL* 42, Sora. *Porzana carolina* (Reed-bird, Carolina rail). . . As a game bird they are considered a great delicacy, as they are always fat.

4 See quot.

1956 *DE Folkl. Bulletin* 1.22 [Black], A chicken and reedbird dinner will be given by the stewardess board of Mt. Carmel Methodist Church. *Ibid,* They aren't birds being served tonight. They're chitlins—going by the name reedbirds!

reed brake n **Sth** Cf **reed 1, reed cane**
A **brake** n[2] b; see quots.

1818 in 1953 McMullen *Topog. Terms FL* 179, The soil of the reed-brakes is very similar to that of the Bay-galls—a loose spongy mass of vegetable mould on a foundation of sand and clay, they differ however essentially from the other kinds of swamp in having the best water of the country—which is found in the center of the reed-brakes, in narrow, deep little channels with clear currents and sandy bottoms. **1849** (1850) Drake *Systematic Treatise Principal Diseases N. Amer.* 197, Sluggish wet-weather streams, with marshy borders, having . . a considerable growth of small cane;—hence they are called 'switch-cane marshes' and 'reed-brakes.' **1854** Davis *Farm Book* 46 **AL** *(DA)*, Planted the Dean cotton on the left side of the reed brake Bridge. **1948** *Carthaginian* (Carthage MS) 19 Aug 4/4, Total of 190 acres, 70 acres of good reedbrake corn land and 70 acres of cotton land. **1986** Pederson *LAGS Concordance* **MS** *(Swamp)* 2 infs, Reed brake(s); 1 inf, Reed brake—grass won't grow, trees and shrubs do; 1 inf, Reed brakes—boggy, soft land, small streams.

Reed canary grass See **canary grass**

reed cane n Also *reed, cane reed (grass)* **Sth, S Midl** Cf **mutton cane 1, reed brake**

Giant cane (*Arundinacea gigantea*).

1817 Brown *Western Gaz.* 78 **IN, KY,** The Reed Cane . . grows south of the ridge of hills. . . The vines of Spain, the silk worm, and the sweet potatoe will flourish wherever the reed cane grows. **1818** Darby *Emigrant's Guide* 77 **LA,** There are two very distinct species of the arundo, or large reed cane, growing in southern Louisiana; the *arundo gigantea,* and the *arundo aquatica.* **1833** Flint *Biog. Memoir D. Boone* 143 **Ohio Valley,** Each is prepared with a bundle of long, dry, reed cane, or other poles, to which are attached splinters of burning pines. **1854** Wailes *Rept. on Ag. & Geol. MS* 345, Reed, Arundo tecta [=*Arundinacea gigantea* subsp *tecta*]. **1890** Johnston *Widow Guthrie* 85 **GA** (as of 1830s), The reed-cane grew out of the blood-red ground not very far below the height reached in the rich alluvium in the bottoms between. **1903** Small *Flora SE U.S.* 161, *Arundinacea tecta* [=*A. gigantea* subsp *t.*] . . Reed. . . *Arundinacea macrosperma* [=*A. gigantea*]. . . Along river banks and swamps. . . Cane. Cane Reed. **1942** Hylander *Plant Life* 516, The Cane-reed (*Arundinacea*) grows in swamplands from Virginia to Florida and Texas . . ; Cane-reeds are tall woody plants reaching a height of thirty feet, with flat leaf blades. **1956** McAtee *Some Dialect NC* 36, Reed . . cane (*Arundinaria gigantea*). **1969** *DARE* (Qu. L8, *Hay that grows naturally in damp places*) Inf **TX**63, Meadow hay; cane-reed grass grows tall in damp places.

reed grass n [*OED2* 1578 →] Cf **salt reed grass, wood ~**
Any of var grasses, spec:

a A grass of the genus *Calamagrostis.* Also called **marsh grass 1;** for other names of var spp see **bluejoint 1, nigger hair 2, pine grass 1a, pony ~, wild redtop**

1795 Winterbotham *Amer. U.S.* 3.401, The States of New-England abound with. . . Reed grass, several species, Arundo, Brome grass [etc]. **1847** Wood *Class-Book* 601, *C[alamagrostis] Canadensis.* . . Reed Grass. . . Wet grounds, N. Eng. W. to Mich. Makes good hay. Common. **1881** Phares *Farmer's Book of Grasses* 39, Our southern species, *C[alamagrostis] coarcatata* [sic], or glaucous small reed grass . . grows in swamps and has attracted no attention. **1948** Blomquist *Grasses NC* 78, Reedgrass. . . Several species of *Calamagrostis* are important forage grasses in the United States. *Calamagrostis canadensis*. . . is an important source of wild hay in the North Central states. Several other species are important range grasses in some of the western and northern Pacific Coast states. **1961** Douglas *My Wilderness* 29 **CO,** The canyons are thick with many grasses, sedges, and rushes. . . Purple pine grass (reed grass) is here too. **1967** *DARE* (Qu. L9a, . . *Kinds of grass . . grown for hay*) Inf **MI**40, Reed grass—in exceptionally low places. **1973** Hitchcock–Cronquist *Flora Pacific NW* 628, Reedgrass. . . The spp. are mostly palatable and nutritious, although not among the best of range grasses.

b A common **reed 1** (here: *Phragmites australis*).

1822 Eaton *Botany* 183, Arundo. . . phragmites [=*Phragmites australis*], . . marsh reed grass. . . About 6 or 8 feet high. Damp. **1837** Darlington *Flora Cestrica* 61 **sePA,** *Phragmites*. . . Reed-grass. . . It is a fine looking plant, somewhat resembling *Broom corn*, in habit. **1868** (1869) *Amer. Naturalist* 2.653 **cMN,** The Reed-grass (*Phragmites communis*) grows in all wet places here. **1920** Saunders *Useful Wild Plants* 218, A good string may also be made by twisting the fiber obtained from the common Reed-grass (*Phragmites communis* . .),—the Carrizo of the Southwest,—whose tall, straight canes crowned with silky, plume-like floral panicles, form a conspicuous feature in swamps and damp places throughout the United States and Canada. **1957** *Plateau* 30.2.34 **AZ, UT,** Along beds of creeks feeding into Glen Canyon and in scattered

spots along the higher banks of the Colorado River itself, great bleached heads of common reedgrass (*Phragmites communis*) rose above the broad green leaves of the new growth. **1976** Bruce *How to Grow Wildflowers* 260, A brackish marsh overrun by the giant Reed-grass *Phragmites communis* verged right up to the roadside.

c =**giant reed a.**

1822 Eaton *Botany* 183, *Arundo*. . . *donax* (reed grass . .). Culm somewhat woody. **1889** Vasey *Ag. Grasses* 60, *Arundo Donax* (Giant Reed Grass). . . It is . . well established on the borders of the Rio Grande River, where it is probably indigenous.

d =**sand reed 2** (here: *Calamovilfa* spp).

1903 Small *Flora SE U.S.* 128, *Calamovilfa*. . . Reed Grass. **1932** Rydberg *Flora Prairies* 98, *Calamovilfa*. . . Reed-grass. Sand-grass. Tall perennials with horizontal rootstocks and elongated narrow leaf-blades. **1945** MI Ag. Exper. Sta. *Technical Bulletin* 201.18, Other plants . . sometimes occurring on sandy soil at inland points are . . long-leaved reed-grass (*Calamovilfa longifolia*) and silver-weed (*Potentilla Anserina*).

e Bermuda grass (*Cynodon dactylon*).

1958 Jacobs–Burlage *Index Plants NC* 101, *Cynodon Dactylon*. . . Reed grass; wire grass; Indian cough grass; dog's tooth grass; Scotch grass.

reed mace n [*OED2* 1548 →]
=**cattail 1.**

1822 Eaton *Botany* 496, *Typha*. . . *latifolia* (cat-tail, reed-mace . .). **1876** Hobbs *Bot. Hdbk.* 97, Reedmace, Cat tail flag, Typha latifolia. **1933** Small *Manual SE Flora* 13, *Typha*. . . Erect herbs with sheathed stems. . . Represented in our range by 2 species widely distributed. . . Cat-tails. Reed-maces. Cooper's reed. Cat-o'-nine-tails. **1974** *WI Acad. Rev.* Summer 20, Cattail (*Typha latifolia*) . . reedmace.

reed manna grass n Cf **reed grass, reed meadow ~**
A **manna grass** (here: *Glyceria grandis*).

1843 Torrey *Flora NY* 2.464, *Glyceria aquatica* [=*G. grandis*]. . . Reed Manna-grass. . . This is a very abundant grass in some places. It is good fodder. **1961** Peck *Manual OR* 94, Reed Manna-grass. . . Swampy ground east of the Cascade Mts., especially northward, to Alaska and the Atlantic states. **1973** Hitchcock–Cronquist *Flora Pacific NW* 643, Reed m[annagrass]. . . G[lyceria] grandis.

reed meadow grass n [*OED2* 1842 at *reed* sb.[1] 14] Cf **meadow grass 2d, reed manna ~**
A **manna grass** (here: *Glyceria grandis*).

1857 Gray *Manual of Botany* 559, *G[lyceria] aquatica* [=*G. grandis*]. . . Reed Meadow-Grass. . . Wet meadows, &c.; common northward. **1889** Vasey *Ag. Grasses* 69, Reed Meadow Grass. . . Widely diffused in the northern portions of the United States and Canada, and in the Rocky Mountains from Mexico to Montana. **1925** *Book of Rural Life* 6.3344, A still larger grass (*G. grandis*), occurring mostly in the East, is called *reed meadow grass*. All three of these grasses look like overgrown specimens of Kentucky blue grass. **1956** St. John *Flora SE WA* 46, Reed Meadow Grass. . . Spikelets mostly purplish. . . In wet places.

reed-pile n Cf **reed brake**
See quot.

1956 McAtee *Some Dialect NC* 36, Reed-pile . . a growth of cane, a small cane-brake.

Reed's canary grass See **canary grass**

reed wren n Also *reed warbler*
The long-billed **marsh wren** (*Cistothorus palustris*).

1883 Nuttall Ornith. Club *Bulletin* 8.77 **RI,** *Telmatodytes palustris* is . . Reed Warbler in Rhode Island. **1917** (1923) *Birds Amer.* 3.197, Long-billed Marsh Wren. . . Reed Wren. . . The canoeist who paddles . . along some sluggish river bordered by broad meadow marshes, may catch sight of a nervous little brown bird hanging to the stems or leaves of rushes, reeds, or cat-tails. **1946** Hausman *Eastern Birds* 446, Reed Wren. . . A very shy, secretive little wren. . . If disturbed it dives into the reeds.

reedy See **redbird 1**

reef v

1 To pull or push (something) vigorously; to tug, use force

(on something). [Ult < *reef* to diminish the size of (a sail) by rolling up a part and fastening it] **chiefly Nth** Cf **reef** n
  1958 McCulloch *Woods Words* 147 **Pacific NW,** *Reef.* . . To pull hard, with the donkey throttle wide open. **1967** *DARE* FW Addit **MI**32, *Reef it* or *give it a reef.* Used by fishermen—"Reef the hell out of it," i.e., jerk on the line to set the hook. Or, "Let's all get behind this car and see if we can reef it out of here." **1969** Sorden *Lumberjack Lingo* 95 **NEng, Gt Lakes,** *Reefing her*—Pushing a boat with a pole. **1999** *NADS Letters* se**MI,** All of us who worked on our hotrods or motorcycles used the term "reef" to reference tightening a bolt as tight as possible without breaking it, usually those that perpetually came loose. (One pulling on wrench, the other says, 'Reef that sucker down'). *Ibid* **nMN, nWI,** To "reef" is common usage in northern Minnesota and Wisconsin in the parlance of fishing and has been since my boyhood. To reef (or to really reef) on a fish means to set the hook very hard in response to a strike or pull really hard to keep a fish out of the rocks or weeds. I've also heard it used to describe pulling hard on a snag to break off. . . I also overheard the mate use the same expression with the same meaning (to set the hook hard) on the headboat "Marathon Lady" out of Marathon, Florida. . . His dialect was decidedly not Inland Northern. **2000** *Ibid* **ME,** Reef as in 'to reef on it hard' 'He was just a reefin' on that old thing with all his might'. Means to pull really hard, maybe in a kind of desperation. I'm born and bred in Maine, I'm a 47 year old woman. I live in Bradford, about 25 miles north of Bangor. I've heard it very frequently here, but don't remember it growing up in the western part of the state, Casco, in the Sebago Lake region about 45 miles from Portland. *Ibid* **swWA,** The word "reef" is often used to describe tugging hard or the extra energy needed to get a stuck part to move, such as "you'll really have to reef on it." It seems to be common to farmers or to those who do labor with their hands. *Ibid* **OR,** I happen to regularly use, and hear other people use, the term "reef" in conversation at work in Albany, Oregon. An example of when I might use it would be to say, "I really reefed on that cupboard door but it is still stuck—can you get it open?" . . I am a twenty-nine year old female who has lived in western Oregon my entire life, although I have heard my relatives from southeastern Idaho and eastern Montana use this term occasionally as well. *Ibid* **ME, MI, OR, WA, WI.**

2 also vbl n *reefing:* See quots. Note: The relation, if any, of these exx to the preceding sense is not clear.
  1889 *Atlantic Mth.* 64.115, When the driver [in a trotting race] moves the bit to and fro in his mouth, the effect is to enliven and stimulate the horse. . . If this motion be performed with an exaggerated movement of the arm, it is called "reefing." **1936** Adams *Cowboy Lingo* 100, The cowboy was said to 'curry him out' when he 'raked' with his spurs; 'reefing' and 'combing' were also terms used. **1968** Adams *Western Words* 246, *Reef*—To slide the legs back and forth along the horse's sides as one spurs.

reef n Cf **reef** v 1
A vigorous tug.
  1958 [see **reef** v 1]. **1967** [see **reef** v 1]. **1979** Lewis *How to Talk Yankee* [29] **nNEng,** *Reef* . . strong tug. "If you'll stop frigging around and take a good reef on that line, we can haul this old scow off the rocks before sunset."

reef bass n
=**red drum.**
  1879 (1972) Kilbourne *Game Fishes* 37, *Sciænops ocellatus.* . . In the Carolinas, Florida, and the Gulf, we meet with the name 'Bass,' and its variations, 'Spotted Bass,' 'Red Bass,' 'Sea Bass,' 'Reef Bass,' and 'Channel Bass.' **1935** Caine *Game Fish* 39, *Sciænops ocellatus.* . . The larger fish assumes a reddish shade all over. . . Reef Bass. **1973** Knight *Cook's Fish Guide* 376, Bass . . Reef . . see Drum, Red.

reefer n Also *reefer jacket, reefing* ~ **esp NEast** See Map *old-fash*
A heavy, usu double-breasted, cloth jacket or short coat.
  1849 Melville *Mardi* 1.62, He was quite as busy with his fingers as ever: . . with great patches from the skirts of a condemned reefing-jacket, panneling the seats of our "ducks;" in short, veneering our broken garments with all manner of choice old broadcloths. **1858** (1929) Taylor *Life on a Whaler* 22, Although his reefing jacket is rather rough, it quite as surely covers a tender spot as does the landsman's finer coat. **1890** *Century Dict.* 5029, *Reefer.* . . A short coat or jacket worn by sailors and fishermen, and copied for general use by the fashions of 1888–90. *Ibid, Reefing-jacket.* . . A close-fitting jacket or short coat made of

strong heavy cloth. **1897** (1968) Sears *Catalogue* 273, *Ladies Spring and Summer Wraps.* . . *A Very Genteel Double Breasted Reefer Jacket,* made of tan imported covert cloth, four white pearl buttons in front and eight on sleeves, lined throughout with fancy figured silk. **1942** ME *Univ. Studies* 56.39, In wind and cold weather officers wore *reefers* or short jackets while on duty. **1950** *WELS (Men's outdoor coats and jackets . . short)* 1 Inf, **cWI,** Reefer—a rough kind of jacket. **1956** Sorden–Ebert *Logger's Words* 27 **MI,** *Reefer,* A jacket or short coat of thick cloth. Same as mackinaw. Called reefer in Michigan. **1965–70** *DARE* (Qu. W4, . . *Men's coats or jackets for work and outdoor wear*) Infs **MA**40, **PA**131, 234, Reefer; **CT**23, Reefer—heavy coat so the winter wind won't go through it; **IL**5, Reefer—buttoned, padded; **IL**23, Reefer—heavy cloth coat; **MA**57, Reefer—made out of heavy wool; women wore them, too; **MA**73, Reefer—made of heavy wool, for work outdoors; had a big collar; **PA**36, Reefer—heavy; **PA**115, Reefer—a weather jacket; **PA**175, Reefer—thigh-length, wool; **RI**17, Reefer—like a pea jacket, worn by sailors. [All Infs old]

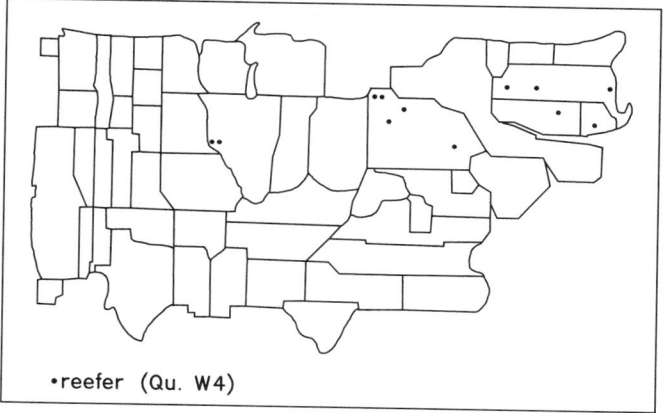
•reefer (Qu. W4)

reef fish n
A **demoiselle 1;** see quots.
  1960 *Amer. Fisheries Soc. List Fishes* 33, Yellowtail reef-fish . . *Chromis enchrysurus.* . . Gray reef-fish . . *Chromis insolatus.* **1986** Pederson *LAGS Concordance (Common . . fish)* 1 inf, **seFL,** Reef-fish—saltwater. **1991** *Amer. Fisheries Soc. Common Names Fishes* 57, *Chromis scotti* . . purple reeffish.

reef goose n
=**Canada goose.**
  1888 Trumbull *Names of Birds* 1 **NC,** *Branta canadensis.* . . At Morehead, North Carolina, *Reef Goose.* **1944** Hausman *Amer. Birds* 514, Goose, Reef—see Goose, Canada.

reefing See **reef** v 2

reefing jacket See **reefer**

reef trout n
=**lake trout 1.**
  1884 Goode *Fisheries U.S.* 1.488 **WI,** "Lake Trout". . . In the vicinity of Two Rivers, Wisconsin, . . [is called] "Reef Trout" . . large and lank, with tough and coarse flesh. **1904** *Salmon & Trout* 287 **MI,** Around and in Traverse Bay, Michigan, the variety taken in shallow water, being long and slender in form, is called "reef trout." **1911** U.S. Bur. Census *Fisheries 1908* 311, *Lake Trout.* . . In different localities the individuals vary greatly in color, size, and shape, and are known by the local names . . "reef trout," [etc]. [**1974** McClane *McClane's New Std. Fishing Encycl.* 529, The humper lake trout, which is known to the commercial fishermen as the "paperbelly" or "bank trout". . . inhabits isolated offshore reefs (banks) surrounded by deep water.]

reegataw See **ringtaw**

reel adj, adv See **real** adj, adv

reel n Also *reel song* **SE** *chiefly among Black speakers*
A dance-song; secular music of any sort.
  1927 Adams *Congaree* 52 **cSC** [Black], Dem niggers been havin' some time eatin' hash and rice, drinkin' liquor, singin' reels and dancin' and gamblin' and fightin'. **1928** Peterkin *Scarlet Sister Mary* 31 **SC,** I told you to kneel down an' thank God an' here you is singin a reel song

an' crossin you feets. Dat's a sin, gal, a pure sin. **1930** *DN* 6.83 **cSC,** *Reel.* . . Any piece of secular music. A negro and po' buckra word. **1939** FWP *Guide TN* 139, In many Negro churches of the rural sections dancing is one of the most important elements in the worship. These dances and the songs accompanying them are called "reels." **1992** in 1993 Adero *Up South* 43 [Black], She hated rhythm and blues records or "reels." **1996** *DARE* File **nwMS** [Black], Reel—any secular music.

reel-footed adj [Scots, Ir dial]
   1984 Wilder *You All Spoken Here* 158 **Sth,** *Reel-footed:* Club-footed.

reel song See **reel** n

reely See **really** adv, adj

ree-rye n [Prob var of nIr dial *ree-raw;* cf *EDD, SND reel rall*]
   1981 *DARE* File **csWI,** Said to be current in Mineral Point, WI: ['ri:ˌraɪ], a state of confusion, a mixup.

reesin See **raisin**

reether See **rather** adv

reezin See **raisin**

reezle n [Ger *Rüssel,* PaGer *riesel*]
   1966–68 *DARE* (Qu. K61, *What do you call the pig's nose?*) Infs **PA**158, **SD**2, Reezle ['rizəl].

refegee, reffygee See **refugee**

refried beans n pl [Calque of MexSpan *frijoles refritos*] **orig chiefly sCA, but now widely recognized** See Map Cf **enchilada**
   Beans that have been boiled, mashed, and reheated by frying.
   1957 *House Beautiful* Sept 126, [Caption:] Main course is a barbecue, Yucatan fashion, accompanied by refried beans. **1960** *NYT Mag.* 1 May 72 **NYC,** The sales of such canned items as tortillas, refried beans and green chilies . . have shown marked increases in recent months. **1965–70** *DARE* (Qu. H50, *Dishes made with beans . . that everybody around here knows*) 12 Infs, 11 **sCA,** Refried beans; **CA**2, Refried beans—Mexican dish; **CA**182, Refried beans—Mexican foods; (Qu. H65, *Foreign foods favored by people around here*) Infs **CA**182, **OR**1, Refried beans; (Qu. I20, . . *Kinds of beans*) Inf **CA**15A, Refried beans. [14 of 17 Infs female, 9 young or mid-aged, 6 comm type 1 or 2] **1976** Turgeon-Birmingham *Sat. Eve. Post All-Amer. Cookbook* 130, California Refried Beans with Cheese. **1999** *DARE* File **csWI,** In the last few years refried beans have become popular far from their source. Grocery stores here have at least half a dozen choices in cans, including those made with no fat, those made with vegetable oil, or those made with the traditional lard.

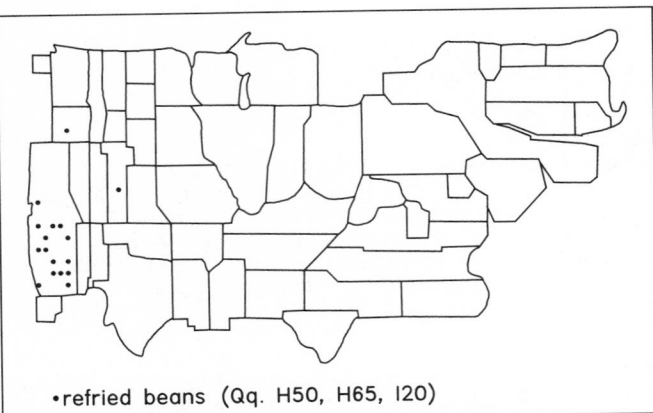

• refried beans (Qq. H50, H65, I20)

refrigeration n Also *refrigerated air* **chiefly SW** *somewhat old-fash*
   Air conditioning; hence adj *refrigerated* air-conditioned.
   1967 *DARE* FW Addit **wTX, eNM,** Refrigerated air—air conditioning; **wNM, AZ,** Refrigeration—air conditioning. **1970** *DARE* File **AZ,** *Refrigerated*—a descriptive term for a house air-conditioned by electricity. Also used for an air-conditioned car. **1998** *NADS Letters* **SW,** When evaporative cooling came in . . , restaurants and motels started advertising that they were "air-cooled." . . When some establishments installed central refrigeration systems to cool the air, they had to distin-

guish this from evaporative cooling, so *refrigerated air* became a strong selling point, including at movie houses. My wife was familiar with the term from California, and it is familiar to me from Texas, though clearly dated. . . I checked the local yellow pages [in AZ] under "Motels" to see if any used the term, and found none. . . To the extent that it is used at all, *air conditioning/-ed* has evidently totally replaced "refrigerated air." *Ibid, Refrigerated, refrigeration* in reference to air conditioning. . . In the Northeast I saw it several decades ago on signs in front of older movie theaters. And I have seen it in a few of the thousands of photographs of urban scenes I have examined. . . [T]hey were not the usual terms for 'air conditioning' and were perhaps mostly used when air conditioning was first being introduced in public commercial spaces. *Ibid* **cNM,** There's 2 types of air-conditioning here in the SW: Swamp-coolers (evaporative coolers) and refrigerated air (forced air central cooling). . . There are 5 'big' ads that specifically list 'refrigerated air' in [the Albuquerque telephone book]. *Ibid* **sCA** (as of 1950s), These terms [=*refrigerated, refrigeration*] were in common usage, especially in the desert areas of Southern California . . [especially] in advertising (motels, restaurants, stores). *Ibid* **OK, TX,** *Refrigerated air* is still used in Texas and Oklahoma for air-conditioning in theaters, small hotels, and motels built prior to about 1950. **1999** *Ibid,* In *The Show Starts on the Sidewalk: An Architectural History of the Movie Theater* (1994) by Maggie Valentine . . [there is a photo of] the Fox Theater, Phoenix, AZ with a banner *"Cooled By Refrigeration."* The movie on the marquee is "Young as You Feel" with Will Rogers released in 1931.

refuge See **refuse** n, adj

refugee v Pronc-spp *refegee, reffygee* **Sth, S Midl**
   1 To make a refugee of; to send to a place of refuge.
   1806 in 1916 Hawkins *Letters* 429 **GA,** It will be some time before the Creek young will get rid of the remains of that alloy which debased the agents and refugeed their associates. **1866** Reid *After the War* 250 **LA,** Many of his pupils were . . negroes that had been "refugeed" from the Red River country. **1874** Collins *Hist. Sketches KY* 1.162, [There have been] about 1,200 deaths . . among the negroes refugeed at Camp Nelson. **c1937** in 1970 Yetman *Voices* 11 **AR** [Black], They had refugeed her children off to different places to keep them from the Yankees. **1945** FWP *Lay My Burden Down* 251 **AR** (as of c1865) [Black], I never seed my father after the closing of the war. He had been refugeed to Texas and come back here, then he went on back to Mississippi.
   2 To flee or live as a refugee. [*OED2* 1750 →]
   1862 (1955) Holmes *Brokenburn* 139 **LA,** The planters generally are moving back to the hills as fast as possible. There are two families refugeeing in our neighborhood. **1887** *Atlantic Mth.* 60.333 **cVA** [Black], De balance o' de young marsters, dey married off an' reffygeed away. **c1937** in 1972 *Amer. Slave* 2.163 **SC,** I refugeed wid Massa. *Ibid* 238 **SC,** My father way when dey been 'rough-few-gieing' (refugeeing) de Beaufort Bridge been burn down. **c1937** in 1977 *Amer. Slave Suppl. 1* 1.169 **AL,** Us refegeed ter Salem, Alabama. **1938** FWP *Guide MS* 410 **cwMS,** During high water in the spring, when the river overflows its banks, a majority of the occupants of the cabins in the river flats "refugee" to the hills. **1957** *NC Hist. Rev.* 34.528 **NC** (as of 1870s), The man in whose care my father left his house when he refugeed to Virginia died and was buried with the key to the house in his pocket.

refuse n, adj Usu |ˈrɛfjus, -juz|; also |ˈrɛfjuǰ, rɪˈfjuz|; for addit varr see quots Pronc-sp *refuge* [Engl dial; cf *EDD refuge* sb.², adj]
   Std senses, var forms.
   1818 Fessenden *Ladies Monitor* 172, Provincial words . . to be avoided. . . *refuge* for refuse. **1905** Wasson *Green Shay* 67 **NEng,** That was all the thing in the shop that was long enough, unless'n I used some old refuge cedar boards that wa'n't hardly fittin'. **1941** *LANE* Map 346 (*Rubbish*) 1 inf, **nwMA,** [ˈrɛfjʊudʒ]; 1 inf, **cwNH,** [ˈrɛfɪdʒ]; [1 inf, [ˈrɛfjus]; 1 inf, [ˈrɛfjuz]]. **1943** in 1944 *ADD* 505 **nWV,** *Refuse* . . [pronounced] *refuge.* **1967** *DARE* Tape **WA**11, That's the refuse [rɪˈfjuz] from what's left after the ore has been smelted off. **1968** *DARE* (Qu. G10) Inf **NC**55, Rake the refuse [rɪˈfjuz] stuff.

regard v, n Pronc-sp *regyard* Cf Pronc Intro 3.I.16
   A Forms.
   1884 *Anglia* 7.255 **Sth, S Midl** [Black], Participial Prepositions: . . regyardin'. **1934** *WV Review* Dec 79, I know a well-educated West Virginian who says *regyard,* but does not use this sounding in other words of this class.
   B As noun.

In phr *in regards to:* About, concerning.   [Prob blend of *in regard to* + *as regards*]

1904 *DN* 2.419 **nwAR,** *In regards to, prep. phr.* In *regard to.* 'I can't give you any answer in regards to that matter.' **1924** Lardner *How to Write* vi, Maybe boys and gals who wants to take up writing as their life work would be benefited if some person like I was to give them a few hints in regards to the technic of the short story. **1928** Weseen *Crowell's Dict. Engl. Gram.* 545, *Regards.* Correctly used in the expression "as regards." . . Unidiomatic in the expression "in regards to," which should be "in regard to." **1989** *Webster's Dict. Engl. Usage* 807, The issue in this case appears to be largely a social one. *In regards to* seems to be an expression heard chiefly from those who speak H.L. Mencken's "vulgate." Most of our citations were taken from phone-in radio programs.

regella See **regular**

reggelation See **regulate**

reggilator See **regulate**

regiment n Pronc-spp *ridgment, rigiment, rigimint, rijiment*
A Forms.

1840–41 in 1944 *ADD* 505, Rijiment. J.F. Cooper. **1861** Holmes *Venner* 1.168 **NEng,** That was shown pretty well in New England two or three generations ago. There were a good many plain officers that talked about their "rigiment" and their "caounty." **1878** *Appletons' Jrl.* 5.416 **Sth,** At the South it is common, if not universal, to hear . . *rigiment* . . for *regiment.* **1887** (1892) Hinman *Corporal Si Klegg* 64, The veterans laughed loudly. . . "Look at the big ridgment o' tenderfoots!" **1891** *DN* 1.159 **cNY,** [rɪdʒmənt] < *regiment.* **1917** in 1944 *ADD* 505 **sWV,** *Regiment* . . rig-. **1921** Haswell *Daughter Ozarks* 27 (as of 1880s), Doc were surgeon of the old rigimint. **1929** *AmSp* 5.130 **ME,** The pronunciations "leftenant," "rigiment," [etc] . . were common. **1942** Hall *Smoky Mt. Speech* 19 **wNC, eTN,** The raising of [ɛ] to [ɪ] was observed also in: . . regiment [rɪdʒ]- (once).
B Sense.

A large number or quantity.

1953 Randolph–Wilson *Down in Holler* 277 **Ozarks,** *Regiment.* . . "We didn't plant no garden this year, but we got a whole regiment of canned stuff in the cellar." The word *nation* is sometimes used with the same meaning. **1966** *DARE* (Qu. LL8b, . . *A large number* . . *"She has a whole _____ of cousins."*) Infs **FL2, WA18,** Regiment.

reglar See **regular**

reglashin See **regulate**

regular adj, adv Usu |ˈrɛgjələ(r)|; also |ˈrɛg(ə)lə(r), ˈræglə| Pronc-spp *regella, reglar, regler, regula, rigilar*
A Forms.

1843 (1916) Hall *New Purchase* 147 **IN,** There was no reglar town of theirn nearer nor twenty miles. **1851** Hooper *Widow Rugby's Husband* 129 **AL,** I'm reglar 'listed in the 'nited States' sarvice. **1853** Simms *Sword & Distaff* 507 **SC,** A gentleman . . who is a rigilar off'cer in the line of the army. **1859** Taliaferro *Fisher's R.* 46 **nwNC** (as of 1820s), I've hearn you was a reg'lar built screamer in that way. **1884** *Anglia* 7.263 **Sth, S Midl** [Black], *Er reg'ler collidge nigger* = an educated negro. **1891** *DN* 1.162 **cNY,** But medial *y,* like medial *w,* suffers ecthlipsis in many cases, as shown by the following: . . [regəlr (reglr)], 'regular.' **1909** *DN* 3.363 **eAL, wGA,** *Reglar.* . . Regular(ly). **1914** *DN* 4.78 **ME, nNH,** *Reg'lar he-un.* . . A big, strong specimen of man or beast. **1921** Haswell *Daughter Ozarks* 29 (as of 1880s), I felt his pulse and hit were as regler as ever I timed. **1939** *LANE* Map 98 (*Frost*) 1 inf, **nwCT,** [rɛglr friz]; 1 inf, **ceMA,** [reˈgjələ frɪz]; 1 inf, **nwMA,** [rɛglr fri·z]. **1941** *Ibid* Map 462, 1 inf, **cCT,** [hiz ə reglə jæŋkɪ]. **1941** *AmSp* 16.9 **eTX** [Black], Regular [ˈrɛglə]. **1942** Hall *Smoky Mt. Speech* 68 **wNC, eTN,** Regular [ˈrɛglɚ], [ˈræglɚ]. **1942** *New Yorker* 11 July 18 **swCA,** She tells me she is prepared to pay even more than what is my regella fee. **1968** *DARE* FW Addit **NY91,** Regular [ˈrɛgələ·]. **1975** Gould *ME Lingo* 230, *Reg'lar-built.* **1982** Chaika [see **B** below].
B Sense.

Of coffee: served in an expected way, usu with milk or cream, but either with or without sugar; see quots.

1963 *DARE* File **Boston MA,** Regular coffee—coffee with cream or milk. **1975** *Ibid* **cMA,** Regular coffee—coffee with cream or milk (heard at a Howard Johnson's on the Massachusetts Turnpike). **1982** Chaika *Speaking RI* [8], *Regula cawfee* = cawfee with cream an' suga. **1982** *Capital Times* (Madison WI) 11 Nov 51/2, He knows no reason

"regular" coffee in New York means with milk or cream while elsewhere it means without. **1993** *DARE* File **RI** (as of c1973), In fact, 'regular coffee' in Rhode Island (at least 20 years ago . .) means coffee with milk and sugar. **1994** *NYT Mag.* 31 July 10, The mere mention of the word "regular" has been known to throw baristas [=coffee-bar tenders] into fits of frustrated rage, because "regular" means "black" in Chicago, "with milk" in Boston, "with milk and sugar" in Rhode Island and just about anything in New York. **1996** *DARE* File, Friends in a New York meeting recently were discussing the different meanings of "regular" coffee. To me it has meant caffeinated rather than de-caf; that was the meaning for members of the group from Vermont, New Hampshire, and Virginia. But in New York it is commonly understood to mean white with no sugar, in Boston black with sugar, and in Providence R.I. with cream and sugar. **1998** *DARE* File **NYC,** I grew up in NY, ordering "regular coffee," meaning coffee with milk and sugar. My father mentioned this term on the phone last night, actually, and I asked him some more about it, and he said that these days he sometimes hears people ordering "regular coffee with sugar" (which he thinks is redundant) or "regular coffee without sugar" (which he said "isn't really a regular coffee, but they do get what they want").

regulate v Usu |ˈrɛgjə̩let|; also |ˈrɛg(ə)̩let| Similarly n |ˈrɛg(ə)̩letə|; pronc-spp *reggilator* (for *regulator*), *reggelations, reglashin* (for *regulation*)
Std sense, var forms.

1843 (1916) Hall *New Purchase* 404 **IN,** A d—d Yankee reg-lashin. **1874** (1895) Eggleston *Circuit Rider* 145 **sOH** (as of early 19th cent), Well, then, I'll let the reggilators know abouten you. **1887** (1892) Hinman *Corporal Si Klegg* 121, I don't reck'n drillin' makes a feller have any more sand, . . but it's reggelations. **1891** *DN* 1.127 **cNY,** Regulate . . reg-. **1936** *AmSp* 11.159 **eTX,** In another group, the medial *u* is pronounced both [jə] and [ə], the latter sound being especially characteristic of less literate speech: . . *regulate.* . . In *regulate* the vowel is also sometimes omitted: [ˈrɛglet]. **1936** *AmSp* 11.310 **Upstate NY,** *Regulate* occurs 102 times with [j], 7 times without it. **1941** *AmSp* 16.9 **eTX** [Black], Regulator [ˈrɛg(ə)letə].

regyard See **regard**

reharsh v [Prob blend of *rehearse* + *rehash*]
To rehearse.

1932 Randolph *Ozark Mt. Folks* 52, One o' my cousins had a plumb good 'un [=a poem to learn]—I remember it yit from hearin' her reharshin' of it day an' night, 'specially on th' way home from school.

rehaul v [Prob blend of *repair* + *overhaul*]
1903 *DN* 2.326 **seMO,** Rehaul. . . Overhaul; repair.

rehaul n, also attrib Cf **haulback**
See quots.

1958 McCulloch *Woods Words* 147 **Pacific NW,** Rehaul. . . Another name for a haulback. . . *Rehaul engine*—A donkey used to pull the main line back to the woods in the period between the use of the line horse and the development of the two-drum yarding engine. Some rehaul engines also had a loading drum.

reight See **right**

rein n
A Form.

Pl: usu *reins;* also *reinge.* Gullah Cf **running range**
1909 *S. Atl. Qrly.* 8.51 **seSC** [Gullah], *Reinge* for *reins.* **1922** Gonzales *Black Border* 323 **sSC, GA coasts** [Gullah glossary], *Reinge*—reins.
B Sense.

A driving rein. **widespread, but somewhat less freq Midl** See Map on p. 554 Cf **checkrein, line** n[1] **1** Note: As *rein* is known everywhere and appears to be virtually the only term used in ref to a saddle horse, only quots that give systematic regional data on the use of *rein* in ref to a harness horse are given here.

1939 *LANE* Map 177 (*Reins*), The map shows the terms *reins, lines, ribbons* and *webbings* . . , denoting the long strap(s) used to guide and restrain one or more horses drawing a vehicle. [*Reins* is very common **throughout NEng;** it is the only or first response of most infs.] **1965–70** *DARE* (Qu. L51, *The leathers or ropes that a driver holds to guide a horse*) 531 Infs, **widespread, but somewhat less freq Midl,** Reins; (Qu. K33, *When you're driving horses [or mules], how do you make them start?;* total Infs questioned, 75) Inf **FL9,** Cluck to them and slap reins on them; **FL**18, Slap reins on their backs; **MS**21, Hit reins and say "Come up"; **MS**39, Slap their backs with the reins and say "Come up"; **MS**66, Shake the reins; (Qu. K34, *What do you say to make the horses stop?*) Inf **FL**12, Tightening reins; (Qq. K35a, b, *What do you say to make the horses or mules turn right [or left]?; total Infs questioned, 75*) Inf **DC**1, Use rein; (Qu. K36a, *What do you say to make a horse go faster?*) Inf **ME**12, Give tweak with reins; **NH**3, Slap with reins; (Qu. K36b, *What do you say to make a horse go backwards?*) Infs **CA**16, **FL**18, Pull reins; **TX**3, Done with reins; **CT**17, Pull back on your reins; **MS**9, Pull on reins; **NY**35, Pull reins in; **FL**17, Use reins; (Qu. Z14a) Inf **CO**27, Gives him free (*or* loose) rein; (Qu. KK28) Inf **MI**108, Straining at the reins. **1971** Bright *Word Geog. CA & NV* 173, *Reins . . for driving or plowing, not riding . . reins 79% [of 300 infs] . . lines 35%.* **1973** Allen *LAUM* 1.269 **Upper MW** (as of c1950), For some infs. the generic term is *lines,* and for others the generic is *reins.* Some use them as interchangeable generics. Some infs. distinguish between use with a saddle horse, for which their term is *reins,* and use with a hitched horse, for which the term is *lines.* Occasionally such an inf., however, will point out that for him *reins* also can be used with a single horse, but *lines* only with a team. In this varied use no marked patterning by either informant type or geographical area emerges in the U[pper] M[idwest]. **1989** Pederson *LAGS Tech. Index* 143 **Gulf Region,** (*Lines* [for driving or plowing]) 392 infs, Line(s); 324 infs, Rein(s).

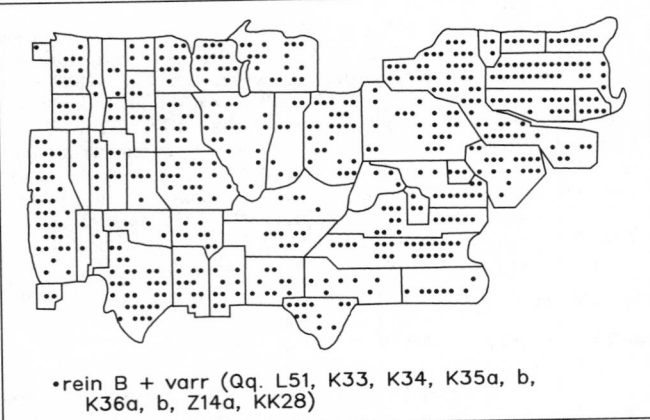

•rein B + varr (Qq. L51, K33, K34, K35a, b, K36a, b, Z14a, KK28)

reina n [Appar Span *reina,* literally "queen"]
A **rockfish 3** (here: *Sebastes elongatus*).
1882 U.S. Natl. Museum *Bulletin* 16.669 **CA,** *S[ebastodes] elongatus. . . Reina. . .* About Monterey and San Francisco; abundant in deep water. **1898** *Ibid* 47.1815, *Reina. . .* Color light red; sides above with irregular horizontal interrupted olive-green bands. **1953** Roedel *Common Fishes CA* 132, *Sebastodes elongatus. . .* Often found in association with the bocaccio and chilipepper as well as other species taken in water of moderate depth. . . *Reina.*

reindeer moss n Also *reindeer lichen* [*OED2 reindeer moss* 1753 →, ~ *lichen* 1770 →] **esp NEast** Cf **moss** n 2c
A lichen of the genus *Cladonia,* esp *C. rangiferina.* Also called **caribou moss, deer ~ 2.** For other names of var spp see **British soldier 2, red-cup moss, star ~**
1846 Emmons *Agriculture NY* 1.5, We find an alpine region, where reindeer-moss and other lichens abound. **1907** Marshall *Mosses* 27, Reindeer-lichen *(Cladonia rangiferina),* covers the ground with a carpet of loveliest grays. . . The reindeer . feed almost entirely upon this lichen. **1942** Hylander *Plant Life* 79, Other lichens are found in the woods of our northern states, where much of the ground is covered with the spongy Reindeer Moss. **1961** Douglas *My Wilderness* 221 **NH,** In the dwarf-birch zone the lichens take over. . . One of the brightest is a gray lichen known as reindeer moss *(Cladonia rangiferina)* often growing in other moss. **1977** *UpCountry* Dec 21 **csME,** Some [Christmas wreaths] are bought by local florists to be embellished with cones and berries and reindeer moss but most are shipped south. **1978** Whipple *Vintage Nantucket* 235 **MA,** Still we saw an infinite variety of flora: woolly pincushions of beach heather, dark-leaved golden heather, carpets of reindeer and Iceland moss—tundra plants that seemed out of place on the warm September beach—as did the bright red British soldier lichens that paraded through the underbrush. **1982** *AK Geographic* 9.3.26, Scattered here and there are patches of reindeer lichen *(Cladonia* sp.), a species sought by several hundred of these animals [=reindeer].

reinge See **rein**

reinikaboo See **ranikaboo**

rein orchid n Also *rein orchis* [See quot 1895]
Any of var orchids, esp those of the genera *Habenaria* and *Platanthera,* but also of the genera *Coeloglossum, Gymnadenia,* and *Piperia.* Note: Many of these latter were at times included in the genus *Habenaria.* For other names of *Coeloglossum viride* see **satyr orchid**
1895 Gray-Bailey *Field Botany* 407, *Habenaria. Rein Orchis.* (Latin *habena,* a rein or thong, from the shape of the lip of the corolla in some species.) **1906** (1918) Parsons *Wild Flowers CA* 98, *Habenaria leucostachys* [=*Platanthera l.*] . . From July to September we may look for the milk-white rein orchis in moist meadows. **1933** Small *Manual SE Flora* 373, *G[ymnadeniopsis] nivea* [=*Platanthera n.*] . . White rein-orchid. . . Low pinelands, acid meadows, and moist hillsides. *Ibid* 374, *G. clavellata* [=*Platanthera c.*] . . Green rein-orchid. . . Moist grounds and swamps. **1950** Correll *Native Orchids* 74, *Habenaria flava* [=*Platanthera f.*] . . The Southern Rein-orchid is an inconspicuous species, . . primarily a plant of the Atlantic Coastal Plain and Gulf Coast. *Ibid* 91, *Habenaria obtusata* [=*Platanthera o.*] . . The One-leaved Rein-orchid is a northerner, . . extending south only to central New England and in the West at high altitudes. *Ibid* 113, *Habenaria unalascensis* var *elata* [= *Piperia elongata* subsp *elongata*]. . . Wood Rein-orchid. **1961** Smith *MI Wildflowers* 81, *Green Rein-orchid . . Habenaria viridis . .* var. *bracteata* [=*Coeloglossum viride*]. . . In rich woods and thickets, meadows, bogs, open grassy swamps, and beach meadows. **1973** Hitchcock–Cronquist *Flora Pacific NW* 702, *Habenaria. . .* Rein-orchid. . . Our spp. with fairly close mutual relationship, but often treated in part under other generic names. **1987** Case *Orchids* 92 **Gt Lakes,** Rein-orchids (platantheras) are erect, glabrous, and leafy-stemmed. . . Many have inconspicuous greenish flowers.

reins n pl [*OED2* 1387 → "Now *arch.*"] Cf **running range**
1960 Criswell *Resp. to PADS 20* **Ozarks,** *Reins . .* used for *kidneys,* only in case of hogs when dressed. These people invariably discarded them. Prob. *rarer* now.

reither See **rather** adv

relation n
1 A person related by blood or marriage; a relative—freq used in pl. [*OED2* 1502 →] **widespread, but less freq Sth, S Midl** See Map Cf **kinfolk**
1899 (1912) Green *VA Folk-Speech* 350, *Relation. . .* A person connected by blood or affinity; a kinsman or kinswoman; a relative. **1941** *LANE* [see **2** below]. c**1955** Reed-Person *Ling. Atlas Pacific NW,* 9 infs, Relations. **1962** Atwood *Vocab. TX* 65, Those related to someone . . are predominantly termed *kinfolks* (71[% of c270 infs]), less often *folks* (14) or *relatives* (11). *Relations* (7) is less current, while *kin* (5) is both rare and archaic. **1965–70** *DARE* (Qu. Z9, . . *Others related to you by blood*) 115 Infs, **widespread, but less freq Sth, S Midl,** (My) relations; 10 Infs, **scattered,** (My) blood relations; **MN**19, **WA**20, Shirttail relations; **WA**20, Bedstead relations; **IL**113, Near relations; **MO**19, Poor relations; 14 Infs, **esp Nth, N Midl,** (My own) relation; **CA**21, **CO**20, **MN**19, 33, **PA**42, Blood relation; (Qu. Z8, *General word for your own immediate family group*) 12 Infs, **chiefly Nth, N Midl,** (My) relations; **IN**28, **PA**237, Blood relations; (Qu. Z7, *Nicknames . . for any other relatives*) Inf **NY**165, Shirttail relation. **1966** Dakin *Dial. Vocab. Ohio R. Valley* 442, *Relatives* and *relation(s)* appear to have come into the Ohio Valley primarily from the North Midland. They are old, long-established terms and have largely replaced the earlier more common *kinfolk(s)* everywhere north of the Ohio except in southwestern Indiana. . . [*Relatives*] is now replacing *relation(s).* The latter term is frequently used by simple folk as an uninflected collective. . . *Relation* is slightly more common in Illinois (6 to 5) and is usual in Indiana (7 to 2) and Kentucky (9 to 6). In Ohio, however, *relations* is more common (8 to 4), with 3 of the 4 uninflected usages appearing in the southwest just across the river from Kentucky. **1971** Wood *Vocab. Change* 37 **Sth,** In the larger sense of "immediate family" *my people* and *my relatives* occur generally; *my relations* are [sic] unreported in Alabama, Mississippi, Louisiana, and Arkansas. For the second sense, "others related by blood," the preferred words are *my kinfolks* and *my relatives,* followed by *my family, my kin,* and *my relations. My people* and *my relation* are less widely reported. **1973** Gawthrop *Dial. Calumet* 79 **nwIN,** Others related by blood: my relatives 98 (of 125 infs), my family 26, my relations 7, my relation 5, my folks 4. **1982** Barrick *Coll.* **csPA,** *Relations*—relatives. **1989** Pederson *LAGS Tech. Index* 238 **Gulf Region**

(Relatives) 38 infs, Relations; 1 inf, Blood relations; 1 inf, [Re]lations; 468 infs, Relatives.

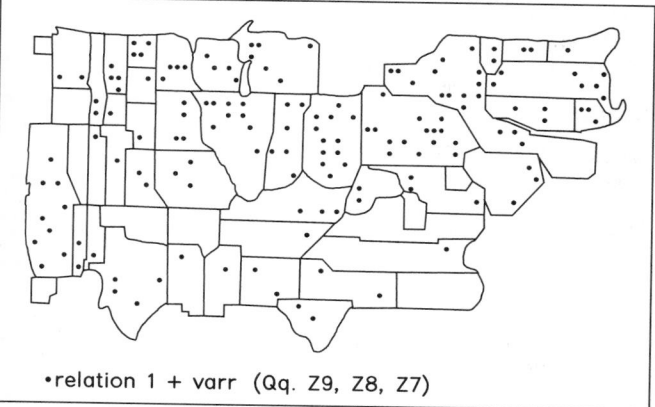

•relation 1 + varr (Qq. Z9, Z8, Z7)

2 used collectively: People related to one, one's relatives. [*OED2* 1653–1702 "*Obs. rare*"]; but the US use may be independent, perh by analogy with *kin* or *kindred*] **scattered, but less freq Sth, S Midl**   See Map

1938 *AmSp* 13.158, Elsie Cather (who is a sister of the novelist Willa) points out that a collective singular *relation*, in place of 'relations,' is now often used by school children and others: 'The relation and friends were invited,' 'After showing talent at this young age his relation sent Alexander Hamilton over here to the United States.' **1941** *LANE* Map 388 *(Relatives)*, [The word *relation* is fairly common **throughout NEng**, usually as a singular collective; only in **MA** and **wCT** is the plural *relations* the more common form.] **1941** Smith *Going to God's Country* 43 **MO** (as of 1890), There were all the relation, neighbors and friends to see us off. **1948** Davis *Word Atlas Gt. Lakes* app qu 90a *(Immediate family)* 30 (of 233) infs, **MI, IL, IN, OH**, Relatives; 5 infs, Relation; 3 infs, Relations. *Ibid* app qu 90b *(Others related by blood)*, 130 (of 233) infs, **MI, IL, IN, OH**, Relatives; 30 infs, Relation; 21 infs, Relations. **1965–70** *DARE* (Qu. Z9, *General word for others related to you by blood*) 11 Infs, **chiefly Nth, Midl**, Relation; CA21, CO20, MN19, 33, PA42, Blood relation; NH14, My own relation. **1966** [see **1** above]. **1971** [see **1** above]. **1973** Allen *LAUM* 1.345 **Upper MW** (as of c1950), Relatives [is] the choice of two-thirds of the infs. . . Its doublets *relation* and *relations* contrariwise seem more homespun or old-fashioned. . . A likely regional contrast is indicated between the collective *relation* and the plural *relations*. . . In the U[pper] M[idwest] it seems that the collective form is dying out among Northern speakers. Its distribution is clearly Midland.

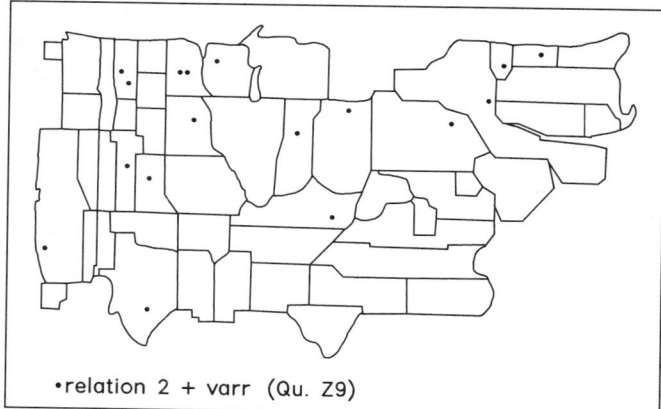

•relation 2 + varr (Qu. Z9)

relative n Usu |ˈrɛlətɪv|; also occas |ˈrælətɪv, rəˈletɪv, rɪ-| [The forms with stress on the second syllable may be by analogy with *relation*.]

Std sense, var forms.

1891 *DN* 1.121 **cNY**, [ˈrælətɪv] . . 'relative.' **1935** Sheppard *Cabins* 277 **wNC**, When Doc Hoppas sings the "Rim Rock Ranch," the lines run thus: Goodbye to my friends and relatives / Goodbye to the girl that I love. **1941** *LANE* Map 388 *(Relatives)* 1 inf, **swNH**, [rɪˈletɪ̬vz]. **1942** Hall *Smoky Mt. Speech* 61 **wNC, eTN**, Relatives is sometimes (but

not frequently) stressed [rəˈleɪtɪvz]. **1968** *DARE* (Qu. Z9) Inf **NH**14, Relatives [rɪˈledɪvz].

relay arm n

In distilling: a pipe for conveying mash from the **relay barrel** back to the still pot.

1968 *Foxfire* 2.3.49 **nGA**, *Still Parts And Tools. . . Relay Arm*—the pipe connection from the bottom of the relay barrel back into the still. **1974** Maurer–Pearl *KY Moonshine* 123, *Relay arm. . .* The connection between the relay barrel and the still through which heated beer is piped.

relay barrel n Also *relay keg*

In distilling: a barrel between the still and the **thump barrel** that returns boiled-over mash to the still or preheats it before it enters the still.

1968 *Foxfire* 2.3.49 **nGA**, *Still Parts And Tools. . . Relay Barrel* or *Dry Barrel*—a fifty gallon barrel with connections for the cap arm, relay arm, and long thump rod. Catches "puke" from the still during boiling and conveys it back into the still. **1974** Maurer–Pearl *KY Moonshine* 123, *Relay barrel* or *keg. . .* A large scale puker combined with a preheater arrangement for preheating beer and charging the still. Seldom used in Kentucky.

rele See **real** adj, adv

release n Also *Billy release* [Cf **relievo** quot 1969] =**ring-a-levio 1.**

1953 Brewster *Amer. Nonsinging Games* 60 **TX**, *Release. . .* For the playing of this game, two teams are needed. Each establishes a "home base." . . Each team now starts out from its home base, either in pairs or singly, to capture the enemy. The capture is made by touching a player three times on the back. The prisoner must now go to the captor's home base, where he waits to be released. His release can be effected by one of his comrades who will touch the enemy home base and shout "Release!" **1957** *Sat. Eve. Post Letters* **MA**, I play a game called "Relievo," formerly "Billy Release" at summer camp. . . We have one base for prisoners, two sides. One side hunts the other putting all prisoners at the base. The prisoners may be released by someone from the "chased" [side] tagging the base. **1968–70** *DARE* (Qu. EE12, *Games in which one captain hides his team and the other team tries to find it*) Infs PA76, 94, Release; (Qu. EE33, *Other outdoor games*) Inf PA93, Release—two teams; players who are caught must stay around the base until they are "released" by a team member; [(Qu. EE1, . . *Games . . in which they form a ring, and either sing or recite a rhyme*) Inf IL116, Release [Inf doubtful]].

relievo n Also *relevo, relievio*; aphet *lievo* [*OED2* 1888 →; cf also quot 1969 below. Ult from arch, chiefly Scots dial *relieve* to release, rescue] **chiefly NEast, esp MA** =**ring-a-levio 1**; also used as a call in the game.

1923 Acker *400 Games* 115, *Relievo*—Sides are chosen and a den is marked out. . . One side waits in the den until the other players are hidden. Then all start out to hunt, except one man who is left to guard the den. . . The object of the game is to bring all those hiding into the den. A member of the group in hiding may free a prisoner in the den by tagging him. . . If successful, he calls out "Relievo! Relievo!" **1954** Forbes *Rainbow* 197 **NH**, When the day was ending and it was getting on, too dark for ball games, we played Hoist the Green Flag, Run, Sheep, Run, Relevo—running games, running through the dusk, and all over the campus. **1957** *Sat. Eve. Post Letters* **NJ** (as of c1900), *Relievio.* The one who was it stood by a stone, against which was propped quite a heavy stick. One of the gang threw the stick and the one chosen to be it ran and brought it back to position while the whole gang ran to hide. Then it was typical hide and seek, but if any one could sneak back and throw the stick, he would shout "Relievio" and every one would rush to hide again as they were all freed so the poor "it" had to start all over again. *Ibid* **Boston MA**, There were many running games such as . . relievo (most popular). *Ibid* **swMA** (as of 1920s), Relievo. *Ibid* **neMA** (as of 1910s), Relievo. **1957** [see **release**]. **1966–69** *DARE* (Qu. EE12, *Games in which one captain hides his team and the other team tries to find it*) Inf **MA**33, [riˈlivo]; **MA**71, [rəˈlivo]; (Qu. EE15, *When he has caught the first of those that were hiding what does . . 'it' call out to the others?*) Inf **MA**11, [rəˈlivo]; (Qu. EE33, . . *Outdoor games . . that children play*) Inf **RI**6, Lievo |ˈlivo|—two teams on opposite sides, one team tries to run through the other without getting caught. [**1969** Opie–Opie *Children's Games* 172, In Scotland, Wales, and the northern half of England, 'Relievo' is the principal seeking game with two sides. . . When a hider is caught he is taken to the den, and it becomes the object of his own side to try and release him. *Ibid* 173, General names: 'Leavo', 'Leavio', 'Rallio', 'Realio', 'Release', 'Releaso', 'Relievo', 'Relievio', 'Rileo', 'Tally-ho'.] **1971** *AmSp* 46.83 **Chicago IL,** Line and running games: . . *relievio.*

relliche See **rolliche**

rellum See **realm**

remanier n
1950 *PADS* 14.56 **SC,** *Remanier* [rɪ'menɪə]: . . A cobbling tailor who mends clothing. Fr. *remanieur.*

remant See **remnant**

rember See **remember**

remblant, rembling See **remnant**

remember v

Pronc-spp *'member, 'membuh, mem'er, rember, renember*
A Forms.

1867 Allen *Slave Songs* 20 **SC coast,** When you get to heaven say you 'member me. **1899** Chesnutt *Conjure Woman* 47 **csNC** [Black], Dey hadn' 'membered right. **1909** *DN* 3.348 **eAL, wGA,** *Member.* . . To remember. **1916** *DN* 4.355, Due, perhaps, to rapid utterance are the following contractions, or assimilatory condensations, frequently heard, and appearing in written form also. . . *Rember,* remember. **1922** Gonzales *Black Border* 168 **eSC** [Gullah], Uh 'membuh de time w'en uh could'uh box'um en' kick'um alltwo one time. **1927** Adams *Congaree* 21 **cSC** [Black], Ef it do you any good, jes 'member I belongs to you. **1931** (1991) Hughes–Hurston *Mule Bone* 53 **cFL** [Black], Yeah, I 'member seein' you comin' down de road. **1939** in 1976 *Weevils in the Wheat* 304 **VA** [Black], I mem'ers so well when dey uster to cut wheat. *Ibid,* I jes don't mem'er any. **1942** Hall *Smoky Mt. Speech* 53 **wNC, eTN,** On a phonograph record, *remember* sounds very much like [ɾ'mɛmbɚ] in the phrase, 'I don't remember . . ' **1942** Faulkner *Go Down* 13 **MS** [Black], You member that. **1950** *WELS Suppl.,* [n] for [m] in first nasal. "I don't just renember now." (I'm sure of this. He used it at least 3 times.) **1967** *DARE* (Qu. JJ28, *If you are afraid you may forget something, you may tell another person, "Before I leave tonight, be sure and _____ [me to do it]."*) Inf **LA8,** Make me member it; (Qu. JJ29, . . *Something that may have happened in the past: "Have you met him before?" "Not that I _____."*) Inf **SC32,** Member. **1970** *AmSp* 45.76 **PA,** Remember. 'Member the mountain home? . . 'Member the day I saw you on Broad Street? . . 'Member last week when I came to see you? [*DARE* Ed: All these exx were heard from White speakers.]
B Senses.

1 To remind. [*OED2* remember v. 7.a c1386 →; "Now *arch.* or *dial.*"; 7.b c1449 →; "Now *dial.*"] *old-fash* Cf **remind**
1817 (1930) Sewall *Diary* 25 **ME,** Such awful and sudden death—is enough to remember us of our own mortality. **1899** (1912) Green *VA Folk-Speech* 350, *Remember.* . . To put in mind of: as, "If you will remember me of it." **1950** *PADS* 14.46 **SC,** *'Member.* . . To remind. "'Member me to call Jenny." **1951** Johnson *Resp. to PADS* 20 **DE** *(If you are afraid you will forget something)* Mind—remember me of it—old-fashioned. **1952** Brown *NC Folkl.* 1.583 **wNC,** *Remember.* . . To remind. **1968** *DARE* (Qu. JJ28, *If you are afraid you may forget something, you may tell another person, "Before I leave tonight, be sure and _____ [me to do it]."*) Inf **NY75,** Remember me of it. [Inf old]

2 To recall (something to someone). [*OED2* remember v. 8.a 1382–1672]
1941 Stuart *Men of Mts.* 28 **eKY,** You hear the bargain, Pewee. . . Now remember it to me when I get into office.

3 in phr *remember of:* See **of** prep **Bb.**

remember n

One's memory; a memory.
1945 Saxon *Gumbo Ya-Ya* 389 **LA,** Her eyes are bad, but she says her 'remember' is still very good. **1986** Pederson *LAGS Concordance,* 1 inf, **cMS,** I done slipped my remember; 1 inf, **nwLA,** It done slipped my remember; 1 inf, **nwAR,** Good remembers = memories.

remember service n Pronc-sp *'member service* Cf **remember** v **A**
1950 *PADS* 14.46 **SC,** *'Member service.* . . A religious service in *remembrance* of the dead, usually held on the first anniversary of death. Negro usage.

remembrance n Also aphet *'memb(r)ance, 'membunce* **S Atl, Gulf States** *esp freq among Black speakers*
Usu with possessive pron: The faculty of memory; recollection.
1838 (1852) Gilman *S. Matron* 28 **SC** [Black], Me an't got no membrance, if me an't member maussa, just like a yesterday. **1883** Harris *Nights with Remus* 203 **GA** [Black], Ef I makes no mistakes wid my 'membunce. **1899** Chesnutt *Conjure Woman* 40 **csNC** [Black], Dat saw . . kyars [=carries] my 'memb'ance back ter ole times. **1922** Gonzales *Black Border* 313 **sSC, GA coasts** [Gullah glossary], *'Memb'unce*—remembrance, remembrances. **1927** Kennedy *Gritny* 128 **sLA** [Black], Put de thing out yo' 'membunce, an' stop worrin' 'bout it. **1937** Hall *Coll.* **wNC,** "I've never seed it in my remembrance"—[used by] "old people." **1946** *PADS* 6.11 **ceNC,** *Delicun squinton* . . : Whisky. "Delicun squinton makes you speak the truth and gives you everlasting remembrance." **1953** Brewer *Word Brazos* 52 **eTX** [Black], Ah wants evuh livin' soul heah tonight to keep dis in yo' 'membrance dat Ah mought gib out, but Ah ain't in no wise evuh gonna gib up. **1966–70** *DARE* (Qu. JJ29, . . *"Have you met him before?" "Not that I _____."*) Inf **MS37,** Have any remembrance of; **FL28,** Not to my remembrance; (Qu. JJ30b, *Other expressions for forgetting: "It _____."*) Infs **GA5, 7, SC26, 69,** Slipped my remembrance. [2 of 6 Infs Black] **1969** *DARE* Tape **GA72,** Years ago in my remembrance . . I can remember people shooting revenuers in this country. **1979** Carpenter *Walton War* 152 **sAppalachians,** "The best I can find out, he has lost his remembrance." "Remembrance" here carried a lot more meaning than memory would have. This man meant his uncle had lost his mind. **1986** Pederson *LAGS Concordance,* 2 infs, **seAL, neMS,** To my (nearest) remembrance. [Both infs Black]

reminant See **remnant**

remind v [*OED2* remind v. 1.a 1645 →; "Now *rare* or *obs.*"]
To remember, recall.
1859 (1968) Bartlett *Americanisms* 360 **NY,** To remind, for remember; as, "the company will please remind." A New York vulgarism. **1902** *DN* 2.243 **sIL,** Remind. . . To call to mind. Always used with negative, as 'I don remind,' i.e. I don't remember. Also always used at the end of the clause, never as in 'I don remind that, etc.' **1952** Brown *NC Folkl.* 1.584, *Remind.* . . To remember.

remnant n Usu |'rɛmnənt, -nɪnt|; also |'rɛmənənt, 'rɛmnɛt, 'rɪmnənt|; for addit varr see quots Pronc-spp *remant, remblant, rembling, reminant, remlet* [For the varr with *-m(b)l-* in place of *-mn-* see *EDD* remlet (also *remlit, rimlet, remlant, remlin(g)*) and cf **chimney**]
Std sense, var forms.
1915 *DN* 4.228 **wTX,** *Remblings.* . . Remnants. "Have you any calico remblings?" **1941** in 1944 *ADD* 506, *Remlet.* . . Remnant. **1941** *AmSp* 16.10 **eTX** [Black], *Remnant* . . ['rɪmnɛt]. **1946** McDavid *Coll.* **GA,** *Remblant* = remnant (of cloth). **1950** *WELS Suppl.* **seWI,** Reminants—cloth scraps. **1965–70** *DARE* (Qu. W25) 117 Infs, **widespread,** Remnant(s) [no pronc recorded]; **CT8, MA3, 4, 64, NY144, VA62, 63, 106,** ['rɛmnənts] (*or* ['rɛmnɪnts]); **CA15, IN35, MI2, 19, VT16,** ['rɛmənənts]; **OH16,** ['rɛmɪnənts]; **RI8,** ['rɛmɪnṇts]; **ND1,** Reminants; **MO2,** ['rɛmnɪts]; **OK6,** ['rɪmnɪts]; **TX26,** ['rɛmnɛts]; **AL39,** ['rɪmnɛts]; **MA48,** ['ræmnɛts]; **IL135,** [rɛmnɪns]; **PA57,** Remants; **MD25,** ['rɛnɪmṇts]. **1981** Pederson *LAGS Basic Materials Gulf Region,* [Proncs of *remnant(s)* were recorded from 13 infs. 7 were of the std type ['rɛmnənt], 3 of the type ['rɪmnənt]. Other proncs recorded once each were: [rɛ^mṇt], ['rĭ˞əmənt], ['rɛmɪnɪnt], and, from an inf who also said ['rɪmnənt], ['rɪ˞mlə̆nts].]

remonia See **pneumonia**

remontha, remoother See **remuda**

rempshion, remption See **rimption**

remuda n Pronc-spp *remontha, remoother, remudo, remutha, remuthar* [MexSpan *remuda;* the form *remontha* in quot 1887 is appar a blend with MexSpan *remonta,* used in the same sense.] Cf **manada, saddle band**
A herd of riding horses (or rarely other work animals) from which those needed at any time can be selected.
1887 *Scribner's Mag.* 2.512 **West,** You will not see these extraordinary foot-coverings if he is whipping up . . a *remontha* (bunch of saddle-

horses), or if he has any other active work to do. **1892** *DN* 1.251 **TX,** *Remúdo or remúda:* a "bunch" of horses, about a score. Usually applied to geldings only. See *manada.* From *remudar* to exchange. The Spanish form is *remuda, remuda de caballos,* a change, a relay of horses. **1907** White *AZ Nights* 92, The leader turned unhesitatingly into the corral. After him poured the stream of the remuda—two hundred and fifty saddle horses—with an unceasing thunder of hoofs. **1920** Hunter *Trail Drivers TX* 211 (as of 1877), It [=lightning] killed seven or eight head of cattle . . and two horses out of the "remuthra," which being interpreted means the saddle horses. **1929** Dobie *Vaquero* 91 **West,** When the remuda was rounded up next morning, six horses were missing. **1932** Bentley *Spanish Terms* 195, *Remuda (Spanish,* [re: mú: ða:]; *English,* [rə mú: ðə]; *also* [rə mú: ðər]) The horses, mules and other riding, pack, or harness animals of a ranching, camping, freighting, or traveling outfit or expedition when considered as a group. **1933** *AmSp* 8.1.30 **nwTX** [Ranch diction], *Remuda.* The small string of horses kept for daily use in a convenient pasture or, on the range or the trail, herded or hobbled. Most *cowmen* who have ventured to spell this word have said "r-e-m-o-o-t-h-e-r", showing the Spanish influence of the soft "d" between two vowels. **1937** *DN* 6.618 **swTX,** A *mount* is one horse put aside for special riding jobs, while a number of horses so corralled compose what is generally termed a *remuda.* **1952** Brown *Trail Driving* 36, The horse herd accompanying a trail drive was known as the remuda (pronounced *remoother* in Texas). *Ibid* 184, The Texas "remuda" had become a "cavvy" [in Wyoming]. **1956** Ker *Vocab. W. TX* 215, For a band of saddle horses the term of Spanish origin *remuda* is most generally current. . . The older informant of Randall county responds *remuthar.* **1962** Atwood *Vocab. TX* 55, For a band of saddle horses, still much used on ranches, the most popular specific word is *remuda* (30[% of 273 infs]). This is current mainly in the old ranch country. **1966** *DARE* Tape **NM**14, Every man was mounted with about eight horses, and we called the horses the remuda [rɪˈmudə]. **1986** Pederson *LAGS Concordance,* 1 inf, **ceTX,** Remuda—only in the movies; 1 inf, **csTX,** Remuda—a big bunch of saddle horses.

remudero n
A person in charge of a **remuda;** also fig.

1920 Hunter *Trail Drivers TX* 56, The first acquaintance I met here [= Dodge City, Kansas] was George W. Saunders, now the president and chief remudero of the Old Trail Drivers'. **1929** Dobie *Vaquero* 91 **West,** With some outfits a *remudero,* or wrangler—"night-hawk," he was often called—herded the horses.

remudo, remutha, remuthar See remuda

rence See rinse 3

rench See rinse 4

renege v Usu |ˌriˈnɪg, ˌrɪˈnɪg, ˈrɪˌnɪg|; *also* |ˌriˈnɛg|; for addit varr see quots Pronc-sp *renig*
Std senses, var forms.

1784 in 1908 Mathews *A. Ellicott* 27 **PA,** The Hussey immediately Reniged and reclaimed the Bed. **1866** Smith *Bill Arp* 153 **GA,** When the Secretary read out my name . . I felt that I was obleged to renig. **1899** (1912) Green *VA Folk-Speech* 350, *Renig.* . . To play a card that is not of the suit led; to revoke. **1903** *DN* 2.326 **seMO,** *Re-nig.* . . To back out. 'We made a fair and square trade but he re-nigged and azzled out of it.' **1907** *DN* 3.235 **nwAR,** *Renig.* . . To back out. *Ibid* 363 **nwAR,** *Renig.* . . To renege. **1907** White *AZ Nights* 180, I must say when I saw her I felt inclined to renig. **1914** *DN* 4.165 **AZ,** *Renig.* . . To back out; 'quit.' **1965–70** *DARE* (Qu. II31, . . *"He saw that he was wrong, so he started to _____."*) 24 Infs, **scattered,** [rɪˈnɪg, ˈrinɪg]; 9 Infs, **scattered,** [rɪˈnɪg]; **AZ**14, 15, **MT**2, **OH**45, **TX**72, 74, [rəˈnɪg]; **SC**24, 45, **TX**1, **WV**18, [rɪˈnɪg]; **MI**92, [reˈnɪg]; **CT**21, **NJ**57, **NY**27, 32, 206, **WA**25, [ˌriˈnɛg]; **AZ**2, **MA**98, [rineg] [stress not recorded]; **MI**13, **WA**33, [rɪˈnɛg]; **VA**43, [riˈneɪg]; **WA**11, [ˈrineɪg].

renember See remember v

renicky(-boo) See ranikaboo

renig See renege

rense See rinse 3

rent n¹ [*OED2* 1466 →; *"Obs. exc U.S. dial."*] **NEng, esp ME** Cf **rent house**
Living quarters that are rented.

1913 *DN* 4.1 **cME,** *Rent.* . . Tenement. "Have you found a rent yet?" **1926** *AmSp* 2.79 **ME,** A Maine Yankee never lives in an apartment. The owner of rentable property always advertises a "rent," whether it be in the nature of an entire establishment or a few rooms for light housekeeping. **1926** *DN* 5.388 **ME,** *Rent.* . . Apartment or rentable house. Universal. **1941** *LANE* Map 355 *(Tenement),* [About 40 infs, all in **nNEng,** and most in **ME,** responded *rent.*] **1943** *New Yorker* 21 Aug 54, Just what in tunket *is* a rent-hunter? [In ref to an editorial in the *Boston Herald* that used this word.] **1966–69** *DARE* (Qu. D24, *Living quarters in a building where several other families live*) Infs **CT**7, 13, **NH**14, **VT**16, Rent; **AL**1, Rent [Inf doubtful]; (Qu. L2, *The extra house on a large farm where a hired man and his family live*) Inf **ME**12, Hired-hand rent. **1966** *DARE* FW Addit **ME,** Rent—an apartment or house to rent. "Have you found a good rent yet?" **1966** *N. Berwick Enterprise* (ME) 29 Apr 5/5, Mr. and Mrs. Gerald Goodwin who have been living in Kenneth Smith's upstairs rent, moved to Somersworth last Saturday. **1975** *DARE* File **ME,** Rent—An apartment or house which is rented. I knew this in Portland, Me. **1998** *Ibid* s**CT,** It sounded odd to me when I first moved here in 1984, but people around here would say, "She's looking for a rent," when I would have said, " . . for an apartment to rent."

rent n² *esp freq among women*
A tear, snag in a piece of fabric.

1965–70 *DARE* (Qu. W27, . . *A three-cornered tear in a piece of clothing from catching it on something sharp*) 14 Infs, **scattered exc Atl,** Rent. [12 Infs female]

rent house n scattered, but esp TX, AR Cf rent n¹ See Map
A house that is rented out.

1965–70 *DARE* (Qu. L2, *The extra house on a large farm where a hired man and his family live*) 22 Infs, 14 **TX, AR,** Rent house; (Qu. D24, *Living quarters in a building where several other families live*) Inf **TX**36, Rent house. [18 of 22 total Infs old; 18 comm type 4 or 5] **1968** *Fredericksburg Std.* (TX) 4 Sept 5/2, [Advt:] *Rent House*—Special Offering—Rent house near school, owners moving out of town, now offering at sacrifice price. **1998** *NADS Letters* nwLA, A friend . . was getting ready to sell a house she had inherited because "It's too hard to keep up a rent house." . . In my parents' generation (both born in south Alabama, 1891 and 1895) the term was important to describe a social class. . . To live in a "paid-for house" was several steps above living in a house with a mortgage, which was several steps above living in a "rent house." *Ibid* c**TX,** Rent House. This is common usage throughout Texas. . . The term applies mostly to small frame houses of the type realtors and developers prefer to call "starter homes." Generally "rent houses" are structures which were built primarily as income producing rent properties rather than for the builder's residence. *Ibid* c**NM,** I had just moved from DC to a 'town' fewer than 1,000 souls to teach school and, upon inquiring into the availability of housing, was directed to a Mr. Warfield, who owned some 'rent houses.' *Ibid* **Sth,** Rent house . . was widely current as recently as late 1970's in northwest Tennessee. . . I have heard the phrase used within the past year in Birmingham, Alabama and the suburbs south of Atlanta, Georgia. *Ibid,* Rent house— Eastern mid-west (Ohio to Missouri) and I've also heard it in Northern Florida (non-urban areas). "We'll be gittin money from three rent (rental) houses next month." *Ibid,* **AR, TX, sTX, eTX, neTX, ceTX,** Rent house.

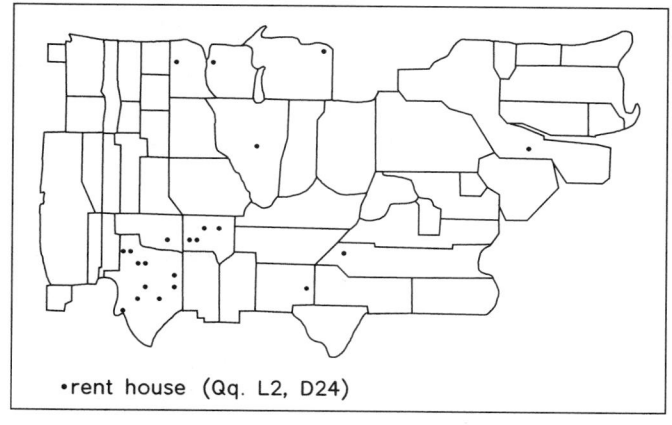

•rent house (Qq. L2, D24)

rent party n Also *rent-raising party* **chiefly NYC** *chiefly among Black speakers*
=**house-rent party.**

1926 Van Vechten *Nigger Heaven* 150 **Harlem NYC,** There were . . the modest rent-parties. **1929** Gordon *Born to Be* 224 **Harlem NYC** [Black], Madge is giving a rent party tonight. . . In Harlem most of the flat rents are so high some people can't make the monthly payments . . they tell all their friends to come over. . . When these people arrive they drop . . money into the box at the door. **1965** Little *Autobiog. Malcolm X* 77 **Harlem NYC,** People offering you little cards advertising "rent-raising parties." I went to one of these—thirty or forty Negroes sweating, eating, drinking, dancing. . . the fried chicken or chitlins with potato salad and collard greens for a dollar a plate, and cans of beer or shots of liquor for fifty cents. **1969–70** *DARE* (Qu. DD34, *A party at which there is considerable drinking*) Inf NY131, Rent party—the colored people have them when things are rough; for a dollar apiece, all you can drink; (Qu. FF2, . . *Kinds of parties*) Inf PA247, Rent-raising parties— the owner of the house has a party to help him raise money for the tenant who is unable to pay his rent. **1980** Banks *First-Person America* 252 **NYC** (as of 1920s) [Black], When I first came to New York from Bermuda, I thought rent parties were disgraceful. **1981** Palmer *Deep Blues* 15 **Chicago IL** (as of 1940s) [Black], I started playing for these rent parties. **1983** Mebane *Mary Wayfarer* 198 **NC,** "The rent's due and I haven't got the money. That's why I'm having this little selling, trying to make the rent." . . I thought, Rent Party! Rent parties were something that used to happen in black urban communities during the Depression. I didn't know they still had them. **1993** Delany–Delany *Having Our Say* 97 **NYC,** The less well-to-do would hold "rent parties," where, for a small entrance fee, visitors would drink bathtub gin and dance until dawn, raising money to pay the landlord.

rep See **reap**

repentant seat n [*repentant* a penitent; *W3* "archaic"]
=**penitent's bench.**

1983 *MJLF* 9.1.53 **ceKY** (as of 1956), *Repentent* [sic] *seats* . . the mourner's bench.

rept See **reap**

rernt See **ruin A2c**

resaca n **TX**
An area of river bed that is flooded in periods of high water; an artificial reservoir.

1930 Dobie *Coronado* 366 **TX,** Resaca, marsh. **1931** Allhands *Gringo Builders* 119 **TX,** After they had plodded along for hours their water ran out, and it could not be replenished until long after nightfall when they ran across a *resaca* containing some rather unpalatable water. **1940** Writers' Program *Guide TX* 514 **csTX,** San Benito . . is both an agricultural and recreational center. Stately palms border its wide streets and edge the banks of a *resaca,* whose waters sparkle in the bright sunshine. **1962** Atwood *Vocab. TX* 40, *Backwater of a river.* . . A word characteristic of Southwest Texas is *resaca* (7 [% of c270 infs]) . . , which still means to some informants the overflow of a river; however, it more often designates a place where water is artificially stored for irrigation or any other purpose. **1967** *DARE* (Qu. C4a, . . *A fairly large body of fresh water*) Inf TX31, Resaca—river has changed course and left inundation behind it; fills with rain; Resaca de la Guerra. **1970** Correll *Plants TX* 778, Zarza. . . Locally abundant in dry lake beds and resacas and other seasonally inundated areas of clay soil. **1986** Pederson *LAGS Concordance* 1 inf, **csTX,** Resaca = lake; 1 inf, **csTX,** Resaca—more like a lake; 1 inf, **csTX,** Resaca—filled with river overflow before levees; 1 inf, **csTX,** Resaca—larger than stream, like lake; water runs.

resate See **receipt**

rescue grass n

1 A **bromegrass** (here: *Bromus catharticus*). [See quot 1884] **chiefly Sth**

1856 *S. Lit. Messenger* 22.176, The mesquit grass, the sweet vernal grass, and the rescue grass have been lately sown, and promise well. . **1861** Wood *Class-Book* 791, *B[romus] unioloides* [=*B. catharticus*]. . *Rescue Grass.* Culm 18′ [=18″] to 3f. **1884** Vasey *Ag. Grasses* 73, Rescue Grass. . . is one of the so-called winter grasses; that is, it makes, in the South, a large share of its growth during the winter months. . . It is said to have been introduced into Georgia by General Iverson, of Columbus, and by him called rescue grass. **1906** *DN* 3.124 **TX,** *Rescue grass.* . . A kind of grass, liked by horses and cattle, which comes up in

November, grows in winter to a height of two feet, and is not affected by frost. **1923** Abrams *Flora Pacific States* 1.226, Rescue Grass. . . Now distributed from Chile to southern United States. **1950** GA Dept. Ag. *Farmers Market Bulletin* 20 Sept. 4/1 *(Mathews Coll.),* Rescue grass has some promise as a volunteering winter grass. **1958** Latham *Meskin Hound* 17 **cTX,** Outside of little patches of rescue grass, young oats were about the only green pickings deer got in the fall.

2 =**fescue.** [Perh folk-etym]
1912 Wooton–Standley *Grasses NM* 123, The Fescue Grasses (*Festuca* spp.) sometimes called Rescue grasses, are moderately common in the upper timbered areas of the State from elevations of 7500 feet (or less for the small annual species) to above timber-line.

resebiler See **reservoir**

reseet See **receipt**

reservoir n Usu |ˈrɛzə(r)ˌvwɑ(r), -ˌvwɔ(r), -ˌvɔ(r)|; also |ˈrɛzə(r)ˌvɔɪ|; for addit varr see quots Pronc-spp *reservoi, rese(r)voy, res'vore;* by folk-etym *razorboiler, resebiler, rizzyboiler*
Std senses, var forms.

1892 *DN* 1.240 **cwMO,** Reservoir. Pronounced in Kansas City [ˈrɛzɚˌvɔɪ]. I have heard this in Concord, N.H., and in Cambridge, Mass., also at Ann Arbor, Mich. [*DN* Ed: I once heard the popular perversion *razor-boiler* at Saginaw, Mich. . . The pronunciation intended above for the places in New England is probably [ˈrɛzəvɔɪ]; this can often be heard in Cambridge.] **1896** *DN* 1.423 **NH, NY,** Reservoir: specifically, a water-tank attached to a stove. Pron. [ˈrɛzəˌvɔɪ(r)], N.H., Westchester Co., Ontario Co., N.Y. Sometimes [ˈrɛzəˌvɔr] is heard. **1901** *DN* 2.146 **AR, TN,** Rizzy-boiler. . . A sheet-iron boiler attached to a wood stove. **1905** *DN* 3.92 **nwAR,** Resebiler. . . Reservoir. Negroism. Used facetiously by whites. **1909** *DN* 3.402 **nwAR,** Reservoi. . . Reservoir. **1914** in 1944 *ADD* 507 **cNY,** [ˈrɛzəvɔɪ]. **1926** Ferber *Show Boat* 63, It's got a stove with a res'vore. **1930s** in 1944 *ADD* 507 **eWV,** Reservoi. **1942** *Sat. Eve. Post* 28 Mar **MS,** Across that Government reservoy up at Oxford? **1942** in 1944 *ADD* 507, [ˈrɛzɪˌvar]. Occas.—[ˌvɔɪ]. **1965–70** *DARE* (Qu. C4a, . . *A fairly large body of fresh water*) Infs CO2, 26, [ˈrɛzɚˌvoɚ(z)]; LA18, [ˈrɛzəvoɚ]; CA156, [ˈrɛsəvɔɪ]; CO18, [ˈrɛsivɔr]; ID3, [ˈrɛzɚvɔɪ]; TX35, [ˈrɛzɚˌvɔɪ]; (Qu. C4b) Inf PA165, [ˈrɛzəvɔɚ]; TX1, [ˈrɛzɚˌvoɚ]; CO11, [ˈrɛzivɔɪr]; NV1, [ˈrɛzivɔɪ]; WY4, [ˈrɛzəˌvɔɪ]; (Qu. C10, *When a river is dammed and the water backs up and spreads out above a dam;* total Infs questioned, 75) Inf DC1, [ˈrɛzɚˌvwoɚ]. **1966–69** *DARE* Tape CA156, There's different reservoirs [ˈrɛzɪˌvɔɪz] around. All of 'em's pretty good fishing; NM2, We have a reservoir [ˈrɛzəˌvɔɪ]. . . they have a outlet. . . valve that they let it out into the ditch out of the reservoir. **1969** *DARE* FW Addit cCA, Reservoir(s) [ˈrɛzəˌvɔɪ(z)]. **1999** Proulx *Close Range* 111 **WY,** This damn everlastin drought it's a sure thing. . . Put in a resevoy tank.

resh See **rush** v, n[1]

residenter n [Scots, nIr, nEngl dial]

1 A resident, inhabitant; esp an early settler; a longtime resident, "old-timer"—often in comb *old residenter.*

1797 in 1916 Hawkins *Letters* 464, By a residenter in the Cherokees, . . I am informed that Colonel Hawkins did not set out for the point where they were to begin runing the line until the 12th of May. **1827** *Western Mth. Rev.* 1.70 **TX,** Hence arose a feud and a collision of authorities between the old and the new 'residenters.' **1828** *Ibid* 2.252 **NY,** But the eye traces in, new villages, neat houses, and establishments strongly contrasting with the old *outre* 'residenter' buildings, that New-England is gradually making its way. **1873** Twain–Warner *Gilded Age* 228, When I tell the old residenters that this thing went through without buying a note or making a promise, they say, 'That's rather too thin.' **1899** Garland *Boy Life* 88 **nwIA** (as of c1870s), You now understand that you are dealing with "an old residenter," not a young and foolish child. **1903** *DN* 2.327 **seMO,** Residenter. . . Citizen; resident. 'He is an old residenter.' **1906** *DN* 3.153 **nwAR,** Residenter. . . Resident. "Mrs. Winters lived here several years ago and is well remembered by our older residenters."—Fayetteville Daily. **1923** *DN* 5.218 **swMO,** Residenter. . . An old settler. **1928** *AmSp* 4.127 **ncNE,** A "residenter" or an "old-timer" [is] one who has lived in the hills many years. **1942** Hall *Smoky Mt. Speech* 66 **wNC, eTN,** [ˈrɛzɚˌdɛntɚ] for *residenter* 'old timer' . . occurs on a phonograph record. **1952** Brown *NC Folkl.* 1.584, *Residenter:* . . A resident. **c1960** Wilson *Coll.* **csKY,** Residenter. . . Resident, native; often *old residenter.* **1968** *DARE* FW Addit **cwNY,** Residenters—residents. **1969–70** *DARE* Tape **AR56,** That township . . is called Kentucky township and it was because . . the old residenters, about ninety percent of 'em come from the state of Kentucky; **NY**183, It wasn't the old-timers . . the residenters, the old ridge-runners. **1983** *Lutz Coll.* **NJ**, Most of our "old residenters" (an expression one of them used) have died.

2 also in comb *old residenter;* Fig: an old animal or thing, esp one that has acquired venerable or impressive qualities through age; an antique, relic. **esp PA**

1912 *DN* 3.585 **wIN**, *Old residenter.* . . Anything that reveals age or the toughness, strength, or wisdom of age. "It's no use to try to catch that fish; the old residenter isn't ready to have us cook him just yet." **1913** *DN* 4.46 **PA**, *Old residenter.* I have heard this in Philadelphia. [*DARE* Ed: This refers to preceding quot.] **1938** Stuart *Dark Hills* 250 **KY**, Some of them snakes was old residenters. They was so old they was scaly. **1971** Tak *Truck Talk* 130 **PA**, *Residenter:* any old tractor still used over the road. **1972** *NYT Article Letters* **PA**, The Pennsylvanian locution "old residenter" for an ancient object (not person, i.e., not "resident") such as a house, a wagon, anything of that sort. Doubtless it may also refer to a person but I have never heard it so used. **1982** *Barrick Coll.* **csPA**, *Residenter*—antique object. "That's an old residenter." Rarely used of people.

resin n Usu |ˈrɛzɪn|; infreq |ˈrɛsɪn, ˈrɛzɪm|; for addit varr see quot 1965–70 [*OED2* 1388 →] **chiefly Nth, N Midl** See Map Cf **rosin**

=**pitch** n¹. Note: The use of *resin* as a technical or commercial term is not illustrated here.

1828 Webster *Amer. Dict., Resin.* . . An inflammable substance, hard when cool, but viscid when heated, exsuding [sic] in a fluid state from certain kinds of trees, as pine, either spontaneously or by incision. **1842** Thompson *Hist. VT* 1.215, The wood is . . on account of the resin it contains much heavier than that of the white pine. **1884** *Harper's New Mth. Mag.* 69.514, I was . . shown into a little doorless cell upstairs, built of new lumber, out of which the resin was exuding in big drops and trickling streams. **1965–70** *DARE* (Qu. T7, *The sticky stuff that comes out of pine trees*) 58 Infs, **esp Nth, N Midl**, Resin [ˈrɛzn, ˈrɛzɪn, ˈrɛzɪn]; **GA**80, 84, **NY**217, **OH**38, **PA**192, **TX**75, [ˈrɛsɪn, ˈrɛsɪn, ˈrɛsən] **CO**22, [rɛzɪm]; **AR**5, **MS**63, Pine resin; **GA**84, Gum resin. **2002** *DARE* File—Internet, *Fabric Stain Guide*—Pine Resin (Sap from Christmas Tree, Wreaths, etc.)

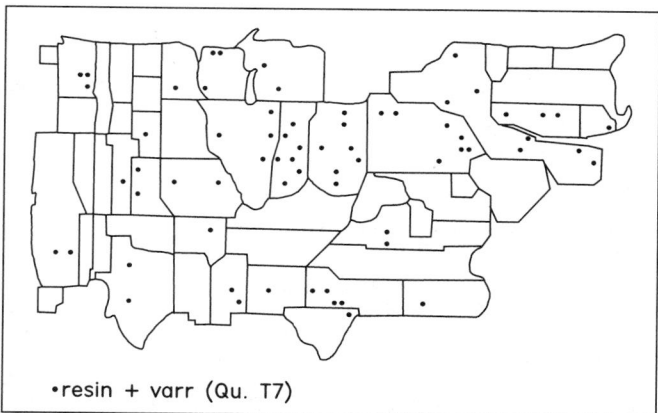

•resin + varr (Qu. T7)

resin birch n

A **dwarf birch** (here: *Betula nana*).

1931 U.S. Dept. Ag. *Misc. Pub.* 101.18, *Resin birch (B[etula] glandulosa [=B. nana]),* . . one of the commonest and most widely distributed western birches, ordinarily does not exceed 6 or 7 feet in height. **1959** Munz–Keck *CA Flora* 900, *Resin Birch.* . . Wet places, 6500–7500 ft. **1972** Viereck–Little *AK Trees* 130, *Resin Birch.* . . Twigs often finely hairy when young, densely resinous with warty glands, with a gray layer of wax.

resin bush n

A **goldeneye 4** (here: *Viguiera stenoloba*).

1970 Correll *Plants TX* 1647, *Viguiera stenoloba.* . . *Resin-bush.* Much-branched shrub about 1 m. high. . . Locally abundant in dry . . areas in the Trans-Pecos and Rio Grande Plains.

resin grass See **rosinweed 1**

resin plant See **rosin plant**

---

resinweed n

1 See **rosinweed 1**.

2 See **rosinweed 2**.

3 A **snakeweed** (here: *Gutierrezia* spp).

1968 Schmutz et al. *Livestock-Poisoning Plants AZ* 40, Resinweed . . (*Gutierrezia microcephala*) . . (*G. sarothrae*). . . Low, perennial half-shrubs growing 1 to 2 feet tall. They are many-branched and quite resinous. **1987** Bowers *100 Roadside Wildflowers* 45 **SW**, Snakeweed is also known as . . resinweed. . . *Gutierrezia sarothrae.*

resk(y) See **risk**

resolute v [Malaprop]

1917 *DN* 4.416 **wNC**, *Resolute.* . . To persevere. "To keep the hogs from resolutin' around."

ress See **rest** v¹ **A1**

resses See **rest** v¹ **A2**

rest v¹

A Forms.

1 pres (exc 3rd pers sg): usu *rest;* also *ress, restes.* **esp Sth, S Midl**

1928 *AmSp* 3.407 **Ozarks**, I allus stops an' restes of a ev'nin'. **1941** O'Donnell *Great Big Doorstep* 46 **sLA**, 'Leave him alone,' Mrs. Crochet complained. 'Leave him ress, darlin.' **1974** Fink *Mountain Speech* 22 **wNC, eTN**, Wait while they restes. **1986** Pederson *LAGS Concordance* 1 inf, **seAL**, His teeth restes on the jowl bone.

2 pres 3rd pers sg: usu *rests;* also *restes, resses.* **esp Sth, S Midl** Cf **-es suff¹ 3a, b**

1947 Ballowe *The Lawd* 81 **LA**, Gwineter sen' Duppy to 'n'int the soles whilest she resses. **c1960** *Wilson Coll.* **csKY**, Rests /ˈrɛstɪz/ fairly common. **1973** Gt. Smoky Mt. Natl. Park *Recordings* 79:1:18 (*Montgomery Coll.*), Some of his relatives have put a little stone up there . . where we know our great grandfather restes on the hillside overlookin' his Sugarlands. **1976** Garber *Mountain-ese* 74 **sAppalachians**, Clem is so short winded he restes ever few steps he takes. **1986** Pederson *LAGS Concordance,* 1 inf, **seMS**, Your shoe restes on the wall; 1 inf, **seLA**, Your leg restes on a strap above stirrup.

B Senses.

1 in phr *rest one's saddle:* To dismount; also fig—used in inviting one who is passing by to stop and visit. Cf **alight and look at one's saddle, light** v² **1**

1966–68 *DARE* (Qu. II15, *When somebody is passing by and you want him or her to stop and talk a while*) Inf **NC**30, Light and rest your saddle; **VA**5, Get down and rest your saddle. **1968** *DARE* FW Addit **cVA**, "Come in and rest your saddle"—old-fashioned; "Come in and rest your hat"—present usage.

2 To take off or hang up (a hat or coat)—used in var polite formulas addressed to a visitor. **chiefly Sth, S Midl**

1895 *DN* 1.374 **seKY, eTN, wNC**, *Rest your hat:* take off your hat. "Won't you come in and rest your hat?" **1897** Lewis *Wolfville* 70 **AZ**, The old lady. . . asks me to rest my hat the second I'm in the door. **1912** Cobb *Back Home* 229 **KY**, Judge Priest . . made him rest his hat and overcoat—"rest" was the word the judge used—and sit down. **1942** Perry *Texas* 134, Our cook invites callers whom she meets at the door to "rest their hats and coats". **1943** *AmSp* 18.237 **neLA** [Black], Won't you rest your coat? **1967** *DARE* (Qu. II15, *When somebody is passing by and you want him or her to stop and talk a while*) Inf **MA**5, Rest your hat—not local. **1967** *DARE* FW Addit **DE**, "May I rest your coat?"—may I take your coat? **1968** *DARE* [**B1** above]. **1973** *Patrick Coll.* **cAL**, *Rest*—put aside, hang up. Let me rest your hat (or coat), sir. **1986** Pederson *LAGS Concordance* 1 inf, **ceTX**, Rest your wrap—"take off your coat"—mother says.

rest n, v² See **risk**

restes See **rest** v¹ **A1, 2**

resting adj Cf **going to bed**

In abundance, galore.

1970 *DARE* (Qu. LL9b, . . *All you need or more* . . *"She's got clothes _____"*) Inf **SC**69, Resting, going to bed.

resting powder n Cf **easing powder, rest powder**

1917 *DN* 4.416 **wNC**, *Restin' powder.* See *easin' powder.* [*Ibid* 411, *Easin'-powder.* . . An opiate.]

resting room See **rest room**

rest one's saddle See **rest** v[1] **B1**

rest part n

The rest, remainder.

1903 DN 2.300 **Cape Cod MA** (as of a1857), *Rest-part.* . . Remainder. 'The rest-part of the day.' **1974** AmSp 49.63 **ME** (as of c1900), He took the rest-part of the money.

rest powder n Cf **resting powder**

Snuff.

1927 AmSp 3.25 **eTX** [Sawmill talk], The saw mill commissary (general store) is called the "Robbersary." Among other things it sells bacon—"sow bosom" and snuff—"rest powder" or "heiffer dust." **1969** Sorden Lumberjack Lingo 96 **NEng, Gt Lakes,** *Rest Powder*—Snuff.

rest room n Also rarely *resting room* **scattered exc NEast, but esp freq S Midl** See Map

An indoor toilet in a house; an outhouse.

1950 WELS (Names . . for an indoor toilet) 10 Infs, **WI,** Rest room. **1965–70** DARE (Qu. F37, . . An indoor toilet) 66 Infs, **scattered exc NEast, but more freq S Midl,** Rest room; **VA9,** Restin' room [Of all Infs responding to the question, 28% were comm type 5, 29% gs educ or less, 29% male; of those giving these responses, 54% were comm type 5, 58% gs educ or less, 43% male.]; (Qu. M21a, *An outside toilet building*) Inf **OK49,** Rest room; (Qu. M21b, *Joking names for an outside toilet building*) Infs **LA8, MS74, SC7, VT10,** Rest room; (Qu. V2b, . . *"I wouldn't trust him _____."*; not asked in early QRs) Inf **VA9,** Till I come back from the restin' room. **1986** Pederson LAGS Concordance **Gulf Region,** 1 inf, Rest room—lavatory, no bathing facilities; 2 infs, Rest room (=bathroom); (Outhouse) 10 infs, Rest room; 3 infs, Outdoor rest room; 2 infs, Rest room—(more) recent; 1 inf, Rest room—modern term; 1 inf, Outside rest room; 1 inf, Inside it's either a rest room or a bathroom; [1 inf, Rest house—laughing;] (Room with a toilet and sink, no bath or shower; this question was asked chiefly in urban areas) 11 infs, Rest room.

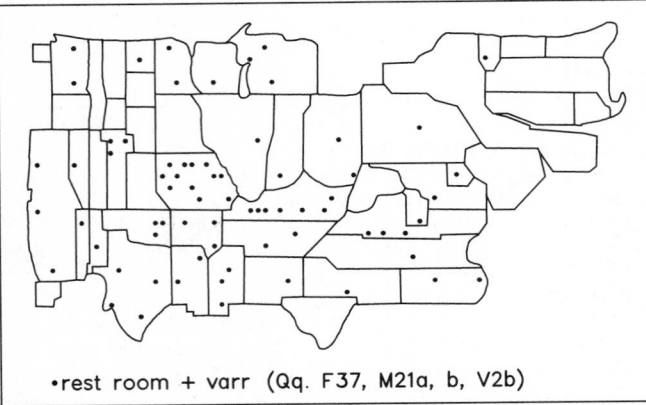

•rest room + varr (Qq. F37, M21a, b, V2b)

rest-time bird n

A **wood thrush** (here: *Hylocichla mustelina*).

1951 AmSp 26.278 **GA,** Two lovely names are given to the wood thrush in Georgia from the times it is chiefly heard to sing, that is, *rest-time bird* (when men are resting from farm work) and *sundown bird*.

restus (plow) See **rastus** n[2]

resty adj [Cf OED2 resty a.[1] 2.a "Disinclined for action or exertion. . . Obs." EDD resty a. "Quiet, full of ease."]

Lazy; inclined to rest; at ease.

1931 Randolph Ozarks 76, The hillman's adjective *resty*, meaning indolent, is another Shakespearian survival. **1933** Williamson Woods Colt 112 **Ozarks,** The old feller likes to take things easy, at the same time he ain't so resty but what he can reach out for a jug o' corn. **1942** (1971) Campbell Cloud-Walking 28 **seKY,** They put him down as being too resty to do no work. *Ibid* 87, He felt more resty going barefooted. *Ibid* 129, I feel too resty with tending that woman down on Piney Creek all day and her bad off.

resurrection fern n Also *resurrection plant* [See quot 1911]

A **polypody** (here: *Pleopeltis polypodioides*).

1875 Amer. Naturalist 9.111, *Polypodium incanium*, the commonest of all the ferns of Florida, is often called the resurrection fern. **1897** Jrl. Amer. Folkl. 10.147 **FL,** *Polypodium* (a Florida species), resurrection fern. . . From its habit of unrolling upon being wet with rain. **1911** Waters Ferns 84, The gray polypody. . . has the habit of curling up when very dry, but it soon revives when moistened. It is one of the many "resurrection plants." **1938** Small Ferns SE States 78, The resurrection fern has the distinction of being the most abundant and common of all the small ferns of the hammocks of our range. **1975** Natl. Audubon Soc. Corkscrew 15 **swFL,** Resurrection Fern. . . During periods of dry weather the leaves are curled, brown, and quite dead looking but after a rain they are as fresh and beautifully green as ever. This accounts for the popular name. **1990** Simpson Gt. Dismal 40 **nNC, sVA,** Stopping there again on a balmy late April day, I saw poison ivy on the gum stump where resurrection fern had been growing before.

resurrection flower n

1 See **resurrection plant 3.**

2 An amaryllis (here: *Amaryllis belladonna*).

1968 DARE (Qu. S26e, *Other wildflowers not yet mentioned;* not asked in early QRs) Inf **CA105,** Amaryllis or naked lady or resurrection flower.

resurrection plant n

1 A spikemoss, usu *Selaginella lepidophylla*. [See quot 1868]

1868 (1870) Gray Field Botany 374, S[elaginella] lepidophylla . . is the "Bird's-Nest Moss," or "Resurrection-Plant." It is a nest-like ball when dry, but when moist it unfolds and displays the . . elegant fern-like branches radiating from a coiled-up central stem. **1893** G.D. Leslie Lett. Marco xviii 119 (DA), 'A resurrection plant' . . some sort of large lichen or spleenwort from Colorado. **1970** Correll Plants TX 39, *Selaginella lepidophylla.* . . Resurrection plant. . . Plant hygroscopic, forming a distinct rosette of bright-green cespitose branches when moist, the branches inrolled to form a tight nestlike ball when excessively dry. . . *Selaginella pilifera.* . . Resurrection plant. Similar in habit and characteristics to *S. lepidophylla* but usually smaller in size.

2 See **resurrection fern.**

3 also *resurrection flower*: A **bitterroot 2** (here: *Lewisia rediviva*).

1947 Nature Mag. 40.444 **MT,** Other common names [for *Lewisia rediviva*] are rock rose, . . resurrection plant [etc]. **1961** Peck Manual OR 304, L[ewisia] rediviva. . . Resurrection flower; Bitter Root. . . Leaves . . withering before flowering time. . . Sterile stony ground, widely distributed east of the Cascades.

res'vore See **reservoir**

ret See **right**

retama n [MexSpan < Span *retama* plant of the genus *Genista*] **TX**

A **paloverde 1,** usu **Jerusalem thorn.**

1891 Coulter Botany W. TX 94, P[arkinsonia] aculeata. . . Throughout southern and western Texas. Often cultivated for ornament and known as "retama." **1892** DN 1.194 **wTX,** *Retáma:* broom sedge. In Western Texas a plant of the family of *leguminosæ (Parkinsonia aculeata).* **1903** 'O. Henry' in Ainslee's Dec. 139/2 (OED2), One December in the Frio country there was a retama tree in full bloom. **1929** Dobie Vaquero 202 **TX,** Here are vast *cejas*—another term of the vaqueros for "thicket," . . —of the wand-like *retama*, green also of bark and leaf, its adder-toothed thorns disguised all summer long under yellow flowers. **1949** Chi. Tribune 20 Feb. 30/3 (DA), Cedar and mesquite alone are costing Texas ranchers 115 million dollars a year. Add the sage and cactus, . . blackjack oak, retama and prickly pear and the toll is terrific. **1975** Lamb Woody Plants SW 72, Parkinsonia aculeata—"Retama"—"Palo verde". **1981** Pederson LAGS Basic Materials, 1 inf, **csTX,** [ri'ta^mə, rɛ'ta^məˣ] has red bark, small leaves, yellow flower; 1 inf, **csTX,** [rɪ'ta^·mə] has a "real fine leaf, clusters of yellow blossoms, real lacy looking. Wherever you see a lot o' retama trees the soil is no good. They either destroy the soil or they grow in bad soil."; 1 inf, **csTX,** [rɪ'ta^·mə]; 1 inf, **csTX,** [lɪ'ta·mə] (Mex[ican] word—No Eng. equiv[alent]); 1 inf, **csTX,** [rɪi'tamə] (with yellow flowers).

retch v See **reach** v[1] **A1, 2a, 3a**

retch n See **reach** n

retched See **reach** v[1] **A2b, 3b**

rether See **rather** adv

ret up See **redd 3a, b**

return thanks v phr Also aphet *'turn thanks* Also in phrr *'turn thanks over* (or *to*) *the table* chiefly **Sth, S Midl**
To say grace before a meal.
  1953 *PADS* 19.14 **wNC,** *'Turn thanks over the table:* . . To say grace. "Miss Smith, will you 'turn thanks over the table?" Rock Creek, Mitchell Co., N.C. **1965** *DARE* FW Addit **OK**1, 2, *Return thanks*—used for "say grace" at a meal. **1982** Mason *Shiloh* 101 **wKY,** As the family sat down, Carolyn realized no one ever asked Pappy to "turn thanks" anymore at holiday dinners. **1984** Wilder *You All Spoken Here* 81 **Sth,** Talk to the table, 'turn thanks to the table. **1986** Pederson *LAGS Concordance* **Gulf Region,** 5 infs, [Re]turn thanks; 3 infs, [Re]turn thanks = (you) say grace; 3 infs, [Re]turn thanks = (same as) ask the blessing; 1 inf, Let's be seated and return thanks; 1 inf, [Does] someone want [to] [re]turn thanks? 1 inf, [Re]turned thanks = said the blessing.

reub See **rube**

Reuben n *old-fash*
  =**rube.**
  [**1804** *The Nightingale* 284 *(DA),* But she, tho' conscious of his worth, Had chose a youth more rare; A rustic Reuben was his name.] **1890** Hall *Turnover Club* 49 **Chicago IL,** And I overheard one of a knot of Reubens standing on a corner. **1909** *DN* 3.415 **nME,** *Reuben.* . . An unsophisticated countryman. **1911** Quick *Yellowstone Nights* 313 **KS,** I took a basket of eggs an' went in among 'em, feelin' like a animal trainer in a circus parade as the Reubens gethered around the train. **1941** *LANE* Map 450 *(A rustic)* **NEng,** 3 infs, Reuben. **1968** *DARE* (Qu. HH1, *Names and nicknames for a rustic or countrified person*) Inf **PA**118, Reuben. **1973** Allen *LAUM* 1.350, *A rustic.* . . reuben [1 inf, **MN**].

revel See **rivel**

revengeance n [*OED2* →1565, but here prob reformed as blend of *revenge* + *vengeance*]
  Revenge.
  1883 (1971) Harris *Nights with Remus* 395 **GA** [Black], He . . do lak he gwine take he revengeance out'n po' ole Brer Tarrypin. **1945** FWP *Lay My Burden Down* 23 **Sth** (as of c1865) [Black], That what the nigger want him to do, and he feel satisfy that the monkey done dead and he have he revengeance.

revengement See **-ment B**

revenoo See **revenue**

revenoo(e)r See **revenuer**

revenue n Pronc-spp *revenoo, revynoo* chiefly **S Midl**
  =**revenuer.**
  a used as a count noun.
  1880 *Daily Inter–Ocean* (IL) 1 June 12/2 **eTN,** Berong's daughter, an intrepid mountain maid of 18 summers, came in and quietly inquired, "Is there revynoos up on the mountain?" **1883** Zeigler–Grosscup *Heart of Alleghanies* 357 **NC, SC,** My pards mout tak' ye fer a revenoo, an' let a hole thro' ye. **1887** (1967) Harris *Free Joe* 125 **cGA,** I tell you, Babe, that ar man is one er the revenues. **1907** Wright *Shepherd* 69 **Ozarks,** Can't tell 'bout revenues. . . Don't you mind how that'n fooled everybody over on th' bend last year? **1913** Kephart *Highlanders* 171 **sAppalachians,** He knows there'd be another revenue 'murdered.' **1931** Goodrich *Mt. Homespun* 45 **sAppalachians,** When he's in jail he can't be killed or crippled in a fight with them revenues.
  b used as a collective or unmarked pl.
  1913 Kephart *Highlanders* 170 **sAppalachians,** You wunt find ary critter as has a good word to say for the revenue. The reason is 't we know them men from 'way back. **c1920** in 1993 Farwell–Nicholas *Smoky Mt. Voices* 134 **sAppalachians,** Up stepped two revenoo right to the door. **1937** *Hall Coll.* **eTN,** The state officers were stricter than the revenue. **1949** *AmSp* 24.9 [Argot of the moonshiner], *Feds.* . . Officers of the Alcohol Tax Unit. . . Also revenoo. **1978** in 1996 Montgomery *Coll.* **eTN,** The revenue has got so smart on that with technical things that they can't operate but a week or two.

revenuer n Pronc-spp *revenoo(e)r, revynor* chiefly **S Midl**
  An officer engaged in enforcing the laws against illegal distilling.
  1880 *Daily Inter–Ocean* (IL) 1 June 12/1 **eTN,** His wife and daughter discharged their conjugal and filial duties by . . watching from their home for the approach of the "Revynors". **1913** Kephart *Highlanders* 123 **sAppalachians,** When a revenner [sic] come sneakin' around, why, whut he gits, or whut we-uns gits, that's a 'fortune of war,' as the old sayin' is. **1933** Rawlings *South Moon* 45 **FL,** I were makin' moonshine whiskey. The revenooers come messin up with me. **1934** Carmer *Stars Fell on AL* 37, Damned if I didn't take yuh fer a couple o' revenuers. **1939** *Hall Coll.* **eTN,** "Shoot him, pappy, he's got shoes on; he's a revenuer." A saying heard at Tellico Plains, Tenn. **1942** Thomas *Blue Ridge Country* 256, The process of capturing the moonshiner has changed considerably from that of other days. Then the revenooer (mountain folk usually call him the law) slipped up from behind the bushes on the offender. **c1960** *Wilson Coll.* **csKY,** *Revenuer* . . usually for fun now. **1968** *Foxfire* 2.342 **nGA,** We moved her [=the still] out *that night*. It was a revenuer all right. **1976** Garber *Mountain-ese* 75 **sAppalachians,** *Revenoor* . . A[lcoholic] B[everage] C[ontrol] officer— The revenoor tore up Jed's still afore he could run off a batch.

reverence v [Weakened from std sense "to show reverence for"]
  1927 *DN* 5.476 **Ozarks,** *Reverence.* . . To tolerate. "Ef a feller done me like Lem done her, I shore would'nt reverence him fer a minute."

reverend adj, n, v Pronc-spp *reb'm, reb'ren', rever(e)nt, reverin, revrunt, revyun, riverind*
  A Forms. Note: For addit exx of *reverent* see **B1, 2** below.
  1837 Sherwood [see **B2** below]. **1894** [see **B2** below]. **1922** Gonzales *Black Border* 322 **sSC,** GA coasts [Gullah glossary], *Reb'ren'*—reverend—used also as a noun, as "de reb'ren'." **1927** Kennedy *Gritny* 217 **sLA** [Black], She didn't want any priest or revyun of any kind to come up in her house. **1941** *LANE* Map 439 *(The Reverend Mr. Simpson),* [In this context the commonest type of pronc is that ending [-(ə)nd], but nearly as common are the types [-(ə)n] and [-(ə)nt]; there are a few examples of [-(ə)nᵊ].] **c1960** *Wilson Coll.* **csKY,** *Reverend* /rɛvɚənt/ common. **1969** Gordone *No Place* 20 **NYC** [Black], Then somebody pro-nounced that reb'm some-Body would pray! **1982** *Barrick Coll.* **csPA,** *Reverend*—pron. révernt. Always used without *the*, unless used alone. "Reverend Jones won't be here today. The reverend is sick." **1982** [see **C** below]. **1997** Hassler *Dean's List* 388 **nMN,** The rev-runt's dead, I s'pose you heard. **1998** Kingsolver *Poisonwood Bible* 21 **GA,** Reverent and Misrus Underdown, who started the African children on going to church way back years ago.

  B As adj.
  1 Extraordinary, powerful.
  1826 Flint *Recollections* 15 **wPA,** A firm push of the iron-pointed pole on a fixed log, is termed a "reverend" set. **1888** *Overland Mth.* (2d ser) 12.508 **sAppalachians,** These hyur young uns haint, nary one of 'em, got ary bit o' sense. The las' one on 'em is stark rever'nt fools, they is. **1891** *PMLA* 6.167 **WV,** *Reverent* is used in the sense of *genuine, thorough;* as, a *reverent scolding,* that is a *thorough scolding.* **1903** *DN* 2.327 **seMO,** *Reverent* (reverend?). . . Extraordinary; distinguished. (Generally, perhaps always, used in a bad sense and preceded by right.) 'My opinion is that he is a right reverent scoundrel.' [*DARE* Ed: Cf **right B**] **1907** *DN* 3.235 **nwAR,** *Reverent.* . . Extraordinary; distinguished. Generally, however, used in a bad sense and preceded by right. "He's a right reverent scoundrel.["] **1982** McCool *Sam McCool's Pittsburghese* 29 **PA,** Reverend: great, extreme, as in "You can tell he hasn't bathed for days by the reverend odor."

  2 Usu of drink: pure, unadulterated; also fig. chiefly **Sth, S Midl**
  1837 Sherwood *Gaz.* GA 71, *Provincialisms.* . . *Reverent,* for strong; *reverent whisky,* . . i.e. not diluted. **1837** Wetmore *Gaz.* MO 336, "Muster courage to take . . a table-spoonful, three times a day."—"Jist reverend, without water, doctor?" **1853** (1854) Baldwin *Flush Times* 306 **AL,** It aint as pleasant as sitting on a log by a camp fire, with a tickler of the reverend stuff. **1864** *Harper's New Mth. Mag.* 28.569, He would put water in his liquor, instead of taking it "reverent." **1887** Amer. Philol. Assoc. *Trans. for 1886* 17.46 **Sth,** List of common Southern expressions—many of them vulgarisms—that have not, so far as I know, either old English or provincial English authority. . . *Reverent* (undiluted, of liquor). **1894** in 1941 Warfel–Orians *Local-Color Stories* 738 **sAR,** Den agin, look lak dat ain't riverind jestice nuther, bein' as I ain't nothin' but he's step-mammy, an' ain't in no way 'spornserble fo' dem twins. **1899** (1912) Green *VA Folk-Speech* 351, *Reverent.* . . Strong; unadulterated liquors. "He took a drink of reverent whiskey." **1936** *AmSp* 11.317 **Ozarks,** *Reverend.* . . Pure, full strength, undiluted. 'Do you want this

here castor oil reverend, or shall I mix some sody-pop in it?' *Ibid* 373 **VA**, A man, when asked if he would have sugar or cream in his coffee, replied, 'No, thank you, I'll take it reverent so.' He meant that he wanted it straight, pure, unadulterated. **1954** *PADS* 21.35 **SC**, *Reverend*: . . Pure, in full strength. To take it without cream and sugar; applied also to whiskey, neat. **1969** *DARE* (Qu. KK61, *Food taken alone, with nothing added: "Would you like milk or lemon in your tea?" "No thanks, I'll take it _____."*) Inf **NC61**, Reverent. **1986** Pederson *LAGS Concordance*, 1 inf, **seAL**, Reverent—"just plain coffee"—nothing in it.

C As verb.

To revere.

1982 Slone *How We Talked* 76 **eKY** (as of c1950), *Burin' ground*— Cemetery, or graveyard. Each family had their own "plot." They "reverined" their dead to almost a worship.

revlet n

1978 *DARE* File **cTX**, Do you have 'revlets' (['rɛvləts]) in *DARE?* I heard it for the first time the other day and have confirmed it twice since. It is Afro-American, child's speech, and refers to the particles of food from one's mouth which find their way into a bottle of soda when one gives another a swig. . . If someone asks for a drink from your soda bottle and that person is eating something at the same time, he's told 'don't get no revlets in my soda!' White friends remember having a word for the same thing, but it wasn't the same word.

Revolution n Also *Revolution(ary) War, War of the Revolution*
Sth, S Midl Cf **Rebellion**

The American Civil War.

1966 Dakin *Dial. Vocab. Ohio R. Valley* 2.516, Some older speakers in the Mountains [of KY]—and a few scattered elsewhere—also seem to say *The War of the Revolution* or (more common) *The Revolution War.* **1967** Fetterman *Stinking Creek* 37 **seKY**, He fought in the old Revolution War and didn't die 'til after I was married. **1983** *MJLF* 9.1.53 **ceKY** (as of 1956), *Revolution War* . . the War Between the States. **1986** Pederson *LAGS Concordance* **Gulf Region** *(Civil War)* 12 infs, (The) revolution; 1 inf, Revolution—[inf] guessing; not familiar with history; 1 inf, Revolution—vague reference; 1 inf, Revolution—name of war; 1 inf, Civil War was revolution; 4 infs, Revolutionary (War); 1 inf, Revolutionary War—not clearly for Civil War; 1 inf, Second Revolutionary War; 1 inf, War of the Revolution.

revrunt See reverend

revynoo See revenue

revynor See revenuer

revyun See reverend

reward v

To offer a reward, or to offer (a certain sum) as a reward, for the arrest of.

1915 Hall *Claib Jones* 26 **KY**, I was rewarded seven hundred dollars and one day at Salt Lick some of the Coburns tried to arrest me. **1924** Raine *Land of Saddle-Bags* 103 **sAppalachians**, "He *rewarded* Bill." This means no gift to Bill, but a reward offered for his apprehension.

rewm See room

rhea See ree adj

rheum n [*OED2 rheum* sb.¹ 2 "Occasionally used = Rheumatic pains"; see esp quots 1667, 1755]

Also pl: Rheumatism; an attack of rheumatism.

1966 *DARE* (Qu. BB8, *When a person's joints and muscles ache and sometimes swell up, especially in damp weather, he may have _____*) Inf **SC4**, The rheums—before his time; **SC10**, We been used to call it a rheum.

rheumatic n Usu |ru'mætɪk, 'rumə₍ₒ₎tɪk|; for varr see quots
Also sp *rheumatick, roomaticks, rumaticks* [*OED2* 1789 →]
old-fash Cf **rheumatiz**

Usu pl; often with *the*; Rheumatism; a rheumatic attack or pain.

1835 in 1838 *S. Lit. Messenger* 4.89 **NEng**, Take my rheumatics and you may have my berth and welcome. **1874** Taylor *Chip Basket* 67 **WI**, This year it [=winter] has come like an attack of the rheumatics. **1883** Zeigler–Grosscup *Heart of Alleghanies* 61 **wNC**, I'd . . hunt from

the day I was big nuff to tote a rifle-gun, ontil old age an' roomaticks fastened on me. **1887** (1892) Hinman *Corporal Si Klegg* 50, It'll help pervent ye ketchin' the rumaticks. **1905** *DN* 3.64 **eNE**, *Rheumaticks, rheumatiz*. . . Current variants for *rheumatism*. **1939** Coffin *Capt. Abby* 186 **ME** (as of 1860s), They said it was getting too cold for her to risk rheumatics. **1941** Stuart *Men of Mts.* 173 **eKY**, Don't you sprawl out there on that damp ground. . . It will give you the rheumatics. **1942** in 1944 *ADD* 509 **wAR**, |ru'mætɪks|. . . Radio. **1943** *LANE* Map 506 *(Rheumatism)*, Our informants treat *rheumatism* regularly as singular . . ; *rheumatics* more often as plural; and *rheumatic* always as singular. . . The forms *rheumatics* and *rheumatic* may be stressed in two different ways: (a) on the second syllable, with or without a secondary stress on the first; (b) on the first syllable, usually with a secondary stress on the third, or equally on the first and third syllables. The position of the main stress(es) is always reflected in the quality of the second vowel: thus [ru'mætɪks] but ['rumətɪks, 'rumə'tɪks], and the like. . . 1 inf, **seNH**, [rʊᵂmətɪz, -tæks, rʌmə- [reported as heard used by others]]. **1953** Stuart *Beatinest Boy* 75 **KY**, Now I've got rheumatics again and my finger joints are swollen. **1960** Criswell [see **rheumatiz**]. **1965–70** *DARE* (Qu. BB8, *When a person's joints and muscles ache and sometimes swell up, especially in damp weather, he may have _____*) 12 Infs, **scattered**, Rheumatics; **GA33, IL46A, NC31**, The rheumatics; **OH15, VT12**, Rheumatics—old-fashioned; **NV2**, The rheumatics—old-timers say; **AZ2**, Rheumatics—humorous use; **HI1**, Rheumatics—may have read this; **LA14**, Rheumatics—the folk may say this; **MI96**, ['rumətɪks]—in the South; **TN3**, Rheumatics—joking term; **TX33**, Rheumatics—long time ago; **MO15, OK13**, Rheumatic; **NC4**, [ru'mætɪk]; **OH95**, The ['rumə,tik]—old-fashioned; **PA130**, The [,ru'mætək]; **PA8**, [ru'mæts] [14 of 30 total Infs comm type 5, 25 old, 16 coll educ]; (Qu. BB4, *. . A pain . . "He's had a _____ in his arm for a week."*) Inf **MO15**, A rheumatic; (Qu. BB49, *. . Other kinds of diseases*) Inf **OR3**, Rheumatics. **1973** [see **rheumatiz**]. **1986** Pederson *LAGS Concordance*, 1 inf, **csTN**, Rheumatics—probably recalling folk term; 1 inf, **swAL**, Rheumatics—old folks say; 1 inf, **nwTN**, Rheumatics—old term for "arthritis"; 1 inf, **nwAR**, Rheumatics—some say; 1 inf, **cwAR**, Rheumatics—most would say; 2 infs, **cwMS, ceTX**, Rheumatic.

rheumatic plant n

A **jimmyweed** (here: *Isocoma veneta* [formerly *Haplopappus v.*]).

1896 *Jrl. Amer. Folkl.* 9.191 **CA**, *Bigelovia venata* [=*Isocoma v.*], . . rheumatic plant. . . Medicinal cure for rheumatism.

rheumatics See rheumatic

rheumatic weed n

An aster (here: *Aster puniceus*); see quots.

1854 King *Amer. Eclectic Dispensatory* 265, The Aster Aestivus [= *Aster puniceus*], named *Rheumatic-weed*, also *Sampson Snakeroot, Starflower,* etc. **1876** Hobbs *Bot. Hdbk.* 97, Rheumatic weed, Sampson's snake root, Aster aestivus.

rheumati(e)s See rheumatiz

rheumatism n Cf rheumatic

Std sense, var syntax.

Used in pl or as pl.

1906 *DN* 3.153 **nwAR**, *Rheumatisms*. . . Rheumatism. **1943** [see **rheumatiz**].

rheumatismed adj

Afflicted with rheumatism.

c1938 in 1970 Hyatt *Hoodoo* 2.1500, Try tuh git holt of a person right-hand glove dat's rheumatismed.

rheumatism root n Cf rheumatism weed

Any of var plants supposed to alleviate symptoms of rheumatism, as:

a =**twinleaf.**

1843 Torrey *Flora NY* 1.34, *Jeffersonia diphylla*. . . *Rheumatism-root*. . . The root. . . is sometimes employed as a remedy in chronic rheumatism. **1847** Wood *Class-Book* 152 **OH**, *J[effersonia] diphylla*. . . A singular plant. . . This plant has in Ohio the reputation of a stimulant and antispasmodic, and is there significantly termed *rheumatism root.* **1897** Creevey *Flowers* 308 **wNY**, Twin-leaf. Rheumatism-root. . . A plant of low growth, not uncommon in the woods of western New York, southward and westward. **1916** Keeler *Early Wildflowers* 89, *Jeffersonia* *diphylla*. . . From its supposed medicinal qualities it is sometimes called Rheumatism-root. **1936** IL Nat. Hist. Surv. *Wildflowers* 116, In rich woods of the central and northern parts of the state, as well as throughout the Great Lakes region and south to Tennessee, grows. . . the Twinleaf or Rheumatism Root. **1971** Krochmal *Appalachia Med. Plants* 146, Rheumatism root. . . The rhizomes and roots have been used to treat chronic rheumatism, dropsy, spasms, and as a gargle.

b A **wild yam** (here: *Dioscorea villosa*).

1887 Bentley *Manual Botany* 706, The rhizome of *D[ioscorea] villosa*, the Wild Yam of the United States, is regarded as a valuable remedy in Virginia in rheumatism, and is hence commonly known as 'rheumatism root.' **1892** (1974) Millspaugh *Amer. Med. Plants* 174-1, *Dioscorea villosa*. . . Rheumatism root. . . Rheumatism Root generally alludes to *Jeffersonia diphylla*. **1930** Sievers *Amer. Med. Plants* 63, *Dioscorea villosa*. . . Rheumatism root. . . is most common in the central and southern portions of the United States. **1974** (1977) Coon *Useful Plants* 128, Rheumatism-root. . . The part used is the smallish root, dried, powdered, and made into a decoction.

c =**spotted wintergreen.**

1900 Lyons *Plant Names* 96, *C[himaphila] maculata*. . . Rheumatism-root. **1979** Erichsen-Brown *Med. N. Amer. Plants* 314, *Chimaphila maculata*. . . Very like pipsissewa except that the leaves are striped white along the midvein and have pointed ends. . . Rheumatism root.

d Either **spreading dogbane** or **Indian hemp 1.**

1936 IL Nat. Hist. Surv. *Wildflowers* 241, *Indian Hemp. Rheumatism Root. Apocynum cannabinum*. . . The root is used to some extent in medicine and consequently accounts for the name Rheumatism Root. **1959** Carleton *Index Herb. Plants* 99, *Rheumatism-root:* Apocynum androsaemifolium; Chelone glabra; Jeffersonia diphylla.

e =**turtlehead** (here: *Chelone glabra*).

1940 Clute *Amer. Plant Names* 29, *C[helone] glabra*. . . Rheumatism-root. **1959** [see **d** above].

f A **colicroot 2** (here: *Aletris farinosa*).

1971 Krochmal *Appalachia Med. Plants* 40, *Aletris farinosa*. . . Rheumatism root. . . The plant . . has been used . . in treating rheumatism, often called ague in Colonial times.

rheumatism weed n Cf **rheumatism root**

Any of several plants supposed to alleviate symptoms of rheumatism, as:

a A **pipsissewa:** usu *Chimaphila umbellata*, but also **spotted wintergreen.**

1784 in 1785 Amer. Acad. Arts & Sci. *Memoirs* 1.444 **NH**, Rheumatism-Weed. Blossoms pale red. In wood land. It abounds near *White-Mountains*. It is said to have been considered by the Indians as an effectual remedy in rheumatisms. **1814** Bigelow *Florula Bostoniensis* 106, *Pyrola umbellata* [=*Chimaphila u.*] . . Unbelled Winter Green. . . [is] known by the names of *Rheumatism weed, Phipsewa* or *Wipsewog, &c.* **1830** Rafinesque *Med. Flora* 2.70, *Pyrola maculata* [=*Chimaphila m.*] . . Wintergreen, . . Rheumatism Weed, &c. [*Ibid* 71, The whole plants. . . have been used in dropsy, nephritis, . . rheumatism, and low fevers.] **1831** Child *Frugal Housewife* 28, Winter evergreen is considered good for all humors, particularly scrofula. Some call it rheumatism-weed. **1911** Henkel *Amer. Med. Leaves* 16, *Chimaphila umbellata*. . . Rheumatism weed. . . Sometimes employed in rheumatic and kidney affections. **1924** *Amer. Botanist* 30.55, *Chimaphila umbellata*. . . really has medicinal qualities as its name [sic] "rheumatism-weed" and "king's cure" attest. **1974** (1977) Coon *Useful Plants* 217, *Chimaphila umbellata* . . rheumatism weed. . . Some Indians used it steeped, for blisters, while others used the dried leaves as an astringent and tonic, or for rheumatism.

b Either **spreading dogbane** or **Indian hemp 1.**

1894 *Jrl. Amer. Folkl.* 7.94 **WV**, *Apocynum androsaemifolium*, . . rheumatism-weed. **1900** Lyons *Plant Names* 40, *A[pocynum] androsaemifolium*. . . Rheumatism-weed. . . *A. cannabinum*. . . Rheumatism-weed. **1930** Sievers *Amer. Med. Plants* 34, *Apocynum cannabinum*. . . Rheumatism weed. . . The plant contains a milky juice. **1974** Morton *Folk Remedies* 27 **SC**, Rheumatism weed. . . *Apocynum cannabinum*. . . The bitter and astringent root is still collected for pharmaceutical use.

rheumatiz n Usu |'ruməˌtɪz|; for varr see quots Pronc-spp *rheumati(e)s, roomatiz, rum'a'tis, rumatiz;* sometimes interpreted as pl, hence sg *rheumaty, rheumety* [*OED2* 1760 →] *old-fash*

Also with *the:* Rheumatism; a rheumatic attack or pain.

1844 *New Englander & Yale Rev.* 2.431, The old woman who went every year to be confirmed, because she found it so good for the "*rheumatiz*," had a view of the subject not a whit more unwarranted or superstitious. **1857** *Putnam's Mag.* 10.350 **NEng,** Brother Eldridge had a "rheumatiz." **1873** Harte *Mrs. Skaggs* 69 **ceCA,** I've got a fevier. And childblains. And roomatiz. **1891** (1967) Freeman *New Engl. Nun* 221, He'd been laid up with the rheumatiz all winter. **1893** Shands *MS Speech* 54, Rumatiz ['rʊmətɪz]. Negro and illiterate white for *rheumatism.* I think that this word is largely used outside of Mississippi. **1899** [see **rheumaty-bud**]. **1902** *DN* 2.243 **sIL,** Rheumatiz. . . Used as a plural, as shown by pronoun and verb. **1903** *DN* 2.294 **Cape Cod MA** (as of a1857), He's keeled up with rheumatis. **1905** [see **rheumatic**]. **1907** *DN* 3.197 **seNH,** I've got rheumatiz the worst way. *Ibid* 225 **nwAR,** Rheumatiz. . . Used as a plural. **1909** *DN* 3.363 **eAL, wGA,** Rheumatiz. . . Rheumatism. **1933** Williamson *Woods Colt* 14 **Ozarks,** I jest thought of a better remedy for them rheumatiz of Ed's. **1937** Eaton *Handicrafts* 145 **TN,** Buckeye, good for 'rheumety.' **1938** Matschat *Suwannee R.* 85 **neFL, seGA,** " 'Pears as if fowkses got their rheumatis most cured." **1940** Stuart *Trees of Heaven* 256 **eKY,** Ground hogs' grease is good medicine fer rheumatiz. **1943** LANE Map 506 (*Rheumatism),* Our informants treat *rheumatism* regularly as singular, very rarely plural; *rheumatiz* as either singular or plural, with singular forms slightly predominating. . . The forms *rheumatism* and *rheumatiz* are regularly stressed on the first syllable, often with a secondary stress on the third syllable. **1956** *Harder Coll.* **cwTN,** [rumə'tɪs]: . . Rheumatism. **c1960** *Wilson Coll.* **csKY,** The rheumatiz. . . Rheumatism. **1960** Criswell *Resp. to PADS 20* **Ozarks,** Rheumatiz. . . For *rheumatiz;* heard now and then but not so common as dialect imitators would have us believe. Rheumatics heard now and then. **1965–70** *DARE* (Qu. BB8, *When a person's joints and muscles ache and sometimes swell up, especially in damp weather, he may have _____*) 48 Infs, **scattered,** Rheumatiz (proncs of the type ['rumə₍₎tɪz]) [9 Infs indicated that this is an older or old-fashioned term; 1 Inf that it is used jokingly]; **IL46, MS51, WI30,** The rheumatiz; **IL135,** The ['rjuməˌtɪz]; **KY70,** ['rumətɪs]; (Qu. BB4, *. . A pain . . "He's had a _____ in his arm for a week."*) Infs **AL33, MA58, WI30,** Rheumatiz; (Qu. BB49, *. . . Other kinds of diseases*) Inf **TX65,** Rheumatiz. **1973** Allen *LAUM* 1.367 **Upper MW** (as of c1950), Two old-fashioned forms [of *rheumatism*] have been carried from the east coast. *Rheumatiz* survives with 15 scattered infs., but only four of them—one in Minnesota and three in Iowa—still use it. All are older infs. Twelve, including some of the preceding, recall the variant *rheumatics,* but only one . . still has it as an active term. *Rheumatics* does not appear in Minnesota or North Dakota. **1975** Chalmers *Better* 33 **wNC, eTN,** The "shot o' rheumaty medicine" ordered by the city doctor was soon given. **1982** Slone *How We Talked* 103 **eKY** (as of c1950), Rum'a'tis—Rheumatism. **1986** Pederson *LAGS Concordance* 35 infs, **Gulf Region,** Rheumatis[m] [8 infs indicate that this used to be said or is used by other people].

rheumaty bud n Cf **rheumatic**

See quot.

1899 Bergen *Animal Lore* 99 **NH,** A gall from the stem of a goldenrod (caused by the sting of *Trypeta solidaginis* or *Galechia galli-solidaginis*) is called a "rheumaty-bud." Each contains a small white grub, and it is believed that as long as the grub remains alive, the one who carries the gall in his pocket will be free from rheumatism.

rheumety See **rheumatiz**

rhinoceros beetle n [*OED2* (at *rhinoceros* sb. 3) "a kind of beetle having a horn" 1681 →]

1 A scarab beetle of the genus *Dynastes,* esp *D. tityus.* Also called **horn beetle 2, unicorn ~**

1890 *Century Dict.* 5152, The common rhinoceros-beetle of the United States, *Dynastes tityus,* the largest of the North American beetles, has two large horns directed forward. **1949** Swain *Insect Guide* 145, Rhinoceros Beetle—*Dynastes tityus.* . . occurs from Arizona eastward throughout the southern United States. **1972** Swan–Papp *Insects* 437, Rhinoceros Beetle: *Dynastes tityus.* . . 1.5–2".

2 A related beetle (*Xyloryctes jamaicensis*).

1954 Borror–DeLong *Intro. Insects* 393, In the rhinoceros beetle, *Xyloryctes satyrus* [=*X. jamaicensis*] . . , the males have a single large upright horn on the head. . . The rhinoceros beetle is an Eastern species, occurring from Connecticut to Texas.

Rhode Island bent n Also *Rhode Island bentgrass*

A **bentgrass 1:** usu *Agrostis capillaris,* but also *A. canina.*

1790 Deane *New Engl. Farmer* 188, The Rhode-Island bent, as it is called, or red-top grass, will do with less drying than some other grasses. **1795** Winterbotham *Amer. U.S.* 3.400, The following are the principal grasses sown in the cultivated ground, or in any way propagated for feed and hay: . . Rhode-Island bent, Agrostis interrupta. **1910** Graves *Flowering Plants* 64 **CT**, *Agrostis canina*. . . Brown Bent Grass. Rhode Island Bent. Local. Meadows. **1922** U.S. Dept. Ag. *Farmers' Bulletin* 1254.33, Rhode Island bent (*Agrostis tenuis* [=*A. capillaris*] . .) is the most common and abundant grass on well-drained soils in New England and New York and is not uncommon south to Virginia and Missouri and west to the Pacific. **1952** Strausbaugh–Core *Flora WV* 112, *Agrostis tenuis*. . . *Rhode Island bent grass*. . . Cultivated for lawns and pastures. **1969** *DARE* (Qu. L9a, . . *Kinds of grass . . grown for hay*) Inf **RI**16, Rhode Island bent. **1976** Bailey–Bailey *Hortus Third* 42, [*Agrostis*] *tenuis*. . . Rhode Island b[ent] g[rass].

Rhode Island clover n
=**oxeye daisy 1.**

   1894 *Jrl. Amer. Folkl.* 7.91 **VT**, *Chrysanthemum leucanthemum*, . . Rhode Island clover, Montpelier, Vt.

Rhode Island johnnycake n Also sp *Rhode Island jonnycake*
esp **NEng** Cf **johnnycake 1**
A small cake made typically with stone-ground white corn-meal and cooked on a lightly greased skillet.

   1895 (1900) Arnold *Century Cook Book* 237, *Rhode Island Johnny-Cake*—For this, Rhode Island meal, ground between stones, is required. Take one pint of meal and one teaspoonful of salt, and scald thoroughly. . . Thin with cold milk . . and drop in tablespoonfuls on a hot buttered griddle. . . Eat with butter. **1932** (1946) Hibben *Amer. Regional Cookery* 16, *Rhode Island Jonny Cake*—2 cups Rhode Island corn meal (the grayish, unbolted variety)[,] 1 teaspoon salt[,] boiling water. . . Have an iron skillet very hot, grease with bacon fat, and drop on the cakes from a spoon. . . In some parts of Rhode Island milk is added after the corn meal has been scalded with boiling water. . . A native Rhode Islander . . would as soon be caught putting sugar in his jonny cake batter . . as adding an *h* to the spelling. **1937** FWP *Guide RI* 113, Rhode Island johnnycake is still made with white corn meal, slowly ground between millstones of Narragansett granite which is of a peculiarly fine grain. **1939** Wolcott *Yankee Cook Book* 132, *Rhode Island Jonnycake*—1 cup Rhode Island white jonnycake cornmeal, not bolted (waterground if you can get it)[,] 1 teaspoon salt[,] 1 cup boiling water[,] ½ cup milk. . . Bake on slightly greased skillet, allowing more time than for frying griddle cakes. **1940** Brown *Amer. Cooks* 736, *Rhode Island Johnnycake*. . . Use water-ground white corn meal. . . The use of this meal finely ground between stones is the secret of success. **1949** Kurath *Word Geog.* 68, In New England and the New England settlement area *johnny cake* means 'corn bread,' but in Rhode Island it refers to a corn griddle cake, which is known as a *Rhode Island johnny cake* in the adjoining parts of Connecticut and Massachusetts.

rhododendron n Cf **hell 1, mock azalea, swamp apple**
Std: a plant of the genus *Rhododendron*. Also called **honeysuckle 3, laurel 3, pink** n[2] **2, rosebay;** for other names of var spp see **blue laurel, buck ~, dwarf ~ 3, dwarf rhododendron, election pink, flame azalea, Florida flame ~, headache flower 2, ivy 3, honeysuckle azalea, jack honeysuckle, June pink, kiss-me-over-the-gate, little laurel 1, mayapple 4, May pink 2, mountain honeysuckle 1, ~ rosebay, pink azalea, pink-shell ~, pinkster 2, red laurel, rhodora, snowbrush, swamp azalea, ~ honeysuckle, ~ pink, wild azalea, ~ honeysuckle**

rhodora n [The genus-name assigned to this plant by Linnaeus in 1765]
A **rhododendron** (here: *Rhododendron canadense*) native to the northeastern US.

   1839 in 1847 Emerson *Poems* 59, I found the fresh Rhodora in the woods. **c1886** in 1924 Dickinson *Complete Poems* 82, The crocus stirs her lids,/ Rhodora's cheek is crimson. **1924** *Amer. Botanist* 30.59, A famous New England plant, immortalized by Emerson, is the "rhodora" called . . *Rhododendron Canadense*. . . The vernacular name has continued unchanged. **1954** Forbes *Rainbow* 86 **MA**, The wild rhodora moves in and the green all but disappears under their purple pink. **1961** Douglas *My Wilderness* 285 **ME**, The rhodora (*Rhododendron canadense)* which stands about knee-high was barely in bloom, showing dark

blue flowers. **1965** *Native Plants PA* 10, Rhodora is the earliest species of native Rhododendron to flower in Pennsylvania.

rhubarb n Usu |'rubɑ(r)b|; also |'rubə(r)b| Pronc-spp *rhuberb, rhubub, rue-bub*
A Forms.

   1929 *AmSp* 5.126 **ME**, "Rhubub" or "pie plant" was rhubarb. **1954** *Harder Coll.* **cwTN**, Rhubarb [rubɜ˞b]. **1967** Fetterman *Stinking Creek* 84 **seKY**, I seen pie plants—some calls them rhubub—big as your arm. **1969** *DARE* (Qu. I30, *Other names for rhubarb*) Inf **RI**1, ['ruubəb]—old-fashioned; **OH**41, 56, Rhuberb. **1975** Gould *ME Lingo* 208, Mainers call rhubarb *pieplant* sometimes, otherwise they call it rue-bub. **1979** *Greenfield Recorder* (MA) 2 June [Hemenway column], Rhubarb was "rhubub."
B Sense.
Std: a plant of the genus *Rheum*. For other names of the garden plant *R. rhabarbarum* see **apple cabbage, apple (of) peru 3, elephant's ear 5, garden sauce, go-quick plant, pieplant, pie stem, sour sticks, wine plant** Cf **Eskimo rhubarb, Indian ~, wild ~**

rhum See **rum** n[3]

riata, riato, riatta See **reata**

riband grass See **ribbon grass 1**

riband snake See **ribbon snake**

rib bacon See **rib meat**

ribbed road n Also *rib road* Cf **hog-rib road, rubboard 2**
A rough road; a road having an irregular or corrugated surface.

   [**1832** (1833) Fidler *Observations* 122 **Upstate NY**, There was a kind of road formed, by round logs of wood laid across. . . Such roads are denominated by the natives, "ribbed or corduroy roads," an appellation not ill chosen.] **1950** *WELS (Names for different kinds of unpaved roads: When they get very rough)* 1 Inf, Ribbed road; [1 inf, **csWI**, Washboard, pitted, ribs]. **1967–69** *DARE* (Qu. N17) Inf **GA**77, Rib road; (Qu. N27b, *When unpaved roads get very rough, you call them _____*) Inf **SC**63, Washboard, rib road; **VT**7, Ribbed.

ribber See **river**

ribbit n[1], v Also *ribbet* [Pronc-spp for *rivet;* cf *EDD* *rebbet*] Cf Pronc Intro 3.I.17
A rivet; hence fig adj phr *weak in the ribbits* weak in the joints.

   1795 Dearborn *Columbian Grammar* 138, *List of Improprieties*. . . Ribbit for Rivet. **1847** Hurd *Grammatical Corrector* 88, *Rivet* ["incorrect" pronc = ['rɪbɪt]; "correct" pronc = ['rɪvɪt]]. **1899** (1912) Green *VA Folk-Speech* 351, Ribbit. . . A form of *rivet*. **1909** *DN* 3.363 **eAL, wGA**, *Ribbet, n* and *v*. Rivet. **1968** *DARE* (Qu. GG26, *A feeling of weakness from fear: "When she saw the dog coming at her she got _____."*) Inf **NC**82, Weak in her tummy, weak in the ribbits ['rɪbɪts]—I guess that means joints.

ribbit n[2] See **rabbit**

ribble See **rivel**

ribble off v phr [*SND* (at *reeble* v. 1) "To reel off in a hurried, expressionless manner"]
To recite quickly, by rote.

   1900 Day *Up in ME* 177, He ribbled off a mess / Of names. **1995** *DARE* File **ME** (as of c1925), *Ribble off*—To speak rapidly (a list or series one knows well). She would ribble off the names of her brothers and sisters.

‡**ribbly** n Also sp *wribbly* Cf **nibby** n[1]
   1991 *DARE* File **cNY**, The article mentioned the term "nibby" as a . . [term for the end slice of a loaf of bread]—well, I grew up with a variant of that—"wribbly" or "ribbly."

ribbon n
1 A rein, esp a driving rein.
   1846 *S. Lit. Messenger* 12.741, The wind, "his whip" then . . holds the ribbons and drives winter at a slapping pace. **1857** (1861) Bates *Incidents* 328 **NEng**, How gracefully she held the ribbons, and with what dexterity she managed her spirited horse. **1908** Johnson *Highways*

Pacific Coast 130 **sCA,** Presently a fellow approached driving a smart span of horses attached to a gig, "Hold on to them ribbons thar!" was the cry from the piazza. **1910** *DN* 3.455 **seVT,** *Ribbons.* . . Reins for driving. **1923** *DN* 5.218 **swMO,** *Ribbon.* . . A bridle rein, or a line. **1930** Shoemaker *1300 Words* 50 **cPA Mts** (as of c1900), *Ribbons*—The reins on a private turnout. **1939** *LANE* Map 177 *(Reins),* The term *ribbons* is often distinguished from the other terms [=*reins, lines,* and *webbings*] by its special connotation. It is described as a sportsman's term . . , as a racing term . . , as a ladies' word . . , as a jocular modern term. . . Once . . ribbons are said to apply especially to the reins of stage-coach horses. [*Ribbons* is found **throughout NEng.**] **1956** Almirall *From College* 353 **CO,** The following day, with Harry on the ribbons and me up beside him on the driver's seat, Minnie and King took us in the spring wagon down to Parshall to meet our guests. **1965–70** *DARE* (Qu. L51, *The leathers or ropes that a driver holds to guide a horse*) Infs **CA**195, **CT**2C, **MI**56, **WA**20, Ribbons; **CA**105, Ribbons—used in old days by stagecoach drivers; **KY**39, Ribbons—old-fashioned "western style"; **MA**75, Ribbons—the fancy name.

2 See quot.

1947 Croy *Corn Country* 223, "Ribbons" are the husks left on an ear.

3 See **ribbon wire.**

ribbon cactus n
=**jewbush.**

1976 Bailey–Bailey *Hortus Third* 832, [*Pedilanthus*] *tithymaloides.* . . redbird cactus, ribbon c[actus].

ribbon cane n Also *ribbon plant cane* [From the longitudinal stripes on the canes]
A variety of sugarcane *(Saccharum officinarum).*

[**1811** Mathison *Notes Jamaica* 65 (DJE), The *riband* or *striped* cane is no longer cultivated by judicious planters. The rind is hard.] **1827** in 1910 Commons *Doc. Hist. Amer. Industrial Soc.* 1.215 **seLA,** Some ribbon plant cane have suckered on the 9th. **1833** Silliman *Manual Cultivation* 10, The varieties of Cane cultivated in the United States, are the Creole, . . the Ribbon Cane [etc]. **1883** *GA Dept. Ag. Pub. Circular No. 26* 8.19, Ribbon cane is the most profitable article raised in this county. **1945** FWP *Lay My Burden Down* 84 **AL** (as of c1865) [Black], 'Sides the crops of cotton and corn and rice and ribbon cane we raised in the bottoms, we had vegetables and sheep and beef. **1949** *AmSp* 24.106 **GA,** *Blue cane.* . . Ribbon cane: the large but easily infected sugar cane. **1967** *DARE* (Qu. H21, . . *The sweet stuff that's poured over these* [*pan*]*cakes*) Inf **AR**52, Ribbon-cane syrup—most highly refined. **1967** *DARE* FW Addit **SC,** Ribbon cane—sugarcane that has no seed (seeded cane), but you must plant the joints. **1968–69** *DARE* Tape **GA**84, We would plant our sugarcane or ribbon cane, and just before frost was potato-digging time, sweet potatoes, and syrup-making time; **LA**29, Sugarcane, sugarcane; we planted no sorghum. . . We just planted sugarcane, ribbon cane what they call it. **1970** *Thompson Coll.* **cnAL** (as of 1920s), Ribbon cane—Stalks are reddish, shading toward brownish purple. . . larger in diameter and having shorter joints than blue cane. **1986** Pederson *LAGS Concordance* Gulf Region, 50 infs, Ribbon cane; 19 infs, Ribbon-cane syrup; 1 inf, Blue-ribbon cane; 1 inf, Blue-ribbon sugarcane; 1 inf, Red-ribbon cane—makes dark syrup; 1 inf, Ribbon cane—sweeter than sorghum; 1 inf, Ribbon cane—used further south; 1 inf, Ribbon cane—better type of syrup; 1 inf, Ribbon cane—more "delicate" than sorghum; 1 inf, Ribbon-cane molasses. **1998** *DARE* File—Internet **AL,** [Advt:] Get yourself and your friends some Carson Ann Syrup. You'll agree with our family, it's the best pure ribbon cane syrup you've ever had! [From a website for the product named]

ribbon fish n [*OED2* 1751 →]
The cutlass fish *(Trichiurus lepturus).*

1842 DeKay *Zool. NY* 4.110, This [=the silvery hair-tail] is known here by the fishermen under the name of *Ribbon-fish.* **1906** NJ State Museum *Annual Rept. for 1905* 247, *Trichiurus lepturus* . . Cutlass Fish. Hair Tail. Ribbon Fish. **1946** Stilwell *Hunting in TX* 40, I have wasted countless hours traveling to flocks of these gulls only to find nothing under them except possibly a school of tiny ribbon fish which were playing around on the surface apparently for the sheer fun of it. **1967** *DARE* (Qu. P4, *Saltwater fish that are not good to eat*) Inf **TX**14, Ribbon fish. [*DARE* Ed: identity of this fish not certain] **1998** *DARE* File **TX** (as of c1955), When my father would take us fishing in the Gulf, sometimes we'd catch long, silvery fish with lots of sharp little teeth. He'd call them ribbon fish. They were no good to eat, and we threw them back.

ribbon grass n

1 also *riband grass:* A **canary grass** (here: *Phalaris arundinacea* var *picta*). [*OED2* 1786 →] Also called **gardener's garters 1, ladies' grass**

1822 Eaton *Botany* 386, [*Phalaris*] *americana* . . ribbon grass, wild canary grass. . . Var. *picta,* leaves variously striped.—This variety is the ribbon grass of the gardens. **1832** *MA Hist. Soc. Coll.* 2d ser 9.153 **cwVT,** Phalaris arundinacea, Ribbon grass. **1836** (1840) Phelps *Lectures on Botany* 124, [*Phalaris*] *americana,* (riband-grass, wild canary-grass). **1876** Hobbs *Bot. Hdbk.* 46, Grass, Ribbon, Striped grass, Phalaris colorata. **1925** *Book of Rural Life* 8.4674, Reed Canary Grass. . . A variegated smaller form is the ornamental ribbon grass often seen in gardens. **1940** Gates *Flora KS* 135, Phalaris arundinacea picta . . Ribbon Grass. **1986** Pederson *LAGS Concordance,* 1 inf, **seMS,** Ribbon grass.

2 =**bear grass 1b.**

1961 Wills–Irwin *Flowers TX* 97, Ribbon-grass, *Nolina* spp., of which there are many species, differs by having narrower, rough-margined, or minutely toothed leaves and papery 3-seeded capsules.

3 =**buckhorn plantain.**

1961 Wills–Irwin *Flowers TX* 210, Ribbon-grass—*Plantago lanceolata.* **1967** *DARE* Wildfl QR (Wills–Irwin) Pl.48A Inf **TX**44, Ribbon grass.

ribbon plant cane See **ribbon cane**

ribbon snake n Also *riband snake*
A **garter snake 1** (here: either *Thamnophis proximus* or *T. sauritus*).

1711 Petiver *Gazophylacii Naturae* 7.69 (OED2), Sir Walter Rawleigh's Ribbond Snake. **1743** Catesby *Nat. Hist. Carolina* 2.50, *Anguis gracilis fuscus.* The Ribbon-Snake. This is a slender Snake. . . The Upper Part of the Body dark brown, with three parallel white Lines, extending the whole Length of the Body; the Belly white. They are very nimble and inoffensive. **1837** (1962) Williams *Territory FL* 68, The Garter, Riband, Green and Grass snakes are occasionally seen, but there are few of either kind. **1838** *MA Zool. & Bot. Surv. Repts. Zool.* 49, The beautiful *garter* and *ribbon* and *green* snake even, are avoided with consternation by not a few. **1891** in 1895 *IL State Hist. Lab. Bulletin* 3.264, *Eutainia saurita* . . Garter Snake, Riband Snake. **1904** (1913) Pringle *Woman Rice Planter* 105 (DAE), There was a small ribbon snake, a foot long and one inch round. **1928** *Baylor Univ. Museum Contrib.* 16.18 **TX,** Long's Garter Snake. . . In some localities it is known as the *Ribbon Snake,* in others as the *Red-striped Garter Snake.* **1966–70** *DARE* (Qu. P25, . . *Kinds of snakes*) Infs **FL**29, **MI**123, **NJ**10, Ribbon snake; **DC**2, Ribbon snake—brownish, olive drab with lighter stripe lengthwise, harmless. **1986** Pederson *LAGS Concordance,* 1 inf, **nwLA,** Ribbon snakes.

ribbon wire n Also *ribbon (steel)*
A usu flat, wide wire used for fencing; see quots.

1940 U.S. Dept. Ag. *Farmers' Bulletin* 1832.7, Flat ribbon wire is used for horse enclosures and by some railroads. **1942** Giese *Farm Fence Hdbk.* 15, [Caption:] An old style ribbon steel fence in Massachusetts. **1965–70** *DARE* (Qu. L63, *Kinds of fences made with wire*) Inf **NY**89, Ribbon fence; **MA**42, Ribbon fence—woven, flat, kind of a fancy fence; strands were ten inches apart—two to three inches wide; **CA**97, Ribbon wire—twisted wire; **CT**17, Ribbon wire—twisted, thick wire with barbs—old-fashioned; **DC**8, Ribbon wire—half-inch wide "rolled"; **MA**68, Ribbon wire—plain wire and no barbs; **TX**6, Ribbon wire—many kinds, as wire developed; **OH**87, Ribbon-wire fence; **NY**219, Ribbon-wire fence—flat, half-inch wide with barbs.

ribbuh See **river**

ribey adj [Cf *SND ribe* n. 2 "A long-legged, thin person. . . Hence *r(e)ibie,* lanky, emaciated"] **sAppalachians, esp WV**
See quots.

1927 in 1944 *ADD* **WV,** Ribey. . . Poor, skinny. **1933** *AmSp* 8.1.25 **Appalachians,** *Ribey looking* is heard in Kentucky and sometimes to the north for what is commonly understood as *seedy looking.* **2000** *NADS Letters* **sWV,** "Ribey." This was a word used by my grandmother who is now in her late 60s. It was often used as an adjective in reference to our back sides: "You kids get your ribey rumps over here." I never knew the exact meaning. "Scrawny" would make sense. *Ibid* **sWV,** Ribey was used to indicate a person or thing that was scrawny. Not merely little, but rather reflecting a condition of being notably thin, poorly fed, or wizened. . . Examples of use would be: "He's a ribey little fellow." "He's a ribey-assed sonofabitch." "Those sure are some ribey cabbage plants."

ribgrass n [*OED2* 1538 →] Cf **dog ribs, ribwort**
A plantain, usu buckhorn plantain.

[**1890** *Century Dict.* 5165, *Rib-grass.* . . The English or ribwort plantain, *Plantago lanceolata.* [*DARE* Ed: This entry goes on to cite the *Edinburgh Review.*]] **1935** (1943) Muenscher *Weeds* 431, Buckhorn plantain, . . Rib-grass, Ribwort [etc]. **1967–68** WI Acad. *Trans.* 56.304, *Plantago lanceolata* . . Ribgrass, Ripplegrass, English Plantain [etc].

rib meat n Also *rib bacon* Cf **side meat**
Bacon.

1967 *DARE* (Qu. H38, . . *Words for bacon [including joking ones]*) Inf **SC**56, Rib meat—a store name; **AR**47, Rib bacon. **1986** Pederson *LAGS Concordance* (A side of bacon) 1 inf, **swMS**, Rib meat.

rib road See **ribbed road**

ribwort n [*OED2* c1440 →] Cf **dog ribs, ribgrass**
A plantain, usu buckhorn plantain.

1814 Bigelow *Florula Bostoniensis* 34 **MA**, *Plantago lanceolata.* . . Ribwort or field plantain. **1894** *Jrl. Amer. Folkl.* 7.96 **WV**, *Plantago lanceolata* . . buck-plantain, buck-horn plantain, ripple, ribwort, English plantain. **1898** (1899) Earle *Home Life* 165 **NEng**, Many home-grown substitutes were used in Revolutionary times for tea: ribwort was a favorite one. **1936** Whitehouse *TX Flowers* 142, Red-Seeded Plantain or Ribwort *(Plantago rhodosperma).* . . The ribwort is a very common weed in sandy soil from Missouri to Texas and Arizona.

Rican n Cf **Portoreek**
A Puerto Rican, or a person of Puerto Rican descent; also a Cuban.

1968–70 *DARE* (Qu. HH28, *Names and nicknames . . for people of foreign background: Puerto Rican*) Infs **NY**249, **SC**65, Rican. **1983** Allen *Lang. Ethnic Conflict* 66, Puerto Ricans . . rican . . spick . . spookerican. **1986** Pederson *LAGS Concordance* (Puerto Ricans) 1 inf, **swFL**, Ricans; 1 inf, **seFL**, Ricans—also used for Cubans.

rice n Usu |raɪs|; also *esp S Atl, Gulf States* |raˑs|; **esp Mid and S Atl** |rɔɪs| Pronc-sp *rass*
A Forms.

1920 in 1944 *ADD* 509 **eVA**, *Rice.* . . [rɔɪs]. [**1955** *PADS* 23.43 **Charleston SC**, Centered beginning of /ai, au/ [əi, əu] before voiceless consonants, as in *knife, ice, out, house* (also e. Virginia and Canada).] **1966** *DARE* Tape **SC**5, [rɛɪs]; **SC**9, [rɑɪs]; **SC**10, [ra·ɪs, rɛˇɪs]; **SC**12, [rɑɑs, rɑ·ɪs, rɑˑs]; **SC**13, [rɛɪs, rɑɪs]. c**1970** Pederson *Dial. Surv. Rural GA* **seGA**, [Of 49 infs who offered proncs of *rice*, 41 proncs were of the type [raɪs, rɑɪs, raɛˆs, rɑɛˆs]; 3 were of the type [ra·s]; 7 were of the type [rɔɪs].] **1989** Pederson *LAGS Tech. Index* 171 **Gulf Region**, [For *rice*, 603 infs offered the pronc [raɪs], 215 [ras].] **1990** Amory *Cat & Curmudgeon* 192 **eTX**, I kept thinking about that East Texas accent. . . "rass" for rice.

B Senses.
1 =wild rice.

a**1665** (1885) Radisson *Voyages* 215 **Gt Lakes**, We had there a kinde of rice, much like oats. It growes in the watter in 3 or 4 foote deepe. . . They have a particular way to gather up that graine. Two takes a boat and two sticks, by wch they gett ye eare downe and gett the corne out of it. **1778** Carver *Travels N. Amer.* 523, [The Indians place] their canoes close to the bunches of rice, in such position as to receive the grain when it falls. **1871** U.S. Dept. Ag. *Rept. of Secy. for 1870* 422, *Wild rice, (Zizania aquatica).* . . An acre of rice is nearly or quite equal to an acre of wheat in nutriment. **1911** NJ State Museum *Annual Rept. for 1910* 215, The Rice sometimes follows the course of small streams for many miles back from the rivers or coast. **1965** *Bee* (Phillips WI) 19 Aug [3/2], Rice beds regulated by the conservation commission are located in Ashland, Bayfield, Burnett, Douglas, Forest, Lincoln, Marinette, Oneida, Polk, Price, Sawyer, Vilas and Washburn Counties. **1982** Elman *Hunter's Field Guide* 326, When an old Connecticut pusher mentions oats, he means wild rice. The best way to hunt soras is to push through rice at high tide.

2 A louse B1. Cf **string of pearls**
1967 *DARE* (Qu. R25, *Joking names for a head louse, or body louse*) Inf **MI**67, Rice—for head louse.

3 See quot.

1970 *DARE* (Qu. HH28, *Names and nicknames . . for people of foreign background*) Inf **NY**239, Rice—West Indian Negro.

ricebird n

1 =bobolink B. chiefly Sth See Map
1731 Catesby *Nat. Hist. Carolina* 1.14, *The Rice-Bird.* In the beginning of *September,* while the Grain of Rice is yet soft and milky, innumerable Flights of these Birds arrive from some remote Parts, to the great detriment of the Inhabitants. **1775** (1962) Romans *Nat. Hist. FL* 114, Meadow larks, fieldfares, rice birds, &c. &c. are very frequently had. **1778** (1930) Mackenzie *Diary* 1.281 **RI**, I shot a bird here this day, which is called here, The Quamquidle, or Bob-o'-Lincoln; but properly the Rice bird. **1815** Lit. & Philos. Soc. NY *Trans.* 1.126, Considerable doubts have also been suggested with respect to that interesting bird called the rice bird, reed bird, or bob lincoln (emberiza oryzivora). I call it interesting on account of the beauty of its plumage, the melody of its notes, and the delicacy of its flesh. **1897** *Oölogist* 14.48, After the "Reed-bird" he [=the bobolink] becomes the "Rice-bird" of the south, then the "Butter-bird" of the West Indies. **1937** Heyward *Madagascar* 32 **sSC coast**, By the tenth of September these same little birds [=May birds] would be back again. They had changed their plumage and were known as rice birds. [Footnote:] In Maryland and Delaware these birds are called reed birds, and in New England they are known as bobolinks. **1950** *WELS* **WI** (*Birds found in your region . . Bobolink*) 6 Infs, Ricebird; 1 Inf, Ricebird—bobolink—South. **1956** [see **reedbird 1**]. **1965–70** *DARE* (Qu. Q14, . . *Names . . for . . bobolink*) 58 Infs, **chiefly Sth**, Ricebird; (Qu. Q10, . . *Water birds and marsh birds*) Inf **SC**9, Ricebird. **1966** *DARE* Tape **SC**16, Many man make a hundred dollars tonight catching ricebird, dollar a dozen. **1984** Joyner *Down by Riverside* 1 **SC coast**, Now the rice fields have been reclaimed by river and swamp; and bobolinks—locally called rice birds—have the banks to themselves. **1986** Pederson *LAGS Concordance,* 1 inf, **ceGA**, Ricebird—a delicacy; 1 inf, **cAL**, Ricebirds; 1 inf, **swLA**, Ricebirds—hunted locally.

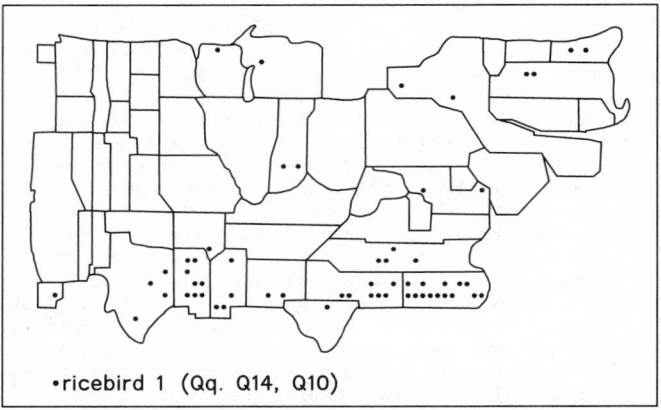

•ricebird 1 (Qq. Q14, Q10)

2 =cedar waxwing.
1917 *Wilson Bulletin* 29.84 **KY**, *Bombycilla cedrorum.*—Rice-bird, paroquet, Hickman, KY.

3 =purple grackle.
1808 in 1810 Schultz *Travels* 2.185 **Lower Missip Valley**, The rice bird is a small species of blackbird. **1911** *Century Dict. Suppl.,* *Rice-bird.* . . In Texas, the crow-blackbird, *Quiscalus quiscula.*

4 =red-winged blackbird. chiefly Gulf States, GA See Map
1851 *De Bow's Rev.* 11.54, *Rice Bird*—1st, gray-brownish, and also the 2d, red-winged; these are migratory, and, I believe, do not build their nests here. **1913** *Auk* 30.498 **Okefenokee GA**, *Agelaius phoeniceus floridanus.* Florida red-wing; 'Rice-bird.' Common on the prairies in the northern portions of the swamp. **1950** *WELS*, 1 Inf, **cwWI**, Red-winged blackbird—the ricebird and reedbird of the South. **1965–70** *DARE* (Qu. Q11, . . *Kinds of blackbirds*) Infs **AL**17, **FL**7, **GA**3, 9, **MS**6, 21, **MO**24, **NC**49, Ricebird; **AL**38, Redwing—also called ricebird; **FL**34, Redwing or ricebird; **FL**35, Redwing or redwing; **GA**28, Ricebird, maybird—same (black with red on wings); **LA**26, Little red-winged ones—called ricebirds; **LA**31, Ricebird = redwing blackbird; **LA**33, Redwing blackbird—called ricebird; [**LA**44, Ricebird—this has gray on him;] **TX**9, Ricebird—red dot on wings; **TX**31, Redwing, ricebird; (Qu. Q14) **LA**29, Ricebird—this is applied to redwing blackbird; **MA**21, Redwing = ricebird.

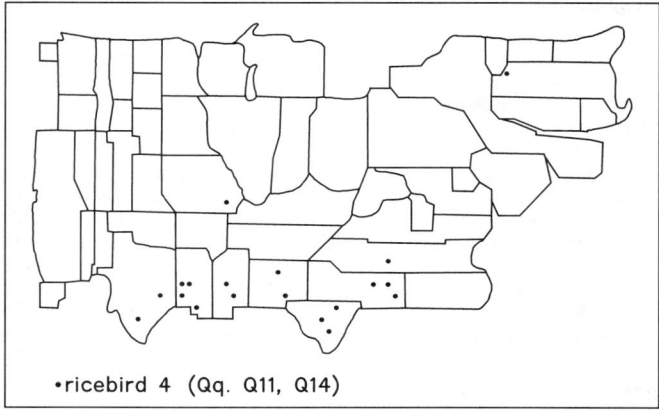

•ricebird 4 (Qq. Q11, Q14)

5 The blue **grosbeak** (*Guiraca caerulea*).   Cf **blue rice bird**

1899 in 1900 LA Soc. Naturalists *Proc.* 108, *Blue Grosbeak*. A most abundant summer resident in some sections of the state, especially in the Florida parishes, where it is generally called "Ricebird." Flocks of thousands descend upon the ripe rice during August and September.

6 A goldfinch 1.

1933 *AmSp* 8.1.51 **Ozarks**, *Ricebird*. . . The American goldfinch, also called the wild canary. The Ozarker does not use this term with reference to the bobolink. **1965–67** *DARE* (Qu. Q14, *. . Names . . for . . goldfinch*) Inf **AR**48, Wild canary or ricebird; **MS**59, Ricebird [Inf queries].

rice corn n

A variety of **Indian corn 1** with long, pointed kernels, used for popcorn.

1849 Emmons *Agriculture NY* 2.265, *Rice corn*. . . is used principally for popping. **1863** Burr *Field & Garden* 600, [In a list of corn varieties:] Rice (White Kernel). . . The kernels are long and slender, angular, sharply pointed at the outward extremity . . extremely hard and flinty. **1938** Damon *Grandma* 168 **CT**, It must be "rice" corn; the sharp spikes made shelling painful, but the flavor was esteemed better. **1942** Amer. Joint Comm. Horticult. Nomenclature *Std. Plant Names* 102, White Durra. . . Rice Corn [etc.]. **1988** Whealy *Garden Seed Inventory* (2d ed) 154, [In a list of popping corn varieties:] White Rice—110 days.

rice cousin n

1 as *rice's cousin:* =**rice cut-grass.**

1892 *AN&Q* 9.18, "Rice's Cousin" is in some parts of this country a popular name for a kind of grass, *Leersia oryzoides*, which resembles the true rice. It is also called white grass, cut grass, etc. It has no special value.

2 =**barnyard grass.**

1916 *Torreya* 16.236 **SC**, *Echinochloa Crus-galli* . . Shank grass, rice cousin, Oakley, S.C.

rice cut-grass n

A **cut-grass 1** (here: *Leersia oryzoides*).   Also called *rice's cousin* (at **rice cousin 1**)

1857 Gray *Manual of Botany* 540, Rice Cut-grass. . . Wet places; common. **1894** Coulter *Botany W. TX* 511, [*Homalocenchrus*] *oryzoides* . . Rice cut-grass. . . Margins of streams, often in shallow water, Texas to Minnesota and eastward. **1946** Tatnall *Flora DE* 35, [*Leersia*] *oryzoides* . . Rice Cut-grass. Common in roadside ditches and on pond margins. **1970** Correll *Plants TX* 114, Rice cutgrass. Perennial with short slender scaly rhizomes. **1985** Madson *Up River* 263 **Upper Missip Valley**, But other rich aquatics took its place—at least seven other species of smartweeds, leafy pondweed, sago pondweed, wild rice, rice cutgrass, wild celery, and the rich beds of American pondweed.

rice duck n

=**coot** n[1] **1.**

1968 *DARE* (Qu. Q9, *The bird that looks like a small, dull-colored duck and is commonly found on ponds and lakes*) Inf **MD**36, Rice duck, coot—same thing.

rice-field rail See **rice rail**

ricegrass n

1 =**mountain rice.**   Cf **Indian rice 2**

1875 *Ladies' Repository* 2.181, *Rice Grass for the Manufacture of Paper*.—Canada rice grass is said to afford an excellent material for the manufacture of paper. . . The plant grows wild and in great abundance in the United States and Canada. **1950** Stevens *ND Plants* 72, *Oryzopsis* [spp]—Ricegrass. *Ibid* 73, *Oryzopsis racemosa* . . Blackseed Ricegrass. **1975** Zwinger *Run River* 226 **UT**, The rice grass, just spreading into bloom, is full of ladybugs. A translucent sheath encases fat white buds striped with pale green, opening into a graceful fine-spun panicle. Indians often ground the seeds, which are high in food value, into flour for bread.

2 A vine mesquite (here: *Panicum obtusum*).

1937 U.S. Forest Serv. *Range Plant Hdbk.* G91, Vine-mesquite. . . is also known, especially in Texas, as grapevine-mesquite and, in the Southwest, as vine panic-grass. Other local names are ricegrass, vine grass, and wire grass.

rice hen n [**rice B1**]   **chiefly Gt Lakes**

1 =**Florida gallinule.**

1888 Trumbull *Names of Birds* 122 **cnIL**, Others . . in these localities and on the Illinois River (in Putnam Co., at least) who are more particular in such matters, distinguish the Gallinule as *Rice-hen*. **1923** U.S. Dept. Ag. *Misc. Circular* 13.44 **IL, IN, WI**, *Florida Gallinule*. . . Vernacular Names. . . *In local use* . . rice-hen. **1932** Bennitt *Check-list* 28 **MO**, Mud-hen; moor-hen; water-hen; rice-hen. **1953** [see **4** below]. **1967–68** *DARE* (Qu. Q5, *. . Kinds of wild ducks*) Inf **MN**2, Rice hen; (Qu. Q9, *The bird that looks like a small, dull-colored duck and is commonly found on ponds and lakes*) Inf **MN**2, Rice hen; **MN**42, Rice hen—have a white tip to the bill. [*DARE* Ed: These Infs may refer instead to other senses below.]

2 =**king rail 1.**

1923 U.S. Dept. Ag. *Misc. Circular* 13.40 **IN**, *King Rail*. . . Vernacular Names. . . *In local use* . . rice-hen. **1953** [see **4** below].

3 =**sora.**

1953 [see **4** below].

4 =**coot** n[1] **1.**

1953 *AmSp* 28.280, *Rice hen*. The only catch in the use of this name is that in the Northern localities here mentioned, the modifier relates to wild rice, but in Mississippi and California to the cultivated sort. On that understanding, we have as *rice hens* the king rail (Ind., Wis., Ill., Miss.), sora (Ill.), common gallinule (Ind., Ill., Wis., Minn., Ontario), and the American coot (Mich., Wis., Minn., Calif.) **1968** *DARE* (Qu. Q9, *The bird that looks like a small, dull-colored duck and is commonly found on ponds and lakes*) Inf **MN**18, Coot or mud-hen or rice hen.

rice hook n esp **SC** *old-fash*

A sickle for harvesting rice.

1855 *De Bow's Rev.* 19.485 **sAL**, It [=indigo] is cut by hand with the hand-sickle, or rice hook. [**1925** *Book of Rural Life* 8.4712, The greater part of the rice crop in the United States is harvested with twine binders, though a small acreage along the Mississippi River in Louisiana is cut with hand hooks.] **1966–67** *DARE* (Qu. L28, *Tools used in the past for cutting grain*) Inf **SC**9, Rice hook [FW illustr: 18-inch curved blade with handle]; **SC**43, Rice hook—for rice, not used now. **1984** Joyner *Down by Riverside* 47 **SC coast** (as of a1866), Standing shoulder-high among the rice plants, the field hands dexterously harvested the grain with sickles known as rice hooks.

rice pea n

A small bean; see quots.

1954 *Harder Coll.* **cwTN**, Rice peas—a small bean resembling rice grains. "Purty little things that take half a day to shell them. We used to raise them little peas." **1966** *DARE* (Qu. I19, *Small white beans with a black spot where they were joined to the pod*) Inf **AR**17, Crowder peas (small peas), rice peas (smaller still); (Qu. I20, *. . Kinds of beans*) Inf **AR**3, Rice peas—very small peas, white.

rice rail n Also *rice-field rail* **LA**

=**sora.**

1916 *Times–Picayune* (New Orleans LA) 2 Apr mag sec 5, Sora Rail . . Rice Rail; Carolina Rail; Ortolan. **1921** LA Dept. of Conserv. *Bulletin* 10.69, The sora rail (*Porzana carolina*), generally referred to as rice rail and sometimes as "ortolan", . . is best known in the rice fields of August and September. **1923** U.S. Dept. Ag. *Misc. Circular* 13.43 **LA**, *Sora*. . . Vernacular Names. . . *In local use* . . rice-field rail, rice rail.

rice root n Also *rice-root lily*   Cf **lily-bulb rice**

A **fritillary.**

1897 Parsons *Wild Flowers CA* 264, Rice-Root. . . Its bulb. . . is pure, shining white, conical in form, and surrounded by many tiny bulblets, like grains of rice, which crumble away from it at a touch. **1915** (1926) Armstrong–Thornber *Western Wild Flowers* 38, Yellow fritillary. . . The smooth bulb is pure white, and made up of a number of rounded, thickish scales not resembling grains of rice, so the name Rice Root is not appropriate and the local Utah names, Crocus, Snowdrop, and Buttercup are absurd. **1938** (1958) Sharples *AK Wild Flowers* 57, *F[ritillaria] camschatcensis* . . "Squaw Lily," "Rice Root," and "Indian Rice" are some of its many vernacular names, suggested by the fact that where it grows in abundance it is a common article of food among the Indians. . . The conical-shaped bulb is entirely covered with numerous bulblets, the whole resembling a cluster of boiled rice. **1940** Writers' Program *Oregon* 21, Along the bluffs of the Columbia . . are the yellow-belled rice root, the blazing star, and the Lewisia and the Clarkia, named for the adventurers who discovered them. **1967** Gilkey–Dennis *Hdbk. NW Plants* 55, Fritillaria lanceolata . . *Rice-root lily*.

rice's cousin See **rice cousin 1**

rich adj See also **rich pine** Cf **fat** adj[1] **1**
Of wood: having a high resin content.
1922 U.S. Dept. Ag. States Rel. Serv. *Exper. Sta. Rec.* 46.313, 'Rich' stumps, containing not less than 60 per cent of very resinous heartwood, probably can be profitably distilled in a commercial plant where the stand of such stumps is dense enough. **c1970** Pederson *Dial. Surv. Rural GA* **seGA** (*What do you call particularly rich pieces of wood that you cut into little slivers to get a fire started?*), [Many infs responded with *fat lightwood*, but none with *rich lightwood*, despite the question text.] **1975** McDonough *Garden Sass* 176 **AR**, Down there [in the Ouachtine] the pines very often became what we called 'rich'. The turpentine and tar in it made it . . 'rich pine,' which is good for pine knot kindling and torches. **1986** Pederson *LAGS Concordance (Fatty kindling sticks for starting a fire)* 5 infs, **csAR, cn,cwLA**, Rich lighterd; 1 inf, **cwAL**, Rich lighterd splinters; 1 inf, **cnFL**, Rich wood—lighterd, deadwood; 1 inf, **seLA**, Rich wood—pine, not sure; 1 inf, **ceTX**, Kindling is usually rich wood cut up fine.

rich as grease See **grease** n B2

richinal See **original**

richleaf See **richweed 3**

Richmond, go to v phr Cf *DS* AA28, **New York B4**
1944 *PADS* 2.48 **csVA**, Richmond, to go to. . . To become pregnant; to be near to giving birth to a child. A localism used mainly by rural Negroes; originating, perhaps, from the fact that many women living in rural sections went to Richmond, Va., to give birth to a baby in a hospital.

rich pine n [**rich**] **chiefly Sth, S Midl** See Map
=**fat pine 2.**
1851 Pickett *Hist. AL* 91, This was performed by puncturing the parts with gar's-teeth, and rubbing in a dye made of the drippings of rich pine roots. **1873** *Appletons' Jrl.* 9.109 **Sth**, On entering it at night, their first act was to raise a light, by means of a splinter or two of rich pine, in the fireplace. **1883** Zeigler–Grosscup *Heart of Alleghanies* 149 **wNC**, Jake threw a rich pine knot on the fire. **1930** Shoemaker *1300 Words* 51 **cPA Mts** (as of c1900), *Rich pine*—Pine knots filled with resin which blaze brightly in camp fires. **1949** Dean *Diamond Bess* 198 **TX**, The gas is made from rich pine and pine knots. **1949** Kurath *Word Geog.* 29, The

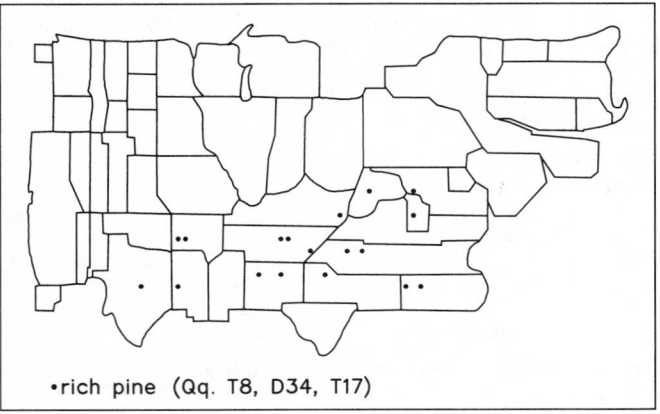

•rich pine (Qq. T8, D34, T17)

Midland term for kindling wood is *pine, fat-pine, rich-pine*. **1967** *DARE* (Qu. T8, *Joints of pine wood that burn easily and make good fuel*) 14 Infs, **chiefly Sth, S Midl**, Rich pine; **DC**8, Rich pine—will burn from a match "as if it had gas to it"; (Qu. D34, . . *The small pieces of wood and other stuff that are used to start a fire*) Inf **AR**53, Rich pine; **SC**32, Rich pine—used for kindling, ignites easily, lots of tar in it; **SC**46, Rich pine—[same as] lightwood pine that burns easily, used for kindling; (Qu. T17, . . *Kinds of pine trees; not asked in early QRs*) Inf **KY**39, Rich pine (pitch pine). **1969** *DARE* Tape NC68, Some calls it lightwood. Some calls it pine. Down east North Carolina they call it lightwood. Through here we call it rich pine. **1970** Tarpley *Blinky* 110 **neTX**, *Wood used to start a fire* . . rich pine [4 of 200 infs]. **1986** Pederson *LAGS Concordance (Fatty kindling sticks for starting a fire)* 51 infs, **chiefly inland Gulf Region**, Rich-pine; 1 inf, **cnGA**, Rich pine-wood; 2 infs, **cnGA, nwMS**, Rich-pine knots; 1 inf, **csAR**, Rich-pine splinters.

richtocrat See **arichtocrat**

rich up v phr
To improve (soil or farmland) by the addition of fertilizer; to fertilize.
1986 Pederson *LAGS Concordance*, 1 inf, **cnTX**, Rich it up—fertilize or enrich it.

richweed n

1 A plant of the genus *Pilea*, esp *P. pumila*. Also called **clearweed, coolweed.** For other names of *P. pumila* see **stingless nettle, toe itch**
1814 Bigelow *Florula Bostoniensis* 220, Urtica pumila . . *Rich-weed.* . . A weed about houses, distinguished by its stem, which is fleshy and almost transparent. **1843** Torrey *Flora NY* 2.223, Adike pumila . . *Richweed. Coolweed.* **1876** [see **4** below]. **1892** IN Dept. Geol. & Nat. Resources Rept. for 1891 152, Pilea pumila . . Richweed. Clearweed. Glass-Nettle. **1943** Fernald–Kinsey *Edible Wild Plants E. N. Amer.* 166, Richweed, Clearweed, *Pilea pumila*. . . It has been suggested that the common Richweed may be an available potherb. **1975** Hamel–Chiltoskey *Cherokee Plants* 52, Richweed . . *Pilea pumila*. . . Infusion to reduce excessive hunger of children.

2 A **boneset 1** (here: *Ageratina altissima*).
1894 *Jrl. Amer. Folkl.* 7.92 **NC**, Eupatorium ageratoides . . richweed. Banner Elk, N.C. **1964** Kingsbury *Poisonous Plants U.S.* 397, *Eupatorium rugosum* . . Snakeroot, white snakeroot, richweed. **1998** (acc) Purdue Univ. Coop. Ext. Serv. *IN Plants* (Internet), White Snakeroot, White Sanicle, Richweed.

3 also *richleaf*: A **horse balm** (here: *Collinsonia canadensis*).
1822 Eaton *Botany* 244, [Collinsonia] canadensis (horse balm, rich weed). . . Strong scented, not unpleasant. Woods. **1828** Rafinesque *Med. Flora* 1.111, Collinsonia canadensis. . . Vulgar Names—Rich-weed, Richleaf [etc]. **1930** Sievers *Amer. Med. Plants* 23, Citronella horsebalm. . . horseweed, richweed, richleaf. . . The entire flowering herb possesses a pleasant, lemonlike odor. **1970** Anderson *TX Folk Med.* 75, Put some rick-weed [sic] . . roots into a jug of whiskey and let them set for about two or three weeks. During the spring, take a tablespoonful each morning. **1970** *DARE* (Qu. S21, . . *Weeds . . that are a trouble in gardens and fields*) Inf **VA**43, Richweed—whitish foliage. [*DARE* Ed: Inf may refer instead to another sense.]

4 A **bugbane 1** (here: *Cimicifuga racemosa*).
1762 Gronovius *Flora Virginica* 79, Actæa racemis longissimis. . . Nostratibus Rich-weed & aliquibus Black-Snake-root. [=Actaea with very long racemes. . . Rich-weed among our people and Black-snake-root among some.] **1828** Rafinesque *Med. Flora* 1.85, Black snake-root. . . Vulgar Names—Squaw root, Rich weed, Rattle weed, Rattle-snake-root [etc]. **1876** Hobbs *Bot. Hdbk.* 98, Richweed, Black cohosh, Cimicifuga racemosa. . . Richweed, Tall ambrosia, Ambrosia trifida. Richweed, Stingless nettle, Urtica pumila. **1892** (1974) Millspaugh *Amer. Med. Plants* 11-1, Cimicifuga [spp]. . . Com[mon] Names.— Black cohosh, Black snake-root, Rich weed. **1930** Sievers *Amer. Med. Plants* 23, Black cohosh, . . richweed, squawroot. **1971** Krochmal *Appalachia Med. Plants* 96, Rattle-top, rattleweed, richweed.

5 =**giant ragweed.**
1876 [see **4** above]. **1900** Lyons *Plant Names* 27, *[Ambrosia] trifida*. . . Bitter-weed, Rich-weed [etc].

rick n

1a rarely *rick stack*: A pile or stack, usu rectangular in plan, of hay, straw, or sheaves—often in comb *hayrick*. [*OED2* a900 →] **scattered, but chiefly Midl** See Map

1853 Simms *Sword & Distaff* 240 **SC**, Much of the roofing had decayed, and the openings were thatched with ricks of broom-grass and pine-straw—a very slight and imperfect shelter for the encounter with our March and September squalls. **1860** in 1986 *This State of Wonders* 68 **cIA**, The passers by stop to look at our cattle and ricks and remark they never saw so nice a fix. **1899** (1912) Green *VA Folk-Speech* 351, *Rick.* . . A heap or pile; specially a pile of hay, grain, or wood. **1902** *DN* 2.243 **sIL**, *Rick.* . . A long, rectangularly-based pile of hay, or grain in the sheaf. Distinct from *stack*, which is round. **1907** *DN* 3.225 **nwAR**, *Rick.* . . A long, rectangular pile of hay, grain, or wood. **1937** *AmSp* 12.106 **eNE** [Farm terms], An oblong stack is a *rick*. **1939** LANE Map 104 *(Haystack; cock)*, Oblong stacks with a ridge-like top are mentioned by [28 infs]; these are called *long stacks* or less commonly *ricks* [by 12 infs]; also *rick stack* [by 1 inf]. **1946** *PADS* 5.34 **VA**, *Rick.* A stack of hay, usually long and rectangular; common everywhere except the Tidewater south of the Rappahannock and the Eastern Shore. **1949** Kurath *Word Geog.* 54, *Hay stack.* . . In an area including all of Virginia, except the Middle Neck and the South Side (the Norfolk area), all of Maryland, as well as Delaware Bay and the Lower Delaware Valley, these rectangular stacks are called *ricks*. Scattered instances of *rick* have been noted in West Virginia and in westernmost North Carolina. **1950** WELS **WI** *(The small piles of hay in the field)* 2 Infs, Hayrick; *(Pile of hay stored outdoors)* 2 Infs, Hayrick—occasionally. **1960** Criswell *Resp. to PADS* 20 **Ozarks**, A *rick* of hay was a rather long (not round) stack put up in the field, used for feeding in the winter. . . It might be weighed down on top and down the sides with wires to which large rocks were attached, to prevent blowing, and it might have a canvas cover on the top. **c1960** *Wilson Coll.* **csKY**, *Hayrick.* . . A large stack or pile of hay, without a pole; usually elongated. **1965–70** DARE (Qu. L14, *A large pile of hay stored outdoors: [Do names differ according to shape?]*) 74 Infs, **chiefly Midl**, (Hay)rick; **MD38, TN62**, Rick of hay; **VA33**, Straw rick; (Qu. L12, . . *The small piles of hay standing in the field*) 11 Infs, **chiefly Midl**, (Hay)ricks; (Qu. L30b, *Then these sheaves . . are set together in piles called* _____) Infs **FL15, LA40, NY123, SC4, TX105**, Ricks. **1968** DARE FW Addit **GA33**, Rick—a small pile of hay. **1973** Allen *LAUM* 1.185 (as of c1950), *Haystack.* . . *(hay)rick* occurs chiefly in southern Iowa, with scattered instances in southern Minnesota and Nebraska. . . Both *stack* and *rick* denote a variety of shapes, although *rick* is favored to signify a square or rectangular pile. *Ibid* 186, *Haycock* (in the field). . . rick. . . hay[rick] [7 infs, **Upper MW**]. *Ibid* 275, *Shock* (of corn, wheat, etc.) . . rick [1 inf, **cwIA**]. **1986** Pederson *LAGS Concordance (Haystack)* 20 infs, **chiefly inland Gulf Region**, Rick(s); 1 inf, **seAL**, Rick—used in other parts of the country; *(Hay barrack)* 14 infs, **chiefly inland Gulf Region**, (A) rick *(or ricks [of hay])*; *(Cock)* 17 infs, **chiefly inland Gulf Region**, Rick(s); *(Shock)* 4 infs, **nwAL, cwGA, cTN, cTX**, Rick(s). [DARE Ed: Most infs described ricks as rectangular or long; some said that hay was stacked around a pole, others specified that no pole was used; others said it was made up of raked-up rows of hay.]

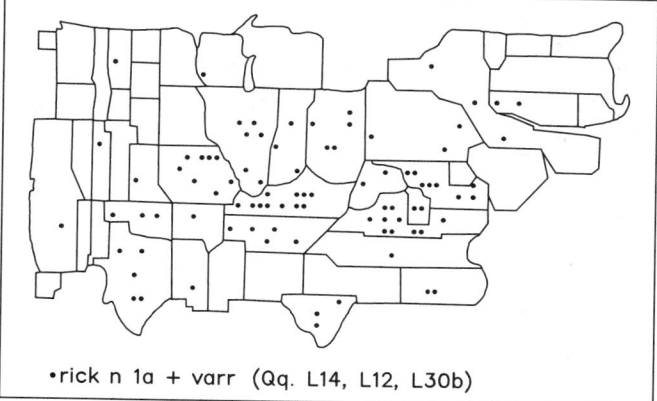

•rick n 1a + varr (Qq. L14, L12, L30b)

b =hay barrack.

1986 Pederson *LAGS Concordance (Hay barrack . . four poles and a sliding roof)* 1 inf, **csTX**, Rick—four poles.

2 A rectangular stack of wood sawn in uniform lengths; esp one that is eight feet long, four feet high, and with a depth equal to the length of the sticks; rarely, a bundle or load of wood.

1899 Garland *Boy Life* 49 **nwIA** (as of c1870s), Afterwards these pieces, split into small sticks ready for the stove, were thrown into a con-

ical heap, which it was Lincoln's business to repile in shapely ricks. **1903** *DN* 2.327 **seMO**, *Rick.* . . Rank or pile of wood. **1904** *DN* 2.420 **nwAR**, *Rick.* . . A measure of firewood. 'Black-jack is a dollar and a quarter a rick.' **1907** [see **1a** above]. **1917** *DN* 4.421 **LA**, *Rick.* . . A pile of wood, eight feet across, four feet high, and of any length. **1923** *DN* 5.218 **swMO**, *Rick*, n. or v. Wood, cut any length, arranged uniformly in a pile eight feet long and four feet high. "I ricked up two ranks o' wood." **1932** Randolph *Ozark Mt. Folks* 123, [In a notice of public sale:] 4 rick of wood. **1956** Sorden–Ebert *Logger's Words* 27 **Gt Lakes**, *Rick*, 1. A pile of wood cut in stove length, usually 16 inches, piled four feet high and eight feet long, three ricks to a cord. In 12 inch length, 4 ricks to a cord. 2. A pile of cordwood stave bolts, or other material split from short logs; a cord eight feet long, four feet high, and of a width equal to the length of one stick. **1959** Robertson *Ram* 93 **ID** (as of c1875), Sometimes there would be ricks containing forty or fifty cords. **1962** Salisbury *Quoth the Raven* 72 **seAK**, [They] made a contract with me to supply 60 ricks of wood—part fir—part cedar, and some hemlock. **1965–67** DARE FW Addit **cNM**, Rick (of wood)—about a "tubful" of 18″ wood (a burro load is three ricks—two on sides, one on top); **eOK**, Firewood is bought by the cord or by the rick. . . A rick is two feet by four feet by eight feet. **1967–68** DARE (Qu. L55, *If the wagon was only partly full . . he had a* _____) Inf **OH10**, Half a rick; **LA15**, Rick—if it was that amount of wood; **LA40**, Rick—this probably wouldn't be a load; (Qu. LL24, *To keep firewood neat you have to cut it, split it, and* _____ *it up*) Inf **OK13**, Put it in ricks. **1973** Allen *LAUM* 1.211 (as of c1950), *Turn* (of corn, wood, etc.) . . the quantity of grain or wood that might be carried in a wagon on one trip. . . *rick* [1 inf, **cnND**]. **1986** Pederson *LAGS Concordance*, 23 infs, **chiefly AR, TN, TX**, Rick(s) *(or rick of wood).* [DARE Ed: Infs differ as to how much wood makes a rick.]

3 =double-runner a. Cf **rack** n[2] **1**, **reach** n **B2**

1969 DARE File **cwIN** (as of early 20th cent), "We used to fly down 18th street on a rick, and it was hard to steer." As far as I could tell, a rick is two sleds joined together by a board—the sleds being placed side-by-side rather than end-to-end.

4 also *saw rick*, *wood* ~: A **sawbuck 1**. Cf **rack** n[2] **2**

1969 DARE (Qu. L59, *An implement with an X-frame . . to hold firewood for sawing*) Infs **OH90, TX57**, (Wood) rick. **1986** Pederson *LAGS Concordance (Sawbuck)* 3 infs, **TN**, Rick; 1 inf, **ceTX**, Saw rick; 1 inf, **neMS**, Wood rick.

5 See **hayrick**.

rick v Usu with *rick* [**rick** n 1, 2] **chiefly W Midl, West** See Map on p. 570

To stack (esp firewood) in an orderly fashion.

1899 (1912) Green *VA Folk-Speech* 351, *Rick.* . . To pile up in ricks. **1904** *DN* 2.420 **nwAR**, *Rick.* . . To arrange in a straight line. 'Do you want me to rick this wood?' **1914** *DN* 4.78 **ME, nNH**, *Rick up.* . . To pile up (brush). **1919** *DN* 5.58 **NW**, *Rick up.* . . To pile. A good supply of wood was *ricked up*. **1923** [see **rick** n 2]. **1937** Sandoz *Slogum* 46 **NE**, Some settler along the river had cut and ricked several loads of ash poles to dry. **1942** Whipple *Joshua* 137 **UT** (as of c1860), These grass sods, one by two feet, ricked up in rows like regular adobes. **1944** *PADS* 2.60 **MO**, *Rick up.* . . To pile wood in a orderly manner. **1953** Randolph–Wilson *Down in Holler* 278 **Ozarks**, *Rick.* . . During World War II, I heard a wounded veteran say, "We killed so many Germans the boys just ricked 'em up like cookwood." **1953** *PADS* 19.13 **sAppalachians**, *Rick up.* . . To stack. "I cut the stove wood and the boys can rick up some by the kitchen door." **1958** McCulloch *Woods Words* 148 **Pacific NW**, *Rick up*—To pile wood. In actual measurement three ricks equal one cord but the term rick up is also used to mean pile up wood in any quantity or shape; as in setting up a stack to be loaded out for donkey fuel. **1965–70** DARE (Qu. LL24, *To keep firewood neat you have to cut it, split it, and* _____ *it up*) 76 Infs, **chiefly W Midl, West**, Rick; (Qu. L15, *When you are putting hay into a building for storage . . you are* _____) Inf **VA75**, Ricking hay. **1967–68** DARE Tape **MD34**, The fodder . . the stalk after the ear is out . . that was ricked in big long ricks and that was feed for what livestock you had . . for the winter; **TX37**, You busted it [=pulpwood] up . . and ricked it up and hogpenned it up for it to dry. **1986** Pederson *LAGS Concordance (Haystack)* 6 infs, **esp inland Gulf Region**, Rick it (up); 1 inf, **cwTN**, Ricked it; 1 inf, **csTN**, Ricked out—no pole; 1 inf, **cwAR**, We ricked some; 2 infs, **nwTN, cMS**, Ricks (it up); *(A turn of . . wood)* 2 infs, **AR**, Rick it; 1 inf, **cnAR**, Rick it off = measure it off—of wood—8′ x 4′; 1 inf, **cwTN**, Ricked it up; 1 inf, **cnLA**, We ricked ours up—piled wood outside the house; 1 inf, **ceAR**, Ricked up; 1 inf, **neAR**, Wood was ricked up in cords; 1 inf, **cTN**, Ricking the wood. **1999** *NADS Letters*

cnAR, In rural West Tennessee when you stack fire wood you "rank" it. . . In Mountain Home, Arkansas, it is called "rick."

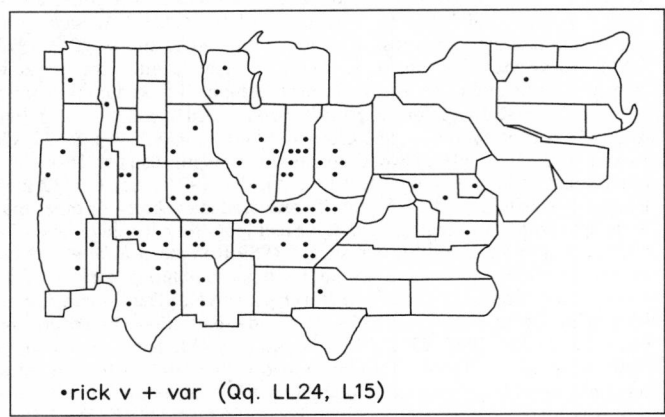

•rick v + var (Qq. LL24, L15)

‡ricket fence n
　1969 DARE (Qu. L62, *A fence made of split logs*) Inf **KY**29, Ricket fence—a few built, rails set on end. [FW illustr: crossed-rail fence]

rickets n Also *ricks* [Cf *EDD* rickets sb. pl. "*Obs.* . . A disease in sheep; the staggers."]
A condition marked by involuntary shaking or trembling.
　1909 DN 3.363 **seAL, wGA,** Rickets. . . St. Vitus's dance.　**1966–70** DARE (Qu. GG13b, *When something keeps bothering a person and makes him nervous . . "It gives me the _____."*) Infs **GA**7, **IL**29, Rickets; (Qu. DD22, *. . Delirium tremens*) Inf **TN**53, Ricks.　**1984** *Annals Internal Med.* 100.899 **wAL,** Patients with *those old leg rickets* have restless shaky legs.

rickety-bang v phr [Echoic]　Cf **rippity slash**
　1914 Whitson *Centennial Hist. Grant Co.* IN 1.136, The straight sides of the poles and log [sic] used were laid together sufficiently close that a horse's foot could not get through between them, and the wagons would "rickety-bang" over them.

rickety-rackety adj Also *ricky-racky*　Cf Intro "Language Changes" I.3
Shaky, dilapidated.
　1968 DARE (Qu. KK20a, *Something that looks as if it might collapse any minute: "That old shed is certainly _____."*) Inf **NY**70, Ricky-racky; (Qu. KK70, *Something that has got out of proper shape: "That house is all _____."*) Inf **NY**70, Rickety-rackety.　**1975** Gould *ME Lingo* 225, *Rickety-rackety* indicates both instability and clatter, as a wheel with loose spokes or a shed door that *chowders* in the wind.

rickididdle n
　1967 DARE FW Addit **cnLA,** Rickididdle [FW: Inf's spelling] ['rɪkɪˌdɪdl]—old-fashioned for dumpling.

ricklety adj [Prob var of *rickety,* but cf *EDD* rickley (at *rickle* sb.¹) "loose, unstable, rickety, dilapidated"]　Cf Intro "Language Changes" I.8, **racklety**
　1969 DARE (Qu. KK20a, *Something that looks as if it might collapse any minute: "That old shed is certainly _____."*) Inf **KY**36, Ricklety ['rɪkəlˌti]; (Qu. KK23, *Weak or unsteady: "I think the footbridge will hold but it is a bit _____."*) Inf **KY**11, Ricklety ['rɪkˌɪdi].

rickolliction See **recollect**

rickrack adj
Of a fence: laid out in a zigzag pattern.
　1968 DARE (Qu. L61, *Fences made of solid logs, now or in the past*) Inf **NC**54, Rickrack fence—made of split logs [FW illustr: zigzag pattern]; (Qu. L64, *The kind of wooden fence that's built around a garden or near a house*) Inf **AK**8, Rickrack fence.　**1986** Pederson *LAGS Concordance* (Rail fence) 2 infs, **cAL, seGA,** Rickrack (fence); 1 inf, **cAR,** Rickrack fence—split trees laid zigzag pattern.　**1988** Tyler *Breathing Lessons* 16 **sePA,** Maggie gazed at a weathered wooden fence that girdled a field. . . "Don't they call that kind of fence 'rickrack'?"

rickrack adv
　1986 Pederson *LAGS Concordance* (Kitty-cornered) 1 inf, **cGA,** Walked rickrack.

ricks See **rickets**

rick stack See **rick** n 1a

rick up See **rick** v

ricky-racky See **rickety-rackety**

ricolec', ricolleck, ricollick, ricollict See **recollect**

ricommend See **recommend**

rictum-dity See **rinktum tiddy**

rid v¹　See **ride** v¹ **A1, 2a, 3b**

rid v²　See **redd 2, 3a, b, 4**

ridd v¹　See **ride** v¹ **A2a**

ridd v²　See **redd 3a**

ridding See **redd 4**

ridding comb See **redding comb**

riddle n¹
Std sense, var form.
Pl: usu *riddles;* also *riddleses.*　Cf Intro "Language Changes" II.3
　1972 Jones–Hawes *Step it Down* xii **eGA** [Black], We would hear all those things—riddleses and stories and different things.

riddle n²　[*OED2* a1100 →]
A coarse-meshed sieve or sifter; hence v *riddle* to sift with such a sieve; n pl *riddlings* siftings; also fig.
　1797 in 1916 Hawkins *Letters* 252 **GA,** I will give . . each a pestle and mortar, a sifter and riddle and fanner, an earth pot, pan and large wooden spoon.　**1848** *Union Mag.* (NY NY) 3.29, Through the steel riddle, more or less coarse, is the arrowy Maine forest . . relentlessly sifted, till it comes out boards, clapboards [etc].　**1849** Wierzbicki *California* 35, On the upper edges of the boards, rests a box of boards, called a sieve or a riddle.　**1899** (1912) Green *VA Folk-Speech* 34, Leak like a riddle. *Ibid* 352, Riddle. . . To sift with a riddle, or coarse sieve. Wheat-riddle. . . Riddlings. . . The coarser part of anything, as grain or ashes, which is left in the riddle after sifting; siftings; screenings.　**1930** Shoemaker *1300 Words* 49 **cPA Mts** (as of c1900), Riddle—A coarse sieve. **c1937** in 1970 Yetman *Voices* 214 **OK** [Black], We'd take corn and beat it in a mortar with a pestle. They took out the husks with a riddle and a fanner. The riddle was a kind of a sifter.　**1939** LANE Map 134 (*Flour sieve*) 5 infs, **CT, MA, ME,** Riddle; 1 inf, **cCT,** [rɪdl], to sift or [wɪnə] grain.　**1951** PADS 15.59 **ceIN** (as of 1890s), With us, the sieve was circular and used by hand, while the riddle was oblong, stood up aslant, and the material to be screened was thrown up against it with a shovel. **1955** Roberts *S. from Hell-fer-Sartin* 47 **seKY,** She said if he would go to the spring and pack 'im some water in a riddle—bucket—that she'd bake it for 'im. Well, he went and he was at the spring and that riddle wouldn't hold water.　**1968–70** DARE (Qu. L32b, *In early days, how was the grain separated from the chaff?*) Inf **UT**4, Through a riddle—they would shake them apart; **VA**68, Riddles or screens in a threshing machine.　**1980** Banks *First-Person America* 82 **IL** (as of 1939), One of my first jobs was to shake the riddle. The riddle is a coarse sieve through which the fine coal is sifted, the fine stuff falling to the ground.

riddle v
1 See **riddle** n².
2 See quots.　Cf **redd 4**
　1851 in 1927 Jones *FL Plantation Rec.* 339 **nwFL,** 4 [hands] Ridling hog Guts.　**1952** Brown *NC Folkl.* 1.584, Riddle. . . To remove fat from the entrails of animals.—Granville county.

riddles(es) See **riddle** n¹

riddlings See **riddle** n²

ride v¹
A Gram forms.
1 pres: usu *ride;* also rarely *rode, rid.*
　1937 in 1976 *Weevils in the Wheat* 73 **VA** [Black], God is jes roding her fer some dem licks and starving she give me.　**1989** Pederson *LAGS Tech. Index* 130 **Gulf Region,** [Infinitive of *ride:*] 1 inf, [rɪd]; 1 inf, [rod].

2 past: usu *rode;* also:

a *rid(d).* [OED2 ride v. A.2.γ, c1489 →; appar still in std use in England in the 19th cent] **now chiefly Sth, S Midl**

1677 (1900) Manning *Sea Jrl.* 6.182 **ME,** Anchored on ye East side in 10 fathõe of water, & there rid all that Night. **1818** Fessenden *Ladies Monitor* 172 **NEng,** Provincial words . . to be avoided. . . *Rid* for rode. **1828** Webster *Amer. Dict., Ride* . . pret. *rode* or *rid;* pp. *rid, ridden.* **1844** Thompson *Major Jones's Courtship* 135 **GA,** He rid rite up and pulled a paper out of his hat. **1893** *DN* 1.277 **nwCT,** Ride—[past, past participle:] rode, [and] rid. **1893** Shands *MS Speech* 53, Rid. . . Negro for *rode.* **1899** (1912) Green *VA Folk-Speech* 351, Rid. **1906** *DN* 3.123 **sIN,** Rid. **1912** *DN* 3.587 **wIN,** Rid. **1923** *DN* 5.219 **swMO,** Rid. **1930** *AmSp* 5.264 **Ozarks,** The hillman usually says *rid* instead of *rode.* **1934** *WV Review* Dec 77. **1940** Faulkner *Hamlet* 19 **MS,** So he rid back to where his niggers had done fetched up the water barrels. **1957** *AmSp* 32.34 **NEng** (as of 1620–1700), To ride, all occurrences [of past tense]: 18; rid(d), 10; rode, 8. **1965–70** *DARE* (Qu. OO27a, *Talking about riding horses: "When she was a girl she _____ horseback."*) 13 Infs, **esp Sth, S Midl,** Rid. [7 of 13 Infs gs educ or less] **1969** *DARE* Tape **KY**16A, He . . rid up and she knowed him, said, "Get down, preacher, and come in." **c1970** Pederson *Dial. Surv. Rural GA* **seGA** (*"Someone _____ the horse yesterday."*) 50 [of 59 infs], Rode [26 infs White, 24 Black]; 9 infs, Rid [1 White, 8 Black]. **1989** Pederson *LAGS Tech. Index* 130 **Gulf Region,** [Past tense of *ride:*] 591 infs, [rod]; 16 infs, [rɪd].

b rarely *ride(d).*

1966–70 *DARE* (Qu. OO27a) Infs **CA**72, **MO**24, **SC**9, 19, 26, Ride; **PA**166, Rided. **1989** Pederson *LAGS Tech. Index* 130 **Gulf Region,** [Past tense of *ride:*] 4 infs, [raɪd].

3 past pple: usu *ridden;* also:

a freq *rode.* [OED2 ride v. A.3.γ, 1597 →] *esp freq among speakers with little formal educ*

1800 (1907) Columbia Hist. Soc. *Records* 10.151 **PA,** He . . brought home Dr. May to dinner, whose horse he had rode to town. **1801** in 1889 MA Hist. Soc. *Proc.* 2d ser 4.132 **MA,** After having rode two or three miles from the town, there is nothing in prospect but land and sky. **1828** (1938) Bolling *Diary* 46.237 **VA,** Mrs. Royall who had rode there behind her husband returned in my carriage. **1829** Kirkham *Engl. Grammar* 146, Ride—rode—rode, ridden [Footnote: Ridden is nearly obsolete]. **1856** Emerson *English Traits* 302 **MA,** The swarms which . . have sailed, and rode, and traded. **1865** (1922) Jackson *Col.'s Diary* 199 **PA,** We left a large number of sick with them that had rode in the supply wagons. **1884** *Anglia* 7.252 [Black], *Pres.* ride—*Past.* rid—*Pass. Part.* rode. **1893** [see A2a above]. **1907** *DN* 3.249 **eME.** **1909** *DN* 3.364 **eAL, wGA,** Rode, pp. of ride. Ridden is rarely heard among the uneducated. **1910** *DN* 3.447 **cwNY.** **1938** Rawlings *Yearling* 405 **nFL,** The hull passel of 'em has rode off. **1953** Atwood *Survey of Verb Forms* 19 **Atlantic,** *Rode* [as past participle] . . predominates rather heavily in n.e. N. Eng. among the older informants . . and is used by about half the younger ones . . as well. In this area many of those who use *rode* also know and use *ridden.* In s. and w. N. Eng. *rode* is more scattered and more characteristic of older informants. Except for n. N.J. and the lower Hudson Valley, where *rode* is rather infrequent, this form predominates very strongly in Type I [=poorly educated] throughout the M[iddle] A[tlantic] S[tates] and the S[outh] A[tlantic] S[tates]; and it is also used by from one half to two thirds of the Type II informants [=of fair education]. **1965–70** *DARE* (Qu. OO27b, . . *"All my life I've _____ [horses]."*) 380 Infs, **widespread,** Rode. [Of all Infs responding to the question, 43% were comm type 5, 36% gs educ or less; of those giving this response, 51% were comm type 5, 53% gs educ or less.] **c1970** Pederson *Dial. Surv. Rural GA* **seGA** (*"Has that horse ever been _____?"*) 27 [of 63] infs, Rode [14 infs White, 13 Black]; 25 infs, Ridden [16 White, 9 Black]; 8 infs, Rid [1 White, 7 Black]; 3 infs, Ride [all infs Black]. **1975** Allen *LAUM* 2.23 **Upper MW** (as of c1950), Although the eastern distribution pattern revealing *rode* as Midland-oriented is perhaps reflected in its concentration in the southern half of Iowa, the more conspicuous U[pper] M[idwest] contrast is between the eastern and the western states of the area. . . *Rode* . . is less frequent in Nebraska and the Dakotas. . . As in the East, *rode* is much more heavily favored by Type I speakers [=old, with little educ], for whom it is the dominant form in each state but South Dakota. The effect of the schools may appear in the rather wide difference between its 59% for Type I and only 21% for Type II [=mid-aged, with approx hs educ], with a somewhat surprising incidence of 19% among the better educated speakers. **1991** *DARE* File **NC,** In addition to feeling "puny, dauncy" . . you can add "rode hard and hung up wet." **1991** Pederson *LAGS Social Matrix* 94 **Gulf Region,** [Of the 594 instances of the past participle of

ride that were collected, *ridden* made up 60% and *rode* 36%. The frequency of *rode* was, however, strongly affected by social factors, most notably education. Among infs in the lowest category, with 0–7 years of schooling, *rode* made up more than 70% of the instances, but only 17% among those with 11–12 years and 6% among those with more.]

b *rid.* [OED2 ride v. A.3.β →1798] *old-fash*

1828 [see **A2a** above]. **1843** (1916) Hall *New Purchase* 335 **IN,** The scampering, and tearing . . as the quadrupeds were "being" rid up to the rack! **1851** Hooper *Widow Rugby's Husband* 91 **AL,** We shouldn't have but one horse that could be rid. **1893** [see **A2a** above]. **1899** Chesnutt *Conjure Woman* 48 **csNC** [Black], Sandy must 'a' clim' up on de tree en jump' off on a mule . . en rid fur ernuff ter spile de scent. **1937** (1963) Hyatt *Kiverlid* 13 **KY,** I never have rid her with a hick'ry. **1953** Atwood *Survey of Verb Forms* 19 **Atlantic,** The archaic *rid* . . occurs in a scattered way in n.e. N. Eng., being confined to informants of Types IA and IIA [=old, with poor or fair education], most of whom also use *rode* or *ridden* or both. Elsewhere in the East *rid* is extremely rare until one reaches the coastal and mountain areas of the South and South Midland. It has its greatest frequency in N.C., where it is used by about one third of the Type I [=poorly educated] informants. **1955** Ritchie *Singing Family* 63 **seKY,** I guess they'd shore have rid me on a rail. **1957** *AmSp* 32.38 **NEng** (as of 1620–1700), To ride, all occurrences [of past pple]: 4; rid(d), 4; ridden, 0. **1965–70** *DARE* (Qu. OO27b, . . *"All my life I've _____ [horses]."*) 16 Infs, **scattered,** Rid. [11 of 16 Infs comm type 5, none young] **c1970** [see **A3a** above]. **1975** Allen *LAUM* 2.23 **Upper MW** (as of c1950), Archaic *rid* . . is reported only once, in the speech of a Type I [=old, with little educ] South Dakotan whose father was born in Vermont.

c rarely *ride, roden.*

1953 Atwood *Survey of Verb Forms* 19, One informant in Georgetown, S.C., uses *ride* as a participle. **1966–67** *DARE* (Qu. OO27b) Infs **SC**9, 26, Ride; **CO**47, Roden. **c1970** [see **A3a** above]. **1989** Pederson *LAGS Tech. Index* 130 **Gulf Region,** [Past participle of *ride:*] 2 infs, [raɪd]; 1 inf, [rɑd].

B Senses.

1 See quots.

1893 Roosevelt *Wilderness Hunter* 216 **nID,** If the tree is too tall it [= a moose] "rides" it, that is, straddles the slender trunk with its fore legs, pushing it over and walking up it until the desired branches are within reach. **1925** Dargan *Highland Annals* 161 **cwNC,** He jest rid the saplin's after them dogs. It was the masterest sight, him goin' over ever'thing like he had wings in his insides. . . He was "riding the saplings" when we saw him.

2a To patrol, inspect (something), usu on horseback.

1897 Hough *Story Cowboy* 48 **West,** At times he must ride the range . . to keep track of the cattle, to see whether any are back in box cañons from which they may be driven, to see whether any are "drifting." **1920** *DN* 5.83 **eOR,** Ride a range, to. To ride over a range. **1929** *AmSp* 5.74 **NE** [Cattle country talk], "Riding the range" nowadays is generally the act of "riding" a long stretch of barb wire fence to see that it is "stock proof." **1940** *AmSp* 15.135 [Tobacco market language], *Riding the territory.* Looking over the fields of tobacco during the growing season or visiting the markets. **1942** Faulkner *Go Down* 99 **MS,** He would pass the house on his mare while riding his crops.

b esp in phrr:

(1) *ride (a or the) fence:* To follow a fence, making repairs as necessary; hence vbl n *riding (the) fence.* **chiefly West** Cf **fence rider 1**

1881 (1882) Chase *Editor's Run* 49 **NM,** Mr. Chase . . has general supervision, with a boss on each ranch, to attend to all details, such as hiring the necessary help to "ride the fences." **1920** *DN* 5.83 **eOR,** Ride a fence, to. To ride along a fence. **1929** *AmSp* 5.57 **NE** [Cattle country talk], "Riding the fence" is continuous on many of the largest ranches which may have several "fence riders," who occasionally use an old automobile rather than a "saddle pony" during the "ride." **1933** *AmSp* 8.1.30 **nwTX** [Ranch diction], *Ride the fence.* To follow the fenceline, with wire-stretchers, hammer, and staples . . for repairing. **1944** Adams *Western Words* 127, Ridin' fence—The duty of keeping the fences in repair. **1966** Barnes–Jensen *Dict. UT Slang* 35, Ride fence . . to ride along the fence of a cattle ranch to keep it in repair. **1994** *DARE* File **MO,** There is an activity here in Missouri called "riding fence," or "checking fence," which means checking your fences out on the farm.

(2) *ride (the) line:* To patrol an unfenced boundary to keep cattle from straying across it; rarely =**ride** v[1] **B2b(1);** hence vbl n *riding line.* **West** Cf **line rider**

1888 Roosevelt in *Century Illustr. Mag.* Mar 669 **ND,** Even for those . . who are not forced to ride the line . . , there is apt to be some hardship.   **1897** Hough *Story Cowboy* 207 **West,** Perhaps his ranch is under fence, and if so he must ride the line to see that the fence is not down at any point.   **1933** *AmSp* 8.1.30 **nwTX** [Ranch diction], *Ride the line.* To ride between two unfenced ranches.   **1936** McCarthy *Lang. Mosshorn* np **West** [Range terms], *Ridin' Line.* Holding a line of cattle in a particular topographical area which is not fenced. A river or a ridge often serves as the line.   **1966** *DARE* Tape **NM**13, The cattle were . . allowed to roam out there on that open range. The man that had them there certainly had to ride line. So-called "riding line" would be to have a certain area where he made his trips backwards and forwards and around day after day, throwing his cattle back—back towards his location.

(3) *ride the ditch:* To oversee an irrigation ditch.

1931 *AmSp* 7.122 **eID** [Irrigation terms], The *ditch rider* is a sort of overseer who *rides the ditch* and allots the water to the farmers.   **1950** *AmSp* 25.164 **eCO,** The 'ditch boss' or the 'ditch rider' . . usually 'rides the ditch' on horseback though he may sometimes 'walk ditch.'

(4) *ride bog:* See quots; hence vbl n *riding bog.*   Cf **bog rider**

1936 McCarthy *Lang. Mosshorn* np **West** [Range terms], *Ridin' Bog.* . . Riding the low range in the spring while the cattle are in poor condition and extricating any animals who have become bogged down.   **1937** *DN* 6.620 **swTX,** *To ride bog* is to ride the banks of the river, usually after a flood, to see if the cows are stuck in the mud.

3 in phr *ride herd:*

a To herd cattle on horseback; with *on:* to herd (cattle) on horseback.   **West**

1911 *Century Dict. Suppl.,* *To ride herd* or *to ride herd on,* in the western United States, to guard cattle by riding on the outer edge of the herd of feeding animals, keeping them from straying and also keeping off wild animals. . . [*"*]Blacknell was *riding herd on* a small bunch of calves who with heels mostly in the air were making life a burden to him and to his wiry cow-pony.["] *J. Bronson,* The Lost River, i [*DARE* Ed: this source not found].   **1913** Cather *O Pioneers* 21 **NE,** So far John had not attempted to cultivate the second half-section, but used it for pasture land, and one of his sons rode herd there in open weather.   **1941** Writers' Program *Guide WY* 464, *Ride herd*—To ride after the cattle.   **1942** Perry *Texas* 12, This was Frank Dobie's land. . . On it he's ridden herd while his fellows slept.

b By ext; with *on,* rarely *over:* to manage, watch over, tend; also fig.   **chiefly West**

1897 Lewis *Wolfville* 235 **AZ,** The way them pore darkened drunkards rides herd on each other . . is as good as sermons.   *Ibid* 303, I'd shorely prefer to try an' hold a bunch of five hundred ponies on a bad night, than ride herd on the heart of one lady.   **1927** *AmSp* 2.278 **Pacific,** *Ride herd*—manage.   **1937** Sandoz *Slogum* 86 **NE,** The locator from the Niobrara would be pretty saddle-galled if he tried to ride herd on the shiftless class of people that homesteaded in this cattle country.   **1939** (1973) FWP *Guide MT* 415, *Ridin' herd on (a woman)*—Courting.   **1944** *Sun* (Baltimore MD) 17 Nov. 8/6 *(OED2),* Her mother-in-law . . and a cousin of her husband . . arrived in Albany to-day to ride herd on the Dewey small fry.   **1966** *DARE* (Qu. Y8, *To keep after a person . . : "He never gets a minute's peace—she's always _____";* total Infs questioned, 75) Inf **DC**6, Riding herd over [him]—outdoors.   **1973** Allen *LAUM* 1.370 **ND** (as of 1950), He is *courting* her. . . Rare but of unusual interest are metaphors reflecting local customs and views. In the North Dakota Badlands a Type I [=old, with little educ] widow of cattle-ranching background has *riding herd on her* and *building her a smoke.*

4 in phr *ride sign:* To patrol a cattle range on horseback watching for the traces of strayed cattle; hence vbl n *riding sign.*   Cf *ride line* (at **B2b(2)** above)

1897 Hough *Story Cowboy* 39 **Plains States,** Each day the cow-punchers "ride sign" around the edge of the agreed territory, turning back or looking up any cattle that seem to be wandering from their proper range.   **1922** Rollins *Cowboy* 192 **West,** There were inspection trips about the Range, so-called "outridings," to . . discover by "riding sign" whether any beasts were straying too far afield.

5 in phr *ride sheriff:* See quot.

1899 (1912) Green *VA Folk-Speech* 352, *Ride* sheriff; to ride about as sheriff for the purpose of collecting taxes from the people. "I rode sheriff in that county five years."

6 To ride at or fill (a specified position) in herding cattle.   Cf *drag rider* (at **drag driver**), *point rider* (at **point B1**), **tail rider**

1916 Sinclair *Phantom Herd* 245 **West,** You see a herd drifting before a storm, maybe,—a blizzard like yesterday, with your pal riding point.   **1922** Rollins *Cowboy* 221 **West,** Quietly there ranged along either side of the herd and from among the circle riders a line of flankers, riders less strategic than . . the lieutenant-generals who "rode tail."   **1954** *True* June 68 **TX,** You'd have a couple of leopard dogs up there riding point.   **1956** Moody *Home Ranch* 24 **CO** (as of 1911), Little Britches can take the south, I'll ride point and let Zeb bring up the drag.   **1971** Adams *Cowman* 28 **West,** On the trail the men who rode drag were said to be "eatin' drag dust."   **1985** [see **point B1**].

7 in phr *ride a log:* See quots.

1905 U.S. Forest Serv. *Bulletin* 61.44 [Logging terms], *Ride a log, to.* To stand on a floating log. (Gen.)   **1969** Sorden *Lumberjack Lingo* 96 **NEng, Gt Lakes,** *Ride a log*—To stand on a floating log.

8 in phr *ride the saw;* In using a two-man crosscut saw: to hang back or bear down in such a way that one's partner does the greater part of the work; hence vbl n *riding the saw;* also fig, to shirk one's share of a job.

1921 (1973) Campbell *Southern Highlander* 2, Pliny did not "ride the saw," but did his full share with his big brother Homer in cutting up the logs for firewood.   **1958** McCulloch *Woods Words* 148 **Pacific NW,** *Ride the saw*—a. To bear down or shove a crosscut saw when cutting. b. To pull to one side to make a crooked cut. c. Said of a greenhorn who cannot do his share of the work, and is accused of climbing on the saw to ride.   **1966** *DARE* Tape **NH**5, It pulled pretty hard, especially if one of the fellows on the other end of the saw had to ride it a little.   **1968** Adams *Western Words* 250, *Riding the saw*—A logger's expression for loafing, said when a partner on a crosscut saw does not do his share of the work.   **1984** Wilder *You All Spoken Here* 153 **Sth,** *Ride the saw:* Make somebody else do the hard work, the dirty work, while you pretend to bear your share of the load. The term comes from using a crosscut saw.

9 To cross (a river) on horseback—used in fig phrr *(someone) to ride the river with* (and varr) (someone) to be relied upon. [Var of the Scots, nEngl phrr *(someone* or *something) to ride the water on* (or *with*) applied literally to a horse that can be trusted in fording a stream and fig to a person or thing that can be relied on]   **West**

1940 *AmSp* 15.220 **cwTX,** If this 'wrangler' is playful but not vicious, the 'pusher' (foreman) may claim that 'he'll do to ride the river with.' The river is the Rio Grande, not Jordan, and this expression means that the 'cow-waddie' could be relied on even for 'rustling' contraband from Mexico to Texas.   **1945** Thorp *Pardner* 155 **SW,** Men who knew him at that time without knowing his past, believed him to be a master cowman (he was), and personally a chap who would do to ride the river with (that was open to serious debate).   **1956** Almirall *From College* 22 **CO,** Dad Elliott, eh? Well, he's a man to ride the river with.

10 in phr *ride circle:* To ride around a section of range to inspect fences or round up cattle.   Cf **circle n 1, circle rider**

1958 Blasingame *Dakota Cowboy* 241 **SD,** Breakfast at dawn, riding circle to throw a roundup together.   **1966** Barnes–Jensen *Dict. UT Slang* 35, *Ride circle* . . to ride around a cattle ranch, to inspect fences, etc.

11 *ride (the) chuck line:* See **chuck line.**

12 in phr *ride shotgun:*

a To ride in a vehicle as an armed guard.   [It is generally assumed that this phr was orig applied to the "shotgun messengers" on Western stagecoaches, but so far no ex earlier than 1954 has been found. It no doubt owes its recent currency, if not its origin, to movie or television "Westerns."]

1954 Horan–Sann *Pictorial Hist. Wild West* 82 **CA,** The drivers picked up their "ribbons," and the messenger, "ridin' shotgun," hooked a high-heeled boot over the seat and cradled his weapon.   **1963** Golden *Forgotten Pioneer* 14, He was as adventurous as the fellow riding shotgun on the stagecoach, or the cowboy.   **1966** *Natl. Observer* 26 Dec 1, The gunships "ride shotgun" on the highly vulnerable, more lightly armed transports.   **1969** *Chicago Tribune* (IL) 27 Apr mag sec 35, Publicity about the possibility of specially trained FAA "sky marshalls" riding shotgun on Miami flights . . is rarely more than that.

b To ride in the seat next to the driver of a car or truck.   Cf **shotgun 2**

1961 *Seattle Daily Times* (WA) 29 Jan 21, Good Ol' Days: Riding Shotgun On Ambulance. . . Riding "shotgun" on our swaying "stagecoach" were various young doctors. **1967** *DARE* File, *Riding shotgun.* . . To ride on the right most side of the front seat of a vehicle. "You drive—I'll ride shotgun." Current in West (reported from California, Texas, Idaho, Indiana, N. Mexico, etc.). **1969** *AmSp* 44.207 [Trucker jargon], *Ride shotgun*—Ride without driving; ride on the right side of the cab; be a passenger. **1999** *Isthmus* (Madison WI) 16 Apr 41/1, My personal chauffeur was behind the wheel. . . Her mother . . was riding shotgun. I was in the back seat. **1999** *DARE* File **sID** (as of 1964), A college friend talked of "riding shotgun" when she meant that she was riding in the front passenger seat. *Ibid,* The term [=*ride shotgun*] was widespread among teenagers in Orlando, Florida, and Jackson, Mississippi, in the mid '50s.

13a To provide a ride for (someone). [Cf *DA* ride v. 1 "To convey or haul in a cart or other vehicle. *Obs*."]

1928 *AmSp* 4.156 **West,** "Can't I ride you down town?" or "Can't I ride you to town?" (meaning "Won't you ride down town with me?" or "Won't you ride to town with me?") asks a hospitable Western rancher as he stops his car beside a stranger trudging along the road. This use is frequent elsewhere. **1938** Rawlings *Yearling* 62 **nFL,** I'll ride him by your place. **1959** *VT Hist.* 27.154 **nwVT,** *Ride*. . . To give someone a ride. Heard in Highgate, Franklin Co. **1964** *Ferhoodled Engl.* [22] [PaGer], You better hitch up the horses and ride her to the dentist. **1966** *DARE* Tape **SC15,** When you see a sea turtle . . get on his back, he ride me. **1968** *DARE* FW Addit **LA32,** I rode him down the street = I gave him a ride. **1972** *Atlanta Letters* **cGA,** You have a friend who calls for you in his/her car to go to work. Another friend asks, "How do you get to work without a car?" You say, "Oh, a friend *rides me* both ways to work & home." **1989** Pederson *LAGS Tech. Index* 352 **Gulf Region** (*[May I] take you home?*) 15 infs, Ride you (home); 1 inf, Ride you a piece. **2000** *NADS Letters* **MS** (as of 1950s), He rode me to the store on his bike.

b Spec: to push (a baby) in its carriage. **chiefly Sth, S Midl** Cf **roll v 1**

1949 [see **roll v 1**]. **1972** [see **roll v 1**]. **1973** Gawthrop *Dial. Calumet* 77 **nwIN,** To _____ the baby (in a vehicle): wheel 53 [of 125 checklist infs], push 25, ride 21. **1989** Pederson *LAGS Tech. Index* 228 **Gulf Region** (*Wheel [the baby]*) 56 infs, Ride; 4 infs, Riding; 1 inf, Go out and ride; 1 inf, Ride (the baby) around; 1 inf, Riding around; 1 inf, Rode.

ride n

In logging: see quots.

1905 U.S. Forest Serv. *Bulletin* 61.44 [Logging terms], *Ride.* . . The side of a log upon which it rests when being dragged. **1956** Sorden–Ebert *Logger's Words* 27 **Gt Lakes.** **1958** McCulloch *Woods Words* 148 **Pacific NW,** *Ride.* . . A flat surface hewed on a log so it would ride better, not roll, when being skidded by bulls.

ride v² See redd 4

ride a cotton bicycle v phr Cf horse B8, saddle n 5

To menstruate; hence vbl n *riding the cotton bicycle.*

1948 *Word* 4.183, Americans appear to phrase their synonyms for menstruation in terms of material culture: *the rag, riding the cotton bicycle* [etc]. **1966–69** *DARE* (Qu. AA27, . . *A woman's menstruation*) Infs **MN35, NJ16,** Riding a (*or* the) cotton bicycle.

ride a cotton pony See pony n²

ride a fence See ride v¹ B2b(1)

ride-a-horse See ridy-horse 1

ride a log See ride v¹ B7

ride and tie v phr, n, adv phr

Of two people or groups of people traveling with a single horse or vehicle: to proceed by alternately riding or driving ahead a certain distance and then walking, leaving the horse or team tied up for the other to use; the act of, or by means of, traveling in this way.

[**1791** in 1945 Paine *Complete Writings* 283, It is like what the country people call, "Ride and tie—You ride a little way, and then I."] **1859** (1968) Bartlett *Americanisms* 365 **MD, VA,** *To ride and tie.* Said of two persons travelling on the same horse, one of whom rides ahead, and at a suitable place ties the horse for his companion; he walks on and his companion rides and ties; and so they continue by turns. **1878** Hart *Sazerac Lying Club* 113 **NV,** To "ride and tie" is for two men with one horse between them to take turn about at riding and walking. **1892** *KS Univ. Qrly.* 1.98 **CO,** *Ride and tie,* verbal phrase, describing a mode of travel in which one vehicle is used by two sets of people, one riding ahead a given distance and tying the team where the others who have walked will come up to it, the first walking on ahead until overtaken and passed by the second, and so on. **1899** (1912) Green *VA Folk-Speech* 352, *To ride and tie,* to ride and go on foot alternately; said of two persons. **1903** *DN* 2.327 **seMO,** The horse wouldn't carry double so we had to ride and tie. **1908** Fox *Lonesome Pine* 331 **KY,** We won't 'ride and tie' back to town—but I'll take turns with you on the horse. **1945** FWP *Lay My Burden Down* 134 **OK** (as of c1865) [Black], We came across some more Negroes who had a horse, and Mammy paid them to let us children ride and tie with their children. **1954** Forbes *Rainbow* 119 **NH,** Chaises and gigs and high-stepping pairs. Some came on horseback, or ride-and-tie. A lot on foot. **1958** McCulloch *Woods Words* 148 **Pacific NW,** *Ride and tie*—A system whereby two men and one horse could cover a lot of ground. One man rode ahead, tied the horse, and walked on. The second man reached the horse, got on, rode past the first man to an agreed point, where he tied the horse and walked on himself. The term has been forgotten since horses ceased to be a means of getting to and from camp.

ride bog See ride v¹ B2b(4)

ride chuck line See chuck line

ride circle See ride v¹ B10

rided See ride v¹ A2b

ride fence See ride v¹ B2b(1)

ride granny's colt See mother's colt, ride one's

ride herd See ride v¹ B3

ride herd on See ride v¹ B3a, b

ride herd over See ride v¹ B3b

ride line See ride v¹ B2b(2)

ride mamma's colt See mother's colt, ride one's

ride one bug-hunting See bug n¹ 14e

ride one's mother's pony See mother's colt, ride one's

ride out v phr

1 in fig phr *ready* (or *about, going*) *to ride out* and varr; of a room or piece of furniture: Very cluttered or disordered. **chiefly NEng**

1855 *Plain Talk* 111 **NEng,** The servants have taken advantage of having no one to oversee them; and such a forlorn-looking house I never saw. The . . kitchen looks as if about to ride out. **1890** *DN* 1.19 **seNH,** *Ride-out.* 'The chairs are riding out.' *Ibid* 79 **Cape Cod MA,** *Ride out.* . . This use is explained by the saying common fifty years ago on Cape Cod: "The room looks as if it was ready to ride out"; every chair saddled and bridled"; used of a room in great disorder. **1892** *DN* 1.218 **swMA,** *Ride out.* . . "This use is familiar in Chicopee, Mass.; as, 'The room looks as if it was going to ride out.'" **1927** *AmSp* 3.136 **ME,** A cluttered room was "ready to ride out." **1945** Colcord *Sea Language* 104 **ME, Cape Cod, Long Island,** This room looks as if it would ride out—it's a regular hóoraw's nest. **1954** *WELS Suppl.,* My parents were from New England. . . An expression I remember when things were not in order in the house was that they looked as if about "to ride out." I cannot recall what the significance of that was. **1970** *DARE* (Qu. E22, *If a house is untidy and everything is upset . . "It's a _____!" or "It looks like _____."*) Inf **MA98,** Grandmother said "looks ready to ride out." **c1974** *DARE* File **cwMA** (as of c1918), *Ready to ride out.* . . An untidy mess. Said of a table, desk, any piece of furniture loaded with various things.

2 with *with:* To court. Cf **walk out**

1941 *LANE* Map 405 (*Keeping company with her*) 1 inf, **nwCT,** Riding out (with her).

ride-out n [ride out v phr]

Fig: a mess.

1890 *DN* 1.19 **seNH,** *Ride-out.* . . 'The room looks like ride-out.'

1942 *Sat. Eve. Post* 5 Sept 88 **FL**, Things look like rideout, round here, but I ain't up to much, yet [after having a baby].

ride out with See **ride out** v phr **2**

ride point See **point** n **B1**

rider n
1 A fence rail, usu supported at one or both ends by crossed stakes, used to heighten or reinforce a zigzag fence or stone wall, or by itself to form a section of fence; hence v *rider* to provide a fence with riders; ppl adj *ridered;* n *rider fence.* Cf **lock** n **1, stake-and-rider fence**
1760 (1925) Washington *Diaries* 1.155 **VA**, Good part of my New Fencing that was not Riderd was leveld. **1779** in 1789 Anburey *Travels* 2.324 **VA**, These rails . . are laid zig zag to the amount of ten or eleven rails in height, then stakes are put against each corner, double across, with the lower ends drove a little into the ground, and above these stakes is placed a rail of double the size of the others, which is termed the rider, which, in a manner, locks up the whole, and keeps the fence firm and steady. **1784** in 1915 *New Engl. Hist. & Geneal. Reg.* 69.297 **MA**, I ridored my wall Round my orchard. **1800** [see **panel fence**]. **1822** (1972) Deane *New Engl. Farmer* 134, Log fences should always be braced with strong stakes across; and heavy riders add strength to a fence. *Ibid* 135, The limbs of trees, with their small branches upon them, laid on a stone wall, make a cheap and effectual guard against the passage of sheep. Riders with some of the limbs on them are best for this purpose. **1869** in 1951 *S. Folkl. Qrly.* 16.147, In Kansas, . . a worm fence must be at least four and a half feet high to the top of the rider, or if not ridered, four and a half feet high to top rails. **1872** *U.S. Dept. Ag. Rept. of Secy. for 1871* 501 **NJ**, About 30 per cent. of inclosures are surrounded by the worm-fence, of chestnut or cedar rails chiefly, which are laid in angles of 25 degrees, with stakes set in the ground, and double ridered. **1899** (1912) Green *VA Folk-Speech* 352, Rider. . . In a snake-fence, a rail or a stake one end of which rests on the ground, while the other end crosses and bears upon the fence-rails at the angle of meeting, and thus holds them in place. **1903** Fox *Little Shepherd* 386 **KY**, The worm fences had lost their riders and were broken down here and there. **1909** *DN* 3.402 **nwAR**, Rider. . . A rail laid above the crossed stakes and parallel to the lower rails. **1940** *U.S. Dept. Ag. Farmers' Bulletin* 1832.6, [Caption:] A Virginia fence of loose stones with stakes and riders to increase height. **1967–70** *DARE* (Qu. L62, *A fence made of split logs)* Inf **CA211**, Rider fence; (Qu. L65, . . *Other kinds of fences, past or present . . you have around here)* Inf **TX35**, Rider fence—made of wood rails [FW illustr: single line of horizontal poles supported by crossed stakes]. **c1970** Pederson *Dial. Surv. Rural GA,* 1 inf, **seGA**, Rail fences had stakes and riders.
2 =**cap** n[1] **12.** Cf **bunk-and-toggle fence, cap-and-stake ~, stake-and-rider ~**
1909 *DN* 3.416 **nME**, *Stake and rider fence. . .* A fence made in the following manner: heavy logs called bunks about two and a half feet long are laid at right angles to the line of the fence. . . Two large holes are bored in each bunk into which are set upright stakes. Rails . . are laid from bunk to bunk between the stakes. Short blocks called toggles are laid on top of the rails between the stakes and other rails are laid on these. Thus the fence is built as high as desired. The stakes are held in place at the top by riders resembling bunks, but lighter.

rider v See **rider** n **1**

‡**rider boys** n [Joc var of *arthritis*] Cf **arthuritis**
1970 *DARE* (Qu. BB28, *Joking names . . for imaginary diseases:* "He must have the _____.") Inf **FL51**, Those rider boys—from "arthritis" [laughter].

ridered, rider fence See **rider** n **1**

rider-horse See **ridy-horse 2**

riders n
In marble play: see quot.
1922 *DN* 5.187, Riders. . . A case when one side has knocked from the ring all the marbles but one, and is allowed to shoot only at the opposing taws.

ride shank's mare See **shank's mare**

ride sheriff See **ride** v[1] **B5**

ride shotgun See **ride** v[1] **B12**

ride sign See **ride** v[1] **B4**

ride the chuck line See **chuck line**

ride the cotton pony See **pony** n[2]

ride the ditch See **ride** v[1] **B2b(3)**

ride the fence See **ride** v[1] **B2b(1)**

ride the line See **ride** v[1] **B2b(2)**

ride the river with See **ride** v[1] **B9**

ride the saw See **ride** v[1] **B8**

ridey-horse See **ridy-horse**

ridgeback n
1 =**razorback hog.** Cf **ridge runner 5**
1872 *Harper's New Mth. Mag.* 44.663 **Alleghany Mts**, She told me it was a 'ridge-back'—a 'jumping alligator,' a 'sub-soiler.'
2 also *ridgeback hard-shell:* A **map turtle.**
1937 Cahn *Turtles IL* 105, *Graptemys geographica.* . . Geographic turtle; map turtle; ridge-back. *Ibid* 113, *Graptemys pseudogeographica.* . . Ridge-back; map turtle [etc]. **c1940** Newman–Murphy *Conserv. Notes* 5 **neLA**, There are . . varied reptiles in the parish. . . Among the varieties of turtles are . . ridgeback hard shell.

ridgeboard n chiefly **Nth**, esp **NEast** *esp freq among older speakers* Cf **ridge roll**
=**saddle board.** Note: This is to be distinguished from the std sense "board running along the ridge of a roof to which the rafters are attached."
1950 *WELS (The strip of wood or metal that covers the ridge of a roof)* 13 Infs, **WI**, Ridgeboard(s). **1965–70** *DARE* (Qu. D30) 61 Infs, chiefly **Nth**, esp **NEast**, Ridgeboard; **NE7, NY218, RI16, SC4**, Ridgeboard [FW sugg]; **MA29, SC38**, Ridgeboard [FW sugg; Inf doubtful]; **CA125**, Ridgeboard [FW sugg]—wood; ridge iron—we use mostly around here; **CT6**, Ridgeboard—used to be the apprentice's job to paint the ridgeboard; don't use them anymore; **IA31**, Ridgeboard—if of wood; ridge roll—if of metal; **IL31, NY4**, Ridgeboard—if (made out of) wood; **MA58**, Ridgeboard; ridge cap—if metal; **MN14**, Ridgeboard; ridge roll—if metal; **NY35**, Ridgeboard—old-fashioned; **NY68**, Ridgeboard—this is wood; ridge roll—this is metal; **NY72**, Ridgeboard—old-fashioned wooden one; **OR5**, Ridgeboard—old-fashioned; ridge roll; **PA164**, Ridgeboard—this is covered over with roofing; **TX13**, Ridgeboard—wood; ridge roll—tin; **WI19**, Ridgeboard; metal ridge; **WI50**, Ridgeboard—two top boards; ridge roll—made of metal. [Of all Infs responding to the question, 76% were old; of those giving this response, 93% were old.] [DARE Ed: Inf **PA164** is probably referring to the interior member to which the rafters are connected, and it is possible that some of the other Infs are also using *ridgeboard* in this sense.]

ridgeling n Also sp *ridgling* Cf **original, rig** n[1]
A male animal with one or both testicles undescended; esp an animal which, because of this condition, has been incompletely castrated.
1790 Deane *New Engl. Farmer* 233, *Ridgling,* a male animal, half-castrated. A horse of this kind is as troublesome as a stallion, but is not fit to be depended on as one. A ridgling-hog will never be fat. . . till his castration be completed, as it may be by making an opening in the belly. **1899** (1912) Green *VA Folk-Speech* 352, *Ridgeling.* . . A horse or mule with one testicle removed or wanting. **1917** *DN* 4.397 **neOH**, *Original, 'riginal.* . . Ridgeling, a horse whose testicles have not descended into the scrotum at the proper time. **1948** Wolfe *Farm Gloss.* 216, *Monorchid Male*—A male animal with only one testicle down in the scrotum. Also called a ridgeling or "rig." **1965–67** *DARE* (Qu. K31, *A horse that's only partly castrated;* total Infs questioned, 75) Infs **AR21, 40, GA9, OK1**, Ridgeling; **DC1**, Ridgeling—not quite a horse, altered; altered stallion sometimes makes trouble. **1968** Adams *Western Words* 248, *Ridgling*—A male horse one or both of whose testicles have not descended within sight.

ridge plow n Also *ridging plow*
=**lister 1.**
1876 Knight *Amer. Mech. Dict.* 3.1939, *Ridge-plow. (Agriculture.)* A double mold-board plow, used in throwing land into ridges for certain kinds of crops. *Ibid, Ridging-plow.* A double mold-board plow, throw-

ing the earth away and serving to ridge up land for beetroot, potatoes, or other plants sown on the ridge, and for opening water-furrows. **1966** *DARE* (Qu. L18, *Kinds of plows used around here, at present and in the past*) Inf **NC**37, Ridge plow.

ridgepole n [Perh by confusion of **ridge roll** and *ridgepole* the timber running along the ridge of a roof to which the upper ends of the rafters are attached] Cf **ridgeboard**

A covering for the ridge of a roof.

    1950 *WELS* **WI** (*The strip of wood or metal that covers the ridge of a roof*) 8 Infs, Ridgepole; 2 Infs, Ridgepole, (ridge) plate; 1 Inf, Ridgepole or covering; 1 Inf, Formerly a ridgepole—a pole cut out in this fashion (end view) [Illustr shows circle with wedge cut out]. Then two boards nailed together as an inverted water trough—same name; each called a saddle board. Now the metal strip is commonly called a ridge roll. **1965–70** *DARE* (Qu. D30) 130 Infs, **scattered**, Ridgepole [Of these Infs, 3 subsequently corrected themselves and 3 were doubtful about the response.]; **CA**79, Ridgepole—if made of wood; **CA**105, Ridgepole; wooden trough in old days; **IL**31, Ridgepole if metal, ridgeboard if made out of wood; **KS**14, Ridge tin, ridgepole; **ME**9, Ridgepole, saddle boards; **MA**72, I've always called it ridgepole, but I think it's actually a ridgeboard; ridge roll for a shingled roof—it is made out of asbestos; **MA**83, Flashing; ridgepole on older houses; **MA**99A, Saddle board; ridgepole—wife [says]; **NC**8, Ridgepole, cap of the roof; **NC**23, Ridgepole, gableboard; **OH**61, Ridgepole, ridge roll, ridge row; **VT**16, Ridgeboard, ridge plate, ridge row, ridge tin, saddle; [**CA**21, Ridgepole—where the rafters join; **NC**31, Ridgepole—center beam; **NY**52, **TX**33, Ridgepole—inside; **VA**33, Ridgepole—under the roof; **WI**5, Ridgepole—the part underneath]. [*DARE* Ed: The bracketed Infs were clearly referring to the interior member to which the rafters are connected; the comments and synonyms recorded from the other Infs suggest that they were indeed referring to an outer covering for the ridge of a roof.]

ridgepole pine n

=**lodgepole pine**.

    1885 Roosevelt in *Century Illustr. Mag.* 30.225 **SD**, The forest was composed mainly of what are called ridge-pole pines, which grow close together, and do not branch out until the stems are thirty or forty feet from the ground.

ridge roll n Also *ridge row*; rarely *ridge rolling* **widespread, but less freq NEast, Gt Lakes, Pacific** See Map Cf **ridgeboard, ridgepole**

A rounded finishing for the ridge of a roof, usu made of metal or metal-covered.

    1890 *Century Dict.* 5172, *Ridge-roll*, a batten with a rounded face, over which the sheathing of lead or other metal is bent on the ridges and hips of a roof. **1927** (1970) Sears *Catalogue* 1083, *Ridge Roll Finial—Galvanized Steel Finial* to be used with our Ridge Roll 48K3337. [*Ibid, Round Roll Ridge Cap*—Diameter of roll, 2 in.; width of apron, 2½ in.] **1950** *WELS* **WI** (*The strip of wood or metal that covers the ridge of a roof*) 11 Infs, Ridge roll; 2 Infs, Ridge roll—(if) metal; 1 Inf, Now the metal strip is commonly called a ridge roll; 4 Infs, Ridge row; [1 Inf, Hip roll]. **1965–70** *DARE* (Qu. D30) 153 Infs, **widespread, but less freq NEast, Gt Lakes, Pacific**, Ridge roll; 52 Infs, **scattered, but less freq NEast, Gt Lakes, Pacific**, Ridge row; **VA**38, Ridge rolling.

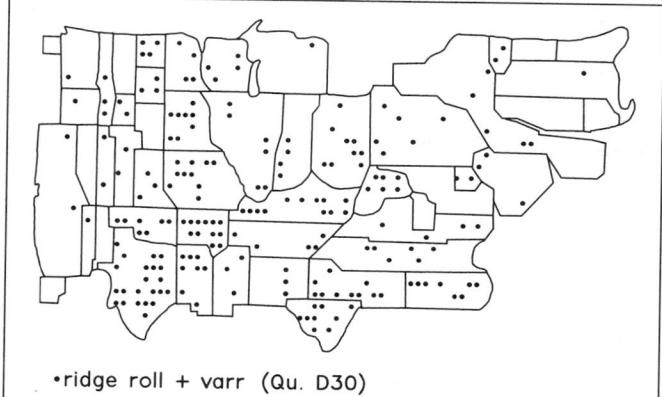

•ridge roll + varr (Qu. D30)

ridge rooter See **ridge runner 5**

ridge row See **ridge roll**

ridge run See **ridge runner 2**

ridge runner n

1 A rustic, esp a mountaineer. **esp Midl**

    1917 in 1944 *ADD* **sWV**, Ridge runner. . . A mountaineer. **1927** *DN* 5.476 **Ozarks**, Ridge runner. . . A derisive term for the mountaineer, as contrasted with the valley farmer. Implies ignorance or stupidity. The word *hill-billy* is used in the same sense. **1933** *AmSp* 8.3.31 [Prison terms], Ridge runner. Originally an Arkansas, rather than a Kentucky, *hill billy*. Any uncouth stupid fellow. [Brought in by the Southerners.] **1933** Williamson *Woods Colt* 183 **Ozarks**, It's all fine empty country, except for a few old-timers prob'ly, a few old ridge-runners that's still cooterin' around. **1948** *AmSp* 23.77 [Army speech], Hill-billy recruits were called 'ridge-runners.' **1963** Edwards *Gravel* 7 **eTN** (as of 1920s), Brother Lawrence Edwards has spent half a century soaking up the lore of his beloved Cumberland wonderland in East Tennessee. . . He can't any more escape it than he can avoid saying "Thang" when he means "Thing." He is a ridge-runner and a cove-ite all kneaded into one, with gravel in his shoes. **1964** *PADS* 42.31 **Chicago IL** [Black], The most characteristic feature of Negro terms for Caucasians is the tendency to expand particularized designations for Caucasians to include all members of the race, e.g. terms for poor Southerners . . *ridgerunner*. **1965–70** *DARE* (Qu. HH1, *Names and nicknames for a rustic or countrified person*) Infs **KY**53, **OH**2, 45, 71, **WV**5, 7, 8, Ridge runner; **MD**9, Ridge runner—from Virginia, West Virginia; **NY**7, Road runners—students who commute to local college and don't live in the town; ridge runners—students at Albany College who live between mountains and city. **1966** Dakin *Dial. Vocab. Ohio R. Valley* 453, A rustic. . . Single instances of *ridge runner* are given in Harlan County, Kentucky, and Washington County, Ohio. **1976** *Capital Times* (Madison WI) 2 Dec 25/1, In 1935 when I came out of the West End, a young ridgerunner from Preston, Wis. **1986** Pederson *LAGS Concordance* (*A rustic*) 3 infs, **ceTN, cnGA, cAR**, Ridge runner; (*Poor whites—white man's terms*) 1 inf, **ceTN**, Ridge runners—from a rough place [*DARE* Ed: Inf Black]; (*Poor whites—black man's terms*) 1 inf, **neTN**, Ridge runner—has only heard this; 1 inf, **csTN**, Ridge runners. **1994** *Jrl.–Patriot* (N. Wilkesboro NC) 25 Aug sec D 5/4 [Logging terms], A "ridgerunner" was a farmer who logged occasionally. **1997** *DARE* File **sOH** (as of c1980), Competing terms [i.e., with *redneck*] were "ridge-runner" and "hill-jack."

2 A person who wanders from place to place, esp someone "on the prowl"; hence v phr *ridge run* to range about; vbl n *ridge running*.

    1930 *DN* 6.88 **cWV**, *Ridge runner*, a "hick" who has become discontented with his job, leaving it to find a new one, and going, of necessity, across the mountainous ridges of this section. *Ridge running*, the act of going across country in search of a new job. **1960** Williams *Walk Egypt* 113 **GA**, A ridge-runner if you wasn't a road-walker. . . A somebody won't stay in one place when two worse places is beyond. I know a somebody-like-you. **1968** *DARE* (Qu. Y29a, *To 'go out' a great deal, not to stay at home much*) Inf **WV**2, Ridge runner. **1975** Gould *ME Lingo* 230, *Ridge runner*. . . A veteran trapper may be a *ridge runner*, but so is a boy who likes to hunt and fish. (Gerald Averill wrote a fine book about his experiences in the Maine woods and titled it *The Ridge Runner*.) Out of the woods, a *ridge runner* is a gay blade on the prowl, just hitting the high spots, and certainly looking for game. **1993** Doig *Heart Earth* 138 **MT**, No, the reading and the rest of it she would not change. She can't feel regret for how any child of hers ridge-runs the country of his head.

3 One who transports or sells illegal liquor.

    1986 Pederson *LAGS Concordance*, 1 inf, **csGA**, Ridge runner—sells "shine." **1992** *Houston Post* (TX) 20 Sept sec A 26 **AL**, Stealing cars and working as a "ridge runner" was his expertise. "I grew up in it. It was just a way of life. Everyone either hauled whiskey or made it."

4 See quots.

    1939 (1973) FWP *Guide MT* 415, *Ridge runner*—Wild horse which keeps to a ridge or high point to watch for danger and warn the herd. **1975** Gould *ME Lingo* 230, *Ridge runner*—A deer *ranging* the beech ridges in the fall, and from that a general term for somebody well versed in the woods.

5 also *ridge rooter*, *~-runner hog*: =**razorback hog**.

    1954 *Sportsman* 2.4.62, The big tuskers, those up to about 250 pounds classed as feral hogs, broadly speaking may be divided into three geographical classes. The first is the wild razorback or "ridge-runner." He is most plentiful in Louisiana, Texas, Mississippi, Tennessee (central to western section), Arkansas, Georgia, South Carolina and in some of the back country of Florida, North Carolina and Virginia. **1982** Powers

Cataloochee 282 **cwNC** (as of a1940), When hogs went wild, they were known as ridge-rooters. **1986** Pederson *LAGS Concordance (Wild hog)* 2 infs, **AR**, Ridge runners; 1 inf, **TN**, Ridge-runner hog—wild hog in the mountains.
6 See quot.
1999 *DARE* File **nwMA**, Ridge runners are hired every summer to patrol sections of the Appalachian Trail. They backpack along their assigned stretch of trail, camping out for a week at a time, doing trail maintenance where needed and assisting hikers.

ridge running See **ridge runner 2**

ridging plow See **ridge plow**

ridgling See **ridgeling**

ridgment See **regiment**

ridgnal See **original**

ridic(k)'lus See **ridiculous**

ridicule n Also *redicule* [Varrs of *reticule*; *OED2* 1805 →; "*Obs. exc dial.*"] *old-fash*
1843 (1916) Hall *New Purchase* 430 **IN**, La! if I ain't dropt my ridicul'! **1899** (1912) Green *VA Folk-Speech* 352, Ridicule. . . A form of *reticule*; a bag in which women carry gloves, handkerchiefs, etc. Redicule. **1917** in 1944 *ADD* **sWV**, Ridicule. . . Cloth handbag with drawstring to carry knitting outfit. **1940** Edmonds *Chad Hanna* 274 **NY**, Her ridicule swinging nervously in her fingers. **1952** Brown *NC Folkl.* 1.584, Ridicule. . . A reticule. **1957** *Sat. Eve. Post Letters* **cnKY**, Ridicule or judicule (big bag) used by my grandmother.

ridiculous adj Pronc-spp *redick(i)lous, ridic(k)'lus* [Engl dial] **chiefly Sth, S Midl**
Shocking; outrageous; indecent.
1832 in 1957 *AmSp* 32.159, These Mingoes act *mighty redick'lous* with women and children. **1853** Simms *Sword & Distaff* 477 **SC**, You would'nt [*sic*] be so onkind and outright redickilous, as to do that—and after all that's [*sic*] she's been a-doing for you. **1887** Amer. Philol. Assoc. *Trans. for 1886* 17.42 **Sth**, In the South we often say, "That's a ridiculous affair," when we really mean outrageous. It seems to be so used sometimes in the North. **1890** *DN* 1.23 **NEng**, Ridic'lus (*i.e.,* ridiculous), meaning detestable, abominable. In rustic use in New England. *Ibid* 79, Ridic'lus. . . Reported in this sense from Kentucky. **1899** (1912) Green *VA Folk-Speech* 352, Ridiculous. . . Abominable; outrageous; shocking. **1903** *DN* 2.227 **seMO**, Ridiculous. . . Outrageous; indecent. This use of the word is almost universal. A country paper stated that the details 'were too ridiculous to be fit for publication.' **1907** *DN* 3.235 **nwAR**, Ridiculous. . . Outrageous, indecent. **1909** *DN* 3.402 **nwAR**, Ridic'lus. . . Detestable. "The way he cut up was something ridiculous." **1922** Gonzales *Black Border* 323 **sSC**, **GA coasts** [Gullah glossary], Ridick'lus—ridiculous, also outrageous, scandalous. (Often so used by illiterate whites). **1926** *DN* 5.402 **Ozarks**, Ridiculous. . . Shocking, outrageous. "Hit was plum ridic'lus how thet feller kilt his pappy." **c1960** Wilson *Coll.* **csKY**, Ridiculous. . . Shocking.

ridie-bob See **ridy-bob**

ridinel See **original**

riding board n Also *riding plank* Cf *DS* EE31
A **seesaw 1**.
c1970 Pederson *Dial. Surv. Rural GA* **seGA** (*What do you call a piece of playground equipment that is made with a long board balanced in the middle? One child sits on one end of the long board and another child sits on the other end, and they go up and down*) 2 infs, Riding board. **1998** *DARE* File, Here are some words. . . from a college-educated male from Purcell, Oklahoma, who was born in 1958: *riding plank*—a homemade seesaw (he says he learned this word from his grandparents, who were born in Tennessee.)

riding bog See **ride** v[1] **B2b(4)**

riding fence See **ride** v[1] **B2b(1)**

riding-horse See **ridy-horse 1, 2**

riding line See **ride** v[1] **B2b(2)**

riding mare n Cf *flying mare* (at *flying horse* 1b), **ridy-horse 3**
1969 *DARE* (Qu. EE32, *A homemade merry-go-round*) Inf **NC72**, Riding mare.

riding plank See **riding board**

riding plow n Also *riding corn plow, ~ sulky plow* **esp Midl, Gt Lakes** See Map Cf **sulky plow, walking ~**
A wheeled plow with a seat for the operator.
1868 *Scientific Amer.* 19.317 **IN**, I claim . . A two-wheel single riding plow. **1911** *Century Dict. Suppl.*, Riding plow. Same as *sulky-plow*. **1924** Croy *R.F.D. No. 3* 24 *(DAE)*, The farmers tried to make up for it with increased machinery—riding plows . . trucks. **1925** *Book of Rural Life* 7.4374, In general, single riding plows are called *sulky* plows, and those with two or more bottoms are *gang* plows. **1927** (1970) Sears *Catalogue* 1060, Riding Attachment for Walking Plows. . . Regular type of riding plow wheels with wide oval tires. **1937** *AmSp* 12.105 **eNE** [Farm terms], A *sulky* plow has wheels and one *bottom*. It is a *riding plow*, not a *walking plow*. **1939** *LANE* Map 166 *(Plow)* 1 inf, **nwCT**, Riding plow. **1965–70** *DARE* (Qu. L18, *Kinds of plows*) 42 Infs, **esp Midl, Gt Lakes**, Riding plow; **NJ16**, Horse riding plow; **MD29**, Riding corn plow; **IN35**, Riding sulky plow; **NJ20**, Three-horse riding plow. **1966–67** *DARE* Tape **IL15**, They had the walking plows, and then they finally got to the riding plows, they had the four-horse plow; **MI12**, [Inf:] They had more riding plows, too, where the person didn't have to walk anymore, so then rode on the plow. [FW:] Just call them riding plows? [Inf:] Yeah, they called them riding plows. **1986** Pederson *LAGS Concordance (Plow)* 2 infs, **TN**, (A) riding plow; 1 inf, **seTX**, Riding plow—had a seat on it; 1 inf, **csGA**, Two-mule riding plow. **1992** Phelps *Famous Last Words* 22 **NEng**, A few years later I learned to plow with a sulky or riding plow which had two bottoms which worked best on level land, as hitting a rock on a side hill could roll them over.

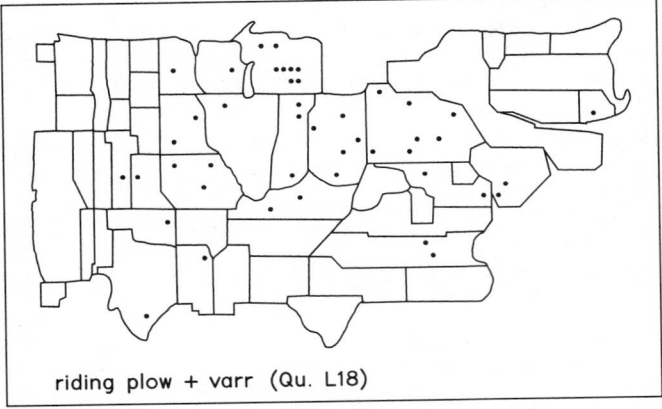

riding plow + varr (Qu. L18)

riding sign See **ride** v[1] **B4**

riding the cotton bicycle See **ride a cotton bicycle**

riding the fence See **ride** v[1] **B2b**

riding the saddle See **saddle** n **5**

riding the saw See **ride** v[1] **B8**

rid off See **redd 3b**

rid up See **redd 3a, b**

ridy-bob n Also *ridie-bob* **esp KY**
A **seesaw 1**.
1969 *DARE* (Qu. EE31, *Playground equipment with a long board for two children to sit on and go up and down in turn*) Infs **KY29, 40**, Ridy-bob. **1982** Slone *How We Talked* 94 **eKY** (as of c1950), A "riddie [*sic*] bob"—See-saw. A plank or pole was placed across a large log so as to balance each end. One or two children would sit on each end. With a slight push with their feet. [*sic*] they could make first one end go up and then the other. As one end went up, the other came down.

ridy-horse n Also sp *ridey-horse*
1 also *ride-a-horse, riding-horse*: Any of var types of usu im-

provised play horses, such as a hobbyhorse or bent sapling; see quots. **chiefly sAppalachians**

1913 Kephart *Highlanders* 259 **sAppalachians,** The children have few toys other than rag dolls . . and such "ridey-hosses" and so forth as they make for themselves. **c1920** in 1993 Farwell–Nicholas *Smoky Mt. Voices* 135 **sAppalachians,** *Ridey-hoss*—Git you a stick for a r[idey]-h[oss]. [**1943** Chase *Jack Tales* 66 **wNC,** I was just a-ridin' it [=a lion] down here to get it broke in for you a ridey-horse.] **1946** TN *Folk Lore Soc. Bulletin* 12, Most every sapling around the school house was converted into a Ride-a-horse when this riding fever would break out. **1964** *McDavid Coll.* **ceSC,** *Riding horse*—We climbed the tall pine saplings and other trees, and bending them down we made *riding horses.* **1986** Pederson *LAGS Concordance,* 1 inf, **ceTN,** Ridy-horse—hobbyhorse; 1 inf, **cnTN,** Ridy-horse—not seesaw, tree bent down to ride on; 1 inf, **neTN,** Ridy-horse—bent over bush, children rode it; 1 inf, **neTN,** Ridy-horse—inclusive term for play horse; 1 inf, **ceTX,** Little-old ridy-horse—apparently, a hobbyhorse; 1 inf, **neTN,** Ridy-horse—sitting on someone's foot.

2 also *rider-horse, riding-horse, ridy-horsey:* A **seesaw 1** or similar recreational device. **chiefly Sth, sAppalachians**

1949 Kurath *Word Geog.* 59, *Seesaw.* . . In the Southern area and in the Appalachians. . . the most widespread regional term is *ridy-horse (riding horse).* It occurs (1) in the Appalachians from central West Virginia southward, and (2) in the coastal area of the Carolinas between the Neuse and the Peedee; and (3) relics of it occur on Albemarle Sound and on upper Chesapeake Bay. **1965–70** *DARE* (Qu. EE31, *Playground equipment with a long board for two children to sit on and go up and down in turn*) 10 Infs, **esp sAppalachians,** Ridy-horse; **NJ69,** Riding-horse. **1966** Dakin *Dial. Vocab. Ohio R. Valley* 172, [Of the 27 infs (out of a total of 246) who responded with *ridy-horse* for a *seesaw,* 24 were from eastern Kentucky.] *Ibid* 174, *Ridy-horse* includes an instance of *riding-horse* and one of *rider-horse.* . . It is clear from the field record comments and sketches that *ridy-horse* is not an exact synonym for *seesaw* = "a plank balanced in the middle on which a child at each end moves alternately up and down." It means rather a plank laid across some type of support with one end permanently fastened in a lower position. The child sits on the high end and "rides" by bouncing up and down. On [sic] Kentucky informant says a *ridy-horse* is also called a *bounce up 'n down.* **c1970** Pederson *Dial. Surv. Rural GA* **seGA** (*What do you call a piece of playground equipment that is made with a long board balanced in the middle? One child sits on one end of the long board and another child sits on the other end, and they go up and down*) 4 infs, Ridy-horse. **1971** Wood *Vocab. Change* 39 **Sth,** Of the playground equipment specifically listed in the questionnaire, *seesaw* was chosen in over three-fourths of all possibilities. East of the Mississippi and including Louisiana, the second is *ridy horse.* **1972** *PADS* 58.16 **cwAL,** *Seesaw.* South and Midland *seesaw* (22 [of 27 infs]) predominates, but two informants gave South Midland and older Southern *ridy-horse.* **1986** Pederson *LAGS Concordance (Seesaw)* 24 infs, **Gulf Region exc TX,** Ridy-horse(s); 1 inf, **seGA,** Ridy-horse—put a board through a rail fence; 1 inf, **seMS,** Ridy-horse—log across pole; 1 inf, **cnAR,** Ridy-horse—up and down through a crack in the fence; 1 inf, **nwFL,** Ridy-horsey; *(They are seesawing)* 3 infs, **seAL, csMS, seMS,** Riding on a (*or* that, their) ridy-horse; 1 inf, **ceGA,** Ridy-horsey. **1991** Still *Wolfpen Notebooks* 47 **sAppalachians,** Young'uns can't think about their text books for wanting to get to the swings and ridey-horses. [*DARE* Ed: This quot may refer instead to another sense.]

3 Any of var other recreational devices; see quots. **esp Sth, sAppalachians** Cf **flying jenny 1, joggling board**

1971 Wood *Vocab. Change* 39 **Sth,** For . . the homemade merry-go-round, whirlygig and ridy horse alternate as first and second choices. **1986** Pederson *LAGS Concordance (Flying jenny)* 2 infs, **c,csGA,** Ridy-horse; 1 inf, **ceTN,** Ridy-horse = homemade merry-go-round; 1 inf, **neGA,** Ridy-horse—heard of; 1 inf, **cnLA,** Ridy-horse—around and around; 1 inf, **cnLA,** Ridy-horse—more like merry-go-round than seesaw; *(Joggling board)* 2 infs, **cnGA, neTN,** Ridy-horse.

ridy-horsey See **ridy-horse 2**

riff v See **rift** v

riff n

1986 Pederson *LAGS Concordance* **seGA** (*Hay barrack*) 1 inf, Riffs—the small piles of hay; *(Cock)* 1 inf, Riffs—small piles in the field to be stacked later.

riffle n[1] Also *ripple* **chiefly West, esp CA** Cf **long tom 2** Also in combs *riffle bar, ~ block;* In gold washing: any of var contrivances placed on the bottom of a sluice box or similar apparatus to capture and retain particles of gold; see quots.

1850 (1914) Kingsley *Diary* 120 **CA,** Finished the riffles to the machine to day. **1866** *Atlantic Mth.* 18.243 **MT,** The constant stream of water carries over the sand, while the gold, being seven times heavier, sinks to the bottom, and is caught by cross bars called *"riffles,"* placed there for the purpose. **1910** Hart *Vigilante Girl* 50 **nCA,** When the miners shut off the water, and began to examine their sluices, sometimes the riffles would be clogged with coarse gold. **1966** Barnes–Jensen *Dict. UT Slang* 36, *Riffle-bar* . . a bar, slat or other obstacle placed at the bottom of a miner's sluice box to arrest particles of gold. **1967–70** *DARE* Tape **AK10,** Then he takes up those ripples that I spoke about and washes them all off. . . In the box. . . the gold hangs on behind; **CA120,** We get all ours right out off riffles on a concentrating table; **CA128,** They put cleats across the bottom [of the sluice box]—that's your riffles—an' let the water run through and they shovel into that, see, an' the gold sticks behind these riffles; **CA137,** Then, that dirt and water run through a box, a sluice box with the riffles in it; and the gold being heavier than the dirt and sand, it settled at the bottom; **CA200,** What they call a riffle. That's a box the water runs in and washes the rocks, and the gold settles on the cross pieces; **OR2,** A long tom is just a long riffle . . shake the loose stuff out of the riffles and let the gold accumulate. **1968** Adams *Western Words* 250, *Riffle bar.* . . Also called *riffle, riffle block.*

riffle n[2] See **rivel**

riffle bar, riffle block See **riffle** n[1]

riffle bug n

A **water strider** (family Veliidae).

1972 Swan–Papp *Insects* 114, Small water strider: *Rhagovelia obesa* (Veliidae). . . Also called riffle bug. **1982** Heat Moon *Blue Highways* 406 **VA,** Water striders and riffle bugs cut angles and arcs on smooth backwaters of the stream. **1998** in 2000 (acc) MN Univ. *Insects Cedar Creek* (Internet), *Family Veliidae*—Riffle Bugs.

riffle, make the v phr Also *ripple, make the* [From *riffle* a rapid; see quot 1860] **orig chiefly West, esp CA; later more widespread**

To succeed at something.

1853 (1930) Buck *Yankee Trader* 130 **CA,** 'Madam La Marquise'. . . built a splendid saloon, opened and flourished for about two months but couldn't make the riffle. **1856** (1930) DeLong *Jrls.* 9.57 **CA,** Went to Camptonville to try and borrow some money could not make the riffle. [**1860** *Harper's New Mth. Mag.* 21.134 **Pacific NW,** "Gentlemen," said the commander [of a steamboat], politely, "I am under the disagreeable necessity of asking your assistance on the [tow] line until we get to yonder point; I am afraid, otherwise, that we can't make the riffle."] **1895** *Overland Mth.* 26.651 **CA,** My boss told me . . that if I could make the riffle he'd have a stack of chips for me. [**1896** *DN* 1.423 **Sth,** *Riffle:* an attempt. "I will at least make a riffle at it."] **1903** *DN* 2.327 **seMO,** *Riffle (to make the).* . . To accomplish what is undertaken. 'He tried but couldn't make the riffle.' **1909** *DN* 3.348 **eAL, wGA,** He couldn't quite make the riffle. **1913** *DN* 3.583 **wIN,** *Make the riffle.* . . To succeed in an undertaking, especially to recover from sickness. "He has typhoid fever, but I guess he'll make the riffle all right." **1939** FWP *ID Lore* 241, *Made the riffle*—was successful. **1942** McAtee *Dial. Grant Co. IN* 42 **AL, wIN** (as of 1890s), *Make the riffle* . . succeed; "He couldn't quite _____". **1949** *PADS* 11.8 **wTX** (as of 1911–29), He wanted to make the team, but he couldn't make the riffle. **1953** Randolph–Wilson *Down in Holler* 263 **Ozarks,** *Make the riffle.* . . To accomplish a given task. **1958** *Sat. Eve. Post Letters* **swIN,** "To make the riffle," had no reference to canoeing in our part of the country, but rather to a skiff or flatboat on the Ohio, the Wabash or the Green River. The expression as we used it referred to failure in a long term undertaking rather than as regards a single incident or episode. For example, we used to say: "She tried mighty hard to catch a beau but she never did make the riffle"; or, "They made quite a few payments on their house but they just couldn't make the riffle." **c1960** *Wilson Coll.* **csKY,** *Make the riffle.* . . To succeed: probably an echo of taking rafts or boats over riffles in the streams, always a difficult task. **1966** Barnes–Jensen *Dict. UT Slang* 30, *Make the ripple:* accomplish an undertaking. "I'd buy that ranch but I couldn't make the ripple n [sic] payments." (Also used as "riffle".)

riffle sucker n
=hog sucker.

1951 Harlan–Speaker *IA Fish* 66, Northern Hog Sucker—Other Names—Black Sucker, spotted sucker, riffle sucker [etc]. **1983** Becker *Fishes WI* 678, Northern Hog Sucker. . . Other common names: hog-molly, . . riffle sucker [etc].

riffraff n, v [Folk-etym for *riprap*]

1968 *DARE* Tape **CT4**, About twenty-five, thirty years ago, these banks were riffraffed with brownstone. The river stays pretty much in its channel today. **1969** *DARE* (Qu. L60, *A fence made of stone or rock without mortar*) Inf **NY226**, Riffraff—perhaps. **1998** *DARE* File **swCA**, On our local TV channel we heard a local workman standing on our rocky seashore, between storms, pointing to some big boulders and saying "We're bringing in some riffraff."

rifle n¹, also attrib [*OED2* 1459 →] chiefly NEast

A tool for whetting a scythe, esp such a tool made of wood coated with sand or emery.

1841 (1969) Emerson *Essays* 189 **MA**, The sound of a whetstone or mower's rifle. **1845** Kirkland *Western Clearings* 58 **MI**, I have never learned to this day why a whetstone should be called a "rifle." **1883** *Narragansett Hist. Reg.* 1.312 **RI**, The day for getting rifle sand (better known as "Beach Pond Day") was the last Saturday of June. **1899** (1912) Green *VA Folk-Speech* 353, *Rifle*. . . An instrument used after the manner of a whetstone for sharpening scythes, and made of a piece of wood coated with sharp sand or emery, with a handle at one end. Also made of a piece of shingle, paddle-shaped, coated with tar and covered with sand. **1911** Essex Inst. *Coll.* 47.13 **eMA**, "Whetting" . . is done by means of a sanded stick called a "rifle." *Ibid*, Nearly all the old grocery stores sold rifle sand. **1949** Kurath *Word Geog.* 19, *Rifle* . . , denoting an emery covered wooden whetter for the scythe, occupies . . the New England coast, Long Island Sound, and East Jersey. **1965–67** *DARE* (Qu. L38, *What do you use . . to sharpen tools in the field?*) Inf **CT14**, Rifle ['raɪfəl]—a stick with emery on each side; **CT17**, Rifle ['raɪfəl]—emery on a stick; **ME5**, Rifle—wooden piece with something abrasive glued on two sides—used to whet a scythe; **NJ1**, Rifle—wooden with emery stone on both sides; **NJ29**, Rifle—has like an emery board on it and you whip the edge of it; **PA201**, Rifle—dry whetstone; **PA230**, Rifle—really a whetstone; **RI12**, Rifle. **1967** Faries *Word Geog. MO* 86, *Whet stone*. . . The Northern *rifle* . . appear[s] once [among c700 infs].

rifle v, n² [*OED2* rifle v.² 1590 →; "*Obs. exc. dial.*"] sAppalachians

To raffle; a raffle.

1913 Kephart *Highlanders* 278 **sAppalachians**, Sounds of *a* are confused with . . *i*, grit (grate), rifle (raffle). **1915** *DN* 4.188 **swVA**, *Rifle*. Variant of *raffle*. **1939** in 1944 *ADD* **nNC**, *Rifle*. . . He won it in a rifle. **1942** Hall *Smoky Mt. Speech* 26 **wNC, eTN**, They're going to ['raɪfəl] it off. **c1960** *Wilson Coll.* **csKY**, *Raffle* is often confused in sound with /'raɪfl/. **1976** Garber *Mountain-ese* 75 **sAppalachians**, They're gonna rifle off a new car fer charity this year.

rifle gun n [Either attrib use of *rifle* "spiral groove in a gun barrel" + *gun* or phonetic reduction of *rifled gun;* in either case, the original form from which *rifle* "gun with a rifled barrel" was abbreviated] now chiefly sAppalachians, Ozarks old-fash

A rifle.

1747 in 1912 Augusta Co. VA *Chronicles* 1.529, They were . . robbed of . . a rifle gun (double tricked). **1775** in 1917 MA Hist. Soc. *Coll.* 72.58, They do Execution with their Rifle Guns at an Amazing Distance. **1805** in 1815 Sutcliff *Travels N. Amer.* 119 **PA**, Considerable business was done in the manufactory of locks, latches, and rifle guns. **1908** Fox *Lonesome Pine* 111 **KY**, I thought yo' fishin' pole was a rifle-gun. **1913** Kephart *Highlanders* 286 **sAppalachians**, Everywhere in the mountains we hear of biscuit-bread, ham-meat, rifle-gun [etc]. **1926** *DN* 5.402 **Ozarks**, *Rifle-gun*. . . A muzzle-loading rifle. **1937** Thornburgh *Gt. Smoky Mts.* 98, The first shoot I've shot with a rifle-gun . . was jes' last week. **1941** Writers' Program *Guide AL* 6 **neAL**, The Alabamians of this region hunt with "rifle-guns." **1949** Webber *Backwoods Teacher* 105 **Ozarks**, "Rifle-gun" (a proper distinction from shotgun) balls run in molds on the "chimley hurth." **1952** Brown *NC Folkl.* 1.584 **wNC**, *Rifle gun*. **1967** *Mt. Life* 43.1.15 **sAppalachians**, He hadn't seed nary another person a-packin a rifle-gun. **1972** *Foxfire Book* 276 **nGA**, I had one a'these old-fashioned rifle guns we used t'call'em.

rift v Pronc-sp *riff* Also with *up* [*OED2* rift v.² a1340 →; "*Now Sc. and north. dial.*"] esp PA

To belch; rarely, to vomit or, of a cow, to regurgitate the cud.

1930 Shoemaker *1300 Words* 50 **cPA Mts** (as of c1900), *Rift*—To belch. **1936** Morehouse *Rain on Just* 19 **NC**, Probably old Sukey [=a cow] had bloated up, eating too much clover, and not rifting right. *Ibid* 133, Women folks . . toting nursing babies who were rifting more than need be, or handing along . . children who might . . holler out. **1939** Aurand *Quaint Idioms* 26 [PaGer], Is it impolite to *rift* (belch) in the presence of company? **1956** McAtee *Some Dialect NC* 57 **seNC**, *Rift*. . . Belch. **1968** *DARE* (Qu. BB17, . . *Vomiting*) Inf **WV4**, Riff up. **1972** *Press* (Pittsburgh PA) 15 Oct 10, You know the lady is a Pennsylvanian if you hear her say she will "redd up" (tidy up) the house. Or a man if he uses "rift" for belch. **1982** *Barrick Coll.* **csPA**, *Rift*—belch—often *rift up.* "I been riftin' up all day." **2000** *DARE* File **cPA**, I was pretty taken back when one of my first patients complained that they "been rift'en and had jags in my leaders"! "Rift'en" was gastric acid reflux, "jags" were sharp shooting pains and "leaders" were the anterior neck muscle groups. *Ibid* **Pittsburgh PA**, *Rift*. . . Many Pittsburghers apparently regard this as a repulsive vulgar word. Still, they use it far more than 'burp' or 'belch', I think. *Ibid* **neOH**, My Akron family used "rift" . . [to mean] "belch."

rift n esp NEast

A patch of broken water; a riffle, rapid.

1727 in 1855 *Documents Colonial Hist. NY* 5.826, The French . . have no way but to come up from Montreal to the Lake against a Violent Stream, all full of Rifts and Falls and Shallows. **1770** in 1889 Washington *Writings* 293 **VA**, The river from Fort Pitt to the Logstown has some ugly rifts and shoals, which we found somewhat difficult to pass. **1817** in 1918 IN Hist. Soc. *Pub.* 6.279 **NY**, We . . ran down the rift. **1845** (1876) Cooper *Chainbearer* 321 **NY**, The most that can be done with it . . will be to float it down to the next rift. **1879** *Scribner's Mth.* 19.21 **MI**, In one hanging rift close by the bank . . I took at five casts fifteen fish. **1968** *DARE* (Qu. C3, *A place in a swift stream where the surface of the water is broken*) Infs **NY93, NJ5, PA119**, Rift(s).

rift up See rift v

rig n¹, also attrib [*OED2* rig sb.³ c1430 →] Cf gellyon, original =ridgeling; occas =stag.

1948 [see ridgeling]. **1966** *DARE* (Qu. K31, *A horse that's only partly castrated;* total Infs questioned, 75) 13 Infs, chiefly FL, GA, Rig. **1967** *DARE* Tape **LA7**, That's the dad of them pigs, that big old guy. He's cut now; that's what you call a rig [rɪg]. . . Now, you cut that little boar pig there, he'll be a barrow. **1967** *DARE* FW Addit **SC19**, Rig (hog)—if one stone remains undescended. Common. **1986** Pederson *LAGS Concordance (Barrow)* 1 inf, **seAL**, Rig—is where he's left one; [1 inf, **csGA**, Rig—castrated when old].

rig n² Cf rig v

1 A joke, prank—often in phrr *have* (or *get*, *run*) *a rig on* to play a joke on, make sport of. [*OED2* rig sb.⁵ 1725 →]

1858 Hammett *Piney Woods Tavern* 139, Don't you go to runnin' any of yer rigs, nor pokin' fun at me. **1859** Taliaferro *Fisher's R.* 30 **nwNC** (as of 1820s), Woe to the man who happened to fall into some ludicrous mishap! He never heard the last of it from Johnson. He had "a rig" on nearly every man. *Ibid* 105, He concluded it was some "rig" the young ladies were running on him. **1892** *DN* 1.231 **KY**, *Rig*. . . He got up a rig on him. **1899** (1912) Green *VA Folk-Speech* 353, *Rig*. . . A frolic; a trick. "They are all the time running rigs on each other." **1916** *DN* 4.328 **KS, NY, eOH**, *Rig*. . . Joke. . . "There was a bunch talking, and they had some sort of a rig on Bud." N.Y. and W. Res.—*have a rig on, v. phr.* Also W. Res. **1940** *Sat. Eve. Post* 10 Feb 85 **Upstate NY**, He knew Chad had run a rig on me. . . That was a smart rig.

2 By ext: a joker, prankster; an outrageous person.

1975 Gould *ME Lingo* 230, *Rig*—An amusing sort of chap, *cuss, joker,* etc: "Oh, that Newt! He's a rig!" **1979** Lewis *How to Talk Yankee* [36] **ME**, *Rig*. . . Outlandish person: "That Peter is an awful rig. He's taking out them two Williams sisters, and I hear they both got a bun in the oven."

rig n³ Cf fix n 2

In phr *in good rig*: In good condition.

1939 (1962) Thompson *Body & Britches* 503 **NY**, From Ontario County, in the Honeoye Valley . . farmers say *in good rig*, when they mean that an animal is in good condition. **1959** *VT Hist.* 27.154, *Rig. . .* Shape; condition. In good *rig.* Occasional. Rural areas. **c1950** *Halpert Coll.* 52 **wKY, nwTN,** In good rig = in good condition.

rig v, hence ppl adj *rigged* Cf **rig** n[2]

To tease, mock, vex; to reprimand; hence n *rigging* a teasing; a scolding.

1883 (1971) Harris *Nights with Remus* 94 **GA** [Black], Now den, Miss Sally'll be a-riggin' me 'bout noddin'. **1892** *DN* 1.231 **KY,** *Rig:* to tell a joke on. "He rigged him good." **1897** *KS Univ. Qrly.* (ser B) 6.56, *Rigged:* plagued, teased, hoaxed; as, "They played a practical joke on the old man and he was terribly rigged about it." *Ibid* 91, *Rig:* to "guy."—General. **1899** A.H. Quinn *PA Stories* 100 *(OED2)*, I rigged him about it once and he said he'd reform. **1912** Croly *Marcus Alonzo Hanna* 460 **OH,** He was continually on the lookout for a chance to joke about the peccadilloes of his friends. There were few of them who escaped some kind of rigging. **1923** *DN* 5.219 **swMO,** *Rig. . .* To deride. **1929** *AmSp* 5.128 **ME,** He might "fly off the handle," or become "so mad he frothed at the mouth" when something "didn't set very well," or "it was thunderin' aggravatin'," and "kind of rigged him," or "it started his temper." **1968–69** *DARE* (Qu. Y6, *. . To put pressure on somebody to do something he ought to have done but hasn't:* "He's a whole week late. I'm going to _____.") Inf **VA24,** Give him a rigging; (Qu. GG32a, *To habitually play tricks or jokes on people:* "He's always _____.") Inf **KY30,** Rigging; [(Qu. GG32b, *To habitually play tricks or jokes on people:* "He's an awful _____.") Inf **NY96,** In the lumber woods—"He's an awful rigging"].

rigging slinger n

In logging: see quots.

1940 Writers' Program *Oregon* 369, Out in the timber a chokerman places a heavy wire slip-loop, or choker, around a log and a rigging-slinger attaches this loop to the main cable. **1942** *AmSp* 17.223 [Loggers' talk], *Rigging slinger.* The assistant supervisor of a *side* in high-lead operation; the man who attaches the chokers to the main yarding line. **1966–67** *DARE* Tape **MT4,** I worked some in . . logging camps on the [Pacific] coast. . . They used steam donkeys then, and had . . usually three chokermen, a rigging slinger, and a hook tender. . . The hook tender, he was—in a way he was a foreman. Chokermen and what they call the rigging slinger, they would clear out and get ready to hook the cables onto the logs. . . The rigging slinger was really the foreman; he'd supervise the work in the woods; **OR**1, [FW:] What occupations fit in under someone working in the woods? . . [Inf:] Well, there's the timber-faller, bull buck, . . choke setters, rigging slingers, . . skid cap drivers. **2001** *DARE* File—Internet, [Job description from national on-line employment agency:] *Rigging Slinger* (Logging). . . Directs *Choke Setters* (logging) in high lead, slack line, or similar log yarding system. Determines sequence of logs to be yarded, according to guidelines established by *Hook Tender* (logging), issues directions to crew regarding logs to be yarded, positioning and securing logs to be yarded, positioning and securing of chokers, and position of crew during movement of logs.

right adv, n, adj Usu |raɪt|; also **esp Sth, S Midl** |rat, ræt, rɑt| Pronc-spp *rat(e), reight, ret*

A Forms.

1899 (1912) Green *VA Folk-Speech* 350, *Reight. . .* For right. **1919** *DN* 5.40 **VA,** *Right. . .* (pronounced ri-eet). This word is used "right much" in the James River country. **1930** in 1944 *ADD* **sNH,** *Right. . .* 'Come in the house rate away.' Rural. **1937** *AmSp* 12.287 **wVA,** *Right . .* [rat]. **c1937** in 1976 *Weevils in the Wheat* 108 **VA** [Black], Got a brother libin'] ret on dis here street. **1941** *AmSp* 16.7 **eTX** [Black], In *right,* [ra:t] and [ræ:t] are typical, but [rart] also occurs. **1942** Hall *Smoky Mt. Speech* 43 **wNC, eTN,** Typical . . *right* [ra·t]. **1964** Jackman–Long *OR Desert* 102, Anyone who got in the cook's way heard about it "rat now." **1967** *DARE* FW Addit **TN,** Common use of "right" [ra:t] as a mildly emphatic form: "right good," "right tired," etc. **1988** Lincoln *Avenue* 202 **wNC** (as of c1940) [Black], Rat nice-lookin' ol' mule you ridin' on. **1990** Amory *Cat & Curmudgeon* 192 **eTX,** He's in the barn with it rat now.

B As adv.

Very; quite. **chiefly Sth, S Midl** See Map on p. 580

1837 Sherwood *Gaz.* **GA** 71, *Right good,* for very good. **1844** (1885) Green *Memoir Otey* 29 **VA,** I had had enough of the romance of a soldier's mode of life to make me right glad . . to find myself in comfortable quarters. **1854** in 1983 *PADS* 70.48 **ce,sePA,** Raind in the afternoon right smart. **1857** (1930) DeLong *Jrls.* 9.145 **NY,** I wanted to go myself right bad. **1871** Eggleston *Hoosier Schoolmaster* 39 **sIN,** Mar-

ried a right rich girl. **1887** (1967) Harris *Free Joe* 67 **GA,** Well, I'm able to get about right lively. **1902** *DN* 2.243 **sIL,** *Right sharply, right smartly.* **1903** *DN* 2.327 **seMO,** *Right. . .* Quite. 'I am not right sure.' 'It's a right warm day!' **1904** *DN* 2.420 **nwAR,** I'm right glad to see you. **1906** *DN* 3.153 **nwAR,** *Right smart. . .* Very clever. **1907** *DN* 3.225 **nwAR.** **1908** Fox *Lonesome Pine* 110 **KY,** She riz up in bed with her eyes right wide. **1909** *DN* 3.363 **eAL, wGA,** He is right much worried over it. **1919** *DN* 5.40 **VA,** *Right. . .* Two phrases are dear to the heart of the Virginian: "Right much," and "right many." In the hills one hears "right regular." **1923** *DN* 5.219 **swMO.** **1926** *AmSp* 1.408 **Okefenokee GA.** **1936** *AmSp* 11.369 **nLA,** It rained right sharp today. **1938** Rawlings *Yearling* 29 **nFL,** We stand a right good chancet o' comin' up with that bear today. **1941** *LANE* Map 426 (*I'm mighty glad to see you*) 1 inf, **sVT,** *Right,* older term. *Ibid* Map 461 (*Lively, spry*) 1 inf, **sRI,** She's right peart; 1 inf, **eMA,** Right peart—only in jest; 1 inf, **cVT,** Right up-and-coming. **1943** *Ibid* Map 716 (*Awfully cold*) 2 infs, **cRI, csMA,** Right. **1956** Algren *Walk on the Wild Side* 12 **wTX,** You right sure that boy got everything he's supposed to have? **1956** McAtee *Some Dialect NC* 36. **1960** Lee *Mockingbird* 81 **sAL,** Mr. Avery'll be in bed for a week—he's right stove up. **1964** in 1982 *Barrick Coll.* **csPA,** *Right—rather*—"She seemd [sic] right jolly last night."[*] **1965–70** *DARE* (Qu. LL35, *Words used to make a statement stronger:* "This cake tastes _____ good.") 35 Infs, **Sth, S Midl,** Right; (Qu. GG29, *To be in a good or pleasant mood:* "This morning he seems to be feeling _____.") 25 Infs, **chiefly Sth, S Midl,** Right good; **WV4,** Right chipper; **IN60,** Right pert; **ID2,** Right smart; **NJ20,** Right well; (Qu. A13, *When something needs to be done immediately . .* "I'll do it _____!") 9 Infs, **scattered Sth, S Midl,** Right quick; **VA13,** Right straight; (Qu. KK27, *A very lively, active old person:* "For his age, he's _____.") Infs **IN40, NY23, SC32, 54, TX4,** Right spry; **SC31, 39, 45,** Right pert; **SC21, 31,** Right active; **TX1, WV4,** Right peart; **OK58,** Right lively; (Qu. A23, *To do something at the very first try:* "He got the right answer _____.") Inf **KY84,** Right quick; (Qu. B1, *If a day is very pleasant . . it's a _____ day*) Infs **PA233, SC9, TN66,** Right nice; **FL29,** Right fitting; **VA42,** Right pretty; (Qu. B2, *If the weather is very unpleasant . . it's a _____ day*) Inf **FL29,** Right nasty; (Qu. B6, *When clouds begin to increase . . it's _____*) Inf **LA3,** Getting right dark; (Qu. L5, *When a farmer gets help on a job from his neighbors . . you call it _____*) Inf **OH45,** Being right neighborly; (Qu. U38a, *Words referring to a great deal of money:* "He's . . _____") Inf **TN65,** Right wealthy; (Qu. W28, *When a woman is in a hurry and has to sew up a torn place quickly . .* "I'll just _____.") Inf **AR47,** Mend this up right quick; (Qu. X52, *. . A person . . who had been sick was looking _____*) Inf **IN32,** Right bad; (Qu. BB38, *When a person doesn't look healthy, or looks as if he hadn't been well for some time . .* "He looks _____.") Infs **AZ2, IN32,** Right puny; (Qu. BB47, *Feeling in the best of health and spirits:* "I'm feeling _____!") Inf **CA199,** Right good; (Qu. DD33a) Inf **MD13,** Right sensible person; (Qu. FF17, *. . A very good or enjoyable time:* "We all had a _____ last night.") Inf **IN32,** Right good time; (Qu. GG16, *. . Finding fault, or complaining:* "You just can't please him—he's always _____.") Inf **IA30,** Plain right onery; (Qu. GG19b, *When you can see from the way a person acts that he's feeling important or independent:* "He seems to think he's _____.") Inf **NM9,** Right important; (Qu. GG26, *A feeling of weakness from fear*) Inf **TN6,** Felt right droopy; (Qu. GG41, *To lose patience easily*) Inf **TN6,** Flies off the handle right quick; (Qu. HH5, *Someone who is queer but harmless*) Inf **MS56,** Not right bright; (Qu. HH13, *Expressions meaning that a person is not very alert or not aware of things:* "He's certainly _____.") Inf **WV16,** Not right bright; (Qu. HH16, *Uncomplimentary words with no definite meaning—just used when you want to show that you don't think much of a person*) Inf **TN26,** Not right bright nohow; (Qu. HH36, *A careless, slovenly woman*) Inf **TN14,** Right sorry dressed; (Qu. II3, *Expressions to say that people are very friendly toward each other:* "They're _____.") Infs **ME19, MO8,** Right good friends; **IN32,** Right friendly; (Qu. II11b, *If two people can't bear each other at all . .* "Those two are _____.") Inf **GA6,** Right unfriendly; (Qu. KK1a, *. . Very good—for example, food:* "That pie was _____.") Infs **IN32, MS88, NC23, VA50,** Right good; **IN32,** Right fitting; **LA17,** Right tasty; (Qu. KK40, *. . 'Usually':* "They come twice a month, _____.") Inf **LA17,** Right regularly; (Qu. LL28, *. . Entirely full:* "The box of apples was _____.") Inf **UT3,** Right full; **NC72,** Right much full; (Qu. MM25, *. . A long distance:* "Texas is a _____ [from here].") Infs **KY33, 41, 60,** Right smart piece; **DE1,** Right far piece. **1966–68** *DARE* Tape **GA7,** All you have to do is mash that bottle right quick; **GA30,** [**GA31:**] You ever seen a right young bear? **MI35,** Not right recently; **TX1,** The main thing, to win the game right quick, was to knock that big one out. **1994** NC

Lang. & Life Project *Harkers Is. Vocab.* 9 **eNC**, She's a right smart worker.

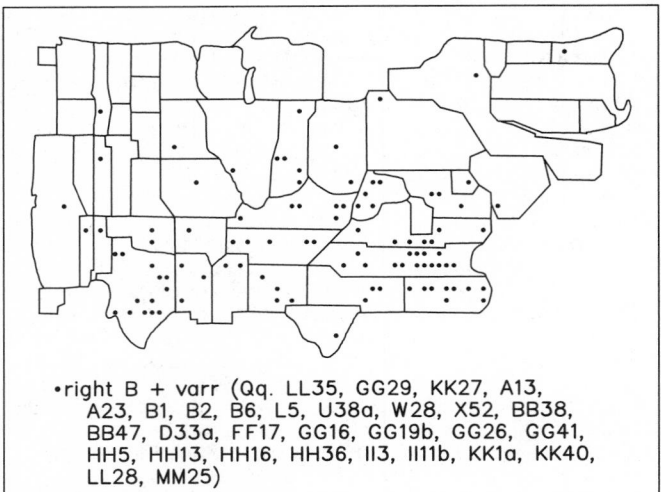

•right B + varr (Qq. LL35, GG29, KK27, A13, A23, B1, B2, B6, L5, U38a, W28, X52, BB38, BB47, D33a, FF17, GG16, GG19b, GG26, GG41, HH5, HH13, HH16, HH36, II3, II11b, KK1a, KK40, LL28, MM25)

C As noun.
A responsibility, obligation.
1933 *AmSp* 8.3.78 **cePA**, At Allentown, Pennsylvania, I have heard the substitution of *have a right to* for *should*. Instances are "I waited an hour for you. You had a right to tell me you would be late." "Willie fell into the pond. I had a right to tell him not to but forgot." **1934** *AmSp* 9.317, The expression *have a right to,* used in the sense of 'should'. . . I have known the expression for at least ten years, learning it from a Colorado friend who had it from her mother, a resident of Illinois. It was always employed to express a strong sense of obligation or admonition.

D As adj.
True, genuine.   Cf **own** adj **1** Note: Exx of this sense as a literary archaism are not illustrated here.
1903 *DN* 2.352, *Right*. . . Own, in expression 'a right brother,' a brother by blood. **1934** Hurston *Jonah's Gourd Vine* 151 **AL** [Black], Lawd, An' Pheemy, Ah got somethin' in mah heart ain't got no name. Ah layin' here right now tryin' tuh find some words for feelin's. Look lak mah right heart ain't beatin' no mo'.

right and left n
1909 *DN* 3.363 **eAL, wGA**, *Rights and lefts*. . . Fruit patties with the dough on both sides, a sort of fruit doughnut.

right-down adv phr, adj phr [*OED2* 1623 →; cf Intro "Language Changes" I.1] **chiefly Sth, S Midl**
Very, truly; genuine, downright.
1828 Royall *Black Book* 2.114 **VA**, He was one of your right down flat-footed ox-drivers. **1832** Trollope *Domestic Manners* (NY) 296, Why, that's right down true. **1843** (1916) Hall *New Purchase* 310 **IN**, But, strangers, you'll find things right down poor here, and have to sleep on the floor. **1851** Burke *Polly Peablossom* 99 **GA**, Now, Judge, you ain't in right down good yearnest, is you? **c1856** in 1993 *DARE* File **VA**, I can not pick up anything worth telling and it is right down drudgery to have to write nothing. **1884** Baldwin *Yankee School-Teacher* 130 **VA**, A right-down sensible person! **1898** Harris *Tales Home Folks* 269, That's a right down pretty baby. **1899** (1912) Green *VA Folk-Speech* 353, *Right-down*. . . Very. "Right-down cold." **1909** *DN* 3.363 **eAL, wGA**, *Right down, adv.* Downright. **1968–70** *DARE* (Qu. Y12b, *A real fight in which blows are struck*) Inf **TX103**, Right-down hard fight; (Qu. GG40, *Words or expressions meaning violently angry*) Inf **NY68**, Right-down terribly mad; (Qu. KK50, *When something is planned out carefully, down to the last detail: "He had it all worked out _____."*) Inf **CA107**, Right-down pat. **1984** Wilder *You All Spoken Here* 194 **Sth**, *Right down:* Downright; very, as in "Talk about nuclear waste disposal is right down serious, I tell you." **2000** *NADS Letters* **sNEng**, The other day, for no reason, I found myself saying "right down" in the sense of "definitely", "to a high degree", in other words, for emphasis. I realized that I had not used it for some time, but I used to hear it when I was a child. That would have been in the 30's in Connecticut or Massachusetts.

right-foot adj, n See **right-handed 1**

right-hand adj
1 See **right-handed 2.**
2 Of a person: born of parents who are married; legitimate. [Cf *OED2* *right-handed* a. 2 "of the right kind"]
1908 Day *King Spruce* 305 **ME**, "Have you any idea what 'Stumpage John' is goin' to do with the other one—the left-hand one [=a child born out of wedlock]?" he inquired, blandly. "Favor each other considerably, don't they? It told the story to me the first time I saw them together, after the right-hand one got there to my place. You can't hardly blame John for not takin' the left-hand one out with him."

right-handed adj
1 also *right-foot*: Roman Catholic; hence nouns *right-foot, right-hander* a Roman Catholic.   Cf **left-hander**
1935 *AmSp* 10.314 **NY**, 'You say that he is an Irishman?' 'Yes.' 'Is he right-handed?' 'Well, he doesn't go to Mass every Sunday but he's right-handed all right.' . . *Right-handed* obviously means 'a good Catholic.' This use is common along the Southern Tier of New York State. **1950** *WELS (Nicknames for different religions)* 1 Inf, **seWI**, Right-handers (Catholics). **1960** Wentworth–Flexner *Slang* 428, *Right-foot* [derog.] *adj.* Roman Catholic. *n.* A Roman Catholic. . . *Right-handed* [derog.] = *right-foot.*
2 also *right-hand*: Used in var combs to refer to a nonexistent item used as the basis of a practical joke.
1966–70 *DARE* (Qu. HH14, *Ways of teasing a beginner or inexperienced person—for example, by sending him for a 'left-handed monkey wrench': "Go get me _____."*) Infs **CT3, FL52, KS18**, Right-handed hammer; **LA37, MD40, PA39**, Right-handed screwdriver; **OK18**, Right-hand screwdriver; **LA8**, Right-handed crescent wrench; **NY27**, Right-handed shovel; **SC21**, Right-handed umbrella.

right-hander See **right-handed 1**

right hand-running adv phr
=**hand running 1.**
1896 *DN* 1.423 **IA, IL**, *Right-hand-running:* for *hand-running.* **1954** *Harder Coll.* **cwTN**, *Right hand-running* . . in succession. " 'Em squirrels went up 'at tree right hand-runnin.' "

rightify v Cf **-ify**
To rectify; to correct.
1916 *DN* 4.292 **sAppalachians**, With the suffix . . *-ify,* we have: *rightify (rectify).* **1953** Randolph–Wilson *Down in Holler* 45 **Ozarks**, I have heard a schoolmarm speak of term papers as being *rectified* when she meant corrected, and the word *rightify* is sometimes used in the same meaning.

right now adv phr **chiefly Sth, S Midl**
Used without ref to the immediate present: instantly; then and there; at that time.
1895 [see **pone** n **3a**]. **1929** Dobie *Vaquero* 10 **TX**, Jack came up from the spring with a bucket of cold water and dashed it on him. The cold water brought George to right now. **1930** Stoney–Shelby *Black Genesis* 190 **seSC**, Br' Rabbit straighten up he face right now. **1938** Rawlings *Yearling* 150 **nFL**, Hit's like not to do no good. A man dies right now, bit in the arm. **1951** *WELS Suppl.* **AK**, "Yesterday I told him to do it, and he did right now". . . Reported by a student as heard in use in Kodiak, Alaska. **1956** [see **papermouth**]. **1957** *Sat. Eve. Post Letters* **ceIL**, About local terms. . . Another is the usage of 'right now', used in place of 'immediately' or 'suddenly'. Such as, 'He went to the hospital and died right now'. This is very common here. **1966–70** *DARE* Tape **GA30**, [I've] saw ducks fly up and start down these runs. . . And I've saw them kites come . . from out of the bushes . . and pick 'em up before you can say scat, and catch 'em right now; **OH32**, Dad just took the towel he had on and wiped the lather off of the other side of his face, and out of there we went right now; **SC17**, You know tobacco is a quick thing. When it do come, it makes right now; **VA96**, You'd go out to spray them and it will just kill them right now. **1969** *DARE* FW Addit **KY48**, That cow got sick right now. [FW: Inf was referring to an event several years past; usage is common, also heard used by other local residents.] **1975** Newell *If Nothin' Don't Happen* 121 **FL**, Uncle Wint said he didn't have a gun with him—which is hard for me to believe—and he had to do something right now because the dogs was

gettin' cut up. **1986** Pederson *LAGS Concordance,* 1 inf, **cnTX,** (He) died right now; 1 inf, **nwMS,** He cooled his fever right now; 1 inf, **cwTN,** It killed her [=a cow poisoned by a farmer] right now. **1988** Lincoln *Avenue* 172 **wNC** (as of c1940) [Black], But he don't make no move to git in the truck an' go rat now.

right on *adv phr* **chiefly Sth**
Anyway, nevertheless, just the same.

1928 Fisher *Walls Jericho* 304 **NYC** [Black], *Right on*—Nevertheless. **1929** Gordon *Born to Be* 20 [Black], Before Maude came, a round of drinks cost a dollar anywhere on the line, no matter if you were alone or ten, a dollar right on. **1960** Williams *Walk Egypt* 15 **GA,** I had me a robin pie last night. They et all my pink camellia buds, but they taste brown right on. *Ibid* 42, It was her fault, her fault right on! **1966** *DARE* [(Qu. X26a, *If a person's eyes look in different directions, looking inward, he's* _____) Inf **FL26,** Cross-eyed;] (Qu. X26b, *If a person's eyes look in different directions, looking outward, he's* _____) Inf **FL26,** Cross-eyed right on. **1979** *NC Folkl. Jrl.* 27.57 **cNC** [Black], Well, I made baskets from that time till you get ready to go pickin' cotton and harvestin' the stuff. We'd make a few right on, but most of the time we didn't make no more till we got through gatherin'. **1986** Pederson *LAGS Concordance,* 1 inf, **cGA,** They're all pigs right on; 1 inf, **ceGA,** I'd say "shrimp" right on; 1 inf, **seGA,** She'd lay eggs right on; 1 inf, **swGA,** Made with meal right on = just the same; 1 inf, **neGA,** Call them relatives right on—close or distant; 1 inf, **csGA,** Corn bread right on = nevertheless; 1 inf, **neGA,** It's liquor right on = nevertheless; 1 inf, **seGA,** Corn bread right on = still called corn bread; 1 inf, **neGA,** It's a water bucket right on = regardless; 1 inf, **seGA,** A little dumb right on = still seems stupid; 1 inf, **neFL,** It would be a kerosene lamp right on; 1 inf, **cnFL,** It would be a road right on = all the same; 1 inf, **cnFL,** We lived on the farm right on; 1 inf, **nwFL,** I might think of it as a gully right on; 1 inf, **neFL,** We call them turtles right on; 1 inf, **csLA,** I got a pair of ox, right on; 2 infs, **cwLA,** It was corn bread right on (= nevertheless); 1 inf, **cwLA,** I call him Scotty right on = I still call him Scotty; 1 inf, **ceLA,** Feed him right on = nevertheless; 1 inf, **neAL,** Well, they're still peanuts right on; 1 inf, **cAL,** Well, that's nicker right on = it's still nicker; 1 inf, **nwMS,** We had several right on = nevertheless; 1 inf, **cMS,** But it's a cemetery right on—i.e. nevertheless. [*DARE* Ed: 22 infs—13 GA, 3 MS, 2 FL, 2 AL, 2 LA—gave a contextless response, *right on,* which was glossed as "nevertheless," "still," "yet," "just the same," or "in any case."]

right smart *adj phr* **chiefly Sth, S Midl**

1 Usu of a measure or quantity: great, considerable; quite a. **[right B + smart]** Cf **chance B1, 3**

1843 (1916) Hall *New Purchase* 92 **IN,** She . . pulled off what she called a "right smart chance of rattles." **1871** Eggleston *Hoosier Schoolmaster* 28 **sIN,** He's got a right smart lot of this world's plunder. **1884** *Anglia* 7.274 **Sth, S Midl** [Black], *Er right smart w'ile* = a good while. **1892** [see **right smart** *n* 1] **1895** *DN* 1.374 **seKY, eTN, wNC,** I got a right smart little bit of roughness in the beastis. **1905** *DN* 3.92 **nwAR,** *Right smart.* . . Great, large, long. 'You gave me a right smart smidgin.' 'It's a right smart piece.' 'He's got a right smart bit of land.' 'I'm in a right smart hurry' is not so usual as 'I'm in a right smart of a hurry.' **1912** *DN* 3.587 **wIN,** *Right smart heap.* . . A good quantity. "There's a right smart heap of hay in the mow yet." **1927** *AmSp* 2.363 **cwWV,** *Right smart spell* . . for a long time. "Aunt Alice has been ailing for a right smart spell." **1941** *AmSp* 16.24 **sIN,** *Right smart.* 'It's a right smart piece over to his place.' **1943** *AmSp* 18.67 [IN sayings used elsewhere], *Right smart* (as in 'a right smart piece to town'). S.C., N.C., Ala., Ky., Tenn., Miss., La. **1944** *PADS* 2.12 **Sth,** *Smart, right.* . . Long, large, extensive. "It's a right smart distance to town." **1952** Brown *NC Folkl.* 1.585, *Right smart, a.* . . A good deal, a great many; quite. "He has a right smart money." [sic] "It's a right smart distance to White Plains."—General. Mainly illiterate. **1956** *DE Folkl. Bulletin* 1.24, I had a right smart time gettin' the consent of my mind to come down this-a-way! **1962** Fox *Southern Fried* 147 **SC,** I'm in the wholesale corn whisky business and . . we've been doing a right smart business up here. **1967–69** *DARE* (Qu. MM25, . . *A long distance: "Texas is a* _____ *[from here]."*) Infs **KY**33, 41, 47, 60, Right smart piece. **1967** *DARE* Tape **AL**15, You'd go to town and you'd have your right smart little bit of money and you'd think, "Well, I'm just gonna buy something." **1976** Garber *Mountain-ese* 75 **sAppalachians,** There's a right-smart pile uv corn left in the crib.

2 Much, many; a lot of.

1899 (1912) Green *VA Folk-Speech* 396, *Smart.* . . *Right smart;* much;

many; a great deal. "There were right smart people at the church." **1914** *DN* 4.160 **cVA,** *Right smart.* . . Very much, very. "Giv [sic] me right smart gravy; Ah'm r[ight] s[mart] hahngry." **1954** Tolbert *Bigamy Jones* 2 **wTX** (as of 1870s), He never got married unless he was on a holiday. "That cowboy took right smart holidays, though," said Grandfather Renfro. *Ibid* 12, Right smart work is piling up for me at Hell-to-Catch when I get off this marrying holiday. **1965** *Dict. Queen's English* 16 **NC,** *Right smart:* A considerable amount. . . He has right smart money. **1965** *DARE* FW Addit **OK**7, "It made right smart hay." Expression common among people from Arkansas, according to Cushing Informant. **1976** Ryland *Richmond Co. VA* 377, *Smart*—right smart means "many."

right smart *adv phr* Rarely *right smartly* **chiefly Sth, S Midl**

1 To a considerable degree, very much, a lot. Cf **right smart** *n* 1

1859 in 1956 Eliason *Tarheel Talk* 290 **neNC,** Andrew is able to help me right smart. **1905** *DN* 3.92 **nwAR,** *Right smartly.* . . Greatly. 'He was right smartly excited.' **1908** Fox *Lonesome Pine* 30 **KY,** Uncle Billy used to drink right smart. **1921** Haswell *Daughter Ozarks* 18 (as of 1880s), I hev travelled around right smart myself. **1938** FWP *Guide DE* 500, Hit favors rain right smart. **1966–67** *DARE* Tape **GA**1, It smell right smart like a skunk; **TN**16, [FW:] Have you done much butchering? [Inf:] Yeah, right smart, done a lot of butchering in my life. **1967** *DARE* (Qu. EE21b, *When boys were fighting very actively . . "For a while those fellows really* _____.") Inf **SC**46, Fighting right smart. **1967–68** *DARE* FW Addit **GA**34, I fish right smart; **swNC,** You've talked to me right smart; **TN**16, That's used right smart. **1985** *Amer. Jrl. Med.* Feb 183 **eTN,** *Right smart* . . a lot; very much—"It hurts right smart."

2 modifying an adj: Very, quite.

1858 Hammett *Piney Woods Tavern* 138 **TX,** Dog-on-my-cat! ef I aint a grown right smartly worn out with the story. **1913** (1941) Burgess *Mother West Wind's Neighbors* 37, Yes, Suh, Ah reckon Ah'm right smart old. **1914** [see **right smart** *adj phr* 2] **1938** Rawlings *Yearling* 54 **nFL,** Howdy, sir. I'm right smart tol'able. **1942** Footner *MD Main* 8, In Baltimore . . the superlative degree good or bad is indicated by "right smart." **1967** *DARE* Tape **TN**16, [FW:] They taste something like bacon? . . [Inf:] No, no, it's right smart different from bacon. **1969** *DARE* FW Addit **cKY,** That tastes right smart good.

right smart *n* [Prob abbr for *right smart chance* and similar phrr; see **right smart** *adj phr* 1 and **chance B1, 3** and cf **considerable** *n*]

1 A great deal; a considerable amount, a lot; rarely, a considerable distance; hence *adv phr a right smart* considerably; quite a bit. **chiefly Sth, S Midl**

1842 Buckingham *Slave States* 2.327, I asked here, whether people made much maple-sugar in this neighbourhood; when the gentlemen . . answered, 'Yes, they do, I reckon, right smart.' **1846** in 1956 Eliason *Tarheel Talk* 290 **ce,neNC,** She has got a right smart of the wherewithal. **1859** *Ibid* 290 **cNC,** Idont git as much [milling] as ican do but git right Smart. **1892** Eggleston *Hoosier Schoolmaster* 71 **IN,** [Footnote:] No phrase of the Hoosier and Southwestern dialect is such a stumbling-block to the outsider as *right smart*. The writer from the North or East will generally use it wrongly. Mrs. Stowe says, "I sold right smart of eggs," but the Hoosier woman as I knew her would have said "a right smart lot of eggs" or "a right smart of eggs," using the article and understanding the noun. A farmer omitting the preposition boasts of having "raised right smart corn" this year. No expression could have a more vague sense than this. **1895** *DN* 1.372 **seKY, eTN, wNC,** There's a right smart of hardness between them two boys. **1902** *DN* 2.243 **sIL,** *Right smart.* . . A great deal, or great quantity. **1903** *DN* 2.327 **seMO,** *Right smart.* . . He raises a right smart of cotton. **1905** *DN* 3.92 **nwAR,** 'He's suffering a right smart.' 'We had a right smart of rain last spring,' Very common. **1906** *DN* 3.123 **sIN,** *Right smart.* . . A great deal. **1908** *DN* 3.297 **eAL, wGA,** *Right smart (chance).* . . A considerable amount. "He's got a right smart (chanst) of cotton." **1908** *German Amer. Annals* 10.41 **sePA,** *Right smart.* Many. "Were many there?" "Yes, right smart." **1909** *DN* 3.363 **eAL, wGA,** He was a right smart hurt. **1910** *DN* 3.457 **KY,** *Right smart of.* . . Considerable quantity or distance. "It's a right smart of a distance to London." "Yes, we raise a right smart of corn in the mountains." **1923** *DN* 5.219 **swMO,** *Right smart,* A great deal, a large amount. Not used with reference to a large number of individual things or objects. 'A right smart of rain or of dry weather or of money or of grain, etc.,' but not 'a right smart of horses,' etc. **1939** *Hall Coll.* **cwNC,** He has a right smart of an age on him. **1940** Faulkner *Hamlet* 20 **MS,** He's setting at breakfast with a right smart of his eyebrows and hair both swinged off. **1952** Giles *40 Acres* 52 **KY,** We could sell it for a right smart. **1966–68** *DARE* (Qu. LL8a, *A large amount or number: More than enough . . "He's got _____ of time.")* Inf **DC**8, Right smart; (Qu. LL9a, *As much as you need or more . . "We've got _____ of apples.")* Inf **LA**17, Right smart; **NY**22, A right smart of apples—that's down South. **1966–70** *DARE* Tape **AR**15, I used to hunt a right smart, then I quit for thirty-three years; **GA**48, We always had a right smart of poles; **KY**56, In this neighborhood they're using gas a right smart; **MS**61, I think it had been pranked with a right smart; **NC**65, It's right smart of a job to learn fishing; **TN**51, I think it has learnt you a right smart of devilment. **1968** *DARE* FW Addit **ceWV,** *Right smart* is used to refer to distance and quantity: "It's a right smart from here." "I've drank a right smart of it." **1995** *Signal Mag.* Dec np **cwTX,** *Right smart*—"They've got right smart of money." A lot.

2 A superior example or specimen.
    1893 Shands *MS Speech* 53, *Right smart. . .* In Mississippi it also means *worthy of consideration;* as, "He is right smart of a man"; i.e. a man who possesses considerable excellence in some line. The expression frequently occurs in *right smart chance.* **1942** Perry *Texas* 135, In the old days when a boastful cowboy moved to a new community and wanted to give himself an all-inclusive recommendation, he would, in less delicate terms, declare that he was: a fornicator, a fighter, a wild horse rider, and right smart of a windmill fixer. **1966** *DARE* Tape **AR**15, I can tell you, if you wanna find out something about fishermen, now, a fellow named Manny. . . he's right smart of a fisherman.

right smartly See **right smart** adv phr

rigid adj [Perh var of *frigid;* but cf *OED2* rigid a. A.2 "Of cold, etc.: Severe, hard, rigorous. *rare.*"; 1611–1726]
    1957 Beck *Folkl. ME* 85, In the winter, too, when it was too "rigid" outside, odds and ends of chores would be done that had waited all summer for time to do them.

rigilar See **regular**

rigiment, rigimint See **regiment**

rig(i)nal See **original**

rignum n [See quot 1821]
    A **horsemint 1** (here: *Monarda punctata*).
    1821 Elliott *Sketch* 1.30 **SC, GA,** *[Monarda] punctata. . . Dotted Monarda. Origanum falsely, and corruptly Rignum.* **1900** Lyons *Plant Names* 251, Horsemint, American Origanum, Rignum.

rigor n Also *the rigors* [*OED2* c1400 →] **esp Gulf States, TX** See Map
    A chill; a shiver, tremor, or shake.
    1806 (1970) Webster *Compendious Dict.* 259, *Rigor. . .* A shivering with cold. [*DARE* Ed: This entry does not appear in Webster's English model.] **1857** *Living Age* 55.78 **PA,** The tumultuous form of nervous action which constitutes a rigor, conveys to those who are the subjects of it, the sensation as of a sudden abstraction of heat. **1905** *DN* 3.92 **nwAR,** *Rigor, . . rigors. . .* A malarial chill which causes the sufferer to shake violently. 'I had a hard rigor yesterday.' 'These rigors are about getting me down.' **1909** *DN* 3.363 **eAL, wGA,** *Rigor. . .* A slight chill, a mild shaking as from malaria. **1965–70** *DARE* (Qu. BB13, *. . Chills and fever*) Infs **AL**8, 30, **NC**33, **TX**32, 37, 71, 74, 86, 98, The rigors; **MS**1, **TX**42, Rigors; **CA**127, The rigors—a back-East word; **TN**27, The rigors—for chills; **MS**51, Rigors; hard rigor; (Qu. P36, *When a hunter sees a deer or other game animal and gets so excited he can't shoot, he has _____*) Infs **MS**21, **TX**32, Rigors; (Qu. DD22, *. . Delirium tremens*) Inf **TN**24, The rigors [FW: This does not seem to be a synonym; Inf used it to describe tremens]. **1984** *Annals Internal Med.* 100.899 **wAL,** A *nervous rigor* may be confused with a chill but is characterized by the patient alternately tensing and relaxing the muscles over the body, shivering, and the absence of fever; it is a type of anxiety attack. **1986** Pederson *LAGS Concordance (Caught a cold)* 1 inf, **csAR,** Took a rigor—involves shaking. **1990** Cavender *Folk Med. Lexicon* 30 **sAppalachians,** *Rigors*—[Cavender: sometimes pronounced "rygors"] a chill accompanied by mild trembling; commonly used as "the rigors." **1993** Mason *Feather Crowns* 298 **KY,** Christie watched

from the window. . . A rigor ran up her spine, turned and dived into her stomach. . . Her heart beat fast.

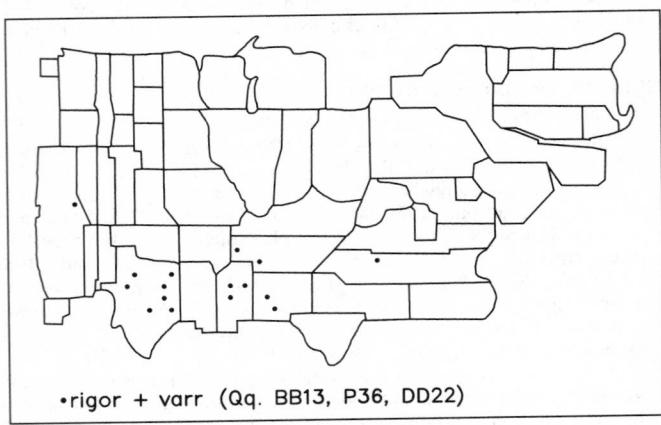

•rigor + varr (Qq. BB13, P36, DD22)

rig-out n [*rig out* to clothe] *old-fash*
    A suit of clothes; an outfit.
    1857 Thompson *Gaut Gurley* 130 **NEng,** "Tomah himself! But what a rig-out! Wife, look here." . . [H]er eyes were greeted with the appearance of a smart-looking and jauntily-equipped young Indian, mounted on the back of a stately, antlered moose. **1899** (1912) Green *VA Folk-Speech* 354, *Rig-out. . .* A rig; an outfit; a suit of clothes; a costume. **1902** (1904) Rowe *Maid of Bar Harbor* 167 **ME,** I hain't no lady, an' I hain't got nobody ter buy me a lady's rigout. **1920** Hunter *Trail Drivers TX* 482, Our way back home was paid by those who employed us. We came back as immigrants, all dressed up in new suit, boots and hat, the rig-out costing about $30. **1929** Suckow *Cora* 158 **IA,** That's quite a rig-out he's got on!

rijiment See **regiment**

‡**rildy** n [Etym unknown]
    1933 *AmSp* 8.1.31 **nwTX** [Ranch diction], *Rildy.* Patch-work quilt, *one your mother made you when you left home.*

riley adj Also sp *rily, ryley* Cf Pronc Intro 3.I.11, **hoist** n, v
1 also *roily;* Of liquids, chiefly water: turbid, muddy; agitated. **Nth, N Midl, West** See Map
    1805 (1965) Ordway *Jrls.* 240, [The water was] verry riley and bad tasted. **1814** in 1947 *AmSp* 22.274, Riley for turbid. **1823** Cooper *Pioneers* 2.14 **NY,** For fear you [=maple sap] should get roily. **1825** Neal *Brother Jonathan* 1.369 **CT,** I swallered pooty nigh a gallon o' ryley water, I guess—right out o' the spring. **1859** (1931) Tuttle *CA Diary* 15.79 **WI,** The water [of the Platte River] is very roily though it tastes very well. **1880** *Scribner's Mth.* 20.484 **NY,** If the water is very roily or brackish. **1905** *DN* 3.17 **cCT,** *Rily. . .* Turbid. **1907** *DN* 3.198 **seNH,** *Rily. . .* Full of sediment. . . "This water is awful rily." **1910** *DN* 3.447 **cwNY,** *Rily. . .* Full of sediment. "How rily the water is!" **1913** (1980) Hardy *OH Schoolmistress* 100, *Riley* was used to mean muddy—of course from *roil.* **1949** in 1986 *DARE* File **MI,** The water is too riley for washing this week. **1960** *VT Hist.* 28.207, If you keep stirring a mud puddle, it will always be riley. **1965–70** *DARE* (Qu. KK39, *Stirred*

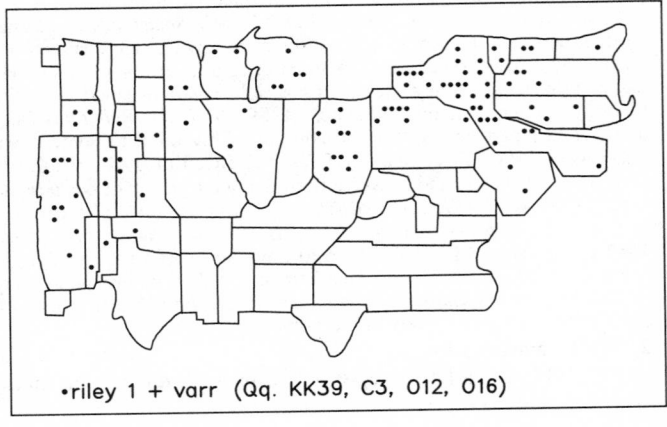

•riley 1 + varr (Qq. KK39, C3, O12, O16)

up, upset: "Because of the storm, the pond was all _____.") 74 Infs, **Nth, N Midl, West,** Riley; 25 Infs, **scattered Nth, N Midl, West,** Roily; (Qu. C3, *A place in a swift stream where the surface of the water is broken*) Inf **CA211,** Roily; (Qu. O12, *A disturbance caused by wind which seems to run and spread quickly along the surface of water*) Inf **NY155,** Riley waves; (Qu. O16, . . *The stirred-up water following a boat*) Inf **CT13,** Roily water.
2 Angry, irritated.
a1824 (1937) Guild *Jrl.* 3.256 **VT,** This made the old man some ryly. **1847** (1962) Robb *Squatter Life* 64 **MO,** The boys and gals kept it up so strong, laffin at my scrape, and the pickle I wur in, that I gin to git riley. **1858** Hammett *Piney Woods Tavern* 101, I guess tain't every day you see a chap so riley as the young man was. **1898** Dunbar *Folks from Dixie* 85, Won't she be riley when she fin's out how mistaken she is? **1941** *LANE* Map 472 *(Angry)* 3 infs, **ME, NH,** Rily. **1967** *DARE* (Qu. K16, *A cow with a bad temper*) Inf **OR10,** Riley.

rill See **real** adj, adv

rillscale n
An **orach** (here: *Atriplex dioica*).
1950 Stevens *ND Plants* 131, *Atriplex dioica* . . Rillscale. Erect, slender, or bushy, rounded plant. **1973** Hitchcock–Cronquist *Flora Pacific NW* 95, Alkaline and badland regions; mostly e[astern] R[ocky] M[ountains], in our area in s[outh] c[entral] Mont[ana]; rillscale.

rilly See **really** adv, adj

rily See **riley**

rim v[1] [Engl dial var of *rime,* itself appar a doublet of *ream;* cf *OED2 rime* v.[4], *rimer* sb.[2], *EDD* **rim** v.[2]]
1 also with *out*: To ream out, enlarge (a hole); hence n *rimmer* a tool for doing this; a reamer.
1863 *Scientific Amer.* 9.330, Among these we noticed a very neat thing in the shape of an expanding rimer [sic]. . . [T]hrough the agency of a simple contrivance the rimmer is made to expand as it wears by use and sharpening. **1865** J.H.A. Bone *Petroleum & Petroleum Wells* 22 (*OED2* at *rimer* sb.[2]), But the hole must be as nearly round as possible, and therefore the tools are taken out, and a 'rimmer', or 'reamer', sent down. **1876** Knight *Amer. Mech. Dict.* 3.1887, *Reamer.* Sometimes, but incorrectly, written *rimmer.* A tool used to enlarge a hole. **1914** *DN* 4.156 **Cape Cod MA,** Rim out. . . To ream. "Rim out the hole a bit if the peg won't fit." **c1960** *Wilson Coll.* **csKY,** Ream: v. is often /rɪm/. **1998** *NADS Letters* **neSC,** As for rim out, my father still says that at 80 yrs. of age, . . to enlarge the hole. I don't remember his using a "rimmer." **1999** *Ibid* **wTX,** My Dad uses this term [=rim out] all the time. He is a retired Oil Field Welder and apparently they used the term in his field work.
2 To cheat, swindle, defraud; hence n *rimming.* [Cf *OED2 ream* v.[3] 4 1914 →]
1937 Sandoz *Slogum* 262 **NE,** And when the land office finally opened, word got around that all the good claims were gone. . . By now the homeseekers were certain they had been rimmed. **1945** V.J. Monteleone *Criminal Slang* 84 (*OED2*), Rim, . . to cheat; to swindle: to defraud. **1950** *WELS Suppl.* **cwWI,** Rimmed—being beaten at cards. **1967–68** *DARE* (Qu. LL22, *Less than you should get: "They'll try to give you _____ every time."*) Inf **OH1,** A rimming; (Qu. LL23, *Cheated, treated dishonestly: "These apples are wormy, I think you got _____."*) Inf **OH17,** Rimmed; **IA46, OH87,** A rimming. **1973** D. Hughes *Along Side Road* vii.54 (*OED2*), Ten bucks? For that old thing? I'd be rimming you, Charles. **1995** *Brophy Coll.* 63 **swMO** (as of c1960), Rim. [T]o cheat, to "job," to ream, "shave."

rim v[2] [Origin unknown; cf *OED2 brim* v.[1] 1 "Of swine: To be 'in heat', rut, copulate."]
See quots.
1923 *DN* 5.219 **swMO,** Rim, v. To be desirous of sexual intercourse, wanting to be bred. Said especially of sows. **1953** Randolph–Wilson *Down in Holler* 107 **Ozarks,** I have heard *rim* and *rimmin'* and *over-rim* used with reference to many females, including young girls. I am not sure just what these words mean, but they are not regarded with favor by respectable country women.

‡**rim** n Cf **kink, nibby** n[1]
1989 *DARE* File **cwAL,** As for the end pieces of a loaf of bread, we

have the terms *heel* and *end* used in Tuscaloosa and *rim* used in Butler, Alabama.

rim ash n [Presumably from its use in making wooden wheels] Cf **hoop ash 3**
A **hackberry** (here: *Celtis occidentalis*).
1900 Lyons *Plant Names* 89, [*Celtis*] *occidentalis*. . . Hoop Ash, Rim Ash. **1960** Vines *Trees SW* 206, Vernacular names are Nettle-tree . . Rim-ash, Hoop ash and One-berry. . . The wood is occasionally used commercially for fuel, furniture, veneer, and agricultural implements.

rim-fire n Also *rimmy* [Transf from *rimfire* of a cartridge: designed to be struck at the rim rather than the center]
A **double-rigged** saddle. **West** Cf **center fire**
1894 *Harper's New Mth. Mag.* 88.350 **SW,** The "punchers" . . regarded my new-fangled saddle with amused glances; indeed . . Tom Bailey called it "a d_____ rim-fire." **1922** Rollins *Cowboy* 123 **West,** The saddle of two cinches was designated technically as "double-rigged" or "double rig"; popularly and in pistol-maker's phrases as "double fire," "rim fire," or "double-barrelled." **1927** (1944) Russell *Trails Plowed Under* 3 **West,** He wasn't so much for pretty; his saddle was low horn, rimfire, or double-cinch. **1936** Adams *Cowboy Lingo* 45, Saddles with two cinches were 'rim-fire,' 'rimmies,' 'double-rigged,' 'double-fire,' and 'double-barreled.' **1956** Almirall *From College* 30 **CO,** Saddles with two cinches were known as rim-fires or "rimmies."

rim, go over the v phr
See quot.
1941 Writers' Program *Guide UT* 299, A *Historical Marker* . . set in a sage-covered valley, indicates the South Rim of the Great Basin. Mormon colonization south of this point in early times was characterized as "going over the Rim," and in colloquial usage the same phrase came to connote violent death.

rimmer See **rim** v[1] 1

rimming n[1]
See quot.
1949 *Amer. Forests* Dec 40 **NEng,** Grouse may often be found in the blackberry patches bordering cover—in New England such spots are called "rimmin's"—where the birds feed on dried blackberry "raisins."

rimming n[2] See **rim** v[1] 2

rimmy See **rim-fire**

rim out See **rim** v[1] 1

rimption n Also *rempshion, remption, rimpshion, rimtion* chiefly **Appalachians**
An abundance; plenty; a large amount or number.
1913 Kephart *Highlanders* 293 **sAppalachians,** If the provender be scant the hostess may say, "That's right at a smidgen," meaning little more than a mite; but if plenteous, then there are rimptions. **1917** *DN* 4.416 **wNC,** Rimpshions. . . Abundance. "There's rimpshions of squirrels in the Hickory Cove." **c1926** Bird *Cullowhee Wordlist* **swNC,** There was rempshions of fish in the river. **1942** in 1944 *ADD* 514, *Rimption*. . . If you ask for [a] rimption in Ga. you are requesting a lot. A. Baer in Syracuse, N.Y. *Herald–Journal* Jly 20. **1952** Brown *NC Folkl.* 1.585 **wNC,** Rimption. . . A good deal. **1967** Williams *Greenbones* 103 **GA** (as of c1910), Len Lobdale's got six young'uns to support, and you know and I know you can't support a rimption of young'uns at a tax desk, not without it's got a crooked drawer. **1969** *DARE* (Qu. LL8a, *A large amount or number: More than enough . . "He's got _____ of time."*) Inf **GA72,** He has a rimption of time; (Qu. LL9a, *As much as you need or more . . "We've got _____ of apples."*) Inf **GA72,** Remption. **1972** Cooper *NC Mt. Folkl.* 95, Rimtion—a great deal. **1988** *DARE* File, An Appalachian term for a whole lot of anything . . is "A whole rimption."

rimptious adj [Cf *EDD rumptious* "Riotous; unruly"]
1975 *Appalachian Jrl.* 2.159 **wNC,** To say a horse is *rimptious* or *foolish* means he is spirited; whereas, a *rank* horse is fast-gaited or spirited.

rimrack v Also *rimreck, rimwrack* [Appar *rim* (of a wheel) + *rack* twist, strain]
To damage or destroy, esp by misuse; fig: to ruin, cheat; rarely,

to behave riotously; hence ppl adj *rimracked* ruined, worn out, rickety; n *rimrack* a foul-up.

1841 in 1842 *Times & Seasons* (Nauvoo IL) 15 Jan 665/2, I am determine by the help of the Lord God of Israel to be one . . to rim rack and centre shake the kingdom of the devil. **1862** in 2001 *DARE* File—Internet, [Letter:] We are about 4 miles from the Shenandoah river in the woods. The hens, turkeys, geese, ducks and pigs get rimracked badly. The boys go right in on their nerve—don't spare anything they want. **1914** *DN* 4.78 **ME, nNH,** *Rimrack.* . . To injure, damage. [**1916** Wallace *Shack Locker* 99 **eCanada,** Her iron work aloft is 'most worn through, an' her whole framin' an' plankin' is rim-racked with Kemble's sail dragging.] **1940** (1978) Still *River of Earth* 120 **KY,** Nary a son I had pleasured himself with shooting off guns, a-rimrecking at Hardin Town and in the camps, a-playing at cards and mixing in knife scrapes. **1950** *WELS* (Weak or unsteady) 1 Inf, **cWI,** Rimracked; (Uneven, not square or at straight angles: "That house is all _____.") 2 Infs, **WI,** Rimracked. **1953** Randolph–Wilson *Down in Holler* 278 **Ozarks,** *Rimreck.* . . To destroy, to dismantle, to ruin. "If we let that feller into the Lodge, he'll rim-reck the whole business inside of a year." **1957** *ME Coast Fisherman* July 21, If nets have been rimracked, (any foul-up is a rimrack in the trawlerman's jargon) it means working on deck under flood repairing nets and gear. *Ibid,* After a few "brokers," a seasoned trawlerman may swear he's going ashore for good. But the chances are even that he'll get rimracked ashore, and come time for departure, there he will be with his seabag back on board. **1967** *DARE* Tape **WA**30, And I looked for that bastard's car for an hour. . . They'd've a had a long walk that night, because I'd've rimracked that thing. **1969–70** *DARE* (Qu. KK20a, *Something that looks as if it might collapse any minute: "That old shed is certainly _____."*) Inf **KY**85, Rimrecked; (Qu. KK70, *Something that has got out of proper shape: "That house is all _____."*) Inf **MI**110, Rimracked. **1969** *DARE* FW Addit **MO,** They thought they'd been rimracked [=cheated]. **1974** Peden *Speak to Earth* 23 **IN,** "They simply rimracked it," Clovis told Dick. . . Any farmer would have known what he meant. The tractor was demolished, ruined, damaged beyond repair. **1975** Gould *ME Lingo* 231, *Rimwracked*—Wagon and buggy wheels were made of four parts: hub, spoke, felloe (rim), and tire. The spokes fitted into holes in the felloe, and in time the holes would wear larger and the spokes would wear smaller. A wheel thus worn was literally *wracked* in the *rim.* So, anything old, past its use, misshapen, toppling, etc., is *rimwracked* in Maine parlance until the word is even applied to a hogging boat, or a shed that is frost-hove on its foundation. A person crippled or aged can be *rimwracked.* **1975** Eaton *Coll.* **Washington Is. WI,** They [the public] will rimwrack her [a wrecked freighter] by Spring. **1983** *MJLF* 9.1.53 **ceKY,** *Rimreck* . . to tear down, destroy, ruin. **1996** *Std.–Times* (New Bedford MA) 14 Jan (Internet), Fishing in largely untested waters, he found a considerable amount of rough bottom and underwater snags to contend with. "It tore the nets and rim-racked them."

rimrack n, **rimracked, rimreck** See **rimrack** v

rimrock v, hence vbl n *rimrocking,* n *rimrocker* **West** *hist*
To destroy (a herd of sheep) by driving it over a cliff.

1941 Writers' Program *Guide WY* 365 (as of c1905), Herds [of sheep] valued at hundreds of thousands of dollars, were dynamited or 'rimrocked'—driven over cliffs by whistling, shouting raiders. **1944** Adams *Western Words* 128, *Rim-rockin' sheep*—Running sheep over a cliff to destruction. This was often done during the wars between the cattle and the sheep factions. **1949** *World–Herald Mag.* (Omaha) 18 Sep. 18/5 *(DA),* Cattle raisers destroyed the flocks [of sheep] by clubbing, shooting, dynamiting, . . poisoning, and stampeding them over cliffs—a practice sometimes called rim-rocking. **1950** *AmSp* 25.305 **CO,** The term *rimrockers* goes back to the days of the cattle–sheep wars, during which it was the custom of the cattlemen to manifest their unfriendly feelings toward sheep herders by *rimrocking* their sheep, pushing a herd over the edge or rim of a mesa to their death below.

rimtion See **rimption**

rimwrack See **rimrack** v

rinch See **rinse 1**

rincon n [Span *rincón* corner] **chiefly SW**
A piece of land, esp one in an alcove, a river bend, or other somewhat secluded place; see quots.

1847 *CA Star* (San Francisco CA) 20 Mar [4]/2, All the ungranted tract . . lying and situated between Fort Montgomery and the Rincon,

and known as the Water and Beach Lots, . . will be surveyed and divided. **1888** *Outing* 13.129 **TX,** Halting for lunch at the *rincon* (Spanish for inner corner) of the range, [I] enjoyed some of the finest scenery outside a modern theatre. **1892** *DN* 1.194 **TX,** *Rincón:* a corner, a nook, a mountain recess, the bend of a river, etc. Often used by surveyors in describing land. **1919** Chase *CA Desert* 243, In a *rincon* or elbow at the foot of the rise lay the hamlet of Banner. **1932** *DN* 6.232 **West,** *Rincon.* Originally meaning a piece of ground or part of one's property, the term is now used for a little round valley, pocket, or hole, generally one in which a man has his house and corrals. It is common enough in New Mexico, Southwestern Colorado, Arizona, and Southern California, but may also be heard in Western Oklahoma and Texas. **1944** (1967) McNichols *Crazy Weather* 179 **SW,** South Boy brought up the end of the line—the place of the second-in-command on a dangerous trail. He sent word traveling ahead to Havek: "There's a rincon in the bluff where the mesa bends. That's a good place." **1956** *Names* 4.230, *Rincon* has essentially the distribution typical of Spanish terms. . . Literally "corner," and usually defined as an angular reentrant in higher land with rimming cliffs, in New Mexico it is also a ridge and a tributary valley, and in south Texas is an angle of coastal lowland. **1971** Bright *Word Geog. CA & NV* 102, *Spanish borrowings.* . . rincon [in ref to a high-altitude basin or enclosed grassy place].

rinctum(-do) See **rinktum**

rind n, v Pronc-sp *rine*
A Form.

1899 (1912) Green *VA Folk-Speech* 354, *Rine.* . . The outside of a water-melon, or a musk-melon. **1909** *DN* 3.363 **eAL, wGA,** *Rine.* . . Rind. Universal. **1912** *DN* 3.587 **wIN,** *Rine.* . . Rind, which is rarely heard. **1917** *DN* 4.399 **neOH,** *Rine.* . . Rind. **1921** Thorp *Songs Cowboys* 90, But he never skinned old longhorn,/ 'Caze he could n't cut his rine. **1942** Warnick *Garrett Co. MD* 2 **nwMD** (as of 1900–18), *Rine* (rind)—Obs. exc. dial.

B As noun.
=hull n B2(a)1.

1967–69 *DARE* (Qu. I39, . . *The thick outside covering of a walnut*) Infs **MA**5, **NY**213, Rind. **1986** Pederson *LAGS Concordance* (Walnut) 1 inf, **nwAL,** Rind—soft outer cover; 1 inf, **neMS,** The black-walnut rind = soft; 1 inf, **cnMS,** Rind—green . . rub on ringworm—cured it; 1 inf, **cnMS,** Rind—hard and green—falls off when dry; 1 inf, **ceTX,** Rind—outside covering.

rine-injin See **rye and Indian (bread)**

riney n Also *riner* [Perh var of **ranny** n 1]
A thin or sickly creature; hence adj *riney* sickly.

1967 *DARE* (Qu. K15, *A thin, bony, or poor-looking cow*) Inf **CO**33, Riney ['raɪnɪ]; **IL**34, Riner ['raɪnɚ]; (Qu. X52, . . *A person . . who had been sick was looking _____*) Inf **CO**33, Pretty riney.

ring n[1] Pronc-sp *rang* Cf **ring** v
A Form.

1963 *Mt. Life* 39.2.51 **sAppalachians,** He's a real rang-tail rouser. **1995** Karr *Liars' Club* 81 **eTX,** Hit was a yellow rang around the moon last night.

B Senses.

1 See **ring duck.**

2 also *ring cake, ringer:* A doughnut or **cruller.**

1941 *LANE* Map 284 (Doughnut), 1 inf, **cCT,** Ringer = cruller; 3 infs, **Nantucket MA,** Doughnut, rings. **1967** Faries *Word Geog. MO* 102, Doughnut. . . The Northern . . *ring* and *ring cake* (1 occurrence each) [out of 700 infs]. **1967** *DARE* (Qu. H27, . . *Joking names for doughnuts*) Inf **MN**2, Sinkers, ringers, fry cakes.

3 also pl; In marble play: any of var games played in an area outlined on the ground. Cf **hole n 4**

1922 *DN* 5.187 **KY,** Ring, n. = *keeps.* Also *ring taw.* [*Ibid,* Keeps. . . A game played for the stakes.] **1949** *PADS* 11.25 **CO,** *Ring.* . . A marble game in which the players try to shoot marbles out of a ring drawn on the ground. **1967** *DARE* Tape **WY**1, Rings was spins in or spins out. . . That was usually the older fellas that was the good shots played that. You'd make a ring about six feet through eight feet in diameter and put the marbles inside, two or three apiece, and then you shot from the outside, knuckles down, and you had to hit one of the marbles in the center and knock it out and leave your taw spinning right in the ring.

4 A group of farmers working collectively; see quots.

1938 FWP *Guide IA* 505, Between Dallas Center and Panora. . . Threshing is a cooperative activity, occurring usually in August. The farmers who help one another form a "ring," hiring or buying a thresher cooperatively; starting at one end of the "run," they proceed from farm to farm, loading the bundles and hauling them from the field, stacking the straw [etc]. **1968** *Budget* (Sugarcreek OH) 18 July 6/5 *sePA*, Threshing wheat is in full swing, and quite a few rings have already finished.

‡**5** pl: A hernia palpably descending through the abdominal rings.

[**1911** *Century Dict.*, Hernia. . . *Inguinal hernia,* a hernia of the intestine or omentum which descends through the abdominal rings.] **1938** Stuart *Dark Hills* 136 **eKY**, Around the pit of the stomach the Doctor examined me carefully to see if I had rings. That is, if I could stand heavy lifting without rupturing myself.

ring v Usu |rɪŋ|; also esp **Sth, S Midl** |rɪŋ, rɛŋ, reŋ, ræŋ|
A Proncs.

1893 Shands *MS Speech* 10, All classes frequently give [ɪ] the sound of [ɛ] in such words as *sing, ring,* . . *sting.* This sound is heard only before *ng.* **1934** *AmSp* 9.210 **Sth**, [the second element being rather light. . . *ring.* **1941** *AmSp* 16.4 **eTX** [Black], Before *ng, nk,* [ɪ] becomes [ē], [ēɪ]: *bring, ring,* . . *wing.* **1942** Hall *Smoky Mt. Speech* 16 **wNC, eTN**, *Ring* is usually [reɪŋ]. **1942** in 1944 *ADD* 514 **AR**, *Ring* [ræŋ]. **1954** *Harder Coll.* **cwTN**, *Ring* v. pres rang.

B Gram forms.

1 past: usu *rang;* also:
a *rung.*

1829 Kirkham *Engl. Grammar* 146, Ring—rung, rang—rung. **1904** Day *Kin o' Ktaadn* 91 **ME**, Till our ears rung an' we got dizzy. **1954** *Harder Coll.* **cwTN**, *Ring* v. . . past: rung, runged (occ[asionally]). **1965–70** *DARE* (Qu. OO20a, *About the school bell ringing: "When it was time for school, the bell* _____ .") 131 Infs, **widespread,** Rung. [Of all Infs responding to the question, 25% were gs educ or less; of those giving this response, 48% were gs educ or less.] **c1970** Pederson *Dial. Surv. Rural GA* **seGA** (*Yes, they* _____ *the bell this morning*) 18 [of 64] infs, Rung.

b *ringed;* infreq *ring(ded), ranged, runged.* esp **Sth, S Midl**

1884 *Anglia* 7.252 [Black], To the regular forms of the Irregular verbs as used by the whites, the Negro adds the following forms of his own. . . Pres. ring—Past. ringed . . , ring', runged—Pass. P. [same forms]. **1896** Harris *Sister Jane* 87 **GA** [Black], De bell done ringded. **1909** *DN* 3.363 **eAL, wGA**, Ranged, pret. and pp. of *ring.* **1954** [see **B1a** above]. **1966–70** *DARE* (Qu. OO20a, *About the school bell ringing: "When it was time for school, the bell* _____ .") Infs **FL52, MD19, MS57, MO16, SC10, 26,** Ring; **GA93, OK42,** Ringed. **c1970** Pederson *Dial. Surv. Rural GA* **seGA** (*Yes, they* _____ *the bell this morning*) 1 inf, Ranged; 1 inf, Ring; 1 inf, Ringed; [1 inf, Been ring;] 1 inf, Runged.

2 past pple: usu *rung;* also:
a *rang.*

1902 *DN* 2.243 **sIL**, Rang. . . For rung, as 'The bell has rang.' **1906** *DN* 3.152 **nwAR**, Rang. . . Rung. "Has the bell rang?" **1909** *DN* 3.362 **eAL, wGA**, Rang, pp. Rung. **1965–70** *DARE* (Qu. OO20b, . . *"Has the bell* _____ *[yet]?"*) 213 Infs, **widespread,** Rang. [Of all Infs responding to the question, 25% were gs educ or less; of those giving this response, 46% were gs educ or less.] **c1970** Pederson *Dial. Surv. Rural GA* **seGA** (*Has that bell been* _____ *today?*) 17 [of 64] infs, Rang.

b rarely *ring(ed), ranged, runged.* esp **Sth, S Midl**

1884 [see **B1b** above]. **1909** [see **B1b** above]. **1966–70** *DARE* (Qu. OO20b, *About the school bell ringing: "It's eight o'clock. Has the bell* _____ *[yet]?"*) Infs **MS57, MO16, NC30, SC10, 26,** Ring; **GA93, MS88, NY24, OK42,** Ringed; **MS60,** Ranged. **c1970** Pederson *Dial. Surv. Rural GA* **seGA** (*Has that bell been* _____ *today?*) 1 inf, Ring.

ring n² Pronc-sp *rang* [Prob folk-etym for *rung*]
The rung of a ladder.

1966–68 *DARE* (Qu. F34, *The wooden cross-pieces that you put your feet on when you go up a ladder*) Infs **LA24, MS73, MA9,** Rings; **IN48,** Rings—old-fashioned; [**MI48,** Rings; rungs—cross out "rings"—I misspoke;] **MI34,** Rangs [ræŋz].

ring-a-lario See **ring-a-levio 1**

ring-a-leavo See **ring-a-levio 2**

ring-a-levio n [*ring* (in ref to the enclosure in which captured players are confined) + varr of **relievo**]

1 also *ring-a-lario, ring releavo,* and varr: A team hiding or chasing game in which players who have been caught must remain in a designated area until released by a teammate. chiefly **NYC** Also called **release, relievo** Cf **prisoner's base**

1891 *Jrl. Amer. Folkl.* 224 **Brooklyn NYC**, *Ring relievo.* The two best runners "count out" to see which shall have the first choice, and this done, these two alternately choose a boy for his side until all are chosen. A course is then determined on, and one side is given a start, which, if the course is around a city block, is usually a quarter of the way round. The start given, the chase commences, and when one of the pursued is captured, he is brought back to the starting-place, where he is placed within a ring marked with chalk or coal upon the pavement. If he succeeds in pulling in one of his opponents while they are putting him in the ring, he becomes free. Or one of his own men will watch his chance to relieve him by running and putting one foot in the ring. The game continues until all players of the side that had the start are made captives. **1901** *DN* 2.146 **Brooklyn NYC**, *Ring alevio.* . . Name of a game; same as run, sheep, run. **1909** (1923) Bancroft *Games* 166, *Ring-a-lievio.* . . This is a form of Hide and Seek in opposing parties. Players who are caught are prisoners. . . The method of capture . . differs from that in some forms of Hide and Seek. **1957** *Sat. Eve. Post Letters* **NYC**, *Ring-a-leave-ee-o:* a game which I believe is also known as Prisoner's Base; **NYC** (as of c1925), *Ring-a-levio* (a kind of tag game); **NYC** (as of c1948), *Ring-a-leevio;* **Boston MA** (as of c1918), *Ring-releavo*—As I recall, the game went something like this—one side was given a specific time to hide or to get some distance away from a ring marked into the earth. . . After the first side . . departed, the second looked for them and, when caught, the captured were brought back and placed within the confines of the ring. One boy would be placed on guard over the prisoners to prevent their being *releaved* [sic]. They could be releaved by one member of their team simply approaching the ring unnoticed and tagging or touching a prisoner. **1968–70** *DARE* (Qu. EE33, . . *Outdoor games . . that children play*) Infs **NY60, 86, 119,** Ring-a-levio; **NY64,** Ring-a-levio—like hide-and-seek, only you tag people; (Qu. EE12, *Games in which one captain hides his team and the other team tries to find it*) Infs **NY37, 42, 44, 241,** Ring-a-levio; **NY250,** Ring-a-lario. **1970** *DARE* FW Addit **ceNC**, *Ring-a-lee-bo* [ˌrɪŋəˈlibo]—a tag game. **1975** Ferretti *Gt. Amer. Book Sidewalk Games* 142 **NYC**, *Ring-a-levio.* . . In this game (also known as Ring-O-Levio, Ringelevio, Ringalario, Ring-O-Leary-O, and Ringoleavo), one team of players hunts, captures, and jails the other team, keeping members of the hunted team imprisoned despite attempts to free them. . . When caught, a player must be held firmly as the Hunter shouts, "Ring-a-levio, 1, 2, 3!" . . A player who is captured can be freed in several ways. . . When all members of one team are caught by the other team—truly a long process, with some chases not completed for days—then the Hunters become the Hunted. **1977** *NY Times* (NY) 6 July 29, It was a game as valid to him and his friends as stoop-ball, kick the can, ring-a-lievio, red rover and salugi were to an earlier generation. **1979** Patrick Pope *Greenwich Village* 257 **NYC**, On a sweltering August night when he was twelve, during a game of ring-a-levio on Carmine Street, he had charged the den and been kicked under the chin in the pileup. **1982** *DARE* File **Manhattan NYC**, *Ring-o-levio.* You're either on the side that's "it" or the side that's not "it". It's usually played on concrete. The purpose of the game is to capture players and hold them down long enough to yell "Ring-o-levio-1-2-3 ring-o-levio-1-2-3 ring-o-levio-1-2-3."

2 as *ring-a-leavo;* By ext: see quot. [Prob with pun on *leave*] Cf **snipe hunt**

1966 *DARE* File **Boston MA**, *Ring-a-leavo* . . a children's game. Hide and seek game played under arc light. Stranger on block would be left hiding eyes at lamppost (a la snipe hunt).

ring and taw See **ringtaw**

ring-a-peg n Also *ring(-the)-peg;* for addit varr see quot 1965–70
The game of horseshoes, **quoits,** or a similar game.

[**1931–33** *LANE Worksheets* **seRI**, Ringing-the-stake—playing horseshoes.] **1965–70** *DARE* (Qu. EE37, *The game where you try to throw metal rings or something similar over a stake in the ground*) Inf **CA9,** Horseshoes, ring-a-peg, ringtoss; **MI44,** Horseshoe, ring-a-peg; **NY37,** Ring-a-peg; **OH70,** Horseshoes, ring-a-peg; **WI5,** Horseshoes; ring-a-peg—old game; **MN**1, Horseshoes; quoits; ring-peg; ringtoss; **NY**68, Horseshoes or ring-the-peg; quoits; **GA**80, Horseshoes; ring-the-pin; **NH**11, Horseshoes; also use a ring—ring-the-pole? **CO**21, Horseshoes; quoits—commercial set with cord rings; metal barrel staves over a stick—hoops; ring-the-stake; **VA**50, Ring-the-stob; horseshoes.

ring-around n Also *ring-round*

1 =runaround 1.

1950 *WELS* (What do you call a hard, painful swelling [often on a finger] that seems to come from deep under the skin?) 3 Infs, **WI**, Ring-around. **1965–70** *DARE* (Qu. BB30) 10 Infs, **scattered**, Ring-around; **NH**16, Ring-round.

2 =runaround 2.

1909 *DN* 3.363 **eAL, wGA**, Ring-round. . . A ring-worm. Universal. **1954** *Harder Coll.* **cwTN**, Run (a)round: . . A skin disease, same as *ring (a)round;* probably shingles. **1999** *NADS Letters*, My deceased father, who was born in 1924 and raised in southeast Ohio, referred to the skin disease known as ringworm as 'ringaround.'

ring-around-a-rosy n Also *ring-around-the-rosy*

Std sense, var forms.

1 *ring-around-(the-)roses, ring-around-the-rosies,* and varr. **scattered, but chiefly Sth, S Midl** See Map

1965–70 *DARE* (Qu. EE1, . . Games . . children play . . in which they form a ring, and either sing or recite a rhyme) 98 Infs, **chiefly Sth, S Midl; also NEng**, Ring-around-the-roses; 23 Infs, **esp Sth, S Midl**, Ring-around-the-(or -a-)rosies; **AR**28, **MS**21, 73, **TN**24, **VA**39, **WV**16, Ring-around-roses; **IN**41, **ME**9, Ring-around-the-rose; (Qu. EE33, *Other outdoor games*) Inf **TX**53, Ring-around-the-rosies. **1968** *DARE* Tape **VA**9, Then we'd play "ring around the rosies, pocket full of tosies, sweet bread, dry bread, squat." We'd have to squat then, the kids would. **1986** Pederson *LAGS Concordance,* 21 infs, **Gulf Region**, Ring-around-the-roses; 1 inf, **swAL**, Ring-around-roses.

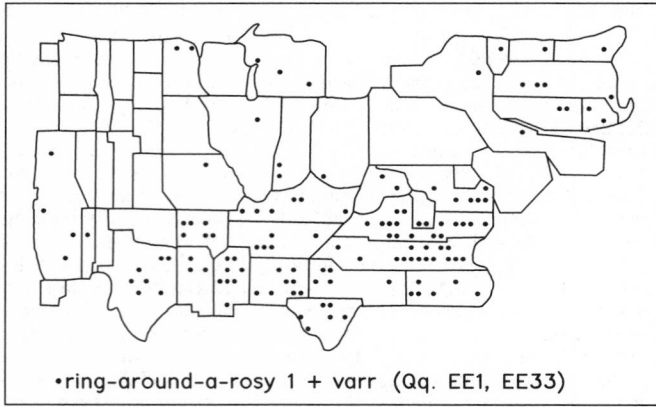

•ring-around-a-rosy 1 + varr (Qq. EE1, EE33)

2 *ring-around-rosy* (or *rosie*).

1965–70 *DARE* (Qu. EE1, . . Games . . children play . . in which they form a ring, and either sing or recite a rhyme) 27 Infs, **scattered**, Ring-around-rosy. [25 of 27 Infs old] **1983** *MJLF* 9.1.53 **ceKY** (as of 1956), Ring around rosie . . a child's game. **1986** Pederson *LAGS Concordance,* 4 infs, **cnGA, seLA, cAR, cTX**, Ring-around-rosy.

3 *ring-around-a-posy, ring-around-the-posy* (or *posies*).

1966–68 *DARE* (Qu. EE1, . . Games . . children play . . in which they form a ring, and either sing or recite a rhyme) Infs **MD**18, **WI**24, Ring around a posy; **AR**24, **WA**20, Ring around the posy; **MO**35, Ring around the posies.

4 addit var.

1968 *DARE* (Qu. EE1, . . Games . . children play . . in which they form a ring, and either sing or recite a rhyme) Inf **LA**20, Ring-a-ring-a-rosy.

ring-around-roses See **ring-around-a-rosy 1**

ring-around-rosie (or rosy) See **ring-around-a-rosy 2**

ring-around-the-roses (or -rosies) See **ring-around-a-rosy 1**

ringbill n

1 also *ringbill bluebill* (or *duck, scaup*), *ring-billed blackhead* (or *duck, shuffler*): **=ring-necked duck.**

1843 Audubon *Birds Amer.* 6.320, In shape, the Tufted Duck, or Ring-bill, as it is called in Kentucky, resembles the Scaup or Flocking Fowl. **1874** NY Acad. Sci. *Annals Lyceum Nat. Hist.* 10.74 **IL,** *[Fuligula] collaris* . . Ring-neck Scaup; Ring-bill. Winter sojourner. **1888** Trumbull *Names of Birds* 61 **neMD**, Ring-necked Duck. . . At the mouth of the Susquehanna commonly known as *Ring-billed Black-head. Ibid* **NC**, At Newberne, N.C., and Wilmington, same state, [the ring-billed duck is called] *ring-billed shuffler.* **1911** *Forest & Stream* 77.173 **WI**, Ring-Necked Duck. . . Ringbill Bluebill, Lake Puqua, Wis. **1921** LA Dept. of Conserv. *Bulletin* 10.60, The ring-necked, or ring-billed duck *(Marila collaris),* known likewise as blackjack and "black duck", is prized greatly by Louisiana hunters. **1946** Hausman *Eastern Birds* 153, Ring-necked Scaup, Ring-necked Blackhead, Ring-billed Blackhead, Ringbill [etc]. **1955** MA Audubon Soc. *Bulletin* 39.315 **MA,** Ring-necked Duck. . . Ring-bill Scaup. **1955** *Oriole* 20.4, Ring-necked Duck. . . *Ring, Ringbill, Ringbill Duck* (from the pale crossband near the front end of the bill). **1977** Bull–Farrand *Audubon Field Guide Birds* 458, This species [=*Aythya collaris*] might better be called the "Ring-billed Duck," for its chestnut neck-ring is usually seen only at close range while the white ring on the bill is a prominent field mark.

2 See **ring-billed gull.**

ringbill bluebill (or duck), ring-billed blackhead (or duck) See **ringbill 1**

ring-billed gull n Also *ringbill (gull)*

A gull (here: *Larus delawarensis*). Also called **gray gull 1, lake ~ 2, winter ~**

[**1831** Richardson *Fauna Boreali-Amer.* 2.421, Ring-billed Mew-Gull. . . The bill . . is of a dutch-orange colour, with a blackish ring near its tip.] **1842** DeKay *Zool. NY* 2.309, The common gull above described, although called the *Ring-billed Gull* in the books, has received no other popular name than *Brown Winter Gull.* . . The ring on the bill is not always found. **1916** *Times–Picayune* (New Orleans LA) 26 Mar mag sec 1, Ring-billed gull. . . bill greenish-yellow, with a black band or ring about it. **1928** Bailey *Birds NM* 289, The Ring-billed Gull . . was one of the most widely distributed of gulls. **1967–70** *DARE* (Qu. Q10, . . *Water birds and marsh birds*) Inf **CA**140, California ringbill; **CO**7, **MI**53, Ringbill gull; **RI**17, **VA**52A, Ring-billed gull. **1977** Udvardy *Audubon Field Guide Birds* 461, Ring-billed Gull *(Larus delawarensis). Ibid* 462, The eye of the slightly larger, darker-mantled California Gull is *dark brown;* whereas eye of Ring-bill is *yellow.*

ring-billed shuffler See **ringbill 1**

ringbill gull See **ring-billed gull**

ringbill scaup See **ringbill 1**

ring-bound adj phr Cf **fat** adj[2]

In marble play: see quot.

1909 *DN* 3.363 **eAL, wGA**, Ring-bound. . . In the game of marbles, when one's taw stops on the line of the ring, he is called *ring-bound* and loses his turn.

ring cake See **ring** n[1] **B2**

ringded See **ring** v **B1b**

ring dog n [*OED2* 1846] Cf **dog** n[1] **B2**

In logging: see quot 1969.

1876 Knight *Amer. Mech. Dict.* 1944, Ring-dogs. Two dogs attached to a ring for hauling timber. **1958** McCulloch *Woods Words* 150 **Pacific NW**, *Ring dog*—A dog with a large ring through the eye, used in rafting. A cable passed through the ring had a certain amount of give as the raft rose and fell, prevented the dog from pulling out. **1965** Needham–Mussey *Country Things* 88 **VT**, A ring dog is used to roll big, heavy logs; it is a ring maybe six inches in diameter with an arm ending in a sharp hook, pivoted so that it will swing parallel to any pole that you stick through the ring. They slide a pole through the ring, . . drive the hook into the under part of a big log, and the butt of the pole rests on the top of the log. They heave up on the pole . . and the hook rolls the log away from them. **1969** Sorden *Lumberjack Lingo* 96 **NEng, Gt Lakes,** *Ring dog*—Any dog attached to a fairly large ring through its eye through which lines were run. Could also be used to roll logs.

ring duck n Also *ring, ringed duck*

=ring-necked duck.

1923 U.S. Dept. Ag. *Misc. Circular* 13.21, Ring-necked Duck. . . Book

Names. . . ring-billed shuffler, ring duck. **1955** *Oriole* 20.4, Ring-necked Duck. . . *Ring, Ringbill*. (from the pale crossband near the front end of the bill). **1967–70** *DARE* (Qu. Q5, . . *Kinds of wild ducks*) Inf **TN**53, Ring duck; [**NY**207, Ring-wing;] **AZ**9, Ringed.

ringed See **ring** v B1b, 2b

ringed crappie n
    The white **crappie** (*Pomoxis annularis*).
    1908 Forbes–Richardson *Fishes of IL* 239, The present species [= *Pomoxis annularis*] is often called the pale crappie, or the white crappie, or the ringed crappie, the last by reason of the more conspicuous vertical bars upon the sides. **1939** *Natl. Geogr. Soc. Fishes* 110, Around the Great Lakes it [=the white crappie] is called ringed crappie, pale crappie, and strawberry bass. **1947** Dalrymple *Panfish* 85, Here, my friend, are the various names by which you would address that little gamester, the Crappie, depending on where you happened to be at the moment: Bachelor . . Ringed Crappie [etc].

ringed duck See **ring duck**

ringed hawk See **ringtail hawk**

ringed king snake n Also *ring king snake*
    A **milk snake** 1 (here: *Lampropeltis triangulum*).
    1928 Baylor Univ. Museum *Contrib.* 16.16 **TX**, Ringed King Snake (*Lampropeltis triangulum gentilis*). . . It is also known as the *Thunder Snake*. **1970** *DARE* (Qu. P25, . . *Kinds of snakes*) Inf **IL**119, Ring king snake.

ringed map turtle See **ringed turtle**

ringed perch n Also *ring perch, ring-tailed perch* [See quot 1882]
    A **yellow perch** (here: *Perca flavescens*).
    1877 Hallock *Sportsman's Gaz.* 272, Yellow Perch; or Ring Perch.— *Perca flavescens*. **1882** U.S. Natl. Museum *Bulletin* 16.524, *Yellow Perch; American Perch; Ringed Perch*. . . sides with 6 or 8 broad dark bars, which extend from the back to below the axis of the body. **1884** Goode *Fisheries U.S.* 1.414, The descriptive names "Yellow Perch" and "Ringed Perch" are in common use. **1938** FWP *Ocean Highway* 171 **NC**, The catches include bass, rock, German carp, mullet, white and ring perch [etc]. **1956** Harlan–Speaker *IA Fish* 145, Yellow Perch—*Perca flavescens*. . . Other Names . . ringed perch, ring-tailed perch, lake perch. **1966–70** *DARE* (Qu. P1, . . *Kinds of freshwater fish . . caught around here . . good to eat*) Infs **IL**9, 81, **NM**6, Ring perch; (Qu. P3, *Freshwater fish that are not good to eat*) Inf **VA**79, Ring perch—lives in brackish water.

ringed plover See **ring plover**

ringed turtle n Also *ringed map turtle, ~ sawback (turtle)*
    A **map turtle** (here: *Graptemys oculifera*).
    1952 Carr *Turtles* 201, No information on the natural history of the ringed turtle is available. **1999** (acc) VA Polytechnic *Endangered Species Info. System* (Internet), Common names—turtle, sawback, ringed; sawback, ringed; turtle, map and ringed. *Ibid*, Other common names for the species are ringed map turtle and ringed sawback. **1999** (acc) U.S. Fish & Wildlife Serv. *Bogue Chitto Natl. Wildlife Refuge* (Internet) **seLA**, Endangered and threatened species on the refuge: Bald Eagle, Ringed-Sawback Turtle [etc].

ringer n
1 also *ringers*: A marble game; see quots.
    1939 *PIC* 25 July 31/1 (*Popik Coll.*), Marbles. . . Ringers. **1940** *Recreation* (NY) 34.109, The game of ringer is used [in the National Marbles Tournament] which . . is an adaptation of the oldest marble game played. *Ibid* 110, Of the towns which play ringer, 80 per cent use a 10-foot ring, with 20 per cent using a ring varying in size from 4 to 15 feet. . . In Cleveland the game of ringer is played in various schools during April and May. **1942** Berrey–Van den Bark *Amer. Slang* 665.1, *Ringer* . . a game in which the players shoot marbles from a "pot" or ring. **1968** *DARE* Tape **IA**40, The marble games that have been played in Council Bluffs are ringers. . . The size of the ring is 10 feet in diameter. In the center of the ring 13 marbles are placed in the form of a cross. . . The shooter will shoot at the 13 marbles in the ring and if he knocks any marble outside the ring and his shooter or taw stays in the ring, he can shoot again. **c1970** Wiersma *Marbles Terms, Ringer*. . . A specific form of marble game using a large circle. **1975** Ferretti *Gt.*

Amer. Book Sidewalk Games 150, *Ringer* . . is governed by strict playing rules. The playing circle is ten feet in diameter, and thirteen marbles are placed in an X shape in the center. When there are two players, the first one to hit seven marbles from the circle wins. As long as the winner continues to hit any marble with his shooter and knock it from the ring, he can keep on shooting (as in a run at billiards), but his shooter must stay within the circle. If it goes out of the ring, the other player shoots. **1976** *WI Acad. Rev.* June 20 (as of 1920s), "Ringers" . . was played from the edges of a ring on the ground three or four feet in diameter. We didn't play this game much, but played a lot of one something like it, on a cement sidewalk square or indoors on a scatter rug of about the same dimensions. Each player made a one or more marble "ante" and the players in turn tried to knock the antes off the square. Shooters were always retrieved, but an ante that got near the edge—not off the square— was fair game for the next player who could move to the edge nearest the off-center ante. **1986** Pederson *LAGS Concordance*, 1 inf, **seFL**, Ringers—marble game.
2 A playing marble; see quots.   Cf **ringman 2**
    1967–69 *DARE* (Qu. EE6b, *Small marbles or marbles in general*) Infs **AR**51, **GA**89, Ringers. **1969** *DARE* Tape **GA**84, They were ringers, the big ones. **c1970** Wiersma *Marbles Terms* **WA** (as of 1959), *Ringer*—lopsided marble, tends to drift around.
3 See **ring** n[1] B2.
4 A complete workweek.
    1969 *AmSp* 44.23 **swWA** [Painter jargon], *Ringer*. . . A complete workweek. . . [A complete] workday or week. Often faced with adverse elements, when the painter gets in a full day or week, [he will] *get in a ringer*. **1970** *DARE* File **San Francisco CA** (as of c1940), *Ringer*—A week in which dock workers can put in full time and get full pay (without layoffs or other interruptions).

ringers See **ringer 1**

ringey See **ringy**

ringeye n
    =**Canada goose**.
    1968 *DARE* (Qu. Q6, . . *Kinds of wild geese*) Inf **LA**31, Canada geese—they call him ringneck or ringeye.

ring grass n Also *ring(-grass) muhly* [See quot 1937]
    A **muhly (grass)** (here: *Muhlenbergia torreyi*).
    1937 U.S. Forest Serv. *Range Plant Hdbk*. G84, Ring muhly, also called ring grass, and ticklegrass, get [sic] its common names from its unusual and characteristic growth habit. As each tuft enlarges, the center dies, leaving a border of tufted grass 2 to 4 inches wide which forms a ring 6 to 18 inches (sometimes a few feet) in diameter. The species occurs from Colorado and Kansas, to Texas and Arizona, being most abundant in New Mexico, Arizona, and southwestern Colorado. **1970** Correll *Plants TX* 231, *Muhlenbergia Torreyi* . . Ringgrass muhly. . . Arid limestone slopes, Trans-Pecos (Hueco and Delaware) mts.

ring king snake See **ringed king snake**

ringler n [*OED2 wringle* v. 2 "*Obs*. . . To move sinuously; to writhe"]
    =**earthworm**.
    1968 *DARE* (Qu. P5, . . *The common worm used as bait*) Inf **NY**41, Ringler.

ringlet n
    =**killdeer 1**.
    1923 U.S. Dept. Ag. *Misc. Circular* 13.69 **NY**, *Killdeer*. . . Vernacular Names. . . *In local use* . . ringlet.

ringman n
1 The ring finger. [*OED2* 1483 →; "*Obs*. exc. *dial*."]   Cf **lingman**
    1987 *NADS Letters* c**UT**, [From a children's song, "Thumbkin Says":] Ring-man says, "I'll dance."
2 A marble, esp a small one.   esp S Midl   Cf **ringer 2**
    1909 *DN* 3.363 e**AL**, w**GA**, Ring-man. . . One of the marbles placed in the ring. **1955** *PADS* 23.28 cw**TN**, Ring-men. . . The marbles that are placed in the ring. **1966–69** *DARE* (Qu. EE6a, . . *Different kinds of marbles—the big one that's used to knock others out of the ring*) Inf **VA**42, Ringman; (Qu. EE6b, *Small marbles*) Infs **AR**51, **GA**9, **KY**11, Ringmen.

3 also *ringmen:* A type of marble game; see quots. **esp S Midl** Cf **ringer 1**

1893 Shands *MS Speech* 59, In playing ring-men, a player is said to have *stakes* when he has knocked three marbles out of the ring. **1969** *DARE* (Qu. EE7, . . *Kinds of marble games*) Inf **KY**11, Ringman—make a square with a marble in each corner and the center; knock out any two or the center marble and you win the game; **KY**24, **TN**37, Ringmen. **1969** *DARE* Tape **TN**37, There's another game of marbles . . called ringmen. It was played more by adults than it was boys. You had a ring, say, about . . three feet around, and you had . . about . . five marbles in there. . . And one, the one in the center, was the largest and the others were 'round different corners. And . . it was generally two to four people played the game, and they would stand at a distance of, say, 10 to 12 feet and shoot their marble and try to hit these marbles in the ring.

ring muhly See **ring grass**

ringneck n

1 See **ring-necked snake.**

2 also *ring-necked blackhead, ~ bluebill, ~ scaup (duck), ringneck scaup:* =**ring-necked duck.**

1838 Geol. Surv. OH *Second Annual Rept.* 187, [Fuligula] rufitorques. The ring-neck is a visiter [sic] early in the spring. Its flesh is hardly eatable. **1874** NY Acad. Sci. *Annals Lyceum Nat. Hist.* 10.389 **IL**, [Fuligula] collaris . . Ring-neck Scaup; Ring-bill. **1887** Ridgway *N. Amer. Birds* 2.164, *Ring-necked Duck.* Popular synonyms. Ring-billed Black-head . . Ring-necked Scaup Duck, or Blue-bill [etc]. **1917** (1923) *Birds Amer.* 1.137, Ring-necked Duck. . . Other Names.—Ring-bill . . Ring-neck [etc]. **1928** Bailey *Birds NM* 138, The male Ring-neck, called also Ring-necked Scaup, Ring necked Black-head, and by hunters, Ring-bill, may be known in life by his "squarish" head [etc]. **1982** Elman *Hunter's Field Guide* 202, Ring-necked Duck. . . Common & Regional Names: ringneck, ringbill, . . ring-necked scaup [etc].

3 Any of several **plovers,** but esp **semipalmated plover;** see quots. Cf **ring-necked plover, ring plover**

1844 DeKay *Zool. NY* 2.209, The *Ring Plover,* or *Ring-neck* as it is commonly called in this State, arrives here about the beginning of May. **1872** Coues *Key to N. Amer. Birds* 244, Piping Plover. Ringneck. . . Eastern and Middle North America; abundant on the Atlantic coast. *Ibid,* Semipalmated Plover. Ring Plover. Ringneck. . . North America, abundant. **1895** (1907) Wright *Birdcraft* 235, Piping Plover: *Aegialitis meloda.* Pale Ring-neck. . . This, the second of the Ring-neck Plovers, comes to us in scattering flocks in late April. **1910** Eaton *Birds NY* 1.353, The Semipalmated plover or American ring-neck, at first sight suggests to the beginner in bird study a diminutive Killdeer. **1923** U.S. Dept. Ag. *Misc. Circular* 13.69, Kildeer. . . Vernacular Names. . . *In local use* . . ringneck (N.Y., La.); ring-necked plover (Mich., Tenn.) [etc]. *Ibid* 70, Piping Plover. . . Vernacular Names. . . *In local use* . . pale ringneck . . (Mass.) . . ringneck (. . R.I., Long I[slan]d, N.Y., Va., N.C.) *Ibid* 71, Wilson Plover. . . *Vernacular Names:* Ringneck, ring plover (Md.) **1928** Beston *Outermost House* 146 **Cape Cod MA**, The first shore birds to pause here on their way back to the Northern country were "ringnecks"—the semipalmated plover, *Charadrius semipalmatus.* **1955** *Oriole* 20.1.7 **GA**, Wilson's Plover.—Ringneck (a larger bird than the last [=the semipalmated plover], with similar neck markings, the dark band broader, black in front, the remainder grayish brown). **1965** Teale *Wandering Through Winter* 153 **TX**, A pugnacious little ringneck, a semipalmated plover that apparently considered the bar its private preserve, dashed endlessly this way and that. **1970** *DARE* (Qu. Q10, . . *Water birds and marsh birds*) Inf **VA**47, Ringneck—semipalmated plover.

4 See **ring-necked goose.**

5 =**mallard 1.**

1923 U.S. Dept. Ag. *Misc. Circular* 13.8 **OH**, Mallard. . . Vernacular Names. . . *In local use* . . ringneck.

6 A **woodpecker.**

1966 *DARE* (Qu. Q17, . . *Kinds of woodpeckers*) Inf **OK**25, Ringneck.

7 =**ring-necked pheasant.**

1967 *PA Game News* Aug 6 **PA**, The Friendly Pheasant. . . A rustling sound behind him . . turned out to be a friendly ringneck, which didn't leave when the hunter started talking to him. **1967** *DARE* Tape **PA**17, [Inf:] Ringnecks'll kill 'em. They're like dang roosters, they'll kill these rabbits. [FW:] Oh, I didn't know that. [Inf:] Yeah, they'll kill the young

rabbits. **1969** *DARE* (Qu. Q7, *Names and nicknames for . . game birds*) Inf **PA**182, Ringneck.

8 See quot.

1969 *DARE* (Qu. P27, . . *Kinds of squirrels*) Inf **CA**163, Ringneck—live in ground.

ringneck dove n

=**spotted dove.**

1944 Munro *Birds HI* 158, Chinese Dove. . . Other names: *Lace-neck* or *Ring-neck Dove.* **1967** *DARE* (Qu. Q7, *Names and nicknames for . . game birds*) Inf **CA**3, Ringneck dove.

ring-necked blackhead (or bluebill) See **ringneck 2**

ring-necked duck n

Std: a **scaup** (here: *Aythya collaris*). Also called **bar-bill, bastard broadbill, black duck 1, blackhead 1, blackie 2, blackjack 1a, blackneck c, bluebill 4, blue bullet 2, broadbill 1, bull duck, bullhead 2c, bullneck 1, coldshin, creek redhead, dogy** n^2, **fall duck, goldeneyes, marsh bluebill 2, moon-bill, mud duck 3, raft ~ a, ringbill 1, ring duck, ringneck 2, tufted duck, whistlewing**

ring-necked goose n Also *ringneck (goose)*

=**Canada goose.**

1911 *Forest & Stream* 77.173 **LA, TX**, (Canada Goose) . . Ring-Neck Goose, Vermillion Bay, La.; Gum Cove, La.; Galveston and Rockport, Tex. **1916** *Times–Picayune* (New Orleans LA) 26 March mag sec 2/7, Canada Goose. . . Outarde; Ring-necked Goose.—The best known and most widely distributed of the geese and the commonest of those that visit Louisiana each winter. **1965–70** *DARE* (Qu. Q6, . . *Kinds of wild geese*) Infs **CA**191, **GA**28, **LA**29, **OH**67, **TX**37, 42, **VA**46, Ringneck geese; **KY**88, **LA**33B, **SC**40, Ringneck; **LA**31, They call him ringneck or ringeye; **MN**10, Ring-necked geese.

ring-necked lizard n **TX**

A **lizard 1** (here: *Crotaphytus collaris*).

1893 in 1900 U.S. Natl. Museum *Annual Rept. for 1898* 253, Dr. C.H. Merriam gives the following account . . of *Crotaphytus collaris:* "The 'ring-necked' lizard does not inhabit . . the Lower Sonoran Zone." **1908** Biol. Soc. DC *Proc.* 21.69 **cnTX**, The handsome ring-necked lizard (*Crotaphytus collaris* Say) has been collected in Coryell County. **1928** Baylor Univ. Museum *Contrib.* 16.10 **TX**, *Crotaphytus collaris.* . . In the granite country of west central Texas it is the *Big Green Lizard* or *Ring-necked lizard.*

ring-necked loon n

A **loon 1** (here: *Gavia immer*).

1917 (1923) *Birds Amer.* 1.12, Loon. . . Other Names.—Common Loon . . Ring-necked Loon [etc]. **1946** Hausman *Eastern Birds* 62, Common Loon. . . Other Names—Big Loon, Ring-necked Loon [etc].

ring-necked pheasant n

Std: an introduced game bird (*Phasianus colchicus torquatus*). Also called **Chinaman 2, Chinese pheasant, chink** n^3 **2, English pheasant, prairie hen 4, ringneck 7, stubble duck**

ring-necked plover n Also *ringneck plover* Cf **ringneck 3, ring plover**

Any of several **plovers,** but esp **semipalmated plover;** see quots.

1791 Bartram *Travels* 296, [Charadrus] minor, the little sea side ring necked plover. **1874** NY Acad. Sci. *Annals Lyceum Nat. Hist.* 10.383, [Ægialitis] hiatacula (L.), var. *semipalmatus.* . . Ring-necked Plover. **1895** (1907) Wright *Birdcraft* 235, Piping Plover. . . This, the second of the Ring-neck Plovers, comes to us in scattering flocks in late April. **1923** U.S. Dept. Ag. *Misc. Circular* 13.69 **MI, TN**, Kildeer. . . Vernacular Names. . . *In local use* . . ringneck plover. **1932** Bennitt *Checklist* 28 **MO**, Killdeer . . Killdee; ring-neck plover; dotterel. **1977** Bull–Farrand *Audubon Field Guide Birds* 375, Semipalmated Plover. . . A dark-backed shorebird with white underparts and a *conspicuous black breast band* from which it gets its common name of "Ring-necked Plover."

ring-necked scaup (duck) See **ringneck 2**

ring-necked snake n Also *ringneck (snake)* [See quot 1974] A common colubrid snake (*Diadophis punctatus*) distinguished by the colored ring behind the head.   Also called **copper-belly 3, corkscrew snake, horse racer 1, racer 1e, ring snake**

1791 Bartram *Travels* 276 **FL, NC, SC,** There are many other species of snakes in the regions of Florida and Carolina; as the . . copper belly, ring neck, and two or three varieties of vipers. [**1834** (1879) Brooks *Zóphiël* 252, The ring-necked serpent is still sometimes seen in North America: it is of a shining black, with a white circle about its neck.] **1853** Baird–Girard *N. Amer. Reptiles* 1.112, *Diadophis punctatus.* . . Ring-necked Snake. **1908** Biol. Soc. DC *Proc.* 21.73, *Diadophis regalis* . . Western Ring-necked Snake. **1947** Pickwell *Amphibians* 41, *Diadophis amabilis,* the Ring-necked Snake . . is one of our smallest Snakes and is easily identified by its collar. **1966–69** DARE (Qu. P25, . . *Kinds of snakes*) Inf **CA**114, Ringneck; **FL**27, Ring snake, ringnecked snake. **1972** GA Dept. Ag. *Farmers Market Bulletin* 19 Apr 1, [Letter:] My son found a small, slender, dull black snake with a red-yellowish belly and a red ring around its head. . . [Response:] The Game and Fish Commission identified your snake as an Eastern ringneck snake. **1974** Shaw–Campbell *Snakes West* 64, Perhaps the most common snake in the American West, or for that matter in the United States, is one few people have seen. . . It is a small snake, most often dark gray on its upper side, but with a ring of bright yellow around its neck immediately behind the head. This ring gives it the common name ringneck snake. **1986** Pederson *LAGS Concordance,* 1 inf, **neFL,** Ringnecks—snakes.

ringneck goose See **ring-necked goose**

ringneck plover See **ring-necked plover**

ringneck scaup See **ringneck 2**

ringneck snake See **ring-necked snake**

ringneck squash n
See quot.
1966 DARE (Qu. I23, . . *Kinds of squash*) Inf **SC**1, Ringneck squash is a yellow crook-necked one.

ring-peg See **ring-a-peg**

ring perch See **ringed perch**

ring play See **play** n **1b**

ring plover n Also *ringed plover* Cf **ring-necked plover**
Any of several **plovers,** but esp **semipalmated plover;** see quot 1955.
1785 Pennant *Arctic Zool.* 485, Ringed . . Pl[over]. . . the neck is encircled with a white ring. **1813** (1824) Wilson *Amer. Ornith.* 7.69, The Ring Plover has a sharp twittering note. **1834** Nuttall *Manual Ornith.* 2.18, Piping Ringed Plover. (*Charadrius melodus*). *Ibid* 25, The Semipalmated Ring Plover, though so well suited for an almost aquatic life, feeds on land as well as marine insects, collecting weavels, and other kinds. **1844** Giraud *Birds Long Is.* 217, Piping Plover. Ring Plover, Charadrius Hiaticula. **1898** (1900) Davie *Nests N. Amer. Birds* 155, Ring Plover—*Ægialitis hiaticula.* **1923** U.S. Dept. Ag. *Misc. Circular* 13.71 **MD,** Wilson Plover. . . *Vernacular names:* Ringneck, ring plover. **1955** Lowery *LA Birds* 236, Piping Plover. . . This is the first of our five so-called "ringed plovers"—plovers that have one or two bands that either partially or completely encircle the birds' neck and chest. The well-known Killdeer, which is in this group, has *two* bands across the chest that join on the sides. In the other four species, the Piping, Snowy, Semipalmated, and Thick-billed Plovers, there is but one band. **1961** Ligon *NM Birds* 112, Semipalmated (Ringed) Plover.

ring releavo See **ring-a-levio 1**

ring-round See **ring-around**

ring shout n
1 See **shout** n **1.**
2 See **shout song.**

ring sing n
=**shout** n **1.**

1931 VA *Qrly. Rev.* Jan 98, As far back as the old people could remember, Whitehall negroes held a ring sing to celebrate, in a spiritual way, the final picking of the cotton crop.

ring snake n
=**ring-necked snake.**
1778 Carver *Travels N. Amer.* 487, The *Ring Snake* is about twelve inches long. **1836** Edward *Hist. TX* 76, One will meet . . at times with that beautiful, small, harmless creature, the ring-snake. **1842** DeKay *Zool. NY* 3.39, The Ring Snake. *Coluber punctatus.* . . Small. Bluish brown; beneath, red; often with a triple row of black dots; a white collar around the neck. Length 12–18 inches. **1891** in 1896 IL State Lab. Nat. Hist. Urbana *Bulletin* 3.300, *Diadophis punctatus* . . Ring Snake. **1966** DARE (Qu. P25, . . *Kinds of snakes*) Inf **FL**27, Ring snake, ring-necked snake.

ring-streaked and striped adj phr Also *ring-streaked and striked* [Prob alter of Genesis 30:35 "ring-straked and spotted"] Cf **streaked and striped**
Irregularly striped.
1885 Twain *Huck. Finn* 196, He was painted all over, ring-streaked-and-striped, all sorts of colors, as splendid as the rainbow. **1909** DN 3.363 **eAL,** *Ring-streaked and striked.* . . Striped irregularly. Sometimes *ring-streaked and striped* is used. The *-ed* is always pronounced as a separate syllable.

ring tag n
=**kiss-in-the-ring.**
1960 Korson *Black Rock* 242 **PA** (as of c1900), The teen-age boys and girls were in a mood to play the game they had been waiting for impatiently all day—the ring game, also known as "kiss ring" and "ring tag."

ringtail n
1 also *ringtail coon:* =**raccoon.**
1844 *N.O. Picayune* 30 Sep. 257/5 (*DA*), It aided the fun not a little to see the mischievous monkey. . . bite into his arm, and hang on like a 'ring-tail' to a bough. [DARE Ed: This quot may refer instead to **2** below.] **1965–70** DARE (Qu. P31, . . *Names or nicknames . . for the . . raccoon*) 81 Infs, **scattered but less freq NEng, West,** Ringtail; **IN**51, **KY**11, **NC**85, **NY**219, Ringtail coon. **1973** Flach *Yankee German–America* 85 **csTX,** "There is a ringtail in the old grain barn. He is stretched out on a rafter and he thinks I cannot see him." "Did you shoot him, Papa?" "No, indeed," with a glance at me. "He catches mice and he should have a fine time. Plenty of mice." **1978** Mullen *Old Fishermen* 134 **seTX,** We'd go out 'possum or ringtail hunting at night. [DARE Ed: This quot may refer instead to **2** below.] **1986** Pederson *LAGS Concordance,* 2 infs, **cTN,** Ringtail coon.
2 See **ring-tailed cat.**
3 See **ring-tailed marlin.**
4 See **ringtail hawk.**

ringtail cat See **ring-tailed cat**

ringtail coon See **ringtail 1**

ring-tailed cat n Also *ringtail (cat)*   esp **CA, TX**
The cacomistle (*Bassariscus astutus*).   Also called **cat squirrel 2, civet cat 1, coon ~ 2, mountain ~ 3, miner's ~, Pacific ~, raccoon fox**
1917 Anthony *Mammals Amer.* 109 **CA,** The American Civet Cat. . . is not a Cat, being more like a weasel. . . [T]he reader may find other references to it as the "Bassaris," "Cat Squirrel" (so called in Texas); "Mountain Cat," and "Ring-tailed Cat" (California) [etc]. **1937** Grinnell et al. *Fur-Bearing Mammals CA* 1.172, The animal has been called in California "civet cat," "coon cat," "band-tailed cat," "miner's cat," "ring-tail," and "coon-fox." However, it is not a true civet, neither is it a cat nor a coon. **1956** Gipson *Old Yeller* 100 **TX,** But the hogs didn't seem to mind the stickers. Neither did . . the little big-eared ringtail cats. **1967–68** DARE (Qu. P31) Inf **CA**87, Ring-tailed cat—has a long, ringed tail—rare; **TX**29, Ringtail cat—this isn't a coon; (Qu. P32, . . *Other kinds of wild animals*) Infs **TX**19, 67, Ringtail; **TX**5, 13, Ringtail cat. **1980** Whitaker *Audubon Field Guide Mammals* 561, In a narrow den often padded with moss, grass, or leaves, the Ringtail sleeps by day. **1981** Pederson *LAGS Basic Materials,* 1 inf, **csTX,** Ringtails—more lanky; heavier and taller than civet cat; rings around tail.

ring-tailed eagle n

The immature phase of the **golden eagle.**

[**1809** Shaw *Genl. Zool.* 7.71, *Ring-Tailed Eagle.* . . It is a native both of Europe and North-America.] **1813** (1824) Wilson *Amer. Ornith.* 7.15, The Ring-tailed Eagle measures nearly three feet in length. **1832** Nuttall *Manual Ornith.* 1.65, The Common, or Ring-tailed Eagle, is now found to be the young of the Golden Eagle. **1869** John Burroughs in *Atlantic Mth.* 23.712 **NY,** One September, while a youth, I saw the ring-tailed eagle, an immense, dusky bird, the sight of which filled me with awe. **1895** Minot *Land-Birds New Engl.* 383, Golden Eagle. Ring-tailed Eagle (young). **1955** Forbush–May *Birds* 115, American Golden Eagle. . . *Other names:* Mountain Eagle; Ring-tailed Eagle; Royal Eagle.

ring-tailed marlin n Also *ringtail, ring-tailed godwit*

=**Hudsonian godwit.**

1844 DeKay *Zool. NY* 2.253, The Ring-Tailed Marlin. . . Tail doubly forked, white at base, the black tipped with white. **1880** *Forest & Stream* 15.4, Hudsonian godwit *(Limosa hudsonica),* ring-tailed marlin; white-tailed marlin; humility; Virginia woodcock. Generally known everywhere as the ring-tailed marlin, so called from the white band crossing the tail feathers. **1923** U.S. Dept. Ag. *Misc. Circular* 13.59, Hudsonian Godwit. . . Vernacular Names. . . *In local use* . . ringtail (Miss.); ring-tailed marlin (R.I., Long I[slan]d, N.Y., N.J., Va.) **1932** Bennitt *Check-list* 32 **MO,** Hudsonian godwit . . Black-tailed or ring-tailed godwit or marlin. **1942** Natl. Park Serv. *Fading Trails* 157, Market hunters of Boston called all godwits "goose birds," but perhaps the most widely used name for the Hudsonian godwit was "ring-tailed marlin" because of the white band on its upper tail coverts.

ring-tailed perch See **ringed perch**

ring-tailed roarer n Also *ringtail roarer, ring-tail(ed) snorter* (or *squealer, tooter*); for addit varr see quots Cf **rip-tail snorter**

A ferocious mythical animal; hence a powerful, violent, or wild person; an extraordinary example of its kind.

1828 *Western Mth. Rev.* 3.15, He was the first, who published the good story of the fight between the Kentuckians, the one half horse and alligator, and the other steam boat and earthquake. The *snapping turtle, the ring tailed painter, the best horse, dog and gun,* &c. have been successive additions. **1830** *Telegraph* (Painesville OH) 15 June 1/5 **GA,** *Ringtailed Roarer*—A most violent fellow, a Crockett. **1832** Paulding *Westward Ho* 124, I got tired of making fun of the ring-tail-roarer. **1837** Bird *Nick of Woods* I.iii.56 *(OED2),* Stranger, my name's Ralph Stackpole, and I'm a ring-tailed squealer! **1859** *Oregon Argus,* Dec. 10 **(1912** Thornton *Amer. Gloss.),* Here lies James D. Porter,/ Who lived as he hadn't orter,/ But as a Methodist exhorter / Was a regular *ringtail snorter.* **1898** Westcott *Harum* 308 **nNY,** "Got you roped in, have they?" he said, using his hat as a fan. "Scat my _____! but ain't this a ring-tail squealer?" "It is very hot," responded John. **1909** Rye *Quirt & Spur* 81 **TX,** Ain't he a 'ring-tail tooter,' boys? **1913** *Sat. Eve. Post* 1 Nov 66 **sCA,** Scotty always said that when he got the dough from his old man's estate he was going to have a ringtail-peeler of a time. **1941** *Jrl. Amer. Folkl.* 54.62 **swTX,** The "Big Bender". . . calls . . an extended inebriation "a ring-tailed tooter." **1950** *PADS* 14.76 **FL,** *Ring-tailed snorter.* . . A person with a high temper and generally obnoxious disposition. **1959** *VT Hist.* 27.158 **cw,neVT,** *Ringtail snorter.* . . A hard thunder shower. Often said by people who are educated and uneducated rural residents in Addison Co. Also Essex. **c1960** *Wilson Coll.* **csKY,** *Ring-tailed screamer*—A loud-mouthed boaster; probably a left-over of actual pioneer boasting. *Ring-tailed snorter* (or *roarer*). . . A mythical monster with which early pioneer bad men were always comparing themselves. *Ring-tailed tooter.* **1963** *Mt. Life* 39.2.51 **sAppalachians,** Elz thanks he's a real rang-tail rouser, a-joggin' along thar on that old stove-up mare. **1968–70** DARE (Qu. Z16, *A small child who is rough, misbehaves, and doesn't obey, you'd call him a* _____) Inf **NJ39,** Ring-tailed snorter; (Qu. CC7, . . *A person who goes to church very seldom or not at all*) Inf **MA123,** Ringtail devil; (Qu. CC17, *Imaginary animals or monsters that people around here tell tales about*) Inf **MA123,** Ringtail devil; **PA223,** Ring-tailed snorter; (Qu. II23, *Joking names for the people who are, or think they are, the best society of a community*) Inf **KY50,** Ring-tailed tooters. **1968** DARE FW Addit **LA17,** Ring-tailed tooter—something extraordinary. **1975** Gould *ME Lingo* 232, You have to go some to keep ahead of him; he's a reg'lar ringtail peeler! **1985** Ladwig *How to Talk Dirty* 36 **Ozarks,** He's a ring-tailed tooter with his tail screwed in . . a hyper person.

ringtail hawk n Also *ringtail, ringed hawk* [*OED2 ringtail* sb. 1.a 1538 →] Cf **sparrow hawk**

Perh the female **marsh hawk 1.**

1709 (1967) Lawson *New Voyage* 143 **NC, SC,** The Ring-tail is a short-wing'd Hawk, preying on Mice, and such Vermine in the Marshes, as in *England.* **1950** WELS (*Kinds of hawks in your neighborhood*) 1 Inf, **cWI,** Ringtail. **1967–68** DARE (Qu. Q4, . . *Kinds of hawks*) Inf **TN6,** Ringtail hawk; **IN19,** Ringed hawk.

ringtail leader n [*ringleader,* infl by **ring-tailed roarer** and varr]

1912 *DN* 3.587 **wIN,** *Ring-tail leader.* . . The leader of the leaders; ring-leader. "You ought to get him; I think he is the ring-tail leader."

ringtail roarer (or snorter, squealer, tooter) See **ring-tailed roarer**

ringtaw n Also *ring and taw,* pronc-sp *reegataw* Cf **taw**

In marble play: a game in which marbles are placed in a ring and knocked out with a **shooter 1.**

1906 Lovett *Old Boston Boys* 43, Then there was "ring taw" and "three holes," and lots of other names which have been forgotten. These games were good fun, and kept boys out of doors as well as out of mischief. **1922** [see **ring** n[1] **B3**]. **1932–34** Hanley Disks **Boston MA,** We played what they called reegataw. . . Place your marble in the ring, then you snap at it, knock it out. **1955** *PADS* 23.28 **cwTN,** *Ring-taw (ring and taw).* . . A game played with marbles. **1967** DARE (Qu. EE7, . . *Kinds of marble games*) Inf **NJ2,** Ringtaw—knock marbles out of places in a board, and then out of a ring.

ring-the-peg See **ring-a-peg**

ringy adj Also sp *ringey, wringy* [Etym uncert; cf **wring-tail,** *EDD wrangy* adj. "Wrong, cross"] **chiefly West**

Nervous; angry; irritable.

1928 Mulford *Mesquite Jenkins* 233 **West,** "All right. Don't get ringy." "_____ _____!" said Jim. "Ain't no need to swear. They won't get away." **1929** Dobie *Vaquero* 288 **West,** The water cooled the yearling down . . but Claude spluttered up the bank as "ringy" as the yearling had been. **1936** Adams *Cowboy Lingo* 226, To be mad was to be 'ringey,' 'riled,' 'on the prod.' **1941** Cleaveland *No Life* 59 **NM,** That outfit was all bowed-up. Every man in it was wringy. You know how we all get in a dry spring trying to work pore cows? **1942** Stegner *Mormon Country* 144 **UT,** The cow was "ringy." She kept looking around suspiciously and switching her matted tail [while being milked]. **1945** *AmSp* 20.306 **SW** (as of 1935), That horse is pretty ringy. (Quite frisky.) **1946** *NYT Mag.* 20 Oct 35 [Rodeo lingo], *Ringy:* frisky, said of a horse (pron. RANG-ee). **1958** Blasingame *Dakota Cowboy* 86 **SD,** They were ringy and hard to hold the whole drive. **1973** Allen *LAUM* 1.359 (as of c1950), He got (became) *angry.* . . Most of the remaining infrequently recorded terms . . are actually widely known, but a few are unusual either as words or as bearers of the meaning "angry." . . *ringy* [1 inf, **ND**].

rinkerhawk, rinklehawk See **wrinklehawk**

rinktum n Also *rinctum(-do)* [Etym unknown] Cf **spizzerinctum**

1 A gadget or contrivance; something whose name is unknown or which one does not want to name.

1896 *DN* 1.423 **MA, cNY,** *Rinctum:* a wrinkle, contrivance, design. **1908** Wasson *Home from Sea* 288 **ME,** Aunt Polly never cal'lated to set stock still with her hands folded, by consid'ble. She was going through her rinktums [=rituals to cast a spell], too, of course, but jest what they was, she always took plaguy good care never to let anybody find out. **1931** *AmSp* 6.258, Indefinite names current in the Central West of the United States. . . rinktum. **1942** McAtee *Dial. Grant Co. IN* 53 (as of 1890s), *Rinktum* . . device, gadget, thingumbob. **1952** Brown *NC Folkl.* 1.585, *Rinctum-do: n.* An unnamed contrivance. "What are you making?" "Oh, a rinctum-do."—Central and east.

2 An unidentified game. Cf **rinktum 4**

1905 *DN* 3.92 **nwAR,** *Rinktum.* . . The name of a game.

3 See quot.

1926 *DN* 5.389 **ME,** *Rinktum.* . . Party or dance. "Are you going to the rinktum to the town hall tonight?" Common.

4 also *rinktums:* =**noogie**—often used as an exclam; see quots. **Sth, S Midl**

1930 *AmSp* 5.331 **TX,** If some one has a fresh haircut, a person may rake him up the back of the head forcibly and say "Rinktums!" or "Rinktums on you!" This can be done only on the first day of the haircut, however. To avoid the experience on the second day one insists that he "slept on his haircut." The custom involving the ejaculation is most common among young people. **1949** *PADS* 11.10 **wTX,** *Rinktums.* . . A word which, if said before the owner of a new haircut can say "Venture rinktums," entitles the one who says it to initiate the new haircut by rubbing his thumb forcefully up the back of the owner's head. **1954** *Harder Coll.* **cwTN,** *Rinktum.* . . An especially hard knuckle blow to someone's head. In a quick motion, the one who gives the blow places his thumb, fist up, on a person's head and scrapes down so that the knuckles hit solidly on the person's head. **1970** *Thompson Coll.* **cnAL** (as of 1920s), *Rinctum on that haircut* . . yelled by boys spotting one with a fresh haircut. The one caught was supposed to submit to a dry-knuckle rub of the area from which hair had been removed. **c1970** *DARE* File **MD** (as of c1915), Back in my youth, when a playmate appeared with a fresh haircut, someone would throw an arm around his neck to hold his head, dig his knuckles into his skull, and cry ['rɪŋktəm]. I can't remember if this was localized to the suburb of Baltimore (Md.) where I lived—West Arlington—or whether I also heard it at school in the city. **1999** *NADS Letters,* When I moved from Connecticut to Clarksville, Arkansas, in 1938, I was surprised one day to have a boy stand up in class and announce, "No rinktum." . . I asked him later what that was about, and he explained that if he didn't say that, some other kid might knuckle his head.

rinktum tiddy n Also *rictum-dity, rinkum tiddy, rum-tum-diddy;* for addit varr see quots [Etym unknown] **esp NEng**

A dish, usu of cheese, tomatoes, onion, egg, and pepper, served over toast.

1911 Williams Pub. Lib. Assoc. *Ariz. Cook Book* 99 *(DA),* Rinktum Ditty. **1913** *Ladies' Home Jrl.* Oct 47, *Rictum-Dity.* One cupful of grated cheese, one teaspoonful of salt, two tablespoonfuls of butter, two eggs, one chopped green pepper, one can of tomatoes, half of a grated onion and a dash of red pepper. Mix the tomatoes, cheese, onion and chopped pepper. Melt the butter in a chafing-dish, add the mixture, and, when heated, add the eggs well beaten and the seasonings. Cook until eggs are of a creamy consistency, stirring all the time. Serve hot. **1920** Kander *Settlement Cook Book* 460, *Rictum-dity* . . tomatoes . . grated cheese . . grated onion . . green pepper . . butter . . eggs . . salt. Mix tomatoes, cheese, onion juice and the pepper, chopped. Melt the butter, in chafing dish, add the mixture and when heated add the eggs well beaten. Cook until eggs are of creamy consistency . . Serve at once on toast. **1940** Brown *Amer. Cooks* 370 **MA,** *Rinktum tiddy*—Heat butter . . slowly fry onion. . . Add seasonings, tomatoes, and sugar. Heat slowly. . . Add grated cheese; heat . . until cheese melts. Add egg . . and take from heat before egg can curdle. Pour over hot buttered toast and eat at once. **1948** *Ada* (Okla.) *Ev. News* 2 July 6/1 *(DA),* We enjoyed Rum-Tum-Diddy, a dish made of corn, bacon, cheese, tomatoes, onions and other mysterious ingredients. **1955** Taber *Stillmeadow Daybook* 269 **swCT,** Soufflé or a rabbit or rinkum tiddy, that happy blend of tomatoes, onion and cheese. **1983** *DARE* File **cnMA** (as of 1915), *Rinktum ditty*—A kind of Welsh rabbit with tomato in it. Served on toast or saltines. A supper dish—or perhaps refreshment for the whist club.

rinse v, n Usu |rɪn(t)s|; for varr see below [All of the var forms noted below are found in Brit dial; cf *EDD range* v.[2], sb.[2], *rench* v., sb., *rinch* v., *ringe* v.[3], sb.[4], and also *SND,* which gives [rɪnz] as the usu Scots pronc]
Std senses, var forms.

1 |rɪnč, rɪnš|; rarely |rɪnč|; pronc-spp *rinch, rinsh.* **chiefly Sth, S Midl** See Map

1906 *DN* 3.153 **nwAR,** Rench, rinch. . . To rinse. **1915** *DN* 4.188 **swVA,** *Rinch.* **1916** [see **4** below]. **1917** *DN* 4.416 **wNC,** *Rinch.* **1927** *DN* 5.470 **Appalachians,** *Rinse*—rensh, rinch. **1930** Shoemaker *1300 Words* 50 **cPA Mts** (as of c1900), *Rinch*—To rinse or lightly wash the hands without soap. **1950** *PADS* 14.57 **SC,** *Rinsh, rensh:* . . To rinse. **1950** *WELS (When you put clothes into clean water to get the soap off)* 1 Inf, **seWI,** Rinse—many people pronounce it rinsh. **1957** *Sat. Eve. Post Letters* **eNM,** "Rinch", always for "rinse." **1965–70** *DARE* (Qu. F43) 90 Infs, **chiefly Sth, S Midl,** Rinch ('em, etc) [proncs of the types [rɪnč, rɪnš]]; **IL91,** Rinch is said by a great many people; **IL113,** Rinch—Inf no longer uses, considers substandard; **IA12,** [rɪnč]; **KY5,** ['rɪnčəm] **KY94,** Rinch—Inf has heard people pronounce word this way; **MI108,** They used to say rinch; **MI111,** Rinch 'em—Inf says

some use, not she; **NJ43,** People say rinch, but better educated say rinse; **NY69,** Rinch—one lady says this; **NC11,** Rinch—heard from old-timers; **NC72,** Rinch—Inf suggests colored would use this; **OH98,** Rinch—common here; **TX33,** Rinch—Inf says this is common around here; **VA28,** Some say rinch 'em; (Qu. G15) 38 Infs, **chiefly Midl, Sth,** Rinch. **1983** Abbott *Womenfolks* 163 **AR,** They "warshed" things out, and then they "rinched" them. **1989** Pederson *LAGS Tech. Index* 70, [For *rinse,* 437 infs gave proncs of the std types [rɪn(t)s]; 219 gave proncs of the types [rɪnč, rɪnš]; 4 [rinč].]

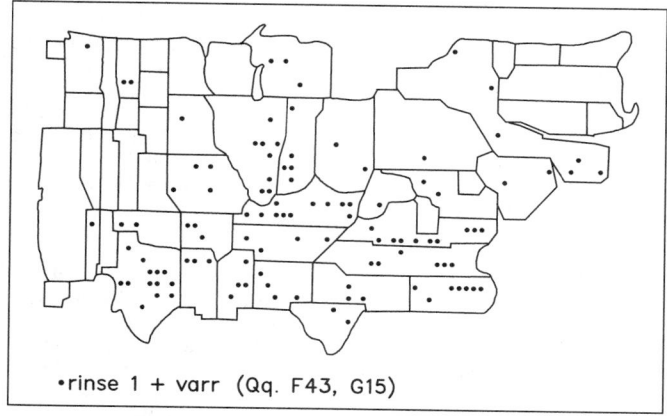

•rinse 1 + varr (Qq. F43, G15)

2 |rɪnz|. **esp Midl, Sth** See Map
1940 *AmSp* 15.85 **neTN,** wi wɔʃt ən rɪnzd ɑr hænz. **1941** *AmSp* 16.119 **VA,** *Rinse* is very often [rɪnz]. **1965–70** *DARE* (Qu. F43) 18 Infs, **esp Midl, Sth,** [rɪnz] ('em). **1989** Pederson *LAGS Tech. Index* 70, [8 infs gave proncs of the type [rɪnz].]

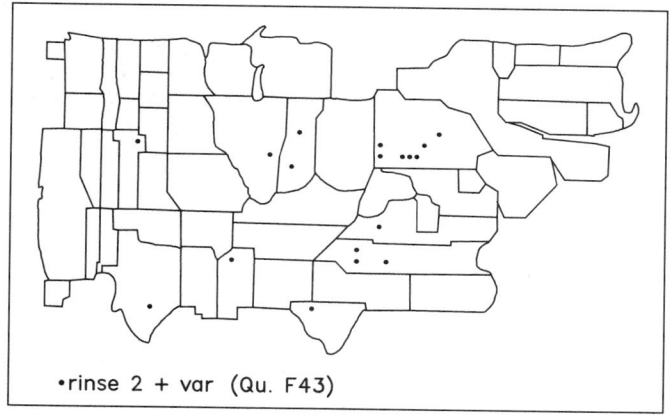

•rinse 2 + var (Qu. F43)

3 |rɛn(t)s|; pronc-spp *rence, rense.*
1867 Lowell *Biglow* xxvii 'Upcountry' **MA,** He changes the *i* into *e* in . . *rense* for *rinse.* **a1883** (1911) Bagby *VA Gentleman* 71, There is always some household business going on here. . . shelling of peas, washing of butter, or rinsing (I'd rather say rensing, yea even renching, if you will allow me) of things. **1890** [see **4** below]. **1891** Cooke *Huckleberries* 9 **NEng,** Jest rence off them teeth. **1892** *DN* 1.241 **cwMO, MI,** Rinse. Generally [rɛns]. **1910** *DN* 3.447 **wNY,** Rense. . . To rinse. **1916** [see **4** below]. **1944** In 1946 *AmSp* 21.53 **nwMN,** To my intense chagrin my younger sister caught me out in the use of 'rinse' for 'rinse' in recent years. **1950** *PADS* [see **1** above]. **1950** *WELS (When you put clothes into clean water to get the soap off)* 1 Inf, **cwWI,** Rense; 1 Inf, **csWI,** Rensing. **1961** Kurath–McDavid *Pronc. Engl.* 130 **Atlantic,** *Rinse*—In *rinse* the vowels /ɪ/ and /ɛ/ are current nearly everywhere; distribution is less in social dissemination. Cultivated speech has predominantly /ɪ/, but instances of /ɛ/ occur. . . In folk speech, *rinse* has predominantly the vowel /ɛ/ of *ten.* . . All in all, there are social gradations in the use of /ɪ/ and /ɛ/ rather than sharp social boundaries, the drift being away from /ɛ/. Other vowels are rare in *rinse.* In the southern Appalachians, the /æ/ of *pan* occurs beside /ɛ/ in folk speech, in eastern North Carolina, the /e/ of *pain.* **1965** *PADS* 43.21 **seMA,** To get soap out of clothes, you _____ them. . . rense [1 of 9 infs; old term]. **1965–70** *DARE* (Qu. F43) 47 Infs, **scattered,** Rense ('em, etc) [proncs of the types [rɛnts, rɛns]]; (Qu. G15) 29 Infs, **scattered,** Rense. **1975** Gould

ME Lingo 230, Be with you soon's I rense my hands. **1989** Pederson *LAGS Tech. Index* 70, [56 infs gave proncs of the types [rɛn(t)s].]

4 |rɛnč, rɛnš|; pronc-spp *(w)rench.* **widespread exc NEng**
See Map

a1824 (1937) Guild *Jrl.* 3.263 **VT,** She would . . stand in the brook and rench her close and come up barefoot. **1827** (1939) Sherwood *Gaz.* GA 139, *Wrench,* for rinse. **1858** in 1983 *PADS* 70.58 **ce,sePA,** They. . . have a machine to wash the cloathes one to wrench them & one to wring and a place to dry them. **a1883** [see **3** above]. **1886** *S. Bivouac* 4.349 **sAppalachians,** Rench (rinse). **1890** *DN* 1.63 **sePA,** *Wrench:* for *rinse,* e.g. "Wrench your mouth out!" Common in the neighborhood of Philadelphia. [Evidently the same word as the New England "rense," for *rinse.* . . .] **1892** *DN* 1.234 **KY,** *Wrench* ([rɛnč]: "did she rench the clothes?") **1899** (1912) Green *VA Folk-Speech* 350, *Rensh.* . . A form of *rinse.* . . Pronounced like *wrench.* **1902** *DN* 2.243 **sIL,** *Rench.* **1903** *DN* 2.237 **swMO,** *Rinse.* . . Pronounced rench. **1906** [see **1** above]. **1906** *DN* 3.123 **sIN,** *Rench.* **1909** *DN* 3.363 **eAL, wGA,** *Rench.* **1912** *DN* 3.587 **wIN,** *Rench.* **1916** *DN* 4.279 **NE,** *Rench* (or *rinsh, rense*) *water.* . . Variants of *rinse.* "Save the rense water." *Ibid* 341 **NY, seOH, LA,** *Wrench.* **1917** *DN* 4.416 **wNC, LA, IL, SC, KS, MA, CA,** *Rench.* **1920** Hunter *Trail Drivers TX* 210 (as of 1877), I got down to pull off my boots and wrench my socks. **1923** *DN* 5.224 **swMO,** *Wrench.* **1927** [see **1** above]. **1941** O'Donnell *Great Big Doorstep* 2 **sLA,** Come and rench out the diaper before T.J. wets the other one. **1958** *Resp. to PADS 29* **WI,** We always wrenched our clothes in the laundry. **1959** *VT Hist.* 27.154 **nVT,** *Rench.* **1965–70** *DARE* (Qu. F43, *After clothes have been washed, what do you do to get the soap off?*) 111 Infs, **widespread exc NEng,** Rench ('em, etc) [proncs of the types [rɛnč, rɛnš]]; IL23, [rɛʲnč]; LA6, [rɛⁱnč]; TN27, [rɛⁱnč] 'em [Many Infs gave this only as a second response. 13 Infs indicated that they heard it from older people or that it is what people "used to say"; 22 indicated in var ways that they heard it from other people but did not use it themselves.]; (Qu. G15, *When you pour hot water on the dishes to get the soap off, you _____ them*) 44 Infs, **scattered, but less freq Nth,** Rench. **1967** *DARE* FW Addit **nwLA,** "I'll get you some water to [rɛʲⁱnč] that coffee down"—Waitress in Natchitoches, La. **1968** *DARE* Tape GA30, That ol' mother alligator will . . hold 'em light in her mouth an' just wash 'im, rench 'im in the water. **1989** Pederson *LAGS Tech. Index* 70, [96 infs gave proncs of the types [rɛnč, rɛnš].]

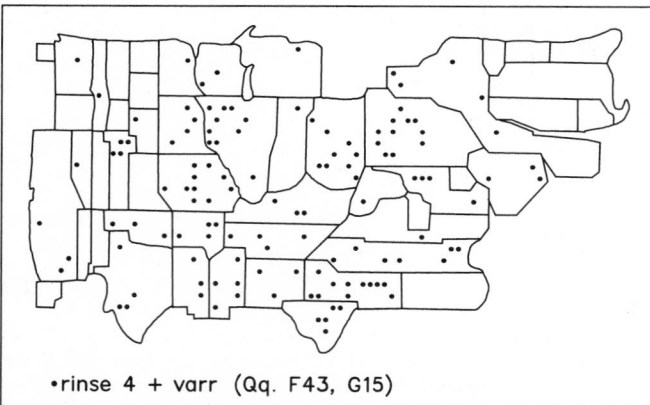

•rinse 4 + varr (Qq. F43, G15)

5 |rænč, rænš, rænts|; also |rɛnč, ren(t)s|; pronc-spp *ra(i)nch.*
1897 *KS Univ. Qrly.* (ser B) 6.56 **KS,** *Rainch:* rinse, rense. **1961** [see **3** above]. **1966** *DARE* FW Addit **cwNC,** Rinse—[rænč] among older folks. **1967–68** *DARE* (Qu. F43, *After clothes have been washed, what do you do to get the soap off?*) Inf **MO38,** [rɛnč] 'em; **AR54,** [rænč]; **GA46,** [rænč]—old-fashioned. **1976** Garber *Mountain-ese* 74 **sAppalachians,** I'll be through with my housework when I ranch the dishes. **1989** Pederson *LAGS Tech. Index* 70, [13 infs gave proncs of the types [rænč, rænš], 5 [rænts], 6 [rɛnč], 2 [ren(t)s].] **2000** *DARE* File **seKY** (as of c1950), Go *ranch* that soap out if [sic] your hair.

rinsh See **rinse 1**

Rio Grande perch n **TX**

A blue-spotted perchlike fish (*Cichlasoma cyanoguttatum*). Also called **guinea perch**

1946 Stilwell *Hunting in TX* 111, One member of the perch family really appeals to me. . . the Rio Grande perch, more frequently called the bullhead or the guinea perch. **1967** *DARE* (Qu. P1, . . *Kinds of freshwa-*

ter fish . . caught around here . . good to eat) Inf **TX**1, Rio Grande perch—goggle-eyed, bites like a trout; **TX**19, Rio grande perch—same as guinea perch.

rip n¹

1 An area of turbulence in the ocean caused by opposing tides or an irregular bottom; hence phr *back of the rip* in a very remote or inaccessible place.

1775 (1962) Romans *Nat. Hist. FL* app 88, You will see a rip appear like breakers; but in the rip is 18 or 20 fathom, and the moment a ship gets into this rip, she jumps out of soundings. **1807** MA *Hist. Soc. Coll.* 2d ser 3.73, Ships in storms get within the dangerous rips which lie off the island [=Chappaquiddick]. **1882** Godfrey *Is. Nantucket* 311 **eMA,** Standing here, one can see the "rips" in the distance, over which break the angry waves. **1916** Macy–Hussey *Nantucket Scrap Basket* 125, *"Back of the rip"*—The dangerous shoals and sandbars [*DARE* Ed: Prob instead the water above the shoals and sandbars] which surround the island are known as "rips"; the islanders have a way of consigning any annoying person or thing to a point beyond these obstructions to navigation, from which it would be difficult if not impossible to return. Example: "I wish he (or it) was back of the rip!" **1967–68** *DARE* (Qu. O15, . . *Names . . for . . kinds of waves . . referring to how the water acts*) Inf **CT**10, Rip—more a current; **MA**55, Chop; rip; (Qu. O18, *Different currents or actions of the water that are important when you're in a boat*) Inf **HI**1, Rip—I don't think we have this here—where changing tide meets.

2 A stretch of rough water in a river or stream; a rapids. **chiefly NEng, esp ME**

a1828 in B. James *Jrnl.* (1896) ii.195 *(OED2)* **ME,** We passed several very dangerous places, which they there [on the Kennebec R.] termed 'rips', which was a confused number of rocks and large stones in the direct way we were obliged to pass, and which generally had a fall of some few feet. **1839** Holmes *Rept. Aroostook R.* 7 **ME,** The existing obstacles which present themselves to the present navigation of the river, are, the "rips," which are occasioned principally by loose boulders of rocks. **1882** Hubbard *Moosehead Lake* 61 *(DA)* **ME,** A canoe would have to be carried around the 'rip.' **1966–68** *DARE* (Qu. C3, *A place in a swift stream where the surface of the water is broken*) Infs **ME**1, 5, **NJ**21, Rips. **1975** Gould *ME Lingo* 232, *Rip*—The word for agitation and turbulence in . . a stream. . . In the woods, a *rip* is less than a rapids, and more than a riffle. **1977** *New Yorker* 9 May 106 **AK,** A couple of tributaries came into the river . . and they deepened the pools and improved the rips. **1979** Lewis *How to Talk Yankee* [31] **nNEng,** We kept to the right hand side in the rips below Russell's Point, found the *heavy water,* and put that 20-foot Guide's Model through there *slicker'n a smelt.* **1982** *Smithsonian Letters* **ME,** *Rips,* where the river goes rapidly over rocks, rapids.

rip n² Cf **Old Rip**

1 often with *old:* A bony or ill-tempered animal, esp a horse. [*OED2* 1778 →]

1883 *Amer. Philol. Assoc. Trans.* 14.52 **Sth,** *Rip,* 'a lean horse,' not uncommon in South, though a low word. "There's an old rip down there in the stable; you may take him and ride him to hell, if you want to," said an irate Carolina farmer to a foraging party during the war. **1905** [see **2** below]. **1915** *DN* 4.200, *Rip,* a reprobate; a screw of a horse. "You old rip! I'll whip you until you know enough to stand still." **1967–69** *DARE* (Qu. K16, *A cow with a bad temper*) Inf **OH**35, Rip; (Qu. K44, *A bony or poor-looking horse*) Infs **SC**34, **VA**24, Rip; **PA**191, Old rip.

2 also rarely *rip-jack;* often in phr *old rip:* A reckless, dissolute, or otherwise disreputable person, esp a woman. [*OED2* 1791 →]

1894 Twain *Pudd'nhead Wilson* 101, What does the old rip want with me? . . Send her in! **1899** (1912) Green *VA Folk-Speech* 355, *Rip.* . . A vicious, reckless, and worthless person; applied to a man or woman of vicious practices or propensities, and more or less worn by dissipation. **1904** *DN* 2.427 **Cape Cod MA** (as of a1857), *Old rip.* . . A disrespectful term for a loud-mouthed woman. **1905** *DN* 3.89 **nwAR,** *Old rip.* . . An ill-tempered person of either sex. 'He's the hatefulest old rip I ever saw.' This can be applied to a horse also. **1907** *DN* 3.195 **seNH,** *Old rip.* . . A shrewish woman of bad reputation. "She's an old rip." **1921** *DN* 5.117 **KY,** *Rip,* a woman of ill repute. **1930** Shoemaker *1300 Words* 50 **cPA Mts** (as of c1900), *Rip*—"Old rip", a hardened old sport or libertine. **c1937** in 1970 Yetman *Voices* 226 **SC** [Black], When Marse Jim's pappy die he leave de whole thing [=plantation] to Marse

Jim, if he take care of his mammy. She sure was a rip-jack. She say niggers didn't need nothin' to eat. Dey just like animals, not like other folks. She whip me, many time . . till I was black and blue. **1941** *LANE* Map 466 *(Slovenly)* 1 inf, **cwMA**, She's a dirty old rip. **1962** Morison *One Boy's Boston* 16, She expressed herself freely on the character of our visitors; one whom she described as an "old rip" was thenceforth regarded with suspicion. **1965–70** *DARE* (Qu. AA7b, . . *A woman who is very fond of men and is always trying to know more—if she's not respectable about it*) Infs **KY**19, **NC**37, 41, **TN**1, (Old) rip; **IA**30, Darned old rip; **NJ**1, She is a rip; (Qu. HH34, *General words . . for a woman, not necessarily uncomplimentary*) Inf **IL**26, Some old rip; (Qu. HH36, *A careless, slovenly woman: "She's just an old _____."*) Infs **IL**126, **IN**25, **NE**1, Rip; (Qu. HH37, *An immoral woman*) Infs **IA**27, **KY**19, 42, **NY**22, **NC**30, **TN**1, **VA**2, (Old) rip; (Qu. HH40, *Uncomplimentary words for an old man*) Infs **CT**13, **OH**37, (Old) rip; (Qu. II36b, *Of somebody who talks back or gives rude answers . . "She certainly is _____!"*) Inf **MO**18, Mean old rip. **1983** *MJLF* 9.1.53 **ceKY** (as of 1956), *Rip . . :* a dissolute woman.

rip n³ See **ripper 2**

rip and rear v phr Also *rip and rar(e)* [Cf *EDD* to rip and rear (at *rip* v.) "to work hard for"]
=**rip and tear 1.**
   1884 *Anglia* 7.270 **Sth, S Midl** [Black], *To rip en' r'ar* = to move excitedly. **1893** Shands *MS Speech* 53, *Rip and rare* [rɪp æn rær]. This term is used by all classes of Mississippians as meaning *to create a violent disturbance*, especially by swearing and cursing. *Rar* [rɑə] is sometimes heard for *rare* among the negroes. **1909** *DN* 3.363 **eAL, wGA**, *Rip and rear. . .* To rip and tear, rage and scold. **1912** *DN* 3.587 **wIN**, *Rip and rear. . .* To rage.

rip and stave v phr
   1915 *DN* 4.188 **swVA**, *Rip and stave. . .* To rage and scold about.

rip and tear v phr
1 To rave, rage; to behave violently. [*EDD* rip and tear (at *rip* v.) "to curse and swear, to behave uproariously"] Cf **rip and rear**
   1873 Twain–Warner *Gilded Age* 249, A man wants rest, a man wants peace—a man don't want to rip and tear around *all* the time. **1885** Twain *Huck. Finn* 179, It was perfectly lovely the way he would rip and tear and rair up behind when he was getting it off. **1899** (1912) Green *VA Folk-Speech* 354, *To rip and tear*, to be violent and furious, as with excitement and rage. **1916** *DN* 4.342 **NY, OH, KS**, *Rip and tear*. To rave. **1952** Brown *NC Folkl.* 1.585 **wNC**, *Rip and tear. . .* To curse, quarrel, to be noisily unpleasant. **1956** McAtee *Some Dialect NC* 37, Rip and tear. . . Curse, speak violently. **1972** Cooper *NC Mt. Folkl.* 95, *Rip and tear*—to raise cain.
2 To go to bed; to retire for the night.
   1937 *Writer* 50.239 **neOH** [Black], *Rip and tear*—to retire for the night. **1967–69** *DARE* (Qu. X40, . . *Ways . . of saying, "I'm going to bed"*) Infs **MA**58, **NY**34, Rip and tear. **a1975** Lunsford *It Used to Be* 174 **sAppalachians**, "Let's rip and tear" means let's go to bed. **1989** *DARE* File **wNC**, *Rip and tear*—Odd as it may seem, I can verify this as a humorous var of *retire*, v, as in "retire for the night." I learned it from an aunt who lived as a member of our family c. 1916 in Burke Co.

ripe adj [*OED2* c1410 →]
Of an abscess, boil, or sore: suppurating; ready to be lanced or discharged.
   1909 *DN* 3.363 **eAL, wGA**, *Ripe. . .* Said of a boil when it is ready to be lanced. **1950** *WELS* (When the core of one of these is ready to come out, you say it is) 45 Infs, **WI**, Ripe. **1966–69** *DARE* (Qu. BB31, *When a swelling begins to get less . . it's _____*; total Infs questioned, 75) Inf **MS**45, Getting ripe; (Qu. BB36, *When there's an open sore and this yellowish stuff is coming out of it . . it's _____*) Infs **IN**54, **LA**11, **MO**21, (Getting) ripe.

riped ppl adj [*OED2* ripe v.¹ 2 "To make ripe" 1398–1591; fig use 1513–1863]
Ripened.
   1946 Stuart *Tales Plum Grove* 93 **seKY**, I picked up the first frost-riped persimmons.

ripgut n
1 A **cordgrass** (here: *Spartina pectinata*). **esp MO**

1920 *Torreya* 20.18 **MO**, *Spartina michauxiana* . . lowland grass, sawgrass, rip-gut, Hartmann, Mo. **1940** *AmSp* 15.376 **NE**, A shiftless trader of the neighborhood was nicknamed 'Ripgut' because of his habit of cutting coarse slough grass, known as 'ripgut,' with which to feed his bony horses. **1967** *DARE* (Qu. L8, *Hay that grows naturally in damp places*) Infs **MO**11, 38, Ripgut. **1995** Brophy Coll. 63 **swMO** (as of c1960), *Ripgut.* = [S]lough-grass—a kind of long sharp grass in river bottoms.
2 also *ripgut brome, ripgut grass*: A **bromegrass**, usu *Bromus rigidus*. **esp CA**
   1923 in 1925 Jepson *Manual Plants CA* 78, *B[romus] rigidus* . . "Ripgut" Grass. . . At maturity nos. 3 to 6 [=*Bromus rubens, B. madritensis, B. rigidus, B. sterilis*] are injurious to grazing animals; the disjointed sharp-pointed florets with their long rough awns penetrate the eyes, nose and mouth parts, causing sores and blindness. **1940** *Jrl. Mammalogy* 21.394 **CA**, Each burrow opening was partly surrounded by small . . stands of rip-gut, rye, barley, oats and vetch. . . There were few sprouted caches except a few of rip-gut grass after the rains began. **1969** *DARE* (Qu. L8, *Hay that grows naturally in damp places*) Inf **CA**136, Ripgut. **1970** Correll *Plants TX* 126, *Bromus rigidus* . . Ripgut. **1998** (acc) U.S. Dept. Ag. *Plants Database* (Internet), *Bromus diandrus* . . ripgut brome.

ripgut fence n Cf **shadback fence**
A type of rail fence; see quots.
   1931–33 *LANE Worksheets* **seRI**, Ripgut equals rail fence. **1934** Hanley Disks **cME**, That was called rip-gut fence. [Inf says it's the same as shad-belly fence.] **1940–41** Cassidy *WI Atlas* **neWI**, Ripgut (fence) (common term). **1949** Kurath *Word Geog.* 55, Other types of fences are built of rails: the *post-and-rail* fence of New England, also known as the *Connecticut rail fence*, in which the rails are inserted in sturdy posts; the *herring-bone fence* = *stake-and-rider fence* = *buck fence* (Eastern Pennsylvania) = *rip-gut fence* in which the rails are supported by crossed stakes. **1968** *DARE* (Qu. L62, *A fence made of split logs*) Inf **UT**9, Ripgut fence. [FW illustr: Drawing in text represents crossed stakes supporting a single line of poles.] **1983** *High Country News* (Paonia CO) 5 Sept 9, I return from a trip to the pinon-juniper mesas of Utah or the Stanley Basin of Idaho with sketches and notes on a particular ripgut fence or a six-rail-buck horse pasture. [*DARE* Ed: Photo shows a fence of crossed stakes with poles between the crotches and three poles angled from the ground to each crotch.]

ripgut grass See **ripgut 2**

rip-jack Se **rip** n² **2**

ripper n
1 Something or someone remarkable for its kind. Cf **piss-ripper**
   1848 in 1935 *AmSp* 10.41 **Nantucket MA**, *Ripper.* Anything very large of its kind. **1899** (1912) Green *VA Folk-Speech* 355, *Ripper,* A very efficient person or thing; one who does great execution: as, he is a regular *ripper.* A big lie. **1930** Henry *Conquering Plains* 65 **TX**, Both drovers and cowboys called an unfortunate transaction "bad medicine" and a bad failure "a ripper." **1939** FWP *Guide TN* 135, Backcountry folk are prone to use parts of speech in strange ways. . . An extravagant lie is a "ripper," a "snorter," a "screamer." **1942** Berrey–Van den Bark *Amer. Slang* 29.2, *Something excellent.* . . ripper; 316.2, *Big lie.* . . "whopper." . . ripper; 395.1, *Superior or admirable person.* . . ripper; 432.2, *Expert.* . . ripper. **1964** Jackman–Long *OR Desert* 394, Ripper—a good big horse with endurance.
2 also rarely *rip*: =**double-runner a.** **esp wMA, CT**
   1943 *LANE* Map 573–574 *(Sled; sleigh)* 5 infs, **wCT, Long Is. NY**, Ripper; 1 inf, **swMA**, Double rip; rips; 1 inf, **nwMA**, Rippers, pair of rippers; [1 inf, **csCT**, Ripper [used of a low sled with solid sides, coming to a point in front]; 1 inf, **csCT**, Ripper, made of two cutters]. **1949** Kurath *Word Geog.* 59, *Bob sled* is the regular term in the Midland and the North for a coasting sled consisting of two short sleds or *bobs* that are fastened together, tandem fashion, with a heavy board. . . *Double ripper*, occasionally shortened to *ripper*, or *double rip*, is found in all of Connecticut and in western Massachusetts. **1957** *Sat. Eve. Post Letters* **MA**, A *"Ripper"* was two sleds joined together by a large plank. **1967** *DARE* (Qu. N40b, . . *Sleighs for carrying people*) Inf **MA**5, Ripper—for kids sliding, 2 sleds joined by one board. **1999** *DARE* File **nwMA** (as of early 20th cent), We used to go sledding on this road, you know. We'd come down on rippers and flexible flyers.
3 See quot.

1968 *DARE* (Qu. N40a, . . *Sleighs . . for hauling loads*) Inf **CT2**, *Ripper*—big heavy sledge.

rippet n Also sp *rippit* [Scots dial; *OED2 rippit* 1508 →] **chiefly S Midl**

A noisy disturbance, dispute, or fight; hence v *rippet* to cause a disturbance; to fight.

1870 (1935) Duval *Advent. Big Foot* 270 **TX**, At last the manager threw his hat among 'em and called out, "Stampede all," and the "rippit" commenced. **1884** Smith *Bill Arp's Scrap Book* 97 **GA**, They all put on their working aprons and went to beating eggs and stirring batter, and some more young ladies dropped in to help and I never heard such a rippet as they kept up all day. **1887** (1967) Harris *Free Joe* 111 **nGA**, Folks has mighty bad luck when they go a-rippitin' hether an' yan on the mounting. **1890** *DN* 1.66 **KY**, *Rippit* . . a great noise. "He made a great rippit." **1909** *DN* 3.364 **eAL, wGA**, *Rippit*. . . A fight, a mix-up. Universal. **1913** Kephart *Highlanders* 294 **sAppalachians**, If he and his neighbor dislike each other, there is a hardness between them; if they quarrel, it is a ruction, a rippit, a jower, or an upscuddle. **1952** Brown *NC Folkl.* 1.585, *Rippit*. . . A fight; to fight. **1968** *DARE* (Qu. KK16, *A great noise or disturbance: "I wish they'd stop making that awful _____."*) Inf **VA21**, Rippet. **1975** *Appalachian Jrl.* 2.157 **wNC**, The many words that mean *fight* attest to the prevalence of the activity. . . A *racket* implies more actual contact, whereas *ruckus* or *rookus, fraction,* and *fray* all mean a fist fight or gun fight. *Rippit* is sometimes used in this connection, but it may also mean, as one man defined the term, "a cuttin' up sort of a night, a rousin' good time, drunk and dancin'."

rippity slash adv phr [Echoic] Cf **rickety-bang**

1913 Johnson *Highways St. Lawrence to VA* 13, Well, what changes have taken place since I was a boy! Gosh! who'd ever think I'd live to see a wagon goin' rippity slash through the street with no horse hitched to it.

ripple n[1] Also *ripple grass*
=**buckhorn plantain.**

1819 *Amer. Farmer* 1.149 **sePA**, My milch cows . . were turned into a field well set with *Rib Plantain* or *Ripple Grass,* as it is generally called. **1894** *Jrl. Amer. Folkl.* 7.96 **WV**, *Plantago lanceolata* . . ripple, ribwort, English plantain. **1967–68** WI Acad. *Trans.* 56.304, *Plantago lanceolata.* . . Ribgrass, Ripplegrass [etc]. **1982** Barrick *Coll.* **csPA**, *Ripple*—lance leaf plantain. Plantago lanceolate [sic].

ripple n[2] See **riffle** n[2]

ripple, make the See **riffle, make the**

rip-roaring adj Also *rip-raring* Cf **ring-tailed roarer, ripsnorter**

Boisterous, unrestrained, very lively; hence adv *rip-roaring* extremely; similarly n *rip-roarer* a very lively time.

1834 Caruthers *Kentuckian* 1.62, There was a rip-roaring sight of slight o' hand and tumblin work there. **1859** Taliaferro *Fisher's R.* 72 **nwNC** (as of 1820s), I . . went to eatin' riproarin' fashion. **1878** Hart *Sazerac Lying Club* 89 **NV**, That thar boy was in a rip-rarin, ragin' fever, and jest a-burnin' up by inches. **1884** Nye *Baled Hay* 231 **WY**, He thought . . Kirke was there . . to give Laramie the grandest, riproaringest tempest of mirth that she had ever experienced. **1905** *DN* 3.64 **eNE**, *Rip-roaring*. . . Strong, intensive. "We had a rip-roaring time." *Ibid* 92 **nwAR**, *Rip-roaring*. . . Excited, angry. 'He was just rip-roaring,' Common. **1912** *DN* 3.588 **wIN**, *Rip-roaring*. . . They were having a rip-roaring time when I saw them." **1965–70** *DARE* (Qu. FF17, *A very good or enjoyable time: "We all had a _____ last night."*) 27 Infs, **scattered**, Rip-roaring (good) time; (Qu. FF18, *Joking words . . about a noisy or boisterous celebration or party: "They certainly _____ last night."*) Inf **IL113**, Had a rip-roaring time; **AL5**, Riproarer; (Qu. GG40, *Words or expressions meaning violently angry*) Inf **CA114**, Rip-roaring mad; (Qu. LL37, *To make a statement as strong as you can: "I could have wrung her neck, I was so _____ mad."*) Inf **MA14**, Rip-roaring. **1986** Pederson *LAGS Concordance*, 1 inf, **ceTN**, Rip-roaring good time.

rip-roodle v Cf **rip and tear 1**

1909 *DN* 3.364 **eAL, wGA**, *Rip-roodle*. . . To romp, go tearing about.

ripsack n [See quot 1874] *hist*
=**gray whale.**

1860 *Merc. Marine Mag.* VII.213 (*DAE*), It being difficult to capture

them, they have a variety of names among whalemen, as 'Ripsack,' . . 'Devil-fish.' **1874** Scammon *Marine Mammals* 24, The habits of the Gray [whale] have brought upon it many significant names, among which the most prominent are . . "Gray-back" and "Rip-sack." *Ibid* 25, "Rip-sack" originated with the manner of flensing. **1911** U.S. Bur. Census *Fisheries 1908* 310, Gray whale. . . also called "devilfish," "hard-head," "grayback," "rip sack," "mussell digger," etc.

‡**ripshack** n Cf **rip** n[2] 1, **ripsack**

1921 *DN* 5.117 **KY**, *Ripshack,* an old sow.

ripshin n **Appalachians**

A thorny or entangling plant; hence comb *ripshin thicket.*

1913 Kephart *Highlanders* 304 **sAppalachians**, Rip Shin Thicket, Dog-hobble Ridge . . they, too, were well and fitly named. **1927** *AmSp* 2.363 **cwWV**, *Ripshin* . . a running brier. "The hill field is full of ripshins." **1936** in 1944 *ADD*, *Ripshin*. . . Dewberry bushes;—so named from the briars, . . W. Va. or Ohio. Reported use c. 1900. **1939** FWP *Guide TN* 430 **ceTN**, Great boulders, left above the ground by erosion, are covered with moss and often lie in "ripshin" thickets of laurel, or rhododendron.

ripsnorter n Cf **ring-tailed roarer**

A violent, wild, extravagant, or striking example of its kind—hence adj, adv *ripsnorting.*

1840 (1955) Crockett *Almanacks* 20 (*OED2*), Of all the ripsnorters I ever tutched upon, thar never war one that could pull her boat alongside of Grace Peabody. **1846** *Yale Lit. Mag.* 336, What a rip-snorting [=extremely] red head you have got! **1859** (1968) Bartlett *Americanisms* 367, Rip-snorter. . . A tearer, driver, dasher. **1889** Munroe *Dorymates* 84 **MA**, Boys, we are in for a regular 'rip-snorter.' I never saw a nastier night. **1905** *DN* 3.64 **eNE**, *Rip-snorter*. . . Terror. "That cowboy was a rip-snorter." **1942** McAtee *Dial. Grant Co. IN* 53 (as of 1890s), *Rip-snorter* . . a violent storm; a tempestuous person or situation; the best or biggest of its kind. Slang. *Ibid, Rip-snortin'* . . having the qualities of a rip-snorter; rip-roaring, violent, superlative. Slang. **1942** Warnick *Garrett Co. MD* 13 **nwMD** (as of 1900–18), *Rip-snorter* . . something unusually violent (Slang). **1956** Ker *Vocab. W. TX* 65, *Strong wind from north* . . rip snorter. [2 of 67 infs] **1965–70** *DARE* (Qu. B25, . . *Joking names . . for a very heavy rain. . . "It's a regular _____."*) Infs **CT17, IA8**, Ripsnorter; (Qu. Y29b, . . *A man who doesn't stay home much*) Inf **MI106**, Ripsnorter; (Qu. BB47, *Feeling in the best of health and spirits: "I'm feeling _____!"*) Inf **ID5**, Ripsnorting; (Qu. FF17, . . *A very good or enjoyable time: "We all had a last night."*) Infs **MN36, NM4**, Ripsnorting time; (Qu. FF18, *Joking words . . about a noisy or boisterous celebration or party: "They certainly _____ last night."*) Inf **CA136**, Had a ripsnorter; **IL113**, Had a ripsnorting time; **TX33**, Ripsnorter; (Qu. KK27, *A very lively, active old person*) Inf **TX70**, Ripsnorter; **WI34**, Ripsnortin'. **1966** Barnes–Jensen *Dict. UT Slang* 36, *Rip snorter:* . . a cantankerous or violent person or thing. "That woman would be a rip snorter as a wife." The words "rip snorter" are sometimes used, also, to indicate a superior person or thing. **1978** *Detroit Free Press* (MI) 14 Apr sec B 15/4, A ripsnorting cockroach race, with the men on their hands and knees, urging their bugs down makeshift lanes.

ripstaver n, hence adj *ripstaving* Also sp *ripstavur*
=**ripsnorter.**

1833 *Sketches D. Crockett* 144, In ten minutes he yelled enough, and swore I was a ripstavur. **1859** (1968) Bartlett *Americanisms* 367, Ripstaver. A tearer, driver, dasher. **1906** *DN* 3.153 **nwAR**, *Rip-staving*. . . Enjoyable, exceedingly good. "We had a rip-staving time." **1995** Brophy *Coll.* 63 **swMO** (as of c1960), Ripstaver. [A] first-rate person or thing, a dashing fellow.

rip-tail snorter n [Blend of *ring-tail* + **ripsnorter**]
=**ring-tailed roarer.**

1895 *DN* 1.399 **cNY**, *Rip tail snorter:* one who attracts much attention, who creates a sensation. "He's an old rip tail snorter." **1968** *DARE* (Qu. B25, . . *Joking names . . for a very heavy rain. . . "It's a regular _____."*) Inf **MD24**, Rip-tail snorter.

ris v See **rise** v A1a, 2b

rise v

A Gram forms. Note: There has been considerable intermingling of the forms of *rise* and *raise,* presumably because of the widespread use of the latter in var intr senses (see **raise** v C).

Because it is generally impossible to determine from an isolated example what other forms a speaker uses, all forms that are historically from *rise* and used in senses in which *rise* is common are treated here, even though some speakers might in fact use *raise* as the present tense. But examples of such forms used in senses in which *raise* is the preponderant verb used are treated at **raise** v A.

1 past: usu *rose;* also:

a *riz, ris(s);* rarely *rizzed.* **chiefly SE, Lower Missip Valley, SW; also NEast** See Map

1704 (1825) Knight *Jrls.* 49 **MA,** From the time I went to bed to the time I Riss. **1836** (1955) *Crockett Almanacks* 54 **wTN,** His dander riz right up. **1843** (1916) Hall *New Purchase* 172 **IN,** I never know'd what to preach about till I riz up. **1843** (1847) Field *Drama Pokerville* 117 **MO,** A sky rocket never *ris* faster. **1851** Hooper *Widow Rugby's Husband* 47 **AL,** I riz right up on a cotton bag. **1890** *DN* 1.71 **LA,** *Riz:* did rise. **1893** *DN* 1.277 **wCT,** Rise [past, past pple:] *riz.* **1893** Shands *MS Speech* 53, *Riz* (riz). Negro for *rose,* the past tense of *rise.* **1903** *DN* 2.327 **seMO,** *Riz, pret.* of rise. **1907** *DN* 3.235 **nwAR,** *Riz, pret.* of rise. **1909** *DN* 3.364 **eAL, wGA,** *Riz, prep.* [sic] and *pp.* of rise. Ibid 415 **nME,** *Riz, v. pret.* and *pp.* Rose or raised. **1920** Hunter *Trail Drivers TX* 487, I have been right here in Texas since the morning star first "riz," and when you publish your next book I hope to be a retired stockman. **1923** *DN* 5.219 **swMO,** *Riz, v.* Raised, or arose. "He riz up in bed an' shore rose hell when Doc set 'is arm." **1929** Sale *Tree Named John* 101 **MS** [Black], Den Ah tell her de creek riz. **1952** Brown *NC Folkl.* 1.585, *Riz* [rɪz]. . . Past tense and past participle of *rise.* . . General. Illiterate. **1953** Atwood *Survey of Verb Forms* 19, *Rise.* . . Only the preterite is recorded. . . The standard . . *rose* . . prevails throughout N. Eng., N.Y., N.J., and Pa. . . *Riz* . . occurs with some frequency in n.e. N. Eng. . . usually alongside *rose.* . . In s. N. Eng. and throughout the whole of the M[iddle] A[tlantic] S[tates] *riz* occurs only in a very scattered way. . . In the S[outhern] A[tlantic] S[tates], however, it is the dominant form [among those of poor education] . . little currency [among those of fair education] . . and most . . Va. and N.C. Negro informants use it. **1962** [see **A1b** below.] **1965–70** *DARE* (Qu. OO6a, *Talking about dough with yeast in it: "The room was warm, so the dough _____ [quickly]."*) 29 Infs, **esp SE, Lower Missip Valley, SW; also NEast,** Riz [Of these 29 Infs, 12 also gave *riz* as the past pple at Qu. OO6b, 11 *risen,* 4 *rose,* and 1 *raised.*]; (Qu. CC11, *When somebody has had a lot of good luck . . he _____*) Inf **SC3,** Riz to the top. **1968** *DARE* Tape **GA30,** The alligator riz an' went on. **c1970** Pederson *Dial. Surv. Rural GA* **seGA** (*Yes, it [=the sun] _____ at six o'clock today*) 10 [of 64] infs, Riz. **1989** Pederson *LAGS Tech. Index* 18 **Gulf Region,** [474 infs, [roz] and varr;] 51 infs, [rɪz]; 1 inf, [rɪzd].

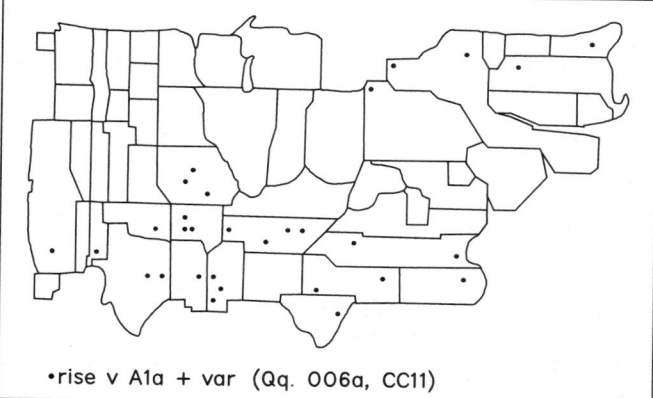

•rise v A1a + var (Qq. OO6a, CC11)

b *rised.*

1943 *LANE* Map 657 (*Rose*) 2 infs, **csVT, csNH,** Rised; 1 inf, **nwMA,** *Rised,* rare. **1962** Atwood *Vocab. TX* 76, *The sun rose.* Those who use the verb *rise* usually from the past with *rose.* . . The Southern form *riz* . . is rare, archaic, and uneducated; *rised* . . is of negligible occurrence. **1965–70** *DARE* (Qu. OO6a, *Talking about dough with yeast in it: "The room was warm, so the dough _____ [quickly]."*) 77 Infs, **scattered,** Rised. [Of these 77 Infs, 16 also offered *raised* and 6 *rose* in resp to this question. 39 offered *risen* as the past participle at Qu. OO6b, 17 *raised,* 14 *rised,* and 7 *rose* or *riz.*] **1967** LeCompte *Word Atlas* 101 **seLA,** *At six in the morning yesterday, the sun _____* . . rised [4 of 21 infs].

1975 Allen *LAUM* 2.23, *Rise.* . . Of the infs. replying with the verb *rise* 90% [of 437] use the standard preterit *rose.* . . *Rised,* also a minor Midland form found in Ohio and Kentucky, occurs in the speech of four . . infs. in Minnesota and South Dakota, two of whom have foreign-language background and two of whom have Ohio parentage. **1989** Pederson *LAGS Tech. Index* 18 **Gulf Region,** 7 infs, [raɪzd].

c *rise.* *esp freq among Black speakers*

1966–70 *DARE* (Qu. OO6a) Infs **FL49, NY35, SC9, 26, 32, 67, 70, VA48,** Rise. [5 of 8 Infs Black] **c1970** Pederson *Dial. Surv. Rural GA* **seGA** (*Yes, it [=the sun] _____ at six o'clock today*) 3 infs, Rise. [All infs Black] **1989** Pederson *LAGS Tech. Index* 18 **Gulf Region,** 6 infs, [raɪz]; 1 inf, [rɑz].

d *risen.*

1884 *Anglia* 7.251 [Black], *Pres.* (a)rise—*Past.* riz, ris'n (de bred ris'n)—*Pass. Part.* rose. **c1970** Pederson *Dial. Surv. Rural GA* **seGA** (*Yes, it [=the sun] _____ at six o'clock today*) 2 infs, Risen. [Both infs Black] **1989** Pederson *LAGS Tech. Index* 18 **Gulf Region,** 3 infs, ['rɪzn].

2 past pple, ppl adj: usu *risen;* also:

a *rose, rosen,* and varr. **chiefly Sth, S Midl** See Map

1781 *PA Jrl. & Weekly Advt.* (Philadelphia) 16 May, One of the most common vulgarisms . . is putting the preterite for the participle . . *rose,* for *risen.* **1884** [see **A1d** above]. **1886** *Overland Mth.* (2d ser) 7.637 **FL** [Black], De moon had rose den, white 'n' clar. **1965–70** *DARE* (Qu. OO6b, . . *"She put the dough in the oven too soon—before it had _____ enough."*) 65 Infs, **chiefly Sth, S Midl,** Rose; **KY22,** Rose up. [Of all Infs responding to the question, 27% were gs educ or less, 32% coll educ; of those giving these responses, 50% were gs educ or less, 12% coll educ. Of these Infs, 51 also gave *rose* as the past tense at Qu. OO6a, 6 gave *rised,* 4 *riz,* and 4 *raised.*] **c1970** Pederson *Dial. Surv. Rural GA* **seGA** (*Has the sun _____ yet?*) 18 [of 64] infs, Rose; [3 infs, Arose;] 1 inf, Rosen. **1989** Pederson *LAGS Tech. Index* 18 **Gulf Region,** [355 infs, ['rɪzn];] 111 infs, [roz]; 3 infs, [rozn]; 2 infs, [ro]; 1 inf, [rod]; 1 inf, [roðn]; 1 inf, [rozd]. **1998** *DARE* File **neTX,** We will never know what heights she would have [rozn] to.

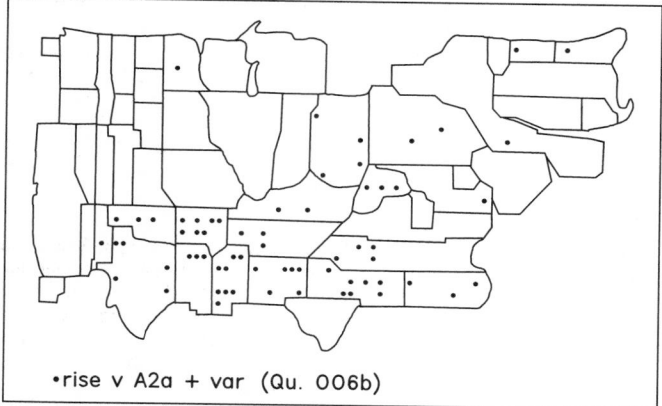

•rise v A2a + var (Qu. OO6b)

b *riz, ris.* **scattered, but esp SE, Lower Missip Valley** See Map on p. 596

1795 Dearborn *Columbian Grammar* 138, *List of Improprieties.* . . *Riz* for Risen. **1841** *Spirit of Times* 27 Mar 42 **AR,** Peltry is worth thirty cents a pound, and coon skins three bits a piece. Jim says if they will only stay "riz," he can make his everlasting fortune. **c1845** in 1981 *AmSp* 56.156 **swIL,** Pants have riz up in the regions of the boots. **1845** Thompson *Pineville* 16 **cGA,** Is [=have] the Ingins ris again? *Ibid* 29, But the Sweeny blood was "riz"—and . . he fought at random with desperation. **1848** Lowell *Biglow* 145 'Upcountry **MA**', Riz, risen. **1859** Taliaferro *Fisher's R.* 86 **nwNC** (as of 1820s), All the limbs on his tree had riz from the yeth two foot. **1870** Alcott *Little Women* 1.167 **MA,** I say, isn't bread "riz" enough when it runs over the pans? **1893** [see **A1a** above]. **1909** [see **A1a** above]. **1952** [see **A1a** above]. **1965–70** *DARE* (Qu. OO6b) 22 Infs, **esp SE, Lower Missip Valley,** Riz. [10 of 22 Infs were gs educ or less. Of these 22 Infs, 12 gave *riz* as the past tense at Qu. OO6a, 6 *rose,* 4 *rise, rised,* or *raised.*] **c1970** Pederson *Dial. Surv. Rural GA* **seGA** (*Has the sun _____ yet?*) 7 infs [of 64], Riz; [2 infs, Been riz] [Both infs Black] **1989** Pederson *LAGS Tech. Index* 18, 37 infs, **Gulf Region,** [rɪz]. **1996** *WI State Jrl.* (Madison) 31 Mar advt suppl 10, Spring has sprung./ The grass has ris./ This is where your new car is.

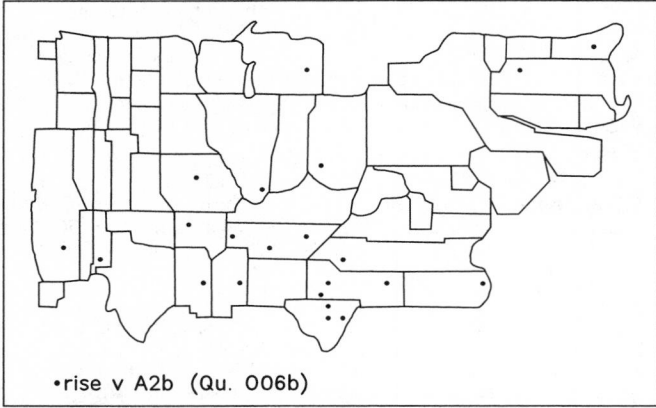

•rise v A2b (Qu. OO6b)

c *rised.*

1965–70 *DARE* (Qu. OO6b, *Talking about dough with yeast in it: "She put the dough in the oven too soon—before it had _____ enough."*) 26 Infs, **scattered,** Rised. [Of these 26 Infs, 14 also gave *rised* as the past tense at Qu. OO6a, 11 gave *rose,* and 2 *raised.*] **1989** Pederson *LAGS Tech. Index* 18, 12 infs, **Gulf Region,** [raɪzd].

d *rise. esp freq among Black speakers*

1966–70 *DARE* (Qu. OO6b, *Talking about dough with yeast in it: "She put the dough in the oven too soon—before it had _____ enough."*) Infs **SC**26, 67, 70, Rise; **OH**42, Would be rose or rise. [3 of 4 Infs Black] **c1970** Pederson *Dial. Surv. Rural GA* seGA (*Has the sun _____ yet?*) 5 infs, Rise; [1 inf, Arise; 1 inf, Been rise]. [All infs Black] **1989** Pederson *LAGS Tech. Index* 18 **Gulf Region,** 4 infs, [raɪz]; 1 inf, [raz].

B Senses.

1 also with *up:* To form an abscess, suppurate; hence ppl adjs *rising, riz(zed), rose.* [Cf *OED2 rise* v. 20.b "Of blisters, etc.: To become prominent on the skin or surface." 1388–1697] **Sth, S Midl** Cf **rising** n **1**

1965–70 *DARE* (Qu. BB36, *When there's an open sore and this yellowish stuff is coming out of it . . it's _____*) Inf **KY**34, Riz; **NC**61, Rising; (Qu. BB37, *When yellowish stuff comes out of a person's ear*) Infs **KY**19, 34, Head's riz; **FL**8, Ear is rising; **GA**3, Rizzed ear; **KY**19, Ear's riz; **KY**28, Rising ear; **NC**55, His ears is rose, his head rose; **NC**82, Ear's rising; **SC**7, Ear is riz. **1986** Pederson *LAGS Concordance,* 1 inf, **csTN,** Rise up—of a boil.

2 =**raise** v **B6.** *arch*

1781 *PA Jrl. & Weekly Advt.* (Philadelphia) 16 May [1]/3, Just as you *rise* the hill. . . [is a "corruption"] much more common in England than America. **1817** in 1866 Essex Inst. *Coll.* 8.230 **MA,** As you rise the eminence above the bridge, you have a most beautiful prospect of the adjacent country. **1832** in 1922 Ontario Hist. Soc. *Papers & Rec.* 19.120 **NJ,** We soon find ourselves rising the "mountain." **1892** Smith *Farm & Fireside* 248 **GA,** I see Tom Barker a risin' of the hill.

3 ppl adj, esp *riz;* Of baked goods: leavened, esp with yeast. **chiefly Nth** Cf **raised 1**

1872 Schele de Vere *Americanisms* 534, *Riz-cake,* for risen cake, is common to all the New England States. **1879** (1965) Tyree *Housekeeping in Old VA* 346, *Risen Cake.* . . Set it where it will rise. In the morning, when well risen, mix in the remainder of the butter and sugar [etc]. **1890** Holley *Samantha among Brethren* 168 **NY,** And now she thinks she can set hens better than I can—and make better riz biscuit. **1891** (1967) Freeman *New Engl. Nun* 183, I thought I'd have some riz biscuit in the mornin'. **1895** *DN* 1.383 **NJ,** *Riz bread:* yeast bread (not raised with soda). **1899** Garland *Boy Life* 335 **nwIA** (as of c1870s), The entire Jennings family joined in the feast of cold chicken, jelly, pickles, "riz" biscuits, dried beef, apple pie, cake, and cheese. **1905** *DN* 3.64 **eNE,** *Riz bread.* . . Light bread. **1907** *DN* 3.198 **seNH,** *Riz bread.* . . Raised bread. **1909** *DN* 3.415 **nME,** *Riz bread.* . . Raised bread. **1932** (1946) Hibben *Amer. Regional Cookery* 6, *Risen Sally Lunn* (Virginia). [*Ibid* 7, *Quick Sally Lunn* (South Carolina).] **1948** Camp *Hunter's Encycl.* 929, Serve this with a green salad with a tart French dressing, hot "rizzen" biscuits, and a glass of light claret. **1948** *WELS Suppl.* **cwWI,** Of course, you are familiar with the Bohemian kolache, as it is Englished? It is riz dough cast in rounds. **1949** Kurath *Word Geog.* 21, For the homemade wheat bread baked in loaves Eastern New England has *white-bread* . . *raised-bread* or *riz-bread.* In the same area doughnuts made of raised dough are called *raised doughnuts* or *riz doughnuts.*

1959 *VT Hist.* 27.154, *Riz doughnuts.* . . Raised doughnuts. Common. Rural areas. **1966–70** *DARE* (Qu. H19, *What do you mean by a biscuit? How are they made?*) Inf **CA**97, Risen biscuits—with yeast; **NY**35, Risen biscuits—put on radiator and rose; **NY**107, Riz biscuit; **PA**200, Risen biscuits—yeast used in them; **SC**21, Rised biscuits—plenty of baking soda; [**VA**98, Unrisen bread;] **WA**6, Yeast or risen biscuits; (Qu. H28, *Different shapes or types of doughnuts*) Inf **WI**20, Riz doughnut. **1974** Fink *Mountain Speech* 22 **wNC, eTN,** *Riz bread* . . risen or yeast bread. **1975** Gould *ME Lingo* 235, *Rose bread* uses yeast, and this term distinguishes it from the numerous favored hot breads which do not. *Raised bread.*

4 Used in var senses where *raise* would be std. Cf **raise** v **C**

1913 *DN* 4.1 **cME,** *Rise.* . . To raise. "Did you rise many ducks?" [**1925** *DN* 5.340 **Nfld,** *Rise,* v.t. Raise.] **c1938** in 1970 Hyatt *Hoodoo* 2.1173 **seGA,** Whenevah de sun rise, dat rises dem [=people who have been conjured]. When de sun goes down . . dey git dat misery worstest shape, much badder shape. **1941** *LANE* Map 281, 1 inf, **seMA,** Bakers rise it with yeast. *Ibid* Map 282, [The same inf] Cream of tartar biscuit, 'they don't rise them'. **1986** Pederson *LAGS Concordance,* 1 inf, **nwTN,** You have to use yeast to rise it—of bread.

rise n

1 in phrr *the rise (of);* rarely *in the rise of:* More (than). **chiefly Sth, S Midl** *old-fash* Cf **rising** adj **1**

1834 in 1925 Bassett *Southern Overseer* 66, I muste plante the rise of a hundred aceres in coten. **1845** Hooper *Advent. Simon Suggs* 157 **AL,** "How many have you?" "The rise of seventy, and three hens a-settin'!" **1851** Hooper *Widow Rugby's Husband* 130 **AL,** Hit's now been thirty years and the rise. **1858** in 1956 Eliason *Tarheel Talk* 290 **neNC** [Black], At Mr Collins thar has bin de rise of A hundred down with the measles. **1884** Smith *Bill Arp's Scrap Book* 31 **nwGA,** It's now the rise of 42 years since I come into this cursed old world. **1899** (1912) Green *VA Folk-Speech* 355, *Rise.* . . Increase beyond a certain number. "He has the rise of fifty sheep." **1911** *DN* 3.539 **eKY,** *Rise of.* More than; e.g., "It's the rise of two miles from here to town." **1915** *DN* 4.188 **swVA,** *Rise of, the.* . . (Slightly) more than. "It's the rise of three miles to the mill." **1917** *DN* 4.416 **wNC,** *Rise of, the.* More than. "A leetle the rise o' six miles." **1939** *Hall Coll.* **wNC,** Hall: "How long have you lived here, Mr. Welch?" Jake Welch: "The rise of fifty years." **1974** Fink *Mountain Speech* 22 **wNC, eTN,** *Rise* . . in excess of. "He had in the rise of 20 hogs."

2 in phr *have the rise on (someone):* To be taller than (someone).

1914 *DN* 4.160 **cVA,** Ah'v got the rise on yo!

rised See **rise** v **A1b, 2c**

rise, make one's v phr Cf **rising** adj **2**

To be promoted to the next grade in school.

[**1859** M. Laborde *Hist. S.C. College* 35 (DA), The first rising examination was held on the 25th November and the several classes were advanced to the next higher grade.] **1959** Faulkner *Mansion* 133 **MS,** That gal . . wasn't trying to do nothing but jest get shut of having to go to school by getting there on time and knowing the lesson to make the rise next year. **1972** *Atlanta Letters* **GA,** Around Jefferson, Georgia at the end of school in May, the most often expression heard is "Did you make your rise?" Of course, it means "Did you get promoted?"

risen See **rise** v **A1d**

rise of the moon n Cf **light of the moon**

The period of the waxing moon.

1904 (1913) Johnson *Highways South* 165 **KY,** Take and boil meat that was killed in the rise of the moon—it don't matter when, if it's only killed before the moon fulls, and that meat will be plump as can be.

rise, Sally, rise n

=**little Sally Water(s).**

1970 *DARE* (Qu. EE1, . . *Games . . children play . . in which they form a ring, and either sing or recite a rhyme*) Inf **VA**54, Rise, Sally, rise.

rise up See **rise** v **B1**

rising n Also sp *rizing*

1 A boil, abscess, or other infected swelling. [*OED2* 1563 →; "Now *dial.* or *U.S.*"] **chiefly Sth, S Midl, TX, OK** See Map Cf **raising 4, rise** v **B1**

1834 (1930) Sewall *Diary* 160 **IL,** Laid up with a bad rising on my hand. **1843** in 1956 Eliason *Tarheel Talk* 290 **nw,cnNC,** I. . . have suffered a great deal with a rising on my gum. **1896** Harris *Sister Jane* 249 **GA,** I ain't never intirely got over that risin' that busted in my head. **1897** *KS Univ. Qrly.* (ser B) 6.56 **KS,** *Risin':* swelling in the head. **1899** (1912) Green *VA Folk-Speech* 355, *Rising.* . . He has a bad rising on his hand. **1902** *DN* 2.244 **sIL,** *Rising.* . . A boil. **1903** *DN* 2.327 **seMO,** *Rising.* . . A swelling; a boil or abscess. **1909** *DN* 3.364 **eAL, wGA,** *Rising.* . . A boil. **1910** *DN* 3.458 **FL, GA,** *Rising.* . . A boil. **1912** *DN* 3.588 **wIN,** *Rising.* . . A boil. **1914** *DN* 4.78 **ME, nNH,** *Risin'.* . . Boil, ulcer, tumor, swelling. *Ibid* 160 **cVA,** *Risin'.* . . Boil. . . Ah got a risin' on mah ankle. **1923** *DN* 5.219 **swMO,** *Risin'.* . . A boil, an abscess. **1929** *AmSp* 5.122 **ME,** A person had a "rising in the ear," the "phthisic" (asthma) or "salt rheum." **1960** Williams *Walk Egypt* 231 **GA,** She was prey to everything, croup and colic, earache and "risings." **1965–70** *DARE* (Qu. BB33a, . . *A swelling under the skin, bigger than a pimple, that comes to a head*) 110 Infs, **chiefly Sth, S Midl,** Rising; (Qu. BB37, *When yellowish stuff comes out of a person's ear, he has a _____*) 86 Infs, **chiefly Sth, S Midl,** Rising (in his ear *or* in his head); NC41, Boil or rising in his head; SC32, Rising in the ear; MO9, Rising of the head; (Qu. BB30, . . *A hard, painful swelling [often on a finger] that seems to come from deep under the skin*) 50 Infs, **chiefly Sth, S Midl, TX, OK,** Rising; (Qu. BB33b, . . *A swelling under the skin—if it is very big or serious*) 17 Infs, **esp S Atl, Lower Missip Valley,** Rising; (Qu. X59, . . *The small infected pimples that form usually on the face*) Inf **TX35,** Risings. **1971** *Today Show Letters* **cnAL** (as of a1940), A pimple was never such, alway was called a "risin'" (rising). **1982** *Smithsonian Letters* **AR,** A rizin' in the head. . . it's a boil inside your head, and it breaks and runs out of your ear. **1994** NC Lang. & Life Project *Harkers Is. Vocab.* 9 **eNC,** *Risin'.* . . A swelling. *She had a risin' on her arm.*

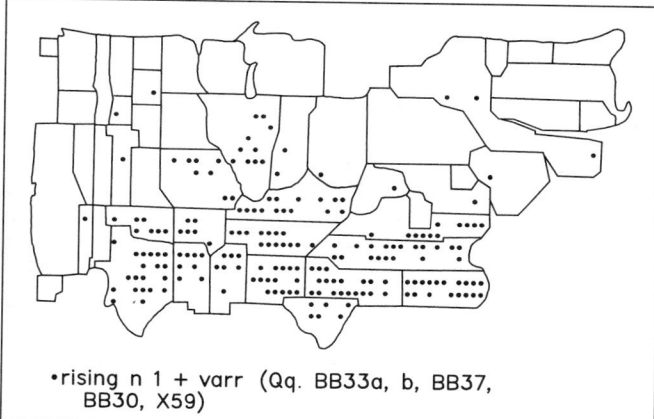

•rising n 1 + varr (Qq. BB33a, b, BB37, BB30, X59)

2 rarely pl; also in combs: Yeast or other leavening agent. [*OED2* 1594 →; "*dial.*"] Cf **lightening, raising 3, salt-rising**
1856 in 1862 Colt *Went to KS* 90 **NY,** I have mixed up some bread, using baking powder for risings, for I could not tend to raising yeast. **1887** (1895) Robinson *Uncle Lisha* 91 **wVT,** Jemimy she allers uses milk risin'; mis'able flat-tasted bread it makes tew. **1899** (1912) Green *VA Folk-Speech* 355, *Rising.* . . That which is used to make dough rise, as yeast or leaven. **1930** Shoemaker *1300 Words* 50 **cPA Mts** (as of c1900), *Risings*—Home-made yeast. **1941** *LANE* Map 290 *(Yeast)* 1 inf, **seMA,** We used to make rising out of potatoes; 1 inf, **neMA,** Rising; 1 inf, **seVT,** The rising; 1 inf, **seNH,** *Rising,* older than yeast. **1942** Whipple *Joshua* 276 **UT** (as of c1860), She also kept on hand cornmeal 'rising' for salt-rising bread. **1959** *VT Hist.* 27.154, *Rising.* . . Leavening. Rare. **1966–70** *DARE* (Qu. H16, *What do people use to raise the bread before it's baked?*) Infs **MD30, MA58,** Rising; **PA72,** Dry rising; **OK53,** Rising cake; **NH11,** Rising yeast; (Qu. H17, . . *Kinds [of yeast]*) Infs **MT2, WI62,** Rising; **ID5, IN34,** Salt-rising; **ME16,** They used to call yeast "risin'."

rising ppl adj See **rise** v **B1**

rising adj

1 often foll by *of*: Exceeding; also as adv: more than. *old-fash* Cf **rise** n **1**
1812 *Eve. Post* (NY NY) 10 Nov 2/2, New Hampshire has chosen . . federal electors for President by a majority rising *Three Thousand!* **1817** Paulding *Letters from South* 2.121 **VA,** How much wheat did you raise this year? "A little rising of five thousand bushels." **1842** Kirkland

Forest Life 2.38 **MI,** Look at the last legislature. They did not hold on above two months, and passed rising of two hundred laws. **1848** Bartlett *Americanisms* 276, *Rising,* or *Rising of.* More than; as, 'There were rising of a thousand men killed at the battle of Buena Vista.' **1859** (1968) *Ibid* 367, James Smithson bequeathed to the United States rising half a million of dollars. **1861** *Oregon Argus* 9 Feb (1912 Thornton *Amer. Gloss.*), Gen. Harney is a little rising fifty years old. **1908** Wasson *Home from Sea* 27 **sME coast,** I been going out of this Cove risin' seventy year now, and this is the first time ever God A'mighty shut the door plumb in my face. **1927** *AmSp* 2.363 **cwWV,** *Rising of* . . more than. "He has been gone rising of two hours."

2 with a noun designating a student of a certain year in school: About to become (a student of that year). [By ext from *rising* approaching (a certain age)] Cf **long B4; rise, make one's**
1959 McAtee *Oddments* 6 **cNC,** *Rising:* . . a local use of this term, perhaps University slang. . . A rising sophomore is one nearing the end of his first year. Similarly "a rising junior," and so on. **1966** *Carteret Co. News-Times* (Morehead City & Beaufort NC) 16 Aug 4/6, The bride is a rising senior at East Carteret High School. **1968** *State* (Columbia SC) 2 May sec B 8, The Erskine College student body has elected editors and business managers for The Mirror, campus newspaper, and The Arrow, college yearbook for the 1968–69 year. Mary McColl, rising senior, was named editor-in-chief of The Mirror.

rising bread n Cf **rise** v **B3**
Bread made with **rising** n **2.**
1933 Miller *Lamb in His Bosom* 54 **GA,** Margot would cook . . spiderfuls of rising-bread. **1966** *DARE* (Qu. H15, *Bread made with wheat flour*) Inf **WA13,** Rising bread. **1976** Garber *Mountain-ese* 76 **sAppalachians,** *Rizin'-bread* . . yeast bread—["]Pludie baked a batch of rizin' bread fer Sunday dinner.["] **1986** Pederson *LAGS Concordance* (*Other kinds of bread made of flour*) 2 infs, **LA,** Rising bread; 1 inf, **ceTX,** Rising bread—made with yeast; (*Other kinds of bread . . made of cornmeal*) 1 inf, **cwFL,** Rising bread.

rising of See **rising** adj **1**

risk n, v Also *resk;* rarely *rist, rest;* similarly adj *resky*
A Forms.
1818 Fessenden *Ladies Monitor* 172 **VT,** Provincial words . . to be avoided. . . *Resk* for risk. **1837** Sherwood *Gaz. GA* 71, *Provincialisms.* . . *Resk,* for risk. **1864** (1868) Trowbridge *3 Scouts* 110 **TN,** If't only was whiskey, 'twould be worth the resk of capturing, I say. **1871** Eggleston *Hoosier Schoolmaster* 180 **sIN,** Ef you don't resk nothin' you'll never git nothin'. **1884** *Anglia* 7.267 **Sth, S Midl** [Black], *To run no resk ef you kin he'p it* = to be very careful. **1888** *Century Illustr. Mag.* 36.551 **GA,** Her appetites, ever since I have knowed her, and special' lately, they has not been large, but they has been resky. **1899** (1912) Green *VA Folk-Speech* 350, *Resk.* . . For *risk.* "I don't think I can take the *resk.*" **1905** *DN* 3.56 **eNE,** The change of *i* to *e,* is seen in . . *resk.* **1906** Johnson *Highways Missip. Valley* 276 **nMN,** "I suppose," said he, "you think it's pretty resky livin' where there's so many Indians around." **1909** *DN* 3.363 **eAL, wGA,** *Resk.* . . A not uncommon pronunciation of *risk.* **1909** *Ibid* 415 **nME,** *Resk.* **1912** Green *VA Folk-Speech* 350, *Resky.* . . Risky. **1914** *DN* 4.78 **ME, nNH,** *Resk.* . . To take a chance. "I'll take an' resk it." **1917** *DN* 4.399 **neOH,** *Resky.* . . Risky. My native pronunciation. . . . General. **1923** *DN* 5.218 **swMO,** *Resk.* . . To chance. "I'll resk 'im a-comin'." **1931** *PMLA* 46.1316 **sAppalachians,** *I,* short, becomes short *e* . . "resk" (risk). *Ibid* 1317, *K* becomes *t* in "rist" or "rest" (risk). **1952** Brown *NC Folkl.* 1.584, *Resky* ['rɛskɪ].

B As noun.
=**mumblety-peg;** also a call or maneuver in that game. Cf *DS* **EE5**
1926 *AmSp* 2.65 [Playground argot], From the sandlot below the window there comes "stab the butcher," "risk," "double risk," "red risk" "over the world," "the five sisters." . . Read the first line to any small boy. If he's big enough to whittle a pink stick, he'll grin and say, "Aw, you're readin' about mumblypeg. . ." *Ibid* 66, "Risk," of course, is a risky throw; "double risk" is twice difficult; "red risk"—why not red for such a dangerous try?—is triply hard. **1983** *DARE* File **VT,** (*Games where you try to make a jackknife stick in the ground*) Risk.

risk a huckleberry to a persimmon See **huckleberry** n **9**

riss See **rise** v **A1a**

rist See **risk**

ristra n [Span "a string (of chilis, garlic, onions, etc)"] **esp NM**
A string of dried chili peppers.

1989 *NY Times* (NY) 22 Nov sec C 1/1 **NM,** In the Indian pueblos and the old Hispanic villages below the mountain range, the smoky fragrance of roasting green chili peppers perfumes the fall air while brilliant ristras, ribbons of ripe red chilis, hang . . drying in the sunshine in the doorways of adobe houses. **1990** *Los Angeles Times* (CA) 7 Oct sec L 3/3 **NM,** The Chile Trail . . winds through adobe huts and mansions decked with chile ristras. . . Roadside fruit stands glow with shiny apples and red chile chains called *ristras.* **1997** *DARE* File **swNM,** Here are three Spanish loanwords that are in very common use among New Mexico Anglos. [R]istra—a string of dried chile peppers—a ristra is often hung from a viga or a portal. **1999** *Williams–Sonoma Holiday* (Catalog) 57, *Orchid Chili Ristra.* . . the 25 mild chilies on this raffia-tied swag may be used in cooking for up to nine months. **1999** *DARE* File **csWI,** A board game about New Mexico that my son played ten years ago had pictures of regional icons, including a beautiful red ristra. Ristras are also sold in a local Tex-Mex restaurant. **2001** *Denver Post* (CO) 9 Sept sec K 1 (Internet) **cCO,** [They] have spent the past decade painstakingly restoring the adobe structures. . . Ristras hang outside the house.

ritchie n, also attrib [Perh a trade name] Cf **rowdy**
A man's heavy jacket; see quots.

1941 Writers' Program *Guide WV* 403 **csWV,** If the weather is cool, he [=a logger] swings across his shoulders a red-green-and-black plaid mackinaw or a gray 'ritchie' flannel coat, the pockets bulging with a miscellany of belongings. **1968** *DARE* (Qu. W4, . . *Men's coats or jackets for work and outdoor wear*) Inf **PA**175, Ritchie—a hunting jacket, wool, bold plaid, waist-length; **WV**2, Ritchie jacket—from company that makes them.

rium See **room**

rival n [By syncope from *revival*] Cf Intro "Language Changes" I.9
c1937 in 1972 *Amer. Slave* 2.32 **SC,** They was havin' a rival (revival) meetin' de night of de earthquake.

rivel n Also *revel, ribble, riffle, rivvel, riwwel* [PaGer *riwwel* < *reiwe* to rub, grate] **chiefly PaGer area** Cf **rubs**
1 A small fragment of noodle-like dough, usu boiled in soup.

1907 in 1953 *PA Dutchman* Apr 5, Add finely cut parsley, pepper, salt, and the inevitable "rivels." If the soup is too thick thin it with water, boil hard for five minutes and serve. **1935** Frederick *PA Dutch* 105, *Rivel Soup*—1 quart milk, 1 egg, 1 cup flour; mix egg and flour, and rub thru hands in small lumps, and let shreds drop into boiling milk. **1939** Berolzheimer *U.S. Cookbook* 271 [PaGer], *Rivel soup*—2 cups sifted flour[,] ½ teaspoon salt[,] 1 egg, well beaten[,] 6 cups chicken or beef broth[.] Combine flour, salt and beaten egg and blend until mixture is crumbly. Pour into boiling broth, and cook 10 minutes. The rivels will look like boiled rice when cooked. **1950** *WELS* (Kinds of soup) 1 Inf, **cnWI,** Revel. **1953** *Reading Times* 26 Jan 9/1 (*Mathews Coll.*) NC, "Riwwels" and "riwwel soup" [are] still so called and enjoyed. **1957** *Sat. Eve. Post Letters* IN, Her cousin used to put "riffles" in diced potatoes (a noodle or dough). **1967–68** *DARE* (Qu. H36, *Kinds of soup*) Inf **IL**9, Rivel [ˈrɪvl] soup—made with noodles; **OH**81, Rivel soup; **PA**159, Rivel soup—egg [beaten], salt, flour, milk; **PA**176, Potato with rivels; (Qu. H45, *Dishes made with meat, fish, or poultry that everybody around here would know, but that people in other places might not*) Inf **OH**75, Thickened milk—same as rivel soup; **OH**80, Rivel soup—chicken stock with a noodle dough cooked right in; **MD**27, Rivels [ˈrɪvl̩z]—egg beaten with flour, boiled in soup. **1968** *DARE* Tape IN3, Well, I told you they was the yeast rivels; **MD**21, Rivels, made out of eggs, flour, and a little bit of salt. . . Put it in with the beans and boil it, maybe ten minutes, so it's cooked down enough. **1977** Anderson *Grass Roots Cookbook* 46 **sePA,** Rivvel (dumpling) soups have a lumpy look and, in fact, rivvel means "lump." . . *To make rivvels:* Combine flour and salt in a . . mixing bowl, add egg and milk and stir briskly and lightly just to make a soft dough. . . [D]rop rivvel dough into soup, scattering it over surface. **1982** *Barrick Coll.* **csPA,** Rivels, ribbles—small lumps of dough cooked in chicken or corn soup; larger lumps of dough are called *dumplings.* **1987** *Jrl. Engl. Ling.* 20.2.173 **ePA,** Riwwel . . [actively used by] 34 [of 100 infs]. . . Although this item was elicited frequently, only five informants are under 30. **2000** *NADS Letters* **sOH,** When making potato soup, riffles were crumbled bits of flour dumpling or biscuit dough dropped into the soup at the very last. . . In calling some older relatives, several variations of the term were mentioned. Some pro-

nounced the word as riffles, some as ripples, but they said the actual correct *spelling* is rivels.
2 Transf: see quots.
[**1924** Lambert *PA Ger. Dict.* 125, Riwwel. . . small roll of dirt formed on the body when washing.] **1968** *DARE* (Qu. E20, *Soft rolls of dust that collect on the floor under beds or other furniture*) Inf **MD**30, Rivels [ˈrɪvl̩z].

river n Pronc-spp *ribber, ribbuh, ruvver* Cf Pronc Intro 3.I.17
Std sense, var forms.
1853 Simms *Sword & Distaff* 116 **SC,** So long as dere's . . duck in de ribber, and fish in de pond—so long, I tell you, Tom will always hab 'nough somet'ing to cook! **1899** (1912) Green *VA Folk-Speech* 362, *Ruvver.* . . River. **1899** Chesnutt *Conjure Woman* 85 **csNC** [Black], Ter go down de ribber. **1922** Gonzales *Black Border* 323 **sSC, GA coasts** [Gullah glossary], *Ribbuh*—river, rivers.

river ash n
1 =**green ash.** [From its preference for stream banks]
1897 Sudworth *Arborescent Flora* 328 **RI,** *Fraxinus pennsylvanica.* . . Common names. . . River Ash. **1910** Graves *Flowering Plants* 317 **CT,** *Fraxinus pennsylvanica.* . . Red, Brown or River Ash. Frequent. Along streams and in swamps, sometimes in drier places. **1950** Peattie *Nat. Hist. Trees* 564, Red Ash. . . Other Names: River, Bastard, Black, or Brown Ash. **1960** Vines *Trees SW* 864, Vernacular names [for the green ash] are Water Ash, River Ash, Red Ash, the Swamp Ash.
2 =**box elder.**
1968 *DARE* (Qu. T13, . . *Other names . . for . . box elder*) Inf **VA**24, River ash.

riverbank grape n Also *river(side) grape*
A **frost grape** (here: either *Vitis riparia* or *V. vulpina*). For other names of the former see **June grape**
1817 Darby *Geogr. Descr. LA* 356, *Vitis riparia* . . River grave [sic] vine. **1830** Rafinesque *Med. Flora* 2.131, *V. riparia* of Pursh, Elliot, Torrey, &c. River Grape. . . On the banks of streams from New York to Carolina. **1872** MO State Entomol. *Annual Rept.* 60, *Vitis riparia,* Michx. River Bank Grape. **1891** Coulter *Botany W. TX* 63, *V. riparia* . . Riverside grape. . . Stream banks or near water, common in most of the watered cañons of western Texas. **1942** Tehon *Fieldbook IL Shrubs* 193, The Riverbank Grape. . . ranges from New Brunswick to Manitoba and south to Virginia and Texas. In Illinois, it is a very common and abundant grape.

river bass n
A **black bass 1:** usu **largemouth bass** or **smallmouth bass.**
1820 Rafinesque *Ohio R. Fishes* 30, Genus. River Bass. *Lepomis. Ibid* 31, Brown River-bass. *Lepomis flexuolaris.* . . Vulgar names, Black Bass, Brown Bass, Black Pearch; &c. *Ibid* 32, Trout River-bass. *Lepomis salmonea.* . . Vulgar names[,] White Trout, . . Black Bass, Black Pearch, &c. *Ibid,* Spotted River-bass. *Lepomis notata.* **1857** *Spirit of Times* 11 April 86 *(DA),* The Oswego (sometimes known as the 'river bass') is the heavier fish, often attaining to eight pounds weight. **1890** Howells *Boy's Town* 30 **sOH,** There were men who were reputed to catch at will, as it were, silvercats and river-bass. **1933** LA Dept. of Conserv. *Fishes* 313, None of our other fresh water fishes has been given so many popular names as our Black Bass. . . [T]hey are here enumerated as follows . . River Bass, Rock Bass [etc]. **1976** Tryckare et al. *Lore of Sportfishing* 101, Smallmouth Black Bass. . . Other common names . . river bass, swago bass [etc]. **1985** Madson *Up River* 136 **Upper Missip Valley,** Upper Mississippi was prime smallmouth-bass territory. . . The smallmouth is more a creature of moving waters than is its bigmouth cousin; one of the aliases of this fish is "river bass."

river birch n
A birch, usu *Betula nigra,* but also **sweet birch** or **western birch.** For other names of *B. nigra,* see **gat brush, red birch 2, water ~**
1848 Gray *Manual of Botany* 422, *B[etula] nigra* . . River or Red Birch. . . Low riverbanks, Massachusetts to Penn., eastward and southward. **1897** Sudworth *Arborescent Flora* 142 **MN,** Sweet Birch. . . Common Names. . . River Birch. **1950** Stevens *ND Plants* 115, *Betula fontinalis.* . . The name "River Birch" is not appropriate in North Dakota. The plants grow in shrubby clumps on wet hillsides along small tributaries of the Missouri River and on the Killdeer Mts. **1961** Douglas *My Wilderness* 198 **MD,** The river birch depends on the waters of the river for propagation. They carry the seeds downstream, leaving them on

muddy banks. **1967–70** *DARE* (Qu. T15, . . *Kinds of swamp trees*) Infs IL26, 119, VA64, River birch. **1985** Madson *Up River* 62 **Upper Missip Valley,** Over on Delphy's Island it was still night back under the river birches and huge old silver maples.

river boss n

1 The person in charge of a **river drive.**

1903 White *Forest* 94 **Nth,** There was Jimmy, the river boss who could not swim a stroke. **1905** U.S. Forest Serv. *Bulletin* 61.44 [Logging terms], *River boss.* The foreman in charge of a log drive. (N[orthern] F[orest]) **1958** McCulloch *Woods Words* 150 **Pacific NW,** *River boss.* . . Back east, the man in charge of river drives; and used in the same sense in the Northwest in early days. **1969** Sorden *Lumberjack Lingo* 97 **NEng, Gt Lakes,** *River boss*—The foreman in charge of a log drive.

2 See quot.

1958 McCulloch *Woods Words* 150 **Pacific NW,** *River boss.* . . In the western woods, it meant the man in charge of river works in splash dam operations.

river brush See river bush

river bug n Also river miller

=**mayfly 1.**

1950 *WELS* (*Large winged insect that hatches in summer in great numbers around lakes or rivers, crowds around lights, lives only a day or so, and is good fish bait*) 1 Inf, **swWI,** River bug—and in Dubuque; 1 Inf, **ceWI,** River miller—gray-brown, like miller, hatch in water and fly up and live a very short time—lay eggs on water. **1967** *DARE* (Qu. R4) Inf MO7, River bugs.

river bush n Also river brush

=**buttonbush 1.**

1824 Bigelow *Florula Bostoniensis* 51, Button bush or river bush is a frequent ornament of the water side. . . The shrub rises five or six feet out of the water. **1901** Lounsberry *S. Wild Flowers* 475, Button, or river, bush. **1960** Vines *Trees SW* 938, Vernacular names for the shrub are Spanish Pincushion, River-brush, Swampwood [etc].

river cat n Also river catfish

Any of several catfish such as **blue catfish 1, flathead catfish 1,** or **white catfish 1.**

1770 (1925) Washington *Diaries* 1.419 **WV,** At this place we . . found a Cat fish of the size of our largest River Cats. **1906** NJ State Museum *Annual Rept. for 1905* 166, *Ameiurus catus* (Linnaeus). . . Big Cat Fish. River Cat Fish. **1948** *Dly. Ardmoreite* (Ardmore, Okla.) 23 April 7/1 *(DA),* Some of the larger, like Sand creek and Caney river, yield big blues and tackle-busting river cats, or Appaluchians. **1966–70** *DARE* (Qu. P1, . . *Kinds of freshwater fish . . caught around here . . good to eat*) Infs KY49, 75, VA46, River cat; [FL6, Suwannee River catfish; VA43, New River cat—same as English Channel cat]. **1972** Hilliard *Hog Meat* 85, The most important food fish in the interior was the catfish. At least one of several species inhabited virtually every stream deep enough to wade in, and many "river cats" reached gigantic proportions. **1973** Knight *Cook's Fish Guide* 377, Catfish . . river [same as] Blue.

river chub n

=**hornyhead c** or a similar chub (here: *Nocomis micropogon*).

1877 NY Acad. Sci. *Annals Lyceum Nat. Hist.* 10.375 **nGA,** We heard several peculiar vernacular names for fishes on the Rock Castle and Cumberland . . River Chub—*Nocomis biguttatus.* **1908** Forbes–Richardson *Fishes of IL* 167, *Hybopsis kentuckiensis* . . River chub; Hornyhead. **1929** OK Univ. Biol. Surv. *Pub.* 1.2.65, *Nocomis biguttatus* . . Western river chub. **1957** Trautman *Fishes* 292 **OH,** References before 1925 to the Hornyhead Chub in Ohio are mostly a composite of this species and the River Chub, for it was not until 1926 . . that both were recognized as distinct species. *Ibid* 295, River Chub—*Hybopsis micropogon.* **1966–69** *DARE* (Qu. P3, *Freshwater fish that are not good to eat*) Inf ME8, River chub; MA26, River chup [sic—FW sp]. **1983** Becker *Fishes WI* 485, Hornyhead Chub. . . Other common names: hornyhead, horned chub, river chub [etc].

river cooter n Also river turtle

A **red-bellied turtle** (here: *Pseudemys concinna*).

1952 Carr *Turtles* 286, River Turtle—*Pseudemys floridana concinna.* . . From Maryland southward to Alabama, mostly east of the

mountains and above the fall line, and into eastern Tennessee. **1958** Conant *Reptiles & Amphibians* 58, *River Cooter.* . . Indigenous to streams of the Piedmont and following such streams to Atlantic Coast. **1972** Ernst–Barbour *Turtles* 156, The river cooter is shy and leaves the water only to bask or nest. **1979** Behler–King *Audubon Field Guide Reptiles* 447, River Cooter. . . The meat is favored locally in the South. **1986** Pederson *LAGS Concordance,* 1 inf, **seMS,** River turtle.

river cottonwood n

A **cottonwood 1** (here: either **Carolina poplar 1** or **swamp cottonwood**).

1882 U.S. Natl. Museum *Proc.* 5.86 **IN,** *Populus heterophylla.* "River Cottonwood"; "Swamp Cottonwood"; "Stumpy Gum." **1932** Rydberg *Flora Prairies* 247, *P. Sargentii.* . . Western or River Cottonwood. River bottoms. **1950** Peattie *Nat. Hist. Trees* 96, Swamp Cottonwood. . . Other Names: Black, Swamp, or River Cottonwood.

river crane n

=**great blue heron.**

1970 *DARE* (Qu. Q10, . . *Water birds and marsh birds*) Inf **KY**86, River crane—some blue, some white.

river crow n

Prob =**fish crow 1.**

1970 *DARE* (Qu. Q11, . . *Kinds of blackbirds*) Inf VA46, Woods crow—highland. River crow—marshes and creeks.

river darter n

A **darter 1** (here: *Percina shumardi*).

1943 Eddy–Surber *N. Fishes* 195, River Darter—*Imostoma shumardi.* **1966** WI Acad. *Trans.* 55.110, River darter. . . a common darter of large rivers such as the Wisconsin and Mississippi. **1991** Amer. Fisheries Soc. *Common Names Fishes* 50, *Percina shumardi* . . river darter.

river drive n chiefly Nth Cf drive n 6, driver 4

The process of floating logs downstream; hence v phr *river drive* to transport logs in such a manner; n *river driver;* vbl n *river driving.*

1848 Bartlett *Americanisms* 276, *River Driver.* A term used by lumbermen in Maine, for a man whose business it is to conduct logs down running streams, to prevent them from lodging upon shoals or remaining in eddies. **1854** Bullard *Now-A-Days* 118 **ME,** River drivin' is the pootiest part of loggin', I think. **1905** U.S. Forest Serv. *Bulletin* 61.44 [Logging terms], *River driver.* One who works on a log drive. **1907** *DN* 3.248 **eME,** *River-driver.* . . A man employed by lumbermen to direct the floating of logs down a stream and prevent them from lodging. **1908** White *Riverman* 50 **Nth** (as of 1870s), How does river-driving strike you? **1925** *AmSp* 1.135 **ME, MI, MN,** In the spring the logs are driven down the rivers to the mills by "river drivers." **1942** *AmSp* 17.223 **Nth** [Loggers' talk], *River drivers.* Loggers who shepherd logs down river to storage boom or mill. **1956** Sorden–Ebert *Logger's Words* 27 **Gt Lakes,** *River-drive,* Taking logs to a mill by floating them down a river. This was the most dangerous part of early logging and many lumberjacks lost their lives on these drives. **1958** McCulloch *Woods Words* 150 **Pacific NW,** *River drive*—To move logs by the high water in a river, not in a raft. **1966–67** *DARE* Tape **ME**19, River drivers' shoes . . had corks on 'em . . so you wouldn't roll a log; **MI**20, Wherever the streams were large enough, they floated the logs down. That's what they called river driving. Of course, that was nothing new here. That was done all over, in the east and wherever they logged. . . No cost to that. . . They'd float the logs down to the mills; **MI**47, A peavey is used extensively in river driving, but not so much in loading logs. **1967** *Warrensburg–Lake George News* (Warrensburg NY) 11 May 4/1, Great preparations were made for the river drivers.

river elm n

A **white elm** (here: prob *Ulmus americanus*). Cf **swamp elm, water ~**

1852 in 1854 U.S. War Dept. *Explor. Red River* 76 **OK,** It is fringed upon each side with . . river-elm, (*Ulmus memoralis* [sic]). **1967** *DARE* (Qu. T11, . . *Kinds of elm trees*) Inf TX29, River elm.

river forest n [From its tendency to form thickets on riverbanks and islands]

A **false indigo 1** (here: *Amorpha fruticosa*).

1959 Carleton *Index Herb. Plants* 99, *River forest:* Amorpha fruticosa.

river grape See riverbank grape

river hawthorn n

=**black haw 3.**

1869 *Amer. Naturalist* 3.406, River Hawthorn (*Crataegus rivularis*). A hawthorn with black berries . . forming a shrubby tree fifteen to twenty feet high. **1897** Sudworth *Arborescent Flora* 215 **UT**, *Crataegus douglasii*. . . River Hawthorn. **1931** U.S. Dept. Ag. *Misc. Pub.* 101.64, River hawthorn (*C. rivularis*) is very close to black hawthorn botanically and by some authors considered a variety of it. **1976** Elmore *Shrubs & Trees SW* 147, River Hawthorn. . . Streambanks, 3,000′–8,500′.

river herring n

A **herring** n[1] **1** such as **alewife**, a **gizzard shad 1** (here: *Dorosoma cepedianum*), or a **skipjack 1b.**

1884 *Century Illustr. Mag.* 27.909 **eMA**, The different townships on Cape Cod protect the alewife, or "river herring." **1906** NJ State Museum *Annual Rept. for 1905* 95, *Pomolobus pseudoharengus* . . River Herring. Herring. Alewife. **1933** LA Dept. of Conserv. *Fishes* 215, The Gizzard Shad has been given many names in Louisiana, chief among them being Hickory Shad . . River Sardine and River Herring. **1945** *Natl. Geogr. Mag.* Sept 262 **neMA**, Springtime drives salt-water alewives upstream to spawn. . . A few, canned, enter the domestic market as "river herring." **1956** Harlan–Speaker *IA Fish* 59, Skipjack Herring—*Alosa chrysochloris* . . Other Names—Shad, river shad, river herring. **1983** Becker *Fishes WI* 270, Skipjack Herring. . . Other common names . . river shad, river herring.

river hog n Also *river pig* **Nth**

One who works on a **river drive.** Also called **driver 4, river jack 2, ~ rat 2**

1902 White *Blazed Trail* 384 **MI**, And now we've gone and bust, just because that infernal river-hog had to fall off a boom. **1921** *DN* 5.113 **CA**, *Riverpig*. . . A lumberman who follows the drive in low water and dislodges logs from bars, mud, etc. Brought by lumbermen from Michigan to California. **1930** Shoemaker *1300 Words* 50 **cPA Mts** (as of c1900), *River-hog*—One who works along rivers helping to float logs. **1942** *AmSp* 17.223 **Nth** [Loggers' talk], *River hog.* A river driver. **1942** Beck *Songs MI Lumberjacks* 77, A "river hog" was a man who drove logs down the streams. **1942** ME Univ. *Studies* 57.133, *River Hog.* Same as a *driver.* **1944** Nute *Lake Superior* 211 **MI, WI, MN**, Along the main stream a well-worn path was beaten by the feet of the river pigs, or river hogs, as the drivers were termed. **1961** Holbrook *Yankee Loggers* 122 **NEng**, *River hog*—A river driver. **1967–68** *DARE* Tape **MI**47, [FW:] Do you know the term river pig? Was it ever used here? [Inf:] Oh, yes. River pig is a fellow that works on the drive, works on the river. [FW:] Was it a term of insult? [Inf:] . . No, not exactly. . . They called them river pigs or river hogs; **NH**14, [FW:] What was that name you had now for, say, an old fellow who's bowlegged? [Inf:] River hog. River driver or river hog. River hog. [FW:] And how does he get to be bowlegged? [Inf:] Well, wearing them driving shoes and standing on a log. 'Course, them driving shoes have got them caulks in 'em. You can stand right on a log, you know. Each foot on the rolling side of a log and you can ride the damn log right down the river. 'Course, that makes 'em bowlegged. **1984** *MJLF* 10.155 **cnWI**, *River hogs.* Men who took the rafts of lumber down the river.

riverind See **reverend**

river jack n

1 See quots.   Cf **jackrock 1, jackstone 2**

1946 *PADS* 6.25 **swVA**, *Riverjack*. . . A rock from a river bed. **1968** *DARE* (Qu. C22, *A piece of stone too big for one person to move easily*) Inf **VA**26, River jack—smoothed off by the water; (Qu. C25, . . *Kinds of stone . . about . . [. . size of a person's head]*) Inf **VA**26, River jack.

2 =**river hog.**

1969 Sorden *Lumberjack Lingo* 97 **NEng, Gt Lakes**, *River jack*—Man who worked on a log drive. River pig, river hog, river rat, river driver, catty man.

river lamprey n

A **lamprey;** see quots.

1896 U.S. Bur. Fisheries *Rept. for 1895* 212, *Ichthyomyzon* [spp] . . River Lampreys. **1906** NJ State Museum *Annual Rept. for 1905* 48, *Petromyzon marinus*. . . Sea Lamprey. Lamper Eel. River Lamprey. **1983** Becker *Fishes WI* 203, In late 1949 numerous "river lampreys" were reported parasitizing fish in Pool 11 of the Mississippi River (opposite Grant County). About 500 silver lampreys . . had done damage to various fish. *Ibid* 208, Chestnut Lamprey. . . Other common names: western lamprey . . river lamprey [etc]. **1991** Amer. Fisheries Soc. *Common Names Fishes* 11, *Lampetra ayresi* . . river lamprey.

river locust n Cf **locust B1**

A **false indigo 1** (here: *Amorpha fruticosa*).

1896 *Bot. Gaz.* 22.479 **MN**, *Amorpha fruticosa* . . river locust. **1922** *Amer. Botanist* 28.72, *Amorpha fruticosa* . . is "lead plant", "river locust" and "false indigo." The locust-like leaves and the plant's habit of growing along river banks makes [sic] the second name appropriate. **1959** Carleton *Index Herb. Plants* 99, *River-locust:* Amorpha fruticosa.

river maple n

=**silver maple.**

1851 (1856) Springer *Forest Life* 25 **NEast**, It is said that the wood of this tree [=the rock maple] may be easily distinguished from the Red, or the River Maple. **1908** Britton *N. Amer. Trees* 645, The Silver maple, or Soft maple. . . is also known as River maple, Water maple, White maple and Creek maple. **1968–69** *DARE* (Qu. T14, . . *Kinds of maples*) Inf **KY**35, River or water maple; **PA**118, River maple—sometimes called butcher-knife maple; **VA**24, River maple—like a white maple or silver maple—a soft maple; **WV**17, River maple; (Qu. T15, . . *Kinds of swamp trees*) Inf **NJ**6, River maple.

river miller See **river bug**

river minnow n

A **mummichog** (here: *Fundulus heteroclitus*).

1906 NJ State Museum *Annual Rept. for 1905* 188, Killy Fish. River Minnow. Mummichog. **1965–69** *DARE* (Qu. P7, *Small fish used as bait for bigger fish*) Inf **OK**11, River minner doesn't glisten—shiner does; **GA**65, **TX**74, River minnow.

river otter n

The North American otter (*Lutra canadensis*), as distinct from the sea otter.   Also called **land otter, water dog**

1928 Anthony *N. Amer. Mammals* 114, *Lutra canadensis*. . . Land Otter; River Otter. **1947** Cahalane *Mammals* 200, Like the sea otter, the river or land otter has the outline of a small seal or a very big weasel. **1980** Whitaker *Audubon Field Guide Mammals* 590, A pair of River Otters may work together to drive a school of fish into an inlet where they can be caught easily.

river pig See **river hog**

river pine n

=**Jersey pine.**

1860 Curtis *Cat. Plants NC* 20, Jersey Pine. . . In some parts of the country it is known also under the names of *Cedar, River,* and *Scrub* Pine. **1908** Britton *N. Amer. Trees* 47, It [=the Jersey pine] is also called by many other names, as Scrub pine, Short pine, Short-leaved pine, Cedar pine, River pine [etc]. **1950** Peattie *Nat. Hist. Trees* 27, Virginia Scrub Pine . . Other Names: Jersey, Nigger, or River Pine.

river pink n

A **pinkster 2** or similar rhododendron.

1892 *Jrl. Amer. Folkl.* 5.100 **VT**, *Rhododendron nudiflorum*. . . river pink. Cavendish, Vt. **1933** Rawlings *South Moon* 164 **nFL**, The river-pinks grew in dense masses, piled as high as small trees.

river rat n

1 A person who lives or works on a river.   *usu derog*

1884 *Harper's New Mth. Mag.* 68.513 **ceMO**, Observe the river-rats clustering about the groggeries. **1896** (1897) Brodhead *Bound in Shallows* 31 **KY**, She was a black-skinned little river-rat living yonder in the boom house. **1937** Sandoz *Slogum* 141 **NE**, Him nothing but a worthless river rat who'd never have a cent. **1953** (1977) Hubbard *Shantyboat* 316 **Missip-Ohio Valleys**, There was no resemblance here to the shiftless hand-to-mouth river rat so often pictured. . . No bartering or bank trade in fish, no gardening, all so common on the Ohio among river people. **1957** McMeekin *Old KY Country* 82, But more familiar to today's waterline scene are the shacks, shantyboats, and ancient houseboats . . where the true folk-of-the-river . . live out their years. River rats, they are called, for they are shy and suspicious, existing in contented squalor, setting trotlines or putting out a few cane poles with a mat of hooks on a hemp string to snag a buffalo or catfish when they "take a notion." **1966** Dakin *Dial. Vocab. Ohio R. Valley* 2.454, General derogatory terms [for a *rustic*] are *white trash* (Ill[inois]); *river rats* (K[entucky]) . . *hoodlum* (K[entucky]). **1967–70** *DARE* (Qu. HH18, *Very insignificant or low-grade people*) Infs **KY**77A, **LA**32, River rats; (Qu. C34) Inf **IL**8, River rats. **1967** *DARE* Tape **IA**13, There's always the ones we call river rats. But the river rats are also very respectable people. . . One that just loves to be on the river . . would rather spend his time being on the river than anything else. **1973** Allen *LAUM* 1.351, *River rat:* Derogatory for dweller on bottomland along the Niobrara River. **1985** Madson *Up River* 95 **Upper Missip Valley,** It was crewed by two young men, scarcely more than boys but already with that indelible river look to them, that indegoddampendent Huck-Finnish aspect that validates the pedigree of a born-and-bred river rat. **1986** Pederson *LAGS Concordance (A rustic)* 3 infs, **AR,** River rat(s); 1 inf, **nwMS,** River rats; 1 inf, **cwMS,** River rat—lives on river; 1 inf, **swGA,** River rat—not too insulting; 1 inf, **nwAL,** River rats—make living from river; 1 inf, **ceAR,** River rats—people that live on river; 1 inf, **ceAR,** River rats—live on back of river, fish and trap; *(Poor whites)* 1 inf, **nwMS,** River rats—peckerwoods in houseboat. **1999** *DARE* File ce**NY** (as of 1950s–60s), Among people who knew men who made their living by hunting and fishing along the upper Hudson River, "river rat" was a descriptive and even complimentary term. To say, "That guy's a real river rat" meant that he knew everything about life on the river.

2 =**river hog.**
    1905 U.S. Forest Serv. *Bulletin* 61.44 [Logging terms], *River rat.* A log driver whose work is chiefly on the river; contrasted with Laker. (N[orthern] F[orest]). **1956** Sorden–Ebert *Logger's Words* 28 **Gt Lakes,** *River-rat,* See river-pig. **1958** McCulloch *Woods Words* 150 **Pacific NW,** *River rat*—A logger working on booms or river drives. **1968** *DARE* FW Addit **WI**59, River rat—nickname for lumberjack.

3 =**muskrat 1.**
    1968–70 *DARE* (Qu. P31, . . *Names or nicknames . . for the . . muskrat*) Infs **MO**36, **TN**65, River rat; (Qu. P32, . . *Wild animals . . around here*) Inf **MA**26, River rat.

river shiner n
A **shiner 1:** usu *Notropis blennius,* but also *Cyprinella whipplei.*
    1891 Jesup *Plants Hanover NH* 59, [Notropis] Whipplei . . Silver-Fin. River-Shiner. Not rare. **1943** Eddy–Surber *N. Fishes* 142, The river shiner ranges from Manitoba through Wisconsin and Ohio to Pennsylvania and southward to Oklahoma. . . This species [=*Notropis blennius*] prefers large streams. **1966** WI Acad. *Trans.* 55.104, The river shiner is found commonly in the Wisconsin and Mississippi Rivers and occasionally in the lower extremities of their tributaries.

river shrimp n **LA, MS, AL**
A freshwater shrimp: either *Macrobrachium ohione* or a **grass shrimp** (here: *Palaemonetes paludosus*).
    1879 U.S. Natl. Museum *Bulletin* 14.260 **New Orleans LA,** River shrimp (*Palaemon* sp.) . . (*Pal. ohionis* Smith). **1884** Goode *Fisheries U.S.* 1.819, The River Shrimps—*Palæmon ohionis,* Smith; *Palæmonetes exilipes,* Stimpson. Only two species of river Shrimp have yet been described from the United States east of the Mississippi River, and they seem to be used as food in only a few localities. At New Orleans, however, one species, the *Palæmon ohionis,* is very much esteemed. **1966–67** *DARE* (Qu. P18, . . *Kinds of shellfish*) Inf **LA**10, River shrimp—people eat these occasionally; **MS**32, River shrimp. **1967** *DARE* Tape **LA**5, Plenty of times you could catch 'em [=catfish] with regular river shrimp. You could bunch on live river shrimp, and yellow cat would hit that pretty good. **1981** Pederson *LAGS Basic Materials,* 1 inf, se**AL,** River shrimp; 1 inf, c**LA,** ['rɪvə swɪmp]—live in fresh water; produce "shrimp moth," which fly 2 days & return to water to become shrimp. **1982** Sternberg *Fishing* 126, Sold as *river shrimp* along the lower Mississippi River, freshwater shrimp spawn in brackish waters. They range widely throughout large river systems, moving upstream as far as the first major dam or obstruction. They often live in connecting lakes, channels or backwaters. **1998** *DARE* File—Internet s**LA** [New Orleans Online], A salad of wild greens, portobello mushrooms and petite river shrimp in a sweet red pepper pesto vinaigrette.

riverside grape See **riverbank grape**

river snapper n
A black **bullhead 1b** (here: *Ameiurus melas*).
    1951 Harlan–Speaker *IA Fish* 94, Northern Black Bullhead. . . Other Names . . catfish, stinger, and river snapper. **1983** Becker *Fishes WI* 697, *Black Bullhead* . . Other common names: . . horned pout, . . river snapper.

river snipe n
=**spotted sandpiper.**
    1917 (1923) *Birds Amer.* 1.249, Spotted Sandpiper. . . Other Names . . Sand Snipe; River Snipe. **1968** *DARE* (Qu. Q10, . . *Water birds and marsh birds*) Inf **CA**105, River snipe.

river trout n
A **walleye**; see quots.
    1927 Weed *Pike* 46 **NC,** *Stizostedion*—Common names of this group are so confused that no attempt has been made to separate the names belonging only to the Saugers from those belonging only to the Walleye. It is probable that practically all the names are applied to either. . . River Trout; North Carolina. **1933** LA Dept. of Conserv. *Fishes* 367, A member of the True Perch Family (Percidae), the Walleye, like so many of our fishes, has come to bear a variety of often meaningless, common names. They are: Walleye . . and River Trout.

river turtle See **river cooter**

riverweed n
1 A small aquatic plant (*Podostemum ceratophyllum*) native to the eastern US. Also called **threadfoot**
    1832 Williamson *Hist. ME* 1.128, We have, also . . *Oar-weed, River-weed,* and *Succory,* as common herbs. **1867** *Atlantic Mth.* 19.280 **SC,** Sometimes a mere dark mass of river-weed would be floated by the tide past the successive stations. **1894** *Outing* 24.366 cn**NY,** They were quite ready to accept Horace Campbell's proposal to . . try for pike at the hour when these fish are most eagerly prowling through their river-weed jungles. **1946** Tatnall *Flora DE* 135, *P[odostemum] ceratophyllum* . . River Weed. On rocks in the Brandywine and Red Clay Creeks (NC); formerly rather frequent, but no longer to be found, having been exterminated by industrial waste in those streams. **1970** Correll *Plants TX* 714, River-weed. . . Attached to rocks in streams . . from Ga., along the Gulf Coast to Okla.

2 =**crownbeard.**
    1920 *Torreya* 20.117 **VA,** The most abundant weed . . was *Actinomeris squarrosa,* often called "river-weed." **1959** Carleton *Index Herb. Plants* 99, *River-weed:* Actinomeris alternifolia.

3 =**tape grass.**
    1941 *Torreya* 41.45 **FL,** *Vallisneria spiralis* . . river-weed, Silver Springs, Fla.

4 Perh a **cow parsnip 1.**
    1969–70 *DARE* (Qu. S21, . . *Weeds . . that are a trouble in gardens and fields*) Inf **KY**47, Hogweed or riverweed; **KY**89, Riverweed—tall, 7–8 feet, large leaves; **VA**38, Riverweed—in rich, low ground; **VA**43, Riverweed.

river whitefish n
A **mooneye 1** (here: *Hiodon tergisus*).
    1983 Becker *Fishes WI* 284, Mooneye—*Hiodon tergisus.* . . Other common names: toothed herring, cisco, river whitefish [etc].

river worm n
See quot.
    1967 *DARE* (Qu. P6, . . *Kinds of worms . . used for bait*) Inf **MO**11, River worms. [FW: When asked about a sign in the neighborhood saying "River Worms," Inf said they were fishworms, perhaps somewhat larger.]

riveter n *joc*
A **woodpecker.**
    1968 *DARE* (Qu. Q18, *Joking names and nicknames for woodpeckers*) Inf **VA**8, Riveter. **1986** Pederson *LAGS Concordance,* 1 inf, cw**TN,** Riveter—woodpecker.

rivvel, riwwel See **rivel**

riz v[1] See **rise** v **A1a, 2b**

riz v[2] See **raise** v **A2**

riz ppl adj See **rise** v **B1, 3**

rizing See **rising** n

rizzed v See **rise** v **A1a**

rizzed ppl adj See **rise** v **B1**

rizzle v [Scots, nEngl dial; *EDD rizzle* v.[1] "To dry by the heat of the sun or fire"]

1897 *KS Univ. Qrly.* (ser B) 6.56 **neMA,** *Rizzle:* to 'loaf' around in the sun.

rizzy-boiler See **reservoir**

roach n[1]

1a Any of var **minnows B1** or other fish of the family Cyprinidae; see below. **chiefly Atlantic**

1637 (1967) Morton *New English Canaan* 227 **NEng,** There are in the rivers, and ponds, very excellent . . Roches, Perches, Tenches, Eeles, and other fishes. **1698** (1848) Thomas *Hist. & Geog. Acct.* 13 **neMD, sePA,** And for Fish, there are prodigious quantities of most sorts, . . Roach, Eels [etc]. **1709** (1967) Lawson *New Voyage* 163, We have the same Carp as you have in *England.* And the same Roach; only scarce so large. **1796** in 1799 Weld *Travels* 80 **VA,** The Patowmac . . abounds with . . shad, roach, herrings, &c. **1832** Williamson *Hist. ME* 1.159, The *Roach,* though rather scarce, is found in fresh ponds. **1966–70** *DARE* (Qu. P7, *Small fish used as bait for bigger fish*) Infs **NJ31, NC49, PA168, VA70,** Roach; **FL48,** Shiners—silverfish and roaches are other names; (Qu. P3, *Freshwater fish that are not good to eat*) Inf **FL7,** Roach. **1981** Pederson *LAGS Basic Materials,* 1 inf, **seAL,** Roach—a shiner; 1 inf, **nwFL,** Roaches = minnows, small fish used for bait.

b Spec:

(1) A **fallfish:** usu *Semotilus corporalis,* but also the creek chub, *S. atromaculatus.*

1842 DeKay *Zool. NY* 3.208, The Roach Dace. *Leuciscus pulchellus.* . . According to Dr. Storer, this species is found in the Eastern States, where it is called *Roach* and *Cousin Trout.* **1854** (1969) Thoreau *Walden* 199 **MA,** There have been caught in Walden . . shiners, chivins or roach [etc]. **1886** Mather *Memoranda* 28 **neNY,** In America there is but one species which grows to a size that entitles it to the notice of the angler. This is the "big chub," "fall fish," "roach," etc. *Semotilus bullaris.* **1890** *Century Dict.* 5199, *Roach.* . . In the United States, one of many different fishes like or mistaken for the roach, as . . the American chub, *Semotilus atromaculatus.* **1891** Jesup *Plants Hanover NH* 59, [*Semotilus*] *bullaris* . . Fall Fish. Chub. Dace. Roach. Abundant. **1911** U.S. Bur. Census *Fisheries 1908* 314, Roach (*Semotilus corporalis*).—The largest chub found east of the Rocky Mountains. It is abundant in the streams of the New England and Middle states east of the Alleghenies. Also called "fallfish," "chub," "dace," etc.

(2) =**golden shiner.**

1884 U.S. Natl. Museum *Bulletin* 27.489, *Notemigonus chrysoleucus* . . Golden Shiner; Bream; Roach. United States, from New England west to Dakota; Mississippi Valley south to Texas; in the Eastern States south at least to Delaware. **1903** NY State Museum & Sci. Serv. *Bulletin* 60.133, The roach, shiner, golden shiner or bream is one of the commonest fishes of the eastern states. It is found from New England to Minnesota and southward. A variety of the roach replaces the common northern form from North Carolina to Texas. **1933** LA Dept. of Conserv. *Fishes* 444, Known under the various names of Roach, Bream, Sunfish, Dace, Bitterhead, Chub, Gudgeon, Young Shad and Wind Fish, this species [=*Notemigonus crysoleucus* [sic]] of the Cyprinid family is northern in distribution. . . In the South it is replaced by a closely related species, *Notemigonus bosci* . . , to which the same popular names have been given. **1983** Becker *Fishes WI* 432, *Golden Shiner.* . . Other common names: bream, American bream, roach, American roach [etc].

(3) A fish of the genus *Hesperoleucus.*

1957 Blair et al. *Vertebrates U.S.* 108, *Hesperoleucus symmetricus* . . California roach. *Ibid, Hesperoleucus navarroensis* . . Navarro roach. *Ibid, Hesperoleucus parvipinnis* . . Shortfin roach. *Ibid, Hesperoleucus mitrulus* . . Northern roach. **1991** Amer. Fisheries Soc. *Common Names Fishes* 20, *Hesperoleucus symmetricus* . . California roach.

2 A **sunfish,** usu **bluegill 1** or **red-breasted sunfish 1.** Cf **johnny roach**

1838 Geol. Surv. OH *Second Annual Rept.* 191, [*Perca*] *vulgaris.* Sunfish, or roach. . . Varieties, or perhaps distinct species, are abundant in all the western waters. **1935** Caine *Game Fish* 26, Red-breasted Sunfish—*Lepomis auritus.* . . Synonyms: Black-eared Bream . . Roach [etc]. **1968** *DARE* (Qu. P1, . . *Kinds of freshwater fish . . caught around here . . good to eat*) Inf **CT14,** Dace—small, silver; roach—deep-bodied fish; **CT17,** Roach or johnny roach or sunfish. **1983** Becker *Fishes WI* 844, *Bluegill.* . . Other common names: bluegill sunfish . . roach [etc].

3 A **spot** (here: *Leiostomus xanthurus*).

1873 in 1878 Smithsonian Inst. *Misc. Coll.* 14.2.27 **VA,** Liostomus Obliquus . . roach (*Northampton County, Virginia*). **1887** Goode *Amer. Fishes* 129 **MD,** The Spot, or Lafayette, *Liostomus xanthurus,* is found along our coast from New England to the Gulf of Mexico, and is known . . in the Chesapeake region also as . . the "Roach." **1902** Jordan-Evermann *Amer. Fishes* 463, The single species, *Leiostomus xanthurus,* is a popular and well-known fish on our South Atlantic and Gulf coasts, under the vernacular names spot, goody, lafayette, roach, chub, chopa blanca, and masooka. **1976** Tryckare et al. *Lore of Sportfishing* 114, Spot . . Other common names: Goody, lafayette, roach, chub [etc].

roach v, hence ppl adj *roached,* vbl n *roaching* Also with *up* [Transf from *roach* to cut (a horse's mane) short so that it stands up] **chiefly Sth, S Midl**

To cut or arrange (the hair) so that it stands up or sweeps back from the forehead.

1833 *Sketches D. Crockett* 38, His hair was roached, and he wore an air of much dignity. **1853** (1854) Baldwin *Flush Times* 108 **AL,** His hair was roached up, and stood as erect and upright as his body. **1865** in 1885 Bagby *Selections Misc. Writings* 2.27 **VA,** You see it in the tie of his cravat, the cut of his coat . . the roaching of his hair. **1874** (1895) Eggleston *Circuit Rider* 294 **sOH** (as of early 19th cent), Brady took a seat opposite to him . . and roached up his iron gray hair uneasily. **1883** (1971) Harris *Nights with Remus* 336 **GA** [Black], Mr. Lion, he roach he ha'r back outen he eyes. **1899** (1912) Green *VA Folk-Speech* 355, *Roach.* . . To cause to stand up or arch; make projecting or convex: as, his hair was *roached* up over his forehead. **1906** Casey *Parson's Boys* 145 **sIL** (as of c1860), As he plastered his hair down on each side of his face, "roaching" it straight up in front, it made his countenance decidedly striking. **1906** *DN* 3.153 **nwAR,** *Roach.* . . To brush the hair on the edge of the forehead straight back. "I hate to have barbers roach my hair." **1909** *DN* 3.364 **eAL, wGA,** *Roach.* . . To comb or brush (the hair) straight back from the forehead; also, to come up out of the water so as to sweep the hair back thus. "Watch me roach my hair, boys." **1915** [see **roach** n[2]]. **1919** *DN* 5.39 **eTN,** *Roach.* . . To comb (the hair) straight back. **1939** Hall *Coll.* **wNC,** "She said she'd be out just as quick as she roached her hair back a little." "Roach your hair back a little." "Old fashioned" according to [1 inf]. **1942** Faulkner *Go Down* 10 **MS,** Her hair was roached under a lace cap. **1946** *PADS* 6.25 **eNC** (as of 1900–10), *Roach.* . . To comb the hair back from the front smooth and straight. . . Common. **1951** *PADS* 15.59 **neIN** (as of 1890s), *Roach.* . . To train the hair in a curved mass. **1952** [see **roach** n[2]]. **1956** [see **roach** n[2]]. **1968** *DARE* (Qu. X3, *When a woman puts her hair up on her head in a bunch*) Inf **IN13,** Roach; (Qu. X5, . . *Different kinds of men's haircuts*) Inf **TX54,** Got roached. [Both Infs old]

roach n[2] **chiefly Sth, S Midl**

A roll or wave of hair; a style of dressing the hair in which it is made to stand up or sweep back from the forehead.

1872 *Harper's New Mth. Mag.* 45.31 **WV,** Nevertheless he must drop every thing . . and then, giving his roach and shirt collar each a sly twig as he passed the fly-specked looking-glass, take his stand behind the counter. **1880** *Scribner's Mth.* 22.244 **GA** [Black], He take en walk up ter de Little Gal, Brer Rabbit did, en pull his roach [Footnote: Top-knot, foretop], en bow, en scrape he foot, en talk mighty nice en slick. **1902** *DN* 2.244 **sIL,** *Roach.* . . A mode of dressing the hair, by parting it on each side, and turning the intervening hair in a large curl down the top of the head. This word has become corrupted to mean any large curl or twist of any portion of the hair. **1907** *DN* 3.225 **nwAR,** *Roach.* . . A mode of dressing the hair by parting it on each side, and turning the intervening hair in a large curl down the top of the head. **1909** *DN* 3.364 **eAL, wGA,** *Roach.* . . A cow-lick, a topknot, a foretop. **1915** *DN* 4.189 **swVA,** *Roach* . . = cowlick (of hair).—v. To comb the hair so that it stays fixed. **1952** Brown *NC Folkl.* 1.585, *Roach.* . . A roll-back wave induced by combing or brushing the hair back; to comb or brush the hair in this manner.—General. **1956** McAtee *Some Dialect NC* 37, *Roach:* . . A roll of hair; and to make such a roll. *Colloq. & Dial.* **c1960** Wilson *Coll.* **csKY,** *Roach.* . . A roll of hair. **1967** *DARE* (Qu. X5, . . *Different kinds of men's haircuts*) Inf **AZ8,** Roach—short, sticks up about an inch; **LA11,** Roach—combed straight back, cut very short. [Both Infs old]

roachback n

1 A **grizzly bear** (here: *Ursus arctos horribilis*).

1887 *Scribner's Mag.* 2.309 **Rocky Mts,** Some men insist that among the gray bear there are no less than three distinct varieties—silvertip, roachback, and grizzly. . . [A]s to these differences of color indicating a distinct variety, I cannot believe it. **1893** Roosevelt *Wilderness Hunter* 266 **NW,** Any bear with unusually long hair on the spine and shoulders, especially if killed in the spring, when the fur is shaggy, is forthwith dubbed a "roach-back." **1900** *Century Illustr. Mag.* Jan 355 **ID, MT,** The Roachbacks, as the Bitter-root Grizzlies are called, are a cunning, desperate race. An old Roachback knows more about traps than half a dozen ordinary trappers; he knows more about plants and roots than a whole college of botanists. **1982** Elman *Hunter's Field Guide* 570, Grizzly Bear. . . Common & Regional Names . . silvertip, roachback [etc]. *Ibid* 574, The surest way to tell a small grizzly from a big black bear is by the grizzly's shoulder hump, which inspired the colloquial name "roachback."

2 See **roachback buffalo.**

roachback buffalo n Also *roachback*   Cf **humpback buffalo, quillback ~, razorback ~ (fish)**
=**smallmouth buffalo.**

   1933 LA Dept. of Conserv. *Fishes* 442, The Smallmouth Buffalo has . . received a confusion of popular names. Included are Razorback Buffalo . . Roachback Buffalo [etc]. **1956** Harlan–Speaker *IA Fish* 73, Smallmouth Buffalo. . . Other Names—Roach-back, razor-back-buffalo fish, and thick-lipped buffalo. **1983** Becker *Fishes WI* 625, Smallmouth Buffalo. . . Other common names: razorback buffalo . . roachback buffalo [etc].

roach comb n Also *roaching comb*
A comb for dressing the hair in a **roach** n². an ornamental comb worn in a **roach** n².

   1884 Harris *Mingo* 43 **GA,** Nor was his ideal of feminine beauty reached by the village belles, with their roach-combs. **1909** *DN* 3.364 **eAL, wGA,** Roach-comb. . . A semi-circular comb used by children (girls) to roach the hair back over the forehead. Formerly common, but now out of style. Sometimes *roaching-comb.* **1950** *PADS* 14.56 **SC,** *Roach comb* . . worn in the hair, and . . more or less ornamental.

roached ppl adj See **roach** v

roaches of the liver n [Folk-etym for *cirrhosis of the liver*]
   1967 *DARE* FW Addit **KY34,** [ˈročɪz əv ðə ˌlɪvɚ]. **1984** Wilder *You All Spoken Here* 203 **Sth,** *Roaches of the liver:* Cirrhosis. **1995** *DARE* File, Self-diagnosed illnesses of emergency room patients. Very-close veins . . roaches of the liver . . sick-as-hell anemia. [*DARE* Ed: From an e-mail communication referring to an article in an unidentified medical journal]

roaching See **roach** v

roaching comb See **roach comb**

roach killer n, also attrib   Cf **cockroach killer, toad-stabber**
A sharp-pointed shoe or boot.
   1970 *DARE* (Qu. W42a, . . *Nicknames . . for men's sharp-pointed shoes*) Inf **NJ67C,** Roach killers. [FW: Aux Inf from **NYC**] **1983** Glimm *Flatlanders* 9 **cnPA,** He wore a ten-gallon hat, them high-heeled roach-killer boots, and a silver belt buckle. [**1999** *DARE* File **swSD** (as of 1978), When I arrived in South Dakota to start a job, I was informed by a local wearing cowboy boots that the reason cowboys wear pointy-toed boots was to kill cockroaches in the corners.]

roach up See **roach** v

road n¹ Usu |ro(ʊ)d|; also |roɛd, roəd|; also esp **NEng** |rʌd, rəd| Pronc-spp *ro-ud, rud*
   A Forms.
   1890 *DN* 1.40 **ME,** *Road* . . [Author's pronc:] originally [rəd]; now [roʊd]. **1907** *DN* 3.248 **eME,** *Road.* . . Pronounced [rəd]. The New England short *o* is almost universal in Eastern Maine. **1909** *DN* 3.415 **nME,** *Road.* . . Pronounced *rod* [*DARE* Ed: prob =[rəd]]. [**1914** *DN* 4.79 **ME, nNH,** *Rudder.* . . A good horse. (Var. of *roader.*)] **1926** *DN* 5.389 **ME,** *Road.* . . [[roʊd], diphthong almost one letter]. Any highway. Common. **1926** *AmSp* 2.77 **ME,** No alien has ever yet been able to master our so-called short *o.* . . [T]ry to enunciate such words as *road, coat, boat, load,* and *stone.* . . After puzzling over the phonetics of these words for some years I have discovered that the difficulty lies in thinking that we are dealing with a single vowel. There is no *o* that represents these words. Instead of a single sound it consists of two actual vowels so rapidly spoken that only one seems apparent. Yet it is the only way that you can manufacture the sound. Thus say very rapidly "ro-ud," "co-ut," "bo-ut," "lo-ud," and "sto-un." **1931** *AmSp* 6.399 **coastal ME,** In *boat* and *road,* [o] is often changed to [ʌ]. **1941** *AmSp* 16.6 **eTX** [Black], *Road,* [roɛd], as well as [ro:d]. **1947** Stegner *Second Growth* 190 **NH,**

Clear around that rud, clean through to the highway. . . She ain't no queerer than the rest on that rud. **1959** *VT Hist.* 27.154 **neVT,** *Road* [rɜd] [*DARE* Ed: prob for [rʌd]] . . pronc. Common. Also [roəd] in northeast Vermont. **1961** Kurath–McDavid *Pronc. Engl.* 111, The dialect of New England possesses a checked mid-back vowel /ɵ/, traditionally called "the New England short *o,*" in such words as *coat, road* . . which does not occur outside the New England settlement area, i.e., the Northern dialect area. . . The checked vowel /ɵ/ is normally a fronted and lowered mid-back [oˬ~ɔˬ] sound, clearly ingliding before alveolar stops, as in *coat, road.* . . This vowel phoneme, a hallmark of the New England dialect, is sharply recessive at the present time and has obviously been receding for several generations. It is preserved most extensively in northeastern New England (from the Green Mountains in Vermont eastward), less so in the southeast. In the lower Connecticut Valley and westward it is now rather uncommon, except among the older generation, and in the New England settlements of Upstate New York, northern Pennsylvania, and east-central New Jersey it survives only as a rare relic. **1964** De Vries *Reuben* 33 **CT,** It [=ˈcal'late"] went with "fust" and "mebbe" and "up the rud a piece" and all the other folk talk no longer in regular use but very helpful in playing the hick to people you are laughing in your teeth at.
   B Senses.
   1 A way, course of travel—freq in phrr *out of the road, in the road* out of the way, in the way.   [Scots, nEngl dial]
   1826 Royall *Sketches* 58 **WV,** For get out of the way, they say get out of the road: Road is universally used for way; "Put them cheers, (chairs) out of the road." **1874** in 1983 *PADS* 70.48 **ePA,** I stopped at Finney's on my road home a while. **1876** *Ibid,* I took Jonathon wife & child out to Harboro this morning on their road to the Centennial to spend their last day there. **1914** *DN* 4.111 **cKS,** *Out of the road* . . out of the way. **1941** in 1944 *ADD* **WV,** *Road.* . . Without [adjustable seats] tall people would have to drive with their knees in the road of their hands. **1944** *AmSp* 19.38 **PA,** In the phrases *in the way, Get out of my way* . . Philadelphians and Pennsylvania Dutch alike say *road* instead of *way.* **1953** *AmSp* 28.253 **csPA,** *Road,* as in 'You are in the road' or 'Get out of my road.' . . It is in general use, along with *way.* **1966** *DARE* (Qu. NN22b, *Expressions used to drive away children*) Inf **NM9,** Git out of the road. **1969** *DARE* Tape **CA172B,** The main danger is to see 'em [=snakes] . . in time so that they have plenty of time to get out of your road or that you'd have plenty of time to get out of their road. **1976** Garber *Mountain-ese* 46 **sAppalachians,** Please don't git in my road or I can't see the TV picture. **1982** Barrick *Coll.* **csPA,** *Road—way—*"You're always in the road." "Get out a my road."
   2 in phrr *give one the road, send one down the road,* and varr: To dismiss or reject (one).   Cf **down the country, give one**
   c1950 Halpert *Coll.* 53 **wKY, nwTN,** He sent her down the road = called off their relationship. **1950** Williams *Rocky Mts.* 234 **CO,** But the operators had a way of meeting this situation. They simply discharged—sent down the canyon, was the way the workers expressed it—any man who joined the U.M.W. **c1960** Wilson *Coll.* **csKY,** *Send him down the road.* . . Jilt him. **1967–70** *DARE* (Qu. AA11, *If a man asks a girl to marry him and she refuses,* . . *she* _____) Inf **TX35,** Sent him on down the road; (Qu. II5b, *When you don't want to have anything to do with a certain person because you don't like him* . . "I'd certainly like to give him the _____.") Infs **KY74, NY96,** Road. **1969** Sorden *Lumberjack Lingo* 106 **NEng, Gt Lakes,** *Sent him down the road—*To discharge a man.
   3a in phrr *on the road, in the ~,* and varr: On the go; gadding about.   Cf **foot** n **C5f, street**
   1965–70 *DARE* (Qu. Y29a, *To 'go out' a great deal, not to stay at home much:* "She's always _____.") Infs **CT36, LA37, MA16, ME13, 21, NY213, RI6, SC32, WI77,** On the road; **KY19,** On the roads; **LA8, SC34,** In the road; **VA65,** In the road a lot; (Qu. Y29b, . . *About a man [who doesn't stay home much]:* "He's always _____.") Infs **IN45, KY72, LA20, 37, MA16, ME13, MN39, NC22, 29,** On the road; **LA8, VA65,** In the road. **1982** Walker *Color Purple* 62 **GA** [Black], Sofia gone six months, Harpo act like a different man. Used to be a homebody, now all the time in the road.
   b in comb with personal name: A gadabout.   Cf **roadrunner 4**
   1966–70 *DARE* (Qu. Y29a, *To 'go out' a great deal, not to stay at home much:* "She's always _____.") Inf **SC26,** She's a regular road Annie; **NC88,** In the street; a road Lucy. [Both Infs Black]

road n² See **rode** n

road apple n   Cf **alley apple 2, horse apple 3**

A lump of horse manure.

1942 Berrey–Van den Bark *Amer. Slang* 124.2, *Dung.* . . Road apples. **1951** M. Spillane *One Lonely Night* v. 112 *(OED2),* Smart? Sure, just like road apples that happen behind horses. **1969** O'Connor *Horse & Buggy West* 95 **AZ,** The horse was no paragon of virtue, safety, or sanitation. Wherever the horse went he urinated and dropped road apples. **1969** *DARE* (Qu. L17, . . *Names . . for manure*) Inf **IL38,** Road apples—horse droppings used to be called road apples. **1988** *DARE* File **TN, TX,** The term "cow chips" is hardly regional, but I never before had heard of a road apple—a single horse turd, fresh or dry. My informer said it was used in Tennessee and in Texas! **1999** *DARE* File **TX,** This morning on National Public Radio, Baxter Black was talking about the effectiveness of the horse's tail in swishing away flies. He wondered aloud why the cow's tail wasn't similarly constructed. Then he remembered that a cow pie is a lot sloppier than a road apple.

road bird n
=**lark sparrow.**

1967 *DARE* (Qu. Q15, . . *Kinds of larks*) Inf **OR5,** Road bird—lark family, small; congregate in dust on road.

road-bunkie n Cf **bunk sled**
In logging: see quot.

1966 *DARE* Tape **MI10,** Out in the woods, the workmen. . . who had more or less menial tasks in the woods, who worked on the sleigh roads, were called road-bunkies.

road cart n Also *road car*
A light, two-wheeled, usu one-horse vehicle, usu for one or two passengers.

1883 *Overland Mth.* (2d ser) 2.8 advt sec 5 **CA,** The party . . started for the ranch house . . in a Petaluma road cart drawn by a span of tough Nevada half-bred horses. **1889** *Century Illustr. Mag.* 37 advt sec 64, *Elkhart Carriage and Harness Manufacturing Co.* . . Road Carts $17. **1902** (1969) Sears *Catalogue* 379, Our Fulton Special Road Cart, $9.75. . . The wheels are . . 46 inches high. . . The cart is very strong . . carrying capacity, two passengers. **1927** (1970) *Ibid* 1044, Phaeton Body Road Cart. . . $29.90. **1938** Hertzler *Horse & Buggy Dr.* 61 **KS** (as of early 20th cent), The means of transportation at the beginning of any practice was preferred in the order named: horse or team and buggy; horse and road cart, a two-wheeled vehicle with a simple and very hard board seat on which no cushion could be fastened. **1965–70** *DARE* (Qu. N41a, . . *Horse-drawn vehicles . . to carry people*) 10 Infs, **chiefly Atlantic,** Road cart; **GA84, 89, MD19, NC50, SC19,** Road cart—two wheels (*or* -wheeled); **MD13,** Road cart—two wheels, one seat—used to break young horses because they could turn quickly without damaging cart; **NY68,** Road cart—two-wheeled cart with one seat; on the same plan as their trotting sulkies, only the wheels was made out of wood; **WI43,** Road cart—used to break colts; **GA7,** Road car—two wheels; **NC87,** Road car—seated one; **SC32,** Road car—two buggy wheels, light—two passengers; (Qu. N41b, *Horse-drawn vehicles to carry heavy loads*) Inf **SC7,** Road cart—two wheels, with a body like a wagon, shorter than a wagon body; (Qu. N41c, *Horse-drawn vehicles to carry light loads*) Inf **SC26,** Road cart—two-wheeled. **1968** *DARE* Tape **IN20,** And I had a big old high-wheel road cart. **1977** Berkebile *Amer. Carriages* 24, *Road cart.* The term was supposedly introduced about 1881; the vehicle was previously known as a sulky. It was intended for use on the road rather than on the track. Some had seating for two. . . For those interested in increased comfort and better appearance, phaeton-body road carts were also available, complete with falling top.

road days n pl
1980 *McDavid Coll.* **ceGA** (as of 1946), *Road days*—Days of labor to maintain public roads, once required of all adult males; later changed to a tax. Mentioned often by Georgia informants. *Ibid* **ceGA** (as of 1946), *Road days*—3 days work a year.

road donkey n Pacific NW Cf **roader 2**
In logging: a **donkey 1** used to drag logs along a **skid road 1.**

1905 U.S. Forest Serv. *Bulletin* 61.44 **Pacific NW,** *Road donkey.* A donkey engine mounted on a heavy sled, which drags logs along a skid road by winding a cable on a drum. It has a second drum for the haulback. **1958** McCulloch *Woods Words* 150 **Pacific NW,** *Road donkey*—A machine which is being rapidly forgotten since truck roads have cut out long yarding shows. In the old days a road donkey was one with large drum capacity (up to 10,000 feet of ⅝-inch haulback). It was used to haul logs from the yarding donkey by fore-and-aft or dirt road, to

within reach of the swing donkey which carried the logs on to the landing.

road duster n
A **grasshopper 1.**

1942 McAtee *Dial. Grant Co. IN* 53 (as of 1890s), *Road-dusters* . . grasshoppers (of the genera *Arphia* and *Hippiscus*) that frequent open places, often roads, from which they make short rattling flights only to alight again nearby.

roade See **rode** n

roader n Pronc-sp *rudder*
1 A horse for driving or riding on a road. **NEng** Cf **roadster 1**

1884 *Boston Jrnl.* 7 June *(DAE),* Any gentlemen wanting to purchase a strictly first-class roader or a trotter call on G.W. Gould. **1906** (1907) Wiggin *New Chron. Rebecca* 134 **ME,** Mr. Simpson had borrowed a "good roader" . . and would himself drive the girl. **1914** *DN* 4.79 **ME, nNH,** *Rudder.* . . A roadster; a good horse. (Var. of *roader.*) "He's a smart rudder." **1939** Coffin *Capt. Abby* 178 **ME** (as of 1860s), The boy Elias was there, with the Old Boy in him bigger than a woodchuck and the new black roader.

2 =**road donkey.**

1925 *AmSp* 1.136 **Pacific NW,** There are generally three donkey engines used to operate a side—a "yarder," a "roader," and a "loader." The yarder may fetch the logs a distance of fifteen hundred feet or more, the roader may take them on for twenty-five hundred feet, and the loader merely swings them up to the "top-loader" and "second-loader" on the cars—"flats" or "trucks." **1958** McCulloch *Woods Words* 151 **Pacific NW,** *Roader*—Same as road donkey. **1967** *DARE* Tape **WA20,** Another donkey we called a roader would hook on to ten, twelve, fifteen [logs]. . . And that way they would pull 'em right into the water.

road grass n
See quots.

1968 *DARE* (Qu. S8, *A common kind of wild grass that grows in fields: it spreads by sending out long underground roots, and it's hard to get rid of*) Inf **MO34,** Road grass. **1969** *DARE* File **TX,** Rye Grass—always called road grass because it was the only thing that would grow in the dirt in the road.

road hog n
=**bush hog** n.

1968 *DARE* (Qu. L35, . . *Tools used for cutting underbrush*) Inf **MO25,** Road hog.

road lizard n Cf **roadrunner 2**
See quots.

1961 *McDavid Coll.* **csOK,** Road lizard—a harmless variety. **1996** McDowell *Leaving Pipe Shop* 151 **AL** [Black] (as of 1960s), But not like the craziness of them Barnes folks. Every one of them is crazy as road lizards. **1998** *DARE* File—Internet **cAK** [Life in the Desert—Interior Alaska], Longtime Delta [AK] farmer, Tom Wilson, described pumping water on a hot day plainly to us: "After you get pumping for awhile, you will be panting like a road lizard," he said.

road maintainer See **maintainer**

road patrolman See **patrolman**

road-patter See **roadrunner 4**

roadrunner n
1 also *roadrunner bird:* A large ground cuckoo of the desert Southwest (*Geococcyx californianus*). [See quot 1940] Also called **Arizona peacock, California ~, chachalaca 2, chaparral cock, cock of the desert, ground cuckoo, lizard bird, medicine ~, Mexican peafowl, paisano 2, prairie cock 2, rattlesnake killer, snake-~, Texas bird-of-paradise, warbird**

1856 *Hutchings' CA Mag.* Nov 201, The Road-Runner is seldom seen on trees, unless pursued very closely. **1897** *Oölogist* 14.68 **CA,** Another of our more common birds is the Road-runner (*Geococcyx californianus*) or Paisano as the Mexicans call it. **1926** TX Folkl. Soc. *Pub.* 5.88, As crazy as a *paisano* (road-runner or chaparral bird). **1940** Writers' Program *Guide TX* 28, The road runner or ground cuckoo. . . is the clown of the highways. With plumage comically ruffled, this large long-legged bird runs swiftly along the ground instead of flying and tries to race ahead of automobiles. **1956** Almirall *From College* 60 **CO,** That's what is specifically described as a chaparral cock, but commonly called a "road runner." **1965–70** *DARE* (Qu. Q7, *Names and nicknames for . . game birds*) Infs **TX**1, 42, Roadrunner; (Qu. Q10) Infs **MI**93, **UT**5, Roadrunner; (Qu. Q14, *. . Names . . for . . birds*) Infs **CA**91, 120, **IL**21, **TX**5, Roadrunner; (Qu. Q16, *. . Kinds of jays*) Inf **TX**66, Roadrunner; (Qu. Q23) Infs **MO**39, **NM**13, Roadrunner. **1968** *DARE* Tape **CA**89, [Inf:] I've seen these roadrunners. . . I've seen them attack snakes. They're quick. . . The last ones that I've seen have been down in the low country. . . [Aux Inf:] They look like a raggedy chicken. [Inf:] Yeah, kinda. They're long-legged and got a sharp bill. **1970** Anderson *TX Folk Med.* 10, *Boils.* . . Fry a roadrunner bird and eat it. **1977** Udvardy *Audubon Field Guide Birds* 505, Roadrunner. . . Famous for its rather unusual behavior. It is a reticent bird that when surprised on a road runs rapidly away (hence its name), vanishing into cover. **1998** *DARE* File—Internet [Desert USA *The Roadrunner*], When the Roadrunner senses danger or is traveling downhill, it flies, revealing short, rounded wings . . otherwise, it runs or walks with a clownish gait.

2 A **whiptail** (here: *Cnemidophorus gularis*).

1928 Baylor Univ. Museum *Contrib.* 16.13, Western Lined Lizard—*Cnemidophorus gularis.* . . I have heard *gularis* called the *Roadrunner,* on account of its scampering along roads in advance of vehicles; and *Black-throated Race-runner* and *Spotted Race-runner* because of its coloration and disposition to "race" with any one pursuing it.

3 See quot. Cf **horse racer 2, racehorse 1**

1968 *DARE* (Qu. R9a, *An insect from two to four inches long that lives in bushes and looks like a dead twig*) Inf **WI**65, Roadrunners; walking-stick.

4 also *road-patter:* A gadabout; a lively person. Cf **road n¹ B3a**

1966–70 *DARE* (Qu. Y29a, *To 'go out' a great deal, not to stay at home much: "She's always _____"*) Infs **IL**140, **MS**37, Roadrunner; **MS**45, Just a roadrunner; **LA**11, Road-patter; (Qu. Y29b, *. . About a man [who doesn't stay home much]: "He's always _____."*) Inf **VA**31, Roadrunner. **1986** Pederson *LAGS Concordance (Quite lively)* 1 inf, **cnGA,** He's a roadrunner.

5 A rustic. Cf **ridge runner 1**

1967 *DARE* (Qu. HH1, *Names and nicknames for a rustic or countrified person*) Inf **NY**7, Roadrunner. **1986** Pederson *LAGS Concordance (A rustic)* 1 inf, **ceTN,** Roadrunner.

roadrunner bird See **roadrunner 1**

roadster n

1 =**roader 1.**

1821 in 1860 Claiborne *Life Quitman* 1.64 **NY,** He has given me some severe falls, but is now a fine roadster. **1856** U.S. Patent Office *Annual Rept. for 1855: Ag.* 39, We have many fine roadsters and saddle horses. **1885** *Wkly. New Mexican Rev.* 2 July 2/4 *(DAE),* Col. Grayson. . . paid the Duncan boys $365 for a span of roadsters. **1899** (1912) Green *VA Folk-Speech* 356, Roadster. . . A good travelling horse is called a good roadster.

2 A touring bicycle.

1880 *Scribner's Mth.* 19.486 **MA,** His saddle had been set well up to the head of his roadster, so that he was nicely poised over the center of his wheel. **1887** *Scribner's Mag.* 1 advt sec 37, The "Cunard"—Light Roadster Bicycles. Full Roadster Bicycles. **1893** *Atlantic Mth.* 71 advt sec 26, The Remington. *Three Styles for 1893.* Light Roadster, Roadster, and Ladies Wheel.

3 A light carriage or buggy.

1892 *Hist. Rev. York Co.* 68 **PA,** The former [repository and office] carries a fine line of . . everything in light and heavy work from the most substantial farm truck to the lightest finished roadster. **1901** *DN* 2.146 **cwNY,** Roadster. . . A vehicle. "I went to a farmer near and hired a young horse and a roadster." Buffalo, N.Y. **1968** *DARE* (Qu. N41a, *. . Horse-drawn vehicles . . to carry people*) Inf **IN**39, Roadster.

road trotter n

=**horned lark.**

1917 (1923) *Birds Amer.* 2.212, Horned Lark. . . Other Names . . Northern Horned Lark . . Road Trotter [etc.].

road wagon n

1 A heavy wagon for transporting loads. **formerly more widespread, but now esp Ohio Valley** See Map

1833 U.S. Congress *Reg. of Debates* 9.2.1320 24 Jan, In 1829, the Kiskiminetas salt works, in Pennsylvania, employed two hundred road wagons. **1868** *Putnam's Mag.* 12.488, The road-wagon was a vast improvement on the pack-train. **1889** *Century Illustr. Mag.* 37.602 **nwCA,** The stout road-wagon was drawn by a good-looking pair of American horses. **1942** Warnick *Garrett Co. MD* 13 **nwMD** (as of 1900–18), *Road-wagon* . . heavy wagon as distinguished from a light, or spring, wagon. **c1960** Wilson *Coll.* **csKY,** Road wagon. . . A farm wagon, distinguished from a spring wagon. Also called a jolt wagon. **1965–70** *DARE* (Qu. N41b, *Horse-drawn vehicles to carry heavy loads*) 10 Infs, **esp Ohio Valley,** Road wagon; **AR**51, Road wagon—standard wagon; **KY**74, Road wagon—heavy wagon; (Qu. L13, *The kind of wagon used for carrying hay: [. . special wagon, or frame put on ordinary wagon]*) Infs **KY**43, **MO**9, Road wagon; **AR**18, Road wagon with a hay frame; (Qu. N40a, *. . Sleighs . . for hauling loads*) Inf **KY**9, Road wagon. [12 of 14 total Infs male]

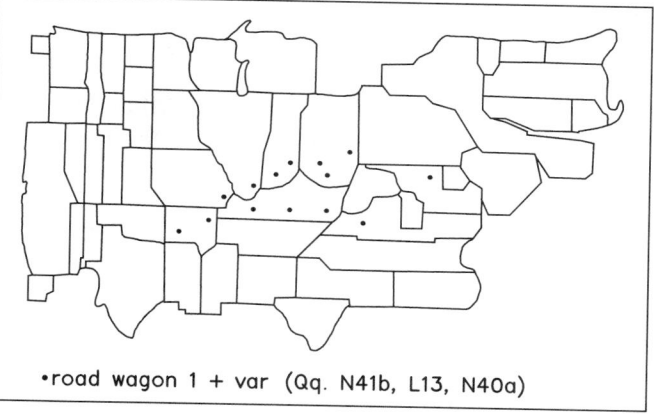

•road wagon 1 + var (Qq. N41b, L13, N40a)

2 A light, four-wheeled, one-horse vehicle used for transporting loads or people.

1868 *Atlantic Mth.* 21.523 **seNY** (as of 1862), His appearance on the course in his road wagon, driving the well-known beauties, detained the whole assembled multitude. **1883** *Harper's New Mth. Mag.* 67.720, There is a place for sulkies and road-wagons. **1901** *Scribner's Mag.* 29.422, He was drawing a light, bicycle-wheeled road-wagon. **1902** (1969) Sears *Catalogue* 363, Our $22.35 Road Wagon. . . Our $23.95 Road Wagon. **1902** *DN* 2.244 **sIL,** Road-wagon. . . Light, spring wagon. This word has recently come into general use. **1907** *DN* 3.226 **nwAR,** Road-wagon. . . Light, spring wagon. **1934** Hanley Disks **csCT,** Then they had what they called road wagons, very light. Some of 'em a one-man wagon. **1965–70** *DARE* (Qu. N41a, *. . Horse-drawn vehicles . . to carry people*) Infs **IL**104, **MO**9, Road wagon; **OH**3, Road wagon—four-wheeled, one seat; **WA**12, Road wagon—cross between wagon and hack; (Qu. N41c, *Horse-drawn vehicles to carry light loads*) Infs **AR**51, **IL**16, **KY**6, 9, **TX**37, Road wagon.

roan lily n

A **lily 1** (here: *Lilium grayi*).

1933 Small *Manual SE Flora* 291, [Lilium] *Grayi* . . Roan-lily, Orange-bell lily. . . Because of its supposed rarity this species is sought by specialists in lily-culture. **1949** Moldenke *Amer. Wild Flowers* 324, A rather unusual lily is the so-called roan lily, *L. grayi,* whose 1 to 3 spreading or slightly drooping flowers are red or yellow-tinged at the base. . . In its native haunts the roan lily occurs only in acid meadows in the mountain fastnesses of North Carolina, Tennessee, and Virginia.

roasting corn n Cf **green corn 2, roasting ear B1, sweet corn**

Corn suitable or ready for human consumption.

1966–70 *DARE* (Qu. I33, *. . Ears of corn that are just right for eating*) Infs **GA**85, **KS**5, **MN**12, **NY**75, **OK**43, **TX**71, **VA**56, Roasting corn; **AL**14, **CA**136, Roastin' corn. **1986** Pederson *LAGS Concordance (Sweet corn)* 7 infs, **AL, FL, GA, TN,** Roasting corn.

roasting ear n Usu |ˈro(ʊ)stɪŋ, -ɪn| *ear;* for varr see **A** below Pronc-spp *roasin' ear, roastin' year, roast-near, ros'in (y)ear;* for addit pronc and sp varr see **A** and **B** below Cf **ear**

A Forms. See also quots at **B** below

1 |ˈro(ʊ)sn̩, -ən, -ɪn, -ɪn| *ear.* **chiefly Sth, S Midl** See Map on p. 606

1965–70 *DARE* (Qu. I33) 103 Infs, **chiefly Sth, S Midl**, ['roʊsn̩, -ən, -ɪn, -m̩, 'rozn̩] ears; (Qu. H50) Inf **GA**46, ['rosn̩] ear(s).

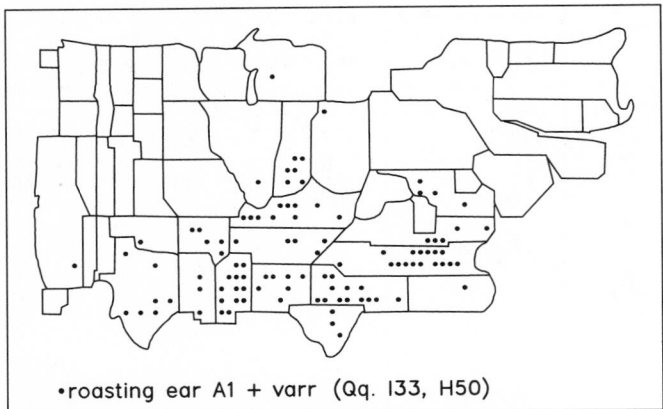

•roasting ear A1 + varr (Qq. I33, H50)

2 |'roʊstɪŋ, -in| *ear.* **scattered, but esp Midl**   See Map
  1965–70 *DARE* (Qu. I33) 34 Infs, **scattered, but esp Midl**, ['roʊstɪŋ, 'roʊstin] ear(s).

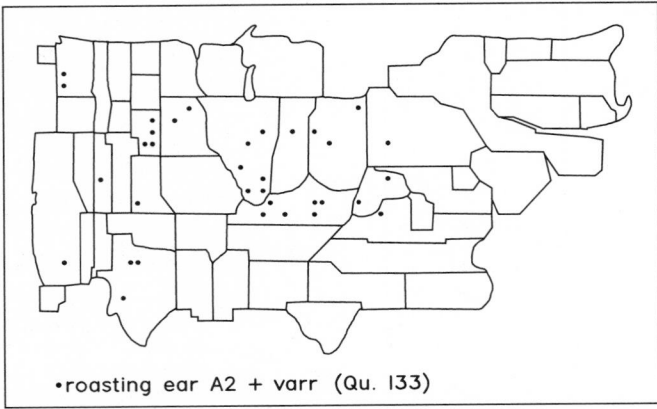

•roasting ear A2 + varr (Qu. I33)

3 |'roʊs, nɪr|. [By metanalysis; cf Intro "Language Changes" I.2] **esp S Midl**
  1967–70 *DARE* (Qu. I33) Infs **AR**56, **DE**3, **LA**32, ['roʊs,nɪɚz]; **LA**2, ['roʊz,nɪɚz] or ['roʊs,nɪɚz]; **TN**30, ['ros,nɪɚz].

4 See quot.   Cf Pronc Intro 3.II.8
  1968 *DARE* (Qu. I33) Infs **MD**28, 50, ['rɛostɪŋ] ears.

B Senses.

1 also rarely *roast ear:* An ear of corn *(Zea mays)* at the stage when it is edible with brief cooking; kernels of corn or a dish prepared from kernels of corn at this stage; occas applied to corn as a crop or to dried ears of corn; hence adj phr *in roasting ear(s)* of corn: suitable for eating. **widespread exc NEast** See Map   Cf **green corn 2; milk, in the; roasting corn; sweet ~; tender ~**
  1650 (1923) Bland *New Brittaine* 10 **VA**, The Inhabitants came, and brought us roasting eares. **1825** (1922) Biggs *Narrative* 28 **IL**, They [=Indians] said if I staid with them until their corn got in roasting ears, then I must take a wife. **1864** (1922) Jackson *Col.'s Diary* 146 **PA**, We find plenty of corn in good condition for roasting ears. **a1883** (1911) Bagby *VA Gentleman* 98, Other vegetables, such as tomatoes, onions, black-eye peas, cymlings, and "rosin" ears, being grown here and there. **1884** Smith *Bill Arp's Scrap Book* 402 **GA**, We had roasten ears for supper and buttermilk and honey. **1894** Riley *Armazindy* 52 **IN**, Roas'in'-yeers. **1895** *DN* 1.393 **wFL**, *Roast'n ear:* green corn, whether on the cob or not; may be in tin cans. **1896** Robinson *In New Engl. Fields* 136, A foraging party repairs to the nearest cornfield for roasting ears, and the hunters shorten the slow night-tide with munching scorched corn. **1899** (1912) Green *VA Folk-Speech* 356, *Roasting-ear.* . . An ear of corn in the green milky state, and fit for roasting for food. "Roasin'-ear." *Ibid* 357, *Rosen-ear.* . . Roasting ear; green corn. Ro's'n. **1903** *DN* 2.327 **seMO**, *Roasting-ears* (often *roastin-ears*). . . Green-corn. **1907** *DN* 3.235 **nwAR**, *Roas(t)ing-ears.* . . Green sweet corn. Also

ros'in years. **1909** *DN* 3.364 **eAL, wGA**, *Roas(t)in(g)-ear.* . . Green corn, usually on the cob, but applied to any sort of dish made of green corn. The almost universal pronunciation is ['rosn̩]-ear. *Rosn-year* is also heard. **1915** *DN* 4.189 **swVA**, *Roas'n year.* . . Any dish made of green corn. *Ibid* 228 **wTX**, *Roast-nears.* . . Roasting ears (of corn). **1916** *DN* 4.328 **KS**, *Roasting ear.* . . Ear of Indian corn or maize at the stage of maturity when the grains contain a milky fluid before full ripeness. It is boiled usually, and rarely roasted, notwithstanding the term. General. **1923** *DN* 5.219 **swMO**, *Roastin' year.* **1944** *PADS* 2.12 **Sth**, *Roasting-ear* ['roʊstn̩,ɪə] ((in Va., N.C. ['rosnjɛə])). . . Ear of green corn, well filled out and suitable for cooking, chiefly by boiling, served with the grain on the ear. ((Still roasted in Va. and N.C. in hot ashes, over hot coals, in a stove, or in the "flue" or the "furnace" of the tobacco barn.)) *Ibid* 60 **MO**, *Roasting-ear* ['rosn̩,ɛr]. **1953** [see **B2** below]. **1959** *Hall Coll.* **wNC, eTN**, *Roastin' ear.* . . A ripe ear of corn. . . Also used of dried corn for cattle feed. **1965–70** *DARE* (Qu. I33, . . *Ears of corn that are just right for eating*) 497 Infs, **widespread exc NEast**, Roasting ears; **GA**13, Roast ears; **MS**79, Roast years; (Qu. H50, *Dishes made with . . corn that everybody around here knows, but people in other places might not*) Inf **GA**46, Roasting ears; (Qu. H56, *Names for . . pickles*) Inf **NC**44, Pickled roasting ears; (Qu. I32, *How do you know when corn is ready to eat?;* total Infs questioned, 75) Inf **OK**43, When the white milk comes out of the grain—it's in roasting-ear stage; (Qu. I34, *If you don't have sweet corn, you can always eat young* _____) Infs **NC**87, **PA**181, Roasting ears; (Qu. L26, *Sayings about corn and other important crops around here;* total Infs questioned, 75) Inf **MS**4, Lay corn by when you can bring roasting ears in for dinner. **1976** Garber *Mountain-ese* 76 **sAppalachians**, *Ros'neers.* **1996** *DARE* File **neTX** (as of 1920s-30s), We had lots of corn on the cob—which I called "roas-sneers." I found out much later that they were "roasting-ears."

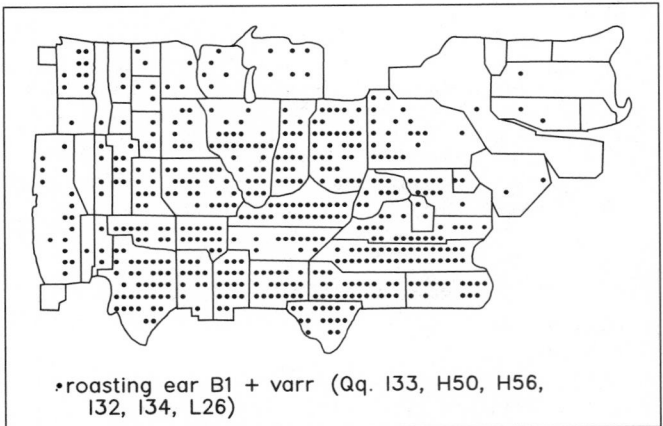

•roasting ear B1 + varr (Qq. I33, H50, H56, I32, I34, L26)

2 attrib or in adj phr *in roasting ear;* Of other plants: mature; esp of legumes: ripe but not dry.   **S Midl**
  1927 *DN* 5.479 **Ozarks**, "The yonkipins is in roastin' ear" means that they [=water lilies] are fully developed—the mature pistil somewhat resembles an ear of corn. **1953** Randolph–Wilson *Down in Holler* 279 **Ozarks**, *Roasting ear, in:* phr. Ripe, mature. Perhaps applied primarily to corn, but used with reference to other plants as well. Fully developed beans, for example, are said to be *in roastin' ear.* Isabel France (*Arkansas Gazette,* August 24, 1947) writes of "crowder peas canned *in the roasting ear.*" **1958** *PADS* 29.15 **csTN**, The term "*rostin' ear peas* [is] used in referring to field peas or black eyed peas that are turning yellow or [are then] just ready to shell." **1966–70** *DARE* (Qu. I15, *Some of the beans that you eat in the pod have yellow pods; you call these* _____) Inf **AR**20, Roasting-ear beans; (Qu. I20, . . *Kinds of beans*) Inf **KY**90, Roastin'-ear beans; **AR**3, Roasting-ear peas—young field peas. **1970** *DARE* FW Addit **KY**85, *Roastin' ear stage* ['rosn̩,ɪɚ]—When beans are mature enough to be shelled out of the pod, but [not] yet dry. **1986** Pederson *LAGS Concordance,* 1 inf, **cwTN**, Roasting-ear bean [and] roasting-ear pea—stage before mature—but tender; 1 inf, **cnAR**, Roasting-ear beans—you shell them; 1 inf, **cnGA**, Roasting-ear peas; 1 inf, **cnAR**, Roasting-ear peas—brown crowder peas; 1 inf, **neAR**, Roasting-ear stage—of any fresh vegetable or fruit.

roasting-ear bread n   Cf **gritted bread**

A type of **corn cake** made with grated kernels of **roasting ears.**
  1905 (1975) Miles *Spirit of Mts.* 32 **eTN**, Odd-looking utensils,

these; . . a huge "gritter" on which green corn is grated in late summer for the making of "roas'n' ear" bread. **1941** Justus *Cabin on Kettle Creek* 35 **eTN,** "Let's have roas'n' ear bread!" . . The two girls . . brought back a sackful of tender green corn. . . They all took turn and turn about grating the ears of corn. . . Mammy put a pinch of salt in it [= the grated corn] and beat the batter with a spoon. Glory greased the griddle. . . Mammy dropped a spoonful of grated corn on it, enough for a cake.

roasting-ear wine n Also *roasting-ear cordial* Cf **corncob wine**

See quots.

1929 *AmSp* 4.387 **KS** [Wet words], The so-called *roasting-ear wine* is not really wine at all, but corn whiskey. **1934** (1940) Weseen *Dict. Amer. Slang* 282, *Roasting-ear wine*—Corn whiskey; any intoxicating liquor. **1941** in **1944** *ADD* **Sth,** *Roasting-ear wine.* Corn whiskey. . . Reported. **1968** *DARE* (Qu. DD28b, . . *Fermented drinks . . made at home*) Inf **AL**39, Roasting-ear wine—white wine out of roasting ears. **1986** Pederson *LAGS Concordance,* 1 inf, **ceGA,** Roasting-ear cordial—cheap whiskey.

roastin' year, roast-near See **roasting ear**

robalo n [Span]

A **snook,** usu *Centropomus undecimalis.*

1882 U.S. Natl. Museum *Bulletin* 16.528, C[entropomus] undecimalis . . *Robalo.* . . A large food-fish, abundant in the West Indies; ranging northward to Lower California, Florida, and Texas. **1887** Goode *Amer. Fishes* 149, The Ravallia or Snook, *Centropomus undecimalis.* . . occurs only along the Gulf coast, where it is known by the Spanish name, "Robalo," with such variations as "Ravaljo," "Ravallie" and "Ravallia." **1902** Jordan–Evermann *Amer. Fishes* 368, The Robalos. . . *Centropomidæ.* . . The species are all of salt or brackish water, and their habits resemble those of the basses, as their common name, robalo, indicates, robalo being the Spanish name of the European bass. **1935** Caine *Game Fish* 119, Until recent years the robalo or snook has not really come into its own as a game fish, but game fish it certainly is, if ever there was one. **1976** Tryckare et al. *Lore of Sportfishing* 95, Snook . . Other common name: Robalo. . . A belligerent fish with a temperament much like that of the muskellunge.

robber bird n Cf **nest robber**

1 also *robber:* =**cowbird 1.**

1967–68 *DARE* (Qu. Q14, . . *Names . . for . . cowbird*) Inf **CT**5, Robber bird; **OH**6, Robber.

2 =**Canada jay.** Cf **camp robber**

1968 *DARE* (Qu. Q16, . . *Kinds of jays*) Inf **WI**58, Whiskey jack—another name for the Canada jay—they are also called robber birds.

robber duck n

=**baldpate 1.**

1962 Imhof *AL Birds* 138, American Widgeon—*Mareca americana.* . . because it cannot dive well, it snatches food from the American Coot, Redhead, Canvasback, and others, and so is called "Robber Duck."

robber fly n [Because it preys on other insects]

An insect of the family Asilidae. Also called **bee catcher 1, hornet fly, mosquito hawk 2d**

1870 (1871) *Amer. Naturalist* 4.686 **MA,** A robber-fly (*Proctacanthus Philadelphicus* . .) . . burrows in the sand of the shores of Plum Island, Mass. **1905** Kellogg *Amer. Insects* 330, The Asilidae, or robber-flies, compose a considerable family—nearly 1000 species occur in this country—of large, swift, hairy, ferocious-looking flies which live wholly by predatory attacks on other insects. **1940** Teale *Insects* 200, Rotting wood is the early home of the fierce hawk-like robber flies. . . The adults are streamlined "insect falcons." **1969** *DARE* (Qu. R12, . . *Other kinds of flies*) Inf **CA**114, Robber fly. [FW: Name . . out of insect book] **1972** *Living Museum* 34.116 **IL,** The robber flies (Family Asilidae) are predacious in both adult and larval stages.

robber gull n

A **jaeger** n[1]; see quots.

1890 *Century Dict.* 5202, *Robber-gull.* . . The skua, or robber jäger. **1962** Imhof *AL Birds* 265, Pomarine Jaeger . . Other name: Robber Gull. . . Outside the breeding season, it prefers to rob other sea birds of their food. *Ibid* 266, Parasitic Jaeger . . Other name: Robber Gull. . .

This jaeger consistently robs other sea birds, usually gulls and terns, of their catch of fish or mollusks.

robber stick n Also *robber's cane*

=**cheat stick.**

1931 *AmSp* 7.47 **Sth, SW** [Lumberjack lingo], Lumberjack society is stratified. . . The "scaler" always carries a "robber stick" and is usually a social outcast although he has the rank of foreman. **1956** Sorden–Ebert *Logger's Words* 28 **Gt Lakes,** Robbers-cane, See scale-rule.

robber vine n

=**dodder.**

1951 *PADS* 15.38, Cuscutaceae . . Love vine; strangle-weed; angel-hair; robber vine.

Robert of Lincoln n Also *Robert, Lincoln, Robert ~* [By facetious folk-etym from *bob-o-lincoln* (at **bobolink A**)]

=**bobolink B.**

1839 *Boston Eve. Transcript* (MA) 8 June 2/4 **NH,** Our old friend, Robert Lincoln, the celebrated musician, better known by the abbreviation of Bob Lincoln or Boblink, is on his usual visit. **1874** Taylor *World on Wheels* 253 **cnNY,** There in the meadow. . . Robert o' Lincoln should ring his chime of bells. **1895** (1907) Wright *Birdcraft* 166, Bryant's poem on Robert of Lincoln contains a good description of the bird's plumage, but is too precise and measured to express the rapture of the song. It may describe a stuffed Bobolink, but never a wild, living one. **1904** Wheelock *Birds CA* 391, While his demure brown sweetheart listens in the long meadow grass, Robert of Lincoln flies upward on quivering wings, exploding with melody. *Ibid,* The mother bird broods alone for thirteen days, while Robert frolics gayly over the fields. **1950** *WELS* (Names . . for . . bobolink) 1 inf, **ceWI,** Robert of Lincoln. **1956** MA Audubon Soc. *Bulletin* 40.130 **MA,** Bobolink. . . Lincoln Short for Bob-o'-Lincoln, sonic. **1969** *DARE* (Qu. Q14, . . *Names . . for . . bobolink*) Inf **RI**15, Robert of Lincoln—a poem about him.

robin n

1 Std: a large thrush (*Turdus migratorius*), gray above and brick-red below, common throughout North America. Also called **Christ bird, fieldfare, Hiawatha's chicken, redbreast 1a, red-breasted robin 1, robin redbreast 1, summer robin**

2 also *robin perch:* A **sunfish:** usu **red-breasted sunfish 1,** but also a **pumpkinseed 1** (here: *Lepomis gibbosus*). **esp NC**

1853 in **1956** Eliason *Tarheel Talk* 290 **NC,** We caught 19 brim & robins. . . I never saw a robin before, they are the prettiest fish I ever saw. **1935** Caine *Game Fish* 26, Red-breasted sunfish. . . *Synonyms:* Black-eared Bream . . Robin[;] Robin Perch. **1946** LaMonte *N. Amer. Game Fishes* 139, Pumpkinseed. . . Names: Common Sunfish . . Robin [etc]. *Ibid,* Yellowbreast Sunfish. . . Names: Long-eared Sunfish . . Robin Perch. **1966–68** *DARE* (Qu. P1, . . *Kinds of freshwater fish . . caught around here . . good to eat*) Inf **NC**10, Robin—a red-breasted perch; **NC**49, Redbreast—a lot of people call it a robin.

3 =**pinfish 1a. esp NC**

1878 U.S. Natl. Museum *Proc.* 1.378 **NC,** *Lagodon rhomboides.* . . Robin; Pin-fish. Taken by the thousands by boys with hook and line, from the wharves. **1884** Goode *Fisheries U.S.* 1.393 **NC,** The "Sailor's Choice" . . bears several other names, being known about Cape Hatteras as the "Robin" and "Pin-fish." **1935** Caine *Game Fish* 55, Salt-water Bream or Sailor's Choice. . . *Synonyms:* Bream . . Robin [etc].

4 =**red-breasted merganser.** Cf **cock-robin duck**

1888 Trumbull *Names of Birds* 68 **MA,** At Rowley, Mass. [the red-breasted merganser is called] *sea-robin,* or *robin* simply.

5 =**knot** n[2].

1888 Trumbull *Names of Birds* 179, At Newport, R.I., on Long Island . . , in New Jersey . . , and at Eastville, Va., [the knot is called] *robin-snipe,* this being shortened (particularly among the Long Island gunners) to *robin.* Again at Moriches, L.I., and at Morehead, N.C., *beach-robin;* at Manasquan, N.J., *robin-breast.*

6 also *robin fish:* A **sea robin 1a** (here: *Prionotus carolinus*).

1870 *Punchinello* 6 Aug 302 **NY,** Changing our location for a change of luck, we captured a superb mess of sea robins and toad fish. . . We didn't have any of our toadies or robbins [sic] cooked, as those "spoils of ocean" . . are not considered good to eat. **1890** *Century Dict.* 5203, *Robin.* . . a sea-robin or flying-robin; one of several kinds of *Triglidae.* **1969** *DARE* (Qu. P4, *Saltwater fish that are not good to eat*) Inf **NJ**56,

Robin-fish—got whiskers—looks like catfish but different.   **1998** (acc)
U.S. Food & Drug Admin. *Seafood List* (Internet), *Prionotus carolinus*. . . Vernacular . . *robin* . . *Carolina robin*.

7 =rufous-sided towhee.

   1917 *Wilson Bulletin* 29.2.83 **WA,** *Pipilo maculatus oregonus*.—
Robin, Oyster Bay.   **1936** *Sun* (Baltimore MD) 17 Feb 7/2 *(Hench
Coll.)*, One side [of Eastern shore ornithologists] asserts it has seen "robins" hopping about in the snow; the opponents are scornful—they're not
robins, but . . bush-birds.   **1968** *DARE* (Qu. Q10, . . *Water birds and
marsh birds*) Inf NC80, Robin—marsh.

8 =brown thrasher.

   1967 *DARE* (Qu. Q14, . . *Names . . for . . brown thrasher*) Infs **AL**32,
35, Robin.

Robin Adair n [Appar in ref to the song of this name]
=jack-in-the-pulpit 1.

   1968 *DARE* (Qu. S1, . . *Jack-in-the-pulpit*) Inf **IN**30, Robin Adair.

robin-breast n
=knot n[2].

   1888 Trumbull *Names of Birds* 179 **NJ,** At Manasquan, N.J., [the knot
is called] *robin-breast.*   **1917** (1923) *Birds Amer.* 1.231, Knot. . . Other
Names . . Robin-breast; Beach Robin [etc]. [*Ibid* 232, A flock of Knots
tripping along the beach in their spring plumage with rufous breasts
gives the observer the impression that some Robins have acquired nautical propensities and come down to the ocean for a change of food.]

robin-dipper n
=bufflehead 2.

   1888 Trumbull *Names of Birds* 82 **ME, MA,** At Bath, Me., and North
Scituate, Mass., [the bufflehead is called] *robin-dipper.*   **1917** (1923)
Birds Amer. 1.140, Buffle-head . . Other Names . . Robin Dipper [etc].
1982 Elman *Hunter's Field Guide* 211, *Bufflehead* . . Common & Regional Names . . robin dipper, Scotch dipper [etc].

robin fish See **robin 6**

Robin Hood n [*OED2* 1844 →]
=herb Robert.

   1969 *DARE* (Qu. S26e, *Other wildflowers not yet mentioned; not
asked in early QRs*) Inf **NJ**56, Robin Hood—stays till Christmas time—
little stalk with flowery top like wild carrot—used in the same customs as mistletoe—looks like crow's foot.   **1998** *DARE* File—Internet
[Weeds—Botanical Names], Geranium robertianum—Herb robert . .
Robin hood.

Robin Hood's barn, go (all the way) around v phr Also *go
round Robin Hood's barn, go (all the way) round Robinson's
barn;* for addit varr see quots [Engl dial; cf *EDD* to go round
by Robin Hood's barn (at *Robin Hood*)] **scattered, but chiefly
Nth, N Midl, C Atl, WV** See Map
To engage in an unnecessarily roundabout course of action;
also fig.

   1797 in 1929 Weems *Mason Locke Weems* 2.77 **MD,** I can sell them
abundantly fast without the trouble of going round Robin Hood's barn.
1836 *S. Lit. Messenger* 2.625, If requests be of any avail as a check, why
go around Robin Hood's barn?   **1909** *DN* 3.415 **nME,** *Robinson's
barn*. . . A circumlocution. "Don't go way round Robinson's barn trying
to tell it."   **1924** *DN* 5.291, *Robin Hood's barn.* Same as Robinson's
barn.   **1928** Lewis *Man Who Knew Coolidge* 17, When it came to *talking,* why say, he wandered all round Robin Hood's barn!   **1951** Wouk
Caine Mutiny 464, I have gone all the way around Robin Hood's barn to
arrive at the old platitudes.   **1951** *Courier–Jrl.* (Louisville KY) 4 Jan
sec 2, Will you please elucidate? But do not go all the way around Robinson's barn, as I have noticed you are sometimes inclined to do.   **1960**
VT Hist. 28.114, All around Robinson's barn. All around Robin Hood's
barn. (To tell a long-winded, repetitious account.)   **1965–70** *DARE* (Qu.
KK52, *To do something in an indirect and complicated way: "I don't
know why he had to go _____ to do that."*) 144 Infs, **scattered, but
chiefly Nth, N Midl, C Atl, WV,** (All the way) (a)round Robin Hood's
barn; 11 Infs, **scattered,** All around Robin Hood's barn; **IL**45, **NY**206,
OH78, All round Robin Hood's barn; **IA**45, **MI**114, **NC**72, (All the
way) round Robin; **MA**73, **WI**34, Way round Robin Hood's barn;
VA58, All the way round Robin Hood's bush; **MD**17, Around Robin
Hood's barn and in the back door; **PA**175, **MI**92, Beat (*or* clear) around
Robin Hood's barn; **WI**51, This way round Robin Hood's barn; **MI**44,

OH72, **RI**6, (All the way) round Robin's barn; **KY**25, **OH**40, (All)
around Robin's barn; **WA**1, All around Robin's hill; **IA**38, 41, **MI**79,
MA48, **OH**38, **PA**122, (All the way) round Robinson's barn; **KS**19, All
around Robinson's barn; (Qu. JJ45, *When someone avoids giving a
definite answer: "We tried to pin him down, but he just kept _____."*)
Infs **NJ**24, **NY**238, **PA**104, **WI**34, Going (*or* taking me) around Robin
Hood's barn; **OH**45, Beating round Robin Hood's barn.   **1985** *DARE*
File **nwMS,** Going "all around Robin Hood's barn" and winding up
without what we were seeking.   [**1988** Kingsolver *Bean Trees* 217 **KY,**
Finding the church turned out to be a chase around Robin Hood's barn.
Mattie's directions were to the old church. The congregation had since
moved its home of worship.]

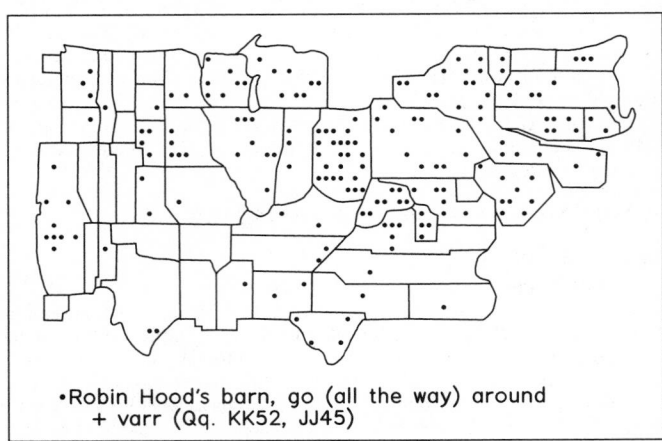

•Robin Hood's barn, go (all the way) around
   + varr (Qq. KK52, JJ45)

robin perch See **robin 2**

robin plover n
=knot n[2].

   1955 *AmSp* 30.181 **MA,** The knot is. . . also known . . as . . *robin
plover.*

robin redbreast n

1 =robin 1.

   1689 (1878) *MA Hist. Soc. Coll.* 5th ser 5.242, Some say they saw a
Robin-Redbrest to-day.   **1774** (1900) Fithian *Jrl.* 1.232 **VA,** Not a bird,
except now & then *Robbin-Redbreast* is heard to sing in this Feverish
Month.   **1803** in 1804 *MA Hist. Soc. Coll.* 1st ser 9.202 **RI,** Among the
birds usually observed in this place are the robin red-breast [etc].   **1858**
Atlantic Mth. 2.598 **MA,** The English Robin Redbreast has been immortalized in song. But the American Robin, *(Turdus migratorius,)* though
surnamed Redbreast, is a bird of different species and different habits.
1933 in 1953 Botkin–Harlow *Treas. Railroad Folkl.* 394, Superstitious
sailors are afraid that bad luck will come from shooting an albatross,
and, by the same token, railroad men refuse to annoy a robin redbreast.
1955 *Oriole* 20.1.11, American Robin. . . Robin Redbreast (general; by
transfer from a similarly confiding but smaller European species of the
same family, which is dusky and reddish-orange below).   **1968–70**
DARE (Qu. Q7, *Names and nicknames for . . game birds*) Inf NC82,
Robin redbreast—robin; (Qu. Q14) Infs **AR**9, **NY**241, Robin redbreast.
1986 Pederson *LAGS Concordance,* 1 inf, **ceFL,** Robin redbreast.

2 =rose-breasted grosbeak. Cf **English robin 6, redbreast 1f**

   1916 *Times–Picayune* (New Orleans LA) 23 Apr mag sec 5/4, Rose-
breasted Grosbeak (Zamelodia ludoviciana). "Robin Redbreast."

3 Perh **=round robin;** see quot.

   1969 *DARE* (Qu. P4, *Saltwater fish that are not good to eat*) Inf
NH18, Robin redbreast.

4 The American bluebird *(Sialia sialis).*

   1890 *Century Dict.* 5203, *Robin redbreast*. . . The American Bluebird,
Sialia sialis: an occasional misnomer.

robin-run-ahead n Also *robin runnel-head* [Engl dial]
=bedstraw. Cf **robin-run-the-hedge 1**

   1896 *Jrl. Amer. Folkl.* 9.190 **swOH,** *Galium* sp., robin-run-ahead,
cleavers, Sulphur Grove.   **1901** *Plant World* 4.144 **csKY,** In Barren
county I heard several local names of plants that were new to me . .
Robin Runnel-head *(Galium),* the four-leaved species used for the bite of
a spider, the six-leaved ones used for hives.

robin-run-around n

A **horsemint 1**; see quots.

1959 Carleton *Index Herb. Plants* 99, *Robin-run-around:* Monarda didyma. **c1985** *Lutz Coll.* **neNJ,** Robin-run-around—A local woman's name for the plant usually known as bee balm or bergamot *(Monarda).*

robin-runaway n Also *robin-runs-away, runaway-robin*

1 =**ground ivy 1. chiefly NEng**

1784 in 1785 *Amer. Acad. Arts & Sci. Memoirs* 1.461 **NEng,** *Glecoma. . .* Ground Ivy. *Gill-go-over-the-Ground. Robin-run-away.* A decoction of the leaves is esteemed by the common people a remedy for the jaundice. **1892** *Jrl. Amer. Folkl.* 4.102 **NH,** *Nepeta Glechoma,* Robin runaway. **1922** *Amer. Botanist* 28.152, "Ground ivy". . . is abundant on both sides of the Atlantic and has a host of common names most of which are of obvious significance as "gill-over-the-ground", "gill-go-by-the-ground", "gill-run-over", "creeping Charley", "creeping Jenny", "wild snake-root" and "robin-runaway." **1945** MA Audubon Soc. *Bulletin* 27.285 **eMA,** I must have been given half a dozen different names for the one plant—robin-runaway, gill-over-the-ground, ground ivy, etc. **1951** Teale *North with Spring* 218 **NC,** Or he may return with juglans, kinnikinnic, hackmatack . . or robin-runs-away. **1961** Douglas *My Wilderness* 252 **ME,** There too are long tangled creepers of ground ivy with their small, rounded leaves and purplish blossoms—the plant known as gill-over-the-ground or runaway-robin. **c1978** *DARE* File **cnMA,** Robin runaway—Name for ground ivy. Elsewhere called *gill-over-the-ground, creeping Charlie.*

2 =**dewdrop.**

1896 *Jrl. Amer. Folkl.* 9.187 **ME,** *Dalibarda repens . .* robin-run-away . . Oxford County. **1950** Gray–Fernald *Manual of Botany* 864, *[Dalibarda] repens . .* Robin-run-away. **1976** Bailey–Bailey *Hortus Third* 361, *Dalibarda . .* False violet, Robin-run-away.

robin-run-by-the-hedge See **robin-run-the-hedge 2**

robin-run-in-the-grass See **robin-run-the-hedge 1**

robin-run-in-the-hedge See **robin-run-the-hedge 2**

robin runnel-head See **robin-run-ahead**

robin-runs-away See **robin-runaway**

robin-run-the-hedge n [Engl dial]

1 also *robin-run-the-edge, ~-in-the-grass:* A **cleavers** (here: *Galium aparine*). [*EDD* 1831 →] Cf **poor robin 1, robin-run-ahead**

1837 Darlington *Flora Cestrica* 101 **sePA,** *[Galium] aparine. . . Vulgò*—Common Cleavers. Goose grass. Robin-run-the-Hedge. **1891** *AN&Q* 7.118, *Singular Plant-names.*—I should like to gather a few of these, and beg leave to open the list with the following: Man of the Earth; Good King Henry; Life of Man; Lad's Love; Seven years' Love; Robin-run-the-edge. [*DARE* Ed: This quot may refer instead to **2** below.] **1940** Clute *Amer. Plant Names* 259, *Galium asprellum.* Kidney vine . . Robin-run-in-the-grass [etc].

2 as *robin-run-in* (or *-by)-the-hedge:* =**ground ivy 1.** [*OED2* 1796 →]

1849 Howitt *Our Cousins in OH* 75, They gathered handfuls of the pretty, blue, scentless violet, the tooth-wort, and robin-run-in-the-hedge, which was dear to their mother, from its old English associations. **1900** Lyons *Plant Names* 174, *[Glechoma] hederacea. . .* Robin-run-away, Robin-run-in-the-hedge. **1940** Clute *Amer. Plant Names* 265, *Nepeta glechoma. . .* Lizzie run in the hedge, Gill go by the hedge, Gill creep by the ground, Robin run by the hedge [etc].

robin sandpiper n

=**knot** n[2].

1884 Coues *Key to N. Amer. Birds* 632, *Tringa. . .* Robin Sandpiper. Bill about as long as, or rather longer than, the head.

robin's nest n Cf **bird's nest 2**

=**thumbprint cookie.**

1949 (1986) Leonard *Jewish Cookery* 327, *Robin's Nests. . .* Shape [cookie] dough into small balls and dip into beaten egg whites then roll in chopped nuts. . . [W]ith the finger made a depression in center of each ball. Bake. . . When cool fill centers with jam or jelly.

robin snipe n

1 =**knot** n[2].

1832 *NY Mirror* 7 Apr 317 **NYC,** In the woods the throstle and on the beach the robin-snipe whistle to the breeze. **1880** *Forest & Stream* 15.4 **Long Is. NY, NJ,** Red-breasted sandpiper. . . Generally known everywhere on Long Island and New Jersey as the robin snipe, so called in the spring, as its brown plumage resembles the red-breasted thrush, or robin. **1888** Trumbull *Names of Birds* 179, At Newport, R.I., on Long Island . . , in New Jersey . . , and at Eastville, Va., [the knot is called] *robin-snipe.* **1946** Kopman *Wild Acres* 48 **LA,** There were numerous other birds of the snipe-plover group to be seen at this time, especially yellow-legs, the now rare knot, or robin snipe, dowitchers, or red-breasted snipe, and occasional curlews. **1949** Kitchin *Birds Olympic Peninsula* 100, Amid these excitables are flocks of red-breasted knots or 'robin snipe.' **1955** *AmSp* 30.181, The knot is *robin-snipe* generally on both the Atlantic and Pacific coasts. **1970** *DARE* (Qu. Q10, . . *Water birds and marsh birds)* Inf **VA**47, Robin snipe—same as knot.

2 =**pectoral sandpiper.**

1880 *Forest & Stream* 15.4 **NJ,** Pectoral sandpiper *(Tringa maculata). . .* On the inland meadows of New Jersey it is known as the robin snipe and meadow snipe.

3 =**dowitcher.** Cf **long-billed beach robin**

1888 Trumbull *Names of Birds* 160 **CT, MA,** In Massachusetts at Salem, Rowley, Ipswitch, in the vicinity of Boston and at Chatham, and in Connecticut at Lyme and Saybrook, [the dowitcher is called] *robin-snipe.* **1917** (1923) *Birds Amer.* 1.229, *Dowitcher. . .* Other Names.—Robin Snipe. **1955** *AmSp* 30.181, The dowitcher is a *robin snipe* rather generally and is the *long-billed beach robin* in North Carolina.

4 The buff-breasted **sandpiper** *(Tryngites subruficollis).* **LA**

1897 *Auk* 14.288 **LA,** *Tryngites subruficollis.* Buff-breasted Sandpiper.—Commonly known as *Churook,* and Robin Snipe. Abundant during spring and fall migration. **1916** *Times–Picayune* (New Orleans LA) 2 Apr mag sec 8/3, Buff-breasted Sandpiper . . Chorook; Robin Snipe.—A rare winter visitor to Louisiana. **1923** U.S. Dept. Ag. *Misc. Circular* 17.64 **LA,** *Buff-breasted Sandpiper. . . Vernacular names. . .* robin snipe.

5 =**Wilson's snipe.**

1923 U.S. Dept. Ag. *Misc. Circular* 13.50 **PA,** Common snipe *(Gallinago gallinago). . . Vernacular names. . .* In local use . . robin snipe.

robin snow n Also *robin storm* Cf **red robin snow**

A light snowfall; a late spring snowfall.

1853 in 1906 Thoreau *Writings* 10.462 **MA,** He says that the most snow we have had this winter (it has not been more than one inch deep) has been only a "robin snow," as it is called, *i.e.* a snow which does not drive off the robins. **1948** Beston *N. Farm* 60 **cME coast,** There is an old expression in use here for a snowstorm which comes after the spring robins return: we call it a "robin storm." **1949** Webber *Backwoods Teacher* 263 **Ozarks,** We had another February snow—a robin snow which came in the night and was gone before noon. **1968** *DARE* (Qu. B39, *A very light fall of snow)* Inf **NJ**42A, If in late winter, early spring . . it's called a robin snow since robins are coming and/or present. **1975** Gould *ME Lingo* 233, *Robin snow*—A light fall of perhaps an inch or two coming in late spring as an afterthought of winter. It is usually fluffy and wet and makes a beautiful morning, but it soon melts. Considered good for the greening landscape, a *robin snow* is also called the *poor man's fertilizer.*

robin's plantain n

1 A **fleabane:** usu *Erigeron pulchellus.* Also called **dog fennel 6, hogweed 2d, poor Robin's plantain 2, rosebetty**

1736 in 1894 *Documents Colonial & Post-Revol. Hist. NJ* 11.446 **NY,** To Drink give a Decoction of Devil's bitt or Robbins Plantain. **1824** Bigelow *Florula Bostoniensis* 302 **MA,** *Erigeron bellidifolium . . Robin's Plantain. . .* Dry fields, Cambridge.—Perennial. **1901** Lounsberry *S. Wild Flowers* 513, It seems strange to see the robin's plantain in blow so early in the season as April when the spring is advanced, for it has much the look of an aster, a tribe of course closely identified with the autumn. **1966** *DARE* FW Addit **KY**17, Dog fennel—robin's plantain *(Erigeron pulchellus).* **1969** *DARE* (Qu. S26e, *Other wildflowers not yet mentioned;* not asked in early QRs) Inf **CT**23, Robin's plantain—spike in center—looks like aster. **1981** *Greenfield Recorder* (MA) 23 May sec A 3, [Ruby Hemenway column:] There were buttercups, some daisies, Robin's plantain, maybe a few jack-in-the-pulpits, or perhaps some swamp pinks.

2 =**hawkweed** (here: *Hieracium venosum).* Cf **poor robin's plantain 1**

1958 Jacobs–Burlage *Index Plants NC* 55, *Hieracium venosum* L. . .

Robin's plantain, rattlesnake weed; veiny hawkweed; poor robin's plantain. **1966** *DARE* (Qu. S20, *A common weed that grows on open hillsides: It has velvety green leaves close to the ground, and a tall stalk with small yellow flowers on a spike at the top*) Inf **NH4**, Robin's plantain.

robin storm See **robin snow**

robin wheat n Also *robin's rye*

A moss n **1**: usu **haircap moss.**

1886 *Pop. Sci. Mth.* 29.368, The birds are not the only harvesters of the pretty moss known as robin-wheat. **1890** *Century Dict.* 5203, *Robin's-rye.* . . The haircap-moss, *Polytrichum juniperinum:* so called, perhaps, as suggesting a miniature grain-field. Also *robin-wheat.* **1892** *Jrl. Amer. Folkl.* 5.105 **OH**, *Bryum* sp., robin-wheat. Mansfield. **1900** Lyons *Plant Names* 301, [*Polytrichum*] *juniperinum* . . Hair-cap Moss, Bear's-bed . . Robin's Rye.

robin worm n

An earthworm.

1946 *PADS* 6.25 **eNC** (as of 1900–10), *Robin worm.* . . A long, slender, reddish worm used for fishing. . . Common. **1949** Kurath *Word Geog.* 49 **NC**, Other expressions for the earthworm are local in character. . . *robin worm* is heard on Pamlico Sound in North Carolina.

roble n [Span "oak"] **esp CA**

Usu =**valley oak.**

1857 in 1941 *AmSp* 16.265 **CA** [Span words used in English], *Roble,* Oak tree. [**1888** Lindley–Widney *CA of South* 334, The Mexican "Roble," *Quercus lobata,* is one of the grandest trees and forms natural parks of great extent.] [**1914** Saunders *With Flowers in CA* 11, In the language of Spanish-Californians the valley oak, which is deciduous, is called *roble.*] **1976** Elmore *Shrubs & Trees SW* 23, Oaks—robles, encinas [etc]. . . *Emory Oak* . . black or blackjack oak; roble negro. . . *Arizona White Oak* . . Arizona oak, roble.

roccous See **ruckus**

rock v[1]

1 See **rock along.**

2 See quot.

1967 *DARE* (Qu. X40, . . *Ways* . . *of saying, "I'm going to bed"*) Inf **AL8**, Retire, hit the sack, rock.

rock n[1]

1 A building stone; stone as a building material—freq used attrib of a building or building element: made of stone or a stone; esp in comb *rock house.* See also **hearth rock, jamb-rock, rock fence**

1701 in 1900 Essex Inst. *Coll.* 36.82 **neMA**, For . . tending the mason and drawing of Rockes and bringing of Clay or brick. **1712** in 1879 MA Hist. Soc. *Coll.* 5th ser 6.344 **Boston MA**, I lay'd a Rock in the North-east corner of the Foundation of the Meetinghouse. **1800** in 1846 MA Hist. Soc. *Coll.* 1st ser 6.219, The inhabitants are supplied abundantly with rocks for building of cellars from the hills. **1926** Roberts *Time of Man* 3 **KY**, The chimney was made outen rocks. *Ibid* 80, The rock doorstep out at Bodines didn't grow e'er bit all the time we lived there. **1942** *Esquire* Sept 173 **KY**, "That's right, Mick," Uncle Uglybird said, pointing . . toward the pile of chimney rocks. *Ibid,* Uncle Uglybird . . hunted among the smart weeds and ragweeds for a foundation rock. **1942** *Sat. Eve. Post* 27 June 111 **GA**, They's a big rock house out on a hill there in Atlanta which the state has provided for its governor to live in. **1966** *Roswell Daily Rec.* (NM) 11 Mar 12/2, Large attractive 4 bedroom, rock home. **1968** *Fredericksburg Std.* (TX) 4 Sept 5/2, [Advt:] *Old Time Rock Houses*—Large home across from Catholic School. . . 2 Story, 2 Bath Near Center of Town. **1968** *DARE* (Qu. M22, . . *Kinds of buildings* . . *on farms*) Inf **VA24**, Rock house—a root cellar; (Qu. EE33, . . *Other outdoor games*) Inf **KY66**, Rock houses—from rocks, played house. **1969** *DARE* Tape **MA30**, It was a rock-built chimney. **1981** *KS Qrly.* 13.2.70 **nNV**, *Rock house* . . house or bunkhouse made of local granite, sandstone, or miscellaneous rubble. **1986** Pederson *LAGS Concordance* **Gulf Region,** 11 infs, Rock chimley(s); 3 infs, Rock chimney(s); 5 infs, Hearth rock; 2 infs, Rock hearth; 1 inf, Rock house—where we stored canned fruit; *(Barn)* 2 infs, Rock house; *(Dairy)* 1 inf, Rock house; *(House)* 3 infs, Rock house; 1 inf, Rock house—square, four rooms; 1 inf, Rock house or a stone house; 4 infs, 3 **AR**, Arch rock [over fireplace]; 1 inf, The hearths was built of rock; 1

inf, There is some homes that has a front is rock; 1 inf, Hearth is brick or rock; 1 inf, Hearth built out of rock; 1 inf, Chimneys were made out of rock and mud; 1 inf, Rock-hearth; 1 inf, Rock fireplace; 1 inf, Fireplaces built out of rock; 1 inf, Chimney made of rock; 1 inf, Hearth made of brick or rock; 1 inf, Rock oven; 1 inf, Rock-stick-and-mud chimneys; 1 inf, Chimney made of rocks and cement; 1 inf, Jamb rocks at sides of the fireplace.

2 Used as the second element in the names of types of stone where *-stone* is std.

1804 (1905) Lewis *Orig. Jrls. Lewis & Clark Exped.* 6.159, [Specimen] found exuding from a Strata of sand rock. **1843** (1916) Hall *New Purchase* 175 **IN**, The devel and his angils pelt them with red hot balls of brimrock and fire! **1885** *Century Illustr. Mag.* 29.466, There are a number of theories concerning the formation of natural gas, and the deposit of the sand-rock in which it is obtained. **1940** (1968) Haun *Hawk's Done Gone* 167 **TN**, I was fixing to scour that second time when Miss Robinson come hunting for what she called antiques. I had sandrock beat up and scattered all over the floor and I had the water nigh hot enough to commence. **1965–70** *DARE* (Qu. C26, . . *Special kinds of stone or rock*) 49 Infs, **esp S Midl**, Sandrock; 21 Infs, **scattered,** Limerock; **FL48, GA1, LA18, OK18,** Ironrock; **GA77, MO20, TN37,** Fieldrock; **NM8,** Cobblerocks; **WV3,** Flagrock; **OH15,** Puddingrock; **NY92,** Rottenrock; **LA11,** Soaprock. **1976** Wells *Barns U.S.A.* np **csIA**, The basement is made of sandrock blocks which were quarried on the farm.

3 A dense natural bed of oysters resembling a rock; see quots. **esp Chesapeake Bay**

1769 Stork *Descr. East FL* 21, The oysters are so plentiful here, that nothing is more common, than at low water, to see whole rocks of them. **1881** Ingersoll *Oyster-Industry* 247, [Glossary:] *Rock.*—A growth of native oysters massed into a rock-like bottom or ledge. **1883** U.S. Natl. Museum *Bulletin* 27.214 **Chesapeake Bay,** Whenever the solid beds or 'Rocks' were encountered, they were found to be long and narrow ridges. **1976** Warner *Beautiful Swimmers* 87 **Chesapeake Bay,** Every waterman knows that oyster beds or "rocks," as they are always called, can be dredged clean and that many years will be required to restore them. **1984** *DARE* File **Chesapeake Bay** [Watermen's vocab], Oyster grounds[,] rock, public rock[,] private grounds.

4a A small piece of stone, such as one may easily carry or throw. **widespread, but less freq NEast** See Map Note: Obviously the line between large and small stones is extremely variable; for the *DARE* quot and Map, only questions eliciting words for a stone that can be thrown have been used; *rock* in resp to other questions, as C22 and C25, does not show significant regionality.

1817 in 1865 Essex Inst. *Coll.* 8.231 **MA**, The people [in Ohio]. . . kept up their carousal through the night, screeching like savages, beating drums, throwing of rocks against buildings. **1823** *Natl. Intelligencer* (DC) 1 May (*DN* 4.47), *Western Dialect.* . . *rock.* . . A small stone. **1837** Sherwood *Gaz.* GA 71, *Provincialisms.* . . *Rock,* for stone;—he threw a *rock* at me; *stone* is the proper word. . . David slung a *stone* at Goliah [sic]; but it would have required Sampson [sic] to have cast a *rock.* **1838** Parker *Jrl. Rocky Mts.* 48, It is one of the peculiarities of the dialect of the people in the westernmost states, to call small stones rocks. And therefore they speak of throwing a rock at a bird, or at a man. **1848** Bartlett *Americanisms* 277, *Rock.* A stone. In the Southern and Western States, stones of any size are absurdly called rocks. **1895** *DN* 1.374 **seKY, eTN, wNC**, *Rock:* stone. "I got a rock in my eye." **1899** (1912) Green *VA Folk-Speech* 356, *Rock.* . . A stone of any size larger than a pebble. **1902** *DN* 2.244 **sIL**, *Rock.* . . For stone, a word which is not used. **1903** *DN* 2.327 **seMO**, He had his pocket full of rocks. **1905** *DN* 3.17 **cCT**, *Rock.* . . A stone. **1907** *DN* 3.216 **nwAR**, *Rock.* . . A stone. *Ibid* 248 **eME**, Us boys were throwing rocks at each other today. **1910** *DN* 3.457 **seKY**, Teacher, Bill Hughes threw rocks at me. [*Ibid* 454 **seVT**, *Rock.* . . Applied to a large, more or less immovable, mass of mineral formation. Almost never is it applied to anything smaller than one's head.] **1915** *DN* 4.189 **swVA**, *Rock.* . . A stone. **1946** *PADS* 5.35 **VA**, *(Throw a) rock:* (Throw a) stone; common everywhere. . . A stone of any size larger than a pebble. **1958** *PADS* 29.10 **TN**, *Flint rock:* A piece of flint. People use "steel to strike sparks from a flint rock." Rep[orted] from Perry, Warren. **1965–70** *DARE* (Qu. C24a, *A small piece of stone that you could easily throw*) 561 Infs, **widespread, but less freq NEast**, Rock; **AR53, CA107, FL35, GA12, LA2, ME1, OH57, OK21,** Small rock; **CA79, KY76, NV1, TN23, TX45,** Little rock; **DC1, LA33,** Big rock; **GA77, NY66,** Hand rock;

UT3, Cobble rock; (Qu. EE30, *Throwing a flat stone over the surface of water so that it jumps several times*) 148 Infs, **widespread, but less freq Nth, N Midl,** Skipping rocks [and other resps including *rock*]; (Qu. V2c, *About a deceiving person, or somebody that you can't trust* . . "*I wouldn't trust him any further than I could _____.";* not asked in early QRs) 25 Infs, **scattered Sth, S Midl, West,** Throw a (*or* that) rock; **TX**94, Further as I could throw a rock; (Qu. V2b, *About a deceiving person, or somebody that you can't trust* . . "*I wouldn't trust him _____.";* not asked in early QRs) Infs **AL**27, 39, **CA**161, 166, **CO**47, **KY**72, 76, 85, **OK**1, As far as I could throw a rock (*or* something); **OK**42, Far as I could throw a rock; **MO**15, Fur as you'd throw a rock; **TX**94, Further as I could throw a rock; (Qu. C24b, "*The dog wouldn't go away, so he took a stone/rock and . . _____ [it at it.]*") Infs **FL**27, **GA**73, **NC**8, 11, 17, Chunked a rock; **NM**11, Bounced a rock. **1968** *PADS* 49.16 **Upper MW,** Vocabularies sometimes change because a word from one dialect appears to have more prestige than that of another dialect. . . *Rock,* a Midland term, is replacing the Northern *stone* in expressions such as "He threw a *rock* at the dog." **1989** Pederson *LAGS Tech. Index* 118 **Gulf Region** (*Rock* [in context "he threw a _____"]) 613 infs, Rock; [95 infs, Stone].

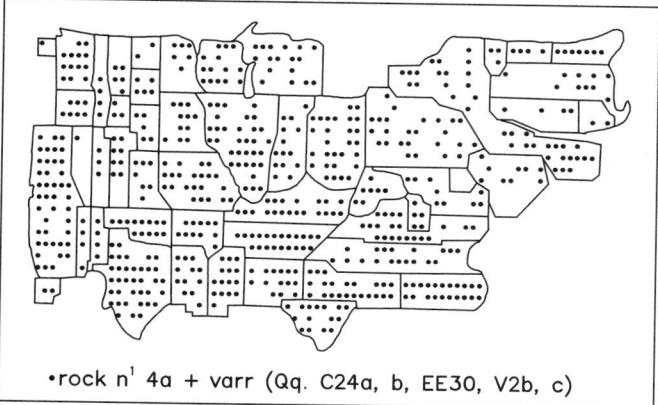

•rock n¹ 4a + varr (Qq. C24a, b, EE30, V2b, c)

b Spec; esp in combs *emery rock, grind(ing) rock, whetrock,* etc: a piece of abrasive stone used for sharpening. **chiefly Sth, S Midl** See Map

1895 *DN* 1.374 **seKY, eTN, wNC,** Grind-rock = grind-stone. **1906** *DN* 3.164 **nwAR,** Whetrock. . . Whetstone. "Where's the whetrock? I want to sharpen the hatchet." **1909** *DN* 3.387 **eAL, wGA,** Whetrock. . . Whetstone. Common. **1913** Kephart *Highlanders* 297 **sAppalachians,** A mountaineer. . . sharpens tools on a grindin'-rock or whet-rock. **1915** *DN* 4.192 **swVA,** Whetrock. . . Whetstone. **1946** *PADS* 5.43 **VA,** Whetrock. . . Whetstone; mostly in the southern part of the Blue Ridge, and the southern Piedmont. **1949** *AmSp* 24.107 **ceGA, nwSC,** *Cradle rock.* . . Whetstone. **1949** Kurath *Word Geog.* 60, *Whet rock* is current in the South, except for the tidewater area, and in the South Midland; *whet stone* is in general use in the North Midland and in the North. *Whet stone,* however, is also the usual term on Chesapeake Bay and in northeastern North Carolina, and is used to some extent throughout the *whet rock* area. **1962** Atwood *Vocab. TX* 51, The stone on which knives are rubbed to sharpen them is usually known as a *whetrock* (56[% of 273 infs]). This term is used about equally in all parts of the state, and extends into adjoining states as well. . . *Whetstone* (35[%]) is in limited use in all age groups and educational types. . . The usual word for the large revolving device for sharpening axes and similar implements is *grindstone* (72[%]). The rather rare *grindrock* (7[%]) is characteristic of older informants. **1965–70** *DARE* (Qu. L38, *What do you use . . to sharpen tools in the field?*) 59 Infs, **chiefly Sth, S Midl,** Whetrock; 6 Infs, **Sth, S Midl,** Wetrock; 25 Infs, **scattered, but esp Sth, S Midl,** Grind rock; **AR**4, **IL**93, **KY**23, 35, **MO**15, **MT**5, **SC**3, 34, **TX**63, Emery rock(s); **AL**55, **GA**60, **LA**10, **SC**7, 12, 43, Grinding rock; **LA**31, **SC**63, Rock; **VA**3, Corbin rock; **SC**34, Cradle rock; **SC**26, Razor rock, rub-rock; **OH**50, Scythe rock; **GA**45, Wedge rock. **1970** Tarpley *Blinky* 134 **neTX,** *Flat piece of stone for sharpening knives.* . . other responses . . sand rock. **1971** *PADS* 56.36 **AL,** Informants with a gradeschool or highschool education use three Southern terms: *nicker, bundle, whet rock.* . . Informants with a college education use three Northern and Midland terms: *whinny, sheaf, whetstone.* **1973** Allen *LAUM* 1.225 (as of c1950) **Upper MW,** Recessive is the South Midland *whetrock,* reported in Iowa and southwestern South Dakota, and as a remembered and heard form in Iowa and Nebraska. **1989** Pederson *LAGS Tech. In-*

dex 88 **Gulf Region** (*Whetstone*) 398 infs, Whetrock; 46 infs, Rock; 19 infs, Emery rock; 6 infs, Razor rock; 6 infs, Sharpen(ing) rock; 26 infs, Carbon (*or* flint, grind, hand, hard, honing, knife, etc) rock. *Ibid* 89, (*Grindstone*) 103 infs, Grind rock; 92 infs, Grinding rock; 8 infs, Emery rock; 7 infs, (Big) whetrock; 3 infs, Rock; 3 infs, Sharpen(ing) rock; 1 inf, Mill rock; 1 inf, Sandrock.

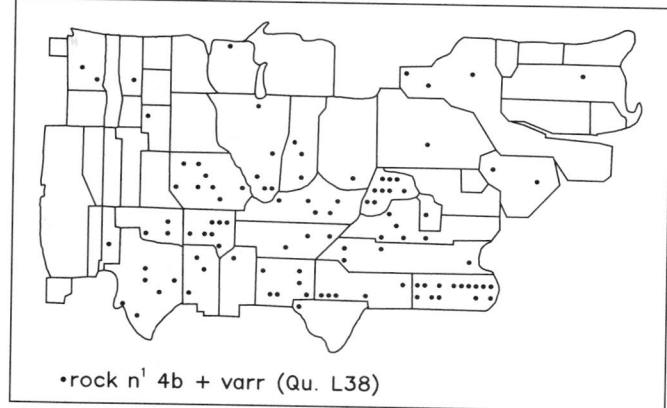

•rock n¹ 4b + varr (Qu. L38)

5 *also pl:* Gravel or crushed stone used as a paving material; hence nouns *rock road,* rarely *rock,* a road paved with gravel or crushed stone. **chiefly Upper Missip and Ohio Valleys, C and S Atl** See Map Cf **rock** v² **2**

1903 *DN* 2.327 **seMO,** Rock road. . . Macadamised road. **1907** *DN* 3.235 **nwAR,** Rock road. . . Macadamized road. **1911** in 1983 Truman *Dear Bess* 44 **MO,** Remember to go south every time the rock road goes south and you can't miss the place. **1941** Faulkner *Men Working* 63 **MS,** Half a mile down the dirt road they came to the gravel highway—The Rock—and Frank wheeled to the left. **1958** McCulloch *Woods Words* 152 **Pacific NW,** Rock road—A gravel road. **1965–70** *DARE* (Qu. N23, *Other kinds of paved roads*) Infs **FL**10, 35, **GA**23, **NC**10, Rock; **FL**33, **MD**4, Rocks; **NC**60, Rock—on asphalt; **VA**70, Rock—little chopped-up rocks and tar; **FL**6, **NC**3, Rock roads; **GA**3, Rock road—tar and gravel; **MO**1, The rock road; **MN**2, Hard rock, oil-dressed; **CA**15, Macadam—rock and gravel, oiled; **NC**76, Rock and tar, or asphalt and rock; **NC**49, Rocktop; **SC**19, Rock and tar; (Qu. N27a, *Names . . for different kinds of unpaved roads*) 12 Infs, **chiefly Upper Missip and Ohio Valleys,** Rock road(s); **MO**32, Basic rock road; **TN**37, Rock road—crushed limestone; **WV**3, Rock-base; **IA**7, Rock-surface; **IA**22, White rock or crushed limestone. **1989** Pederson *LAGS Tech. Index* 114 **Gulf Region** (*Road materials/surfaces*) 80 infs, Rock (road).

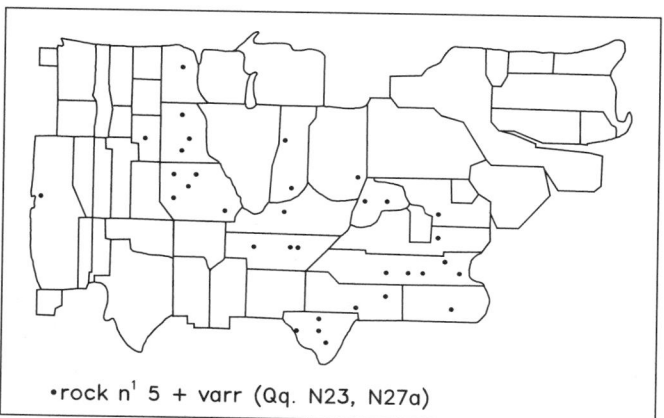

•rock n¹ 5 + varr (Qq. N23, N27a)

6 A peach pit. Cf **stone**

1943 Chase *Jack Tales* 158 **sAppalachians,** I couldn't find a thing but some peach seed where I been eatin' peaches and saved the pits to take home and plant. Jack . . says, "Hand here one of them peach rock." *Ibid* 160, You remember that swag where I shot at all them deer with them peach rock you had? **1967–69** *DARE* (Qu. I50, . . *The hard center of a peach*) Inf **KY**28, Rock; (Qu. I52, *The kind of a peach where the hard center is tight to the flesh*) Inf **KY**34, Tight-rock peach.

7 See **rockfish 1.**

rock v[2]

1 To throw stones at, pelt; to throw stones; hence n, vbl n *rocking.*   **chiefly Sth, S Midl**

1836 *Pub. Ledger* (Philadelphia PA) 30 Aug 1/4, 'Rock him! rock him!' cried the boys, 'rock him round the corner'. . . The wearer was 'rocked' till he turned his cloak inside out. **a1848** in 1848 Bartlett *Americanisms* 277, They commenced *rocking* the Clay Club House. **1899** (1912) Green *VA Folk-Speech* 356, *Rock*. . . To throw rocks. "You boys stop rocking." **1903** *DN* 2.327 **seMO**, *Rock*. . . Throw stones at. 'The boys were rocking each other.' **1904** *DN* 2.420 **nwAR**, *Rock*. . . To stone. 'You could sorter keep the hogs away in daytime by rocking them and sicking the dogs on them.' **1905** *DN* 3.92 **nwAR**, *Rock*. . . Primarily, to stone; secondarily, to pelt with other missiles than stones. 'He rocked me with cobs.' Common. **1909** *DN* 3.364 **eAL, wGA**, *Rock*. . . Stone. "They picked up a lot of rocks and rocked the chickens out of the patch." **1910** *DN* 3.457 **seKY**, *Rock*. . . "They rocked him on the way home from the party." **1913** Kephart *Highlanders* 259 **sAppalachians**, A prime amusement of the small boys is "rocking" (throwing stones at marks or at each other), in which rather doubtful pastime they become singularly expert. **1918** *DN* 5.19 **NC**, *Rock*, to throw rocks at. **1923** *DN* 5.219 **swMO**, *Rock*. . . To attack with stones. "I rocked 'im off o' the place." **1943** *LANE* Map 667 *(Threw)* 1 inf, **neMA**, To rock 'em, the Marblehead term for stoning strangers; 1 inf, **neMA**, In Marblehead they'd say they . . rocked you; 1 inf, **cMA**, He rocked 'im. **1966–69** *DARE* (Qu. C24b, *"The dog wouldn't go away, so he took a stone/rock and _____ [it at it.]"*) Infs **NM11, TN11**, Rocked; (Qu. Y10, *To throw something . . "The dog came at him, so he picked up a stone and _____ it at him."*) Inf **IL96**, Rocked him. **1968** Haun *Hawk's Done Gone* 205 **TN**, A bunch of boys around here had made it up to rock him. *Ibid* 212 **eTN**, He would just git him a big crowd together and give that upstart a good rocking. **1984** Gilmore *Ozark Baptizings* 173 **MO**, At a church service in Stone County a woman was prostrated with fear when a group of boys rocked the church house.

2 To pave (a road or street) with gravel or crushed stone; hence ppl adj *rocked,* vbl n *rocking.*

1935 *AmSp* 10.235 **VA**, The town of Blacksburg is paving streets that have recently been rocked. The portion of the street in front of the old school building and at the side of the Episcopal Church are being paved at present by relief workers. Other streets will be paved when the rocking is complete. **c1940** Eliason *Word Lists FL* 3 **nwFL**, *Rocked*. . . Paved. Probably derived from the usual paving of roads in that section; white slag. "Be glad when that road's rocked." **1958** McCulloch *Woods Words* 152 **Pacific NW**, *Rock a road*—Putting rock on a dirt road to make an all-weather road. **1967** *Smith Co. Pioneer* (Smith Center KS) 26 Oct 8/2, The only other east and west road north of it, which is . . rocked, is . . a distance of six miles. **1969** *DARE* (Qu. N23, *Other kinds of paved roads*) Inf **IL108**, Rocked roads.

rock n[2]

See quot.

1930 Woofter *Black Yeomanry* 221 **seSC**, Although dancing is frowned on by the church, the few "ungodly" have occasional dances at private homes or lodge halls. These are accurately termed "rocks."

rock n[3] See rack n[1] 2

rockachaw See racacha

rock along v phr Also *rock (on)*   **chiefly S Midl**

Fig: to go on steadily, continue without change.

1898 Lloyd *Country Life* 19 **AL**, His mother didn't take the yarn about the dew and the grass exactly like he gives it to her, but she didn't have no dead sure proof, and so she lets things rock along so till further notice. **1906** *DN* 3.153 **nwAR**, *Rock along*. . . To continue unsettled, remain neglected. "So the matter rocked along and nothing was done." **1946** *Sun* (Baltimore MD) 10 Oct 2/1 *(Hench Coll.)*, The creation of a new board or administrator . . would permit the program to rock along much as it is now. **1959** in 1972 Hall *Sayings Old Smoky* 115 **wNC, eTN**, *Rockin' along*. Going along as usual. "Everything is rockin' along just like when Lena was here." **1965** *DARE* Tape **MS1**, [They] would go to Taylor's and get drunk on Saturdays, and raise Cain. . . They'd stop on the way back . . and . . make bonfires out of the man's rail fence, . . cuss all night, and then drive by his house and cuss him out and go on home. Well, it rocked on and rocked on, and that fella just got his belly full of it. **1967** *DARE* (Qu. KK47, *Something that is left undecided or unfinished: "Perhaps we'd better just _____."*) Inf **SC34**, Let it rock. **1981** Harper-Presley *Okefinokee* 65 **seGA** (as of a1948), It

was a big meetin' time—it just kept in motion, you know. It rocked on till about Friday. **1986** Pederson *LAGS Concordance*, 1 inf, **cnFL**, He rocked on—went on and on.

rock bait See rock worm

rock bass n

1 A fish of the genus *Ambloplites,* esp *A. rupestris.*   For other names of *A. rupestris* see **bream B3, frogmouth perch, goggle-eye 1a(1), lake bass 2, mud sunfish 2, redeye 1a, redeyed bass 2, ~ bream, ~ sunfish 1, redeye perch, rockfish 11, rock sunfish**

1811 Lesueur *Hist. Poissons* 3.88 *(DAE)*, Le centrarchus. . . sous le nom anglais de 'rock basse.' [=The centrarchus. . by the English name 'rock basse.'] **1817** Rafinesque in *Amer. Monthly Mag. & Crit. Rev.* 2.120, *Bodianus rupestris*. . . Its vulgar name is Rock Bass, and in Canada *Crapet*. It is found in all the lakes of New-York, Vermont, Canada, &c., affording a good food. **1877** U.S. Natl. Museum *Bulletin* 9.22, The name "Red-Eye" in the region which this fish is supposed to inhabit is chiefly applied to the Rock-Bass (*Ambloplites rupestris*). **1902** Jordan-Evermann *Amer. Fishes* 338, *Genus Ambloplites* . . The Rock Basses. *Ibid* 339, The common rock bass is one of our most familiar panfishes. It is found from Vermont and New York westward to Manitoba and south to Louisiana and Texas. **1943** Eddy-Surber *N. Fishes* 219, The rock bass is found from the Dakotas and southern Canada southward in the Mississippi drainage to North Carolina and northern Arkansas. . . Although it is supposed to inhabit rocky streams only, it is found commonly as well in many lakes of moderate size. **1965–70** *DARE* (Qu. P1, *. . Kinds of freshwater fish . . caught around here . . good to eat*) 37 Infs, **scattered**, Rock bass; **AR22**, Rock bass—same as goggle-eye; **GA72**, Rock bass—dark skin, red rings around eyes; **VA8**, Rock bass = red-eye; (Qu. P3, *Freshwater fish that are not good to eat*) Inf **MN35**, Rock bass. [*DARE* Ed: Some of these Infs may refer instead to other senses below.] **1986** Pederson *LAGS Concordance*, 10 infs, **AR, TN, AL**, Rock bass; 1 inf, **nwAR**, Rock bass = goggle-eyes.

2 A fish of the family Serranidae (here: *Paralabrax* spp).   **CA** For other names of var spp see **ground bass, Johnny verde, kelp bass, sand ~ 1, sugar ~**

1884 Goode *Fisheries U.S.* 1.413 **CA**, The Cabrilla—*Serranus clathratus.* This species is called at Monterey, where it is not common, the "Kelp Salmon;" farther South it is known to the "Americans" usually as "Rock Bass." *Ibid,* The Johnny Verde—*Serranus nebulifer.* . . This species receives the name "Rock Bass" and "Cabrilla" with the other species. **1911** U.S. Bur. Census *Fisheries 1908* 308 **CA**, Cabrilla—A name applied indiscriminately to several serranoid fishes of the southern coast of California. They are also called "rock bass," "kelp salmon," "Johnny Verde," "lockee cod" (Chinese), etc. **1933** John G. Shedd Aquarium *Guide* 102 **CA**, Kelp Bass; Rock Bass; Cabrilla. . . the most common species of the genus on the California coast. **1946** LaMonte *N. Amer. Game Fishes* 48 **CA**, California Kelp Bass—*Paralabrax clathratus.* . . Names: Rock Bass, Sand Bass, Cabrilla. *Ibid* 49, Red-Spotted Rock Bass—*Paralabrax maculatofasciatus.* **1968** *DARE* (Qu. P2, *. . Kinds of saltwater fish caught around here . . good to eat*) Inf **CA65**, Rock bass—pier and beyond the kelp.

3 =black sea bass 1.

1884 Goode *Fisheries U.S.* 1.407 **seMA**, In the Middle States the Sea Bass is called "Black Will," "Black Harry," and "Hannahills"; about Newport and New Bedford, "Bluefish," and at New Bedford also "Rock Bass." **1946** LaMonte *N. Amer. Game Fishes* 48, Sea Bass—*Centropristes striatus.* . . Names: Blackfish, Black Sea Bass . . Rock Bass. . . A Northern fish, both inshore and offshore. Apt to be found near or among rocks. Off New England is most abundant from July through September.

4 =largemouth or smallmouth bass.

1887 Goode *Amer. Fishes* 56, The Small-mouth shares with the Large-mouth in the Southern States the names "Jumper," "Pearch" and "Trout". . . "Marsh Bass," "River Bass," "Rock Bass" [etc] are other names applied to one or both species. **1933** LA Dept. of Conserv. *Fishes* 313, None of our other fresh water fishes has been given so many popular names as our Black Bass. For the sake of making all these often confusing designations available to the reader, they are here enumerated as follows: Large-mouthed Black Bass . . Rock Bass [etc].

5 Any of several closely related sunfish: **bluegill 1, pumpkinseed 1,** or a **warmouth** (here: *Chaenobryttus gulosus*).

1909 Holder-Jordan *Fish Stories* 240, But finer than any trout is the old-fashioned green and golden sunfish with a black ear trimmed with scarlet. . . Some of these are called blue-gills, dollardee, red-eye, rock-bass, grass-bass. **1967** Cross *Hdbk. Fishes KS* 257, Most or all "rock bass" caught in these and other Kansas lakes are *C[haenobryttus] gulosus* rather than *Ambloplites rupestris*. **1968–69** DARE (Qu. P1, . . *Kinds of freshwater fish . . caught around here . . good to eat*) Inf CT9, Rock bass = bluegill; GA25, Warmouth perch is rock bass back north; GA41, Rock bass (warmouth); VT12, Punkinseed = rock bass; VT16, Punkinseed—rock bass.

6 The black **crappie**. Cf **rockfish 8**

1933 LA Dept. of Conserv. *Fishes* 335, The Calico Bass or Rock Bass. . . Few of our Louisiana fresh water fishes have received so many popular names as has the Calico Bass, one of the many Crappies that afford good sport.

7 A **striped bass** (here: *Morone saxatilis*). Cf **rockfish 1**

1890 *Century Dict.* 5205, *Rock-bass*. . . The striped-bass. **1968** DARE (Qu. P2, . . *Kinds of saltwater fish caught around here . . good to eat*) Inf GA41, Sheepheads, flounder, rock bass—come to fresh water to spawn. **1986** Pederson *LAGS Concordance,* 1 inf, **neFL**, Rock bass—saltwater fish; 1 inf, **cFL**, Rock bass.

rock bed See **rock boat**

rock bells n

A **wild columbine** (here: *Aquilegia canadensis*).

1930 OK Univ. Biol. Surv. *Pub.* 2.61, *Aquilegia canadensis* . . Wild Columbine. Rock-bells. **1961** Smith *MI Wildflowers* 139, Wild Columbine, Rock-bells, Meetinghouses.

rockberry n [See quot 1924]

A **bearberry 2** (here: *Arctostaphylos uva-ursi*).

1900 Lyons *Plant Names* 44, [*Arctostaphylos*] *Uva Ursi*. . . Bearberry, . . Rock-berry [etc]. **1924** *Amer. Botanist* 30.13, The rather large bright red and attractive fruits are devoid of juice which accounts for "meal-berry" and "meal plum." Such names as "rock-berry," "crow-berry," . . and "mountain cranberry" are self-explanatory and mostly indicate a confusion of this with the true cranberry.

rockbird n

1 =**purple sandpiper**. [Because it inhabits rocky shorelines]

1888 Trumbull *Names of Birds* 182 **MA**, [Footnote:] I have heard it [= the purple sandpiper] called Winter Rock-bird at Ash Point, Me . . ; and it is the Rock-bird, Rock Plover, and Rock Snipe at Rowley and Salem, Mass. **1917** (1923) *Birds Amer.* 1.232, Purple Sandpiper. . . *Other Names.*—Rock Sandpiper; Rock Snipe; Rock Plover; Rock-bird; Rock-weed Bird; Winter Rock-bird. **1956** MA Audubon Soc. *Bulletin* 40.19 **NEng**, *Purple Sandpiper*. . . Rock Bird (Maine, N.H., Mass.)

2 =**ruddy turnstone**.

1923 U.S. Dept. Ag. *Misc. Circular* 13.71 **ME**, *Common Turnstone*. . . Vernacular Names. . . *In local use*. . . rock-bird.

rock boat n Also *rock bed, ~ drag* Cf **drag** n **2**

=**stoneboat**.

1842 *New Engl. Farmer* 30 Nov 174, [Soil] may be taken out, . . thrown directly on to a drag or rock-boat, and hauled to the upland. **1843** *Ibid* 6 Sept 78, What in one county is called a *harrow*, is in another county called a *drag*—and the *drag* of one place, is the *rock-boat* of another. **1967–69** DARE (Qu. L57, *A low wooden platform used for bringing stones or heavy things out of the fields*) Infs **IN**17, 25, **OR**13, **WY**4, Rock boat; **KY**64, Rock bed. **1966** *Cynthiana Democrat* (KY) 28 Apr 6/7, *Public Auction* . . -A-harrow; rock drag; 2 hand sheep shears. **1981** *PADS* 67.26 **neMN**, *Stone boat*. . . The Northern *stone boat* (or *bolt*), almost unanimous among other Minnesota informants, is the usual Iron Range expression. . . *Rock boat* (1 occ[urrence]).

rock brake n

Any of var ferns, as:

a A **cliff brake**, usu *Pellaea atropurpurea*.

1822 Eaton *Botany* 414, [*Pteris*] *atropurpurea* (rock brake). . . From three to ten inches high, bluish green, leaves stiff. **1847** Wood *Class-Book* 632, [*Pteris*] *atropurpurea*. Rock Brake. . . Fern 6–10′ [DARE Ed: =inches] high, growing on rocks. **1876** Hobbs *Bot. Hdbk.* 57, Indian dream, rock brake, Pteris atropurpurea. **1906** Rydberg *Flora CO* 4, *Pellaea* [spp] . . Rock-Brake. **1953** Nelson *Plants Rocky Mt. Park* 34, The *rock brake* or *Brewers cliffbrake, Pellaea breweri* . . , has been reported for this region.

b A **polypody**, usu *Polypodium virginianum*.

1876 Hobbs *Bot. Hdbk.* 202, Polypodium incanum, Rock brake,

(Bracken). *Ibid*, Polypodium Virginianum, Polypody, Rockbrake. **1900** Lyons *Plant Names* 301, Common Polypody . . Rock Brake [etc]. **1938** Small *Ferns SE States* 73, Being such a wide-spread fern it [= *Polypodium virginianum*] has received many common names. Some of these are: My Many-feet, . . Sweet-fern, Rock-brake.

c The parsley fern *(Cryptogramma acrostichoides)*.

1911 Waters *Ferns* 112, Closely allied to the slender cliff-brake is the parsley-fern, or rock-brake, which is found to the northward and westward from the northern shore of Lake Huron. **1953** Nelson *Plants Rocky Mt. Park* 34, *Parsley fern* or *American rockbrake, Cryptogramma acrostichoides*. . . This is a rock-loving fern of the subalpine zone and is often found in full sun.

rock brush n

Either a **kidneywood** (here: *Eysenhardtia texana*) or a **naked-wood 1** (here: *Colubrina texensis*).

1920 Pellett *Amer. Honey Plants* 223, Rockbrush (*Eysenhardtia amorphoides*) . . is a small shrub common to southern and western Texas, and extending into Mexico. It blooms after heavy rains, several times during the year, and yields honey in surplus quantity. . . *Colubrina Texensis*, an entirely different shrub, which is common from the Colorado River to the Rio Grande and west to New Mexico, is also know by the name of rockbrush. **1960** Vines *Trees SW* 528 **TX**, Texas Kidneywood. . . It is also known as Rock Brush in the Texas hill country.

rock cat n

A catfish: perh **blue catfish 1** or **white catfish**.

1857 *Harper's New Mth. Mag.* 14.442 **NC**, The refuse fish commonly taken are sturgeon, rock-cats, trout [etc]. **1986** Pederson *LAGS Concordance,* 1 inf, **nwAR**, Rock cat.

rock cedar n **TX**

A **mountain cedar** (here: *Juniperus ashei*).

1908 Rogers *Tree Book* 108, The Rock Cedar (*Juniperus sabinoides* . .) is a considerable tree in the lowlands of the central counties of Texas, but dwindles in size as it ascends the mountains. **1945** Wodehouse *Hayfever Plants* 27, The most important in hayfever is the mountain cedar, Mexican cedar or rock cedar. . . This species is extremely abundant on the lime-stone hills of Texas. **1970** Correll *Plants TX* 79, *Juniperus Ashei*. . . Rock cedar, post cedar. . . In central and west Texas the wood of this species is the main source of fence posts which are extremely durable when in contact with the soil.

rock chestnut oak n Cf **mountain oak a**

Usu a **swamp chestnut oak** (here: *Quercus prinus*), but also **chinquapin oak 1**.

1810 Michaux *Histoire des Arbres* 1.23, *Rock chesnut oak* . . seul nom donné a cette espèce dans les Etats de New-York et de Vermont. . . *Rock et rocky oak* . . dans cette même partie des États-Unis. [=*Rock chesnut oak* . . only name given to this species in New York and Vermont. . . *Rock* and *rocky oak* in the same part of the United States.] **1837** Darlington *Flora Cestrica* 535 sePA, Mountain Quercus. *Vulgò*—Rock Chesnut-Oak. . . Hilly, rocky woodlands: frequent. **1860** Curtis *Cat. Plants NC* 34, *Rock Chestnut Oak*. . . This is sometimes called *Rock Oak* and *Chestnut Oak*, and is found as far north as New England. **1917** (1923) Rogers *Trees Worth Knowing* 53, "Rock chestnut oak" is a title that lumbermen have given to the oak with exceptionally hard wood, heavy and durable in soil, adapted for railroad ties, posts, and the like. **1980** Little *Audubon Guide N. Amer. Trees E. Region* 405, Chestnut Oak—"Rock Chestnut Oak."

rockchuck n Also *rock woodchuck* **NW, Rocky Mts**

A **marmot a** (here: *Marmota caligata* or *M. flaviventris*).

1893 Roosevelt *Wilderness Hunter* 124 **nMT**, We heard the shrill whistling of hoary rock-woodchucks. **1913** *Outing* Jan 451 **nwWY**, [Caption:] Not a woodchuck but a "rockchuck." **1950** FWP *Guide ID* 81, The rockchuck (often mistakenly called woodchuck) favors as its home piles of slide-rock near succulent meadows. All three species of marmot are found in Idaho. . . The hoary keeps to the highest peaks; the brown (woodchuck is the common name) prefers deep forests . . ; and the yellow (rockchuck) chooses the rocky flanks. **1961** Douglas *My Wilderness* 22 **CO**, This is the yellow-belly marmot. . . These animals—locally known as woodchucks, rock chucks, and whistle-pigs—are fat, saucy, and inquisitive. **1966–67** DARE (Qu. P31, . . *Names or nicknames . . for the groundhog*) Infs **MT**4, **OR**10, Rockchuck; (Qu. P32, . . *Other kinds of wild animals*) Inf **ID**1, Rockchuck. **1982** Elman *Hunter's Field Guide* 419, The true rockchucks are the yellow-bellied, or yellow-footed, marmot *(Marmota flaviventris)* and the hoary marmot *(Marmota caligata).*

rock cliff n **chiefly sAppalachians** Cf **cliff, rock house 1**

A cliff; a shallow cave beneath an overhanging cliff.

1913 Kephart *Highlanders* 106 **sAppalachians,** I fell over a rock clift twenty feet down. **1926** Roberts *Time of Man* 291 **KY,** And now I am on the top of a rock-cliff and I can see the hickory trees down past the rock shoulder. **1939** *Hall Coll.* **eTN,** We trailed him around and jumped him under some rock cliffs. **1941** Stuart *Men of Mts.* 226 **KY,** I walk over across the creek to a rock cliff. **1953** *Hall Coll.* **wNC,** He come across a big rock cliff and his dog got to barkin' into it around in there. **1954** *Harder Coll.* **cwTN,** *Rock-clift:* cliff. **c1960** *Wilson Coll.* **csKY,** *Rock clift* [sic]. . . A cliff or overhang or rock-house. **1986** Pederson *LAGS Concordance (Cliff)* 11 infs, **inland Gulf Region,** Rock cliff(s).

rock cockle n [Because it burrows in gravel and coarse sand] **Pacific**

A **littleneck 2;** see quots.

1921 CA Fish & Game Comm. *Fish Bulletin* 4.37, Rock Cockle— *Paphia staminea.* . . Other names—Little-neck. *Ibid* 40, In Tomales Bay the rock cockle is found in the greatest abundance and here they are more important commercially than in any other bay on the California coast. **1949** Palmer *Nat. Hist.* 358, Rock Cockle. *Protothaca laciniata.* . . From Unalaska, Alaska, to San Diego, Calif.

rock cod n

1 A variety of Atlantic cod *(Gadus morhua)* found in shallow water and often of a red or reddish color.

1634 Wood *New Engl. Prospect* 42, Besides here is a great deale of Rock-cod and Macrill. **1807** in 1815 MA Hist. Soc. *Coll.* 2d ser 3.56 **Martha's Vineyard MA,** The rock cod is taken in autumn. **1839** MA Zool. & Bot. Surv. *Fishes Reptiles* 120, Several varieties . . are known by the names of 'Rock Cod,' 'Shoal Cod,' &c. **1887** Goode *Amer. Fishes* 338, The fishermen recognize several varieties of Cod for which they have different names. Rock Cod are those which are found in shoal water among the reefs and ledges, and which usually are of a dark color; these fish are often brilliant red in color, owing to the fact that the small animals upon which they live feed upon the red algae, abundant in those localities, from which they have absorbed the red coloring matter into their tissues. **1933** John G. Shedd Aquarium *Guide* 64, Large Cod from deep water are usually a gray or brown mottled with irregular darker spots. Smaller Cod from the rocky banks in shallow water are often bright red or reddish brown with the spots darker red or yellow and are known as Rock Cod. **1966–70** *DARE* (Qu. P2, . . *Kinds of saltwater fish caught around here . . good to eat)* Inf **MA**97, Rock cod; **ME**22, Rock cod—red, near shore. **1975** Evanoff *Catch More Fish* 207, The codfish *(Gadus morhua)* is also called the rock cod, and young ones are often called "scrod" by commercial fishermen.

2 also *rock codfish:* **=greening.** *DARE* Ed: Some of these quots may refer instead to **3** below.

1838 Parker *Jrl. Rocky Mts.* 198 **OR, WA,** The rock codfish were not known to inhabit the waters about the mouth of the Columbia, until the present year. **1884** Goode *Fisheries U.S.* 1.267, *Spotted Rock Trout (Hexagrammus decagrammus . .).* The name "Boregata" is applied to this species by the Italians on Puget Sound. The name "Rock-cod" is also given to it. **1886** Turner *Contribs. AK* 95, *Hexagrammus asper.* . . This fish is known to the English-speaking people of Saint Michael's and Unalashkan [sic] districts as "Rock-cod." **1913** London *Valley of Moon* 236 **cwCA,** An' we used to go out on the Rock Wall an' catch pogies and rock cod. **1994** Guterson *Snow Falling* 296 **nwWA,** At full dusk or thereabouts he ate three rice balls, a slab of rock cod, and two windfall apples.

3 **=rockfish 3. esp CA**

1876 U.S. Natl. Museum *Bulletin* 6.64 **Pacific,** Fishes, (western coast:) . . Rock fish or "rock cod," *(Sebastomus rosaceus* and species of *Sebastosomus, Sebastichthys,* &c.) **1884** [see **rockfish 3**]. **1911** U.S. Bur. Census *Fisheries 1908* 310, The name "grouper" is also applied to the rock cod of southern California. **1928** Pan-Pacific Research Inst. *Jrl.* 3.3.13, Scorpaenidae. The rock-cods. . . *Sebastodes alutus . .* Long-jaw rock-cod. . . *Sebastodes proriger . .* Rock-cod. . . *Sebastodes pinniger . .* Orange rock-cod [etc]. **1965–70** *DARE* (Qu. P2, . . *Kinds of saltwater fish caught around here . . good to eat)* 9 Infs, **CA,** Rock cod; (Qu. P14, . . *Commercial fishing . . what do the fishermen go out after?)* Infs **CA**15, 31, 168, Rock cod; (Qu. X9, *Joking or uncomplimentary words for a person's mouth)* Inf **CA**107, He's got a mouth on him like a

rock cod—jokingly—means his lips stick out like a rock cod. **1999** *DARE* File—Internet [Southern California Hot Page—Ocean Rept.], All boats are reporting good rock cod action from Morro Bay to San Diego.

rock codfish See **rock cod 2**

rock cony n Cf **coney** n[1] **1**

=pika.

1958 Barnes *Nat. Hist. Wasatch Autumn* 29 **UT,** Mammals sometimes select strange habitats, but none perhaps more unattractive than the high mountain slide-rock chosen by the pika. . . Rock conies they are sometimes called.

rock crab n [Because it is found on rocky shores or bottoms]

1 The Atlantic crab *Cancer irroratus.*

1837 (1962) Williams *Territory FL* 105, The Rock Crab is common on the Atlantic coast. **1871–72** in 1884 Goode *Fisheries U.S.* 1.766 **seMA,** The common 'Rock Crab,' *Cancer irroratus,* is generally common under the large rocks near low-water mark, and often lies nearly buried in the sand and gravel beneath them. **1901** Arnold *Sea-Beach* 277, *[Cancer] irroratus,* the rock-crab. This is the common crab of the New England coast. It ranges from Labrador to South Carolina, but is rare south of New Jersey. **1976** Warner *Beautiful Swimmers* 10 **ME,** Perhaps as tasty as these, although taken in much lesser numbers, are the Florida stone crab and the rock and Jonah crabs of Maine. **1986** Pederson *LAGS Concordance,* 1 inf, **neFL,** Rock crab.

2 The Pacific crab *Cancer antennarius.*

1883 U.S. Natl. Museum *Bulletin* 27.109, The most valuable of these [=crabs] are . . the Common Crab, Rock Crab, and Red Crab *(Cancer magister, antennarius, productus),* of the Pacific Coast. **1901** Arnold *Sea-Beach* 280, *[Cancer] antennarius,* the rock-crab of the Pacific coast. This species of the California coast inhabits rocky bottoms below low-water mark. **1939** Natl. Geogr. Soc. *Fishes* 235, The rock crab. . . is seldom seen in the fish stalls, probably because commercial fishermen find it unprofitably difficult to catch. . . The shores which it inhabits are too rocky. **1981** Meinkoth *Audubon Field Guide Seashore* 641, Pacific Rock Crab. . . On rocky shores, kelp beds, gravel bottoms.

rock cranberry n

A **mountain cranberry 1** (here: *Vaccinium vitis-idaea*).

1900 Lyons *Plant Names* 386, *[Vaccinium] Vitis-Idaea.* . . Mountain Cranberry, Rock Cranberry [etc]. **1939** Medsger *Edible Wild Plants* 70, Mountain or Rock Cranberry. . . Like the cranberry, the fruit is not good raw but when properly sweetened is excellent for sauce and jelly. In fact it grows in rather dry rocky soil, and the berries are apparently larger and better far north. **1955** U.S. Arctic Info. Center *Gloss.* 53, *Mountain cranberry.* . . Also called 'alpine cranberry,' . . 'rock cranberry' [etc]. **1974** (1977) Coon *Useful Plants* 136, *Vaccinium vitis-idea*—Rock cranberry, cowberry, lingenberry, mountain cranberry.

rock crib See **rock jack**

rock currant n

A **currant B1** (here: *Ribes cereum* var *pedicellare*).

1931 U.S. Dept. Ag. *Misc. Pub.* 101.41 **West,** Wax currant *(Ribes cereum)* . . and squaw currant *(R. inebrians),* the latter frequently known also as rock currant and wine currant, . . are two of the commonest and most widely distributed species of this genus. **1937** U.S. Forest Serv. *Range Plant Hdbk.* B131 **West,** Squaw currant . . , also known as rock currant and wine currant, . . occurs in the Rocky Mountains and eastward, ranging from South Dakota to western Nebraska, New Mexico, central California, and Idaho.

rock daisy n

1 **=mountain daisy 2.**

1936 Whitehouse *TX Flowers* 169, Rock Daisy *(Melampodium cinereum)* is very abundant on limestone slopes and in dry soil from Texas to Arkansas, Kansas, and Arizona. **1961** Wills–Irwin *Flowers TX* 230, Mountain Daisy also has the common names Blackfoot Daisy, Prairie Daisy, and Rock Daisy, and is found throughout Texas west of Wilbarger, Bell, and Jim Wells counties.

2 A **desert star** (here: *Monoptilon bellioides*).

1971 Dodge *100 Desert Wildflowers* 82, *Desertstar*—Also known as "desert daisy" and "rock daisy," this dwarf winter annual grows on sandy or stony mesas. **1995** *Smithsonian* Mar 80 **AZ,** [There are] a few outcrops of glossy black volcanic rock, now prettily grouted with rock daisies.

rock drag See **rock boat**

rock duck n [*OED2* 1704 →]
=harlequin duck.

[**1884** in 1888 Trumbull *Names of Birds* 91, Harlequin Duck. . . known about Mud and Seal Islands, Yarmouth Co., Nova Scotia, as *Rock Duck.*] **1925** (1928) Forbush *Birds MA* 1.259, Harlequin Duck. *Other names:* Rock Duck; Lord and Lady; Squealer; Sea Mouse. **1949** Kitchin *Birds Olympic Peninsula* 52, Western Harlequin Duck. . . Other common names: Lord and Lady, Painted Duck, Rock Duck. **1982** Elman *Hunter's Field Guide* 223, Harlequin Duck . . Common & Regional Names: painted duck . . rock duck [etc].

rock eagle n
=duck hawk.

1955 MA Audubon Soc. *Bulletin* 39.442 **ME, NH,** Peregrine Falcon. . . Rock Eagle (Maine, N.H. From a nesting site and its dominating, predatory habits.)

rocked See **rock** v² **2**

rock elm n

1 also *rockwood:* An elm (*Ulmus thomasii*) whose wood is hard and difficult to split. [*DCan* 1830 →] Also called **cork elm 1, hickory ~, ironwood ~, wahoo**

1898 Sudworth *Forest Trees* 60, Ulmus racemosa. . . Names in use . . Rock Elm (R.I., W.Va., Ky., Mo., Ill., Wis., Iowa, Mich., Nebr.) **1938** Brown *Trees NE U.S.* 231, Rock Elm, Cork Elm. . . Wood hard, heavy, strong, coarse-grained, tough, difficult to split. . . Considered superior to that of other American elms. **1950** *WELS* (*Different kinds of elm trees: [Include all names used]*) 18 Infs, **WI,** Rock elm. [*DARE* Ed: Some of these Infs may refer instead to **2** or **3** below.] **1960** Vines *Trees SW* 213, Rock Elm—*Ulmus thomasi.* . . An elm confined mostly to the Eastern and Northern states, but found in northern Arkansas also. **1965–70** *DARE* (Qu. T11, . . *Kinds of elm trees*) Infs **IA**13, **MI**27, 110, **MN**36, Rock elm; **AR**16, Rock elm—same as ironwood elm; **OH**69, Rock elm—old-fashioned; **MS**16, Rockwood. [*DARE* Ed: Some of these Infs may refer instead to other senses below.] **1970** *DARE* Tape **MI**125, They bought a lot of rock elm—they call them ship timbers. . . as far as forty, fifty feet. **1984** *MJLF* 10.150 **WI,** Rock elm, a favorite for barn timbers, being long and straight. Also called "bastard elm".

2 A **white elm** (here: *Ulmus americana*).

1846 Browne *Trees* 499, *Ulmus americana* . . American White Elm, Canadian Elm, White Elm, Rock Elm. **1897** Sudworth *Arborescent Flora* 181, White Elm. . . Common Names. . . Rock Elm. **1960** Vines *Trees SW* 209, American Elm—*Ulmus americana.* . . Vernacular names are Rock Elm, Common Elm [etc]. **1968** *DARE* (Qu. T11, . . *Kinds of elm trees*) Inf **WI**43, Rock elm, white elm—same thing?

3 A **slippery elm** (here: *Ulmus rubra*).

1897 Sudworth *Arborescent Flora* 180 **TN,** Slippery Elm. . . Rock Elm. **1960** Vines *Trees SW* 208, Slippery Elm—*Ulmus rubra.* . . Vernacular names are Rock Elm, Red Elm [etc]. **1966–68** *DARE* (Qu. T11, . . *Kinds of elm trees*) Inf **MI**14, Rock elm—same as piss elm; **MN**19, Rock elm or red elm.

4 also *southern rock elm:* **=cedar elm.**

1960 Vines *Trees SW* 210, Cedar Elm—*Ulmus crassifolia.* . . Vernacular names are Scrub Elm . . and Southern Rock Elm. **1980** Little *Audubon Guide N. Amer. Trees E. Region* 420, *Cedar Elm* . . "Southern Rock Elm." **1986** Pederson *LAGS Concordance*, 1 inf, **cLA,** Rock elm. [*DARE* Ed: This inf may refer instead to another sense above.]

rocket n

1 **=hooded merganser.**

1923 U.S. Dept. Ag. *Misc. Circular* 13.7 **FL,** Hooded Merganser (*Lophodytes cucullatus*). . . Vernacular Names. . . *In local use.* . . Rocket.

2 **=submarine sandwich.** Cf *DS* H42

1967 *AmSp* 42.282, *Terms Used for Submarine Sandwich in One Hundred American Cities.* . . Rocket—Cheyenne [WY], Cincinnati [OH].

rock farm n Cf **rock rancher**
A farm with very rocky soil.

1970 *DARE* Tape **MA**74, I had a pretty good farm up there and—rocky, it was a rock farm, but it was good in the days that I farmed.

rock fence n **widespread exc NEast, Gt Lakes** See Map Cf **rock wall, stone fence**
A low wall made from stone, usu without mortar, that serves as a fence.

1862 in 1885 U.S. War Dept. *War of Rebellion* 1 ser 13.229, I ordered my men to direct their fire on the force on the east and southeast and gain the rock fence. **1896** *DN* 1.423 **cNY,** *Rock fence:* a stone wall. **1905** *DN* 3.92 **nwAR,** *Rock fence*[b] *rock wall.* . . Stone wall. The 'rock fence' or 'rock wall' is quite different from the New England 'stone wall.' The Arkansan variety consists of split stone laid closely together and evenly faced. 'Rock fences are not very common.' **1909** *DN* 3.364 **eAL, wGA,** *Rock fence*[b] *rock wall.* . . Stone wall. **1946** *PADS* 5.35 **VA,** *Rock fence.* . . A fence of loose stone; everywhere, but not common north of the Rappahannock. **1949** Kurath *Word Geog.* 40, *Rock fence* . . is another Southern term that is fully established in the South Midland and the Shenandoah Valley. In West Virginia the Southern *rock fence* and the Midland *stone fence* occur side by side on the Monongahela and the upper reaches of the Potomac. The Midland term has been carried southward along Chesapeake Bay, nearly eliminating the Southern *rock fence* north of the Potomac and restricting its use on Delamarvia. **c1960** [see **rock wall**]. **1962** [see **rock wall**]. **1965–70** *DARE* (Qu. L60, *A fence made of stone or rock without mortar*) 194 Infs, **chiefly W Midl, West,** Rock fence; **TX**69, Stacked rock fence; (Qu. L60b, *A fence of stone built with mortar;* total Infs questioned, 75) Infs **AR**29, **GA**5, **NM**3, **OK**27, 43, 52, Rock fence; (Qu. L65, . . *Kinds of fences*) Infs **CA**117, 156, **CO**22, **OH**77, **OK**14, **TX**63, **VA**68, Rock fence. **1967** Faries *Word Geog. MO* 78, Stone fence. A fence composed of stones is referred to by a majority of the Missouri informants as a *rock fence* . . 314 [of 700 infs]. . . less common . . *rock wall* . . 139 [of 700 infs]. **1970** *DARE* Tape **CA**201, There was a couple of rock fences that were made. And they were made from the coolie labor. They'd pick up the rocks, haul 'em off on sleds, and build fences with them. **1971** Bright *Word Geog. CA & NV* 153, Stone wall. . . rock fence 34% [of 300 infs]. **1981** *PADS* 67.23 **Mesabi Iron Range MN,** *Stone fence.* . . The common term for Iron Range informants . . is the North Midland *stone fence,* which is usual for other Minnesota informants. . . One-fourth of the Range informants use the Southern *rock fence,* an infrequent variant . . for other Minnesota informants. **1986** Pederson *LAGS Concordance,* 222 infs, **Gulf Region,** Rock fence(s).

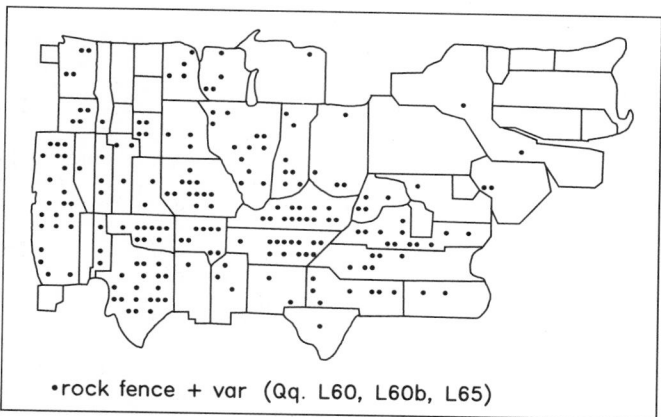

•rock fence + var (Qq. L60, L60b, L65)

rock-fence lizard n
Prob **=fence lizard 1.**

1961 Seeman *In Arms of Mt.* 55 **eTN,** Tracy's as cold as a rock-fence lizard—and twict as poison.

rock fern n

1 A **maidenhair fern** (here: *Adiantum capillus-veneris* or *A. pedatum*).

1828 Rafinesque *Med. Flora* 1.30, *Adiantum pedatum.* . . Vulgar Names—Maiden-hair, Rock-fern, Sweet-fern. **1900** Lyons *Plant Names* 15, *A. pedatum.* . . Hair Fern, Rock fern. **1951** *PADS* 15.26 **TX,** *Adiantum capillus-veneris* . . rock fern. **1974** (1977) Coon *Useful Plants* 198, Maidenhair fern, Venus' hair, rock fern, duddergrass.

2 A **polypody** such as the **licorice fern.**

1898 Davidson *CA Plants* 72, The rock fern or Polypodium came above ground so quickly that it was hard to catch the leaves unrolling. **1898** *Plant World* 2.198 **swPA,** Rock Fern for *Polypodium vulgare.* . . Very abundant on the summits and sides of rocks and boulders. **1938** (1958) Sharples *AK Wild Flowers* 108, [Polypodium] occidentalis. "Rock Fern," "Licorice Fern". . . Southwestern and Southeastern Alaska.

rockfish n

1 also *rock:* A **striped bass,** usu *Morone saxatilis.* **chiefly C**

and S Atl   Note: Some of these quots may refer instead to other senses below.

1605 in 1843 *MA Hist. Soc. Coll.* 3.8.134 **ME,** We got about thirty very good and great lobsters, many rockfish . . and fishes called lumps. **1698** (1848) Thomas *Hist. & Geog. Acct.* 14 **ePA,** There are prodigious quantities of. . the large sort of Fish, as Whales . . Rock, Oysters. **1787** Gesellschaft Naturforschender Freunde *Schriften* 8.160 **NY,** Rock-Fish. Striked [sic] Bass. . . Es ist ein sehr gemeiner Fisch, welcher sich das ganze Jahr an der Kuste von Neuyork aufhalt. Im Winter wird er in grossen Haufen, aber tod, zu Markt gebracht. [=Rock-Fish. Striked Bass. . . It is a very common fish, which lives all year off the coast of New York. In winter it is brought dead to market in great quantities.] **1815** *Lit. & Philos. Soc. NY Trans.* 1.413, Mitchill's Perch, Striped Basse, or Rock Fish. . . With eight parallel lines from head to tail. One of the most large, distinguished, and excellent of the New-York fishes. **1875** Scott *Fishing Amer. Waters* 47, This fish is known south of New Jersey as the rockfish; but as no two ichthyologists agree upon a classical name for the fish, it had probably best be called by the name by which it is known where the greatest numbers are taken, and there it is known only as the *striped bass.* **1884** Goode *Fisheries U.S.* 1.425, The Striped Bass . . occurs in all the waters of our coast from latitude 50° to latitude 30°. In the North it is called the "Striped Bass," in the South the "Rock Fish," or the "Rock." The neutral territory where both these names are in use appears to be New Jersey. The fishermen of the Delaware use the latter name, those of the sea-coast the former. **1899** (1912) Green *VA Folk-Speech* 356, *Rock.* . . A fish, the striped bass. **1906** *Forest & Stream* 29 Dec 1021 **Chesapeake Bay,** In the fall "rock," or striped bass, come into the creeks till the water is alive with them. **1946** Roberts *Lake Pontchartrain* 317 **sLA,** The rockfish or Atlantic striped bass is the largest game fish encountered in the fresh waters of Louisiana. **1965–70** *DARE* (Qu. P2, . . *Kinds of saltwater fish caught around here . . good to eat*) 14 Infs, **chiefly C Atl,** Rock; **MD34,** Rock—also called striped bass; **NJ22,** Rock; striper; 12 Infs, **chiefly C Atl,** Rockfish; (Qu. P1, . . *Kinds of freshwater fish . . caught around here . . good to eat*) 13 Infs, **chiefly C and S Atl,** Rockfish; **MD36,** Rockfish—both fresh and salt water . . also called striped bass; **SC11,** Rockfish—the channel bass coming up to spawn—rockfish are landlocked in Lakes Marion and Moultrie—only place in the world; **MD48, NC8, 10, 18, 21, 85, SC40,** Rock; (Qu. P14, . . *Commercial fishing . . what do the fishermen go out after?*) 12 Infs, **DE, MD, NC, VA,** Rock; **MD10, NC13, 15, VA47, 55, 110,** Rockfish; **NJ16,** Rock or striped bass; (Qu. H45, *Dishes made with meat, fish, or poultry that everybody around here would know, but that people in other places might not*) Infs **NC14, 18,** Rock muddle; **NC16,** Rock muddle—rockfish cooked and seasoned with onion, bacon grease, salt and pepper and parsley—some put potatoes and boiled eggs in it; **NC8,** Baked or stewed rockfish; **NC82,** Stewed rock; (Qu. P4, *Saltwater fish that are not good to eat*) Inf **NJ56,** Rockfish. [*DARE* Ed: Some of these Infs may refer instead to other senses below.] **1966–68** *DARE* Tape **DE2,** If we're buying fish, we usually buy either rock or flounder; **GA3,** If you're bottom fishing. . . you don't catch any . . freshwater bass, . . but you do catch a lot of rockfish and stag bass, and whities also. **1976** Warner *Beautiful Swimmers* 10 **Chesapeake Bay,** Most prized by both sport and commercial fishermen is the striped bass, always called rockfish in the Bay country. **1986** Pederson *LAGS Concordance,* 1 inf, **neFL,** Rockfish.

2 A **grouper 1a** (here: *Epinephelus striatus*) or **grouper 1b.** [*OED2* 1697 →]

[**1734** Royal Soc. London *Philos. Trans.* 38.316, The *Rock-Fish.* This *Fish* is reckon'd the most poisonous of any among the *Bahama* Islands. Many of these *Fish,* which are poisonous in one Place, are not so in another; and tho' the Inhabitants can give a near Guess, yet they are sometimes miserably deceiv'd.] **1876** U.S. Natl. Museum *Bulletin* 5.56, The Rock-fish attains the length of four or five feet, and is one of the choicest of table-fishes, though Catesby declares that his "Rock-fish," which seems most probably the same, "has the worst character for its poisonous quality of any other among the Bahama Islands". **1896** Jordan-Evermann *Check List Fishes* 374, *Mycteroperca bonaci.* . . *Marbled Rockfish.* West Indies, Pensacola to Brazil. **1911** U.S. Bur. Census *Fisheries 1908* 310, Grouper (*Epinephelus*).—A food fish found off the south Atlantic coast and in the Gulf. The different species are known as "red grouper" . . "rockfish," etc. **1946** LaMonte *N. Amer. Game Fishes* 51, *Mycteroperca venenosa apua* . . Names: Bonaci Cardinal, Red Grouper, Rockfish [etc]. *Ibid* 53, Nassau Grouper. . . Names: Hamlet . . Rockfish [etc].

3 A fish of the genus *Sebastes.*   For other names of var spp see **black rockfish 1, chilipepper, Chinafish, chucklehead 4,**

filione, **flag rockfish, fly-fish, garrupa, gopher rockfish, grass ~, grouper 2, honeycomb rockfish, jack** n[1] 24b(2), **ocean perch, orange rockfish, rasher** n[2]**, redfish b, red rock cod 1, red rockfish, ~ snapper 2, reina, rock cod 3, rosefish, Spanish flag, tambor, tomcod, treefish, widow rockfish, yellowtail ~**

1876 U.S. Natl. Museum *Bulletin* 6.64, Fishes, (western coast:) . . Rock fish or "rock cod," (*Sebastomus rosaceus* and species of *Sebastomus, Sebastichthys,* &c.) **1884** Goode *Fisheries U.S.* 1.26 **Pacific,** These fishes [=Scorpaenidae] are universally known by the names of Rock-fish and rock-cod. The latter name is the one most commonly heard, the other name being apparently a reaction against the obvious error of calling these fish "Cod." **1911** U.S. Bur. Census *Fisheries 1908* 314, Rockfish (*Scorpaenidae*). . . There are a large number of species, known to the fishermen as "priest fish," "rock cod," and "rockfish," with many qualifying prefixes. . . The name is also applied to the striped bass (*Roccus lineatus*) along the Atlantic coast; to the groupers (*Epinephelus*) about Key West and in the Gulf of Mexico; to the log perch (*Percina caprodes*). **1953** Roedel *Common Fishes CA* 120, Rockfishes—Genus *Sebastodes.* . . There are about 60 species of rockfish on the Pacific coast of North America and at least 50 of these are found in California. . . *Note:* some of the rockfishes are at times confused with the kelp and sand basses (*Paralabrax*) by Southern California fishermen. **1975** Evanoff *Catch More Fish* 107, Along the Pacific Coast. . . are the so-called rockfishes. . . Some of the more popular ones are the bocaccio, chilipepper, yellowtail rockfish, black rockfish, orange rockfish, vermilion rockfish, and the sculpin.

4 The blacknose **dace** (*Rhinichthys atratulus*).

1877 NY Acad. Sci. *Annals Lyceum Nat. Hist.* 10.332 **nwGA,** *Rhinichthys obtusus.* . . Most of my specimens were taken in Mobley's "Spring Branch," which flows into Silver Creek, near Rome, Ga. The species is known locally as Rock Fish.

5 A female **killifish 1** (here: *Fundulus majalis*). [See quot 1908]

1878 U.S. Natl. Museum *Proc.* 1.384 **NC,** Hydrargyra majalis . . *Rock Fish* [Female]. **1908** NJ State Museum *Annual Rept. for 1907* 155, May Fish. About Sea Isle City the fishermen call the females "rock fish," as the dark longitudinal lines suggest the striped bass. The males are thought by some fishermen to be a different species.

6 A **log perch** (here: *Percina caprodes*).

1882 U.S. Natl. Museum *Bulletin* 16.499, [*Percina*] *caprodes* . . Log Perch; Rock-fish; Hog-molly; Hog-fish. **1911** [see **3** above]. **1983** Becker *Fishes WI* 907, Logperch. . . Other common names: zebra fish, Manitou darter, rockfish [etc].

7 A **greenling** (here: *Hexagrammos decagrammus*).

1946 LaMonte *N. Amer. Game Fishes* 90, California Sea Trout . . Names: Rock Trout, Rockfish, Greenling [etc]. **1953** Roedel *Common Fishes CA* 142, Greenling Seatrout. . . Unauthorized Names: Rock trout, rockfish, bluefish. **1955** Zim–Shoemaker *Fishes* 142, The Kelp Greenling . . is sometimes called Sea Trout or Rockfish, though both these names are misleading. **1968** *DARE* (Qu. P2, . . *Kinds of saltwater fish caught around here . . good to eat*) Inf **AK1,** Rockfish. [*DARE* Ed: This Inf may refer instead to **3** above.]

8 =**crappie.**   Cf **rock bass 6**

1947 Dalrymple *Panfish* 85, Here, my friend, are the various names by which you would address that little gamester, the Crappie, depending on where you happened to be at the moment: Bachelor . . Rockfish [etc].

9 =**lake sturgeon.**

1951 Harlan–Speaker *IA Fish* 35, *Lake Sturgeon.* . . Other Names—Rock sturgeon, rock fish, rubber-nose. **1983** Becker *Fishes WI* 221, *Lake Sturgeon.* . . Other common names: freshwater sturgeon, . . rock sturgeon (usually the long-snouted, obviously plated young), . . rock fish [etc].

10 See quots.   Cf **rock** n[1] **3**

1967 *DARE* (Qu. P18, . . *Kinds of shellfish*) Inf **CA25,** A rockfish is a shellfish. **1986** Pederson *LAGS Concordance,* 1 inf, **cnGA,** Rockfish—a river oyster.

11 =**rock bass 1.**

1967 *DARE* (Qu. P1, . . *Kinds of freshwater fish . . caught around here . . good to eat*) Inf **PA28,** Rockfish—rock bass. **1986** Pederson *LAGS Concordance,* 3 infs, **TN,** Rockfish; 1 inf, **swLA,** Rockfish = sunfish.

12 =**pike perch.**   Cf **rock pike**

1968 *DARE* (Qu. P1, . . *Kinds of freshwater fish . . caught around here . . good to eat*) Inf **PA**136, Rockfish—dark, stripes—I call them pickerel.

rock fishing vbl n Cf **handfish, noodle** v[1]

1970 *DARE* (Qu. P13, . . *Ways of fishing . . besides the ordinary hook and line*) Inf **KY**72, Rock fishing—stick in your hand; when your finger gets bit, pull out what bit you.

rock garden n Cf **marble orchard**

1968 *DARE* (Qu. BB61a, *Other words . . for a cemetery*) Inf **CT**3, Rock garden; (Qu. BB61b, . . *Joking names for a cemetery*) Infs **CT**3, **NY**68, Rock garden.

rock geranium n [See quot 1953] **Sth**
=**alumroot 1.**

1903 Small *Flora SE U.S.* 503, *Heuchera* [spp]. . . Alum-root. Rock Geranium. **1953** Greene–Blomquist *Flowers South* 44, Alum-Roots, Rock-Geraniums (*Heuchera*)—The alum-roots are typically inhabitants of rocky ground, blooming in spring or early summer. They have basal rosettes of geranium-like leaves. **1967** *DARE* Wildfl QR Pl.89 Inf **SC**41, Rock geranium—alum root—hillsides.

rock grape n

A **sand grape** (here: *Vitis rupestris*).

1862 U.S. Patent Office *Annual Rept. for 1861: Ag.* 485, "Rock grape," *Vitis rupestris*. . . grapes small, black. **1891** Coulter *Botany W. TX* 63, Rock, or Sand, or Sugar grape. . . In the valley of Devil's River and westward into the mountains west of the Pecos. . . Also called "mountain grape." **1922** Hedrick *Cyclop. Hardy Fruits* 229, Mountain Grape. Rock Grape [etc]. . . Its favorite places are gravelly banks and bars of mountain streams or the rocky beds of dry watercourses. **1960** Vines *Trees SW* 729, Vernacular names are Sand Beach Grape, July Grape, Currant Grape, Rock Grape, and Bush Grape.

rockhead n [From the **lucky stone** found in the head] Cf **jewelhead**
=**freshwater drum.**

1967 *DARE* (Qu. P1, . . *Kinds of freshwater fish . . caught around here . . good to eat*) Inf **TX**1, Gaspergou—rockheads.

rock hind n

A **grouper 1a** (here: *Epinephelus adscensionis*). Also called **polka dot**

1896 U.S. Natl. Museum *Bulletin* 47.1152, *Epinephelus adscensionis* . . Rock Hind. **1933** John G. Shedd Aquarium *Guide* 97, Rock Hind. Widely distributed throughout the warm parts of the western Atlantic as well as in the West Indies. **1946** LaMonte *N. Amer. Game Fishes* 56, *Rock Hind*. . . Names: Cabra Mora, Grouper, Hind, Speckled Hind, Polka Dot.

rock hoof n

A type of horse's hoof suitable for rocky terrain.

1971 Green *Village Horse Doctor* 305 **cwTX** (as of 1940s), The walls of the hooves of horses become thicker and tougher to withstand the wear of pebbly rocks, hard ground, and the rimrock of the canyon regions as well as the rocky surfaces of the mountains. As this occurs through several generations of horses, the hoof becomes much smaller in width and the sole of the hoof becomes much more concave, which enables the walls to better protect the sole of the hoof. . . After a few generations, the hoof on a horse of such regions is referred to by horsemen as a desert hoof, rock hoof, or sometimes a mountain hoof.

rock house n

1 A cave or shelter beneath an overhanging cliff. **Appalachians, Ozarks** Cf **rock cliff**

1860 *S. Lit. Messenger* Aug 127 **wNC, eTN**, [Alum Cave] is not strictly a cave, it is what they call in mountains "a rock-house,"—that is, a precipice so far projecting over its base, as to shelter the space beneath from rain and snow. **1883** Smith *Rept. for 1881 & 1882* 438 **nwAL**, Underneath the overhanging cliffs, or "rock houses," as they are locally termed, grow abundantly some of our rarest and most beautiful ferns. **1923** *DN* 5.219 **swMO**, Rock house. . . A deep shelter beneath an overhanging cliff. **1933** *AmSp* 8.1.51 **Ozarks**, Rock house. . . A shallow cave or shelter under an overhanging bluff. Hillmen often speak of storing their hay in a rock house, or of using a rock house as a stable. **1952** Brown *NC Folkl.* 1.585 **cw,nwNC**, Rock house. . . A rock cave; an open-

ing under a rock.—Caldwell and Swain counties. **c1960** *Wilson Coll.* **csKY**, Rock house. . . A cave-like overhang of rock strata, as at Sand House Cave. **1981** *High Coll.* **ceKY** (as of c1930), Rock house . . a shallow cave under an overhanging rock or cliff. In the Gorge, these formations have been used for camping, keeping stock, or storing materials. Commonly found throughout the area. **1983** *MJLF* 9.1.53 **ceKY** (as of 1956), Rock house . . a shallow cave, or a shelter underneath an overhanging cliff, used to house cattle.

2 See **rock** n[1] 1.

rocking vbl n See **rock** v[2] 1, 2

rocking n See **rock** v[2] 1

rocking board n

A **seesaw 1.**

1909 *DN* 3.417 **nME**, Teeter. . . A rocking board. **1966** *DARE* (Qu. EE31, *Playground equipment with a long board for two children to sit on and go up and down in turn*) Inf **SC**19, Rocking board.

rocking-chair money n Also *rocking-chair check,* ~ *pay* Cf **happy pappy**

Unemployment compensation or another benefit paid to someone who is not working.

1944 *AmSp* 19.156 **sIN**, Rockin' chair money (unemployment compensation). **1946** Richmond *Times–Dispatch* (VA) 16 Jan 5/2 *(Hench Coll.)*, An increase in 'rocking chair money' for the State's unemployed. *Ibid* 26 Dec 1/3 *(Hench Coll.)*, 'Rocking Chair' Checks Sent To 66,627. **1946** *Hall Coll.* **wNC, eTN**, Rocking chair money. "Well, I haven't looked for a job yet, but I guess we could get one. I have been drawing rocking chair money." **1958** McCulloch *Woods Words* 152 **Pacific NW**, Rocking chair money—Unemployment compensation. **1963** *Western Folkl.* 22.267 **CA**, The popular *Rockin' chair money* is used when a person draws unemployment compensation when he is out of a job. **1965** Bowen *Alaskan Dict.* 28, Rocking chair money. United States Government Unemployment Insurance payments. Since much labor in Alaska is seasonal, many men draw wages totaling $10,000 to $15,000 a season in construction, and during the long winter months sit back and draw rocking chair money while awaiting the next construction season. **1970** *Thompson Coll.* **seMI, swCA** (as of 1950s–60s), Rocking-chair (money) . . social security, unemployment, disability insurance, pension, and similar payments. Detroit 1950's, Los Angeles 1960's. **1976** Garber *Mountain-ese* 76 **sAppalachians**, Caleb hain't struck a lick since he started drawin' his rockin'-cheer pay from the guvment.

rock jack n Also *rock crib,* ~ *trap*

See quot 1991.

1977 Jones *OR Folkl.* 41, Rock jacks (also known as rock cribs, or rock traps) . . are structures used with barbwire fences where the ground is too hard to dig postholes and sink posts. **1991** *DARE* File **cID**, A rock jack is a crib of rocks spaced between the posts of a barbed wire fence, and used to keep the wire tight by providing a firm anchorage in scab land where fence posts cannot be sunk deeply into the ground.

rockle v [Frequentative of *rock*]

To rock back and forth.

1943 Chase *Jack Tales* 18 **wNC** (as of 1880s), He cloomb on up on the scaffle, rockled and reeled this-a-way and that-a-way. **1955** Ritchie *Singing Family* 133 **seKY**, He showed me the best rocks to step on, the ones that wouldn't rockle and make me lose my stand and fall into the branch.

rock lettuce n

1 A **live-forever 4** (here: *Dudleya cymosa setchellii*).

1925 Jepson *Manual Plants CA* 453, [*Cotyledon*] *laxa* . . Rock Lettuce. . . Rocky ground, 300 to 5500 ft. **1949** Moldenke *Amer. Wild Flowers* 54, Owing to their large size, chalky white color, and red flowers, the plants of this species [=*Cotyledon*] are striking features of the rocky seaward hillsides. . . [I]n the rocklettuce, *C. laxa*, the flowers are clear yellow or orange.

2 See quot.

1968 *DARE* (Qu. S26e, *Other wildflowers not yet mentioned; not asked in early QRs*) Inf **VA**25, Rock lettuce = chickory—some cook it for greens.

rock lily n

1 A **wild columbine** (here: *Aquilegia canadensis*).

1892 *Jrl. Amer. Folkl.* 5.91 **NH**, *Aquilegia Canadensis* . . rock-lily. Mason, N.H. **1910** Graves *Flowering Plants* 192 **CT**, *Aquilegia canadensis* . . Wild or Red Columbine . . Rock Lily.

2 =pasqueflower.

1896 *Jrl. Amer. Folkl.* 9.179 **WI**, *Anemone patens*, var *Nuttalliana* . . wind-flower, rock-lily, wild crocus, Madison, Wis.[;] rock-lilies, Brodhead, Wis. **1937** U.S. Forest Serv. *Range Plant Hdbk.* W159 (leaf 2), Although pasqueflower is the common name most widely used, such other appellations as April-fools, Easter-flower, hartshorn, headacheplant, Mayflower, rocklily, wild-crocus, and windflower have variously designated this species.

3 An **evening primrose a.**

1924 *Amer. Botanist* 30.33 **West**, *Oenothera pallida* is generally called "tall white primrose" to distinguish it from the stemless species which are locally called "rock lily."

4 See quot.

1966 *DARE* FW Addit **WA**12, Rock lily—big thick fleshy leaf, several blooms to a stem, cream color to pink. Only in Tumwater Canyon, west of Leavenworth.

rock liver n
=hard liver.

1966 *DARE* (Qu. DD24, *Other diseases that come from continual drinking*) Inf **MS**6, Rock liver.

rock lizard n Also *rock swift* **SW**
A lizard such as the collared lizard, earless lizard, or **swift**; see quots.

1904 *Amer. Inventor* 15 Apr 176 **SW**, Those lizards popularly known through many parts of Texas, New Mexico, Arizona, and contiguous regions, as rock lizards, belong to the genus *Crotaphytus*. **1928** Baylor Univ. Museum *Contrib.* 16.11 **TX**, Texan Spotted Lizard . . In middle and western Texas, where this species is very common, it is variously known as the *White Lizard, Rock Lizard, Zebra-tailed Lizard,* and *Dog Lizard. Ibid*, Yarrow's Brown-shouldered Lizard. . . In the canyon region of northwestern Texas, this species is sometimes known as the *Little Rock Lizard. Ibid* 12, Poinsett's Lizard. . . Southwestern and western Texas names for this species are *Big Rock Lizard, Black-collared Lizard, Collared Rock Lizard,* and *Rock Swift.* **1966** *DARE* (Qu. P32, . . *Other kinds of wild animals*) Inf **NM**3, Mountain boomer—same as rock lizard. **1987** *Smithsonian* Aug 83 **Desert SW**, Like geckos, many of the rock lizards are small, quick insect hunters.

rock maple n

1 A **sugar maple** (here: *Acer saccharum*) or the closely related **black maple**. **chiefly NEng** See Map Cf **hard maple, hardrock ~**

1775 in 1867 RI Hist. Soc. *Coll.* 6.4 **NEng**, The timber [is] large and of various kinds, such as Pine, Oak, Hemlock and Rock Maple. **1810** Michaux *Histoire des Arbres* 1.31, A[cer] saccharinum. *Sugar maple*. . . *Rock maple* (Erable des rochers), nom qui prévaut dans tous les Etats situés au nord de la rivière Hudson, ainsi que dans le District de Maine, la Nouvelle–Brunswick et la Nouvelle-Ecosse. [=A[cer] saccharinum. *Sugar maple*. . . *Rock maple* (Maple of the rocks), the name that prevails in all the states north of the Hudson river, as well as in the District of Maine, New Brunswick, and Nova Scotia.] **1812** *Ibid* 2.238, Dans le Génésée . . , on ne fait au contraire aucune distinction entre ces deux espèces [=*A. saccharinum* and *A. nigrum*], et on les désigne également par les noms de *Rock maple* et de *Sugar maple*. La cause de cette confusion . . vient probablement de ce que cette portion de l'État de New-York a été, en grande partie, peuplée par des émigrans des Etats du Nord, qui auront donné à l'espèce dont il est ici question [=*A. nigrum*], le même nom qu'à l'autre, parce qu'ils avoient trouvé son bois propres aux mêmes usages, et qu'ils en retiroient une égale quantité de sucre. [= In the Genesee region . . , on the other hand, no distinction is made between these two species [=*A. saccharinum* and *A. nigrum*], and both are equally known as *Rock maple* and *Sugar maple*. The cause of this confusion is probably the fact that this part of New York State was settled, for the most part, by emigrants from the northern states, who gave to the species in question [=*A. nigrum*] the same name as to the other because they found its wood suitable for the same purposes and extracted from it the same amount of sugar.] **1884** Sargent *Forests of N. Amer.* 48, Sugar Maple. Sugar Tree. Hard Maple. Rock Maple. **1923** in 1931 McCorrison *Letters Fraternity* 49 **NEng** (as of 1878), Now the oak and hemlock are all gone, and most of the rock maple; only here and there a tree that we used to tap in that long ago. **1947** *PADS* 8.3 **VT**, The sugar maple

(commonly known as the rock or hard maple). **1949** Kurath *Word Geog.* 22 **NEng**, Rock maple . . is the distinctive name given to the sugar maple in Eastern New England, including the upper Connecticut valley. *Sugar maple* is of course also used in this area. **1965–70** *DARE* (Qu. T14, . . *Kinds of maples*) 34 Infs, **chiefly NEng**, Rock maple; **CT**17, Rock maple = sugar maple in Vermont; **MI**10, Most call it hard maple; maybe a few stray people call it rock maple; (Qu. T3, *The tree that produces syrup and sugar*) 25 Infs, **chiefly NEng**, Rock maple; (Qu. T4, *The place where . . trees grow together and sap is gathered*) Inf **MA**42, Rock maple grove; (Qu. T16, . . *Kinds of trees . . 'special'*) Inf **NJ**39, Rock maple. [36 of 47 total Infs male, none young] **1966–67** *DARE* Tape **ME**18, When it was dry, when there was no snow, we'd use what they call a scoot. . . Then they'd take a yellow birch, a rock maple, beech—beech made good what they call shoes to put on right underneath; **MA**92, The rock maple is a harder wood than ash. **1973** Allen *LAUM* 1.335 **Upper MW**, Nine hundred six respondents, even where the sugar maple does not grow, encircled their word for it on the checklist. . . Six scattered respondents use *rock maple*. **1975** Gould *ME Lingo* 233, Mainers do know it [=*Acer saccharum*] as sugar maple but more readily identify it as *rock maple* to distinguish it from six other maples found in the state. **1999** *DARE* File **NEng**, The terms rock maple, hard maple, and sugar maple all refer to the same tree.

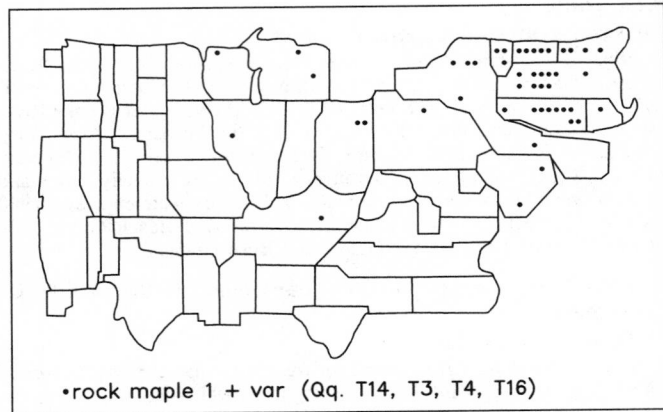

•rock maple 1 + var (Qq. T14, T3, T4, T16)

2 =dwarf maple.

1931 U.S. Dept. Ag. *Misc. Pub.* 101.98, *Rocky Mountain maple* . . , also called dwarf maple . . and sometimes known as mountain maple and rock maple, varies in size from a bush about 7 feet high to a small tree.

rock minnow n
=longnose dace.

1963 Sigler–Miller *Fishes UT* 85, Longnose Dace . . Common Names: Longnose dace, rock minnow. **1967** *DARE* (Qu. P3, *Freshwater fish that are not good to eat*) Inf **WY**1, Rock minnow.

rock moss n
A **stonecrop** (here: *Sedum pulchellum*).

1896 *Jrl. Amer. Folkl.* 9.188 **swMO**, Sedum pulchellum . . rock moss. **1937** Stemen–Myers *OK Flora* 186, *Sedum pulchellum* . . Rock-moss. . . on rocks or rocky soil. Wichita and Arbuckle Mountains. **1979** Niering–Olmstead *Audubon Guide N. Amer. Wildflowers E. Region* 480, Rock Moss (*S. pulchellum*), found from Virginia southwest to Texas and Kansas, has rose-pink flowers and linear leaves.

rock oak n

1 A **swamp chestnut oak** (here: *Quercus prinus*). **chiefly NEast** Cf **hard oak, mountain ~ a**

1699 in 1868 CT (Colony) *Pub. Rec.* 4.304, Running eastward three hundred rod to a rock-oak tree markt. **1773** in 1887 *Ibid* 14.172, Resolved . . that the rock-oak tree aforesaid with stones about it is the southwest corner of Midletown. **1810** [see **rock chestnut oak**]. **1822** Eaton *Botany* 421, [*Quercus*] *montana* . . Rock oak, chesnut oak, mountain oak. **1860** Curtis *Cat. Plants NC* 34, *Rock Chestnut Oak*. . . This is sometimes called *Rock Oak* and *Chestnut Oak*, and is found as far north as New England. It is an inhabitant only of high rocky or gravelly situations. **1897** Sudworth *Arborescent Flora* 156, *Quercus prinus*. . . Rock Oak (N.Y., Del., Pa.) *Ibid* 160, *Quercus douglasii* . . (California) Rock Oak. **1950** Peattie *Nat. Hist. Trees* 206, Chestnut Oak—*Quercus montana* . . Other Names: Rock or Mountain Oak. **1965–70** *DARE* (Qu.

T10, . . *Kinds of oak trees*) 14 Infs, **chiefly NEast,** Rock oak; **MD**18, Rock oak—bark used to tan leather; **NJ**1, Rock oak—rough bark, grows on mountainous ledges, rounded lobes to the leaves; **NY**191, Rock or chestnut oak; **WV**7, Rock oak—get tanning bark from; (Qu. T16, . . *Kinds of trees* . . *'special'*) Inf **NY**206, Rock oak.

2 Any of var other **oaks** such as **blue oak 2, chinquapin oak 1, Lacey oak,** or **Texas oak.**

1860 Greeley *Overland Journey* 349 **CA,** Black and rock-oak are found in some of the mountain valleys. **1897** [see **1** above]. **1960** Vines *Trees SW* 193, Texas Oak. . . Also known under the names of Texas Red Oak, Rock Oak [etc]. *Ibid* 194, Graves Oak. . . Vernacular names are Chisos Oak . . Rock Oak [etc]. **1968** *DARE* (Qu. T10, . . *Kinds of oak trees*) Inf **CA**87, Maple oak—leaf like a holly leaf—also called rock oak (drops leaves). **1979** Little *Checklist U.S. Trees* 232, *Quercus glaucoides* . . Lacey oak. . . Other common names—rock oak, canyon oak, smoky oak. *Ibid* 237, *Quercus muehlenbergii* . . chinkapin oak. . . Other common names . . rock chestnut oak, rock oak [etc].

rock old-squaw n [See quot] Cf **old-squaw**
=**northern phalarope.**

1956 MA Audubon Soc. *Bulletin* 40.21 **ME,** *Northern Phalarope.* . . Jersey Goose, Rock Old-squaw (Maine. The last two are facetious names comparing the phalarope to much larger species.)

rock on See **rock along**

rock onion n
A **wild onion** (here: *Allium macrum*).

1923 Abrams *Flora Pacific States* 1.385, *Allium macrum* . . Rock Onion. . . Barren rocky soil . . Blue Mountains of eastern Washington and Oregon. **1973** Hitchcock–Cronquist *Flora Pacific NW* 682, Dry gravelly soil . . rock o[nion]. . . *A[llium] macrum.*

rock on the chest n Also *rock on the box, rocks in one's lungs*
West Cf **miner's consumption**
Any of several pulmonary diseases caused by the inhalation of silica dust.

1949 Emrich *Wild West Custom* 165, *Widow makers* were the early compressed-air drills creating the dust which caused silicosis. And a miner with silicosis had *rock on the chest, rock on the box, the miner's con* or, succinctly, *the miner's.* **1967** *DARE* (Qu. BB10, . . *Names or nicknames* . . *for tuberculosis*) Inf **NV**2, He's got rocks in his lungs; **CA**148, Rock on the chest—Inf thinks this is different from T.B. [**1993** Doig *Heart Earth* 67 **West** (as of c1945), "Could hear it in her." The miner knocks on his own chest. "Got a chuteful of rocks, don't she, there in her lungs. She's young to have it like that."]

rock oyster n
1 An **oyster** B1 growing in a **rock** n¹ **3.**
1716 Petiver *Petiveriana* 2/1.130, *This resembles the* Virginia *Rock-Oyster.* **1881** Ingersoll *Oyster-Industry* 148 **DE,** The natural beds of oysters—"rock-oysters" is the local term—are confined practically to the shore between the mouth of Mahon river and Bombay hook.

2 Any of var oyster-like bivalves of the Pacific coast, as:
a A **pecten** *(Hinnites giganteus).*
1882 Nash *2 Yrs. OR* 85, The tide has run nearly out this evening: a good chance for some rock-oysters. **1911** Keep *West Coast Shells* 48, Our oddest relative is the rock-oyster, or winter shell, as some people call him. . . He may be found all along the coast of California. **1913** London in *Cosmopolitan* Aug 367 **CA,** Some oysters first—I want to compare them with these rock-oysters.

b A **jingle shell** (here: either *Anomia peruviana* or *Pododesmus macroschisma*).
1921 CA Fish & Game Comm. *Fish Bulletin* 4.26, Rock Oysters—*Anomia peruviana* . . *Monia macroschisma.* . . Habitat and habits—Attached to stones between or below tides. **1949** Palmer *Nat. Hist.* 356, Rock Oyster, Jingle Shell, Pearly Monia. *Pododesmus macroschisma.* . . Rough outside but pearly inside. . . Pribilof Islands to Sea of Okhotsk and Lower California. At Puget Sound at 100–250 ft. down. **1989** Mickelson *Nat. Hist.* 26 **csAK,** Common clams . . include: butter, softshell and little-neck clams, macoma clams, cockles, and rock oysters.

c A **jewel box 1** (here: *Chama arcana*).
1949 Palmer *Nat. Hist.* 356, Agate Chama, Rock Oyster. *Chama pellucida.* . . Looks like nubbin of rock or like limpet. . . On pilings and breakwater rocks from Oregon to Chile.

rock partridge n
The chukar *(Alectoris chukar).*

1953 Jewett *Birds WA* 227, Rock Partridge. *Alectoris graeca.* **1982** Elman *Hunter's Field Guide* 37, *Chukar Partridge* . . Common & Regional Names: red-legged partridge, redleg, Indian hill partridge, rock partridge [etc].

rock pike n
=**pike perch.**
1927 Weed *Pike* 46 **VT,** Stizostedion [spp]. . . Rock Pike: St. Johnsbury, Vermont.

rock pilot n
=**demoiselle 1.**
1905 Jordan *Guide to Fishes* 2.381, The *Pomacentridæ,* called rock-pilots or damsel-fishes, are exclusively marine. **1933** John G. Shedd Aquarium *Guide* 137, The demoiselles or rock pilots are sprightly little fishes of the tropical seas. . . [T]hey are all very active and add much to the life and color of the coral reefs and rocks, where they abound.

rock pine n
Any of several **pines 1,** as:
a =**jack pine 1.**
1894 *Jrl. Amer. Folkl.* 7.100 **cME,** Pinus Banksiana. . . shore-pine, rock-pine, Grand Lake section of Penobscot River.
b =**ponderosa pine 1.**
1897 Sudworth *Arborescent Flora* 20, Pinus ponderosa scopulorum . . Rock Pine. **1952** Peattie *Black Hills* 23 **SD,** Rock pine, bull pine, western yellow pine—but ponderosa is their right name, according to the scientific folk who should know.
c A **slash pine** (here: *Pinus elliottii*).
1933 Small *Manual SE Flora* 4, [*Pinus*] *caribaea.* . . Slash-pine. Caribbean-pine. Rock-pine.

rock pink n
1 also *rock pink fameflower:* A **fameflower** (here: esp *Talinum calicynum*). **esp KS, MO**
1896 *Jrl. Amer. Folkl.* 9.183 **MO,** *Talinum calycinum* . . rock pink, Greene County, Mo. **1940** Steyermark *Flora MO* 185, Rock Pink, Fame Flower (*Talinum* [spp]). *Ibid,* Rock Pink . . (*Talinum parviflorum*). *Ibid,* Rock Pink . . (*Talinum calycinum*). **1948** Stevens *KS Wild Flowers* 135, Talinum calycinum—Rock-pink Fameflower. . . suitable for planting in the rock garden. **1968** Barkley *Plants KS* 140, Rockpink Fameflower.
2 =**moss pink 1.**
1952 Gleason *New Britton & Brown* 3.97, *Phlox subulata* L. Moss Pink. Rock Pink. . . Sandy or gravelly soil and rock-ledges.
3 A **wire lettuce** (here: *Stephanomeria parryi*).
1941 Jaeger *Wildflowers* 310 **CA, NV,** Parry Rock-Pink. . . A rather coarse perennial, of the mountains bordering or in the desert.

rock pink fameflower See **rock pink 1**

rock plover n
1 =**purple sandpiper. NEng**
1888 [see **rockbird 1**]. **1956** MA Audubon Soc. *Bulletin* 40.19 **ME, MA, RI,** *Purple Sandpiper* . . Rock Plover.
2 =**ruddy turnstone.**
1899 Howe–Sturtevant *Birds RI* 55, Turnstone. *Rock Plover.* . . A common migrant to the rocky shores, and Cormorant Rock. **1923** U.S. Dept. Ag. *Misc. Circular* 13.71 **ME, RI,** *Ruddy turnstone.* . . Vernacular Names. . . *In local use.* . . rock-plover. **1969** Longstreet *Birds FL* 61, Ruddy Turnstone—*Other names:* Brant Bird . . Rock Plover.

rock pocketbook n **Upper Missip Valley** Cf **pocketbook 1**
A **freshwater clam** (here: *Arcidens confragosus*).
1979 *WI Week-End* 6 Apr 6, Do you know what a white heel splitter is? How about a three-horned warty back, a rock pocketbook or a fat mucket? These are the names of some of the fresh water clams which can still be found in the Mississippi River. **1982** U.S. Fish & Wildlife Serv. *Fresh-Water Mussels* 2.37, *Rockshell.* Rock Pocketbook. Historically widespread, common; now much less so. **1991** IL Nat. Hist. Surv. *Biol. Notes* 137.11, The rock pocketbook seldom occurs in large numbers although it is widely distributed in Illinois. **1992** [see **rock shell**].

rock portulaca n

A **fameflower** (here: *Talinum teretifolium*).

1933 Small *Manual SE Flora* 494, Rock-portulaca. . . Rocks, rocky soil, and sand, various provinces, rarely Coastal Plain, Ga., Fla. (?) to Ala., Tenn. and Pa. **1975** Duncan–Foote *Wildflowers SE* 32, Talinum; Rock-portulaca. . . Thin soil on dry rocks, dry sand.

rock post n Cf driprock

1983 *MJLF* 9.1.53 **ceKY** (as of 1956), *Rock post . . a stalagmite*.

rock ptarmigan n chiefly AK

A **ptarmigan** (here: *Lagopus mutus*).

1839 Audubon *Synopsis Birds* 208, Lagopus rupestris . . Rock Ptarmigan. . . Breeds from Labrador to the Arctic Seas. Rocky Mountains. Abundant. **1886** Turner *Contribs. AK* 154, Lagopus rupestris . . *Rock Ptarmigan.* . . At Unalashka [sic] they seem to prefer the high, rocky ledges, but everywhere come down to the low, narrow valleys to roost and rear their young. **1917** (1923) *Birds Amer.* 2.22, The Rock Ptarmigan is common on the mainland of Alaska where it is to be found chiefly on high ground in the summer months. **1963** Murie *Birds Mt. McKinley* 39 **AK,** Usually the rock ptarmigan are quite tame. . . In August flocks may be seen feeding on high rocky slopes where the vegetation is sparse.

rock rabbit n

1 =pika.

1878 Beadle *Western Wilds* 457 **CO,** The rock rabits [sic] (conies?) ran from covert to covert with a peculiar low moaning cry. **1881** Farrow *Mt. Scouting* 207, The *rock rabbit* is very small, being only five or six inches long and has pointed ears. **1913** *Outing* 61.450 **nwWY,** [Caption:] One of the oddest citizens of the Park is this little chap—also known as Coney or Rockrabbit. **1947** Jones *Evergreen Land* 67 **WA,** The jack rabbits and the tiny rock rabbits, the gophers and the rattlesnakes had all moved back over the hills. **1966** Barnes–Jensen *Dict. UT Slang* 40, Starved rat . . a name sometimes given to the pika. . . The little mammal is also sometimes called coney or rock-rabbit. **1966** *DARE* (Qu. P30, . . *Wild rabbits*) Inf **WA**12, Rock rabbits—coneys.

2 See quot.

1966 *DARE* (Qu. P30, . . *Wild rabbits*) Inf **SD**8, Cottontail—also called rock rabbits.

rock rancher n [In joc imitation of compounds like *chicken rancher, hay ~* (at **rancher**)] Cf **rock farm, stump ranch**

1967 *DARE* (Qu. HH1, . . *A rustic or countrified person*) Inf **OR**1, Stump rancher, rock rancher.

rock rattlesnake n Also *rock rattler*

A **rattlesnake 1,** as:

a =timber rattlesnake. **WI**

1928 Pope–Dickinson *Amphibians* 71 **WI,** *Banded Rattlesnake. Crotalus horridus.* . . Other common names for this snake are Common Rattlesnake, Timber Rattlesnake, Rock Rattlesnake, Yellow Rattlesnake and Black Rattlesnake. **1967–68** WI Acad. *Trans.* 56.29 **WI,** The timber rattlesnake, also known as the banded, yellow, mountain, and rock rattlesnake, is rarely found far from rock outcrops, and in Wisconsin rock rather than timber would be a more appropriate name. **1999** *DARE* File **WI** (as of c1980), A friend who farms near Dodgeville told us of all the rock rattlesnakes he had caught in the area from boyhood on. As he said, "The sun comes out warm in late winter, and them rock rattlers jes' lay up on the rocks. They're kinda slow then, but you still have to be careful when you catch 'em."

b A similar snake (here: *Crotalus lepidus*). **esp TX** Also called **green rattlesnake, pink rattler**

1937 Pope *Snakes Alive* 225 **SW,** Rock rattlesnake *(C. lepidus).* Two subspecies of this snake have recently been diagnosed, one *(lepidus)* occurring in southwestern Texas to but not including the El Paso region, the other *(klauberi)* found from the El Paso region of extreme western Texas into southwestern New Mexico and southeastern Arizona. **1969** *DARE* (Qu. P25, . . *Kinds of snakes*) Inf **TX**67, Rock rattler. **1974** Shaw–Campbell *Snakes West* 223, One of the smaller rattlesnakes, an adult rock rattlesnake *(Crotalus lepidus)* is from fifteen to thirty inches long. . . As its name suggests, it is found mostly in rocky habitats, among boulder piles, or on rock ledges. **1998** *DARE* File—Internet **TX** [Pitter Patter Pets], Venomous [Snakes] (In Season)—Trans Pecos Copperheads, Black Tailed Rattlesnakes . . Rock Rattlesnakes.

c A **prairie rattlesnake 1** (here: *Crotalus viridis*). **CA**

1956 Klauber *Rattlesnakes* 23 **CA,** The snake that I shall call the

northern Pacific rattlesnake *(Crotalus viridis oreganus)* is variously known, in different parts of California, as the black, black diamond, diamondback, green, gray, mountain, rock, and timber rattlesnakes, to mention only a few of its names. **1970** *DARE* (Qu. P25, . . *Kinds of snakes*) Inf **CA**207, Rock rattler.

rock road See rock n¹ 5

rock-roller n

1 =hellgrammite 1.

1965 *DARE* (Qu. R3, *Whitish, worm-like creatures, found in ponds, that hatch into dobsonflies, and are commonly used for fish bait;* total Infs questioned, 75) Inf **UT**3, Rock-rollers. **1999** *DARE* File **WY,** [A friend], who grew up in Wyoming, referred to the larva of the helgramite as a "rockroller."

2 A **stone roller** (here: *Campostoma anomalum*).

1967 *DARE* (Qu. P3, *Freshwater fish that are not good to eat*) Inf **SC**40, Rock-rollers—a hornyhead; up to 6″—used for bait.

rockrose n

1 A plant of the genus *Helianthemum*, esp *H. canadense*. [*OED2* 1731 →] Also called **frostweed 2.** For other names of *H. canadense* see **frost flower 2, ~ plant, frostwort 1, holly rose, ice plant 4, scrofula ~ 2**

1822 Eaton *Botany* 238 **CT,** *[Cistus] canadensis* (rock rose, frost plant). . . At the foot of the Pine-rock, New-Haven, the barren plains produce great quantities of this plant. **1830** Rafinesque *Med. Flora* 2.209, *Frostwort, Rock rose.* Used by empirics for curing scrofula, in decoction and cataplasms. The roots throw off small white icicles. **1901** Lounsberry *S. Wild Flowers* 345, Rock-rose. Sun Rose. *Helianthemum Carolinianum.* **1953** Greene–Blomquist *Flowers South* 73, The Carolina rock-rose grows in dry pinelands of the Coastal Plain n. Fla. to e. Tex. and N.C. **1974** (1977) Coon *Useful Plants* 97, *Helianthemum canadense*—Frostweed, frostwort, ice plant, rockrose [etc].

2 A **Saint-John's-wort** (here: *Hypericum prolificum*).

1860 Curtis *Cat. Plants NC* 109, *Hypericum.* Of this we have five woody species, all with yellow flowers, one of which, (H. prolificum,) is occasionally cultivated under the name of *Rock Rose.* **1960** Vines *Trees SW* 756, Shrubby St. John's-wort. . . It is also known as Broom-brush, Paint-brush, and Rock-rose.

3 A **gilia** (here: *Leptodactylon californicum*).

1897 Parsons *Wild Flowers CA* 208, Prickly Phlox. *Gilia Californica.* . . In some localities they are called "rock-rose," an unfortunate name in two respects: it has long belonged to a yellow flower of an entirely different family—*Helianthemum;* and these blossoms do not in the least resemble a rose.

4 =evening primrose a. **West**

1932 Rydberg *Flora Prairies* 575, *Pachylophus* [spp] . . Rock Rose, Mountain Primrose. . . Petals white, turning pink, showy. **1963** Craighead *Rocky Mt. Wildflowers* 121, Evening primrose—*Oenothera caespitosa.* . . Other names: Sandlily, Rockrose, Morning Primrose, Gumbo Primrose. **1967** Dodge *Roadside Wildflowers* 52, Tufted evening-primrose—Stemless primrose, rockrose, sandlily.

5 A **bitterroot 2** (here: *Lewisia rediviva*). **NW**

1935 Davis *Honey* 254 **OR,** Wild hollyhocks and delicate pink-white rock-roses, bird-bills and lupin. **1941** Writers' Program *Guide WA* 21, In the eastern part of the State, where the rainfall is somewhat heavier, grasses and flowering plants increase. . . the low rose-red bitterroot, often called the rockrose, which springs forth on the driest hillsides or nestles among the rocks. **1966** *DARE* (Qu. S3, *A flower with a large violet with a yellow center and small ragged leaves—it comes up early in spring on open, stony hilltops*) Inf **MT**5, Rockroses. **1966–67** *DARE* FW Addit **OR**12, Bitterroot (*Lewisia redivivia* [sic]) (rockrose, or red-headed Louisa) locally—sand lily; **WA**10, *Lewisia rediviva*—Bitterroot; rockrose, food plant of Indians; **WA**12, Montana bitterroot or rock-rose—thick, fleshly [sic] leaf, comes up in early spring and blooms in May and June.

6 A **mallow B** (here: *Pavonia lasiopetala*). **esp TX**

1936 Whitehouse *TX Flowers* 73, Rock Rose. Pavonia. Pink Mallow *(Pavonia lasiopetala).* . . is found in dry, rocky woods from Central Texas to Mexico. **1998** *DARE* File—Internet **sTX** [Watersaver Native Plants], Rock Rose *(Pavonia lasiopetala)* . . pink flowers spring to fall.

rock sallet n [By folk-etym from *rocket*]

Arugula (*Eruca vesicaria* subsp *sativa*).

1969 *DARE* Tape **KY**41, [Inf:] Yes, there was a thing a-called—for salad of course—rock sallet. It was kind of, oh, this one had the purple flower on it. Hit grew up—the flower would grew up a foot high, an' it was sort of sprangled out. And it grew around where there might be a cliff, in the mountains or something. . . [FW:] What kind of leaves does it have at the bottom? [Inf:] They were just a little bit sprangly. It's not a smooth leaf at all. . . [FW:] When does it blossom? [Inf:] Oh, . . it's early, . . before very much vegetation begins to grow up in the hills. **2000** *NADS Letters,* I've heard this term used to describe a bitter salad green that I know as Arugula or by its french name Rockette (there are other spellings of this last name.) This plant has a purplish flower when it goes to seed. My great grandmother from Kentucky used this green, as did relatives in West Virginia. *Ibid* **NC,** *Rock sallet*—My mother used to refer to a particular garden green as "rocket" and told us about her grandmother calling it "rock sallet." Her grandmother was born in 1872 in Beaufort County, North Carolina.

rock school n Also *rock teacher* **chiefly Sth, S Midl**
=**school.**
   1967–70 *DARE* (Qu. EE33, . . *Outdoor games . . that children play*) Inf **MA**8, Rock school—played on steps; **MO**30, Rock school; **TN**46, Rock teacher—play school where children are promoted by guessing which one of the teacher's hands had a rock in it; **NY**130, Stone school—you sit on a step and the teacher holds a pebble in her hand and if you guess which hand holds the stone, you go up a step or a grade. [3 of 4 Infs Black] **2000** *NADS Letters* **seTN,** We played "rock school" when I was a little girl—1940's—in Chattanooga, Tennessee. *Ibid* **cnAL,** I am a 59 year old white male born and raised in Birmingham, Alabama. We used to play "rock school" frequently as children in the 1940's and 1950's and it was played just as you describe. *Ibid* **cnNC,** I used to play "rock school" as a child in Burlington, NC. I am a Caucasian (very WASP) female and played the game with my neighborhood girlfriend and her older sisters in the mid-'50s when I was 5–7 years old. *Ibid* **cwNC,** I used to play rock school at my grandmother's home in Peachtree community near Murphy, N.C. I am 59 years old. **2001** *Ibid* **cTX,** Rock School was a common neighborhood game when I was a small child in the late 1940s in Midlothian (Ellis Co.), Texas. . . Many of the old timers there were of Scottish descent, but I don't know if this was the origin or not. *Ibid* **ceTX** [Black], I remember playing this game as a child in Marshall, Texas. . . It was called "rock school" and was played exactly as described, though, I may add, in our version, the "teacher" presented his/her hands to the "pupils" crossed at the wrists. I'm a black male approaching his 64th birthday, so the relevant years are approximately 1940–1947. In those days, segregation was total in Marshall. . . As a consequence, I have no idea as to whether the game was also played by local white children.

rock shell n **Missip Valley**
A **freshwater clam** (here: *Arcidens confragosus*).
   1941 *AmSp* 16.156 **Missip Valley,** There are many varieties of freshwater mussels, but the button-cutter is ignorant of any technical terminology for them. . . The following list gives the common names as applied by the cutter and fisher of shells. . . Rock-shell [etc]. **1982** [see **rock pocketbook**]. **1992** Cummings–Mayer *Field Guide Freshwater Mussels MW* 88, Rock-pocketbook. . . Other common names—Rock-shell, grandmaw, bastard, black pocketbook, queen. . . Extirpated from Ohio. Threatened in Wisconsin. Rare in Missouri.

rocks in one's lungs See **rock on the chest**

rock sled See **sled**

rockslide daisy n
A **fleabane** (here: *Erigeron leiomerus*).
   1953 Nelson *Plants Rocky Mt. Park* 165, Rock-slide daisy, *Erigeron leiomeris* . . is a low-growing plant of sub-alpine and alpine zones usually found in loose rocks where its long, stout taproot anchors itself at considerable depth.

rock snake n
=**night snake.**
   1915 *Copeia* 15.4 **CA,** The following snakes were observed within one-half day's walk of the city of Los Angeles during the years 1913 and 1914. . Rock Snake, *Hypsiglena ochroryncha* [etc]. **1928** Baylor Univ. Museum *Contrib.* 16.17 **TX,** Spotted Night Snake. . . On account of its being found under stones on hill and mountain sides, this small species is frequently called *Rock Snake.* **1952** Ditmars *N. Amer. Snakes* 152, Rock Snake, Spotted Night Snake. . . Central Texas northwestward to southern Idaho; central and southern California.

rock snipe n
1 =**purple sandpiper.** [See quots 1835, 1956]
   1835 Audubon *Ornith. Biog.* 3.558, Their marked predilection for rocky shores has caused them to be named "Rock Snipes" by the gunners of our eastern coast. **1888** Trumbull *Names of Birds* 182 **MA,** [Footnote:] I have heard it [=the purple sandpiper] called . . Rock-bird, Rock Plover, and Rock Snipe at Rowley and Salem, Mass. **1956** MA Audubon Soc. *Bulletin* 40.19 **ME, MA,** *Purple Sandpiper* . . Rock Snipe (Maine, Mass. It frequents sea-washed rocks.)
2 =**ruddy turnstone.**
   1923 U.S. Dept. Ag. *Misc. Circular* 13.71 **WA,** *Ruddy turnstone.* . . Vernacular Names. . . *In local use.* . . rock snipe.

rock spirea n
=**ocean spray.**
   1931 U.S. Dept. Ag. *Misc. Pub.* 101.58 **West,** Rockspireas (*Sericotheca* spp.) *Ibid,* Bush rockspirea (*S. dumosa*). **1937** U.S. Forest Serv. *Range Plant Hdbk.* B147, As its common name indicates, bush rockspirea grows in rocky sites, usually in dry or moderately dry soils . . , frequently in the niches of rocky ledges and cliffs. **1963** Craighead *Rocky Mt. Wildflowers* 84, Mountainspray. . . *Other names:* Oceanspray, Rock-spirea, Creambush. **1974** (1977) Coon *Useful Plants* 226, *Holodiscus discolor*—Rock spirea, mountainspray [etc]. . . A spreading, much branched tall shrub found on the West Coast.

rock squirrel n **West, esp TX** Cf **desert rock-squirrel**
A **ground squirrel b**, esp *Spermophilus variegatus*.
   1855 U.S. War Dept. *Rept. Explor. Railroad* 1.532 **ID, MT,** We observed to-day . . a species of the large rock squirrel, a specimen of which we preserved. *Ibid,* We observed also many blue jays, small rock squirrels, rabbits, and mountain weasel, or mink. **1917** Anthony *Mammals Amer.* 184, Rock Squirrels nearly always live in rocky mountains, the ledged and boulder-strewn sides of canyons, the bare rocky slopes along the base of the foothills, and the rim rock of outlying mesas and buttes being especially frequented. **1951** Martin *Amer. Wildlife & Plants* 247, California Ground Squirrel. . . It is known locally, as the Beechy ground squirrel, digger squirrel, or, because of its partiality to rocky places, the rock squirrel. **1959** Barnes *Nat. Hist. Wasatch Winter* 80 **UT,** Scampering over the deep snow of the hillside, is a Utah rock squirrel (*Citellus variegatus utah*). . . The rock squirrel may, indeed, make its permanent home in a hollow tree a rod above ground; but it usually burrows a nest beneath a boulder or under some brookside labyrinth. **1966–70** *DARE* (Qu. P27, . . *Kinds of squirrels*) Infs **TX**54, 67, 81, 88, Rock squirrel; **NM**3, Rock squirrel—brown, larger [than ground squirrel]; **TX**4, Black squirrel—rock squirrel; **TX**26, Gray squirrel = rock squirrel. **1980** Whitaker *Audubon Field Guide Mammals* 403, Rock Squirrel (*Spermophilus variegatus*). . . The common name is apt, for it is often seen sitting on rocks; it runs among them and makes its den in a burrow beneath them. **1986** Pederson *LAGS Concordance,* 1 inf, **cTX,** Rock squirrel—mountain squirrel, dark gray; 1 inf, **csTX,** Rock squirrel = black squirrel, mountain squirrel.

rock's throw n Also *rock throw* [Var of *stone's throw*]
A short distance.
   1953 *Hall Coll.* **wNC,** I was born in a log cabin within a rock throw of where the hotel at Walland [TN] now sits. **1966–67** *DARE* (Qu. MM6, . . *'Very close' or 'only a short distance away'*) Inf **TX**37, Rock's throw; (Qu. MM24, . . *'A short distance'*: "The river is just a _____ from the house.") Inf **ID**1, Rock's throw.

rock sturgeon n
=**lake sturgeon.**
   1877 Hallock *Sportsman's Gaz.* 329, Rock Sturgeon.—*Acipenser rubicundus*. . . This is the sturgeon of the great lakes. **1903** NY State Museum & Sci. Serv. *Bulletin* 60.66, This is known as the lake sturgeon, Ohio river sturgeon, rock sturgeon [etc]. . . It inhabits the Mississippi and Ohio rivers and the Great lakes, and is abundant in the Allegheny. **1933** LA Dept. of Conserv. *Fishes* 412, The Lake Sturgeon. . . Known also as the Rock Sturgeon, Red Sturgeon, and Rubber-nose Sturgeon. **1983** Becker *Fishes WI* 221, Lake Sturgeon. . . Other common names . . rock sturgeon (usually the long-snouted, obviously plated young).

rock sunfish n
=**rock bass 1.**
   1935 Caine *Game Fish* 24, Rock Bass. . . *Synonyms:* Bream . . Rock Sunfish [etc]. **1951** Harlan–Speaker *IA Fish* 121, *Northern Rock Bass*. . . Other Names—Redeye, redeye bass, rock bass, goggleeye, rock

sunfish. **1983** Becker *Fishes WI* 852, Rock Bass. . . Other common names: northern rock bass, redeye, redeye bass, goggle eye, rock sunfish.

rock swift See **rock lizard**

rock teacher See **rock school**

rock throw See **rock's throw**

rock trap See **rock jack**

rock tripe n

A lichen of the genus *Umbilicaria* or *Gyrophora.*

1866 Lindley–Moore *Treas. Botany* 1172, *Tripe de Roche.* This name, or that of Rock Tripe, is given in North America, in consequence of the blistered thallus, to several species of lichens belonging to *Gyrophora* or *Umbilicaria*, but especially to the latter. **1907** Marshall *Mosses* 85, Rock Tripe, *Umbilicaria vellea.* . . On rocks in high mountains. *Ibid* 174, [Caption:] Rock Tripe, *Umbilicaria Muhlenbergii.* **1942** Hylander *Plant Life* 83, [Caption:] Rock Tripe *(Umbilicaria)* is a smooth dark green lichen with a sooty black undersurface. **1998** *DARE* File—Internet [Rocky Mountain Survival Group *Primitive Wilderness Survival Guide*], Gyrophora—Rock Tripe: The lichen is edible, especially when boiled with meat. . . Umbiliceria [sic]—Rock Tripe. . . They are said to be mucilaginous, great for thickening stews.

rock trout n
=**greenling.**

1879 U.S. Natl. Museum *Bulletin* 14.35 **CA,** *Chirus constellatus* . . "Rock Trout." Coast of California. **1902** Jordan–Evermann *Amer. Fishes* 502 **Pacific coast,** *[Hexagrammos] superciliosus,* the red rock-trout, occurs from Bering Island to Monterey Bay. **1939** Natl. Geogr. Soc. *Fishes* 238, [Caption:] Often incorrectly called rock trout, *Greenlings* . . are valued as filets on the Pacific coast. Anglers seek them around rocky headlands and sometimes in the surf near reefs. **1955** U.S. Arctic Info. Center *Gloss.* 67, Rock trout. An Alaskan term for several marine food fishes of the genus *Hexagrammos* of the North Pacific coasts, especially the kelp greenling and the Atka mackerel.

rock wall n **chiefly Sth, S Midl, West** See Map Cf **stone wall**
=**rock fence.**

1862 Pierson *Jefferson* 113 **VA** (as of c1805), When I was there, the President's house was surrounded with a high rock wall, and there was an iron gate immediately in front of it. **1905** [see **rock fence**]. **1909** [see **rock fence**]. **c1960** *Wilson Coll.* **csKY,** *Rock fence* was the term used, but such fences were very rare, in the area. *Rock wall* was fairly common. **1962** Atwood *Vocab. TX* 49, *Wall (or fence) made of rocks (or stones).* A barrier built of rocks is usually known as a *rock wall* (45 [% of 273 infs]) or a *rock fence* (38 [% of 273 infs]). . . None of these expressions are characteristic of any particular area or age group. **1965–70** *DARE* (Qu. L60, *A fence made of stone or rock without mortar*) 70 Infs, **chiefly Sth, S Midl, West,** Rock wall; **HI**12, Dry laid rock wall; (Qu. L60b, *A fence of stone built with mortar;* total Infs questioned, 75) Infs **GA**1, 9, **OK**52, Rock wall; (Qu. L65, . . *Kinds of fences*) Infs **CA**1, 11, Rock wall. **1966** Dakin *Dial. Vocab. Ohio R. Valley* 109, *Rock wall,* scattered and rare in Virginia but fairly common in parts of North Carolina, also appears in the Ohio Valley. This term is less common and more scattered than *stone wall* but instances of its use appear in Indiana, Ohio, and Kentucky. **1967** [see **rock fence**]. **1968**

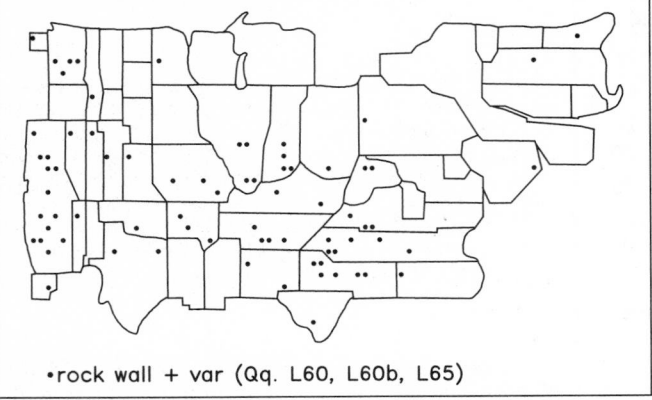

•rock wall + var (Qq. L60, L60b, L65)

Mt. Home News (ID) 8 Feb 8/7, Eight days after No. 10 was involved in the Boise accident he lost control of his car and slammed into a rock wall. **1970** *DARE* Tape **CA**201, There's a lot of rock walls and things like that that they [=coolies] built. **1971** Bright *Word Geog. CA & NV* 153, *Stone wall . . rock wall* 14% [of 300 infs]. **1983** *MJLF* 9.1.53 **ceKY** (as of 1956), *Rock wall . .* a rock fence. **1988** Pederson *LAGS Genl. Index* 318 **Gulf Region,** [158 infs, Rock wall(s); [1 inf, Rock wall fence]].

rockweed n

An alga of the genera *Fucus* or *Ascophyllum,* which grows on tidal rocks.

[1626 Smith *Accidence* 29, [In a list of nautical commands and terms:] Rocke-weede, adrift, or flotes.] **1698** in 1894 Providence RI Rec. Comm. *Early Rec.* 6.198, My son Elisha shall have free Egress & Regress . . to fetch Rockweede for his vse at any time on the said Neck. **1790** Deane *New Engl. Farmer* 148, I have sometimes defended the plants . . by encircling them with rock-weed. **1839** MA Ag. Surv. *Rept. for 1838* 89, [Caption:] Result of ten experiments of seeding Potatoes, twenty hills each, manured with a small handful of Rock-weed. **1879** U.S. Natl. Museum *Bulletin* 14.265, *Employed in the manufacture of fertilizers, iodine [etc].* . . Rockweed *(Fucus vesiculosus)* . . New England coast. **1901** Arnold *Sea-Beach* 72, Genus *Fucus.* . . The rockweeds. . . The plants are attached by sucker-like discs to the rocks, from which they hang like fringe when the tide recedes. **1928** Beston *Outermost House* 192 **Cape Cod MA,** Here have the tides strewn a moist tableland with lumpy tangles, wisps, and matted festoons of ocean vegetation— with common sea grass, with rockweed olive-green and rockweed olive-brown . . and bleached sea moss. **1966–69** *DARE* Tape **ME**24, [FW:] What's the rockweed like? [Inf:] Rockweed got a little . . bulb. . . we call it rockweed, I guess the name of it is seaweed; **RI**8, Rockweed, what we call rockweed. . . It's seaweed with little bubbles on it full of water, and when it gets hot they break, and they keep making steam so that everything [in a clambake] has a nice sea taste to it. **1983** Beyle *How Talk Cape Cod* 32, Rockweed is the seaweed that's flat and tough and has oval air sacs along its ribs and at the branching ends. It attaches itself to rocks and pilings. **1989** Mickelson *Nat. Hist.* 21 **AK,** A brown alga, rockweed . . attaches with holdfasts to intertidal rocks.

rockweed bird n [Because it feeds on marine creatures found in **rockweed**]
=**purple sandpiper.**

1917 (1923) *Birds Amer.* 1.232, Purple Sandpiper. . . *Other Names.* . . Rockweed Bird [etc]. **1955** Forbush–May *Birds* 194, Purple sandpiper. . . *Other names:* Rock-bird, Rockweed Bird; Rock Plover; Rock Snipe. **1956** MA Audubon Soc. *Bulletin* 40.19, *Purple Sandpiper.* . . Rockweed Bird (Maine, Mass. From its frequenting growths of rockweed or common seaweed, *Fucus.*)

rock willow n
=**heartleaf willow.**

1923 Abrams *Flora Pacific States* 1.507, *Salix vestita* . . Rock Willow. . . rocky places, mountains. **1924** Hawkins *Trees & Shrubs* 62, Rock willow (Salix petrophila). . . "Petrophila" means lover of rocks and it is on dripping rocks that it most often is found. **1953** Nelson *Plants Rocky Mt. Park* 56, The *rock willow* or *skyland willow,* Salix petrophila . . may be recognized by its dark green shiny leaves, pale beneath, which have distinctly yellow petioles. **1973** Hitchcock–Cronquist *Flora Pacific NW* 69, Rock w[illow]. . . S[alix] vestita.

rockwood See **rock elm 1**

rock woodchuck See **rockchuck**

rock worm n Also *rock bait* Cf **periwinkle** n[2] **2**
The larva of a caddis fly *(Trichoptera);* rarely, a **hellgrammite 1.**

1948 Baumann *Old Man Crow's Boy* 49 **ID,** We turned over the rocks in the stream-bottom to get the bugs and worms on which they fed: periwinkles, which we called "rock-worms" on account of the little cases or houses which they made out of rock particles and cemented about themselves. **1966–69** *DARE* (Qu. P6, . . *Kinds of worms . . used for bait*) Inf **GA**72, Rock bait—same as sandstoodle; build nests in sand; (Qu. P13, . . *Ways of fishing . . besides the ordinary hook and line*) Inf **NC**37, Rock bait. **2000** *Atlanta Jrl.–Constitution* (GA) 7 Sept Home & Garden sec 5/2, I fish with what I call a "rock worm" in the Flint River, which is the larva stage of the dobsonfly. **2000** *NADS Letters* **CO** (as of 1950s), My father called the little worms you described, who wrapped themselves in sand grains "rock worms." He is a Colorado native, age 92. He didn't mention that they might be used as bait. I had found some near a creek bank, and asked him what they were. **2001** *DARE* File—Internet **CA,** The rock worm is a generic term for the ubiquitous uncased *Rhyacophila* and *Hydropsyche* caddis larvae.

rock wren n [See quot 1977]

A grayish-brown sparrow-sized wren of the western US (*Salpinctes obsoletus*).

1838 Audubon *Ornith. Biog.* 4.443, Rock Wren. *Troglodytes Obsoletus,* Say. **1858** Baird *Birds* 357, Rock Wren. . . High central plains through the Rocky mountains to the Coast and Cascade ranges. **1923** Dawson *Birds CA* 2.685, The Rock Wren is nestled among the most impressive surroundings, yet he gives no evidence of a chastened spirit. **1949** Guthrie *Way West* 193, Rock loped after some little birds—ground sparrows or rock wrens or something kin to them. **1977** Bull–Farrand *Audubon Field Guide Birds* 620, The Rock Wren has the unusual habit of laying down a path of small pebbles in front of its nest; this little "pavement" often simplifies an observer's effort to locate a nest.

rocky adj

Obscene, off-color.

1906 Canfield *Diary Forty-Niner* 75 **CA,** [The men] told stories, some of them pretty rocky. **1951** *PADS* 15.60 **neIN** (as of 1890s), *Rocky.* . . Off-color. "A rocky story." **c1960** *Wilson Coll.* **csKY,** *Rocky.* . . Off color, obscene.

rocky-horse n Cf ridy-horse

A **seesaw 1** or similar recreational device; see quots.

1968 *DARE* (Qu. EE31, *Playground equipment with a long board for two children to sit on and go up and down in turn*) Inf **MD**38, Rocky ['rakı]-horse. **1986** Pederson *LAGS Concordance* (Seesaw) 3 infs, **TN,** Rocky horse; 2 infs, **TN,** (A-)riding a rocky horse; (*Flying jenny*) 2 infs, **TN, GA,** Rocky horse; (*Joggling board*) 1 inf, neMS, Rocky horse—homemade.

Rocky Mountain bee plant n West

A **spiderflower** (here: *Cleome serrulata*). Also called **bee plant 1,** ~ **flower 2,** ~ **spiderflower,** ~ **weed 2a, guaco, skunkweed 3, stinking clover, stinkweed**

1892 WY Ag. College *Annual Rept. for 1891, Cleome integrifolia* [Rocky Mountain Bee Plant.]—This plant grows in great abundance in many parts of the plains, the long racemes of large, showy, reddish-purple flowers being visible for a long distance. **1895** Gray–Bailey *Field Botany* 68, [*Cleome*] *integrifolia* . . wild in Minn. to Kans., and cult. in gardens, also for bees under the name *Rocky Mountain Bee Plant.* **1939** *Natl. Geogr. Mag.* Aug 227, *Pink Cleome.* . . Bees are attracted in such great numbers to the nectar secreted abundantly by these dainty blossoms of prairie and roadside that the species is often called "Rocky Mountain bee plant" and has been cultivated for many years as a source of commercial honey. **1957** Barnes *Nat. Hist. Wasatch Spring* 44 **UT,** Returning after an interesting day we find just below Park City beds of pink cleome, stinkweed or Rocky Mountain bee plant . . in full bloom. **1982** *Plants SW* (Catalog) 27, Rocky Mountain Beeplant. . . In times of severe food shortages, the Navajos made a meal out of the ground seeds.

Rocky Mountain bluebird See mountain bluebird

Rocky Mountain brook trout See Rocky Mountain trout

Rocky Mountain canary See mountain canary

Rocky Mountain clematis n Cf mountain clematis

A **virgin's bower** (here: *Clematis pseudoalpina*).

1950 Stevens *ND Plants* 145, *Clematis pseudoalpina* . . Rocky Mountain Clematis. . . I found this first in 1935 at Killdeer Mts. where it is fairly common on upper, steep slopes and rocky ridges. **1975** Lamb *Woody Plants SW* 44, Rocky Mountain clematis may have violet, purple, or white flowers. . . It occurs in the higher mountains of our area.

Rocky Mountain cottontail n Also mountain cottontail

A **cottontail** (here: *Sylvilagus nuttallii*).

1928 Anthony *N. Amer. Mammals* 498, [*Sylvilagus*] *Nuttalli* Group.—Rocky Mountain Cottontails. *Ibid* 499, Rocky Mountain Cottontail—*Sylvilagus nuttalli pinetis.* **1952** Burt *Field Guide Mammals* 147, Mountain cottontail. *Sylvilagus nuttalli.* . . In the *mountains* of the west lives this *grayish* cottontail, washed with *pale yellowish.* **1980**

Whitaker *Audubon Field Guide Mammals* 352, Nuttall's Cottontail—"Mountain Cottontail."

Rocky Mountain egg n Cf Alabama egg

1980 *DARE* File **csWI,** The best thing about camping is eating breakfast. We usually make what we call "Rocky Mountain eggs"—that's when you cut a hole in the center of a piece of bread and fry an egg in the hole.

Rocky Mountain goat n

=**mountain goat.**

1842 DeKay *Zool. NY* 1.112, [*Capra*] *americana.* . . *Rocky Mountain Goat.* . . Color white, with long straight hair. Larger than the common goat. **1884** *Century Illustr. Mag.* 29.193 **Rocky Mts,** *Hunting the Rocky Mountain Goat.* . . As a popular name mountain antelope or antelope-goat might be suggested. **1917** Anthony *Mammals Amer.* 56, Rocky Mountain Goat.—*Oreamnos montanus montanus.* . . Ranges in the Cascade Mountains north to British Columbia. **1982** Elman *Hunter's Field Guide* 518, Mountain Goat. . . Common & Regional Names: *Rocky Mountain goat, white goat.*

Rocky Mountain grasshopper See Rocky Mountain locust

Rocky Mountain iris n Cf mountain lily 5

An **iris B1** (here: *Iris missouriensis*).

1880 Meehan *Native Flowers* 2d ser 1.103, As it is the only species of *Iris* found there, the common name of "Rocky Mountain Iris" has suggested itself to us. **1936** McDougall–Baggley *Plants of Yellowstone* 41, Rocky Mountain iris (*Iris missouriensis*).—The slender shoot grows from a stout underground stem and bears one or two large, light blue flowers. **1963** Craighead *Rocky Mt. Wildflowers* 34, Rocky Mountain Iris. . . Roots were ground by the Indians, mixed with animal bile, then put in the gall bladder and warmed near a fire for several days. Arrow points were dipped in this mixture, and it is reported by old Indians that many warriors only slightly wounded by such arrows died within 3 to 7 days.

Rocky Mountain jay n Cf mountain jay

A **Canada jay** (here: *Perisoreus canadensis capitalis*).

1898 (1900) Davie *Nests N. Amer. Birds* 328, Rocky Mountain Jay. . . This bird is called the White-headed Jay or Rocky Mountain Whisky Jack—a race of the Canada Jay, but very much different. It is peculiar to the Rocky Mountain region, and is especially common in Northern New Mexico and Colorado. **1941** Writers' Program *Guide CO* 19, Camprobber. . . Rocky Mountain jay. **1965** Bailey–Niedrach *Birds CO* 2.553, There are several races of the Camp Robber, but the one in the mountains of the West is, appropriately, the Rocky Mountain Jay (*Perisoreus canadensis capitalis*). **1967** *DARE* (Qu. Q16, . . *Kinds of jays*) Inf **TX5,** Rocky Mountain jay.

Rocky Mountain lily See mountain lily 2, 4

Rocky Mountain locust n Also Rocky Mountain grasshopper

A **grasshopper 1** (here: *Melanoplus spretus*).

1876 Wheeler *Iron Trail* 36 **cCO,** "Tell us, somebody," cried June, brushing a Rocky Mountain grasshopper from her sandwich, "how this chasm was made." **1882** (1903) Treat *Injurious Insects* 269, It is usually called the Rocky Mountain Locust, but is sometimes known as the "Hateful Grasshopper." This insect has visited Kansas, Nebraska and other Western States with most destructive effect, the recital of which reminds one of the accounts of the plagues of Egypt. **1926** Essig *Insects N. Amer.* 84, The Rocky Mountain locust . . is the most famous of all the destructive, migrating locusts of this country. . . It breeds in the higher foothills region of the eastern slopes of the Rocky Mountains. **1937** (1943) Dick *Sod-House Frontier* 202, As early as 1857 the grasshoppers, or Rocky Mountain locusts as they were called, made incursions into the little cultivated area along the Missouri River. **1980** Milne–Milne *Audubon Field Guide Insects* 422, The "Grasshopper Glacier" near Cooke, Montana, contains millions of embedded Rocky Mountain Grasshoppers, presumably from swarms that settled on the glacier and froze.

Rocky Mountain maple n Cf mountain maple

Usu = **dwarf maple,** but also a bigtooth **maple** (here: *Acer saccharum* subsp *grandidentatum*).

1911 *Century Dict. Suppl., Maple* sb.¹ . . Rocky Mountain maple, the dwarf maple. **1930** OK Univ. Biol. Surv. *Pub.* 2.71, *Acer grandidentatum* . . Rocky Mountain Maple. **1931** U.S. Dept. Ag. *Misc. Pub.* 101.98, Rocky Mountain maple . . also called dwarf maple . . and sometimes known as mountain maple and rock maple, varies in size from a bush about 7 feet high to a small tree. **1975** Lamb *Woody Plants SW* 85, Rocky Mountain maple occurs in the high mountains throughout the western two-thirds and northeastern New Mexico, and in Arizona from the southeast corner north and west to the Grand Canyon.

Rocky Mountain oyster See **mountain oyster**

Rocky Mountain swallow n
=**cliff swallow.**

1917 (1923) *Birds Amer.* 3.84, Cliff Swallow—*Petrochelidon lunifrons lunifrons.* . . Crescent Swallow; Rocky Mountain Swallow; Moon-fronted Swallow. **1944** Hausman *Amer. Birds* 527, Swallow, Rocky Mountain—see Swallow, Cliff.

Rocky Mountain trout n Also *Rocky Mountain brook trout*
=**cutthroat trout.**

1882 U.S. Natl. Museum *Bulletin* 16.314, *S[almo] purpuratus* . . Salmon Trout of the Columbia; Yellowstone Trout; Rocky Mountain Brook Trout; Lake Trout. . . The common trout of the Rocky Mountains and Cascade region, abounding in all the streams of Alaska, Oregon, and Washington, where it descends to salt water, and reaches a weight of 20 pounds. **1949** Caine *N. Amer. Sport Fish* 79, Cutthroat Trout. . . *Colloquial Names* . . Rocky Mountain Brook Trout [etc]. **1972** Sparano *Outdoors Encycl.* 356, *Cutthroat Trout*—Common Names . . mountain trout, Rocky Mountain trout [etc].

Rocky Mountain whitefish n Cf **mountain whitefish**
1 A **whitefish** (here: *Prosopium williamsoni*).

1882 U.S. Natl. Museum *Bulletin* 16.297, [*Coregonus*] *williamsoni* . . *Rocky Mountain White-fish.* . . Clear streams and lakes from the Rocky Mountains to the Pacific; abundant in the Sierra Nevada. **1902** Jordan–Evermann *Amer. Fishes* 120, Though this species is most widely known as the mountain herring, it is also called Williamson's whitefish, Rocky Mountain herring, Rocky Mountain whitefish, and in some places grayling. **1949** Caine *N. Amer. Sport Fish* 165, A freshly caught Rocky Mountain whitefish is hard to beat for its sweet delicate flavor.

2 =**grayling.**

1949 Caine *N. Amer. Sport Fish* 92, Montana grayling. . . *Colloquial Names*—Rocky Mountain Whitefish [etc]. [*Ibid*, The Montana grayling is often confused with the Rocky Mountain whitefish.]

roday-o See **rodeo**

rode n Also sp *road(e)*, *rood* [Appar swEngl (Devon) dial < ME *rode rope;* see 1965 *Mariner's Mirror* 51.115–16, 1966 *Ibid* 52.87–9] **chiefly NEng** Cf **killick**, **roding**, *DNE*
A rope, esp one attached to a boat anchor.

1628 in 1843 MA Hist. Soc. *Coll.* 3d ser 8.166, At length I caused our killick (which was the anchor we had) to be cast forth, and one continually to hold his hand upon the rood or cable, by which we knew whether our anchor held or no. **1634** Wood *New Engl. Prospect* 40, They are constrayned to . . hale their Boats by the sealing, or roades. **1679** in 1881 Boston Registry Dept. *Records* 7.135, A roade taken out of his Boate in the time of ye fire, & made use of to pull downe houses. **1726** Penhallow *Indian Wars* 58 (*DAE*), [They] quit one of their boats by cutting the roads and lashings. **1865** Essex Inst. *Coll.* 7.36 **NEng**, Another old word unnoticed by lexicographers is the "rood" mentioned by Levett. This is the cable or hawser of the killick; and the boatman speaks of the *"rode"* (as it is pronounced) to his killick, but never the *cable,* which is larger and belongs with the anchor. **1896** *DN* 1.423 **neMA,** *Rode, rood* [rōd], a light line attached to a killick. Marblehead, Mass. **1905** Wasson *Green Shay* 219 **ME,** All the way ever I can account for it is that there's folks must been aboard strippin' of her afore she got clear from the "Pup," and ef she had a kaidge ahead of her then, no doubt but what they might have cut the road [Footnote: Cable] and lugged it off along of 'em; kaidge and all, maybe! **1918** *DN* 5.16 **Martha's Vineyard MA,** *Rode.* . . A rope, especially an anchor rope. **1950** Moore *Candlemas Bay* 40 **ME,** His anchor and rode were stowed away under the stern. **1960** *Washington Post & Times Herald* (DC) 22 Nov np, At high tide last Wednesday he was plying the Potomac off Collingwood. . . Suddenly the craft struck a submerged piling, was holed, and sank. . . Rusokoff grabbed his anchor rode and made shore where . . the rode was made fast to a stump. [*DARE* Ed.: The final ed. changed *rode* to *rope*.] **1963** Rowland *North Advent.* 147 **N Atl**, With both hooks down and a good scope of rode she should be able to ride out anything. **1965** *Mariner's Mirror* 51.115 **seMA,** Gershom Bradford tells me that when he

heard the word [=*rode*] in Duxbury, Mass. as a boy, it meant a light rope in a small boat. He says, 'By the time the size of the boat reaches the necessity of using chain, the term should be cable. I never heard chain-cable referred to as *rode*. . . I never heard it used at sea.' (Bradford first went to sea in 1898.) *Ibid* 116, Initially, the word [=*rode*] was a local term on the east coast, but it has since been widely disseminated by the activities of U.S. Power Squadrons and Canadian Power Squadrons—organizations interested in educating the boating public.

rode v See **ride** v[1] **A1, 3a**

rodee-o See **rodeo**

roden See **ride** v[1] **A3c**

rodeo n Usu |ˈrodiˌo|; also esp CA, SW |ˌroˈde-o|; pronc-spp *rodee-o, roday-o* For addit pronc and sp varr see **A** below
A Forms.

1932 *AmSp* 7.451, The word *rodeo* . . is pretty young to have yet achieved a standard pronunciation. There are regional differences to be taken into account. On the Pacific Coast and in the Southwest, and in cities where the shows have been presented, the pronunciation is usually *roday*ʹ-o. Since the word is Spanish, this accentuation is the book accentuation and it is that of the performers. . . In the Central West and the East where there is less consciousness of Spanish and aquaintance with the word is eye-acquaintance, the first syllable is stressed, *ro*ʹ-deo. . . One hears from some speakers, a half-Americanized pronunciation, *rodee*ʹ-o. **1936** McCarthy *Lang. Mosshorn* np **West** [Rodeo terms], *Rodeo.* The Mexican word for roundup. It is pronounced ro-day-o, with the accent on the second syllable, in the south. In Montana and Wyoming, it is pronounced ro-de-o with the accent on the first syllable. The southern expression is sometimes used humorously in the north. **1938** D. Coolidge *Arizona Cowboys* ii.27 (*OED2*), The round-up had just begun. They call it *rodéo*, in Spanish. . . The contest riders of today have given it another twist and call it ró-deo. **1943** *CA Folkl. Qrly.* 2.42, Perhaps an Easterner becomes a Californian when it is natural for him to say *rodáy-o*. Across the Mississippi it is always *ró-dio*, and the Spanish pronunciation is an affectation. **1946** *NYT Mag.* 20 Oct 35 [Rodeo lingo], *Rodeo:* exhibition of cowboy prowess in riding, roping, etc. (pron. roh-dee-oh by professionals, not roh-*day*-oh). **1965–70** *DARE* (Qu. FF16) 105 Infs, **scattered, but chiefly West,** [Proncs of the types [ˈro(ʊ)diˌo(ʊ), ro(ʊ)dɪˌjo(ʊ)]]; 12 Infs, **chiefly Pacific, esp CA,** [Proncs of the types [ˌroˈde-o(ʊ)]]; CA18, 32, 65, [ˈrode(ɪ)-o]. **1971** Bright *Word Geog. CA & NV* 108, Generally speaking, *rodéo* was more accepted in California, with heavy concentration along the central and southern coasts from Monterey-Salinas south—in other words, the old Spanish settlement area. . . On the other hand, in Nevada and along the northern border of California, *ródeo* was the commonly accepted form. Except for the specific areas mentioned, competition between the two forms is apparent in both states. **1981** Pederson *LAGS Basic Materials,* 1 inf, **csLA**, [ˈroˑˌdɪoˑ]; 1 inf, **nwLA**, [ˈroˑʊdɪˌoˑʊ]; 1 inf, **csTX**, [roˈˑdeɪˌoˑ]; 1 inf, **cwLA**, [ˈroˢʊdɪˌoˢ]; 1 inf, **csAL**, [ˈroˢʊˑˌdɪˌoˢʊˢz].

B Sense.

Also attrib: a usu competitive exhibition of skill in tasks associated with the traditional cattle **roundup 1,** esp roping and riding; transf to var other exhibitions of skill; see quots. [Span *rodeo* a cattle roundup] **orig chiefly West, esp TX; now more widely recognized** See Map

1912 (1914) Sinclair *Flying U Ranch* 16 **MT,** They have them rodeos on a Sunday, mostly, and they invite everybody to it, like it was a picnic. **1927** *AmSp* 2.278 **CA** [Stanford expressions], *Rodeo*—a wild west show. **1936** *LA Conserv. Rev.* July 1, The Louisiana Tarpon Rodeo at Grande Isle will next September celebrate its ninth year. **1941** Writers' Program *Guide WY* 464, *Rodeo*—A Western celebration, featuring bucking, roping, and bulldogging. **1949** *Daily Progress* (Charlottesville VA) 22 Aug 9/1, Entries for the fishing rodeo for youngsters here must be in by Thursday. **1964** Jackman–Long *OR Desert* 393, Rodeo—Public display of horsemanship. Originally a roundup. **1965–70** *DARE* (Qu. FF16, . . *Local contests or celebrations*) 121 Infs, **chiefly West, esp TX,** Rodeos; LA40, Fishing rodeo; IL27, Fishing rodeo—give prize for the biggest fish caught on Labor Day; PA72, Car rodeo—feats of driving skill—used to promote safe driving; CA142, Folsom rodeo; TX73, Horse show and rodeo; OK20, Jay-cee rodeo; KS13, Little britches rodeo—for children; goattail tying; calf roping; barrel racing; LA37, Redfish rodeo; MO30, Rodeo circus; AZ11, Rodeo parade; OK51, State prison rodeo and parade; LA32, Tarpon rodeo. **1966** Barnes–Jensen *Dict. UT Slang* 36, *Rodeo.* . . a public exhibition of lassoing, horsemanship, and other features of the round-up. It is a Spanish word meaning round-up, and is gradually supplanting the words "wild west show" in Utah and adjoining states. **1966–70** *DARE* Tape **AZ4,** I never did contest in these rodeos ['rodjoz]; **CA136,** These rodeo ['rodi-ou] riders, they . . grip their legs some, but it's more just getting in rhythm with the horse, that makes them top riders; **CA164,** I have ridden in the parades at the fair, not in the rodeos ['rodi⋎-o⁵uz]; **CA210,** The rodeos ['rodi-ouz] here are the same as they'd be every place, you have your main events—bronc riding, bull riding, bareback bronc riding, and your calf roping, team roping, bulldogging. **1986** Pederson *LAGS Concordance,* 3 infs, **LA,** 1 inf, **TX,** Rodeo; 1 inf, **csAL,** Rattlesnake Rodeos, held in Opp, AL.

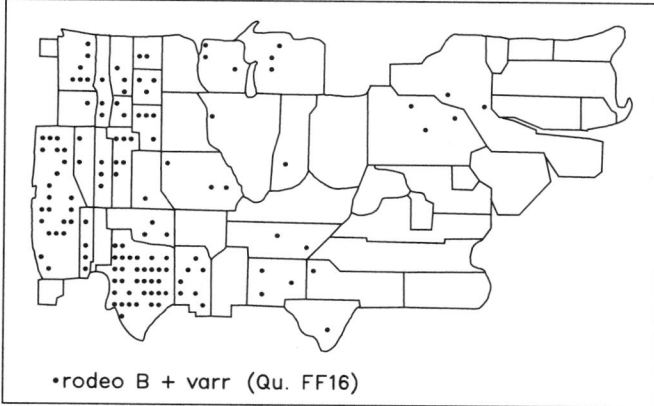

•rodeo B + varr (Qu. FF16)

roder v |'ro͵de| [Fr *roder*] Pronc-sp *rodey* **LA**
To roam, prowl about.

   1983 *Reinecke Coll.* 10 **LA,** *Roder* ['ro͵de]. . . to roam, ramble, walk about, esp. at night. From same word in St[andard] French. "Why don't he stay home instead of *rodeying* around?" Relatively common. **1992** Scott *Cajun Vernacular Engl.* 49, *Roder.* . . Used as a verb in C[ajun] V[ernacular] E[nglish], this word takes the same inflectional suffixes as a regular English verb: *roders* ("He just *roders* all the time."), *roder-ed* ("They *roder-ed* all night long."), and, *roder-ing.* As one informant was heard to say, "I didn't do any homework last night. I spent my time running the roads and rodé-ing with my friends."

roding n
=**rode** n.

   1896 (1897) Kipling *Captains Courageous* 57, Dan . . twitched once or twice on the roding, and . . the anchor drew up at once. [*DARE* Ed: Kipling was a US resident in 1896, and had worked on an American schooner on the Grand Banks.] [**1911** *Century Dict. Suppl., Roding.* . . A rope attached to the anchor of a dory or small fishing-boat. [*Century* Ed: Bay of Fundy].] [**1916** Wallace *Shack Locker* 127 **Nova Scotia,** Thomas hove the dory anchor over and paid out the roding to the bitter end.] **1944** Ashley *Ashley Knots* 537, To *scow a grapnel.* This method is used in small-boat fishing on rocky bottoms. . . The roding or warp is led tightly around the crotch and is stopped to the ring with a single rope yarn. *Ibid* 602, *Roding:* Originally the anchor warp or cable of a coasting schooner, nowadays of any small craft. Derived from roadstead and roadster.

roe v [Perh by back-formation from *roed* full of roe (*OED2* 1611 →)]
Of a female fish: to become full of roe.

   1965 *DARE* Tape **FL22,** Any ways from May until October till the fish begin to roe, the mullet begin to roe, you'll see 'em fishing on the outside. . . because they want to get the roe out of the fish. Most of 'em catch the fish and take the roe out and just throw the fish away because they're so plentiful they didn't want them.

roebuckers n pl [From Sears-*Roebuck,* the mail-order house]
Cf **Sears-Roebuck 2**
False teeth.

   1968 *DARE* (Qu. X13b, *Joking names for false teeth*) Inf **PA162,** Roebuckers. **1984** Wilder *You All Spoken Here* 37 **Sth,** *Roebuckers:* False teeth. Probably from the catalog. **1987** Robertson *Ideal Genuine Man* xix **ME,** I will not dissect *The Ideal Genuine Man* for you, any more than I would chew your food for you if you had any working teeth

left in your head (or even a good set of what the old folks used to call "Roebuckers").

rogation flower n [*OED2* 1597 → for *Polygala vulgaris*] Cf **procession flower**
A **milkwort** (here: *Polygala incarnata*).

   1900 Lyons *Plant Names* 299, *P[olygala] incarnata* . . eastern U.S. to Mexico, Pink Milkwort. (American) Rogation-flower. **1949** Moldenke *Amer. Wild Flowers* 52, A dainty little pink- or rose-flowered species, *P. incarnata,* with slender usually unbranched few-leaved stems 1 or 2 feet tall. It is often called *processionflower* or *rogationflower,* and blooms continuously throughout the year in the southern part of its range. **1959** Carleton *Index Herb. Plants* 100, *Rogation-flower:* Polygala [spp].

roger v [From earlier slang *roger* penis (*OED2* a1700 →)]
To have sexual intercourse with (a woman); to copulate; rarely, to rape.

   1710 (1941) Byrd *Secret Diary* 278 **VA,** I went to bed again and lay till 7 and rogered my wife. **1850** in 1956 Eliason *Tarheel Talk* 186 **c,csNC,** That they, by lecherous feelings led / Would lie and sleep, in the same bed;/ That Albert Pearson, for the Dollars,/ Would often Roger Fanny Rogers. **1899** (1912) Green *VA Folk-Speech* 356, *Roger.* . . To copulate. **1930** Shoemaker *1300 Words* 50 **cPA Mts** (as of c1900), *Roger*—To rape, to take advantage of forcibly. **1944** *PADS* 2.48 **NC, VA,** *Roger.* . . To copulate. **1977** Randolph *Pissing in the Snow* 35 **Ozarks,** An honest folklorist cannot substitute . . *copulate* when his informant says *fuck, diddle, roger,* or *tread.*

Roger(-Roger)-over n, exclam [Varr of **Antony-over**]

   1967 *DARE* (Qu. EE22, . . *The game in which they throw a ball over a building . . to a player on the other side*) Inf **NY30,** Roger-Roger-over; (Qu. EE23a, *In the game of andy-over . . what . . you call out when you throw the ball*) Inf **NY30,** Roger-over [FW sugg].

rogerry n Cf **roger**

   1899 (1912) Green *VA Folk-Speech* 356, *Rogerry.* . . The penis.

rogue n

1 A scoundrel, cheat, thief; a difficult or mischievous person.
chiefly Sth, S Midl See Map on p. 626 *esp freq among rural speakers and speakers with little formal educ* Note: Only clearly non-literary examples are included here. Cf **roguish 1, roguy**

   1939 *Hall Coll.* **wNC,** When he found the rogue who stole those things, he didn't do nothin'. *Ibid* **eTN,** I think more of a rogue than of a man who'd lie. **1965–70** *DARE* (Qu. V6, . . *Words . . for a thief*) 64 Infs, **chiefly Sth, S Midl,** Rogue; **TX106,** A plumb rogue [Of all Infs responding to the question, 29% were comm type 5, 26% gs educ or less; of those giving these responses, 53% were comm type 5, 50% gs educ or less.]; (Qu. U17, *Names or nicknames for a person who doesn't pay his bills*) Inf **PA245,** Rogue; (Qu. U36a, . . *A person who saves in a mean way or is greedy in money matters:* "He's an awful _____.") Inf **TX106,** Rogue; (Qu. V2a, . . *A deceiving person, or somebody that you can't trust*) Infs **AL3, GA19,** 30, 36, 84, **NC40, NJ33,** Rogue; **KY44,** Horse-rogue; (Qu. V3, . . *A thoroughly dishonest person* . . "He's a _____."; total Infs questioned, 75) Inf **MS45,** Big rogue; (Qu. V7, *A person who sets out to cheat others while pretending to be honest*) Infs **IN19, KY40, LA8, MO8, NJ28, PA244, SC26, WV3,** Rogue; (Qu. Z12, *Nicknames and joking words meaning 'a small child':* "He's a healthy little _____.") Inf **ME21,** Rogue; (Qu. AA6b, . . *A man who is fond of being with women and tries to attract their attention—if he's rude or not respectful*) Infs **CA169, GA33, IL97, IN35,** 60, **PA221, WA20,** Rogue; (Qu. GG38, *Somebody who is usually mean and bad tempered:* "He's an awful _____.") Inf **MO39,** Rogue; (Qu. HH16, *Uncomplimentary words with no definite meaning—just used when you want to show that you don't think much of a person:* "Don't invite him. He's a _____.") Inf **MO39,** Rogue; (Qu. II21, *When somebody behaves unpleasantly or without manners:* "The way he behaves, you'd think he was _____.") Inf **MO39,** Rogue; (Qu. II35, *A person who is disliked because he seems to think he knows everything*) Inf **MO39,** Rogue; (Qu. KK37, *Words to describe a very sly person:* "He's _____.") Inf **MA24,** Rogue; (Qu. NN9b, *Exclamations showing great annoyance:* "He's run off with my hammer again, _____!") Inf **LA8,** Rogue. **1986** Pederson *LAGS Concordance* (*The poor whites*) 1 inf, **cnAL,** A rogue—from mountains; 1 inf, **cMS,** They rogue [sic]; (*Derelict*) 1 inf, **swTN,** Rogues; 1 inf, **swGA,** Rascal or rogue—angry terms for Negro; 1 inf, **cnGA,** Rogue stole my pencil; (*Varmint*) 1 inf, **ceGA,** A person would be a rogue.

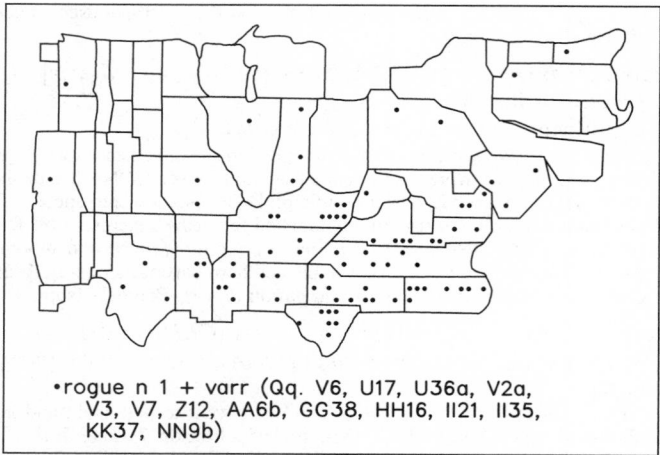

•rogue n 1 + varr (Qq. V6, U17, U36a, V2a,
V3, V7, Z12, AA6b, GG38, HH16, II21, II35,
KK37, NN9b)

2 An animal with a bad disposition or one inclined to break out of enclosures.
　1896 *DN* 1.423 **wCT**, *Rogue* . . a horse that has the habit of getting out of his pasture, and cannot be restrained by ordinary fences. **1915** *DN* 4.189 **swVA**, *Rogue.* . . Applied to animals that break through or jump fences. **1923** *DN* 5.219 **swMO**, *Rogue.* . . Any breachy animal. [*Ibid* 202 **swMO**, *Breachy.* . . Given to breaking through or throwing down or jumping over fences.] **1966–68** *DARE* (Qu. K16, *A cow with a bad temper*) Inf **AR40**, She's a rogue; (Qu. K37, . . *A horse of mixed colors*) Inf **IN49**, Rogue; (Qu. K42, *A horse that is rough, wild, or dangerous*) Inf **IN44**, Rogue.

rogue v **Sth, S Midl**
1 To steal (something)—also in phrr *rogue one out of (something)* to rob one of (something); *rogue (it)* to be a **rogue n 1.**
　1896 *DN* 1.423 **swNC**, *Rogue.* . . To thieve. "The cat is roguing it some." **1939** *Hall Coll.* **wNC, eTN**, *Rogue.* . . To steal. "He rogued me out of it," [=he stole it from me]. **1968** *DARE* (Qu. V4, . . *Words for stealing something valuable* . . "*Yesterday somebody _____ my watch.*") Infs **GA19, 30**, Rogued. **1986** Pederson *LAGS Concordance*, 1 inf, **neTN**, He rogued it = stole it. **1992** in 1996 *Montgomery Coll.* **eTN**, *Rogue* v.i . . to stray off course.
2 as vbl n *roguing;* Of wild animals: preying on domestic animals.
　1981 Pederson *LAGS Basic Materials*, 1 inf, **seAR**, And they do their roguing at night—wild animals that preyed on stock.

rogue adj See **roguish 2**

roguing See **rogue** v **2**

roguish adj **Sth, S Midl**
1 Scoundrelly, mischievous, thievish. [*OED2 roguish* a. 2 1596 →] Note: Only clearly non-literary examples are included here. Cf **rogue n 1**
　1937 in 1976 *Weevils in the Wheat* 249 **VA** [Black], Cutting the nails of a nursing infant will make it "rougish" [sic]. **1952** in 1968 Haun *Hawk's Done Gone* 290 **TN**, "I wouldn't have him [=a witch doctor] as long as I could keep spells off myself," Jake said. "For they say he's turned roguish." **1967–68** *DARE* (Qu. U36a, . . *A person who saves in a mean way or is greedy in money matters:* "*He's an awful _____.*") Infs **GA19, 30**, Roguish fellow; (Qu. V7, *A person who sets out to cheat others while pretending to be honest*) Inf **LA6**, Roguish. **1984** Wilder *You All Spoken Here* 17 **Sth**, Roguish: Thieving; mischievous.
2 also *rogue:* Of a domestic animal: unruly; inclined to break out of enclosures. Cf **breachy 1, rogue n 2**
　1931 *PMLA* 41.1304 **sAppalachians**, That cow has turned roguish, and is up to meanness. (A 'roguish' cow is one that jumps fences, etc.) **1953** Randolph–Wilson *Down in Holler* 279 **Ozarks**, *Roguish.* . . Term applied to cattle that break through fences. **1954** *Harder Coll.* **cwTN**, *Roguish.* . . Term applied to cattle that break through fences. **1974** Fink *Mountain Speech* 22 **wNC, eTN**, *Roguish* . . descriptive of a cow inclined to jump the fence or stray from the pasture. **1986** Pederson *LAGS Concordance*, 1 inf, **cnAR**, A pretty roguish animal—ornery rather than wild; 1 inf, **ceTN**, A roguish cow would jump fences; 1 inf, **neGA**, Roguish cows won't stay in pasture; 1 inf, **swAR**, Got rogue

= became wild; of a sheep. **1995** in 1996 *Montgomery Coll.* **eTN**, Roguish.

roguy adj Also sp *rogy* [*OED2 roguy* a. 2 c1610 →; "*Obs.*"] Cf **rogue n 1**
Scoundrelly, mischievous.
　1899 (1912) Green *VA Folk-Speech* 356, *Roguy.* . . Knavish; dishonest. "He has a roguy look." **1929** *WV Review* Oct 9, Curiosity induced me to inquire into the word *rogy*, which I once heard an old woman say. I found it in the sense in which she had used it to be an old word for mischievous.

roily See **riley**

rok See **rake** v[1] **A2**

roke See **rake** v[1] **A1, 2**

roley-holey See **rolly-holey**

roley-poley See **roly-poly**

roll v **Sth, S Midl**
1 To push (a baby) in its carriage. [*OED2 roll* v.[2] 1.c "to convey in a wheeled vehicle"; →1889] Cf **ride** v[1] **B13b**
　1949 Kurath *Word Geog.* 77, *Wheel the baby.* . . The Southern area, except for South Carolina, has the two expressions, *roll the baby* and *ride the baby* side by side. . . In the Virginia Piedmont it [=*ride*] is now rare. It has been superseded by *roll*, which is current in the entire Southern area and is gaining ground in the Blue Ridge as well. *Roll the baby* is the only expression used in South Carolina (except the Peedee Valley, where *ride* survives), and on the Georgia coast. **1972** *PADS* 58.22 **cwAL**, *Wheel the baby*. Southern *ride the baby* (3 [of 27 infs]) and *roll the baby* (1) were found together with a number of other terms: *walk* (5), *stroll* (5), *take* (5), *carry* (3), *push* (2), and *tote* (1). **1989** Pederson *LAGS Tech. Index* 228 **Gulf Region** (*Wheel [the baby]*) 119 infs, Roll; 22 infs, Roll (the baby) around; 8 infs, Rolling; 3 infs, Roll (the baby) out; 1 inf, Roll (the baby) in the sun.
2 To prepare (a packed lunch).
　1971 *Thompson Coll.* **cnGA**, To pack, "fix" a lunch, as in "she's done got where she don't even get up and roll his lunch no more." **1984** Wilder *You All Spoken Here* 86 **Sth**, *Roll your lunch:* Pack your lunch.

roll-a-bat n Also *roll-(to-)the-bat*　esp **S Atl**　Cf **hit-the-bat**
A bat-and-ball game; see quot 1966–68.
　1964 Tyler *If Morning Ever Comes* 150 **NC**, You weren't just a little boy to play roll-a-bat with any more. **1966–68** *DARE* (Qu. EE11, *Bat-and-ball games for just a few players [when there aren't enough for a regular game]*) Inf **GA54**, Roll-to-the-bat; **NC47**, Roll-a-bat; **SC3**, Roll-a-bat—fielders can roll or toss ball at the bat placed flat on the ground; if it hits it, the fielder goes to bat; if it's caught in the air or on first bounce, i.e. a batted ball or a missed pitch, the fielder goes to bat; no special positions except catcher and pitcher, who exchange places with the batter if they retire him; **SC31**, Roll-a-bat—batter must lay bat down after hitting; the one who fields ball can roll to it; if he hits bat he bats; **NC53**, Roll-the-bat.

rolla-cheese See **rolliche**

roll and toss v phr Also *roll and tumble*　esp **S Midl**
To be restless (in bed); to toss and turn.
　1929 in 1983 Taft *Blues Lyric Poetry* 208, And I rolled and I tumbled : and I cried the whole night long. **1942** McAtee *Dial. Grant Co.* IN 53 (as of 1890s), *Roll and toss* . . be restless in bed. **1956** McAtee *Some Dialect NC* 37, *Roll and toss.* . . be restless in bed. **c1960** *Wilson Coll.* **csKY**, *Roll and toss:* To be restless and "sick-abed". **1966** Barnes–Jensen *Dict. UT Slang* 36, *Roll and toss, to* . . to be restless. "That camp ground was so hard, that I rolled and tossed all night." **1967–70** *DARE* (Qu. OO32b, *If a person can't sleep steadily but keeps on waking* . . "*Every night this week I've _____ [several times].*") Infs **GA44, KY74, NC41**, Rolled and tumbled; **TN1, WI33**, Rolled and tossed. **2001** *NADS Letters* **cNY**, We say it: "I rolled & tossed all night"; so did my parents—Central NY, Syracuse area. I'm sure I've heard others use it.

rollaway See **rollway 2**

roll-bug n Cf **roly-poly 6**
=**sow bug.**

1999 in 2001 *DARE* File—Internet, I hear these phrases, and my mind closes up like a roll-bug. **2000** Launspach *ID Dial. Project* 5 **seID,** *(The little black insect that curls up when you touch it)* 1 inf, Roll bug.

roll dam See **rolling dam**

rolle bolle n, also attrib Also *rol(l)y-bol(l)y* [Cf Du *rollebol* in ref to any of several games] **chiefly Upper Missip Valley; in Dutch and Belgian settlement areas**

A game similar to lawn bowling or boccie, but using heavy disks instead of balls.

1939 FWP *Guide IL* 463 **nwIL,** In the portion of Henry County near Annawan, Atkinson, and Kewanee, Belgian settlers play a game called *rolle bolle.* The game, which is played with heavy discs of wood, combines certain features of bowling and horseshoe pitching. So popular is the game in the region that the Henry County Fair, held annually at Cambridge, features a Rolle Bolle Day. **1945** Le Sueur *North Star Country* 319 **MN, WI, nIA,** The Hollanders say there are no young men this year to play rolly-bolly, a Dutch game of horseshoe. **1947** Croy *Corn Country* 242, Garretson, South Dakota, was originally settled by Belgians and there still exist some of the manners, customs, and games of that country. Once a year, in the summer, there is "Roly-Boly Day," but such good times are had that it usually lasts two or three. "Roly-Boly" is a bit like horseshoes. **1998** *Star* (Kansas City MO) 5 June 28/2, The Rolle-Bolle competition . . involves tossing a black wheel-type disc at pins. The sport, sort of a cross between bowling and horseshoes, hails from Belgium. **2000** *NADS Letters,* My grandparents were Belgian and lived in Moline, Illinois. The East End Club in Moline was one of the centers of rolle bolle (We said "rolly bolly.") I remember watching the old guys play rolly bolly in the '50s and '60s but I think the game is still played there. The disks were rolled not tossed as you would toss a horseshoe. They were rolled toward a mark or an area at the other end of the lane. I think the lanes were clay, not dirt.

rollejee See **rolliche**

roll-'em-up n Cf **roly-poly 6**
=**sow bug.**

1966 *DARE* (Qu. R27, . . *Kinds of caterpillars or similar worms*) Inf NC24, Roll-'em-ups—rolls up in a tiny hard ball at a touch.

roller n[1] See **roller shade**

roller n[2] See **rolling** vbl n

roller bird n
=**blue jay 1.**

1956 Rayford *Whistlin' Woman* 229 **AL,** In the vicinity of Dothan, Alabama, bluejays are often called "roller birds," because when chinaberries are ripe, they sit in the trees and gorge themselves on chinaberries until they grow drunk. Then they tumble out of the trees and roll on the ground, and the cats creep out and eat them as they lie there.

roller blind See **roller shade**

roller broom n esp Nth

A carpet sweeper.

1971 *Today Show Letters* **neIL,** My mother from the South said "Carpet Sweeper"—in Chicago it was "Roller Broom." **2000** *NADS Letters* **WA** (as of 1930s), My maternal grandmother had a Bissell carpet sweeper she called a roller broom. It was a housing with two brushes that rotated when you pushed it back and forth and threw the dirt into a central holding area that you could then dump out. . . My grandmother came from Moweaqua, IL where my mother was born. I think they came to Washington state around 1920 but can't be sure about that. *Ibid* **PA,** My mom used to use this term [=*roller broom*] to describe a device like a broom. It rolled on rollers and picked up the dirt, then you tipped it over to empty it. She is in her 70's and grew up in PA. *Ibid* **MI,** A roller broom is a common term for a sweeper used in Detroit, particularly by the older generations of Polish descent. *Ibid* **TX, OK,** Roller-broom—I've heard this term used a couple of times in Texas, Oklahoma and the US expat community in Honduras (I believe the person I had in mind was from Minnesota). **2001** *Ibid* **NJ,** Roller broom. . . It's a mechanical device still in use (the cleaning lady here at my office uses one). It's not a vacuum cleaner or a regular broom, but a device on wheels with a long handle that, when pushed, rotates the bristles and causes it to brush up dirt. The power comes from the person pushing it. . . My mother used it frequently. She grew up in Maryland, and lived as an

adult in NJ & PA. *Ibid* **OR** (as of 1960s), My mother always used to call our carpet sweeper a roller broom. *Ibid* **IL, IN.**

roller cart n

A type of **log cart;** see quot.

1956 *AmSp* 31.282 **sAL** (as of c1900), Timber carts were of two kinds—roller carts and terry-rig carts. . . A roller cart was a two-wheeler and so called because it had on its hounds one or two cast-iron rollers each securely mounted and having on its barrel or body a place to attach a chain. At one end it had a ratchet arrangement and provisions for the insertion of a handspike, a "jacking stick," into its barrel or body. When the cart had been brought over the approximate center of a saw log, the operator with chains and jacking stick hoisted the log beneath the iron axle of the cart. Two good-sized logs were the usual load.

roller curtain See **roller shade**

roller-holley See **rolly-holey**

roller shade n Also *roller (blind),* ~ *curtain, roll shade*

An opaque window covering attached to a spring roller.

1941 *LANE* Map 327 *(Window shades)* 5 infs, **CT, RI, seMA,** Roller curtain(s); 1 inf, **nwCT,** Roller shades; 1 inf, **ceRI,** Roll shades; 1 inf, **seCT,** Rollers = window shades; 1 inf, **swCT,** Roller shades are recent. **1949** Kurath *Word Geog.* 28, The modern expression *roller shades* has taken its [=*blinds*] place in Philadelphia and among the Pennsylvania Germans. *Ibid* 52, Roller shades are a recent invention. The term *(roller) shades* has general currency in the Hudson Valley, the Virginia Piedmont, and the greater part of the Carolinas, and it is widely used in urban areas elsewhere. **1950** *WELS* *(Strips of stiff material that you pull down on the inside of a window to keep the light out)* 1 inf, **cwWI,** Roller shade—occasional. **1966–68** *DARE* (Qu. E12, *Pieces of stiff material that you pull down on the inside of a window to keep the sun out)* Infs **NC79, SC19,** Roller shades; **MA72, SD1,** Roller curtains. **1967** Faries *Word Geog. MO* 72, *Roller shades.* Only one-fourth of the [700] Missouri informants use the general term *roller shades* and its simplex *shades* for window coverings on rollers. . . *roller curtains, roller blinds* . . occur a few times. **1973** Allen *LAUM* 1.167 **Upper MW** (as of c1950), Roller curtain [4 infs, **MN, ND, SD**]. . . roller [1 inf, **MN**]. **1986** Pederson *LAGS Concordance Gulf Region* *(Window shades)* 7 infs, Roller shade(s); 2 infs, Roller curtains. **1988** Lincoln *Avenue* 47 **wNC** (as of c1940) [Black], Dr. Tait pulled the string on the roller shade that hung inside his front door until the sign saying *The Doctor is Out* was centered in the middle of the door glass.

roller towel n Also *rolling towel* **chiefly Nth, Midl, West**

An endless towel hung from a roller.

1845 *Knickerbocker* 25.444 **NEng,** Beside the window was the linen roller-towel. **1869** Stowe *Oldtown Folks* 263 **NEng,** We performed our morning ablutions, refreshing our faces and hands by a brisk rub upon a coarse rolling towel of brown homespun linen. **1882** Terhune *Eve's Daughters* 409, She had . . a roller-towel rack screwed upon the wall at one side. **1902** *Harper's Mth. Mag.* 104.977, [They] dried themselves on a common roller-towel. **1937** Sandoz *Slogum* 20 **NE,** They sloshed themselves with water in the row of tin basins along the wall and wiped noisily on the clean roller towels. **1963** Owens *Look to River* 19 **TX,** He stopped long enough to wet his face and hands and dry them on a roller towel. **1965–70** *DARE* (Qu. G17, . . *Kinds of towels*) 39 Infs, **Nth, Midl, West,** Roller towel; **MS73,** Rolling towel. **1986** Pederson *LAGS Concordance (Bath towel)* 1 inf, **swTN,** Roller towel—in the wall.

roller worm n [Because it lives in nests of rolled or tied leaves]

The larva of the long-tailed skipper (*Urbanus proteus*).

1899 U.S. Dept. Ag. *Yearbook for 1898* 259, A caterpillar known as the bean leaf-roller or "roller worm" is injurious in the Gulf States to leguminous plants. **1911** *Century Dict. Suppl., Long-tailed skipper,* an American hesperiid butterfly, *Eudamus proteus,* ranging from New York southward into Mexico. In the south its larva, known as the *roller-worm,* is a pest in vegetable-gardens, eating the leaves of beans, turnips, and cabbages. **1966–67** *DARE* (Qu. P6, . . *Kinds of worms* . . *used for bait)* Infs **GA1,** Roller worms—found in wet, decayed leaves; **SC32,** Roller worm—looks like a maggot; found near branches where leaves and sand are mixed together—one and one-half inches.

rolliche n Also *relliche, rolla-cheese, rollejee, rollichie, ruletji, rullichie* [Du *rolletje,* dimin of *rol* roll (in many spec senses, including that given below)] **NY, NJ** Cf **rullepolse**

A dish made of seasoned beef wrapped in tripe, and usu boiled, pickled, and cut into rounds.

1830 *Boston Eve. Transcript* (MA) 21 Dec 2/2 **NY,** If reading the above has given you the lock-jaw, why then certes, you will lose your share of the *oley cooks, ruletjis, smoked geese and sour krout.* **1847** (1852) Crowen *Amer. Cookery* 69 **NY,** Rolla-cheese.—Take the skirts of beef, cut it in narrow strips, and lay it, fat and lean, on pieces of prepared tripe, the rough side in, season with pepper and salt . . ; roll each piece of tripe up, with a portion of the meat in it . . ; draw the edges together, and sew them with a strong thread, making them in rolls; sew up the ends; after all are made, drop them into a pot of hot water, and let them boil gently, until a straw will easily penetrate them; then take them from the water, and lay them in a vessel or tub side by side, lay a board and weight over them, to press them flat; when cold keep them in vinegar and water. Cut them in thin slices, for breakfast, supper, or luncheon. **1848** Bartlett *Americanisms* 280, *Rullichies.* (Dutch.) Chopped meat stuffed into small bags of tripe, which are then cut into slices and fried. An old and favorite dish among the descendants of the Dutch in New York. **1881** Vanderbilt *Social Flatbush* 105 **Brooklyn NYC,** "Rolliches" were made of fat and lean beef cut in pieces somewhat larger than dice, highly seasoned, served in tripe, and boiled for several hours. These were then placed under a press and were eaten cold. **1895** *DN* 1.383 **NJ,** *Rollejees* [rɑlɪčiz]: chopped meat, stuffed in "sausageskins" to be sliced and cooked. **1896** (1968) Earle *Colonial NY* 143, Two purely Dutch dishes were *rolliches* and head cheese. [**a1949** (1964) Storms *Jersey Du. Vocab.* np, *Rull*—Roll. Rulletje—Sour meat.] **1949** Kurath *Word Geog.* 24, Some food terms of Dutch origin have spread beyond the Dutch area [=the Hudson Valley, Catskills, and upper Delaware] . . , but others, such as . . rollichies for meat roulades . . have probably always been Dutch family words and are disappearing fast. **1969** *DARE* Tape **NY220,** Of course, regarding food some of the old Dutch relliches ['rɛlɪčəz]. Do you know what relliches are? That's a meat dish. It's made from the stomach of a cow. The tripe had to be cleaned, which was a very long process, and then of course you used good beef in those days, not the kind you buy now. And my mother would fix it, sew it up in a ball, and put it in the juice—out where it's cold.

rollicky adj [Engl dial] Cf rollix

Boisterous; merry.

1854 *S. Lit. Messenger* 20.230, His cheerful, rollicky manner, and pleasant, kind tones revived the desponding and brought hope to the despairing. **1872** *Appletons' Jrl.* 8.157, But out of this simple, rollicky tune, the glamour of the voice wove a whole mocking world of rebuke. **1942** Berrey–Van den Bark *Amer. Slang* 278.20, *Hilarious.* . . rollicky. **1953** Randolph–Wilson *Down in Holler* 279 **Ozarks,** *Rollix.* . . To frolic, to carouse, to philander. . . There is an adjective, too, which sounds like *rollicky.* **1954** Tolbert *Bigamy Jones* 64 **wTX** (as of 1870s), Bigamy had given her the hat as a souvenir—"a souvenir of rollicky days," he said. **1959** Lahey–Hogan *As I Remember It* 27 **swKS** (as of 1894), But they were very rollicky that evening, I suppose because they had been confined in the house all day, owing to the cold outside.

rollies See rolls

rolling n

1 also attrib: =logrolling 1.

1819 in 1920 *WI Mag. Hist.* 3.463 **VT,** Attend a rolling bee this morning. **1843** (1916) Hall *New Purchase* 203 **IN,** Now, it is to a clearing the log-rolling, or, for brevity's sake, "a rolin," pertains. In . . the rolling the owner has all prostrate trunks cut into suitable lengths, and the bushy tops preserved for fuel to the log-heaps; still many trees remain to be prepared even on the grand rolling day. **1847** Howe *Hist. Coll. OH* 358, Many times were we called from six to eight miles to assist at a rolling or raising. **1922** Herndon *Centennial Hist. AR* 1.209, The trees were felled, cut or burned into lengths so that they could be handled, and then the neighbors were invited to the "rolling."

2a pl: =makings.

1931 *AmSp* 7.52 **Sth, SW** [Lumberjack lingo], "Rollins" is the tobacco for a cigarette. **1940** *AmSp* 15.213 [C.C.C. slang], The day before payday, the camp's 'smoking' has become scarce and 'rollings' or 'makings' are at a premium. **1941** *AmSp* 16.168 [Army slang], *Rollings.* Cigarette tobacco.

b Transf: the amount of tobacco required to make one cigarette.

1913 *Collier's* 1 Feb 28, Forty "rollings" in each 5 cent muslin sack [of tobacco].

rolling vbl n

=barrel-dogging; hence n roller.

1954 *Courier–Jrl.* (Louisville KY) 25 Apr Mag sec 8/1, Barrel dogging—also called steaming, burning, sweating and rolling—really has come into its own. **1984** Wilder *You All Spoken Here* 138 **Sth,** Barrel dogger, steamer, roller, sweater, burner: One who steams used whiskey barrels, fresh from legal distilleries, to extract whiskey that has been absorbed in the aging process in the white oak barrel staves.

rolling adj See rolling fat

rolling bank n Cf bank (at banking ground(s))

=rollway 1.

1901 NY Forest Fish & Game Comm. *Annual Rept. for 1900* 259, Logs . . were cut and skidded in the fall, were hauled during the winter to the banks of the streams, where they were piled in huge tiers on the "banking ground," as it was called on the Susquehanna, or "rolling bank" in Northern New York.

rolling dam n Also roll dam

Esp in logging: a dam designed so that the surplus water flows over the crest.

1815 Lit. & Philos. Soc. NY *Trans.* 1.151, A rolling dam was made over the river, and a canal of one hundred rods was cut. **1905** U.S. Forest Serv. *Bulletin* 61.45 [Logging terms], *Rolling dam.* A dam for raising the water in a shallow stream. It has no sluiceways, but a smooth top of timber over which, under a sufficient head of water, logs may slide or roll. (Gen[eral]) **1913** Bryant *Logging* 350, "Roll dams" which have no gates or sluiceways are also built to raise the stream level. The water and logs pass over the crest of the dam. **1916** in 1924 Gray *Songs ME Lumberjacks* 22, He started out to break a jam / That had formed upon a rolling dam. **1957** Beck *Folkl. ME* 230, Dams were erected—some, known as "rolling" dams, increased the depth of the water and allowed the logs to roll over them. **1969** Sorden *Lumberjack Lingo* 97 **NEng, Gt Lakes,** *Roll dam*—A dam built without gates. The logs floating over the dam caused a roll after which the dam took its name.

rolling fat adj phr Also rolling

Very fat.

1861 *S. Lit. Messenger* 33.140 **VA,** When I sen dis horse away, he was rolling fat. **1924** *DN* 5.295 **csNH,** *Rolling fat.* . . Extremely fat. **1937** in Lib. of Congress *Amer. Memory: WPA Life Hist.* (Internet) **cTX,** The hogs were always rolling fat from feeding on the pecans and acorns that grew in abundance in those bottoms. **1942** Perry *Texas* 65, His hogs . . had greedily devoured a crop of corn and were "rolling" fat. **1966** *DARE* (Qu. X50, *Names or nicknames for a person who is very fat*) Inf **IL50,** Rolling. **1967** Green *Horse Tradin'* 111 **TX,** The man had a good bay horse, rolling fat, with a few cockle burrs in his mane.

rolling store n

A wagon or truck modified to serve as a mobile store.

1937 Hall Coll. **wNC, eTN,** *Rolling store.* . . A small store on wheels which came to mountain communities. **1938** FWP *Guide CT* 409 **cwCT,** The traveling blacksmith and the rolling store are often seen in this back-country, catering to the needs of the farm folk who, facing starvation, still cling to rough hilltop acreage. **1941** Writers' Program *Guide AR* 379 **seAR,** Some of the trade, however, is carried on by "rolling stores," necessary institutions in rural Arkansas. These trucks, outfitted with stocks of manufactured goods, groceries, and farm implements, chug up to the farmers' doors. The drivers take payment in kind. **1966–68** *DARE* (Qu. U6, *Someone who sells vegetables or other articles from a wagon or truck, going from house to house*) Inf **FL26,** Rolling store—sell dry goods and/or groceries; go out in country; **GA23,** Rolling store—small items of all kinds. **1970** *Thompson Coll.* **cnAL** (as of 1930s), *Rolling store* . . a store on a truck chassis. **1988** Palmer *Lang. W. Cent. MA* 49, [rolɪŋ stɔr]—That used to come after the store left [closed down]. We used to trade blueberries for whatever we wanted. . . it was like a big U-Haul truck, with shelves in it, and it came to your door. You bought what you wanted off of it. They'd buy, too. That was in the late 20's. **1988** *DARE* File **nwMA** (as of 1915), The wagon used by one who sold vegetables or other articles door to door was called the rolling store. **1989** Flynt *Poor But Proud* 80 **ceAL** (as of 1910–30), The monopoly of the country merchant was occasionally interrupted by the "rolling store." Sometimes operated by a Jewish peddler who added an exotic dimension to rural life, the rolling store was a wagon or truck modified as a mobile store. It roamed backcountry dirt roads, offering cloth, needles, thread, and a variety of other sundries and food-stuffs.

rolling tier n Cf rolling bank
=rollway 1.

1844 *N. Amer. Rev.* 58.333 **ME,** But who could impeach his integrity, since the proprietor's *sealer* [*DARE* Ed: perh error for *scaler*] came to the *rolling-tier.* [Footnote: Place at the stream-end of his road, which he prepares in order to get his logs from the land upon the ice.] **1870** *Overland Mth.* 5.57 **WA,** With a shout and a spur from his goad, the team all pull together, and the log is soon hauled to the "rolling-tier."

rolling towel See roller towel

roll-in-the-hole n Also *roll-in-hole* Cf rolly-holey
A marble game; see quots.

1935 *AmSp* 10.159 **seNE,** *Roll-in-the-hole.* . . Played entirely with *commies,* the object being to roll them into a small hole some distance away. The first marble in takes all that have rolled away. **1968** *DARE* (Qu. EE7, . . *Kinds of marble games*) Inf **NJ53,** Roll-in-hole—make a hole in the ground and try to roll marbles into it from behind a line; winner is one with most marbles in the hole; he takes all the others; hole about 5 inches in diameter; roll from at least 10 feet.

rollix v [Var of *rollick*] Cf *mommix, mummox* (at mammock v), rallack, rollicky
1927 *DN* 5.476 **Ozarks,** *Rollix.* . . To carouse, or to philander. "Doc Yancey he jes' lef' his woman at home an' went a-rollixin' 'round th' country."

roll landing n Cf rollway 1
A **landing 1** designed so that logs may be rolled directly onto railroad cars.

1958 McCulloch *Woods Words* 152 **Pacific NW,** *Roll landing*—a. A landing built to handle long logs; had big brow logs down both sides of the track level with the car bunks. b. Sometimes used to mean a landing where logs were still rolled on cars, at the time when overhead loading first came into use. **1962** *AmSp* 37.134 **nwCA,** *Roll landing.* . . A landing with big logs down both sides of the track which was level with the car bunks—used to roll logs onto the train cars.

rolls exclam Also *rollies, rollsies*
In marble play: a call that permits or requires a marble to be rolled; see quots.

c1970 Wiersma *Marbles Terms* **swMI,** *Rollies.* . . A call made by the player which allows him to roll his marble into his opponent's piece rather than use the traditional stand-and-throw shot. *Ibid* **swMI,** *Rolls.* . when the opponent['] s marble is close to the intended marble, you can call "rolls" and he must roll his marble instead of tossing it. Eg. "'Rolls' on you; yours is too close." *No rolls* . . in the above situation (rolls), if the opponent calls "no rolls" before "rolls" is called he may play through as he wishes. Eg. I called "no rolls"—it['] s my play! **1973** Ferretti *Marble Book* 51, *Rollsies!* A defensive call to force a player to roll his shooter in a bowling marbles game rather than throw it.

roll shade See roller shade

rollsies See rolls

roll the bed v phr Cf roll and toss
To toss and turn (in bed).

1938 Matschat *Suwannee R.* 161 **neFL, seGA,** But one dark night, when she rolled the bed, a-worrin', a bright cloud 'peared outside her window. **1965** *DARE* File **sWV** (as of 1930s), *Roll the bed.* . . Sleep poorly, toss and turn. "I rolled the bed all night."

roll-(to-)the-bat See roll-a-bat

rollway n

1 In logging: a natural or prepared slope down which logs may be rolled; an area on or adjacent to such a slope where logs are stacked prior to transport; a stack of logs awaiting transport. Cf **banking ground(s), landing 1, rolling bank, roll landing, skidway**

1855 in 1882 MI Laws *Genl. Statutes* 1.994, Such corporations shall have authority to make and construct all . . necessary rollways. *Ibid* 995, It shall be lawful for such company to cause such rollways or jams to be broken. **1888** *Scribner's Mag.* 4.655 **neNY,** The logs . . are piled

in great roll-ways either on the ice or on a high bank. **1895** *Outing* 26.392 **MI,** The banks . . were . . lined with roll-ways, piled high with thousands of logs. **1902** White *Blazed Trail* 92 **MI,** The rollways are then broken, and the saw logs floated down the river to the mill. **1905** U.S. Forest Serv. *Bulletin* 61.41 [Logging terms], *Landing.* . . A place to which logs are hauled or skidded preparatory to transportation by water or rail. . . Syn[onyms]: bank, banking ground, log dump, rollway, yard. **1913** Bryant *Logging* 332, Where water storage is used the track is built along the bank of the stream or pond, or else extended over the water on piling. In the former case it is necessary to construct an inclined rollway over which the logs may be rolled into the water. This consists of a framework composed of three parallel sets of stringers . . which extend along the water's edge for from 400 to 600 feet. . . Heavy . . timbers . . are placed on top of and at right angles to the stringers, and serve as a bed over which the logs are rolled. **1926** Rickaby *Ballads Shanty-Boy* 236 **MI, MN, WI** (as of a1920), *Roll-way.* Logs or trimmed trunks laid down, twelve or fifteen feet apart, to receive the logs piled at the landings. They facilitated piling or decking the logs through the winter and breaking them out and rolling them into the river in the spring. **1942** Beck *Songs MI Lumberjacks* 46, It was on the first of April / the birds began to sing;/ We began to break the rollways,/ So I thought it must be spring. **1958** McCulloch *Woods Words* 153 **Pacific NW,** *Rollway*—a. A landing where logs are piled up waiting loading or river driving. b. In some places a log dump is called a rollway. **1961** Labbe–Goe *Railroads* 259 **Pacific NW,** *Rollway:* A sloping deck of poles or logs, usually at a landing, for storing logs. Logs were rolled aboard the cars by hand and by gravity.

2 also *rollaway:* An outside entrance to a cellar. **chiefly NEng, esp ME**

1901 *DN* 2.146 **sME coast,** *Roll-way.* . . A cellar-way. **1904** Day *Kin o' Ktaadn* 9 **ME,** Acres poured their bounty through barn doors and down the cellar roll-way. **1907** *DN* 3.249 **eME,** *Rollway.* . . An outside cellar-entrance with nearly horizontal double doors. "They laid planks from the top of the rollway down through the cellar-door into the cellar; then they rolled the hogshead in." **1909** *DN* 3.415 **nME,** *Rollway,* or *rollaway.* . . The outside entrance to a cellar. **1910** *DN* 3.454 **seVT,** *Roll-way.* . . The door-way of a cellar usually having the door-sill below the surface of the ground, and a short flight of steps or a gentle incline leading down. **1966–70** *DARE* (Qu. D20, *Names for a sloping outside cellar door*) Inf **ME15,** Rollaway; rollway; **WV14,** Rollaway.

rolly-bolly See rolle bolle

rolly-holey n Also *roly-pol(l)y,* **chiefly S Midl, esp KY** *rollyhole;* for addit varr see quots **scattered, but chiefly Sth, S Midl** See Map on p. 630 Cf **hole n 4, holey n 1, knuck n[1] 2a, roly-poly 1**
A marble game that usu involves a series of holes into which marbles must be rolled in sequence.

1892 Smith *Farm & Fireside* 267 **GA,** What glorious sport in playing town-ball and bull-pen and cat and rolly-hole and knucks and sweepstakes. **1906** *DN* 3.153 **nwAR,** *Roly-holy.* . . A game of marbles in which the players roll from one hole to another in a series of holes. *Ibid* 154 **nwAR,** *Roly-poly.* . . A game of marbles. **1915** *DN* 4.189 **swVA,** *Roly-hole* . . =*knucks,* a game of marbles. **1940** *Recreation* (NY) 34.110, Games of marbles played throughout the country . . Roller holley. **1947** Lomax *Advent. Ballad Hunter* 14 **TX** (as of c1880), We children never played games on Sunday, not even . . roley-holey. **1957** *Sat. Eve. Post Letters* **wKY** (as of early 1930s), "Roly-holy". . . resembled croquet. Three holes in a straight line about a yard apart were dug, and a starting line drawn about a yard ahead of the first hole. The first player shot for the first hole; if he made it he was allowed to move his marble a span and shoot for the second hole and so on until he missed. When a player got to the third hole he started back down the line. . . The first player to make the circuit three times won the game. **1965–70** *DARE* (Qu. EE7, . . *Kinds of marble games*) 41 Infs, **scattered, but esp Sth, S Midl,** Rolly-holey; 12 Infs, **chiefly S Midl, esp KY,** Rolly-hole; **AR52,** Holey-rolly—you dig a chain of holes in the ground. **1968–70** *DARE* Tape **AL39,** [Inf:] That's rolly-holey, where you made little holes . . one here and one around like this . . and you'd shoot . . to roll the marbles in the hole. . . [Aux Inf:] And you went to one and then to the other . . and you had to follow a specific pattern. . . You had these certain holes to go to . . before you got back. [Inf:] It was kinda like playing croquet; **IA37,** Rolly-holey marbles was, you drew a circle about a foot in diameter, took your heel and made a hole in the center of the circle. Then you stood back about ten or fifteen feet and you pitched marbles to see who could get 'em into the hole in the center of the circle.

And you kept pitching marbles until . . someone got one in the, roll in the hole. And then whoever was the first to do that picked up all the marbles that were on the ground around the hole; **TN**37, One was called rolly-holey. There were three holes as I recall them, and boys would shoot these marbles with their fingers, and try to see who could get in the three holes first. And the one that accomplished this and got back, made the three holes and back, he was the winner; **TX**99, And the other one was rolly-holey, where you'd dig five little holes in the ground so far apart, . . then each one would just shoot and try to hit those holes and the one that hit the most holes won the game; **TX**100, Mostly we would play what you call rolly-holey. . . You'd dig your bunch of holes there, and you'd shoot at those holes and it would count so much, you know, you'd have points on it, you know. **1973** Ferretti *Marble Book* 86, Rolly-polly. This five-hole marbles game was popular in the Philadelphia–Central New Jersey area. Five holes, up to four inches deep, are dug in a line, three feet apart. The players shoot from a starting line about 10 feet from the first hole and make their way through the five holes. Once through they become "Killer" or "Poison" and can shoot their fellow players out of the game. **1986** Pederson *LAGS Concordance,* 4 infs, **swGA, cwAR**, Roly-holey—marble game (*or* marble-playing word); 1 inf, **cnAL**, Roly-poly—shoot marbles into a series of holes; 1 inf, **ceLA**, Roly-poly—game with marbles; 1 inf, **csTX**, Roly-poly—roll marbles into hole.

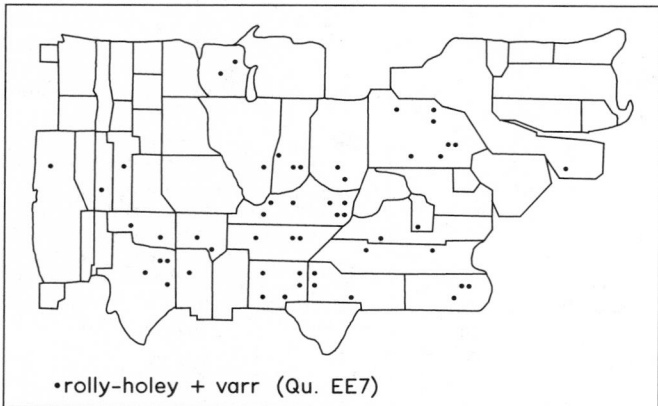

•rolly-holey + varr (Qu. EE7)

rolly-polly See **roly-poly**

roly-boly n[1] See **rolle bolle**

roly-boly n[2] Cf **rolly-holey**
A marble game; see quot.
    1968 *DARE* (Qu. EE7, . . *Kinds of marble games*) Inf **IN**49, Roly-boly; **LA**25, Roly-boly—three marbles in a small ring, roll for a line and roll it back to shoot.

roly-hole See **rolly-holey**

Roly Holer n Also *Roly Holy* [Joc metath of *Holy Roller*]
    1967–70 *DARE* (Qu. CC4, . . *Nicknames . . for various religions or religious groups*) Inf **KY**84, Roly Holers, Holy Rollers—Pentecostal or Holiness; **TX**37, Roly Holers; **LA**11, Roly Holy; Roly Holies; **LA**14, Roly Holies.

roly-holy n[1] See **rolly-holey**

Roly Holy n[2] See **Roly Holer**

roly-polly See **rolly-holey**

roly-poly n Also sp *roley-poley, rolly-polly* [OED2 *roly-poly* sb. 2.a "The name of various games, in most of which the rolling of a ball is the chief feature"; 1713 →]
1 also *rol(e)y-hol(e)y, roly-hole:* A game in which each player stands by a small hole in the ground, one player tries to roll a ball into one of these holes, and the player into whose hole the ball rolls tries to hit one of the other players with the ball. Cf **dolly in the blanket, nigger baby** n **2a**
    1891 *Jrl. Amer. Folkl.* 4.234 **Brooklyn NYC**, *Roley poley.* . . Each player digs a hole three or four inches in diameter. If this is impossible, hats are used instead of holes in the ground. A medium-sized rubber ball is used, and one of the players stands at a distance of about twenty feet,

and tries to roll it into one of the hats or holes. All the others stand by their holes; and when the ball enters one of them, its owner must throw the ball at the player nearest to him. Meantime, when a boy sees the ball rolling into any near hole, he will run away to escape being hit. The boy who is hit must put a stone into his hole; but if the thrower is unsuccessful in hitting any one, the stone must go into his own hole. The game continues until one of the players gets ten stones in his hole. Then he has to stand up with his back against a wall or fence, and let each boy take three shots at him with the rubber ball. **1896** *DN* 1.423 **IA, cNY**, *Roly-poly:* a game played with a rubber ball and small holes dug in the ground. **1897** (1952) McGill *Narrative* 32 **ceSC**, In "Roley Holey," in which each had a hole dug in the ground, we stand around them, as a player rolls the ball confined between two poles, and before it settles in any hole the more excitable boys dash away, and being called to, return only to find the ball in their hole, and the other players beyond the reach of his ball as he throws. For every out a chip is put in his hole, three outs putting you out the game. The last in the game being the winner, has a ten step throw at the open hand of each player, resting on the wall of the house. **1899** Champlin–Bostwick *Young Folks' Games* 585, *Roly-poly, or nine holes,* a game of ball played by any number of persons, generally nine. As many holes as there are players . . are dug about a foot apart, the whole forming a square. **1940** *Hench Coll.* **ceNC**, Rolly-polly. . . Boys dug as many holes . . in a row as there were boys. Each boy was given a hole, called his hole. Then some one chosen rolled the ball and it fell into one of the holes. Immediately the boy whose hole it was hurriedly picked up the ball and threw at any of the other players that he could. . . If he hit him, he (the thrower) in turn ran away as fast as he could, because the one hit had to get the ball and hit some one else. **1967–68** *DARE* (Qu. EE16, *Hiding games that start with a special, elaborate method of sending the players out to hide*) Inf **LA**34, Roly-poly; (Qu. EE33, . . *Outdoor games . . that children play*) Inf **SC**31, Roly-holy—each man digs a ball-sized hole; one rolls the ball, and if it goes in a hole he can throw it at that man whose hole it is and try to hit him. **1968** *DARE* Tape **LA**34, Roly-poly is a game you play with a ball. . . You dig a hole in the ground, about the same size as the ball, for each player. And then you get two people on the end to roll the ball. Now everyone is standing alongside their hole. When they roll the ball, if it would fall in a person's hole, he would have to put his foot over his hole, count to ten, and say "stop." In the meantime, the others would be running for a good place to hide. Now when he'd holler "stop," the player could swivel more or less on one foot, but he had to stay more or less stationary in that one spot and the fella would throw the ball at him and try to hit him with it. **1986** Pederson *LAGS Concordance,* 1 inf, **swAL**, Roly-poly—dig holes; run; throw ball at others; 1 inf, **swMS**, Roly-hole [Pederson: =poly]—game; rolling ball into holes.

2 See **rolly-holey**.

3 A game resembling hopscotch played with a ball; see quots.
    1957 *Sat. Eve. Post Letters* **Detroit MI**, *Roly-poly*—Divide 2 concrete squares of the sidewalk in 8 smaller squares, with chalk; number them 1–8. Roll ball first to square #1 & bounce ball around rest of squares, etc. *Ibid* **Providence RI** (as of c1927), *Roly-poly*—A sort of cross between hopscotch and a bouncing ball game. Using the blocks of a cement walk, preferably two wide by three long, we played "oneses, twoses and threeses" up to "sixes" by rolling a tennis ball into one square after the other by set rules about stepping on lines, balancing on one foot etc. **1998** *DARE* File **NYC** (as of 1950s), This was a girls' game called *roly-poly* . . played usually by two or three with a ball, preferably a pink Spalding, on 6 numbered squares. It was rather like hopscotch in that you had to enter each box in turn, but instead of throwing down a small object, you had to roll the ball into the right box, bounce it the right number of times and proceed to the next box in the specified manner: walking, jumping, hopping as the game went on.

4 A meat dish consisting of a flattened, filled, and rolled-up steak, or of meat and vegetables rolled up in a casing of dough; see quots.
    1890 James *Mother James' Cooking* 60, *Roly Poly.* Procure a good round steak, and after beating thoroughly well, lay flat on board; make a dressing of Irish potato, . . bread crumbs . . [and seasonings]. Spread this mixture on the steak, roll over and over like a jelly cake, and fasten with skewers or sewing. Place in a baking tin with a little water, place in a hot oven. **1967–69** *DARE* (Qu. H44) Inf **WI**76, Roly-poly—(Scandinavian dish) made with beef flank (or veal); cut, trim, put in pork, roll up and sew, put in salt brine, then boil, and press it with heavy stone; (Qu. H45, *Dishes made with meat, fish, or poultry that everybody around here would know, but that people in other places might not*) Inf **CO**47, Roly-poly—boiled meat and vegetable roll; pastry dough rolled out flat (suet

in the dough), filled with meat and vegetables (cubed), rolled up and placed in muslin or cheesecloth bag, placed in a kettle of simmering water on the back of a cookstove for at least five hours; sliced and broth served on or with [it]. **2000** *NADS Letters* **Long Is NY,** Roly-poly: this is what we called rouladen (German dish) in our household when we were small. This may just be a children's word, though.

5 A confection, as:

a also attrib: A rectangle made of dough that is spread with fruit or preserves, rolled up, and baked, steamed, or boiled. **chiefly Nth**

1895 (1900) Arnold *Century Cook Book* 443, Roly-Poly Pudding. . . [S]pread it [=dough] with any kind of berries. . . Then roll it, and tie it in a cloth, . . and boil or steam it. **1920** Kander *Settlement Cook Book* 287 **seWI,** *Roly Poly*—Make a dough. . . Roll out ½ inch thick. Spread with chopped apples, raisins, sugar and cinnamon, or with jam; roll. . . [B]ake in a hot oven, basting often, with the sauce in the pan. **1939** Wolcott *Yankee Cook Book* 198 **NEng,** *Rhubarb Roly Poly.* . . Knead [dough] on slightly floured board and roll ⅛-inch thick. Spread with rhubarb, dot generously with butter, sprinkle with sugar and roll like a jelly roll. Bake in a moderate oven. **1940** Brown *Amer. Cooks* 389 **MA,** *Roly-Poly Puddings*—Prepare biscuit dough same as for Blackberry Roll, spread with any desired ripe or cooked fruit, roll like a jelly roll, and sew pudding in cloth. . . Boil or steam 1 hour. Cherries make delicious roly-poly. **1952** Tracy *Coast Cookery* 153 **NY,** Peach Poly. . . Roll as a jelly roll. . . Place on clean muslin . . and wrap loosely. . . Place on a rack in boiling water to cover. **c1965** Randle *Cookbooks* (Ask Neighbor) 4.73 **neOH,** *Raisin Roly Poly.* . . Roll up the dough. . . Place in buttered pan, and pour over 1 and 1½ [sic] cups of cold water. . . Put in hot oven. **1967** *DARE* (QR, near Qu. H45) Inf **CO47,** [FW:] Inf's mother made a jelly-filled roly-poly on the same basic principle [as described in **4** above]. **2000** *NADS Letters* **csIA** (as of c1940), My grandmother made a dish with rhubarb she called Roly Poly. *Ibid* **CO,** My family uses the term roly-poly. A roly-poly is made using leftover pie crust scraps. After the pies are made, you take the extra pie dough and roll it out flat. You then sprinkle it with cinammon [sic] and sugar and roll it up like a jelly-roll and then slice it into one inch thick pieces. They form sort of a snail shape after they are baked. *Ibid* **NYC,** My Great-Grandmother used to use the term *Roly-Poly* to describe her Apple Schtreudel. It was your basic long, somewhat flattened pastry filled with an unknown mixture of apple, sliced nuts and other sugary indredients. She was a Russian Jew who was probably born a bit before the turn of the 20th century. She lived in New York City for at least half her life until she died around 1970. *Ibid* **RI,** My mother (she's 45) always made "roly-poly"s [sic] by making a dough like a pie crust, rolling it out flat. Then she would sprinkle cinnamon, sugar, and sometimes raisins on it. She would then roll it up and cut slits all along it, but not cut it all the way through. She would then bake it, let it cool and cut the pieces through all the way to make little pieces called "roly-polys". *Ibid* **wMA,** Roly-poly—I seem to recall hearing this used when I was a boy visiting relatives in Lee, (Western) Massachusetts, in the fifties. It was not a food item I was familiar with, but I had the impression that it referred to a sort of jelly roll from my peers (6–8 years old). **2001** *NADS Letters,* My wife uses the term "roly-poly" to refer to miniature "cinnamon roll"-like items made with leftover pie crust dough. The dough is rolled flat, sprinkled with cinnamon and sugar, then rolled into a cylinder, which is then cut into short sections and baked.

b See quots.

2000 *NADS Letters,* I used to make blackberry roly-poly in NC in the early 80's. I think I was taught to make it by our next-door-neighbor, a farmer's wife in her late 60s or early 70s. You take blackberries and sugar and cook them in a saucepan, and then drop biscuit dough into it. It was like a cobbler, but done on the stovetop, not baked. *Ibid* **cePA,** A "roly-poly" is an apple dumpling, composed of a peeled, cored apple baked in its own little pie crust, and usually served with ice cream. (Rural PA near Quakertown, 1972–80). **2001** *Ibid* **csAL** (as of 1950s), Roly-Poly was, when I was a boy, a cathead biscuit with a hole poked in it with your finger and then filled with cane syrup. That was back in the fifties.

6 also *roly-poly bug:* **=sow bug.**

1968 *DARE* FW Addit **New Orleans LA,** Roly-poly—alternate term for the little bugs with a lot of legs that roll up into a ball. **1986** Pederson *LAGS Concordance,* 1 inf, **csTX,** Roly-poly bugs. **1994** *DARE* File **KY,** We called pill bugs roley poleys. . . Or sow bugs. *Ibid* **LA,** Growing up in LA of Arkansas hillbilly heritage, surrounded by other Arkies and Okies in Wilmington . . I called them sow bugs as the 'serious' name, roly polies as a kind of 'cute' name. *Ibid* **MS,** That crit-

ter that Wayne wrote about, that curls up when you touch it—looks like a trilobyte, right?—is a sow bug around here. . . No, no—it's a rolypoly! **1998** *Ibid* **nwLA,** A small gray worm with a hard shell . . commonly lives under damp rocks in the south. When you turn the rock over they roll into a ball. Hence they are called *roley-poleys.* **2000** Launspach *ID Dial. Project* 5 **seID,** *(The little black insect that curls up when you touch it)* 15 infs, Roly poly bug. **2000** *NADS Letters,* 8 **Sth, S Midl,** 5 **NCent, Cent,** 4 **CA,** 3 **NEast,** Roly-poly.

romal n Also *ramole* [Var of Span *ramal* a strand (of a cord)] **West**

A whip usu braided to the end of a pair of reins.

1920 *DN* 5.83 **NW,** Ramole. Whip used for driving cattle while riding horseback. **1922** Rollins *Cowboy* 143 **West,** The reins . . were, at the saddle end, either "tied," *i.e.,* fastened together (if so, not uncommonly continuing into a flexible whip which thus attached was called a "romal"), or else they were left "untied." **1927** (1944) Russell *Trails Plowed Under* 2, Texas an' California . . cowpunchers . . west of the Rockies rangin' north. . . were generally strong on pretty, usin' plenty of hoss' jewelry . . instead of a quirt, [they] used a romal, or quirt braided to the end of the reins. **1932** Bentley *Spanish Terms* 191, *Ramal* English modification, *romal.* . . From *rama,* branch. A thong usually braided and divided into lashes, attached to the saddle or reins and used as a "quirt." **1940** Writers' Program *Guide NV* 75, The bridle, consisting of headstall, bit, and reins, has several appendages—the *bozal* or braided rope band, the *romal,* a heavy whip attached to the end of the reins. **1953** *Western Folkl.* 12.185, In the West the bridle reins were woven together to form a romal, used as a quirt. **1964** Jackman–Long *OR Desert* 392, *Romal*—A weighted end to joined reins.

Roman bean n Cf **cranberry bean**

See quots.

1968–70 *DARE* (Qu. I14, *Kinds of beans that you eat in the pod before they're dry*) Inf **PA135,** Roman bean; (Qu. I17, *Beans . . that are dark red when they are dry*) Inf **PA235,** Roman beans. **1998** (acc) ID Dept. Ag. Bean Commission *Varieties* (Internet), *Cranberry* [bean]—Deep red markings, pink skin. A favorite for Italian cuisine. Also known as Roman beans. Loses streaks when cooked.

Roman cannon n **Sth, S Midl** See Map

A Roman candle or similar firework.

1965–70 *DARE* (Qu. FF28, . . *Kinds of fireworks;* not asked in early QRs) 10 Infs, **Sth, S Midl,** Roman cannons; (Qu. FF14, . . *Kinds of firecrackers*) Infs **GA28, KY5,** Roman cannons; **KY23,** Roman cannons—old-fashioned. [9 of 12 total Infs comm type 5, 10 gs educ] **c1991** in 2001 *DARE* File—Internet **cKY,** When I was growing up, at my uncle George Daughtery's store, there was always a big crowd of boys, and they was shooting firecrackers and Roman cannons. We would have those Roman cannon fights, shoot at one another. **2000** *NADS Letters* **nwFL, sAL,** We always used . . to diffentiate [sic] between a roman candle, a firecracker which creates beautiful colors but no sound, and a roman cannon, a firecracker with the same kind of color as a roman candle but with a loud bang. I am 32 years old. My mother, father and maternal grandparents all used this term. It came up during the 4th of July—naturally—at our beach house in Northwest Florida. The people at the beach always seemed to use this differentiation too. By the way, several people I know in South Alabama use this differentiation as well. *Ibid* **cMS** (as of c1980), I was living in Jackson, Mississippi . . and some

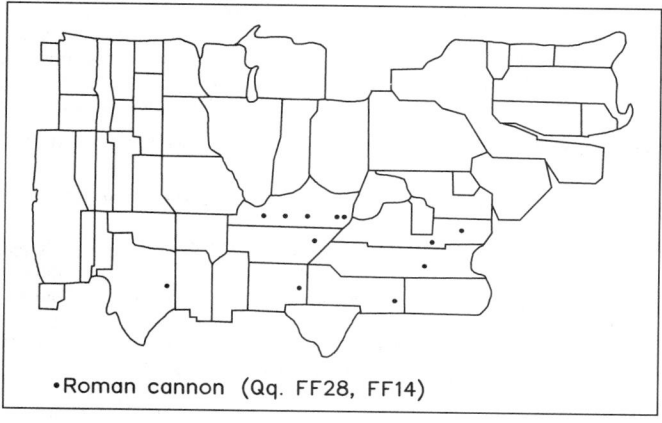

•Roman cannon (Qq. FF28, FF14)

kids across the street called the Roman candle fireworks "Roman cannons." *Ibid* **seVA,** Roman cannon . . [used by] old people. It is the same as a roman candle. **2001** *Ibid* **csTN** (as of 1940s), As a boy . . Roman cannon was the only name I ever heard for the firework. I had to relearn the name as Roman candle after growing up and moving away.

romance v

1 See quots. [Cf *EDD* romance v. 2 "To exaggerate" and 3. "To be delirious"]

1903 *DN* 2.327 **seMO,** *Romance.* . . To talk extravagantly; to utter nonsense. Often said of a person who is 'flighty' with fever. 'His fever riz and he got to romancin.' **1907** *DN* 3.235 **nwAR,** *Romance.* . . To talk extravagantly; to talk in delirium.

2 also with *around:* To play; to loaf. [Cf *EDD* romance v. 5 "To play in a foolish manner; to caper around"]

1902 *DN* 2.244 **sIL,** *Romance.* . . To play sportively, as children. 'They're jes romancin.[']' **1952** Brown *NC Folkl.* 1.585, *Romance around.* . . To loaf.—Central and east.

Roman wormwood n Also *Roman wormweed*

A **ragweed 2** (here: *Ambrosia artemisiifolia*).

1784 in 1785 Amer. Acad. Arts & Sci. *Memoirs* 1.489, *Ambrosia* . . Conot-Weed. Roman Wormweed. . . It is used in antisceptic fomentations. **1814** Bigelow *Florula Bostoniensis* 221, Ambrosia elatior. *L. Tall Ambrosia.* Roman Wormwood. **1892** Coulter *Botany W. TX* 210, *A[mbrosia] artemisiaefolia* . . Roman wormwood. . . A common weed of waste grounds. **1937** St. John *Flora SE WA & ID* 411, *Ambrosia artemisiifolia* . . var. *elatior* . . Roman Wormwood. . . It produces large quantities of pollen, and this is a frequent cause of hay fever. **1966–69** *DARE* (Qu. S20, *A common weed that grows on open hillsides: It has velvety green leaves close to the ground, and a tall stalk with small yellow flowers on a spike at the top*) Inf **ME20,** Wormwood . . Roman wormwood? (Qu. S21, . . *Weeds . . that are a trouble in gardens and fields*) Infs **ME12, 14,** Roman wormwood; **MA68,** Roman wormwood = ragweed.

romeo n Cf **juliet**

A type of slipper, usu for men.

1895 (1969) Montgomery Ward *Catalogue* 514, Men's Leather Sole Romeo. . . This slipper is made of one piece of black felt. . . Ladies' Romeo. . . Made of toilet felt. **1926** Ferber *Show Boat* 5, A brown cashmere skirt, very bustled and bunchy; a pair of scuffed tan kid bedroom slippers (men's) of the sort known as romeos. **1952** Bissell *Monongahela* 205 **PA,** While sitting on the bunk pulling on your romeos you wonder what side of the family this madness comes from that makes you live like this. **1965–70** *DARE* (Qu. W21, *Soft shoes that people wear only inside the house*) 10 Infs, **scattered,** Romeos. **1997** *DARE* File **seWI** (as of c1965), My father was very fond of his slippers, which he called "romeos." These were mahogany-colored leather with elastic panels in the sides.

romero n [MexSpan < Span "rosemary"] CA

A **blue curls 1** (here: usu *Trichostema lanatum*).

[**1878** *Amer. Naturalist* 12.654, *Trichostemma lanatum.*—By Mexicans and the Indians of Southern California, it is called *Romero.* It is used by them to impart a dark or black color to the hair, and to promote its growth.] [**1897** Parsons *Wild Flowers CA* 316, Among the Spanish-Californians it [=*Trichostema lanatum*] is known altogether by the musical name of "Romero," and is one of their most highly valued medicinal herbs, being considered a panacea for many troubles. Fried in olive oil, it becomes an ointment which alleviates pain and cures ulcers; dried and reduced to powder, it is a snuff very efficacious for catarrh; and made into a tincture it is used as a liniment.] **1959** Munz–Keck *CA Flora* 693, *T[richostema] lanatum* . . Woolly Blue-curls. Romero.

rommegrot n [Norw *rømmegrøt* cream porridge] esp MN, WI

A porridge or pudding of which cream is the principal ingredient.

1951 Tufford *Scandinavian Recipes* 25 **MN,** *Rømmegrøt* (Cream mush) [Ingredients include sweet milk, flour, salt.] . . Combine and cook until well done, stirring continuously. In another kettle add . . flour to . . sour cream and put on to cook. . . When butter forms, remove it and save. When no more butter can be obtained combine the two mixtures. . . Add a little more salt . . and sugar. Serve hot with melted butter, sugar and cinnamon. **1967–68** *DARE* (Qu. H63, *Kinds of desserts*) Infs **MN14, 42,** Rommegrot; **MN13,** Rommegrot [rʌməgrəd]—a cream pud-

ding with the butter ladled off and served with brown sugar and the butter put back on; (Qu. H65, *Foreign foods favored by people around here*) Infs **MN14, 16,** Rommegrot; **MN6,** Rommegrot ['rʊməgryt]. **1981** Hachten *Flavor WI* 309, *Romme Grot* (Norwegian) [Ingredients include soured cream, flour, milk, salt, Sugar, Cinnamon.] . . [A] staple in Norwegian households. . . It was also served with honey or maple syrup for breakfast. **1983** *Capital Times* (Madison WI) 11 May 19 **csWI,** "Who is going to make Norwegian goodies after we are gone?" asked Oyvind Wikum of rural Stoughton, who is making rommegrot (cream pudding) for this year's smorgasbord. **1995** *WI State Jrl.* (Madison) 20 Aug sec C 1/2 **csWI,** "They're out of rommegrot?! They can't be out. . . That's all I've been waiting for [at a Norwegian-American Fest]." . . Rommegrot is a sweet creamy porridge and a favorite among festival attendees who wanted to get a taste of home.

romp v

1 with *around:* To tumble (one) about boisterously; hence ppl adj *romped* tumbled, rumpled.

1887 (1967) Harris *Free Joe* 103 **nGA,** I'm a-gittin' too ole fer ter be romped aroun' by a great big double-j'inted gal like Babe. **1937** Gardner *Folkl. Schoharie* 79 **NY,** But she did find the beds romped, the blankets and sheets thrown about, and the curtains clawed and blooded by the witches.

2 with *on:* To attack (someone), esp verbally. [Cf *EDD* ramp v.[2] 1 "to use violent language"]

1933 Rawlings *South Moon* 295 **nFL,** Then when things gits bad agin, time enough for me to romp on him to git to work. God knows I cain't keep him at it all the time. **1938** Rawlings *Yearling* 189 **nFL,** "Your Ma wouldn't romp on your Pa while he was ailin', would she?" "She don't never romp on him with nothin' but talkin'."

romp around, romped See **romp 1**

romp on See **romp 2**

ron See **run** v A1a

roncadina n Also *roncodina* [Span dimin of *roncador*] Cf **roncador, ronco**

A **croaker** n[1] **1a(1)** (here: *Micropogonias undulatus*).

1898 U.S. Natl. Museum *Bulletin* 47.1461, *Micropogon undulatus* . . Croaker; Roncadina; Corvina. . . South Atlantic and Gulf Coasts of the United States . . a food fish of some importance. **1946** LaMonte *N. Amer. Game Fishes* 83, Croaker . . Names: Corvina, Roncadina, Ronco [etc]. . . Cape Cod, Massachusetts, to Texas. **1949** Caine *N. Amer. Sport Fish* 61, Croaker. . *Synonyms* . . Roncodina [etc].

roncador n [Span, literally "snorer," from the noise it makes] Cf **little roncador, red ~, roncadina, ronco, yellow roncador**

1 also *ronky:* A Pacific sciaenid fish (here: *Roncador stearnsi*). Also called **black croaker, croaker** n[1] **1a(2), golden ~ 2, red roncador 2**

1882 U.S. Natl. Museum *Bulletin* 16.572, *[Sciaena] stearnsi.* . . Roncador. . . Coast of California, north to Point Concepcion; a large and valued food-fish, singularly distinguished by its black pectoral spot. **1884** Goode *Fisheries U.S.* 1.379, The Roncador—Roncador Stearnsi. This species is generally known as the "Roncador" . . and is always considered the genuine Roncador, the other Sciaenoids being to the fishermen bastards. . . It makes a very distinct grunting noise, probably with its air-bladder, on being taken from the water. **1968–70** *DARE* (Qu. P4, *Saltwater fish that are not good to eat*) Inf **CA65,** Tomcod or roncador; ronkies—old Spanish name for [them]; they're wormy—Chinamen eat [them]; **CA176,** Ronky—related to bonefish.

2 =**little roncador.**

1953 Roedel *Common Fishes CA* 100, White Croaker—*Genyonemus lineatus.* . . Unauthorized Names: Tomcod, herring, roncador, tommy.

‡ronch v

1978 *DARE* File **Haden AL** (as of 1890s), They *drenched* a sick horse, and if a cow quit chewing the cud, they did something like *ronching* her. It might have been *ronch, raunch,* or *runch.* It had something to do with the first stomach being too full, and they forced a fake cud into her mouth to promote the natural process.

ronchen See **raunch**

ronco n [Span, literally "hoarse," from the noise it makes] Cf **roncadina, roncador**

1 also *roncho, ronker:* A **croaker** n[1] **1a(1)** (here: *Micropogonias undulatus*).

1882 U.S. Natl. Museum *Proc.* 5.282, Micropogon undulatus . . *Croaker; Ronco.* . . Very common; a food-fish of considerable importance, although reaching but a small size. **1884** Goode *Fisheries U.S.* 1.378 **TX**, The Croaker . . ranges from New York at least to the Gulf of Mexico. . . In Texas it is called "Ronco." **1890** *Century Dict.* 5219 **seTX**, *Roncho.* . . The croaker, *Micropogon undulatus.* [*Century* Ed: Galveston, Texas.] **c1940** Eliason *Word Lists FL* 11 **wFL**, *Ronker* [rɔŋkɚ]. . . A fish similar to a red-fish that makes a noise very much like the sound of the name that is given him. It is a salt-water species. **1946** [see **roncadina**].

2 freq in combs: A **grunt** n **1** (here: *Haemulon* spp).

1887 Goode *Amer. Fishes* 80 **FL**, Stearns mentions the Black Grunt as abundant at Key West among the reefs, and as frequently seen in the markets. It is there known as the "Ronco Grande." **1902** Jordan–Evermann *Amer. Fishes* 421, *Genus Haemulon.* . . The Roncos or Grunts. *Ibid* 424, Bastard Margaret; Ronco—*Haemulon parra.* . . This grunt, also known as sailor's-choice, ronco blanco, ronco prieto, and arrayado, occurs from southern Florida to Brazil. **1946** LaMonte *N. Amer. Game Fishes* 66, Yellow Grunt—Names . . Ronco Amarillo. . . Common around the Keys. **1999** (acc) U.S. Food & Drug Admin. *Seafood List* (Internet), Market Name: *Grunt.* Scientific Name: *Haemulon bonariense.* . . Vernacular: *Ronco prieto. Ibid*, *Haemulon parra.* . . *Ronco* . . *Ronco blanc* [sic] . . *Ronco prieto. Ibid*, *Haemulon plumieri.* . . *Ronco ronco.*

roncodina See **roncadina**

ronker See **ronco 1**

ronky See **roncador 1**

-roo See **-eroo**

rooch See **rutch**

roocus See **ruckus**

rood See **rode** n

roody See **ruddy**

roof n, v Usu |ruf|; also esp **NEng, Upper MW** |rʊf|; also *old-fash* |rʌf| Pronc-spp *ruf(f), rufe* Cf **food, hoof A, root A** Std senses, var forms.

1771 in 1915 *New Engl. Hist. & Geneal. Reg.* 69.14 **MA**, James [Dickinson] & I was Boarding ye Ruff of my Barn. **1795** Dearborn *Columbian Grammar* 138, *List of Improprieties.* . . Ruff for Roof. **1827** (1939) Sherwood *Gaz. GA* 139, *Erroneous Pronunciations.* . . Ruff, for roof. **1856** in 1956 Eliason *Tarheel Talk* 317 **c,csNC**, Ruf. **1890** Holley *Samantha among Brethren* 62 **NY**, He yells at 'em enough to raise the ruff. **1892** *DN* 1.212 **ceMA**, I say (or said before making a conscious change) . . [rʊf], [sʊn], [rʊm], for . . *roof, soon, room.* **1912** Green *VA Folk-Speech* 359, *Rufe.* . . For roof. "Rufe of the mouth." *Ibid, Ruff.* . . Roof. "The ruff of his mouth." **1921** Haswell *Daughter Ozarks* 107 (as of 1880s), Hit kin be closed in and the ruff onto hit by come this day a week. **1950** *WELS Suppl.*, 2 Infs, **swWI**, [rʊf]; 1 Inf, **seWI**, Both [ruf] and [rʊf] are heard; latter more frequent. **1952** Brown *NC Folkl.* 1.586, *Ruff* [rʌf]: pronc. *Roof* of the mouth.—Central and east. **1954** *Harder Coll.* **cwTN**, *Roof* [rʊf]. **c1960** *Wilson Coll.* **csKY**, *Roof* is always /ruf/. **1961** Kurath–McDavid *Pronc. Engl.* 154, *Roof.* . . /u/ is current to some extent in nearly all sections of the Eastern States. . . It is universal in the Lower South and . . in the Upper South, as far north as Baltimore. It predominates decisively in Pennsylvania and in Metropolitan New York . . and is rather common in large parts of New England. In Upstate New York and the adjoining counties of Pennsylvania, /ruf/ is in the minority, as also in Connecticut and parts of eastern Massachusetts. . . *Roof* with the vowel /ʊ/ of *wood* is largely confined to three areas: (1) New England and its settlements to the west, (2) Delaware Bay, and (3) West Virginia north of the Kanawha. . . Scatterings of /rʊf/ survive along the Southern coast from Chesapeake Bay to the Neuse in North Carolina, and in the Valley of Virginia and the Pennsylvania settlements in the upper Piedmont of North Carolina. In areas where both /ruf/ and /rʊf/ are common, the former is apt to be used by the better educated speakers. . . The pronunciation of *roof* as /rʌf/ occurs only in folk-speech; as such it is not too uncommon in northern New England, on Delmarva and Albemarle Sound, and in the Southern Appalachians, but rare elsewhere. **1966–70** *DARE* (Qu. M1) Infs **MI**97,

NY224, [ruf]; **CT**2, 17, [rʊf]; (Qu. X45) Inf **NC**61, Knocking the [rʌf] in; (Qu. AA27) Inf **MI**75, [rʊf]; **IN**1, [rʊf]; (Qu. FF18) Infs **LA**2, **MA**14, **MI**18, **PA**234, **TX**29, [rʊf]; **NJ**48, [ruf]. **1968** *DARE* FW Addit **ceMI**, *Roof*—[rʊf]. **1973** *PADS* 60.49 **seNC**, Roof. . . It seems . . quite straightforward [sic] to find ten informants saying [ʊ] or [ʊ‹] while only two say /u/. **1976** Allen *LAUM* 3.252 (as of c1950), In the U[pper] M[idwest] /rʊf/ is dominant as the choice of two-thirds of all infs., with its lowest incidence in Iowa. The form with the vowel /u/ of *food* is conversely most frequent in Iowa, with its low point in Nebraska. . . A northern New England and eastern Maryland nonstandard relic pronunciation, /rʌf/ rhyming with *stuff*, is barely preserved in Iowa and Nebraska. **1989** Pederson *LAGS Tech. Index* 45 **Gulf Region**, Roof. [620 infs offered the pronc [ruf], 102 the pronc [rʊf]]. **1990** Pederson *LAGS Regional Matrix* 31, [Of the 102 infs who gave proncs of the type [rʊf], 40 were in **AR** and the eastern third of **TN**.]

roof ball n Cf *over-the-roof* (at **over E1**)
=**Antony-over A.**

1970 *DARE* (Qu. EE22, . . *The game in which they throw a ball over a building . . to a player on the other side*) Inf **PA**247, Roof ball.

rook n[1]
=**ruddy duck.**

1888 Trumbull *Names of Birds* 112 **DC**, In the markets of Washington the Ruddy is known as rook. Just think of it, a duck called a rook under the very shadow of the Smithsonian.

Rook n[2] [Trademark, 1912 →] **scattered, but chiefly Sth, S Midl** See Map
A card game played with a special proprietary deck of cards.

1942 Faulkner *Go Down* 155 **MS**, She had attended a club rook-party that afternoon and had won the first, the fifty-cent, prize. **1954** *Harder Coll.* **cwTN**, *Rook* /ruk/. . . Card game. **c1960** *Wilson Coll.* **csKY**, *Rook.* . . A formerly popular and common card game, not banned as were spot cards. **1965–70** *DARE* (Qu. DD35, . . *Card games*) 122 Infs, **esp Sth, S Midl**, Rook; (Qu. DD37, . . *Table games played a lot by adults*) 11 Infs, **scattered**, Rook; (Qu. EE40) Infs **FL**6, **TX**61, Rook; (Qu. FF2, . . *Kinds of parties*) Infs **LA**12, **MD**35, **MS**56, **VA**80, Rook parties; (Qu. FF22a, . . *Clubs and societies . . for women*) Inf **AR**52, Rook clubs. **1976** Brown *Gloss. Faulkner* 164, *Rook-party* . . a party to play rook, a card-game played with a deck of 56 cards in four suits distinguished only by color. The cards have only numbers on them—no pips or faces. The game is played primarily by churchly old ladies who think ordinary playing cards are wicked. **1986** Pederson *LAGS Concordance (Games)* 1 inf, **ceTN**, Rook.

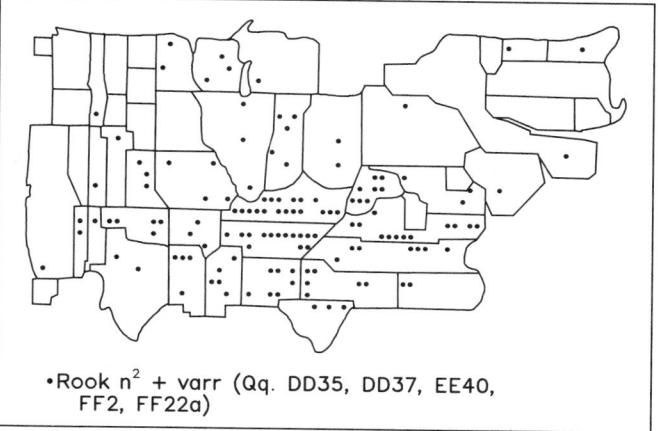

•Rook n[2] + varr (Qq. DD35, DD37, EE40, FF2, FF22a)

‡rookie, play v phr [Alter of *hooky,* prob infl by *rookie* a novice] Cf *DS* JJ6
To be truant.

1998 *DARE* File **OK**, To play rookie—meaning to play hookey (skip school). Used by white male from Oklahoma City—two years college—born 1958. Strongly insisted it was "play rookie" *not* "play hookey."

rookus See **ruckus**

room n Usu |rum|; also **scattered, but esp NEng, Mid and S Atl, Gulf States** |rʊm|; also rarely |rʌm| Pronc-spp *rewm, rium, rum*

A Forms.

1887 Kirkland *Zury* 146 **ceIL,** They returned to the "sett'n' rewm." **1890** *DN* 1.24 **cSC,** *Room* . . [rʌm]. **1891** *PMLA* 6.165 **WV,** Here belongs that peculiar pronunciation of *room* (rium) . . in rhyme with *perfume.* **1892** [see *roof*]. **1927** Shewmake *Engl. Pronc. VA* 30, Two . . sounds . . of which there is lack of uniformity . . are represented by the words *pool* and *pull.* . . The words in which these sounds vary. . . *aloof* . . *roof* . . *room* . . *woof.* **1931** *AmSp* 6.165 **seVA,** In these records *room* is usually [rʊm]. Elsewhere in the South, I have heard only [rum]. **1942** *AmSp* 17.40 **seNY,** *Living room* . . [u] 28 [persons] . . [ʊ] 2 [persons]. . . *Room* . . [u] 143 [persons] . . [ʊ] 14 [persons]. **1943** [see **B1** below]. **1955** *PADS* 23.43 **e,cSC, eNC, seGA,** /ʊ/ in *room, broom,* along with /u/. (/ʊ/ dominant in n.e. New England, e. Virginia, and the Buffalo-Rochester area.) **1961** Kurath–McDavid *Pronc. Engl.* 152, The word *room* exhibits a very similar pattern [to that of *broom*] in the dissemination of /u/ and /ʊ/. [*Ibid, Broom* with the vowel /ʊ/ . . is largely restricted to three subareas of the Atlantic seaboard: New England, Eastern Virginia, and the Lower South.] **1965** Carmony *Speech Terre Haute* 111 **IN,** In the pronunciation of . . *room* . . , /u/ is the predominant vowel. . . Informant 16 [of 16 infs] uses /ʊ/ in the word *room.* The phonemic status of the vowel of *room* is difficult to determine in the record of informant 11. **1966** *DARE* Tape **FL**41, We call this our sitting room [ruˇm] here, because we stay back here all the winter, you know. And up in the livin' room [rʊˆm], of course, I have a 'lectric heater. And we have oil heaters around in the other rooms [ruˇmz]; **MS**15, This child ought to be in down at the class, down in my room [ruˆm], you see. . . When eight o'clock comes, my room [rʊuˆm] is going to be, school's going to start; **SD**8, The ranching business is a nice free business. You see, you're your own boss, to a great extent, and you got room [rʊm] to move around. **1966–68** *DARE* FW Addit **SC,** Rooms [rʊˆmz]; **LA**22, Room [rʊm]—very short and much reduced; approaches [rʌm]; **csLA,** Rooms [rʊmz]; **ceMI,** Room [rʊm]. **1974** Gilbreth *Dictionary* 14 **seSC,** *Rum:* An enclosed space within a building. **1989** Pederson *LAGS Tech. Index* 36 **Gulf Region,** [In *bedroom* there were 709 exx of proncs of the type [-rum], 49 of the type [-rʊm], and 6 of the type [-rʌm].]

B Senses.

1 in phrr *in (the) room of:* Instead of, in place of. [*OED2 room* sb.¹ 13.c, d 1489 →] **chiefly NEng, S Midl**

1744 in 1985 Lederer *Colonial Amer. Engl.* 198 **NY,** In Room and Stead of [three others]. **1767** *Ibid* 131 **MA,** There is a certain herb . . which begins already to take Place in the Room of Green tea. **c1801** in 1956 Eliason *Tarheel Talk* 281 **swNC,** Lifted this Deed . . & gave him a Deed for 311 acres in room of it. **1859** *Ibid* 291 **cnNC,** I had rather you would come up in the room of writing. **1914** *DN* 4.79 **ME, nNH,** *Room of, in.* . . In place of. "I gin you jell in room o' plums." **1921** *DN* 5.119 **KY,** *Room of.* . . Instead of; in the place of. Cf. balladry, "In the room of me." **1932** Wasson *Sailing Days* 46 **cME coast,** In room of saltin' down a dollar for a rainy day, . . I misdoubted if he didn't go astern [=go into debt] the heft o' the time. **1943** *LANE* Map 726 (*Instead of*), Eight informants offered the phrase *in room of* as an equivalent expression. [2 infs used proncs of the type [rum], 6 of the type [rʊm]; 1 inf, Used by old people; 1 inf, Old-fashioned.] **1952** Brown *NC Folkl.* 1.585, *Room, in the _____ of.* . . In the place of. **1959** *VT Hist.* 27.154, *In room of.* . . In place of. Rare.

2 A reason, right (to do something). [*EDD to have room to talk* (at *room* sb.¹ 2.(2)) "to have a right to speak"; cf also *OED2 room* sb.¹ 4]

1942 (1960) Robertson *Red Hills* 174 **SC,** It wasn't long before the whole of Texas was on to that fellow's tactics. Uncle Stevie, tell me what room has any of them to say such things. **1999** *DARE* File, Phrases like "Where does he get room to say that?" and "He has no room to say that" are usually expressed with some indignation. My sister and I, who grew up in California in the 1950s and 1960s, both remember these phrases, and my niece, who now lives near Sacramento, says they are perfectly familiar to her.

3 See quot. [*EDD room* sb.¹ 3 "The best sitting room."]

1946 *PADS* 5.35 **VA,** *(The) room.* . . The living room; among older people, rare.

4 A section or **bay** of a tobacco barn. [Cf *OED2 room* sb.¹ 8 "Formerly also, a compartment, bay, stall (of a barn, stable, etc.)" and *EDD room* sb.¹ 4 "A compartment for smoking fish in a fish-house"] Cf **bay** n², **bent** n² 2

1967 Key *Tobacco Vocab.* **KY, TN,** Room [=bent]. *Ibid* **MD,** [Each part of the barn] is called a room, like a 10 room barn, a 20 room barn. *Ibid* **NC,** You fill it, one room at a time, till the barn's full. [**1969** *NC*

Folkl. 17.33 **wNC,** Tobacco barns were outfitted with *tierpoles* running the length and height of the structure. . . A set of tiers extending from the top to the bottom of the barn was called a *room.*]

5 in phr *room to cuss a cat* and varr: Adequate space.

1921 Thorp *Songs Cowboys* 31 **NM,** On a range so badly crowded / There ain't room to cuss a cat. [**1946** *PADS* 6.41 **NC,** This room is too small to cuss a cat in without getting hairs in your mouth ((teeth)).] **1972** *Atlanta Letters* **cnGA,** Speaking of your request for Sou[thern] colloquialisms. . . Not room to cuss a cat. **1984** Wilder *You All Spoken Here* 71 **Sth,** *Room enough to cuss a cat without getting fur in your teeth:* Elbow room; opposite of not enough room to change your mind.

roomaticks See **rheumatic**

roomatiz See **rheumatiz**

room to cuss a cat See **room B5**

roont See **ruin A2b**

Roosevelt n Also *Roosevelt building, ~ hideout, ~ house, ~ toilet, ~ monument* [Franklin D. *Roosevelt,* US President 1933–45; see quot 1973] Cf **Eleanor, hideout 2**
An outdoor toilet.

c1955 Reed–Person *Ling. Atlas Pacific NW,* 1 inf, Roosevelt house. **1966–68** *DARE* (Qu. M21a, *An outside toilet building*) Inf **MS**1, Roosevelt house; (Qu. M21b, *Joking names for an outside toilet building*) Infs **AZ**9, **CO**3, **IN**17, **KS**6, **UT**7, Roosevelt building (*or* hideout, monument, toilet); **IN**30, **SD**2, Roosevelt. **1973** Allen *LAUM* 1.180 (as of c1950), *Privy.* . . Roosevelt. . . During the second administration of Franklin D. Roosevelt, the Works Project Administration sought to alleviate unemployment by the mass production of sturdy cement-based outdoor toilets. *Ibid* 182, [1 inf, **ND**] says that this term [=*Roosevelt*] is common around here because of a WPA project.

Roosevelt weed n
A **groundsel tree** (here: *Baccharis salicina*).

1970 Correll *Plants TX* 1561, *Baccharis neglecta* . . Roosevelt weed, New Deal weed.

Rooshan, Rooshian See **Russian**

Rooshy See **Russia**

Roosian See **Russian**

Rooskie See **Russki**

roost n

1 The upper balcony of a theater. **chiefly Gulf States, SC, TX, W Midl, esp IN** See Map *old-fash* Cf **buzzard roost 2**

1905 *DN* 3.92 **nwAR,** *Roost.* . . Theatre balcony. . . 'The roost was full at the "opera house" last night.' Common. **1915** *DN* 4.228 **wTX,** *Roost.* . . The "peanut" gallery of a theatre. **1965–70** *DARE* (Qu. D40, *Names and nicknames . . for the upper balcony in a theater*) 48 Infs, **chiefly Sth, S Midl, TX,** Buzzard('s) roost; 19 Infs, **esp Gulf States, SC, TX, W Midl, esp IN,** Roost; **AR**55, **IL**64, **IN**49, **SC**69, **TX**29, 31, Chicken roost; **AR**38, 52, **IN**82, **MO**38, **OH**1, Pigeon(s') roost; **FL**15, **TX**5, 31, **VA**44, Peanut roost; **MS**13, 22, **OH**38, **SC**43, Crow(s') roost;

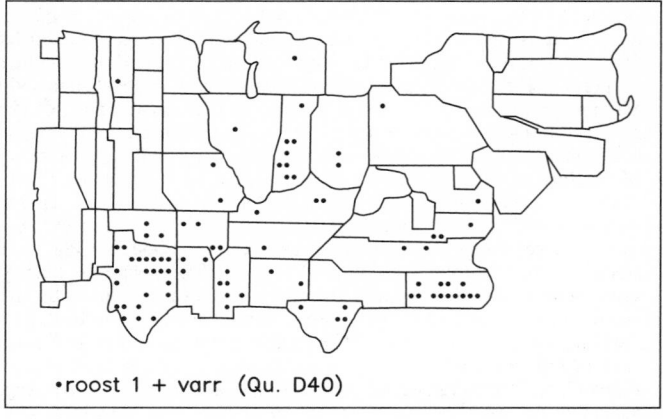

•roost 1 + varr (Qu. D40)

MT1, Lovers' roost; SC69, Monkey roost; PA193, Turkey roost. [68 of 84 total Infs old]

2 A toilet, esp one outdoors.

1968 *DARE* (Qu. M21b, *Joking names for an outside toilet building*) Inf CA87, Roost; NY123, Uncle Sam's roost. **1975** Gould *ME Lingo* 234, *Roost*—Another Maine obliqueness for the toilet. The *roost* was a spruce pole offering multilateral accommodations for lumber camp crews, and because the clientele was men only, the approach side was often open. Such a pole-backhouse, which was the more formal term for the *roost*, survives occasionally at abandoned logging sites, but here and there a sporting camp will still have an outhouse which is not truly a *roost* but is so labeled out of, perhaps, respect for the traditions. *Roost* appears frequently in upstate remarks as a synonym for a *convenience* of any style.

rooster n

1 The hammer of a firearm; hence v *rooster* to cock (the hammer of a firearm); ppl adj *roostered* cocked; also fig. **chiefly sAppalachians, Ozarks** *euphem*

1856 *Porter's Spirit of Times* 1 Nov 140 **OH**, Well now, daddy, says he, I lost the *rooster* off the lock of my gun. **1913** Kephart *Highlanders* 101 **sAppalachians**, Then the dad-burned gun wouldn't stand roostered [Kephart: cocked]; the feather-spring had jumped out o' place. **1928** *DN* 6.59 **Ozarks** [Verbal modesty], Such expressions as *I roostered my ol' hawg-leg* are not at all uncommon . . and when a hillman says *I pulled back both roosters* he means only that he cocked both barrels of his shotgun. **1952** Brown *NC Folkl.* 1.585 **wNC**, *Rooster a gun.* . . To cock a gun. Perhaps an example of verbal modesty or humor. **1972** Cooper *NC Mt. Folkl.* 95, *Rooster a gun*—to cock a gun. **1999** Proulx *Close Range* 42 **WY**, Night perfs had their own hot charge, the glare, the stiff-legged parade of cowboy dolls in sparkle-fringed chaps into the arena, the spotlight that bucked over the squinting contestants and the half-roostered crowd. They were at the end of the night now, into the bullriding, with one in front of him.

2 usu pl; also *rooster bloom, ~ violet*: Any of several **violets**, but esp *Viola palmata*. [From the children's game played with the flowers; see quot 1901] Cf **gallito 1, hen B2, hens and roosters, rooster fight 1, ~ head 1**

1893 *Jrl. Amer. Folkl.* 6.138 **VT, NY**, *Viola palmata*, roosters. Ferrisburgh, Vt. *Viola palmata* var. *cucullata* . . roosters. N.Y. **1901** Lounsberry *S. Wild Flowers* 347, [*Viola*] *palmata.* . . These are the violets which generally in parts of the south are called "little roosters," while the blossoms of the bird's-foot violet are designated as "big roosters." Often the young people take them as opponents and fight them in the way of game cocks until one or the other has lost its head. **1959** Carleton *Index Herb. Plants* 100, *Roosters:* Viola cucullata. **1965–70** *DARE* (Qu. S3, *A flower like a large violet with a yellow center and small ragged leaves—it comes up early in spring on open, stony hilltops*) Inf GA18, Rooster violets; NY219, Blue violet—blue roosters—have a hook on the end of flower; (Qu. S11, . . *Blue violet*) Infs KY28, MS70, Rooster violet; MO37, Hen-and-rooster—purple ones are roosters; NY219, Blue rooster; TN13, Roosters—children's term—played games with the flowers; WI70, Blue roosters; (Qu. S26c, *Wildflowers that grow in woods*) Inf LA12, Roosters. **1967** *DARE* FW Addit AR51, Rooster bloom—a violet-like flower . . with what looks like a little hook-shaped pod under the flower—this is the sheath that encases the immature petals. Boys hook the hooks together and jerk to see which flower will pull the head off the other. **1975** Dwyer *Thangs* 37 **Sth, S Midl**, *Little roosters*—early blue violets. **1978** *Our Smokies Heritage* June 146 **wNC, eTN**, To mountain children the violet was known as "roosters." A favorite game resulted, "rooster fights", in which two violets were hooked in the crooks of their stems and pulled; the winner pulled off the flower of the opposing violet.

3 pl: A **dogtooth violet** (here: *Erythronium albidum*).

1898 *Jrl. Amer. Folkl.* 11.281 **IL**, *Erythronium albidum* . . roosters, Hillsboro, Ill.

rooster bloom See **rooster 2**

rooster comb n Also *rooster's comb*

Perh =**cockscomb 2**, but cf **rooster head**.

1964 in 1970 Johnson *White House Diary* 142, One little girl . . offered me a bunch of red and yellow wildflowers—"snake tongue" and "rooster comb". **1966–70** *DARE* (Qu. S26e, *Other wildflowers not yet mentioned*; not asked in early QRs) Inf TN22, Cockscomb—more polite to say "rooster comb"; VA69, Rooster's comb.

roostered See **rooster 1**

rooster egg See **rooster's egg**

rooster fight n

1 also *rooster fighter:* Any of several **violets**, but esp *Viola palmata*. [From the children's game played with these flowers; cf *EDD* cock-fighters (at *cock* sb.[1] 2.(5)) "the seed-stems of *Plantago lanceolata*."] **S Midl, esp KY** Cf **chicken fight 1, rooster 2**

[**1884** *Harper's New Mth. Mag.* 69.94 **NY**, Purple violets . . were slaughtered by hundreds, for the projecting spur under the curved stem at the base of the flower enabled the boys to hook them together and "fight roosters," as they termed it.] **1916** *DN* 4.345 **TN**, *Rooster-fight.* . . A violet: so called from the practice of 'fighting' them together to see which would pull the other's head off. **c1960** *Wilson Coll.* **csKY**, Rooster (or rooster fight): violet. Children often carried on rooster fights by hooking violets together and pulling; the tougher violet won the fight. **1965–70** *DARE* (Qu. S11, . . *Blue violet*) Infs IN48, KY11, 68, 74, 77, MO8, Rooster fight; OK28, Wild violets—also called rooster fights; KY5, Rooster fighter—old-fashioned; kids' nickname. **1967** *DARE* FW Addit nwAR, A violet-like flower . . with what looks like a little hook-shaped pod under the flower . . [is called] *rooster fight* . . by people in the Paron–Lake Winona area.

2 also *rooster fighting:* Any of var contests in which the object is to throw one's opponent off balance. Cf **chicken fight 2**

1940 Harbin *Fun Encycl.* 189, *Rooster fight.* . . Hands on ankles. Players jostle one another with the shoulder. The point is to make the opponent lose his balance or loosen his hold on his ankles. **1945** Boyd *Hdbk. Games* 32, *Rooster Fight*—Two players, with arms folded, hop on one foot, each trying to make the other put his foot to the floor. **1946** TN Folk Lore Soc. *Bulletin* 12, "Whip-Crack," "Rooster Fighting," and other games were played in this rougher list. **1953** Brewster *Amer. Nonsinging Games* 171 **IL**, *Rooster-Fighting.* . . This game is played by two boys at a time. Each bends his arms so that the right hand grasps the left arm just above the elbow and the left hand grasps the right arm at the same point. Then the two sidle up to each other, swinging their folded arms sidewise, and try to strike each other in the ribs with their elbows. **1968** *DARE* (Qu. EE28, *Games played in the water*) Inf WV11, Rooster fights—girls on boys' shoulders; two teams; girls try to knock others off shoulders. **1969** Sorden *Lumberjack Lingo* 62 **NEng, Gt Lakes**, *Rooster fight:* A broom handle was placed under the knees of a squatting man with his hands tied to it on either side. Two men tied in this fashion butted each other to see who would get tipped over first.

rooster fighter See **rooster fight 1**

rooster fighting See **rooster fight 2**

rooster head n

1 also *rooster heads, ~ hoods, rooster's head:* A **violet** of the genus *Viola*.

1892 *Jrl. Amer. Folkl.* 5.92 **NC**, *Viola* (sp. unknown), rooster hoods. Buncombe Co., N.C. **1954** *Harder Coll.* **cwTN**, Rooster's head . . Johnny-jump-up (viola tricolor)—Yellow, purple, white. **1966–70** *DARE* (Qu. S3, *A flower like a large violet with a yellow center and small ragged leaves—it comes up early in spring on open, stony hilltops*) Inf AR28, Rooster heads; (Qu. S11, . . *Blue violet*) Inf KY74, Rooster heads. **1984** Wilder *You All Spoken Here* 176 **Sth**, *Rooster heads:* Birdfoot violets.

2 also *roosters' heads:* A **shooting star**, esp *Dodecatheon meadia*. **esp CA**

1894 *Jrl. Amer. Folkl.* 7.94 **CA**, *Dodecatheon Meadia*, var. shooting stars, roosters' heads, Santa Barbara Co. **1897** Parsons *Wild Flowers CA* 206, Among the children the various forms [of *Dodecatheon*] are known by a number of names, such as "mad violets," "prairie pointers," "mosquito-bills," and "roosters'-heads." The latter is said to be the designation of prosaic little boys who seek in these blossoms gaming possibilities, and who love to hook them together and pull to see which head will come off first. **1898** *Jrl. Amer. Folkl.* 11.274 **CA**, *Dodecatheon* (sp.) . . roosters' heads. **1920** Rice-Rice *Pop. Studies CA Wild Flowers* 86, Children . . have invented rather pert little names [for *Dodecatheon* spp]. . . The most common of these are Shooting Stars, Mad Violets, Mosquito Bills, Sailors' Capes, Rooster Heads, and Prairie Pointers. **1959** Carleton *Index Herb. Plants* 100, *Rooster-head:* Dodecatheon meadia.

3 A **lousewort 1.** Cf **chicken head 1**

1954 *Harder Coll.* **cwTN,** Rooster head. . . weed, also known as chicken head. **1966** *DARE* (Qu. S26e, *Other wildflowers not yet mentioned;* not asked in early QRs) Inf **WA1,** Chicken head, rooster head—grows on a slender stem, lavender blossom like rooster's comb.

rooster heads (or hoods) See **rooster head 1**

rooster's ass n Also *rooster's pitcher* Cf **chicken butt**

1965–69 *DARE* (Qu. X34, . . *Names and nicknames for the navel*) Infs **IN18, OK7,** Rooster's ass; **GA72,** Rooster's pitcher.

rooster's comb See **rooster comb**

rooster's egg n Also *rooster egg*

An egg regarded as special or unusual; rarely, a fertilized egg; see quots.

1899 Bergen *Animal Lore* 12 **IL,** A "luck egg" is the egg of a rooster; also called "rooster's egg." *De Kalb Co., Ill.* **1899** (1912) Green *VA Folk-Speech* 357, Rooster's egg. . . A small hen's egg. **1912** Green *VA Folk-Speech* 357, Rooster's egg. . . A small imperfect egg, differing in size, shape and colour from the usual hen eggs. Produces roosters. Said sometimes to be laid by roosters. **1914** *DN* 4.152 **ME,** Rooster's egg. . . A fertilized egg. . . In Mass[achusetts] rooster's egg is used facetiously for a large egg. **1942** McAtee *Dial. Grant Co. IN* 24 (as of 1890s), *Egg, rooster's* . . faceitous [sic] for a small or abnormal hen's egg. **1947** (1964) Randolph *Ozark Superstitions* 43, Unusually long eggs, or eggs with shells noticeably rough at one end, are also regarded as "rooster eggs." **c1960** *Wilson Coll.* **csKY,** Rooster's eggs. . . An oddly-shaped egg. At Fidelity we thought a biggish egg would hatch out a rooster. **1980** Koch *Folkl. KS* 374, Large eggs that have two yolks are rooster eggs.

rooster's head See **rooster head 1**

roosters' heads See **rooster head 2**

rooster's pitcher See **rooster's ass**

rooster spur (pepper) n **SE**

A small hot pepper (here: *Capsicum annuum* var).

1966–70 *DARE* (Qu. I22a, . . *Peppers—small hot*) Inf **AL15,** Rooster spur; **MS87,** Rooster-spur peppers; **FL8,** Rooster spur—hot, green, finger-size; (Qu. I22b, . . *Peppers—large hot*) Inf **GA46,** Rooster spur.

rooster supper n

1941 Street *In Father's House* 137 **MS,** Mama gave a rooster supper on Saturday night. A rooster supper is when you have only men at the table.

rooster violet See **rooster 2**

root n¹, v Usu |rut|; also *esp* **NEng, Upstate NY, Upper MW** |rʊt|; less freq |rɪut, rʌt|; for addit varr see quots Pronc-sp *rute*
A Forms.

1818 Fessenden *Ladies Monitor* 172 **VT,** *Rutes* for roots. **1890** *DN* 1.41 **ME,** I say [rut] . . for *root.* **1892** *DN* 1.212 **ceMA,** I say (or said before making a conscious change) [rʊt] . . for *root.* **1942** *AmSp* 17.40 **seNY,** Root . . [u] 82 [informants] . . [ʊ] 5. **1950** *WELS Suppl.* **csWI,** Root . . pronounced [rʊt]. **c1955** Reed–Person *Ling. Atlas Pacific NW,* Roots /u/ [25 infs]. . . Roots /ʊ/ [21 infs]. **c1960** *Wilson Coll.* **csKY,** Root /rut/ only. . . Roots. . . /ruts/ only local pronunciation. **1961** Kurath–McDavid *Pronc. Engl.* 155, Root. . . The vowel /u/ . . is universal in the South and South Midland, and nearly so in the North Midland, the lower Hudson Valley with Metropolitan New York, and southeastern New England. . . In the remainder of New England and in the New England settlements to the west, /ʊt/ is either in the minority or of rare occurrence. . . The vowel /ʊ/ . . is largely confined to the New England settlement area. It predominates decisively in Connecticut, central and western Massachusetts, New Hampshire, Vermont, and Upstate New York, less so in Maine. **c1970** Pederson *Dial. Surv. Rural GA* **seGA** (*The parts of a tree that are under the ground are its _____*), [58 infs [of 63] offered proncs of the type [rʊuts]; 2 infs, proncs of the type [ruts]; 1 inf, [ruts], corrected to [rʊuts]; 1 inf, [rʊut]; 1 inf, [ro^ʊˇots].] **1973** *PADS* 60.50 **seNC,** Root. . . The Carteret County informants with only one exception said [u] or [u<]; the exception's vowel was [ʊ^], markedly raised, which may be an idiosyncratic case of lowered /u/. **1976** Allen *LAUM* 3.252 (as of c1950), In the U[pper] M[idwest] . . the /rʊt/ pronunciation has spread widely. . . The form /rʊt/ . . is . . most frequent in southern Iowa and Nebraska. **1989** Pederson *LAGS Tech. In-*

dex 216 **Gulf Region,** *Roots* [720 infs offered proncs of the type [rut(s)]; 54 infs offered proncs of the type [rʊt(s)]; 42 infs, proncs of the type [rɪut(s)]; 3 infs, proncs of the type [rʌt(s)]; 1 inf, [rɪts].]
B As noun.

1 A plant root believed to have magical power, esp as used to harm someone; broadly, =**hoodoo** n **1a**—often in phrr *work the root(s) on, put the roots on* to harm by means of **hoodoo** n **1a. Sth** *chiefly among Black speakers* Cf **conjure bag, root doctor 2, ~ man, ~ work**

1895 *S. Workman* 24.117 **VA,** Love affairs gave plenty of employment to the conjure doctors, as they were believed to be able to "work their roots" so to make one person return another's affection. **1926** Puckett *Folk Beliefs S. Negro* 231, Goofering is walking over a root-bag or goofer-bag. On the outside is goofer-root, then cloth, then more root, then another layer of cloth, and inside is the goofer—strands from your hair, broken needles and graveyard dirt. **1931** [see **B2** below]. **c1938** in 1970 Hyatt *Hoodoo* 1.59 **seSC** [Black], She say, well, dat hen, if anybody put down any *roots* or anything fer 'er, dat hen would scratch 'em up. *Ibid* 256 **seMD** [Black], I gon'a work mah *roots* on you. *Ibid* **ceVA** [Black], I'm going to chew a *root* for you. . . I'll do that on a dark night—when the moon changes you'll be changed too, when I *fix* my *root* for you. **1954** *Greensboro Daily News* (NC) 26 Aug (*Mathews Coll.*), A Goldsboro Negro and his son were charged in a fight Saturday, which began when the son accused his father of "putting the roots" on his girl friend. **1962** *Jrl. Amer. Folkl.* 75.313 **cNC,** Negroes who become insane, die under mysterious conditions, have strange afflictions . . are also thought to be under the influence of some form of evil magic. Local synonyms for the spell are "curse," "trick," "fix," "conjure," "root," and "hoodoo." **1966** *DARE* (Qu. CC14, . . *Where one person supposedly casts a spell over another*) Inf **SC26,** Worked the root on. [Inf Black]

2 pl: Folk medicine. Cf **root doctor 1**

1931 *Jrl. Amer. Folkl.* 44.317, "Roots" is the Southern Negro's term for folk-doctoring by herbs and prescriptions, and by extension, because all hoodoo doctors cure by roots, it may be used as a synonym for hoodoo.
C As verb.

Also with *at:* To work **hoodoo** n **1a** on; hence vbl n *rooting.* *among Black speakers* Cf **root work**

1962 *Jrl. Amer. Folkl.* 75.316 **cNC,** Melville was told that he could not stay away from the woman who had "rooted him". **1968–70** *DARE* (Qu. CC14, . . *Where one person supposedly casts a spell over another*) Inf **SC69,** Rooted; **GA42,** Rooted at you. [Both Infs Black] **1968** *DARE* FW Addit **PA66,** *Rooting (someone)*—the practice of sprinkling a special type of dirt (from Georgia?) on a person's doorstep. The first person to step on the dirt will fall in love with the one who sprinkled it there. [Inf Black]

root n² [Cf **rooter 3, snooter**]

A nose, snout.

1915 *DN* 4.245 **MT,** Root. . . Nose. "Jane, how came that scale on your root?" **1965–70** *DARE* (Qu. K61, . . *The pig's nose*) Infs **MS60, MO37, SC9,** Root.

root n³ See **route A1**

rootabaga See **rutabaga**

root at See **root v C**

root-beer tree n

=**sassafras B1.**

1973 *Foxfire 2* 49 **sAppalachians,** Sassafras (*Sassafras albidum*) . . (white sassafras, root beer tree, ague tree, saloop).

root cellar n Also *root cave* **widespread, but less freq Sth, S Midl, SW** See Map Cf **cellar** n¹ **B1, root house**

An underground storage area for root vegetables and similar perishables.

1851 Norton *Notes* 14 **NEast,** It is easy to have a root cellar and a boiler near by, for their special accommodation. **1867** Beecher *Norwood* 535 **NEng,** The grain-room, the root-cellars, the straw-sheds, the mill-room . . seemed like parts of a city rather than of a barn. **1910** *Outlook* 25 June 367, No sooner . . are the foundations laid than the housewife sees that a root cellar must be added. **1923** *DN* 5.219 **swMO,** Root cellar. . . An underground storage room for vegetables. **1937** Sandoz *Slogum* 51 **NE,** A big root cellar that kept carrots and turnips, even squash, sound and firm into April. **1941** *LANE* Map 248 (*Roots*) 1 inf, **ceMA**, Root cellar, place where vegetables are stored. **1950** *WELS Suppl.* **cnWI**, Root [rut] *cellar*—Where convenient, the same structure as the storm cellar. . . Also called *vegetable cellar.* **1965–70** *DARE* (Qu. M19, *A place for keeping carrots, turnips, potatoes, and so on over the winter*) 269 Infs, **widespread, but less freq Sth, S Midl, SW**, Root cellar; [**OH**57, Root storage;] (Qu. D22, *Underground place to go to in case of a violent windstorm*) 13 Infs, **esp Upper MW, Gt Lakes, NEng**, Root cellar; (Qu. D10a, *The place to keep food cool, usually with ice, so that it won't spoil*) Infs **CT**2, **ME**20, Root cellar; (Qu. D16, . . *Parts added on to the main part of a house*) Inf **MI**104, Root cellar; (Qu. D18, *The part of the house below the ground floor*) Inf **MI**110, Root cellar; (Qu. M12, *What do you keep food for the cattle in over winter?*) Inf **AK**8, Root cellar; (Qu. M22, . . *Kinds of buildings . . on farms*) Inf **CT**22, Root cellar. **1967** *DARE* File **IL**, *Root* [rut] *cellar* or wind cave—where you keep vegetables, bulbs, etc. and/or where you go in case of tornado. **1969** Sorden *Lumberjack Lingo* 98 **NEng, Gt Lakes**, *Root cellar*—A cavelike depression, usually dug into the side of a small hill or knoll near the camp, shored up and roofed over with log rafters and earth in which perishable foodstuffs such as onions, potatoes, etc. were kept from freezing in the winter. **1975** *Appalachian Jrl.* 2.155 **wNC**, Women would dry apple slices and beans and store them in the loft of the house or in the *sass hole*, also known as the *root cellar* or *can house;* and they would be ready for use during the winter. **1983** *MJLF* 9.1.53 **ceKY** (as of 1956), *Root cellar* . . a warm house. **1986** Pederson *LAGS Concordance* 15 infs, **Gulf Region**, Root cellar(s).

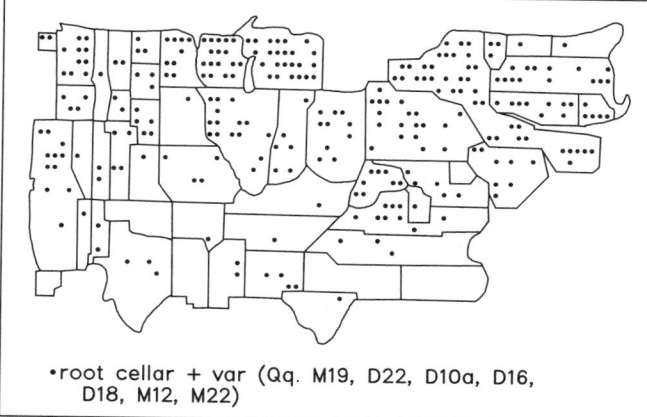

•root cellar + var (Qq. M19, D22, D10a, D16, D18, M12, M22)

rootch See **rutch**

rootchy See **rutch 1**

root doctor n Note: It is sometimes difficult to distinguish between senses **1** and **2** in the quots below.

1 One who treats illness with roots and herbs; hence vbl n *root doctoring.* Cf **root** n[1] **B2**

1821 Howison *Upper Canada* 195 **CT**, "Oh," said the woman, "if I had but the *root* doctor that used to attend our family at Connecticut; he was a dreadful *skeelful* man." **1840** [see **rattlesnake violet 2**]. **1843** Torrey *Flora NY* 1.425, This plant [=*Lobelia inflata*] is well known for its acrid and emetic qualities, and for being the chief remedy of those empirics called *botanic physicians,* and *root-doctors.* **1890** *NY Age* (NY) 19 Apr 1, Carmier was what people call down here a root doctor. . . He only rode around the country . . and made his living curing the sick and selling his medicine. **1931** *Jrl. Amer. Folk.* 44.441 **Sth**, Nearly all of the conjure doctors practice "roots," but some of the root doctors are not hoodoo doctors. **1934** Carmer *Stars Fell on AL* 214, Wade decided he didn't want to work. So he has taken a cabin back in Chambers County and turned to doctoring, mostly root doctoring for venereal diseases. **1950** *PADS* 14.57 **SC**, *Root doctor:* . . One who heals or pretends to heal by means of medicinal roots and herbs. **1981** Pederson *LAGS Basic Materials,* 1 inf, **cnFL**, Root doctor—a gatherer of roots and herbs who makes medicine; 1 inf, **ceGA**, Colored people used roots for medicine. They had root doctors. **1993** Delany–Delany *Having Our Say* 31 **cNC** [Black], Mr. Miliam was a root doctor. He was always messing around with different herbs and roots and things, looking for cures.

2 A practitioner of **hoodoo** n **1a**. [**root** n[1] **B1**] **Sth** *esp freq among Black speakers*

1900 *Jrl. Amer. Folk.* 13.228 **GA**, I didn't get any better, and went and saw a root-doctor, who told me he could take off the conjure, he gave me a cup of tea to drink and biled up something . . to wash my feet and legs with, but it ain't done me much good, he ain't got enough power. . . They say root-doctors have power over spirits, who will tell them who does the conjuring; they generally uses yerbs gathered on changes of the moon. **1926** Puckett *Folk Beliefs S. Negro* 201, The term "root-doctor" is common through the South, as is also "hoodoo-doctor." **c1938** in 1970 Hyatt *Hoodoo* 1.160 **Richmond VA** [Black], He called hisself to be a *root doctor* and also a preacher. **1939** FWP *Guide FL* 131, Since voodooism is an unwritten form of the occult, it varies greatly according to the environment. Its commonest exponent is the 'root doctor.' His medications may run from harmless nostrums to lethal powders, the latter to be given an enemy with appropriate abracadabra. **1940** Writers' Program *Guide GA* 260, Root doctors and "cunjur" folk ply their trade for a small fee, and at some shops can be purchased . . Lucky Mojoe Drops of Love . . to bring love and luck to the buyer and confusion to his enemies. **1962** *Jrl. Amer. Folk.* 75.316 **cNC**, Later, when sober, he found that he missed his watch. He went to a root doctor and was told that for fifteen dollars she would get his watch back for him. **1966–70** *DARE* Tape **SC**25, [Inf:] They [=Black people] still have the root doctors, and they still use the roaches and dried frogs. [FW:] . . What do they use it for? [Inf:] Put on a sore or something, or if someone they feel they've done them a great injustice they want to fix; they go to a root doctor and get the root doctor to prescribe some medication; **VA**40, You find a lot of them believe in what they call the root doctor. **1985** Wilkinson *Moonshine* 90 **neNC**, Conjure doctors are also called root doctors because they sell Adam and Eve roots, which they collect from ditch banks and bottle up in little vials. Putty root is what they are.

root doctoring See **root doctor 1**

rootebagger See **rutabaga**

rooter n

1 also *hill rooter, long ~, mountain ~, prairie ~, rooter hog, wild rooter, wood(s) ~*: =**razorback hog. chiefly SE** Cf **piney-woods rooter**

1872 IL Dept. Ag. *Trans. for 1871* 204, The old fashioned "prairie rooter and elm peeler" are banished from the country. **1928** *AmSp* 4.130 **cnNE**, Wild hogs are "prairie rooters." **1938** [see **piney-woods rooter**]. **c1960** *Wilson Coll.* **csKY**, Hill-rooter. . . A lean long-nosed, bony hog, usually one half wild. **c1970** Pederson *Dial. Surv. Rural GA* **seGA** (*What do you call a long-legged hog that has a thin body and a long snout?*) 1 inf, Rooters. **1975** Dwyer *Thangs* 27 **Sth, S Midl**, Razorback hogs, called "long rooters" are variously colored, long-snouted, long-tailed, long-bodied, long-legged, long-tusked, even long in the squeal. . . His long snout can scent like a cat's yet it can burrow, uproot, and overturn heavy objects. **1986** Pederson *LAGS Concordance,* 7 infs, **GA, MS, TX**, Rooter(s); 1 inf, **cTN**, Rooters—sleep in daylight and roam at night; 1 inf, **seMS**, Rooter hog—longer teeth than ordinary hogs; 4 infs, **GA, AL**, Mountain rooter(s); 1 inf, **swTN**, Hill rooters— sharp nose, long legs, high backs; 1 inf, **cnGA**, Wild rooters; 2 infs, **AL, TX**, Wood(s) rooters.

2 See **rooter skunk**.

3 A hog's snout; transf, a human nose. **chiefly Sth, S Midl** See Map

1954 *Harder Coll.* **cwTN**, Rooter. . . A pig's nose. **c1960** *Wilson Coll.* **csKY**, Rooter. . . A hog's snout. **1965–70** *DARE* (Qu. K61, . . *The*

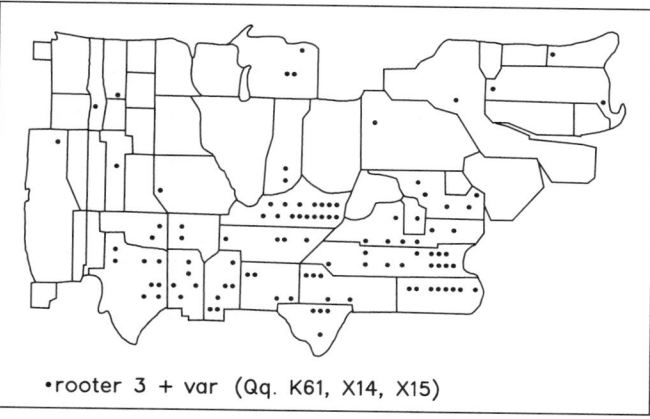

•rooter 3 + var (Qq. K61, X14, X15)

pig's nose) 101 Infs, **chiefly Sth, S Midl,** Rooter [Of all Infs responding to the question, 66% were male, 36% gs educ or less, 77% comm type 4 or 5; of all Infs giving this response, 76% were male, 63% gs educ or less, 89% comm type 4 or 5.]; (Qu. X14, *Joking words for the nose*) Infs **FL**48, **MD**19, 41, **ME**5, **MA**40, **SC**29, 34, 46, **VA**69, Rooter; (Qu. X15, . . *Kinds of noses, according to shape or size*) Inf **SC**3, Rooter, hog rooter—an especially long nose. **1972** *Foxfire Book* 205 **nGA,** Lot'a people throwed away that they called th' rooter. Oh I forbid that. I'd rather have that as any part a'th'hog. Oh that's good eatin'. **1983** *MJLF* 9.1.53 **ceKY** (as of 1956), Rooter . . a hog's snout. **1986** Pederson *LAGS Concordance,* 1 inf, **ceTN,** Rooter—snout.

rooter skunk n Also *rooter*
=**hognose skunk.**

1957 Blair et al. *Vertebrates U.S.* 756, Genus *Conepatus* . . Rooter skunks. . . Snout long, projecting well beyond lower jaw and with thickened, naked pad on upper side. *Ibid, Conepatus mesoleucus* . . Western rooter skunk. *Ibid, Conepatus leuconotus* . . Tamaulipan rooter skunk. . . East coast of Mexico through brushlands of southern Texas. **1960** Natl. Geogr. Soc. *Wild Animals N. Amer.* 204 **SW,** Hog-nosed skunk. . . has a long flexible muzzle similar to the snout of a hog. It uses this to root for insects, hence the name "rooter skunk." **1968** *DARE* (Qu. P26, *Names and nicknames . . for a skunk*) Inf **TX**54, Rooter. **1980** Whitaker *Audubon Field Guide Mammals* 588, Hog-nosed Skunk—"Rooter Skunk". . . Sign: Extensive patches of ground torn up and pitted by rooting.

root fellow See **root man**

root for the peg See **root the peg**

root, hog, or die phr Also *root, (little) pig, or die;* for addit varr see quots [*hog* (or *pig*) was originally vocative, but later freq reinterpreted as a verb. The latter interpretation is implicit in constrs such as "he had to root, hog, or die"; in other cases only intonation patterns would allow one to determine which interpretation is implied.] Cf **die, dog, or eat the hatchet; eat, pig, or die**

Work hard or suffer the consequences—often used attrib or as a quasi-noun or adv; hence, as v phr, to work hard or suffer the consequences; to fend for oneself, struggle for existence.

1834 Crockett *Narrative* 60 **TN,** It looked like it was to be starvation any way; we therefore determined to go on the old saying, root hog or die. **1836** in 1973 Porter *Quarter Race* 18 **KY,** After another toss for choice of tracks, and another for the word, the horses walked off towards the head of the stretch. Now it was, "Hurra, my Popcorn—I believe in you—come it strong, lumber—go it with a looseness—root little pig, or die." **1845** *St. Louis Reveille* (MO) 5 Jan 1/6, I . . determined to reach the springs "come what may"—"root pig or die." **1857** Paige *Dow's Patent Sermons* 3.195, They are obliged to go upon the root-hog-or-die principle. **1886** Poore *Reminiscences* 1.97 **DC** (as of 1829) *(Mathews Coll.),* When the *Telegraph* was asked what these men could do to ward off starvation, the insolent reply was, "Root, hog, or die!" **1909** *DN* 3.364 **eAL, wGA,** Root hog or die. . . To work for oneself or perish. "He had to root hog or die." Very common. **1915** *DN* 4.189 **swVA,** Root hog or die. . . Look out for yourself or die. **1929** *AmSp* 5.123 **ME,** The frequent expressions . . "wait until the cows come home," . . "root hog or die," . . "I'd give my eye-teeth," need no explanation. **[c1937** in 1976 *Weevils in the Wheat* 53 **VA** [Black], When de war wuz ovuh, de govu'ment jes let de slaves drop. Den ye had tuh "root like a pig er die."**] 1941** Street *In Father's House* 346 **MS,** Of course, it's root hog or die and we have to do a lot of rooting. But we get plenty to eat. **1942** McAtee *Dial. Grant Co. IN* 53 (as of 1890s), *Root hog or die* . . do that to which there is no alternative, work out one's own salvation. **1951** *DE Folkl. Bulletin* 1.4, Root hog or lose your tater (you must dig for what you get). **1966** *DARE* Tape **FL**42, I stayed on the farm until I was fourteen, and then I had to get out and root, hog, or die. **1986** Pederson *LAGS Concordance,* 1 inf, **neTN,** Root, hog, or die—take care, you're on your own; 1 inf, **ceAR,** Root, hog, or die—do your best to survive; 1 inf, **cLA,** It was root, hog, or die—animals had to rough it. **1989** Mosher *Stranger* 247 **nVT,** It was root, hog, or starve, with maybe a country cowboy song or two throwed into it to make us proud of being poor.

root house n **chiefly Nth, esp Gt Lakes, WA** See Map Cf **root cellar**
A building for the storage of foodstuffs.

1790 *PA Packet & Daily Advt.* (Philadelphia) 30 Mar 4/2, On the premises are . . two arched stone root houses. **1872** U.S. Bur. Indian Affairs *Rept. for 1871* 432 **MT,** [I] have constructed two root-houses for stowing away vegetables. **1949** Arnow *Hunter's Horn* 191 **KY,** Aunt Marthie's rose-of-Sharon bushes were blooming out by the tumble-down root house. **1949** Peattie *Cascades* 44 **Pacific NW** (as of 1890s), Had plenty of food. Fresh fish, game, canned meat, pheasant, wild rabbit. Had own smokehouse for fish, bacon, ham. Root-house full of vegetables, preserves. **1965–70** *DARE* (Qu. M19, *A place for keeping carrots, turnips, potatoes, and so on over the winter*) 22 Infs, **esp wGt Lakes, WA,** Root house; (Qu. M22, . . *Kinds of buildings . . on farms*) Inf **NH**5, Root house.

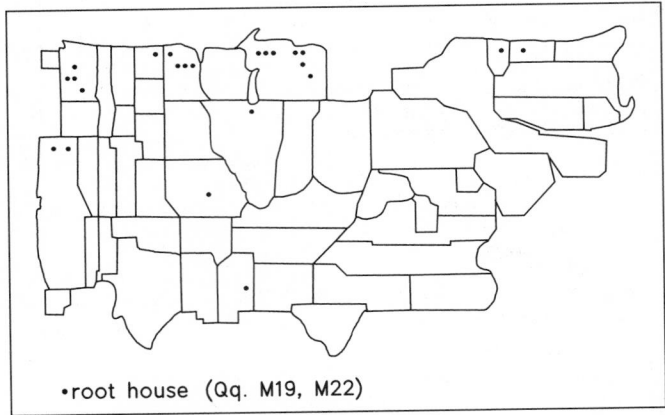

•root house (Qq. M19, M22)

rooting See **root** v C

rootle v [Engl dial]
To root; to grub; fig, to poke about.

1903 *DN* 2.300 **Cape Cod MA** (as of a1857), Rootle. . . To root. **1916** *DN* 4.265 **Cape Cod MA,** Pigs on Cape Cod do not *root,* for that suggests a staccato movement; they *rootle.* **1997** *DARE* File **seWI,** My grandmother and great grandmother (Milwaukee, of Norwegian descent, early–mid 1900s) used to use the term "rootle" . . which means to look through or sort through things. My grandmother would say, "I was up in the attic rootling around and found. . ." or "It's a good day to rootle"—meaning that there is nothing pressing to do, so going through "stuff" would be a good use of extra time. . . "Root" rhymes with "put." . . The "t" is actually pronounced as a "d."

root, little pig, or die See **root, hog, or die**

root man n Also *root fellow,* pl *root people* [**root** n[1] **B1**] *among Black speakers*
=**root doctor 2.**

c1938 in 1970 Hyatt *Hoodoo* 1.53 **seNC** [Black], (What will you do with that dirt [from a whirlwind caused by a wandering spirit]?) Carry it to de man—*root man. Ibid* 185 **neFL** [Black], She been gone three months. Ah went to diff'rent *root people,* ah been all over. Dere's plenty of dem here in dis town—plenty of 'em tell yo' dey kin do things, whether they done do it er not. *Ibid* 457 **cwFL** [Black], A *root fellah* tole me de way he done tuh keep 'em [=hostile spirits] off him. **1942** Rawlings *Cross Creek* 276 **nFL** [Black], "I wisht I could find me a good root man, to find out is something buried under my house." "A conjur bag?" "Yessum."

root, pig, or die See **root, hog, or die**

roots(c)h See **rutch**

root-soaker n **Sth, S Midl**
A very heavy rain.

c1960 *Wilson Coll.* **csKY,** Root-soaker. . . A big rain. **1966** Dakin *Dial. Vocab. Ohio R. Valley* 2.21, Severe rainstorm . . *ground soaker, root soaker* (once each, southernmost Mountains). **1966–70** *DARE* (Qu. B25, . . *Joking names . . for a very heavy rain. . .* "It's a regular _____.") Infs **KY**66, **MS**45, **NC**1, 13, 20, **VA**69, Root-soaker.

root the peg n Also *root for the peg* **esp Gulf States, S Atl**
=**mumblety-peg.**

1901 *DN* 2.146 **Long Is. NY,** Root the peg. . . A variety of mumblety-peg. **1966–69** *DARE* (Qu. EE5, *Games where you try to make a jack-*

knife stick in the ground) Infs **LA**34, **SC**26, 44, 54, Root the peg; **GA**82, Root for the peg.   **1986** Pederson *LAGS Concordance,* 1 inf, **swAL,** Root the peg—flip knife and make it stick.

root work n [Cf phr *work the root(s) on* at **root** n[1] **B1**]   Sth esp freq among Black speakers

The practice of **hoodoo** n 1a; hence n *root worker* =**root doctor** 2; v *root-work* =**root** v C; ppl adj *root-worked.*

c1938 in 1970 Hyatt *Hoodoo* 1.329 **seNC** [Black], I was *hurt* once by a *rootworker.* I was *hurt* in mah right leg.   *Ibid* 2.1175 **seGA** [Black], Yo' take another *root-worker,* well, if he got a crystal ball dere, yo' know, he kin jes' be settin' down dere [Hyatt: at home] lookin' right at chew.   *Ibid* 1181 **seGA** [Black], An' while yo' are doin' dis kinda work, dese candles are a cover-up to yo', yo' see, cover [Hyatt: for] other *root-works* an' things.   *Ibid* 1190 **seGA** [Black], Well, yo' take a lotta *root-workers* dey'll take a root from any kinda—which dey go out in de woods an' dig up herbs an' diff'rent kinda *roots,* yo' know, an' make yo' medicine fo' yo' to take an' run de *miseries* out.   *Ibid* 1538 **ceGA** [Black], If a person is *rootworked* or if dey is *witchcrafted* an' dey wanta git bettah, git up in de mawnin' 'bout fo' or five a'clock an' go down to a runnin' stream of watah an' jes' set dere an' hold dat foot in de watah.   *Ibid* 1543 **ceGA** [Black], If anybody wanta *rootwork* yo' or *witchcraft* yo', if yo' wear a dime aroun' yore laig, . . dat dime will turn black.   **1967** *Psychosomatic Med.* 484, Root work treatment is an even more nebulous point. Some root workers seem to be very well thought of. . . Treatment probably includes a root worker's listening to the patient's complaints, certain incantations, use of powders or liquids to counter the spell, and specific advice for further behavior. . . Root work survived in the twentieth century . . among the poorest, least educated, and most deprived Southerners.

rootybagger See **rutabaga**

rope n   scattered, but chiefly **Nth, N Midl, Pacific**   See Map   Cf **el ropo**

Tobacco; a cigar.

1899 (1977) Norris *McTeague* 81 **San Francisco CA,** The smoke of his cheap tobacco drifted into the faces of the group. . . "If you've got to smoke rope like that, smoke it in a crowd of muckers; don't come here amongst gentlemen."   **1934** H. McLellan in *Detective Fiction Weekly* 10 Nov. 29/2 *(OED2),* He jerked a cigar out of her mouth. . . 'It burns my stomach to see a dame smoking a rope.'   **1940** *AmSp* 15.335 **NE** [Smokers' slang], Tobacco is . . rope. . . A cigar is *rope.*   **1965–70** *DARE* (Qu. DD6a, *Other names or nicknames for cigars*) 72 Infs, **scattered, but chiefly Nth, N Midl, Pacific,** Rope; **VT**12, Hunk o' rope; (Qu. DD7, *Different names for cigars . . according to size, shape, or the way they're made*) Infs **FL**28, **WI**64, Rope; **NY**40, Dago rope.   **1978** Wouk *War & Remembrance* 66, Carter Aster was smoking a long brown Havana tonight. That meant his spirits were high; otherwise he consumed vile gray Philippine ropes.

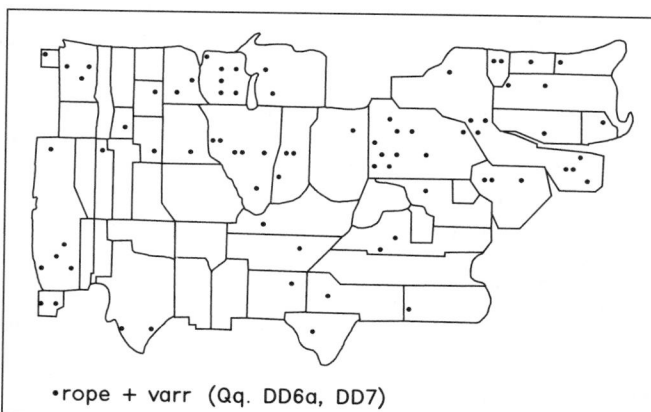

• rope + varr (Qq. DD6a, DD7)

ropebark n [See quot 1828]

A **leatherwood** 1 (here: *Dirca palustris*).

1828 Rafinesque *Med. Flora* 1.158, *Dirca Palustris.* . . Vulgar Names—Leatherwood, Moosewood, Swampwood, Ropebark. [*Ibid* 159, The bark is very tough, can hardly be broken, and tearing in long stripes [sic] is used as yet in many parts for ropes, a practice borrowed from the Indian tribes.]   **1876** Hobbs *Bot. Hdbk.* 98, Rope bark, Leatherwood, Dirca palustris.   **1892** (1974) Millspaugh *Amer. Med. Plants*

146–1, Dirca Palustris. . . Com[mon] Names.—Leatherwood, Moosewood, Wicopy, Rope Bark, Swampwood, Thong Bark [etc].   **1940** Clute *Amer. Plant Names* 96, [*Dirca] palustris.* . . rope-bark.   **1976** Bailey-Bailey *Hortus Third* 391, [*Dirca] palustris* . . Wicopy, Ropebark, Moosewood.

roper n   Cf **goat roper**

1998 *DARE* File **TX,** Here is another word that seems pretty well known in Texas—*roper* for a rustic. It is short for *goat roper* which is well known in both Oklahoma and Texas.

rope yarn Sunday n   Also *rope yarn holiday*   Cf **every hair a rope yarn**

Among sailors: a period of relative leisure on shipboard; see quots.

1852 *S. Lit. Messenger* Apr 195, This is "rope-yarn Sunday." The ordinary work of the ship is suspended as far as practicable, and the day is allotted to the men for the purpose of making and mending their clothes.   **1914** *DN* 4.151 [Navy slang], *Rope yarn holiday.* . . A half holiday.   **c1929** Bowen *Sea Slang* 113, *Rope Yarn Sunday.* . . The Americans use the term for Saturday afternoon when there are no drills or inspections, but ship's work is done. Their make and mend is on Wednesday, known as *Rope Yarn Holiday.*   **1957** Beck *Folkl. ME* 171, Now and then the captain would call "rope yarn Sunday" a day of general rest and relaxation when the crew would mend torn clothes, cut hair, indulge in games, usually feats of strength and agility, write home or wash their clothes in the barrel of urine kept by the fo'c'sle door for such purposes.

rosa de montana See **mountain rose 2**

rosary pea n

=**crab's eye.**

[**1866** Lindley–Moore *Treas. Botany* 854 *(OED2),* Pea, Rosary, the seed of *Abrus precatorius.*]   **1923** Amer. Joint Comm. Horticult. Nomenclature *Std. Plant Names* 2, *Abrus precatorius* . . Rosary-pea.   **1953** Greene–Blomquist *Flowers South* 61, Crab's-eye, Indian-Licorice, Rosary-Pea. . . It is native to Europe but has become naturalized in peninsular Fla.   **1965** Neal *Gardens HI* 455, Rosary-pea, black-eyed susan, bead vine, pukiawe-lei.

rosberry, rosbry See **raspberry**

rose v[1], ppl adj   See **rise** v A2a, B1

rose v[2]   See **raise** v A2

rose acacia n   Also *rose (acacia) locust*

A **locust** B1 (here: *Robinia hispida* or *R. viscosa*).

1833 Eaton *Botany* 306, [*Robinia] hispida* . . rose locust, rose acacia.   **1897** Sudworth *Arborescent Flora* 263 **PA, RI, VT,** *Robinia viscosa* . . Rose Acacia.   **1901** Lounsberry *S. Wild Flowers* 275, *R. hispida,* rose acacia or bristly locust, is really the moss locust, holding among the acacias the same place as the moss rose does among roses.   **1922** *Amer. Botanist* 28.28, Two other species of *Robinia* are known as "clammy locust" (*R. viscosa*) and "bristly locust" (*R. hispida*). . . On account of their rosy flowers both are also known as "rose acacia."   **1941** Walker *Lookout* 47 **TN,** It sometimes has an unrelated companion growing with it known as rose acacia.   **1960** Vines *Trees SW* 567, Rose-acacia Locust—*Robinia hispida.*

roseate spoonbill n

Std: the southern spoonbill (*Ajaia ajaja*) with brilliant pink plumage and white neck and back.   Also called **pink bird, ~ crane, ~ curlew**

rosebay n

Std: =**rhododendron,** esp *Rhododendron macrophyllum* or *R. maximum.*   For other names of these spp see **mountain laurel 2;** for other names of *R. maximum* see **big laurel 2, cow plant, deer laurel, deer-tongue ~, great ~, horse-~, laurel 3, rose tree, spoonhutch**

rosebetty n

A **robin's plantain** 1 (here: *Erigeron pulchellus*).

1784 in 1785 *Amer. Acad. Arts & Sci. Memoirs* 1.480, *Erigeron.* . . Rosebetty. Blossoms in the circumference purple; those in the center yellow.   **1830** Rafinesque *Med. Flora* 2.218, [*Erigeron] bellidifolium,* called *Rosebety* [sic] and *Robert's plantain,* is bitterish, pungent, used for hard tumors, and for the bite of snakes. **1900** Lyons *Plant Names* 148, *E. pulchellus*. . . Robert's Plantain, Rose-Betty. **1931** Harned *Wild Flowers Alleghanies* 559, Robin's Plaintain. . . A very common perennial known also under the familiar names, Blue Spring Daisy, Poor Robin, Rose-petty [sic] and Poor Robin's Plantain.

rosebird n
=**rose-breasted grosbeak.**

1955 Lowery *LA Birds* 473, The male "rosebird," as it is often called, is black and white, except for a prominent patch of rose-red in the center of its breast.

rose breast n
1966 DARE FW Addit **MA6**, *Rose breast*—A double breast—i.e. one growing abnormally under another—not full size, but having a nipple much inclined to leak when mother was nursing. Inf says nipple has more holes than usual. After birth of child, this third breast must be emptied regularly with a breast pump or caking and painful clogging occur.

rose-breasted grosbeak n Also *rosebreast*
Std: a grosbeak *(Pheucticus ludovicianus)*, the black-and-white male of which has a rose-red patch on the breast and underwing. Also called **English robin 6, grosbeak, peabird 1, potato-bug bird, redbreast 1f, robin redbreast 2, rosebird, throat-cut**

rose-breasted nuthatch n
=**red-breasted nuthatch.**

1969 DARE (Qu. Q23, *The insect-eating bird that goes headfirst down a tree trunk*) Inf **VT13**, Rose-breasted nuthatch.

rose campion n
=**corn cockle.**

1837 Darlington *Flora Cestrica* 281 **sePA**, *[Agrostemma] Githago*. . . *Vulgò*—Cockle. Corn Cockle. Rose Campion. **1840** MA Zool. & Bot. Surv. *Herb. Plants & Quadrupeds* 87, *[Agrostemma] githago*. . . A well-known weed of wheat fields, hairy and bearing fine rose-colored flowers, and often called *Rose Campion*. **1910** Graves *Flowering Plants* 177 **CT**, *Agrostemma Githago*. . . Rose Pink or Campion.

rose-comb lightwood (knot) n Also *rose-comb pine knot* esp Gulf States
A piece of **lightwood** n[1]; see quots.

1967 DARE Tape **AL20**, [FW:] Do you know what rose-comb lighterwood is? [Inf:] Yes, sir, rose-comb lightwood. . . [FW:] Or is it roostercomb, or is it rose-comb, which is it? [Inf:] Well, I always thought they said rose-comb, but it must have been named after a rooster, like his comb. . . It's a knot out of a lightwood tree where it's just lain in the weather so long, a little hard knot, and it'll be like a fish fin on a fish's back. . . That's where it gets its name, rose-comb, rooster-comb. [FW:] Is it kind of red? [Inf:] No, it'll be bleached white. **1967** DARE FW Addit **AL**, Rose-comb lighter (or lighterd) knot or heart pine. After pine rots, the red heart remains full of pitch. It is a rose color like a rooster's comb. **1968** DARE (Qu. T8, *Joints of pine wood that burn easily and make good fuel*) Inf **LA15**, Rose-comb pine knots. **1981** Pederson *LAGS Basic Materials*, 1 inf, **cwFL**, Rose-comb lighterd knots.

rose crown n Cf king's crown, queen's ~ 2
A **stonecrop** (here: *Sedum rhodanthum*).

1961 Douglas *My Wilderness* 19 **CO**, Queen's (or rose) crown *(Sedum rhodanthum)* has a rounded head of pink flowers. **1963** Craighead *Rocky Mt. Wildflowers* 70, Rosecrown—*Sedum rhodanthum*. . . A dense cluster of rose-colored flowers is at the top of the stem and superficially resembles red clover. **1979** Spellenberg *Audubon Guide N. Amer. Wildflowers W. Region* 471, Red Orpine or Rose Crown *(S. rhodanthum)* has deep pink to nearly white flowers.

rosefish n [See quot 1884]
A **rockfish 3** (here: *Sebastes marinus*). Also called **bream B4, hemdurgan, ocean perch, redfish b, red perch 2, snapper**

1731 in 1906 Essex Inst. *Coll.* 42.223 **MA**, Wee spy'd the Fin of a Whale . . & Supposing it to be a Rose fish, ran forward to see it. **1839** MA Zool. & Bot. Surv. *Fishes Reptiles* 26, S[ebastes] Norvegicus. . . *The Norway Haddock*. . . By our fishermen it is known by the names of "*Rose fish*," "*Hemdurgan*," and "*Snapper*." **1884** Goode *Fisheries U.S.* 1.260, The Rose-fish, *Sebastes marinus*, is conspicuous and unique

among cold-water fishes by its brilliant scarlet color. **1933** John G. Shedd Aquarium *Guide* 128, The Rosefish is abundant on both shores of the north Atlantic in rather deep water. It is an important food fish in New England and in Europe. **1966** DARE (Qu. P2, . . *Kinds of saltwater fish caught around here . . good to eat)* Inf **ME22**, Rosefish (old name); redfish (common now); ocean perch (when sold in stores).

rose gentian n
=**marsh pink 1.**

1923 Amer. Joint Comm. Horticult. Nomenclature *Std. Plant Names* 456, *Sabatia* [spp] . . Rosegentian. **1949** Moldenke *Amer. Wild Flowers* 228, Another very showy group of gentian relatives is the rosegentians, *Sabbatia*. **1979** Ajilvsgi *Wild Flowers* 226, Prairie rose-gentian—*Sabatia campanulata*.

rose laurel n
=**calico bush 1.**

1830 Rafinesque *Med. Flora* 2.16, Kalmia latifolia. Names. . . *Vulgar.* Laurel, Mountain Laurel, Rose Laurel [etc]. **1892** (1974) Millspaugh *Amer. Med. Plants* 103–1, *Mountain Laurel.* . . Com[mon] Names.—Mountain Laurel, American Laurel, Calico-bush, Spoonwood, Big Ivy, Rose Laurel [etc]. **1911** Henkel *Amer. Med. Leaves* 17, Mountain Laurel. *Kalmia latifolia* . . Other common names.—Broad-leaved laurel . . rose laurel [etc].

rose locust See rose acacia

rose mallow n Cf mallow rose
=**hibiscus.**

1857 Gray *First Lessons* 68, *Hibiscus* [spp] . . Rose-Mallow. *Ibid, H. Moscheutos* . . Swamp Rose-Mallow. **1901** Lounsberry *S. Wild Flowers* 336, *H. Moscheutos*, rose mallow, or swamp mallow. . . In August it blooms through swamps, and often side by side with the pink form will be seen a white one. **1924** *Amer. Botanist* 30.106, Far more partial to wet grounds than the marsh mallow are the various species of *Hibiscus*. Though occasionally called "marsh mallows," they are more often known as "rose mallows." **1949** Moldenke *Amer. Wild Flowers* 111, Residents of areas adjacent to salt and brackish marshes on the eastern coastal plain from Massachusetts to Florida and Texas are well acquainted with the popular swamp rosemallow, *Hibiscus moscheutos* . . , easily the showiest of its tribe. **1966–69** DARE (Qu. S21, . . *Weeds . . that are a trouble in gardens and fields)* Inf **MA6**, Mallow—also rose mallow; (Qu. S26b, *Wildflowers that grow in water or wet places)* Inf **RI15**, Rose mallow in salt marshes. **1967** DARE Wildflower QR Pl.149 Inf **SC41**, Rose mallow. **1969** DARE FW Addit **NC**, Rose mallows—plant common [on] Hatteras Island. **1976** Bruce *How to Grow Wildflowers* 183, In midsummer no flower quite enlivens the landscape so much as the big and showy Rose-mallow, *Hibiscus palustris*.

rose mandarin n
A **twisted-stalk** (here: *Streptopus lanceolatus* var *roseus*).

1933 Small *Manual SE Flora* 298, *[Streptopus] roseus.* . . Rosy-Twisted-stalk, Rose-bells. Rose-Mandarin. . . Woods, Blue Ridge and more northern provinces, Ga. to Mich., Ore., Alas[ka]. **1961** Smith *MI Wildflowers* 53, Rosy Twisted-stalk, Rose Mandarin. . . In moist woods and thickets. Flowering April to July. **1976** Bailey–Bailey *Hortus Third* 1081, *[Streptopus] roseus* . . Rose mandarin. . . N. Ore. to Alaska. Var. *perspectus* . . s. to Penn. and w. to Mich.

rosemary pine n Also *rosemary* chiefly Sth, esp NC
Any of three **pines 1: loblolly pine 1, longleaf pine 1,** or **shortleaf pine 1.**

1859 Perry *Turpentine Farming* 161 **NC**, Rosemary, or spruce pine.— There is less of this kind than any other, and its nature falls between the two preceding descriptions, except that it has the shortest, finest straw. **1897** Sudworth *Arborescent Flora* 25, *Pinus taeda*. . . Rosemary Pine (Va., N.C.) *Ibid* 30, *Pinus palustris*. . . Rosemary Pine (N.C.) **1901** Lounsberry *S. Wild Flowers* 6 **NC**, *Pinus Taèda*. . . By many this tree is known as the frankincense pine, and when growing in swampy ground, the North Carolina woodsmen call it rosemary pine. **1922** U.S. Dept. Ag. *Farmers' Bulletin* 1256.2, In South Carolina and Georgia the original-growth slash pine is sometimes called "rosemary," a name applied, however, in different sections to large trees of several other species of pines. **1966–68** DARE (Qu. T17, . . *Kinds of pine trees*; not asked in early QRs) Infs **NC24, 49, TX37**, Rosemary pine. **1971** Krochmal *Appalachia Med. Plants* 192, *Pinus palustris*. . . Rosemary pine. . . in southern Appalachia is a valuable source of turpentine, pine oil, tar, pitch, and rosin. **1986** Pederson *LAGS Concordance*, 2 infs, **nwFL, ceLA**, Rosemary pine; 1 inf, **swGA**, Rosemaries (short-needled pines).

rose moss See **moss rose 2, 3**

rosen n See **rosin A1a**

rosen v See **rise** v **A2a**

rose of Plymouth n [See quot 1901]
A **marsh pink 1** (here: *Sabatia stellaris*).

1890 *Century Dict.* 5286, The flowers are usually numerous and handsome, marked by a small central yellow star, and in the largest species, *S[abbatia] chloroides*, are about 2 inches across. This species, from its color and locality, is known as the *rose of Plymouth*. **1901** Lounsberry *S. Wild Flowers* 427, *S[abbatia] stellaris*, sea or marsh pink, the familiarly known member of the genus, extends from Florida along the coast as far northward as Maine. Locally it is much beloved, and called the rose of Plymouth in accordance with the tradition that there the pilgrims first beheld it on the Sabbath day. **1912** Baker *Book of Grasses* 214, They are slender grasses, blossoming in midsummer and later when the beautiful sea-pink, or rose of Plymouth, blooms in salt meadows. **1949** Moldenke *Amer. Wild Flowers* 229, The *rose-of-Plymouth* or *seapink*, *S[abatia] stellaris*, and the *slender marshpink*, *S. campanulata*, inhabit salt meadows and coastal marshes from Maine to Florida and Louisiana. Their pink flowers have a yellow, star-shaped "eye" in the center, which is often bordered with red.

rose of Sharon n
1 A **hibiscus** (here: *Hibiscus syriacus*).

1859 (1880) Darlington *Amer. Weeds* 67, *Syrian Hibiscus*. Rose of Sharon. Shrubby Althæa. **1901** Lounsberry *S. Wild Flowers* 337, As examples [sic] of the family seen in cultivation is the beautiful rose of Sharon, Hibiscus syriacus. **1966** *DARE* Wildflower QR Pl.129 Inf **NC28**, Rose of Sharon, [corr to] mallows—grow in white and pink along rivers; **SC49**, Rose of Sharon—Althea. **1968–70** *DARE* (Qu. L65, . . *Kinds of fences*) Inf **OH78**, Rose of Sharon hedge; (Qu. T16, . . *Kinds of trees . . 'special'*) Inf **MD22**, Rose of Sharon—gives purple, white, pink flowers—large bush; **NC87**, Rose of Sharon, cotton blossom—names for bush.

2 A **locust B1** (here: *Robinia hispida*). Cf **rose acacia**

1901 Lounsberry *S. Wild Flowers* 275, *R[obinia] hispida*, rose acacia, or bristly locust, is really the moss locust. . . Occasionally we hear it erroneously called the Rose of Sharon.

3 A **globe mallow 1** (here: *Sphaeralcea incana*).

1967 Dodge *Roadside Wildflowers* 41, Soft globemallow—false mallow, wild hollyhock, rose-of-Sharon[.] Abundant on road shoulders, globemallows of many species grow throughout the Southwest at all elevations up to 8,000 feet.

rose-of-the-mountain See **mountain rose 2**

rose pine n
Perh =**loblolly pine 1**.

1970 *DARE* (Qu. T17, . . *Kinds of pine trees*; not asked in early QRs) Inf **VA46**, Rose pine—same as spruce pine—cones rose-shaped.

rose pink n
1 A **marsh pink 1** (here: usu *Sabatia angularis*, but also *S. campestris*).

1830 Rafinesque *Med. Flora* 2.76, Sabatia angularis. *Names*. . . *Vulgar*. Rosepink, Wild Succory, Bitterbloom. **1910** Shreve *MD Plant Life* 470, Rose Pink. Coastal and Midland Zones. **1936** IL Nat. Hist. Surv. *Wildflowers* 235, Rose Pink—*Sabatia angularis*. . . The fragrant rosy flowers are produced in July and August. **1979** Ajilvsgi *Wild Flowers* 225, Rose-pink. . . *Flower:* pink or rose, rarely white, with greenish central star, delicately fragrant.

2 =**corn cockle**.

1910 Graves *Flowering Plants* 177 **CT**, *Agrostemma Githago*. . . Rose Pink or Campion. . . In the West, where it is often abundant, its seeds injure the appearance and quality of grain.

rose pogonia n
Std: an orchid of the eastern US (*Pogonia ophioglossoides*) bearing a single fragrant rose-pink flower. Also called **adder's mouth 2, grass pink 2, snakemouth**

roseroot n
Std: a **stonecrop** (here: *Rhodiola rosea*) whose root has the smell of roses. Also called **heal-all 6, hen and chickens 1a(3), king's crown, queen's ~ 2, scurvy grass 1**

rose tree n
A **rosebay** (here: *Rhododendron maximum*).

1899 Woerner *Rebel's Daughter* 298 **Ozarks**, "Rose-tree, did you say?" the rejoicing young man inquired with a deferential show of curiosity. "I thought it was an oleander." "So it is," Miss Waldhorst responded.

rosette n chiefly **WI, MN**   *esp in Scan settlement areas*
A crisp pastry made by dipping a usu rose-shaped, heated timbale iron into batter and then into deep fat, and usu served sprinkled with confectioners' sugar.

1950 *WELS* (Foods made with dough and cooked in deep fat) 11 Infs, **WI**, Rosettes; 1 Inf, **cWI**, Rosettes (Norwegian); 1 Inf, **seWI**, Rosettes—made with an iron—fancy shape, dip in batter and fry. **1966** *Stoughton Courier* (WI) 1 Dec sec 2 [12/3], Rosettes are another crisp cookie that can be served in many ways. They are fried in deep fat with a floral shaped iron. When cool and brittle crisp they are sprinkled with confectioner's sugar or filled. **1966–68** *DARE* (Qu. H28, *Different shapes or types of doughnuts*) Inf **VA33**, Rosette—shaped like a figure eight; (Qu. H32, . . *Fancy rolls and pastries*) Inf **MN39**, Rosettes—made on an iron; (Qu. H63, *Kinds of desserts*) Inf **WI72**, Rosettes; (Qu. H65, *Foreign foods favored by people around here*) Inf **WI58**, Rosettes—Swedish; (Qu. H31, *Other foods made with dough and cooked in deep fat;* total Infs questioned, 75) Inf **MS46**, Rosettes—make for other people; **MS65**, Rosettes [FW sugg]. **1967** *DARE* Tape **MN6**, We also made rosettes, which are made on a rosette iron and then they are dipped in sugar after they are done. **1981** Hachten *Flavor WI* 301, *Rosettes (Swedish). . .* Beat eggs; add sugar, milk, flour, salt, and vanilla and beat. . . Heat rosette iron by dripping [sic] into heated shortening. . . Dip heated iron into batter . . ; dip into hot shortening. . . Remove cookie from fat . . and sprinkle with confectioners' sugar. **1983** *Capital Times* (Madison WI) 11 May 19, Passing culinary heritage from generation to generation prompts the Sons of Norway Mandt Lodge, Stoughton, to host a smorgasbord. . . Pastries include . . rosettes. **1989** Karni-Jarvenpa *Sampo* 327 **MN**, My grandmother fed me Rosettes:/ deep fried batter butterflies / and flowers / sprinkled with white powdered sugar / to make my blood sparkle / and bloom flesh. **1991** [see **sandbakkel**].

rose willow n
A **dogwood 1** (here: *Cornus amomum* or *C. sericea*).

1815 Drake *Natural View Cincinnati* 83, [The] rose willow, leather wood and aspen, seem to be confined to the more northern portions of this tract. **1873** in 1976 Miller *Shaker Herbs* 254, Willow, Rose—*Cornus Sericea*. . . Bitter, astringent, detergent, and antiperiodic. Used occasionally as a substitute for quinine. **1940** Clute *Amer. Plant Names* 97, *C[ornus] amomum*. . . red osier, red-brush, red willow, rose willow [etc].

rose-wings n
=**grass pink 1**.

1933 Small *Manual SE Flora* 376, Grass-pinks. Rose-wings. **1953** Greene–Blomquist *Flowers South* 24, Rose-Wings (*Calopogon pulchellus*).

rosin n Usu |'rɑzɪn, -ɪn, -ən, -n̩|; for varr see **A** below Cf **resin**
A Forms. Note: In interpreting the distribution of forms, it is important to be aware that the sense in which *rosin* was most freq elicited is itself strongly regional; see **B1** below.
1a |'rɔzɪn|; pronc-sp *rosen*. chiefly **Sth, S Midl** Note: It is possible that this pronc-sp represents a different pronc.

c1930 Swann *Lang. Circus Lot* 15, *Rosen back:* Horse for bare-back riding. **1965–70** *DARE* (Qu. T7, *The sticky stuff that comes out of pine trees*) 90 Infs, chiefly **Sth, S Midl**, Rosin ['rɔzɪn, -ɪn, -ən, -n̩, 'rɔzɪn, -n̩, 'rɑzən, -n̩]; (Qu. T8) Inf **MN12**, Rosin ['rɔzɪn]. **1972** Hilliard *Hog Meat* 73, Much of the coastal South has never seen the plow, only the blade of the "rosen" (naval stores) and lumber men.

b |'rɔuzɪn, 'rauzɪn|. esp **Sth, S Midl**

1966–70 *DARE* (Qu. T7) Inf **IN9**, ['rɔu,zən]; **IN11**, ['rau,zɪn]; **LA28**, ['rɔuzn̩]; **SC3**, [rɔuzɪn]; **SC7**, [rɔuzɪn]; **SC11**, [rauzɪn]; **TN62**, ['rauzən].

2a |'rɑzəm, 'rɔz-|; pronc-spp *rawsum, rosim, ros(o)m, rosum, rozom, rozzum*. chiefly **Sth, S Midl**

1795 Dearborn *Columbian Grammar* 138, *List of Improprieties*. . . Rozom for Rosin or Resin. **1843** (1916) Hall *New Purchase* 421 **IN**, Dan was, truly, no niggard of "rosum." **1867** Harris *Sut Lovingood Yarns* 185 **TN**, Thar's more rosim in hell than thar's in all Noth Caliny.

1872 Schele de Vere *Americanisms* 536, *Rosum* is a common corruption of *rosin*, which is almost universally pronounced *ros′m* by the mass of people. **1891** *PMLA* 175 **TN**, *Rosin* is [pronounced] *rosum* or *rawsum*. **1893** Shands *MS Speech* 54, *Rozzum* [razm̩ or rozm̩]. Negro for *rosin*. Used also in Tennessee. **1899** (1912) Green *VA Folk-Speech* 357, *Rosum*. . . Rosin. **1909** *DN* 3.364 **eAL, wGA**, *Rozum*. . . Resin, rosin. **1912** *DN* 3.588 **wIN**, *Rosum*. . . Rosin, which is rarely heard. **1915** *DN* 4.189 **swVA**, *Rosum*. Rosin. **1917** *DN* 4.399 **neOH**, *Rosm* [rozm̩]. . . Rosin. Also La., Ill., Vt., Kan., Ky. [razn̩] and [razɪn] are acquired. **1922** Gonzales *Black Border* 323 **sSC, GA coasts** [Gullah glossary], *Rozzum*—rosin. **1965–70** *DARE* (Qu. T7, *The sticky stuff that comes out of pine trees*) 57 Infs, **Sth, S Midl**, Rozzum ['razəm, -ɪm, 'rozəm, -ɪm, -m̩]; (Qu. T8) Inf **DC5**, ['rozəm]; **SC10**, ['razəm]. **1968** *DARE* FW Addit **LA29**, *Rosum* [rozəm] = the hard substance from dried pine sap. **1972** Cooper *NC Mt. Folkl.* 95, *Rosm*—resin or rosin. **1974** Fink *Mountain Speech* 22 **wNC, eTN**, *Rosum* . . resin. **1982** Powers *Cataloochee* 364 **cwNC**, The fiddler was 'Mericus Hall . . and you should have heard and seen him putting rosom (resin) on the bow.

b ['rouzəm, 'rauzəm].
1968–70 *DARE* (Qu. T7, *The sticky stuff that comes out of pine trees*) Infs **TN26, VA38**, ['rouz(ə)m]; **VA2**, ['rauzm].

3 ['rasɪn, 'rɔs-]. **scattered, but esp Sth, S Midl** Note: These may well be spelling-proncs.
1965–70 *DARE* (Qu. T7, *The sticky stuff that comes out of pine trees*) 14 Infs, **scattered, esp Sth, S Midl**, Rosin ['rasɪn, -ən, 'ras(ə)n, 'rosɪn, -ɪn, -(ə)n, 'rɔsɪn].

4 ['rasəm, 'rɔs-]; pronc-sp *rossum*. **scattered Sth, S Midl, SW**
1866 Reid *After the War* 416 **seLA, sMS**, The rossum heels live in thar [=in pine barrens]. **1899** [see **B1a** below]. **1965–70** *DARE* (Qu. T7, *The sticky stuff that comes out of pine trees*) 13 Infs, **scattered Sth, S Midl, SW**, Rossum ['rasəm, 'rasəm, 'rɔsəm, -ɪm, -ɪm, -ɛn, 'rɒsm̩]; (Qu. T8) Inf **IN44**, Rossum sticks; (Qu. BB50c) Inf **GA77**, Pine rossum.

5 Addit varr; see quots.
1957 *Sat. Eve. Post Letters* **WI**, And how about an old tin can with a string coated with rosing, used as a noisemaker. **1966–68** *DARE* (Qu. T7) Inf **OK20**, [rozəm]; **PA95**, [risən]; **SC24**, [rozɪn], [rizɪn], or whatever you call it.

B Senses.
1a =**pitch** n¹. **chiefly Sth, S Midl** See Map
1888 Johnston *Mr. Absalom Billingslea* 137 **GA**, The only use he had ever known rawsom put to was chewing, and of that he admitted that from a child he had been fond. **1899** (1912) Green *VA Folk-Speech* 361, The rossum runs out of the wood with the hot sun. **1965–70** *DARE* (Qu. T7, *The sticky stuff that comes out of pine trees*) 280 Infs, **chiefly Sth, S Midl**, Rosin [and varr]; [**SC43**, Rosin—left over after making turpentine;] (Qu. BB22, . . *Home remedies . . for constipation*) Inf **NC88**, Pine rosin—chip the tree, catch the sap, let it congeal, give it to kids to chew; good also for worms and upset stomach; sweet-gum rosin; (Qu. BB50a, . . *Favorite remedies . . for a cough*) Inf **AL48**, Pine rosin—put in spoon, heat, mix with water, stir with a toothpick; (Qu. BB50c, *Remedies for infections*) Inf **GA77**, Pine rosum, sugar, lard, baking soda, mixed together and put on wound; **MI96**, Rosin salve; **VA42**, Pine-rozum salve; (Qu. BB51a, . . *Cures for corns or warts*) Inf **KY34**, Rosum—from pine trees. **1966** *DARE* Tape **FL17**, The pines were very big, and they had to, men to go and take the face off, put cups on 'em, and get the turpentine out, get the rosin ['rozən] . . still the turpentine;

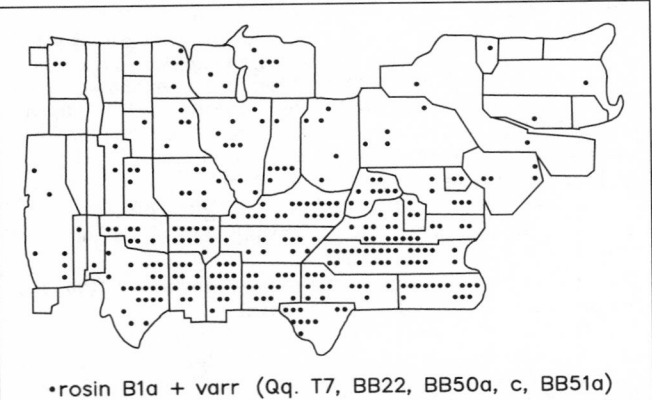

•rosin B1a + varr (Qq. T7, BB22, BB50a, c, BB51a)

GA7, We don't work any black pine; it wouldn't run. . . It usually wouldn't produce a little ['razm̩] or something like that. **1969** Sorden *Lumberjack Lingo* 96 **NEng, Gt Lakes**, Resin or rosin—Pitch. A secretion of the evergreen tree. Secretion of balsam fir generally called rosin.
b attrib; Of pine wood: very resinous—freq in combs *rosin pine, ~ joint, ~ knot, ~ stick*.
1967–69 *DARE* (Qu. T8, *Joints of pine wood that burn easily and make good fuel*) Infs **IA34, IL11, 66, MS47, MO38, NY101**, Rosin pine; **IL104, MN12**, Rosin joints; **DC5, MO37**, Rosin knots; **IN44**, Rosin sticks. **1981** Pederson *LAGS Basic Materials (Lightwood)* 1 inf, **swMS**, ['rɔˠʌˀzlm̩, ˌpʰaˀɪn]; 1 inf, **neLA**, [riˀ·l rɪˀtʃ rɒ·zm̩ pʰaˀɛn].
2 The gum exuded by certain broadleaf trees.
1967–70 *DARE* (Qu. BB22, . . *Home remedies . . for constipation*) Inf **NC88**, Sweet-gum rosin; (Qu. BB51a, . . *Cures for corns or warts*) Inf **MO38**, Take rosin out of peach trees; put it on a knife and drag it through that wart and that will kill it.

rosin belly See **rosin heel**

rosin brush n
A **groundsel tree** (here: *Baccharis sarothroides*).
1931 U.S. Dept. Ag. *Misc. Pub.* 101.160, Broom baccharis (*B. sarothroides*), locally called greasewood and rosin brush, ranges from Lower California and islands to southern California, southwestern New Mexico, and Sonora. . . The herbage has a resinous-bitterish taste and is normally unpalatable to grazing animals. **1949** Curtin *By the Prophet* 65 **AZ**, Rosinbrush grows in the bottom-lands and on the hillsides up to 4,000 feet altitude. **1960** Vines *Trees SW* 972, Broom Baccharis. . . It is also known under the vernacular names of Greasewood, Desert-bloom, Rosin-brush, and Groundsel.

rosin chewer n *esp freq among Black speakers*
A rustic.
1981 Pederson *LAGS Basic Materials (A rustic)* 1 inf, **nwAL**, ['rɒˀzm̩z ˈtʃoˠʌəz]; 1 inf, **cAL**, ['rɔˠɔˀzn̩ ˈtʃɪ̈ˀu<ə]—insulting [used of a White person]; 1 inf, **cAL**, [ˌrɒˀˠˀzn̩ ˈtʃɒˀɔˠəz] [synonym for *peckerwood*]; 1 inf, **ceMS**, ['rɔˠɔˀzm̩ ˌtʃɵ̈ᵻ̈ə or ˌtʃɔˠ·ɔˀə]. [All infs Black]

ros'in ear See **roasting ear**

rosin heel n Also *rosin belly* **Gulf States** Cf **rosin chewer**
See quots.
1826 Flint *Recollections* 319 "**West FL**" [now **sMS**], They are a wild race, with but little order or morals among them; they are generally denominated "Bogues," and call themselves "rosin heels." **1866** [see **rosin A4**]. **1927** *AmSp* 3.24 **eTX** [Sawmill talk], The common laborer is variously known as a "lumber rustler," "rosum belly," or "sawdust eater." **1949** *AmSp* 24.26, To this list [of opprobrious nicknames] may be added *Fly-up-the-creek*, *Bogue*, and *Rosin-heel* for a Floridian.

rosin joint (or knot) See **rosin B1b**

rosin pine n
1 A **longleaf pine 1** or similar pine.
1966 *DARE* (Qu. T17, . . *Kinds of pine trees*; not asked in early QRs) Inf **DC5**, ['rozəm ˌpaɪn].
2 See **rosin B1b**.

rosin plant n Also *resin plant*
A **rosinweed 1** (here: usu *Silphium compositum*).
1839 in 1856 MI State Ag. Soc. *Trans. for 1855* 7.419, *Silphium gummiferum*. . . Rosin-plant. **1901** Lounsberry *S. Wild Flowers* 517, Resin Plant . . *Silphium terebinthinaceum*. . . The whole genus . . is possessed of a resinous juice, which, especially of the species Silphium laciniatum, is obtained and considerably used by country people. **1953** [see **rosinweed 1**].

rosin stick See **rosin B1b**

rosinweed n
1 also *resin grass, resinweed*: A plant of the genus *Silphium*, esp *S. laciniatum*. For other names of the latter see **compass plant 1, gopher ~ 3, polar ~**; for other names of var spp see **cup plant 1, gum ~ 4, pilot weed, prairie dock 1, ragged cup, rosin plant, turpentine weed**.
1831 *Jamestown Jrl.* (Chautauqua Co. NY) 13 July 1 **WI**, Sun flowers and rosin-weed . . abound. **1833** (1834) Schoolcraft *Narr. Exped. Upper Missip.* 297 **nwIL**, Among the flowers, the plant called rosin-weed

attracts attention by its gigantic stature. **1852** Mackinnon *Atlantic & Transatlantic* 1.268 **WI,** I found that he had spoken the truth, and that the resin grass, or weed, had peculiar leaves which always grew in the same direction. **1856** Ferguson *America* 372 **csIL,** The most prominent plant is the resin-weed. It has a palmated leaf, and grows to a considerable height. . . It exudes a resin, and is aromatic to the taste. **1869** Porcher *Resources* 460 **Sth,** Rosin Weed, (*Silphium laciniatum*). . . Asthma or heaves in horses is said not to exist in the prairies where this plant grows. **1953** Greene–Blomquist *Flowers South* 137, Rosin-Weeds, Rosin-Plants (*Silphium compositum*). . . often seen in summer on forest margins in various districts from Ga. to Ala., n. to Tenn. and s.e. Va. **1966–70** *DARE* (Qu. S26a, . . *Wildflowers. . . Roadside flowers*) Inf **KS**16, Rosinweed—a species of sunflower; (Qu. S26d, *Wildflowers that grow in meadows;* not asked in early QRs) Infs **GA**91, **IA**3, 8, **NY**84, **PA**35, Rosinweed; (Qu. S26e, *Other wildflowers not yet mentioned;* not asked in early QRs) Inf **OK**52, Rosinweed—in hay meadows. [*DARE* Ed: Some of these Infs may refer instead to other senses.]

2 also *resinweed:* **=gum plant 1,** esp *Grindelia robusta* and *G. squarrosa.*

1869 (1870) Parkman *Discovery Gt. West* 206, The meadows . . spangled with the yellow blossoms of the resin-weed and the Rudbeckia. **1897** Parsons *Wild Flowers CA* 176, The *Grindelias* are especially characteristic of the region west of the Mississippi River, and are all known as . . "resin-weed," owing to the balsamic exudation which is found mostly upon the flower-heads. **1930** OK Univ. Biol. Surv. *Pub.* 2.85, *Grindelia lanceolata* . . Narrow-leaved Gum-plant or Rosin-weed. *Grindela squarrosa* . . Broad-leaved Gum-plant or Rosin-weed. **1963** Craighead *Rocky Mt. Wildflowers* 213, *Grindelia squarrosa.* . . Resinweed. . . The heads of this plant, and usually leaves also, are very sticky. **1973** Hitchcock–Cronquist *Flora Pacific NW* 523, *Grindelia.* . . Resinweed. . . Our spp. gen[erally] fl[owering] midsummer to fall.

3 A bitterweed (here: *Hymenoxys acaulis*).

1937 U.S. Forest Serv. *Range Plant Hdbk.* W6, Stemless actinea. . . has not acquired a well-established common name but is known by a great variety of (and often misapplied) local names, such as cloth-of-gold, golden-daisy, golden-head, Indian-tobacco, ironweed, ray-flower, rosinweed, and yellow-aster.

4 A goldeneye 4 (here: *Viguiera multiflora*).

1937 U.S. Forest Serv. *Range Plant Hdbk.* W204, Showy goldeneye, a perennial herb with golden-yellow, sunflowerlike, flower heads, is sometimes known as rosinweed. . . This species has no well-established common name.

5 A jimmyweed (here: *Isocoma pluriflora* [formerly *Haplopappus p.*]).

1937 U.S. Forest Serv. *Range Plant Hdbk.* B13, Jimmyweed, a dull green, bushy halfshrub growing 1 or 2 (occasionally 4) feet high, is also known as rayless-goldenrod and rosinweed.

6 =Saint-John's-wort.

1940 Clute *Amer. Plant Names* 261, *Hypericum perforatum.* Tipton-weed, rosin-weed, Klamath-weed [etc].

7 A golden aster 1 (here: *Chrysopsis villosa*).

1940 Clute *Amer. Plant Names* 80, [*Chrysopsis] villosa.* Golden Aster. Rosin-weed.

rosinwood n Cf **rosinweed 7**
A golden aster 1 (here: *Chrysopsis villosa*).

1850 (1854) Bartlett *Personal Narr.* 1.94 **TX,** Rosin wood, or creosote plant, a most disgusting, strong-smelling shrub. **1896** *Jrl. Amer. Folkl.* 9.191 **ND,** *Chrysopsis villosa* . . rosinwood.

ros'in year See **roasting ear**

rosm, rosom See **rosin A2a**

rossel See **wrestle**

rossum See **rosin A4**

rosum See **rosin A2a**

rostle See **rustle** v

Rosy nosy See **nosy Rosy**

rot v Cf **rotten** adj **1**
Of ice: to disintegrate, become porous; to cause (ice) to become porous.

1871 *Galaxy* 11.520, If this does not prove sufficient to thaw or at least

to rot and loosen the surface ice, it would be likely to give way beneath the influence of the sun. **1889** *New Engl. Mag.* 7.70, The water beating against a rotting fringe of ice that dureth still. **1950** *Eaton Coll.* **Washington Island WI,** *Rot* . . of ice in Spring—to become porous and unable to bear weight. **1968** *DARE* FW Addit **DE,** Rotting ice. **1977** *New Yorker* 20 June 86 **AK,** Snow was melting. Ice was beginning to rot.

rotary n Also *rotary circle* **chiefly NEng** See Map Cf **traffic circle**
A road junction in which traffic moves in one direction around a circular island.

1940 Geddes *Magic Motorways* 92 **NY,** Progress around the rotary is slow, for all cars have to weave from lane to lane and are slowed down by the cars feeding in ahead. **1955** *New Yorker* 12 Mar 38, At eight the next morning we came to the first traffic rotary outside New York, in New Jersey. **1965–70** *DARE* (Qu. N20, . . *A circular arrangement on one level at a big intersection, where cars can go around till they come to the road they want*) 61 Infs, **chiefly NEng,** Rotary; **ME**19, **VT**16, Rotary circle. **1966** *PMLA* 81.2.11, In my lifetime I have seen the *traffic circle* of the Middle Atlantic States become the *rotary* of Eastern New England. **1983** Beyle *How Talk Cape Cod* np, Take route 6 and, at the Orleans Rotary, turn toward Orleans about ½ mile.

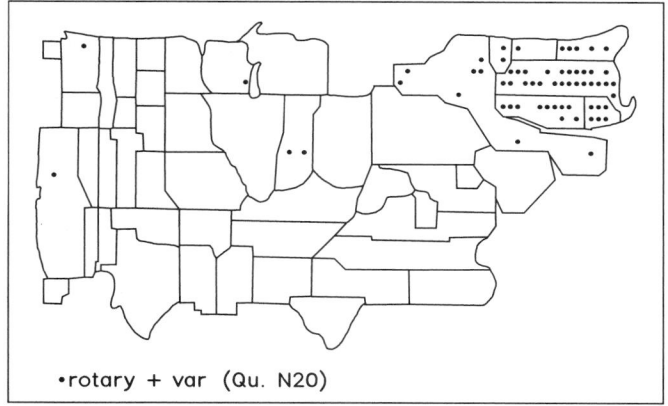

•rotary + var (Qu. N20)

rotch n Also *rotch(i)e* [*OED2* a1809 →]
=dovekie.

1890 *Century Dict.* 5237, Rotche. . . The little auk, auklet, dovekie, or sea-dove, *Mergulus alle* or *Alle nigricans. Ibid,* Rotchie. . . Same as rotche. **1917** (1923) *Birds Amer.* 1.31, *Dovekie.* . . *Other Names.*—Little Auk; Sea Dove; Alle; Rotch; Ice-bird. **1946** Hausman *Eastern Birds* 337, *Dovekie.* . . Other Names—Sea Dove, Little Auk, Alle, Pine Knot, Knotty, Rotch, Little Ice Bird, Ice Bird.

rote n [*OED2* 1610 →] **coastal NEng** Cf **rut,** *DNE*
The roar of breaking waves.

1847 [see **rut**]. [**1855** Haliburton *Nature* 210 **Nova Scotia,** When . . the rote is on the beach, it tells me it is the voice of the south wind giving notice of rain.] **1864** Lowell *Fireside Travels* 185 **MA,** X. walked away, rumbling inwardly like the rote of the sea heard afar. **1875** *Atlantic Mth.* 35.608 **seNH,** Slowly the coast-lights fade, and now the rote of the sea among the lonely ledges of the shoals salutes his attentive ear. **1900** *Atlantic Mth.* 86.153 **ME,** I can hear the rote o' them old black ledges way down the thoroughfare. **1908** Wasson *Home from Sea* 13 **sME coast,** You take it out abreast of his place there on the aidge of the hollow, and you'll get the rote double and thribble as plain as what we do here. **1932** Wasson *Sailing Days* 125 **cME coast,** On Isle au Haut, as upon the northern coast, and on board vessels, the rumbling noise of the sea, charging upon rocky shores, was universally known as the "rote." Every man on vessels approaching shore, when weather was so often "thick-o'-fog," listened intently to "make the rote" on various ledges or islands as a means of identifying position. **1942** ME Univ. *Studies* 56.60, Another omen of bad weather was the *rote,* or peculiar dull sound of the waves breaking on the beach, a forerunner of a storm coming from the sea. **1965** *Amer. Neptune* Oct 236 **ME,** Often have I heard a Maine man say, 'Sea's making up. Hear that rote!'

roten See **rotten** v

rot foot n esp **S Midl** Cf **hoof rot**
An infection of the foot.

1960 Williams *Walk Egypt* 280 **GA,** You want the hens should get rot-foot from the damp? **1967–70** *DARE* (Qu. K28, . . *Chief diseases that cows have*) Infs **IN**13, **KY**27, 35, 93, **LA**18, **MA**15, Rot foot; (Qu. K47, . . *Diseases . . horses or mules commonly get*) Inf **TN**17, The rot foot.

rotine See **routine**

rotn, rotnin(g) See **rotten** v

rotten adj

1 Of ice: crumbling, becoming porous, disintegrating. **scattered, but esp C Atl, N Cent** See Map Cf **porridge ice, rot, rubber ice**

1746 in 1940 *AmSp* 15.229 **NEng,** *Rotten,* weak, of ice. 'Went over ye River upon ye ice. It grew very rotten.' **1810** Pike *Expeditions* 87, The ice [was] very dangerous[,] being rotten. **1861** *Harper's New Mth. Mag.* 22.350, Oh, Rupert Clare! Where are your eyes?/ *The rotten ice* before us lies! **1935** *Monthly Weather Rev.* (Washington) LXII.133/1 *(OED2),* The boatman, fisherman, and lots of others . . swear that at this season [*sc.* spring] surface ice becomes rotten, or honeycombed, and sinks. **1965–70** *DARE* (Qu. B35, *Ice that will bend when you step on it, but not break*) 10 Infs, **scattered, but esp C Atl, N Cent,** Rotten ice; **DE**1, Rotten ice—when it's thawing in the spring; **NY**230, Rotten ice—unsafe spring ice; it's just starting to go out; (QR, near Qu. B35) Inf **IA**8, Rotten ice—ice that gets honeycombed in the spring. [10 of 13 Infs old, 10 male] **1966** *DARE* File **sIN,** Limber belly ice (rubber ice) [is] rotten ice in Southern Indiana. **1967** *DARE* Tape **MI**55, The ice would be too rotten to travel on. **1999** *WI State Jrl.* (Madison) 28 Dec sec B 2/2, A few inches of new ice may be enough to support a person, while a foot or more of old "rotten" ice may not.

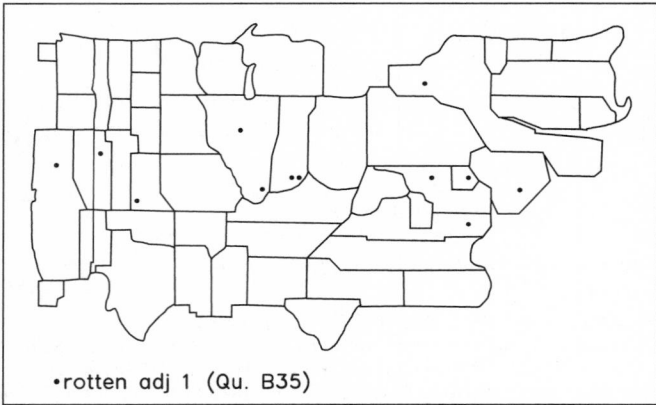

•rotten adj 1 (Qu. B35)

2 Of the weather: disagreeable, unpleasant. [*OED2* 1599 →] **chiefly Nth, N Midl** See Map Cf **rough** adj **1**

1950 *WELS* (*If the weather is unpleasant, you say it's*) 1 Inf, **csWI,** Rotten. **1965–70** *DARE* (Qu. B2, *If the weather is very unpleasant . . it's a _____ day*) 30 Infs, **chiefly Nth, N Midl,** Rotten; **IA**32, Rotten day out.

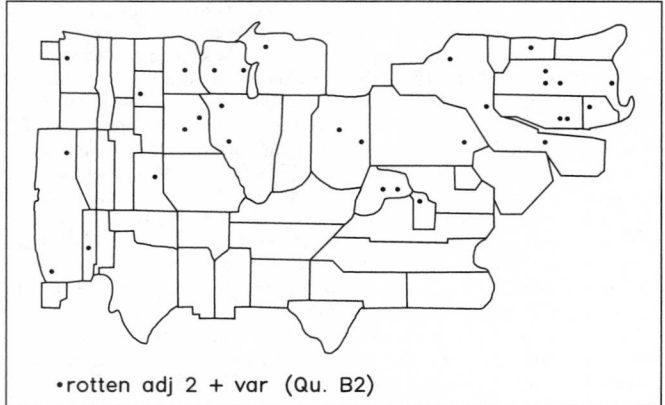

•rotten adj 2 + var (Qu. B2)

3 Of a child: spoiled, coddled, or pampered to an excessive degree. **chiefly Sth, S Midl** See Map Cf **rotten spoiled**
Note: The phrase *spoiled rotten* in this sense is widespread.

1912 Green *VA Folk-Speech* 358, *Rotten.* . . In a superlative degree, in the expression: "That child is spoilt so he's rotten." **1954** *Harder Coll.* **cwTN,** *Rotten.* . . Spoiled, pampered, of a child. **c1960** *Wilson Coll.* **csKY,** *Rotten:* adj. Spoiled or, as an adv., to intensify spoiled itself. **1965–70** *DARE* (Qu. Z14b, *If a child expects to have its own way or have too much attention . . "That child is _____."*) 48 Infs, **Sth, S Midl,** Rotten; **NC**55, **SC**19, Spoiled till he's (*or* it's) rotten; **NC**88, Rotten to the core. [24 of 50 total Infs young or mid-aged]

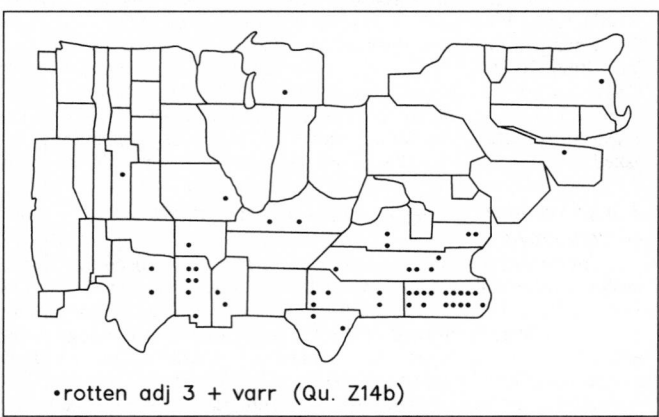

•rotten adj 3 + varr (Qu. Z14b)

4 Of the ground: soft, boggy. **esp VA**

1649 in 1940 *AmSp* 15.386 **VA,** Part of which is likewise Rotten Marsh amounting to three hundred and fifty acres. **1840** *S. Lit. Messenger* 6.155 **VA,** The ground she trod on was rotten, and quaked beneath her feet; and the slightest indiscretion of a young man, whom she held only by the slender tie of honor, might precipitate her . . into the mire of infamy and disgrace. **1940** *Hench Coll.* **VA,** Rotten—of ground: deep in mud. Told me by Lee Runk . . , who now runs a farm in the county (Albemarle) and who gets about the state a good deal. Runk says he hears the expression rather widely. "The ground was rotten in Virginia all early February."

rotten v Also sp *rot(e)n* Used esp in pres pple *rottening*, pronc-spp *rot(t)ning* [Cf -en suff[5]] **scattered, but chiefly Sth, S Midl, NEast** See Map Cf **hotten**
To decay; to cause to decay, spoil; also fig: hence n *rotnin* rot, rotten part; rarely ppl adj *rottening* rotten, darned.
1902 *DN* 2.244 **sIL,** *Rotnin.* . . For rotting. **1903** *DN* 2.327 **seMO,** *Rottening.* . . Rotting. **1906** *DN* 3.123 **sIN,** *Rotnin.* . . Regular form for *rotting.* **1907** *DN* 3.226 **nwAR,** *Rotnin'.* . . Rotting. *Ibid* 235 **nwAR,** *Rottening.* . . Rotting. **1909** *DN* 3.364 **eAL, wGA,** *Rot(t)en.* . . To rot. "That roof will rotten out in less 'n a year." Common, especially in the ppr. *rottnin(g). Ibid* 403 **nwAR,** *Rotnin'.* . . Rotten part. "The apples are rotning; cut out the rotnin'." **1915** *DN* 4.189 **swVA,** *Rotten.* . . To rot. "My taters are all-a-rott'nin.'" **1937** (1963) Hyatt *Kiverlid* 68 **KY,** I'll make one fatty dodger, but they ain't no use a rottenin' shad with spilin' in no sich a-way. **1942** Warnick *Garrett Co. MD* 1 **nwMD** (as of 1900–18), *Rotnin* (rotting). **1950** *PADS* 14.57 **SC,** *Rotten.* . . To spoil. "You sho' gonna rotten dat chile." Mostly Negro usage. *Rottening.* . . Rotting, becoming rotten. **c1960** *Wilson Coll.* **csKY,** *Rottening.* . . Rotting, decaying. **1965–70** *DARE* (Qu. KK7, *When wood . . is starting to decay inside . . "It's _____ inside."*) 41 Infs, **scattered, but**

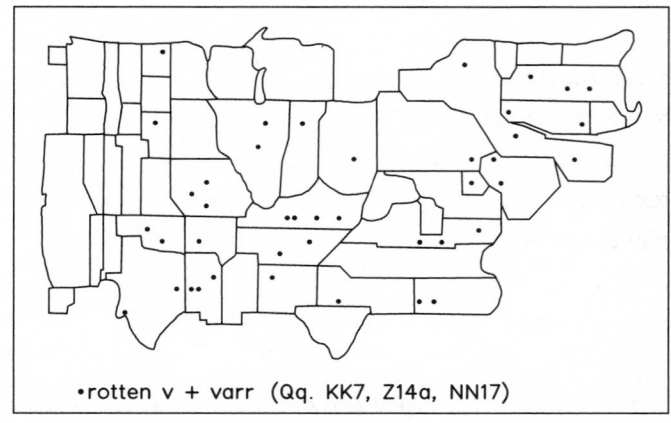

•rotten v + varr (Qq. KK7, Z14a, NN17)

chiefly **Sth, S Midl, NEast,** Rottening; **MO**8, Began to rotten; (Qu. Z14a, *To give a child its own way or pay too much attention to it: "Everyone _____ that child."*) Inf **GA**57, Rottens; (Qu. NN17, *Something that keeps on annoying you—for example, a fly that keeps buzzing around you: "That _____ fly won't go away."*) Inf **VA**39, Rottening. [13 of 44 total Infs Black] **1965** *DARE* FW Addit **OK**52, Rottening— used for "rotting." **1986** Pederson *LAGS Concordance,* 1 inf, **nwTN,** the house was a-rottening down; 1 inf, **cnAR,** Put water on ashes for lye soap rottening them.

rottendy adj Cf **flowerdy, rotten** v
Rotten, rickety.
1945 FWP *Lay My Burden Down* 100 **MS** (as of c1865) [Black], He live in a big old rottendy house, but he ain't farming none of the land.

rotten egg n
1 also as exclam; Any of var games: see quots; a call used in a game.
1942 Warnick *Garrett Co. MD* 7 **nwMD** (as of 1900–18), Games (children's): Bat, button, hot pot, hot socket, hull gull, Jack-in-the-bush, rotten egg. **1946** TN Folk Lore Soc. *Bulletin* 12, We had a game called "Rotten Egg." It must have belonged just to our group since I don't recall having seen it played anywhere else. It took a person with pretty good grip in his hands to hold when he was being shaken by the cooks to see if he was sound or rotten. **1950** WELS Suppl. **ceWI,** Rotten egg—Ball rolls back in Anty-Anty-over. **1957** Sat. Eve. Post Letters **CO,** Some of the games I remember from my Rocky Ford and Fort Morgan, Colorado childhood (I was born in 1913) are: Anty Over, Rotten Egg . . O' Larry; **WI,** Games we often played here in Red Mound over 60 years ago . . 'Rotten Egg'. **1968** *DARE* (Qu. EE33, . . *Outdoor games . . that children play*) Inf **PA**74, Rotten egg. [FW: Guessing colors, but that is all Inf remembers.] **1968** *DARE* FW Addit **VA**13, Rotten egg—a tin can was set up in a circle and members of the group tried to force each other to touch the can. If they did, he was a rotten egg and out of the game. The game proceeded till all but one was a rotten egg. **2000** NADS Letters **cnAL,** Rotten egg—The game which this refers to is a trampoline game where one person (the rotten egg) balls him or herself up by locking their hands and arms around their folded knees while one or more others try to bounce the person in the middle until they "pop" or became the rotten egg. I heard this used as a child (10 years ago) in Birmingham, Alabama.
2 pl: Perh =**owl's clover.** Cf **butter-and-eggs 3**
1969 *DARE* (Qu. S26a, . . *Wildflowers. . . Roadside flowers*) Inf **CA**127, Rotten eggs—yellow and bloom in spring.

rottening See **rotten** v

rotten-logging vbl n **West**
Necking, courting.
1931 *AmSp* 7.22 [Yellowstone Park language], *Rottenlogging*—dating or necking. **1936** McCarthy *Lang. Mosshorn* np **West** [Range terms], *Rotten Loggin'.* The comparatively rare practice of romantic couples sitting on a log in the moonlight and sparking. **1940** *AmSp* 15.443 **swUT,** At Zion (reached by a mile-long automoblie tunnel, where the hotel is situated near the log-strewn shores of the Virgin River, and a nearby not-too-steady bridge), spooners are said to be *tunnelling, swinging bridging,* or *rotten-logging.* **1959** Martin *Gunbarrel* 23 **WY,** We had a lingo all our own in Yellowstone. . . We didn't "spoon" or "neck" in Yellowstone; we went out "rotten logging." **1982** Brooks *Quicksand* 328 **swUT** (as of 1932), Here we did our first love-making, but by whatever name it is currently called—"sparking," "spooning," "petting," "necking," "pitching-the-woo," "rotten-logging"—it all adds up to the same thing in the end: an engagement to be married.

rotten on it intj Cf *rottening* ppl adj (at **rotten** v)
See quots.
1956 Ker *Vocab. W. TX* 385, Expressions of mild disgust. . . 1 inf, Rotten on it, stinken on it. **1970** Tarpley *Blinky* 300 **neTX,** *Mild expression of disgust* . . other responses [include] rotten on it.

rotten spoiled adj phr
=**rotten** adj **3.**
1950 PADS 14.57 **SC,** Rotten. . . Spoiled, pampered, especially of children or young people. *Rotten spoiled.* **1965–70** *DARE* (Qu. Z14b, *If a child expects to have its own way or have too much attention . . "That child is _____."*) 15 Infs, scattered, Rotten spoiled; **CA**97, Rotten spoiled—people around here [FW: Not used by Inf]; **MD**9, Rotten spoiled—other people say; **OH**17, Rotten spoiled [laughter]; **SC**11, 42,

Rotten spoiled—[FW sugg]; **SC**44, Rotten spoiled [FW sugg; Inf has heard]. **1997** *DARE* File **nKY** (as of c1972), A neighbor in Louisville frequently entertained me with tales of her two adolescent granddaughters who, she informed me, were "rotten spoiled." The girls' indulgent father provided for their every whim.

rottning See **rotten** v

rotydid n
Prob = **katydid B1.**
1967 *DARE* (Qu. R8, . . *Kinds of creatures that make a clicking or shrilling or chirping kind of sound*) Inf **NE**9, Rotydids.

ro-ud See **road** n¹

rouen See **rowen**

rouge plant n
1 also *rougeberry:* A shrub native to the south central US (*Rivina humilis*), noted for its bright red berries. Also called **baby pepper, inkberry 5, pigeonberry 10, pokeberry 2, pokeweed 3, pokeroot 3**
1890 Century Dict. 5240, *Rouge-berry* . . A shrub, *Rivina laevis* (including *R. humilis*), of tropical America, often grown in hothouses. . . Also *rouge-plant.* **1936** Whitehouse *TX Flowers* 21, Rouge Plant. . . The low plants, a foot or more high, grow profusely in woods in Central Texas, but may be found from Arkansas to the tropics. **1953** Greene-Blomquist *Flowers South* 30, Baby-Pepper, Rouge-Plant . . A relatively small, often partially woody plant. . . Seen all year throughout its range from Fla. to Tex. and Ark. **1991** Hiaasen *Native Tongue* 166 **FL,** He parked on the side of the road and watched a pair of mustard-colored bulldozers plow a fresh section of hammock, creating a tangled knoll of uprooted tamarinds, buttonwoods, pigeon plums and rougeberry.
2 A **mullein** (here: *Verbascum thapsus*).
1968 *DARE* (Qu. S20, *A common weed that grows on open hillsides: It has velvety green leaves close to the ground, and a tall stalk with small yellow flowers on a spike at the top*) Inf **WI**50, Mullein, rouge plant.

rough adj
1 Of weather: inclement; unpleasant; stormy. [*OED2* →1852] **chiefly Sth, S Midl, West** See Map Cf **rotten** adj **2**
1939 LANE Map 88 (*A cloudy day*) 1 inf, **cME coast,** Rough. **1950** WELS (*If the weather is unpleasant, you say it's*) 1 inf, **cwWI,** Rough. **1956** Ker *Vocab. W. TX* 60, *Storm with rain and thunder and lightning. . . rough rain.* [1 of 67 infs] **1961** Folk *Word Atlas N. LA* map 104, Storm with much thunder and lightning . . [less freq responses include] rough weather. **1965–70** *DARE* (Qu. B2, *If the weather is very unpleasant . . it's a _____ day*) 33 Infs, **chiefly Sth, S Midl, West,** Rough; **AZ**7, **CA**129, **KY**10, **OK**51, Pretty rough; **NC**1, 13, It's rough outside; **LA**2, Kinda rough; **AR**56, Sure a rough day; (Qu. B3, *If a day is very hot . . it's [a] _____*) Inf **TX**42, Rough; **GA**13, Rough day; (Qu. B5, *When the weather looks as if it will become bad . . it's _____*) Infs **KS**6, **LA**15, Looking rough; **MN**38, Going to get rough; **NH**14, Gonna be rough weather; **NC**49, Looks like rough weather; **GA**19, Looks pretty rough; **MN**34, Looks rough out; **NJ**17, Rough weather ahead; (Qu. B6, *When clouds begin to increase . . it's _____*) Inf **LA**11, Beginning to look rough; (Qu. B8, *When clouds come and go all day . . it's _____*) Inf **MD**31, Rough day; (Qu. B12, *When the*

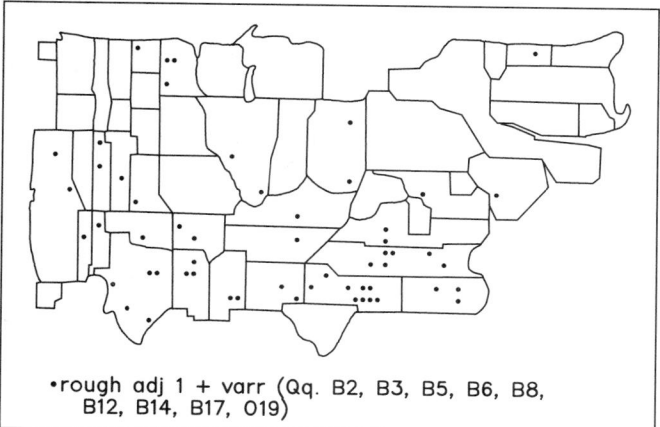

•rough adj 1 + varr (Qq. B2, B3, B5, B6, B8, B12, B14, B17, O19)

wind begins to increase . . it's _____) Inf **IL**93, **UT**5, Getting rough; **MD**26, Getting rougher; **MS**11, Rough; (Qu. B14, *When the wind is blowing unevenly, sometimes strong and sometimes weak, . . it's* _____) Infs **IL**71, **OH**4, Rough; (Qu. B17, *A destructive wind that blows straight*) Inf **OH**45, Rough wind; (Qu. O19, . . *Kinds or degrees of wind that are important when you're in a boat*) Infs **CO**22, **NM**8, Rough wind. [44 of 56 total Infs old, 42 male] **1986** Pederson *LAGS Concordance* **Gulf Region** *(It's a gloomy day)* 10 infs, (A) rough day; 1 inf, It's just a rough day; 1 inf, It's a rough-looking day; 1 inf, Rough outside; 1 inf, A rough, rainy day; 1 inf, Real rough—of the weather; 1 inf, Rough weather; *(The weather is changing)* 4 infs, (Weather is) getting rough; 1 inf, Rough; 1 inf, A rough day; 1 inf, Going rough; 1 inf, Going to be some rough weather coming in; *(Thunderstorm)* 1 inf, Rough weather; *(The wind is picking up)* 4 infs, Getting rough(er) *(It's rather cold)* 4 infs, Pretty rough; 3 infs, Kind of rough; 1 inf, Pretty rough time.

2 Of manure: see quot.

1966–68 *DARE* (Qu. L17, . . *Names . . for manure used in the fields*) Inf **NC**49, Rough manure—out of stalls; **SC**3, Rough manure; **SC**47, Rough manure—same as compost.

rough n Also sp *ruff* [*OED2 rough* sb.¹ 2.b 1600 →; "Now *local*"] **chiefly S Midl** Cf **slick** n

Also pl: An area covered with trees or brush.

1779 in 1940 *AmSp* 15.386 **VA**, To a post white oak in a Ruff. **1859** *Ibid* **VA**, Beginning at a beech and two spotted oaks, on the top of the Locust rough. **1915** Hall *Claib Jones* 28 **KY**, The next day we struck a bear's track and the bear had gone into a big ruff. It fell to my lot to go through the ruff. **1927** in 1929 Dobie *Vaquero* 259 **West**, I finally caught the buck [antelope] after turning it into the roughs. *Ibid* 260, I ran across two panthers out on the flat . . but lost them in the roughs. **1939** *Hall Coll.* **eTN**, I crawled through the roughs and got up there to 'im, nearly to 'im; **wNC**, We had some old trained bear hounds 'at (that) turned off into the roughs, the La'rel, on the Bear Creek side. **1953** *Ibid* **wNC**, The bear had left to go up to his denning place, or up to his lying place up in the rough. **1953** Randolph–Wilson *Down in Holler* 279 **Ozarks**, *Rough.* . . A grove, a thicket. Judge John Turner White, of Jefferson City, Mo., told me that two groves on the old White farm were known as the *Big Rough* and the *Little Rough*. "Where we got those names, I do not know," he added. [**1968–70** *DARE* (Qu. C28, *A place where underbrush, weeds, vines and small trees grow together so that it's nearly impossible to get through*) Inf **NC**49, Rough land; **TN**66, A rough spot.]

rough-bark elm See **rough elm**

rough box n

An outer case into which a casket is placed at burial.

1950 *WELS (The box that a body is put into for burial)* 5 infs, **WI**, Rough box; 1 inf, swWI, Coffin and rough box or vault; 1 inf, seWI, Rough box—the wooden box that holds a coffin is a "rough box." If of concrete, etc., it is a "vault." **1959** Lahey–Hogan *As I Remember It* 19 **swKS** (as of 1890s), One morning Uncle Jimmie and Johnnie O'Dea rode to the graves and found where the coyotes had dug a big hole, exposing the rough box of Uncle John's grave. **1965–66** *DARE* (Qu. BB59, *The box that a body is put into for burial;* total Infs questioned, 75) Inf **OK**7, Rough box—wooden box into which velvet covered casket was put; **OK**18, Rough box—put casket or coffin inside. **1966** *DARE* Tape **MI**24, So we got a rough box from one of the undertakers, and Sunday morning we went out and dug up the remains. **1967** *DARE* FW Addit **IA**, *Rough box*—outer box into which coffin was placed—old-fashioned. **1973** Allen *LAUM* 1.367, *Casket.* . . 2 infs, **MN**, **SD**, Rough box. [The **SD** inf characterized this as old-fashioned.] **1986** Pederson *LAGS Concordance (Casket),* 1 inf, **nwFL**, Rough box. **1987** *DARE* File **csPA**, Rough box = vault; outside casing in a grave, into which the coffin is placed. Originally of "rough" lumber, these are now of reinforced concrete. 1930–40, but still used by older residents.

rough elm n Also *rough-bark elm*

A **slippery elm** (here: *Ulmus rubra*).

1941 Writers' Program *Guide AR* 297, The women wear sunbonnets, and many of them use snuff, taking a small quantity on the end of a "rough elm toothbrush," and chewing it like plug tobacco. **1966–70** *DARE* (Qu. T11, . . *Kinds of elm trees*) Inf **AR**28, Rough-bark elm; **LA**8, Rough elm—hard to split; **VA**38, Rough elm.

rough feed n esp **S Midl**
= **roughness 1.**

1863 in 1889 U.S. War Dept. *War of Rebellion* 1st ser 23.1.16, Our train was out for rough feed where I had previously found it. **1906** *DN* 3.154 **nwAR**, *Rough feed.* . . Corn-husks, straw, etc. **1909** *DN* 3.364 **eAL, wGA**, *Roughage.* . . Coarse feed for cattle, horses, etc., as hay, fodder, shucks. Also called *rough-feed.* **1917** in 1944 *ADD* **sWV**, *Rough feed.* **1952** Brown *NC Folkl.* 1.586, *Rough feed.* . . Fodder, hay, and other heavy feed for cattle. **1956** McAtee *Some Dialect NC* 37, *Rough feed.* . . Roughage as fodder, hay, etc., for stock feed.

rough-leaved white oak See **rough oak**

roughleg n

Usu = **rough-legged hawk;** rarely, the closely related *Buteo regalis*.

1890 *Century Dict.* 5241, *Roughleg.* . . A rough-legged hawk. **1917** (1923) *Birds Amer.* 2.79, *Rough-legged Hawk.* . . When mice are abundant one or two Rough-legs will hunt for weeks in the vicinity, effectually controlling these pests and saving many fruit trees, especially the young ones, from destruction. **1928** Bailey *Birds NM* 172, *Ferruginous Rough-leg.* . . The feathered tarsus of the two Rough-legs, however, when it can be seen, separates them from the Western Red-tail and Swainson. **1963** Murie *Birds Mt. McKinley* 29, The rough-leg is a large soaring hawk with long, broad wings and a tail that is broad and rounded. The legs are feathered to the toes.

rough-legged hawk n Also *rough-legged buzzard,* ∼ *falcon, roughleg hawk, rough-shinned* ∼

A large hawk *(Buteo lagopus sanctijohannis)* with legs feathered to the talons. Also called **black buzzard 1,** ∼ **eagle 3,** ∼ **hawk 1, gopher hawk, mouse** ∼ **1b, roughleg**

1811 Wilson *Amer. Ornith.* 4.59, Rough-legged Falcon. *Falco Lagopus. Ibid* 60, The Rough-legged Hawk measures twenty-two inches in length. **1844** DeKay *Zool. NY* 2.8, The *Rough-legged Buzzard,* or *Black Hawk,* is a northern species, rarely found beyond Carolina. . . Its usual haunts are low grounds, where it preys upon mice, small birds, frogs, etc. **1858** Baird *Birds* 32, *Archibuteo Lagopus* . . Rough-legged Hawk. **1917** (1923) *Birds Amer.* 2.79, Rough-legged Hawk. *Archibuteo lagopus sancti-johannis. . . Other Names.*—American Rough-legged Hawk; Rough-leg; Rough-legged Buzzard. **1965–70** *DARE* (Qu. Q4, . . *Kinds of hawks*) Infs **CO**7, **IA**3, **WI**12, Rough-legged hawk; **PA**155, Roughleg hawk; **ME**8, Rough-shinned hawk.

rough lock n **chiefly West**

A chain (or rarely rope) arranged so as to immobilize a wheel of a wagon and sometimes also to drag beneath it, or fixed under or around a sled runner or a log being skidded, and serving as a brake on a steep descent.

1886 *San Jose (Calif.) Mercury* June 3/1 *(DA)*, If he thinks the logs will slide and overtake his team, he puts a chain around some of them, making what he calls a rough lock. **1913** in 1991 Tabbert *Dict. Alaskan Engl.* 214, I told her to be kerful when she come about half way,/ To cut her dogs out, fix her rough-lock, and she'd sail down all O.K. **1923** Ezra G. Wade *Early Days at Paonia* (MS) 2 *(DA)* **CO**, We put chain rough-locks on each rear wheel. **1958** [see **rough-lock** v]. **1958** McCulloch *Woods Words* 153 **Pacific NW**, *Rough lock*—a. A brake such as a rope passed around a log to prevent it from running ahead into the animals in ox team days. b. A rope wound on a wagon wheel to lock it so it skids, acting as a brake. **1967** *AK Sportsman* 12 (Tabbert *Dict. Alaskan Engl.*), I stopped and fastened creepers over my mukluks and put the rough-lock on the sled. **1967** Fetterman *Stinking Creek* 47 **seKY**, This is the "rough lock," a length of chain secured to a front standard of the sled and allowed to drag under a runner. It acts as a brake, slowing the sled as it is brought down from the high places. **1993** *DARE* File **wID** (as of c1940), This subject reminds me of another way of braking a wagon that I have seen used. . . Dad called it a "rough lock," and we used it when we were hauling sacks of wheat. . . For this technique to work, the descent has to be quite steep because what is involved is the use of a log chain to immobilize the rear wheels of a wagon by threading this heavy chain through the spokes and around the axles so that the wheels simply skid.

rough-lock v

1 To apply a **rough lock** n to; to employ a **rough lock** n; hence vbl n *rough-locking.* **chiefly West**

1859 (1965) Marcy *Prairie Traveler* 93 **West**, When the declivity is . . very abrupt, requiring great effort on the wheel animals to hold the wagon, the wheels should be rough-locked by lengthening the lock-chains so that the part which goes around the wheels will come directly upon the ground, and thus create more friction. . . Rough-locking is a very safe method of passing heavy artillery down abrupt declivities. **1884** Shepherd *Prairie Exper.* 197 **CA,** The hind-wheels were rough-locked, that is, a large linked chain was tied round the rim of the wheel in such a way that the wheel rides upon the chain, which drags along and cuts into the ground. **1888** Cody *Story Wild West* 548 **CO,** We locked both wheels on each side, and then rough-locked them. We now started the wagon down the hill. **1913** Browne *Conquest Mt. McKinley* 201 **AK,** On the first steep pitches we had to double "rough-lock" our sleds or they would have overrun the dogs. We used heavy dog-chains for the purpose. **1944** Botkin *Treas. Amer. Folkl.* 331 **WV,** Cultivation on these slopes is so difficult that the native son at times will say with a perfectly straight face that he has to roughlock his harrow to get it down off the hill. **1950** Stuart *Hie Hunters* 249 **eKY,** Do be keerful to rough-lock down hills so the sled won't hit Dinah's heels. **1956** Almirall *From College* 144 **CO,** "Goin' 'round that shoulder and downgrade, which must run 16 to 20 per cent, sure had these broncs settin' on their haunches, even though I'd rough-locked the rear wheels." That meant he'd fixed them with chains he carried, so they wouldn't turn. **1958** *AmSp* 33.271 **eWA** [Ranching terms], *Rough lock.* 1. *v.* To secure one wheel of a wagon with a chain through the spokes, around the rim, and fast to the wagon. 2. *n.* Such a device, used as a brake to hold a load, usually on a grade. **1959** Robertson *Ram* 155 **ID** (as of c1875), Coming down the mountain on a narrow snow road with a big load was exciting. Nobody bothered to rough-lock, so it was a mad race with the teams at full gallop to escape being run over by their own loads. **1967** *AK Sportsman* May 12 (Tabbert *Dict. Alaskan Engl.*), I rough-locked the sled and we slid down at a very fast clip. **1976** Garber *Mountain-ese* 76 **sAppalachians,** The hill was so steep we had to rough-lock two wheels uv the wagon.

2 as ppl adj *rough-locked;* Fig: see quot.
1984 Wilder *You All Spoken Here* 97 **Sth,** Rough-locked: Mated.

rough-locking See **rough-lock** v **1**

roughneck n

In oil-drilling: a laborer on an oil rig, esp a member of a drilling crew; hence v *roughneck* to work as such a laborer.
1917 *DN* 4.421 **LA,** Roughneck. . . A man who works about an oil derrick. **1932** *AmSp* 7.270 [Oil field language], *Roughneck.* . . The regular term for a member of a driller's crew on a rotary rig; not applied to the driller. . . To work as a member of a rotary driller's crew. **c1939** in 1984 Lambert–Franks *Voices* 74 **OK,** I'll get you on as a roughneck with me and give you some experience, and we'll see if you can make the grade. **1942** Perry *Texas* 178, The roughnecks, the workers on the drilling rigs, were the skilled, happy-go-lucky, whisky-drinking, fist-fighting crew. **1966** *Daily Oklahoman* (Oklahoma City OK) 11 Dec mag sec 11/4, A "roughneck" works on a rotary rig and is supposed to have acquired the name because of his rough language. **1969** *DARE* FW Addit **CA114,** Roughneck—a skilled member of a drilling crew. **1973** *Cook Inlet Courier* (Kenai AK) 20 Sept 3/1, Since moving to Alaska, Glad has been employed as a heating service repairman, . . a roughneck and roustabout, a platform operator, a labor foreman, and a chemical plant operator. **1973** *DARE* File **nwCO,** Roughneck. . . worker at the drilling rig, in oilfields. **1980** Banks *First-Person America* 85 **OK** (as of 1939), I dressed tools, roughnecked, roustabouted, or done anything that had to be done. **1986** *DARE* File **neOK** (as of 1979), In 1979 when I visited there, the professional soccer team in Tulsa, Oklahoma, was known as the Tulsa Roughnecks because of the community's emphasis on the oil-drilling industry. **2000** *Ibid* **TX** (as of c1950), My brother talked about daytime, evening, and midnight towers (shifts) on oil rigs when he was a roughneck in the early 1950s in Texas.

roughness n Also sp *ruf(f)ness*

1 Coarse fodder, roughage. **Sth, S Midl,** esp **Appalachians** Cf **rough feed**
1813 (1939) Hartsell *Memora* 99 **eTN,** Did not draw aney rufness for our teeme. **1859** in 1942 Hafen *Overland Routes* 11.78 **VA,** We left camp at nine thirty, our destination being "roughness" for our cattle. **1884** Smith *Bill Arp's Scrap Book* 61 **nwGA,** He said he wanted to buy some ruffness, and I agreed to bring him a load of shucks for two dollars. **1895** *DN* 1.374 **seKY, eTN, wNC,** Roughness: coarse fodder, hay, shucks, and the like, in contrast with grain. **1903** *DN* 2.327 **seMO,** Roughness. . . Coarse feed, as hay, fodder, etc. 'I have plenty of oats and corn, but no roughness for your horses.' **1904** (1913) Johnson *Highways South* 142 **eTN,** "I got to go up over the mountain to-day," said Andy, "to git some roughness"—that is, cow-fodder or hay. **1906** *DN*

3.154 **nwAR,** Roughness. . . Coarse feed. **1913** Kephart *Highlanders* 38 **sAppalachians,** Corn is topped for the blade fodder, the ears gathered from the stalk, and the main stalks afterwards used as "roughness" (roughage). **1938** Stuart *Dark Hills* 88 **neKY,** We don't feed the cattle anything but roughness. **1940** Hall *Coll.* **wNC, eTN,** Roughness. . . Old people call feed *roughness. Roughness* means corn-tops; some people call it *fodder.* **1949** *PADS* 11.10 **wTX** (as of 1921–29), Roughness. **c1960** Wilson *Coll.* **csKY,** Roughness. **1974** Fink *Mountain Speech* 22 **wNC, eTN,** Roughness . . fodder, food. "I was gathering roughness for my stock."

2 also *rough stuff;* Transf: fibrous foods for human consumption.
1906 *DN* 3.154 **nwAR,** Roughness. . . Green salad, such as lettuce. (Jocose.) **1965** *DARE* FW Addit **neMS,** Rough stuff—A generic term for home-grown vegetables. I never heard this except in Iuca, Mississippi, but I was invited for meals if I would like to join the people for rough stuff. I heard this term used by several different families in Iuca.

rough oak n Also *rough(-leaved) white oak*
A **post oak 1a** (here: *Quercus stellata*).
1850 Emerson *Rept. Trees & Shrubs* 133, Post Oak or Rough Oak. . . It resembles the white oak, but is distinguished at once by its mode of branching, by the density of its foliage, and by the stiffness and peculiar form of its rough leaves. **1859** (1880) Darlington *Amer. Weeds* 308 [*Quercus*] *obtusiloba.* . . Barrens White Oak, Post Oak. Rough Oak. . . The wood is very durable. **1890** Newhall *Trees NE Amer.* 104, Post Oak, Iron Oak, Rough-leaved White Oak. . . *Leaf,* four to six inches long; *rough* above and below; thick and coarse. **1940** Clute *Amer. Plant Names* 163, *Q[uercus] stellata.* Post Oak. Iron oak, rough oak . . rough white oak. **1960** Vines *Trees SW* 155, Post Oak. . . Vernacular names are Iron Oak, Cross Oak, Branch Oak, Rough Oak, and Box Oak.

rough room n Cf **mud room**
1914 *DN* 4.156 **Cape Cod MA,** Rough-room. . . An unfinished room 'in' back of the kitchen, used for the heavier household work, such as the weekly washing, the churning, *etc.* "Pa's out in the rough-room washing the separator."

rough root n
=**blazing star 3,** esp *Liatris spicata.*
1830 Rafinesque *Med. Flora* 2.237, *Liatris* [spp]. . . Many vulgar names, *Backache root* . . *Rough root,* &c. All have a tuberous medical root, acrid, bitterish, pungent, spicy, smelling like turpentine or juniper. **1876** Hobbs *Bot. Hdbk.* 100, Rough root, Button snake root, Liatris spicata. **1900** Lyons *Plant Names* 212, [*Laciniaria*] *spicata* . . Devil's-bit, Rough-root, Sawwort [etc].

rough-scuff n Also *roughscruf, ruff-scuff*
1 Riffraff, the rabble; a disreputable, common, or lower-class person.
1831 *Boston Eve. Transcript* (MA) 1 Oct 1/2, The roughscruf of St. Louis called my deliverer a Watchenago. **1844** Stephens *High Life in NY* 2.15, No ginuine gentleman ever gits mad with sich a ruff-scuff. **1859** (1968) Bartlett *Americanisms* 371, Rough-scuff. The lowest people; the rabble. **1899** (1912) Green *VA Folk-Speech* 358, Rough-scuff. . . A rough coarse fellow; a rough; collectively, the lowest class of people; riff-raff; the rabble. **1905** *DN* 3.17 **CT,** Rough-scuff. . . The lowest people; the rabble. **1941** *LANE* Map 415 (*The whole crowd*) 1 inf, **nME,** Rough scuff.

2 Poor fodder. Cf **rough feed,** *rough stuff* (at **roughness 2**)
1902 Day *Pine Tree Ballads* 4 **ME,** Drat the man who feeds out ruff-scuff, wood and wire from the swale,/ 'Cause he wants to press his herds'-grass, send his clover off for sale.

rough-shinned hawk See **rough-legged hawk**

rough side of one's tongue n [*OED2* a1733 (at *lick* sb. 1.a), 1820 (at *tongue* sb. 4.b)] Cf **tongue**
A scolding; in phr *lick with the rough side of the tongue* to deliver a scolding.
[**1889** *Harper's New Mth. Mag.* 78.631 **NYC** [Irish immigrant], That was the ould girl that run that hashery, an' she always had a lick o' the rough side of her tongue for me whiniver she seen me.] **1946** *PADS* 6.39 **eNC** (as of 1900–10), To lick with the rough side of the tongue. (A sarcastic way of threatening to "polish a person off.") . . Common among bullies. **1965** *DARE* FW Addit **nMS,** Rough side of her tongue—a tongue lashing or scolding. Occasional. **2002** *DARE* File

NYC, When Mike Walsh laid the rough side of his tongue on a person, it generally smarted some.

rough string n West

A group of unbroken or partly broken horses; hence *rough string rider* the person in charge of such horses.

  1934 (1940) Weseen *Dict. Amer. Slang* 105, *Rough string*—A group of partly broken horses. **1940** Writers' Program *Guide NV* 76, A *rough-string,* the spoiled, unbroken horses taken on the roundup, are usually assigned to the care of one or two men. **1944** Adams *Western Words* 132, *Rough-string rider*—A professional bronc buster. Of necessity all cowboys are good riders, but the men who handle the rough strings have to be bronc busters, and they draw a few extra dollars a month for this perilous work. **1958** Blasingame *Dakota Cowboy* 16 **SD,** I went to South Dakota—in charge of the horses and mules—as "rough-string" rider for the new setup. **1966** *DARE* Tape **ND**5, They gave me fifty dollars to ride nineteen heads of them [=colts] on round up. Well, it's what you'd call the rough string, to make it plain. Some of those boys didn't want to ride.

rough stuff See **roughness 2**

rough white oak See **rough oak**

rough-wing See **rough-winged swallow**

rough-winged hawk n Also *ruffed-wing hawk*
  Prob =**rough-legged hawk**
  1968–70 *DARE* (Qu. Q4, . . *Kinds of hawks*) Inf **CT**5, Rough-winged hawk; **MA**78, Ruffed-wing hawk. **1997** in 2000 *DARE* File—Internet **CA,** December 97 Stanislaus Audubon Bird Sightings. . . Del Puerto Canyon. All along the first 2 miles. Rough-winged hawk. **1997** in 2001 *Ibid* **nwGA,** This is the Georgia Rare Bird Alert for Saturday evening, March 15, 1997. . . Aubrey Scott and Michael Vale reporting a *rough-winged hawk* flyover 8–10 miles NE of Rome, in Floyd County. **2000** *NADS Letters* **cMA,** The term ruffed wing hawk refers to a regular square tail hawk. When you look at the bird from below, the wings appear to be "rough-winged." **2001** *DARE* File—Internet **cwTX,** Brian Cassell reports a Rough-winged Hawk near the Belding area.

rough-winged swallow n Also *rough-wing; ruffed-winged swallow*

A brown and dusky-colored swallow (*Stelgidopteryx ruficollis*) distinguished by tiny hooks on the outer primary feathers. Also called **bank swallow 2, bridge ~, gully martin, sand ~ 2**

  1838 Audubon *Ornith. Biog.* 4.595, In its general appearance . . the Rough-winged Swallow is extremely similar to the Bank Swallow. **1913** Bailey *Birds VA* 261, The earliest swallow to depart in the fall . . and the earliest to arrive in the spring . . is the Rough-winged. **1923** Dawson *Birds CA* 2.531, Unlike the Bank Swallows, the Rough-wings do not colonize to any great extent, but are rather solitary. **1955** Lowery *LA Birds* 372, The Rough-wing winters in small numbers in southern Louisiana. **1967–68** *DARE* (Qu. Q20, . . *Kinds of swallows and birds like them*) Inf **WI**58, Rough-wing swallow; **CA**78, **IA**20, Rough-winged swallow; **IA**3, **MN**18, Ruffed-winged swallow.

roun' See **round**

rounance See **roundance**

rounce n Also *rouncin's, rounds, rounses, rowance* [*EDD roonses* int. "A marble-playing term: the exclamation made by a player when he wishes to claim his right to shift to a better position at an equal distance from the ring"—reported from Aberdeenshire. Cf *SND round* n. 9, where *roonses* is interpreted as a double plural ("roundses").]

In marble play: =**roundance 1.**
  1855 *N&Q* 11.352 **NY** (as of 1810s), In playing marbles—seizing the moment of making a shot, to regulate the next shot by claiming or forbidding a certain indulgence if needed—the formula was "rowance," evidently "allowance" for claiming. **1888** *Century Illustr. Mag.* 36.78 **IL,** Their cries of "rounses," "taw" . . and "vent" might often be heard. **1922** *DN* 5.187 **KY,** *Rounce.* . . A call given when one's taw is so placed that he cannot shoot at the ring or at an opponent. If he calls "Rounce" he may select a convenient place to shoot from, unless his opponent first calls, "Vence ye rounce." Also *rouncin's,* n. **1958** *Resp. to PADS* 29 **wKY** (as of c1930), These [=*rounds* and *cleaning*] were both privileges [sic] that the shooting player could take after claiming *Ventures. Rounds*

meant to move his shooting taw along the circumference of the circle whose center was the marble in the ring at which he intended to shoot. **1968** *DARE* (Qu. EE7, . . *Kinds of marble games*) Inf **IN**46, Rounds. **1976** *WI Acad. Rev.* Mar 9/1 (as of 1920s), If you wanted a position advantage at the marbles in the ring and shouted "rounds" . . , you could then move your shooter from one side of the ring to another, but no closer than your original position.

round n Also sp *roun'*

1 also *cross round:* A rung (of a ladder); a stretcher, spindle. [*OED2* 1548 → in ref to a ladder rung]
  1806 (1970) Webster *Compendious Dict.* 261, *Round, n.* a . . rundle. [*DARE* Ed: This entry was carried over from Webster's English model.] **1816** in 1824 Knight *Letters* 29 **Boston MA,** They [=Philadelphians] say . . rungs for rounds of a ladder. **1855** Douglass *My Bondage* 37 **MD** (as of 1820s), This ladder was really a high invention, and possessed a sort of charm as I played with delight upon the rounds of it. **1876** Knight *Amer. Mech. Dict.* 3.1994, *Round.* . . *(Joinery.) a.* The *rung* or *rime* of a ladder which forms a step. . . *b.* The round rail joining the legs of a chair. **1899** (1912) Green *VA Folk-Speech* 358, *Round.* . . A round, cylindrical, part or piece of something. *Round* of a ladder; *round* of a chair. . . The step in a ladder between the side-frames. **1903** *DN* 2.300 **Cape Cod MA** (as of a1857), *Round.* . . Rung. **1907** *DN* 3.207 **nwAR,** *Round.* . . Rung. **1909** *DN* 3.364 **eAL, wGA,** *Roun(d).* . . A rung. **1915** *DN* 4.189 **swVA,** *Roun'.* . . Rung (of a ladder). **1934** Stribling *Unfinished Cathedral* 159 **AL,** He . . hitched his heels self-consciously on the second round of his chair. **1940** Weygandt *Down Jersey* 271 **sNJ,** Throughout most of New Jersey and Pennsylvania we speak of chair rungs and ladder rungs rather than the "rounds" we always hear them called in our summer home in central New Hampshire. That "rounds" for "rungs" is but one out of a score of instances in which we come upon Down East influence in South Jersey. **1965–70** *DARE* (Qu. F34, *The wooden cross-pieces that you put your feet on when you go up a ladder*) 227 Infs, **widespread,** Rounds; **FL**19, Cross rounds; **NM**8, Ladder rounds; (Qu. FF21b, . . *About old jokes people say: "The first time I heard that one _____"*) Inf **AR**31, I kicked the round out of my cradle.

2 in combs *over-round, under-round:* An **earmark** made by taking a semicircular section out of the upper or lower edge of the ear of a cow.
  1936 Adams *Cowboy Lingo* 132, The 'over-round' was made by cutting a half-circle from the top of the ear; the 'under-round' by cutting the half-circle from the bottom.

3 See quot.
  1982 *Barrick Coll.* **csPA,** *Round*—slice (of bread).

4 pl; also *round(s)ies:* =**rounders 1.**
  1912 *DN* 3.568, *One-old-cat.* . . Called . . *rounds* in Illinois and Missouri. **1953** Brewster *Amer. Nonsinging Games* 81 **IA,** Rounds—[Iowa]—This ball game is particularly popular with small groups which do not have enough players for baseball. . . Each time an out is made, players advance in position and the batter takes the last place in the field. This order is followed unless a flyball is caught. In that event the player who caught the ball becomes batter and the batter takes the former's position. **1968–69** *DARE* (Qu. EE11, *Bat-and-ball games for just a few players*) Infs **PA**95, 196, Roundies; **PA**76, Roundsies; **IL**63, Rounds.

5 pl: See **rounce.**

6 also in phr *a round:* For each of a number of items, apiece.
  1809 (1890) Cutler *Life & Times* 97 **CT,** Sold to Mr. Maurice Baker five head at $17 round. **1967** Green *Horse Tradin'* 180 **TX,** I said to him: "I guess then, that you are figuring these horses at about $60 a round." He said, "No, but if a man would take a bunch of them, they ought to be worth around $75 a round."

round adj [Cf *EDD round* adj. 4 "Coarse, thick" (the ex quoted refers to "a pair of rounder knitting needles")]

Large in diameter—freq in phr *as round as* as big around as.
  1896 *Scribner's Mag.* 19.493, Chadwick . . looked gravely at a sunspot as round as a dollar dancing on the floor. **1968** *DARE* Tape **MD**24, Well, the sweeping end was just the long handle—was the stick of hickory. He would always try to find a young hickory tree that was about as—well, it was a little rounder than most of our brooms would be now, but then after you'd whittled the one end up real fine . . why you had a really bushy end on that that made a nice broom. **1998** *NADS Letters* **NJ,** These were hollow, ribbed pasta shapes, about as round as a pencil. **2001** *DARE* File—Internet, Magnet Sensor Sizes—Dog: As round as a quarter and 1/2″ thick.

roundabout n
=**rounders 1.**

1950 *PADS* 14.57 **SC,** *Roundabout.* . . A ball game in which each player successively occupies each position on the team. When a batter is put out, he takes to the field, a fielder takes third base, the third baseman moves to second and so on to first, pitcher, catcher, and batter.

roundance n Also *rounance, roundems, roundence, roundings, round'unce* **chiefly Sth, S Midl**

1 In marble play: the privilege of moving around the ring to a better position for shooting—freq used as a call claiming this privilege.   Also called **rounce, rounders 2, roundsters**

1883 Newell *Games & Songs* 186, When a lad wishes to change his position, so that, while preserving the same distance from his mark, he may have a more favorable position, he exclaims, "Roundings." If, however, his antagonist is quick enough, he will cry "Fen [defend] roundings." **1890** *DN* 1.66 **KY,** *Round'unce:* for *round once;* used in a game of marbles. **1893** Shands *MS Speech* 75, *Roundance.* A term used in playing marbles. By crying out *roundance* the player obtains the right to move around to a more favorable position for shooting. I think that the word is merely an abstract noun formed from the adjective *round.* **1897** (1952) McGill *Narrative* 33 **SC,** Some boys would claim slippance and there was none, violating the orders "knuckle down and fire hard," no fudging, no clearance nor roundance and no extension of the span towards the ring or a man. **1906** *DN* DN 3.154 **nwAR,** *Roundin's.* . . A term used in playing marbles. The players, if they change their position, must always remain at the same distance from the target or marble aimed at. **1909** *DN* 3.364 **eAL, wGA,** *Rounance.* . . A term used in the game of marbles for permission to move around to a more suitable position. **1926** *AmSp* 2.66 [Playground argot], Hear the chatter that comes out of a marble-shooting ring. "Straights," "vent," "knuckle down," "three knuckles down," "in the country," "roundings," "vent everything," the youngsters cry. **1950** *PADS* 14.70 **SC,** *"Venture roundance!"* pronounced by an opponent deprives the player from moving in an arc around his target for a better shot. The player can retain his right to roundance by saying "Roundance no lose." If he fails to add the last two words, his opponent may by saying "lose two yards" force him to withdraw that distance before he shoots. **1950** *WELS (Cries or calls used in playing marbles—to get the right to do something)* 1 Inf, **cwWI,** Roundings—to move to different part of circle to shoot. **1955** *PADS* 23.28 **cwTN,** *Roundings: interj.* Same as *rounce.* . . *heard.* **1957** *Sat. Eve. Post Letters* **OK** (as of 1890s), If the shooter said "anys" before "vents" was spoken . . , he could have a choice of any of a number of advantages. . . He could for instance exercise "roundance" which meant that he could move his taw or shooting point to another position the same distance from the objective. *Ibid* **sIN** (as of c1905), At the call of "Roundems" the shooter was allowed to move his taw to a more advantageous, but not closer, spot. **c1960** *Wilson Coll.* **csKY,** *Roundance.* . . A term in marbles, used to indicate going to a more advantageous position.

2 in phrr *take (a) roundance:* To avail oneself of the privilege of **roundance 1;** by ext: to avoid an obstacle or problem by going around it.   Cf **rounders 3**

1884 Smith *Bill Arp's Scrap Book* 31 **nwGA,** I thought the Confederacy would be calling 'em up to 45 [=years] before long, so I took roundence and fudged on 'em and managed to get on one of their ding'd old staffs. **1892** Smith *Farm & Fireside* 246 **GA,** And so Uncle Tom was advised to take roundance and never tackle the crossroads. **1915** *DN* 4.191 **swVA,** *Take roundins.* . . In marbles, to change positions with reference to the ring or another taw. **1941** Writers' Program *Guide AR* 97, While the panting woodsman was praying for his second wind, he came to a large white oak; here he took roundence. The snake, instead of swerving, rolled into the tree. **1956** *Hall Coll.* **wNC, eTN,** *Take a roundance on it.* . . To wind around in going to the top of a mountain; to climb a mountain by winding around it to the top, as cattle do. **1995** *Brophy Coll.* 63 **swMO** (as of c1960), *To take roundance* =[T]o take a circular route, to go around.

round ball n Also *round base* **Nth**
=**rounders 1.**

1834 R. Carver *Bk. of Sports* (*OED2*), This game is known under a variety of names. It is sometimes called 'round ball', but I believe that 'base', or 'goal ball' are the names generally adopted in our country. **1841** *Daily Picayune* (New Orleans LA) 25 May 2/2 **nOH,** We would go to Cleveland ourselves just for one game of round ball, provided we could not enjoy it at less cost. [*DARE* Ed: Reprinted from *Cleveland Herald*] **1856** *Porter's Spirit of Times* 27 Dec 276 **Boston MA,** I have

thought . . a statement of my experience as to the Yankee method of playing "Base," or "Round" ball, as we used to call it, may not prove uninteresting. **1867** *Ball Players Chron.* 18 July 4/2 (*DAE*), This game of rounders. . . was brought to our country by the early emigrants, and was called here 'base ball' or 'round ball.' **1871** Cutting *Student Life* 112 **MA,** "Wicket" and "Round Ball," were quite common once, though of late years, "Base Ball" has entirely superceded them. **1907** *DN* 3.249 **eME,** *Round base.* . . Primitive game of baseball, such as the present standard game seems to have been developed from. Among the players were the *thrower* (pitcher), *catcher, striker* (batsman), and two *tenders,* one of whom assisted the *catcher* and one the *thrower.* The bases were called *gools.* **1950** *WELS (Bat-and-ball games for a few players, [when you don't have enough for a regular game])* 1 inf, **seWI,** Round ball.

round barn n **chiefly Nth, N Midl**
A barn constructed in a circular shape.

1859 *Scientific Amer.* 5 Feb 178, We cannot advise you to build a round barn, because it is troublesome to match the doors and other timbers. We prefer the rectangular form. **1890** WI Ag. Exper. Sta. *Annual Rept. for 1890* 192, The floor space of the round barn is larger. **1950** *WELS Suppl.,* Round barn. **1965–70** *DARE* (Qu. M1, . . *Kinds of barns . . according to their use or the way they are built*) 27 Infs, **chiefly Nth, N Midl,** Round barn; **IA12,** Round barn—built of tile; **IA19,** Round barn—so the cows wouldn't do it in the corner; **MI12,** Round barn—had one, but it's gone; **MN7,** Round barn—a regular barn as far as uses are concerned; **OK43,** Round barn—made of sheet iron with steel framing, igloo. **1967** Sloane *Age of Barns* 53, Round Barns . . the first American "Modern Architecture." *Ibid* 54, The first big round barn of stone was built by the Shakers at Hancock, Massachusetts, in 1826. "The interior," they said, "was designed so that a great number of workers might be simultaneously engaged at their tasks and no person be in another's way." It had a fortlike security in its nearly yard-wide walls; it held fifty-two head of cattle; and there was an immense hay-storage area in its center. . . Countless other smaller round barns were built, . . and many of them still remain—mostly in Vermont—and operate efficiently. **1967** (1970) Jackman-Scharff *Steens Mt.* 144 **seOR,** There seems to be no exact date established when the [Barton Lake Ranch] round barn was built, but it was finished and being used in 1884. It is a hundred feet in diameter, and has a sixty-foot round stone corral in the middle, with an outer circle paddock twenty feet wide for working horses. . . Evidently the purpose was to use it for breaking horses in winter.

round base See **round ball**

round clam n **esp CT**
A **quahog 1** (here: *Mercenaria mercenaria*).

1843 DeKay *Zool. NY* 6.217, *Venus mercenaria.* . . This species is the common *Round Clam,* much prized as an article of food, and so savory in some localities as to be equally valued with the *Oyster.* Its aboriginal name of *Quahog* has now fallen into disuse. **1872** Schele de Vere *Americanisms* 29, The more costly beads came from the largest shells of the *Quahaug* or *Cohog,* a whelk, known in the Middle and Southern States as the Round Clam. **1911** U.S. Bur. *Fisheries 1908* 314, *Quahaug.* . . It is also called "hard clam," "round clam," "bull-nose," "little neck," etc. **1939** *LANE* Map 235 (*Round clam*) 32 infs, **sNEng, esp CT,** Round clam. **1949** Kurath *Word Geog.* 21, The large clam, known as the *round clam* in most of Connecticut, has generally retained its Indian name [=*quahog,* with varr *quohog* and *cohog*] from New London to Nantucket and from Cape Cod to Maine. **1970** *DARE* (Qu. P18, . . *Kinds of shellfish*) Inf **CT42,** Round clams.

round dock n [*OED2* 1825 →]   Cf **dock** n¹
A **mallow B** (here: *Malva rotundifolia* or *M. sylvestris*).

1900 Lyons *Plant Names* 238, [*Malva*] *sylvestris.* . . Pancake plant, Round Dock [etc]. **1924** *Amer. Botanist* 30.106, The "high mallow" is *M. sylvestris.* . . Though several names have been derived from the circular cluster of ovaries the name of "round dock" probably refers to the leaves which are roundish, though the term would be better applied to *M. rotundifolia.*

roundems, roundence See **roundance**

rounders n pl but sg in constr

1 A bat-and-ball game with few players; see quots.   Cf **move-up, one old cat, work-up** [Cf *OED2* rounders (at *rounder* sb. 2.a) → for a team bat and ball game akin to baseball] **esp N Cent**

1950 *WELS (Bat-and-ball games for a few players [when you don't have enough for a regular game]),* 1 Inf, **swWI,** Rounders. **1957** *Sat.*

Eve. Post Letters **seWI**, *Rounders*—Positions same as in base ball, chosen by players—at least three "inners". When one was put out he went to the field and the catcher became "inner" etc. Same as "work up." **1965–70** *DARE* (Qu. EE11, *Bat-and-ball games for just a few players [when there aren't enough for a regular game]*) Infs **IL**135, **IN**69, **MO**7, **OH**82, **PA**71, **UT**3, Rounders; **OH**42, Rounders—like work up. **1965** *DARE* File **ceMO** (as of c1930), *Move-up, rounders*—Elementary baseball game for a few players; the batter runs to first base (the only one) and back to make a run. Fly balls caught or the ball thrown to home base put batter out. No strikes counted. Players "move up" to get turns at bat.

2 also *roundies;* In marble play: = **roundance 1.**

1950 *WELS* (*Cries or calls used in playing marbles—to get the right to do something*) 1 Inf, **swWI**, Rounders—to get right to go around tree etc; 1 Inf, **seWI**, Roundies. **1958** *Resp. to PADS 29* **cnOK**, Advantage could be gained by being the first to cry. . . Rounders—Moving about on the circumberance [sic] of a circle whose center was the object marble in order to clear an obstruction. **1970** *DARE* (Qu. EE7, . . *Kinds of marble games*) Inf **KY**84, Rounders—some rule whereby you go closer to the inner ring or could get a second shot. [FW: Inf not sure] **1973** [see **roundsters**].

3 in phr *take rounders:* See quot. Cf **roundance 2**

1933 *AmSp* 8.1.53 **Ozarks**, *Take rounders.* . . To walk around an obstacle, rather than scale it. *Bee Bluff is so dang steep we generally allus tuck rounders on it.* **1955** Dykeman *French Broad* 330 **wNC**, You cannot know this river by simply sitting on the level banks of its lower body or by striking out on any straight road up its course; you must judge the "lay of the land" and follow a wandering path that will take "rounders" on its sources high in the mountains.

round eyes n pl, but sg in constr Also *round eye* Cf **slant eyes**

A Caucasian.

1972 McCormick *Vocab. HI* 74, *Round-eyes*—Caucasian, haole. **1986** Chapman *New Dict. Amer. Slang* np, *Round-eye* . . esp Korean War armed forces—A Caucasian as distinct from an Asian.

roundfish n

Perh a **redhorse 1;** see quot.

1970 *DARE* (Qu. P1, . . *Kinds of freshwater fish . . caught around here . . good to eat*) Inf **VA**38, Roundfish—same as sawhorse . . long, round, funny round mouth.

round forty n Cf **long forty, rubber forty** *hist*

A forty-acre timber cut that has been intentionally enlarged by an unscrupulous logger; also in joc v phr *cut a round forty* to cut "around" forty acres.

1938 (1939) Holbrook *Holy Mackinaw* 93 **MI, WI** (as of c1890), If they [=lumbermen] couldn't get all they wanted at a dollar and a quarter an acre, they might get a "Round Forty" and cut it. This Round Forty business was the classic joke of the era and founded on sober fact. . . A boss logger. . . might buy forty acres, which was the smallest unit . . [of] timber. . . He'd send in the boys to cut it, telling his foreman to "log around [approximately] forty acres." So, the boys would cut . . a round forty. First, the forty acres to the north, then to the east, the south, the west. **1956** Sorden–Ebert *Logger's Words* 28 **Gt Lakes**, *Round-forty,* About forty acres of land. To cut a round forty meant that cutting was done over the line into the next forty. **1964** Hargreaves–Foehl *Story of Logging* 61 **MI** [Glossary], *'Round forty*—A dishonest way to cut timber. A logging company, after purchasing a piece of land, would not only cut the timber on that piece, but dishonestly cut trees on land surrounding it. Legislation, making the practice illegal, was effective in 1903—but it was too late to benefit the State of Michigan. Most of the white pine had been cut. **1969** Sorden *Lumberjack Lingo* 99 **NEng, Gt Lakes**, *Round forty*—About forty acres of land. To cut a round forty meant that the cutting crossed the line into the next forty. The practice was to cut to the line plus as far as a man could throw his ax. Same as "he logs on section 37."

roundhead n

1 A person of Northern or Eastern European birth or background.

1895 *DN* 1.393 **NW**, *Roundhead:* a Swede. **1931** 'D. Stiff' *Milk & Honey Route* iii.38 *(OED2)*, Swedes are 'roundheads' or 'salve eaters'. **1938** (1964) Korson *Minstrels Mine Patch* 317 **nePA**, *Roundhead:* Nickname for Slavic immigrants. **1950** *WELS* (*Names and nicknames for people of foreign background*) 1 inf, **cwWI**, Roundhead—German.

1956 Sorden–Ebert *Logger's Words* 28 **NEng, Gt Lakes**, *Round-head,* A Scandinavian lumber-jack. **1966–69** *DARE* (Qu. HH28, *Names and nicknames . . for people of foreign background*) Infs **MI**28, 47, 101, **MN**10, **WA**20, Roundhead—Swedish; **MN**2, Roundhead—Norwegian; **PA**227, Roundhead—Polish; **VA**5, Roundhead—Finnish.

2 = **hardhead 7.** Cf **niggerhead 1**

1950 *WELS* (*Names for . . stones of particular size*) 1 Inf, **seWI**, Roundhead. **1965–70** *DARE* (Qu. C25, . . *Kinds of stone . . about . . [. . size of a person's head], smooth and hard*) 9 Infs, **scattered**, Roundhead.

3 A **kingfish 1.**

1939 Natl. Geogr. Soc. *Fishes* 93, The kingfish [=*Menticirrhus saxatilis*] has two immediate relatives [=*M. americanus* and *M. littoralis*] on the Atlantic coast with which its range overlaps. These relatives are so close that fishermen generally do not distinguish the three, and therefore they have no distinctive common names. The group as a whole is well supplied with local or common names. Besides kingfish they are called whiting, . . roundheads, sea minks, and sea mullets. Wherever the three species occur together, the local names apply alike to each. **1968** *DARE* (Qu. P2, . . *Kinds of saltwater fish caught around here . . good to eat*) Inf **NC**80, Roundheads—same as kingfish. **1969** *DARE* FW Addit **eNC**, *Roundheads*—also called sea mullet. **1984** *DARE* File **Chesapeake Bay** [Watermen's vocab], Sand mullet / sea mullet / Virginia mullet / roundhead / whiting.

roundhead buffalo n

= **bigmouth buffalo.**

1933 LA Dept. of Conserv. *Fishes* 439, The Common Buffalofish or Redmouth Buffalo . . has come to be known under many popular names [including]. . . Gourd Seed Buffalo, Round Head Buffalo [etc]. **1983** Becker *Fishes WI* 615, Bigmouth Buffalo. . . Other common names: redmouth buffalo . . roundhead buffalo [etc].

round herring n [See quot 1906]

A clupeid fish of the genus *Etrumeus*, esp *E. teres*. For other names of var spp see **makiawa**

1873 in 1878 Smithsonian Inst. *Misc. Coll.* 14.2.32, *Etrumeus teres* . . Round herring. Cape Cod to Havana. **1906** NJ State Museum *Annual Rept. for 1905* 93, Genus Etrumeus . . The Round Herrings. . . Distinguished from all our herrings by the rounded belly. **1926** Pan-Pacific Research Inst. *Jrl.* 1.5, Dussumieriidae. The Round Herrings. **1999** (acc) U.S. Food & Drug Admin. *Seafood List* (Internet), Market Names: Herring. . . Common Name: Round herring[·] Vernacular: Atlantic round herring . . red-eyed round herring.

round-hog buy n Cf **pig in a poke 1**

1967 *DARE* FW Addit **cLA**, *Round-hog buy*—you agree to accept it regardless of how bad or good it is.—No grade or quality stipulated.

roundies n[1] See **rounders 2**

roundies n[2] See **round 4**

roundings See **roundance**

round meat See **round steak**

round note n

A musical note with an oval head, as contrasted with a **shape note.**

1913 (1980) Hardy *OH Schoolmistress* 5, He had a beautiful tenor voice and was very fond of singing. Later . . he had acquired the ability to read "round note." **1942** (1960) Robertson *Red Hills* 291 **SC**, We still sing from music books printed with shaped notes instead of round notes—with shaped diamonds, circles, squares, and triangles as William & Smith devised them at Philadelphia in 1798.

round pompano n

A **pompano 1** (here: *Trachinotus falcatus*). Also called **dory n[1] 3, oldwife 1c, palometa**

1884 Goode *Fisheries U.S.* 1.329, The Round Pompano, in the South sometimes called the "Shore Pompano," is known in the Bermudas by the name "Alewife." **1933** John G. Shedd Aquarium *Guide* 82, *Trachinotus falcatus*—Round Pampano. More southern in its range than the Common Pampano. **1955** Zim–Shoemaker *Fishes* 95, *Permit* resembles the pompano and is sometimes called Round Pompano. **1976** Tryckare et al. *Lore of Sportfishing* 108, Atlantic Permit . . *Trachinotus falcatus*—Other common names: Round pompano, Indian River permit.

round potato n esp C Atl Cf **long potato**
=**white potato.**

a1782 (1788) Jefferson *Notes VA* 40, Round potatoes. Solanum Tuberosum. **1864** Morris *How to Get a Farm* 248 **NJ,** His wheat crop has been 20 bushels per acre, 75 of shelled corn, 200 of round potatoes, 100 of sweet, [etc]. **1899** (1912) Green *VA Folk-Speech* 358, *Round-potatoes. . .* Irish potatoes, distinguishing from *long-potatoes,* or sweet-potatoes. **1913** Johnson *Highways St. Lawrence to VA* 209 **ceNJ,** The "white" or "round" potatoes, as they called the Irish variety, were six inches high. **1970** *DARE* (Qu. I9, . . *Names [including nicknames] for potatoes)* Inf **VA51,** Round potatoes—Irish potatoes.

round robin n

A **mackerel scad** (here: *Decapterus punctatus*). Also called **cigarfish, scad**

[**1873** in 1878 Smithsonian Inst. *Misc. Coll.* 14.2.25, *Decapterus punctatus . .* Dotted scad; round robin *(Bermudas).* Cape Cod to Florida.] **1879** U.S. Natl. Museum *Bulletin* 14.42, Round Robin.—West Indian Fauna and north to Massachusetts. **1902** Jordan-Evermann *Amer. Fishes* 302, The genus *Decapterus* contains the mackerel scads. . . One of these, *D. punctatus,* known as the scad, round robin, or quia-quia, is common on the coasts of Florida. **1933** John G. Shedd Aquarium *Guide* 84, Scad; Cigarfish; Round Robin. **1968** *DARE* (Qu. P1) Inf **NC80,** Round robin—against the law to sell in market.

‡**round row** n

A circle.

c1938 in 1970 Hyatt *Hoodoo* 1.843 **cwMS,** When you giving a party and you wanta have luck and success in your party, . . you get you seven candles . . and set 'em on your table *in a round row* [Hyatt: circle].

round saucer squash See **round squash**

round-shave n

A tool with a curved blade that cuts a concave channel as it is drawn toward the user.

1703 in 1886 NC *Colonial Rec.* 1.591, Henry Norman [shall] pay . . one Drawing Knife one Round Shave. **1859** Perry *Turpentine Farming* 28, Among the various causes of the wood of a pine looking white at the spot where it is chipped with the round-shave, may be enumerated the following. **1952** Brown *NC Folkl.* 1.586, *Round-shave. . .* 1 . . . A concave iron tool used to round out the inside of barrel staves. . . Yancey county. 2. . . A long-handled iron tool used to chip turpentine pines.— South and central. **1969** *DARE* Tape **GA48,** He made his tools; he could make a round side on the outside, make a round side inside. . . I believe he called it a round-shave.

roundsies See **round 4**

round snow n Cf **corn snow**

See quot.

1894 *DN* 1.342 **wCT,** *Round snow:* hard, hail-like snow which falls when a snow-storm is just turning to rain.

roundsomes See **roundsters**

round square n Also *round straightedge* **esp Nth** See Map Cf **half-round square**

A nonexistent item used as the basis for a practical joke.

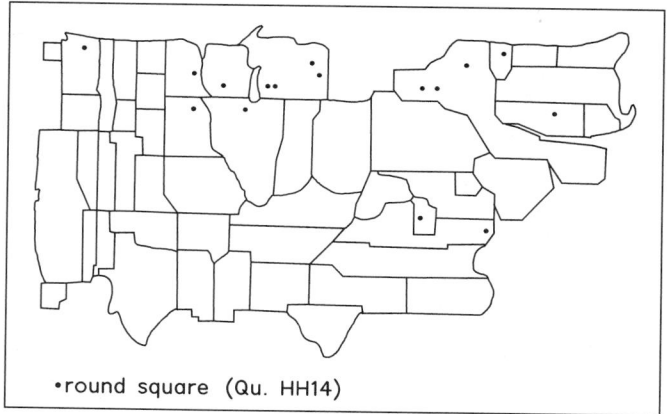

•round square (Qu. HH14)

1896 *DN* 1.423 **wNY, IA,** *Round square:* to send a boy after a *round square* is to send him on a fruitless errand (as a joke). **1921** *DN* 5.95, *Round square.* Carpenter's joke word. **1960** *VT Hist.* 28.219, To go for a round square. (To go on a foolish errand.) **1965–70** *DARE* (Qu. HH14, *Ways of teasing a beginner or inexperienced person—for example, by sending him for a 'left-handed monkey wrench':* "Go get me ———.") 16 Infs, **esp Nth,** Round square. [13 of 16 Infs old] **1973** *DARE* File **cwIL,** Round straight-edge. . . Non-existent tool which a greenhorn is sent to fetch. . . Among bricklayers; Macomb IL.

round squash n Also *round saucer squash,* ~ *white squash, white round squash* **chiefly Sth, S Midl** See Map
A **summer squash,** esp **pattypan squash.**

1965–70 *DARE* (Qu. I23, . . *Kinds of squash)* Infs **AR51, GA1, NC14,** 30, **TX26,** 31, Round squash; **AL11,** Round squash—white; **TN24,** Round squash [FW illustr: a squash similar to a pattypan squash]; **KY90,** Round saucer squash; **NC3,** Round white squash; **GA3,** White round squash; **VA74,** White round squash [FW illustr: a squash with scalloped edges]. **1986** Pederson *LAGS Concordance* **Gulf Region,** 6 infs, Round squash; 1 inf, Round squash—green; 1 inf, Round squash— white; 1 inf, Round squash—it makes a neck.

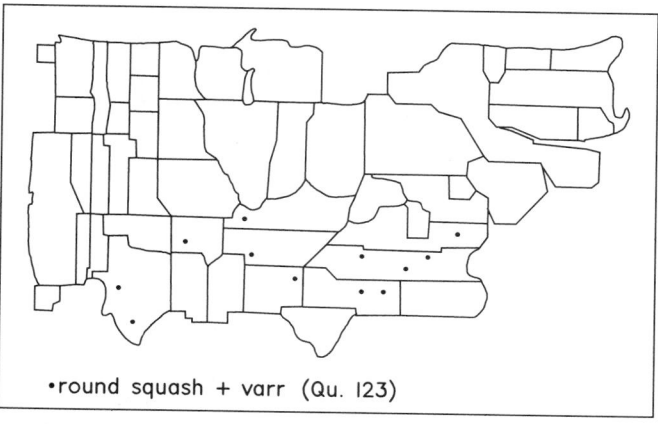

•round squash + varr (Qu. I23)

round steak n Also *Polish round steak, round meat* Bologna.

1972 Shafer *Dict. Prison Slang* 33, Round steak—bologna. **1982** Slone *How We Talked* 43 **eKY** (as of c1950), "Round meat"—bologna. **1987** *DARE* File **seWI,** I have heard ring bologna called round steak and Polish round steak.

roundsters n Also *roundsomes*
=**roundance 1.**

1927 *88 Successful Play Activities* 29, "Roundsters"—Circling—The act of selecting the best location for a knuckle down out side of ring during a turn. **1932** (1953) Smith *Games* 226, [From the "Official Interstate Tournament Rules":] "Roundsters" is the privilege of taking a different position on the Ring Line for shooting and is permitted only at the start of the game or on a turn after a shooter has passed out of the Ring. **1958** *PADS* 29.40, Roundsomes. . . Same as *roundems* (Ohio). **c1970** Wiersma *Marbles Terms,* Roundsters. . . Going around the circle to select the best shot. **1973** Ferretti *Marble Book* 51, Roundsters. Circling around the playing ring, seeking the best shooting position. Also called Rounders.

round straightedge See **round square**

round sunfish n

Either of two **sunfishes:** the **flier 2** or a **pumpkinseed 1** (here: *Lepomis gibbosus*).

1896 U.S. Natl. Museum *Bulletin* 47.988, *Centrarchus macropterus . . .* Round Sunfish; Flier. . . Lowland streams and bayous from Virginia southward to Florida and Louisiana; northward in the Mississippi valley to southern Illinois. **1946** LaMonte *N. Amer. Game Fishes* 143, Flier . . Round Sunfish. . . Greenish, with broken lines of round dark dots. **1949** Caine *N. Amer. Sport Fish* 43, Pumpkinseed. . . Round Sunfish. **1983** Becker *Fishes WI* 828, Pumpkinseed. . . Other common names . . common sunfish, sunfish, round sunfish.

round table n

A table with a built-in lazy Susan.

1921 *DN* 5.119 **KY**, *Round table.* . . A sort of two pieced, round dinner table, once very common in the mountains. Dishes of food are placed on the top piece, which revolves. The plates are placed on the larger section, beneath this.

roundtail n

1 A **minnow B1,** as:

a also *roundtail chub: Gila robusta.*

1896 U.S. Natl. Museum *Bulletin* 47.227, *Gila Robusta* . . Roundtail. . . the flesh full of small bones and nearly worthless as food. **1900** *Land of Sunshine* 13.436, The Gila is a hump-back chub, about a foot and a half long, with a low, large mouth and a long, broad tail. It is popularly known as Bony-Tail, Gila Trout and Round-Tail; and is about as poor eating as a fish can be. **1935** Pratt *Manual Vertebrate Animals* 69, *G. robusta* . . Roundtail. . . Colorado and Gila Rivers; very common. **1964** Lowe *Vertebrates* 140 **AZ**, *Gila robusta* . . the roundtail, generally inhabits major tributaries of the Gila and Colorado rivers. **1983** *Audubon Field Guide N. Amer. Fishes* 416, Roundtail Chub . . *Gila robusta.* . . Warm, often turbid waters of large rivers, creeks, pools, and lakes.

b A **squawfish** (here: prob *Ptychocheilus lucius*).

1967 *DARE* (Qu. P3, *Freshwater fish that are not good to eat*) Inf **CO**41, Roundtail—not good to eat—looks like a trout—gets up to 12–15 pounds; also called squawfish.

2 A mule. Cf **broomtail 2, hardtail 4, pestle-tail,** *DS* K50

1940 *AmSp* 15.447 [TN mountain speech], *Round tail.* Mule. 'Pearl rode to the store on a round tail.'

roundtail chub See **roundtail 1a**

round-tailed muskrat n

A swamp-dwelling vole of Florida and Georgia *(Neofiber alleni)*, smaller than the true muskrat. Also called **Florida water rat, muskrat 2, water rat**

1917 Anthony *Mammals Amer.* 256, Round-tailed musk-rat. . . While called a Musk-rat, this less familiar animal occupies a group by itself, intermediate between the smaller Mice and its big cousin the common Musk-rat. . . It is at home in both the fresh and salt-water ponds, and marshes of Eastern Florida. **1938** Matschat *Suwannee R.* 31 **neFL, seGA,** Recently the round-tailed muskrat, or Florida water rat, has been found in Okefenokee, the only place it is known to exist in Georgia. **1980** Whitaker *Audubon Field Guide Mammals* 507, *Round-tailed Muskrat.* . . "Florida Water Rat."

round-town n Also *round-town ball* chiefly S Midl, esp KY Cf **one old cat, scrub 2, town ball, work-up** =**rounders 1.**

1938 Stuart *Dark Hills* 237 **KY**, The dead were now being buried on the ground where we used to play Fox and Dog, Jail, Among the Little White Daisies, London Bridge, and Round-town Ball with a twine ball. **1964** *Mt. Life* Summer 41 **eTN**, In the summer we played roundtown, or long cat or short cat, or drop-the-hat or hot pepper. **1968–69** *DARE* (Qu. EE11, *Bat-and-ball games for just a few players [when there aren't enough for a regular game]*) Infs **KY**40, 41, 72, **OH**48, 74, **VA**30, Round-town; **NC**69, Round-town—pitcher and catcher and a fielder or several—like work up. **1982** Slone *How We Talked* 94 **eKY** (as of c1950), A game we played which we called "round town" was very much like baseball, with a batter, pitcher, and first, second and third base, homeplate and striking out. **1983** *MJLF* 9.1.53 **ceKY** (as of 1956), *Round town* . . one man in town, a game of baseball, [also known from] VA.

round tree See **roundwood**

round turn n esp ME

A turnaround at the end of a road; also fig.

1905 U.S. Forest Serv. *Bulletin* 61.45 **Gt Lakes, NEng** [Logging terms], *Round turn.* A space at the head of a logging-sled road, in which the sled may be turned round without unhitching the team. **1942** ME Univ. *Studies* 57.133, *Round Turn.* The terminus of a road constructed in circular form so that teams or tractors hauling sleds can turn around without backing. **1969** Sorden *Lumberjack Lingo* 99 **NEng, Gt Lakes,** *Round turn*—The loop at the end of a sleigh road where the driver could turn around without backing. **1975** Gould *ME Lingo* 235, *Round turn.* . . In lumbering, a *round turn* was provided at a dead end logging road, so teams could come about—a rotary. Thus a person who finds a way out of a difficulty has a *round turn.*

round'unce See **roundance**

roundup n West

1 also attrib: A cooperative activity in which **cowhands** drive large numbers of range cattle to a central point where they are segregated by owner for purposes of counting the herd, branding calves, or shipping cattle to market; the horses and riders involved.

1873 in 1927 *Annals WY* 5.74 [sic *OED2*—quot not found], The herders of this Co. start a Round-up tomorrow. . . Each man picks out his stock and drives them in. **1878** Beadle *Western Wilds* 437 **wTX**, These cattle, having run wild . ., are collected by a grand "round-up." **1878** in 1939 *Colorado Mag.* 16.152, Most of the round-up gone; a few still lingered at the bar; two of whom inspired by bad whiskey . . spurred their horses up onto the hotel piazza. **1887** *Overland Mth.* (2d ser) 9.231 **West**, About May or June . . the whole country is searched, and the cattle appertaining to a district driven together into one vast herd, from whence the different ranchmen separate their own animals . . each owner takes his herd back to the home range, brands the calves, turns them loose, and does not see them again collected until the next round up. **1893** in 1932 *AmSp* 7.259 **NE** [Cowboy terms], *Round-up*—the driving in together of all the cattle from a large territory, participated in by all owners, each of whom then brands the stock to which he is entitled, the calf being given a like brand as that borne by the mother. **1893** Roosevelt *Wilderness Hunter* 23 **nRocky Mts**, Close beyond the trees . . stood the two round-up wagons. **1910** Hart *Vigilante Girl* 114 **nCA**, A rodeo is a round-up. . . A round-up is—why, at a round-up all the animals in a district are gathered together by the *vaqueros,* or cowboys, and the different owners' cattle are separated and branded. **1913** *DN* 4.28 **NW**. **1920** Hunter *Trail Drivers TX* 310 (as of c1883), The largest "round up" that I ever saw . . was the C.C. Slaughter "round up," . . estimated at 100,000 head of cattle. *Ibid* 311, These cattle in this round up were not owned by one individual, but belonged to ranches from a radius of many, many miles. . . Cattle were known to drift as far as 150 miles north. . . This made it necessary to have the "round up," and to get the different brands of cattle to their respective owners and ranches. **1921** Chapman *Cactus Center* 18 **SW**, And we got word to the round-ups, and they let the brand-irons lie. *Ibid* 12, There was n't much work doin' in the round-up gang for days. **1929** *AmSp* 5.68 **NE** [Cattle country talk], The "round-up" occurs in the spring and in the late summer or early fall—in March and in September or October, when all the animals grazing on the "ranges" of the ranch are "herded" or "driven" to a single point. **1939** (1973) FWP *Guide MT* 415. **1966–70** *DARE* Tape **CA**192, They had a great big roundup, and then they'd have lots of fun and games, and competitive sports; **NM**13, So we had to stay at the wagon unless you wanted to ride your roundup horse, or your cutting horse they called 'em away from there; **NM**14, In that roundup we'd have anywhere from three to five thousand cattle. **1986** Pederson *LAGS Concordance,* 1 inf, **csTX**, Roundup—ten men needed for 15–20,000 acres; 1 inf, **csTX**, Roundup—of cattle, four to five days.

2 A community festival that includes a **rodeo B.**

1914 *World's Work* 27.444 **neOR**, During the three days of The Round-Up a constant stream of humanity pours into Pendleton. **1948** *Great Falls* (Mont.) *Tribune* 18 Sep. 5/4 *(DA)*, Malta is preparing to welcome at least 5,000 people this weekend when the two-day fall roundup will be staged. **1999** *DARE* File—Internet **neOR** [Welcome to Pendleton Oregon], *Pendleton Roundup* . . it's billed as the USA's best rodeo. Established in 1909, the celebration includes an old-fashioned rodeo, cowboy breakfasts, a parade, a country music concert [etc]. *Ibid* [Rodeo Sport Tours], American's [sic] Classic Rodeo—that's the Pendleton Round-up. In the summer of 1910 [sic], a group of area ranchers and farmers gathered in Pendleton to celebrate the end of the harvest. This was the beginning of the world famous Pendleton Round-up. Seven major . . events are run each day on a grass arena, plus pony express races, Indian and baton races, wild horse races, wild cow milking, and much more.

3 in phrr *last* (or *grand, great*) *roundup*: Fig: death. Cf **go west,** *DS* BB56

1908 (1966) Thorp *Songs Cowboys* 19 **West**, I hear there's to be a grand round up / Where cow-boys with others must stand / To be cut out by the riders of judgment / Who are posted and know all the brands. **1915** (1922) Clark *Sun & Saddle* 40 **West**, When my earthly trail is ended / And my final bacon curled / And the last great roundup's finished / At the Home Ranch of the world. **1936** *AmSp* 11.200 [Euphemisms for dying], Went to the last roundup. **1940** *Hoofs & Horns* Dec 11/1 **West** (*AmSp* 17.213), Tom Mix . . has laid down his honors won through the years and *taken the sunset trail* that leads to *the Last Roundup.* **1942** Berrey–Van den Bark *Amer. Slang* 117.1, *Death . .* last roundup. **1958** Blasingame *Dakota Cowboy* 317 **SD**, I expect to keep a good cowhorse under me and a saddle rope in my hand until I, too, reach the Great Roundup.

round whitefish n
A **whitefish** (here: *Prosopium cylindraceum*). Also called **frostfish 5, grayback 3c, menominee, pilotfish 3, shad waiter**
1883 WI Chief Geologist *Geol. WI* 1.431, *[Coregonus] quadrilateralis . .* Round white fish. Lake Michigan. This species spawns . . just outside the stony ridge north of Racine. **1978** *AK Fishing Guide* 81, *The round whitefish . .* is distributed across the northern slope of the Brooks Range, through the Brooks Range, on the Seward Peninsula and the drainages of the Yukon and Kuskokwim rivers.

round white squash See **round squash**

roundwood n Also *round tree* [Var of **rowan** + *wood, tree; round* is prob a folk-etym spelling representing [raʊn]; cf the spp *rountree* and *rown* in *OED2* (at *rowan-tree* and *rowan*).]
A **mountain ash 1** (here: *Sorbus americana*).
1848 *Union Mag.* (NY NY) 3.179 **ME**, The wood was chiefly yellow birch, spruce, fir, mountain-ash, or round-wood, as the Maine people call it, and moose-wood. **1916** *Torreya* 16.238 **ME**, *Pyrus americana . .* Roundwood or roundwood tree, Matinicus I[slan]d. **1928** in 1931 McCorrison *Letters Fraternity* 177 **ME**, There were two kinds of trilliums . . ladies slipper, violets of several colors, star flowers, dog wood, moss wood, bass wood, round wood and numerous other kinds of a dwarf nature. **1930** Sievers *Amer. Med. Plants* 7, American Mountain-ash . . *Other common names.*—Roundwood, round-tree, American rowan tree. **1979** Little *Checklist U.S. Trees* 277, *American mountain-ash. . .* roundwood.

rounses See **rounce**

roup-garou n Also *rugaroo, rugarue* [Varr of **loup-garou**]
An imaginary monster.
1939 (1962) Thompson *Body & Britches* 299 **NY**, Newcomers have been warned . . against the ferocious *rugarues*—perhaps related to the *loup-garou* (werewolf) of the French "Canucks". **1952** Dorson *Bloodstoppers* 74 **MI**, But Aunt Jane's choicest mysteries are reserved for the *roup-garou* (the St. Ignace corruption of *loup-garou*). "Seventy-five years ago," she recalls, "if the people see a man look into the house and disappear, they lock all doors and shut up the windows, and even stuff up the cracks. He might be a *roup-garou* who would throw some medicine into the house. We never hear anything of that any more; all those *roup-garou* people are dead." [**1967** LeCompte *Word Atlas* 396 **seLA**, A tormented soul in the body of an animal . . *roup-garou* [17 of 21 infs]; *loup-garou* [2 of 21 infs].] **1988** Erdrich *Tracks* 170 **ND**, Your mother had played this with you before, curled her fingers in claws, pretended to be a dangerous rugaroo.

roust v Also sp *rowst* [Perh blend of *rouse* + **rout**; *OED2 roust* v.[2] 1 1658 → "orig. *dial.* and *U.S.*"]
1 with *out, up:* To search out, dig up.
1845 Kirkland *Western Clearings* 179 **MI**, You ha'n't hid nothing, have ye? If you have, you'd better rowst it out at once't! **1871** Hay *Pike Co. Ballads* 14 **IL**, We rousted up some torches,/ And sarched for 'em far and near. **1905** Lincoln *Partners* 115 **NEng**, Roust out that bottle and heave it overboard.
2 usu with *out, up:* To rouse, waken (someone or something); to cause to stir; to stir up; hence ppl adj phr *rousted up* stirred up, excited. **chiefly Sth, S Midl**
1850 (1852) Colton *Deck & Port* 299, We rousted our anchors this afternoon from the bed in which they have slumbered for the last six weeks. **1883** *Peterson's Mag.* June 469 **NY**, Awhile ago you was all rousted up about goin' to New York village. **1909** *DN* 3.364 **eAL, wGA**, *Roust. . .* To rouse, stir about vigorously. "They rousted us up before day." *Ibid* 403 **nwAR**, *Roust. . .* To rouse. "We'll go and roust him out." **1912** *DN* 3.588 **wIN**, *Roust. . .* To arouse. "It's midnight, but let's roust them out." **1922** *DN* 5.184 **GA**, *Roust. . .* Arouse. "But I couldn't roust you outer bed." **1928** in 1952 Mathes *Tall Tales* 67 **sAppalachians**, I dreamp me a dream last night, that we rousted up Ol' Lucky, that main big b'ar that killed them five dawgs last winter. **1946** *PADS* 6.25 **eNC**, *Roust out. . .* To wake a person early and get him out of

bed. . . Among men. Occasional. **1951** *PADS* 15.60 **neIN** (as of 1890s), *Roust. . .* To rouse, rout out. . . To us it usually meant getting a person out of bed. **1954** *Harder Coll.* **cwTN**, *Roust him out . .* to get someone out of bed in the morning. "Roust 'im outta thair 'fore I wash 'is face in col(d) water." **1965–69** *DARE* (Qu. P39a, *When a hunter or a dog finds a game animal and makes it start running . . he _____ it*) Inf **GA**72, Rousted it; (Qu. X44, *To get somebody out of bed early in the morning: "I had to _____";* total Infs questioned, 75) Inf **OK**11, Roust him out; **MS**6, Roust him up. **1972** *Atlanta Letters* **cnGA**, You have "rousted" me up. **1972** *Foxfire Book* 169 **sAppalachians**, Y'get up and roust up your fire. **1986** Pederson *LAGS Concordance*, 1 inf, **ceTX**, Roust him out of bed. **1987** Childress *Out of the Ozarks* 62, Dad's two dogs . . were investigating clumps of Bermuda grass, perhaps in hopes of rousting a field mouse.
3 with *out, up:* To wake, stir oneself.
1884 Harris *Mingo* 162 **cGA**, It twon't never do in the roun' worl' for to be a-makin' faces at 'im frum the groun'. Roust up, roust up. **1887** (1967) Harris *Free Joe* 222 **GA** [Black], Atter w'ile, yer come daylight, en den I rousted out, I did, en built me a fire. **1900** (1901) Munn *Uncle Terry* 172 **ME**, I ginerally roust out by daylight. **1912** Wason *Friar Tuck* 67 **WY**, I knew it was my duty to roust up an' keep Horace from gettin' more sleep'n my treatment for his nerves called for.
4 with *around:* To rummage about, root around.
1941 Street *In Father's House* 19 **MS**, Suppose you were a dominecker . . hen. . . And you were in a coop and just outside the coop was a heap of grass that you wanted to roust around in.

roustabout n [*roustabout* an unskilled or semi-skilled laborer]
In tobacco processing: =**flunky 1c.**
1966 *PADS* 45.21 **cnKY**, *Roustabout . .* flunky. **1967** Key *Tobacco Vocab.* **MO, TN**, *Flunky. . .* Also *Roustabout.*

roust around See **roust 4**

rousted up See **roust 2**

rouster n **chiefly Lower Missip Valley**
A deckhand or longshoreman; a roustabout.
1883 *American* 6.40, Men . . who used to be rousters, and are now broken down and played out. **1929** Burman *Mississippi* 47, A rouster, with two coffee sacks tied around his body . . lay on the boiler deck strumming a guitar. **1929** *Sat. Eve. Post* 17 Aug 11 **LA**, Old Folks, [who is] an ex-roustabout, long since too old and infirm for the heavy labor of the rouster. **1932** Stribling *Store* 143 **AL**, I suppose we could start now. . . I'll have to hustle up some rousters. **1947** Ballowe *The Lawd* 72 **LA**, The rousters began to fetch baggage and pile it on top of the levee.

roust out (or up) See **roust 1, 2, 3**

rout v
1 also with *out, up:* To rouse, stir from sleep or concealment. Cf **roust 2**
1787 (1888) Cutler *Life* 1.287 **NJ**, The people at the White House were gone to bed, but I soon routed them. **1856** Stowe *Dred* 2.81 **NC**, I took a notable turn, this morning, and routed them up to an early breakfast. **1892** *N.Y. Sun* 8 May 2/7 (*DAE*), He ran to a neighbouring farmhouse, routed out the people. **1927** *Ruppenthal Coll.* **KS**, To rout . . one out of bed. . . To call or otherwise cause one to get out of bed, esp. at an unusual hour, or where the sleeper is reluctant to arise. We were routed out of bed shortly after midnight. **1933** Rawlings *South Moon* 239 **FL**, They saw the man, asleep. . . Lant said to Zeke, "Go out there man." **1966–69** *DARE* (Qu. P39a, *When a hunter or a dog finds a game animal and makes it start running . . he _____ it*) Infs **PA**185, 188, 198, Routed; **PA**132, Rout; **PA**163, Routing; (Qu. P39b, *If a hunter or a dog makes a bird or a covey fly*) Inf **IL**48, Routed it out; (Qu. X44, *To get somebody out of bed early in the morning: "I had to _____";* total Infs questioned, 75) Inf **DC**6, Rout him out.
2 with *out:* To dig out, find after some effort. Cf **roust 1**
1938 Rawlings *Yearling* 31 **nFL**, He dashed in to his room and routed out his heavy cowhide brogans from under the bed.
3 with *out:* To clear out, remove accumulated junk from.
1950 Moore *Candlemas Bay* 127 **ME**, Ordinarily, he would have enjoyed routing out the fishhouse.
4 To till (soil); hence n *routing plow* a type of cultivator.
1940 *Hench Coll.* **ceVA** [Black], [She] asked me if I would like

Alonzo (colored man) to "rout, as he calls it" the earth in my garden. She meant to go over the ground with a harrow—the kind that is made of a frame of wood with big steel spikes stuck through the wood. . . This morning Alonzo was looking at my garden and said, "Any time you want me to rout the part there . . , just let me know." **1943** *Ibid* **ceVA,** Mr. McCauley plowed part of my garden today with what he called a "routing plow," that is, one with two small plow points which do not go as deeply into the ground as the normal plow does. A routing plow can be used to plow up potatoes.

rout n See **route A2**

route n

A Forms. Note: In interpreting the maps, it is important to note that the sense in which *route* was chiefly elicited is itself strongly regional; see **B1** below.

1 |rut| **chiefly NEast, C Atl** See Map

1892 [see **A2** below]. **c1955** Reed–Person *Ling. Atlas Pacific NW,* 11 [of 52] infs, Paper route /uw/. **1965–70** *DARE* (Qu. N18) 228 Infs, **chiefly NEast, C Atl,** [rut]; (Qu. N28) Inf **MO39,** [ruˇu:t]; (Qu. U6) Inf **VT3,** [rut]; (Qu. KK52) Inf **MO14,** [ruˇut]. **1966–69** *DARE* Tape **AK9,** All mail, the same [rut], he could haul it; **CA142,** That was the original Pony Express [rut]; **FL20,** This is the main [rut]. **1967–68** *DARE* FW Addit **sePA,** Well-traveled route [rut]; **ceMI,** *Route*—[rut] highway, [rɑut] paper. **1975** Gould *ME Lingo* 235, *Route*—Maine people usually say *Route* One or devious *route* as in "root." . . But in speaking of the R.F.D. *route,* or a paper *route,* Mainers often say "rout."

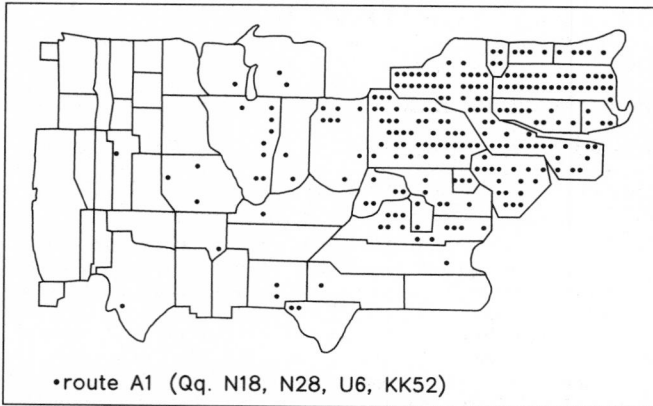

•route A1 (Qq. N18, N28, U6, KK52)

2 |raut, ræut|; pronc-spp *rout, rowt.* [*OED2* route "Down to *c* 1800 the usual spelling was *rout.* The pronunciation (raut), which appears in early 19th cent. rimes, is still retained in military use, and by many speakers in the U.S. and Canada."] **scattered, but chiefly IL, OH, wPA, WV, MD** See Map

1814 (1922) Tatum *Jrl.* 7.79 **NC,** The Commanding General immediately ordered Captain Denkin to proceed with the artillery, by the rout we had entered the Town. **1828** Webster *Amer. Dict.,* Rout. . . The course or way which is traveled or passed. **1892** *DN* 1.241, All but universally [raut] in Kansas City. [*DN* Ed: [raut] is yielding to [rut] in Michigan. . . Both are used in New England.] **1899** (1912) Green *VA Folk-Speech* 358, Rout. . . A way, road; path; a line of travel, passage, or progression; the course passed or to be passed over in reaching a destination. **1913** Wharton *Custom of Country* 332 **NY,** "The Twentieth Century's generally considered the best route to Dakota," explained Mr. Spragg, who pronounced the word *rowt.* **1933** *AmSp* 8.2.44 **neNY,** *Route* is sometimes [ræut]. **1941** *AmSp* 16.7 **eTX** [Black], [au]—In Negro speech this diphthong is not often flattened to [æu] as in 'hill type' speech, but retains its standard form, with lengthening of the first element. . . *route.* **1942** Hall *Smoky Mt. Speech* 45, The following words almost always have [æu] rather than [au]: . . *route.* **c1955** Reed–Person *Ling. Atlas Pacific NW,* 34 [of 52] infs, Paper route /aw/, news route /aw/. **1965–70** *DARE* (Qu. N18) 143 Infs, **scattered, but chiefly IL, OH, wPA, WV, MD,** [rut, raut]; (Qu. N28) Inf **AR51,** [raut]; (Qu. N37) Inf **IL97,** [raut]; (Qu. X31) Infs **NY10, OR3,** [raut]; (Qu. HH1) Inf **IN61,** [raut]; (Qu. II29a) Inf **CA189,** [raut]. **1966–70** *DARE* Tape **AZ14,** That meant building one on the Southern [raut]; **AR52,** My mother's people were the ones who came the other [raut] into Arkansas; **CA69,** The access road . . will in part go through National Forest land, one portion of the [raut]; **CA113,** It was on the [raut] of the Butterfield

stages; **CA159,** They're over . . along the [raut] of the Highway 99; **CA181,** I run a paper [raut] . . for about a year; **MI44,** They are now laying out trails and [rauts] for them; **SD1,** The government . . established Highway 81 on practically the same [raut]. **1967–68** [see **A1** above]. **1975** [see **A1** above]. **1981** Pederson *LAGS Basic Materials,* [*Route* was elicited from 75 infs in a variety of contexts. All but one apparently pronounced it with the vowel of *out*—most often represented as [ao], [æo], or [au]. 1 inf, **ceTX,** used [ʊʉ].]

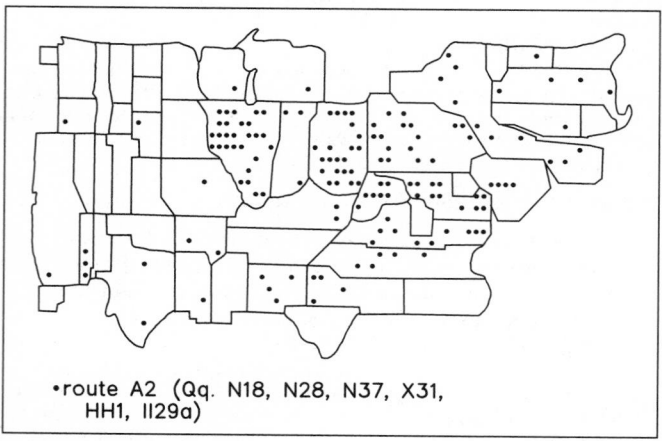

•route A2 (Qq. N18, N28, N37, X31, HH1, II29a)

B Senses.

1 Used in referring to a specific numbered or lettered main road. **chiefly NEast, WV, OH, IL, C Atl** See Map and Map Section Cf **highway**

1924 *NY Times* (NY) 21 Dec sec 8 9/7, Route 2 is the high-way from Scranton Pa. . . to Montreal. **1938** *Travel* June 37/1 (*OED2*), From New York there are three delightful motor routes . . all picking up Route 6. **1965–70** *DARE* (Qu. N18, . . *Roads that have numbers or letters. For example, if someone asked directions* . . *"Take _____"*) 370 Infs, **chiefly NEast, WV, OH, IL, C Atl,** Route (*or* route *or* route + number *or* route + number + compass direction). **1970** *Washington Post & Times Herald* (DC) 30 Sept sec B 4/1, Fredricksburg location is just off route 95.

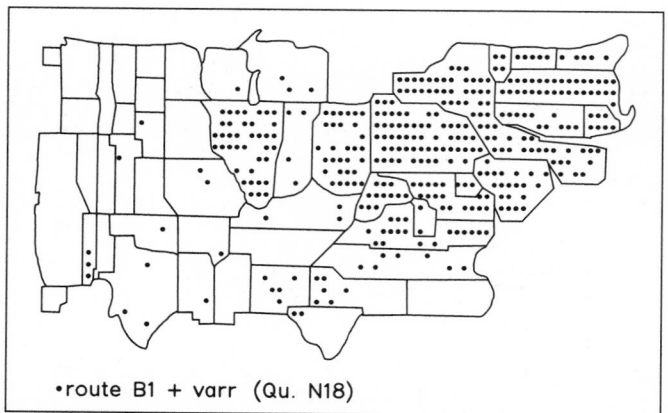

•route B1 + varr (Qu. N18)

2 In logging: see quots.

1938 (1939) Holbrook *Holy Mackinaw* 263, *Route.* Total length of time at any given camp; viz., a *long route* means a long stretch of employment on one job. **1941** *AmSp* 16.233 **MT** [Lumberjack lingo], *Long route.* An employee *on the long route* is one who works a long time for one outfit to garner a *grub stake.* He is the opposite of a *boomer. Ibid* 232, *Boomer.* [An itinerant worker who works but a few days.]

routine n Usu |ˌruˈtin|; also |ˈrauˌtin, ˌrauˈtin, ˈroˌtin| Pronc-sp *rotine*

A Forms.

1847 Hurd *Grammatical Corrector* 88, *Routine* ["incorrect" pronc = [ˈrautin]; "correct" pronc = [ruˈtin]]. **1891** *DN* 1.143 **cNY,** [ˈrotin] < [Fr] *routine.* **1941** [see **B** below]. **1981** Pederson *LAGS Basic Materials,* 1 inf, **seLA,** [ˌraˆʊ<ˈtiˑn].

B Sense.

A sequence of things; hence phr *in routine* in a row, in sequence.

1927 *DN* 5.476 **Ozarks,** *Rotine.* . . A series of connected items. "They's a hull rotine o' thet 'ar ballet, but I caint sing hit no more." This means merely that the song has many verses, but that the speaker has forgotten them. 1941 in 1944 *ADD* **eWV,** ['ro'tin]. 'In rotine' = in rotation, in order. 1968 *DARE* (Qu. KK33, . . *'In succession':* "He had a cold, then the measles, then chicken pox _____.") Inf **NJ8,** In routine.

routing plow See **rout** v 4

rout out See **rout** v 1, 2, 3

rout up See **rout** v 1

rover n Also *old rover* Cf **ral**

1995 *Brophy Coll.* 64 **swMO** (as of c1960), *Rover.* [S]yphilis, "the old rover" (wanderer), so called from its contagious nature. "[O]ld Rover bit him."

rover, red rover See **red rover**

roving Charley n
=**ground ivy 1.**

1940 Clute *Amer. Plant Names* 227, *Nepeta hederacea.* Roving Charley.

row n

1 in phrr *a hard* (or *tough*) *row* (*to hoe*) and varr: A difficult task or situation to contend with.

1835 Crockett *Account* 69, I never opposed Andrew Jackson for the sake of popularity, I knew it was a hard row to hoe; but I stood up to the rack, considering it a duty I owed to the country that governed me. 1848 Lowell *Biglow* 145 **'Upcountry' MA,** Row, a long row to hoe, *a difficult task.* 1905 *DN* 3.11 **cCT,** *Hard row to hoe.* . . A difficult matter to accomplish. 1907 *DN* 3.213 **nwAR,** *Hard row to hoe.* . . A difficult matter to accomplish. *Ibid* 216 **nwAR,** *Row to hoe.* . . Task to perform. 1910 *DN* 3.443 **wNY,** *Hard row to hoe.* . . A difficult task to perform; serious trouble or misfortune to bear. "That poor fellow has a hard row to hoe." 1927 *AmSp* 2.356 **cwWV,** She has had a hard row to hoe since her husband died. 1927 *AmSp* 3.140 **eME,** *Hard row to hoe.* 1946 *PADS* 6.41 **eNC** (as of 1900–10), *To have a bad row to hoe.* (To have many kinds of difficulties to contend with.) . . Occasional. 1948 *Sat. Eve. Post* 14 Aug 106, I'd like to be a surgeon, but it's a long row to hoe. 1965–70 *DARE* (Qu. CC12a, . . *Bad luck* . . *"Poor Joe. He's really been having _____."*) Inf **TX3,** Hard row to hoe; **IL102,** Rough row to hoe; **OR13,** Tough row; (Qu. CC12b, . . *If a person has a lot of bad luck* . . *"He's been _____."*) Inf **TX80,** Having a tough row to hoe; **WI30,** He's really had a hard row; **MI110,** Hoeing a tough row; (Qu. KK8, . . *Succeeding, especially in spite of difficulty:* "He had a hard time, but at last he _____.") Inf **NY219,** Had a hard row to hoe; (Qu. KK41, *Something that is very difficult to do:* "I managed to get through with it, but it was _____.") Infs **MI15,** 102, **MS14, TX5,** 81, Tough (or hard) row to hoe. 1986 Pederson *LAGS Concordance,* 1 inf, **ceFL,** They got a hard row to hoe—hard time ahead.

2 in phrr *hoe one's* (*own*) *row:* To work unassisted; to tend to one's business.

1841 *Knickerbocker* 17.362, Our American pretender must, to adopt an agricultural phrase, 'hoe his own row,' . . without the aid of protectors or dependents. 1872 Schele de Vere *Americanisms* 608, To *hoe one's own row* is an admonition equal to minding one's business. 1895 *Century Illustr. Mag.* 50.378, I would n't marry a man that could n't work in open daylight for a livin'. I'd ruther hoe my own row. 1905 *DN* 3.11 **cCT,** *Hoe one's row.* . . To do one's own work. 1907 *DN* 3.213 **nwAR,** *Hoe one's row.* . . To do one's own work. 1927 *AmSp* 2.357 **cwWV,** *Hoe your own row* . . take care of yourself. "I have hoed my own roe [sic] since I was twelve years old." 1930 Stoney–Shelby *Black Genesis* 62 **seSC,** If you wants to git 'long wid me, you mind you' manners, an' hoe you' row, an' don't bodder me wid all o' dat. 1967 *DARE* (Qu. II22, *Expressions to tell somebody to keep to himself and mind his own business*) Inf **IL5,** Hoe your own row. 1984 Wilder *You All Spoken Here* 21 **Sth,** *Chew your own tobacco:* Hoe your own row.

3 in phrr *a hard row of stumps* (or *to stump*) and varr: A troublesome or difficult situation. **Sth, S Midl**

1863 in 1943 Wiley *Life Johnny Reb* 346 **LA,** If the Confederacy has no better soldiers than those we are in A bad roe for stumps. 1890 *DN* 1.66 **KY,** *Stumps.* "He is in a bad row of stumps," means to be in trying places. Comes from the trouble one has in plowing in stumpy land.

1893 Shands *MS Speech* 60, *Stumps.* . . The phrase *in a bad row of* [or *for*] *stumps,* meaning in an unfortunate plight, is used by all classes. It is probably derived from ploughing in *new ground,* where stumps are sometimes very troublesome. 1897 *KS Univ. Qrly.* (ser B) 6.58 **KS,** *Stumps,* in a hard row of: an unfortunate condition; as, We're in a hard row of stumps. 1905 *DN* 3.82 **nwAR,** *Hard row of stumps.* . . Trouble. 'He's in a hard row of stumps.' 1908 *DN* 3.319 **eAL, wGA,** *Hard row of stumps.* . . Trouble, a difficulty. 1912 *DN* 3.579 **wIN,** He's been in a hard row of stumps since both of his barns burned. 1915 *DN* 4.184 **swVA,** *Hard row of stumps, in a.* . . In a bad way. 1927 *AmSp* 2.356 **cwWV,** *Hard row of stumps* . . a job which presents many difficulties. "This contract has certainly been a hard row of stumps." 1942 McAtee *Dial. Grant Co.* IN 53 (as of 1890s), *Row of stumps,* . . in a bad. 1946 *PADS* 6.41 **eNC** (as of 1900–10), *To be in a bad row of stumps.* (To be in difficulties—bad health, debts, etc.) . . Occasional. 1960 Criswell *Resp. to PADS 20* **Ozarks,** *Hard row of stumps, a.* . . A very difficult project or situation. Very frequent years ago and still used now and then. "That fellow is in a hard row of stumps. I don't think he'll be able to pay it off." 1969 *DARE* FW Addit **KY**20, Someone who's had tough luck or a hard life with many problems has had a hard row to stump. 1970 *DARE* (Qu. CC12a, . . *Bad luck* . . "Poor Joe. He's really been having _____.") Inf **KY84,** Hard row to stump. 1984 Wilder *You All Spoken Here* 150 **Sth,** *In a bad row of stumps:* In trouble; in an unpleasant situation.

4 in phrr *not to amount to* (or *not to be worth*) *a row of pins* (or *beans*): To be of little or no value. **chiefly Nth, Atlantic, Gulf States** See Map

1863 in 1903 Norton *Army Letters* 169 **PA,** He worries himself homesick and isn't worth a row of pins. 1903 *NY Post* (NY) 18 Sept 12/4, The work doing from Ann Street to Bowling Green does not amount to a row of pins. 1903 *NY Times* (NY) 17 Sept 14/4 **NY,** The letter of Buchanan suspending us doesn't amount to a row of beans. 1942 McAtee *Dial. Grant Co.* IN 53 (as of 1890s), *Row of beans* . . a very little, in the expression, "don't amount to a _____". (Md., Va.) 1951 Johnson *Resp. to PADS 20* **DE,** An idle, worthless person: "He doesn't amount to a row of pins." 1956 McAtee *Some Dialect NC* 37, *Row of pins* . . very little, in the expression: "don't amount to a row of pins." 1965–70 *DARE* (Qu. HH20b, *Of an idle, worthless person* . . "He doesn't amount to _____.") 168 Infs, **chiefly Nth, Atlantic, Gulf States,** Row of pins; 35 Infs, **scattered,** Row of beans; **AZ**3, **NY**84, Row; **CT**23, **IN**19, **NY**34, 232, **PA**118, Row of shucks (*or* blue beans, peanuts, peas); (Qu. HH20c, *Of an idle, worthless person* . . "He isn't worth _____.") Infs **MA**53, **NC**87, **VT**16, Row of beans; **MD**9, **NJ**15, **PA**122, Row of pins; (Qu. KK17, . . *'Worthless':* "It isn't worth _____."; total Infs questioned, 75) Inf **FL**17, Row of pins.

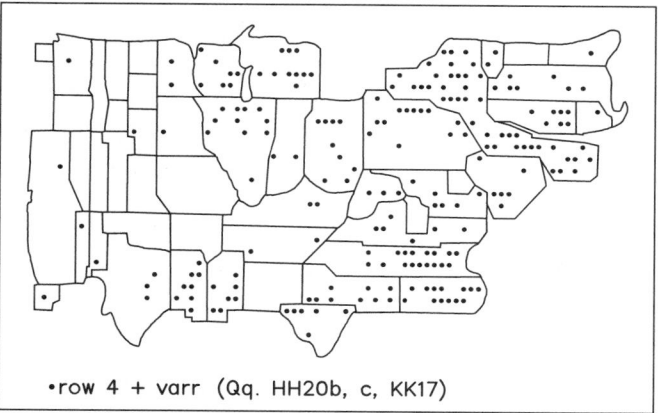

•row 4 + varr (Qq. HH20b, c, KK17)

5 in phr *end of one's row:* See **end of one's row.**

rowan n[1] Also *rowan bush,* ~ *tree* [*OED2* rowan-tree 1548 →, rowan 1804 →; "north. and Sc."]
=**mountain ash 1.**

[1848 Gray *Manual of Botany* 130, American Mountain-Ash. . . Very much like the European Rowan-tree.] 1880 *Scribner's Mth.* 20.141 **SC,** The rowan bushes, scarlet with berries. 1908 Rogers *Tree Book* 294, The Rowan Tree or European mountain ash (*Sorbus Aucuparia* . .), is the one people usually plant on their lawns in this country. 1930 Shoemaker *1300 Words* 49 **cPA Mts** (as of c1900), *Rowan*—The mountain ash; the leaves and berries are a charm against the hechs, the berries make excellent jelly when served with game. **1991** Still *Wolfpen Note-books* 163 **sAppalachians,** *Rowan tree:* mountain ash (*Sorbus americana*).

rowan n² See **rowen**

rowan bush See **rowan** n¹

rowance See **rounce**

rowan tree See **rowan** n¹

rowboat n Cf **canal boat, flatboat** n 3, **gunboat** 1

An especially large foot.

1950 *WELS* (*Humorous or uncomplimentary names for big feet*) 1 Inf, **nwWI,** Rowboats. **1968** *DARE* (Qu. X38, *Joking names for unusually big or clumsy feet*) Infs **MI**116, **MO**10, **NY**68, Rowboats.

rowdy n Cf **ritchie**

An overall jacket.

1942 *AmSp* 17.129 **nwPA,** The janitor of the college building, having misplaced his keys, announced later that he had discovered them in the pocket of his *rowdy.* . . I found that he referred to the jacket of his over-alls. . . An English born janitor . . said in the old country a *rowdy* was something like a mackinaw. . . The manager of the Penney Store . . says that the word is commonly used for a jumper or jacket for an overall suit and that he has never heard the term outside of this locality. **1998** *DARE* File **nOH, ePA,** The minute you said "rowdy," a picture of a blue denim jacket came into my mind. I think it was a brand name.

rowen n Usu |ˈrɑu(w)ən, ˈrɑu-, -ɪn|; for varr see quots Also *rouen, rowan, rowen crop* **chiefly NEng** See Map Cf **aftermath, second cutting**

A second growth or crop of hay in one season; also fig.

1743 in **1911** Dow *Holyoke Diaries* 35 **MA,** Began to mow Rowens. **1831** *Genesee Farmer* 1.247 **NEng,** There are but few objects connected with the management of a farm of more importance than that of obtaining good crops of rouen, after math, or second crops of grass. **1844** (**1969**) Emerson *Essays 2d Ser.* 261 **MA,** The frugal farmer takes care that his cattle shall eat down the rowan. **1888** VT State Bd. Ag. *Rept. for 1887–88* 36, Feed hay . . till rowen is large enough, then rowen till fodder corn comes to maturity. **1903** *DN* 2.300 **Cape Cod MA** (as of a1857), *Rowen* [ˈrɑuɛn]. . . A second crop of clover. **1915** (**1916**) Johnson *Highways New Engl.* 243, The man has married a second time and got some young children—kind of a rowen crop. **1939** *LANE* Map 125 (*Second crop*), [*Rowen* is found **throughout NEng, but less freq ME;** it occurs most often in proncs of the types [ˈrɑu(w)ɪn, ˈrɑowɪn, ˈræwɪn, ˈrɑwən], but there are also exx of the types [ˈrɑwɪn, ˈrɑuɪn] as well as the following: 7 infs, 6 **NH,** Proncs of the types [ˈrɑwɪt, ˈrɛwɪt, ˈtʌwɪt]; 8 infs, 7 **ME,** Proncs of the types [ˈrɑwɪl, ˈræwɪl, ˈrɛwɪl]; 1 inf, seNH, [ˈrɛᵛʊɪdʒ].] **1949** Kurath *Word Geog.* 16, The New England settlement area has a variety of terms for the second crop of hay that do not occur elsewhere in the Eastern States. Of these expressions *rowen* . . and *rowen crop* . . are common in all of New England except Maine, and in New York State; and relics of it are found in the Western Reserve of Ohio. *Ibid* 67, *Rowen* (riming with *plowin'*). **1959** *VT Hist.* 27.154, *Rowen* [ˈrɑuʃn]. . . The season's second crop of hay. **1965–70** *DARE* (Qu. L10, *After hay has been cut, then it grows back and you cut it again*) 21 Infs, **chiefly NEng,** Rowen [ˈrɑuwən, ˈrɑu(w)ən, -ɪn, -ɪn, -ŋ]; 11 Infs, **NEng,** Rowen [ˈrɑuwɛn, ˈrɑuɛn]; **ME**5, Some call it [ˈruwɪn];

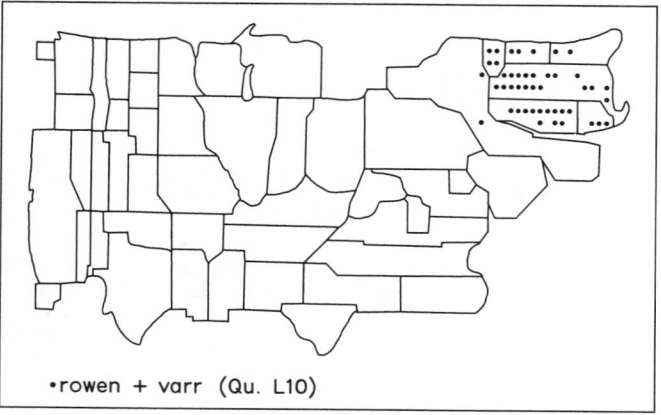

•rowen + varr (Qu. L10)

MA6, [ˈrɑuwən]—nice and tender, cattle can chew it better; **MA**25, [ˈrɑuwən]—old-fashioned [FW: overheard in local restaurant]; **MA**31, [ˈrɑuwən]—old-fashioned; **MA**55, [ˈrɑuwən]—conversation; **MA**72, [rɑuɪn, rowɪn]—I'm gonna make a guess at that; **NH**3, [ˈrowɛn, ˈrɑuwɛn]; **NY**68, [ˈruwɛn, ˈrɑuwɛn]—old-fashioned; [FW: Inf uncertain of pronunciation]; **RI**2, [ˈrɑuɪn]—only grass, not for alfalfa; **RI**15, [ˈræwɪn]; **RI**16, [ˈræŋ]; **VT**2, [ˈræwɛn]; **VT**12, [ˈrɛɑuən]. [41 of 45 total Infs old, 40 male] **1967** *DARE* Tape **VT**1A, [FW:] What do you call the second crop, or the last crop of hay? [Inf:] The rowen [ˈrɑuwɪn]—yes, after it's been cut, you mean, and then it comes up. **1967** Faries *Word Geog. MO* 97, Second crop. . . *Second cutting* and *rowen crop* are . . infrequently used. **1971** Wood *Vocab. Change* 298 **Sth,** 3 [of approx 1000 infs] Rowen.

row, get one's ducks in a See **duck** n 9

row's end n Cf **end of one's row**

Fig: the limits of one's endurance; the end of one's life.

1965–70 *DARE* (Qu. GG22a, *When you have come to the end of your patience* . . *"Well that's the _____."*) Inf **GA**28, My row's end; **MS**63, Row's end; (Qu. X48b, . . *If a person is not so young any more* . . *"He's _____."*) Inf **KY**85, About to the row's end; **MS**50, At his row's end.

rowst See **roust**

rowt See **route** A2

Roxbury waxwork n [*Roxbury* Massachusetts + *waxwork* from the waxy aril of the fruit]

A **bittersweet** (here: *Celastrus scandens*).

1870 (**1871**) *Amer. Naturalist* 4.215, Bittersweet (*Celastrus scandens*), also called Roxbury Waxwork, . . is a hardy climber. **1892** *Jrl. Amer. Folkl.* 5.94 **eMA,** *Celastrus scandens,* Roxbury wax-work. **1960** Vines *Trees SW* 660, American Bitter-sweet. . . Known also by the vernacular names of . . Roxbury-waxwork [etc].

royal eagle n [*OED2* 1575 → (as *eagle royall*)]

=**golden eagle.**

1832 Nuttall *Manual Ornith.* 1.62, Royal or Golden Eagle. . . About 30 miles inland from the Mandan Fort on the Missouri, I once had occasion to observe the eyry of this noble bird. **1955** Forbush–May *Birds* 115, American Golden Eagle. . . *Other names:* Mountain Eagle; Ring-tailed Eagle; Royal Eagle.

royal fern n Also *royal flowering fern*

A **flowering fern** (here: *Osmunda regalis*). Also called **bog onion** 1, **buckhorn brake** 1, **hartshorn bush, hog onion** 2, **locust fern**

1878 Williamson *Ferns KY* 133, *Osmunda regalis* . . Royal Flowering Fern. **1889** *Century Dict.* 4167, Six species are known, of which three are found in North America, *O. regalis* being the royal fern or osmund royal, also called *bog-onion, buckhorn-brake, ditch-fern,* and *king-fern.* **1911** Waters *Ferns* 298, In open woods or wet thickets, or even in moist hillside pastures, the reddish green of the uncoiling fronds of the royal fern gives a pleasing touch of color early in the spring. **1968** McPhee *Pine Barrens* 131 **cNJ,** Wherry pointed out . . bold and lacy royal ferns.

royal palm n

A tall and graceful palm (*Roystonea elata*) native to Florida.

1861 Smithsonian Inst. *Annual Rept. for 1860* 440 **FL,** The Palm mentioned by Nuttall . . is found, as I was informed by several persons, in large groves, between Capes Sable and Romano, and one tree three miles north of Fort Dallas. It was called "Royal Palm," and said to grow 120 feet high. **1908** Rogers *Tree Book* 119, The Royal Palm . . is one of the noblest of tropical trees, bearing its abundant crown of foliage, each leaf 10 to 12 feet long, and bending gradually outward and down-ward, with a grace peculiarly its own. . . The trees grow from Bay Biscayne around the southern points of Florida and on Long's Key, the vanguard of a host that inhabits central America and the West Indies. **1929** Neal *Honolulu Gardens* 45, Like a graceful column carved in long symmetrical curves, the royal palm raises its smooth, whitened, faintly ringed shaft, which terminates in a bunch of immense dark-green plumes. **1960** McGeachy *Hdbk. FL Palms* 30, Royal Palms are among the handsomest of all Palms. Their smooth, cylindrical trunks look more like gray concrete pillars than living structures. **1966** *DARE* (Qu. T16, . . *Kinds of trees* . . *'special'*) Infs **FL**39, **SC**4, Royal palm. **1966** *DARE* Tape **FL**5, Of course, the royal palm is a very tall and stately—

oh, there must be hundreds of different kinds of palms. **1986** Pederson *LAGS Concordance,* 2 infs, **FL,** 1 inf, **TX,** Royal palm.

royal poinciana n

A wide-spreading, flat-topped tropical tree *(Delonix regia)* with showy, orange-red flowers. Also called **flamboyant-tree, flame tree, poinciana**

1908 Britton *N. Amer. Trees* 546, Flame Tree. . . This deciduous tree, also called Flamboyant and Royal poinciana, is. . . spontaneous in southern peninsular Florida and on the Keys. **1929** Neal *Honolulu Gardens* 147, Royal poinciana, flame tree, flamboyant, peacock flower. . . One of the best-loved trees in Honolulu is the poinciana. **1953** Greene–Blomquist *Flowers South* 80, Native of Madagascar, royal poinciana has become naturalized in the Caribbean area where its aggressive roots constantly break up sidewalks. In June, Miami, Palm Beach, and Ft. Myers are wonderlands of this royal flame flower. **1966–67** *DARE* (Qu. T15, . . *Kinds of swamp trees)* Inf **FL4,** Royal poinciana; (Qu. T16, . . *Kinds of trees . . 'special')* Infs **FL23, HI2,** Royal poinciana.

royal tern n [See quot 1969]

A large, chiefly Atlantic **tern** *(Sterna maxima).* Also called **gannet striker, redbill 1, Spanish gull**

1858 Baird *Birds* 859, *Sterna Regia* . . The Royal Tern. . . Atlantic coast of the southern and middle States and California. **1916** *Times-Picayune* (New Orleans LA) 26 Mar mag sec 2/5, Royal Tern. . . Although similar to the Caspian tern in general appearance, the royal is far more common along the coasts. **1969** Longstreet *Birds FL* 69, The royal tern, one of the commonest members of the family, lives along Florida's coast, and is the commonest tern that stays in the state during winter. . . In summer the bird's head is crowned with a black crest that gives the species its regal name. **1970** *DARE* (Qu. Q10, . . *Water birds and marsh birds)* Inf **VA52,** Royal tern.

royal walnut moth n

Std: a large saturniid moth *(Citheronia regalis)* whose larvae feed on the leaves of walnut, hickory, and persimmon trees, among others. For other names of the larva of this moth see **hickory horned devil, 'simmon bull**

royo See arroyo

rozom, rozzum See rosin A2a

rub v chiefly Sth, S Midl Cf dip v 1, snuff rubber, ~ stick

To apply (snuff) to the gums or inside of the lips; to take snuff in this way; hence n *rubber* one who takes snuff in this manner; n *rub(ber)* an amount of snuff taken at one time in this way.

1825 (1832) Pickering *Inquiries* 107, One [practice is] in common use in the Eastern part of Maryland, of girls taking a "rubber" of snuff—that is, taking as much snuff as will lie on the end of the forefinger out of a box, and rubbing it round the inside of the mouth. **1849** *Knickerbocker* 34.117 **GA,** The 'gude woman' sat in the corner 'rubbing snuff,' or 'dipping.' **1853** *Putnam's Mag.* 1.142 **VA,** This neat, orderly, sin-exterminating woman, rubbed snuff! She kept a snuff-box in her right pocket, filled with the strongest and most pungent Scotch snuff; and she went about all day, brandishing a dangerous-looking hickory stick, with a mop end, which she was constantly dipping into the huge black horn snuff-box. **1942** Warnick *Garrett Co. MD* 13 **nwMD** (as of 1900–18), *Rub snuff* . . take snuff (probably referring to the manner in which used). [**1944** *PADS* 2.65 **S Midl,** *Dip.* . . To rub snuff on the gums.] **1951** Johnson *Resp. to PADS* 20 **DE** *(A person who uses snuff)* A rubber of snuff. . . One hears: "She rubs snuff." **1965–70** *DARE* (Qu. DD3b, *How . . people take snuff)* [62 Infs, **chiefly Sth, S Midl,** Rub it on the gums with a snuff stick [and var phrr: see *DS*];] **PA175,** Rub; **DE7, MD15, MA55,** Rub (it *or* snuff); (Qu. DD3a, . . *A person who uses snuff)* Infs **DE1, 3, MD15, 22, 40, 42, NE3, PA93, 134, WV2,** (Snuff) rubber; **DE1, GA68, MD18, 34, PA209,** Rubs snuff; **MD43,** Rubs. **1984** Wilder *You All Spoken Here* 195 **Sth,** *A little rub:* A dip of snuff.

rubbage n Also sp rubbi(d)ge [Varr of rubbish, perh infl by garbage; OED2 (at rubbish sb. 1.a) 1551–52 →, EDD] Cf skirmish A

1815 Humphreys *Yankee in England* 108, Rubbige, rubbish. **1899** Chesnutt *Conjure Woman* 98 **csNC** [Black], It wuz a good riddance er bad rubbage. **1899** (1912) Green *VA Folk-Speech* 359, Rubbage. . . Rubbish. **1905** *DN* 3.17 **CT,** Rubbage. **1907** *DN* 3.216 **nwAR,** Rub-

bage. **1922** Gonzales *Black Border* 323 **sSC, GA** coasts [Gullah glossary], Rubbidge. **1923** *DN* 5.219 **swMO,** Rubbage. **c1938** in 1970 Hyatt *Hoodoo* 2.1097 **cSC,** Go somewhere where somebody cleanin' a flo'. . . Git a roll of dat rubbage off any kinda flo', whether it's pine or oak or whatevah it is. **1941** *LANE* Map 346 *(Rubbish)* 18 infs, **NEng,** Rubbidge. **1946** McCullers *Member* 30 **AL,** And a good riddance to a big old bad rubbage. **c1960** *Wilson Coll.* **csKY,** Rubbish /'rʌbɪdʒ/. **1967** *DARE* (Qu. F25, *The container for kitchen parings and scraps—out of doors)* Inf **NY9,** Rubbage can. **1982** Barrick *Coll.* **csPA,** Rubbage—rubbish. **1986** Pederson *LAGS Concordance,* 1 inf, **seAL,** Rubbage = rubbish.

rubber n

1 A rubber band.

1965–70 *DARE* (Qu. F49, . . *Rubber band;* not asked in early QRs) 22 Infs, **scattered,** Rubber. **1973** Allen *LAUM* 1.397 **Upper MW** (as of c1950), *Rubber band.* . . Rubber [4 infs, **MN,** 1 inf, **SD,** 3 infs, **ND**]. **1986** Pederson *LAGS Concordance (Rubber band)* 7 infs, **Gulf Region,** (A) rubber; 1 inf, **cAR,** A plain rubber (i.e., without band); 1 inf, **cwFL,** Put a rubber (a)round it.

2 See **rub** v.

rubber v Also with in; also rubberneck; hence vbl nouns rubbering, rubbernecking [By ext from rubber(neck) to gape, gawk with great curiosity] esp wInland Nth

To eavesdrop on a telephone party line; to listen to (a telephone conversation); hence n *rubbering switch* a device to conceal one's eavesdropping.

1920 Lewis *Main Street* 189 **MN,** These goats are always rubbering in on party-wires. **1950** *WELS Suppl.* **csWI,** Rubber. . . Short form of rubber-neck; specifically, to listen in on a party line. "He told them if they'd stop rubbering all the time, their batteries wouldn't wear out so quick." **1950** Reeves *Man from SD* 160 **SD,** The telephone was screwed firmly to the wall at a Spartan height, and at the base of the oaken box there was a jutting shelf on which short people could chin themselves to reach the mouthpiece and talk. On the side of the box was the "rubbering switch," a device which kept our voices off the line while we listened to things which were none of our affair. **1970** *DARE* File **csWI,** Lord knows we haven't anything to conspire about. . . They are surely wasting their time if they are—as Frank used to say about the people who listened in on the party line—rubbernecking. **1980** *DARE* File **nCA** (as of early 20th cent), Though all bells rang on all phones, your private ring told everyone the call was for *you*—and listening in on a private conversation—called "rubbernecking"—was strictly forbidden. **1984** Doig *English Creek* 284 **nMT,** "Rubber that, will you, Jick," called my mother from whatever chore she was on elsewhere in the house. . . I went to the wall phone and put the receiver to my ear. Rubbering, which is to say listening in, was our way of keeping track of matters without perpetually traipsing back and forth between the house and the ranger station.

rubberback turtle n [Because the shell is covered with soft, leathery skin instead of horny scutes]

Prob =**leatherback 1.**

1970 *DARE* (Qu. P24, . . *Kinds of turtles)* Inf **VA47,** Rubber-back turtle—five hundred pounds.

rubber bass n

See quot.

1968 *DARE* (Qu. P1, . . *Kinds of freshwater fish . . caught around here . . good to eat)* Inf **MN38,** Bullheads or rubber bass—if you're from Iowa, you'll eat [them].

rubber binder n Also binder scattered, but esp MN

A rubber band.

1950 *WELS Suppl.* **cwWI, Minneapolis MN,** Binder—meaning rubber-band. . . "The boys are using binders to shoot paper wads." **1958** *Ibid* **cwWI** (as of 1940s), "Rubber-binder" was at least as familiar to us as "rubber-band." **1967–70** *DARE* (Qu. F49, . . *Rubber band;* not asked in early QRs) Infs **IN66, MS85, TX17, 36,** Rubber binder; **IN28,** Rubber band; rubber binder [FW sugg]; **MN34,** Rubber band; binder—hear in Minneapolis—most common term there; rubber binder; **WV3,** Rubber band, rubber binder—old-fashioned. **1978** *AP Letters* **swMN,** My wife, a native Minnesotan (Montevideo), still says "rubber binder" for rubber band. . . Certain areas of Minnesota and the Dakotas are the only regions where "rubber binder" is used. **1993** *DARE* File **MN,** I lost my rubber binder. **1997** Keillor *Wobegon Boy* 166 **MN,** Dad died on the next-to-top basement step on his way upstairs from having taken to the basement a box of rubber binders that Mother had told him to get rid of.

rubber boa n Also *rubber snake* [From its ability to roll itself into a compact ball or from its "rubbery" appearance] **West, esp CA**

A nonpoisonous blunt-tailed snake *(Charina bottae)* found in the moister regions of western North America. Also called **silver boa, two-headed snake, worm snake**

1897 CA Acad. Sci. *Occas. Papers* 5.156, The Rubber Snake . . is not rare in the moister portions of California. **1931** *Copeia* 7 **CA**, The rattlers did not stir for an hour after the rubber snakes retired. **1952** Ditmars *N. Amer. Snakes* 173, Rubber Boa . . . If much disturbed, it may roll the body into compact loops like a ball, hiding the head in the center of its folds. **1957** Barnes *Nat. Hist. Wasatch Summer* 71 **UT**, It is hardly believable that we have in the mountains hereabout a real boa constrictor, yet there it is in a hat box on the front porch, the second for identification in a single year. It is a rubber boa, silver snake, two-headed snake or worm snake *(Charina bottae utahensis),* as it is variously called, taken from the Bonneville shore line only a few hundred rods away. **1969–70** *DARE* (Qu. P25, . . *Kinds of snakes)* Inf **CA**114, Rubber boa; **CA**75, Rubber snake. **1974** Shaw–Campbell *Snakes West* 52, The name "rubber boa" is quite fitting. Heavy-bodied and blunt at both ends, the snake resembles a tubular section of rubber.

rubber brush n [See quot 1967]
A **rabbit brush 1b.**

1941 Jaeger *Wildflowers* 266, Rubberbrushes are all handsome plants in autumn when covered with yellow bloom, especially when, as often happens, they occur in large, dense aggregations. [*Ibid,* The Paiute Indians chewed the wood and bark of this plant [=*Chrysothamnus teretifolius*] to get a crude chewing gum containing rubber.] **1967** Dodge *Roadside Wildflowers* 76, The name "chamiso" . . is applied to rabbit-brush in many parts of the pinyon-juniper belt. . Because their sap contains latex, several species are called rubberbrush.

rubber bush See **rubber plant 2**

rubber elastic See **elastic (band)**

rubber forty n Cf **long forty, round ~** *hist*

1958 McCulloch *Woods Words* 153 **Pacific NW**, Rubber 40—A timber grab in the early days when timber was plentiful and accurate surveys were scarce. A crooked buyer would purchase 40 acres of land, and then stretch it, logging as far as he could in all directions until caught, or until he ran out of timber.

rubber ice n Also *India-rubber ice* **chiefly Nth, wN Midl**
See Map Cf **bender 1, bendy leather, cracky benders, green ice, gummy** adj, **hickory bender, kittly-bender, leathery ice, limber ice, pompey** adj, **tiddly-bender**
Thin, flexible ice on water.

1896 *DN* 1.423 **NY, seMI**, *Rubber ice:* thin ice that bends when skated upon. **1905** *DN* 3.93 **nwAR**, *Rubber ice.* . . Ice that bends but does not break under a person's weight. Common. **1916** *Ladies' Home Jrl.* Apr 101, "Soft as cheese!" Doctor Rolfe concluded. "Rubber ice and air holes!" **1940** Stong *Hawkeyes* 253 **IA**, I broke through the ice three times in one day skating the edges and bouncing on "rubber-ice." **1942**

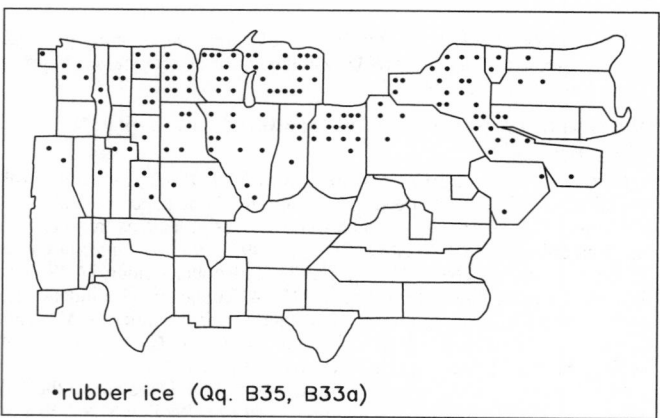

•rubber ice (Qq. B35, B33a)

McAtee *Dial. Grant Co. IN* 53 (as of 1890s), *Rubber-ice* . . ice that bends but does not break under skaters. **1951** *PADS* 15.66 **cwNH**, *India-rubber ice.* . . Ice that bends but does not break under skaters. **1954** *WELS Suppl.* **nwWI**, There are many words to describe the ice. . . Hard, smooth ice—"glare ice" or "iron ice"; softer ice—"rubber ice," "sponge ice." **1965** Bowen *Alaskan Dict.* 28, *Rubber ice.* . . New *sea ice* which bends under a man's weight and lets him down into the water more casually than brittle river or lake ice would. Rubber ice is dangerous. **1965–70** *DARE* (Qu. B35, *Ice that will bend when you step on it, but not break)* 143 Infs, **chiefly Nth, wN Midl,** Rubber ice; [31 Infs, **esp N Cent, Upper MW,** Rubbery (ice);] (Qu. B33a, *The first thin ice that forms over the surface of a pond or pool)* Infs **MI**1, 90, 98, Rubber ice. **1979** *NYT Article Letters* **swCT**, "Rubber ice" was when the ice began to melt and you'd feel a dip as you skated over it. This was also very rare but we considered it fun.

rubber in, rubbering (switch), rubberneck(ing) See **rubber** v

rubber-nose sturgeon n
=**lake sturgeon.**

1933 LA Dept. of Conserv. *Fishes* 412, Known also as the Rock Sturgeon, Red Sturgeon and Rubber-nose Sturgeon, the Lake Sturgeon has been recorded as reaching a length of nine feet and a weight of over 100 pounds. **1951** Harlan–Speaker *IA Fish* 47, *Lake Sturgeon.* . . *Other Names:* Rock sturgeon, rock fish, rubber-nose and black sturgeon. **1985** Madson *Up River* 106 **Upper Missip Valley,** Biggest of the bunch was the lake sturgeon or "rubbernose sturgeon," a primitive giant that has reportedly reached eight feet in length and three hundred ten pounds.

rubber pine n
=**whitebark pine.**

1948 *Pacific Discovery* Nov–Dec 20, Short needles, short cones, and a rubbery stem are equipment with which the white-bark pine resists a constant wind; and its stems are so tough that the mountaineers call it the "rubber pine."

rubber plant n

1 A **bitterweed:** usu **pingue,** but also *Hymenoxys odorata.* [Because the sap contains latex]

1906 Rydberg *Flora CO* 380, *Hymenoxys* [spp] . . Colorado Rubber Plant. **1909** [see **pingue**]. **1940** Gates *Flora KS* 238, Actinella odorata . . Bitterweed, Colorado Rubber Plant. . . Dry plains. **1967** Dodge *Roadside Wildflowers* 90, Pingwing, also called rubberweed and Colorado rubber plant, is a tufted perennial with a woody crown and branched stems.

2 also *rubber bush:* A **guayule:** usu *Parthenium argentatum,* but also *P. incanum.* [Because the sap contains latex]

1913 Wooton *Trees NM* 145, *Parthenium incanum.* . . is a near relative of the guayule or Mexican rubber plant found in Western Texas and northern Chihuahua. **1931** U.S. Dept. Ag. *Misc. Pub.* 101.165, Mariola *(Parthenium incanum),* known also as horsebrush, . . New Mexican rubberbush, and sage, is a shrubby plant, growing scatteringly but commonly . . from extreme western Texas to southern Arizona and south into Mexico. . . Its congener, guayule, or Mexican rubberbush *(P. argentatum),* occurs indigenously as far north as western Texas and produces rubber. **1936** Whitehouse *TX Flowers* 176, The silver-leaved guayule or rubber plant *(Parthenium argentatum)* found in West Texas and Mexico. . . is a commercial source of rubber but is not yet profitable, as the plants are of slow growth. **1960** Vines *Trees SW* 1018, *Parthenium argentatum.* . . is the well-known Rubber Plant of the Southwest. **1981** Benson–Darrow *Trees SW Deserts* 298, Mariola is of interest as a relative of the Mexican rubber plant, guayule *(Parthenium argentatum).*

3 A **pussytoes** (here: *Antennaria plantaginifolia).*

1940 Steyermark *Flora MO* 530, Pussy Toes, Ladies' Tobacco, Rubber Plant, Everlasting *(Antennaria plantaginifolia).*

4 also *rubber bush:* A **sangre de drago** (here: *Jatropha dioica).* [Because the stem is flexible]

1939 Tharp *Vegetation TX* 60, Rubber-bush *(Mozinna* [=*Jatropha])*. . . So-called because of the pliability and toughness of the stems, which permit them to be tied in knots. **1960** Vines *Trees SW* 625, Rubber-plant—*Jatropha dioica.* **1970** Correll *Plants TX* 954, *Jatropha dioica* . . Sangre de drago, leather stem, rubber-plant. . . In scrub in s. and w. Tex.

5 A **milkweed 1** (here: *Asclepias syriaca).* [Because the sap contains latex]

1968 *DARE* Wildfl QR Pl.175 Inf **OH**82, Milkweed or rubber plant.

rubber rabbit-brush n Also *rubber yellowbrush*
A **rabbit brush 1b** (here: *Ericameria nauseosa*).
1931 U.S. Dept. Ag. *Misc. Pub.* 101.161, Rubber rabbit brush (*C[hrysothamnus] nauseosus*), known also as fetid rayless-goldenrod, rubber yellowbrush, and white sage (brush) . . ranges from British Columbia to northern California, Utah, and Alberta. **1967** Dodge *Roadside Wildflowers* 46, Rubber rabbitbrush—Chamiso. **1989** Mayes–Lacy *Nanise* 87, Rubber rabbitbrush is a fairly densely branched, gray-green shrub growing up to about 5 feet in height.

rubber root n
=**butterfly weed 1.**
1971 Krochmal *Appalachia Med. Plants* 70, *Asclepias tuberosa* . . Common names: Butterfly milkweed . . rubber root [etc].

rubbers n pl Freq with *the* [Ult from the proverb "They who play at bowls must look for rubbers" and varr (*OED2* rubber sb.² 1.b), where *rubbers* is an erron alteration of earlier *rubs* (*OED2* at rub sb.¹ 2.a). In most of the exx quoted below, the sense of *rubbers* has been reinterpreted on the analogy of phrr such as **flint mill, go through the.**]
Fig: misfortune, bad luck—usu in phrr *meet with (the) rubbers, pass through the rubbers.*
1776 in 1901 *Documents Colonial & Post-Revol. Hist. NJ* 1.217, And I am mistaken if they don't meet some severe rubbers. **1890** *DN* 1.19 seNH, *Rubbers:* misfortune, ill-luck. The phrase is, 'to meet with the rubbers.' *Ibid* 79 **Cape Cod MA**, *Rubbers.* . . The phrase *to meet with the rubbers* is known on Cape Cod in this sense. **1892** *DN* 1.218 ceMA, TN, *Rubbers.* . . Quite common in parts of Middle Tennessee, where the phrase is *to pass through the rubbers.* . . "To meet with the rubbers was common in Boston in my youth." **c1950** Halpert Coll. wKY, To pass through the rubbers = to have ill luck, misfortune. **1968** *DARE* (Qu. CC12b, . . *If a person has a lot of bad luck* . . "*He's been* _____.") Inf NJ22, Hit with the rubbers.

rubber snake See **rubber boa**

rubbertail n
=**green sunfish 1.**
1951 Harlan–Speaker *IA Fish* 115, Green Sunfish . . Other Names—Rubber tail, green perch [etc]. **1983** Becker *Fishes WI* 822, Green Sunfish. . . Other common names: green perch . . rubbertail [etc].

rubber vine n
Any of several apocynaceous plants native to southern Florida, as **devil's potato**, *Angadenia berteroi*, or *Rhabdadenia biflora*.
1933 Small *Manual SE Flora* 1062, *R[habdadenia] biflora.* . . Rubber-vine. *Ibid* 1063, *Echites umbellata* . . Devil's-potato. Rubber-vine. **1949** Moldenke *Amer. Wild Flowers* 163, In southern peninsular Florida and on the Keys. . . The yellow rubbervine, *Rhabdadenia corallicola*, also has yellow flowers. . . The white rubbervine, *R. biflora*, has white flowers. . . The stems of both are greatly elongated and the sap is rubbery. **1971** Craighead *Trees S. FL* 202, Rubber vine, *Rhabdadenia biflora*.

rubberweed n [Because the sap contains latex]
1 A **bitterweed**: usu **pingue**, but also *Hymenoxys odorata*.
1913 (1979) Barnes *Western Grazing* 269, The rubber weed is a small plant, bearing a bright yellow flower about three-fourths of an inch in diameter, growing in the semi-desert ranges. Under commercial treatment it produces small quantities of a rather low grade of crude rubber. **1937** U.S. Forest Serv. *Range Plant Hdbk.* W5, The whole rubberweed group should be regarded with suspicion since bitter rubberweed (*A[ctinea]* [= *Hymenoxys] odorata* . .), locally known as bitterweed and limonillo, and pingüe (*A. richardsoni* . .), often called Colorado rubberweed, abundant over large areas, are poisonous to livestock. **1967** [see **rubber plant 1**].
2 A **rabbit brush 1b** (here: *Ericameria nana*).
1960 Abrams *Flora Pacific States* 4.282, *Haplopappus nanus* [= *Ericameria nana*] . . Rubber Weed. . . Common through the Great Basin to Utah and the Snake Plains of Idaho. **1973** Hitchcock–Cronquist *Flora Pacific NW* 524, Rubber-weed . . [*Haplopappus] nanus*.

rubber yellowbrush See **rubber rabbit-brush**

rubbi(d)ge See **rubbage**

rubbing board See **rubboard 1**

rubbing doctor n Also *rub doctor*
See quot 1929.
1929 Ruppenthal Coll. **KS**, *Rubbing doctor.* . . One who relieves or professes to relieve physical ills by rubbing the part affected, or by massage, or by manipulating some part of the body. Applied to osteopaths, and also, loosely, to chiropractics. **1967** *DARE* (Qu. BB53a, . . *Joking names* . . *for a doctor*) Inf **KS5**, Rub doctor—if he's an osteopath; **IL30**, Rubbing doctor—for an osteopath. **1971** *Foxfire* Spring–Summer 36 **nGA**, Those girls, they just fell down like dead. By God, I thought we'd never get 'em back t'th'house. We toted 'em and ruffed 'em around. Even got a rubbin' doctor from Pine Mountain when they come to.

rubboard n
1 also *rubbing board:* A washboard. **now chiefly Sth, S Midl** Cf **battling block, scrubboard 1**
1845 U.S. Democratic Rev. 17.227 **IL**, She was clad in a dress which had once been printed, but yielding to the pressing solicitations of the rubbing boards, had parted with its colors. **1864** *Scientific Amer.* new ser 10.408, Washing Machine.—Joel Lee, Galesburg Ill.: I claim the . . rub-board frame, B, rub-board, C, washing rolls, FF [etc]. **1895** *New Engl. Mag.* 18.501, Grandma was up to her elbows in the suds, vigorously rubbing up and down the fluted wash-board granther's begrimed shirt sleeves. . . Zinc rubbing-boards and patent soap powders were unknown then. **1949** in 1986 *DARE* File **GA**, The road is like a rubboard. **1954** Harder Coll. cwTN, *Rub-board.* . . A washboard. "I as soon have a good rub-board as that old washing-'chine." **1966** *Good Old Days* 2.11.13 **nwAR** (as of early 20th cent), Mother did the family wash down by the spring on a rub board. **1966–67** *DARE* (Qu. N27b, *When unpaved roads get very rough, you call them* _____) Infs **AR33, SC26**, (Rough just) like a rubboard; **SC42**, Just like a wash and rubboard. **1966–69** *DARE* Tape **AL1**, She had a wash-bench down there, and a washpot, and two, three old tubs, and a wooden rubboard, and a battling stick; **CA138**, I washed and ironed several of those for the museum. And I wondered how they ever did it with the old-fashioned sadirons and the rubboard. **1977** *Mais Jamais* 27 **LA**, They would pump water into a tub, and rub the clothes along with the lye soap on a rubbing board. **1986** Pederson *LAGS Concordance* **Gulf Region**, 66 infs, Rub board(s); 3 infs, Rubbing board; 1 inf, **cwAL**, Rub board—to rub clothes on when washing outside; 1 inf, **cnAR**, Rub board = scrubboard; 1 inf, **cnFL**, Rub board—for rubbing clothes on after beating; 1 inf, **cnFL**, Used to wash clothes on the rub board; [1 inf, **cnFL**, [Of rub boards:] You had to rub it, soap it;] 1 inf, **swGA**, Rub them by the rub board; 1 inf, **ceLA**, Battling block replaced by rub board; 1 inf, **csMS**, Rub board—battling board—beat clothes to clean; 1 inf, **neTN**, Washed them on a rub board; 1 inf, **cnTX**, Rub board = scrubboard, washboard. **1989** Flynt *Poor But Proud* 202 **ceAL**, You rubbed 'em [=the clothes] on a rub board and boiled 'em in the pot. You'd build you a fire around that, the old metal pot, . . we called it the black pot. You'd build your fire and heat your water . . and you had a rub board, a wash board, you'd call it.
2 Transf: a rough, unpaved road; hence adj *rubboardy*. **esp Gulf States, TX, AR**
1965–70 *DARE* (Qu. N27b, *When unpaved roads get very rough, you call them* _____) 10 Infs, **esp Gulf States, TX, AR**, Rubboard; **TX89**, Rubboardy.

rub close v phr
To cut (something) close.
1890 *DN* 1.19 seNH, *Rub the time close:* allow little time. 'Aren't you rubbing the time too close?'

rub doctor See **rubbing doctor**

rube n, also cap Also sp *reub;* also *country rube, hay* ~ [Abbr for **Reuben**] **widespread, but less freq Sth, S Midl** See Map on p. 660
A farmer or rustic; a hick; an unsophisticated or boorish person.
1890 (1891) Bunner *Short Sixes* 101, If the boys [=circus employees] was here, and I [=circus proprietor] hollered 'Hey Rube!'—there would n't be enough of yer to spread a plaster fer a baby's bile! **1896** (1898) Ade *Artie* 8 **neIL**, If I had time I'd go over to that church and make a lot o' them Reubs look like thirty-cent pieces. **1897** *KS Univ. Qrly.* (ser B) 6.91, *Rube:* a farmer.—General. **1900** *DN* 2.40 [College slang], *Hay rube.* . . Country-man, farmer. [Northwestern Univ., Evanston, Ill.] *Ibid*

56 [College slang], *Rube. . .* 1. A farmer. 2. A green, boorish, unsophisticated fellow. **1900** Willard *Tramping* 396, [Glossary:] *Rube:* a "hoosier," or "farmer." **1918** in 1983 Truman *Dear Bess* 263 **MO,** It's rather funny for an old rube to be handing knowledge (of a sort) to the Harvard and Yale boys, but it's happening now. **1919** *DN* 5.67 **NM** [Among hs students], *Rube,* a countryfied person; a hay-seed. "All the rubes came in to see the circus." **1926** in 1931 McCorrison *Letters Fraternity* 91 **NEng,** The Rube abroad, arrived home from Portland all right—with no mishap. **1941** *LANE* Map 450 **NEng,** 52 infs, Rube; 2 infs, Country rube. **c1955** Reed–Person *Ling. Atlas Pacific NW (A rustic)* 3 infs, Rube. **1965** *PADS* 43.21 **seMA,** Joking or uncomplimentary names a city person may have for a country person . . rube [1 of 9 infs]. **1965–70** *DARE* (Qu. HH1, *Names and nicknames for a rustic or countrified person*) 106 Infs, **widespread, but less freq Sth, S Midl,** Rube; **AL20, OH8, PA27, 242, VT7,** Country rube [Of all Infs responding to the question, 63% were old; of those giving these responses, 82% were old.]; (Qu. HH3, *A dull and stupid person*) Infs **CA169, NY153, PA126,** Rube; (Qu. HH15, *A very inexperienced person, one who is just learning how to do a new thing*) Inf **OH94,** Rube; (Qu. HH18, *Very insignificant or low-grade people*) Inf **MS30,** Rube; (Qu. HH21, *A very awkward, clumsy person*) Inf **MI65,** Rube; (Qu. II21, *When somebody behaves unpleasantly or without manners:* "*The way he behaves, you'd think he was _____.*") Infs **IL46, MT4, UT6,** Rube. **1986** Pederson *LAGS Concordance* **Gulf Region** *(A rustic)* 9 infs, Rube; 1 inf, Country rubes—used to say.

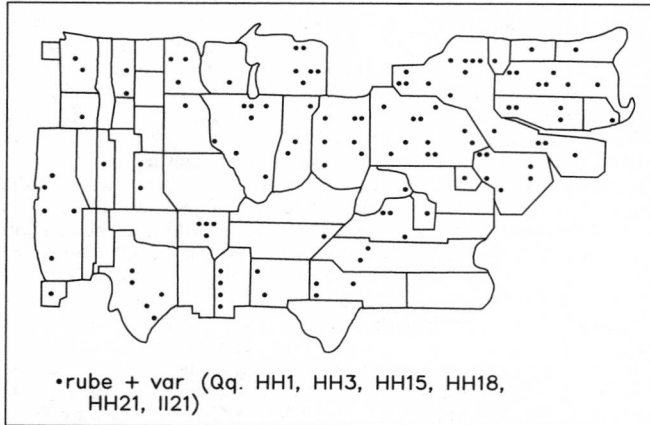

•rube + var (Qq. HH1, HH3, HH15, HH18, HH21, II21)

rubrock See **rubstone**

rubs n pl Cf **farmer's rice, rivel 1**
1967 *DARE* File **csWI,** *Rubs*—a mixture of egg and flour made very stiff and then crumbled and put in soup the last few minutes of cooking time.

rubstone n Also *rubrock* [*OED2* 14 . . →]
A whetstone.
1687 in 1886 MA Hist. Soc. *Coll.* 6th ser 1.75, Send me for my own proper accountt. . . six duz of rub stones. **1759** *Newport Mercury* (RI) 3 July 5/3, Just Imported. . . Sealing Wax, Snuff Boxes, Rubstones, Nails. **1876** Knight *Amer. Mech. Dict.* 3.1998, *Rub-stone.* The flat stone on which the currier's knife is ground to an edge. **1939** *LANE* Map 159 *(Whetstone)* 1 inf, **swCT,** Cf. rub stone; 1 inf, **cwCT,** Cf. rub stone, 'if it's stone'; 1 inf, **cCT,** Rifle, 'pretty good to sharpen a scythe.' 'The real rub stone will put on a delicate edge.' **1951** *NY Folkl. Qrly.* 7.187 **NY,** The Finger Lakes area has . . relic occurrences of *rubstone* for whetstone. **1966** *DARE* (Qu. L38, *What do you use . . to sharpen tools in the field?*) Inf **SC26,** Rubrock. **1986** Pederson *LAGS Concordance,* 1 inf, **cnGA,** Rubstone = whetstone.

ruby bead See **bead ruby**

ruby lily n
=**chaparral lily.**
1897 Parsons *Wild Flowers CA* 72, Ruby Lily. Chaparral Lily. Redwood Lily. . . These are at first pure white, dotted with purple, but they soon take on a metallic luster and begin to turn to a delicate pink, which gradually deepens into a ruby purple. **1949** Moldenke *Amer. Wild Flowers* 324 **CA,** The ruby lily or chaparral lily, *L[ilium] rubescens,* of California, has nearly white flowers, somewhat dotted with brown, aging to rose-purple.

ruby spot n
A **damselfly** (here: *Haeterina americana*), the male of which has ruby-red spots at the base of its clear wings.
1980 Milne–Milne *Audubon Field Guide Insects* 383, When the male Ruby Spot flies through a shaft of sunlight, its red color shows spectacularly. If it suddenly flits into the shade, it seems to vanish.

ruby-throated hummingbird n Also *ruby-throat*
Std: a **hummingbird 1** (here: *Archilochus colubris*), the male of which has a brilliant patch of red at the throat. Also called **bee bird 3, bumblebee 4, hominy bird 1, honeysucker 2**

rucas See **ruckus**

ruch See **rutch**

ruck n[1] [*OED2 ruck* sb.[2] →1787]
See quots.
1828 Webster *Amer. Dict.* np, *Ruck. . .* A wrinkle; a fold; a plait. **1899** (1912) Green *VA Folk-Speech* 359, *Ruck. . .* A fold, crease, or pucker in the material of a garment, resulting from faults in the making.

ruck n[2] [*OED2 ruck* sb.[3] "dial." →1869]
A rut; hence adj *rucky* full of ruts.
1899 (1912) Green *VA Folk-Speech* 359, *Ruck. . .* A narrow track worn or cut in the ground; especially, the hollowed track made by a wheel in passing over the ground. The road is full of *rucks;* it is very *rucky.*

ruck v[1] See **rake** v[1] **A2**

ruck v[2] [Cf *EDD ruck* sb.[6] 4 "Noise, racket"]
1952 Brown *NC Folkl.* 1.586, *Ruck. . .* To rattle, make a noise. "I could hear my hack ruckin'."—Central and east.

rucket n [*EDD rucket* sb.[2] 1 "A loud, confused noise"]
=**ruckus.**
c1940 Hall *Coll.* **wNC, eTN,** Raise a ruckus, a rucket. To raise a rumpus, make a lot of noise. (*Ruckus* is pronounced ['rukəs], and *rucket* ['rʌkət].)

ruckuhnize See **recognize**

ruckus n Usu |'rʌkəs|; also **esp Sth, S Midl** |'rukəs, 'rukəs| Pronc-spp *roccous, roocus, rookus, rucas, rucus, rukus*
A noisy disturbance, row, fight—freq in phr *raise* (or *make*) *a ruckus* create a commotion or disturbance.
1890 *DN* 1.66 **KY,** *Rucas* [rukəs]: for *rumpus.* **1892** *Century Illustr. Mag.* 44.159 **GA** [Black], He ain' try ter hender me, an' he better not, 'cause ef 'e had, deir 'd er b'en er rookus right deir. **1892** *KS Univ. Qrly.* 1.98 **KS,** *Rucus:* quarrel, rumpus. **1893** Shands *MS Speech* 53, *Rookus* [rukəs]. A word signifying a quarrel or row. Used principally by negroes and illiterate whites, and occurring most frequently in the southern central part of the State. **1902** *DN* 2.244 **sIL,** *Rukus* [rukəs]. Same as racket. **1903** *DN* 2.327 **seMO,** *Rucas* [rukəs]. . . Quarrel. 'He raised a rucas every time he got drunk.' **1906** *DN* 3.123 **sIN,** *Rukus* ['rukəs]. . . Racket . ; fight, disturbance. **1907** *DN* 3.235 **nwAR,** *Rucas. . .* Quarrel. **1909** *DN* 3.365 **eAL, wGA,** *Rucas, rucus. . .* A row, an open quarrel, a disturbance. **1912** *DN* 3.588 **wIN,** *Rucus. . .* A noisy quarrel or disturbance. "What kind of a rucus are they having in there, anyhow?" **1914** *DN* 4.78 **ME, nNH,** *Rookus. . .* Fight, disturbance. **Ibid** 111 **cKS,** *Rookus. . .* Disturbance; uproar. Also *rukus.* **1923** *DN* 5.219 **swMO,** *Rookus. . .* Ruckus, an altercation. **1927** Kennedy *Gritny* 29 **sLA** [Black], Raisin' a roocus w'en I refuse to leave him put on de w'ite folks clo'se. **1929** Gordon *Born to Be* 113 [Black], This little roccous was very interesting to me, because it was the first time I had heard my new boss reprimand anyone. **1940** Writers' Program *Negro in VA* 95 (as of c1936) [Black], Sometimes feel like raisin' a ruckus—make plenty noise wid de winders wide open, shout clap and sing. **1942** Hall *Smoky Mt. Speech* 70 **wNC, eTN,** *Ruckus* ['rukəs]. **1950** *PADS* 14.57 **SC,** *Rookus* ['rukəs]. . . A row, disturbance, uproar. **Ibid,** Ruckus ['rʌkəs, 'rukəs]. . . Same as *rookus.* **1953** Randolph–Wilson *Down in Holler* 279 **Ozarks,** *Ruckus* ['rukəs]. . . A scuffle, a fight in which more than two persons are involved, a free-for-all. Sometimes one hears this pronounced *rookus,* but ordinarily the *u* is short. "Take care the jug don't get busted, fellers! Looks like there's goin' to be a little ruckus here." **1965–70** *DARE* (Qu. KK16, *A great noise or disturbance:* "*I wish they'd stop making that awful _____.*") 40 Infs, **scattered,** Ruckus; **GA31, TN52, TX39,** ['rukəs]; **VA15,** ['rukəs]—old-

fashioned pronunciation; **LA2**, ['rʊkəs]; (Qu. KK15, *A disagreement or quarrel: "They had _____ about where the fence was to be."*) 21 Infs, **scattered,** A ruckus; **IL116, KY40, NM4, OK27, SC40, VA15,** A ['rʊkəs]; **AR55, GA7,** A ['rʊkəs]; **NC31,** A ['rʊkɨs]; (Qu. KK11, *To make great objections or a big fuss about something: "When we asked him to do that, he _____."*) Infs **AR22, 36, CA195, MA1, MI72, 106, TN31, 35, 46, WV1,** Raised a ruckus; **AR6, FL31, GA1, NC79, OK9,** Raised (*or* made) a ['rʊkəs]; **GA67, SC11, VA15,** Raised a ['rʊkəs]; **MS69,** Raised a ['rʌkəs]; (Qu. FF18, *Joking words . . about a noisy or boisterous celebration or party: "They certainly _____ last night."*) Infs **AR3, 33, VA41,** Raised a ruckus; **AR15, TN56, TX3,** Raised a ['rʊkəs]; **KY87, TN36,** Had a ruckus; **KY40, TN56,** Had a ['rʊkəs]; **TN33, TX64,** Made a (lot of) ruckus; (Qu. Y12a, *A fight between two people, mostly with words*) Inf **SC19,** ['rʊkɨs]; (Qu. Y12b, *A real fight in which blows are struck*) Inf **NY205,** ['rɪkəs]; **SC64,** Ruckus; (Qu. Y13, *A fist fight with several people in it*) Infs **FL31, IL25, OK31,** (Kind of a) ['rʊkəs]; **MA127,** ['rʌkəs]; **VA5,** Ruckus. **1967–69** DARE Tape **CA21,** It makes a ruckus ['rʊkəs] all right. . . They [=missiles] make a noise, a roar, as they go up, and the windows all rattle; **IL77,** When the ruckus ['rʊkəs] come up with Korea, then they called him back again. **1986** Pederson *LAGS Concordance,* 1 inf, **cAR,** Never raised a ruckus; 1 inf, **cLA,** Ruckus; (*A dance*) 1 inf, **nwFL,** Ruckus.

ruckus juice n Cf ruckus

Liquor, esp when of an inferior quality or illegally made.

1929 *AmSp* 4.385 **KS** [Wet words], Such terms as *rookus juice . . joy water . .* and *bust-head* are evidently references to the potency or the effect of the liquor designated. **1949** Emrich *Wild West Custom* 65 **West,** Early whisky in the frontier West was rightly named—Tangle-Leg, Forty Rod, Tarantula Juice, Rookus Juice. **1966–70** DARE (Qu. DD21a, *General words . . for any kind of liquor*) Inf **GA72,** Ruckus juice; (Qu. DD21b, *General words . . for bad liquor*) Inf **TN53,** Ruckus juice; (Qu. DD21c, *Nicknames for whiskey, especially illegally made whiskey*) Inf **GA72,** Ruckus juice; **NC37,** ['rukɨs] juice; (Qu. DD27, . . *Nicknames . . for wine*) Inf **TN53,** Ruckus juice; (Qu. DD28b, . . *Fermented drinks . . made at home*) Inf **TN53,** Ruckus juice. **1968** Foxfire Fall–Winter 101 **nGA,** Various names given moonshine include: ruckus juice (pronounced "rookus"). **1970** Thompson *Coll.* **seMI** (as of 1960s) [Black], *Ruckus juice . .* alcoholic beverages. **1974** Dabney *Mountain Spirits* 26 **Sth,** Another ghetto nickname, again suggesting the power of the drink, is "ruckus juice" (pronounced *rookus*). "When you drink it, you will want to start a ruckus," says Atlanta black preacher, Rev. William Holmes Borders. **1985** Wilkinson *Moonshine* 28 **neNC,** "After that they'd serve you North Carolina Corn." It is called . . ruckus juice.

rucky See ruck n²

ruction n Also rarely rumption, runction [Engl, Scots, Ir dial, cf EDD; perh altered aphet form of insurrection] Cf ruckus

A noisy disturbance, row, fight.

1844 *Spirit of Times* 28 Dec 517 (*AmSp* 40.26), Ruction. **1893** *KS Univ. Qrly.* 1.141 **KS,** Ruction: a quarrel. **1899** (1912) Green *VA Folk-Speech* 359, Ruction. . . A vexation or annoyance; also, a disturbance; a row or rumpus. **1903** *DN* 2.327 **seMO,** Ruction. . . An outbreak; a row. **1907** *DN* 3.235 **nwAR,** Ruction. **1907** Mulford *Bar-20* 122 **West,** My friends know where I am an' they'll come down here an' raise a ruction if I don't show up. **1921** *DN* 5.117 **eKY,** Ruction, a rough-and-tumble, free-for-all fight. **1927** *AmSp* 3.140 **eME,** "Ruction" (provincial English and Scotch) is an uproar or quarrel. **1942** McAtee *Dial. Grant Co. IN* 53 (as of 1890s), Ruction . . noisy outbreak, row, fight. Chiefly dial. **1945** FWP *Lay My Burden Down* 116 **LA** [Black], Some the niggers what work for the white folks from the North act pretty uppity and big, and come pestering round the dance places and try to talk up ructions amongst us, but it don't last long. **1952** Brown *NC Folkl.* 1.586, Ruction. . . A quarrel, a fight.—Central and east. *Ibid* 587, Ruction. . . A noise. **1966–67** DARE (Qu. KK15, *A disagreement or quarrel: "They had _____ about where the fence was to be."*) Infs **AR31, DC1,** (A) ruction. **1967** DARE FW Addit **TN23,** Rumption ['rʌmpšən]—a fuss, an argument. "Stir up a rumption," "have a rumption." Common. **1975** Gould *ME Lingo* 226, Raise a ruction—To start a fuss, by one person or by several. Tax bills come out, and everybody raises a ruction. Ruction usually suggests a big stew over some small matter. **1978** Doig *This House* 46 **MT,** Oh, he could handle us 'rangutangs, all right . . no ructions on a crew of your daddy's. **1991** Heat Moon *PrairyErth* 470 **ceKS,** The *Banner* pumped Sam's projects and promoted women's rights, a cause that drew him into as many ructions as had abolition.

ructious adj Also sp rukshus, ruxious [ruction]

Annoyed; vexatious; distressing.

1830 *Phila. Chronicle* 12 Aug. 1/6 (*DA*), 'Swapp'd, ructious, and something clever—O I understand you now,' said I. **1833** Neal *Down-Easters* 1.14 **NEng,** Ryled—ructious—there ye go agin! . . jest as eff you never heerd o' bein' ryled afore? **1897** *Kissimmee* (Fla.) *Valley* 3 March 1/6 (*DAE*), T.P. Howard is having a ruxious old time splitting rails . . as the timber is so tough. **1955** Ritchie *Singing Family* 192 **seKY,** Mom said it [=shooting a gun to celebrate Christmas] just sounded plain rukshus to her, just blasphemous. **1957** *Time* 18 Feb 69, Perhaps the greatest expert on those teasing, furniture-tossing, ructious ghosts called poltergeists was the late British Jesuit, Father Herbert Thurston.

rucus See ruckus

rud See road n¹

rudder adv See rather adv

rudder n See roader

rudder duck n Also rudder bird [From the narrow, stiff tail feathers]

=ruddy duck.

1884 Coues *Key to N. Amer. Birds* 715, *Erismatura,* . . Rudder Ducks. Remarkably distinguished from other *Fuligulinae* . . by the stiffened, linear-lanceolate tail-feathers. **1923** U.S. Dept. Ag. *Misc. Circular* 13.31 **UT,** Ruddy Duck. . . Vernacular Names. . . *In local use.* . . rudder bird, rudder duck [etc].

rudderfish n

Any of var fishes noted for following vessels or floating debris, as:

a also *black rudderfish:* An Atlantic **butterfish 1** (here: *Hyperoglyphe perciformis*). Also called **logfish 1**

1818 Mitchill in *Amer. Monthly Mag. & Crit. Rev.* 2.244 **NY,** Rudderfish, or Perch Coryphaena—*Coryphaena perciformis;* with zig-zag impressions adown his sides . . and a faint radiation around the eyes. **1884** Goode *Fisheries U.S.* 1.334, The Black Rudder-fish—*Lirus perciformis.* . . The habits of this fish are peculiar in the extreme. They are almost always found in the vicinity of floating barrels and spars, sometimes inside of the barrels; hence the fishermen often call them "Barrel-fish," though the most usual name is "Rudder-fish." *Ibid,* They doubtless have gained the name of Rudder-fish from the sailors who have seen them swimming about the sterns of becalmed vessels. **1933** John G. Shedd Aquarium *Guide* 81, *Palinurichthys perciformis*—Rudderfish; Logfish; Black Pilot. **1991** Amer. Fisheries Soc. *Common Names Fishes* 165, Rudderfish[₅] . . black—see barrelfish.

b also *banded rudderfish:* An **amberfish** (here: *Seriola zonata*). Also called **jack n¹ 24b(1)(b), jackfish 2b, pilotfish 2, shark pilot 1**

1842 DeKay *Zool. NY* 4.129, They [=*Seriola zonata*] are called *Rudder-fish* by the fishermen, who apply the same name to other fishes. **1884** Goode *Fisheries U.S.* 1.331, The Banded Rudder-fish—*Seriola zonata.* . . It is called in Southern New England the "Rudder-fish" on account of its resemblance to the rudderfish of the ocean. **1933** John G. Shedd Aquarium *Guide* 83, *Seriola zonata*—Pilotfish; Rudderfish. This fish, which is restricted to the Atlantic coast of the United States, resembles the Shark-pilot. **1991** Amer. Fisheries Soc. *Common Names Fishes* 52, *Seriola zonata* . . banded rudderfish.

c A **harvest fish** (here: *Peprilus alepidotus*).

1903 NY State Museum & Sci. Serv. *Bulletin* 60.457 **SC,** At Charleston the fish [=*Rhombus paru*] is called rudderfish. **1906** NJ State Museum *Annual Rept. for 1905* 269, *Seserinus paru* . . Rudder Fish.

d A fish of the family Kyphosidae, esp the Bermuda chub (*Kyphosus sectatrix*).

1903 NY State Museum & Sci. Serv. *Bulletin* 60.569, The Bermuda chub grows to the length of 18 inches. . . Its name of rudder fish refers to its habit of following vessels, presumably to secure the waste food thrown from them. **1921** *Copeia* 91.9 **MA,** The Rudderfish, sometimes called Bermuda Chub (*Kyphosus sectatrix*), is not common in southern Massachusetts and is not observed every year at Woods' Hole. On October 15, one was taken in a trap in Buzzard's Bay. **1946** LaMonte *N. Amer. Game Fishes* 72, Rudderfish. . . Eats algae chiefly. The fish gets its name from its habit of following vessels for long distances, presumably feeding on their waste.

ruddle n [Etym unknown]
The attic of a house.

1963 Haywood *Yankee Dict.* 133, *Ruddle*—The attic of a house. **1967** *DARE* (Qu. D4, *The space up under the roof, usually used for storing things*) Inf **MA**72, Ruddle. **1999** *NADS Letters* neMA, I have heard ruddle, *very* infrequently, but I'm from Beverly, MA, 2 towns away from Lynn . . well, maybe 3 towns away. But still very close by. And I've only heard it once or twice.

ruddock n [*OED2* c1000 → for the robin, *Erithacus rubecula;* "Now chiefly *dial.*"]
=cardinal 1.

1953 Randolph–Wilson *Down in Holler* 279 **Ozarks**, *Ruddock*. . . The redbird or cardinal *(Richmondena cardinalis).* Louise Platt Hauck, of St. Joseph, Mo., says this word was common at Blue Eye, near the Missouri–Arkansas line, in the early nineteen thirties.

ruddy n Also *roody, buck ruddy*
=ruddy duck.

1893 *Outing* 23.68, She described the duck closely and I guessed that they were "ruddies." **1911** *Forest & Stream* 77.173 **WI**, Ruddy Duck. . . Buck Ruddy (not meaning the male only as might be supposed, but applied to all ruddy ducks), Lake Puqua and Delavan Lake, Wis. **1917** (1923) *Birds Amer.* 1.152, Ruddy Duck. . . *Other Names* . . Rook; Roody [etc]. **1923** Dawson *Birds CA* 4.1841, His flesh, therefore, has been generously voted "tough" and "stringy"; *and* you must *not* shoot a Ruddy, please! **1965** Herlan *NV Highway Bird Watcher* 9, At a distance both male and female Ruddys appear to be small, compact, unpatterned dark birds.

ruddy diver n Cf diver
=ruddy duck.

1867 (1868) Samuels *Ornith. & Oology New Engl.* 525, The Ruddy Duck. . . is so expert a diver that sportsmen recognize it by the name of "Ruddy Diver" and "Dipper;" and all attest to the difficulty with which it is shot. **1917** (1923) *Birds Amer.* 1.152, Ruddy Duck. . . Other Names. . . Ruddy Diver [etc]. **1953** Jewett *Birds WA* 151, Northern Ruddy Duck. . . Other names: Wire-tail . . Ruddy Diver [etc].

ruddy duck n
Std: a small, broad-billed duck *(Oxyura jamaicensis),* the male of which has chestnut-colored breeding plumage. Also called **beaver duck, biddy** n[1] **2, blackjack 1b, bluebill 2, bobbler, booby** n[1] **2, bristletail 2, broadbill 3, bubby duck, bull-neck 2, bumblebee coot, ~ duck 2, butterball 2, butter-bowl, cockmantail, coot** n[1] **2b, cootie** n[2]**, dapper 2, daub-duck, deaf duck 1, dickey** n[1]**, dinky** n[1] **2, dipper 5, dip-tail diver, diver, dopper** n[1] **2, dumb bird, dumpling duck, dunbird, dun diver 1, fool duck 1, frost ~, goddam, goose teal, ~ widgeon, gray teal, greaser B3, hardhead 5a, hardtack 5, heavy-tailed duck, hickoryhead, horse-turd coot, Johnny Bull 2, leatherback 3, leather breeches** n pl **3, lightwood knot 2, mud dipper, ~ hen 2b, murre 2, muskrat duck, noddy 2, paddy** n[1] **6, pintail 2, pond coot 1, quilltail, raft duck b, rook** n[1]**, rudder duck, ruddy, ~ diver, saltwater teal 1, shanty duck, shot-pouch, sinker 4, sleeper, sleepyhead, soldier duck, spatterer, splatter-ass, spiketail, spinetail, spirit duck, spoonbill, spoon-billed butterball, sprigtail, steelhead, sticktail, stifftail, stub-and-twist, stubtail, tough-head, water partridge, wedge-ass, widgeon, ~ coot, wiretail**

ruddy plover n
=sanderling.

[**1785** Pennant *Arctic Zool.* 2.486, *Ruddy. Pl[over]*. . . Inhabits Hudson's Bay.] **1813** (1824) Wilson *Amer. Ornith.* 7.135 **NJ**, This bird . . has hitherto been named the Ruddy Plover. **1898** (1900) Davie *Nests N. Amer. Birds* 142, The Sanderling, Ruddy "Plover" or "Beach Bird," is a species of wide distribution. **1917** (1923) *Birds Amer.* 1.239, Sanderling. . . *Other Names.*—Ruddy Plover [etc]. **1969** Longstreet *Birds FL* 65, Sanderling—*Other names:* Beach Bird . . Ruddy Plover.

ruddy turnstone n
Std: a stocky, red-legged shore bird *(Arenaria interpres)* that winters on the Atlantic, Gulf, and California coasts. Also called **brant-bird 1, calico-back 1, chicaric, chicken** n **B2, ~ bird 1, chickling, chuckatuck, gannet 3, heart bird, horsefoot snipe 1, jenny 3, king-crab bird, maggot-eater, maggot snipe, maybird 5, oxeye 1a, oysterbird 2, pigeon, plover, red-legged ~, rockbird 2, rock plover 2, ~ snipe 2, saltwater partridge, sand runner 1, sea quail 1, sparked-back, stone-pecker, streaked-back, whalebird**

rue v Also with *back* [Scots, nIr, nEngl dial] **chiefly Sth, S Midl**
Also in phrr *rue (a) bargain:* To back out of an agreement or bargain; hence vbl n *ruing back;* n *rue-bargain* a bargain that one regrets.

1826 (1933) Sibley *Santa Fe Diary* 153, Bot 2 mules for $70. But the man rued and took one deal. **1860** *Harper's New Mth. Mag.* 20.281, Our friend issued a license for the marriage of John Murphy and Mary Manning, both natives of the Emerald Isle. . . But the intended bride 'rued.' **1891** *PMLA* 6.3.174 **TN**, To *rue back* is to *back out,* and is used in such examples as, "he cheated me and I want to rue back." **1893** Shands *MS Speech* 54, *Rue back*. . . Used by all classes to mean *to back out of a trade, to trade back.* When a man is not satisfied with a purchase, but returns it and gets his money back, he is said to *rue back. Rue back* applies also to a swap or any kind of a trade. **1902** *DN* 2.244 **sIL**, *Rue.* . . To dissolve a contract, as to *rue* a bargain. *Rue back*. . . To trade back; to reëxchange commodities. **1903** *DN* 2.328 **seMO**, *Rue* or *rue back*. . . To trade back. 'We traded yesterday and he wanted to rue to-day.' **1909** *DN* 3.365 **eAL, wGA**, *Rue back*. . . To seek to withdraw from a bargain, back down from one's bargain. "We swapped knives, and then he wanted to rue back." **1915** *DN* 4.189 **swVA**, *Rue back*. . . To 'back down' from a bargain. **1926** *DN* 5.402 **Ozarks**, We done swapped fa'r an' squa'r, an' now Ed he's a-tryin' t' rue back on me. **1944** *PADS* 2.48 **NC**, *Rue-bargain*. . . A bad bargain; to withdraw from a bargain made in good faith. **1952** Brown *NC Folkl.* 1.586, Rue back. **1954** Harder *Coll.* **cwTN**, Rue back. **1965** Davis *Summer Land* 107 **cnNC**, Wash overheard him and rolled his eyes like he was about to rue back on his trade, but he shook Jimroe by the hand and took the blind mare. **1982** Slone *How We Talked* 5 **eKY** (as of c1950), Another well-known custom: if you asked a price for something, and someone offered to give you what you had asked, you must take this price, even if you had later changed your mind and did not want to sell at that price. It was counted very shameful if you did not, and was called "ruing back." **1983** *MJLF* 9.1.54 **ceKY** (as of 1956), *Rue back* . . to go back on a trade. . . *Rue bargain* . . same as above.

rue anemone n
A **meadow rue** (here: *Thalictrum thalictroides*). Also called **mayflower 3c, wild potato, windflower**

1822 Eaton *Botany* 174, [*Anemone*] *thalictroides* . . rue anemone. **1861** Wood *Class-Book* 203, Rue Anemone. . . A fine little plant of early spring. **1901** Lounsberry *S. Wild Flowers* 180, Rue-Anemone. . . Almost as perishable and very like those of the wind flower are this plant's blossoms, while its leaves resemble the foliage of the meadow rue. **1967** *DARE* Wildfl QR Pl.68B Inf **MI**57A, Rue anemone. **1968** *DARE* (Qu. S2) Inf **PA**70, Rue anemone. **1979** Niering–Olmstead *Audubon Guide N. Amer. Wildflowers E. Region* 729, The leaves of Rue Anemone are similar to those of the Meadow Rues.

rue back, rue bargain See rue

rue-bub See rhubarb

ruf(e), ruff n[1] See roof

ruff n[2] See rough n

ruffed grouse n Also *ruff grouse, ruffle(d) grouse* Pronc-sp *ruffid grouse* **chiefly Nth** See Map Cf **partridge B2, pheasant 1a**
A brown, chicken-like gamebird *(Bonasa umbellus* and var races) with ruffs of black feathers at the sides of the neck. Also called **biddy** n[1] **2, drummer 4, fool hen 1, French ~, gray partridge 2, hen B4, Hungarian partridge 2, moun-**

tain pheasant, partridge B2, pat n³, pheasant 1a, pine pheasant, willow grouse, woodcock, wood hen, ~ pheasant

[**1752** G. Edwards *Gleanings Nat. Hist.* I.79 *(DAE),* The Ruffed Heath-cock, or Grous.] **1812** Wilson *Amer. Ornith.* 6.45, *Ruffed Grous.. .* This is the *Partridge* of the eastern states, and the *Pheasant* of Pennsylvania and the southern districts. **1839** Audubon *Synopsis Birds* 202, Tetrao Umbellus . . Ruffed Grouse. . . Common from Maryland to Labrador, and in the interior from the mountainous districts to Canada and the Saskatchewan. **1848** in 1850 Cooper *Rural Hours* 13 **NY,** Our Partridge or Pheasant, or Ruffed Grouse, as we should rather call it, is a more hardy bird. **1874** *Forest & Stream* 1.411 **Baltimore MD,** [Letter:] I am glad that sportsmen are awaking to the idea that birds, fish and animals should be called by their right names. . . Here they call the quail a partridge . . they call a ruffed grouse a pheasant [etc]. **1896** Robinson *In New Engl. Fields* 183, The ruffed grouse bursts into view, in full flight with the first strokes of his thundering pinions. **1944** Nute *Lake Superior* 295 **MI, WI, MN,** That same day I saw many ruffed grouse. **1961** Douglas *My Wilderness* 117 **nMN,** I saw two partridges or ruffed grouse on one portage, the male making a big fan of his tail and ruffing his collar. **1965–70** DARE (Qu. Q7, *Names and nicknames for . . game birds*) 11 Infs, **chiefly Nth,** Ruffed grouse; **ME8,** Partridge—really a ruffed grouse; I've heard natives call the ruffed grouse a ruffled grouse—more common; **NY92,** Partridge or ruffed grouse; 11 Infs, **chiefly NEast,** Ruffled grouse; **KY24,** Ruffled grouse . . used to be called and frequently still is called pheasant; **NH4,** Ruffled grouse—same as partridge; **MA78, MI14,** 112, **NY133, OH82, RI4, WI58,** Ruff grouse; **GA76,** Ruff grouse—same as mountain pheasant; **MI10,** Ruff grouse—call these "pats," from "partridge"; of "ruff grouse" and "partridge," I think "ruff grouse" is winning; **MI42,** Ruff grouse is called partridge around here; **MA68,** Ruff grouse—same as partridge; **MI2,** Partridge—that is the ruff grouse; **NY6,** Ruffid grouse, ruffle grouse.

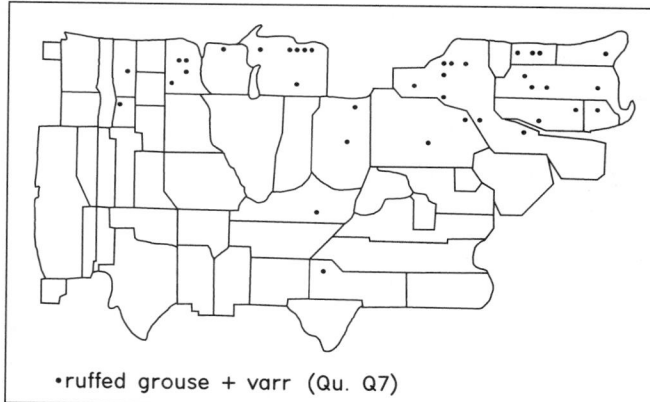

•ruffed grouse + varr (Qu. Q7)

ruffed-winged swallow See **rough-winged swallow**

ruffed-wing hawk See **rough-winged hawk**

ruff (or ruffid, ruffle(d)) grouse See **ruffed grouse**

ruffledy adj Cf **flowerdy, rottendy**
Ruffled.
1984 Burns *Cold Sassy* 201 **nGA** (as of 1906), There were ruffledy yellow and brown checked curtains at the windows.

ruffles n pl Cf **wrinkles**
=**chitterlings 1.**
1969 *This Week Mag.* 12 Oct 14/3 *(Mathews Coll.)* **Sth** [Black], My husband demanded at least two sessions with the "ruffles" every winter, and—to my disgust—all three of our daughters loved "ruffles," too. *Ibid* 15/2, "Ruffles" and "wrinkles" are two of the pet names for chitterlings. **1969** DARE File, *Ruffles* = chitterlings. Said to be a recent term among Negroes now that whites have taken to eating chitterlings. **2001** NADS *Letters,* "Ruffles", generally "hog ruffles", meaning chitterlings occurs with some frequency in piedmont Virginia. I have heard it from both black and white in the last 20 years.

ruf(f)ness See **roughness**

rufous-sided towhee n
Std: a **towhee** (here: *Pipilo erythrophthalmus* and var races)

with cinnamon-rufous patches on the flanks.   Also called **brownbird 2, bush bird, Cherokee robin, chewink, fox bird 2, go-wank, grasset 1, ground chippy 2, ~ robin 1, jo-wheet, joe-lee, joree** n 1, **joritte, marsh robin, nigger-head 5, pewit 3, red-eyed towhee, robin 7, shitbird 2, swamp robin, turkey sparrow, white-eyed towhee, wood robin**

rugaroo, rugarue See **roup-garou**

rugged adj **chiefly NEng**
Healthy; in good health.
1814 in 1947 *AmSp* 22.274 **NH** [Americanisms noted by Thomas Elwyn], *Rugged* . . for hardy or robust. **1846** Worcester *Universal Dict.* 622, *Rugged.. .* Hardy; healthy.—Colloquial, U.S. **1872** Holmes *Poet* 399 **MA,** I'm getting along in life, and I ain't quite so rugged as I used to be. **1890** *Harper's New Mth. Mag.* 80.747 **CA,** She is not what you could call a rugged-looking baby. **1905** *DN* 3.17 **cCT,** *Rugged.. .* Hardy, robust. **1908** Wasson *Home from Sea* 208 **sME coast,** Myry was . . always a little grain sickly like; that is, maybe not so very sickly, but a good deal same 's her brother Abner; noways rugged. **1927** *AmSp* 3.140 **eME,** When asked how they are, people still respond in these terms "Poorly," "not very rugged," "kind of slim," "first-rate," "nicely." **1941** LANE Map 460, 1 inf, **cME,** Rugged = healthy; 1 inf, **RI,** Rugged, of a healthy child. **1968–69** DARE (Qu. Z12, *Nicknames and joking words meaning 'a small child': "He's a healthy little _____."*) Inf **CT36,** Rugged little cuss; [(Qu. HH27a, *A very able and energetic person who gets things done*) Inf **NH14,** He's a rugged lad (or boy).

rug rat n Cf **ankle-biter**
A small child.
[**1967** DARE (Qu. Z16, *A small child who is rough, misbehaves, and doesn't obey, you'd call him a _____*) Inf **TX33,** Rug ape.] **1970** *Current Slang* 4.3–4.23 [NM State Univ slang], *Rug rat.. .* A small child. **1980** DARE File **Madison WI,** It's a restaurant we like because there aren't usually any rug rats there. **1984** Weaver *TX Crude* 123, *Rug-rat.* A child. **1987** DARE File **WI,** We can't get in the swimming pool 'til after 4. Right now it's full of rug rats. **1997** *Ibid* **eTN** (as of c1985), Rug rat—same as an ankle-biter. **1998** *WI State Jrl.* (Madison) 2 Jan sec D 3/1, Founded 18 years ago, [Nickelodeon] is the undisputed leader of the pack, commanding nearly 60 percent of the children's ad market. Its signature shows, "Rugrats" and "Hey Arnold," are enormous hits.

ruin v
A Forms.
1 pres: usu |'ruən|; rarely |rɝ·n|; pronc-sp *rurn.*
1942 [see A2c below]. **2000** [see B2 below].
2 past, past pple, ppl adj: usu *ruined;* also:
a *ruin.*   Cf Pronc Intro 3.I.22
1986 Pederson *LAGS Concordance* **Gulf Region** (The meat is spoiled) 4 infs, Ruin = ruined; 1 inf, Ruin meat; 2 infs, It's (nearabout) ruin; 1 inf, They like to [=almost] ruin that old boy; 1 inf, Like to ruin it = almost ruined it.
b |'ruint|, rarely |runt|; pronc-spps *roont, ruint.*   **chiefly Sth, S Midl, TX, OK**   See Map on p. 664
1884 *Anglia* 7.262 **Sth, S Midl** [Black], To be in er fa'r way ter git *ruint* = to be on the road to ruin. **1903** [see B1 below]. **1907** *DN* 3.235 **nwAR,** *Ruint.. .* Injured; not necessarily spoiled. **1913** [see B1 below]. **1923** *DN* 5.219 **swMO,** *Ruint.. .* Ruined. "Dry weather like to 'a' [sic] ruint me." **1932** (1974) Caldwell *Tobacco Road* 139 **GA,** It's already ruint, sister. **1942** [see A2c below]. **1955** Roberts *S. from Hell-fer-Sartin* 158 **seKY,** He cut ole Shorty's long smooth tail off right behind his years. Just like to ruint my dog. **1965–70** DARE (Qu. Y35, *To spoil something so that it can't be used . . "My new coffee pot—it's completely _____."*) 54 Infs, **chiefly Sth, S Midl, TX, OK,** Ruint; **OK42,** [runt]; (Qu. I8, *When root vegetables get old and tough and are not good to eat*) Inf **KY69,** Ruint; (Qu. Z14b, *If a child expects to have its own way or have too much attention . . "That child is _____."*) Infs **GA37, KY10,** 77, **MS72, SC10, TN27,** Ruint; **NJ69,** Ruint to death. **1974** Fink *Mountain Speech* 22 **wNC, eTN,** They ruint me. **1976** Garber *Mountain-ese* 76 **sAppalachians,** Someone spilled ink on my new dress and ruint it. **1997** DARE File—Internet **cePA** [Coal-Speak], I fell in the crick and now my hair is roont!

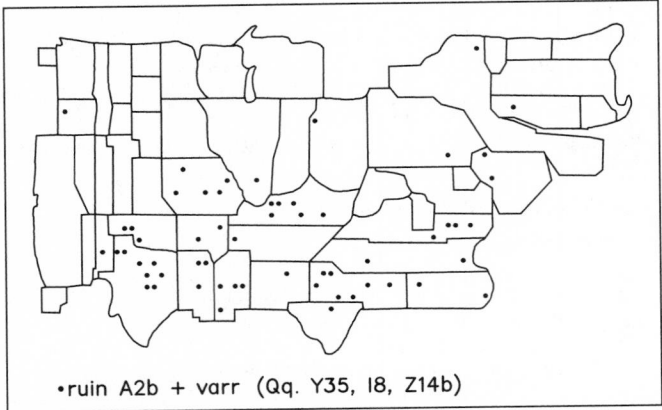

•ruin A2b + varr (Qq. Y35, I8, Z14b)

c |rɜ·nt|; pronc-spp *rernt, rurned, rurnt.* **Sth, S Midl**
1942 Hall *Smoky Mt. Speech* 38 **wNC, eTN,** *Ruined,* past tense of
ruin, is [rɜ·nt] (once [rĕə·nt]), and occasionally ['ru,ɪnt]. The present
tense is usually [rɜ·n]. **1961** *Mt. Life* 37.1.6 **sAppalachians,** Frequently
r is inserted in other words . . *breakferst, terbaccer, rurnt* (ruined).
1969 *DARE* FW Addit **seGA,** *Ruined* ['rɜ·nt]—said several times. **1981**
Pederson *LAGS Basic Materials,* 1 inf, **neMS,** [rɜ·nt]—probably facetious. **1982** Powers *Cataloochee* 93 **cwNC,** "Major" complained to
Professor Hall about the new hunting rules imposed on him. "(The Park)
has rernt this country. They have us hemmed in, 'n you cain't kill a
thing." **1983** Allin *S. Legislative Dict.* 26 **Sth,** *Rurned:* damaged or
soiled beyond repair. "Dog if I ain't rurned this shirt." **2000** [see **B2** be-
low].
B Senses.
1 To harm, injure seriously.
1903 *DN* 2.328 **seMO,** *Ruint* (ruined). . . Injured; not necessarily
spoiled. 'The hail ruint my wheat so it won't make over half a crop.'
1907 [see **A2b** above]. **1913** Kephart *Highlanders* 294 **sAppalachians,**
"I'm bodaciously ruint" (seriously injured). **1956** *Hall Coll. (Montgomery Coll.)* **eTN,** I bumped my toe, and I cut the nail off of it and I
grabbed my foot up and I said, "God damn, I've ruint my foot."
2 To spoil (a child); to treat (a child) with undue leniency;
hence ppl adj *ruined.* **chiefly Sth, S Midl** See Map
1965–70 *DARE* (Qu. Z14b, *If a child expects to have its own way or
have too much attention . . "That child is _____.")* 28 Infs, **chiefly
Sth, S Midl,** Ruined; **MD40,** Being ruined; **GA37, KY10,** 77, **MS72,
SC10, TN27,** Ruint; **NJ69,** Ruint to death; (Qu. Z14a, *To give a child its
own way or pay too much attention to it: "Everyone _____ that
child.")* 19 Infs, **chiefly Sth, S Midl,** (Just) ruins. [Of all Infs responding to these questions, 27% were gs educ or less; of those giving these
responses, 47% were gs educ or less.] **2000** *DARE* File **seKY** (as of
c1950), *Rurn—(Ruin)* "That candy will Rurn yore supper". Also a
Rurned child is a spoiled child.

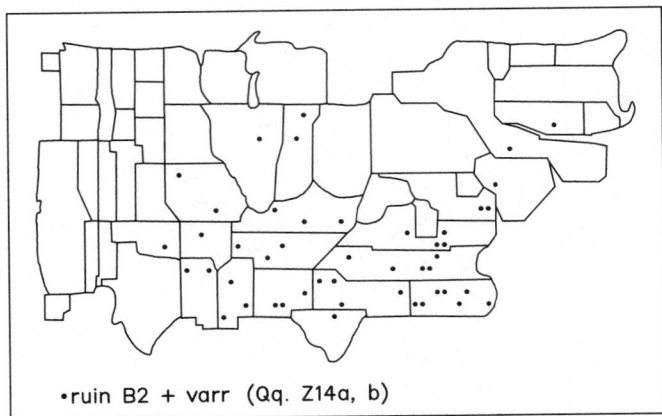

•ruin B2 + varr (Qq. Z14a, b)

3 To become spoiled; to become incapable of proper functioning. **Sth, S Midl**
1935 *AmSp* 10.156 **NC,** During a stay in North Carolina it was my
good fortune to lodge in the house of a woman whose speech was strikingly rich in local idiom. . . She would bring in my milk from the porch,

which I had neglected to do, saying that she 'knew it would ruin' out
there in the hot sun. **1946** *AmSp* 21.191 **seKY,** *Ruin* . . spoil. 'Them
peaches 'll ruin if I don't can 'em right soon.' **1947** *AmSp* 22.156 **sIN,**
The following words, with the same meanings as in [quot 1946
above] . . have been perfectly familiar to me for more years than I like to
remember: . . *ruin* [etc]. **1965** *DARE* (Qu. K7, *What sickness can a cow
get in her udder—for example, if she's left unmilked too long?)* Inf
MS58, Bag ruins. **1986** Pederson *LAGS Concordance (The meat is
_____)* 1 inf, **ceAR,** How come it ruined; 1 inf, **swGA,** It ruined; 1
inf, **swTN,** It ruins; 1 inf, **neTX,** Done already ruined; [Other contexts:]
1 inf, **ceAL,** It'll ruin; 1 inf, **neAR,** Or else it would mold and ruin—of
hay; 1 inf, **seMS,** That's goin' ruin; 1 inf, **nwMS,** Like to ruin = almost
ruined; 1 inf, **seAR,** Like to ruined; 1 inf, **swGA,** Done ruined; 1 inf,
cTN, They ruined; 1 inf, **cnTX,** Ruining—shriveling.

ruinate v, hence ppl adj *ruinated* [*OED2* "In very common use
from c1550 to 1700; now rare."] **chiefly Sth, S Midl** *old-fash*
To ruin.
1806 (1970) Webster *Compendious Dict.* 262, *Ruinate* . . to ruin, sub-
vert, bring to poverty. [*DARE* Ed: This entry was carried over from Webster's English model.] **1844** Thompson *Major Jones's Courtship* 81
GA, Come out here a tryin to ruinate some pore innocent gal. **1858**
Hammett *Piney Woods Tavern* 148, I'm killed! I'm ruinated! **1899**
(1912) Green *VA Folk-Speech* 359, *Ruinate.* . . To bring to ruin; overthrow; undo. **1917** *DN* 4.416 **wNC,** *Ruinate.* . . To ruin. **1927** *AmSp*
2.363 **cwWV,** Jim ruinated a good game when he got that hand. **1931**
Randolph *Ozarks* 69, He come a-junin' in all narvish-like an' tetchous,
an' rid th' pore ol' trollop a bug-huntin'—jes' plum bodacious hipped an'
ruinated her. **1933** Williamson *Woods Colt* 115 **Ozarks,** Maybe thar's
too much fire under the b'iler, an' you got to slack up or ruinate the hull
[=whole] dang mess. **1952** Brown *NC Folkl.* 1.586, *Ruinate.* . . To ruin.
c1960 *Wilson Coll.* **csKY,** *Ruinate.* . . To ruin in any sense. **1979** *AmSp*
54.99 **ME** (as of 1899–1910), *Ruinate.* . . Ruin.

ruined See **ruin B2**

ruing-back See **rue**

ruint See **ruin A2b**

ruk(e) See **rake** v[1] **A2**

rukshus See **ructious**

rukus See **ruckus**

rule n **chiefly Nth, esp NEng** *old-fash*
A recipe.
1847 (1852) Crowen *Amer. Cookery* 436 **NY,** *A general rule for making sponge cake.* Take the weight of the eggs used in sugar, and half the
weight of flour, beat the yolks and sugar together [etc]. **1896** (c1973)
Farmer *Orig. Cook Book* 413 **MA,** Count out number of eggs required . . , separating yolks from whites if rule so specifies. **1936** Lutes
Country Kitchen 148 **sMI,** I guess we all know about your sour-
cream cookies, Miz' Thompson. I wisht you'd give me the rule for 'em.
1939 Wolcott *Yankee Cook Book* 212, Wherever he has gone, the New
Englander's "rule"—not "recipe"—book has accompanied him. **1940**
Brown *Amer. Cooks* 540 **NH,** Early New Hampshire ladies went by rule
and not by recipe! **1950** *WELS (Written directions for cooking a dish,
baking a cake, etc)* 4 Infs, **WI,** Rule(s). **1951** Johnson *Resp. to PADS*
20 **DE** (*The written directions for making a dish, baking a cake, etc*)
Rule (old-fashioned). **1953** *PADS* 19.13 **sAppalachians,** *Rule* . . I'd
like your rule for grape-leaf pickle. **1959** *VT Hist.* 27.154. **1962**
Carrell *Autobiog.* [33] **ceMA,** Mother fed them well, I think you have
her rule for molasses blueberry ginger bread. **1965–70** *DARE* (Qu.
H79, . . *The exact directions for cooking a certain dish, making a cake,
and so on*) 10 Infs, **chiefly Nth, esp MA,** Rule. [All Infs old] **1999**
Berkshire Eagle (Pittsfield MA) 21 July np, I supposed it was a recipe
known only to the pre-1900 women of my family—except they would
have called it a "rule."

rule G n Also *big G*
In railroading: the general regulation prohibiting the use of alcohol or narcotics on the job.
1929 *Bookman* 69.527 [Railroad lingo], *Rule G:* In all railroad rule
books, prohibiting the use of intoxicants. **1932** *RR Mag.* Oct 369, *Rule
G*—Thou shalt not drink. **1945** Hubbard *Railroad Ave.* 358, *Rule G*—
"The use of intoxicants or narcotics is prohibited"—one of twelve general rules in standard code adopted by Association of American Rail-

roads, based upon previous regulations made by individual companies. Countless thousands of railroad men, especially *boomers,* have been discharged for violation of *Rule G;* not because of railroads' objection to liquor itself but because a man under the influence of liquor is not to be trusted in a job involving human lives and property. **1976** Gould *Blackie's RR Hdbk.* 14, *Railroad rule against alcoholic beverage use:* Rule "G"—Big "G".

rule-of-five n

A **waterleaf** (here: *Hydrophyllum virginianum*).

1974 Peden *Speak to Earth* 63 **cIN,** Waterleaf, which I never really wanted in the first place, just appeared one year in the wildlife corner. It is also called rule-of-five, which is appropriate because it is dominated by fives. The leaves, shaped like geranium leaves dusted with blight, are divided into five points, some even into five panels. The pale lilac-blue, cuplike flowers have five petals and when these have fallen, a five-pronged star-shaped calyx remains, green-white at the center. The foot-high watery green stalks with their hairy covering are ridged into five sides.

ruler's root n Also *ruler of the earth,* ~ *world*

A root used in **hoodoo** n **1a;** perh a **Solomon's seal** (here: *Polygonatum biflorum*).

1931 Hurston in *Jrl. Amer. Folkl.* 44.413 **LA** [Black], World-wonder Root. It is used in treasure hunts. Bury a piece in the four corners of the field; also hide it in the four corners of your house to keep things in your favor. Ruler's Root. Used as above. **c1938** in 1970 Hyatt *Hoodoo* 1.244 **ceNC** [Black], Yo' know, *Adam an' Eve, devil's-shoestring,* and de *ruler of de earth* . . dey talks to each other. Yo' put 'em in dat perfume an' puts 'em all togethah. *Ibid* 652 **SC** [Black], Ah git some *root* dey call de *High John de Conker,* an' *Ruler of de Worl'* an' *King of Man.*

ruletji See rolliche

ruling day n sAppalachians

A day, often one of the first twelve days of the year, whose weather is believed to foretell the weather at some later period.

[**1888** *Overland Mth.* (2d ser) 12.506 **sAppalachians,** The weather during each of the first twelve days of the year is, consecutively, a fair sample of the weather that will prevail during each month of the year.] **1905** (1975) Miles *Spirit of Mts.* 107 **eTN,** But he and Arth do not disagree about certain weather signs their mother had taught them when they were "shirt-tail boys," signs about Groundhog Day, for example, and the Ruling Days, the twelve days from the twenty-fifth of December to Old Christmas, each of which rules the weather of a month of the coming year. **1940** (1978) Still *River of Earth* 140 **KY,** I recollect it was Ruling Day in February, years ago. *Ibid* 223, The robins came back in February. . . The cold spells at Old Christmas and during the week Ruling Day fell were the only times I had need to put on my red woven coat. **1970** *NC Folkl.* 18.51, Weather on each of the ruling days, January 1–12, was sign of same sort of corresponding month. *Ibid,* The twelve Ruling Days contain important indications as to the future. **1986** *DARE* File **wNC** (as of 1912–20), This use of January 1–12 as *ruling days,* indicating the kind of weather to be expected in the respective months of the ensuing year, was known . . in my childhood. **2001** *NADS Letters* **sKY,** My mother (67 yrs old) has used the term ruling days ever since I was a boy. She is from southern KY, about 15 miles from the TN state line. The ruling days are the first 12 days after Christmas.

rullepolse n [Norw *rullepølse*] esp in Norw settlement areas Cf rolliche

A dish made of meat that is rolled, pressed, boiled, and cut into rounds.

1952 Tracy *Coast Cookery* 174 **ND,** Rullepolse . . beef or mutton flank . . pork . . Salt, pepper . . Ginger . . Allspice . . Onion . . Bouillon or stock. . . Cut the pork into strips. Lay them on the flank and season with the spices and chopped onion. Roll tightly, sew up with strong cord, and wind a cord around to hold it together. . . Simmer. . . Place under a heavy weight while cooling. Cut into thin slices for serving. **1966** *Badgerland* (Stoughton WI) 15 Oct 8/2, So the . . committee planned the menu of lefse, flotegrot (cream pudding), Norse cookies [etc]. . . Mrs. Anfin Moen suggested "Rulle Polse." **1966** Tufford *Scandinavian Recipes* 56, *Rullepølse* (Mutton Rolls)—Cut mutton flank into pieces. . . On each piece place smaller pieces of veal and pork. Season. . . Shape into rolls. Sew each roll firmly with cord. . . Make a solution of . . salt . . sugar . . water. . . [P]our over rolls. Store in cool place. When rolls are to

be served, take out of solution and boil until tender. . . When done, remove from kettle and put into a press for several hours. Slice thinly and serve with bread and butter. **1967–68** *DARE* (Qu. H43) Inf **MN39,** Rullepolse [FW: Inf has eaten—never made]; (Qu. H65, *Foreign foods favored by people around here*) Inf **OR4,** Rullepolse—beef and pork made into long rolls.

rullichie See rolliche

rullion n [Scots dial; cf *SND rullion* (at *rivlin* n. 4)]

1953 Randolph–Wilson *Down in Holler* 279 **Ozarks,** Rullion. . . A coarse, tough, unkempt person; I believe it is usually applied to unattractive women of low origin and loose morals. Pronounced to rhyme with *scullion.*

rullock n¹ [Var of *rowlock*]

An oarlock.

1827 Cooper *Red Rover* 1.118 (as of c1770), The chap in boots, who was for shoving his oar into another man's rullock. **1899** (1912) Green *VA Folk-Speech* 360, Rullock. . . Rowlock.

rullock n² |ˈrʌlək| Also *rulluck* [Cf *EDD rallock* "Of meat: a piece. . . A tattered garment; a rag"; perh pronc var of *relic*]

See quots.

1899 (1912) Green *VA Folk-Speech* 360, Rullock. . . A tattered garment; a rag. Rullucks. A form of *relics.* Odds and ends of dolls' clothes. Old clothes. "Rullucks and jullucks." **1932** *AmSp* 11.16 **eTX,** |ˈrʌləks| for *relics,* meaning old, ragged clothes. **1941** *LANE* Map 346 *(Rubbish)* 1 inf, **neMA,** Rubbish, sculch, rullocks.

rum n¹

1 Used as a generic, often derog, term for liquor—freq in combs such as *rum blossom* a pimple on the nose caused by excessive drinking; a nose having such pimples; *rum hound* a habitual heavy drinker; *rum joint* a saloon or speakeasy; *rum-pot* a drunkard; *rum runner* a smuggler of illegal liquor; for addit combs see quots. **scattered, but chiefly NEast, Mid Atl** See Map on p. 666 Cf **rum-dum** adj, **rum-dum** n, **rummy 1, stump rum**

1858 Holmes *Autocrat* 219 **MA,** Rum I take to be the name which unwashed moralists apply alike to the product distilled from molasses and the noblest juices of the vineyard. Burgundy . . is rum. Champagne . . is rum. Hock . . is rum. **1859** (1860) Creecy *Scenes South* 259, Cold water is just as valuable when applied externally as when taken internally; and rum-suckers and tobacco victims should know that fact. **1859** (1968) Bartlett *Americanisms* 181, *Groggery.* A place where spirituous liquors are sold and drank; a grog-shop. In the West, often called a Doggery or Dog-hole, and in New York a Rum-hole. *Ibid* 374, *Rum-Sucker.* An habitual drinker, a toper. **1873** Twain–Warner *Gilded Age* 302, Industry and economy soon enabled him to start a low rum shop in a foul locality. **1899** (1912) Green *VA Folk-Speech* 360, Rum-blossom. . . A pimple on the nose caused by excessive drinking. **1904** *DN* 2.427 **Cape Cod MA** (as of a1857), Rumhole. . . A liquor saloon. **1909** *DN* 3.415 **nME,** Rumhole. . . A liquor saloon. **1914** *DN* 4.79 **ME, nNH,** Rum. . . Generic name for all kinds of liquor. **1920** *NY Times* (NY) 19 Sept 6/1, The Detroit rum runners have had a good deal of notoriety. **1929** *AmSp* 4.440, Some names for intoxicants of various grades and potencies are: rum—a favorite blanket word of the old-time reformers, its use at times approaching slang. **c1940** Eliason *Word Lists FL* 11 **wFL,** Rum-head: A person who continually drinks bad liquor. **1965–70** *DARE* (Qu. DD12, . . *A person who drinks steadily or a great deal*) 11 Infs, **scattered Atlantic,** Rum hound; **NY94, TX5,** Rumpot; **SC10,** Rum drunker; **LA2,** Rum head; (Qu. DD32, *A person who sells illegal liquor*) 13 Infs, **esp NEast,** Rum runner; (Qu. DD21a, *General words . . for any kind of liquor*) Infs **DE7, MA11, 30, 72, NJ28, PA245, VT4,** Rum; **NY62,** Just plain rum; **MD15,** Demon rum; (Qu. X15, . . *Kinds of noses, according to shape or size*) Infs **MA40, NY233,** Rum blossom; **ID5,** Rum; (Qu. X53b, *An oversize stomach that results from drinking*) Infs **MA68, NY73,** Rum belly; **NJ2,** Rum tummy; [**DE5,** He would be a rummer;] (Qu. X59, . . *The small infected pimples that form usually on the face*) Inf **PA223,** Rum blossoms; (Qu. BB28, *Joking names . . for imaginary diseases:* "He must have the _____.") Inf **RI6,** Rum puckeroo; (Qu. DD13, *When a drinker is just beginning to show the effects of the liquor . . he's _____*) Inf **NY10,** Got a rum nose; (Qu. DD21c, *Nicknames for whiskey, especially illegally made whiskey*) Inf **AL16,** Rum—illegally made whiskey; (Qu. DD22, . . *Delirium tremens*) Inf **ME16,** Rum horrors; (Qu. DD24, . . *Diseases that come from continual* *drinking*) Inf **VA**15, Rum blossom; (Qu. DD30, *Joking names for a place where liquor is [or was] sold and consumed illegally*) Infs **CT**4, **ME**19, **NJ**47, **NY**70, Rum shop (*or hole, joint*); (Qu. DD34, *A party at which there is considerable drinking*) Infs **MD**36, **ME**6, **MA**11, 40, **NC**1, Rum party; **NY**37, Rum fest; **NJ**16, Rum suckers. **1968** McPhee *Pine Barrens* 60 **cNJ**, Fred Brown . . may be the only man in the pines who calls whiskey rum. **1968** *DARE* Tape **PA**81, [FW: From Inf's grandmother's 1903 journal:] Rum blossoms grow on the nose. . . They are produced by too much blood in the blood vessels. This is one of the bad results of alcohol! **1986** Pederson *LAGS Concordance*, 1 inf, **ceGA**, Rum—popskull or white lightning; 1 inf, **seAL**, Rum—homemade whiskey; moonshine; 1 inf, **nwFL**, Rum—moonshine; 1 inf, **swFL**, Rum hound—speaking of his father, an alcoholic.

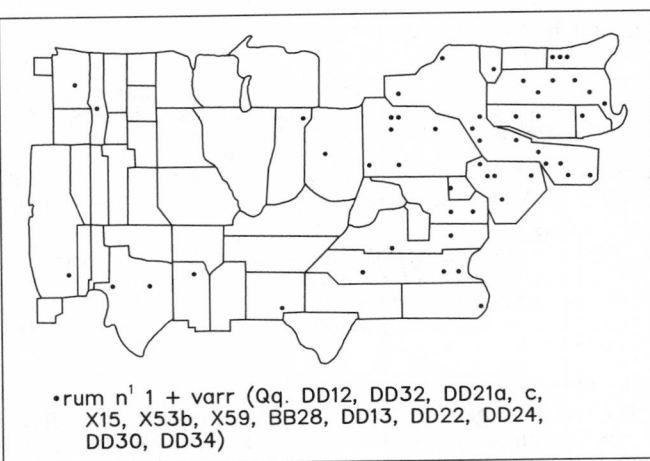

•rum n¹ 1 + varr (Qq. DD12, DD32, DD21a, c, X15, X53b, X59, BB28, DD13, DD22, DD24, DD30, DD34)

2 See **rummy 2.**

rum n² See **room**

rum n³ Also *rhum* [Varr of *rummy*] **NCent, PA** See Map
Any of var card games in which the object is to meld runs or flushes of three or more cards.
1910 *Sun* (N.Y.) 10 Sept. II. 3/1 [sic *OED2*—quot not found], The leader this season seems to be a new round game that is called rum. **1913** *Chicago Record-Herald* 2 Mar. v. 6/1 (*OED2*), I never found on one of them The kale I lose at rhum. **1965–70** *DARE* (Qu. DD35, . . *Card games*) Infs **IL**21, **IN**49, 80, **MI**49, 76, 109, **OH**56, Rum; **PA**94, 134, Five hundred rum; **OH**61, Contract rum; **IN**42, Keck rum; **PA**25, Royal rum; **PA**165, Shanghai rum. [11 of 13 Infs male]

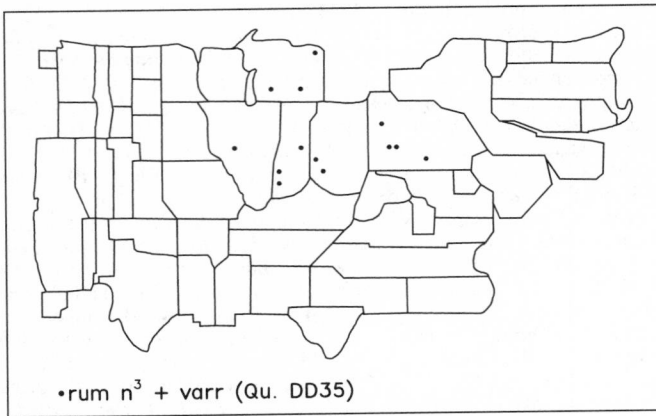

•rum n³ + varr (Qu. DD35)

rum'a'tis, rumatiz See **rheumatiz**

rumba, rumble See **rumpus**

rumbled up adj phr Also *rumbled* [Engl, Scots dial; cf *SND rummle* v., n.¹ (also *rumble*) I.7 "Also in Eng. dial. Vbl.n. *rumbling*, stirring, agitation, of water"; II.6 "anything confused or disordered, as a heap of articles"]
Jumbled; stirred up; also fig.
1968–69 *DARE* (Qu. Y38, *Mixed together, confused:* "The things in the drawer are all _____.") Inf **KY**51, **SC**64, Rumbled (up together);

(Qu. KK39, *Stirred up, upset:* "Because of the storm, the pond was all _____.") Infs **GA**84, Rumbled up. **2000** *NADS Letters* **MN**, All rumbled up—all stirred up (about something exciting or irritating). *Ibid* **cMS**, Rumbled up. Means messed up. I heard it used in my family for messed up hair (your hair is all rumbled up) but more often laundry (I was to fold the laundry after it finished in the dryer, and not let it get all rumbled up). I never heard it used for anything like an unmade bed or wadded up paper, though. **2001** *Ibid* **seKY**, Rumbled (up)—stirred up into a pile—my aunt uses this sometimes.

rum blossom See **rum** n¹ **1**

rumbunctious See **rambunctious**

rum cherry n [Because its fruit may be used to make or flavor alcoholic beverages; see quots] Cf **whiskey cherry**
=**black cherry.**
1822 Eaton *Botany* 411, [*Prunus*] *virginiana* . . wild cherry, rum cherry, cabinet cherry. **1908** Britton *N. Amer. Trees* 506, Wild cherry. . . This well-known tree, also called the Black, Cabinet, or Rum cherry, is abundant in mixed forests and neglected clearings. . . The fruit is used to some extent for making jellies and as a flavoring for alcoholic liquors. **1929** *Torreya* 29.150 **ME**, Prunus serotina, "Rum Cherry,"—rum was added and the cherries left in the bottle. **1939** Medsger *Edible Wild Plants* 48, Black Wild Cherry, or Rum Cherry. . . In years gone by, the fruits were much esteemed for flavoring rum and whisky, making what is known as "cherry bounce." **1967–69** *DARE* (Qu. I46, . . *Kinds of fruits that grow wild around here*) Inf **MA**68, Rum cherries—same as black cherries; **MA**72, Chokecherries, wild cherries or rum cherries.

rum-dum adj Also *rum-dumb, rum-dumm*
Stupid, apathetic, or confused with, or as if with, liquor.
1891 *Brooklyn Eagle* 11 Sept. 2/4 (*OED2*) **NYC**, Rum-dumb. . . stupid with continual drinking. **1922** Lewis *Babbitt* 99, Don't faint with surprise if some of those rum-dumm liars get one good swift poke from Mike. **1927** *DN* 5.461 [Underworld jargon], Rum-dum. . . Intoxicated sufficiently to be silly yet not enough to lose the power of locomotion. **1938** *AmSp* 13.156 [Airplane factory terms], Rum-dum. Stupid, blasé. **1939** Steinbeck *Grapes* 215, Can't get a word out of 'im. Jus' rum-dumb. **1944** *AmSp* 19.104 [Vocab of sailors], *Gassed up, gas-hound, gheed up, rumdum,* and *goofed up* are cognate and self-explanatory. **1956** Algren *Walk on the Wild Side* 35 **wTX**, Fritz was playing the fool for the same gang of cactus-headed rundums [sic] for whom he always played the fool. **1965–70** *DARE* (Qu. DD13, *When a drinker is just beginning to show the effects of the liquor . . he's* _____) Inf **PA**1, Rum-dum; (Qu. DD15, *A person who is thoroughly drunk*) Infs **MI**47, **MT**4, Rum-dum; (Qu. GG2, . . '*Confused, mixed up*': "So many things were going on at the same time that he got completely _____.") Infs **TX**71, **WA**9, Rum-dum; (Qu. HH13, *Expressions meaning that a person is not very alert or not aware of things:* "He's certainly _____.") Infs **GA**11, **MS**1, Rum-dum.

rum-dum n Also *rum-dumb*
1 also *rum-dummer:* An alcoholic; a stupid person. **scattered, but esp NEast, C Atl** See Map Cf **rummy 1, 2**
1891 *Brooklyn Eagle* 11 Sept. 2/4 (*OED2*) **NYC**, Rum-dumb. . . an habitual soak. **1939** *AmSp* 14.240 [Hotel slang], Rum-dumb. Person habitually stupid or vague from drink. **1942** Footner *MD Main* 98, There was old Charlie Lee . . who . . was a very untidy dresser and fond of his

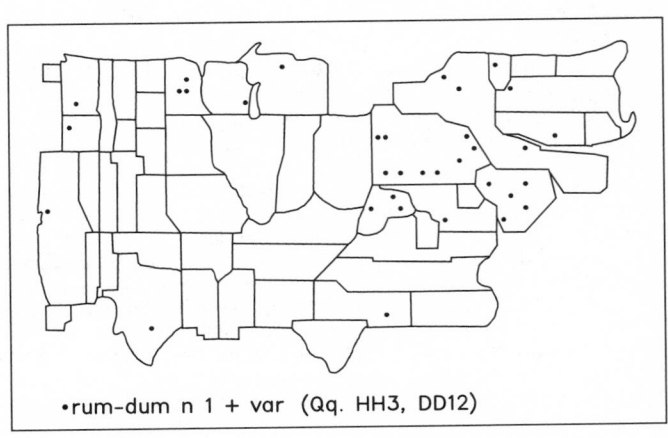

•rum-dum n 1 + var (Qq. HH3, DD12)

dram—a "rum-dum" as they say in Belair. **1965–70** *DARE* (Qu. HH3, *A dull and stupid person*) 21 Infs, **scattered, but esp NEast, C Atl**, Rum-dum; **MI**17, Rum-dum [FW sugg]; (Qu. DD12, . . *A person who drinks steadily or a great deal*) 12 Infs, **esp NEast, C Atl**, Rum-dum; **PA**177, Rum-dummer. **1979** Lewis *How to Talk Yankee* [29] **nNEng**, Rumdum . . a sot.

2 See quots.

1927 *AmSp* 2.389 [Vagabond argot], Rum-dumb is a condition of hopeless intoxication. **1968** *DARE* (Qu. DD24, . . *Diseases that come from continual drinking*) Inf **WV**2, Shakes; rum-dum.

rum-dumb adj See **rum-dum** adj

rum-dumb n See **rum-dum** n

rum-dumm See **rum-dum** adj

rum-dummer See **rum-dum** n 1

rum horrors See **horrors** 2

rum hound (or joint) See **rum** n¹ 1

rum mad adj phr
Fig: emotionally intoxicated.

1931 in 1996 Horton *Island Out of Time* 114 **Chesapeake Bay MD**, I am sixteen and they say that at that age you get rum mad over love.

rummage pickle n Cf **end-of-the-garden pickle, last-of-the-garden**
A relish of mixed vegetables; see quots.

1939 Wolcott *Yankee Cook Book* 293 **MA**, Rummage Pickles [Ingredients include green tomatoes, ripe tomatoes, green or red peppers, onions, cabbage, celery, cauliflower, sugar, vinegar, salt, pepper, mustard.] . . Put all vegetables through food chopper, add salt, let stand overnight and drain. Heat sugar, vinegar and spices to boiling; add vegetables. Simmer 5 minutes and seal. **1967** *DARE* (Qu. H57, *Tasty or spicy side-dishes served with meats*) Inf **MA**83, Rummage pickle—old-fashioned relish; green and red tomatoes, cabbage, celery, onions. **2000** *DARE* File—Internet **IL**, Rummage Pickle (Relish)—Green tomato, vinegar, cabbage, ripe tomato, onion, celery, brown sugar, sweet red pepper, salt, & ground mustard. A variation of this relish appeared in Comfort Magazine, Sept. 1931. . . The original recipe calls for celery root.

rummit See **runnet** 2

rummy n

1 An alcoholic; a habitual drinker. **chiefly NEast, C Atl** See Map

1850 Green *12 Days* 55 **NYC**, The court adjourned, and the rummies repaired to *another bar* to congratulate each other upon the success of the morning. **1907** *DN* 3.198 **seNH**, Rummy. . . A drunkard. **1922** *Lit. Digest* 30 Dec 32, The lying labels, proclaiming to the trusting rummies that the whiskey is "pure and unadulterated, soothing as mountain dew, guaranteed 110 proof," etc., are pasted on the hooch. **1930** *AmSp* 5.392 [Language of N Atl fishermen], Rummy. . . Anyone who is habitually drunk. **1934** *AmSp* 9.288 **PA** [Black student slang], Rummy. One who drinks intoxicants to excess. **1965–70** *DARE* (Qu. DD12, . . *A person who drinks steadily or a great deal*) 28 Infs, **chiefly NEast, C Atl**, Rummy. [24 of 28 Infs male, 15 young or mid-aged] **1986** Pederson *LAGS Concordance (Drunk)* 1 inf, **cAR**, Rummy—usually derelict type.

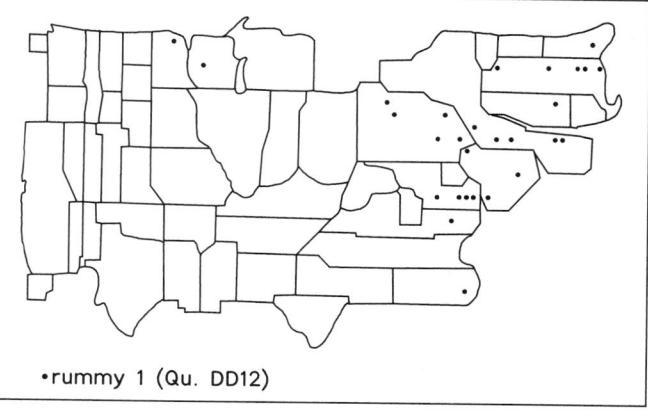

•rummy 1 (Qu. DD12)

2 also *rum:* A stupid person; an unlucky person; a sucker.
1911 in 1983 Truman *Dear Bess* 38 **MO**, I can sympathize with these western rummies now who can never raise a garden. Ours is a total failure. **1912** Ade *Knocking* 108, She extracted a promise from Cousin and several other Desperate Characters that they would come out into the Wilderness and give the Rummies a Touch of High Life. **1915** *DN* 4.202, Rummy, rum, weak-minded person. "Just see all them rummies a goin' to church." **1937** *New Yorker* 7 Aug 23, Most rummies never discover they have been rooked. **1968** *DARE* (Qu. HH3, *A dull and stupid person*) Inf **WI**57, Rummy.

rumpelkammer n [Ger "junk room"] **esp WI** Cf **kram** n
A storage closet or similar space in a house.
1948 *WELS Suppl.* **ceWI**, My mother would speak of the "Kram-kammer," also calling the same room a "Rumple-kammer" [sic]. **1950** *Ibid* **seWI**, A word for storage closet we use is rumpelkammer. Even our German girls to whom German is a foreign language use it. *Ibid* **seWI**, Rumpelkammer—place to hide things in a house. **1968** *DARE* (Qu. E22, *If a house is untidy and everything is upset* . . *"It's a _____!" or "It looks like _____."*) Inf **WI**13, Rumpelkammer. **1986** Pederson *LAGS Concordance (Junk room)* 2 infs, **AR, TX**, Rumpelkammer. **2000** *NADS Letters* **MI**, I grew up in the German speaking community of Frankenmuth, Michigan, in the late 1930s and early 1940s. . . [E]ach . . farm had—and still has—a Rumpelkammer, the small entry at the back of the house where the farmer . . would take off his dirty boots and soiled jackets to avoid getting the kitchen (to which the rumpelkammer opened) dirty. The rumpelkammer might also be the place to store milk pails and small utensils until they were needed the next day again.

‡rumpityfetida n [Euphem var of **asafetida**]
1944 *PADS* 2.21 **sAppalachians**, Rumpityfetida [ˈrʌmpɪtɪˌfɪtɪdɪ]: *n.* Asafetida—and a more polite word than the latter!

rumpot See **rum** n¹ 1

rump-sprung adj
Of a garment: stretched out of shape in the rear.
1967 *DARE* FW Addit **MO**, Rump-sprung [heard in conv]—a skirt stretched at the rump. **1984** Wilder *You All Spoken Here* 32 **Sth**, *Rump sprung:* A dress or trousers stretched out of shape across the rear. **1999** *DARE* File **ID** (as of c1970), My aunt bought a beautiful knit suit at a classy San Francisco store and was appalled when, after one wearing, the back of the skirt was stretched out and no longer hung straight. She exclaimed, "Why, it's rump-sprung!"

rumption See **ruction**

rumpus n Also *rumba, rumble* [Joc varr of *rump*] Cf **berumpus**
1968 *DARE* (Qu. X35, *Joking words for the part of the body that you sit on* . . *"He slipped and came down hard on his _____."*) Infs **IA**17, **VA**31, Rumpus; **GA**43, Rumba; **VA**13, Rumble. **1999** *DARE* File **cwCA** (as of c1955), When I was a child, kids would talk about falling down on their seater-rumpuses. I guess neither *seater* nor *rumpus* seemed enough by itself.

rum runner See **rum** n¹ 1

rum-sucker n
1 A **haircap moss** (here: *Polytrichum commune*). [See quot]
1892 *Jrl. Amer. Folkl.* 5.105 **NH**, *Polytrichum commune* . . rum-suckers. Stratham, N.H. [Footnote to *rum-sucker:*] So called from the supposed spirituous taste of the pasty mass of unripe spores.
2 See **rum** n¹ 1.

rum-tum-diddy See **rinktum tiddy**

run v
A Gram forms.
1 past: usu *ran;* also:
a *run,* rarely pronc-sp *ron.* *esp freq among speakers with gs educ or less*
1637 in 1871 MA Hist. Soc. *Coll.* 5th ser 1.247, They left me and runn. **1686** in 1878 *Ibid* 5th ser 5.128, [I] went and run the Line between us and Tho. Faxon. **1774** (1957) Fithian *Jrl. & Letters* 187 **CT**, On this side She waked her husband, who run to his Gun. **1800** (1907) Columbia Hist. Soc. *Records* 10.127 **PA**, The water run over the back of his horse, & into the top of his boots. **1859** (1931) Tuttle *CA Diary*

15.83 **WI**, I expected to see the whole [wagon] train smashed up as all run head long into the Platte. **1884** Smith *Bill Arp's Scrap Book* 78 **GA**, At the first crack of the whip they . . got loose and run away. **1903** *DN* 2.239 **seMO**, My clock run as well as ever after I put coal-oil through her. *Ibid* **Cape Cod MA** (as of a1857). **1905** *DN* 3.59 **eNE**. **1909** *DN* 3.365 **eAL, wGA**. **1909** *S. Atl. Qrly.* 8.44 **sSC coast** [Gullah], De buttah melt; eh ron een 'e yeye an' 'im yez. **1953** Atwood *Survey of Verb Forms* 20, The preterite *ran* . . predominates rather strongly in e. N.Y. and n. N.J.; it occurs in about half the communities of s. N. Eng. and Pa. Elsewhere it is more or less sharply limited by the form *run* . . predominates among the more old-fashioned informants in s. N. Eng. and among all the noncultured types in n. N. Eng. . . North and east of the Merrimack *ran* hardly occurs at all outside of cultivated speech. . . In general, south of the Potomac . . the form *ran* does not occur except in cultured speech. **1965–70** *DARE* (Qu. OO28a, *Talking about running: "John was so scared he _____ [all the way home]."*) 190 Infs, **widespread, but less freq Inland Nth**, Run; **CO**33, **IA**11, **IL**4, **OH**23, **TX**101, Run like hell (*or* a bat out of hell, a rabbit, a streak of lightning, scared) [Of all Infs responding to the question, 29% were gs educ or less; of those giving the responses *run, run like*, etc, 62% were gs educ or less.]; (Qu. II17, *If you happen to meet someone that you haven't seen for a while: "Guess who I _____ this morning."*) 75 Infs, **scattered**, Run across (*or* acrost, afoul of, into, onto, upon) [Of all Infs responding to the question, 25% were gs educ or less; of those giving the responses *run across*, etc, 41% were gs educ or less.] [Further exx throughout *DS*] **1966–69** *DARE* Tape AR51, They run that wolf little over an hour; **CA**100, He run up and got the shovel and come down; **LA**1, One of them run five and a half hours; **MA**22, He run the boarding house for all these ore teamsters; **MI**8, The cutter upset and the horse run away. **1975** Allen *LAUM* 2.24 **Upper MW** (as of c1950), The conflict between the school insistence upon historical *ran* and the powerful leveling tendency toward use of analogical *run* has led a rather high proportion of speakers to be uncertain about which form is "correct." . . *Run* as preterite . . connotes both lack of formal education and extreme conversational informality, sometimes only the second. Among all types the evidence for the use of *run* is found primarily in free conversation. **1990** Pederson *LAGS Regional Matrix* 242 **Gulf Region**, [For the preterite, 458 infs offered *ran*, 319 infs, *run*.]

b *runned.*   **chiefly Sth, S Midl**   Cf **-ed 2**

1843 (1916) Hall *New Purchase* 227 **IN**, He was so sker'd he didn't see where he runn'd. **1884** *Anglia* 7.253 [Black], To the regular forms of the Irregular verbs as used by the whites, the Negro adds the following forms of his own. . . *Pres.* run—*Past.* runned. **1899** Chesnutt *Conjure Woman* 17 **csNC** [Black], De gemman's hoss runned away. **1907** Mulford *Bar-20* 11 **West**, I runned into him on th' other side o' th' pass. **1909** *DN* 3.365 **eAL, wGA**, Run. . . Sometimes *runned* is heard in pret. and *pp*. "We lack to got runned over." **1937** in 1976 *Weevils in the Wheat* 86 **VA** [Black], We runned away and came to Hampton. **1953** Brewer *Word Brazos* 11 **eTX** [Black], He runned off from de plannuhtation time an' time again. **1955** Roberts *S. from Hell-fer-Sartin* 134 **seKY**, And he runned over there and tried to wake that other man up. **1965–70** *DARE* (Qu. P39a, *When a hunter or a dog finds a game animal and makes it start running . . he _____ it*) Inf **VA**55, Runned; (Qu. Y26b, *To walk very quietly: "The children filled their pockets and _____ out the back way."*) Inf **MO**16, Runned; (Qu. Y46a, *To get hurt with something sharp . . "He _____ a thorn into his hand."*) Inf **WA**17, Runned; (Qu. II17, *If you happen to meet someone that you haven't seen for a while: "Guess who I _____ this morning."*) Inf **NY**24, Runned onto; (Qu. KK53, *When one thing suddenly hits hard against something else: "He ran _____ into a car."*) Inf **TN**13, Runned; (Qu. OO28a, *Talking about running: "John was so scared he _____ [all the way home]."*) Infs **KY**21, 94, **MO**16, **VA**50, 54, Runned. **1966–70** *DARE* Tape AL1, But this water runned all the time; **MS**76, When the frog git out, he runned; **VA**55, My sister's son, he runned into a buoy. **1986** Pederson *LAGS Concordance* (*Principal parts of run* [preterit]) 14 infs, **coastal Gulf Region**, Runned (*or* runned away, etc). [9 infs Black]

c *ranned.*   Cf *doved* (at **dive 1**).

1986 Pederson *LAGS Concordance*, 1 inf, **seMS**, She ranned away. [Inf Black]

‡d *runded.*   Cf *drownded* (at **drown 3**), **-ed 1**

1896 Harris *Sister Jane* 139 **GA** [Black], De reason I ast . . was dat I run de [fortune-telling] kyards 'bout you . . , an' dey runded mighty quare.

2 past pple: usu *run;* also:

a *ran.*

1835 *S. Lit. Messenger* Jan 206, On a day, when the war of words had ran unusually high, there was a momentary . . quietude. **1852** *S. Qrly. Rev.* July 83, [Footnote:] He said his aide had ran off with his horse! **1862** Gatlin *Immortal Hero* 9 (*Montgomery Coll.*), "Merciful God," exclaimed Mr. Elmore. "Keelan, have you went to sleep on the road . . and has the train ran over you?" **1960** Criswell *Resp. to PADS 20* **Ozarks**, *Run*. . . He had run, the commonest form then and now. *Had ran* used only by somewhat illiterate people trying to be correct. **1965–70** *DARE* (Qu. OO28b, *Talking about running: "He was out of breath because he had _____ [so fast]."*) 185 Infs, **widespread**, Ran. **1990** Pederson *LAGS Regional Matrix* 242 **Gulf Region**, [*Run*. . . For the past participle, 75 infs offered *ran*, 360 infs *run*.]

b *runned.*   **esp Sth, S Midl**

1884 *Overland Mth.* (2d ser) 4.487 **sCA**, The strange new life into which Fate had led her footsteps on that Summer's afternoon, when she had "runned away." **1899** Chesnutt *Conjure Woman* 47 **csNC** [Black], He 'lowed Sandy had runned away. **1909** [see A1b above]. **1940** (1968) Haun *Hawk's Done Gone* 189 **eTN**, If I hadn't dodged out of the way he would have runned right smack-dab over me. **1954** *Harder Coll.* **cwTN**, Run. . . Past ppl: run, runned (Occ[asionally]). **1967** *DARE* Tape **TX**26, The wagonyard was runned and owned by Mr. Woody. **1969–70** *DARE* (Qu. OO28b, *Talking about running: "He was out of breath because he had _____ [so fast]."*) Infs **KY**94, **NC**61, Runned. **1986** Pederson *LAGS Concordance* (*Principal parts of run* [past participle]) 2 infs, **swGA, cwMS**, Runned; 1 inf, **csLA**, Runned a mile; 1 inf, **seLA**, Runned over. [All infs Black]

B Senses.

1 To pursue, chase; also fig.

1841 Catlin *Letters Indians* 1.219, On this journey we saw immense herds of buffaloes; and although we had no horses to *run* them, we successfully *approached* them on foot. **1843** (1940) Ruxton *Rocky Mts.* 197 **NY**, Indians and others . . kill deer or buffalo by running them on horseback. **1939** *Hall Coll.* **wNC**, I could hear the bear run 'em [=hunting dogs] and snap his teeth. *Ibid* **wNC**, I'll continue a story of a panther a-runnin' a feller. *Ibid* **wNC**, They haint one dog in a hundred that will run a panter. . . But then, pretty near any of 'em will run a wolf, though. **1944** *AmSp* 19.148, A Negro witness said, 'He run me with a knife.' My southern friends say that they would immediately understand this to mean, 'He chased me with a knife.' **1961** *McDavid Coll.* **OK**, A trashy dog will run anything. **1962** Fox *Southern Fried* 140 **SC**, I traded that hog and I got me a dog for the plain and simple reason that I can't go running no fox with no hog. **1965–70** *DARE* (Qu. P35b, *Illegal methods of shooting deer;* not asked in early QRs) Inf **MO**17, Run 'em here with dogs; **PA**168, Running them; **WI**22, Running with dogs; (Qu. P39a, *When a hunter or a dog finds a game animal and makes it start running . . he _____ it*) Infs **CA**95, **NC**63, **NY**123, 191, **VA**43, 64, 101, Ran; **CA**211, **IL**46, **MD**42, **NJ**41, **NY**1, 92, Runs; **TN**26, Run; **VA**55, Runned; **MO**5, **NY**219, Running; **KY**39, A-running; **NJ**10, Dog runs; (Qu. AA5, *If a woman seems to be going after one certain man that she wants to marry: "She's _____ him."*) Infs **OH**97, **VA**69, Running; **NJ**59, He's running her. **1966–69** *DARE* Tape AR15, You want to start 'em [=puppies] around about six months old with your old dogs that run fox; **DC**9, We don't want our hounds to run deer, although they will run deer if they get on 'em; **CA**89, You run this rabbit till he begin to get kind of tired; **CA**145, We ran a chipmunk down this log and he ran in this woodpecker hole; **FL**36A, She [=a cow] run me around and around and around and around that stump. I thought I never would get away from her. **1975** Gould *ME Lingo* 237, A hound dog *runs*, and if his nose is good he *runs* very well, as when he *runs* a rabbit. **1982** Ginns *Snowbird Gravy* 14 **nwNC**, Now, a gray fox, I have killed a few of them. 'Cause they're hateful to run, anyway. They just get in the bush just like a rabbit. Run around and around. The dogs can't run 'em.

2 To thrust or drive (a sharp object). [*OED2 run* v. 48.a, 1480 →] **chiefly Inland Nth, N Midl, West**   See Map   Cf **job** v² **1, stick**

1806 (1970) Webster *Compendious Dict.* 262, Run. . . pierce or stab. [*DARE* Ed: This sense does not appear in Webster's English model.] **1876** in 1983 *PADS* 70.49 **ce,sePA**, Brother John met with an accident today by falling on a fork and run the prong deep into his arm. **1902** *DN* 2.244 **sIL**, Run in. . . To pierce or prick, which words are not used. 'To run a needle or brier in the finger.' **1907** *DN* 3.226 **nwAR**, Run in. . . To pierce or prick. **1965–70** *DARE* (Qu. Y46a, *To get hurt with something sharp . . "He _____ a thorn into his hand."*) 246 Infs, **Inland Nth, N Midl, West**, Ran; 83 Infs, **chiefly Nth, N Midl, West**, Run; **WA**17, Runned; (Qu. Y46b, *To get hurt with something sharp . . "She _____ herself with a needle."*) [Infs **OH**76, **PA**190, Ran;]

CO20, **NJ**28, Ran a needle (in herself); **NY**10, Run a needle in her finger; **SC**58, Run a needle in her hand.

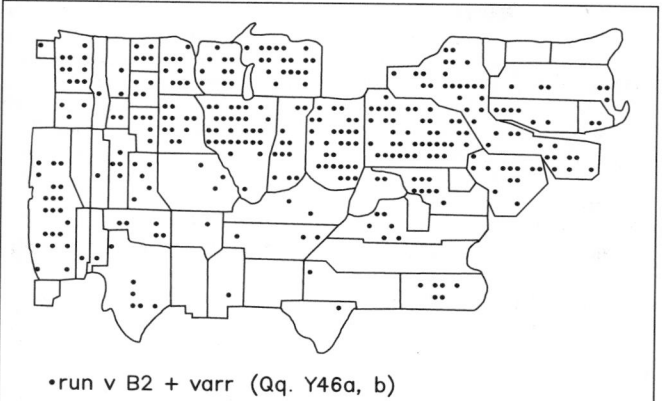

•run v B2 + varr (Qq. Y46a, b)

3 To drive (one), cause (one) to be (crazy, out of one's mind, etc.). [*OED2* run v. 44.b, 1621] **Sth, S Midl** Cf **run-mad**

1845 *Amer. Whig Rev.* 2.180, I must go down and stop that, or it'll run me crazy sure enough. **1861** *S. Lit. Messenger* 32.190, Andrew Jackson Roselius, carry that fly-brush b-a-c-k into the dining room—you children will run me crazy. **1899** (1912) Green *VA Folk-Speech* 361, That sort of thing would run me mad. **1924** (1926) Vollmer *Sun-Up* 13 **wNC**, Neither one of us is got 'nough [learning] to run us crazy. **1928** Peterkin *Scarlet Sister Mary* 288 **SC**, It'll run you crazy if it don' kill you. **1940** Stuart *Trees of Heaven* 20 **eKY**, Some say whiskey will run a man crazy. **1942** *Sat. Eve. Post* 22 Aug 12, Fink's meanness had run his wife out of her head. *Ibid* 42, Pap . . whose slippers air them that's run mommy crazy? **1942** in 1944 *ADD* **cAR**, I should think it would run you crazy. **1986** Pederson *LAGS Concordance,* 1 inf, **cnAL**, It'll run you nuts; 1 inf, **cwMS**, Almost run me nuts; 1 inf, **nwMS**, Run me plumb crazy; 1 inf, **ceTX**, He like to run me crazy.

4 To graze (livestock); to provide grazing for (livestock). [*OED2* run v. 43.c, 1812 →]

1907 White *AZ Nights* 76, I didn't see them any more after that until I'd hit the Lazy Y, and had started in runnin' cattle in the Soda Springs Valley. **1942** Whipple *Joshua* 195 **UT** (as of c1860), His sheep were American Rambouillets, mostly 'run for wool'. **1966** Barnes–Jensen *Dict. UT Slang* 36, *Run cattle* . . care for, range or graze cattle. "I run my cattle in the Henry mountains." **1966–70** *DARE* Tape **CA**135, We don't run horses on the range anymore; **MD**26, [FW:] How many cattle did you have? [Inf:] Oh, I run about thirty, thirty-five . . around there; **SD**8, I've never lost in excess of two percent in one year, . . so it's a safe place to run cattle; **TX**24, Of course they tromped out a whole lot more country that way than they do this way, and your country wouldn't run as many sheep; **TX**69, He learned . . that it was possible to run sheep and cattle on the same land, successfully; **TX**100, We have a few people that run two, three hundred head cattle; **WA**8, We run livestock for a few years. **1981** *KS Qrly.* 13.2.70, *Run cattle* . . to be in the cattle ranching business. **1986** Pederson *LAGS Concordance,* 1 inf, **cwGA**, We run cows; 1 inf, **cLA**, I've run cows; 1 inf, **ceMS**, Used to run cattle; 1 inf, **csTX**, How many head of cattle do you run?

5 To drive or herd (livestock).

1916 *DN* 4.348 **cTX** (as of 1896), *Run*. . . To drive (cattle), not necessarily fast. **1929** Dobie *Vaquero* 13 **TX**, When we gathered cattle, we said we were on a "cow hunt," a "cow work," a "work," or a "cow drive," or maybe we said we were out running cattle. **1929** *AmSp* 5.74 **NE** [Cattle country talk], To "run cattle" is to change them from one range or pasture to another, as "It's a good day to run 'em over to the winter range." **1937** *Hall Coll.* **wNC**, Our dog has been teached to run the cattle. **1958** Blasingame *Dakota Cowboy* 107 **SD**, I got on him and followed the stampede. We ran steers and horses the rest of the night.

6 To go along (a gill net, **trotline**, trapline, or the like) checking for captured fish or animals; broadly, to set up and maintain (a **trotline**, trapline, etc.).

1880 *Harper's New Mth. Mag.* 60.855 **Chesapeake Bay**, The boatman . . turns directly back and "runs the net"—passing the cork line through the hands—readily detecting the presence of the fish. . . The shad, whenever found, are "ungilled" and thrown into the boat, and the net drops away again. *Ibid* 856, The net is "run" twice or three times

and is then taken up. **1938** Burman *Blow for a Landing* 274 **MS**, Toward evening, when he rowed out on the misty river to run his lines, she would sit in the bow, rolling the bread balls that served as bait. **1942** Faulkner *Go Down* 222 **MS**, They were swampers: gaunt, malaria-ridden men appearing from nowhere, who ran trap-lines for coons. **1949** Faulkner *Knight's Gambit* 81 **MS**, Didn't you ever run a trotline, a trotline right at your camp? You don't paddle, you pull the boat hand over hand along the line from one hook to the next. **1950** *Chicago Daily Tribune* (IL) 3 Aug sec 1 6/4, A few years ago when farm boys found it profitable to run lines of traps to catch foxes they could get a fair price for pelts. **1954** *Harder Coll.* **cwTN**, *Run a trot*. . . To place a trot-line . . in a stream; to take fish off a trot-line. **1967–68** *DARE* (Qu. P13, . . *Ways of fishing . . besides the ordinary hook and line*) Inf **LA**40, Set lines—you put 'em out, tie them to something, then you go run the lines; **MO**12, Limb line is just a piece of a branch off of a tree, stuck into the side at the bank with your line on it, and you put those in in the evening about dusk, then you run 'em during the night or early in the morning. **1976** Warner *Beautiful Swimmers* 148 **eMD**, The actual running of the trotlines is not difficult. . . But the preparation or laying and relaying and baiting and rebaiting of the lengthy lines is hard and messy work. Given the choice, most crabbers prefer to work with pots. **1998** *DARE* File **nWI** (as of c1960), In the evenings they would often come in to supper talking about having run their traplines, i.e. having gone out to check the traps and bring in whatever fur-bearing animals had been caught. **1999** *NADS Letters* **seMI** (as of 1940s), We used the term "to run a trapline" to mean that we regularly placed a series of traps in a given waterway rather than the actual checking of the traps. *Ibid* **ceTX**, Run some crab traps. . . I always inferred it meant to 'lay down' or 'put,' but you are right in that I've heard people use it to also mean to check on the item in question. *Ibid* **nwTN**, I can attest common usage of "run a trotline" and "run traps", both meaning to check either contraption to see if you've caught anything, from the mid-1950's to the present in northwest Tennessee. In addition, the act of setting out a trotline was also referred to as "running a trotline." *Ibid* **ceMS** (as of 1940s), "Running a trotline" meant to establish it (put it in place) and/or to tend it. *Ibid* **cMI** (as of c1950), Running a trapline . . was like having a herd of milking cows. . . One had to do it every day, day after day.

7 in phr *run a set:* To perform the figures of a dance. **sApalachians**

1930 *VA Qrly. Rev.* 6.241, We set by the fire whilst they run a set or two, then Sally leaned over to me and says, 'Abe, why can't we run a set too?' . . So we run a set. **1942** (1971) Campbell *Cloud-Walking* 123 **KY**, The young folks run sets till daybreak and then the crowd broke up. **1953** *PADS* 19.13 **sAppalachians**, *Run a set.* . . Used in reference to folk dance or square dance. "When John's old Ned gets tuned up we'll run a set." **1955** Ritchie *Singing Family* 53 **seKY**, Soon I was playing for the dancing. They'd say, "Balis, Sal said for me to tell you we aim to run some sets tonight at the stir-off. Bring your bucket and your fiddle!"

8 also with *up:* To plow (land); to cultivate (a crop).

1941 Ward *Holding Hills* 72 **IA**, One year I visited him on the Fourth; in the morning he was running for the "third and last" time some tall corn close to the house. [Footnote to *running:*] The common word is "plowing" corn, but we also say "running" it and we understand the old word "cultivating." **1969** *NC Folkl.* 17.31 **wNC**, The cultivator was distinguished from the *hill-turner,* used to break ground, and from the *single-foot,* the plow used to *run-up* ground. **1986** Pederson *LAGS Concordance,* 1 inf, **ceAR**, Run the middles (in plowing); 1 inf, **neTX**, Running middles.

9 in var phrr (see below): To come across, meet unexpectedly. Note: The combs *run into* and *run across* are widespread and std. Cf **afoul of**

a *run up with.* **chiefly Sth**

1884 *Anglia* 7.270 **Sth, S Midl** [Black], *To run up wid* = to meet. **1929** Wolfe *Look Homeward* 478 **NC**, You never know who you'll run up with on a train. **1955** *PADS* 23.42 **e,cSC, eNC, seGA**, I . . *ran up with* . . him. **1966** [see **B9c** below]. **1966–67** *DARE* (Qu. II17, . . "*Guess who I _____ this morning.*") Infs **GA**7, **SC**34, Ran up with. **1968** *DARE* Tape **GA**35, Five and a half to six feet normally's about as big as they [=diamondback rattlesnakes] get. Of course, sometimes you run up with one longer than that. **1969** *DARE* FW Addit **cwNC**, I run up with him in town—meet, run into. **1986** Pederson *LAGS Concordance (I ran across him)* 8 infs, **Gulf Region**, Run up with him (*or* people, etc.).

b *run onto, ~on to; rarely ~on.* **scattered, but more freq Nth, N Midl**

1902 Wister *Virginian* 18 **WY,** Meet a man once and you're sure to run on to him again. **1941** *LANE* Map 422 *(I ran across him)* 22 infs, **esp nNEng,** (Ran) onto. **1960** Criswell *Resp. to PADS* 20 **Ozarks,** *(If you happened to meet someone that you hadn't seen for a while: "Guess who I _____ this morning!")* Run onto. **1966** Dakin *Dial. Vocab. Ohio R. Valley* 2.218, The third most common expression [after *run into* and *run across*] is *run on to*—rarely *run on*. *Run on to* is in common use along the Ohio River from the Scioto to Pennsylvania but is extremely rare in the interior counties or elsewhere in this state. *Run on to* is fairly common again in Indiana west of the Whitewater Valley—but does not appear around Evansville or Indianapolis—and is the most common expression in Illinois between the Wabash and the Kaskaskia. South of the Ohio River *run on to* is rare. **1966–68** *DARE* (Qu. II17, *If you happen to meet someone that you haven't seen for a while: "Guess who I _____ this morning."*) Inf **OH**44, Ran onto; **NY**24, **ND**1, Run(ned) onto. **1967–69** *DARE* Tape **TX**24, I run on to him, oh, thirty years later, I say, "Tank, you remember?" **MA**30, I was looking through Shakespeare and . . I run onto that expression very similar. **1969** *DARE* FW Addit **VT,** Guess who I run onto. **1986** Pederson *LAGS Concordance (I ran across him)* 2 infs, **TN,** Onto him; 1 inf, **ceAR,** Run onto—met by chance; 1 inf, **cwAR,** Ran onto you; 1 inf, **csTX,** A pilot I ran onto.

c *run up on, ~ upon.* **chiefly Sth, S Midl**

1941 *LANE* Map 422 *(I ran across him)* 1 inf, **ceMA,** (Ran) upon; 1 inf, **cVT,** Ran upon—perhaps affected. **1966** Dakin *Dial. Vocab. Ohio R. Valley* 2.220, Kentucky has in contrast [to *run on to*] its own expression with *run—run upon*—which is not used north of the Ohio. This expression which is sometimes pronounced *'run ,up 'on* and sometimes *,run 'up ,on,* is used by some older speakers in the Bluegrass in addition to other expressions, and in the eastern Knobs and the northern Mountains as the only expression attested. Farther south in eastern Kentucky one speaker says *run up to* and another says *run up with*. *Run upon* is also used in the Pennyroyal-Purchase area on both sides of the Cumberland and Tennessee Rivers. **1966–70** *DARE* (Qu. II17, . . *"Guess who I _____ this morning."*) Infs **GA**9, **KY**85, **TX**98, Run up on. **1967–69** *DARE* FW Addit **Okefenokee GA,** *Run up on*—meet unexpectedly; **LA**6, *To run up on*—to find accidentally, to "come across" something. "I was looking for something else and run up on 'em"; **neNC,** "I run up on a deer"—man from Currituck Co. **1986** Pederson *LAGS Concordance (I ran across him)* 36 infs, **Gulf Region,** Run up on him (*or* them, etc); 7 infs, Run (*or* ran) upon him (*or* them, etc).

d *run (up) against.*

1941 *LANE* Map 422 *(I ran across him)* 14 infs, **scattered, but more freq nNEng,** Ran against (*or* agin); 6 infs, Ran up against (*or* agin). [4 infs call it old-fashioned or rare.]

e *run up to.*

1966 [see **B9c** above]. **1986** Pederson *LAGS Concordance,* 1 inf, **seGA,** Run up to him = ran into him.

10 To apply (a brand); to use a **running iron** to make or alter (a brand); also fig. **West**

1885 Siringo *TX Cowboy* 85, The way I would go about it would be to rope and tie down one of the longeared fellows and after heating the straight piece of round, iron bolt, in the brush or "cow-chip" fire, "run" my brand on his hips or ribs. **1894** *McClure's Mag.* July 101 **West,** [The brand] is simply drawn, or "run" upon the hide, using a long, sharp-pointed, hot iron rod for a pencil; and those so made are called "running brands." **1897** Lewis *Wolfville* 179 **AZ,** 'That's straight,' says Dave Tutt, 'you-alls can't run no brand on melodies.' **1920** Hunter *Trail Drivers TX* 298, A "running iron" is a branding iron made of a straight piece of iron with a curve at one end. This end is heated red hot and the branding artist is thus enabled to "run" any letter he wishes to put on the side of the animal. **1931** *AmSp* 7.120 **eID,** To *run a brand* is to disguise it by branding over it. **1939** in Lib. of Congress *Amer. Memory: WPA Life Hist.* (Internet) **TX,** That was his iron, and nobody else run it 'til he went in partners with old Col. Jot Gunter. **1967** *DARE* Tape **TX**24, [FW:] If you're branding the cows, . . what did you do just besides run the brand on 'em? [Inf:] Well, we run the brand on 'em, castrate the bulls. Earmarked 'em. . . Past time, a whole lot of these old-time cow thieves burn those brand, . . turn 'em into something else. [FW:] And run 'em, yeah. [Inf:] They call it running a brand. Some old boy figured out, made a five-pointed star. . . a decent-looking five-pointed star out of that XIT.

11 also with *on* or *upon:* To denigrate; tease; to make fun of; hence vbl n *running upon*.

1828 Webster *Amer. Dict., To run on.* . . To press with jokes or ridicule; to abuse with sarcasms. **1835** (1927) Hone *Diary* 1.151 **NYC,** This is a club . . where they sup, drink . . and run each other good-

humoredly. **1852** Baldwin *Southern & SW Sketches* 137 **AL,** He is a quiet, good-natured, inoffensive sort of chap—one of those who will stand "running upon" as long, if not longer, than most of men, but who is a perfect "Bengal tiger" when his passions are once aroused. **1873** (1891) Holley *My Opinions* 411, 'But,' says I, not wantin' to run anybody to thier [sic] backs, 'she thought it was her spear to marry.' **1905** *DN* 3.17 **cCT,** *Run* or *run on*. . . To make a butt of. **1912** Green *VA Folk-Speech* 361, *Run*. . . To harrass [sic]; to make a butt of. "The other boys are always running that one." "You ought not to run him like that."

run n

1 Any of var types of watercourses, as:

a A small stream. [nEngl dial; cf *EDD run* sb. 26] **scattered, but chiefly wPA, OH, WV, MD** See Map Cf **branch 1, brook, creek** n[1] **B2, drain** n[1] **C2**

[**1605** in 1843 *MA Hist. Soc. Coll.* 3d ser 8.146 **ME,** Searching up in the island, we saw it [=a pond] fed with a strong run.] **1634** in 1940 *AmSp* 15.386 **VA,** From the runn that falleth down by the Easter side of a peece of land knowne by the name of the woodyard. **1703** in 1894 Providence RI Rec. Comm. *Early Rec.* 5.179, The said ffifty acres of land . . is at the head of a Run of Water which Runneth through Timothy Sheldon his land on which he now liveth. **1800** (1907) Columbia Hist. Soc. *Records* 10.117 **PA,** Joe. . . said they had liked to have been lost in Pohick run on the other side of Alexandria—Saw a horse near Shore that had been drowned there. **1818** in 1824 Knight *Letters* 106 **KY,** They here call a river, a run. **1843** (1916) Hall *New Purchase* 79 **IN,** He lives rite fornence the tan house over the run. **1899** (1912) Green *VA Folk-Speech* 360, *Run*. . . A small stream of water running in one direction; a rivulet; a brook. **1908** Palmer *Life Palmer* 277 **neMA,** With us. . . that which runs swiftly a part of the year, and shows a dry bed for the remainder we fittingly call a run. **1917** *DN* 4.399 **neOH,** *Run*. . . In accordance with the differing topography from that of Indiana [*DARE* Ed: cf quot 1912 at **1c** below], *run* in N.E. Ohio connotes a living stream. Witness such names as Furnace Run, Boston Run, Robinson Run, streams in Summit Co. Also W. Va., Ky. **1929** *AmSp* 5.123 **ME,** A small brook was a "run." **1933** *AmSp* 8.1.51 **Ozarks,** *Run*. . . A small stream, a spring branch. Generally used in connection with a specific name, as Puckett's Run, Starbuck's Run, etc. **1942** Footner *MD Main* 36, In Maryland speech "branch" is an inlet from tidewater while "run" is the running stream that empties into it. **1945** *CA Folkl. Qrly.* 4.320 **CO** [Mining terms], *Run:* Creek. **1949** Kurath *Word Geog.* 13, The line between Northern *brook* and Midland *run*, reflecting a settlement boundary, is rather sharply defined, but the Midland *run* has acquired currency in the northern counties of Pennsylvania. *Ibid* 32, *Run* appears in the names of many small streams throughout the North Midland, so that even those who no longer use *run* as a common noun have occasion to refer to a particular stream in the neighborhood as *the run*. **1958** *Resp. to PADS 29* **cwPA,** We also have always referred to a small stream of water as a "run", and throughout Western Pennsylvania all little streams go by such names as "Slippery Rock Run", . . yet in Cleveland, Ohio, the people thought that was a strange way to refer to a "brook". **1965–70** *DARE* (Qu. C1, . . *A small stream of water not big enough to be a river*) 69 Infs, **scattered, but chiefly wPA, OH, WV, MD,** Run; **GA**80, Spring run; **OH**87, Wildcat run; (Qu. C4a) Inf **NC**49, Old runs; (Qu. C4b) Inf **PA**184, A run into lake of fresh water; **OH**26, Lake has run of fresh water. **1995** *NY Times* (NY) 11 July sec A 14/6 **VA,** One stream, Indian Gap Run, burbles 100 feet from the . . bungalow.

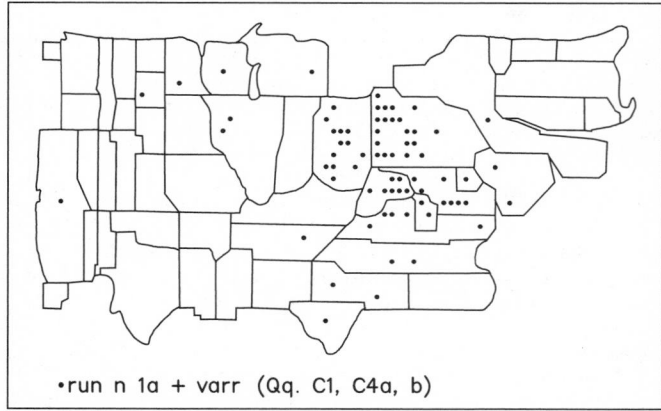

•run n 1a + varr (Qq. C1, C4a, b)

b A channel of water in a swamp or tidal flat. **esp seGA, FL** Cf **drain** n[1] **C4**

1651 in 1940 *AmSp* 15.400 **VA**, To the Maine Swamp Upon the head of Ware river and down the said swamp runn and river. **1926** *AmSp* 1.417 **Okefenokee GA**, Hyere the lake [scratching a diagram on the ground], an' hyere's a little run [Footnote: Channel]—goes out erbout thirty yards broad. **1939** [see **1c** below]. **1954** *Living Wilderness* Autumn 4 **Okefenokee GA**, Waterscapes . . covered with . . maiden cane and purple bladderwort, impassible except through "runs" or alligator trails. **1966** *Fishing World* 13.6.51 **FL**, On falling tide, always pay close attention to any "runs" or sloughs which are slightly deeper than surrounding flats, and which the fish might use as avenues to deep water. **1966–68** *DARE* Tape **FL**19, They [=snakes] came . . through our garden and onto a little run-like, was a little farther down, with the trees . . and brush in it; **GA**30, I've saw 'em [=fork-tailed kites] setting outside of these runs, in the swamp. . . where the water runs.

c infreq *runway*: A valley or depression between hills; a swale or marshy area; a channel or ravine cut by water, whether containing water or not.   Cf **coulee 1, drain** n[1] **C3**

1663 in 1940 *AmSp* 15.386 **VA**, Thence over a small run or Bottom and a ridge. **1719** *Ibid*, Beginning on the run or Swamp . . South . . to the head of the southern runn or the meadow. **1912** *DN* 3.588 **wIN**, *Run*. . . A slight depression or valley. The term is not applied to a stream of water. **1917** Garland *Son Middle Border* 92 **IA**, It was an unpainted square cottage and stood bare on the sod at the edge of Dry Run ravine. **1937** *Hall Coll.* **wNC**, Run—"a sort of marshy place; any kind of little stream." *Ibid*, "Drains or runs"—"a drain is a soft place in bottom-land where water [collects]." **1939** *LANE* Map 29 (*Meadow; swale*), Swale and *run* usually denote a more or less swampy and rough depression in a meadow or field, in which water gathers or through which it drains off. . . 1 inf, **seCT**, *Run*, a narrow valley; 1 inf, **neMA**, *Swale = run*; *swale*, more 'high-toned'; 1 inf, **seNH**, *Run*, in a meadow; 1 inf, **sME**, *Run*, a narrow strip of flat land along a brook; 1 inf, **sME**, *Run*, fresh grass land between hills; 1 inf, **sME**, *Swale = run*; 1 inf, **wME**, *Run*, a small valley on a hillside; 1 inf, **csME**, *Swale, run*, drier than a meadow; 1 inf, **seME**, *Swale = run = bog*. *Ibid* Map 37 (*Gully, washout*), The fieldworkers were instructed to record terms for 'a channel cut by a stream of water in a field or across a road.' . . *Run*, [is] commonly used both of a washout and of a permanent drain in a field or meadow. . . Instead of *run*, one informant [**sME**] uses *runway*. **1960** Hall *Smoky Mt. Folks* 59, *Run*: a marshy place or small stream. **1966–68** *DARE* (Qu. C21, *A deep place cut in sloping ground by running water*) Infs **ME**5, **PA**92, Run. **1973** Allen *LAUM* 1.235 (as of c1950), *Coulee*. . . dry [run] [12 infs, 11 **seMN, nwIA**].

2 An enclosed area for domestic animals or fowl to feed or range.   [*OED2 run* sb. 21.b, 1856 →]   Cf **lot** n **1a, pound** n[2] **1**

1884 Roe *Nature's Serial Story* 49 **seNY**, Fowls are restricted to a narrow yard or run. **c1933** in 2000 *DARE* File, Rath Meat Packing Company, Cantilevered Hog Run, Sycamore St. . . Waterloo, Black Hawk County, IA. **1933** Rawlings *South Moon* 186 **nFL**, Piety and Kezzy leaned over the edge of the hog-run on an afternoon in a late November. **1938** Burman *Blow for a Landing* 135 **MS**, And right out there by that live oak, we'll have the chicken run and the stable. **1954** (1955) Grau *Black Prince* 39 **eTN**, The people prefer pork. Each family keeps enough razorbacks in a run of bark palings. **1966** Dakin *Dial. Vocab. Ohio R. Valley* 2.84 **KY**, Hog run . . used once in the Bluegrass. **1967–70** *DARE* (Qu. M13, *The space near the barn with a fence around it where you keep the livestock*) Inf **MN**2, Barn run; **MA**75, Cow run; (Qu. M14, *The open area around or next to the barn*) Inf **MN**2, Cow run; **GA**19, Run; **PA**135, Run for the animals; (Qu. M15, *The place outdoors where pigs are kept*) Inf **MD**31, Hog run; **HI**2, Pig run; **GA**19, Run; (Qu. M16, *The small shelter for a hen that can be moved about from place to place*) Inf **NY**9, Chicken run; run; (Qu. M17, *A building where chickens or hens are kept*) Infs **CA**7, **HI**2, Chicken run; (Qu. M22, . . *Kinds of buildings . . on farms*) Inf **WI**65, Turkey run. **1973** Allen *LAUM* 1.188 **Upper MW** (as of c1950), Shelter and enclosure for hogs and pigs. . . hog run [2 infs]. *Ibid* 189, Enclosure only. . . hog run [1 inf]. **1975** Gould *ME Lingo* 237, *Run*. . . A dog will have an enclosure which is a *run*. **1986** Pederson *LAGS Concordance*, 2 infs, **AL**, Chicken run; 1 inf, **nwAL**, Hog run—large area.

3 A stampede (of cattle).

1903 (1965) Adams *Log Cowboy* 38 **West**, This herd is breaking into trail life nicely. If we'll just be careful with them now for the first month, and no bad storms strike us in the night, we may never have a run the entire trip. **1920** Hunter *Trail Drivers TX* 179 (as of c1880), We had our first stampede in the Blue Mounds country, north of Fort Worth, and from there on it was a run night after night, with but short intermissions.

4 See quot.

1984 *MJLF* 10.155 **cnWI**, *Run*. The distance between the runners on a sleigh, its width. "An eight foot run". [Used by] 2nd, 3rd [generations].

5 A trapline.   Cf **run** v **B6**

1999 *NADS Letters* **PA**, As I recall, trappers (mink, muskrat, etc.) in the mountains around Johnstown, PA, used to talk about *run* as a noun ("I set a run" or "I need to check my run") indicating a series of traps set along a known path [or] creek.

6 also *running, run-off*; In moonshining: a single cycle of distillation; the finished product.   **esp Sth, S Midl**

1934 Carmer *Stars Fell on AL* 41, "Reckon you inherited that charred keg," he said. "Been in there three months," said Henry. "My own run. Have one, perfesser?" **1953** *PADS* 19.13 **sAppalachians**, *Run-off* . . A batch of illicit liquor. "They always give a signal when they make a run-off." **1968** *Foxfire* 2.3.101 **nGA** [Stilling terms], A "Run"—an expression meaning to run the contents of the still through the whole operation once. Gave rise to expressions like, "There's gonna be a runnin' tomorrow," "He'll make us a run," etc. **1974** Maurer–Pearl *KY Moonshine* 124, *Run*. . . A cycle of whiskey. **1974** Dabney *Mountain Spirits* xxiv **sAppalachians**, *Run*: One whiskey distilling cycle. "We're going to have a run today." **1982** Slone *How We Talked* 69 **eKY** (as of c1950), *A run off*—the whole process of cooking the mash and collecting the finished product, the whiskey. **1984** Wilder *You All Spoken Here* 137 **Sth**, *Run*: A moonshiner makes a run when he completes a single distilling operation—when he fills, or charges, his still pot with the proper amount of fermented mash and converts the mash into booze.

7 in phr *hard run of stumps*: =*a hard row of stumps* (at **row 3**).

1954 *Harder Coll.* **cwTN**, *Hard run of stumps*. . . A sequence of misfortunes.

8 with *the*; also *the rush*: See quot.

1996 Horton *Island Out of Time* 20 **Chesapeake Bay MD**, A great wave has been building. It usually starts in April, down in the shallow coastal bays and sounds of the Carolinas, rolling up through the Chesapeake, cresting throughout Tangier Sound by mid-May, reaching nearly to New England before it is spent. It is called in these parts simply "the run," or "the rush."

run against See **run** v **B9d**

runagate n Also *runnygade* [Engl dial; *OED2 runagate* sb. 3 "A vagabond, wanderer; a run-about"; 1547 →]
A gossiping woman; a gadabout.
1895 *DN* 1.393 **cwIN**, *Runagate*: woman who neglects her household affairs to go gossiping about the neighborhood. [**1927** *AmSp* 3.139 **eME**, *Runnygade*.] **1968** *DARE* (Qu. Y29a, *To 'go out' a great deal, not to stay at home much:* "She's . . _____.") Inf **PA**134, [A] runagate; **OH**48, [A] runnygade.

runago See **running go**

run-a-mile n [Cf *SND rin-a-mile* (at *rin* v. B.1.(4)(i)) 1930 →]
A hide-and-seek game.
1891 *Jrl. Amer. Folkl.* 4.227 **Brooklyn NYC**, *Run a mile*. The boy who is "it" runs from one street corner to another, and while he runs, the others go hide. The first boy spied is "it," unless he can get in and touch the base before the spy. **1940** Mencken *Happy Days* 29 **Baltimore MD**, Every boy knew it as familiarly as he knew the rules of run-a-mile or catty. **1969** *DARE* (Qu. EE13a, *Games in which every player hides except one, and that one must try to find the others*) Inf **NY**126, Run-a-mile; (Qu. EE16, *Hiding games that start with a special, elaborate method of sending the players out to hide*) Inf **PA**200, Run-a-mile. [Both Infs old]

run-an(d)-go See **running go**

run a rig on See **rig** n[2] **1**

runaround n

1 also *run-round*: A swelling or infection in a finger, esp surrounding the nail.   **scattered, but chiefly Sth, S Midl, SW** See Map on p. 672   Cf **ring-around 1**

1857 *Knickerbocker* 49.97, There comes us a 'run-round' on the end of our pen-finger. **a1872** Talmage *Sermons* (1st ser) 224 **NJ**, Some hypochondriac with a run-around or a hang-nail. **1899** (1912) Green *VA Folk-Speech* 361, *Runaround*. A disease of the finger where the inflammation *runs around* the nail. **1913** London *Valley of Moon* 352, His finger was hurting too much, he said. . . "It might be a run-around." **1965–70** *DARE* (Qu. BB30, . . *A hard, painful swelling [often on a* *finger] that seems to come from deep under the skin*) 27 Infs, **scattered, but chiefly Sth, S Midl, SW,** Runaround; **GA**89, **MS**51, **SC**24, **TX**18, Runaround—around the (finger)nail; **CA**87, Felon, runaround, bone felon; **ME**4, Run-round goes around finger; **NM**9, Runaround—a big yellow spot that came up and ran around the finger . . removed fingernail; **NY**64, Felon, runaround—an infection that comes from the corner of the fingernail being infected; **SC**46, [rʌn raʊn]; **TN**16, Runaround—milder than felon; **UT**3, Runaround—on your nail; **UT**3, Runaround [about the same as] felon; **VA**13, Runaround—if around a nail or joint. **1979** *Greenfield Recorder* (MA) 4 Aug sec A 4, What would an old time "run around" that was a terribly painful infection on one side of a thumb in my grandmother's case, be called today? She said they used bread poultices . . to bring it to a head. There was a bad scar on one side of her thumb and a disfigured nail. **1997** *DARE* File, [Query:] I just heard the noun "run-arounds" used to describe cuticle infections. Any one else familiar with this? [Reply:] I'm pretty sure this is the term we used in the early 1940s when I had several of these as a kid between 10 and 12 in Texas. **1999** *NADS Letters* **eTN** (as of c1945), Recently, I developed a painful infection around my fingernail, which the doctor diagnosed as paronychia. When I told my mother the symptoms, she said that when she was school aged (in east Tennessee) this infection was called a "runaround."

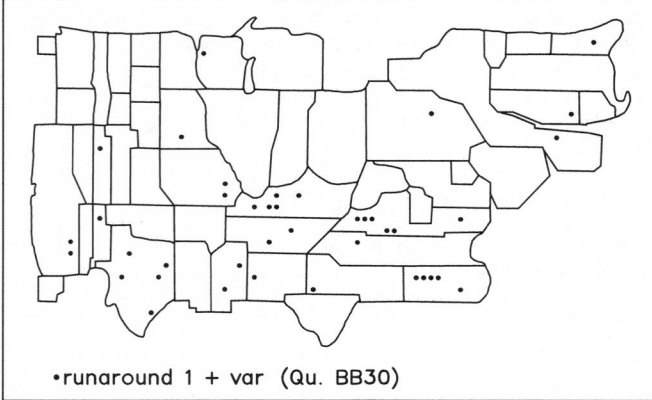

•runaround 1 + var (Qu. BB30)

2 also *run-round;* also with *the:* A skin disease; see quots. Cf **ring-around 2**

1954 *Harder Coll.* **cwTN,** *Run (a)round:* . . A skin disease, same as *ring-(a)round;* probably shingles. **1967** *DARE* FW Addit **PA,** *The runaround*—an inflamed face; something like eczema. **1970** *DARE* (Qu. BB25, . . *Common skin diseases around here*) Inf **NC**83, Runaround—a skin disease, oval sores. **2000** *NADS Letters* **NEast,** I recall an older woman in hospital once saying she had "the runaround". I assumed she meant "the runs" but she was referring to the case of shingles which started along her spine and had extended to her abdomen.

3 A temporary dam built around a leak in a **levee** n¹ **1a.** Cf **boil** n¹ **C2, sand boil**

1923 *DN* 5.244 **LA,** *Run-arounds.* . . Rows of cribbing which are filled with sand bags to close a crevice in the levee. **1941** Percy *Lanterns* 246 **MS,** What you do, if you have the gumption of a catfish, is build with sacks of earth a little "run-around"—that is, a small levee around the geyser to the height of its jet. That stabilizes the pressure, and the boil is safe.

run a sandy (on or over) See **sandy** n¹

run a set See **run** v **B7**

runaway-Jack n
=**ground ivy 1.**
1897 *Jrl. Amer. Folkl.* 10.53 **MA,** *Nepeta Glechoma* . . run-away Jack, blue bells, Cambridge, Mass.

runaway-Nell n
=**ground ivy 1.**
1897 *Jrl. Amer. Folkl.* 10.53 **MA,** *Nepeta Glechoma* . . run-away Nell, Medford, Mass.

runaway-robin n See **robin-runaway**

runboat n
A boat that collects the catches of individual fishermen.

1940 Writers' Program *Guide MD* 411 **csMD,** Until about 1920 most of the oysters caught in the river and sound were sent on sailing vessels up the 40 miles of river to Seaford, where they were shucked and packed for shipment north by rail. Now most of the local oysters go . . on refrigerated trucks and vessels. Many other oysters from this section are sold to 'run-boats' from Baltimore and Washington. **1964** Will *Hist. Okeechobee* 71 **FL,** They all got on the runboat . . for the day long run to Ft. Meyers. **1965** Will *Okeechobee Boats* 1 **FL,** Gasoline engined boats hauling freight and passengers too, and run boats for to fetch catfish to town, and tugs to tend the floating dredges. **1984** *DARE* File **Chesapeake Bay** [Watermen's vocab], Run boat.

runction See **ruction**

runded See **run** v **A1d**

rundlet See **runlet**

run down v phr *esp freq among Black speakers*
To explain (something); to make (a situation) clear; to expatiate on a subject.
1964 *MA Rev.* Summer 622 [Black], I tried to figure out the best way to run it down to this girl right quick that they didn't have to live in this town. **1970** Major *Dict. Afro-Amer. Slang* 98, *Run it down:* to tell the whole truth of whatever is in question. **1972** Kochman *Rappin'* 48 [Black], This gesture of lowering the lip is a result of the emphatic manner in which they are "running it down". *Ibid* 48, [Footnote:] "Running it down" is a manner of talking or rapping. **1972** Claerbaut *Black Jargon* 78, *Running (something) down.* . . explaining an issue; verbally relating a situation. **1980** Folb *Runnin' Down* 91 **Los Angeles CA** [Black], Run down some heavy lines, tell 'im what's happenin'. . . Run down the basic fundamentals to d' dude. *Ibid* 252, *Run (it) down* See *break it down.* [*Ibid* 231, Break it down 1. Explain. 2. Set one straight. 3. Present in detail.] **1994** Smitherman *Black Talk* 69, *Break it down*—To explain something; to simplify a thing. Also *run it down.*

run-down n
A **surf clam** (here: *Spisula solidissima*).
1913 *DN* 4.57 **seMA,** *Run-down.* . . A large clam not usually seen in markets, larger than the "sage-clam" . . but smaller than the sea-clam: so-called from the popular saying that it burrows deeper as one digs for it. "Dig quick or you'll lose him; he's a run-down." **1935** Lincoln *Cape Cod Yesterdays* 49 **eMA,** At the inner edge, bordering the clumps of coarse beach grass, were the "sedge clams", little fellows, tender and just right for a bake or a boil. Farther out were the "rundowns", the big chaps with their shells snowy white. Rundowns were best in a chowder.

run down at the heels adj phr [Blend of *run down* + **down at the heel(s)**]
1970 *DARE* (Qu. BB5, *A general feeling of discomfort or illness that isn't any one place in particular*) Inf **TX**98, Run down at the heels; (Qu. KK30, *Feeling slowed up or without energy: "I certainly feel _____."*) Inf **MI**114, Run down at the heels.

run emptins See **emptins 2**

run fox run n Also *running the fox*
Prob = **fox and hounds 1.**
1967 *DARE* (Qu. EE33, . . *Outdoor games . . that children play*) Inf **IL**11, Run fox run; **LA**6, Running the fox.

rung See **ring** v **B1a**

runged See **ring** v **B1b, 2b**

runlet n Also *rundlet, runlit* [*OED2 runlet* sb.¹ 1394→; "Now only *arch.* or *Hist.*"] **chiefly NEng** *old-fash*
A small keg or cask.
1633 in 1867 NH *Prov. & State Papers* 1.77, 1 runlett with bone ashes and crucibles. **1636** in 1869 Winthrop *Life & Letters* 2.151 **NEng,** There is in one of them a rundlet of honey. **1708** in 1859 Essex Inst. *Coll.* 1.172 **MA,** The same sloop took . . twelve four gallond Runlits. **1757** (1901) Hempstead *Diary* 687 **CT,** I sent adam over to Stonington to Carry a Rundlet of Tarrwater for Joshua. **1845** (1969) Hooper *Advent. Simon Suggs* 72 **AL,** They come from the runaway Seminole and the runlet-making Cherokee! **1898** (1899) Earle *Home Life* 305 **NEng,** The dish-turner and cooper were artisans of importance in those days; piggins, noggins, runlets, keelers, firkins, buckets, churns, dye-tubs, cowles, powdering-tubs, were made with chary or no use of metal.

1901 *DN* 2.146 **NY,** *Runlet.* . . A small barrel or keg in which to carry water to laborers in the field. **1931–33** *LANE Worksheets* **RI,** *Rundlet.* . . A one gallon measure. **1958** Babcock *I Don't Want* 40 **eSC,** I forgot to say, by the way, that in the case of Scuppernong *vs.* Muscadine, it was the considered opinion of the jury . . that a runlet of blackberry wine had a slight edge over both.

run-mad adj Cf **run** v **B3**
Rabid; deranged.
　　1928 in 1944 *ADD* **NC,** You sailed on [into] him like a run-mad man. **1946** *PADS* 6.26 **ceNC,** *Run-mad dog.* . . A mad dog. Pamlico [Co.] Mainly among children. **1986** Pederson *LAGS Concordance,* 1 inf, **csLA,** A run-mad dog—rabid.

runned See **run** v **A1b, 2b**

runner n

1 A locomotive engineer; an operator of a **donkey 1.** Cf **driver 6**
　　1874 (1875) Forney *Catechism Locomotive* 547, Every locomotive runner should. . . have an exact knowledge of the engine entrusted to him. **1901** *Munsey's Mag.* 25.749, A new express locomotive . . under the hand of . . one of the most experienced runners on the road. **1945** in 1953 Botkin–Harlow *Treas. Railroad Folkl.* 340, In the halcyon era when runners were assigned to regular locomotives and virtually owned them . . every division of the Southern . . pikes had its notable "musicians." **1958** McCulloch *Woods Words* 154 **Pacific NW,** *Runner*—a. Donkey puncher. b. Locie engineer. **1962** *AmSp* 37.135 **nwCA,** *Runner.* . . A locomotive engineer.

2 One who solicits customers as an agent for a business.
　　1824 *Microscope* (Albany, N.Y.) 21 Feb. 183/3 *(OED2),* Our wholesale property-speculators and their gentry in livery, called *runners.* **1840** (1841) Dana *2 Yrs.* 453 **Boston MA,** The landlords, runners, and sharks in Ann Street learned that there was a rich prize for them down in the bay. **1859** (1968) Bartlett *Americanisms* 375, *Runner.* A person whose business it is to solicit passengers for steamboats and railroads. Numbers of these men are always found about the wharves, shipping, railroad stations, and hotels of our principal cities, trying to induce travellers or emigrants to travel by the routes they recommend. **1883** *Harper's New Mth. Mag.* 67.814 **NEast,** The runners for several livery-stables offered to provide special transportation. **1946** in 1953 Botkin–Harlow *Treas. Railroad Folkl.* 182, Runners from all the hotels met all the trains. **1948** *Chelsea* (Mass.) *Rec.* 30 Nov. 817 *(DA),* Unethical lawyers, plus their hired 'runners,' probation officers, jail attaches and police officers were 'selling' justice in the courthouse corridors to ignorant criminal defendants.

3 A traveling salesman. Cf **drummer 6**
　　1903 *DN* 2.352 **seIA,** *Runner.* . . A traveling salesman. **1911** *DN* 3.546 **NE,** *Runner.* . . Traveling-man. "There were three runners on the train." **1912** *DN* 3.588 **wIN,** *Runner.* . . A traveling salesman. **1975** Gould *ME Lingo* 82, *Drummer*—A travelling salesman. . . Another Maine term for a drummer is "runner."

4 =**racer 1a.** [So called from its swiftness] **formerly more widespread, but now chiefly Sth** See Map Section Cf **gray runner**
　　1795 in 1809 Williams *Nat. & Civil Hist. VT* 1.485, In a field in Connecticut, . . I approached with caution within twenty feet of a black snake, about seven feet long, having a white throat, and of the kind which the people there call runners, or choking snakes. **1855** Simms *Forayers* 549 **SC,** We got glimpse of a few runners [black-snakes], but they were quite too swift of foot for the hunters. **1908** *DN* 3.291 **cAL, wGA,** *Black-runner.* . . A black snake noted for fleetness. **1965–70** *DARE* (Qu. P25, . . *Kinds of snakes*) 17 Infs, **chiefly Sth,** Black runner; 10 Infs, **chiefly Gulf States,** Blue runner; **TX37,** Gray runner; **MD31,** Horse runner; **TX13, 19,** Prairie runner; **MS63, MA5,** Runner; **IN68,** Runners. **1986** Pederson *LAGS Concordance* **Gulf Region,** 9 infs, Black runner(s); 1 inf, Blue runners; 1 inf, Runner; 1 inf, Speckle runner—snake; not dangerous.

5 =**rainbow runner.**
　　1884 Goode *Fisheries U.S.* 1.332, The Runner—Elagatis pinnulatus. This West Indian fish, known at Key West as "Skipjack" or "Runner," and at Pensacola as "Yellow-tail" or "Shoemaker," is, according to Stearns, "abundant on the western and southern coasts of Florida." **1946** LaMonte *N. Amer. Game Fishes* 37, Rainbow Runner . . Names: Runner, Yellowtail, Skipjack, Shoemaker. **1976** Tryckare et al. *Lore of Sportfishing* 108, Rainbow Runner . . Other common names: Hawaiian salmon, runner, prodigal son [etc].

6 also *runner fish:* A **crevalle a:** usu **hardtail 1,** but also *Caranx ruber.*
　　1896 Jordan–Evermann *Check List Fishes* 346, Caranx crysos . . *Hardtail; Runner.* . . Cape Cod to Brazil. **1939** Natl. Geogr. Soc. *Fishes* 205, A much smaller fish is the Runner *(Caranx ruber . .*) which inhabits the open waters, bays, and inlets from the Carolinas to the West Indies. **1946** LaMonte *N. Amer. Game Fishes* 34, Blue Runner—*Caranx crysos* . . Names: Hardtailed Jack, Jack, Yellowjack, Hardtail, Runner [etc]. **1986** Pederson *LAGS Concordance* **FL,** 3 infs, Blue runner(s); 1 inf, Runner fish. **1991** Amer. Fisheries Soc. *Common Names Fishes* 51, *Caranx crysos* . . blue runner.

7 =**leatherjacket 2.**
　　1896 U.S. Natl. Museum *Bulletin* 47.898, *Oligoplites saurus* . . Leather Jacket; Runner [etc]. . . along the Florida Coast, ranging north to New York and Lower California.

8 also *runner peanut, running ~:* =**peanut 1.** **esp GA**
　　1925 *Book of Rural Life* 7.4199, Varieties of peanuts grown in the United States are divided into two groups, *bunch* and *runner.* . . The runner varieties have a spreading habit of growth, forming pods along the lateral stems. **1946** *Democrat* 16 May 1/1 *(DA)* **swAL,** If you do not have sufficient running peanuts to fatten all of your hogs you should plant grain sorghum. **1968** *DARE* (Qu. I42, . . *Names or nicknames . . for peanuts)* Inf **GA17,** Runners—small. **1986** Pederson *LAGS Concordance,* 1 inf, **ceGA,** North Carolina runner peanut; 1 inf, **swGA,** Runner peanut (ordinary peanut); 1 inf, **swGA,** Runners—a kind of peanut; 1 inf, **swGA,** Dixie runner—peanut; North Carolina runners—peanuts—old-timey variety; 1 inf, **swGA,** Runner-type peanuts; 1 inf, **seGA,** Running peanut—pinder; 2 infs, **seAL, nwLA,** Running peanut(s).

9 A **lae** (here: *Scomberoides sancti-petri*).
　　1960 Gosline–Brock *Hawaiian Fishes* 169, Scomberoides sancti-petri (Lae, Leatherback, Runner).

runner fish See **runner 6**

runner oak n
A **post oak 1a** (here: *Quercus margarettiae*).
　　1970 Correll *Plants TX* 477, *Quercus Margaretta* . . Sand post oak, runner oak. Low or moderate-sized shrubs branched from the base. . . Low woodlands in deep sandy soil in cen. and e. Tex.; e. to the Atl. and n. to Va. and Okla. **1979** Little *Checklist U.S. Trees* 242, *Quercus stellata* var. *margaretta* . . dwarf post oak, post oak, runner oak [etc].

runner peanut See **runner 8**

runnet n [Engl dial var of *rennet;* cf *EDD*]
1 Rennet.
　　1790 Deane *New Engl. Farmer* 237, *Runnet,* or *Rennet,* an acid juice, contained in the maw of a calf that has fed on nothing but milk. **1859** MI State Ag. Soc. *Trans. for 1857* 144, Warm some cream, add runnet in the proportion of a spoonful to a pint. **1917** *DN* 4.416 **IL, wNC,** *Runnet.* . . Variant of rennet. **1922** (1926) Cady *Rhymes VT* 259, For instance, runnet crocks and whey / Are simply words to Bridgeport May.

2 also *rummit, runnich:* The stomach of an animal; hence used vaguely in ref to the human entrails—often in phr *bust one's runnet.*
　　1932 Stribling *Store* 69 **AL,** "Ye-es," drawled the preacher, "oncet I stood up an' said whut I thinks, an' dat white man nea'ly busted my runnet." **1936** *AmSp* 11.317 **Ozarks,** *Runnet.* . . The stomach, or sometimes the gall-bladder. Used in a jocular fashion. [4]"Look out thar, Jim! You'll fall down an' bust your runnet!" **1939** (1962) Thompson *Body & Britches* 65 **NY,** He did not hesitate to fire upon a doe and her two fawns—the little chaps' runnets would bring fifty cents each. **1941** *AmSp* 16.21 **sIN,** *Bust your runnet.* Usually said to children. 'If you don't stop eating, you're going to bust your runnet.' **1947** McDavid *Coll.* **seGA,** Runnich—Negro name for entrails. St. Simons Is[land]. **1969** *DARE* (Qu. BB28, *Joking names . . for imaginary diseases: "He must have the _____.")* Inf **NY186,** Pantod on the rummit. **1981** Harper–Presley *Okefinokee* 99 (as of a1929), He said they "grow in the deer's runnet, right where his swaller [esophagus] goes into his maw [stomach]."

running See **run** n **6**

running bean n [Var of *runner bean*] **esp Gulf States**
A cultivated pole bean.
　　1863 Burr *Field & Garden* 481, Pole or Running Beans. **1966–68** *DARE* (Qu. I20, . . *Kinds of beans)* Inf **GA55,** Running beans—plant on

a fence; **LA**12, Running beans—they run up on a stick or pole; (Qu. I14, *Kinds of beans that you eat in the pod before they're dry*) Inf **MS**23, Running beans; (Qu. I17, *Beans . . that are dark red when they are dry*) Inf **GA**3, Running pole beans.   **1979** *Descant* 10.3–4.26 [Black], She pass up for some reason, maybe not seeing them or because her plate is limber and won't hold no more, the runnin beans.   **1986** Pederson *LAGS Concordance* **Gulf Region,** 32 infs, Running bean(s); 6 infs, Running butter bean(s); 1 inf, Green running bean; 1 inf, Pole beans called running beans; 1 inf, Running bean—kind of butter bean; 1 inf, Running snap beans.

running berry See **running blackberry**

running birch n [See quot 1924] Cf **running tea**
A **wintergreen** (here: *Gaultheria hispidula*).
   1894 *Jrl. Amer. Folkl.* 7.93 **VT,** *Chiogenes serpyllifolia* . . running birch.   **1924** *Amer. Botanist* 30.56, *Chiogenes hispidula* best known as "creeping snow-berry" or "running birch." Its foliage has the same flavor as the aromatic wintergreen and the black birch, which accounts for the last-mentioned name.   **1979** Erichsen-Brown *Med. N. Amer. Plants* 312, Creeping snowberry. . . Common names. Moxie, ivory plums, . . running birch [etc].

running blackberry n Also *running berry* Cf **running brier**
=**dewberry 1.**
   1814 Bigelow *Florula Bostoniensis* 122, *Rubus trivialis.* . . Low or running blackberry. Dew-berry. . . Stems . . running several yards upon the ground. . . Fruit large, black, sweet.   **1840** MA *Zool. & Bot. Surv. Herb. Plants & Quadrupeds* 59, *R[ubus] trivialis* . . Running Blackberry, Dewberry. Characterized by its name, bears large black berries, very excellent when fully ripe.   **1899** (1912) Green *VA Folk-Speech* 361, *Running-blackberry.* . . The dewberry; it trails on the ground, bearing small blackberries.   **1901** Lounsberry *S. Wild Flowers* 238, Low running blackberry. *Rubus villosus. Ibid, [Rubus] hispidus,* running swamp blackberry, also trails along the ground mostly in low wet places.   **1935** (1943) Muenscher *Weeds* 295, *Rubus flagellaris.* . . Dewberry, Running blackberry.   **1967–69** *DARE* (Qu. I44, *What kinds of berries grow wild around here?*) Inf **NY**205, Running berry or running blackberry—vine grows along ground; **SC**39, Dewberries—a running blackberry.

running box n Cf **boxberry 2**
A **partridgeberry 1** (here: *Mitchella repens*).
   1950 Gray–Fernald *Manual of Botany* 1327, *[Mitchella] repens* . . Two-eyed-berry, Running Box.—Dry or moist knolls in woods.   **1971** Krochmal *Appalachia Med. Plants* 176, *Mitchella repens* . . Common names: Partridgeberry . . running box [etc].

running brand See **running iron**

running brier n Cf **running blackberry**
=**dewberry 1.**
   1837 Darlington *Flora Cestrica* 308 se**PA,** Trivial Rubus. *Vulgò*— Dew-berry. Running Brier. . . The plough-boy is apt to get well acquainted with this species,—by the long trailing stems, with their recurved prickles, drawing across his naked ankles! *expertus loquor.*   **1895** U.S. Dept. Ag. *Farmers' Bulletin* 28.28, Running briar, dewberry, low blackberry . . *Rubus canadensis.*   **1910** Graves *Flowering Plants* 239 **CT,** *Rubus villosus.* . . Dewberry. Running Brier. Running or Low Blackberry.   **c1938** in 1970 Hyatt *Hoodoo* 2.936 ce**VA,** Whut did I get? *Runnin' brier* an' pokeberry [Hyatt: poke or pokeweed] root.

running buddy See **running mate**

running buffalo clover n Also *running clover* Cf **buffalo clover 1**
A white-flowered perennial clover *(Trifolium stoloniferum)* with long basal runners.
   1847 Wood *Class-Book* 227, [Trifolium] stoloniferum. . . *Running Buffalo Clover.* . . Fields and woods, Western States.   **1881** Phares *Farmer's Book of Grasses* 8, Running Buffalo Clover. This is much like, and may be a variety of number 3 [=buffalo clover].   **1933** Small *Manual SE Flora* 685, *[Trifolium] stoloniferum.* . . Buffalo-clover. Running-clover.   **1953** Strausbaugh–Core *Flora WV* 544, Running Buffalo Clover. . . along Back Fork of Elk River, Webster County.

running cedar n
1 =**creeping juniper.**

   1916 *Torreya* 16.236 **ME,** *Juniperus horizontalis* . . Ground or running cedar, Matinicus I[slan]d, Me.
2 A **club moss.**
   1959 Carleton *Index Herb. Plants* 101, *Running-cedar:* Lycopodium obscurum.   **1976** Bruce *How to Grow Wildflowers* 23, Perhaps I would see the club mosses called Ground-pine and Running-cedar.

running clover See **running buffalo clover**

running go n Also *runago, run-an(d)-go* s**Appalachians**
A running preparation for a leap or attack—usu in phr *take a running go.*
   1915 *DN* 4.189 sw**VA,** *Run-an'-go.* . . A run before leaping.   **1937** (1963) Hyatt *Kiverlid* 64 **KY,** Ol' Baldy wus done fer when the bull backed up fer a main run-an'-go!   **1939** Hall *Coll.* w**NC,** e**TN,** *Run-ago.* . . An it (a bear) wheeled back on the dogs. He [=a man] took a run-ago an' run his arm into that hole he cut into it, an' run it up about his heart.   **1950** Stuart *Hie Hunters* 10 e**KY,** Did gripped the vine, took a run-and-go, and swung across the hollow beside Sparkie.   **1955** Ritchie *Singing Family* 23 se**KY,** I snatched up an old broom handle lying in the yard and took a runago at the homemade screen door and rammed that stick plum through.   **1956** Hall *Coll. (Montgomery Coll.)* e**TN,** She took a runnin'-go at him.   **1984** Wilder *You All Spoken Here* 67 **Sth,** *Run-ago:* A running jump, as in "He took a run-ago an' cleared that there rail fence there an' hit the groun' a-runnin'."   **1991** Haynes *Haywood Home* 55 w**NC,** Ice skating on the branches and creeks was fun. . . Of course we didn't have ice skates, so we'd take a running go and slide on our shoe soles.

running iron n **West** Cf **stamp iron**
A branding iron that allows brands to be drawn freehand on an animal's hide; hence *running brand* a brand so made.
   1894 *McClure's Mag.* July 101 **West,** The running-irons . . are now considered bad form by progressive cattlemen.   **1907** White *AZ Nights* 317, That vehicle, furthermore, transported such articles as the blankets, the tarpaulins under which to sleep, the running irons for branding, the cooking layout, and the men's personal effects.   **1920** Hunter *Trail Drivers TX* 298, A "running iron" is a branding iron made of a straight piece of iron with a curve at one end. This end is heated red hot and the branding artist is thus enabled to "run" any letter he wishes to put on the side of the animal.   **1924** in 1975 White *Git Along* 117 **West,** Oh, they taken their hosses and runnin' irons / And mabbe a dawg or two.   **1929** *AmSp* 5.69 **NE** [Cattle country talk], A "running iron," used like a pencil and producing a "running brand."   **1933** *AmSp* 8.1.30 nw**TX** [Ranch diction], *Running iron.* Branding iron curved at the end.   **1935** Davis *Honey* 187 **OR,** As soon as he got where there was a running-iron and a branding-chute to run the mare into, he would.   **1941** Writers' Program *Guide WY* 464, *Running iron*—Ring or bar, or even piece of wire, or tool used for branding in emergency.   **1967** *DARE* FW Addit **CO,** Running iron—circular or J shaped iron that could be used to make up any or change any brand.   **1967** *DARE* Tape **CO**4, [Inf:] But as a whole, a running iron wasn't used steady or regular. [FW:] A running iron became sort of basic equipment for rustlers, I understand. [Inf:] Well, that's true; very true.   **1981** *KS Qrly.* 13.2.70 n**NV,** Running iron . . small piece of iron or special branding iron in one of several simple shapes used to alter marks (brands) on cattle or to put another brand on strays; a cinch ring is sometimes used.

running ivy n
=**poison ivy 1.**
   1895 *Auk* 12.33 **MA,** Consequently there is but little verdure, running ivy *(Rhus radicans)* and sand reed or beach grass *(Ammophila arundinacea).*   **1940** Clute *Amer. Plant Names* 270, *Rhus toxicodendron.* Climbing sumach, poison creeper, running ivy [etc].

running jack n
=**hardtail 1.** Cf **runner 6**
   1935 Caine *Game Fish* 48, Blue Runner—*Caranx crysos.* . . Synonyms: Cojinua . . Running Jack [etc].

running mate n Also *running buddy, ~ partner*
A close friend or associate; a sweetheart or spouse.
   1911 *Munsey's Mag.* Mar 865, His running-mate, Elizabeth Brice, in spite of the eyes she makes, also inspires liking.   **1941** *LANE* Map 399 *(Her sweetheart)* 1 inf, s**ME,** Better half; runnin' mate.   **1944** Adams *Western Words* 134, *Runnin' mate*—Used by the cowboy to refer to his pal or his wife.   **1967–70** *DARE* (Qu. I11, *. . A close friend . . "He's my*

_____.") Inf **TX**33, Running mate; (Qu. II2b, *When two people have become friendly . . "It's been quite a while that Mary and Jane have been _____."*) Inf **MS**88, Running pardners; (Qu. II3, *Expressions to say that people are very friendly toward each other: "They're _____."*) Inf **DC**11, Running buddy. **1970** *Current Slang* 5.2.12 [Black Univ student slang], *Running partner. . .* A close friend and companion.

running myrtle See **myrtle** n[1] **B3**

running oak n

1 A low-growing **oak** (here: *Quercus pumila*).

1676 in 1878 MA Hist. Soc. *Coll.* 5th ser 5.26, There saw Acorns upon bushes about a foot high, which they call running Oak. **1812** Michaux *Histoire des Arbres* 2.84, Quercus pumila. Running Oak. . . De toutes les espèces de Chênes qui existent dans les Etats-Unis, et même qu'on a trouvées jusqu'à présent dans les autres parties, soit de l'ancien, soit du nouveau continent, il n'en est aucune qui s'élève si peu que le *Quercus pumila;* car il a rarement plus de 20 pouces (55 centim.) de hauteur, sur 2 lignes (4 millim.) de diamètre. [Quercus pumila. Running Oak. . . Of all the varieties of oak which exist in the United States, and also those currently known in other places, either in the old or new world, there is none which grows so low as the *Quercus pumila;* for it is rarely more than 20 inches (55 cm) in height, or more than 2 lignes (4 mm) in diameter.] **1860** Curtis *Cat. Plants NC* 37, There is a dwarf variety of this [=upland willow oak], called *Running Oak* and *White Oak Runners . .* which is, I believe, the smallest Oak known. It rarely reaches a height of 3 feet, and bears a profusion of acorns at the height of 15 and 20 inches. **1901** Lounsberry *S. Wild Flowers* 130, Q[uercus] pumila, running oak, is a shrub which spreads itself by stolons and covers acres and acres of sandy, barren soil along the coast region. **1941** Ward *Holding Hills* 15 **IA** (as of early 20th cent), Even the north side of that hill ran into brush, into hazel and running-oak and a second crop of hickory. That side would have been hard to plow. **1966** Grimm *Recognizing Native Shrubs* 99, Running Oak. . . North Carolina south to Florida, west to Mississippi. **1966–68** *DARE* (Qu. T10, *. . Kinds of oak trees*) Inf **OK**18, Running oak; **GA**25, Running oak—they make bushes, not trees.

2 =**mountain misery 1.**

1925 Jepson *Manual Plants CA* 500, [Chamaebatia] foliosa. . . Also called Bear-mat, Bear-clover, Tarweed, Jerusalem Oak and Running Oak.

running off (at the bowels) n Also *run off(s);* for addit varr see quots **widespread exc NEast, C Atl, Gt Lakes** See Map Diarrhea; dysentery; a bout of diarrhea or dysentery.

1902 *DN* 2.244 **sIL,** Runnin off. . . Diarrhea or dysentery. **1906** *DN* 3.123 **sIN,** *Runnin off to bowels. . .* Diarrhea. **1907** *DN* 3.226 **nwAR,** *Runnin' off. . .* Diarrhœa or dysentery. **1909** *DN* 3.403 **nwAR,** *Runnin' off 't t' bowels. . .* Diarrhœa. "Fresh pork always give me a runnin' off (a)t' t'(he) bowels." **1910** *DN* 3.447 **wNY,** *Running off. . .* Diarrhea. **1945** FWP *Lay My Burden Down* 111 **LA** (as of c1865) [Black], My mammy knowed just what root to go out and pull up to knock the chills right outen me. And the bellyache and the running off the same way, too. **1954** *Harder Coll.* **cwTN,** *Running off.* Chicken diarrhea. Them chickens got the old running off. **c1960** *Wilson Coll.* **csKY,** *Running off of the bowels. . .* Diarrhea. **1960** Criswell *Resp. to PADS 20* **Ozarks,** *Running-off. . .* Dysentery. "A, [or] the running off." Common of old and still used though many now use the more refined term. **1965**

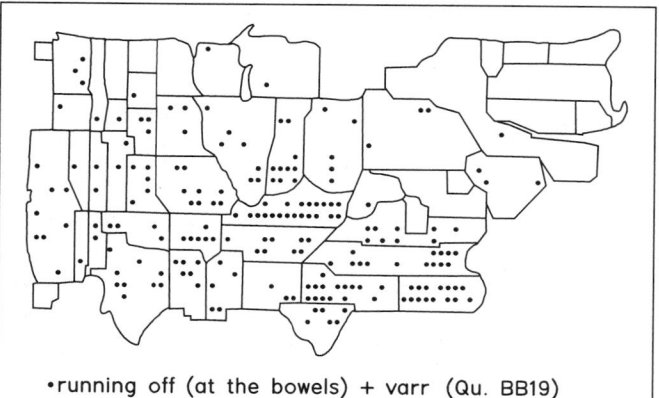

•running off (at the bowels) + varr (Qu. BB19)

Weller *Yesterday's People* 119 **sAppalachians,** She discovered that "running off" is a term for diarrhea. **1965–70** *DARE* (Qu. BB19, *Joking names for looseness of the bowels*) 174 Infs, **widespread exc NEast, C Atl, Gt Lakes,** Running off; 11 Infs, **scattered,** Run-off(s); **AR**33, **CA**80, 106, 127, **KY**81, 86, **NC**55, **SD**5, Running off (at) the bowels; **CA**166, **CO**20, **LA**18, **NC**79, **VA**74, Running off of (*or* on) the bowels; **CO**3, Running off at bowels; **GA**13, Running offs; **NV**8, Run off at the bowels. **1982** Slone *How We Talked* 102 **eKY** (as of c1950), *Running off* (diarrhea). **1986** Pederson *LAGS Concordance,* 1 inf, seMS, The runoff—diarrhea. **1990** Cavender *Folk Med. Lexicon* 30 **sAppalachians,** *Running off*—diarrhea; also "the runs."

running off at the head See **head** n **B2**

running okra n [Because the young fruits are eaten like okra] A gourd (*Luffa* sp).

1971 GA Dept. Ag. *Farmers Market Bulletin* 21 Apr 1/3 **ceGA,** [Letter:] Is running okra as good to eat as other okra? . . [Response:] According to our area horticulturist, running okra is not okra but a member of the gourd family. It is edible when the fruit is in an immature stage but is tough and full of fibers when the fruit is mature. *Ibid,* Running okra is harvested and prepared as regular okra but is known as a novelty. **1986** Pederson *LAGS Concordance,* 1 inf, **ceMS,** The vegetable is called running okra. **1990** *Seed Savers Yearbook* 269, *Luffa sponge (Vine Okra) . .* a.k.a. Running Okra, plant on fence or trellis, ready to eat when 8–10″ long, fry as any other okra, very good.

running partner See **running mate**

running peanut See **runner 8**

running pine n Also, perh erron, *running vine*

A **club moss:** usu *Lycopodium clavatum* but also *L. complanatum*.

1890 *Century Dict.* 3552, L[ycopodium] clavatum is the common club-moss, or running pine, which is extensively employed in decorations. **1896** Robinson *In New Engl. Fields* 254, The lesser growths of the old woods. . . as . . the decorative running pine. **1897** *Jrl. Amer. Folkl.* 10.147 **VT,** Lycopodium complanatum . . trailing, running, or creeping vine, Ferrisburgh. **1946** Tatnall *Flora DE* 8, [Lycopodium] complanatum . . Running Pine. **1961** Douglas *My Wilderness* 268 **nME,** Granite rocks, bunchberry, and the moss known as ground (or running) pine, because of its shape, meant [Mt.] Katahdin. **1961** Peck *Manual OR* 58, L. clavatum . . Ground- or Running-pine. Elk Moss. . . Alaska to Ore., east to the Atlantic coast. **1985** Rattray *Advent. Dimon* 236 **Long Is. NY,** I picked a good bunch and left them to get on my way home, on a slab of bark with some running pine and damp moss, saving one for my buttonhole.

running range n [Prob pronc-sp for *running reins;* cf **rein A, reins**]

Gonorrhea.

1931 *Jrl. Amer. Folkl.* 44.414 **Sth** [Black], Prescriptions of root doctors. . . For Running Range (Claps).

running side n

The side of a log on which it will be most stable when skidded.

1979 Carpenter *Walton War* 125 **cwNC** (as of early 1900s), If a log's running side was not judged right and it rolled one way or another while being dragged, the grab chain and spikes could end up on the side or the bottom and it would either fail to "track" with the rest of the logs or catch the spike on the crosspoled road and make the whole thing too hard to pull.

running tea n Cf **ground tea, running birch**

A **wintergreen** (here: *Gaultheria hispidula*).

1897 *Jrl. Amer. Folkl.* 10.49 **ME,** Chiogenes serpyllifolia . . running tea, Bethel, Me.

running the fox See **run fox run**

running tomato n

A kind of **tomato** (*Lycopersicon lycopersicum*); see quot 1986.

1965 *DARE* (Qu. I21, *Names or nicknames for tomatoes;* total Infs questioned, 75) Inf **FL**18, Other types are apple tomato, running tomato. **1986** Pederson *LAGS Concordance* **Gulf Region,** 2 infs, Running tomato(es); 1 inf, Running tomato—small ones—perhaps called; 1 inf, Running tomatoes—small ones.

running upon See **run** v **B11**

running vine n
1 See **running pine.**
2 A **morning glory 1.**

1966–70 *DARE* (Qu. S5, . . *Wild morning glory*) Inf **GA**11, Running vine; **NC**49, Just a running vine; (Qu. S21, . . *Weeds . . that are a trouble in gardens and fields*) Inf **DC**13, Running vines. 1981 Pederson *LAGS Basic Materials*, 1 inf, seGA, Running vine—grows on the house.

running white oak n
=**chinquapin oak 2.**

1940 Clute *Amer. Plant Names* 163, [*Quercus*] *prinoides*. Scrub Oak. . . running white oak. 1960 Vines *Trees SW* 153, Dwarf Chinquapin Oak. . . It also has the vernacular names of Scrub Chestnut Oak . . Running White Oak [etc].

runnygade See **runagate**

run off v phr
To survey (land).

1748 (1925) Washington *Diaries* 1.8 **VA**, We began at ye. Boundary Line. . . and run of two Lots. 1903 *DN* 2.328 seMO, Run off. . . To survey (land). 'He ought to have his land run off before he builds his fence.' 1907 *DN* 3.235 nwAR, Run off. . . To survey (land). 1909 *DN* 3.365 eAL, wGA, Run off. . . To survey (land).

run off n
1 See **running off (at the bowels).**
2 See **run** n **6.**

run off at the jibs See **jib** n[1] **1b**

run offs See **running off (at the bowels)**

run off the jibs See **jib** n[1] **1b**

run on See **run** v **B9b, 11**

run (one) around the stump v phr
To deceive (someone); to give (someone) the runaround.

1945 Partridge *January Thaw* 82 **CT**, I want you to get it straight that we got legal rights same as you have, and we don't mean to be outsmarted or thimblerigged or run around the stump.

run one down the country See **down the country, give one**

run one's face See **face, run one's**

run one's mouth v phr Also *run one's mouth off,* ~ *head,* ~ *lip,* ~ *tongue,* ~ *trap* **chiefly Sth, S Midl** See Map
To talk excessively.

1940 *Sat. Eve. Post* 23 Nov 39 **MS**, Drunk still and running his mouth. 1952 Brown *NC Folkl.* 1.587, Run (one's) lip. . . To scold; to talk a great deal without saying anything. 1953 *PADS* 19.13 sAppalachians, Run (one's) tongue: . . To be overly talkative. "Can she talk! You ought to hear her run her tongue!" 1956 McAtee *Some Dialect NC* 37, Run one's tongue. . . Be very talkative. 1962 Faulkner *Reivers* 81 **MS**, All

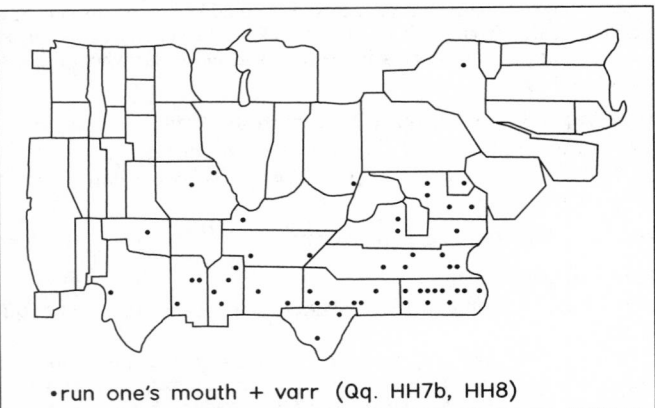

•run one's mouth + varr (Qq. HH7b, HH8)

right. Jump out. You want to visit Alabama. You done already made yourself fifteen minutes late running your mouth. 1965–70 *DARE* (Qu. HH7b, *Someone who talks too much, or too loud: "He's always _____."*) 47 Infs, **chiefly Sth, S Midl**, Running his mouth (*or* head, tongue, trap); **GA**30, 36, **TN**24, Running his mouth off; (Qu. HH8, *A person who likes to brag*) Inf **FL**4, Running his big mouth. [26 of 51 Infs young or mid-aged] [1967 *DJE* 388, *Run (one's) mouth*. . . Yu run yu mout fe not a ting, all de talk yu talk fe nutten. Man, to chat or gossip—run mouth.] 1970 Major *Dict. Afro-Amer. Slang* 98, *Run (one's) mouth:* to talk excessively; to complain.

run onto (or on to) See **run** v **B9b**

runout n
A flash flood.

1953 (1977) Hubbard *Shantyboat* 291 **Lower Missip R**, It is . . a creek flowing down from the hills, subject to treacherous runouts. . . The lamplighter . . told us about the runouts, but with the river as high as it was the rush of water down from the hills after a storm would be checked by the backwater from the river long before it reached us.

run-round See **runaround 1, 2**

runs n pl Usu with *the* Also *G.I. runs;* for addit varr see quot 1965–70 **widespread, but chiefly Nth, N Midl, West** See Map Cf **G.I's, Lucy Bowles**
An attack of diarrhea; also frequent urination.

1950 *WELS* (*Joking or nicknames for diarrhea or looseness of the bowels*) 26 Infs, **WI**, (The) runs; 2 Infs, **WI**, G.I. runs. 1965–70 *DARE* (Qu. BB19, *Joking names for looseness of the bowels*) 264 Infs, **widespread, but chiefly Nth, N Midl, West**, Runs; **PA**243, Fast runs; **MD**9, **MA**69, **MO**26, (Got) the runs; **NJ**41, Lucy runs; **PA**223, Twenty-four-hour runs; (Qu. BB20, *Joking names or expressions for overactive kidneys*) 15 Infs, **scattered**, Runs; **MO**2, Bathroom runs. 1970 *DARE* FW Addit **OH**95, Runs, the—remedy for "the runs"—hasty-pudding (milk, flour, salt). 1971 Malamud *Tenants* 214 **NYC**, Sam Clemence . . despite a bad case of the runs . . stands up for his friend Willie.

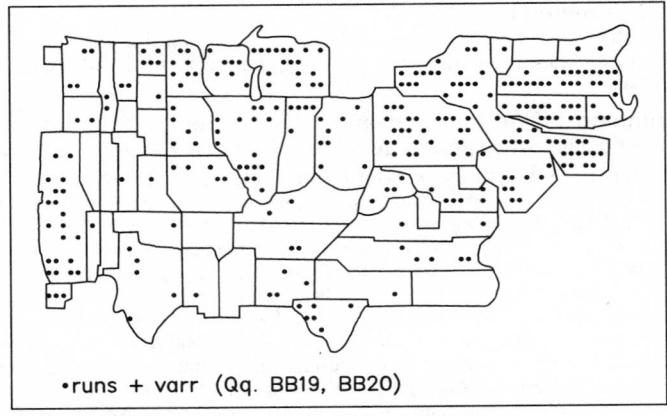

•runs + varr (Qq. BB19, BB20)

run sheep run n Also *run sheepie run;* for addit varr see quots
A hiding game typically involving two teams, in which the leader of the hiding team accompanies the searchers, communicating with the hiders by means of a prearranged code, and the hiders, at a signal from their leader, must race the other team to a home base; also used as the call signaling that they should run. [Perh of Scots origin, though earlier attested in this country; cf *SND* (at *rin* v. B.1.(4)(v)) and 1969 Opie–Opie *Children's Games* 183.] **chiefly Nth, N Midl, West** See Map Cf **cabbage and cornbread, go-sheep-go, hoist the (green) sail, lay low sheepie**

1903 Norris *Pit* 150 **Chicago IL**, The sidewalks were filled with children clamoring at "tag", "I-spy", or "run-sheep-run." 1905 *DN* 3.93 nwAR, Run, sheep, run. . . A kind of hide and seek in which the participants hide together. 1909 (1923) Bancroft *Games* 170, Run, Sheep, Run! This is a form of hide-and-seek, but the hiding and seeking are done by parties instead of individually, each party acting under the direction of a captain. 1928 Aldrich *Lantern* 5 **NE**, Children at the north end of town played "Run, Sheep, Run," in her yard. 1940 Harbin *Fun Encycl.* 173, Run, sheep, run. . . Two equal sides, each with a captain. A home base is indicated. One group becomes the "sheep." They go out and hide. Their leader comes back, when they are ready, and goes with the opposing side as it hunts for the "sheep." When the leader thinks the opportune time has come he yells "Run, sheep, run!" All the "sheep" immediately rush for home base, as do the "hunters." If the "sheep" beat the "hunters" to home base, they hide again. If not, the "hunters" become "sheep" in turn. **1953** Brewster *Amer. Nonsinging Games* 40 **IN**, *Run, Good Sheep, Run.* . . [The players] are divided into two groups, each of which chooses a leader or "shepherd." It is his job to make a code . . to inform his group of the location of those on the other side. One group remains at the base; the other leaves to hide. The leader of the latter group takes his players on a meandering course. . . When they have been safely hidden, he returns to the base. . . The opposing group then starts out to find the hiders, and the captain of the latter accompanies them, calling out his code along the way. . . When the searchers are far enough away, the leader of the hiding group yells "Run, good sheep, run!" His players immediately run for the base, and the others try to tag them. **1957** *Chicago Daily News* (IL) 12 Oct 3/4, Outside we played tag, blind . . run-she-brun (run, sheep run). **1963** *North Rascal* 27 **WI** (as of 1918), Girls had to wear swimming suits and come in earlier from our evening games of prisoner's base and run-sheep-run. **1965–70** *DARE* (Qu. EE12, *Games in which one captain hides his team and the other team tries to find it*) 203 Infs, **chiefly Nth, N Midl, West,** Run sheep run; 26 Infs, **chiefly Nth, N Midl,** Run sheepie run; **MA**21, **WI**29, 40, 64, 71, Run my (good) sheep run; **CO**26, **CT**42, **OH**89, 90, Run sheep; **PA**45, Run the sheepies; **DC**2, Sheep-sheep-run; **DC**8, Run black sheep run; **MN**37, Run run sheep; **CA**174, Hail-oh, run sheep run; **MS**65, **NC**40, Running the sheep; **NY**152, Running sheep; **VA**18, Sheepie-run; (Qu. EE1, . . *Games . . children play . . in which they form a ring, and either sing or recite a rhyme*) Inf **WA**1, Run sheep run; (Qu. EE2, *Games that have one extra player—when a signal is given, the players change places, and the extra one tries to get a place*) Inf **MT**3, Run sheep run; (Qu. EE4, *Games in which one player's eyes are bandaged and he has to catch the others and guess who they are*) Inf **MO**36, Run sheep run; **IL**30, Run sheep run—but that doesn't have a blindfold; **WI**40, Run my good sheep run; (Qu. EE13a, *Games in which every player hides except one, and that one must try to find the others*) Infs **CA**59, **MT**3, **NY**2, Run sheep run; (Qu. EE15, . . *What does the player who is 'it' call out to the others?*) Infs **CA**59, **WA**16, Run sheep run; (Qu. EE16, *Hiding games that start with a special, elaborate method of sending the players out to hide*) Infs **NE**9, **WA**6, Run sheep run; **IN**58, Run sheepie run; (Qu. EE27, *Games played on the ice*) Inf **MA**128, Run sheep run—few people are chosen as sheep; few are chosen as wolves; obj[ect is to] see who catches who; (Qu. EE33, . . *Outdoor games . . that children play*) Infs **CA**9, 15, 24, 112, **ID**1, **IL**26, 40, **PA**74, Run sheep run.

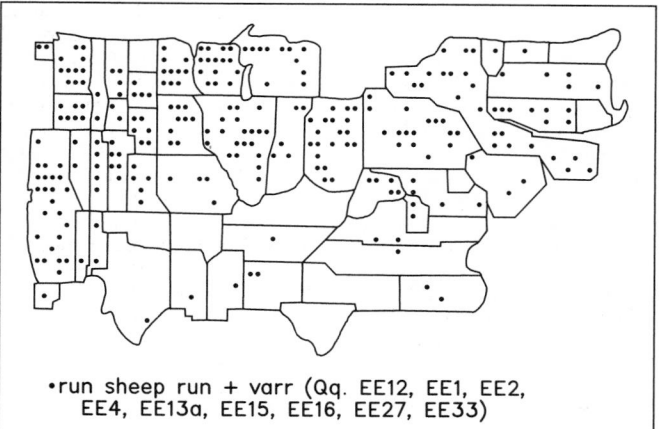

•run sheep run + varr (Qq. EE12, EE1, EE2, EE4, EE13a, EE15, EE16, EE27, EE33)

run the mill See **mill** n[1] 4

‡**run the ridge** v phr Cf **ridge runner** 2
To run away.
  1968 *DARE* FW Addit **VA**4A, *Run the ridge* = run away. "If that happens to me again, I'm-a-going a run the ridge."

run to emptins See **emptins** 2

run up v phr
1 To flush (a game animal).

1966–69 *DARE* (Qu. P39a, *When a hunter or a dog finds a game animal and makes it start running . . he _____ it*) Infs **GA**16, **KY**56, Run him (*or* it) up.
2 Of a person: to grow rapidly. **esp Sth, S Midl**
  1969 *DARE* (Qu. OO23a, . . *"Billy has to have new clothes—during the summer he _____ [two inches]."*) Inf **GA**72, Run up; **NC**62, Ran up; (Qu. OO23b, . . *"You wouldn't think a child could have _____ [so fast]."*) Inf **GA**72, Run up. **1986** Pederson *LAGS Concordance*, 1 inf, **neTN**, Run [preterite] up = grew rapidly; 1 inf, **cGA**, When he started running up = growing up; 1 inf, **cnAR**, You've run up = grown rapidly—[of a] child or crop; 1 inf, **ceTX**, Run up = grew.
3 See **run** v B8.

run up against See **run** v B9d

run up on See **run** v B9c

run upon See **run** v B9c, 11

run up to See **run** v B9e

run up with See **run** v B9a

runway n
1 In logging: see quot 1969. Cf **drag road, dray ~, gutter ~**
  1905 U.S. Forest Serv. *Bulletin* 61.39 [Logging terms], *Gutter road.* The path followed in skidding logs. . . Syn[onyms]: drag road, runway, skidding trail, snaking trail. **1969** Sorden *Lumberjack Lingo* 100 **NEng Gt Lakes**, *Runway*—A long skid road from woods to skidway. Same as drag road, dray road, gutter road, travois road.
2 See **run** n 1c.

runza n [Now a trademark; prob < Ger *Ranzen* a satchel] **chiefly Upper MW, esp NE**
A pocket of bread or pastry dough traditionally stuffed with ground beef, cabbage, onions, and spices.
  1998 *DARE* File—Internet, *Runza Casserole.* Ingredients include hamburger, cabbage, chopped onion, salt, pepper, garlic powder, Pillsbury Crescent Rolls, shredded cheese.] . . I tried making traditional runzas . . using frozen bread dough and it just didn't seem to work. Brandon salvaged the mess by turning it into a casserole. **2001** *DARE* File **seNE**, Runza = cabbage and beef stuffed in a roll. A brand name for the Runza Hut drive-in but evidently widely used before that. The public schools served "Runzas" though they later (c late 1970's) started calling them something else. Also, Geier's Bakery, run by a branch of my wife's family, served 'Runzas' though they too had to change the name. *Ibid* **seNE**, A runza is a sandwich-like closed pocket of fried dough similar to a Polish pierogi, though a little doughier. . . The fillings [were] . . often potatoes and ground beef, sauerkraut and cheese or cottage cheese. *Ibid* **seNE** (as of c1978), When the schools in Lincoln stopped using the term "Runza" [because of its copyright], they replaced it with "krautburger." Of course, they didn't stop serving them. . . Needless to say, we kept using "Runza" for both the restaurant and the school cafeteria varieties. **2001** *DARE* File—Internet **NE** [Runza® Restaurants], The Runza® Sandwich is made from fresh ground beef, onions and special spices baked inside home made bread. . . The Runza® Sandwich has German-Russian roots stretching back to the 18th century. . . It made its commercial debut in Lincoln, Nebraska . . when the first Runza® Drive-Inn [opened] in 1949. . . Runza® Restaurants has grown into a regional chain of Over [sic] 60 restaurants in Nebraska, Iowa, South Dakota, Kansas and Colorado. *Ibid* **MN**, The Runza Society of the Greater Twin Cities Metropolitan Area (a.k.a. Minnesotans for Nebraska) encourages you to proudly serve up a heapin' helpin' of Husker hospitality the next time you host a football gathering. Runzas that is. Our recipe . . makes about 20 Runzas. . . "Runzas to the Left, Runzas to the Right. Stand Up. Sit Down. Bite, Bite, Bite."

rural n **chiefly Sth** *chiefly among Black speakers*
Also pl: The country—usu in phrr *(out) in the rural(s).*
  1965 Belfrage *Freedom Summer* 74 **MS** [Black], It [=a car] almost never worked, though once in a while it briefly decided to, and the whole family would pile in for an excursion to "the rural." **1968** *DARE* FW Addit **nwLA**, I live out in the rural. **1979** *NC Folkl. Jrl.* 27.56 **cNC** [Black], He didn't get to town with 'em [=baskets], just sold 'em out there in the rural. **1986** Pederson *LAGS Concordance*, 1 inf, **seAL**, The rural; out in the rural; 1 inf, **ceAR**, In the rural; 1 inf, **neMS**, Out in the rurals; 1 inf, **seMS**, In the rural we had; 1 inf, **seMS**, The rural; 1 inf, **ceTX**, Out in the rural; people in the rurals. [5 of 6 infs Black] **1998**

DARE File **nwMS** [Black], Here are . . words I know from black people of Marks. . . in the rural—out in the country.

rurn See **ruin A1**

rurned, rurnt See **ruin A2c**

rush v, n[1] Usu |rʌš|; also |rɛš, rɝ·š| Pronc-spp *resh, rursh* Cf **brush** n, v[1] **A1, 4**

A Forms.

1848 Lowell *Biglow* 145 'Upcountry MA', Resh, rush. **1916** *DN* 4.340 **seOH,** The sound of *r* is usually inserted between certain *u* or *e* sounds and *sh* (=[š]). For example, . . *rursh* (rush). **1923** (1946) Greer-Petrie *Angeline Steppin'* 36 **csKY,** He reshes up and interduces hisse'f. **1930s** in 1944 *ADD* **eWV,** 'Don't get in a rursh.' 'Don't rursh.' |rɝʃ|. **1942** Hall *Smoky Mt. Speech* 41 **wNC, eTN,** In unschooled speech [ʌ] is sometimes replaced by [ɛ], as in . . *rush.*

B As noun.

Std: a plant of the genus *Juncus.* Also called **wire grass.** For other names of var spp see **black grass, frog rush, joint ~, needlegrass 4, niggerhead 3i, nut grass 2, poverty ~ 2g, salt hay, sugar grass, whip, wildcat grass**

rush n[2] See **run** n **8**

rush bird n
=**bobolink B.**

1968 *DARE* (Qu. Q14, . . *Names . . for . . bobolink*) Inf **IN33,** Rush bird.

Rushea See **Russia**

rush grass n
=**dropseed 3.**

1832 MA Hist. Soc. *Coll.* 2d ser 9.151 **cwVT,** Juncus effusus, . . Juncus setaceus, . . Juncus nodosus, . . Juncus tenuis, . . Juncus campestris, Rush grass. **1897** IN Dept. Geol. & Nat. Resources *Rept. for 1896* 598, [*Sporobolus*] *asper* . . Rough Rush-grass. Sandy banks and hillsides. **1914** Georgia *Manual Weeds* 47, Small Rush-grass . . *Sporobolus neglectus.* **1930** OK Univ. Biol. Surv. *Pub.* 2.53, *Sporobolus angustus* . . Dense Rush-grass. *Ibid,* *Sporobolus asper* . . Long-leaved Rush-grass. *Ibid, Sporobolus clandestinus* . . Rough Rush-grass. *Ibid, Sporobolus neglectus* . . Small Rush-grass. **1937** U.S. Forest Serv. *Range Plant Hdbk.* G108, Most of the dropseeds are bunchgrasses, but a few of the perennial species, such as Mississippi dropseed, or rushgrass (*S. macrus*) and seashore dropseed, or rushgrass (*S. virginicus),* have creeping rootstocks. **1973** Hitchcock–Cronquist *Flora Pacific NW* 670, *Sporobolus* [spp] . . Dropseed. Rush-grass.

rush lily n
A **blue-eyed grass 1;** see quots.

1884 Miller *Dict. Engl. Names of Plants* 119, Rush-Lily. The genus *Sisyrinchium.* Purple. *Sisyrinchium grandiflorum.* White. *Sisyrinchium grandiflorum var album.* **1938** (1958) Sharples *AK Wild Flowers* 140, *Sisyrinchium* [spp]. . . "Blue-eyed Grass," "Rush Lily," "Grass Widow."

rush nut See **nut rush 2**

rush pea n
A plant of the genus *Hoffmannseggia.* Also called **mesquite weed.** For other names of var spp see **hog potato 4, pignut 7**

1968 Barkley *Plants KS* 191, Hoffmanseggia jamesii . . Rush Peg [sic]. **1970** Correll *Plants TX* 798, *Hoffmannseggia drepanocarpa* . . Sicklepod rush-pea. . . In sandy or limestone soils in w. Tex. **1970** Kirk *Wild Edible Plants W. U.S.* 255, *Hoffmannseggia densiflora* . . Camote-de-Raton, Hog Potato, Rushpea.

rush pink n
A **skeletonweed 3.**

1935 (1943) Muenscher *Weeds* 510, Lygodesmia juncea. . . Skeletonweed, Rush pink, Wild asparagus, Devils shoestring. **1963** [see **skeletonweed 3**]. **1970** Kirk *Wild Edible Plants W. U.S.* 149, Rush-Pink is found in dry, sandy or gravelly soil . . throughout the west except for Washington, Oregon, California, and western Nevada. **1973** Hitchcock–Cronquist *Flora Pacific NW* 537, Lygodesmia [spp]. . . Rush-pink.

rush sparrow n
=**field sparrow a.**

1832 Nuttall *Manual Ornith.* 1.499, Field or rush sparrow. . . This small species, in size and general color, is scarcely distinguishable from the Chipping Sparrow. **1841** (1949) Thoreau *Jrl.* 1.265 **MA,** The rush sparrow sings still unintelligible. **1917** (1923) *Birds Amer.* 3.44, Thoreau says: "The Rush Sparrow [a local name for the bird in his time, and one still sometimes used] jingles her small change, pure silver, on the counter of the pastures." **1944** Hausman *Amer. Birds* 527, Sparrow, Rush—see Sparrow, Field.

rush the growler See **growler** n[2] **1**

Russell Barlow knife See **barlow knife**

Russia n Usu |'rʌšə|; also |'rušə, 'ruši|; for addit varr see quots Pronc-spp *Rooshy, Rushea*
Std sense, var forms.

1785 in 1956 Eliason *Tarheel Talk* 291, Rushea Duck. **1862** *Vanity Fair* 25 Jan 50, A Minister to Rooshy. **1904** *DN* 2.423 **Cape Cod MA** (as of a1857), Russia (Rooshy). **1939** *LANE* Map 26 *(Russia)* **NEng,** [Proncs of the type ['rušə, 'ruši, 'rʌʃi] are found scattered throughout the region and are characterized by 40 infs as older but still in use. The pronc ['rušiə] is also found, though much less frequently.] **1973** *PADS* 60.45 **seNC,** Russia. . . [T]he vowel /ʌ/ of *rush* is regularly used by the cultured and most of the middle group. The Carteret County informants all said [ʌ] or [ʌ‹], except one who used [u]. **1981** Pederson *LAGS Basic Materials,* 1 inf, **cGA,** ['rʌ^ʃ,ɪ̯ɝ]; 1 inf, **nwAR,** ['ru‹u‹ʃə] (facetious); 1 inf, **ceTX,** ['rʉʉʃi] (uncle called it this).

Russian adj, n Usu |'rʌšən|; also |'rušən, -ɪn| Pronc-spp *Rooshan, Roos(h)ian*
Std senses, var forms.

1848 Lowell *Biglow* 57 'Upcountry' **MA,** The Rooshian black eagle looks blue in his eerie. **1939** [see **Russian boar**]. **1941** in 1944 *ADD,* Russia. . . There'll be a rush of Rooshian films after Jan. 1. **1942** Hall *Smoky Mt. Speech* 41 **wNC, eTN,** [Footnote:] *Russian hog* is ['rušən 'hɔg]. **1948** [see **Russian boar**]. **1954** (1962) *Catahoula Hog Dog* 3, I have hunted . . the 250-pound "Rooshans" along the North Carolina–Tennessee line. **1957** *Sat. Eve. Post Letters,* My father came from Malone, Franklin Co., N.Y. and now at 96 he still says 'Roosians' for Russians. **1967–68** *DARE* (Qu. S21) Infs **CO4,** 20, ['rušən] thistle; (Qu. HH28) Infs **CA106, NE3,** 6, ['rušən(z)]; **IN5,** ['rušɪnz]. **1979** *AmSp* 54.93 **sME** (as of 1899–1910) Roosian.

Russian boar n Also *Russian (wild boar),* ~ *(wild) hog* chiefly **Sth**

A wild boar introduced to Hooper's Bald, North Carolina, c1910; the offspring of such an animal and a domestic pig.

1939 FWP *Guide TN* 128, For Tennessee's newest big game animal—the Russian wild boar, locally called "Rooshian" wild hog—the ancient sport of boar hunting has been revived. . . When jumped by the dogs, the "Rooshians" strike through brush-grown ravines and over laurel-covered mountain slopes. **1948** Camp *Hunter's Encycl.* 40, Short-sighted and ill-tempered, the Russian fights at close range. *Ibid* 43, On arriving at an area which a boar is known to be using, the dogs are cast and the hunters take it easy until a "Rooshian" is jumped. **1966–68** *DARE* (Qu. P32, . . *Other kinds of wild animals*) Inf **GA19,** Russian hog; **NC36,** Russian boar. **1984** *DARE* File **wNC,** Russian boar—a wild boar. **1986** Pederson *LAGS Concordance,* 2 infs, **cwGA, swAR,** Russian wild boar; 1 inf, **cnGA,** Russian boar—stocked in North GA; 1 inf, **seTN,** Russian boars; 1 inf, **csTX,** Russian boars—400–600 pounds—temperamental. **1998** *DARE* File—Internet [All Outdoors *Understanding and Hunting the Wild Boar*], When many of us think about wild boar, we think of one thing—Russian boars. These are the fierce, huge-tusked, heavy-bodied boars we see in the hunting magazine ads.

Russian cactus See **Russian thistle**

Russian cat n
=**flathead catfish 1.**

1896 U.S. Natl. Museum *Bulletin* 47.143, *Leptops olivaris* . . Mud Cat, Yellow Cat, Bashaw, Russian Cat. . . Rivers of the Mississippi Valley and Southern States, southwest to Chihuahua. **1902** Jordan–Evermann *Amer. Fishes* 33, The names Bashaw and Russian cat are sometimes heard, but their origin has not been explained. **1976** Tryckare et al. *Lore of Sportfishing* 79, Flathead catfish . . Other common names: Mud catfish . . Russian cat [etc].

Russian coupling n
In logging: see quots.

1950 *Western Folkl.* 9.381 **neCA** [Lumberjack language], *Russian* *coupling.* Occurs when two logs are not completely sawed through. **1958** McCulloch *Woods Words* 154 **Pacific NW,** *Russian coupling*—A log which the bucker did not completely cut off from the next one.

Russian hog See Russian boar

Russian peanut n

A dried sunflower seed; less freq a dried watermelon seed.

1938 FWP *Guide ND* 81 **csND,** A favorite delicacy of the Russo-Germans, also typically Russian, is the sunflower seed, known as the "Russian peanut." **1950** Bracke *Wheat Country* 79 **cKS,** Sunflower seeds, frequently called Russian peanuts after they have been dried, are also widely eaten. **1959** Tallman *Dict. Amer. Folkl.* 257 **KS,** "Russian peanuts"—The people of Ellis County, Kansas, gave this name to the dried sunflower seeds which were popular in that area. They also included dried watermelon seeds.

Russian pigweed n Cf pigweed 2

An annual herb *(Axyris amaranthoides)* of the family Chenopodiaceae.

1914 Georgia *Manual Weeds* 119, Russian pigweed. . . A native of Siberia, first appearing in this country in 1886, in Canada near Winnipeg, Manitoba; since when the plant has spread very rapidly, east, west, and south. **1925** *Book of Rural Life* 4844, Russian pigweed . . an introduced annual weed that occurs from New Brunswick to Manitoba, Minnesota and South Dakota. **1935** (1943) Muenscher *Weeds* 205, *Axyris amaranthoides* [sic] . . Russian pigweed. . . Grain fields, roadsides and along railroads and waste places.

Russian rabbit n Cf marsh rabbit 2

=**muskrat 1** when regarded as food.

1969 *DARE* (Qu. P31, . . *Names or nicknames . . for the . . muskrat*) Infs **MI108,** Russian rabbit—when served at a meal.

Russian rat n NC Cf neutral

The nutria *(Myocaster coypus).*

1969 *DARE* (Qu. P32, . . *Other kinds of wild animals*) Inf **NC60,** Russian rats—imported from Russia, running rampant now. **1969** *DARE* FW Addit **NC,** Russian rat—A South American rodent introduced by a rod & gun club; so called by natives. A nutria. Found on Hatteras Island, N.C. **1994** NC Lang. & Life Project *Dial. Vocab.* Ocracoke 15 **eNC,** *Russian rat.* . . A large rodent found on Ocracoke, technically known as a *nutria. We have lots of Russian rats and mink on the island.*

Russian thistle n Also Russian cactus, ~ tumbleweed

An annual thorny weed *(Salsola kali* var *tenuifolia)* of high arid western lands. Also called **pigweed 3, tumbleweed, wind witch**

1893 U.S. Dept. Ag. *Farmers' Bulletin* 10.3 **NW,** The Russian thistle or Russian cactus is really neither a thistle nor a cactus. . . Under any name, however, it is one of the worst weeds ever introduced into the wheat fields of America. . . To the farmers of the Northwest, who are best acquainted with the troublesome plant, it will probably continue to be known as the Russian thistle until finally exterminated. **1894** U.S. Dept. Ag. Div. Botany *Bulletin* 15.7, This plant is generally called Russian thistle in South Dakota and Russian cactus in North Dakota. Russian tumbleweed and other appropriate names have been suggested, but have not met the approval of popular usage. **1908** NM Univ. *Biol. Ser.* 3.1.83 **cNM,** [Salsola] *Kali,* var. *tragus.* The Russian Thistle, "*Tumble Weed.*" This spiny plant is too common around Albuquerque, especially on the western edge of the mesa and where the soil has been disturbed by grading or along trails. **1935** (1943) Muenscher *Weeds* 214, *Salsola Kali . . var. tenuifolia* . . Russian thistle, Saltwort, Prickly glasswort, Russian cactus, Russian tumble weed [etc]. **1937** Sandoz *Slogum* 205 **NE,** Every day the girl seemed more like a Russian thistle in the fall, russet and soft to the eye but prickly and unyielding, and vacillating in every wind. **1965–70** *DARE* (Qu. S21, . . *Weeds . . that are a trouble in gardens and fields*) 27 Infs, **chiefly West,** Russian thistle(s); **CO20,** Russian thistle—more stickery—when dry called tumbleweeds; **ID1,** Russian thistle—very tall with lavender blossom at top; **MT3,** Russian thistle—becomes tumbleweed in fall; (Qu. I28b, *Kinds of greens that are cooked)* Inf **CO20,** Russian thistles—about 4 feet high; (Qu. S14) Inf **OR1,** Russian thistle—blue flower; (Qu. S15, . . *Weed seeds that cling to clothing)* Infs **CA181, 195,** Russian thistle; (Qu. S20) Inf **IL44,** Russian thistle. **1966** *DARE* Tape **SD3,** They used Russian thistles for hay. . . It is a great big thistle. Never would think of using it otherwise, but they made hay out of it. Cut it when it was real green. Russian thistles really thrived in that kind of weather and they'd blow. You could go

along your fence line after they'd got broken loose from the roots and they'd just pile up on the fences. You'd go along the fences and pick up your Russian thistles and put them in a haystack. **1966** *DARE* FW Addit **WA12,** Russian thistle—a tumbleweed—grows up & forms a ball shape—prickly. In fall wind breaks it loose & it rolls. **1986** McPhee *Rising from the Plains* 74 **WY,** Spheres of tumbleweed, tumbling east, came at us on the interstate at high speed, like gymfuls of bouncing basketballs dribbled by the dexterous wind. "It's a Russian thistle". . . "It's one of nature's marvels. As it tumbles, seeds are exploded out."

Russian turnip n Also Russia turnip Cf Swedish turnip =rutabaga B.

1819 *Plough Boy* 1.46 **ceNY,** There were six competitors for the premium offered for the best acre of the *Ruta Baga* or *Russian turnip.* **1822** Cobbett *Year's Residence U.S.A.* 48, The *Ruta Baga* is a sort of turnip well known in the State of New York, where, under the name of *Russia* turnip, it is used for the Table from February to July. **1863** Burr *Field & Garden* 86, Ruta-baga, or Swede Turnip. Russian Turnip. French Turnip. **1968** *DARE* (Qu. I3, . . *The large yellowish root vegetable, similar to a turnip, with a strong taste)* Inf **NY43,** Russian turnip.

Russian wild boar (or hog) See Russian boar

Russia turnip See Russian turnip

Russki n Also Rooskie [Russ *Russkiy; OED2* 1858 →] Cf Norski

A Russian or person of Russian descent.

1919 in 1972 *AmSp* 47.93 (as of 1917–19) [Slang of Amer Forces in Europe], Large numbers of lowly 'Rooskies' plodded through the weary days. **1967–68** *DARE* (Qu. HH28, *Names and nicknames . . for people of foreign background: Russian)* Infs **MI67, OH42,** Russki. **1986** Pederson *LAGS Concordance* **Gulf Region** *(Russians;* this question was asked chiefly in urban areas) 18 infs, Russki(es); 1 inf, Russki—only term she has heard; not insulting; 1 inf, Russkies—used by his grandfather's friends.

russle v See rustle v

russle n See rustle n

rusticator n ME

A vacationer, esp a summer boarder.

1869 *Harper's New Mth. Mag.* 39.653 **NY,** It is its romantic wooded rock scenery, dark caverns, [etc] . . that render the Helderberg interesting to artist, author, poet, tourist, or rusticator. **1884** in 1953 Johnson *Sullivan* 127 **ME,** Affording superior accommodations at reasonable charges to families, tourists and rusticators, and all those seeking a healthful and pleasant place during the summer months. **1908** Wasson *Home from Sea* 148 **sME coast,** Of course they're chock-a-block full of their cranky idees, else they would n't be rusticators. . . You let her tell it, and all the rest-part of the rusticators that has to pack up their dunnage and be off to them city-places afore ever the leaves has turned. **1941** *LANE* Map 449 *(Tourist)* 10 infs, **ME,** Rusticator; 1 inf, **ME,** Rusticator, one who stays several weeks in the country; 1 inf, **ME,** Rusticator, older term. **1971** *Courier–Gaz.* (Rockland ME) 15 Aug 24 **cME coast,** Harbor scene at Owls Head, one of the coast's earliest gathering places for summer "rusticators." **1975** Gould *ME Lingo* 237, *Rusticator—A summer complaint,* but the derivation of the word suggests the farm rather than the seashore or the woods.

rusticrat n [Prob blend of rusticator + aristocrat] Cf arichtocrat

1895 *DN* 1.393 **ME, DE,** *Rusticrat:* summer visitor of the richer class. Mt. Desert, Me.; Del.

rustle v Pronc-spp rostle, russle

A Transitive senses.

1 also with *up:* To get by foraging; to obtain or assemble by one's own efforts; rarely, to search (an area) for. **formerly chiefly West, now widespread**

1844 *Spirit of Times* 14 Sept 343 **MS,** He nailed my thumb in his jaws, and rostled up a handfull of dirt and throwed it in my eyes. **1889** U.S. Natl. Museum *Annual Rept. for 1887* 2.451 **Plains States,** His first care is to start out with his largest gunning-bag to "rustle some buffalo chips" for a camp-fire. **1893** in 1932 *AmSp* 7.260 **NE** [Hobo terms], *Rustle a meal*—hunting something to eat. **1903** (1965) Adams *Log Cowboy* 332 **West,** The work was divided up . . , Honeyman being excused on agreeing to rustle the wood and water. **1919** *DN* 5.37 **OK,** *Rustle.* . . To hunt, or find. "He lit out and rustled up the 'kale-seed' (money)." **1935** Davis *Honey* 12 **OR,** She helped them guess about the meaning of the fires on Round Mountain while she rustled their supper. **1942** Kennedy *Palmetto Country* 237 **FL,** As cattle king Hendry has written, "The razorback . . rustles the marshes for wampee, a root similar to the arrow." **1943** Howard *Montana* 150, The Texas dogies would stand around the ranch house and bawl for their food instead of going out and rustling it for themselves. **1951** West *Witch Diggers* 12 **IN,** A couple of jumbles, . . if you can rustle them up, wouldn't be bad either. **1956** Sorden–Ebert *Logger's Words* 28 **Gt Lakes,** *Rustle wood.* . . To bring the wood inside the logging camp ready to be fed into the stove. **1969** *DARE* (Qu. H7, *When a housewife is about to prepare a meal* . . *"I have to go and _____ supper."*) Infs **NC72, VT16,** Rustle up. **1969** *DARE* Tape **CA159,** We were all born there at the old home place. Born without a doctor, no birth certificate; every one of us had to rustle up a birth certificate in late years.

2a To make to move rapidly; to hustle (someone).

1882 *Century Illustr. Mag.* 24.508, 'Rustle the things off that table,' means clear the table in a hurry. **1966–68** *DARE* (Qu. A19, . . *"I'm late, I'll have to _____."*) Inf **MI22,** Rustle my bones; (Qu. A20, *Joking ways of telling somebody to hurry*) Infs **CA15, NY49,** Rustle your bustle; (Qu. X44, *To get somebody out of bed early in the morning: "I had to _____"*; total Infs questioned, 75) Inf **AR28,** Rustle him out of bed; (Qu. Y23, . . *To* . . *get yourself in motion: "I was so stiff I could hardly _____."*) Inf **CA15,** Rustle your bustle. **1999** *DARE* File **cwCA** (as of c1960), *Rustle your bustle* was a phrase used to urge someone to hurry.

b also with *in, up:* To drive or round up (livestock); to herd; rarely, to round up the animals in (an enclosure). **chiefly West**

1896 Dice *Life* 30, I . . 'rustled' up a good big herd of cattle which we shipped to the Kansas City market. **1902** McElrath *Rustler* xi **West,** Then the cowpuncher who had used to go out and "rustle" mavericks for his employer became on his own account a "rustler." **1903** (1965) Adams *Log Cowboy* 53 **West,** Our foreman, as though fearful of the loss of a moment's time, sent Honeyman to rustle in the horses before we had finished our dinners. **1919** *DN* 5.37 **OK,** *Rustle.* . . To herd (cattle). **1921** Chapman *Cactus Center* 5, But he [=a reporter from the East] wrote, with good intentions, as most everyone allows,/ "Our townsman, Poker Johnson, has gone South to rustle cows";/ He meant to say that Poker was a-roundin' up his brand,/ For he didn't know that "rustle" meant to "thieve" in Cattle Land. **1933** *AmSp* 8.1.30 **nwTX** [Ranch diction], *Rustle.* To tend the *remuda*; to steal cattle on the range. **1967** *DARE* Tape **TX47,** I've worked with sheep. Rustled sheep, tended sheep. **1968** Adams *Western Words* 262, *Rustle the pasture*—A cowboy's expression for bringing in the saddle horses in preparation for the roundup.

3 To convey illicitly, steal (esp cattle); rarely, to rob; hence vbl n, ppl adj *rustling.* **formerly chiefly West, now widespread** Cf **rustler 3**

1879 Lew Wallace *MS* 23 March (In Lib. Ind. Hist. Soc., Indianapolis) (*Mathews Coll.*), Rustling Bob (found dead in the Pecos killed by his own party). **1893** in 1932 *AmSp* 7.259 **NE** [Cowboy terms], *Rustle*—to steal. **1895** [see **B1** below]. **1897** Lewis *Wolfville* 18 **AZ,** 'If this yere industrious hold-up keeps up his lick,' says Texas Thompson about the third time the stage gets rustled, 'an' heads off a few more letters of mine, . . my wife back in Laredo ain't goin' to onderstand it none.' **1897** *KS Univ. Qrly.* (ser B) 6.91 **West,** *Rustle:* to run off cattle. **1907** Mulford *Bar-20* 59 **West,** Mebby he rustled some grub out with him—I saw him tiptoein' out of th' gallery this mornin'. *Ibid* 60, I'd shore look nice askin' th' *boss* if he'd rustled my whisky, *wouldn't I?* **1909** *DN* 3.403 **OK,** *Rustle.* . . To steal. "He has a right smart bunch of calves, but we think he rustled most of them." **1921** [see **A2b** above]. **1933** [see **A2b** above]. **1936** *Sun* (Baltimore MD) 9 Feb 2/6 (*Hench Coll.*) **NY,** Every time he returned Walter found he had less money than the cost of the food—the boys had been rustling the tray. **1937** *Ibid* 23 Oct 3/2 (*Hench Coll.*), Battle front of the cotton-rustling racket—offspring of nearly defunct cattle and liquor smuggling operation—is the Fabens Island area along the Rio Grande. **1940** *AmSp* 15.220 **cwTX,** If this 'wrangler' is playful but not vicious, the 'pusher' (foreman) may claim that 'he'll do to ride the river with.' . . [T]his expression means that the 'cow-waddie' could be relied on even for 'rustling' contraband from Mexico to Texas. **1963** *Wall St. Jrl.* (NY NY) 11 Oct 4 (*Hench Coll.*), Growers Move to Thwart Florida Orange 'Rustlers.' . . Add "orange rustling" to the list of crimes against society. **1967** *DARE* (Qu. V4, . . *Stealing something valuable* . . *"Yesterday somebody _____ my watch."*) Inf **TN1,** Rustled.

4 To catch, "nab."

1906 *DN* 3.154 **nwAR,** *Rustle.* . . To catch and shake out. "As soon as the dog saw the rabbit he rustled it." **1934** *Sun* (Baltimore MD) 8 Aug 5/6 (*Hench Coll.*), Painesville, Ohio . . —Two men shot and killed a young heifer, then were rustled as they attempted to pack it into a big sedan.

5 See quots.

1940 *RR Mag.* April 51, *Rustling the bums*—Searching a freight train for hobos. **1945** Hubbard *Railroad Ave.* 358, *Rustling the bums*—Searching a freight train for hobos. In bygone days it was common practice for trainmen to collect money from freight-riding 'bos, often at the rate of a dollar a division.

B Intransitive senses.

1 also with *(a)round:* To work energetically, hustle, bustle, esp in difficult circumstances; hence vbl n, ppl adj *rustling.* Cf **rustler 1**

[**1872** Johnson *Very Far West* 191 **British Columbia Canada,** There is the middle-class rustler, who starts a store . . upon credit. *Ibid,* 'Rustling' is an Americanism, denoting the process of fighting against odds for a living. *Ibid* 195, I've rustled upwards from a picayune printin' office down to New Orleans.] **1881** *NY Times* (NY) 18 Dec 4/3 **MT,** *Rustle.*—Grappling with circumstances. Rising superior to all contingencies of "luck." Cattle, in Winter, "rustle" for food by nosing through the snow to the dried grass beneath. **1882** *Century Illustr. Mag.* 24.508 **ND,** To rustle around is to bestir one's self in a business way. *Ibid,* To do a rustling business is to carry on an active trade. **1884** *Anglia* 7.274 **Sth, S Midl** [Black], *To russle 'roun'* = to bustle. **1885** *Harper's New Mth. Mag.* 71.190 **MT,** Rustle now, boys, rustle! for you have a long and hard day's work before you. **1885** Twain *Huck. Finn* 100 **MO,** We'll rustle around and gether up whatever pickins we've overlooked in the staterooms, and shove for shore and hide the truck. **c1895** (1914) Norris *Vandover* 95 **San Francisco CA,** You bet I've been working . . working like a dog. A man's got to rustle if he's going to make a success at law. **1895** *DN* 1.393 **West,** *Rustle* (a): to be active = hustle; (b) to steal. *Rustler,* (n.) to both meanings. **1909** *DN* 3.365 **eAL, wGA,** *Rustle.* . . To hustle. *Ibid* 403 **nwAR,** *Rustle.* . . To be active. "I'll rustle around and get up the money to pay that note." "You'll have to rustle if you make your train." **1935** in 1983 Taft *Blues Lyric Poetry* 23, I'm a rustling man : I rustle night and day / Just as soon as I get my money : I won't have to rustle this a-way. **1942** Perry *Texas* 157, I rustled around my hog herd [=circle of acquaintances] and raised about seven hundred dollars. **1968** *DARE* (Qu. A19, *Other ways of saying "I'll have to hurry": "I'm late, I'll have to _____."*) Inf **KS14,** Rustle.

2 also with *about:* To search, forage (for); of livestock: to live off the land without supplemental feed; hence ppl adj *rustling.* **chiefly West**

1881 [see **B1** above]. **1890** [see **rustler 2**]. **1890** *Stock Grower & Farmer* (Las Vegas NM) 29 Mar 4/2 **WY,** The condition of rustling animals is . . deplorable. **1911** (1916) Porter *Harvester* 6 **IN,** Do I go on as I have ever since mother left me, rustling for grub, living in untrammelled freedom? **1925** *AmSp* 1.150 **West,** "Rustle for your bacon" is much more than a quaint Westernism; it is the expression of a people still close to their grim struggle with an unrelenting wilderness. **1927** Siringo *Riata* 187 **TX,** Many of these Indians had never seen or heard of cattle before, . . so muley and her calf were turned out on the tall grass to rustle for themselves. **1929** *AmSp* 5.68 **NE** [Cattle country talk], "To rustle" as applied to cattle, means to let the cattle hunt their own feed in the "winter pasture" or "range" under the snow. Some cattle are "good rustlers." **1935** Sandoz *Jules* 108 **wNE** (as of 1880–1930), Cattle men from Dakota said this was more like the old days, when stock rustled all winter and came through strong and in good meat. **1956** Gipson *Old Yeller* 88 **TX,** We never fed them [=hogs], unless maybe it was a little corn that we threw to them during a bad spell in the winter. The rest of the time, they rustled for themselves.

3 Among miners: to look for work; to ask for work at (a particular mine); hence vbl noun *rustling,* often attrib; see quots.

1939 (1973) FWP *Guide MT* 71 (as of c1912), The mines adopted the "rustling card" system under which company-owned employment offices issued cards granting permission to "rustle" (ask for work) at the mines. Before a card could be issued, the applicant was required to give his personal history. Upon taking a job he had to surrender his card. **1950** Jensen *Heritage Conflict* 323 **MT,** On December 1, 1912, the Anaconda Copper Mining Company established its "rustling office." In order to secure employment a man had to procure a "rustling card" which gave him the right to go to the mines to rustle for work. **1950** *Western Folkl.* 9.21 **MT,** One of the best of the group of rustling songs is "The

Butte Miners' Rustling Song," as sung by George Prescott. *Ibid* 22, [Lyrics:] Well now, I've rustled the High Ore, I've rustled the Bell;/ I've rustled the Diamond, I've rustled like hell;/ I've rustled the Mountain Con, Mountain View, too,/ And I landed a job in the El-ler-mer-loo.

rustle n Also sp *russle*

1 A hustle—in phr *get a rustle on* to get a move on.   Cf **rustle** v **B1**

1896 Crane *Maggie* 101 **NYC,** Hi, you, git a russle on yehs! **1899** C.W. Gordon *Sky Pilot* xxi *(DAE),* It's about time for me to get a rustle on.

2 An illegitimate or abandoned child.   Cf *DS* Z11a, b

1944 *Collier's* 23 Sept 12 **Harlem NYC,** A drop or a rustle is a boy of completely undetermined parentage. *Ibid* 13, A professional granny accepting anywhere from twenty-five cents to a dollar a week for taking in drops, rustles, fetches or whatever you've a mind to call them.

rustle around See **rustle** v **B1**

rustle in See **rustle** v **A2b**

rustler n

1 An energetic, ambitious person.   Cf **rustle** v **B1**

[1872 see **rustle** v **B1.**] **1881** *NY Times* (NY) 18 Dec 4/3 **MT,** *Rustler.*—One who never succumbs to circumstances. This is about the highest compliment that can be paid to a man who, failing in one thing, finds something else available for his support. **1882** *Century Illustr. Mag.* 24.508, He was evidently what they call in Dakota a "rustler." To say that a man is a rustler is the highest endorsement a Dakotan can give. It means he is pushing, energetic, smart, and successful. **1895** [see **rustle** v **B1**]. **1909** *DN* 3.403 **nwAR,** *Rustler.* . . An active person. "He's a rustler. He made a thousand dollars in three years." **1935** Sandoz *Jules* 37 **wNE** (as of 1880–1930), Naw, you got the wind wrong. The parson ain't a rustler, he's a *rustler*—works hard scratching souls together for Kingdom Come. *Ibid* 195, "Jules's wife sure cleaned him up. She must be a rustler," the neighbors were remarking. **1942** Whipple *Joshua* 424 **UT** (as of c1860), 'Has 'Sheba cleaned house yet?' asked Pal, puffing along. Clory nodded absently. 'My, she's certainly a rustler!' Lucy was admiring. **1967** *DARE* (Qu. HH27a, *A very able and energetic person who gets things done*) Inf **CA24,** Rustler.

2 A nominally domestic animal that survives by foraging for itself.   Cf **rustle** v **B2**

1881 Romspert *W. Echo* 190 **TX,** He is a good rustler and will find enough to live on. **1890** *Harper's New Mth. Mag.* 80.689, The California sheep . . are . . known as "rustlers," because they must rustle about for their food. **1929** [see **rustle** v **B2**]. **1956** Almirall *From College* 55 **CO,** Herefords, the breed of cattle I knew were considered, and proved to be, the best rustlers on open range. Rustlers in this case meant critters which were able to keep themselves in good shape even when grazing was none too good. **1966** Barnes–Jensen *Dict. UT Slang* 37, *Rustler:* . . (a) a cattlethief; (b) a grazing animal that is good at finding food for itself. **1969** *DARE* (Qu. J6, *A cat that catches lots of rats and mice* . . "*She's a good _____*.") Inf **CA131,** Rustler.

3 A thief, robber, esp a cattle thief.   **formerly West, now widespread**   Cf **rustle** v **A3**

1878 in 1954 *AmSp* 29.15, Dolan, Captain Jesse Evans (of the Banditti) came up to Ft. Stanton and stopped there where they could get protection from the military, while the Rustlers, as they called themselves robbed the citizens. **1882** *Blackwood's Edinburgh Mag.* 131.273, A gang of "rustlers" [=train robbers]—as the lawless desperadoes who abound in Arizona, New Mexico, and Texas are called. **1883** *The Vindicator* (Los Lunas, New Mexico) Oct. 27 *(Century Dict.),* A horde of rustlers who are running off stock. **1889** Nelson *50 Yrs.* 364 **SD,** These men, however, must not be confounded with another class of desperadoes—*i.e.* those who would not work and were what is termed "Rustlers" or house [=*DARE* Ed: prob for *horse*] thieves. **1893** in 1932 *AmSp* 7.258 **NE,** Hence the only way of preventing the true ownership of a calf from being known, is to separate it from the cow, to do which the latter is not infrequently killed by the *rustlers* or *Maverick thieves.* **1895** [see **rustle** v **B1**]. **1929** *AmSp* 5.58 **NE** [Cattle country talk], Formerly "waddie" meant a "rustler," a stealer of others' cattle. **1931** *AmSp* 7.120 **eID,** A *slow elk* is the cattle *rustler's* (cattle thief's) term for a calf. **1935** Sandoz *Jules* 121 **wNE** (as of 1880–1930), The cattlemen from the mountains of Wyoming to the corn lands of Nebraska organized against rustlers. **1936** McCarthy *Lang. Mosshorn* np **West** [Range terms], *Rustler.* . . An "appropriator" of cattle. **1963** [see **rustle** v **A3**]. **1966–70** *DARE* (Qu. V6, . . *Words . . for a thief*) Infs **CA87, NM12,** Rustler; **IL136,** Cattle rustler. **1970** Green *Ely* 101 **eTN**

[Black] (as of c1910), I dismounted and sneaked around the shoulder of the canyon . . , only to find it was old man Wat Cannon, who Grandpa had call [sic] him a hog rustler.

4 A ranch cook or **camp tender 1.**   Cf **rustle** v **A1**

1887 *Scribner's Mag.* 2.508 **West,** The cook on a ranch used to be called a "rustler." **1913** (1979) Barnes *Western Grazing* 157, With each outfit is a camp rustler, or tender, who goes ahead of the sheep, picks out a camping place, keeps the camp stocked with food and supplies. . . Where one owner has several bands one rustler can take care of more than one.

5 See quot.   Cf **rustle** v **A2b**

1933 *AmSp* 8.1.30 **nwTX** [Ranch diction], *Rustler.* One who tends the *remuda;* a cattle thief.

6 in comb *lumber rustler:* See quot.

1927 *AmSp* 3.24 **eTX** [Sawmill talk], The common laborer is variously known as a "lumber rustler," "rosum belly," or "sawdust eater."

7 =**sea catfish.**   [Perh by ext from **2** above].   Cf **turd-rustler**

1967 *DARE* (Qu. P4, *Saltwater fish that are not good to eat*) Inf **TX19,** Saltwater catfish—also called hardhead and rustler.

rustle round See **rustle** v **B1**

rustle up See **rustle** v **A1, 2b**

rustling See **rustle** v **A3, B1, 2, 3**

rust robin n

=**brown thrasher.**

1950 *WELS* (*What other names are used for . . Brown thrasher*) 1 Inf, **csWI,** Rust robin. **1995** *DARE* File **csWI** (as of 1940s), It [=brown thrasher] was also known as a rust robin in Cottage Grove, Wisconsin.

rusty adj[1] [Cf *OED2* rusty a.[1] 3 "Of persons: Presenting an appearance suggestive of something old and rusted"] **West**   Cf **dogie 1**

Runty, stunted; hence n *rusty* a stunted or low-grade beef animal.

1936 McCarthy *Lang. Mosshorn* np **West** [Range terms], *Rusties.* . . Cattle of slight value for any purpose. **1944** Adams *Western Words* 135, *Rusties*—Culled, wild, or lean cattle. **1961** Adams *Old-Time Cowhand* 158 **West,** A scrawny, poorly developed animal was a "rusty." *Ibid* 211 **West,** No matter how much he paid for the bull that sired his calves, they'd become dogied and rusty.

rusty adj[2] [*OED2* rusty a.[2], var of *resty* < Fr *resté* left over, 1515 →; "Very common in the 17th and 18th centuries, and still wide-spread in dialect use."]   **esp Sth**

Of meat, esp bacon: rancid.

1790 Deane *New Engl. Farmer* 280, The pork should be kept continually under pickle; for if it be exposed ever so little to the air, it will become rusty and unpalatable. **1855** Douglass *My Bondage* 76 **MD,** The water, in which meat had been boiled, was as eagerly sought for by me. It was a great thing to get the privilege of dipping a piece of bread in such water; and the skin taken from rusty bacon, was a positive luxury. **1859** (1860) Creecy *Scenes South* 106 **Sth,** I had never fallen in with any cooking so villanous. Rusty salt pork, boiled or fried, "solitary and alone," . . and musty corn-meal dodgers. **1899** (1912) Green *VA Folk-Speech* 362, *Rusty.* . . Rancid: "rusty bacon." **1986** Pederson *LAGS Concordance* (*The meat is _____*) 1 inf, **nwFL,** Rusty.

rusty adj[3] [*OED2* rusty a.[3] "Of horses: Restive. In phr *to ride,* or *run, rusty.* Freq of persons: To become intractable or obstinate; to be angry or annoyed; to take offence."]

In phr *cut up rusty:* To become obstreperous.

[1891 Farmer–Henley *Slang* 2.243, *Cut up* [*rough, rusty, savage, stiff, ugly,* etc.], *verbal phr.*—To become quarrelsome or dangerous. [*DARE* Ed: No ex of *cut up rusty* is quoted; the exx of the other phrr are from Dickens, Thackeray, and Trollope.]] **1899** (1912) Green *VA Folk-Speech* 362, *Rusty.* . . Unruly; ill-humoured; "he cut up rusty"; applied to persons or horses.

rusty n[1] See **rusty** adj[1]

rusty n[2] [The phr *cut a rusty* is prob an alteration, infl by such phrr as *cut a caper,* of *cut up rusty* (at **rusty** adj[3]), from which the noun sense has been abstracted.]   **chiefly Sth, S Midl**
Note: This treatment expands and improves that at **cut a rusty.**

An instance of violent, outrageous, or exuberant behavior; a caper, prank, trick—freq in phrr *cut (up) rusties, cut a rusty* to engage in such behavior.

1835 Bird *Hawks* 2.245 **ePA,** "I hit the 'oss on the 'ead, and cuss the bit of his master! Neversomever, I'll try for a spell ag'in, and the next'll be a right-down rusty." . . With these words he spurred his horse into the river. **1838** Neal *Charcoal Sketches* 111 **sePA,** It won't do for us to be cutting rusties here at this time o' night. **1853** *S. Lit. Messenger* 19.602 **AL,** We cut up our rusties at his *hotel.* **1872** Schele de Vere *Americanisms* 537, *Rusties,* in Pennsylvania and Ohio, the name given to the restive movements of an unquiet horse. **1911** *DN* 3.539 **eKY,** *Rusty.* . . A prank or caper; used chiefly in the phrase "cut a rusty," meaning play a prank or a "stunt." **1927** *DN* 5.473 **Ozarks,** *Cut a rusty.* . . To do something foolish or improper. "I sure did cut a rusty when I showed th' ol' woman thet 'ar letter." **1933** *AmSp* 8.1.31 **nwTX** [Ranch diction], *Cut a rusty.* To do something clever or pert. **1939** *AmSp* 14.90 **eTN,** *Cut a rusty.* To have an outburst of anger. 'He cut a rusty when he was talking to his papa.' **1940** (1978) Still *River of Earth* 37 **KY,** I like a wild living bird a sight more than a tame one keeping house in a gourd. Wild ones got a bushel more sense. They kin cut rusties same as a man. It's onbelieving what some kin do. . . Fletch and I hid behind the woodpile, trying to think of a rusty to pull on Uncle Jolly. **1940** *AmSp* 15.215 **FL,** *Cut a rusty* . . refers to a fit of joy. **1941** *Esquire* May 63 **KY,** Mom said not to step in and cut a rusty at Dollie and Eif's wedding, 'cause she didn't want no trouble. **1941** *AmSp* 16.22 **sIN,** *Cut a rusty.* Make an exhibition of oneself. 'Now ain't you cuttin' a rusty?' **1944** *PADS* 2.48 **NC, NJ, VA,** *Rusty, to cut a.* . . To cut a caper. **1966–68** *DARE* (Qu. KK11, *To make great objections or a big fuss about something: "When we asked him to do that, he _____.")* Infs **AL3, WV3,** Cut a rusty. **1991** Still *Wolfpen Notebooks* 124 **sAppalachians,** Too much chicanery goes on and sometimes people get hurt. A rusty is one thing and chicanery is another. *Ibid* 163, *Rusty:* prank.

rusty back See **rusty lizard**

rusty blackbird n Also *rusty-winged blackbird, rusty crow blackbird*

A robin-sized blackbird (*Euphagus carolinus*) of the eastern US, with juveniles and adults in winter having a rust-brown color. Also called **rusty grackle, thrush blackbird**

1832 Nuttall *Manual Ornith.* 1.199, Rusty Blackbird. . . Glossy-black, more or less skirted with ferruginous. **1844** DeKay *Zool. NY* 2.137, The Rusty Crow Blackbird. . . Glossy black, more or less rusty. . *Young,* dusky brown. **1851** (1874) Glisan *Jrl. Army Life* 89, Of the birds and animals not usually eatable, there are the . . rusty-winged blackbird, blue-bird, buzzard, crow. **1917** (1923) *Birds Amer.* 2.264, The full-plumaged male Rusty Blackbird is almost pure black with a greenish gloss, while the young bird in autumn is mainly rusty-brown. **1962** Imhof *AL Birds* 509, The Rusty Blackbird is appropriately named, for immature birds show a great deal of *rusty-brown* in their plumage, and the song of the male sounds like the squeaking of a rusty hinge. **1965–70** *DARE* (Qu. Q11, . . *Kinds of blackbirds*) Infs **CT5, IA3, 20, ME8, MI120, MA67, NY22,** Rusty blackbird; **PA23,** Black rusty blackbird; **OH98,** Old rusty blackbird.

rusty buck See **rusty lizard**

rusty crackle See **rusty grackle**

rusty crow blackbird See **rusty blackbird**

rusty cuss See **rusty lizard**

rusty dab n Also *rusty flatfish, ~ flounder* [See quot 1842] A **flounder** n B (here: *Limanda ferruginea*). Also called **sand dab 1a**

1839 MA Zool. & Bot. Surv. *Fishes Reptiles* 141 **neMA,** P[latessa] ferruginea. . . The Rusty Dab. . . This species is occasionally brought to our market, in the winter season only. **1842** DeKay *Zool. NY* 4.297, The Rusty Flat-fish. Platessa ferruginea . . Head and body greenish, with numerous irregular, crowded, chocolate or rust-colored spots, giving a rusty hue to the animal. **1872** Schele de Vere *Americanisms* 384, The *Rusty Dab* (Platessa ferruginea) is the popular name of one of the flatfishes, caught on the coasts of Massachusetts and New York. **1884** Goode *Fisheries U.S.* 1.197, The Sand Dab, or Rough Dab, *Hippoglossoides platessoides*, also sometimes known as the Rusty Flounder, is taken in winter by the line fishermen of New England. **1946** LaMonte

N. Amer. Game Fishes 100, Rusty Dab. . . body and fins covered with rusty red dots.

rusty dusty n *among Black speakers*
The buttocks.

1948 Hurston *Seraph* 292 **FL** [Black], Shake your rusty-dusty down there! I'm hungry as hell. **1953** Burroughs *Junkie* 42, A Negro voice was singing, "Get up, get up, woman, off your big fat rusty-dusty." **1970** Major *Dict. Afro-Amer. Slang* 99, *Rusty dusty:* (1940's–50's) the buttocks. **1986** Pederson *LAGS Concordance,* 1 inf, **cwFL,** Sit on your rusty dusty. [Inf Black]

rusty flatfish (or flounder) See **rusty dab**

rusty grackle n Also *rusty crackle*
=**rusty blackbird.**

1811 Wilson *Amer. Ornith.* 3.41 **PA,** [The] *Rusty Grakle.* . . frequents corn fields. **1838** Geol. Surv. OH *Second Annual Rept.* 162, Quiscalus ferrugineus . . *Rusty Grakle.* **1872** Coues *Key to N. Amer. Birds* 159, *Rusty Grackle.* [Male] in summer lustrous black, the reflections greenish . . in general simply glossy black, nearly all the feathers skirted with warm brown above, and brownish-yellow below. **1931** LA Dept. of Conserv. *Bulletin* 20.540, An extremely abundant wintering blackbird . . is the so-called Rusty Blackbird or "Rusty Crackle," as some term it. **1955** Forbush–May *Birds* 471, Rusty Blackbird. . . *Other names:* Rusty Grackle; Thrush Blackbird.

rusty gut (or jack, jenny) See **rusty lizard**

rustyleaf n
=**fool's huckleberry.**

1925 Jepson *Manual Plants CA* 742, [*Menziesia*] *ferruginea* . . Rustyleaf. Slender shrub 6 to 15 ft. high. **1942** Hylander *Plant Life* 420, Rusty leaf is a taller shrub of the Pacific coast, with rusty hairs on the uppersurface [sic] of the leaves and . . greenish purple flowers. **1964** Kingsbury *Poisonous Plants U.S.* 254, Mock azalea, rustyleaf. . . In woods along the coast from northern California to Alaska, eastward at lower elevations in mountains to Montana.

rusty lizard n Also *rusty back, ~ buck, ~ cuss, ~ gut, ~ jack, ~ jenny, ~ scorpion* [From the dark brown color] **AL, AR, GA, LA, TX**
A **fence lizard 1** (here: *Sceloporus undulatus*).

1909 *DN* 3.365 **eAL, wGA,** *Rusty-cuss.* . . A dark-colored, rusty-looking lizard. Also called *rusty-back, rusty-buck.* **1928** Baylor Univ. Museum *Contrib.* 16.3 **LA, TX, AR,** When one hears negroes call a Fence Lizard "Rusty Jack" at Shreveport, Louisiana, then again at Texarkana, Texas, and later in numerous localities in the states of Louisiana, Texas, and Arkansas, he realizes that these people are familiar with a folk name which has wide circulation. *Ibid* 11 **eTX,** The Fence Lizard is abundant in the timbered regions of extreme eastern Texas. Here it is known as the *Pine Lizard, Rusty Lizard,* and *Rusty Scorpion.* **1930** *Copeia* 4.154 **swGA,** Pine lizard . . Local names are 'rusty Jenny' and 'rustygut.' **1955** *Clarke Co. Democrat* (Grove Hill AL) 8 Sept 4/5 (*Mathews Coll.*), Probably the most common of the lizards is the one which is given the book name of fence lizard, but which I have always known as the rusty lizard. **1967** *DARE* (Qu. P32, . . *Other kinds of wild animals*) Infs **TX11, 13,** Rusty lizard. **1968** *DARE* FW Addit **LA40,** Rusty buck—a lizard that lives around aging wood and somewhat resembles a chameleon. [FW: This seems to be the common fence-post lizard, though I did not see one to verify the description.] **1986** Pederson *LAGS Concordance,* 1 inf, **cwAR,** Old rusty lizard.

rusty mockingbird n Also *rusty mock* Cf **mockingbird 2**
=**brown thrasher.**

1917 *Wilson Bulletin* 29.2.84 **VA,** *Toxostoma rufum* . . rusty-mock, Wallops I[slan]d, Va. **1919** Pearson et al. *Birds NC* 311, The Thrasher, "Brown Thrush," or "Rusty Mockingbird," is a common summer resident throughout North Carolina. **1970** *DARE* (Qu. Q14, . . *Names . . for . . brown thrasher*) Inf **VA47,** Rusty mock.

rusty scorpion See **rusty lizard**

rusty-winged blackbird See **rusty blackbird**

rut n [*DNE* 1612 →; *OED2 rut* sb.[3] "Now *U.S.* and *dial.*"] **coastal NEng**
=**rote.**

1847 in 1857 Webster *Private Corresp.* 2.262 **eMA,** I hear the sea, very strong and loud at the north. . . They call this the rote or rut of the sea. **a1862** (1865) Thoreau *Cape Cod* 89 **eMA,** The old man said that this was what they called the "rut," a peculiar roar of the sea before the wind changes. **1892** *DN* 1.211 **seMA,** *Rut:* the noise of the waves on the beach.

rutabaga n Pronc-spp *rootabaga, rootebagger, rootybagger, ruta-begger* Cf **baga**

A Std sense, var forms.

1909 *DN* 3.365 **eAL, wGA,** *Ruta-begger.* **1922** (1926) Sandburg *Rootabaga Stories.* **1965–70** DARE (Qu. I3, . . *The large yellowish root vegetable, similar to a turnip, with a strong taste*) 547 Infs, **widespread,** [proncs of the types ['rudɑˌbe(ɪ)gə, 'rutə-, 'rutə-, -ˌbɛgə]]; 85 Infs, **scattered,** [proncs of the types [-be(ɪ)gɚ, -bɛgɚ]]; 43 Infs, **scattered,** [proncs of the types [-bɛkɚ, -bekɚ, -bɛkə, -bekə]]; 28 Infs, **scattered,** [proncs of the types [-bækə, -bægə]]; 14 Infs, **scattered,** [proncs of the types [-bɛgɪ, -begɪ, -begɪ, -begɪ]]; 11 Infs, **scattered,** [proncs of the types [-bɑgə, -bagə]]; **CA**10, **CO**47, **DE**3, **GA**8, **IL**26, **ME**1, **TN**1, [proncs of the types [rutɪ-, rudɪ-]]; **IA**2, 9, **MI**102, **MN**11, **MS**73, [proncs of the types [rutə-, rudə-]]; **GA**1, **IA**43, **KY**40, **NJ**3, [proncs of the types [-bæg, -bɛg, -beg]]; **AL**46, 52, **KY**66, **TX**39, **VA**2, [proncs of the type [-bægə]]; **CA**196, **CO**30, 45, **NJ**46, [proncs of the types [rutə-, rudə-]]; **NY**66, **PA**166, ['rutəˌbəgə]; **CT**9, **IA**30, [rutebegə]; **CT**21, **MI**93, [proncs of the types [rʌtə-, rʌdə-]]; **CT**6, ['rudəˌbʌgə]; **PA**178, [rudəbaigə]. [DARE Ed: Primary stress is usually on the first syllable but occasionally occurs on the third syllable.] **1976** Garber *Mountain-ese* 77 **sAppalachians,** We raised a fine crop of rootebaggers in our garden this year. **1984** Wilder *You All Spoken Here* 204 **Sth,** *Against:* Injurious, as in "Eatin' rootybaggers is against you."

B Sense.

Std: a large, yellow-fleshed winter turnip (*Brassica napa* Napobrassica Group). Also called **cow beet, hanover 1, Russian turnip, Swede, Swedish turnip, turnip, wild ~**

rutch v Usu |ruč, ruč|; also |ruts, rʌts| Also sp *rooch, root(s)ch, rootsh, ruch, rutsch, rutz* [Ger *rutschen,* PaGer *rutsche*] **chiefly Ger settlement areas, esp PaGer area**

1 usu with *around:* To slide about; esp to wriggle, squirm, fidget; hence vbl n *rutching around;* adjs *rutschi, rootchy, rutzy* restless, fidgety.

1916 *DN* 4.328 **NE,** *Rutch.* . . To crawl, esp. in a hesitating way. "The child was just old enough to rutch round on the floor." **1937** *AmSp* 12.205 [Engl of PaGer area], The verb 'rutch' (to slide, as in 'Don't rutch around in your chair') occurs only in speech. **1939** Aurand *Quaint Idioms* 18 [PaGer], You never saw a baby *rootsh* (crawl or squirm) so much. **1954** WELS Suppl. **csWI,** Grandmother would say, "Stop rutching around—haven't you got any sitzlädder?" **1955** *Reading Times* (PA) 30 Aug 13/1 *(Mathews Coll.),* There'd always be two or three new pairs of knickerbockers, . . whose seats would shine like mirrors after a few weeks of "rutching" around school desks. **1960** Korson *Black Rock* 238 **PA** [PaGer], Children . . were told not to *ruch* and that was that they weren't to squirm or fidget. **1964** *Ferhoodled Engl.* [16] [PaGer], Now you children sit still onct and don't Rootsch (squirm) around so much. **1968** *Helen Adolf Festschrift* 36 **PaGer area,** *Rutsch* and *rutschi*—The verb *to rutsch* . . meaning 'to slide (as on a chair),' is still often used. . . The adjective *rutschi* . . meaning 'fidgety,' is frequently used in speaking of a small child that is nervous and restless. **1968** DARE File **NC,** *Rutch*—squirm, wriggle. Commonly used in Hickory, North Carolina. **1980** *NYT Article Letters* **csPA,** I am a native of . . the Harrisburg area. . . Unspoken in Philadelphia, just a hundred miles from where I grew up, are "strubbly", "rooching around", and "fressing." **1982** *Barrick Coll.* **csPA,** Stop rootchin' around when I'm tryin' to comb your hair. **1987** *Jrl. Engl. Ling.* 20.2.173 **ePA,** *Rutch (around)* 'to slide, to squirm'. . . [Actively used by] 52 [of 100 infs]. **1997** DARE File **wNY,** "Rootchy" (. . 'root' is pronounced like 'foot'). I grew up in the Buffalo, NY area and my parents used this word. It means restless, fidgety, unable to sit still. I've noticed that people outside the area don't know its meaning. **1998** *Ibid* **KY,** When I was a child, I was often admonished not to "rootch" or squirm when I was bored or restless. . . It seemed a local rather than a family usage. *Ibid* **PA,** *Rooch*—In the mid 1950s in Johnstown, Pennsylvania the word meant to wriggle into position; to move restlessly as if you had ants in your pants. *Ibid* **csWI,** My late grandmother, b. 1888 in Madison of Irish descent, always used the word "rootch," as in "He rootched [ručt] around in bed last night." **2000** *NADS Letters* **csPA,** Nurses in the hospital will tell

patients to "rutch over on the bed." **2001** *Ibid* **sePA** (as of 1970s), "Rutz around" is to wiggle, also referred to as "rutching around." A child in church is told to not be so "rutzy."

2 with *up:* To slide (something); to pull (something) into or out of place.

1978 *Capital Times* (Madison WI) 9 Nov 49/5, Her skirt gets ruched up around her hips, and the slip she shows is stained and grey. [**1999** DARE File **Canada,** In Lunenburg County, Nova Scotia, among older and rural people. . . a hospital patient speaking to a nurse: "Rutch me up in bed" . . meaning to correct that inevitable state of having gradually slid down in a hospital bed that has the head cranked up.]

3 with *around:* To root around, rummage; to putter about.

1991 DARE File **ceWI,** To rutz [rʌts]—to rummage, as *rutzin' around.* **2000** *NADS Letters* **csPA,** "Rutching" around in handbags or purses. *Ibid* **GA,** My husband used to use a word with the same senses as you give for ratch [=to search, root about], but he pronounced it to rhyme with "butch." I believe he got it from his mother who was born in 1907(?) and raised in Georgia. *Ibid* **ceWI,** Rutz around: pronounced "rootz" (rhymes with puts and foots). I grew up in Sheboygan, Wisconsin (born 1933). My mother, who was full-blooded German often used this expression. . . An example of "rutzing around." Digging around in a drawer, looking for something, and usually leaving the drawer in a mess. *Ibid* **MN,** Rutz around = putz around—putter. **2001** *Ibid* **sePA** (as of 1970s), "Rutz around" also refers to rummaging, used like "What are you rutzing around in my drawers for?" *Ibid* **Upstate NY,** My mother uses the term "rutz around" to mean "rummage" or "wander". She's in her early 40s and from upstate New York; she might've picked up the term from her own family (far northern New York, near Canada, of Irish descent) or from my father's family (Pennsylvania German).

rutch around See **rutch 1, 3**

rutchie n |'ruči| Also sp *rutchee, rutschi* [Appar dimin of PaGer *rutsch* sliding place] **sePA**

A slope used for sledding.

1914 *DN* 4.158 **PA,** *Hivvely.* . . Rough. "A hivvely rutschi." *Ibid, Rutschi.* . . A sliding-pond. **1937** *AmSp* 12.205 [Engl of PaGer area], 'Rutchie' appears regularly in print . . , as in this typical head-line from the Reading *Times*: 'City Police to Patrol Eight Rutchie' (streets for the use of sleds). **1955** *Reading Times* (PA) 14 Jan 1/3 *(Mathews Coll.),* Police announced that the following streets have been set aside today from 4 p.m. to 10 p.m. as "rutchies," or sledding areas. **1971** *Today Show Letters* **sePA,** The place where we used our sleds was known as a *rutchee,* rhyming with butchee. **1987** *Jrl. Engl. Ling.* 20.2.174 **ePA,** *Rutschi* 'a hill for coasting or sledding'. . . [N]ot one informant from Berks County (or anywhere else) used the term. In fact, only two [of 100] informants acknowledged hearing it—two Lancaster County residents, ages 39 and 73.

rutching around See **rutch 1**

rutch up See **rutch 2**

rut cutter See **rutter** n[1]

rute See **root** n[1], v

Ruth and Jacob See **Jacob and Rachel**

ruther adv See **rather** adv

ruther n See **rather** n

Rutland beauty n
=hedge bindweed 1.

1847 Wood *Class-Book* 444, [Calystegia] sepium . . *Rutland Beauty.* . . A vigorous climber, in hedges and low grounds, Can[ada] to Car[olina], W. to Ill[inois]. . . It is cultivated as a shade for windows, arbors, &c. **1892** *Jrl. Amer. Folkl.* 5.101 **NH,** *Convolvulus sepium* . . Rutland beauty. Temple, N.H. **1897** *Ibid* 10.51 **OH,** Rutland beauty, Kentucky hunter, pea vine, Sulphur Grove, Ohio. **1914** Georgia *Manual Weeds* 323, Rutland Beauty. . . Nearly as obnoxious as the smaller Field Bindweed, and about as hard to control. **1976** Bailey–Bailey *Hortus Third* 208, [Calystegia] sepium . . Wild morning-glory, bindweed . . Rutland-beauty. . . Weedy.

rutsch See **rutch**

rutschi n See **rutchie**

rutschi adj See **rutch 1**

rutter n[1] Also *rut cutter*

In logging: a device for cutting ruts in an **ice road.**

1905 U.S. Forest Serv. *Bulletin* 61.45 [Logging terms], *Rutter.* . . A form of plow for cutting ruts in a logging road for the runners of the sleds to run in. **1913** Bryant *Logging* 168, The snowplow is followed by the rutter which cuts a square or round rut for the sled runners. The machine is mounted on a heavy set of runners and has two chisel-like blades which may be raised or lowered so that a rut of any desired depth can be secured. Snowplows and rut cutters are often combined in one machine. **1942** ME Univ. *Studies* 57.42, After the road is well iced, such a rutter as the one shown in Figure 34 is used. A good road can be obtained with this machine in one passing, and it serves equally well for a plow after heavy storms. **1966–68** *DARE* Tape MI27, In the wintertime I was on the sprinklers, making ice roads. . . And when the ruts got too full, well, they had a rig they called a rutter. . . They had knives on it, and you'd cut the ice out. . . Every other night you'd run the rutter and the sprinkler both; **WI**59, To keep from sliding off . . the logging roads . . , they would use what they call a rutter. And they would go down the road and it would cut a little groove into this ice, so there would be no way of the load of logs going off and into the ditch.

rutter n[2] [See quot 1975] **sOH**

A lazy, slovenly, ignorant person.

1968 *DARE* (Qu. HH18, *Very insignificant or low-grade people*) Inf **OH**47, Rutter. **1975** *DARE* File **OH**, According to a story in the Dec. 3, 1974 "Columbus Sunday Dispatch," *DARE* language surveyors in southeastern Ohio found: "rutter [is a term] for a person with poor personal hygiene." . . I believe that this connotation comes directly from a rural family named Rutter who was allergic to work, washing, schooling, and most of civilization's amenities. Now, this family has died out. . . Nevertheless, the derogatory appellation lingers on, especially in Athens County where that Rutter family once lived. **1997** *Ibid* **sOH**, Competing terms [i.e., with *redneck*] are "rutter" (after a local family name), "wanker" (from British slang?) or "plugger" (from use of chewing tobacco?)

rutz See **rutch**

rutz around See **rutch 1, 3**

rutzy See **rutch 1**

ruvver See **river**

ruxious See **ructious**

ruz See **raise** v A2

ryaninjun See **rye and Indian (bread)**

rye See **ryegrass 1**

rye and Indian (bread) n Pronc-spp *rine-injin, ryaninjun* **NEng** Cf **Indian** n B1, **Indian bread 2**

Bread made from a mixture of rye and cornmeal.

1840 *Knickerbocker* 16.18 **MA**, There were eggs and fried ham . . rye-and-Indian bread. **1844** *Daily Picayune* (New Orleans LA) 16 Jan 1/6, She [=a woman from Massachusetts]'s got *every thing* that ever was perduced for sich pupposes. . . kittels, pots, a jonny-cake board, troth to mix rine-injin bread in. **1895** Brown *Meadow-Grass* 118 **NH**, "I dunno's I ought to ha' stirred up rye 'n' Injun," she went on. . . "Some might say the steam was bad for your lungs." **1909** *DN* 3.415 **nME**, *Rye-and-*

Indian (Injun). . . A kind of bread made of a mixture of corn meal and rye flour. **1929** *AmSp* 5.121 **ME coast**, "Rye and Injun bread" was familiar, and so was "posy." **1947** Bowles–Towle *New Engl. Cooking* 67, But you still have a few things to do before you can slide your loaves of "ryaninjun" from the wooden peel—a long-handled shovel—into the cavern [=a brick oven]. **1967–69** *DARE* (Qu. H14, *Bread that's made with cornmeal*) Inf **MA**5, Rye 'n' injun ['rɑɪn 'ɪnjʲən]—old-fashioned brown bread baked in brick ovens with rye and cornmeal; (Qu. H18, . . *Special kinds of bread*) Inf **MA**58, Rye and injun (rye and cornmeal).

rye chops See **chop** n[1] **1**

ryegrass n

1 also *rye:* A grass of the genus *Lolium,* esp *L. perenne.* For other names of the latter see **English bluegrass 1**; for other names of var spp see **cheat 2, darlen, poison darnel, Randall grass**

1749 in **1905** Franklin *Writings* 2.384 **sePA**, I sowed an Acre more with two bushells of Rye-Grass Seed. **1812** (**1944**) *Thomas Jefferson's Garden Book* 474 **VA**, E. Vineyard. Mar. 26. . . W. end. Rye grass. **1881** U.S. Dept. Ag. *Rept. of Secy. for 1880* 385, Lolium perenne.—Rye grass, and Italian Rye grass. **1922** U.S. Dept. Ag. *Farmers' Bulletin* 1254.32, Perennial rye-grass . . is also known as English or Australian rye-grass. **1937** Sandoz *Slogum* 75 **NE**, He went after the rye grass creeping in at the upper edges of his garden, chopping with his hoe at the roots that were like wet string. **1965–70** *DARE* (Qu. L9a, . . *Kinds of grass . . grown for hay*) 28 Infs, **scattered,** Ryegrass; 15 Infs, **scattered,** Rye; **ND**1, Canadian ryegrass; **GA**84, Oats and ryegrass; (Qu. L9b, *Hay from other kinds of plants [not grass];* not asked in early QRs) 13 Infs, **scattered,** Rye; **MA**58, Rye—early green feed; **VA**20, Rye hay; (Qu. L8, *Hay that grows naturally in damp places*) Inf **IN**35, Ryegrass; (Qu. L21, . . *Kinds of grain grown around here;* total Infs questioned, 75) Inf **MS**1, Ryegrass; (Qu. L34, . . *Most important crops grown around here*) Infs **AL**26, **NV**2, Ryegrass; (Qu. S9, . . *Kinds of grass that are hard to get rid of*) Infs **CA**157, 179, **GA**70, **NE**9, Ryegrass; (Qu. S21, . . *Weeds . . that are a trouble in gardens and fields*) Inf **MI**67, Ryegrass. **1967** *DARE* Tape **TX**8, It's been my experience that in feedin' cattle and seedin' these rice fields with clover that it doesn't pay off on a cattle operation either. 'Bout the only type of winter grass that I plant is the red rolled common ryegrass, or winter grass. **1969** *DARE* File **TX**, Rye Grass—always called road grass because it was the only thing that would grow in the dirt in the road. **1982** *Plants SW* (Catalog) 36, Ryegrass—*Lolium.* . . Not to be confused with rye *(Secale)* or wild rye *(Elymus).* European, naturalized throughout cool temperate North America. **1986** Pederson *LAGS Concordance,* 7 infs, 5 **MS**, Ryegrass.

2 =**wild rye. esp Pacific**

1847 Wood *Class-Book* 621, [Elymus] villosus . . *Rye Grass.* . . Dry grounds, Free States. **1889** Vasey *Ag. Grasses* 77, *Elymus Canadensis* (Wild Rye; Rye Grass; Lyme Grass). A perennial, coarse grass, growing on river banks and in rich, shaded woods. *Ibid, Elymus condensatus* (Giant Rye Grass). . . Mr. W.C. Cusick, of Oregon, says: This is a very valuable grass, commonly known as rye grass. **1923** Abrams *Flora Pacific States* 1.251, *Elymus virescens* . . Pacific Rye-grass. *Ibid, Elymus hirsutus* . . Northern Rye-grass. *Ibid* 252, *Elymus glaucus* . . Western Rye-grass. **1947** Jones *Evergreen Land* 29 **WA**, She did not really break at all until her first-born daughter was drowned in the creek near the Whitman mission, there in the valley of the rye grass. **1961** Thomas *Flora Santa Cruz* 87 **cwCA**, [Elymus] glaucus . . Western Rye Grass, Blue Wild Rye. A common grass of wooded and brush-covered slopes.

ryley See **riley**

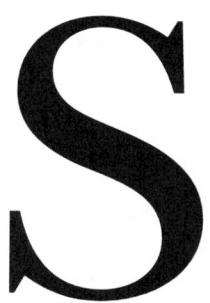

-s suff[1] [OE *-es,* the genitive sing ending of several noun-classes, used to mark nouns used adverbially or as the object of the prep *to* in adv phrr, and then widely extended, esp in ME, as an adverbial marker (see *OED2 -es* suff[1]). The non-std exx treated here are of diverse history; some (e.g. **noways**) are survivals of old forms; others are more recent (and in some cases perhaps idiolectal) analogical formations.] See also **abouts, adays, aftertimes, a lots, a nights, anyways, anywheres, barebones, before-times, betimes, bumpity-bumps, bys, by times, double-tides, elseways, everyways, everywheres, flugens** adv, **footermans, hindside-backwards, late years, latterdays, leastways,** *lives* (at **lief** adv), **noways, nowheres, offtimes, otherways, somehows, someways, somewheres, yonders**

Used to form adverbs, esp those expressing place, direction, time, or manner; see quots.

1638 in 1898 *Springfield MA First Century* 1.164, It is ordered . . not to sell or any ways pass away any Cannoe . . untill it be five years old. **1775** in 1877 *Essex Inst. Coll.* 13.171, Your house will be as safe as anywheres to put the Candles in. **1867** Twain *Jumping Frog* 15, Fellers that had travelled and been everywheres. **1905** *DN* 3.57 eNE, The adverbial *-s* is added very commonly in the familiar *somewheres, anywheres, leastways, anyways,* etc. **1919** Mencken *Amer. Lang.* 229, It goes without saying that the common American tendency to add *-s* to such adverbs as *towards* is carried to full length in the vulgar language. One constantly hears, not only *somewheres* and *forwards,* but even *noways* and *anyways.* Here we have but one more example of the movement toward uniformity and simplicity. *Anyways* is obviously fully supported by *sideways* and *always.* **1928** Ruppenthal *Coll.* **KS,** After the tornado the trees lay every which ways. **1931** *PMLA* 46.1320 s**Appalachians,** These forms are common: "somehows," "some'eres," "anywheres," "nowheres," "nohows," due to fondness for the *s.* **1940** *AmSp* 15.52 s**Appalachians, Ozarks,** Adverbial *-s* survives in: nowheres, anywheres, ever'-which-aways. **1942** Hall *Smoky Mt. Speech* 92 wNC, eTN, Most Smokies speakers prefer to pronounce [z] in the adverbs compounded with *-ward, -where* . . nowhere, somewhere ['sʌmɚz]. Perhaps by the influence of these words, the intensive *no-way* often appears as [noʊ weɪz]: 'We didn't have no use fer it noways.' **1948** Manfred *Chokecherry* 248 **nwIA,** Yellow jackets! . . See if there's one somewheres here in my neck. **1965–70** *DARE* (Qu. MM11, . . "*I must have left it _____.*") 120 Infs, **widespread,** Somewheres (around here, *etc*); (Qu. MM15, *If a carpenter nails a board crossing another board at an angle* . . "*He nailed the board on _____.*") 9 Infs, **chiefly W Midl, NW,** Slanchways; **AL**51, **CO**7, **NC**15, **SC**69, Slantways; **NE**11, **OH**31, **WI**52, Right-angles; **WA**1, **PA**242, Cross-angles; **MD**17, Biasways; **NY**173, Cornerways; **MI**40, X-ways; (Qu. B5) Inf **MN**23, Storm brewing somewheres; (Qu. B14, *When the wind is blowing unevenly*) Inf **NY**66, Blowing whichways; (Qu. U40, *Somebody who is temporarily out of money* . . "*At the moment he's _____.*") Inf **VT**8, Broke (he's badly bent anyways); (Qu. Y45) Inf **MD**20, Went everywheres; (Qu. Y47) Inf **OH**89, Hid somewheres; (Qu. JJ15a, . . "*He hasn't sense enough to _____.*") Inf **AL**16, Know if he's going forward or backs; (Qu. KK68, . . "*We agree on most things, but on politics we're _____.*") Inf **TN**31, Far aways; (Qu. LL32) Inf **PA**240, Nowheres near; (Qu. MM2, . . "*Look, you've got your dress on _____.*") Inf **LA**45, Backways; **NY**30, Hindside backways; (Qu. MM3, . . "*This is the front, you've got the whole thing turned _____.*") Inf **LA**45, Backways; (Qu. MM4, . . "*The mail box is just _____ the pine tree.*") Inf **IN**5, A piece aways from; (Qu. MM12a, . .

"*He shot into a flock of birds and they went _____.*") Infs **MD**32, **VA**46, (Scattered) everywheres; **NJ**50, All overs; **IL**39, All which ways; **VA**15, Everwheres; **MD**13, Everways; **NJ**31, Every which ways; (Qu. MM12b, . . "*She broke her beads and they went _____.*") Inf **NJ**50, All overs; **MA**33, Everyways; **VA**15, Everywheres; **MD**26, Scattered everywheres; (Qu. MM14, *If a drugstore is on one corner of a square and a gas station is on the far corner* . . "*The drugstore is _____ the gas station.*") Infs **ME**12, **NY**108, **PA**1, Cornerways (from); **DE**7, **IL**138, **MN**19, Cross-corners from; **TX**36, Catty-cornereds from; **SC**11, Cattyways; (Qu. NN26b) Inf **MO**16, Go lay down somewheres. **1986** Pederson *LAGS Concordance,* 1 inf, seLA, I couldn't find it noways; 1 inf, neMS, She didn't have to move nowheres else.

-s suff[2] [Perh of multiple origin, but prob chiefly from the pl *-s*] Cf **-ie** suff[3], **-ies** suff 2 See also **abbers; achins; aikie(s); allies; all mines; anys; anythings; baby fingers; back-licks; borrows; bunches; burns; burnings; checks; cleaners; clearance(s); clears; crooks; dib** n[1] 2; **doubles** exclam; **dribbles; drubs; dubs** exclam; **ducks** exclam, n[2]; **everlastings; evers; eye-drops; eyes** exclam; **fairs, no; fibs; fingers; fins; flees; flips; fourbs; fubs; fudgings; goods; grindins; halvers** 1; **hikes;** *histings* (at **hoist** C1d); **hunch** n 2a; *hunchings* (at **hunch** v 2a); **hunks** exclam; **inching; knee drop;** *knuckles* (at **knuckle shot**); **lasts; lay** n[1] 3; **nose-drops; nothings; nudges; overs; picks; pigtail** exclam; **placings;** *rounds* (at **rounce**); *roundings* (at **roundance**); **rounders** 2; **slippins; slips; straights; toe-drops; trades;** *vents* (at **ven**)

In children's games, esp marbles, and other ritualized activities: used to form names of actions and situations as well as exclams claiming or denying specific privileges or enforcing specific rules.

1843 (1916) Hall *New Purchase* 42 **IN,** Man-lay!—Clearings!—'fen!—knuckle down!—. . histings!—comins about! **1883** Foote *Led-Horse* 62 **CO,** 'What is it the boys say when they play marbles?—"Fend" something.' . . 'Fend dubs?' Hilgard suggested. **1890** *DN* 1.24 **KY,** To "take everys" or "evers" is to move around so as to get *every* "man" in range. **1896** *DN* 1.412 ceNY, Ben nuggins ['nʌjɪnz]: a term in marbles. **1922** *DN* 5.187 **MA,** Nothings. . . A call which gave no privileges, whereas *everythings* gave all. **1939** Hench *Coll.* **PA,** Exclamations in games. . . No fairs. . . Shouted whenever a boy thought another boy wasn't playing correctly or fairly. **1942** Berrey–Van den Bark *Amer. Slang* 665.6, Marbles. . . Overs!, *called for permission to shoot over.* **1950** *WELS* **WI** (Cries or calls used in playing marbles) 1 Inf, Evers, roundings, evers on pards; 1 Inf, Dibs; 1 Inf, Roundings; 1 Inf, Nuts, kings, clicks; 1 Inf, Eyes; 1 Inf, Kicks, rounders; 1 Inf, Placings; 1 Inf, Nothings, anythings; 1 Inf, No sets, sets, dribbles; 1 Inf, Fan dubs; 1 Inf, Eye drops, no kicks. **1965–70** *DARE* (Qu. EE17, *In a game of tag, if a player wants to rest, what does he call out so that he can't be tagged?*) 56 Infs, **scattered,** Times out; 53 Infs, **scattered,** Times ex; **NJ**43, **NY**34, 37, 42, 78, Fins; **MI**8, 45, **MN**11, Borrows; **IL**97, Checks; **NY**44, Fingers; **NY**119, Five fingers; **NY**341, I got fins; **IA**46, Times ex; **WI**47, Toots; **CA**15, Vents; [**TX**9, Vince;] (Qu. V5b, . . "*Before anybody else gets it, I'm going to _____ this.*") Infs **IL**97, **WI**57, Get dibs on; **KS**10, Put my dibbies on; **MN**30, Put my nibs on; (Qu. EE15, *When he has caught the first of those that were hiding what does the player who is 'it' call out to the others?*) Inf **MI**108, Firsties; (Qu. EE20, *When two boys are fighting, and the one who is losing wants to stop, he calls out, "_____."*) Infs **NY**186, **SC**31, **TX**35, **VA**54, Times; **KY**94,

MS90, Times out; **NY**119, Fins; **PA**76, Gives; (Qu. EE23b, *In the game of andy-over . . if you fail to get the ball over the building . . what do you call out?*) Infs **IA**29, 46, **MN**28, **SD**2, Pigtails; **GA**23, Slips.

-s suff[3] Cf **-es** suff[1] **2** See also **child A3, deer B, gentleman A2, man** n **B2, ox A2a**

Used as a redundant plural-forming suffix; see quots.

   1827 (1939) Sherwood *Gaz.* GA 139, *Oxens* for oxen. **1890** (1895) Riley *Rhymes of Childhood* 18 **cIN**, 'Cause all the little childerns there's so straight an' strong an' fine. **1915** in 1944 *ADD* 462 **wTX**, Deers. . . Sheeps. **1928** Peterkin *Scarlet Sister Mary* 31 **SC** [Gullah], Here you is singin a reel song an' crossin you feets. *Ibid* 114, De womens don' let him rest. **1966** *DARE* Tape LA5, The commercial fishermens around here . . catches 'em. **1986** Pederson *LAGS Concordance*, 2 infs, **LA**, Teeths.

-s suff[4] [Engl dial; cf *EDG* §435] See also **come** v **A1, do** v **B2, fetch** v **A1, get** v **A1, go** v **A1, have** v[1] **B2, keep** v **A2, know** v **B2a, leave** v **A1, live** v **B1, say** v **B1, 3**

Used to make finite forms of the present tense other than the 3rd sing.

   1823 in 1944 *ADD* 169, I doesn't. J.F. Cooper. **1843** (1916) Hall *New Purchase* 55 **IN**, The stranger and his woman-body thinks themselves mighty big-bugs. *Ibid* 150, Then I goes to the fire and sits down. *Ibid* 433, Keep rite even on strate ahead till you gits to Rock-Ford. *Ibid* 437, I holds it down this a way. **1899** Chesnutt *Conjure Woman* 78 **csNC** [Black], I wants yer ter run dis yer plantation. **1921** Haswell *Daughter Ozarks* 107 (as of 1880s), I lives on the Bryant Fork over in Douglas County. **1927** Adams *Congaree* 18 **cSC** [Black], Ellen oughts to love you. **1952** Brown *NC Folkl.* 1.587, *-s, -es: suffix.* Third person plural of present tense. This usage may be a survival from the northern Middle English.—Mainly west. Illiterate. **1953** Atwood *Survey of Verb Forms* 26, *I work, we work. . .* The inflected form *I works* does not occur in N. Eng., though one informant gives *we works* and one, *they works. . .* 53 field records, scattered through all parts of the S[outh] A[tlantic] S[tates], were made before the items were eliminated from the work sheets. The results, though not conclusive, are highly suggestive. . . We might state tentatively that *we works* is fairly common in Type I [=infs with little education] in the S.A.S., that *I works* occasionally occurs, and that both are in pretty general use among the more old-fashioned Negroes. *Ibid* 29, *They say. . .* In the M[iddle] A[tlantic] S[tates] and the S.A.S. the present tense plural form is recorded in the context "They (say) he did it." In contrast to the predominant use of the singular in *people thinks,* the plural form *say* /se/ is almost universally used. . . There are only 14 occurrences of *says* /sɛz/, scattered very widely through the S.A.S. **1966–70** *DARE* Tape GA71, We got several bear, some people hunts 'em. I never hunt bear; **NC**9, Some people puts salt, some don't, some people just puts a little water; **SD**8, Most of our storms here comes from the northwest; **VA**2, The railroad cars comes in; **VA**112, They get weaker as the times comes on. **1986** Pederson *LAGS Concordance,* 1 inf, **neLA**, I keeps my milk up in the icebox; 1 inf, **nwFL**, People keeps them in toolboxes; [25 infs used *knows* as the present tense form in situations where *know* is standard;] 1 inf, **cLA**, You leaves; 1 inf, **ceTX**, I loves everybody; 1 inf, **cFL**, Spanish people really loves gopher.

-s suff[5] [Ger dial] **esp in Ger settlement areas**

Used with a man's first name to signify his immediate family; see quots.

   1996 Huth *Famil. Words* 108 **csPA**, Nancy's Pennsylvania Dutch family used the singular possessive form of a male's first name to denote his entire family (wife and children). . . Here are a few examples: *1944* Irvin's took Mother down to see Harry's and we are glad she was able to go. . . *1960s* Budmond's are /'bʌmənz/ are coming. (Common phrase used by Verda Frye when her son Budmond and his family were going to visit) **1998** *DARE* File, My Pennsylvania Dutch inlaws refer to their respective families by the genitive alone: "When John's come to visit. . ." meaning John, his wife and children. *Ibid,* The usage was alive in rural Iowa at least as late as my grandparents' generation. On a visit there in the late 60s I noticed my great aunt . . referring to her sons and their families as "Verlin's" and "Dale's." My father (who grew up in Des Moines) confirms that the usage was . . fairly widespread, though mostly rural. *Ibid* **sID** (as of 1950s), My relatives talked of inviting Milt's for dinner, meaning, of course, Milt and his family. They were all from Nebraska.

-s suff[6] [Relic of the Ger genitive ending used in certain expressions of time] **PaGer area**

Used with days of the week; see quots.

   1908 *German Amer. Annals* 10.34 **sePA**, *Mondays, etc.* Monday. The days of the week used in plural when but one day is referred to. "I'll start to-morrow and get back Mondays." . . fr. Pa. Ger. *Mondōgs,* etc., so used. Possibly a loose use of Ger. genitive. **1914** *DN* 4.157 **sePA**, A sort of genitive of time is found in this sentence: "She came Saturdays and left Mondays." In each instance this means one particular day.

sa See **saw** exclam

saa'b See **serve**

saa'bint See **servant**

saabis See **serve**

saa'bunt See **servant**

saach See **search**

saadie See **saddy**

saa'pint, saa'punt See **serpent**

saa't'n See **certain**

Sabbada(y), Sabbady See **Sabbath-day**

sabbath berry n [Prob by folk-etym]
   A **serviceberry** (here: *Amelanchier arborea*).
   1984 *DARE* File **csPA**, Sabbath berry—tree with small white blossoms early in spring . . "The sabbath berry's the first tree in the woods to bloom." [*DARE* Ed: Enclosed leaf was identified as *Amelanchier arborea.*]

Sabbath-day n Pronc-spp *Sabbada(y), Sabbady, Sabberday, Sabby-day* **chiefly NEng** *arch*
   Std sense, var forms.
   c1772 in 1920 *Essex Inst. Coll.* 56.292 **MA**, Thare was in the yeare 1738 a great athcak [sic] one sabbady. **1815** Humphreys *Yankey in England* 108, *Sabba-da,* Sabbath-day. **1844** Stephens *High Life in NY* xi, *Sabberday.* The Sabbath day. **a1861** (1880) Eastman *Poems* 116 **VT**, One Sabba' day, just after "Old Mortality" was sung. **1867** Beecher *Norwood* 47 **NEng**, Duties never conflict, you said, only Sabby-day morning last. **1871** (1882) Stowe *Fireside Stories* 113 **MA**, Don't you 'member the sermon Parson Lothrop preached about hastin' to be rich, last sabba'day? **1904** *DN* 2.427 **Cape Cod MA** (as of a1857), *Sabba' day pucker. . .* Sunday state and circumstance. 'There she goes all of a Sabba' day pucker,' all fixed up as for Sunday. **1935** Lincoln *Cape Cod Yesterdays* 5 **MA**, I knew that, when I next dressed, it would be in the prim and stiff and spotless garments befitting what Grandmother often said her mother used to call "Sabba' Day."

saberbill n Also sp *sabrebill* Cf **sicklebill**
   =**long-billed curlew.**
   1877 Hallock *Sportsman's Gaz.* 172, *Numenius longirostris. . .* Long-billed Curlew. Sickle-bill. Sabre-bill. **1880** *Forest & Stream* 15.4, Long-billed curlew . . sabre-bill. **1890** *Century Dict.* 5287, *Saberbill. . .* A curlew: same as *sicklebill.* **1923** U.S. Dept. Ag. *Misc. Circular* 13.65, *Long-billed Curlew. . .* Sabre-bill.

saber fish n Also sp *sabre fish* [*OED2* 1863 →]
   The cutlass fish (*Trichurus lepturus*).
   1882 U.S. Natl. Museum *Proc.* 5.267 **TX**, *Trichurus lepturus. . .* Sabre-fish. . . Rather common about Galveston. **1884** Goode *Fisheries U.S.* 335, *Trichurus lepturus. . .* is . . known . . on the coast of Texas as "Sabre-fish." **1890** *Century Dict.* 5287 **TX**, *Saber-fish. . .* The hairtail or silver-eel, *Trichiurus lepturus.*

sabina n[1]
   Either **cherrystone juniper** or a similar western **juniper 1** (here: *Juniperus osteosperma*).
   1913 Wooton *Trees NM* 23, The Cedar or Sabina (*Sabina* [=*Juniperus*] *monosperma*) is the common low tree of the drier mountain slopes of the northern part of the State. . Another species very similar in appearance is *Sabina utahensis* [=*Juniperus osteosperma*], which grows mostly in the northwestern part of the State and passes under the same names. **1960** Vines *Trees SW* 34, Other vernacular names [for *Juniperus monosperma*] are Cherrystone Juniper . . and Sabina. **1976** Elmore *Shrubs & Trees SW* 15, Western juniper, sabina. . . *Juniperus osteosperma.* . . In appearance is similar to that of the one-seed juniper. *Ibid* 17, Cherry-stone or redberry juniper; sabina. . . *Juniperus*

monosperma. . . The characteristic juniper of northern Arizona and New Mexico.

sabina n[2] Also *sabino* Pronc-sp *savina* [Span *sabina, -o*] **West**

An animal with a red-roan coat, esp one with white markings.

1944 Adams *Western Words* 135, Sabinas (sah-bee′nas)—A Spanish word used to describe cattle with red and white peppered and splotched coloring. . . Sabino (sah-bee′no)—Usually used in referring to a horse with a peculiar shade of light reddish, almost pinkish, roan-colored body and pure white belly. **1964** Jackman–Long *OR Desert* 123, Charlie was riding a big, fine-looking, bald-faced roan, a "savina" horse. [Footnote:] I am not sure how this is spelled or where the word came from, but it was in common use on the desert and meant a bald-faced, red roan with white stockings and sometimes a pinto spot on the side or belly. **1967** *DARE* (Qu. K39, . . *Names . . for horses according to their colors*) Inf **CO**33, Savina [′sɑvinə]—roan horse with a bald or white face.

sabine n [From the *Sabine* River] **LA** Cf **red bone 1**

A member of a mixed-race group inhabiting southern Louisiana.

[**1931** Read *LA French* 182, In Lower Louisiana *Sabine* designates a person of mixed negro and Indian blood, doubtless because this kind of half-breed was first observed in the vicinity of the Sabine River. Here Sabine is used as an adjective or as a noun, masculine or feminine.] **1945** *Progressive* 12 Feb 8, With 20,000 other Creoles, Cajuns, Islenos, Dalmatians, Sabines—the mixed folk of south Louisiana—Alcee is going to trap muskrats. **1946** *Social Forces* 24.445 **LA,** *Red Bones of Louisiana.* . . The parishes of Natchitoches, Vernon, Calcasieu, Terrebonne, La Fourche, and St. Tammany. The term "Red Bone" is derived from the French Os Rouge, for persons partly of Indian blood. Also called "Houmas" along the Coast and "Sabines" farther west. In Natchitoches are the "Cane River Mulattoes." **1947** *Chicago Tribune* (IL) 21 Dec mag sec 9/2, With the approval of the Southern Baptist Convention, he began missionary work among the Sabines, a term used colloquially for the forgotten people of Bayou Grand Caillou and Bayou du Large, the swamp rivers running to the Gulf of Mexico. **1963** Berry *Almost White* 27 **LA,** Along the bayous and deep in the marshy fringes near the Gulf of Mexico, there are the so-called Houma Indians, known locally as Sabines. **1968** *DARE* (Qu. HH29a, . . *People of mixed blood—part Indian*) Inf **LA**35, Sabines [sɑbinz]—mixture of French, Negro, and Indian; (Qu. HH29b, . . *People of mixed blood—part Negro*) Inf **LA**35, Sabines. **1979** Hallowell *People Bayou* 88 **sLA,** One group whose members *are* excluded from the definition [of "Cajun"] are the Sabines—a generally derogatory term (but there is no other) for those few people who have a sprinkling of American Indian, black, and Chinese genes. **1986** Pederson *LAGS Concordance*, 1 inf, **seLA,** Sabines—half Negro, half French or white.

Sabine's gull n

Std: a **gull** (here: *Xema sabini*). Also called **fork-tailed gull, hawk-tailed ~**

sabino n[1] [MexSpan]

1 A **bald cypress,** usu *Taxodium mucronatum.* **esp TX**

1900 Lyons *Plant Names* 365, T[axodium] distichum. . . Sabino-tree. **1946** Reeves–Bain *Flora TX* 18, In . . southern Texas is also T[axodium] mucronatum . . "Sabino", distinguished by its branchelets [sic] falling the second season. **1970** Correll *Plants TX* 76, Taxodium mucronatum. . . Sabino. . . Along the Rio Grande and occasionally along resacas . . in the Rio Grande Valley. **1980** Little *Audubon Guide N. Amer. Trees E. Region* 303, "Sabino" *Taxodium mucronatum.* . . Trunk enlarged at base with ridges above; sometimes small "knees" project from submerged roots.

2 A **mountain cedar** (here: *Juniperus ashei*).

1960 Vines *Trees SW* 33, *Juniperus ashei.* . . Names used are Mountain Cedar, Cedar Brake, Texas Cedar, Sabino [etc].

sabino n[2] See **sabina** n[2]

sable n Pronc-sp *saple* [*OED2* 1423 → for *Mustela zibellina*] **chiefly NEng**

=**pine marten.**

1674 in 1889 Gt. Brit. Pub. Rec. Office *Calendar State Papers Colonial Ser. Amer. for 1669–74* 581, The natural inhabitants of the woods, hills, and swamps [in Maine include] . . musquashes, sables, [and] squirrels. **1765** Rogers *N. Amer.* 263, The *Martin,* or *Sable,* lives principally among the mountains. **1784** in 1877 Belknap *Papers* 2.392 **NH,** Along

this road yesterday and this morning we saw the culheags, or log-traps, which the hunters set for sables. **1842** DeKay *Zool. NY* 1.33, The Sable is exceedingly active, and destroys great quantities of squirrels. **1887** (1895) Robinson *Uncle Lisha* 122 **wVT,** They [=deer] wa'n't wuth skinnin' fur their skins, say nothin' baout the meat, which the' wa'n't 'nough on tew carcasses tu bait a saple trap. **1947** Cahalane *Mammals* 174, For durability, softness and beauty, the fur of the marten ranks very high. It is frequently called the American sable. The famous sable is only a larger marten that lives in the pine-fir forests of Siberia. **1966** *DARE* Tape **ME**26, Saple—there's a stray one once in a while. . . The saple is small—isn't any bigger than a mink. He looks just like a little fox. He lives on squirrels. **1980** Whitaker *Audubon Field Guide Mammals* 569, *Marten* "Pine Marten" "American Sable."

sablefish n [*sable* black + *fish,* devised as a commercial name; see quot 1925]

A saltwater fish of the family Anoplopomatidae, usu *Anoplopoma fimbria* of the Pacific coast. For other names of *A. fimbria* see **beshow, black cod, candlefish 2, coalfish 3, horse mackerel 6, skilfish**

1918 *Copeia* 54.29 **CA,** *Anoplopoma fimbria* . . is now being largely pushed under the name of "Sablefish" and is, by the way, both fresh and smoked a real addition to our food-supplies. **1925** *Book of Rural Life* 4854, Later, when commercial fishing became important on the North Pacific coast, the "black cod" was something of a nuisance to the fishers for cod and herring, because they caught it, but could not sell it. But, by the co-operation of the U.S. Bureau of Fisheries, the fish has been renamed *sablefish*. Many people have learned that it is "one of the richest and fattest of American fishes." **1929** Pan-Pacific Research Inst. *Jrl.* 4.4.9 **CA,** Anoplopomidae [=Anoplopomatidae]. The Skil Fishes; Sable Fishes. **1968** *DARE* (Qu. P1, . . *Kinds of freshwter fish . . caught around here . . good to eat*) Inf **AK**1, Sablefish—black cod. **1983** *Audubon Field Guide N. Amer. Fishes* 724, The Sablefish spawns during the winter, and the eggs drift near the surface. . . Smoked and sold for food, it is very important commercially.

sabrebill See **saberbill**

sabre fish See **saber fish**

sacahuista n Also *sacahuiste, sachehuiste, sacuista* [Mex-Span *zacahuiscle,* ult of Nahuatl origin]

1 =**bear grass 1b,** esp *Nolina microcarpa* and *N. texana.* **SW**

1880 (1883) U.S. Census Office *Rept. Ag.* 970 **TX,** Other grasses named are the sachehuiste, wild rye, and wire grass. **1896** *Houston* (Tex.) *D. Post* 19 April *(DA),* For some four or five hours my pony stumbled around in the sacuista grass. [*DARE* Ed: This quot may refer instead to **2** below.] **1931** U.S. Dept. Ag. *Misc. Pub.* 101.15, Plants of the related genera, sotol (Dasylirion) and sacahuista or beargrass (Nolina), are also sometimes machine-cut or shredded, like soapweed, as emergency feed or silage, especially for cattle. **1945** Benson–Darrow *Manual SW Trees* 76, *Nolina microcarpa.* . . *Sacahuista.* . . Plant resembling a large, coarse grass. **1968** Schmutz et al. *Livestock-Poisoning Plants AZ* 98, *Beargrass,* sacahuista, sacahuiste, nolina (*Nolina microcarpa* and *N. texana*). . . The small, white to greenish flowers appear in May and June. **1985** Dodge *Flowers SW Deserts* 27, Yuccas are often confused by newcomers to the desert with . . *Nolinas* ("beargrass, sacahuista"). *Ibid* 29, Sacahuista, Beargrass . . *Nolina microcarpa . . Nolina parryi . . Nolina erumpens.* . . Leaves are browsed by livestock in times of drought, sometimes harmful results in the case of sheep or goats.

2 A **cordgrass** (here: *Spartina spartinae*). **chiefly TX** Cf **thatch grass**

1939 Tharp *Vegetation TX* 46, *Spartina spartinae* . . [?] the sacahuiste of the coastal vaquero, is the most conspicuous grass along the immediate Texas coast throughout that coast's extent. Growing in dense clumps sometimes three feet across, its stiff spine-tipped leaves deal misery to the legs as one makes his way through it. Though coarse and tough in age, it is tender and palatable when young. **1942** *Torreya* 42.158 **LA,** *Spartina spartinae.* . . Sacahuista. **1946** Stilwell *Hunting in TX* 246, We were hunting in the sacahuiste grass, country we never hunt unless we have to. There are thousands and thousands of acres of this stiff, heavy, thorny grass along the submarginal salt flats near the Texas coast. **1950** Writers' Round Table *Padre Is.* 135 **seTX,** Captain Andy Anderson and also W.S. Rankin remembered the great amount of hay which was cut along the *sacahuista,* or salt grass, area at Shamrock Point. **1967** *DARE* Tape **TX**24, Sacahuista grass. . grows up in a bunch. . . about two and a half, three feet long. . . It's a stem about . . the size of a small lead pencil on down at the root. . . They chop it off at the roots and tie it in bundles. **1970** Correll *Plants TX* 250, *Spartina spartinae*. . . Sacahuista. . . Extremely abundant near the coast.

sacalait n [LaFr, by folk-etym (appar meaning "milk bag") from Choctaw *sakli;* see quot 1938 at **1** below]

1 also *sacalait perch, sac au lait:* The white **crappie** *(Pomoxis annularis)*. **chiefly LA**

[**1802** Baudry des Lozières *Voyage LA* 175, Je puis dire seulement qu'on y prend l'esturgeon, le faisan d'eau, . . les sacalés, les patasses [etc]. [=I can only say that they catch there sturgeon, water pheasant, sacalés, patassas [etc].]] **1865** Norris *Amer. Angler's Book* 112 **LA,** This graceful fish [=*Pomoxis annularis*] is known by the creoles of Louisiana as the "Sac-à-Lai [sic]," where it is also sometimes called "Chinkapin Perch." **1896** U.S. Natl. Museum *Bulletin* 47.987, *Pomoxis annularis*. . . Sac-a-lait. . . Color silvery olive, mottled with dark green. **1931** Read *LA French* 67, In Louisiana the final *t* of *sacalait* is silent and the word is pronounced by the French in French fashion; by the English approximately like *sackalay*, with the chief stress either on the first or on the last syllable. **1938** *Zeitschrift für französische Sprache* 61.82, *Sacalait.* The Louisiana name for the Crappie (*Pomoxis annularis* Raf.), commonly thought to have been suggested by the beautiful white flesh or the silvery appearance of this fish. The actual source of the name is Choctaw *sakli,* "trout," French *sac-à-lait* being merely a typical example of folk etymology. **1960** (1966) Percy *Moviegoer* 150 **New Orleans LA,** We found a hole under a fallen willow—a good place for *sac au lait* if ever I saw one. . . So I said, go ahead, right down through the leaves—that's the way you catch *sac au lait.* **1967–68** *DARE* (Qu. P1, . . *Kinds of freshwater fish* . . *caught around here* . . *good to eat*) Infs **LA3,** 14, 26, 34, 40, Sacalait; **LA7,** Sacalait perch. **1967** *DARE* Tape **LA5,** I don't fool with sport fishing . . even if we . . catch the fish . . we gotta throw 'em right back into the water. . . They have sacalait. **1967** *DARE* FW Addit **sLA,** Sac-a-lait ['sɑkə,leɪ], ['sækə,leɪ]—local word for crappie. **1986** Pederson *LAGS Concordance* 12 infs, **LA,** Sacalait(s); 1 inf, **cnLA,** Sacalait = white crappie, catfish; 1 inf, **csLA,** Sacalait—large perch; 1 inf, **neLA,** Sacalait—French call freshwater crappie; 1 inf, **csMS,** Sacalait = white perch; 1 inf, **swMS,** Sacalait fish—French name common here; 1 inf, **ceTX,** Sacalaits—in LA, same as white perch, crappie.

2 A **warmouth** (here: *Chaenobryttus gulosus*).
1933 LA Dept. of Conserv. *Fishes* 342, *Chaenobryttus gulosus*. . . has come to bear many confusing popular names. These are: Warmouth, . . Sac-a-lait [etc]. **1946** LaMonte *N. Amer. Game Fishes* 142, *Warmouth*. . . *Names* . . Sac-à-lait, Indianfish [etc]. . . Deep holes, muddy water, weed beds, around bridges. **1976** Tryckare et al. *Lore of Sportfishing* 102, *Warmouth Bass*. . . Sac-a-lait. . . Coloration: olive brown to a brassy hue with darker blotches or mottling.

3 =**flier 2.**
1938 Schrenkeisen *Field Book Fishes* 258, *Centrarchus macropterus*. . . Sac-a-lait. . . Color yellowish-green with rows of dark spots along the sides.

4 A **killifish 1** such as *Fundulus grandis* or *F. similis.*
1884 Goode *Fisheries U.S.* 1.466 **FL,** *Fundulus grandis,* is known at Pensacola by the name "Sac-a-lait." **1911** U.S. Bur. Census *Fisheries 1908* 312, *Poeciliidae* [here: =Cyprinodontidae]. . . Along the eastern coast they are known as . . "killifish . . ;" on the Gulf as "sac-à-lait;" and in the interior as "minnows."

sacalait perch n See **sacalait 1**

sacapellote n
A composite plant *(Acourtia microcephala)* native to California.
1925 Jepson *Manual Plants CA* 1014, *P[erezia] microcephala* [=*Acourtia m.*]. . Sacapellote. . . Chaparral belt, rather common. **1960** Abrams *Flora Pacific States* 4.550, Sacapellote. . Stout erect perennials. . . corollas lavender-pink to white. . . Common on dry slopes.

sac-a-plomb n [LaFr, literally "bag of lead," from its habit of sinking rapidly when alarmed] **LA**
=**pied-bill(ed) grebe.**
1916 *Times–Picayune* (New Orleans LA) 26 Mar mag sec 1, *Pied-billed Grebe*. . Sac-a-plomb. **1967** LeCompte *Word Atlas* 206 **seLA,** This bird [=*Podilymbus podiceps*] also goes by the name *sac à plomb.* **1983** Reinecke *Coll.* 10 **LA,** Sac-a-plomb ['sækəplõ]. . . the pie-billed

grebe, hell-diver, because of its habit of dropping below surface for long periods. Chiefly Cajun.

sacasil n [MexSpan]
A **hedgehog cactus 3** (here: *Echinocereus poselgeri*).
1960 Vines *Trees SW* 770, *Wilcoxia poselgeri* [=*Echinocereus p.*] . . is also known under the vernacular names of Sacasil and Lead Pencil Cactus. **1970** Correll *Plants TX* 1095, Sacasil. . . In s. Tex. near the Rio Grande.

sacate n Also *zacate* [MexSpan *zacate* < Nahuatl *zacatl*]
Grass, hay, esp such as grows naturally.
1848 (1962) U.S. Army Corps Topog. Engineers *Abert's NM Rept.* 41, As there were no pasture grounds near the village, I was forced to buy "zacate" for my mules. **1891** U.S. Dept. Ag. Div. Botany *Bulletin* 12.2, [Facing Pl. XX:] [*Sporobolus wrightii* is] a tall coarse grass, growing in dense tufts, commonly called Saccaton or Zacate. **1892** *DN* 1.195 **TX,** *Zacáte:* grass, fodder. **1894** *DN* 1.325 **TX,** Sacáte. See *zacate.* **1932** Bentley *Spanish Terms* 217, Zacate—English modification *sacate.* . . "Wild hay," i.e., grass harvested from swales, mesas, etc., where it grows naturally. . . Grama grass seems to be the favorite variety for wild hay.

sacaton n Also *saccatoa, saccaton(e), saccato(o), zacaton* [MexSpan *zacaton* augmentative of *zacate;* cf **sacate**]
Any of var grasses of the western US, as:
a A **dropseed 3,** usu *Sporobolus wrightii* or *S. airoides.*
[**1863** U.S. Congress *Serial Set* 1174.1.16 **Mexico,** "Sacaton" indicates water near surface.] **1873** Army *Interesting NM* 27, The "sacaton" a grass growing 6 feet high also abounds [in the bottomlands of the Red River]. **1894** Coulter *Botany W. TX* 520, *S[porobolus] Wrightii*. . . Bunch grass. Zacaton. . . In adobe soil, along streams, western Texas to southern California. **1913** (1979) Barnes *Western Grazing* 43, There is also sacaton (Sporobolus airoides). *Ibid* 54, There are great areas along the rivers and in the alkali lands which grow a fine crop of sacaton (Sporobolus). . . Sacaton (sac-ah-tone) starts very early in the spring and while young is relished by all classes of stock. . . I have seen a herd rounded up on a sacaton flat for several days at a time. **1929** Bews *World's Grasses* 201, Two species of the S.W. States are important forage grasses in the arid or semi-arid regions of Nebraska, Arizona, and Texas—*S[porobolus] wrightii* Munro, 'Saccaton,' and *S. airoides* Torr., 'Alkali Saccaton' or 'Alkali Drop-seed.' **1942** Castetter–Bell *Pima & Papago Ag.* 22 **AZ,** Along the edges and in the openings of the forests of these two drainages, sacaton grass *(Sporobolus Wrightii)* thrives. **1967** *DARE* FW Addit **neCO,** Alkali Sacaton—Native Colorado grass. Common. **1970** Correll *Plants TX* 219, *Sporobolus Wrightii*. . . Sacaton. . . Mostly near the Rio Grande or near the coast. . . *Sporobolus Tharpii*. . . Coastal sacaton. . . Near the coast, s.e. Tex. and Rio Grande Plains. . . *Sporobolus airoides*. . . Alkali sacaton. . . Plains Country and Trans-Pecos, often very abundant.
b A **muhly (grass)** (here: either *Muhlenbergia distichophylla* or *M. rigens*).
1890 U.S. Dept. Ag. Div. Botany *Bulletin* 1.i, [Facing Pl. XXV:] *Muhlenbergia distichophylla* [=*M. asperifolia*]. . . is one of the grasses called saccato. *Ibid* [Facing Pl. XXVII:] *Epicampes macroura* [= *Muhlenbergia rigens*]. . . is another of the grasses called saccato, or saccatone. **1932** Bentley *Spanish Terms* 217, Zacaton—English modification *sacaton.* . . Literally, a large *zacate* or grass. *Zacaton* is applied to a particular kind of grass probably (*Epicamper* [sic] *rigens*) that grows in tussocks or "hills" along river bottoms and other lower land. . . This grass is usually referred to as "zacaton grass" or "basket grass."
c A **mountain rice** (here: *Achnatherum hymenoides*).
1880 (1883) U.S. Census Office *Rept. Ag.* 961 **sCA,** *Eriogoneæ cuspidata* [=*Achnatherum hymenoides*] is one of the valuable bunch grasses. . . It runs into several varieties, one of which is called in southern California saccatoo or saccatoa.

sac au lait See **sacalait 1**

saccato(a) See **sacaton**

saccato gordo n Also *zaccato gordo* [Appar varr of MexSpan *zacate* or *zacaton* (see **sacate, sacaton**) + *gordo* fat]
A **fiddleneck 1** (here: either *Amsinckia douglasiana* or *A. menziesii* var *intermedia*).
1915 (1926) Armstrong–Thornber *Western Wild Flowers* 428, *Amsinckia intermedia* [=*A. menziesii* var *intermedia*]. . . Very abundant in southern Arizona and . . valued as a grazing plant for stock and . .

therefore known as Saccato Gordo, which means "fat grass." **1925** Jepson *Manual Plants CA* 844, *A[msinckia] douglasiana.* . . Also called Fireweed and Zaccato Gorda [sic].

saccaton(e), saccatoo See **sacaton**

sacer See **saucer**

sachehuiste See **sacahuista**

sachet See **sachet kitten**

sachet bush n Cf **polecat tree 2, spicebush**

A **false indigo 1** (here: *Amorpha fruticosa*).

   1940 Clute *Amer. Plant Names* 251, *Amorpha fruticosa.* . . Sachet-bush.

sachet kitten n Also *sachet (kitty),* ~ *pussy, sashay kitty* Cf **perfume(d) pussy**

=**skunk 1.**

   1921 *DN* 5.114 **CA,** *Sachet kitten, sachet pussy.* . . Pole cat. **1944** Adams *Western Words* 135, *Sachet kitten*—Cowboy's name for a skunk. **1946** Peattie *Pacific Coast* 90, Shunned because of their mephitic odor and potentiality for malicious mischief, these animals are called by a number of humorous nicknames—sachet pussy, perfume merchant . . but a skunk by any other name . . ! **1967–70** *DARE* (Qu. P26, *Names and nicknames . . for a skunk*) Infs **MD**29, **PA**234, **TX**9, Sachet kitten; **OH**42, **PA**128, **TX**11, Sachet kitty; **NY**123, Sachet. **1982** *Ft. Myers News–Press* (FL) 24 Jan sec F 5, The car had just run over a skunk. . . I dropped off that tainted car smelling like a sashay kitty and headed for the shop to get warm.

sack n

1 A container of heavy paper permanently closed on the sides and bottom. **widespread, but less freq NEng, sPA** See Map Cf **poke** n[1] **1a**

   1903 *DN* 2.352 **WA,** *Sack.* . . A bag of any material, and of any size. A paper bag is here called a sack. At the grocery, 'I'll put these eggs in a sack, and send them round.' **1904** *DN* 2.420 **nwAR,** *Sack.* . . Bag. 'Put the apples in a paper sack.' **1909** *DN* 3.365 **eAL, wGA,** *Sack.* . . A bag of any kind. "Put it in a paper sack." Universal. **1928** *DN* 6.60 **Ozarks,** A paper bag is always a *sack* or a *poke,* since *bag* means scrotum in the hill country. **1946** McAtee *Dial. Grant Co. IN Suppl. 3* 8 (as of 1890s), *Paper sack* . . paper bags ordinarily seen in stores. **1946** *PADS* 5.31 **VA,** *Paper sack* (see *poke*): A paper bag; not common. **1965–70** *DARE* (Qu. F22a, *A smaller paper container for bringing groceries home from the store*) 339 Infs, **widespread, but less freq NEast,** (Paper) sack; 14 Infs, **scattered,** Grocery sack; (Qu. F22b, *A smaller paper container for carrying a lunch: "He had his lunch in a _____."*) 346 Infs, **widespread, but less freq NEast,** (Paper) sack; **TN**66, Lunch sack; (Qu. F21, *A cloth or paper container that you buy flour in*) 19 Infs, **scattered,** Paper sack; **IL**134, Grocery sack; **TX**91, Poke sack—old-fashioned; (Qu. F17) Infs **MO**15, 39, **OH**84, **PA**131, Sack; **MO**14, Paper sack; (Qu. F24, *The container for kitchen parings and scraps—inside the kitchen*) Infs **CA**59, **MI**94, **OH**78, Paper sack; (Qu.DD1, *What different forms does chewing tobacco come in around here?*) Infs **IA**11, **KY**85, **MD**20, **OH**41, **TN**26, Sack; **OH**23, Cans and sacks; **PA**57, Loose in a paper sack. **1972** *PADS* 58.15 **cwAL,** *(Paper) bag* (18 [of 27 infs] is more common than *(paper) sack* (8). [**1986** *AmSp*

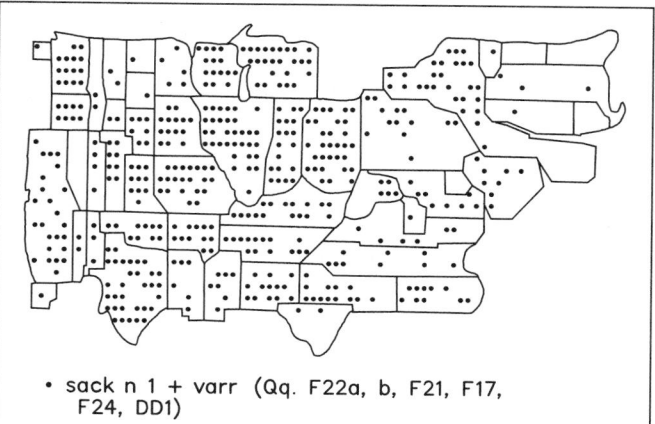

• sack n 1 + varr (Qq. F22a, b, F21, F17, F24, DD1)

61.205 **IN,** There is no consensus in Bloomington, Indiana, about the term for a paper container. Epitomizing the indecision is a sign outside the cafeteria at Eigenmann Hall, an Indiana University dormitory: "Sack lunch bags may not be taken into the cafeteria."] **1994** *NC Lang. & Life Project Dial. Dict. Lumbee Engl.* 10 **seNC,** *Sack.* . . Paper bag. Generally replaced by *bag,* but still used to a limited extent by older speakers. Help me with this sack of groceries, will you?

2a also *milk sack:* An udder. **chiefly S Midl** See Map

   1903 *DN* 2.328 **seMO,** *Sack.* . . Bag. 'The cow has a full sack.' **1915** *DN* 4.180 **swVA,** *Bag.* . . Udder. Also *sack.* **1949** Arnow *Hunter's Horn* 107 **KY,** From the way their sacks were hardening up, it looked as if several would lamb anyway. **1950** *WELS (The cow's udder is called)* 2 Infs, **WI,** Sack. **c1960** Wilson Coll. **csKY,** *Sack:* a cow's udder. **1965–70** *DARE* (Qu. K4, *The cow's udder*) 43 Infs, **chiefly S Midl,** Sack; **MO**5, 39, **OH**31, Milk sack; (Qu. K7, *What sickness can a cow get in her udder—for example, if she's left unmilked too long?*) Inf **IN**45, Caked sack; (Qu. K9, *If one quarter of a cow's udder does not give milk . . she's _____*) Inf **IN**17, Has a spoiled sack; **MO**9, Spoil sack; **SC**34, Quarter of her sack's ruined. **1983** *MJLF* 9.1.54 **ceKY, seMO,** *Sack* . . the udder of a cow.

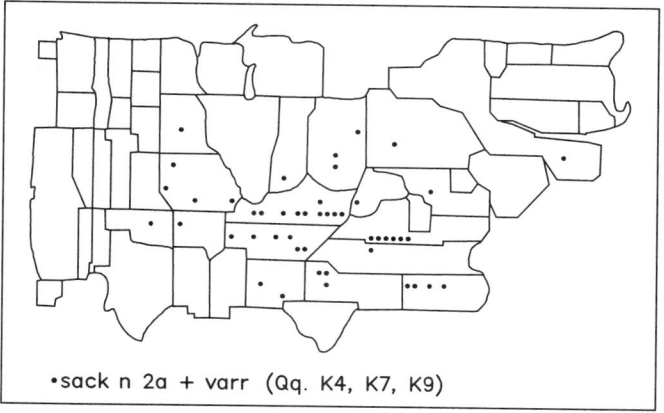

•sack n 2a + varr (Qq. K4, K7, K9)

b A woman's breast. Cf *milk bag* (at **milk B2**)

   1968 *DARE* (Qu. X31, . . *A woman's breasts*) Infs **MD**19, **NY**55, Sacks.

3 A woman—freq in phr *old sack.* **derog**

   1927 *AmSp* 3.131 [College slang], If the student finds his companion lacking in the qualities that he admires she may be called: "a flat tire," "a flop," "a crock," "a high hig," or "a sack," or she deserves "thumbs down." **1928** *AmSp* 3.220 **KS** [University slang], *Sack.* . . An unpopular, unattractive woman; decidedly not a good date. **1968–69** *DARE* (Qu. HH34, *General words . . for a woman*) Inf **TX**72, Old sack; (Qu. HH36, *A careless, slovenly woman: "She's just an old _____."*) Infs **MD**31, **TX**72, Sack.

4 in var phrr where *bag* is customary, as:

a *hold the sack:* To bear alone the consequences that should be shared by others; to possess what remains after others have taken whatever is of value; to be in a predicament.

   [**1897** Lummis *King of Broncos* 44 **NM,** Ef they hain't gi'n me the sack to hold!] **1904** Smith *Promoters* 343 **OH,** They are the ones that are always left to hold the sack. **1916** *DN* 4.324 **KS, NE,** *Hold the sack.* . . To be the loser, esp. thru the plans or connivance of others,—in allusion to the practical joke in which the victim is led to hold a sack over the opening in which a 'snipe' or some animal or fabulous thing is concealed, and the jokers profess to go to drive the animal out from the other end of the log, etc., but in fact, leave the victim to 'hold the sack.' General south. **1929** *Univ. Kansas Graduate Mag.* Apr. *(OED2),* We will be holding the sack for an additional . . deficit of nearly $1000. **1949** *Chicago Daily News* (IL) 8 Aug 10/4, It seems . . that Uncle Sam is holding the sack right now. **1954** Faulkner *Fable* 176 **MS,** You might leave your own kinfolks holding the sack, but these are the sheriff's friends. **c1960** Wilson Coll. **csKY,** Hold the sack (or bag). . . Take the rap, be deserted by one's gang. Probably related to the age-old *Snipe Hunt,* designed to catch yokels rather than snipe. **1966** Barnes–Jensen *Dict. UT Slang* 43, *To hold the sack* . . to be left in the lurch; to hold what's left after others have taken everything of value.

b *let the cat out (of) the sack:* To disclose a secret.

   1967–68 *DARE* (Qu. JJ43, *To give away a secret or tell a piece of* news too soon: "He wasn't supposed to know. Somebody must have _____.") Infs **OH**81, **SC**32, Let the cat out (of) the sack.

c *in the sack:* Thoroughly drunk. Cf *in the bag* (at **bag** n **B1**)

1969 *DARE* (Qu. DD15, *A person who is thoroughly drunk*) Inf **CT**35, In the sack.

sack v

1 In logging:

a To follow a log drive, returning to the main stream those logs that have become lodged or stranded—usu in phrr *sack the river, ~ (the) rear, sack logs,* etc; hence vbl n *sacking,* n *sacker.* Cf **drive** n **6, pick** v **3c, rear** n¹ **1**

1868 *Harper's New Mth. Mag.* 36.422 **MN,** Another frequent and laborious part of the "drive" is "sacking." This takes place when the logs . . have been thrown up and lodged upon the shore. **1878** *Lumberman's Gaz.* 11 June 518/2 **WI,** It has been a much cleaner drive than was expected. The last work was finished this week, sacking the main river down to the rear of the drive. **1893** *Scribner's Mag.* 13.715 **MI,** Thus, wading and "sacking" logs, the rear crew works wet to the waist from daylight to dark until the drive is down. **1902** White *Blazed Trail* 334 **MI,** Intense rivalry existed as to which crew "sacked" the farthest down stream in the course of the day. *Ibid* 360, It was noon. The sackers looked up in surprise. **1905** U.S. Forest Serv. *Bulletin* 61.45 [Logging terms], *Sack the rear, to.* To follow a drive and roll in logs which have lodged or grounded. (Gen.) **1907** *DN* 3.249 **eME,** *Sack the rear.* . . (Of river-drivers.) To follow an entire drive of logs and see that none are left behind. **1942** ME Univ. *Studies* 57.134, *Sacking the Rear.* Removing *pulpwood* or *logs* from banks, rocks, *logans,* etc., at the *rear* of a *drive.* **1942** Beck *Songs MI Lumberjacks* 199, De foreman come; he say go sak [sic]./ You got in de watair all over your back. **1958** McCulloch *Woods Words* 155 **Pacific NW,** *Sack.* . . To chase stray logs behind the drive. *Sack the banks*—To hunt for hung-up logs along the river banks following a drive. . . *Sacker*—The tail end man on a river drive. **1966** *DARE* Tape **ME**26, [FW:] Ever run the logs down the river? [Inf:]. . . There's one fella there; put him sacking rear 'cause he couldn't ride the lumber. . . Rear. . . That's the stack that's left behind the main drive, the stack that you kick out and goes, strays, see, in the bushes and like that.

b in phr *sack the slide:* To return logs to a slide from which they have become dislodged.

1905 U.S. Forest Serv. *Bulletin* 61.45 [Logging terms], *Sack the slide, to.* To return to a slide logs which have jumped out. (Gen.) **1958** McCulloch *Woods Words* 155 **Pacific NW,** *Sack the slide*—To replace logs which have jumped out of a chute or slide.

2 To carry, lug, tote (esp something heavy); hence *sack off* carry off, steal. **ME, NH**

1907 *DN* 3.249 **eME,** *Sack off.* . . Carry off surreptitiously. "Somebody has sacked your team off," i.e., has run away with your horse and carriage. **1914** *DN* 4.79 **ME, nNH,** *Sack.* . . To carry. **1939** *LANE* Map 165 (*Lugged*) 2 infs, **nME,** Sacked. **1975** Gould *ME Lingo* 239, Mostly, as used in Maine, *sack* is a verb interchangeable with *tote, lug, carry,* and *haul* where something is moved with the hands or on the back. A load is *sacked* into camp; meaning it was *toted. Sack* does suggest a little more difficulty with the task.

3 with *out:* See quots; hence vbl n *sacking out.*

1936 McCarthy *Lang. Mosshorn* np **West** [Rodeo terms], *Sackin' Out.* Tying the hind leg of a horse and waving a saddle blanket over its eyes in order to gentle down for riding. **1939** (1973) FWP *Guide MT* 415, *Sack out*—To break a shying horse by tying him up and throwing sacks at him until he no longer shies. **1961** Adams *Old-Time Cowhand* 96 **West,** They [=slickers] was good for sackin' out a green colt.

sack bag n

A large, cloth bag; see quots.

1842 (1940) Arnold *Diaries* 160 **VT,** Mr. Gleason borrowed a sack bag to carry up his cocoons in. **1899** (1912) Green *VA Folk-Speech* 363, *Sack-bag.* . . A bag holding three bushels of grain. **1946** *PADS* 5.35 **VA,** *Sack bag.* . . A large bag made of coarse canvas; rare. **1949** *AmSp* 24.113 **SC,** *Sack bag.* . . Burlap bag. **1968** *DARE* (Qu. F20, *A cloth container for feed*) Inf **NY**61, Sack bags; (Qu. F23, *A container made of rough, loosely-woven, brown cloth; commonly used for potatoes, etc*) Inf **DE**3, One old man said grass sack bag; **MD**44, Sack bag, burlap bag.

sack clover n

A clover with an inflated calyx (here: either *Trifolium depauperatum* or *T.d.* var *amplectens*).

1944 Abrams *Flora Pacific States* 2.537, *Trifolium amplectens* [=*T. depauperatum* var. *a.*] . . Pale Sack Clover. . . The standard much inflated in age. *Ibid* 538, *Trifolium depauperatum.* . . Dwarf Sack Clover. . . Calyces inflated and reflexed in fruit. **1961** Thomas *Flora Santa Cruz* 214 **cwCA,** *T[rifolium] depauperatum.* . . Dwarf Sack Clover. . . *T. amplectens.* . . Pale Sack Clover.

sacker, sacking vbl n See **sack** v **1a**

sacking n Cf **dog pile, monkey ~**

A type of horseplay; see quot.

1957 *Sat. Eve. Post Letters* **IN** (as of c1900), One of the favorite sports at school was "sacking" (a favorite probably because the teachers frowned on it). This started by "dogging" the victim. One boy would jump on the victims [sic] back, another would jump on his back and the third & so on. Finally something would have to give and when they fell everyone yelled "sack" and piled on. Strangely the bottom layer felt very little weight—but the second layer was pretty rugged.

sacking out See **sack** v **3**

sack logs See **sack** v **1a**

sack louse n

1990 Cavender *Folk Med. Lexicon* 30 **csAppalachians,** *Sack lice*—lice in the pubic area.

sack man n

A hobgoblin.

1966 Dakin *Dial. Vocab. Ohio R. Valley* 520, *The devil.* . . The precise meaning of several other Kentucky terms is uncertain, but it seems they are imaginary demons rather than "the devil." . . *the sack man* . . Harlan County. **1968** *DARE* (Qu. EE41, *A hobgoblin that is used to threaten children and make them behave*) Infs **LA**40, 43, Sack man.

sack off See **sack** v **2**

sack out See **sack** v **3**

sack (the) rear, sack the river See **sack** v **1a**

sack the slide See **sack** v **1b**

Sacramento cat n Also *Sacramento catfish*
=**brown bullhead 1.**

1882 U.S. Natl. Museum *Bulletin* 16.104 **CA,** *Sacramento Cat.* Color dark yellowish brown, more or less clouded. . . Introduced into the rivers of California, where it has rapidly multiplied. **1949** Caine *N. Amer. Sport Fish* 148, *Brown Bullhead.* . . *Colloquial Names* . . Sacramento Catfish [etc]. **1973** Knight *Cook's Fish Guide* 377, Catfish . . sacramento see Bullhead, Brown.

Sacramento perch n

A freshwater fish (*Archoplites interruptus*) native to California.

1882 U.S. Natl. Museum *Bulletin* 16.466 **CA,** *A[rchoplites] interruptus.* . . *Sacramento Perch.* . . Sacramento and San Joaquin rivers; abundant; the only fresh-water percoid west of the Rocky Mountains. **1946** LaMonte *N. Amer. Game Fishes* 138, *Sacramento Perch.* . . Varies from almost wholly black to almost wholly silvery; alternating pale and dusky blotches on the sides. **1963** Sigler–Miller *Fishes UT* 139, The Sacramento perch is not an important fish in Utah because it occurs only in Garrison Reservoir. **1983** *Audubon Field Guide N. Amer. Fishes* 550, The Sacramento Perch. . . has been introduced into some western lakes that are too alkaline for other fishes.

Sacramento pike n Cf **pike** n¹ **3**

A **squawfish** (here: either *Ptychocheilus grandis* or *P. oregonensis*).

1882 U.S. Natl. Museum *Bulletin* 16.226, *P[tychocheilus] oregonensis.* . . *Sacramento "Pike".* . . Rivers of the Pacific slope, chiefly west of the Sierra Nevada. **1911** U.S. Bur. Census *Fisheries 1908* 315, *Sacramento pike (Ptycocheilus* [sic] *oregonensis* and *P. grandis*).—A chub of the Sacramento and Columbia. **1946** LaMonte *N. Amer. Game*

Fishes 158, *Sacramento Pike—Ptychocheilus grandis.* . . Eats young trout.

Sacramento salmon n Also *Sacramento River salmon* =chinook salmon.

1879 U.S. Natl. Museum *Bulletin* 14.58, *Oncorhynchus quinnat.* . . *Sacramento Salmon.*—Northwest Coast of America; south to California. **1904** *Salmon & Trout* 154, The quinnat salmon . . bears a number of different names in different regions, such as . . Sacramento salmon. **1953** Roedel *Common Fishes CA* 40, *Oncorhynchus tshawytscha.* . . Quinnat salmon, . . Sacramento River salmon [etc].

Sacramento squawfish n Cf Sacramento pike, squawfish

A **squawfish** (here: *Ptychocheilus grandis*).

1944 (1967) McNichols *Crazy Weather* 53 **SW**, The fish was no salmon, although it was popularly so called all along the river. It was a great chub, first cousin to the minnows found in all eastern streams, and an own brother to the Sacramento squawfish. **1983** *Audubon Field Guide N. Amer. Fishes* 452, This fish was once considered a major predator of young salmons, but while both fishes may compete for food and space, most waters inhabited by Sacramento Squawfish are too warm for young salmons and trout.

Sacramento sucker n

A **sucker** (here: *Catastomus occidentalis*) native to the western US.

1882 U.S. Natl. Museum *Bulletin* 16.128 **CA**, *C[atostomus] occidentalis.* . . *Sacramento Sucker.* . . Abundant in the Sacramento and San Joaquin. **1939** Natl. Geogr. Soc. *Fishes* 279, Sacramento suckers may reach a length of nearly two feet, but average about 15 inches. **1957** Blair et al. *Vertebrates U.S.* 88, Sacramento sucker. Head small. Mouth rather small, . . lips rather thin.

sacred bark n [Calque of AmSpan *cascara sagrada*]

The medicinal bark of **cascara 1**.

1891 *Century Dict.* 5294, *Sacred bark*, cascara sagrada bark. **1929** in 1950 *Western Folkl.* 9.340, Medicinal herbs of early days in use and collected in the San Antonio Mission District. . . Cascara Sagrada . . or Sacred Bark, or California Coffee: for Rheumatism, Poison Oak, or as Purgative. **1930** Sievers *Amer. Med. Plants* 21, *Rhamnus purshiana.* . . Sacred bark. . . Cascara bark must be aged at least one year before it is used. If collectors in removing the bark allow enough to remain to prevent the tree from dying it will develop new bark, thus prolonging the natural supply of this valuable drug which is gradually being exhausted.

sacred bug n

A **conenose** (here: *Triatoma protracta*).

1926 Essig *Insects N. Amer.* 355, *Triatoma protracta* . . is also known by various other common names as big bedbug . . and sacred bug. . . It is common throughout California. . . It frequently invades the beds of campers as well as residences and is often responsible for painful bites to humans.

sacred harp n attrib [The shape-note hymnals of this name in current use are descended from the *Sacred Harp* of B.F. White and E.J. King, first published in 1844, but there were several earlier ones with this title.] chiefly Sth Cf harp n 4, fasola

Appearing in or employing a **shape-note** hymnal—often in combs *sacred harp sing(ing)*.

1940 Writers' Program *Guide GA* 127, An interesting development of this rural music is the Sacred Harp singing, in which performers read from shaped note song books. **1940** Writers' Program *Guide TX* 380, A typical Sacred Harp gathering is an all-day affair; folk from far and near arrive early and bring picnic lunches. *Ibid* 399, The rural folk cling to old customs, have Sacred Harp singing conventions, religious revival meetins, and in some areas, hold wakes. **1978** Wolfe *I'm On My Journey Home* 6/2, [Liner notes:] The words "Jesus, my all, to Heaven is gone" appear in a number of Sacred Harp songs and have become almost a commonplace line. **1986** Pederson *LAGS Concordance* 1 inf, **cMS**, Sacred Harp sings. **1989** Flynt *Poor But Proud* 229 **ceAL** (as of 1910–30), [The event was] variously called a Sacred Harp sing (for the name of the oblong songsters), a Fasola sing . . or a Shaped Note sing. . . Alabama mountain song: "Sacred Harp Singin'/ Dinner-on-the-grounds / Whiskey in the woods / An' the devil all around."

sacrifice service n

1959 Lomax *Rainbow Sign* 181 **TX** [Black], When we begin a revival, we have a week's sacrifice service. Those who smoke, don't smoke. Those who dip snuff, don't dip no more. We don't buy luxuries and we eat just common.

sacuista See sacahuista

sad adj [*OED2* 1688 →; "Now *dial*."] chiefly Midl, Sth

Of bread, cake, or the like: heavy, dense, soggy.

1886 *S. Bivouac* 4.343 **sAppalachians**, Sad (of bread, heavy). **1890** *DN* 1.76 **seNJ**, *Sad*: heavy as applied to bread, as 'the bread is sad.' **1899** (1912) Green *VA Folk-Speech* 363, *Sad*. . . Heavy; sobby: as bread. **1903** *DN* 2.328 **seMO**, *Sad*. . . Soggy. 'This bread is sad.' **1905** *DN* 3.93 **nwAR**, *Sad*. . . Heavy, soggy. [*·*]The bread . . [or] cake is sad.' Common. **1906** *DN* 3.154 **nwAR**, *Sad cake is the best cake of all.* Said of soggy cake. **1909** *DN* 3.365 **eAL, wGA**, *Sad*. . . Soggy. "This cake is sad, but it's good." **1935** *AmSp* 10.172 **PA** [Engl of PA Germans], Cakes which don't rise properly are spoken of as *sad cakes.* **1944** *PADS* 2.48 **NC, VA**, *Sad*. . . Heavy; said of bread, cake, etc. Several Southern states. Older people. **1949** Webber *Backwoods Teacher* 204 **Ozarks**, That there cake of mine is mighty sad [heavy] lookin'. **1967** *DARE* Tape **PA**14, They say if you lift the lid, that . . makes your dumplings sad. **1987** Kytle *Voices* 32 **NC**, As a treat for me, then, sometimes she'd put in what she called "too much" shortening and sugar and make a sad cake. She knew I put a high rating on the heavy, nearly soggy cakes. **1991** Still *Wolfpen Notebooks* 163 **sAppalachians**, Sad (referring to bread dough): won't rise.

Sadaday See Saturday

‡sadaddle adv Cf wrong-sedadus

1970 *DARE* (Qu. MM2, *Suppose a little girl accidentally gets her dress on wrong so that the back part is turned around* . . *"Look, you've got your dress on _____."*) Inf **TX**92, Sadaddle [ˌsəˈdædəl].

Saday, Sadday See Saturday

saddity See siditty

saddle n

1 In logging: a notch cut in one of the transverse logs forming a **skid road 1** intended to guide the logs being skidded; hence v *saddle* to cut such a notch in (a skid).

1905 U.S. Forest Serv. *Bulletin* 61.45 **Pacific NW** [Logging terms], *Saddle*. . . The depression cut in a transverse skid in a skid road to guide the logs which pass over it. **1913** Bryant *Logging* 149 **Pacific NW**, Skid roads built for animal snaking in the Northwest are carefully located. . . Skids 10 feet long and from 10 to 14 inches in diameter are laid across the completed grade at 10-foot intervals, and are partly buried in the ground. . . A "saddle" is adzed out of the center of each skid and in this the log rides. **1956** Sorden-Ebert *Logger's Words* 29 **Gt Lakes**, Saddle the skids, v., To hew cut one side of the skids so that the logs would pass over without slipping sideways. **1958** McCulloch *Woods Words* 155 **Pacific NW**, *Saddle*. . . A scooped-out place in the middle of skids laid across the skidroad. It kept the logs from rolling off the skid. In some incline systems where logs were roaded downhill between the rails, the ties were also saddled. . . *Saddle a skid*—To chop a saddle in a skid or timber.

2 The central support of a corn shock formed by twisting a number of cornstalks together. Cf **saddle bunch**

1968 Allen *It Happened* 204 **sIL** (as of c1900), A shock row regularly included sixteen rows of corn. Shocks were spaced about twenty paces apart. At the spot where the shock was to form, a "saddle" was tied. This was done by bending a number of stalks in the middle rows together and fastening their tops by twisting them. Several armfuls of corn were cut, placed on end about the saddle, and tied at the top with a bent cornstalk. After a few armloads were in place, this core of the stock [sic] was bound with a stalk.

3 See quot.

1945 Thorp *Pardner* 258 **SW**, A young horse, unaccustomed to weight would tire easily, so the first day's ride (called a "saddle") was usually not more than three or four miles.

4 also *saddling*: A covering for the ridge of a roof. scattered, but esp Sth See Map on p. 692 Cf **saddle board**

1965–70 *DARE* (Qu. D30, *The strip of wood or metal that covers the* *ridge of a roof*) 23 Infs, **scattered, but esp Sth,** Saddle [FW sugg]; **SC**19, Ridgerow—the "right" name, but we call it a saddle; **WI**29, Roof saddle; **NC**81, Saddling. **1986** Pederson *LAGS Concordance* (Eaves trough) 1 inf, **swMS,** A saddle—on roof.

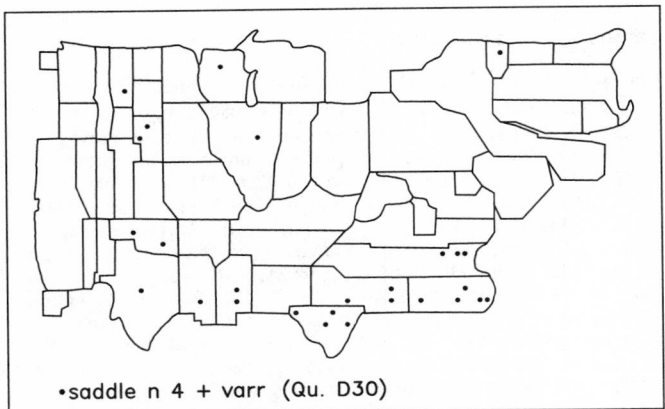

•saddle n 4 + varr (Qu. D30)

5 A sanitary napkin—usu in phrr *in* (or *riding*) *the saddle:* menstruating. Cf **back in the saddle (again)**
1954 *AmSp* 29.298 **TX, OK, FL** [Vernacular of menstruation], *Reference to material culture . . candy bar (M[en]); rag (M[en]); saddle (M[en] and W[omen]); back in the saddle (M[en] and W[omen]).* **1966–70** *DARE* (Qu. AA27, . . *A woman's menstruation*) Infs **CA**94, **KY**84, **MS**16, **OH**84, In the saddle; **MO**26, She's ridin' the saddle.

saddle v See **saddle** n 1

saddleback n
1 See **saddleback gull.**
2 See **saddleback caterpillar.**
3 See quot.
1967 *DARE* (Qu. Q21, . . *Kinds of sparrows*) Inf **TX**5, Saddleback.
4 =**camelback 3.** [Cf *OED2* saddle-backed a. 2 1675 →]
[**1899** (1912) Green *VA Folk-Speech* 363, *Saddle-backed. . .* Hollow-backed; sway-backed; said of a horse.] **1968** *DARE* (Qu. K44, *A bony or poor-looking horse*) Infs **NH**14, **NY**99, Saddleback.

saddleback caterpillar n Also *saddleback, saddlebag worm* [From the markings on its back]
The larva of a small brown moth *(Sibine stimulea).* Also called **packsaddle worm**
1890 Packard *Insects* 146, *The Saddle-back Caterpillar. . .* The caterpillar is of strange form, being short and thick. . . The hairs fringing the sides of the body sting severely. **1938** Brimley *Insects NC* 292, *S[ibine] stimulea . . Saddle-back Caterpillar.* **1948** *S. Folkl. Qrly.* 12.171 **AL, GA,** His description of the packsaddle [see **packsaddle worm** quot 1884] corresponds to that of the saddlebag worm, still found in cotton and cornfields in Alabama and Georgia, which gets its name from the fact that it has a brown saddlebag upon its green back. **1966–68** *DARE* (Qu. R21, . . *Other kinds of stinging insects*) Inf **FL**16, Saddleback caterpillar; (Qu. R27, . . *Kinds of caterpillars or similar worms*) Infs **PA**17, **SC**57, Saddleback; **SC**2, Saddleback caterpillar. **1968** *PA Game News* Sept 6 **PA,** This morning I found a saddleback caterpillar, his legless belly pressed against a jewelweed leaf. **1984** Covell *Field Guide Moths* 412, *Saddleback Caterpillar Moth. . .* Larva *(Saddleback Caterpillar . .)* can inflict a painful *sting* with sharp bristles on its body. *Range:* Mass. to Fla., west to e. Mo. and Tex. **1995** in 1998 (acc) OH State Univ. *Ohioline: Insect & Pest Ser.* HYG–2130–95 (Internet), *Saddleback Caterpillar*—Larvae are slug-like, about one inch long and 3/8 inch wide full-grown, brown at both ends . . , green around the middle "saddle blanket," with a purple-brown oval spot "saddle" edged with white in the center of the back.

saddleback gull n Also *saddleback* [*OED2* 1770 →]
=**great black-backed gull.**
1844 Giraud *Birds Long Is.* 362, The Black-backed or "Saddle Back Gull," is said to be an inhabitant of various parts of the northern shores of the American continent. At the approach of winter, it migrates to the extreme southern part of the United States. **1872** Coues *Key to N. Amer. Birds* 312, Great Black-backed Gull. Saddle-back. Coffin-carrier. Cobb.

1898 (1900) Davie *Nests N. Amer. Birds* 30, The large and powerful Black-backed Gull, or Saddle-back, inhabits the Atlantic waters of Europe and North America. **1925** (1928) Forbush *Birds MA* 1.69, *Larus marinus. . .* Saddle-back. **1956** MA Audubon Soc. *Bulletin* 40.22, *Great black-backed gull. . .* Saddle-back (Mass.; also in British provincial use. In allusion to the black mantle.); Saddle-back Gull (Maine).

saddleback house See **saddlebag house**

saddlebag n
1 See **saddlebag** v.
2 See **saddlebag house.**
3 A **skimmer 3** (here: *Tramea lacerata*).
1980 Milne–Milne *Audubon Field Guide Insects* 380, *Jagged-edged Saddlebag (Tramea lacerata).* *Ibid* 381, Saddlebags are named for the large saddle-shaped mark on the hind wings.

saddlebag v Also *saddlebaggs*
Of a boat, barge, or raft: to become snagged on an obstruction so as to be swung or doubled around it by the current; hence n *saddlebag* something that has doubled around an obstruction.
1863 in 1904 *DN* 2.388 [Oil industry language], A boat. . . laden with 1,500 barrels of oil saddle-bagged on pier of Oil Creek bridge. Boat and contents a total loss. **1885** Twain *Huck. Finn* 106, They lost their steering-oar, and swung around and went a-floating down, stern-first, about two mile, and saddle-baggsed on the wreck. . . and it was so dark we didn't notice the wreck till we was right on it; and so we saddle-baggsed. **1901** NY Forest Fish & Game Comm. *Annual Rept. for 1900* 254, Sometimes the long floating mass would swing in the wind and current so that it would 'saddle-bag' on the head of the bar below the dam. **1905** U.S. Forest Serv. *Bulletin* 61.45 [Logging terms], *Saddlebag. . .* As applied to a boom, to catch on an obstruction and double around it. (Gen[eral]) **1930** Shoemaker *1300 Words* 51 **cPA Mts** (as of c1900), *Saddle-bagged*—When a pair of rafts becomes caught on a high stump or snag in the river. **1945** Fugina *Lore Lure* 65 **WI,** The raft was caught in a cross-current and saddle-bagged (piled up) on the towhead. **1956** Sorden–Ebert *Logger's Words* 29 **Gt Lakes,** Saddle-bag, A float of lumber that has become doubled around a tree or a sand bar or island when going down the river, or balanced sideways on a rock or bar in a river.

saddlebag house n Also *saddlebag;* rarely *saddleback house* [From the shape] **Sth, S Midl** Cf **breezeway, dogtrot, double-pen(ned), Texas house**
A house consisting of two parts separated by a central space or by a large fireplace with a central chimney and covered by a single roof.
1925 in 2001 *DARE* File—Internet, A two-pen or Southern saddlebag house is just what its name implies, two cabins set in line with each other about 10 feet apart and one roof extending over the two pens. The space between the two cabins in the South is called a gallery, in other places an areaway, and in the North a hallway. In this case the hall is open at both ends. A saddlebag makes a most delightful summer camp. **1934** Carmer *Stars Fell on AL* 37, In its center stood a "saddlebag" house. [*Ibid* 38, The right wing, usually one room, is a complete unit. So is the left wing—which usually contains the kitchen and chimney. Between the two wings—with the roof above and the porch floor below—is nothing.] **1940** Writers' Program *Guide GA* 452 **cw,swGA,** In the thinly settled farm region surrounding Lumpkin are many good examples of the breezeway (also known as dogtrot or saddlebag) type of house, in which two units are connected by a roof built across an open central passageway. **1941** Johnston–Waterman *Early Architecture NC* 7, *Double-cabin, central-chimney type*—Commonly called Saddle-Bag house. Each part, or "pen," was as large as could be built conveniently from logs. **1941** Writers' Program *Guide AR* 103, Usually the new dwelling was in the style most commonly known as dogtrot, but sometimes called saddlebag, breezeway, or "three P's" (two pens and a passage). **1961** Folk *Word Atlas N. LA* map 314 A house with open hall or breezeway separating it into two parts . . saddle bag house 17% [of 275 infs]. **1976** Montell–Morse *KY Folk Architecture* 22, The saddlebag house consists of two rooms built back to back against a large chimney serving fireplaces in both halves of the house. . . Some folk call this house a double-fireplace; some actually use the term saddlebag; others have no special term for it. **1984** Joyner *Down by Riverside* 119 **SC coast,** Several double-pen cabins are visible in the old photographs of Waccamaw slave streets, all of them examples of the saddlebag-type, with the additional room added to the chimney end, resulting in a double-pen cabin with a central chimney. **1991** Williams *Homeplace* 27

swNC, Of the larger folk houses, the saddlebag plan with its rooms of equal size on either side of a central chimney was the most prevalent. **2000** *NADS Letters,* I lived in a saddlebag house or also called a dog trot when I was a child in Eastern Kentucky. The purpose was to separate the living quarters from the cooking quarters and allow the breeze to cool both rooms. *Ibid,* I have heard "saddleback house" in panhandle OK with the meaning you give the term "saddlebag house." This from people born there about 1900, talking of their early housing.

saddlebag worm See **saddleback caterpillar**

saddle band n West Cf **cavvy 1**
=**remuda.**

   1888 *Century Illustr. Mag.* 35.655 **West,** Near the middle of the glade stands the . . horse-corral . . and a wing built out from one side of the gate entrance, so that the saddle band can be driven in without trouble. **1936** Adams *Cowboy Lingo* 80 **NW,** This term [=*caballado*] was used in the Southwest, but the term more commonly used was 'saddle band' in the Northwest. **1942** Berrey–Van den Bark *Amer. Slang* 916.20 **West,** Saddle band, a herd of saddle horses. **1942** Dale *Cow Country* 47 **West,** The band of horses was variously known as the *remuda,* "saddle band," or the *caballado.*

saddle blanket See **blanket 3, 4**

saddle board n scattered, but esp NEng, Gulf States See Map
One of a pair of boards covering the ridge of a roof.

   1856 Robinson *Kansas* 50, The house being so unfinished, the saddleboards not yet on the roof, . . and no back door, my presence was needed in several places at the same moment. **1931–33** *LANE Worksheets* **MA,** Saddle boards . . used to cover the ridge of a shingle roof. **1950** *WELS* (*The strip of wood or metal that covers the ridge of a roof*) 1 Inf, **nwWI,** Saddle boards. **1965–70** *DARE* (Qu. D30) 19 Infs, **scattered, but esp NEng, Gulf States,** Saddle board(s); **AL1,** Saddle boards [FW sugg]; **KS11,** Saddle boards [FW: Inf's husband says this is the word used here.]; **ME5,** Saddle boards—the two boards—one 5″, one 6″; **UT4,** Ridge roll—if it's metal; saddle boards—if it's wood; **VA69,** Saddle boards [FW: Inf says it's the main name]. **1986** Pederson *LAGS Concordance* (*Eaves trough*) 1 inf, **swMS,** Saddle board—over top of roof, sheds water; 1 inf, **swMS,** Saddle board—on roof.

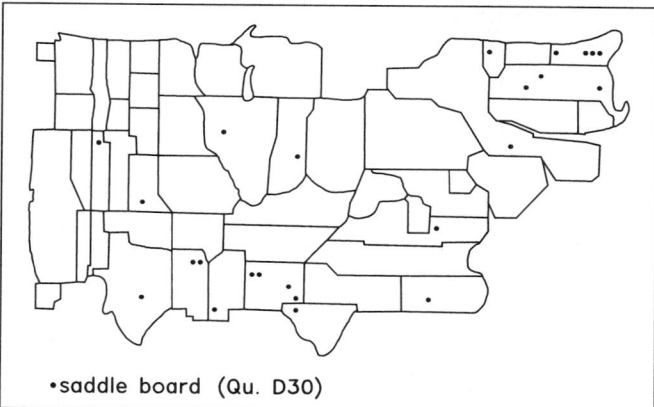

•saddle board (Qu. D30)

saddle bum n Also *saddle stiff,* ~ *tramp* **chiefly West** Cf *chuck line rider* (at **chuck line**)
An out-of-work cowboy who drifts from ranch to ranch subsisting on free meals.

   1932 Tooné *Yankee Slang* 32, *Saddle tramp:* Horseman who rides from ranch to ranch asking for work, and praying that he won't find any; a drifter—a mounted bummer. **c1936** in Lib. of Congress *Amer. Memory: WPA Life Hist.* (Internet) **cnTX** (as of c1870s–1900), Every ranch house, cook shack, and chuck wagon had it's [sic] latch string on the outside and a man was welcome to stop and stay as long's he wanted to, providing he done the right thing. . . When they didn't take a job, they were called 'Saddle Bums,' of which there were plenty. . . When they made a locality too many times . . they were told to get after they'd got a meal. *Ibid* **TX** (as of c1880), I wanted to see the country so became a saddle bum, a chuck line rider, for a spell. **1956** Ker *Vocab. W. TX* 194, *Saddle tramp*—worn out cowboy [1 of 67 infs]. **1968** Fulbright *Cow-Country Counselor* 195 **AZ,** Apsey hired only cowboys drifting from

one ranch to another seeking employment. They were called saddle tramps.   **1984** Doig *English Creek* 13 **nMT,** Alec, you will End Up as Nothing More Than a Grimped-Up Saddle Stiff.

saddle bunch n Cf **cap** n[1] **1, saddle** n **2**
=**cap bundle.**

   1968 *DARE* (Qu. L31, . . *The top bundle of a shock*) Inf **SC57,** Saddle bunch—flatten 2 bundles to shed water.

saddle flower See **sidesaddle flower**

saddle horse n [Because the driver sometimes rides the (rearmost) left hand horse or mule; cf PaGer *saddelgaul* (rearmost) left hand horse in a team; Ger *Sattelpferd*] **scattered, but esp C and Mid Atl** See Map
=**near horse;** the rearmost near horse in a team of more than one pair; similarly n *saddle mule.*

   1861 *Scientific Amer.* 23 Nov 332, Some [mules] plunge and rear all the time . . ; others kick out of the traces, face on driver riding the saddle mule, rear up and viciously strike at him with their fore feet. **1875** *Atlantic Mth.* 35.557 **West,** Rising on his saddle he launches his ubiquitous whip at the off wheeler and the swing mules, pounds his saddle mule with his heels, and vents a peculiar, vivifying shriek at the distant ears of his leaders. **1948** Davis *Word Atlas Gt. Lakes* app qu 57 (*Horse on the left side in plowing or hauling*), 4 (of 233) infs, **IN, MI, OH,** Saddle horse. **1949** Kurath *Word Geog.* 66, *Near-horse.* . . In parts of the German settlements in Eastern Pennsylvania, in the Shenandoah Valley, and on the Yadkin the near-horse is called the *saddle horse.* This term is modeled on the German *Sattelgaul.* **1961** Folk *Word Atlas N. LA* map 814, Horse on left side in hauling . . [less freq responses include] saddle horse. **1965–70** *DARE* (Qu. K32b, *The horse on the left side in plowing or hauling*) 13 Infs, **scattered, but esp C and Mid Atl,** Saddle horse; **NC49,** Saddle mule; (Qu. K32a, *With a team of horses, . . the horse on the driver's right hand*) Infs **SC57, WV69,** Saddle horse. [15 of 16 Infs old] **1966** Dakin *Dial. Vocab. Ohio R. Valley* 2.294, *Nigh horse.* . . Scattered but rare usages of *saddle horse,* originally from the German settlements in southeastern Pennsylvania, appear in Ohio, Kentucky, and Illinois. **1967** Faries *Word Geog. MO* 96, *Near horse.* . . Other regional expressions are known to a few of the informants . . *saddle horse. Ibid* 147, *South and Midland Expressions* . . saddle horse—10 [of c700 infs]. **1970** Greatman *Dial. Atlas MD* 139, *Pennsylvania German* Definitive Items . . saddle horse . . 4 [of 50 infs]. **1981** *PADS* 67.32 **Mesabi Iron Range MN,** *Near-horse.* . . Another Range informant . . remembers hearing the Midland-Southern *saddle horse* used in the logging camps of the old days. **1985** *AmSp* 60.234 **sePA,** *Saddle horse*—Left horse of a team . . 3.3% [of 60 infs]. Even though there is now a general unfamiliarity with the practice of using a team of horses for plowing, among those individuals who are still knowledgeable about terminology relating to the practice, the variant *saddle horse* . . is almost extinct.

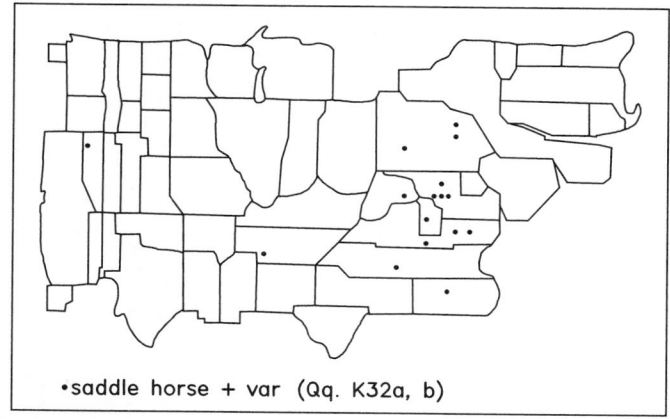

•saddle horse + var (Qq. K32a, b)

saddle-horse ant n Cf **horse ant**
See quot.

   1968 *DARE* (Qu. R17, . . *Names . . for the big black ants that sting*) Inf **CA87,** Saddle-horse ant—the big black [ant]—no sting Inf knows of.

saddleleaf n Also *saddle tree* [See quots 1866, 1931]
=**tulip tree.**

   1820 in 1839 Mathews *Memoirs* 3.149, If you have not got any in the grounds, a saddle-leaf tulip is beautiful. **1843** *Penny Cyclop.* 25.341, In America where it [=Liriodendron tulipifera] is a native, it is also known by the names White wood, Canoe wood, Saddle-tree. **1866** Lindley–Moore *Treas. Botany* 688, The leaves large, . . four-lobed and somewhat like a saddle in shape; hence the tree is sometimes spoken of as the Saddle-tree. **1890** *Century Dict.* 5298, *Saddletree.* . . The American tulip-tree, *Liriodendron tulipifera:* name suggested by the form of the leaf. Also *saddle-leaf.* **1910** Graves *Flowering Plants* 194 **CT,** *Liriodendron tulipifera.* . . Saddle Tree. . . The inner bark is medicinal. **1931** Clute *Common Plants* 39, The tulip tree *(Liriodendron tulipifera)* was called saddle-leaf because the young leafblades in the bud were bent back across the petiole in such a way as to retard the growth of the tip and make it appear as if cut square across. **1960** Vines *Trees SW* 280, Tuliptree. . . Other vernacular names in use are . . Saddle-tree [etc].

saddle mule See **saddle horse**

saddle plant See **sidesaddle flower**

saddle pocket n

A saddlebag.

1857 *Putnam's Mag.* 9.456 **West,** They can only beat us by starving us out; and, by filling your saddle-pockets with dried meat, that will be guarded against. **1873** Custer in *Galaxy* 15.781, All the horses . . were to be newly shod, and an extra fore and hind shoe fitted to each horse; these, with the necessary nails, were to be carried by each trooper in the saddle pocket. **1894** *Scribner's Mag.* 15.55 **Sth,** What you reckon you've been sitt'n' on in one of them saddle pockets all the way from Suez? **1930** Dobie *Coronado* 208 **AZ,** He gathered enough of the nuggets to fill his saddle pockets. **1981** *High Coll.* **ceKY** (as of c1930), *Saddle-pocket doctors.* . . expression used for physicians who traveled through the mountains on horseback, often for great distances. **2001** *DARE* File—Internet, The saddle pocket has always been an important part of the cowboys [sic] riding gear. These are very useful either on horseback or when carried full of ammo to the firing line. Two sizes available.

saddle tree See **saddleleaf**

saddling See **saddle** n 4

saddy exclam Also *saadie, sahdie* [Etym unknown, but see quots 1859, 1924] **chiefly PA**

Thank you; hence n *saddy* a formal acknowledgement of thanks; rarely v *saddy* to curtsy; vbl n *sadying* curtsying. Note: the only evidence for the verb and vbl noun is quot 1835 Crockett and Bartlett's interpretation of it; it is possible, however, that *sadying* in 1835 is to be explained otherwise, perh as an error for *sashying* (cf **sashay** v 1).

1835 Bird *Hawks* 1.155 **PA** [Black], "Come now, my old boy, here's a dollar. . . " "Saddy, massa; God bless massa!" **1835** Crockett *Account* 34, It would do you good to see our boys and girls dancing. None of your stradling, mincing, sadying; but a regular sifter, cut-the-buckle, chicken-flutter set-to. [**1848** Bartlett *Americanisms* 281, *Sadying.* A simple and unaffected mode of dancing, practised by novices in the art. [Followed by the Crockett quot given above].] **1859** (1968) Bartlett *Americanisms* 375, *To saddy.* To bob up and down; to curtsy like a child. Probably a child's corruption of *Thank ye,* applied to the curtsy which accompanies the phrase. [Followed by the Crockett quot given above]. **1870** *Nation* 28 July 56 **PA,** And what is the origin of the word "saddy," which Bartlett guesses to be a child's corruption of "thank ye" . . ? He would seem to do better in his definition of the word, which he makes a verb that means "to bob up and down, to courtesy like a child." But it used to be almost always a noun in Pennsylvania, our writer says; the child was directed to "made a saddy." Yet he admits that among Quaker children in Philadelphia "to this day the only known word for 'thank you' is 'saddy.'" . . We should say, to help conjecture, that in pronouncing the word the first syllable (whose flatness is marked by the double d) is lengthened out to four times the length of the last syllable. **1882** (1971) Gibbons *PA Dutch* 391, And what is the derivation of *"Sahdie?"* so much used by children for "Thank you." **1889** *AN&Q* 4.35 **PA,** Has an explanation ever been given of the word *saadie,* which was always used by children, when I was young, by way of thanks for a gift? It was a word peculiar to childhood. Does it still survive? That it is not utterly obsolete, I know. Within a year or two, a policeman, to whom, for some trifling attention, a cigar had been offered, accepted the gift, and said with a smile, "Saadie, sir," **1890** *Ibid* 4.211, *Saadie.* . . I am informed this word prevails in the South, so far even as New Orleans. Is consid-

ered of a negro origin. **1890** *DN* 1.76, **MD, seNJ,** *Saddie:* used by children in thanking another for a gift. **1892** *KS Univ. Qrly.* 1.98 **PA,** *Saddy:* thanks, thank you. **1908** *German Amer. Annals* 10.41 **sePA,** *Saddy.* Thank you. (Used only by and to children.) "When he gives you anything, you must say saddy." **1916** *DN* 4.338 **Philadelphia PA,** *Saddy* ['sædɪ]. Thank you: used by negroes and children. "When he gives you anthing, you must say, Saddy." [**1924** Lambert *PA Ger. Dict.* 129, *Saddi* . . thank you (usually used by elders in reminding a small child to say "thank you"). Probably a corruption of "sag Dank."] **1960** Korson *Black Rock* 238 **PA** [PaGer], To say "saddy" was to say an infantine "Thank you." Nobody knows why, what saddy was or anything about it, except that it was something you taught to children. [**1991** Beam *Revised PA Ger. Dict.* 183, *Thanks.* . . *cf* saeddi—Thank you! *(Usually used by elders in reminding a small child to say "Thank you!")*]

Saddy See **Saturday**

sadiddy See **siditty**

sadiron n *old-fash*

A flatiron.

1761 *Newport Mercury* (RI) 3 Nov 4/3, To be sold by Naphtael Hart, jun. . . Sad Irons, Telescopes [etc]. **1815** *Niles' Weekly Reg.* 9.94, The following articles of American manufactures were to be had last year. . . sad irons [etc]. **1903** *DN* 2.328 **seMO,** *Sad-iron.* . . Flatiron. **1907** *DN* 3.235 **nwAR,** *Sad-iron.* . . Flatiron. **1927** (1970) Sears *Catalogue* 970, Mrs. Potts Pattern Asbestos Lined Sadirons $2.40 Complete. . . Set of 3 Common Pattern 7-Lb. Sadirons . . $2.25. **1965–70** *DARE* (Qu. F29, *Different kinds of irons—not electric—used . . for smoothing clothes after they're washed*) 354 Infs, **widespread,** Sadiron; **MA57, PA9,** Mrs. Potts sadiron; **MO39,** Mrs. Potter's sadiron. [Of all Infs responding to the question, 72% were old; of those giving these responses, 84% were old.] **1967** LeCompte *Word Atlas* 134 **seLA,** *Device /not electric/ to smooth clothes after washing.* . . sadiron [2 of 21 infs]. **1967** *Smith Co. Pioneer* (Smith Center KS) 26 Oct 12/8, *Public auction.* . . Electric kitchen clock; throw rugs; picture frames; set sad irons & holder. **1968** *NJ Herald* (Newton) 23 June 18/1, *Public Auction.* . . Paintings, sad irons, frames, china wash bowls, Victrola with horn, bamboo book shelf, stools. **1971** Bright *Word Geog. CA & NV* 158, *Flat iron* . . sad iron 21% [of 300 infs]. **1981** *High Coll.* **ceKY** (as of c1930), *Sadiron.* . . a heavy flatiron. . . "We washed ever week and used a sadiron on our clothes." **1986** Pederson *LAGS Concordance* 10 infs, **Gulf Region,** Sadiron(s).

saditty See **siditty**

sadying See **saddy**

safe n

1 A usu free-standing cabinet or cupboard, esp one of which all or part is ventilated with screen wire or perforated sheet metal for the storage of foodstuffs—freq in combs *pie safe, kitchen safe.* **chiefly Sth, S Midl, TX** See Map

1649 in 1850 CT (Colony) *Pub. Rec.* 1.496, *An Inventory of the Estate of Mr. William Whiting.* . . a clock, a safe, a bedstead. **c1770** in 1833 Boucher *Glossary* 1 **MD,** Old Johnny Two-shoes . . / Sent me a 'possum, dead indeed, but whole;/ . . all full of maggots in the *safe* it lies. **1815** *View N.Y. State Prison* 35 *(DAE),* Wheelbarrows, swifts, safes, tables, and indeed almost everything appertaining to the business [of carpentering] are manufactured. **1899** (1912) Green *VA Folk-Speech* 363, *Safe.* . . A receptacle [sic] for the storage of meat and provisions. Usually a skeleton frame of wood covered with a fine wire-netting to keep out insects. **1905** *DN* 3.85 **nwAR,** *Kitchen-safe.* . . Portable kitchen cupboard. **1909** *DN* 3.365 **eAL, wGA,** *Safe.* . . A portable cupboard. *Cupboard* is never heard except in nursery rimes. **1933** Rawlings *South Moon* 79 **nFL,** She foraged in the kitchen safe and fried the boy cold biscuits. **1941** Street *In Father's House* 30 **MS,** We've got one of the biggest safes in the county. . . It's in the corner of the kitchen, on the other side of the room from the big stove, so the heat from the stove won't hurt the food. The top of the safe opens out like a cabinet. . . Mama keeps the knives and forks in the drawers. **1942** Hurston *Dust Tracks* 27 **FL** (as of c1910) [Black], In the dining-room there was an old "safe," a punched design in its tin doors. **1944** *PADS* 2.58 **nwMO,** *Kitchen safe.* . . A cupboard. . . Rural. **1946** *AmSp* 21.99 **sIL,** Among farmers, a 'mantel' is known as a *fireboard,* and a 'cupboard' as a *safe.* **1950** *WELS Suppl.* **cwWI,** A cupboard with slat shelves and screened sides and front, used until the days of cream separators for storing milk and cream. Also to store foods in winter like frozen pies. Sometimes the screening was pierced tin sheets. **1965–70** *DARE* (Qu. D9, *To prevent bread and cake from drying, you put them in a* _____) 33 Infs, **chiefly Sth, S Midl, TX,** Safe; **KY**5, **LA**2, **OH**61, **VA**42, Safe—old-fashioned; **AR**34, Safe—old term; **FL**3, Safe—had two sections, bottom was a cupboard, top had wire to keep the flies out; **FL**49, Safe—used to put them in the safe; safes were like ice boxes and refrigerators; plain wooden cabinets that stood on the floor; **GA**13, Safe—old days; **NC**20, Safe—with a tin door, punctured with holes for ventilation; **NC**62, Safe—made of pine; quite large . . with panelled double doors, covered with tin, perforated; perforations were often in a design; **SC**11, Safe—an upright piece of furniture with screened-in double doors for keeping pie, cake, bread, and all sorts of eats; **VA**58, Safe—years ago bread, pies, etc., were stored in shelved compartments—situated on the back porch—called "safes"; safes were about the size of a large bookcase . . made of wood with a metal door which had been pierced with holes usually forming a design—for ventilation; 11 Infs, **esp Sth, S Midl,** Pie safe; **IL**7, Pie safe—old-fashioned [FW: Inf has a pie safe—it is large (size of a breakfront) made of wood and has perforated, metal sides, and rows of shelves.]; **AL**61, **GA**67, **NY**34, **TX**38, **WV**11, Kitchen safe; **TX**1, Kitchen safe—6′ x 4′ x 18″, 2 doors, drawers, dishes and food kept; **TX**39, Kitchen safe—big cabinet with shelves, perforated metal doors; **TX**45, Kitchen safe—old-fashioned—screen doors at top, solid doors below, ca. 6′ high; **TN**37, **WV**5, Bread safe; **FL**35, Hanging safe—kept outside for milk; (Qu. E5, *A piece of furniture with a flat top for keeping tablecloths, dishes, and such*) Infs **AL**1, **IN**19, Safe; **FL**49, Safe—they call anything—buffet, china closet, etc., a safe; **LA**9, Safe—for dishes and food; straight and tall; **NC**50, Safe—glass doors and dishes inside drawers in bottom; **TX**32, Safe—for dishes only; **VA**8, Safe—in kitchen; old-fashioned; **VA**74, Safe—old-fashioned; pie safe; **LA**2, Dish safe; **VA**6, Kitchen safe—old-fashioned; 2 types—10-door safe, glass door cupboard; (Qu. D10a, *The place to keep food cool, usually with ice, so that it won't spoil*) Infs **CA**125, **FL**26, 29, 35, Safe; **CA**19, Safe—a square thing with screen sides, tops, etc., hung on back porches—worked on same principle as cooler—the cool air would move through it; **TX**36, Safe—no ice; (Qu. M18, . . *Where milk is kept cool*) Inf **LA**3, Before refrigeration we used to keep it in a safe—article of furniture with screened doors and shelves. **1980** *DARE* File **Brooklyn NY** (as of c1920), In the shed [behind a "Brooklyn Brownstone" house] was the "safe" for meat etc. It is smaller, but similar to a southern "pie safe." However, it is screened. **1986** Pederson *LAGS Concordance* **Gulf Region** *(Pantry),* 5 infs, (A) pie safe; 1 inf, Pie safe—wire screen in front, for china too; 1 inf, Pie safe—a cabinet with screened door; 1 inf, Pie safe—like cabinet, doors screened or tinned; 1 inf, Pie safes—mother used before refrigerators; 1 inf, Pie safes—like china cabinets, screened doors.

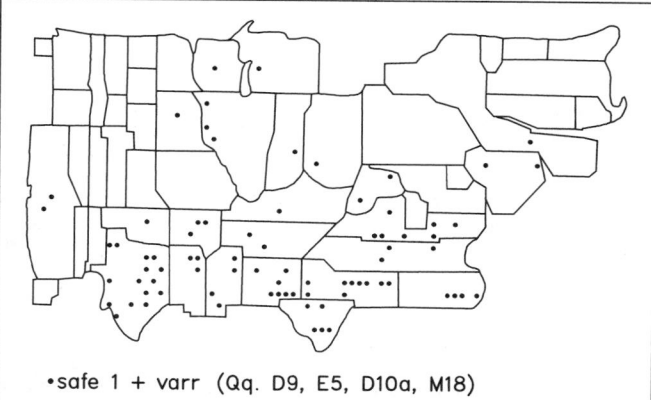

•safe 1 + varr (Qq. D9, E5, D10a, M18)

2 in comb *cake safe:* A covered cake-plate or tray.

1965–70 *DARE* (Qu. D9, *To prevent bread and cake from drying, you put them in a* _____) Inf **MO**27, Cake safe for a cake; **NC**71, Cake safe [FW illustr]; **NY**93, Cake safe—has a cover that goes on [FW illustr]; **OR**1, Cake safe—smaller than bread box; **PA**110, Cake safe [FW illustr].

saffron n [Appar from the color of the flowers]
A **butterfly bush 1** (here: *Buddleja marrubiifolia*).
1960 Vines *Trees SW* 873, *Buddleia marrubiifolia.* . . Also known by the vernacular names of Saffron [etc]. . . Used as a bath for rheumatic disorders, and as an aperitive and diuretic.

saffron bread n **Nth, esp MI** See Map
Bread that is colored and flavored with saffron; similarly, *saffron bun,* ~ *cake,* ~ *roll.*
1869 Wright *Book of Receipts* 252, *Saffron cake.* Hay saffron . . petals of safflowers . . rape oil. . . Make them into a cake. **1939** Wolcott *Yankee Cook Book* 353, *Saffron Bread.* **1940** Brown *Amer. Cooks* 412 **MI,** *Saffron Bread Or Rolls*—The Cornish like saffron in bread and cakes, and they use it lavishly, turning out a product dyed a deep yellow and tasting, to those not accustomed to it, a little on the medicinal side. **1952** Dorson *Bloodstoppers* 107 **MI,** Cornish folk have other sacred food loves: their scroll pilchard, saffron buns, and scalded cream. **1965–70** *DARE* (Qu. H18, . . *Special kinds of bread*) Infs **IL**3, **MI**13, 22, 43, 46, **NJ**9, **SD**5, Saffron bread; **CA**146, Saffron cake; (Qu. H19, *What do you mean by a biscuit? How are they made?*) Inf **MI**43, Saffron buns; (Qu. H32, . . *Fancy rolls and pastries*) Inf **MI**94, Saffron buns; **MI**46, Saffron rolls; (Qu. H63, *Kinds of desserts*) Infs **CA**146, **MI**13, 34, 43, **MA**40, **PA**110, Saffron cake; **MI**34, Saffron bread. **1967** *DARE* Tape **MI**43, [FW:] What other Cornish dishes or Cornish recipes do you still work with here? [Inf:] Oh, I make saffron buns and seedy buns, myself. [**1981** Hachten *Flavor WI* 22, A kitchen redolent with cardamon and almond flavoring was usually, but not exclusively, Norwegian; with saffron, Cornish.]

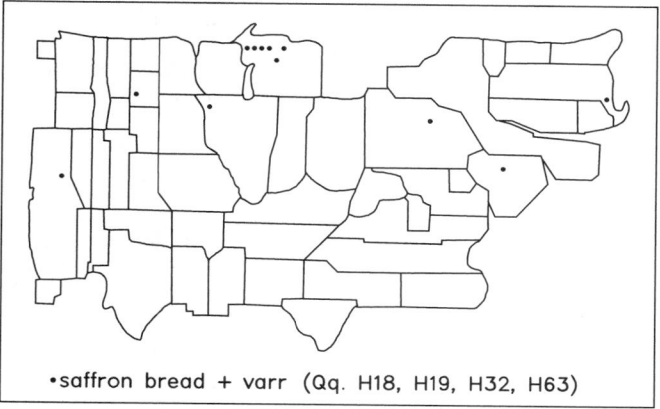

•saffron bread + varr (Qq. H18, H19, H32, H63)

saffron plum n
A small tree *(Sideroxylon celastrinum)* native to Florida and Texas. Also called **coma, downward plum.**
1884 Sargent *Forests of N. Amer.* 103, *Saffron Plum.* A small tree, rarely exceeding 4 meters in height. **1933** Small *Manual SE Flora* 1033, *Saffron-plum.* . . The light-brown, hard, heart-wood is used for cabinet-work. The flowers are fragrant. **1971** Craighead *Trees S. FL* 94, Some of the more characteristic trees and shrubs of the beaches and coastal ridges are . . bay cedar, beachberry, . . and saffron plum.

saffron roll See **saffron bread**

saft adj |sæft| [Scots dial var of *soft*] **chiefly Sth, Midl** Cf **crop** n A, **drop** A
1815 in 1947 *AmSp* 22.284, *Saft.* Soft. **1823** *Natl. Intelligencer* (DC) 1 May (*DN* 4.47), *Saft.* . . Soft. **1837** Sherwood *Gaz. GA* 71, *Provincialisms. . . Saft,* for soft. **1843** (1916) Hall *New Purchase* 291 **IN,** His face was near on about as saft as yourn. **1856** Simms *Eutaw* 184 **SC** [Black], Is he worth picking? Is thar anything to pick? Is he saft? **1893** Shands *MS Speech* 11, In the negro dialect short (o) is sometimes changed into (æ), as . . [sæft] for *soft.* **1899** (1912) Green *VA Folk-Speech* 363, *Saft.* . . For *soft.* **1909** *DN* 3.365 **eAL, wGA,** *Saft* [sæft]. . . Soft. . . Rare. **1912** *DN* 3.588 **wIN,** *Saft.* . . Soft. **1930** Shoemaker *1300 Words* 60 **cPA Mts** (as of c1900), *Saft*—Weak, silly, characterless. **1936** *AmSp* 11.26 **eTX,** *Soft* is pronounced [sæːft], [sæ˔ːft] only by older people who have not had formal education. **1952** Brown *NC Folkl.* 1.587, *Saft* [sæft]. . . Soft.

safte adj |seft| [Var of *safe;* cf Intro "Language Changes" I.8] Cf *clift* (at **cliff**), *acrost, clost* (at **close** adj, adv), **crost,** *doste* (at **dose**), **skift** n[1], n[2], v[1], v[2]
1891 *DN* 1.165 **cNY,** *T* is escrescent in: . . ['seftɚ] < *safer.* **1903** *DN* 2.328 **seMO,** *Safte* [seft]. . . Safe. 'I can make you safte for your money.' Meaning 'I can give good security.' **1907** *DN* 3.235 **nwAR,** *Safte* [seft], adj. Safe. **1913** Johnson *Highways St. Lawrence to VA* 227 **DE**

[Black], Elizabath / W. Maull / died in / 1896 Dec./ 9 / Age 44 / Safte in / the / Arms of / Jesus.

sag n Cf **swag**

1 A depression on a ridge or mountainside; a **gap** n[1] **1.**

1727 in 1940 *AmSp* 15.387 **VA,** Thence along the North Side of the Mountains . . to a Corner Several Saplins by a Sagg. **1869** Bowles *New West* 107 **Rocky Mts,** We suddenly came out of the trees into . . a gap or sag in the mountains. **1880** in 1925 Stuart *40 Yrs.* 2.118 **MT,** There are plum bushes in every sag and ravine. **1901** Woods *Albemarle* 14 **VA,** Here and there occur low depressions in its crown, which supply a natural and convenient way for roads. North of the Rivanna are three of these depressions—the most northerly, the Turkey Sag, so named from Turkey Run, a branch of Priddy's Creek which rises at its western base, the next, Stony Point Gap, [etc]. **1927** Mason *Lure Great Smokies* 22, Many of these 'wallows' are scattered at intervals on high, isolated ridges and 'sags' in the thick laurel. **1932** *DN* 6.233 **West,** *Sag.* This word is sometimes used for a notch in a line of hills, or even for the slope of a hill. **1938** Stuart *Dark Hills* 133 **eKY,** The loamy sags with the heavy tobacco crop . . , are they not worth fighting for? **1940** *Hench Coll.* **VA,** Today I asked . . [a] student . . if he knew what a place name in the mountains such as Turkey Sag would mean. "Why yes," he said, "a sag is a low place in the mountains. It's also called a 'swayback' or a 'saddle'." **1940** Writers' Program *Guide GA* 476 **cnGA,** South of Snake Mountain the crest of the Blue Ridge falls to a relatively low "sag," which in mountaineer dialect is known as the "Swag of the Blue Ridge." **1958** [see **2** below]. **1970** *DARE* (Qu. C15, *A place in mountains or high hills where you can get through without climbing over the top*) Inf **NY233,** Pass, sag.

2 A low, often damp, area in relatively flat land; a gentle slope.

1741 in 1940 *AmSp* 15.387 **VA,** To two Hiccory's on the side of a Sagg. [*DARE* Ed: It is possible that this quot belongs at **1** above.] **1850** U.S. Patent Office *Annual Rept.: Ag. for 1849* 443, Strawberries are met with . . on the edges of "sloughs" or "saggs," where the soil is deep and moist. **1932** [see **1** above]. **1936** McCarthy *Lang. Mosshorn* np **West** [Range terms], Sag. . . A gentle slope. **1958** McCulloch *Woods Words* 155 **Pacific NW,** *Sag.* . . b. A low spot in the ground, or in a track. c. A saddle or pass in the mountains. **1968** *DARE* (Qu. C19, . . *Low land running between hills*) Inf **MN42,** Sag, such as the Watson Sag. [FW: It appears to be the flat depression between hills that is used for overflow during high water. It looks much like an old river bottom. . . The Watson Sag usually has standing water at one end of it. It is called Watson Sag on the highway sign.] **1997** *Montgomery Coll.* **eTN,** Stay away from that sag at the end of the field.

3 A low point on a roadway.

1911 *Century Dict. Suppl., Sag.* . . In railroad construction, a depression in the grade of a road. **1937** *AmSp* 12.154 [Railroad terms], *Sag.* Bottom of a down grade. **1958** [see **2** above].

sagaciate v Also *sagashawate, (sa)gashuate, sagatiate, segaciate, segashuate;* for addit varr see quots **chiefly Sth, S Midl** *esp freq among Black speakers; joc; old-fash* Cf **corporosity, suffancified**

1 To fare, get on; to bear, endure—usu used in facetious inquiries about someone's health.

1832 *Boston Eve. Transcript* (MA) 2 Aug 2/3 [Black], Sambo. Well, Clem, how do you sagatiate dis lubly wedder? **1843** in 1956 Eliason *Tarheel Talk* 127 **NC,** [From a schoolboy's letter:] How does your coporosity seem to sagaticate. I will now conversate a little on the proximosity of nonsense. **1883** (1971) Harris *Nights with Remus* 80 **GA** [Black], One day he meet Brer Tarrypin en he ax 'im how he seem te segashuate en he fambly en all his chilluns. [Footnote to *segashuate:*] An inquiry after his health. Another form is: "How does yo' corporosity seem ter segashuate?" **1884** *Anglia* 7.267 **Sth, S Midl** [Black], *How duz yo' sym'tums segashuate?* = how are you? **1890** *Jrl. Amer. Folk.* 3.311 **Philadelphia PA,** *Sagatiate.* . . came into use between 1853 and 1859, being used only in the phrase, "How does your corporosity sagatiate the inclemency of the weather?" **1893** Shands *MS Speech* 54, *Sagashuate* [se'gæʃjuet]. This word is used by negroes in the sentence: "How does your corporosity seem to sagashuate?" and is a common way of inquiring after anybody's health. . . *Sagashuate,* as far as I know, is not used outside of this or similar expressions, and here it would seem to mean *to thrive* or *prosper.* **1899** (1912) Green *VA Folk-Speech* 363, *Sagaciate.* . . To do or be in any way; think, talk, or act, as indicating a state of mind or body: as, "How do you sagaciate this morning?" **1903**

DN 2.329 **seMO,** *Segaciate.* . . To fare; to get on. (Humorous.) 'Well, how do you-uns segaciate to-day?' **1906** *DN* 3.154 **nwAR,** *Sagashuate[b] sagashawate.* . . To get on. "How are you sagashawatin'?" Negroism. **1907** *DN* 3.236 **nwAR,** *Segaciate.* . . To fare; to get on. Facetious. "How does your caparistis seem to gashuate?" **1909** *DN* 3.365 **eAL, wGA,** *Sagashuate.* . . To get on. Often in the facetious greeting, 'How does your corporosity seem to sagashuate?' Also *segashuate.* **1945** Street *Gauntlet* 125 **MO** (as of 1920s), "Well, well, hello, Preacher," he said, and slipped into the chair next to London. "How's your corporosity segaciating?" **1953** Randolph–Wilson *Down in Holler* 282 **Ozarks,** *Segashiate.* . . To move about; to progress. Usually jocular or factious. **1979** *NYT Article Letters* **neOH** (as of 1930s), My aunt . . who was driving to or from school . . picked up an old colored woman. As the woman laborously [sic] climbed into Aunt Jeannette's car she asked: "How's your Corporosity segash′ēāting?"

2 To associate.

1883 (1971) Harris *Nights with Remus* 102 **GA** [Black], Dey wuz times . . w'en de creeturs 'ud segashuate tergedder des like dey ain't had no fallin' out. **1922** Talley *Negro Folk Rhymes* 200, One, two, three, fo', five, six, seben;/ All de good chilluns goes to Heaben./ All de bad chilluns goes below,/ To segashuate wid ole man Joe. [Footnote: Segashuate means associate with.]

sagah See **sager**

sagashawate, sagashuate, sagatiate See **sagaciate**

sage n

1 Std: a plant of the genus *Salvia.* [*OED2* a1310 →] Also called **purple sage 1, wild salvia;** for other names of var spp see **black sage 2, blue ~ 1, cancerweed 1, chia, clary** n[2]**, clear-eye, desert sage, firecracker plant 3, fourth-of-July plant, horsemint 5, hummingbird sage, Indian fire 1, mealy-cup sage, mountain ~ 3, pitcher ~ 2, red ~ 2, scarlet ~, silver ~, thistle ~, white ~, wild clary, ~ sage**

2 also *sagebush:* =**sagebrush 1.** **chiefly West**

1805 (1904) Lewis *Orig. Jrls. Lewis & Clark Exped.* 2.29 **MT,** The wild hysop sage . . and some other herbs also grow in the plains and hills. **1806** (1807) Gass *Jrl.* 204 **WA,** Sage bushes . . grow in great abundance on some parts of these plains. **1837** Irving *Rocky Mts.* 2.49 **seID,** The country . . [had] a considerable quantity of sage or wormwood. **1845** Frémont *Rept. Rocky Mts.* 124, The road . . was made extremely rough by the stiff tough bushes of *artemisia tridentata,* in this country commonly called sage. **1866** U.S. Bur. Indian Affairs *Report* 125 **UT,** Some twenty-five acres of land have been cleared from thick sage bushes. **1894** *Jrl. Amer. Folk.* 7.91 **MN,** *Artemisia Ludoviciana,* . . sage. **1902** *Harper's Mth. Mag.* 269 **CA,** He started on a run, racing in and out among the sage-bushes. **1924** *Amer. Botanist* 30.32, *Western Plant Names.* . . Now as to the species of *Artemisia.* I do not believe any of them are ever called "wormwood" by westerners, all of them are "sage." *Artemisia frigida* is "Rocky Mountain sage." . . *A. ludoviciana* is often called "wooly sage." **1950** Stevens *ND Plants* 289, *Artemisia*—Wormwood. "Sage." . . Bitter aromatic herbs or shrubs. . . Sage of culinary use is a species of *Salvia.* **1967–68** *DARE* (Qu. S17, . . *Kinds of plants . . that . . cause itching and swelling*) Inf **CO4,** Sage; (Qu. S26e, *Other wildflowers not yet mentioned;* not asked in early QRs) Inf **NV5,** Sage—state flower—grows anyplace; (Qu. BB50b, *Remedies for chest colds*) Inf **NV8,** Sage tea; (Qu. BB50d, *Favorite spring tonics*) Infs **CA87, CO10,** 47, Sage tea; **UT12,** Sage. [*DARE* Ed: Some of these Infs may refer instead to **1** above.] **1981** *KS Qrly.* 13.2.70, *Sage, sagebrush* . . a tough desert plant, shrub-like, sometimes reaching six feet in height, which when dry makes fuel for fast and hot cooking or warming fires for working buckaroos; the main plant in the Nevada landscape.

3 A **guayule** (here: *Parthenium incanum*).

1931 U.S. Dept. Ag. *Misc. Pub.* 101.165, *Parthenium incanum . . ,* known also as . . sage, is a shrubby plant, growing . . from extreme western Texas to southern Arizona and south into Mexico. Despite its peculiar taste and its rubber content the tender new shoots and the flower head are sometimes nibbled by goats, cattle, and sheep.

4 See **sedge.**

5 See **sedge grass 2.**

6 See **sage tree 2.**

7 See **sage rabbit 2.**

8 See **salt sage 1.**

sage broom See **sedge grass 2**

sagebrush n

1 Any of var plants of the genus *Artemisia*. **chiefly West** See Map Cf **mugwort, wormwood** Also called **hickory B10, sage 2**; for other names of var spp see **black sage 1, blue ~ 2, bud sagebrush, cudweed 3, dogwood 6, estafiata, fringed sagebrush, ghost plant 3, greasewood 1, hyssop, Indian hair tonic, mountain fringe 2, ~ sage 1, mugwort, old man 1a, povertyweed 1j, sand sage, white ~, wild ~**

1852 (1919) Akin *Jrl.* 16 **WY**, Not much grass plenty sage brush for use. **1861** in 1917 Twain *Letters* 1.54 **NV**, On the plains, sage-brush and grease-wood grow about twice as large as the common geranium. **1890** Custer *Following* 71 **KS**, The dull sage-brush, or grease-root, or the sparse buffalo-grass, were all that the sun spared from its scorching rays. **1907** White *AZ Nights* 27, Onpeaceable citizens Texas Pete used to plant out in the sage-brush. *Ibid* 193, Denton and I hurried back to find him on his hands and knees behind a sage-brush, clawing away at the sand. **1917** Webster *Gold Seekers* 84 **CA** (as of 1849), We were compelled to tie our mules to sage brush to keep them from straying away. **1942** Whipple *Joshua* 14, The wild, keen fragrance of burning sagebrush plucked at Clory's empty stomach. **1965–70** *DARE* (Qu. C28, . . *Underbrush*) Inf **CA30**, Sagebrush; (Qu. C29, *A good-sized stretch of level land with practically no trees*) Inf **CO11**, Sagebrush flats; (Qu. L36, . . *When you dig out roots and underbrush to make a new field*) Inf **ID3**, Sagebrush beater; (Qu. S20) Inf **CO20**, Sagebrush; (Qu. S21, . . *Weeds . . that are a trouble in gardens and fields*) Infs **CA1**, 207, **OK20**, Sagebrush; **TX68**, Sand sagebrush; (Qu. S26a, . . *Wildflowers . . Roadside flowers*) Infs **CA94, NV5**, Sagebrush; (Qu. S26c) Inf **UT3**, Sagebrush; (Qu. T15) Inf **WY1**, Sagebrush; (Qu. T16, . . *Kinds of trees . . 'special'*) Infs **NV8, WY1**, 4, 5, Sagebrush; (Qu. BB50d, *Favorite spring tonics*) Inf **NV2**, Sagebrush tea. **1969** *DARE* Tape **CA136**, It's timberland, and what isn't timber is a bunch of rocks on it and sagebrush; **CA166**, And these great big mounds with sagebrush and everything. **1990** *Plants SW* (Catalog) 65, *Artemisia ludoviciana—Prairie Sagebrush.* . . This plant is a wonderful switch hitter as it grows from deep in the mountains all the way to the harsh, dry High Plains.

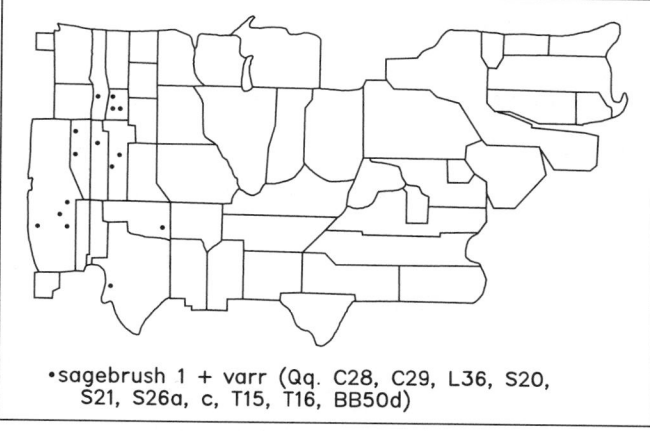

•sagebrush 1 + varr (Qq. C28, C29, L36, S20, S21, S26a, c, T15, T16, BB50d)

2 The four-wing **saltbush 1** *(Atriplex canescens).*

1913 Wooton *Trees NM* 66, *Atriplex canescens.* . . In many localities where there is no true sage brush this plant is incorrectly referred to under this name, though it is in no way related to the sage brushes. **1960** Vines *Trees SW* 236, *Atriplex canescens.* . . is known also by the vernacular names of . . sage-brush [etc].

3 See **sedge grass 2.**

sagebrush chippy n Cf **sage sparrow**

Brewer's sparrow *(Spizella breweri).*

1904 Wheelock *Birds CA* 229, Wherever in California there is sagebrush there is Brewer Sparrows. . . It resembles the chipping sparrow, and. . . is sometimes called the "Sagebrush Chippie."

sagebrusher n **West**

A tourist; a camper.

1908 *Sat. Eve. Post* 29 Aug 4, [In Yellowstone Park] a Sagebrusher is a person who takes in his own camping outfit. **1931** *AmSp* 7.22 [Yellowstone Park language], *Sagebrushers*—tourists who travel through the

Park in their own cars or who camp out. **1936** McCarthy *Lang. Mosshorn* np **West** [Range terms], *Sagebrusher.* A tourist into the west. **1940** *AmSp* 15.443 **nAZ, sUT**, In the vast canyon lands. . . Let not the tourist smirk over the names applied to the *help*—for, unbeknownst to him, he is also classified, as . . a *sage-brusher* (a tourist driving his own car but stopping at the park hotel). **1949** *Natl. Geogr. Mag.* June 750, We made assorted and innumerable new friends of the road. "Sagebrushers" such traveling campers are called in western lingo. **1966** Barnes–Jensen *Dict. UT Slang* 37, *Sage brusher.* . . one who takes his own camping outfit with him.

sagebrush grass See **sedge grass 2**

sagebrush lizard n

A **swift** (here: *Sceloporus graciosus*) native to the western US.

1946 Smith *Lizards* 248, *Sagebrush Lizard.* . . Widely distributed from southwestern Montana to northern Arizona, and western Colorado to extreme eastern California, and from southern Oregon to northwestern New Mexico. **1964** Lowe *Vertebrates* 162, Sagebrush Lizard. . . Primarily on the ground in basin sagebrush *(Artemisia tridentata)* and other shrub cover . . in the open desert. **1979** Behler–King *Audubon Field Guide Reptiles* 521, Sagebrush Lizard. . . Primarily terrestrial, these lizards occasionally climb trees or bushes in pursuit of insect prey.

sagebrush violet n [See quot 1973]

A **violet** (here: *Viola trinervata*).

1951 Abrams *Flora Pacific States* 3.125, *Viola trinervata.* . . Sagebrush or Howell's Violet. **1973** Hitchcock–Cronquist *Flora Pacific NW* 296, Petals bicolored, upper pair deep reddish-violet, lower 3 pale to fairly deep lilac, . . sagebr[ush] flats and rocky hillsides where moist early in spring. . . Sagebr[ush] v[iolet].

sagebush See **sage 2.**

sage buzzard n

=**sage grouse.**

1982 Elman *Hunter's Field Guide* 26, *Common & regional names.* . . For sage grouse . . *sage buzzard.* *Ibid* 34, In parts of the West an old prejudice inveighs against eating "sage buzzard" but it is as tasty as the other species [of grouse]. Primarily an eater of leaves and shoots, its chief food is sage.

sage chicken n Rarely *sage turkey* **esp Rocky Mts** Cf **prairie chicken 1, 6**

A grouse, usu the **sage grouse.**

1850 *Alta California* (S.F.) 6 Oct. 2/3 *(DA),* For the last week we have been feasting on sage-chicken and wild-ducks. **1873** in 1885 Custer *Boots & Saddles* 293 **seMT**, A pair of sage-chickens, a pair of curlew, and a jack-rabbit complete my present collection. **1902** Wister *Virginian* 53 **WY**, At our noon meal we killed a rattlesnake and shot some young sage chickens, which were good at supper. **1909** in 1914 Stewart *Letters* 5 **WY**, There is a saddle horse . . and a little shotgun with which I am to kill sage chickens. **1923** U.S. Dept. Ag. *Farmers' Bulletin* 1375.13 **CO**, No open season: . . sage chicken. **1956** Almirall *From College* 250 **CO**, Lower down on the sagebrush flats, there were nice, big, clumsy, sage chickens and their young to stalk. **1966–67** *DARE* (Qu. Q7, *Names and nicknames for . . game birds*) Inf **CO46, SD5, WY5**, Sage chicken. **1967** *DARE* Tape **WY2**, Oh, yes, when we lived up there on the ranch . . sage chickens were very plentiful. **1982** Elman *Hunter's Field Guide* 26, *Common & regional names.* . . For sage grouse . . *sage chicken, sage turkey.*

sage clam See **sedge clam**

sage cock n

=**sage grouse,** esp the male.

1839 in 1840 Wislizenus *Ausflug Felsen-Gebirgen* 49 **ND**, Ganz ähnlich schmeckt ein Vogel, der sich von dieser Pflanze nährt, der sogenannte *sage cock, cock of the plains.* [=A bird that feeds on this plant, the so-called *sage cock* or *cock of the plains,* tastes exactly the same.] **1852** U.S. Army Corps Topog. Engineers *Exped. Gt. Salt Lake* 319, *Tetrao urophasianus.* . . Cock of the Plains, or Prairie Cock; Sage Cock. . . It is found on the plains skirting the Rocky Mountains, seldom coming down to the Missouri, except far to the north. . . abundant along the Columbia River. Its flesh is not usually considered edible, from feeding so much upon the artemisia or sage. **1874** Coues *Birds NW* 406, Even those who are familiar with the appearance of the "drums" of the common Pinnated Grouse . . , may fail, without actual inspection, to form a fair idea of the enormous yellow sacs of the Sage Cock in their condition of greatest distension. **1918** Grinnell *Game Birds* 564, *Sage-hen. . . Other names*—Sage Grouse; Sage Cock. **1951** Porter *Ragged Roads* 20 **OK,** Just when the rosebuds were swelling and the sage cocks were drumming and the plains were being clothed in verdant green grass for the teams, here came the "kivvered" wagon folks. **1959** Barnes *Nat. Hist. Wasatch Winter* 47 **UT,** There is no doubt that this large game bird should be called "sage grouse". . . S.F. Baird was as much in error in designating it "sage cock" as sportsmen . . were in naming it "sage hen", doubtless because its cluck reminded them of the barnyard fowl.

saged adj Cf **loco** v

1929 *AmSp* 5.68 **NE** [Cattle country talk], "Saged" and "locoed" cattle are those stiffened and crazed by eating sage brush and loco weed.

sage fowl n
=**sage grouse.**

1869 (1870) *Amer. Naturalist* 3.82 **MT,** Sage Fowl (*Centrocercus urophasianus*). . . is very rare [near Fort Benton]. **1874** Coues *Birds NW* 407, The young Sage Fowl shows features parallel with those of the young Sharp-tailed [Grouse], as might be expected from the affinity of the two. **1953** Jewett *Birds WA* 215, *Centrocercus urophasianus plaios*. . . Sage Fowl.

sage grass See **sedge grass**

sage grass broom See **sedge grass 2**

sage grouse n

A large grouse (*Centrocercus urophasianus*) native to the western US. Also called **chicken B1, cock of the plains, prairie cock 1, ~ chicken 6, sage buzzard, ~ chicken, ~ cock, ~ fowl, ~ hen** n[1]

1876 Dodge *Black Hills* 124 **SD,** Packs of the sage grouse are occasionally encountered. **1904** Wheelock *Birds CA* 128, As the name implies, the Sage Grouse loves the barren alkalai plains, . . where no green thing can grow save the sagebrush and the cacti. **1928** Bailey *Birds NM* 212, The extermination of the Sage Grouse in New Mexico is most unfortunate and it should be reinstated and given absolute protection. **1966–69** *DARE* (Qu. Q7, *Names and nicknames for . . game birds*) Infs **CA136, ND5,** Sage grouse. **1968** *Recorder–Herald* (Salmon ID) 25 Jan 8/1, Work on sage grouse resumes this week when Owyhee Mountain wintering ranges are located for study purposes. **1978** Doig *This House* 19 **MT,** Sage grouse nearly as large as hen turkeys whirred from their hiding places.

sage hare See **sage rabbit 1**

sage hen n[1] [**sage 2**] **Pacific, Rocky Mts**
=**sage grouse.**

1843 Williams *Narr. Tour IN to OR* 14, The sage hen is found here also. **1861** Berkeley *Engl. Sportsman* 25 (*OED2*) **West,** There is a certain bird of the grouse species . . called the 'sage hen.' **1878** Hart *Sazerac Lying Club* 17 **NV,** The sage-hen, so-called, is a bird of the grouse family, inhabiting Nevada, and feeds on the sage-brush which, in the main, constitutes the vegetation of the "Silver State." **1923** U.S. Dept. Ag. *Farmers' Bulletin* 1375.3, Nevada shortened the season on prairie chickens 3 months and on sage hens 15 days. **1965** Herlan *NV Highway Bird Watcher* 33, *Sage Grouse*. . . Better known among hunters as "Sage Hen," this grouse spends its entire life among sagebrush. **1965–70** *DARE* (Qu. Q7, *Names and nicknames for . . game birds*) 20 Infs, **chiefly Pacific, Rocky Mts,** Sage hen. **1982** Elman *Hunter's Field Guide* 26, *Common & regional names*. . . For sage grouse—*sage hen*.

sage hen n[2] See **sedge hen**

sage-leaf(ed) willow See **sage willow b**

sage mocker n Cf **mountain mockingbird**
=**sage thrasher.**

1953 Jewett *Birds WA* 506, *Oreoscoptes montanus*. . . Sage Mocker. [*Ibid* 507, The sage thrasher is famous for its song, which is reminiscent of that of the mockingbird.]

sage orange n [Aphet form of **Osage orange**]

1965–70 *DARE* (Qu. T13, . . *Names . . for . . osage orange*) Infs **KY9, 80, VA38,** Sage orange.

sage peter See **sedge peter**

sager n |ˈseɪǰə(r)| Also *country sager;* pronc-sp *sagah* **Sth, S Midl**

A rustic; a poor White person.

1893 Shands *MS Speech* 54, *Sager* [seǰə]. Illiterate white for backwoodsman, rustic. It is probably derived from *sedge* (pronounced [seǰ]), and refers to one coming from a sedge-grass region, i.e. from the country. Its use is confined almost exclusively to South Mississippi. **1915** Hall *Claib Jones* 28 **KY,** We reached Beech mountain, stayed all night with an old sager. We laid in our bread and hired him and his horse to take us to the Beech mountain. **a1929** (2000) Wolfe *O Lost* 359 **NC** (as of c1916) [Black], "Git away f'm me!" she said loudly, protestingly. "Yo' low-down white sagah!" **1943** Korson *Coal Dust* 5, Full-time miners naturally resented them [=farmer-miners] and expressed their distrust by calling them "winter diggers," "wheats," "corncrackers," "hay johns," "pumpkin rollers," "clodhoppers," "greenies," "scissorbills," and "sagers." **1945** *Hench Coll.* swVA, A poor white is called a sager. **1949** *AmSp* 24.107 cnGA, Country sager. . . A rustic ('new'). **1953** in 1965 *DARE* File seKY, *Sager* [ˈseɪǰɚ] = hick, country bumpkin. **1970** Green *Ely* 42 **TN,** As we started through the park a white man of the sager class or poor white trash, so called by the Negros and the aristocrats, walked up to us. **1986** Pederson *LAGS Concordance (Poor Whites)* 2 Infs, **AL, TN,** (Poor) sagers; 1 inf, **eTN,** Sager—father used this for poor whites; 1 inf, **csTN,** Sager—pejorative used by Blacks; *(Caucasian)* 1 inf, **cAL,** Sager—insulting; *(A rustic)* 1 inf, **swGA,** A sager; 1 inf, **nwGA,** A country sager; 1 inf, **neTN,** An old sager = mountaineer; 1 inf, **ceTN,** Sager—he used as a boy for "poor whites"; 1 inf, **cwGA,** Country sager—poor white trash; 1 inf, **ceTN,** Sagers— white people.

sage rabbit n

1 also *sage hare:* A cottontail rabbit of the western US, usu *Sylvilagus nuttallii.* [**sage 2**]

1846 Sage *Scenes Rocky Mts.* 31, [The] sage rabbit. . . is nearly three times the size of the common rabbit, and of a white color, slightly tinged with grey. **1859** Baird *Mammals N. Amer.* 602 **West,** *Lepus Artemisia,* Bachman. Sage Rabbit. **1868** (1869) *Amer. Naturalist* 2.536 **MT,** [The] Sage Hare (*Lepus Artemisia*). . . is more rare near Fort Benton. **1879** U.S. Natl. Museum *Bulletin* 14.20, *Lepus sylvaticus* . . var. *nuttalli.—* Sage Rabbit.—United States west of 97th meridian.

2 also *sage:* A cottontail rabbit; see quots. [Cf **sedge grass 1, 2**] Cf **canecutter, marsh rabbit 1**

1969 *DARE* (Qu. P30, . . *Wild rabbits*) Inf **GA76,** Sage rabbit. **1969** *DARE* Tape **GA86,** We have two kinds here; this was the cotton tail, sage rabbit, we would call it. And course in the swamps you'd have buck rabbits, which was a little larger rabbit . . but, sages, that was the main rabbit that we had.

sage sparrow n [**sage 2**]

A sparrow of the genus *Amphispiza,* usu *A. belli.*

1884 Coues *Key to N. Amer. Birds* 375 **SW,** *Amphispiza*. . . Sage Sparrows. **1898** (1900) Davie *Nests N. Amer. Birds* 386, *Sage Sparrow. Amphispiza belli nevadensis*. . . This bird abounds in the sage-brush deserts of Nevada, Utah, New Mexico and Arizona. **1904** Wheelock *Birds CA* 237, Truly well named is the little gray bird called the Sage Sparrow. Everywhere in the sagebrush district his metallic call may be heard. **1928** Bailey *Birds NM* 735, The Sage Sparrows were . . found among the sparse vegetation of the open desert. **1968** *DARE* (Qu. Q21, . . *Kinds of sparrows*) Infs **CA78, NV6,** Sage sparrow. **1977** Udvardy *Audubon Field Guide Birds* 610, *Amphispiza belli*. . . The Sage Sparrow is secretive . . except during the spring breeding season, when the males sing from a sagebrush perch to announce their territory.

sage thrasher n [**sage 2**]

A **thrasher** (here: *Orescoptes montanus*) native to the western US. Also called **gray bird a, mountain mockingbird, sage mocker, ~ thrush**

1884 Coues *Key to N. Amer. Birds* 249 **West,** Sage Thrasher. **1898** (1900) Davie *Nests N. Amer. Birds* 462, Sage Thrasher. . . is exclusively an inhabitant of the sage-brush region of the West, and is partial to the lower portions of the country, though not infrequently met with in the open mountains. **1928** Bailey *Birds NM* 561, The grayish brown Sage Thrasher, next to the Sage Grouse the largest of the characteristic birds of the sagebrush country, may be seen perching on bowlders or running over the ground. **1961** Ligon *NM Birds* 229, Few birds have been more appropriately named than has the Sage Thrasher. Its summer and nesting range . . is confined almost wholly to the big or purple sage *(Artemisia tridentata)* area. **1977** Bull–Farrand *Audubon Field Guide Birds* 623, On its breeding grounds the Sage Thrasher is wary and difficult to approach.

sage thrush n
=**sage thrasher.**

1917 (1923) *Birds Amer.* 3.174, Sage Thrasher. . . Other Name.—Sage Thrush. **1964** Jackman–Long *OR Desert* 105, A little bird we called the sage thrush would sing occasionally with surpassing sweetness.

sage tree n
1 =**chaste tree.**

1898 *Jrl. Amer. Folkl.* 11.277 **TX**, *Vitex Agnus-castus*, . . sage tree, Waco, Tex. **1960** Vines *Trees SW* 899, *Vitex agnus-castus*. . . Vernacular names are . . Sage-tree [etc]. **1970** Correll *Plants TX* 1340, *Sage-tree*. . . Widely cult., escaped in every part of Tex. except Trans-Pecos and Plain Country. **1986** Pederson *LAGS Concordance* 1 inf, **cwMS**, Sage tree.

2 also *sage:* A **lantana** (here: *Lantana involucrata*) native to Florida and Texas.

1897 *Jrl. Amer. Folkl.* 10.52 **FL**, *Lantana involucrata*, . . var Floridana, sage tree, Florida keys. **1933** Small *Manual SE Flora* 1142, *L[antana] involucrata*. . . *Sage*. . . Pinelands, hammocks, sand dunes, S pen[insular] Fla. and Florida Keys; S Tex.

sage turkey See sage chicken

sage willow n
A **willow:**

a =**prairie willow.** [See quot 1846]

1846 in 1850 Emerson *Rept. Trees & Shrubs* 255, The Sage Willow. *Salix tristis* [=*S. humilis*]. . . Conspicuously grayish and sage-like in its appearance, . . sage willow is a slender, hoary plant, or a spreading tufted bush, one or two feet high, growing in the openings and on the borders of dry, sandy woods. **1901** Lounsberry *S. Wild Flowers* 109, *Sage Willow*. . . This fluffy little one of the shrubs which grows through the barren and dry soil of the mountains blooms very early in the spring. **1938** Van Dersal *Native Woody Plants* 352, Sage willow (*Salix humilis, Salix candida*). **1966** Grimm *Recognizing Native Shrubs* 84, *Salix humilis* var. *microphylla*. . . Also known as the Dwarf Prairie Willow, Dwarf Pussy Willow, and Sage Willow. **1973** Stephens *Woody Plants* 42, Sage willow. . . *Leaves* . . upper surface light yellowish-green, glossy or dull, . . lower surface silvery white pubescent.

b also *sage-leaf(ed) willow:* The hoary **willow** *(Salix candida).* [See quot 1891]

1891 *Jrl. Amer. Folkl.* 4.148 **NH**, One species was *Sage Willow*, because of its sage-like leaves. **1942** Tehon *Fieldbook IL Shrubs* 57, The Sage Willow . . is a low, very branchy shrub generally 8 to 10 inches, rarely 3 feet, high, with long, narrow, densely white-tomentose leaves. **1952** Gleason *New Britton & Brown* 2.18, *Salix candida* Fluegge. Sage-leafed Willow. Hoary Willow. Shrub 2–10 dm. tall; branches divaricate, brownish, glabrous. **1972** Viereck–Little *AK Trees* 115, Sage willow. . . An erect shrub . . with an overall silvery appearance. **1998** (acc) U.S. Dept. Ag. *Integrated Taxonomic Info. System* (Internet), *Salix candida*— Vernacular Name: sageleaf willow.

sago n
1 See **sego lily.**
2 See **sago pondweed.**
3 The white **crappie** *(Pomoxis annularis).*

1972 Sparano *Outdoors Encycl.* 361, *White Crappie*. . . *Common Names:* White crappie, . . sago, grass bass.

sago lily See sego lily

sago pondweed n Also *sago (grass), sego pondweed*
A **pondweed** (here: *Potamogeton pectinatus).*

1913 *Torreya* 13.226 **MN**, *Potamogeton pectinatus*. . . Sago, Duluth, Minn. **1923** in 1925 Jepson *Manual Plants CA* 65, *Potamogeton pectinatus*. . . Sago Pondweed. . . The rootstocks bear tubers about the size of a pea, which are fed upon by the Canvas-back and Broad-bill. **1938** FWP *Ocean Highway* 171 **NC**, The marshes and waters of the sound, covered with wild celery, pond-weed, and sago grass, form a rendezvous for millions of migratory waterfowl. **1950** Gray–Fernald *Man-

ual of Botany* 70, *P[otamogeton] pectinatus*. . . "Sago." . . Saline, brackish or calcareous waters of coast and interior. **1961** Thomas *Flora Santa Cruz* 66 **cwCA**, Sego or Fennel-leaved Pondweed. Fairly common in reservoirs, lakes, ponds, and quiet pools along streams. **1970** Correll *Plants TX* 88, Sago pondweed. Rhizome creeping, much-branched, . . bearing terminal tuberous bulblets.

saguaro n Also *sahuaro;* for addit vars see quots [MexSpan *saguaro, sahuaro,* prob < Opata (a Piman lang) *sahuaro*]

A **cactus B1** (here: *Carnegiea gigantea*) native to the southwestern US; hence *saguaro apple* the fruit of this cactus. Also called **giant cactus, harsee, Indian fig 2, organ cactus, pitahaya 1, umbrella cactus**

1856 *Wide West* (S.F.) Oct. 4/6 *(DA)*, There are in this region a few Indian rancharies, to which the *Papagos* resort to gather the fruit of the *sugarro.* **1864** Mowry *AZ & Sonora* 161, Gradually appear the palo verde, the mesquit, and a greater variety of cacti, and on the hills scattered saguaras (Cereus giganteus). **1884** Sargent *Forests of N. Amer.* 90, *Suwarrow. Saguaro. Giant Cactus.* Wood . . used in the region almost exclusively for the rafters of adobe houses, for fencing, and by the Indians for lances, bows, etc. **1906** NM Ag. Exper. Station *Bulletin* 60.120, *Saguarro.* . . This familiar and conspicuous giant cactus of Arizona . . may be fed to stock with very little difficulty. **1907** White *AZ Nights* 220, This wasn't no such tur'ble long a snake, but he was more'n a foot thick. Looked just like a sahuaro stalk. **1942** Hylander *Plant Life* 312, Spines have been known to persist unchanged on the trunk of giant Suaharos several centuries old. **1942** *Western Folkl.* 1.289 **Desert SW**, *Zahuaro, sahuara, saguaro, saguero, sahuero, sajuaro, seguarro.* . . An arborescent cactus of desert regions in the S.W. U.S. **1957** Jaeger *N. Amer. Deserts* 65, Long hooked sticks are employed in jarring loose the sahuaro "apples" from the tall branches. The fruit pulp is eaten raw or stewed, and sometimes is permitted to ferment to form an intoxicating drink. **1979** *AZ Daily Star* (Tucson) 1 Apr (Advt. Section) 16/7, This parcel [of land] is dotted with native sahuaro. *Ibid*, You want beautiful desert vegetation including Saguaros.

saguaro woodpecker n
=**Gila woodpecker.**

1884 Coues *Key to N. Amer. Birds* 488 **SW**, Saguaro Woodpecker. **1917** (1923) *Birds Amer.* 2.162, *Centurus uropygialis*. . . Saguaro Woodpecker. . . The peculiarity [of this woodpecker] . . is its apparent preference for the stem of the giant cactus as a home-site. **1944** Hausman *Amer. Birds* 532, Woodpecker, Saguaro.

sahdie See saddy

sahnt See send 2

saht'n See certain

sahuaro See saguaro

sahvant See servant

sail See sailfish 1

sail bird n
The eastern **meadowlark 1.**

1923 WV State Ornith. *Birds WV* 47, The Meadowlark is also called the "sail-bird" by some gunners. He raises from the ground much like the quail, but not so swiftly. Then he sails a short distance, when he again uses his wings to propel him.

sail cat n
=**gaff-topsail catfish.**

1966 DARE (Qu. P4, *Saltwater fish that are not good to eat*) Inf **FL29**, Sail cat.

sailfish n
1 also *sail;* Std: a saltwater fish of the family Istiophoridae, usu *Istiophorus platypterus.* Also called **billfish 1, spearfish, spikefish**
2 A carpsucker: usu *Carpiodes velifer,* but also *C. cyprinus.*

1882 U.S. Natl. Museum *Bulletin* 16.119, *C[arpiodes] cyprinus*. . . *Sail-fish.* . . [Footnote:] Possibly two or three species are here included: *velifer,* with the anterior dorsal rays longer than the fin; *cyprinus,* with them somewhat shorter; and *cutisanserinus,* with a blunter snout and the dorsal rays very long. **1902** Jordan–Evermann *Amer. Fishes* 43,

C[arpiodes] velifer, the . . sailfish, . . is a small species found pretty well throughout the Mississippi Valley. It is distinguished from other species in the same waters by the produced first dorsal ray and the character of the lower lip whose halves meet at an acute angle. **1983** Becker *Fishes WI* 638, *Carpiodes velifer*. . . sailfish. . . Dorsal fin long, falcate.

sailor n Cf **marsh rabbit 1, swamp ~.**

A cottontail (*Sylvilagus* spp).

1966 *DARE* (Qu. P30, . . *Wild rabbits*) Inf **MS6**, Cottontails, dodger, hillbillies, sailor [are the] same.

sailorcaps See **sailor's caps**

sailor-in-a-boat n

=Moses-in-the-bulrushes 1.

1955 *S. Folkl. Qrly.* 19.233, *Moses in the Bullrushes*. . . bears its tiny white flowers in a boat-shaped bract. . . Perhaps a devotee of fishing is responsible for renaming the plant *Sailor in a Boat*, which is just as apt as *Moses in the Bullrushes*.

sailor's buttons n

See quot.

1950 *WELS Suppl.* **csWI**, Sailor's buttons—small bright yellow perennials with waxy leaves and flowers. They spread like wildfire once they get into your garden.

sailor's caps n Also *sailorcaps* **CA**

A **shooting star**, usu *Dodecatheon hendersonii*.

1901 Jepson *Flora CA* 376, *D[odecatheon] Hendersoni*. . . *Sailors Caps*. . . Petals purple with a transverse yellow band at base. **1920** Rice–Rice *Pop. Studies CA Wild Flowers* 86, *Dodecatheon*. . . Children seem to have . . invented rather pert little names . . to suit the flowers. The most common of these are Shooting Stars. . . Sailor's Capes [sic], . . and Prairie Pointers. **1949** Moldenke *Amer. Wild Flowers* 235 **CA**, In . . *D[odecatheon] patula*, the flowers are white. . . In the *mosquitobills* or *sailorcaps*, *D. hendersonii*, the corolla is purple, with a transverse yellow zone at the base edged above with white and bounded below by a black-purple band. Both are natives of California.

sailor's choice n

1 Any of several **grunts 1**; see below.

a A **pigfish c** (here: *Orthopristis chrysoptera*).   **esp NC, SC.**

1850 in 1945 Easterby *SC Rice Plantation* 102, Alick has given us fish nearly every day, but not very choice ones, today he has brought a whiting and a sailors choice for the first. **c1860** in 1884 Goode *Fisheries U.S.* 1.399 **NC, SC**, The 'Sailor's Choice' makes its appearance in our waters about the month of April and continues with us until November, when the largest are taken. **1902** Jordan–Evermann *Amer. Fishes* 435 **NC, SC**, Large numbers [of *Orthopristis chrysoptera*] are taken along the Carolina coast. It is very highly valued as a pan-fish, and is known in some places as the sailor's-choice. **1911** [see **2** below]. **1967** *DARE* (Qu. P2, . . *Kinds of saltwater fish caught around here* . . *good to eat*) Inf **SC63**, Sailor's choice. **1973** Knight *Cook's Fish Guide* 388, Sailor's Choice [=*Haemulon parrai*] or see Pigfish [=*Orthopristis chrysopterus*] or see Pinfish [=*Lagodon rhomboides*].

b A **grunt 1** (here: *Haemulon parra*) of southern Florida waters.   Also called **margaretfish 2, ronco 2**

1887 Goode *Amer. Fishes* 80 **FL**, At Key West. . . *D[iabasis] chromis* [=*Haemulon parra*] [is called] the "Sailor's Choice." **1902** Jordan–Evermann *Amer. Fishes* 424, *Haemulon parra*. . . This grunt, also known as sailor's-choice, . . occurs from southern Florida to Brazil. **1935** Caine *Game Fish* 79, *Haemulon parra*. . . Sailor's Choice. . . Rocky shoals, channels and deep holes, and under mangrove roots. **1976** Tryckare et al. *Lore of Sportfishing* 113, *Haemulon parra*. . . The sailor's choice is medium sized, somewhat elongate, compressed, with a moderate sized mouth and a long snout. . . Takes a bait and offers good sport on light tackle.

c =**margaret grunt.**

1935 Caine *Game Fish* 85, *Haemulon album*. . . Sailor's Choice. . . Found from Florida south to Brazil. **1946** LaMonte *N. Amer. Game Fishes* 64, *Haemulon album*. . . Sailor's Choice. . . Averages 1 to 2 pounds; runs up to 10 pounds and a length of over 2′.

d =**pompon 1.**

1935 Caine *Game Fish* 114, *Anisotremus surinamensis*. . . Sailor's Choice. . . *Average size:* 1 to 2 lbs. **1946** LaMonte *N. Amer. Game*

Fishes 67, *Anisotremus surinamensis*. . . Sailor's Choice. . . *Distribution:* North to Florida.

2 =**pinfish 1a.**

1879 U.S. Natl. Museum *Bulletin* 14.46, *Lagodon rhomboides*. . . *Sailor's Choice.*—West Indian Fauna and north to Cape Cod. **1911** U.S. Bur. Census *Fisheries 1908* 315, *Sailor's Choice* (*Lagodon rhomboides*).—A food fish found on the Atlantic coast south of Cape Hatteras and in the Gulf. . . the name is also applied to the pigfish (*Orthopristis chrysopterus* [sic]) in South Carolina. **1933** LA Dept. of Conserv. *Fishes* 195, Porgies . . are good food fishes. The most common of these is the Pinfish or Sailor's Choice, *Lagodon rhomboides*. **1976** Tryckare et al. *Lore of Sportfishing* 115, *Pinfish*. . . Other common names . . bream, . . sailor's choice.

sailor's purse n Also *sailor's pocket*

The egg case of a skate or shark; see quots.

1890 *Century Dict.* 5306, *Sailor's-purse*. . . An egg-pouch of oviparous rays and sharks, which is mostly found empty on the sea-shore. **1895** *Funk & Wagnalls Std. Dict.* 1572, *Sailor's-pocket*. . . The egg-case of a skate or oviparous shark. *sailor's-purse*. **1974** McClane *McClane's New Std. Fishing Encycl.* 615, *Mermaid's purse*. . . It is also called "sea purse" and "sailor's purse." The capsules are 3–8 inches in length and contain one or more eggs. **1978** Whipple *Vintage Nantucket* 237 **MA**, Just above the tide line was the usual litter of skates' egg cases, black rectangles with tiny protuberances at all four corners. Sometimes called "mermaid's pouches" or "sailor's purses," these hollow parchments serve to protect the skate's eggs, and attach themselves to rocks or floating weed.

sai-min n [Prob Cantonese; see quots 1972, 1986] **HI**

A kind of noodle soup.

1972 Carr *Da Kine Talk* 91 **HI**, *Saimin*, a richly flavored, uniquely Hawaiian noodle concoction that is today the most popular quick-lunch snack in the islands. *Ibid* 99, The Cantonese word *min* 'noodles' introduces another complex of delicacies. The best known is *saimin*, a noodle soup which is disclaimed by both the Chinese and Japanese. . . The best judgment as to a Chinese origin. . . is that *sai* is a Cantonese rendering of the word 'water' and that *saimin*, therefore means 'water noodles' or 'noodle soup.' **1975** Sunset *HI Guide* 8, Many hole-in-the-wall places feature *saimin*, a filling noodle soup that borrows from both Chinese and Japanese cuisines but is unique to the Islands. **1981** *Pidgin To Da Max* np **HI**, *Saimin*. . . When nothing else looks good, there's always saimin. **1986** *12000 Words* 170, *Sai-min* . . [prob. fr. Chin (Cantonese) *sai mîn*, lit., fine noodles]: an Hawaiian noodle soup.

saint n esp **UT** *old-fash* Cf **gentile**

A member of the Church of Jesus Christ of Latter-day Saints; a Mormon.

1833 *Eve. and Morning Star* (Independence MO) July 111 (*DA*), The saints must shun every appearance of evil. **1877** *Scribner's Mth.* 14.396 **UT**, That these murders were committed, neither Saint nor Gentile denies. **1878** Hart *Sazerac Lying Club* 131 **NV**, The committee . . instructing me to forthwith wait on the Mormon family. . . I wended my way to the spot where the family of Saints and Saintesses were camped. **1900** *Atlantic Mth.* 85.271 **UT**, When two peoples fall foul of each other, the quicker they make trial of strength, the better for both. As with Boer, so with Mormon; the Saint must shortly be beaten. **1965** Rice *Ambassador* 62 **sUT** (as of 1908), People of the community . . stared at me as I walked down the street. . . It was not pleasant . . for one who felt that he had come as a friendly ambassador to the people who called themselves saints. **c1971** Hall *Snake River Valley* **sID**, (*Terms for Mormons*) 2 [of 68] infs, Saints. **2000** Launspach *ID Dial. Project* 6 **seID**, (*Terms for Mormons*) 3 [of 99] infs, Saints.

Saint-Andrew's-cross n [See quot 1848]

A **Saint-John's-wort** (here: *Hypericum hypericoides*) native chiefly in the South and Midland.

c1738 (1929) Byrd *Histories* 155 **NC, VA**, We saw . . the Fern Rattlesnake Root, which is said to be the strongest Antidote against the Bite of that Viper. And we saw St Andrew's-Cross almost every Step we went, which serves for the same Purpose. **1848** Gray *Manual of Botany* 52, *A[scyrum] Crux-Andreæ* [=*Hypericum hypericoides*]. . . St. Andrew's Cross. . . Petals scarcely exceeding the outer sepals, approaching each other in pairs over them, in the form of a St. Andrew's cross. **1901** Lounsberry *S. Wild Flowers* 344, The little plant commonly known as St. Andrew's cross. . . is a low plant, spreading well over the ground.

1941 Walker *Lookout* 50 **TN,** Saint Andrews cross, Saint Peterswort, wild stonecrop . . are abundant. **1964** Batson *Wild Flowers* SC 75, *St. Andrew's Cross* . . is generally smaller [than *St. Peter's-wort*] and more generally distributed. **1979** Niering–Olmstead *Audubon Guide N. Amer. Wildflowers E. Region* 560, St. Andrew's Cross. . . is found on sandy sites from Massachusetts south to Florida. In the north it may form a mat on the ground.

Saint Augustine grass n [From *St. Augustine,* Florida]

A perennial grass *(Stenotaphrum secundatum)* common esp in the South Atlantic and Gulf States, but cultivated also in California and Hawaii. Also called **buffalo grass c, California ~, manienie 2**

1894 Coulter *Botany W. TX* 511, *S[tenotaphrum] secundatum. . . St. Augustine grass. . .* Near the coast. Cultivated in Florida. **1929** Pope *Plants HI* 28, *Stenotaphrum secundatum. . .* This grass. . . was found in the vicinity of St. Augustine, Florida, at a very early date and from that place is supposed to have spread to most of the southern states, being generally known as St. Augustine grass. **1948** Blomquist *Grasses NC* 123, *Stenotaphrum secundatum . . ,* called St. Augustine grass . . is cultivated to a considerable extent as a lawn grass. **1966–69** DARE (Qu. L9a, *. . Kinds of grass . . grown for hay)* Inf **TX**36, San [sic] Augustine grass; (Qu. S8, *A common kind of wild grass that grows in fields: it spreads by sending out long underground roots, and it's hard to get rid of)* Inf **AR**55, Saint Augustine grass; **FL**39, Saint Augustine grass—used for lawns; (Qu. S9, *. . Kinds of grass that are hard to get rid of)* Inf **TX**60, Saint Augustine. **1966** DARE Tape **FL**5, Yes zoysia—We've tried zoysia, St. Augustine, and centipede [grass]. **1986** Pederson *LAGS Concordance,* 7 infs, **Gulf Region,** Saint Augustine (grass).

saint heart See sand tart 1

Saint-Jacob's-dipper n Also *Saint-John's-dipper*

A **pitcher plant 1** (here: *Sarracenia purpurea*).

1931 Clute *Common Plants* 78, Saint's [sic] names have been attached to various indigenous species through sheer fancy. This is probably true of Saint Jacob's dipper *(Sarracenia purpurea).* **1959** Carleton *Index Herb. Plants* 102, *St. Jacob's dipper:* Sarracennia [sic] purpurea. . . *St. John's-dipper:* Sarracenia purpurea.

Saint-Jacob's-quinine n Cf wild quinine

Perh a **feverfew 3.**

1945 Saxon *Gumbo Ya-Ya* 529 **LA,** St. Jacob's quinine grows mos' everywhere, an' that's good for fevers.

Saint-John's-dipper See Saint-Jacob's-dipper

Saint John's lily n [From *St. John's* River, Florida]

A **swamp lily** (here: *Crinum americanum*).

1901 Lounsberry *S. Wild Flowers* 67, *St. John's Lily. . . Crinum Americanum. . .* One of the most potent charms of the unusual scenery along the banks of the St. John's river in Florida is the tangled masses of this plant's milk-white and intensely fragrant flowers. **1938** Baker *FL Wild Flowers* 43, *St. John's Lily. . .* This beautiful wild crinum blooms chiefly in spring and summer, but flowers are found even in midwinter in the southern part of the state.

Saint-John's-weed n Also *Saint-John-weed, ~-John's-root* chiefly SE

A **Saint-John's-wort;** see quots.

1933 Small *Manual SE Flora* 873, *H[ypericum] perforatum. . . St. John's-weed. . .* Nearly throughout U.S. and S. Can. **1937** *Hall Coll.* **eTN,** Saint John weeds with dew on 'em makes sores, not biles [Hall: = boils] and risin's. **1970** *NC Folkl.* 8.28, An ointment made from small twigs of St. John's root and combined with calves' feet oil relieved pains and joints. **1974** Morton *Folk Remedies* 75 **SC,** *St. John's weed. . . Hypericum hypericoides. . .* South Carolina (Current use): Decoction of plant, medium-warm applied to burns and swellings. . . The plant has astringent properties.

Saint-John's-wort n

Std: a plant of the genus *Hypericum.* Also called **John's-wort;** for other names of var spp see **broom brush 1, flower-cross, goatweed 5, goldwire, ground pine 1, guinea cypress, hundred holes, Klamath weed, louseweed, nits-and-lice, nitweed, orange grass, paintbrush 2, pine tassel, pine-**

weed 1, poverty grass 2f, rock rose 2, rosinweed 6, Saint-Andrew's-cross, ~-John's-weed, ~-Peter's-wort, sandweed, speckled John, tinker's penny, witches' herb

Saint-John-weed See Saint-John's-weed

Saint-Margaret's-flower n

A **false dragonhead 1,** (here: *Physostegia virginiana*).

1959 Carleton *Index Herb. Plants* 102, *St. Margaret's-flower:* Physostegia virginiana.

Saint Paul goose n Cf Irish goose, nigger ~ 1 =double-crested cormorant.

1956 *AmSp* 31.182 **WI,** St. Paul goose [=] Double-crested cormorant.

Saint Paul sandwich n

A sandwich with multiple fillings, one of which is egg.

1943 *AmSp* 18.308 **wLA, eTX** [Cafe terms], *St. Paul sandwich.* Sandwich made of four pieces of bread, with sliced chicken between two pieces and egg between the other two. **1967–70** DARE (Qu. H45, *Dishes made with meat, fish, or poultry that everybody around here would know, but that people in other places might not)* Inf **MO**29, Saint Paul sandwich; **NE**11, Saint Paul sandwich—made of hamburger and egg and served on a bun. **1999** DARE File—Internet **ceMO,** The St. Paul Sandwich is a culinary curiosity that has nothing to so with St. Paul, Minnesota. This quite wonderful specialty of St. Louis, Missouri, consists of egg foo yung on Wonder Bread, served up with lettuce, tomato and mayo. **2001** *NADS Letters* **KY** (as of 1960), One of my classmates mentioned "St. Paul sandwich" as being a fried egg sandwich.

Saint-Peter's-cabbage n

A **saxifrage** n^2 (here: *Saxifraga virginiensis*).

1933 Small *Manual SE Flora* 595, *M[icranthes] virginiensis* [=*Saxifraga v.*] *. . St. Peter's-cabbage. . .* Dry hillsides and rocks, various provinces. **1953** Greene–Blomquist *Flowers South* 45, *St. Peter's-Cabbage. . .* is the commonest and most widespread of the saxifrages, growing on stream banks, shallow soil surrounding rock exposures, and dry soil of poor drainage.

Saint Peter's mudhole See Peter's mudhole

Saint-Peter's-wort n Also *Peterwort* [*OED2* (at *peter* 8.c) 1552 →]

A **Saint-John's-wort:** usu *Hypericum crux-andreae,* but also *H. hypericoides.*

1785 Marshall *Arbustrum* 13, *Ascyrum* [=*Hypericum*]. *St. Peter's Wort. Ibid* 14, *Ascyrum Hypericoides* [=*H. hypericoides*]. *St. Peter's Wort. . .* is a small shrubby plant, growing naturally in low moist ground. . . The flowers . . have somewhat the appearance of those of St. John's wort. . . *Ascyrum villosum* [=*H. crux-andreae*]. *Villose St. Peter's wort. . .* The leaves are oblong and hairy. . . The flowers are produced at the top of the stalks, resembling those of St. John's wort, but have only four petals. **1843** Torrey *Flora NY* 1.84, *Ascyrum stans* [= *Hypericum crux-andreae*]. . . Upright St. Peter's Wort. **1869** Porcher *Resources* 83, *St. Peter's-wort. . .* Collected in pine land soils. . . The taste is somewhat acrid. **1891** Coulter *Botany W. TX* 34, *St. Peter's-wort. . . A[scyrum] hypericoides. . . A. stans. . .* Atlantic and Gulf States, and extending to . . Texas. **1901** Mohr *Plant Life AL* 619, *Ascyrum hypericoides. . . Southern St. Peter's-Wort. . .* South Carolina to Florida, west to Texas and southern Arkansas. **1931** Clute *Common Plants* 78, Saint's [sic] names have been attached to various indigenous species through sheer fancy. This is probably true of. . . our St. Peter's wort *(Ascyrum stans)* and the St. Andrew's cross *(Ascyrum hypericoides)* [which] are scarcely better situated since they are not the original plants so named but are obliged to bear names transferred from European species. **1960** Vines *Trees SW* 752, Atlantic St. Peter's-wort—*Ascyrum stans. . .* Flaxleaf St. Peter's-wort—*Ascyrum linifolium* [=*Hypericum hypericoides*]. **1974** Morton *Folk Remedies* 75 **SC,** Peterwort; St. Peter's wort. . . Hypericum hypericoides. . . Flowers . . with 4 bright-yellow, oblong petals in "X" formation. . . South Carolina (Current use): Decoction of plant, medium-warm applied to burns and swellings. **1979** Niering–Olmstead *Audubon Guide N. Amer. Wildflowers E. Region* 560, St. Peterswort (Hypericum stans). . . This . . has only 4 petals instead of the usual 5, and the sepals are of very unequal sizes. St. Andrew's cross *(H. hypericoides)* is similar.

Saint-Peter's-wreath n

A **spirea** (here: *Spiraea hypericifolia*).

1847 Wood *Class-Book* 256, S[piraea] hypericifolia. *St. Peter's Wreath.* . . Cultivated in gardens and shrubberies. . . Flowers white, in numerous umbels, terminating the short, lateral branches. **1895** Gray–Bailey *Field Botany* 149, *S. hypericifolia.* . . *St. Peter's Wreath.* Shrub . . with long recurved branches. **1951** Hough *Singing in Morning* 41 **Martha's Vineyard MA,** There are some fifty members of the spiraea family to which the bridal wreath belongs. . . the bridal wreath, also called St. Peter's wreath.

sairse, saisse See **sauce**

sake-a See **senkah**

sal See **salmagundi**

salad n Usu |'sæləd|; also esp **Sth, S Midl** |'sælət, -lɛt, -lɪt| Pronc-spp *salat, sal(l)et, sallit*

A Forms.

1622 in 1918 *John Pory's Plymouth Colony* 41 **MA,** After their powdred sallets . . they may refresh and quench their thirst. **1806** (1970) Webster *Compendious Dict.* 264, *Salad, Sallet.* **1859** Taliaferro *Fisher's R.* 143 **nwNC** (as of 1820s), My sallet were meltin' away mighty fast. **1902** *DN* 2.244 **sIL,** *Sallit.* **1917** *DN* 4.416 **wNC,** *Salat.* **1927** *DN* 5.470 **Appalachians,** *Salad.* . . *sallet.* **1928** *AmSp* 3.404 **Ozarks** (as of 1916–27), *T* replaces the final *d* in words like *salad, ballad,* [etc]. **1965** *Dict. Queen's English* 4 **NC,** *Salet* (for salad): Garden greens, i.e., turnip salad. I'm going to cook up a mess of salet for dinner. **1965–70** *DARE* (Qq. I28a, b, *Greens*) 10 Infs, **chiefly S Midl,** Poke sallet; **VA**35, 42, Cressy sallet; **KY**40, Plantain sallet; **AR**47, Poke ['sælɪt]; **KY**5, Poke ['sælət]; **KY**42, **SC**32, Sallet; **VA**40, ['sæələt]; **SC**34, Sallet greens; **KY**34, Sticky sallet; **SC**3, 46, **VA**35, 42, Turnip sallet; **KY**85, Wild sallet; (Qu. BB50b) Inf **VA**42, Poke sallet. **1965** *DARE* File **cnIA,** Sallet ['sælət]. **1989** Pederson *LAGS Tech. Index* 192 **Gulf Region,** 124 infs, (Collard *or* green, mustard, poke, rape, turnip) sallet; 1 inf, Sallet part.

B Senses.

1 Edible greens, green vegetables (whether eaten raw or cooked); an edible green. [Cf *OED2 salad* sb. 2 "Any vegetable or herb used in a raw state as an article of food"; c1460 →] **chiefly Sth, S Midl, TX** See Map

1622 [see **A** above]. [**1781** *PA Jrl. & Weekly Advt.* (Philadelphia) 23 May 1, *Raw salad* is used in the South for *salad.* N.B. There is no salad boiled.] **1819** (1821) Nuttall *Jrl.* 107 **AR,** I met with a new species of *Sysimbrium.* . . [which] might perhaps be better worth cultivating as an early sallad, than the *Barbarea americana,* or winter sallad. **1860** Mordecai *Virginia* 211 *(DAE),* A few vegetables also volunteered their verdure; such as dandelions—an excellent salad—butter cups [etc.] **1886** Smith *Hist. KY* 157, The indigenous salads and early berries came next, and finally the feast of garden vegetables. **1899** (1912) Green *VA Folk-Speech* 364, *Sallet.* . . Applied to fresh, green herbs that are cooked for food: as, "turnip-*sallet.*" **1901** *DN* 2.328 **seMO,** *Sallet* (salad). . . Greens. 'We had boiled sallet for dinner.' **1902** *DN* 2.244 **sIL,** *Sallit.* . . Salad; greens. **1907** *DN* 3.226 **nwAR,** *Sallit.* . . Salad; greens. **1908** *DN* 3.314 **eAL, wGA,** *Garden-sass.* . . Vegetables, particularly greens, salads, etc. **1915** *DN* 4.189 **swVA,** *Sallet.* . . Greens. **1917** *DN* 4.416 **wNC,** *Salat* . . =greens. **1923** *DN* 5.219 **swMO,** *Salat.* . . Salad, greens. **1944** *PADS* 2.12 **AL, LA,** *Salat* ['sælɪt]. . . Cooked greens, as *turnip salat.* . . Turnip greens. **1946** *AmSp* 21.99 **sIL,** A *mess* of early spring 'greens' cooked with a piece of fat and served with vinegar is called *sallet* in rural communities. **1946** *PADS* 5.35 **VA,** *Sallet:* Greens cooked for food; common everywhere except west of the Blue Ridge. **1949** Kurath *Word Geog.* 73, *Greens.* . . The distinctive Virginia Piedmont term is *salad,* more commonly pronounced *salat* in the speech of the folk. It is universal here and predominates over *greens* in adjoining parts of Maryland and North Carolina as well. In the greater part of the Carolinas *salad* and *greens* stand side by side, many persons using both terms. In the Virginia Tidewater *salad* has almost eliminated *greens,* but it has not crossed the Bay to the Eastern Shore. **1965–70** *DARE* (Qu. I28a, . . *Kinds of things . . you call 'greens' . . [Those that are eaten raw]*) 33 Infs, **chiefly Sth, S Midl,** Poke salad; **SC**32, **TX**33, Poke sallet; 16 Infs, **chiefly Sth, S Midl,** Salad(s); **AR**52, Salad—usually greens around here is cooked; **LA**4, Salad—this is the general word for green things eaten raw; **NC**12, Salad—term for any and *all* greens; **VA**40, Sallet; **SC**32, Sallet—off of turnips; **MS**60, Salad greens—all greens are called salad greens; **MD**28, Salad plant—served with hot

dressing over it; **PA**132, Salad plant—a "salad plant" is any one that is eaten raw; **NY**49, Field salad—green leaf—eaten in December; **CA**17, Green salad—lettuce; **IL**68, **KY**22, **NY**159, **TN**24, Lettuce salad; **MS**59, Turnip salad; **PA**206, Wild salad; **AR**20, Wild salad—lamb's tongue; **KY**85, Wild sallet—similar to turnip greens—cooked—wild green; (Qu. I28b, *Kinds of greens that are cooked*) 22 Infs, **chiefly Sth, S Midl,** Poke salad; 10 Infs, **scattered Sth, S Midl,** Poke sallet; **VA**35, 42, Cressy sallet; **SC**57, **VA**40, Mustard salad; **VA**35, Mustard sallet; **KY**40, Plantain sallet—wild green; **VA**40, Salad; **SC**22, Salad—mustard greens; **AL**1, **MS**60, **NC**1, 8, 76, 81, Salad green(s); **KY**42, **SC**32, Sallet; **SC**34, Sallet greens; **KY**34, Sticky sallet—same as cow thistle—cook and then fry; **MS**16, **NC**5, **TN**24, 37, **VA**40, 46, Turnip salad; **SC**3, 46, **VA**35, 42, Turnip sallet; **AR**20, Wild salad—lamb's tongue; (Qu. H54, . . *Kinds of 'greens' . . eaten . . ; total Infs questioned, 75*) 13 Infs, **esp MS,** Poke salad; 11 Infs, **esp FL,** Salad; **GA**13, Mustard sallet, turnip sallet, kale sallet; (Qu. BB50d, *Favorite spring tonics*) Infs **GA**84, **MD**5, **NC**30, **SC**39, **TX**95, 104, Poke salad; **VA**42, Poke sallet; **MS**1, Pokeberry root and poke salad; **TX**62, Pokeweed salad; (Qu. I4, . . *Vegetables . . less commonly grown around here*) Inf **GA**9, Turnip salad; (Qu. S21, . . *Weeds . . that are a trouble in gardens and fields*) Infs **AR**49, **GA**84, **TX**51, Poke salad. **1989** Pederson *LAGS Tech. Index* 192 **Gulf Region,** 45 infs, Salad; 76 infs, Collard (*or* green, mustard, onion, poke, rape, turnip) sallet; 48 infs, Sallet; 1 inf, Sallet part.

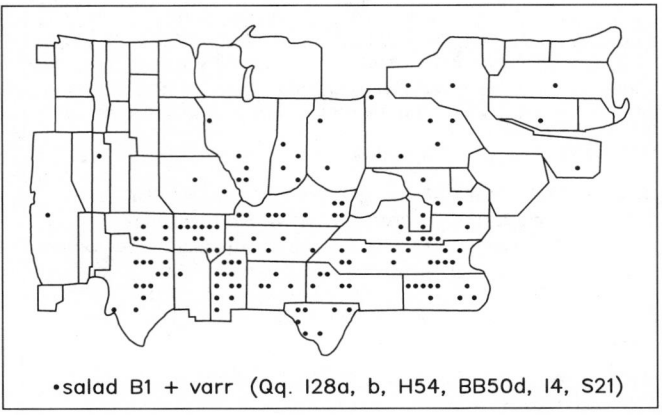

•salad B1 + varr (Qq. I28a, b, H54, BB50d, I4, S21)

2 Spec:

a also *garden salad:* Lettuce. [Engl dial.; PaGer *(Gaarde) salaat* lettuce] Cf **salad bird**

1741 in 1974 Franklin *Sayings Poor Richard* 119 **PA,** When is the best time to cut hair, trim cocks, or sow salad? **1769** in 1911 Dow *Holyoke Diaries* 71 **MA,** Sallad up in the garden. **1801** (1898) Hunt *Diary* 5 **PA,** This day I . . sowed some salled & radishes. **1849** Howitt *Our Cousins in OH* 131, Willie wrote down . . all the vegetable produce of their garden. . . It . . was as follows: . . salad, . . canteleup-melons, squashes, or vegetable marrow. **1851** (1976) Melville *Moby-Dick* 110, A king's head is solemnly oiled at his coronation, even as a head of salad. **1859** (1968) Bartlett *Americanisms* 377, *Salad.* In the Northern States often used specifically for *lettuce,* of which salad is frequently made. [**1969** *DARE* (Qu. I28a, . . *Kinds of things . . you call 'greens' . . [Those that are eaten raw]*) Inf **KY**22, Wilted salad—pour hot grease over fresh lettuce.] **1987** *Jrl. Engl. Ling.* 20.174 **ePA,** *Salad* 'lettuce' (cf. PaGer *Salaat*). . . 21% (22), ages 21–101. . . Of the twenty-two informants, only five are under 40. Three informants used the term in the compound *salad greens,* and one in the compound *garden salad* (cf. PaGer *Gaardesalaat*).

‡b Celery.

1901 *DN* 2.146 **cNY,** *Sallet.* . . Celery. . . Formerly common.

salad bird n **PA** Cf **lettuce bird, salad B2a**

A **goldfinch 1** (here: *Carduelis tristis*).

1808 Wilson *Amer. Ornith.* 1.21, [Goldfinches] pass by various names expressive of their food . . such as Sallad-bird. **1890** Warren *Birds PA* 231, The Salad-bird . . is fond of feasting on the blossoms of apple, cherry and maple trees; the seeds of the dandelion, thistle and sunflower enter largely into his bill of fare. **1919** Burns *Ornith. Chester Co. PA* 74, Saladbird. . . Common resident, though many migrate in severe winters. **1966–69** *DARE* (Qu. Q14, . . *Names . . for . . goldfinch*) Infs **PA**1, 89, 126, 147, 155, 169, 205, Salad bird. **1982** *Barrick Coll.* **csPA,** *Salad bird—goldfinch.* Spinus tristis. Any yellow bird.

salad onion n chiefly Sth, S Midl

A **green onion 1** or similar **onion** n B.

1941 *LANE* Map 258 (*Scallion, spring onion*) 1 inf, seNH, Salad onions; 2 infs, seNH, Sallet onion. **1965–70** *DARE* (Qu. I5, . . *Kind of onions that keep coming up without replanting year after year*) Infs KY90, NC5, 50, TN26, VA42, 46, Salad onions; (Qu. I6, *The kind of onions that come up fresh early in the year, and you eat them raw*) Infs GA12, KY90, NC50, 68, Salad onions. **1966** Dakin *Dial. Vocab. Ohio R. Valley* 367, Miscellaneous terms. . . *Salat (salad) onions.* **1986** Pederson *LAGS Concordance* Gulf Region, 8 infs, Salad onion(s); 1 inf, Salad onion—winter onion, doesn't make a head; 2 infs, Sallet onion(s); 1 inf, Sallet onion—blade was foot high, hot onion; 1 inf, Sallet onion—grows all winter and summer.

salad pea n chiefly sAppalachians

A **garden pea** with an edible pod.

1982 Powers *Cataloochee* 352 cwNC (as of a1940), I think sallet peas is one of the best vegetables in the world. We always grew some and made enough to can. . . They're edible pods. Some think you have to pick 'em real early before their maturity, y'know. But these edible peas, they're not too particular. **2000** *NADS Letters* eKY, Salad or sallet pea has been used in rural Eastern Kentucky to describe early peas that are picked and cooked whole. They are very sweet and tender, sometimes called English peas. If you raised them to hull out and eat only the pea, you would be very tired as the pea inside the shell is very small. *Ibid* wNC, eTN, "Sallet peas" are the first garden items next to spring onions to come in season. . . They can be cooked early in the pod, or when mature they can be shelled. They are green and sweet. *Ibid* swVA, My mom says it is called a "salad pea" (pronounced "sallet") because it can be put in salads. However, it is frequently eaten as a side dish. It is the only pea with a pod tender enough to eat. *Ibid* eTN, I heard my mother's, and granmother's, voice. . . "Now Bobby, you eat chure sallet peas. They're good for you." I believe that "sallet peas" are just a regionalism for "salad peas." In other words, green pea pods so young and tender that they could be placed in a salad raw. *Ibid* sAppalachians, AR, AZ, MA, Salad (*or* sallet) peas.

salad tree n

A **redbud** (here: *Cercis canadensis*).

[**1709** (1967) Lawson *New Voyage* 106, The Red-Bud-Tree bears a purple Lark-Heel, and is the best Sallad of any Flower I ever saw.] [**1756** Kalm *Rese* II.204 *(DA)*, Sallad-trä. . . i god jord. [=Salad tree. . . in good soil.]] **1813** Muhlenberg *Catalogus Plantarum* 42 PA, Cercis Canadensis. Red bud, Judas tree (salad tree). **1897** Sudworth *Arborescent Flora* 252 DE, *Cercis canadensis.* . . Salad Tree. **1940** Clute *Amer. Plant Names* 17, *C[ercis] Canadensis.* . . Salad tree.

salaeratus See **saleratus**

salal n |sə'læl| Also sp *sallal* [Chinook Jargon]

A **wintergreen 1** (here: *Gaultheria shallon*) native chiefly to the Pacific Northwest; hence n *salal(-berry), salalle-berry* the fruit of this plant. Also called **shallon**

[**1805** (1905) Clark *Orig. Jrls. Lewis & Clark Exped.* 3.274 nwOR, An old woman presented . . a kind of Surup made of Dried berries which is common to this Countrey which the natives Call Shele wele (*She-well*).] [**1825** (1959) Douglas *Jrl.* 104, *Gaultheria shallon;* called by the natives 'Salal,' not 'Shallon'.] **1833** in 1963 Tolmie *Jrls.* 230 swWA, Have supped on Sallal & at dusk, shall turn in. **1838** Parker *Jrl. Rocky Mts.* 202, The salalberry is a sweet and pleasant fruit, of a dark purple color, and about the bigness of a grape. **1855** (1874) Glisan *Jrl. Army Life* 249 swOR, Berries afford them a good substitute for bread; such as the blackberry, . . salalle-berry, salmon-berry [etc]. **1935** Davis *Honey* 91 OR, The stunted firs ended and they came into a great spread of waist-high salal. **1951** Morgan *Skid Road* 6 WA, The trees grew to the edge of the bluff, a thick stand of giant evergreens rising out of a tangle of underbrush—ferns and wild rose bushes and salal and Oregon grape. **1967** *DARE* (Qu. I44, *What kinds of berries grow wild around here?*) Infs OR4, WA19, Salal-berries; (Qu. BB50c, *Remedies for infections*) Inf WA19, Boil down skunk cabbage roots or salal-berry, use as poultice. **1977** Gillis *Killers Starfish* 79 WA, She started to lead the way through Mike's pile of salal cuttings. *Ibid* 77, High walls of salal so tangled and thick a rabbit couldn't get through it. **1994** Guterson *Snow Falling* 153 nwWA, Everything was familiar and known to her here . . the upturned root wads hung with vine maple, the toadstools, the ivy, the salal, the vanilla leaf, the low wet places full of devil's club.

2000 *DARE* File cOR, My aunt used to talk about picking salal [sə'læl] berries.

salamagundy See **salmagundi**

salamander n

1 Std: an amphibian of the order Caudata. Also called **lizard 2**; for other names of var of these see **ghost lizard, ground lizard 1, ~ puppy 1, hellbender 1, Hoosier salamander, leadback 2, man-eater 2, mole salamander, mud puppy, red-backed salamander, red ~ 1, 2, spring lizard, ~ salamander, tiger salamander, water dog, ~ puppy, ~ lizard, wood lizard, zigzag salamander**

2 pronc-sp *sallymander:* A **pocket gopher 1** (here: *Geomys* spp). Sth, S Midl, esp Gulf States Cf **sandy mounder**

1805 (1904) Lewis *Orig. Jrls. Lewis & Clark Exped.* 1.289, Their work resembles that of the salamander common to the sand hills of the States of South Carolina and Georgia. **1825** in 1974 *Fauna Americana* 153, *Geomys cinereus.* . . Vulgarly *Sand-rat, Goffer, Pouched-rat, Salamander,* &c. **1827** Williams *View W. FL* 27, The Salamander is a large mole, about half the size of a rat. It penetrates the earth in every direction, especially the pine barrens. **1884** Henshall *Camping in FL* 40, The surface of the ground was also perforated in many places with the holes of "salamanders." **1939** FWP *Guide FL* 25, The small rodent oddly termed 'salamander' is actually the pocket gopher. . . The salamander builds the countless little white mounds of sand that are a familiar sight in Florida. **1965–70** *DARE* (Qu. P29, . . *'Gophers'* . . *other name* . . *or what other animal are they most like*) Infs AR52, 55, FL16, LA12, 29, OK23, TX19, 32, 33, 37, 62, Salamander; AR51, Salamander—they are most like a mole or ground squirrel; most people know them only as salamanders; LA14, Salamander—very small pouch gophers; LA15, Salamander—they are not called gophers; FL7, Sallymander—the animal that burrows. **1966** *DARE* Tape FL16, Also, a pocket gopher in this area is called a salamander. . . And of course in the north a salamander you think of as being a water lizard. But here it's strictly a fur-bearing animal. **1975** Newell *If Nothin' Don't Happen* 114 nwFL, What we call a salamander is sort of like a big old brown mole that digs tunnels and throws the sand out into little hills a foot high or so. You'll see 'em all over the sand-hill country. **1986** Pederson *LAGS Concordance*, 8 infs, Gulf Region, Salamander(s); 1 inf, swAL, Salamander—locally—digs holes like chipmunk; 1 inf, cwFL, Salamander—proper name for gopher? 1 inf, cwLA, Salamander—similar to mole, lives underground.

salamander mussel n [See quot 1982]

A **freshwater clam** (here: *Simpsonaias ambigua*).

1982 U.S. Fish & Wildlife Serv. *Fresh-Water Mussels* 2.43, *Salamander Mussel* [=*Simpsonaias ambigua*]. Usually in colonies beneath rocks, the habitat of its host, the Mudpuppy, a salamander. **1991** IL Nat. Hist. Surv. *Biol. Notes* 137.17, *Simpsonaias ambigua.* . . Three museum records of the salamander mussel may be attributable to the Sangamon River. . . The Sangamon River basin is well within the historical range of the salamander mussel. **1992** Cummings–Mayer *Field Guide Freshwater Mussels MW* 90, *Salamander Mussel.* . . Small, thin, elliptical shell, poorly developed teeth.

salary n[1]

A sum of money pledged to a church; a tithe.

1970 *DARE* (Qu. CC11, *When somebody has had a lot of good luck . . he _____*) Inf VA41, Must a been paying his salary at church. [Inf Black] **1970** *DARE* FW Addit VA39, *Salary*—pledge of money to the church—tithe. Common. [Inf Black]

salary n[2] See **celery**

salat See **salad**

salatarus, salaterus See **saleratus**

sale n Cf **cry** v 1, **vendue**

An auction; hence n *sale-caller* an auctioneer; *sale-crying* conducting an auction.

1774 (1900) Fithian *Jrl.* 1.235 VA, And what in New-Jersey we call a Vendue here they call a "sale". **1941** Writers' Program *Guide IN* 416, After one week of instruction [in the Auctioneering School] the students are given practical experience, 'crying' public sales in the streets of Decatur. **1944** Wellman *Bowl* 46 KS, Len LeForce can give cards an' spades to any other sale-caller hereabouts. *Ibid* 162, Sale-crying in itself required ability of an unusual kind, coupled with sedulous practice. The auctioneer's song was an accomplishment denied most men. *Ibid* 167, Many never before had heard LeForce "call a sale." **1958** Randolph *Sticks* 101 **Ozarks,** One of 'em was a doctor, and the other fellow used to cry sales. **1960** Criswell *Resp. to PADS 20* **Ozarks,** *Cry a sale.* **1968** *DARE* Tape **IN30,** On a given day, which they called sale day, the settlers would go to Crawfordsville to the land office to buy land. They would bid against each other, but the land had to bring one dollar and twenty-five cents [per acre]. **1976** *PA Folklife* Spring 25, Over the years the salebill has developed distinctive . . characteristics. . . The title at the top is almost invariably *Public Sale,* a term that displaced the older *Public Vendue* early in the 19th Century. . . Chuck Bricker, an auctioneer in Mechanicsburg, titles his salebill *Outstanding Public Sale* when a large estate lot of valuable antiques is involved. **1982** *Barrick Coll.* **csPA,** *Sale bill*—broadsheet advertising an auction.

sale day n Also *sales day;* also with a day of the week specified, as *sales Monday* **esp Sth, S Midl** Cf **first Monday, trade day**

A day fixed for the buying, selling or bartering of goods; a market day.

1840 *Spirit of Times* 25 Apr 90/2, Sale days. **1877** VT Dairymen's Assoc. *Report* 8.19, Attempts have been made . . to falsify the truth of history, by representing that the first effort to establish 'sales days' or a country cheese market was made at Utica in 1870. **1887** *Century Illustr. Mag.* Apr 841 **cGA,** Only last sale-day you mighty nigh jolted the life out of Bill-Tom Saunders with the big end of a hickory stick. **1905** *DN* 3.93 **nwAR,** *Sales-day.* . . Market-day; trading-day; a day set aside at irregular intervals for buying, selling, and bartering. 'Yesterday was sales-day in Rogers.' Rare. **1938** Stuart *Dark Hills* 305 **KY,** It was so warm and pretty today and everybody stirring around in Greenup at the sales day. **1967** *DARE* File **neAL,** We visited Scottsboro, Alabama for their "First Monday" sale day. . . Around the courthouse square . . [was] the most awesome collection of people, iron ware, glass, pictures, coffee mills, chickens, rabbits, . . clothes, chairs, auto parts, . . silver, shotguns, and only the Lord knows what else. **1984** Wilder *You All Spoken Here* 75 **Sth,** Sales Monday; swap day; trade day; boneyard day: The first Monday in the month and time for trading livestock in sales usually near the county courthouse.

salem grass n

A **velvet grass** (here: *Holcus lanatus*).

1749 in 1905 Franklin *Writings* 2.386, I threw in . . a bushell of Salem Grass or Feather-Grass. **1881** Phares *Farmer's Book of Grasses* 81, *H[olcus] lanatus.* . . In the eastern States this grass is called Salem Grass and White Timothy. **1912** Baker *Book of Grasses* 134, *Salem Grass.* . . *Holcus lanatus.* . . Meadows, waysides, and waste places. May to August.

saleratus n, freq attrib Also sp *salaeratus* Also by metath *salatarus, salaterus* **chiefly Nth, esp NEast** *old-fash*

Potassium or sodium bicarbonate (baking soda) esp when used as a leavening agent.

1837 S. Graham *Treatise on Bread* 46 *(DAE),* Pearlash or saleratus is also used by them [*sc.* public bakers] in considerable quantities. **1846** *Knickerbocker* 27.510 **NEng,** The white sal-aeratus cake . . [is] quickly devoured. **1857** *Lawrence* (Kan.) *Republican* 11 June 4 *(DAE),* Saleratus is becoming almost as necessary with our people in the production of bread, as flour. **1859** in 1942 Hafen *Overland Routes* 11.154 **VA,** We pass a saleratus lake. **1871** (1975) Levy *Jewish Cookery* 67, *Saleratus Fritters.* . . A teaspoonful of saleratus . . flour . . milk . . salt . . eggs . . mix all together, and fry with plenty of butter or sweet oil to a light brown color. *Ibid* 128, *A Good and Sure Cure for Measles.* . . Have ready another bath, with a quarter pound of saleratus in hot water. **1898** Smith *Caleb West* 35 **NEast,** Set out before him were fried eggs sizzling in squares of pork; hashed potatoes, browned in what was left of the sizzle; saleratus biscuit, full of dark spots; and coffee in tin cups. **1904** Day *Kin o' Ktaadn* 97 **ME,** A dozen clothes-pins and a package of saleratus—all neatly tiered. **1915** *DN* 4.228 **wTX,** *Salatarus.* . . Soda. "You put too much salatarus in the biscuits." **1926** *AmSp* 2.78 **ME,** I must not forget what is most important of all, the hot "saleratus biskits." **1931–33** *LANE Worksheets* **ceMA,** A bannock contains no saleratus. **1941** *LANE* Map 282 *(A pan of biscuit[s])* 1 inf, **cwCT,** [sæl̩ˈretəs ˌbɪskɪt]; 1 inf, **swMA,** [ˌsæˈlə˰ˈre·təs ˌbɪskɪt]. *Ibid* Map 290 *(Yeast)* 1 inf, **cwCT,** We got snowed in for a week and got out of [ˈsalr̩etəs]. **1950** *WELS Suppl.* **csWI,** *Salaterus.* . . Baking soda. Pronounced

[ˈsæləˈtɛrəs]; **csWI,** *Saleratus.* . . Soda. **1968–69** *DARE* (Qu. H19, *What do you mean by a biscuit? How are they made?*) Infs **MN13, MA40, 69, NY92,** Saleratus biscuits; (Qu. BB22, . . *Home remedies . . for constipation*) Inf **MA14,** Saleratus and hot water. **1968** *DARE* Tape **NY88,** [FW:] What did you use to raise them [=buckwheat pancakes] with? . . [Inf:] Soda. . . And they called it saleratus [ˈsæləˌerɪts]. **1979** Flagg *Cape Cod Cooking* 217 **MA,** The saleratus and cream of tartar of grandmother's recipe has been replaced by the double acting baking powder of today. **1979** *UpCountry* Jan 38 **ME,** Nor was there agreement on what hot bread should be the Saturday night companion of the baked beans and pickles. . . Others preferred corn bread or saleratus biscuits. **1991** *DARE* File **seNY,** Saleratus = baking powder. Needed to make crullers.

salet See **salad**

salf See **self**

salivate v [From the archaic technical sense "to treat with a medicine—usu one containing mercury—that causes an excessive secretion of saliva" *(OED2* 1669 →)]

1 To make severely (or fatally) ill; hence ppl adj *salivated.*

1984 *Annals Internal Med.* 100.6.900 **cwAL,** Being *salivated* now means to be devastated by an illness, but in the last century it referred to the copious flow of saliva caused by mercury poisoning, often due to overzealous purging with calomel. **1988** *DARE* File **wNC** (as of c1910), I knew *salivate* . . with reference to fatal kinds or combinations of food. "That will salivate you if you eat it."

2 To shoot full of holes; to kill with violence. [Orig in facetious allusion to the double sense of *blue pill* a mercury-containing pill once widely used as a laxative, and **blue pill** a bullet]

1932 Tooné *Yankee Slang* 32, *Salivate:* Kill. **1934** Hurston *Jonah's Gourd Vine* 110 **AL** [Black], Nex' time he fool wid me, Ah bet Ah'll try mah bes' tuh salivate 'im. **1936** *AmSp* 11.200 [Euphemisms for hanging], Salivate. *Ibid* 317 **Ozarks,** *Salivate.* . . To mangle, to tear apart. 'Tom he jest salivated that thar dawg with a load o' buckshot.' **1939** (1973) FWP *Guide MT* 415, *Salivate*—To "liquidate"; to shoot full of holes. **1940** Stuart *Trees of Heaven* 65 **eKY,** I'll git 'im before he ever has time to draw a gun on me if he's in my reach. I'll knock 'im cold as a cucumber. I'll salivate 'im. **1956** Almirall *From College* 64 **CO,** Yellow, huh? I figured you was. Maybe just as well, because I'd sure hate like hell to have had to salivate you if you'd gone for your iron.

salivated See **salivate 1**

sallal See **salal**

sallet, sallit See **salad**

sally crab n Cf **jimmy 3**

A female blue crab *(Callinectes sapindus).*

1984 *DARE* File **Chesapeake Bay** [Watermen's vocab], Sally crabs—she-crabs—sooks.

Sallygodlin See **Sarahgodlin**

Sally in the saucer See **little Sally Water(s)**

Sally Lightfoot n

A red crab *(Grapsus grapsus)* native to Florida.

1937 *Natl. Geogr. Mag.* 71.210 **FL,** Tropical rock crabs, the "Sally Lightfoot" *(Grapsus grapsus),* swiftly scamper over the rocks in all directions, especially where they are drenched by salt spray. **1981** Meinkoth *Audubon Field Guide Seashore* 648, *Sally Lightfoot.* . . Mottled dark red and pale green, or solid red, with many white speckles. . Speed, agility, and keen eyesight make this large and colorful crab extremely hard to catch. **1999** *DARE* File **sFL,** There were Sally Lightfoots scuttling about on the rocks at Everglades City in January.

Sally Lunn n Also *Sally Lund, Sally Lunn bread* [*OED2 Sally Lunn* sb. 1.a 1780 →]

1 A rich, usu sweet, yeast bread or its quick-bread counterpart; see quots. **esp NC, VA** See Map

1847 (1979) Rutledge *Carolina Housewife* 207, *Sally Lunn.* Two eggs, two small cups of cream, two cups of loaf sugar, one pint of flour, half a pound of butter, one tea-spoonful of mace. . . add a tea-spoonful of tartaric acid, one and a half tea-spoonfuls of soda. **1853** (1982) Lea *Domestic Cookery* 76, *Sally Lunn.* Warm a quart of milk with a quarter of a pound of butter, and a heaped spoonful of sugar; beat up three eggs, and put in, with a little salt, and flour enough to make it stiffer than pound-cake; beat it well; put in a tea-cup of yeast, and let it rise; butter a fluted pan and pour it in; bake it in a quick oven, slice and butter it. **1879** (1965) Tyree *Housekeeping in Old VA* 34, *Sally-Lunn.* [4 recipes are given for yeast-leavened breads.] *Ibid* 36, *Quick Sally-Lunn* [leavened with soda and cream of tartar]. **1887** *Century Illustr. Mag.* 35.16 **VA,** A procession of little darkies . . was seen to pass and repass, supporting plates of hot batter-cakes, muffins, Sally Lunns, rice waffles. **1932** (1946) Hibben *Amer. Regional Cookery* 6 **VA,** *Risen Sally Lunn.* *Ibid* 7 **SC,** *Quick Sally Lunn.* **1940** Brown *Amer. Cooks* 637 **NC,** *Old-Fashioned Sally Lunn* . . flour . . salt . . sugar . . yeast cake . . milk . . eggs . . butter. . . Cover and let rise. . . Pour into buttered funnel cake pan. . . Turn out and carry to the tea table at once. *Ibid* 846 **VA,** *Sally Lunn* . . flour . . sugar . . baking powder . . salt . . milk . . eggs . . butter. . . Bake in a well buttered funnel pan, or in muffin pans. Eat with tea. All of the old-time Sally Lunns were made with yeast, and many were as sweet and rich as cake. **1965–70** *DARE* (Qu. H18, . . *Special kinds of bread*) Infs **VA4,** 83, 98, 104, 108, Sally Lunn (bread); **TN5,** Sally Lund; **VA33,** Sally Lunn—made in a loaf; eaten hot, and broken off in chunks; never cut; **NC36,** Sally Lunn bread—risen, baked in a round tube pan—light and sweet; **VA23,** Sally Lunn bread—between a cake and a bread; used for Sunday night supper; **VA42,** Sally Lunn bread—cake-like; **VA74,** Sally Lunn bread—old-fashioned. [8 of 11 Infs coll educ] **1986** Pederson *LAGS Concordance* (*Kinds of bread made of flour*), 3 infs, **AL, GA, TN,** Sally Lunn (bread). **1988** Lincoln *Avenue* 222 **wNC** (as of c1940) [Black], She was an excellent cook, turning out extraordinary cakes and pies or Sally Lunn or Charlotte Russe with effortless perfection.

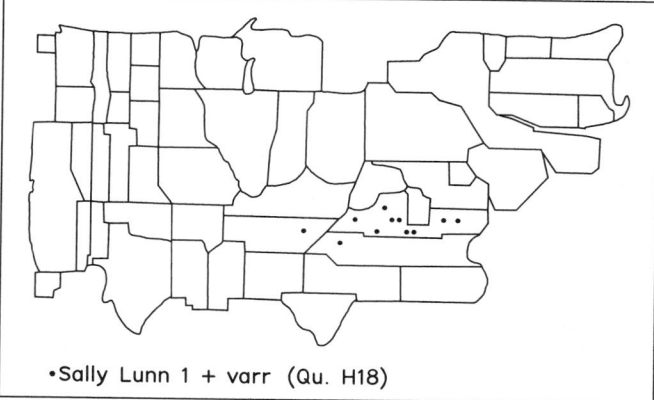

•Sally Lunn 1 + varr (Qu. H18)

2 See quots.
1966–69 *DARE* (Qu. H14, *Bread that's made with cornmeal*) Inf **IL55,** Sally Lunn—more like a pudding, made with cornmeal; (Qu. H63, *Kinds of desserts*) Inf **FL15,** Sally Lunn—whipped cream with sponge cake served in deep dish—old-fashioned. **1986** Pederson *LAGS Concordance* (*Kinds of bread . . made from cornmeal*) 1 inf, **csGA,** Sally Lunn = spoon bread; VA corn bread dish.

sallymander See **salamander 2**

Sally Walker See **little Sally Walker**

Sally Water See **little Sally Water(s)**

salmagundi n Also *sal(a)magundy;* abbr *sal* [OED2 1674 →] Cf **hushmagundi**
A cold plate of chopped or sliced meats, fish, eggs, and vegetables, usu artfully arranged and topped with a vinegar dressing; by ext, a meal consisting of a variety of dishes; a **potluck meal.**
1848 Bartlett *Americanisms* 291, *Salmagundi.* A Dutch dish common in New York. It is made of pickled or smoked shad, cut into thin slices or shreds, and sliced onions. The whole is then acidulated with vinegar. This dish is generally used at tea. **1871** (1975) Levy *Jewish Cookery* 25 **Philadelphia PA,** *Salamagundy.* . . Chop separately the white part of cold chicken or veal, yolks of eggs, boiled hard, the whites of eggs, parsley, half a dozen anchovies, red beet root, pickled cabbage, smoked beef, grated tongue, or anything well flavored and of a good color, a little onion, if desirable. . . The salamagundy may be laid in rows. **1967–68**

DARE (Qu. H45, *Dishes made with meat, fish, or poultry that everybody around here would know, but that people in other places might not*) Inf **NY66,** [sælməngʌndɪ]; (Qu. H70, *When people bring baked dishes, salads, and so forth to a meeting-place and share them together, that's a _____ meal*) Inf **NE3,** Salamagundy [ˈsɛləməˌgʌndɪ]. **1980** *Morning Call* (Allentown PA) 24 Nov B 4, [Column *Es Deitsch Schtick:*] We asked about something which one makes of beef, onions and vinegar. A couple of persons wrote us about it, . . [calling it] *Salmagundy.* **1991** *DARE* File **NE** (as of 1930s), In York, Nebraska, we used to call a potluck meal a *sal,* short for [ˌsæləməˈgʌndi].

salmon n Usu |ˈsæmən|; also |ˈsælmən, ˈsaɪmən| Pronc-sp *si-mon*

A Forms.
1899 (1912) Green *VA Folk-Speech* 388, *Simon.* . . Salmon. The upper bricks in a kiln . . so called from their colour. **1900–20** in 1944 *ADD* **cNY,** *Salmon.* . . [sælmən]. **1906** *DN* 3.154 **nwAR,** *Salmons.* . . Pronounced by the ignorant [saɪmənz]. **1941** *AmSp* 16.5 **eTX** [Black], *Salmon,* [ˈsaɪmənz]. **1942** in 1944 *ADD* **WV,** *Salmon.* . . [sælmən].

B Senses.   Cf **salmon trout**
1 Any of several fishes of the family Salmonidae, as:
a Std: a fish of the genus *Salmo,* esp *S. salar,* a food and game fish of North Atlantic waters and of freshwater. [OED2 13 . . →] For other names of *S. salar* see **black salmon 1, jack n[1] 24b(4), lake salmon 2, ~ trout 4, landlocked salmon 1, leaper 1, native trout, racer 2b, Schoodic salmon, Sebago ~, togue**
b Any of var fishes of the genus *Oncorhynchus* of chiefly Pacific waters and freshwater, but usu the anadromous **chum salmon, humpback salmon, sockeye salmon, chinook salmon,** or **coho salmon.** Note: The last two, as well as **rainbow trout,** have also been introduced into the Great Lakes. Cf **salmon trout 1c, e**
[**1759** Venegas *Hist. CA* (transl. Anon.) 1.47, Father Antonio de la Ascencion, speaking of the bay of San Lucas [Lower California], says, "With the nets which every ship carried, they caught a great quantity of fish of different kinds, and all wholesome and palatable: particularly holybuss, salmon, turbots, skates, pilchards [etc.]."] **1806** (1905) Lewis *Orig. Jrls. Lewis & Clark Exped.* 4.163 **nwOR,** The common Salmon and red Charr are the inhabitants of both the sea and rivers. **1828** *Western Mth. Rev.* 2.139, [The Shoshoni] lived indolently on dried venison and salmon, and prairie potatoes. **1860** in 1960 *Seattle Daily Times* (WA) 1 Jan mag sec 7 **cwWA,** Swan dined with Old Skipping, evidently a Clallam, "on mussel, skates, salmon and other Indian fixings." **1886** Turner *Contribs. AK* 110, *Onchorynchus gorbuscha.* . . This salmon is the smallest of all the species in this genus. **1908** Johnson *Highways Pacific Coast* 258 **OR,** The salmon have been kind o' played out the last few years up here. **1938** Schrenkeisen *Field Book Fishes* 49, Fresh steelhead [=*Oncorhynchus mykiss*] is an excellent table salmon. **1947** Hubbs–Lagler *Fishes Gt. Lakes* 34, Local names applied to some of these trout can be confusing. For example, a rainbow trout which has run into the Great Lakes and developed into a silvery fish with a steely blue colored head is called a "steelhead," and sometimes even a "salmon" by an over-enthusiastic angler. **1968** *DARE* Tape **CA**100, They're quite full of, there's some salmon in here. **1989** Lesley *River Song* 169 **cnOR** [Amer Ind speaker], "What do you think he saw?" "I don't know," Danny said. "Salmon, maybe." Willis nodded. "Thousands of them. . . Those big Chinooks that used to go a hundred pounds."
c =**lake trout 1.** Cf **salmon trout 1b**
[**1787** Pennant *Arctic Zool. Suppl.* 139 **Canada,** The Namaycush Salmon.] **1842** DeKay *Zool. NY* 4.240, The Mackinaw Salmon. *Salmo amethystus* [=*Salvelinus namaycush*]. *Ibid* 241, This magnificent Trout . . exists in all the great lakes lying between the United States and the Arctic ocean. . . Its flesh is reddish. **1870** McClung *MN in 1870* 180, *Varieties* [of fish]. . . Salmon or Mackinaw trout. **1886** Mather *Memoranda* 17 **Adirondacks NY,** The lake trout is miscalled "salmon" in many parts of this region. This error comes from the fact that in some places the lake trout is called the "salmon trout," and to distinguish the fish from the brook trout they call the latter simply "trout," and the former "salmon." *Ibid* 22, The "salmon" of the Adirondacks, which one hears so much of here, is simply the lake trout, sometimes called salmon-trout, and often the first part of the name only is used.
2 Any of var fishes of other families; see below.
a Any of several freshwater fishes, as:

(1) A fish of the genus *Stizostedion,* usu the **walleye** *(S. vitreum).*

1765 Rogers *N. Amer.* 177, In the rivers round Lake Ontario are salmon in great plenty. **1818** *Amer. Monthly Mag. & Crit. Rev.* 3.354, I have pretty nearly explored the ichthyology of the river Ohio, and the following catalogue of its fishes, is complete. . . Perca Salmonea [= *Stizostedion vitreum*]. . . Salmon [etc]. **1856** *Porter's Spirit of Times* 20 Dec 253/2 **Gt Lakes,** The same kind of fish [as in the Ohio River], is brought from the lakes and sold in our markets [in Cincinnati], and the fishermen tell me that on the lake shore they are called lake pickerel, but here salmon. **1865** Norris *Amer. Angler's Book* 120, *Lucioperca Americana* [=*Stizostedion vitreum*]. . . Of the many misnomers given to fish, that of "Salmon," as applied to this, is the most inappropriate. **1884** *Century Illustr. Mag.* Apr 908/1, The pike-perch becomes a "salmon" in the Susquehanna, Ohio, and Mississippi rivers. **1927** Weed *Pike* 29, In the southern streams where this fish [=*Esox masquinongy*] is called "Pike," the Walleye *(Stizostedion)* is generally called "Salmon." **1935** Caine *Game Fish* 31 **Sth,** Wall-eyed Pike—Stizostedion vitreum. . . *Synonyms:* . . Salmon.

(2) =**largemouth bass.** Cf **salmon trout 1f**

1856 *Porter's Spirit of Times* 25 Oct 129/2, There was not, never had been, and never could be a salmon within a thousand miles of the Kentucky River, and . . the fish so called by the people of that State is either the pike-perch . . or another analogous fish, sometimes called the growler, the *Gristes Salmoeides* [=*Micropterus salmoides*] of authors. **1933** LA Dept. of Conserv. *Fishes* 313, None of our other fresh water fishes has been given so many popular names as our Black Bass. . . It will be seen that such completely inaccurate designations as "Salmon," "Perch" and "Trout" have all been applied to this fine species.

(3) A squawfish (here: *Ptychocheilus lucius*). **esp AZ, UT**

1896 U.S. Natl. Museum *Bulletin* 47.225, *Ptychocheilus lucius.* . . The largest of the American *Cyprinidæ,* reaching a weight of 80 pounds, and having considerable value as a food-fish. Known locally as *"Salmon."* **1944** (1967) McNichols *Crazy Weather* 53 **AZ,** "Salmon," he gasped. . . The fish was no salmon, although it was popularly so called all along the [Colorado] river. It was a great chub, first cousin to the minnows found in all eastern streams, and an own brother to the Sacramento squawfish. **1963** Sigler–Miller *Fishes UT* 81, Typically, the "salmon" are said to lie in deep holes, especially below riffles, but when the [Colorado] river level rises they come in close to shore to feed on drift material. **1964** Lowe *Vertebrates* 141 **AZ,** *Ptychocheilus lucius.* . . This large minnow . . has nearly disappeared from the Arizona fauna, although a few adults have been caught in recent years in the lower Colorado River. . . A hundred years ago it was still common in San Pedro River (tributary to Gila River) near Charleston in Cochise County, where the residents called it "Salmon." The species is known only from the Colorado River basin, inhabiting the main channel and the larger tributaries.

b A **weakfish** (here: *Cynoscion nebulosus*) of Atlantic waters and freshwater. Cf **Santa Catalina salmon, salmon trout 2**

1884 Goode *Fisheries U.S.* 1.365, The Spotted Squeteague—*Cynoscion maculatum* [=*C. nebulosus*]. . . Owing to its shape and the presence of well-marked spots on the sides it is usually known on the Southern coast as the "Salmon" or "Spotted Trout." **1935** Caine *Game Fish* 145, Spotted Weakfish—Cynoscion nebulosus. . . Synonyms: Salmon [etc].

salmon bass n Cf **salmon B2a(2)**

Prob = **largemouth bass.**

1966 *DARE* (Qu. P1, . . *Kinds of freshwater fish . . caught around here . . good to eat*) Inf **AL2,** Salmon bass.

salmonberry n

A **raspberry B,** as:

a A shrub *(Rubus spectabilis)* native chiefly to the Pacific Northwest and Alaska, which produces usu orange fruits; also the fruit itself. [See quots 1934, 1937] Also called **salmon brush**

1844 in 1933 OR Hist. Soc. *Hist. Qrly.* 34.359, A salmon berry. . . being put into the mouth of a fish [*sc.* a salmon], destroys the charm. **1875** in 1962 FitzGerald *Army Doctor's Wife* 148 **AK,** I have just washed and put away some salmon berries. Did you ever see any? . . They are something like a raspberry and something like a blackberry, not being quite as sweet and good as either. **1890** *Century Dict.* 4966, *R[ubus] Nutkanus* is a similar western species [to *R. odoratus*] with white flowers; also, and better, called *salmon-berry.* **1915** (1926) Armstrong–Thornber *Western Wild Flowers* 236, *Rubus spectabilis.* . . It is

rather confusing that this should be called Salmon-berry in the West, for in the East that is the common name of *Rubus parviflorus.* **1929** Raine *Famous Sheriffs* 267 **wWA** (as of 1902), Walking up from Renton . . , Tracy met Miss May Baker, Mrs. McKinney, and young Jerrolds picking salmonberries. **1934** Haskin *Wild Flowers Pacific Coast* 173, *Rubus spectabilis.* . . There are three possible reasons why this plant came to be called salmon-berry. The first is from the fact that, in the fishing taboos of the Chinook Tribes, the salmon-berry held a large place. Coyote, according to one of their myths, was fishing for salmon. . . [and was told]: "When you kill a salmon go and pick some salmon-berries. When you have caught many salmon put salmon-berries in the mouth of each." The second possible reason is that the bark, which is astringent, was used by early explorers as a remedy for certain digestive disorders brought on by eating too largely of salmon. The third reason is the clear salmon-yellow color of some of the fruit. **1937** U.S. Forest Serv. *Range Plant Hdbk.* B140, *Rubus spectabilis.* . . Salmonberry, so called because of its large, juicy, typically salmon-colored fruit, is an attractive, erect, vigorous-growing shrub. **1966–68** *DARE* (Qu. I44, *What kinds of berries grow wild around here?*) Inf **AK3,** Salmonberries—looks like a flat loganberry, red or yellow—a weed; **WA**1, 19, 25, Salmonberries; **CA**105, Red salmonberries, yellow salmonberries—resembles salmon roe. [*DARE* Ed: Some of these Infs may refer instead to other senses below.] **1977** Churchill *Don't Call* 73 **nwOR** (as of c1918), Salmonberry was in the green bud stage, soon to be followed by its handsome, shy lavender flowers, the forerunner of breakfast berries. **1994** Guterson *Snow Falling* 120 **nwWA,** They ate their lunch there in the shadows of the hemlocks and gathered salmonberries.

b A red-fruited **thimbleberry** (here: *Rubus parviflorus*) native chiefly to the western US, Alaska, and the Upper Midwest.

1915 (1926) Armstrong–Thornber *Western Wild Flowers* 238, Thimble-berry—*Rubus parviflorus.* . . In shady mountain woods we find this attractive plant, which is called Salmon-berry farther east. . . This is found as far east as Michigan. **1937** U.S. Forest Serv. *Range Plant Hdbk.* B139, *Rubus parviflorus.* . . Thimbleberry, . . sometimes erroneously called salmonberry. . . [has] flattened fruiting-disks (receptacles), in contrast to the typical *Rubus* . . which has . . convex fruiting-disks. **1967** Harrington *Edible Plants Rocky Mts.* 273, *Rubus parviflorus* . . Salmonberry. *Ibid* 275, The Indians ate the fruits [of *Rubus parviflorus*] fresh, or managed to dry them for storage. They often ate them in the Northwest with half-dried salmon eggs (hence the common name salmonberry). **1967** *DARE* FW Addit **swWA,** Chills—new roots of the salmonberry; the Indian word was *chits* from which white kids developed *chills.* Old-fashioned. (Same as Thimbleberry.)

c =**cloudberry.** **chiefly AK**

1869 U.S. Dept. Ag. *Rept. of Secy. for 1868* 178, The salmon-berry . . *(Rubus chamaemorus).* All these berries, but especially the salmon-berry or *"morosky"* of the Russians *(Rubus chamaemorus,)* are excellent antiscorbutics. **1901** Brooks et al. *Reconnaissances AK* 170 **swAK,** *Rubus chamaemorus.* . . Salmon berry. . . Differs from the salmon berry of the States in that it has a solid core like the blackberry, while the salmon berry of the States is a cap, like the raspberry. . . Probably the most important food plant of Seward Peninsula. **1947** Bowles–Towle *New Engl. Cooking* 159, Blueberries, huckleberries, raspberries, and the less-known amber-colored baked-apple berries and salmon berries were all used for pies. **1979** *Theata* 7.37 **AK,** Salmon berries are small and round and look a little like a cluster of eggs. Within each individual berry are the salmon seeds and juice. When the berry isn't ripe, it is green and is covered with small leaves. When it is ready to ripen, the leaves come off, and the berry turns red to a reddish-orange. When it is fully ripe, the berry is yellowish. Usually one to two larger leaves are under the berry, and the leaves faintly resemble the raspberry leaves. **1982** *Alaska Wild Berry Guide and Cookbook* 1 (Tabbert *Dict. Alaskan Engl.*), The salmonberry of Western Alaska is "cloudberry" or "baked apple berry" in Southcentral Alaska. It is *Rubus chamaemorus.*

salmon brush n

=**salmonberry a.**

1940 White *Wild Geese* 345 **AK** (as of 1890s), Through the forest back of the house? That was tough going: "A tangle of salmon brush and devil's club, thicker'n hair." *Ibid* 349, The salmon brush did not look particularly unfriendly, but when they tried to buck it they had to lean their whole weight to move at all.

salmon-eater n Also *salmon-cruncher*

A person from the Pacific Northwest.

1947 Jones *Evergreen Land* 1 **WA,** I have been to other States and lived in some of them. I have even liked them. But I remain unregenerate, a Salmon Eater, an Apple Knocker, a Rain Worshipper, a Sage-brusher, and a Whistle Punk from the Big Woods. In brief, a Pacific Northwesterner. **1965** Bowen *Alaskan Dict.* 28, *Salmon cruncher*—A derogatory term for a *native,* probably derived from the native custom of rotting salmon until they are tender and then crunching open the heads for the partly liquified matter inside, which is a dainty.

salmonfly n West Cf willow fly

Any of several stoneflies (Plecoptera), esp *Pteronarcys californica.*

1926 Essig *Insects N. Amer.* 167, The salmon fly, *Tæniopteryx pacifica* [=*Pteronarcys californica*] . . is a black species with red and yellow markings and measures 13 mm. to the tips of the folded wings. **1948** Baumann *Old Man Crow's Boy* 48 **ID**, At the end of the high water in early summer, when the salmon flies were thick, we picked them off the willows and fished for trout of goodly size. **1967–69** DARE (Qu. R4, *A large winged insect that hatches in summer in great numbers around lakes or rivers, crowds around lights, lives only a day or so, and is good fish bait*) Infs **CA**136, 137, 145, 162, 171, **OR**1, 13, Salmon fly. **1972** Swan–Papp *Insects* 84, *California Salmonfly: Pteronarcys californica.* . . Anglers use the adults for bait; Indians used them for food, scooping up large numbers from streams after shaking the overhanging bushes. **1982** Sternberg *Fishing* 84, The salmon fly . . is a large species of stonefly that hatches in huge swarms on western streams. **1995** DARE File, Stonefly—called willow fly in the West and salmonfly in Montana. **1997** DARE File—Internet **swMT**, The salmonfly hatch begins during the first two weeks in July, starting below Livingston and progressing upstream into the canyons of Yellowstone Park.

salmon grouper n

A **rockfish 3** (here: *Sebastes paucispinus*).

1953 Roedel *Common Fishes CA* 121, *Bocaccio—Sebastodes paucispinis.* . . *Unauthorized Names:* Grouper, salmon grouper.

salmon-killer n

A **stickleback** (here: *Gasterosteus aculeatus*).

1882 U.S. Natl. Museum *Bulletin* 16.396, *Salmon-killer; Stickleback.* . . Very abundant northward [of Alaska]. **1903** NY State Museum & Sci. Serv. *Bulletin* 60.341, In the North Pacific and Bering sea there is a . . species [*of Gasterosteus*] . . which has been styled the salmon killer.

salmon of the Ohio See Ohio salmon

salmon shark n

A **mackerel shark 1** (here: *Lamna* spp).

1903 NY State Museum & Sci. Serv. *Bulletin* 60.40, The porbeagle, salmon shark, or mackerel shark [=*Lamna nasus*] is a very powerful and destructive species, and it has a wide distribution. **1928** Pan-Pacific Research Inst. *Jrl.* 3.3.11, *Lamna nasus.* . . Salmon Shark. Has been recorded from California and Alaska (perhaps erroneously). **1953** Roedel *Common Fishes CA* 15, *Salmon Shark—Lamna ditropis.* . . Coastal north Pacific from Alaska south to Southern California.

salmon-snatcher n Cf mackerel-snapper

1968 DARE (Qu. CC4, . . *Nicknames . . for various religions or religious groups*) Inf **WI**24, Salmon-snatchers—Catholics.

salmon trout n Cf salmon

1 Any of var freshwater or anadromous fishes of the family Salmonidae, as:

a Std: =**brown trout 1.** [*OED2* 1421 →]

b Usu **lake trout 1,** but occas also **brook trout.** [See quot 1938] **Gt Lakes, NEast** Cf **salmon B1c**

1705 *Boston News–Letter* 22 Oct. 2/1 [sic *DAE*—quot not found], Our men were refresh'd with variety of Fish, especially Salmon Trouts, some whereof 2 foot long. **1792** Belknap *Hist. NH* 3.179, Salmon trout. . . The *trout* is found in all the streams which flow from the mountains, and very near their summits. **1823** Cooper *Pioneers* 2.55 **cNY**, Bull-pouts, salmon-trouts, and suckers. **1842** DeKay *Zool. NY* 4.238, This [= *Salvelinus namaycush*] is the well known *Lake Salmon, Lake Trout* or *Salmon Trout* of the State of New-York. **1876** WI Comms. Fisheries *Annual Rept. for 1875* 8, 250,000 of the spawn of the salmon-trout [were stocked in Lake Geneva]. **1886** Mather *Memoranda* 21 **Adirondacks NY**, *Salvelinus namaycush.* . . Salmon trout. Parts of New York. **1908** Forbes–Richardson *Fishes of IL* 56, In our Illinois markets it is known almost wholly by the name of lake trout, but farther north the names of Mackinaw trout, salmon-trout, and namaycush are sometimes

used. **1938** Schrenkeisen *Field Book Fishes* 53, Its [=lake trout's] meat is frequently pink, whence the name Salmon Trout. **1966–67** DARE (Qu. P1, . . *Kinds of freshwater fish . . caught around here . . good to eat*) Infs **MI**44, **MA**6, Salmon trout. **1983** Becker *Fishes WI* 323, *Salvelinus namaycush namaycush.* . . Salmon trout.

c =**rainbow trout.** orig **West;** now also **Gt Lakes** Cf **salmon B1b**

1806 (1905) Clark *Orig. Jrls. Lewis & Clark Exped.* 4.166, The *Salmon Trout* are seldom more than two feet in length, they are narrow in purportion to their length. . . their jaws are nearly of the same length. . . at the Great Falls [of the Columbia River] are met with this fish of a silvery white colour on the belly and sides, and a blueish light brown on the back and head. . . in this neighbourhood we have met with another species which does not differ from the other in any particular except in point of colour. this last is of a dark colour on the back, and its sides and belley are yellow with transverse stripes of dark brown. **1896** U.S. Bur. Fisheries *Rept. for 1895* 291, *Salmo gairdneri* [=*Oncoryhncus mykiss*]. . . "Salmon Trout." . . Especially abundant in the lower Columbia, ascending Snake River as far as Angier Falls and headwaters of Salmon River, Idaho. **1904** *Salmon & Trout* 165, The steelhead . . , while in reality a trout, is popularly regarded as a salmon, and on the west coast is known as . . salmon-trout. *Ibid* 208, In every section of the country, on the Pacific slope as well as on the Atlantic, whenever a big steelhead, cut-throat, rainbow, or any other trout, sea-run or otherwise, of unusual size is taken, it is baptised at once a "salmon-trout," without designation of species; and the same popular name is given in the Middle West and East to the Great Lake trout or togue. **1938** Schrenkeisen *Field Book Fishes* 49, *Steelhead Salmon.* . . *Common Names.* . . Salmon Trout. . . When their run starts in late winter, they are the first fresh salmon shipped east from the Pacific coast. **1966** DARE (Qu. P1, . . *Kinds of freshwater fish . . caught around here . . good to eat*) Inf **NM**6, Salmon trout. [DARE Ed: This Inf may refer instead to sense **1e** below.] **1976** DARE File **nwMI**, At Rock Harbor [on Isle Royale] salmon trout are called channel trout. Salmon trout spawn in channels near the island. They are big, silver, almost speckled.

d =**Dolly Varden 1.** [See quot 1939] **West, esp AK**

1880 (1884) U.S. Census Office *Rept. Population Industries Resources AK* 73, In the lakes [of the Kuskokwim district], . . the salmon-trout is quite plentiful throughout the winter, and is secured by the natives with hooks and lines or dip-nets through openings in the ice. **1886** Turner *Contribs. AK* 104, *Salvelinus malma.* . . The Salmon trout is a resident of the smaller streams of the mainland and islands. **1907** U.S. Dept. Commerce Bur. Fisheries *Document* 618.63 **AK**, Some [species of trout] occur in extraordinary numbers—for instance, the Dolly Varden, or salmon trout, as it is known locally. **1939** Natl. Geogr. Soc. *Fishes* 293, The flesh [of *Salvelinus malma*], which is delicious when properly cooked, is often of a pale pink color similar to that of the Yellowstone blackspotted trout [=*Oncorhynchus clarkii*]. Thus both of these species are known in some localities as "salmon trout." **1946** Dufresne *AK's Animals* 234, In southeastern Alaska the principal form of the Dolly Varden spends a large part of its adult life in or near salt water, and is often referred to as the "salmon trout." **1991** Tabbert *Dict. Alaskan Engl.* 139, In North American English *salmon trout* has been long and widely used to name various large fishes, including the lake trout, the cutthroat trout, and the steelhead. In Alaskan writing *salmon trout* has frequently been applied to the Dolly Varden, though it is seldom used now.

e =**cutthroat trout.** [See quot 1939] **West** Cf **salmon B1b**

1882 U.S. Natl. Museum *Bulletin* 16.314, *S[almo] purpuratus* [= *Oncorhynchus clarkii*]. . . *Salmon Trout of the Columbia; Yellowstone Trout; Rocky Mountain Brook Trout.* . . Back and caudal peduncle profusely covered with rounded black spots of varying size. . . The red blotches on the lower jaw between the dentary bones and the membrane joining them is very constant and characteristic. **1904** [see **1c** above]. **1939** [see **1d** above].

f =**largemouth bass.** Cf **salmon B2a(2)**

1934 Vines *Green Thicket* 4 **cnAL**, He told her of the many red horses and black horses and salmon trout, red suckers and black suckers, buffaloes and drums, blue cats and yellow cats, he had caught.

2 A **weakfish** (here: *Cynoscion nebulosus*). **Mid Atl** Cf **salmon B2b**

1873 in 1878 Smithsonian Inst. *Misc. Coll.* 14.2.26, *Cynoscion carolinensis* [=*C. nebulosus*]. . . Salmon-trout; spotted sea-trout *(south coast).* **1882** U.S. Natl. Museum *Proc.* 5.607 **eSC**, *Cynoscion maculatum* [=*C. nebulosus*]. . . *Salmon Trout.* An abundant food-fish, caught with seines in muddy channels in the [Charleston] harbor. **1899** (1912) Green *VA Folk-Speech* 364, *Salmon-trout. . . A fish in Virginia waters which resembles both a salmon and a trout.* **1968** *DARE* (Qu. P2, . . *Kinds of saltwater fish caught around here . . good to eat*) Inf **MD**45, Speckled trout—same as salmon trout. **1984** *DARE* File **Chesapeake Bay** [Watermen's vocab], Spotted trout / speckled trout / salmon trout.

saloogie See **saluggi**

salpa n

A saltwater **sculpin 1** such as the **cabezon** or a **midshipman.**

1884 Goode *Fisheries U.S.* 1.259, *Sculpins of the Pacific Coast.*—The Cottidae . . are represented on the Pacific coast by about eighteen species, known by such names as "Sculpin," . . "Salpa," [etc]. . . "Salpa" is a Spanish word for toad, and applied also to species of Batrachidae.

salsa n Also sp *salza* [Span *salsa* sauce] **orig CA, SW, but now widely recognized**

A spicy condiment of which the main ingredients are tomatoes, onions, and hot peppers.

1895 *Overland Mth.* (2d ser) 25.485 **CA,** I'm so sorry for ye, too. Life without love is like eatin' bull-beef jerky without *salsa!* **1923** Wyman *Los Angeles Times Prize Cook Book* 114 (*Popik Coll.*), *Salza Sauce*— Take a cupful each of tomatoes, onions and a green pepper. . . [C]hop all together, add salt and enough olive oil to moisten. **1935** (1937) Steinbeck *Tortilla Flat* 292 **CA,** Her two sons . . carried a washtub of *salsa pura* between them. **1970** *DARE* (Qu. H57, *Tasty or spicy side-dishes served with meats*) Inf **CA**194, Salsa—made with tomatoes, onions, . . chilis, vinegar, oil. **1970** *DARE* Tape **CA**193, The other thing we used to make was the salsa. That was chili and tomato, chopped together very fine. Makes a regular sauce. . . You eat it with the meat. **1978** *Tucson Mag.* Dec. 84/3 (*OED2*), Steak and salsa rate high. **1986** *12000 Words* 170, *Salsa. . . a spicy sauce of tomatoes, onions, and hot peppers.* **1989** *Parade* 12 Nov 9, The Mexican food boom has everyone eating burritos, quesadillas, homemade tortilla chips and salsa.

salsify n

A **goatsbeard 1,** usu *Tragopogon porrifolius,* but also, usu with modifying adj, *T. dubius* or *T. pratensis.*

1822 Eaton *Botany* 488, *Tragopogon . . porrifolium* (vegetable oyster, goat-beard, salsify.) **1842** *S. Lit. Messenger* 8.203, Salsify, which we fondly call the oyster plant, . . is but an infant. **1856** *Harper's New Mth. Mag.* 12.855 **KY,** Davy's mistress sent him to market for some *salsify,* a delightful vegetable not much known at the North. **1876** Hobbs *Bot. Hdbk.* 219, Tragopogon pratensis, Meadow salsify, . . eaten as food. **1932** Rydberg *Flora Prairies* 888, *Tragopogon. . . Salsify.* **1957** Roberts–Nelson *Wildflowers CO* 56, *Salsify, Tragopogon dubius. . . This plant grows from 1 ½ to 2 ½ feet tall. . . There are two other species, one with yellow heads . . and one with purple rays.* **1960** Abrams *Flora Pacific States* 4.584, *Tragopogon pratensis. . . Meadow Salsify. Ibid* 586, *Tragopogon dubius. . . Yellow Salsify.* **1965–70** *DARE* (Qu. I4, . . *Vegetables . . less commonly grown around here*) 60 Infs, **scattered,** Salsify; (Qu. H36, *Kinds of soup*) Infs **MO**5, **OH**4, Salsify; (Qu. I5, . . *Kind of onions that keep coming up without replanting year after year*) Inf **MA**6, Salsify; (Qu. I7, *The small plants like onions with hollow green leaves that are cut up in a salad*) Inf **WA**30, Salsify; (Qu. S21, . . *Weeds . . that are a trouble in gardens and fields*) Inf **NY**103, Salsify; (Qu. S26a, . . *Wildflowers. . . Roadside flowers*) Inf **MO**38, Salsify. **1967** Harrington *Edible Plants Rocky Mts.* 220, *T[ragopogon] pratensis* and *T. dubius,* . . very similar to each other in general appearance . . , often called "wild salsify" or "goatsbeard," are preferred by some to the purple-flowered one. **1994** (1995) Snead *Hollow Boy* **nVA** (as of c1930), We usually had three or four vegetables, corn on the cob, string beans cooked with fat back, salsify once in a while, and always mashed potatoes and gravy. *Ibid* 111, I enjoyed about everything that we grew in our garden except salsify, which had an oyster-like flavor.

salt n

1 usu pl: A salt marsh; a coastal area where the streams are salt or brackish. **esp SC, GA coasts**

1674 (1912) Alvord–Bidgood *First Explor.* 223 **SC,** They went down ye river and came to ye mouth of ye salts. **1686** in 1940 *AmSp* 15.388 **VA,** Tobacco that grows on low Lands as far as the Salts. **1709** (1967) Lawson *New Voyage* 106 **SC,** The Birch grows all on the Banks of our Rivers, very high up. I never saw a Tree on the Salts. **1789** Morse *Amer. Geog.* 447 **eGA,** Immediately after you leave the salts, begin the valuable rice swamps. **1859** (1968) Bartlett *Americanisms* 162, The

lands in Talbot County, Md., are divided into freshes and salts. **1922** Gonzales *Black Border* 159 **sSC, GA coasts,** Most of them came from about Toogoodoo, "down on de Salt," as the inland negroes designate the sea coast and the contiguous lands lying along the salt rivers and creeks. **1942** (1965) Parrish *Slave Songs* 238 **GA coast,** All white residents who could leave fled at nightfall to the "salts"—as the sea marshes were called. **1990** Burke *Morning for Flamingos* 20 **seLA,** You would not guess that she had witnessed a massacre in her Salvadoran village, or that I had pulled her from a pocket of air inside a crashed plane, carrying illegal refugees, out on the salt.

2 See **salt grass a(1).**
3 An **oyster B1;** see quot. Cf **floater 7**
1968 *DARE* File **NJ,** Salts—small, firm oysters; oysters that are not placed in freshwater.

salt v, hence vbl n *salting* **orig West**
To place precious metals or minerals in (a mining claim) to make it seem more valuable than it is; to "plant" (such minerals) in a mine.

1852 in 1855 *Pioneer* (San Francisco CA) 3.146, The quicksilver which was procured at the Rancho, for the testing of the quartz, the victims declare was 'salted,' and they accused the *Rancheros* of conniving at the fraud. **1863** Goode *Outposts of Zion* 415 **CO,** The grounds have been "salted"—gold dust scattered to deceive. **1877** Wright *Big Bonanza* 405 **West,** Mr. Fair was close upon the heels of the men who put up the great Arizona diamond swindle and prospected their "salted" ground about as soon as the "salt" was sown. **1902** *Everybody's Mag.* Feb 188 **sCA,** We'll salt Barney's claim for him. . . and set him a-finding of it. **1929** *AmSp* 5.147 **CO** [Mining expressions], *Salting a mine* is accomplished by placing good mineral specimens in a poor mine in order to deceive a purchaser. **1939** FWP *ID Lore* 244, Mining jargon in the Pierce City area:—*Salt*—to salt is to place gold on a worthless prospect to deceive the unwary into investing. The deception is still practiced. **1949** *Natl. Geogr. Mag.* May 569 **Rocky Mts,** One group salted a Rocky Mountain mine with uncut stones bought in Rotterdam and sold stock in this "diamond mine." **1968** *Mojave Desert News* (CA) 4 Jan 4/6, It would seem that since the big gold rush of "49", every known method of salting a gold property had been used and public awareness would make it virtually impossible to salt a property today.

salt-and-pepper n Also *salt-and-pepper plant*
A **plantain** (here: *Plantago patagonica*).
1940 Steyermark *Flora MO* 497, *Salt-and-Pepper Plant* (*Plantago Purshii* [=*P. patagonica*]). . . Flowering stems longer than the leaves; flowers in long or short dense heads, none of the leaf-like bracts conspicuous. **1967** *DARE* Wildfl QR Pl.6a Inf **OH**14, Salt-and-pepper?

salt-and-pepper snake n
A **king snake 1** (here: *Lampropeltis getulus holbrooki*).
1929 Bell *Some Contrib. KS Vocab.* 189, Salt and pepper snake. . . Cited from Larned [KS] as applied to a snake. **1958** Conant *Reptiles & Amphibians* 169, *Speckled Kingsnake. . . The "salt-and-pepper snake"* with a profusion of white or yellowish spots scattered more or less at random over all the black or dark brown colored surfaces. **1998** *DARE* File—Internet, The speckled king snake (a.k.a. Salt and Pepper Snake), *Lampropeltis getula* [sic] *holbrooki* . . ranges from Southern Iowa to the Gulf of Mexico and West into Eastern Texas. This is a dark brown to black snake with a light yellowish or whitish spot on each scale.

salt back n
=**salt pork.**
1956 Ker *Vocab. W. TX* 268, *Salt pork . . salt back* [2 of 67 infs]. **1973** Allen *LAUM* 1.290 **Upper MW** (as of c1950), *Salt pork. . . Salt back,* not reported in the East, is the term of a western South Dakota cattleman of Ohio and Wisconsin parentage. **1986** Pederson *LAGS Concordance* **seMS** (*Salt pork*) 1 inf, Salt back; 1 inf, Salt back—lean and fat; thicker than bacon.

salt bacon n Also *salted bacon* **chiefly Sth, S Midl** Cf **salt back**
=**salt pork.**
1849 *Living Age* 23.156, The transition[s] from our luxurious home fare . . to pickled pork and salt bacon . . are . . not easily to be conceived. **1899** *Overland Mth.* (2d ser) 33.155, Much of the provisions that were to have been for use during the voyage were in some inaccessible recess of the hold, necessitating the appearance at meals of salt pork with a reg-

ularity that was not altogether appreciated by the many who did not possess a co-ordinate appetite for fat salt bacon. **1956** Ker *Vocab. W. TX* 268, *Salt pork* . . salt bacon [2 of 67 infs]. **c1960** Wilson *Coll.* **csKY,** *Salt bacon*—Hog meat that has been preserved by salt. **1961** Folk *Word Atlas N. LA* map 1015, Salt pork. . . dry salt bacon 15% [of 275 infs]. **1965** Carmony *Speech Terre Haute* 32 **cwIN,** *Salt pork.* . . Several terms are used . . for the sides of pork preserved in brine. The most frequent . . [is] the New England *salt pork.* . . Other forms . . *salt bacon* (1 [of 16 infs]). **1966** Dakin *Dial. Vocab. Ohio R. Valley* 2.334, *Bacon* usually means "smoked"—but that it does not always is shown by the terms *fresh bacon* and *salt bacon.* [*DARE* Ed: It is not possible to determine how many of the 246 infs responded with *salt bacon* in reply to the question re *salt pork,* as that response has been mapped (see Figure 111) in combination with *salt pork, salt meat, salt side,* without distinguishing among them.] **1967** *DARE* (Qu. H38, *. . Words for bacon [including joking ones]*) Infs **CO20, SC46, TX**12, Salt bacon; (Qu. BB50c, *Remedies for infections*) Inf **MO**5, Piece of salt bacon; **TX**12, Salt bacon poultice. **1971** Wood *Vocab. Change* 44 **Sth,** *Meat from hogs.* . . To return to the salted product. . . Among volunteered words, *streak-o-lean* and *salt bacon* may serve to identify linguistic subareas. **1973** Allen *LAUM* 1.290 **Upper MW** (as of c1950), *Salt pork.* . . Bacon = *salt bacon* [1 inf **ND**]; Salt bacon [2 infs **IA,** 1 inf **NE**]. **1986** Pederson *LAGS Concordance,* 27 infs, **Gulf Region,** Salt bacon; 1 inf, **neTN,** Salt bacon—very fat; 1 inf, **ceTX,** Salt bacon—very little lean; 1 inf, **seGA,** Salted bacon.

salt banking vbl n Cf **banker 2,** *DCan* salt-banker, *DNE* salt trip

Making an extended fishing voyage to the Newfoundland banks, during which the fish are preserved by salting.

1952 (1973) Thomas *Fast & Able* 7 **neMA,** In 1903 and 1904 Capt. Gayton took her salt banking.

saltbird n
=**red crossbill.**

1959 Natl. Geogr. Soc. *America's Wonderlands* 427 **wNC, eTN,** But I did see red crossbills. At Round Bottom a flock few in to take over our camp before the pack horses were loaded. Sam told us they used to swarm around salt licks for the cattle, so the mountain people call them "salt birds." **1960** Stupka *Gt. Smoky Mts.* 41, In years gone by when cattle ranged on the high mountain meadowlands, the herders knew this [=the red crossbill] as the "salt bird." Crossbills are exceptionally fond of salt, and since they were very approachable while feeding on the salt which had been distributed for the benefit of the cattle, the name they were known by was entirely appropriate. **1982** Powers *Cataloochee* 478 **cwNC,** The red crossbill, which is known by the locals as the saltbird because of its habit of staying by the licklogs where salt was put out for cattle.

saltbox n attrib [From the shape; see quot 1963] orig **NEng,** now more widely known

Being or having an asymmetrical sloping roof; hence nouns *saltbox (house)* a house, typically having two stories in front and one in back, covered by such a roof.

1842 Thompson *Hist. VT* 3.146, This fort was 120 feet long by 80 wide, and was built of yellow pine timber . . laid up about 16 feet high,—the houses were built against the wall, with a roof slanting up, (called a salt-box roof,) to the top of the wall. **1876** Ingram *Centennial Exposition* 717, One of the chief oddities of the Exhibition—the Hunter's Cabin. It was built of logs in the "salt-box" style and entirely open in front. **1900** Shelton (title), *The Salt-Box House: Eighteenth Century Life in a New England Hill Town (DAE).* **1944** *Sat. Review* 2 Sept 30, [Advt:] New England saltbox in scenic New York setting. **1951** Graham *My Window* 39 **ME,** It is a saltbox type, two stories in front sloping to one in the back. **1963** Haywood *Yankee Dict.* 138, *Salt Box House*—The ordinary man built a two and a half story house with rooms on each side of the front door. Later, if he prospered, he might enlarge by extending the rear slope of the roof down to the first floor level, thus providing rooms in back. . . Because the top of an old fashioned salt box for the table had about the same slope, this design came to be called the "salt box house." It is common in houses built in colonial times and has been widely copied in recent years. **1966** *DARE* FW Addit **MS,** *Saltbox house*—Very sloping roof. One side slopes lower than the other side. (I was told this term was common all over, but I have never heard it!) **1968** *DARE* Tape **CT**4, The saltbox house is common to New England. Originally it came as a part of a shed attached to the back of a house. . . I believe also there was some connection there with taxation. . .

They didn't tax some real estate at all, as real estate. . . depending on the number of cooking fireplaces you had in the house; **CT**5, On a house like this, where it's a so-called saltbox, more accurately called a lean-to house, the main house . . was a two room downstairs, two up, house originally. . . The saltbox, the old saltbox, was shaped like this. . . You opened up one side, and that's how it got its name, saltbox. **1976** *New Yorker* 22 Mar 125 **NYC,** Cunningly combining painted backcloths, a two-story saltbox frame, and picturesque detail . . Ming Cho Lee's decor . . was . . romantic. **2001** *DARE* File—Internet **MI,** Solve your outdoor storage problems with a new englander salt box shed. The unique slant-back roof-line creates a look all its own.

saltbrush See **saltbush 1, 2, 3**

saltbush n [*AND* saltbush 1846 →]

1 also *saltbrush:* Any of var plants of the genus *Atriplex* native chiefly to the western US. Also called **shad scale.** For other names of var spp see **buckbrush 3q, cattle spinach, chamise 2, cenizo 1, cornflake bush, desert holly 2, ~ saltbush, duck lettuce, fat hen 1, goose weed 1, greaseweed 1, greasewood 2b, hard-iron, hopsage 2, orach, pinkweed 3, poison clover, quailbrush 1, sagebrush 2, salt sage 1, saltweed, sheep fat, white sage, ~ thistle, wingscale**

1898 Davidson *CA Plants* 118, *Atriplex.* Salt Bush. Annual or perennial herbs or shrubs, more or less mealy or scurfy. **1920** Saunders *Useful Wild Plants* 54 **West,** Similarly useful [as food] to desert Indians are the seeds of species of Saltbush (*Atriplex canescens,* . . *A. lentiformis,* . . *A. Powellii,* . . *A. confertifolia*). **1940** Writers' Program *Guide NV* 13, The desert plants are the salt bushes, grease wood, seep weed, iodine bush. **1957** *Plateau* 30.2.33 **AZ, UT,** Shrubby plants dot both the terraces and the higher plateaus. Perhaps the most common are the various species of saltbush or shadscale. **1967** *DARE* FW Addit Inf **CO**7, Saltbush—an *Atriplex*—*A. canescens.* **1970** Kirk *Wild Edible Plants W. U.S.* 59, *Atriplex* species . . Saltbush. . . The leaves and young shoots may be used as greens; they have a distinct salty taste. . . Saltbush is widely scattered throughout the West in arid, alkaline, or saline soil. **1976** Elmore *Shrubs & Trees SW* 37, Four-wing Saltbush . . saltbrush. . . It is used extensively—and highly prized—by the Navajos as forage for their cattle, sheep and goats, especially in winter and early spring when other forage is scarce. **1990** *Plants SW* (Catalog) 66, Four-wing Saltbush makes an excellent cover for small wildlife. **1999** *DARE* File **UT,** Saltbrush—grows in the southern part of the state.

2 also *saltbrush:* A related plant of the western US, such as a **hopsage 1** (here: *Grayia spinosa*) or a **sea blite** (here: *Suaeda moquinii*). See also **gray saltbush**

1931 U.S. Dept. Ag. *Misc. Pub.* 101.33, Spiny hop-sage [=*Grayia spinosa*]. . . is a small bushy shrub, . . known also as . . Gray's saltbush, spiny sage, horsebrush, and saltbrush. . . The species is distributed from Washington to California, Utah, Wyoming, and Montana. **1949** Curtin *By the Prophet* 71 **AZ,** *Suaeda torreyana* [=*S. moquinii*]. . . Saltbush. . . A clammy shrub . . which grows in saline and alkaline soils. . . *Chuchk onk* [=Pima name for *S. moquinii*], meaning 'black salt,' produces flavor in cooking.

3 also *saltbrush:* A **groundsel tree** (here: *Baccharis halimifolia*).

1951 *PADS* 15.42 **TX,** *Baccharis halimifolia.* . . Salt bush. **1974** Morton *Folk Remedies* 35 **SC,** *Salt Bush.* . . *Baccharis halimifolia.* . . Abundant in salt marshes, lowlands, coastal hammocks, roadsides. . . All except extreme west of South Carolina and North Carolina. **1979** Little *Checklist U.S. Trees* 59, *Baccharis halimifolia.* . . Saltbrush. . . Range— Coastal Plain generally near coast. **1982** *Naples Now* May 37 **sFL,** Also found in the scrub zone is . . the *saltbrush* or *sea myrtle,* a shrub or occasionally small tree to 12 feet. Female plants produce mature seeds with silky white hair or "paintbrushes" in the fall.

4 A **marsh elder 1** (here: *Iva frutescens*).

1960 Vines *Trees SW* 997, *Iva frutescens.* . . Shrub of saline marshes. *Ibid* 998, *Iva frutescens.* . . Vernacular names are High Water Shrub, Salt Bush [etc].

salt cedar n

1 also *saltwater cedar:* =**tamarisk.** chiefly **SW, Gulf States**

1881 *Harper's New Mth. Mag.* 62.731, Salt cedars and stunted live-oaks . . were the only trees growing from the thin soil. **1895** U.S. Dept. Ag. *Yearbook for 1894* 425, Along the Gulf coast of Texas and the shores of southern California "salt cedar" is doubtless a good sand binder. **1929** Dobie *Vaquero* 290 **West,** The salt-cedars are low, and for hundreds of miles not a tree marks the course of the river. **1965–70** *DARE* (Qu. T5, . . *Kinds of evergreens, other than pine*) Infs **NM2, OK25, TX11**, 13, 16, 18, Salt cedar; (Qu. T13, . . *Names . . for . . tamarack*) Infs **AZ9, NM6**, Salt cedar; (Qu. T15, . . *Kinds of swamp trees*) Infs **NM13, TX78**, Salt cedar; (Qu. T16, . . *Kinds of trees . . 'special'*) Infs **TX5, 26**, Salt cedar. **1969** *DARE* Tape **TX72**, The salt cedar tree, down here, use up a tremendous amount of water. **1970** Correll *Plants TX* 1068, *Salt Cedar*. . . Planted for windbreaks and for sand binding. Most have become naturalized in such places as along streams (especially if saline), in and about salt flats and in waste places generally. **1986** Pederson *LAGS Concordance (Local trees)* 1 inf, **swLA**, Saltwater cedars.

2 See **salt-cedar grass**.

salt-cedar grass n Also *salt cedar*
=**salt grass a(6)**.

1911 *Century Dict. Suppl.* (at *cedar*), *Salt cedar*, creeping wiry grass, *Monanthochloë littoralis*, with many short bristle-pointed leaves on short branches, forming a good sand-binder. It is found along the coast of southern California and Lower California, and in southern Texas and southern Florida. **1950** Writers' Round Table *Padre Is.* 132 **csTX**, The sour wiry grass which Samuel Reid described may have been . . salt cedar grass (*Monanthochloe littoralis*) which is a fine creeping grass and is more notable for its artistic pattern than for nourishment.

salt-cedar weed n [See quot]
=**jointweed 1**.

1951 *PADS* 15.30, *Polygonella* sp.—Salt-cedar weed, from resemblance of the branches to those of *Tamarix*.

saltcellar n Also *cellar old-fash*
A saltshaker. Note: *Saltcellar* in ref to a small, open vessel used at the table for holding salt is widespread.

1950 *WELS Suppl.* **ceWI**, Salt shaker—old term. Salt cellar—now heard for shaker (also older term for open small dish). **1960** Criswell *Resp. to PADS 20* **Ozarks**, *Salt cellar*. Salt shaker. It was capped, but I believe *salt cellar* was used for both the capped and the open receptacle. **1965–70** *DARE* (Qu. G4, *A container for salt that has a cover with holes in it*) 148 Infs, **widespread, but more freq Nth, N Midl**, Saltcellar; **CO6, CT42, IN82, MI94, MA58, NY88, 205**, Cellar. [Of all Infs responding to the question, 70% were old; of those giving these responses, 80% were old.]

saltchuck n [*salt* + Chinook Jargon **chuck** n⁴] Cf **skookum chuck**, *DCan*
A body of salt water, esp an inlet or salt lagoon.

1868 Whymper *Travel AK* 45, An Indian, paddling in his 'frail kanim' on the great 'salt chuck' or sea, was swallowed—canoe and all—by a great fish. **1899** U.S. Fish & Wildlife Serv. *Fishery Bulletin* 18.72 **AK**, Into this salt chuck another stream empties. **1909** Denny *Blazing the Way* 120 **wWA**, The fish, of many excellent kinds, from the "salt chuck," brought fresh and flapping to our doors, in native baskets by Indian fishermen. **1930** Williams *Logger-Talk* 21 **Pacific NW**, *Chuck*: A body of water, as in *salt chuck* for Puget Sound. **1951** *AK Sportsman* April 28, Any salt chuck is a lagoon near enough to sea-level that the flow of its outlet stream is reversed by the rising tide. **1958** McCulloch *Woods Words* 156 **Pacific NW**, *Saltchuck*—The ocean. **1990** *AK Fish & Game* 22.3.4, Roosevelt Lagoon is an estuary influenced both by the ocean via a salt chuck at the head of Naha Bay and by the Naha River.

salt clover n
A **sour clover** (here: *Trifolium obtusifolium*).

1902 U.S. Natl. Museum *Contrib. Herbarium* 361, *Trifolium obtusiflorum*. . . very distinctly characterized by the peculiar sticky exudation which even at midday in June covers the flower heads and growing stems like dew. This exudation has a strong acid taste and on this account the clover is variously known as "sour" or "salt" clover. **1911** *Century Dict. Suppl.* (at *clover*), Salt clover. See sour clover. [*Ibid*, Sour clover. . . *T[rifolium] obtusifolium*, a species having an acid taste and clammy with an acid exudation. The Indians regard it as one of the best for eating.] **1920** Saunders *Useful Wild Plants* 140 **CA**, Next to this [=*Trifolium virescens*] in favor [with the Indians of Mendocino County] is the "sour" or "salt clover" (*T. obtusiflorum* . .) with narrow, saw-toothed leaflets, whitish blossoms with purple centers, and a clammy, acidulous exudation that covers the leaves and flowers.

salt dip See dip n¹ 8

salted bacon See salt bacon

salter n
1 A **brook trout** found in, or returning from, the sea.

1890 *Century Dict.* 5319 **NEng**, *Salter*, . . a trout about leaving saltwater to ascend a stream. **1904** *Salmon & Trout* 321, Along the New England shores, particularly those of Massachusetts in Barnstable County and in the salt estuaries and bays of Long Island, . . the river-trout will be found in salt water, remaining there for some months and returning to fresh water when the spawning instinct impels them. . . In Massachusetts these salt-water migrators are called "salters"; in all other sections, "sea-trout."

2 A small vessel used at the table for holding salt; rarely, a saltshaker. Cf **saltcellar**

1959 Tallman *Dict. Amer. Folkl.* 260, *Salter or salt cellar*—In colonial times. . . the salter was placed in the center of the table in continuance of a custom started in England where the position of the salter indicated the relationship of the diners. **1967–69** *DARE* (Qu. G3, *A container for salt that's put on the table—if it's open [without a cover]*) Infs **IL45**, 103, **KS1, VA31**, (Individual) salters; **IA25**, Salter—old-fashioned; **OH8**, Salter; **OH84**, Salters—old-fashioned; (Qu. G4, *A container for salt that has a cover with holes in it*) Inf **IA7**, Salter; **NY65**, Pepper and salter. **1967** *DARE* FW Addit **OR**, Salter—an open salt dish. Common.

salt farmer See saltwater farm

salt grass n Cf **marsh grass**
Any of var plants common to alkaline or brackish areas, such as:

a Any of var grasses, as:

(1) A **cordgrass**, esp *Spartina patens*. **chiefly coastal regions** Cf **red salt, thatch grass, white salt**

1704 in **1894** Providence RI Rec. Comm. *Early Rec.* 5.224, The which sd Cove is a place of salt Grass called Thatch. **1822** Eaton *Botany* 337, *Limnetis*. . . *juncea* [=*Spartina patens*] . . rush salt grass. *Ibid* 338 **NY**, [*Limnetis*] *polystachia* [=*S. cynosuroides*] . . many-spiked saltgrass. . . Very abundant near the Patroon's mansion house in Albany. **1875** *Fur Fin & Feather* 119 **cAtl**, Very soon after feeding on the succulent salt-grasses . . [the ducks] acquire the delicious flavor for which they are so highly esteemed. **1884** Vasey *Ag. Grasses* 45, *Spartina juncea* [=*S. patens*] (Marsh grass, Salt grass, Rush salt grass.) . . Usually 1 to 2 feet high. . . This grass forms a large portion of the salt marshes near the seacoast. It makes an inferior hay, called salt-hay. **1939** Tharp *Vegetation TX* 46, Salt grass, tall (*Spartina spartinae*) . . is the most conspicuous grass along the immediate Texas coast throughout that coast's extent. Growing in dense clumps sometimes three feet across. . . [and] though coarse and tough in age, it is tender and palatable when young. **1948** Pearson *Sea Flavor* 118 **NH**, Above the thatch-grass area is the zone of . . the salt grass. . . Here . . one can find three grasses—fox grass [=*Spartina patens*], spear grass [=*Puccinellia maritima*], and spike grass [=*Distichlis spicata*]. They grow from 10 to 15 inches tall. **1965–70** *DARE* [see **a(2)** below]. **1986** [see **a(2)** below].

(2) A grass (*Distichlis spicata*) found throughout much of the US. Also called **alkali grass 1, marsh ~, marsh spike-~, spike-~, wire ~** Cf **marsh hay, salt ~**

1774 (**1884**) Hutchinson *Diary* 1.240 **MA**, The grass appears unlike our salt grass: more like what some call bastard grass, when fed. **a1816** in **1848** GA Hist. Soc. *Coll.* 3.1.43, Such is the attachment of horses to this moss, or as the traders call it, salt grass, that when they are removed, they retain so great a fondness for it, that they will attempt, from any distance within the neighboring nations, to return to it. **1852** Stansbury *Expedition* 235 **WY**, The only vegetation, to-day, has been a little dwarf artemisia, grease-bush, rabbit-bush, [and] salt-grass. **1894** *Jrl. Amer. Folkl.* 7.104 **nwNE**, *Distichlis spicata*, . . salt-grass. **1910** Hart *Vigilante Girl* 350 **SW**, The little stream . . ran from the spring through bunches of salt grass. **1937** St. John *Flora SE WA & ID* 40, *Salt Grass*. . . Alkaline shores and flats, in the scabland along the western border. **1951** Martin *Amer. Wildlife & Plants* 438, *Saltgrasses—Distichlis*. . . are confined to salty areas . . and for this reason are conspicuous only in the West and in seaboard marshes. In coastal areas they often occur in a zonal association with cordgrass. **1965–70** *DARE* (Qu. L8, *Hay that grows naturally in damp places*) Inf **CT6**, Swamp grass—called "salt grass" along the seashore; **ME5**, Salt grass—cut near ocean in salt marshes; **NY48**, Salt grass—hay grew wild in salt water; (Qu. L9a, . . *Kinds of grass . . grown for hay*) Inf **KS6**, Salt grass; **TX12**, Salt grass—winter pasture; (Qu. S8, *A common kind of wild grass that grows* *in fields: it spreads by sending out long underground roots, and it's hard to get rid of*) Infs **CA**2, 157, **KS**6, **NM**9, **UT**4, Salt grass; **MT**5, Salt grass—grows along alkali cricks; (Qu. S9, . . *Kinds of grass that are hard to get rid of*) Inf **CA**65, Salt grass—breeds ladybugs—plow under, comes up again; **CO**31, Salt grass or wild grass—in the lawn; **KS**15, **MA**124, Some kind of salt grass near the beaches; **NM**2, Salt grass—comes up early—good grazing—a prairie grass; **NM**9, Salt grass—similar [to crab grass]—found where there's more moisture; **NV**8, Salt grass or joint grass—a pest; **SD**8, Salt grass; (Qu. S26e, *Other wildflowers not yet mentioned;* not asked in early QRs) Inf **TX**19, Salt grass—grows on salty land. [*DARE* Ed: Some of these Infs may refer instead to other senses.] **1986** Pederson *LAGS Concordance* 1 inf, **cFL,** Salt marshes with salt grass; 1 inf, **ceTX,** Salt grass—the land itself; 1 inf, **ceTX,** Salt grass—used as cattle feed—grows in marsh.

(3) =dropseed 3. West

1886 Havard *Flora W. & S. TX for 1885* 529, *Sporobolus airoides,* the Salt Grass of the Pecos; grows on all the low saline prairies of that stream and farther west and north. It purges at first, and may cause severe colic in horses and mules; cattle are but slightly affected, and seem to relish it. **1889** Vasey *Ag. Grasses* 107, *Sporobolus airoides.* . . is common on the arid plains of the West, is sometimes called salt grass, and affords persistent pasturage where other grasses are trampled out. **1913** (1979) Barnes *Western Grazing* 54, There are great areas along the rivers and in the alkali lands which grow a fine crop of sacaton (Sporobolus), sometimes but erroneously called salt grass. **1937** U.S. Forest Serv. *Range Plant Hdbk.* G109, *Sporobolus airoides.* . . also known as . . finetop saltgrass, . . is a robust, perennial grass, widely distributed from Washington to South Dakota, western Texas, and California. . . In the Southwest it . . is of considerable importance as a forage plant. . . This species . . is eaten freely by cattle and horses. **1951** Porter *Ragged Roads* 65 **OK,** The salt-grass-levels here seemed low and quiet and the sun beat down without mercy through the mottled shade.

(4) as *Mexican salt grass*: A **lovegrass** (here: *Eragrostis obtusiflora*).

1912 Wooton–Standley *Grasses NM* 120, *Mexican Salt Grass* is the name given to *Eragrostis obtusiflora* which occurs on the playas at the extreme southwestern corner of the State in alkaline soil. This might easily be mistaken for ordinary salt grass [=*Distichlis spicata*] which it resembles in many respects but the inflorescence is somewhat different. It is of some importance in the region mentioned and may . . [have] been overlooked on account of its similarity to Salt Grass.

(5) A **sprangletop** such as *Leptochloa fascicularis* or *L. mucronata.* Cf **salt-meadow grass b**

1930 OK Univ. Biol. Surv. *Pub.* 2.51, *Leptochloa fascicularis.* . . Clustered Salt-grass. . . *Leptochloa filiformis* [=*L. mucronata*]. . . Feather or Salt-grass. **1933** Small *Manual SE Flora* 118, *Leptochloa.* . . Salt-grasses. **1973** Hitchcock–Cronquist *Flora Pacific NW* 647, *L[eptochloa] fascicularis.* . . Clustered salt-grass. . . Coastal, in brackish water; . . inl[and] in moist habitats.

(6) A low-growing perennial grass *(Monanthochloe littoralis)* of salt marshes, native to Florida, Louisiana, Texas, and California. Also called **salt-cedar grass**

1939 Tharp *Vegetation TX* 46, Salt grass, fine *(Monanthochloa* [sic] *littoralis).* . . is found in wet flat saline situations along the coast, and inland to Gonzales County. . . It is . . important . . locally . . , but it is too tough and salty to be of any value for grazing.

(7) An **alkali grass 2** (here: *Puccinellia maritima*). Cf **salt-meadow grass c**

1948 [see **a(1)** above].

b =glasswort.

1942 *Torreya* 42.159 **CA,** *Salicornia* spp. . . Salt-grass, San Luis Obispo. **1954** Sprunt *FL Bird Life* 480, These sparrows [=*Ammodramus maritimus mirabilis*] lived in isolated small colonies in patches of tall marsh grass *(Spartina patens juncea)* and in salt grass *(Salicornia)* on Cape Sable.

salt hay n **chiefly N Atl** See Map   Cf **marsh hay, meadow hay, ~ musk**

Hay made from plants of brackish coastal areas, esp **black grass, cordgrass,** or **salt grass a(2).**

1648 in 1852 MA Hist. Soc. *Coll.* 4th ser 1.204, Salt hay and fresh there thousands of acres I doe deeme. **1732** (1901) Hempstead *Diary* 23 Sept 252 **seCT,** I went to Mamacock & fetch a Ld of Salt hay alias Rushes that grew on Capt Houghs Medow. **1790** Deane *New Engl. Farmer* 191, Salt hay should not be cut when the full or the change of

the moon is approaching, lest the tides should be high, before it can be got off the marsh. **1843** *Knickerbocker* 22.34 **NY,** Range your eye along the summits of the salt-hay stacks. **1872** Schele de Vere *Americanisms* 408, *Salt-Hay,* a very important product of salt-marshes, is of two principal sorts, called *salt-grass* and *black-grass.* **1884** [see **salt grass a(1)**]. **1885** Jewett *Marsh Is.* 41 **ME,** The men folks would all be off about the salt hay. **1907** *DN* 3.179 **seNH,** *Salt hay.* . . Hay from salt marshes on the coast. "He went every year to Salisbury Ma'sh to cut salt hay." **1911** NJ State Museum *Annual Rept. for 1910* 233, The green carpet which covers miles upon miles of our coastal marshes consists mainly of the three species above mentioned [=*Spartina patens, Distichlis spicata,* and *Juncus gerardi*], and the "salt hay" that the farmers along the shore are in the habit of gathering is composed of the same plants. **1928** Beston *Outermost House* 29 **Cape Cod MA,** The seaside sparrow keeps more to the marsh rim and the salt-hay mowings. **1945** Beck *Jersey Genesis* facing 82 **seNJ,** [Caption:] Charlie Weber, last of the salt hay men to use a barge on the Mullica. **1965–70** *DARE* (Qu. L8, *Hay that grows naturally in damp places*) Infs **CT**17, **MA**40, **NJ**16, 22, **NY**36, 79, 107, Salt hay; (Qu. L9a, . . *Kinds of grass . . grown for hay*) Inf **MA**55, Around here there's salt hay—grows near salt water; **NJ**22, Salt hay; (Qu. L9b, *Hay from other kinds of plants [not grass];* not asked in early QRs) Inf **NJ**53, Salt hay; (Qu. C6, . . *A piece of land that's often wet, and has grass and weeds growing on it)* Inf **NJ**15, In South Jersey the meadows are salt marshes along the coast; salt hay was harvested here. **1968** *DARE* Tape **CT**14, This hay is supposed to have no weed seed in it. You see, it's a salt hay and people use it to mulch, to cover strawberry beds and one thing and another. **1986** Pederson *LAGS Concordance,* 2 infs, **nwFL, swGA,** Salt hay.

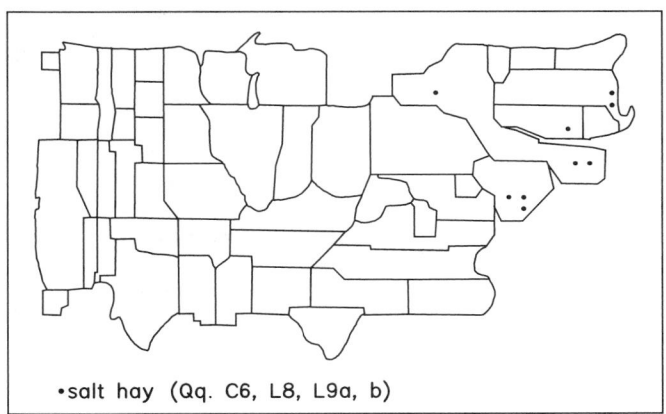

•salt hay (Qq. C6, L8, L9a, b)

salt hole n **NEast**

A small depression, esp in a salt marsh, that fills with salt water.

1691 *Jamaica* (L.I.) *Rec.* I.391 *(DA)* **seNY,** What salt holles shall fall in ye sd. meadow ye sd. Mr. Whitte to make up with mowable meadow. **1894** *DN* 1.333 **NJ,** *Salt holes:* pool holes of small size filled with salt water. Frequent in marshes. **1913** *DN* 4.57 **seMA,** *Salt-hole.* . . (1) Any depression in which salt water is left by the ebbing tide. (2) A depression in a salt marsh which is flooded only by "high-course" tides and in which the water stagnates between "high-course" and "high-course." "Look out you don't let the horse get in a salt-hole if you use him to mow the salt-meadow!"

salt horse n [*OED2* (at *salt* a. 2.b) 1836 →] **esp NEng** Cf **salt junk**

Salt beef.

1847 Melville *Typee* 1, There is nothing left us but salt-horse and sea-biscuit. **1864** in 1983 *PADS* 70.49 **ce,sePA,** Next (this) morning they. . . gave us a breakfast of clear hot coffee, bread, & 'salt hoss'. **1888** *Century Illustr. Mag.* 36.467, He knew that "salt-horse" and "cow-feed" were nicknames [among Civil War soldiers] for corned-beef and vegetables. **1905** Lincoln *Partners* 96 **Cape Cod MA,** If you're dyin' to eat salt-hoss and smell bilge, you can go in. **1922** *DN* 5.189, *Salt horse.* Corned beef. **1936** *AmSp* 11.44 [Soda jerker jargon], *Salt horse.* Corned beef. **1938** Tripp *Flukes* 33 **MA,** He had a voice that sounded like a rasp which he attributed to the tons of salt horse that had slid down his throat during his seafaring days. **1941** *LANE* Map 303 *(Dried beef, smoked beef), Corned beef* . . 1 inf, **Cape Cod MA,** Salt horse; 1 inf, **Cape Cod MA,** Salt horse—sailor's term for beef pickled in saltpeter. **1942** ME Univ. *Studies* 56.37, Their meat was "salt horse," or salt beef, tough and red with saltpeter. **1947** Bowles–Towle *New Engl. Cooking* 47, Cooks on Nantucket whalers and other seagoing vessels frequently served lobscouse, a dish made of salt beef—familiarly known as "salt horse"—potatoes, onion, and pepper stewed together. **1957** Beck *Folkl. ME* 194, Generally the salt beef was not dignified with the name beef, but was referred to as "salt horse."

salting See **salt** v

salt junk n [From *junk* old rope; cf *OED2 junk* sb.² 3]
=**salt horse**.
   1792 in 1888 Cutler *Life* 1.486, I had infinitely rather sit down with you to a piece of salt junk at one o'clock than be tormented with the parade. **1852** U.S. Army Corps Topog. Engineers *Exped. Gt. Salt Lake* 171, A very few days' immersion . . [changed] its character from corned beef to what the sailors called "salt junk." **1858** in 1966 Boller *MO Fur Trader* 41 **MO,** For the best part of the time we have had nothing but salt junk to eat. **1926** Ashley *Yankee Whaler* 139, *Salt Horse:* The common name aboard ship for salt beef: similar to corned beef but more briny. . . *Salt Junk:* Another name for the above. **1929** Dobie *Vaquero* 25 **TX** (as of c1870s), Any man with a herd of cattle that he could not dispose of otherwise might set up a packery in which to take off their hides and make "salt junk" of their meat.

salt log n
=**lick-log 1**.
   a1816 in 1848 GA Hist. Soc. *Coll.* 3.1.45, The range is a good one for stock. The owners of horses have a place called a *stomp*. They select a place of good food, cut down a tree or two, and make salt logs. **1966** *DARE* FW Addit **OK23,** *Salt-log*—a log with notches cut into it to hold salt for cattle. **1968** Adams *Western Words* 177, *Lick log*. . . Also called *salt log*.

salt-marsh See **salt-marsh grass**

salt-marsh bulrush n
   A bulrush (*Bolboschoenus robustus*) native chiefly to Atlantic, Gulf, and Pacific coastal areas. Also called **angle grass, coco ~ 2, goose ~ 1d, nut ~ 2, spurt ~, three-cornered ~, three-square, turk's head, wild chufa**
   1901 Jepson *Flora CA* 87, *S[cirpus] robustus* [=*Bolboschoenus r.*] . . *Salt-Marsh Bulrush* . . Rootstock stout, often forming hard woody tubers. . . Common in brackish marshes along the coast, and in moist alkaline soils in the interior. **1911** NJ State Museum *Annual Rept. for 1910* 270, *Scirpus robustus*. . . *Salt Marsh Bulrush*. . . Common all along the coast and the bay shore, in salt marshes. **1946** Tatnall *Flora DE* 55, *Salt Marsh Bulrush*. Common in salt marshes of the Coastal Plain. **1975** Duncan–Foote *Wildflowers SE* 234, *Saltmarsh Bulrush*. . . Common. Brackish marshes and ditches; se Tex into Fla and Mass; Cal. July–Sept.

salt-marsh caterpillar n [See quot 1980]
   The larva of a **tiger moth** (here: *Estigmene acrea*).
   1852 Harris *Treatise Insects* 269 **MA,** The salt-marsh caterpillar, an insect by far too well known on our seaboard, and now getting to be common in the interior of the State, whither it has probably been introduced, while under the crysalis form, with the salt hay annually carried from the coast by our inland farmers, closely resembles the yellow bear in some of its varieties. **1854** Emmons *Agriculture NY* 5.225, *Spilosoma acrea*. Saltmarsh Caterpillar. **1949** Swain *Insect Guide* 96, Salt-marsh Caterpillar—*Estigmene acrea*—Found throughout our region, the larvae being destructive chiefly in the late summer. **1980** Milne–Milne *Audubon Field Guide Insects* 788, Because these caterpillars [=*Estigmene acrea*] often feed on grasses in salt marshes, they are sometimes called "Salt Marsh Caterpillars."

salt-marsh cordgrass See **salt-marsh grass**

salt-marsh fleabane n
   A **marsh fleabane 1** (here: *Pluchea camphorata* or *P. odorata* var *odorata*).
   1848 Gray *Manual of Botany* 217, *P[luchea] camphorata*. . . *Salt-marsh Fleabane*. . . Salt marshes, Massachusetts to New Jersey and southward. **1901** Lounsberry *S. Wild Flowers* 515, *Salt-marsh Fleabane. Pluchea camphorata*. . . In the salt marshes we see the pale bloom of this plant, which is credited with emitting an odour much like that of camphor and is therefore sought to keep away moths. **1946** Tatnall

Flora DE 266, *P[luchea] purpurascens* [=*P. odorata* var *odorata*]. . . *Salt Marsh Fleabane*. Common in salt marshes, and on the shores of Delaware River and Bay, and Atlantic Ocean; less frequent in fresh to brackish estuaries along Chesapeake Bay. **1996** *Audubon Mag.* 98.53 **seCT,** We began to encounter brackish-water species—salt-marsh fleabane, now in pink bloom, riversedge, rough cordgrass, sea lavender, and water smartweed.

salt-marsh grass n Also *salt-marsh (cordgrass)* Cf **salt-meadow grass a**
   A **cordgrass**, usu *Spartina alterniflora*.
   1829 *S. Agriculturist* Feb 96, Can any of your readers inform me of the relative advantages of using Salt Mud, and Salt Marsh, cut green. **1848** Gray *Manual of Botany* 586, *S[partina] glabra* [=*S. alterniflora*]. . . *Smooth Salt-Marsh Grass*. . . Muddy salt and brackish marshes, common on the coast. **1869** Porcher *Resources* 679 **Sth,** *Salt Marsh Grass (Spartina glabra)*. . . This plant is greedily eaten by horses and cattle; and though it affords a good pasturage for out-door stock, yet it is remarkable for a strong, rancid and peculiar smell, affecting the breath, the milk, butter and even the flesh of animals that feed on it. **1894** Coulter *Botany W. TX* 527, *S. stricta* [=*S. alterniflora*]. . . *Salt marsh-grass*. . . Salt marshes, mostly near the coast. **1932–34** *Hanley Disks* **Cape Cod MA,** We use what they call the salt marsh—no taste to that— . . salt marsh is a kind of a dry (grass). *Ibid* **coastal ME,** We have the salt mash fed to cattle. **1933** Small *Manual SE Flora* 114, *S[partina] patens*. . . *Salt Marsh-grass*. . . Salt marshes, along the coast, Fla. to Tex. and Newf. **1942** *Torreya* 42.158 **SC,** *Spartina alterniflora*. . . Salt-marsh, coastal South Carolina. **1951** Martin *Amer. Wildlife & Plants* 439, Cordgrasses form a major part of the vegetation of our brackish coastal marshes. . . The two most important species are the medium-tall, tidewater plant, salt-marsh cordgrass (*Spartina alterniflora*), and the smaller . . *S. patens*.

salt-marsh hen n Cf **sedge hen**
=**clapper rail**.
   1888 Trumbull *Names of Birds* 127, Clapper rail . . salt-marsh hen. **1925** (1928) Forbush *Birds MA* 1.354, *Rallus crepitans crepitans*. . . *Salt-marsh hen*. . . In salt marsh or on coastal islands, rarely in upland fields. **1932** Howell *FL Bird Life* 205, *Northern Clapper Rail*. . . *Salt-marsh Hen*. . . Breeds in salt marshes of the Atlantic coast, from Connecticut to southern Virginia. . . Winters south to the Carolinas and Florida. **1953** *AmSp* 28.281 **MA,** Marsh hen . . salt . . Clapper rail.

salt-marsh mallow n Cf **marshmallow**
   A **mallow B** (here: *Kosteletzkya virginica*).
   1933 Small *Manual SE Flora* 859, *K[osteletzkya] virginica*. . . *Salt-marsh mallow*. . . Marshes and wet hammocks, Coastal Plain and rarely adj. provinces. **1953** Greene–Blomquist *Flowers South* 72, *Salt-marsh . . Mallow*. . . Anyone who has visited the coast during the summer months has undoubtedly seen the pink, mallow-like flowers in brackish marshes between the dunes and along borders in inlets among salt-marsh rushes and saw-grasses. **1972** Brown *Wildflowers LA* 110, *Salt Marsh-mallow*. . . Fresh to saline marshes, abundant in lower Louisiana. Also Texas and Mississippi.

salt-marsh mosquito n Cf **saltwater mosquito**
   Any of several **mosquitoes** n¹ **B1,** but usu those of the genus *Aedes*, esp *A. sollicitans* of the Atlantic and Gulf coasts and *A. dorsalis* and *A. squamiger* in the West.
   1873 U.S. Bur. Fisheries *Rept. for 1871 & 1872* 466 **eMA,** In these brackish pools and ditches we find. . . the larva of the salt-marsh musquito [sic] (*Culex*, sp.,) . . and the adults in August, September, and October, so swarm in these marshes as to render it extremely unpleasant to go on or near them. **1904** NY State Museum & Sci. Serv. *Bulletin* 79.293, *Culex cantator* Coq. *Brown salt marsh mosquito*. . . [is] largely confined to the coast. *Ibid* 296, The salt marsh mosquito is somewhat unique on account of its traveling long distances. *Ibid* 301, *Culex taeniorhynchus* Wied. *Small salt marsh mosquito*. . . [has a] banded proboscis. *Ibid* 332, *Culex salinarius* Coq. *Unbanded salt marsh mosquito*. . . is closely related to C. pipiens. **1926** Essig *Insects N. Amer.* 537, *The brown salt marsh mosquito, Aedes dorsalis* . . is one of the most common and troublesome insects along the Pacific coast. . . The larvae live in ground and rock pools, brackish water, and salt marshes. The adults are often carried by the wind into towns and cities. *Ibid* 538, *The California salt marsh mosquito, Aedes squamiger*. . . The larvae inhabit salt marshes and tide pools along the coast of middle and southern California. The adults invade cities and towns, particularly in the San

Francisco Bay region. **1932** *Sun* (Baltimore MD) 23 Aug 4/7, The salt marsh mosquito causes intense discomfort, both along the seashore and many miles inland. **1949** Swain *Insect Guide* 189, Salt Marsh Mosquito—*Aedes sollicitans*—This is the famous "New Jersey mosquito" which breeds in the salt marshes of our Atlantic and Gulf coasts. **1954** Borror–DeLong *Intro. Insects* 596, Some of the salt-marsh mosquitoes (for example, *Aedes sollicitans* . .) may travel many miles from the larval habitat. **1968** *DARE* (Qu. R15a, . . *Names or nicknames . . for mosquitoes*) Inf DE4, Salt-marsh mosquitoes and freshwater mosquitoes. **1980** Milne–Milne *Audubon Field Guide Insects* 640, *Golden Saltmarsh Mosquito (Aedes solicitans* [sic]). . . Near brackish and salt water; larvae also in swimming pools. *Ibid* 641, The Black Saltmarsh Mosquito *(A. taeniorhynchus)*. . . is black with broad white bands.

salt marsh shrew See **marsh shrew**

salt-marsh snake n

A **water snake** (here: *Nerodia clarkii, N. fasciata,* or *N. sipedon*).

1953 Schmidt *N. Amer. Amphibians* 163, *Natrix sipedon taeniata.* . . Common names.—Atlantic salt marsh snake. *Natrix sipedon clarkii.* . . Common name.—Gulf salt marsh snake. **1979** Behler–King *Audubon Field Guide Reptiles* 635, Gulf Salt Marsh [Snake]. . . Gulf coast, nw. Florida to se. Texas. . . Atlantic Salt Marsh [Snake]. . . Coastal Florida, from near Daytona Beach to Vero Beach. *Ibid* 638, Carolina Salt Marsh [Snake]. . . Outer Bank islands and mainland coast of Pamlico and Core sounds, North Carolina.

salt-marsh terrapin n Also *salt-marsh turtle* Cf **saltwater terrapin**
=diamondback terrapin.

1872 *Amer. Philos. Soc. Proc.* 12.475, The salt-marsh terrapin. **1911** U.S. Bur. Census *Fisheries 1908* 317, *Malaclemmys palustris* [=*Malaclemys terrapin*]. . . also called "salt-marsh turtle" and "diamond-back." **1935** Pratt *Manual Vertebrate Animals* 234, Salt marsh turtles. . . Feet large and webbed.

salt-marsh wren See **saltwater marsh wren**

salt meadow See **meadow B1**

salt-meadow grass n Cf **salt-marsh grass**
A grass of alkaline or brackish areas, as:

a also *salt-meadow cordgrass:* A **cordgrass** (here: *Spartina patens*). **Atlantic and Gulf coasts**

1842 Hawes *Sporting Scenes* 1.193 **Long Is. NY,** Lie down in the bottom of the boat, in the dry salt-meadow grass. **1910** Graves *Flowering Plants* 68 **CT,** *Spartina patens.* . . Salt Meadow Grass. . . Furnishes much of the hay cut on the salt meadows. **1947** *Jrl. Wildlife Management* 2.52 **LA, eTX,** Early in spring they [=snow geese] graze more on new foliage of salt-meadow cordgrass *(Spartina patens)* and saltgrass in burned marshes. **1949** Moldenke *Amer. Wild Flowers* 376, Our salt meadows and sandy beaches provide the favorite haunts of the extremely prolific *saltmeadowgrass, S[partina] patens*—a low plant of only 1 to 3 feet in height. **1958** Thomson *Changing Face New Engl.* 94, The lower part of the sward is covered with salt meadow grass *(Spartina patens).* **1970** Correll *Plants TX* 250, *Spartina patens.* . . *Saltmeadow cordgrass.* . . Sandy seasonally moist soil near the coast, . . common. **1976** Bruce *How to Grow Wildflowers* 205, Slightly back from the water Black Rush *(Juncus gerardii)* and Salt-meadow Grass *(Spartina patens)* form a flat, low expanse of grayish green.

b A **sprangletop** (here: *Leptochloa fascicularis*).

[**1912** Baker *Book of Grasses* 166, Salt-meadow leptochloa [=*Leptochloa fascicularis*] is a low grass that grows in tufts in brackish marshes or meadows and also on saline soil toward the interior of the country.] **1940** Gates *Flora KS* 130, Leptochloa fascicularis. . . Salt Meadowgrass. . . Brackish meadows, ditches, alkali flats or shallow water. **1968** Barkley *Plants KS* 49, Leptochloa fascicularis. . . Salt Meadowgrass. Bearded Sprangletop.

c An **alkali grass 2** (here: *Puccinellia airoides*).

1950 Stevens *ND Plants* 57, *Puccinellia nuttalliana* [=*P. airoides*]. . . *Salt Meadowgrass. Alkaligrass.* . . Common, usually in scattered tufts at edges of ponds or on saline, wet flats.

salt meat n **Lower Missip Valley, esp LA** See Map Cf **meat n 2, side meat**
=salt pork.

1961 *PADS* 36.13 **LA, sAR,** A word that has spread somewhat farther to the north than to the west is *armoire* for a large wardrobe. . . Another of the same sort, but with a somewhat wider spread, is *salt meat* for salt pork, which is fairly common in southern Arkansas. **1961** Folk *Word Atlas N. LA* map 1015 *(Salt pork),* Salt meat. [*DARE* Ed: This response has the highest frequency among the "other" responses.] **1962** Atwood *Vocab. TX* 89, *Louisiana Words.* . . Spreading northward, well into southern Arkansas, but not into Texas, we find *salt meat* for salt pork. **1965–70** *DARE* (Qu. H38, . . *Words for bacon [including joking ones]*) 11 Infs, **LA, MS, OK,** Salt meat; **LA11, MS23,** Dry salt meat; (Qu. BB50c, *Remedies for infections*) Inf **LA37,** Salt meat fat. **1966** Dakin *Dial. Vocab. Ohio R. Valley* 2.335, *Salt pork.* . . Side pork, salt meat, and *salt side* . . are fairly common in southern Illinois and the latter two are also used in sections of Ohio and Kentucky. **1989** Pederson *LAGS Tech. Index* 158, *(Salt pork)* 128 infs, *(Dry)* salt meat. [Of these infs, 103 are from the **Lower Missip Valley,** 47 of whom are from **LA.]**

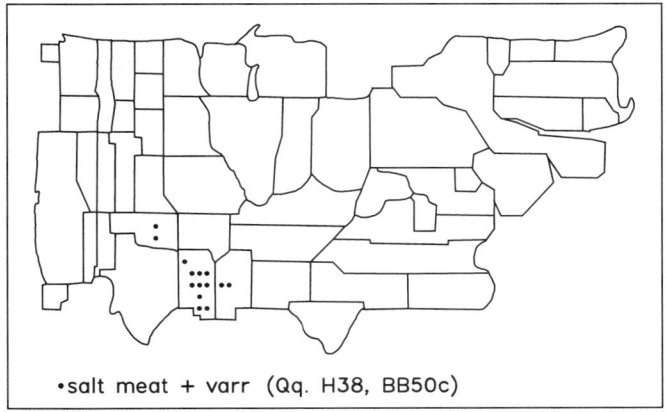

•salt meat + varr (Qq. H38, BB50c)

salt mullet See **saltwater mullet**

salt pork n Also *salt pork bacon* **scattered, but somewhat more freq NEng, Upstate NY** See Map on p. 714 Cf **bacon B, salt back, ~ bacon, ~ meat, ~ side, side meat**
The back or sides of a hog cured in salt or brine.

1723 *New-Engl. Courant* (Boston MA) 16 Sept 1/2, She knows . . who makes Broth of Salt Pork and a Pudding Bag. **1871** Eggleston *Hoosier Schoolmaster* 81 **IN,** Floating islands of salt pork [were] fished out of oceans of hot lard. **1934** Carmer *Stars Fell on AL* 40, We . . sat down to a steaming mess of salt pork, collard greens, cowpeas and corn bread. **1949** Kurath *Word Geog.* 69, *Salt pork* is current in New England and in the New England settlements of New York State as far west as the Finger Lakes. **1965** Carmony *Speech Terre Haute* 32 **cwIN,** *Salt pork.* . . Several terms are used . . for the sides of pork preserved in brine. The most frequent . . [is] the New England *salt pork.* **1965–70** *DARE* (Qu. H38, . . *Words for bacon [including joking ones]*) 30 Infs, **scattered,** Salt pork; **LA14,** Dry salt pork; **NM12,** Salt pork bacon; **NC14,** Salt porks; (Qu. BB50c, *Remedies for infections*) 17 Infs, **chiefly Nth, esp wNEng, Upstate NY,** Salt pork; **MI92,** Iodoform on salt pork; **NH2,** Piece of salt pork; **CT39,** Salt pork and pepper; **OH87,** Salt pork and turpentine; **MA24,** Salt pork rind; (Qu. H37, . . *Words . . for gravy*) Inf **VT16,** Salt pork gravy; (Qu. H47, *Kinds of fried potatoes*) Inf **NH15,** Salt pork hash; (Qu. H50, *Dishes made with beans . . that . . people in other places might not [know]*) Inf **NY43,** Baked beans and salt pork and molasses; **CA107,** Beans cooked with ham or salt pork; **IN70,** Salt pork and navy beans; (Qu. P8, . . *'White bait';* total Infs questioned, 75) Inf **ME20,** Salt pork; (Qu. BB34b, *What is a poultice made with?;* total Infs questioned, 75) Inf **FL39,** Salt pork; (Qu. BB50a, . . *Favorite remedies . . for a cough*) Infs **NH6, NY27,** Salt pork; **OH15,** Salt pork bound around the throat with pepper; **NM12,** Salt-pork plaster; **MA57,** For sore throat—scraped salt pork, put on a cloth, and pinned around the throat; (Qu. BB50b, *Remedies for chest colds*) Inf **NJ1,** Red flannel and strip of salt pork (or sour pickle) around sore throat; **CT12,** Salt pork and pepper; (Qu. BB51a, . . *Cures for corns or warts*) Inf **MI96,** Tie salt pork on a wart; (Qu. BB51b, . . *'Magical' cures for corns or warts*) Inf **RI12,** Rub with salt pork, then plug through the window; **RI10,** Steal a piece of salt pork, put it in ground; **NJ8,** Tie a piece of salt pork. **1969** *DARE* FW Addit **CT,** *Salt pork gravy*—cream gravy made with salt pork drippings—a poor family's supper. **1981** *PADS* 67.34 **Mesabi Iron Range MN,** *Salt pork.* . . All of the Iron Range respondents use the Northern *salt pork,* recorded also for five of six other Minnesota informants.   **1989** Pederson *LAGS Tech. Index* 158 **Gulf Region,** *(Salt pork)* 153 infs, Salt pork.

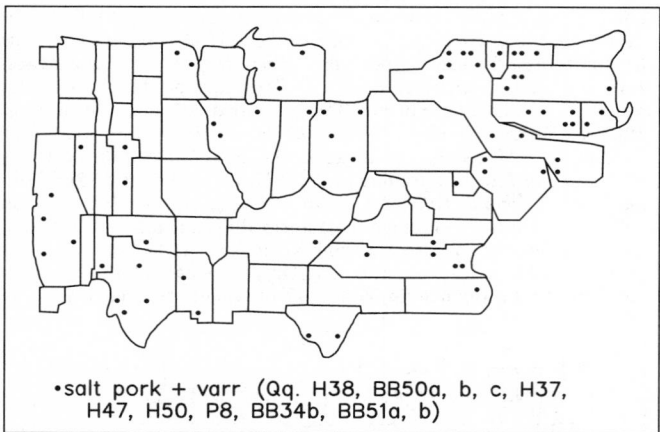

•salt pork + varr (Qq. H38, BB50a, b, c, H37, H47, H50, P8, BB34b, BB51a, b)

salt potato n esp Syracuse NY

A small potato cooked in brine until crusted with salt.

1986 Hendrickson *Amer. Talk* 15, The signs pitching "Lobster and Salt Potato—Only $6.95" along the Boston Post Road in Connecticut, . . puzzled me until I learned that the red-skinned potatoes are so called because they are cooked in salted water.   **1993** *DARE* File, Does anyone outside of Central New York know about salt potatoes (small potatoes cooked in brine until they are crusted with salt on the outside—must be served with lots of cold beer)?   *Ibid,* [A Rhode Island native talking to a former Upstate New York native:] How about salt potatoes and Heid's hotdogs? Ever have those in Syracuse?   **2000** *Ibid* **cNY,** In Syracuse ("Salt City") they make and eat something called a "salt potato." A small potato, grown specially for the purpose, is boiled in salty water. As a non-native I don't see anything special about them but the natives think it is a great delicacy.   *Ibid* **cNY,** Since Syracuse was known as the "salt city" because of the salt mines here . . I suspect salt potatoes date back to the 18th/19th century. . . The tiniest potatoes . . are boiled whole and eaten dipped in butter.   *Ibid,* Syracuse NY used to be known as the Salt City because of all the "salt blocks" (boiling hearths) along the shores of Onondaga Lake. Here salt was manufactured by boiling the water from the many local salt springs. At noontime the workers dropped small potatoes (1–2 inch diameter) into these salt blocks as lunch. There is still a market for "salt potatoes" in the area. No local picnic or clam bake would be complete without them.   *Ibid* **Syracuse NY,** Salt potatoes . . were a common part of picnic/barbecue type of meals. . . The potatoes themselves are usually red, thin-skinned "new potatoes" and if you buy them as "salt potatoes" from a store in central NY you get an envelope of rock salt with the bag of potatoes. Then they are boiled with the salt until they are tender. The brine is then drained off and the potatoes saturated with butter.

salt reed grass n Cf salt-marsh grass, salt-meadow ~ a

A **cordgrass** (here: *Spartina cynosuroides*).

1848 Gray *Manual of Botany* 586, S[partina] polystachya [=S. cynosuroides]. . . *Great Salt Reed-Grass.* . . Salt or brackish marshes, within tide-water.   **1901** Mohr *Plant Life AL* 374, *Spartina polystachya.* . . *Salt Reed Grass.* . . Southern New England, coast of New York to Florida, west to Louisiana.   **1912** Baker *Book of Grasses* 162, Salt Reed-grass *(Spartina cynosuroides).* . . On the Jersey marshes, acres are covered by this grass, which sometimes attains a height of ten feet, with stems an inch in diameter at the base.   **1946** Tatnall *Flora DE* 34, *Salt Reed Grass.* Common; saline shores and marshes of the Coastal Plain.   **1950** Gray–Fernald *Manual of Botany* 179, *Salt Reed-Grass.* . . Brackish or fresh tidal marshes.

salt rheum n chiefly Nth

Any of var cutaneous inflammations.

1809 Kendall *Travels* 1.325 **Nth,** [The disease] of which I heard the name in every one's mouth, is the *salt rheum.*   **1831** *Genesee Farmer* 1.58 **wNY,** A few weeks ago, a member of my family had *salt rheum* on the hands, of more than a months continuance; and latterly it formed a spot of an inch diameter, on the face.   **1872** McClellan *Golden State* 168 **sCA,** [The grindelia] has long been known to the Indians and native Spanish of California . . as a cure . . in many skin diseases, as salt-rheum, nettle-rash, and many others.   **1929** *AmSp* 5.122 **ME,** A person

had a "rising in the ear," the "phthisic" (asthma) or "salt rheum."   **1950** *WELS (Common skin diseases)* 1 Inf, **seWI,** Salt rheum—itchy, skin gets dry.   **1967–69** *DARE* (Qu. BB25) Inf **MA5,** Salt rheum—scaly, white, itchy; **WI30,** Salt rheum—old-fashioned; roughness of the skin in patches; (Qu. BB27, *When somebody pretends to be sick . . he's _____*) Inf **NY196,** Got the salt rheum.   **1970** *NC Folkl.* 18.30, A remedy for open scorbutic sores is nightshade leaves or for salt rheum if applied continually.   **1981** *DARE* File **cnMA** (as of c1915), It occurred to me the other day, as I looked at a bit of rough reddish skin on my cheek, that my grandmother would have said, looking at it, "Just a bit of salt rheum."

salt-rheum weed n [From its use to treat salt rheum]

A **turtlehead** (here: *Chelone glabra*).

1847 Wood *Class-Book* 400, C[helone] glabra. . . *Salt-rheum Weed.* . . A plant of brooks and wet places (Can. and U.S.) with flowers shaped much like the head of a snake, the mouth open and tongue extended.   **1930** Sievers *Amer. Med. Plants* 58, Salt-rheum weed. . . *Part used.*— The herb, especially the leaves. . . In reasonably constant demand.   **1971** Krochmal *Appalachia Med. Plants* 84, Salt-rheum weed. . . The leaves have been used for reducing inflammation, and as an anthelmintic and tonic.

salt-rising n, also pl, but sg in attrib use Also salt-rise scattered, but more freq W Midl, Gt Lakes See Map Cf emptins, rising n 2

A leaven prepared by making a mixture of flour or cornmeal, water or milk, usu salt, and occas other ingredients, and allowing it to ferment; bread made with such a leaven; also adj *salt-risen.*

1838 *Greeley's New-Yorker* 28 July 290, At table there was always the large loaf of salt-risen bread.   **1846** Farnham *Life in Prairie Land* 138 **IL,** When tea-time approached . . the "salt-risin" loaf . . [was] put to baking.   **1863** *S. Lit. Messenger* 37.305 **VA,** She had more kinds of bread than any woman I ever heard of; splendid, hot, high, light bread . . and rolls, and biscuit, and . . pone, and ash-cake, and hoe-cake, and "salt risen" bread, and apple-bread, and cracklin bread . . and many others.   **1864** *Atlantic Mth.* 14.692 **NEng,** There is, however, one species of yeast . . against which I have to enter my protest. It is called salt-risings, or milk-risings, and is made by mixing flour, milk, and a little salt together, and leaving them to ferment.   **1880** *Scribner's Mth.* 19.426 **NEng,** The whole feminine conclave launched out into a . . discussion of the relative merits of salt-risin's, milk-emptin's, and potato yeast.   **1890** James *Mother James' Cooking* 169, *Salt-rising bread.* . . Take a quart dish and scald it out; then put in a pint of warm water, put in a teaspoonful of salt, stir flour enough in to make a thick batter, set the dish in a kettle of warm water. . . If the flour is good it will be very light in two hours.   *Ibid, Salt-rising bread.* Take a pint of boiling sweet milk and thicken it with meal; keep it in a warm place all night; next morning add a teacupful of lukewarm water, using flour enough to make a stiff batter. Place this in a kettle of warm water to rise; it will be light in two hours.   **1905** *DN* 3.93 **nwAR,** *Salt-risin' bread.* . . Wheat bread. Common.   **1909** *DN* 3.365 **eAL, wGA,** *Salt-risin(g) bread.* . . A slow-rising bread, so called because the yeast is set with salt. Rare.   **1923** *DN* 5.236 **swWI,** *Salt-rising.* . . Bread made from dough, part of [sic] all of which has been allowed to ferment. "Livin' on salt-risin' and sow belly."   **1939** Wolcott *Yankee Cook Book* 146 **MA,** *Salt-Rising Bread.* . . Scald [4 tablespoons] cornmeal, [2 tablespoons] sugar and ½ teaspoon of salt with

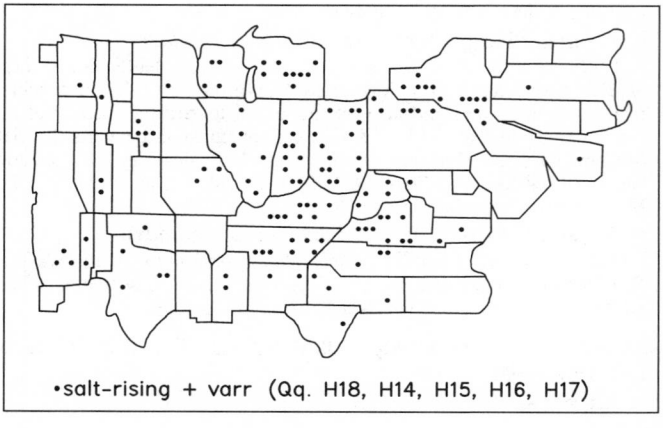

•salt-rising + varr (Qq. H18, H14, H15, H16, H17)

milk. Let stand in a warm place overnight or until fermented. Into this "yeast" stir shortening, . . salt, lukewarm water and . . flour. **1965–70** *DARE* (Qu. H18, . . *Special kinds of bread*) 126 Infs, **scattered, but more freq W Midl, Gt Lakes,** Salt-rising bread; **NY75,** Salt-raising bread; (Qu. H14, *Bread that's made with cornmeal*) Infs **IL34, MI100, OH8,** Salt-rising bread; (Qu. H15, *Bread made with wheat flour*) Infs **AL11, TN5, 11, 23,** Salt-rising bread; (Qu. H16, *What do people use to raise the bread before it's baked?*) Inf **TX42,** Salt-rise; **IN7,** Salt-rising bread; (Qu. H17, . . *Kinds [of yeast]*) Infs **ID5, IN34,** Salt-rising. [110 of 129 total Infs women] **1986** Pederson *LAGS Concordance* **Gulf Region,** 18 infs, Salt-rising bread; 2 infs, Salt-rising light bread.

salt rush n

A rush: either *Juncus lesueurii* in the western US or *J. roemerianus* of the Atlantic coast.

   1901 Jepson *Flora CA* 93, *J[uncus] Lesueurii* [sic]. . . *Salt Rush.* . . Salt-marshes and alkali soils; not uncommon. **1901** Mohr *Plant Life AL* 432, *Juncus roemerianus.* . . *Salt Rush.* . . Seashore of New Jersey to Florida, west to Texas. . . Salt and brackish swamps, covering the large salt marshes, overflowed by the tide. **1942** *Torreya* 42.158 **SC,** *Juncus roemerianus.* . . Salt rush, coastal South Carolina. **1973** Hitchcock–Cronquist *Flora Pacific NW* 569, Coastal marshes and dunes; s BC to Cal; salt r[ush]. . . *J. lesueurii.*

salt sage n

1 also *(salty) sage:* A **saltbush 1,** usu *Atriplex canescens, A. confertifolia,* or *A. gardneri.* **West**

   1898 *Jrl. Amer. Folkl.* 11.277 **CO,** *Atriplex canescens,* . . salty sage. *Ibid* 278 **WY,** *Atriplex Nuttallii* [=*A. gardneri*], . . salt sage. **1913** (1979) Barnes *Western Grazing* 57, There are many varieties of sage in the southern ranges. . . Salt sage (Atriplex) is the one most generally called by the generic name sage by stockmen all over the West. **1931** U.S. Dept. Ag. *Misc. Circular* 101.28, *Atriplex canescens.* . . Other names in more or less common use are chamiza (New Mexico), . . salt sage [etc]. *Ibid* 30, *A. confertifolia* . . frequently known locally with other species of Atriplex as salt sage, is one of the most important native species of this genus. **1950** Stevens *ND Plants* 132, *Atriplex nuttallii.* . . *Salt Sage.* . . is an important forage plant for sheep in the plains area. **1967** *DARE* FW Addit **CO15,** Cornflake bush . . name for salt sage; **CO29,** Cornflake bush . . name for salt sage because it looks like it's strung with cornflakes. **1973** Hitchcock–Cronquist *Flora Pacific NW* 95, Saltsage. . . *A. nuttallii.* **1986** McPhee *Rising from the Plains* 79 **WY,** From the ranch buildings, by Muskrat Creek, the Wind River Basin reached out in buffalo grass, grama grass, and edible salt sage across the cambered erosional swells of the vast dry range.

2 =**marsh elder 1.**

   1932 Rydberg *Flora Prairies* 763, *Iva.* . . Marsh Elder, Bozzleweed, Salt Sage, Poverty Weed. **1940** Clute *Amer. Plant Names* 262, *Iva axillaris.* . . Salt sage.

salt shake n Also *shake* **scattered, but esp S Midl** See Map Cf **flyswat**

A saltshaker.

   1965–70 *DARE* (Qu. G4, *A container for salt that has a cover with holes in it*) 24 Infs, **esp S Midl,** Salt shake; **MI51,** Saltcellar, or a shake, salt shake, and some people even call 'em saltshakers; **CT26,** Shaker, shake. [16 of 26 Infs comm type 5, 15 gs educ or less] **1983** *MJLF* 9.1.54 **ceKY** (as of 1957), *Salt shake* . . a salt shaker.

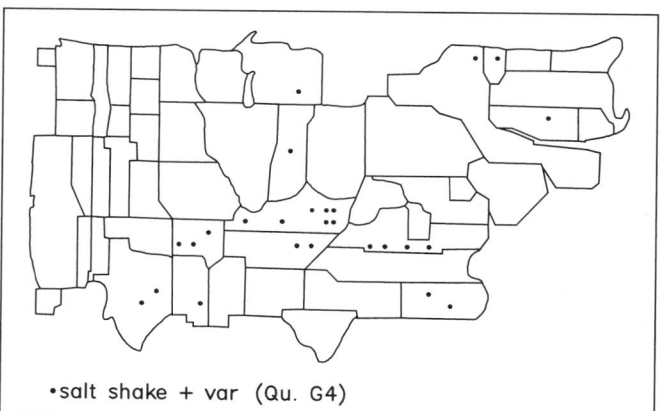

•salt shake + var (Qu. G4)

salt side n esp **CO** Cf **fresh side, salt meat, side ~, sowbelly** =**salt pork.**

   1929 Ellis *Ordinary Woman* 111 **CO** (as of early 20th cent), We took a piece of salt side, which we called 'sow-belly.' **c1955** Reed-Person *Ling. Atlas Pacific NW,* 2 infs, Salt side. **1960** Criswell *Resp. to PADS* 20 **Ozarks,** Salt side—Salt pork or salt side, a large slab about two inches thick covered with salt, sold in the spring in grocery stores. **1961** *AmSp* 36.266 **CO,** The term *salt side* is probably a . . blend of Northern *salt pork* and Midland *side meat,* terms for bacon. . . *Salt side* might have developed . . as far east as Ohio. **1966** Dakin *Dial. Vocab. Ohio R. Valley* 2.335, Salt pork. . . Side pork, salt meat, and *salt side* . . are fairly common in southern Illinois and the latter two are also used in sections of Ohio and Kentucky. **1967** Faries *Word Geog. MO* 156, Salt side (2 [of 700 infs]). **1967–68** *DARE* (Qu. H38, . . *Words for bacon [including joking ones]*) Infs **CO5, 11, 27, 40, MD33,** Salt side; **CO30,** Salt side—the back side, not the bacon end; **CO47,** Salt side—not smoked; **OH78,** Salt side—fatter than bacon. **1986** Pederson *LAGS Concordance* (*A side [of bacon]*) 1 inf, **ceGA,** Salt side; (*Salt pork*) 1 inf, **nwFL,** Salt side—not sure.

salts water n esp **Sth, S Midl**

A solution of Epsom salts.

   [**1899** (1912) Green *VA Folk-Speech* 364, *Salts.* . . Epsom salt, taken as a medicine.] **1965–70** *DARE* (Qu. BB50a, . . *Favorite remedies . . for a cough*) Inf **TX32,** Salts water; (Qu. BB50c, *Remedies for infections*) Infs **AR47, KY6, LA12, OH53, TX32,** Salts water; **LA28, MO19,** Hot salts water; **NC16,** Dip it in salts water; **TX98,** Soak it in hot salts water. **1968** *DARE* Tape **OH60,** [FW:] What kind of a thing did they use for infections, to draw out the poison? [Inf:] Salt and salts water. If you had a cut, that's what you used.

salt thatch n Cf **creek thatch**

A **cordgrass** (here: *Spartina alterniflora*).

   [**1843** Torrey *Flora NY* 2.449, *Spartina alterniflora.* . . For thatching, it much outlasts wheat straw.] **1958** Thomson *Changing Face New Engl.* 94, On the slope of this bluff . . grows a pure stand of tall, coarse salt thatch or saltwater grass (*Spartina alterniflora*).

saltwater See **saltwater mosquito**

saltwater bass n Cf **sea bass** =**red drum.**

   1935 Caine *Game Fish* 39, *Sciaenops ocellatus.* . . Red Drum . . Salt-Water Bass. **1969–70** *DARE* (Qu. P2, . . *Kinds of saltwater fish caught around here . . good to eat*) Infs **MS81, MA55, NH18,** Saltwater bass. **1986** Pederson *LAGS Concordance,* 1 inf, **neFL,** Saltwater bass.

saltwater blackbird n =**boat-tailed grackle.**

   1932 Howell *FL Bird Life* 432, *Boat-tailed Grackle.* . . *Other Names* . . *Salt-water Blackbird.* . . [O]ccurs commonly on the Kissimmee Prairie, the St. Johns marshes, the prairies of Lee and Hendry Counties, the Everglades, and along all coasts. **1955** *Oriole* 20.1.12 **GA,** *Boat-tailed Grackle.* . . *Salt-water Blackbird* (its habitat is mostly near the coast). **1969** Longstreet *Birds FL* 143, *Salt-water Blackbird.* . . The bird obtains much of its food along the muddy borders of ponds, sloughs, and tidal creeks, often wading belly-deep in the water, and at times submerging its head in search of small fishes, crabs, shrimps, and crawfishes.

saltwater bream n Also *sea bream* Cf **bream B2**

1 =**pinfish 1a.**

   1787 Gesellschaft Naturforschender Freunde *Schriften* 8.151, *Sparus rhomboides.* . . Saltwater Bream. In Amerika. **1884** Goode *Fisheries U.S.* 1.393 **SC,** *Lagodon rhomboides.* . . bears several other names, being known . . at Charleston as the "Salt-water Bream." **1946** LaMonte *N. Amer. Game Fishes* 71, Bream—*Lagodon rhomboides.* . . Salt-water Bream, . . Sea Bream. **1966** *DARE* (Qu. P2, . . *Kinds of saltwater fish caught around here . . good to eat*) Inf **GA3,** Sea brim. **1986** Pederson *LAGS Concordance,* 1 inf, **seAL,** Saltwater bream.

2 =**pompon 1.**

   1935 Caine *Game Fish* 114, *Anisotremus surinamensis.* . . Salt-Water Bream[,] Sea Bream.

saltwater bush n

Either a **groundsel tree** or a **marsh elder 1.**

   1838 (1863) Kemble *Jrl. Georgian* 17, I met with . . a most beautiful species of ivy, . . growing in profuse garlands from branch to branch of some stunted evergreen bushes which border the dike, and which the people call salt-water bush. **1916** *Torreya* 16.235 **VA,** On Revels Id., Va., the staminate plant of *Baccharis halimifolia* is known as salt water bush, and the pistillate plants . . as kinks bushes. **1926** *Torreya* 26.6, *Iva* spp. . . *Baccharis* spp. . . The two plants are confused . . as salt-water bush.

saltwater catfish n Also *saltwater cat*

Either the **gaff-topsail catfish** or a **sea catfish** (here: *Arius felis*).

    1814 in 1815 *Lit. & Philos. Soc. NY Trans.* 433, *Salt-water Catfish.* (*Silurus marinus* [=*Bagre m.*].) A splendid fish, twenty inches long. . . Two whiskers, between five and six inches long, projecting from the upper lip, near the corners of the mouth. **1877** in 1879 *U.S. Natl. Museum Proc. for 1878* 1.278 **AL,** The Salt-water Catfish is very abundant everywhere on the Gulf coast. **1884** Goode *Fisheries U.S.* 1.629, *Arius felis.* The Salt-water Catfish is found along the coasts of the Gulf of Mexico to as far north as Cape Hatteras. **1905** NJ State Museum *Annual Rept. for 1904* 165, The Gaff Topsail Cat Fishes. *Felichthys marinus.* . . Salt Water Cat. . . Dr. C.C. Abbott records this fish from the lower Delaware waters, though it is unusual out of salt-water. **1966–70** *DARE* (Qu. P2, . . *Kinds of saltwater fish caught around here . . good to eat*) Infs **MS81, SC69, VA55,** Saltwater catfish; **SC43,** Saltwater cat; (Qu. P4, *Saltwater fish that are not good to eat*) Infs **FL16, MS73, TX19,** Saltwater catfish—also called hardhead and rustler; (Qu. P14, . . *Commercial fishing . . what do the fishermen go out after?*) Inf **VA55,** Saltwater catfish. **1986** Pederson *LAGS Concordance,* 3 infs, **TX,** Saltwater catfish; 1 inf, **seMS,** Saltwater cat.

saltwater cedar See **salt cedar 1**

saltwater chub n
=**tautog.**

    1884 Goode *Fisheries U.S.* 1.268 **Chesapeake Bay,** *Tautoga onitis.* . . is called . . at the mouth of the Chesapeake "Salt-water Chub." **1939** Natl. Geogr. Soc. *Fishes* 66, The tautog has several names. . . In Chesapeake Bay it occasionally is called blackfish, other names being chub, saltwater chub, and black porgy.

saltwater cordgrass See **saltwater grass**

saltwater crane n
=**wood ibis.**

    1926 *AmSp* 1.418 **Okefenokee GA,** They wuz there frum Salt-water Cranes [Footnote: Wood Ibises]—right down ter little fellers. **1969** *DARE* FW Addit **GA51,** Saltwater crane = wood ibis (white back, wings tipped with black).

saltwater crow n Cf **tidewater crow**

The common crow *(Corvus brachyrhynchos).*

    1967 *DARE* (Qu. Q10, . . *Water birds and marsh birds*) Inf **SC62,** Saltwater crow = marsh crow—a scavenger.

saltwater farm n **NEng, esp ME**

A farm directly on the seacoast; hence nouns *salt(water) farmer.*

    1939 *Harper's Mag.* 178.441 **ME,** The saltwater farms hereabouts give ample evidence that their owners have a great deal on their minds. . . With the whole sea bottom to rake, he isn't going to spend all his time weeding a bean row. **1995** *WaveLength Paddling Mag.* Apr.–May (Internet) **ME,** His marine origins date back to his "saltwater farmer" ancestors who came over to the new world in colonial times. After graduating college . . he became a professional boat builder in Ipswich and Gloucester (Maine). **2000** *Yankee* Dec 65 **NEng,** Matthias Tibbetts, the youngest son of a salt farmer, becomes a ship's captain, but—knowing where his heart lies—returns to his island home. **2001** *DARE* File—Internet **ME,** I married the brother of a colleague, and moved Downeast to live on an eight-generation salt-water farm. . . where I learned to milk cows (60 of them). *Ibid* **ME,** We are a family with five children who live in Kennebunkport, Maine on a saltwater farm. We raise sheep and chickens and have a small farm stand.

saltwater gar n

A **needlefish 1** (here: *Strongylura* spp).

    1946 LaMonte *N. Amer. Game Fishes* 18, *The Needlefishes* . . *Strongylura.* . . *Names:* Gar, Salt-water Gar [etc]. [*Ibid* 19, Both jaws prolonged into long, thin, fine-toothed and rather fragile beaks; long nar-

row bodies.] **1986** Pederson *LAGS Concordance,* 1 inf, **csGA,** Saltwater gar.

saltwater grass n Also *saltwater cordgrass*

A **cordgrass** (here: *Spartina alterniflora*) or similar grass.

    1950 Gray–Fernald *Manual of Botany* 179, S[*partina*] *alterniflora.* . . Salt-water C[*ordgrass*] . . Odor strong and rancid. **1958** Thomson *Changing Face New Engl.* 94, Above the band of saltwater grass there is an abrupt transition to smooth, almost level meadow. **1968** *DARE* (Qu. L8, *Hay that grows naturally in damp places*) Inf **AK4,** Saltwater grass. **1968** *DARE* Tape **AK4,** We used to cut on the tide flats out here what we call saltwater grass.

saltwater marsh hen n Also *saltwater hen* Cf **freshwater marsh hen, marsh hen 1**
=**clapper rail.**

    1835 Audubon *Ornith. Biog.* 3.35, The Salt-water Marsh Hen swims with considerable ease. **1872** Coues *Key to N. Amer. Birds* 273, *Salt-water Marsh-hen.* . . Salt marshes of Atlantic States, extremely abundant southerly. **1910** Eaton *Birds NY* 1.273, The . . Salt-water marsh hen[s] . . remain under the cover of the dense sedge grass during the greater part of the day or when danger is near, and it is almost impossible to flush them, except at high tide when the marshes are flooded. **1938** Oberholser *Bird Life LA* 200, The Louisiana Clapper Rail, commonly known also as 'marsh hen' or 'salt water marsh hen', is one of the most abundant birds on the coastal marshes of the Gulf of Mexico. **1946** Hausman *Eastern Birds* 237, *Northern Clapper Rail.* . . Saltwater Hen. **1953** *AmSp* 28.281 **NY, MD,** Marsh hen . . (salt-water)—Clapper rail.

saltwater marsh wren n Also *salt-marsh wren* Cf **freshwater marsh wren**

The long-billed **marsh wren** *(Cistothorus palustris).*

    1917 (1923) *Birds Amer.* 3.197, Long-billed Marsh Wren. . . Other Names . . Salt-water Marsh Wren. **1946** Hausman *Eastern Birds* 446, Long-Billed Marsh Wren. . . Other Names . . Marsh Wren, Salt-Marsh Wren.

saltwater meadow hen n Cf **freshwater meadow hen, meadow hen 1**
=**clapper rail.**

    1844 DeKay *Zool. NY* 2.259, *The Saltwater Meadow-hen.* . . Appears along the shores of this State about the latter end of April, and, after raising its brood, departs for the South in October. **1888** Trumbull *Names of Birds* 127, Clapper rail . . Salt-water meadow hen. **1953** *AmSp* 28.281 **NY,** Meadow hen . . (salt-water)—Clapper rail.

saltwater minnow n

A **mummichog** (here: *Fundulus heteroclitus*).

    1882 U.S. Natl. Museum *Bulletin* 16.336, F[*undulus*] *heteroclitus.* . . Salt-water Minnow. . . Maine to Mexico, everywhere very common in brackish waters. **1903** NY State Museum & Sci. Serv. *Bulletin* 60.310, The killifish [=*Fundulus heteroclitus*]. . . is frequently called . . salt-water minnow. [*Ibid* 311, The range of the species is from Maine to South Carolina, usually in shallow salt or brackish water, but sometimes ascending streams beyond tidewater.]

saltwater moccasin n Cf **moccasin 1b, water moccasin**

A **water snake** (here: *Nerodia fasciata*).

    1970 *DARE* (Qu. P25, . . *Kinds of snakes*) Inf **VA55,** Saltwater moccasin.

saltwater mosquito n Also *saltwater* Cf **salt-marsh mosquito**

A **mosquito** n[1] **B1** such as *Aedes cantator* or *A. sollicitans.*

    1946 *PADS* 6.26 **ceNC,** *Salt-water mosquito.* . . A small mosquito that thrives in salt-water marshes or brackish water marshes. Does not produce malaria. (*Culex cantator, Culex sollicitans.*) . . Common. **1966** *DARE* Tape **NC25,** These saltwater mosquitoes, old big mosquitoes. . . The big saltwater don't hurt you as those little ones do. **1967** *DARE* (Qu. R15b, . . *An extra-big mosquito*) Infs **LA12, TX12,** Saltwater mosquito. **1986** Pederson *LAGS Concordance,* 1 inf, **cnLA,** Saltwater mosquito (will eat you up—no malaria).

saltwater mullet n Also *salt mullet, saltwater mulley* Cf **sea mullet**

A **mullet** n[1] **1** (here: *Mugil* spp).

1970 *DARE* (Qu. P2, . . *Kinds of saltwater fish caught around here . . good to eat*) Inf **SC**69, Saltwater mulley. **1986** Pederson *LAGS Concordance,* 1 inf, **neFL,** Saltwater mullet; 1 inf, **csGA,** Salt mullet.

saltwater muskellunge n

The great **barracuda** *(Sphyraena barracuda).*

1946 LaMonte *N. Amer. Game Fishes* 15, *Sphyraena barracuda. . .* The barracudas . . are all pikelike in shape. . . *Names . .* Salt-water Muskellunge.

saltwater myrtle n Cf myrtle n¹ B9

Usu a **groundsel tree,** esp *Baccharis halimifolia,* but also a **marsh elder 1.**

1926 *Torreya* 26.6 **GA,** *Iva* spp.—Salt-water myrtle, to distinguish it from the sweet myrtle (myrica), Sapelo Id., Ga. . . *Baccharis* spp. . . Salt water myrtle, Sapelo Id., Ga. **1977** Kibler *Simms as Naturalist* 2 **SC,** Water-myrtle appears only once in the Revolutionary novels [of William Gilmore Simms] and may possibly be the wax-myrtle or more likely the *Baccharis halimifolia,* called locally "saltwater-myrtle," "silverling," or "groundsel."

saltwater partridge n

=**ruddy turnstone.**

1888 Trumbull *Names of Birds* 187, At St. Augustine, Fla. (to some native gunners at least), [*Arenaria interpres* is called] *salt-water partridge.* **1932** Howell *FL Bird Life* 224, *Ruddy Turnstone. . . Salt-water Partridge. . .* Frequents ocean beaches and sandy flats in the coastal bays and lagoons. **1946** Hausman *Eastern Birds* 259, Salt-water Partridge. . . A variegated black, white, and chestnut shore bird with a black bill and orange-red legs and feet.

saltwater perch n Cf perch n¹ 6

=**cunner** n¹ **1.**

1889 (1971) Farmer *Americanisms* 141, *Chogset. . .* In New York it is known as the *burgall* or *blue fish . . ,* also as the *salt water perch.* **1920** Packard *Old Plymouth* 163 **seMA,** In the beginning of things were the cunners, known along Massachusetts Bay mainly as perch. Names are good only in certain localities. . . Down at Newport, R.I., they catch cunners and if you talk salt-water perch to them it is at your peril.

saltwater pigweed n

A **goosefoot** (here: *Chenopodium rubrum*).

1951 Graham *My Window* 47 **ME,** They say salt-water pigweed's good to eat.

saltwater pike n [Appar from the resemblance to a pike n¹ 1] Cf sea pike

1 =**pike perch.**

1927 Weed *Pike* 198 **NC,** [*Stizostedion:*] Saltwater Pike, Pasquotank River.

2 A **snook** (here: *Centropomus undecimalis*).

1935 Caine *Game Fish* 118, *Robalo (Snook). . .* Salt-water Pike. **1975** Evanoff *Catch More Fish* 218, The snook *(Centropomus undecimalis)* is also called . . salt-water pike. . . Found in Florida, the Gulf of Mexico, and in other tropical waters.

3 The great **barracuda** *(Sphyraena barracuda).*

1946 LaMonte *N. Amer. Game Fishes* 15, *Sphyraena barracuda. . .* The barracudas . . are all pikelike in shape. . . *Names . .* Salt-water Pike.

saltwater tad n

=**horned grebe.**

1970 *DARE* (Qu. Q10, . . *Water birds and marsh birds*) Inf **VA**47, Salt-water tad—eared grebe.

saltwater tailor n Cf freshwater tailor

=**bluefish 1.**

1859 (1968) Bartlett *Americanisms* 469 **MD, VA,** *Tailor.* A fish resembling the shad, but inferior to it in size and flavor. In the towns on the Potomac, the Blue fish is called a *Salt-water tailor.* **1884** U.S. Natl. Museum *Bulletin* 27.448, *Pomatomus saltatrix. . .* Salt-water Tailor. . . This is a food fish of great importance. **1911** U.S. Bur. Census *Fisheries 1908* 308, Young bluefish are called . . "salt-water tailors" in some parts of New England.

saltwater teal n

1 =**ruddy duck.**

1844 Giraud *Birds Long Is.* 326, *Ruddy Duck. . .* In Massachusetts Bay it is frequently met with, but in the Chesapeake Bay it is more common, and is known to the gunners by the name of "Salt-water Teal." **1888** Trumbull *Names of Birds* 111 **NJ,** "Ruddy". . . At Red Bank (Monmouth Co.), N.J., *salt-water teal.* **1926** (1986) Phillips *Nat. Hist. Ducks* 4.159, *Oxyura jamaicensis. . .* Salt-water Teal. **1955** Forbush–May *Birds* 88, *Ruddy Duck. . .* Salt-water Teal. . . In marshes and sloughs.

2 =**bufflehead 2.**

1880 *Forest & Stream* 23 Dec 406, *Bucephala albeola. . .* Salt-Water Teal. . . It does not often, on the Atlantic Coast, pay much attention to decoys.

saltwater terrapin n Cf freshwater terrapin, salt-marsh ~

=**diamondback terrapin.**

1829 in 1836 NY Acad. Sci. *Annals Lyceum Nat. Hist.* 3.113, *Testudo centrata,* Daudin. . . Salt-water Tarapin of the southern states. . . It is found from New-York to Florida, and even in the West Indies, in salt water and always in the neighborhood of marshes. **1842** DeKay *Zool. NY* 3.11, This species [=*Malaclemys terrapin*] is the well known and justly prized Terrapin of epicures. It is well distinguished as the Salt-water Terrapin, for it is found exclusively in salt or brackish streams near the seashore. They bury themselves in the mud during the winter, from which they are taken in great numbers, and are then very fat. **1884** Goode *Fisheries U.S.* 1.156, The "Diamond-back," or "Salt-water Terrapin," is common along our entire Atlantic coast from Nantucket and New Bedford, in Massachusetts, to Texas. **1906** Gregory *Woman's Cookbook* 86, The kind [of terrapin] most in demand is the "diamondback," or salt-water terrapin, and is never found far from the seacoast. Rarely does their length exceed ten inches, and their weight about eight pounds. **1911** U.S. Bur. Census *Fisheries 1908* 317, The salt-water terrapin *(Malaclemmys palustris* [=*Malaclemys terrapin*]) is very highly prized for food. It is found in salt marshes along the coast . . , but those which enter into commerce are principally from Chesapeake Bay and the Carolina coast. **1945** McCauley *Reptiles MD & DC* 163, Salt-water terrapin. . . A moderately large turtle, attaining a maximum carapace length of about 9 inches. **1970** *DARE* (Qu. P24, . . *Kinds of turtles*) Inf **VA**47, Saltwater terrapin ['tɛrɪpɪn]—six inches—in marshes.

saltwater trout n Also *salty trout* S Atl, Gulf States

A **weakfish,** usu *Cynoscion nebulosus* or *C. regalis.*

1737 (1911) Brickell *Nat. Hist. NC* 234, The *Salt-Water Trouts . .* are exactly shaped like the *Trouts* with us, only these have blackish and not Red Spots. They are in great plenty in the Sounds, near the Inlets, and Salt Waters. **1873** in 1878 Smithsonian Inst. *Misc. Coll.* 14.2.26, *Cynoscion regalis. . .* Salt-water trout . . *(southern coast).* **1935** Caine *Game Fish* 144, *Cynoscion regalis. . . Cynoscion nebulosus. . .* Salt-Water Trout. *Ibid* 146, In the South they are known almost solely as salt-water trout. . . Although they do not belong to the trout family, they do bear a marked resemblance to this speckled beauty. The salt-water trout is probably our most popular salt-water game fish. **1965–67** *DARE* (Qu. P2, . . *Kinds of saltwater fish caught around here . . good to eat*) Infs **FL**7, 17, 39, **GA**3, 16, **TX**9, Saltwater trout. **1986** Pederson *LAGS Concordance,* 2 infs, **TX,** Saltwater trout; 1 inf, **swMS,** Salty trout—from Gulf.

saltwater turkey n

1 The Atlantic cod *(Gadus mohrua).* Cf **Cape Cod turkey, Marblehead ~**

1966 *Fishing World* 13.6.7, "Salt-water turkey" will be the main dish of anglers working the ocean grounds during November and December. This description of the codfish goes back to we don't know when, but every year come Election Day the salt-water fishermen turn their attention to their heavy tackle, insulated underwear and foulweather gear.

2 See **turkey.**

saltweed n

Usu a **saltbush 1,** esp *Atriplex argentea;* occas a related plant of the family Chenopodiaceae such as a **glasswort** (here: *Salicornia rubra*).

1837 Irving *Rocky Mts.* 1.167 **ID,** There was abundance, too, of the salt weed; which grows most plentiful in clayey and gravelly barrens. It resembles pennyroyal, and derives its name from a partial saltness. **1881** *Macmillan's Mag.* 44.237 **WY,** Vegetation wholly fails [in the Badlands of Wyoming], save here and there a bunch of salt-weed or a bush of the ubiquitous sage-brush. **1920** *Torreya* 20.20 **UT,** *Salicornia europaea* [=*S. rubra*]. . . Saltweed, Salt Lake Valley. **1930** OK Univ.

Biol. Surv. *Pub.* 2.60, *Atriplex argentea.* . . Saltweed. **1936** *Winter Plants NE* 194, *A[triplex] argentea.* . . Saltweed. In dry and saline soils. **1944** Abrams *Flora Pacific States* 2.78, *Atriplex Gmelinii.* . . Gmelin's Saltweed or Orache. . . On or near the seashore, . . Alaska to central California. **1968** *DARE* (Qu. S21, . . *Weeds* . . *that are a trouble in gardens and fields*) Inf **CA91**, Saltweed—has to be cut out or it will be pesty; a large-growing weed—the leaves taste salty.

saltwort n
=pickleweed 3.

1890 *Century Dict.* 5320, *West Indian saltwort, Batis maritima* of the West Indies and Florida. **1900** Lyons *Plant Names* 59, *Batis.* . . Jamaica Saltwort or Samphire. . . Maritime shrub. **1903** Small *Flora SE U.S.* 404, *Batis maritima.* . . In sand along the coast and in salt-marshes, North Carolina to Florida and Texas. . . *Salt-wort.* **1944** Abrams *Flora Pacific States* 2.115, Salt-wort. . . A . . strong-scented woody plant. . . On the Pacific shores. **1964** Munz *Shore Wildflowers* 89, Another inconspicuous but locally common maritime plant [is] *Saltwort.* . . Growing on the strand and in salt marshes of southern California, it occurs also on the Atlantic Coast. **1974** Munz *Flora S. CA* 242, *Saltwort.* . . Ventura Co. to L. Calif.

salty adj

1 Ill-tempered, angry, resentful. See also **jump salty** *esp freq among Black speakers*

1936 Adams *Cowboy Lingo* 235, A peevish person was 'techy as a teased snake,' or, if extremely so, was 'salty as Lot's wife.' **1944** C. Calloway *Hepsters Dict. (OED2)*, *Salty,* angry, ill-tempered. **1945** *AmSp* 20.83 **TX**, Less warm is such an expression as 'don't you get salty,' meaning 'don't get tough with me.' It is used mostly by Negroes, but some white persons find it valuable. **1952** Brossard *Who Walk* 67 **NYC**, Why do you have to get so salty when people want to have fun? **1967** Williams *Man Who Cried* 187 **NYC** [Black], Oops! The dozens, is it? I made you salty eh? **1970** Major *Dict. Afro-Amer. Slang* 100, *Salty:* . . irritated; ill-tempered; angry. **1971** *Today Show Letters* **DC** [Black], *Salty* (I was feeling salty about it)—Annoyed, disgusted, put-upon, put-down. **2000** *DARE* File **VA**, *Salty* has been used in the African-American community for decades, meaning angry or mad.

2 Of a horse or its behavior: wild, unmanageable. **West**

1936 McCarthy *Lang. Mosshorn* np **West** [Range terms], *Salty.* . . If speaking of . . a horse, it means "He's a hard bucker." **1937** *DN* 6.618 **swTX**, A *salty* horse is a vicious beast. **1940** Writers' Program *Guide NV* 76, A horse that likes to buck is *salty.* **1940** *AmSp* 15.220 **cwTX**, If this particular cowboy has committed all the vices either inside or outside the law, it is said that he has, like a 'salty' (wild) horse, 'gone the gaits.' **1941** Writers' Program *Guide WY* 464, *Salty*—Mean, applied to a horse. **1958** Blasingame *Dakota Cowboy* 203 **SD**, A handsome black, and full of salty action as ever a horse could be. **1970** *DARE* (Qu. K42, *A horse that is rough, wild, or dangerous*) Inf **CA210**, Salty horse.

3 Expensive. [Cf *OED2* salt a. 6 "*slang* and *dial.* Of expense, cost: Excessive in amount; costly, dear"; 1710 →]

1974 Peden *Speak to Earth* 23 **IN**, In this community when something costs too much the farmers say, "It's pretty salty." **1982** *Barrick Coll.* **csPA**, *Salty*—expensive.

salty sage See **salt sage 1**

salty trout See **saltwater trout**

salud intj [Span, literally "health"] Cf **scat** intj
Used as an expression of good will toward one who has sneezed.

1967 *DARE* (Qu. NN18, *When somebody sneezes, what do people say to him?*) Infs **TX**3, 4, 31, 41, Salud.

saluggi n |ˌsəˈluǰi| Also *s(a)loogie, salugie, salugi* [Etym unknown] **NYC** Cf **monkey-in-the-middle**
An unorganized game among children in which an article is snatched away from a victim and tossed back and forth among the tormentors; also used as a call in the game.

1975 Ferretti *Gt. Amer. Book Sidewalk Games* 169, *Saluggi,* or *Saloogie,* is another rather simple game that derives from torment. Two or more players simply take something . . virtually anything that can be construed as something of a treasure . . from another kid and throw it back and forth . . while the owner tries desperately to get back his or her property. The only rules are that whoever catches the item must shout, "Saloogie on Chris's knife!," . . or whatever and that the victim must be angry, which is not at all difficult. It is not necessary to choose up for a game of Saloogie; rather, the predators have to decide on a victim, which is not difficult. **1977** *NY Times* (NY) 6 July 29, It was a game as valid to him and his friends as stoop-ball, kick the can, ring-a-lievio, red rover and salugi were to an earlier generation. **1985** *DARE* File **NYC** (as of c1920), [səˈluːǰi]. . . was what we called a nasty little practice in grade school when children—when, the boys—got out. . . Someone would say, "Let's play [səˈluːǰi]!" And he would grab the cap off the head of the nearest boy. . . and he would *fling* the cap to someone . . across the way. The boy whose cap it was would go *rushing* after it, and of course the recipient [would] . . fling it off to someone else. And this kept on until the boy was in tears, or until he got so angry that he started to beat people. . . Sometimes. . . after the person was in despair . . somebody would [say] "*Ah!* give it to him!" **1987** *Ibid* **Bronx NYC** (as of 1955), *Salugi* [ˌsəˈluǰi]—an unorganized torment "played" by boys, which involved snatching the cap or hat off one boy's head and tossing it back and forth between confederates until the victim either retrieved his cap or was reduced to tears or the use of his fists. Although the cap was the article most frequently snatched, any small article would do. The victim received no warning—all of a sudden he would hear the cry "Salugi!" and his cap would be gone. **1993** *Ibid* **NYC**, [Re descriptions of saluggi:] Sounds like saloogie/sloogie all right! Did I tell you it's also known as Monkey In The Middle? *Ibid* **NYC**, Salugi is/was a rather malicious "game" . . that *must* have a victim, one who is not a willing player. At least for me, monkey-in-the-middle has no such constraints. *Ibid* **NYC**, I grew up in Brooklyn, but learned the "game" in Manhattan and the Bronx. It is that fine old vicious childhood game of stealing a kid's hat. . . Usually the kid is fat or short or weak or the wrong sex or wrong color—in any case it is certainly a Persecution Model game. . . I learned the word [=saluggi], then, in Northern New York City in the 1950s, and have heard it nowhere else.

salute n scattered, but more freq NEast, rare West See Map
Often in combs: A noise-making firework.

1923 U.S. Dept. Commerce *Regulations for Transportation of Explosives: Pamphlet 10* 11 (*W3* File), Giant firecrackers, bombs, and salutes. **1950** Natl. Fireworks Corp. *Catalog* 8 (*W3* File), This old reliable item needs little description. One of our best noise makers. *2" National Flash Salutes.* **1953** *Springfield Union* (MA) 30 June 6, Youngsters armed with salutes tossed them from their hands or lit them in trees or on curbstones in many parts of the city. **1965–70** *DARE* (Qu. FF14, . . *Kinds of firecrackers*) 88 Infs, **scattered, but more freq NEast, rare West**, Salutes; **NY73**, Cherry salutes; **CT73**, Giant salutes; **MN36**, Minnesota salute; **IL72**, Victor salutes; (Qu. FF28, . . *Kinds of fireworks;* not asked in early QRs) Infs **IN68, LA35**, Salutes. **2000** *DARE* File—Internet [Dyberry Fireworks], 21st Century Salutes (1–⅝").

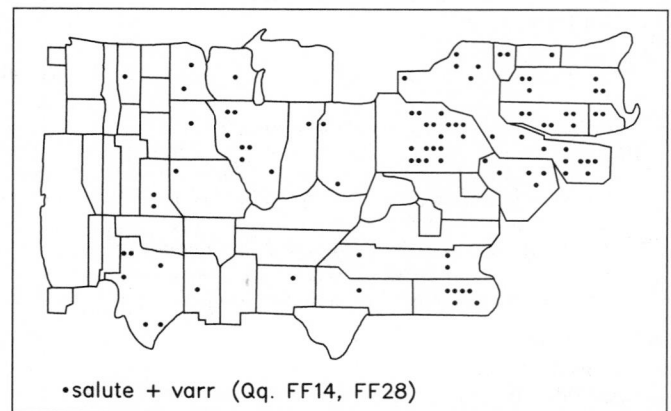

•salute + varr (Qq. FF14, FF28)

salvagerous See **savagerous**

salve bug n
An isopod (*Aega psora*) or similar crustacean; see quots.

1890 *Century Dict.* 5322, *Salve bug.* . . A parasitic isopod crustacean, *Æga psora,* and some similar forms. One of these, parasitic on the cod, is *Caligus curtus,* sometimes used as an unguent by sailors. **1935** Pratt *Manual Invertebrate Animals* 435, *A[ega] psora.* . . Salve bug. . . Parasitic on the skate, cod, halibut, and other fishes; used as a salve by fishermen; Long Island Sound to Greenland; Gulf of Mexico; Europe.

salvia n
In combs *old-field salvia, pasture* ~: **=blue toadflax.**

1951 *PADS* 15.40 **TX**, *Linaria texana* [=*Nuttallanthus canadensis*]—Harebell . . pasture, or old-field, salvia.

salvy adj Pronc-sp *savvy* [Cf *EDD salvy* adj. 1 "Greasy, oily, soapy; of the complexion: pale, sickly"]

See quots.

1859 in 1861 IL State Ag. Soc. *Trans.* 4.103, Care should be taken not to work it too much, as it will hurt the grain of the butter and make it salvy. **2000** *DARE* File **nwMA** (as of c1910–present), Salvy ['sævi] means neither hard nor soft, more gluey. If you put flour in the filling of a fruit pie instead of tapioca, it'll be salvy. *Ibid* **ME**, Have you heard of . . "savvy" to mean sweaty? This word is used in South Bristol, Maine . . by dialect speakers.

salza See **salsa**

sam n[1] See **psalm**

Sam n[2] [Abbr for **Sambo** n[1]] *now chiefly among Black speakers*

A Black person.

1867 Dixon *New Amer.* 470, What negro dares to put his feet on the white man's steps? Sam likes his free condition . . but he also loves his skin. **1928** Fisher *Walls Jericho* 304 **NYC** [Black], Sam—See *boogy*. *Ibid* 297, [*Boogy*]—Negro. A contraction of *Booker T.*, used only of and by members of the race.] **1937** *Writer* 50.239 **neOH**, *Sam*—Negro's name for Negroes. **1938** *AmSp* 13.152 [Black], *Sam*. A negro who demeans himself to secure favor with white people.

Sam n[3]

1 in phrr *cut up* (or *raise*) *Sam:* To be noisy or rowdy; to cause a disturbance. Cf *cut up jack* (at **jack** n[1] **14**), **raise sand**

1945 *AmSp* 20.83 **TX**, Many Texans spend happy leisure hours 'goin' out tonkin'.' This means they go to 'honky-tonks.' Sooner or later, being extremely high-spirited, they will start 'cuttin' up Sam,' and eventually somebody will call 'the laws.' **1968** *DARE* FW Addit **GA33**, *Raise Sam*, meaning: "raise hell, cause a disturbance."

2 =**opossum.** [Prob abbr for **poor Sam**]

1968 *DARE* (Qu. P31, . . *Names or nicknames . . for the . . opossum*) Inf **IN46**, Sam.

Sambo n[1] [From a personal name of Afr origin; cf Wolof *Samb(a)*, Mandingo *Sambu*, Hausa *Sambo*] *often derog or joc* Cf **Sam** n[2]

Used as a nickname for a Black man or as a personification of Black people in general.

[**1704** *Boston News–Letter* (MA) 2 Oct 2/2, There is a Negro man taken up supposed to be Runaway from his Master . . calls himself *Sambo*.] **1806** Fessenden *Democracy Unveiled* 24, Our *daughters* and our *wives.* . . Will strengthen Jefferson's resources / By Sambo's social intercourses. **1841** *Daily Picayune* (New Orleans LA) 12 Jan 2/2, Literally speaking, the Sambos and their 'lubly' Dinahs were going the whole figure. **1853** Simms *Sword & Distaff* 199 **SC**, Sambo seldom troubles himself to look out for the morrow. **1857** Long *Pictures Slavery* (2d ed) 145 **MD**, The negro was the sure crop, though he sold cheap. If the master wanted to build a new house, he sold one or two negroes. If he bought a fine carriage, poor Sambo had to look out. **1864** in 1947 Ayers *Diary* 6, Oh wont Rebs here sware if they have to be garded by sambo. **1877** Rusling *Gt. West* 318, As the ocean receives all rains and rivers, and yet shows it not, so America receives the Saxon and the Celt, the Protestant and the Catholic, and can yet receive Sambo and John, and absorb them all. **1885** in 1894 Lowell *Letters* 2.301, Haven't they resuscitated Sambo in a shape as *descomunal* as ever, after we had dismounted him once and for all? **1941** *LANE* Map 452b *(Nicknames for a Negro)* 4 infs, **CT, NH, MA**, Sambo. **1948** Faulkner *Intruder* 154 **MS**, The postulate that Sambo is a human being living in a free country and hence must be free. **1966** Dakin *Dial. Vocab. Ohio R. Valley* 2.448, Some older informants, chiefly from more isolated rural areas where their contact with Negroes is very infrequent, still use *nigger* in this neutral way. The aged southerner—isolated and nearly illiterate—in Brown County, Indiana . . is an example. . . His derogatory terms are *coon* and *Sambo*. **1967–70** *DARE* [(Qu. C34, *Nicknames for nearby settlements, villages, or districts*) Inf **TX42**, Sambo;] (Qu. HH28, *Names and nicknames . . for people of foreign background: Negro*) Inf **MA128**, Black Sambo; **GA83**, Sambo. **1971** Bright *Word Geog. CA & NV* 115 **CA**, *(Negro/derogatory)* Sambo 2 [infs, both Black] Los Angeles and East Bay. **1986** Pederson *LAGS Concordance*, 3 infs, **GA, TX**, Sambo(s); 1 inf, **cwMS**, Sambo—older term; 1 inf, **seLA**,

Sambo—derogatory; 1 inf, **cnTX**, Little Black Sambo—derogatory. [5 of 6 infs White]

Sambo n[2] Cf **poor Sam, Sam** n[3] **2**
=**opossum.**
1927 [see **poor Sam**].

sambo n[3] [Appar var, by folk-etym, of **song bow**]
=**mouth bow.**
1989 *DARE* File **cnNC**, One informant here tells me about the "sambo": "It's got one string. You rive you out a piece of pine and you make it like a bow and arrow. You put one string across it and you pick it like you do a jew's-harp." . . But—I've not found anybody playing it any more.

sambridge See **sandwich**

Sam Day n
=**menhaden 1.**
1894 *DN* 1.332 **NJ**, *Menhaden:* called . . "Sam Days," . . in Cape May County. **1945** Beck *Jersey Genesis* 147 **NJ**, "We've called 'em [=menhaden] mossybunkers, greentails, and Sam Days, too." Some say the name is that of a man who was in the business; others have told me Sam Day is the modern variation that began with *samedi*, but the significance has been lost.

same like conj phr, prep phr, adj phr (also used absol) Pronc-sp *same lukkuh* [Engl dial] **chiefly Sth** *esp freq among Black speakers*

In the same manner as; just like; same, identical.

1861 *Harper's New Mth. Mag.* 23.395 **GA** [Black], Same like me now got dis possum swinged and ready fur de pot. **1887** *Catholic World* 44.777 **NC** [Black], You talk like you want Uncle Ryal fed up an' pompered up the same like . . he were a fightin'-cock. **1922** Gonzales *Black Border* 324 **sSC, GA coasts** [Gullah glossary], *Same lukkuh* . . same like, like, resembling. **1928** Peterkin *Scarlet Sister Mary* 47 **SC** [Gullah], E weddin-dress fits em same like a green shuck fits a young ear o' corn. *Ibid* 207, If you cry here on dis wood-pile to-day I'll lay down on de ground an' holler same like a dog. *Ibid* 227, "How you do to-day?" . . "Fine. . . Same like a lamb a-jumpin." **1934** Carmer *Stars Fell on AL* 182 [Black], You got de same like red 'roun' your th'oat. **1986** Pederson *LAGS Concordance*, 1 inf, **cGA**, In the same like manner that you do wheat. [Inf Black] **1991** Still *Wolfpen Notebooks* 26 **sAppalachians**, Personally, I've never been bothered about being called a "hillbilly" or "briar." They're synonomous [sic]—the "samelike," as we say.

same old six and seven, the phr Also *the same old seven and six, ~ seventy-six, ~ sixes and sevens* [*seven and six* is the older form, and originally stood for "seven shillings and sixpence"; the reverse order is prob due to the infl of *at sixes and sevens*. Cf the now obsolete (at least in the US) expressions *the same old sixpence, ~ two and sixpence* and Brit Engl *the same old six and eightpence*.]

Much as usual, the same as always.

1863 in 2001 *DARE* File—Internet **sIN**, [Civil War diary entry:] The same old seven and six. I am on camp guard today. **1915** *DN* 4.190 **swVA**, Six and seven, same old, phr. 'Same old' routine, story, etc. **1935** in 2001 *DARE* File—Internet **ceMS**, The Key Brothers indicated as heretofore, "It's the same old seven and six up here." **1963** Wright *Lawd Today* 63 **Chicago IL** [Black], "How's yourself?" "Aw, pretty good. What you know?" "Nothing. Same old 6's and 7's. What you know?" **1981** *Verbatim Letters* **TX**, I first heard this expression in a variation, "the same old seven and six." Between 1934–1938 while a student at Baylor University, Waco, Texas. It was usually given in response to the inquiry of "How are you" or "How's things?" and usually given when a period of time had elapsed between meetings of the two persons involved. It meant that there are seven days in a week and you have been working six days a week but nothing interesting or unusual had happened since the last encounter. *Ibid* **IN**, My husband . . says, "the same old seventy-six" when referring to a boring, routine day. *Ibid*, I have always heard "the same old seven and six" rather than the other way around. **1981** *DARE* File **nwKS** (as of c1900), "The same old six and seven" . . was my grandfather's answer to the question, "How are things?" My father uses this expression and I picked it up from him. **1984** Wilder *You All Spoken Here* 198 **Sth**, *Same old six and seven:* The same as always—it still adds up to thirteen and no luck. **1986** Pederson *LAGS Concordance*, 1 inf, **cTX**, Same old six and seven—i.e., nothing new. **2001** *DARE* File—Internet **CA,** It's the same old six and seven . . those who 'get it,' *get it,* and those who don't, continue to claim personal rights to use synthetic scents.

same quill, of the See **quill** n 6

Sam hill crane See **sandhill crane**

sammidge, sammitch See **sandwich**

samp n [Of Algonquian origin; cf Narraganset *nasaump* "softened by water"] **chiefly NEast** Cf **hominy B1**
Whole hulled corn or coarsely ground cornmeal, esp when prepared as porridge.

[**1634** Wood *New Engl. Prospect* sig O2ᵛ, [From a vocabulary of "the Natives Language":] *Nasamp*—pottage.] **1643** Williams *Key into Language* 11 **RI,** *Nasàump,* a kind of meale pottage, unparch'd. From this the *English* call their *Samp,* which is the *Indian* corne, beaten and boild, and eaten hot or cold with milke or butter. **1672** Josselyn *New-Englands Rarities* 53, The blew Corn . . is light of digestion, and the *English* make a kind of Loblolly of it, . . which they call *Sampe.* **1713** (1901) Hempstead *Diary* 5 Dec 30 **seCT,** I was at home al day fixing Sampmorter & killing Sheep. **1761** in 1888 Huntington NY *Town Rec.* 2.448, Jacob Brush should have Lyberty to Build a samp Mill in the Meeting house Brook. **1830** *VA Lit. Museum* 1.479, *Samp.* "Corn broken coarsely, boiled and mixed with milk." *Indian.* **1893** *Harper's New Mth. Mag.* 88.33 **NYC,** Then a canvas-back apiece . . with samp, of course, and a mayonnaise of celery. **1898** (1899) Earle *Home Life* 131 **NEng,** The various foods which we use to-day made from Indian corn are all cooked just as the Indians cooked them at the time of the settlement of the country; and they are still called with Indian names, such as hominy, pone, suppawn, samp, succotash. **1932** *DN* 6.284 **swCT,** *Samp.* Whole corn soaked in weak lye, a hominy to be eaten with milk. **1939** Wolcott *Yankee Cook Book* 106, Both hulled corn and hominy (samp) may be purchased today in two forms—hulled and ready to cook . . or in tins, all cooked. **1940** Brown *Amer. Cooks* 375 **MA,** *Sampit* [sic] *bread*—2 tablespoons butter₍,₎ ½ cup cooked hominy₍,₎ 2 eggs, beaten light₍,₎ ⅝ cup corn flour₍,₎ ½ teaspoon salt₍,₎ milk. **1941** *LANE* Map 288 *(Corn meal mush)* 4 infs, **CT, ME, VT,** Samp; 1 inf, **swCT,** Samp—of whole crushed corn; 1 inf, **swMA,** Samp—of coarse meal; 1 inf, **seME,** Samp—of hulled corn. **1967–69** *DARE* (Qu. H24, . . *Names or nicknames . . for boiled cornmeal*) Infs **NY34,** 72, 220, **NC41,** Samp; **MI68,** Samp—Indian name for cornmeal mush. **1991** *DARE* File **seNY,** Samp = hulled Indian corn, coarsely cracked. Also called samp porridge and Sam Porridge. **1998** *Yankee* Nov 20, Hasty pudding was originally an English porridge of wheat flour cooked in hot water or milk. . . When the Pilgrims arrived on these shores and learned about corn from the Indians, it was only natural for them to use the familiar name for a dish that differed only in the choice of starch employed. The locals called the stuff *na'samp* or *nausamp,* which the visitors shortened to *samp.* Later generations said cornmeal mush.

Sam Patch n Also *Sam Scratch* [Amer daredevil who died on Nov 13, 1829, attempting to jump the Genesee Falls near Rochester, New York] Cf **Old Scratch**
Used as a euphem for the devil or hell; see quots.

1892 *Atlantic Mth.* 70.794 **sCA,** Letterlone; she's as cross as Sam Patch. **1905** *DN* 3.64 **eNE,** Sam Patch, Sam Scratch. . . "I feel like Sam Scratch." **1906** *DN* 3.154 **nwAR,** Sam Patch. . . In the expression, "What in Sam Patch?" "What in Sam Patch are you all doing?" **1947** *AmSp* 22.204, Sam Patch. . . Equiv. of . . Sam Hill . . still in colloq. use in Middle West, in mild expletive 'What the Sam Patch!' **1951** *PADS* 15.60 **ceIN** (as of 1890s), Sam Patch. . . Euphemism . . for the devil. . . "What the Sam Patch is goin' on here?"

Sam Peabody See **peabody bird**

samphire n [*OED2* 1545 → for the European plant *Crithmum maritimum,* 1703 → for "various other maritime plants, esp. the glasswort"]
1 Either **glasswort** or a plant of the related genera *Arthrocnemum* and *Sarcocornia.*

[**1794** Barham *Hortus Americanus* 165, *Sampier. . .* There is another sort, which resembles the English *kali, kelp,* or glass-wort; another sort hath a thick juicy saltish leaf, in shape of purslane . . ; another sort hath a turnsole leaf.] **1822** Eaton *Botany* 440, *Salicornia. . . herbacea* (samphire, glasswort . .). It grows in salt marshes along the sea board. . . It is used for pickles and for making soda. **1897** Parsons *Wild Flowers CA* 387, The samphire, or glasswort, is the source of a wonderful glory in

our marshes in the autumn. **1910** Graves *Flowering Plants* 168 **CT,** *Salicornia. . .* Samphire. . . Frequent or common on salt marshes and shores. **1943** Fernald–Kinsey *Edible Wild Plants E. N. Amer.* 183, "Samphire," . . *Salicornia* (various species). . . The name "Samphire" is in colloquial use in America for these plants, but they should not be confused with the quite different samphire of Europe. **1970** Correll *Plants TX* 548, *Salicornia utahensis. . . Utah samphire. . .* Edge of saline lakes and along shores and on islands, Ut., N.M. and Tex. **1974** Welsh *Anderson's Flora AK* 106, *Salicornia pacifica* [=*S. virginica*]. . . *Pacific Samphire. . .* Saline tidal flats and beaches.

2 =**pickleweed 2.**

1931 U.S. Dept. Ag. *Misc. Pub.* 101.36 **SW,** Pickleweed *(Allenrolfia occidentalis),* known . . frequently, but erroneously, as samphire, is a fleshy, jointed, and practically leafless undershrub of the Great Basin and Southwest.

sample house n Also *sample home*
A model house.

1890 *Overland Mth.* 15.671 **San Francisco CA,** Portable Cottages! Can be put up and taken down at will. . . Sample house to be seen on Van Ness Avenue, just north of McAllister Street. **1952** *Reading Eagle* 13 July 39/5 *(Mathews Coll.)* **PA,** Sample home open daily and Sunday, 12 p.m. to 8 p.m. *Ibid* 39/6, Sample House—College Heights—Open Sunday 3:00 to 8:00 p.m. **1986** *DARE* File **sePA, sNJ,** Sample House—Used in the Philadelphia/South Jersey area for a Model House in a new development. I've not seen the term used elsewhere.

sample room n
A saloon, barroom.

1856 *Programme* (N.Y.) 18 Dec. 3/2 *(Mathews Coll.),* In a well arranged Sample Room in the rear, may also be found Wines, Liquors, and Cordials of the finest qualities imported. **1865** Sala *Diary in Amer.* 2.46 **NYC,** Sometimes the bar is at the side, screened off, and genteelly disguised under the name of "sample room." **1885** *South Fla. Sentinel* (Orlando) 29 April 3/1 *(DAE),* A gentleman from Georgia is about to start a sample and billiard room. **1896** *Chicago Rec.* (IL) 13 Jan 11/6, For Sale—Corner Sample-room. . . license paid. **1931** *AmSp* 7.86 [Prohibition terms], Places of business for illegal traffic in liquor. . . Sample room. **1935** in 1953 Botkin–Harlow *Treas. Railroad Folkl.* 77 **NEng,** The reporters were in no shape to write their copy until they had been treated at the nearest sample room by the populace. **1938** Hart *New Yorkers* 180, The "quiet trade" sipped their gin at "sample rooms" such as Haan's on the site of the present Hotel McAlpin. **1946** Driscoll *Country Jake* 19 **KS** Not only did Johnny Mahan have the agency for Anheuser–Busch beers and some of the best Kentucky whiskies; he also owned most of the saloons, or "sample rooms," in which these beverages were dispensed.

Sampson n¹, v See **Samson** n¹

Sampson n² See **Sampson's snakeroot**

Sampson fox n Also sp *Samson fox* [In allusion to Judges 15:4, because of the singed appearance of the fur]
A red fox with woolly or otherwise abnormal fur; see quots.

1903 Rhoads *Mammals PA & NJ* 148, The red fox is nowhere common in N.J. as in Pa. . . A Samson fox is merely one whose pelage has become worn, thin, curly or crisp. . . It indicates a run-down or depauperate condition, or may sometimes result from being caught in forest fires. **1915** (1916) Johnson *Highways New Engl.* 57, Sometimes too, we'd shoot what we called a Samson fox that you'd think, to see it, had been in the fire and got its fur singed. It looked so mean that the hide wasn't worth much. **1961** Jackson *Mammals WI* 299, Vernacular names [for *Vulpes vulpes*]. . . Sampson . . fox (color and pelage-condition phase). *Ibid* 300, Rarely, a red fox lacks some or all of the guard hairs, and the woolly animal may be called a Sampson fox. **1982** Elman *Hunter's Field Guide* 362, When a hunter or trapper speaks derisively of a Sampson . . fox, he means an animal with a skin affliction which halts the development of guard hairs, rendering the pelt worthless.

Sampson root n

1 See **Sampson's snakeroot 1.**

2 A **purple coneflower** (here: either *Echinacea angustifolia* or *E. pallida*). Cf **black sampson**

1900 Lyons *Plant Names* 69, B[rauneria] pallida [=*Echinacea p.*] . . Sampson-root. *Root* alterative; remedy for snake-bite. **1930** Sievers *Amer. Med. Plants* 27, *Brauneria angustifolia* [=*Echinacea a.*] . . Sampson-root. . . *Part used.*—The root, collected in autumn. In reasonably constant demand. **1936** Whitehouse *TX Flowers* 175, *Sampson's Root. . . (Echinacea angustifolia). . .* is hard to distinguish from the pale purple cone-flower *(Echinacea pallida).*

Sampson's snakeroot n Also *Sam(p)son, Sampson snakeroot, Samson('s)* ~ Cf **black sampson, Sampson root, strong man Sampson**

1 also *Sampson root:* Any of several **gentians,** but usu *Gentiana andrewsii, G. catesbaei, G. saponaria,* or *G. villosa.* **chiefly Sth**

1830 Rafinesque *Med. Flora* 2.223, *Gentiana. . . G. ochroleuca* [=*G. villosa*] and *G. catesbei* often called *Simpson* [sic] *root* or *Snake root* in the South, nauseous, used for bites of snakes, nervous fevers, pneumonia, &c. **1854** King *Amer. Eclectic Dispensatory* 494, *Gentiana ochroleuca* [=*G. villosa*]. . . This plant is likewise known by the names of *Marsh Gentian,* . . *Sampson Snakeroot,* etc. . . Also used for bites of snakes, and in typhus fevers, pneumonia, etc. **1869** Porcher *Resources* 554 **Sth,** Sampson's Snakeroot . . *(Gentiana Catesbaei).* **1876** Hobbs *Bot. Hdbk.* 101, Sampson root, Sampson snake root, Gentiana ochroleuca. **1901** Lounsberry *S. Wild Flowers* 430, *G[entiana] Saponaria. . .* This gentian and the species, *[Gentiana] villosa,* . . also the closed or blind one [=*Gentiana andrewsii*], seem all to be indiscriminately called through the mountains Samson's snakeroot, and decoctions made from them are taken in great doses as a remedy for dyspepsia and are favourably regarded as powerful tonics to invigorate the system. . . They use it for their horses also. . . The negroes, on the other hand, have really faith that the gentians can cure snake-bite. **c1938** in 1970 Hyatt *Hoodoo* 2.934 **cVA,** This here's a Samson [Hyatt: or Sampson—sometimes called Sampson snakeroot]. *Ibid* 1741 **seGA,** An' de first root he give me an' tole me tuh chip some off an' put in de pot wus *John de Conker.* De next one wus de Samson snakeroot. Wel, dem two wus put in dere. **1938** in 1972 *Amer. Slave* 2.1.24 **SC,** De people never didn' put much faith to de doctors in dem days. Mostly, dey would use de herbs in de fields for dey medicine. Dere two herbs, I hear talk of. Dey was black snake root en Sampson snake root. **1953** Greene–Blomquist *Flowers South* 100, *Samson's-Snakeroot (Gentiana villosa)* One of the most widely distributed gentians which is fairly frequent although never especially abundant. **1986** Pederson *LAGS Concordance,* 1 inf, **cAL,** Sampson snakeroot—medicinal root; 1 inf, **swAL,** Sampson snakeroot—for medicinal tea, stimulates; 1 inf, **ceMS,** Sampson snakeroot; 1 inf, **seMS,** Sampson snakeroot—for colic; 1 inf, **csTN,** Sampson snakeroot. [*DARE* Ed: Some of these infs may refer instead to senses below.]

2 =**cocash 2.**

1854 King *Amer. Eclectic Dispensatory* 265, The Aster Aestivus, named *Rheumatic-weed,* also *Sampson Snakeroot, Star-flower,* etc., resembles the above plant [=*Aster puniceus*]. **1876** Hobbs *Bot. Hdbk.* 97, Rheumatic weed, Sampson's snake root, Aster aestivus. *Ibid* 101, Sampson snake root, Aster aestivus.

3 A **scurf pea** (here: *Orbexilum pedunculatum*). **chiefly Sth, S Midl**

1892 (1894) Foster *Illustr. Encycl. Med. Dict.* 4.2660, *P[soralea] eglandulosa* [=*Orbexilum pedunculatum*]. Samson's snakeroot. **1901** Lounsberry *S. Wild Flowers* 260, *Samson's Snakeroot. Psoralea pedunculata. Ibid* 261, Although the common name of this rather unattractive plant seems undoubtedly to be Samson's snakeroot, it is the one which the mountaineers of the south reserve exclusively for the blue gentian. **1922** *Amer. Botanist* 28.76, In all probability the name "Sampson snakeroot" applied to *Psoralea pedunculata* is derived from "sainfoin." **1937** in 1987 *Hall Coll.* **wNC, eTN,** Samson's snakeroot—plant used in the treatment of colic. "It has a little long blossom that blooms in September, a little pod, an' hit blue." **1941** Walker *Lookout* 48 **TN,** Among the wild plants once employed as antidotes for the bites of poisonous reptiles, are rattlesnake master, blacksnake root, rattlesnake-weed, Samson snakeroot, or scurfy. **1953** Greene–Blomquist *Flowers South* 56, *Sampson's-Snakeroot . . (Psoralea psoralioides). . .* Ranges in the Coastal Plain from Fla. to Tex. n. to Ind. and Va. **1970** *NC Folkl.* 8.16, Sampson snakeroot tea was used to treat colic (bellyache).

4 A **wild ginger** (here: *Hexastylis arifolia*).

1974 Morton *Folk Remedies* 73 **SC,** Wild Ginger. Old plants with large leaves sometimes called *"Sampson's snakeroot,"* a name applied to several different plants in the South. *Hexastylis arifolia.*

Samson n[1] Also sp *Sampson* Also *Samson pole* [In allusion to the strength of the Biblical *Samson:* cf Judges 13–16] **Nth, esp NEng** Cf **kilhig**

In logging: any of var contrivances, usu involving a massive lever, for applying an extraordinary force, esp one used to di-

rect the fall of a tree; hence v *Sampson* to move with such a contrivance.

1905 U.S. Forest Serv. *Bulletin* 61.45 **nNEng, nNY** [Logging terms], *Sampson. . .* An appliance for loosening or starting logs by horsepower. It usually consists of a strong, heavy timber and a chain terminating in a heavy swamp hook. The timber is placed upright beside the piece to be moved, the chain fastened around it, and the hook inserted low down on the opposite side. Leverage is then applied by a team hitched to the upper end of the upright timber. *Ibid, Sampson a tree, to.* To direct the fall of a tree by means of a lever and pole. **1913** Bryant *Logging* 83, *Kilhig* or *Sampson. . .* It consists of a pole . . from 8 to 16 feet long, either sharpened or armed on one end with a spike. In operation the pointed end of the pole is placed in a notch in the tree trunk from 5 to 8 feet above ground. The free end projects downward to a point 10 or 12 inches above the ground where it is supported on a peavey handle or a pole the lower end of which is firmly planted in the ground. A laborer grasps the free end of the peavey handle and by pressing forward is able to exert a very strong pressure against the bole of the tree. **1958** McCulloch *Woods Words* 156 **Pacific NW,** *Sampson. . .* A pry to help shove over a tree which is difficult to fall. . . *Sampson a tree*—To shove a tree toward the desired line of fall with a lever. **1966** *DARE* FW Addit **nME,** Samson—a type of lever for making a tree fall in a certain direction. **1971** *Chr. Sci. Monitor* (Boston MA) 13 May **NEng,** Then comes into use the Samson pole. . . By rigging two lengths of poles, the men contrive a simple leverage, and they can push the tree the way they want it to go, and get their saw out.

Samson n[2] See **Sampson's snakeroot**

Samson fox See **Sampson fox**

Samson pole See **Samson** n[1]

Samson('s) snakeroot See **Sampson's snakeroot**

samwich, samwidge See **sandwich**

san' See **sang** n

Sancho n[1] [From the character in J.W. Cunningham's didactic novel *Sancho, or the Proverbialist* (London, 1816)] **esp MA** Cf **Sanko** n

In phr *act like Sancho* and varr; Of a child: to act in an unruly or mischievous way; hence n *sancho* an unruly, mischievous child.

[**1855** *U.S. Democratic Rev.* 36.338 **NYC,** He inaugurates a system of neighborhood donations, of creature comforts, and of personal coddlings, that finds the Reverend gentleman, with little Sancho at least, "making much of himself."] **1862** *Atlantic Mth.* 10.588 **MA,** They thought we were going to find them little monsters, which their motherly hearts were persuaded they were not, though they behaved like little sanchos at home. **1869** Alcott *Little Women* 2.141 **MA,** Had a lively time in my seminary, this morning, for the children acted like Sancho. **1874** (1969) Coffin *Caleb Krinkle* 69 **MA,** They were compelled to put up with it, because it was Mr. Meek's boy that did it. "He is a little Sancho," said Dan Dishaway, comparing him not to the jolly esquire of "Don Quixote," but adopting a name which popularly was supposed to have reference to the father of all mischief. **1909** *DN* 3.407 **nME,** *Act like Sancho. . .* To misbehave, of a child. **1913** *DN* 4.55 **seMA,** *Act like Sancho. . .* To behave very badly. "Pa, I don't know what to do with Caleb: he's acted like Sancho all day."

sancho n[2] [MexSpan] **West** Cf **dogie**

A runty animal, esp an orphaned one; see quots.

1929 Dobie *Vaquero* 212 **West,** A few of the cows were so wild that they would not come to the pens even for their calves. In that event the calves might be released to their mothers, or they might be suckled to other cows and thus raised as *sanchos* (dogies). **1966** *DARE* (Qu. K65, *A sheep that's kept as a pet;* total Infs questioned, 75) Inf **NM3,** Sancho ['sančo]—Mexican.

Sanctified (Church) n Also *Sanctification* Pronc-sp (by assim) *Sanctify;* abbr *Sanct* [See quot 1980] **Sth, S Midl** *chiefly among Black speakers*

Any of several fundamentalist churches emphasizing holiness and sanctification; a member of such a church.

1938 FWP *Ocean Highway* 203 **SC,** In this little building which was once a country store, worship a group of Negroes who call themselves "The Sanctify." **1942** *Jrl. Amer. Folkl.* 55.218 **LA** [Black], The name

[=*Easter rock*], as the first deacon . . explains it, is derived from the fact that "everything rocks." The sancts rock; the church . . rocks; the earth rocks; and the sun rocks as it comes over the horizon.   **1965–70** DARE (Qu. CC3, . . *Religions that have come in recently . . or are a bit different from the common ones*) Infs **FL**33, **MS**80, 88, **MO**23, **NC**87, **TN**53, **VA**50, **WV**20, Sanctified (Church); **SC**10, Holy Sanctify—one that has "shouting," guitars, and more excitement; (Qu. CC2, . . *Predominant religious denominations*) Infs **FL**51, **VA**69, Sanctification; **MO**29, Sanctified; **TN**48, Sanctified Church; (Qu. CC4, . . *Nicknames . . for various religions or religious groups*) Inf **FL**51, Holy-rollers (Sanctification)—dance and shout; Saints (Sanctification)—don't wear any kind of makeup, long dresses; **TN**53, Sanctified Church; **VA**41, Sanctified—ingroup word; [**SC**64, Sanctity Church]. [14 of 15 total Infs Black]   **1969** DARE File **St. Louis MO** [Black], *Sanctified.* . . The Church of God in Christ. "When we really wanted a good sermon we went to the Sanctified." Very fundamental Negro Church. Sanctified generally used in place of correct name. Used by members only.   [**1980** Mead *Hdbk. Denominations U.S.* 81, *Christ's Sanctified Holy Church*—This church began with the preaching of holiness and sanctification in the Colored Methodist Episcopal Church in Louisiana by a small body of white evangelists; it was organized in 1904 as the Colored Church South.]   **1986** Pederson *LAGS Concordance (Baptist)* 1 inf, **csLA**, Sanctified; 1 inf, **cnLA**, Sanctified Church—Pentecostal, Holiness; *(They joined the church)* 1 inf, **cGA**, Sanctified; 1 inf, **seFL**, Sanctified Church; *(Protestants)* 1 inf, **cAR**, Sancfify [sic]; 1 inf, **cAR**, Sanctified—where people shout and clap hands; 1 inf, **nwLA**, Sanctified. [All infs Black]

sanctum suly n   Also *sankumsuly, sanctum sully*
In moonshining: see quots.
   1944 PADS 2.30 **KY**, *Sanctum suly* ['sæŋktəm 'sulɪ]. . . Good whisky. Used by a Ky. moonshiner in describing his product. Perhaps derived from Latin. The mountaineer, however, was illiterate.   **1962** Mt. Life 38.4.12 **sAppalachians**, If the vintage is raw and fiery it is said to be "as strong as akyfortis," but if it has mellowed in the moonlight it is sometimes referred to sweetly as "samkumsuly."   **1984** Wilder *You All Spoken Here* 138 **Sth**, *Sanctum sully:* Whiskey that drinks mighty easy.

sand n
1 Courage; tenacity; stamina—freq in phr *have sand in one's craw* and varr: to be courageous, tenacious, or energetic; hence adj *sandy* brave, resolute.   **chiefly Sth, S Midl**
   1867 Harris *Sut Lovingood Yarns* 102 **TN**, I tell yu, he hes lots ove san' in his gizzard; he is the bes' pluck I ever seed.   **1878** Hart *Sazerac Lying Club* 50 **NV**, He was one of them fellers what aint afraid of nothin' what walks or talks, but the quietest, silentest critter you ever seed, and he had so little to say, even when he was drinkin', and was always so good-natured and smilin' like, that a stranger would a' thought thar warn't no sand in him, and he wouldn't fight nothin'.   **1881** NY Times (NY) 18 Dec 4/3 **MT**, *Sand.*—To have "sand in one's craw." To be determined and plucky. Equivalent to "grit."   **1887** Kirkland *Zury* 538 **IL**, *Sand.* . . Courage, determination, obstinacy, perseverance, grit.   **1887** Francis *Saddle & Mocassin* 147 **swNM**, He's got all Sam's sand [Footnote: Pluck], and is cooler.   **1899** Garland *Boy Life* 224 **nwIA** (as of c1870s), And the hired man took a malicious delight in taunting the boys with lacking "sand."   **1904** Illustr. *Sporting News* 11 June 8/1, In Winslow she had a "sandy" and determined captain.   **1907** White *AZ Nights* 256, I'm looking for a man with sand and *sabe* of the country enough to lead a posse after cattle-rustlers into the border country.   **1909** DN 3.365 **eAL, wGA**, *Sand in one's craw.* . . Courage, tenacity.   **1910** Youth's Companion 15 Sept 477, It was sandy of Sheldon to go into that thing all by himself. It took nerve.   **1912** DN 3.589 **wIN**, *Sand in one's craw.* . . Courage. "He won't do it; he hasn't any sand in his craw."   **1923** DN 5.219 **swMO**, *Sand, no sand in his craw,* Nerveless, fearful, cowardly.   **1956** McAtee *Some Dialect NC* 38, *Sand.* . . courage.   **2001** DARE File **csWI** (as of c1960), My father used to say that if you had enough sand in your ass, you could take on anybody.
2 also *sand-dust:* the gritty matter that forms in the eyes when one is sleepy or sleeping.   [Cf *sandman* a folklore character who is supposed to make children sleepy by sprinkling sand in their eyes]
   1977 Morrison *Song of Solomon* 43 [Black], Well, before we could get the sand rubbed out of our eyes and take a good look around, we saw him sitting there on a stump.   **1981** AmSp 56.80 **MD**, Everybody in Frederick and Baltimore in my childhood knew what that gritty residue in the eyes was: it was *sand*, left there by the sandman, whose only function, as far as I knew, was to put it there.   **1981** Mebane *Mary* 15 **cnNC**, My eyes would have sand in them and Mama would tell me to go to bed.   **1983** DARE File **MN, VT**, *(The stuff in the corner of your eyes*

when you wake up in the morning) Sand.   **1984** Ibid **UT**, Sand-dust. Ibid **nIL, CO, UT**, Sand.   **1985** Ibid **MD, NJ**, Sand.   **1986** Ibid **VA, MD**, Sand.
3 in phr *raise sand:* See **raise sand**.

sand adder n   Cf **adder 1, sand viper**
=**hognose snake**.
   1879 Scribner's Mth. 18.650 **NJ**, Truth compels us also to admit that sand-adders are quite partial to the Hook [=Sandy Hook, New Jersey].   **1945** McCauley *Reptiles MD & DC* 63, *Heterodon contortrix contortrix.* . . Sand adder. . . A very stout-bodied snake attaining a length of three feet.   **1966–68** DARE (Qu. P25, . . *Kinds of snakes*) Inf **MN**42, Sand adder—lies in gravel pits—brown, spotted, also called blow snake; **SD**8, Sand adder.

sand-and-clay road n   Also *sand-clay road*   **chiefly S Atl, VA**
See Map
   1965–70 DARE (Qu. N27a, *Names . . for different kinds of unpaved roads*) Infs **MI**109, **MS**1, **SC**31, **VA**42, 46, 64, 96, Sand-and-clay road; **FL**7, **GA**84, 89, **NC**36, 52, Sand-clay road.

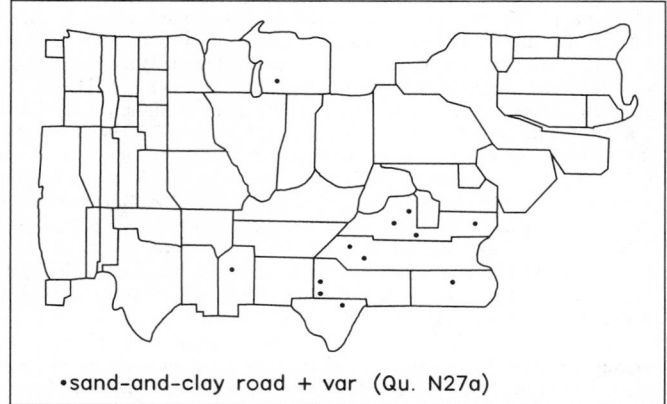

•sand-and-clay road + var (Qu. N27a)

sand ant n
1 A mound-building ant *(Formica exsectoides).*
   1966–69 DARE (Qu. R18, . . *Kinds of ants*) Infs **IN**62, **MN**2, **NJ**6, **NY**35, Sand ant(s); **IA**22, Sand ant—a red ant; **MI**24, Sand ants—build sand piles, sort of brown.
2 See quot.
   1966–67 DARE (Qu. R17, . . *Names . . for the big black ants that sting*) Infs **GA**13, **LA**8, Sand ant.

sand auger n   **SW**
=**dust devil 1**.
   1900 Nation 15 Nov 390, One of those little, waltzing whirlwinds so characteristic of the Southwest, and known to frontiersmen of our speech as "sand-augers."   **1968** Adams *Western Words* 266, *Sand auger*—A cowman's name for a little sand whirlwind.   **1982** TWA Ambassador July 47, *Dust devil.* . . In Death Valley, California, it is sometimes called a *sand auger.*

sandbag n   [Cf OED2 *sandbag* sb. 3 "The stomach of a crab"]
The stomach of a **terrapin** or a lobster; see quots.
   1888 Gossler *Turnpike-Road* 52 **eMD**, People ta'ks a mighty lot dis way 'n' dat 'bout de propah mannah o' cookin' of de tah'pin. . . When I wash a little shaver, . . people use' to wrap 'em in wet paper to keep out de grit, 'n' kiver up in de hot ashes on de hea'th; let him ros' dar til he well done, den take off de bottom shell, take out de bones, de sand-bag 'n' de gaul, chop up de res', eggs 'n' all, in de top shell.   **1929** Mod. Priscilla Cookbook 89, Open the [lobster's] body by splitting down the center. Remove the feathery, gill-like portions, sometimes referred to as "fingers," . . and also the sandbag, stomach, or "lady" as it is often called. This sandbag is found in the center of the body; it is tough and cartilaginous, grayish green in color.

sandbakkels n |'sɑnd'bɑkəls| Also *sandbakkelse, sandbakkel* (back-formation from *sandbakkels,* understood as pl)   Pronc-sp *sun buckle*   [Norw *sandbakkels(e)* sand cookie]   **MN, WI**
A butter cookie traditionally baked in a small, fluted tin.
   1966 Tufford *Scandinavian Recipes* 33 **MN**, *Sand Bakkels* (Sand Tarts) . . butter . . sugar . . flour . . eggs . . vanilla. Cream butter until

soft, beat in sugar . . add egg yolks and beat until creamy. Gradually stir in flour. . . Take a small piece of dough and press into fluted Sand Bakkels pans. . . This makes a cup shaped cookie. Bake in moderate oven. **1967** *DARE* Tape **MN**6, And then there are sand bakkelse ['sɑnd 'bɑkəlsə] which are made in a little sand bakkelse tin. **1981** Hachten *Flavor WI* 302, *Sand Bakkels* (Norwegian). . . Lacking a Sand Bakkels pan, the dough may be rolled out thinly and baked on cookie sheets. Some recipes call for topping the baked Sand Bakkels with chopped nuts, after brushing with egg whites. **1983** *Capital Times* (Madison WI) 11 May PM sec 19/2, Pastries include . . sand bakkelse. **1991** *Star Shopper* (Stoughton WI) 19 Nov 4, [Advt:] Let Us Help With Your Christmas Baking. . . Try These Norwegian Specialties. . . *Rosettes . . Berliner Kranser . . Sandbakkels.* **1994** *Courier Hub* (Stoughton WI) 12 May Special marketing sec 7/2, *Sun Buckles (Norwegian Sandbakkel-cookies).* **1998** *DARE* File **WI**, My mother-in-law, who grew up in a very Scandinavian small town in Wisconsin, still makes sandbakkels. In her usage the singular (and attributive) form is sandbakkel ['sɑnd,bɑkl]. **2000** *Ibid* **seWI** (as of c1950), Sandbakkels ['sɑnd'bɑkəls] were a common after-school treat at the homes of my playmates of Scandinavian heritage. Mrs. Fetters, a neighbor, frequently urged me to have "just one more sandbakkels" before going out to play.

sandbar willow n Cf **ditch willow, dog ~, frog ~**

1 A **willow** (here: *Salix exigua*) widely distributed throughout the US except in parts of the Southeast. Also called **coyote willow, gray ~, red ~ 1, silver ~, white ~**

1884 Sargent *Forests of N. Amer.* 168, *Salix longifolia* [=*S. exigua*]. . . Sand-Bar Willow. . . Very common throughout the Mississippi River basin, and reaching its greatest development in the valleys of Oregon and northern California. **1924** Deam *Shrubs IN* 46, The sandbar willow takes its name from the fact that it occurs commonly on sandbars and mudbars in streams and is one of the plants to occupy new-made bars. **1953** Strausbaugh–Core *Flora WV* 280, *Salix interior* [=*S. exigua*]. . . *sandbar willow.* . . Forming dense thickets on gravel, sand, and mud bars along streams, common in the Ohio Valley. **1968** *DARE* (Qu. T15, . . *Kinds of swamp trees*) Inf **WI**12, Sandbar willow. **1972** Viereck–Little *AK Trees* 126, Sandbar willow is an occasional pioneer on the sand and silt bars of the rivers of interior Alaska, where it is often the first willow to invade a newly exposed bar. **1974** Davis *Near Woods* 64 **WI**, A natural hedge of sandbar willows accompanied us for twenty or so yards into the lake. **1981** Benson–Darrow *Trees SW Deserts* 362, *Salix exigua.* . . *Sandbar Willow.* . . Along streams and bottomlands in all the deserts, the grasslands, all the woodlands and chaparrals, and the lower montane forests.

2 Either of two similar **willows:** *Salix sessilifolia* of the Pacific Northwest or *S. hindsiana* of California and Oregon.

1910 Jepson *Silva CA* 178, *Salix sessilifolia.* . . *Sandbar Willow.* . . Abundant in stream beds of the Coast Ranges, Great Valley, and Sierra foothills northward into Oregon. **1923** in 1925 Jepson *Manual Plants CA* 264, *S[alix] sessilifolia . . var. hindsiana.* . . *Sandbar Willow.* . . Abundant in flood beds of streams of the Coast Ranges, Great Valley, and Sierra Nevada foothills. **1959** Munz–Keck *CA Flora* 913, *S. hindsiana.* . . *Sandbar Willow.* . . Common locally along ditches, on sand bars, etc., below 3000 ft. **1981** Benson–Darrow *Trees SW Deserts* 362, *Salix sessilifolia . . var. leucodendroides.* . . *Sandbar Willow.* . . Along streams and arroyos.

sand bass n

1 also *sandy:* A **rock bass 2,** usu *Paralabrax nebulifer.* **CA**

1946 LaMonte *N. Amer. Game Fishes* 48, *California Sand Bass—Paralabrax nebulifer.* . . Over sandy bottom in shallow water. . . *California Kelp Bass—Paralabrax clathratus.* . . Sand Bass. . . Commonest in the kelp beds. **1953** Roedel *Common Fishes CA* 74, *Sand Bass—Paralabrax nebulifer.* . . A desirable sport species but of far less importance than is the kelp bass. **1955** Zim–Shoemaker *Fishes* 108, Kelp Bass [=*Paralabrax clathratus*]. . . is rare north of Monterey. Another sea bass of the Pacific is the Sand Bass, more common in the south than the Kelp Bass. **1970** *DARE* (Qu. P2, . . *Kinds of saltwater fish caught around here . . good to eat*) Inf **CA**181, Sand bass. **1999** *DARE* File—Internet **CA**, Sandbass. . . *Scientific Name*—Paralabrax nebulifer, family Serranidae (sea basses). . . *Common Names*—sand bass, sandies, cabrilla (Mexico). . . In some years, in certain locations, barred sand bass can comprise as much as 17% of all fish taken by the southern California marine recreational catch.

2 =**green sunfish 1.**

1951 Harlan–Speaker *IA Fish* 115, *Lepomis cyanellus.* . . Sand bass. . . This little sunfish is often mistaken for the bluegill . . Like the war-

mouth and rock bass, its body is rather short and stocky. **1983** Becker *Fishes WI* 822, *Lepomis cyanellus.* . . Other common names . . blue bass, . . sand bass.

3 also *sandy (bass):* A **white bass** (here: *Morone chrysops*). esp **OK, TX**

1949 Caine *N. Amer. Sport Fish* 122, *Colloquial Names* [for *Morone chrysops*] . . Gray Bass, . . Sand Bass [etc]. **1965–69** *DARE* (Qu. P1, . . *Kinds of freshwater fish . . caught around here . . good to eat*) Infs **OK**11, 25, 42, Sand bass; **TX**74, Sandy bass. **1968** *DARE* File **OK**, Sandy, sandies—sand bass. Term comes from area where there is much lake fishing, sand bass primary catch. Cf. National Sand Bass Festival—annual event at Lake Tecoma. **1974** *DARE* File **OK**, White bass are known as sandies to those Oklahomans who like to catch them on their spawning runs. **1986** Pederson *LAGS Concordance*, 1 inf, c**TX**, Sand bass—freshwater; 1 inf, ce**TX**, Sand bass. **1999** *DARE* File—Internet **TX**, The sandbass . . are also schooling on the south end of the lake . . Bill Young. . . and his family recently caught 60–70 sandies . . schooling on the top, near the dam.

sand bee n

Perh a **sweat bee.**

1967 *DARE* (Qu. R21, . . *Other kinds of stinging insects*) Inf **IL**26, Ice-cream bees or sand bees.

sand bells n

1 A perennial herb *(Nama hispidum)* having flowers with bell-shaped corollas.

1936 Whitehouse *TX Flowers* 111, Sand bells *(Nama hispidum)* has small, reddish-purple, bell-shaped corollas.

2 A **globe mallow 1** (here: *Sphaeralcea coccinea*).

1966 Barnes–Jensen *Dict. UT Slang* 37, Sand bells . . a local name for the Red False Mallow *(Sphaeralcea coccinea dissecta).*

sandberry n

1 A **bearberry 2** (here: *Arctostaphylos uva-ursi*).

1907 *Auk* 24.123 ne**IL**, The dunes and ridges are covered with . . sand berries *(Arctostaphylos uva-ursi).* **1925** Jepson *Manual Plants CA* 748, *A[rctostaphylos] uva-ursi.* . . *Sand-berry.* . . Berry typically brilliant red or pink. . . Sand-dunes along the ocean shore. **1973** Hitchcock–Cronquist *Flora Pacific NW* 342, Sandberry; one of the finest ground covers known, esp for dry banks.

2 A **sandburr;** see quot.

1967–68 *DARE* (Qu. S13, . . *A common wild bush with bunches of round, prickly seeds; when they get dry they stick to your clothing*) Inf **MO**3, Sandberries; (Qu. S15, . . *Weed seeds that cling to clothing*) Inf **WI**37, Sandberries. [FW: Inf's grandfather used to call sandburrs "sandberries."]

3 See **sand blackberry.**

sand bird n

1 A small shore bird, usu any of var **sandpipers.** now esp **NEng**

1709 (1967) Lawson *New Voyage* 154 **NC, SC**, The Sand-Birds are about the Bigness of a Lark, and frequent our Sand-Beaches; they are a dainty Food, if you will bestow Time and Ammunition to kill them. **1745** *London Mag.* Aug 396 se**GA**, [Footnote:] There is a very extraordinary Bird in this Country, which frequents the Sea Beaches, &c., call'd a Sand-Bird, which almost melts in the Mouth. **1832** Williamson *Hist. ME* 1.149, All the species of the *Tring Kind* are unwebbed, and not large bodied. . . A *Beach,* or *Sand-bird* is about the size of a swallow, coloured white and gray. **1869** Alcott *Little Women* 2.197 **MA**, [A] sand-bird came tripping along the beach. **1874** Coues *Birds NW* 483, In the little Sand-bird's [=least sandpiper's] life. . . stretches of sand, or pebbly shingle, or weed-loaded rocks, or muddy flats bestrewn with wrack, invite, and are visited in turn. **1917** (1923) *Birds Amer.* 1.234, *White-rumped Sandpiper.* . . *Other Names.* . . Sand-bird. . . Usually found among the Least and Semipalmated Sandpipers tripping over awash seaweed or running along the shore. **1917** *Wilson Bulletin* 29.2.80 **ME**, *Actitus macularia.*—Sandbird, Matinicus I[slan]d, Me. **1956** MA Audubon Soc. *Bulletin* 40.17, *Spotted Sandpiper.* . . Sand Bird (Maine). *Ibid* 19, *White-rumped Sandpiper.* . . Sand Bird (Mass.) . . *Least Sandpiper.* . . Sand Bird . . (Maine). *Ibid* 21, *Sanderling.* . . Sand Bird (Maine). **1966** *DARE* (Qu. Q7, *Names and nicknames for . . game birds*) Inf **ME**22, Sand birds.

2 =**bank swallow 1.** Cf **sand martin 1**

1956 MA Audubon Soc. *Bulletin* 40.84 **ME**, *Bank Swallow.* . . Sand Bird.

sand blackberry n Also *sandberry*

A blackberry (*Rubus cuneifolius*).

1843 Torrey *Flora NY* 1.217, *Rubus cuneifolius. . . Sand Blackberry. . .* Fruit large, black, abundant and well flavored. Sandy fields. **1896** *Jrl. Amer. Folkl.* 9.187 **MO,** *Rubus cuneifolius,* . . sand blackberry. **1910** Shreve *MD Plant Life* 442, Sand Blackberry. . . In open dry situations; preferring sandy soil; common. **1933** Small *Manual SE Flora* 621, Fruit black, rather dry, but well-flavored. . . *Sand-blackberry.* **1969** *DARE* (Qu. I44, *What kinds of berries grow wild around here?*) Inf **GA**72, Sandberries—seeds are like sand in your mouth. **1976** Fleming *Wild Flowers FL* 25, Sand blackberry grows in sandy woodlands and fields throughout the coastal plain from Florida to Alabama and northward. . . The . . ripe fruits . . make good pie or jam. **1986** Pederson *LAGS Concordance* 1 inf, **ceLA,** Sandberry = sand blackberry.

sandblow n Cf sand boil

An eruption of sand caused by an earthquake; the mound resulting from such an event.

1869 *Atlantic Mth.* 24.555, Reelfoot Lake, near the Mississippi River, in the State of Kentucky . . was formed by a "sand blow," or the eruption of a great amount of sand. . . This extensive body of water had no existence until the earthquake shock. **1903** *DN* 2.329 **seMO,** *Sand-blow. . .* A small mound raised by gas blowing up through sandy soil during earthquakes. They are very common in the vicinity of New Madrid, Missouri.

sand boil n Cf boil n[1] C2, run-around 3

See quot 1976.

1937 *Daily Progress* (Charlottesville VA) 2 Feb 1/8 *(Hench Coll.),* Dread "sand boils" bursting up in the heart of . . Cairo [IL] forewarned of deeply undermined barriers guarding the . . city today. . . The eruptions . . sprang from the terrific pressure of the flooded Ohio River waters slowly eating their way beneath the . . levees. **1939** Faulkner *Wild Palms* 28 **MS,** Even those who . . had probably never before seen more water than a horse pond . . could (and did) talk glibly of sandboils. **1951** *Sun* (Baltimore MD) 16 July 1/1 *(Hench Coll.),* But inside the barrier there was danger from sand boils—geysers of water breaking through the ground surface. **1976** Brown *Gloss. Faulkner* 167, When the water inside a *levee* is much higher than the land outside, water may be forced underground for considerable distances, and begin to come up, bringing sand with it, on the landward side of the levee, or even at some distance inland from it. The place where it comes up, and the phenomenon itself, are both called sandboils. A sandboil must be neutralized promptly. This is done by building a wall of sandbags around it so that a column of water will be built up above it to equalize the pressure.

sand brier n

1 A **horse nettle 1** (here: *Solanum carolinense*). **chiefly S Midl**

1819 *Western Rev.* 1.93 **KY,** [Among] the trees and plants peculiar to this region . . [is] *Solanum Carolinianum,* Sand Briar. **1894** *Jrl. Amer. Folkl.* 7.95 **WV,** *Solanum Carolinense,* . . sand-brier. **1898** *Ibid* 11.276 **KS,** *Solanum Carolinense,* . . sand brier. **1935** (1943) Muenscher *Weeds* 410, *Solanum carolinense. . .* Sand brier. . . Native in the southern states; . . locally abundant and spreading in the central and eastern states. **1968–70** *DARE* (Qu. S21, . . *Weeds . . that are a trouble in gardens and fields*) Inf **VA**34, Sand brier; **MD**49, Sand briers; (Qu. S15, . . *Weed seeds that cling to clothing*) Inf **VA**30, Sand briers; (Qu. S17, . . *Kinds of plants . . that . . cause itching and swelling*) Inf **VA**43, Sand briers. **1968** *DARE* FW Addit **VA**26, Sand brier—horse nettle. **1974** Morton *Folk Remedies* 147 **SC,** *Sand Brier. . .* bears many yellowish bristles. . . Leaves . . have spines protruding from both surfaces of veins, midrib and petiole. . . Common around old horse stables.

2 A **greenbrier.**

1970 *DARE* (Qu. S21, . . *Weeds . . that are a trouble in gardens and fields*) Inf **VA**38, Sand briers—same as cat briers.

sand bug n

A **mole crab** (here: *Emerita talpoida*).

1817 Acad. Nat. Sci. Philadelphia *Jrl.* 1.161, Known generally on the coast by the name of *Sand-bug,* and may be found burrowed in the sand of the beach, at the recess of the tide; its exuviæ is frequent on the line formed by the extreme wave. **1884** Goode *Fisheries U.S.* 1.779, *The Sand Bug. . .* is rather an odd species of Crab, related to the Hermit Crabs, from which, however, it differs greatly in appearance. . . The Sand Bug ranges from Cape Cod to Florida, but is much more abundant toward the South than at the North. **1901** Arnold *Sea-Beach* 268, *H[ippa] talpoida* [=*Emerita t.*]. This animal, commonly known as the "sand-bug," . . burrows with great rapidity into the loose and shifting sands, using . . the appendages . . for pushing and digging. **1965** McClane *McClane's Std. Fishing Encycl.* 560, The sandbug . . is popular among pompano fishermen. These little, hardshelled animals, seldom more than 1 ½ inches long, are dug from ocean beaches at the tideline with a wire-mesh scoop that is pulled through the soft sand.

sand bugger n

1938 Rawlings *Yearling* 12 **nFL,** His mother had cooked a supper good enough for the preacher. There were poke-greens with bits of white bacon buried in them; sand-buggers made of potato and onion and the cooter he had found crawling yesterday. . . He was torn between his desire for more biscuits and another sand-bugger.

sand bunchgrass See sand grass 1h

sandburr n Also sp *sandbur* Cf burr n[1], mock sandburr, sandspur

1 Any of var plants which usu produce spiny burrs; also the burr itself. **chiefly West, Upper MW, N Cent, C Atl** Note: Some of these quots may refer spec to senses below.

1834 Pike *Prose Sketches* 48 **West,** To add to our comforts, the ground here was covered with sand-burs. **1859** in 1942 Hafen *Overland Routes* 11.151 **VA,** Saw several handsome flowers peculiar to these sand ridges, on which, by the way, the "sand burr" flourishes. **1896** *NY Voice* (NY) 12 Mar 4/4, "The Prohibitionists of the state [=Kansas] are soon to meet at Topeka again and feed sand-burs to Governor Morrill."—*Wichita Eagle.* If Governor Morrill can swallow Frank Burt . . he can probably digest the "sand-burs." **1943** Hamner *Short Grass* 249 **TX,** They made bedfellows of the sandburs in the breaks. **1957** Eiseley *Immense Journey* 69, There passed before my eyes the million airy troopers of the milkweed pod and the clutching hooks of the sandburs. **1965–70** *DARE* (Qu. S15, . . *Weed seeds that cling to clothing*) 117 Infs, **chiefly West, Upper MW, N Cent, C Atl,** Sandburr(s); (Qu. S13, . . *A common wild bush with bunches of round, prickly seeds; when they get dry they stick to your clothing*) 13 Infs, **esp N Cent,** Sandburr(s); (Qu. S14, . . *Prickly seeds, small and flat, with two prongs at one end, that cling to clothing*) Infs **AZ**10, **CA**7, **CO**20, **CT**2, **IL**26, **KS**7, **MO**20, Sandburr(s); (Qu. S21, . . *Weeds . . that are a trouble in gardens and fields*) Infs **IN**70, **TX**5, Sandburrs; (Qu. N37, *Joking names for a branch railroad that is not very important or gives poor service*) Inf **KS**12, Sandburr special. **1986** Pederson *LAGS Concordance,* 1 inf, **cwAR,** Sandburs—in Texas; 1 inf, **neTX,** Sandburs.

2 Spec:

a also *sandburr grass:* =**burr grass.**

1830 (1940) Ferris *Rocky Mts.* 28, These grass-knots, are called "Sandburrs." **1892** *Jrl. Amer. Folkl.* 5.105, *Cenchrus tribuloides,* sand-burr. Ill. and westward. **1897** *Ibid* 10.146 **TX,** *Cenchrus tribuloides,* . . sand bar [sic], Waco, Tex. **1920** U.S. Natl. Museum *Contrib. Herbarium* 22.50, In the United States they [=*Cenchrus* spp] are commonly called sandburs. **1935** (1943) Muenscher *Weeds* 147, *Cenchrus pauciflorus* [= *C. incertus*]. . . Sandbur, . . Sandbur-grass. . . Reproducing by seeds in the spiny burs. **1950** *WELS* **WI** (*Other weed seeds that cling to clothing*) 8 Infs, Sandburr(s); 1 Inf, Sandburr—low plant has spikes with many small burrs covered with many sharp thorns; 1 Inf, Sandburr—¼ inch diameter or over, very sharp hooked spines; 1 Inf, Sandburrs—larger [than beggar's lice], sharp and painful; 1 Inf, Sandburr—smaller than a thistle burr; 1 Inf, Sandburr—burr size of pea, very sharp piercing spines. **1950** *WELS Suppl.* **cWI,** Sandburr—very sharp and painful; grow in sandy areas. **1965–70** *DARE* (Qu. S15, . . *Weed seeds that cling to clothing*) Infs **CO**22, **MD**42, Sandburrs; **CA**24, Sandburrs—by the dunes—looks like a quack grass, has small burrs; **CA**60, Sandburrs—grows flat on the ground in a crabgrass sort of plant; **CO**31, Sandburrs—sits in a crabgrass type of plant; **IA**36, Sandburrs—little seed with pricklies all over—about the size of a farmer-match head; **IA**45, Sandburrs—just a little round burr with stickers on it—grows along plants on the ground; **IL**33, Sandburrs—small, prickly all the way around, grow where it's real sandy; **IL**45, Sandburrs—little round ball full of prickers, beige color, the color of sand; **IN**26, Sandburrs—small with prongs, ⅛-inch long, all over—light brown in color; **KS**15, Sandburrs—little, round, tan, almost like a cuckleburr, only smaller; **NM**9, Sandburrs—starts out like grass, grows low, sends out long shoots with tiny gray seeds; **NM**13, Sandburrs, a grass—burr is small and round with many sharp stickers, hard on animals who eat them—they stick behind tongue; **OK**22, Sandburrs—like a cuckleburr, but smaller and rounder, grow close to ground; **OK**32, Sandburr—round, size of a pea, has burrs all around it; **OK**42, Sandburr or grass burr—size of a match head, round, covered with needles; **OK**52, Sandburrs—size of a small match head, many thorns, hard to pull out; **TX**73, Sandburrs— "grass burrs"—tiny, sharp, grow in grass; **TX**78, Sandburr—"grass burrs"; **WI**66, Sandburrs—about as big as a pea with real sharp spines on it; **WV**2, Sandburrs—light tan, small, grow in sand; (Qu. S14) Inf **MD**42, Sandburr—round, very sharp, found in sandy ground or beaches; **NJ**6, Sandburrs—round, small, light-colored, with "pickers," hooks; (Qu. S9, . . *Kinds of grass that are hard to get rid of*) Inf **CO**22, Sandburr—grows on grasslike blade; **OK**18, Sandburr grass; (Qu. S13) Inf **MO**11, Sandburr—grow close to ground. **1970** Kirk *Wild Edible Plants W. U.S.* 189, After thorough singeing in open flames to remove the spiny bristles, the seeds may be ground into meal. . . Sandbur is found in sandy or gravelly places throughout the West.

b A **burr sage,** usu *Ambrosia acanthicarpa* or *A. dumosa.* esp **CA**

1898 *Jrl. Amer. Folkl.* 11.229 **CA,** *Franseria Hookeriana* [=*Ambrosia acanthicarpa*], . . sand burr. **1925** Jepson *Manual Plants CA* 1108, *F[ranseria] dumosa* [=*Ambrosia d.*]. . . Burro-weed. . . Also called Sand-bur. **1931** U.S. Dept. Ag. *Misc. Pub.* 101.154, White bur-sage (*F. dumosa* . .), locally known as burroweed and sand bur, is a . . somewhat spiny-twigged bush, ranging from southwestern California to southwestern Utah. **1945** Wodehouse *Hayfever Plants* 145, *F[ranseria] acanthicarpa*. . . is . . specially common . . principally west of the Mississippi River. . . On account of its spiny fruits and preference for sandy soils it is sometimes called sandbur. *Ibid* 147, The . . sand bur (*F. dumosa* . .) is a low grayish shrub. . . [which] grows in great abundance in the Colorado and Mohave deserts. . . [Another is the beach sandbur (*F. bipinnatifida* . .). It . . is common on sea beaches and sand dunes . . from Lower California to British Columbia. **1974** Munz *Flora S. CA* 109, *A[mbrosia] acanthicarpa*. . . Sand-Bur. . . Common weed of sandy plains, stream bottoms, etc.

c Usu **=buffalo burr,** but occas also the related **horse nettle 1** (here: *Solanum carolinense*).

1900 Lyons *Plant Names* 350, *S[olanum] rostratum*. . . Sand-bur, Buffalo-bur. **1914** Georgia *Manual Weeds* 368, *Solanum rostratum*. . . Sand Bur. . . This is one of the weeds frequently transported in baled hay. **1940** Clute *Amer. Plant Names* 51, *S[olanum] rostratum*. . . Sand-bur. *Ibid* 168, Sand-bur. *Tribulus terrestris*. *Ibid* 272, *Solanum Carolinense*. . . Sand-bur. **1950** *PADS* 14.69 **SC,** *Solanum caro-linense*. . . Sand-bur. **1950** *PADS* 14.69 **SC,** . . The sand-bur; the North American nightshade. **1950** *WELS (Other weed seeds that cling to clothing)* 1 Inf, **WI,** Sandburr—one mean one—blue blossom.

d A **ratany** (here: *Krameria lanceolata*).

1931 U.S. Dept. Ag. *Misc. Pub.* 101.82, *Trailing ratany . . ,* also called sand bur and Texas ratany, which occurs from Kansas to New Mexico. . . would theoretically appear to be palatable to livestock. **1936** Whitehouse *TX Flowers* 51, *Prairie Sand-Bur*. . . (*Krameria lanceolata*) is not the sand-bur of the grass family with which all children of the South are familiar; however, the burs are just as spiny, but are densely covered with white hairs.

e =**puncture vine.** Cf **Mexican sandburr**

1939 Tharp *Vegetation TX* 59, Sand-bur (*Tribulus*); in sand or limestone soil. **1940** [see **2c** above]. **1966–67** *DARE* (Qu. S15, . . *Weed seeds that cling to clothing*) Inf **AZ**2, Goatheads, sandburrs—same here; **OK**28, Grass burrs or sandburrs—small, round, covered with stickers, but have two extra-long ones, might grow a foot high; **TX**40, Sandburrs run on ground, same as goathead; (Qu. S21, . . *Weeds . . that are a trouble in gardens and fields*) Inf **CO**4, Texas sandburr—will puncture a tire. **1983** *DARE* File **nCO,** The scientific name of . . "sand burr" . . is *Tribulus terrestris*.

f A **panic grass** (here: *Dichanthelium oligosanthes*).

c1967 GA Univ. *Weeds S. U.S.* 26, *Panicum pauciflorum* [=*Dichanthelium oligosanthes*] field sandbur. . . Floral spike short, spikelets enclosed in sharp, spiny burs, with two to three seed [sic]. Found in cultivated fields, roadsides, fencerows, lawns.

sandburr grass See **sandburr 2a**

sand burr oak n Cf **burr oak**

A **post oak 1a** (here: *Quercus stellata*).

1921 Deam *Trees IN* 114, This species [=*Quercus stellata*] in some localities is called iron oak, and in Gibson County on the sand dune area it is called sand bur oak.

sand cake See **sand tart 1**

sand cat n

Perh a **blue catfish 1.**

1967–69 *DARE* (Qu. P1, . . *Kinds of freshwater fish . . caught around here . . good to eat*) Infs **GA**84, **SC**32, Sand cat(s).

sand cedar n

A **juniper 1** (here: *Juniperus virginiana* var *silicicola*) native to the southeastern US.

1970 Correll *Plants TX* 80, *Juniperus silicicola* [=*J. virginiana* var *s.*] . . *Southern red cedar, sand cedar*. . . Usually in sandy soils in s.e. Tex. **1980** Little *Audubon Guide N. Amer. Trees E. Region* 310, *Southern Redcedar* "Sand-cedar". . . This southeastern coastal [tree] . . is distinguished by its often drooping foliage and smaller "berries." **2002** *DARE* File—Internet **TX,** *Southern Red Cedar, Sand Cedar* . . *Juniperus silicicola*. . . Grows near water or in areas with a very shallow water table. It is found in southeastern Texas in moist, sandy soils.

sand cherry n Cf **sand plum, sandhill ~**

1 A cherry (*Prunus pumila*) or a var thereof, native to much of the northern US east of the Rocky Mountains; also its fruit. Also called **dwarf plum, sandhill ~**

1778 Carver *Travels N. Amer.* 30, Near the borders of the Lake [=Lake Michigan] grow a great number of sand cherries. [*Ibid,* As they grow only on the sand . . they are called by the French cherries de sable, or sand cherries.] **1796** Morse *Amer. Universal Geog.* 1.168, On its [= Lake Huron's] banks are found amazing quantities of sand cherries. **1844** Lapham *Geogr. Descr. WI* 79, *Cerasus pumila*, . . sand cherry. **1893** *Jrl. Amer. Folkl.* 6.140, *Prunus pumila,* sand cherry. **1935** Sandoz *Jules* 211 wNE (as of c1900), In less than a week he was back with the hind quarter of an antelope sewed into canvas and in his hunting coat a jar of purple sand-cherry jam for Mary. **1950** *WELS (Fruits that grow wild in your neighborhood)* 1 Inf, **WI,** Sand cherry. **1961** Douglas *My Wilderness* 242 **ME,** Sand cherry (*Prunus pumila*) heavy with black fruit formed low hedges along the river's banks. **1966–67** *DARE* (Qu. I44, *What kinds of berries grow wild around here?*) Infs **IL**50, **NE**3, 8, 10, **SD**8, Sand cherries; (Qu. I46, . . *Kinds of fruits that grow wild around here*) Inf **CO**3, Sand cherries; (Qu. I53, . . *Fruits grown around here . . special varieties*) Inf **ND**9, Sand cherries. [*DARE* Ed: Some of these Infs may refer instead to other senses below.] **1987** Kindscher *Edible Wild Plants* 173, The sand cherry, *P. pumila* var. *besseyi*. . . loves sandy areas and is quite common in the Nebraska Sand Hills. It is used like a plum, although its fruit, which varies in quality, is more like a tart cherry in shape and taste.

2 A similar **wild plum** such as *Prunus americana* or *P. angustifolia* var *watsoni*.

1930 OK Univ. Biol. Surv. *Pub.* 2.65, *Prunus angustifolia* var. *watsoni*. . . Sand Plum, Sand Cherry. **1987** Kindscher *Edible Wild Plants* 170, Sand cherry . . *Prunus americana*. . . Shrubs or small trees, . . usually forming thickets.

3 A **serviceberry** (here: *Amelanchier canadensis*).

1893 *Jrl. Amer. Folkl.* 6.141 **MT,** *Amelanchier Canadensis*. . . Sand cherry. **1936** Winter *Plants NE* 61, *A[melanchier] canadensis*. . . Service-berry. Sand-cherry. Occasional along streams and in woods in eastern Nebr. . . Fruit ripe June–July.

sand chicken n **SC** Cf **sand bird 1, ~ peep**

A small shore bird, esp any of var **sandpipers.**

1910 Wayne *Birds SC* 50, *Least Sandpiper*. . . All of the smaller species of shore birds are known on this coast as "Sand Chickens," and this species [=*Calidris minutilla*] is best known to nearly all the inhabitants of the coast. **1949** Sprunt–Chamberlain *SC Bird Life* 243, *Least Sandpiper*. . . *Local Names:* Sandchicken, Peep. . . It is very tame and one can come surprisingly close to it at times. *Ibid* 244, *Red-backed Sandpiper*. . . *Local Names:* Sandchicken, Peep. . . It is an abundant bird in South Carolina. *Ibid* 248, *Semipalmated Sandpiper*. . . *Local Names:* Peep, Sandchicken. . . In stormy weather the birds . . huddle in close groups. *Ibid* 251, *Sanderling*. . . *Local Names:* Sandchicken. . . One of the most attractive of the sandpipers.

sand clam n

1 also *sand shell clam:* =**soft-shell clam.**

1792 Belknap *Hist. NH* 3.183, Sand Shell Clam, *Sabella granulata* [= *Mya arenaria*]. **1809** Kendall *Travels* 2.144 **MA,** Rich . . in fish and in

sand-clams *(sabella granulata.)* **1949** Palmer *Nat. Hist.* 360, *Sand or Soft-shelled Clam. . . Mya arenaria. . .* Common between tide lines, in shallow water and mud flats. **1967** *DARE* (Qu. P18, . . *Kinds of shellfish*) Inf **MA**72, Sand clams—in flats.

2 See **sand shell.**

sand-clay road See **sand-and-clay road**

sand collar n Also *sand saucer* [*OED2 sand saucer* (at *sand* sb.² 10.b) 1885]

The egg mass of a marine snail of the family Naticidae. Also called **lamp-chimney, tommy-cod house**

    1891 *Century Dict.* 5332, *Sand-saucer. . .* A popular name for the egg-mass of a naticoid gastropod, as *Lunatia heros,* commonly found on beaches, resembling the rim of a saucer or lamp-shade broken at one place and covered with sand. **1914** *DN* 4.155 **Cape Cod MA**, *Lamp-chimney. . .* Sand-saucer. **1935** Pratt *Manual Invertebrate Animals* 618, *Naticidae. . .* Eggs deposited in a "sand collar," a thin collar-shaped lamella formed by agglutinating grains of sand together by means of mucus. **1981** Rehder *Audubon Field Guide Seashells* 484, Females [of the family Naticidae] embed egg capsules into thin, flattened spiral masses of sand grains, which are bound together by secreted mucus; the mass then hardens. These are the "sand collars" frequently encountered on beaches and sandy shores. **1989** Mickelson *Nat. Hist.* 45 **AK**, Moon or sand-collar snails are common on sand flats. Their egg cases may be 6 or 7 in. in diameter and look like discarded rubber plungers.

sand coon n

An albinic **raccoon 1**; see quot.

    1973 *WI Acad. Trans.* 61.82, Henry Murphy, formerly of Belleville, . . caught one [=a raccoon] that was light yellow with pink eyes and called a "sand coon."

sand-corn n

A **death camas** (here: *Zigadenus paniculatus*).

    1923 in 1925 Jepson *Manual Plants CA* 212, *Z[igadenus] paniculatus. . . Sand-corn. . .* Sagebrush hills. **1959** Munz–Keck *CA Flora* 1334, *Sand-Corn. . .* Dry places, . . May–June. **1968** Schmutz et al. *Livestock-Poisoning Plants AZ* 126, Sandcorn. . . Resembling wild onion but lacking the onion smell. . . Flowers are pale yellow and occur in elongate clusters at the ends of seed stalks.

sand crab n

Any of var crabs, as:

a Usu the **ghost crab**; occas a related crab of the family Ocypodidae.

    [**1743** Catesby *Nat. Hist. Carolina* 2.35 **Bahamas**, *Cancer arenarius. The Sand Crab. . .* hath eight Legs and two Claws, one of which is twice the Bigness of the other. . . The Head has two square Holes which are Receptacles for its Eyes. . . Their Abode is on the Sandy Shoars.] **1854** Wailes *Rept. on Ag. & Geol. MS* 339, *Ocypode arenaria* [=*Ocypode quadrata*]. Small sand-crab. **1881** *Harper's New Mth. Mag.* Apr 745 **LA**, Dina bestowed as much attention as possible on the bereft sand-crab. **1901** Arnold *Sea-Beach* 282, *O[cypoda] arenaria* [=*O. quadrata*], the sand- or ghost-crab. . . Colored almost exactly like the sand, . . it inhabits sandy beaches above tide-mark from Long Island to Brazil, and subsists largely upon beach-fleas. **1935** Pratt *Manual Invertebrate Animals* 466, *O[cypode] albicans. . .* Sand crab. . . New Jersey to Florida and southwards . . ; a very active crab which has become a terrestrial animal. **1986** Pederson *LAGS Concordance,* 1 inf, **cnGA**, Sand crabs—in Florida; 1 inf, **csTX**, Sand crabs. **1999** *DARE* File—Internet **FL**, Ghost or sand crab.

b =**lady crab.**

    1817 *Acad. Nat. Sci. Philadelphia Jrl.* 1.4.7, The exuvia of this beautiful species [=*Ovalipes ocellatus*] is extremely common on the sea beach. It is known to the inhabitants by the name of *Sand Crab,* and is not used for food. **1884** Goode *Fisheries U.S.* 1.774, The "Lady Crab," or "Sand Crab," is abundant on nearly all our sandy shores from Cape Cod to Florida, and in the Gulf of Mexico. . . When living at low-water mark on the sand beaches, it generally buries itself up to its eyes and antennae in the sand, watching for prey. **1901** Arnold *Sea-Beach* 276, The lady-crab or sand-crab. . . is found among the loose sands at low-water mark, even on the most exposed beaches, and also is abundant on sandy bottoms offshore.

c =**mole crab** (here: *Emerita* spp). Cf **sand bug, ~ dab 2**

    1935 Pratt *Manual Invertebrate Animals* 458, *E[merita] talpoidea. . .*

The sand crab. . . Cape Cod to Florida; Pacific Coast; very common on sand bottoms and beaches, in which it burrows with great rapidity. **1999** (acc) CA Univ. Ocean Discovery Center *Ocean Sea Life* (Internet) **sCA**, Sand Crab . . Emerita analoga. . . Common intertidal inhabitant of all sandy beaches in Southern California, especially along Santa Monica Beach. **1999** *DARE* File—Internet **Pacific NW**, The Pacific mole crab, or "sand crab" (Emerita analoga), is so significant in the surfperch's diet that anglers often gauge the potential of any beach by the density of mole crabs found there.

sand crane n

Perh =**sandhill crane 1.**

    1820 in 1908 *MO Hist. Soc. Coll.* 3.20 **NJ**, Saw some wolves & sand cranes. **1846** in 1848 Emory *Notes Reconnoissance* 40 **SW**, Swarms of wild geese and sand cranes passed over camp. **1966** *DARE* (Qu. Q10, . . *Water birds and marsh birds*) Inf **FL**34, Sand crane.

sand cress n

A **pussypaws** (here: *Cistanthe monandra*).

    1941 Jaeger *Wildflowers* 63 **Desert SW**, *Sand-cress. Calyptridium monandrum* [=*Cistanthe m.*] . . A sprawling fleshy-leaved plant of the desert.

sand cricket n Cf **Jerusalem cricket**

Any of several **grasshoppers 1** of the genus *Stenopelmatus*.

    1884 Kingsley *Std. Nat. Hist.* 2.185, Throughout the Rocky Mountain region . . are found several species of large, fierce-looking insects. . . popularly known as sand-crickets. **1905** Kellogg *Amer. Insects* 157, On the Pacific Coast occurs a large, awkward, thick-legged, transversely striped form, Stenopelmatus, called sand-cricket or Jerusalem cricket. **1947** *Desert Mag.* Jan. 22/3 *(DA)*, It appears that the Babyface is actually our old friend the yellow-and-black striped Jerusalem-cricket or sand-cricket. **1966** *DARE* (Qu. R8, . . *Kinds of creatures that make a clicking or shrilling or chirping kind of sound*) Inf **OK**25, Sand cricket. **1972** Swan–Papp *Insects* 79, *Stenopelmatus fuscus. . .* Also called sand cricket. . . West of the Mississippi River, common along the Pacific coast. . . They bite but are harmless.

sand dab n

1 A **flounder B,** as:

a In Atlantic waters, usu the American plaice *(Hippoglossoides platessoides),* but occas the **rusty dab** or the **windowpane.**

    1839 *MA Zool. & Bot. Surv. Fishes Reptiles* 143, *Platessa dentata* [= *Hippoglossoides platessoides*]. . . known by the fishermen as the *"Sand-dab"* in the Boston market. **1843** DeKay *Zool. NY* 5.178, Those [= mollusks] . . were found in the stomachs of the *P[latessa] dentata,* or *Sand-dab.* **1891** *Century Dict.* 5329, *Sand-dab. . .* A kind of plaice, the rusty dab, *Limanda ferruginea* [=*Pleuronectes ferrugineus*], found along the Atlantic coast of the United States, especially northward. **1902** Jordan–Evermann *Amer. Fishes* 525, The sand-dab, or rough-dab, *H. platessoides,* is found in the North Atlantic, and as far south as Woods Hole. . . It is found off the New England coast in rather deep water. **1903** *NY State Museum & Sci. Serv. Bulletin* 60.726, *Limanda ferruginea* . . Sand Dab. **1933** John G. Shedd Aquarium *Guide* 68, *Lophopsetta maculata* [=*Scophthalmus aquosus*]—Window-pane; *Sand Dab. . .* It is prettily marked to resemble the coarse sand over which it is found. **1955** Zim–Shoemaker *Fishes* 77, *American Plaice,* or *Sand Dab* . . is common at 20 to 100 fathoms on muddy or sandy bottoms. . . Feeds on sea urchins, sand dollars, and other bottom-dwellers.

b In Pacific waters, a fish of the genus *Citharichthys.*

    1914 *DN* 4.164 **CA**, *Sand-dab. . .* Applied to a Pacific Coast fish. **1928** Pan-Pacific Research Inst. *Jrl.* 3.3.16 **OR, WA**, *Citharichthys sordidus. . .* Sand dab. . . *Citharichthys stigmaeus. . .* Speckled sand dab. **1939** Berolzheimer *U.S. Cookbook* 624 **Pacific,** The sand dab, cousin of the Norfolk spot, very thin and about 3 inches in diameter, is a great treat when fried like chicken Maryland. **1953** Roedel *Common Fishes CA* 51, The sanddabs . . are in the lefteyed flounder family. *Ibid* 52, *Citharichthys sordidus. . .* Two other species of sanddab are found in California. The speckled sanddab, *Citharichthys stigmaeus . . ,* ranges along the entire coast. . . The longfin sanddab, *Citharichthys xanthostigma . . ,* ranges from Southern California south to the Gulf of California. **1954** Steinbeck *Sweet Thursday* 155 **cwCA**, Joe Elegant ordered sand dabs for supper. **1968–69** *DARE* (Qu. P2, . . *Kinds of saltwater fish caught around here . . good to eat*) Inf **AK**1, Sand dab; (Qu. P14, . . *Commercial fishing . . what do the fishermen go out after?*) Inf **CA**168, Sand dabs.

2 A **mole crab** (here: *Emerita analoga*). Cf **sand crab c**
1968 *DARE* (Qu. P18, . . *Kinds of shellfish*) Inf **CA**80, Sand dab—looks like a tiny armadillo—not the sand dab fish.

sand daisy n

A **lazy daisy 1**.
1937 Stemen–Myers *OK Flora* 556, *Aphanostephus humilis* [=*A. ramosissimus* var *h.*] . . *Sand-daisy*. . In dry soil. Spring and summer. **1967** *DARE* (Qu. S26e, *Other wildflowers not yet mentioned;* not asked in early QRs) Inf **CO**7, Sand daisies.

sand darter n

A **darter 1**, usu of the genus *Ammocrypta*.
1886 Mather *Memoranda* 7 **Adirondacks NY**, I was expecting to find some of the little sand-darters [Mather: Family Etheostomatidæ, genera several, but one of the species of *Boleichthys* in particular]. **1887** (1888) Jordan *Sci. Sketches* 32, Our little friend was the Pellucid Darter (*Ammocrypta pellucida* . .), better called the "Sand Darter." **1906** NJ State Museum *Annual Rept. for 1905* 299, *Boleosoma nigrum olmstedi* [=*Etheostoma n.*] . . Darter. Sand Darter. [*Ibid* 301, They are found most frequently . . in the smaller streams, usually with sandy bottoms.] **1929** OK Univ. Biol. Surv. *Pub.* 1.101, *Ammocrypta vivax* . . (Arkansas sand darter)—Red River system in Arkansas. **1955** Carr–Goin *Guide Reptiles* 99 **FL**, *Ammocrypta beani* . . Naked Sand Darter. **1967** Cross *Hdbk. Fishes KS* 299, Sand darters usually inhabit shallow water in large streams. . . *A[mmocrypta] clara*, like others of its genus, partly buries itself in sand when resting. **1983** Becker *Fishes WI* 920, The sand darter. . . because of its small thin body . . is not a suitable bait fish.

sand devil n [*OED2* (at *sand* sb. 10.a) "in Africa, a small whirlwind" 1901 →]

=**dust devil 1**.
1944 Wellman *Bowl* 10 **KS**, The towering "sand devils" which sucked up the powdered earth in their whirlwinds and scattered it afar over the dry landscape.

sand diver n

A lizardfish (*Synodus intermedius*).
1896 U.S. Natl. Museum *Bulletin* 47.535, *Synodus intermedius*. . *Sand Diver*. . Coast of southern Florida . . ; the most brightly colored of our species. **1933** LA Dept. of Conserv. *Fishes* 268, The Sand Diver, . . which may grow as large as fifteen inches . . is known from Brazil to North Carolina. **1991** Amer. Fisheries Soc. *Common Names Fishes* 29, *Synodus intermedius*. . A[tlantic] . . sand diver.

sand dock n

A **dock n¹** (here: *Rumex venosus*).
1915 (1926) Armstrong–Thornber *Western Wild Flowers* 88, *Sand Dock*. . is a very handsome member of a rather plain genus. **1937** St. John *Flora SE WA & ID* 125, *Rumex venosus*. . *Sand Dock*. . In sandy soil especially on sand dunes, where it is a natural sand-binder. **1957** Barnes *Nat. Hist. Wasatch Spring* 53 **UT**, We find on a cindered, graveled railroad-embankment the blood-red fruits of the sand dock (*Rumex venosus*).

sand dollar n

1 Std: any of var flattened sea urchins of the class Echinoidea, such as the common *Echinarchnius parma*. For other names of *E. parma* see **dollarfish 4**
2 A **gaillardia B**.
1967 *DARE* (Qu. S26e, *Other wildflowers not yet mentioned;* not asked in early QRs) Inf **TX**15, Sand dollars . . red and yellow, grow on beach.
3 A **cactus B1** (here: *Astrophytum asterias*).
1976 Bailey–Bailey *Hortus Third* 127, [*Astrophytum*] *asterias*. . *Sand-dollar*. . Spring, S. Tex., n. Mex.
4 A **tickseed** (here: *Coreopsis nuescensis*).
2001 *DARE* File—Internet **TX**, *Coreopsis nuescensis*. Sand-Dollars. . It produces a perennial rosette of bright green, deeply cut leaves and long stems topped by yellow, daisy-like flowers. A pale lavender-colored line runs about midway across each petal, completely circling the flower.

sand down a rathole, pound See pound sand down a rathole

sand dropseed n Also sand dropseed-grass

A **dropseed 3** (here: *Sporobolus cryptandrus*).

1903 Porter *Flora PA* 27, *Sporobolus cryptandrus*. . . *Sand Dropseed*. . In sandy soil, coast of N. Eng., along all the Great Lakes, west to N. Dak. south to Tex. and Mex. **1937** U.S. Forest Serv. *Range Plant Hdbk.* G110, Sand dropseed. . . is common in all the western range States, except California. . . It most commonly appears at lower elevations and, as the common name implies, on sandy soils. **1951** Martin *Amer. Wildlife & Plants* 374, The seeds of dropseedgrasses are important to ground-feeding birds. Sand dropseedgrass . . is outstanding in extent of use. **1967** *DARE* File **CO**, Sand dropseed—native Colorado grass. Common. **1973** Hitchcock–Cronquist *Flora Pacific NW* 670, Most of the US except the extreme se; sand d[ropseed]. . . *S[porobolus] cryptandrus*.

sand-dust See sand 2

sand eel n [*OED2* 1307 →]

A **sand lance** (here: *Ammodytes americanus*).
1873 in 1878 Smithsonian Inst. *Misc. Coll.* 14.2.29 **NEng**, *Ammodytes americanus*. . . Sand-eel. **1884** Goode *Fisheries U.S.* 1.244, Of all the small species of fishes occurring in the North Atlantic there is probably none more important to man than the Lant—Launce, as it is called in Europe, frequently also the Sand-eel both in Europe and America. **1928** Beston *Outermost House* 178 **Cape Cod MA**, It was the familiar sand eel or sand launce, *Ammodytes americanus*, of the waters between Hatteras and Labrador. This is no kin of the true eels, though he rather resembles one in general appearance, for his body is slender, eel-like, and round. **1933** John G. Shedd Aquarium *Guide* 150, *Ammodytes americanus*. . . Sand Eel. . . They have the habit of burying themselves in the sand in shallow water to escape the hordes of fishes that feed on them.

sander n

=**sandpiper**; see quot.
1930 *AmSp* 5.392 [Language of N Atl fishermen], *Sanders*. . . Sandpipers, especially young ones.

sanderling n

Std: a small **sandpiper** (*Calidris alba*) common in coastal areas of the US. Also called **bull peep 2, clam chaser, grayback 1f, ghost bird 5, oxeye 1a, peeper n¹ 3, ruddy plover, sand bird 1, ~ chicken, ~ peep, ~ snipe, sea chicken, stib, strand snipe, surf ~, wave chaser, white bird, ~ plover, ~ sea-chicken, ~ snipe, whitey, whiting**

sand fiddler n Sth, esp NC

A **fiddler crab** such as *Uca pugilator*.
1852 Wiley *Life in South* 30 **NC**, Sand fiddler. . . the local name for a small animal of the shell-fish kind, and which abounds on the beach. **1863** *Harper's New Mth. Mag.* Aug 356 **NC**, The grotesque amphibious "sand-fiddlers" and the little darkeys are the only exponents of energy. **1946** *PADS* 6.26 **ceNC**, Sand fiddler. . . A small, crab-like crustacean that uses in the sands of the ocean, sounds, and creeks. . . Common. **1967** LeCompte *Word Atlas* 218 **seLA**, Small crab with one pincer smaller than the other . . sand fiddler. **1967–68** *DARE* (Qu. P6, . . *Bait*) Inf **TX**14, Sand fiddler—little crab; (Qu. P19, . . *Small, freshwater crayfish*) Inf **NC**80, Sand fiddlers—looks like a crab—can stay on land or water. **1969** *DARE* FW Addit **NC**, Sand fiddler—little crab that digs in sand. **1973** *PADS* 60.1 **ceNC**, The long beaches are left to the sun and the surf, the sand fiddlers, the gulls and the pelicans. **1981** Meinkoth *Audubon Field Guide Seashore* 654, Sand Fiddler (*Uca pugilator*).

sandfish n

1 A fish of the family Trichodontidae, usu *Trichodon trichodon* of the Pacific coast.
1882 U.S. Natl. Museum *Bulletin* 16.626, Trichodontidæ. (The Sandfishes.) *Ibid* 627, *T[richodon] stelleri* [=*T. trichodon*]. . . *Sand-fish*. . . Coast of Alaska, south to San Francisco, burying itself in the sand near the shore. **1928** Pan-Pacific Research Inst. *Jrl.* 3.3.15 **OR, WA**, Trichodontidæ. The sandfishes. . . *Trichodon trichodon*. . . Sandfish. **1991** Amer. Fisheries Soc. *Common Names Fishes* 61, *Trichodon trichodon* . . P[acific] . . Pacific sandfish.
2 A fish of South Atlantic and Gulf waters, as:
a A **sand perch 2b** (here: *Diplectrum formosum*).
1896 U.S. Natl. Museum *Bulletin* 47.1207, *Diplectrum formosum*. . . *Sand-fish*. . A handsome fish, common on the South Atlantic and Gulf coasts of the United States on rocky or sandy shores.

b also *sand tilefish:* A **tilefish** (here: *Malacanthus plumieri*).

1933 John G. Shedd Aquarium *Guide* 118, *Malacanthus plumieri—Sandfish.* . . A small, shore fish. . . [I]t frequents shallow water. **1983** *Audubon Field Guide N. Amer. Fishes* 589, *Sand Tilefish (Malacanthus plumieri).* . . Over sand and rubble to about 25 fathoms. . . From Cape Lookout, North Carolina, to . . Gulf of Mexico.

c A small serranid *(Serranus subligarius)* of Atlantic waters.

1983 *Audubon Field Guide N. Amer. Fishes* 547, *Belted Sandfish (Serranus subligarius).* . . Around rock jetties and over sand. From North Carolina to Florida; Gulf of Mexico. . . Of no commercial value.

sand flea n

1 A crustacean, as:

a Any of var crustaceans of the family Orchestiidae.

1807 *MA Hist. Soc. Coll.* 2d ser 3.54 **seMA,** The sand flea is abundant on the beach: carcases left there are soon devoured by them. **1818** *Acad. Nat. Sci. Philadelphia Jrl.* 1.5.385, The . . animals of this genus [=*Talorchestia*] . . do not inhabit the waters, but are found in considerable numbers upon sandy beaches of the sea, and are well known to every observer by the name of *sand flea;* they leap about with great agility, feed upon and conceal themselves under the rejectamenta of the sea, and for repose and security dig a hole in the sand, to which they skip at the approach of danger. **1844** DeKay *Zool. NY* 6.35, *Orchestia longicornus* [=*Talorchestia l.*] . . These small crustaceans are well known under the name of *Sand-flea,* or *Beach-flea,* occurring along the shores of Long Island. **1884** U.S. Natl. Museum *Bulletin* 27.130, *Orchestia agilis.* . . Sand-flea. Atlantic coast. . . Scavengers. **1889** Munroe *Dorymates* 138 **MA,** The sand-fleas have made a meal off of him [=a fish]. . . just . . as you may see almost any time hopping on a beach. **1928** Beston *Outermost House* 183 **Cape Cod MA,** Once this living light [=a luminous tide] has seeped into the beach, colonies of it speedily invade the tissues of the ten thousand thousand sand fleas which are forever hopping on this edge of ocean. Within an hour the grey bodies of these swarming amphipods *(Orchestia agilis; Talorchestia megalophthalma),* show phosphorescent pin points.

b A scud n[1] (here: *Gammarus* spp.).

1939 Natl. Geogr. Soc. *Fishes* 70, The [Atlantic] salmon. . . feeds extensively on crustaceans, the sand flees [sic] (Gammarus), and shrimp being among the important ones.

c A mole crab (here: *Emerita talpoida*). Cf **sand bug,** ~ **crab c**

1966 *Fishing World* 13.6.8 **FL,** Pompano prefer small jigs or sand fleas. **1974** McClane *McClane's New Std. Fishing Encycl.* 560, The sandbug, erroneously called "sandflea," is popular among pompano fishermen. *Ibid* 839, *Sandbug—Hippa talpoida.* . . In Florida, where they are known as sandfleas, these crustaceans are of great importance in catching pompano.

2 A flea such as *Tunga penetrans,* but also a **black fly** or a **punkie** n[1] **1,** or a **harvest mite;** see quots. [*OED2* at *sand sb.*[2] 10.b 1796 for *Tunga penetrans*]

1859 (1968) Bartlett *Americanisms* 77, *Chigoe,* spelt also *chigre, chigger, jigger,* etc. *(Pulex penetrans.)* Sand-fleas, which penetrate under the skin of the feet, particularly the toes. **1916** Kephart *Camping & Woodcraft* 1.254, The chigoe or sand-flea . . is a larger and more formidable pest than our little red-bug. It attacks, preferably, the feet, especially under the nail of the great toe, and between the toes. **1929** *AmSp* 5.76 **NE** [Cattle country talk], A fast running horse or man is "foggin'," "goin' like the sand fleas are after 'im." **1939** FWP *Guide FL* 6, The native Floridian . . is likely to be guilty of the abysmal ignorance that causes the Yankee to refer to . . sandflies as 'sandfleas.' **1950** *WELS (A very tiny fly that you can hardly see but that stings sharply)* 1 Inf, **WI,** Sand flea. **1965–70** *DARE (Qu. R11, A very tiny fly that you can hardly see, but that stings)* Infs **CA167, MD9, MI106, NJ1, NY20, 44, SC69,** Sand flea; **MI65,** Sand flea—they're not a fly, but they bite; *(Qu. R12, . . Other kinds of flies)* Inf **MA98,** Sand flea—on beach; *(Qu. R21, . . Other kinds of stinging insects)* Infs **IL119, MI93, RI15, TX37, WI68,** Sand flea; **IA22,** Sand fly or sand flea—looks like a small bee; **MI9,** We have sand fleas—they hop and they bite; *(Qu. R22, Very small red insects, almost too small to see, that get under your skin and cause itching)* Infs **CA207, MI116, NH5,** Sand fleas; *(Qu. R23a, Insects or other creatures that fasten themselves to the skin and suck blood—on land)* Infs **IL58, NY2,** Sand fleas; **CT8,** Sand fleas—at the seashore. **1972** Swan–Papp *Insects* 659, *Tunga penetrans.* . . Also called such names as sand flea, . . and jiggers. . . Southern United States sporadically. **1986** Pederson *LAGS Concordance,* 3 infs, **swAL, seFL, cwGA,** Sand flea(s);

1 inf, **cwFL,** Sand flea—like chigger, found around beaches; 1 inf, **csTX,** Sand flea—bite is similar to chigger/red bug.

sand flirt n Cf **sandlapper 4**

A **whiptail.**

1949 *PADS* 11.10 **wTX,** *Sand flirt.* . . A sand-colored, long-tailed lizard.

sand flounder n

1 =**windowpane. N Atl**

1842 DeKay *Zool. NY* 4.296, *Platessa Pusilla* [=*Pleuronectes americanus*]. . . This small flat-fish is taken in the shallow bays about New-York, in September. It is little valued as an article of food, as [sic] is known in the markets under the name of *Sand Flounder. Ibid* 302, The Spotted or Watery Turbot [=*Scophthalmus aquosus*]. . . is sometimes called the *Watery Flounder,* and more frequently the *Sand Flounder.* **1873** in 1878 Smithsonian Inst. *Misc. Coll.* 14.2.17, *Lophopsetta maculata* [=*Scophthalmus aquosus*]. . . Windowpane *(New Jersey);* sand flounder *(New York).* **1905** NJ State Museum *Annual Rept. for 1904* 390, Window Light. . . Sand Flounder. . . A small thin flounder, notable for its translucent appearance. . . On our coast it is abundant. **1911** U.S. Bur. Census *Fisheries 1908* 310, Spotted sand flounder.

2 Any of var other **flounders B** such as *Paralichthys albigutta* of Gulf waters or *Psettichthys melanostictus* of Pacific waters.

1842 [see **1** above]. **1973** Knight *Cook's Fish Guide* 381, Flounder, . . sand—Gulf Flounder [=*Paralichthys albigutta*] or see Sole, Sand [=*Psettichthys melanostictus*]. **1991** Amer. Fisheries Soc. *Common Names Fishes* 135, Flounder, sand—see gulf flounder . . sand sole.

sand fly n

1 Any of var usu bloodsucking or biting dipterous insects of the families Ceratopogonidae, Psychodidae, and Simuliidae such as a **black fly** or a **punkie** n[1] **1. scattered, but esp Sth, TX, Upper Missip Valley** See Map Cf **sand flea 2,** ~ **gnat**

1736 (1909) Wesley *Jrl.* 1.191 **GA,** I wrapped myself up . . in a large cloak, to keep off the sand-flies. **1743** Catesby *Nat. Hist. Carolina* 2.xxxvii **NC, SC,** I concluded to take Notice only of the particular Genus's I observed in *Carolina.* . . [as] The Sand-fly. **1822** in 1929 Weems *Mason Locke Weems* 3.345 **GA,** Those day & night tormentors of men & beast, the *sand flies & musquitoes,* drove me back. **1842** Harris *Treatise Insects* 405, They [=black flies] are followed, however, by swarms of midges, or sand-flies *(Simulium nocivum),* called no-see-'em . . on account of their minuteness. **1886** *Forest & Stream* 26.349 **Lake Superior,** The [mosquito] bar is no protection . . from sandflies or "no-see-ems" and the black fly. **1901** Howard *Insect Book* 120, *Simuliidae.* . . These insects, known as black flies, sand flies or buffalo gnats, are small, stout, hump-backed biting flies. **1939** [see **sand flea 2**]. **1950** *WELS (A very tiny fly that you can hardly see but that stings sharply)* 2 Infs, **WI,** Sand fly *(or flies).* **1954** Borror–DeLong *Intro. Insects* 590, *Psychodidae.* . . Most of the Northern species of this family are harmless to man, but the species in the genus . . *Phlebotomus* [=*Lutzomyia*], often called sand flies, are blood-sucking; these occur in the Southern states and in the tropics. **1965–70** *DARE (Qu. R11, A very tiny fly that you can hardly see, but that stings)* 36 Infs, **scattered, but esp Sth, Gt Lakes,** Sand fly *(or flies);* **GA11, 28, 35,** Sand fly = sand gnat; **ME3,** Sand flies—same as midges; **MN2,** Sand flies—don't sting, they bite; *(Qu. R12, . . Other kinds of flies)* Infs **AL6, FL9, IN1, MI27,**

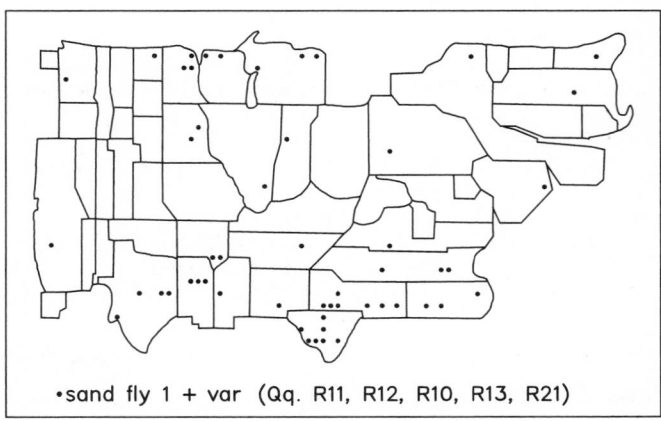

•sand fly 1 + var (Qq. R11, R12, R10, R13, R21)

NJ67, **SC**63, **TN**1, **WI**58, Sand fly (*or* flies); **MN**2, Sand fly—bites; (Qu. R10, *Very small flies that don't sting, often seen hovering in large groups or bunches outdoors in summer*) Infs **LA**3, **NC**41, **ND**3, **TX**35, Sand fly (*or* flies); (Qu. R13) Inf **NY**28, Sand fly; (Qu. R21, . . *Other kinds of stinging insects*) Inf **IA**22, Sand fly or sand flea—looks like a small bee; **MA**122, Sand flies on the beaches sting like blazzers [sic]; **MN**5, Cockeyed sand flies. **1966** *DARE* Tape FL45, When I got in there, they had what they called a sand-fly net, was fastened on the framework [of a bed]. **1972** Swan–Papp *Insects* 595, *Ceratopogonidae.* . . The biting midges. . . include some very annoying pests, variously called no-see-ums, punkies, sand flies, moose flies, and gnats. **1986** Pederson *LAGS Concordance,* 9 infs, **Gulf Region,** Sand fly (*or* flies); 1 inf, **cwFL,** Sand flies—in salt water; 1 inf, **swMS,** Sand flies = "jiggers", small, white wings.

2 A mayfly **1.** **Gt Lakes**

1868 *Scientific Amer.* 12 Aug 102, Chicago was visited July, 21st, by countless numbers of the sand-fly, an insect about the size of the gallinippers which infest the Southern swamps. . . Wherever a light was placed the flies gathered around it in millions, and covered the glass in the windows so as to render it almost an impossibility to see the gas jet. **1949** *WELS Suppl.* swWI, Along the north shore [of Lake Michigan] they [=mayflies] are known as "Sand flies." **1950** *WELS* (*Large winged insect that hatches in summer in great numbers around lakes or rivers, crowds around lights, lives only a day or so, and is good fish bait*) 1 Inf, **WI,** Sand fly. **1967–70** *DARE* (Qu. R4) Infs **MI**109, **NY**231, Sand fly; **NY**227, Sand flies—see them at night; **IL**4, Sand fly, shad fly—alternative names.

3 A fly such as those of the families Muscidae or Tabanidae; see quot. Cf **dog fly 1**

1966–70 *DARE* (Qu. R12, . . *Other kinds of flies*) Inf **LA**23, Sand fly—same size as housefly; **SC**7, Sand fly—same as dog fly; **SC**19, Sand fly—stings, smaller than housefly; (Qu. R13, *Flies that come to meat or fruit*) Inf **SC**69, Sand fly—not as big as a housefly.

sand food n Also *sandroot, sand sponge*

A parasitic plant (*Pholisma sonorae*) native to Arizona and California that produces edible stems. Also called **camote**

1871 U.S. Dept. Ag. *Rept. of Secy. for 1870* 424, *Sand food.* . . This herbaceous and fleshy plant is of a dull orange color, parasitic on the roots of an unknown shrub. **1920** Saunders *Useful Wild Plants* 39, Another subterranean parasite, though not a fungus, that is of genuine worth as an edible, is the curious Sand Food (*Ammobroma Sonorae* . .). The subterranean stem is tender, juicy and sweet—a refreshing and luscious morsel, meat and drink in one. It may be eaten either raw or roasted, and is relished by redmen and white alike. **1931** U.S. Dept. Ag. *Misc. Circular* 101.154 **West,** *White bur-sage.* . . is one of the two chief host plants of the curious, parasitic . . sandroot (*Ammobroma sonorae* [=*Pholisma s.*]), known also as sandfood . . , whose succulent stems with a flavor reminiscent of sweetpotatoes, are a valuable source of food supply to the Cocopa Indians and to desert travelers. **1941** Jaeger *Wildflowers* 180 **Desert SW,** *Sand-food, sand-sponge.* . . Following a wet winter the parasitic sand-sponge is plentiful on the Algodones sand hills west of Yuma and at the head of the Gulf of California. **1970** Kirk *Wild Edible Plants W. U.S.* 237, Sand Food, Sand Root. . . The long, succulent, underground stems of this root parasite were once used by the Papago Indians as a very nutritious food.

sand gnat n **scattered, but chiefly SE** See Map Cf **sand flea 2, ~ fly 1**

Any of var dipterous insects of the families Ceratopogonidae or Simuliidae such as a **black fly** or a **punkie** n[1] **1.**

1877 *Scribner's Mth.* 13.749, We were surrounded and harassed all the morning by innumerable sand-gnats, which darted into our eyes, crawled into our nostrils, buzzed in our ears, and wriggled down our necks in a most annoying fashion. **1928** Beston *Outermost House* 195 **Cape Cod MA,** The sand quivers with insect lives. On such days, . . sand gnats or "no-see-ums" gather in myriads on the sun-drenched south wall of the house. **1933** Rawlings *South Moon* 124 **nFL,** The sand-gnats were troublesome and mosquitoes were plentiful. *Ibid* 297, Sand gnats swarmed in clouds and passed the sore-eyes from one baby to another. **1965–70** *DARE* (Qu. R11, *A very tiny fly that you can hardly see, but that stings*) 32 Infs, 21 **SE,** Sand gnat; (Qu. R12, . . *Other kinds of flies*) Inf **FL**22, Sand gnats. **1975** Newell *If Nothin' Don't Happen* 238 **nwFL,** The sand gnats was awful bad. **1986** Pederson *LAGS Concordance,* 4 infs, **cFL, seGA,** Sand gnat(s).

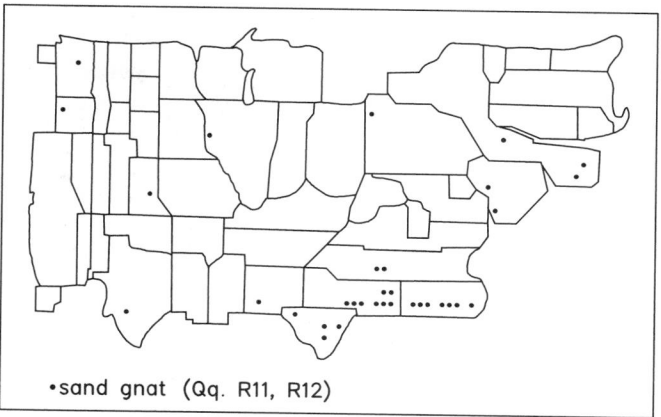

•sand gnat (Qq. R11, R12)

sand grape n

A **grape** (here: *Vitis rupestris*) native to much of the South and Midland; occas another **grape** such as *V. acerifolia* or *V. aestivalis.* For other names of *V. rupestris* see **currant grape, July ~, mountain ~ 1, rock ~, sugar ~**

1856 Ferguson *America* 273, In 1799 . . a Frenchman . . was making several barrels of wine every year, out of grapes that were found growing wild and abundantly, on the heads of the islands on the Ohio river, called sand-grapes. **1872** MO State Entomol. *Annual Rept. for 1871* 60, *Vitis rupestris.* . . Bush Grape or Sand Grape. **1891** Coulter *Botany W. TX* 62, *V[itis] aestivalis.* . . Abounding in the sandy post-oak woods of eastern Texas it is called . . "sand-grape." *Ibid* 63, *V. rupestris.* . . *Sand* . . *Grape.* . . Berries rather small, sweet, in very close bunches.—In the valley of Devil's River and westward into mountains west of the Pecos. **1893** *Jrl. Amer. Folkl.* 6.139 **WV,** *Vitis rupestris,* sand grape. **1938** Van Dersal *Native Woody Plants* 337, Grape, Sand (*Vitis lincecumii* [=*V. aestivalis*], *Vitis aestivalis*). **1960** Vines *Trees SW* 725, *Vitis . . longii* [=*V. acerifolia*]. . . Also known by the vernacular names of . . Sand Grape [etc]. . . The fruit is sometimes gathered to make pies and homemade wine in the Texas Panhandle area. *Ibid* 729, *Sand Grape—Vitis rupestris.* . . Sand Grape succeeds in poor calcareous and sandy soils. **1969** U.S. Dept. Ag. *Ag. Hdbk. No. 356* 222, Two other common species are bushy sand grape, *V. rupestris* Scheele, of sandy streambanks, with more or less glabrous foliage . . and frost grape.

sand grass n

1 Any of var grasses, as: see below.

a A sand-binding grass of the genus *Triplasis,* usu *T. purpurea* of the eastern two-thirds of the US.

1857 Gray *First Lessons* 556, *T[riplasis] purpurea.* . . *Sand-Grass.* . . In sand, Massachusetts to Virginia along the coast, and southward. **1882** McCabe *NY by Sunlight* 110 **seNY,** The sand grass and brambles grow thickly over the lowly, lonely graves. **1894** Coulter *Botany W. TX* 539, *S[ieglingia] purpurea.* . . *Sand grass.* . . Sandy shores, eastern Texas to Michigan and along the Gulf and Atlantic coasts. **1912** Baker *Book of Grasses* 171, Sand-grass, thick and rigid of leaf, is a tufted plant of the beaches, and, like a few other salt-water grasses of the Atlantic coast, it is also found on Western ranges. **1936** Winter *Plants NE* 26, *T[riplasis] purpurea.* . . *Sand-grass.* In the sand-hills. **1946** Tatnall *Flora DE* 25, Sand Grass. Frequent on maritime sands of the Coastal Plain. **1970** Correll *Plants TX* 217, *Triplasis purpurea.* . . *Purple sandgrass.* . . Open areas of loose sand.

b A **beach grass** (here: *Ammophila arenaria*). [*OED2* at *sand* sb.[2] 10.c 1857]

1889 Vasey *Ag. Grasses* 48, *Ammophila arenaria.* . . Sand Grass. . . grows on sandy beaches of the Atlantic, at least as far south as North Carolina, and on the shores of the Great Lakes, but has not, so far, been recorded from the Pacific coast. . . This grass has no agricultural value, but . . its utility in binding together the loose sands of the beach, and restraining the inroads of the ocean, has been recognized.

c =**sand reed 2,** usu *Calamovilfa gigantea* or *C. longifolia.* **ND, Plains States**

1894 *Jrl. Amer. Folkl.* 7.104 **NE,** *Calamagrostis longifolia* [=*Calamovilfa l.*], . . sand-grass, central Neb. **1906** Rydberg *Flora CO* 32, *Calamovilfa.* . . Reed-Grass, Sand-Grass. **1937** U.S. Forest Serv. *Range Plant Hdbk.* G43, Prairie sandgrass [=*Calamovilfa longifolia*] . . occurs chiefly in sandy soil . . on plains and hills east of the Rocky Mountains. . . It produces a considerable amount of forage which cures on the ground and is an important source of winter cattle feed. . . It is also cut for hay. **1940** Gates *Flora KS* 125, Calamovilfa gigantea. . . Sandgrass. Sanddunes. . . Calamovilfa longifolia. . . Sandgrass. Sanddunes and sand prairie. **1950** Stevens *ND Plants* 70, *Calamovilfa longifolia. . . Big Sandgrass. . .* Common on prairie and roadsides, especially in dry, sandy soils. It is too wiry to be a good forage grass but is useful to check soil blowing. **1966** *DARE* (Qu. L9a, . . *Kinds of grass . . grown for hay*) Inf **ND5,** Sand grass—not considered very good; (Qu. S15, . . *Weed seeds that cling to clothing*) Inf **ND1,** Sand grass. **1968** Barkley *Plants KS* 41, Calamovilfa gigantea. . . Sandgrass. . . Calamovilfa longifolia. . . Sandgrass.

d A **bluegrass 1** (here: *Poa douglasii*).

1901 Jepson *Flora CA* 66, *P[oa] Douglasii. . . Sand-grass. . .* Apparently peculiar to California.

e =**beardgrass.**

1903 Small *Flora SE U.S.* 60, Andropogon. . . Beard Grass. Broom Grass. Sand Grass. **1911** *Century Dict. Suppl., Sand-grass. . . Colorado sand-grass,* one of the beard-grasses, *Andropogon Hallii,* found in the sandy regions of the western United States. It resembles big blue-stem, *A. furcatus,* and is likely to be of considerable value for hay. **1933** Small *Manual SE Flora* 43, *Andropogon. . . Sand-grasses. . .* Some species are important forage grasses.

f A **burr grass** (here: *Cenchrus incertus*).

1912 Baker *Book of Grasses* 83, *Bur-grass. Sand-grass. . . Cenchrus carolinianus* [=*C. incertus*]. . . Sandy soil. . . Maine and Ontario to South Dakota, south to Florida, Texas, and southern California.

g A **needlegrass 2** (here: *Aristida adscensionis*).

1914 Georgia *Manual Weeds* 42, *Sand-Grass—Aristida fasciculata* [= *A. adscensionis*]. *Ibid* 43, In the hot, arid regions of the Southwest, . . the Sand-grass is not called a weed, for its thin, wiry stems afford some grazing where otherwise there might be none.

h also *sand bunchgrass, sand rice:* A **mountain rice** (here: *Achnatherum hymenoides*).

1920 Saunders *Useful Wild Plants* 56, A Southwestern grass of wide distribution, particularly in the deserts, in sandy places . . and on arid hillsides, is the . . Sand-grass (*Eriocoma cuspidata* [=*Achnatherum hymenoides*] . .). It is a. . . desert grass with edible seeds. **1923** in 1925 Jepson *Manual Plants CA* 124, *O[ryzopsis] hymenoides. . . Sand Bunch Grass. . .* Deserts and plains, Mohave Desert and northw. **1937** U.S. Forest Serv. *Range Plant Hdbk.* G88, *Oryzopsis hymenoides. . .* is locally called sandgrass, sandrice, and silkygrass. . . It characteristically grows on dry sandy soils, sometimes even in sand dunes: hence the local name sandgrass. **1957** Jaeger *N. Amer. Deserts* 94, The most conspicuous of these [plants in the Algodones Dunes] is a sand grass (*Oryzopsis hymenoides*) and a large shrubby wild buckwheat.

i =**blowout grass 2.**

1932 Rydberg *Flora Prairies* 108, *Redfieldia. . . Blow-out Grass, Sand-Grass. . .* Sand hills: S.D.—Colo.—Wyo. **1940** Gates *Flora KS* 136, Redfieldia flexuosa. . . Blowout Grass, Sandgrass. Sandhills.

j A **needlegrass 1** (here: *Hesperostipa comata*).

1937 U.S. Forest Serv. *Range Plant Hdbk.* G116, Needle-and-thread [=*Hesperostipa comata*]. . . is also called . . sandgrass. . . This grass is very widely distributed over the Western States and the Great Plains and also occurs in the upper valley of the Yukon. It is common on sandy, or gravelly plains, mesas and foothills and sometimes extends into the mountains.

2 A **jointweed 1** (here: *Polygonella articulata*).

1894 *Jrl. Amer. Folkl.* 7.97 **MA,** Polygonella articulata, . . sand-grass, Wellfleet, Mass.

sand heath n

=**beach heather.**

1940 Weygandt *Down Jersey* 29 **sNJ,** I remember how easy it was to be tripped by sand heath and by grass that had been looped by blowing sand.

sand herring n Cf herring n[1] 1

A **cisco** (here: *Coregonus artedi*).

1983 Becker *Fishes WI* 341, *Cisco or Lake Herring. . .* Other common names . . sand herring.

sand hickory n

A **hickory B1** (here: *Carya pallida*) native to much of the South and Midland areas of the US. Also called **pignut 1**

1953 Peattie *Nat. Hist. W. Trees* 133, The Sand Hickory has no illustrious history like so many of its close relatives; probably only squirrels, boys, and botanists are epicures of its nuts. **1962** Kurz–Godfrey *Trees N. FL* 47, Sand hickory. . . has roughish, ridged and furrowed bark with a more or less diamond-like pattern. **1980** Little *Audubon Guide N. Amer. Trees E. Region* 353, Sand Hickory. . . Nut tree with *tiny, silvery or yellowish scales* on twigs, buds, and undersurface of leaflets.

sand hill n

1 A hill or dune composed largely of sand—freq used in pl in ref to areas of the southern coastal plain and of western Nebraska characterized by such hills. Cf **chophill**

1622 Mourt's Relation *Iournall Plimoth* 3, [They found] the ground or earth, sand hils, much like the Downes in *Holland.* **1731** Catesby *Nat. Hist. Carolina* 1.32 **NC, SC,** [Larks] frequent the Sand Hills upon the Sea-shore of *Carolina.* **1806** in 1852 U.S. Congress *Debates & Proc.* (App.) 16.1134 **Cent,** The great chain or dividing ridge, [is] commonly known by the name of the sand hills. **1846** Sage *Scenes Rocky Mts.* 36 **NE,** Ranges of broken sand-hills mark the transition to the high arid prairies in the rear. **1899** Chesnutt *Conjure Woman* 10 **NC** [Black], I lives des ober yander, behine de nex' san'-hill. **1949** *Prairie Schooner* Spring 27 **seMT,** This sheep camp at the mouth of Reno Creek is one of several which dot this valley and the adjoining sandhills of the Cheyenne country. **1966–69** *DARE* (Qu. C17, . . *A small, rounded hill*) Inf **OK25,** Sand hill; **NC60,** Sand hill—10–20 feet high; **NE2,** Knob—here it's a "sand hill"; (Qu. C29, *A good-sized stretch of level land with practically no trees*) Inf **NC41,** Sand hills. **1967–69** *DARE* Tape **NE2,** [Inf:] She handles the truck pretty well over these sandhill roads. [FW:] Now, this sand hill. This word keeps cropping up. . . I was wondering what that name really means. [Inf:] It is sand. [FW:] Mainly sand? [Inf:] I wouldn't describe it in any other manner. . . The sand hills are sand. . . Have you been out in the sandhill area at all? **TX71,** Well, 'course the Indians lived in the sand hills, and we'd just go out in the sand hills and just walk. **1986** Pederson *LAGS Concordance* (*Loam*) 3 infs, **FL, GA,** Sand hill(s); (*Hill*) 4 infs, **FL, GA,** Sand hill(s).

2 often sp solid; attrib:

a Esp of a person or animal: belonging to or coming from an area of sand hills—sometimes derog, esp in ref to the sandhill areas of the southern coastal plain. Cf **sandhiller 1**

1813 *Raleigh* (N.C.) *Minerva* 19 Nov. (*DAE*), Arrived . . transport fleets of gigs, single and double chairs, and sand-hill ponies. **1858** *S. Lit. Messenger* 26.230 **sGA,** We had . . a class of sand hill boys and gopher trapping girls, ranging in age from fourteen to twenty years. **c1885** in 1981 Woodward *Mary Chesnut's Civil War* 64 **SC** (as of 1861), Thirty of Tom Boykin's company came home from Richmond. . . They were sandhill tackies, those fastidious ones. Not very anxious to fight with anything—or in any way, I fancy. *Ibid* 420 (as of 1862), Mrs. Izard witnessed two instances of patriotism in the caste called "sandhill tackies." One forlorn, chill-and-fever, freckled creature, yellow, dirty, and dry as a nut, was selling peaches at ten cents a dozen. Soldiers collected around her cart. She took the top off and cried, "Eat away—eat your fill, I never charge our own soldiers anything." **1935** Sandoz *Jules* 84 **wNE** (as of 1880–1930), Now the last sandhill taboo was broken and the cattlemen, crowded out by settlers east of the sandhill country, . . moved into this, their last stronghold. **1944** Wellman *Bowl* 17 **KS,** We've combed this country for names until I think we've got just about every nester an' sand hill rat in the district. **1958** Humphrey *Home from the Hill* 66 **neTX,** He had little trouble convincing himself that Theron was accepted on his own merits, that his qualities would have been recognized had he been the ditch-edge child of some share-cropping sandhill tacky. **1963** Berry *Almost White* 35 **NJ,** Geography frequently furnishes them with a name. For instance, . . New Jersey [has] its Sand Hill Indians. **1967–69** [see **1** above].

b also *sandhills:* Containing or characterized by sand hills—usu used in ref to western Nebraska. Cf **sandhiller 2**

1913 (1979) Barnes *Western Grazing* 65, These latter species are the well-known western prairie grasses, of which A. hallii is the most common grass in the sandhill region of western Nebraska. **1929** *AmSp* 5.53 **NE** [Cattle country talk], "Cattle range" or "cattle country" generally means the entire grazing area of the West. But these terms are commonly used in Nebraska as synonyms for the "sandhills" or "sandhill country." **1939** FWP *Guide NE* 7, The Sandhills region in the north central and central western part of the State is the most clearly defined topographic subdivision and occupies about 20,000 square miles, including some small outlying areas. It is more suitable for grazing than cultivation. The surface is a rolling plain of wind-blown sand and dunes lying on ridges and hills of eroded bedrock formations.

3 See **sandhill crane.**

sandhill cherry See **sandhill plum**

sandhill crane n Also *sand hill;* also, by folk-etym, *Sam Hill crane*

1 also *sandyhill crane:* A tall, long-legged, long-necked crane (*Grus canadensis* and subspp) with mostly gray plumage and a red forehead. Also called **blue crane 3, brown ~, gray ~, little blue ~ 2, little brown ~, Irish snipe 2, kronky, lord god 3, red shitepoke, stork, upland crane, whooping ~ 2**

  1805 (1904) Lewis *Orig. Jrls. Lewis & Clark Exped.* 2.255, Saw several of the large brown or sandhill Crain today with their young. **1826** Biggs *Narrative* 21 **IL** (as of 1788), I had a plenty to eat while I remained with the baker—good light bread, bacon and sandy-hill crains, boiled in leyed corn, which made a very good soup. **1838** Geol. Surv. OH *Second Annual Rept.* 184, The sand-hill or whooping crane, the adjutant bird, occasionally visits Ohio. **1886** *Forest & Stream* 26.348 **IL,** *Sandhill Crane.* . . This bird has evidently taken a more western path in its migrations, although it has not altogether deserted the Illinois River route. . . The sandhill weighs perhaps fifteen pounds or thereabouts and its flesh is preferred by some to that of the wild goose. **1913** *Pacific Coast Avifauna* 9.22 **CA,** *Sandhill Crane.* . . Our cranes first arrive in September and are fairly common in suitable places all through the winter. **1951** *AmSp* 26.91, Variations in pronunciation seem to be the major source of folk etymology. Among other instances in bird names . . [is] *Sam Hill crane* (Texas) for the sand-hill crane. **1965–70** *DARE* (Qu. Q10, . . *Water birds and marsh birds*) 17 Infs, **scattered,** Sandhill crane; (Qu. Q7, *Names and nicknames for . . game birds*) Infs **MI**2, 96, **NM**3, Sandhill crane; (Qu. Q5) Inf **AK**9, Sandhill crane; (Qu. Q14) Inf **TX**1, Crane—sandhill crane. **1969** *DARE* FW Addit **Okefenokee GA,** Pinkroot—an Okefenokee prairie plant; sandhill cranes feed on the roots. **1977** Udvardy *Audubon Field Guide Birds* 425, *Sandhill Crane.* . . In winter the Sandhill chooses not only marshes but also extensive prairies and fields, where it thrives on spilled grain. **1999** *Isthmus* (Madison WI) 2 Apr 11/1 **WI,** Allow, for the first time, the hunting of sandhill cranes.

2 =**great blue heron** or other long-legged wading bird.

  1897 *Oölogist* 14.33, There are probably a million people in America who from poor judgment or no reasoning at all, call the Great Blue Heron the Sandhill, and others who apply the name to most any longlegged bird. **1898** (1900) Davie *Nests N. Amer. Birds* 114, The Great Blue Heron is often erroneously called "Sand-hill Crane" or "Blue Crane"—in fact it is better known by either of these names than it is by its proper vernacular name. **1955** MA Audubon Soc. *Bulletin* 39.312 **ME,** *Great Blue Heron.* . . Sandhill Crane. . . Probably by transfer from the generally similar bird, properly so-called, which is now of only accidental occurrence in New England. **c1960** *Wilson Coll.* **csKY,** Sandhill crane—a name often used to mean any large heron. The actual sandhill crane has been recorded in the area only five or six times in thirty years. **1969** *DARE* (Qu. Q10, . . *Water birds and marsh birds*) Inf **CA**120, Heron—we call them Sam Hill cranes.

3 Fig: see quot.

  1995 Brophy *Coll.* 65 **swMO** (as of c1960), *Sandhill crane.* [A] tall slim awkward person.

sandhiller n

1 A poor White person from one of the sandhill regions of the southern coastal plain. **Sth, esp GA, SC** *derog* Cf **sand hill 1, 2a**

  1848 U.S. Congress *Congressional Globe* (App.) 26 Jan 137, The thing is whispered even among the *sandhillers* of South Carolina. **1850** Burke *Reminiscences of GA* 205, These people are known at the South by such names as crackers, clay-eaters, and sand-hillers. **1856** Olmsted *Journey Slave States* 506 **SC,** The sand-hillers. . . are small, gaunt, and cadaverous, and their skin is just the color of the sand-hills they live on. **1860** Hundley *Social Relations S. States* 257, Every where they are just alike, possess . . the same habits; although in different localities, they are known by different names. Thus, in the extreme South and South-west, they are usually called Squatters; in the Carolinas and Georgia Crackers or Sandhillers . . but every where, Poor White Trash. **1872** *KS Mag.* Mar 238, Who that has seen the "clay-eater," the "sandhiller," or the "piney woods cracker" of the South, does not know that it is impossible to exaggerate the sinfulness which looks out through the loop-holes of his red apologies for eyes. **1887** *Amer. Philol. Assoc. Trans. for 1886* 17.35 **Sth,** A gentleman from Ohio . . has attempted to indicate for me the words that were imported during or after the war from the South into

Southern Ohio. . . He mentions as recently imported . . *sandhillers* (inhabitants of sandy districts). **1947** Lumpkin *Making Southerner* 151 **SC,** With their pasty faces, scrawny necks, angular ill-nourished frames, straw-like hair, they seemed to me no different from the real "sandhillers." **1958** Babcock *I Don't Want* 155 **SC,** Barefooted and shirtless, the sandhiller was sprawled listlessly on the porch when I arrived.

2 An inhabitant of the sandhill region of western Nebraska. **NE** Cf **sand hill 1, 2b**

  1928 *AmSp* 4.132 **cnNE,** "On pump" is the "sandhiller's" term for buying necessities at the inland store on credit. **1929** *AmSp* 5.73 **NE** [Cattle country talk], The following is a partial list of words and expressions current on Nebraska ranches. Many of them now form part of the "talk" of the "sandhillers," the farmers of the "sandhill region," and many have been absorbed into the speech of "easterners," those living on the farms and in the towns of eastern Nebraska. **1935** Sandoz *Jules* 356 **wNE** (as of 1880–1930), Two sandhillers clashed on the streets of Gordon. **1939** FWP *Guide NE* 108, "The Kinkaider's Song," still popular at sandhill picnics and reunions, is sung to the tune of "My Maryland." . . In parodies, however, the sandhiller spared neither truth nor feelings. **1973** Allen *LAUM* 1.349 **Upper MW** (as of c1950), Homesteaders in the Nebraska sandhill country are known as *sandhillers.*

sandhill gentian n

A **gentian** (here: *Gentiana autumnalis*).

  1953 Greene–Blomquist *Flowers South* 100, *Pinebarren-Gentian, Sandhill-gentian.* . . This remarkable flower is a surprise to anyone seeing it for the first time.

sandhill milkweed n Also *sand milkweed*

A **milkweed 1** such as *Asclepias amplexicaulis, A. arenaria,* or *A. humistrata.*

  1930 OK Univ. Biol. Surv. *Pub.* 2.76, *Asclepias arenaria.* . . Sand-hill Milkweed. **1953** Greene–Blomquist *Flowers South* 102, Sandhill-milkweed (*A[sclepias] humistrata*) is. . . one of the most distinctive plants frequenting dry pinelands, scrub, and sandhills. **1964** Batson *Wild Flowers SC* 95, Sand Milkweed: *Asclepias amplexicaulis.* . . Dry fields and open woods mostly in the eastern two-thirds of the state. **1968** Barkley *Plants KS* 275, *Asclepias arenaria.* . . Sand milkweed. Sandy soil.

sandhill pavement n

  1933 *AmSp* 8.1.80 **NE** [Sandhill talk], *Sandhill pavement* is a term which puzzles a newcomer to the Nebraska sandhills. This expression does not refer to hard-surfaced or graveled roads. Because of the excessively hot, dry weather of the summer the roads become so very sandy that they would be almost impassable if the ranchers did not spread hay upon them. These hay-covered roads are *sandhill pavement.*

sandhill pine See **sand pine 1**

sandhill plum n Also *sandhill cherry* Cf **sand cherry 1, 2, sand plum 2**

A **wild plum** such as *Prunus americana,* **sand cherry 1,** or **Chickasaw plum;** see quots.

  1871 U.S. Dept. Ag. *Rept. of Secy. for 1870* 418, *Prunus pumila.* . . The plant thrives in sandy wastes, and is sometimes called sand-hill plum. **1879** (1880) Johnson *Hist. NE* 84, The sand-hill cherry, so famous on our western plains, is really . . a dwarf plum. It . . is found over the greater part of the western half of the State, on the sand-hills and very sandy land. It is a prolific fruit, about the size of the domestic cherry, and is very finely flavored. **1966–68** *DARE* (Qu. I46, . . *Kinds of fruits that grow wild around here*) Inf **KS**8, Sandhill plums; **OK**27, Sandhill plums—looks [sic] like cherry; **OK**32, Wild sandhill plums. **1973** Stephens *Woody Plants* 282 **Upper MW, Plains States,** *Prunus angustifolia.* . . is the common plum in sandy areas and is appropriately known as the sandhill plum. . . This is excellent cover for small birds and also produces a quantity of fruit for human consumption. **1987** Kindscher *Edible Wild Plants* 170, *Common Names* [of *Prunus americana*] . . sandhill plum, . . sand cherry [etc].

sandhill racer See **racer 3**

sandhill redbird See **redbird c**

sandhills See **sand hill 2b**

sandhill sage See **sand sage**

sandhills hornet See **sand hornet**

sandhill turtle See **sand turtle**

sandhill violet See **sand violet**

sand holly n

A **holly** n¹ **1** (here: *Ilex ambigua*).

1960 Vines *Trees SW* 654, *Ilex ambigua*. . . Vernacular names are Sand Holly and Possum Holly. **1970** Correll *Plants TX* 995, *Ilex ambigua*. . . Carolina holly, sand holly. Shrub or small tree. . . In sandy woods, along streams and in hammocks in e. Tex.

sand hornet n Also *sandhills hornet* Cf **sand wasp**

A **yellow jacket** such as *Vespa crabro* or *Vespula arenaria,* or a wasp of the family Sphecidae.

1881 *Harper's New Mth. Mag.* 64.75 **NH,** The fluttering butterfly . . is pounced upon in mid-air by the great sand-hornet. *Ibid,* This sand-hornet . . is built for a professional murderer. He carries two keen cimeters besides a deadly poisoned poniard, and is armed throughout. . . Not even the butcher-bird hankers after him. **1969** *DARE* (Qu. R21, . . *Other kinds of stinging insects*) Inf **KY**47, Sand hornet. **1980** Milne–Milne *Audubon Field Guide Insects* 837, *Sandhills Hornet (Vespula arenaria). . .* Sandy country.

sand house n

=**rock house 1.**

1969 *DARE* File **KY,** *Sand house*—a cliff that hangs over. Also called a *rock house.* Hence *Sandhouse Cave.*

sand jack n

1 =**bluejack 1.** esp **TX**

1884 Sargent *Forests of N. Amer.* 153, *Quercus cinerea* [=*Q. incana*]. . . Sand jack. . . Sandy barrens and dry upland ridges. **1897** Sudworth *Arborescent Flora* 176 **TX,** *Quercus cinerea.* . . Sand Jack. **1946** Reeves–Bain *Flora TX* 220, Sand Jack. . . Small tree with stout branches. . . Usually dry sandy soil. **1967** *DARE* (Qu. T10, . . *Kinds of oak trees*) Inf **TX**33, Sand jack. **1970** Correll *Plants TX* 485, *Quercus incana.* . . Sand jack. . . Low trees or shrubs to 8 m. tall. **1986** Pederson *LAGS Concordance,* 2 infs, **TX,** Sand jack; 1 inf, **cwLA,** Sand jack acorn tree.

2 A **willow oak** (here: *Quercus phellos*).

1960 Vines *Trees SW* 177, *Quercus phellos.* . . Other local names are Water Oak, . . Sandjacks [sic] Oak, . . and Pin Oak. . . Other oaks which are apt to be confused with the Willow Oak [=*Q. phellos*] are . . Bluejack Oak [etc].

‡**sand jigger** n Cf **jig-stick**

1970 *DARE* (Qu. L18, *Kinds of plows*) Inf **TX**78, Sand jigger . . shaft with rotating teeth to turn up wet dirt.

sand lamprey n

A young **lamprey** (here: *Petromyzon marinus*).

1938 Schrenkeisen *Field Book Fishes* 5, The young [of *Petromyzon marinus*]. . . are called "mud-eels" or "sand lampreys" and make good bait. They probably enter the sea when about 6 inches long.

sand lance n

Std: a fish of the genus *Ammodytes.* For other names of American spp see **lant, needlefish 3, sand eel**

sandlapper n

1 One who eats dirt; by ext, a low-class or countrified White person. [See quot 1942] chiefly **S Atl** *derog* Cf **clay-eater 1**

1836 Simms *Mellichampe* 1.83 **seSC,** He is some miserable overseer—a sand-lapper from Goose Creek. **1854** Simms *Scout* 153 **SC,** He was a little, dried-up withered atomy—a jaundiced "sand-lapper" or "clay-eater," from the Wassamasaw country. **1906** *DN* 3.155 **nwAR,** *Sand-lapper.* . . A man from the swamps or low land (as opposed to the "hill-billy"). **1936** Smith–Sass *Carolina Rice* 76 **SC,** He had dismounted from his horse and stood over a half dozen jugs and demijohns . . while two sad-looking "sandlappers" and a small covered wagon stood by. **1942** Kennedy *Palmetto Country* 65 **AL, FL, GA,** Before the Civil War, crackers were often called "sandlappers," because their children "contracted the habit of eating dirt." This "habit," now known to be a symptom of hookworm infection, has by no means disappeared. **1960** Williams *Walk Egypt* 35 **GA,** A picture of the Watts children came to her, ricketty-jointed and ragged, sand-lappers for sure.

1966–68 *DARE* (Qu. C35, *Nicknames for the different parts of your town or city*) Inf **SC**51, The Sandlappers—for Melrose Heights; (Qu. HH1, *Names and nicknames for a rustic or countrified person*) Inf **FL**16, Florida sandlapper.

2 also attrib: A native of South Carolina. Cf **clay-eater 2**

1904 (1913) Johnson *Highways South* 290 **SC,** A South Carolinian who was one day enlightening me on the habits of the countryside mentioned that the people of his state were often nicknamed "sandlappers." "They call us that," he explained, "because sand is so powerful plenty." **1943** Wiley *Life Johnny Reb* 339 **Sth** (as of 1861–65), Provincialism likewise found expression in the nicknames applied by soldiers of one state to those of another. Virginians were called the "Buttermilk Brigade"; South Carolinians, "Sand Lappers." **1948** Mencken *Amer. Lang. Suppl. 2* 608, Their State [=South Carolina] has also been called the *Rice State,* the *Iodine State,* the *Swamp State* and the *Sand-lapper State.* **1984** Wilder *You All Spoken Here* 121 **Sth,** Ms. Rita Jenrette, whose husband represented Horry County [SC] in Congress and was tagged in the Abscam affair, brought chicken bog to national attention when she said she was fed up to here with Sand-lapper political excursions featuring chicken bog, alligator shoes, polyester suits, and Moose Lodge ceremonies with members parading with antlers on their heads.

3 A homesteader in Oregon; see quot.

1964 Jackman–Long *OR Desert* 37, With the wave of homesteaders, each week showed new shacks sprouting in the sand. . . The old-established livestock men, with irrigated land, didn't believe in plowing up the desert and called this army of newcomers "sandlappers." This was partly contemptuous, partly just good-natured, and the drylanders retaliated by calling owners of grass meadows "tule rooters."

4 also *sand sifter:* A **whiptail:** usu *Cnemidophorus sexlineatus,* but also *C. gularis.* [See quot 1928]

1909 *DN* 3.365 **eAL, wGA,** *Sand-sifter.* . . A small fleet-footed lizard. Also called *racer, swift, swift-jack, swift-jenny.* **1918** *Copeia* 53.23 **VA,** Brown, with six white stripes. Tail brown. "Sand-lapper." *Cnemidophorus sexlineatus.* **1928** Baylor Univ. Museum *Contrib.* 16.12 **TX,** *Sandlapper.* This name is applied to the Six-lined Lizard and the related *Cnemidophorus gularis* on account of the peculiar habit they have of frequently dipping up sand with their mouths. . . This vernacular name is widely used in many of the Southern States. **1967** Huheey–Stupka *Amphibians Reptiles Gt. Smoky Mts.* 50, The Six-lined Racerunner, known locally as "Sandlapper," is abundant.

sand lark n [*OED2* at *sand lark* sb. 1 1800 → for "some of the smaller limicoline birds"]

=**spotted sandpiper.**

1842 DeKay *Zool. NY* 2.246, The Spotted Sand-Lark. *Totanus macularius.* **1872** Coues *Key to N. Amer. Birds* 260, *Spotted Sandpiper.* . . Familiarly known as the sandlark, . . tip-up, etc. **1904** (1910) Wheelock *Birds CA* 72, *Actitis macularia.* . . Sandlark. . . Found along almost every beach and river and lake of California. **1932** Bennitt *Check-list* 29 **MO,** *Spotted sandpiper.* . . Sand-lark. **1956** MA Audubon Soc. *Bulletin* 40.17 **MA,** *Spotted Sandpiper.* . . Sand Lark.

sand leaf See **sand lug**

sand lily n **West**

1 An **evening primrose a** (here: *Oenothera cespitosa*).

1892 *Atlantic Mth.* 70.306 **CO,** Down the road presented an enchanting procession of flowers, which changed from day to day as the season advanced: to-day the scarlet castilleia . . , tomorrow the sand lily lifting its dainty face above the bare sand. **1963** Craighead *Rocky Mt. Wildflowers* 121, *Oenothera caespitosa.* . . Sandlily. . . A large white flower close against the ground, 2–4 in. broad, composed of 4 petals that turn pink to red as they mature. **1966** Barnes–Jensen *Dict. UT Slang* 37, *Sand lily* . . local name for the evening primrose. **1967** Dodge *Roadside Wildflowers* 52 **SW,** *Sandlily.* . . The blossoms are delicately fragrant and often grow en masse along roadsides. . . Distributed from Minnesota to Washington State, south to New Mexico and California. **1967** *DARE* FW Addit **OR**12, Evening (desert) primrose—locally: sand lily.

2 A liliaceous plant (*Leucocrinum montanum*) of the western US. Also called **mountain lily 2, soaproot, star lily, star-of-Bethlehem, wild hyacinth, ~ tuberose**

1913 (1919) *WNID, Sand lily.* A white-flowered scapose liliaceous plant (*Leucocrinum montanum*) of the western United States. **1923** in 1925 Jepson *Manual Plants CA* 213, *Sand Lily.* . . Plentiful in its special localities but the localities few. **1950** Stevens *ND Plants* 103, *Leu-*

cocrinum montanum. . . Sand Lily. . . Flowers pure white. . . It is a good plant . . and can be increased from the black seeds which are borne in capsules just under ground. **1973** Hitchcock–Cronquist *Flora Pacific NW* 691, Sand lily. . . In sandy to rocky areas or in fairly heavy soil; . . Ore, to Cal, e across Ida to Mont and SD, and s to NM. **1979** Spellenberg *Audubon Guide N. Amer. Wildflowers W. Region* 584, *Sand Lily. . .* With its flowers nestled among the leaves, this distinctive little Lily is unmistakable.

3 A **stickleaf,** esp *Mentzelia decapetala.*

1940 Gates *Flora KS* 218, Mentzelia decapetala. . . Sand Lily. . . Plains and hills. West half. **1949** Moldenke *Amer. Wild Flowers* 33, *Nuttallia nuda* and *N. stricta* [=*Mentzelia nuda*]. . . are usually called *sandlilies,* and occupy hillsides and plains from western Nebraska to Colorado and Wyoming. **1967** *DARE* FW Addit **OR**12, Blazing star, . . Stick leaf, locally Sand lily. **1973** Hitchcock–Cronquist *Flora Pacific NW* 300, Sand lily, evening star . . *M*[*entzelia*] *decapetala.*

4 =**mariposa lily.**

1966–67 *DARE* FW Addit **WA**12, Sand lily (or mariposa) grows on tall slender stalk, bloom is like flock of butterflies; **OR**12, Sego lily— mariposa lily (state flower of Utah)[₂] local name: sand lily.

5 =**bitterroot 2.** Cf **sand rose**

1967 *DARE* FW Addit **OR**12, Bitterroot (Lewisia Redivivia [sic]) (Rock rose, or Redheaded Louisa) locally—sand lily.

sand lizard n Cf **sandlapper 4, sand swift**

Any of var **lizards 1,** esp a **whiptail** (here: *Cnemidophorus sexlineatus*).

1910 Ditmars *Reptiles World* 173, The *Sand Lizard* or *Striped Race-Runner C. sexlineatus,* is the only species of its genus ranging into the southeastern portion of the United States. **1928** [see **sand swift 1**]. **1935** Sandoz *Jules* 166 **wNE** (as of 1880–1930), Shooting, knifing, and disappearances became common as sand lizards and wind. **1954** Stebbins *Amphibians Reptiles W. N. Amer.* 224, Buried sand lizards can sometimes be frightened from the sand. **c1955** Reed–Person *Ling. Atlas Pacific NW,* 1 inf, Sand lizzard [sic].

sand lug n Also *sand leaf* Cf **lug** n² **1**

A lower leaf of a tobacco plant; see quots.

1950 *PADS* 14.58 **SC,** *Sand lugs. . .* Lowest grade of tobacco leaves, growing low on the plant, and having sand beaten upon them by rains. **1966–70** *DARE* Tape **FL**26, The bottom leaves are called sand leaves— you take them off. And if they're good you can save 'em, but if they kinda holey or got a good bit of grit on 'em, you just drop them on the ground right there; **NC**8, The first picking or gathering is called the sand lugs. . . "Sand" because they're very sandy; they're dirty; **SC**24, [Inf:] And when it begins to ripen they take off the lugs. The first leaves are called lugs. [FW:] Oh, sand lugs? [Inf:] Um-hum, sand lugs. And they cure them of course, but they are cheap tobacco; **VA**75, [Inf:] Pulled all the leaves off. You'd have certain grades for it. You'd have sand leaves in one pile, next grade to that, then a better grade to that—about three grades. . . [FW:] What are the sand leaves? [Inf:] Sand leaves is the leaves next to the ground. **1967** Key *Tobacco Vocab.* 135 **PA,** *Sand leaf* . . the lower leaves of the plant; **GA, NC,** *Sand lugs.*

sand lupine n

A **lupine** native to the western US: either *Lupinus formosus* of California or *L. ammophilus.*

1896 *Jrl. Amer. Folkl.* 9.186 **CA,** *Leguminosa formosus* [=*Lupinus f.*], sand lupine. **1898** Davidson *CA Plants* 201, Some of these native spring-time weeds are, the poppy, . . owl's clover, sand-lupines, chili-cothe. **1999** (acc) U.S. Dept. Ag. *Integrated Taxonomic Info. System* (Internet), *Lupinus ammophilus*—Vernacular Name: *sand lupine.*

sand martin n Cf **martin**

1 =**bank swallow 1.** [*OED2* at *sand* sb. 2 10.b 1668 →]

[**1743** Catesby *Nat. Hist. Carolina* 2.xxxvi, European *Land-Birds inhabiting* America. . . The Sand-Martin [etc.].] **1813** (1824) Wilson *Amer. Ornith.* 5.46, Bank Swallow, or Sand Martin. *Hirundo Riparia.* . . This appears to be the most sociable with its kind and the least intimate with man. . . They are particularly fond of the shores of rivers, and in several places along the Ohio, they congregate in immense multitudes. **1875** Flagg *Birds Seasons New Engl.* 251 **NEng,** Of all the Swallows the Sand-Martins afford the most amusement for small boys in the vicinity, who employ themselves in digging out their nests, which are sometimes less than two feet under the surface. **1938** Oberholser *Bird Life LA* 405, *Riparia riparia maximiliani.* . . is sometimes called . . 'sand

martin', because of its nesting habits. **1956** MA Audubon Soc. *Bulletin* 40.84, *Bank Swallow.* . . Sand Martin (General; also in British folk use.) **1962** Imhof *AL Birds* 362, Sand Martin. . . Common and abundant on the Gulf Coast and in the Tennessee Valley, especially in fall.

2 =**rough-winged swallow. SE**

1913 Bailey *Birds VA* 261, *Rough-winged Swallow.* [Sand Martin]. . . The earliest swallow to depart in the fall, August 5th, and the earliest to arrive in the spring, March 25th. **1954** Sprunt *FL Bird Life* 305, *Riparia riparia riparia.* . . *Local Names:* Sand Martin. (Also the local name of the Rough-winged Swallow, which breeds. This one does not.) **1962** Imhof *AL Birds* 364, *Rough-winged Swallow.* . . *Other names:* Sand Martin [etc.]. . . The nest is usually in a burrow in an exposed bank.

sand mat n

1 A plant of the genus *Chamaesyce.*

1941 Jaeger *Wildflowers* 130, Small-seeded sand-mat. *Euphorbia polycarpa* [=*Chamaesyce p.*] *Ibid* 131, Rib-seeded sand-mat. *Euphorbia glyptosperma* [=*Chamaesyce g.*] . . Death Valley sand-mat. *Euphorbia vallis-mortae* [=*Chamaesyce v.-m.*] . . New Mexico sand-mat. *Euphorbia neomexicana* [=*Chamaesyce serpyllifolia*]. . . A flat, spreading species, with maroon leaves. . . Sonoran sand-mat. *Euphorbia micromera* [= *Chamaesyce m.*]. . . This and other milky-juiced sand-mats were considered valuable as snake-bite remedies by the Indians. . . *Bristle-lobed sand-mat. Euphorbia setiloba* [=*Chamaesyce s.*] **1965** Teale *Wandering Through Winter* 22 **CA,** We encountered . . the red sand-mat . . which becomes a mass of glittering droplets of collected moisture after a rain. **1973** Doran *Something Swans* 55, Probably now even the illusion of emptiness is gone, so busily and speedily have men possessed the Southern California desert. . . When I was first there, they had settled on its western parts only as the little desert sand-mats do, fitfully, here and there, easily pulled up by the single root.

2 A low, mat-forming plant (*Cardionema ramosissimum*) native to the western US.

1944 Abrams *Flora Pacific States* 2.114, *Cardionema ramosissima* [sic]. . . Sand Mat. . . Stems numerous, forming mats 10–15 cm. across. **1973** Hitchcock–Cronquist *Flora Pacific NW* 113, Sandmat. . . Sandy beaches along the coast.

sand milkweed See **sandhill milkweed**

sand mullet n

1 =**striped mullet.**

1884 Goode *Fisheries U.S.* 1.449 **NC,** The Striped Mullet, *Mugil albula* [=*M. cephalus*]. About Cape Hatteras the names "Jumping Mullet" and "Sand Mullet" occur.

2 A **kingfish 1.**

1968 *DARE* (Qu. P2, . . *Kinds of saltwater fish caught around here . . good to eat*) Inf **MD**36, Sand mullet or kingfish. **1984** *DARE* File **Chesapeake Bay** [Watermen's vocab], Sand mullet / sea mullet / Virginia mullet / roundhead / whiting.

sand myrtle n

1 A low evergreen shrub (*Leiophyllum buxifolium*) native chiefly to the central and south Atlantic parts of the US. Also called **mountain heather 1, ~ myrtle 2**

1814 Pursh *Flora Americae* 1.301 **NJ,** Ammyrsine . . *Ledum buxifolium.* . . being known by the name of *Sand-myrtle* among the inhabitants of New Jersey. **1860** Curtis *Cat. Plants NC* 100, Sand Myrtle. . . grows in sandy woods of Brunswick county, and on the rocky summits of our Mountains, from the Grandfather to Whiteside. **1882** *Harper's New Mth. Mag.* June 71 **sNJ,** Of the smaller shrubs now in bloom we find the sand-myrtle, with its terminal umbel-like clusters of small pinkish flowers. **1956** Savage *River* 266 **SC,** Beyond lay . . white-flowered pixie moss, miniature rhododendrons called sand myrtles, bright blue clumps of lupine [etc]. **1979** Niering–Olmstead *Audubon Guide N. Amer. Wildflowers E. Region* 502, *Sand Myrtle.* . . Height: 4–20″. . . Rocky or sandy woods and bluffs.

2 A **groundsel tree** such as *Baccharis halimifolia.*

1942 *Torreya* 42.165, *Baccharis halimifolia.* . . Sand myrtle, coastal South Carolina. **1960** Williams *Walk Egypt* 106 **GA,** The edge selvaged with willow and sand myrtle and hickory. A man could hide in those thickets.

3 A **fire thorn** (here: *Pyracantha coccinea*).

1930 in **1972** *Hench Coll.* **cVA,** The plant in front of our house was called in Fluvanna County where Mrs. Mickie got it, firethorn, or pyracanthus [sic]. Its name in Charlottesville is sand myrtle. **1934** *Ibid*

seVA, Sand myrtle, thorn oak—Mrs. Mickie tells me that these are variant names for a bush that grows around Virginia Beach. It is a bush with an evergreen-appearing leaf and has thorns on it.

sand oak n Cf sand jack 1

Either **myrtle oak** or a **shinnery oak** (here: *Quercus havardii*).

1960 Vines *Trees SW* 167, *Quercus havardii*. . . Vernacular names are Shinnery Oak, Sand Oak [etc]. *Ibid* 180, *Quercus myrtifolia*. . . is also known as . . Sand Oak.

sand owl n

=**burrowing owl.**

1986 Pederson *LAGS Concordance,* 1 inf, **cFL,** Sand owl—lives in the sand.

sand oxeye n Cf oxeye 1a

Either the **semipalmated sandpiper** or the **least sandpiper.**

1917 (1923) *Birds Amer.* 1.238, *Semipalmated Sandpiper*. . . *Other Names.* . . Sand Ox-eye. **1946** Hausman *Eastern Birds* 286, *Semipalmated Sandpiper*. . . Sand Oxeye. . . This species, so similar to the Least Sandpiper, is more of a sea-beach sandpiper and is less commonly found inland on muddy shores. **1956** MA Audubon Soc. *Bulletin* 40.19 **ME,** *Least Sandpiper.* . . Sand Oxeye. *Ibid* 20 **ME, MA,** *Semipalmated Sandpiper.* . . Sand Oxeye.

sand oyster n Cf rock oyster 1

A type of **oyster B1** (here: *Crassostrea virginica*).

1881 Ingersoll *Oyster-Industry* 247 **Chesapeake Bay,** *Sand-oysters.* Single scattered oysters found on leeward sandy shores.

sandpaper aster n Also sandpaper starwort

An asterlike plant *(Ionactis linariifolius).*

1940 Clute *Amer. Plant Names* 76, *A[ster] lineariifolius* [sic]. . . Sandpaper starwort. **1948** Wherry *Wild Flower Guide* 135, *Aster linariifolius* [=*Ionactis l.*] . . This is also known as *Sandpaper Aster,* in reference to the rough herbage.

sandpaper oak n [See quot 1960]

A **scrub oak** (here: *Quercus vaseyana*).

1960 Vines *Trees SW* 168, *Quercus pungens*. . . The rough feel of the leaf surface, because of the stiff, short hairs, has given it the name of Sandpaper Oak. **1980** Little *Audubon Guide N. Amer. Trees W. Region* 409, Sandpaper Oak is one of a few species of shrubby oaks in the Southwest; most do not usually attain tree size.

sandpaper starwort See sandpaper aster

sand pea n

1 =**goat's rue.**

1938 Baker *FL Wild Flowers* 107, *Sand Peas* . . Genus *Cracca* [=*Tephrosia*]—Our most common plants of this genus . . bear . . small flowers that usually open about noon; at that time they are white, by sunset they have changed to pale pink, and the following day are crimson.

2 =**beach pea.**

1944 Abrams *Flora Pacific States* 2.623, *Lathyrus maritimus* [=*L. japonicus* var *maritimus*]. . . Beach or Sand Pea. . . Beach and sand dunes along the coast.

sand peep n esp NEng Cf peep n 2, sand bird 1

Any of var small **sandpipers,** but esp the **least** and **semipalmated sandpipers;** also fig.

1868 *Atlantic Mth.* 21.12 **NEng,** He . . was only waiting, with his fowling-piece, for Lucian, before going down to the shore to bag sandpeeps. **1872** Coues *Key to N. Amer. Birds* 254, *Least Sandpiper.* . . This species and the last [=*Calidris pusilla*] are usually confounded under the common name of "sandpeeps," and look much alike. **1874** (1969) Coffin *Caleb Krinkle* 463 **MA,** The sand-peeps and the gulls came circling through the air. **1923** U.S. Dept. Ag. *Misc. Circular* 13.55, *Least Sandpiper.* . . *Vernacular Names.* . . *In local use.* . . Sand peep (Long Id., N.Y., Calif.) *Ibid* 57, *Semipalmated Sandpiper.* . . Sand peep (Mass., Long Id., N.Y.) . . *Sanderling.* . . Sand peep (Fla.) **1935** Lincoln *Cape Cod Yesterdays* 130 **seMA,** Another delicacy, so he said, which was always served in that camp once a season, was a sandpeep pie. **1940** White *Wild Geese* 86 **AK,** And so I've told these poor timid sand peeps plain enough. **1956** MA Audubon Soc. *Bulletin* 40.17, *Spotted Sand-*

piper. Big Sand Peep (Maine. Peep is a general cognomen for small shore birds, sonic for some of them.) *Ibid* 18, *Solitary Sandpiper.* . . Sand Peep (Maine.) *Ibid* 19, *Least Sandpiper.* . . Sand Peep (Maine.) *Ibid* 20, *Stilt Sandpiper.* . . Sand Peep (Maine.) . . *Semipalmated Sandpiper.* . . Sand Peep (Maine, Mass., Conn.) **1963** Gromme *Birds WI* 217, Sandpeep (Least and Semipalmated Sandpipers). **1966–70** DARE (Qu. Q7, *Names and nicknames for . . game birds*) Inf **MA**72, Sand peep; (Qu. Q10, *. . Water birds and marsh birds*) Infs **ME**6, **MA**98, Sand peep.

sand perch n

1 A freshwater fish, as:

a The black **crappie** *(Pomoxis nigromaculatus).*

1877 Hallock *Sportsman's Gaz.* 378, Sand Perch, or Bachelor Perch. . . Apparently a cross between the yellow belly and silver perch. **1890** *Century Dict.* 5331 **Sth,** *Sand-perch.* . . The grass-bass, *Pomoxys hexacanthus.* **1935** Caine *Game Fish* 16 **Sth,** Sand Perch. . . *Calico Bass.* **1946** Richmond (Va.) *Times–Dispatch* 4 Aug iv.4–D/2 (*OED2*), There is always the likelihood of catching . . sand perch and blue-nosed perch [=*Lepomis macrochirus*]. **1967–68** DARE (Qu. P1, *. . Kinds of freshwater fish . . caught around here . . good to eat*) Inf **GA**28, Sand perch; **SC**40, Sand perch—like bass. **1968** DARE Tape **GA**20, [Inf:] I do a good bit of fishing. . . catfish, we got what we call a sand perch, in here, some people call 'em shriners [sic]. Uh, thin gizzards. [FW:] Thin gizzard? That's the same as a shriner? [Inf:] Yeah. **1976** Tryckare et al. *Lore of Sportfishing* 102, *Black Crappie.* . . Other common names . . sand perch. **1986** Pederson *LAGS Concordance,* 1 inf, **nwFL,** Sand perch—freshwater fish; 1 inf, **seFL,** Sand perch.

b =**log perch.**

1905 NJ State Museum *Annual Rept. for 1904* 299, *Percina caprodes.* . . Hog Fish. Sand Perch. This, the largest of the darters, may be distinguished from our other species by the . . pig-like projecting snout.

c A **pumpkinseed 1** (here: *Lepomis gibbosus*).

1938 Schrenkeisen *Field Book Fishes* 246, *Lepomis gibbosus*. . . *Common names.* . . Sand Perch. [*Ibid* 247, It spawns in summer, . . commonly making its nest . . in clay, sand, or gravel bottoms.] **1976** Tryckare et al. *Lore of Sportfishing* 102, *Lepomis gibbosus.* . . Sand perch. . . One of the commonest and most widely distributed of the sunfishes.

2 A saltwater fish, as:

a =**mademoiselle.**

1942 Chesapeake Biol. Lab. *Pub. 53* 17, The sand perch, or mademoiselle, *Bairdiella chrysura,* was a frequent captive [in crab pots]. **1953** MD Dept. Educ. *Our Underwater Farm* 15, On the Western Shore [of Chesapeake Bay] the common white perch is called a black perch, and the sand perch is a white perch.

b A small serranid fish of the genus *Diplectrum,* usu *D. formosum* of Atlantic and Gulf waters. For other names of *D. formosum* see **sandfish 2a, squirrelfish**

1968 *Sports Afield* June, Sand perch. . . In the Atlantic, the name applies to one of the small sea basses, sometimes called a sandfish. In the Pacific it's a regional name for a barred surfperch. **1974** McClane *McClane's New Std. Fishing Encycl.* 840, *Sand Perch—Diplectrum formosum.* An Atlantic marine species of little angling value. **1983** *Audubon Field Guide N. Amer. Fishes* 538, *Sand Perch (Diplectrum formosum).* . . From Virginia to Florida, throughout Gulf of Mexico. . . *Dwarf Sand Perch (Diplectrum bivitattum)* . . occurs over mud or sand from North Carolina throughout Gulf of Mexico. Rather common in certain areas, this little sea bass [=*D. formosum*] is often caught by anglers who are pursuing something larger. **1986** Pederson *LAGS Concordance,* 1 inf, **nwFL,** Sand perch—small baitfish.

c A **surfperch** (here: *Amphistichus argenteus*).

1968 [see **2b** above].

sand peter n

=**least tern.**

1925 Bailey *Birds FL* 9, Least tern. . . *Sterna albifrons antillarum* (Sand peter, Kill peter, Sea swallow, Little striker). . . They arrive in April (5th) on the East Coast, and. . . spend the winter farther south.

sand phlox n

A **phlox** (here: *Phlox bifida*).

1933 Small *Manual SE Flora* 1103, *P[hlox] bifida.* . . *Sand-phlox.* . .

Exposed slopes and cliffs in rocky or sandy, sterile soil. **1951** Voss-Eifert *IL Wild Flowers* 40, *Phlox bifida.* . . Like crisp embroidery or delicate lace, the flowers of sand phlox are draped over sandy slopes, in sandy woods, along roads, on sandstone cliffs. **1966** *DARE* Wildfl QR Pl.178 **WI**80, Sand phlox. **1979** Niering–Olmstead *Audubon Guide N. Amer. Wildflowers E. Region* 698, Sand Phlox *(P. bifida)*, occurs in sandy habitats in the Midwest and has petals with notches.

sand pike n

A **sauger** n[1], usu *Stizostedion canadense*.
1877 U.S. Natl. Museum *Bulletin* 10.72 **TN**, *List of Fishes of Nashville, as given by a Fisherman.* . . Sand Pike. Pike. . . Gar [etc]. **1884** Goode *Fisheries U.S.* 1.424, The "Sauger" . . [is] known also as the . . "Sand Pike." . . The common Sauger or Sand Pike of the Lakes . . should bear the name of *Stizostedion canadense*, var. *grisea.* . . The 'Sand Pike' of the Upper Missouri averages rather slender, with a long, slender nose and more flattened and snake-like head. **1908** Forbes-Richardson *Fishes of IL* 274, *Stizostedion canadense griseum.* . . *Sand-pike.* . . Length: 1 to 1 ½ feet. **1927** Weed *Pike* 45, *Stizostedion*—Common names of this group are so confused that no attempt has been made to separate names belonging only to the Saugers from those belonging only to the Walleyes. It is probable that practically all the names are applied to either. . . Sand Pike; general. **1935** Caine *Game Fish* 31, *Wall-eyed Pike*—*Stizostedion vitreum.* . . Sand Pike. **1939** Natl. Geogr. Soc. *Fishes* 134, The sauger or sand pike. . . has the same general distribution as the wall-eyed pike, that is in the Great Lakes basin and upper Mississippi Valley. **1966–68** *DARE* (Qu. P1, . . *Kinds of freshwater fish* . . *caught around here* . . *good to eat*) Inf **MN**21, Sand pike—common name here for sauger; **MN**22, Sand pike—like a little pike, caught near shores; **ND**1, Sauger or sand pike. **1983** Becker *Fishes WI* 880, *Stizostedion canadense.* . . Sand pike, river pike.

sand pine n

1 also *sandhill pine:* A **pine 1** (here: *Pinus clausa*) native to the southeastern US. Also called **pitch pine b(5), scrub ~, spruce ~**
1884 Sargent *Forests of N. Amer.* 199, *Pinus clausa.* . . Sand Pine. . . Florida, shores of Pensacola bay, south, generally within 30 miles of the coast. . . Occasionally used for the masts of small vessels. **1938** Rawlings *Yearling* 3 **nFL**, Where he walked now, the scrub had closed in, walling in the road with dense sand pines, each one so thin it seemed to the boy it might make kindling by itself. **1966–69** *DARE* (Qu. T5, . . *Kinds of evergreens, other than pine*) Inf **FL**34, Sand pine; (Qu. T17, . . *Kinds of pine trees; not asked in early QRs*) Infs **FL**34, **NC**60, Sand pine. **1986** Pederson *LAGS Concordance* **FL**, 1 inf, Sand pine—small, tiny pinecones, in sandy areas; 1 inf, Sand pine; 1 inf, Sandhill pine.
2 =**lodgepole pine.**
1897 Sudworth *Arborescent Flora* 23 **OR**, *Pinus contorta.* . . Sand Pine. **1967** Gilkey–Dennis *Hdbk. NW Plants* 29, *Pinus contorta.* . . Lodgepole pine. . . Sand . . pine. Scrubby trees, usually less than 20 m. . . Common along sea-coast.

sand pink n

=**moss pink 1.**
1966 *DARE* Wildfl QR Pl.178 **WI**80, Sand pinks.

sandpiper n

Std: any of var limicoline birds of the family Scolopacidae. For other names of these see **brownbird 1, bull peep, cherook, grass bird 2, grayback 1b, kittledee 2, knot** n[2], **least sandpiper, oxeye 1a, pectoral sandpiper, peep** n **2, pennywinkle 4, pin snipe, purple sandpiper, red-backed ~, robin snipe 4, sand bird 1, ~ chicken, sander, sanderling, sand peep, ~ snipe, semipalmated sandpiper, solitary ~, spotted ~, stilt ~, upland plover, white-rumped sandpiper**

sand plum n

1 =**beach plum.**
1843 Torrey *Flora NY* 1.194, *Prunus maritima.* . . Beach Plum. Sand Plum. [*Ibid* 195, When fully ripe and growing in exposed situations, particularly on the sides of sand-banks, the fruit is agreeably flavored, but much of it is acerb and astringent.] **1859** (1880) Darlington *Amer. Weeds* 116, *P[runus] maritima.* . . Beach Plum. Sand Plum. **1968** *DARE* (Qu. I46, . . *Kinds of fruits that grow wild around here*) Inf **CT**2, Sand plums—near water—out now [=no longer found locally].

2 A **wild plum:** usu a var of **Chickasaw plum** (here: *Prunus angustifolia* var *watsoni*), occas also *Prunus gracilis* or other sp. **esp Plains States, OK, TX** Cf **sand cherry 2, sandhill plum**
1894 *Garden and Forest* 7.134, This plant [=*Prunus watsoni*] . . is the Sand Plum of southern and south-eastern Nebraska and central Kansas. **1898** Bailey *Sketch Native Fruits* 218, The Sand plum of Nebraska and central Kansas is the most important of the plums which we have not yet discussed. So recently has this plum come to be known that it has never had a specific name until Professor Sargent described it as *Prunus Watsoni*, four years ago. . . The inhabitants of those parts of the West where this plum is native collect the better forms in large quantities for domestic consumption, and even sell the fruits in the towns. **1916** *Torreya* 16.238, *Prunus gracilis.* . . Sand plum, Lincoln Co., Okla.; prairie cherry, Games Creek, Ark. **1930** OK Univ. Biol. Surv. *Pub.* 2.65, *Prunus angustifolia* var. *watsoni.* . . Sand Plum, Sand Cherry. **1938** Van Dersal *Native Woody Plants* 349, Plum, Sand *(Prunus texana)*. **1951** Porter *Ragged Roads* 80 **OK**, On the opposite side there was a level plot some three or four rods wide with sand-plum bushes. **1959** Lahey–Hogan *As I Remember It* 104 **swKS** (as of 1890s), The wild sand plums . . grew wild in the valleys between the hills where people from the north, including ourselves, went . . to pick the fruit in the late summer and fall. **1965–68** *DARE* (Qu. I46, . . *Kinds of fruits that grow wild around here*) Infs **CO**20, **KS**1, 11, **OK**3, Sand plums. **1973** Stephens *Woody Plants* 286, *Prunus gracilis* . . Sand plum, Oklahoma plum. . . Dry, sandy soil. . . Kansas, Oklahoma, Texas, and New Mexico. **1980** Little *Audubon Guide N. Amer. Trees E. Region* 494, *Chickasaw Plum*—"Sand Plum"—*Prunus angustifolia.* **1997** *DARE* File **c,wOK**, In central and western Oklahoma there is a kind of wild fruit tree called sand plum.

sand puffs n

=**sand verbena 1.**
1915 (1926) Armstrong–Thornber *Western Wild Flowers* 104, Sand Puffs—*Abronia salsa* [=*A. elliptica*]. . . This plant is . . most attractive, particularly against the sandy soil where it grows. . . The flowers are numerous, . . in handsome roundish clusters, . . with a papery, pinkish or yellowish involucre. **1932** Rydberg *Flora Prairies* 308, *Abronia.* . . Sand Verbena. Sand Puffs. . . *Tripterocalyx.* . . Sand Puffs. **1999** (acc) U.S. Dept. Ag. *Integrated Taxonomic Info. System* (Internet), *Tripterocalyx carnea*—Vernacular Name: winged sandpuffs.

sand rat n

=**pocket gopher 1.**
1825 in 1974 *Fauna Americana* 153, *Geomys cinereus* [=*G. bursarius*]. . . Vulgarly *Sand-rat, Goffer, Pouched-rat, Salamander*, &c. **1846** in 1848 Emory *Notes Reconnoissance* 388 **wKS**, Piles of loose earth, like small ant hills . . are formed by the sand rats or gophers. **1867** *Amer. Naturalist* 1.394 **AZ**, Only one, the Red Sand-rat, (*T[homomys] fulvus*) is at all common. **1928** Anthony *N. Amer. Mammals* 283, *Douglas Pocket Gopher or Columbia Sand Rat.—Thomomys douglasii douglasii* [=*T. bulbivorus*]. . . Found along the Columbia River near Vancouver, Washington. **1967** *DARE* (Qu. P29, . . *'Gophers'* . . *other name* . . *or what other animal are they most like*) Inf **OR**1, Sand rat. **1968** *Edgerton Enterprise* (MN) 25 July sec 2 2/6, For example, take the sand rat. This animal lives in an extremely austere environment. It lives where the soil is salty and plants have a high salt content.

sand rattler n

Either the **massasauga** or a **diamondback rattlesnake** (here: *Crotalus atrox*).
1969 *DARE* (Qu. P25, . . *Kinds of snakes*) Inf **MI**101, Brush rattler, sand rattler [FW: Inf thinks these are the same]; **TX**72, Diamondback is sand rattler.

sand reed n

1 also *sand reed grass, sea sand reed (grass):* =**beach grass.** [*OED2* at *sand* sb.[2] 10.c 1805 →]
1822 Eaton *Botany* 183, *A[rundo] arenaria* [=*Ammophila a.*] . . (sand reed grass . .) panicle spiked. **1861** Wood *Class-Book* 778, *C[alamagrostis] arenaria.* . . *Sand Reed.* . . Of great value in confining loose, sandy beaches. **1881** Phares *Farmer's Book of Grasses* 39, The *C. arenaria*, beach grass, mat grass, sea-sand reeds [sic] grass, of no agricultural interest, is yet very valuable in many parts of the world, doing what King Canute could not. **1912** Baker *Book of Grasses* 128, Sea

Sand-reed. Ammophila arenaria. . . Sandy beaches along the coast. **1950** Gray–Fernald *Manual of Botany* 159, *Ammophila.* . . *Sand-Reed.* . . Coarse perennials of Eu. and Atl. N. Am.

2 A plant of the genus *Calamovilfa.* Also called **reed grass d, sand grass 1c**

   1937 U.S. Forest Serv. *Range Plant Hdbk.* G43, Prairie sandgrass [= *Calamovilfa longifolia*], a tall, coarse, tough, perennial grass also known as sandreed, is a drought-resistant species which occurs chiefly in sandy soil . . on plains and hills east of the Rocky Mountains. . . It is the most widespread species of *Calamovilfa,* a genus . . restricted to North America. **1939** FWP *Guide KS* 11, In western Kansas the short grasses dominate. . . Sand reed and turkeyfoot grow in the semi-arid southwest, and saltgrass and alkali sacaton in the alkaline soils. **1954** Harrington *Manual Plants CO* 80, *Calamovilfa.* . . *Sandreed.* . . Leaf blades long . . and tapering to tip. **1968** Barkley *Plants KS* 41, Calamovilfa gigantea. . . Big Sandreed. . . Calamovilfa longifolia. . . Prairie Sandreed.

sand reed grass See **sand reed 1**

sand rice See **sand grass 1h**

sandridge See **sandwich**

sand rocket n

Std: an introduced wall rocket *(Diplotaxis muralis).* Also called **flixweed 2**

sand roller n

=**trout-perch.**

   1896 U.S. Natl. Museum *Bulletin* 47.783, *Percopsidae. (The Sand Rollers).* . . Small fishes of the fresh waters of the cooler parts of America. *Ibid* 784, *Percopsis guttatus* [=*P. omiscomaycus*]. . . Sand Roller; Trout Perch. . . Length 6 inches. Spawns in spring. **1933** John G. Shedd Aquarium *Guide* 67, *Percopsis omiscomaycus* . . *Sand-roller.* The Trout-Perch is abundant in the Great Lakes region. . . It is too small to be of value as food. **1957** Blair et al. *Vertebrates U.S.* 160, *Columbia transmontana* [=*Percopsis t.*]. . . Sand roller. Columbia River Basin in Oregon, Washington, and western Idaho. **1983** Becker *Fishes WI* 741, *Percopsis omiscomaycus.* . . Sand roller.

sandroot See **sand food**

sand rose n

A **bitterroot 2** (here: *Lewisia rediviva*).

   1947 *Nature Mag.* 40.444 **MT,** Other common names [of *Lewisia rediviva*] are rock rose, sand rose [etc].

sand runner n

1 =**ruddy turnstone.**

   1877 Hallock *Sportsman's Gaz.* 164, *Strepsilas interpres.* . . Sand-runner. **1917** (1923) *Birds Amer.* 1.268, *Ruddy Turnstone.* . . *Other Names.* . . Sand-runner. **1946** Hausman *Eastern Birds* 259, *Ruddy Turnstone.* . . Some twenty-five or more local names, among which are: Chicken Plover, . . Sand Runner, Stone-pecker.

2 also *sand skeeter:* A **whiptail** (here: *Cnemidophorus sexlineatus*). Cf **skeet** v **1**

   1945 McCauley *Reptiles MD & DC* 36, *Cnemidophorus sexlineatus.* . . Racerunner, . . sand skeeter. **1955** *Clarke Co. Democrat* (Grove Hill AL) 8 Sept 4/5 *(Mathews Coll.),* Still another lizard is the six-lined lizard which I as a boy knew as a sand runner.

sand sage n Also *sand sagebrush, sandhill sage*

A **sagebrush 1** (here: *Artemisia filifolia*).

   1960 Vines *Trees SW* 967, *Sand Sage-brush.* . . Rounded, aromatic shrub. **1961** Ligon *NM Birds* 90, The sand . . sage *(Artemisia filifolia),* found throughout practically all of the original [Lesser Prairie] Chicken range, . . constitutes a major part of their diet in winter and during periods of drought. **1968** Abbey *Desert Solitaire* 28 **seUT,** Sand sage or old man sage, a lustrous windblown blend of silver and blue and aquamarine, gleams in the distance, the feathery stems flowing like hair. **1968** Barkley *Plants KS* 370, Artemisia filifolia. . . Sandhill Sage. Sand Sagebrush. High plains.

sand saucer See **sand collar**

sand scrub n

1 A **ceanothus** (here: *Ceanothus dentatus*).

   1938 Van Dersal *Native Woody Plants* 87, *Ceanothus dentatus.* . . *Sand*

scrub. . . A small, densely-branched shrub; . . occurs on sandy and other soils.

2 =**shinnery oak.** Cf **sand oak**

   1960 Vines *Trees SW* 167, *Quercus havardii.* . . Vernacular names are Shinnery Oak, Sand Oak, . . and Sand Scrub.

sand shark n

1 A small shark of the genus *Odontaspis,* usu *O. taurus.*

   1873 U.S. Bur. Fisheries *Rept. for 1871–72* 813 **ME,** *Eugomphodus littoralis* [=*Odontaspis taurus*]. . . Sand shark; shovel-nose. **1884** Goode *Fisheries U.S.* 1.671, The Sand Shark—*Odontaspis littoralis.* This species . . is found on our coast from New England southward to Charleston. **1905** NJ State Museum *Annual Rept. for 1904* 52 **NJ,** *Carcharias littoralis.* . . Sand Shark. . . Reported to me from Stone Harbor. **1921** *Copeia* 100.77, An unusually large specimen of the Sand Shark *(Carcharias taurus)* was captured on August 25, 1921, by Captain Charles Hurd of Clinton, Connecticut. **1966** DARE Tape **FL**45, Something wiggled and stirred up the mud and he saw a small sand shark. **1967–70** DARE (Qu. P4, *Saltwater fish that are not good to eat)* Infs **MA**32, 97, 123, **NJ**60, **WA**28, Sand shark(s).

2 A **dogfish 1** (here: *Squalus acanthias*).

   1935 Caine *Game Fish* 156 **Sth,** Sand Shark—*Squalus acanthias.* . . Probably the most numerous of the shark family, . . [it] also is the most annoying to the angler, especially the surf-caster. **1984** DARE File **Chesapeake Bay** [Watermen's vocab], Dog shark—dog fish—sand shark.

sand shell n Also *sand clam*   **chiefly Missip-Ohio Valleys**

A **freshwater clam:** either *Ligumia recta* or a clam of the genus *Lampsilis,* esp *L. teres.*

   1900 (1906) *Webster's Internatl. Dict. Suppl.* 183, *Sand shell* . . , a yellow river mussel, or naiad *(Lampsilus* [sic] *anodontoides),* of the Mississippi River, valuable for the manufacture of pearl buttons. Applied also to other allied species, as the black *sand shell (L. rectus),* used for the same purpose. **1908** Kunz–Stevenson *Book of the Pearl* 73, The sand shells *(Lampsilis)*—of which there are several species—do not occur in large beds. **1941** Writers' Program *Guide AR* 207 **neAR,** Dredging the White River and its tributaries for fresh-water mussels used for button making affords farmers a part-time occupation. . . Most prized is the rare sand shell, sold to European markets for use on knife handles and for other decorative purposes. **1953** (1977) Hubbard *Shantyboat* 211 **Missip-Ohio Valleys,** We learned that there are many classes of shells, of different value. Those called sand and niggerhead shells bring the highest price. **1966** *WI Conserv. Bulletin* 31.3.26 **WI** (as of 1900–10), Clamming was big business. Hundred of clam boats dragged the bottom . . bringing up . . species such as muckets, sand shells, and "pocketbooks." **1991** IL Nat. Hist. Surv. *Biol. Notes* 137.12 **IL,** Matteson collected 69 yellow sandshells, all of them at a single station on Sugar Creek "north." . . The species was present in good numbers in all but Sugar Creek "south" and the South Fork Sangamon River. **1992** *Nature Conserv. Mag.* 42.6.22, Yellow sandshell, *Lampsilis teres;* . . black sandshell, *Ligumia recta.* **1992** Cummings–Mayer *Field Guide Freshwater Mussels MW* 148, *Yellow sandshell—Lampsilis teres.* . . *Other common names* . . slough sandshell, . . sand clam. . . *Habitat* Medium to large rivers in sand or fine gravel.

sand shell clam See **sand clam 1**

sand shiner n [See quot 1951]

A **shiner 1** (here: *Notropis stramineus*).

   1943 Eddy–Surber *N. Fishes* 144, *Northern Sand Shiner—Notropis deliciosus stramineus* [=*N. stramineus*]. . . The most common form found in the Great Lakes area. **1951** Harlan–Speaker *IA Fish* 97, The sand shiner is abundant in most Iowa waters. . . They are often observed over sand bars or in shallow water where they are more secure from their enemies. **1967** Cross *Hdbk. Fishes KS* 133, The sand shiner is one of the commonest fishes in Kansas, inhabiting streams throughout the State. **1983** Becker *Fishes WI* 565, The sand shiner probably serves as an important forage fish because of abundance in certain areas.

sand shrimp n [See quots 1873, 1901]

A shrimp of the genus *Crangon,* usu *C. septemspinosa.*

   1873 U.S. Bur. Fisheries *Rept. for 1871–72* 339, The common "sand-shrimp," *Crangon vulgaris* [=*C. septemspinosa*], . . always occurs in great numbers on the sandy flats and in the tide-pools and rivulets. **1901** Arnold *Sea-Beach* 260, *C[rangon] vulgaris,* the common sand shrimp. It ranges from Labrador to North Carolina on the Atlantic coast and from Alaska to southern California on the Pacific coast. . . Upon the sandy shores it is translucent, pale in color, and often speckled, closely resembling the sand. **1974** McClane *McClane's New Std. Fishing Encycl.* 558, Shrimp are one of the most widely used natural baits in the Southern United States, and they are used to some extent in the Northeast and on the Pacific Coast. . . Various sand shrimp *(Crangon)* . . are commonly used as bait. **1981** Meinkoth *Audubon Field Guide Seashore* 618, Sand Shrimp *(Crangon septemspinosa). Ibid* 619, Sand shrimps have a great tolerance for variations in salinity. . . *C. franciscorum.* . . is trawled commercially in San Francisco Bay.

sand sifter See **sandlapper 4**

sand skeeter See **sand runner 2**

sand snake See **sand viper**

sand snipe n
Any of var **sandpipers,** but esp the **spotted sandpiper.**
   1806 (1905) Lewis *Orig. Jrls. Lewis & Clark Exped.* 4.135, The common snipe of the marshes and the small sand snipe are the same of those common to the Atlantic Coast tho' the former are by no means as abundant here. **1840** *Knickerbocker* 16.27 **MA,** We were all despatched . . on different errands; some to shoot sand-snipe, and others to collect drift-wood for fuel. **1880** *Forest & Stream* 15.4/3 **Chesapeake Bay,** In addition to these [=bay snipe] there are . . the tiny sand pipers, such as the ox-eyes, sand-snipe, shore birds and peeps, excellent when roasted, but only fit for little beginners to pop away at. **1913** Bailey *Birds VA* 71, *Actitis macularia.* . . Sand Snipe. . . This little shore bird . . is a most common bird with us during the entire year. **1923** U.S. Dept. Ag. *Misc. Circular* 13.54, *Pectoral Sandpiper.* . . *Vernacular Names.* . . *In local use.* . . Sand snipe (Ark.) *Ibid* 55, *Least Sandpiper.* . . Sand snipe (Md.) *Ibid* 57, *Semipalmated Sandpiper.* . . Sand snipe (Md.) . . *Sanderling.* . . Sand snipe (Va.) *Ibid* 64, *Spotted Sandpiper.* . . Sand snipe (N.J., Md., Va., Ind.) **1954** Sprunt *FL Bird Life* 185, *Red-backed Sandpiper.* . . *Local Names:* Sand-snipe; Peep. *Ibid* 192, *Sanderling.* . . *Local Names:* Sand Snipe. **1966–68** *DARE* (Qu. Q10, . . *Water birds and marsh birds*) Inf **PA**155, Sand snipe; **SC**21, Sand snipe—beach bird.

sand sole n
A **sole** (here: *Psettichthys melanostictus*) native to the Pacific coast.
   1953 Roedel *Common Fishes CA* 60, Sand Sole—*Psettichthys melanostictus.* . . Alaska to Southern California. . . Forms a minor portion of the sole catch in California, but is considered a desirable species. **1973** Knight *Cook's Fish Guide* 381, Flounder, . . sand—Gulf [flounder] or see Sole, Sand.

sand sparrow n
=**Ipswich sparrow.**
   1946 Hausman *Eastern Birds* 589, *Passerculus princeps.* . . The Sand Sparrow is an almost strictly ground bird, seldom or never alighting in a tree, but running about on the open sand and among the grasses and weeds of the dunes above the high-tide lines.

sand sponge See **sand food**

sandspur n Also *sandspur grass, ~ weed, sandy spur* **SE** See Map Cf **grass burr**
=**burr grass;** the sharp penetrating burr produced by such a plant.
   1890 *FL Ag. Exper. Sta. Gainesville Bulletin* 8.15, Rating weeds in order of badness, I would give Sandspurs the first place. They are bitter grasses eaten only as a last resort by cattle, and all other weeds in the State combined do not cause as much pain, profanity and danger to life, as these worthless grasses. **1897** *Jrl. Amer. Folkl.* 10.146 **FL,** *Cenchrus tribuloides,* . . sand spur. **1939** FWP *Guide FL* 6, The native Floridian . . is likely to be puzzled at the abysmal ignorance that causes the Yankee to refer to . . sandspurs as 'sandburs.' **1946** *PADS* 6.26 **NC,** *Sand spur.* . . The spiny bur of beach grass. Carteret Co., N.C., Common, 1940. **1948** Hurston *Seraph* 38 **wFL,** His worries . . followed him everywhere. . . It was like a sandspur sticking in his skin. **1960** Williams *Walk Egypt* 51 **GA,** There was sandspurs all over the cuffs. **1965–70** *DARE* (Qu. S15, . . *Weed seeds that cling to clothing*) 50 Infs, **SE,** Sandspurs; **FL**48, Sandy spurs; (Qu. S9, . . *Kinds of grass that are hard to get rid of*) Inf **GA**7, Sandspur; **FL**6, Sandspur grass; (Qu. S12b, . . *The sharp points along the stems of rose bushes, berry bushes, and so on . . small ones*; total Infs questioned, 75) Inf **FL**17, Sandspurs; (Qu.

S13, . . *A common wild bush with bunches of round, prickly seeds; when they get dry they stick to your clothing*) Infs **AL**15, **FL**29, 39, Sandspur; (Qu. S14, . . *Prickly seeds, small and flat, with two prongs at one end, that cling to clothing*) Infs **GA**20, 35, Sandspur(s); (Qu. S21, . . *Weeds . . that are a trouble in gardens and fields*) Infs **FL**11, 29, **GA**7, Sandspurs. **1966** *DARE* Tape **FL**45, We would . . borrow some fisherman's boat and go all the way across the river and then fight the sandspurs, the mosquitoes, and the palmettoes to get across into the ocean beach itself. **1986** Pederson *LAGS Concordance,* 15 infs, 14 **AL, FL, GA,** Sandspur(s); 1 inf, **cnFL,** Sandspur grass; 1 inf, **nwFL,** Sandspur weeds. **1994** NC Lang. & Life Project *Harkers Is. Vocab.* 9 **eNC,** *Sandspur.* . . Small, round, prickly fruit of a certain weed which grows well in sand. The prickles of sandspurs are very sharp.

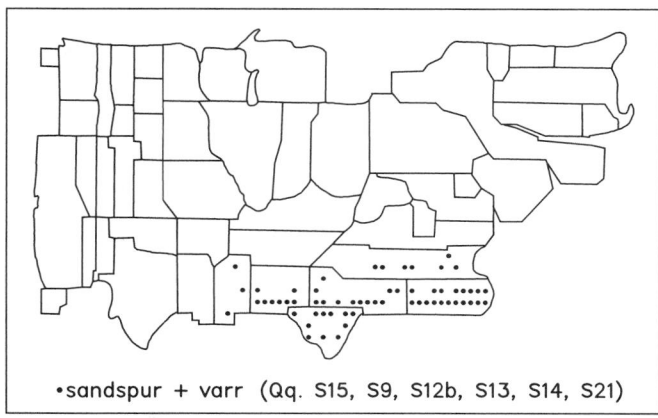

•sandspur + varr (Qq. S15, S9, S12b, S13, S14, S21)

sandstoodle n
The larva of a caddisfly (Trichoptera).
   1969 *DARE* (Qu. P6, . . *Kinds of worms . . used for bait*) Inf **GA**72, Sandstoodle—same as rock bait—build nests in sand. [**1972** Swan-Papp *Insects* 192, *Caddisfly.* . . The majority [of caddisfly larvae] construct portable cases—in an amazing variety of shapes—from stones, leaves, sticks, or sand, held together with a cement-like secretion and silk threads.]

sand sturgeon n esp Upper Missip Valley
A **shovelnose sturgeon** (here: *Scaphirhynchus platorhynchus*).
   1933 LA Dept. of Conserv. *Fishes* 414, *Scaphirhynchus platorhynchus.* . . Known also as the . . Sand Sturgeon, the Shovelnose shares with the Paddlefish first honors for odd appearance among North American fresh water fishes. **1951** Harlan–Speaker *IA Fish* 36, *Shovelnose Sturgeon.* . . *Other Names*—Sand sturgeon. . . The flesh is delicious and is prepared by deep-fat frying, broiling or smoking. **1971** *WI State Jrl.* (Madison) 29 Aug sec 4 5/1, Between the four of us we caught one small walleye, . . and a hackleback sturgeon, also known as a sand sturgeon. **1983** Becker *Fishes WI* 227, Sand sturgeon. . . This species inhabits deep channels of large rivers over sand or gravel in the presence of some current. **1985** Madson *Up River* 240 **Upper Missip Valley,** A few little hackleback (sand) sturgeon were beginning to show up at the fish market, but Curt hadn't been taking any because he hadn't been making any drifts over the sandbars where you would expect to find hacklebacks that time of year.

sand swallow n [*OED2* (at *sand* sb.² 10.b) 1797] Cf **sand martin 1**
=**bank swallow 1.**
   1838 Geol. Surv. OH *Second Annual Rept.* 162, Hirundo riparia. . . *Sand Swallow.* **1950** *WELS* **WI** (*Kinds of swallows around your locality*) 2 Infs, Sand swallow—same as bank swallow; 2 Infs, Sand swallow(s). **1965–70** *DARE* (Qu. Q20, . . *Kinds of swallows and birds like them*) Infs **CT**22, **IA**20, **MI**101, **ND**1, **NY**10, 52, 71, **SC**62, **VT**16, Sand swallow; (Qu. Q14) Inf **CT**22, Sand swallow.

sand swift n Cf **sand lizard**
1 A **whiptail** (here: *Cnemidophorus gularis* or *C. sexlineatus*).
   1928 Baylor Univ. Museum *Contrib.* 16.12, *Sand Lizard, Sand Swift,* and *Striped Sand Lizard* are names used in Texas for this species [= *Cnemidophorus sexlineatus*] on account of its habit of burrowing in sand

banks. . . *Cnemidophorus gularis.* . . I have also heard all of the names listed under the Six-lined Lizard used in referring to this species.

2 A **lizard 1** of the genus *Holbrookia.*

1930 OK Univ. Biol. Surv. *Pub.* 2.230, *Holbrookia.* Spotted Lizard; Sand Swift.

sand swiper See **sand viper**

sand tart n

1 also *sand cake,* and, by folk-etym, *saint heart:* A cookie dusted with sugar and cinnamon. [Ger *Sandtorte, Sandkuchen*] **esp in PaGer settlement areas**

1896 (c1973) Farmer *Orig. Cook Book* 409, *Sand Tarts* [Recipe includes butter, sugar, egg, flour, baking powder, almonds, sugar, cinnamon]. . . Brush over with white of egg, and sprinkle with sugar mixed with cinnamon. . . Place on a buttered sheet, and bake . . in a slow oven. **1932** Stieff *Eat in MD* 227, *Sand Tarts* [Recipe includes flour, sugar, butter, eggs, almonds]. . . Sift sugar and cinnamon over each cake. . . Bake in quick oven. **1935** *Sun* (Baltimore MD) 9 Dec 4/5 *(Hench Coll.),* Hail, Happy Sand Cakes, Emblem Of Our Joy. . . The old-fashioned sand cake . . with a fine layer of sugar and cinnamon. . . Why my old German aunt always called them sand tarts I never could tell. **1948** Hutchison *PA Du. Cook Book* 176, *Aline Dillinger's Sand Tarts* . . sugar . . flour . . butter . . eggs. . . Spread a little egg on top of each cookie, then sprinkle with sugar, cinnamon, and chopped nuts. **1952** *PA Dutchman* Sept 4, We were almost drooling by the time we heard about the wash baskets full of Leckerli, lard cans filled with Lebkuchen and mounds of Sandtarts. **1957** Showalter *Mennonite Cookbook* 274 **MD, PA,** *Sand Tarts or Saint Hearts.* . . Brush tops with rich milk and sprinkle with sugar and cinnamon. . . The oldest recipe books call these cookies Saint Hearts. **1969** *DARE* FW Addit **ceNY,** *Sand tarts*—little cookies brushed with egg white and sprinkled with almonds. **1970** *DARE* (Qu. H32, . . *Fancy rolls and pastries)* Inf **PA**242, Sand tarts—a Christmas cookie. **1999** Millersville Univ. Center for PA Ger. Studies *Jrl.* Fall 18, The Harmony Society, which founded the village of Economy, PA in 1824, was a German-speaking group, dedicated to communal living. Their meals reflected their southern German background, which is demonstrated by the cookbooks used by community members. . . Recipes include dishes such as . . little sand cakes, stollen, and baked elderberry blossom.

2 =**sandbakkels.**

1968 *DARE* (Qu. H32, . . *Fancy rolls and pastries)* Inf **MN**17, Sand tarts—a Swedish cookie—a sugar cookie dough; lots of butter; baked as a shell with fruit inside.

sand terrapin See **sand turtle**

sand tilefish See **sandfish 2b**

sand toad n Also *sandy toad*

A **horned toad 1.**

1870 Beadle *Life in UT* 471, The "horned toad" or "sandy toad," scientifically ranked *Phrynosoma,* is found on all the high, dry plains. . . [and] is calloused on the belly like an alligator. **c1955** Reed–Person *Ling. Atlas Pacific NW,* 1 inf, Sand toad. **1966** *DARE* (Qu. P23, *Names for the animal similar to the frog that lives away from water)* Inf **OK**25, Sand toad.

sand trout n **TX**

A **weakfish:** *Cynoscion arenarius* or the similar *C. nothus.*

1931 *Copeia* 2.50 **TX,** *Leptecheneis naucrates* [=a remora]. . . Said to have been attached to a young 'sand trout' (probably *Cynoscion nothus*). **1933** LA Dept. of Conserv. *Fishes* 186, *Cynoscion arenarius.* . . Mr. Isaac Ginsburg of the Bureau of Fisheries. . . states that in Texas it is known as Sand Trout and in Florida as White Trout. **1946** LaMonte *N. Amer. Game Fishes* 76, *Cynoscion arenarius.* . . Sand Trout. . . This fish . . is the larger and more common of two species found on the Gulf coast. . . The other species is . . *Cynoscion nothus.* . . Sand Trout. **1967–70** *DARE* (Qu. P2, . . *Kinds of saltwater fish caught around here . . good to eat)* Infs **TX**9, 14, 19, 88, Sand trout. **1967** *DARE* FW Addit **TX,** Kinds of fish caught in surf: sand trout [etc]. **1986** Pederson *LAGS Concordance,* 3 infs, **TX,** Sand trout.

sand turtle n Also *sandhill turtle, sand terrapin* Cf **land turtle**

=**box turtle.**

1937 Cahn *Turtles IL* 84, *Terrapene carolina carolina* . . Common box

turtle; sand turtle. [*Ibid* 94, The nest is usually made in sand.] *Ibid* 96, *Terrapene ornata* . . Painted box turtle; sand turtle. **1965–70** *DARE* (Qu. P24, . . *Kinds of turtles)* Infs **CO**20, **CT**42, **MN**42, **NE**1, 10, **NC**60, **TX**26, **UT**3, **WI**50, Sand turtle; **CO**4, Sandhill turtle—a land turtle. **1973** Allen *LAUM* 1.328 **Upper MW** (as of c1950), Two others [=infs] in the Nebraska sandhill region use *sand turtle.* . . *Sand terrapin* [is also used by one inf] . . in Nebraska. **1986** Pederson *LAGS Concordance,* 1 inf, **cLA,** Sand turtle.

sand verbena n

1 A plant of either of the western genera *Abronia* or *Tripterocalyx.* [See quot 1936] Also called **sand puffs;** for other names of var spp of *Abronia* see **heart's-delight, snowball**

1897 Parsons *Wild Flowers CA* 146, *Abronia latifolia.* . . The fragrant blossoms of the yellow sand-verbena may be found upon the beach at almost any time of year. **1915** (1926) Armstrong–Thornber *Western Wild Flowers* 106, *Yellow Sand-Verbena.* . . Pretty at a distance, but rather coarse close by. **1936** Whitehouse *TX Flowers* 19, *Narrow-leaved Sand-Verbena (Abronia angustifolia)* is a low plant with a dense head of pink flowers which are so fragrant that one plant will perfume the air for some distance. . . It is called sand-verbena because of the verbena-like clusters. **1966** *Silver City Press Frontier* (NM) 21 Mar 1/4, The California deserts welcomed the new season with carpets of desert primrose and sand verbena bursting into bloom. **1966–70** *DARE* (Qu. S26a, . . *Wildflowers. . . Roadside flowers)* Infs **CA**2, 94, **NV**8, **NM**6, Sand verbena(s); (Qu. S26e, *Other wildflowers not yet mentioned;* not asked in early QRs) Infs **CA**24, 60, 189, Sand verbena. **1966** *DARE* Wildfl QR Pl.8A (Wills–Irwin) Inf **TX**44, Sand verbena. **1970** Correll *Plants TX* 598, *Abronia carnea* [=*Tripterocalyx c.*] . . Winged sand verbena. . . In dry places, early spring to late summer. **1995** *Smithsonian* Mar 80 **Desert SW,** There are carpets of shocking-magenta desert sand verbena.

2 =**devil's bouquet.**

1951 *PADS* 15.31 **TX,** *Nyctaginia capitata.* . . Devil's bouquet; . . sand verbena.

sand vine n

A twining vine *(Cynanchum laeve)* native to much of the eastern half of the US. Also called **devil's shoestring 4, honey vine, vine milkweed, wild sweet potato vine**

1900 Lyons *Plant Names* 29, *Ampelanus* [=*Cynanchum*]. . . Sandvine. . . Herbaceous twining vines. **1936** Winter *Plants NE* 111, *G[onolobus] laevis* [=*Cynanchum laeve*]. . . Sand Vine. . . Frequent in southeast Nebr. along rivers. **1938** Madison *Wild Flowers OH* 90, *Sandvine.* . . White. . . Thickets, river banks. **1948** Stevens *KS Wild Flowers* 187, *Sandvine.* . . This . . twining vine grows to many feet in length. . . Flowers having the odor of lilacs occur in clusters. . . The plant is attractive enough to be welcome in the flower garden. **1970** Correll *Plants TX* 1234, *Cynanchum laeve.* . . Sand-vine. . . In silty clay or sand in low moist woods or fields, often weedy and climbing on shrubs or fences.

sand violet n Also *sandhill violet* **esp NEng, WI**

Any of var **violets,** but esp **bird's-foot violet 1.**

1880 *Harper's New Mth. Mag.* 62.87 **NEng,** When I was married to Ethan . . he didn't fetch me a big bunch of sand-violets. **1931** Fassett *Spring Flora* 114 **WI,** *V[iola] adunca.* Sand Violet. . . Dry sand and ledges. **1950** *WELS* **WI** (*A flower like the violet)* 2 Infs, Sand violet; 1 Inf, Sand violet or birdsfoot; 1 Inf, Sandhill violet. **1966–70** *DARE* (Qu. S3, *A flower like a large violet with a yellow center and small ragged leaves—it comes up early in spring on open, stony hilltops)* Inf **CT**30, Sand violet—same as bird-foot violet; **MA**100, Sand violet; (Qu. S11, . . *Blue violet)* Inf **CT**11, Sand violet (when it grows in the sand—it's paler); **MA**6, Sand violet—is yellow and grows high; **WI**43, Sand violet—yellow, grows in sandy places; (Qu. S26c, *Wildflowers that grow in woods)* Infs **CT**23, **MA**49, Sand violet(s).

sand viper n Also *sand snake, ~ (s)wiper* Cf **sand adder**

=**hognose snake.**

1891 *Century Dict.* 5333, *Sand viper* . . a hog-nosed snake. . . [*Century* Ed: Local, U.S.] **1928** Pope–Dickinson *Amphibians* 50, *Hog-nosed Snake—Heterodon contortrix* [=*H. platyrhinos*]. . . This snake is also known under various names in different localities, such as . . Sand Viper . . and Blow Snake. **1958** Conant *Reptiles & Amphibians* 138, Hog-nose Snakes. . . As a result of their behavior these harmless snakes have earned such dangerous-sounding names as "hissing adder," . . "hissing sand snake." **1968** *DARE* (Qu. P25, . . *Kinds of snakes)* Inf **NJ**17, Sand wiper, sand swiper; **NY**80, Sand snake. **1974** Shaw–Campbell *Snakes*

West 69, When it is encountered in the wild in a place where it cannot readily escape, the hognose snake [here: =*Heterodon nasicus*]. . . will hiss or blow loudly and strike out savagely toward the attacker. . . in an altogether convincing performance that has earned it the names "puff adder," . . [and] "sand viper." . . The hognose snake generally inhabits country that is flat and sandy with much open space. . . It is fond of sunning itself on the sand.

sand wasp n Cf digger wasp, sand hornet

Any of var sphecid wasps, esp those of the genus *Bembix*. For other names of *Bembix* spp see **horse guard**

1869 U.S. Dept. Ag. *Rept. of Secy. for 1868* 310, The several families of sand wasps, mud-daubers, &c., build their nests in the earth. **1872** Schele de Vere *Americanisms* 391, *Yellow-jacket* is the familiar and descriptive name of a small hornet (Pelopsus) and of the Sand-wasp (Ammophila). **1907** *St. Nicholas* June 748, [Caption:] The sand wasp using a tool. Pounding down the earth with a small pebble. **1926** Essig *Insects N. Amer.* 580, In Oregon it [=a tachinid fly] has been reared from the giant sand wasp, *Sphecius speciosus*. **1939** *LANE* Map 239 (*Wasp*) 2 infs, cw,ceCT, Sand wasp . . a very large wasp which burrows in sand. **1969** *DARE* (Qu. R21, . . *Other kinds of stinging insects*) Inf KY40, Sand wasp. **1972** Swan–Papp *Insects* 562, *Mud Daubers, Sand Wasps, and Cicada Killers (Sphecidae).* This is a large family of solitary wasps that build their nests in the soil . . and provision their nests with paralyzed insects or spiders. *Ibid* 565, *Sand Wasp: Sphex (Ammophila) urnarius.* . . This is the celebrated "tool user" that has attracted much attention for its habit of using a pebble or other small object . . to tamp the dirt sealing off the burrow. *Ibid* 567, Sand Wasp: *Bembix pruinosa*. **1980** Milne–Milne *Audubon Field Guide Insects* 841, *Eastern Sand Wasp (Bembix americana spinolae).* . . Sandy meadows, lakeshores, and beaches.

sandweed n [See quot 1933]

A **Saint-John's-wort**, usu *Hypericum fasciculatum*.

1933 Small *Manual SE Flora* 872, *H[ypericum] fasciculatum.* . . *Sand-weed.* . . A growth of this shrub in a pond indicates a hard sand bottom, hence the common name. It often reaches tree-like form in swamps near the gulf coast. **1966** Grimm *Recognizing Native Shrubs* 199, *Sandweed—Hypericum fasciculatum.* . . Coastal plain; South Carolina south to Florida, west to Texas. . . *Sandweed—Hypericum nitidum.* . . *Sandweed—Hypericum reductum.* . . *Sandweed—Hypericum lloydii.* . . Similar to *H. fasciculatum*. **1970** Correll *Plants TX* 1064, *Hypericum fasciculatum.* . . *Sand-weed.* . . In wet places about ponds and lakes. **1979** Ajilvsgi *Wild Flowers* 198 **TX**, *Sand-weed— Hypericum fasciculatum.* . . Erect, commonly moundlike, woody, much-branched shrub to 40 in. tall, often lower.

sand whiting n

A **kingfish 1** (here: *Menticirrhus americanus*).

1898 U.S. Natl. Museum *Bulletin* 47.1474, *Menticirrhus americanus.* . . *Carolina Whiting; Sand Whiting.* . . Very common on the sandy coasts of our Southern States, where it is a food-fish of some importance. **1933** John G. Shedd Aquarium *Guide* 116, *Sand Whiting.* Small fishes, abundant on the sandy shores of eastern United States in shallow water. . . The Sand Whiting rarely goes north of Chesapeake Bay. **1946** LaMonte *N. Amer. Game Fishes* 86, Sand Whiting. . . Very much like the Whiting [=*Menticirrhus saxatilis*]. . . Sandy coasts.

sandwich n Usu |ˈsæn(d)wɪč|; also |ˈsæmɪǰ|; for addit varr see quots   Pronc-spp *sambridge, sammidge, sammitch, samwich, samwidge, sandridge, sandwidge, sangwich, sanich*

Std sense, var forms.

1897 *KS Univ. Qrly.* (ser B) 6.91 **KS**, *Samwich*: sandwich. **1931** *AmSp* 6.348, The assimilation is commoner in current colloquial speech than might be thought, at least in the Central Western region. . . In the not very frequent *sambridge* for *sandwich*, the substitution of *br* for *dw* accounts for the *m* from *n*. **1949** in 1965 *DARE* File, "Malted milk anna ham san'ich," he muttered. **1950** Bissell *Stretch on River* 166 **Missip Valley**, Want some pie or a samwidge or sumpthing? **1966–68** *DARE* (Qu. H18, . . *Special kinds of bread*) Inf **DC**4, Sandwich [ˈsænwɪǰ] bread; (Qu. H41, . . *Kinds of roll or bun sandwiches . . in a round bun or roll*) Inf **IN**7, Fish [ˈsændwəčɪs]; **SC**56, Barbecue [ˈsæmwɪš]; (Qu. H42, . . *[A sandwich] . . in a much larger, longer bun, that's a meal in itself*) Inf **NJ**1, Guinea sandwidge. **1981** Pederson *LAGS Basic Materials*, 1 inf, **ceMS**, [ˈsæᵋmɪdʒ]. **1982** Chaika *Speaking RI* [8], Sangwich. **1982** McCool *Sam McCool's Pittsburghese* 31 **PA**, *Sammitches*: a quick meal—"Mom's making jumbo sammitches."

1989 Nicholson *Field Guide S. Speech* 57, Sammidge. **1990** Smith *Understanding Speaking S. Lang.* 7, Sammitch. **1998** *DARE* File—Internet **cePA** [Language of the Hayna Valley], Sangwich—Sandwich. **1999** *DARE* File—Internet **eMA** [Boston Online *Wicked Good Guide to Boston English*], Sangwich—Sandwich.

sand wiper See sand viper

sandworm n chiefly N and C Atl   Cf bloodworm 1, mussel worm, redworm 2, sea worm

A clam worm of the genus *Nereis*, esp *N. virens*.

1965–70 *DARE* (Qu. P5, . . *The common worm used as bait*) Infs **MA**40, **NY**47, 57, 76, Sandworm; **NY**40, Sandworm—for salt water; **NY**44, Sandworm—dug out of the bay, with hairs; **TX**26, Sandworm—big; (Qu. P6, . . *Kinds of worms . . used for bait*) Infs **NY**44, 66, 118, Sandworm; **CA**23, Sandworm—dig along beach; **CT**10, Sandworm—on the shore; **CT**13, Sandworm—in salt water; **ME**10, Sandworm—4–6″ long, saltwater worm, good for striped bass; **ME**22, Sandworm—marine worm; **NJ**21, Sandworm—very similar to bloodworm; **NJ**36, Sandworms and bloodworms for salt water; (Qu. P8, *Do fishermen around here use 'white bait'? If . . 'yes', what is it?*; total Infs questioned, 75) Inf **FL**26, Sandworm. **1966** *DARE* Tape **ME**24, They call 'em sandworms and bloodworms. Larger ones are sandworms, large brown ones, and the smaller ones they call bloodworms. **1970** Tarpley *Blinky* 67 **neTX**, *Worms used for fish bait* . . sand worm. **1995** *USA Today* (Arlington VA) 9 June, Eastern Maine sandworm diggers went on strike, demanding a dime per worm, up from 7 ½¢. Bloodworm diggers stopped work last week. Bait shop owners said anglers will turn to other baits. **1999** (acc) VA Polytechnic *Marine & Coastal Species Info. System* (Internet), The sandworm [=*Nereis virens*] is a burrowing polychaete that is often one of the most abundant animals in intertidal flat communities. It may reach a length of 35 inches and is harvested commercially for the bait worm industry. **2001** *Yankee* Mar 46 **ME**, Sandworms and bloodworms are a $3.9 million annual business in Maine. All 700,000 pounds of these worms are hand-harvested from mudflats by 1,000 licensed diggers.

sandwort n

Std: a plant of the genus *Arenaria* or of a related genus such as *Moehringia* or *Minuartia*.   For other names of var plants of these genera see **chickweed 1e, sandywinks, sparkles**

sandy n¹ [Etym unknown]

A deception, trick—freq in phr *run a sandy* to bluff; to play a trick on someone; in phrr *run a sandy on* (or *over*) to trick, cheat, dupe.

1897 *KS Univ. Qrly.* (ser B) 6.56 **KS**, *Run a sandy:* to 'bluff' (poker term.) **1914** *DN* 4.112 **cKS**, *Run a sandy on.* . . To mislead; delude. **1916** *DN* 4.328 **cKS**, *Sandy.* . . A joke.—*run a sandy on.* . . To make (one) the subject of a joke, esp. of a practical joke. **1923** *DN* 5.219 **swMO**, *Run a sandy over.* . . To mislead by trickery. **1932** Toone *Yankee Slang* 58 [Criminal slang], *Run a Sandy:* Put across swift action, pull a fast act, hoodwink a rival. **1953** Randolph–Wilson *Down in Holler* 280 **Ozarks**, *Sandy.* . . A trick, a bluff. "He run a sandy on me" means that he fooled me somehow or bluffed me into doing something against my inclination. **1954** *Harder Coll.* **cwTN**, *Sandy.* . . A trick, a bluff. **1958** McCulloch *Woods Words* 153 **Pacific NW**, *Run a sandy*—To play a trick on a man. **1995** Brophy *Coll.* 65 **swMO** (as of c1960), *Sandy.* [A] trick, hoax, swindle. *[T]o run a sandy on* = to cheat, to hoodwink (West).

sandy adj See sand 1

sandy n²

1 See **sand bass 1**.
2 See **sand bass 3**.

sandy bass See sand bass 3

sandyhill crane See sandhill crane 1

sandyland sage n

A **horsemint 1** (here: *Monarda punctata*).

1946 Reeves–Bain *Flora TX* 162, *M[onarda] punctata.* . . Perennial Sandyland Sage. . . Sandy soil; prairies, open woods, and roadsides.

sandy mockingbird n Also *sandy mocker* chiefly Sth   Cf mockingbird

=**brown thrasher.**

1858 Baird *Birds* 353, *Harporhynchus rufus.* . . Thrasher; Sandy Mocker; French Mocking Bird. **1883** Nuttall Ornith. Club *Bulletin* 8.75 DC, *Harporhynchus rufus.* . . Its strong color and mimicking voice gives [sic] us . . *Sandy Mockingbird.* **1904** (1905) Dugmore *Bird Homes* 51 VA, In Virginia he [=the brown thrasher] is known as the Sandy Mocking-bird. **1924** Howell *Birds AL* 330, The brown thrasher. . . pours forth a rich, musical medley which compares very favorably with the song of his famous cousin, the mockingbird. His relationship to the latter bird is expressed in the popular name of "sandy mocker," prevalent in some parts of the South. **1955** *Oriole* 20.1.11 GA, *Brown Thrasher.* . . *Sandy Mocker* (from its tawny-rufous color . .). **1969** Longstreet *Birds FL* 117, *Sandy Mocker.* . . plainly shows its kinship to the mocker, . . by its shape, habits, actions, and song.

sandy mounder n [Folk-etym for **salamander 2**] Cf **sand rat**
A **pocket gopher 1** (here: *Geomys* spp).

1979 *DARE* File nwFL, In Milton, Florida in about 1952 I met a man who called pocket gophers "sandy mounders" because of the little piles of sandy soil they leave behind. The term made especially good sense when I learned that other people in the area call these animals "salamanders."

sandy Pete See **santapee**

sandy-river bell n
A **harebell 1** (here: *Campanula divaricata*).

1968 *DARE* FW Addit VA15, Sandy-river bell—roadsides—old-fashioned; book term is southern harebell.

sandy spur See **sandspur**

sandy toad See **sand toad**

sandywinks n
A **sandwort** (here: *Minuartia obtusiloba*).

1963 Craighead *Rocky Mt. Wildflowers* 48, *Arenaria obtusiloba* [= *Minuartia obtusiloba*]. . . Sandywinks. . . A low mat-forming plant with . . small solitary white and green flowers.

sang n Also *san', seng, shang* [Aphet forms of *ginseng*; cf **ginseng A**] **chiefly S Midl** Cf **bogue-sang**
=**ginseng B1.**

1843 (1916) Hall *New Purchase* 133 IN, Once on bringing his stock of ginseng to our tannery . . Mr. Ashford . . thus began: "Well . . what do you allow sang's (ginseng) done with out thare in Chi-ne?" **1886** *S. Bivouac* 4.350 sAppalachians, 'Sang (ginseng). **1903** *DN* 2.329 seMO, *Sang.* . . Ginseng. *Sang-diggers* or *sang-hunters.* . . Persons who make a business of digging ginseng roots. Only the poorest people follow the business, as the plant is rare and grows only in remote places. The root when dried is worth from three to five dollars a pound. **1907** *DN* 3.205 nwAR, *Sang.* . . Ginseng. **1911** *Century Dict. Suppl.*, *Seng.* . . An abbreviation of *ginseng*. [*Century* Ed: Local, U.S.] **1923** *DN* 5.236 swWI, *Sang*, clipped form of *ginseng*. **1927** *DN* 5.477 Ozarks, *Sang root*. **1932** Kelley *Inchin' Along* 51 AL, I go up on de hill to dig san' yarbs. **1937** in 1987 *Hall Coll.* wNC, Ther used to be a good big scope of seng thar on that mountain. **1939** *Ibid* eTN, Fifty cents a pound fer seng in them days. **1950** *WELS Suppl.* WI, Ginseng: *ginsang, ginshang, shang*—forms of word used in Wis. **1968** *DARE* FW Addit VA, Sang [sæŋ] or ginseng ['jɪnsæŋ]—sold for $30 a pound. **1969** *DARE* (Qu. S26c, *Wildflowers that grow in woods*) Inf KY40, Sang; (Qu. S26e, *Other wildflowers not yet mentioned;* not asked in early QRs) Inf KY21, Sang. **1970** *NC Folkl.* 18.10, Ginseng (sang) tea was good tonic and appetite builder. **1971** *Foxfire* 5.18 nGA, They'd get lots'a sang. . . Forty dollars a hundred. **1982** *Newsweek* 8 Nov 62 cWI, Marathon County has grown ginseng—"shang" in local parlance—since the turn of the century and now accounts for about 90 percent of the United States' annual crop. **1983** *MJLF* 9.1.54 ceKY (as of 1956), *Sang root*. **1986** Pederson *LAGS Concordance*, 4 infs, GA, Sang; 4 infs, TN, Sang roots; 1 inf, neTN, Sang—medicinal, harvested locally; 1 inf, neTN, Hit was high sang.

sang v[1], hence vbl n *sanging* [**sang** n] **esp sAppalachians**
To gather **ginseng B1**; hence n *sanger* one who gathers it.

1848 Bartlett *Americanisms* 282, *Sang.* An abbreviation of *ginseng*. It is or was also used in Virginia as a verb; *to go a sanging*, is to be engaged in gathering ginseng. **1859** (1968) Bartlett *Americanisms* 379, *Sang.* . . In Alleghany Co., Maryland is *Sang Run* near which is a well

known "*sanging* ground." **1877** *Field & Forest* 3.40 sAppalachians, Why, I have 'sanged' all over it [=a mountain]. **1892** (1972) Allen *Blue-Grass Region KY* 231, In the wildest parts of the country . . entire families may still be seen "out sangin'." **1923** *DN* 5.236 swWI, *Sang* . . to dig ginseng root. "What you doin'?" "Sangin'." **1924** Raine *Land of Saddle-Bags* 229 sAppalachians, Going "sanging" (to dig wild ginseng) used to be a common and profitable recreation which brought one a good bit of money as well as a pleasant ramble in the open woods. **1931** *PMLA* 46.1306 sAppalachians, Sis has been a-sangin' (hunting ginseng) all day. **1939** *Hall Coll.* wNC, eTN, Sangin'. . . Gathering ginseng. **1976** Garber *Mountain-ese* 77 sAppalachians, Pa spent the entire Sattiday out sangin' in the mountains. **1995** *NC Folkl. Jrl.* 42.57 NC, Ginseng buyers in the United States take these circumstances into account when buying from sangers and cultivators.

sang v[2] See **sing** v A1, 2

sanged See **sing** v A2

sang hoe n Also *sanging hoe* **esp sAppalachians**
A short-handled, narrow-bladed hoe for digging **ginseng B1** and other roots.

1859 (1968) Bartlett *Americanisms* 379, *Sang-Hoe.* The implement used in gathering ginseng. **1888** *Congressional Record* 1 May 19.4.3587 KY, The "sang hoe" is a small hoe of domestic manufacture, with which the people dig ginseng root, which is the only agricultural staple of a portion of the mountain district in Southeastern Kentucky. **1921** Haswell *Daughter Ozarks* 126 (as of 1880s), On this particular morning these two had taken their " 'Sang hoes" upon their shoulders and entered the forest to dig for Ginseng, Seneca Snake root, or other of the medicinal roots with which the Ozarks abound. **1923** *DN* 5.236 swWI, *Sang-hoe.* . . A narrow hoe used in digging ginseng root. **1974** Fink *Mountain Speech* 23 wNC, eTN, *Sanginghoe* . . special implement for digging ginseng—narrow blade, short handle. **1982** Slone *How We Talked* 133 eKY (as of c1950), *Sang hoe*—a very short-handled hoe with a narrow, sharp blade, used to dig gensing and other roots that were to be sold for medicine and dyes. **1986** Pederson *LAGS Concordance*, 1 inf, neTN, Sang hoes—to dig up plant for roots.

sanging vbl n See **sang** v

sanging n See **singing** n 1

sanging hoe See **sang hoe**

sango See **sanko** v

sangre de cristo n [MexSpan, literally "blood of Christ"]
An **Oregon grape** (here: *Mahonia repens*).

1947 (1976) Curtin *Healing Herbs* 201 NM, *Sangre de cristo*— Mahonia repens. **1976** Elmore *Shrubs & Trees SW* 123, Sangre de Cristo. . . *Berberis repens.* . . This barberry . . seldom grows over a foot high.

sangre de drago n [MexSpan, literally "dragon's blood," in ref to the red sap of the root]
A woody shrub native to the Desert Southwest: usu *Jatropha cardiophylla, J. cuneata,* or *J. dioica*. For other names of the last see **drago, leather plant 2, rubber ~ 4**

1886 Havard *Flora W. & S. TX for 1885* 513, *Mozinna spathulata.* . . Sangre de Drago, or simply Drago. . . The stems, . . as well as the roots, contain a reddish, astringent juice . . , and are employed by the natives as a remedy to cleanse the teeth and harden the gums. The juice can also be used to make indelible marks on linen. **1924** Austin *Land of Journeys' Ending* 283 TX, It goes on still and forever, this silent working together of man and the grass of the field. . . osha, with its healing, the light, springy wood of the sahuaro and the Joshua-tree, hohoba, sangre de drago, the enduring dye and incomparable honey pasture of the Rocky Mountain bee-weed. **1947** Carr *Desert Parade* 72 Desert SW, When the roots . . are broken, the sap issues forth like blood, and thus another name is "sangre de drago," dragon's blood. **1970** Correll *Plants TX* 954, *Jatropha dioica.* . . Sangre de drago. . . In scrub in s. and w. Tex. **1981** Benson–Darrow *Trees SW Deserts* 114, The plant [=*Jatropha cardiophylla*] is called . . sangre de drago, for the reddish sap of the roots, which supply tanning and dyeing material.

sang-sign n Also *sang-sign plant* **sAppalachians** Cf **indicator**
Any of several plants thought to indicate the presence of **sang**

n, as **bloodroot 1, goldenseal 1,** a grape fern (*Botrychium virginianum*), a **maidenhair fern** (here: *Adiantum pedatum*), **white baneberry,** or a **yellowroot** (here: *Xanthorhiza simplicissima*).

1901 *Plant World* 4.144 **wKY,** In Barren county I heard several local names of plants . . sang-sign (*Botrychium*), it being believed . . that the apex of the leaf points to a "sang" (ginsing) plant. **1911** Waters *Ferns* 341 **KY,** A writer in the "Fern Bulletin" states that in parts of Kentucky the rattlesnake-fern [=*Botrychium virginianum*] is known as "sang sign" because it is believed that the tip of the frond always points towards a ginseng plant. **1968** *Foxfire* 2.2.15 **nGA,** Certain plants that grow . . in close association with the ginseng . . are known as "sang-sign." They are indicators of where sang is found. . . Best known as sang-sign is the "little brother of the ginseng", the golden seal. *Ibid* 47, True yellowroot (Xanthorhiza) . . was also . . a sang-sign plant. . . Another sang-sign plant . . is the white baneberry (Actaea), the "doll's-eyes" of the mountain healers. *Ibid* 50, Bloodroot (Sanguinaria) is possibly the most common of the sang-sign plants. *Ibid* 51, Two ferns [=*Adiantum pedatum* and *Botrychium virginianum*] mark the site of ginseng and are found in close association with the other sang-sign plants. The rattlesnake fern (Botrychium virginianum) is known as the "hope of ginseng."

sang-tree n

A **hop tree** (here: *Ptelea trifoliata*).

1900 Lyons *Plant Names* 309, *P[telea] trifoliata*. . . Sang-tree. **1930** Sievers *Amer. Med. Plants* 36, Hoptree. . . *Other common names*. . . Sang-tree, pickaway-anise. . . Both leaves and flowers have an unpleasant odor. The . . fruits. . . have a bitter taste.

sanguillah n **SC**

=**orchard oriole.**

1809 Ramsay *Hist. SC* 2.333, Of the birds of Carolina the following are the principal: Bald eagle, fishing hawk, . . nut-hatch great and small, sanguillah, wild pigeon. **1910** Wayne *Birds SC* 110, *Icterus spurius*. . . This oriole is a summer resident known on the coast as the "Sanguillah." Dr. Ramsay, in his History of South Carolina, published more than a hundred years ago, gives the above name to this species. **1949** Sprunt–Chamberlain *SC Bird Life* 495, Orchard Oriole. . . One name which is sometimes heard in the Low-country, though not often, is the Indian name "Sanguillah."

sangwich, sanich See **sandwich**

sanicle n Cf **false sanicle, Indian ~, white ~**

1 Std: a plant of the genus *Sanicula*. Also called **black snakeroot 2, snakeroot;** for other names of var spp see **footsteps-of-spring, gamble weed, nigger baby 5, sticktights, turkey pea, yellow mats**

2 An **alumroot 1,** usu *Heuchera americana* or *H. villosa*.

1828 Rafinesque *Med. Flora* 1.241, *Heuchera acerifolia*. . . *Vulgar Names*—Alumroot, Sanicle, Ground Maple [etc]. [*Ibid* 242, All the species of this very natural genus have the same properties, and are used indiscriminately under the name of Alumroot.] **1837** Darlington *Flora Cestrica* 175 **sePA,** *H[euchera] americana*. . . Alum-root. American Sanicle. . . The *root* of this is considerably astringent; and is one of the *Indian remedies* reputed to cure cancers, and other ill-conditioned ulcers. **1933** Small *Manual SE Flora* 593, *H[euchera] villosa*. . . Hairy-alumroot. Rock-sanicle. **1975** Hamel–Chiltoskey *Cherokee Plants* 23, Alum-root, american sanicle . . *Heuchera americana*. . . Chew root to take coat off tongue.

sanker See **sanko** v

sankfield See **cinquefoil**

sankle See **sanko** v

Sanko n Also *Old Sanko* [Etym unknown; perh infl by **Sancho**] **NEast**

The devil, a de⟨v⟩il; also fig.

1856 *Porter's Spirit of Times* 18 Oct 109 **MA,** I can't boast of owning matched family horses, but I *will* bet that I can show the handsomest pair of matched family *puppies* that there is in this State—perfect little sankoes, seven weeks old. **1860** Street *Woods & Waters* 15 **neNY,** 'Up with yer here!' says he, ' . . or I'll give the whull consarn to Old Sanko!' *Ibid* 52, And, sanko! how the sparks flew! *Ibid* 219, Bimeby the deer come like old Sanko, and a leetle after 'im come Watch [=a dog], and I

tell yer, he went so fast 'twas as much as I could do to see 'im. *Ibid* 244, But the Old Sanko unly knows what the critters hatch at all fur. **1930** Shoemaker *1300 Words* 44 **cPA Mts** (as of c1900), *Old Sanko*—A mountaineer name for the deil, or satan. **1941** *LANE* Map 474 (*He ran like a house afire*) 1 inf, **csCT,** He ran like Sanko [sæŋkoᵁ].

sanko v Often with *along, around;* hence vbl n *sankoing* (*around*) Also *sango, sanker, sankle* [Etym uncert; cf **ankle**] chiefly **sAppalachians, Ozarks**

To saunter, stroll; to loaf, idle.

1937 (1977) Hurston *Their Eyes* 176 **csFL** [Black], Therefore Janie drank her coffee and sankled on back to her room without asking her landlady anything. **1949** Hornsby *Lonesome Valley* 18 **eKY,** His feet begged him to hurry, but he made them take their time. He sankoed out toward the gate. *Ibid* 180, Uncle Lihugh was coming from the barn, sankoing along and looking at the pasture and the sky and the woods. *Ibid* 297, Johnny looked at him. . . saw him eyeing a dommer rooster sankoing across the yard. **1953** *Courier–Jrl.* (Louisville KY) 27 Jan sec 2, "When I was growing up in Jackson County," reports Mrs. Evelyn Reed, Louisville, "my mother often asked people who dropped by the house: 'What's So-and-So doing?' And often the answer was: 'Oh, just sankoing around.' I haven't heard the expression lately." **1953** Randolph–Wilson *Down in Holler* 280 **Ozarks,** *Sanko* ['sæŋko]. . . To walk silently, to pussyfoot around with no apparent purpose. Joe Beaver, of Eureka Springs, Ark., told me that he "used to sanko around in the woods" when he was a boy. Sometimes it means to assume a solemn manner, like that of a country preacher. "Deacon Jeems come a-sankoin' round, but I never paid no attention." **1963** *Mt. Life* 39.2.52 **sAppalachians,** I'd jis' sanker aout to that road and pull 'im offen thar and shake 'im till his toenails rattled. **1979** Carpenter *Walton War* 152 **sAppalachians,** "I hain't been doin' nothin', jest sangoin around." "Sangoin" seems to be one of those words created by the mountaineer for his own purpose. It means loafing, sashaying; maybe "hanging" around. **1983** *MJLF* 9.1.54 **ceKY,** *Sankoing around* . . loafing, loitering. **1995** in 1996 *Montgomery Coll.* **wNC, eTN,** Sango (around).

sankumsuly See **sanctum suly**

sanky See **zanja**

sanky poke n Cf **thanky poke**

1944 *PADS* 2.48 **NC,** *Sanky poke* ['sæŋkɪ]. . . A traveling bag. Caldwell Co., N.C. Reported.

sannup n [Algonquian; Narraganset *sannop*, Abnaki *senanbe* a married male member of the community] **nNEng**

A scamp, mischievous boy; see also quot 1959.

[**1634** Wood *New Engl. Prospect* sig O3ʳ, [From a vocabulary of "the Natives Language":] *Sannup*—a man / *Squaw*—a woman.] **1939** Coffin *Capt. Abby* 56 **ME** (as of 1860s), There's that young sannup of a Sam going home crying again like a bullefant. I guess he got his going-home-a-crying at school today. **1947** Coffin *Yankee Coast* 63 **ME,** A boy. . . is a *sannup,* the old Algonkian for warrior, if he misbehaves. **1959** *VT Hist.* 27.155 **cs,seVT,** *Sarnup* [sic]. . . Anything vicious, such as a cross setting hen. Rare. Windsor. **1975** Gould *ME Lingo* 241, *Sannup.* . . loosely used throughout Maine for a boy-child and usually a mischievous one: "You sannup, you! Stop plaguing that poor cat!"

San Pedro quail n

=**mountain quail 1.**

1982 Elman *Hunter's Field Guide* 92, Common & regional names. . . For mountain quail . . *San Pedro quail*.

Santa Ana n Usu |'sæntə 'ænə|; also |ˌsæn'tænə|; for addit varr see quot 1965–70 Also *Santa Ana wind, Santana (wind)* [See quot 1887] chiefly **sCA** See Map on p. 742

A strong wind usu from the east or northeast that brings hot, dry air to coastal southern California; also transf.

1887 *Ann. Meteorol. Rev. Calif. 1886* (Calif. State Agric. Soc.) 128 (*OED2*), Another health-giving, but extremely disagreeable wind, is the 'Santa Ana', or 'norther'. *Ibid.* The 'Santa And' [sic] wind receives its name, because it frequently issues from the Santa Ana Pass. **1915** *Nature & Sci.* 22, Known locally as Santa Anas, these wind storms constitute the most disagreeable feature of the weather in the great valley of the south. **1939** FWP *Guide CA* 630, East winds seldom occur, but when they do Los Angeles wilts under blistering "Santa Anas," dry wind storms. **1965–70** *DARE* (Qu. B18, . . *Special kinds of wind*) Infs **CA38, 82,** ['sæntə ˌænə]; **CA4,** Santa Ana or Santana ['sæntə ˌænə, 'sæntænə] (winds from North—hot or cold—strong wind into valleys); **CA**35, Santa Ana—dry, heavy winds—dangerous in southern California; **CA**48, ['sæntə ˌænə] or ['sæntænə]—a warm, dry wind from the desert—a gravitational wind; used to be called Riversiders (because [they] came from Riverside, California, to Santa Ana); **CA**52, ['sæntænə]—the correct one, or ['sæntə ˌænə]; **CA**62, ['sænti ˌænə]—a northwest wind—some cold as the devil, but all dry; **CA**80, Santa Ana—affects people's personalities—kids are hard to manage, violent crimes, etc; hot, dry wind; **CA**87, Santa Ana—a hot, dust-laden wind; **CA**173, East winds, older expression; or Santa Anas, more recent expression—a hot, dry wind off the desert; **CA**6, Santa Ana wind = hot blow; **CA**10, Hot wind (Santa Ana wind); **CA**30, A Santa Ana wind—Santana; warm, northeastern wind; raises dust, causes haze; **CA**181, Santana wind or Santa Ana wind; **CA**189, [sænə ænə]; (Qu. B12, *When the wind begins to increase . . it's _____*) Inf **CA**82, Santa Ana condition, if from the east; (Qu. B17, *A destructive wind that blows straight*) Inf **CA**80, ['sæntə ˌænə]; **CA**87, ['sænti ˌænə]. [14 of 15 total Infs old or mid-aged, 14 hs or coll educ] **1978** *New Yorker* 4 Dec 49 **sCA**, The foothill wind that blew seasonally from the interior, beginning with autumn and going on through the late winter . . had a name we learned with dread—Santa Ana. It blew through the canyon of Santa Ana and was capable of putting enough sand in the air to take the paint off your car. **1980** *NV State Jrl.* (Reno) 25 Aug 19/2, It's early July, and the Santana winds are racing across the Great Basin up the timbered slopes of the Sierra. **1980** Benford *Timescape* 287 **CA**, A Santa Ana wind was blowing outside. It pushed with a dry, heavy hand through the low coastal mountain passes, bringing the desert's prickly touch. . . The red wind, some natives called it. . . *Must be the air in here,* he thought. That, and the Santa Ana. **1985** *DARE* File **sCA**, Santa Ana [sæn'tænə]. **1997** *WI State Jrl.* (Madison) 2 Feb sec G 1/4, Very recently, after blowing around California like strong-scented Santa Ana winds for the last few years, aromatherapy has hit the Madison area.

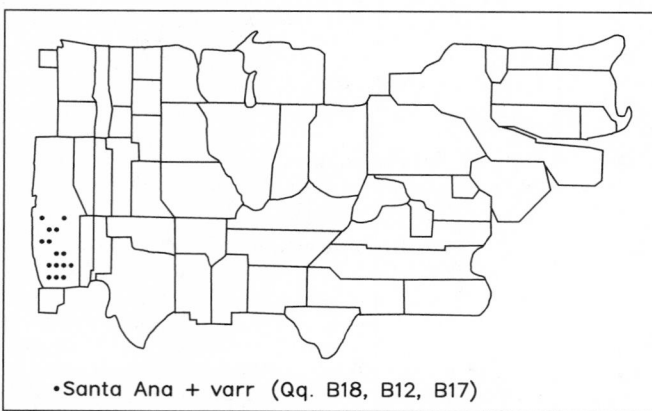

•Santa Ana + varr (Qq. B18, B12, B17)

Santa Anna's revenge n [Antonio López de *Santa Anna* (c1794–1876) Mexican general and political figure, captured at the Battle of San Jacinto, April 21, 1836, by Sam Houston]
=Montezuma's revenge.

1967 *DARE* (Qu. BB19, *Joking names for looseness of the bowels*) Inf **TX**28, Santa Anna's revenge. **1969** *DARE* FW Addit **TX**, *Santa Anna's revenge*—jocular for loose bowels. Occasional.

Santa Catalina salmon n
=white sea bass.

1902 Jordan–Evermann *Amer. Fishes* 459, This fish [=*Atractoscion nobilis*] is a beautiful creature in bronze and old-gold tints, and is well called the Santa Catalina salmon, having a close resemblance to that fish and being its equal in every way. **1946** LaMonte *N. Amer. Game Fishes* 78, *California White Sea Bass. . . Names* . Santa Catalina Salmon. . . Reaches 80 pounds. Said to grow much larger.

Santa Claus whiskers n
The comae or the comose seeds of **milkweed 1** (here: *Asclepias* spp); see quot.

1968 *DARE* (Qu. S15, . . *Weed seeds that cling to clothing*) Inf **MD**9, Santa Claus whiskers—same thing as milkweed pod, fuzzy remnant of milkweed that has gone to seed; floats through air, cottony consistency.

santafee See santapee

Santa Lucia fir n
The bristlecone fir (*Abies bracteata*).

1897 Sudworth *Arborescent Flora* 56, *Abies venusta* [=*A. bracteata*]. . . Santa Lucia Fir. **1910** Jepson *Silva CA* 124, The Santa Lucia Fir inhabits the moist bottoms of cañons and dry rocky summits and is found only in the Santa Lucia Mountains of Monterey County. **1948** *Sierra Club Bulletin* Mar 137 **sCA**, Among these were the Santa Lucia fir, *Pinus sabiniana* (Digger pine), *Pinus monticola*, and hosts of others. **1967** *DARE* Tape **CA**69, You ought to read this about the Santa Lucia fir . . ; it's in this one [=an issue of *National Geographic*] right here.

Santa Maria n Also *Santa Maria feverfew*
A **guayule** (here: *Parthenium hysterophorus*).

1930 OK Univ. Biol. Surv. *Pub.* 2.86, *Parthenium hysterophorus*. . . Santa Maria. **1968** Barkley *Plants KS* 360, Parthenium hysterophorus. . . Santa Maria. Scattered in east half, especially in southeast. **1970** Correll *Plants TX* 1627, *Parthenium Hysterophorus*. . . *Santa Maria feverfew*. . . Locally very abundant in disturbed ground.

santapee n Also *santafee, santerfee, santiped(e), santy fay;* folk-etym *sandy Pete* [Varr of *centipede;* cf AmSpan *cientopié*]
1 A centipede.

1889 in 1944 *ADD* 103, Sandy Pete. **1919** *DN* 5.38 **OK**, Santerfee. . . Centiped. Also *santiped*. **1923** *DN* 5.219 **swMO**, Santy fay. . . Centiped. **1927** *DN* 5.472 **Ozarks**, "This hyar arbuckle started from a santy-fay bite, Doc." A santy-fay is a centipede. **1967–70** *DARE* (Qu. R21, . . *Other kinds of stinging insects*) Infs **HI**4, **NY**183, Santapee; **LA**18, **NJ**69, **TX**71, Santipede. **1979** Jordan *Yesterday in TX Hill Country* 72, The Hill Country . . has many insects . . [including] centipedes (we call them "santafees" in English).

2 Transf: a **scorpion B1** (here: *Centruroides* spp).

1950 *PADS* 14.77 **FL**, *Santa-pee*. . . The small scorpion found in decaying wood.

Santiam lily n [See quot 1950]
A **lily 1** (here: *Lilium washingtonianum*).

1934 Haskin *Wild Flowers Pacific Coast* 21, In the north it [=*Lilium washingtonianum*] is known as the Mount Hood lily; in California as the Shasta lily; . . and in the central Willamette Valley as the Santiam lily. In intermediate points it bears other local names, each region hoping thus to gain virtue by adopting this flower as its own. **1950** *Nature Mag.* 43.1.40 **OR**, Near the headwaters of the Santiam River, it becomes "Santiam lily."

santiped(e), santy fay See santapee

sap n[1] See sap gum 1

sap v
1 To gather tree sap; to gather sap from (a tree).

1966 *Carroll Co. Independent & Pioneer* (Center Ossipee NH) 22 Apr 8/6, While sapping in his wood lot on Moose Mountain, Mr. Albert Wiggin of Sanbornville saw a very large bobcat. **1969** *DARE* FW Addit **KY**42, Sapping in the spring—getting the sweet sap of the birch tree. **1981** *High Coll.* **ceKY** (as of c1930), Sap a birch . . to peel off the bark of a sweet birch (*Betula lenta*) and scrape the sap to eat as a kind of natural candy, a treat to children in the Gorge. . . "We'd sap a birch, and it'd come out in strings and be a little chewy and real sweet, and had a teaberry flavor like teaberry gum."

2 To milk (a cow); to do the milking. **esp Pacific** See Map

1965–70 *DARE* (Qu. K8, *Joking terms for milking a cow: A farmer might say, "Well, it's time to go out and _____."*) Infs **AZ**10, **CA**195, 210, **IA**8, **OR**2, **WA**30, **WI**21, Sap the cow(s) (*or* bossies, Jerseys, sallies, sookies); **CA**136, 138, 163, Sap. **1967** *DARE* File **WA**, *Sap the cow*—farmer's expression for milking.

sap n[2] [*EDD sap* sb.[1] 4 "Juice, gravy."] Cf **sop**
Gravy.

1896 *DN* 1.423, *Sap:* gravy.

sap beer n NEng, esp VT
A fermented beverage made from maple sap.

1950 Nearing–Nearing *Maple Sugar* 202 **VT**, The other maple product is sap beer. **1965** Needham–Mussey *Country Things* 42 **VT**, In the old days they used to make a barrel of sap beer. They boiled it down a while to give it more pep; then they let it ferment, just the same as you make cider. **1969** *DARE* (Qu. DD28b, . . *Fermented drinks . . made at home*)

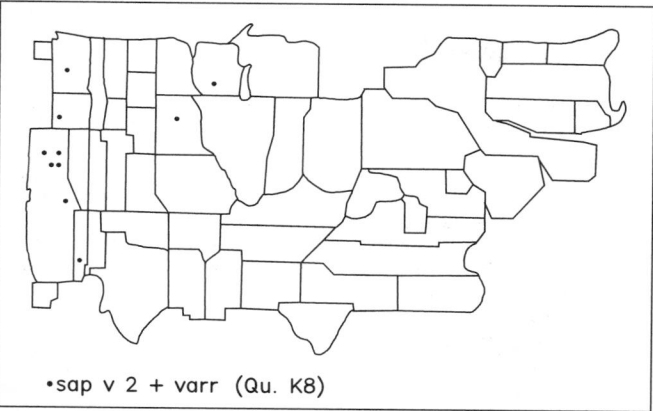

•sap v 2 + varr (Qu. K8)

Inf **MA**25, Sap beer.   **1986** Strickland *Vermonters* 99, My great-uncle used to make sap beer a lot out of maple sap in the spring. My father used to make it every year at the tail end of the sugar season when the sap tasted like bud run and didn't make good syrup. . . [Y]ou'd save all that sap and boil it down . . until it began getting quite red. Then strain it and put it in a barrel. Maybe put yeast in it to make it work. It was real powerful. A nice smooth drink which didn't take effect right off.

sap bucket See **bucket 2c**

sap bush n [Du *sap bosch,* literally "sap grove"; see quot 1949]
chiefly cNY Cf **bush** n[1] **B1a**
=**sugar bush.**
  1828 *New Engl. Palladium* (Boston MA) 18 Apr 2/4, The daughter of Mr. Hunsinger, of Camillus, Onondagua County, N.Y. . . , was burnt to death last week, in consequence of her clothes taking fire in a *sap bush.* This is understood to be a temporary settlement for boiling the sap of the maple tree into sugar.   **1884** Weed *Life* 1.12 **cNY** (as of 1808), I now look with great pleasure upon the days and nights passed in the sap-bush.   **1894** Frederic *Marsena* 104 **nNY,** The dense, big-leafed foliage of a sap-bush, sheltered in the basin.   **1913** *DN* 4.54 **cNY,** *Sap-bush.* . . A place where maple sap is gathered, with especial reference to trees. "Sam Jones has quite a large sap-bush."   **1913** Johnson *Highways St. Lawrence to VA* 36 **csNY,** I was settin' by the window lookin' up toward the sap bush when it started, and I see the big maples bend over nearly to the ground.   **1941** *LANE* Map 247 *(Sugar maple grove)* 7 infs, 4 **wCT,** Sap bush.   **1949** Kurath *Word Geog.* 25, The Hudson Valley has two expressions for the sugar maple grove, *sugar bush* and *sap bush.* . . *Sap bush.* . . occurs only in the valleys of the Hudson and the Mohawk. *Sap bush* is an Anglicized form of the Dutch term.   **1950** WELS (*To do something in an unnecessarily roundabout way:* "*I don't know why he had to go _____ to do that.*") 1 Inf, **cnWI,** All around the sap bush. **1955** Potter *Dial. NW OH* 89, Maple grove . . bush (with the qualifiers *sugar* and *sap*).   **1967** Faries *Word Geog. MO* 114, *(Sugar) maple grove.* . . Northern terms occur in scattered use throughout the state: . . *sap bush.*   Ibid 135, Sap bush—1 [of 700 infs].   **1967–69** *DARE* (Qu. T4, *The place where . . trees grow together and sap is gathered)* Infs **MA**15, **NC**48, **NJ**31, **NY**73, 107, 126, 176, Sap bush.   **1973** Gawthrop *Dial. Calumet* 73 **nwIN,** Place Where Sap Is Gathered . . sap bush 3 [of 125 infs].

sap garden See **sap yard**

sap grove See **sap orchard**

sap gum n **Sth**
1 also *sap (tree):* =**sweet gum.**
  1940 Clute *Amer. Plant Names* 263, *Liquidambar styraciflua.* . . Sap, sap-gum.   **1956** Ker *Vocab. W. TX* 83, The responses *sap tree, gum tree,* and *sweet gum,* [were] offered by one or two informants.   **1968–69** *DARE* (Qu. T15, . . *Kinds of swamp trees)* Inf **GA**89, Sap gum—same as sweet gum; **LA**15, Sweet gum or sap gum—has no heartwood, has several points on leaves.   **1974** Morton *Folk Remedies* 91 **SC,** *Sapgum . . Liquidambar styraciflua.* . . In warmest regions, aromatic balsamic resin flows from cuts; like thin honey, light amber but darkening as it stiffens into a soft gum.   **1980** Little *Audubon Guide N. Amer. Trees E. Region* 453, "Sapgum"—*Liquidambar styraciflua.*
2 A **tupelo gum** (here: *Nyssa aquatica*).
  1940 Clute *Amer. Plant Names* 265, *Nyssa aquatica.* . . Sap-gum,

swamp black gum.   **1958** Jacobs–Burlage *Index Plants NC* 71, *Nyssa aquatica.* . . Tupelo gum; . . sap gum.

sap house n **chiefly NEng**
A building in which maple sap is boiled.
  1869 *Harper's New Mth. Mag.* 39.667 **MA,** Maple-sugar making is another industry common here. In frosty spring, smoke rising here and there over the woods tells of the fires crackling and flaming under the great iron kettles in the open forest, or . . in a well-built sap house.   **1917** Canfield *Understood Betsy* 140, The sap-house, where Cousin Ann and Uncle Henry were making syrup.   **1939** Wolcott *Yankee Cook Book* 338, A whole building . . is set aside for the exclusive use of the god of sapping and his priests. . . Any one who participates in the rites of sugaring-off becomes a quiet fanatic who yearly . . returns to the sap house with a lilting heart.   **1946** Gould *Yankee Storekeeper* 56 **ME,** The hemlock thicket was on the lower side of the sap berth near the sap house. **1968–69** *DARE* (Qu. M22, . . *Kinds of buildings . . on farms)* Inf **MA**37, Sap house; (Qu. T4, *The place where . . trees grow together and sap is gathered)* Inf **NH**14, Sap house.

saple See **sable**

sapling n
1 See **sapling pine.**
2 A **pine 1;** see quot.
  1915 *Brooklyn Museum Qrly.* 2.231 **Okefenokee GA,** Presently, after passing on our right a group of particularly tall slash pines, we pointed our boat's prow toward another pine that towered above the far southern horizon. These 'saplin's' (for in the native speech every pine in the swamp, be it ever so tall, is a 'saplin' ') serve as familiar landmarks for Dave and his brothers in their journeys between Billy's Island and the northern border of the swamp.

sapling pine n Also *sapling* **chiefly nNEng** *obs* Cf **pumpkin pine, sap ~**
A **white pine** (here: *Pinus strobus*) characterized by a relatively high proportion of sapwood and a coarse grain.
  1809 Kendall *Travels* 3.145 **ME,** I have referred the *sapling* [=a white pine of upland, dry situations] of the lumberers to the yellow, red or Norway pine; but this is a mistake.   **1810** Michaux *Histoire des Arbres* 1.103, *Pinus strobus. The White Pine.* . . [E]lle reçoit cependant encore quelquefois dans le New-Hampshire et dans le district de Maine, les dénominations secondaires de *Pumpkin pine* . . et de *Sapling pine.* [= *Pinus strobus. The White Pine.* . . It sometimes, however, also receives in New Hampshire and the district of Maine the secondary designations of *Pumpkin pine* . . and of *Sapling pine.*]   Ibid 109, Mais, lorsqu'il croît dans des terreins secs et élevés, son bois est plus ferme et plus résineux, son grain est plus grossier, ses couches concentriques sont très-espacées, et alors on l'appelle *Sapling pine.* [=But, when it grows in dry and elevated regions, its wood is firmer and more resinous, its grain is coarser, its concentric rings more widely spaced, and then it is called *Sapling pine.*]   **1850** Emerson *Rept. Trees & Shrubs* 63 **ME,** Standing nearly by itself, or surrounded by deciduous trees, especially on the boundaries between high lands and swamps, it [=*Pinus strobus*] grows rapidly, is usually full of knots and resin, has much sap-wood, and thence receives the name of sapling pine. Bull sapling resembles the pumpkin pine in all respects save the color of the wood, which is a clear white. These names are little used, except in Maine.   **1851** (1856) Springer *Forest Life* 41 **ME,** The sap or outside of the sapling Pine is much thicker than that of the pumpkin Pine.   **1868** *Harper's New Mth. Mag.* 36.419 **MN,** Intermixed with the most valuable pines in the American forests are many trees of the character I have just described. The lumbermen call them 'saplings,' and generally regard them as different in species from the true white pine, but botanists are unable to establish a distinction between them.

sap molasses n Cf **molasses C1**
Maple syrup.
  1926 *DN* 5.389 **ME,** *Sap 'lasses.* . . Maple sirup. Obsol.   **1941** *LANE* Map 307 *(Maple syrup)* 1 inf, **nwCT,** Maple molasses, sap molasses.

sap neck-yoke See **sap yoke**

sap orchard n Also *sap grove*
=**sugar bush.**
  1861 *Boston Herald* 12 April 2/6 (*DAE*), Owners of sap orchards can afford to work day and night.   **1941** *LANE* Map 247 *(Sugar maple grove)* 2 infs, **eME,** Sap grove.   **1949** Kurath *Word Geog.* 22, Sap or-

chard . . for the sugar maple grove (in the upland of New Hampshire and Maine). **1966** Dakin *Dial. Vocab. Ohio R. Valley* 417, *Maple grove*. . . Attested only once: *sap orchard.* **1966–70** *DARE* (Qu. T4, *The place where* . . *trees grow together and sap is gathered*) Infs **CA**11, **IA**41, **ME**21, **NY**86, 209, **WV**21, Sap orchard. **1967** Faries *Word Geog. MO* 114, *(Sugar) maple grove*. . . Northern terms occur in scattered use throughout the state: *sap orchard* [etc]. *Ibid* 135, Sap orchard—25 [of 700 infs]. **1973** Gawthrop *Dial. Calumet* 73 **nwIN**, Place Where Sap Is Gathered . . sap orchard 3 [of 125 infs].

sapote See chapote

sapphire grass n

A lilyturf (here: *Liriope spicata*).

1954 *PADS* 21.36 **SC**, Sapphire grass. . . The *liriope spicata.* So called because of the *sapphire* berries at its base. . . It forms a favorite evergreen border.

sap pine n Cf sapling pine

Either **pitch pine a(1)** or **loblolly pine 1.**

1810 Michaux *Histoire des Arbres* 1.92, Sur les montagnes et dans les terreins secs et graveleux, il est très-résineux . . , ce qui lui a fait donner le nom de *Pitch pine* . . , dans les marais, au contraire, il est tendre, léger et encore plus chargé d'aubier; alors il est désigné sous celui de *Sap pine.* [=In the mountains and on dry and gravelly land it is very resinous . . , which has caused it to be called *pitch pine* . . ; in the swamps, on the other hand, it is soft, light, and even more abounding in sapwood; thus it is called *sap pine*.] **1810** Pike *Expeditions* 1 app 54 **Upper Missip Valley**, The whole of this course lays through ridges of pines or swamps of pinenet, sap pine, hemlock, &c. **1857** Long *Pictures Slavery* (2d ed) 257 **MD**, Here is our old-fashioned worm-fence, made of sap pine rails, that has to be mended every year. **1896** Mohr–Roth *Timber Pines* 106 **NC, VA**, The Loblolly Pine. . . Common or local names. . . Sap Pine. **1916** *Torreya* 16.236 **VA**, *Pinus taeda*. . . Sap pine, Wallops I[slan]d, Va. **1950** Peattie *Nat. Hist. Trees* 20, Pitch Pine—*Pinus rigida*. . . Black, Torch, or Sap Pine. **1968–70** *DARE* (Qu. T17, . . *Kinds of pine trees;* not asked in early QRs) Infs **CT**2, **NJ**22, **NY**233, **TN**65, Sap pine(s). **1969** Sorden *Lumberjack Lingo* 102 **NEng, Gt Lakes**, *Sap pine*—An inferior pine—heavy, knotty, and pitchy compared with the white pine monarchs. A term used mainly in Canada.

sapsuck See sapsucker 1, 4

sapsucker n

1 also *sapsuck:* Any of var usu smaller **woodpeckers**, esp those of the genus *Sphyrapicus*, but also such others as **downy woodpecker, flicker n²1, hairy woodpecker, red-bellied woodpecker**, or **red-cockaded woodpecker.** For other names of *Sphyrapicus* spp see **peck-sap, red-breasted woodpecker, red-headed ~ 4, red-throated ~, yellow-bellied ~**

1805 (1905) Clark *Orig. Jrls. Lewis & Clark Exped.* 6.187, [I saw] the small woodpecker or *sap-sucker* as they are sometimes called. **1838** Geol. Surv. OH *Second Annual Rept.* 179, *P[icus] pubescens* [= *Dryobates p.*]. The sap-sucker. This small bird is one of the most destructive enemies of our orchards. . . I am inclined to believe with the popular opinion that it does it for the sake of sucking the juices of the trees. **1848** in 1850 Cooper *Rural Hours* 301 **NY**, The downy woodpecker, and the hairy woodpecker. . . are called sap-suckers by the country people. **1880** *Cimarron News & Press* 23 Dec. 1/4 (*DAE*), Of the several small species commonly called 'sap suckers,' a variety of the yellow-bellied is perhaps the most striking. **1891** *Leighton News* (AL) 3 July np, *Southern Hairy Woodpecker*. . . This is one of the five varieties of black and white speckled Woodpeckers found here, all of which are commonly called "Sapsuckers." **1894** Riley *Armazindy* 149 **IN**, The Sap-suck, and the Wren. **1900** *Wilson Bulletin* 31.9, The Flicker. . . *Sapsuck, Sapsucker.* Southern States. From the belief that it extracts sap from the trees in which it bores. Misnomer. **1910** [see **2** below]. **1949** Webber *Backwoods Teacher* 56 **Ozarks**, [W]e saw swarms of butterflies sucking at the juice which oozed from the tree where something—"sapsuckers," the children said—had injured the bark. **1950** *WELS* **WI** (*Different kinds of woodpeckers*) 9 Infs, Sapsucker(s); 6 Infs, Yellowbellied sapsucker; 1 Inf, Downy or sapsucker. **1962** Imhof *AL Birds* 329, *Woodpeckers*. . . These far-ranging woodland birds are called Peckerwoods and Sapsuckers in the South. **1965–70** *DARE* (Qu. Q17, . . *Kinds of woodpeckers*) 194 Infs, **widespread, but somewhat more freq Sth, S Midl**, Sapsucker(s); 16 Infs, **scattered**, Yellow-bellied sapsucker; **CT**5, Red-bellied sapsucker; **MS**81, Redhead sapsucker;

AL17, Red-headed sapsucker; **TX**32, Sapsuck; **CT**5, Yellow sapsucker; **GA**3, Yellowbelly sapsucker; (Qu. Q18, *Joking names and nicknames for woodpeckers*) 11 Infs, 10 **Sth, S Midl**, Sapsucker; (Qu. Q14) Inf **IN**69, Sapsucker; (Qu. Q19, . . *Birds similar to the whippoorwill;* total Infs questioned, 75) Inf **AR**39, Sapsucker; (Qu. Q23, *The insect-eating bird that goes headfirst down a tree trunk*) Inf **TX**59, Yellow-bellied sapsucker. **1986** Pederson *LAGS Concordance* **Gulf Region**, 95 infs, Sapsucker(s) [Comments indicating that this refers to a class or species of woodpecker are recorded from 22 infs.]; 1 inf, Guinea sapsucker; 2 infs, Red-breasted sapsuckers—black-and-white checked; 2 infs, Redhead(ed) sapsucker(s); 1 inf, Redhead sapsuckers—large, about size of chickens; 1 inf, Striped sapsucker; 1 inf, Yellow-bellied sapsucker; 1 inf, Yellow-breasted sapsucker.

2 =**nuthatch.**

1846 in 1848 Emory *Notes Reconnoissance* 502, This morning I got a little sapsucker, "sitta Carolina." **1862** in 1865 IL Dept. Ag. *Trans.* 5.731 **seWI**, All of our spotted *Woodpeckers*, and even the *Nuthatchers* [sic], are, by many, indiscriminately called Sap-Suckers. **1883** Nuttall Ornith. Club *Bulletin* 8.76, In *Tomtit* (Ohio Valley) and *Sapsucker* (Maryland) for these birds [=nuthatches], other errors are indicated. **1910** KY Hist. Soc. *Register* 8.15, *Sitta carolinensis*. . . This Nut-thatch [sic] is popularly "lumped" with that imaginary group, the "Sap-suckers;" i.e., the smaller woodpeckers. **1919** Burns *Ornith. Chester Co. PA* 108, *Sitta carolinensis carolinensis*—White-breasted Nuthatch, "sapsucker," "woodpecker." . . *Sitta canadensis*—Red-breasted Nuthatch, "sapsucker." **1950** *WELS* **WI** (*Insect-eating bird that goes head first down a tree*) 3 Infs, Sapsucker; 1 Inf, Sapsucker—slate blue or gray, slender, active, a little larger than wren. **1965–70** *DARE* (Qu. Q23, *The insect-eating bird that goes headfirst down a tree trunk*) 42 Infs, **scattered**, Sapsucker. [*DARE* Ed: 7 of these Infs expressed doubt about the response. Of the rest, it is impossible to determine how many actually meant to equate *sapsucker* with the nuthatch. It is clear that many Infs did not understand this question; more than half gave no response, and many of the responses that were given clearly do not refer to the nuthatch, including 65 instances of *woodpecker* (or *peckerwood*) alone or in var combs.] **1986** Pederson *LAGS Concordance*, 1 inf, **neAR**, Sapsucker—different from peckerwood; 1 inf, **swAR**, Sapsucker—black and gray; 1 inf, **nwMS**, Sapsucker—gray with longer bill than peckerwood; 1 inf, **cwMS**, Sapsucker—different from peckerwood; 1 inf, **nwFL**, Sapsucker—little, gray.

3 Occas another bird that resembles one of the above in color or habit, such as the **black-and-white warbler** or a **chickadee n¹1**; see quots.

1919 Burns *Ornith. Chester Co. PA* 89, *Mniotilta varia*—Black and White Warbler, . . "little sapsucker." *Ibid* 108, *Penthestes atricapillus atricapillus* [=*Parus a. a.*]—Chickadee, . . "sapsucker." . . Tolerable common winter visitant. *Ibid* 109, *Penthestes carolinensis carolinensis* [=*Parus c. c.*]—Carolina chickadee, . . "sapsucker." **1986** Pederson *LAGS Concordance*, 1 inf, **cwLA**, Sapsucker—brown bird.

4 also *sapsuck:* Used as a term of abuse for a person.

1906 *DN* 3.154 **nwAR**, Sapsucker. . . A term of contempt. "I'll pay you back, you old sapsucker, you." **1926** Hoffman *Gun Gospel* 224 (*Mathews Coll.*), "Scared stiff, that's what they are," grumbled the veteran puncher. "A bunch of sapsuckers." **1972** Cooper *NC Mt. Folkl.* 95, *Sapsuck*—sapsucker; a half-wit. **1995** McCormack *Fields Pastures* 225 **TN**, "Let go of my golf club, you little sapsucker!" I growled, using one of my father's favorite words. The term "sapsucker" is about as strong a word as he ever used. If he called something or somebody a sapsucker, then they were pretty rotten and worthy of future avoidance.

sap tree n

1 A **sugar maple** such as *Acer saccharum*.

1843 *Knickerbocker* 22.161 **VT**, One felled the proper trees, taking care to leave the sap-trees, the sugar-maple, untouched. **1846** Browne *Trees* 83, The Sugar Maple. Synonymes. . . Rock Maple, Hard Maple, . . Sap-tree. **1941** *LANE* Map 247, 1 inf, **cwCT**, Sap tree [heard from others]; 1 inf, **cCT**, Sap tree—general term, including hard maples; [1 inf, **ceMA**, Sap maple]. **1966** Dakin *Dial. Vocab. Ohio R. Valley* 2.413 **swIL**, *Sap tree* and *syrup tree* are both given in addition to *hard maple* by a speaker in the American Bottom, where *sugar tree* does not seem to be current. **1970** *DARE* (Qu. T3, *The tree that produces syrup and sugar*) Inf **TN**46, Sap tree. **1973** Allen *LAUM* 1.335 **Upper MW** (as of c1950), *Sugar maple*. . . A scattered few other infs. use simple *maple, sap tree* [etc]. **1986** Pederson *LAGS Concordance* (*Sugar maple*) 1 inf, **ceAL**, Sap tree.

2 See **sap gum 1.**

sapwood pine n Cf **sapling pine, sap ~**
=**Jeffrey pine.**
   1897 Sudworth *Arborescent Flora* 22 **CA**, *Pinus jeffreyi.* . . Sapwood
Pine. **1908** Britton *N. Amer. Trees* 25, *Pinus Jeffreyi* . . , also known
as . . Sapwood Pine, occurs on dry volcanic mountains from southern
Oregon through California . . , often forming pure forests. . . The wood
is coarser and more resinous [than that of *Pinus ponderosa*].

sap woods See **sap yard**

sap works n esp **NEast**
=**sugar camp;** also fig.
   1831 *Genesee Farmer* 1.310 **NY**, Our Sap Works were in a hollow of
the breast of the 'Hog Back' Ridge, or Hill, and never were there happier
evenings, than occurred in that grove of gigantic sugar maples. **1832**
(1961) Strang *Diary* 15 **NY**, The people want their boys to work in the
sapworks. **1849** *Knickerbocker* 33.279, 'The Sugar Bush' has vividly
recalled to memory . . the pale-blue smoke curling up from the 'sapworks.' **1959** *VT Hist.* 27.155, All over the sap works . . var. All over
the sugar bush. Where the maple sugar trees grow and where the sugar-
ing takes place; hence, everywhere. Common. **2001** *DARE* File **cVT**,
Sap works is still used in Central VT and in the same context as "the
whole nine yards" or "the whole shooting works". An expression might
be, "you can take the whole sap works".

sap yard n Also *sap garden, ~ woods*
=**sugar bush.**
   1950 *WELS Suppl.* **ceNH**, *Sap yard*—Grove of trees from which maple sugar is taken. Also sometimes *maple orchard.* **1966–69** *DARE*
(Qu. T4, *The place where . . trees grow together and sap is gathered*) Inf
AL11, Sap garden; [**NY209**, Sap places;] **NY69**, Sap woods.

sap yoke n Also *sap neck-yoke*   chiefly **NEast**
A yoke for carrying buckets of maple sap on the shoulders.
   1878 VT State Bd. Ag. *Report* 5.105, The sap was lugged with sap
yoke and pails on their shoulders. **1923** Adams *Pioneer Hist. Ingham
Co.* 312 **MI**, One neighbor whittled out brooms for several families. Another gauged the sap yokes, and another made ox yokes. *Ibid* 315, I recall things of long ago . . the dash churn, spinning wheel, pod augur
[sic], sap neck-yoke. **1930** Shoemaker *1300 Words* 52 **cPA Mts** (as of
c1900), *Sap-yoke*—A yoke used to carry buckets of maple sap from the
sugar bush to the boilers. **1948** *McDavid Coll.* **cnNY**, *Sap yoke*—[used]
to carry sap buckets—across a man's shoulders. **1959** *VT Hist.* 27.155,
Sap yoke. . . A frame fitting the neck and shoulders of a person, used for
carrying a pair of sap buckets in collecting maple syrup. Old fashioned.
1965 Needham–Mussey *Country Things* 40 **VT**, A lot of people in
Gramp's time used wooden sap yokes, pieces of wood hollowed out to
fit over your shoulders, with a semi-circle cut out for the neck, and a
piece sticking out from the shoulder at each end. You would take two of
your wide-bottomed wooden buckets, and hang them by cords on the
ends of the yoke, and go to a tree. **1966** *DARE* Tape **NH5**, When we
used to use an old-fashioned sap yoke to gather the sap and lug it
around, it was not near so much lugging now, because . . instead of sap
buckets we have what they call plastic tubing.

sarabacca See **asarabacca**

Sarady See **Saturday**

Sarah n Cf **benjamin**
A **trillium** (here: *Trillium undulatum*).
   1894 *Jrl. Amer. Folkl.* 7.102 **ME**, *Trillium erythrocarpum* [=*T. undulatum*], . . Sarah, Penobscot Co., Me. . . *Trillium erectum* is here called
Benjamin, and children every spring go hunting Benjamins and Sarahs.
1940 Clute *Amer. Plant Names* 232, *Trillium undulatum*. Sarah, painted
lady.

Sarahgodlin adj, adv Also *Sallygodlin*
=**antigodlin 1.**
   1950 *PADS* 14.58 **SC**, *Sarahgodlin, Sallygodlin*. . . Same as *antigodlin*. . . Apparently these variants arise from a mistaken understanding
of *antigodlin*, as if it were *aunty-godlin*.

sarana n Also *saranna* [Russ *sarana*, of Tatar orig] **AK**
A **fritillary** (here: *Fritillaria camschatcensis*).
   1955 U.S. Arctic Info. Center *Gloss.* 69, *Saranna*. . . The Kamchatka
lily. **1968** Hultén *Flora AK* 308, *Fritillaria camschatcénsis*. . . Kamchatka Fritillary, Saraná. . . The bulblets are dug in the fall, dried, and

used in stews or powdered into flour. **1987** Hughes–Blackwell *Wildflowers SE AK* 74, Chocolate Lily, Kamchatka Lily, . . sarana, black lily
[etc]. . . The large, nodding and bell-like flowers have a strong, unpleasant odor.

sarape See **serape**

sarce See **sauce**

sarcelle n [Fr "teal"] **LA**
Either the **green-winged teal** or the blue-winged teal *(Anas
discors)*.
   1897 *Auk* 14.286 **LA**, *Anas carolinensis*. . . Green-winged Teal.—
Commonly known as *sarcelle*. The most abundant winter resident of all
the ducks. **1911** *Forest & Stream* 77.173 **LA**, Green-winged Teal. . .
Sarcelle . . , Blue-winged Teal. . . Sarcelle. [**1916** *Times–Picayune*
(New Orleans LA) 26 Mar mag sec 2, Green-winged Teal. . . Sarcelle;
Sarcelle d'hiver. . . This favorite of the sportsmen is here in great numbers every winter, but it is never as common as the blue-winged teal. . .
Blue-winged Teal . . Sarcelle Autonniere; Sarcelle Printanniere.—Although a summer breeder in this state, this duck is here mostly in win-
ter.]

sarcer See **saucer**

sarch See **search**

sarcumstance See **circumstance**

sardine n [*OED2* c1430 for *Sardina pilchardus* or some other
related fishes of chiefly European waters]
1 Any of var fishes of the family Clupeidae, spec:
a =**menhaden 1.   esp Gulf States**
   1850 *De Bow's Rev.* 9.289 **LA**, The fish are catfish, casseburgo or
sheep head, sardine, . . flounder, grand ecaille, . . and the sturgeon.
1877 Bartlett *Americanisms* 551, Sardines. . . Menhaden prepared in resemblance to the sardines prepared in Europe. **1878** *Amer. Naturalist*
12.736, Among the manufacturers in Port Monmouth, N.J., who prepare
the menhaden as an article of food, a number of trade names are in use,
such as "American sardine" (in distinction from the European fish which
is prepared in a similar manner). **1884** Goode *Fisheries U.S.* 576, The
Gulf Menhaden has several vernacular names. At Key West it is called
'Sardine,' in common with other fish of the same general appearance. . .
At New Orleans the names 'Sardine' and 'Alewife' are both in use, the
latter perhaps more generally. On the Texas coast it is known as 'Herring,' 'Alewife,' 'Sardine,' and 'Shad,' each locality having its peculiar
name. **1921** LA Dept. of Conserv. *Bulletin* 10.143, Partial investigation
into the food habits of the pelican in Louisiana show that in summer at
least it feeds largely on the menhadden [sic], or "sardines," of the Gulf,
with a slight addition of mullet. **1986** Pederson *LAGS Concordance
(Saltwater fish)* 2 infs, **MS**, Sardine(s); *(Small fish used as bait)* 3 infs,
seFL, seMS, cTX, Sardine(s).

b The Atlantic **herring** n[1] 1 *(Clupea harengus).*   **esp ME**
   [**1872** *Appletons' Jrl.* 13 Apr 7.412 **Canada**, Another kind of fishing,
very profitable to the *habitans* and quite new to the tourists, is the sardine and smelt fishing.] **1949** Palmer *Nat. Hist.* 440, Atlantic Herring.
Clupea harengus. . . Fry 3–4 in.; . . larger, canned as "sardines". **1966**
DARE (Qu. P2, . . *Kinds of saltwater fish caught around here . . good to
eat*) Inf **ME6**, Sardines; (Qu. P14, . . *Commercial fishing . . what do the
fishermen go out after?*) Inf **ME10**, Sardines (herring); **ME16**, Sardines.
1966 *DARE* Tape **ME17**, [Inf:] Sardines. They go after sardines. . .
[FW:] What kind of fish make sardines? [Inf:] Herring. Small herring.
1974 McClane *McClane's New Std. Fishing Encycl.* 63, Atlantic Herring. . . Young herring, sometimes known as sardines, are important
commercially, while the adults form the basis of one of the world's largest commercial fisheries. Some are canned, smoked, and sold fresh or
salted.

c A common small fish *(Sardinops sagax)* of the Pacific coast.
Also called **pilchard 2**
   1863 Hittell *Resources CA* 145, The sardine (*Meletta cerulea* [=
Sardinops sagax]) is abundant from Humboldt Bay to San Diego. **1882**
U.S. Natl. Museum *Bulletin* 16.265, *C[lupea] sagax*. . . California Sardine. . . Resembles the European Sardine (*C. pilchardus*), but has no
teeth and the belly less strongly serrate. **1892** *Overland Mth.* (2d ser)
20.154 **CA**, Barracuda, herrings, sardines, and anchovies are abundant in
season. The sardine is almost exactly the same as the sardine of Europe,
and might make a great canning industry if developed. **1953** Roedel
Common Fishes CA 33, *Sardinops caerulea*. . . Sardines, other than

those taken for bait, normally enter the fishery when two or three years old and eight or nine inches long. **1967** *DARE* (Qu. P2, . . *Kinds of saltwater fish caught around here . . good to eat)* Inf **CA**31, Sardines. **1974** McClane *McClane's New Std. Fishing Encycl.* 735, Young sardines are used as live bait, principally for tuna and mackerel.

2 usu pl, but sg in constr; also *sardines in a box:* A game of hide-and-seek in which one person hides from several who try to find him and, when they do so, hide with him until all the seekers are crowded into the same hiding place.

1909 (1923) Bancroft *Games* 172, *Sardines.* . . The player chosen to be It . . goes out himself to hide, while all of the other players stay at the goal. . . After counting, they . . all start out to hunt for the hider. Any player discovering him must . . hide in the same place with the hider. **1940** Harbin *Fun Encycl.* 158, *Sardines.* **1965–70** *DARE* (Qu. EE12, *Games in which one captain hides his team and the other team tries to find it)* Infs **NY**81, 123, 144, Sardines; **CT**8, Sardines in a box—whole team must hide in one place; (Qu. EE13a, *Games in which every player hides except one, and that one must try to find the others)* Inf **FL**28, Sardines; **IL**37, Sardines—one person would hide and anyone who found him squeezed in; the last person to find the others was "it"; **PA**49, Sardines—when they catch all before starting again, it was called sardines; (Qu. EE16, *Hiding games that start with a special, elaborate method of sending the players out to hide)* Inf **CA**190, Sardine—one goes out and hides and each player, as he finds the original hider, joins him. Game is over when last person finds the whole pack; **NY**199, Sardines—one hides, the rest separately try to find; as each finds, he crawls in and also hides; **OH**63, Sardines—they all get in one bunch to be found; **OH**87, Sardines—they all hide in the same spot; (Qu. EE17) Inf **CA**50A, Sardines—one hid and as the others found her, they climbed in with her (like sardines). **1967** *DARE* Tape **PA**49, One person hides and then all the others start out to hunt him, and when you find the person you stay there so that eventually everybody is collected in one place. Now, that's sardines. . . Because by the end of the game everybody's packed in like sardines. **1975** *Ford Times* Mar 22 (as of 1940s), Sardines was our hands-down favorite indoor winter game, but we rarely got to play it. . . Who wouldn't want 15 or 20 children tramping through the house . . seeking out the smallest possible hiding place that would hold them all? **1988** Fulghum *All I Really Need* 58, In Sardines the person who is It goes and hides, and everybody goes looking for him. When you find him, you get in with him. . . Pretty soon everybody is hiding together, all stacked in a small space like puppies in a pile. And pretty soon somebody giggles and somebody laughs and everybody gets found.

3 pl, but sg in constr: See quot.

1976 Sublette Co. Artist Guild *More Tales* 347 (as of c1900), At one party in our home we played "Sardines". Everyone circled around one blindfolded person who had to find, in the dark, the person who held one particular card, the ace of spades. We all hid—some under beds, some in closets or other hiding places.

sardines in a box See **sardine 2**

sargo n [Span]

1 Either a **pinfish 1a** or a related fish such as *Diplodus holbrooki.*

[**1873** in 1878 Smithsonian Inst. *Misc. Coll.* 14.2.27, *Lagodon rhomboides.* . . Sargo *(Cuba).*] **1896** Jordan–Evermann *Check List Fishes* 390, *Diplodus argenteus.* . . *Sargo.* West Indies; Florida and the Bermudas. **1933** John G. Shedd Aquarium *Guide* 110, *Diplodus argenteus.* . . *Sargo.* . . *Diplodus holbrooki* . . *Sargo.* The Sargos are silvery fishes, the young of which show numerous black bars which disappear with age. **1935** Caine *Game Fish* 55 **Sth**, *Salt-water Bream or Sailor's Choice—Lagodon rhomboides.* . . *Synonyms* . . Sargo. **1946** LaMonte *N. Amer. Game Fishes* 71, *Lagodon rhomboides.* . . Sargo. . . North to Cape Cod, Massachusetts; very common southward and on the Gulf coast of Florida. **1976** Tryckare et al. *Lore of Sportfishing* 115, *Lagodon rhomboides.* . . sargo. . . Abundant on shallow and grassy flats. . . Used as live baits by anglers, and popular locally as small panfish.

2 A **grunt 1** (here: *Anisotremus davidsoni)* of the Pacific coast. Also called **Chinese croaker 2, perch** n[1] **7**

1882 U.S. Natl. Museum *Bulletin* 16.551, *P[omadasys] davidsoni.* . . *Sargo.* Grayish silvery, dark above. . . Pacific coast, from Santa Barbara Islands southward. **1884** Goode *Fisheries U.S.* 1.400, *California Grunts.* . . One, known to the fishermen by the name "Sargo," *Pristipoma Davidsoni,* . . feeds on crustaceans and is a good pan-fish. **1946** LaMonte *N. Amer. Game Fishes* 68, *Sargo—Anisotremus davidsoni.* . . North to San Diego, California. . . Not taken abundantly; usually in sum-

mer and fall. **1953** Roedel *Common Fishes CA* 93, *California Sargo.* . . A minor sport fish caught in fair numbers in Newport Bay.

sarment, sarmin(t), sarmon(t), sarmun See **sermon**

sarpent, sarpint, sarpunt See **serpent**

sarsaparilla n Usu |ˌsæsp(ə)ˈrɪlə, ˌsɑrspəˈrɪlə|; also (perh infl by *sassafras)* |ˌsæsfəˈrɪlə| Pronc-spp *sasparilla, sasparilly, sassafrilla, sass(a)parilla, sassyperiller;* for addit pronc and sp varr see quots below

A Forms.

1851 in 1927 Jones *FL Plantation Rec.* 440 **nwFL**, Received from George Jones Esqr. one Bottle of Sands sarsapariler. **1862** (1864) Browne *Artemus Ward Book* 124, Old man Townsin's Fort was to maik Sassyperiller. **1892** *DN* 1.241 **cwMO**, *Sarsaparilla* [sæsprɪlə]. [*DN* Ed: In Michigan [sæs(ə)ˈprɪlə]]. **1905** *DN* 3.58 **eNE**, *Sassaparilla* (sassafrilla). **1907** *DN* 3.198 **seNH**, *Sasparilla* [sæspəˈrɪlə]. **1909** *DN* 3.366 **eAL, wGA**, *Sassyparilla.* . . Sarsaparilla. **1909** in 1914 Stewart *Letters* 40 **WY**, He was full of surprise [that] he didn't "git some cherry bark and some sasparilly and bile it good and gin it to him." **c1910** in 1944 *ADD* **NYC**, *Sarsaparilla.* . . [sæsəˈprɛlə]. **1912** *DN* 3.588 **wIN**, *Sassaparilla.* **1917** *DN* 4.399 **neOH**, *Sassparilla.* . . Pronounced [sæspəˈrɪlə] [*DN* Ed: also Pa., N.Y., Ill.], [sæsfəˈrɪlə], [sɑrsfəˈrɪlə]. **1938** Berger *Bowleg Bill* 135, Comes the hurricane, and it blows, and now all my forty-odd voyages on the deep water is teacakes and sarsprilly. **1941** *LANE* Map 312, 2 infs, **CT**, [sæsprɪlə]; 3 infs, **CT, RI**, [sæsp(ə)rɪlə]; 4 infs, **CT, RI**, [sæsf(ə)rɪlə]; 2 infs, **MA, RI**, [sæsəˈprɪlɛ]; 1 inf, **cMA**, [saˈsprɪlə]. **1965–70** *DARE* (Qu. BB50d, . . *Spring tonics)* Infs **MD**17, **MO**8, **MA**6, [ˈsæspɑrɪlə]; **MI**115, **MO**9, **TN**3, [sæs(ə)fɑrɪlə]; **MI**93, [ˈsɑsəpɑrɪlə]; **MA**14, [ˌsæspɑˈrɛlə]; **NY**69, [ˌsæsəpəˈrɪlə] [sic]; **SC**19, [sɔspəˈrɪlə]; **WI**76, [ˈsɑrsəspəˈrɪlə]; (Qu. I44, . . *Kinds of berries)* Inf **LA**33, [ˌsæspəˈrɪlə]. **1969** *DARE* Tape **KY**5, He'd get cherry bark, and wild cherry . . and he'd get sarsaparilla [ˈsæːsˌpɑrɪˈlə]. **1981** Pederson *LAGS Basic Materials,* 1 inf, **cwGA**, [sæᵋspɑrɪˈlə]; 1 inf, **cnTN**, [sæᵗspɚˈɪˈlə]; 1 inf, **swAL**, [sæˈsfɑrɪˈlə]; 1 inf, **nwLA**, [sæᵋfəˈrɪᵗlə]; 1 inf, **cLA**, [sæˈⱽˈsˈprɪˈlə]; 1 inf, **cLA**, [sæsfəˈrɪᵗlə]; 1 inf, **neTX**, [sæᵗspəˈrɪᵗlə]; 1 inf, **cwMS**, [sæᵋsfəˈrɪᵗlə]; 1 inf, **cwMS**, [sæᵋsˈⱽˈrɪᵗlə]; 1 inf, **cwMS**, [sæˈⱥsbəˈrɪᵗlə].

B Senses. Cf **false sarsaparilla, wild ~, yellow ~**

1 also *sarsaparilla vine:* Any of several **greenbriers,** esp *Smilax glauca* or *S. walteri;* also the root of such a plant. [*OED2* 1577 → for *Smilax officinalis* and related plants]

[**1731** Miller *Gard. Dict.* (*OED2*), *Smilax* . . Rough Virginian Bindweed, with a smooth Ivy Leaf, commonly call'd Zarzaparilla.] **1737** (1911) Brickell *Nat. Hist. NC* 22, *Sarsaparilla, White Hellebor,* and several sorts of *Thistles.* **1785** Marshall *Arbustrum* 142, Smilax Sarsaparilla [=*S. glauca*]. *Ivy leaved rough Bindweed, or Sarsaparilla.* This grows naturally in Virginia and to the southward. **1860** Curtis *Cat. Plants NC* 116, *Sarsaparilla* (S[milax] glauca . .). The root of this is sometimes used in the composition of diet drinks. It is not the Sarsaparilla of the Druggists, but is said to be often mixed with it. **1876** Hobbs *Bot. Hdbk.* 7, Bamboo brier, Southern states sarsaparilla,[,] Smilax sarsaparilla. **1901** Torreya 1.115 **GA**, *Smilax Walteri.* . . Sarsaparilla. Sumter [and] Coffee [Counties]. **1933** Small *Manual SE Flora* 313, *S[milax] Walteri.* . . Sarsaparilla. *Ibid* 314, *S. pumila.* . . Sarsaparilla-vine. **1938** Van Dersal *Native Woody Plants* 353, Sarsaparilla (Smilax lanceolata [= *S. smallii*], Smilax walteri). . . Sarsaparilla vine (Smilax pumila). **1958** Jacobs–Burlage *Index Plants NC* 135, *Smilax glauca.* . . Sarsaparilla. . . This species grows in thickets and old fields and along hedge rows . . throughout North Carolina. *Ibid* 136, *Smilax sarsaparilla.* . . Sarsaparilla. . . It has the same uses as commercial sarsaparilla except that its action is weaker; not much is known regarding its properties. **1960** Williams *Walk Egypt* 127 **GA**, Oak and hickory laced with heart-leafed sarsaparilla vine and goldenseal. **1966** *DARE* (Qu. S26e, *Other wildflowers not yet mentioned;* not asked in early QRs) Inf **AR**24, Sarsaparilla—a vine you make whiskey from. **1974** (1977) Coon *Useful Plants* 176, *Smilax (various species).* . . sarsaparilla. . . Medicinally most have qualities known as "alterative." One species has a mild sarsaparilla flavor and has been used as a substitute for same. **1986** Pederson *LAGS Concordance,* 1 inf, **swAL**, Sarsaparilla—used for medicinal tea, stimulates; 1 inf, **cwGA**, Sarsaparilla—used in tanning leather; 1 inf, **cLA**, Sarsaparilla roots = sassafras roots, made tea; 1 inf, **cnLA**, Sarsaparilla vines—roots used for medicine; 1 inf, **nwLA**, Sarsaparilla—used for medicine in home remedies; 1 inf, **cwMS**, Sarsaparilla tea; 1 inf, **cwMS**, Sarsaparilla tea—made from a vine; 1 inf, **cwMS**, Sarsaparilla vine—used for tea; 1 inf, **ceTX**, Sarsaparilla—grandfather would use; 1 inf, **neTX,** Sarsaparilla roots for medicinal tea; 1 inf, **cnTN,** Sarsaparilla roots—grow on ground, have vine. [*DARE* Ed: Some of these infs may refer instead to other senses below.]

2 A **spikenard:** usu *Aralia hispida* or *A. nudicaulis,* but also *A. racemosa.*   For other names of *A. hispida* see **dwarf elder, pigeonberry 3, wild elder**

1637 (1967) Morton *New English Canaan* 66, There is abundance af Sassafras and Sarsaperilla.   **1672** Josselyn *New-Englands Rarities* 59, We have in *New-England* two Plants, that go under the name of Sarsaparilla.   **1778** Carver *Travels N. Amer.* 512, *Sarsaparilla.* The root of this plant, which is the most estimable part of it, is about the size of a goose quill, and runs in different directions, twined and crooked, to a great length in the ground; from the principal stem of it springs many smaller fibres, all of which are tough and flexible. . . The bark of the roots, which alone should be used in medicine, is of a bitterish flavour, but aromatic. It is deservedly esteemed for its medicinal virtues, being a gentle sudorific, and very powerful in attenuating the blood when impeded by gross humours.   **1792** Belknap *Hist. NH* 3.125, The former [= the black elder] is too well known to need any description; as are the *maiden-hair (adianthus pedatuus)* the *sarsaparilla (aralia)* [etc].   **1828** Rafinesque *Med. Flora* 1.53, *Aralia nudicaulis.* . . Sassaparil, Sarsaparilla. *Ibid* 54, All the plants of this genus [=*Aralia*] . . have active properties. Two other American species *A. racemosa* and *A. hispida,* have the same properties as this [=*A. nudicaulis*], and may be used for each other. . . This species [=*A. nudicaulis*] is often called Sarsaparilla, the root being similar to that article, and having similar properties.   **1837** Darlington *Flora Cestrica* 209 **sePA,** *A[ralia] nudicaulis.* . . Sarsaparilla. . . The *root* of this has a somewhat aromatic but mawkish taste; and is often used as a substitute for the *Sarsaparilla* of the shops, in making popular diet-drinks.   **1894** *Jrl. Amer. Folkl.* 7.89 **NC,** *Aralia nudicaulis,* . . sassafariller, Banner Elk, N.C.   **1896** *Ibid* 9.189 **ME,** *Aralia nudicaulis,* . . sasapril or sasafril, Me. saxapril and sasafafarilla, Bath, Me.   **1911** (1916) Porter *Harvester* 452 **IN,** He drove through the woods to the sarsaparilla beds. He noticed the beautiful lobed leaves . . and the heads of lustrous purple-black berries.   **1929** *Torreya* 29.150 **ME,** Aralia nudicaulis, *"Sassafrilla".*   **1958** Jacobs–Burlage *Index Plants NC* 17, *Aralia hispida.* . . Sarsaparilla. . . This species grows in rocky places in New England, the middle states, and in the mountains of North Carolina. . . *Aralia nudicaulis.* . . Sarsaparil; sarsaparilla. . . This aralia is found in moist high woodlands and mountains from New England to Carolina to Missouri and is abundant in North Carolina.   **1968–70** *DARE* (Qu. I44, *What kinds of berries grow wild around here?*) Inf **LA33,** Sarsaparilla berries; (Qu. S26a, . . *Wildflowers.* . . *Roadside flowers*) Inf **MN14,** Sarsaparilla; (Qu. S26c, *Wildflowers that grow in woods*) Inf **MA100,** [sæsˈpʌrɪlə], [-ˈpɪrələ] (Qu. S26e, *Other wildflowers not yet mentioned;* not asked in early QRs) Inf **VT10,** Sasparilla.   **1979** Erichsen-Brown *Med. N. Amer. Plants* 351, *Aralia nudicaulis.* . . American sarsaparilla. *Ibid* 448, *Bristly Sarsaparilla—Aralia hispida.* . . Common names. . . Rough sarsaparilla.

3 also *Texas sarsaparilla:* =**moonseed 1.**

1836 Edward *Hist. TX* 43, Let us look at some of the roots and plants below, such as . . the sarsaparilla.   **1854** King *Amer. Eclectic Dispensatory* 630, *Menispermum canadense.* . . This plant is also known by the names of *Sarsaparilla, Moonseed, Vine Maple,* etc.   **1896** *Jrl. Amer. Folkl.* 9.180 **IN, OH,** *Menispermum Canadense,* . . sarsaparilla, Parke County, Ind., Sulphur Grove, Ohio.   **1930** Sievers *Amer. Med. Plants* 42, *Menispermum canadense.* . . Texas sarsaparilla. . . *Part used.*— The rootstock, collected in autumn.   **1960** Vines *Trees SW* 277, *Menispermum canadense.* . . Some vernacular names for the vine are Texas Sarsaparilla [etc]. . . The rhizome, now thought to be inert, was at one time used as a substitute for sarsaparilla. . . The fruit is considered poisonous to human beings.   **1974** (1977) Coon *Useful Plants* 187, *Menispermum canadense.* . Texas sarsaparilla. . . A woody, twining, perennial vine common in the eastern United States of which a tincture of the fresh root has been used as a diuretic and stomachic, and sometimes as a substitute for sarsaparilla. But against this is the fact that the berries are poisonous and should never be used.

4 A **birthwort 1** (here: *Aristolochia macrophylla*).

1900 Lyons *Plant Names* 45, *A[ristolochia] macrophylla.* . . Dutchman's-pipe, . . Big Sarsaparilla.

5 Either **moonseed 2** or **snail-seed.**

1920 *Torreya* 20.21 **TX,** *Cocculus carolinus.* . . Sarsaparilla, used as a tonic.   **1960** Vines *Trees SW* 276, *Cocculus diversifolius.* . . Also known under the vernacular name of Sarsaparilla.

6 =**pepper vine.**

1939 Tharp *Vegetation TX* 61, Cow-itch; sarsaparilla *(Ampelopsis).*

7 =**spreading dogbane.**

1940 Clute *Amer. Plant Names* 251, *Apocynum androsaemifolium.* Sarsaparilla, bitter dogbane, cruel plant, honey-bloom.

sarsaparilla vine See **sarsaparilla B1**

sarse See **sauce**

sartain See **certain**

sartainly See **certainly**

sartan, sarten, sartin(g) See **certain**

sart(i)nly See **certainly**

sarvant See **servant**

sarve, sarvice n¹ See **serve**

sarvice n², **sarviceberry** See **serviceberry**

sarviceable See **serve**

sarvint See **servant**

sarvis n¹ See **serve**

sarvis n², **sarvisberry** See **serviceberry**

sarviss See **serve**

sas See **sauce**

sasafrac See **sassafras**

saseadg See **sausage**

saser See **saucer**

sashay v Also *sashy, sashshay, shasha;* also with *around;* hence vbl n *sashaying around* [By metath from Fr *chassé*] Cf **chassay**

1 In dancing: to perform a chassé or similar sliding step; also fig.

1836 *Franklin Repository* (Chambersburg, Pa.) 4 Oct. 1/3 *(DA),* If you don't sashay across, button your lip, and go home quietly, you and I will have to promenade all round, and swing corners into the watch house.   **1838** (1852) Gilman *S. Matron* 76 **SC** [Gullah], Ladies change—turn you partner at de corner—shasha all round.   **1861** Holmes *Venner* 1.125 **NEng,** The Doctor looked as if he should like to rigadoon and sashy across.   **1891** Johnston *Primes & Neighbors* 127 **GA,** Sashay W'all!   **1905** *DN* 3.65 **eNE,** Sashay. . . Term in dancing. . . "They sashayed back and forth to beat the band."   **1909** *DN* 3.364 **eAL, wGA,** Sashay. . . A term in dancing, same as *chassé.*   **1915** *DN* 4.228 **wTX,** Sashshay. . . To bow to one's partner in a figure in a square dance. [*DARE* Ed: prob erron]   **1926** *DN* 5.402 **Ozarks,** Sashay. . . To move briskly about. Used chiefly in calling country dances.   **1933** Rawlings *South Moon* 28 **nFL,** They sashayed, swung their partners.   **1938** Matschat *Suwannee R.* 113 **neFL, seGA,** Now ye sashay back agin. . . All sashay!   **1942** Perry *Texas* 274, He would strike up a jig and sashay in semicircles about his doomed fellows.   **2001** *DARE* File **nwMA,** Yes, *sashay* is still a standard dance call, in both square and contra dancing. It's a sort of sideways gallop.

2 To walk or go, esp in a conspicuous, bold, or easy manner; to strut, flounce, saunter, "waltz."

1878 Hart *Sazerac Lying Club* 83 **NV,** "S'pose, gentlemen, that we sashay up to the bar." And they all "sashayed."   **1903** *DN* 2.328 **seMO,** Sashay. . . To start out. (Facetious.)   **1905** *DN* 3.65 **eNE,** Sashay. . . go consciously or conspicuously. . . "She sashayed uptown."   **1906** *DN* 3.154 **nwAR,** Sashay around. . . To trifle, to "cut up". "None of your sashayin' around here."   **1907** *DN* 3.235 **nwAR,** Sashay. . . To set out. "I reckon I better sashay off some."   **1909** *DN* 3.364 **eAL, wGA,** Sashay. . . To move consciously, go in ostentatious way, put on airs in moving; also to court, act the gallant. Often with *around.*   **1910** McCutcheon *Rose* 263 **NYC,** Then he up and sashayed to New York.   **1912** *DN* 3.588 **wIN,** Sashay. . . To rush; to dash. "He sashayed right through the crowd."   **1944** *PADS* 2.60 **nwMO,** Sashay. . . To parade, to strut about. "I saw you sashaying up the street yesterday." . . Uneducated.   **1949** *PADS* 11.25 **CO,** Sashay out. . . To sidle out. An uncomplimentary way of describing a Mae West gait. . . To make a haughty exit; to flounce out. "She sashayed out with her nose in the air." **1966–70** *DARE* (Qu. Y22, *To move around in a way to make people take notice of you: "Look at him _____."*) Infs **CA**173, **NJ**59, **VA**101, **WA**33, Sashay; **FL**27, Sashaying around. **1976** Garber *Mountain-ese* 77 **sAppalachians**, Joe jist sashayed right up to Sue and axed her fer a date. **1980** *AZ Highways* Feb 7, They went out of their way to present a distinctive appearance and thought nothing of sashaying into town once or twice a year to spend hard-earned pay on fancy clothes and other trappings for themselves and their horses. **2001** *DARE* File **nwMA**, [He] once told a group of town office workers, all women, who had come to a meeting to protest sexist treatment at work, not to come sashaying into his office every time some little thing went wrong. It was not a clever thing to say to people there to complain of sexism.

3 To weave, move (back and forth).

1941 *Time* 17 Feb 58 **NYC**, He contrived a clockwork mechanism to make the bird flap its wings, sashay back & forth, and open its beak. **1949** *PADS* 11.25 **CO**, Sashay. . . To travel in diagonals; to weave from side to side. "He sashayed up the timber." "The car sashayed off the road." **1969** Kantor *MO Bittersweet* 102, Instant recollection of a certain old man at home. He used to sashay over the sidewalk, stepping on ants, and counting aloud the ones he squashed. **1995** McCormack *Fields Pastures* 201 **TN**, The old truck in front of me frequently fishtailed and sashayed around when its wheels ran out of the watery ruts created by previous vehicles. *Ibid* 260 **TN**, I had already found that efforts to pass nasogastric tubes in blue-nosed mules frequently resulted in severe damage to the front side of the tube manipulator's body. . . "Awright now, Mr. Kent. You've got to hold on to this twitch and stand around here on the off side while I try to work from the other side. Carney, one of y'all might ought to steady his rear end in case he starts to sashay around."

sashay n

A walk; an excursion, foray.

1900 Ade *More Fables* 184, Lutie never got out of her Dream until she made a bold Sashay with a Concert Company. **1935** Davis *Honey* 15 **OR**, If you yank him out for any all-night sashay on these roads, you ought to be ashamed of yourself. **1941** *Sat. Eve. Post* 16 Aug 68 **Sth**, On my first sashay into the flying field. **1949** *PADS* 11.25 **CO**, Sashay. . . A walk taken by travelling in diagonals. "He took a sashay up the mountain." **1952** in 1976 White *Letters* 355 **NEast**, Spring is making little sashays about coming to town, but it has been a fairly unconvincing demonstration so far.

sashay(ing) around See **sashay** v

sashay kitty See **sachet kitten**

sashiate v Cf **sagatiate**
=**sashay** v **1**.

1913 Kephart *Highlanders* 263 **sAppalachians**, Eight hands up and go to the left; half and back; corners turn; partners sash-i-ate. . . Gents stand and ladies swing in the center; own partners and half sash-i-ate. **1926** *DN* 5.402 **Ozarks**, Sashiate. . . To move briskly about. Used chiefly in calling country dances. **1995** in 1996 *Montgomery Coll.* **wNC, eTN**, Sashiate . . used in calling figures in square dance.

sashimi n Also *sashime* [Japanese; *OED2* 1880 →] **orig HI, but now more widely recognized** Cf **sushi**

A dish of thin slices of raw fish served with condiments and soy sauce.

1940 Bazore *Hawaiian Foods* 68 **HI**, Sashime—Raw fish sliced very thin, and served with shoyu sauce, grated daikon, or grated fresh ginger. **1967** *DARE* (Qu. H45, *Dishes made with . . fish . . that everybody around here would know, but that people in other places might not*) Inf **HI**1A, Sashimi—raw fish, much eaten here. **1972** Carr *Da Kine Talk* 91 **HI**, Sashimi 'raw fish', served with sauces and condiments, and *sushi* are prime favorites with Asians and Westerners. **1981** *Pidgin To Da Max* np **HI**, Sashimi. . . Raw fish. Good with shoyu and mustard and beer.

sashshay See **sashay** v

sashy See **sashay** v

saskatoon n Also *saskatoonberry, saskatoon serviceberry* [Of Algonquian orig; cf quot 1910; *DCan* 1810 →] **NW, Upper MW**

A **serviceberry**, usu *Amelanchier alnifolia*.

[**1910** Hodge *Hdbk. Amer. Indians* 2.468, Saskatoon. A name used in the Canadian N.W. for the service berry . . : probably a corruption of *misâskwatomin*, which is the name applied to the fruit in the Cree dialect of Algonquian.] **1928** Rosendahl–Butters *Trees MN* 213, *Amelanchier.* . . Saskatoon. *Ibid* 216, *Amelanchier florida* [=*A. alnifolia*]. . . Saskatoon. **1936** McDougall–Baggley *Plants of Yellowstone* 78 **nwWY**, Saskatoon (*Amelanchier alnifolia*). . . The fruit is purple when ripe and is sweet and juicy. Also called *serviceberry* [etc]. **1938** FWP *Guide MN* 282 **ceMN**, The saskatoon, which resembles the juneberry, is found here [=on Isle Royale]. **1950** Stevens *ND Plants* 174, *Amelanchier alnifolia.* . . Saskatoon. . . Common in woods, coulees or sometimes on open hillsides. **1955** U.S. Arctic Info. Center *Gloss.* 69 **AK**, Saskatoon berry. The serviceberry. **1962** Stegner *Wolf Willow* 121 **nMT**, Sunk solitary as a bear in a spider-webby, sweaty, fruit-smelling saskatoon patch in Chimney Coulee on a hot afternoon, I might have felt . . the presence of the traders. **1967–68** *DARE* [(Qu. I44, *What kinds of berries grow wild around here?*) Inf **WI**52, Juneberries are called saskatoons in Canada;] (Qu. I46, . . *Kinds of fruits that grow wild around here*) Inf **OR**6, Saskatoon—little blue berry—serviceberries. **1973** Stephens *Woody Plants* 226 **Upper MW**, *Amelanchier alnifolia.* . . Saskatoon service berry. . . The fruits of the Amelanchiers are often used for making jam, the one main objection being the numerous seeds. **1980** Little *Audubon Guide N. Amer. Trees E. Region* 459, "Saskatoon" . . *Amelanchier alnifolia.* . . The fruit of this and related species are eaten fresh, prepared in puddings, pies, and muffins, and dried like raisins and currants.

sasparilla, sasparilly See **sarsaparilla**

Sasquatch n [Salish "wild man"; *OED2* 1929 →] **Pacific NW** Cf **Bigfoot, skunk ape**

A large, hairy, man-like creature reported as living in the forests and mountains of the northwest United States and Canada.

[**1964** *Western Folkl.* 78, The Sasquatch . . became well known to Canadian whites during the nineteenth century.] **1974** *New Yorker* 25 Feb 92 **cwOR**, The Northwest's legendary Sasquatch, a huge, humanoid seven-or-so-foot creature akin to the Abominable Snowman of Tibet. **1987** *Los Angeles Times* (CA) 28 June sec 1 3/1 (Internet) **WA**, What is unusual is these 4 ½-inch footprints. . . belong to Sasquatch—also known as Big Foot. **1989** Lesley *River Song* 180 **cnOR**, "Red Shirt scared me with Sasquatch," Danny said. "Sometimes when he'd show me one of those big cornhusk bags the old Nez Perce women made, he said it was a Sasquatch bag—just the right size for children. He had a bunch of Sasquatch stories but always told one about the big ugly sisters who carried children way off into the woods and ate them." **1995** Lesley *Sky Fisherman* 208 **OR**, He was gone a few moments, then reappeared wearing an oversize hooded shaggy coat. "For Christ sakes, get the gun! It's a Sasquatch!" Sniffy's eyes widened in mock terror. **2000** *Denver Post* (CO) 24 Oct sec B 1 (Internet) **swWA**, Researchers in the Pacific Northwest believe they've obtained the first clear body imprint of a sasquatch. . . The imprint was found by a team of researchers in a mud wallow near Mount Adams in southern Washington. **2000** *DARE* File **cwCA** (as of 1960s), I remember hearing stories about Sasquatch sightings in the mountains of northern California and Oregon in the sixties.

sass See **sauce**

sassafras n Also *sassaf(r)ac, -fracks, sassifax, saxafrax, -fridge, saxifrage, -fras, -f(r)ax;* for addit varr see **A** below [Span *sassafrás* (of uncert orig). Many of the non-std forms show varying degrees of assimilation to *saxifrage*.] Cf **sass tea**

A Forms.

1622 in 1910 Smith *Travels & Wks.* 1.260 **eMA**, About three hogsheads of Beuer skins and some Saxefras. **1670** (1937) Denton *Brief Descr.* 4, The greatest part of the Island is very full of Timber, as . . Maples, Cedars, Saxifrage, Beach. **1684** [see **B1** below]. **1728** *Boston Rec.* 222 (DAE), No Popler. . . Sassifax, . . or Ceder Shall be Corded up. **1845** Judd *Margaret* 24 **NEng** (as of 18th cent), "That's saxifax," said her companion, striking his spade into the roots of a well-known shrub. **1847** Hurd *Grammatical Corrector* 89, Sassafras ["incorrect" pronc = ['sæsæfæks]; "correct" pronc = ['sæsæfæs] [sic]]. **1854** [see **B1** below]. **1860** Hundley *Social Relations S. States* 261 **S Atl**, A little "swat'ning" to put in their coffee or their "sassefack" tea. **1887** (1967) Harris *Free Joe* 223 **cGA** [Black], Ef dey hadn't er been . . so many sassyfac saplin's. **1891** *AN&Q* 7.128 **TN**, I never heard it [=sassafras tea] called Sass, but sometimes jocularly *saxifrax*, in allusion to the story of the old countrywoman who asked her guests if they would take

"Saxifrax or Sage?" **1897** Sudworth *Arborescent Flora* 202, Sassafac (W. Va.) Sassafrac (Del.) **1909** *DN* 3.366 **eAL, wGA**, *Sassafac*. . . Sassafras. **1915** *DN* 4.189 **swVA**, *Sassafac*, [sɛəsɪfæk]. **1922** Talley *Negro Folk Rhymes* 17, My ole Mosser say to me,/ Dat I mus' drink sassfac tea. **1924** Raine *Land of Saddle-Bags* 26 **sAppalachians**, Ye cross the branch and go through a patch o' saxifras. **1930** Shoemaker *1300 Words* 57 **cPA Mts** (as of c1900), *Sassafrack*. **1936** *AmSp* 11.155 **eTX**, *Sassafras* is almost universally ['sæɹɪs,fræɹɪs]. **c1938** in 1970 Hyatt *Hoodoo* 1.234 **New Orleans LA** [Black], Get you some sasafax and boil that sasafax. *Ibid* 2.1295 **New Orleans LA** [Black], I go an' get me some sasifak. **1942** Hall *Smoky Mt. Speech* 60 **wNC, eTN**, ['sæsɪfæk] 'sassafras'. **1950** *PADS* 14.77 **FL**, *Sassafracks*. **1953** Randolph–Wilson *Down in Holler* 280 **Ozarks**, *Sassafrack*. . . Sassafras. Used facetiously, or when talking with children. **c1960** *Wilson Coll.* **csKY**, *Sassafac*. . . Humorous for sassafras or sassafras tea. **1967** Williams *Greenbones* 83 (as of c1910), Some call it saxifrage or cinnamon wood, smelling-stick or ague tree. **1969** *DARE* FW Addit **CT**, *Sassafras* (tree or tea) called *sassy-ass* or *hackamatack*. **1972** Cooper *NC Mt. Folkl.* 95, *Sassafras*. **1974** Morton *Folk Remedies* 139 **SC**, *Sassafras; "satifek;" sassafrax*. **1976** Garber *Mountain-ese* 77 **sAppalachians**, *Sassafack*. **1977** *Greenfield Recorder* (MA) 12 Feb 8, [Ruby Hemenway column:] For a hot drink at dinner they had what he called "saxafridge" tea (sassafras) sometimes called "saxafrax" also. **1986** [see **B1** below]. **1993** Mason *Feather Crowns* 404 **KY**, Hit was stupid to sell sass'ras in a bottle when anybody in his right mind would just go dig up a sass'ras root and not be out a dollar for a bottle of tonic.

B Senses. Cf **swamp sassafras**

1 An aromatic tree or sometimes shrub *(Sassafras albidum)* native to much of the eastern half of the US; also the wood, bark, or root of this plant. Also called **ague tree, cinnamon wood, gumbo filé 3, hackmatack 3, mitten tree, root-beer ~, smelling-stick**

[**1577** (1925) Monardes *Joyfull Newes* (transl. Frampton) 1.99, [Title:] Of the Tree that is brought from the Florida, whiche is called Sassafras. *Ibid* 104, The name of this Tree as the Indians dooeth name it, is called Pauame, and the Frenche menne doeth call it Sassafras. . . Our Spaniardes . . doeth corrupte it, and calleth it Sassafragia.] **1602** Brereton *Discouerie VA* 12, *The finder of our Sassafras in these parts, was one Master* Robert Meriton. **1650** in 1901 Portsmouth RI *Early Rec.* 378, James Sands . . haue sould . . fortie fower acres of land . . [bounded] South west with a Sassafrax tree. **1684** in 1896 *Academy* 49.36 **Philadelphia PA**, The trees that grow here are the Mulberry, . . Chesnut, Ash, Sarsafrax. **1792** Belknap *Hist. NH* 3.97, *Sassafras (laurus sassafras)* is commonly found in moist land. It does not, in this State, grow to a large size. Its root, bark and leaves have an aromatic smell. **1854** *Spirit of Times* 4 Nov. 447/3 *(DAE)*, Presently we cum to a sassafrac bush. **1903** Fox *Little Shepherd* 19 **KY**, He came upon a cow browsing on sassafras-bushes right in the path. **1963** Owens *Look to River* 126 **TX**, They were following the brushy turnrow of a field left to lie out so long that sassafras and persimmon sprouts grew in patches waist high. **1965–70** *DARE* (Qu. BB50a, . . *Favorite remedies . . for a cough*) 32 Infs, **scattered, but least freq NEast, West**, Sassafras tea; **IL**7, Sassafras roots; (Qu. T16, . . *Kinds of trees . . 'special'*) 26 Infs, **chiefly Midl, N Cent**, Sassafras (bush *or* tree); (Qu. H82b, *Kinds of cheap candy that used to be sold years ago*) Infs **NY**230, **SC**29, Sassafras; **IN**48, **OH**52, Sassafras sticks; **NY**230, Sassafrat [sic] root; (Qu. I35, . . *Kitchen herbs . . grown and used in cooking around here*) Infs **CA**205, **CT**2, **LA**33, **MS**1, **PA**245, Sassafras; **PA**150, Sassafras tea; (Qu. S26e, *Other wildflowers not yet mentioned;* not asked in early QRs) Inf **GA**80, Sassafras; **OH**82, Sassafras roots; (Qu. T13) Inf **CT**31, Sassafras, also called sassy-ass; (Qu. T15, . . *Kinds of swamp trees*) Infs **DE**5, **NJ**66, **PA**126, **RI**15, Sassafras; (Qu. BB22, . . *Home remedies . . for constipation*) Inf **CA**188, Sassafras; **IL**9, 25, **MI**50, **VA**5, Sassafras tea; **GA**77, Sassafras-root tea; (Qu. BB50b, *Remedies for chest colds*) Inf **OK**31, Sassafras; **FL**51, **SC**55, **WA**9, Sassafras tea; (Qu. BB50c, *Remedies for infections*) Infs **AL**27, **OK**31, Sassafras; **AL**27, **IL**11, **MD**50, **SC**3, **WA**6, Sassafras tea; (Qu. DD3b, *How . . people take snuff*) Inf **KY**65, Put in cheek with sassafras twig that has frayed end. **1966–70** *DARE* Tape **AL**1, We had tea, made out roots you got out of the field. . . ['sæsɪfæk] root; **KY**34, They'd gather pennyroyal, willow, and ['sæsəfæk], and ['sæsə,fæs] wood. . . And that cured your meat. . . If you didn't put any ['sæsə,fræs], why, you got a hickory taste to your meat; **TX**89, They have pine and they have gum and they have oak . . and they have sassafras. **1982** *Greenfield Recorder* (MA) 2 Jan sec A 4/3, Sassafras bush. It is easily recognized by its mitten-shaped leaves. **1986** Pederson

LAGS Concordance **Gulf Region**, 279 infs, Sassafras; 67 infs, Sassafras tea; 60 infs, Sassafras root(s); 15 infs, Sassafras tree(s); 2 infs, Sassafras sprouts; 1 inf, Sassafras bushes; 1 inf, Sassafras leaf; 1 inf, Sassafras root; 1 inf, Sassafras worms; 1 inf, Sassa[fras] tree.

2 as *California(n) sassafras:* =**California laurel**. Cf **sassafras laurel**

1897 Sudworth *Arborescent Flora* 203, *Umbellularia californica*. . . Californian Sassafras. **1911** *Century Dict. Suppl., Sassafras*. . . *California sassafras*, the California laurel, *Umbellularia Californica*.

sassafras laurel n
=**California laurel**.

1859 Emory *Rept. U.S. Mex. Boundary* 190 **CA**, *Oreodaphne Californica*. . . In various parts of California, especially mountainous districts. . . Besides the popular names of the plant mentioned in the report here quoted, it is also called Sassafras-Laurel, Cajeput Tree and California Olive. **1906** (1918) Parsons *Wild Flowers CA* 379, This tree [= *Umbellularia californica*] is known in different localities by a variety of names, such as . . "sassafras laurel."

sassafras sprout n Cf *DS* HH1

1995 *Brophy Coll.* 65 **swMO** (as of c1960), *Sassafras sprout.* [A] hillbilly child.

sassafrilla See **sarsaparilla**

sassage See **sausage**

sassanger See **sassinger**

sassaparilla See **sarsaparilla**

sass-box n Also *sass-bucket*, *~-pot*, *sassy-box* **widespread exc NEng** See Map Cf **saucebox**
An impudent person, esp a child.

1871 Eggleston *Hoosier Schoolmaster* 99 **IN**, Yes, I war too, you little sass-box! What did I take you fer? Hey? **1907** *DN* 3.198 **seNH**, *Sàss-box* [*DARE* Ed: =[sas]]. . . A saucy or pert woman or child. **1919** *DN* 5.65 **NM**, *Sass-box*, an impudent person. "Mary has become a little sass-box." **1937** (1963) Hyatt *Kiverlid* 67 **KY**, I'll let pappy take you down a few notches fer bein' a sass-box. **1965–70** *DARE* (Qu. II36a, *Somebody who talks back or gives rude answers: "Did you ever see such a _____?"*) 51 Infs, **widespread exc NEng**, Sass-box; **AK**5, **CA**169, **MN**15, Sass-pot; **IL**5, Sass-bucket; **AL**33, Sassy-box.

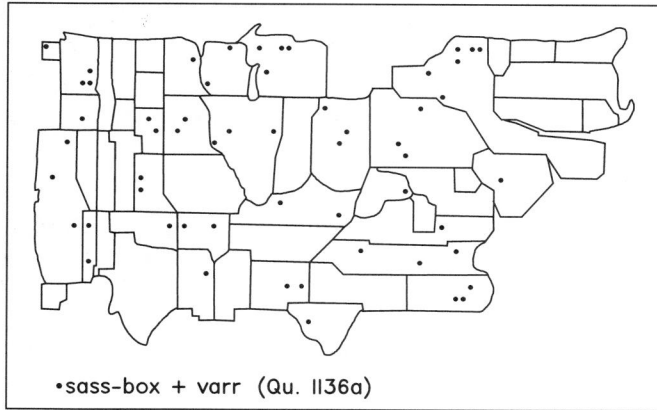

•sass-box + varr (Qu. II36a)

sassenger See **sassinger**

sasser See **saucer**

sassfac See **sassafras**

sass hole n
A place to store **sauce B1**.

1906 Casey *Parson's Boys* 214 **sIL** (as of c1860), The Parson prepared half a dozen "sass-holes" about the garden, in which were stored plentiful supplies of cabbage, beets, turnips, potatoes and other vegetables. **1917** in 1944 *ADD* **sWV**, Sass hole. . . Go to the sass hole & get some taters. **1975** *Appalachian Jrl.* 2.155 **wNC**, Women would dry apple slices and beans and store them in the loft of the house or in the *sass hole*, also known as the *root cellar* or *can house;* and they would be ready for use during the winter.

sassidge See **sausage**

sassifax See **sassafras**

sassige See **sausage**

sassinger n Also *sassanger, sassenger, sausenger, sausinger*
[Cf *EDD sausinger*] Cf **sausage**

A sausage.

1844 Thompson *Major Jones's Courtship* 74 **GA,** I haint seed nothin but hogs . . for more'n a week, and I know I haint eat nothin but backbone and turnips, and spare-ribs, and sassingers, and cracklin-bread. *Ibid* 141, In come Pete with his . . lips stickin out like a link of green sassengers. **1851** Burke *Polly Peablossom* 70 **MS,** All sorts of good things—bacon, an' possum fat, an' ash cake, an' a great big sausenger, 'bout as big as your arm. **1859** *Unsworth's Burnt Cork Lyrics* 20, Her market stall, where she sold fresh tripe, and sassangers, likewise liver. **1862** (1864) Browne *Artemus Ward Book* 184, Go home. . . go to bilin' sope—stuff sassengers. **1894** *Century Illustr. Mag.* 48.869 **swIN,** No types can express, however, the long-drawn flatness of the accented vowel in apast, yander, and paster, or for that matter in "pasnips" for parsnips, in "passell" for parcel, in "sassers" for saucers, and in "sassingers" for sausages. **1899** (1912) Green *VA Folk-Speech* 366, *Sassinger.* . . Sausage. **1899** Garland *Boy Life* 222 **nwIA,** He could return to breakfast, which consisted of home-made sausages ("snassingers [sic]," the boys called them) and buckwheat pancakes. **1916** *DN* 4.305, *Sassinger.* . . Sausage: used without facetiousness in Dover, N.H., some generations ago. **1927** *AmSp* 2.363 **cwWV,** We had buckwheat and sassengers for breakfast. **1941** *LANE* Map 304 *(Sausage),* Sausingers in various pronunciations, are natural to some informants, but are usually regarded as old-fashioned or reported as having been current in earlier days. [29 infs, **CT, MA, ME, NH,** offered proncs of the type [sæsɪndʒə, sɔsɪndʒɹ, sɑsndʒə].]

sassparilla See **sarsaparilla**

sass-pot See **sass-box**

sass'ras See **sassafras**

sass tea n [Abbr for **sassafras B1**] chiefly **Sth, S Midl**

1847 (1962) Robb *Squatter Life* 72 **MO,** In the morning Hoss Allen became "dreadful poorly," . . the matron of the house boiled him some hot "sass-tea," which, the old man said, relieved him mightily. **1872** Schele de Vere *Americanisms* 395 **Sth** (as of c1860), The question "Will you have a cup of tea?" was very apt to elicit the counter-question, "What kind of tea have you got? sage- or sass- or store-tea?" **1891** *AN&Q* 7.67, Sassafras bark or leaves, largely used in the Southern States by poor people, who prepare from it what is called *sass tea.* **1981** Pederson *LAGS Basic Materials,* 1 inf, **cnLA,** ['sæˀ ˌti>ɨ] (sassafras tea). **1982** Parris *Here's How (Montgomery Coll.)* **wNC, eTN,** Sassafras tea is "sass" tea.

sassy v

To speak impudently to.

1883 (1971) Harris *Nights with Remus* 366 **GA** [Black], Dar 'uz Mr. Hawk sailin' 'roun' an' 'roun'. Time he see 'im, Brer Rabbit 'gun ter kick up an' sassy 'im. **1909** *DN* 3.365 **eAL, wGA,** Don't you come sassying me. *Ibid* 366, *Sassy.* . . To talk saucily to.

sassy-box See **sass-box**

sassy jack n

A **spurge** (here: *Euphorbia lathyris*).

1942 *Torreya* 42.162 **VA,** *Euphorbia lathyris.* . . Sassy Jack, mountains of Virginia.

sassyparilla, sassyperiller See **sarsaparilla**

sat See **set** v[1] **A2b**

satchel See **satchel foot**

satchel-ass n, also attrib

A fat person.

1968 *DARE* (Qu. X50, *Names or nicknames for a person who is very fat*) Inf **WI12,** Satchel-ass. **1984** Doig *English Creek* 246 **nMT,** "You satchel-ass old son of a frigging goddamn"—Wisdom's was a rendition I have always wished I'd had time to commit to memory.

satchelbill n

The California brown pelican *(Pelecanus occidentalis).*

1946 Peattie *Pacific Coast* 99, California brown pelicans. . . can be observed closely . . along the coast. . . Satchelbills they are often called, and [they have] huge bills, with great pouches below.

satchel foot n Also *satchel*

A large foot; also *satchel feet:* a person with large feet; hence adj *satchel-footed* having large feet.

1934 (1940) Weseen *Dict. Amer. Slang* 241, *Satchel feet.* . . A heavyweight prizefighter. **1946** *Richmond Times–Dispatch* (VA) 9 Dec 11/5 *(Hench Coll.),* "Satchel-foot" Carrera. . . is gunning for the world's heavyweight wrestling championship. **1949** *Daily Progress* (Charlottesville VA) 15 Oct 3/3, It has been some years since Murray had to wear out his own dancing pumps steering satchel-footed pupils around the floor. **1969–70** *DARE* (Qu. X38, *Joking names for unusually big or clumsy feet)* Inf **WA20,** Satchel foot; **CA107, MD15, NY127,** Satchels; **CA65, DC6,** Satchel; **CT30,** Satchels—not here [resp to FW sugg].

satchel mouth n

1 =**goosefish**.

1906 NJ State Museum *Annual Rept. for 1905* 425, *Lophius piscatorius.* . . Bellows Fish. All Mouth. . . Satchel Mouth. [*Ibid* 426, This large fish is abundant on our coast and is. . . noted for its great voracity and exceptional ugliness of appearance.]

2 See quot 1934.

1934 *AmSp* 9.288 **PA** [Black student slang], *Satchel-mouth.* A person with an unusually large mouth. **1969** in 1999 Armstrong *Louis Armstrong* 21, New Orleans always was a town where Nick Names Originates. Even in my young days I accumulated several Nick Names. . . Satchelmouth—like a Dr's valise. In fact that's how the name *Satchmo* was Originated.

Sat'd'y See **Saturday**

saterfaction, saterfy, satifaction, satify See **satisfy**

Satiddy See **Saturday**

satin bell(s) n

A **mariposa lily** (here: *Calochortus albus*).

1897 Parsons *Wild Flowers CA* 54, *Calochortus albus.* . . They have received a variety of common names in different localities, being known as . . "satin-bell," . . and "white globe-tulip." **1920** Rice–Rice *Pop. Studies CA Wild Flowers* 28, This lovely little flower [=*Calochortus albus*] is also called the "Satin Bell" . . but . . is not bell shaped. The tips of its petals are prettily crossed. **1923** in 1925 Jepson *Manual Plants CA* 238, [*Calochortus albus:]* Also called Snow-drops, Indian Bells, and Satin Bells.

satin curls n [See quot 1955]

A **virgin's bower** (here: *Clematis catesbyana*).

1933 Small *Manual SE Flora* 525, *C[lematis] catesbyana.* . . Satin-curls. . . Fla. to La. and S.C. **1949** Moldenke *Amer. Wild Flowers* 7, Sandy woods on the coastal plain . . are the habitat of the *satincurls, C. catesbyana.* **1955** *S. Folkl. Qrly.* 19.232, Satin Curls (Clematis Catesbyana) is a vine named for the long plumose style.

satinfin shiner n Also *satinfin minnow*

A **shiner 1** (here: either *Cyprinella analostana* or *C. spiloptera*).

1918 *Copeia* 53.11, The . . so-called swift gravelly group begins with the small mouth bass followed by the satin-fin minnow. **1947** Hubbs-Lagler *Fishes Gt. Lakes* 67, Satinfin Shiner—*Notropis analostanus.* . . Chiefly frequenting creeks and reservoirs. **1983** Becker *Fishes WI* 549, *Notropis spilopterus.* . . Satinfin minnow. . . Living fin silvery, underlaid with a bluish cast on back and sides. **1983** *Audubon Field Guide N. Amer. Fishes* 432, *Notropis analostanus.* . . The Satinfin Shiner breeds from May to August. Spawning males defend their territory against other males.

satinflower n

1 A **chickweed 1a** (here: *Stellaria media*). [*OED2* 1854]

1876 Hobbs *Bot. Hdbk.* 103, Satin flower, Chickweed, Stellaria media. **1973** *Foxfire 2* 70 **sAppalachians,** Chickweed *(Stellaria media)* . . satinflower. **1999** *DARE* File—Internet [Green Tree Nutrition], The scientific name for chickweed is Stellaria media. . . Other common names include mouse-ear, Adder's mouth, satin flower [etc].

2 =**fringed polygala.**

1940 Clute *Amer. Plant Names* 124, *P[olygala] pauciflora.* . . Satinflower. **1959** [see **3** below].

3 A **farewell-to-spring,** usu *Clarkia amoena.*
1959 Carleton *Index Herb. Plants* 103, *Satin-flower:* Godetia (v); . . Polygala pauciflora; . . Stellaria media. **1968** *DARE* (Qu. S26e, *Other wildflowers not yet mentioned;* not asked in early QRs) Inf **CA97,** Three or four species of *Godetia* [=*Clarkia*], especially *amoena,* which is put in gardens and called satin flower. **1999** (acc) ID Univ. *Plant Viruses Online* (Internet), *Clarkia amoena* (syn. *Godetia amoena*) Satin flower.

satin grass n *West*
Any of several **muhly (grasses);** see quots.
1923 Abrams *Flora Pacific States* 1.139, *Muhlenbergia racemosa.* . . Wild Timothy, Satin-grass. . . Moist meadows and low ground. **1930** OK Univ. *Biol. Surv. Pub.* 2.51, *Muhlenbergia tenuiflora.* . . Slender Satin-grass. **1940** Gates *Flora KS* 131, *Muhlenbergia mexicana.* . . Satin Grass, Wirestem Muhly. Wet meadows, thickets and waste places. **1961** Peck *Manual OR* 128, *M. racemosa.* . . *Satin Grass.* . . Cascade Mts., to B.C., Calif. and across the continent. **1968** Barkley *Plants KS* 52, Muhlenbergia frondosa. . . Satin grass. **1973** Hitchcock–Cronquist *Flora Pacific NW* 651, Satin-grass. . . *M[uhlenbergia] racemosa.*

satinleaf n [See quot 1946]
A tree *(Chrysophyllum oliviforme)* native to southern Florida.
1896 U.S. Dept. Ag. *Yearbook for 1895* 172, The satin leaf (*Chrysophyllum oliviforme*), probably having the most beautiful foliage of any native tree of Florida, was frozen down about Rockledge, its northern limit. **1946** West–Arnold *Native Trees FL* 176, *Satinleaf.* . . *Leaves* . . dark green and shining above, covered with satin-like rust-colored down beneath. . . In a breeze it turns to a mass of shimmering golden brown, as the lower sides of the leaves are exposed. **1971** Craighead *Trees S. FL* 152, The more common trees in the pine stands are Dade County pine, rough leaf, . . blolly, . . satinleaf [etc.].

satintail n [Perh from the silky panicle]
A grass *(Imperata brevifolia)* native to much of the southwestern US.
1950 Hitchcock–Chase *Manual Grasses* 737, *Imperata brevifolia.* . . *Satintail.* . . Desert regions, western Texas to southern California, Utah, and Nevada. **1959** Munz–Keck *CA Flora* 1549, *Satintail.* . . Panicle somewhat tawny or pinkish, soft-silky. **1970** Correll *Plants TX* 189, *Satintail.* Perennial with short hard scaly rhizomes.

satinwood n
A **prickly ash 1,** usu *Zanthoxylum flavum,* native to Florida; esp the wood of such a tree.
1792 Imlay *Western Terr.* 214 **KY,** Satin-wood tree—Not classed. **1827** Williams *View W. FL* 99, Sattin Wood.—It does not grow large, but makes beautiful furniture. **1884** Sargent *Forests of N. Amer.* 30, *Xanthoxylum Caribæum.* . . Satin Wood. Semi-tropical Florida. . . A small tree, 6 to 10 meters in height. **1897** Sudworth *Arborescent Flora* 266 **FL,** *Xanthoxylum cribrosum.* . . Satinwood. **1933** *Small Manual SE Flora* 757, *Z[anthoxylum] flavum.* . . Satin-wood. The heart-wood, exceedingly hard and heavy, is orange-colored. **1962** Harrar–Harrar *Guide S. Trees* 394, Satinwood—*Zanthoxylum flavum.* [*Ibid* 395, This species produces a hard, rich, golden-yellow, highly figured wood that at present is not infrequently used in American cabinet shops for the fabrication of modern furniture.] **1986** Pederson *LAGS Concordance,* 1 inf, **ceFL,** Satinwood—tree.

satisfactory adj Also *satisfactch'll, satisfactional, satisfactionary, satisfactionate, satisfactual, sattafactual*
Std sense, var forms.
1845 *Amer. Whig Rev.* 2.545, "The Two Camps" is much finer—more "consistive and satisfactional," as the clown says in the Old Play. **1883** *Century Illustr. Mag.* 26.186 **nGA,** I'm willin' to extracise my bes' judgment. It mayn't be satisfactual, but me and Sis is mighty long-headed when we pulls together. **1891** *PMLA* 6.167 **WV,** *Satisfactual* is a vulgarism for satisfactory. **1903** *DN* 2.328 **seMO,** *Satisfactional.* . . Satisfactory. **1916** *DN* 4.281 **NE,** *Satisfactionary.* . . Satisfactory. **1927** Kennedy *Gritny* 213 **sLA** [Black], Felo came in from the kitchen, smiling, wanting to know if everything wasn't "sattafactual." **1946** Wrubel–Gilbert *Zip-A-Dee-Doo-Dah* 2, [Song lyrics:] It's the truth, it's "act-ch'll,"/ Ev-'ry-thing is "sa-tis-fact-ch'll." **1972** Cooper *NC Mt. Folkl.* 95, *Satisfactionate* . . satisfactory.

satisfy v, hence ppl adj *satisfied* Pronc-spp *satify, sattafy, sat(t)erfy* Similarly nouns *saterfaction, satifaction, sattafaction, sattifackshun* Cf *sattafactual* (at **satisfactory**)

Std senses, var forms. **Sth, S Midl** *esp freq among Black speakers*
1884 Murfree *TN Mts.* 280, He war sati'fied that Caleb never gin his wife nuthin' ter hurt. **1888** Jones *Negro Myths* 51 **GA coast,** Eh gone eenside an fassen up de do, an mek ehself saterfy. *Ibid* 92, Buh Rabbit fine eh cant git no saterfaction outer Buh Elephunt. **1892** (1969) Christensen *Afro-Amer. Folk Lore* 39 **seSC,** But 'e fader aint sati'fy yet. **1906** Johnson *Highways Missip. Valley* 93 **TN** [Black], De hoodoo doctor he listen an' lif' his eyebrows; but he 'pear not to be sati'fied yit. **1917** *DN* 4.416 **wNC,** Satify, satifaction. **1922** Gonzales *Black Border* 324 **sSC, GA coasts** [Gullah glossary], Sattifackshun—satisfaction. **1927** Kennedy *Gritny* 18 **sLA** [Black], She ain' sattafy havin' seven head o' chillun to wait on her. *Ibid* 23, You kin eat 'fo de fire to yo' sattafaction. **1929** Sale *Tree Named John* 34 **MS** [Black], He . . got mo' uv eve'thing 'n whut anybody ilse is got en ain' satterfied.

Sattady See **Saturday**

sattafactual See **satisfactory**

sattafy, satterfy, sattifackshun See **satisfy**

Saturday n Usu |'sætə(r),dɪ, -dɪ|; also |'særdɪ, 'sædɪ|; for addit varr see quots Pronc-spp *Sadaday, Sad(d)ay, Saddy, Sarady, Sat'd'y, Satiddy, Sattaday, Sattyday*
Std sense, var forms.
1847 Hurd *Grammatical Corrector* 89, Saturday ["incorrect" pronc = ['sɑtedi] [sic]; "correct" pronc = ['sætə-de]]. **1890** *DN* 1.69 **KY,** Sad'day. **1893** Shands *MS Speech* 54, Saddy [sædɪ]. Illiterate white and negro for Saturday. **1899** (1912) Green *VA Folk-Speech* 363, Sadday. **1909** *DN* 3.365 **eAL, wGA,** Sadday. . . Saturday. Very common. *Ibid* 403 **nwAR,** Sad'day. . . Saturday. **1922** Gonzales *Black Border* 324 **sSC, GA coasts** [Gullah glossary], Sat'd'y, Sattyday—Saturday. **1937** *Natl. Geogr. Mag.* 71.271 **MS,** "Sadaday" night is traditional "darkey night" up-State. **c1937** in 1976 *Weevils in the Wheat* 89 **VA** [Black], Slaves always wanted to marry a gal on 'nother plantation cause dey could git a pass to go visit 'em on Saddy nights. *Ibid* 252, She had jus' made 'em for de quiltin' spree which was to be held Saday night. **1939** *LANE* Map 70 (*Saturday*) **NEng,** The pronunciation varies greatly with the care and speed of utterance. In rapid speech (especially in phrases like *Saturday morning, Saturday night*) the dissyllabic form, with syncope of the second syllable, is common [*DARE* Ed: e.g., ['særdi, 'sætdi, sæˀʔdɪ]]; but in view of several comments characterizing this 'fast form' as older or old-fashioned, it appears to be losing ground. Pronunciations with a vowel or diphthong of the type [e, eɪ] in the final syllable are usually to be associated with slow, careful or emphatic utterance. . . Pronunciations with some variety of [a, ɑ] in the first syllable are regarded as older or old-fashioned but still in use by . . [7 **NH** and 10 **ME** infs]. Dissyllabic pronunciations are regarded as older though still in use by . . [2 **CT,** 4 **MA,** 3 **VT,** 2 **NH,** and 3 **ME** infs]. **1940** Faulkner *Hamlet* 18 **MS,** So it come Sat-dy and the wagon druv up to the store. **1947** Ballowe *The Lawd* 119 **LA** [Black], Scott Gardner givin' a big to-do on Happy Dream, come Sadd'y. **1948** Manfred *Chokecherry* 74 **nwIA,** What's wrong with those you wore Satiddy night? **1958** Humphrey *Home from the Hill* 7 **neTX,** Still sleeping off their Saddy night Sweet Lucy. **1966** *DARE* Tape **SC10,** Saturday ['sæ·ɐtde]. **1967–69** *DARE* FW Addit **seAR,** Saturday ['sæ·dɪ]; **MA68,** Saturday [sæˀʔdi]; **NY70,** Saturday ['sædɪ]. **1968** *DARE* (Qu. W24a) Inf **VA18,** ['sæədeɪ]. **1984** Burns *Cold Sassy* 152 **nGA** (as of 1906), Son, what's today? Sarady? **1989** Pederson *LAGS Tech. Index* 16 **Gulf Region,** [480 Infs gave proncs of the type ['sætɚdɪ]; 138 infs, ['sædɚdɪ]; 85 infs, ['særdɪ, særde]; 51 infs, ['sætɚde]; 4 infs, [sɛrdɪ]; 1 inf, ['sɪdɪ]; addit minor pronc varr also appear.] **1990** Smith *Understanding Speaking S. Lang.* 7, Sattady—Day before Sunday. **2000** *DARE* File **wPA,** I can do it if it's on Saturday ['sæɚdɪ].

Saturday is longer than Sunday See **Monday comes before Sunday**

Saturday night special n Also *Saturday night knife* [Cf *Saturday night special* a cheap, small handgun] Cf **nigger killer 3**
A large folding knife or switchblade.
1958 Humphrey *Home from the Hill* 62 **neTX,** It was five inches long, closed—a nigger knife, the kind they call a Saturday Night Special, one of those in the shape of a woman's leg in a high-heeled shoe, with a push-button to spring the blade. **1967** *DARE* (Qu. F39, *A large pocket knife with blades that fold in and out*) Inf **TX38,** Saturday night knife—the Negroes say.

satyr orchid n

A **rein orchid** (here: *Coeloglossum viride*).

1950 Correll *Native Orchids* 114, *Habenaria viridis* . . var. *bracteata* [=*Coeloglossum viride*]. . . Satyr Orchid. . . Lip narrowly oblong-spatulate. . . Spur scrotiform. **1952** Strausbaugh–Core *Flora WV* 260, *H[abenaria] viridis*. . . Satyr orchid. . . Shenandoah Mountain.

satyr's beard n

A hedgehog **mushroom B1** (here: *Hericium erinaceus*).

1980 Marteka *Mushrooms* 96, All of these white mushrooms (*Hericium*) are edible. . . One, the satyr's beard, truly looks like a white beard. **1981** Lincoff *Audubon Field Guide Mushrooms* 430, *Hericium erinaceus*. . . Also called . . the "Satyr's Beard," . . it is only a choice edible when young and very fresh, because it turns sour with age.

sauce n

Usu |sɔs|; also **chiefly Inland Nth, N Cent, West** |sɑs|; also **chiefly Sth, S Midl** |sɔus, sɑus|; for addit varr see **A** below Pronc-spp *sairse, saisse, sarce, sarse, sas(s)* Note: The var *sass* |sæs| appears to be esp freq in the senses entered at **B** below, and in the widespread fig sense "impudence, back talk," which is now thought of as a separate word by many speakers.

A Forms.

1771 in 1956 Eliason *Tarheel Talk* 317 **c,cnNC,** *Sauce pan*—saspan. **1801** *Spirit Farmers' Museum* 235 **NH,** Set the cups, and beaker glass,/ The pumpkin, and the apple sauce. **1815** Humphreys *Yankey in England* 41, Long sairse and short sairse; consisting of a variety of leetle notions too tedious to mention. *Ibid* 108, *Saisse,* or *sairse,* sauce. **1834** Davis *Letters Downing* 211 **NEng,** Sass for the goose ought to be sass for the gander too. **1837** (1955) *Crockett Almanacks* 91 **wTN,** Greatest chaps in creation for brag and sarce. **1844** Stephens *High Life in NY* xi, *Sarce.* Sauce. **1848** Lowell *Biglow* 145 **'Upcountry' MA,** Sarse, *abuse, impertinence.* **1892** *DN* 1.231 **KY,** *Sass:* sauce (impertinence). **1896** *DN* 1.423 **seMI, cNY,** *Sass:* small talk, empty talk. **1905** *DN* 3.18 **cCT,** *Sass.* . . Sauce. *Ibid* 65 **eNE,** *Sass.* . . Impertinence. **1928** *AmSp* 3.404 **Ozarks** (as of 1916–27), *Sauce* . . becomes *sass.* **1960** Carpenter *Tales Manchaca* 138 **cTX,** Thereafter my husband rarely fretted me with male sass. **c1960** *Wilson Coll.* **csKY,** *Apple-sass.* . . Rarely heard now. **1965–70** *DARE* (Qu. H66a, *The sweet liquid that you pour over a pudding*) 419 Infs, **widespread,** [sɔs, sɒs]; 78 Infs, **chiefly Inland Nth, N Cent, West** [sɑs]; 66 Infs, **scattered,** [sɔɒs, sɒɑs, sɔɪs]; 62 Infs, **chiefly Sth, S Midl,** [sɔus, saus, sɑus, sɒus, sɒus]; **CA1, IN1, WV3, 8, 12,** [sɑəs]; **VA23,** [sɔɒs]; **UT4,** [saz]; **TX38,** [sɑɔɒs]; **NC18,** [sɔz]; **NJ69,** [sɔɒs]; **MS72,** [sɔlts].

B Senses.

1 Vegetables, esp garden vegetables. [Engl dial] **chiefly NEng, Sth, S Midl** See also **garden sauce, long ~, short ~**

1775 in 1912 Essex Inst. *Coll.* 48.43 **MA,** Steven Barker come down & brought us som sas. **1814** in 1947 *AmSp* 22.274 **NH,** Sauce for roots & vegetables. **1816** in 1824 Knight *Letters* 29 **Philadelphia PA,** They say . . sauce for vegetables. **1825** Neal *Brother Jonathan* 1.72 **CT,** Sweet corn, pumpkin pies, and *sarse* (vegetables). **1836** (1861) Tucker *Partisan Leader* 2.124 **VA,** The fellow talked to me about living at home on codfish, and potatoes, and cider, and pies, and *all sorts of sass.* **1843** (1916) Hall *New Purchase* 155 **IN,** But who can tell of the "sasses?" for we had [ˠ]biled petaturs!"—and "smashed petaturs!"—and "petatursis!" **1899** (1912) Green *VA Folk-Speech* 365, *Sass.* . . Vegetables, particularly those used in making sauces: as garden *sass.* Same as *sauce.* **1909** *DN* 3.365 **eAL, wGA,** *Sass.* . . Sauce: chiefly in *garden-sass.* **1915** *DN* 4.189 **swVA,** *Sass.* . . Vegetables for the table. **1937** (1963) Hyatt *Kiverlid* 79 **KY,** I like this wild sass . . rather'n I do the gyarden sass. **1939** *LANE* Map 121 (*Vegetable garden*) 1 inf, **seMA,** Sauce yard; 1 inf, **ceMA,** Sauce hole. **1941** *Ibid* Map 253 (*Garden vegetables*) 1 inf, **seMA,** [soˇ·s]—Mother used to call 'em *sauce*; 1 inf, **csRI,** A mess of green sauce [sɒəs]. **1952** Brown *NC Folkl.* 1.587, *Sass.* . . Shortened form of *garden sass*; garden vegetables.—General. **1954** Forbes *Rainbow* 129 **NH,** But by then it was our table's turn to be fed the salt cod, sass and gingerbread. **c1960** *Wilson Coll.* **csKY,** *Sass.* . . Garden vegetables. **1966** Dakin *Dial. Vocab. Ohio R. Valley* 2.352, *Vegetables.* . . *Garden sass* (in the Mountains simply *sass*). **1969** *DARE* FW Addit **KY5,** Sass—same as salats or salad or greens. Old-fashioned. **1973** Allen *LAUM* 1.302, *Homegrown vegetables.* . . sass [2 infs, **IA, NE**]. **1982** Slone *How We Talked* 30 **eKY** (as of c1950), *Sass*—all the food put away for winter, except meat and corn. **1986** Pederson *LAGS Concordance* (*Vegetables*) 2 infs, **GA,** Sass; (*Greens*) 2 infs, **AL, TN,** Sass. **1991** Still *Wolfpen Notebooks* 20 **sAppalachians,** I had a garden full of sass—sweet corn, beans, squash, okra, cushaw, tomatoes, cucumbers and cabbage.

2 Stewed or preserved fruit served as a condiment or as dessert; fresh berries served as dessert—also in comb *orchard sass.* Note: Combs such as *applesauce, cranberry sauce,* or *rhubarb sauce* are regarded as std and not included here. **chiefly Nth**

1844 Thompson *Major Jones's Courtship* 64 **GA,** Peach sas, made out of the large English white reserve peaches. **1894** *DN* 1.342 **wCT,** *Sass* [sæs]: stewed or preserved fruit. **1910** *DN* 3.447 **wNY,** *Sauce.* . . Stewed fruit. "Let's have some pear sauce for supper." **1948** *WELS Suppl.* **csWI,** Apple sauce was "sauce" to me, while any canned fruit was "sauce" to him. **1949** in 1986 *DARE* File **WI,** "We'll have peach sauce for dessert." Sauce is used to signified [sic] that the fruit is canned, or to distinguish it from fresh fruit. **1950** *WELS Suppl.* **cWI,** *Sauce*—Peaches, pears, berries—any kind of fruit in a sweet syrup. **1954** *Ibid* **cwWI,** A native of Indiana said, "You people here in Wisconsin call canned fruit 'sauce.' Never heard it called that in Indiana." **1957** *Sat. Eve. Post Letters* **MI,** *Sauce*—any cooked fruit. **c1960** *Wilson Coll.* **csKY,** *Sass.* . . Apple sass. **1966** *AmSp* 41.74 **nIL,** "*Sauce*". . . My informant invited me to eat in his Ogle County farmhouse. After a good lunch, he asked me if I would like some sauce for dessert. . . I was greatly surprised . . to be served a dish of home-canned peaches. . . For "A Dish of Fruit Eaten at the End of the Meal". . . this meaning for *sauce.* . . cluster[s] . . in the upper Midwest. . . Some people made a further distinction. Some indicated that *sauce* referred only to home canned fruit. Some included commercially canned fruit in their definition. Some included fresh fruit when peeled, sliced, and served in a dish. **1967** *Weston Chron.* (MO) 8 Sept 4/6, Mrs. Burns has fourteen varieties of garden and orchard "sass" in the cellar. **1967** *DARE* File **MA** (as of c1915), *Sauce* = fruit served as dessert. . . My grandmother's generation (but not my mother's) put up all available fruit in summer so there was a wide choice of sauces in the cellar. "What kind of sauce shall I bring up?" one might call up the cellar stairs. . . We meant home-canned fruit. A bowl of fresh raspberries . . *might* be sauce, i.e. it was served as supper dessert. **1968** *Harmony News* (MN) 11 Jan 2/6, Tuesday: Rice-hamburger hot dish, carrot and celery sticks, cinnamon bread, peach sauce and milk. **1975** Gould *ME Lingo* 241, *Sauce*—Almost unknown in Maine as the word for gravy, *sauce* is rather the term for dessert. Preserved pears, peaches, and berries will be served in a *sauce dish.* **1998** *DARE* File, Our Minnesota family called all such mashed or cooked fruit desserts "sauce"—raspberry sauce, peach sauce, cranberry sauce, apple sauce. . . But when I use such terms down here in Ohio, people seem puzzled, apparently thinking of 'sauce' only as a topping for meats or fish.

saucebox n [*OED2* 1588 →] **chiefly NEast** See Map Cf **box** n **5a**

=**sass-box.**

1800 (1980) Brown *Arthur Mervyn* 383 **Baltimore MD,** "Run with my compliments to him, wench. Tell him, please walk up." "It is not Mr. Somers, ma'am." "No! Who then, saucebox?" **1902** (1904) Rowe *Maid of Bar Harbor* 55 **ME,** You sauce box! **1965–70** *DARE* (Qu. II36a, *Somebody who talks back or gives rude answers: "Did you ever see such a _____?"*) Infs **CT39, IA34, MI45, MA5, NY22, 105, PA19, 105, 118,** Saucebox. [8 of 9 Infs old, all female] **1975** *DARE* File **cnMA** (as of c1915), I was called a little sauce-box, as I recall, rather frequently.

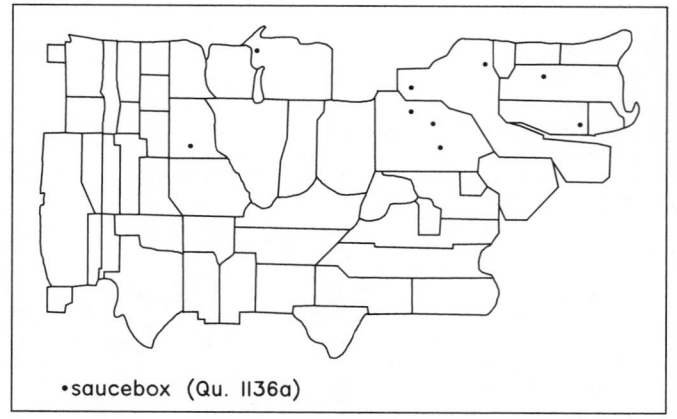

•saucebox (Qu. II36a)

saucedish n **chiefly Nth, N Midl, West** See Map

A small, shallow bowl for serving **sauce B2** or other food.

1861 in 1903 Norton *Army Letters* 12 **PA**, A boy would . . turn out a beautiful salt-cellar . . a sauce-dish, or whatever the mold happened to be. **1895** (1969) Montgomery Ward *Catalogue* 540, *The Vigilant Glass Assortment.* . . one 8-inch berry dish, six small sauce dishes. **1927** (1970) Sears *Catalogue* 927, *7-Piece Footed Iridescent Berry Set.* . . The set consists of one 8-inch footed berry bowl and six 4 ¾-inch sauce dishes. **1965–70** *DARE* (Qu. G6, . . *Dishes that you might have on the table for a big dinner or special occasion—for example, Thanksgiving*) 29 Infs, **chiefly Nth, N Midl, West,** Saucedish(es). [25 of 29 Infs old, none young] **1969** *DARE* FW Addit **cwNY,** *Sauce* (served in *sauce-dishes*)—canned (as in put up) fruit poured on bread and butter. **1975** Gould *ME Lingo* 241, *Sauce.* . . is . . the term for dessert. Preserved pears, peaches, and berries will be served in a *sauce dish.* **2000** *DARE* File **ID** (as of c1960), My grandparents had saucedishes that were the shape of a pear. They served canned fruit, applesauce, or (if we were lucky) ice cream in them.

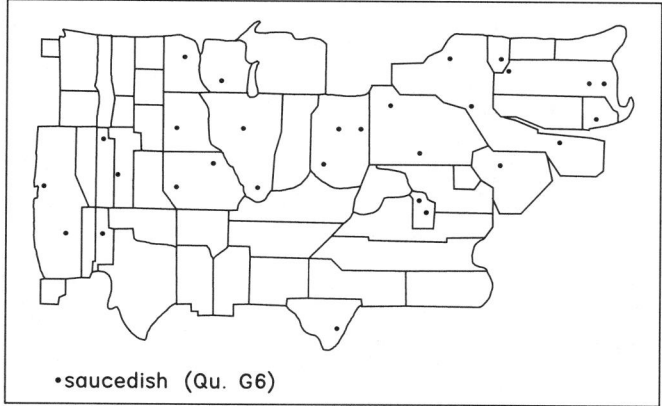

•saucedish (Qu. G6)

saucer n, v Usu |ˈsɔsə(r)|; also |ˈsæsəˈ, ˈsɑsəˈ| Pronc-spp *sa(r)cer, sas(s)er*

A Forms.

1837 Sherwood *Gaz. GA* 71, *Sacer,* for saucer. **1843** (1916) Hall *New Purchase* 133 **IN,** Chany tea cups and sassers. **1851** Hooper *Widow Rugby's Husband* 91 **AL,** He had the Injun ager 'twell his eyes was big as sassers. **1858** Hammett *Piney Woods Tavern* 114, Vittles, cups, sassers. **1894** *Century Illustr. Mag.* 48.869 **swIN,** I give "sassers" for extreme Hoosier, but I find "sasers" in a Connecticut inventory before 1650, in the time of American phonetic spelling. **1899** (1912) Green *VA Folk-Speech* 362, *Sacer.* . . Sasser. Saucer. **1907** Lincoln *Cape Cod* 264 **MA,** I make up my mind I wouldn't drink out of my sasser if I scalded the lining off my throat. **1911** (1916) Porter *Harvester* 342 **IN,** Bile tea in them, make grease sassers of them, and use them to dish up the bakin' on! **1958** Hale *New Engl. Girlhood* 64 **MA** (as of c1900), I mostly drink it from the sarcer. **c1960** Wilson *Coll.* **eKY,** *Saucer*—/ˈsæsəˈ/ or /ˈsɑsəˈ/. **1969** *DARE* FW Addit **MA**15, [ˈsæˌsəˈ] = saucer. **1975** *Appalachian Jrl.* 2.151 **wNC,** Diphthongs yield considerable variety of pronunciation. *Real* becomes *rail;* . . *saucer, sasser.* **1982** Slone *How We Talked* 33 **eKY** (as of c1950), *Sasser*—saucer.

B As noun.

1 also *berry saucer, fruit ~:* =**saucedish.** [This is essentially the original sense of *saucer* (*OED2* 13.. →), "a dish for sauce," although the sense of *sauce* has changed.]

1895 (1969) Montgomery Ward *Catalogue* 530, Fruit Saucers, 4-inch. **1897** (1968) Sears *Catalogue* 686, *Berry Set.* . . 1 large dish and 6 saucers. **1902** (1969) *Ibid* 799, *Our $1.75 40-Piece Glass Outfit.* . . 12 Berry Saucers, 1 Large Berry-Bowl. **1948** *Hench Coll.* **Charleston SC,** A mother gives her child an extra spoonful of ice-cream in her saucer and says, "That's for broadus." **1948** *WELS Suppl.* **VA,** It was quite all right for me to call a "sauce dish" a "saucer" because it holds "sauce," while *he* always held only a cup saucer was a "saucer." **1967–68** *DARE* (Qu. G6, . . *Dishes that you might have on the table for a big dinner*) Inf **NC**46, Plate, saucer, salad bowl; **PA**95, Saucers for vegetables; **PA**248, Vegetable dishes, saucers, plates. [*DARE* Ed: Only cases where *saucer* was not juxtaposed with *cup* are recorded here.]

2 also *flying saucer, saucer-sled, snow saucer:* A metal or plastic coasting sled in the shape of a shallow, circular bowl. **esp NEast, N Cent** See Map

1965–70 *DARE* (Qu. EE24a, *When there's snow, children go down the*

hill on a _____) Infs **CT**16, **IL**97, **MI**78, **MN**11, **NJ**13, **OH**70, **WI**5, Saucer; **MN**15, 34, **NY**94, Flying saucer; **MA**128, Snow saucer; (Qu. N40b, . . *Sleighs for carrying people*) Inf **NJ**12, Children now ride on sleds or saucers; **WI**57, A saucer; (Qu. EE26, . . *Games* . . *children play in the snow*) Inf **KY**11, Saucer. **2001** *DARE* File **csWI** (as of c1960), I remember "saucers" from when I was a kid. They were made of aluminum, maybe 30 inches in diameter, and with two canvas strap handles. They were impossible to steer, and after a few trips down Scholl's hill, they usually had the dents to prove it. *Ibid* **csWI** (as of c1965), I had an aluminum saucer-sled; now they come in bright orange plastic.

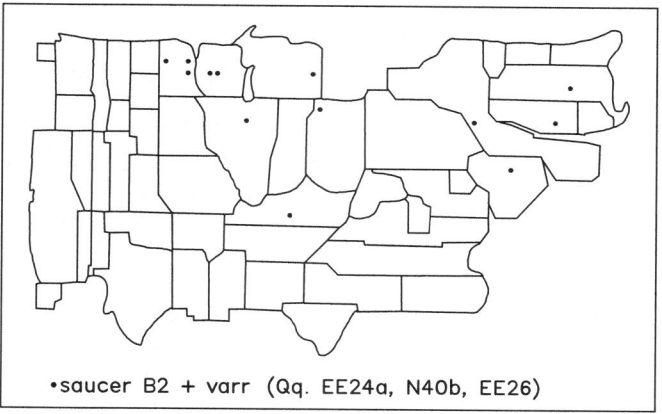

•saucer B2 + varr (Qq. EE24a, N40b, EE26)

3 In marble play: a shallow hole.

1973 Ferretti *Marble Book* 46, *Hole.* . . Holes in marble games can vary in depth. . . Shallow holes are called saucers.

C As verb.

Pronc-sp *saucy:* To pour (a hot liquid) into a saucer to cool; hence ppl adj phr *saucered and blowed* cooled by having been poured out and blown upon; fig: ready, in order. **esp sAppalachians**

1938 *Atlantic Mth.* 162.552 **Ozarks,** Want a sasser o' sorghum. . . The visitor would 'sasser' some sorghum. **1950** Stuart *Hie Hunters* 213 **eKY,** "I didn't mean to backsass, Peg," Arn apologized, as she saucered her coffee. **c1950** *Halpert Coll.* 55 **wKY, nwTN,** It's all saucered and blowed = everything is ready [Originally referred to coffee.] **1951** Craig *Singing Hills* 31 **sAppalachians,** Saucy your coffee, boy! Ain't you got no manners? **1953** *PADS* 19.13 **sAppalachians,** Sister, we ain't given to waitin' on no one; jest sasser your coffee and make yourself to home. **1966** *Good Old Days* Feb 6 **St. Louis MO,** Remember the saucered coffee days? Nobody could endure their Arbuckles if it was hot. It had to be poured into a saucer. **1978** *New Yorker* 9 Jan 41, Have you ever heard the old Texas expression 'saucered and blowed'? . . If a cowboy's coffee is too hot, he puts some in a saucer and blows on it. A cowboy will say to a friend, 'Take mine, it's already saucered and blowed.' Jim needs to get the energy bill saucered and blowed, and that press conference was a step. **1981** *NC Folkl.* 29.82 **sAppalachians,** Excuse me, ma'am, but since you're in such a allfard hurry I'd be right proud to trade with you. Mine's already sassered and blowed. **1984** Wilder *You All Spoken Here* 90 **Sth,** *Saucered an' blowed:* Coffee that's been cooled down; you've poured some from cup to saucer and funneled your breath across it. Also means everything is hunky-dory, on schedule, on the beam, A-OK. **1986** Pederson *LAGS Concordance,* 1 inf, **cwTN,** Saucer your coffee; 1 inf, **ceGA,** Saucered your coffee—into saucer to cool it; 1 inf, **neTN,** Saucering your coffee—pouring in saucer to cool it. **1994–95** in 1996 *Montgomery Coll.* **eTN,** He always sassered his coffee so it can be more comfortably drunk. **1999** *DARE* File **neAL,** Is the contract ready for the boss'[s] signature? Has it been reviewed by all the departments? If so, it's "done saucered and blowed."

saucereye porgy n

A porgy n[1] **1b(4)** (here: *Calamus calamus*).

1896 U.S. Bur. Fisheries *Rept. for 1895* 389, *Calamus calamus.* . . *Saucer-eye Porgy.* . . North to Florida Keys. **1902** Jordan–Evermann *Amer. Fishes* 438, *Saucer-eye Porgy. Ibid* 439, At Key West the conchs assure you that its English name is correctly pronounced sasser-eye. . . It is an excellent food fish and always commands a good price. **1933** John G. Shedd Aquarium *Guide* 110, The porgies . . are small shore fishes fairly abundant . . on our south Atlantic shore. . . *Calamus calamus—Saucer-eye Porgy.* **1975** Evanoff *Catch More Fish* 208, The southern porgy, jolthead porgy, and saucer-eye porgy [are] found in southern waters.

saucer flower n

A **miner's lettuce** (here: *Claytonia perfoliata*).

1920 Rice–Rice *Pop. Studies CA Wild Flowers* 89, A striking and attractive feature of . . the Miner's Lettuce . . is furnished by the two-stemmed leaves, which unite directly under the blossoms, forming a perfect saucer in shape; in fact, I have known children to call them . . "saucer flowers."

saucer-sled See saucer B2

saucer squash n Also *flying saucer* esp Sth, S Midl

=**pattypan squash.**

1966–70 *DARE* (Qu. I23, . . *Kinds of squash*) Inf **AL**1, Saucer squash; **NY**36, Saucer squash—whitish, like a flying saucer, two inches thick, flat and round with scalloped edges; **SC**9, Saucer squash—flat; **SC**43, Saucer squash—round, flat; **KY**90, Round saucer squash. **1986** Pederson *LAGS Concordance (Squash)* 1 inf, **csGA**, Saucer squash; 1 inf, **cLA**, Flying saucers—joking term for white flat ones; 1 inf, **cnMS**, A crookneck and a saucer squash.

saucy See saucer C

sauerbraten n [Ger] esp N Cent, Upper Missip Valley See Map

A dish of beef marinated in a vinegar solution; see quots.

1889 (1906) Kramer *"Aunt Babette's" Cook Book* 62, Sauerbraten. . . Take a solid piece of meat . . put it in a deep earthen jar and pour enough boiling vinegar. . . turn it daily. . . three or four days. **1920** Kander *Settlement Cook Book* 140 **Milwaukee WI**, *Beef A La Mode Or Sauerbraten.* **1923** *Ladies' Home Jrl.* Mar 133 **sePA**, A demure little Mennonite maid, who will invite you cordially to "sit up" to a table arrayed with the wealth of cup cheese and . . *sauerbraten* . . and all the rest of the savory dainties . . on the menu of a Pennsylvania Dutch family. **1940** Brown *Amer. Cooks* 215 **IA**, Sauerbraten. *Ibid* 890 **WI**, Sauerbraten. **1964** Bellow *Herzog* 80 **Chicago IL**, We eat in twenty minutes. Good chow. Sauerbraten. **c1965** Randle *Cookbooks* (Ask Neighbor) 3.88 **Cleveland OH**, Sauerbraten . . lean English cut or pot roast . . vinegar . . white wine . . bay leaf . . peppercorns . . onion. Rub beef with garlic, salt and pepper. . . Heat . . wine, vinegar . . water. Add remaining ingredients. Pour over beef. Cover. Place in refrigerator for at least a week. . . Drain beef. Flour lightly and brown in large frying pan. Add a cup of the stock. . . Cover and simmer until tender. **1965–70** *DARE* (Qu. H65, *Foreign foods favored by people around here*) 11 Infs, **scattered, but esp N Cent, Upper Missip Valley,** Sauerbraten; (Qu. H45, *Dishes made with meat . . that everybody around here would know, but that people in other places might not*) Infs **CA**167, **IA**32, **IL**3, 91, **MN**23, 37, 42, **PA**5, Sauerbraten. **1978** *Detroit Free Press* 16 Apr. (Detroit Suppl.) 28/2 *(OED2)*, Sauerbraten, the German version of roast beef, is always good, marinated with a vinegar mixture which later is used to make the rich brown gravy. **1981** Hachten *Flavor WI* 204, Sauerbraten (German) . . pot roast or beef . . vinegar . . sugar . . onion . . salt . . peppercorns . . cloves . . bay leaves . . shortening . . butter . . flour . . ginger snaps. **1986** Pederson *LAGS Concordance,* 1 inf, **swTN**, Sauerbraten.

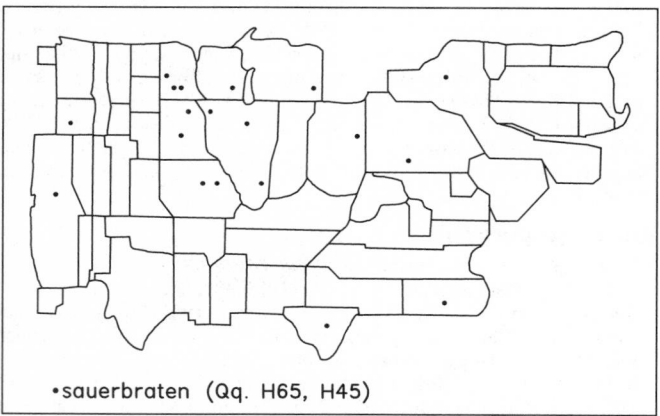

•sauerbraten (Qq. H65, H45)

sauerkraut n Also sp *sauerkrout, sourcrout, sourkraut, sourkrout*

1 Thinly sliced cabbage fermented in brine. **scattered, but chiefly Nth, N Midl** See Map Cf **kraut** n **1**

1776 Leacock *Brit. Tyranny* 30 **Boston MA,** Don't leave me, and you shall have plenty of porter and sour-crout. **1806** *Balance* (Hudson NY) 5.25, Some of his neighbors might have spoken of him as . . making excellent *sour krout.* **1857** (1928) Twain *Advent. Snodgrass* 38, The Dutch was friz to the sour-kraut kegs. **1888** *Century Illustr. Mag.* 35.807, It is not the descendants of the "Mayflower," in short, who are the representative Americans of the present day; it is the Micks and the Pats, the Hanses and the Wilhelms, redolent still of the dudeen and the sauerkraut barrel. **1944** *Amer.–German Rev.* 10.5.28 **seWI,** Sauerkraut and Salzgurken (cucumbers) were pickled and packed in earthen crocks. **1947** Croy *Corn Country* 241, Not far away is Ackley, Iowa, which was settled by Germans whose descendants still carry on the early traditions. "Sauerkraut Day!" . . Barrels and barrels of sauerkraut are given away and pounds and pounds of frankfurters are dumped into huge vats, steamed, and served free. **1960** Criswell *Resp. to PADS 20* **Ozarks,** Kraut, sometimes called sauerkraut, made from long ago. **1965–70** *DARE* (Qu. H65, *Foreign foods favored by people around here*) 23 Infs, **esp Nth, N Midl,** Sauerkraut; **NM**5, **NY**109, Sauerkraut and wieners; **IL**131, Wieners and sauerkraut; **PA**167, Kolbasy and sauerkraut; **PA**131, 135, Sauerkraut and pork (and wieners); **OK**9, Sauerkraut and wienies; (Qu. H52, *Dishes made with fresh cabbage*) 22 Infs, **esp Nth, N Midl,** Sauerkraut; **CA**113, **IL**40, Sauerkraut salad; (Qu. H36, *Kinds of soup*) Inf **WA**18, Spare ribs with sauerkraut; (Qu. H45, *Dishes . . that everybody around here would know, but that people in other places might not*) Inf **PA**221, Russian sauerkraut; **PA**26, Sauerkraut; **NY**70, Sauerkraut and spareribs; (Qu. H50, *Dishes . . that everybody around here knows, but people in other places might not*) Inf **PA**41, Pork and sauerkraut; **MI**96, Sauerkraut and wieners; (Qu. H51, *Dishes made with cooked cabbage;* total Infs questioned, 75) Infs **FL**3, 6, Sauerkraut; (Qu. H57, *Tasty or spicy side-dishes served with meats*) Inf **IN**70, Sauerkraut; **PA**176, Sauerkraut and fresh cold sage; (Qu. I28a) Inf **WI**13, Sauerkraut; (Qu. BB22, . . *Home remedies . . for constipation*) Infs **CA**4, **NY**2, Sauerkraut; **NY**1, 80, Sauerkraut juice; **MD**9, Sauerkraut and beer; (Qu. BB50a, . . *Favorite remedies . . for a cough*) Inf **WA**18, Sauerkraut; (Qu. BB50d, *Favorite spring tonics*) Inf **WA**18, Sauerkraut; (Qu. HH30, *Things that are nicknamed for different nationalities—for example, a 'Dutch treat'*) Inf **PA**71, German sauerkraut. **1986** Pederson *LAGS Concordance,* 2 infs, **GA, TX,** Sauerkraut.

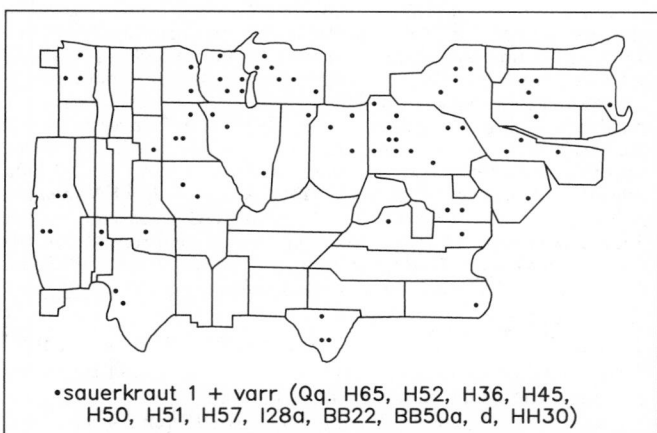

•sauerkraut 1 + varr (Qq. H65, H52, H36, H45, H50, H51, H57, I28a, BB22, BB50a, d, HH30)

2 also *sauerkrauter eater:* A German or person of German ancestry—also used as a nickname for such a person. **chiefly Nth, esp NW, Upper MW** See Map Cf **kraut** n **2**

1841 Mercier–Gallop *Life Man-of-War* 232 **Boston MA,** Yes, old sour-crout, and you'd be *dirty too* if you were . . in that infernal shot-locker as long as these fellows have been. **1858** Stone *Put's Golden* 41 **CA,** Sauer-Kraut was looking for a Justice of the Peace. **1909** *Sat. Eve. Post* 3 July 7, I'll expurgate you, you old Dutch Sauerkrout! **1918** in 1919 Cowing–Cooper *Dear Folks* 217 **MT,** We will scatter those "sauerkrauter eaters" before the summer is over. **1965–70** *DARE* (Qu. HH28, *Names and nicknames . . for people of foreign background: German*) 10 Infs, **esp NW, Upper MW,** Sauerkraut; [**WI**44, Dutch as sauerkraut;] (Qu. C35, *Nicknames for the different parts of your town or city*) Inf **PA**200, Sauerkraut Hill—German section of town; (Qu. II25, *Names or* nicknames for the part of a town where the poorer people, special groups, or foreign groups live) Inf **PA**200, Sauerkraut Hill—for Germans. [10 of 11 total Infs old]

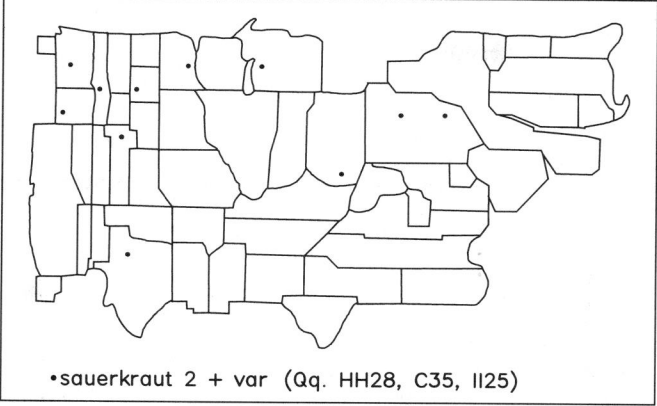

•sauerkraut 2 + var (Qq. HH28, C35, II25)

3 also *sauerkraut candy:* See quots. **esp WI**

1915 *West Bend Cook Book* 385 **WI**, *Sauer Kraut Candy*. Cook one pound brown sugar and enough milk to moisten, for about five minutes, stirring all the time, then add one-quarter pound cocoanut, stir well and turn on buttered paper. **1950** *WELS* (*Kinds of candy often made at home in your neighborhood*) 1 Inf, **seWI**, "Sauerkraut" candy (a brownsugar candy with coconut). **1970** *DARE* (Qu. H82b, *Kinds of cheap candy that used to be sold years ago*) Inf **TN**49, Sauerkraut—a strip of vanilla, chocolate and strawberry, coconut. **2001** *DARE* File **ceWI**, One of my favorite treats as a child in the 1950s was sauerkraut candy. This common confection was a cooked mixture mostly of brown sugar and coconut—it looked something like a bit of sauerkraut. I have seen it in other places called "haystacks" and "coconut clusters."

sauerkrauter eater See **sauerkraut 2**

sauga See **massasauga**

sauger n[1] Usu |ˈsɔgɚ, ˈsagɚ|; also |ˈsaugɚ| Also *sauger jack,* ~ *pike* [Etym unknown]

A **pike perch:** usu *Stizostedion canadense,* occas also a **walleye** (here: *Stizostedion vitreum vitreum*). For other names of the former see **blue pike 1, dory** n[1] **2, gray pike 1, ground pike, hornfish 2b, horsefish 3, jack** n[1] **24a(2), jackfish 1b, jack salmon 1, pickerel 3, pickering, pike** n[1] **2, rattlesnake pike, salmon 2a(1), sand pike, walleye**

1877 U.S. Natl. Museum *Bulletin* 10.44, Among the species of *Stizostethium* [sic], there are two well-marked groups, known to our lake fishermen respectively as the "Saugers" and the "Pikes." *Ibid* 45, Of American species I know certainly . . the Sauger or Gray Pike (*Stizostethium griseum* or *canadense*). **1884** Goode *Fisheries U.S.* 1.424, *Stizostedium canadense.* . . The "Sauger," known also as the "Gray Pike," . . "Pickerel," and "Horse-fish," has its habitat . . in the Saint Lawrence River, Great Lake region, Upper Mississippi, and Upper Missouri Rivers, also in the Ohio. **1902** Jordan–Evermann *Amer. Fishes* 364, A few years ago the sauger was, to the few elect who knew where to find it, the choicest game-fish of the lower Wabash River; and we knew a minister who always went "saugering" when he failed in other ways to get the proper inspiration for his next Sunday's sermon. **1927** Weed *Pike* 45, *Stizostedion*—Common names of this group are so confused that no attempt has been made to separate names belonging only to the Saugers from those belonging only to the Walleyes. It is probable that practically all the names are applied to either. . . Sauger; general. Sauger Pike. **1950** *WELS Suppl.*, Sauger, sand pike—same—a small river pickerel. Mississippi River. **1965–70** *DARE* (Qu. P1, . . *Kinds of freshwater fish . . caught around here . . good to eat*) Infs **IN**22, **IA**22, **ND**9, Sauger(s); **OH**58, 67, Sauger(s) [FW sp: sogger(s)]; **KY**60, **ND**1, **TN**1, 14, [ˈsɔgɚ]; **TN**65, [ˈsagɚ]; **MI**103, [ˈsaugɚ] pike. **1971** *WI Conserv. Bulletin* 36.6.23 **WI**, Lake Winnebago ice fishermen generally pursue the popular walleye and sauger. **1981** Pederson *LAGS Basic Materials* (*Common freshwater fish*) 1 inf, **nwAL**, Sauger [ˈsɔᵛɔ^gɚ]; 1 inf, **ceTN**, Sauger jack [ˌsɔ^ᵒ‹gɚˈdʒæᵋk].

sauger n[2] See **massasauga**

sauger jack (or pike) See **sauger** n[1]

saunt See **send 2**

saurel n

A fish of the genus *Trachurus,* usu **jack mackerel 2.**

1882 U.S. Natl. Museum *Bulletin* 431, *Trachurus.* . . Saurels. *Ibid* 432, T[rachurus] *saurus.* . . Horse Mackerel; Skip Jack; Saurel. **1902** Jordan–Evermann *Amer. Fishes* 302, The xurel or saurel, T[rachurus] *symmetricus,* is common on our Pacific coast. . . In summer it is abundant in the San Francisco markets where it is regarded as a good foodfish. **1946** LaMonte *N. Amer. Game Fishes* 40, *Trachurus symmetricus.* . . Saurel. . . The fish is mackerel-shaped.

sausage n Usu |ˈsɔsɪ̆dʒ|; also |ˈsɑsɪ̆dʒ, ˈsæsɪ̆dʒ|; for addit varr see quots Pronc-spp *saseadg, sassage, sassi(d)ge* Cf **sassinger** Std sense, var forms.

1835 in 1956 Eliason *Tarheel Talk* 292 **ceNC**, Saseadg stoffer [an item in a sales list]. **1862** (1864) Browne *Artemus Ward Book* 222, We'll be chopt into sassige meat before we'll exhibit our coat-tales to the foe. **1864** (1868) Trowbridge *3 Scouts* 116 **VT**, It's an almighty stout cask, and a fellow stuffed in in that shape, as you'd stuff a sassidge, can't get no purchase with his legs. **1891** *DN* 1.121 **cNY**, [sæsɪdʒ] . . sausage. **1899** (1912) Green *VA Folk-Speech* 366, Sassage. **1904** Day *Kin o' Ktaadn* 82 **ME**, Ah, he rose as calm's a sassige jest as soon's them lawyers quit. **1922** (1926) Cady *Rhymes VT* 116, The vinegar made boiled dish fine,/ Whilst sassage lived for pepper. **1961** Kurath–McDavid *Pronc. Engl.* 162, *Sausage* . . the rounded vowels /ɔ ~ ɒ/ predominate everywhere except in tidewater Virginia and in Maryland, being nearly universal in New York State, most of Pennsylvania, and the South Midland. . . Unrounded [ɑ ~ ɑ̈ ~ a] . . appear with greatly varying frequency in most parts of the Eastern States. On both sides of Chesapeake Bay, /ɑ/ is in rather general use. . . In the Midland and in New England, /ɑ/ is rather infrequent and cultured speakers avoid it. . . [A]nother phoneme . . /æ/ . . occurs with some frequency in the folk speech of northeastern New England; only scattered relics remain elsewhere. **1967** *DARE* Tape **KY**34A, And you ground that malt corn up on a [ˈsɔsɚ̆j] mill. **1967–69** *DARE* FW Addit **neLA**, Sausage [ˈsasɪj]; **MA**68, [ˈsæsəjɛz] sausages. **1976** Garber *Mountain-ese* 77 **sAppalachians**, *Sassage* . . sausage—It takes a lot uv sage to make a real good batch uv sassage. **1989** Pederson *LAGS Tech. Index* 160, [654 infs gave proncs of the type [ˈsɔsɪj]; 265 infs [ˈsasɪj]; 2 infs [ˈsæsɪč]; addit minor pronc varr also appear.]

sausage grass n
=**glasswort.**

1941 *Torreya* 41.47 **SC**, *Salicornia* spp.—Sausage grass. **1954** Sprunt *FL Bird Life* 479, The type of marsh they [=*Ammospiza maritima*] frequent is rather drier than that of other seaside sparrows, and the so-called "sausage-grass" (*Salicornia*) is a typical growth.

sausage tree n [From the shape of the fruits]

An evergreen tree (*Kigelia africana*) introduced in Florida; see quots.

1939 FWP *Guide FL* 335 **swFL**, Adjoining the fairway . . is the Key West Botanical Garden . . , planted with thousands of exotic trees and shrubs. . . Among them are the sausage tree, bearing hard sausagelike fruit on long slender stems. **1944** *Sun* (Baltimore MD) 6 Dec 8/3 (*Hench Coll.*), An "Admirer Visiting in Florida" sends me a colored picture postal-card view of a sausage tree, such as has been referred to several times recently by correspondents to the column. There they hang, the sausage-like pods, amid a background of wonderful green foliage. **1982** Perry–Hay *Field Guide Plants* 32, Sausage tree. . . *Fruits:* large, sausage-shaped. . . They sometimes weigh over 7 kg (15 lb) each. **2000** *DARE* File **swFL**, On the grounds of the Thomas A. Edison winter home in Fort Myers, there is a large sausage tree much admired by the many visitors.

sausenger, sausinger See **sassinger**

savage n Cf **cedar savage, jackpine ~, sawdust ~**
A logger; see quots.

1925 *AmSp* 1.135 **Pacific NW**, Never call the worker in the woods of the Pacific Northwest "lumberjack." In certain humors he may admit being a timber beast or a savage, but "logger" is the name he has made for himself. He uses the term "lumberjack" only in referring to the worker in the "toothpick" timber, the small second-growth pine and hemlock, in Minnesota, Michigan and Maine. **1930** Williams *Logger-Talk* 28 **Pacific NW**, *Savage:* A logger's self-characterization.

savagerous adj, adv Also *salvagerous, se(r)vagerous, sevagarous* [Etym uncert; usu explained as a derivative of *savage,* but this is not consistent with the pronc implied by the early sp *sevagarous.* Cf **servigrous, vigrous**] **esp Sth, S Midl**
Fierce, violent, vigorous; fiercely, violently, vigorously.

1832 Trollope *Domestic Manners* (NY) 116 **West,** The visitor took it [=a dagger] up, and examining it with much emotion, exclaimed, "What! do you really jab this into yourself sevagerous?" **1837** Bird *Nick of Woods* 1.96 **KY,** The strongest man in Kentucky, and the most sevagarous at a tussel [sic]. **1843** *Spirit of Times* 25 Aug (1912 Thornton *Amer. Gloss.*), The Editor [of the *Age*] calls his savagerous enemy a remarkably pious and moral young man. **1845** (1852) Simms *Wigwam & Cabin* (2d ser) 82 **SC,** "A madman, eh?" "Yes, and a mighty sevagerous one at that. . . He's kill'd two men already." **1851** Burke *Polly Peablossom* 149 **MS,** Arch he . . looked me right plum in the face as savage as er meet axe! . . I 'termined to give him as good as he sent; so I looked at him sorter servagerous like, and, sez I, "Look here, hoss, how can you have the face to talk to me?" **1857** Gladstone *Englishman* 206 **KS,** My white brother was not very communicative, but, on being pressed, said he was "took aback some, just a spot; he'd never sot eyes on such a salvagerous set of coons." **1866** Smith *Bill Arp* 54 **GA,** It is, perhaps, *when suspended,* the most savagerous beast that ever got after tories and traitors. **1927** *AmSp* 2.363 **cwWV,** Servagerous . . very active. "That is a servagerous coon dog." **1975** Gainer *Witches* 16 **sAppalachians,** Servagerous . . , very active. "That youngun is too servagerous to suit me. I can't keep up with him."

savanna See **savannah**

savannah n Also sp *savanna* **chiefly S Atl** Cf **bay** n¹ 3, **bay** n³, **pocosin** 1
An expanse of low-lying marshy ground; a marsh.

1671 in 1897 SC Hist. Soc. *Coll.* 5.333, You will finde . . great Creeks, mar[s]hes, or Savanoes on the other side. **1741** GA Hist. Soc. *Coll.* 2.249, The savannahs, (so they call the low watery meadows which are usually intermixed with pine lands). **1791** [see **savannah cricket**]. **1814** (1922) Tatum *Jrl.* 7.69 **NC,** Took up the line of march . . through poor, Pine woods interspersed with ponds, or savanna's, to Cochran's Cowpens. **1905** U.S. Forest Serv. *Bulletin* 64.7 **eTX,** Loblolly is the first pine to take possession of the savannas, or marshy prairies, when the latter are sufficiently drained to allow of tree growth. **1934** *Sun* (Baltimore MD) 16 Feb 10/6 *(Hench Coll.),* In the Carolinas there are 3,000 shallow pits, unique features of the landscape which the Carolinians call "savannas," "pocosins" or "bays." **1940** Weygandt *Down Jersey* 326 **sNJ,** Here on the sea islands off Jersey we have savannas between the dunes and the bayshore. The savannas are low places, above high tide mark, but depressed enough to catch rain and to keep rain water to the depth of a few feet, two, say, or three. It was the sweet grass that grew in the savannas after the rain water seeped away that made these sea islands so good cattle runs in old time. **1949** Kurath *Word Geog.* 61 **cs,seNC, ceSC,** *Bottom land. . . Savannah,* from the lower Neuse to the Peedee, for low lying grassland. **1966–69** *DARE* (Qu. C6, . . *A piece of land that's often wet, and has grass and weeds growing on it)* Inf **FL29,** Savannah—a long strip of marshy land with water on it, sawgrass, weeds, lilies, but no trees; good fishing; (Qu. C7, . . *Land that usually has some standing water with trees or bushes growing in it)* Inf **NJ55,** Savannah land. **1967** *DARE* FW Addit **SC19,** Bay—a small swamp of cold water confined to an area, also [called] *savannah.* **1986** Pederson *LAGS Concordance (Marshes)* 1 inf, **ceGA,** Savanna.

savannah cricket n Also *savannah cricket frog*
=**cricket frog.**

1791 Bartram *Travels* 278 **PA,** There is yet an extreme diminutive species of frog, which inhabits the grassy verges of ponds in savannas: these are called savanna crickets, are of a dark ash or dusky colour, and have a very picked nose. **1842** DeKay *Zool. NY* 3.70, *Hylodes gryllus. . .* At the South, it is called *Savannah Cricket.* **1882** *Amer. Naturalist* 16.707, One of the earliest indications of returning spring is the clear, bell-like note of the little batrachian, called by many the "Savannah cricket," known in New Jersey as the "peeper." **1932** Wright *Life-Hist. Frogs* 156, *Acris gryllus. . . Common Names . .* Savannah Cricket. Savanna Cricket. . . Savannah Cricket Frog.

savannah orchid n
A **fringed orchid** (here: *Platanthera nivea*).

1950 Correll *Native Orchids* 89, *Habenaria nivea. . .* Savannah Orchid. . . The Big Savannah in Pender County, North Carolina, and the

extensive savannahs around Brunswick, Georgia, as well as in other southern regions, often contain large colonies of this species.

savannah sparrow n
A sparrow (*Passerculus sandwichensis* and races) widely distributed throughout much of the US. Also called **field sparrow c, grass bird 1b, ~ finch 2, ~ sparrow c, ground bird d, ~ sparrow b, marsh sparrow 2, meadow ~, stinkbird**

1811 Wilson *Amer. Ornith.* 3.55, The female of the Savannah Sparrow is five inches and a half long. **1858** Baird *Birds* 442, Savannah Sparrow. . . Feathers of the upper parts generally with a central streak of blackish brown. **1899** in 1900 LA Soc. Naturalists *Proc.* 106, Savanna Sparrow. An abundant winter resident throughout the state. **1928** Beston *Outermost House* 30 **Cape Cod MA,** I whirred up groups of savannah sparrows. **1948** Pearson *Sea Flavor* 43, Those who like the beaches, dunes, and drumlins in the marshes, are certain to get acquainted with the savanna sparrow. **1967–69** *DARE* (Qu. Q21, . . *Kinds of sparrows)* Infs **IN69, MA50,** Savannah sparrow. **1977** Bull–Farrand *Audubon Field Guide Birds* 531, *Savannah Sparrow. . .* Fields, prairies, salt marshes, and grassy dunes. . . Shows a great deal of color variation over its wide range.

save v
A Gram form.
Past: usu *saved;* rarely *seft.*
1995 *DARE* File **csWI** (as of c1945), I seft five dollars on it.
B Senses.
1 To harvest, gather, or store (a crop). [Cf *EDD save* v. 3] **Sth, S Midl**
1847 in 1927 Jones *FL Plantation Rec.* 273 **nwFL,** 23 hands saveing foder. *Ibid* 295, 2 [hands] saving hay, 3 braking corn, 6 halling corn. **1899** (1912) Green *VA Folk-Speech* 366, Save. . . To house a crop. "I have finished saving my corn." "The fodder is all saved." **1921** *DN* 5.119 **KY,** Save. . . To make, or gather. "The whole family's a-savin' hay and punkins to-day." **1966–70** *DARE* (Qu. L15, *When you are putting hay into a building for storage . . you are* ____) Infs **FL26, TN62, 53,** Saving hay. **1976** Ryland *Richmond Co. VA* 376, Save—harvest; "We saved the beans." **1984** Wilder *You All Spoken Here* 131 **Sth,** Save: When a barn of tobacco is saved, it has been harvested and cured without having been destroyed by barn burning, hail, worms, or other pestilences that bug tobacco farmers.
2 To put away. [Calque of LaFr *sauver;* see quot 1984] **c,sLA**
1968 *DARE* FW Addit **csLA,** To save—To pick up and put away. "Save those toys" means to get them off the floor and into the toy box. This is said to be most characteristic of people of French descent around Franklin. [**1984** Daigle *Dict. Cajun Lang.* 2.144, *Sauver. . .* To save, to rescue, to preserve, to keep, to put away.] **1992** Scott *Cajun Vernacular Engl.* 40, Save—In C[ajun] V[ernacular] E[nglish], this verb means "to put away" or "to put up" in addition to its usual meaning in other English dialects, "to rescue." The following are examples of common CVE uses of *to save.* Save those cans of beans in the cabinet. I have to save the clothes before I can leave. Do you want me to save those flowers? (Clerk at florist shop.) Mais, it's your turn to save the dishes. **1998** *DARE* File **cLA,** I remember an expression my godmother used once when commenting on someone whose housekeeping she didn't admire. "She never saves her dishes," she said. "Save" here means to put them away once you've washed them after a meal. **2000** *NADS Letters* **csLA,** All over the Acadiana area people of all ages use "save" to mean put away. We save the dishes or clothes for example.

sa'vent See **servant**

savig(e)rous See **servigrous**

savin n
1 A **juniper 1:** usu *Juniperus virginiana,* but also *J. communis* or *J. horizontalis.* [*OED2* c1000 → for *Juniperus sabina*] Cf **horse savin**
1642 (1908) Winthrop *Jrl.* 2.62 **nNEng,** Within 12 miles of the top was neither tree nor grass, but low savins. **1672** Josselyn *New-Englands Rarities* 3 **NH,** In these Gullies grow *Saven* Bushes, which being taken hold of are a good help to the climbing Discoverer. **1709** (1967) Lawson *New Voyage* 97 **NC, SC,** Last of Bushes, (except Savine, which grows every where wild) is the famous *Yaupon.* **1774** (1900) Fithian

Jrl. 1.141, The Land . . produces in very great quantities shrubby *Savins.* *Ibid* 143, Amongst them interspers'd the gloomy Savin. **1822** Eaton *Botany* 325, *[Juniperus] prostrata* [=*J. horizontalis*] (american savin . .). A shrub. **1864** (1868) Trowbridge *3 Scouts* 138, Carl's genial countenance peered through the savins. **1901** Lounsberry *S. Wild Flowers* 18, *J[uniperus] Virginiana*, red cedar, or savin, has perhaps the happiest knack of versatility of all the trees. **1930** Shoemaker *1300 Words* 55 **cPA Mts** (as of c1900), *Savin*—A bush grown in yards of backwoods cabins for the purpose of birth control. **1979** Little *Checklist U.S. Trees* 157, *Juniperus virginiana.* . . Savin.

2 =stinking cedar 1.

1827 Williams *View W. FL* 76, And some of the burnt barrens will not produce even pine or scrub oaks, but are usually partially covered with clumps of savin. [*DARE* Ed: This quot may refer instead to another sense.] **1884** Sargent *Forests of N. Amer.* 186, *Torreya taxifolia.* . . *Stinking Cedar. Savin.* . . Wood . . susceptible of a beautiful polish, . . largely used locally for fence posts, etc. **1885** *Bot. Gaz.* 10.253 **FL,** It [=*Torreya taxifolia*] is called *Savin*, or *Stinking Cedar* . . , names also applied . . to the Florida Yew *(Taxus Floridana).* **1946** West–Arnold *Native Trees FL* 14, *Torreya taxifolia.* . . *Savin.* . . The range . . is very limited, including only a small area on the banks of the Apalachicola River.

3 =Florida yew.

1885 [see **2** above]. **1908** Britton *N. Amer. Trees* 124, *Taxus floridana.* . . A much smaller tree [than *Taxus brevifolia*], often a shrub, occurring with Torreya on river banks, in a limited area of Gadsden county, Florida, where it is also called Yew and Savin. **1946** West–Arnold *Native Trees FL* 13, *Taxus floridana.* . . *Savin.* . . Limited to ravines in a small area of the Apalachicola River Valley.

savina See **sabina** n[2]

savvy See **salvy**

savvy cow See **know cow**

saw n See **sawbuck 3**

saw exclam |sɔ, sɑ|; for addit proncs see quots   Also sp *sa* **chiefly Sth, S Midl, TX**   See Map   Cf **so, soo**

Stand still!—used to a cow during milking; hence rarely v *saw* to stand still.

1906 *DN* 3.154 **nwAR,** *Saw, saw, bos.* Command to a cow to stand still when she is being milked. **1909** *DN* 3.366 **eAL, wGA,** *Saw.* . . A command to make a milch-cow stand still. Often followed by the derogatory use of *madam.* "Saw, madam! I'll bust you open ef you don't saw." **1912** *DN* 3.588 **wIN,** *Saw.* . . A command to a cow to stand still. "Saw, Daisy, saw!" **1915** *DN* 4.189 **swVA,** *Saw.* . . Command to a cow to stand still during milking. **1942** Warnick *Garrett Co. MD* 13 **nwMD** (as of 1900–18), *Saw* . . a command to a cow to stand still while being milked. **1944** *PADS* 2.48 **sVA,** *Sa, madam* ['sɑˌmædəm]: A command to a cow to stand in a better position to be milked. . . Obsolescent. **1949** Kurath *Word Geog.* 64, Calls to Cows during Milking. . . *saw!* . . is current everywhere south of Pennsylvania, except Delmarvia, and in south-central Pennsylvania also (as far north as the fork of the Susquehanna). In the greater part of this large area *so!* and *saw!* stand side by side. **1955** in 1966 Goldstein–Byington *Two Penny Ballads* 160 **PA,** To make a cow be at ease while milking her, say "saw-saw." **1956** McAtee *Some Dialect NC* 38, *Saw* . . command to a cow to stand still for milking. **1965–70** *DARE* (Qu. K81, *To make a cow stand still—for example, when milking her—you say, "_____."*) 154 Infs, **chiefly Sth, S Midl, TX,** Saw; 40 Infs, **scattered Sth, S Midl,** [sɔ(ː)]; **GA7, KY29, MD15, SC3, 40, 57, VA32,** [sɑː]; **PA80, 212,** [sɑ] boss (*or* now); **CO22, 44, GA84,** [sɔ(ː)] boss; **MI87, MS60,** [sɔ(ː)ɪ]; **NM13,** [sɒːw]; **NM3,** [sɑːw]; **OK10, 43, TN30,** [sɑ(ː)ɪ] (now); **OK27,** [sɔːɚ]; **MS46, 53, OK33, 52,** [sɔːə]; **NY66,** Saw bess; **MO21, TX6,** Saw boss(y); **GA68,** Saw calf saw; **KY43, LA10, MS87, MO17, VA40,** Saw cow; **TN14,** Saw heifer; **OK43, TN2, TX37,** Saw jersey; **KY43,** Saw now; **DC8,** Saw suk saw suk; **GA77,** [sɒ:] there; [(Qu. K80, *The call that's used . . to get the cows in from the pasture*) Inf **MS9,** Saw cow; (Qu. K83, *To call a calf to you at feeding time*) Infs **MS9,** 53, Saw (calf)]. **1972** *PADS* 58.18 **cwAL,** Calls to cows during milking. Midland and Southern *saw* . . is usual. **1983** *MJLF* 9.1.54 **ceKY** (as of 1956), *Saw* . . a call to a cow during milking. **1986** Pederson *LAGS Concordance* **Gulf Region** (*Calls to cows—to make them stand still during milking*) 192 infs, Saw; 60 infs, Saw baby (*or* Bess, Betsy, bossy, cow, gal [etc]).

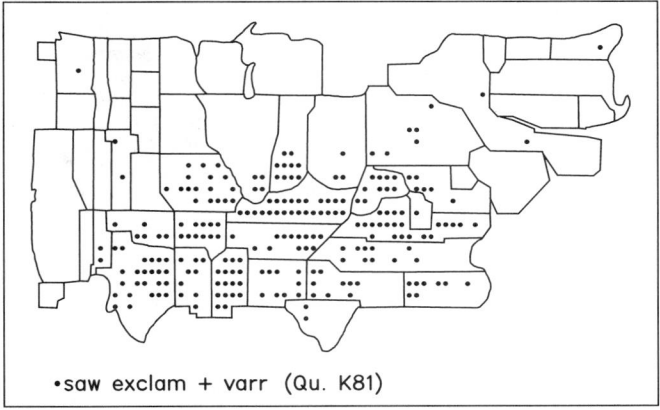

•saw exclam + varr (Qu. K81)

saw v See **see** B3a

sawback n [See quot 1958]
=map turtle.

1937 Cahn *Turtles IL* 113, *Graptemys pseudogeographica pseudogeographica* . . Saw-back. . . Carapace with a conspicuous persistent vertebral ridge. **1952** Carr *Turtles* 186, Genus *Graptemys*—The Map Turtles and Sawbacks. *Ibid* 192, This sawback [=*Graptemys barbouri*] prefers creeks and rivers, ideally with clear water and rocky bottom. **1958** Conant *Reptiles & Amphibians* 49, Sawbacks. . . These are lake and river turtles. . . All have dorsal keels; in several there are projections upward from the keel (hence the name Sawbacks). **1972** Ernst–Barbour *Turtles* 131, *G[raptemys] oculifera* is most closely related to the other narrow-headed sawbacks.

saw bean n
See quot.

1988 Erdrich *Tracks* 63 **ND,** They could be counted on to bring a torte or flummery, a chicken cut to pieces and cooked pale, a pot of saw beans.

sawbelly n

1 A **herring** n[1] **1:** either an **alewife** (here: *Alosa pseudoharengus*) or **glut herring.** [See quot 1950]

1873 in 1878 Smithsonian Inst. *Misc. Coll.* 14.2.33 **ME,** *Pomolobus pseudoharengus.* . . Alewife, sawbelly, cat-thresher. **1884** Goode *Fisheries U.S.* 1.583, The *C[lupea] aestivalis.* . . around the Gulf of Maine . . is also known by the names . . "Saw-belly," and "Cat-thresher." Although the coast fishermen of Massachusetts and Maine claim to distinguish the two species [=*Alosa aestivalis* and *A. pseudoharengus*] . . I have frequently had them sort out into two piles the fishes which they distinguish . . , and found their discrimination was not at all reliable. The features to which they mainly trusted in the determination of *C. aestivalis* are the bluer color of the back and the greater serration upon the ventral ridge. **1950** Everhart *Fishes ME* 12, *Pomolobus pseudoharengus.* . . The alewife is characterized by a row of spiny scutes along the midline of the belly which are strong and sharp and have led to the use of the common name "sawbelly" in some sections. **1957** Trautman *Fishes* 180 **OH,** On December 27, 1942, following a high wind storm, several fishermen found their gill nets, . . which they had previously given up as lost. In these nets were two kinds of "sawbellies," of which one Gizzardshad and two Alewives [=*Alosa pseudoharengus*] . . were sent to me. **1976** Tryckare et al. *Lore of Sportfishing* 70, *Alosa pseudoharengus.* . . Sawbelly.

2 A **gizzard shad 1** (here: *Dorosoma cepedianum*).

1874 U.S. Bur. Fisheries *Rept. for 1872–73* 35 **Gt Lakes,** From twenty fathoms to the shore are found the most numerous assemblage of species: The lawyer, . . the saw-belly [etc]. **1947** Hubbs–Lagler *Fishes Gt. Lakes* 34, "Saw-belly" refers to the gizzard shad, which is still generally known by that name in Lake Erie. **1957** [see **1** above]. **1983** Becker *Fishes WI* 273, *Dorosoma cepedianum.* . . Sawbelly.

saw bench n esp **S and Mid Atl**   See Map on p. 758
=sawbuck 1.

1860 Todd *Young Farmer's Manual* 230, On this platform should be kept the shovel and spade, the auger and spud, the crowbar and spoon, and the rammer . . and it should be borne in mind, that this little light bench is not strong enough to be used as a heavy *saw* bench.

1949 Kurath *Word Geog.* fig 81 (*Saw horse*), [The map shows *saw bench* chiefly in eNC, eVA, and eMD.] **1965–70** *DARE* (Qu. L58, *An implement with an A-shaped frame . . that you put boards on to saw them*) Infs **GA**5, 12, **NC**68, **RI**15, **SC**7, Saw bench; (Qu. L59, *An implement with an X-frame . . to hold firewood for sawing*) Infs **GA**19, 28, 80, **MD**38, **NC**44, 85, **SC**7, Saw bench. **1986** Pederson *LAGS Concordance* (*Sawbuck*) 9 infs, **GA**, Saw bench; 4 infs, **eFL**, Saw bench; 2 infs, **AL**, Saw bench. [Of those infs who offered a description, 9 described it as A-frame(d) or A-shaped, 2 as X-shaped, and 1 as A- or X-framed.]

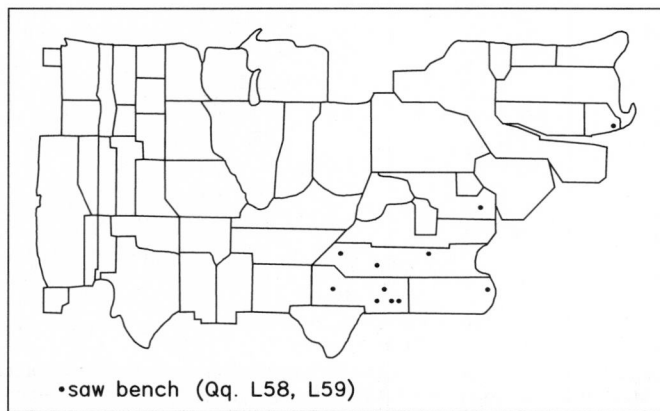

• saw bench (Qq. L58, L59)

sawbill n Also *sawbill duck* [See quots 1949, 1982] Cf **bec-scie, sawbill diver**
=**merganser.**

1827 McKenney *Sketches* 249 **Gt Lakes,** The ducks we have seen are all, or nearly all, of one species. They are the saw-bill. **1839** *Knickerbocker* 13.432 **nMI,** The sportsmen of our party here brought us the partridge, pigeon, and saw-bill duck. **1876** *Forest & Stream* 7.276 **eCT,** *Mergus merganser, Mergus serrator.* . . Saw bill, merganser. **1888** Trumbull *Names of Birds* 65, Other names by which our three mergansers . . have been more or less loosely known, are *Fish-duck* . . and *Saw-bill.* **1949** Kitchin *Birds Olympic Peninsula* 57 **WA,** *Lophodytes cucullatus.* . . This little saw-bill is only half the size of the other two that are found in the United States. . . Both birds [=male and female] have the long narrow bill with saw-like edges. **1966–69** *DARE* (Qu. Q5, . . *Kinds of wild ducks*) Infs **FL**9, **MI**2, 107, Sawbill. **1975** Newell *If Nothin' Don't Happen* 34 **nwFL,** By this time we'd picked up two pintails, leavin' the sawbill for the turtles. **1982** Elman *Hunter's Field Guide* 226, *Mergus merganser* . . sawbill. *Ibid* 227, The mandibles [of *M. merganser*] are "sawtoothed" and the bill is long, narrow, almost cylindrical, hook-nailed. *Ibid* 228, *Lophodytes cucullatus* . . sawbill, lake sawbill. *Ibid* 230, *Mergus serrator* . . sawbill.

sawbill diver n Cf **diver, sawbill**
=**hooded merganser.**

1888 Trumbull *Names of Birds* 73, *Hooded Merganser.* . . In Connecticut at Milford and Stratford, *Saw-bill diver.* **1938** Oberholser *Bird Life LA* 142, *Lophodytes cucullatus.* . . This bird, sometimes called . . 'sawbill diver,' is one of our handsomest ducks.

sawbill duck See **sawbill**

sawbones n

1 also *sawbone*: A doctor or surgeon. [*OED2* 1837 →] *joc* or *derog*

1850 *U.S. Democratic Rev.* 27.35 **NYC,** Here is an interesting sketch of the notorious Doctor's riot. . . Hearken to the Saw-bone's mob. **1851** Burke *Polly Peablossom* 89 **SC,** A village . . cumbered by a wag of a young doctor, or perhaps it were better to say, that it contained a bran new, bright, and polished journeyman sawbones, just out of his time. **1930** Shoemaker *1300 Words* 52 **cPA Mts** (as of c1900), *Sawbones*—A country surgeon or doctor. **1931** *AmSp* 7.48 **Sth, SW** [Lumberjack lingo], The hospital surgeon is "Saw Bones." **1939** *AmSp* 14.91 **eTN,** *Saw-bones.* A physician. 'When I have a bad hurting I send for my sawbones.' **1941** Writers' Program *Guide WY* 464, *Sawbones*—A doctor. **1945** Hubbard *Railroad Ave.* 359, *Sawbones*—Company doctor. **1965–70** *DARE* (Qu. BB53a, . . *Joking names . . for a doctor*) 318 Infs, **widespread,** Sawbones; **MO**16, **WY**5, Sawbone; (Qu. BB53b, . . *A doctor who is not very capable or doesn't have a very good reputation*) 10 Infs,

scattered, Sawbones; **WI**76, Old sawbones. **1976** Garber *Mountainese* 78 **sAppalachians,** Saw-bones . . doctor, surgeon—We had to take Jake to the saw-bones to have his laig set.

2 =**rawbones.**

1967–68 *DARE* (Qu. K44, *A bony or poor-looking horse*) Infs **MO**5, **NY**48, Sawbones.

saw brier n Also *saw(tooth) briar* **chiefly S Midl**

Usu a **greenbrier,** esp *Smilax glauca;* occas a similar plant such as a **mimosa 1** (here: *Mimosa microphylla*).

1806 in 1852 U.S. Congress *Debates & Proc.* 1142, The saw briar, single rose briar, and china root briar [grow near the Washita River]. **1819** (1821) Nuttall *Jrl.* 180 **AR,** This route was . . often entangled with brambles, and particularly with the tenacious "saw-brier" (*Schrankia horridula* [=*Mimosa microphylla*]). **1859** Taliaferro *Fisher's R.* 60 **nwNC** (as of 1820s), I felt suthin rakin' my feet wusser than sawbriers. **1914** Georgia *Manual Weeds* 83, Saw Brier—*Smilax glauca.* **1936** *Esquire* Nov 56 **KY,** It's right close . . to where I was raised—old yellow hills and saw-briar thickets. **1937** Thornburgh *Gt. Smoky Mts.* 23, A few of the more common vines you may encounter . . are . . Dutchman's pipe, trumpet vine, crossvine, virgin bower, woodbine, muscadine, and greenbrier, which is also called saw brier, cat brier and bamboo brier. **1942** (1960) Robertson *Red Hills* 199 **SC,** It was a quiet meditative place, . . brightened with yellow mullein and saw briers and wild eglantine roses. **1967** *Ozark Visitor* (Point Lookout MO) Feb 6, Saw brier spread its lacy leaves in intermittent patches to support magenta blossoms which looked like delicate golf balls gone modern in color. As I moved through these sensitive plants they folded their leaves in protest against an animal in their plant world. **1977** Randolph *Pissing in the Snow* 59 **Ozarks,** The old man . . cut him a saw-tooth briar. **1986** Pederson *LAGS Concordance* 3 infs, **TN, AR,** Saw brier(s). **1992** *Houston Chron.* (TX) 5 Apr sec G, *Smiling.* . . Like a jackass eating saw briars.

sawbuck n

1 A sawhorse, esp one with X-shaped end pieces. **chiefly Nth, N Midl, West** See Map Cf **buck n[1] 4, wood horse**

1851 *Amer. Temperance Mag.* July 12 **NY,** Noon came and he sat down on his saw-buck to eat his frugal Christmas dinner. **1862** U.S. Patent Office *Annual Rept. for 1861: Ag.* 141, The sheep is then laid upon his back in a kind of saw-buck. **1877** Burdette *Rise & Fall* 308, You might as well tell a joke to a sawbuck as to his wife, for she hadn't as much conception of geniune humor as a cow. **1904** *DN* 2.421 **nwAR,** *Saw-buck.* . . Saw-horse. "You can't buy no saw-buck here; you'll have to get a carpenter to make one." [*DN* Ed: Known to me in early years in eastern Iowa. . . Common in eastern Kansas.] **1948** *Sat. Eve. Post* 10 July 83 **SW,** I'd roped everything around the ranch—calves, hounds, horses, fence posts, sawbucks. **1949** Kurath *Word Geog.* 59, *Saw buck, wood buck,* sometimes simply *buck,* are characteristic of the entire German settlement area in Eastern Pennsylvania, western Maryland, the Shenandoah Valley, the upper reaches of the Potomac in West Virginia, and on the Yadkin in North Carolina. These expressions are clearly modeled on German *Sägebock, Holzbock.* Saw buck also has rather general currency in the entire Dutch settlement area from Long Island and eastern New Jersey to Albany, whence it was carried into the rest of New York State, into the Housatonic Valley, along Long Island Sound into Connecticut, and into western Vermont. Here *saw buck* has the Dutch prototype *zaagbock.* **1965–70** *DARE* (Qu. L59, *An implement with an X-frame . . to hold firewood for sawing*) 288 Infs, **chiefly Nth, N Midl, West,** Sawbuck; (Qu. L58, *An implement with an A-shaped frame . . that you put boards on to saw them*) 74 Infs, **chiefly Nth, N Midl, West,** Sawbuck. **1981** *PADS* 67.27 **Mesabi Iron Range MN,** Saw horse. . . There are two common racks used for cutting wood; one has X-shaped endpieces, and the other has endpieces shaped like inverted V's. The rack with X-shaped uprights is usually called a *saw buck* by both Iron Range . . and other Minnesota . . informants. **1985** *AmSp* 60.34 **sePA,** *Saw buck.* . . Device used for holding wood while it is being cut ([*saw*] *horse* 59% [of 60 infs], *saw buck* 20% [of 60 infs]. . . [O]ne can no longer accept Kurath's claim . . that [*saw*] *horse* "is in rather general use throughout the Eastern States except for the greater part of Pennsylvania east of the Alleghenies, . . where *saw buck* dominates.") **1986** Pederson *LAGS Concordance* **Gulf Region,** 66 infs, Sawbuck(s). [46 infs described it as "X-frame" or "X-shaped"; 2 infs as "A-frame(s)".] **1999** Millersville Univ. Center for PA Ger. Studies *Jrl.* Fall 6 (as of 1930s), At home the logs were sawed by hand on a sawbuck to stove length and then split.

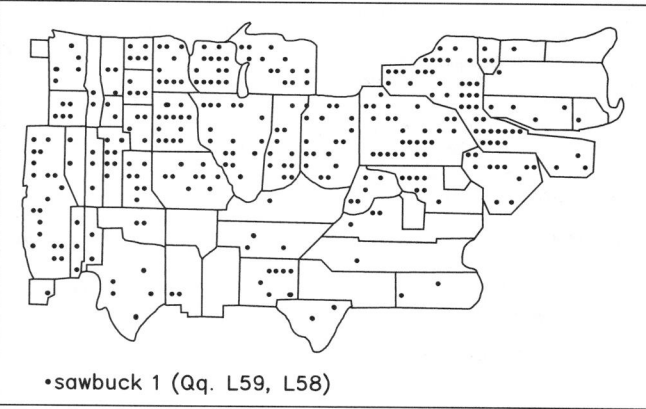

• sawbuck 1 (Qq. L59, L58)

2 also *sawbuck (pack)saddle:* A packsaddle with an X-shaped frame.   **West**

1880 (1881) Nye *Bill Nye & Boomerang* 67 **WY,** This summer, however, I will get me a little blue jackass and put a sawbuck on his back. **1907** White *AZ Nights* 17, We skirmished around and found a condemned army pack saddle with aparejos, and a sawbuck saddle with kyacks. On these we managed to condense our grub and utensils. **1913** *Outing* 61.425, The most practical equipment for pack animals is the ordinary crosstree or sawbuck pack saddle for all-round use. The . . sawbuck . . is used almost exclusively in the United States by forest rangers, cowboys, prospectors and pack travelers generally. **1936** Thompson *High Trails* 138 **MT,** If you are going on a camping trip you utter an instinctive protest as your packer cinches up the "sawbuck" packsaddle and loads his animal. **1958** *AmSp* 33.268 **eWA** [Ranching terms], *Alforkus . . Sawbuck.* A packsaddle. **1969** O'Connor *Horse & Buggy West* 121 **AZ,** Uncle Jim had a romantic barn full of hay, a tack room with saddles, bridles, saddle blankets, rifle scabbards, curry combs, a couple of sawbuck pack saddles, pack boxes cleverly contoured on one side to fit the shape of a horse's ribs. **1978** Doig *This House* 8 **MT,** The only thing we could get you on was a sawbuck pack saddle. You know what they are, like a little sawhorse setting on top of the saddle rigging. Hard as a rasp to sit on, but you straddled in there like it was the only thing going.

3 also *saw(ski):* A ten-dollar bill; ten dollars; occas a bill of another denomination.   Cf **double sawbuck**

[**1850** *Knickerbocker* 36.297, Send me the two double 'saw-bucks'.] **1852** *OR Statesman* (Oregon City OR) 13 Nov 1/1 **KY,** Dod rabbit it, thar goes another 'saw-buck,' on the plag'uey jack. **1912** *DN* 3.589 **wIN,** *Sawbuck.* . . A ten dollar bill. The X in the corner is shaped like a sawbuck. **1927** *AmSp* 2.282 [Prison lingo], *A sawbuck*—Ten dollars. **1931** *AmSp* 6.335 [Circus and carnival slang], *Saw-buck,* or *saw.* . . A ten-dollar bill. "I just saw two saws and a fin in that sap's roll." **1932** *AmSp* 7.312, A $20 bill was originally called a saw-buck, because on the old large size currency its denomination was noted by the Roman numeral XX which resembles a carpenter's saw-buck. The term then became applied to a $10 bill with the single Roman numeral X. In a gangster play I have heard a $20 bill referred to as a double saw-buck. **1953** *AmSp* 28.118 **Pacific coast** (as of late 1940s) [Carnie talk], *Sawbuck, sawski.* . . A ten-dollar bill. 'A double sawski,' a twenty-dollar bill. **1965–70** DARE (Qu. U28b, . . *A ten-dollar bill*) 182 Infs, **widespread,** Sawbuck; **MA3,** Sawski; **SC55,** Single saw; (Qu. U8a, . . *"It cost me ten dollars."*) Infs **MA3,** 7, **WV13,** Cost (me) a sawbuck; **DC12,** It cost me a sawbuck; (Qu. U26, *Names or nicknames . . for a paper dollar*) Infs **KS12, MO3,** 11, Sawbuck; **OK7,** Sawbuck, or is that a five? **TX76,** Sawbuck—for any denomination; (Qu. U27, . . *A silver dollar*) Inf **AL50,** Sawbuck [Inf doubtful]; (Qu. U28a, . . *A five-dollar bill*) Infs **GA89, WA11,** Half a sawbuck; **OK7, WA19,** Sawbuck [Infs doubtful]; **MN2,** Sawbuck; **NY68,** Is that a sawbuck or is that a ten? **1986** Pederson *LAGS Concordance,* 3 infs, **AR, TN,** Sawbuck (ten-dollar bill).

4 The common **merganser** (*Mergus merganser*) Cf **sawbill, sawbill diver**

1923 U.S. Dept. Ag. *Misc. Circular* 13.5 **IL,** *Vernacular Names* [for *Mergus merganser*]. . . *In local use.* . . Sawbuck. **1932** Bennitt *Check-list* 21 **MO,** *American merganser.* . . Saw-buck.

sawbuck (pack)saddle   See **sawbuck 2**

saw cabbage palm n Also *saw cabbage* [See quot 1908] Cf **cabbage palm**

The Everglades palm (*Acoelorraphe wrightii*).

1908 Britton *N. Amer. Trees* 141, Saw Cabbage Palm. . . *Paurotis Wrightii.* . . The dark brown leaf-stalks are about as long as the [leaf] blades, concave on the upper side, their margins armed with stout curved spine-like teeth. **1933** Small *Manual SE Flora* 242 **FL,** *Saw-cabbage-palm.* . . Hammocks and low savannahs. Big Cypress and S. Everglades, Fla. **1960** McGeachy *Hdbk. FL Palms* 9, The Saw Cabbage. . . have as their foliage small, stiff, fan-shaped leaves. These leaves are divided about half way into numerous segments which are in turn deeply split.

sawd   See **see B2d, 3d**

sawder   See **solder**

sawdust eater n

A sawmill worker.

1927 *AmSp* 3.24 **eTX** [Sawmill talk], The common laborer is variously known as a "lumber rustler," "rosum belly," or "sawdust eater." [**1935** Davis *Honey* 146 **OR,** That sawdust hog [=son of a sawmill owner] that was here last night said you offered him twenty dollars for his gun.] **1938** (1939) Holbrook *Holy Mackinaw* 263, *Sawdust eater.* One of those fellers who works in a sawmill. **1942** *AmSp* 17.223 [Loggers' talk], *Sawdust eater.* Any sawmill employee. **1950** *Western Folkl.* 9.122 **nwOR** [Sawmill workers' speech], *Sawdust eater.* A sawmill worker. **1959** *AmSp* 34.79 **nwCA** [Logger lingo], *Sawdust eater.* . . A sawmill employee. **1966** DARE Tape **MI10,** A sawmill hand who preferred to live out in town was known as a sawdust eater.

sawdust gravy n Cf **sawmill gravy**

See quots.

1966 Adams *Mt. LeConte* 37 **wNC, eTN,** We ate well that night—fried squirrels, boiled potatoes, fresh green beans, "sawdust" gravy, bread and coffee. **2001** DARE File (as of c1970), Friends who were natives of Tennessee, but living in Kentucky at the time, invited us for a real 'down home' meal which included "sawdust gravy." This seemed to be a somewhat gritty, thickened red-eye gravy. The texture may have come from cornmeal.

sawdust pudding n

A dish consisting primarily of coarsely ground meal; see quots.

1729 in 1841 *S. Lit. Messenger* 7.596, [Quoting Benjamin Franklin:] My friends, any man who can subsist on sawdust pudding and water, as I can see, needs no man's patronage. **1950** *WELS* (*What names do you have for . . Fried corn meal: [Include joking names]*) 1 Inf, **seWI,** Sawdust pudding.

sawdust savage n Cf **savage**

=**sawdust eater.**

1930 Williams *Logger-Talk* 28 **Pacific NW,** A mill-hand is sometimes called a *sawdust savage.*

sawed adj Cf **hacked** ppl adj[1]

Embarrassed, confused, flustered.

1843 (1847) Field *Drama Pokerville* 199 **MO,** The thoroughly "sawed" victim made way for him. **1940** *AmSp* 15.447 **eTN,** *Sawed.* Embarrassed. 'Clyde was sawed.'

sawed v See **see B2d, 3d**

saw-filer n

=**saw-whet owl.**

1927 Forbush *Birds MA* 2.211, *Cryptoglaux acadica acadica* [= *Aegolius acadicus*]. . . *Saw-filer.* . . Smallest New England owl. [*Ibid* 212, *Voice.*—Sharp whistles resembling saw filing.] **1932** Bennitt *Check-list* 38 **MO,** *Cryptoglaux acadica acadica.* . . Saw-filer. **1956** MA Audubon Soc. *Bulletin* 40.81, *Saw-whet owl.* . . Saw-filer.

sawfish n

1 =**bowfin.** Cf **sawyer 3**

1967 DARE Tape **LA5,** Choupique. . . well plenty of 'em call it a green cypress trout. . . lot of people call it sawfish around here.

2 Perh a **gizzard shad 1** (here: *Dorosoma cepedianum*).   Cf **sawbelly 2**

1969 *DARE* (Qu. P1, . . *Kinds of freshwater fish . . caught around here . . good to eat*) Inf **IN**58, Sawfish; (Qu. P3, *Freshwater fish that are not good to eat*) Inf **IN**58, Sawfish.

saw frame n esp SE   See Map

=sawbuck 1.

1899 *Living Age* 223.167 **Missip Valley,** One of them [=a flying squirrel] ran up an upright of the saw-frame and took his flight from the top of that Pisgah. **1965–70** *DARE* (Qu. L59, *An implement with an X-frame . . to hold firewood for sawing*) 18 Infs, **esp SE,** Saw frame; (Qu. L58, *An implement with an A-shaped frame . . that you put boards on to saw them*) Inf **GA**77, Saw frame. [17 of 18 total Infs male, 17 old or mid-aged] **1986** Pederson *LAGS Concordance (Sawbuck)* 3 infs, **GA, TN,** Saw frame(s).

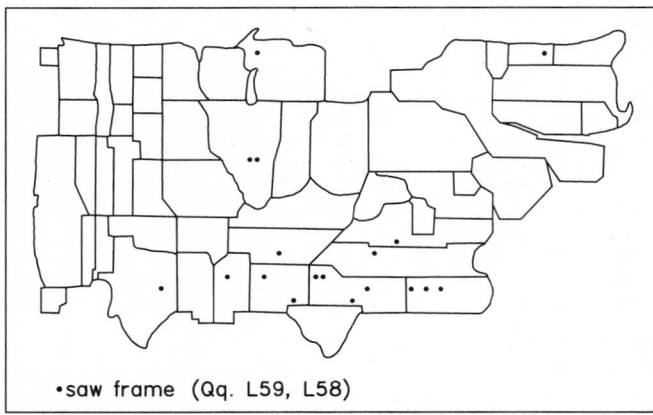

•saw frame (Qq. L59, L58)

saw gourds See gourd 3

saw grass n

1 A sedge of the genus *Cladium,* esp *C. mariscus.* [See quot 1975] **chiefly S Atl, Gulf States**   For other names of *C. mariscus* See **redtop 3**

1822 Simmons *Notices E. FL* 24, They were obliged to defend their horses' feet with wrappings of cow-hide, in order to prevent their being injured by the sharp saw grass, a species of triaugular [sic] reed, with which this watery desart is thickly overgrown. **1848** *S. Lit. Messenger* 14.531 **FL,** The saw grass was at least four feet above the heads of the men seated in the boats. **1894** *Jrl. Amer. Folkl.* 7.103, *Cladium effusum,* . . saw-grass, Fla. and other Southern States. **1941** O'Donnell *Great Big Doorstep* 3 **LA,** The girls waded gingerly over the saw-grass marsh, avoiding the tall graceful blades which could inflict deep cuts if brushed the wrong way. **1966** *DARE* (Qu. S9, . . *Kinds of grass that are hard to get rid of*) Inf **FL**35, Saw grass. **1966–68** *DARE* Tape **FL**39, [Inf:] There you'll see the great acres of saw grass. [FW:] Is that the stuff that's supposed to cut you? [Inf:] It sure will. If you go through it, it doesn't make you hemorrhage, but it'll scratch you up pretty badly; **LA**31, We have saw grass. That's long-stemmed and it has a rough saw-edge to it. Sharp point on the end. **1975** Natl. Audubon Soc. *Corkscrew* 8, *Sawgrass* (*Mariscus jamaicensis* [=*Cladium mariscus*]). . . The name is derived from three rows of fine saw teeth, one on each edge and another on the back of the mid-rib. Walking through thick growths of saw-grass is very unpleasant due to these teeth which cause painful cuts. **1986** Pederson *LAGS Concordance,* 1 inf, **ceFL,** Saw grass—in swamps or marshes; 1 inf, **ceFL,** Saw grass—when it blooms, hurricane will come; 1 inf, **nwLA,** Saw grass; 1 inf, **swLA,** Saw grass—grew in marshes, burned off when dry; 1 inf, **ceAL,** Saw-grass flats. **1990** Burke *Morning for Flamingos* 273, There're a lot of abandoned housing developments in the Everglades. So they use these paved roads out in the saw grass for airstrips.

2 A plant such as a **cordgrass** (here: *Spartina pectinata*), a **nut rush 1** (here: *Scleria triglomerata*), or a **tearthumb** (here: *Polygonum sagittatum*); see quots.

1913 *Torreya* 13.230 **SC,** *Polygonum sagittatum.* . . Cut or saw grass, Santee Club, S.C. **1920** *Ibid* 20.18 **MO,** *Spartina michauxiana* [=*S. pectinata*]. . . Lowland grass, sawgrass, rip-gut, Hartmann, Mo. **1927** Boston Soc. Nat. Hist. *Proc.* 38.247 **Okefenokee GA,** *Scleria (trichopoda?)* [=*Scleria triglomerata?*] 'Little-bladed saw-grass'. . . *Cladium effusum* 'Big-bladed saw-grass'. *Ibid* 351, I found a nest of *Oryzomys,*

built among fern and 'little-bladed saw-grass' at a height of about 6 inches from the surface of the prairie. **1965–70** *DARE* (Qu. L8, *Hay that grows naturally in damp places*) Infs **IN**32, 45, Saw grass; (Qu. L9a, . . *Kinds of grass . . grown for hay*) Inf **LA**44, Saw grass; (Qu. S15, . . *Weed seeds that cling to clothing*) Inf **CT**2A, Saw grass—mostly in swamps or along brooks, etc; (Qu. S21, . . *Weeds . . that are a trouble in gardens and fields*) Inf **NY**207, Saw grass—broad, sharp-edged leaf; **RI**4, Saw grass—good to chew on. [*DARE* Ed: Some of these Infs may refer instead to **1** above.]

sawing horse n [*OED2* sawing horse (at sawing vbl. sb. 3) 1846]

1967–68 *DARE* (Qu. L58, *An implement with an A-shaped frame . . that you put boards on to saw them*) Infs **NC**54, **TN**16, Sawing horse(s).

sawing rack See saw rack

sawjack n

=sawbuck 1.   Cf **jack** n[1] **6**

1948 Davis *Word Atlas Gt. Lakes* app qu 59a, 3 (of 233) infs, **IL, MI,** Saw jack. **1950** *WELS* (*To hold wood when you're going to saw it*), 1 Inf, **seWI,** Sawjack. **1955** Potter *Dial. NW OH* 127, *Saw buck* (for holding fire-wood). . . *Saw jack* appeared once in the youngest group and twice in the oldest. **1962** Atwood *Vocab. TX* 51, The x-shaped device used to hold logs in place . . *saw jack* (2.2[% of 273 infs]). **1965–70** *DARE* (Qu. L59, *An implement with an X-frame . . to hold firewood for sawing*) 13 Infs, **scattered,** Sawjack; (Qu. L58, *An implement with an A-shaped frame . . that you put boards on to saw them*) Infs **IL**134, **NC**8, 76, 80, **OK**20, **VT**2, **WI**63, Sawjack. **1971** Wood *Vocab. Change* 50 **Sth,** If the wood to be sawed is firewood, the supports of the frame are shaped like an X. . . *Buck, jack, saw jack, trestle,* and *wood buck* occur in scattered distributions. If the piece of wood is a board, the appropriate equipment has the form of an A. . . Scattered terms—*jack, rack, sawbuck, saw jack,* and *trestle*—do not exceed one-tenth of the choices made in any state [covered in the survey]. **1973** Allen *LAUM* 1.221 (as of c1950), *Sawbuck.* . . Saw jack [3 infs, **NE, ND**]. **1986** Pederson *LAGS Concordance (Sawbuck)* 6 infs, **AL, FL, TN, TX,** Saw jack. [4 of the 6 infs describe it as an X-frame.]

sawleaf daisy n

A **gum plant 1** (here: *Grindelia papposa*).

1961 Wills–Irwin *Flowers TX* 224, *Prionopsis ciliata* [=*Grindelia papposa*]. . . Saw-leaf Daisy, or Golden-weed, as it is sometimes called, is a drought-resistent plant . . found . . northwestward to the Panhandle.

saw logs v phr Also cut logs; for addit varr see quot widespread exc NEast   See Map   Cf saw wood

To snore.

1949 in 1986 *DARE* File **MI,** John was certainly sawing the logs last night. A proverbial expression which means to snore. **c1950** *Halpert Coll.* 37 **wKY, nwTN,** He's sawin' logs = snoring. **1960** Criswell *Resp. to PADS* 20 **Ozarks,** *Sawing logs* . . [refers to snoring]. **1965–70** *DARE* (Qu. X45, . . *Joking expressions . . about snoring*) 278 Infs, **widespread exc NEast,** Sawing logs; **CA**118, Sawing a log; **AR**37, Sawing big logs; **NY**34, Sawing logs and stacking them; **CO**33, Sawing some logs; **MI**67, Sawed a log; **MO**21, Sawing the log; **MO**25, Saw logs; **NE**8, **TN**50, Cutting logs; **SC**3, Cuttin' logs; (Qu. X40, . . *Ways . . of saying, "I'm going to bed"*) Inf **TX**28, Going to saw some logs.

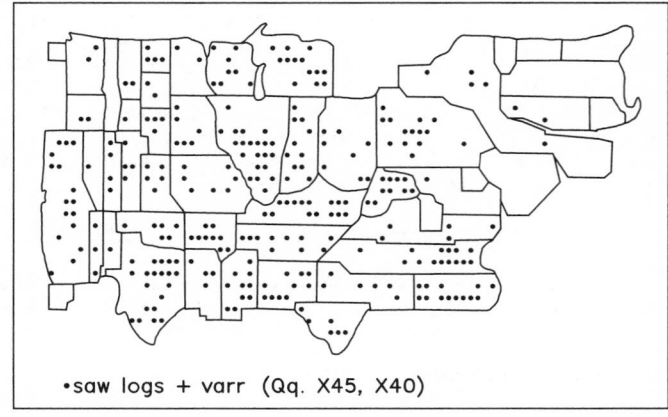

•saw logs + varr (Qq. X45, X40)

sawmill, born in a adj phr Also *raised in a sawmill;* for addit varr see quots **chiefly NEast, C Atl** See Map
=**raised in a barn.**

1878 *Scribner's Mth.* 16.515 **NEng,** It is often said of one who leaves outer doors open in cold weather, "Guess he was brought up in a sawmill, where there wa'n't no doors." **1950** *WELS* (When somebody behaves unpleasantly or without manners: "He must have been _____.") 3 Infs, **WI,** Brought up in (or born and raised in) a sawmill. **1965–70** *DARE* (Qu. II21) 15 Infs, **chiefly NEast, C Atl,** Born (or brought up, raised, reared) in a sawmill; **NY75,** Brought up in sawmill—if someone goes out without closing the door; **MD30,** Raised on the sawmill. [15 of 17 Infs old]

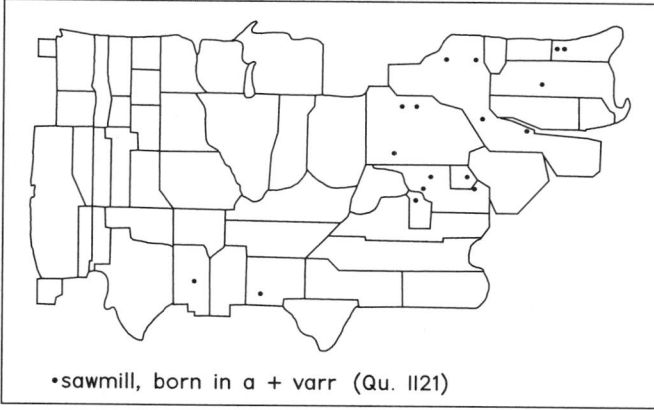

•sawmill, born in a + varr (Qu. II21)

sawmill chicken n Also *sawmill turkey*
Salt pork.

1967–68 *DARE* (Qu. H38, . . *Words for bacon [including joking ones]*) Inf **GA24,** Sawmill chicken; **TN1,** Sawmill turkey—because sawmill workers ate so much of it. **1986** Pederson *LAGS Concordance* (Salt pork) 1 inf, **csGA,** Local restaurant calls side meat sawmill chicken.

sawmill coffee n
Very strong coffee.

1970 *DARE* (Qu. H74a, . . *Coffee* . . *very strong*) Inf **TN44,** Sawmill coffee. **1986** Pederson *LAGS Concordance,* 1 inf, **cwTN,** Sawmill coffee—extremely strong.

sawmill gravy n **chiefly sAppalachians** Cf **sawdust gravy**
A thick gravy; see quots.

1940 *AmSp* 15.447 **eTN,** Saw mill gravy. Thick gravy. **1965** *West Time Was* 28 **nwNC,** The gravy had been made by frying flour in pork grease for body, then stirring in milk while the gravy thickened. . . She smiled. . . "Anybidy that's had as much practice doin a job as I've had makin sawmill gravy is bound to be a expert or crazy as a bedbug." **1966–69** *DARE* (Qu. H37, . . *Words* . . *for gravy. Any joking ones?*) Infs **GA19, 70, KY37, NC37, 41,** Sawmill gravy; **NC44,** Sawmill gravy—white; **NC48,** Sawmill gravy—thick; **TX33,** Sawmill gravy—cream gravy. **1977** *Foxfire 4* 315 **swNC,** She would make them [=loggers] a big pan of sawmill gravy. She'd have a great big skillet and she'd put some meal or flour in it. You could make it out of corn meal or flour, but . . generally . . flour. She'd put that flour in that pan and she'd let it brown a little bit. Then she'd dump milk in there—or water if she didn't have milk. So they'd have gravy. **1983** *DARE* File **cNC,** From a restaurant breakfast menu: Sawmill gravy. [Cook's description:] "Take the fat from fried meat, stir in flour and brown. Add milk and serve with hot biscuits." **1985** Madson *Up River* 244 **Upper Missip Valley,** Cooks like "Big Tit Mary" created such appealing viands as "Dead Man's Leg" (a dessert often made of leftovers), "Barge Line Buzzard" (chicken), and "Sawmill Gravy," which was gravy of the lumpier, sorrier sort, resembling sawdust mixed with engine oil. **1987** *DARE* File **seAL,** Sawmill gravy: flour browned in fat, made into gravy with little pieces of sausage (patty) in it. Eaten over biscuit. **1989** Smith *Flyin' Bullets* 55 **TN,** Corn bread might be eaten for breakfast with "saw mill gravy," a gravy made of corn meal. **1993** *DARE* File **seTN,** Sawmill gravy. Made with corn-meal mixed with a little flour and browned in ham or bacon drippings thinned with water or milk. *Ibid,* [Menu item:] Two Homemade Butter-milk Biscuits served with Sawmill Gravy. **1996** Adams *Piano Lessons* 73 **MS,** I'm eating sawmill gravy and grits, and there's Faulkner's nephew over there. **1997** Frazier *Cold Mountain* 262 **NC,** His hair was

the next thing to white and his skin was greyish, so that overall he gave the impression of a china plate filled with biscuit and sawmill gravy.

Sawmill Hollow n Cf **mill town**
1966–68 *DARE* (Qu. C35, *Nicknames for the different parts of your town or city*) Infs **NC30, VA2,** Sawmill Hollow.

sawmill license n
A "license" for a common-law marriage.

1968 *DARE* (Qu. AA19, . . *A man and woman who are not married but live together as if they were*) Inf **GA23,** Sawmill license. **1986** Pederson *LAGS Concordance (Married)* 1 inf, **swGA,** Sawmill license—common-law marriage; popular.

sawmill, raised in a See **sawmill, born in a**

sawmill turkey See **sawmill chicken**

sawn See **see** B2e, 3e

sawney n Also sp *sawny* [Scots dial; *OED2* →1882]
A foolish or indolent person; a lanky person.

1950 *WELS Suppl.* **cwWI,** A gangly person or goof is called a sawny. **1974** *DARE* File, A low-down, lazy, no-good bum is a "sawney." This came from a New Englander transplanted to Rochester, Wis. in 1880.

saw owl See **saw-whet owl**

saw palmetto n

1 A **palmetto B** (here: *Serenoa repens*).   Also called **scrub palmetto**
1797 in 1916 Hawkins *Letters* 85 **GA,** The whole country was a pine barron, with wiregrass and saw palmetto. **1837** (1962) Williams *Territory FL* 290, The mouth of the [Caloosahatchee] river is chequered with mangrove islets. . . The banks covered with tall pines and saw palmet-toes. **1869** Porcher *Resources* 604 **Sth,** Saw palmetto, (*Chamoerops serrulata,* L. [=*Serenoa repens*]). . . The pulp is very sweet, but is possessed of a purgative property, often producing a copious evacuation attended with griping. **1894** Torrey *FL Sketch-Book* 3, The ground [was] covered thickly with saw palmetto. **1913** *Auk* 30.483 **Okefenokee GA,** The islands. . . are covered for the most part with pine barrens. . . Beneath the pines is an abundant and practically continuous growth of saw-palmetto (*Serenoa serrulata*). **1938** Rawlings *Yearling* 317 **nFL,** They [=bears] were eating the berries of the saw palmetto. **1967** *DARE* (Qu. T16, . . *Kinds of trees* . . *'special'*) Inf **SC63,** Saw palmetto. **1982** *Naples Now* May 37 **sFL,** Then, there's the *saw palmetto,* resistant to fire, drought, and cold. The fan shaped leaves of this plant can be three feet wide and are mounted on stiff slender stems.

2 The Everglades palm (*Acoelorraphe wrightii*).   Cf **saw cabbage palm**
1965 Neal *Gardens HI* 97, Saw palmetto. *Paurotis* [=*Acoelorraphe*] *wrightii.* **1979** Little *Checklist U.S. Trees* 44, *Acoelorrhaphe wrightii.* . . Silver-saw-palmetto.

saw rack n Also *sawing rack, wood saw rack* **chiefly Sth, S Midl** See Map on p. 762
=**sawbuck 1.**

1936 *LAMSAS Materials* **wNC** (Montgomery Coll.), Sawrack. **c1960** *Wilson Coll.* **csKY,** Sawrack. . . Sawhorse. **1961** Folk *Word Atlas N. LA* map 616, Wooden rack for sawing planks . . [less freq responses include] sawing rack. **1965–70** *DARE* (Qu. L59, *An implement with an X-frame* . . *to hold firewood for sawing*) 34 Infs, **Sth, S Midl,** Saw rack; **KY29, OK14, TN16,** Sawing rack; **NC15,** Wood saw rack; (Qu. L58, *An implement with an A-shaped frame* . . *that you put boards on to saw them*) Infs **GA77, KY86, SC19,** Saw rack. [37 of 39 total Infs comm type 4 or 5, 32 male] **1966** Dakin *Dial. Vocab. Ohio R. Valley* 2.168, Racks of both types [=X-frame and A-frame] are called *sawhorse,* or simple *horse,* . . but *sawbuck* . . *saw rack,* and *rack* are more common names for Type A [=A-frame]. *Ibid* 169, Throughout Kentucky generally, the most common name for the *sawbuck* (Type A) is *wood rack, saw rack.* . . North of the river . . *saw rack* [is] scattered in the counties along the Ohio from the Big Sandy to Pennsylvania, and in the interior counties in Illinois. **1971** *PADS* 56.13 **AL,** Saw rack . . *Rare.* **1973** Allen *LAUM* 1.221 (as of c1950), Sawbuck. . . saw rack [1 inf, **IA**]. **1986** Pederson *LAGS Concordance* **Gulf Region** (*Sawbuck*) 44 infs, Saw rack(s); 2 infs, Sawing rack. [Of those infs who offered a description, 31 described it as an X-frame or X-shaped; 2 infs as an X- or A-frame, and 1 inf as a modified A-frame.]

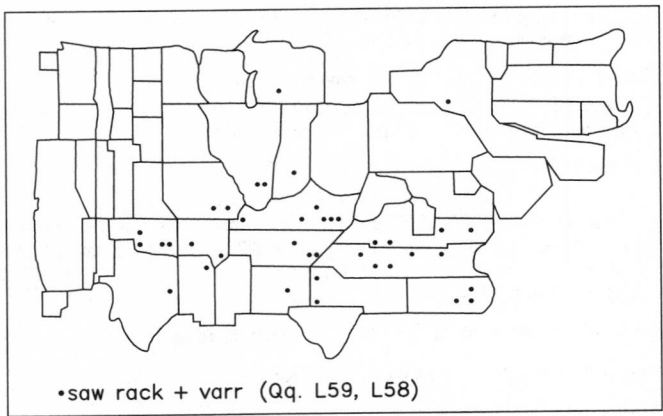

•saw rack + varr (Qq. L59, L58)

saw rick See **rick** n 4

saw-set mark n Also *saw-set (earmark)* [From the resemblance to an old-fashioned saw set]

An **earmark** n; see quots.

1943 *Democrat* 14 Jan 4/6 (*DA*), Reddish brindle muley-headed yearling . . swallowfork and under sawset in right. **1944** *Ibid* 13 April 4/4 (*DA*), One yellow heifer . . marked crop the right, swallow fork and saw set in the left. **1968** *DARE* (Qu. K18, . . *Kind of mark . . to identify a cow*) Inf **LA**29, Crop and saw-set mark—saw-set is the slit underneath the ear. [FW illustr] **1968** Adams *Western Words* 267, *Saw-set earmark*—An earmark made by cropping the ear and then cutting out the center in the shape of a rectangle; sometimes called *crop and mortice*.

sawski See **sawbuck** 3

sawtooth briar See **saw brier**

saw vine n

Prob a **saw brier.**

1967 *DARE* (Qu. S21, . . *Weeds . . that are a trouble in gardens and fields*) Inf **AR**55, Saw vine.

saw-whet owl n Also *saw-whet(ter), saw owl, whet-saw* [See quot 1834] **chiefly Nth, esp NEng, NY** See Map

A small, dark brown owl (*Aegolius acadicus*) native to much of the US. Also called **Acadian owl, barn ~ 2, mouse ~, saw-filer, screech owl 2b, sparrow ~, stone ~, white-fronted ~**

1834 Audubon *Ornith. Biog.* 2.567, The Little Owl is known in Massachusetts by the name of the "Saw-whet," the sound of its love-notes bearing a great resemblance to the noise produced by filing the teeth of a large saw. **1844** DeKay *Zool. NY* 2.30, The *Little Owl*, or *Saw-whet* as it is called in Massachusetts and this State, is found in every part of the Union. **1858** Baird *Birds* 58, Saw-whet Owl. . . The smallest owl found in the eastern and middle States of North America, and is probably an inhabitant of the entire temperate regions of this division of the continent. **1875** Flagg *Birds Seasons New Engl.* 282, *The Acadian Owl, or Saw-whetter*. **1911** Howell *Birds AR* 43, The saw-whet . . in the lower Mississippi Valley is a rare or accidental winter visitant. **1941** *LANE*

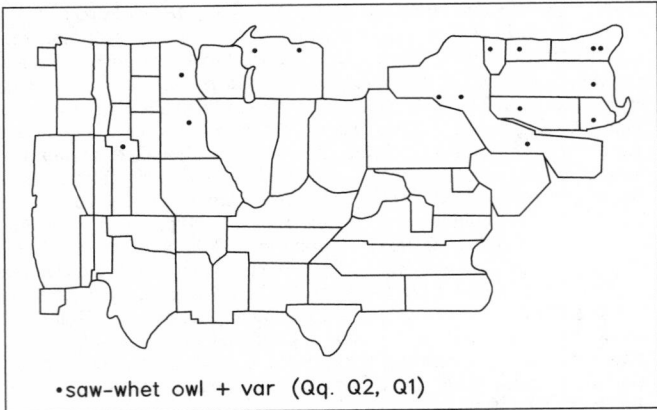

•saw-whet owl + var (Qq. Q2, Q1)

Map 230, 2 infs, **NEng**, Saw-whet (owl). **1956** MA Audubon Soc. *Bulletin* 40.81, Saw-whet owl. . . Saw-whet (Maine, Vt., Mass.); . . Saw-whetter (Mass.); Whet-saw (Maine). **1965–70** *DARE* (Qu. Q2, . . *Kinds of owls*) 11 Infs, 10 **NEast, N Cent**, Saw-whet owl; **NY**66, Saw owl; (Qu. Q1, . . *Kind of owl that makes a shrill, trembling cry*) Infs **CO**7, **ME**8, **NH**5, Saw-whet owl. [14 of 15 Infs old] **1977** *New Yorker* 5 Sept 24 **NYC**, Saw-whet owls and long-eared owls roost in evergreens in winter.

saw wood v phr Also *chop wood, cut timber, cut wood;* for addit varr see quots **widespread, but less freq S Atl, Inland Sth, Lower Missip Valley** See Map Cf **saw logs**

To snore.

1858 Hammett *Piney Woods Tavern* 126, They was in full blast . . sawin' wood and snortin' like troopers' horses. **1942** McAtee *Dial. Grant Co. IN* 54 (as of 1890s), Saw wood . . snore. Slang. **c1950** Halpert *Coll.* 37 **wKY, nwTN**, He's sawin' logs = snoring. . . Var[iant] . . [Sawing] Wood. **c1960** Wilson *Coll.* **csKY**, Cutting big timber: . . Snoring loudly, sawing gourds. **1965–70** *DARE* (Qu. X45, . . *Joking expressions . . about snoring*) 353 Infs, **widespread, but less freq S Atl, Inland Sth, Lower Missip Valley**, Sawing wood; 15 infs, **scattered, but esp Nth, N Midl**, Cutting wood; **MI**93, 105, 120, Buzzing wood; **KY**94, **MN**37, **MO**26, Chopping wood; **IL**30, Pounding wood; **CO**33, 47, Sawing some (*or* the) wood; **NY**205, Sawing woods; **FL**27, **WI**74, Saw(s) wood; **AR**18, **IL**96, **MO**15, Sawin(g) boards; **FL**39, Saw lumber; **AR**56, **MD**9, **NC**61, **NY**7, 86, **SC**32, **WA**28, Cutting (big) timber; **FL**22, **KY**45, **NC**30, Sawing timber; (Qu. X40, . . *Ways . . of saying, "I'm going to bed"*) Infs **MN**10, **PA**165, 195, (Going to) saw wood.

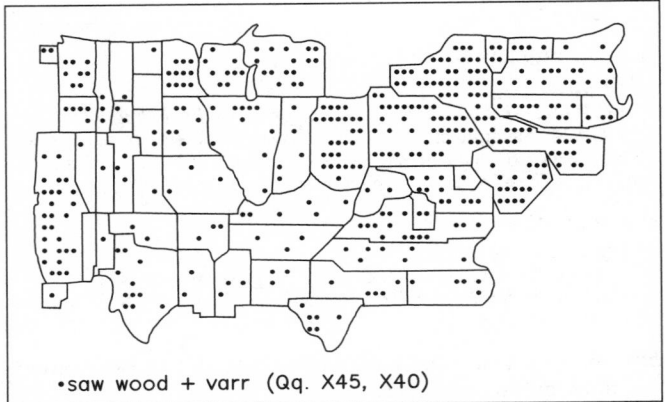

•saw wood + varr (Qq. X45, X40)

sawworm n

A **flatheaded borer;** see quot.

1885 Thompson *By-Ways* 36, [The ivory-billed woodpecker's] principal food is a large flat-headed timber-worm known in the South as *borer* or *saw-worm*.

sawwort n

A **blazing star 3,** usu *Liatris spicata*.

1830 Rafinesque *Med. Flora* 2.237, Liatris. . . Throatwort, Sawort [sic], *Button Snakeroot*. . . All have a tuberous medical root. **1876** Hobbs *Bot. Hdbk.* 103, Saw-wort, Button snake root, Liatris spicata. **1900** Lyons *Plant Names* 212, Liatris spicata. . . Rough-root, Sawwort.

sawyer n

1 also *log* (or *pine, wood*) *sawyer, sawyer beetle, ~ bug*: Any of several wood-boring beetles or larvae of the families Cerambycidae and Buprestidae, but usu a larva of *Monochamus* spp. **chiefly S Atl, Gulf States** See Map

1780 in 1789 Anburey *Travels* 2.452 **VA**, The log huts in which the soldiers reside . . [have been] nearly destroyed by an insect that . . preys upon the solid part of the timber; and these insects . . have the appellation of sawyers. **1890** Packard *Insects* 675, The most insidious and widely destructive kinds are the timber-borers, and of these the grub or larva of *Monohammus confusor*, called in the Southern pine districts "the sawyer," does the most damage. **1892** *Jrl. Amer. Folkl.* 5.111 **Baltimore MD**, If it [=a baby] teeths very hard tie a "sawyer-bug" around its neck, and when the bug dies the tooth will come through. **1905** Kellogg *Amer. Insects* 285, The sawyers, various species of the genus Monohammus, are beautiful brown and grayish beetles with extremely long delicate antennae; the larvae bore in sound pines and firs and do great damage to evergreen forests. **c1938** in 1970 Hyatt *Hoodoo* 1.229 **AL,** [They] looked lak young dirt daubers but dey were log sawyers—dey had dat little brown tip on der haids, flat. **1946** Kopman *Wild Acres* 46 **LA,** Red-cockaded woodpeckers. . . belonged as much to their environment as . . the "sawyers," or beetle larvae, that bored in diseased or fallen trees. **1958** Babcock *I Don't Want* 158 **eSC,** To be sure, you will find zealous advocates of wood sawyers, crickets, cockroaches [as bait for bream]. **1965–70** *DARE* (Qu. P6, . . *Kinds of worms . . used for bait*) Inf **LA7,** Sawyer—a white worm, lives in bark; **LA15,** Sawyer—they come out of them pine logs; **LA29,** Sawyer—a white worm with brown head that works the bark off timber; **MS72, TX35,** Sawyers; **PA166,** Sawyers—big white grubs found in hardwood; **SC7,** Sawyer—in rotten logs only, same as commercial "golden grub"; **SC43,** Sawyer—a worm in rotten wood; **LA8,** Wood sawyer—come from rotten logs; **NC44,** Wood sawyer—white worm, brown head; (Qu. P5, . . *The common worm used as bait*) Inf **MS81,** Sawyer worms; (Qu. P13, . . *Ways of fishing . . besides the ordinary hook and line*) Inf **GA5,** Flathead sawyer—a white worm one inch long, lives in dead pines; (Qu. R3) Inf **FL17,** Sawyers—on pines, under dead bark; **OK23,** Wood sawyers—found in trees; (Qu. R8, . . *Kinds of creatures that make a clicking or shrilling or chirping kind of sound*) Inf **MI2,** Pine sawyer—hard, green, one-half inch long, click every time they bite a chunk of wood; (Qu. R27, . . *Kinds of caterpillars or similar worms*) Inf **LA15,** Sawyer—in pine logs; (Qu. R30, . . *Kinds of beetles; not asked in early QRs*) Inf **MN14,** Sawyer beetle—bores trees. **c1970** Pederson *Dial. Surv. Rural GA,* 1 inf, **seGA,** We uses sawyers [as bait]. **1986** Pederson *LAGS Concordance,* 1 inf, **csAR,** Sawyer—type of worm; 1 inf, **swAR,** Sawyers used for bait, type of worm; 1 inf, **cFL,** Sawyer—a wood worm; 1 inf, **cwFL,** Sawyer—good worm for fishing, lives in tree bark; 1 inf, **ceFL,** Sawyer—white worm found in dead trees, good bait; 1 inf, **ceGA,** Wood sawyer—little white worm, chews into wood; 1 inf, **csGA,** Sawyer—larger than earthworm; 1 inf, **neGA,** Sawyers—from old decaying pine trees; 1 inf, **seGA,** Sawyers make good fishing bait, can cut wood; 2 infs, **cLA, cMS,** Sawyers; 1 inf, **ceLA,** Sawyer—from bark of dead trees; 1 inf, **csMS,** Sawyers—under bark of dead trees, flat heads; 1 inf, **seMS,** Sawyer—small white worm that bores in trees.

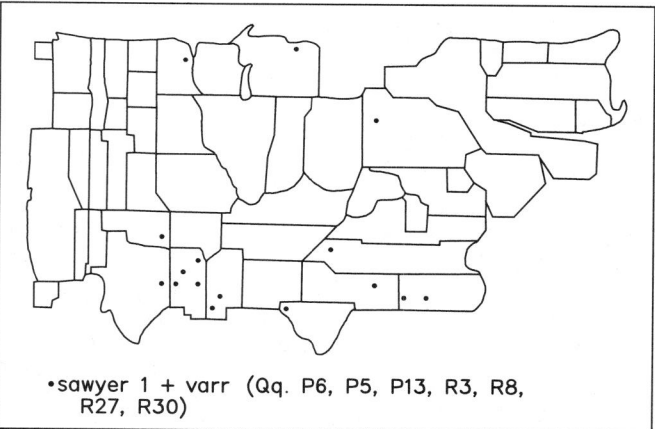

•sawyer 1 + varr (Qq. P6, P5, P13, R3, R8, R27, R30)

2 A **grasshopper 1** of the family Tettigoniidae, usu a **katydid B1. esp VA**

1804 (1905) Lewis *Orig. Jrls. Lewis & Clark Exped.* 6.127, The green insect known in the U'States by the name of the *sawyer* or *chittediddle.* **1816** in 1824 Knight *Letters* 62 **VA,** The tops of the trees are vociferous with sawyers, other larger insects of the locust tribe, called also *katy dids.* **1912** Green *VA Folk-Speech* 366, *Sawyer. . .* A kind of locust that saws off small branches of trees. **1970** *DARE* (Qu. R6, . . *Names . . for grasshoppers*) Inf **VA40,** Sawyer—the green one. **1986** Pederson *LAGS Concordance,* 1 inf, **cTN,** The big grasshopper, his name is sawyer. . . Sawyer—big, two inches long, red, stripes on wing.

3 =**bowfin. Cf sawfish 1**

1884 Goode *Fisheries U.S.* 1.659, *Amia calva. . .* occurs in the Great Lakes, where it is called "Dogfish" and "Sawyer". **1911** U.S. Bur. Census *Fisheries 1908* 308, *Bowfin. . .* "Sawyer".

4 A menace to navigation consisting of a log or tree caught in a river in such a way that its top bobs up and down with the current. **esp Missip-Ohio Valleys Cf planter 1**

1786 in 1877 *Mag. Amer. Hist.* 1.312, Arrived at Guyandot this evening and lay all night off its mouth in rapid water—obliged to make fast to a sawyer. **1804** *Philadelphia Med. & Phys. Jrl.* 1.1.96 **sePA,** This morning we had like to have run foul of a *Sawyer.* These are old trees which lie in the river fast at the roots, and from the manner of their tops rocking up and down, they are called Sawyers. They are deemed very dangerous. **1843** (1916) Hall *New Purchase* 43 **Ohio Valley,** A *sawyer* is either a long trunk, or more commonly an entire tree, so fixed that its top plays up and down with the current and the wind, and is therefore periodically perilous to the navigator. **1851** Burke *Polly Peablossom* 188 **IL,** Oh, sometimes we run foul of a snag, or sawyer; then again, we occasionally collapse a boiler and blow up sky high. **1903** *DN* 2.328 **seMO,** *Sawyer. . .* A snag, generally a whole tree, one end of which is fixed and the other floating. The up and down movement caused by the current gives it its name. **1953** (1977) Hubbard *Shantyboat* 268 **Missip-Ohio Valleys,** Some of the trees were leaning, and disappeared under the surface and rose above it with a slow rhythm as if worked by a giant machine. These are called sawyers; the stationary ones are called planters. **1957** McMeekin *Old KY Country* 83, The snags and sawyers . . were the natural river hazards. **1985** Madson *Up River* 45 **Upper Missip Valley,** "Sawyers" were logs also embedded in the river bottom, but with one end free and pointing upstream, the current imparting a bobbing motion as if it were "sawing."

sawyer beetle (or bug) See **sawyer 1**

Sawyer's, lean toward See **lean v B3**

saw yucca n

A **sotol** (here: *Dasylirion texanum*).

1951 *PADS* 15.29 **TX,** *Dasylirion texanum. . .* Saw yucca. A source of fibers and an emergency cattle feed.

saxafrax, saxafridge, saxifax See **sassafras**

saxifrage n[1] See **sassafras**

saxifrage n[2]

Std: a plant of the genus *Saxifraga.* For other names of var spp see **beefsteak plant 3, groundhog salad, lettuce saxifrage, mayflower 5, mountain lettuce, pussyfoot 1, red moss, Saint-Peter's-cabbage, spider plant, swamp beet, ~ saxifrage, sweet Wilson, wild beet, yellow mountain saxifrage**

saxifras, saxifrax See **sassafras**

say v

A Pronc varr.

1 *says:* Usu |sɛz|; also |sez|; pronc-sp *sayz.*

1949 in 1986 *DARE* File **Sth,** He *says* [sez] that it can be done. **1956** Algren *Walk on the Wild Side* 65 **TX,** "What do the sign sayz, mister?" . . "[I]t *sayz* to scoff up here all you want 'n thank the citizens of San Anton' for it."

2 *said:* Usu |sɛd|; pronc-spp *sade, sayed.* old-fash; now esp in representations of Black speech

1636 in 1927 Orbeck *Early New Engl. Pronc.* 25, Saide. **1647** *Ibid,* Seid. **1679** *Ibid,* Sayed. **1701** *Ibid,* Sade. **1723** in 1894 *New Engl. Mag.* 17.310 **eMA,** He immediately produced the aforesaid bill . . and withall sayed she might inform herself of the goodness of the bill by inquireing of her neighbours. She made reply to him and said what's the matter of the bill? **1829** Kirkham *Engl. Grammar* 192 **NEng,** I axt him for't, and he sade no. **1875** *Harper's New Mth. Mag.* 51.310 **GA** [Black], I found dem in Mr. Boyds pen; he sayed he buyed dem from Mr. Twiggs. **1891** *Atlantic Mth.* 68.47 **AR,** Maw sayed she never *would* sell him. **1937** in 1976 *Weevils in the Wheat* 29 **VA** [Black], Wen he come down, all de overseers sayed dey was going to shoot an dey fired on a man at South Carolina named Anderson. **1940** Writers' Program *Negro in VA* 95 (as of c1936) [Black], Marsa ain't sayed we cain't have no dance an' he ain't sayed we can.

B Gram forms.

1 pres (exc 3rd pers sg): Usu *say;* also

a *says* (eye-dial sp *sez*), used esp in historical present, often in inverted phr *says I.*

1795 Dearborn *Columbian Grammar* 138, *List of Improprieties. . .* Says I for Said I. **1818** Fessenden *Ladies Monitor* 172 **VT,** *Says I,* for I said. **c1840** in 1936 *Jrl. Amer. Folkl.* 49.234, Crack my whip and the leader sprung / I says "day-day" to the wagon tongue. **1860** *Harper's New Mth. Mag.* 20.302 **ME,** "Keep still, Cap'n," says I, "he's after that lucive." **1885** Twain *Huck. Finn* 349 **MO,** "*I* hain't ben nowheres," I says, "only just hunting for the runaway nigger." **1907** White *AZ Nights* 76, "Well," says I to the carcass, "no one's goin' to be able to swear whether you're a maverick or not." **1909** *DN* 3.366 **eAL, wGA,** Says I [sɛzaɪ]. Used in reporting direct discourse after the analogy of *says he.* **1914** Dickinson *WI Plays* 24, I was just sayin', I said so to Jake only this mornin'. I says, "Jake," I says, "I'm gettin' so that I'm su'prised whenever I wake up alive. Whenever I do it," I says, "it's like every blessed mornin' of my life was a genu-ine resurrection for me." **1929** (1954) Faulkner *Sound & Fury* 268 **MS,** "Been much busy?" Earl says. "Not much," I says. **1931** *AmSp* 6.205 **MO** [Univ slang], *Says you:* You say no, but I don't believe you. "Says me" is the answer. **1932** Tooné *Yankee Slang* 32, *Sez me:* Says me. *Ibid, Sez you:* Says you. **1939** *Hall Coll.* **wNC, eTN,** Bowles says, 'I'll shoot if it catches us both.' I says, 'Cut loose after I take care of myself and you take care of yourn.' **1953** Atwood *Survey of Verb Forms* 26, *I says* 'said' . . In N. Eng., only, the first person singular form is recorded as a narrative form in reporting conversations, in such contexts as "I (said) to him" and "(Said) I." In n. N. Eng. . . (*I says,* or, much more frequently, *says I*) occurs in nearly every community. It is used freely by both old-fashioned and modern informants, though not commonly by cultured ones. In s. N. Eng. (except for Cape Cod and the islands) this form is considerably less common and is more clearly characteristic of old-fashioned speech. Here the order is usually *I says* rather than *says I.* **1962** *Mt. Life* Spring 18 **KY,** He begin to pull back, and I says, 'You want me to sqush yer head wi' this hyar .45?' **1965–68** *DARE* Tape **CA5,** So after we got through eatin', I says—that was later on—I says, "Well, I'm here tonight." Well she says, "Get busy, then"; **MA30,** I says to my wife . . , "We'd better get down cellar"; **IN13,** And so—by Jacks he come back and I says to him, I says, "Old George," I says, "has treed the coon round there." **1968** *DARE* FW Addit **CT**14, 15, *Says I*—used for I said. **1986** Pederson *LAGS Concordance* **Gulf Region,** 16 infs, I says; 1 inf, I says—used habitually in recounting dialogue; 1 inf, I told her I says you can do that at night; 2 infs, I says (no)—historical present; 1 inf, I told her, I says now; 1 inf, I says, "Son you ain't letting us down at all."; 1 inf, You says.

b in historical present *say(s) I* and narrative *said I,* often contracted to *s'I, si'I, s'y, sye I.*

1883 (1971) Harris *Nights with Remus* 263 **GA** [Black], I mighty glad you come, en I sez ter de gals, s'I, " 'Fo' de Lord, gals! dar come Brer Fox, en yer we is a-gigglin' en a-gwine on scan'lous; yit hit done come ter mighty funny pass," s'I, "ef you can't run on en laugh 'fo' home folks," s'I. Dat des 'zactly w'at I say, en I leave it ter old Brer Rabbit an de gals yer ef 't aint. **1887** (1967) Harris *Free Joe* 129 **GA,** When your pappy got tetchy, I thes says to myself, s'I, 'Ef I'm wuth havin', I'm wuth scramblin' atter.' **1929** *AmSp* 5.131 **ME,** Old persons frequently interpolated "si'I," . . when telling stories. **1930** *Herald–Advt.* (Huntington WV) 30 Nov sec 3 6/7 **ceKY,** With the mountaineer "s'y" does not merely mean "say" but carries the meaning of "I said". . . Example: "Si, 'Tom, you'd better not do that'." **1952** *AmSp* 27.237 **nwMO,** As a boy I was greatly puzzled by a word which my great-grandmother was constantly throwing into her speech. . . It was the word *sy* [saɪ]. It was years before I figured out this was merely a slurring together of the words *says I.* My sister had a similar experience with another grandmother, one of whose cronies had a farm near by and a son named Chris. This woman was always telling our grandmother what she had said to Chris about this thing or that: 'Sy, Chris, you're going to have to get more than that for those shoats'; 'Sy, Chris, that hay's going to get wet if you don't get it in this afternoon'. My sister told me that for years she thought the man's name was Sy Chris. **1957** *Sat. Eve. Post Letters* **MA,** Expressions my grandmother often used. Instead of "I said" or "I told him," she would say "S'I". I remember asking my mother about it and being told it was . . very old-fashioned. **1967** *DARE* FW Addit, *S'I* [saɪ]—for *says I* in rapid speech. Said by old man. **1972** *Atlanta Letters* **nwGA,** Sye I—said I. **1974** Fink *Mountain Speech* 23 **wNC, eTN,** *'S' I* . . said I. "Your[sic]'re crazy, 's' I."

2 pres 3d pers sg: Usu *says;* also

a *say*—used also in historical present. *esp freq among Black speakers*

1836 *S. Lit. Messenger* 2.493 **SC** [Black], Then I see the fire in his eye, and he say, bridling up jest like him, I would not fill my mouth with any of their good things. **1837** *Ibid* 3.174 **cnVA** [Black], Becase you did'nt [sic] come home last night. . and he say he can't put up no longer with sich tricks. **1878** *Atlantic Mth.* 41.577 **eTN,** Rick *say* he never tuk the filly. **1887** *Ibid* 59.486 **VA** [Black], She say he bring

preacher wid him next time sho. **1899** Chesnutt *Conjure Woman* 20 **csNC** [Black], She . . po'd some out . . fer Henry ter drink. He manage ter git it down; he say it tas'e like whiskey. *Ibid* 26, Dey ain' nuffin pertickler de matter wid 'im—leastways de doctor say so. **1931** (1991) Hughes–Hurston *Mule Bone* 56 **cFL** [Black], Well, she say to tell you when she come. **1982** Heat Moon *Blue Highways* 70 **SC** [Black], I says, 'How that water gone get up to me?' He say with a lectric pump. I says, 'We drink water what comes up of his own mind.' **1986** Pederson *LAGS Concordance* **Gulf Region,** 1 inf, And my mother say you got one bucket of lard; 2 infs, He say; 1 inf, Old nigger say; 1 inf, Mamma say; 3 infs, She say; 1 inf, She say she would; 1 inf, The Bible say you must not use the term. [7 of 10 infs Black]

b in historical present, inverted phr *says he* contracted to *s'ee.*

1926 *AmSp* 2.82 **ME,** In telling a story he uses a contraction of the often iterated *says he* as "s'ee." Thus, "John sez, s'ee—."

3 3d pers pl: usu *say;* also *says* (eye-dial sp *sez*).

1832 *New Engl. Mag.* 3.116 **MA,** My wife and my wif's muther thinks its no Use to deel til the Comeat cums Along. they says the Hotness will sour the bere. **1866** Lowell in *Atlantic Mth.* 17.642 **'Upcountry' MA,** They sez, "Be gin'rous, let 'em swear right in." **1887** (1967) Harris *Free Joe* 104 **GA** [Black], Some sez he likes Babe, an' some sez he likes Susan's fried chicken. **1899** Chesnutt *Conjure Woman* 60 **csNC** [Black], Folks sez dat de ole school'ouse . . is gwine ter ha'nted. **1913** Kephart *Highlanders* 380 **sAppalachians,** The Bible says they're human—leastways some says it does. **1945** FWP *Lay My Burden Down* 36 **TX** [Black], There am . . folks . . what says we-uns believes in superstition. **1953** Atwood *Survey of Verb Forms* 29, *They say.* . . the plural *say* . . is almost universally used with *they.* . . There are only 14 occurrences of *says* . . scattered very widely through the S[outh] A[tlantic] S[tates]. **1967** *DARE* Tape **AZ**1, There's two or three doctors here says folks don't . . die from snakebite. **1986** Pederson *LAGS Concordance* **Gulf Region,** 10 infs, People says he did (*or* he do, he does, he has); 9 infs, Some says; 5 infs, Some of them says; 4 infs, Some people says; 1 inf, Her daughters says I made 10,000 gallons of gravy; 1 inf, Lots of people says dishcloths; 1 inf, Men all says; 1 inf, Most of them just says; 1 inf, Most people says; 1 inf, People says they will sting you; 1 inf, Some folks says; 1 inf, Some people says they using you; 1 inf, Some says "aunt" and some says "auntie"; 1 inf, Some says "I swear to God"; 1 inf, The Negroes says "my auntie"; 1 inf, The people here in Georgia says; 1 inf, The people says he's guilty; 1 inf, When people says "good day"; 1 inf, That's what people says happened; 1 inf, Well, some says harp; 1 inf, You know, ninety percent of your colored people says that.

C Sense.

Also *say not;* as a tag question: Isn't that so? **PaGer area** Cf **ainna**

1948 *AmSp* 23.237 [Engl of PA Germans], It should be mentioned also that *say* as an interrogative, if used with a rising inflection, is meant to anticipate an affirmative answer, like Fr. *n'est-ce pas,* H.G. *nicht wahr,* P.G. *net.* **1986** Hendrickson *Amer. Talk* 167 [Pennsylvania German], Nice crop of wheat, say not? (It's a nice crop of wheat, isn't it?) **1998** Millersville Univ. Center for PA Ger. Studies *Jrl.* Summer 17, Have you ever hard [sic] a Pennsylvania Dutch farmer say, "Throw the cow over the fence some hay?" "Tie the dog loose" is another obvious phony. How about "Come quick onct, Pop half et already?" That's dumb, say? **2000** *NADS Letters,* Here in Eastern PA (PA "Dutch" territory), the word *"say"* is used in place of "isn't it so?" . . That was a good movie, say?

say conj Also sp *suh* [From any of several W Afr languages; see quot 1949; cf *DBE say, DJE se*] **Gullah**

Used with verbs of speech or thought to introduce direct or indirect discourse; see quots.

1888 Jones *Negro Myths* 27 **GA coast,** Buh Rabbit bin spicion say de Gal guine tell Buh Wolf. **1909** *S. Atl. Qrly.* 8.49 **seSC,** An odd usage is that of *say* auxiliary to all verbs of speech or thought. . . In Gullah the use is: '*De angel tell John say 'No man can't count 'em!' [']* . . *Buh Rabbit t'ink say 'Oho! huccum?'* This usage has maintained, unaltered, at least, for seventy-five years; a record of 1835, made by a South Carolinian, shows it identically: *"Me heart t'ink say 'He gwine soon.'"* **1922** Gonzales *Black Border* 119 **sSC, GA coasts** [Gullah], W'en Dry Drought come, bullfrog know suh alligettuh cyan' mek'um fuh wedduh. *Ibid* 168, Da' 'oman t'ink suh him lick me, Gin'ul, but enty you know suh him oughtuh tengk Gawd fuh sabe'-um? **1935** Hurston *Mules & Men* 217 **FL,** Told him say, "Go down dere, boy." **1949** Turner *Africanisms* 211, The word [sɛ] (also pronounced [se]) is used in Gullah after verbs of saying, thinking, and wishing and introduces objective clauses. . . [Turner's transcr:] [den dɪ cɪlən dɛ in ɲu yɒk sɛn wʌd sɛ de ẽ gɒɪn gɪt nʌtɪn] 'Then the children there in New York sent word saying (or that) they were not going to get anything'; [dɪ pɪpl kʌm hom nekɪd . . tɛl mi ɑftə sɛ de cɛc bʌd] 'The people came home naked . . told me afterward that they caught birds'; [de lɔ sɛ wi tu ol] 'They admit that we are too old.' The use of [sɛ] or a synonym of it is common in many West African languages. . . Twi. . . Ibo. . . Ewe. . . Mende. **1987** Jones-Jackson *When Roots Die* 142 **sSC coast** [Gullah], The word *say* is most commonly used in Gullah to introduce a direct quotation and is repeated before each clause, group of words, or single utterance, in order to assure that the listeners will recognize what follows as the exact words of another speaker. . . Gullah: He tell em, say, "E ain't no deer round here." Say, "Where you de hunt?" English: He told him, "There aren't any deer around here." He asked, "Where are you hunting?"

sayed See **say** v **A2**

say grace over v phr **Sth, S Midl**

In phrr *all* (or *more than*) *one can say grace over:* As much as (or more than) one can handle; a lot.

1941 *AmSp* 16.21 **sIN,** *All I can say grace over.* All I can find time for. **1943** *AmSp* 18.66 **SC,** *All I can say grace over.* **1979** *DARE* File **TX,** [Ambassador Robt. Strauss on national television show:] I've got all I can say grace over, and the Secretary [of State] has all he can say grace over. **1982** *DARE* File **AR,** They've got more than I can say grace over. **1986** Pederson *LAGS Concordance,* 1 inf, **ceTX,** More than you could say grace over = a great many. **1995** Brophy *Coll.* 1 **swMO** (as of c1960), *All one can say grace over.* [A]ll one can cope with. **1996** *Verbatim* Autumn 1 **Sth,** "She has more than she can say grace over," was another expression which seems to have disappeared. Even though it refers to grace before meat and thus means that the materfamilias has more people to feed than she can manage, the term was used in many situations of someone whose load was too heavy.

saying over vbl n

Scolding, reprimanding; swearing.

1905 Wasson *Green Shay* 65 **NEng,** You let us work chock out to our gear on one of them kind of chances, jest to find everything picked clean as a hound's tooth, and there's liable to be some pretty tall sayin' over aboard this packet! [Footnote to *sayin':* Swearing, scolding, berating] **1974** *AmSp* 49.63 **sME coast** (as of c1900), *Saying-over. . .* Reprimand. "The captain gave him a good saying-over."

say not See **say** v **C**

says See **say** v **B1a, 3**

says I See **say** v **B1a**

say-so n [LaFr *say-so (de crème).* This is generally regarded as from Engl *say so,* but the sense remains unexplained.]

An ice-cream cone.

[**1931** Read *LA French* 116, *Say-so. . .* English "say so," used in various ways. *Un say-so de crème,* for example, is the equivalent of "a cone of ice-cream."] [**1939** *AmSp* 14.200 **sLA,** The following English words have passed into the active French vocabulary with pronunciations approximately English. . . *Say so* [seso]. An ice-cream cone.] **1967** *DARE* FW Addit **LA**14, A *say-so* ['seɪ,sou]—old-fashioned—for ice-cream cone. **1981** *DARE* File **seTX** (as of c1930), As a child growing up in the Gulf Coast region near the Louisiana border I frequently went to the local drugstores to purchase a "say-so" (I never knew how it was spelled) which was an ice-cream cone. I have always suspected it was of Cajun origin.

says which See **say which**

say what interrog exclam *orig esp freq among Black speakers, but now more widely known* Cf **do what, say which**

Used to request the repetition of something improperly heard or understood; also used as an expression of incredulity; see quots.

1968–70 *DARE* (Qu. X18, . . *When one person doesn't quite hear what another person said, what does he say?*) Infs **NC**88, **OK**57, **PA**76, Say what? **SC**70, Say what again? [3 of 4 Infs Black] **1983** Allin *S. Legislative Dict.* 26 **Sth,** Say what?: (see Do what?) **1986** Pederson *LAGS Concordance (What's that?—failing to hear someone's utterance)* 37 infs, **Gulf Region,** Say what? 1 inf, **swGA,** Say what?—blacks say. [19 of 38 infs Black] **1988** Tyler *Breathing Lessons* 168 **sePA** [Black],

"I made it up." . . Lamont said, "Say what?" "I fibbed," Maggie said blithely. **1994** Smitherman *Black Talk* 198, Say what? A response questioning the validity of what somebody has said. Crossover expression.

say which interrog exclam Also *says which*
=**say what.**

1931 *AmSp* 6.205 **MO** [Univ slang], Says which?: What do you say? **1941** in 1944 *ADD* **Sth,** 'Say which?' = What did you say?

sayz See **say** v **A1**

scab n Cf **tail end**

A cow or steer less than one year old.

1907 Love *Deadwood Dick* 52 **West,** Short yearlings were those over one year old and short of two years, long yearlings those two years and short of three years, tail end and scabs mean nearly the same thing, and comprise all the very young stock of all classes not yet reached the dignity of yearlings.

scabbard fish n [See quot 1884]

The cutlass fish *(Trichiurus lepturus).*

1879 U.S. Natl. Museum *Bulletin* 14.39, *Trichiurus lepturus. . .* Hairtail; *Scabbard-fish.*—Temperate and Tropical Atlantic. **1884** Goode *Fisheries U.S.* 1.335, *Trichiurus lepturus. . .* "Scabbard-fish". . . In shape and general appearance it looks very much like the metallic scabbard of the sword. **1902** Jordan–Evermann *Amer. Fishes* 290, *Trichiurus lepturus,* known as the . . scabbard-fish, . . a long, slender, ribbon-like fish, . . is taken occasionally in the lower Chesapeake and along the South Atlantic coast. . . Though not abundant enough to be of commercial importance, it is nevertheless an excellent food fish. **1933** LA Dept. of Conserv. *Fishes* 163, With the setting in of the ebb tide there was a strong movement of 'Cutlass' or 'Scabbard' Fishes from the lakes—which the Tarpon tribe learned centuries ago to lie in wait for. **1976** Tryckare et al. *Lore of Sportfishing* 123, Scabbardfish. . . A voracious small marine predator that is occasionally caught on shrimp or small fish bait, or artificial lures.

scabbish See **scabish** 1, 4

scaber See **scaper** v

scabious n Cf **scabish**

1 Std: a plant of the genus *Scabiosa.* Also called **scabish 4**
For other names of var spp see **mourning bride, pincushion 1a, sweet scabious**

2 A **fleabane:** esp a **horseweed 1** (here: *Conyza canadensis),* but also var spp of *Erigeron.* Cf **sweet scabious**

1828 Rafinesque *Med. Flora* 1.164, *Erigeron heterophyllum* [=*E. annuus*]. . . *Erigeron Canadense* [=*Conyza canadensis*]. . . A multitude of vulgar names are applied to these plants [=the above as well as *Erigeron philadelphicus* and others of this genus]. Fleabane is the true English name. . . Scabious is erroneous, since they are nothing like the genus *Scabiosa.* **1876** Hobbs *Bot. Hdbk.* 103, Scabious, Canada fleabane, Erigeron Canadense. *Ibid* 172, Erigeron annuum [sic], Scabious. . . Erigeron heterophyllum, Scabious. . . Erigeron strigosum, Scabious. **1892** (1974) Millspaugh *Amer. Med. Plants* 80–1, *Canada Fleabane. . .* Com[mon] Names. . . horse-weed, . . scabious. [*Ibid* 80–2, The decoction [of this plant] has proven tonic . . and been found useful. . . *E. heterophyllum,* and *Philadelphicum* have, however, greater power than *Canadense* in this direction.] **1911** Henkel *Amer. Med. Leaves* 38, Horseweed, . . scabious. . . [is] common in fields and waste places and along roadsides almost throughout North America. **1937** U.S. Forest Serv. *Range Plant Hdbk.* W67, It [=*Conyza canadensis*] is . . also known as Canada fleabane and, for some unknown reason, is often misnamed scabious. This annual is native to the eastern United States and is now diffused almost universally.

3 An **evening primrose a** (here: *Oenothera parviflora).*

1916 *Torreya* 16.239 **ME,** *Oenothera muricata* [=*O. parviflora*]. . . Scabious, Matinicus I[slan]d, M[ain]e.

scabish n Cf **scabious**

1 also *scabish tree, scabbish, scurvish:* An **evening primrose a,** usu *Oenothera biennis.* [See quot 1814] **esp NEng**

1814 Bigelow *Florula Bostoniensis* 90 **MA,** *Œnothera biennis. . .* In the country it is vulgarly known by the name of *Scabish,* a corruption probably of *Scabious,* from which however it is a very different plant. **1822** Eaton *Botany* 364, [*Oenothera*] biennis (scabish . .) . . Phosphorescent. *Ibid* 365, *[O.] chrysantha* [=*O. perennis*] . . dwarf scabish. **1833** Beck *Botany N. & Middle States* 118, *Œ. biennis*. . . Scabish-tree. **1840** MA *Zool. & Bot. Surv. Herb. Plants & Quadrupeds* 47, *Oe[nothera] biennis*. Scabish. . . Roots farinaceous. . . *Oe. pumila* [=*O. perennis*]. . . Low scabish. Is common over dry fields. **1892** *Jrl. Amer. Folkl.* 5.96 **NH,** *Oenothera fruticosa,* scabbish. **1893** *Ibid* 6.142 **NH,** *Oenothera biennis,* scurvish. Franconia, N.H. **1896** *Ibid* 9.188 **ME,** *Oenothera biennis,* . . scabish, South Berwick, Me. **1911** Henkel *Amer. Med. Leaves* 14, *Oenothera biennis*. . . Scurvish, scabish. . . It has been used for coughs and asthmatic troubles. **1974** (1977) Coon *Useful Plants* 197, *Oenothera biennis* . . scabish. . . is a weedy growing, tallish biennial with bright yellow flowers.

2 usu as *skevish:* A **fleabane** (here: *Erigeron philadelphicus*).

1828 Rafinesque *Med. Flora* 162, *Erigeron philadelphicum* [sic]. . . *Vulgar Names*—Skevish, Scabish. **1876** Hobbs *Bot. Hdbk.* 106, Skevish, Philadelphia fleabane, *Erigeron Philadelphicum*. **1910** Graves *Flowering Plants* 387 **CT,** *Erigeron philadelphicus*. . . Skevish. . . The herb is medicinal. **1914** Georgia *Manual Weeds* 437, *Erigeron philadelphicus*. . . Skevish. . . Often spoken of as the "common" Fleabane, but not usually an abundant weed. **1930** OK *Univ. Biol. Surv. Pub.* 2.84, *Erigeron philadelphicus*. . . Philadelphia Fleabane. Skevish. **1968** *DARE* (Qu. BB50c, *Remedies for infections*) Inf **NC**79, ['skeɪvɪš] root.

3 =**cocash 2.** Cf **meadow scabish**

1891 *Jrl. Amer. Folkl.* 4.149 **NEng,** A very rough, coarse, rank-growing weed in the swamps, which I think now was some kind of Aster, grandmother called *Scabish*.

4 also *scabbish:* =**scabious 1.**

1940 Clute *Amer. Plant Names* 105, *S[cabiosa] arvensis*. . . Scabish. **1959** Carleton *Index Herb. Plants* 103, *Scabbish:* Oenothera biennis; Scabiosa (v).

scabland n

A region of flat rock covered with a patchy layer of topsoil and little vegetation; hence n *scabrock* the rock underlying such land.

1923 *Jrl. Geol.* 31.617, The terms "scabland" and "scabrock" are used in the Pacific Northwest to describe areas where denudation has removed or prevented the accumulation of a mantle of soil, and the underlying rock is exposed or covered largely with its own coarse, angular débris. **1941** Writers' Program *Guide WA* 312, According to geologists, this silty depression among the scablands, known locally as Dry Alkali Lake, is a part of the Hartline Basin. . . As US 10 continues across the ancient lake bed, the scablands appear again, and plant and animal life are limited. *Ibid* 420, Scattered farmhouses surrounded by small fields of wheat, patches of scrub pine, and stretches of scabland border the highway. **1947** Jones *Evergreen Land* 57 **WA,** A high-falutin national politician who ventured into the scablands and spoke feelingly of the Grand Coulee, with a broad "a" . . would get mighty few votes. *Ibid* 118 **WA,** There are . . prehistoric pools in the deep caverns of the scab rock. **1991** *DARE* File **cID,** Buck and pole fences and jack and pole fences are useful in scab land (land with a thin layer of topsoil such that fence posts can't be dug into the ground) because they support themselves with bucks and don't have to be dug in. **2000** Launspach *ID Dial. Project* 3 **seID,** (*Stretch of bad soil with little vegetation*) 1 inf, Scab land.

scace See scarce

scad n Cf big-eyed scad

Also with modifier: =**round robin.**

1873 in 1878 Smithsonian Inst. *Misc. Coll.* 14.2.25, *Decapterus punctatus*. . . Dotted scad. **1882** U.S. Natl. Museum *Bulletin* 16.432, *D[ecapterus] punctatus*. . . Scad; Round Robin. Bluish above, silvery below; a dark opercular spot. **1902** Jordan–Evermann *Amer. Fishes* 302, The genus *Decapterus* contains the mackerel scads. . . One of these, *D. punctatus,* known as the scad, . . is common on the coasts of Florida. **1919** *Copeia* 71.57 **Long Is. NY,** *Decapterus punctatus*. Scad. From June 18 to late August there were numerous young, less than 2 inches in length, in the Sound. **1933** John E. Shedd Aquarium *Guide* 84, Scad; Cigarfish; Round Robin. **1983** *Audubon Field Guide N. Amer. Fishes* 596, *Decapterus punctatus*. . . Although used as food in some areas, the Round Scad is primarily a bait fish.

scadoodles n pl Also sp *skadoodles* [Blend of *scad(s)* + *oodles*]

Great quantities.

1869 *Overland Mth.* 3.131 **TX,** A Texan never has a great quantity of any thing, but he has "scads" of it, or "oodles," or . . "scadoodles." **1905** *DN* 3.95 **nwAR,** *Skadoodles of money*. . . Much money. **1911** *DN* 3.546 **NE,** *Scadoodles*. . . Same as *scads*. "Scadoodles of money." **1953** Randolph–Wilson *Down in Holler* 281 **Ozarks,** *Scadoodles*. . . A very large number, or a very large amount. "I seen scadoodles of mussels in White River, just below Cotter." Perhaps a combination of *scads* and *oodles,* both of which are used in this region to mean large quantities. **1954** *Harder Coll.* **cwTN,** *Scadoodles*. . . A very large number or large amount.

scaff See scarf n[2]

scaffle See scaffold n

scaffling See scaffold n

scafflings See scaffold n B1

scaffold n Usu |'skæfəld, 'skæfold|; also esp S Midl |'skæf(ə)l| Pronc-spp *scaffle, skaffle* Similarly n *scaffling*

A Forms.

1899 (1912) Green *VA Folk-Speech* 367, *Scaffling*. . . Scaffolding. Materials for scaffolds. A scaffold for building. **1942** Hall *Smoky Mt. Speech* 91 **wNC, eTN,** [d] is frequently unsounded after . . [l], as in . . scaffold. **1943** Chase *Jack Tales* 18 **wNC** (as of 1880s), He cloomb on up on the scaffle, rockled and reeled this-a-way and that-a-way. **1944** [see **B2** below]. **1966** [see **B1** below]. **1969–70** [see **B2** below]. **1971** [see **B1** below]. **1975** [see **B1** below]. **2001** [see **B1** below].

B Senses.

1 also *scafflings, scaffoldings:* A raised platform or loft in a barn used for storing hay or grain; rarely, the attic of a house; also fig. **chiefly NEng**

1745 in 1915 NH *Prov. & State Papers* 33.71, [We] have Set off to Susanna. . . The South Part of the Barn . . and the East Scaffold for hay. **1806** (1970) Webster *Compendious Dict.* 140, *Hayloft* . . a scaffold for hay. **1874** VT *State Bd. Ag. Rept. for 1873–74* 522, The single cow is . . fed from the scaffold of choice hay. **1917** *DN* 4.399 **neOH, NEng, NY,** *Scaffold*. . . A loft for grain, often with removable sleepers and boards, and located over the driveway of a barn. . . "He has his haymows and both scaffolds full." **1949** Kurath *Word Geog.* 53, The smaller New England barns often have a raised platform over the cow stalls or at one end for storing hay or grain, which is known as the *scaffold* (usually pronounced *scaffle*). This expression is found also on the Mohawk and in the northern counties of Pennsylvania. **1966** Dakin *Dial. Vocab. Ohio R. Valley* 2.69, *Loft*. . . The occasional Northern term *scaffold* for a raised platform over the stalls or at one end of the barn appears, but it is rare. Always pronounced [skæfl] it is known in Jackson County, Illinois, as an old term for a temporary support for hay in a barn, and in the Purchase as a temporary support in a tabacco [sic] barn. An informant in the southern Mountains says that a *skaffle* is the overhead section of a house. **1966–69** *DARE* (Qu. M3, *The place inside a barn for storing hay*) Infs **MA**58, 68, Scaffold; **MA**42, Scaffold—half a bay—over cows; **MA**74, Scaffold—in older barns; (Qu. M5, . . *The hole for throwing hay down below*) Inf **ME**24, Scaffold hole. **1971** Wood *Vocab. Change* 47 **Sth,** *Storage places*. . . The upper part of a barn is one such. . . *Barn chamber*. . and *scaffold* are reported less often. . . In passing, note *scaffle* [skæfəl] which may have a wider distribution than is shown by the responses to the spelling *scaffold*. **1975** Gould *ME Lingo* 243, *Scafflings*—From scaffoldings; an extra barn mow over the big front doors and inside the gable. Often the *scafflings* was a pole mow and unless needed for an unusually big crop of hay, it remained a catch-all for odds and ends. "Up on the *scafflings*" means out of sight, out of mind, and, considering the location of the *scafflings,* often out of reach. To go up on the *scafflings* is to go into retirement. Family treasures, laid away as heirlooms, can be said to be on the *scafflings*. **1986** Pederson *LAGS Concordance (Loft)* 1 inf, **cGA,** Scaffold. **2001** *DARE* File **nwMA,** It [=scaffold] was, to him, a *temporary* raised platform. And, as such, he said, it was often a practice to jerry-rig some kind [sic] platform to put the hay on so that it would be elevated during storage, and that that cobbed structure was often referred to as a *scaffold*. The more permanent kind was called a *mow*. . . Grandma asked her old buddy . . who has never in her life left farms of one type or another, and she agreed with Doug, (without knowing what he'd said) that one fixed up a scaffold to store hay. . . We always pronounce it *skaffle*.

2 A standing framework for drying fruits or plants (esp tobacco) outdoors; hence v *scaffold* to place or hang a fruit or plant on such a frame; vbl n *scaffolding.* **esp S Midl**

1784 Smyth *Tour U.S.A.* 2.134 **VA,** When the tobacco plants are cut and brought to the scaffolds. **1868** in 1927 Jones *FL Plantation Rec.* 177 **nwFL,** Cato's crowd is the only one which will have no scaffold for sunning cotton. If plank can be spared from the large scaffold, it might be used for that purpose. **1939** *Hall Coll.* **wNC** (Montgomery Coll.), *Scaffold.* . . We used to dry our fruit. We'd gather our apples in of a day and peel our apples of a night and put them out on a scaffold. . . We'd fill our scaffold about every three days. When it got pretty dry, we'd take it off on a cloth and lay it out in the sun and fill our scaffold again. **1944** *PADS* 2.70 **S Midl,** *Scaffle* ['skæfl]. . . Scaffold. Framework for holding or hanging tobacco while curing. **1966** *PADS* 45.21 **cnKY,** *Scaffold.* . . A frame designed to support sticks of freshly cut tobacco in the field while it is wilting. . . To hang freshly cut tobacco on scaffolds. . . "I scaffold my tobacco to make it wilt quicker." **1967** *Key Tobacco Vocab.* 187 **GA, MD, KY, PA, TN,** *Scaffold.* . . A frame designed to support sticks of freshly cut tob[acco] in the field while it is wilting. **1968** *KY Folkl. Rec.* 14.40 **KY,** An early favorite way of curing tobacco made use of a *scaffold.* This was a framework of poles erected on posts in the *tobacco patch.* The sticks, filled with tobacco plants, were hung on the scaffold for several days for the tobacco to *cure.* **1969** *NC Folkl.* 17.33 **cwNC,** Some farmers were proponents of sticking as opposed to *scaffolding* (allowing the tobacco to hang on a temporary scaffold in the open air several days before housing it). . . Some farmers claimed burley "just naturally *kyored* (cured) *up* prettier" if it was stuck or scaffolded before it was housed. **1969–70** *DARE* Tape **GA71,** She just strings the beans and . . puts 'em on what we call a scaffold of a thing and dries 'em; **VA75,** We'd put up a scaffold ['skæ^ɛfəl]; you'd take and put down four posts and you put long poles on those posts and then you'd cut the 'bacco and put it on a—you had a thing you called a horse, would hold a stick; . . you'd take the stick and put it on the scaffold and leave it out in the field until it cured good before you carry it to the barn. **1974** Cates et al. *S. Appalachian Heritage* 63 (Montgomery Coll.), Dolly would see that the chickens were fed . . and the drying fruit put on the scaffold in the hot sun and brought in before the evening dew began to fall.

3 also *log scaffold, wood ~, scaffolding:* **=sawbuck 1.** **chiefly Gulf States, esp LA**

1967 LeCompte *Word Atlas* 154 **seLA,** *Wooden rack for sawing planks.* . . scaffold [2 of 21 infs]. **1968** *DARE* (Qu. L58, *An implement with an A-shaped frame . . that you put boards on to saw them*) Inf **LA29,** Scaffold. **1970** Tarpley *Blinky* 136 **neTX,** *Wooden rack for sawing planks* . . scaffold [rare]. **1986** Pederson *LAGS Concordance* (Sawbuck) **Gulf Region,** 12 infs, Scaffold(s); 5 infs, Scaffolding; 2 infs, Log (or wood) scaffold. [11 infs described it as an A-frame, 5 as an X-frame.]

scaffold v See **scaffold** n B2

scaffolding n See **scaffold** n B3

scaffolding vbl n See **scaffold** n B2

scaffoldings See **scaffold** n B1

scag See **skag**

scaid See **scare** B

scairse See **scarce**

scairt See **scare** B

scaise See **scarce**

scalawag n, also attrib Also sp *scallawag, scallywag, skal(l)awag* [Etym uncert]

1 A rogue; a good-for-nothing; a deceiver. *old-fash*

1848 Bartlett *Americanisms* 284, *Scalawag.* A favorite epithet in western New York for a mean fellow; a scape-grace. **1869** Browne *Adventures* 183, She . . had been eight days at this infernal place among a set of scallywags who didn't understand her lingo. **1885** Jewett *Marsh Is.* 17 **ME,** I asked that young scalawag who drove me over this noon. **1903** *McClure's Mag.* Sept 462 **Chicago IL,** The honest, conservative . . citizen remains at home and plays with his babies, while the able scalawag runs his organization. **1905** *DN* 3.18 **cCT,** *Scallawag.* . . A scamp. *Ibid* 64 **eNE,** *Skalawag.* . . Rascal. **1907** *DN* 3.216 **nwAR,**

Scallawag. . . A scamp. Used especially of Southern-born men who held office under the reconstruction régimes. **1912** *DN* 3.588 **wIN,** *Scalawag.* . . A scamp. **1927** *AmSp* 3.140 **eME,** "Mealy-mouthed," "soft soap," "scaly trick," "slippery customer," scalawag . . all show the hard-headed New Englander. **1965–70** *DARE* (Qu. V7, *A person who sets out to cheat others while pretending to be honest*) 13 Infs, **scattered,** Scalawag; 9 Infs, **scattered,** Scallywag; (Qu. U17, *Names or nicknames for a person who doesn't pay his bills*) Infs **MT2, TN65,** Scalawag; (Qu. V2a, . . *A deceiving person, or somebody that you can't trust*) Infs **CA36, 79, LA40, SC4,** Scalawag; **GA72, NC16,** Scallywag; (Qu. V3, . . *A thoroughly dishonest person* . . "He's a _____"; total Infs questioned, 75) Inf **OK51,** Scalawag; (Qu. Z16, *A small child who is rough, misbehaves, and doesn't obey, you'd call him a _____*) Inf **GA13,** Scalawag; (Qu. HH18, *Very insignificant or low-grade people*) Inf **MS71,** Scallywag; (Qu. HH20a, *An idle, worthless person:* "He's a _____.") Infs **IN32, MD31,** Scalawag; (Qu. HH37, *An immoral woman*) Inf **KS18,** Scallywag; (Qu. HH44, *Joking or uncomplimentary names for lawyers*) Inf **OR4,** Scallywag. [31 of 37 Infs old] **1976** Garber *Mountain-ese* 82 **sAppalachians,** *Skallawag* (n) cheat, menace—Don't ever trade with that feller, he's jist a plain skalawag. **1986** Pederson *LAGS Concordance* (A rustic) 2 infs, **AL,** (A) scalawag; (The poor whites) 1 inf, **swGA,** Scalawag—no-account white; 2 infs, **LA, MS,** Scalawags; 1 inf, **ceTX,** Scalawag going on = dishonest dealings; 1 inf, **neTN,** Someone who's kind of a scalawag.

2 An animal of poor quality or little value.

1854 *NY Tribune* (NY) 24 Oct 8/3, The truth is that the number of miserable "scallawags" is so great, that . . they tend to drag down all above themselves to their own level. **1872** VT State Bd. Ag. *Report* 1.312, Valuable sheep have been messed with the skalawags of the flock. **1878** IL Dept. Ag. *Trans. for 1876* 14.286, The cows in the Northwest, as a whole, are "scalawags." **1902** (1903) Lorimer *Letters* 15 **Chicago IL,** Like feeding his weight in corn to a scalawag steer that won't fat up. **1920** Hunter *Trail Drivers TX* 379 (as of 1874), We had a few old trouble-makers in the herd, which, if they had been shot when we first started, would have saved us a lot of worry. They ran so much they became regular old scalawags. **1929** Dobie *Vaquero* 29, Yet some of the slaughter houses continued operating for several years, utilizing old cows, rough stags, cripples, lump-jawed steers, and "scalawag" stuff in general. **1968** *DARE* (Qu. J2, . . *Joking or uncomplimentary words . . for dogs*) Inf **MD19,** Scalawag; (Qu. K55, *A pig that doesn't grow well and is not worth keeping*) Inf **NJ17,** Scalawag.

3 A **sculpin** (here: *Myoxocephalus* spp).

1924 *DN* 5.288 **Cape Cod MA,** Jelly fish are 'sunsqualls' for some unknown reason, and a sculpin is a 'scalawag'.

scald n

1 A patch of bare, infertile soil. [*OED2 scald* sb.[2] 4 "A patch of land scorched by the sun. *Local.*"] Cf **bald** n, **fire scald**

1865 IL State Ag. Soc. *Trans. for 1861* 5.170, A stratum of hardpan, . . when exposed, or the surface soil washed from it, is known as the "scalds." **1871** IL Dept. Ag. *Trans. for 1869–70* 8.205, In the northeastern portions of the county, however, are occasional "scalds," caused by the removal of the surface soil from a finely comminuted arenaceous subsoil. **1883** Zeigler-Grosscup *Heart of Alleghanies* 68, There are other bare spots on these mountains known as scalds, and like this old field, situated in the heart of fir forests. **1937** *Hall Coll.* **wNC,** Scald . . "a place that's wore out," . . (when asked what 'wore out' meant, he said "eroded, where it goes to washin'.") **1939** *Ibid* **wNC,** Scald on a hill, nothin' grows on it; where they ain't no weeds nor nothin' on it; just a bare place.

2 in phrr *get a good* (or *poor*) *scald on* and varr: To make a good (or poor) job of. [From hog-butchering, where the ease with which the hair can be scraped off depends on how well it has been scalded]

1893 *KS Univ. Qrly.* 1.141 **KS,** *Scald:* preparation, as 'I didn't get a good scald on that speech.' **1906** *DN* 3.154 **nwAR,** *Scald.* . . In the phrase, "to get a good scald on," i.e., to do something well. "I got a good scald on that job." **1914** *DN* 4.112 **cKS,** *Scald.* . . In the phrase *to get a good scald on,* to have good results with:—perhaps because a good scalding permits the easy scraping away of hog bristles. "I baked bread today and got a pretty good scald on it." **1917** *DN* 4.392 **neOH,** *Get the right scald on.* . . To be fortunate in doing something just right. From scalding hogs in dressing them, an operation requiring experience. "I got just the right scald on that." **1923** *DN* 5.220 **swMO,** *Scald.* . . Satisfactory accomplishment. "I got a good scald on that job." **1927** *AmSp*

2.355 **cwWV,** *Get the right scald on* (verb phrase), to do the matter under consideration exactly right. "We got the right scald on that haystack." **1950** *WELS* (In good condition) 1 Inf, **cwWI,** Got a good scald on it. Old-fashioned. **1958** *AmSp* 33.270 **eWA** [Ranching terms], *Good (or poor) scald, a.* A good (or bad) job. The term comes from hog killing. **1969** *DARE* (Qu. KK4, *When things turn out just right . . "Everything is _____ now."*) Inf **KY60,** Sure got a good scald on that—from scalding butchered hogs; a good scald, then the hair comes off good. **1969** *DARE* Tape **ID11,** Now, if I cooked something especially nice, Mom'll say, "You really got a good scald on that," and this comes from when they slaughter pigs. **1979** *NYT Article Letters* **sOH,** To "get a good scald" on something is another one of my uncle's expressions from southern Ohio. It means getting the taste, the seasonings, the proportions of a certain dish just right—usually a favorite family food for which there is no recipe! *Ibid* **TX,** My father . . spoke about "getting a good scald" on things, meaning to do something to perfection, as in, "Honey, you sure got a good scald on that chili." **1986** *DARE* File **cIA,** The expression "get a good scald on" is used in my family to describe something which turns out particularly well, often due to chance or accident. For example, in making baked goods, if one batch of something turned out exceptionally well, we would say, "You got a good scald on it that time."

scalded (corn) bread n Also *scald-bread, scalded hoecake* esp **Sth, S Midl** Cf **hot-water corn bread**
A **corn bread** made with **scalded meal.**

1906 *DN* 3.155 **nwAR,** *Scalded bread. . .* Corn bread made of scalded meal. "Scalded bread tastes better than cold water bread." **1940** Brown *Amer. Cooks* 464 **MS,** *Scalded bread*—Mix and sift 2 cups corn meal with ½ teaspoon salt; add 1 cup boiling water, or more if necessary. Stir in 1 tablespoon melted fat, or ¼ cup broken "cracklings," and mix well. Shape into oblong pones. . . Bake 30 minutes. **1947** Bowles–Towle *New Engl. Cooking* 9, *Scalded Corn Bread* [Recipe includes cornmeal, water, salt, butter, eggs, buttermilk, soda]. . Scald the corn meal with enough boiling water to moisten. **1966** Dakin *Dial. Vocab. Ohio R. Valley* 2.315, *Corn bread. . .* Miscellaneous terms . . *pan bread* (Ind., Ky.) . . *scalded (corn) bread* (Ky.); *sour bread* (Ky.) **1967** *DARE* (Qu. H24, . . *Names or nicknames . . for boiled cornmeal*) Inf **LA9,** Scald-bread. **1982** Slone *How We Talked* 57 **eKY** (as of c1950), By using hot water to make cornbread we made what we called "scalded bread." **1986** Pederson *LAGS Concordance* (Kinds of bread and cakes made of cornmeal) 1 inf, **nwMS,** Scalded bread—pone of corn bread; hot-water bread; 1 inf, **cnLA,** Scalded bread—hot water and meal; 1 inf, **csTN,** Scalded hoecake—meal/water/salt/in skillet; scalded hot hoecake—in shallow baker. **1995–97** Montgomery *Coll.* **wNC,** *Scalded bread . .* cooked in form of a pone; meal and hot water cooked in greased skillet. *Ibid* **eTN,** Scalded bread.

scalded egg n Also *scalt egg* Cf **scalt**
A poached egg.

1934 *AmSp* 9.93 **NEng,** Other expressions for 'poached eggs' [collected in the fieldwork for the *Linguistic Atlas of New England*]. . . *Scalded eggs* is given as the first response by the informant in Standish (Cumberland County, Me.), who calls *dropped eggs* "modern"; and *scalt eggs* is reported as heard regularly from a neighbor by one informant in Rowley (Essex County, Mass.)

scalded hoecake See **scalded (corn) bread**

scalded meal n Also *scald-meal* Cf **scalded (corn) bread**
Cornmeal to which boiling water has been added.

1860 *Scientific Amer.* 2.135, If mixed with scalded meal or shorts, or with sour milk, the hens will eat it readily. **1906** [see **scalded (corn) bread**]. **1967** *DARE* (Qu. H14, *Bread that's made with cornmeal*) Inf **TX4,** Scald-meal [bread]; (Qu. H24, . . *Names or nicknames . . for boiled cornmeal*) Inf **LA9,** Scalded meal.

scale v[1] Usu with *off, up* [Scots, nEngl dial *scale, skail* to disperse, depart] **NEng**
Of bad weather: to clear off, lift.

1898 Smith *Caleb West* 60 **NEast,** The storm was still raging, the wind beating in fierce gusts against the house and rattling the window panes. . "Turrible dirty, ain't it? . . I guess she'll scale off; it's hauled a leetle s'uth'ard since daylight." **1957** Beck *Folkl.* **ME** 168, The natives might remark that a man was coming along "handsomely," very well, when he disappeared in a "dungeon of fog," thick fog, which later "browned off" or "scaled up." **1966** *DARE* (Qu. B19, *When fog begins*

to go up into the air . . it's _____) Inf **ME22,** Lifting, scaling. **1975** Gould *ME Lingo* 243, *Scale*—Sea fog which lifts is said to *scale* off. When Tudor Gardiner was campaigning for governor, he rowed out to Beal Island in a dense fog and found everybody downcast, all sitting in their bait houses to wait out a fogmull. Tudor asked one lobsterman, "Are you interested in politics?" He answered, "I ain't int'risted in a gahdam thing till this fog scales off!"

scale n esp **NEast, Sth** See Map *somewhat old-fash* Cf **shell** n[1] **3**
The first thin coating of ice on a body of water; hence adj *scaly* of ice: thin; ppl adj phr *scaled over* covered with a thin coating of ice.

1896 *DN* 1.423 **c,wNY,** *Scaly ice:* ice through which the skate cuts. **1943** *LANE* Map 648 (Froze), A milder degree of freezing. . . 6 infs, **VT, MA,** Scaled over. **1950** *WELS Suppl.* **ceWI,** *Scale*—Of thin ice on a lake. **1965–70** *DARE* (Qu. B33a, *The first thin ice that forms over the surface of a pond or pool: "There's just a _____ of ice."*) 13 Infs, esp **NEast, Sth,** Scale; **PA92,** Light scale; **MS55,** Thin scale; (Qu. B33b, *Talking about the first thin ice that forms over the surface of a pond or pool: "The pond is just _____ over."*) Infs **CT36, MS55, NY3, 84, 116, 200, SC26,** Scaled; **NY106,** Scale. [14 of 17 Infs old] **1973** Allen *LAUM* 1.157 **Upper MW** (as of c1950), First thin coating of ice. . . scale of ice [2 infs, **IA, ND**]. **1986** Pederson *LAGS Concordance,* 1 inf, **cLA,** Scale—of ice; 1 inf, **cwMS,** Scale of ice; 1 inf, **cAL,** Thin scale of ice. [All infs old]

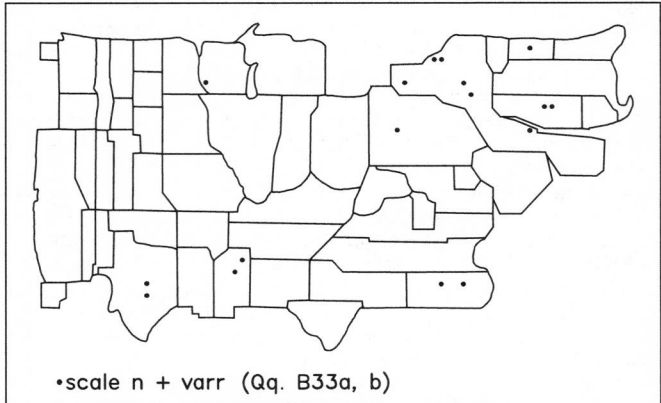

•scale n + varr (Qq. B33a, b)

scale v[2], hence vbl n *scaling*
1 intr: To skim through the air; to skip, bounce; esp of a bird: to glide.

a1870 Chipman *Notes on Bartlett* 382 (*DAE*), *To scale.* 1. To go, or make go, sideling. 2. To skip, ricochet, or cause to do so.—New England. **1948** Camp *Hunter's Encycl.* 254, Once the course is set, it [=a ring-necked pheasant] flaps and sails, then sets its wings and planes. . . The planing or scaling often gives an illusion of being level, but the bird is really pitching. *Ibid* 260, The stricken bird [=a ring-necked pheasant] may fly for a mile or more before scaling to earth. **1999** *DARE* File **ME** (as of 1970s), Once in the air a partridge will often glide between the trees with its wings set, changing direction by angling its body one way or the other. Everyone I knew would refer to this motion by saying, "The partridge scaled off into the woods."

2 tr: To skim (a flat object) through the air; to skip (a flat stone) on a body of water; hence n *scaler* a stone suitable for skipping. **chiefly NEng, NY** See Map

a1870 [see **1** above]. **1877** Bartlett *Americanisms* 644, *Scaling stones* (upon the water) was a common New England expression for what English boys call "making ducks and drakes." **1965–70** *DARE* (Qu. C24b) Inf **MA100,** Scale a stone = skip a stone; (Qu. EE30, *Throwing a flat stone over the surface of water so that it jumps several times*) Infs **CT23, ME19, NY37,** Scaling; **MA82, NH17, NY211, RI3,** Scaling (it, stones, *or* the stone); **ME15,** Scaling or skipping rocks; a good rock is a scaler. **1986** *DARE* File **eMA** (as of 1955), *Scale . .* sail, skim (e.g., a piece of cardboard in the air, a stone on water, etc.) Current in N.E.—spec. Boston area. *Ibid* **cnUT.** **1987** *Ibid* **NY,** Cow chips—Dried cow turds sufficiently thin and of the right size and shape to scale. **1999** *Ibid* **nwMA,** "Scaling a rock across the water" is certainly familiar sounding, and "scaling a rock at a dog" is also familiar. . If I were to scale a rock

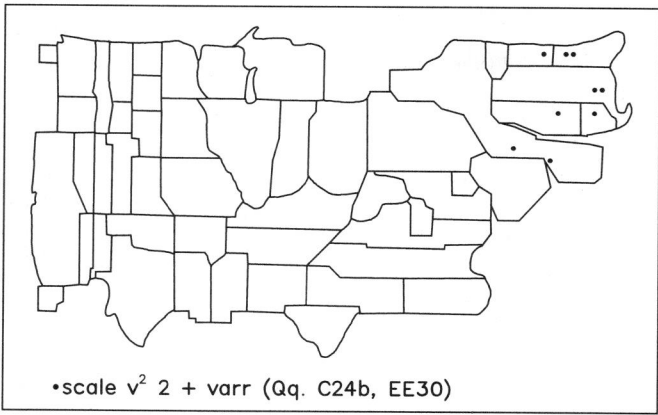

•scale v² 2 + varr (Qq. C24b, EE30)

at a dog, I would expect to do it sidearm, imitating the motion used to skip a rock across the water, not overhand as with a baseball.

scale carp n Also *scaled carp*

A var of the common carp *(Cyprinus carpio)*; see quots.

1880 U.S. Bur. Fisheries *Rept. for 1878* 6.xlii **MD,** About half of the scale carp . . remained in Baltimore. **1883** GA Dept. Ag. *Pub. Circular No. 34* 8.12, Three varieties of carp are cultivated, which are thus described by Dr. Hessel, Superintendent of the United States' carp ponds at Washington, D.C.: 1. *Cyprinus carpio communis,* the scale carp, with regular, concentrically arranged scales. . . 2. *Cyprinus carpio specularis,* the mirror carp; thus named on account of the extraordinarily large scales, which run along the sides of the body in three or four rows, the rest of the body being bare. 3. *Cyprinus carpio coriaceus sive nudus,* the leather carp; which has on the back either only a few scales or none at all, and possesses a thick, soft skin, which feels velvety to the touch. **1908** Forbes–Richardson *Fishes of IL* 105, The first successful introduction of carp into the United States was made in 1877, when R. Hessel . . brought 345 carp to this country. Of these, . . 118 were scale-carp. . . The introduction of carp into the waters of Illinois began . . [in] 1879 . . , and in 1880 scaled carp to the number of 800 were received from the U.S. Fish Commission.

scaled ling n Cf **ling**
=**bowfin.**

1938 Schrenkeisen *Field Book Fishes* 21 **NY,** *Amia calva.* . . Scaled Ling. **1949** Caine *N. Amer. Sport Fish* 133, *Colloquial Names* . . Bowfin . . Scaled Ling. . . General aspect is a muddy green made faintly iridescent by coarse scales. **1983** Becker *Fishes WI* 251, *Amia calva.* . . Scaled ling. . . Scales "polygono cycloid," large, 63–70 in lateral line.

scaled over See **scale** n

scaled quail n Also *scale quail, scaled partridge, scaly ~*
[See quots 1961, 1977]

A bluish-grey ground bird *(Callipepla squamata)* with a white-tipped crest native to the southwestern US. Also called **blue racer 2, ~ quail, cactus quail, cottontop 2, Mexican quail 2, whitetop**

1858 Baird *Birds* 646, *Callipepla squamata.* . . *Scaled or Blue Partridge.* . . Valley of the Rio Grande of Texas. . . Most abundant on the high broken table lands and mezquite plains. **1874** Coues *Birds NW* 441, The Blue is also called the Scaled Quail, from the peculiar appearance of the plumage of the under parts, which is seemingly abnormal in texture or disposition; but this is merely an optical effect of the singular coloration of the feathers, simulating imbricated scales or tiles. **1907** Anderson *Birds IA* 232, *Scaled Partridge.* A single specimen of this southwestern bird, shot at Tabor, Iowa, May 2, 1889, . . was doubtless a straggler. **1953** Jewett *Birds WA* 223, *Callipepla squamata.* . . Scaly Partridge. . . Introduced permanent resident in Yakima County. . . This quail has been moderately successful in Yakima and some adjoining counties, standing hard shooting during several open seasons. **1961** Ligon *NM Birds* 96, So alike in appearance are the male and female Scaled Quail that it is difficult to determine the sex. . . The designation *squamata,* squamous, . . has reference to the pattern of the breast feathers, which has given the bird its common name. **1967** *DARE* (Qu. Q7, *Names and nicknames for . . game birds)* Inf **TX5,** Scale quail. **1977** Udvardy *Audubon Field Guide Birds* 534, *Scaled Quail.* . . Bluish-gray feathers of breast and mantle have black semicircular edge, creating

scaled effect; belly also has brown "scales". . . North to southeastern Arizona, New Mexico, Utah, southern Colorado, and parts of Texas.

scale duck n Cf **shelduck 1**
=**red-breasted merganser.**

1982 Elman *Hunter's Field Guide* 230, Red-breasted merganser . . Common & regional names: . . scale duck.

scale off See **scale** v¹

scale quail See **scaled quail**

scaler See **scale** v² 2

scale up See **scale** v¹

scaling See **scale** v²

scallawag See **scalawag**

scallion n Usu |ˈskæljən|; also **esp NEast** |ˈskʌljən| Pronc-spp *scellion, scullion, skellion, skillion;* for addit pronc and sp varr see quots [*OED2* scallion 13.. → for *Allium fistulosum*] **scattered, but chiefly NEast, S Atl** See Map on p. 770 Cf **cullion, multiplying onion, potato ~, rareripe 2, scunnion**

An **onion** n B: usu a small-bulbed, long-necked onion (here: *Allium cepa* var *cepa);* occas also a leek *(A. porrum),* chive *(A. schoenoprasum),* or other similar **onion** n B. For other names of *A. cepa* var *cepa* see **bunch onion, green ~ 1, salad ~, shallot B, spring onion**

1790 Deane *New Engl. Farmer* 196, When onions are thick necked, do not incline to bottom, but rather to be what are vulgarly called scallions, the more care should be taken to harden the ground about them. . . After they are pulled up. . . the scallions should . . be hung up in some dry place in small bunches. **1843** (1844) Johnson *Farmer's Encycl.* 862, At present all onions that have refused to bulb, and formed lengthened necks and strong blades in spring and summer, are scallions. **1863** Burr *Field & Garden* 125 **NEng,** The Leek, . . when full grown, much resembles what are commonly known as "Scallions;" the lower, blanched portion being the part eaten. *Ibid* 143, Allium Ascalonicum. The Shallot. . . The specific term . . [is] derived from Ascalon, a town in Syria: hence also the popular English name, "Scallion." **1890** *DN* 1.59 **SC,** *Scellion* or *skellion,* if my memory fails not, is a rare word in Charleston, S.C., meaning an onion or leek. The French is *échalote,* a plant belonging to the leek family. It is derived from the Latin *ascalonia,* and that from *Ascalo,* a city in Phœnicia, whence the plant came. The older form is *escalone,* whence the Charlestonian *scellion.* Two persons from Maine have told me that they have always called poor onions that grow up to stalk, with no bulbs, *scullions.* This may be the same word, though I am inclined to think it is simply the word *scullion, kitchen-servant,* used in the sense of a scullion among onions. **1896** *DN* 1.424 **NY,** *Scullions:* small onions. **1932** Tooné *Yankee Slang* 75, Some words in general use in the United States of America, but not in England:—*America*—Scallions. *England*—Spring onions. **1941** *LANE* Map 258 *(Scallion, spring onion),* The map shows the terms *scallion, scullion, rareripe, . . spring onion, green ~, . .* denoting either a shallot . . or a variety of the onion *(allium cepa),* usually characterized by a small bulb and a long fleshy stem and eaten raw. . . A scallion or scullion is described by more than sixty informants in all parts of New England (few in R.I. and Conn.) as consisting chiefly of a fleshy stem or stalk, with only a small bulb. Typical comments are that it 'runs to top' or 'grows to stem' or 'won't bottom'. Others describe a scallion as a misshapen or imperfect onion . . , as a soft, loose onion 'with no insides' . . , as an onion that will not mature . . , as an undeveloped . . or unripe onion . . , or simply as a small onion. . . Several say that scallions are the culls or discards from graded onions. . . Some informants say that a scallion is useless—that it cannot be marketed . . or that it cannot be kept during the winter without rotting. . . It is, however, widely used as a salad delicacy. . . Finally, scallions are described as growing from seeds . . , from bulbs . . , from onion sets . . , or from old onions. **1965–70** *DARE* (Qu. I6, *The kind of onions that come up fresh early in the year, and you eat them raw)* 128 Infs, **chiefly NEast, S Atl,** Scallions [ˈskæljənz, -jɪnz, -iənz]; **CA178, MA58,** [ˈskælənz]; **SC21, 22, 62,** [ˈskæjənz, -jɪnz]; **CA15, HI1, MA3, NH5,** Scallions; **UT6,** Scallions [ˈskæiljənz]—they call them that back in New York, but not around here; 46 Infs, **chiefly NEast,** Scullions [ˈskʌljənz, -jɪnz]; **PA52, 60,** [ˈskʌjənz]; **VA48,** [ˈskʌlɪnz]; **MI34,** The English plant [ˈskʌljənz]; **SC19,** Skillions [ˈskɪljənz]; **SC46,** Skellions [ˈskɛljənz]; (Qu. I7, *The small plants like onions with hollow green leaves that are* *cut up in a salad*) 36 Infs, **chiefly Nth, esp NEast,** Scallions; **NY52,** Scallion tops; **CT2, MA4, TX4, WI29,** Scullions; (Qu. I5, . . *Kind of onions that keep coming up without replanting year after year*) 16 Infs, **chiefly NEast, S Atl,** Scallions; **MA3,** [skalijɔnz]; **NJ31,** Top-set scallions; 16 Infs, **chiefly NEast, S Atl,** Scullions; **PA2,** [ˈskʌjənz]; **GA3,** [ˈskɛ‿ˤljənz]; **LA12,** [ˈskɛljɨnz]; (Qu. I28a, . . *Kinds of things . . you call 'greens' . . [Those that are eaten raw]*) Infs **MA3, NJ30, TX38,** Scallions; (Qu. I35, . . *Kitchen herbs . . grown and used in cooking around here*) Infs **IL99, NY65,** Scallion(s); **MA29,** Scullions. **1970** U.S. Dept. Ag. *Yearbook for 1969* 189, Green onions, shallots, and leeks are sometimes called "scallions." **1986** Pederson *LAGS Concordance* 68 infs, **Gulf Region,** Scallion(s).

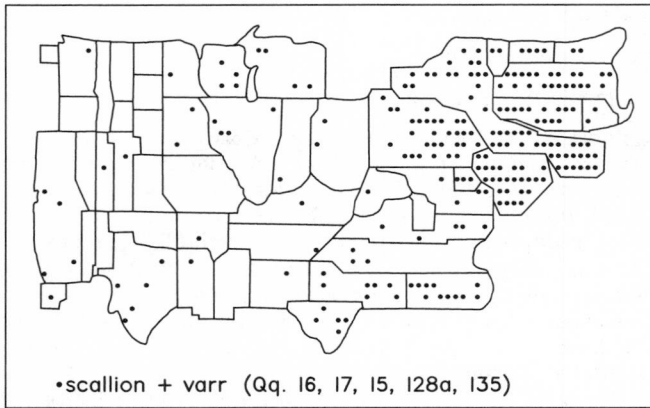

•scallion + varr (Qq. I6, I7, I5, I28a, I35)

scallop See **scallop squash**

scalloped oak See **scallop oak**

scalloped squash See **scallop squash**

scallop oak n Also *scalloped oak*

Appar an **oak** with wavy-edged leaves.

1967–68 *DARE* (Qu. T10, . . *Kinds of oak trees*) Inf **CT4,** Scallop oak; **SC41,** Scalloped oak.

scallop squash n Also *scallop(ed squash), scolloped (squash)* Cf **cymling 1, pattypan squash**
=**pattypan squash.**

1843 (1844) Johnson *Farmer's Encycl.* 1009, Mr. Kendrick, of Boston, notices the following varieties [of squash]: . . Early scallop . . Acorn . . Long yellow crook neck [etc]. **1863** Burr *Field & Garden* 210, Like the Summer Crookneck, the scolloped squashes are used while young or in a green state. *Ibid* 211, Green Bush Scolloped. . . Fruit similar in size and form to the Yellow or White Bush Scolloped. **1895** Gray–Bailey *Field Botany* 191, C[ucurbita] Pepo. . . The chief types are . . the *Bush Scallop Squashes* with white or yellow fruit flattened endwise and the vines scarcely running. **1910** Graves *Flowering Plants* 372 **CT,** *Cucurbita Pepo* . . var. *condensa*. . . Scallop Squash. **1925** *Book of Rural Life* 9.5251, Of summer squashes the chief varieties are the White and Yellow Bush Scallops, or Pattypans, and the Crooknecks. **1950** *WELS* **WI** (*Kinds of squash that grow in your neighborhood*) 1 Inf, Scallop squash; 1 Inf, Scallop squash—yellow; 1 Inf, Scalloped—round saucer shape. **1965–70** *DARE* (Qu. I23, . . *Kinds of squash*) Infs **CA144, CT39, IN7, KY81, MI53, MA68, NM12, TX37,** Scallop squash; **AL52, CO27, KY84, 90,** Scalloped squash; **LA40,** White scalloped squash; **CA132,** Scarlip [sic—FW sp] squash—greenish with indentation all around. **1976** Bailey–Bailey *Hortus Third* 343, [*Cucurbita*] *Pepo*. . . 'White Bush Scallop', *pattypan squash, scallop s[quash]*, fr[uit] white, disc-shaped, ribbed, to 3 ½ in. high and 9 in. in diam[eter], flesh creamy-white. *Ibid* 928, Summer squash includes fruits with a range of shapes and colors, from the white scallops or pattypans to the cylindrical solid green zucchinis or striped cocozelles and the yellow straightneck and crookneck types. **1986** Pederson *LAGS Concordance,* 1 inf, **cAR,** Scallop squash; 1 inf, **nwFL,** Scallop squashes—pound [sic], flat; 1 inf, **cLA,** Scallop squash = white squash; 1 inf, **cLA,** Scallop squash—small, green; 1 inf, **ceTX,** Scallop squash—white round variety.

scallyhoot v Also sp *schalahoot, skallyhoot* [Cf *SND skelli-hewit* "A row, a noisy quarrel, din, rumpus"] **esp West** Cf **ballhoot, gallihoot**

To go or depart quickly; to gallivant.

1862 in 1881 *Hist. Buchanan Co. IA* 202, They [=jiggers] don't like soap, and will "schalahoot" in short metre. **1869** *Overland Mth.* 3.128 **SW,** In fact, a mustang is not "worth shucks." He will run "sky-godlin" . . ; lie down and roll over; then "get up and scallyhoot" a short distance. **1909** Porter *Roads of Destiny* 96 **TX,** Same old Whipperwill Creek skallyhootin' in and out of them motts of timber. **1935** Davis *Honey* 108 **OR,** Clay not only urged, but ordered him to stay where he was and not go skallyhooting around the country wearing down his horse when there was no use in it. **1942** McAtee *Dial. Grant Co. IN* 30 (as of 1890s), Go scallyhootin' . . go fast. **1971** Adams *Cowman* 5 **West,** [The expression] "they came skally-hootin' into town" paints a complete picture of men riding recklessly down the dusty street and drawing their sweating horses to a slithering halt before the hitch rack.

scallyhoot n Cf **run sheep run**

1967 *DARE* (Qu. EE12, *Games in which one captain hides his team and the other team tries to find it*) Inf **MI65,** Scallyhoot [ˌskælɪˈhut]—the "it" team would chant: "Holler, holler, or I shan't foller."

scallywag See **scalawag**

scallywhampus adj Cf *DS* KK1a

1913 *DN* 4.25 **NE,** Scallywhampus. Splendid, fine. Facetious. Used in Nebraska. "Those apples are scallywhampus." "This pie is scally-whampus." "We had a scallywhampus time."

scalp n, v Pronc-spp *sculp, ske(l)p, skulp*

A Forms.

1676 *New Further Narr. State New-Engl.* 14, They knockt one Youth of the Head, and laying him for dead, they flead (or skulp'd) his head of skin and hair. **1709** (1967) Lawson *New Voyage* 207 **NC, SC,** [They] never miss Skulping of them, as they call it, which is, to cut off the Skin from the Temples, and taking the whole Head of Hair along with it. **1758** in 1881 *Essex Inst. Coll.* 18.180 **MA,** They obtained fifty-two Sculps & two Prisoners. **1834** Caruthers *Kentuckian* 1.61, I wish I may be horn swoggled, if ever I thought to live to see the day when I should *'sculp'* a Christian man. **1843** (1916) Hall *New Purchase* 227, [H]e tells them as how the Injins . . had . . tuk his skulp! **1853** Simms *Sword & Distaff* 283 **SC,** You don't mind much ef we was all killed and sculped. **1858** Hammett *Piney Woods Tavern* 125, If I don't show ye his bare sculp afore mornin' then I ain't a namesake of that unfortnet critter that got himself made a martyr on. **1859** (1965) Marcy *Prairie Traveler* 212, Don't they kill and sculp a white man when-ar they get the better on him? **1874** (1895) Eggleston *Circuit Rider* 111 **sOH** (as of early 19th cent), And then, if . . the Indians should come and skelp us, they'd be precious few left. **1878** Hart *Sazerac Lying Club* 103 **NV,** They come mighty nigh nailin' my skelp, too. **1899** (1912) Green *VA Folk-Speech* 389, Skelp. . . To remove the *skelp,* or scalp. **1902** [see **B1** below]. **1903** [see **B2** below]. **1907** [see **B1** below]. **1923** *DN* 5.221 **swMO,** Skelp, v. or n. Scalp. Also, Ske'p.

B As verb.

1 To skin an animal. [Cf *DNE sculp* (also *scalp*) 1 "To cut the skin and attached blubber from a harp or hooded seal"; 1819 →; 2 "To skin and quarter a beaver or deer"; 1872 →]

1902 *DN* 2.245 **sIL,** Skelp, v. tr. . . To skin a small place by a glancing blow; to skin an animal. **1907** *DN* 3.226 **nwAR,** Skeep [sic for *skelp*]. . . To skin a small place by a glancing blow; to skin an animal.

2 To graze, mark in passing. Cf **scamp** v[4], **scape** v

1902 [see **B1** above]. **1903** *DN* 2.329 **seMO,** Skelp. . . To mark slightly. 'The bullet just skelped his cheek.' **1907** [see **B1** above].

C As noun.

See quot. [Cf *DNE sculp* (also *scalp*) "The skin of a harp or hooded seal with the blubber attached"; 1826 →]

1902 *DN* 2.245 **sIL,** Skelp. . . A pelt.

scalt past ppl, ppl adj [Pronc-sp for *scalded*] **esp ME, MA**

1795 Dearborn *Columbian Grammar* 138, List of Improprieties. . . Scalt for Scalded. **1903** *DN* 2.328 **seMO,** Scalt. . . Scalded. **1914** *DN* 4.152 **cME,** Scalt. . . Scalded. "The dishes are washed and scalt but not wiped." Common throughout Central Maine. Also used in Mass. **1934** [see **scalded egg**]. **1979** *AmSp* 54.94 **sME** (as of 1899–1910), Nonstandard past participles . . *scalt* 'scalded.'

scalt egg See **scalded egg**

scaly See **scale** n

scalyback n

1 A **fence lizard 1** (here: *Sceloporus undulatus*).
1934 *Natl. Geogr. Mag.* 65.609 **Okefenokee GA,** The fence lizard, or scalyback, is a familiar sight about old cabins and on pine or oak trunks and logs, where its rough, grayish upper parts enable it to simulate a dead stick.

2 A particular size of **diamondback terrapin;** see quot.
1970 *DARE* Tape **VA**52A, [FW:] Do you have a name for different sizes . . ? [Inf:] Well, a six-inch on up to seven is what we call a six-inch terrapin, very few sevens. And then from six-inch down to five-and-a-half is what we call a scalyback.

scaly bark n Also *scaly-bark hickory*   **chiefly SE, Lower Missip Valley**   See Map   Cf **shagbark hickory, shellbark ~**
Usu a **shagbark hickory** (here: *Carya ovata*), but also a **shellbark hickory** (here: *Carya laciniosa*); also the nut of such a tree.

1775 Adair *Amer. Indians* 360, Filberts . . are as sweet and thin-shelled, as the scaly bark hiccory-nuts.   **a1782** (1788) Jefferson *Notes VA* 37, Scaly bark hiccory. Juglans alba cortice squamosa.   **1810** Michaux *Histoire des Arbres* 1.190, *Juglans squamosa* [=*Carya ovata*]. . . La disposition assez singulière qu'offre l'écorce de cette espèce de Noyer, lui a fait donner les noms de *Shell bark Hickery*, de *Scaly bark*, de *Shag bark Hickery*, Hickery à écorce écailleuse. [= *Juglans squamosa* [=*Carya ovata*]. . . The rather unusual arrangement which the bark of this species of walnut presents, has caused it to be given the names *Shell bark Hickery, Scaly bark, Shag bark Hickery,* Hickery with scaly bark.] *Ibid* 199, *Juglans laciniosa* [=*Carya l.*] . . Cette espèce, qui a beaucoup de rapport avec celle qui a été précédemment décrite [=*Carya ovata*], est fréquemment confondue avec elle, par les habitans des contrées de l'Ouest, qui lui donnent le même nom. [= *Juglans laciniosa* [=*Carya l.*] . . This species, which is very similar to that which has been previously described [=*Carya ovata*], is frequently confused with it by the inhabitants of the western regions, who give it the same name.]   **1851** (1874) Reid *Desert Home* 187, At length, we saw him descend a tree, whose bark was exceedingly rough—in fact, crisped outward in great, broad pieces, or scales of a foot long, and several inches broad, that looked as though they were about to fall from the tree. For this reason, the tree is known among backwoodsmen as the 'scaly bark.'   **1883** (1971) Harris *Nights with Remus* 359 **GA** [Black], One en deze yer great big scaly-bark trees. De tree wuz des loaded down wid scaly-barks, but dey wa'n't ripe, en de green hulls shined in de sun des lak dey ben whitewash'.   **1893** Shands *MS Speech* 54, *Scaly-bark.* . . A name applied by all classes to a species of hickory tree, as well as to the nuts that grow thereon.   **1898** Lloyd *Country Life* 53 **AL,** I had went down in the cellar before I started and filled my pockets full of scalybarks and peanuts and some swivelled up apples of my own raisin.   **1906** *DN* 3.155 **nwAR,** *Scaly-bark.* . . A kind of hickory tree and its nut.   **1909** *DN* 3.366 **eAL, wGA,** *Scaly-bark.* . . A small soft-shelled hickory nut; also the tree on which it grows.   **1921** Deam *Trees IN* 68, This hickory [=*Carya laciniosa*] is also known as the big scalybark hickory and hard-head hickory. The nuts are an article of commerce . . although . . hard to crack.   **c1940** Newman–Murphy *Conserv. Notes* 7 **neLA,** The scaly-bark hickory tree grows but scantily in this section.   **1950** *PADS* 14.36 **SC,** *Hickory nut.* . . The *scaly bark* . . is a smaller nut with the general shape of the hickory nut, but with a much thinner shell and larger kernel.   **1965–70** *DARE* (Qu. I43, *What kinds of nuts grow wild around here?*) 16 Infs, **chiefly SE, Lower Missip Valley,** Scaly-

bark nuts; **GA**9, **MS**45, **SC**57, **TX**51, Scaly barks; **KY**74, **MO**20, Scaly-bark hickory nut; **MS**60, Scally bars [sic—FW sp]—like a hickory nut, but the shell is thin; **TN**24, Scaly bar [sic—FW sp]—a kind of hickory nut that is thin-hulled; (Qu. T16, . . *Kinds of trees . . 'special'*) Infs **AL**2, **IL**119, **NC**72, **SC**29, Scaly bark; **LA**2, **TN**30, 37, 65, Scaly-bark hickory; (Qu. T15, . . *Kinds of swamp trees*) Infs **MS**63, **SC**46, Scaly-bark tree.   **1986** Pederson *LAGS Concordance* **Gulf Region,** 46 infs, Scaly bark(s); 3 infs, Scaly-bark hickory; 5 infs, Scaly-bark hickory nut(s); 3 infs, Scaly-bark tree(s).

scaly-bark birch n
See quot.
1970 *DARE* (Qu. T15, . . *Kinds of swamp trees*) Inf **VA**79, Scaly-bark birch.

scaly-bark hickory See **scaly bark**

scaly lizard n   Cf **scalyback 1**
Any of var **swifts** of the genus *Sceloporus*.
1908 Biol. Soc. DC *Proc.* 21.72, *Sceloporus spinosus.* . . *Texas Scaly Lizard.* . . Abundant along the wooded banks of rivers and streams.   **1916** Acad. Nat. Sci. Philadelphia *Proc. for 1915* 124, *Sceloporus undulatus.* . . Abundant throughout the higher and drier portion of the Okefinokee and called by the natives "scaly lizard."   **1947** Carr *Desert Parade* 53 **Desert SW,** Handsome in a full-bodied sort of way, the scaly lizard (=*Sceloporus jarrovi*) has a black collar, large dark blue-black back scales with a white spot upon the center of each scale, which aid one greatly in identification.   **1953** Schmidt *N. Amer. Amphibians* 124, *Sceloporus jarrovi jarrovi.* . . Yarrow's scaly lizard. . . *Sceloporus poinsetti.* . . Red scaly lizard. . . *Sceloporus cyanogenys.* . . Blue scaly lizard.

scaly partridge See **scaled quail**

scammony n   Also *scammony root, wild scammony (root)*
=**man-of-the-earth 1.**
[**1828** Rafinesque *Med. Flora* 1.125, Our *C[onvolvulus] panduratus* has also been mistaken for Scamony, Rhubarb and Mechoacan.]   **1876** Hobbs *Bot. Hdbk.* 103, Scammony root, Wild potato, Convolvulus panduratus. *Ibid* 131, Wild scammony root, Wild potato, Convolvulus panduratus.   **1900** Lyons *Plant Names* 203, Conv[olvulus] panduratus. . . Scammony-root, Wild Scammony. *Tubers* feebly cathartic.   **1974** (1977) Coon *Useful Plants* 119, *Ipomoea pandurata* . . scammony. . . Possible to use as a food, but . . it has a reputation as a strong purgative, and is not recommended.

scamp n   [See quot 1882]
A **grouper 1b** (here: *Mycteroperca phenax*).
1882 U.S. Natl. Museum *Proc.* 5.273, *Trisotropis falcatus* [=*Mycteroperca phenax*]. . . is one of the best food-fishes, more delicate than the other "groupers." It is called "*Scamp*" from its way of flapping when touched after lying apparently dead on the deck.   **1902** Jordan–Evermann *Amer. Fishes* 394, The scamp reaches a length of 2 feet and a weight of 12 pounds or more, though those seen at Key West do not usually exceed 2 or 3 pounds.   **1933** John G. Shedd Aquarium *Guide* 101, *Mycteroperca phenax.* . . Called Scamp on the coast of Florida.   **1966** *Fishing World* 13.6.47 **AL,** Suddenly the sea was boiling alive with red snappers, brown triggerfish, . . and even the much sought-after "scamp" . ., favorite food fish of the Alabama reefs.   **1991** Amer. Fisheries Soc. *Common Names Fishes* 46, *Mycteroperca phenax* . . scamp.

scamp v¹   [Prob Scots, Engl dial; cf *SND scamp* v. "To go about in an idle manner, to roam, rove around, with *aboot, through,* often with the idea of intended mischief"; *EDD scamp* v.¹]
With *around:* To gallivant.
1960 Williams *Walk Egypt* 296 **GA,** You belong to be in bed, not scamping around.

scamp v²   [Prob Engl dial; *OED2* →1888]
To do (a job) carelessly or badly; to scrimp on (materials).
1905 Chesnutt *Col.'s Dream* 20 **GA,** The old house had been built of the best materials, and its woodwork dowelled and mortised and tongued and grooved by men who knew their trade and had not learned to scamp their work.   **1934** Stribling *Unfinished Cathedral* 144 **AL,** The way they scamped their material and their work made me sick.   **1951** West *Witch Diggers* 334 **IN,** Get on back to the barn. You scamped your work there.   **1966** *DARE* (Qu. KK49, *When you don't have the time or ambition to*

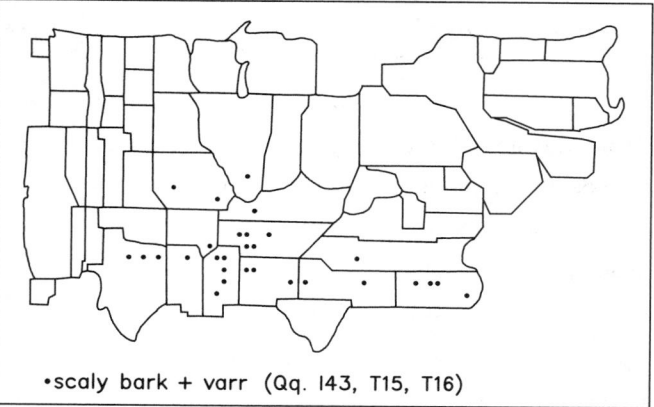

•scaly bark + varr (Qq. I43, T15, T16)

do something thoroughly: "I'm not going to give the place a real cleaning, I'll just _____.") Inf **MS39,** Scamped [skɛmpt] it.

scamp v³ [Etym unknown; cf *OED2 scamp* sb. "A highway robber. *arch.*"]
To cheat; to steal.
   1909 *DN* 3.415 **nME,** Scamp. . . To cheat. **1947** (1962) Henry *Misty* 115 **eVA,** He was wearing nothing but Grandpa's jacket over his underwear. He grinned at Grandpa. Grandpa winked back. "I see you scamped my belongings," he chuckled.

scamp v⁴ [Etym unknown] Cf **scalp B2, scape** v
To graze, deliver a glancing blow to.
   1911 *DN* 3.539 **eKY,** Scamp. . . To strike slightly, to graze; e.g., "The tree fell and just scamped my shoulder." **1915** *DN* 4.189 **swVA,** *Scamp* . . =graze, to touch lightly in passing. "That rock scamped my hat." **1919** *DN* 5.35 **seKY,** Scamp. . . To touch, or barely glance. "Jep cut drive with a big rock an' scamped Dish."

scamp around See **scamp** v¹

scanalous See **scandalous**

Scandahoovian See **Scandihoovian**

scandal n Pronc-spp *scannel, scannle* Cf **scandalous**
A Forms.
   1936 *AmSp* 11.234 **eTX,** ['skjæn!], ['skjænləs] . . for *scandal, scandalous* . . should be noted as widespread illiterate pronunciations in East Texas. **1955** Ritchie *Singing Family* 67 **seKY,** Scannle and shame! **1965** [see **B** below]. **1981** [see **B** below].
B Sense.
A scoundrel, rascal, "varmint." [By folk-etym from **scoundrel** (esp as pronounced ['skaunəl])] **esp Sth, S Midl**
   1965 Davis *Summer Land* 42 **cnNC,** When Fax asked him how come him to change his mind, you know what that scannel said? **1969** *DARE* (Qu. V6, . . *Words* . . *for a thief*) Inf **TX58,** Dirty scandal. **1981** Pederson *LAGS Basic Materials,* 1 inf, **cnGA,** That ['skæ·nnl] was here before we moved in—speaking of a dog; 1 inf, **cwFL,** Little old ['skæᵋnl]; 1 inf, **cwTN,** Them ['skæᵋnɬz] = wild hogs; 1 inf, **cwMS,** Trifling, good for nothing, [skænᵈl].

scandalize v [*OED2 scandalize* v.¹ 3 1566 →; "Now somewhat *rare*"] **chiefly Sth, S Midl**
To slander, malign, or defame—esp in phr *scandalize (some)one's name.*
   1844 *Ladies' Repository* 4.79, It [=the theater] *ridicules,* it *scandalizes* my Church; yes, and worse, it *blasphemes* my God! **1861** *Harper's New Mth. Mag.* 23.251 **MA,** They fell to scandalizing poor little Mrs. DeCroix. Such things as they told—things that I would blush to repeat. **1952** Brown *NC Folkl.* 1.587, Scandalize. . . To cause a scandal to one. **1958** Robeson *Here I Stand* 50, The white newspapers of this country . . never miss an opportunity to scandalize my name. **1966–70** *DARE* (Qu. Y3, *To say uncomplimentary things about somebody*) Infs **SC26, VA11,** Scandalize (his name); **FL51,** ['skænəlaz]; [**MO1,** Scandal or irritate; **OH44,** Gossip, scandal]. **1976** Garber *Mountain-ese* 78 **sAppalachians,** *Scandalize* . . bemean, ridicule—Those rumors were just meant to scandalize my good name. **1984** Wilder *You All Spoken Here* 46 **Sth,** *Scandalize his name:* Put the bad mouth on him. **1996** *Montgomery Coll.* **wNC, eTN,** Scandalize. **2000** in 2002 *DARE* File—Internet **AZ,** We've got the friendliest church in the world . . , but we're just as likely as the next guy to badmouth a brother, or scandalize a sister with a juicy tidbit of gossip.

scandalous adj, adv Usu |'skændələs, -dləs|; also **esp S Midl** |'skænləs|; for addit varr see quot 1936 Pronc-spp *scan(a)lous, scandless, scandulous*
A Std senses, var forms.
   1902 *DN* 2.244 **sIL,** Scandalous [skænləs]. **1903** *DN* 2.329 **seMO,** *Scandalous* (often scanlous). **1906** *DN* 3.155 **nwAR,** *Scan'alous.* **1907** *DN* 3.235 **nwAR,** *Scan(da)lous.* **1909** *DN* 3.367 **eAL, wGA,** *Scan(a)lous.* . . Scandalous. **1911** *DN* 3.546 **NE,** *Scanlous.* **1936** [see **scandal A**]. **1996** McDowell *Leaving Pipe Shop* 174 **AL** (as of 1960s) [Black], How can you be drinking whiskey on a Sunday? It's a [sic] scandless.
B As adv.

Very, exceedingly; excessively; see quots. **esp sAppalachians**
   1884 *Century Illustr. Mag.* 28.700 **LA,** 'Taint so scandalous far 'awa-a-ay' as you talk like. **1913** Kephart *Highlanders* 121 **sAppalachians,** We can't git a doctor up hyar less'n three days; and it costs scand'lous. **1931** Hannum *Thursday April* 55 **wNC,** But they do say he treats his women scandulous mean. **1974** Fink *Mountain Speech* 23 **wNC, eTN,** *Scandalous* . . very, exceedingly. "Clothes costes scandalous high these days." **1976** Garber *Mountain-ese* 78 **sAppalachians,** *Scandalous* . . very great—Food prices are scandalous high in them big city food stores.

Scandihoovian n, adj Also *Scandahoovian, Scandihuvian, Scandinoovian, Skandihoovian;* abbr *Scandie* [Joc varr of *Scandinavian*] **chiefly Upper MW, Pacific** See Map Cf **herring choker 2, Scowegian, snooser, squarehead**
   1901 *Bulletin* (San Francisco CA) 24 Feb 12 *(Zwilling Coll.),* [In cartoon "The Gin Bums' Crusade":] And raid the joint of a poor Scandahoovian. **1930** Williams *Logger-Talk* 16 **Pacific NW,** *Scandihoovian:* A Scandinavian. **1936** (1947) Mencken *Amer. Lang.* 296, For Scandinavian . . *scandihoovian, scandinoovian.* **1942** [see **Scandihoovian dynamite**]. **1950** *WELS (Names and nicknames for people of foreign background: Norwegian)* 3 Infs, **WI,** Scandihoovian(s). **1958** McCulloch *Woods Words* 166 **Pacific NW,** *Skandihoovian*—A logger from Scandinavia. **1964** *PADS* 42.39 **Chicago IL,** Applied to all Scandinavians . . were scoop, Scandihuvian, and Scandie. **1965–70** *DARE* (Qu. HH28) Infs **CA87, ND9, PA199,** Scandihoovian—Norwegian; **CO7, MT4, WI65,** Scandihoovian—Norwegian and Swedish; **CA161, MN6, 16,** Scandihoovian—Scandinavians [in general]; **WA16,** Scandihoovian—Norwegian, Swedish, Danes, and Finns; **TX18,** Scandihoovian—Swedish; (Qu. DD3a, . . *A person who uses snuff*) Inf **MN36,** Scandihoovian. **1998** Leary *WI Folkl.* 62 **nwWI** (as of 1950s), Just as we cheerfully admitted we were "micks," "harps," "Paddies," and "fish-eaters," we knew that Swedes and Norwegians alike might be teased as "herring chokers," "Scandihoovians," "snoose chewers," and "squareheads." **2000** *DARE* File **CA** (as of c1965), My father, who grew up in the Pacific Northwest and whose mother was a Swede from Nebraska, used to joke about our being Scandihoovians.

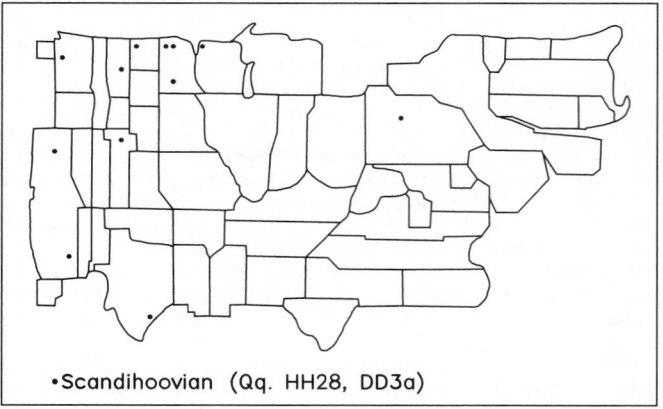

• Scandihoovian (Qq. HH28, DD3a)

Scandihoovian dynamite n
Snuff.
   1942 *AmSp* 17.223 **Nth** [Loggers' talk], *Scandahoovian dynamite.* A pet name for *snoose.* **1968** *AmSp* 43.303, His [=the Northwest logger's] 'snuff' is *Scandihoovian dynamite.* **1969** Sorden *Lumberjack Lingo* 104 **NEng, Gt Lakes,** *Scandihoovian dynamite*—Snoose, snuff.

Scandihuvian, Scandinoovian See **Scandihoovian**

scandless, scanlous, scandulous See **scandalous**

scannel, scannle See **scandal**

scapaug See **scuppaug**

scape v Cf **scalp B2, scamp** v⁴
   1909 *DN* 3.366 **eAL, wGA,** Scape. . . To graze, mark slightly. "The bullet just scaped his scalp." Cf. *skelp* in same sense.

scape n See **skep** n¹

scapegallows n Also, by folk-etym, *scrapegallows* Pronc-sp *scapegallus*

A scoundrel, rascal; hence v phr *scapegallows around* to go about in an idle or reprehensible manner.

1799 in 1893 Washington *Writings* 14.154 **VA**, None but the riff-raff of the Country, and the scape-gallowses of the large cities will be to be had. **1854** Smith *'Way Down East* 132 **ME**, You are a scoundrel and a scape-gallows and an infernal small piece of a man, I think. **1884** Jewett *Country Dr.* 62 **ME**, I can put up with her pranks; 't is of pore old Mis' Thacher I'm thinkin'. She's had trouble enough without adding on this young 'scape-gallows. **1899** (1912) Green *VA Folk-Speech* 367, *Scape-gallows.* . . One who has escaped the gallows though deserving; a villain. **1946** *PADS* 6.26 **ceNC** (as of 1900–10), *Scrapegallows.* . . A man given to various kinds of skulduggery. Applied to a person like a forger of checks. . . Occasional. **1953** Randolph–Wilson *Down in Holler* 281 **Ozarks**, *Scape-gallows.* . . To idle about, to loaf. "Jim got let out of the army to work on his farm. But he don't do no work. He's out there now, just scape-gallowsin' around." Rufe Scott, of Galena, Mo., heard this term in his neighborhood, and says that it means "just keepin' ahead of the hangman." **1983** *Lutz Coll., Scapegallows* (scapegallus)— [A woman from] Suffern, N.Y., used this word for a man who got drunk, drove cars wildly, and so on. When I asked what the word meant, she said it was someone always in mischief. She pronounced the word *scapegallus*.

scapegrace See **cape-race**

scaper v Also *scaber* [Cf *SND scape* v. 2 "To run at large, to scamper."]

To dash, romp; with *around*: to gad about.

1933 Rawlings *South Moon* 18 **nFL**, 'Tain't mannerly no-ways to go scaperin' acrost to the men-folks that-a-way. **c1938** in 1970 Hyatt *Hoodoo* 1.185 **Jacksonville FL**, She was stayin' tuh her aunty a while, stayin' over tuh her cousin a while—see jest scabering aroun' jest like somebody goin' away when she got her own home dere to stay tuh. But dey put a spell on her—she couldn't he'p it. **1938** Rawlings *Yearling* 198 **nFL**, We was mighty lucky 'twas a young bear like this un come scaperin' under our noses.

scaper n [Perh agent noun < *scape* v as in **scapegallows**, **scapegrace**, but perh < **scaper** v] esp **FL, GA**

A rascal; a critter, varmint.

1933 Rawlings *South Moon* 82 **nFL**, Hit must be 'possums. They's dirty scapers. *Ibid* 145, "What you gittin' for 'em?" "Dime or so a pound. Wisht I'd been huntin' when them passenger boats was on the river. They quit runnin' 'bout the time I commenced huntin' reg'lar. Them scapers paid forty cents a pound." **1938** Rawlings *Yearling* 13 **nFL**, You sly scaper. . . That's the first I knowed you been off. You gittin' slick as a clay road in the rain. **c1960** *Mathews Coll.* **AL** (as of c1900), *Scaper*—Common in Ala. of 1900 with reference to a rascal, shaver,—a kind of affectionate diminutive. **1960** Williams *Walk Egypt* 27 **GA**, Hunting him all over creation, and you know where the scaper was? **1975** Newell *If Nothin' Don't Happen* 6 **nwFL**, When he were just a shirttail boy he were a scrappy little scaper and didn't take nothin' from nobody. *Ibid* 96 **nwFL**, It probably weren't the looks of old man Shorter that turned back the skeeters—them scapers go more by scent than sight. **2001** *NADS Letters* **csAL**, I am 52 years old, from Butler County, Alabama (South Alabama). "Scaper" has always meant something like rascal ever since I can remember. Such as, "Some scaper has done come along and left the gap down."

scaper around See **scaper** v

scarapin See **scorpion**

scarce adj, adv, v Usu |skɛ(r)s|; also |ske(r)s, skæ(r)s, ska(r)s, skɜ(r)s|; for addit varr see quots Pronc-spp *kace, scace, scai(r)se, scarct, scase, scurse, skace, skase, skearce, skeerce, skerse, skirs, skurce, skurse*

A Forms.

1795 Dearborn *Columbian Grammar* 138, *List of Improprieties,* commonly called *Vulgarisms,* which should never be used in *Speaking, Reading, or Writing.* . . *Skase* for Scarce. **1837** Sherwood *Gaz.* **GA** 71, *Provincialisms.* . . *Scace,* for scarce. **1843** (1916) Hall *New Purchase* 150 **IN**, Game was mighty skerse. **1850** in 1956 Eliason *Tarheel Talk* 317 **c,cNC**, *Scase.* **1867** Lowell *Biglow* 18 'Upcountry' **MA**, Green ones is plentife enough, skurce wuth a nigger's getherin'. **1871**

Eggleston *Hoosier Schoolmaster* 40 **sIN**, Schools was skase in them air days. **1887** (1892) Hinman *Corporal Si Klegg* 23, Farm hands is gittin' skurce. **1893** Shands *MS Speech* 44, Make one's self skase [skes]. **1899** (1912) Green *VA Folk-Speech* 368, *Scase.* . . A form of *scarce. Ibid* 389, *Skearce.* . . For *scarce.* **1903** *DN* 2.328 **seMO**, *Scase.* **1904** Day *Kin o' Ktaadn* 154 **ME**, He says they's scurse a stormy night the tarnal witch don't come. **1906** *DN* 3.154 **nwAR**, *Sca'ce* [skeɪs]—*skirs* [skirs]. **1909** *DN* 3.366 **eAL, wGA**, *Scase* [skes]. **1910** *DN* 3.458 **Chicago IL**, *Skurser* than hens' teeth. **1913** Johnson *Highways St. Lawrence to VA* 233, It's pretty skearce around here now. **1915** *DN* 4.189 **swVA**, *Scarce* [skes]. **1922** Gonzales *Black Border* 308 **sSC, GA coasts** [Gullah glossary], *'Kace*—scarce. **1923** *DN* 5.221 **swMO**, *Skace.* **1928** *AmSp* 3.401 **Ozarks** (as of 1916–27), The vowel in *care, share* and *scarce* is pronounced almost exactly as though the words were spelled *keer, sheer* and *skeerce.* **1938** Rawlings *Yearling* 275 **nFL**, The creeturs is so scarct now and the hides so pore, hit's no use. **1942** Perry *Texas* 23, The fact that such logs are growing "skase" does not shatter his inner serenity. **1952** Brown *NC Folkl.* 1.587, *Scase* [skes]. **1961** Kurath–McDavid *Pronc. Engl.* 150, *Scarce* . . has the vowel phoneme /e/ of *eight* in the South and the southern sector of the South Midland. This pronunciation, resulting from the early loss of /r/ before /s/, is especially common in the Carolinas and in Georgia, and only less so along Chesapeake Bay. /skes/ is rarely used by cultured speakers and is not as frequent in the speech of the middle group as among the folk. This expression was not investigated in New England. **1965–70** *DARE* (Qu. LL11a, *In short supply—hard to get:* "Good men are _____ these days.") 291 Infs, **widespread**, [skɛ(r)s]; 111 Infs, **scattered, but chiefly N Midl, C and S Atl, Atl**, [ske(ɪ)s, skejɚs]; 9 Infs, **esp S Atl**, [ske(ɪ)s, skejəs]; 48 Infs, **scattered**, [skæ(r)s]; 9 Infs, **esp NEng**, [ska(r)s]; **TN31, 33, 35, 36, VA2**, [skɑrs]; **CT25, FL17, KY34, MA5, 128, NJ19, TX92, VA21**, [skɜ(r)s]; **VA15**, [skjɚs]; **AZ9, DC8, FL38, MA71, SC32**, [skɪə(r)s]; (Qu. LL11b) **Inf KY34**, [skɜ˞s]; (Qu. LL14, *None at all, not even one:* "This pond used to be full of fish but now there's _____ left.") **Inf VA99**, [skɛs] a one. **a1975** Lunsford *It Used to Be* 162 **sAppalachians**, Rocks are pretty scaise around here. **1989** Pederson *LAGS Tech. Index* 348 **Gulf Region**, *Scarce* . . 346 infs, [skɛrs]; 144 infs, [skæ(r)s]; 75 infs, [skeɜs]; 54 infs, [skers]; 46 infs, [skes]; 33 infs, [skɪrs]; 15 infs, [skjers, skjærs, skjɪrs]; 10 infs, [skæɜs]; 6 infs, [skɪɜs]; 5 infs, [skes]; 2 infs, [skʌrs]; 1 inf, [skɪs]; 1 inf, [skjɪɜs]; 1 inf, [skjɪrs]. **1989** *DARE* File **cnNC**, The term "scase" (pron. as in *base* or *race*) is still in use among older Blue Ridge people in this area. Meaning *scarce,* of course.

B As adj.

Poorly supplied with some commodity; usu with *of*: short of, deficient in; hence n *scarce-of-fat* a skinny person. [*OED2 scarce* a. 5. 1541 →; "Now *rare* or *obs.*"]

1810 Pike *Expeditions* 3.253 **TX**, This route . . is very scarce of water. **1813** (1939) Hartsell *Memora* 11.112 **PA**, I told them that I wold tell to them that we had bought Some when we was Scarce. **1864** (1922) Jackson *Col.'s Diary* 158 **PA**, Our men were very scarce of meat. **1910** Johnson *Highways Rocky Mts.* 40, This is a pretty good farm except that we sometimes run skurce of water. But there's wells within a mile that never fail. **1938** Stuart *Dark Hills* 355 **KY**, All they tell me is they are scarce of money and thousands are asking for credit. **1941** Ward *Holding Hills* 84 **IA** (as of early 20th cent), The youngest of these three men is what we call a "scarce-of-fat." . . He is as slender as a rail.

C As verb.

With *up*: To decline in abundance, become rare.

1967 *DARE* File **ME**, A program on TV the other night, deploring the growing scarcity of lobsters along the Maine coast, had the reporter asking a fisherman the cause of all this. He replied that the waters are overfished and the lobsters are 'scarcein' ['skɪrsən] up.'

scarcely adv Pronc-spp *cacely, kacely, scasely, scurcely, skeersely*

Std sense, var forms.

1837 Sherwood *Gaz.* **GA** 71, *Skeersely,* scarcely. **1888** Jones *Negro Myths* 103 **GA coast**, Buh Rabbit mek answer een er woice so leely you cacely kin yeddy um. **1890** *DN* 1.62 **swOH**, *Scasely:* for *scarcely.* **1892** *DN* 1.234 **KY**, *Scasely.* **1893** Shands *MS Speech* 55, *Scasely* [skeslɪ]. Negro for *scarcely.* **1899** (1912) Green *VA Folk-Speech* 368, *Scasely.* . . A form of *scarcely.* **1905** *DN* 3.58 **eNE**, *Scasely.* **1908** Lincoln *Cy Whittaker* 38 **MA**, There wan't a breath scurcely. **1922** Gonzales *Black Border* 308 **sSC, GA coasts** [Gullah glossary], *'Kacely*—scarcely, hardly.

scarce of (fat) See **scarce B**

scarce up See **scarce C**

scarct See **scarce**

scare n, v

A Pronc forms.

Usu |skɛə(r), skæə(r)|; also |skeə(r)|; also **chiefly Sth, S Midl** |skɪə(r)|; for addit varr see quots   Pronc-spp *skear, skeer, skere* Cf **scary**

1843 (1916) Hall *New Purchase* 225 **IN,** Let's you and me make out to be Injins, and skere them doctur fellers. **1858** Hammett *Piney Woods Tavern* 126, Old Pond . . catched enough of his words to skear him into chicken fits. **1877** Wright *Big Bonanza* 54 **West,** We nat'rally had to keep stirrin' about to try to skeer up somethin' that would do to eat. **1878** *Appletons' Jrl.* 5.416 **Sth,** At the South it is common, if not universal, to hear . . *skeer* for *scare*. **1891** *DN* 1.125 **cNY,** Occasionally . . [skæər], [skɪər], 'scare'. **1893** Shands *MS Speech* 55, *Scare* [skeə]. This pronunciation of *scare* is used by negroes and illiterate whites, and even by educated people sometimes. **1899** (1912) Green *VA Folk-Speech* 389, *Skeer, v.* and *n.* A form of *scare*. **1903** *DN* 2.328 **seMO,** *Scare*. . . Pronounced *skeer*. **1905** *DN* 3.18 **cCT,** *Scare* or *skeer*. . . A fright. **1907** *DN* 3.235 **nwAR,** *Scare*. . . Pronounced [skɪr]. **1908** Fox *Lonesome Pine* 15 **KY,** An' I don't waste time skeering folks. **1909** *DN* 3.366 **eAL, wGA,** *Scare*. . . Pronounced skeer. **1927** Shewmake *Engl. Pronc. VA* 33, *Scare*. . . scae-uh. **1936** *AmSp* 11.20 **eTX,** Educated speech . . is by no means free from such forms as . . [skeə], [skɛɚ], for . . *scare*. . . These pronunciations are used chiefly by less literate speakers. Educated people do not use the forms . . [skɪə], [skɪɚ], which are widespread among the less literate. **1938** Rawlings *Yearling* 176 **nFL,** Don't skeer him. **1941** *AmSp* 16.5 **eTX** [Black], *Scare* [skjɛə]. **1942** Hall *Smoky Mt. Speech* 25 **wNC, eTN,** By less well educated speakers . . [ɪ] . . may appear also in . . *scare*. **1946** *AmSp* 21.98 **sIL,** *Skeer, scare*. **1949** Webber *Backwoods Teacher* 11 **Ozarks,** He jist likes to skeer folks. **1965** *Dict. Queen's English* 10 **NC,** A sight like that is enough to skeer a man. **1967–68** *DARE* (Qu. GG24, . . *To frighten: "Now don't let those fellows _____ you."*) Infs **GA30, LA2,** Skeer [skɪr].

B Gram forms.

Past, past ppl, ppl adj: usu *scared;* pronc-spp *scaid, scairt, sca't, skear(t), skeered, skeert;* for addit varr see quots

1795 Dearborn *Columbian Grammar* 138, *List of Improprieties*. . . *Skeer'd* for *Scar'd*. **1815** Humphreys *Yankey in England* 108, *Scart,* scared. **1843** (1916) Hall *New Purchase* 145 **IN,** A leetle skur'd. *Ibid* 149, I gits bodaciously sker'd. **1848** Lowell *Biglow* 146 **'Upcountry MA',** *Skeered,* scared. **1853** Simms *Sword & Distaff* 446 **SC,** Ef you skear, nebber le' Miss Ellen see you skear. **1858** Hammett *Piney Woods Tavern* 129, They was all so most amazin' skeart. **1864** (1868) Trowbridge *3 Scouts* 19 **TN,** Ever since Tildy come home, . . you've been as scaret as any of us. **1871** (1882) Stowe *Fireside Stories* 172 **MA,** Jest then the meetin'-house bell begun to ring, and that scart 'em. **1883** Harte *In Carquinez Woods* 4, What in thunder skeert the hosses? Did you see or hear anything? **1884** Jewett *Country Dr.* 8 **ME,** We shall get to telling over ghost stories if we don't look out, and I for one shall be sca't to go home. **1884** *Anglia* 7.263 **Sth, S Midl** [Black], *Skeered outen his skin*. **1893** Frederic *Copperhead* 133 **nNY,** "I wasn't born in the woods to be skeert by an owl!" replied Abner. **1893** Shands *MS Speech* 55, *Scare*. . . *Skered* is the ordinary past tense of this word, but negroes sometimes say *sked*. **1899** (1912) Green *VA Folk-Speech* 389, *Skeart*. . . A form of *scared*. **1906** Johnson *Highways Missip. Valley* 213 **IA,** They [=men in an automobile] stopped that time they scat Sarah Colton's horse. **1906** *DN* 3.155 **nwAR,** *Scaret* [skæət]. . . Scared. **1907** *DN* 3.249 **eME,** *Scat*. . . Scared, afraid of. "I ain't scat the rain." **1909** *DN* 3.366 **eAL, wGA,** He was nigh skeert out'n his wits. *Ibid* 370 **nAL, wGA,** *Skeart, skeared, pret.* and *pp.* of *scare* or *skeer. Ibid* 415 **nME,** *Scairt*. . . Scared. **1910** *DN* 3.454 **seVT,** He was scat out of his wits. **1915** (1916) Johnson *Highways New Engl.* 60, The feller who was watchin' was so scat he didn't know where they'd gone nor nothin'. **1921** Haswell *Daughter Ozarks* 82 (as of 1880s), Law, Mr. Haberton, how ye skeered me! **1922** Gonzales *Black Border* 326 **sSC, GA coasts** [Gullah glossary], *Skay'd—scared*. **1923** *DN* 5.221 **swMO,** *Skeer*. . . Past tense, *Skeert*. **1925** in 1953 Botkin–Harlow *Treas. Railroad Folkl.* 228, Holy Smokes! I was scairt. **1927** Kennedy *Gritny* 141 **sLA** [Black], I was so sk'yeard, Unc' Nat, I start to run an' holler for help. **1927** Shewmake *Engl. Pronc. VA* 14, *Skeart* for *scared*. **1930** *AmSp* 5.201 **Ozarks,** *Scared* is usually *skeert* or *scairt* in the Ozark country—

both very old English forms. **1934** *WV Review* Dec 77, *Sceart*. **1938** Rawlings *Yearling* 31 **nFL,** You'll not be scairt when we come up with him, Pa? *Ibid* 84, How come some is skeert and some is bold? **1941** Smith *Going to God's Country* 147 **MO** (as of 1896), He was so sceard that he jumped on his horse and started to El Remo. **1942** Hall *Smoky Mt. Speech* 25 **wNC, eTN,** To run like a ['skɪə·d 'hæᵉnt]. **1963** Owens *Look to River* 123 **TX,** I'm scaid. **1967–68** *DARE* FW Addit **LA40,** Was you scairt? **cnNY,** Scairt me out of 7 years growth.

scared-cat n Also *scare-cat, scary-cat* [Varr of *scaredy-cat*] Cf *fraid cat* (at **fraidycat**)

A fearful person.

1897 *KS Univ. Qrly.* (ser B) 6.91 **neKS,** Scare cat: "fraid cat." A timid person. **1936** *Sun* (Baltimore MD) 30 Jan 1/2 *(Hench Coll.)*, Most of the "scare cats," which is the name applied to those Senators who, against their convictions and entirely through fear, voted to override the President's veto, realize they have made an unpleasant spectacle of themselves. **1950** *WELS (Names and expressions for a coward)* 2 Infs, **WI,** Scare-cat; 1 Inf, **csWI,** Scared-cat. **1966–69** *DARE* (Qu. HH10, *A very timid or cowardly person: "He's _____."*) Infs **IL4, ME6, MN2, NJ39, OH38,** Scared-cat; **MI67, NY66, TX36, WI70,** Scary-cat; **CA158, LA40, MI55,** Scare-cat.

scared water n

Weak coffee.

[**1942** Berrey–Van den Bark *Amer. Slang* 92.3, *Soft, or weak, inferior drink*. . . *frightened water*. . . *spoiled water.*] **1960** Criswell *Resp. to PADS* 20 **Ozarks,** *Scared water*. . . Weak coffee. Still used. **1967–69** *DARE* (Qu. H74b, . . *Coffee . . very weak*) Infs **CA59, CO11, 27, KS1, MO39, OR4, PA186,** Scared water. **1980** *NADS Letters* **TN,** "Scared water". . . used by an elderly snuff-chewing mountain woman living in Clinton, Tennessee, to describe her daughter's weak coffee.

scaredy adj [Perh by back-formation from *scaredy-cat,* but cf Intro "Language Changes" III.1] Cf **fraidy, scary**

Afraid, fearful.

1955 Ritchie *Singing Family* 11 **seKY,** 'Law no, Mom, I couldn't stay, with all these four little uns—' 'You with no lantern either, and them all scaredy—'. **1968–70** *DARE* (Qu. HH10, *A very timid or cowardly person: "He's _____."*) Infs **KY6, PA98, WI44,** Scaredy; [**NY73,** A scaredy]. **2000** Humphreys *Nowhere* 20 **csNC** (as of c1865), But I don't mean Boss was scaredy or girlish.

scares See **scours**

scaret See **scare B**

scare the daylights out of one See **daylight 1**

‡scare toad n Cf *DS* HH10

=**scared-cat**.

1941 *LANE* Map 475 *(Afraid)* 1 inf, **seRI,** Scared, a child's word, used by adults only in jest; cf *scare toad,* a child's nickname for one who is easily frightened.

scareweed n

A **wild indigo 1** (here: *Baptisia simplicifolia*) native to Florida.

1933 Small *Manual SE Flora* 675 **FL,** *B[aptisia] simplicifolia*. . . *Scare-weed*. . . Pinelands. . . Plants dry black. **1949** Moldenke *Amer. Wild Flowers* 135, *B. simplicifolia,* the *scare-weed,* with the flowers in terminal racemes and the foliage drying black.

scarf n¹ **chiefly Sth, S Midl** See Map

A decorative cloth furniture-covering.

1895 (1969) Montgomery Ward *Catalogue* 23, *Fringed Scarfing*. A novelty in linen, for making tray cloths, table, sideboard or dresser scarfs. **1897** (1968) Sears *Catalogue* 537, *Upright Piano Scarfs*. . . Piano Scarf, made of finest quality of felt . . plush front, fine embroidery . . with cord and tassels. **1927** (1970) *Ibid* 566, *Scarfs*. . . Dresser. . . Piano. . . Radio Cabinet. . . Table. **1965–70** *DARE* (Qu. E10, *Knitted or crocheted pieces placed on the back and arms of a chair for decoration and cleanliness*) 10 Infs, **Sth, S Midl,** Scarfs; **GA8,** Chair scarfs; **LA20, 38, NC50, ND2, OH7, PA239, SC46, TX87,** Scarves; **VA76,** Chair scarves; **WI76,** Arm scarves, crocheted scarves. **1986** Pederson *LAGS Concordance,* [1 inf, **swGA,** A scarf [=a pillow sham];] 1 inf, **cMS,** Chifforobe scarf, dresser scarf. **2001** *DARE* File **nwMA,** I wonder what ever happened to that bureau scarf I started embroidering when I was a girl.

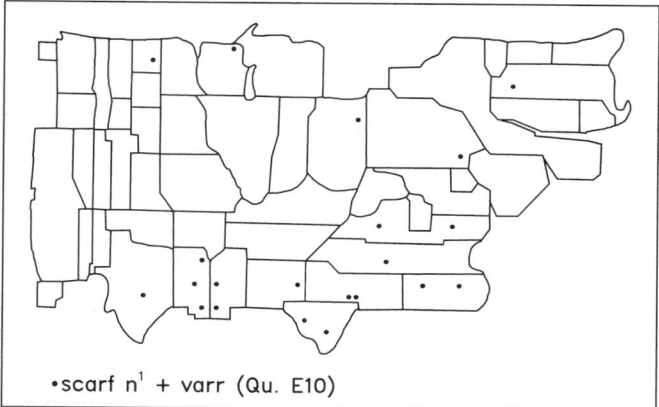

•scarf n¹ + varr (Qu. E10)

scarf n² Pronc-sp *scaff* [Prob by confusion of *carf* (var of **kerf**) with *scarf* a notch or taper made in the end of a timber to allow it to be joined to another similarly shaped timber.] Cf *AND, DNZE*

A cut or notch, as:

a A groove or notch made by an ax or saw; a kerf; esp an undercut made to direct the fall of a tree; the cut surface of a stump or the butt of a log; hence v *scarf* to make a groove or undercut in. **chiefly NEng**

1843 *Amer. Pioneer* 2.448 **OH,** The ash beyond the house crossed the scarf and fell on the cabin, but without damage. **1888** Billings *Hardtack* 180 **MA,** When an army first went into camp trees were cut with the scarf two or three feet above the ground, but as the scarcity increased these stumps would be chipped down. **1957** Beck *Folkl. ME* 230, Once it [=a tree] was properly "scarfed" (notched on one side) the choppers fell to with a will and in a short time it would come down. **1958** McCulloch *Woods Words* 157 **Pacific NW,** *Scarf* a. An undercut. b. To cut a deep groove around the end of a large log to hold the butt chain, prevent it slipping off, in the days before big steam power in the woods. **1966–68** *DARE* Tape **ME**18, They'd cut that scarf [skɑf] round where they wanted it. . . We'd scarf 'em on the side where we wanted to go; cut in a couple inches and wedge 'em; **ME**19, They'd scarf [skɑf] 'em. . . they would start above and make a scarf right down in; **NH**14, Say a tree stand straight, you could fall it in any direction, whichever way you wanted to. . . "Put a scarf [skɑf] in it," all the older people used to say. **1966** *DARE* FW Addit **ME**5, A scaff—notch cut into side of tree to make it fall in a certain direction. Verb—to scaff a tree. **1969** Sorden *Lumberjack Lingo* 104 **NEng, Gt Lakes,** *Scarf*—Surface of the undercut in falling trees. **1972** *Yesterday* Mar–Apr 23 **Nth,** In the hands of real expert such a tool [=a well-tuned ax] used on a clear grained "punkin" pine would leave a "scarf" or notched surface as smooth as a planed board. **1975** Gould *ME Lingo* 152, *Kerf*—The educated forester's uppity word for what every Maine chopper and sawyer calls the *scarf*. It is the cut or groove made by the ax to direct the falling tree in the right direction; and it is also the cut made by a saw in the log at the mill. . . old Maine sawmills took out a ¼-inch *kerf/scarf*.

b A cut made in a whale's body to allow large slabs of blubber to be peeled off; hence v *scarf* to make such a cut; to make such a cut in.

1851 (1976) Melville *Moby-Dick* 303, The blubber in one strip uniformly peels off along the line called the "scarf," simultaneously cut by the spades of Starbuck and Stubb, the mates. *Ibid* 304, And thus the work proceeds; . . the mates scarfing, . . and all hands swearing occasionally. **1874** Scammon *Marine Mammals* 63, A scarf is cut along the body and through the blubber. **1887** Goode *Fisheries U.S.* 5.2.278, The second mate 'scarfs,' or cuts the body blubber. **1926** Ashley *Yankee Whaler* 139, *Scarf*: The line or score around a whale made by the spades in cutting-in. It is the dividing line between two blankets.

scarf v See **scarf** n² **a, b**

scarlet berry n

A **bittersweet** (here: *Solanum dulcamara*).

1830 Rafinesque *Med. Flora* 2.86, *Solanum dulcamara*. . . Names. Bitter-sweet Nightshade. . . Scarlet Berry. . . Woody vine. . . Berries oval, of

a bright scarlet. **1898** U.S. Dept. Ag. *Farmers' Bulletin* 20.53, *Bittersweet. Solanum dulcamara*. . . *Other names* . . scarlet berry [etc]. . . The berry, though its taste is not remarkably disagreeable, is somewhat poisonous. **1935** (1943) Muenscher *Weeds* 411, *Solanum dulcamara*. . . Scarlet berry. . . Most common in the eastern and north central states; local on the Pacific coast. **1959** Carleton *Index Herb. Plants* 104, *Scarletberry:* Solanum dulcamara.

scarlet bugler n [See quot 1914]   **West**

Any of several red-flowered **beardtongues,** esp *Penstemon centranthifolius*.

1897 Parsons *Wild Flowers CA* 358, The tall spires of the scarlet bugler are such familiar sights . . that people almost forget the enthusiastic admiration their bright beauty first elicited. **1914** Saunders *With Flowers in CA* 117, One [species of *Penstemon*] bearing panicles a foot or two long of vivid scarlet trumpet-shaped flowers, which have suggested the popular name, scarlet bugler. . . is *Penstemon centranthifolius,* and its colonies brighten the chaparral sometimes by the acre. **1915** (1926) Armstrong–Thornber *Western Wild Flowers* 484, *Scarlet Bugler—Penstemon Eatoni*. . . Very beautiful, . . with a bright scarlet, funnel-shaped corolla. . . These graceful wands of vivid color are conspicuous in the Grand Canyon. **1959** Martin *Gunbarrel* 154 **WY,** On the steep arid hillsides among the rocks, the same colors were repeated in stonecrop, scarlet bugler, harebells, and locoweed. **1967** Dodge *Roadside Wildflowers* 41 **SW,** The name scarlet bugler has been applied to several of the beardtongues which have brilliant red flowers. One of these . . is. . . *Penstemon barbatus*. **1968** *DARE* (Qu. S26a, . . *Wildflowers*. . . *Roadside flowers*) Inf **CA**87, Scarlet buglers—look like little red bugles. **1979** Spellenberg *Audubon Guide N. Amer. Wildflowers W. Region* 769, *Scarlet Bugler (Penstemon centranthifolius)*. . . in certain situations . . will produce extensive, nearly solid patches of brilliant red.

scarletbush n

=**fire bush 1.**

1946 West–Arnold *Native Trees FL* 199, The scarletbush, *Hamelia patens* . . , is set off by bright-red flowers and flower stalks, black berries . . , and thin, pointed leaves. **1979** Little *Checklist U.S. Trees* 144, *Hamelia patens*. . . Scarletbush. . . Commonly a shrub in Fla. but recorded also as a small tree in Fla. Keys.

scarlet creeper n

A **cypress vine 1** (here: *Ipomoea coccinea*).

1846 Thorpe *Mysteries* 50, The scarlet creeper and fragrant jasmine . . shed upon . . Rousseau a shower of fragrance. **1970** Correll *Plants TX* 1250, *Ipomoea coccinea*. . . Scarlet creeper. Low-climbing vine; . . corolla orange-red or red with yellow tube. **1987** Bowers *100 Roadside Wildflowers* 62 **SW,** Scarlet creeper . . is typical of hummingbird flowers. A vine of roadsides and woodland clearings, scarlet creeper occurs from western Texas to Arizona. . . *Ipomoea coccinea.*

scarlet cup n

1 An **Indian paintbrush 1** (here: *Castilleja affinis*).

1901 Jepson *Flora CA* 412, *C[astilleja] affinis*. . . Scarlet Cup. . . Best known by its bright scarlet pediceled flowers.

2 =**summer cypress.**

1975 Logan *Land Remembers* 165 **swWI** (as of c1920), We argued half the summer about whether the red flowers should be called Indian paintbrush, red-hot poker, fireball, or scarlet cup.

scarlet gilia n

Std: a **gilia** (here: *Ipomopsis coccinea*). Also called **fairy trumpet 1, fox fire 5, honeysuckle 5i, polecat plant, skunk flower 2, skyrocket, timpiute, trumpet phlox, wild cypress, ~ honeysuckle**

scarlet haw n Also *scarlet hawthorn*   Cf **red haw 1, scarlet thorn**

Any of several **hawthorns,** esp *Crataegus chrysocarpa*.

1860 Curtis *Cat. Plants NC* 83, Scarlet Haw. (Crataegus coccinea, Linn. [=*C. chrysocarpa*]). . . The fruit is bright red, ½ inch or more long, and eatable. **1897** Sudworth *Arborescent Flora* 219, *Crataegus coccinea*. . . Scarlet Haw (N.H., Mass., N.Y., N.J., Pa., N.C., S.C., Miss., Ark., Mo., Ill., Nebr., Iowa, Minn.). *Ibid* 221, *Crataegus mollis*. . . Scarlet Haw. **1908** Rogers *Tree Book* 309, Scarlet Haw (C[rataegus] pruinosa . .) . . is one of the handsome native thorn trees, a long time confused with *C. coccinea. Ibid* 312, Scarlet Haw (C. Ellwangeriana [=*C. pedicellata*] . .). . . Fruits . . bright crimson, . . flesh thin, sour, *juicy.* **1921** Deam *Trees IN* 214, *Crataegus Phaenopyrum. . . Scarlet Haw. . .* Its scarlet autumn foliage and beautiful little scarlet fruit persist for a long time. **1950** Grimm *Trees PA* 236, *The scarlet hawthorns. . .* are small trees or shrubs. . . The fruits are . . scarlet in color, and usually have a thick, soft, juicy flesh. **1980** Little *Audubon Guide N. Amer. Trees E. Region* 467, *Scarlet Hawthorn—Crataegus coccinea. . .* S. Quebec south to Maine and New York, west to Iowa, and north to SE. Minnesota . . local south in mountains to W. North Carolina. One of the three native [i.e., to the US] hawthorns described by Linnaeus in 1753.

scarlet king snake n

A **milk snake 1** (here: *Lampropeltis triangulum* subsp).

1935 Pratt *Manual Vertebrate Animals* 211, *L[ampropeltis] t[riangulum] amaura. . .* Scarlet king-snake. Ground color yellow; bands bright red. . . Mississippi to Texas. **1952** Ditmars *N. Amer. Snakes* 103, *Scarlet King Snake . . , Lampropeltis elapsoides elapsoides. . .* Red, yellow and black encircle the body with the typical form. *Ibid* 146, *Scarlet King Snake . . Lampropeltis triangulum amaura. . .* Southeastern United States to Kansas; southward to Texas. **1967** Huheey–Stupka *Amphibians Reptiles Gt. Smoky Mts.* 66, In the Scarlet Kingsnake *(L[ampropeltis] triangulum elapsoides),* the body is ringed by wide bands of red and narrow bands of yellow bordered by black. **1969** *DARE* (Qu. P25, . . *Kinds of snakes*) Inf **GA**76, Scarlet kingsnake. **1979** Behler–King *Audubon Field Guide Reptiles* 623, Scarlet Kingsnake *(L. t. elapsoides),* . . snout red, bands usually continue across belly; North Carolina south through Florida Keys, west to the Appalachians and the Mississippi River in s. Mississippi and adjacent Louisiana, north through ne. Mississippi, c. Tennessee, and sc. and e. Kentucky.

scarlet larkspur n

A **delphinium** (here: *Delphinium cardinale*) native to California.

1897 Parsons *Wild Flowers CA* 364, The brilliant spires of the scarlet larkspur . . sometimes rise to a height of ten feet! **1944** Abrams *Flora Pacific States* 2.181, Scarlet Larkspur. . . Plants with stout fascicled roots and hollow stems. **1982** *Plants SW* (Catalog) 16 **CA,** *Scarlet Larkspur. . .* Bright orange-red flowers attract hummingbirds. Blooms in late spring–early summer.

scarlet lightning n

=Maltese cross.

[**1892** *Jrl. Amer. Folkl.* 5.93, *Lychnis chalcedonica. . .* Scarlet lightning. Hemmingford, P[rovince] Q[uebec]. . . Probably a corruption for *Lychnis.*] **1902** Earle *Old Time Gardens* 443 **NEng,** Scarlet Lightning . . has five deeply-nicked petals. **1940** Clute *Amer. Plant Names* 62, *L[ychnis] chalcedonica. . .* Scarlet lightning.

scarlet maple n

A **red maple** (here: *Acer rubrum*).

1768 Miller *Gardener's Dict.* **VA,** *Acer.* I have observed, upon cutting off branches from the scarlet Maple in February, a great quantity of a very sweet juice hath flowed out. **1813** Muhlenberg *Catalogus Plantarum* 95 **PA, OH,** *Maple* (scarlet, white, red, or soft). **1848** in 1850 Cooper *Rural Hours* 64 **NY,** The sugar, the scarlet, and the silver maples, are assuredly very fine trees. **1850** Emerson *Rept. Trees & Shrubs* 483 **MA,** *Acer rubrum. . .* The Red Maple, called also . . the Scarlet . . Maple, is a tree of middling size, growing abundantly . . in most parts of the State. Its flowers, which appear in April or May, before the leaves, are of a bright crimson or scarlet, and make a striking appearance . . on the scarlet or purple branches. **1897** Sudworth *Arborescent Flora* 290 **TX,** *Acer rubrum. . .* Scarlet Maple. **1922** Sargent *Manual Trees* 696, *Scarlet Maple. . . Leaves . .* turning in the early autumn to brilliant shades of scarlet and orange, or clear bright yellow. **1950** Grimm *Trees PA* 284, The Red Maple is also known as the . . Scarlet . . Maple. **1967–69** *DARE* (Qu. T14, . . *Kinds of maples*) Infs **IL**26, 27, **PA**223, **TN**22, Scarlet maple. **1986** Pederson *LAGS Concordance,* 1 inf, **cwAR,** Scarlet maple.

scarlet oak n

1 Std: an **oak** (here: *Quercus coccinea*) native to much of the US east of the Missip River. Also called **bastard oak 4, black ~, ink-ball ~, red ~ 2e, Spanish ~, spotted ~**
2 **=Shumard oak.** [See quot]

1913 TX Acad. Sci. *Trans. for 1910–12* 12.73, *Quercus Schneckii* [= *Q. shumardii*]. . . Also called Scarlet Oak, locally, on account of the fact that it is our only oak that has a brilliant foliage after the first frosts.

scarlet paintbrush n Also *scarlet painter's brush* [See quot 1915] **West**

Any of var **Indian paintbrushes 1;** see quots.

1897 Parsons *Wild Flowers CA* 344, Scarlet Paint-brush. *Castilleia parviflora. . .* Most of their brilliancy is due not to the corollas, but to the large petal-like bracts under the flowers and to the calyxes. **1898** Davidson *CA Plants* 142, The other flower . . has several common names, painted cup, scarlet painter's brush, Indian plume, etc. **1906** (1918) Parsons *Wild Flowers CA* 350, Scarlet Paint-brush. *Castilleia latifola. . .* We have many species of *Castilleia,* closely resembling one another. **1915** (1926) Armstrong–Thornber *Western Wild Flowers* 472, Scarlet Paint Brush—*Castilleja pinetorum* [=*C. applegatei* subsp *pinetorum*]. . . This . . gives much the effect of a brush dipped in red paint, for the yellowish bracts are beautifully tipped with scarlet and the flowers are also bright red. **1936** Whitehouse *TX Flowers* 133, Scarlet Paint-Brush (*Castilleja indivisa*) is. . . one of the most inspiring landscape displays of native flowers. . . The eastern or swamp scarlet paintbrush (*Castilleja coccinea*) . . has similar flower clusters but grows in swampy places. **1940** Fergusson *Our Southwest* 234 **NM,** Michaelmas daisies and scarlet paintbrush form soft tapestries against the warm gray of chamiso tipped with sunny yellow. **1967** *DARE* Wildfl QR (Wills–Irwin) Pl.45C.1 Inf **TX**44, Scarlet paintbrush.

scarlet painted cup n

An **Indian paintbrush 1,** usu *Castilleja coccinea* native chiefly east of the Missip River.

1848 Gray *Manual of Botany* 308, *C[astilleja] coccinea. . .* Scarlet Painted-cup. . . A variety is occasionally found with the bracts dull yellow instead of scarlet. **1938** Madison *Wild Flowers OH* 102, Scarlet Painted Cup. *Castilleja coccinea.* Corolla greenish yellow. . . Bracts and calyx scarlet. **1949** Moldenke *Amer. Wild Flowers* 273, Most popular . . is the *scarlet paintedcup, C. coccinea,* our only eastern species, living in meadows and moist thickets from Ontario to Saskatchewan, south to Georgia and Texas. **1954** Sharpe *101 Wildflowers* 26 **WA,** Scarlet Paintedcup—*Castilleja miniata. . .* Grows in profusion near timberline in August and September.

scarlet painter's brush See **scarlet paintbrush**

scarlet pea n

A **coral tree** (here: *Erythrina herbacea*).

1966 *DARE* Wildfl QR (Wills–Irwin) Pl.20A Inf **TX**34, Scarlet pea.

scarlet pimpernel n

An introduced creeping plant (*Anagallis arvensis*) widespread throughout most of the US. Also called **devil's-weed 1, eyebright 10, poison chickweed, red ~**

1818 Eaton *Botany* 134, *Anagallis. . . arvensis . . .* scarlet pimpernell. . . petals entire flat, with hairs at the margin. **a1862** (1865) Thoreau *Cape Cod* 154 **eMA,** The scarlet pimpernel, or poor-man's weather-glass (*Anagallis arvensis*), greets you in fair weather. **1903** Porter *Flora PA* 244, *Anagallis arvensis. . .* Scarlet Pimpernel. . . In waste places. **1915** (1926) Armstrong–Thornber *Western Wild Flowers* 362, Scarlet Pimpernel. . . The flowers and leaves are usually in pairs, the seed-vessels on the tips of slender stems, curving around and toward each other, as if the plant were stretching out its little hands. **1940** Steyermark *Flora MO* 410, *Scarlet Pimpernel. . .* Scattered in southern and central Mo. **1961** Thomas *Flora Santa Cruz* 269 **cwCA,** Scarlet Pimpernel. . . Plants with flowers can be found at most times of the year. **1979** Spellenberg *Audubon Guide N. Amer. Wildflowers W. Region* 687, Scarlet Pimpernel . . (*Anagallis arvensis*). . . The name Scarlet Pimpernel is not entirely apt, for the flowers are pinkish-orange, and there is even a rarer blue phase.

scarlet runner n

1 also *scarlet runner bean:* A cultivated runner bean (*Phaseolus coccineus*). [*OED2* at *scarlet* adj. B.4.c 1786 →] chiefly **NEng**

1806 McMahon *Amer. Gardener's Calendar* 580, Bean, The Dwarf Kidney. . . *Running Kinds. . .* Scarlet Runners. **1863** Burr *Field & Garden* 497 **MA,** Scarlet-Runner. [*Ibid* 498, The plants are twelve feet or more in height or length, with deep-green foliage and brilliant scarlet flowers.] **1871** *Harper's New Mth. Mag.* Aug 385 **NEng,** He stopped by the window and peeped through the scarlet runners. **1899** Jewett *Queen's Twin* 107 **ME,** Scarlet-runner beans made haste to twine themselves to a line of strings for shade. **1925** *Book of Rural Life* 8.4922, *Scarlet Runner Bean,* a plant that is both a flower and a vegetable. The flowers are bright scarlet, as are the pods which follow them. **1931–33**

LANE Worksheets **nw,cnCT,** Scarlet runner—a variety of bean; **seRI,** Scarlet bean. **1966** *Monadnock Regionaire* Summer 22 **swNH,** Plan now to make your reservations for the 25th Annual Revival of *"The Old Homestead."* As "Uncle Josh" says: "Come on, all of ye, and let the scarlet runners chase you back to childhood." **1968** *DARE* (Qu. I17, *Beans . . that are dark red when they are dry*) Inf **CA**101, Scarlet runner beans; (Qu. I20, *. . Kinds of beans*) Inf **NY**106, Scarlet runner beans. **1988** Whealy *Garden Seed Inventory* (2d ed) 73, *Scarlet Runner . .* Food & ornamental, . . enjoys cool weather, . . attracts hummingbirds.

2 The bedbug (*Cimex lectularius*). Cf **crimson rambler, redcoat 1**

 1950 *WELS* (*Other names [include joking and nicknames] for bedbugs*) 1 Inf, **seWI,** Scarlet runners.

scarlet runner bean See **scarlet runner 1**

scarlet sage n chiefly Sth

A **sage 1,** usu *Salvia coccinea*.

 1824 Elliott *Sketch* 2.32 **S Atl,** [*Salvia*] *coccinea. . . Corolla* bright scarlet. . . Grows on the southern islands of Georgia. In the streets of Beaufort [SC], common. Flowers through the whole summer. *Scarlet Sage.* **1953** Greene-Blomquist *Flowers South* 111, Scarlet-sage (*S[alvia] coccinea*) is the only red-flowered native sage which is both conspicuous and easily recognized. . . It frequents roadsides and waste places in the Coastal Plain, Fla. to Tex., S.C. and Mex. **1961** Wills-Irwin *Flowers TX* 195, Scarlet Sage—*Salvia coccinea. Ibid* 197, Scarlet Sage or Indian-fire, with bright red flower from April to October, grows mainly south of Travis and Harris counties. . . The Scarlet Sage offered by seedsmen is *S. splendens . . ,* a native of Brazil. **1966** *DARE* Tape **NC**31, Asters are my favorite, but we grow roses, snapdragons . . petunias, salvia, which we call scarlet sage. **1967** *DARE* Wildfl QR (Wills-Irwin) Pl.52A Inf **TX**44, Scarlet sage. **1974** (1977) Coon *Useful Plants* 163, *Salvia officinalis*—Garden sage, scarlet sage. . . This is the sage used by all cooks for flavoring meat and medicinally as sage tea.

scarlet skyrocket See **skyrocket**

scarlet snake n

1 A red-, black-, and yellow-banded burrowing snake (*Cemophora coccinea*) native chiefly to the southern US. Also called **coral snake 2b**

 1842 Holbrook *N. Amer. Herpetology* 3.127, *Rhinostoma coccinea* [= *Cemophora c.*] . . The Scarlet Snake. *Ibid,* The 'Couleuvre écarlate' (Scarlet Snake) of Bosc is quite another animal, doubtless the Calamaria elapsoidea [=*Lampropeltis triangulum* subsp]. **1930** *Copeia* 2.34 **OK,** Scarlet-snake. . . The belly is immaculate white, in contrast to the black checkered markings of the red milk-snake. **1955** Carr-Goin *Guide Reptiles* 282 **FL,** Scarlet Snake. . . A small, slim snake with bright red, yellow, and black crossbands, a pink nose, and a plain belly. . . Usually found burrowing in leaf mold, rotten logs, moist loam, or even muck and peat soil. **1979** Behler-King *Audubon Field Guide Reptiles* 593, Scarlet Snake. . . Often mistaken for Coral Snake, but Scarlet's wide red bands are separated by much narrower black-bordered yellow bands. *Bands do not encircle body.*

2 A **milk snake 1** (here: *Lampropeltis triangulum* subsp).

 [**1842** see **1** above.] **1891** *Century Dict.* 5381, Scarlet snake, *Osceola elapsoidea* [=*Lampropeltis triangulum* subsp], of the southern United States, which is bright-red with about twenty black rings, each inclosing a white one. It thus resembles a poisonous snake of the genus *Elaps,* but is quite harmless. **1908** Biol. Soc. DC *Proc.* 21.75 **TX,** *Lampropeltis doliatus doliatus* [=*L. triangulum* subsp]. . . Scarlet Snake. **1935** Pratt *Manual Vertebrate Animals* 212, *L[ampropeltis] elapsoides.* . . Scarlet snake. . . Southeastern and Gulf States, from Maryland to Louisiana.

scarlet sumac n Also scarlet sumach Cf red sumac =smooth sumac.

 1846 Browne *Trees* 184, *R[hus] . . glabra. . . Scarlet Sumach,* with glabrous leaves, and fruit covered with red, silky hairs. **1901** Lounsberry *S. Wild Flowers* 306, *R[hus] glabra,* smooth upland, or scarlet sumac, . . over its extended range . . is generally known, and mostly by its dense, beautiful clusters of crimson velvety drupes. **1920** Pellett *Amer. Honey Plants* 251, The red or scarlet sumac . . (*Rhus glabra*) is most common, being found from New England west to Saskatchewan, Colorado and Arizona, and south to Florida and Louisiana. **1951** Abrams *Flora Pacific States* 3.50, Smooth or Scarlet Sumac. . . Shrub or small tree. . . A variable and widely distributed species. **1980** Little *Audubon*

Guide N. Amer. Trees E. Region 548, "Scarlet Sumac". . . The most common sumac.

scarlet tanager n

Std: a tanager (here: *Piranga olivacea*), the male of which in breeding plumage is red with black wings and tail, native to much of the US from the Missip-Ohio Valleys eastward. Also called **dogwood-winter bird, English robin 3, firebird 2, pocket bird, redbird c, red linnet 1**

scarlet thorn n Cf scarlet haw

A **hawthorn** (here: *Crataegus coccinea*).

 1897 Sudworth *Arborescent Flora* 219 **VT, MA, RI, NJ, DE,** *Crataegus coccinea. . .* Scarlet Thorn. **1921** Deam *Trees IN* 209, *Crataegus coccinea. . . Scarlet Thorn. . .* Bark light gray, spines stout, curved. **1931** Harned *Wild Flowers Alleghanies* 246, Scarlet Thorn. . . A beautiful shrub or small tree characterized by its reddish branches. . . Fruit round or pear-shaped, scarlet red to dark crimson, ripe and edible in late September–October.

scarlet trumpet n Also scarlet trumpet honeysuckle =trumpet honeysuckle.

 [**1709** (1967) Lawson *New Voyage* 102, The Scarlet Trumpet-Vine bears a glorious red Flower, like a Bell or Trumpet, and makes a Shade inferiour to none that I ever saw; yet it leaves us, when the Winter comes, and remains naked until the next Spring. It bears a large Cod, that holds its Seed.] **1900** Lyons *Plant Names* 229, *L[onicera] sempervirens. . .* Scarlet Trumpet Honeysuckle. **1940** Clute *Amer. Plant Names* 263, *Lonicera sempervirens.* Scarlet trumpet. **1960** Vines *Trees SW* 957, Vernacular names [for *Lonicera sempervirens*] are . . Scarlet Trumpet, Honeysuckle [etc].

scarpion See **scorpion**

scarripin n

 1890 *DN* 1.66 **KY,** Scarripin [skǽrɪpɪn]: for *terrapin.* By negroes and illiterate persons.

scarry See **scary**

scart See **scare B**

scary adj Pronc-spp scarry, skeary, ske(e)ry, skurry Cf scare A Forms.

 1841 [see **B** below]. **1843** (1916) Hall *New Purchase* 226 **IN,** But it's not a bit more skery than our bullits. **1859** [see **B** below]. **1892** [see **B** below]. **1903** *DN* 2.328 **seMO,** Scary or skeary. . . Frightful. 'It was a skeery sight.' **1905** [see **B** below]. **1907** *DN* 3.235 **nwAR,** Scary, skeary. . . Frightful, terrible. **1909** *DN* 3.366 **eAL, wGA,** Skeery. **1976** Garber *Mountain-ese* 82 **sAppalachians,** Skeery.

B Sense.

Easily frightened, fearful, afraid. **scattered, but chiefly Sth, S Midl; also NEast** See Map on p. 778

 1800 in 1929 Weems *Mason Locke Weems* 2.160 **MD,** I have always been very scary about our monies. **1841** (1952) Cooper *Deerslayer* 222 **NY,** I thought . . that you was a gal not to be frightened by the sound of a bursting we'pon. No, I didn't think you so skeary! **1859** Boucicault *Octoroon* 16 **MA,** I'm the skurriest crittur at a fight you ever see; My legs have been too well brought up to stand and see my body abused. **1892** (1893) Botume *First Days* 13 **seSC,** I is mighty skeery myself, an' I has all my t'ings pick up. *Ibid* 45 **seSC,** The mothers, who had been watchful to protect their children, now turned around and berated them well for "being so *scarry.*" **1899** (1912) Green *VA Folk-Speech* 368, *Scary. . .* Inclined to be scared; subject to scares; timid. *Ibid* 389, *Skeery. . .* A form of *scary,* shying, easily scared. "The horses were very skeery." **1905** *DN* 3.18 **cCT,** Scary or skeery. . . Timorous. **1907** *DN* 3.216 **nwAR,** Scary skeery. . . Timorous. **1909** *DN* 3.370 **eAL, wGA,** Skeery. . . Scary, easily scared. **1909** in 1914 Stewart *Letters* 30 **WY,** Night had already fallen. I began to get scary. **c1937** in 1972 *Amer. Slave* 2.251 **SC,** Is de black man nervous or is he natchally scary? **1941** *LANE* Map 475 (*Afraid*) 24 infs, **chiefly ME, NH,** Scary. **1947** Ballowe *The Lawd* 8 **LA** [Black], She [=a mule] was scary only at night when the spirits were abroad. **1965–70** *DARE* (Qu. HH10, *A very timid or cowardly person: "He's _____."*) 15 Infs, **chiefly Sth, S Midl, C Atl,** Scary; **LA**8, ['skɪɚ·ɪ]; (Qu. P36, *When a hunter sees a deer or other game animal and gets so excited he can't shoot*) Inf **GA**19, He's scary. **1986** Pederson *LAGS Concordance* **Gulf Region,** 47 infs, Scary—(a person) easily frightened; 6 infs, Scary person—one who is easily frightened; 3 infs, I'm (too) scary—frightened, too afraid; 1 inf, Real scary—of one easily frightened; 1 inf, She was scary—she was scared; 1 inf, So scary—afraid of everything; 1 inf, They were so afraid, and people was scary to go out on it.

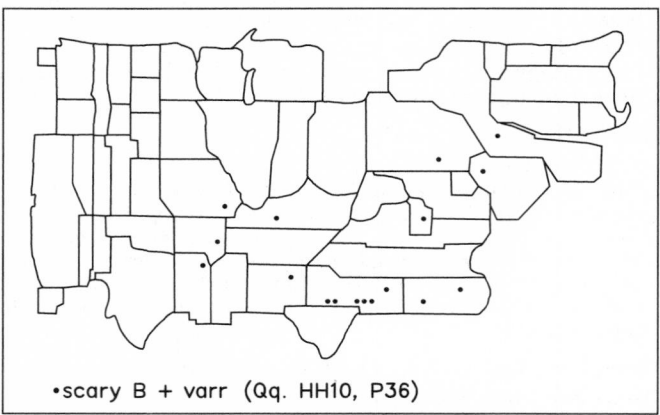

•scary B + varr (Qq. HH10, P36)

scary-cat See **scared-cat**

scase See **scarce**

scasely See **scarcely**

scat intj [Prob < *scat* begone! Perh in ref to the belief that the devil enters the body when a person sneezes, but numerous phrasal refs to cats suggest another source] **Sth, S Midl, TX** See Map and Map Section   Cf **gesundheit, get** v D1b

Often in phrr: Used as a response when someone sneezes; see quots.

1890 *DN* 1.66 **KY,** *Scat!* [skæt]: to a child on sneezing. **1899** (1912) Green *VA Folk-Speech* 368, *Scat.* . . Said to a person when he sneezes. **1909** *DN* 3.403 **nwAR,** *Scat.* . . Sometimes said when one sneezes. Synonyms are *shoo! git! God save you! God bless us!* Addressed to the Devil or his angels, who try to creep into the body of the person sneezing. **1909** *DN* 3.366 **eAL,** *Scat.* . . Said to a child when it is about to sneeze. **1915** *DN* 4.189 **swVA,** *Scat.* . . Said not only to a cat, but when one is about to sneeze. **1946** *PADS* 6.26 **eNC** (as of 1900–10), *Scat.* . . Said to a small child who has just sneezed. . . Common. **1947** *PADS* 8.15 **sIN** (as of early 1900s), *Scat:* Also Scat, you bitch, your tail's afire! **c1950** *Halpert Coll.* 61 **wKY, nwTN,** Scat, Tom! Your tail's on fire! = said when you sneeze. **1965–70** *DARE* (Qu. NN18, *When somebody sneezes, what do people say to him?*) 95 Infs, **Sth, S Midl, TX,** Scat; **AL**16, **AR**27, **KY**10, 84, **VA**2, Scat Tom; **AR**47, **GA**72, 77, **KY**11, **NC**30, 55, Scat there(, your son bit your tail off); **LA**17, **TX**32, Scat cat(, your tail's on fire); **KY**85, Scat kitty; **NC**61, Scat the cat; **MS**64, Scat Tom, your tail is afire; **VA**93, Scat-you; **LA**12, **VA**15, Scat, (damn you,) your tail's afire. [Of all Infs responding to Qu. NN18, 67% were comm type 4 or 5; of those Infs giving these responses, 89% were comm type 4 or 5.] **1968** *DARE* FW Addit **cAR,** Scat Tom, your tail's in the gravy = said when someone sneezes. **1973** *Patrick Coll.* **cAL,** *Scat your tail out of the butter*—said when someone sneezes. **1982** *Smithsonian* June 14, "Scat" is an abbreviation of the phrase "Scat cat, your tail's on fire," as my East Texas mother has al-

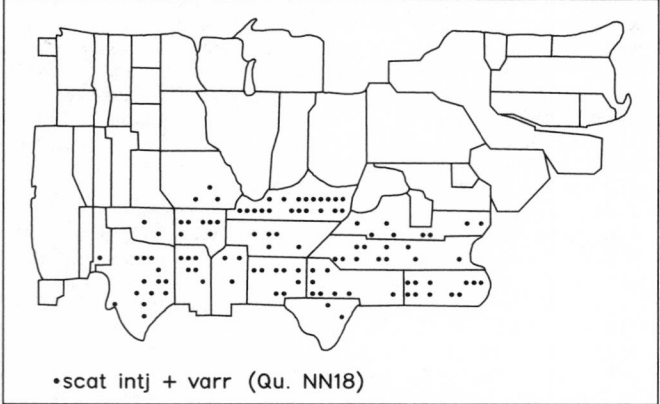

•scat intj + varr (Qu. NN18)

ways said when I sneeze. **1984** Wilder *You All Spoken Here* 157 **Sth, Scat:** *Gesundheit;* God bless you. Sneezing babies and cats that go "pfth" sound the same. A sneeze of man-sized proportions will scatter cats four ways from Sunday. **1997** *DARE* File **eTN,** I've run the "Scat cat! Get your tail out of my gravy!" by several people from all over East Tennessee, and they all remember it. . . Some people just said, "Scat, Cat!" whenever anyone sneezed. They also said, "Scat there!" I'm not sure if I'm right in this perception or not, but it seems the "Scat, Cat! Get your Tail out of my gravy!" was used more in familiar settings, as a mother to a child, etc. In my mind, men seemed to more often use the shorter version. I can still hear my grandfather saying, "Scat there!" when somebody sneezed.

scat n [From *scat* shoo! taken as an example of a very short utterance]

1 in phrr *like scat, quicker than* (or *quick as) scat, before one can say scat* and varr: Very quick; very quickly.

1860 Jones *Green Mt. Boy* 13, I'll have the square discharge him quicker than s'cat. [Play first performed in 1833] **1889** Twain *CT Yankee* 480, But the scheme fell through like scat. **1897** Robinson *Uncle Lisha's Outing* 86 **wVT,** One o' the boys . . hed his fork into 't . . quicker'n scat. **1909** Porter *Girl Limberlost* 325 **cwIN,** Quicker 'an scat there was her ma a-whirling. **1927** *AmSp* 3.139 **eME,** A neighbor often said "well, I must be mogging along," mog meaning to move slowly, to depart. If [in] a hurry he must "cut along" or "marvel" or go "quick as scat." **1942** Whipple *Joshua* 275 **UT** (as of c1860), Before Abijah could say scat! there was this Cecil making eyes at Sis and Miny. **1956** Moody *Home Ranch* 51 **CO** (as of 1911), He ain't goin' high, but he'll be a sidewindin' son-of-a-gun, and quicker'n scat. **1967** *DARE* (Qu. A14, *Referring to a very short period of time: . . "It won't take any longer than _____."*) Inf **MO**38, To say scat. **1968** *DARE* Tape **GA**30, Pick 'em up before you can say "Scat, hog." **1987** *DARE* File **ceNY** (as of 1932), We may saddle some country phrases on hired men. The one who brags that he is "quicker than scat" may prove to be "slower than molasses in January."

2 in phr *say scat:* To say the slightest thing.

1941 Stuart *Men of Mts.* 322 **neKY,** I never could understand why we grieve over the whole and never say 'scat' about one of the parts. **1941** *S. Rev.* 7.75 **TN,** Then he went out through the kitchen without saying "scat" about what she should do.

sca't v See **scare** B

scat'ring See **scattering**

scatter-barrel (shotgun) n esp **TX**
A shotgun.

1966–67 *DARE* (Qu. P37b, *Nicknames for a shotgun*) Infs **MS**6, **TX**1, 11, 26, 35, Scatter-barrel. **2001** *NADS Letters* **OK, TN,** A scatter barrel is a shotgun. I know my Dad used the word. He was born in Oklahoma in 1919—I'm pretty sure that some of my relatives there used it too. My dad and mom moved to Galveston TX after WWII and then to Memphis in the early 1950's. I've also heard it here in Memphis, where I now live. In addition, I've heard "scatter barrel shotgun" as one phrase, rather than just scatter barrel. *Ibid eTX,* I know "scatter-barrel" from my childhood and youth in eastern Texas. It often occurred, redundantly (it would seem) as an epithet:"scatter-barrel shotgun."

scattering adj Pronc-spp *scattern, scat'ring* [*OED2 scattering* ppl. a. 1.b 1610 →] **formerly widespread, now chiefly Sth, S Midl**
Widely and sparsely distributed; scattered, sparse, occasional.

1666 in 1897 *SC Hist. Soc. Coll.* 5.63, [I found] on the Outside of the woods some single scattring Pine trees. **1713** (1901) Hempstead *Diary* 19 **CT,** Some Scatering Snow. it Snowed at night also a little. **1766** in 1850 Adams *Works* 2.185 **MA,** There were six different hats with votes for as many different persons, besides a considerable number of scattering votes. **1856** Olmsted *Journey Slave States* 642, Washington is a mean, scattering village. **1904** *McClure's Mag.* Mar 557 **TX** (as of 1860s), In them days . . ranches were scatterin'. **1912** Green *VA Folk-Speech* 368, *Scattering.* . . Few: "Herring and shad are very scattering as yet." **1927** Kennedy *Gritny* 15 **sLA** [Black], A cheap li'l thing like a few scat'ring vi'lets. **1931** Goodrich *Mt. Homespun* 77 **sAppalachians,** "Christians is mighty scatterin' around here," said aunt Cinthy, "but the'll be several out to hear elder Ryan." **1949** Kurath *Word Geog.* 79, Scattering instances of *lay out* and *laid out* have also been noted on the James and the Rappahannock. **1950** *Western Folkl.* 9.119 **nwOR** [Logger speech], *Scarce and scattering.* A very thin stand of marketable trees. **1955** Ritchie *Singing Family* 262 **seKY,** No one set much store by the scattern tales spread about, that a railroad was coming through Perry County. **1966–68** *DARE* (Qu. B10, . . *Long trailing clouds high in the sky*) Inf **NC49,** Scattering; broken clouds; (Qu. B29, *A frost that does not kill plants*) Inf **NC49,** ['skædɪn] frost; **SC9,** Scattering frost; (Qu. B39, *A very light fall of snow*) Inf **SC9,** Scattering snow. **1967** Will *Dredgeman* 133 **FL,** These capes . . were free from mangroves. . . Instead, there were scattering trees of other kinds. **1975** *Appalachian Jrl.* 2.152 **wNC,** The corn is *scatterin'* this year if there are only a few years, or if most of it is only *nubbins.*

scatterings n pl *chiefly* **NEast** Cf **scatter rake**
Remnants of hay or grain in the field after the main harvesting.
  1917 *DN* 4.399 **neOH,** Scatterings. . . Stray grain or hay left on the field after the main crop has been removed. *To rake scatterings* = "to gather the scatterings with a hand- or horse-rake." "I guess I'll leave the scatterings in that lot." "He's down there raking scatterings." Also N. Eng., Ill., N.Y. **1929** *AmSp* 5.124 **ME,** It takes a good man to rake the scatterin's. **1967** *Amer. Agric. & Rural New Yorker* 164.6.30 **ME,** [In a list of old words not now commonly known:] Jack or loafer rake—a rake for raking scatterings. **1967–69** *DARE* (Qu. L16) Inf **MA5,** Bull rake—used to rake scatterings; **MA42,** Bull rake rakes up scatterings from loading it on [a] rack. **1967** *DARE* Tape **MA5,** The big rake that they raked the scatterings with . . came after the horse rake. **1988** Palmer *Lang. W. Cent. MA* 31, ['skætɚɪŋz]—The hay that's left by the plow or tractor is called the 'scatterings'. . . You would go through the field with the plow or tractor first, then rake up the scatterings, but now you can't afford to rake them up.

scatterment See **-ment B**

scattern See **scattering**

scatter rake n, hence n *scatter raker* Cf **scatterings**
  1984 Doig *English Creek* 34 **nMT,** As a scatter raker Alec was working the job for more than it was worth. *Ibid* 224 **nMT,** A scatter rake simply resembles a long axle—mine was a ten-foot type—between a set of iron wheels, high spoked ones. . . The "axle," actually the chassis of the rake, carries a row of long thin curved teeth, set about a hand's width apart from each other, and it is this regiment of teeth that rakes along the ground and scrapes together any stray hay lying there. . . Midway between the wheels a seat stuck up for the rake driver . . to ride on, and a wooden tongue extended forward for a team of horses to be hitched to.

scatters n Cf **skitters**
  1949 *PADS* 11.10 **wTX,** Scatters. . . Diarrhea, particularly of animals; scours. "The new calf has the scatters this morning."

scauer See **scour** adj

scaup n
Std: a duck of the genus *Aythya.* Also called **blackhead 1, bluebill 1, broadbill 1, bullneck 1, dos gris, nun 1, quindar, sea duck, ~ widgeon;** for other names of var spp see **canvasback duck, greater scaup, lesser ~, redhead 1a(1), ringnecked duck**

scauppaug See **scuppaug**

scavenger n
1 also *scavenger man:* A privy-cleaner; see quot 1906; hence n *scavenger wagon* the wagon driven by a privy-cleaner. **AR**
  1906 *DN* 3.155 **nwAR,** Scavenger. . . Privy-cleaner; public official who superintends privy-cleaning. In the expression of contempt, "I wouldn't vote for him for scavenger." **1986** Pederson *LAGS Concordance,* 1 inf, **cAR,** Scavenger wagon—comes to clean outhouse; 1 inf, **neAR,** Scavenger wagons—driven by outhouse cleaners; 1 inf, **ceAR,** Scavenger man—clean toilet, with wagon.
2 also attrib: A private garbage collector.
  1950 *PADS* 14.58 **SC,** Scavenger cart: . . A garbageman's cart. Now obsolescent, since the coming of the truck. **1967** *DARE* FW Addit **IL,** Scavenger service = garbage truck (private). **1969** *DARE* File, [From a pamphlet published by the Downers Grove, Illinois, Chamber of Commerce, describing village services:] Garbage: Disposal by 3 private scavengers.

scavenger hunt n Also *scavenger (game),* ~ *party* **scattered, but chiefly** **NEast, N Cent** See Map

A game in which participants go in search of predetermined articles that are hidden or difficult to acquire.
  1933 *Sun* (Baltimore MD) 30 Oct 16/4 *(Hench Coll.),* The "scavenger game," an up-to-date version of a treasure hunt, was brought to the attention of the Central district police. . . The players are sent out to collect certain articles, and at this party it was stipulated that the players bring back a patrolman's badge. **1940** *Ibid* 1 Nov 7/3 *(Hench Coll.),* Eight young persons on a scavenger hunt sponsored by a Westport High School sorority went to the Sixty-third street police station . . to obtain signatures of policemen. **1940** Harbin *Fun Encycl.* 587 **cFL,** A Scavenger Party—Meeting at the home of the recreation leader . . the group was assigned to cars, about six in each one, and given a list of objects to be obtained from any place possible within a given time. . . The group having the largest collection of the articles exactly as listed . . won. **1965–70** *DARE* (Qu. EE3, *Games in which you hide an object and then look for it*) 66 Infs, **scattered, but chiefly** **NEast, N Cent,** Scavenger hunt; **NJ2, NY44,** 195, **PA124,** 200, **VT16, WV1,** Scavenger; **PA138,** Scavenger or treasure hunt; (Qu. EE16, *Hiding games that start with a special, elaborate method of sending the players out*) Infs **MI78, NY184,** Scavenger hunt; (Qu. EE33, . . *Outdoor games . . that children play*) Inf **OR15,** Scavenger hunt; (Qu. FF2, . . *Kinds of parties*) Inf **SC54,** Scavenger hunts. [39 of 77 total Infs coll educ, 21 comm type 1 or 2] **1967** *Galena Gaz. & Advt.* (IL) 29 June, Team Centers On Scavenger Hunt. **1968** *Athens Messenger* (OH) 28 May 3/4, The [Cub Scout] group planned three outings for the summer: . . Mother and Son scavenger hunt.

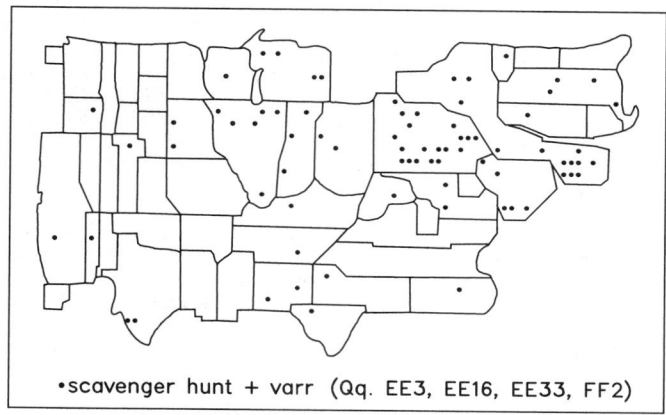

•scavenger hunt + varr (Qq. EE3, EE16, EE33, FF2)

scavenger man See **scavenger** n **1**

scavenger party See **scavenger hunt**

scavenger wagon See **scavenger** n **1**

scawgin See **scoggin 2**

sceard, sceart See **scare B**

scellion See **scallion**

scenery n Usu |'sinəri|; also |'sinri, 'sinjɚ| *Pronc-sp seenyuh*
A Forms.
  1917 [see **B1** below]. **1942** Hall *Smoky Mt. Speech* 64 **wNC, eTN,** Scenery ['sinrɪ]. *Ibid* 66, ['sinjɚ] for *scenery,* heard now and then.
B Senses.
1 A picturesque view; a sight; a spectacle. [Cf *OED2 scenery* sb. 4 "A landscape or view; a picturesque scene. . . Now rare."] **esp sAppalachians**
  1896 *DN* 1.423 **swNC,** Scenery: picturesque spot. "This here's quite a scenery." **1917** *DN* 4.416 **wNC,** Scenery. . . Curio. "He jes' wanted the skull fer a scenery." *Ibid, Seenyuh.* . . Scene or scenery. "Thar's a right smart seenyuh thar, too." **1922** in 1985 *TN Civil War Veterans* 5.1453, A beautiful scenery all around a nice cemetary [sic] on the place & a Baptist Church in sight. **1936** *AmSp* 11.373 **cwVA,** Another man, who did not write easily, was telling of signing his name to some document. He said, 'It's a scenery to see me write my name.'
2 See quot.
  1933 *AmSp* 8.1.51 **Ozarks,** Scenery. . . A picture, usually a photograph. Rose Wilder Lane, Mansfield, Mo., writes me that she has heard hillmen say: *That shore is a right purty scenery of them children.*

scent bottle n

A **fringed orchid** (here: *Platanthera dilatata*).

1950 Gray-Fernald *Manual of Botany* 472, H[abenaria] dilatata [= *Platanthera d.*] . . Scent-bottle. . . Flowers . . strongly spicy-fragrant. **1963** Craighead *Rocky Mt. Wildflowers* 38, Scent-bottle. . . Occurs in wet soil of swamps, bogs, banks of springs and streams. **1973** Hitchcock-Cronquist *Flora Pacific NW* 703, Fl[ower]s white or pale greenish. . . Scent-bottle.

schaefchen n [Ger *Schäfchen* lamb, little sheep]

=dust bunny.

1950 WELS *Suppl.* seWI, Schaefchen (Little sheep). Rolls of dust on the floor.

schafskopf n Also *schafkopf, schapskopf*; for addit varr see quots [Ger *Schafskopf*, literally "sheep's head"] **chiefly WI** See Map

=sheepshead 5.

1913 *Official Rules of Card Games* 205, Schafkopf—(Sheepshead.) . . 32-card pack, 7's low. . . *Object of the Game.*—To win in tricks certain cards of counting value as follows: A's, 11, 10's, 10, K's, 4, Q's, 3, and J's, 2. **1950** WELS (*Card games played a good deal in your neighborhood*) 8 Infs, WI, Schafskopf; 2 Infs, WI, Schafko(p)f; 2 Infs, WI, Schaskopf; 1 Inf, ceWI, Schafskof; 1 Inf, ceWI, Schaufskopf; 1 Inf cWI, Shaafs-kopf. **1966** *Tomahawk Leader* (WI) 3 Mar sec 2 [2/6], Mrs. Roy Larson was hostess to club members at her home Feb. 24. Schafskopf was played and a lunch was served by the hostess. **1968–69** DARE (Qu. DD35, . . *Card games*) Inf MN36, Schafkopf; WI9, [šafskʌp]; WI12, [šapskoᵊpf]; WI30, [šafs,kəv]; WI40, Sheepshead—same as schapfska—a Polish [sic] word; WI48, ['šapskʌp]; WI51, Shapskopf; WI60, ['šafskap]; WI63, ['šaskəp]; WI77, ['šɔs,kɒf]. [All Infs old or mid-aged, 9 of 10 male] **1977** *Capital Times* (Madison WI) 16 Sept 2/5, The city of Jefferson will put its best Germanic foot forward tonight through Sunday when it celebrates its well known Gemuetlichkeit Days with a variety of activities to include rolling pin throwing and chicken flying contests, bike rally plus euchre and schapsfkopf tournaments. **2001** DARE File cWI (as of 1944), As a small child at family gatherings, I was allowed to watch the adults and older children play Schafskopf in the evenings if I was quiet. Amost everyone played this card game and commonly called it ['ša:s'kʌp]. It was also referred to by many others, usually people who spoke German as well as English, as ['šafs'kʌp]. Some few used the 'correct' German pronunciation of ['šafs'kʌf]. My parents, born 1908 and 1912, played Schafskopf from childhood on.

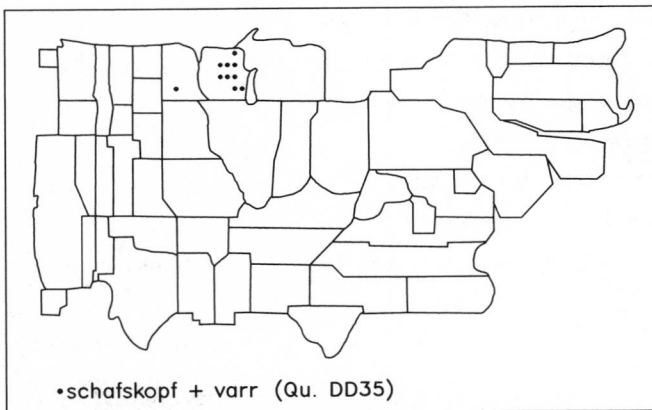

•schafskopf + varr (Qu. DD35)

schalahoot See **scallyhoot** v

schap(p)s See **chaps**

schapskopf See **schafskopf**

schemy adj Also *scheme*; also sp *scheemy* **esp Mid and S Atl**

Scheming; devious.

1888 Jones *Negro Myths* 2 GA coast [Gullah], Buh Rabbit bin der watch um all de time. Buh Rabbit too scheemy. **1891** French *Otto* 250 AR, He was powerful schemy! But I was schemy, too. That's how I got out. **1892** (1969) Christensen *Afro-Amer. Folk Lore* 76 seSC, Br'er Rabbit, you too scheme. **1922** Gonzales *Black Border* 324 sSC, GA coasts [Gullah glossary], Schemy—scheming, tricky. **1923** Parsons

Folk-lore Sea Islands 7 csSC, Ber Rabbit is a very schemy man. **1966** DARE (Qu. II33, *To get an advantage over somebody by tricky means:* "I don't trust him, he's always trying to _____.") Inf SC19, Pull something over you; he's schemy; (Qu. KK37, *Words to describe a very sly person:* "He's _____.") Infs LA14, VA25, 39, Schemy.

schimmel n Also sp *shimmel* [Ger *Schimmel*] **chiefly in Ger settlement areas**

A white or gray horse.

[**1871** Leland *Breitmann Ballads* 108, O, vere I on my schimmel grey,/ Mein sabre in my hand.] **1950** WELS *Suppl.* cWI, Schimmel. . . A gray or white horse. Heard in Waupaca County. . . My mother specifies that it means an old gray horse. **1952** Brown *NC Folkl.* 1.589, Shimmel. . . A white horse. **1965–70** DARE (Qu. K38, *A horse of a dirty white color*) Infs IL87, MI93, NY65, 117, PA1, WI14, 51, Schimmel; MD3, NY205, TX54, WI10, 58, Schimmel [FW sugg]; [IL33, MN37, WI24, Schimmel—[in] German; (Qu. K37, . . *A horse of mixed colors*) Inf IL65, Schimmel—but that's German]. [14 of 16 Infs old] **2001** DARE File cWI (as of c1945), When I was about four, my uncle put me up on Molly, one of his big plow horses. He was especially proud of this horse because she was a 'schimmel'—she had been born with a dark coat, then turned dapple grey, and finished almost white. *Schimmel* was a common term for a horse of such a color among most farmers at that time.

schitzel See **schnitzel** v

schlacht n [Ger, literally "battle, slaughter"; cf Ger *Schlachtfest* a festival held at the time of pig slaughtering] **esp WI**

A drinking party.

c1965 DARE File **Milwaukee WI**, Schlacht is well documented in Milwaukee for a drinking party. **1968** DARE (Qu. DD34, *A party at which there is considerable drinking*) Infs WI12, 51, [šlak(t)]; IN35, [šlɔxt]; WI48, [šləkt]. **2001** DARE File cWI (as of c1950s), My father often referred to a sort of drinking party as a "Schlacht." This was usually one which had got rough or out of hand and sometimes taken on the aspects of a bar brawl. Some of his friends used the term as well. The usage certainly went back at least as far as their college days in the early 1930s.

schlep See **schlepp** n 2, **schlepper**

schlepp v, hence n vbl n *schlepping* Freq with *around;* also sp *shlepp* [Yiddish *shlepn* to drag] **chiefly NYC, but becoming more widely used**

To haul, to lug (someone or something); to drag oneself about; also fig.

1931 Steffens *Autobiog.* 137, By this means the tuglike *Schlepper* schlepped a string of cargo boats up the Neckar to Heilbron. [**1946** (1949) Clifford *Go Fight City Hall* 149 NYC [Speaker from "the old country"], I have to get all dressed up, and *shlepp* myself on the subway.] **1975** *New Yorker* 11 Aug 32, When her husband, Sidney, was alive he sustained a rupture, and Mrs. Singer says she had to schlepp him in and out of bed several times a day. **1985** *NYT Mag.* 1 Dec 16, [William Safire column:] The Presidentially schlepped Yiddishism [= "stop this *futzing* around"] . . is a good example of a word that has been cleaned up. **1987** *Capital Times* (Madison WI) 17 Dec sec 5 9/1 ?NYC, What's a millionaire to do? All those bluebloods on the holiday-giving list and not a second to waste schlepping around from store to store. **1987** *Isthmus* (Madison WI) 9 Oct 11/1, I am a Madisonian born and bred, and it seems to me that the women in this city lack an original style. This isn't a commentary on the women I saw who were wearing their normal, schlepping-around clothes. **1989** Piesman *Unorthodox Practices* 154 NYC, Her notebook looked like something a shopping bag lady would schlepp around the city with her. **1998** Kahn *Fax Bagel* 163, The phone's too expensive to use, anyway. I only got it because I was logging so many miles schlepping to my work sites.

schlepp n [schlepp v]

1 See **schlepper.**

2 also *schlep, shlepp:* A difficult or troublesome trip; also fig. **esp NYC**

1968 *NY Times* (NY) 8 Apr 55 NYC, Why live in Wantagh and do the 'schlepp' [trek] if you don't have the kids? **1976** *Natl. Observer* 4 Dec B 19 NYC, Anybody who has ever tried to make even a small amount of a classic brown sauce from scratch would probably agree with Liederman's assessment that "it's the ultimate schlep." **1993** Isaacs *Af-*

ter All 43 **Long Is. NY,** The easiest route was down the flight of wooden stairs at the end of our back lawn, onto the beach, across the sand, and then up the Tillotsons' stone staircase to the back of their house—a schlepp when one of us ran out of ketchup. **2001** *Boston Herald* (MA) 3 May 37 (Internet), And talk about a shlep. You don't have to change planes, but even so, between the round trip and the orbiting, you're traveling 2.5 million miles. **2001** *DARE* File **NYC** (as of c1970s), "That's quite a shlepp"—meaning "That's quite a difficult job"—was commonly heard.

schlepp around See **schlepp** v

schlepper n Abbr *schlepp;* also sp *s(c)hlep, shlepp(er)* [**schlepp** v] **orig NYC; now more widely used**

An idler; a worthless or ineffectual person; an oaf, slob, jerk.

1934 *AmSp* 9.284 **NYC,** A customer who shops from store to store continually trying on shoes but not buying is known as a *shlepper.* In Yiddish the word means a mean fellow. **1939** *News Letter & Wasp* 23 June 13 (OED2), The name of the radio character known to thousands, Schlepperman, is evidently a personification of 'schlep', which means a poor slob. [*DARE* Ed: The character "Schlepperman" first appeared on *The Jack Benny Program* January 27, 1935.] **1947** *Holiday* Apr 65 **NYC,** In vain I protested that my dependents would be reduced to beggary; the editor's face remained flinty. "About time those *schleppers* went to work," he grunted. **1960** Wentworth–Flexner *Slang* 446, *Schlep. . .* A stupid or awkward person. **1968** *DARE* (Qu. HH16, *Uncomplimentary words with no definite meaning—just used when you want to show that you don't think much of a person: "Don't invite him. He's a _____."*) Inf **NY**81, Bore, creep, cretin, schlep, jerk, ass. **1968** *New Yorker* 27 July 52, [Movie review of *The Graduate:*] Benjamin—evidently head of the debating club, campus editor, captain of the cross-country team, social chairman of his house—transformed into a somnambulistic, clowny schlepp and, again, into an aggressive tiger. **1987** *Milwaukee Jrl.* (WI) 19 May Xtra sec 18, Ernest works as a handyman in a camp, but what he really wants to do . . is to be a counselor and shape young minds. . . but he's such a shlep he always gets turned down. **2001** *Boston Globe* (MA) 21 Sept sec C 5 (Internet), [Review of the film *Haiku Tunnel:*] Underling would be a step up for Josh Kornbluth's schlep. . . He's a temp . . he's also commitment-shy. Ordinarily, he'd flee the prospect of switching from temp to "perm" at a San Francisco law firm. But when he learns his employer will pay his psychotherapy bills, he . . accepts. **2001** *DARE* File **NYC** (as of c1970s), Shlepp . . [in the sense of] an "oaf"—also not uncommon.

schlepping See **schlepp** v

schlut See **shlook**

schmear See **smear**

‡**schmoozle** v [Prob < Ger *schmusen* to cuddle]

1967 *DARE* (Qu. AA8, *When people make too much of a show of affection in a public place . . "There they were at the church supper _____ [with each other]."*) Inf **CA**4, Schmoozle. [*DARE* Ed: Inf's grandparents on both sides were German immigrants.]

schmutz v, hence vbl n *schmutzing* Pronc-sp *smutz* [PaGer *schmutze* to kiss] **chiefly PaGer area**

To kiss; to caress.

1939 Aurand *Quaint Idioms* 26 [PaGer], Some girls like fellows who can *schmutz* (i.e. give rather wet kisses). **1964** *Ferhoodled Engl.* [10] [PaGer], After all—"Knoatching und Schmutzing" may not sound very romantic to us: but to the young folks in the Pennsylvania Dutch country it means hugging and kissing. That can be fun in any language. **1968** *Helen Adolf Festschrift* 36 **cePA,** Smutz or *schmutz*—The verb *to smutz* (also *to schmutz*), derived from Pennsylvania German *schmutze,* is still used . . in the area as a substitute for the verb 'to kiss' or 'to caress.' **1996** Huth *Famil. Words* 109 **csPA,** Schmutz /'ʃmʊts/ . . to kiss.

schnabel n Also *schnobie, shnovvel* [Ger *Schnabel* beak, bill; mouth]

The nose.

1901 *Bulletin* (San Francisco CA) 15 Dec 12 (*Zwilling Coll.*), Rap him on de schnobie. **1939** Aurand *Quaint Idioms* 20 [PaGer], A man's *shnovvel* (beak, nose) may be the measure of his character; even noses may be the means to making a fortune! **1968** *DARE* (Qu. X14, *Joking words for the nose*) Inf **WI**47, Schnabel.

schnecke n Also *schneck;* pl usu *schnecken,* also *schnecks* [Ger *Schnecke,* literally "snail," pl *Schnecken;* from the shape] **esp in Ger settlement areas**

A type of cinnamon roll.

1920 Kander *Settlement Cook Book* 356 **seWI,** *Cinnamon Rolls or Schnecken.* **1935** Frederick *PA Dutch* 116, Schnecken . . [includes milk, yeast, flour, sugar, raisins, salt, egg, butter, and almonds, shredded]. . . Roll dough ½ inch thick, brush with melted butter, sprinkle with sugar and cinnamon mixed, raisins, and almonds. Roll up like jelly roll and cut in 1 inch pieces. Place pieces in pan . . flat side down. . . To give the Schnecken a bun-like stickiness put brown sugar and butter on bottom of pan before putting Schnecken in. **1940** Brown *Amer. Cooks* 922 **WI,** Schnecken. **1942** *AN&Q* 2.107 **NY,** Until the outbreak of the present war, the bakeries in the Cushman chain in New York used the German name of *Schnecke* for the coil-like "snail." **1950** *WELS* (*Kinds of fancy home-baked rolls and so forth in your neighborhood*) 2 Infs, **WI,** Schnecken; 1 Inf, **cWI,** Schnecken . . also called snails; 1 Inf, **seWI,** Schnecks. **1965–70** *DARE* (Qu. H32, . . *Fancy rolls and pastries*) 9 Infs, **scattered,** Schnecken; **MI**108, Schnecken; **NY**65, Schnecken; **WI**47, Schnecks. **1989** *DARE* File **Milwaukee WI,** Schneck—a piece of bakery. **1992** *Woman's Day* 22 Dec 127, Julia Naughton's *Schnecken.*

schneider n Pronc-spp *sneeder, snyder* [Ger *Schneider* tailor, also applied to the **daddy longlegs 1** and to var insects, including the **dragonfly**] Cf **ear sewer 1, sewer, stitcher**

A dragonfly.

1950 *WELS* (*Other names for the dragonfly*) 1 Inf, **ceWI,** Sneeder or darning needle. **1950** *WELS Suppl.,* Schneider—dragonfly. They sewed up your ears with a darning needle. **1968** *DARE* (Qu. R2, . . *The dragonfly*) Inf **WI**48, Snyder—from "Schneider"—German for "tailor."

schnibble n Also *schnipfel, s(ch)nipple, schnivvle, schnuffel, s(c)hnibbel, snibble, snibblin, snipsle* [Ger *Schnippel* a scrap] **chiefly in Ger settlement areas**

A scrap; a small piece; hence v *schnibble* to chop (meat) into small pieces.

1948 *WELS Suppl.* **cWI,** [She] also offered the word *shnibbel* which seems to mean small pieces of cloth (like pieces left over when cutting out garments). *Ibid,* Snipples is a common word among Michigan people of Holland background. **1950** *Ibid* **seWI,** Schnipples—cloth scraps; **csWI,** Snipsles—ends and pieces of cloth; **IA,** Snipsles in Sioux Co., Iowa; **seWI,** Snibbles—scraps after sewing. **1965–70** *DARE* (Qu. W25, *When a woman is cutting out a dress to sew . . the little scraps of cloth left over*) Infs **AL**6, **PA**36, 203, **WI**47, Schnibbles; **CA**4, Schnipfels; **AL**6, **PA**54, 154, 242, Snibbles; **OH**98, Snibblins; **PA**18, Snipples. **1983** *Barrick Coll.* **csPA,** Schnibbles—diced meat; also v.t. *schnibble,* "to dice." **1995** *DARE* File **Milwaukee WI** (as of 1969), One of the localisms I picked up upon moving to Wisconsin was *schnivvle* [šnɪvl] for a small, torn off piece of paper. **1998** *DARE* File **Milwaukee WI** (as of c1960), I remember my mother (and I think her German mother too) referring to little bits and pieces of things—often paper or cloth cut with a scissors—as "schnuffels" with a *u* as in put. **2001** *DARE* File **nOH** (as of c1945), Schnibbles. My grandparents and parents used this word to refer to food on my plate that I had left uneaten. . . Our ancestors emigrated from Wurtemburg, Germany. *Ibid* **cwMT,** [Advt:] *Schnibbles* [=name of store] Flowers, Gathered Bits, Inspirations.

schnickelfritz n Also *s(ch)nicklefritz, snicke(l)tyfritz, snigglefritz* [Perh < Ger dial *Schnickel, Schniggel* little boy's penis + the common name *Fritz*] Cf **hanswurst**

A mischievous little boy; a scamp—usu used endearingly; by ext, a sweetheart.

[**1872** *Galaxy* 14.105, No name, unless matched by deeds, can be despotic in the arena of business. If there be force and courage behind it, Ichabod Snicklefritz—certainly not a title to melt the muses . . would be esteemed and honored of his kind.] **1905** *DN* 3.65 **eNE,** Snicklefritz, snigglefritz. . . About the same as *skeezicks.* **1916** *DN* 4.281 **NE,** Snicketyfritz, snickeltyfritz. = snigglefritz. . . [*DN* Ed: The latter also in Ill.] **1967** *DARE* (Qu. AA3, *Nicknames or affectionate names for a sweetheart*) Inf **CA**4, Schnicklefritz. **1973** *DARE* File **swPA** (as of 1920s), Snickle-fritz. . . Endearing epithet for a child. **1975** *Studies in Honor of Kasten* 30 **swIL,** Schnicklefritz, snicklefritz [< *Schnickele* + *Fritz*]: term of endearment to small male children ("little guy"). **1983** *DARE* File **ceWI,** Snicklefritz . . usually a little rascal. **2000** *DARE* File **seWI** (as of c1950), When we visited my Uncle Valentine on his farm, he often greeted my brother with, "Ah, there's the little Schnickelfritz!"

This was said affectionately, but reflected also his opinion that my brother was something of a scamp who frequently "got into things". *Ibid* **ceWI** (as of c1955), When I was growing up in Oshkosh, people used to call a little kid a *schnickelfritz* as an endearment. *Ibid* **Detroit MI** (as of c1950), My father's term for a small child was *schnickelfritz*; his parents were from the German community in St. Louis. **2000** *DARE* File—Internet **MN** [Winona Post], *Rediscovering Schnickelfritz* . . Schnickelfritz was the moniker adopted by Freddie Fisher, a musician originally from Iowa. . . [H]is band [was] a forerunner of the Spike Jones type of entertainers. . . Schnickelfritz . . signed a contract for a movie in the late 1930s.

schnipfel, schnipple See **schnibble**

schnittlauch n For var spp see quots [Ger *Schnittlauch*] esp **WI**

Chives *(Allium schoenoprasum)*.

  1950 *WELS* **WI** (The small plants like onions with hollow green leaves that are cut up in salad) 2 Infs, Schnitlau—German; 1 Inf, Chives, schnitlach; 1 Inf, Schnittluk—it may not be spelled correctly, but sounds like schnitluk. **1968** *DARE* (Qu. I7, *The small plants like onions with hollow green leaves that are cut up in a salad*) Inf **NY79**, Schnitlock; **WI58**, Schnitlof; (Qu. I5, . . *Kind of onions that keep coming up without replanting year after year*) Inf **WI13**, Schnittlauch; (Qu. I35, . . *Kitchen herbs . . grown and used in cooking around here*) Inf **WI13**, Schnittlauch. **1988** Whealy *Garden Seed Inventory* (2d ed) 256, *Chives* (. . Schnittlauch, Grass Onion . .). Delicate onion flavor, once established will last many years.

schnitz n[1] Also sp *schnitts, snits, snitz, snitzen(s)* [PaGer *snitz* dried apples < sGer dial *Schnitz* a piece; a slice (of fruit)] chiefly **PA** See Map

Used as mass noun or pl: Slices or sections of fruit, esp apples dried in slices; hence, by back-formation, sg *snit* a slice of usu dried fruit.

  1848 *Knickerbocker* 31.222 **Upstate NY**, A Dutchman smiles when he sees snits and scralls. **1869** *Atlantic Mth.* 24.483 **PA**, The rest of the family gathered in the kitchen, and labored diligently in preparing the cut apples, so that in the morning the "schnitz" might be ready to go in. **1872** Haldeman *PA Dutch* 58 [English influenced by German], *Snits*, a *snit* (G. schnitz, a cut), a longitudinal section of fruit, particularly apples, and when dried for the kitchen. The term is in use in districts where German is unknown. **1886** *Amer. Philol. Assoc. Proc.* 17.xii **ePA**, "Snitz," from *Schnitz*, a 'slice,' is a word so common that the village grocer would be surprised to have a customer ask him for dried apples. **1903** *McClure's Mag.* Dec 217 **PA**, Don't eat them snits. **1908** *German Amer. Annals* 10.43 **sePA**, *Snits.* . . Dried fruit, usually apples. When used of other fruit, the name is given, as "peach snits." **1916** *DN* 4.339 **PA, KS**, *Snits.* . . Pieces of fruit quartered and dried. "You can make pies of apple snits." **1927** *AmSp* 2.364 **cwWV**, *Snits* . . apples quartered for drying or for apple-butter. "How many snits do we have cut?" **1931** *Sun* (Baltimore MD) 3 Oct 8/7 (Hench Coll.), Uncle Pilduzer says since they have abandoned the gold standard in so many places he expects they will have to come down to it in the park and adopt the apple-snitzen ratio. **1937** *AmSp* 12.287 **wVA**, A *snit* is a slice, as of an orange. **1937** *Sun* (Baltimore MD) 24 Nov 10/5 (Hench Coll.), I saw in a Washington county paper the other day a reference to apple "snitzens." . . The apples are peeled and cut in thin slices from the quarters and dried on the roof. **1946** *PADS* 5.39 **VA**, *Snits*: Apples cut in quarters and dried; in the northern part of the Blue Ridge, rare. **1965–70** *DARE* (Qu. H18, . . *Special kinds of bread*) Inf **MI108**, Schnitz bread; [**MO12**, Schnittsbrot;] (Qu. H32, . . *Fancy rolls and pastries*) Inf **NC52**, Snit pie—same as hoecake [*DARE* Ed: At Qu. H30, Inf described *hoecake* as "apples . . inside and fried."]; (Qu. H45, *Dishes made with meat . . that everybody around here would know, but that people in other places might not*) Infs **MD27, PA**1, 2, 22, 52, 242, Schnitz (*or* snitz) and knepp; **PA72**, Schnitz; (Qu. H50) Inf **PA159**, Schnitz and knepp; (Qu. H63, *Kinds of desserts*) Inf **PA1**, Schnitz pie—dried apples. **1968–70** *DARE* Tape **IN3**, And of course, dried apples was called snits. And dried apple pie was pretty good eating, too, especially when they made fried kinds; **MD27**, Apple snits are apples sliced and dried; **PA242**, Schnitz and knepp is a Lancaster County dish, which you take ham and dried apple snits, which are apples that are dehydrated by a drying process like prunes are dried, and then these are boiled with the . . ham; **SC57**, Snits is dried fruit . . like I was cutting them peaches here this morning? It's like that, I just cut 'em in certain size, peaches about the size of my finger. **1982** *Barrick Coll.* **csPA**, Snit—slice of apple or other fruit; e.g.,

peach snits. [A]lso schnit. **1984** *DARE* File **csPA**, Snit—grapefruit or orange sections: "The skin peels right off and the snits come right apart." **1986** Pederson *LAGS Concordance (Snits)* 2 infs, **TX**, Apple schnitts; 5 infs, **AL, GA, TX**, Snits; 1 inf, **ceTN**, Snits is fruit. **1996** Huth *Famil. Words* 111 **csPA**, *Snit* /snɪts/ . . dried apple slices.

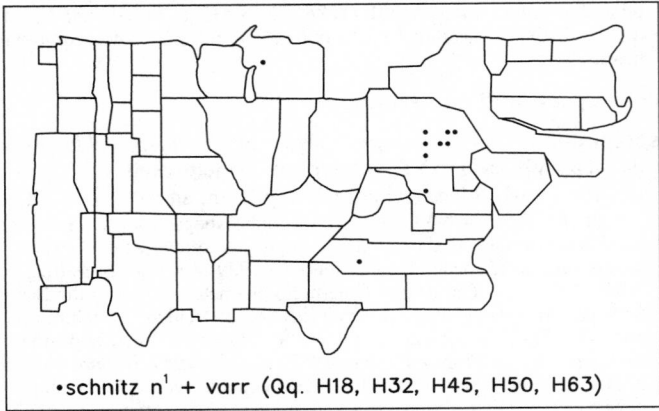

• *schnitz* n[1] + varr (Qq. H18, H32, H45, H50, H63)

schnitz v, hence vbl n *schnitzing* Also *snitz* [PaGer *schnitze*] Cf **apple bee**

To cut (fruit) into pieces; hence n *schnitzing*, pronc-spp *schnitzen, schnitz-in* a social gathering at which apples are sliced for drying.

  1879 *St. Nicholas* June 529 **wPA**, A *schnitzen* is a party where the invited guests are expected to help in paring the apples, and cutting them for drying; each apple is cut into about eight pieces. After a couple of hours of this work, the apples are put aside, and a bountiful supper is served; and the evening is finished with games or dancing. **1891** *Jrl. Amer. Folkl.* 4.116 **cPA**, A "schnitz-in" was held. . . and boys and girls vied with each other in speed and neatness of paring and quartering the apples. **1907** Wayland *Ger. Element* 197 **nwVA**, The whole family . . would be "peeling" and "schnitzing" the apples. **1907** (1970) Martin *Betrothal* 108 **sePA**, She was snitzing the apples and cut herself so ugly in the thumb I'm writing for her. **1964** *Ferhoodled Engl.* [5] [PaGer], The whole family is busy schnitzin' apples. **1977** Anderson *Grass Roots Cookbook* 47 **sePA**, How to "Schnitz" Apples. . . When the Pennsylvania Dutch talk about "schnitzing" apples, they mean peeling, coring, slicing, and drying them.

schnitz n[2] See **snit**

schnitzel n Also *snitsle* [Ger *Schnitzel* a bit, a scrap] =**schnibble**.

  1950 *WELS Suppl.* **swWI**, Snitsles—Fragments of clothing after cutting. **1968** *DARE* (Qu. W25, *When a woman is cutting out a dress to sew . . the little scraps of cloth left over*) Inf **NJ36**, Schnitzel [šnɪtzl].

schnitzel v Also *schitzel* [Ger *schnitzeln*] Cf **schnitz** v

To cut (a vegetable) into shreds.

  1942 in 1944 *ADD* **nwVA**, Snitz. . . Try schnitzeling the [string] beans (cutting them in thin strips) & cooking them with carrot strips. **1973** Allen *LAUM* 1.409 (as of c1950), Schnitzel. To cut (green beans). "[T]o schnitzel beans" [1 inf, **MN**]. Also: schitzel [1 inf, **NE**].

schnitzen, schnitz-in, schnitzing vbl n, n See **schnitz** v

schnivvle See **schnibble**

schnobie See **schnabel**

schnozzle n Also *schnoz(z), schnozzler, shnozz* [Etym uncert; prob pseudo-Yiddish alter of *nose* or *nozzle*] chiefly **Nth, N Midl, West** See Map Cf **snozzle** Note: *Schnozzola*, made famous as the sobriquet of Amer entertainer James Francis (Jimmy) Durante's (1893–1980) large nose, is found scattered throughout the US and has not been entered.

A nose; also transf.

  1930 *Variety* 26 Feb 56 **NYC**, "Roadhouse Night" . . brings Jimmy Durante to the screen. Admirers of his peculiar madness usually fear for its reception by a general public . . but the Schnozzle's first screen appearance removes any doubts that might have been entertained. **1932**

AmSp 7.335 [Johns Hopkins jargon], *Schnozzle*—nose. **1937** *Amer. Mag.* May 61, A youngster like me [=Jimmy Durante] whose schnozzle could be seen two blocks away. . . When we admit our schnozzles . . we begin to laugh. **1942** *New Yorker* 13 June 15, I see she's not occupied excep' she's powderin' her schnoz. **1965–70** *DARE* (Qu. X14, *Joking words for the nose*) 76 Infs, **chiefly Nth, N Midl, West,** Schnozzle; 35 Infs, **esp PA, NY, Gt Lakes,** Schnozz; LA31, Schnozzler [ˈšnɑzlɚ]; (Qu. X15, . . *Kinds of noses, according to shape or size*) Infs **MI**67, **NY**209, **WI**43, (Jewish) schnozzle; (Qu. K61, . . *The pig's nose*) Inf **IN**35, Schnozzle. **2000** Bourdain *Kitchen Confidential* 42, The intimidating old French master would look down his Gallic shnozz and unload the most withering barrage of scorn. **2001** *DARE* File **wNY,** Schnozz . . the nose.

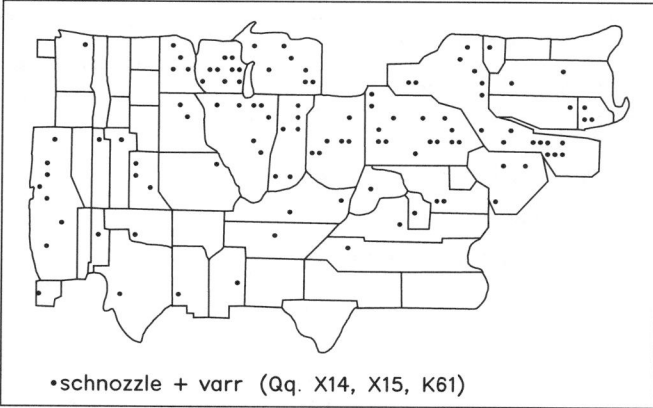

• schnozzle + varr (Qq. X14, X15, K61)

schnuffel See **schnibble**

scholar n [*OED2 scholar* sb. 1.a "Now somewhat *arch*."] **scattered, but esp Atlantic, N Cent** See Map *old-fash* Cf **scholard**

One who attends school; a student, pupil.

1825 in 1894 Stockbridge *Model Pastor* 45 **NH,** In the morning attended Sunday school. . . [O]ur scholars number one hundred and nineteen. **1857** in 1983 *PADS* 70.49 **ce,sePA,** There are such few scholars. **1876** in 1988 Palmer *Lang. W. Cent. MA* 27, Went up to Cheapside to see Mattie and her school—has 40 scholars. **1890** Howells *Boy's Town* 203 **OH,** One awful morning at school, it suddenly became so dark that the scholars could not see to study their lessons. **1906** Johnson *Highways Missip. Valley* 137 **Ozarks,** They [=school directors] jis' got somebody no account to beat and thump, and who didn't learn the scholars a thing. **1924** (1946) Greer-Petrie *Angeline Gits an Eyeful* 16 **csKY,** All of us *scholars* had to git our ha'r clipt to *git shet* of the nits. **1939** Griswold *Sea Is. Lady* 547 **csSC,** The chief purpose of Penn School was to train teachers for the county schools and prepare "scholars" for the county examinations. **1941** *LANE* Map 445 *(Student),* [Of the 24 *scholar* responses given in the commentary, all but 4 were either irrelevant or unidentifiable as to sense:] 1 inf, **swCT,** Scholar goes to school; 1 inf, **cnCT,** Student in college, scholar in school; 1 inf, **RI,** Scholar in grammar school; 1 inf, **ceVT,** Scholar, a young child in school. **1955** Ritchie *Singing Family* 48 **seKY,** Nick [=the teacher] told the scholars to study away while he talked with the men. **1959** *VT Hist.* 27.156,

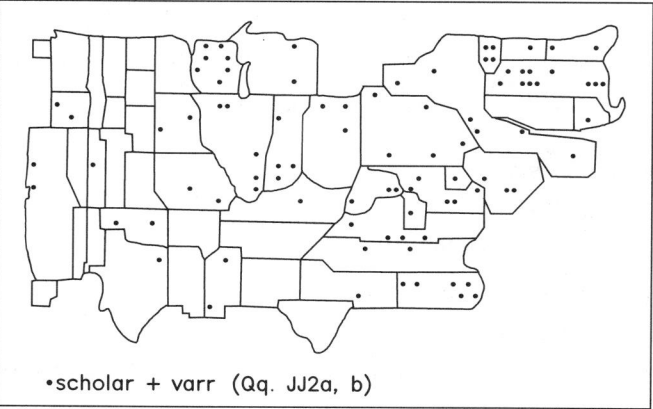

• scholar + varr (Qq. JJ2a, b)

Scholars . . school children. Old fashioned. Rare. **1965–70** *DARE* (Qu. JJ2a, *A child going to school, one in the lower grades*) 64 Infs, **scattered, but esp Atlantic, N Cent,** Scholar; VA42, Grammar scholar; VA25, Primary scholar; (Qu. JJ2b, *A person who attends high school*) 36 Infs, **scattered,** Scholar; MS61, VA25, High school scholar. [Of all Infs responding to Qq. JJ2a and JJ2b, 63% were old; of those giving these responses, 77% and 92% respectively were old.] **1968** *DARE* Tape **CA**103, I was one of the first scholars to enter the school in this town; **VA**9, He got paid for teaching me and five families of other scholars. **1982** *Barrick Coll.* **csPA,** *Scholars*—pupils (in one-room schools, esp.). The usual academic meaning of the word is unknown here. **1986** Pederson *LAGS Concordance* Gulf Region, [Of the 160 *scholar* responses, 54 were unidentifiable as to sense, and 68 were, on the basis of the inf's or fieldworker's remarks, irrelevant. Of the remaining responses, 21 restricted *scholar* to a grammar and/or high school student and 6 to a college student, 6 characterized it as an "old term," and 5 offered it as equivalent to "pupil" or "student."]

scholard n Also *schollard, scol(l)ard* [Engl dial]
A scholar; a student.

1815 Humphreys *Yankey in England* 108, Scholard, scholar. **1823** Cooper *Pioneers* 193 **NY,** You've forgot your schooling, and the young mistress is a great scollard. **1830** *MA Spy & Worcester Co. Advt.* (Worcester MA) 28 July 4/1, *Drap* your Yankee phrases, and talk like a *scholard*. **1916** *DN* 4.335 **Nantucket MA,** Scholard. . . Scholar. Hibernian. **1921** Haswell *Daughter Ozarks* 81 (as of 1880s), To-day she were a'talkin' to me and some other of the largest schollards. **1927** *AmSp* 2.363 **cwWV,** John is a fine scholard in his books. **1929** *AmSp* 5.131 **ME,** Maine folk spoke of a "scolard" or "scholard" (Prov. Eng.) when referring to one who was well educated or a student, that is, a scholar. **1939** in 1944 *ADD* **wWV,** Scholard. . . Any pupil or student, however young. Not freq. except among old people.

scholar's companion n Also *school companion* old-fash
A box in which school supplies are kept.

1895 (1969) Montgomery Ward *Catalogue* 118, Scholar's Companions. . . Whitewood Box Scholar's Companion; furnished with lead pencil, pen, penholder, slate pencil and six inch wood ruler. **1897** (1968) Sears *Catalogue* 354, Scholar's Companions. . . Unique Scholar's Companion, varnished maple box, with sliding cover, 9-inch ruler attachment with scale, fitted with lead pencil, slate pencil and pen holder. . . Magic Combination Lock, Scholar's Companion. **1943** *AN&Q* 3.73 **NEng,** When I first went to school, about 1906, a scholar's companion was a small box containing pen, pencil, eraser, short ruler, perhaps a penwiper, etc. *Ibid* **NEng,** [The scholar's companion] was a small box about eight inches long, two inches wide, and an inch or so in depth. It had a cover hung on metal hinges and a "real" lock and key. The cover usually carried a picture in gay colors. . . No grade-school youngster . . was considered properly equipped at the opening of school each September unless he had his scholar's companion. But it was . . beneath the dignity of a high-school student to carry one. **1955** *Sun* (Baltimore MD) 12 Sept Edition B 10/7 (*Hench Coll.*), I was born and grew up in Frederick county [MD]. Our pencil boxes were always called "scholar's companions." . . I attended public school here in Wilmington [DE]. We called our pencil boxes "school companions." . . Fifty or more years ago [every] child on the Eastern Shore of Virginia had to have . . a "scholar's companion." **1970** *DARE* FW Addit **MA**79, Scholar's companion. . . Pencil box popular in the early 20th century; had drawers in it; held pencils, a compass, a ruler (usually 6″ long), colored pencils, an inkwell, a folding drinking cup; the more drawers it had, the better; the "show-off" at school had the biggest.

schollard See **scholard**

schonocker See **shonicker**

Schoodic salmon n Also *Schoodic trout* [From *Schoodic Lakes,* Maine]
The lake-dwelling Atlantic **salmon B1a** (*Salmo salar*).

1873 *NY Ag. Soc. Trans. for 1871* 352, An eleven pound Schoodic salmon is the largest on record. **1884** Goode *Fisheries U.S.* 1.470, The "Land-locked" or "Fresh-water" Salmon . . [is] known . . in different parts of Maine as "Schoodic Trout." **1902** Jordan–Evermann *Amer. Fishes* 169, In Maine the original habitats were Presumpscot River or Sebago Lake basin . . and St. Croix River basin which includes the Schoodic Lakes from which the fish derives also the name of "Schoodic salmon". **1975** Evanoff *Catch More Fish* 77, The landlocked salmon (*Salmo salar sebago*) is also called the . . Schoodic salmon.

school n Also *schoolhouse* Cf **Chinese school, dummy ~, rock ~**

A children's guessing game; see quots.

1957 *Sat. Eve. Post Letters* Philadelphia PA, *School*—This game was played on steps with a piece of stone. Each child in turn hides the stone in one of his fists which are then held out for the teacher or guesser to give his answer as to which hand holds the stone. Depending on a correct or incorrect answer the student either ascends to another grade or remains where he is. The winner of course, is the first to go up and back down all the steps. **1970** *DARE* (Qu. EE33, . . *Outdoor games . . that children play*) Inf **OH**98, School—you move up steps if you guess what is held in the other's hands behind his back. **2000** *NADS Letters* NJ (as of c1965), I also played schoolhouse on my front steps using small rocks as you described. . . We called it either schoolhouse, or shortened it to school. The person to reach the top step first became the teacher for the next round. **2001** *Ibid* Phildelphia PA, "School" is the name my friends and I called the popular game you describe as "Rock School." All of the elementary-school-aged boys and girls played it and called it "School." (Philadelphia mixed ethnicity neighborhood, 1968–74).

school bass n

A small **red drum.**

1884 Goode *Fisheries U.S.* 1.372, In the Carolinas, Florida, and the Gulf, . . many persons suppose 'Channel Bass' to be a characteristic name [for *Sciaenops ocellatus*], but . . the term is applied properly only to large individuals . . ; wherever this name is used, the smaller fish of the species are called simply 'Bass,' or 'School Bass.' **1935** Caine *Game Fish* 39 **Sth,** *Sciaenops ocellatus.* . . School Bass. **1986** Pederson *LAGS Concordance (Fish)* 1 inf, **seGA,** School bass.

school-bell fever n Also *school-bus cramps, ~ fever*

Fig: an illness feigned to avoid having to go to school.

1967–70 *DARE* (Qu. BB27, *When somebody pretends to be sick . . he's _____*) Inf **RI**17, School-bell fever; **NY**234, School-bus fever; (Qu. BB28, *Joking names . . for imaginary diseases: "He must have the _____."*) Inf **NY**27, School-bus cramps.

school breaking n Also *school break* Cf **break v C3, school closing**

The end of the school year, freq marked by a public program displaying the students' accomplishments.

1927 *AmSp* 2.363 **cwWV,** *School break* . . the last day of school. "I am going to the school break to-morrow." **1952** Brown *NC Folkl.* 1.588, *School breaking.* . . Commencement, the close of the school year.—General. **1954** *PADS* 21.31 **SC,** *School breaking.* . . Same as *school exhibition.*

school-bus cramps (or fever) See **school-bell fever**

school butter exclam [*OED2* (at *school* sb.¹ 19) 1593 →. The earliest exx are allusive, but it seems likely that the orig sense was "a whipping received at school."] **Sth, S Midl**

Used as a taunting call to schoolboys; see quots.

1835 Longstreet *GA Scenes* 84, Ding his old red-headed skin . . to go and kick me right in my sore belly, where I fell down and raked it, running after that fellow that cried 'school-butter.' [Footnote:] I have never been able to satisfy myself clearly, as to the literal meaning of these terms. They were considered an unpardonable insult to a country school, and always justified an attack by the whole fraternity, upon the person who used them in their hearing. **1887** *Amer. Philol. Assoc. Trans. for 1886* 17.46 **Sth,** List of Southern expressions. . . *School-butter* (challenge to country school). **1890** *DN* 1.66 **KY,** *School-butter:* the direst insult to a country school-boy. To cry out *school-butter* to a lot of boys is to invite a fight. **1893** Shands *MS Speech* 55, *School-butter.* . . This word, when yelled out by one school-boy to another, is regarded as the direst insult and as calling for immediate fight. **1899** (1912) Green *VA Folk-Speech* 369, *School-butter.* . . A word of obscure origin and meaning but of the greatest insult to schoolboys. When called out to them by a passer of the old country school-house he could only save himself by flight from their wrath. "A flogging." **1909** *DN* 3.366 **eAL, wGA,** *School butter.* . . A teasing call to school children. Not heard in some localities, but common in others. **1912** *DN* 3.588 **wIN,** *School butter.* . . A term of reproach applied to school children. "When he yelled *school butter* at us, we yanked him off the wagon and blacked his eyes." **1915** *DN* 4.189 **swVA,** *School butter.* . . Used as a term of reproach to school children. "A man hollered out *school butter* to us and we grabbed him and giv' him a good duckin'." **a1975** Lunsford *It Used*

to Be 176 **sAppalachians,** "School butter" is an epithet of offense to a school group in rural western North Carolina. I know nothing about its origin. It has a tendency to provoke the school into taking the offender to a nearby branch and ducking him. **1996** *DARE* File **eTN** (as of 1920s), 'School butter.' I heard this one from my mother-in-law, who was originally from East Tennessee (Johnson City), who said this was what the Big Kids used to call after the new pupils as they walked into the school. My husband recalls that . . [his mother] woke him up on the day he was going off to first grade in 1942, with a smile and "Get up, School Butter."

school closing n

=**school breaking.**

1967 Green *Horse Tradin'* 283 **TX,** She told me the coming Friday night was school-closing. There was going to be a big country play and an ice cream and cake supper after the play was over. **1967** *DARE* (Qu. FF16, . . *Local contests or celebrations*) Inf **SC**46, School closing—girls did flower drills (marching), picnic, recitations. **1986** Pederson *LAGS Concordance,* 1 inf, **csAR,** School-closing programs end [the] school year.

school companion See **scholar's companion**

schoolhouse See **school**

school is out phr Cf **church is out**

Fig: the truth has come out and the consequences must be faced; the time for restraint is over.

1958 McCulloch *Woods Words* 158 **Pacific NW,** *School's out*—There's hell to pay. **1965** Davis *Summer Land* 184 **cnNC,** He drove the nail out of sight, whipped up the plank—and school was out. They emptied the cache in a wink. Wash and Arch Davis both laid a hand on every quart as it came out, to make it legal. **1999** *DARE* File **nKY** (as of 1950s), In my basketball playing days (and even after), the phrases "School is out" and "Church is out" referred to "intense periods of play or feverish activity in a game (or even in a fight), when the participants tried their hardest." Such phrases were even used as encouragement to fellow players. "OK, school's out. Let's get in there and kick ass." It seemed also (as my invented routine suggests) to indicate that any delicacy was about to be discarded.

schoolmarm n Also *schoolma'am, school mom* [See quot 1975] **chiefly Nth**

A forked tree; a forked pole or log.

1930 Williams *Logger-Talk* 28 **Pacific NW,** *Schoolma'am:* A forked tree. **1938** (1939) Holbrook *Holy Mackinaw* 263, *Schoolmarm.* A crotched log, consisting mostly of two trunks. **1939** FWP *ID Lore* 244, Lumberjack jargon in the St. Maries area and elsewhere: . . *School mom*—a tree that forks; forked pole used in loading. **1950** Eaton *Coll.* **Washington Is. WI,** Schoolma'am . . a tree with double trunk. **1950** *Western Folkl.* 9.119 **nwOR** [Logger speech], *Schoolmarm:* Two trees growing from the same trunk or stump, supposedly resembling the trunk and legs of a woman. **1954** *WELS Suppl.* **cWI,** The term "schoolmarm" or "schoolma'am" as applied to a forked tree is a common term among sawyers and other woodsmen around Wausau. . . As you probably know, its origin is a very earthy one which I don't care to put into words. . . I will say it does not refer to the schoolteacher's "upraised arms." **1975** Gould *ME Lingo* 244, *Schoolmarm*—A forest tree which has suffered some damage to its top and as a consequence has developed into two tops. . . The suggestion of a lady with both legs in the air must have occurred to the first Maine woodsman who likened such a tree to a *schoolmarm.* **1977** Churchill *Don't Call* 42 **nwOR** (as of c1918), A schoolmarm, Mother learned, was a tree that started out with a single stem, then branched out into a double. **1982** *Smithsonian Letters* **ME,** *Schoolma'am,* a pine that has branched into two parallel trunks somewhat above the ground.

schoolmaster n

Std: a **snapper** (here: *Lutjanus apodus*) native esp to coastal South Atlantic waters. Also called **black snapper 1, dog ~, gray ~, lawyer B6**

school mom See **schoolmarm**

schooslich See **schussel v 1**

schottische n widespread exc Appalachians, Mid and S Atl See Map

A round dance with hopping steps performed to a stately four-count rhythm.

1851 *S. Lit. Messenger* 17.377 **Sth,** The "fine looking women" are . . showing off the steps of Saracco in the schottische but with a freedom of their own. **1852** *Knickerbocker* 39.155 **ME,** The 'Schottische,' [was] danced by one of *our* ladies and a blushing young man. **1902** Wister *Virginian* 116 **WY,** Miss Wood . . was dancing the schottische. **1933** Rawlings *South Moon* 11 **nFL,** A bass fiddle was playing a schottische. **1954** Piper–Piper *175 Folk Dances* 17, Schottische—*Basic Step*—1, 2, 3, hop; 1, 2, 3, hop; step-hop, step-hop, step-hop, step-hop. **1965–70** *DARE* (Qu. FF5a, . . *Different steps and figures in dancing—in past years*) 215 Infs, **widespread exc Appalachians, Mid and S Atl,** Schottische; **CO**31, **OH**74, Dip schottische; **MA**73, Five-step schottische; [**CA**123, Scottish] [Of all Infs responding to the question, 64% were old; of those giving these responses, 81% were old.]; (Qu. FF5b, *More recent dance steps*) Infs **IL**4, **OK**18, Schottische. **1966–70** *DARE* Tape **MI**115, The schottische had gone out of style; that was in my mother and father's day; **ND**2, Waltzes and polkas and schottisches; dances were very popular; **TX**3, We had two-step, and put-your-little-foot, and schottische, and polka, waltz. **1973** Flach *Yankee German-America* 79 **csTX,** The orchestra alternated old-time music and the modern kind. There was "Put Your Little Foot," the Schottische, the fast German waltz, "Ten Pretty Girls." Modern dances at that time were the fox trot and the slow waltz. **1986** Pederson *LAGS Concordance* (*A dance*) 1 inf, **seTX,** Schottische; 1 inf, **csTN,** Schottische—formerly aristocratic; 1 inf, **csTX,** Schottische—he likens it to polka; 1 inf, **csTX,** Schottische—old type of dancing; 1 inf, **seLA,** Schottische—dance music in her day; 2 infs, **TN, TX,** Schottische(s). **2001** *DARE* File **ME** (as of 1977–78), I followed the Maine Country Dance Orchestra around Maine to wherever they were holding a dance. We danced contra dances, circle dances, and always one polka and one schottische each time. The schottische seemed like a very formal dance to me.

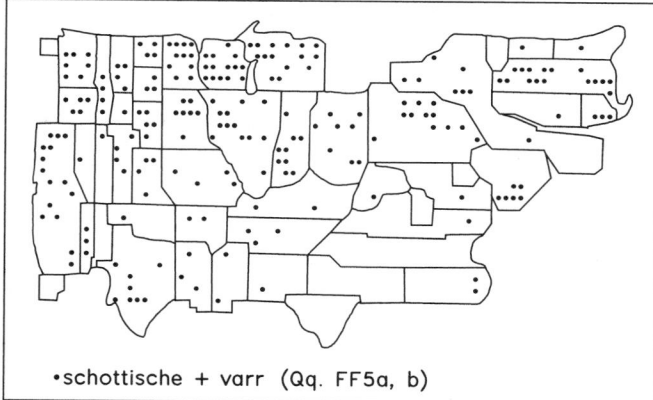

•schottische + varr (Qq. FF5a, b)

schrod(e) See **scrod**

schrooch See **scrooch 5**

schrowd See **scrowd**

schtroobly, schtruvely See **strubbly**

schussel n Usu |ˈʃʊsəl|; for varr see quot 1968–70 Also *schussel-ass, schussle* [PaGer *schussel* a hasty, flighty person] **PA** Cf **doppich**

A hasty, clumsy person.

1914 *DN* 4.158 **PA,** Schussle. . . One who in hurrying falls over his own feet. **1968–70** *DARE* (Qu. A21, *When someone is in too much of a hurry . . "Now just slow down! Don't _____."*) Inf **PA**242, Don't be a schussel [ˈʃʊzəl]; too much in a hurry; he'll mess up; (Qu. N12, . . *Somebody who drives carelessly or not well*) Inf **PA**199, Schussel [ʃʊsəl]; (Qu. HH21, *A very awkward, clumsy person*) Inf **PA**151, Schussel [ʃʊsəl]; **PA**199, Schussel-ass.

schussel v [PaGer] **PaGer area**

1 To rush; to do something in a quick and sloppy way; hence adjs *schooslich, schusslig, schussely* hasty, clumsy, sloppy.

1935 *AmSp* 10.170 **PA** [Engl of PA Germans], Other German words used in English are. . . *Schussel,* to hurry, 'She schusseled to get ready.' **1939** Aurand *Quaint Idioms* 19 [PaGer], I've seen lots of people in my

time but never such a *schooslich* person (one who pokes along, or stumbles over everything; hands the wrong things; dresses indifferently; doesn't know what he is saying, etc.; a very descriptive word, hard to define in English). **1940** in 1944 *ADD,* Schussely. . . Untidy. . . [ˈʃʊsəli]. Reported as Penn. Dutch. **1967–68** *DARE* (Qu. A21, *When someone is in too much of a hurry . . "Now just slow down! Don't _____."*) Inf **PA**18, [ˈʃʊsəl]; **PA**156, Be so schusslig [ˈʃʊsˌlɪk]; (Qu. KK63, *To do a clumsy or hurried job of repairing something: "It will never last—he just _____."*) Inf **MD**30, Schusseled [ʃʊsl̩d] over it; **PA**25, [ʃʊsələd] [sic] over; **PA**150, [ʃʊsəld] through—sloppy. **1968** *Helen Adolf Festschrift* 36 **PaGer area,** *Schussel*—The verb *schussel* is often used, particularly by the older inhabitants in the area, as a substitute for the verb 'to hurry.' **1987** *Jrl. Engl. Ling.* 20.2.174 **ePA,** *Schussel* 'to hurry'. . . 4.5% [of all resps] ([actively used by] 5 [of 100 infs]), ages 21–80. . . [S]chussel is rarely used, even by older speakers, to whom it is largely confined.

2 To wiggle; to fidget.

1996 Huth *Famil. Words* 109 **csPA,** Schussel. . . to be active or restless as in class. Stop schusseling!

schussel-ass See **schussel** n

schussely See **schussel** v 1

schussle See **schussel** n

schusslig See **schussel** v 1

Schuylkill cat n

Either of two related fishes: **brown bullhead 1** or **white catfish 1.**

1882 *U.S. Natl. Museum Bulletin* 16.104, [Ameiurus] catus. . . *Bullhead . . Small Cat-fish; Schuylkill Cat.* **1884** *U.S. Natl. Museum Bulletin* 27.491, *Amiurus* [sic] *catus. . . Schuylkill Cat. . .* This is one of the best known and most esteemed of our cat-fish. . . In the markets of Philadelphia, Baltimore, and Washington it is extensively sold. **1902** Jordan-Evermann *Amer. Fishes* 26 **PA,** *Amiurus nebulosus.* . . In the East and North it is the common bullhead or horned pout; in Pennsylvania it is the Schuylkill cat; and everywhere, the small catfish. **1903** NY State Museum & Sci. Serv. *Bulletin* 60.86 **Philadelphia PA,** This [=*Ameiurus catus*] is the white cat or channel cat, in Philadelphia distinguished as the Schuylkill cat.

schwartemagen n Also *schwademage(n), schwatamagen, schwatermakin* [Ger *Schwartenmagen* brawn; chopped, cooked, molded pork parts]

=**headcheese 1** or a similar dish.

1914 *DN* 4.112 **cKS,** Schwartemagen. . . Boiled scraps of pork stuffed in a preserved hog's stomach. "After every butchering, they made schwartemagen." **1967–68** *DARE* (Qu. H43, *Foods made from parts of the head and inner organs of an animal*) Inf **OH**80, Schwademage—same as headcheese; **MN**37, Schwatamagen; **MO**12, Schwatermakin [ˈʃwɑrɚˌmɑkɪn]. **1986** Pederson *LAGS Concordance* (*Headcheese*) 1 inf, **csTX,** Schwademagen [ˈʃlɑˤt̠rəˌmãˢə]; (*Liver sausage*) 1 inf, **cTX,** Schwademagen [ˈʃwɑt̠ɚˌmʌˤŋ].

science n, v See **scion**

science adj Also *scienced* [*OED2* →1836]

1926 *DN* 5.403 **Ozarks,** *Science.* . . Skillful, proficient, expert. "Jim shore is a plum science fiddler." Sometimes a final *d* or *t* is pronounced, and the word becomes *scienced.*

scient See **scion**

scimption See **skimption**

scion n, v Also sp *cion* Pronc-spp *science, scient, sign* [See *OED2 scion* sb. 1.a.γ, c for 16th- and 17th-cent exx of sg *scient* and pl *sciences*]

A Forms.

1894 *DN* 1.329 **sNJ,** Cions, scions: pron. science [saɪəns]. . . Young growth of oak timber. Pines and cedars have no scions. To "science" (verb) is to cut off these sprouts. **1899** (1912) Green *VA Folk-Speech* 369, Science. . . A scion; a shoot. **1903** *DN* 2.328 **seMO,** Scient. . . Scion. 'My onions growed from scients.' **1976** [see **B2** below].

B As noun.

1 A shoot, tree sprout. [*OED2 scion* sb. 1.a "A shoot or twig;

also, a sucker. *Obs. exc. fig.*"; c1305 →] Note: The restricted sense "a slip for grafting or planting" is std and is not illustrated here.

1894 [see **A** above]. **1899** [see **A** above]. **1940** [see **C** below]. **1982** *McDavid Coll.* **eNC,** *Scions*—shoots from a stump (used as switches to punish children).

2 A seedling tree or bush intended for transplanting.

1785 (1925) Washington *Diaries* 349 **VA,** Thursday 10th. . . Sent my Waggon . . to Occoquaw for the Scion of the Hemlock. . . Friday 11th. . . Planted the Hemlock Scions . . in the shrubbery. . . Brought 9 scions of the Portugal Peach from Mr. Cockburn's with me. . . Monday 14th. . . Planted the young peach Trees which I brought from Mr. Cockburn's in the No. Garden. **1976** Ryland *Richmond Co. VA* 376, *Sign*—scion, shoot of a bush or tree which can be dug up and planted.

3 An onion set.

1903 [see **A** above].

C As verb.

As *science:* To cut tree shoots, clear brush from (a roadway); broadly, to improve a road. **esp sNJ**

1894 [see **A** above]. **1940** Weygandt *Down Jersey* 100 **sNJ,** After trying a road . . that had not been brushed out or "scienced" for years, and finding it impassable, we returned to the through road. *Ibid* 102, We had given up the following of "unscienced" roads, roads along which the bushes or the "scions" from the roadside trees had not been cut away. **1968** McPhee *Pine Barrens* 59 **cNJ,** When highway workers do anything to a road, they are said to be sciencing it.

scissor n[1]

1 A pair of scissors.

1948 *WELS Suppl.* **WI,** "Hand me a scissor." I've heard this here and there in the state. **1950** *Ibid* **csWI,** *Scissor*—used always in singular form. "What became of the scissor that was in that box?" **2001** *NADS Letters* **cTX,** In eastern Texas (specifically the small town of Weimar . .) during the 1950s and 1960s, the use of "a scissor" to mean 'a pair of scissors' was quite common. My mother, an English teacher in the local high school, always regarded the construction as a shibboleth marking the local descendants (first-, second-, and third-generation) of Czech immigrants—of whom there were many in the area. *Ibid* **Chicago IL,** The Italian-American girls I played with often said *scissor* (singular) for a pair of scissors. *Ibid* **RI,** I have definitely heard "scissor" used instead of "a pair of scissors." *Ibid* **IA** (as of c1980), He would say . . "Hand me a scissor" or "I need a plier to do this." *Ibid* **OR,** My grandmother . . would ask me "Richard, bring me that scissor, there." *Ibid* **NJ,** My grandparents use the term "scissor" for "pair of scissors." They are in their mid-70s, . . [and] are both of Italian descent.

2 See **scissorbill 2a.**

scissor n[2] See **sizzer** n[1]

scissorbill n Also *scissorsbill;* also sp *scizzorbill, sizzerbill*

1 The black **skimmer 1** (*Rynchops niger*). [*OED2* 1839 → (at *scissors* sb. 5) for *Rynchops* spp] **S Atl, Gulf States**

1921 *LA Dept. of Conserv. Bulletin* 141, One of the most entertaining birds of the Louisiana coast is the black skimmer (*Rhynchops nigra*), known familiarly as . . "scissor-bill". . . Its lower mandible, or lower part of the bill, averages nearly an inch longer than the upper mandible. Both mandibles are compressed laterally to the shape and dimensions of small blunt knife blades. **1924** Howell *Birds AL* 34, The black skimmer, more often known in Alabama as . . "scissor-bill," is common along the coast beaches both in summer and winter. **1946** Kopman *Wild Acres* 27 **LA,** The purpose of the shape and structure of the bill [of the black skimmer] . . is to allow the bird to submerge the lower mandible at a shallow and fixed angle to the water . . ; thus . . it shears . . almost horizontally. It is from this unique adaptation that the bird gets the popular names of "shearwater" and "scissors-bill." **1954** Sprunt *FL Bird Life* 226, *Rynchops nigra nigra. . . Local Names* . . Scissorbill. **1969** *DARE* (Qu. Q5) Inf **NC72,** Scissorbill.

2 A contemptible person, spec:

a also *scissor, sizzer:* One regarded as foolish, incompetent, or inexperienced.

1916 *DN* 4.328 **KS,** *Scissors, n. pl.* Applied to persons in disparagement. Also *scissors-bills.* **1919** *DN* 5.58 **WA,** *Scissorsbill.* . . If the scissorbills can't get their crops garnered for lack of help. **1925** *AmSp* 1.151 **West,** "Scissorbill," which referred originally to a worker lacking

in class consciousness . . now is a synonym for a general know-nothing. **1930** *RR Man's Mag.* June 472, *Scissor-bill*—Applied to either yard or road brakeman and a term which is not considered complimentary; a student in train service. **1931** *AmSp* 7.52 **Sth, SW** [Lumberjack lingo], A "scissor bill" is a lumberjack off stripe in any way. **1932** *Santa Fe Mag.* Jan 34, A new brakeman, or a beginner, is a *sizzer* or a *whicker bill.* **1932** *RR Mag.* Oct 369, *Scissor-bill* or *sizzer-bill*—Yard or road brakeman; not complimentary. **1940** *Ibid* April 52, *Scizzor-bill.* . . Any individual holding a job for which he is unfitted, due to lack of training or mental ability, usually both. **1943** Korson *Coal Dust* 5 **Midl,** Full-time miners naturally resented them [=farmer-miners] and expressed their distrust by calling them . . "greenies," "scissorbills," and "sagers." **1944** Botkin *Treas. Amer. Folkl.* 548 **Chicago IL,** Some sign painters couldn't dot the letter "i" without a pounce to go by. It was enough to make a dog laugh to see some poor scissorsbills wrestling around with a pounce. **1948** *McDavid Coll.* **cnNY,** *Scissor bill, whistle punk*—poor workman. **1965** Bowen *Alaskan Dict.* 28, *Scissor Bill*—A derogatory term used by Indians for Caucasians. **1966** *DARE* Tape **NC30,** In this area a greenhorn at a logging camp or a sawmill is called a scissorbill. **1978** Doig *This House* 13 **MT,** The winter of 'twenty-one, I helped that scissorbill feed his cattle. **1995** *Brophy Coll.* 65 **swMO** (as of c1960), *Scissorbill.* [A]n awkward person, a country jake.

b One regarded as a traitor to his class or associates.

1913 *Industrial Worker* (Spokane, Washington) 1 May 5/3 [sic *OED2*—quot not found], Scissorbill is a localized slang term. Here it refers to the 'home-guard' worker, who is filled with bourgeoise [sic] ideas and ethics. It ordinarily describes a worker who has some source of income other than his wages. **1925** [see **2a** above]. **1926** *AmSp* 1.652 [Hobo lingo], *Scissor bill*—one without knowledge of the labor problem. A farmer who can clip coupons. One who has struck oil. **1930** Williams *Logger-Talk* 18 **Pacific NW,** *Scissor-bill:* According to the I.W.W., a laboring man who is not "class conscious." **1938** (1939) Holbrook *Holy Mackinaw* 263, *Scissorbill.* A worker who is not filled with spirit for the Revolution. **1940** Cottrell *Railroader* 135, *Scissors bill*—A railroad detective; a propensity for sticking his nose into other people's business develops that organ (until it is a bill). **1943** Korson *Coal Dust* 180, Some worked in the mine on Sundays, holidays, and other idle days without compensation, piling up coal for future loading, but were rewarded with extra turns when work was resumed. Men guilty of these practices were characterized by the miners as "free clickers," "free turn men," "scissorbills," and "coal hogs." **1958** McCulloch *Woods Words* 158 **Pacific NW,** *Scissor bill*—A non-union man. **1970** *Current Slang* 5.1.12 [Jargon of railroad employees], *Scissorbill.* . . Strikebreaker, scab.

scissors n Also *crossed scissors, passing the scissors, scissors game*

A game in which a pair of scissors is passed among the players; see quots.

1935 Mason–Mitchell *Social Games* 213, *Crossed Scissors.* . . There are two ways of passing the scissors, crossed and uncrossed. **1952** Brown *NC Folkl.* 1.41 (as of c1921), *Scissors.* . . Several people are seated in a circle. The leader crosses her legs, says, "I received them crossed and I pass them uncrossed," uncrosses her legs, and hands the scissors to the player sitting next to her. The scissors pass clear around the circle, and the joke is to see how many fail to cross and uncross the legs. **1953** Brewster *Amer. Nonsinging Games* 124 **AR,** *Scissors.* **1966–67** *DARE* (Qu. EE3, *Games in which you hide an object and then look for it*) Inf **CO3,** Scissors game—crossed, uncrossed—legs as clue; (Qu. EE40) Inf **FL2,** Passing the scissors—pass them on and say I pass the straight (or crossed) and you open or close them and you cross your fingers or legs. The next person has to say I receive them straight or crossed. **1997** *NADS Letters* **NEng** (as of c1960), Passing the scissors is a "game" where a group of people sit in a circle. The group consists of at least one person who knows the game and new players who don't know the rules. Scissors are passed around the circle, the person saying "Crossed" or "Uncrossed" when they are passed. The object is for the newcomers to figure out when "Crossed" is correct and "Uncrossed" is the right thing to say. The players in the know, use ruses (such as elaborate arm motions, opening and closing the scissors) to confuse the new players. Most new players concentrate on the scissors (are they opened or closed?) or the arm movement (or a combination of the two). In fact, the real answer is whether one's legs are crossed (crossed-ankles alone count). *Ibid* **eCT,** I have heard of passing the scissors. . . I learned this game in Voluntown (Eastern) CT around 1980–81. My Junior high schoolteachers taught it to me. *Ibid* **csWI,** Passing the Scissors. . . I remember playing this game with my Grandmother (German ancestry) and my parents, aunts and uncles, sometime in the mid to late 50's. . . It was usually played when someone was visiting who didn't know the game.

scissorsbill See **scissorbill**

scissors game See **scissors**

scissortail n

1 also *scissors-tail (bird), scissortail bird, scissor-tail(ed) fly-catcher, scissortail swallow:* A **flycatcher 1a:** usu *Tyrannus forficatus,* which has a very long, deeply forked tail and is native chiefly to the south-central US; occas also a **kingbird 1** (here: *Tyrannus tyrannus*). [See quot 1858] **esp TX, Cent** See Map   For other names of the former see **kingbird 2, Mexican mockingbird, sizzletail, Spanish mockingbird, swallow-tailed flycatcher, Texas bird-of-paradise**

1858 Baird *Birds* 169 **West,** *Milvulus forficatus* [=*Tyrannus f.*] . . This exquisitely beautiful and graceful bird is quite abundant on the prairies of southern Texas. . . It is usually known as the scissor-tail from the habit of closing and opening the long feathers of the tail like the blades of a pair of scissors. **1872** Schele de Vere *Americanisms* 379, The proud name of *King-bird* is very fairly given to the bravest of birds, the *Scissor-tail* (Tyrannus carolinensis [=*T. tyrannus*]), who comes to us in summer from the far South. **1899** in 1900 LA Soc. Naturalists *Proc.* 103, *Milvulus forficatus.* . . *Scissor-tailed Flycatcher.* . . October 6, 1889 . . I saw a flock of ten near Kenner. **1955** in 1958 Brewer *Dog Ghosts* 39 **TX** [Black], Unkuh Josh say de las' time dey seed dat ball a scissors-tail bird was cuttin' at hit. **1960** Peterson *Field Guide Birds TX* 153, *Scissor-tailed Flycatcher—Muscivora forficata.* . . A beautiful bird . . with an extremely long scissor-like tail. Usually the "scissors" are folded. **1964** Wallace *Frontier Life* 53 **swOK** (as of 1893–1906), We watched the hummingbird, the scissors-tail, and heard the first emulating notes of the mockingbird. **1965–70** DARE (Qu. Q20, . . *Kinds of swallows and birds like them*) 27 Infs, 24 **TX, Cent,** Scissortail; TX28, Scissors-tail; **TX84,** Scissortail flycatcher; **TX91, WV14,** Scissortail swallow; (Qu. Q14) Inf **TX66,** Scissortail; **AR51,** Scissortail. **1993** Kingsolver *Pigs in Heaven* 176 **OK,** As he nears the Arkansas River and Cherokee county, the fields give way to trees and . . scissortail birds snipping over the meadows catching bugs, and big-headed kingfishers sitting on high lines.

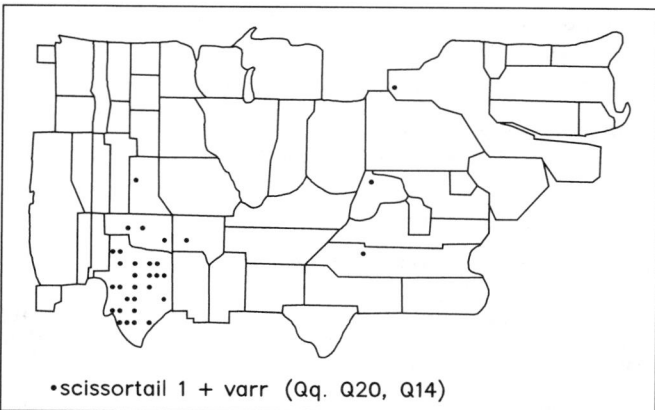

•scissortail 1 + varr (Qq. Q20, Q14)

2 =**man-o'-war bird.** Cf **hurricane bird**

1978 Mullen *Old Fishermen* 56 **seTX,** There is another bird, related to the albatross, which is variously called a storm bird, scissortail, storm king, or water turkey. It is always prophetic of a storm or bad weather: "When the scissortail or storm bird comes across the Gulf, you can look out for bad weather."

scissortail bird, scissortailed flycatcher See **scissortail 1**

scissor-tailed kite n

=**swallow-tailed kite.**

1941 Faherty *Big Old Sun* 32 **sFL,** You made five dollars for scissor-tailed kite's egg.

scissortail flycatcher (or swallow) See **scissortail 1**

scizz See **sizz**

scizzorbill See **scissorbill**

scizzor See **sizzer** n[1]

scobolotch n Also *scobblotcher, skoplotch* [Appar AmInd] =**mayfly 1.**

c1942 in 1965 *DARE* File **swWI,** Scobolotch ['skɑbələč]—mayfly—term used by an elderly informant of French-Indian origin. **1950** *WELS Suppl.,* I asked two friends, sisters whose childhood was spent in Redwing, Minnesota, what they called them, and they recalled both mayflies and cisco flies. Then one of them added, without my mentioning anything of the sort: "The Indian children called [them] *skoplotch.*" **1968** *DARE* (Qu. R4, *A large winged insect that hatches in summer in great numbers around lakes or rivers, crowds around lights, lives only a day or so, and is good fish bait*) Inf **MN36,** Scobblotcher ['skɑb,blɑčɚ]; **WI66,** Scobolotch.

scoffle v [*scoff* + frequentative *-le*] To speak contemptuously or mockingly.

1927 *DN* 5.477 **Ozarks,** Scoffle. . . To ridicule, to scoff. "Maggie kep' a-scofflin' at me—allus a hell-raisin' 'bout somthin'."

scoff off v phr [Cf *scoff off* to dismiss with derision] Of the moon: to keep bad weather away.

1939 *LANE* Map 89, 1 inf, **ceMA,** When the moon fulls, we may not have a storm after all: the moon may [skɒf it ɒ·f]. **1957** Beck *Folkl. ME* 191, There won't be no weather on a night like this. The moon will scoff it off.

scoggin n Also *scoggins* [Prob < *OED2 scoggin* sb. "*Obs.* . . A coarse jester, buffoon" (after a court jester of this name, supposed author of a popular jest-book first published 1566), with shift of sense to 'a grotesque figure; an object of ridicule.' Cf also *EDD scoggin* "A vane, weathercock"]

1 An object of ridicule.

1890 *DN* 1.23 **Provincetown MA** (as of 1888), *Scoggins* [skɔgınz]: a *butt* (for ridicule and tricks). "There was a fellow abroad [sic for *aboard*] that they made a kind o' scoggins out of." **1938** Matschat *Suwannee R.* 160 **neFL, seGA,** "Guess we better call Ab a five-shot scoggin! I remember my pappy sayin' it was a waste of good lead to use it on a b'ar." *Ibid* 289, Scoggin: a butt for ridicule. **2000** *NADS Letters,* The other terms I have heard of are "Scoggins" which I learned from my uncle. It is in reference to a really stupid person, or a stupid comment someone makes. I still use it today. My uncle (50 years old) grew up on Long Island, N.Y., and I am not sure where he learned the term. **2001** *Ibid* **seKY,** Scoggin(s)—I was called this once in school . . (I had no idea what it meant).

2 also *scawgin, scroggin(s), skoggin, squagin:* Any of var birds of the family Ardeidae. **chiefly S Atl** Cf **gray scoggin, night scoggins, pond scoggin**

1913 *Auk* 30.492 **Okefenokee GA,** Little Blue Heron. 'Blue Scoggin.'—Common. A colony of several hundred birds was reported nesting in Cowhouse Bay in May. **1926** *AmSp* 1.417 **Okefenokee GA,** I reckon there wuz five er six hunderd birds around the edge er that lake—scoggins [Footnote: herons], blue an' white uns, an' all kinds. **1945** *AmSp* 20.230, Scoggin . . This term, also used in plural form with singular meaning, is prevalent on the shores of the great sounds of eastern North Carolina and has spread some distance both north and south. It is applied to herons, sometimes with qualifying prefixes by those who recognize the diversity of these birds. **1950** *PADS* 14.77 **FL,** Scoggin. . . Any pond bird. **1955** *Oriole* 20.1.2, Louisiana Heron . . *Skoggin. Ibid,* Little Blue Heron. . . *Skoggin; White Crane.* **1959** *Names* 7.116, Of the heron family, the American bittern shares with its cousins a number of names, strict application of which has not been achieved. . . The southeastern term, scoggin, and variants, also has due usage. . . Scoggin, simply, has been heard as a bittern name in South Carolina; and as scroggin (Del.), scroggins (Fla.), and squagin and ma'sh scawgin (N.C.) **1966–68** *DARE* (Qu. Q8, *A water bird that makes a booming sound before rain and often stands with its beak pointed almost straight up*) Inf **GA20,** Scoggins—nickname for any kind of water bird; (Qu. Q10, *Water birds and marsh birds*) Inf **NC21,** Herons—scoggins or scouts or johnny gonkers; **NC24,** Scoggin—a white heron [DARE Ed: The immature little blue heron is white; there is also a white form of the great blue heron.] **1968** *DARE* FW Addit **GA25,** "Scoggin" ['skɑgın]—nickname for small blue heron.

scoke n Also *scoke-berry;* also sp *skoke* [See quot 1910]
=**pokeweed 1a.**

1778 Carver *Travels N. Amer.* 517, *Gargit* or *skoke* is a large kind of weed, the leaves of which are about six inches long. **1848** Gray *Manual of Botany* 385, P[*hytolacca*] *decandra* [=*P. americana*]. . . *Scoke.* . . A smooth plant, with a rather unpleasant odor. **1850** *Knickerbocker* 36.335 **NY,** A 'curt notelet' . . indited in the red juice of the scoke, or poke-berry, the *phytolacca decandra* of science. *Ibid,* With voice triumphant, sweet and clear,/ 'Scoke-berry! Scoke-berry!' **1873** Howells *Poems* 87, When the pheasant booms from your stealthy foot in the cornfield,/ And the wild-pigeons feed, few and shy, in the scoke-berry bushes. **1910** Hodge *Hdbk. Amer. Indians* 2.595, *Skoke.* A New England name for the pokeberry. . . Probably derived from Massachuset *m'skok,* that which is red (Trumbull), or *m'skwak.* **1969** *DARE* (Qu. S21, . . *Weeds . . that are a trouble in gardens and fields*) Inf **NY**150, Scoke. **1974** Morton *Folk Remedies* 109, Pokeweed; "poke;" poke salad, pokeberry; skoke; pigeonberry; ink berry; cancer root; wild spinach.

scolard See **scholard**

scoldenore n Also *scolder* [*scoldenore* is prob pronc-sp for *scolding whore*]
=**old-squaw.**

1870 *Atlantic Mth.* 25.210 **NH,** Boats go out . . after sea-fowl, . . [among which are] oldwives, called by the natives *scoldenores,* with clean white caps. **1888** Trumbull *Names of Birds* 89, Other odd names [for the old-squaw] met with among old New England gunners are *Scoldenore,* at Portsmouth, N.H., and at . . Plymouth, Mass. . . we hear . . also, *Scolder,* a term much more easily understood. **1955** MA Audubon Soc. *Bulletin* 39.375, *Old-squaw.* . . Scolder (Mass.); Scoldenore (Maine, N.H. These two also are "garrulity" names.) **1982** Elman *Hunter's Field Guide* 232, *Oldsquaw . . Common & regional names . . scolder.* . . Accompanied by noisy gabbling, . . little foraging bunches flit a few yards above the water.

scolding locks n pl
Hair or curls that do not stay in place.

1942 Whipple *Joshua* 8 **UT** (as of c1860), Her white skin and the scolding-locks of her black hair crisping on her soft neck below her bob. **1942** Berrey–Van den Bark *Amer. Slang* 121.48, *Scolding locks,* curls that can't be kept in place. **1954** *WELS Suppl.* **cWI,** Scolding locks. . . Short, straight ends of hair that fell below hair line—very ugly unless pinned up; **neWI,** Scolding locks—hairs too short to stay in place when the owner (female) wags and shakes her head in scolding someone. They were sometimes very becoming, no implication of ugliness as I understood it from my elders; **WI,** Scolding locks was a familiar term in my childhood for wayward hairs and curls; **seWI,** *Scolding locks* we still use, but then, we have long hair! **1955** in 1968 *DARE* File, *Scolding locks*—Familiar to, used, and cherished by Miss Kay . . 50ish, New England background. Esp. for stragglers from a fixed hairdo. **1957** *Hand Coll.* **neOH,** *Scolding locks*—The loose locks of hair that fall on the neck when the hair is done up on the head—these were called "scolding locks."

scollard See **scholard**

scolloped (squash) See **scallop squash**

sconion See **scunnion**

scooch v Also *scooge, scoosh, scootch, scouch, scutch, skootch, skutch* [Appar *EDD* *scouch* "To crouch, stoop, bend over," perh infl by **scrooch;** senses **2, 3,** and **4** have been infl by *scoot*]

1 also with *down, up:* To crouch, squat; to compress oneself so as to fit in a small space. **scattered, but somewhat more freq NEng** Cf **scoocher, scooch-tag, scoot v 3**

1858 *Atlantic Mth.* 2.421 **wCT,** She scooched down on the floor and pulled my two hands away. **1890** *DN* 1.19 **seNH,** *Scooch:* crouch. 'To scooch down in the corner.' In New York City *scouch* [skauč] is said to be used. **1895** *New Engl. Mag.* 17.697, Scooch down under that fence, an' run. **1903** *DN* 2.301 **Cape Cod MA** (as of a1857), *Scooch.* . . To crouch under or down. **1907** *DN* 3.249 **eME,** *Scooch.* . . To crouch, to squat. "He scooched down and I couldn't see him." **1916** *DN* 4.281 **NE,** *Scooch.* . . Probably echoic composite, built on *crouch* and *scoot,* etc. "He scooched down and scrooged under." **1931** *AmSp* 6.231 **cnNE,** *Skutch.* Crouch. "So when we saw the deer we sort of skutched

down so they wouldn't see us." **1943** *LANE* Map 581 *(Crouch),* [113 instances of *scooch down* and 25 of *scooch* were recorded in **NEng**; it is found in all the states except **RI,** but it is particularly common in **ME.**] **c1960** *Wilson Coll.* **csKY,** Scooch (or *scooch down*). . . To squeeze oneself into a small space. **1965–70** *DARE* (Qu. Y32, *To squeeze yourself into a small space:* "*If you're going to fit in there you'll have to _____.*") 12 Infs, **scattered,** Scooch; **AL**6, Scooch; shrink up; **CO**27, Scooch; fold your legs; make yourself like an accordion; **MA**46, Scooch—esp lowering yourself; **IN**60, **OH**17, 98, **OK**1, **PA**193, **VT**8, **WY**4, Scooch down; **TN**42, Scooch down is to squat as if to pick up something; **MI**112, **VA**73, Scooch up; **KY**10, Draw up; scrooch up; scooch up; **VA**69, Draw up; scooch yourself up—said esp about fitting people into a car; **OR**16, Scooge [skuǰ]. **1975** [see **scooch-tag**]. **1978** *UpCountry* May 46 **Friendship ME** (as of c1910), She spied me scooching by the syringa. **1986** Pederson *LAGS Concordance (Crouch)* 1 inf, **ceTN,** Scootched. **1992** *DARE* File **cnCO,** I . . use or have heard 'scooch down' to mean 'crouch down and make yourself smaller in order not to be observed.'

2 See quot.

1897 *KS Univ. Qrly.* (ser B) 6.56 **KS,** Scooch—to hasten, run.

3 =**scoot v 2.**

1965–70 *DARE* (Qu. Y52, *To move over—for example on a long bench:* "*. . . Can you _____ [a little]?*") Infs **CA**65, **CO**27, **IL**28, 45, 98, **MI**75, **NV**9, **OH**61, **OR**1, Scooch over; **NY**7, **VA**101, Scooch; **IA**27, Scooch down; move over [9 of 12 Infs young or mid-aged, 9 female]; [(Qu. Y34a, *When somebody moves on his hands and knees:* "*He was down in the bushes, _____ around.*") Inf **MI**108, Scooching;] (Qu. Y34b, *What babies do before they walk*) Inf **CA**65, Crawl; scooch—some do. **1982** Slone *How We Talked* 32 **eKY** (as of c1950), *Scutch*—move over. **1992** *DARE* File **cnCO,** 'Scoot over' is a bigger move for me than 'scooch over'. 'Scooch over' is cuter, a littler move, and more endearing. I don't think I have as much occasion to use it as 'scoot over'. **1996** Huth *Famil. Words* 109 **csPA,** *Skootch* . . to scoot over and out of the way. **1998** *WI State Jrl.* (Madison) 3 May sec G 1/1, When some fans tend toward the callipygian, bench seats can be tweaked—Can you scoosh over a bit?

4 with *over:* To move (something) a short distance.

1990 Smith *Understanding Speaking S. Lang.* 8, *Skootch over*—To move something a *skoash* or more. **1994** in 1996 Huth *Famil. Words* 110 **csPA,** Now all we need to do is skootch it over.

5 ppl adj *skootched up:* Snuggled together. Cf **scrooch 3**

1990 Smith *Understanding Speaking S. Lang.* 8, *Skootched up*—Very close together; necking.

scooch down See **scooch 1**

scoocher n [**scooch 1**]

1890 *DN* 1.19 **seNH,** *Scoocher:* to 'take a scoocher' is to slide down a snow-slope in a squatting position.

scooch over See **scooch 4**

scooch owl n Cf **scrooch owl, scooch 1**
A **screech owl 1** (here: *Otus asio*).

c1940 *LAMSAS Materials,* 3 infs, **MD, SC, GA,** Scooch owl. **1966** Dakin *Dial. Vocab. Ohio R. Valley* 2.386, Kentucky west of the Mountains and south of the Bluegrass has *scrooch owl* and *scooch owl* (less commonly), variants which also have some currency between the Little Wabash and the Kaskaskia and in the hills and the Pocket of Indiana south of the White River (East Branch). . . The Jackson Purchase has *scrich owl . . scooch* ~. **1967** *DARE* (Qu. Q1, . . *Kind of owl that makes a shrill, trembling cry*) Inf **TN**22, Scooch owl [ˈskuč ˌaul]—common pronunciation for "screech owl." **1973** Allen *LAUM* 45.7 **Upper MW** (as of c1950), For the small harsh-sounding owl *(Otus asio).* . . *scooch owl . .* is used by a southeast Iowa farmer with a Kentucky and Tennessee background.

scooch-tag n [**scooch 1**]
=**squat-tag.**

1975 Gould *ME Lingo* 244, *Scooch.* . . means to hunker down, to sit on your heels. Maine children play *scooch*-tag, a schoolyard game in which a child saves himself from being "it" if he *scooches* before being tagged.

scooch up See **scooch 1**

scooge See **scooch**

scoom See **skim** v **A**

scoop n

1 also *cellar scoop, drag ~, dump ~, horse ~, pond ~, scoop shovel:* A device for excavating and earth-moving, consisting in its simplest form of a shallow pan with a sharp lip in front, a bail to which a draft animal can be hitched, and a pair of rearward projecting handles. **scattered, but esp NY, PA, IN** See Map Cf **fresno 2, slip**

1925 *Book of Rural Life* 8.4751, The scrapers include machines for moving earth a considerable distance. The simplest form is the *slip,* or *scoop,* scraper. This implement is simply a large scoop arranged with a bail for drawing, and handles for dumping. **1958** McCulloch *Woods Words* 158 **Pacific NW,** *Scoop. . .* A horse-drawn slip for moving dirt in the days before bulldozers. **1965** West *Time Was* 245 **nwNC,** Will worked a one-mule scoop. . . The scoop was shaped something like a huge, square-lipped spade with two wooden handles extending backward. A flat steel bail was attached just forward of the center on each side, and the singletree was attached to the center of this bail. **1965–70** *DARE* (Qu. L41, *A device for moving dirt*) Infs **IN**80, **OH**95, **PA**75, 174, **TX**31, Scoop; **NY**93, **PA**80, Scoop [FW illustr]; **IN**54, Scoop [FW: Inf said that horses were used with scoops]; **MO**5, Scoop—pulled by two horses; **NY**75, Scoop—hitched a horse to it [FW illustr]; **NY**230, Scoop—horse; **PA**235, Scoop—two wheels, handles; scoop it in dirt and pull back on handles and wheel it away; **RI**8, Cellar scoop; **NY**200, Dump scoop; **IN**67, Rolling scoop; **DC**2, Scoop shovel with two horses; **IN**54, Scoop with wheels. [14 of 16 Infs old] **1968–69** *DARE* FW Addit **TN**26, Pond scoop. [*DARE* Ed: Photograph shows a shallow scoop with a bail in front and a pair of wooden handles projecting rearward.]; **MA**40, Drag scoop—more or less the same shape as a shovel only larger. On the front was an open lip. On the sides were two handles. When you lifted up on the handles it nosed the lip into the ground. It was pulled by a horse and was the way cellars for houses were dug. **1968** *DARE* File **DE,** Scoop = horse- or mule-drawn dirt-moving implement. [FW illustr] **1978–79** *Midwest. Lang. & Folkl. Newsl.* 1–2.20 **ME,** In Maine the "fresno" is called a "horse scoop." **1986** Pederson *LAGS Concordance* 1 inf, **cTN,** Scoops = earthmovers.

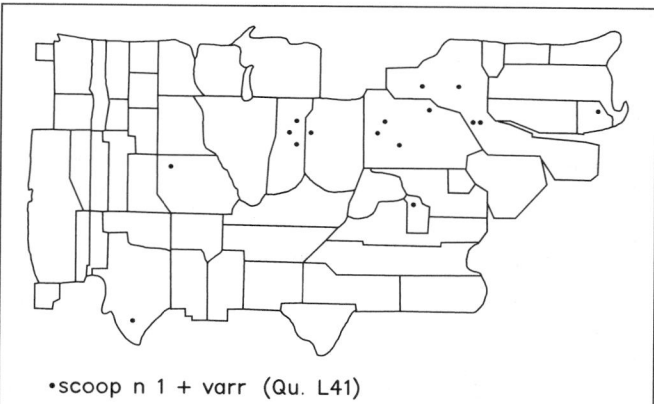

•scoop n 1 + varr (Qu. L41)

2 A cranberry rake. **esp MA**

1913 *DN* 4.57 **seMA,** *Scoop. . .* A large boxlike implement, with one open end, with the bottom formed by long, parallel, wooden teeth, and having the top furnished with a large double handle by which the whole is pushed through the vines. Unlike the "rake" and "snap," it is entirely of wood. "Picked five barrels o' berries yesterday with my new thirty-six-tooth scoop." **1950** *WELS Suppl.,* I notice that a cranberry *rake* (Wis.) is called a cranberry *scoop* in Mass. I wonder if there are any *scoops* here? **1970** *DARE* Tape **MA**102, Perhaps I should tell you about a hand scoop before I try to describe a picker. . . the old wooden scoop was. . . twenty-four inches wide and had long curved teeth on it about eight inches long, with two handles, one in back and one in front; and in back of the teeth there was a solid portion of the box, and the scoop was curved on the bottom.

3 A ravine; a hollow. [*OED2 scoop* sb.² 2.a. 1762 →] **NEng** **a1817** (1821) Dwight *Travels* 1.110 **NEng,** Beautiful swells [in the landscape], and elegant scoops, of every form, are in a sense innumerable. **1854** in 1894 Lowell *Letters* 1.216 **NEng,** You get a gleam of sea through some scoop in the woods. **1938** FWP *Guide NH* 455 **cwNH,** The middle peak, Baldface, is the highest elevation in this part of the

State. The mountain is steep-sided, dropping almost perpendicularly for 1200 feet into the forests below, while the spurs from the flanking peaks, running out to the east, enclose a vast ravine, or scoop.

scoop v, hence vbl n *scooping*

To shovel (snow); to shovel snow from.

1978 *DARE* File **cwIL,** Scooping snow is known around here too [= Jacksonville, IL]. After I had given a talk to a local group about dialects, a young woman, native of Springfield, came up and said she used the term. **1981** [see **scoop shovel 1**]. **1987** Mohr *How Minnesotan* 125 **MN,** Hardly a day passes when Kyle doesn't say to his wife, "If we'd just have about two or three inches of snow every so often so I could help scoop the walks here in Sunshine Village, I think I'd be happier."

scoop board n

A board at the rear of a wagon that can be let down to facilitate the removal of its load; hence fig, a drop seat in a pair of underwear.

1895 (1969) Montgomery Ward *Catalogue* 581, *Our Scoop Board. . .* The simplest, best, cheapest and strongest board made; used for corn, potatoes, turnips, cobs, etc.; wood bottom, steel sides, iron braces and supports. [Illustration in text] **1914** *DN* 4.112 **cKS,** *Scoop-board. . .* A board projecting at the rear of a farm wagon. **1923** *DN* 5.221 **swMO,** *Scoop board. . .* A broad board used to facilitate the unloading of grain from a wagon. **1965** *Good Old Days* Dec. 7 **nwIL,** He was wearing red woolen underwear. . . [M]other. . . called to him to pull up his "scoop board", that was what we called the rear of the panties.

scooper n [See quots] **=shoveler.**

1962 Imhof *AL Birds* 139, *Spatula clypeata. . .* Spoonbill, Scooper. . . This medium-sized duck has a *tremendous bill,* longer and wider than its head, and usually held pointed downward at an angle. **1982** Elman *Hunter's Field Guide* 160, *Shoveler. . . Common & regional names . .* scooper. [*Ibid* 163, The shoveler paddles about, head partially submerged, so that algae, vegetable debris, or any other edible particles flow into its large open bill.]

scooping See **scoop** v

scoop shovel n

1 A shovel with a deep scoop used primarily to shovel grain or other loose materials; also fig. **esp Cent, Upper MW**

[**1843** in 1850 Hines *Voyage Round World* 160, With the help of . . a couple of scoop-shovel canoes, we succeeded in crossing without accident.] [*DARE* Ed: The reference is to a canoe suggestive of a scoop-shovel in shape.] **1855** Thomson *Doesticks* 218 **NYC,** [The picture] is either a female rag-picker with a scoop-shovel, or a Virginia wench with a hoe-cake in her hand. **1902** (1969) Sears *Catalogue* 668, *Scoop Shovels. . .* Steel Scoop. . . A first class farmer's scoop. [Illustration in text] **1928** *Ruppenthal Coll.* **KS,** *Scoop shovel. . .* A shovel of large capacity by having high sides and back. However large the area of the flat part of a shovel, it is not called a scoop or scoop shovel unless both sides and the back part towards the handle are relatively high to the flat part. **1937** *AmSp* 12.103 **eNE** [Farm terms], The compound *scoop-shovel* refers to the tool used in scooping grain. **1938** Hertzler *Horse & Buggy Dr.* 73 **KS** (as of early 20th cent), I may mention incidentally that when the snow was deep, a scoop shovel, wire cutters and a hammer were as much a part of my equipment as was my Colt six-shooter and medicine and instrument bags. **1942** Warnick *Garrett Co. MD* 13 **nwMD** (as of 1900–18), *Scoop-shovel . .* scoop. **1942** McAtee *Dial. Grant Co. IN* 55 (as of 1890s), *Scoop-shovel . .* this example of tautology was always used in specifying a certain type of shovel. **1966** *DARE* Tape **OK**40, [FW:] How does that scoop race work? [Inf:] You just tie a rope to a scoop and a little boy gets in it and rides it. . . and that horse will run it. Just sit down in a old scoop shovel and rides it. **1967–70** *DARE* (Qu. EE24a, *When there's snow, children go down the hill on a _____*) Inf **IL**113, Scoop shovel; (Qu. LL4, *Very large: "He took a _____ helping of potatoes."*) Inf **MO**21, Scoop shovel. **1968** *DARE* Tape **IN**42, I think right now that we have one scoop shovel. We use it in case of an absolute emergency. **1973** Allen *LAUM* 1.219 **Upper MW** (as of c1950), *Sled. . .* Terms for a vehicle traveling over snow. . . scoop shovel [3 infs, **ND**]. **1981** *DARE* File **cIA, csWI,** *Scoop shovel. . .* Used currently, I believe; certainly in the 50's and 60's. A grain shovel of hollowed-out shape, the shovel part about 16″ wide and 20″ long, used to "scoop" shelled or ear corn, oats or soybeans from or into a wagon or bin. Also used to scoop feed or even snow. The term describes what you do with the shovel. The two words are inseparable when referring to this kind and size of shovel. You might shovel corn, of course, but most farmers would scoop it with a scoop shovel, I'd guess.

2 See **scoop** n **1**.

scoosh See **scooch**

scoot v

1 To eject (a liquid) in a jet; with *down:* to wash (something) with a jet of water. [Scots, nEngl, nIr dial *scoot, scout*] **esp Sth** Cf **scoot horn, scoots, skeet** v **4**

1909 *DN* 3.366 **eAL, wGA,** *Scoot.* . . To squirt, eject forcibly. **1967** *DARE* FW Addit **AR55,** I don't know whether it'd burn in that safe or not. They'd scoot [skut] water on it. **1971** O'Connor *Complete Stories* 493 **cGA,** "Claude scoots them [=hogs] down with the hose every afternoon and washes off the floor." . . "I know I wouldn't scoot down no hog with no hose." **1990** *DARE* File **FL, GA,** *Scoot* . . 'to eject or squirt.' Now, friends of mine (one from Panama City, Florida; the other from Savannah, Georgia) . . have just that usage.

2 intr (rarely refl): To slide oneself along; esp to move (over, down, etc) on a bench or the like so as to make room for another person. **widespread exc NEast, C Atl** See Map

1937 *Hall Coll.* **wNC, eTN,** *Scoot.* . . To move, make room. Scoot over, like you had a family. (Request to make room, as at table, when others come in unexpectedly—request to make room for others). **1950** *WELS (To move over (for example, on a long bench) without getting up: "Can you _____ and make room for one more?")* 1 inf, **cWI,** Scoot over—occasional. **1954** *Harder Coll.* **cwTN,** *Scoot over.* . . To move over. "Scoot over so's I can set down." "Scoot yeself over 'n make some room." **c1960** *Wilson Coll.* **csKY,** *Scoot over*—move over. **1965–70** *DARE* (Qu. Y52, *To move over—for example on a long bench: ". . . Can you _____ [a little]?"*) 193 Infs, **widespread exc NEast, C Atl,** Scoot over; 27 Infs, **chiefly Sth, S Midl,** Scoot down; 19 Infs, 13 **IN, MO,** Scoot; **MI116, NM2,** Scoot along [Of all Infs responding to the question, 36% were young or mid-aged; of those giving these resps, 48% were young or mid-aged.]; (Qu. Y34b, *What babies do before they walk*) Infs **CA59, KY28, 94, PA134, VA102,** Scoot; **CA53,** Scoot on their behinds; **CO20,** Some scoot; **CO47,** Scoot on their ass—some do; **OK31,** Scoot—the way a baby moves sitting up and wiggling. [All 9 Infs at Qu. Y34b also offered the resp "crawl."] **1986** Pederson *LAGS Concordance (The baby crawls)* 2 infs, **TN, TX,** Scoot; 1 inf, **cwTN,** Scoot (on the floor); 1 inf, **neLA,** Scoot (along the floor . . crawl rapidly).

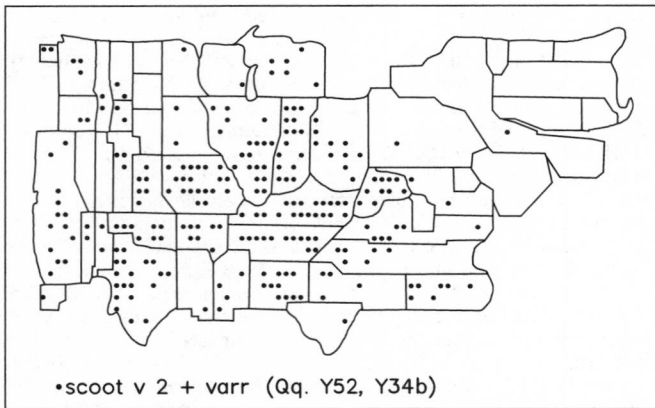

•scoot v 2 + varr (Qq. Y52, Y34b)

3 usu with *down:* To crouch down, compress oneself. [Infl by **scooch 1**]

1943 *LANE* Map 581 *(Crouch),* 2 infs, **MA,** Scoot down. **1967** *DARE* (Qu. Y32, *To squeeze yourself into a small space: "If you're going to fit in there you'll have to _____."*) Inf **OH4,** Scoot down; **WA26,** Crunch down; scoot. **1986** Pederson *LAGS Concordance (Crouch),* 2 infs, **FL, MS,** Scoot down; 1 inf, **ceTN,** Scooted down.

scoot n[1] Also *scooter*

1 also *log scoot, scoot sled:* A stout sled with a single pair of runners used for hauling logs or other heavy objects. **chiefly NEng** Cf **bob** n[3] **1, crotch** n[1] **3, dray** n **1**

1905 U.S. Forest Serv. *Bulletin* 61.46 [Logging terms], *Scoot.* . . Dray. **1907** *DN* 3.249 **eME,** *Scoot.* . . Same as *bob.* **1965** [see **scow** n[1] **1**]. **1966–69** *DARE* (Qu. N40a, . . *Sleighs . . for hauling loads*) Inf **MA23,**

Log scoot; **NH10,** Scoot—for logging; **ME5,** Scoot sled—for logging—even on bare ground—wooden runners; (QR near Qu. N41b) Inf **MN19,** Scoot—for short heavy loads—also called stone-boat; **MA36,** Scoot—sleds used for logging. **1966** *DARE* Tape **ME6,** [FW:] And on these scoots or sleds that carry them on, what were they built like? [Inf:] They built 'em out of just wood with sides about 12–14 inches high [with] bunks on 'em. . . That's a crossbeam between the two sides of your scoot, roll your logs onto 'em. *Ibid* **ME18,** Course, when it was dry when there was no snow we'd use what they'd call scoot that was made out of planks sawed out of, well, [we] most always used spruce. **1969** Sorden *Lumberjack Lingo* 104 **NEng, Gt Lakes,** *Scoot.* . . A sled used to haul logs out of the woods by placing one end of the log on the sled. **1971** *DARE* File **cwWI,** Scoot or jumper. . . It is homemade with narrower runners than the stoneboat and . . sometimes shod with strap iron. Rather than being long, it was square, and had built-up sides (boxed) all round deep enough so a plank could be laid across for a seat. **1975** Gould *ME Lingo* 244, *Scoot*—A farm and timberland vehicle without wheels which slides on bare ground much as a toboggan or sled would. A *stone boat* (stone drag) is a kind of *scoot* and is often called a stone *scoot.* In the *twitching* of logs, a single log would usually be pulled from the woods to the brow by a team. The *scoot* would have several logs loaded on it to be drawn forth by the same horse-power. There was a considerable coefficient of friction to a *scoot,* but its advantage was in its closeness to the ground; logs could be rolled on and off easily with a *canthook,* and no rollway was needed. **1981** *Blair & Ketchum's Country Jrl.* June 7 **ceVT,** "These logs come from quite a ways up the hill whar they ain't no roads," he replied. "We can't use wagons. . . Besides the scooter works as well on leaves and sech as it would on snow. . . We call this a scooter up here. I made it myself. Oak runners and ash shoes."

2 A sled used for coasting on snow. **chiefly NEast**

1943 *LANE* Maps 573–574 *(Sled; sleigh)* A crude small sled with a barrel-stave runner . . scooter [3 infs, **VT,** 1 inf, **NH,** scoot [1 inf, **NH,** 1 inf, **ME**] . . a low sled with solid sides coming to a point in front, often home-made . . scooter [1 inf, **VT**]. **1967–69** *DARE* (Qu. EE24a, *When there's snow, children go down the hill on a _____*) Infs **NY23, VT16,** Scooter; **CT23,** Scooter—tin pan or any piece of metal; **IA3,** Scooter—nowadays; **NY92,** Scooter—barrel stave with an upright piece and a seat nailed to it; **OH70, WI29,** Scoot.

scoot n[2]

A piece of inferior or defective lumber.

1932 Wasson *Sailing Days* 20 **cME coast,** Slightly defective lumber known as "scoots," . . was also often thrown overboard from the mills or sold locally for a nominal sum. *Ibid,* Good-looking houses in coast towns many miles distant were pointed out with a grin as being built entirely of "scoots" from "Bangor River." **1956** Sorden-Ebert *Logger's Words* 30 **Gt Lakes,** *Scoot.* . . An inferior and practically worthless piece of hardwood lumber. **1964** Clarkson *Tumult* 370 **WV,** *Scoot*—Lumber that is very defective and practically worthless. **1975** Gould *ME Lingo* 245, *Scoots*—Reject lumber (it was tossed on a *scoot* to be hauled away from the mill carriage). Either given away or sold cheaply, *scoots* were a speculation cargo for Maine vessels. With good lumber in the hold, and a load of *scoots* on deck, the captain might turn a penny on the *scoots* and keep it for himself.

scoot n[3] [Cf *EDD scoot* sb.[2] "A term of contempt applied to both men and women"] Cf **scutter** n[1]

A rascal.

1906 *DN* 3.155 **nwAR,** *Scoot.* . . Rascal. "He's an old scoot." **1967** *DARE* (Qu. Z12, *Nicknames and joking words meaning 'a small child': "He's a healthy little _____."*) Inf **OH25,** Scoot.

scoot n[4]

1 also *scoot train:* A train; see quots.

c1870 Chipman *Notes on Bartlett* 385 (*DAE*), 'Scoot train,' one that omits stopping at a particular station; an express train. New England. **1907** *DN* 3.249 **eME,** *Scoot (train).* . . Suburban railway train. "He was killed by the scoot as he was crossing the track." **1943** *AmSp* 18.169, *Scoot.* Shuttle train. **1950** *WELS (A train that stops at every station along the way)* 1 inf, **seWI,** Scoot. **1968** *DARE* (Qu. N37, *Joking names for a branch railroad that is not very important or gives poor service*) Inf **WI72,** Bayfield scoot.

2 See **scooter** n[2].

scootberry n [See quot 1891]

A **twisted-stalk** (here: *Streptopus amplexifolius* and *S. lanceolatus*).

1891 *Jrl. Amer. Folkl.* 4.149 **MA,** *Streptopus roseus* [=*Streptopus* lanceolatus] I learned to call Scoot-berry long before I understood why it was so called. The sweetish berries were quite eagerly eaten by boys, always acting as physic, and as the diarrhoea was locally called "the scoots," the plant at once received that name. **1943** Fernald–Kinsey *Edible Wild Plants E. N. Amer.* 136, *Streptopus* (2 species). . . The pulpy, pendulous, red or scarlet berries . . are known to country boys in other parts of northern New England as *Scoot-berries*. . . The berries are cathartic. **1976** Bailey–Bailey *Hortus Third* 1081, [*Streptopus*] *amplexifolius*. . . Amer. plants . . have been distinguished as var. *americanus* . . *scootberry*.

scootch See **scooch**

scoot down See **scoot** v 1, 3

scooter n¹

1 also *scooter plow, scooting* ~, also sp *scouter, scuter*: A type of plow with a narrow share; see quots. **chiefly S Atl** See Map Cf **bull tongue 1**

1820 *Henderson's N.C. Almanac* (1823) 25 *(DA)*, The ridges are opened with a small plow called a scooter, something like a shovel plow. **1842** in 1969 Turner *Cotton Planter's Manual* 55 **AL**, The next operation to be performed . . is to plough out the middles *well* . . with a good shovel-plough, having first run around the young plant with a scooter-plough. **1851** in 1927 Jones *FL Plantation Rec.* 439 **nwFL**, Rec'd 6 scooter Ploughs, three axes and one Bush knife. *Ibid* 118 **nwFL**, 18 scuter ploughs. **1867** *Harper's Weekly* 2 Feb 69 **AL**, A small plow called a "scouter" is then used to cut the furrows for the seed. **1883** GA Dept. Ag. *Pub. Circular No. 34* 8.35, I . . ridged with small scooter furrow and bedded with turning plow, and run in bottom of furrow with scooter deep. Broke out middles with scooter. . . First plowing done with sweeps, second with small scooter. *Ibid* 37, When the wheat had attained a height of 2 ½ feet it was thoroughly plowed with a scooter. **1909** *DN* 3.366 **eAL, wGA**, Scooter. . . A kind of narrow plow,—so called because it makes the earth 'scoot.' **1927** Jones *FL Plantation Rec.* 589 **nwFL**, Scooter ("scuter"): a bull-tongue ploughshare which when used alone makes a narrow furrow. For cultivating the crop a scooter is often bolted upon a "scrape", which has slanting horizontal wings. The scooter facilitates control of depth, while the scrape breaks the crust in a considerable swath. **1947** Lomax *Advent. Ballad Hunter* vii **TX** (as of 1870s), Years ago I used to chant this rhyme as I dropped seed corn into a freshly turned furrow. I followed close behind a scooter, pulled by two sturdy mules, that ripped open a trench in the warm earth. **1965–70** *DARE* (Qu. L18, *Kinds of plows*) Infs **FL**50, **GA**9, 14, 22, **OK**14, **SC**19, 47, Scooter; **FL**37, Scooter plow; **LA**18, Scooter stock; (Qu. L25, *The implement used to . . loosen the earth*) Infs **GA**16, 77, 87, Scooter; **AL**15, Scooter and a sweep. **1972** *Atlanta Letters* **neGA**, A scooter is something you plow with. **1973** *DARE* File **swGA**, Scooter—A type of plow the share of which is supported by a running wheel, the "scooter," the setting of which regulates the depth of the penetration of the share in the soil. Sumter Co., Ga. **1986** Pederson *LAGS Concordance* **Gulf Region**, 22 infs, (A) scooter; 10 infs, Scooter plow(s); 6 infs, Scooters; 1 inf, Scooting plow; 1 inf, Single scooter.

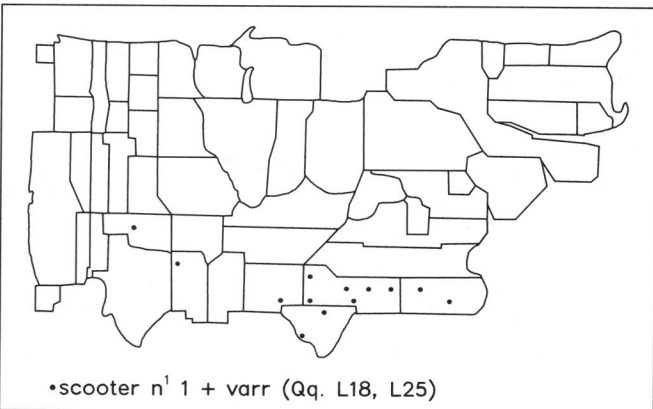

• scooter n¹ 1 + varr (Qq. L18, L25)

2 See **scoot** n¹.

scooter n² Also *scoot*

A **barracuda** (here: *Sphyraena argentea*).

1946 LaMonte *N. Amer. Game Fishes* 18, *Sphyraena argentea*. . . Scoots, Scooters. . . Most abundant off California in spring and summer.

scooter n³ [Prob folk-etym]
=**scoter.**

1911 *Forest & Stream* 77.453, Local North Carolina names . . are as follows: . . Scooters. **1918** Grinnell *Game Birds CA* 195, Scooters. . . from their habits . . are often called "Scooters." Typical sea ducks, they are to be found almost entirely on salt water. **1923** U.S. Dept. Ag. *Misc. Circular* 13.27 **CT, NY, NC**, Scooters. . . Collective Vernacular Names. . . In local use. . . Scooters. **1953** Jewett *Birds WA* 147, *Melanitta deglandi dixoni*. . . Scooter. *Ibid* 148, *Melanitta perspicillata*. . . Scooter. *Ibid* 150, *Oidemia* [=*Melanitta*] *nigra americana*. . . Scooter; Scooter. **1966** *DARE* Tape **ME**10, We have what we call scooters; they're sea birds. . . These . . scooters are diving birds. There's, oh, several different species. **1982** Elman *Hunter's Field Guide* 237, American Scoter. . . Common & regional names . . scooter. *Ibid* 240, Surf Scoter . . scooter.

scooter n⁴ See **scutter** n¹

scooter plow See **scooter** n¹ 1

scoot horn n Also *scout horn* [Prob from **scoot** v 1; cf *OED2 skeet* sb. and **skeet** v 4]
See quot 1884.

1855 Hammett *Wonderful Advent.* 183 **Long Is NY**, He contented himself with . . keeping his hands busy with the scoot-horn wetting the sails. **1884** U.S. Natl. Museum *Bulletin* 27.779, *Scout-horn.* A wooden pole having a piece of a leather boot-leg fastened to one end so as to form a scoop. . . Used in former years to wet the sails of small vessels in order to make them set flat and hold the wind when sailing close-hauled. **1896** *DN* 1.423 **MA**, *Scoot-horn:* a leather cup with a long handle, for throwing water from the sea to the mast-head. Marblehead, Mass.

scooting plow See **scooter** n¹ 1

scoots n pl, but sg in constr; freq with *the* Also *backdoor scoots* [Cf *EDD scoot* sb.⁶ 9 "Diarrhœa, esp in cattle."] Cf **backdoor trot, scoot** v 1
Diarrhea.

1891 [see **scootberry**]. **1950** *WELS (Joking names for . . looseness of the bowels)* 1 Inf, **swWI**, Scoots. **1965–70** *DARE* (Qu. BB19) Infs **CA**87, 123, **CO**14, **IL**126, **KS**15, **NY**105, **OH**70, **SD**8, (The) scoots; **CA**127, Backdoor scoots. **1975** *AmSp* 50.65 **AR** (as of c1970), Scoots . . Diarrhea—"Eating Pomfret [Hall] food gives me the scoots." [**1995** Brophy *Coll.* 65 **swMO** (as of c1960), Scoots, the. [D]ysentery.]

scoot sled See **scoot** n¹ 1

scoot train See **scoot** n⁴ 1

scope n [Ir dial; cf *OED2 scope* sb.² 10, *EDD scope* sb.¹ 2] **Sth, S Midl**
A tract, expanse, patch (of land, woods, etc).

1895 *DN* 1.374 **seKY, eTN, wNC**, Scope of land: tract of land. "My brother has a big scope o' land." **1930** *VA Qrly. Rev.* 6.244 **AR**, An up-country Arkansawyer . . may own a scope of land. **1936** *AmSp* 11.317 **Ozarks**, Scope. . . A large area or extent. 'They got a big scope o' road t' grade up this winter.' **1939** *Hall Coll.* **eTN**, You go through a scope of woodland. *Ibid* **wNC**, A scope of seng. **1941** *Hench Coll.* **ceAL**, 'Scope' of woods. . . The word describes a patch that can be seen around. **c1960** *Wilson Coll.* **csKY**, Scope. . . "A fine scope of timber." **1965** Will *Okeechobee Boats* 8 **FL**, That made him the owner of a huge scope of territory. **1966–70** *DARE* (Qu. C29, *A good-sized stretch of level land with practically no trees*) Infs **GA**3, **NC**87, (Clear) scope of land; (Qu. T1, . . *A bunch of trees growing together in open country, especially on a hill*) Inf **MS**1, Scope of trees; **TN**62, Scope; (Qu. T2a, . . *A piece of land covered with trees . . only a few acres*) Infs **GA**77, **TN**30, Scope of woods. **1974** (1975) Shaw *All God's Dangers* 23 **AL** [Black], Got to the woods that day. . . Place we called Cold Tree, in a big scope of woods cuttin ties for Mr. Jim Flint. **1986** Pederson *LAGS Concordance*, 1 inf, **csTN**, Scope of timber—stand of woodland; 1 inf, **nwLA**, Scope of woods—narrow area between two fields; 1 inf, **neAL**, Scope of woods—small patch of woods. **1995** Brophy *Coll.* 65 **swMO** (as of c1960), Scope. [A] stretch or piece of land.

scopeberry n Cf **scootberry**
See quots.

1941 *LANE* Map 274 **cCT**, Names of berries incidentally recorded. . . Scopeberries [skoᵁpbɛrɪz]. **1969** *DARE* (Qu. BB19, *Joking names for* *looseness of the bowels*) Inf **MI**110, Loose as a goose in scopeberry time.

scorch v[1] [*EDD scorch* v.[1] 1 "To shrivel up, caused by frost or cold"; cf also *OED2 scorch* v.[1] 1.d]
To shrivel or nip with cold; hence ppl adj, adv *scorching;* n *scorcher* a killing frost; a period of very cold weather.

1806 in 1965 *AmSp* 40.199 **NY,** Now we have a very cold spell to day Simon Voris has my mare to go to York & he will be Schorched with the cold. [*DARE* Ed: The author of this diary was born and raised in Ireland, but had been in the US since at least 1790.] **1856** in 1927 Jones *FL Plantation Rec.* 472 **nwFL,** Cotton is scorched by the frost. **1876** in 1969 *PADS* 52.54 **seIL,** Another scortching [*sic*] cold morning. **1890** *Harper's New Mth. Mag.* 81.862, But the scorching frost deters: we prefer to remain in the cozy 'Yokohama'. **1916** *DN* 4.281 **NE,** Scorcher. . . Used in expressions like "That was the coldest winter we ever had. It was a scorcher." [*DN* Ed: Also N. Car., Pa., Ill., Kan.] **1967** *DARE* FW Addit **LA**11, Scorched—darkened by frost. Common. **1968** *DARE* (Qu. B30, *A frost that kills plants is a* _____) Inf **UT**5, Scorcher. **2000** *NADS Letters* **cnPA,** We often said that plants were "scorched" by frost. However, I am not familiar with "scorcher" meaning a period of cold weather. *Ibid* **IN,** Scorch—"extreme *cold*"—one student from Terre Haute had grandparents, also from Indiana, who used *scorch* in this way. *Ibid* **nwTN,** After a frost the plants that were killed would have been said to be scorched. *Ibid* **csIL,** Scorch in the sense of "damaged by frost" is known to me from my farm-boy days in northern Pope County, IL. No one ever said "scorcher" for a cold spell. . . I remember it in the past tense, as in "The frost scorched the tomato plants last night." *Ibid* **cCA,** I have heard almond growers in my area of Calif. to refer to frost damage to almond tree leaves as being "scorched."

scorch v[2] [Perh folk-etym from aphet *'scort,* or generalized from *'scort you* pronounced ['skoɚˈču]]
To escort.
1934 Hurston *Jonah's Gourd Vine* 114 **AL** [Black], Mis' Potts, kin Ah scorch Mis' Lucy home? **1948** Hurston *Seraph* 6 **wFL,** It called for lots of persistence and a thick hide to "scorch" Arvay Henson home.

scorch v[3] See **scotch** v[1] 1

scorch n See **scotch** n

scorch cloth n
1985 *Amer. Jrl. Med.* Feb 183 **eTN,** Scorch cloth . . a cloth that has been burnt to the point of charring and that is believed to be beneficial in drawing out corruption.

scorcher, scorching See **scorch** v[1]

scoria lily n
A **stickleaf** (here: *Mentzelia decapetala*).
1950 Stevens *ND Plants* 210, *Mentzelia decapetala.* . . *Evening Star.* "Scoria Lily." . . On buttes in burned, crumbled clay ("scoria"), or on clay slopes.

scoripin See **scorpion**

scorn v
1 To ridicule, show contempt for. [*OED2 scorn* v 2 "Obs.";
→1631]
1933 *AmSp* 8.1.51 **Ozarks,** Scorn. . . To ridicule, or even to slander. *That Baines gal jest scorns her kinfolks somethin' turrible, ever' chancet she gits.*
2 in phr *scorn one's name up:* To incur disgrace, expose oneself to condemnation.
1931 Hughes–Hurston *Mule Bone* 122 **cFL** [Black], An' Daisy better not leave them white folks' house today to come traipsin' over here scornin' her name all up wid dis nigger mess. **1934** Hurston *Jonah's Gourd Vine* 218 **AL** [Black], Dey tell me you eben drawed uh knife on yo' son John, 'cause he tried tuh keep dat strumpet out his mama's feather bed . . and nobody but uh low-down woman would want you scornin' yo' name all up lak dat.

scorn n Also *scorning play*
A kissing game; see quots.
1883 Newell *Games & Songs* 126 **NEng,** Scorn. . . An amusement of a not very agreeable nature, familiar at children's parties in New England. A girl was seated on a chair in the middle of the room, and one child after another was led to her throne. She would turn away with an expression of contempt, until someone approached that pleased her, who, after a kiss, took her place. **1975** McDonough *Garden Sass* 180 **AR** [Black], We used to play Scornin' Plays . . you put the two chairs together—side by side—one facing one way and one facing the other. A girl sits in one chair looking straight ahead and a boy comes up, sits down in the other chair, and tries to kiss her. If the girl doesn't want the boy to kiss her she turns away (scorns him), and another boy comes. When she lets a boy kiss her she leaves and another girl comes and sits down.

scorn one's name up See **scorn** v 2

scorpion n Usu |'skɔrpɪən|; also |'skɑrpɪən|; also **scattered Sth, S Midl, SW** |'skɔrpən, -pɪn, -pin|; for addit varr see quots Pronc-spp *scarapin, scarpion, scorpeen, scor(r)ipin, skyarpin*
A Forms.
1837 Sherwood *Gaz.* GA 71, *Scoripin, scorpion.* **1890** *DN* 1.66 **KY,** *Scorripin* [skɔrɪpɪn]: scorpion. **1899** Bergen *Animal Lore* 62, Skyarpin (for scorpion), a common lizard, *Sceloporus. Southern.* **1909** *DN* 3.366 **eAL, wGA,** *Scorripin.* . . Scorpion. Rare. **1915** *Copeia* 18.6 **cwVA,** *Eumeces fasciatus.* . . "Scorpion" or "scarapin." **1926** TX Folkl. Soc. *Pub.* 5.61, The red-headed skink, or "scarpion," is common in the timbered regions of the South. . . In the negro vernacular, scorpion, or "scarpion," means a poisonous animal. **1942** Hall *Smoky Mt. Speech* 65 **wNC, eTN,** Scorpion ['skɔɚpən]. **1965–70** *DARE* (Qu. R21) Infs **AL**29, 30, 32, ['skɑrpɪən]; **AL**6, [skɑrpɪn]; **CA**136, Scorpeen ['skɔrpɪn]; **GA**77, ['skɔrpɪn]; **IN**3, [skɔrpɪn]; **OK**13, [skɑpən]; **SC**3, ['skɔɚpɪn]; **SC**46, ['skɔɚpən]; **TX**32, [skɔrpɪn]; **TX**71, ['skɔrpənz]; **TX**73, ['skɔərpɪn].
B Senses.
1 Std: an arachnid of the order Scorpiones, or a similar arachnid of such orders as Amblypygi, Pseudoscorpionida, Solifugida, and Uropygi. Also called **alacran, hot tail 1, santapee 2, scroncher, stinging lizard, stinging scorpion;** for other names of var of these see **vinegarone, wind scorpion**
2 also *scorpion lizard:* Any of var **lizards 1,** esp a **blue-tailed skink,** a **fence lizard 1** (here: *Sceloporus undulatus*), or a **green lizard 1** (here: *Anolis carolinensis*). **chiefly Sth, Midl** Cf **blue scorpion, red-head(ed)** ~
1709 (1967) Lawson *New Voyage* 136 **NC, SC,** The Scorpion Lizard is no more like a Scorpion than a Hedge-Hog; but they very commonly call him a Scorpion. He is of the Lizard Kind, but much bigger; his Back is of a dark Copper-Colour; his Belly an Orange; he is very nimble in running up Trees, or on the Land, and is accounted very poisonous. He has the most Sets of Teeth in his Mouth and Throat, that ever I saw. **1797** (1905) Latrobe *Jrl. of Latrobe* 110 **VA,** The steep gravelly knoll . . abounds in snakes and scorpions, as a poisonous lizard with a red head and a green body is here very improperly called. **1827** Williams *View W. FL* 28, The largest [lizard] is about seven inches long. . . The old inhabitants call him the scorpion. **1851** *De Bow's Rev.* 11.53 **LA,** Lizards, . . of four kinds, 1st, copper-headed, brown bodied, called scorpions, 2d, blue-tailed, striped bodied, also called scorpions. **1859** Gosse *Letters from AL* 188, A day or two since I had the pleasure of discovering, in a little hollow, beneath a decaying log, a nest of our commonest lizard (*Agama undulata* [=*Sceloporus u.*]), vulgarly called here the Scorpion. **1894** U.S. Natl. Museum *Proc.* 17.321 **FL,** *Eumeces fasciatus.* . . This lizard is rather common in south Florida under rotten logs and stumps and similar places. . . Strange to say, it is called "scorpion," . . and regarded as "awfully poisonous." **1899** [see **A** above]. **1903** *DN* 2.328 **seMO,** Scorpion. . . A small lizard. **1907** *DN* 3.235 **nwAR,** Scorpion. . . A small lizard. **1916** *DN* 4.270 **sLA,** Scorpion. . . Misnomer for a certain small lizard (*Oligosoma laterale* [=*Scincella l.*]). **1925** TX Folkl. Soc. *Pub.* 4.51 **nwLA,** In the folk-tales of northern Louisiana there seems to be no particular distinction between the several species of lizards—all are "scorpions" and poisonous. **1927** *AmSp* 2.363 **cwWV,** Scorpion . . a little lizard. "See that scorpion on the fence." **1931** Randolph *Ozarks* 70, A *scorpion* is not a scorpion, either, but a little blue-tailed skink, quite harmless—the real scorpion is known as a *stingin'-lizard!* **1943** Weslager *DE Forgotten Folk* 179, If a scorpion lizard crawls completely around your waist, you will die. When a scorpion lizard gets mad his tail flies off. A new one will soon grow on the stump. **1955** *DE Folkl. Bulletin* 1.17, As she stooped to pick up a certain piece [of firewood] she saw a blue-throated "scorpion lizard" (fence lizard) resting on it. The male lizard is thought to be poisonous. **c1960** *Wilson Coll.* **csKY,** Scorpion—the blue-tailed skink (*Eumeces*

fasciatus), regarded as very poisonous. The real scorpion, though found occasionally in the area, is probably not known to two dozen people. **1966–70** *DARE* (Qu. R21, . . *Other kinds of stinging insects*) Inf **IN**3, Scorpion—refers to a lizard; **SC**3, Scorpion—blue and white-striped supposed to be very poisonous—red-headed; **KY**28, Blue scorpion; **VA**46, Red-headed scorpion; (Qu. P32, . . *Other kinds of wild animals*) Inf **SC**63, Scorpion—a lizard—harmless. **1999** *DARE* File **seMO** (as of 1950s), I encountered "scorpion" used to refer to a skink (reptile, lizard). Concurrent (and obviously needed) was the use of "stingin' lizard" to refer to the poisonous arachnid. . . The skink does not sting, though it will bite if you succeed in catching one.

3 A turtle such as the **spotted turtle**; see quots.

1952 Carr *Turtles* 118, Elsewhere [=not in upper NY] it [=*Clemmys guttata*] is called "scorpion," adding another and most extraordinary misuse to that much-abused term. **1968** *DARE* (Qu. P24, . . *Kinds of turtles*) Inf **DE**1, Scorpion—I don't know what that is, but it's a kind of turtle.

4 Any of var fishes; see below. **Pacific**

a A **scorpion fish** (here: *Scorpaena guttata*).

1882 *U.S. Natl. Museum Bulletin* 16.679, *S[corpaena] guttata*. . . Scorpion. . . Coast of California, . . very abundant. **1884** [see **B**4b below]. **1898** *U.S. Natl. Museum Bulletin* 47.1847, *Scorpaena guttata*. . . Scorpion. . . Cranial spines high, bluntish. . . A good food-fish.

b A **sculpin 1** of the family Cottidae, usu the **cabezon.**

1884 Goode *Fisheries U.S.* 1.259, *Scorpaenichthys marmoratus*. . . The names "Cabezon," "Sculpin," "Scorpion," . . and "Biggy-head" are applied to this species. . . The names "Sculpin," "Scorpion" . . are applied to various other species, and are rather collective than specific names. *Ibid* 263, *Scorpaena guttata*. . . is known by the names . . "Scorpion," and "Sculpin."

c A **thornyhead** (here: *Sebastolobus alascanus*).

1953 Roedel *Common Fishes CA* 136, *Channel Rockfish—Sebastolobus alascanus*. . . *Unauthorized Names:* Idiot, channel cod, scorpion.

scorpion bile n Also *scorpion juice*
Whiskey, esp of an inferior kind.

1865 in 1926 Twain *Sketches* 163 **ceCA**, Our reserve [voters were] . . full of chain lightning, sudden death and scorpion-bile. **1966** *DARE* (Qu. DD21c, *Nicknames for whiskey, especially illegally made whiskey*) Inf **OK**42, Scorpion juice; (Qu. DD31, *Joking names for homemade hard liquor;* total Infs questioned, 75) Inf **OK**42, Scorpion juice. **1968** Adams *Western Words* 270, Scorpion Bible [sic]—A logger's name for inferior whisky. **1974** Dabney *Mountain Spirits* 25 **sAppalachians**, The names [=for corn whiskey] go on: "scorpion juice." **1989** Oliver *Hazel Creek* 26 **wNC** (as of c1900), He made periodic visits to Hazel Creek and once told my grandmother . . that some of his "scorpion juice" would be good for what ailed her.

scorpion fish n
Std: any of var fishes of the family Scorpaenidae, esp those of the genus *Scorpaena*. For other names of these see **nohu 2, ocean catfish 2, scorpion B4a, sculpin 2**

scorpion grass n [*OED2* 1578 →] Cf **scorpionweed 1**
=**forget-me-not 1a.**

1814 Bigelow *Florula Bostoniensis* 47, *Myosotis scorpioides*. . . *Mouse ear Scorpion grass*. . . Flowers pointing one way, small, rose coloured. **1901** Lounsberry *S. Wild Flowers* 446, *Spring Scorpion-grass*. . . Earlier in the season than any other of its relatives, this pubescent little thing unfolds its bloom on dry hillsides. **1933** Small *Manual SE Flora* 1124, *Myosotis*. . . About 35 species, of wide geographical distribution. . . *Scorpion-grasses*. **1946** Reeves–Bain *Flora TX* 138, Scorpion Grass. . Dry soil, often in woods. Spring. **1973** Hitchcock–Cronquist *Flora Pacific NW* 395, *Myosotis*. . . Scorpion-grass.

scorpion juice See **scorpion bile**

scorpion lizard See **scorpion B2**

scorpion mouse n **SW**

1 =**grasshopper mouse.**

1890 *Stock Grower & Farmer* (Las Vegas NM) 4 Jan 7/2, The most curious of all was a little beast that I shall name the "scorpion mouse," because it appears to feed upon scorpions exclusively. **1947** Carr *Desert Parade* 21 **Desert SW**, Grasshopper Mouse, Scorpion Mouse. [*Ibid* 22, The grasshopper mouse. . . feeds upon insects, including grass-

hoppers, and, as might be expected from one of its names, it will also eat poisonous scorpions—a strange diet, to say the least, but food is where one finds it!] **1980** Whitaker *Audubon Field Guide Mammals* 482, The Scorpion Mouse digs its burrows or appropriates those of other small mammals. . . Before killing scorpions, the deadly tail is immobilized.

2 A **white-footed mouse** (here: *Peromyscus maniculatus*).

1947 Cahalane *Mammals* 463, One of its [=grasshopper mouse's] alternate names is "scorpion mouse," acquired from its habit of preying on those fearsome creatures. (For the same reason, this name is even more frequently applied to the Sonoran white-footed mouse.)

scorpionweed n

1 =**forget-me-not 1a.** Cf **scorpion grass**

1818 Eaton *Botany* 325, *Myosotis*. . . *scorpioides* . . scorpion weed. **1897** *Jrl. Amer. Folkl.* 10.51 **West**, *Myosotis*, sp., scorpion weed.

2 A plant of the genus *Phacelia*. [See quot 1985] **chiefly West** Also called **blue curls 3, fiddleneck 2, wild heliotrope;** for other names of var spp see **Aunt Lucy 2, blue spiderweed, California bluebell 2, caterpillar B1, johnny-jump-up 2c, Miami mist, snail flower, spiderflower, wild Canterbury bell**

1935 (1943) Muenscher *Weeds* 377, *Phacelia Purshii*. . . Scorpion weed, a native annual, is locally common in gardens, grain fields, clover fields and waste places in the north central states. **1940** Gates *Flora KS* 177, *Phacelia hirta*. . . Scorpionweed. Dry soil in open woods, ravines, and thickets along streams. **1954** Harrington *Manual Plants CO* 451, *Phacelia*. . . Scorpion Weed. **1970** Kirk *Wild Edible Plants W. U.S.* 74, *Phacelia ramosissima*. . . Scorpionweed. . . The plant may be used as cooked greens. **1975** Zwinger *Run River* 218 **UT**, Clusters of white mustards, wild four o'clock, skeleton plant and purple scorpionweed are a startling green against the pallid ground. **1985** Dodge *Flowers SW Deserts* 109, *Phacelia* . . Scorpionweed. . . The name scorpionweed comes from the curling habit of the blossoming flower heads which somewhat resemble the flexed tail of a scorpion in striking position.

scorripin See **scorpion**

scotch v[1]

1 also *scorch:* To prevent (esp the wheel of a vehicle) from moving by use of a chock. [*OED2 scotch* v.[2] 1 1642 →] **chiefly Sth, S Midl** Cf **scotch** n

1860 (1861) *U.S. War Dept. Instruction Field Artillery* 64, Should there be anything at hand, the wheels may be scotched. *Ibid* 134, Nos. 6 and 7, after scotching the wheels, go to the trail [of the gun carriage] to assist in raising it. **1899** (1912) Green *VA Folk-Speech* 370, Scotch. . . To prop or block, as the wheel of a coach or waggon, with a stone or other obstacle. **1945** FWP *Lay My Burden Down* 116 **LA** (as of c1865) [Black], All the nigger men have to push on the wheels while the mules pull and then scotch the wheels while the mules rest. **1949** in 1986 *DARE* File **MO**, He was speaking of the tire on his car when he said, "I thought someone had scotched it." **1955** Hench *Coll.* **cVA**, Another person said that in this part of Va. it [=to scotch] meant to prop [a wagon] or keep [a wagon] from rolling down hill by putting a stone behind one or more of the wheels. **1966** Adams *Mt. LeConte* 37 **wNC, eTN**, I "scotched" the car, jacked up the wheel, removed the outer tire rim, pulled out the tube and applied a cold patch. **1972** *Atlanta Letters* **cnGA**, Scotch/To Brace—To put a block under a wheel to keep it from rolling. **1982** *Barrick Coll.* **csPA**, Scorch—v.t. block a wheel; n. a block under a wheel. **1984** Head *Brogans* 116 **eKY, eTN**, To "scotch" a wheel meant to put a rock under it to keep it from rolling. **1991** [see **scotch** n]. **1998** *Appalachian Jrl.* 25.157, The very next Christmas I was trying to help Daddy work on a car. He said, "Scotch that tarh." The car started to roll, and Daddy hollered "Scotch hit!" **1999** *NADS Letters* **ceMS** (as of c1945), When a wagon (or any vehicle) was on a slope and needed to be kept in place one was asked to scotch one wheel, placing a large rock or piece of wood downside of the wheel. **2000** *Ibid* **KY**, "Would you please scotch that tire so the car won't roll back?" Or "Would you scotch a door or shutter to keep it from blowing around?" *Ibid* **csKY**, My husband still uses the term *scotch* meaning to make something sturdy. . . Putting a small piece of wood in a space to make it sturdy . ., he would "scotch" it. *Ibid* **GA, KY, TX, WV**, Scotch a tire (or wheel).

2 Fig: to block, obstruct. [Cf *EDD scotch* v.[1] 4 "To stop, to give up; to hinder"]

1966 Dykeman *Far Family* 211 **swNC**, But I thought it was the Bludsoes themselves scotching your way.

3 refl: To hold (oneself) immobile.

1949 Hornsby *Lonesome Valley* 115 **eKY,** They [=grasshoppers] fluttered from among the briers and sprouts in the pasture, going far enough up to get a good look at everything around and then scotching themselves. They stayed in one spot by whizzing their wings, and pretty soon darted back down to the ground.

4 To support, second; to provide assistance (for one); with *out:* to help out, fill in; hence n *scotcher.*   **Sth, S Midl**

1860 *Harper's New Mth. Mag.* Jan 279 **KY,** The Rev. Judson Nott, a local Methodist preacher in the town of _____, in Southern Kentucky. . . was a good singer, could pray long and loud, and was one of the best "Scotchers" that occupied the "Amen corner" [at a church in another town]. **1890** *DN* 1.66 **KY,** *Scotch the preacher,* to: to say "Amen" and grunt frequently during the sermon. **1909** *DN* 3.366 **eAL, wGA,** *Scotch.* . . To assist one in an undertaking, help out in a minor way. "You go ahead with the job, and I'll scotch for you." **1915** *DN* 4.189 **swVA,** *Scotch for* (one). . . To help out. "I'll scotch for you, if you need me." **1986** Pederson *LAGS Concordance,* 1 inf, **ceAL,** She'd scotch out—of substitute teacher.

5 of a horse: ?To straddle; to splay out the legs.   [Cf *EDD scaut* v. 1 "to dig the feet into the ground in order to gain resistance; to stretch the legs out violently"; *OED2 scotch* v.² 3]

1969 Green *Wild Cow Tales* 104, When you are ridin' a horse in a run and he hits a spot of slick rock, it is natural for him to "scotch" in order to steady himself, which increases the possibility of his falling. *Ibid* 294, We cowboys didn't dare try to hurry our horses as they were scotchin' to try to keep from fallin'.

scotch n Also *scorch* [*OED2 scotch* sb.² 1601 →]   **chiefly Sth, S Midl**   Cf **scotch** v¹ 1

A chock used to keep something, esp the wheel of a vehicle, from moving.

1847 in 1956 Eliason *Tarheel Talk* 149 **nwNC,** [The horse] was fastened to the wheel and the howgs rooted the *skoth* [sic] from under the wheel and frightened him. **1899** (1912) Green *VA Folk-Speech* 370, *Scotch.* . . A prop put behind or before a wheel, to prevent its moving, or placed under a log to keep it from rolling. **1982** [see **scotch** v 1]. **1991** Weals *Last Train* 69 **eTN** (as of 1925), "Then he said to me, 'Kick the scotches out.'" So Walter kicked away the rocks that were put in front of and behind both landing wheels to "scotch" them and keep the plane from rolling. **2000** *NADS Letters* **swGA,** When one is changing a flat while on a slope, one uses a "scotch" behind one of the wheels to prevent the vehicle from rolling. *Ibid* **WV,** Get a scotch for that back tire.

scotch v², hence vbl n *scotching* Also *scutch* [From arch *scotch* to cut, score, which has var specialized senses in Scots, Engl dial, as, to trim a hedge, to dress a stone roughly (*EDD scotch* v.¹ 1, *scutch* v.³ 3; *SND scutch* v.³ 1, 2)]   ?obs

To roughhew (usu one side of) a log.

1843 (1916) Hall *New Purchase* 93 **IN,** The orders of cabin architecture are various like those of the Greek; for instance—*the Scotched Order.* In this, logs are hacked longitudinally and a slice taken from one side, the primitive bark being left on the other sides. The scotching, however, is usually done for pastime by the boys and young women. . . But our abode was, from necessity, of the *Rough Order*—its logs being wholly unhewed and unscotched. **1907** Cockrum *Pioneer IN* 186, The first thing to do was to cut three large logs the length the building was wanted and scutch one side and lay them so they were level, on a range with each other. **1914** Whitson *Centennial Hist. Grant Co. IN* 1.55 (as of c1840), The school houses of that day . . were generally built of round logs and hewed or 'scutched' down after being put up.

Scotch adj Also *Scotchy, Scottish*   **esp Nth, N Midl, Plains States**   See Map

Frugal, stingy; straitlaced; hence v *Scotch* to act in a frugal or stingy way.

1932 *AmSp* 7.403 [Orphanage argot], *Scotch.* . . 1. Stingy. 2. Strict. "Mr. _____, if you weren't so Scotch we could have a good time here." **1965–70** *DARE* (Qu. U36b, . . *A person who saves in a mean way or is greedy in money matters:* "She certainly is _____.") 52 Infs, **esp Nth, N Midl,** Scotch; **NY**219, Scotchy; (Qu. U35, . . *Thrifty but not in a complimentary way:* "She's not a bad housekeeper, but very _____.") 16 Infs, **scattered,** Scotch; **CO**20, Scotchy; **NY**29, 75, Scottish; (Qu. U33, *Names or nicknames for a stingy person*) Infs **IL**46,

NJ45, **WA**6, **WI**48, Scotch; (Qu. U36a, . . *A person who saves in a mean way or is greedy in money matters*) Inf **OK**47, Scotch. **1973** Allen *LAUM* 1.355 **Upper MW** (as of c1950), *Stingy.* . . scotch [4 infs, **MN, IA, ND, SD**] . . scotchy [1 inf, **IA**]. **1986** Pederson *LAGS Concordance* (He is a tightwad) 2 infs, **AR, LA,** Scotch. **1999** *NADS Letters,* My background is Penn. Dutch and we always used the term Scotch like "Don't Scotch on good food or on quality etc." It meant don't go the cheap route or don't be too cheap. My grandmother used it so you can safely say it was used 100 years ago. **2000** *Ibid* **wSD,** "Scotchy"—used on Indian reservations, at least around western South Dakota, as an adjective denoting someone who is not generous.

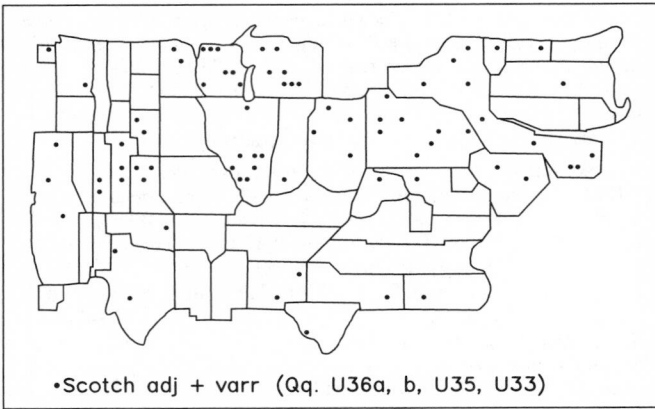

•Scotch adj + varr (Qq. U36a, b, U35, U33)

Scotch bellflower n Also *Scotch bell*   Cf **Scotch bluebell**

A **harebell 1** (here: *Campanula rotundifolia*).

1840 MA Zool. & Bot. Surv. *Herb. Plants & Quadrupeds* 109, *C[ampanula] rotundifolia.* . . Hair Bell, or Scotch Bell. A beautiful and slender plant, with fine blue flowers. **1973** Hitchcock–Cronquist *Flora Pacific NW* 459, Scotch b[ellflower]. . . *C[ampanula] rotundifolia.*

Scotch blessing n   Cf **blessing**

A severe scolding or reprimand.

1907 *DN* 3.198 **seNH,** *Scotch blessing.* . . A stern reprimand. "When his father heard of it, he gave him a Scotch blessing." **1966–67** *DARE* (Qu. HH30, *Things that are nicknamed for different nationalities—for example, a 'Dutch treat'*) Inf **IL**25, Scotch blessing—a tongue lashing; (Qu. II27, *If somebody gives you a very sharp scolding* . . "I certainly got a _____ for that.") Infs **ID**1, **IL**25, Scotch blessing. **1974** *DARE* File **UT** (as of c1920), *Scotch blessing*—A severe scolding. **1982** Brooks *Quicksand* 196 **swUT** (as of c1916), A woman in anger at her husband might *Give him a good dressing-down, A Scotch Blessing,* or a *raking over the coals.*

Scotch bloom n [Prob by folk-etym]
=**Scotch broom.**

1919 *DN* 5.58 **NW,** *Scotch bloom.* Scotch broom. Very common error.

Scotch bluebell n [See quot 1963]   Cf **Scotch bellflower**

A **harebell 1** (here: *Campanula rotundifolia*).

1937 St. John *Flora SE WA & ID* 400, *Campanula rotundifolia.* . . *Scotch Bluebell.* . . Meadows or rocky slopes. **1961** Douglas *My Wilderness* 35 **WY,** I circled the lake to find several plants of yellow bush cinquefoil in bloom and even a bed of Scotch bluebells, past their peak. **1963** Craighead *Rocky Mt. Wildflowers* 185, *Campanula rotundifolia.* . . Scotch Bluebell. . . The flowers are violet-blue, bell-shaped. *Ibid* 186, This same plant is found in Scotland, hence the common name Scotch Bluebell. **1966–67** *DARE* Wildfl QR Pl.218 Infs **AR**44, **OH**14, Scotch bluebell.

Scotch broom n

1 A naturalized woody shrub (*Cytisus scoparius*) common in much of the western and eastern US.   Also called **hayweed, Indian sage 2, Scotch bloom**

1806 in 1944 *Thomas Jefferson's Garden Book* 323, The upper third is chiefly open, but to the South is covered with a dense thicket of Scotch broom (Spartium scoparium Lin.) **1822** Eaton *Botany* 471, *Spartium.* . . *scoparius* (scotch broom . .) leaves ternate and solitary, oblong: flowers axillary. **1862** *S. Lit. Messenger* 34.670 **VA,** Scotch broom, which seems to haunt, with its funeral shade, the spots where the dead have lain, choked up the trenches. **1868** (1870) Gray *Field Botany* 100, *Scotch Broom.* . . Hardy in gardens N.; running wild in Virginia: fl[owers] early summer. **1899** (1912) Green *VA Folk-Speech* 370, Scotch-broom. . . A plant, the common broom. **1915** (1926) Armstrong–Thornber *Western Wild Flowers* 264, *Scotch broom.* . . This is said to have been brought to California by Cornish miners. **1967–69** *DARE* (Qu. S26a, . . *Wildflowers.* . . *Roadside flowers*) Inf **WA28**, Scotch broom; (Qu. S26e, *Other wildflowers not yet mentioned;* not asked in early QRs) Infs **CA140, SC36**, Scotch broom. **1994** Guterson *Snow Falling* 119 **nwWA**, He followed . . certain remnants of trail that gave out suddenly . . in fields of unexpected Scotch broom.

2 =forsythia.

1898 *Jrl. Amer. Folkl.* 11.274 **VA**, *Forsythia viridissima,* . . Scotch broom.

Scotch cap n Also *Scots cap* Cf **blackcap 1**

A **raspberry B**; see quots.

1828 in 1918 Dale *Ashley–Smith Explor.* 245, The timber . . is principally hemlock, pine, and white ceadar . . the under brush, hazle, oak, briars, currents, goose berry, and Scotch cap bushes. **1900** (1906) *Webster's Internatl. Dict. Suppl.* 186, *Scotch cap* . . the wild black raspberry (*Rubus occidentalis*); also, the salmon berry (*R. parviflorus,* syn. *R. Nutkanus*). **1941** *LANE* Map 276 **nwCT**, 1 inf, Scotch cap, a black raspberry; 1 inf, Thimbleberries = Scotch caps, black; 1 inf, Scotch caps, as a boy; 1 inf, Scots caps, Scotch caps, black. **1967–68** *DARE* (Qu. I44, *What kinds of berries grow wild around here?*) Inf **CT11**, Scotch caps—look like a raspberry but littler; (Qu. I46, . . *Kinds of fruits that grow wild around here*) Inf **MI53**, Scotch cap.

Scotch chenille n [Folk-etym for *cochineal*]

1931 Goodrich *Mt. Homespun* 16 **sAppalachians**, For the scarlet wool in a coverlet made in the eighties was used what the weaver called "Scotch chenille" (cochineal?). *Ibid* 74, A bright scarlet cover was colored by a great-aunt, so Cousin Mag said, with "Scotch chenille."

Scotch clipper n

1970 *DARE* (Qu. L18, *Kinds of plows*) Inf **OH95**, Walking plow—Scotch clipper.

Scotch dipper n Also *Scotch duck, ~ teal, Scotchman* =**bufflehead 2.**

1888 Trumbull *Names of Birds* 83, At Wilmington, N.C. [the bufflehead is called] *Scotch-duck, Scotchman, Scotch-dipper,* and *Scotch-teal;* the latter name being a favorite with hucksters, "Teal" being always in demand. **1982** Elman *Hunter's Field Guide* 211, *Bucephala albeola.* . . Scotch dipper, Scotch teal.

scotcher See scotch v¹ 4

Scotch harrow n

Perh a **drag n 1.**

1968 *DARE* (Qu. L20, *The implement used in a field after it's been plowed to break up the lumps*) Inf **PA106**, Scotch harrow—over potatoes—pins down through wood. **1973** Allen *LAUM* 1.218 (as of c1950), *Harrow.* . . Scotch [harrow] [1 inf, **ND**].

Scotch hobble n Cf **crow hobble**

A hobble for a horse; see quot; hence v phr *Scotch hobble* to restrain.

1944 Adams *Western Words* 139, *Scotch hobble*—A hobble made with a large loop that will not slip, placed around the horse's neck and arranged so that a bowline knot lies back on one shoulder. The long end of the rope is then placed around a hind leg just below the ankle joint and the end is run back into the neck loop and tied, just short enough so that the foot, when the animal is standing, will be three or four inches off the ground. To keep the horse from kicking out of the rope, it is usually necessary to take an extra turn about the ankle or twist the rope back on itself. **1995** Brophy *Coll.* 65 **swMO** (as of c1960), *Scotch-hobble* . . punish or restrain severely.

scotching See scotch v²

Scotch kiss n

1916 *DN* 4.329 **KS**, *Scotch kiss.* . . A kiss with the cheeks drawn between the jaws (teeth).

Scotchman n

1 See **Scotch dipper.**

2 =lingcod 1.

1960 Amer. Fisheries Soc. *List Fishes* 67, Scotchman—see lingcod.

Scotch marriage n [*W3* scotch marriage. . . "Common-law-marriage."]

1966–68 *DARE* (Qu. HH30, *Things that are nicknamed for different nationalities—for example, a 'Dutch treat'*) Inf **AL10**, Scotch marriage; **CA15**, Scotch marriage—girl is knocked up; **IA45**, Scotch marriage—if you're thrifty.

Scotch mist n

1 A drizzling rain or heavy fog. Cf **Oregon mist**

1844 *Littell's Living Age* 1.139, She left Kezia staring through a haze, damp as a Scotch mist. **1896** *Pop. Sci. Mth.* 48.465 **cNJ**, From July 6 to October 31, 1895, . . there were . . three days . . when the fog condensed and for a brief time a drizzle or "Scotch mist" prevailed. **1939** *LANE* Map 96 (Fog; foggy) 1 inf, **nwCT**, Scotch mist, a heavy fog. **1966** *Western Folkl.* 25.39, *Scotch mist.* "A dense mist-like fine rain." . . But also sometimes a heavy rain. **1967–68** *DARE* (Qu. B21, *When fine drops of moisture are falling . . it's doing what?*) Infs **CA97, MN15**, Scotch mist; (Qu. B23, . . *A light rain that doesn't last . . it's just a* _____) Inf **MI47**, Scotch mist.

2 See **mist 1.**

Scotch movies n pl

1978 *New Yorker* 6 Feb 28, "They just thought he was watching the Scotch movies," Mr. Hensley will say. By this he means the passing scene that can be watched for nothing.

scotch out See scotch v¹ 4

Scotch sea trout n Cf **sea trout, Sebago salmon** =**brown trout 1.**

1950 Everhart *Fishes ME* 22, *Salmo trutta.* . . Much interest has centered around the so-called "scotch sea-trout" frequently taken near Orland, Maine. These "scotch sea-trout" are sea-run brown trout. Few people can distinguish between these sea-run trout and the Atlantic salmon.

Scotch teal See **Scotch dipper**

Scotchy See **Scotch** adj

scoter n

Std: a duck of the genus *Melanitta*. Also called **black duck 1, booby n¹ 3, brown coot, bucket 9, coot n¹ 2a, deaf duck 2, gray coot, horse duck 2, Indian ~, iron pot, muscovy, nigger duck 2, scooter n³, scovy 2, sea coot 1, squaw duck, surf ~, tar bucket;** for other names of the American scoter (*M. nigra*) see **beetlehead 2, black butterbill, black coot, broad-billed ~, butterbill ~, butternose ~, coppernose 1, dumb coot, fizzy n¹ 1, gray duck g, hollow-billed coot, king ~, pumpkin-blossom ~, red-billed ~, sleighbell duck, smutty coot, whistling ~, whistling duck, willowlegs, yellowbill, yellownose;** for other names of var spp see **surf scoter, white-winged ~**

Scots cap See **Scotch cap**

Scottish See **Scotch** adj

scouch See **scooch**

scouck n Also sp *skouk, skowk* [Echoic] Cf **cow-cow 1, scout n, scow n²** =**green heron.**

1792 Belknap *Hist. NH* 169, Skouk, *Ardea virescens* [=*Butorides striatus*]. **1794** Morse *Amer. Geog.* 1.165, Green Bittern. Poke. Skouk. *Ardea virescens.* **1917** *Wilson Bulletin* 29.2.78 **VA**, *Butorides virecens* [sic]—Scouck, Wallops I[slan]d, Va. . . All these names are onomatopoeic. **1955** MA Audubon Soc. *Bulletin* 39.312 **ME**, *Green Heron.* . . Skowk (Maine. . . In imitation of a cry often made by the bird when it is flushed).

Scouler willow n

Std: a **willow** (*Salix scouleriana*) native to the western US. Also called **black willow 1, diamond ~, fire ~, mountain ~, pussy ~** n[1]

scoundrel n Usu |'skaʊndrəl|; also |'skaʊn(d)əl|; for addit varr see quots Pronc-spp *scounde(r)l, scoun'el, scoun'l* Cf **scandal B**

Std sense, var forms.

1909 *DN* 3.367 eAL, wGA, *Scounde(r)l*. . . Scoundrel. **1936** *AmSp* 11.234 eTX, ['skjæʊnl] . . *scoundrel*. **1940** (1941) Bell *Swamp Water* 23 **Okefenokee GA,** A hog ner cow wasn't to be trusted out, till Gen'l Floyd run them scoun'ls to Florida. **1960** (1966) Percy *Moviegoer* 98 **New Orleans LA,** Why that scoun'l beast Jack Bolling knows more about selling open-ends than anybody on Carondelet Street. **1966** *DARE* (Qu. V2a) Inf **SC26,** ['skaʊnl]—used in conversation. **1975** Newell *If Nothin' Don't Happen* 137 **nwFL,** Most always canvasbacks have to run a little piece on top of the water, like coots, to take off. But not that day! That wind would pick 'em up time they took two steps. Then them flat-headed scoun'els would really carry the mail. **1981** Pederson *LAGS Basic Materials* **Gulf Region,** [Of proncs recorded for *scoundrel,* 6 were of the type ['skæɔndr(ə)l, 'skaɔn-, 'skæʊn-, 'skaʊn-], 2 of the type ['skaʊnr̩l, 'skæən-], 2 of the type ['skæʊndl̩], 3 of the type ['skaʊnl̩, 'skaɔn-], and 2 of the type ['skændr̩l].]

scour v chiefly N Cent, Upper MW, Cent

Of a plowshare: to cut a furrow so that the share becomes polished and earth does not adhere to it, resulting in efficient plowing; also fig: to succeed.

1856 *Scientific Amer.* 1 Nov 59 **csWI,** Such a plow will not *scour* here; the soil will stick to it like pitch to a monkey's paw. **1871** Hutchinson *Resources KS* 268, Nearly all plows scour in this soil. **1871** in 1928 *AmSp* 3.199 **IA,** The galoot who stole Frank Redner's watch is known, and unless the chap returns it soon he will find that such thievish pranks will not scour in this soil. **1887** W.H. Lamon in *Washington Critic* 3 Sept. 3/1 *(OED2)* **IL** (as of 1863), He [sc. Lincoln] said to me on the stand, immediately after the [Gettysburg] speech: 'Lamon, that speech won't scour. It is a flat failure, and the people are disappointed.' **1917** *DN* 4.399 **neOH,** *Scour*. . . To become polish [sic] by friction against the soil. Of a plow or harrow. "My mulboard [sic] won't scour." Also Ill., Ia., N.Y., Kan., Ky. **1929** *AmSp* 5.44 **NE,** In Nebraska when the plow moves along smoothly and steadily, leaving behind it a broad ribbon of overturned prairie sod or a well-turned furrow of rich black crumbling soil and emerges at the end of the furrow as unsullied as a lady's silver mirror, then the plow is *scouring* well, and the farmer's heart rejoices. When the earth is too wet, however, and the soil gums around the share, then the plow jerks to one side or the other, or refuses to bite into the soil. . . Some farmers rub the share with a piece of fresh sod before starting work, to ensure the smooth slicing of sod or soil. **1930** *AmSp* 5.282, Faculty who were reared on farms in New Jersey, Ohio, Indiana, Illinois, Minnesota, Wisconsin, Iowa, and Missouri report that "the plow scours[*]" or "the plow does not scour" are the usual if not the only expressions for the fact that the soil slips or does not slip smoothly from the plow. One member of the faculty from Georgia, however, reports that the word is not used in Georgia so far as he knows. **1937** *AmSp* 12.105 **eNE** [Farm terms], If the dirt passes smoothly off the *moldboard,* the plow is *scouring.* **1941** Ward *Holding Hills* 97 **IA** (as of early 20th cent), If he was smart, he would begin to look to a full outfit of his own, a team, a set of old harness pieced together, an old plow that could by labor be got to scour. **1944** Wellman *Bowl* 130 **KS,** Pulling a sod-buster in buffalo grass turf, dry as it was, would wear down any team, in spite of the fact that the plow was scouring beautifully. **1995** (1998) Brophy *Coll.* 65 **swMO,** *Scour.* [T]o cut clean (of a plow), not collect soil on the share. **1999** *Washington Post* (DC) 18 Sept (Internet), "Why don't these guys 'fess up?" asks Begala, a Gore supporter who nonetheless feels the image of young Gore at the plow won't scour. **2001** in 2002 *DARE* File—Internet **IL** [Troubleshooting section of a plow owner's manual], Bottoms not scouring—Clean bottoms frequently until land polish is obtained. *Ibid* **CT,** I looked into selfish molecules and found that that theory "Won't scour."

scour adj Also sp *scauer* [Perh rel to Scots *scourie* shabby, ragged]

1917 *DN* 4.435 **eVA,** *Scour*. . . The adjective *scour,* pronounced like the verb, occurs in Eastern Virginia in the sense of *untidy.* "That looks very scour"—said by a lady upon opening a drawer in untidy condition.

A spelling *scauer* is found. Instances of this use, as well as its origin, are requested.

scour broom See **scouring broom**

scour grass See **scouring rush**

scouring See **scours**

scouring broom n Also *scour broom, scouring mop* Sth, S Midl Cf *shuck broom* (at **shuck** n[1] **1b(2)**)

A usu homemade broom for scrubbing floors.

1904 (1913) Johnson *Highways South* 308 **NC,** Several brooms were scattered about the kitchen, all of them of home manufacture. The biggest one was a "scouring broom" made of a five-foot stick of hickory. At one end the stick had been whittled down in shavings that were not quite severed from it, and then these hangings were tied about with a string to keep them in a bunch that could be used effectively. **1967–69** *DARE* (Qu. F36, . . *Kinds of brooms*) Inf **KY25,** Scouring broom—old floor brooms used to scrub; **SC29,** Scouring broom—oak splits (shavings) put on a handle and used to scrub floors; **VA13,** Scouring broom—homemade; **TN27,** Scouring mop. **1986** Pederson *LAGS Concordance,* 1 inf, **neTN,** Scour broom—scouring broom for scrubbing floors; 3 infs, **AL, MS, TN,** Scouring mop(s); 1 inf, **swGA,** Scouring mop—made of corn shucks; 1 inf, **seAL,** Scouring with scouring mop filled with shucks.

scouring brush See **scouring rush**

scouring mop See **scouring broom**

scouring rush n Also rarely *scour grass, scouring brush* =**horsetail 1,** esp *Equisetum hyemale.*

1804 *Philadelphia Med. & Phys. Jrl.* 1.1.148, A plant called the Scour-Grass is very common in many parts of the United States, &c. It is the Equisetum hyemale of Linnaeus. **1822** Eaton *Botany* 273, [*Equisetum*] *hyemale,* . . scouring rush. **1848** Emory *Notes Reconnoissance* 13, We find in the bottoms [of the Arkansas River] . . scouring rush, (equisetum hyemale,) a powerful diuretic upon horses. **1858** *Ladies' Repository* 18.594, The largest representative in this country of the ancient equisetaceæ, are the scouring rushes—coarse, reed-like plants, growing on damp, shady hill-sides, and used by many persons for cleaning wooden-ware. **1929** *Torreya* 29.149 **ME,** The curious Equisetum arvense might not attract every child's attention, but it did mine. . . Not until many years later did I know it as "Scouring Rush." **1937** [see **scrub grass**]. **1952** Strausbaugh–Core *Flora WV* 2, *E[quisetum] hyemale.* . . *Scouring rush.* . . Sections of this plant were bound into small bundles that were used by pioneer families for scouring floors, table tops, etc., whence the common name. **1966** *DARE* FW Addit **WA10,** *Equisetum*—horsetail or scouring rush. **1974** Munz *Flora S. CA* 15, *Equisetum.* . . Horsetail. Scouring-Rush. **2001** *DARE* File **NEng** (as of late 1960s), I used to lead nature walks for younger children. I'd put several tarnished pennies in my pocket, and when we got to a patch of horsetails, I'd pick a stem. Crushing it in my fingers, I'd rub the pennies with it. The kids were always amazed to see the bright copper shine appear. I'd tell them that in the olden days that's why it was called *scouring rush;* that the pioneers used bunches of horsetails to clean their copper kettles.

scours n pl but sg in constr Freq with *the* Also *scouring;* pronc-sp *scares* [Transf from *scours* diarrhea or dysentery in cattle] **scattered, but esp Sth, S Midl** See Map Diarrhea.

1942 Whipple *Joshua* 213 **UT** (as of c1860), More corn-meal mush. It was a vicious circle—you ate and got the scours, which made you so weak and empty that you ate some more. **1950** *WELS* (*Joking or nicknames for diarrhea or looseness of the bowels*) 2 Infs, **WI,** Scours. **1954** *Harder Coll.* **cwTN,** *Scours.* . . Same as bowel complaint. " 'At young'un's got tem scours, jist a-runnin' off all time." **1965–70** *DARE* (Qu. BB19, *Joking names for looseness of the bowels*) 11 Infs, **scattered, but esp Sth, S Midl,** The scours; **LA6,** The scours—occasionally said of babies; **TN44,** The scours—mostly in animals; **AL4, AZ2, GA74, MN12, SC34, TX86, WV7,** Scours; **NV8,** Scouring. **1990** Cavender *Folk Med. Lexicon* 30 **sAppalachians,** *Scours*—[commonly pronounced "scares"] diarrhea. **1997** Frazier *Cold Mountain* 286 (as of c1866), The Georgia boy. . . put a hand to his belly and stiffened up as if someone had run a pointed stick through his vitals.—If I'd known I'd have the scours this bad I'd not have eat one mouthful of that venison, he said.

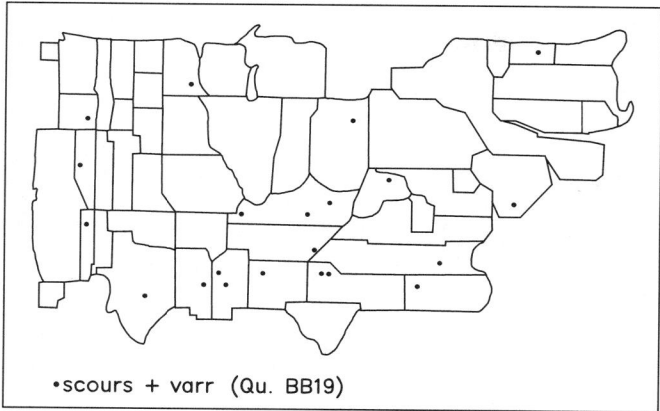

•scours + varr (Qu. BB19)

scout v [*OED2 scout* v.[1] 1.b 1577 →; "*Obs.* exc. *dial.*"] **sAppalachians**
To elude arrest, hide out.

1913 Kephart *Highlanders* 296 **sAppalachians,** Many common English words are used in peculiar senses by the mountain folk, as . . scout for elude. **1927** Mason *Lure Great Smokies* 170 (as of 1860s), A pa'cel of us was scoutin' t' keep outen the armies an' we was havin' a shootin'-match 'r some such er matter to pass the time in th' woods. **1938** Bowman *Land High Horizons* 21 **wNC, eTN,** Many mountaineers avoided serving in the war by "scouting" in the mountains, as they called their method of hiding in the wildernesses of laurel and rhododendron that flourish in the highlands. **1975** *Appalachian Jrl.* 2.153 **wNC,** To scout from the Army is quite different from to scout for the Army; the former means that the man is AWOL. **1976** Garber *Mountain-ese* 78 **sAppalachians,** Kenny has been scoutin' in the mountains since he was indicted. **1994** *Montgomery Coll.* **eTN,** "He had to scout most of his life" (=to live by himself in a remote area in order to conduct moonshining without detection).

scout n [Echoic] **esp Mid Atl** Cf **scouck, scow** n[2]
A bird of the family Ardeidae; see quots.

1913 Bailey *Birds VA* 47, Green Heron. . . Fly-Up-the-Creek. Little Crane. Scout. Scow. **1917** *Wilson Bulletin* 29.2.78 **eVA,** *Butorides virecens* [sic]. . . Scout, Smith I[slan]d, Va. . . All these names are onomatopoeic. **1966–68** *DARE* (Qu. Q3, . . *Birds that come out only after dark*) Inf **MD45,** Scout—looks like a crane but gray; (Qu. Q10, . . *Water birds and marsh birds*) Inf **NC21,** Herons—scoggins or scouts or johnny gonkers. **1970** *DARE* Tape **VA112,** The marsh hens, what you call marsh hens, and these other kind with them long bills, scouts, they call 'em, that place is full of 'em.

scout car n
A police patrol car.

1933 *Sun* (Baltimore MD) 5 May 11/2, The busiest car was scout car No. 5, operating in the Northeastern district. . . This car responded to fifty-seven calls in the month. Nearly as busy was scout car No. 7. **1950** *WELS Suppl.* **seWI,** Scout car. **1967–70** *DARE* (Qu. N4, *A police vehicle with a red, blue, or yellow flashing light on top*) Infs **DC11, MI67, 73, NY132, VA41,** Scout car. **1986** Pederson *LAGS Concordance* (Police sedan) 3 infs, **AL,** 2 infs, **TX,** Scout car(s).

scouter See **scooter** n[1] 1

scout horn See **scoot horn**

scout, on the adj phr Cf **scout** v
Eluding arrest, hiding out.

1891 O'Beirne *Leaders Indian Terr.* 74, Paul was arrested and Ben Dillard fled from the locality, and spent some four years on the scout, after which he gave himself up. **1968** Adams *Western Words* 211, On the scout—On the dodge. **1995** (1998) *Brophy Coll.* 65 **swMO,** Scout, on the. [A]cting as an outlaw (1920s-30s).

scovey duck, scovia See **scovy**

Scoville-hoe n Also *Scovil hoe, Scoville*
See quot 1909.

1909 *DN* 3.367 **eAL, wGA,** Scoville-hoe. . . Also simply *Scoville.* A hoe largely used in the South, especially in chopping cotton, invented by

and named after a young man from Connecticut who settled about 1850 in Eufaula, Ala., as a clerk in a supply store. The hoes in use previously were of soft iron and became easily dulled. Scoville conceived the idea of a hoe with a thin plate of steel on the inner side, so arranged that the softer metal on the outer side would wear away more rapidly and thus keep the edge constantly sharpened. **1986** Pederson *LAGS Concordance* 1 inf, **cnGA,** Scovil hoe—type of hoe; 1 inf, **cAL,** Scovil hoes.

scovy n Also *scov(e)y duck, scoby (duck), scovia* [Aphet forms of *muscovy*] **esp Mid and S Atl**
1 A domestic duck *(Cairina moschata).*

1899 (1912) Green *VA Folk-Speech* 370, Scovy. . . A Muscovy duck. **1969–70** *DARE* (Qu. K76, . . *Kinds of poultry . . raised around here*) Inf **NC85,** Scoby duck—scoby is larger than white Pekin—dark blue with red heads; (Qu. Q5) Inf **GA80,** Scovy duck—bluish head, red markings on neck. **1970** *DARE* Tape **VA47,** [Inf:] There's people that's put scovy duck eggs under wild ducks, and taken wild duck eggs, you know. . . [FW:] What's a scovy duck? [Inf:] He's a muscovy, I guess you'd call him. He's a domestic duck right here, but I guess in Mexico and different places I understand he was wild. **1982** *Barrick Coll.* **csPA,** Scovey duck—Muscovey duck.

2 A **scoter,** usu the **surf scoter.** Cf **muscovy**

1917 *Wilson Bulletin* 29.2.77 **VA,** *Oidemia perspicillata* [=*Melanitta p.*]—'Scovy, Wallops I[slan]d, Va. **1966–70** *DARE* (Qu. Q5, . . *Kinds of wild ducks*) Inf **FL26,** Scovia; **NC80,** Scovy duck; **PA245,** Scoby duck.

scow n[1]
1 also *stone scow:* =**stoneboat;** hence v *scow* to transport (something) in a **stoneboat. NEng** Cf **flatboat** n 2

1714 (1901) Hempstead *Diary* 1.38 **seCT,** I fetched ye Scow load of Railes & Posts. **1737** (1901) *Ibid* 314 **seCT,** I was at home al day Splitting & hewing peices for a Stone Scow. **1751** (1899) MacSparran *Letter Book* 58 **RI,** He and a Boy . . were Scowing wood. **1939** *LANE* Map 168 *(Stone boat)* 3 infs, **MA,** Scow. **1965** Needham–Mussey *Country Things* 88 **VT,** It was only when they begun using horses that they would cut the tree up into twelve-foot lengths on the spot, and use a scow or a scoot.

2 A large foot or square-toed shoe. Cf **flatboat** n 3

[**1924** in 1952 Mathes *Tall Tales* 23 **sAppalachians,** Of evenings in the bunk-house the favorite program would open with the strains of "Sourwood Mountain" or "Arkansaw Traveler" . . or perchance a clog dance by Nigger Pete, whose immense scow-bottom feet flopped and shuffled on the boards like an earthquake set to music.] **1942** Berrey–Van den Bark *Amer. Slang* 121.30, *Feet, esp. large ones.* . . scows. **1950** *WELS (Humorous or uncomplimentary names for big feet)* 2 Infs, **WI,** (Pair of) scows. **1967–70** *DARE* (Qu. W42b, . . *Nicknames for men's square-toed shoes*) Infs **MD49, NY92,** Scows; (Qu. X38, *Joking names for unusually big or clumsy feet*) Infs **AK1, IL7, NJ39, VA48,** Scows.

scow v See **scow** n[1] 1

scow n[2] Also *scower, skeow, skow* [Echoic] **esp S Atl** Cf **scouck, scout** n
A bird of the family Ardeidae, usu the **green heron.**

1910 Wayne *Birds SC* 31, Green Heron. . . It is universally known on this coast as the "Skeow," from its note, and it breeds abundantly. **1911** *Forest & Stream* 77.174 **NC,** *Nycticorax nycticorax nævius.* . . Scow . . Currituck Sound, N.C. **1913** Bailey *Birds VA* 47, Green Heron. . . This heron, commonly called "Scow," remains through the milder winters with us. **1954** Sprunt *FL Bird Life* 35, Usually, the harsh, raucous shriek is given as the bird [=green heron] flushes, this note resulting in the local name of "Skeow." **1955** *Oriole* 20.1.2 **GA,** Green Heron. . . Skow (imitation of a cry often made when the bird is flushed). **1966** *DARE* (Qu. Q10, . . *Water birds and marsh birds*) Inf **NC13,** Cranes or scowers.

scow-bang v, hence vbl n *scow-banging* [Var of *OED2 scowbank* "to loaf"; 1868 →; < *scowbanker* "a loafer"; 1750 →]
To search idly along a beach for anything edible or otherwise of value.

1949 in 1983 Beyle *How Talk Cape Cod* 28, "Scow-banging" is as gypsy-like an occupation as it sounds. If you go off to the beach with certain paraphernalia you can consider yourself "scow-banging". However, you must carry gear for gunning, fishing, and raking clams, and be on the lookout for anything you can salvage from the beach. **1988**

Nickerson *Days to Remember* 77 **Cape Cod MA** (as of c1915), It's [sic] name is "scow-banging". I first heard this word from my father. He defined it this way, "In the early morning you start out with your skiff or little sailboat. Aboard you have a clam hoe, a quohog scratcher, fishing lines, a pair of binoculars, and maybe a gun and some decoys. You're gone all day. Late in the day you return home. You don't know where you've been, you don't know what you've done, but you've had a wonderful day. And in the boat you've brought home something to eat."

Scowegian n Also *Scowoogian* [Blend of *Scandinavian* + *Norwegian*] Cf **Scandihoovian** *joc or derog*
A Scandinavian.
   1919 Kyne *Capt. Scraggs* 93 **CA,** You dirty Scowegian ingrate. **1936** (1947) Mencken *Amer. Lang.* 296, For Scandinavian: *scowegian, scowoogian.* **1950** *WELS Suppl., Scowegian*—A Norwegian or other Scandinavian. **1995** *Brophy Coll.* 65 **swMO** (as of c1960), *Scowegian.* [A] Scandinavian (humorous).

scower See **scow** n[2]

scowl n [Var of *scow*]
   1778 in 1789 Anburey *Travels* 2.162 **sePA,** We crossed the river in scowls, which are flat bottom boats, large enough to contain a waggon and horses. *Ibid* 183, The scowl that I crossed over in had several narrow escapes. **1796** Wansey *Excursion U.S.* 56 **MA,** While our coachee, and all its passengers were passing this fine river in a scowl. **1957** Battaglia *Resp. to PADS 20* **eMD,** *(Names or nicknames for an old, clumsy rowboat)* Scowl; *(Humorous or uncomplimentary names for big feet)* Scowls. **1989** (1990) Baden *Maryland's E. Shore* 53, The *Upper Ferry,* a flat bottomed scowl with a steel cable that clangs across each side of the deck on rollers and runs athwart of the river bed.

Scowoogian See **Scowegian**

scrabble n Also *scrabble pudding* [Varr of **scrapple**]
   1967–70 *DARE* (Qu. H24, . . *Names or nicknames . . for boiled cornmeal*) Inf **PA242,** Scrabble—mush cooked in broth from ground pork (called *puddin' broth*); (Qu. H25, . . *Names or nicknames . . for fried cornmeal*) Inf **ID5,** Scrabble—with meat in it; (Qu. H43, *Foods made from parts of the head and inner organs of an animal*) Inf **IN54,** Scrabble—includes lots of liver, fried with corn meal [FW: Inf thinks scrabble may be more eastern Pennsylvanian than midwestern.]; **PA242,** Scrabble ['skræbəl]—with corn meal, ground pork, heart, liver, and maybe kidneys. **1970** *DARE* Tape **PA242,** Another dish which I didn't have quite the ability to digest was the scrabble pudding which is ground pork. . . The Pennsylvania Dutch farmers . . would often have cornmeal cooked into a cake like, which was then fried and dressed with ground pork. **1986** Pederson *LAGS Concordance (Headcheese)* 1 inf, **cwMS,** Scrabble; *(Scrapple)* 1 inf, **neFL,** Scrabble.

scrabble log n
=**prize log.**
   1969 Sorden *Lumberjack Lingo* 104 **NEng, Gt Lakes,** *Scrabble logs*—Logs which came to the sorting jack without marks denoting ownership. Same as prize logs.

Scrabble Town n [Prob *scrabble* to struggle (as to make a living under difficult circumstances)] **esp MA** Cf **hardscrabble 2**
See quots.
   1947 Botkin *Treas. New Engl. Folkl.* 805, Nomenclature descriptive of local and group traits, both depreciatory and affectionate, has given rise to an extensive mythology of nicknames of states, towns, neighborhoods, sections of the population, etc . . Scrabbletown (the lower end of Chatham). **1968–69** *DARE* (Qu. C34, *Nicknames for nearby settlements, villages, or districts*) Inf **MD12,** Scrabble Town; (Qu. C35, *Nicknames for the different parts of your town or city*) Inf **MA55,** Scrabble Town; (Qu. II25, *Names or nicknames for the part of a town where the poorer people, special groups, or foreign groups live*) Inf **MA30,** Scrabble Town. **1988** Nickerson *Days to Remember* 205 **Cape Cod MA** (as of c1870), It was against this background of high competition between crews of "wreckers" and high risks in saving lives with no reward except in heaven, that the part of Chatham near the twin lights and facing the bars came to be known as "Scrabbletown".

scrag n[1] Also sp *skrag* [*OED2 scrag* sb.[1] "A lean person or animal. (In depreciatory use.)"; →1845]

A scrawny or scruffy-looking person or animal, hence used as a general term of derogation for a person.
   1845 Judd *Margaret* 275 **swME,** We are going to catch every scrag that comes this way from the Pest. **1951** Johnson *Resp. to PADS 20* **DE,** *(A thin, bony, or poor looking cow)* Scrag; *(A bony or poor looking horse)* Scrag. **1969–70** *DARE* (Qu. K15, *A thin, bony, or poor-looking cow*) Inf **VA105,** Scrag; (Qu. HH37, *An immoral woman*) Inf **NY156,** Scrag. **1996** Horton *Island Out of Time* 242 **Chesapeake Bay MD,** My little shanty became the takeup place for the other young men, where we would gather to pass the evening, making pots, griping about the skrags, and just watching the tide run and the stars come out. [Footnote to *skrag:*] inept waterman who horns in on your good fishing spot.

scrag n[2] See **scrog** n

scraggie n [Cf *EDD scrag* sb.[1], adj. 5 "Useless, inferior."]
A kind of playing marble; see quot.
   1958 *Sat. Eve. Post Letters* **swMO** (as of c1914), Scraggies or china's [sic] were white with red stripes around them and very soft and not round. This was the lowest priced marble and never used in a game, only by smaller boys learning to play.

scramble See **scramble dinner**

scrambled eggs n Cf **butter-and-eggs**
Any of several yellow-flowered plants as:
a A **gold fields 1** (here: *Lasthenia californica*).
   1921 *DN* 5.114 **CA,** Scrambled eggs. . . Sunshine, or fly-flower (*Baeria gracilis* [=*Lasthenia californica*]).
b An **owl's clover** (here: *Orthocarpus erianthus*).
   1921 *DN* 5.114 **CA,** Scrambled eggs. . . Also butter-and-eggs (*Orthocarpus erianthus*).
c Any of several plants of the genus *Corydalis;* see quots. **Sth**
   1933 Small *Manual SE Flora* 550, Capnoides [=*Corydalis*]. . . Scrambled-eggs. **1936** Whitehouse *TX Flowers* 35, Plains Scrambled-Eggs (*Capnoides montanum* [=*Corydalis curvisiliqua*]) is a common plant throughout the central and western parts of the state, ranging to Arizona and Montana. . . The short-podded scrambled-eggs (*Capnoides crystallinum* [=*Corydalis crystallina*]) comes into the northern part of the state from Kansas and Missouri. **1949** Moldenke *Amer. Wild Flowers* 31, The yellow species [of *Corydalis*] are often called *scrambledeggs.* **1955** *S. Folkl. Qrly.* 19.232 **FL,** Scrambled Eggs (*Capnoides Halei* [= *Corydalis micrantha*]) . . [is] named from the object they most resemble. **1970** Correll *Plants TX* 667, *Corydalis.* . . Scrambled Eggs.
d =**butter-and-eggs 1.**
   1970 *DARE* (Qu. S11, . . *Wild snapdragon*) Inf **NC87,** Scrambled egg [sic].
e A **daffodil 1.**
   1978 *DARE* File **SC,** Scrambled eggs—late-blooming double daffodils.

scramble dinner n Also *scramble (supper)* [Cf *OED2 scrambling* ppl. a. 1. "applied to a meal at which the partakers help themselves to what they can get"; 1607 →] **esp nIL**
A potluck supper.
   1968 *DARE* File **cnIL,** Scramble—A pot-luck supper. **1972** *Eve. Telegraph* (Dixon IL) 29 Apr 4/8, A scramble dinner is planned by the Dixon Travel Club for 6:30 p.m. . . and members are asked to provide food and table service. **1972** *NYT Article Letters* **cnIL,** Only in Dixon, Ill., my home town, is a potluck or pitch-in dinner or supper referred to as a *scramble* dinner or supper. True for 50 years that I know of. **1972** *DARE* File **neIL,** I could not find an example of *scramble supper,* but it is common, too. . . I can recall the *scramble* usages for more than fifty years. **2001** *Ibid* **cnIL,** Potluck. . . in my family, we refer to it as a 'scramble dinner' (or supper) depending on the time of day the meal is served. We have used this term since I can remember (40–50 years). *Ibid* **neIL,** I have often heard potluck dinners referred to as "scrambles," by my Girl Scout troop leader.

scranch See **scronch** v 1

scrap n Also *scrap leaf,* *~ tobacco* **chiefly Midl, Gt Lakes**
See Map Cf **lug** n[2] 1
A fragment of tobacco left as a byproduct of cigar manufac-

ture and sold as smoking and chewing tobacco; a poor grade of tobacco.

1937 *AmSp* 12.273 [Cigar industry language], *Short filler* or *shorts* were either *scraps,* tobacco leaves broken up intentionally or unintentionally (hail-damaged tobacco was often cured and turned into scraps.) or *cuttings,* ends of cigars which the cigar maker cuts off, pieces of wrappers and binders. **1940** *AmSp* 15.135 [Tobacco market language], *Scraps.* Broken pieces of leaves. **1960** Heimann *Tobacco* 164, The last and least category, scrap, was a byproduct of cigar manufacture; these cigar cuttings (leaf ends) and clippings (cigar ends) were both chewed and smoked. *Ibid* 237, It is interesting that scrap tobacco was included with smoking tobacco figures by the Internal Revenue Bureau until 1930, while after that it was lumped with chewing. Assuming scrap to be half smoked and half chewed, the use of pipe tobacco passed the chewing habit sometime in 1921 or 1922. **1965–70** *DARE* (Qu. DD1, . . *Forms* . . *[of] chewing tobacco*) 73 Infs, **chiefly Midl, Gt Lakes,** Scrap (tobacco); **DE**1, Beechnut scrap; **IN**68, Scrap leaf; **IL**14, **MN**8, Scraps. [70 of 77 Infs old, 68 male] **1970** *DARE* Tape **VA**38, [FW:] What were the grades you divided 'em into? [Inf:] Divided 'em into? Well, we usually had what we'd call a scrap, and then we'd call a lug, and if we had a leaf of tobacco mixed in with it, you'd call 'em wrappers. . . Like your lug grade, it would bring maybe a little more, and if you had a wrapper grade, it would bring a little more, and what you'd call a scrap grade would bring in a little less.

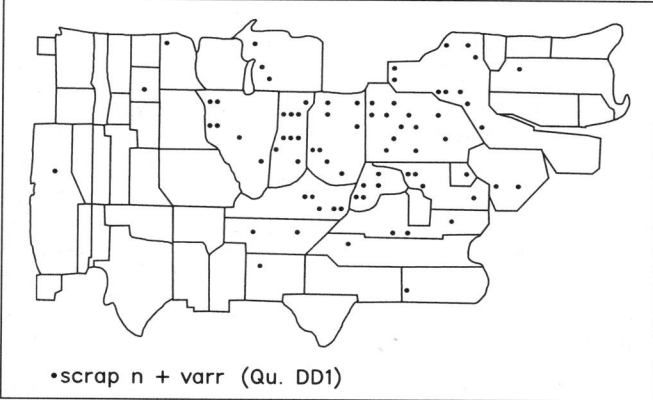

•scrap n + varr (Qu. DD1)

scrap v, hence vbl n *scrapping*

To glean (the remainders of a crop, esp cotton).

1965 *DARE* (Qu. L27) Inf **OK**16A, Scrapping—that's when you get the last of the cotton. **1966–68** *DARE* Tape [**DE**1, They picked up any scrap corn that was left in the field;] **MS**75, Well, it was working for the White people, on the farm, and when they have, they crop together all their corn crops and then we'd go out and scrap corn, what we could find, you see, and shell it, shuck it and shell it, and then you could take it to town. **1987** *Decatur Daily* (AL) 20 Sept 1/1, [Caption to photo of a man in a harvester:] Gene Burgreen shown "scrapping," or harvesting an already-picked cotton field in Limestone County. **1998** *DARE* File **nwMS** [Black], Here is another word about picking cotton from the black people of northwestern Mississippi: to scrap—to pick cotton by hand in a field that has already been picked by machine.

scrape v, hence vbl n *scraping*

A Forms.

1 past: usu *scraped;* also *scrope.*

1895 *DN* 1.393 **NYC,** *Scrope:* pret. of *scrape.*

2 past ppl: usu *scraped;* also *scrup.* Cf **break** v A3, **take**

1949 Webber *Backwoods Teacher* 193 **Ozarks,** Got most of the [hogs'] hair off—shaved off, not scrup out with the roots like hit'd ort to be.

B Senses.

1 also with *down, out, up:* To thin or weed (esp cotton) by hoeing or plowing. **chiefly Sth, S Midl** Cf **chop** v B1, **scrape** n 1

1827 [see **scrape** n 1]. **1835** in 1976 Rose *Doc. Hist. Slavery* 318, It [=cotton] is thinned out, or as it is called, "scraped." During scraping time there is one constant rush, and every hand that can use a hoe is brought into the field. **1858** Hammett *Piney Woods Tavern* 117 **TX,** They looked like a nigger's face in cotton scrapin' time. **1903** *DN*

2.328 **seMO,** *Scrape* (cotton). . . To hoe cotton. **1907** *DN* 3.235 **nwAR,** *Scrape* (cotton). . . To hoe cotton. **1909** *DN* 3.367 **eAL, wGA,** *Scrape*. . . To plow cotton, etc., with a scrape: sometimes with *up.* **1944** *PADS* 2.70 **sVA,** *Scrape down*. . . To pull away with a hoe the surface dirt on the tobacco hill. **1986** Pederson *LAGS Concordance* (*To thin small cotton plants or weed the area*) 4 infs, **LA,** Scrape (it); 1 inf, **cnGA,** Scrape—hoe, thin cotton out; 1 inf, **nwTN,** After cotton came up you had to scrape it; 1 inf, **cwMS,** Scrape means "hoe"—said in old days; 1 inf, **cLA,** Scrape with a hoe; 1 inf, **csLA,** Scrape it with harrow; 1 inf, **cnMS,** Scrape that cotton with one horse plow; 1 inf, **csLA,** Scrape that cotton to get young grass from rows; 1 inf, **swTN,** Scrape that cotton and chop it out—remove some; 1 inf, **swMS,** Scrape the cotton out with a hoe removing grass; 6 infs, **LA, MS, TX,** Scraping; 2 infs, **LA, MS,** Scraping—thinning; 2 infs, **LA,** Scraping—"chopping"; 1 inf, **ceLA,** Scraping cotton to get rid of grass; 1 inf, **swMS,** Scraping cotton—thinning, former more common; 1 inf, **swMS,** Scraping cotton—thinning it out; 1 inf, **csMS,** Scraping cotton—chopping cotton; 1 inf, **csMS,** Scraping cotton—weeding with hoe; 1 inf, **swMS,** Scraping cotton—scraping dirt away.

2 To dredge with a **scrape** n 3; to catch with a **scrape** n 3; hence comb *scraping boat* a boat employed in doing this. **Chesapeake Bay** Cf **scraper** n[1] 2

1880 *Bradstreet's* 15 Sept 8/1, It is noted that in Chesapeake waters there are . . 550 scraping-boats. **1881** Ingersoll *Oyster-Industry* 161 **MD,** Scraping, which is simply dredging on a smaller scale, both as to the size of the boat and the dredge, is conducted only in shallow water. *Ibid* 162, The above figures . . , while they embrace all vessels that are licensed, they by no means include all that are scraping. . . I feel safe in placing the number of scraping-boats at 550. **1939** *Sun* (Baltimore MD) 21 July 2/5 (*Hench Coll.*), Magistrate Fred N. Holland today postponed hearing for more than a score of fishermen charged with scraping crabs while using a power boat. **1976** Warner *Beautiful Swimmers* 212 **eMD,** Marsh scrapes six days a week from late May until the middle of September. *Ibid* 231, Morris Goodwin went on to tell me that for a time scraping had fallen off quite a bit.

scrape n

1 also *scraper, scraping scooter:* A plow or plowshare for shallow cultivation, esp of cotton. **chiefly Sth, S Midl** Cf **middlebuster 1**

1827 *Western Mth. Rev.* 1.82 **LA,** The cotton. . . is thinned carefully, and plows, in the form of scrapers, are used, as the technical phrase is, *to scrape it out.* **1850** in 1969 Turner *Cotton Planter's Manual* 117, I have used the scraper for ten years, and believe I had the first one ever tried in Mississippi. **1909** *DN* 3.367 **eAL, wGA,** *Scrape*. . . A wide-winged plowshare used for shallow cultivation or for merely 'scraping' the crust: often used for breaking middles in cotton culture. Also *right-winged scrape, left-winged scrape,* etc. **1944** Clark *Pills* 282 **Sth,** By colloquial designations the various strange shapes were known to the trade as . . buzzard wings, scrapers, and subsoilers. **1965–69** *DARE* (Qu. L18, *Kinds of plows*) Inf **FL**17, Scrapes—old-fashioned; **SC**52, Scrapes—for cultivating; **SC**23, Scraper—for siding cotton after the middles have been busted; (Qu. L25, *The implement used to clean out weeds and loosen the earth between rows of corn*) Inf **GA**87, We used scooter and scrape—old-fashioned; **NJ**25, Scrapers—in long lines. **1986** Pederson *LAGS Concordance* (*Plow*) 5 infs, **AL,** Scrape(s); 1 inf, **seAL,** Scrapes—used to "side" peanuts or cotton; 1 inf, **ceAL,** A big scrape on it (describing middlebuster); 2 infs, **AR, TN,** Scraper; 1 inf, **cwGA,** I'd use a scooter and a scrape; 1 inf, **cAL,** Scrape—cuts top; 1 inf, **cwAL,** Eel scrape—goes around plants, doesn't disturb; 1 inf, **ceGA,** Little scrape; 1 inf, **seGA,** Scraping scooter—for cotton cultivation; (*Harrow*) 2 infs, **GA,** Scrape(s); 1 inf, **ceAL,** Scrape—used on plow stock; 1 inf, **cwGA,** Scrapes—attached to foot of plow or scooter; 2 infs, **AL, TN,** (Cotton) scraper; 1 inf, **cwTN,** Cotton scraper—simplified hoeing cotton.

2 also *scraping:* In turpentine production: raw turpentine that hardens on the tree and is collected by scraping. **S Atl** Cf **dip** n[1] 4

1832 Browne *Sylva* 232 **S Atl,** The *scraping* is a coating of sap which becomes solid before it reaches the boxes, and which is taken off in the fall and added to the last runnings. **1856** Olmsted *Journey Slave States* 343 **NC,** It is occasionally . . scraped off, and barreled by itself. It is, therefore, known in the market as "scrape." **1859** Perry *Turpentine Farming* 123, There are but two natural qualities of turpentine, commonly known as hard and soft; the hard sticks on the face or scarred surface of the pine, and is called 'scrape,' but the soft runs in the box, and is called 'dip.' **1884** Sargent *Forests of N. Amer.* 517, "Scrape" or "Hard turpentine"—the product of the scrapings of the boxes. **1966–68** *DARE* Tape **GA**7, We don't usually get as much for that scrape as we do if it's gum. You pay a different price for it; **GA**23, The white stuff that falls off the faces, they call that scrapin'.

3 A dredge or dredgelike implement for taking crabs and mollusks; hence *scrape boat* a boat employed in fishing with such an implement. **Chesapeake Bay** Cf **crab scrape, scrape v B2, scraper** n¹ **2**

1881 Ingersoll *Oyster-Industry* 160 **MD**, This license shall hold good for one year, and authorizes said vessel to be used in catching oysters with scoop, scrape, drag, dredge or any similar instrument. **1933** *Sun* (Baltimore MD) 26 Jan 20/8 *(Hench Coll.)*, There had been an exchange of shots between his vessel and the crew of one of several boats caught gathering oysters with "scrapes" and "devil-divers." **1953** MD Dept. Educ. *Our Underwater Farm* 29 **Chesapeake Bay,** Most of these [crabs] are caught by a scrape. This is a net on a rectangular metal frame which is pulled across the bottom on shallow, grassy flats. **1970** *DARE* Tape **VA**112, They got a four foot scrape . . that's got a bar on it . . and a frame, and they got a knitted bag behind it. **1976** Warner *Beautiful Swimmers* 217 **eMD**, There was young Larry Evans . . starting off with a brand new scrape boat. **1996** Horton *Island Out of Time* 46 **Chesapeake Bay MD,** Nowadays, scrape boats got an engine and they pull two scrapes, which is similar to small dredges, and think they are doing something. *Ibid* 61, Unlike a dredge, a scrape has no teeth. It slides across the bottom, breaking the sea grass off at its stem rather than uprooting it.

scrape down See **scrape v B1**

scrape-fire n [From the action of the lock]
A flintlock firearm.
1917 *DN* 4.416 **wNC**, Scrape-fire. . . Flint-lock.

scrapegallows See **scapegallows**

scrapegoat n [Folk-etym for *scapegoat*] Cf *scrapegallows* (at **scapegallows**)
[**1899** *Living Age* 220.251, "I wish you would speak to my son. . . He's turning out a regular scrapegoat." . . The word intended was scapegoat, the meaning of which the speaker had confused with scapegrace.] **1955** *Hench Coll.*, One of the speakers at the sectional meeting of the College English Assoc. (speaking of inaccurate comprehension and its result) mentioned a student's spelling of *scape-goat: scrape-goat.* **1966–69** *DARE* (Qu. II34, *If you think somebody is trying to use you to his advantage: "I'm not going to be his _____."*) Infs **CA**128, **FL**5, **KS**8, **OH**45, 88, Scrapegoat.

scrape out See **scrape v B1**

scraper n¹
1 See **scrape** n **1.**
2 In fishing for crabs or shellfish:
a =**scrape** n **3.**
1881 Ingersoll *Oyster-Industry* 247 **NEng**, Scraper.—A small dredge. Chiefly spoken of with reference to scallops. **1887** Goode *Fisheries U.S.* 2.571 **RI**, For a rocky bottom a dredge is used which has the blade immovably fastened to the arms; otherwise it does not differ from the 'kettle-bail' and it is known as a 'scraper.' **1934** *Sun* (Baltimore MD) 21 July 2/5 *(Hench Coll.),* Maryland law prohibits taking crabs with scrapers from any but sailboats.
b A person who fishes with a **scrape** n **3.** **Chesapeake Bay** Cf **crab scraper**
1881 Ingersoll *Oyster-Industry* 162 **MD**, Socially and morally the scrapers are somewhat superior to the dredgers. **1933** *Sun* (Baltimore MD) 27 Nov 16/2 *(Hench Coll.),* Records . . were broken last week as tongers, scrapers and dredgers had their busiest week of the season getting enough bivalves for Thanksgiving dinners throughout the State and neighboring sections. **1976** Warner *Beautiful Swimmers* 232 **eMD**, There is at least a forty-to-one chance, in fact, that the next soft shell crab you eat . . comes from the hard toil of Eastern Shore scrapers.
c A boat employed in fishing with a **scrape** n **3.** Cf **crab scraper**
1976 Warner *Beautiful Swimmers* 208 **eMD**, A number of the older scrapers still in use, he said, had been directly converted from sailing craft.

scraper n² Also *scraper frog* [?Echoic]
A **tree frog** (here: either *Hyla femoralis* or *H. squirella*).
1932 Wright *Life-Hist. Frogs* 272 **Okefenokee GA**, *Hyla femoralis.* . . "Scraper Frog." *Ibid* 310, *Hyla squirella.* . . "Scraper Frog." *Ibid* 312, On June 22, 1922, a boy at Camp Pinckney brought me a Scraper taken in his own house. *Ibid* 316, In 1921 a great chorus of "scrapers" came August 5. They were calling during the rain or because of rainy weather. . . A very regular and mostly continuous call.

scrape up See **scrape v B1**

scraping n
1 See **scrape** n **2.**
2 pl; also *scrappings;* Fig: the poorest part. **esp Sth, S Midl**
1966–70 *DARE* (Qu. HH18, *Very insignificant or low-grade people*) Inf **GA**1, Scrapings; **AR**39, **VA**93, Scrapings of the earth; **SC**34, Rakings and scrapings of the earth; **VA**35, The scrapings; **TN**53, Scrappings of the earth.

scraping vbl n See **scrape v**

scraping boat See **scrape v B2**

scraping scooter See **scrape n 1**

scrap iron n esp **SE** *esp freq among Black speakers*
Liquor, esp when illegally made or of poor quality.
1942 *Amer. Mercury* July 55.85 **Harlem NYC** [Black], Maybe a shot of scrap-iron or a reefer. **1947** Boulware *Jive & Slang* [7] [Black], Scrap iron . . Whiskey. **1958** *Washington Post & Times Herald* (DC) 1 Nov 1/1 *(Hench Coll.)* **SC**, A trio of investigators warned the drinking public . . to beware of a new bootleg concoction, "scrap iron," noted more for its voltage than vintage. Composed chiefly of rubbing alcohol and mothballs, plus some yeast and cracked corn or corn meal—and sometimes a dash of the cleaning fluid Chlorox—it is made in galvanized drums, which give it a "scrap iron" taste. **1966–70** *DARE* (Qu. DD21b, *General words . . for bad liquor*) Infs **SC**26, 69, Scrap iron; (Qu. DD21c, *Nicknames for whiskey, especially illegally made whiskey*) Inf **SC**68, Scrap iron; (Qu. DD27, . . *Nicknames . . for wine*) Inf **GA**11, Scrap iron [*DARE* Ed: The Inf may have understood "wine" in the sense of **low wine,** here the inferior product of the first distillation in the moonshining process]. [3 of 4 Infs Black] **1970** Major *Dict. Afro-Amer. Slang* 101, Scrap iron: (1940's) bad liquor (Southern Negro college student use). **c1970** Pederson *Dial. Surv. Rural GA (What do you call cheap whiskey?)* 1 inf, **seGA**, Scrap iron ['skræp͟ˌaɪ]. [Inf Black] **1986** Pederson *LAGS Concordance (Cheap whiskey and . . home-brewed beer or whiskey)* 2 infs, **AL, GA**, Scrap iron; 1 inf, **swAL**, Scrap iron—modern term for homemade whiskey. [2 of 3 infs Black]

Scrap Islander n
1916 Macy–Hussey *Nantucket Scrap Basket* 143, *"Scrap Islander"*— The name applied to a Nantucketer by the people of Martha's Vineyard.

scrap johnnycake n Cf **crackling bread**
1903 *DN* 2.310 **seMO**, *Cracklin' bread.* . . Corn bread with 'cracklins.' In the North it is called 'scrap-johnnycake.'

scrap leaf See **scrap n**

scrapping See **scrap v**

scrappings See **scraping n 2**

scrapple n [Dimin of *scrap;* cf *EDD* scrappling "pl. Scraps, odds and ends. . . The renderings of lard."] **scattered, but chiefly Midl, esp PA, MD, C Atl** See Map Cf **panhas, souse**
A dish of meat scraps, usu pork, boiled with corn meal or flour, shaped into loaves, and freq sliced and fried.
1855 *Moore's Rural New Yorker* 10 Feb 47/3 **PA**, I observe a call for a recipe for making "Scrapple," and some other homely dishes. **c1870** Chipman *Notes on Bartlett* 387 *(DAE)* **PA**, Scrapple, equal parts of buckwheat flour and wheat flour boiled in the liquor produced in making 'Head-Cheese,' and used as 'Hasty Pudding' after cooling. **1890** *DN* 1.75 **PA**, Scrapple: a favorite Philadelphia dish, consisting of bacon chopped up and mixed with cornmeal, and fried in cakes. **1908** *German Amer. Annals* 10.41 **sePA**, Scrapple. Same as *ponhaws.* **1935** *AmSp* 10.172 **PA** [Engl of PA Germans], Scrapple, made of meat and corn meal, is sold everywhere. **1939** FWP *Guide NJ* 651 **cwNJ**, Fried scrapple, the inevitable breakfast dish of the country side. Made from

odd scraps of pork at winter "hog killings" and mixed with water-ground corn meal, scrapple is delicately flavored with a carefully compounded mixture of spices and herbs. It is sliced when cold and then fried. **1946** *PADS* 6.24 **swVA**, "Scrapple." "Solidified liquid leavings from liver pudding, etc., cooked (fried) with corn meal." Rural region. **c1955** Reed–Person *Ling. Atlas Pacific NW* 17 infs, Scrapple. [Made of corn meal, meat juice, and scraps]. **1965–70** *DARE* (Qu. H43, *Foods made from parts of the head and inner organs of an animal*) 151 Infs, **scattered, but chiefly Midl, esp PA, MD, C Atl,** Scrapple; **IN**3, Hard scrapple; (Qu. H25, . . *Names or nicknames . . for fried cornmeal*) Infs **CA**80, 101, **DC**7, **MO**7, **MA**122, **OH**66, **OR**1, **PA**134, Scrapple; (Qu. H45, *Dishes made with meat, fish, or poultry that everybody around here would know, but that people in other places might not*) Infs **PA**143, 171, 181, 200, 248, Scrapple; (Qu. H65, *Foreign foods favored by people around here*) Inf **PA**181, Scrapple. **1967** Faries *Word Geog. MO* 123, *Ponhaws. . . Scrapple* seems to be the prevalent term (60 percent) in Missouri. **1977** Anderson *Grass Roots Cookbook* 160 **nwAR,** *Arkansas Sausage Scrapple. . . Scrapple* is usually considered a Pennsylvania Dutch dish, yet it's popular in the Ozarks, too. Here is Mrs. Hatfield's favorite recipe, which she serves for breakfast drizzled with maple syrup or spread with peanut butter. **1986** Pederson *LAGS Concordance* **Gulf Region,** *(Scrapple)* [40 infs replied that they had heard of it but never had it, had never heard of it, or knew it only from a cookbook; 26 infs simply provided the term *scrapple;* 7 infs associate the dish with Pennsylvania, specifically Philadelphia, and 1 inf, **seGA,** calls it, "a Yankee dish." Of those infs familiar with the dish, 6 are from **TN,** 3 from **GA** and **TX,** and 2 each from **AL, FL,** and **LA,** and described it variously as "like souse, without vinegar, eaten fried"; "made from hog's head, sliced and fried"; "trimmings mixed with cornmeal"; "ground liver mixed with meal and fried"; or as equivalent to *souse meat* or *hoghead cheese.*]

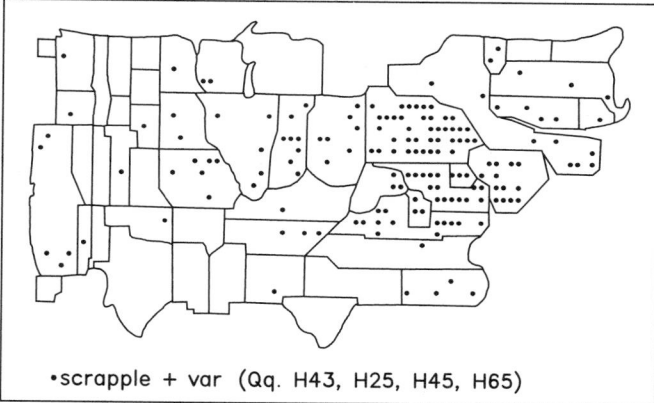

•scrapple + var (Qq. H43, H25, H45, H65)

scrap tobacco See **scrap** n

scratch v

1 See quot.

1908 *German Amer. Annals* 10.41 **sePA,** *Scratch.*—To itch. "My ear scratches." . . fr. Pa. Ger. *krŏdsa,* which means *scratch* or *itch;* Ger. *kratzen* has sometimes both meanings.

2 To incite (a horse) to buck by raking its sides in a kicking motion with the spurs; hence vbl n *scratching,* comb *scratching match* a bucking contest. **West** Cf **screw down**

1929 *AmSp* 5.59 **NE** [Cattle country talk], The "riders" often wear on their high heeled boots or shoes, "grappling-irons," spurs, pieces of metal pointed or holding serrated disks used to "scratch," "rowl," or "rake" a horse, in order that the "bronc" will "pitch" or run. **1935** Sandoz *Jules* 409 **wNE** (as of 1880–1930), Sundays, when the ground was n't frozen, became ranch days, with a crop of Kinkaider cowboys to show off before the native daughters at the scratching matches. **1936** Adams *Cowboy Lingo* 100, 'Scratching' was the act of keeping the feet moving in a kicking motion in riding bucking horses, and one of the acts necessary to win at any real bucking contest. **1937** Sandoz *Slogum* 291 **NE,** The little Sunday rodeos where the young fellows in secondhand hair pants showed off the powers of their long legs to scratch anything that walked on four feet and burned grass. **1941** Writers' Program *Guide WY* 465, *Scratching*—Scratching a horse with spurs while the animal is bucking.

scratch n[1]

1 In marble play: =**lag line.** Cf **taw line**

c1960 *Wilson Coll.* **csKY,** *Scratch.* . . The beginning point of a game, as of marbles. **1967–68** *DARE* (Qu. EE8, *The line toward which the players roll their marbles before beginning a game, to determine the order of shooting*) Infs **CA**15, **OH**56, Scratch. **1973** Allen *LAUM* 1.405 **Upper MW** (as of c1950), *Starting line* in marbles. In some marble games the players toss, throw, shoot, or "lag" the taw marble from a line scratched in the ground. . . scratch [1 inf, **IA**].

2 also *scratch feed,* ~ *grain:* Cracked or coarsely ground grain, esp corn. **esp Mid and S Atl**

1925 *Book of Rural Life* 8.4481, The prevailing practice . . is to feed the birds scratch grain in deep litter. . . A very efficient grain ration . . is composed of equal parts of cracked corn, wheat and heavy oats. **1938** in Lib. of Congress *Amer. Memory: WPA Life Hist.* (Internet) **FL,** So one day I drove her ole flivver to town, makin out I wuz goin for scratch feed. **1940** *Daily Progress* (Charlottesville VA) 13 Nov 5/1, At the time of the first trip to the laying house in the early morning, measure the scratch . . and scatter it well over the floor. . . In the afternoon, an hour or two before dark, give the hens a heavy feeding of scratch grain and see about the water supply again. **1968** *DARE* Tape **GA**21, Just straight corn or scratch and let it sour. **1969** Lyons *My Florida* 219, You'd be amazed at how much chicken scratch our feed stores and chain stores sell to people who use it to feed wild birds and squirrels. **1985** Wilkinson *Moonshine* 20 **neNC,** Because corn meal is expensive, bootleggers often start their mash with scratch feed—that is, hog feed or chicken feed—which has corn meal in it. **1986** Pederson *LAGS Concordance,* 1 inf, **neFL,** Scratch feed—coarse meal for chickens.

Scratch n[2] Also sp *Skratch* [*OED2* →1873] **esp Sth** Cf **Cratch** n[2], **Old Scratch**

The devil.

1856 in 1927 Jones *FL Plantation Rec.* 167 **nwFL,** The New Grounds cotton was the best cotton in this Country but is all torn to peases with limes [i.e., limbs] and treas and that which was not hurt with timber is Split all to Skratch. **1909** *DN* 3.367 **eAL, wGA,** *Scratch.* . . The devil; often with *Old.* **1969–70** *DARE* (Qu. CC8, . . *The devil*) Infs **GA**56, **WI**57, Scratch. **1970** Tarpley *Blinky* 279 **neTX,** *Who is supposed to "get" little children who aren't good?* . . No one under 60 says *Scratch*—another name for the devil—which is used exclusively by non-city men, chiefly those in the lowest educational division. **1974** *AmSp* 49.63 **sME coast** (as of c1900), *Scratch* . . Satan. **1986** Pederson *LAGS Concordance (Devil)* 1 inf, **cnGA,** Scratch.

Scratch-ankle n Also *Scratch-ankle Holler*

1965–70 *DARE* (Qu. C33, . . *Joking names . . for an out-of-the-way place, or a very small or unimportant place*) Inf **FL**17, Scratch-ankle—first name of Milton because of briars; (Qu. C34, *Nicknames for nearby settlements, villages, or districts*) Inf **FL**17, Scratch-ankle; **TN**44, Scratch-ankle Holler; (Qu. C35, *Nicknames for the different parts of your town or city*) Inf **TN**23, Scratch-ankle—poor White.

scratchback n **Sth**

A kind of **corn pone 1.**

1940 Brown *Amer. Cooks* 845 **VA,** *Scratch Backs*—2 cups . . corn meal—2 teaspoons salt—boiling water—Sift meal and salt together and pour boiling water over it very slowly, beating vigorously as water is added. . . Have cooky sheet very hot and well greased. Drop batter on it with a dessertspoon and bake in a very hot oven until a delicate brown. **1943** *Sat. Eve. Post* 15 May 58 **FL,** Hoecake, ashcake, journeycake, or johnnycake, corndodger and scratchback—they are all corn bread in its simplest form and as thoroughly American as corn itself. **1951** Hench *Coll.* **cVA,** Armistead Gordon happened to be talking of corn-pones and said that sometimes in his house they had fried corn-pones called scratch-backs. When I asked Mrs. Michie (sp?) if she knew what a scratch-back was, she said "Of course. It's a corn pone fried in a pan. You score it with a knife and it looks like something to scratch your back with." **1954** *Ibid* **AL,** Scratchback—recipe given to Virginia Hench. . . Ingredients . . cornmeal . . salt . . melted bacon grease (this gives a good flavor) or Crisco. . . Stir [cornmeal, salt and water] and beat vigorously until light and smooth. . . Put in the bacon grease. . . Then take a tablespoon and get a rounded spoonful of the mush. Drop on tin. . . Do this with the others. . . Temperature of oven 500 degrees for the first 20 minutes and then turn down to 450 and should take from 45–50 minutes to cook. . . Serve immediately with butter. **1999** *NADS Letters,* Scratchback—so characterized because the dried cornmeal was of coarse quality and when baked into cornbread, was "scratchy" to the tongue. . . I first heard the term in a book. . . I liked Southern tales as a kid.

scratch boss n Also *scratch foreman*
=**straw boss.**

  1965–69 *DARE* (Qu. HH43b, *The assistant to the top person in charge of a group of workmen*) Infs **MA**4, **MS**30, **NY**205, Scratch boss; **GA**19, Scratch foreman.

scratcher n

1 =**scratch harrow.** esp **Gulf States, TN**

  1954 *Harder Coll.* **cwTN**, Scratcher. . . A small v-shaped harrow, drawn by one mule or horse, used to tear out weeds and loosen the soil between rows of corn. **1966–70** *DARE* (Qu. L18, *Kinds of plows*) Inf **MS**81, Scratchers—past; **AL**33, Scratcher; (Qu. L20, *The implement used in a field after it's been plowed to break up the lumps*) Inf **TX**38, Scratcher; (Qu. L25, *The implement used to clean out weeds and loosen the earth between rows of corn*) Inf **FL**12, Harrow, scratcher; **GA**33, **TX**32, Scratcher. **1971** Wood *Vocab. Change* 371 **Sth**, Additional volunteered words: *drag harrow, drag tooth harrow, . . scratcher.* **1986** Pederson *LAGS Concordance*, 1 inf, **nwTN**, Scratcher—with fine teeth; *(Plow)* 5 infs, **AL**, (A) scratcher; 2 infs, **AL**, Scratchers; *(Harrow)* 1 inf, **ceAL**, Scratcher—some call spring tooth harrow; 1 inf, **csTN**, Scratchers—small, give, bounce up if hit rock.

2 also in combs *chain scratcher, dish ~, metal ~, pan ~, pot ~, wash ~:* A scouring pad. **scattered, but esp Midl, SE** See Map   Cf **scratch pad**

  1965–70 *DARE* (Qu. G14, *The rough metal pad that's used to scour pots and pans*) 42 Infs, **scattered, but esp Midl, SE**, Scratcher; 15 Infs, **scattered**, Pot (*or* chain, dish, metal, pan, wash) scratcher. [50 of 57 Infs female] **2001** *DARE* File **seWI** (as of c1960), When my brother Craig and I would do the dishes, we always used a scratcher on the burned pots.

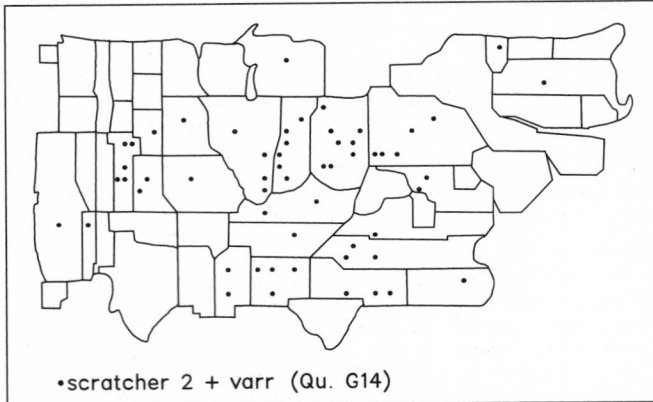

•scratcher 2 + varr (Qu. G14)

scratch feed See **scratch** n[1] **2**

scratch foreman See **scratch boss**

scratch grain See **scratch** n[1] **2**

scratch grass n

1 A **tearthumb:** usu *Polygonum sagittatum,* occas also *P. arifolium.*

  1790 Deane *New Engl. Farmer* 114, There are several other grasses produced in this country, as quitch grass, dogs grass; and scratch grass, resembling arsmart, on the uplands. **1824** Bigelow *Florula Bostoniensis* 158, *Polygonum sagittatum.* . . Scratch Grass. Stem prickly backward. **1891** *Jrl. Amer. Folkl.* 4.148 **NEng**, P[olygonum] sagittata [sic] [was] *Scratch-grass.* **1910** Graves *Flowering Plants* 163 **CT**, *Polygonum sagittatum.* . . Scratch Grass. Frequent. Swamps and wet places. **1933** Small *Manual SE Flora* 458, *Tracaulon* [=*Polygonum*] arifolium. . . Scratch-grass. **1950** Gray–Fernald *Manual of Botany* 587, Scratchgrass. . . *P[olygonum] sagittatum.* . . *P. arifolium.*

2 also *scratchgrass muhly:* A **muhly (grass)** (here: *Muhlenbergia asperifolia).* **West**

  1940 Gates *Flora KS* 131, Muhlenbergia asperifolia. . . Scratchgrass. . . Damp or marshy, often alkalin [sic] soils along streams and ditches. **1952** Davis *Flora ID* 114, *M[uhlenbergia] asperifolia.* . . Scratchgrass. . . Ill. and B.C., south to Tex., Calif., and Mex. **1961** Peck *Manual OR* 128, Scratchgrass. Perennial from hard tough rootstocks, . . pale green. **1968** Barkley *Plants KS* 52, Muhlenbergia

asperifolia. . . Scratchgrass. Alkali Muhly. **1970** Correll *Plants TX* 233, *Scratchgrass Muhly.* . . Moist alluvial soil near streams and ditches.

scratch gravel v phr

To hurry; to work hard.

  1834 *Richmond* (Ind.) *Palladium* 18 Jan. 1/1 *(DA)*, I thought I'd go home—and so I *scratched gravel* for Tennessee. **1883** (1971) Harris *Nights with Remus* 88 **GA** [Black], Ole Brer Rabbit, he'd bin a-pushin' 'long atter Brer Fox, but he des hatter scratch gravel fer ter keep up. **1887** (1892) Hinman *Corporal Si Klegg* 189, He tramped away with a determination to keep up with the old soldiers. . . "[W]e kin scratch gravel jest's well's they kin." **1898** Westcott *Harum* 226 **NY**, Trouble with me was . . that till I was consid'able older 'n you be I had to scratch grav'l like all possessed, an' it's hard work now sometimes to git the idee out of my head but what the money's wuth more 'n the things. **1950** *WELS* (*To run very fast, especially running away from something*) 1 Inf, **cwWI**, Scratched gravel; (*If somebody has been doing poor work or none at all.* . . "He was pretty careless at first, but I made him _____.") 1 Inf, **csWI**, Scratch gravel. **1959** *VT Hist.* 27.156, *Scratch gravel.* . . To get busy; to work. Occasional. **c1960** *Wilson Coll.* **csKY**, *Scratch gravel.* . . To exert oneself, as a team of mules would in pulling a heavy load up a gravelly hill. **1973** *DARE* File **Ozarks** (as of c1910), When one traveled in a hurry he was scratching gravel.

scratch harrow n Also *scratching harrow* esp **NEast** Cf **scratcher 1**

A toothed harrow or cultivator.

  1939 *LANE* Map 167 *(Harrow)* 1 Inf, **RI**, Scratching harrow. **1968–69** *DARE* (Qu. L20, *The implement used in a field after it's been plowed to break up the lumps*) Inf **NJ**20, Scratch or cut harrow; **NJ**22, Scratch harrow—had teeth, used behind disks; **NJ**58, Scratch harrow—teeth only 3 inches.

scratching See **scratch** v **2**

scratching harrow See **scratch harrow**

scratching match See **scratch** v **2**

scratch ivy n

A **poison ivy 1** (here: *Toxicodendron pubescens*).

  1960 Vines *Trees SW* 638, *Toxicodendron.* . . *quercifolium* [=*T. pubescens*]. . . Also known locally as Poison-wood, . . Scratch-ivy.

scratch pad n esp **N Cent** Cf **scratcher 2, scrub pad**

A scouring pad.

  1957 Battaglia *Resp. to PADS 20* **eMD**, (*A pad of rough metal used to scour pots and pans*) Scratch pad. **1967–70** *DARE* (Qu. G14, *The rough metal pad that's used to scour pots and pans*) Infs **IN**3, **MI**95, **OH**24, 48, 96, Scratch pad.

scratchweed n [*OED2* at *scratch* sb.[1] 12.b 1855 →]

A **cleavers** (here: *Galium aparine*).

  1940 Clute *Amer. Plant Names* 52, G[alium] aparine. . . Scratch-weed. **1971** Krochmal *Appalachia Med. Plants* 126, Galium aparine. . . Scratchweed. . . An annual that has a weak, reclining, bristly 4-angled stem, with hairy joints. . . Fruit is very bristly.

scraunch v See **scronch** v **1**

scraunch n See **scronch** n

scrauncher, scraunching See **scronch** v **2**

scrawn n [Etym uncert; cf *SND scrawn* (at *scran* n. 2 "Any kind of discarded refuse or rubbish which may be picked up by a beggar or scrounger")]

See quots.

  1950 Moore *Candlemas Bay* 191 **ME**, Lord, I couldn't let the poor old scrawn burn her tongue off. **1955** Adams *Grandfather* 259 **NY** (as of 1830s), He was a pawky young scrawn, puffed up with vainglory but plainly nervous.

scrawnty adj Cf Pronc Intro 3.I.23

  1954 *DE Folkl. Bulletin* 1.16, Scrawnty (puny or runty—as in "I take note the chickens hatched in the dark of the moon are kind of scrawnty.")

screak v Also sp *screek, skreak, skreek* [*OED2* a1500 →] Cf
screak owl

1 To shriek, screech, or scream; hence (vbl) n, ppl adj *screak-ing.* **chiefly Sth, S Midl**
1860 Street *Woods & Waters* 222 **NY,** There was an awful skreekin'
and howlin' in the bushes, and about twenty of the fightin' characters of
the Carry Tribe bust in. **1899** (1912) Green *VA Folk-Speech* 371,
Screak. . . To utter a sharp, shrill sound or outcry; also, to creak, as a
door or wheel. *Ibid, Screak.* . . Anticipating pain with fear; imitating
the noise made. **1942** Hall *Smoky Mt. Speech* 100 **wNC, eTN,** *Squeak*
was heard only as [skrik], which seems to be a blend of *squeak* and
screech or *shriek.* [Footnote:] The usual meaning of [skrik] is 'squeak,'
but the sense 'shriek' is evident in the lines from 'Pretty Polly': He saw
his pretty Polly come flowing in her blood,/ And [skrikən] she banished
[sic] away. **1967** *DARE* (Qu. KK16, *A great noise or disturbance: "I
wish they'd stop making that awful _____.")* Inf **AR47,** Screaking
noise. **1976** Ryland *Richmond Co. VA* 376, *Screak*—cross between
shriek and squeak. **1980** *DARE* File **AR, wKY, wTN, eTX,** Screak =
screech. **1989** Gurganus *Oldest Confederate Widow* 283 **Sth,** A shrill
cry lifts from out the woods. . . Such ghosty screeking, "Heeere y'all,
heeere y'all!" Cassie soon says, "It [is] peacocks."

2 To squeak, squeal, creak; to grate; hence n *screaking,* ppl
adj *screaking.* **chiefly S Midl**
1843 *New Englander & Yale Rev.* 1.506, You have set the senses laboriously to work to fill the hopper with their coarse grains . . , then
hoisted the gate, and with deafening screakings and monotonous scran-
nel pipings, you have produced—meal? **1883** (1971) Harris *Nights
with Remus* 70 **GA** [Black], All day long Brer Rabbit en Brer Fox keep
de front gate a-skreakin'. **1899** [see **1** above]. **1925** Dargan *Highland
Annals* 223 **cwNC,** "Anybody," he said, "that would take pay from Viny
fer the leetle mite she eats would be so stingy they'd screak." **1929**
Wolfe *Look Homeward* 72 **NC,** The other [trolley] car . . curved with a
skreeking jerk into the switch. **1942** [see **1** above]. **1950** Stuart *Hie
Hunters* 46 **eKY,** Did listened to the barn door screak on its rusty
hinges. **1955** Ritchie *Singing Family* 125 **seKY,** A door screaked, a
chest-lid fell shut, and then soon he was back down with a crackly
folded paper in his hand. **1982** Slone *How We Talked* 19 **eKY** (as of
c1950), A stingy person was described as. . . So tight he screaks when
he walks. **1986** Pederson *LAGS Concordance,* **chiefly Inland Gulf Region,** 10 infs, Screaking—squeaking; 1 inf, Screaking frog; 1 inf, Got to
screaking—began squeaking; 1 inf, Screaking on the blackboard with
[a] piece of chalk; 1 inf, Screaks—squeaks. **1993** Mason *Feather
Crowns* 236 **KY,** All of the babies were sick. They were feverish and
hot, with wrinkled, red faces and feeble, screaking cries.

screak n Also sp *screek, skriek*

1 A shriek, scream. *?obs* Cf **screak v 1**
a1820 in 1895 *New Engl. Mag.* 18.413 **MA,** We were alarmed in the
night by the Screaks of his Sister, his Mother being in a Strong fit.
1864 Brownell *Indian Races* 726 **MN,** A smothered skriek from the sur-
vivors, followed each dull, crushing blow of the weapon, as they, powerless with terror, awaited their turn.

2 A squeak. Cf **screak v 2**
1857 *N. Amer. Rev.* 84.351, With the mind's ear they distinguish the
spirit-stirring screak of the fiddle. **1936** Greene *Death Deep South* 14,
The taller girl finished her drink with a shrill screak of the straw.

screaking (vbl) n, ppl adj See **screak v 1, 2**

screak owl n Also sp *screek owl* Cf **screak v 1**
A **screech owl 1** (here: *Otus asio*).
c1940 *LAMSAS Materials,* 2 infs, **wVA,** Screak owl. **1966** Dakin *Dial.
Vocab. Ohio R. Valley* 2.386, The Jackson Purchase has . . *screek owl,*
and *screet ~.* The latter two terms are each attested only one time else-
where—*screek owl* in Vinton County, Ohio, and *screet owl* in Johnson
County, Kentucky. **1986** Pederson *LAGS Concordance,* 1 inf, **neTN,**
Screak owl.

screaky adj Also sp *skreaky, skreeky, skrieky* [**screak v 2**]
esp S Midl
Squeaky; creaky.
1885 Twain *Huck. Finn* 232, They had borrowed a melodeum—a sick
one; and when everything was ready, a young woman set down and
worked it, and it was pretty skreeky and colicky. **1890** (1895) Riley
Rhymes of Childhood 60 **IN,** An' Mother settin' here / Darnin' socks, an'
rockin' in the skreeky rockin'-cheer. **1892** *DN* 1.231 **KY,** Skrieky

[skriki]: creaky. **1909** *DN* 3.405 **nwAR,** Skreaky. . . Squeaky, from
screech for shriek. "My shoes are skreaky." "I hate skreaky doors."
1986 Pederson *LAGS Concordance,* 1 inf, **cwMS,** Screaky—squeaky.

scream v Usu with *on;* also *scream cold on esp freq among
Black speakers* Cf *play the dozens* (at **dozen n B1**), **signify 1**
To insult or disparage (someone), esp in a ritualized exchange
of insults; hence vbl n *screaming (on)* exchanging ritualized
insults; insulting someone publicly.
1970 *Current Slang* 5.2.12 [Black Univ student slang], Scream on. . .
To speak in a derogatory manner about. **1971** Roberts *Third Ear* np
[Black], *Screaming on.* . . telling someone off. . . embarrassing someone
publicly. **1972** Kochman *Rappin'* 274, The oldest terms [sic] for the
game of exchanging ritualized insults is "the dozens." . . The term
"sounding" is by far the most common in New York. . . "screaming" in
Harrisburg. **1980** Folb *Runnin' Down* 253 **cwCA** [Black], Scream,
scream on, scream cold on—See *holler* [=Disparage, ridicule, or con-
front with particular force.]

screamer n Cf **buster 1, ripper 1**
An extraordinary person, animal, or thing; see quots.
1818 Weems *Drunkard's Looking Glass* 18, Here I come! a screamer!
yes, d_____n me, if I an't a proper screamer; just from Bengal. **1834**
Life Andrew Jackson 16, At a cokfite he was a rale screamer, who cou'd
grin the bark off a tree. **1837** in 1968 Bartlett *Americanisms* 386,
Screamer. . . The folks are all waiting to see the fast steamer . . Ah, here
she is now; you, sir, ain't she a *screamer?* **1899** (1912) Green *VA Folk-
Speech* 371, *Screamer.* . . Something very great, excellent or exciting; a
thing that attracts the attention or draws forth screams of astonishment,
delight, etc.; a whacker, a bouncer. **1939** FWP *Guide TN* 135, Back-
country folk are prone to use parts of speech in strange ways. . . An extravagant lie is a "ripper," a "snorter," a "screamer." **1995** *Brophy Coll.*
66 **swMO** (as of c1960), *Screamer.* [A] bouncing fellow or girl, a strong
man.

scream on See **scream**

screech v Cf **scrinch 2, scrooch 2b, squinch**
To narrow the eyes; hence *screech-eyed* having the eyes narrowed.
1968 *DARE* (Qu. X25, *To close your eyes part way—for example,
when looking at the sun)* Inf **SC58,** Screech; **GA34,** Screech-eyed.

screech cat n
1956 Sorden–Ebert *Logger's Words* 30 **Gt Lakes,** Screech-cat, A high
stump, usually from a windfall, which has splinters that whistle or sing
in the wind.

screecher n

1 A **screech owl 1** (here: *Otus asio*).
1939 *LANE* Map 230 *(Screech owl)* 1 inf, **wCT,** Screecher—a little
devil, but he's got claws!

2 =**long-billed curlew.**
1955 MA Audubon Soc. *Bulletin* 39.446, *Long-billed Curlew.* . .
Screecher (Mass. Its call is harsh and loud.)

screech-eyed See **screech**

screeching owl n
A **screech owl 1** (here: *Otus asio*).
1939 *LANE* Map 230 *(Screech owl)* 1 inf, **wMA,** Screeching owl.
c1940 *LAMSAS Materials,* 2 infs, **SC, GA,** Screeching owl. **1956** MA
Audubon Soc. *Bulletin* 40.81, *Screech Owl.* . . Screeching Owl. **1966-
69** *DARE* (Qu. Q1, . . *Kind of owl that makes a shrill, trembling cry)*
Infs **CA107, NJ10, SD5,** Screeching owl; **SC46,** Screeching owl—foretells a death if he takes up near your house. **1986** Pederson *LAGS Concordance* **Gulf Region** *(Screech owl)* 10 infs, Screeching owl(s).

screech owl n

1 A small eared owl of the genus *Otus,* usu *O. asio.* For
other names of the latter see **barn owl 4, booby ~, cat ~,
chouette, cold owl, cussie ~, death ~, digdee ~, Florida
screech ~, freeze ~, gimme bird, graveyard owl 2, gray
~ 2, hooping ~, hoot ~ 1, horned ~, katydid B3, kitten-
head, laughing owl, little horned ~, mottled ~, night ~ 1,
pigeon ~, quivering ~, rat ~ 1, red ~, scooch ~, screak ~,
screecher 1, screeching owl, screet ~, scrinch ~, scritch ~,**

scrooch ~, scroonch ~, scrunch ~, shiveling ~, shimmering ~, shivering ~ 1, shriek ~, sparrow ~, squeak ~, squeech ~, squinch ~, squitch ~, whinnering ~, whispering ~, whoop ~; for other names of *O. trichopsis* see **whiskered owl**

1671 Ogilby *America* 147, The Birds both common and peculiar [to New England] are thus recited: . . The long-liv'd Raven, th'ominous Screech-Owl,/ Who tells, as old Wives say, disasters foul. **1812** Wilson *Amer. Ornith.* 5.83, Red Owl. . . This is . . well known by its common name, the *Little Screech Owl*. **1884** *Century Illustr. Mag.* Nov 121 **GA**, The screech-owl would shake and shiver in the depths of the woods. **1892** Torrey *Foot-Path Way* 177 **NEng**, On moonlight evenings the tremulous, haunting cry of the screech-owl comes to your ears, always from far away. **1929** *KY Folkl. & Poetry Mag.* 4.1.14, The hoot of a screech owl is a sign of death. **1950** *WELS (The kind of owl that makes a trembling cry)* 43 Infs, **WI**, Screech owl; *(What are some of the birds that stay all winter in your neighborhood?)* 1 Inf, **WI**, Schrech [sic] owl. **1965–70** *DARE* (Qu. Q1, . . *Kind of owl that makes a shrill, trembling cry*) 697 Infs, **widespread**, Screech owl; **SC34**, Screech owl—supposedly foretells a death in a family—pull your shoe off and turn it bottom up to get rid of him; red-hot poker—just heat it while he's sitting and he'll leave; **SC40, 41**, Screech owl—foretells death (in family); **CA78**, California screech owl; (Qu. Q2, . . *Kinds of owls*) 26 Infs, **chiefly Missip-Ohio Valley, Sth**, Screech owl; (Qu. Q3, . . *Birds that come out only after dark*) Inf **CT5**, Screech owl. [*DARE* Ed: Some of these Infs may refer instead to senses below.] **1986** Pederson *LAGS Concordance Gulf Region*, 469 infs, Screech (owl)(s); 36 infs, Screech owl—(very) small (*or* little) (owl); 14 infs, Screech owl—foretells death (*or* someone will die, *or* bad luck); 3 infs, Screech owl—silence it by tying knots in sheets (*or* hand towel); 2 infs, Screech owl = hoot owl; 1 inf, Screech owl—high shrill call, not a barn owl; 1 inf, Screech owl—screech means weather will change; 1 inf, Screech owl = chouette; 1 inf, Screech owl—turn shoes over when you hear one; 1 inf, Screech owl = shivering owl; 1 inf, Screech owl—makes a whistling sort of noise; 1 inf, Screech owl—little, sounds like horse whinnying; 1 inf, Screech owl—live in trees. [*DARE* Ed: Some of these infs may refer instead to senses below.]

2 Any of several other owls, as:

a =**barn owl 1**.　[*OED2* 1593 →]
1839 Audubon *Synopsis Birds* 25, Strix americana [=*Tyto alba*]. . . American Screech-Owl.—Barn Owl. **1939** *LANE* Map 230 (*Screech owl*) 1 inf, **neMA**, Barn owl = screech owl; 1 inf, **cwRI**, Snap owl = screech owl, nests in the barn or in a tree hollow. **c1940** *LAMSAS Materials*, 1 inf, **OH**, Screech owl—big. **1967** *PA Game News* Nov 13 **PA**, The barn or screech owl is often called the "feathered cat" because it is a great foe of mice. **1986** Pederson *LAGS Concordance (Screech owl)* 4 infs, 2 **LA**, 1 **seAL**, 1 **cAR**, Screech owl = barn owl; 1 inf, **neTN**, Screech owl—a big white owl.

b =**saw-whet owl**.
1838 Geol. Surv. OH *Second Annual Rept.* 161, Strix acadica [=*Aegolius acadicus*]. . . *Little screach* [sic] *Owl*. Ibid 179, *S*[*trix*] *acadica*. Both this species and the *S. asio* [=*Otus asio*] exist among us, but they are commonly blended together as one under the name of *Screach Owl*. **1890** Warren *Birds PA* 152, Saw-whet Owl. . . This pigmy mass of owl-life is . . the species which was regarded as not destructive to poultry and game by the author of the "Scalp Act [=a Pennsylvania game law enacted in the 1880s that provided for bounties on some animals and birds of prey]," when he introduced therein a clause exempting "The Acadian Screech or Barn Owl."

c =**great horned owl**.
1939 *LANE* Map 230 (*Screech owl*) 1 inf, **eME**, Screech owl—as big as a turkey, with eyes like an ox; 1 inf, **seNH**, The screech owl kills chickens. **1986** Pederson *LAGS Concordance (Screech owl)* 1 inf, **seAL**, Screech owl = horn owl; 1 inf, **neGA**, Screech owls—catch chickens.

d =**burrowing owl**. esp **TX**
1981 Pederson *LAGS Basic Materials*, 1 inf, **seTX**, Screech owl—lives in ground in armadillo hole; 1 inf, **csTX**, Screech owl—lives in holes in the ground; 1 inf, **ceTX**, Screech owl—dark color, goes boo, boo, boo.

screek v See **screak** v

screek n See **screak** n

screek owl See **screak owl**

screench owl See **scrinch owl**

screen house n Cf **safe 1**
See quots.
1969 Green *Wild Cow Tales* 25 **TX** (as of 1930s), Another means of protecting meat was by constructing . . a screen house. Such a building would be located where there was usually a breeze and would have a roof and be closed in all the way around with screen wire to let the air blow freely, and with the exception of the very hottest of weather, this was a satisfactory way in dry climates to protect fresh meat for several days until it could be used. **1981** Pederson *LAGS Basic Materials*, 1 inf, **nwFL**, We'd have a screen house to put our corn in.

screet owl n [Cf *EDD screet* v. "To screech, scream; to make a shrill sound."]
A **screech owl 1** (here: *Otus asio*).
c1940 *LAMSAS Materials*, 6 infs, 5 **NY**, Screet owl. **1966** [see **screak owl**].

screw n
1 also *cheap screw*: A stingy, miserly person; a sharp bargainer.
1899 (1912) Green *VA Folk-Speech* 372, Screw. . . A stingy fellow; a close or penurious person; one who makes a sharp bargain; an extortioner; a miser; a skinflint. **1919** *DN* 5.64 **NM**, Cheap-skate, -screw, a stingy person. **1932** Toone *Yankee Slang* 32, Screw: Money lender. **1966–70** *DARE* (Qu. U33, *Names or nicknames for a stingy person*) Inf **GA3**, Cheap screw; **PA245**, Screw. **1986** Pederson *LAGS Concordance (He is a . . tightwad)* 1 inf, **swGA**, Cheap screw.
2 A cowboy. Cf **top screw**
1920 Hunter *Trail Drivers TX* 298, Ordinarily, a cowboy is a "waddy" or "screw" or "buckaroo." **1933** *AmSp* 8.1.30 **nwTX** [Ranch diction], *Screw*. The ordinary *cowpuncher*.
3 See **screw cut**.

screw- prefix See **skew-**

screw auger n
A **ladies' tresses** (here: *Spiranthes cernua*).
[**1894** *Jrl. Amer. Folkl.* 7.101, Spiranthes cernus (?), . . screw-auger, Nova Scotia.] **1900** Lyons *Plant Names* 180, G[*yrostachys*] *cernua* [=*Spiranthes c.*] . . Screw-auger. **1950** Gray-Fernald *Manual of Botany* 479, *S*[*piranthes*] *cernua*. . . Screw-auger. . . Wet to dryish open soil or in bogs, low thickets or on shores. **1961** Smith *MI Wildflowers* 85, *Screw-auger* . . *Spiranthes cernua*. . . Flower small, creamy or white, usually with a vanilla-like odor, in 2–4 spiral or nearly vertical rows forming a rather compact spike. **1976** Bailey-Bailey *Hortus Third* 1066, [*Spiranthes*] *cernua*. . . *Screw-auger*. . . Early summer–early autumn. U.S. Canada.

screw-awed See **skew- b**

screw bean n Also *screwbean mesquite, screw(-pod) ~, screwwood* [See quot 1985]
A **mesquite B1**: usu *Prosopis pubescens* of the southwestern US, but also *P. reptans* in Texas; also their fruit. Also called **tornillo**; for other names of *P. pubescens* see **mescrew 1**
1844 Gregg *Commerce* 2.78 **TX**, In the immediate vicinity of El Paso there is another small growth called *tornillo* (or screw-wood), so denominated from a spiral pericarp. **1866** Lindley-Moore *Treas. Botany* 930 **SW**, *P*[*rosopis*] *pubescens*, . . is the Screw-bean or Screw Mezquit of the Americans. **1873** Army *Interesting NM* 110, *Mezquite*, or *screw bean*.—This in the valleys of the Gila becomes a considerable tree. **1884** Sargent *Forests of N. Amer.* 62, *Prosopis pubescens*. . . Screw Bean. *Screw-pod Mesquit*. . . The pods used as fodder, and sometimes made into flour by the Indians. **1931** U.S. Dept. Ag. *Misc. Pub.* 101.77, *Screwbean (Strombocarpa . . pubescens)*, or screwbean mesquite. . . *Dwarf screwbean (S. cinerascens* [=*Prosopis reptans*]), sometimes called ballhead screwbean, . . occurs in southwestern Texas. . . Its very small size (mostly 6 to 12 inches high) . . , would provide far less forage than does the common screwbean. **1941** Writers' Program *Guide UT* 19, The screwpod mesquite is a peculiar shrub that grows in the dry, sandy soil of desert canyons. It bears numerous spirally-twisted pods containing ten or twenty beanlike seeds. **1966** *Julian Apple Day* [19] **csCA**, He sandblasts manzanita and collects screwbeans and the unusual desert ornamentals. **1967** *DARE* (Qu. S26e, *Other wildflowers not yet mentioned;* not asked in early QRs) Inf **CA4**, Mesquite—screwbean and

several varieties on sand dunes. **1985** Dodge *Flowers SW Deserts* 85, Fremont Screwbean, Screwpod Mesquite. . . *Prosopis pubescens*. . . Although the screwbean, so called because of the tight spiral curl formed by the seed pod, is not as common as honey mesquite, it is nearly as widespread.

screw bill n

A crossbill (*Loxia* spp).

1956 MA Audubon Soc. *Bulletin* 40.254 **ME,** Red Crossbill. . . Screw Bill (. . . The crossed mandibles are employed in "screwing" into the cones of pine and allied trees to extract their seeds.) . . *White-winged Crossbill*. . . Screw-bill.

screw cut n Also *screw (haircut)* [Prob varr of *crew cut;* cf Intro "Language Changes" II.8]

1965–68 *DARE* (Qu. X5, . . *Different kinds of men's haircuts*) Infs **KS**7, **NY**82, **PA**139, Screw; **MS**60, Screw cut; **OK**42, Screw haircut.

screw down v, hence vbl n *screwing down* Cf **scratch** v 2

See quots.

1936 Adams *Cowboy Lingo* 100, 'Screwing down' was the act of sinking the spurs into the cinch and failing to move the feet in kicking motion as provided by rodeo rules. **1936** McCarthy *Lang. Mosshorn* np **West** [Rodeo terms], Screwin' Down. A rider who comes out of the chute with knees clamped tightly to saddle and both spurs digging in.

screw-eyed See **skew- h**

screw fly See **screwworm**

screw-gee(d), screw-gied See **skew- a**

screw haircut See **screw cut**

screw-haw(ed) See **skew- b**

screwing down See **screw down**

screw-jawed See **skew- c**

screwman n Gulf States, esp LA

A stevedore who loads and unloads cotton bales.

[**1852** in 1927 Jones *FL Plantation Rec.* 72 **nwFL,** I will Commence getting timbers for the Screw [Footnote: I.e., the cotton baling-press] Next Week.] **1856** (1857) Nordhoff *9 Yrs. Sailor* 38 **AL,** A lighter-load of cotton came down, and with it, a stevedore and several gangs of the *screw men,* whose business it is to load cotton-ships. **1941** Writers' Program *Guide LA* 74, The cotton screwmen organized in 1851 and struck successfully in 1854 and 1858 for higher wages. They became the aristocrats of the river front and by striking in 1866 secured a raise in pay from $2.50 and $3.00 a day to $5.00 and $7.00. **1945** Saxon *Gumbo Ya-Ya* 60 **LA,** Screwmen—who 'screwed' or packed the cotton into the ship's hold. **1981** Pederson *LAGS Basic Materials,* 1 inf, **seLA,** Screwmen—longshoremen who "screw the cargo up in the ship." [*DARE* Ed: Inf was recounting jobs held by his father.]

screw mesquite See **screw bean**

screw pine n

1 Std: a tree of the genus *Pandamus,* usu *P. tectorius.* For other names of this sp see **hala, lauhala;** for names of its fruit see **key 6**

2 =**lodgepole pine.**

1908 Rogers *Tree Book* 50, Lodgepole pine. . . I well remember the curious rustic chairs and seats at the Dome Lake Club House in the Big Horn Mountains in Wyoming, made of the extravagantly twisted branches of this tree. They called it "screw pine," I remember.

screw-pod mesquite See **screw bean**

screw-shy See **skew- h**

screwstem n

An herbaceous plant of the genus *Bartonia,* often with a twisted stem, native to much of the eastern half of the US.

1822 Eaton *Botany* 202, Bartonia. . . paniculata . . screwstem. . . Stem sub-ramose, 4-sided and becoming spirally twisted. **1900** Lyons *Plant Names* 58, Bartonia. . . Two or three species, eastern U.S. . . Screwstem. **1968** Radford et al. *Manual Flora Carolinas* 844, B[artonia] panicu-lata. . . Screw-stem. Stems erect, sprawling or twining, usually pur-

plish. . . Bogs, marshes and pocosins. **1970** Correll *Plants TX* 1209, Bartonia paniculata. . . Screw-stem. . . Flowers to about 5 mm. long . . , creamy-white.

screw the pooch v phr Cf **fuck the dog, jack the dog, poke the puppy**

1991 *DARE* File **cnAL, neOH,** I know the term to mean "to mess up" or "to contaminate," as in, "If she includes that inaccurate data in her study, it will screw the pooch." or, "He really screwed the pooch when he pulled the pin on the grenade too early." . . I am 48 years old, grew up in Cleveland, Ohio, and have learned that a 47 year old woman from Birmingham, Alabama, knows the term in the same way as I; she also never recalls it being used with a sexual or provocative connotation.

screw-wood See **screw bean**

screwworm n

A blowfly larva, usu *Cochliomyia hominivorax,* formerly common esp in Florida and Texas; hence *screw(worm) fly* the adult of such a fly.

1855 *Scientific Amer.* 13 Oct 35 **TX,** I noticed . . an article on the "blow fly," stating that the eggs were hatched after a deposit. This is not the case with the blow-fly, or screw-fly (so called here,) so well known and dreaded by Texas stock raisers. **1872** Morrell *Flowers & Fruits* 381 **TX,** A Texan at once thinks, from this description, of a "screw worm." **1884** (1966) Aldridge *Life on a Ranch* 191 **TX,** We were a good deal troubled in the summer of 1882 by what is called 'screw-fly,' an insect which lays eggs on any raw place that an animal may happen to have, from which are hatched out a number of screw-worms. **1905** Kellogg *Amer. Insects* 344, A flesh-fly of serious importance is the terrible screw-worm fly, *Compsomyia macellaria* [=*Cochliomyia m.*] . . As a pest of domestic animals the greatest injuries have been caused in Texas. **1944** (1967) McNichols *Crazy Weather* 15 **SW,** Every newborn calf had to be found and have its navel doctored with antiseptic and pine-tar salve against screw-fly blow, so the screw-fly patrol was a tediously regular, unending job. **1965–70** *DARE* (Qu. R12, . . *Other kinds of flies*) 25 Infs, **chiefly Sth, TX,** Screwworm fly; **AL**25, **GA**7, **TN**56, Screw fly; (Qu. R13, *Flies that come to meat or fruit*) Inf **AR**28, Screw fly; **MO**39, Screwworm; **FL**32, Screwworm fly; (Qu. K28, . . *Chief diseases that cows have*) Infs **GA**22, **TX**69, 75, Screwworm. **1967–69** *DARE* Tape **CO**4, Texas and Oklahoma and Arizona and those places, they have what you call the screwworm. And . . they—just like maggots—they got to be taken care of; **TX**69A, A screwworm is a little worm that is laid by a fly. The eggs are laid on live flesh, a live animal . . this egg hatches into a worm and that worm eats flesh. . . They'll finally kill the animal. . . We've eliminated that particular fly now. **1986** Pederson *LAGS Concordance,* 6 infs, 3 **TX,** Screwworm(s); 1 inf, **cwLA,** Screw flies.

screwy adj [Appar *screwy* twisted, infl by *askew, skewed*] Cf **ascrew**

Askew.

1950 *WELS* (*What do you say about a necktie that is out of place?*) 1 Inf, **cwWI,** Screwy; (*Out of shape: "Now you've knocked it all _____"*) 1 Inf, **seWI,** Screwy. **1965–70** *DARE* (Qu. KK70, *Something that has got out of proper shape: "That house is all _____."*) Infs **GA**31, **MI**82, **NV**9, **WI**52, Screwy; (Qu. MM13, *The table was nice and straight until he came along and knocked it _____*) Infs **MI**111, **MA**56, **PA**190, **RI**8, **WA**11, Screwy; [**NC**9, Cock-screwy].

scribbet n Cf **schnibble**

A scrap, fragment.

1968 *DARE* (Qu. W25, *When a woman is cutting out a dress to sew . . the little scraps of cloth left over*) Inf **CT**11, Scribbets ['skrɪbɪts]. **1978** *Yankee* Apr 126 **NH,** If you cut up or bone your own meats, simmer all bones and "scribbets" for broth.

scribe n Also *scriber* [*OED2 scribe* sb.¹ 6 "Now somewhat arch."] esp Appalachians, Ozarks

A penman; see quots.

1903 *DN* 2.328 **seMO,** Scribe. . . Writer. 'I can read writin, but I'm a mighty poor scribe.' **1904** *DN* 2.421 **nwAR,** Scribe. . . Penman. 'He's the best scribe in our township; he writes a beautiful hand.' **1924** (1946) Greer-Petrie *Angeline Gits an Eyeful* 6 **csKY,** And her a good scribe too! **1926** *DN* 5.403 **Ozarks,** Scriber. . . Writer. "He's a right good scriber" means that his *handwrite* is easily legible. **1939** *Hall*

Coll. **wNC,** He's a pretty good scribe, he writes a nice hand. **1967** *Ibid* **eTN,** His father was a pretty good scribe . . [he] could write quite well.

scrich owl See **scritch owl**

scrid n Also sp *skrid, squid* [Varr of *screed* a fragment] **chiefly NEng**

A piece, scrap, bit.

   1860 *Atlantic Mth.* 5.7 **NEng,** They're glass chips, and brittle shavings, slender pinkish scrids. **1869** *Harper's New Mth. Mag.* 39.56 **NEng,** Little Gab sat thoughtfully . . , knitting her pretty brows over the scrid of patchwork I had prepared for her. **1877** *Atlantic Mth.* 40.72 **CT,** The wailing day-old baby was brought . . , a mere scrid and atom of humanity. **1914** *DN* 4.79 **ME, nNH,** *Skrid, squid.* . . A lump. A little bit. "He was all a skrid o' fat." "He et every skrid." **1979** Lewis *How to Talk Yankee* [30] **nNEng,** *Scrid* . . tiny portion. "Want a little more of this roobub pie?" "Well, I might take just a scrid, thank you." **1982** *DARE* File **coastal ME,** Scrid: a small piece or bite. **2002** *DARE* File—Internet **cwCA,** The easy fix . . is to make a new pin that's a scrid longer. [*DARE* Ed: Writer learned term from person from ME.] *Ibid* **PA** [Susquehanna University Web Central], How can one ever hope to find that annoyingly evasive scrid of information . . in such a large pool of digital information?

scriffen See **striffen**

scrimage, scrimitch, scrimmage See **skirmish**

scrimption n Also *scrimshun, scrumption, scription* [Engl dial] **chiefly Sth, S Midl** Cf **scrimptom, skimption**

A very small piece or quantity; a bit, scrap.

   [**1834** *Life Andrew Jackson* 33, An affair requirin so much dexterity, every scrimptius bit on't havin tu be worked with master skill.] **1867** Harris *Sut Lovingood Yarns* 46 **TN,** A crazy organ-grinder cum a-pas' yere jis' a small scrimpshun slower nur chain litenin. **1886** *S. Bivouac* 4.349 **sAppalachians,** Scrimshun (scrimption, a very little). **1887** (1967) Harris *Free Joe* 181 **GA,** No vittels would she git from me,—not a scrimption. **1899** (1912) Green *VA Folk-Speech* 372, Scrimption. . . A small portion; a pittance; as, just a *scrimption* of salt. **1909** *DN* 3.367 **eAL, wGA,** Scrimption. . . A small amount, a bit. "You never had a scrimption of sense." **1911** *DN* 3.547 **NE,** Scrimption. . . A small quantity, "A scrimption of cloth," "Use just a scrimption." **1912** *DN* 3.589 **wIN,** Scrimption. . . A very small bit. "When the cake was passed I didn't get even a scrimption." **1942** Warnick *Garrett Co. MD* 13 **nwMD** (as of 1900–18), Scrimption . . a small quantity. **1952** Brown *NC Folkl.* 1.588, Scrimption. . . A small amount. **1966–68** *DARE* (Qu. LL1, *Something very small:* "I only took a _____ one.") Inf **NJ20,** Scrimption ['skrɪmpšən]; (Qu. LL6b, *A small, indefinite amount*) Inf **MS42,** Scrumption. **1967** Williams *Greenbones* 95 **GA** (as of c1910), We got to change before we go visiting. And if you got a scription of soap. **1986** *DARE* File **wNC** (as of c1920s), "There was no butter left, not a scrimption." "Give me a little milk, just a scrimption."

scrimptom n Also *scrimton, skimptum*

=**scrimption.**

   1904 Day *Kin o' Ktaadn* 45 **ME,** Not a scrimptom for any of the folks out your way. *Ibid* 150, He has n't got a scrimtom of his plug left. **1907** *DN* 3.249 **eME,** *Skimptum.* . . Same as *dite.* [*Ibid* 243, *Dite.* . . A very small amount, a little bit.]

scrimshauling vbl n [Prob from *scrimshaw* to employ oneself in making scrimshaw (decorative carvings, esp on whalebone), but cf *scrimshank* to shirk one's duty]

   c1965 *DARE* File **seMA,** Scrimshauling ['skrɪm,šɔlɪŋ] . . complaining, griping, grousing. "I'm tired of listening to all his scrimshauling."

scrimshun See **scrimption**

scrimton See **scrimpton**

scrimy adj |'skraɪmi| [Etym unknown] **sNEng**

1 Stingy, niggardly; meager, skimpy.

   1943 *LANE* Map 484 *(Miser, tightwad),* Stingy. . . 5 infs, **CT,** Scrimy. **1969–70** *DARE* (Qu. U33, *Names or nicknames for a stingy person*) Inf **MA76,** Scrimy ['skraɪmi]; **MA40,** ['skraɪni] [sic]; (Qu. U35, *Words meaning thrifty but not in a complimentary way:* "She's not a bad housekeeper, but very _____.") Inf **MA41,** Scrimy ['skraɪmi]; (Qu. U36b, . . *A person who saves in a mean way or is greedy in money matters:* "She certainly is _____.") Inf **MA76,** Scrimy; **MA40,**

['skraɪmi] [sic]; (Qu. LL13, *Not full or sufficient:* "She gave us a _____ meal.") Inf **MA77,** Scrimy [skraɪmi]. **c1974** *DARE* File **cnMA,** I've heard my sister, who has always lived in Massachusetts, use it [=*scrimy*] in recent years, but I don't remember it earlier. **1985** *Ibid* **CT,** Some years ago, we camped next to a family from Connecticut. In the course of our conversation we described the servings at a local restaurant as "chintzy." In their area, the word is "scrimy" (long 'i') meaning scimpy [sic].

2 Dirty, contemptible, mean.

   1931 Taylor *Cape Cod Mystery* 219 **eMA,** It was a scrimy thing to do. **1969** *DARE* FW Addit **CT,** Pretty scrimy [FW suggests] bunch of kids— pretty grubby. **1994** *DARE* File **csMA** (as of c1950), When my father referred to a man of contemptible, mean-minded dishonesty he called him "scrimy." I assume it is a portmanteau word from scruffy or scroungy + slimy. This was in Southridge, Massachusetts.

scrinch v

1 usu with *up, down:* To draw oneself in, crouch; to crowd together. [Cf *EDD* scrinch v.² "To draw the shoulders together; to cringe." Prob a var of **scringe**]

   1870 (1871) Whitney *We Girls* 108 **NY,** Nor have to scrinch all up . . for fear she'd touch us. **1968–70** *DARE* (Qu. Y32, *To squeeze yourself into a small space:* "If you're going to fit in there you'll have to _____.") Infs **GA84, IL97, NY240, PA72, WI57,** Scrinch up; **PA175,** Scrinch; (Qu. Y52, *To move over—for example on a long bench:* ". . . Can you _____ [a little]?") Inf **KY94,** Scrinch up. **1986** Pederson *LAGS Concordance (Crouch)* 2 infs, **cnGA, seAL,** Scrinch down.

2 To narrow the eyes; hence adj *scrinch-eyed,* having the eyes narrowed. [Prob var of **squinch**] **esp S Midl** Cf **screech**

   1967–70 *DARE* (Qu. X25, *To close your eyes part way—for example, when looking at the sun*) Infs **NC49, SC64, TN27, VA35,** Scrinch; (Qu. X21b, *If the eyes are very sharp or piercing*) Inf **SC40,** Scrinch-eyed.

scrinch down See **scrinch 1**

scrinch-eyed See **scrinch 2**

scrinch owl n Also sp *skrinch owl;* pronc-sp *screech owl;* for addit varr see quot 1986 **Sth, S Midl** Cf **scrinch** v 1, **scroonch owl**

A **screech owl 1** (here: *Otus asio*).

   c1937 in 1976 *Weevils in the Wheat* 247 **VA** [Black], Ef you wonna stop a screech owl from squenching, jes' tro a bit o' salt on de fire an' let it burn. It sho' stops 'em; I done it many times. **c1940** *LAMSAS Materials,* [Scrinch owl was given as a response by 14 infs, chiefly in coastal NC, SC, and GA. 6 of them were Black.] **1955** *PADS* 23.47 **e,cSC, eNC, seGA,** Skrinch owl 'screech owl'. **1966** Dakin *Dial. Vocab. Ohio R. Valley* 2.386, Scrinch owl . . [is] limited to the southern and central Bluegrass. **1967–70** *DARE* (Qu. Q1, . . *Kind of owl that makes a shrill, trembling cry*) Infs **MO8, VA46,** Scrinch owl. **1986** Pederson *LAGS Concordance (Screech owl)* 29 infs, **Gulf Region,** Scrinch owl; 1 inf, **cMS,** Scrinching owl—screams; 1 inf, **nwAL,** 1 inf, **nwMS,** Skrinch owl(s); 1 inf, **cwAL,** Skrink owl.

scrinch up See **scrinch 1**

scringe v Also sp *skringe*

1 To cringe, flinch. [*OED2* a1825 →] **chiefly Sth, S Midl**

   1804 Rhoads *New Instructor* 25, *Correct.* . . crĭnge, ["*Error*":] skrĭnge. **1848** Lowell *Biglow* 146 'Upcountry MA', Scringe, *cringe.* **1869** *Overland Mth.* 3.131 **TX,** In Texas "scringe" means *to flinch.* **1895** *DN* 1.376 **seKY, eTN, wNC,** *Scringe* = cringe. **1915** *DN* 4.189 **swVA,** *Scringe.* . . To cringe. **1936** *AmSp* 11.239 **eTX,** *Cringe* . . [skrɪndʒ]. **1938** Hench *Coll.* **nwSC,** He heard a negro woman say: The way people handle those flowers just makes me scringe. **1939** FWP *ID Lore* 242, *Scringe*—to cringe. **1941** *Sat. Eve. Post* 22 Mar 125 **TX,** How a woman would scringe away from him. **1943** *LANE* Map 581 *(Crouch)* 1 inf, **Long Is. NY,** Scringe down. **1944** *PADS* 2.49 **NC, sVA,** *Scringe.* . . To shrink from because of fear or dislike. **1956** McAtee *Some Dialect NC* 38, *Scringe.* . . cringe, flinch. **c1960** Wilson *Coll.* **csKY,** Cringe is sometimes /skrɪndʒ/. **1968** *DARE* (Qu. BB2, *If a person is careful not to put much weight on his injured leg, you might say he was _____ that leg*) Inf **MO9,** Stiff in that leg; crippled in that leg; scringing. **1974** Fink *Mountain Speech* 23 **wNC, eTN,** *Scringe* . . cringe. "I seen him scringe when he heared it." **1995** Brophy *Coll.* 66 **swMO** (as of c1960), *Scringe.* [T]o make a face; to cringe, wince.

2 See quot.   Cf **scrinch 2**
1968 *DARE* (Qu. X25, *To close your eyes part way—for example, when looking at the sun*) Inf **GA**28, Scringe.

scripter See **scripture**

scription See **scrimption**

scriptuh, scriptur See **scripture**

scriptural cake See **scripture cake**

scripture n Usu |ˈskrɪptʃɚ|; also |ˈskrɪptə| Also *scripter, scriptuh, scriptur* Cf **creature, picture**
A Forms.
  1823 Cooper *Pioneers* 465 **NY**, You have scripter gospels for it.   **1860** Hundley *Social Relations S. States* 89, They [=elderly slaves] . . are great on quotations from "scripter", and oftentimes aspire to become preachers or exhorters.   **1861** Holmes *Venner* 1.165 **NEng**, I shall continoo myself to give Sahbath Scriptur'-readin's to the young ladies.   **1884** Smith *Bill Arp's Scrap Book* 73 **GA**, This is what I call successful farmin—multiplying and replenishing according to Scripter.   **1913** (1980) Hardy *OH Schoolmistress* 86, His strong point, however, was prophecy, and "argyin' scripter."   **1922** Gonzales *Black Border* 324 **sSC, GA coasts** [Gullah glossary], *Scriptuh*—Scripture—the Bible.   **1927** *DN* 5.470 **Appalachians**, *Scripture*—Scripter.   **1956** Algren *Walk on the Wild Side* 142 **New Orleans LA**, The scripters says it's a sin to eat anything that parts the hoof or don't chew cood.   **c1960** *Wilson Coll.* **csKY**, *Scripture* [ˈskrɪptə] among some oldsters.
B Sense.
See **scripture measure.**

scripture cake n Also *scriptural cake*
A cake made with ingredients mentioned in the Bible and referred to in the recipe by the relevant Biblical passage.
  1906 Gregory *Woman's Cookbook* 220, Scripture Cake. Four and one-half cups of I Kings 4:28, flour; one and one-half cups of Judges 5:25, butter, L[ight] C[ream], two cups of Jeremiah 6:20, sugar; . . season to taste with 2 Chronicles 9:9, spices; six of Jeremiah 17:11, eggs; a pinch of Leviticus, salt; one and one-half cups of Judges 4:19, milk, L.C.; two teaspoonfuls of Amos 4:5, baking-powder. Follow Solomon's prescription for making a good boy by Proverbs 23:14—"thou shall beat him well with a rod"—and you will have a good cake.   **1939** Wolcott *Yankee Cook Book* 257, Vermont Scripture Cake.   **1940** Brown *Amer. Cooks* 85 **CT**, Scripture Cake (A favorite colonial recipe not only in Connecticut Colony but throughout New England.)   **1975** McDonough *Garden Sass* 141 **AR**, One of the favorite dishes for any church social was a Bible cake or Scripture cake. . . For the Bible-reading women of yesteryear the only part necessary was the amount and name of each scripture.   **1996** *People Pleasing Recipes* 41 **WI**, Scriptural Cake [Recipe includes Judges V 25 (butter), Jeremiah VI 20 (sugar), Judges IV 19 (milk), etc]. . . Follow Solomon's prescription for making a good boy and you will have a good cake.

scripture measure n Also *scripture* Cf **gospel measure**
As much of a commodity as promised or more; full or generous measure.
  1850 Stacy *Memoirs* 290 **NY**, A Methodist sister, who had partaken with us, having received Scripture measure, *full and shaken down*, it *ran over*, and the tongue of eloquence had to relieve the surcharged heart.   **1874** Taylor *World on Wheels* 84, The wind . . has chucked your hat into the bank, and filled it with snow, Scripture measure.   **1950** *WELS* (*Good measure, generous measure:* "He gave me _____ on those cherries.") 1 Inf, **cnWI**, Scripture.   **1968–69** *DARE* (Qu. U15, *When you're buying something, if the seller puts in a little extra to make you feel that you're getting a good bargain*) Inf **MI**92, Scripture measure; (Qu. LL28, . . *Entirely full:* "The box of apples was _____.") Infs **MA**58, **WI**44, Scripture measure.

scritch v [*OED2* a1250 →] Cf **scritch owl**
To screech; hence adj *scritchy* screechy.
  1892 *Harper's New Mth. Mag.* 86.77 **KY**, " 'Y George! hyear thet woman scritch!"   **1959** in 1965 *DARE* File **AR**, Uncle Finner. . . can't abide hearing a scritchy voiced woman a singing.

scritch n
  1969 *DARE* (Qu. BB3a, . . *A pain that strikes you suddenly in the neck*) Inf **WV**18, Scritch.

scritch owl n Also sp *scrich owl*   [*OED2* scritch-owl "arch. exc. *Southern U.S.*"]   **chiefly S Midl, Mid Atl**   See Map
A **screech owl 1** (here: *Otus asio*).
  1897 *Century Illustr. Mag.* 54.477 [Black], Big Nancy 'lowed 't wa'n't no use; scritch-owl flewed in they house las' week, en lit on Jim's hat hanging upside the wall, en she say she knowed then it his t'un nex.   **1913** *Auk* 30.504 **Okefenokee GA**, *Otus asio floridanus*. . . 'Scrich Owl.' Found in small numbers in the swamp.   **c1940** *LAMSAS Materials*, [*Scritch owl*, given as a response by 10% of all LAMSAS infs, is found in all the Atl states south of PA except for DE (and FL, where only 9 infs were interviewed), but it is particularly common in VA and nNC.]   **1944** *PADS* 2.49 **NC, VA**, *Scritch-owl.* . . Screech-owl. South. Common.   **1960** Williams *Walk Egypt* 269 **GA**, Mary Morning cried, "I seen something sliding." "A rat. A scritch-owl."   **1963** TN Folk Lore Soc. *Bulletin* 29.4.81, *Screech Owl*—This is one bird that everybody knew, chiefly by his quivering call; he was a . . *scritch owl* from his voice.   **1965–70** *DARE* (Qu. Q1, . . *Kind of owl that makes a shrill, trembling cry*) 14 Infs, **chiefly S Midl, Mid Atl**, Scritch owl.   **1966** Dakin *Dial. Vocab. Ohio R. Valley* 2.386, *Scrich owl* is common in the Mountains and southern Kentucky generally. It is not common in the Bluegrass but reappears in southwestern Ohio on both sides of the Miami River. Eastern Indiana has *scrich owl* only rarely, but it is common from the Vincennes Trace to the Ohio. It is not used in Illinois.   **1981** Harper–Presley *Okefinokee* 96 (as of a1951), According to Jack Mizell and Arthur Hickox, a "scrich owl" will stop making its dreadful noise if you pull your pocket inside out.   **1982** Slone *How We Talked* 46 **eKY** (as of c1950), *Scritch owl*—screech owl. If one of these called close to the house, it was the sign of death.

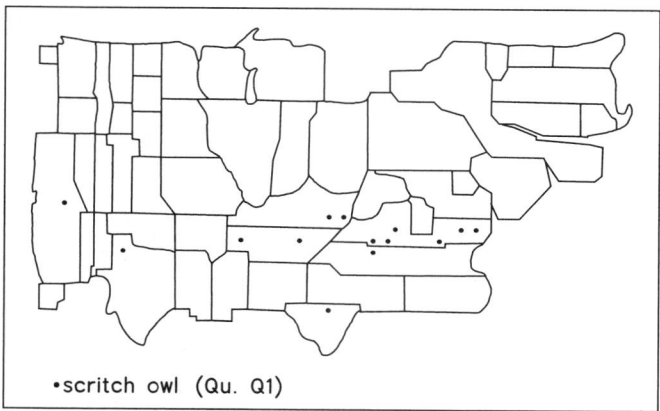

•scritch owl (Qu. Q1)

scritchy See **scritch** v

scriveled See **shrivel** v[1]

scrivin See **striffen**

scrod n, also attrib Also *scrode, schrod(e)*   [Perh orig ppl adj < Corn dial *scraw, scroe;* cf *EDD* scraw v.[2] "Fish are scrawed when they are prepared in a particular way for cooking. This scrawing consists in cutting them flatly open and then slightly powdering them with salt and sometimes with pepper. They are then exposed to the sun and air, that as much as possible of the moisture may be dried up. In this state they are roasted over a clear burning coal or wood fire. Thus prepared and smeared over with a little butter they are said to be 'scrawed'."]   **esp eMA, ME**   Cf *DNE*
A small cod or similar fish (as haddock, hake, or pollock) esp as prepared for food, traditionally by being split, lightly salted, and broiled.
  1841 *Spirit of Times* 16 Oct. 396 *(DA)*, Supplied with a few ship biscuit, a dried scrod, a bottle of good swizzle [etc].   **1846** Worcester *Universal Dict.*, Schrode. . . A young or small cod fish, split and salted for cooking:—written also *scrode.*   **1856** Reynolds *Peter Gott* 92 **neMA**, He had a pile of nice scrods.   **1884** Goode *Fisheries U.S.* 1.201, In the vicinity of Cape Ann the young Cod, too small to swallow a bait, are sometimes known to the fishermen as "Pickers," and throughout all Eastern Massachusetts the name "Scrod," or "Scrode," is in common use. In its primary meaning it seems to refer to these small fish slightly corned, in which condition they are a favorite article of food, but the name is

also transferred to the young fish themselves. **1896** (c1973) Farmer *Orig. Cook Book* 148, *Broiled Scrod.* A young cod, split down the back, and backbone removed, except a small portion near the tail, is called a scrod. Scrod are always broiled, spread with butter, and sprinkled with salt and pepper. Haddock is also so dressed. **1930** *AmSp* 5.392 [Language of N Atl fishermen], *Schrod.* . . Haddock which are too small to be filleted. **1939** Wolcott *Yankee Cook Book* 43, In the fish industry, scrod has come to mean haddock under 2½ pounds. The correct definition of scrod is a small fish prepared for planking. **1951** *Boston Herald* (MA) 19 Dec, Scrod . . refers to the cut of a fish and not to any specific fish itself. In fish pier parlance, it refers, also, to the weight of a fish. . . Any fish weighing two and a half pounds or under, is a scrod fish. The two most common scrod fish in the Boston market are haddock scrod and cod scrod, and it is haddock scrod that supports the Boston fishermen. Whether haddock or cod, scrod is that part of the fish between the body cavity and the tail filleted or split into two equal sections. **1962** Morison *One Boy's Boston* 32 (as of 1890s), My grandfather stoutly maintained that a scrod was, or should be, a small codfish that had been split and slack-salted the night before. **1967** *DARE* (Qu. P14, . . *Commercial fishing . . what do the fishermen go out after?*) Inf **MA**50, Scrod. **1975** Gould *ME Lingo* 245, Until its late and lamentable disappearance in Bangor's renewal program, the Penobscot Exchange Hotel always meticulously stated on its restaurant menu just which fish was being offered each day as *scrod.* **1993** *FDA Consumer* Sept 14, Scrod is not a type of fish. The term originated in the Boston area to describe the catch of the day. It is a fish under two and a half pounds that is either cod, haddock or pollock. Such fish should be labeled in the market or listed in a restaurant as "scrod cod," "scrod haddock," or "scrod pollock." **1999** *DARE* File—Internet **eMA** [Boston Online *Wicked Good Guide to Boston English*], Scrod—A small, ambiguous piece of fish that never knows if it's cod or haddock. Some people claim that "scrod" is a young cod, while "schrod" is a young haddock, but, in fact, there's no difference—it's basically whatever's cheaper at the fish pier that day.

scrofula n Usu |'skrɔfjələ, 'skraf-|; also |'skrɔfjulo, 'skrafjəlo| Pronc-sp *scrofulo* Cf **cupola A, fistula, gondola 1**
Std sense, var forms.

1892 *DN* 1.234 **KY**, Scrofula [skrɔfjulo]. **1893** Shands *MS Speech* 75, *Scrofulo* [skrɔfjulo]. Scrofula is very frequently so called by the uneducated. **1929** *AmSp* 5.20 **Ozarks**, Scrofulo. . . Scrofula. The final *o* is long. **c1960** *Wilson Coll.* **csKY**, Scrofula ['skrɑfjə,lo].

scrofula plant n Also sp *scrophula plant*
1 A **figwort 1** (here: *Scrophularia marilandica*).
1876 Hobbs *Bot. Hdbk.* 103, Scrofula plant, Scrophularia Marilandica. **1910** Graves *Flowering Plants* 351 **CT**, Scrophularia marilandica. . . Scrofula Plant. . . The herb and root are medicinal. **1923** *Amer. Botanist* 29.61, The European plant, *Scrophularia nodosa,* is the one to which all the common names really belong, though our plant *(S. marilandica)* shares them. . . The name "scrofula-plant" . . alludes to the reputation of the plant in the cure of other ills. **1958** Jacobs–Burlage *Index Plants NC* 204, Scrophularia marilandica. . . square stalk; scrofula plant; pile wort. **1974** (1977) Coon *Useful Plants* 246, Scrophularia marilandica . . scrophula plant. . . The many names . . indicate long-known medicinal values.
2 A **rock rose 1** (here: *Helianthemum canadense*).
1876 Hobbs *Bot. Hdbk.* 104, Scrofula plant, Frostwort, Helianthemum Canadense. **1900** Lyons *Plant Names* 185, H[elianthemum] Canadense. . . Scrofula plant. . . Herb, astringent, alterative. **1974** (1977) Coon *Useful Plants* 97, *Helianthemum canadense*—Frostweed . . scrofula plant. . . a North Carolina authority credits it as a "valuable remedy in scrofula, syphilis, cancerous affections, and as a gargle." Other reports which counter this indicate it should always be used with care, and is not, therefore, an important medicinal plant.

scrofularoot n
=**dogtooth violet.**
1876 Hobbs *Bot. Hdbk.* 104, Scrofula root, Adders' tongue, Erythronium Americanum. **1900** Lyons *Plant Names* 151, E[rythronium] Americanum. . . Scrofula-root. **1949** Moldenke *Amer. Wild Flowers* 328, *Erythronium*, of which we have 17 kinds, . . are commonly known under the . . names of *adderstongue* . . and *scrofula-roots*.

scrofulaweed n Also sp *scrophulaweed* [See quot 1830]
A **rattlesnake plantain 1** (here: *Goodyera pubescens*).
1822 Eaton *Botany* 294, *Goodyera. . . pubescens* . . scrophula-weed. . .

Said to be useful in scrofula. **1830** Rafinesque *Med. Flora* 2.224, *Goodyera pubescens.* . . *Scrofula weed.* Deemed by some empirics a specific for the scrofula, the fresh leaves are applied bruised to the sores, renewed every 3 hours, and the warm infusion used as tea freely, also to wash the sores. **1910** Graves *Flowering Plants* 135 **CT**, *Goodyera pubescens.* . . Scrofula-weed. . . All plants of this genus are considered medicinal, the whole plant being used. **1924** *Amer. Botanist* 30.151, *Epipactic* [=*Goodyera*] *pubescens.* . . "Scrophula weed" alludes to reputed medicinal properties. **1979** Erichsen-Brown *Med. N. Amer. Plants* 297, *Goodyera pubescens.* . . *Common names.* Networt, adder's violet, scrofula weed [etc].

scrofulo See **scrofula**

scrog n Also *scrag* [Engl dial. Cf *DNE scrag* "Tree stump; small burnt or broken tree or bush"]
A stunted bush or tree; a standing dead tree.
1975 Gould *ME Lingo* 246, *Scrog*—A wind-stunted bush, shrub, and tree that *hangs tough* on a Maine headland. **2000** *NADS Letters* **NY**, Scrag (rhymes with drag)—In central New York State the term means a tree usually solitary, tall, obviously dead, large enough to be a landmark.

scrog v, hence ppl adj *scrogged*, often with *up* [Cf *EDD scrogged* ppl. adj.² "'Cleaned out,' bankrupt"] **NEng**
To damage, wreak havoc with.
1975 Gould *ME Lingo* 246, *Scrog.* . . Today, it also means anything wrongly done, hanging together bravely, and sort of fouled up. Have you ever seen a shed that was *scrogged* up by a two-foot overhang on one side and a flush eave on the other? **2000** *NADS Letters* **CT**, My husband was born in Groton, Connecticut, and his family is from the Jamestown, NY area. The first time I heard him use the term [=scrog], I laughed because it sounded so close to "scrod". He uses it in the sense of something being really screwed up. ("You should have seen that wreck [sic]—his car was scrogged!" "I don't see how anyone could scrog something that badly!") *Ibid* **MA**, I recall using "scrog" as a verb at MIT in the late 60's and early 70's. We applied it to bugs in computer programs that destroyed data, as in "Something scrogged the payroll totals." (We wouldn't have said "scrogged up".) To me, it had connotations of utter destruction, not just a matter of "off by one". *Ibid* **CT**, I remember using "scrogged up" in the "something fouled up" sense when I was growing up in Madison, Connecticut from 1970–1976. . . I got a paper route (30–40 customers spread over 8 miles of road, on my bicycle, including the Sunday newspaper). I needed to stop to rest or drink water sometimes (or warm up in the winter), so I would talk with all the old Yankee farmer types. . . I think I got the term "scrogged up" . . from them.

scroggin(s) See **scoggin 2**

scronch v
1 Also *scranch, scraunch*: To crush; to crunch, grind between the teeth; by ext, to eat. [*OED2 scranch* [skrɔ:nʃ] 1620 →; "*Obs.* exc. *dial.*"] Cf **craunch, scrunch** v
1828 Webster *Amer. Dict.*, *Scranch* [*DARE* Ed: Diacritics indicate that the *a* is pronounced as in *father.*] . . To grind with the teeth, and with a cracking sound; to craunch. [Webster: *This is in vulgar use in America.*] **1845** Judd *Margaret* 172 **NEng**, Here also they encountered a troop of boys and girls coasting. Some were coming up the hill, goring and scranching the crust with their iron corks. **1859** Elwyn *Glossary* 97, *Scranch.* To grind any hard or crackling substance between the teeth. (Brockett.) The Scotch use this, as well as the North of England; and I have heard it, though not often, in this country. **1867** Harris *Sut Lovingood Yarns* 183 **TN**, The shoes wud scronch the bar toes in dancin. **1899** (1912) Green *VA Folk-Speech* 371, *Scraunch.* . . To grind with the teeth, with a crackling sound; craunch. **1929** *AmSp* 5.130 **ME**, The word . . is known to me only as "scrunch," "scraunch" with the meaning to crunch. **2000** *NADS Letters* **GA**, My mother who is from Medder, GA . . [says], "Bill, go scraunch the garbage down; I can't fit any more in the can." *Ibid* **cPA**, My father-in-law . . lives and grew up in rural (central) PA. As one of thirteen children on a farm, he has about a sixth grade education. He just turned 85 years old. When he says scraunch— (au as in caught)—he means eat. As in, "Let's get some food out here. It's time for us to scraunch."
2 as vbl n *scraunching*: Performing the **scronch** n; hence nouns *scrauncher, scroncher. among Black speakers*
1926 Van Vechten *Nigger Heaven* 281 **NYC** [Black], [⁴] 'Toly, you sho' is one bardacious scroncher.[ⁿ] [⁴]You's goin' git scronched.[ⁿ] **1930**

in 1983 Taft *Blues Lyric Poetry* 109 [Black], Down in Dixie: there's a dance that's new / Ain't much to it: it is easy to do / You wiggle and you wobble: and you move it around /. . . / I know a gal: by name of Lizzie Brown / She do that scraunch: she's the best in town/. . . / Find her doing that scraunch: on a Saturday night / My little gal: know what scraunching means /. . . / Standing on the levee: in New Orleans / Find the best scraunchers: the world ever seen.

3 To have sexual intercourse with (a woman); hence vbl n *scronching.*

1926 [see **2** above]. **1999** *DARE* File **cIL**, The term 'scronch,' as I understand it, has to do with . . sexual intercourse. I have heard my father and his brothers . . talk about . . some of the 'scronchin' they did back when they were young enough to participate in such an act. . . My father assures me that the term was common in his youth.

4 To defeat (in a game).

1934 *AmSp* 9.290 **PA** [Black student slang], *Scraunch.* To overcome an opponent, particularly in basketball. Cries of *Scraunch him!* ring out on every side during a particularly rough basketball game in the *Scraunchemhall.*

scronch n Also *scraunch, scrunch among Black speakers* Cf **scronch** v **2**

A dance; see quots.

1926 Van Vechten *Nigger Heaven* 286 [Black], *Scronch:* a dance. **1930** [see **scronch** v **2**]. **1942** Hurston *Dust Tracks* 190 **FL** [Black], Polk County in the jooks. Dancing the square dance. Dancing the scronch. Dancing the belly-rub. **1970** Major *Dict. Afro-Amer. Slang* 101, *Scrunch:* (1900's–30's) a slow, dragged-out dance.

scroncher n[1] See **scronch** v **2**

scroncher n[2]

A scorpion **B1**.

1950 *PADS* 14.77 **FL**, *Scroncher.* . . A scorpion.

scronching See **scronch** v **3**

scronchous adj Also sp *scrontious*

1 Enjoyable.

1935 Hurston *Mules & Men* 54 **FL** [Black], And what make it so cool, we close enough to you to have a scronchous time, but never no halter on our necks.

2 Fleshy; stout.

1947 Ballowe *The Lawd* 228 **LA** [Black], Ma pa wuz a preacher. . . Bein' a scrontious man, po'tly, . . he was a sweater f'um way back, an' when he got goin' good the water drapped f'um his shirttails.

scroobly See **strubbly**

scrooch v Also *schrooch, scru(t)ch, skrootch, skrutch* [Prob orig < *crooch* (dial var of *crouch*) + excrescent *s-*, infl, esp in senses other than the first, by **scrouge, scrunch** v, or other similar words. Attested earliest in the U.S., but prob of Scots, nEngl dial origin] Cf *EDD, SND,* Intro "Language Changes" I.8

1 often with *up*: To crouch, cringe, draw oneself in; to shrink (back, down, etc); hence ppl adj phr *scrooched up* hunched up. Cf **scooch 1**

[**1844** Stephens *High Life in NY* 2.229, The white figger at t'other eend the entry was kinder half hid in the dark, and lookin kinder scroochy, as if she felt ashamed of standin there all unkivered.] **1860** Street *Woods & Waters* 221 **NY**, Hopsy she scrooched right down to her pa's feet . . , and she cries and she begs, but massy, Mr. Smith, twant no use. **1869** Twain *Innocents* 229, He cuts a corner so closely, now and then . . that I feel myself "scrooching," as the children say, just as one does when a buggy wheel grazes his elbow. **1872** *Appletons' Jrl.* 7.637 **ceMA**, Peter *scrooched* in by the old dog, and the old dog just watched him, and Peter passed on a little farther, and the old dog followed Peter. **1872** (1973) Thompson *Major Jones's Courtship* 90 **GA**, I scrooch'd down in the bag and didn't breathe louder nor a kitten. **1892** *KS Univ. Qrly.* 1.98 **KS**, *Scrooch* or scrooge: to cringe. **1892** *DN* 1.218 **AR, NC**, *Scooch* [see quot 1890 at **scooch 1**]. . . "Instead of this we have scrooch, which is quite common." . . "Here called scrooch." **1898** *Harper's New Mth. Mag.* 98.53 **LA** [Black], Ef she was to study about *gittin' married,* she'd marry *somebody*—not a po' little cross-eyed scrooched-up someth'n' 'nother like me. **1899** (1912) Green *VA Folk-Speech* 372, *Scrooch.* . . To draw up in a small space. "You sit scrooched up in the cornder."

1909 *DN* 3.367 **eAL, wGA**, *Scrooch.* . . To crouch down or under. **1910** *DN* 3.455 **seVT**, *Scrooch down* . . [skrutʃ]. . . To cringe or stoop down. **1912** *DN* 3.588 **wIN**, *Scrooch.* . . To crouch. **1912** *DN* 4.58 **eTN**, *Skrutch.* . . To crouch: noted repeatedly in the vicinity of Knoxville. "Skrutched on his hunkles (haunches).[*]" **1915** *DN* 4.189 **swVA**, *Scrutch* [skrutʃ]. . . To crouch. **1923** [see **scrooch 2**]. **1929** Wolfe *Look Homeward* 156 **NC**, Wonder broken only by . . her commands to him to "scrooch up" when the conductor came through for the tickets. **1942** Hall *Smoky Mt. Speech* 92 **wNC, eTN**, She was all [skrutʃt] up behind a tree. **1943** *LANE* Map 581 *(Crouch),* [58 instances of *scrooch down* and 43 of *scrooch* were recorded in **NEng**; it was found in all parts, but was rare in **ME**, **eNH**, and **cMA**]; 1 inf, **cCT**, [skruʃ] down; 1 inf, **seCT**, [skrʌtʃ]; 1 inf, **Block Island**, [skrutʃ]; 1 inf, **seMA**, Cf *scrooch* = bend forward (over a book); 1 inf, **seMA**, He scrooched with pain. **1944** [see **scrooge 2**]. **1944** *PADS* 2.49 **wNC, sVA**, *Scrooch, scrooge, scrooch, scrunch* [skrutʃ, skraudʒ, skruntʃ, skruntʃʃ]: . . To crouch, to crowd, to crowd oneself into. **1946** in 1954 *Harder Coll.* **cwTN**, [Letter:] Givie was in her din scruched up like a Ground hog when somebody try to smoke them out. **1946** *PADS* 5.36 **VA**, *Scrooch down, scrutch down:* Crouch down; common everywhere. **1951** *West Witch Diggers* 124 **IN**, He don't need to scrooch back there behind the stove to do it. **1965–70** *DARE* (Qu. Y32, *To squeeze yourself into a small space: "If you're going to fit in there you'll have to _____.")* 38 Infs, **scattered, but esp Midl**, Scrooch up; 19 Infs, **scattered**, Scrooch; 16 Infs, **scattered**, Scrooch down; **IA32**, Scrooch in; **MS71**, Scrooch over; **NJ9**, Scrooch under. **1967** Will *Dredgeman* 55 **FL**, He had to navigate the length of West Lake, then, scrooching low in his boat. **1986** Pederson *LAGS Concordance* **Gulf Region** *(Crouch),* 19 infs, Scrooch down; 6 infs, Scrooch(ed); 3 infs, Scrooch up; 1 inf, You scrooch up when it gets cold; 2 infs, Scrooched down; 3 infs, Scrooched up; 1 inf, Scrooches up; 1 inf, Scrooching; 2 infs, Scrooching down *(or* up); 1 inf, He's all scrooched up.

2a also with *down, up*: To contract, squeeze, draw up (esp a part of the body); hence ppl adj phr *scrooched up* contracted, squeezed. **chiefly Sth, S Midl**

1851 Hooper *Widow Rugby's Husband* 88 **AL**, With that old long bonnet on . . and her mouth skrootched up . . the go-to-meetin' way. **1877** *Galaxy* 23.49 **NY**, When they put out a hand to feel her condition she [= a cow] would "scrooch" down her back, or bend this way or that, as if the hand were a branding iron. **1929** (1951) Faulkner *Sartoris* 282 **MS**, He be back. . . He right dar now, watchin' dis lantern wid his eyes scrooched up, listenin' to hear ef de dawgs wid us. **1958** McCullers *Square Root* 46, When I hear the words agony or labor, it make me scrooch up my behind. **1965** Davis *Summer Land* 61 **cnNC**, Sometimes . . he would scrooch up his shoulders and blow through his moustaches. "By God, boys, my wounds hurt me today." **1967** *DARE* Tape **TX29**, I once said to him, "Why do you scrooch your cards up like that? Why don't you spread 'em out?" **1973** *DARE* File **swPA** (as of 1920s), If we cried when we were kids, my mother always said, "Quit scrooching your face up." **1995** Brophy *Coll.* 66 **swMO** (as of c1960), *Scrooch.* . . [T]o squeeze, squash, hunch.

b intr: To narrow the eyes, squint. Cf **screech** v

1965–69 *DARE* (Qu. X25, *To close your eyes part way—for example, when looking at the sun*) Infs **MS63, NC68, SC58**, Scrooch.

3 intr: To force or squeeze one's way; to crowd (over); with *up*: to huddle up, crowd together; hence ppl adj phr *scrooched up* huddled together; of a space: crowded. **chiefly Sth, S Midl** Cf **scrouge** v **2a**

1909 *DN* 3.367 **eAL, wGA**, *Scrooch.* . . To push or squeeze in, scrouge. **1927** Kennedy *Gritny* 40 **sLA** [Black], Workin' up in Miss Newgeem scrooched-up kitchen. **1930s** in 1944 *ADD* **eWV**, Scrooch up a little closer to me. **1944** [see **1** above]. **1954** *Harder Coll.* **cwTN**, *Scrooch up.* . . To squeeze into a small space: "Scrooch up in that bed so's 'll be more room." **1954** [see **scrouge** v **1a**]. **1955** Ritchie *Singing Family* 8 **seKY**, That's when we'd begin scrooching in close to the fire, elbowing silently for good safe places. **1963** Watkins–Watkins *Yesterday Hills* 15 **cnGA**, Students straggled in from play, stood around the room, and scrooched up several to each desk. **1965–70** *DARE* (Qu. Y52, *To move over—for example on a long bench: ". . . Can you _____ [a little]?"*) 10 Infs, **scattered**, Scrooch over; **IN56, WI71**, Scrooch; **MS30, TN30**, Scrooch up. **1976** Garber *Mountain-ese* 79 **sAppalachians**, Make Jamie scrooch over, he is scrouging me. **1979** Carpenter *Walton War* 164 **sAppalachians**, "The younguns was all scrootched up in the bedstid."—A mountain woman talking about her children. "Scrootched" means cuddled together for warmth. **2000** *NADS Letters* **wNC**, I remember as a child spending the night with my great grandma. She would turn off her heat at night and we would curl up in the center of her feather bed to keep warm. I remember her saying, "Let's scrooch up." **2001** *DARE* File **wNY**, Schrooch—v., to edge or wiggle sideways, awkwardly, while seated, as in "Schrooch over so there's room on the couch."

4 To crush, push.

1943 *LANE* Map 581 *(Crouch)* 1 inf, **seCT**, Cf. scrooch = *crush.* **1955** Ritchie *Singing Family* 65 **seKY**, We scrooched the beds back against the wall.

5 also sp *schrooch;* also with *around:* To fidget, squirm; hence adj *scrootchy* fidgety. [Perh infl by PaGer *rutsch*]

1939 Aurand *Quaint Idioms* 19 [PaGer], Stop your darn *schrooching* (twisting or squirming) around. **1942** Warnick *Garrett Co. MD* 13 **nwMD** (as of 1900–18), *Scrooch around* . . to twist about while sitting. **1996** Huth *Famil. Words* 109 **csPA**, *Scrootch* /skɹuːtʃ/skɹutʃ/ . . to wiggle; to fidget. *Scrootchy.* . . "The kids could be kind of anxious and scrootchy."

scrooch down See **scrooch 2a**

scrooched up See **scrooch 1, 2a, 3**

scrooch owl n Also sp *scrootch owl;* for addit varr see quot c1940 *LAMSAS Materials* [Perh infl by **scrooch** v 1] **chiefly Sth, S Midl** See Map

Usu a **screech owl 1** (here: *Otus asio*); occas another owl.

1933 Rawlings *South Moon* 196 **FL**, She were jest a-settin' there, lookin' big-eyed and skeert, like a leetle ol' scrooch-owl on a limb in the day-time. **1934** Vines *Green Thicket* 85 **cnAL**, "Oh, listen, there's an old scrootch owl," she said. "The little old shivelin owl," Clay replied. **c1940** *LAMSAS Materials,* [*Scrooch owl,* given as a response by 10% of all LAMSAS infs, is found in all the Atl States south of PA; it is particularly common in Delmarva, and in NC and SC, but is absent from most of VA. Single instances occur of the varr *scrooching owl* (NC), *scrutch owl* (NC), and *scrotch owl* (WV).] **c1940** Eliason *Word Lists FL* 11, *Scrooch owl* [skrutʃ]: The screech owl. **1956** McAtee *Some Dialect NC* 38, *Scrooch owl* . . the screech owl *(Otus asio).* **c1960** Wilson *Coll.* **csKY**, *Scrooch owl.* . . The screech owl because of his seeming to withdraw into as small a space as possible. **1963** TN Folk Lore Soc. *Bulletin* 29.4.81, *Screech Owl*—This is one bird that everybody knew, chiefly by his quivering call; he was a *scrooch owl* from his habit of sitting *all scrooched up.* **1965–70** *DARE* (Qu. Q1, . . *Kind of owl that makes a shrill, trembling cry*) 24 Infs, **chiefly Sth, S Midl**, Scrooch owl; **MS**1, Scrooch owl ['skrutʃ]; (Qu. Q2, . . *Kinds of owls*) Infs **AR**5, 20, 35, **GA**7, **MS**63, Scrooch owl; (Qu. C34, *Nicknames for nearby settlements, villages, or districts*) Inf **KY**88, Scrooch owl grove. [25 of 31 Infs comm type 4 or 5] **1970** *NC Folkl.* 8.58, When you hear a "scrooch" owl hollering in the night, tie a knot in your shirt tail and he will hush. **1972** *PADS* 58.21 **cwAL**, Screech owl (14 [of 27 infs]) is most frequent, but variants occur:. . *scrooch owl* (3); . . *shivering owl* (1, Negro); . . *squinch owl* (1, Negro); and . . *squeech owl* (1, Negro). **1986** Pederson *LAGS Concordance* **Gulf Region**, 107 infs, Scrooch owl(s); 14 infs, Scrooch owl—larger than barn owl.

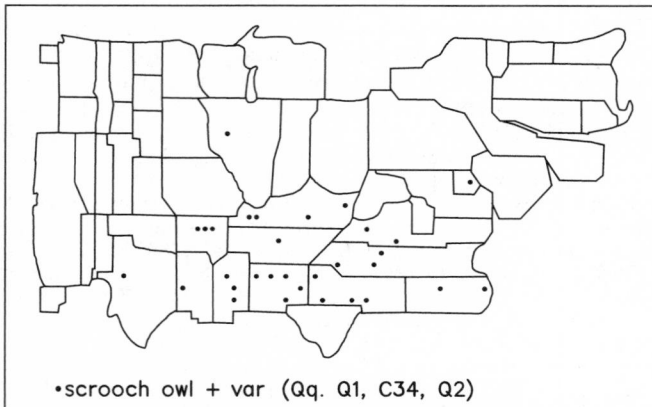

•scrooch owl + var (Qq. Q1, C34, Q2)

scrooch up See **scrooch 1, 2a, 3**

scrooge v Also *scrudge* [Varr of **scrouge**, possibly in sense **1** and very probably in sense **2** infl by **scrooch**. *OED2* (at *scrouge* v. 1.b, corresponding to sense **1** below) 1873 →]

1 To squeeze one's way; to crowd, push; with *up:* to crowd together. Cf **scrouge** v **2a**

1904 Day *Kin o' Ktaadn* 152 **ME**, Scrudge over there, boys. **1909** *DN* 3.367 **eAL, wGA**, *Scrouge, v.i.* and *tr.* To push or crowd; squeeze in. Also pronounced *scrooge* [skrug] [sic]. "Keep back! don't scrooge so!" **1918** *DN* 5.19 **NC**, [skruʒ] [sic—prob for [skruʒ]], to crowd close together. **1927** *DN* 5.477 **Ozarks**, *Scrooge.* . . To squeeze or crowd in. "I'll jes' scrooge in hyar 'long side o' th' school-marm." **1970** *DARE* (Qu. Y52, *To move over—for example on a long bench: ". . . Can you _____ [a little]?"*) Inf **TN**58, Scoot over, scoot down; scrooge up.

2 also with *up:* To crouch, cringe, draw oneself in; to shrink (back, down); hence ppl adj phr *scrooged up* hunched up, huddled. Cf **scrooch 1**

1892 [see **scrooch 1**]. **1905** *DN* 3.64 **eNE**, There I was, all scrooged up in a corner. **1937** *Atlantic Mth.* 160.685 **ceMA**, So he sort of scrooged back in a corner and waited his chance. **1943** *LANE* Map 581 *(Crouch)* 2 infs, **cCT, seMA**, Scrooge. [One inf indicated that this was heard from others, the other that it was "less common."] **1944** *PADS* 2.12 **AL, GA, MS**, [skrutʃ, skrudʒ]: *intr. vb.* To squeeze into small space, crouch. Used chiefly of people, with *up* or *down* indicating posture. . . Rabun Co., Ga.; e. cent. Ala.; n. Miss. Rural. Popular. **1968–69** *DARE* (Qu. Y32, *To squeeze yourself into a small space: "If you're going to fit in there you'll have to _____."*) Inf **IN**35, Scrooge; **VA**5, Scrooge, squeeze; **GA**82, Squinch up, squeeze up, scrooge up; **KY**24, Scrooge up; **NY**205, Scrooge down. [*DARE* Ed: Some of these Infs may belong instead at **1** above.] **1979** Swarthout *Skeletons* 298, I scrooged down in my chair, laid my head back, stretched out my legs.

scroogy adj Cf **scrooch** v **1**, **scrooge** v **2**

1911 *DN* 3.547 **NE**, *Scroogy.* . . Uncanny, horrid, weird. "It was rather dark and scroogy up in the attic." Not common.

scroonch v Also with *up* Cf **scrunch** v **2**

To crouch, hunch; to shrink or squeeze oneself (down, in, etc).

1925 Dargan *Highland Annals* 161 **cwNC**, "Scroonch up to that poplar," called Snead, "an' they'll pass us." **1933** Williamson *Woods Colt* 260 **Ozarks**, The woods colt goes sneakin' up towards the smokehouse, kind of scroonchin' down to the ground. **1943** *LANE* Map 581 *(Crouch)* 1 inf, **swCT**, [skruntʃ]. **1944** [see **scrooch** v **1**]. **1965–70** *DARE* (Qu. Y32, *To squeeze yourself into a small space: "If you're going to fit in there you'll have to _____."*) 8 Infs, **scattered**, Scroonch down; **CO**15, **IL**76, **IN**56, **KS**2, **PA**126, Scroonch up; **NE**8, **TN**53, **TX**9, Scroonch in.

scroonch owl n [Cf **scrooch owl, scroonch**] **S Atl**

A **screech owl 1** (here: *Otus asio*).

c1940 *LAMSAS Materials,* [*Scroonch owl* was the response of 10 infs in NC, SC, and GA.] **1986** Pederson *LAGS Concordance,* 1 inf, **nwFL**, Scroonch owl.

scroonch up See **scroonch**

scrootch owl See **scrooch owl**

scrootchy See **scrooch 5**

scrop n [Pronc var of *scrap;* cf *EDD scrap* sb.¹ [skrap]] Cf **crop** n A, v, **drop** A

1912 Green *VA Folk-Speech* 372, *Scrop.* . . For *scrap.* **1923** (1946) Greer-Petrie *Angeline Steppin'* 31 **csKY**, The table scrops they was a-throwin' away. **1931** Goodrich *Mt. Homespun* 75 **wNC, eTN**, Scrop quilt.

scrope See **scrape** v **1**

scrophula plant See **scrofula plant**

scrophulaweed See **scrofulaweed**

scrotch owl See **scrooch owl**

scrouch v

1 also with *up:* To squeeze in, crowd together; hence ppl adj *scrouched* crowded. Cf **scrouge** v **2a**

1844 Stephens *High Life in NY* 2.196, When she did kinder start up, it was jest to scrouch a leetle closer to me than she was afore. **1943** *Esquire* 19.59 **eKY**, When he scooted Mercedes over on the seat, I scrouched up closter to her. **1953** Randolph–Wilson *Down in Holler* 281 **Ozarks**, *Scrouch,* pronounced to rhyme with *crouch,* is also common. A woman who kept a boardinghouse in Stone County, Mo., often spoke of people being *scrouched* at her table; she meant that they were crowded, that their chairs were too close together. **1986** Pederson *LAGS Concordance,* 1 inf, **ceTN,** Scrouch in = fit yourself in at the table.

2 To crouch, hunch, draw oneself in. Cf **scrooch 1**

1885 Twain *Huck. Finn* 22 **MO,** We scrouched down and laid still. **1890** *DN* 1.79, *Scooch* [see quot 1890 at **scooch 1**]. . . Isn't this a variant of the more common [?] *scrouch* (also pronounced [skrauč])? **1923** *DN* 5.221 **swMO,** *Scrooch,* or *scrouch.* . . To crouch. **1940** McCullers *Lonely Hunter* 179 **Sth,** Father, you been scrouched over that desk since five o'clock. **1943** *LANE* Map 581 *(Crouch),* 3 infs, **CT, MA,** Scrouch (down). **1967–70** *DARE* (Qu. Y32, *To squeeze yourself into a small space: "If you're going to fit in there you'll have to _____."*) Inf **NC86,** Scrouch [skrauč]; **TX43,** Scrouch [skræuč]; **OH70,** Scrouch down. **1977** *UpCountry* Nov 12 **VT,** I kind of scrouched down, so's not to scare him [=a fox], but there wasn't no need for it. **1986** Pederson *LAGS Concordance (Crouch)* 2 infs, **FL, GA,** Scrouch; 1 inf, **ceTN,** Scrouched; 1 inf, **cwAR,** Scrouching.

scrouched, scrouch up See **scrouch 1**

scrouge v Also *scrow(d)ge, scrowj, skrouge* [*OED2 scrouge* v. 1.a (=**1a, b** below) 1755 →]

1a tr: To crowd, push against; to force (into, out of, etc, a crowded space); hence ppl adj phr *scrouged (up)* crowded together. **chiefly S Midl**

1789 Webster *Dissertations Engl. Lang.* 111, *Skroud* and *skrouge* for *croud,* are sometimes heard among people that should be ashamed of the least vulgarism. **1830** *NY Constellation* (NY) 11 Sept 2/5, The room was so completely crowded, that one could not have scrowged the little end of nothing sharpened, between them. **1843** (1847) Field *Drama Pokerville* 15 **MO,** Both ladies were obliged to stand up and be *scrouged* until chairs could be brought from the hotel. **1847** Hurd *Grammatical Corrector* 63, *Scrouge,* as a verb, for *crowd;* as, "Do not scrouge me." "You scrouge me so that I cannot write." Very common in Pennsylvania—There is no such word. **1848** Lowell *Biglow* 92 'Upcountry' **MA,** An' ez the North hez took to brustlin'/ At bein' scrouged frum off the roost,/ I 'll tell ye wut 'll save all tusslin'. **1890** *DN* 1.62 **swOH, TN,** *Scrouge* or *scrowdge,* trans. and intrans.: to crowd. Common. [Also reported from the Seguachee Valley, Tenn. . . "Don't scrowdge me so" = "give me more room."] **1899** (1912) Green *VA Folk-Speech* 372, *Scrouge.* . . To squeeze; press; crowd. **1942** (1971) Campbell *Cloud-Walking* 99 **seKY,** A house with more windows than one and more rooms for living in 'thout being scrouged. **1942** Hall *Smoky Mt. Speech* 92 **wNC, eTN,** Quit ['skræudʒən] me! **1944** *PADS* 2.12, *Scrouge* [skraudʒ]: *tr. vb.* To crowd, pack together, squeeze into or out of. "He just scrouged them into the wagon." "They scrouged me out of the bus." E. cent. Ala.; Rabun Co., Ga.; n. Miss. Popular. **1945** Street *Gauntlet* 45 **MO** (as of 1920s), "Seats about three hundred," Honeycutt said. "He can scrouge in a right smart more, with chairs." **1954** *Harder Coll.* **cwTN,** *Scrouge* [skraudʒ] *up.* . . "They['re] all scrouged up in ner now; ain't no room for no more." Same as *scrooch up.* **1969** *DARE* FW Addit **TN30,** "Scrouge" means to crowd somebody. **1976** Garber *Mountain-ese* 79 **sAppalachians,** We jist kaint scrouge another person in the front seat. **1976** [see **scrooch 3**].

b Fig: to encroach on, take advantage of, cheat; hence ppl adj *scrouged* pressed by circumstances, hard put.

1884 Smith *Bill Arp's Scrap Book* 140 **nwGA,** I don't know of but a few who are making more than a good fair living, and there's ten to one who are powerfully scrouged to do that. **1888** Eggleston in *Century Illustr. Mag.* 36.534 **IL,** You know what *I* am—a good, stiddy-going, hard-working farmer—shore to get my sheer of what's to be had in the world without scrouging anybody else. **1890** [see **scrouge** n **1**]. **1916** Macy–Hussey *Nantucket Scrap Basket* 164, "Scrouge" is another survival, meaning "to squeeze, to press, to crowd." **1924** Raine *Land of Saddle-Bags* 144 **sAppalachians,** We hain't had much schoolin', and when judges and lawyers with heaps o' larnin' scrouges a pore ignorant jury, what can ye do? **1944** Smith *Strange Fruit* 307 **Sth,** There'll be lynchings long as white folks and black folks scrouge each other—everybody scrambling for the same penny.

2a intr: To force or squeeze one's way; to crowd, push; with *up:* to crowd together; hence vbl n *scrouging.* **chiefly S Midl**

1798 *Aurora* (Philadelphia) 13 Dec. 2/1 (*OED2*), Upstairs I scrouged to the front. **1843** (1916) Hall *New Purchase* 303 **IN,** And then we separated; but after hard "scrouging" each way some hundred yards . . we came together and held a council. **1885** Twain *Huck. Finn* 258 **MO,** At

last they got out the coffin, . . and then such another crowding, and shouldering, and shoving as there was, to scrouge in and get a sight, you never see. **1890** [see **1a** above]. **1903** *DN* 2.328 **seMO,** *Scrouge,* v.i. Crowd; to push. **1907** *DN* 3.236 **nwAR,** *Scrouge.* . . To crowd; to push. "Said the ant to the elephant . . 'Quit yo' scrougin'.'" **1909** [see **scrooge 1**]. **1913** Kephart *Highlanders* 75 **sAppalachians,** Git up, pup! you've scrouged right in hyur in front of the fire. **1920** *DN* 5.86 **NC,** *Scrowj.* **1929** (1951) Faulkner *Sartoris* 226 **nMS,** One or two of 'em made to break away, but Cunnel drawed his pistols and let 'em off, and they come back and scrouged in amongst the others. **1940** Faulkner *Hamlet* 351 **nMS,** I could lay my ear to her belly and hear Eula kicking and scrouging like all get-out, feeling the moon. **1942** (1971) Campbell *Cloud-Walking* 38 **seKY,** Viny's three other younguns and five of Shade's and Marthy's scrouged up in the sled. **1943** *Esquire* 19.143 **KY,** Three hundred people couldn't easily scrouge out at one door. **1943** Chase *Jack Tales* 42 **wNC,** So the old dog scrouged under the gate. **1944** [see **scrooch v 1**]. **1960** Hall *Smoky Mt. Folks* 63 **wNC, eTN,** In asking someone on a couch or porch swing to move over to make room for others, one could say, "Scrouge over like you had a family." **1965–70** *DARE* (Qu. Y32, *To squeeze yourself into a small space: "If you're going to fit in there you'll have to _____."*) Infs **GA19, 30, TN13,** Scrouge [skræuʒ] in; **MS1,** Scrouge up; **MS60,** Scrouge; (Qu. Y52, *To move over—for example on a long bench: ". . . Can you _____ [a little]?"*) Inf **LA11,** Scrouge up, move over, move up; **MS59,** Scrouge [skrauʒ] up, move over, slide over; **TN65,** Scoot over—to move over when there is plenty of room; scrouge up—[when it's] crowded; **AL10, MS1,** Scrouge over. [*DARE* Ed: It is possible that the resps *scrouge (up)* at Qu. Y32 belong instead at **3** below.] **1986** Pederson *LAGS Concordance,* 1 inf, **cwTN,** Hogs will scrouge under barbed wire.

b Fig: to be pushy or demanding; to struggle against difficulties; with *in:* to encroach (on).

1830 *MA Spy & Worcester Co. Advt.* (Worcester MA) 28 July 4/1 **Sth,** You're too monstrous inquisitive—you scrouge too hard. **1851** Hall *College Words* 266, *Scrouge.* To exact; to extort; said of an instructor who imposes difficult tasks on his pupils. **1884** Smith *Bill Arp's Scrap Book* 140 **nwGA,** Nobody growing rich, but many scrouging to keep up appearances. **1905** *DN* 3.64 **eNE,** Encroach in mean or petty fashion. . . "He scrowged in on the others."

3 To crouch; hence ppl adj *scrouged up* huddled. [Prob infl by **scrooch 1** or **scrouch 2;** cf **scrooge 2**]

1930 Shoemaker *1300 Words* 52 **cPA Mts** (as of c1900), *Scrouge*—To stoop down or hide oneself; to crowd. **1940** McCullers *Lonely Hunter* 167 **Sth,** He was scrouged up in a corner. **1944** [see **scrooch 1**]. **1986** Pederson *LAGS Concordance (Crouch)* 1 inf, **GA,** Scrouge down; 1 inf, **GA,** Scrouged down.

4 ppl adj phr *scrouged up;* Of the eyes: contracted, narrowed. [Prob infl by *scrooched up* (at **scrooch 2a**)]

1909 Wason *Happy Hawkins* 162 **IN,** The old man looked at me with his little shiny eyes all scrouged up.

scrouge n

1 also sp *scrowdge:* See quot. [**scrouge** v **1b**]

1890 *DN* 1.62 **NEng,** *Scrouge* or *scrowdge.* . . In New England it is in use, pronounced [skrauʒ] . . as a noun, meaning one who drives a hard bargain; and as a verb, to drive a hard bargain with, to overreach one in trade; as "he's an old scrouge," "he'd scrouge you out of your eye-teeth."

2 Room, space—in phr *give one some scrouge.*

1967 *DARE* (Qu. Y52, *To move over—for example on a long bench: ". . . Can you _____ [a little]?"*) Inf **LA2,** Give me some scrouge [skrauʒ]. **1996** *DARE* File **neTX** (as of 1920s–30s), *Give me some scrouge*—meant move over and give me some room.

3 See quot.

1954 *Harder Coll.* **cwTN,** *Scrouge.* . . A push or shove: "Give him a scrouge so's you git through there."

scrouged See **scrouge** v **1a, b**

scrouged up See **scrouge** v **1a, 3, 4**

scrouge in See **scrouge** v **2b**

scrouge up, scrouging See **scrouge** v **2a**

scrounch v
=**scrouch 2.**

1968–69 *DARE* (Qu. Y32, *To squeeze yourself into a small space:*

"If you're going to fit in there you'll have to _____.") Inf **IA**43, Scrounch; **NY**221, Scrounch down.

scrounge v [Engl dial]

1 To force or squeeze one's way; to encroach (on). Cf **scrouge** v **2a, b, scrouch 1**

1953 *Hall Coll.* **wNC**, Scrounge. . . To crowd, encroach on. [In the early days] Indians had the upper end of Deep Creek. The whites kept scroungin' on 'em. **1967–69** *DARE* (Qu. Y32, *To squeeze yourself into a small space: "If you're going to fit in there you'll have to _____."*) Infs **OH**11, **RI**15, Scrounge (over); (Qu. Y52, *To move over—for example on a long bench: ". . . Can you _____ [a little]?"*) Inf **CA**97, Scrounge [skrɔunʤ]—people around here say.

2 To crouch. Cf **scrouge** v **3, scrouch 2, scrooge** v **2**

1950 *WELS* (To double up, or go down on your heels: "_____ down so they can't see you.") 1 inf, **seWI**, Scrounge. **1958** *DE Folkl. Bulletin* 1.32, Scrounge down (hunch down, hide yourself, get out of the way).

scrowd v Also sp *schrowd, skroud*

To crowd.

1789 [see **scrouge** v **1a**]. **1818** in 1824 Knight *Letters* 107 **KY**, Some words are used, even by genteel people, from their imperfect educations, in a new sense; and others, by the lower classes in society, pronounced very uncouthly, as . . schrowd. **1913** *DN* 4.43, Scrowd. . . To crowd. "I'll scrowd in this seat." From *squeeze* and *crowd*.

scrowdge v See **scrouge** v

scrowdge n See **scrouge** n **1**

scrowge, scrowj See **scrouge** v

scrub n

1 An area of scrubby trees and vegetation; a thicket. [Cf *OED2 scrub* sb.¹ 2 1805 →, chiefly Austr, NZ] **chiefly FL**

1933 Rawlings *South Moon* 2 **nFL**, The Florida scrub was unique. . . The growth repelled all human living. The soil was a tawny sand, from whose parched infertility there reared . . so dense a growth of scrub pine . . that the effect of the massed thin trunks was of a limitless, canopied stockade. It seemed impenetrable. **1938** Rawlings *Yearling* 19 **nFL**, The scrub's a fitten place for the game to raise, and all the wild things. Foxes and deer and panther-cats and rattlesnakes. I cain't raise young uns in a pure thicket. **1966–68** *DARE* (Qu. C28, *A place where underbrush, weeds, vines and small trees grow together so that it's nearly impossible to get through*) Inf **FL**6, The scrub; **FL**29, Scrub; thicket; **FL**32, A scrub—on higher land; **FL**34, Hammock if big trees in with it, if not, a scrub; **GA**22, Scrub; scrubby place; **GA**31, Scrub; jungle. **1975** Newell *If Nothin' Don't Happen* 8 **nwFL**, Where the palmettos, scrub oaks and scrub pines grow real thick, we just call it scrub. *Ibid* 96, We all moved over to the Sulphur Island scrubs and camped in a old, deserted homesteader's shack. Things wasn't too comfortable in that camp . . the weather had turned off warm, so the skeeters was really bad.

2 also *scrub ball, scrub-bat, scrubby, scrub up,* and varr: A baseball game with fewer than the regular number of players in which the players play for themselves and rotate through the limited positions. **chiefly NEast, N Cent, TX, Gulf States** See Map Cf **one old cat 1, town ball, work-up**

1892 *DN* 1.214, "Scrub" in New England is that form of base ball played when there are too few players to have opposing sides. **1896** (1909) White *Real Issue* 66 **KS**, Just before school was called Piggy Pennington was playing "scrub". *Ibid* 67, Whirling . . toward the ball ground, shouting "scrub—first bat, first bat, first bat," . . Piggy made four tallies that recess, and the other boys couldn't have put him out. **1896** *DN* 1.424 **sCT, eMA, cwNY**, *Scrub:* a game of baseball among schoolboys, in which the players rotate positions. **1906** *DN* 3.155 **nwAR**, Scrub-bat. . . A game of base-ball which may be played by as few as five players, two basemen, a pitcher, a catcher, and a batsman. *Scrub(by).* . . Ball game known in southeastern New Hampshire as "old cat." **1909** *DN* 3.366 **eAL, wGA**, Scrub. . . A ball game played as a substitute for base ball when there are not enough players to make up two sides. There are two batters, and when one is put out, the catcher goes to the bat, and each out-player moves up one position. In case of an out on a fly, the batter exchanges places with the one who catches the fly. **1910** *DN* 3.447 **wNY**, Scrub. . . A game of baseball played by a half dozen or more persons (when there are not enough to "choose up" for two nines), in which the players move up as a batter is retired. **1946**

TN *Folk Lore Soc. Bulletin* 12, The ball games of "Stray Cat" and "Scrubby Nine" were usually for boys. **1957** *Sat. Eve. Post Letters* **MA**, Around Boston circa 1910 we boys used to play "scrub" for the one old cat or rounders type of baseball—individuals at bat and trying to remain there as contrasted to the regular team vs. team game. *Ibid* **Chicago IL** (as of c1915), "Scrub" was a baseball game played with a hard ball. When the batter was put out, he went to the outfield and worked back to batter again by progression through all the positions as other outs were made. This game was also called "work up" at times. *Ibid* **sIN** (as of c1910), Varieties of baseball depended on the number of players available. Six or less played "town ball". . . With a few more available we would play "cross-out". . . A few more and we played "scrub"—which is called "work-up" now. **1965–70** *DARE* (Qu. EE11, *Bat-and-ball games for just a few players [when there aren't enough for a regular game]*) 123 Infs, **chiefly NEast, N Cent, TX, Gulf States,** Scrub; 11 Infs, **scattered,** Scrub [FW sugg]; **AL**10, Scrub—same as one-eyed cat—three bases; **FL**19, Scrub—the batter hits the ball and the pitcher or outfielder who catches it rolls it back to the batter and tries to hit the bat (which the batter lays on the ground); **MA**42, Scrub—played with homeplate and first base only; **NY**98, Scrub—a rotation game; **OK**28, Scrub—"workout" or "scrub"—players take turns pitching, batting, and fielding; they change when batter gets three strikes; **OK**52, Scrub—players take different positions in rotation; **AR**51, **MI**67, **PA**124, Scrub ball; **IL**76, Scrub ball or move up base; **NC**41, **NY**12, Scrub team; **SC**54, Scrub-a-hole; **WI**60, Scrub first. **1988** Nickerson *Days to Remember* 53 **Cape Cod MA** (as of c1915), For those not on a team there was plenty of informal "scrub up" baseball.

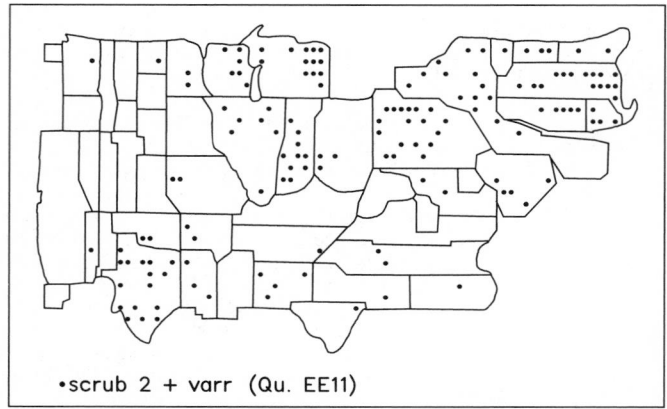

•scrub 2 + varr (Qu. EE11)

scrubbing board See **scrubboard 1**

scrubbing broom See **scrub broom**

scrubbing pad See **scrub pad**

scrub birch n

Usu a **dwarf birch** (here: *Betula nana*), but also a **swamp birch** (here: *B. pumila*).

1822 Eaton *Botany* 204 **MA**, [*Betula*] *glandulosa* [here: =*B. pumila*] (scrub birch). . . From 2 to 8 feet high. Very abundant in the marshes about Stockbridge, Mass. **1894** *Jrl. Amer. Folkl.* 7.98 **MI**, *Betula glandulosa* [here: =*B. pumila*], . . scrub birch. **1910** Jepson *Silva CA* 201, *Betula glandulosa* [here: =*B. nana*]. . . Scrub Birch. . . High mountains of northern Sierra Nevada . . and northward to subarctic regions where it covers vast tracts of country. **1959** Anderson *Flora AK* 186, *B[etula] glandulosa* Michx. [here: =*B. nana*] Glandular Scrub Birch. A shrub 5–15 dm. tall; twigs densely glandular and covered with a thin waxy layer. **1973** Hitchcock–Cronquist *Flora Pacific NW* 73, Scrub b[irch]; 2 vars.

scrubboard n

1 also *scrubbing board:* A washboard. **esp Sth** Cf **rubboard 1**

1889 *Century Illustr. Mag.* 38.84 **Sth,** Her great black, muscular arms drooped towards the scrubbing-board that reclined in the tub. **1966** *DARE* Tape **SC**3, I used to wash on a scrubboard in the tub. **1969** Pinto *Treen* 155, It is believed that ribbed wooden scrubbing boards . . originated in Scandinavia and the manufacture spread to other countries during the 19th century. **1986** Pederson *LAGS Concordance* **Gulf Region,**

9 infs, Scrubboards; 3 infs, Scrubbing boards; 1 inf, Women used to wash with scrubboards; 2 infs, Scrubboard; 1 inf, Scrubboard—used in washing process; [3 infs, Scrubboard(s) [sense uncertain]].

2 A baseboard. Cf **mopboard, washboard**
   1950 Burke et al. *Architectural & Building Trades Dict.* 274, *Scrub Board:* A finishing board placed around a room next to the floor to protect the wall finish. **1966–67** *DARE* (Qu. D37, *The strip of wood about eight inches high along the bottom of the wall [inside a room] joining to the floor*) Infs **CO7, KS1, OK42,** Scrubboard.

scrub broom n Also *scrubbing broom* [*OED2* 1675 →] esp **Midl** See Map
=scouring broom.
   1839 Kirkland *New Home* 118 **MI,** Fetch the broom, Betsey! and the scrub-broom, Betsey! **1890** *Century Dict.* 5427, *Scrub-broom. . .* A coarse broom used on board ships for scrubbing decks. **1937** (1963) Hyatt *Riverlid* 46 **KY,** I reckon you ha'n't got a rooster you'd keer to swap fer a good oak-split scrub broom? **1965–70** *DARE* (Qu. F36, . . *Kinds of brooms*) 13 Infs, **esp Midl,** Scrub broom; **IN23, MA34, NY153, TX26,** Scrubbing broom; [**NC82,** Scrub mop]. **1983** *MJLF* 9.1.54 **ceKY** (as of 1956), *Scrub Broom* . . a long-handled device with a wooden block, for scrubbing. **1986** Pederson *LAGS Concordance,* 7 infs, 6 **eTN,** Scrub broom(s); 1 inf, **neTN,** Scrub broom—was used to make the floors white; 1 inf, **ceTX,** Homemade scrub brooms—made from corn shucks.

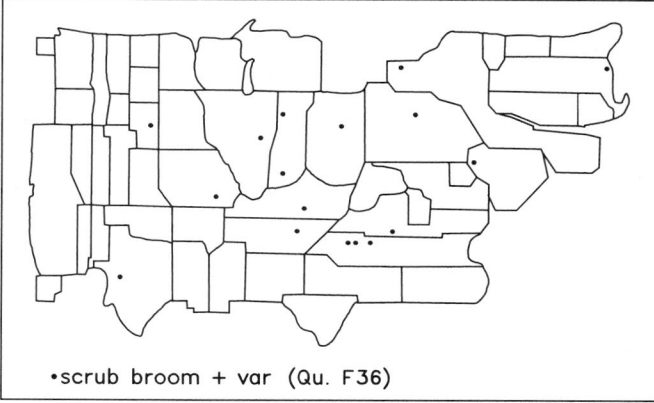

•scrub broom + var (Qu. F36)

scrub bucket See **bucket 2g**

scrubby See **scrub 2**

scrub cabbage n Cf **cabbage** n **B5, cabbage palm**
   A **palmetto B** (here: *Sabal etonia*).
   1933 Small *Manual SE Flora* 240, *S[abal] Etonia. . . (Scrub-palmetto. Scrub-cabbage.)*—Dry pinelands and scrub, pen[insular] Fla.—The bud is eaten like cabbage.

scrub cedar n
   A **tamarisk.**
   1966 *DARE* (Qu. T5, . . *Kinds of evergreens, other than pine*) Inf **OK25,** Scrub cedar—salt cedar (larger, has a "red deal" that hangs down).

scrub elm n
   A **cedar elm** or similar elm.
   1960 Vines *Trees SW* 210, *Ulmus crassifolia. . .* Vernacular names are Scrub Elm, Lime Elm [etc]. . . It is often planted as a shade tree, but the wood is considered inferior to other elms. **1966–69** *DARE* (Qu. T11, . . *Kinds of elm trees*) Infs **AR10, KY53,** Scrub elm; **KY65,** Scrub elm—a fine shade tree.

scrub gopher n
   A **ground squirrel b** (here: either *Spermophilus franklinii* or *S. variegatus*).
   1917 Anthony *Mammals Amer.* 183, *Citellus grammurus* [=*Spermophilus variegatus*]. . . Scrub Gopher. *Ibid* 184, In early October, the "Scrub-Gopher" makes itself safe against unfavorable weather and enemies by plugging up the various entrances to its home with earth, and enters into its night of six months. **1961** Jackson *Mammals WI* 138,

Citellus franklinii [=*Spermophilus f.*] . . *Vernacular names. . .* Line-tailed squirrel, prairie squirrel, and scrub gopher.

scrub grass n Cf **scouring rush**
=horsetail 1, esp *Equisetum hyemale.*
   1814 Brackenridge *Views of LA* 206, Through all these islands, and on the Missouri bottoms, there are great quantities of rushes, commonly called scrub grass. **1819** Thomas *Travels W. Country* 44, Scrub Grass is called, in Scipio, 'Rushes.' Both names are improper, the plant belonging to the . . genus *Equisetum.* **1820** Heckewelder *Narrative* 354 **Canada** (as of 1784) [Writer from **PA**], Two deers . . were shot; they being opened to see what they had fed upon, it was found, that their stomachs were filled with the *scrub grass,* (Equisetum hyemale.) [Footnote: Scrub, and scour grass, so called, as it is made use of in scouring pewter, etc.] **1937** FWP *Guide ID* 104, Less lovely but more widely distributed in Idaho is the scouring-brush, one of the commonest of the large horsetails. Its rough silicious fiber used to be widely favored in the scouring of pots and pans. . . Known variously as scrub-grass, snake-rush, gun-bright, snake-grass, and winter-rush, it is used in Holland to prevent erosion, and was shipped to England as scouring material and took the name of Dutch clean-rush.

scrub hickory n
   A **hickory B1** (here: *Carya floridana*) native to Florida.
   1883 Smith *Rept. for 1881 & 1882* 226 **nAL,** *Barrens soil* from near Cluttsville, Madison county. . . Vegetation [includes] . . scrub hickory, wild gooseberry, blackberry. **1933** Small *Manual SE Flora* 407, *H[icoria] floridana. . . Scrub-hickory. . .* Sandy ridges and scrub. **1946** West–Arnold *Native Trees FL* 21, *Carya floridana. . .* The scrub hickory is a small tree characteristic of the coastal dunes . . and of the scrubs in the interior. **1962** Kurz–Godfrey *Trees N. FL* 42, Scrub hickory. . . is a small tree or shrub. **1980** Little *Audubon Guide N. Amer. Trees E. Region* 346, *Scrub Hickory . . Carya floridana. . .* Range: Central Florida.

scrub jay n
   A **jay** (*Aphelocoma coerulescens*) native to the western US and central Florida. Also called **Florida jay 2, jaybird 1a, Mexican jay, mountain ~ 2**
   1917 (1923) *Birds Amer.* 2.221, *Aphelocoma cyanea* [=*A. coerulescens*]. . . Scrub Jay. . . One of the crestless Jays, . . his preferred habitat is scrub-oak woodland. **1938** Rawlings *Yearling* 182 **nFL,** Scrub jays cried shrilly. **1951** Teale *North with Spring* 59 **FL,** Like the burrowing owls of the Kissimmee Prairie, these Florida or scrub jays underscore the geology of ornithology. **1966–69** *DARE* (Qu. Q16, . . *Kinds of jays*) Infs **CA140, FL34, NV6,** Scrub jay. **1977** Bull–Farrand *Audubon Field Guide Birds* 484, Scrub Jay (*Aphelocoma coerulescens*).

scrub maple n
   The bigtooth **maple** (*Acer grandidentatum*).
   1976 Elmore *Shrubs & Trees SW* 133, Dwarf or scrub maple . . *Acer grandidentatum. . .* It can grow to small-tree size of about 35 feet . . (or it can be a large, usually several-stemmed shrub 8 to 12 feet tall).

scrub oak n Cf **shrub oak**
   Any of var small or shrubby **oaks;** see quots.
   1766 (1942) Bartram *Diary of a Journey* 42 **nFL,** About one o'clock we came to Round-Lake, . . almost surrounded with palmetto, pine, and scrub-oak. **1796** in 1916 Hawkins *Letters* 16 **SC,** The lands in this vale, not rich, the timber small and mostly scruboak. **1872** Schele de Vere *Americanisms* 418, All the smaller, and some more or less dwarfish, varieties [of oaks], are comprehended under the familiar name of *Scrub Oaks.* **1894** *Jrl. Amer. Folkl.* 7.99 **CA,** *Quercus agrifolia,* . . scrub oak, evergreen oak. **1897** Sudworth *Arborescent Flora* 153 **NM, AZ, CO, OR, NV, UT,** *Quercus gambelii. . .* Scrub Oak. *Ibid* 155 **NE, MN,** *Quercus macrocarpa. . .* Scrub Oak. *Ibid* 157 **NY,** *Quercus acuminata* [=*Q. muhlenbergii*]. . . Scrub Oak. *Ibid* 160, *Quercus undulata* [=*Q.* x *pauciloba*]. . . Scrub Oak. *Ibid* 162, *Quercus dumosa. . .* Scrub Oak. *Ibid* 174 **SC,** *Quercus marilandica. . .* Scrub Oak. **1933** Small *Manual SE Flora* 426, *Q[uercus] minima. . .* Shrub, . . the branches less than 1 m. tall. . . Flat pinelands, Coastal Plain, Fla. to Ga. *Ibid* 427, *Q. Chapmanii. . .* Shrub, or tree becoming 15 m. tall. . . *Scrub-oak. . .* Hammocks and scrub, Coastal Plain, Fla. to S.C. . . *Q. Rolfsii* [=*Q.* x *rolfsii*]. . . Shrub, or small tree 7 m. tall. . . *Scrub-oak. . .* Hammocks, and scrub, lower E. coast, Fla. . . *Q. myrtifolia. . .* Shrub, or tree becoming 6 m. tall. . . *Scrub-oak. . .* Sandy hammocks, scrub, and sand ridges, Coastal Plain, Fla. to La. and S.C. *Ibid* 430, *Q. laevis. . . Scrub-oak. . .* Dry pinelands and acid sand-ridges, Coastal Plain and

rarely Piedmont, Fla. to La. and Va. **1947** Collingwood–Brush *Knowing Trees* 216, *Bur Oak—Quercus macrocarpa.* . . may on unfavorable sites live for years in thickets without attaining heights of more than six to eight feet. Under such conditions it is frequently referred to as "scrub oak." *Ibid* 227, *Chinquapin Oak—Quercus muehlenbergi.* . . Throughout the Atlantic States . . on dry hillsides and rocky ridges . . it makes poor growth and is small in size. . . Other names applied to the tree are . . yellow oak and scrub oak. **1960** Vines *Trees SW* 166, *Quercus mohriana.* . . Vernacular names are Scrub Oak [etc]. *Ibid* 167, *Quercus undulata* [=*Q.* x *pauciloba*]. . . Also known as Scrub Oak. *Ibid* 168, *Quercus grisea.* . . Vernacular names are Shin Oak, Scrub Oak [etc]. *Ibid* 169, *Quercus pungens.* . . Also known as Scrub Oak. **1965–70** *DARE* (Qu. T10, . . *Kinds of oak trees*) 166 Infs, **widespread,** Scrub oak; [**FL**17, Oak scrubs;] **SC**24, Scrub; **GA**20, Scrub oak—same as blackjack; **LA**15, Blackjack or scrub oak; **MI**10, Pin [oak]—limited amount, also called "scrub" oak; **NY**36, Scrub oak—on Long Island, in the center part—used to be called the "scrub oaks"—it was covered with good-for-nothing oaks 4–5 ft. high, growing in sandy soil; (Qu. S21, . . *Weeds* . . *that are a trouble in gardens and fields*) Inf **CA**140, Scrub oak; [(Qu. T1, . . *A bunch of trees growing together in open country, especially on a hill*) Inf **GA**28, Oak scrub beds;] (Qu. T2a, . . *A piece of land covered with trees* . . *only a few acres*) Inf **CA**53, Scrub oak acreage; (Qu. T5, . . *Kinds of evergreens, other than pine*) Inf **CA**181, Scrub oak; (Qu. T16, . . *Kinds of trees* . . *'special'*) Inf **PA**245, Scrub oak, scrub pine—that's all that's here. **1968** Pochmann *Triple Ridge* 85, The term "scrub oak" is loosely applied to small- and medium-sized oaks that run apace up the hillsides and across abandoned fields over much of our nation. **1980** Little *Audubon Guide N. Amer. Trees E. Region* 385, "Scrub Oak" *Quercus chapmanii. Ibid* 393, "Scrub Oak" *Quercus laevis. Ibid* 400, "Scrub Oak" *Quercus myrtifolia.* **1980** Little *Audubon Guide N. Amer. Trees W. Region* 395, "Scrub Oak" *Quercus dumosa. Ibid* 402, *Gray Oak* "Scrub Oak" . . *Quercus grisea. Ibid* 405, "Island Scrub Oak" *Quercus macdonaldii. Ibid* 406, "Scrub Oak" *Quercus mohriana. Ibid* 409, "Scrub Oak" . . *Quercus pungens. Ibid* 413, "Scrub Oak" *Quercus turbinella.* **1986** Pederson *LAGS Concordance* 10 infs, 7 **FL, GA,** Scrub oak(s); 1 inf, **ceFL,** Scrub oak trees; 1 inf, **swGA,** Scrub oak—[same as] blackjack oak; 1 inf, **neMS,** Post-oak land—grows scrub oak—poor land.

scrub pad n Also *scrubbing pad* **chiefly Sth, S Midl, TX**
See Map Cf **scratch pad**

1965–70 *DARE* (Qu. G14, *The rough metal pad that's used to scour pots and pans*) 22 Infs, **chiefly Sth, S Midl, TX,** Scrub pad; 9 Infs, **chiefly Sth, S Midl,** Scrubbing pad.

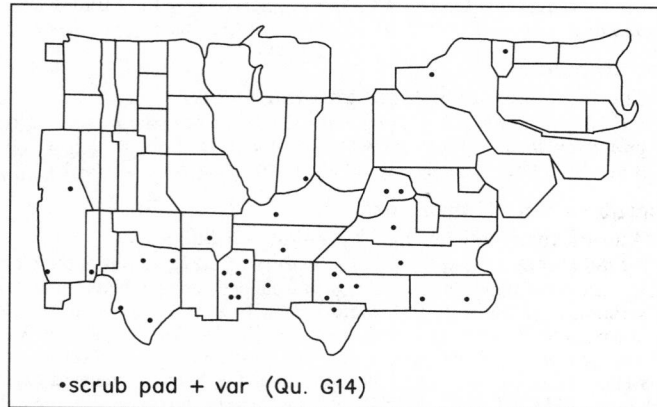

•scrub pad + var (Qu. G14)

scrub pail See **pail** n 2e

scrub palmetto n **chiefly FL**

A low-growing **palmetto B:** usu **blue palmetto 1,** a **dwarf palmetto 1,** or **saw palmetto 1.**

1901 Lounsberry *S. Wild Flowers* 28, *Saw Palmetto. Scrub Palmetto.* . . *Serenoa serrulata* [=*S. repens*]. . . All through swampy places in its natural habitat, . . this low and spreading palm is as distinctive a feature of the undergrowth as is the palmetto of arborescent-life. **1903** Small *Flora SE U.S.* 223, *Sabal megacarpa* [=*S. etonia*]. . . In the scrub or coral sand, peninsular Florida. *Scrub Palmetto.* **1938** Rawlings *Yearling* 40 **nFL,** Pushing through the low scrub oaks, the scrub palmettos, the gallberry bushes and the ti-ti, was less laborious than crossing the swamp. **1942** Hylander *Plant Life* 526, The common Scrub Palmetto of

the Florida pinelands has folded and recurved leaves with thready frayed margins; the stem is subterranean and often spirally twisted. *Ibid* 679, Scrub Palmetto—Sabal etonia. **1967** *DARE* (Qu. T16, . . *Kinds of trees* . . *'special'*) Inf **SC**63, Scrub palmetto = saw palmetto. **1975** Newell *If Nothin' Don't Happen* 9 **nwFL,** There's several kinds of scrub palmettos, including saw palmettos and needle palmettos. Either kind makes real rough goin' for a huntin' dog, because the stems of the saw palmettos will cut him and the spines of the needle palmettos will punch out his eyes if he ain't careful. **1986** Pederson *LAGS Concordance,* 1 inf, **ceFL,** Scrub palmetto.

scrub pine n

A small or shrubby pine; often a **Jersey pine** in the eastern US, a **sand pine 1** or a **shortleaf pine 1** (here: *Pinus echinata*) in the South, a **jack pine 1** in the North, or a **lodgepole pine, knobcone pine,** or **whitebark pine** in the West; see quots.

[**1791** in 1934 Champlain Soc. Toronto *Pub.* 21.517 **Canada,** A high point of Rocks & scrub pine.] **1825** (1832) Pickering *Inquiries* 73 **cwNY,** This peninsula varies in width from a few rods to a mile or two; much covered with fine timber, scrub pines and cedar only. **1860** Curtis *Cat. Plants NC* 20, *Jersey Pine.* . . in some parts of the country . . is also known under the names of *Cedar, River,* and *Scrub* Pine. a**1862** (1864) Thoreau *ME Woods* 275, A peculiar evergreen overhung our fire, . . the *Pinus Banksiana,* . . also called Scrub Pine, Gray Pine, &c. **1897** Sudworth *Arborescent Flora* 30 **ME, VT, NY, WI, MI, MN, Ontario,** *Pinus Banksiana.* . . Scrub Pine. **1901** Lounsberry *S. Wild Flowers* 2, Scrub Pine. Bull Pine. *Pinus echinata.* . . Through the south, from the mountains to the coast-line, there is seen an abundance of this fine, sturdy pine. **1910** Jepson *Silva CA* 104, The Knob-cone Pine. . . Its inferior stature and unattractive appearance is expressed in the folk-name, Scrub Pine, by which it is best known in the mountains. **1921** Deam *Trees IN* 25, *Pinus virginiana.* . . Scrub Pine. . . In its native habitat on the exposed summits of the "knobs" it is usually a small tree about . . 10 m. high. **1965–70** *DARE* (Qu. T17, . . *Kinds of pine trees;* not asked in early QRs) 109 Infs, **widespread, but chiefly east of Missip R,** Scrub pine; **NC**48, **VA**24, Virginia scrub pine; **MD**9, Scrub pine—also called bull [pine]; **MA**30, Jack, scrub [pines]—the same; **NJ**21, Scrub pine or bull pine; **TN**14, Scrub pine—called bull-dick pine; (Qu. T16, . . *Kinds of trees* . . *'special'*) Infs **DC**2, **PA**245, Scrub pine. **1967** Gilkey–Dennis *Hdbk. NW Plants* 29, *Pinus contorta.* . . Lodgepole pine. Scrub . . pine. Scrubby trees, usually less than 20 m. **1980** Little *Audubon Guide N. Amer. Trees W. Region* 268, "Scrub Pine" . . *Pinus albicaulis.* . . Tree with short, twisted or crooked trunk and irregular, spreading crown; a shrub at timberline. **1980** Little *Audubon Guide N. Amer. Trees E. Region* 286, "Scrub Pine" . . *Pinus banksiana.* . . sometimes a shrub. *Ibid* 287, "Scrub Pine" . . *Pinus clausa. Ibid* 298, "Scrub Pine" . . *Pinus virginiana.* . . often a shrub. **1986** Pederson *LAGS Concordance,* 4 infs, **Gulf Region,** Scrub pine(s).

scrub up See **scrub 2**

scruch See **scrooch**

scrudge See **scrooge**

scruff n [Engl dial var of *scurf*]

1 Scurf, dandruff.

1899 (1912) Green *VA Folk-Speech* 372, *Scruff.* . . Scurf; dandruff. **1902** *DN* 2.244 **sIL,** *Scruff.* . . Scurf. **1907** *DN* 3.226 **nwAR,** *Scruff.* . . Scurf.

2 Fig: scum, dregs; a contemptible person.

1929 *AmSp* 5.130 **ME,** The "scruff of the earth" (Prov. Dial.) was sometimes used for the commoner "scum of the earth." **1946** Driscoll *Country Jake* 14 **KS,** They are the scruff of scurf. They are reeking with the drivel of their own imbecility. **1968** *DARE* (Qu. HH18, *Very insignificant or low-grade people*) Infs **PA**76, 94, Scruffs.

scrum(m)age, scrummish See **skirmish**

scrumption See **scrimption**

scrunch v

1 To crunch, crush, squeeze; also fig.

1851 *Harper's New Mth. Mag.* 3.63, Another limb was scrunched from his body [by a shark]. **1873** *Manufacturer & Builder* 5.128, Everything seems to have been twisted and scrunched and hurled and piled together. **1899** (1912) Green *VA Folk-Speech* 373, *Scrunch.* . . To crush as with the teeth; crunch. To squeeze; crush. **1901** *DN* 2.146 **NY,**

Scrunch. . . "To scrunch the farmers" = to oppress them. **1923** *DN* 5.220 **swMO,** *Scrunch.* . . To crunch or mash. **1931** Randolph *Ozarks* 68, Thet 'ar pore susy hippoed woman o' hisn was . . a-scrunchin' cheenches on th' puncheon. **1940** *AmSp* 15.336 **NE,** When you have finished with your cigarette, you may . . *scrunch it out.* **1950** *PADS* 14.59 **SC,** *Scrunch.* . . Usually with *down;* to crush, crunch, break to pieces or flatten under pressure. **1954** *Harder Coll.* **cwTN,** *Scrunch.* . . crunch, crush. **1968–69** *DARE* (Qu. KK21, *When something hollow is crushed by a heavy weight, or by a fall:* "They ran the wagon over the coffee pot and _____.") Infs **IN5, MN21, NY131, WI47,** Scrunched it; (Qu. Y32, *To squeeze yourself into a small space:* "If you're going to fit in there you'll have to _____.") Infs **HI1, KY9,** Scrunch yourself in (*or* together); **CT8,** Scrunch yourself.

2 also *scrunge;* also with *up;* intr: To crouch, cringe, hunch; to shrink or squeeze oneself (down, back, etc); hence ppl adj *scrunched (up)* huddled, squeezed.

1870 *Harper's New Mth. Mag.* 40.708 [Black], An' I jes scrunched down by her piller, an' I went in for't, an' I tole her all Phil had said. **1885** Twain *Huck. Finn* 19 **MO,** Dont scrunch up like that, Huckleberry—set up straight. **1906** Twain in *Harper's Mth. Mag.* 113.335, The surgeon . . began to sew it up; it had to have a lot of stitches, and each one made her scrunch a little. **1931** *VA Qrly. Rev.* Jan 106 [Black], The twins lay upon the spare bed. . . 'Look at dis'n all scrunchedup.' **1939** Steinbeck *Grapes* 8 **OK,** Scrunch down on the running-board till we get around the bend. **1943** *LANE* Map 581 *(Crouch)* 3 infs, **RI, seMA,** Scrunch down; 1 inf, **RI,** Scrunched up = all drawn together. **1951** Capote *Grass Harp* 63, We scrunched together to make a place for Riley. **1962** Faulkner *Reivers* 158 **MS,** Otis was scrunched back against the wall. **1965–70** *DARE* (Qu. Y32, *To squeeze yourself into a small space:* "If you're going to fit in there you'll have to _____.") 28 Infs, **scattered,** Scrunch up; 26 Infs, **chiefly Nth, N Midl,** Scrunch; 15 Infs, **scattered, but esp Nth, Midl,** Scrunch down; **WA37,** Scrunch in; **RI12,** Scrunge down; (Qu. Y52, *To move over—for example on a long bench:* ". . . Can you _____ [a little]?") Infs **IL97, WA33,** Scrunch over; **GA82,** Scrunch up; **LA14,** Scrunch down. **1986** Pederson *LAGS Concordance* **Gulf Region** *(Crouch)* 9 infs, Scrunch (down); 1 inf, Scrunch up; 2 infs, Scrunched (down); 2 infs, Scrunching (up).

scrunch n See **scronch** n

scrunched (up), scrunch up See **scrunch** v 2

scrunch owl n Cf **scroonch owl**

A **screech owl 1** (here: *Otus asio*).

1932 Bennitt *Check-list* 37 **MO,** *Otus asio naevius.* . . Mottled owl; red owl; scrunch owl. **1986** Pederson *LAGS Concordance,* 1 inf, **cnLA,** Scrunch owl.

scrunge See **scrunch** v 2

scrunt n [Scots, nEngl dial] **esp PA**

A runt; hence adj *scrunty* stunted; runty; measly.

1889 *Century Illustr. Mag.* 38.897 **cGA,** How I gwine fin' out 'bout what mek yo' watermillions so runty an' so scrunty? **1967–69** *DARE* (Qu. K54, . . *The smallest pig in a litter*) Infs **PA13, 29,** Scrunt; **NE8,** Scrunty pig; (Qu. K55, *A pig that doesn't grow well and is not worth keeping*) Inf **PA13,** Scrunt; **PA141,** Scrunty; (Qu. LL2, . . *Too small to be worth much:* "I don't want that little _____ potato.") Inf **PA207,** Scrunty.

scrup See **scrap** v

scrutch See **scrooch**

scrutch owl See **scrooch owl**

scud n[1] [See quot 1873]

A crustacean of the order Amphipoda such as those of the genus *Gammarus.* For other names of var of these see **sand-flea 1b**

1873 U.S. Bur. Fisheries *Rept. for 1871–72* 1.125, **Martha's Vineyard MA,** A much larger species . . is the *Gammarus ornatus.* . . They swim rapidly in a gyrating manner back downward, or sideways. . . The only good English name that I have ever heard for these creatures is that of "scuds" given by a small boy, in reference to their rapid and peculiar motions. **1951** Harlan–Speaker *IA Fish* 148, Gammarid or Scud. . . Some of the smaller crustaceans. . . of this group range in size up to one-half inch in length and are common in Iowa waters. **1974** McClane *McClane's New Std. Fishing Encycl.* 858, Scuds. . . Erroneously called

freshwater shrimp. The order of amphipods includes marine forms as well as most terrestrial species which live near the high water mark. . . There are about 50 species of scuds in North American freshwaters. **1981** Meinkoth *Audubon Field Guide Seashore* 604, Scud (*Gammarus oceanicus*). . . Arched, sides flattened. . . 2 pairs of *equally long antennae.* . . 7 pairs of walking legs. **1982** Sternberg *Fishing* 126, Common to many trout streams, scuds thrive in any cool, unpolluted water that is rich in oxygen and has ample rooted vegetation. They are sometimes called *sideswimmers* because they swim with their bodies turned sideways.

scud n[2] See **scut** n[2]

scud n[3] [Var of *scad* a great number, a large amount]

1968 *DARE* Tape **MD37,** He's had a scud of occupations. **1969–70** *DARE* (Qu. LL8b, . . *A large number* . . "She has a whole _____ of cousins.") Inf **KY84,** Scud [skʌd]; (Qu. U38a, . . *A great deal of money:* "He's got _____ [of money].") Inf **KY89,** Scuds [skʌdz]; (Qu. U38b, . . *A great deal of money:* "He made a _____ [of money].") Inf **MO37,** Scuds of money.

scudder n[1] See **scutter** n[1]

scudder n[2] See **scutter** n[2]

scudsy See **scutzy**

scuffle v, hence vbl n *scuffling* **Okefenokee GA**

Of a nesting turtle: to stir up the earth away from the nest to divert predators from the actual nest.

1926 *AmSp* 1.415 **Okefenokee GA,** I had . . to stumble upon a Soft-shelled Turtle in the act of depositing its eggs. This . . species comes upon the land at this season, finds a patch of soft ground, excavates a hole with its hind feet, lays its complement of eggs therein, carefully fills up the hole with earth, and makes for its home in the water. . . But after going a few yards, it pauses to vigorously scratch up the ground, scattering the earth about and so leaving a conspicuous trace of its presence. This shrewd act, known to the Okefinokee hunters as 'scufflin', naturally tends to draw the attention of marauding animals away from the exact spot where the eggs have been concealed. *Ibid* 416, Them Yaller-bellied Tarrapins, they jest lay their aigs anywhere. Don't scuffle a-tall. . . When I find where a turtle has scuffled, I don't dig fer the aigs; I take me a stick an' find the hole. **1934** *Natl. Geogr. Mag.* May 610 **Okefenokee GA,** I soon learned that the swamp hunters were familiar with this trick of "scufflin'," as they call it, and that they were positive in their interpretation of it as a device to baffle the predacious animals that seek the turtle's eggs.

Scuffletonian n esp **GA** Cf **Scuffletown**

A person of racially mixed ancestry (Black and White, or Black and American Indian).

c1970 Pederson *Dial. Surv. Rural GA* **seGA** *(A person whose skin is brown or black—neutral term)* 1 inf, Scuffletonians [ˌskʌfəˈtoʊnɨˈᵊnz, ˌskʌfəˈdoʊnɨᵊnz]. **1986** Pederson *LAGS Concordance* *(A child born of a racially mixed (black and white) marriage)* 1 inf, **csGA,** Scuffletonian [Inf is Black]; 1 inf, **ceGA,** Scuffletonians—blacks, Indians from NC intermarry.

Scuffletown n esp **Mid Atl**

Used as a nickname for a poor or disreputable town or district.

1941 *Sun* (Baltimore MD) 25 Dec 10/7, It reminds me of a Tar Heel friend's definition of Scuffletown, in that state. Scuffletown . . is reputedly an extremely tough district, inhabited by a populace that commands no admiration whatever. Everyone has heard of it and admits its character. The difficulty is in locating it. My friend asserts that he has found by personal investigation that Scuffletown is always four miles down the road until you have proceeded a certain distance when you suddenly discover that it is four miles up the road. **1967–70** *DARE* (Qu. C34, *Nicknames for nearby settlements, villages, or districts*) Inf **GA31,** Scuffletown—a rather rough area, famous for moonshining; **NC49,** Scuffletown—Pembroke; **SC43,** Scuffletown—rough town inhabitants—Big Bay Vat was the old name; **VA42,** Scuffletown—because the folks had such a time a-living; White; on very edge of Chatham; (Qu. C35, *Nicknames for the different parts of your town or city*) Inf **VA8,** Scuffletown—Radio Heights; **VA42,** Scuffletown—White. **1968** *DARE* FW Addit **csNC,** *Scuffletown*—nickname for Pembroke, N.C., perhaps because there used to be so much fighting there. **1998** Avail *Over the James* (Phonodisc), Scuffletown—There's kepone in the river / But the river's still / Flowing east Ethyl dozed the planet / In an attempt to keep /

The downtown clean / Still it's a beautiful day / And the sun is shining Over the James. [*DARE* Ed: The band is from Richmond VA]

scuffling See **scuffle**

sculch n Also sp *skulch* [Engl dial var of **culch;** cf Intro "Language Changes" I.8] **NEng**
Refuse, junk, swill; also fig.

1890 *Jrl. Amer. Folkl.* 3.64 **MA,** Sculch.—Food unfit to eat, or good food served too often. **1900** Day *Up in ME* 91, That harrycane... It picked up sculch and dirt. **1909** *DN* 3.415 **nME,** Sculch... Same as culch. **1914** *DN* 4.79 **ME, nNH,** Skulch... Refuse, swill. **1927** *AmSp* 3.139 **eME,** "Orts," now familiar through cross word puzzles, is archaic for refuse, and this and "culch" or "sculch" were common. **1949** Kurath *Word Geog.* 22, Other "Down East" expressions . . *culch, sculch* . . for junk, trash (from Massachusetts Bay to Maine and northwestward to northeastern Vermont). **1950** Perrin *Coll.* **NEng,** Skulch—trash, worthless stuff—This word, natural in my New England days, has usually roused questions . . in other parts of the country. **1974** *AmSp* 49.63 **sME coast** (as of c1900), Sculch . . Refuse, rubbish. **1988** *Yankee* Aug 22 **NH,** My mother used to say, "Clean out the skulch in your room," or ask Dad to take skulch to the dump.

sculjo See **skulljoe**

scullcap See **skullcap 2**

scullion See **scallion**

sculljoe, scully-joe See **skulljoe**

scully pit See **skelly 1**

sculp See **scalp**

sculpin n

1 Std: any of numerous fishes of the family Cottidae. Also called **biggyhead, bullhead 1a.** For other names of var of these see **cabezon, Cape Cod clergyman, daddy sculpin, democrat 2, drummer 2, goblin** n[1]**, grubby 2, gruntfish 2, Irish lord, johnny 1, miller's thumb 1, mottled sculpin, muddler, muffle-jaw, pigfish a, poison fish, salpa, scalawag 3, scorpion B4b, sea horse 2, ~ raven, ~ toad 1, spoonhead, stargazer**

2 A **scorpion fish** (here: *Scorpaena guttata*) native to California.

1882 U.S. Natl. Museum *Bulletin* 16.679, S[corpaena] guttata . . . Sculpin. Brown, irregularly mottled and blotched with rosy purplish and pale olive. **1898** *Ibid* 47.1847 **CA,** Scorpaena guttata... Sculpin... Very abundant about San Diego; a good food-fish. **1953** Roedel *Common Fishes CA* 137, Scorpaena guttata... Not a true sculpin but a member of the rockfish family... Sold entirely in the fresh fish markets. Considered a desirable species by sportsmen.

3 Used as a derog term for a person or animal. **NEng**

1836 (1838) Haliburton *Clockmaker* (1st ser) 258, Go along, you old sculpin [=a horse], and turn out your toes. **1877** Jewett *Deephaven* 88 **ME,** Ye see the miser'ble sculpin thought I'd never stop to open the goods. **1913** *DN* 4.57 **seMA,** Sculpin... Scalawag; rascal. "Don't have no dealings with him; he's a reg'lar sculpin!" **1916** Lincoln *Mary-'Gusta* 101 **MA,** Did I understand you to say that Mary-'Gusta was with you when that sculpin come to borrow my gun? **1924** *DN* 5.288 **Cape Cod MA,** A sculpin is a 'scalawag'. **1932** Tooné *Yankee Slang* 32, Sculpin: Back-biter, mischievous gossip.

scum n chiefly **Nth, N Midl** See Map Cf **scum** v[1] **2, skim** n **2**

Also in combs *scum of ice, scum ice:* A thin layer of ice on a body of water.

1845 *Littell's Living Age* 5.65, In the centre of this iceberg was found a pool of most delicious water, over which was a scum of ice. **1885** *Century Illustr. Mag.* 30.90, As soon as the surface of the sound was still for any length of time, a thin scum of ice formed over it. **1943** *LANE* Map 648 *(Froze)* 1 inf, **swCT,** The lake had a scum of ice on it. **1950** *WELS* (*The first thin ice that forms on a pond or pool: A* _____ *of ice.)* 5 Infs, **WI,** Scum. **c1960** Wilson *Coll.* **csKY,** Scum... Thin, maybe broken, first ice, on pond. **1964** O'Hare *Ling. Geog. E. MT* 62, The first thin coating of ice... scum ([of] ice) [2 of 12 infs]. **1965–70** *DARE* (Qu. B33a, *The first thin ice that forms over the surface of a pond or*

pool: "*There's just a* _____ *of ice.*") 62 Infs, **chiefly Nth, N Midl,** Scum. **1973** Allen *LAUM* 1.157 **Upper MW** (as of c1950), First thin coating of ice... *Scum,* the most frequent form, has fairly even distribution... Mail responses generally confirm the field data, with *scum* having 44% [of 1064 checklist infs]... Scum ice [1 inf]; [scum] of ice [52 infs]. **1973** Gawthrop *Dial. Calumet* 77 **nwIN,** *First thin layer of ice on lake or pond:* .. scum 2 [of 125 infs].

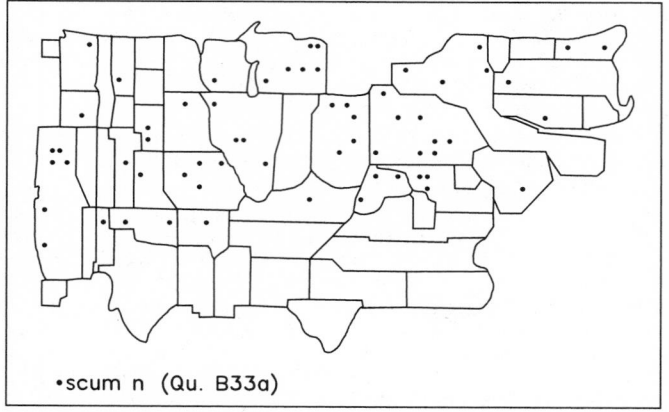

•scum n (Qu. B33a)

scum v[1] Also sp *skum*

1 To remove a floating layer from (a liquid); to skim; hence ppl adj *skummed.* [*OED2 scum* v. 1 1398 →; "*Obs.*"]

1909 *DN* 3.367 **eAL, wGA,** Skum(med), pret. and pp. of *skim.* **1917** in 1944 *ADD* **sWV,** Skummed milk. **1968** *DARE* Tape CA90, Then you scummed the scum off the top of that.

2 with *over:* Of a body of water: to become covered by a thin layer of ice; hence ppl adj phr *scummed over.* Cf **scum** n, **skim** v **B**

1943 *LANE* Map 648 *(Froze)* 5 infs **CT, MA,** Scummed over; 1 inf, **swCT,** [skuᵛmd] over [in context "the pond _____ last night."] **1950** *WELS* (*The first thin ice that forms on a pond or pool .. The pond is just* _____ *with ice.*) 2 Infs, **WI,** Scummed over; 1 Inf, **ceWI,** Scumming over. **1965–70** *DARE* (Qu. B33b, *Talking about the first thin ice that forms over the surface of a pond or pool: "The pond is just* _____ *over.")* 19 Infs, **esp Nth, N Midl,** Scummed. [18 of 19 Infs comm type 4 or 5, 16 old] **1973** Allen *LAUM* 1.157 **Upper MW** (as of c1950), The lake *froze over* last night... Scummed over [2 infs, **ceMN, cNE**].

scum v[2] See **skim** v **A, B**

scum ice See **scum** n

scummed over See **scum** v[1] **2**

scum of ice See **scum** n

scum over See **scum** v[1] **2**

scun See **skin** v **A**

scunner v Also *scunder* [Scots, nEngl dial]
To cause disgust; hence ppl adj *scunnered* disgusted.

1910 *Univ. NC Mag.* 40.3.7 **Hatteras Is. NC,** I inadvertently mentioned the young man's name to the lady's mother, who said, "Oh, he scunners me," meaning "He disgusts me," which would seem to be a causative use of what meant "to loathe." **1938** FWP *Ocean Highway* 189 **NC,** "Don't fault me if I'm scunnered" means "Don't blame me if I'm disgusted." **1943** in 1944 *ADD* **wPA** (as of 1900), Scunner... I'm completely scundered with her.

scunner n [Scots, nEngl dial]
A dislike, aversion, prejudice.

1868 *Galaxy* 5.499, But cultivated and well-meaning people sometimes take a scunner against some particular word or phrase. **1890** *Catholic World* 52.288, To whom .. is he responsible for the tissue of malevolent misrepresentation of the Catholic Church... The writer was evidently predetermined in his scunner at the priesthood. **1933–35** in 1944 *ADD* **NEng,** Scunner... I took a scunner to that man. **1946** Hench *Coll.*, Ned Lehmann .. UVa medical faculty, Charlottesville, Va: Chan has a scunner against the book. **1947** *AmSp* 22.21 [Gaelic loanwords in American], Scunner (an instinctive dislike). **1965** Hench *Coll.*

swPA, Pud McKnight . . said to me: I got a scunner against Shakespeare right from the start.   **1980** *DARE* File **WI,** He must have taken a scunner to you from the start.

scunnered See **scunner** v

scunnion n Also *sconion* [Appar blend of **scallion** + **onion**]
An **onion** n B such as a **scallion.**

1968–70 *DARE* (Qu. I6, *The kind of onions that come up fresh early in the year, and you eat them raw*) Inf **VA71,** Scunnions [skʌnjənz]; (Qu. I7, *The small plants like onions with hollow green leaves that are cut up in a salad*) Inf **MA7,** Scunnions ['skʌnjənz].   **1986** Pederson *LAGS Concordance,* 1 inf, seFL, Sconions [=scallions + onions]; 1 inf, nwLA, Sconions.

scup n Cf **scuppaug**

1 A **porgy** n[1] **1b(2)** (here: *Stenotomus chrysops*) of the Atlantic coast. [See quot 1903] **chiefly seNEng** Also called **bream B2, fair maid, ironsides 1, maiden, pogy 2, scuppaug**

1848 Bartlett *Americanisms* 257, *Porgy,* or *Paugie.* . . A fish of the *sparus* family, common in the waters of New England and New York. . . It is singular that one half the aboriginal name, *scup,* should be retained in Rhode Island for this fish.   **1903** NY State Museum & Sci. Serv. *Bulletin* 60.559, Scup is an abbreviation of scuppaug. . . The scup comes into our northern waters in great schools, the large spawning fish coming first, making their appearance in New York waters in May.   **1939** *LANE* Map 233 *(Porgy, pogy),* Stenotomos argyrops (a sparoid), a common food fish found from Cape Cod southward. . . This fish is called *porgy* . . or *poggy* in Conn., *scup* or (rarely) *scuppaug* in R.I. and southeastern Mass. North of Cape Cod, where the fish is not found, the term *scup* is known by hearsay to some of our informants.   **1965** *PADS* 43.16 seMA, Fish common in this area . . scup [7 of 9 infs].   **1969** *DARE* (Qu. P2, . . *Kinds of saltwater fish caught around here . . good to eat*) Inf **CT31,** Porgie = scup; **MA40, 55,** Scup; (Qu. P14, . . *Commercial fishing . . what do the fishermen go out after?*) Infs **MA55, RI15,** Scup.   **1983** *Audubon Field Guide N. Amer. Fishes* 616, Scup *(S[tenotomus] chrysops)* lacks bars and humeral spot; occurs from Nova Scotia to North Carolina.   **1984** *DARE* File **Chesapeake Bay** [Watermen's vocab], Scup, porgy, maiden, fairmaid.

2 =**pinfish 1a.**

1884 Goode *Fisheries U.S.* 1.393 **FL,** The Sailor's Choice—*Lagodon rhomboides.* This species, which bears considerable resemblance in its form to the scuppaug, . . bears several other names, being known . . in the Indian River region as the "Sailor's Choice," "Scup," and "Yellowtail."   **1935** Caine *Game Fish* 55 **Sth,** Lagodon rhomboides. . . Scup. . . Food value: Excellent.   **1946** LaMonte *N. Amer. Game Fishes* 71, Lagodon rhomboides. . . Scup. . . Very common southward and on the Gulf coast of Florida.

scupnong See **scuppernong**

scuppaug n Also *scapaug, scauppaug, scuppeag, skapaug* [See quot 1884] **chiefly seNEng** Cf **skippaug**
=**scup 1.**

1787 Gesellschaft Naturforschender Freunde *Schriften* 8.169, Zu einem der vorhergehenden Geschlechter, *ex. Ord. Thoracic,* gehöret wahrscheinlich folgender Fisch. . . *Scuppaug* zu Rhode Island. . . Der Kopf ist etwas platt gedrückt und glatt, aber doch mit Schuppen belegt. [=The following fish probably belongs to one of the previous genera, *ex. Ord. Thoracic.* . . *Scuppaug* in Rhode Island. . . The head is somewhat flattened and smooth, but nevertheless covered with scales.]   **1807** in 1815 MA Hist. Soc. *Coll.* 2d ser 3.57 **Martha's Vineyard MA,** The skapaug in shape somewhat resembles the roach.   **1815** in 1816 *Ibid* 2d ser 4.255 **seMA,** Tataug, scauppaug, eels, are the most common fish near the shores.   *Ibid* 289 **seMA,** At Wareham [are found] tataug, sheep's head . . squitteag, scuppeag, eels.   **1838** MA Zool. & Bot. Surv. *Repts. Zool.* 38, The *Pagrus argyrops*—*scapaug*—[is] a very common and useful species in the south-eastern markets of the State.   **1860** *Harper's New Mth. Mag.* 21.755 **Nantucket MA,** We . . spent two hours or more in pulling out scuppaug. This is a species of perch, plump and white, weighing from one to three pounds.   **1884** Goode *Fisheries U.S.* 1.386, The Scup, which in many respects resembles the Sheepshead, is often known in New England as the "Scuppaug," this word being an abbreviation of *Miscuppauog,* the name applied to it by the Narragansett Indians.   **1939** *LANE* Map 233 *(Porgy, pogy),* This fish [=*Stenotomos argyrops*] is called . . *scup* or (rarely) *scuppaug* in R.I. and southeastern Mass. . . *Scuppaug* and *menhaden* are stressed on the second syllable.

1975 Evanoff *Catch More Fish* 208, The northern porgy *(Stenotomus chrysops)* is also called . . scauppaug.

scuppernong n, also attrib Also sp *scupnong, scupplenong, scuppe(r)non'* [From *Scuppernong* River, North Carolina; see quot 1860] **chiefly SE, esp SC, GA** See Map
A **muscadine (grape)** (here: *Vitis rotundifolia*); also cultivars of this grape, its fruit, or the wine made therefrom.

1811 *Raleigh Star* (NC) Mar 40/2, Doctor James Mease . . having seen Mr. Blount's account of the Scuppernong Grape . . has requested of us to procure for him some specimens of the vine.   **1825** *Catawba Jrnl.* 2 Aug. *(DAE),* The editor . . having had a taste of the Scuppernong wine from North-Carolina, extols it in the highest terms.   **1846** *Spirit of Times* 25 Apr 97/1, A keg of 'Scuppernong' is on the way to us, having been shipped from Wilmington, N.C.   **1860** Curtis *Cat. Plants NC* 114, For the following history of the *Scuppernong* . . , I am indebted to Rev. E.M. Forbes, who . . has taken much pains to obtain an authentic account of this Vine. Two men, of the name of Alexander, while clearing land near Columbia, . . which stands on the east side of Scuppernong River, discovered this Grape, and were so much pleased with it, that they preserved the Vine and the tree upon which it grew. . . [T]hey subsequently named the Grape from the River upon which it was found. . . A tradition is furnished me by Dr. Hunter, that "about the year 1774, the Rev. Charles Pettigrew found it on the low grounds of Scuppernong River, and planted out several vines."   **1899** Chesnutt *Conjure Woman* 13 csNC [Black], Mars Dugal' made a thousan' gallon er scuppernon' wine eve'y year.   **1904** (1913) Johnson *Highways South* 308 **NC,** For dessert I was introduced to a scuppernong pie. It was the first grape pie I had ever eaten.   **1960** (1962) Lee *Mockingbird* 40 **AL,** Getting a squirt from Miss Maudie Atkinson's cow on a summer day, helping ourselves to someone's scuppernongs was part of our ethical culture, but money was different.   **1965–70** *DARE* (Qu. I46, . . *Kinds of fruits that grow wild around here*) 25 Infs, **chiefly SE, esp SC, GA,** Scuppernong(s); **FL26,** Scupnongs ['skʌpnɔŋz]; (Qu. I53, . . *Fruits grown around here . . special varieties*) 14 Infs, **SE, esp SC,** Scuppernongs; **MS73,** Scuppenons; **GA28,** Scuppernong grapes; (Qu. DD28b, . . *Fermented drinks . . made at home*) 16 Infs, **SE, esp SC,** Scuppernong wine; **NC80,** Scupplenong wine; (Qu. I44, *What kinds of berries grow wild around here?*) Infs **AL6, 25, FL15, GA16,** Scuppernongs; **FL8, GA8,** Scuppernong grapes; (Qu. DD27, . . *Nicknames . . for wine*) Inf **NC80,** Scupplenong [skʌplnɔŋ].   **1969** *DARE* Tape **GA51,** We got white grapes, scruppernon ['skrʌpənɑn] [sic] I call it.   **1986** Pederson *LAGS Concordance* **Gulf Region,** 27 infs, Scuppernong(s); 7 infs, Scuppernong arbor (*or* grape, jelly, pie, vine, wine).   **1989** Whealy *Fruit Inventory* 248, *Scuppernong*—Oldest, best known and most widely grown variety of muscadine.

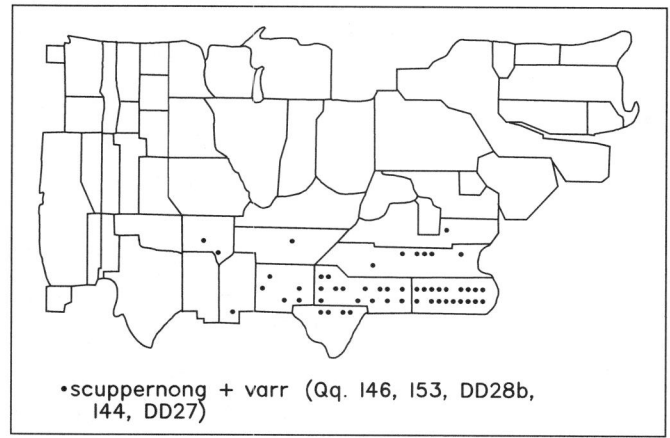

•scuppernong + varr (Qq. I46, I53, DD28b, I44, DD27)

scuppers to adj phr, adv phr Also *scuppers under*
Of a ship: with the scuppers at or beneath the waterline; fig, of a person: fully loaded; weighted down.

[**1899** *Century Illustr. Mag.* 58.697 **Nova Scotia,** Her bellying sail swept the sea as she rolled scuppers under.]   **1905** Wasson *Green Shay* 186 **NEng,** That craft is scand'lous deep loaded. She's a-near scuppers to [Footnote: Loaded, scuppers to the water], that packet is, and it's rough as a grater out there.   **1932** Wasson *Sailing Days* 131 **cME coast,** She [=an aging vessel] was considered none too ripe for the stone business, and was often loaded "scuppers to", with paving or huge blocks of granite. **1996** Horton *Island Out of Time* 238 **Chesapeake Bay MD,** Ladies arrive back from Christmas shopping "scuppers under" with packages, like boats in danger of sinking.

scupplenong See **scuppernong**

scurce See **scarce**

scurcely See **scarcely**

scurf pea n Also *scurfy (pea), scurvy ~* [See quot 1922]
Any of var plants of the genera *Hoita, Orbexilum, Pediomelum, Psoralidium,* or *Rupertia.* Note: These genera were formerly included in *Psoralea.* For other names of var of these see **buck root, congo ~, French grass 1, holy hay, Indian breadroot, ~ turnip 2, leatherroot 1, Sampson's snakeroot 3, tumbleweed, wild alfalfa**

    1848 Gray *Manual of Botany* 105, *Psoralea. . . Scurfy Pea. . .* Perennial herbs, usually sprinkled all over or roughened . . with glandular dots or points. **1900** Lyons *Plant Names* 309, Other indigenous species are . . *P[soralea] floribunda* [=*Psoralidium tenuiflorum*] . . and *P. tenuiflora* [=*Psoralidium t.*] . . , both called Scurfy Pea. **1922** *Amer. Botanist* 28.76, *Psoralea floribunda* and *P. tenuiflora* are known as "scurvy-pea". This name has nothing to do with scurvy, however, but refers to the white-hoary covering of the young plants and should properly be written "scurfy pea!" **1937** U.S. Forest Serv. *Range Plant Hdbk.* W157, Scurfpeas possess but little forage value, having a palatability of from practically worthless to poor, rarely fair, for sheep and cattle. **1941** Walker *Lookout* 48 **TN,** Among the wild plants once employed as antidotes for the bites of poisonous reptiles, are rattlesnake master, blacksnake root, rattlesnake-weed, Samson snakeroot, or scurfy. **1961** Wills–Irwin *Flowers TX* 136, *Scurvy-pea . . Pediomelum cuspidatum. . .* The Scurvy-peas are perennial herbs with enlarged tap roots. **1970** Kirk *Wild Edible Plants W. U.S.* 256, *Psoralea esculenta, megalantha, mephitica* and *epipsila* [=*Pediomelum esculentum, P. megalanthum, P. mephiticum*] . . Bread Root, Scurf Pea, Indian Turnip. . . These . . species have tuberous roots that are edible when cooked. **1973** Hitchcock–Cronquist *Flora Pacific NW* 272, *Psoralea. . .* Scurf-pea. *Ibid* 273, Cal[ifornia]-tea s[curf-pea] . . *P[soralea] physodes* [=*Rupertia p.*] **1979** Niering–Olmstead *Audubon Guide N. Amer. Wildflowers E. Region* 537, *Psoralea argophylla* [=*Pediomelum argophyllum*].

scurryfunge v [Engl dial or slang in var senses; cf *OED2 scurrifunge* a. "To scrub, scour"; 1789; *DNE scurrifunge* 1. "To clean thoroughly, scour"]
    1975 Gould *ME Lingo* 246, *Scurryfunge*—A hasty tidying of the house between the time you see a neighbor coming and the time she knocks on the door. This tends to be coastal. The upland version would be to *teakittle* up: "You scurryfunge your house and I'll teakittle up mine!"

scurvish See **scabish 1**

scurvy See **scurvy grass 1**

scurvy berry n
A **false lily-of-the-valley** (here: either *Maianthemum canadense* or *M. racemosum*).
    1943 Fernald–Kinsey *Edible Wild Plants E. N. Amer.* 135, *Scurvy-berries, Smilacina . . racemosa* [=*Maianthemum r.*] . . The juicy red berries . . are somewhat palatable, bitter-sweet, suggesting bitter molasses, but they are cathartic and should be eaten with caution. *Ibid* 136, *Scurvy-berries, Maianthemum . . canadense. . .* The cherry-red berries . . last over winter and have a not unpalatable bitter-sweet taste.

scurvy grass n [*OED2* a1597 → for *Cochlearia groenlandica*]
1 also *scurvy:* Any of var plants thought to have antiscorbutic properties; see quots.
    1830 Rafinesque *Med. Flora* 2.264, *Sisyrinchium. . . Lily grass, Scurvy grass. . .* Decoction purgative, said by empirics to be antidote of sublimate! and used as eq. of *Cochlearia!* **1892** (1974) Millspaugh *Amer. Med. Plants* 24–2, The fresh plants [of *Brassica nigra*], soon after their appearance, while the leaves are yet young and tender, are used by the laity in many parts of this country as a pot-herb ("greens"). This relish is termed at that stage of its growth, *scurvy-grass,* though the true Scurvygrass is *Sinapis arvensis.* **1900** Lyons *Plant Names* 58, *B[arbarea] vulgaris. . .* Yellow Scurvy-grass. . . *Plant* antiscorbutic, sometimes used for salad. *Ibid* 68, *B[rassica] nigra. . .* Scurvy. *Ibid* 100, *C[hrysopsis] graminifolia* [=*Pityopsis g.*] . . Scurvy-grass. **1935** (1943) Muenscher

Weeds 257, *Brassica nigra. . .* Scurvy. . . Widespread and locally common throughout the United States and Canada. **1943** Fernald–Kinsey *Edible Wild Plants E. N. Amer.* 167, *Mountain Sorrel, "Scurvy-Grass", Oxyria digyna. . . Uses:* salad, potherb, purée. *Ibid* 168, The *Mountainsorrel,* which resembles a miniature rhubarb, . . has always been highly esteemed in the Arctic regions as a "scurvy-grass", the new growth up to flowering time being eaten raw. *Ibid* 224, *Roseroot, Scurvy-grass . . (Rhodiola Rosea). . . Uses:* salad, potherb. **1953** (1962) Heller *Wild Plants AK* 52, *Sea purslane, scurvy grass, sea chickweed—Honckenya peploides. . .* Perennial; fleshy, succulent, much branched, often forming large loose mats; . . sandy beaches. **1959** Carleton *Index Herb. Plants* 104, *Scurvy-grass:* Chrysopsis graminifolia; Cochlearia officinalis.
2 Spec: **a** **winter cress,** usu *Barbarea verna.*
    1876 Hobbs *Bot. Hdbk.* 104, Scurvy grass, Barbarea præens [sic]. **1891** *Century Dict.* 6944, The early winter-cress . . is cultivated and sometimes spontaneous in southern parts of the United States, there called *scurvy grass.* **1900** [see **1** above]. **1910** Graves *Flowering Plants* 208 **CT,** *Barbarea verna. . .* Scurvy Grass. . . Cultivated fields, waste places and roadsides. **1949** Moldenke *Amer. Wild Flowers* 39, The *early wintercress* [=*Barbarea verna*]. . . is called *scurvygrass* in the southern states. **1986** Pederson *LAGS Concordance,* 1 inf, **nwFL,** Scurvy grass—used for medicine; 1 inf, **cnGA,** Scurvy grass—make tea for people with flu; 1 inf, **csMS,** Scurvy grass—is blue grass, makes purgative. [DARE Ed: Some of these infs may refer instead to **1** above.]

scurvy pea See **scurf pea**

scused, scusin See **excusing** prep

'scusshun, scussion See **excursion**

scut n[1] See **scutch** n

scut n[2] Also *scud* [*OED2 scut* sb.[4] 1873 →; "*dial.* or *slang*"] *derog* or *joc* Cf **scutter** n[1]
A rascal, fellow.
    1916 *DN* 4.338 **cs,sePA,** *Scud. . .* A little boy. "Did you see that little scud throw a stone?" **1953** *AmSp* 28.253 **csPA,** *Scut. . .* A mildly pejorative term for a little boy, roughly equivalent to *rascal, rapscallion.* It appears almost invariably accompanied by the adjective *little.* 'Which one of you little scuts threw that snowball?' Popular speech. **1986** Safire *Take My Word* 327 **NYC,** When I was a boy in the late thirties, I lived adjacent to an Irish neighborhood. One of my friend's grandmother would refer to us as lazy or nasty scuts, depending on the degree we'd irritated her. **1995** Brophy *Coll.* 66 **swMO** (as of c1960), *Scut, scutter, scudder.* [A] scamp, a mild scoundrel.

scutch v[1] Also *skutch* [*OED2 scutch* v.[1] 1611 →; "Now chiefly *dial.*"] **esp PA**
To beat, whip; hence n *scutching* a beating, whipping; by ext: a tongue lashing.
    c1900 in 1944 *ADD* **wPA,** *Scutch. . .* To thrash soundly. . . 'I'll scutch him.' Commoner as in 'I'll give you a good scutching.' **1916** *DN* 4.341 **seOH,** *Scutch. . .* To thrash soundly. **1930** Shoemaker *1300 Words* 52 **cPA Mts** (as of c1900), *Scutching*—A whipping; knocking chestnuts off a tree. **1939** in 1944 *ADD* **swPA,** *Scutch. . .* Current. **1952** *DE Folkl. Bulletin* 1.12, A twig used to punish a youngster was always referred to as "a gad to skutch th' young 'un." . . "I just skulked into the woods, cut myself a gad, and give myself a dern good skutching." **1968** *DARE* (Qu. Y16, *A thorough beating: "He gave the bully an awful _____.")* Inf **PA152,** Scutching ['skʌčən]; one would also [skʌč] a fellow; (Qu. II27, *If somebody gives you a very sharp scolding . . "I certainly got a _____ for that."*) Inf **PA135,** Scutching.

scutch v[2] See **scotch** v[2]

scutch v[3] See **scooch**

scutch n Also *scut* [Perh varr of *scud(s)*] Cf **skirt**
A light dusting or flurry of snow.
    1951 *DE Folkl. Bulletin* 1.7, *Scutch* (a small flurry—as of snow). **1968** *DARE* (Qu. B39, *A very light fall of snow*) Inf **DE1,** Scut of snow—old-fashioned [laughter].

scutch grass n Also *scutch* [Var of **quitch grass;** *OED2* 1685 → in ref to *Elytrigia repens*]
Bermuda grass (*Cynodon dactylon*).
    1857 Gray *Manual of Botany* 554, Bermuda Grass. Scutch-Grass. . . *C[ynodon] Dactylon. . .* Penn. and southward; troublesome in light soil.

1880 *Amer. Agric.* 64, Bermuda-Grass, or Scutch-Grass in our Southern States, Creeping Dog's-tooth-Grass in England, Chiendent in France . . are different common names for the grass called by botanists *Cynadon* [sic] *Dactylon.* **1933** Small *Manual SE Flora* 112, Bermuda-grass. Scutch-grass. . . Fla. to Tex., Calif., Ore., and Mass. **1971** GA Dept. Ag. *Farmers Market Bulletin* 24 Nov 8 **GA,** The beautiful grasses of the South are predominantly Cynodon dactylon, otherwise known as wire grass, Bermuda grass, Bahama grass, or scutch.

scutching See **scutch** v[1]

scuter See **scooter** n[1] **1**

scutter n[1] Also *scooter, scudder* [Etym unknown; cf **cutter** n[1] **3** and *cutter* (at **critter**), **scaper** n, **scut** n[2]] **chiefly Sth, S Midl**
1 A scoundrel, rascal, fellow.   *derog* or *joc*
   1934 Vines *Green Thicket* 62 **cnAL,** The scutter's no 'count, Lat. He won't work. He eats too much. That's all that's the matter with him. **1952** Brown *NC Folkl.* 1.588, Scutter ['skʌtə, -ɚ]. . . "A very mischievous person."—Johnston county. **1954** Harder Coll. **cwTN,** Scutter. . . Someone who is rowdy, mean. **1960** Williams *Walk Egypt* 50 **GA,** You oughta seen them scutters jump. **1965–70** DARE (Qu. Z12, *Nicknames and joking words meaning 'a small child': "He's a healthy little _____."*) Infs **NC**55, **SC**40, 44, Scudder; **KY**5, **TN**41, Scutter ['skʌtɚ]; **VA**13, Scutter; **SC**10, Scooter [skudɚ]; **SC**42, Scooter [skudɚ]; (Qu. HH40, *Uncomplimentary words for an old man*) Inf **IN**45, Old scudder. **1967** Williams *Greenbones* 219 **GA** (as of c1910), Someone burn a cross in your pasture? Why, the scutters. **1972** *Atlanta Letters* **cnGA,** That "scudder" did a mean trick on me. **1995** [see **scut** n[2]].
2 A varmint, critter.   *derog* or *joc*
   1940 *Sat. Eve. Post* 3 Feb 14 **sMS,** That frazzling old scutter [=a large bullfrog] jumped. **1958** Babcock *I Don't Want* 164 **eSC,** "Right humorsome old scutter," I commented. [DARE Ed: Referring to a bird dog] **1962** Fox *Southern Fried* 142 **SC,** That dog was a loner, too. . . From the day that scutter was weaned he slept by himself outside the box.
3 A thing, object, thingamabob.   *joc*
   1962 Fox *Southern Fried* 112 **SC,** I'd get out in a drain ditch and I'd keep playing and messing around with that little scudder until the sun came out. Lord. . . I loved that little horn. **1967** DARE FW Addit **LA**7, Scudder—nominative with no particular meaning, with slightly humorous connotations: "Nail that scudder on there."
4 An admirable example of its kind; see quots.   [Perh infl by *scutter* to scurry]
   1941 Street *In Father's House* 30 **MS,** Mama is a root, leaf and berry cook and a scutter when it comes to making good things out of herbs and other green stuff. *Ibid* 120, Aunt 'Tunia is a scutter when it comes to lookin' through a feller. *Ibid* 302, Kink's a scutter with babies. **1954** Harder Coll. **cwTN,** Scutter. . . A person who is quick. **c1960** Wilson Coll. **csKY,** Scutter. . . A fine-appearing person or animal, like the horses in Oklahoma.

scutter n[2] Also *scudder* [By rhotacism from *scuttle*]
   1961 *Mt. Life* 37.1.7 **sAppalachians,** In a few words *r* is substituted for *l*: *frail* (flail), *scudder* (scuttle), and *warnut* (walnut). **1965–67** DARE (Qu. F44, . . *A container for coal to use in a stove*) Inf **AZ**1, [skutɚ]; **MS**60, Coal scutter. **1986** Pederson *LAGS Concordance* (Coal scuttle) 1 inf, **ceAR,** Scutter = scuttle.

scutters n pl [Cf *EDD* scutter sb. 13]
=skitters.
   1966 DARE (Qu. BB19, *Joking names for looseness of the bowels*) Inf **MI**24, ['skʌtɚz]; **NH**2, The scutters.

scuttle n Also *scuttle hole, scutty ~* [*OED2* scuttle sb.[2] **2** 1707 →] **NEng, Sth, S Midl** See Map
A usu small opening through a roof, floor, or rarely wall, often covered by a trapdoor; esp in comb *scuttle hole:* a hay chute; by ext, a small storage space accessed by such an opening.
   1828 (1970) Webster *Amer. Dict., Scuttle*—A square hole in the roof of a house with a lid. **1833** *Farmers' Reg.* Oct 308, The attic should have a board flooring, with a scuttle door for entrance. **1860** *Harper's New Mth. Mag.* 21.428 **Nth,** There was a scuttle-door in the roof of the house, with a convenient stairway leading to it. **1932–34** Hanley Disks *Eastham* **MA,** The [bresh?] and all goes down through the scuttle. **1939** FWP *Guide FL* 165 **swFL,** For additional ventilation 'scuttles' were installed on roofs along with a platform and 'mirador,' from which

to sight ships in distress. **1946** *PADS* 6.26 **eNC,** *Scuttle.* . . An opening in a floor for a flight of steps; a stairway. . . Occasional. **1946** Stuart *Tales Plum Grove* 178 **eKY,** The lightnin' flashed in at our upstairs scuttle-hole we had fer a winder. **1950** Stuart *Hie Hunters* 18 **eKY,** Sparkie climbed up on the manger, put his hands up through the scuttle-hole, and pulled himself up into the barn loft. **1965–70** DARE (Qu. M5, . . *The hole for throwing hay down below*) 32 Infs, **NEng, Sth, S Midl,** Scuttle hole; **CT**22, **MO**36, **MA**42, **NH**12, **RI**15, **VT**2, Scuttle; **KS**1, **NC**21, Scutty hole; (Qu. D4, *The space up under the roof, usually used for storing things*) Inf **LA**2, Attic—you go through the scuttle hole to get there; (Qu. D7, *A small space anywhere in a house where you can hide things or get them out of the way*) Infs **GA**72, **KY**76, Scuttle hole. [33 of 42 total Infs male] **1986** Pederson *LAGS Concordance (Attic)* 1 inf, **swGA,** Scuttle hole—through ceiling; 1 inf, **neAR,** Scuttle hole—entrance to attic, with ladder; 1 inf, **neLA,** Scuttle hole—storage place above living area; 1 inf, **cLA,** Scuttle hole—of a potato pump; 1 inf, **cTX,** Scuttle hole; 1 inf, **ceTN,** Scuttle holes—hatches for access to attic. **1994** NC Lang. & Life Project *Dial. Vocab.* Ocracoke 15 **eNC,** *Scuttle.* . . A hole in a wall or roof covered by a door. **1999** DARE File **nIL,** I learned "scuttle hole" from the carpenter who back in 1960 built a garage for me. . . [H]e had what I assumed was a southern Illinois accent.

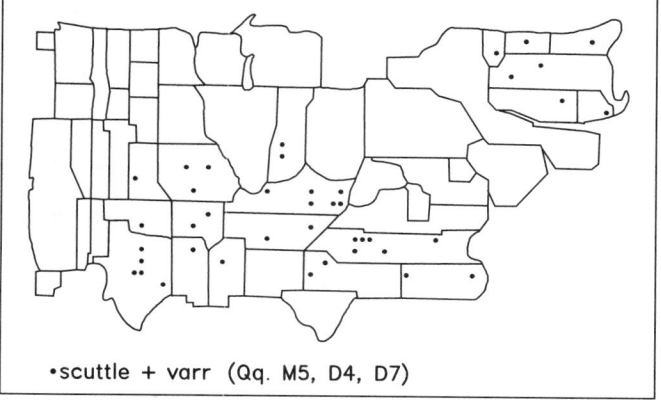

•scuttle + varr (Qq. M5, D4, D7)

scuttle bug n
=whirligig beetle.
   1947 NY Entomol. Soc. *Jrl.* 55.205, A swift darting in intersecting curves . . accounts for . . such terms as scuttle bugs, whirligigs, and whirligig beetles. *Ibid* 206 **NJ,** Scuttle bug.

scuttler n
A **whiptail** (here: *Cnemidophorus sexlineatus*).
   1887 Amer. Philol. Assoc. *Trans. for 1886* 17.46 **Sth,** List of common Southern expressions—many of them vulgarisms—that have not, so far as I know, either old English or provincial English authority. . . *Scuttler* or *streakfield* (striped lizard).

scutty hole See **scuttle**

scutzie See **scutzy**

scutz work n Also *scuz(z) work* [Varr of *scut work*]
Menial or unpleasant work.
   1991 Isaacs *Magic Hour* (paperback ed) 69 **Long Is. NY,** When she wasn't involving herself in rich lives by zipping up their dresses or stroking their embossed names on their charge cards, she was busting her chops doing scutz work for their charity groups. [DARE Ed: The hard cover ed has *scut work;* correspondence from the author confirms that *scutz work* was intended.] **2000** *NADS Letters* **MD,** "Scutz-work," or more commonly "scuz-work," was pretty common usage to me some thirty to forty years back in my home town of Baltimore. It meant what might also be called "grunt work." That is the hard, dirty, boring, menial work that has to be done, but why, oh lord, can't it be done by someone else! *Ibid* **OH,** We always pronounced it "scuz (rhymes with fuzz) - work", as in "Why do I have to clean the toilet and do all the scuz-work and Patty gets off?" My family has always used it (central Ohio) and my grandmother's family (southern Ohio). *Ibid* **PA,** Scutzwork. . . is the crap that's not fun and that no one with any self respect will do willingly. *Ibid* **NY,** Scutz-work. . . I heard this one when I was a teen in the Palmyra region of upstate NY in the 70's. **2002** DARE File—Internet,

OS, EC, and PSA will thus be freed to get development work done (although they are certainly welcome to do scuzz work if they wish!)

scutzy adj Also *scudsy, scutzie* [Varr of *scuzzy*] Cf **scutz work**

Contemptible; disgusting; unacceptable.

1996 *DARE* File **UT,** [She taught me that] I should never do it [= swear], or else I will sound "hard and scudsy." **2000** *NADS Letters* **FL,** In the early 1980's, one of my (white) co-workers . . came in one day very annoyed at her teenage son, . . because the previous day she had stopped to make some purchases at a local K-Mart (a discount store) and he refused to even go into the store, saying, "I'm not going into that scutzie store—I wouldn't want anything from them." I subsequently heard other young people, not necessarily teenagers, in Florida refer to "scutzie" . . whatevers: schools, classes, clothes . . always with the meaning of lowclass, unfashionable, unacceptable. . . I myself have used the term scutzie for years to refer to places like stores or motels that were not well maintained and rather disordered or even somewhat dirty, not necessarily lowclass or unfashionable. *Ibid* **csWI,** I know of a word similar [to *scutz work*] that I use and hear used frequently. That word is "Scutzy." It means that something is, "icky. . . less than good." If someone hands in a bad report for instance, it is scutzy.

scuz(z) work See **scutz work**

scythe n[1] Usu |saɪð|; also |saɪθ, saɪ| Pronc-spp *scy, sigh, sive, size, sy(e);* by folk-etym, *side;* for addit pronc and sp varr see quots [Cf *EDD side* sb.[5], *sive* sb., *sy* sb. 1]

Std sense, var forms.

1891 *DN* 1.166 **cNY,** [saɪz] < scythes. **1899** (1912) Green *VA Folk-Speech* 386, Side. . . A scythe. "Side-blade," scythe-blade. *Ibid* 388, Sive. . . For *scythe*. **1936** Reese *Worleys* 40 **MD** (as of 1865) [Black], To-morrow I gits out my sye an' I cuts down dat fusin' flowah. **1937** *AmSp* 12.103 **eNE** [Farm terms], Foreigners usually omit the *th* in *scythe*, much to the amusement of the native. **1939** *LANE* Map 159 **NEng,** 25 infs, [saɪð, saɪð, saɪð, saɛð, saeð]; 4 infs, [saɪθ, saɪθ, saeθ]. **1942** *AmSp* 17.247, 'Scy'—'Scythe' . . The curious abridged form *scy* or *sy* [saɪ] for *scythe* seems to have fairly wide currency. Surprised to hear a student from South Dakota so pronounce the word when reading it, I asked him whether this was the usage of his region. He had 'never heard the word pronounced in any other way,' he said. Another Dakota student gave the same testimony. Since then I have found a dozen or more Nebraskans who are familiar with the curtailed form. A person of Maine provenience told me that it was known to him in Maine. **1953** Randolph–Wilson *Down in Holler* 32 **Ozarks,** I have heard old men say *sigh* when they meant scythe. **1959** *VT Hist.* 27.156 **cw,swVT,** Scythe [sī] . . pronc. Rare. **1965–70** *DARE* (Qu. L28, *Tools used in the past for cutting grain*) 262 Infs, **widespread,** Scythe [saɪð, saɪð, saɪð]; 104 Infs, **widespread,** Sy [sa(ɪ), sɑ(ɪ), saɪ]; 52 Infs, **scattered,** [saɪθ, saɪθ]; 10 Infs, **scattered,** [saɪz, saɪz] [*DARE* Ed: Prob pl of *sy*]; **MD**13, 38, **NC**76, **NJ**67, [sa(ɪ)v]; **LA**15, **MO**14, **NY**67, **WA**4, 8, [sɪθ, sɪθ]; **LA**39, **MS**87, **VA**40, Side blade; **MN**2, **NJ**6, [si(z)]; **DC**5, Grass side; **VA**40, Side [saɪd]; **MS**81, [saɪf]; **NY**140, [saɪs]; **TX**33, [skaɪθ]; **VA**70, Slide blade; [*DARE* Ed: For the following Qq., responses where only the std spelling was recorded have been ignored.] [(Qu. L37, *A hand tool used for cutting weeds and grass*) 90 Infs, **scattered,** Scythe [saɪð, saɪð, saɪð]; 58 Infs, **scattered,** Sy [sa(ɪ), sɑ(ɪ), saɪ]; 19 Infs, **scattered,** [saɪθ, saɪθ]; 11 Infs, **scattered,** [saɪz, saɪz] [*DARE* Ed: Prob pl of *sy*]; **KY**6, [saɪf]; **MD**13, [saɪv]; (Qu. L35, *Hand tools used for cutting underbrush and digging out roots*) 29 Infs, **scattered,** Scythe [saɪð, saɪð, saɪð]; 13 Infs, **scattered,** Sy [sa(ɪ), sɑ(ɪ), saɪ]; **IA**33, **NY**127, **OH**6, 15, **TN**1, [saɪð, saɪθ]; **KY**46, **PA**136, **TN**44, [saɪz, saɪz] [*DARE* Ed: Prob pl of *sy*]; **DC**5, Side [saɪd]; **MD**13, (Qu. L38) **CA**161, **MI**23, 47, Sy [saɪ]; **PA**51, [saɪθ]; **PA**3, Side [saɪd].] **1976** Garber *Mountain-ese* 82 **sAppalachians,** *Size* (n) mowing scythe—Lemuel, get the size and cut them big bull weeds behind the barn. **1981** Pederson *LAGS Basic Materials* **Gulf Region,** [3 infs offered proncs of the type [saɪθ(s)]; 3 infs offered proncs of the type [sa(ɪ), saᶜ]; 1 inf, [saˀɪf]; 1 inf, [sa˃ɪs] = scythes; 1 inf, Scythes rock [sa·ᶓz rɑ˃k].] **1983** Lutz *Coll., Scythe* (pronounced sye). In singing the ballad "Springfield Mountain," Everett Pitt said, "He laid his sye down on the ground." . . When I called attention to this pronunciation in my Ramsey (NJ) High School classroom, one day about 1950, one of the boys snorted, "Well, how else would you say it?" To him a *scythe* was a *sye*. **1984** *MJLF* 10.158 **cnWI,** *Sy.* The scythe.

scythe n[2], v See **sithe**

scythe-whet n
=veery.

lose half its summer charm were I to miss that shy anchorite, the Wilson's thrush, nor hear in haying-time the metallic ring of his song, that justifies his rustic name of "scythe-whet."

scythe-whetter n
=**flicker** n[2] **1.**

[**1878** *Harper's New Mth. Mag.* 56.858, We have amongst the *Clamatores* several species which merit more or less the distinction of being called "songsters," of which we may mention . . the "flicker" (*Colaptes auratus*) among the woodpeckers, with his scythe-whetting tune.] **1930** OK Univ. Biol. Surv. *Pub.* 2.150, *Colaptes auratus auratus. . . Flicker. . . Local Names . .* scythe whetter. . . . The calls of the flicker are varied from "Chee-ah" and "Yuck-ah" to "Whic-ka-ah."

sea arrow n [*OED2* at *sea* sb. 22.d 1851]

A **flying calamary** (here: *Illex* spp) or a similar squid such as *Loligo pealei.*

1935 Pratt *Manual Invertebrate Animals* 690, *Ommastrephes. . .* Sea arrows. Flying squids. **1949** Palmer *Nat. Hist.* 368, *Sea Arrow—Loligo pealei. . .* Swims by quick expelling of water or, if in danger, of ink, and by use of fins, with body being held horizontally.

sea ash n

1 A **prickly ash 1,** usu *Zanthoxylum clava-herculis.*

1876 Hobbs *Bot. Hdbk.* 104, Sea ash, Southern prickly ash, Xanthoxylum Carolinianum [=*Zanthoxylum clava-herculis*]. **1897** Sudworth *Arborescent Flora* 265 **MS, FL,** Xanthoxylum Clava-Herculis. . . Sea Ash. **1933** Small *Manual SE Flora* 675, Sea Ash. . . Woods and hammocks, Coastal Plain, mostly near the coast. . . The bark is used medicinally. **1986** Pederson *LAGS Concordance (Common trees in the community)* 1 inf, **swGA,** Sea ash tree.

2 =**Hercules'-club 1.**

1900 Lyons *Plant Names* 42, *A[ralia] spinosa. . .* Sea Ash. **1940** Clute *Amer. Plant Names* 251, *Aralia spinosa.* Monkey-tree, sea ash.

sea bass n

1 Any of var fishes of Atlantic waters, as:

a A **black sea bass 1** or similar serranid.   **chiefly N Atl**

1760 (1775) Burnaby *Travels* 63 **Upstate NY,** These waters afford various kinds of fish, black fish, sea bass, sheeps-heads, rock-fish, lobsters, and several others. **1765** Rogers *N. Amer.* 68 **Long Is. NY,** In the sea adjacent to this island are sea-bass and black-fish in great plenty; which are very good when fresh. **1807** in 1815 MA Hist. Soc. *Coll.* 2d ser 3.56 **Martha's Vineyard MA,** The sea bass is caught in every season except winter. **1842** DeKay *Zool. NY* 4.25, This [=*Centropristis striata*] is one of the most savory and delicate of the fishes which appear in our markets from May to July. Its most usual name with us is *Sea Bass.* **1884** Goode *Fisheries U.S.* 1.407, The Sea Bass, *Serranus atrarius* [=*Centropristis striata*], known south of Cape Hatteras as the "Blackfish," is the most important species on our coast. **1905** NJ State Museum *Annual Rept. for 1904* 304, *Family Serranidae.* The Sea Bass. *Ibid* 308, *Centropristes striatus* [sic]. . . Sea Bass. **1965–70** *DARE* (Qu. P2, . . *Kinds of saltwater fish caught around here . . good to eat*) 19 Infs, **chiefly Atl, esp N Atl,** Sea bass; (Qu. P14, . . *Commercial fishing . . what do the fishermen go out after?*) Infs **NJ**55, 60, **NY**36, 76, Sea bass. [*DARE* Ed: Some of these Infs may refer instead to senses below.] **1976** Warner *Beautiful Swimmers* 134 **Chesapeake Bay,** He diversifies, making strong rectangular pots for the ocean capture of "blackfish" or sea bass, as practiced in the Carolinas. **1986** Pederson *LAGS Concordance (Kinds of fish)* 1 inf, **ceTX,** Sea bass—weighs 250 pounds, saltwater.

b =**red drum.**

1873 in 1878 Smithsonian Inst. *Misc. Coll.* 14.2.27 **SC,** *Sciaenops ocellatus. . .* Bass; red bass; sea-bass; spotted bass. **1884** Goode *Fisheries U.S.* 1.372, In the Carolinas, Florida, and the Gulf, we meet with the names [for *Sciaenops ocellatus,* of] 'Bass,' and its variations 'Spotted Bass,' 'Red Bass,' 'Sea Bass,' 'Reef Bass,' and 'Channel Bass.' **1935** Caine *Game Fish* 40 **Sth,** The channel bass, or redfish, or red drum, or spot, or sea bass, or what have you, is the gamey individual that is responsible for bringing surf-casting to the fore as a popular type of angling. **1966** *DARE* (Qu. P2, . . *Kinds of saltwater fish caught around here . . good to eat*) Inf **MS**73, Redfish, sea bass—same. **1986** Pederson *LAGS Concordance (Kinds of fish)* 2 infs, **ceAL, seTN,** Sea bass; 1 inf, **ceAL,** Sea bass—come up river and spawn locally; 1 inf, **neTX,** Sea bass—saltwater fish.

c A **striped bass** (here: *Morone saxatilis*).

1967 *DARE* (Qu. P1, . . *Kinds of freshwater fish . . caught around here . . good to eat*) Inf **SC**40, Striped/sea bass—comes upstream to spawn; some stay all year round—called rock(fish) usually.
2 Any of several fishes of Pacific waters, but usu **white sea bass,** a **grouper 1a,** or the **giant sea bass 1;** see quots. **chiefly CA**

1884 Goode *Fisheries U.S.* 1.378, *Cynoscion nobile* [=*Atractoscion nobilis*]. . . This species is everywhere known as the "Sea Bass" . ., sometimes as "White Sea Bass," to distinguish it from the Black Sea Bass, or Jew-fish. . . It ranges from Cape Mendocino southward to below San Diego. **1890** *Century Dict.* 5438, *Sea-bass.* . . The sturgeon, *Acipenser transmontanus.* . . [*Century Dict.* Ed: Pacific coast, U.S.] **1899** Norris *Blix* 128 **CA,** There were . . sheaves of fishing-rods, from the four-ounce wisp of the brook-trout up to the rigid eighteen-ounce lance of the king-salmon and sea-bass. **1929** Pan-Pacific Research Inst. *Jrl.* 4.4.7 **sCA,** *Epinephelidae.* The Sea Bass; Groupers; Garrupas. **1933** John G. Shedd Aquarium *Guide* 99, *Stereolepis gigas—California Jewfish; Sea Bass.* . . is one of the great game fishes that have made Catalina Island famous. **1935** Caine *Game Fish* 94, *Promicrops itaiara* [=Epinephelus itajara]. . . Black Sea Bass. . . Giant Sea Bass. . . Frequently believed to be the same as . . *Stereolepis Gigas* . ., but such is absolutely *not* the case. **1949** *L.A. Times* 5 May IV.3/8 (*DA*), Sea-bass schools are showing up, too, with catches being made in Catalina waters. **1961** Herald *Living Fishes* 192, The genus *Cynoscion* includes . . the California white sea bass, *C. nobilis.* **1965–70** *DARE* (Qu. P2, . . *Kinds of saltwater fish caught around here . . good to eat*) Infs **CA**23, 31, 109, Sea bass; (Qu. P14, . . *Commercial fishing . . what do the fishermen go out after?*) Infs **CA**15, 36, Sea bass. **1967** *Honolulu Star–Bulletin* (HI) 31 May sec F 1/4, Hapuupuu—Sea Bass. **1972** Sparano *Outdoors Encycl.* 381, *California White Sea Bass*—Common Names: . . sea bass [etc].
3 In the waters of Alaska usu a **black rockfish 1,** but also a **greenling** (here: *Pleurogrammus monopterygius*).

1946 Dufresne *AK's Animals* 286, The black rockfish, pest of the commercial salmon trollers, so often caught around kelp patches in Alaska . . [is] generally miscalled "black bass" or "sea bass." **1955** U.S. Arctic Info. Center *Gloss.* 70, *Sea bass.* A local name for the Atka mackerel. **1978** *AK Fishing Guide* 87, The red rockfish of Alaska, as well as the black rockfish [=*Sebastes melanops*] (which is often called black bass or sea bass) are excellent eating.

sea bat n

1 =**flying gurnard.** [*OED2* at *sea-bat* 1 1611 →]

1884 Goode *Fisheries U.S.* 1.255, The most striking of them all [= Triglidae] is the Sea-bat or Flying Gurnard, *Dactylopterus volitans,* which is remarkable on account of its enormous spreading fins, larger than those of a flying-fish. . . It is found along our entire coast south of Cape Cod.
2 A **batfish 1,** usu *Ogcocephalus vespertilio.* [*OED2* *sea-bat* 2 1756 →]

1873 in 1878 Smithsonian Inst. *Misc. Coll.* 14.2.14, *Malthe cubifrons* [=*Ogcocephalus radiatus*]. . . Box-headed sea-bat. Labrador. *Malthe notata* [=*O. notatus*]. . . Spotted sea-bat. Southern Atlantic coast. **1882** U.S. Natl. Museum *Bulletin* 16.850, *Malthe* [=*Ogcocephalus*]. . . Sea Bats. . . Body stoutish; head very broad and depressed, triangular in form. **1898** *Ibid* 47.2736, *Ogcocephalus.* . . Sea-Bats. . . Small fish of singular form, often regarded by the ignorant as venomous.
3 =**devilfish 1.** Cf **bat ray**

1933 LA Dept. of Conserv. *Fishes* 240, Mantas, also known under the names of . . Blanket Fish, . . Devilfish, and Sea Bats, are in reality gigantic members of the Ray family. *Ibid* 241, Sea Bat—*Manta birostris.* . . This huge ray, known to reach a spread of twenty feet, is a common fish of the Louisiana Gulf Coast.
4 A **sea robin 1a** (here: *Prionotus carolinus*).

1911 U.S. Bur. Census *Fisheries 1908* 315, Sea robin (*Prionotus carolinus*).—This fish is found along the eastern coast south of Cape Cod. They are also called . . "sea bat," etc.

sea bean n

1 =**cowitch 1** or its seed.

1900 Lyons *Plant Names* 254, *M[ucuna] pruriens.* . . Seeds are called Sea-beans. **1933** Small *Manual SE Flora* 717, *M[ucuna] Sloanei* [=*M. pruriens*]. . . Sea-bean. . . Hammocks, Everglade Keys, pen. Fla. . . The seeds are used as beads and ornaments for watch-chains.
2 also *seaside bean*: A **jack bean 1** (here: *Canavalia rosea*).

1913 *Torreya* 13.231 **FL,** *Canavalia obtusifolia* [=*C. rosea*]. . . Sea

bean, St. Vincent I[slan]d, Fla. **1959** Carleton *Index Herb. Plants* 105, *Sea-side-bean:* Canavalia obtusifolia.

sea biscuit n *euphem* Cf **biscuit 5**

In phr *son of a sea biscuit:* =**sea cook.**

1968–70 *DARE* (Qu. NN24, *Humorous substitutes for stronger exclamations: "Why the son of a _____!"*) Infs **IN**42, **MD**16, **MA**14, **PA**133, 247, Sea biscuit.

sea blite n [*OED2* at *sea* sb. 22.f 1762 → for *Suaeda fruticosa*]
Std: a plant of the genus *Suaeda.* Also called **seepweed;** for other names of var spp see **desert blite, inkweed 2, iodine bush 2, pahute weed, quelite, saltbush 2**

sea bob n [See quot 1979] esp **LA**

A shrimp (*Xiphopenaeus kroyeri*).

1949 *Commercial Fisheries Rev.* 11.3.1, Only four of the numerous species of shrimp found along the South Atlantic and Gulf coasts are of commercial importance. These are: The common shrimp (*Penaeus setiferus*); The grooved shrimp (*Penaeus aztecus,* and *Penaeus duorarum*); The sea-bob (*Xiphopenaeus kroyeri*). **1974** McClane *McClane's New Std. Fishing Encycl.* 874, Last pair of walking legs very long and slender. . . sea bob (*Xiphopenaeus kroyeri*). **1979** Hallowell *People Bayou* 130 **sLA,** Pink shrimps, royal reds, and sea bobs (a bastardization of the French words *six barbes*) also are penaeids. **1986** Pederson *LAGS Concordance (Kinds of seafood)* 1 inf, **seLA,** Sea bob—small shrimp used as fertilizer. **2000** (acc) TX Parks & Wildlife—Fishing *TX Shrimp Fishery* (Internet), Seabob (*Xiphopenaeus kroyeri*) . . and roughback shrimp (*Trachypenaeus* sp.) are landed in small quantities.

sea brant See **brant 2**

sea bream See **saltwater bream**

sea burdock See **burdock 2**

sea cane n

A **cordgrass** (here: *Spartina alterniflora*).

1942 *Torreya* 42.158 **LA,** *Spartina alterniflora.* . . Sea cane, . . coastal Louisiana.

sea captain n Also *sea cat,* ~ *dog,* ~ *wolf;* for addit varr see quots

=**sea cook.**

1942 Berrey–Van den Bark *Amer. Slang* 396, *Terms of disparagement.* . . Son of a sea-going rum scutch. **1965–70** *DARE* (Qu. NN24, *Humorous substitutes for stronger exclamations: "Why the son of a _____!"*) Infs **NY**200, **TX**70, Sea captain; **WV**1, Sea cab; **MO**17, Sea cat; **NC**61, Sea chicken; **NY**45, Sea cliff; **SC**40, Sea crab; **SC**44, Sea dog; **MA**8, Seagull; **WV**12, Seaweed; **MS**69, Sea wolf. [5 of 11 Infs young]

sea catfish n Also *sea cat*

Either the **gaff-topsail catfish** or the similar *Arius felis.* For other names of the latter see **hardhead 2e, rustler 7, saltwater catfish, silver** ~ **2**

1855 Smithsonian Inst. *Annual Rept. for 1854* 341, *Ailurichthys marinus.* . . Sea Cat-Fish. . . The flesh is very indifferent. **1882** U.S. Natl. Museum *Proc.* 5.245, *Arius felis.* . . Sea cat-fish; Blue cat. . . Very common on the sandy beaches. It is seldom brought into the markets, and is eaten chiefly by the negroes. *Ibid* 246, *Ælurichthys marinus.* . . Sea kitten; Sea cat-fish; Gaff-top-sail cat. . . Generally abundant. **1884** Goode *Fisheries U.S.* 1.628 **FL,** The Gaff-topsail Catfish. . . is not uncommonly taken at Arlington, Florida, and Empire Point. It is known here and at Pensacola as the "Sea Cat." **1933** LA Dept. of Conserv. *Fishes* 253, *If:* Your Sea Cat has two barbels on the lower jaw . . then your fish is the Gaff Topsail. . . *But if:* Your Sea Cat has four barbels on the lower jaw . . then your fish is . . *Galeichthys felis* [=*Arius f.*] **1968** *DARE* (Qu. P2, . . *Kinds of saltwater fish caught around here . . good to eat*) Inf **LA**26, Sea cats. **1986** Pederson *LAGS Concordance,* 1 inf, **csLA,** Sea cat—from Gulf; 1 inf, **neLA,** Sea catfish—saltwater.

sea chicken n esp **NC** Cf **sand chicken**

A small shore bird such as the **least sandpiper, semipalmated** ~, **spotted** ~, **white-rumped** ~, or **sanderling.**

1911 *Forest & Stream* 77.174, *Pisobia fuscicollis* [=*Calidris f.*].—White-Tailed Sea-Chicken. . . *Pisobia minutilla* [=*Calidris m.*].—Smallest Sea-Chicken. . . *Ereunetes pusillus* [=*Calidris p.*].—Medium Sea-Chicken. . . *Calidris leucophæa* [=*C. alba*].—White Sea-Chicken. Currituck Sound, N.C. . . The term "sea-chicken" . . is applied to all of the smaller shore-birds at Currituck Sound. **1917** *Wilson Bulletin* 29.2.80, *Actitis macularia.* . . This and other small sandpipers are known as . . sea-chickens at Beaufort, N.C. **1919** Pearson et al. *Birds NC* 131, On the coast it [=least sandpiper] occurs in great numbers, and is often called "Sea Chicken." **1953** *AmSp* 28.279, Sea chicken . . Small shore birds . . N.C., S.C. **1968** *DARE* (Qu. Q10, . . *Water birds and marsh birds*) Inf **NC**80, Sea chicken.

sea chickweed See **chickweed 1e**

sea clam n
Any of several clams, as:

a A **surf clam**, usu *Spisula solidissima.* **chiefly NEng**
1765 (1942) Bartram *Diary of a Journey* 16 **S Atl**, There is many clam shels of different sises cast on ye shore by ye waves[,] ye very same with our sea clams: very white: & perfect as if ye fish was just taken out but thay have lost ye fine violet color within side. **1782** Crèvecoeur *Letters* 135 **Nantucket MA**, The shores of this island abound with the soft-shelled, the hard-shelled, and the great sea clams. **1802** MA Hist. Soc. *Coll.* 1st ser 8.192 **seMA**, The sea clam, which is at present called the *hen*, the quahaug having lost that appellation, is bivalve . . and oval. **a1862** (1865) Thoreau *Cape Cod* 78 **eMA**, Our host told us that the sea-clam, or hen, was not easily obtained. **1891** *Auk* 8.3.280, These Scoters . . frequent the New England coast, collecting in greater or less numbers wherever their favorite food can be procured,—the black mussel . . , small sea clams *(Spisula solidissima)* [etc]. **1935** Lincoln *Cape Cod Yesterdays* 49 **eMA**, Away out, along the outer bar, almost two miles from shore and only get-at-able when the tide was at full ebb, were the large "sea clams". *Ibid* 51, There is little real digging in a sea-clam hunt. These big, three-cornered fellows. . . are tough. The fish like them and they are gathered principally for bait. **1939** *LANE* Map 235 **NEng**, The *sea clam* . . [8 infs] and the *beach clam* . . [2 infs] are larger than these [=quahogs]. **1967–70** *DARE* (Qu. P18, . . *Kinds of shellfish*) Infs **MA**40, 55, 72, 97, **RI**15, Sea clams. **1974** McClane *McClane's New Std. Fishing Encycl.* 141, Baits for the ocean-run fish include the sea clam or skimmer, hardshell clam, and a piece of shedder crab.

b Any of var clams of Arctic waters such as a **surf clam** (here: *Mactromeris polynyma*), a **soft-shell clam** (here: *Mya truncata*), or **quahog 2.**
1884 Kingsley *Std. Nat. Hist.* 1.278, *Mactra solidissima* and the closely allied *M. ovalis* [=*Mactromeris polynyma*] are known along our northern coasts as hen-clam, sea-clam, and surf-clam. **1884** U.S. Natl. Museum *Bulletin* 27.232, *Cyprina islandica* [=*Arctica i.*] . . This clam is the "sea-clam" or "false quahaug." It is found in deep water from Block Island to the Arctic. **1890** *Century Dict.* 5439, *Sea-clam.* . . *Arctic sea-clam, Mya truncata,* the chief food of the walrus.

c A **razor clam** (here: *Siliqua lucida* or *S. patula*).
1920 CA Fish & Game Comm. *Fish Bulletin* 4.50, *Siliqua lucida. . . Siliqua patula.* . . At present canned in Alaska and Washington and sold under the name sea clam though this term was not heard on the California coast. **1949** Palmer *Nat. Hist.* 360, Sea Clam, Razor Shell. *Siliqua patula.* . . Delicious. . . Canned in Alaska and Washington.

sea cock See **sea cook**

seacoe See **sego lily**

sea colander n Also *colander* [From the round holes in the fronds]
A brown alga of the genus *Agarum.*
1866 Lindley–Moore *Treas. Botany* 1043, Sea-colander. The American name in the North-eastern States of *Agarum Turneri* [=*A. cribrosum*]. **1870** (1871) *Amer. Naturalist* 4.295, Piles of seawrack can display something similar in the highly curious sea colander *(Agarum Turneri)*. **1884** U.S. Natl. Museum *Bulletin* 27.618 **MA**, *Agarum Turneri* [=*A. cribrosum*]. . . Sea-colander. Nahant, Massachusetts. **1949** Palmer *Nat. Hist.* 44, Sea Collanders [sic] *Agarum cribrosum*. . . This species from Bering Sea to San Juan Island, Wash., with the related *A. fimbriatum* from Puget Sound to San Pedro. *A. cribrosum,* from Massachusetts to Ellesmere Island. . . The common name collander [sic] probably refers to the fact that the blade resembles the kitchen colander in its sieve-like appearance. **1989** Mickelson *Nat. Hist.* 180, *Agarum cribrosum*—colander.

sea cook n Also *sea cock, ~ crook, sea-going cook* **widespread exc Sth, S Midl** See Map *euphem* Cf **sea biscuit, ~ captain, ~ crab**

In phr *son of a sea cook* and var: Used as a term of abuse for a man.
1851 *Amer. Whig Rev.* 13.509, "I didn't do it, sir; indeed I didn't." "You did, you son of a sea-cook!" **1878** *Appletons' Jrl.* 5.346 **eMD**, You need not blame me . . something has given way, and, being the son of a sea-cook, I can't tell what it is. **1894** *Overland Mth.* (2d ser) 23.106, He would never go into the woods again with any sturgeon-livered son of a sea cook. **1942** ME Univ. *Studies* 11, The epithet "son-of-a-seacook" was offensive though meaningless. **1965–70** *DARE* (Qu. NN24, *Humorous substitutes for stronger exclamations: "Why the son of a _____!"*) 130 Infs, **widespread exc Sth, S Midl**, Sea cook; **CA**105, **OR**1, **SD**3, **TX**28, Sea cock; **CT**36, Sea crook; **FL**16, Sea-going cook; (Qu. NN20a, *Exclamations caused by sudden pain—a blow on the thumb*) Inf **SC**21, Son of a sea cook.

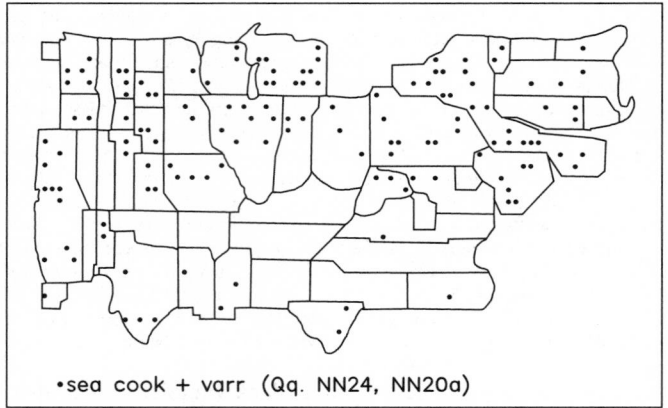

•sea cook + varr (Qq. NN24, NN20a)

sea coot n
1 =**scoter.** Cf **coot** n[1] **2a**
1834 Nuttall *Manual Ornith.* 2.417, The Surf Duck or Sea Coot . . is said to make a nest of grass, lining it with down or feathers. **1888** Trumbull *Names of Birds* 96, The three following species [=*Melanitta fusca, M. perspicillata, M. nigra*] . . , known as . . "sea coots," . . cannot be regarded as general favorites for the table, and we can fully understand the reason when we attempt the mastication of one of mature years. **1911** *Forest & Stream* 77.453 **NC**, Scooters [sic]. . . Sea Coot, North Carolina coast (to distinguish them from the grebes, which also bear the name of coot around New Bern and on the waters below there). **1919** Pearson et al. *Birds NC* 83, "Sea Coot" is the common local name for this [=*Melanitta nigra*] and the following two species [=*M. fusca* and *M. perspicillata*]. All three of the scoters occur regularly during the winter. **1940** Gabrielson *Birds OR* 168, The big, clumsy, heavy-bodied White-winged Scoter, or Sea Coot, is the most abundant of the three species represented in the great rafts found along the Oregon coast. *Ibid* 169, Surf Scoter; Sea Coot . . *Melanitta perspicillata.* **1955** MA Audubon Soc. *Bulletin* 55.376, *White-winged Scoter.* . . Sea Coot (Mass.) *Ibid* 377, *Surf Scoter.* . . Sea Coot (All [states]). . . *American Scoter.* . . Sea Coot (R.I.) **1962** Imhof *AL Birds* 156, *White-winged Scoter.* . . Sea Coot. *Ibid* 157, *Surf Scoter.* . . Sea Coot. **1982** Elman *Hunter's Field Guide* 237, *American Scoter.* . . *Common & regional names* . . sea coot. *Ibid* 240, *Surf Scoter* . . sea coot. *Ibid* 250, *White-winged Scoter* . . sea coot.

2 The common **eider duck** *(Somateria mollissima).* Cf **coot** n[1] **2c**
1876 *Forest & Stream* 7.276 **CT**, *Somateria mollissima.* Eider; sea coot. **1982** Elman *Hunter's Field Guide* 214, *American Eider.* . . *Common & regional names* . . sea-coot.

sea crab n
=**sea cook.**
1967 *DARE* (Qu. NN24, *Humorous substitutes for stronger exclamations: "Why the son of a _____!"*) Inf **SC**40, Sea crab.

sea craw n Cf **crawfish** n **B2**
A **lobster B1** (here: *Homarus americanus*).
1884 Goode *Fisheries U.S.* 1.783 **RI**, On the coast of Rhode Island, Lobsters are sometimes called "Sea-craws," from their resemblance to the fresh-water Cray-fish.

sea cress n
A **glasswort.**

1920 *Torreya* 20.20 **VA**, *Salicornia* sp.—Sea cress, Wallops I[slan]d, Va.

sea crook See **sea cook**

sea crow n [*OED2* 1579 → for var birds]
Any of var birds, as:

a A **coot** n[1] **1** (here: *Fulica americana*). Cf **mud crow, pond ~**

1888 Trumbull *Names of Birds* 118 **NEng**, To some at Buzzard's Bay, Mass., and commonly at East Haddam, Conn., [*Fulica americana* is] *Sea-crow*. . . [Footnote:] A name given by many people along the coast from Cape May to Cape Charles to Black Skimmer, *Rynchops nigra* (not included in this book). 1955 Forbush–May *Birds* 168, *American Coot*. . . *Other names* . . Sea-crow. . . A rather clumsy, simple bird with a gawky, silly expression of countenance.

b The black **skimmer 1** (*Rynchops nigra*). Cf **sea dog**
1888 [see **a** above].

c A **murre 1** (here: *Uria lomvia*).
1899 Howe–Sturtevant *Birds RI* 27, *Uria lomvia*. . . *Brünnich's Murre. Sea Crow. Foolish Guillemot*. . . An irregular winter visitant along the coast.

d An **oyster-catcher** (here: *Haematopus palliatus*). **esp VA**
1913 Bailey *Birds VA* 80, *Hæmatopus palliatus*. . . *Oyster-catcher*. [*Sea Crow*]. . . This large, showy bird fell an easy mark to the spring gunners. 1923 U.S. Dept. Ag. *Misc. Circular* 13.72 **VA**, *American Oyster-catcher*. . . Sea-crow. 1970 *DARE* (Qu. Q10, . . *Water birds and marsh birds*) Inf **VA47**, Sea crow—oyster-catcher.

e =**razor-billed auk.** [*OED2* 1813]
1925 (1928) Forbush *Birds MA* 1.43, *Razor-billed Auk*. . . *sea crow*. . . Head and upper neck all around and other upper plumage generally dark brown or slaty-black.

f =**double-crested cormorant.**
1955 MA Audubon Soc. *Bulletin* 39.312 **CT**, *Double-crested Cormorant*. . . Sea-crow (Conn. A black bird, often seen at sea; it is, however, little like a crow.)

sea dahlia n [See quot 1897]
A **tickseed** (here: *Coreopsis maritima*) native to California.
1897 Parsons *Wild Flowers CA* 146, *Sea-dahlia. Leptosyne maritima* [=*Coreopsis m.*]. . The large yellow flowers. . . closely resemble the yellow single dahlias of our gardens, but the foliage is cut into long lobes, and has the appearance of a coarse, very open lace. 1915 (1926) Armstrong–Thornber *Western Wild Flowers* 540, *Sea Dahlia—Coreopsis maritima*. . . A magnificent plant, forming large clumps, two feet high, but not at all coarse in character. 1960 Abrams *Flora Pacific States* 4.131, *Coreopsis maritima*. . . Sea-dahlia. . . Beaches and coastal bluffs and hillsides.

sea daisy n [Cf *OED2* 1838 → for *Armeria maritima*] Cf **seaside daisy**

1 A **sea lavender 1** (here: *Limonium carolinianum*).
1940 Clute *Amer. Plant Names* 263, *Limonium Caroliniana* [sic]. Sea daisy, marsh pink.

2 also *seaside daisy*: =**sea oxeye.**
1971 Craighead *Trees S. FL* 103, Two species of plants form most of the cover on these praries [sic], *Spartina spartinae* . . , locally called switch grass, and *Borrichia frutescens*, seaside daisy or blueweed. *Ibid* 199, Blueweed (sea daisy), *Borrichia frutescens*. 1976 Fleming *Wild Flowers FL* 56, *Borrichia frutescens*. . . Sea daisy blooms in spring and summer along sea beaches, mangrove areas, and salt marshes from Florida to Texas and Virginia.

sea devil n [*OED2* 1634 → for "various ugly fish" at *sea-devil* sb. 2] Cf **devilfish**

1 =**goosefish.** [*OED2* a1672 for *Lophius piscatorius*]
1814 in 1815 *Lit. & Philos. Soc. NY Trans.* 466, He [=*Lophius americanus*] is called by some the *bellows-fish*, from some resemblance his figure bears to a bellows, and from a power to inflate or swell. . . They have named him also the *sea-devil*, on account of his ugliness. 1873 in 1878 Smithsonian Inst. *Misc. Coll.* 14.2.14, *Lophius americanus*. . . Sea-devil, &c.

2 =**devilfish 1**, esp *Manta birostris*. [*OED2* 1666 →]
1842 DeKay *Zool. NY* 4.377, The Sea Devil, *Cephaloptera vampirus* [=*Manta birostris*], . . is one of those huge monsters of the deep, which are occasionally captured along our shores. 1882 U.S. Natl. Museum

Bulletin 16.52, *M[anta] birostris*. . . *Sea Devil; Devil Fish; Manta*. . . North to North Carolina and San Diego. 1905 NJ State Museum *Annual Rept. for 1904* 80, *Mobulidæ*. The Sea Devils. . . Enormous rays, among the largest of all fishes. 1933 LA Dept. of Conserv. *Fishes* 240, Mantas, also known under the names of Blanket Fish, Sea Devils, Devilfish, and Sea Bats, are in reality gigantic members of the Ray family. 1935 Caine *Game Fish* 152, The devil ray [=*Manta birostris*] is variously known as devilfish, sea devil, giant ray and manta.

sea didapper n Cf **didapper 1**
=**horned grebe.**
1962 Imhof *AL Birds* 62, *Horned Grebe*. . . *Other name:* Sea Didapper.

sea dog n [From its call; cf quot 1949] Cf **sea crow b**
The black **skimmer 1** (*Rynchops nigra*).
[1916 *Times–Picayune* (New Orleans LA) 26 Mar 1/7, Skimmers have a curious note, said by some to resemble the baying of a pack of hounds.] 1949 Sprunt–Chamberlain *SC Bird Life* 283, The familiar, yelping note, so like that of a small dog that fishermen often called the Skimmer "Sea-dog," is a characteristic sound of the night marshes. 1950 *PADS* 14.59 **SC**, *Seadog*. . . The black skimmer, shearwater. 1954 Sprunt *FL Bird Life* 226, *Black Skimmer*. . . Local Names: Shearwater; Scissorbill; Sea-dog.

sea dove n
=**dovekie.**
1834 Nuttall *Manual Ornith.* 2.531, *Little Auk*, or *Sea Dove*. . . This neat and singular little bird, with a quaint resemblance to the Columbine tribe. . . inhabits, however, a region where the gentle cooing of the Dove is never heard. 1844 DeKay *Zool. NY* 2.280, The Sea Dove. *Mergulus alle* [=*Alle a.*] *Ibid* 281, This little *Sea Dove* . . is but rarely seen on our coast. 1884 U.S. Bur. Fisheries *Rept. for 1882* 335 **NEng**, *Little guillemot* or *sea dove* (*Mergulus alle*). . . Frequently seen on the banks in winter, more particularly in the vicinity of field ice. . . It is fond of staying close to a fishing-vessel at anchor, it being attracted by the offal that is thrown over. 1946 Hausman *Eastern Birds* 337, *Dovekie*. . . *Other Names*—Sea Dove [etc]. . . The smallest of the sea birds along our winter coasts, in size halfway between an English Sparrow and a Robin, but round and chunky.

sea drake n Cf **sea duck**
The male **eider duck** (here: *Somateria mollissima*).
[1862 Acad. Nat. Sci. Philadelphia *Proc. for 1861* 240 **Labrador**, [Eider ducks] are universally known as "Sea-ducks," the males being always distinguished as "Sea-drakes."] 1888 Trumbull *Names of Birds* 94, *American Eider*. . . very generally known along the coast from New Brunswick to Rhode Island as *Sea duck*, or *Sea . . drake*.

sea drum n
A **drum 1** (here: *Pogonias cromis*).
1878 U.S. Natl. Museum *Proc.* 1.377 **NC**, *Pogonias chromis* [sic]. . . Sea Drum. Very common. 1933 LA Dept. of Conserv. *Fishes* 179, One of the largest and most interesting of the Croakers, the Sea Drum ranges from Massachusetts to the Rio Grande and as far south as the coast of Argentina. 1955 Carr–Goin *Guide Reptiles* 30 **FL**, *Pogonias cromis* . . Sea Drum. . . A humpbacked fish with chin whiskers. . . Salt water, invading fresh water in large rivers. 1972 Sparano *Outdoors Encycl.* 382, Sea drum. . . *Pogonias cromis*. . . Not so popular a gamefish as is the red drum. . . Centers of abundance include North Carolina, Florida, Louisiana, and Texas.

sea duck n [*OED2* *sea-duck* sb. 1 1753 →] Cf **sea coot**
A duck that frequents the sea; sometimes applied spec to various of these, esp the common **eider duck**.
1792 Belknap *Hist. NH* 3.168, Sea Duck, *Anas mollissima*. 1832 Nuttall *Manual Ornith.* 1.416, *Fuligula perspicillata* [=*Melanitta p.*] . . This species of Sea Duck . . may be properly considered as an American species. . . During summer they feed principally in the sea; they also commonly frequent shallow bars and surf-lashed shores and bays in quest of various kinds of small shell-fish. 1832 Williamson *Hist. ME* 141, On our coast is seen a much greater number of the *Duck kind* than of any other fowl; there being no less than nineteen species. 1. The *Brant*; . . 7. the *sea Duck*. . . [Footnote:] *Duck*.—1. Anas Bernicla. . . 7. Anas Mollissima. 1862 [see **sea drake**]. 1869 (1870) *Amer. Naturalist* 3.226 **NEng**, Their numbers were immensely reinforced by myriads of sea-ducks from more northern seas . . designated by fishermen and gunners as "Coots." 1888 Trumbull *Names of Birds* 55, I have heard the

term "black-head" [for *Aythya marila*] as far south as St. Augustine [FL], though *sea-duck* and *raft-duck* are names better understood by St. Augustine natives. *Ibid* 94, *American Eider* . . very generally known along the coast from New Brunswick to Rhode Island as *Sea duck,* or *Sea* . . *drake.* **1923** U.S. Dept. Ag. *Misc. Circular* 13.9, *Anas rubripes*. . . *Vernacular Names*. . . *In local use*. . Sea duck (R.I.) *Ibid* 30, *Surf Scoter.* . . Black sea-duck (Long I[slan]d., N.Y., N.J.) **1955** MA Audubon Soc. *Bulletin* 39.314, *Black Duck.* . . Sea Duck . . (All [states]). *Ibid* 375 **ME,** *Old-squaw.* . . Sea Duck. *Ibid* 376, *American Eider.* Black-and-white Sea Duck (Mass.); . . Sea Duck (All) *Ibid* 377 **ME,** *American Scoter.* . . Sea Duck. **1966–68** *DARE* (Qu. Q5, . . *Kinds of wild ducks*) Infs **MD**42, **ME**22, Sea ducks. **1982** Elman *Hunter's Field Guide* 214, *Somateria mollissima* . . *Common & regional names:* common eider, . . sea duck.

sea eel n

1 A **conger eel 1** (here: *Conger conger*).

1905 NJ State Museum *Annual Rept. for 1904* 122, *Leptocephalus conger* [=*Conger conger*]. . . Conger Eel. Sea Eel. **1918** *Copeia* 57.53 **Long Is. NY,** *Leptocephalus conger*. . . The local name is "Sea-eel."

2 The California moray *(Gymnothorax mordax).*

1933 John G. Shedd Aquarium *Guide* 41, *Gymnothorax mordax—California Moray; Sea Eel*. . . A large food fish of the southern California coast.

sea fig n

1 A plant of the genus *Carpobrotus.* [See quot 1915]

1901 Jepson *Flora CA* 190, *M[esembryanthemum] aequilaterale* [=*Carpobrotus a.*] . . *Sea Fig*. . . The fruits, which "taste like salted apples," are eaten by schoolboys in Southern California. **1915** (1926) Armstrong–Thornber *Western Wild Flowers* 110, *Sea Fig* . . *Mesembryanthemum aequilaterale*. . . This accommodating plant . . may be seen hanging its long stems over the sea-cliffs all along the coast. . . The fruit is edible, with pulp and tiny seeds something like a fig. **1964** Munz *Shore Wildflowers* 30 **CA,** *Sea-Fig* is *Mesembryanthemum chilense* [=*Carpobrotus c.*] . . The rose-magenta flowers are one to two inches broad. . . Sea-Fig ranges from Oregon to Lower California. **1974** (1977) Coon *Useful Plants* 53, *M[esembryanthemum] edule* [=*Carpobrotus e.*] . . sea fig. . . Planted as erosion controls along the coasts of California.

2 An **ice plant 1** (here: *Mesembryanthemum crystallinum*).

1970 Kirk *Wild Edible Plants W. U.S.* 226, *Mesembryanthemum crystallinum*. . . Ice Plant or Sea Fig. . . Widely naturalized in coastal dunes.

sea foam n

1 also *ocean foam:* Homemade candy made by pouring hot sugar syrup into beaten egg whites. **esp PA, Mid and C Atl, N Cent** See Map Cf **divinity**

1905 *New Engl. Cook Book* 154, Strawberry Short-cake, No. 2.—Take one quart of flour and sift into it two teaspoonfuls of sea-foam. **1920** Kander *Settlement Cook Book* 449 **Milwaukee WI,** *Sea Foam*. . . Boil sugar, corn syrup and water until mixture forms a soft ball when dropped into cold water. Pour slowly into beaten egg whites, beating constantly. . . When it begins to stiffen, add vanilla and nuts, broken in rather large chunks, and drop by the spoonful on oiled paper. **1939** Wolcott *Yankee Cook Book* 348, *Butternut Sea Foam* [A Vermont recipe]. **1957** *Sat. Eve. Post Letters* ceIN, My mother use to make "sea foam" candy—divinity fudge. **1965–70** *DARE* (Qu. H80, *Kinds of candy . . made at home*) 67 Infs, **esp PA, Mid and C Atl, N Cent,** Sea

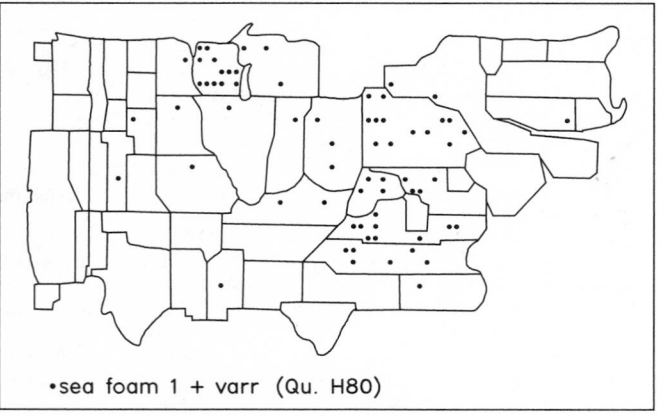

•sea foam 1 + varr (Qu. H80)

foam; **MO**1, Sea foam, foam; **WI**70, Ocean foam. **1969** *DARE* FW Addit **KY**50, Sea foam—old-fashioned homemade candies.

2 A **goatsbeard 2** (here: *Aruncus dioicus* var *vulgaris*).

1967 Gilkey–Dennis *Hdbk. NW Plants* 199, *Aruncus sylvester* [=*A. dioicus* var *vulgaris*]. . . Goat's beard. Sea-foam. . . Flowers very small; . . cream colored. . . Often seen growing on new road grades, or on the upturned roots of spruces unearthed by storms.

sea gannet n

A **gannet 1** (here: *Morus bassanus*).

1925 Bailey *Birds FL* 15, *Sula bassana* (Sea gannet). **1969** *DARE* (Qu. Q10, . . *Water birds and marsh birds*) Inf **NC**60, Sea gannet.

seago n

A type of rope; see quots.

1924 in 1975 White *Git Along* 117 **West,** Now one fine day ole Sandy Bob,/ He throwed his seago down. *Ibid* 124, *Seago*—a "lass rope" made of fiber something like maguey. **1944** Adams *Western Words* 139, *Seago*—From *la soga.* A rope. Applied more particularly to a loosely twisted hemp rope which is used for lassoing purposes. **1980** *AZ Highways* Feb 7, Others preferred the *seago* for their roping.

sea-going cook See sea cook

sea goose n

1 =**phalarope.** [See quots 1891, 1918]

1835 Audubon *Ornith. Biog.* 3.118 **ME,** The gunners of Eastport, who knew them under the name of Sea Geese, spoke of them as very curious birds. **1844** DeKay *Zool. NY* 2.269 **ME,** *Lobipes hyperboreus* [= *Phalaropus lobatus*]. . . occurs abundantly in Maine (where they are termed *Sea Geese*), and farther north. **1880** *Harper's New Mth. Mag.* 61.504 **ME,** A quaint apparent exception, and the only one, to the universal rule of rapine . . was a little bird somewhat larger than a sandpiper—the sea-goose, so-called. **1891** Goss *Hist. Birds KS* 148, *Phalaropus lobatus*. . . These birds. . . ride the waters lightly, drifting upon its surface like a feather, . . in actions much like the true Brant, *Branta bernicla,* and for this reason are known to the sailors as "Sea Geese." **1918** Grinnell *Game Birds CA* 328, Among the fishermen of the North Pacific Ocean these birds [=*Phalaropus lobatus*] together with the Red Phalaropes [=*P. fulicarius*] are known as. . . "Sea Geese" because of the erect posture of their head and neck while they are on the water. **1953** Jewett *Birds WA* 285, *Red Phalarope*. . . Other names . . Sea Goose. *Ibid* 287, *Northern Phalarope*. . . Sea-goose. **1956** MA Audubon Soc. *Bulletin* 40.21, *Red Phalarope*. . . Sea Goose (Maine, Mass. A name usually heard in the plural . .). *Wilson's Phalarope*. . . Sea Goose (Maine, Mass.) . . *Northern Phalarope*. . . Sea Goose (Maine, Mass.)

2 =**double-crested cormorant.**

1946 Hausman *Eastern Birds* 90, *Double-crested Cormorant*. . . *Other Names* . . Nigger Goose, Sea Goose. . . Often fly in long lines, in single file, close to the surface of the water.

sea grape n

A plant of the genus *Coccoloba,* usu *C. uvifera,* native to Florida. Also called **seaside plum;** for other names of *C. uvifera* see **hoopwood 3, mangrove 2a, platter-leaf;** for other names of *C. diversifolia* see **pigeon plum 1**

[**1696** (1945) Dickinson *Jrl.* 50 **FL,** He got some seaside-grapes.] **1775** (1962) Romans *Nat. Hist. FL* xix se**FL,** At the back of a high sand hill . . we called Grooper-Hill . . is a remarkable land, *cabbage* trees, *cocoplumbs,* and sea grapes are here in abundance, as are venison and other meat. **1834** Audubon *Ornith. Biog.* 2.385 s**FL,** When the seagrape is ripe, they [=pigeons] feed greedily upon it. **1897** Sudworth *Arborescent Flora* 191 **FL,** *Coccolobis* [sic] *uvifera.* . . Sea Grape. **1941** Faherty *Big Old Sun* 178 **FL,** The boat was tied to a sea grape bush and was in partial shade of the round leaves. **1943** Pratt *Barefoot Mailman* 4 **FL,** On the other [side] was a tangled vegetation of sea grapes, beach lavender, flowering Spanish bayonet, and a half dozen kinds of palms. **1962** Harrar–Harrar *Guide S. Trees* 271, *Pigeon Seagrape—Coccoloba laurifolia* [=*C. diversifolia*]. **1966** *DARE* (Qu. I46, . . *Kinds of fruits that grow wild around here*) Infs **FL**3, 11, 23, 31, Sea grapes. **1992** Hoffman *Turtle Moon* 13 ce**FL,** Each and every one of them was shocked to discover that . . the sea grape, which grew wild along the beach, could pull their children right into the thicket if they didn't keep to the wooden paths.

sea grass n [*OED2* 1578 → for var grasses, grasslike plants, or seaweeds]

=ditch grass 2.

1900 Lyons *Plant Names* 328, *R[uppia] maritima.* . . Sea-grass. **1933** Small *Manual SE Flora* 15, *R[uppia] maritima.* . . Sea-grass. . . Commonly in extensive dense masses just below the surface of the water. **1939** Tharp *Vegetation TX* 42, Sea-grass *(Ruppia maritima);* in quiet shallow protected sea water along the whole coast.

sea grass sack See **grass sack**

sea greens n

Perh a sea purslane (here: *Sesuvium portulacastrum*).

1950 *PADS* 14.77 **FL,** *Sea greens.* . . A small, tender green vine which grows on sandy beaches. When cooked it tastes much like mustard.

sea hawk n

1 The skua *(Catharacta skua)* or a **jaeger** n[1]. [*OED2* 1852 at *sea-hawk* sb. 2]

[**1851** *Harper's New Mth. Mag.* 3.470, The screaming sea-hawk again descended from the regions of immensity.] **1878** *Appletons' Jrl.* 5.396, On a sudden he turns; with a sea-hawk scream, and a gibe, and a song. *Ibid,* And a sea-hawk flung down a skeleton fish as he flew. **1910** Eaton *Birds NY* 1.114, The Skua or Sea-hawk may be recognized from the other jaegers by its greater size and robustness. **1925** (1928) Forbush *Birds MA* 1.50, *Stercorariidæ.* . . All birds of this family are virtually sea-hawks. . . They are the most predatory of all sea-birds. . . *Catharacta skua.* . . Sea-hawk. **1951** Pough *Audubon Water Bird* 345, Sea hawk. See Jaegers, Skua, and Osprey. **1953** Jewett *Birds WA* 289, *Stercorarius parasiticus.* . . Sea Hawk. . . The unusual habits and appearance of the parasitic jaeger, which is not uncommon in the [Puget] Sound country during migration, have attracted attention from fishermen and others, and have given rise to numerous local names. **1955** Forbush–May *Birds* 215, *Catharacta skua.* . . Sea-hawk. . . Powerful of wing, it rides unharmed upon the storm, and so it keeps the sea—a great, dour, somber bird, the embodiment of predatory might. It is not very rare on the fishing-banks off the New England coast.

2 =**fish hawk 1.**

1946 Goodrich *Birds in KS* 316, Hawk, sea—osprey. **1951** [see **1** above]. **1966–70** *DARE* (Qu. Q10, . . *Water birds and marsh birds*) Infs **CA**191, **FL**16, Sea hawk. [*DARE* Ed: These Infs may refer instead to **1** above.]

sea hen n

1 Usu the skua *(Catharacta skua),* but occas a **jaeger** n[1].

1854 *Putnam's Mag.* 3.316, As we still ascend from shelf to shelf, we find the tenants of the tower serially disposed in order of their magnitude:—gannets, black and speckled haglets, jays, sea-hens, sperm-whale-birds, gulls of all varieties. **1879** U.S. Natl. Museum *Bulletin* 15.94, *Buphagus skua.* . . "Sea-hen" of whalemen. **1884** U.S. Bur. Fisheries *Rept. for 1882* 323 **NEng,** The Great Skua Gull *(Megalestris skua).* This is known to the fishermen as the sea-hen, and is, perhaps, one of the most interesting species that occurs on the fishing-banks. *Ibid* 324, Western part of Grand Banks—during a northwest gale saw a sea-hen which came near the vessel. **1917** (1923) *Birds Amer.* 1.33, *Skua.* . . Other Names. . . Sea Hen. . . Much given to robbing the smaller sea birds. **1946** Hausman *Eastern Birds* 303, *Catharacta skua.* . . Sea Hen. . . Seen most often off the fishing banks of the New England coast and farther out on the ocean. **1953** *AmSp* 28.282, Sea hen. . . Parasitic jaeger—Mass., Labrador. . . Skua—Maine, Mass., Labrador, Newfoundland. American coot—Ky. **1955** Forbush–May *Birds* 216, Sea-hen. . . A bird of the . . fishing banks. . . subsisting on fish and flesh, with a partiality for eggs.

2 =**coot** n[1] **1.**

1953 [see **1** above].

sea hollyhock n

A **hibiscus** (here: *Hibiscus moscheutos*).

1900 Lyons *Plant Names* 190, *H[ibiscus] Moscheutos.* . . Brackish marshes, Massachusetts to Florida. . . Sea Hollyhock. **1950** Gray–Fernald *Manual of Botany* 1006, *H. palustris [=H. moscheutos* subsp *moscheutos].* . . Sea-Hollyhock. . . Saline, brackish, or fresh marshes. **1976** Bailey–Bailey *Hortus Third* 562, Sea hollyhock. . . Petals white, pink, or rose.

sea horse n

1 =**fulmar.**

1917 (1923) *Birds Amer.* 1.80, Fulmar. . . Other Names.—Fulmar Petrel; . . Sea Horse.

2 A **sculpin 1** (here: *Rhamphocottus richardsoni*).

1928 Pan-Pacific Research Inst. *Jrl.* 3.3.14, *Rhamphocottus richardsoni.* . . "Sea horse".

sea island myrtle n

=**groundsel tree.**

1937 *Torreya* 37.101 **GA, SC,** *Baccharis* spp.—Cotton-bush, sea-island myrtle.

sea jack See **jack** n[1] **24b(1)(b)**

sea kitten n Cf **sea catfish**

=**gaff-topsail catfish.**

1882 U.S. Natl. Museum *Proc.* 5.246, *Ælurichthys marinus.* . . Sea kitten.

seal n[1]

1 =**cedar waxwing.** [See quot 1969] Cf **waxbird**

1932 Howell *FL Bird Life* 371, Cedar Waxwing. . . *Other Names:* Cedar Bird; Seal. . . An abundant migrant and moderately common winter resident over most of the State. **1962** Imhof *AL Birds* 417, Seal, Cedar Bird, Hammerlock. . . A trim, silky-brown, *crested* bird. . . A red spot, which looks like a drop of sealing wax, is usually present on the tip of a few secondaries. **1969** Longstreet *Birds FL* 124, Seal. . . Some of the wing feathers, and rarely the tail feathers have small, seed-like tips that resemble tiny drops of red sealing wax. These curious appendages give the bird its name.

2 In the practice of conjuration or sympathetic magic: see quot. Cf **hand** n **B4**

c1938 in 1970 Hyatt *Hoodoo* 1.644 **New Orleans LA,** Take dirt dauber's nest and mix with mostly any oil that you want to. and [sic] make like a *seal* for yourself. Understand. Just write . . like this were—like a *seal* that's made on de *Sixth and Seventh Book of Moses.* Well, you take that and beat it out, you know, press it. Well it gets hard. . . Then you write just whomsomever you want—a person you want upon there—and wear it upon you, just like I'd come to you for a favor or anything. *Ibid* swTN, ([Hyatt:] If I want a *seal,* just how would I do that?) Well, yo' write chur own *seal.* Yo' take yore birth, de day yo' was bo'n, an' de 118 or 'long somewhere lak dat in Psalms. . . Fold it very even an' pin it somewhere down heah in de front. . . An' den yo' might write one an' put it in yore right shoe. . . Dat keep anyone from harmin' yo' dat's tryin' tuh harm yo'. *Ibid* 2.1173 **seGA,** Yo' make dat cross in dere you see. Well, yo' take an' put dat *seal* on de ground. Well, yo' put dat envelope whut chew got dat *graveyard dirt* an' dat photograph in dere—yo' puts dat down on top of dat *seal* [Hyatt: cross drawn on paper]. . . Yo' say, "O.L. Youngs . . yo' to come to me an' do as ah say to yo'." *Ibid* 2.1244 **neFL,** If a person steal anything from yo' an' yo' want it returned, yo' kin write chew a *seal;* an' write on de *seal* what day dat chew want de person to return dat. . . Place it ovah de do' or de windah whichever dat de person went out, an' 'fore de relapse [sic] of 48 hours time dat person will bring de goods back.

seal n[2] See **sele**

seal v Also with *up;* also n, vbl n *sealing* esp **UT, ID** Cf **spiritual wife**

Among Mormons: to bind (a person, usu a woman) spiritually to another, or (a couple) to one another, for eternity, according to the rites of the faith.

1833 in 1937 *UT Geneal. & Hist. Mag.* 28.43, The Lord heard their prayers and moved upon his servant, Lyman, by the power of the Holy Ghost, to seal them up unto eternal life. **1845** *Quincy Whig* (IL) 5 Nov 3/4, Men's wives and daughter were secretly married at night-time to this Young, H.C. Kimball, William Richards, and others, and, in the dark night, were attendidg [sic] the secret lodges until most of the "Seventies" were thus sealed. **1852** in 1855 *Putnam's Mag.* 6.147 **UT,** These extra wives are known by sundry designations—some call them "spirituals," others, "*sealed ones;*" our landlady is fond of calling them "*fixins,*" . . It seems these left-hand marriages are termed *sealings;* the woman is said to be *sealed* to the man. **1922** *Nation* 28 June 768 **UT,** A celestial marriage is a secret Temple rite wherein men have dead women "sealed" to them as their wives for eternity, and unattached women are sealed to dead husbands. **1931** *AmSp* 7.119 **eID,** *Sealed* is the Mormon term for married, sometimes to a mate in the spirit world. **1942** Stegner *Mormon Country* 178, Those are the first processes—baptism and the sealing of one's wife and family. **1948** *Jrl. Amer. Folkl.* 61.28 **UT,** An illegitimate child appeared thrice in a dream, each time insisting that it be sealed legitimately to the family in appropriate temple ceremonies. **1959** Robertson *Ram* 117 **ID** (as of c1875), His wife would be *sealed* to him in the temple for time and eternity. He might be sealed to other women in eternity, even though he could have but one wife on earth so long as mother was alive—but never could she be sealed to another man. His children, too, would be sealed to him and forever and forever they would be jewels in his crown. **1965** *DARE* Tape UT1, [FW:] Well, what does it mean to have your children sealed to you? [Inf:] . . If you're married in the temple, they are officially sealed to you. [FW:] So, that this doesn't have to be done separately. [Inf:] No, up until the time they're eight years old, and then that's when they're supposed to be baptized, themselves. **1983** *Salt Lake Tribune* (UT) 29 May sec B 19/5, Born April 13, 1904. . . Married . . November 9, 1929, at Paris, Idaho. They were later sealed in the Logan LDS Temple.

sea lamprey n

A **lamprey** (here: *Petromyzon marinus*).

1787 Gesellschaft Naturforschender Freunde *Schriften* 8.184, *Petromyzon marinus. . . Sea-Lamprey,* zu Neuyork. Der Körper ist rund, einen halben bis einen Fuß lang, schlüpfrig und schleimig. [=*Petromyzon marinus. . . Sea-Lamprey,* at New York. The body is round, a half to a foot long, slippery and slimy.] **1838** MA Zool. & Bot. Surv. *Repts. Zool.* 47, And the *Petromyzon marinus*—Sea-lamprey—is highly esteemed there, as an article of food. **1903** NY State Museum & Sci. Serv. *Bulletin* 60.12, The sea lamprey or lamprey eel inhabits the north Atlantic, ascending streams to spawn and sometimes becoming landlocked. **1918** *Copeia* 64.93, In the lakes and streams of the United States East of the Rocky Mountains, five species of Lamprey are known to occur, beside the Sea Lamprey (Petromyzon marinus L.), which enters the streams to spawn. **1983** Becker *Fishes WI* 211, The sea lamprey occurs in Lakes Michigan and Superior and in numerous tributaries to these lakes.

sea lavender n

1 A plant of the genus *Limonium,* esp *L. carolinianum.* Also called **beach lavender, cankerroot 2, marsh rosemary;** for other names of *L. carolinianum* see **flax blossom, inkroot, marsh pink 2, sea daisy 1**

1830 Rafinesque *Med. Flora* 2.93, *Statice caroliniana* [=*Limonium c.*] . . Sea Lavender. . . Root perennial, . . purplish brown. . . Petals blue. **1879** *Harper's New Mth. Mag.* 59.550 **NJ,** We added to our treasures . . great bunches of the fragile-looking yet hardy sea-lavender, that gives its purple coloring to the patches of meadow fringing the Shrewsbury River. **1901** Lounsberry *S. Wild Flowers* 411, Sea Lavender. Limonium Carolinianum. . . This pretty little plant . . grows in salt marshes along the coast. **1949** Moldenke *Amer. Wild Flowers* 233, The sea-lavender usually grows in large colonies and, seen from a little distance, the myriads of tiny flowers, borne on loosely spreading branches, give the haunting appearance of low-lying, bluish gray mist blown in over the marshes from the close-by sea or of the fine salt spray itself. . . A similar plant, the *California sea-lavender, L. californicum,* spreads its violet-purple haze over salt marshes and sea beaches in California. **1967** *DARE* Wildfl QR Pl.166B Inf **OH**14, Sea lavender. **1968** *DARE* (Qu. S26b, *Wildflowers that grow in water or wet places*) Inf **NJ**39, Sea lavender. **1974** Morton *Folk Remedies* 89 **SC,** Sea Lavender. . . *Limonium carolinianum. . . (Current use):* Roots are gathered in winter, boiled, and the liquid drunk as a remedy for colds and fever, and especially for diarrhea. **1996** *Audubon Mag.* Nov–Dec 53 **seCT,** A few steps into the marsh, freshwater plants gave way, and we began to encounter . . rough cordgrass, sea lavender, and water smartweed.

2 A maritime shrub (*Argusia gnaphalodes*) native to Florida.

[**1696** (1769) Plukenet *Almagestum* 2.182, Heliotropium Gnaphaloides litoreum fruticescens *Americanum,* Sea-Lavender *Barbadensibus* dictum. [=The littoral American frutescent Heliotropium Gnaphaloides, called Sea-Lavender by the Barbadians.]] **1933** Small *Manual SE Flora* 1130 **FL,** M[allotonia] gnaphalodes [=*Argusia g.*] . . Sea lavender. . . Coastal sand-dunes, S pen[insular] Fla. and the Keys. **1971** Craighead *Trees S. FL* 94, Some of the more characteristic trees and shrubs of the beaches and coastal ridges are . . seven-year apple, sea grape, . . sea lavender [etc].

sea lawyer See **lawyer B6**

sea lettuce n

1 A green alga of the genus *Ulva.* Also called **pussley 3**

1899 Going *Field Flowers* 385, We may notice a green film which is caused by the growth of some tiny and humble cousins of the rich green "sea-lettuces" which float at the edges of tidal pools on rocky coasts. **1928** Beston *Outermost House* 192 **Cape Cod MA,** Here have the tides

strewn a moist tableland with lumpy tangles, wisps, and matted festoons of ocean vegetation—with common sea grass, . . with the crushed and wrinkled green leaves of sea lettuce . . and bleached sea moss. **1976** [see **pussley 3**]. **1989** (1990) Baden *Maryland's E. Shore* 21, The middle beach is a maze of translucent sea lettuce entangled in . . ugly rockweed and equally ugly brown algae, sargassum.

2 A **live-forever 4** (here: either *Dudleya caespitosa* or *D. farinosa*). Cf **bluff lettuce**

1944 Abrams *Flora Pacific States* 2.337 **CA,** Dudleya caespitosa. . . Sea Lettuce. . . Bluffs along the coast. **1961** Thomas *Flora Santa Cruz* 189 **cwCA,** D[udleya] farinosa. . . Sea Lettuce, Bluff Lettuce, Powdery Dudleya. Rocky slopes and bluffs along the coast. July–August.

seal herb n

=**goldenseal 1.**

1940 Clute *Amer. Plant Names* 261, Hydrastis Canadensis. Seal-herb.

sealing See **seal** v

sea lion n Cf **coaster** n[2]

A Texas longhorn steer from the Gulf coast region.

1890 *Stock Grower & Farmer* (Las Vegas NM) 16 Feb 3/3 *(DA),* The purchase, in 1886, of ten thousand head of scrubby south Texas cattle, 'dogies' or 'sea lions,' at very high prices, was the cause of the great losses by the Delano-Dwyer company. **1892** *Scribner's Mag.* 11.738 **TX,** Drovers made a business of going from ranch to ranch and purchasing the marketable beeves. "Dogies," "sea-lions," and "long-horns" were favorite nicknames for the cattle. **1929** Dobie *Vaquero* 20 **TX,** The "coasters" or "sea lions," as people sometimes called the longhorned cattle of the coast country, could swim like ducks and were as wild.

seal up See **seal** v

sealwort n [*OED2* 1863]

A **Solomon's seal** (here: *Polygonatum biflorum*).

1900 Lyons *Plant Names* 299, P[olygonatum] biflorum. . . Dwarf Solomon's-seal or Sealwort. . . *P. commutatum* [=*P. biflorum* var *c.*] . . Sealwort. **1971** Krochmal *Appalachia Med. Plants* 202, Polygonatum biflorum. . . Sealwort. . . Roots and rhizomes are mildly astringent.

sea lyme grass n

A **wild rye** (here: *Leymus mollis* subsp *mollis*).

1912 Baker *Book of Grasses* 247, The Sea Lyme-grass [=*Leymus mollis* subsp *mollis*] . . is found in America, but only on the colder shores, where it is as valuable as the Marram Grass which it somewhat resembles. **1961** Thomas *Flora Santa Cruz* 88 **cwCA,** Sea Lyme or American Dune Grass. Sand dunes along the coast. **1976** Bruce *How to Grow Wildflowers* 213, From coastal Massachusetts northward grows the Sea Lyme Grass or Strand Wheat, a handsome and hardy beach grass whose large seeds are a source of flour.

sea mantis n [*OED2* at *sea* sb. 22.d 1835]

A **mantis shrimp 1** (here: *Squilla empusa*).

1884 Goode *Fisheries U.S.* 1.823, The Mantis Shrimp, or Sea mantis—*Squilla empusa. . .* This species of *Squilla* ranges from Cape Cod to Florida. . . It is probably very abundant in some localities.

sea martin n [See quot 1946]

A **storm petrel** (here: *Oceanites oceanicus*).

1925 (1928) Forbush *Birds MA* 1.149, *Oceanites oceanicus. . .* Wilson's stormy petrel; sea martin. **1946** Hausman *Eastern Birds* 78, *Oceanites oceanicus. . .* These birds beat swallow-fashion over the waves (hence the name Sea Martin), sweeping and fluttering with a graceful flight.

sea matweed n [*OED2* at *sea* sb. 22.f 1843]

=**beach grass.**

1890 *Century Dict.* 3664, Matweed. . . A grass, Ammophila arundinacea (Psamma arenaria): so called from its use in making mats. Also called *sea-mat-weed.* **1933** Small *Manual SE Flora* 106, A[mmophila] breviligulata. . . Sea-mat Weed. . . Sandy beaches and dunes, Coastal Plain and New England Coast, N.C. to Newf[oundland]; also Great Lake [sic] Lowland, Ind. to Wis. and Mich. **1945** Wodehouse *Hayfever Plants* 51, American beachgrass (Ammophila breviligulata . .), also called . . sea-mat weed, . . is a tough coarse perennial. . . On the Pacific coast, possibly also partly along the Atlantic, its place is taken by the very similar European beachgrass (*A. arenaria* . .) which has also been successfully used as a sand binder.

sea mink n

A **kingfish 1** (here: *Menticirrhus saxatilis, M. americanus,* or *M. littoralis*).

1887 Goode *Amer. Fishes* 123 **NC,** The King-fish, *Menticirrus* [sic] *nebulosus* [=*M. saxatilis*], [is] also known as . . the "Sea Mink" in North Carolina. **1939** Natl. Geogr. Soc. *Fishes* 93, This kingfish [=*Menticirrhus saxatilis*] has two immediate relatives [=*M. americanus* and *M. littoralis*] on the Atlantic coast with which its range overlaps. These relatives are so close that fishermen generally do not distinguish the three. . . Besides kingfish they are called . . sea minks and sea mullets. **1951** Taylor *Surv. Marine Fisheries NC* 131, The sea mullet taken commercially in North Carolina includes at least two species, *M[enticirrhus] americanus* and *M. saxatilis.* Other names for these fish are kingfish, sea-mink and hake.

seam-needle n

In phrr *come to* (or *reach*) *the seam-needle:* See quot.

1944 *PADS* 2.49 **NC,** Seam-needle, to come to (or *reach*) *the.* . . To reach a good stopping place. Duplin Co., N.C. Rare. Reported.

sea moss n

A seaweed, esp **Irish moss 1.**

1849 *Ladies' Repository* 9.127, Ten thousand thanks to our fair correspondent, who sends us a small book of impressions of sea mosses. **1860** *Ibid* 26.417, But it is after these storms that the greatest number, and the most perfect specimens of the beautiful sea-mosses are found. These "Algæ" are of three colors, green, olive, and red. . . The green grow near high-water mark; the olive lower down, and the red Algæ, or sea moss, as I prefer to call it, has its home yet further down. **1868** *Atlantic Mth.* 22.181, The major . . had here the opportunity to gratify another of his passions in gathering sea-mosses, or *algæ,* of which he already had a splendid collection. **1892** *Overland Mth.* (2d ser) 20.471 **CA,** The green or gray colors [of fish] match the colors of the sand and kelp; the red ones harmonize with the red sea-mosses among which the red fishes live. **1906** Gregory *Woman's Cookbook* 314, Sea-Moss Blanc-mange. Procure sea-moss at druggist's. Wash a handful in several waters to remove grit. Throw it in a quart of boiling milk, stir until the sea-moss has been absorbed to make it thick, which can be determined by trying a little in a cold dish. Add a pinch of salt and any desired flavoring. Strain into molds and serve cold with sugar and cream. **1916** Dunham *How to Know Mosses* 5, Sea mosses *(Algae).* . . grow in salt water. . . Irish moss used in cooking is an alga. **1928** Beston *Outermost House* 192 **Cape Cod MA,** Here have the tides strewn a moist tableland with lumpy tangles, wisps, and matted festoons of ocean vegetation— with common sea grass . . and bleached sea moss. **1948** Pearson *Sea Flavor* 53 **neMA,** On the rocks the sea moss dries its outer leaves in the sun. **1969** *New Engl. Galaxy* Winter 67 **seMA,** I don't recall the trade name, but we spoke of the pudding we made from it as "sea-moss farine".

sea mouse n [See quot 1925]

=**harlequin duck.**

1917 (1923) *Birds Amer.* 1.142, Harlequin Duck. . . Other Names. . . Sea Mouse. **1925** (1928) Forbush *Birds MA* 1.261, *Voice.* . . males have a "low piping whistle"—probably the note that gives bird name of Squealer or Sea Mouse by which it is often known on Maine coast where gunners say they "squeak like mice." **1982** Elman *Hunter's Field Guide* 226, The colloquial name "sea-mouse" refers to the squeaks of harlequins. They also produce hoarse, whistling squeals, harsh grunts, oinks, and quacks.

seam squirrel n Also *seam rat*

A louse; occas a flea or bedbug.

1899 Skinner *Hist. Fourth IL Volunteers* 129, When it was first rumored that the old confederate seam squirrel had invaded our quarters, a small panic seized many. **1919** in 1972 *AmSp* 47.97 (as of 1917–19) [Slang of Amer Forces in Europe], An hour chasing seam-rats. **1927** *DN* 5.462 [Underworld jargon], Seam squirrel. . . A louse. **1928** Ruppenthal *Coll.* **KS,** Seam squirrel. . . (army) a louse. **1933** *AmSp* 8.3.31 [Prison terms], Seam-squirrel. Louse or flea. **1941** Writers' Program *Guide WY* 465, Seam squirrels—cooties. **1950** *WELS* (Other names [include joking and nicknames] for body and head lice) 1 Inf, **csWI,** Seam squirrel. **1956** Almirall *From College* 233 **CO,** Just about to agree, I heard him snore, and so I muttered to myself, "To hell with these seam squirrels (cowboy lingo for bedbugs). I'm too damn tired." **1966–69** *DARE* (Qu. R25, *Joking names for a head louse, or body louse*) Infs **CA3, MN14, NY52, PA1, 34, 180, 223, TN22,** Seam squir-

rel. **1982** *Smithsonian Letters* **Pacific NW,** I was raised in the lower Columbia river logging country. . . The living conditions in the logging camps of the early 1900's was very crude. Usually the men lived in small . . "bunk houses" and one of the worst pests were bedbugs known as "seam squirrels".

seamster n [*OED2* "arch."] esp **Sth, S Midl**

A seamstress.

1868 *Ladies' Repository* 1.191, D'ye think . . that Fanny and Kate will go out as helps or seamsters? **1917** in 1944 *ADD* **sWV,** Seamster. . . A seamstress. **1927** Kennedy *Gritny* 156 **sLA** [Black], They spoke of her as a "natchal bawn seamster." **1945** FWP *Lay My Burden Down* 123 **LA** (as of c1865) [Black], He say, "Now, honey, I fotches that gal just for you, 'cause she a fine seamster." **1986** Pederson *LAGS Concordance,* 1 inf, **neAR,** Seamster = seamstress; repeated three times.

sea mullet n

1 A **kingfish 1** (here: *Menticirrhus saxatilis, M. americanus,* or *M. littoralis*). **esp NC** Cf **sea mink**

1878 U.S. Natl. Museum *Proc.* 1.378 **NC,** *Menticirrus* [sic] *littoralis.* . . *Sea Mullet.* Rather common. The young abundant in the surf on the outer beach. **1939** [see **sea mink**]. **1951** Taylor *Surv. Marine Fisheries NC* 273, Three species of *Menticirrhus* are present in North Carolina waters. The most numerous [is] *M. americanus.* . . *M. saxatilis* . . is not common south of Chesapeake Bay. *M. littoralis* ranges from Chesapeake Bay south to the Gulf coast. . . The species are all lumped together under the name sea mullet by commercial fishermen. **1966–70** *DARE* (Qu. P2, . . *Kinds of saltwater fish caught around here . . good to eat*) Infs **NC12, 21, VA46,** Sea mullet; **NC80,** Sea mullet = kingfish; **NC82,** Sea mullet, sound mullet—different taste; **NC85,** Sea mullet— not the same as freshwater mullet. **1984** *DARE* File **Chesapeake Bay** [Watermen's vocab], Sand mullet, sea mullet, Virginia mullet, roundhead, whiting.

2 =**striped mullet.**

1884 Goode *Fisheries U.S.* 1.453 **FL,** In the Saint Mary's River. . . the "Sea Mullet" [here: *Mugil cephalus*] ranges from eight to eighteen inches, weighing from eight ounces to two pounds. They never leave this region, but spend the whole time in the salt-water bayous along the coast. They frequently run up into brackish or almost fresh water, probably for the purpose of feeding.

sea myrtle n

1 A **groundsel tree** (here: *Baccharis halimifolia*). Cf **myrtle** n[1] **A, B9, sea island myrtle**

1883 Shields *Hunting* 195 **West,** Within the space of this five acres may be found . . sea myrtle, grape vine and ivy of several varieties. **1938** Rawlings *Yearling* 279 **nFL,** The October blooming of dog-fennel and sea-myrtle had turned to a feathery fluff. **1974** Morton *Folk Remedies* 35 **SC,** Sea muckle; sea myrtle. . . *Baccharis halimifolia.* . . All except extreme west of South Carolina and North Carolina; also north to Massachusetts, down to central Florida, and west to Texas. . . Root decoction taken for colds and for pain in stomach. **1977** *Mais Jamais* 17 **LA,** The herbs and roots they had to collect [to make a cough syrup] were mamou roots, . . Sea Merkle roots, Blue Brier roots [etc]. **1982** *Naples Now* May 37 **swFL,** Also found in the scrub zone is . . the *saltbrush* or *sea myrtle,* a shrub or occasionally small tree to 12 feet.

2 =**joewood.** Cf **myrtle** n[1] **B7**

1922 Sargent *Manual Trees* 804 **FL,** *Jacquinia keyensis.* . . Joe Wood. Sea Myrtle. . . Flowers appearing in Florida from November until June.

sea needle n [*OED2* at *sea* sb. 22.d 1603 → for *Belone belone*]

A **needlefish 1.**

1787 Gesellschaft Naturforschender Freunde *Schriften* 8.194, *Syngnathus acus.* . . Seaneedle, zu Neuyork. Der langgestreckte Körper ist bis zum After eigentlich sechseckig. [=*Syngnathus acus.* . . Sea-needle, at New York. The long body is actually six-sided as far as the vent.] **1890** *Century Dict.* 5445, Sea-needle. . . Same as *garfish (a)* [= Belonidae]: so called from the slender form and sharp snout.

sea nettle n [*OED2* 1601 → for "certain radiate marine animals of the class *Acalephæ,*" 1835 spec for jellyfish] **chiefly Chesapeake Bay**

A stinging jellyfish, esp *Chrysaora quinquecirrha* and related spp; see quots.

1844 *S. Lit. Messenger* 10.405, Navigators have often met with vast numbers of young sea-nettles (medusæ) drifting along with the Gulf

Stream. **1871** *Harper's New Mth. Mag.* 43.705 **Chesapeake Bay,** But those of us who plunged into the tepid tide were so sharply stung by sea-nettles that we came out again in no very comfortable plight. **1931** *Sun* (Baltimore MD) 12 Mar 8 *(Hench Coll.)* **MD,** The waters of the Chesapeake Bay . . are alive with sea nettles which are clogging the pound nets. . . Sea nettles have never been known to be so dense in the upper bay waters as they are at present. . . It is believed the nettles have migrated to the headwaters of the bay, seeking fresh water. **1932** *Ibid* 15 Aug 6 *(Hench Coll.)* **MD,** Mr. Hoover . . is to spend a week fishing in the teeming Chesapeake [Bay]. . . Surely there is none who will wish him less than a fair catch . . and a plague on the jellyfish. . . To call them sea nettles is but to make the metaphor more painful. **1966–68** *DARE* (Qu. R23b, *Blood-sucking creatures—in water*) Inf **DC2,** Sea nettles—have stinging tentacles; **DC8,** Sea nettles; **MD13,** Sea nettle—makes red spot; **MD45,** Sea nettles or jellyfish. **1970** *DARE* Tape **VA113,** Some of them sea nettles, they'll sting the devil out of you if they get on you . . set you afire, almost. . . A sea nettle has a long thing hanging from it; a jellyfish is just a raft-like jellyfish. **1981** Meinkoth *Audubon Field Guide Seashore* 361, *Sea Nettle (Chrysaora quinquecirrha)*. . . Bell covered with fine warts. . . Long, yellow tentacles alternate with marginal sense organs between lobes. Feeding tube extends well below bell margin as *4 long, ruffled, lacy lips*. *Ibid* 362, Floats near surface. . . Cape Cod to Florida and Texas. Abundant in Chesapeake Bay. . . *Mildly toxic.* Contact with a Sea Nettle usually results in a mild itchy irritation. . . The Lined Sea Nettle *(C. melanaster)* is often washed ashore from Alaska to southern California. . . It may also sting severely. **1996** Horton *Island Out of Time* 201 **Chesapeake Bay MD,** It'd show how the men fight the heat and flies and sea nettles all day long, and still sometimes get no more than a hot dog and chips from their wives when they get home.

sea o, sea oar See **sea ore**

sea oat(s) n Also *seaside oat(s)*   Cf **oat grass d**
A **spike-grass** (here: *Uniola paniculata*).
1730 Royal Soc. London *Philos. Trans.* 36.429, Sea-side Oat. **1890** *Century Dict.* 5831, *Spike-grass.* . . The genus *Uniola*, especially *U. paniculata* (also called *sea* or *seaside oats*), a tall coarse grass with a dense heavy panicle, growing on sand-hills along the Atlantic coast southward. **1894** Coulter *Botany W. TX* 545, *U[niola] paniculata.* . . *Sea oats.* . . Drifting sand along the coast, southern Texas to New Jersey. **1912** Baker *Book of Grasses* 184, Seaside Oats *(Uniola paniculata)* is a southern beach grass, growing in drifting sands from Chesapeake Bay southward, and taking the place of the Marram Grass of more northern coasts. **1969** *DARE* (Qu. S26e, *Other wildflowers not yet mentioned; not asked in early QRs*) Inf **NC60,** Sea oat; (Qu. T16, . . *Kinds of trees . . 'special'*) Inf **NC76,** Sea oats. **1986** Pederson *LAGS Concordance,* 2 infs, **FL,** Sea oats; 1 inf, **seMS,** Sea oats—not marsh grass, grow in sandy soil. **1989** (1990) Baden *Maryland's E. Shore* 69, The recoil [of the punt gun] would have done in the hunter for sure had he not packed sea oats and pine needles around the barrel to absorb the shock.

sea-ore n Also *sea oar, ~ o*   [*OED2 ore* sb.[5], also *sea-ore*, "local. . . Seaweed, esp. such as is cast on the shore and gathered for manure"; 1592 →]   **esp Chesapeake Bay**
=**eelgrass 1.**
1762 Gronovius *Flora Virginica* 142, *Zostera.* . . Alga marina graminea, Sea Oar vulgo. In littoribus marinis & fluviorum ostiis ubique reperitur. Pluviis & insolatu nigrescit. [=*Zostera.* . . Grasslike seaweed, popularly called Sea Oar. It is found everywhere along the seacoast and in the mouths of rivers. It blackens with exposure to rain and sun.] **1937** *Torreya* 37.95, *Zostera marina.* . . Sea-oar, coast of Maryland, Virginia, and North Carolina. **1984** *DARE* File **Chesapeake Bay** [Watermen's vocab], Eelgrass, sea o's, seaweed, sea ore, grass. **1991** *NADS Letters* **eVA,** When her friend was unhappy with her hair she'd say it looked like "dog hair and sea ore". **1996** Horton *Island Out of Time* 134 **Chesapeake Bay MD,** They would go ashore on the marsh and cover up in sea oars [masses of dried eelgrass washed ashore] to keep warm, and go to sleep while they waited.

sea oxeye n Also *sea-oxeye daisy*
A plant of the genus *Borrichia*, usu *B. frutescens*.   For other names of this sp see **blueweed 5, sea daisy 2**
1857 Gray *First Lessons* 213, *Borrichia.* . . Sea Ox-eye. . . Shrubby low maritime plants, . . with . . terminal heads of yellow flowers. **1903** Small *Flora SE U.S.* 1262, *Borrichia.* . . Sea Ox-eye. **1953** Greene–Blomquist *Flowers South* 139, Sea Ox-eye *(Borrichia frutescens)*. . .

Grows in salt marshlands on the coast with salt-marsh grasses and glassworts. . . A larger and more variable species *(B. arborescens)* grows in s. Fla. **1974** Morton *Folk Remedies* 37 **SC,** Sea ox-eye; sea ox-eye daisy—*Borrichia frutescens.* . . The leaves have a balsam-like, somewhat bitter flavor.

sea parrot n [*EDD* at *sea* sb. 2.(27) 1822 for *Fratercula arctica*]   Cf **parrotbill**
A **puffin** of the genus *Fratercula*.
1835 Audubon *Ornith. Biog.* 3.105, The Sea Parrot, as this bird [= *Fratercula arctica*] is usually called on the eastern coasts of the United States, . . sometimes proceeds as far south as the entrance of the River Savannah in Georgia. **1859** U.S. War Dept. *Rept. Explor. Railroad* 10.3.75 **cwCA,** *Mormon cirrhatus.* . . This curious, odd-looking, and interesting species was observed on the Farrallones, and known by the inhabitants as the sea parrot. **1870** *Atlantic Mth.* 25.210 **NH,** Little auks, stormy-petrels, loons, grebes, lords-and-ladies, sea-pigeons, sea-parrots, various guillemots, and all sorts of gulls abound [on the Isles of Shoals]. **1904** Wheelock *Birds CA* 3, The name "sea parrot" is applied to all puffins on account of their curious parrot-like bill. **1940** Gabrielson *Birds OR* 323, So far as is known these odd-appearing little Sea Parrots [=*Fratercula cirrhata*] do no harm to anything of economic consequence to man and therefore can well be allowed to remain as an attractive feature of the Oregon shore line. **1956** MA Audubon Soc. *Bulletin* 40.80, *Common Puffin* [=*Fratercula arctica*]. . . Sea Parrot (Maine, N.H., Mass.; also in British folk use.)

sea parsley n [*OED2* at *sea* sb. 22.f 1843]
A **lovage** (here: *Ligusticum scoticum*).
1876 Hobbs *Bot. Hdbk.* 104, Sea parsley, Lovage, Ligusticum Levisticum. **1910** Graves *Flowering Plants* 310 **CT,** *Ligusticum scothicum* [sic]. . . Sea Parsley. Scotch Lovage. Rocky shores of the Sound. Occasional from East Lyme . . eastward. **1991** Tabbert *Dict. Alaskan Engl.* 173, A traditional source of dietary greens in coastal areas is *Ligusticum scoticum*, named "officially" *beach lovage*, but also called popularly *wild parsley, sea parsley, Scotch lovage,* etc.

sea partridge n Cf **partridge duck, water partridge**
Perh =**green-winged teal.**
1970 *DARE* (Qu. Q5, . . *Kinds of wild ducks*) Inf **VA79,** Sea partridge.

sea pea n Also *seaside pea* [See quot 1922]
=**beach pea.**
1840 MA Zool. & Bot. Surv. *Herb. Plants & Quadrupeds* 64 **eMA,** *P[isum] maritimum* [=*Lathyrus japonicus*]. . . Sea Pea. Found on marshes about salt water in the vicinity of Boston, and described by Dr. Bigelow as a Lathyrus. **1900** Lyons *Plant Names* 216, *L[athyrus] maritimus.* . . Sea or Seaside Pea. **1922** *Amer. Botanist* 28.73, Because of its fondness for growing in sterile places near the water, *Lathyrus maritimus* is known as the . . "seaside pea". **1973** Hitchcock–Cronquist *Flora Pacific NW* 262, Sea p[ea] . . *L[athyrus] japonicus.*

sea peach n Cf **sea potato 1** [See quot 1981]
Usu a sea squirt of the genus *Halocynthia*, esp *H. pyriformis*; occas another tunicate.
1888 Kingsley *Riverside Nat. Hist.* 3.57, The fishermen call some of the species of the genus *Cynthia* by the rather appropriate name 'sea peach'. **1901** Arnold *Sea-Beach* 476, *C[ynthia] pyriformis* [=*Halocynthia p.*]. Body globular . . ; hard, velvety, whitish surface, with pink cheeks. . . It . . is sometimes found at low-water mark on the northern New England coast. Commonly called the sea-peach. **1981** Meinkoth *Audubon Field Guide Seashore* 742, *Sea Peach (Halocynthia pyriformis)*. . . The shape, color, and fuzzy surface of this handsome solitary tunicate are reminiscent of a peach. **2000** (acc) *Center for Coastal Studies* (Internet) **neMA,** Some tunicates common to the area are stalked tunicate, . . sea peach *(Halocynthia pyriformis)* (5″ or 127 mm long), and northern white crust.

sea perch n [*OED2* at *sea* sb. 22.d 1601 →]   Cf **perch** n[1]
Any of var fishes that are perch-like in either appearance or habit, as:
a =**cunner** n[1] **1.**   **esp NEng**
1765 in 1903 Rowe *Letters* 86 **eMA,** We caught above sixteen dozn of pond & sea perch. **1839** MA Zool. & Bot. Surv. *Fishes Reptiles* 16 **neMA,** The Greenland Sculpin . . I have . . often taken, while fishing from the rocks there [at Nahant], for the *Sea-perch* or *Conner.* **1855** *Putnam's Mag.* 5.636 **Cape Cod MA,** The bottom being sandy, I could

see the sea-perch swimming about. **1884** Goode *Fisheries U.S.* 1.273 **Cape Cod MA,** *The Chogset or Cunner.* . . At Provincetown they are called "Sea-perch," and at the Isle of Shoals and occasionally on the adjoining mainland . . "Perch." **1894** *New Engl. Mag.* 17.39 **ME coast,** Sometimes the fishermen use "cunners" or sea perch for bait; these may be caught in great number at the harbor. **1933** John G. Shedd Aquarium *Guide* 142, *Tautogolabrus adspersus* . . *Sea Perch.* This little fish is extremely abundant along the Atlantic coast. . . It swarms around the rocks and wharfs where it is a pest to fishermen.

b =tripletail. esp Sth

1840 (1965) Moore *Map & Descr. TX* 36, Among these are red fish, grundiquoit, mullet, sea perch, sea trout, &c. **1882** U.S. Natl. Museum *Proc.* 5.604 **eSC,** *Lobotes surinamensis.* . . *Sea Perch.* Occasionally taken. **1935** Caine *Game Fish* 138 **Sth,** *Tripletail.* . . *Sea Perch.* . . Around wrecks, pilings, jetties, and buoys. **2000** *DARE* File—Internet **sLA,** Surf fishermen take speckled trout, redfish and flounder, while anglers on the bridge connecting Grand Isle to the mainland cast for croakers, white trout, Spanish mackerel, sea perch and sheepshead.

c A white perch (here: *Morone americana***).**

1935 Caine *Game Fish* 18 **Sth,** *Morone americana.* . . *Sea Perch.* . . *Waters frequented:* Both fresh and salt water, prefers brackish rivers. **1976** Tryckare et al. *Lore of Sportfishing* 98, *Morone americana.* . . Sea perch. . . In fresh and salt water along the Atlantic coasts of North America, ranging parts of Great Lakes region, the St. Lawrence River, and south to South Carolina. **2000** (acc) WI Univ. Sea Grant Inst. *Fish Gt. Lakes* (Internet), *Morone americana.* . . White perch, . . sea perch. . . *Native to Atlantic coastal regions,* white perch invaded the Great Lakes through the Erie and Welland canals in 1950.

d Any of var surfperches. Pacific

1953 Roedel *Common Fishes CA* 102, The Surfperches, Family Embiotocidae. . . These fish are not true perches but form a distinct family. . . [T]he six species most closely associated with surf are called "surfperch," those associated with the ocean, but not primarily with the surf, are "seaperch," while those of varying habitat are simply "perch." **1969** *DARE* (Qu. P14, . . *Commercial fishing* . . *what do the fishermen go out after?*) Inf **CA**168, Sea perch. **1983** Audubon Field Guide N. Amer. Fishes 640, Anglers fishing from rocky shores, piers, and small boats catch about 100,000 Striped Seaperches each year in northern and central California. **2000** *DARE* File—Internet **WA,** Saltwater Perch. Sea perch and surf perch are widely available in Washington's marine waters. The three most popular are pile perch, striped seaperch and redtailed surf perch.

sea pigeon n [*OED2* 1620 →]

Any of var birds, as:

a Either the black guillemot (*Cepphus grylle***) or the pigeon guillemot.**

[**1862** Acad. Nat. Sci. Philadelphia *Proc. for 1861* 256, They [= *Cepphus grylle*] are universally known to the natives and fishermen [of Labrador] as "Sea-pigeons."] **1868** Cronise *Nat. Wealth CA* 479, The Pacific Sea Pigeon (. . *Uria Columba*) is as large as the land-pigeon, black with white on the wings, and red feet. It lays and sits on three eggs at a time. **1872** Coues *Key to N. Amer. Birds* 345, *Black Guillemot. Sea Pigeon.* . . N. Atlantic, very abundant. . . *[Cepphus] grylle.* **1910** Eaton *Birds NY* 1.106, The Black guillemot, sometimes called Sea pigeon, is an uncommon winter visitant south of Cape Cod. **1917** (1923) *Birds Amer.* 1.24, Along the coast of Maine the numerous rocky islands . . afford favorite nesting places for numerous sea-fowl, among which the Black Guillemot, or "Sea Pigeon," is by no means rare. **1953** Jewett *Birds WA* 320, The pigeon guillemot is a friendly species, known to many who love the water as the sea pigeon. **1977** Bull–Farrand *Audubon Field Guide Birds* 347, *Black Guillemot.* . . Locally called Sea Pigeon.

b The long-billed dowitcher (*Limnodromus griseus***). esp NJ**

1888 Trumbull *Names of Birds* 161 **NJ,** Dowitcher [=*Limnodromus griseus*]. . . More commonly termed, however, at Cape May City, *sea-pigeon.* (It is scarcely necessary to mention that the latter is a guillemot name, as guillemots are not liable to be confused with birds that interest gunners and sportsmen.) **1937** (1965) Stone *Bird Studies* 1.479 **NJ,** *Limnodromus griseus griseus.* . . The Dowitcher or "Sea Pigeon" of the local gunners, . . is now a common and regular transient about Cape May. **1946** Hausman *Eastern Birds* 283, *Limnodromus griseus.* . . Sea Pigeon. . . They feed and fly in close flocks and allow the observer to approach quite closely before taking wing.

c =black tern.

1924 Howell *Birds AL* 33, Black Tern; "Sea Pigeon". . . I found a flock of more than a hundred of these terns in their handsome black spring dress, standing quietly in close ranks on a mud flat. **1955** Forbush–May *Birds* 239, *Black Tern.* . . Sea Pigeon. . . It appears in considerable numbers on the South Atlantic and Gulf coasts . . during its periodic migrations, but at all other times it is a bird of the interior. **1968–70** *DARE* (Qu. Q10, . . *Water birds and marsh birds*) Inf **MA**78, Sea pigeon is an American tern; **NY**47, Sea pigeon [*DARE* Ed: This Inf may refer instead to another sense].

d A gull such as Bonaparte's gull (*Larus philadelphia***).**

1917 (1923) *Birds Amer.* 1.52, *Bonaparte's Gull.* . . *Other Names.* . . Sea Pigeon. **1946** Hausman *Eastern Birds* 316, *Larus philadelphia.* . . Sea Pigeon. . . A small gull, only about half as large as the Herring Gull. **1950** Writers' Round Table *Padre Is.* 119 **csTX,** The wings of "sea pigeons" (gulls) made up most of the cargo. These lonely sailboats are not now plying the Laguna Madre nor supplying milady with feathered ornaments, as protective laws have been passed. **1953** Jewett *Birds WA* 304, *Larus philadelphia.* . . Sea Pigeon.

e =harlequin duck. obs

1792 Belknap *Hist. NH* 168, Lord and Lady, or Sea pigeon, *Anas histrionica?*

sea pike n [*OED2* 1601 → for "one of various fishes"] Cf **saltwater pike**

1 A needlefish 1, usu *Strongylura marina.*

1787 [see **sea snipe 2**]. **1855** Smithsonian Inst. *Annual Rept. for 1854* 346 **PA,** *Belone truncata* [=*Strongylura marina*]—The Bill-Fish—Sea-Pike—Silver Gar-Fish. . . They have been seen at Columbia, Pennsylvania, in the Susquehanna. **1859** (1968) Bartlett *Americanisms* 32, *Billfish.* (*Belone truncata.*) A small sea-fish fond of running up into freshwater during the summer, and often taken a considerable distance from the ocean. Also called Sea-pike, Silver Gar-fish, etc. **1906** NJ State Museum *Annual Rept. for 1905* 204, *Tylosurus marinus* [=*Strongylura marina*] . . Sea Pike. . . A good food-fish, but avoided usually on account of the greenish color of the bones and flesh, especially by the ignorant, who regard it as poisonous. **1946** LaMonte *N. Amer. Game Fishes* 18, The Needlefishes—Genera: *Strongylura; Ablennes.* . . Names: Gar, . . Sea Pike.

2 A snook, usu *Centropomus undecimalis.*

1890 *Century Dict.* 5445, *Sea-pike.* . . A fish of the family *Centropomidae.* . . They . . resemble the pike in the elongation of their form. . . The oldest known species is *Centropomus undecimalis.* **1933** LA Dept. of Conserv. *Fishes* 69, The Snook—*Centropomus undecimalis.* . . Sergeant Fish, Robalo and Sea Pike are among the species' popular names. . . Occurs in the Gulf of Mexico from Florida to Texas and extends southward in the Atlantic.

sea pink n Also *seaside pink* [*OED2* 1731 → for *Armeria maritima*]

A marsh pink 1, usu *Sabatia stellaris.*

1901 Lounsberry *S. Wild Flowers* 427, *S[abatia] stellaris,* sea or marsh pink, . . extends from Florida along the coast as far northward as Maine. Locally it is much beloved. **1911** NJ State Museum *Annual Rept. for 1910* 639, *Sabatia stellaris.* . . Sea Pink. . . Their stems and leaves are somewhat inconspicuous, and it sometimes looks as if the pink stars might have been scattered broadcast over the low coarse grass and rushes of the meadow. . . *Sabatia gracilis.* . . Slender Sea Pink. . . Local and not always clearly distinct from the last. **1948** Pearson *Sea Flavor* 54 **NH,** Anyone who walks on the salt meadows in midsummer knows the friendly rosy faces of the sea pinks, or marsh pinks as they are commonly called. **1953** Greene–Blomquist *Flowers South* 99, Seaside-Pink (*Sabatia stellaris*)—This is one of the showiest flowers at the seacoast, growing in brackish marshes but more often seen hiding and back of the dunes. **1976** Bruce *How to Grow Wildflowers* 205, Out in the meadow among the rough Black Rush and Cordgrass blooms the soft blue Sea-lavender (*Limonium carolinianum*) in company with starry Sea-pinks (*Sabatia stellaris* and *S. campanulata*) the color of pink nougat.

sea plover n [*OED2* at *sea* sb. 22.c 1682 "a local name for *Squatarola helvetica*"]

=phalarope.

1937 (1965) Stone *Bird Studies* 2.516, *Phalaropus fulicarius.* . . The fishermen of the [Cape Cod] fleet were all familiar with the phalaropes [that they saw near Cape May, New Jersey] and called them "Bull-birds," "Sea Geese" and "Sea Plover," names which they apparently applied as well to the small species.

seapoose n Also *sea pouce*, ~ *purse*, ~ *puss*, *sepoose* [Partial folk-etym of an Algonquian word; cf Delaware *sepus* small brook] **esp seNY, neNJ**

1 An inlet of the sea, esp an artificial channel connecting a body of water with the sea; a pond so connected.

1650 in 1874 Southampton NY *Records* 1.69, [They] are to have for their paines 3s per day at the seapoose. **1658** *Ibid* 132, It was granted by the towne that Mr Raynor and Iohn Iessup shall have 6 acres granted them . . instead of the meadow which was digged vp for the west sepoose. **1874** *Ibid* 69, "Seapoose" is an Indian word and signifies "little river" as found iv [sic] these records it almost always refers to the inlet connecting Meacox bay with the ocean. **1939** *LANE* Map 40, 1 inf, **eLong Is. NY,** [ˌsij'puws], a pond with an artificial outlet to the sea (for drainage).

2 A whirlpool, undertow.

1842 Hawes *Sporting Scenes* 1.102 **seNY,** I kept watch of him—when I came to a sea poose—I went in to the east of it. **1860** *Daily True Amer.* (Trenton NJ) 14 Aug 3/1 **ceNJ,** Both had nearly reached their friends, when they were swept away into the deep current and eddies between the shore and the sand bar over which the surf breaks, and which is known to the Long Branch fishermen as the "sea-poose." **1890** *Scribner's Mag.* 8.102, As the word is ignored by Webster, I shall invent my own spelling and write it "sea-poose." This term is loosely used on different parts of the coast, but the true significance of it is briefly this: There will sometimes come, at every bathing-ground, days when the ocean seems to lose its head and to act in a very capricious way. On such occasions it often happens that the beach is cut away at some one point, presumably where the sand happens to be softer and less capable of resisting the action of the water. There will then be found a little bay indenting the shore, perhaps ten feet, perhaps ten yards. The waves rolling into such a cove are deflected somewhat by its sides and "set" together at its head, so that two wings of a breaker, so to speak, meet and, running straight out from the point of junction, form a sort of double "under-tow," which will, if the conditions that cause it continue, cut out along its course a depression or trench of varying depth and length. It can be readily understood that such a trench tends to strengthen the current that causes it, and these two factors, acting and reacting upon each other, occasion what might be called an artificial "under-tow" which is sometimes strong enough to carry an unwary bather some distance out. **1890** *Century Dict.* 5445, *Sea-purse.* . . A swirl of the undertow making a small whirlpool on the surface of the water; a local outward current, dangerous to bathers. Also called *sea-pouce* and *sea-puss*. [*Century* Ed: New Eng. and New Jersey coasts.] **1899** *Century Illustr. Mag.* 58.213, One day, while bathing off Long Branch, Richard Stockton . . of Trenton, New Jersey, found himself suddenly caught in a sea-puss . . Just after he had saved himself he heard an outcry from the water. Turning, he saw another man being drawn under by the treacherous eddy. **1904** *NY Tribune* (NY) 29 May sec 2 7/1 **Queens NYC,** McDonald was a good swimmer, but, getting caught in a sea puss, was shot out to the deep sea with great velocity. **1939** *LANE* Map 40, 1 inf, **eLong Is. NY,** ['sijpuws], a whirlpool in the sea at the outlet of a pond.

sea poppy n [*OED2* at *sea* sb. 22.f 1562]

A **horn poppy,** usu *Glaucium flavum*.

1903 Porter *Flora PA* 145, *Glaucium Glaucium.* . . *Yellow Horned or Sea Poppy.* . . Long Island and southward near the coast to Va. **1949** Moldenke *Amer. Wild Flowers* 29, Conspicuous and very showy in waste places and especially near the coast . . is the *seapoppy, Glaucium flavum*. **1976** Bailey–Bailey *Hortus Third* 512, *Glaucium.* . . Horned poppy, sea p[oppy].

sea pork n [See quot 1981]

A colonial sea squirt of the genus *Amaroucium*.

1885 in 1888 Kingsley *Riverside Nat. Hist.* 3.58, *Amarœcium*, a genus [of compound ascidians] common on our coasts, forms large colonies. . . The general color is much like that of boiled salt pork, . . and the fishermen . . call them sea-pork. **1935** Pratt *Manual Invertebrate Animals* 742, *A[maroucium] stellatum.* . . Colonies large, . . enclosed by a common gelatinous tunic, and called "*sea pork*" by fishermen; color pale bluish or pinkish; . . common from Cape Cod to North Carolina. **1981** Meinkoth *Audubon Field Guide Seashore* 730, *Northern Sea Pork.* . . Cream-colored with red or orange individuals. *Colony fleshy, soft,* with long, slender individuals embedded vertically in the soft substance. . . A large colony of this compound tunicate resembles a piece of

salt pork. A related species, the Common Sea Pork . . , is similar in color and in range, but . . is more firm and rubbery. . . These fleshy colonies are sometimes hooked and brought up by fishermen.

sea possum n Also *possum ray*

A **skate** n[1] (here: *Raja eglanteria*).

1906 NJ State Museum *Annual Rept. for 1905* 72, *Raja eglanteria.* . . Skate. Brier Ray. Possum Ray. Sea Possum. Bob Tailed Skate.

sea potato n

1 A sea squirt of the genus *Boltenia*. Cf **sea peach**

1874 *Harper's New Mth. Mag.* 49.226, The sea-potato is not remotely a relative, but the likeness of *Boltenia reniformis* to that esculent is very noticeable. Its stem looks like one of those roots which are occasionally attached to a potato. **1890** *Century Dict.* 5445, *Sea-potato.* . . An ascidian of some kind, as *Boltenia reniformis* or *Ascidia mollis*. [*Century* Ed: Local, U.S.] **1939** Natl. Geogr. Soc. *Fishes* 318, Young of the tall *Sea Potato*, or "sea squirt" . . , swim about when first hatched like tadpoles. **2000** (acc) *Center for Coastal Studies* (Internet) **eMA,** Some sea squirts common to the area are stalked tunicate, also known as sea potato (*Boltenia ovifera*) (body 3″ or 76 mm long, stalk 12″ or 30 cm long) [etc].

2 A marine alga (*Leathesia difformis*).

1942 Hylander *Plant Life* 38, *Leathesia* is known as the Sea Potato because of its brown color and tuberous appearance. It is a widely distributed marine plant found attached to rocks around low tide mark throughout the North Atlantic. . . The soft, rounded "potatoes" are frequently washed up on the beaches after storms and very high tides. **2000** *DARE* File—Internet **eNY,** Leathesia difformis—Sea potato; rats brains.

sea pouce, sea purse See **seapoose**

sea purslane n [*OED2* at *sea* sb. 22.f 1548 →]

An **orach** (*Atriplex hortensis*).

1944 Abrams *Flora Pacific States* 2.77, *Atriplex hortensis.* . . Garden Orache or Sea Purslane. . . Low ground. . . Introduced about Klamath Falls, Oregon, and in the San Francisco Bay region. **1959** Anderson *Flora AK* 202, *A[triplex] hortensis.* . . Sea Purslane. . . Introduced at Fairbanks. **1973** Hitchcock–Cronquist *Flora Pacific NW* 95, Occ[asional] escape reported from various parts of our area . . garden o[rache], sea purslane.

sea puss See **seapoose**

sea quail n

1 =**ruddy turnstone.** [See quot 1955]

1888 Trumbull *Names of Birds* 186 **CT,** In Connecticut at Saybrook and Lyme, [the turnstone is called] *sea quail*. **1910** Eaton *Birds NY* 358, The Turnstone, Calico-back, . . and Sea quail as this species is called, . . is primarily a beach bird and a maritime species. **1925** (1928) Forbush *Birds MA* 1.478, *Ruddy Turnstone.* . . *Sea-quail.* . . Quite a common bird in migration along much of the New England coast. . . In the autumn it often becomes very fat and in excellent condition for the table. **1955** MA Audubon Soc. *Bulletin* 39.446, *Ruddy Turnstone.* . . Sea Quail (Mass., Conn. This name may refer to its full breast and partially ruddy plumage).

2 An auklet, esp Cassin's auklet (*Ptychoramphus aleuticus*) or the crested auklet (*Aethia cristatella*). [See quot 1917]

1917 (1923) *Birds Amer.* 1.20, *Cassin's Auklet.* . . Pacific coast of North America. . . Because of its plump shape and size, it has been called a "Sea Quail." *Ibid* 21, *Crested Auklet.* . . Sea Quail. . . Coasts and islands of Bering Sea and north Pacific. **1955** U.S. Arctic Info. Center *Gloss.* 71, *Sea quail.* A common name for any of the small auklets, particularly the 'crested auklet.'

3 A **dowitcher** (here: *Limnodromus griseus*). Cf **sea pigeon b, quail snipe**

1923 U.S. Dept. Ag. *Misc. Circular* 13.51 **NY,** Dowitcher (Limnodromus griseus). . . Vernacular Names. . . In local use. . . Sea-quail (Long Id., N.Y.)

sea raven n

A **sculpin 1** (here: *Hemitripterus americanus*).

[**1672** Josselyn *New-Englands Rarities* 29, Sea Raven.] **1836** Richardson *Fauna Boreali-Amer.* 3.50, *The Sea-raven* . . inhabits the cod-banks on the coast of New York, Nova Scotia, and the Gulf of St. Lawrence. **1873** in 1878 Smithsonian Inst. *Misc. Coll.* 14.2.23, *Hemitripterus acadianus* [=*H. americanus*]. . . Sea-raven; yellow sculpin.

Newfoundland to Cape Hatteras. **1921** *Copeia* 99.73 **Long Is. NY,** *Hemitripterus americanus.* Sea Raven. **1933** John G. Shedd Aquarium *Guide* 133, Although a northern fish, the Sea Raven is common at Cape Cod in the winter and is even seen as far south as New York. **1955** Zim–Shoemaker *Fishes* 125, *Sea Raven,* a larger sculpin up to 20 in. long and weighing up to 5 lb., has large teeth and can bite severely when caught. The mottled skin is prickly. The Sea Raven swells up when caught.

search n, v Usu |sɜ(r)č|; also **chiefly Sth, S Midl** *old-fash* |sɑ(r)č| Pronc-spp *saach, sarch* Cf **learn**
Std senses, var forms.
   1813 in 1956 Eliason *Tarheel Talk* 317 **NC,** Sarch. **1823** Cooper *Pioneers* 2.233 **cNY,** They are wilcome to sarch among the coals and ashes. **1886** *S. Bivouac* 4.349 **sAppalachians,** Sarchin' (of medicine). **1893** Shands *MS Speech* 54, *Sarch* [sɑːč]. Negro and illiterate white for *search.* **1899** (1912) Green *VA Folk-Speech* 365, *Sarch.* . . Search. **1909** *DN* 3.365 **eAL, wGA,** *Sarch,* v. and n. Search. **1922** Gonzales *Black Border* 324 **sSC, GA coasts** [Gullah glossary], *Saa'ch*— search, searches, searched; searching; also examine, examined, etc. **1924** (1946) Greer-Petrie *Angeline Gits an Eyeful* 2 **csKY,** S'archin' around in the grass to see whur they'd lit. **1942** McAtee *Dial. Grant Co. IN Suppl. 1* 8 (as of 1890s), *Sarchin'* . . searching. **1942** Hall *Smoky Mt. Speech* 42 **wNC, eTN,** [ɑɚ] for [ɚ] is rapidly becoming obsolete. Nevertheless, it is preserved in the speech of a few old people, who may use it in *learn* . . *search.* . . (Mount) *Sterling.* **a1975** Lunsford *It Used to Be* 158 **sAppalachians,** The word "sarch" is for "search." **1991** *Macoupin Co. Enquirer* (Carlinville IL) **cwIL** 6, [From a 1961 issue quoting "oldsters":] Specimens are not as scarce as hen's teeth and those who sarch keerfully will oncover them.

searcy See **sirsee**

searer See **sierra**

sea robber n Cf **robber gull**
   =**pomarine jaeger.**
   1917 (1923) *Birds Amer.* 1.33, *Pomarine Jaeger.* . . Sea Robber. [*Ibid* 34, A Tern which had just caught a fish. . . might dart and dodge, [but] the Jaeger followed every move, and by savage attacks finally compelled it to drop the fish. Then by a spectacular swoop the robber would seize the booty in mid-air.] **1946** Hausman *Eastern Birds* 300, *Stercorarius pomarinus.* . . Sea Robber. . . Our largest jaeger.

sea robin n
   1 Any of var fishes, as:
   a A gurnard of the family Triglidae, usu of the genus *Prionotus.* For other names of those of this genus see **flying fish 2, grumbler 1, grunter 1;** for other names of var spp of this genus see **pigfish b, robin 6, sea bat 4, wingfish**
   1814 in 1815 Lit. & Philos. Soc. NY *Trans.* 1.430, *Gurnard, or Sea Robin.* (*Trigla lineata* [=*Prionotus evolans*].) With a line from head to tail along and below the lateral line. **1844** *Amer. Jrl. Science* 47.59 **CT,** Prionotus strigatus. . . Sea Robin, Grunter. **1884** Goode *Fisheries U.S.* 1.255, *The Sea-robin or gurnard family*—Triglidae. This family is represented on our Atlantic coast by several species, some of them being quite abundant. **1894** *Outing* 24.263 **seNY,** Here's a sea-robin! A curious, grunting fellow he was, perhaps ten inches long, with a great fin, like a butterfly's wing, projecting from each side of his throat. **1968–70** *DARE* (Qu. P4, *Saltwater fish that are not good to eat*) Infs **NJ21, 22, 39, NY76, VA41,** Sea robin; **NJ60,** Sea robin—fins spread like wings; **NY118,** Sea robins—all bony. [*DARE* Ed: Some of these Infs may refer instead to other senses below.] **1968** *DARE* Tape **DE3,** [Inf:] We have sea robins, they're another fish that annoys you quite a lot, that are something like a flying fish. . . [FW:] They've got those wide wings on the side. **1983** *Audubon Field Guide N. Amer. Fishes* 720, *Triglidae.* . . The bottom-dwelling searobins are small to medium-sized fishes, variably colored, and easily recognized by . . the usually large, winglike pectoral fins. *Ibid* 721, *Prionotus carolinus.* . . is thought to be the most common searobin in Chesapeake Bay. . . Searobins are a good food fish rather similar to goosefishes in taste. **1998** *DARE* File **Philadelphia PA,** About 45–50 years ago, when I and my dad fished in a bay near the Atlantic seacoast, we routinely caught a fish that we called a sea robin. About 6–8 inches long, with muted brown, yellow, and red splotches and a paunch, this fish made sounds when we brought it out of the water and into the boat and then released it—to us, it was a novelty, not food.
   b A **toadfish** of the genus *Opsanus.*

1879 U.S. Natl. Museum *Proc.* 2.336 **FL,** These fish were called in Pensacola by the names "Sea Robin" and "Sarpo." **1884** Goode *Fisheries U.S.* 1.251, A form found only in the Gulf, *Batrachus pardus* [= *Opsanus p.*] . . is known to the fishermen as the "Sarpo" and the "Searobin." **1911** U.S. Bur. Census *Fisheries 1908* 315, Sea robin. . . The name is also applied to the toadfish (*Opsanus tau*) in the Gulf.

   c =**flying gurnard.** Cf **flying robin**
   1933 John G. Shedd Aquarium *Guide* 136, *Dactylopterus volitans*— Flying Sea Robin. In the Flying Sea Robins, the pectorals are very much longer than in the other Sea Robins. . . While this fish is able to move in the air for short distances, it can not accomplish long flights like those of the true Flyingfish. **1949** *Sun* (Baltimore MD) 17 Sept 10/8 (Hench Coll.), Miller . . reported catching a sea robin, which is very much like a flying fish.

   d A **puffer** n[1] **1,** prob either *Sphoeroides maculatus* or *Lagocephalus laevigatus.* Cf **blowfish 1**
   1968 *DARE* (Qu. P4, *Saltwater fish that are not good to eat*) Inf **NJ41,** Sea robin—same as blowfish; used to be considered inedible, now considered a delicacy.

   2 =**red-breasted merganser.**
   1888 Trumbull *Names of Birds* 68 **MA,** Red-breasted merganser. . . At Rowley, Mass., sea-robin or *robin* simply. **1982** Elman *Hunter's Field Guide* 230, *Mergus serrator.* . . Sea robin. . . The drake's black-speckled, reddish-brown breastband under a white collar is an aid to identification.

   3 =**knot** n[2]. Cf **beach robin, robin 5, robin snipe 1**
   1966 *DARE* (Qu. Q10, . . *Water birds and marsh birds*) Inf **NC12,** Sea robin or beach robin.

Sears See **Sears-Roebuck 1**

Sears-and-Roebuck See **Sears-Roebuck**

Sears-and-Roebuck teeth See **Sears-Roebuck 2**

Sears and Sawbuck n Cf **Monkey Ward**
   The mail-order house of Sears, Roebuck and Company.
   1964 Jackman–Long *OR Desert* 334, Of course, everyone had catalogs from Monkey Ward and Sears and Sawbuck. **1995** *DARE* File **csWI** (as of 1940s), Sears and Sawbuck.

Sears-Roebuck adj Also *Sears-and-Roebuck*
   1 also *Sears;* in phrr *Sears building, Sears-Roebuck headquarters* (or *house, library, storeroom*): An outdoor toilet. [From the use of catalog pages as toilet paper] *joc*
   1950 *WELS* (An outside toilet building: Joking names) 1 inf, **cWI,** Sears-Roebuck headquarters. **1954** Harder Coll. **cwTN,** Sears-Roebuck house, Sears-Roebuck storeroom. . . Joking name for an outdoor toilet. **1966–69** *DARE* (Qu. M21b, *Joking names for an outside toilet building*) [Inf **PA226,** Sears and Roebuck;] **MI19,** Sears-Roebuck library. **1986** Pederson *LAGS Concordance* (Outhouse) 1 inf, **csMS,** Sears building, catalog was kept there.
   2 in phrr *Sears-(and-)Roebuck teeth:* False teeth. Cf **I-bought-you teeth, roebuckers**
   1967–70 *DARE* (Qu. X13b, *Joking names for false teeth*) Infs **GA84, LA11, MS86, NJ67, OH27, TX54,** Sears-(and-)Roebuck teeth.
   3 Inexperienced; incompetent. Cf **mail-order cowboy**
   1917 in 1972 *AmSp* 47.97 [Slang of the AEF], Two tents of Shavetails (i.e. Reverse Officers, Ninety-Day Wonders, Sears & Roebuck Specials, Goldbricks, As-You-Weres, etc.) have been attached to us for instruction purposes. **1927** *DN* 5.462 [Underworld jargon], Sears Roebuck detective. . . A rural Sherlock Holmes. **1930** *AmSp* 5.385 [AEF English], A Sears and Roebuck lieutenant. A new lieutenant. **1932** *AmSp* 7.270 [Oil field language], Sears-Roebuck driller. . . An inexperienced and incapable driller. [**1942** *AmSp* 17.104 [Truck driver lingo], Sears, Roebuck license. Poor driver.] [**1966–68** *DARE* (Qu. N12, . . *Somebody who drives carelessly or not well*) Inf **NJ10,** Bought your license at Sears-Roebuck; **NH1,** He got his license from Sears and Roebuck.] **1968** Adams *Western Words* 271, Sears Roebuck guy—A logger's name for a novice.

Sears-Roebuck headquarters (or house, library, storeroom) See **Sears-Roebuck 1**

Sears-Roebuck teeth See **Sears-Roebuck 2**

sea sage n
   A **groundsel tree** (here: *Baccharis halimifolia*).

1974 Morton *Folk Remedies* 35 **SC,** *Sea sage. . . Baccharis halimifolia. . .* Leaves . . elliptic to obovate, . . dull, dark-green on upper side, lighter below. . . Abundant in salt marshes [etc]. . . Decoction of leafy branch tips taken as remedy for fever.

sea sand reed (grass) See **sand reed 1**

seasash n Cf **ambrosia 1**

A **Jerusalem oak 1.**

1919 *DN* 5.32 **eKY,** *Amberosia. . .* Metathesis for ambrosia, an odorific yard flower, sometimes called "seasash." **1940** (1978) Still *River of Earth* 72 **KY,** They carried yard flowers and wild blooms in their arms: honeysuckle and Easter flowers, and seasash.

seaside bean See **sea bean 2**

seaside daisy n

1 A **fleabane** (here: *Erigeron glaucus*) native to California and Oregon. [See quot 1906] Also called **beach aster**

1906 (1918) Parsons *Wild Flowers CA* 312, *Seaside Daisy. Erigeron glaucum* [sic]. . . Almost anywhere upon our Coast, "within the roar of a surf-tormented shore," we can find the beautiful blossoms. . . They present a most delightful combination of color in their old-gold centers, violet rays, and rather pale foliage. **1934** Haskin *Wild Flowers Pacific Coast* 367, *Seaside Daisy. . .* This is neither an aster or a daisy, but a fleabane. **1954** CA Div. Beaches & Parks *Pt. Lobos Wild Flowers* 19, Seaside Daisies are seldom found more than half a mile from shore. . . Seaside Daisies . . begin to bloom by the middle of April. **1973** Hitchcock–Cronquist *Flora Pacific NW* 514, Seaside d[aisy] . . *E[rigeron] glaucus.*

2 See **sea daisy 2.**

seaside goldenrod n

A **goldenrod 1** (here: *Solidago sempervirens*) of the Atlantic and Gulf coasts.

1848 Gray *Manual of Botany* 212, *S[olidago] sempervirens. . . Seaside Golden-rod. . .* Salt marshes, or rocks on the shore, Maine to Penn. and southward. **1902** (1909) Mathews *Field Book Amer. Wild Flowers* 476, *Seaside Golden-rod. . .* A species frequenting salt-marshes and sea-beaches. **1948** Pearson *Sea Flavor* 148 **NH,** When summer draws on toward fall, the first copper-gold tints of *Solidago sempervirens,* the seaside goldenrod, begin to knit mufflers around the necks of marshes where they fit into the mainland. **1972** Brown *Wildflowers LA* 220, *Seaside Goldenrod. . .* Widespread and abundant along the Gulf Coast . . in fresh to saline marshes.

seaside oat(s) See **sea oat(s)**

seaside pea See **sea pea**

seaside pink See **sea pink**

seaside plum n

=**sea grape.**

1775 (1962) Romans *Nat. Hist. FL* 21, Coccoloba, or sea side plumb, growing in bunches, an almost round veined leaf, & the fruit blue, inclined to purple. **1898** Sudworth *Forest Trees* 63 **FL,** *Coccoloba uvifera. . .* Southern Florida. . . *Names in use.*—Sea Grape (Fla.); Seaside Plum.

seaside sparrow n

A sparrow *(Ammodramus maritimus)* of the Atlantic and Gulf coasts. Also called **meadow chippy**

1886 Amer. Ornith. Union *Code* 269, Seaside Sparrow . . Salt marshes of the Atlantic coast. **1899** in 1900 LA Soc. Naturalists *Proc.* 107, *Ammodramus maritimus. . . Seaside Sparrow.* Very common on the coast, especially in the salt marshes and on the borders of the lakes. **1914** Eaton *Birds NY* 2.299, *Seaside Sparrow. . .* Rarely seen far from the cover of the rank grasses which cover its chosen habitat. . . It has a chippering song of no great melody. **1937** Natl. Geogr. Soc. *Book of Birds* 2.272, *Northern Seaside Sparrow. . .* Never yet have I seen one except within sight or sound of the ocean. One may never expect to find them except in a salt marsh, or perhaps in vegetation growing on the sands in the immediate vicinity of the marsh. **1970** *DARE* (Qu. Q21, . . *Kinds of sparrows*) Inf **VA47,** Seaside sparrow. **1978** C. Harrison *Field Guide Nests, Eggs & Nestlings N. Amer. Birds* 394 *(OED2),* Seaside Sparrow . . breeds on salt marshes.

sea smelt n Cf **smelt**

A **kingfish 1** (here: *Menticirrhus americanus*).

1935 Caine *Game Fish* 148 **Sth,** *Menticirrhus americanus. . .* Sea Smelt. . . *Waters frequented:* All along the surf, especially in sloughs.

sea snipe n

1 Any of var shore birds, as:

a =**marbled godwit.**

1897 *Auk* 14.288 **LA,** *Marbled Godwit.*—Commonly known as *Bècassine;* also as Sea Snipe. Quite common during the winter along the coast. **1916** *Times–Picayune* (New Orleans LA) 2 Apr 8, *Marbled Godwit. . .* Sea Snipe.—A large bird with a long bill that curves upward to a slight degree. . . Game bird.

b =**bluestocking 2.**

1916 *Times–Picayune* (New Orleans LA) 2 Apr 8, *American Avocet* (Recurvirostra americana). . . Blue Stockings, Sea Snipe.—The long slender bill that curves upward at the end at once identifies this webfooted wader.

c A phalarope, usu either the **northern phalarope** or the **red phalarope.** Cf **sea goose 1**

1897 *Atlantic Mth.* 80.392, The birds seen at the Isles of Shoals were doubtless either red phalaropes or northern phalaropes,—or, not unlikely, both,—"sea snipe" as they are often called. **1923** U.S. Dept. Ag. *Misc. Circular* 13.47 **seNY,** *Phalaropes. . . Vernacular Names. . .* Sea snipe (Long Id., N.Y.) **1956** MA Audubon Soc. *Bulletin* 40.21, *Red Phalarope. . .* Sea Snipe (Mass. These birds spend much time on the open sea.) . . *Northern Phalarope. . .* Sea Snipe (Mass.)

d =**Hudsonian curlew.**

1923 U.S. Dept. Ag. *Misc. Circular* 13.66 **LA,** *Hudsonian Curlew. . . Vernacular Names. . . In local use. . .* Sea snipe.

2 A **needlefish 1** (here: *Strongylura marina*).

1787 Gesellschaft Naturforschender Freunde *Schriften* 8.177, *Sea pike, Sea Snipe,* zu Neuyork. Es scheint dieser Fisch dem Esox Belone L. [= *Strongylura marina*] zunächst verwandt zu seyn. [=*Sea pike, Sea Snipe,* at New York. This fish appears to be most closely related to Esox Belone L. [=*Strongylura marina*].] **1911** U.S. Bur. Census *Fisheries 1908* 310, *Garfish (Tylosurus marinus* [=*Strongylura m.*]) . . is also called "needle-fish" in the Gulf of Mexico, . . and "tea-snipe [sic]," "silver gar," and "billfish" in different localities.

season n[1] **Sth, S Midl**

1 A seasonable rain or rainy spell, esp one that is opportune for crops or for tobacco-stripping.

[**1707** Sloane *Voyage* 1.xv **Jamaica,** After Seasons, *i.e.* three or four, or more days Rain, all manner of Provisions, Maiz, *Guinea* Corn, Pease, Patatas . . &c. are planted.] **1800** in 1969 Herndon *Wm. Tatham Tobacco* 14, The term, *season* for planting, signifies a shower of rain of sufficient quantity to wet the earth to a degree of moisture which may render it safe to draw the young plants from the plant bed, and transplant them into the hills which are prepared for them in the field, . . and these seasons generally commence in April, and terminate with what is termed the *long season in May;* which . . very frequently happens in June; and is the opportunity which the planter finds himself necessitated to seize with eagerness for the *pitching* of his crop. **1828** in 1956 Eliason *Tarheel Talk* 292 **cwNC,** If we could have seasons I do not regret our move. **1851** in 1927 Jones *FL Plantation Rec.* 380 **nwFL,** June 14th, a good season of Rain in the evening. **1856** *Ibid* 156 **nwFL,** The Seasons has bin good up to this time tho wee have every apearence of a drouth now. **1899** (1912) Green *VA Folk-Speech* 373, *Season* is a shower, or spell of rain. "Long season in May." **1903** *DN* 2.328 **seMO,** *Season. . .* A soaking rain. **1909** *DN* 3.367 **eAL, wGA,** *Season. . .* A heavy rainfall, rain sufficient to make the moisture of the top soil penetrate to the moisture of the subsoil. **1918** *DN* 5.19 **NC,** This cotton needs a good season. **1934** Hench Coll. **cVA,** *Long season*—long stretch of rainy weather. "Well, I think this is the long season, don't you?" a man said to me today, meaning that he thought that a stretch of rainy weather was beginning. **1944** *PADS* 2.70 **S Midl,** *Season. . .* Proper amount of moisture in the air to put tobacco in condition to handle without crumbling. **1950** Stuart *Hie Hunters* 110 **eKY,** "We've got to work while we got a season," Peg said. "That's the reason we're workin' early and late hours to get this [=stripping tobacco] done." **1986** Pederson *LAGS Concordance* (A steady drizzle) 1 inf, **ceMS,** Season; 1 inf, **neLA,** Get season enough to make it grow. **1986** *DARE* File **cnTN** (as of c1920), After an adequate rain at a time when crops needed periodical rains to grow, it would be said, "Hit come a right good 'season'". *Ibid* **wNC** (as of c1920s), "We've had good season"; "we've had no season, the corn's mostly dried up." **1991** *Ibid* **cMD** (as of c1930), And the flower seeds are in, and soon they are up, and before you can turn around comes a "loblolly rain" and behold, there's a "season." . . No gardener thinks of meals or mending or any such unnecessary things when there is "season."

2 in phr *in good season:* In good condition for planting. [*OED2 season* sb. 3.b "*local*"]

1966 *DARE* (Qu. L26, *Sayings about corn and other important crops around here;* total Infs questioned, 75) Inf **FL27**, Plant when ground is in good season, [when] moisture and temperature are just right.

season n² [*OED2 season* sb. 19 "*Obs.*"]
Seasoning.

1966–70 *DARE* Tape **CA193**, And we used this mint for season; we used this oregano for season, you know; **FL36A**, I got a food mill; . . run it through that and put my season in it, which is onions. . . I get celery, . . green peppers . . and vinegar. **c1970** Pederson *Dial. Surv. Rural GA,* 1 inf, **seGA**, You got the right season there, you got something good to eat. **1986** Pederson *LAGS Concordance,* 1 inf, **cnLA**, Onion season—used in preparing chitterlings.

season v
To add cream or sugar to (tea or coffee); hence ppl adj *seasoned;* n *seasoning* cream or sugar as an ingredient in tea or coffee.

1897 *KS Univ. Qrly.* (ser B) 6.56 **KS**, *Seasoning*—sugar and cream in coffee. **1967** *DARE* FW Addit **cePA**, To *season*—one can *season* tea, i.e., put in sugar. She said, "The tea is seasoned."

seasoning vbl n [Transf from std sense in ref to lumber]
Drying by exposure to air; see quot.

1979 *DARE* File **cSC** [Black], *Seasoning*—Good and dry. Let the clothes stay on the line; they need *seasoning.*

seasoning n See **season** v

seasoning meat n Sth, S Midl
Salt pork or bacon.

1966 Dakin *Dial. Vocab. Ohio R. Valley* 2.333, The following are all used by some speaker for side meat in all three conditions—salted, smoked, and fresh: *bacon . . seasoning meat . . boiling meat.* **1966** *DARE* (Qu. H38, . . *Words for bacon [including joking ones]*) Inf **MS23**, Seasoning meat. **1971** Wood *Vocab. Change* 369 **Sth**, [Blocks of meat cut from the sides of a hog and salted:] Volunteered words: *fatback . . seasoning meat . . hull.* **1986** Pederson *LAGS Concordance* **Gulf Region** *(Salt pork)* 7 infs, Seasoning meat; 1 inf, **ceTN**, Seasoning meat (= streak of lean); 1 inf, **cTN**, Seasoning meat—with some lean; 1 inf, **seLA**, Seasoning meat—modern term.

sea speargrass n
An **alkali grass 2** (here: *Puccinellia fasciculata*).

1848 Gray *Manual of Botany* 594, S[clerochloa] *arenaria* [=*Puccinellia fasciculata*]. . . Sea Spear-grass. . . Branches of the panicle spreading when young. **1912** Baker *Book of Grasses* 217, *Sea Spear-grass.* . . Salt marshes and sea beaches. . . Labrador to New Jersey. **1948** Pearson *Sea Flavor* 149 **NH**, Only a few times a year do the surging tides roll up over the level stretches where the fox, sea spear, and spike grasses, which combine to make marsh hay, grow.

sea spinach n CA
A naturalized plant *(Tetragonia tetragonioides)* that can be cooked like spinach.

1901 Jepson *Flora CA* 189, Sea Spinach. Succulent perennial herb. . . Beaches of San Francisco Bay. **1961** Thomas *Flora Santa Cruz* 157 **cwCA**, Sea Spinach. . . Sandy soils and salt marshes along the coast and San Francisco Bay. **1974** Munz *Flora S. CA* 58, *Sea-Spinach.* . . Natur[alized] along beaches and near salt marshes along the coast to Ore.

sea squab n Cf **sea robin 1d**
A **puffer** n¹ **1** (here: *Sphoeroides maculatus*).

1952 Tracy *Coast Cookery* 296, *Swellfish.* . . Also known as sea squab in some restaurants and fish markets. **1968** *DARE* (Qu. P4, *Saltwater fish that are not good to eat*) Inf **MD36**, Sea squab—same as blowfish—

now people eat them, but they didn't in past; [(Qu. P2, . . *Kinds of saltwater fish caught around here . . good to eat*) Inf **MD45**, Swimming toad—also called sea squash [skwɔš]]. **1973** Knight *Cook's Fish Guide* 387, Puffer. . sea squab provençal. **1976** Warner *Beautiful Swimmers* 13 **Delmarva**, The blowfish. . . [or] the delicious sea squabs, as they are known on the market, have been a good late summer fishery. **1983** *Audubon Field Guide N. Amer. Fishes* 761, The Northern Puffer is used as food and marketed as "sea squab."

sea star n Cf **sea pink**
A **marsh pink 1** (here: either *Sabatia campestris* or *S. stellaris*).

1936 Whitehouse *TX Flowers* 98, *Sabbatia* [sic] *campestris* . . is also known as . . sea star. It . . is found on moist prairies throughout Central Texas from April to June. **1959** Carleton *Index Herb. Plants* 105, *Sea star:* Sabatia stellaris.

sea swallow n [*OED2* at *sea-swallow* 2.a "from their general resemblance to swallows" 1647 →]
A **tern,** esp the common *Sterna hirundo.*

1791 Bartram *Travels* 295, Sterna stolida [=*Anous s.*], the sea swallow, or noddy. **1813** (1824) Wilson *Amer. Ornith.* 7.80, From their long pointed wings they are generally known to seafaring people, and others residing near the sea shore, by the name of Sea-swallows. **1904** (1910) Wheelock *Birds CA* 45, Sea Swallow and Little Striker are the common names applied to this little tern [=*Sterna antillarum*], although sea swallow is used of all terns. The Least Tern is said to feed upon insects, and has the peculiar darting, skimming flight of swallows; hence the appellation "sea swallow" is particularly appropriate to it. **1916** *Times–Picayune* (New Orleans LA) 26 Mar mag sec 1, *Forster Tern* (Sterna forsteri) Sea Swallow; Pigeon Mer (a name applied to all the small terns). **1966–70** *DARE* (Qu. Q10, . . *Water birds and marsh birds*) Infs **GA11, NC85, NY34**, Sea swallow; **MI53**, Sea swallow—in this area it's called the tern; **MS81**, Sea swallow—on the coast; (Qu. Q20, . . *Kinds of swallows and birds like them*) Inf **NH18**, Sea swallow. **1977** Bull–Farrand *Audubon Field Guide Birds* 450, *Common Tern.* . . A grasp of the field marks of other terns is best gained by comparison with these most common of "sea swallows." . . They are seen flying gracefully over the water, searching for small fish and shrimp, which they capture by diving from the air.

seat back exclam
=**place back(s).**

1998 *DARE* File **nIN**, *Place backs!* I have heard this used among my friends here in the dormitory, but we primarily use . . "tap-tap-seatback." **2000** *Ibid* **cMN**, I work at a Bible Camp in central Minnesota and we have a variation of this [=*place backs*]. When someone gets up from his or her seat and wishes to return to it shortly, he or she must say, "Quack, quack, seat back," in order to get it back.

seater See **sitter**

sea tick See **seed tick 1**

sea tiger n Also *tiger of the sea* [*OED2* at *sea* sb. 22.d 1924 →]
A **barracuda** (here: *Sphyraena barracuda*).

1939 Natl. Geogr. Soc. *Fishes* 188, The tiger-of-the-sea is itself a savage fighter when hooked. *Ibid* 193, Well deserving its nickname of "Tiger of the Sea," the carnivorous *Barracuda* (Sphyraena barracuda) darts at its prey on sight and kills fish many times its own size. **1946** LaMonte *N. Amer. Game Fishes* 15, Great Barracuda. . . Names . . Tiger of the Sea, Sea Tiger. . . This is the largest of the barracudas. It averages from 5 to 10 pounds and has been known to weigh 100 pounds.

sea toad n [*OED2* "A name given to several fishes, as . . *Lophius piscatorius*" 1558 →]
1 A **sculpin 1;** see quots.

1787 Gesellschaft Naturforschender Freunde *Schriften* 8.145, Cottus Scorpius [=*Myoxocephalus aeneus*]. . . In Neu-York wird diese Art *Sea-toad* genannt; in Neufundland, wo sie häufiger und größer seyn sollen, nennt man sie *Scolping.* [=*Cottus Scorpius* [=*Myoxocephalus aeneus*]. . . In New York this species is called *Sea-toad;* in Newfoundland, where they are supposed to be more common and larger, they call them *Scolping.*] **1842** DeKay *Zool. NY* 4.52, This species [=*Myoxocephalus octodecemspinosus*], which, on account of its uncouth form, is regarded with aversion by fishermen, is nevertheless not a bad article of food. . . It is known under the various popular names of *Sculpin*, . . *Sea Toad*, and *Pig Fish*. . . It ranges from Virginia to Newfoundland, and perhaps still farther north. **1884** Goode *Fisheries U.S.* 1.258, *Cottidae*. . . On our Atlantic coast are found several species of this family, generally known by the name "Sculpin," and also by such titles as "Grubby," . . "Sea-toad," and "Pig-fish."

2 A **toadfish** (here: *Opsanus tau*). Cf **mud toad, oyster ~**

1890 *Century Dict.* 5449, *Sea-toad*. . . The toadfish, *Batrachus* [= *Opsanus*] *tau*.

sea trout n
Any of var fishes, as:

a =weakfish.

1769 Stork *Descr. East FL* 1.52, Those mostly made use of . . [include the] cat-fish, sea-trout, and black-fish. **1840** (1965) Moore *Map & Descr. TX* 36, Among these are red fish, grundiquoit, mullet, sea perch, sea trout, &c. **1874** *Forest & Stream* 1.411 **eMD**, Here [=in Baltimore] they call . . the weakfish sea trout. **1884** Goode *Fisheries U.S.* 1.362, *The Squeteague—Cynoscion regale*. . . In the Southern Atlantic States . . and with the other members of the genus [it] is spoken of under the name "Sea Trout" and "Salt-water Trout," though, of course, distinct from the "trout" of the fresh waters of the South, the large-mouth Black Bass. **1902** Jordan–Evermann *Amer. Fishes* 456, *Sea-trout—Cynoscion regalis*. . . Although essentially a coast and still-water fish, [it] . . sometimes runs up tidal waters and prefers the vicinity of river-mouths. Though seen in the markets everywhere, this fish is not much valued in the North, but in the South it is highly prized. *Ibid* 458, Owing to its shape and spots, it [=*Cynoscion nebulosus*] is known on the Southern coast as salmon or spotted sea-trout, names wholly inappropriate. **1931–33** *LANE Worksheets* **CT**, Chickrod [=*Cynoscion* spp] is known commercially as sea trout. **1936** Barnhart *Marine Fishes S. CA* 44, *Cynoscion parvipinnis*. . . has been called Sea-trout in southern California for so long that the official name, "Short-fin Sea-bass," is seldom used. **1951** Taylor *Surv. Marine Fisheries NC* 276, Sea Trout . . *Cynoscion regalis*. . . There are big runs from May to October off Long Island and New Jersey. . . Probably more than one species is found off North Carolina, but the only differentiation by fishermen is between this and the spotted trout, . . *Cynoscion nebulosus*. . . This [latter] fish . . runs somewhat smaller than the sea trout, with which fishermen and anglers confuse it. **1967–70** *DARE* (Qu. P2, *Kinds of saltwater fish caught around here . . good to eat*) Infs **CA25, CT42, NJ67**, Sea trout; **MD36**, White fish, sea trout—same thing. **1986** Pederson *LAGS Concordance* (*Saltwater fish*) 1 inf, **csAR**, 1 inf, **cwMS**, Sea trout; 1 inf, **nwFL**, Sea trout—Gulf fish; 2 infs, **seFL, neLA**, Sea trout—saltwater; 1 inf, **neTN**, A speckle sea trout; 1 inf, **ceTX**, Sea trout—in Gulf. **2000** *Houston Chron.* (TX) 22 Mar (Internet), Spotted seatrout (speckled trout), the backbone of the inshore sport fishery, should be a no-brainer.

b =brook trout.

1873 in 1878 *Smithsonian Inst. Misc. Coll.* 14.2.32, *Salmo immaculatus* [=*Salvelinus fontinalis*]. . . Sea Trout. Labrador to Nova Scotia. **1904** *Salmon & Trout* 320, There is no anatomical difference in the structure of the Eastern sea-trout from that seen in the Eastern speckled trout, hence the former has no specific classification other than *Salvelinus fontinalis*. *Ibid* 321, In Massachusetts these salt-water migrators are called "salters"; in all other sections, "sea-trout." **1974** *WI Univ. Fish Lake MI* 24, *Brook Trout—Salvelinus fontinalis* . . common names . . square-tail, sea trout.

c Any of var fishes found chiefly in California waters, as:

(1) =white sea bass.

1882 *U.S. Natl. Museum Bulletin* 16.579, *A[tractoscion] nobile*. . . White Sea Bass; Sea Trout. . . Pacific coast north to San Francisco; one of the largest and most valuable of our . . fishes, reaching a weight of 60 to 70 pounds. The flesh is firm and rich. **1884** Goode *Fisheries U.S.* 1.378, *White Sea Bass*. . . Everywhere known as the "Sea Bass" ("Sea Trout"). . . The young, while yet banded, are known as "Sea Trout," and generally considered a distinct species. **1953** Roedel *Common Fishes CA* 95, *White Seabass*. . . *Unauthorized Name*: Sea trout.

(2) A **greenling**: usu *Hexagrammos decagrammus*, but also *H. lagocephalus*.

1884 Goode *Fisheries U.S.* 1.267, *Green Rock Trout* (*Hexagrammus lagocephalus* . .). This species is confounded with others of this genus under the names of "Rock Trout," "Sea Trout" [etc]. . . *Spotted Rock Trout* (*Hexagrammus decagrammus* . .). From San Francisco southward, the names "Rock Trout" and "Sea Trout" are common. **1953** Roedel

Common Fishes CA 142, *Greenling Seatrout—Hexagrammos decagrammus*. . . This fish is usually called "seatrout" by California fishermen. In the Pacific Northwest "greenling" prevails. . . The fish is not remotely related to the trouts. **1955** Zim–Shoemaker *Fishes* 142, The Kelp Greenling . . is sometimes called Sea Trout or Rockfish, though both these names are misleading.

(3) =queenfish 1.

1953 Roedel *Common Fishes CA* 94, *Queenfish—Seriphus politus*. . . Central California south at least to San Juanico Bay, Baja California. . . Taken commercially chiefly with bait nets. . . *Unauthorized Names*: Herring, tomcod, shiner, seatrout.

(4) A **kingfish 1** (here: *Menticirrhus undulatus*).

1972 Sparano *Outdoors Encycl.* 386, California corbina, . . whiting, sea trout. . . *Menticirrhus undulatus*. . . from the Gulf of California north to Point Conception.

d =coho salmon.

1974 *WI Univ. Fish Lake MI* 17, *Coho Salmon* . . common names: coho, silver salmon, sea trout, blueback. **1983** Becker *Fishes WI* 307, *Oncorhynchus kisutch*. . . Sea trout, blueback. . . Inhabits Lakes Michigan and Superior and a number of their tributary streams.

sea turn n NEng
A wind off the ocean, often accompanied by fog or rain.

[**1643** Williams *Key into Language* 86, This Southwest wind is called by the New-English, the Sea turne, which comes from the Sunne in the morning, about nine or ten of the clock Southeast, and about South, and then strongest Southwest in the after-noone, and towards night, when it dies away.] **1690** (1892) Hammond *Diary* 154 **MA**, Fair weather & seaturns every day. **1792** Belknap *Hist. NH* 3.23, Sometimes the extreme heat of several days, produces, in the maritime parts, a sea turn, and in the inland parts, a whirlwind. **1815** (1846) *MA Hist. Soc. Coll.* 2d ser 3.216, The extreme heat of summer is mitigated by sea turns. **1883** *Atlantic Mth.* 25.765, A dull morning when the sea-turn was beginning to break in a thin, chilly rain. **1896** Jewett *Pointed Firs* 134 **ME**, No surprises of sea-turns or south-west sultriness might be feared. **1939** *LANE* Map 93 (*Shower*) 1 inf, **seMA**, Sea turn [si tɜn], a light rain liable to turn into a northeast storm. **1952** Smiley *Gloss. New Paltz NH*, New Hampshire Expression[:] "A sea turn"—Fog comes in from sea when wind changes. **2001** *NADS Letters* **MA**, Sea turn—I've heard this used down around Scituate, MA on the South Shore south of Boston, MA and north of Sagamore, MA. It was in reference to weather and the gentlemen had to have been middle aged, but that was ten or fifteen years ago.

sea watch n
An **angelica 1a** (here: *Angelica lucida*).

1961 Peck *Manual OR* 569, *A[ngelica] lucida*. . . Sea-watch. . . High banks and bluffs above the sea, to Alaska and Calif. **1973** Hitchcock–Cronquist *Flora Pacific NW* 320, Siberia to n Cal, also from Lab to NY; sea-watch. . . *A[ngelica] lucida*.

seaweed fern n [EDD at sea sb. 1.(14) 1865]
=hart's tongue 1.

1890 *Century Dict.* 5350, *Seaweed-fern*, the fern *Scolopendrium vulgare* [=*Asplenium scolopendrium*]. **1938** *Small Ferns SE States* 148, *Sea-weed fern*. . . Among rocks in shaded ravines and under limestone cliffs, Tenn., N.Y., Ont., and N.B.; also naturalized in Md.

sea widgeon n
1 =pintail 1. Cf **gray widgeon 2, kite-tail(ed) ~, widgeon**

1624 Smith *Genl. Hist. VA* 171, Neither hath the aire for her part been waiting with due supplies of many sorts of Fowles, as . . Sea-wigions, Gray-bitterns, Cormorants [etc]. **1888** Trumbull *Names of Birds* 38 **CT**, At Essex, Conn., . . the species [=*Anas acuta*] goes by the name of *sea widgeon*. **1925** (1928) Forbush *Birds MA* 1.222, *American Pintail. Other names* . . sea widgeon.

2 =scaup.

1895 *Funk & Wagnalls Std. Dict.* 1611, *Sea-widgeon, n. 1.* The pintail duck. *2.* The scaup-duck.

3 The black guillemot (*Cepphus grylle*).

1956 *MA Audubon Soc. Bulletin* 40.80, *Black Guillemot*. . . Sea Widgeon (Maine. ?Corruption of the preceding name [=*sea pigeon*]; however, "widgeon" is applied to a variety of medium-sized water birds.)

sea worm n [OED2 at sea-worm sb. 1 1681 →] NEng, esp MA Cf redworm 2

A marine annelid such as a **sandworm.**

1948 Beston *N. Farm* 194 **cME coast,** There are diggers of the seaworms which are used for bait. **1967–70** *DARE* (Qu. P5, . . *The common worm used as bait*) Infs **MA4,** 123, Sea worm; **MA55,** Sea worm—fly 'em up from down Maine; **MA80,** 97, Sea worm—for saltwater; (Qu. P6, . . *Kinds of worms . . used for bait*) Infs **MA27, NH18,** Sea worm; (Qu. R27, . . *Kinds of caterpillars or similar worms*) Inf **RI15,** Sea worm. **1989** *Yankee* July 18 **ME,** "We looked at all the symbols of Maine—moose, fish, seaworm," says one of the teachers.

Sebago salmon n Also *Sebago (trout)* [From *Sebago* Lake, Maine] Cf **landlocked salmon 1, Schoodic ~**

The lake-dwelling Atlantic **salmon B1a** (*Salmo salar*).

1873 Hallock *Fishing Tourist* 31, The Sebago Trout (*Salmo sebago*) is a monster trout. **1879** U.S. Natl. Museum *Bulletin* 14.57, *Salmo salar,* var. *sebago. . . Sebago Salmon* (land-locked).—St. Croix River and Sebago Lake. Introduced into other lakes. **1884** *Century Illustr. Mag.* Apr 905 **ME,** The land-locked salmon, called . . the "Sebago salmon," is . . distinguishable from the sea-going salmon. **1886** Mather *Memoranda* 14 **ME,** I have seen a Sebago salmon thirteen inches long with the dark bars on the sides still very distinct. **1902** Jordan–Evermann *Amer. Fishes* 168, The Sebago salmon received this name from Sebago Lake, the locality from which it was first described. It originally occurred in 4 river basins in Maine and perhaps in a few lakes in the British Provinces. **1966** *DARE* (Qu. P1, . . *Kinds of freshwater fish . . caught around here . . good to eat*) Inf **ME10,** Sebago salmon. **1974** WI Univ. *Fish Lake MI* 23, *Salmo salar . . common names: . .* sebago, sebago salmon. **1991** Amer. Fisheries Soc. *Common Names Fishes* 28, Lake populations of Atlantic salmon are variously known as ouananiche, lake Atlantic salmon, landlocked salmon, and Sebago salmon.

seben, sebm(ty), seb'n(teen), seb'nty, sebun, se'm See **seven**

secketary, seckytairy See **secretary**

second n Cf **pink sign**

A blue crab (*Callinectes sapidus*) that is a week or less away from shedding.

1976 Warner *Beautiful Swimmers* 27 **Chesapeake Bay,** Then there are also individual . . peelers of both sexes. In time-honored Chesapeake practice, Mike reads these crabs by examining the translucent next-to-last segment of their swimming legs. Some will be. . . "pink signs" or "seconds," which will do it [=molt] within a week. **1984** *DARE* File **Chesapeake Bay** [Watermen's vocab], Pink sign . . second.

second bottom See **bottom** n **1b**

second breakfast n Cf **first breakfast**

A second meal taken in midmorning. Note: *Second breakfast* in ref to a midday meal is not treated here.

1868 *Overland Mth.* 1.161, Although it was but two hours since we had left camp, there was not one in the party who did not enjoy this second breakfast. **1891** *N. Amer. Rev.* 152.138, We enjoyed our second breakfast that morning. **1963** North *Rascal* 154 **WI** (as of 1918), Come on, boy! Come on, 'coon! Milking's done. Time for second breakfast.

second Christmas (Day) n [Calque of Ger *zweiter Weihnachtstag,* PaGer *zwette Grischdâk,* or Du *tweede Kerstdag*]

The day following Christmas Day.

1857 Ritter *Hist. Moravian Church* 131 **Philadelphia PA,** Any that ever were participants of its offerings, temporal and spiritual, must remember the joyful gathering, and the sunny smiles of a Second Christmas Day in the Moravian Church. **c1860** (1890) Gumaer *Hist. Deerpark NY* 175, The day preceding Christmas, preparations were made . . by baking cakes, boiling doughnuts, &c., on which to feast, especially the second Christmas day, when neighbors visited each other and partook of the good victuals. . . The first Christmas was kept holy and reverential as Sunday, and the second as mentioned, on the evening of which the young people generally had a dance. **1894** (1895) Hoover *Enemies* 201 **sePA,** If I live I'll be seventy-six on Second Christmas. **1908** *German Amer. Annals* 10.41 **sePA,** Second Christmas. Day after Christmas. "Come and see us on second Christmas." . . fr. Pa. Ger. *zwědă Krishdog.* The day after Christmas is also kept as a holiday, and is a great day for visiting. **1940** *Sun* (Baltimore MD) 24 Dec 8/1 **MD,** The Day After Christmas. . . What we used to call Second Christmas Day. **1979** [see **second Easter**]. **2002** *DARE* File **WI** (as of c1940), When I was a very young child, we often had Christmas Eve with one

set of grandparents, Christmas Day with the other set, and then "Second Christmas" at home. By about 1950, as we and the grandparents had grown older, they came to us instead for "Second Christmas," December 26th. All of our family and many of their friends always celebrated "Second Christmas," and there were gifts to be opened specifically on that day as well as special foods for the occasion. My own children, born in the 1970s, also experienced "Second Christmas."

second cutting n Also *second cut* **widespread, but less freq nNEng** See Map and Map Section Cf **rowen**

A second crop of hay in one season.

1874 *Amer. Cyclop.* 8.168, It [=*Poa pratensis*] . . is used for hay, its after-math or second cutting being heavier than the first. **c1928** in Lib. of Congress *Amer. Memory: Hist. Amer. West* (Internet) **CO,** [Caption:] Second cutting. [*DARE* Ed: Photo is of an alfalfa field with a man standing next to a waist-high pile.] **1949** Kurath *Word Geog.* 66, *Second crop* (of hay). . . *Second crop* is the regular expression employed with reference to hay and clover in the South and the Midland. *Second cutting* competes with it only . . in the coastal area from Delaware Bay to the Neuse in North Carolina, and . . in the Ohio Valley. . . *Second cutting* competes with *second crop* in New York State and is now also used by some in western Connecticut. **1965–70** *DARE* (Qu. L10, *After hay has been cut, then it grows back and you cut it again*) 439 Infs, **widespread, but less freq nNEng,** Second cutting; **AL43, CA199, IN77, NC54, NY27, PA75, UT3, VA7, WA20,** Second cut. [**1970** *AmSp* 45.62 **England,** Of the several names for the second crop of hay current on this side of the Atlantic, the *SED* [=*Survey of English Dialects*] records . . *second cut* in East Anglia, and in Hampshire-Surrey.] **1972** *PADS* 58.19 **cwAL,** Second crop. Southern and Midland *second crop* was given by three informants (and four others responded to it as a suggested form). Coastal Southern and Ohio Valley *second cut(ting)* (11) is most common. **2000** *DARE* File—Internet **NE** [Oxbow Pet Products], We now have a very early First Cutting timothy that looks and feels like second cutting. . . There is also the current Second Cutting timothy.

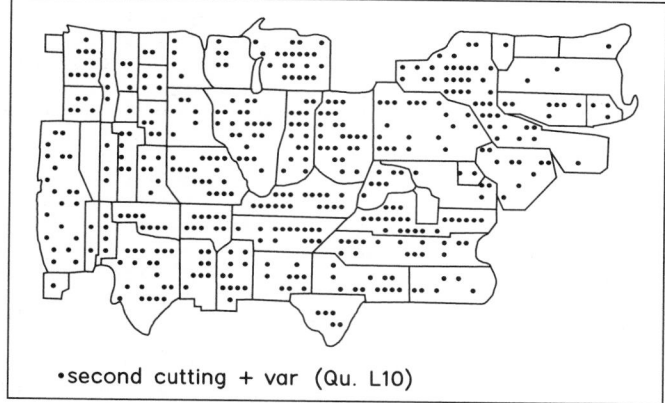

•second cutting + var (Qu. L10)

second day See **first day 1**

second Easter n Cf **second Christmas (Day)**

1979 Jordan *Yesterday in TX Hill Country* 123, The day after Easter was "Second Easter". . . Like "Second Christmas" this was a holiday, and most of the people spent the day visiting friends and relatives.

second-handed adj [*OED2* 1682–1842; "Now chiefly *dial.*"] *somewhat old-fash*

Secondhand; also fig, of a person: inferior; shabby.

1834 *New Engl. Mag.* 7.184, The arguments, which failed to pervert the wise, are lavished by him, second-handed, upon the foolish. **1858** *Harper's New Mth. Mag.* 16.553, We have had to create our wealth. Power has not come to us as a second-handed thing. It has not been inherited. **1892** *DN* 1.211 **seMA,** *Second-handed:* second-hand. **1899** (1912) Green *VA Folk-Speech* 374, *Second-handed. . .* At second hand. "Second-handed clothes." **1906** *DN* 3.155 **nwAR,** *Second-handed. . .* Second-hand. "The only baby-buggy we have left is second-handed." **1909** *DN* 3.367 **eAL, wGA,** *Second-handed. . .* Second-hand. Common. **1921** Haswell *Daughter Ozarks* 44 (as of 1880s), Some of these second-handed fellers was at Red Bird to-night. **c1960** Wilson *Coll.* **csKY,** *Second-handed. . .* Used things offered for sale. **1965–70** *DARE* (Qu. U3, *A coat, dress, or other garment that is passed on from one person to another [or an older child to a younger one]*) 20 Infs, **scattered,** Second-handed. [16 of 20 Infs old] **1982** *Barrick Coll.* **csPA,** *Second-handed*—used.

second joint n

The thigh of a cooked fowl.

1856 *Harper's New Mth. Mag.* 12.436, Who would not rather drink in the songs of the bird than eat him up, wings and "second joint?" **1870** *Appletons' Jrl.* 3.39 **eVA,** Mrs. Smith chose the wing of a chicken, Mrs. Brown a second joint. **1889** *New Engl. Mag.* 7.358, But I do not think that you know the full enjoyment of your favorite morsel,—say that square inch on the side bone, after the second joint has been given to some guest,—unless you have roved with the turkey himself on the downs of Southern Rhode Island. **1994** *DARE* File **Brooklyn NYC,** I can still hear my father . . asking—as he carved a roast chicken—who wanted the "second joint." (A few years ago I was asked if I wanted to be served a thigh. A *what?* Who knew chickens had thighs?) **1999** *NADS Letters* **AL, MS,** "Second joint". . . This is a phrase that is used daily here in Tuscaloosa, Alabama and I have heard it in the "Delta" of Mississippi . . as recently as last year. . . It is my understanding that it was used because it was not considered polite to mention body parts in the company of ladies. . . However, the leg of a chicken was and is always called "[the] leg." *Ibid* **MI,** Second joint was a common term for the thigh of a chicken in central Michigan where I lived from 1936 . . to 1954. *Ibid* **nNJ** (as of 1950s), My mother's family . . called the thigh of a chicken or turkey the "second joint." We also called the drumstick the "first joint." *Ibid* **OH,** My great aunt . . always used the term second joint for chicken thighs. . . She was born 1883 in St. Henry, Ohio . . and came to Cincinnati at 17. **2000** *Ibid* **CT, IL, LA, MA, NC, NY, PA.**

second line n **New Orleans LA**

The unofficial group of persons following the band in a parade; hence v phr *second line* to follow the parade band; vbl n *second lining* following the parade band while doing a particular dance step; n *second liner* a parade-band follower.

1939 (1959) Ramsey-Smith *Jazzmen* 27 **New Orleans LA,** The funerals and parades always had a "second line" which consisted of the kids who danced along behind. **1947** *True* 32.100 **New Orleans LA** [Black], The second line (Cats) . . consisted of raggidy guys who hung around pool rooms and etc. **1954** Armstrong *Satchmo* 24 **New Orleans LA** [Black], When I was in church and when I was "second lining"—that is, following the brass bands in parades—I started to listen carefully to the different instruments. **1955** Shapiro-Hentoff *Hear Me Talkin'* 30 **New Orleans LA,** I was a "second-line" kid. That meant I'd follow the big bands down the streets, and, man, what a thrill when Tio or George Baquet would let me carry their cases while they played! **1972** *Rolling Stone* 11 May 16 **New Orleans LA,** These "second liners" wave handkerchiefs and umbrellas and . . break into a dipping, funky-butt step—half shimmy, half strut—that is known as "second lining." *Ibid,* The second line beat is clearly discernible. *Ibid,* As long as there's a Mardi Gras or a second line funeral, you're gonna have the New Orleans beat. **1984** Stall *Proud New Orleans* 168, Funeral parades with jazz bands have customarily been followed by what has been termed a "second line." The second line is made up of people who are not an official part of the parade but who join in spontaneously to show their enthusiasm for the music. **1987** Rose *I Remember Jazz* 124, He sang and danced a strange little second-line style dance. Anyone could see he was a rhythm man.

second lunch n Cf **first lunch, lunch** n 1

1907 *DN* 3.249 **eME,** *Second lunch.* . . Woodsmen's second breakfast, eaten at 9 A.M.

second month See **first month**

secretary n Usu |'sɛkrə‚tɛrɪ|; for addit varr see quots Pronc-spp *secketary, seckytairy, secutary* Cf Pronc Intro 3.I.22

Std senses, var proncs.

1858 Hammett *Piney Woods Tavern* 68, They called a meetin', and they made chairmin and secketaries. **1891** *DN* 1.163 **cNY,** [sɛkə'tɛrɪ] 'Secretary.' **1894** *Harper's New Mth. Mag.* 89.796 **Sth** [Black], An' dere's a letter for you . . somewhar in he ole secketary. **1916** *DN* 4.280 **NE,** *Secketary.* . . Common for *secretary.* [*DN* Ed: Also Kan.] Also *secutary.* **1924** (1946) Greer-Petrie *Angeline Gits an Eyeful* 6 **csKY,** [She] hors (hires) a seckytairy to print 'em fur her. **1989** Pederson *LAGS Tech. Index* 247 **Gulf Region,** *Secretary.* . . [Of 914 primary infs, 294 offered proncs of the type ['sɛkrətɛrɪ, 'sɛkrɪtɛrɪ]; 231 infs, proncs of

the type ['sɛkətɛrɪ, 'sɛkɪtɛrɪ]; 18 infs, proncs of the type ['sɛkətɛrɪ]; 6 infs, proncs of the type ['sʌkrətɛrɪ, 'sʌkrɪtɛrɪ(z), 'sʌkrɪtʌrɪz]; 2 infs, proncs of the type ['sʌkɪtɛrɪz]; 3 infs, proncs of the type ['sɪkətɛrɪ, 'sɪkɪtʌrɪ]; 2 infs, proncs of the type ['sɛkjətɛrɪ, 'sɛkjətɛrɪ].]

section harrow n chiefly Lower Missip Valley, SE See Map

A spike-tooth harrow consisting of one or more separate rectangular sections.

[**1895** (1969) Montgomery Ward *Catalogue* 583, Three sections to any one of our harrows costs [sic] one-half more than two sections. Four sections cost twice as much as two sections. Drawbar furnished to match number of sections ordered.] **1965–70** *DARE* (Qu. L20, *The implement used in a field after it's been plowed to break up the lumps*) 8 Infs, **SE, AR,** Section harrow; **AL2,** Section harrow—same as spike harrow; **LA15,** Section harrow—square metal frame has solid spikes; **OK52,** Section harrow—factory-made; **SC12,** Section harrow—for leveling—had spikes for teeth; (Qu. L18, *Kinds of plows*) Infs **AR51, MS81,** Section harrow; (Qu. L25, *The implement used to clean out weeds and loosen the earth between rows of corn*) Inf **KY75,** Section harrow. **1966** *DARE* Tape **OK43,** Then they take a disc harrow or a section harrow and they get this land on level. **1979** *NADS Letters* **MS,** A section harrow . . is a big harrow, with spike-teeth, dragged behind mules, horses, or tractors. **1986** Pederson *LAGS Concordance* **Gulf Region** (*Harrow*) 48 infs, Section harrow(s); 1 inf, Section harrow—flat, no handles; 1 inf, Section harrow—loosens dirt from clods; 1 inf, Section harrow—did 3–4 rows at [a] time.

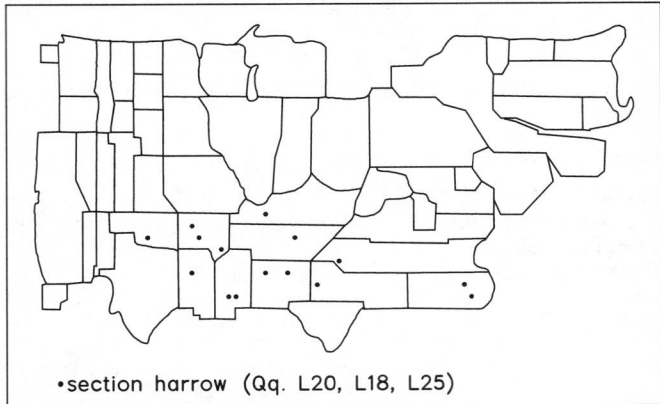

•section harrow (Qq. L20, L18, L25)

section road n Also *section-line (road)* Cf **line road**

A road built along a section line.

1873 *Winfield* (Kan.) *Courier* 11 Jan. 3/3 (*DAE*), Section line roads of Lucious Hubbard and others was laid over under the rule. **1919** McCarter *Cornerstone* 22 (*DA*), He is trying to get Mrs. Helm and her son to shut up our road and force us to sell this little place to him and Mrs. Helm so they can run section-line roads. **1948** Jacobs *We Chose Country* 24 **csWI,** We bowled along, climbing past snatches of woods and the straight section-line roads to a high plateau. **1950** *WELS* **WI** (*A road that follows the survey divisions*) 10 Infs, Section line road; 2 Infs, Section road. **1965–70** *DARE* (Qu. N26, *A road that follows surveyors' divisions;* total Infs questioned, 75) 12 Infs, 9 **OK,** 3 **MS,** Section-line (road); **FL15,** Section road. **1973** Allen *LAUM* 1.241 **Upper MW** (as of c1950), *Byway.* . . Section line road [1 inf, **MN**]; [Section] road [1 inf, **SD**]. **1994** *DARE* File, Section road—heard in Colorado.

section 37 n

Among loggers: see quots.

1958 McCulloch *Woods Words* 159 **Pacific NW,** *Section 37*—The usual township contains 36 sections, and 37 is not supposed to exist. . . Section 37 is a term used to describe something queer, something unusual. **1969** Sorden *Lumberjack Lingo* 105 **NEng, Gt Lakes,** *Section 37.* . . Where all good loggers go when they "cash in their chips." No underbrush there; every tree is big, tall, and straight. No scalers are allowed. **2001** *DARE* File **cnWI,** Frederic has called everyone he can think of and found only a few replies. Most had never heard of it, not only surveyors but logging men also. Here's what he heard. Greenhorns were sent to Section 37, If you were stealing timber you cut it in Section 37, Going to Section 37 was a night at the tavern.

secundo See **segundo**

secutary See **secretary**

sedge n Pronc-sp **chiefly Sth, S Midl, NEng** sage Cf Pronc Intro 3.I.5.b, **edge A**

A Forms.   For addit exx see **sedge grass 2, sedge hen**
    1864 [see **sedge grass 2**]. **1913** DN 4.57 **Cape Cod MA,** *Sage-grass. . .* Sedge: used only of salt-water grasses which remain erect after the tide has ebbed. "You'll find a lot o' sand-eels over in amongst that sage-grass." **1916** DN 4.265 **Cape Cod MA,** "Sedge" has been lengthened into "sage," has lost its significance to the popular mind, and has been expanded into "sage-grass." **1933** Hanley Disks **MA,** You feed 'em on sage—sage hay—and you'll taste it pretty quick (in the milk). **1953** AmSp 28.280, Elsewhere, especially in the Southeast, the modifying term, which is usually written *sedge* but often pronounced 'sage,' relates to marshy growth, collectively dubbed 'sedge.' **c1960** Wilson Coll. **csKY,** Sedge in the Mammoth Cave area is "sage." **1965–70** DARE (Qu. F36, *. . Kinds of brooms*) Infs **AL30, 33, GA81, IN48, MS48, 79, NC55,** Sage broom; **LA3,** Sagebresh broom; **OK21,** Sage-brush grass broom; (Qu. L9a, *. . Kinds of grass . . grown for hay*) Inf **OK52,** Sage grass; (Qu. Q9, *The bird that looks like a small, dull-colored duck*) Inf **NC49,** Sage hen; (Qu. Q5, *. . Kinds of wild ducks*) Inf **NC80,** Sage peter; (Qu. Q10, *. . Water birds and marsh birds*) Infs **MD36, MS60, NC1, VA46, 84,** Sage hen; (Qu. S8, *A common kind of wild grass*) Inf **KY18,** Sage grass; (Qu. S9, *. . Kinds of grass that are hard to get rid of*) Infs **AR35, 52, KY24, 89, VA2,** Sage grass; (Qu. S20, *A common weed*) Inf **MD20,** Sage grass; (Qu. S21, *. . Weeds*) Inf **LA10,** Sage grass; (Qu. OO35b, *. . "That land is poor."*) Inf **TN1,** It wouldn't grow sage grass. **2000** DARE File **Cape Cod MA,** I e-mailed a friend about sage/sedge grass and she responded: Yes, I've always heard it referred to as sage grass. If you had asked me how to spell it, I would have said "sage", so I've learned something new today!

B Senses.

1 also *sedge grass;* Std: any of var coarse plants usu of the family *Cyperaceae* and esp of the genus *Carex,* but also **sweet flag** or an **iris B1** (here: *Iris pseudoacorus*).   For other names of var of the family *Cyperaceae* see **cotton grass, galingale, horned rush, nut grass 1, 2, ~ rush 1, 2, pine grass 4, rabbit ~ 1, redtop 3, three-square, umbrella grass, wool ~;** for other names of var spp of *Carex* see **blackhead 4, fox sedge, iron grass 2, niggerwool 1, pinegrass 4, sour grass** Cf **broom sedge, corn ~, creek ~**

2 See **sedge grass 2.**

sedge clam n Pronc-sp *sage clam* [**sedge B1**]
A **surf clam** (here: *Spisula solidissima*).
    1913 DN 4.57 **Cape Cod MA,** *Sage-clam. . .* Small soft clams growing in the "sage-grass," *q.v.* "Didn't get no cohogs nor run-downs, but got a lot o' sage-clams." **1935** Lincoln *Cape Cod Yesterdays* 49 **MA,** Our wide flat stretches of flats were habited by clams, thousands and thousands of them. At the inner edge, bordering the clumps of coarse beach grass, were the "sedge clams," the little fellows, tender and just right for a bake or a boil. . . Away out . . were the large "sea clams." *Ibid* 51, Digging for sedge clams . . the digger works faster. And he gets fewer clams at a time.

sedge grass n Pronc-sp *sage grass* Cf **sedge A**
1 Std: see **sedge B1.**
2 also *sedge;* pronc-spp *sage (grass);* rarely *sage-brush (grass):* A **beardgrass,** esp **little bluestem** or *Andropogon virginicus*—often in comb *sage(-grass) broom.* **chiefly Sth, S Midl** Cf **broom sedge**
    1857 TX Almanac for 1858 126, He found that the hog-wallow prairie and the rank, coarse sedge grass, common in that part of the State, did not suit sheep. **1864** in 1891 U.S. War Dept. *War of Rebellion* 1st ser 32.1.64 **VA,** We now commenced to advance through an old sage-grass field under fire of their artillery. **1880** (1883) U.S. Census Office *Rept. Ag.* 960, *Andropogon scoparius. . .* It is returned as sage-grass, broom-grass, and even under other names. *Ibid* 970 **csTX,** The sand region in northern Cameron is principally covered with a species of *sage-grass,* affording good pasture never affected by drought. **1886** U.S. Bur. Foreign Commerce *Consular Repts.* Jan 40, Those hundreds of thousands of acres of once valuable Southern lands . . [are] now lying to waste in worthless 'sage grass.' **1891** Leighton News (AL) 1 June np, This . . "Rabbit Hawk," . . is often seen flying low over the fields, searching every patch of sedge grass very carefully for its favorite food. **1893**

Scribner's Mag. 13.801 **TN,** To inhale the odor of . . pungent aromatic things in the tall "Sage-grass." **1903** DN 2.328 **seMO,** *Sage-grass. . .* Sedge-grass. Also called 'broom-sage.' *Sage-field. . .* An old field grown up with sedge-grass. **1907** DN 3.235 **nwAR,** *Sage-grass. . .* Sedge-grass. *(Broom)-sage. . . Sage-field. . .* An old field grown up with sedge-grass. **1912** Wooton–Standley *Grasses* NM 27, *Andropogon. . .* is the *Tall Sage Grass. . . Schizachyrium* is the smaller *Sage Grass.* **1943** Caldwell *GA Boy* 117, Handsome was in and out of the house all morning, scrubbing the floor and splitting fat-pine lighters and sweeping the yard with the sedge broom. **1947** Bedichek *Advent. TX Naturalist* 23 **TX,** In the ill-kept paths of this burial ground and in the right-of-way I see the sage grass (*Andropogan* [sic] *saccharoides*) growing. **1949** Arnow *Hunter's Horn* 179 **KY,** Suse . . ran up over a low sagegrass knoll and down to the edge of the steep wooded banks and ledges that lay above the river. **1950** Faulkner *Stories* 313 **MS,** They were both squat men. . . Their hair looked like sedge grass on burnt-over land. **c1960** Wilson Coll. **csKY,** *Broom sage. . . Andropogon. . .* Also called *sage grass. Ibid, Broomsage broom. . .* Coarse home-made broom to sweep porches. More often sage-grass broom. **1965–70** DARE (Qu. F36, *. . Kinds of brooms*) Infs **AL30, 33, GA81, IN48, MS48, NC55,** Sage broom; **MS79,** Sage broom—people in country used to make brooms out of sage, a form of grass; **LA3,** Sagebresh broom; **OK21,** Sage-brush grass broom—they used to use sagebrush grass brooms, but I never did; (Qu. L9a, *. . Kinds of grass . . grown for hay*) Inf **OK52,** Sage grass; (Qu. S8, *A common kind of wild grass that grows in fields: it spreads by sending out long underground roots, and it's hard to get rid of*) Inf **IA13,** Sedge grass; **KY18,** Sage grass; (Qu. S9, *. . Kinds of grass that are hard to get rid of*) Infs **AR35, 52, KY24, 89, VA2,** Sage grass; **MD49, TN22,** Sedge grass; (Qu. S20) Inf **MD20,** Sage grass; (Qu. S21, *. . Weeds . . that are a trouble in gardens and fields*) Inf **LA10,** Sage grass; (Qu. OO35b, *Talking about vegetables thriving: "That land is poor."*) Inf **TN1,** It wouldn't grow sage grass. **1986** Pederson *LAGS Concordance* **Gulf Region,** 1 inf, Sage; 1 inf, Sage—broom made of; 1 inf, Broom made of sage or pine straw; 1 inf, Sage—used to make homemade brooms; 8 infs, Sage broom(s); 1 inf, Sage broom = yard broom; 1 inf, Sage broom—handmade; 1 inf, Sage broom—made of broom sage; 3 infs, Sage field; 1 inf, Sage field—where broomstraw was gathered; 1 inf, Sagebrush—used for both yard and house brooms; 9 infs, Sage grass; 1 inf, Sage grass—produced by unfertilized soil; 1 inf, Some brooms made of sage grass; 2 infs, Sage-grass broom(s); 1 inf, Sage straw. **1995** McCormack *Fields Pastures* 73 **TN,** I could see an elderly black woman with a blue bandana around her head sweeping the bare-earthed yard with a homemade broom made of sage grass tied onto a four-foot hickory stick.

sedge hen n Pronc-sp *sage hen* [**sedge B1**] **chiefly Mid and S Atl**

1 Any of var **rails** n[2], such as the **clapper rail, king rail 1, sora,** or **Florida gallinule.**
    1824 Latham *Genl. Hist. Birds* 9.421 **GA,** In Georgia it [=*Gallinula carolina*] is seen frequently in the marshes, and sides of ponds, but is not very common; is known there by the name of Water-Hen, or Sedge-Hen, also the Water-Rail. **1888** Trumbull *Names of Birds* 127, *Clapper rail. . .* At Pocomoke City, Md., and at Eastville, Va., *sedge-hen;* very generally so called in these localities. **1890** St. Nicholas June 638 **VA,** We got forty-two sedge-hens, on a high tide. **1913** Bailey *Birds VA* 56, *Clapper Rail. . .* Sage Hen. . . Numerous pairs of these birds are scattered over every salt marsh. **1953** AmSp 28.280, *Sage hen. . .* Especially in the Southeast, the modifying term, which is usually written *sedge* but often pronounced 'sage,' relates to marshy growth, collectively dubbed 'sedge.' The birds known by this moniker comprise the green heron (Va.), American bittern (D.C., N.C.), clapper rail (Md., Va., N.C.), king rail (N.C., Ill.), sora (Ga.), and common gallinule (Va.) **1966–69** DARE (Qu. Q9, *The bird that looks like a small, dull-colored duck and is commonly found on ponds and lakes*) Inf **NC49,** Sage hen; (Qu. Q10, *. . Water birds and marsh birds*) Inf **LA20,** Sedge hen—it's brown, about as big as a fryer, with a long neck and sharp bill; **NC13,** Sedge hen; **NC78,** Sedge hens—in the marsh; **VA84,** Clapper—sage hen.

2 A **green heron, night heron, bittern,** or other marsh bird.
    1953 [see **1** above]. **1965–70** DARE (Qu. Q8, *A water bird that makes a booming sound before rain and often stands with its beak pointed almost straight up*) Inf **NC82,** Sedge hen; (Qu. Q10, *. . Water birds and marsh birds*) Infs **MS60, NC1,** Sage hen; **MD36,** Sage hen—looks like small crane; **VA46,** Sage hen—brown bird, size of bantam hen. **1976** Warner *Beautiful Swimmers* 123 **Delmarva,** The night herons, locally known as sedge hens or "bumcutters," are seldom allowed to share the best [tree] branches.

sedge peter n Also *sage peter* Cf **blue peter 1, marsh ~, sedge A, B1, sedge hen**

Probably either the **Florida gallinule** or the **purple gallinule**.

1968 *DARE* (Qu. Q5, . . *Kinds of wild ducks*) Inf **NC80**, Some call the sedge peter a sage peter.

sedge wren n [**sedge grass 2**]

The short-billed **marsh wren** (*Cistothorus platensis*).

1955 Lowery *LA Birds* 393, *Cistothorus platensis*. . . The suggestion has been made that it be called the Sedge Wren. In the upland areas, at least, it is found in dry, grassy fields, especially those with stands of "broom sedge," which the Leconte, Henslow, and Grasshopper Sparrows also frequent. **1962** Imhof *AL Birds* 393, *Short-billed Marsh Wren*. . . Other name: Sedge Wren.

seditty See **siditty**

see v

A Form.

In combs *see him, see 'em*: pronc-sp *shum*. *Gullah* Cf **him pron B3, 4**

1856 Simms *Eutaw* 174 **SC** [Gullah], "And the major has not been here, Benny?" "Who, Mass Willie?" "Yes." "No! I no sh'um [Simms: see 'em]." **1867** Allen *Slave Songs* xxv **seSC** [Gullah], *"Sh'um,"* a corruption of *see 'em*, applied (as *'em* is) to all genders and both numbers. **1883** (1971) Harris *Nights with Remus* 200 **GA** [Black], 'E do say 'e bin know gal sem lak dat, 'e is bin shum befo'. **1892** (1969) Christensen *Afro-Amer. Folk Lore* 7 **seSC**, 'E look down by de mile pos' an' dere 'e shum Cooter da wait for um. **1922** Gonzales *Black Border* 148 **sSC, GA coasts,** Uh yeddy 'bout 'um but uh nebbuh shum. *Ibid* 152, "Wuh kinduh clawt' you got?". . . "What kind you want?" "Lemme shum." **1930** Woofter *Black Yeomanry* 48 **seSC** [Gullah], Yunnah shum deh on de deah, enty? [=You see it on the deer, don't you?] **1939** Griswold *Sea Is. Lady* 131 **csSC** (as of 1865) [Gullah], Leola, ain' you know Maus' Steve when you shum? [=Leola, don't you know Marse Steve when you see him?] **1949** Turner *Africanisms* 272 [Gullah], [dɪ ʃʌm ɒl reɪt] [=I see him all right].

B Gram forms.

1 pres (exc 3rd pers sg): usu *see;* also *sees.*

1843 (1916) Hall *New Purchase* 312 **IN**, I sees you wants to do what's right. **1853** Simms *Sword & Distaff* 565 **SC**, Plank 'em down, and when I sees 'em, then you shill see the papers. **1986** Pederson *LAGS Concordance*, 1 inf, **neMS**, These youngsters sees; 1 inf, **ceAR**, I sees in the stores; 1 inf, **neLA**, They sees.

2 past: usu *saw;* also:

a *see*. [The forms *see, seed,* and *seen* are well attested in Brit dial; for their distributions see *EDD* and 1970 *AmSp* 45.67.] **scattered, but chiefly Atl, esp NEast**

1781 *PA Jrl. & Weekly Advt.* (Philadelphia) 16 May 1/2, I *see* him yesterday, or I *see* him last week, for I *saw* him. **1843** (1916) Hall *New Purchase* 145 **IN**, That's his skin . . you see tother day. **1884** Jewett *Country Dr.* 265 **ME**, You're the smartest young woman I ever see. **1884** *Anglia* 7.269 **Sth, S Midl** [Black], *Dan I mos' ever see* = than I ever saw. **1890** Holley *Samantha among Brethren* 57 **NY**, I felt like a fool. For I knew she had heard every word, I see she had by her looks. **1893** *DN* 1.276 **nwCT**, The town is one remote from railroads, and city boarders do not reach it; the older inhabitants speak with considerable uniformity the same dialect as our subject. . . [W]ith the single exception of *see*, . . the preterit and past participle are in all [other] cases alike. *Ibid* 277, See—[past] see, p.p. seen. **1899** Chesnutt *Conjure Woman* 50 **csNC** [Black], W'en Tenie see so many things happenin' ter de tree, she 'cluded she'd ha' ter turn Sandy ter sump'n e'se. **1902** [see **B2b** below]. **1904** (1913) Johnson *Highways South* 204 **WV**, I looked out and see thirteen Rebel bushwhackers on their horses. **1907** [see **B2b** below]. **1907** White *AZ Nights* 8, I worked all the morning down at the bottom of the shaft, and when I see by the sun it was getting along towards noon, I put in three good shots. **1953** Atwood *Survey of Verb Forms* 20, See. . . The uninflected preterite *see* . . is by far the most common variant form in N. Eng. . . See also prevails in N.Y. and the northernmost edge of Pa. . . It predominates over other variants in the Piedmont area of Va. and part of the Tidewater area, as well as in parts of n.e. N.C. **1966–70** *DARE* (Qu. OO45a, *About seeing somebody: "He thought nobody was looking but I _____ [him hide it]."*) Infs **MA58, 76, NH14, NY75, SC10, 26,** See. **1968** *DARE* FW Addit **neNY**, See—preterite of *see*. **1979** Lewis *How to Talk Yankee* [29]

nNEng, You can't imagine what *rigs* they wear down in the city. I see one feller with a long black cloak, gum rubbers, a coonskin hat—and ear rings! **1989** Pederson *LAGS Tech. Index* 362 **Gulf Region,** *See*. . . [preterite] See . . 3 [infs].

b *seed*. [See **B2a** above] **chiefly Sth, S Midl** See Map

1795 Dearborn *Columbian Grammar* 138, *List of Improprieties*. . . Seed for Saw. **1829** Tenney *Female Quixotism* 2.86 **Philadelphia PA**, I seed your father as plain as I see you this minute. **1838** (1843) Haliburton *Clockmaker* (2d ser) 13, I looked round and I seed two niggers bringin in the breakfast. **1843** (1916) Hall *New Purchase* 212 **IN**, I. . . seed him a readin on it! **1851** Hooper *Widow Rugby's Husband* 39 **AL**, Then he turned round and seed Dick and his boys. **1893** Shands *MS Speech* 55, Seed. . . Negro and illiterate white for *saw*. **1902** *DN* 2.244 **sIL**, See, seen, seed. Preterits for see. **1903** *DN* 2.328 **seMO**, Seed, pret. and pp. of see. **1907** *DN* 3.227 **nwAR**, See, seen, seed, pret. v. **1909** *DN* 3.367 **eAL, wGA**, Seed, pret. and pp. of see. Very common among the illiterate. **1912** *DN* 3.588 **wIN**, Seed, pret. of see. **1923** *DN* 5.221 **swMO**, Seed. . . Saw. **1931** (1991) Hughes–Hurston *Mule Bone* 125 **cFL** [Black], I ast you whut you seed. **1953** Atwood *Survey of Verb Forms* 20, The weak preterite *seed* . . occurs once in N. Eng.; otherwise there are no occurrences north of the Pa.–Md. boundary. In the mountain areas south of the Kanawha this form becomes quite common. . . *Seed* extends more or less all across N.C., in some areas being the only preterite form in use other than *saw*. *Seed* also occurs in a rather scattered way in S.C. and e. Ga. **1965–70** *DARE* (Qu. OO45a, *About seeing somebody: "He thought nobody was looking but I _____ [him hide it]."*) 15 Infs, **esp Sth, S Midl**, Seed; (Qu. II17, *If you happen to meet someone that you haven't seen for a while: "Guess who I _____ this morning."*) Infs **GA72, IN32, NC69,** Seed. [16 of 17 total Infs comm type 4 or 5] **1966** *DARE* Tape **ME26**, I seed one stable. **1989** Pederson *LAGS Tech. Index* 362 **Gulf Region,** *See*. . . [preterite] Seed . . 44 [infs].

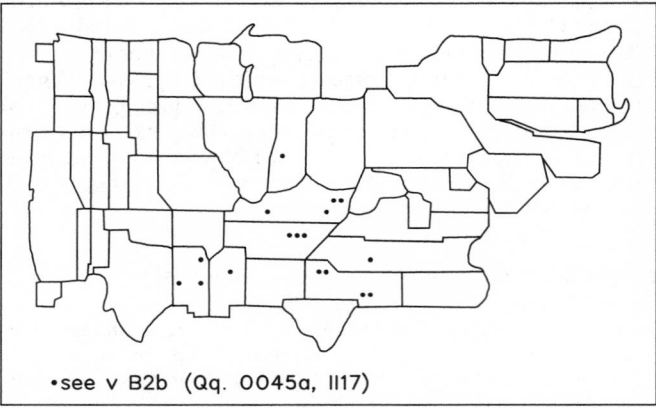

•see v B2b (Qq. OO45a, II17)

c *seen*. [See **B2a** above] **widespread** *esp freq among rural speakers and those with little formal educ*

1818 in 1824 Knight *Letters* 107 **KY**, Some words are used, even by genteel people, from their imperfect educations, in a new sense; and others, by the lower classes in society, pronounced very uncouthly, as . . I seen. **1851** Hooper *Widow Rugby's Husband* 45 **AL**, That's the last time I seen my face. **1871** Eggleston *Hoosier Schoolmaster* 197 **sIN**, He seen ole man Pearson. **1895** *DN* 1.376 **seKY, eTN, wNC**, Well, if it ain't the purtiest critter ever I seen. **1902** [see **B2b** above]. **1905** *DN* 3.18 **cCT**, I seen him do it. **1907** [see **B2b** above]. **1909** *DN* 3.367 **eAL, wGA**, Seen, pret. of see. **1909** *Ibid* 415 **nME**, Seen, v. pret. Saw. **1913** Kephart *Highlanders* 284 **sAppalachians**, In many cases a weak preterite supplants the proper strong one . . seen or seed. **1941** *AmSp* 16.157 **NYC** [New York dialect], I seen—I saw. **1942** *AmSp* 17.169 **sIL**, Some of the common verb forms noted are, for example: . . *I seen* and *I have saw* (for 'I saw'). **1953** Atwood *Survey of Verb Forms* 20, See. . . The preterite. . . The form seen. . . strongly predominates in the Midland area—including most of N.J., the southern three fourths of Pa., W. Va. (except a small southern portion), most of Del. and Md., part of n. and w. Va., some portions of N.C., and all of S.C. and e. Ga. **1965–70** *DARE* (Qu. OO45a, *About seeing somebody: "He thought nobody was looking but I _____ [him hide it]."*) 123 Infs, **widespread,** Seen [Of all Infs responding to the question, 68% were comm type 4 or 5, 28% gs educ or less; of those giving this response, 82% were comm type 4 or 5, 56% gs educ or less.]; (Qu. II17, *If you happen to meet someone that* *you haven't seen for a while:* "Guess who I _____ this morning.") 57 Infs, **esp Sth, S Midl,** (Just) seen [Of all Infs responding to the question, 68% were comm type 4 or 5, 28% gs educ or less; of those giving these responses, 89% were comm type 4 or 5, 61% gs educ or less.] **1966–70** *DARE* Tape CA205, We seen some beautiful country; MI36, Yes, I seen that too; NV8, He says, "As I seen it." As he seen it—why, cripes, I can go back thirty year beyond him; PA17, He seen the deer. **1989** Pederson *LAGS Tech. Index* **Gulf Region,** *See. . .* [preterite] Seen . . 216 [infs]. **1997** *DARE* File—Internet e**PA** [CoalSpeak], *Seen:* Commonly used instead of "saw." "Don't tell me yiz wasn't dere, I seen yiz wit my own eyes!"

d *sawd, sawed.* **Sth, S Midl**

1884 *Anglia* 7.253 **Sth, S Midl** [Black], *Pres.* see—*Past.* seed, see, sawed, seen—*Pass. Part.* [same as past]. **1927** Adams *Congaree* 30 c**SC** [Black], He raise up an open he eyes an' sawed no people. **1937** in 1976 *Weevils in the Wheat* 73 **VA** [Black], So when she raised up and sawd who hit was she say, "Lawd, Lawd, whar did you come from?" **1969–70** *DARE* (Qu. OO45a, *About seeing somebody:* "He thought nobody was looking but I _____ [him hide it].") Infs **GA**84, **KY**11, 84, Sawed. **1989** Pederson *LAGS Tech. Index* 362 **Gulf Region,** *See. . .* [preterite] Sawd . . 1 [inf].

e *sawn.*

1943 *Sat. Eve. Post* 17 Apr 101 **ID,** It was that there hog! . . I sawn her! **1966–68** *DARE* (Qu. OO45a, *About seeing somebody:* "He thought nobody was looking but I _____ [him hide it].") Inf **LA**46, Sawn.

f *seend, seent.*

1953 Brewer *Word Brazos* 40 e**TX** [Black], In 'bout five minutes mo' Unkuh Ebun seent anothuh star shoot crost de heabuns rat 'fo' his gaze. **1989** Pederson *LAGS Tech. Index* 362 **Gulf Region,** *See. . .* [preterite] Seend . . 1 [inf].

3 past pple: usu *seen;* also:

a *saw.* **widespread, but less freq NEast, Gt Lakes, CA** See Map *esp freq among rural speakers and those with little formal educ*

1829 Kirkham *Engl. Grammar* 193 **PA,** Have you saw him? Yes, I have saw him wunst; and that was before you seed him. **1876** in 1969 *PADS* 52.54 se**IL,** They have not saw Hood yet. **1894** Riley *Armazindy* 48 **IN,** Like you've saw Custard-pie with no crust. **1902** *DN* 2.244 s**IL,** *Saw.* Past participle for seen. **1903** *DN* 2.328 se**MO,** *Saw,* pp. of see. Seen. 'I haven't saw him.' Deplorably common. **1904** *DN* 2.421 nw**AR,** *Saw,* pret. for pp. Seen. 'Have you saw Bud?' Very common among the uneducated. **1913** *DN* 4.55 c**NY,** *Saw.* . . Seen; noted as common in this district to an unusual degree. **1941** Faulkner *Men Working* 33 **MS,** How-some-ever, I've saw them. **1942** [see **B2c** above]. **1965–70** *DARE* (Qu. OO45b, *About seeing somebody:* "Many's the time I've _____ him hide things.") 104 Infs, **widespread, but less freq NEast, Gt Lakes, CA,** Saw [Of all Infs responding to the question, 68% were comm type 4 or 5, 28% gs educ or less; of those giving these responses, 80% were comm type 4 or 5, 46% gs educ or less.]; (Qu. KK20b, *Something that looks as if it might collapse any minute:* "Our old washing machine is _____.") Inf **OK**31, Has saw its best days; (Qu. NN10a, *Expressions [such as 'hello'] used when you meet somebody you know quite well*) Inf **OK**52, Haven't saw you in a month of Sundays. **1966–68** *DARE* Tape FL26, But I don't believe so far this winter we've saw a woodpecker out there;

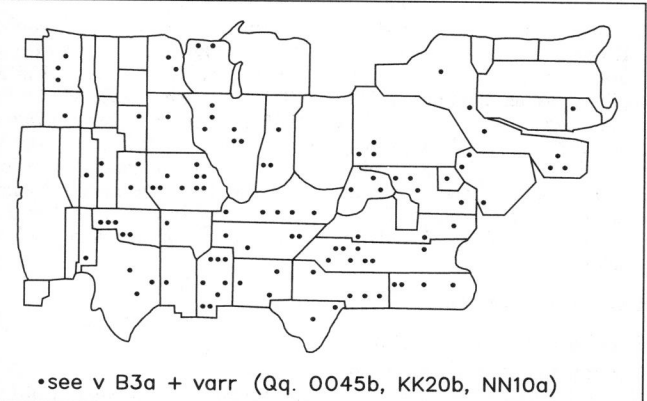

•see v B3a + varr (Qq. OO45b, KK20b, NN10a)

GA7, I have saw times . . when I was small, that we'd already be dipped out; GA30, I've saw 'em do it; TN15, I'd never seen a violin before. Mother had a uncle. . . He played the violin but I'd never saw it. **1989** Pederson *LAGS Tech. Index* 362 **Gulf Region,** *See. . .* [past participle] Saw . . 96 [infs].

b *seed.* [This form is widespread in Brit dial; see *EDD*.] **chiefly Sth, S Midl** See Map

1903 [see **B2b** above]. **1909** [see **B2b** above]. **1929** Sale *Tree Named John* 40 **MS** [Black], You is de no-sensedes' nigger man Ah ever is seed in all my life. **a1930** in 1991 Hughes–Hurston *Mule Bone* 29 c**FL** [Black], Ah aint seed it on no map. **1945** FWP *Lay My Burden Down* 84 **AL** [Black], I've seed the biggest herds of deer following the way the Indians drifted. **1965–70** *DARE* (Qu. OO45b, *About seeing somebody:* "Many's the time I've _____ him hide things.") 17 Infs, **Sth, S Midl,** Seed; (Qu. KK20b, *Something that looks as if it might collapse any minute:* "Our old washing machine is _____.") Inf **GA**31, Seed its best days. [16 of 18 Infs comm type 4 or 5] **1989** Pederson *LAGS Tech. Index* 362 **Gulf Region,** *See. . .* [past participle] Seed . . 44 [infs]. **2000** *DARE* File **GA** (as of c1940), A patient came in and said she "hadn't seed anything."

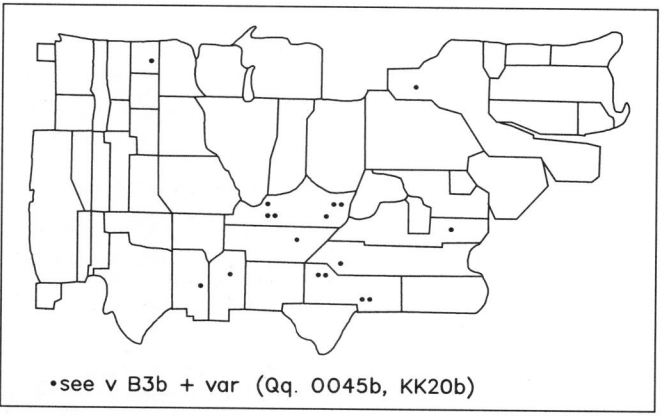

•see v B3b + var (Qq. OO45b, KK20b)

c *see.*

1928 Peterkin *Scarlet Sister Mary* 161 se**SC** [Gullah], Dey ain' never see one annudder. **1965–68** *DARE* (Qu. OO45b, *About seeing somebody:* "Many's the time I've _____ him hide things.") Infs **NY**75, **SC**10, 26, See. **1989** Pederson *LAGS Tech. Index* 362 **Gulf Region,** *See. . .* [past participle] See . . 1 [inf].

d *sawd, sawed.*

1970 *DARE* (Qu. OO45b, *About seeing somebody:* "Many's the time I've _____ him hide things.") Inf **KY**84, Sawed [FW: used in conv]. **1989** Pederson *LAGS Tech. Index* 362 **Gulf Region,** *See. . .* [past participle] Sawd . . 1 [inf].

e *sawn.*

1968 *DARE* (Qu. OO45b, *About seeing somebody:* "Many's the time I've _____ him hide things.") Inf **IN**26, Sawn. **1998** *DARE* File cs**WI,** I've sawn 'em seed or patch in sod and charge it to another account.

f *seend.*

1989 Pederson *LAGS Tech. Index* **Gulf Region,** *See. . .* [past participle] Seend . . 1 [inf].

s'ee v phr See **say** v **B2b**

seed n

1 The hard center of a peach, plum, or cherry. **widespread exc Nth** See Map on p. 840 and Map Section Cf **kernel 1, pit** n[2] **1, stone**

1899 (1912) Green *VA Folk-Speech* 315, *Peach-seed.* . . The hard nut enclosing the seed or kernel within the fruit of the peach. **c1960** *Wilson Coll.* cs**KY,** *Cherry seed* is almost universal; *pit* and *stone* are known but rarely used. **1965–70** *DARE* (Qu. I49, . . *The hard center of a plum*) 486 Infs, **widespread exc Nth,** Seed; (Qu. I50, . . *The hard center of a peach*) 431 Infs, **widespread exc Nth,** Seed; (Qu. I48, *The hard center of a cherry*) 316 Infs, **widespread exc Nth,** Seed. **1968** *PADS* 49.16 **Upper MW,** Vocabularies sometimes change because a word from one dialect appears to have more prestige than that of another dialect. . . The Midland *peach) seed* appears to be replacing the Northern *peach) stone;*

peach) pit, another Northern term is perhaps also on the increase (field informants, 31%; students, 49%). **1972** *PADS* 57.40 **Marietta OH** [Older native speakers], *Seed*—The hard part inside a peach in the Midland and South is a *seed.* **1989** Pederson *LAGS Tech. Index* 180 **Gulf Region** *(Cherry seed)* 460 infs, Seed; 18 infs, Cherry seed; *(Peach seed)* 482 infs, Seed; 115 infs, Peach seed.

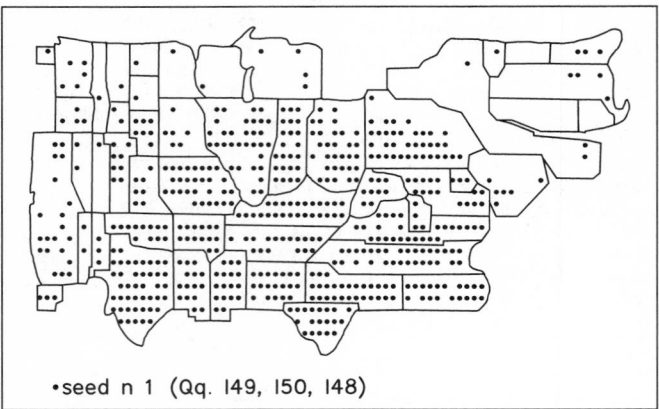

•seed n 1 (Qq. 149, 150, 148)

2 in combs *seed horse, ~ bull, ~ ox,* etc: An uncastrated male (domestic animal), esp one kept for breeding.   [*seed* semen; cf **seed-folks**]

1793 Morse *Amer. Universal Geog.* 485 **VA,** The gentlemen . . have taken much pains to raise a good breed of horses. . . They will give 1000*l.* sterling for a good seed horse. **1857** in 1941 Raymond *Bark Shanty Times* 6 **seMI,** He tells us the reason why pork is so scarce & dear. It is this that it has been so cold out west that all the seed pork is froze and those that did not freeze shook off their stones last dog days and consequently they have run out of seed. **1914** *DN* 4.112 **cKS,** *Seed-horse.* . . Stallion. **1925** in 1976 *PA Folklife* Spring 26, *Public Sale.* . . One pure bred Seed Hog, the balance are shoats weighing from 40 to 100 pounds. **1932** Hemingway *Death in Afternoon* 118, The usual ranch has two hundred cows and four seed bulls. **1939** *LANE* Map 190 *(Bull)* 1 inf, **seNH,** Seed ox. *Ibid* Map 197 *(Stallion)* 2 infs, **NH,** Seed horse. *Ibid* Map 206 *(Boar)* 2 infs, **NH, RI,** Seed hog. **1949** Webber *Backwoods Teacher* 134 **Ozarks,** Euphemisms are used in referring to male animals. . . A boar is a "male hog" or a "seed hog." *Ibid* 246, Hit's a boar's tush. . . A big old wild seed-hog's. **1968–70** *DARE* (Qu. K22, *Words used for a bull*) Inf **TN42,** Seed bull; **IN13,** Seed ox; (Qu. K52, *A male pig kept for breeding*) Infs **NJ10, 16,** Seed hog; **PA230,** Seed boar. **1999** *Cattle Today* Feb (Internet) **TX,** I have marketed . . commercial cattle, commercial seed stock, registered seed stock . . and high-dollar, silk-stocking seed stock to the players in breeds new and old.

3 A testicle.   **chiefly Sth, S Midl**

1927 Ruppenthal *Coll.* **KS,** *Seed.* . . a testicle of a male animal. **1937** *AmSp* 12.104 **eNE** [Farm terms], There are other terms used only by men as a rule that apply to livestock, such as *cut* for *castrate, seeds* or *nuts* for testicles, and *comin' round* for entering the period of sexual susceptibility. **1942** McAtee *Dial. Grant Co. IN Suppl. 1* 8 (as of 1890s), *Seeds* . . testicles. **1946** *AmSp* 21.271 **neKY,** *Seed.* . . Testicle (human). 'I been injured; I got one seed as big's your fist.' **1956** Gipson *Old Yeller* 94 **TX,** Let a boar hog get grown without cutting his seeds out, and his meat is too tough and rank smelling to eat. **c1960** Wilson *Coll.* **csKY,** *Seeds.* . . Testicles. **1968–69** *DARE* (Qu. K70, *Words used . . for castrating an animal*) Inf **MD22,** Take the seeds out; **IN80,** Cut his seeds out; **NC49,** Take their seed out. **1983** *MJLF* 9.1.54 **ceKY,** *Seeds* . . testicles of an animal. **1986** Pederson *LAGS Concordance* *(Haslet)* 1 inf, **ceAR,** Seeds—edible testicles of [a] hog; *(Chitterlings)* 1 inf, **swMS,** Hog seeds; *(Castrate)* 1 inf, **ceAR,** Cut him; get the seeds out; 1 inf, **swGA,** Cutting his seeds out; 1 inf, **cTN,** Get them seeds out; 1 inf, **cnGA,** You take his seeds out. [4 of 5 infs Black] **1990** Cavender *Folk Med. Lexicon* 31 **sAppalachians,** *Seed(s)*—a. semen. b. testicles: "The pain goes down to my seeds."

4 also attrib: Small **oysters B1** suitable for transplanting; an individual oyster of this size.   [Cf *OED2* 1721 at *seed* sb. 6] Cf **set n¹ 1**

1859 *Scientific Amer.* 1.70 **NY,** There is an excellent seed-oyster raked up from a small bay near Sing-Sing, on the Hudson river, which, when it is about the size of a quarter, is transferred to Long Island Sound. **1877**

Scribner's Mth. 15.227 **CT,** There were among the oystermen of Norwalk two young men . . who held possession of a few acres of oyster ground, which they annually replenished with seed brought from the Hudson River. **1881** Ingersoll *Oyster-Industry* 248, *Seed.*—Infant or young oysters suitable or intended for transplanted growth in artificial beds. **1887** Goode *Fisheries U.S.* 2.524, The cultivation of oysters transplanted when young (termed "seed") from the natural reefs where they were spawned to inshore, proprietary grounds, . . has long been followed in the United States. *Ibid* 540, In the South the name "blister" . . is given to the infant oyster, and serves to distinguish it from "seed," "cullens," and "oysters," which represent the successively larger sizes and stages of growth. **1891** *Scribner's Mag.* 10.471 **sNJ,** The Association sets apart certain natural beds for the use of the planters where the seed is obtained. **1948** *AmSp* 23.297 **Puget Sound WA,** The *seed* is the young oyster that, having finished its roving stage while it was looking for a suitable location, has at last settled down into a fixed abode but is not yet big enough to be marketable. Small oysters after they have *stooled* or *struck* or *spatted* down are *seed.* **1951** Taylor *Surv. Marine Fisheries NC* 147, Through trial-and-error methods and observation, oystermen have discovered the most favorable times to plant shells, to secure seed oysters and transplant young oysters. *Ibid* 154, The production of seed requires preparations to secure a set of oysters. **1970** *DARE* Tape **VA79,** Now on private oyster ground they get seed oysters from the James River, which are small oysters. **1995** in 2000 (acc) **VA** Marine Resources Comm. *Regulation Index* (Internet) **VA,** This Regulation. . . establishes as Oyster Management Areas those shell and seed oyster planting locations made during 1993 and in subsequent years. . . All areas planted with oyster shell and seed . . shall be considered Oyster Management Areas.

5 A burning coal covered with ashes to preserve a fire overnight.

1931 Goodrich *Mt. Homespun* 68 **sAppalachians,** I keep the seed of my fire all night, so the corner here is warm a plenty for the pot.

6 A rustic; hence adj *seedy* countrified.   [Prob abbr for **hay- seed 1**]

1900 *DN* 2.58 [College slang], *Seed.* . . A student from the country. . . *Seedy.* . . Countrified. **1900** *Century Illustr. Mag.* 61.292 **CO,** Who is the old seed [=an English cricket player] with the long goatee? **1967– 69** *DARE* (Qu. HH1, *Names and nicknames for a rustic or countrified person*) Inf **MI104, WV12,** Seed; **IL73, MN3,** Seedy. **1986** Pederson *LAGS Concordance* (A rustic) 1 inf, **csTX,** Seed.

seed v See **see B2b, 3b**

seed beer n
=**beer seed.**

1970 *DARE* (Qu. DD28b, . . *Fermented drinks . . made at home*) Inf **KY90,** Seed beer—non-alcoholic. **1986** Pederson *LAGS Concordance,* 1 inf, **ceMS,** Seed beer, California seed beer.

seedbird n
A **myrtle warbler** or similar bird.

1917 *Wilson Bulletin* 29.2.84 **VA,** *Dendroica coronata.*—Seed-bird, Revels I[slan]d, Va. **1968** *DARE* (Qu. Q14) Inf **MD36,** Wild canary— not identical with goldfinch; also called seed bird, eats sunflower seeds; small, yellow and white, sometimes a little black on wings.

seedbox n [See quot 1936]
A **false loosestrife,** usu *Ludwigia alternifolia.*

1821 Barton *Flora* 1.49, *Ludwigia macrocarpa* [=*L. alternifolia*] Large-capsuled Seed-box, or Ludwigia. **1869** Porcher *Resources* 60, *Seed Box, (Ludwigia alternifolia . .).* A decoction of the root is employed as an unfailing emetic. **1893** *Jrl. Amer. Folkl.* 6.142 **WV,** *Ludwigia alternifolia,* seed-box. **1936** IL Nat. Hist. Surv. *Wildflowers* 208, The Seedbox grows 2–3 feet high in swamps and low wet woods. . . The fruit is a cubical capsule about one-quarter inch long, which contains many seeds and is the source of the plant's common name. **1972** Courtenay–Zimmerman *Wild Flowers* 75, Seedbox, Ludwigia alternifolia. . . L. palustris: . . both species have square seed capsules.

seed bull See **seed n 2**

seed eater n Cf **seedbird**
A **goldfinch 1** (here: *Carduelis tristis*).

1917 *Wilson Bulletin* 29.2.83 **swKY,** *Astragalinus tristis* [=*Carduelis tristis*]. . . Seedeater.

seeder See **seed lobster**

seed-folks n pl Also with *old;* also *seed fathers* **NEng, esp ME** Cf **seed** n 2

Ancestors; old-timers; also fig.

1905 Wasson *Green Shay* 15 **sME coast,** The heft of the old seed-folks lays up back o' the meetin'-house; all the young fry that amounts to shucks has to git out of this for a livin'. **1908** Wasson *Home from Sea* 11 **sME coast,** It was the old-seed folks that turned to and built clean away in back here, to commence with. **1927** *AmSp* 3.139 **eME,** Ancestors were "the old seedfolks." **1954** Forbes *Rainbow* 197 **NEng,** Others must have joined us, for we played three-o'-cat and rounders. Not baseball, for it weren't invented yet—games we played were baseball's seed fathers. **1975** Gould *ME Lingo* 195, *Old seed-folks*—The ancestors and original Mainers; now any old-timers who are native born.

seed horse See **seed** n 2

seed lobster n Also *seeder*

An egg-carrying **lobster B1** (here: *Homarus americanus*).

[**1884** Goode *Fisheries U.S.* 1.798, Lobster spawn is variously designated on different parts of the [eastern] coast as "spawn," "roe," "eggs," "berry," "seed," "pea,' "sweetbread," "coral," etc.] **1930** *AmSp* 5.393 [Language of N Atl fishermen], *Seed-lobster.* . . A female lobster carrying eggs under her tail. **1966** *DARE* Tape **ME**17, Seed lobsters got a vee in the tail so that we all know that that's a seeder. **1975** Gould *ME Lingo* 247, *Seeder*—A female lobster the law requires be returned to the water when caught so she may replenish the Gulf of Maine. **2000** ME Dept. Marine Resources *Lobster Newsl.* Spring (Internet), The committee brought up the poor condition of seed lobsters when liberated. *Ibid,* The majority of seeder [sic] have been liberated in the Eastern end of the Coast.

seed moss n Cf **feather moss, swamp ~**

Perh a **moss 1** of the family Hypnaceae.

1939 FWP *Guide TN* 426 **nwTN,** "Seed moss," a filmy iridescent green carpet, grows in and around the twisted and grotesque cypress knees in shallow places.

seed of paradise See **paradise seed**

seed onion n esp **Nth** Cf **green onion, salad ~, scallion, spring onion**

A **green onion 1** or similar **onion** n **B.**

1965–70 *DARE* (Qu. I6, *The kind of onions that come up fresh early in the year, and you eat them raw*) Infs **IA**19, **MA**6, **NY**107, 139, 224, **PA**13, **UT**13, **WI**46, Seed onions. **1966** Dakin *Dial. Vocab. Ohio R. Valley* 2.367, *Green onion, spring onion,* and *young onion* seem most often to mean the onions which are planted in the spring and grow singly. . . Numerous miscellaneous terms are used by scattered speakers: *pull onions,* . . *seed onions* [etc]. **1973** Allen *LAUM* 1.308 **Upper MW** (as of c1950), Infs. also offered terms for other varieties of onion or of related plants, apparently because of some similarity to green onions. . . [such as] *seed onions,* with the synonymous *set onions.*

seed ox See **seed** n 2

seed-sower n Also *seed-strower* [From the resemblance of shot to seed] **SE**

A shotgun.

1965–70 *DARE* (Qu. P37b, *Nicknames for a shotgun*) Infs **GA**89, **MS**6, 60, 89, **SC**32, 34, Seed-sower; **GA**89, Seed-strower.

seed tick n

1 pronc-sp *see tick;* folk-etym *sea tick:* A tick of the family Ixodidae, often the larva or nymph. **chiefly Sth, S Midl** See Map Cf **yearling tick**

1705 Beverley *Hist. VA* 4.66, Seed-Ticks, and Red-Worms are small Insects, that annoy People by day, as Musketaes, and Chinches do by Night. **1779** in 1789 Anburey *Travels* 2.395 **cVA,** There are two sorts of insects extremely troublesome, which are the woodtick, and the seed-tick; . . the latter derive their name from not being much larger than small seed. **1859** Gosse *Letters from AL* 220, The first season they are called Seed-ticks . . the next year they become Yearling-ticks; and the third, Old-ticks. **1887** Custer *Tenting* 139 **sLA,** Two pests of that region, the seed-tick and the chigger. **1899** (1912) Green *VA Folk-Speech* 374, *Seed-tick.* . . Usually "see'tick." A young or small tick. **1903** *DN* 2.329 **seMO,** *Seed-tick.* . . The common wood-tick. **1907** *DN* 3.236

nwAR, *Seed-tick.* . . The common wood-tick. "I went into the woods and got covered with seed ticks and yearling ticks." **1925** Glasgow *Barren Ground* 118 **VA,** I got some seed ticks on me when I went down to the old spring in the pasture yesterday, and they've been eating me up ever since. **1935** Hurston *Mules & Men* 133 **nFL,** Ah see a chigger . . and a seed tick. **c1960** *Wilson Coll.* **csKY,** Seed ticks. . . Immature ticks, very numerous in the woods. **1965–70** *DARE* (Qu. R23a, *Insects or other creatures that fasten themselves to the skin and suck blood—on land*) 33 Infs, **chiefly Sth, S Midl,** Seed ticks; **FL**20, Sea tick (small); **MD**13, Sea tick—very small, not common, land bug despite its name; **NC**80, Sea tick (small tick); (Qu. R22, *Very small red insects, almost too small to see, that get under your skin and cause itching*) Infs **MO**35, **PA**138, Seed ticks; **PA**9, Sea ticks; (Qu. R23b, *Blood-sucking creatures—in water*) Inf **NC**60, Sea tick, sea lice. [31 of 39 total Infs old] **1986** Pederson *LAGS Concordance* (Small insects that burrow in your skin and raise welts) 30 infs, **Gulf Region,** Seed tick(s).

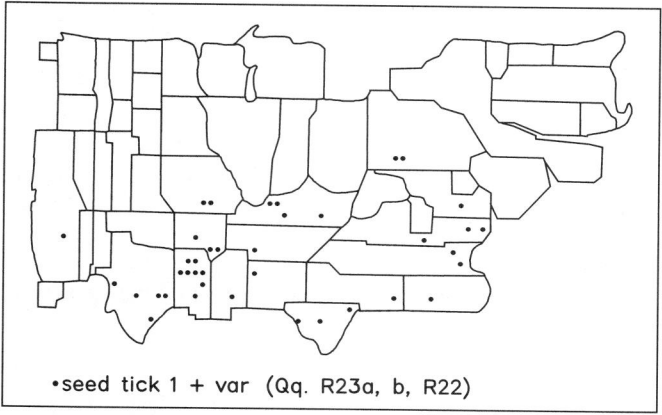

•seed tick 1 + var (Qq. R23a, b, R22)

2 =**tick trefoil.**

1912 Blatchley *IN Weed Book* 91, Seventeen species of these tick-trefoils are known from the State. . . All are vile weeds commonly known as "seed ticks."

3 A **wild carrot** (here: *Daucus pusillus*). [Appar from the resemblance of the seed to **1** above]

1936 Whitehouse *TX Flowers* 90, Beggar's Ticks. Seed-Ticks. Bird's Nest Carrot (*Daucus pusillus*). . . The clusters of seeds resemble a bird's nest. The fact that the seeds are covered with several rows of barbed prickles makes them very difficult to remove from clothing. Their presence in wool renders it inferior in quality. **1961** Wills–Irwin *Flowers TX* 168, A common weedy plant of roadsides and waste places, the Wild Carrot, or Seed-ticks, is nonetheless possessed of singular delicacy of structure.

seed wart n

A wart with a rough surface resembling a group of seeds.

1948 *Courier–Jrl.* (Louisville KY) 3 Mar, When I was a boy. . . I had five or six warts on my hands. One was a seed wart, nearly as big as a grain of corn. **1954** *PADS* 21.36 **SC,** *Seed wart.* . . A wart which shows the seed-like papillae on its surface. **1954** Harder *Coll.* **cwTN,** Seed wart. **1955** McAtee *Dial. Grant Co. IN Suppl.* 6 [2], *Seed wart:* . . one with a rugged surface, suggesting in texture, if I may say so, a bit of cauliflower. **1956** McAtee *Some Dialect NC* 39, *Seed wart* . . a rough one presenting a surface like a group of seeds. **c1960** *Wilson Coll.* **csKY,** *Seed wart.* . . A wart with a rough surface.

seedy See **seed** n 6

seegar n |'sigɑr| Also *seegyar* [Pronc-spp for *cigar*] **scattered, but more freq Sth, S Midl** See Map on p. 842

1858 *Harper's New Mth. Mag.* 16.283 **GA,** Kin enny one of you gentlemen favor me with a *seegar?* **1883** *Century Illustr. Mag.* 26.616, Ole Brer Rabbit, . . he des tuck'n go in de kitchen en light he seegyar. **1885** Twain *Huck. Finn* 97, Seegars, I bet you—and cost five cents apiece, solid cash. **1891** Page *Elsket* 127 **VA** [Black], Heah come P'laski . . wid a creevat! an' a cane! an' wid a seegar! **1899** Chesnutt *Conjure Woman* 25 **csNC** [Black], Mars Dugal' ax 'im ter hab a seegyar. **1902** *DN* 2.231 **sIL,** Cigar. . . Pronounced ['sigɑr] with accent on first syllable. **1903** *DN* 2.309 **seMO,** Cigar. . . seegar. **1906** *DN* 3.131 **nwAR,** Cigar ['sigɑr]. **1960** Criswell *Resp. to PADS* 20 **Ozarks,** Seegar, fairly common. **c1960** *Wilson Coll.* **csKY** ['si,gɑr]. **1965–70**

DARE (Qu. DD6a, *Other names or nicknames for cigars*) 51 Infs, **scattered, but more freq Sth, S Midl, N Cent, PA,** Seegar. **1966** *DARE* Tape **FL9,** [ˈsigɑrz]. **1989** Pederson *LAGS Tech. Index* 197 *(Cigars)* 74 infs, **Gulf Region,** [ˈsigɑr(z)].

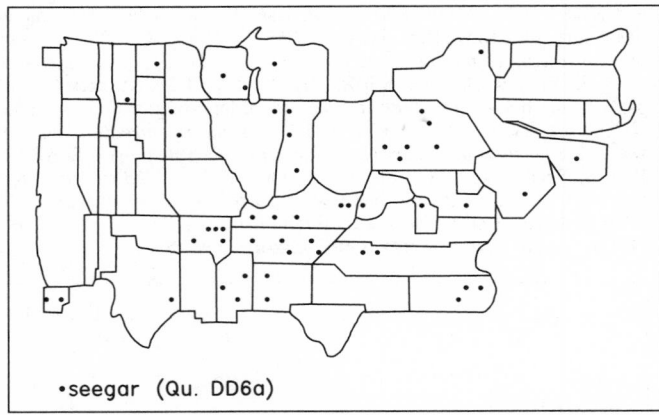

•seegar (Qu. DD6a)

seegoo, seegose See **sego lily**

seegyar See **seegar**

seeing stars See **see stars**

seek v, hence n *seeker;* vbl n *seeking*   **chiefly Sth, S Midl**   *esp freq among Black speakers*
To earnestly pursue religious experience; to "seek religion."
1801–3 J. Lyle *Diary* (MS.) 39 *(DAE),* When I spoke to seekers I cautioned them against depending on a Jesus yet unknown. **1816** in 1824 Knight *Letters* 75 **VA,** With the field-slaves, Sunday is usually a holiday; wherein they deck themselves out for frolic, or for their unintelligible methodist meetings; where those, who are tender in spirit, are said to be 'seeking.' **1838** (1852) Gilman *S. Matron* 270 [Black], Months, often years, elapse before a seeker is considered a fit subject by the leader to be presented to his pastor as a candidate for the communion. **1859** Taliaferro *Fisher's R.* 40 **nwNC** (as of 1820s), He joined . . [a] church. . . The great Goliath . . was now a humble penitent and a devout "seeker." **1884** *Anglia* 7.265 **Sth, S Midl** [Black], *To be a Seekin'* = to seek 'religion'. **1893** Shands *MS Speech* 55, *Seeker* [sikə]. This word is used without modifiers of any sort to mean a penitent, one who is sorry for sin and desires to become religious. **1901** Harben *Westerfelt* 269 **nGA,** "Are you a seeker, John Westerfelt?" she asked, with a sneer. **1928** Peterkin *Scarlet Sister Mary* 172 **SC,** To join the church and be saved from sin. She'd have to seek. That meant praying night and day until Jesus sent her a sign that her sins were forgiven. **1930** Woofter *Black Yeomanry* 226 **seSC,** Candidates for membership [in a church] were instructed by "class leaders" and tested by dreams and visions. This process, in the Sea Islands, is termed "seeking." **c1937** in 1976 *Weevils in the Wheat* 278 **VA** [Black], Uncle John is a devout Baptist, and he says religion isn't what it used to be. Colored people use to starve themselves and pray and seek sometimes a month or more.

seelectman See **selectman**

see monkeys See **monkey** n[1] **B4a, 5**

seen See **see B2c**

seena See **senna** n[1]

seend See **see B2f, 3f**

seenie bean See **siene bean**

seent See **see B2f**

seeny n[1] [Aphet form of **cassena**] **GA**
A **holly** n[1] **1** such as a **yaupon** (here: *Ilex cassine*).
1927 [see **seeny bear**]. **1934** *Natl. Geogr. Mag.* 65.598 **seGA,** The Okefinokee prairies. . . are also dotted here and there with wooded islets—the so-called prairie "heads"—of cypress, slash pine, "seeny" *(Ilex cassine),* . . and other trees. **1968** *DARE* FW Addit **GA25,** "Seeny tree" [ˈsinɪ]—nickname for the white holly.

seeny n[2] See **senna** n[1]

seeny bear n Also *cassenyie bear* [**seeny** n[1]]   Cf **hog bear, Seneca ~**
The black bear *(Ursus americanus).*
1927 Boston Soc. Nat. Hist. *Proc.* 38.281 **Okefenokee GA,** The majority opinion among the best-informed local authorities seems to favor the existence of two kinds or species of Bears in the Okefinokee region: a small brown 'Hog Bear,' and a large black 'Cassenyie Bear' or 'Seeny Bear' (so called from cassena or 'seeny,' *Ilex Cassine*).

seenyuh See **scenery**

seep n Also *seep spring;* also rarely sp *sipe* [*EDD seep sb.* 5 "A small spring"; *sipe sb.* 7]   **chiefly Sth, S Midl, West**   Note: It is unclear whether the sp *sipe* actually represents a var pronc; *sipe* (or *sype*) is well attested in Brit dial, but see quot 1892.   Cf **seep** v, **sipe** n **1**
A place where water oozes out of the ground; a sluggish spring; hence adjs *seepy, seepish* of land: constantly damp.
1859 (1968) Bartlett *Americanisms* 393 **MD, VA,** *Seepy.* Seepy land is land under cultivation that is not well drained. **1881** in 1940 *AmSp* 15.390 **swVA,** Much salt has been made there by boiling the water caught at one of the brine seeps. **1892** Amer. Soc. Civil Engineers *Trans.* 26.568, The water which thus transpires through the soil is called . . by the Americans of the Mississippi Valley "sipe water" (pronounced *seep*). **1901** in 1961 Biggers *Chronicle* 38 **TX,** Bull Run was nothing more than a little sipe spring tributary of the Concho, and during the most favorable seasons afforded only a few little pools of water near its head. **1902** *Nature* (London) 4 Dec 113 **swTX,** At Comanche Spring, a small "seep," seven miles north of the Rio Grande, the limestone bluffs have been covered in a number of places with rude paintings of characteristic Indian design. **1909** *DN* 3.403 **nwAR,** *Seep.* . . A low wet place. **1932** *DN* 6.233 **West,** *Seep.* A *seep* is a place, usually in a pocket, or a draw, or near a spring, where the water seeps out of the hillside and gathers in a pool below. The term is used all over the West. **1933** *AmSp* 8.1.52 **Ozarks,** *Seep.* . . A wet spot produced by a spring which does not quite reach the surface. Some very fine springs are brought to light by digging into these seeps. **1935** Davis *Honey* 305 **OR,** Heavy pelicans from the timbered lakes to the west flapped awkwardly up from the fresh-water seeps at the edge of the tule-beds. **1948** Baumann *Old Man Crow's Boy* 118 **ID,** The bottom of the draw held the seeps or springs which fed that fork of Skunk Creek. **1956** Gipson *Old Yeller* 76 **TX,** I finally came across her, . . close to a little seep spring. **c1960** Wilson *Coll.* **csKY,** *Seep.* . . A small spring. **1965–70** *DARE* (Qu. C6, . . *A piece of land that's often wet, and has grass and weeds growing on it*) Infs **OK25, TN7,** Seep; **MO34, OK42, TX5,** Seepy (land); **WY5,** Seepy; (Qu. C7, . . *Land that usually has some standing water with trees or bushes growing in it*) Inf **NE7,** Seep land; (Qu. C11, *Soft, wet sand in streams or wet places, that draws people and things down into it*) Inf **NM11,** Seep. **1986** Pederson *LAGS Concordance* *(Meadow)* 1 inf, **cwLA,** A seepy place; *(Swamp)* 1 inf, **swMS,** Seepish land—seeps water all the time; 1 inf, **cnTN,** A seepy place; *(Marshes)* 1 inf, **ceTX,** Seep; [1 inf, **cnMS,** A spring seep]; *(Creek)* 1 inf, **neTN,** A seep—smaller than a branch; 1 inf, **neGA,** Small stream or seep—smaller than branch.

seep v
1 also *sipe;* also rarely with *out:* To undergo or subject (something) to soaking in hot liquid.   Note: For the var *sipe* see the note at **seep** n.
1886 in 1890 *Century Dict.* 5652 , The leaves are boiled in fresh cow's milk, and, after boiling a moment, the infusion is allowed to stand and sipe for ten minutes, when it is strained, sweetened, and drank while warm. **1965–70** *DARE* (Qu. H72, . . *Preparing tea: "Pour on the water and let it _____."*) 57 Infs, **scattered,** Seep; **SC43,** Seep out; (Qu. H73, . . *Preparing coffee: the housewife says, "I think I'll go and _____ some coffee."*) Inf **ME19,** Seep.
2 To suppurate; to ooze.   **esp N Midl**   See Map
1965–70 *DARE* (Qu. BB36, *When there's an open sore and this yellowish stuff is coming out of it . . it's _____*) 12 Infs, **esp N Midl,** Seeping.

seepish See **seep** n

seep out See **seep** v **1**

seep spring See **seep** n

seepweed n
=**sea blite.**

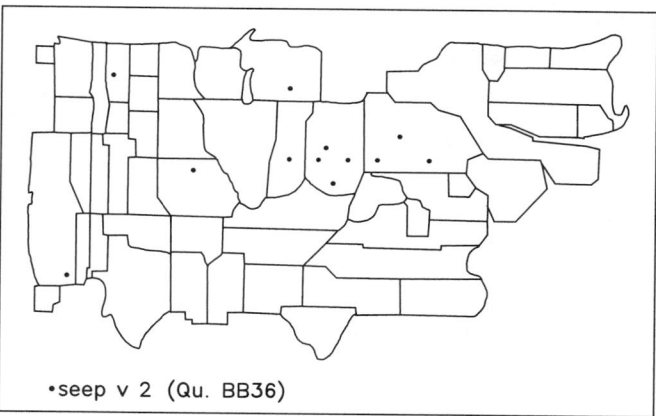

•seep v 2 (Qu. BB36)

1940 Writers' Program *Guide NV* 13, The desert plants are the salt bushes (Atriplex canescens and Grayia spinosa), grease wood (Sarcobatus vermiculatus), seep weed *(Dondia occidentalis),* [etc]. **1970** Kirk *Wild Edible Plants W. U.S.* 62, *Suaeda* species. . . The Seep Weeds are found in alkaline and saline soil throughout the West. **1985** Dodge *Flowers SW Deserts* 14, Seepweed, which is usually an indicator of alkaline soil, is browsed to some extent by cattle when other feed is scarce. . . Flowers of the seepweed are small, greenish, and without petals. . . It is . . common in moist locations through the Southwest.

seepwillow n

A **groundsel tree** (here: *Baccharis glutinosa*) of the western US. Also called **false willow, Gila ~, water motie, ~ willow, ~ wally**

1931 U.S. Dept. Ag. *Misc. Pub.* 101.158, Seepwillow (B[accharis] glutinosa) . . is a bush—occasionally only half-shrubby—3 to 12 feet high, with viscid, willow-like leaves. **1937** U.S. Forest Serv. *Range Plant Hdbk.* B33, Seepwillow . . is a graceful, willowy shrub. . . The use of seep and water as part of the local names refers to the common occurrence of this bush around springs and streams. **1981** Benson–Darrow *Trees SW Deserts* 335, The seep willow is of importance in control of streambank erosion, because it often forms dense thickets along watercourses or intermittent streams.

seepy See **seep** n

see roses v phr Cf **flower** n B1, *DS* AA27

To menstruate.

1990 Cavender *Folk Med. Lexicon* 31 **sAppalachians,** *Seeing roses*—menstruation. [**2000** *DARE* File **GA** (as of c1940), A patient came in and said she "hadn't seed anything." I checked her eyes and found nothing wrong. It took me a long time to figure out that she was afraid she was pregnant because she hadn't seen any blood.]

seers n Also *eye-seers*

1966–67 *DARE* (Qu. X23, . . *Joking words . . for eyeglasses*) Infs **GA9, SC55,** Seers; **MS6,** Eye-seers.

sees See **see** B1

seesaw n

1 A plank that is balanced on a center support and that swings up and down when riders on the ends push against the ground with their feet; the action of riding on such a plank; also v *seesaw* to play on such a device. [*OED2* 1821 →] **chiefly Atlantic, Sth, S Midl, SW** See Map and Map Section Cf **ridy horse 2, teeter-totter**

1834 Smith *Letters Jack Downing* 7 **ME,** Jest like two boys playin see-saw on a rail. First one goes up, then 'tother. **1847** *S. Qrly. Rev.* 11.450, New means were furnished them for swinging on beams, and playing see-saw with the boards. **1859** in 1956 Eliason *Tarheel Talk* 292 **nw,cnNC,** She fell off the plank when we were *sesawing.* **1890** (1972) Howells *Boy's Town* 84, There were plenty of boards for teeter and see-saw. **1899** (1912) Green *VA Folk-Speech* 374, *See-saw.* . . A sport in which two children sit one at each end of a board or long piece of timber balanced on some support, and move alternately up and down. **1937** Crane *Let Me Show You VT* 35 **VT,** The seesaw is called *seesaw* in all parts of the state, but the word *teeter-totter* (imported from southwestern Connecticut) occurs twice. **1941** *Language* 17.33 **WI,** *See-*

saw. . . Despite some opinion to the contrary, *seesaw* is clearly an innovation: mentioned by only 12 per cent of the oldest but 56 per cent of the middle [aged] informants; the young informant uses this alone. **1949** Kurath *Word Geog.* 16, In the North *seesaw* is distinctly a book word, which, however, has attained rather general currency in urban areas. *Ibid* 58, The word *seesaw* is used everywhere [in the eastern United States], but in the New England settlement area other expressions are more widely current than *seesaw.* The same is true of the South and the South Midland. It is only in Pennsylvania, and the greater parts of northern Maryland, Virginia, and South Carolina that *seesaw* is not paralleled by other terms. . . In the Southern area and in the Appalachians *seesaw* is in rather general use on all social levels. **1965–70** *DARE* (Qu. EE31, *Playground equipment with a long board for two children to sit on and go up and down in turn*) 602 Infs, **chiefly Atlantic, Sth, S Midl, SW,** Seesaw. **1968** *PADS* 49.17 **Upper MW** (as of c1950), As a term for the pieces of playground equipment the Northern *teeter-totter* is increasing, while the Southern and Midland *see-saw* is used by a small percentage of each group. **1989** Pederson *LAGS Tech. Index* 86 **Gulf Region,** Seesaw . . ridy-horse (29 [infs]) . . seesaw (771 [infs]) . . teeter-totter (44 [infs]).

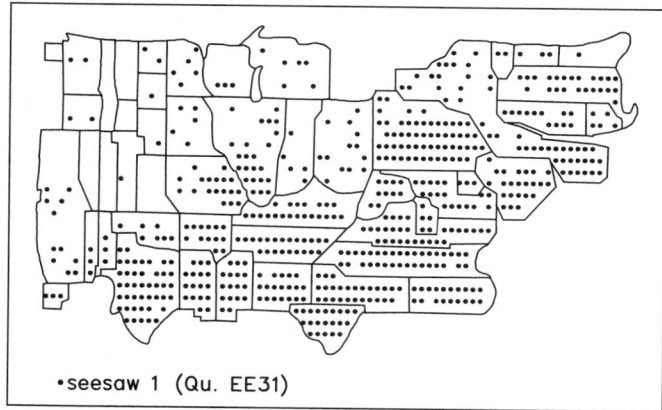

•seesaw 1 (Qu. EE31)

2 =**spotted sandpiper.** Cf **teetertail, tip-up**

1917 (1923) *Birds Amer.* 1.249, Spotted Sandpiper. . . *Other Names.* . . See-saw. *Ibid* 250, The Spotted Sandpiper . . is popularly nicknamed . . from its nervous habit of constantly tilting its body. **1951** Teale *North with Spring* 257, Each time they fluttered down to a mossy log or bit of mud, they teetered violently as they came to rest. Their numerous common names—teeter, teetertail, teeter snipe, teeter-bob, tiptail, and seesaw—are derived from this habit.

seesta See **siehst du**

see stars v phr, hence vbl n *seeing stars*

To participate (as an unwitting victim) in a practical joke; see quots.

1909 *DN* 3.421 **Cape Cod MA** (as of a1857), *See stars.* . . The expression . . refers to a trick practised upon children. The child who admits that he wishes to *see stars* is led into a dark room and asked to look up a coat sleeve or something similar. A dipper of water is then poured down. **1950** *WELS Suppl.* **swWI,** *Seeing stars through a coatsleeve*—One player is in a closet or seperate [sic] room as another stands outside the closed door [who] is called the "door tender" and that [one] knows the "game or joke" along with the one in the room. The "door tender" then chooses or asks just "one" in the roomful of players to come in the closet and see "stars through a coat sleeve". As one goes in the "door tender" enters also. Closing the door [he] throws a coat over the players [sic] head as he sits on a stool or low seat, one [*DARE* Ed: presumably the door tender's confederate] holds the coat sleeve up so the player can see up through it. Then told to keep looking for stars, as a thimble of water is poured down through the sleeve. Play over until all are chosen.

see the elephant See **elephant 1**

see the monkeys See **monkey** n[1] **B5**

see tick See **seed tick 1**

seeve See **sieve**

seewee bean See **sieva bean**

see you in church exclam **chiefly Nth, Upper Missip Valley**
See Map *joc*
Used as an expression of farewell.

1950 *WELS (Informal ways of saying "good-bye")* 5 Infs, **WI,** See you in church. **c1960** *Wilson Coll.* **csKY,** See you in church. . . Facetious farewell. **1965–70** *DARE* (Qu. NN11, *Informal ways of saying 'good-bye' to people you know quite well*) 45 Infs, **chiefly Nth, Upper Missip Valley,** See you in church; [CT6, I'll meet you in church]; **WI26,** See you in church, if you set by the window.

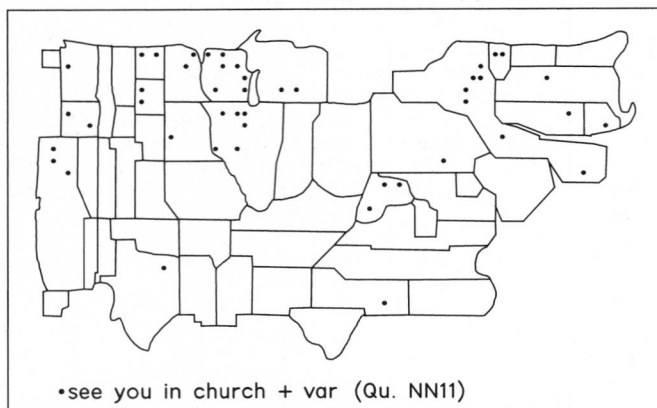

•see you in church + var (Qu. NN11)

sef(f) See **self**

seft See **save A**

segaciate, segashuate See **sagaciate**

sego lily n Also *sago (lily), seacoe, se(e)gose, seegoo, sego(se), sigo* [Paiute *sego;* the var *sago* is prob by confusion with the edible starch of that name] Cf **poison sego, swamp ~**
A **mariposa lily,** esp *Calochortus nuttallii;* also the edible bulb of such a plant.

1851 Howe *Hist. Coll. Gt. West* 432 **nUT,** Hogs fatten on a succulent bulb or tuber, called the Seacoe, or Seegose Root. **1852** Stansbury *Expedition* 160 **UT,** [Frémont] island . . abound[s] in prodigious quantities of the wild onion, wild parsnip, and *sego, (Calochortus luteus.)* The latter is a small bulbous root, about the size of a walnut, very palatable and nutritious, and is much used by the Indian tribes as an article of food. **1861** Burton *City Saints* 396 **UT,** Carrington Island. . . is rich in plants and flowers, as the sego, also spelt sigo, seacoe, and segose, (*Calochortus luteus,* an onion-like bulb or tuber, about the size of a walnut, more nutritious than palatable, much eaten as a table vegetable by the early Mormons and the root-digging Indians, and even now by white men when half-starved . .). **1896** *Garden and Forest* 9.292, Sego (Calochortus Nuttalli).—A Pai Ute word generic with these Indians and others of the same (Shoshonean) linguistic stock, for edible bulbous roots. The word is sometimes spelled Sago. **1901** U.S. Dept. Ag. Div. Botany *Bulletin* 26.52 **MT,** Quamasia and Calochortus . . were commonly known as camas and wild sego, and were much used for food both by the Indians and by travelers. **1903** (1950) Austin *Land of Little Rain* 83 **neCA,** The seegoo establishes itself very readily in swampy borders. **1920** Rice–Rice *Pop. Studies CA Wild Flowers* 30, C[alochortus] nuttali [sic], commonly called the "Sego Lily," is the State flower of Utah, where it is highly esteemed . . because its edible corms formed a substantial part of the diet of the early Mormon pioneers when they crossed the desert. . . Through a misunderstanding of the word, the Mormons formerly pronounced it "Sago Lily," but "Sego" was the Ute term. **1965–68** *DARE* (Qu. S4) Inf **NM9,** Sego lily; (Qu. S26b, *Wildflowers that grow in water or wet places*) Infs **NM9, UT3,** Sego lily; (Qu. S26c, *Wildflowers that grow in woods*) Inf **UT10,** Seagull [sic] lilies. **1967** *DARE* FW Addit **OR12,** Sego lily. **1973** Hitchcock–Cronquist *Flora Pacific NW* 686, *Calochortus* . . Mariposa or Sego Lily. . . Most spp. propagate freely from seeds, but it takes 3–5 years for seedlings to grow into fl[ower] bulbs.

sego pondweed See **sago pondweed**

segose See **sego lily**

seguarro See **saguaro**

segundo n Also *secundo, el segundo* [Span] **esp SW**
A foreman; an underboss.

1903 (1965) Adams *Log Cowboy* 299 **NM,** Flood inquired of their outfit if there was any sub-foreman, or *segundo* as they were generally called. **1936** Adams *Cowboy Lingo* 137, The crew [on a cattle drive] consisted of the 'trail boss,' his assistant, the 'secundo' or 'straw boss,' the cook [etc]. **1937** *DN* 6.621 **swTX,** The Mexican word *segundo* (Spanish for "second") is often used instead of foreman, who is second in command to the rancher. **1949** *Boston Sun. Globe Mag.* 3 April 1/2 *(DA),* What have you got a segundo for? **1967** *DARE* (Qu. HH43a, *The top person in charge of a group of workmen*) Inf **TX4,** El segundo; (Qu. HH43b, *The assistant to the top person*) Inf **TX29,** El segundo. **1970** *DARE* FW Addit, 1 inf (husband of **TX80**), Segundo—means second in Spanish; used here in the fields.

sekker See **senkah**

sele n Also sp *seal* [Engl dial *(give one) the sele of the day* and varr, *(to give one) good day*]
1936 *AmSp* 11.191 **seWY,** Sele. (Mr. Dean gave this as seal, but it must be sele.) 'The sele of the day,' salutation, 'I wouldn't give him the sele of the day.' (I.e., I wouldn't speak to him.)

selectman n Pronc-spp *seelectman, selec' man* **chiefly NEng**
A member of a board of town officers.

1635 in 1846 Frothingham *Hist. Charlestown MA* 51, An order [was] made by the inhabitants of Charlestowne at a full meeting for the government of the Town by Selectmen. **1792** Belknap *Hist. NH* 3.282, Three or five *Selectmen* are annually chosen in each town, who are entrusted with its general concerns. **1811** in 1957 Old *Farmer's Almanac Sampler* 51 **NEng,** If you find near your house a gully in the road or a small hole in the bridge, do not wait for the surveyor or selectman to give orders, but hasten and repair the breach. **1825** Neal *Brother Jonathan* 1.62 **CT,** 'Squire, 'squire!—I'd as lief be anointed "moderator;" "se-lect-man," as you call it, or corporal, or deacon. **1892** in 1986 Brewer *Easthampton Town Lodging House* 4 **cwMA,** A detailed report of these expenditures has been transcribed on an Inventory Book, in Selectmen's room, and is open for the inspection of the voters. **1905** *DN* 3.18 **cCT,** Selectman. . . A town magistrate. **1907** *DN* 3.199 **seNH,** Selectman. One of a board of three principal officers of a New Hampshire town. **1929** *AmSp* 5.124 **ME,** We heard much of "selec' men," "selec' man" and "town meeting." **1949** Kurath *Word Geog.* 20, The *selectmen* are the chief town officers in all of the New England states except Rhode Island, where they are known as *councilmen*. In Maine, New Hampshire, and northeastern Massachusetts (from Concord northward) *selectmen* is stressed on the first syllable (which is usually pronounced as *seal,* less commonly as *sill* or *sell*), elsewhere on the second. **1967–69** *DARE* Tape **CT9,** We have a board of selectmen [sǝˈlɛktmɛn], board of finance, school board . . they really control the town; **MA58,** Well, the selectmen [sǝˈlɛktmɛn], too. They wanna speak, they usually rise and address the moderator; **MI62,** And also it was determined by the selectmen [sǝˈlɛktmɛn] of the village that the main street should be one hundred feet wide, primarily so that they could turn their wagons around in the center of the street. **1969** *DARE* (Qu. N33, *A man whose job is to take care of roads in a certain locality*) Infs **CT22, 29, 36, VT16,** Selectman; **CT23,** First selectman. **1969** *Std.–Times* (New Bedford MA) 22 Jan 1, Middleboro—They haven't done so yet, but perhaps the Board of Selectmen here will be forced to erect "Caution—House Crossing" signs throughout the town. **1975** Gould *ME Lingo* 247, Seelectman—Mainers always give a hearty "see" sound to the first syllable. **2001** *DARE* File **nwMA,** Went to town meeting last night. . . Big discussion over the transfer of Southworth School from the School Committee to the Selectmen.

self pron Usu |sɛlf|; also **Sth, S Midl** |sɛ(ǝ)f| Pronc-spp *salf, sef(f), selth, silf* Cf **help** v A1b
A Pronc varr.

1788 in 1956 Eliason *Tarheel Talk* 317 **NC,** Salf. **1827** *Ibid* 317, Silf. **1834** *Ibid* 317, Seff. **1852** *Ibid* 317, Selth. **1853** [see **B** below]. **1887** *Scribner's Mag.* 2.479 **AR,** I seen ye, myseff, feedin' up that innercent chile on gouber peas an' hogs' melts! **1895** in 1944 *ADD* **sIL,** [ˈmaɪ sɛǝf]. **1909** *DN* 3.367 **eAL, wGA,** Sef. . . Self. **1915** *DN* 4.189 **swVA,** Self [sɛf]. **1923** *DN* 5.213 **swMO,** "I made a jedge o' m'se'f," i.e., made a fool of myself. **1923** *DN* 5.220 **swMO,** Se'f. **1931** *PMLA* 46.1303 **sAppalachians,** Negro influence has crept in in such words as: . . se'f, self. **1936** *AmSp* 11.247 **eTX,** Myself and self usually have only one form: [mǝsɛǝf], [sɛǝf]; but in less literate speech, the *self* words, when unstressed, may be [sɛf].   **1947** Ballowe *The Lawd* 3 **LA,** Some o' the people whut . . run hawg wild found theyse'fs runnin' up the road.   **1949** Turner *Africanisms* 260 **sSC** [Gullah], [sɛf-reɪzɪn] [= self-rising].   *Ibid* 276, [hɪsɛf] [=herself].   **c1960** *Wilson Coll.* **csKY,** *Self* is often /sɛf/.   **1995** McCormack *Fields Pastures* 172 **cwAL** (as of 1960s), Then git y'all's se'f off'n my property!

B Gram form.

Usu in comb with pl pronoun, sg *self* used for pl *selves;* see quots.   **chiefly Sth, S Midl**

   1853 Simms *Sword & Distaff* 76 **SC,** Better we bury wese'f up to de neck in de swamp, where we knows de varmints, dan le' 'em carry we off to de British Hulk, I'm a t'inking.   **1922** Gonzales *Black Border* 325 **sSC GA coasts** [Gullah glossary], '*Self*—himself, herself, itself, themselves.   *Ibid* 338, *We'self*—ourselves.   **1932** Randolph *Ozark Mt. Folks* 22, When I was a young feller we was more serous-like, an' we tuck a interest in book-l'arnin', an' was allus a-tryin' for t' improve ourse'f some way.   **1937** NE Univ. *Univ. Studies* 37.111 [Terms from play-party songs], *Ourself,* pron. (For rhyme with "yourself.") Ourselves. "We'll bet you five dollars we'll better ourself."   **c1937** in 1976 *Weevils in the Wheat* 227 **VA** [Black], Dey was peach trees . . dat us could have fo usself. Co'se us had watermellons en mush mellons also.   **1967–68** *DARE* (Qu. Y18, *To leave in a hurry: "Before they find this out, we'd better* _____*!"*) Inf **MA5,** Make ourself scarce; (Qu. AA8, *When people make too much of a show of affection in a public place . . "There they were at the church supper* _____ *[with each other]."*) Inf **MD19,** Making a fool of theirself; (Qu. AA15a, . . *Joking ways . . of saying that people got married . . "They* _____*."*) Inf **MI96,** Got themself in the soup; (Qu. II18, *Someone who joins himself on to you and your group without being asked and won't leave*) Inf **TN15,** Push theyself; (Qu. JJ7, . . *Cheating in school examinations*) Inf **TN13,** They're just hurting theyself.   **1986** Pederson *LAGS Concordance,* [16 infs, **Gulf Region,** Ourself = ourselves;] 3 infs, **AL, MS,** Y'all (*or* you-all) help yourself; 1 inf, **swLA,** Lot of you had a lot of chance, you never done a damn thing with yourself; 1 inf, **ceLA,** Y'all going have your coffee by yourself.   **1989** Pederson *LAGS Tech. Index* 151 **Gulf Region,** *[They've got to look out for] Themselves* . . their own self . . (5 [infs]); their own selves (2 [infs]); theirself . . (125 [infs]); theirselves (135 [infs]); themself . . (63 [infs]); themselves (423 [infs]).

self-binder n   Also *self-binding harvester*
A harvesting machine that binds the grain it cuts.
   1877 in 1937 Ruede *Sod-House* 113 **KS,** Henry and John went to see a selfbinder at work.   **1883** *Scientific Amer.* 3 March 138 **MN,** An improved bundle separating attachment for self-binding harvesters.   **1925** *Book of Rural Life* 4.2511, The Modern Harvester, or Self-binder. . . The self-binder is one of the most complicated machines used on the farm, and considerable skill is necessary to operate the machine efficiently.   **1943** Crow *Gt. Amer. Customer* 186, The machine bore little resemblance to a modern self binder which had not yet been dreamed of.   **1968** *DARE* (Qu. L28, *Tools used in the past for cutting grain*) Inf **WI30,** Self-binder.   **1984** *MJLF* 10.155 **cnWI,** *Self-binder.* A reaper that both reaps and ties the grain into bundles.

self-brag n   Also *self-bragger*
A braggart; a conceited person.
   c1960 *Wilson Coll.* **csKY,** *Self-brag.* . . A person who worships an idol, himself, and expects other worshipers to follow suit.   **1966–69** *DARE* (Qu. HH8, *A person who likes to brag*) Infs **MO37, OK18,** A self-brag (brags on himself); **VA11,** Self-brag; **GA77,** Self-bragger.

self-catch See **catch** n 2

self-conceity adj phr   Cf **self-brag**
   1969 *DARE* (Qu. II36b, *Of somebody who talks back or gives rude answers . . "She certainly is* _____*!"*) Inf **MO19,** Self-conceity.

self-feeder See **feeder 5**

self-greaser n   Cf **greasy bean**
   1967 *DARE* (Qu. I20, . . *Kinds of beans that are grown around here*) Inf **KY34,** Greasy grits or self-greasers.

self-heal n
Std: a naturalized perennial plant (*Prunella vulgaris*) formerly used as a remedy in throat ailments.   Also called **blue curls 2,** **~ Lucy 1, bumblebee weed, carpenter ~, cure-all 4, dragonhead 3, figwort 2, groundhog plantain, heal-all 2,**
heartsease 3, snakeweed, square-weed, thimbleflower, wild sage

self-planted See **self-sown**

self-rake n   Also *self-rake reaper, self-raker*
A harvesting machine or attachment to a harvesting machine for cutting grain and depositing it in piles; see quot 1925.
   1856 *WI Farmer & NW Cultivator* Feb 91, The question with every man is, which one he had better buy?—whether a Self-Raker, or simply a reaper.   **1857** *IL State Ag. Soc. Trans. for 1856–57* 2.120, A self raker . . *may* be just as simple in its structure as some *hand raker.*   **1879** *Scribner's Mth.* 19.134 **KS,** The self-raker . . drops it [=wheat] in convenient little bunches.   **1925** *Book of Rural Life* 4.2508, The self-rake reaper is a machine for cutting grain and leaving it in unbound bunches in the field. It consists of a cutter bar with a platform directly to the rear, upon which the cut grain falls and from which it is swept at intervals with the rake.   **1967** *DARE* FW Addit **CO3,** *Self-rake*—a reel came around and brushed cuttings off the cradle.—"Platform to winrows."   **1968–70** *DARE* (Qu. L28, *Tools used in the past for cutting grain*) Inf **OH95,** Self-rake: predecessor of binder; a mowing machine; **PA141,** Self-rake; (Qu. L29, *Machines now used for cutting grain*) Inf **NJ10,** Self-rake reaper.

self-sown adj phr   Also *self-planted, ~-seed(ed), ~-seeding, ~-sowed*   **chiefly NEast, Gt Lakes**   See Map   Cf *catch crop* (at **catch** n 2), **volunteer**
Of a plant: sown, propagated, or capable of being propagated without human agency; hence, by back-formation, v *self-sow;* n *self-seeder.*
   1853 *Lit. World* 13 Aug 40, The bud that came / Self-sown in your poor garden's borders.   **1909** *Country Life* Aug 394, Annuals that "self-sow" are welcome.   **1950** *WELS* **WI,** (*A crop (or part of a crop) that springs up and grows by itself from old seed*) 5 Infs, Self-seeded (crop); 4 Infs, Self-sown; 1 Inf, Self-planted; 1 Inf, Self-seeder; 1 Inf, Self-seeding; 1 Inf, Self-sowed.   **1960** Bailey *Resp. to PADS 20* **KS,** (*A crop (or part of a crop) that springs up and grows by itself from old seed*) Self-sowed; self-sown.   **1965–70** *DARE* (Qu. L24) 37 Infs, **NEast, Gt Lakes,** Self-sown (*or* -seeded, -sowed); **NY92, 123,** Self-seeder; **NJ2,** Self-planted; **MA47,** Self-seed; **NY27,** Self-seeding; (Qu. L8, *Hay that grows naturally in damp places*) Inf **NY96,** Self-seeded.   **1986** Pederson *LAGS Concordance* 1 inf, **ceTX,** Self-sown—crop not planted.

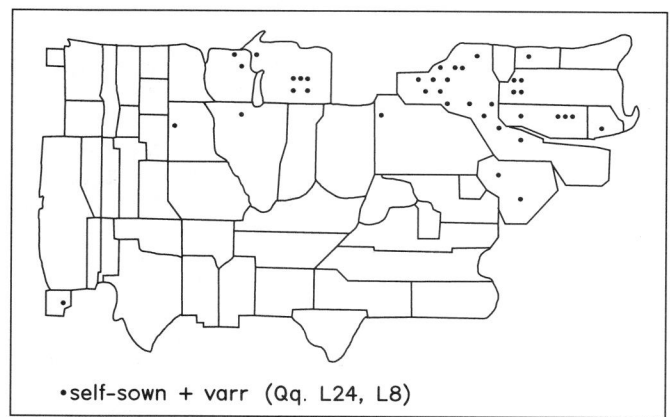

•self-sown + varr (Qq. L24, L8)

sell v   Also with *out*   [*OED2* →1893]
To deceive, cheat, trick.
   1856 Derby *Phoenixiana* 224, "Remember the fate of the first practical joker and profit thereby;" I ventured humbly to ask him who this was; "Judas Iscariot," he replied with bitterness, "he *sold* his master, and you know well what came of it."   **1858** Hammett *Piney Woods Tavern* 85, Sech a yellin' and cursin' . . as thar war when they diskivered how they'd been sold.   **1859** in 1966 Boller *MO Fur Trader* 88 **MO,** When there is nothing else, a good practical joke is got off; I was "sold" once, and have done my full share in "selling" others.   **1884** *Anglia* 7.272 **Sth, S Midl** [Black], To sell er man out = to deceive.   **1967** *DARE* (Qu. II20b, *A person who tries too hard to gain somebody else's favor: "He's always trying to* _____ *the boss."*) Inf **NC45,** Sell; (Qu. KK36, *Talking about a person who is easily fooled: "It's easy to* _____*."*) Inf **OH24,** Sell him.   **1998** in 1999 Millersville Univ. Center for PA

Ger. Studies *Jrl.* Summer 2, My father and mother always spoke to us children in English. "Dutch" was spoken between themselves and their friends. . . I can carry on a conversation to a degree when spoken to in "Dutch." I am not fluent, but they can't "sell me" as the saying goes!

sell n [*OED2* 1853 →]
A deception; a (practical) joke; something that disappoints expectations.
  1876 in 1969 *PADS* 52.55 **seIL,** Our snow turned out to be a sell last night and a person can't see any snow at all this morning. **1899** (1912) Green *VA Folk-Speech* 375, *Sell.* . . An imposition; a cheat; a deception; a trick played at another's expense. **1900** Day *Up in ME* 189, I thought for jest a sell / I'd make believe we'd run away. **1901** Harben *Westerfelt* 285 **nGA,** "I believe, on my soul, it's a sell," he said, in a tone of vast relief. **1915** (1916) Johnson *Highways New Engl.* 210, The signs were printed with a rubber type outfit and included not only poetry but jokes, sells, and conundrums. [**1966** *DARE* (Qu. KK42a, *Expressions about a person who does something very easily:* "For him that would be _____.") Inf **AR41,** A sell.]

sell one's papers See **peddle a**

sell out v phr
1 See **sell** v.
2 To depart, usu hastily; to run away; to skedaddle. **esp Sth, S Midl**
  1934 *AmSp* 9.290 **PA** [Black student slang], *Sell out.* To get up and go; to move out. **1936** *AmSp* 11.369 **nLA,** *Sell out.* To leave quickly; as, "He sold out when he saw his daddy coming." **1938** Hall *Coll.* **wNC, eTN,** *Sell out.* . . To leave in a hurry; to depart quickly. **1942** Rawlings *Cross Creek* 214 **nFL,** When she cooks 'em [=chitterlings], I just sell out and leave home for a day or two. **1942** *Amer. Mercury* 55.223.96 **Harlem NYC** [Black], *Sell out*—run in fear. **1966–70** *DARE* (Qu. Y18, *To leave in a hurry:* "Before they find this out, we'd better _____!") Infs **MD36, SC19,** Sell out; (Qu. Y19, *To begin to go away from a place:* "It's about time for me to _____.") Inf **MD36,** Sell out; (Qu. Y20, *To run fast:* "You should have seen him _____!") Infs **MD36, PA237,** Sell out. **1980** Weals *Strangers* **eTN** (Montgomery *Coll.*), He'd have me use the smoker, and when a bee'd get under my veil, I'd sell out, doctor. I'd get out of there a-flying. **1986** Pederson *LAGS Concordance*, 1 inf, **neAL,** He'd sell out down the path—of a shepherd dog.

selth See **self**

semaphore n [Transf from the application to a now obsolete type of traffic signal that had a moving arm like a railroad semaphore]
A traffic light.
  1965–68 *DARE* (Qu. N9, *The colored lights that control the cars at busy road crossings*) Infs **MN35, 42, UT3, 4, 5, WI70,** Semaphore(s). **1969** *DARE* FW Addit **cnUT,** Semaphore—alternate form of "traffic light."

'semblymen See **assemblyman**

semi n Usu |'sɛmaɪ|; also |'sɪmaɪ|; infreq |'sɛmi|; for other varr see quot 1965–70 Also *semitruck* **scattered, but chiefly N Cent, Upper MW, West** See Map Cf **tractor-trailer, trailer truck, transfer ~**
A semitrailer; a semitrailer hitched to a tractor truck.
  1942 Berrey–Van den Bark *Amer. Slang* 81.16, *Semi* . . a two-wheeled truck. **1955** *AmSp* 30.92 [Truck driver's language], *Semi* . . A semitrailer. **1961** *AmSp* 36.272 **NW** [Truck driver's language], It is common to call a tractor a *horse* and a trailer a *semi*. **1965–70** *DARE* (Qu. N11, *A very large truck used to haul freight, new cars, and other big loads*) 139 Infs, **scattered, but chiefly N Cent, Upper MW, West,** Semi [with proncs of the type ['sɛmaɪ]]; 21 Infs, **esp N Cent, West,** Semi; 17 Infs, **esp N Cent,** Semi [with proncs of the type ['sɪmaɪ]]; **FL11, IL11, PA128, 131,** ['sɛmi]; **NY164,** ['sɛmɪ]; **IN42, TN18,** ['sɛmɑ]; **SD8,** ['sɪmaɪ]; **AZ7, IL114, IN1, IA32, MI56,** Semitruck. **1969** *AmSp* 44.208 [Trucker jargon], *Semi*—Semitrailer; loosely, tractor and semitrailer unit. **1986** Pederson *LAGS Concordance*, 1 inf, **cnGA,** Semi—large tractor-trailer truck; 1 inf, **neFL,** Semi—big, heavy truck. **1999** *WI State Jrl.* (Madison) 17 Mar sec A 1/2, [Caption:] The wreckage of Amtrak's City of New Orleans train stretches across the railroad tracks . . after a Monday night collision with a semitruck. **2000** *DARE*

File **AZ,** Here in the Southwest, where we are overrun with these things, I hear them referred to only as ['sɪmaɪz] or ['sɛmaɪz]. *Ibid,* For me [= speaker orig from **sIN**] the ['sɪmaɪ] pronunciation is categorical for trucks. *Ibid,* I (originally from New York, but most of my adult life in Texas and Alabama) favor . . ['sɛmaɪ] . . as a noun.

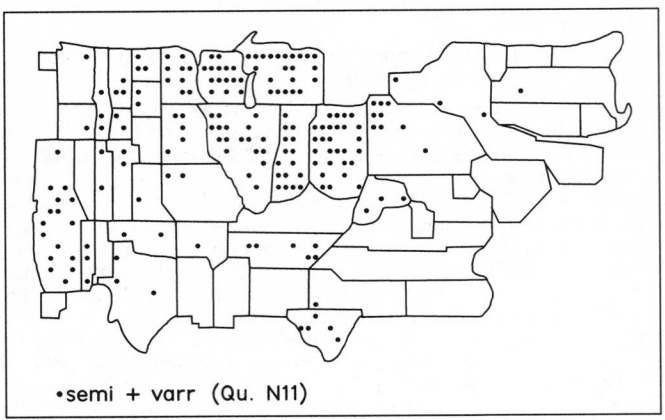

•semi + varr (Qu. N11)

Seminole See **Seminole rattler**

Seminole bread n [See quot 1960]
=**coontie.**
  1960 McGeachy *Hdbk. FL Palms* 53, *Zamia integrifolia.* . . Coontie. . . The large underground stems contain a starch-like substance that the Seminole Indians have utilized for a kind of bread. This has given the Coontie its nickname "Seminole Bread." **2000** *DARE* File—Internet, Z[amia] pumila. . . has several common names, such as Arrowroot, Coontie, Comfortroot, Compties, Contis and Seminole Bread. . . The plant was once used by the Seminole Indians as a main source of starch.

Seminole pumpkin n
A **winter squash** (here: *Cucurbita moschata*).
  1933 Small *Manual SE Flora* 1287, The so-called crookneck, (*Pepo moschata* . .), with fruits of many shapes, known in Florida as the Seminole-pumpkin, may be found growing wild about Indian settlements and abandoned camp sites.

Seminole rattler n Also *Seminole (rattlesnake)* **seGA**
A **timber rattlesnake** (here: *Crotalus horridus*).
  1926 *AmSp* 1.416 **Okefenokee GA,** One of the deadly reptiles of the Okefinokee—the so-called 'Seminole Rattler' (*Crotalus horridus*). **1938** Matschat *Suwannee R.* 27 **neFL, seGA,** More than two dozen species of snakes are known to live in the hammocks and piney woods. . . Six are deadly poisonous; three kinds of rattlesnakes—the diamondback, the timber or Seminole . . , and the small ground rattler [etc]. **1968–69** *DARE* Tape **GA35,** This one here is a timber rattler, or Seminole, or often called canebrake; **GA48,** The diamondback. . . they're more vicious. . . but those Seminole will let you run over them a whole lot of times . . you 'bout have to step on him to make him bite you; **GA51,** There's two kind of rattlesnakes—the . . diamond-backed and the Seminole. The Seminole is a bright-colored rattlesnake.

semipalmated plover n
Std: a **plover** (*Charadrius semipalmatus*) common esp in Alaska and coastal regions of the US. Also called **beachcomber, bull peep 1, cou blanc, redeye 2b, ringneck 3, ringnecked plover, ring plover**

semipalmated sandpiper n
Std: a **sandpiper** (*Calidris pusilla*) common esp in Alaska and coastal regions of the US. Also called **bumblebee peep, hawk's-eye 2, little peep, mudsucker 2, oxeye 1a, peep n 2, pea snipe, pennywinkle 4, sand bird 1, ~ chicken, ~ oxeye, ~ peep, ~ snipe, sea chicken**

semitruck See **semi**

semmel n Pronc-sp *zemmel* [Ger *Semmel*] **esp in Ger settlement areas**
A bread roll, esp one with a crisp crust.
  1932 (1946) Hibben *Amer. Regional Cookery* 27 **PA,** While the sem-

mels are still hot, brush with melted butter and dust over with powdered sugar. Butter Semmels, like Sugar Cake, are eaten fresh from the oven with coffee at 4 o'clock "companies" or "gatherings." Both are typical Moravian delicacies. **1940** Brown *Amer. Cooks* 922 **WI,** Semmel— Take wheat bread dough; when ready to shape into loaves, cut into small, even pieces. Knead into rounds 1 inch high, 3 inches wide. Set 2 inches apart in shallow pan. Let rise slightly. Dip handle of knife in flour. Press down through center . . making a deep crease through middle of each piece. Let rise again. Brush top with egg yolk mixed and beaten with a little cold water. Bake. **1948** Hutchison *PA Du. Cook Book* 25, *Butter Semmel* (Butter Rolls). [Ingredients include mashed potatoes, sugar, yeast, water, milk, eggs, butter, salt, flour.] . . Brush with butter as soon as taken from the oven, and sprinkle with powdered sugar. **1949** (1986) Leonard *Jewish Cookery* 105, *Zemmel* (Crisp Rolls)—Use basic recipe for bread. When ready . . cut into pieces the size of an apple. Knead each piece and shape into flat cakes 1 inch thick and about 3 inches in diameter. Place on a . . baking sheet 2 inches apart. Press a crease in the centers with back of a knife. Let rise. . . Before baking, brush with egg yolk and water. Bake . . until crisp and nicely browned. **1950** *WELS (Fancy home-baked rolls)* 1 Inf, **seWI,** Semmel. **1969** *DARE* (Qu. H19) Inf **MI**108, Zemmel—rolls with a crisp crust ['zɛməl].

sen See **send 1**

senaca See **cienaga**

Senagambian See **Senegambian**

sence See **since**

send v

Std sense, var forms.

1 present: usu *send;* also *sen, sent, sind.*

1854 in 1956 Eliason *Tarheel Talk* 317 **cnNC,** Sind. **1884** *Anglia* 7.253 [Black], To the regular forms of the Irregular verbs as used by the whites, the Negro adds the following forms of his own. . . *Pres.* sent— *Past.* sont, saunt—*Pass. Part.* sont. **1933** Rawlings *South Moon* 89 **nFL,** Tell him to . . sent a barrel every Wednesday until I tell him different. **1937** in 1976 *Weevils in the Wheat* 153 **VA** [Black], Jes' sen' me an envelope lak you said an' I'll write it all down an' sen' it to you. Be good.

2 past, past pple: usu *sent;* also **Sth, S Midl** *esp freq among Black speakers, sahnt, saunt, sont.*

1883 (1971) Harris *Nights with Remus* 13 **GA** [Black], Brer Rabbit . . he say dat 'er pa, he sont 'im out dar. **1884** [see **1** above]. **1890** *DN* 1.71 **LA,** Sont: sent. Used mainly by negroes. **1893** Shands *MS Speech* 58, *Sont* [sɑnt]—Negro for *sent.* **1899** Chesnutt *Conjure Woman* 84 **csNC** [Black], He wuz only sont ober on trial. . . So he tied 'im up en sont 'im back ter Mars Dunkin. **1909** *DN* 3.373 **eAL, wGA,** *Sont, pret.* and *pp.* of *send.* **1913** Kephart *Highlanders* 284 **sAppalachians,** A strong preterite with dialectical change of the vowel . . saunt (sent). **1914** Furman *Sight* 62 **KY,** And straight way he sont for a tooth-dentist. **1930** *VA Qrly. Rev.* 6.246 **S Midl,** There are sundry preterites with dialect changes: . . saunt for sent. **c1938** in 1970 Hyatt *Hoodoo* 1.73 **Waycross GA** [Black], So he sont us back. **1939** in 1976 *Weevils in the Wheat* 124 **VA** [Black], Slaves was sont to dese places for whuppin'. **1942** Faulkner *Go Down* 145 **MS** [Black], She sont me. **1952** Brown *NC Folkl.* 1.593, *Sont* [sɑnt]. . . Past tense and past participle of *send.*— Mainly illiterate Negroes. **1964** Will *Hist. Okeechobee* xi **c,ceFL,** *Sont*—sent. **1983** *DARE* File **nwMS,** Sent (sahnt). This pronunciation (almost always with black speakers) really seems to convey the past tenses with a touch of class. . . Example: "I'm going to send him a thank-you note for the watch he sahnt me for Christmas."

sendero n Pronc-sp *sendera* [Span *sendero* path] **TX**

A path; a clearing.

1892 *DN* 1.252 **TX,** *Sendéra:* a path, a foot-path. Spanish *senda* and *sendero.* **1929** Dobie *Vaquero* x **swTX,** So, sometimes riding with John Young and sometimes picking a course on foot far behind him, I have sought to open a *sendero,* as we say on the border—a clearing—that will allow people to behold some of the secrets that the brush has hidden. **1931** Allhands *Gringo Builders* 126 **TX,** In September, 1906, T.F. Lovett started throwing up a grade north from section thirty on the branch, now the city of San Juan, but at that time nothing more than a wide *sendero.* **1932** *DN* 6.233 **wTX,** Sendero. A clearing, especially in brush country. A Spanish word, perhaps borrowed only in Western Texas where there is a good deal of such country. **1936** Adams *Cowboy Lingo* 202, A 'sendero' meant a path through the brush. **1986** Pederson

LAGS Concordance (Lane) 1 inf, **csTX,** Sendero—just inside [the] fence next to [the] highway.

send one down the road See **road** n[1] **B2**

Seneca See **Seneca snakeroot**

Seneca bear n Cf **seeny bear**

The black bear *(Ursus americanus).*

1924 (1925) Stansbury *Lake of Gt. Dismal* 96 **VA,** There are also hog bear (from the size), Seneca bear (white breast), [etc]. **1927** Boston Soc. Nat. Hist. *Proc.* 38.281 **Okefenokee GA,** Hamp Mizell gives the maximum weight of the . . 'Seneca Bear,' as he calls it[,] . . as 500 or 600 pounds.

Seneca grass n

A **holy grass** (here: *Hierochloe odorata).*

1814 Bigelow *Florula Bostoniensis* 245, *Holcus odoratus* [=*Hierochloe o.*] . . *Seneca grass.* . . It is a thriving, and early grass, being usually in flower by the middle of May. It is sweet and tender, and in drying exhales a fragrant odour. **1815** Lit. & Philos. Soc. NY *Trans.* 1.72, There is a highly aromatic plant collected by the Indians in small quantities, called the Seneca grass. . . Holcus fragrans. **1844** Lapham *Geogr. Descr. WI* 83, Hierochloa borealis . . , Seneca grass—sweet scented grass. **1891** Jesup *Plants Hanover NH* 52, H[ierochloe] borealis. . . (Vanilla or Seneca Grass.) Hanover, etc. **1910** Graves *Flowering Plants* 59 **CT,** Vanilla or Seneca Grass. . . A very fragrant grass, used by the Indians in basket-making. **1914** Georgia *Manual Weeds* 37, *Hierochloe odorata.* . . Seneca-grass. [*Ibid* 38, The Indians of the Northwest make baskets and mats of it; . . but as hay or forage it has no value.] **1973** Hitchcock–Cronquist *Flora Pacific NW* 645, Seneca grass . . H[ierochloe] odorata.

Seneca snakeroot n Also *Seneca (root),* ~ *rattlesnake root;* also *Seneka, Senega* (and combs); rarely pronc-spp *Cinacy, Senicker, Senic(k)y*

A **milkwort** (here: *Polygala senega)* formerly used as a remedy against snakebite and var illnesses; also the dried root of this plant. Also called **milkweed 7, mountain flax 2, rattlesnake root 2c,** ~ **weed 11**

1738 *VA Gaz.* (Williamsburg) (ed. Parks) 30 June 4/2, The *Seneca Rattle-Snake Root* must be of more extensive Use than any Medicine in the *Materia Medica.* **1744** (1841) Byrd *Westover MSS* 42, But there is another sort preferred by the northern Indians, that they call Seneca rattlesnake root, to which wonderful virtues are ascribed in the cure of pleurisies, fevers, rheumatisms, and dropsies; besides it being a powerful antidote against the venom of the rattle-snake. **1789** Morse *Amer. Geog.* 415 **NC,** Among others are the ginseng, Virginia snake root, Seneca snake root, an herb of the emetic kind. **1804** *Philadelphia Med. & Phys. Jrl.* 1.1.82, The Seneca Snake-root (Polygala Senega) may be mentioned in this place. **1806** *Thomas' MA Spy or Worcester Gaz.* (MA) 30 Apr, Seneca, . . or rattle snake root . . has been celebrated as a specific in the cure of croup. **1830** Watson *Annals Philadelphia* 616, About the year 1739, I saw much said in the Gazettes of the newly discovered virtues of the Seneka rattlesnake root. **1834** (1927) Rodman *Diary* 132 **MA,** Ipecacuanha was substituted for the hive syrup and seneka root. **1840** [see **rattlesnake root 2c**]. **1876** Hobbs *Bot. Hdbk.* 72, Mountain flax, Seneca root, Polygala Senega. **1896** *Garden and Forest* 9.292, Senega, or Seneka—Polygala Senega, from the use of its root as a remedy for snake bite among the Seneka Indians, attracted the attention of Dr. Tennant, of Virginia, in 1734, who brought it to the notice of Dr. Mead, of London, in 1738. It was at that time called Senega snakeroot. **1953** Randolph–Wilson *Down in Holler* 12 **Ozarks,** Seneca is the common name of a medicinal herb *(Polygala senega),* but the plant is sometimes called *senicker* in southwest Missouri. Often, however, it is *senicky,* and I have seen it spelled *senicy* or *cinacy* in the local papers. **1967** *DARE* Tape **TX**1A, Seneca snakeroot was what you used when you was snakebit. **1979** Erichsen-Brown *Med. N. Amer. Plants* 360, *Common names* [of *Polygala senega*]: Senega root, rattlesnake root, mountain flax.

Senegambian n Also *Senagambian* [*Senegambia* the region bordering the Senegal and Gambia rivers in west Africa] Cf **Ethiopian 1**

A Black person.

1900 *DN* 2.59 **New Orleans LA,** Senegambian. . . A negro or negress. **1920** *Collier's* 11 Dec 21, A little bimbo . . is struttin' around and bellerin' about the undaunted white race to a big fat grinnin' Senegambian porter. **1931–33** *LANE Worksheets* **CT,** *Senagambian. . .* Nickname for a negro. **1943** *Pittsburgh Courier* (PA) 11 Sept 13/7, There are thousands of Negroes living in similar or better houses, despite the race hustling talk about the "horrible houses" of Harlem. All the civilized Senegambians live in good homes. [*DARE* Ed: Writer is Black] **1946** *PADS* 6.26 **swVA,** *Senagambian. . .* A Negro boy ten to fifteen years old. Salem, as late as 1890. Reported, 1940. [**1947** *PADS* 8.36 **VA,** *Senegambian:* I am acquainted with this word as meaning a Negro from Senegambia—whether ten, fifteen, or fifty years old. Used as a term of contempt.]

Seneka See **Seneca snakeroot**

senellier n [LaFr *cenellier* < Fr *cenelle* hawthorn berry]
A **hawthorn** (here: *Crataegus viridis*).
    1897 Sudworth *Arborescent Flora* 232 **LA,** *Crataegus viridis. . .* Senellier.

seng See **sang** n

senhalenac n Also *senhalanac*
=**smooth sumac.**
    1893 *Jrl. Amer. Folkl.* 6.149 **VT,** *Rhus glabra,* senhalenac. Ferrisburgh, Vt. . . Name for the Saranac River comes from this. **1979** Erichsen-Brown *Med. N. Amer. Plants* 115, Smooth Sumac. . . *Common names:* Senhalanac, Shoe-make. **2000** *DARE* File **seWI** (as of c1945), As we listened to the radio in the evenings, we often heard advertisements touting some patent nostrum which contained "senhalenac" ['sɛnhə,lɛnək]. This, especially if taken together with aspirin, would soon remedy any of the common minor everyday ailments.

Senicker, Senic(k)y See **Seneca snakeroot**

senita n Also *sinita* [MexSpan *sinita, senita,* dimin of *sina* in same sense]
A **cactus B1** (here: *Pachycereus schottii*). Also called **old-man cactus 2, whisker ~**
    [**1859** Emory *Rept. U.S. Mex. Boundary* 2.1.45, C[ereus] Schottii. . . Sierra di Sonoyita, and southeast towards Santa Magdalena, Sonora, where it is named *Zina,* or *Sina,* or *Sinita* by the inhabitants.] **1907** Mearns *Mammals* 66 **SW,** Cereus schottii Engelmann. Schott Cactus. Sinita. **1932** AZ Ag. Exp. Sta. *Bulletin* 141.24, The cactus family is represented in our flora by nearly a hundred kinds, including . . pitahaya, or organ pipe cactus, and senita, or old man; the two latter found only in our warmest canyons and foothills. **1965** Teale *Wandering Through Winter* 74 **sAZ,** Of the more than thirty species of cacti native to the Organ Pipe monument, the rarest of all . . is the senita, the "old one". . . The tips of all the larger stems are tufted with masses of fine gray, whisker-like spines. **1985** Dodge *Flowers SW Deserts* 51, *Lophocereus schottii. . .* The name "senita" (meaning old age) refers to the long, gray, hairlike spines covering the upper ends of the senita stems. [**1988** Schoenhals *Span.-Engl. Gloss.* 98 **Mexico,** Senita. . . *Lophocereus* spp., e.g., L. schotti. *Ibid,* Sina. . . *Cereus* spp. . . Locally, may be applied to other genera of cactii [sic].]

senkah conj, prep Also *sake-a, sekker, senker, sic-a, sukkuh* Gullah Cf **sicarum**
As, like.
    1867 Allen *Slave Songs* xxvi **seSC,** Him an' me grow up sic-a brudder an' sister. **1888** Jones *Negro Myths* 122 **GA coast,** Buh Wolf house buil on de groun senker hog pen. **1908** *S. Atl. Qrly.* 7.333 **sSC** [Gullah], Trouble bun 'pon topper we senkah dut an' flea 'pon topper dorg! **1909** *Ibid* 8.40 [Gullah], *The same liked: i.e., the same as, (this is the same like that),* has by elisions . . and by an obscure nasalization of *m,* become *senkah,* [Footnote:] Un-nasalized variants *sic-a* and *sake-a* are noted, at St. Helena's Island, Georgia; *senkah* is Georgetown idiom. **1922** Gonzales *Black Border* 188 **sSC, GA coasts,** Missis, dem plat-eye t'ick 'puntop da' beach sukkuh fiddluh crab' t'ick een de maa'sh w'en tide low! **1938** in Lib. of Congress *Amer. Memory: WPA Life Hist.* (Internet) **Edisto Is. SC,** The devil the man for blame, not me. He tricky sekker (the same as) snake.

senna n[1] Usu |'sɛnə|; also |'sɪnɪ, -ə, 'si-| Pronc-spp *seena, seeny* [*seeny,* attested also in Engl dial, is a survival of EModE *sene* (*OED2 sene* sb.[4] c1400–1658) < OF *sené* (> Fr *séné*). The Latinized form was earlier *sena,* prob pronounced with a long

first vowel in English, and this form remained common through the 18th cent.]
A Forms.
    1828 Webster *Amer. Dict., Senna. . .* The common pronunciation, *seena,* is incorrect. **1850** *Amer. Whig Rev.* 11.620, The very *thought* of it is worse than a dose of seeny and salts. **1872** (1873) Shillaber *Partingtonian Patchwork* 174 **NEng,** "Have you seena?" asked Mrs. Partington of the apothecary. "Seen whom?" said he. . . "Why, seena and manners," replied she, calmly, "for a gentle purgatory." "Oh, senna and manna!" he repeated *sotto voce,* and procured it for her. **1874** (1875) Diaz *Schoolmaster's Trunk* 51, Mrs. Melendy's . . Dicky was taken ill in the night; and there was an agonizing delay in steeping the "seeny," on account of Mr. Melendy's having forgotten to "split the kindling over night." **1965–70** *DARE* (Qu. BB22, . . *Home remedies . . for constipation*) 30 Infs, **scattered,** Senna (tea *or* leaves, etc), [proncs of the type ['sɛnə]]; **GA**89, 91, 92, **KY**70, 74, **SC**46, Senna tea (*or* leaves, -leave tea), [proncs of the type ['sɪnə, 'sɪnə]]; **KS**5, [,sɪni 'ti]; **TX**42, ['sĭnɪ] tea; **GA**77, **ME**4, Seeny ['sini] (tea *or* leaves); **NH**6, Figs and [sini]; [corr to] [sɛni]; **IA**34, ['sɛnə ti]—but we call it ['sini] tea; **AL**34, ['sɪnɪ] tea; **SC**32, 39, ['sɪnɪ] tea; **OK**2, Seena tea; **GA**82, ['sinə] tea; **UT**7, [,sinə 'ti].
B Senses.
1 Std: a plant of the genus *Senna.* For other names of var spp see **candlestick tree, candle tree 3 coffeeweed 1b, locust plant, magdad coffee, negro ~, negro weed, rattleweed g, rattlebox 1j, sicklepod 2, stinking toe, styptic weed, teaweed, wild indigo, ~ senna**
2 A **false indigo 1** (here: *Amorpha herbacea*).
    1916 *Torreya* 16.238 **SC,** *Amorpha herbacea. . .* Senna.

senna n[2] See **siene bean**

señorita n
Any of var fishes of California kelp beds, usu a small **wrasse** (here: *Oxyjulis californica*), but also another **wrasse** (here: *Halichoeres semicinctus*) or a **kelpfish c** (here: *Gibbonsia elegans*).
    1882 U.S. Natl. Museum *Bulletin* 16.604, P[seudojulis] modestus [= *Oxyjulis californica*]. . . *Señorita. . .* 7 inches. Pacific coast; abundant southward. **1896** Jordan–Evermann *Check List Fishes* 413, *Iridio semicinctus* [=*Halichoeres s.*]. . . Kelpfish; Señorita. . . Santa Barbara Islands to Cerros Island. *Ibid, Oxyjulis modestus. . .* Señorita. . . Monterey to Guadalupe Island. *Ibid* 467, *Gibbonsia evides* [=*G. elegans*]. . . Kelpfish, Señorita. . . south to Point Conception. **1898** U.S. Natl. Museum *Bulletin* 47.2352, *Gibbonsia evides* [=*G. elegans*]. . . *Kelpfish; Señorita. . .* abundant in the kelp, rarely in rock pools. **1930** *Copeia* 1.11, They were to be seen on any clear day while fishing for . . señorita (*Oxyjulis californica*). **1953** Roedel *Common Fishes CA* 116, *Señorita. . .* Considered a pest by many sportsmen because of its penchant for stealing bait. . . *Rock Wrasse—Halichoeres semicinctus. . .* Resembles the señorita but is less slender and lacks the black spot at base of caudal fin. **1976** Tryckare et al. *Lore of Sportfishing* 119, *Halichoeres semicinctus. . .* Kelpfish, señorita. **1983** *Audubon Field Guide N. Amer. Fishes* 652, Anglers catch Señoritas using very small hooks, but few are retained because they are not considered edible. **2000** *DARE* File—Internet **CA,** In the Southern Channel Islands. . . other commonly encountered species include California Sheepshead . . and Señorita (*Oxyjulis californica*).

sense v
1 To understand the meaning of.
    1859 (1968) Bartlett *Americanisms* 394 **NEng,** *To sense.* To comprehend; as, "Do you sense that?" **1895** *DN* 1.393 **Long Is. NY,** Sense . . to understand. **1903** *DN* 2.329 **seMO,** Sense. . . To understand; to comprehend. 'I read the letter but I couldn't sense it.' **1907** *DN* 3.237 **nwAR,** Sense. . . To comprehend; to understand. "I can sorter sense the Dago, but I can't talk it any."
2 in phr *sense (one) into (something):* To cause (one) to understand (something).
    1933 Hurston in *Story* Aug 63 **FL** [Black], Good Lawd, Missie! You womens sho is hard to sense into things. **1934** Hurston *Jonah's Gourd Vine* 25 **AL** [Black], We ain't had de same chance dat white folks had. Look lak Ah can't sense you intuh dat.

sense adv, prep, conj See **since**

sensitive brier n Sth, S Midl Cf **yellow sensitive brier**

A **mimosa 1**: usu *M. microphylla*, but also other spp such as *M. nuttallii* or *M. roemeriana*. For other names of var of these see **cat's claw, gander teeth, pink mimosa 1, saw brier, sensitive plant 1, shame brier, sleepy vine, stingy vine** Note: these spp were formerly included in the genus *Schrankia*.

1803 Ellicott *Jrl.* 287, The sensitive briar, *(mimosa instia,)* this beautiful and singular plant, is common to the poor, sandy land. **1829** Eaton *Botany* 383, [*Schrankia*] *uncinata* [=*Mimosa microphylla*] . . sensitive briar . . leaflets small, . . irritable. **1847** Wood *Class-Book* 238, *S. uncinata*. . . Sensitive Brier. . . Southern States. Stem . . with the petioles and peduncles armed with short, sharp prickles turned downwards. **1890** FL Ag. Exper. Sta. Gainesville *Bulletin* 8.10, Schrankia uncinata. . . Sensitive Briar. **1896** *Jrl. Amer. Folkl.* 9.186 swMO, *Schrankia uncinata*, . . sensitive brier, shame-faced brier. **1940** Steyermark *Flora MO* 288, Sensitive Brier . . (*Schrankia Nuttallii* . .). Leaves divided . . into many small leaflets which close when touched. **1941** Walker *Lookout* 58 TN, Sensitive brier's runners cling to the ground and are tough and spiny. The leaflets fold quickly, following a sudden jar. **1967** *DARE* Wildfl QR (Wills–Irwin) Pl.15B Inf **TX**44, Sensitive brier. **1967** *DARE* File **SC** (as of c1850), Sensitive brier—said to be a sure cure for cancer: roots baked slowly until brittle enough to be pulverized. **1979** Ajilvsgi *Wild Flowers* 158 seTX, Little-leaf sensitive brier. . . Plants armed with prickles mostly throughout. . . Leaflets closing at dusk, during cloudy weather, or at slightest touch. . . Uncommon in the Big Thicket.

sensitive fern n [See quot 1911]

A fern *(Onoclea sensibilis)* native to much of the eastern two-thirds of the US.

1814 Bigelow *Florula Bostoniensis* 257, *Onoclea sensibilis*. . . Sensitive fern. **1843** Torrey *Flora NY* 2.499, Sensitive Fern. . . Moist woods and thickets: common. **1858** *Atlantic Mth.* 2.11 **ME**, Horehound, horsemint and the sensitive fern grew close to the edge. **1878** Williamson *Ferns KY* 109, The common name of Sensitive Fern . . conveys no idea whatever of its peculiar character, as sensibility is the very least of its attributes. **1911** Waters *Ferns* 265, The name sensitive fern seems a very inappropriate one to apply to such a large, coarse-looking plant, and. . . it has been suggested that the name was given because the fronds wither so soon after being cut, or because they are killed by the earlier frosts. **1950** Stevens *ND Plants* 43, Sensitive Fern. A coarse plant with broad, thick, coarsely lobed leaves. **2000** *DARE* File—Internet **WI**, While scouting a cranberry bed for disease and insect pests, identify weed populations as they arise. . . Example: 10% sensitive fern, 20% boneset and joe-pye weed mix.

sensitive grass n

A **partridge pea** (here: *Chamaecrista nictitans*).

1967 *DARE* Wildfl QR (Wills–Irwin) Pl.105A Inf **TX**34, Sensitive grass.

sensitive pea n [See quot 1949]

=**partridge pea**, usu *Chamaecrista fasciculata* or *C. nictitans*.

1843 Torrey *Flora NY* 1.190, *Cassia Chamaecrista* [=*Chamaecrista fasciculata*]. . . Sensitive Pea. . . Sandy fields: Staten Island; Long Island; in the neighborhood of New-York; and along the Hudson to Troy. **1901** Lounsberry *S. Wild Flowers* 261, Its [=*Chamaecrista fasciculata*'s] leaflets also are curious, being very sensitive. *C. nictitans*, . . sensitive pea, is known by its small flowers. **1949** Moldenke *Amer. Wild Flowers* 125, Partridgepeas. . . Their pinnately compound leaflets are often very sensitive and will fold up tightly against the central rachis when touched. . . One of the largest flowered is *C[hamaecrista] fasciculata*, the *large-flowered sensitivepea*. **1970** Correll *Plants TX* 790, *Cassia* [=*Chamaecrista*] *nictitans*. . . Sensitive Pea. . . Leaves . . somewhat touch-sensitive. **1999** *DARE* File—Internet **OK**, Sensitive Pea. . . *Cassia nictitans*. . . A small spreading legume. . . Leaves may close partially when touched.

sensitive plant n

1 Std: = **mimosa 1**, esp *Mimosa pudica*. Cf **sensitive brier, ~ rose**

2 A **partridge pea**, usu *Chamaecrista fasciculata* or *C. nictitans*. [See quot 1922] Cf **wild sensitive plant**

1829 Phelps *Familiar Lect.* 63, Compound leaves possess this property [=irritability] in the greatest degree; as the sensitive plant *Mimosa*

sensitiva; and the American sensitive plant, *Cassia nictitans*. **1876** Hobbs *Bot. Hdbk.* 105, Sensitive plant, Cassia [=*Chamaecrista*] nictitans. **1901** Lounsberry *S. Wild Flowers* 259, *C[assia] Chamaecrista* [=*Chamaecrista fasciculata*], large sensitive plant, or partridge pea, is considerably smaller than the wild senna. . . Its leaflets also are curious, being very sensitive. **1922** *Amer. Botanist* 28.30, The classic "sensitive plant" is . . *Mimosa pudica*. . . As soon as the leaves are touched they close, the leaflets folding togeather [sic] and the leaf itself drooping. In our own region other less active sensitive plants are found. . . *Cassia nictitans* is also called "sensitive plant" . . but it only tardily responds to a stimulus. Its near relative, *Cassia chamaecrista* is still less sensitive though it folds its leaves at night and is occasionally known as "sensitive plant". **1966–67** *DARE* Wildfl QR Pl.105A [= *Chamaecrista nictitans*] Inf **SC**41, Sensitive plant; Pl.105B [=*C. fasciculata*] Infs **AR**44, **WA**10, Sensitive plant; (Wills–Irwin) Pl.16C [=*C. fasciculata*] Inf **TX**34, Sensitive plant.

sensitive rose n [See quot 1856] Cf **sensitive brier, ~ plant 1**

A **mimosa 1** (here: *Mimosa microphylla*).

[**1856** in 1862 Colt *Went to KS* 64, And the sensitive plant, with its slightly briery running stalk, covered all over with flowers of pink balls dotted with yellow, and its tiny leaves that shrink from the least touch, sends out its scent of otto of roses to meet your olfactories, some rods before you reach it.] **1892** *Jrl. Amer. Folkl.* 5.95, *Schrankia uncinata* [=*Mimosa microphylla*], sensitive rose. West and South. **1896** *Ibid* 9.186 SD, *Schrankia uncinata*, . . sensitive rose, Burnside, S. Dak. **1922** *Amer. Botanist* 28.30, A well known member of this group [=sensitive plants] is the "sensitive rose" . . whose scientific title is *Schrankia uncinata*. **1929** Bell *Some Contrib. KS Vocab.* 189, Sensitive plant. . . Often called *sensitive rose*. Very characteristic of Kansas. **1966** *DARE* (Qu. S26d, *Wildflowers that grow in meadows;* not asked in early QRs) Inf **OK**32, Sensitive rose.

sent See **send 1**

sent for and couldn't come adj phr esp Sth, S Midl

Indisposed, out of sorts, exhausted—usu in phrr *look* (or *feel*) *like one was sent for and couldn't come* and varr.

1843 (1846) Haliburton *Attaché* (1st ser) 258 **NEng**, [He] fell right in on the floor, on his face . . a groanin' and a moanin' . . lookin' . . as a critter that was sent for, and couldn't come. **1844** Thompson *Major Jones's Courtship* 129 **GA**, Why he looks like he was sent for and don't want to go. **1939** *AmSp* 14.264 swIN, Ill health or just 'puniness' is indicated by such expressions as . . 'like I'd been sent for and couldn't come.' **1952** Brown *NC Folkl.* 1.472, You look like you were sent for and couldn't come. **1970** *DARE* (Qu. BB38, *When a person doesn't look healthy, or looks as if he hadn't been well for some time . . "He looks _____."*) Inf **KY**77, Like he's been sent for and couldn't come. **1991** *DARE* File **NC**, Feeling like "you were sent for but never got there." **1993** *Ibid* **IL**, My mother, who lived most of her life in Illinois, often said "Sent for and couldn't come" to describe herself or someone else in a sort of snit and unable to perform normally due to circumstances beyond their control; you know how some days one is just not up to snuff, perhaps what younger people nowadays call "a bad hair day."

sent-for-nothing n

=**black-bellied plover**.

1956 *AmSp* 31.186 **NC**, Sent-for-nothin' . . Black-bellied plover . . In reference to its restless flying about for no apparent reason.

sep See **except(ing)**

separate v, hence n *separation* [Folk-etym for *suppurate*]

1968–69 *DARE* (Qu. BB35, *The yellowish stuff that comes out of a boil when the head breaks*) Inf **CT**16, Separation; (Qu. BB36, *When there's an open sore and this yellowish stuff is coming out of it . . it's _____*) Infs **IN**22, **NY**139, Separating; (Qu. BB37, *When yellowish stuff comes out of a person's ear, he has a _____*) Inf **CT**16, Separating ear.

sepoose See **sea poose**

seps See **except(ing)**

September elm n

An elm (here: *Ulmus serotina*) native chiefly to the southern US. Also called **red elm 2**

1938 Van Dersal *Native Woody Plants* 353, September elm (*Ulmus* *serotina).* **1960** Vines *Trees SW* 211, *September Elm.. .* Tree to 60 feet and 3 ft in diameter. The branches are rather short. **1973** Wharton–Barbour *Trees KY* 519, *September Elm* . . flowers in the fall instead of the early spring when other elms flower. It is a southern species, . . [and] in Kentucky it is widely scattered. **1980** Little *Audubon Guide N. Amer. Trees E. Region* 424, September Elm . . *Ulmus serotina. Ibid* 425, Although similar to American Elm, it is distinguishable by its flowers, which appear in September. . . The common name refer[s] to this late blooming.

September weed n

An aster such as **cocash 2.**

1873 in 1976 Miller *Shaker Herbs* 156, *Aster puniceus.. .* September Weed. The warm infusion is used for colds, rheumatism, nervous debility, headache, and menstrual irregularities. **1968** *DARE* (Qu. S25, . . *The small wild chrysanthemum-like flowers . . that bloom in fields late in the fall*) Inf **VT**10, September weed—blue blossom; (Qu. S26e, *Other wildflowers not yet mentioned;* not asked in early QRs) Inf **VT**10, September weed.

sequia n Also *sequi(e), zequia* [Aphet forms of *acequia*]

An irrigation ditch.

1846 (1848) Bryant *What I Saw in CA* 396, The Pimos Indians . . irrigate the land by water from the Gila . . the remains of whose sequias, or little canals, were seen by us. **1859** (1968) Bartlett *Americanisms* 2, *Acequia.. .* The word is sometimes spelt *azequia* or *zequia.* As the mustang sprang over the *zequia*, the flowing skirt of the manga was puffed forward.—*Mayne Reid, The War Trail.* **1870** Ludlow *Heart of Continent* 183 **CO,** I found a number of "sequis," or distributing ditches, already run. **1958** *AmSp* 33.106, When the Rocky Mountain Project is completed, it will show where, in terms of linguistic geography . . water ditches are called *irrigation ditches, government canals,* or *acequias* ('sequies').

sequoia n

Std: Usu a large evergreen tree *(Sequoiadendron giganteum)* native to California, but also a **redwood 2** (here: *Sequoia sempervirens).* For other names of *S. giganteum* see **mammoth tree.**

serape n Also sp *sarape, zarape* [MexSpan *sarape, zarape*] **chiefly West, esp SW**

A blanket used as a cloak by Mexicans or Mexican-Americans.

1834 Pike *Prose Sketches* 138, Everything is new, strange, and quaint; . . the zarape or blanket of striped red and white. **1860** in 1948 *Western Folkl.* 7.18 **sCA,** The Mexican drew a knife from beneath his serape. **1887** *Scribner's Mag.* 2.509 **West,** He sits out on his *piazza,* with a light *serape* of striped woollen thrown over his shoulders. **1892** *DN* 1.194 **TX,** *Serápe:* a Mexican blanket, generally woven by hand by Indian women, with stripes of variegated colors. The *serape* has no opening or slit for the head, like the *poncho,* but is worn by men only, thrown across the shoulders. **1910** Hart *Vigilante Girl* 75 **nCA,** Then on and back of the *aparajo* he bound a *serape* and some other of the dead woman's wraps to make a couch. **1916** Bower *Phantom Herd* 68 *(DA),* He had finished with an old Mexican serape draped around his person for warmth. **1968** *DARE* Tape **CA**90, And I had a serape or what we call a blanket—laid down on that. **1985** Fierman *Guts & Ruts* 49 **SW** (as of c1870), The man's face was covered by a *sarape,* but Nathan could see that he was wearing a blue cavalry coat.

serenade n chiefly Appalachians, Atlantic exc sNEng See Map *old-fash* Cf belling vbl n[2], horning n 1, shivaree n B1, 2

A noisy, prankish demonstration, esp following a wedding or as a Christmas celebration; hence v *serenade* to entertain or annoy (a person) with such a demonstration; also vbl n *serenading.*

1849 in 1956 Eliason *Tarheel Talk* 141 **NC,** A parcel of noisy students have got their instruments and are giving us what is called a . . serinade, some hwoping, some playing on instruments, others ringing the bell, and a general confusion throughout. **1859** (1860) Creecy *Scenes South* 50 **New Orleans,** The wild and screeching, thundering serenade is continued night after night until the worn down victim of an unequal marriage either runs away, "slopes for Texas," or parts unknown—wife, money,

and all—or pays the demand. **1883** Eggleston *Hoosier Schoolboy* 92 **IN,** The boys had resolved to have a demonstration. . . They would serenade him. . . [One boy] was going to pound on his mother's bread-pan. Every sort of instrument for making a noise was brought into requisition. Dinner-bells, tin-pails, conch-shell dinner-horns, tin-horns, and even the village bass-drum, were to be used. **1937** *Hall Coll.* **wNC, eTN,** *Serenade. . .* A celebration held after a wedding. Much noise is made with cow-bells, tin-pans, gun-shots, etc. **1949** Kurath *Word Geog.* 78, *Serenade* . . The serenading of newlyweds has been largely abandoned, but the memory of this old folk custom still stirs the hearts of the older folk in the rural areas of all the Eastern States. *Serenade* is the usual term among the folk in Eastern New England and in the South Atlantic States, and it is widely known and used elsewhere in the Eastern States. **1965–70** *DARE* (Qu. AA18, . . *A noisy neighborhood celebration after a wedding)* 134 Infs, **chiefly Appalachians, Atlantic exc sNEng,** Serenade; **MD**30, Serenading [Of all Infs responding to the question, 66% were old; of those giving these responses, 81% were old.]; (Qu. FF2, . . *Kinds of parties)* Inf **AR**52, Serenades—young ones went around waking the people up, like at Halloween or Christmas, only in honor of some event like twins. **1967** *Nauvoo Independent* (IL) 20 July 5/3, A crowd of employees from the Academy works serenaded James Foster and bride last night. **1967** *DARE* Tape **AL**15, They call it serenading. . . Didn't sing. They just went on those horses and maybe they'd holler, the men as they went along . . riding. Sometimes they walked and sometimes they'd go on a wagon with two horses or mules hitched to it; **PA**9, [FW:] Have you ever heard of a callithumpian band? . . Do they use the term around here? [Inf:]. . . Well, they use it when they write special articles in the newspaper about it, but we used to call them serenading. . . [FW:]. . . The callithumpian band serenaded, is that it? [Inf:] Yes, they always serenaded a newlywed couple. **1969** *DARE* FW Addit **cNC,** A time of noisemaking after a wedding. Begins around midnight of the wedding day at newlywed's house. One trick was to tie a string to a house with a nail and pull rosum along it. It's supposed to make the house sound like it's about to fall down. **1975** Gould *ME Lingo* 248, *Serenade*—The favored Maine word for a little party to honor newlyweds; shivaree. **1982** Barrick *Coll.* **csPA,** *Serenade*—v.t., and n. shivaree. **1986** Pederson *LAGS Concordance* **esp TN, GA, AL, FL,** *(Shivaree)* 44 infs, (To) serenade them; 36 infs, Serenading; 1 inf, **nwAL,** Serenading—on Christmas; 1 inf, **neAL,** Serenading—also at Christmas; 1 inf, **neAL,** Serenading—after weddings and at Christmas; 1 inf, **neAL,** Serenading—especially at Christmas time; 7 infs, Serenaded (them *or* him and his wife, etc.).

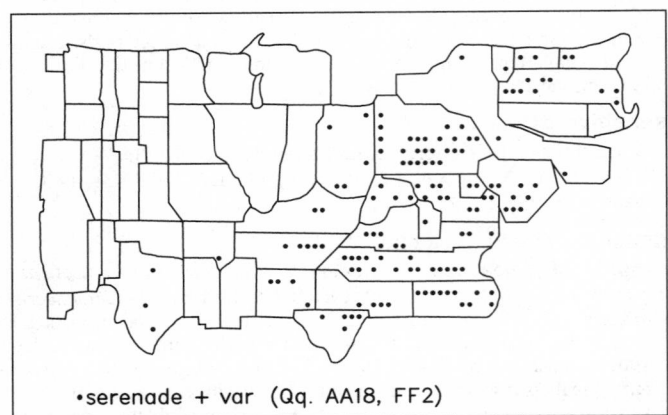

•serenade + var (Qq. AA18, FF2)

sergeantfish n Cf sergeant major

1 =cobia.

1873 *Forest & Stream* 1.258 **FL,** Cobia, Crab-Eater, or Sargent [sic] Fish. . . This fish. . . derives its trivial name from a black stripe running along its silvery sides . . like that on the trowsers of a sergeant. **1882** U.S. Natl. Museum *Bulletin* 16.909, *Elacate canada* [=*Rachycentron canadus*] is known in Florida as "Sergeant-fish", from its lateral stripes. **1933** LA Dept. of Conserv. *Fishes* 197, The Cobia, *Rachycentron canadus . . ,* is invariably known in Louisiana as the Ling or Lemon Fish, in Florida as the Crabeater or Sergeant Fish. . . The term Sergeant Fish is more usually given to the true Snook [=*Centropomus undecimalis*]. **1951** Taylor *Surv. Marine Fisheries NC* 269, Cabio, also called cobia, . . sergeant-fish. . . A very popular gamefish of no commercial value. **1958** *Washington Post* (DC) 24 Sept 1/2 *(Hench Coll.),* An unusually fine run of cobina (the sergeant fish) in the waters of Chesapeake Bay recently has caused big game fishermen to toss caution to the gods of Izaak Walton.

2 A snook (here: *Centropomus undecimalis*).

1933 LA Dept. of Conserv. *Fishes* 69, *Centropomus undecimalis*. . . A silvery fish, pikelike in appearance. . . Sergeant Fish, Robalo and Sea Pike are among this species' popular names. *Ibid* [see **1** above]. **1966** *DARE* (Qu. P2, . . *Kinds of saltwater fish caught around here . . good to eat*) Inf **FL29,** Snook or sergeantfish. **1975** Evanoff *Catch More Fish* 218, The snook. . . is also called the sergeant fish.

sergeant major n Cf night sergeant, sergeantfish

A **demoiselle 1** (here: *Abudefduf saxatilis*).

1876 U.S. Natl. Museum *Bulletin* 5.38, *Glyphidodon saxatilis* [= *Abudefduf s.*] . . The fish is sometimes called the "Sergeant-major," in allusion to the chevron-like bands of yellow on the sides. . . Its accidental occurrence at Newport, R.I., has been recorded. **1884** Goode *Fisheries U.S.* 1.275, Among the reefs of Florida two or three species of the family *Pomacentridae* are abundant. Most prominent among these is the "Sergent Major," . . called in Bermuda the "Cow-pilot." **1933** John G. Shedd Aquarium *Guide* 138, The Sergeant Majors. . . gather in swarms around the piles of wharfs as well as in the coral reefs and tide pools. **1955** Zim–Shoemaker *Fishes* 132, *Sergeant-major,* named for its stripes, and Reef Fish, common on coral reefs, are in the damselfish family.

sergiverous See servigrous

serin See sierra

sermon n Usu |ˈsɜ(r)mən|; also chiefly Sth, S Midl |ˈsɜ(r)mənt|; *old-fash* |ˈsɑrmən(t)| Pronc-spp *sarment, sarmin(t), sarmon(t), sarmun, serment, sermint, sermond, sermont* Cf Intro "Language Changes" I.8, Pronc Intro 3.I.1.f

Std sense, var forms.

1803 Davis *Travels* 237 **VA** [Black], It was as good as any sarment. **1803** in 1956 Eliason *Tarheel Talk* 317 **c,cwNC,** Serment. **1827** *Ibid* 317 **nw,cwNC,** Sermont. **1827** (1939) Sherwood *Gaz. GA* 139, *Sarment,* for Sermon. **1836** (1955) Crockett *Almanacks* 49 **wTN,** He got up and went out to see what it meant, intending to preach them a sarmont against gambling. **1843** (1916) Hall *New Purchase* 147 **IN,** I used to larn sarmins by heart. **1846** in 1956 Eliason *Tarheel Talk* 317 **nw,cwNC,** Sermond. **1893** Shands *MS Speech* 54, *Sarmint* [sɑːmɪnt]. Illiterate white for *sermon.* Negroes generally say *sarmun* [sɑrmn]. **1899** (1912) Green *VA Folk-Speech* 365, *Sarment*. . . A sermon. Sarmon. **1903** *DN* 2.329 **seMO,** Serment. **1907** *DN* 3.236 **nwAR,** Sermint. **1921** Haswell *Daughter Ozarks* 25 (as of 1880s), I was jest on the way to preach a sarment at Red Bird big meetin'. **1930** Shoemaker *1300 Words* 60 **cPA Mts** (as of c1900), *Sarment*—A sermon. **1934** Carmer *Stars Fell on AL* 60, They don't get their sermonts ready. **c1960** Wilson *Coll.* **csKY,** Sermon is frequently /sɜmənt/. **1981** Pederson *LAGS Basic Materials,* 1 inf, **cTN,** [sɝmn̩t].

sermon tack n

A paper fastener consisting of a flat head and two flexible metal strips.

1988 *DARE* File **ceNY,** I enclose one of my precious "sermon tacks". I heard the word first used in Albany NY about 1918 when we moved there from New York City. In New York I had never heard the term. I have also heard them called sermon tacks by younger people than I who came from Eastern New York State. . . This style of paper fasteners seems to be passing out of use. . . Formerly all were made of brass but now some are brass and some plated steel. And they used to come in a large number of sizes.

serpent n Pronc-spp *saa'pint, saa'punt, sarpent, sarpint, sarpunt* *old-fash* Cf Pronc Intro 3.I.1.f

Std sense, var forms.

1815 Humphreys *Yankey in England* 108, Sarpent, serpent. **1841** (1952) Cooper *Deerslayer* 211 **nNY,** Off with it, Sarpent—off with it. **1859** Taliaferro *Fisher's R.* 50 **nwNC** (as of 1820s), The reader shall soon have abundant evidence of this admission in his numerous and rapid flights from "sarpunts." **1871** Eggleston *Hoosier Schoolmaster* 108 **sIN,** Didn't you see the Sarpent inspirin' him? **1903** *DN* 2.290 **Cape Cod MA,** In 1840 the younger and older generations differed most strikingly in their pronunciation of the vowels before *r* plus a consonant. Old folks still pronounced *er* as *ar.* Thus they said . . *sarve,* . .

---

sarpint. **1905** *DN* 3.56 **eNE,** Sarpint. **1922** Gonzales *Black Border* 32 **sSC, GA coasts** [Gullah glossary], *Saa'pint, saa'punt*—serpent (Biblical). **1930** Shoemaker *1300 Words* 59 **cPA Mts** (as of c1900), *Sarpent*—A snake. **1938** Matschat *Suwannee R.* 115 **neFL, seGA,** A pesky sarpent bit him on the heel.

serpent fern n

A fern *(Phlebodium aureum)* native to the southeastern US.

1938 Small *Ferns SE States* 82, *P[hlebodium] aureum*. . . Rootstock stout, creeping serpent-like, copiously fuzzy with red scales. . . Serpentfern. **1942** Hylander *Plant Life* 112, Another epiphytic fern of Florida and near-by states, found on palm trunks, is the Golden Polypody or Serpent Fern.

serpent grass n

A bistort (here: *Polygonum viviparum*).

1890 *Century Dict.* 5512, Serpent-grass. . . The alpine bistort, *Polygonum viviparum.* It is a dwarf herb, 4 to 8 inches high. **1949** Moldenke *Amer. Wild Flowers* 75, Coloring the far northern wastes . . , the higher summits of the White Mountains in New Hampshire, and the Rockies, is the charming *serpentgrass, Bistorta vivipara.* **1963** Craighead *Rocky Mt. Wildflowers* 42, *Polygonum bistortoides*. . . has narrow tapering leaves . . and a thick, twisted, snakelike root. Serpentgrass *(P. viviparum)* is similar, but the root is not so elongated.

serpentine n *obs*

=**Indian pink 1.**

1830 Rafinesque *Med. Flora* 2.91 **CA,** A good worm syrup is also made with it [=*Spigelia marilandica*], united to mild purgatives. Much used in Louisiana, where it is called *Serpentine.*

serpent's tongue n Cf adder's tongue 1

A **dogtooth violet** (here: *Erythronium americanum*).

1959 Carleton *Index Herb. Plants* 105, Serpent's tongue: Erythronium americanum.

servagerous See savagerous

servant n Usu |ˈsɜ(r)vənt|; also *old-fash* |ˈsɑ(r)vənt| Pronc-spp *saa'bint, saa'bunt, sahvant, sarbant, sarvant, sarvent, sarvint, sa'vent* Cf Pronc Intro 3.I.1.f

Std senses, var forms.

1784 in 1956 Eliason *Tarheel Talk* 317 **NC,** Sarvent. [**1789** Webster *Dissertations Engl. Lang.* 105, Another very common error, among the yeomanry of America, and particularly New England, is the pronouncing of *e* before *r,* like *a;* as *marcy* for mercy.] **1815** Humphreys *Yankey in England* 108, Sarvant, servant. **1843** (1916) Hall *New Purchase* 386 **IN,** The Lord's sarvints. **1853** Simms *Sword & Distaff* 132 **SC,** We creep up, and Pomp say—'Da's maussa, Tom, me fellow sarbant!' **1867** Lowell *Biglow* xix **'Upcountry' MA,** Sarvant. **1893** Shands *MS Speech* 54, Sarvant [sɑːvnt]. Negro for *servant.* **1899** Woerner *Rebel's Daughter* 117 **Ozarks** [Black], De Lawd hab heard de pra'er ob his unwuthy sa'vent. **1899** (1912) Green *VA Folk-Speech* 365, Sarvant. . . A form of *servant.* **1922** Gonzales *Black Border* 323 **sSC, GA coasts** [Gullah glossary], *Saa'bint*—(also "saa'bunt") servant, servants. **1930** in 1944 *ADD* **eVA** [Black], *Servant*. . . sahvant [sɑvənt].

serve v Usu |sɜ(r)v|; also |sɑ(r)v| Pronc-spp *saa'b, sarve* Similarly n *saa'bis, sarvice, sarvis(s),* adj *sarviceable*

A Forms.

1815 Humphreys *Yankey in England* 108, Service, service. **1832** *New Engl. Mag.* 309 **ceMA** (as of 1774), Pratt immediately rejoined "I wo'n't *sarve.*" . . Many persons have often heard the anecdote related by Revere. **1841** (1952) Cooper *Deerslayer* 114 **nNY,** I'll just make sartain of your rifle, and then come back and do you what sarvice I can. *Ibid* 211, Doublets of skins, tough leggings, and sarviceable moccasins. **1843** (1916) Hall *New Purchase* 171 **IN,** During "sarvice" . . no despicable noise . . was maintained. *Ibid* 321, Some gravely said . . that teachers and professors in the "people's college ought to sarve for the honour!" **a1861** (1880) Eastman *Poems* 188 **VT,** The mince-pie cooled and the pudding sarved. **1893** Shands *MS Speech* 54, Sarve [sɑ·v]. Negro for *serve.* **1899** (1912) Green *VA Folk-Speech* 365, . . For *serve.* Sarvis. . . Service. **1901** *DN* 2.183 **neKY** [Black], *Serve*—sarve. **1903** [see **serpent**]. **1913** Kephart *Highlanders* 123 **sAppalachians,** Thar's only one sarviceable wagon in this whole settlement. *Ibid* 170, He's been eight years in government sarvice. **1915** *DN* 4.189 **swVA,**

Service [sɑrvɪs]. **1922** Gonzales *Black Border* 323 **sSC, GA coasts** [Gullah glossary], *Saa'b*—serve, serves, served, serving. *Ibid* 324, *Saa'bis*—(also sarbis) service, services, use. **1927** *DN* 5.470 **Appalachians,** *Service*—sarviss. **1942** Hall *Smoky Mt. Speech* 42 **wNC, eTN,** [ɑ˞] for [ɝ] is rapidly becoming obsolete. Nevertheless, it is preserved in the speech of a few old people, who may use it in . . *serve*. . . An old farmer of the Big Creek area was heard to say: ['hæv jɪ 'bɪn wɛl 'sɑ˞vd].

B Senses.

1 To put food on (a plate), fill (a plate) with food.

1941 Faulkner *Men Working* 26 **MS,** Maw worked between stove and table, serving the plates with warmed-over turnip greens and pone bread. **1948** Faulkner *Intruder* 114 **MS,** The sheriff served the plates with his uncle and Legate passed theirs and the sheriff's cup to Miss Habersham. **1986** Pederson *LAGS Concordance (Help yourself)* 1 inf, **cFL,** Serve your plate; 1 inf, **cMS** Serve my plate. **2001** *DARE* File **cwCA** (as of c1960), My mother, who heard this from her Nebraska-born mother, would say "May I serve your plate?" or "I'll serve the plates in the kitchen," where *serve* means 'fill.'

2 See quot.

1944 *AmSp* 19.38 **Philadelphia PA,** *Serve,* 'carry, deliver,' as the mail, newspapers, or anything carried and delivered on a more or less regular route. [Footnote to *serve:* I believe this term may occasionally be heard elsewhere, but here it is used habitually. A colleague who comes from Wilmington, on the outskirts of the dialect area, tells me that you can *serve* the paper, which comes regularly to each subscriber, but not the mail, as there is no predicting when or whether any person will get a letter. But in Chester they *serve* everything.] Thus, the boy next door *serves* the Saturday Evening Post, a farmer *serves* butter and eggs to us.

serviceberry n Also *service, ~ apple, ~ bush, ~ tree* Pronc-spp *sarvice, sarvis* (and combs); for addit varr see quots. [Transf from *service* the Eurasian *Sorbus aucuparia* and its fruit, appar because of the similar appearance of the tree in flower and of the fruit; cf **service tree 2**]

A plant of the genus *Amelanchier;* also the fruit of such a plant.   **chiefly S Midl, Pacific NW, Rocky Mts**   See Map Also called **Juneberry 1, shad 8, shadberry, shadblossom, shadblow, shadbush, shadflower 2, shad tree;** for other names of var spp see **arrowwood h, currant B3, dogwood 5, French pear, grape ~, heathberry, Indian cherry 2, ~ pear 1, juice pear, June plum, Mayberry 2, May cherry, medlar bush, pigeonberry 6, sand cherry 3, sabbath berry, saskatoon, sugarberry, sugar pear, ~ plum, wild currant, ~ pear**

1784 (1821) Asbury *Jrl.* 31 July 1.370, The child he fed with . . sawice [sic—prob for *service*] berries. **1785** Marshall *Arbustrum* 90, Mespilus nivea [=*Amelanchier canadensis*]. *Early ripe, Esculent fruited Medlar, or wild Service.* . . The fruit is ripe in June, pretty large and of an agreeable taste. **1805** (1807) Gass *Jrl.* 136 **sWA,** I saw service-berry bushes hanging full of fruit. **1805** (1904) Lewis *Orig. Jrls. Lewis & Clark Exped.* 2.239, The survice berry differs somewhat from that of the U. States. **1805** (1965) Ordway *Jrls.* 266, Our Intrepter & wife . . found a great quantity of Servis berrys. **1844** Lapham *Geogr. Descr. WI* 79, Amelanchier Canadensis, . . June berry, shad berry, service tree, &c. **1860** Curtis *Cat. Plants NC* 68, Service Berry. . . Universally known in our Mountains under the name of *Services*. In the Lower District it is called *Service Tree*. **1899** (1912) Green *VA Folk-Speech* 375, *Service-tree*. . . A tree bearing small pear-shaped or apple-shaped fruit. . . *Service apples*, the fruit of the service-tree. **1905** *DN* 3.93 **nwAR,** *Service-berry*. . . June-berry. . . Common. **1910** Johnson *Highways Rocky Mts.* 204, Did you notice the bushes along the roadside all white with blossoms? They'll be loaded with berries later—service berries. . . They're awful good to eat raw. **1914** in 1914 Stewart *Letters* 19 **WY,** There were . . service-bushes and birches that shut off the ugly hills on the other side. **1923** *DN* 5.219 **swMO,** *Sarvice berry*. . . Service berry. **1924** Raine *Land of Saddle-Bags* 22 **sAppalachians,** In the spring. . . the feathery white blossoms of the "sarviss," are succeeded by the redbud's blaze of purple. **1939** in 1987 Hall *Coll.* **wNC,** They found one [=bear] lappin' on sarvis. They went back, watched the sarvis tree two days. **1958** *PADS* 29.15 **TN,** *Services:* Fruit of the service berry tree. **1965–70** *DARE* (Qu. I44, *What kinds of berries grow wild around here?*) 22 Infs, **chiefly S Midl, Pacific NW, Rocky Mts,** Serviceberries; **CA136, 155, CO45, KY5, 44, 74, SD5, 8, VA13,** Serviceberries; **KY17,** Services; (Qu. I46, . . *Kinds of fruits that grow wild around here*)

Inf **NC30,** Sarviceberries; **MD24, OH49, WV13,** Serviceberries; **OR6,** Serviceberry; (Qu. I53, . . *Fruits grown around here . . special varieties*) Inf **NC33,** Sarviceberries; (Qu. T16, . . *Kinds of trees . . 'special'*) Inf **VA21,** Sarviceberry = serviceberry [FW: [The latter] is a book word, but given by Inf.]; **KY34,** Sarvice tree. **1969** *SC Market Bulletin* 11 Sept 4/5, Rhododendrons $1.50 ea.; Greybeards $1 ea.; Sarvis trees $1 ea. **1974** Fink *Mountain Speech* 23 **wNC, eTN,** *Services* . . serviceberries or trees. **1982** *Barrick Coll.* **csPA,** Sarvis berry. **2001** House *Clay's Quilt* 211 **eKY,** The first trees to show their new colors—sarvis, redbud, and dogwood—were in bloom.

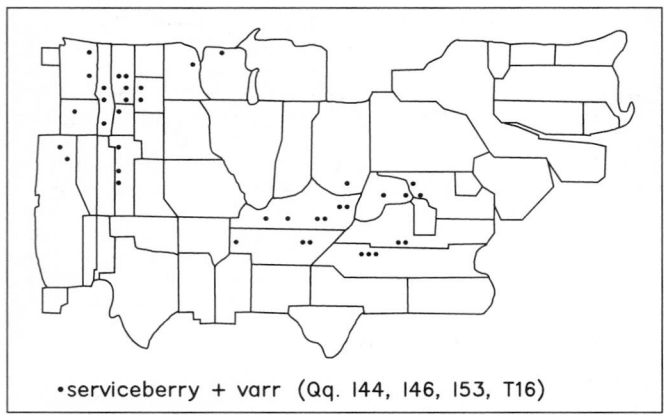

•serviceberry + varr (Qq. I44, I46, I53, T16)

service car n esp **OK**

A taxi; a car used to provide an unofficial bus service.

1965 *DARE* FW Addit **OK23,** *Service car*—a taxicab. Old-fashioned but still used. **2000** *NADS Letters,* I recall that my grandmother and mother used this [=*service car*] to mean a taxi. My grandmother was born in Cleburne, TX in 1870 and lived in Oklahoma (Indian Territory) and in Collin County and Cooke County Texas most of her adult life. My Mother was born in Jack County, Texas in 1896 and spent her formative years in North Texas (Gainesville and McKinney) and Oklahoma (Atoka, Snyder, Crystal). I spent my early years in Harris County, Texas and Del Rio, Texas, and never heard anyone else use it in that sense. [*Ibid,* My father-in-law, who . . grew up near Seminole, OK, knows this term [=*service car*] from his childhood as a vehicle used to haul vegetables to market. He has never heard the term used as a synonym for taxicab.] **2000** *DARE* File—Internet **OK,** [He] reminisced about the days when he used to run a 'Service Car' in Roosevelt [OK] in 1916–18. If it surprises you to know that Roosevelt had taxi service back in those days, it might also surprise you to know just how good a business it was. **2001** *NADS Letters* **ceMO,** In the 1950's, when I lived in Saint Louis, Missouri, a "service car" provided an inexpensive limousine service, available only in black neighborhoods, that *competed* with taxicabs. Service cars traveled a fixed route, like a bus, but could be flagged down, like a taxicab, anywhere along that route, and carried whatever number of people were willing to squeeze in. Service cars were less expensive and more convenient than buses and were *far* less expensive than taxicabs, since, like regular public transportation, their fee was fixed, regardless of the distance that you traveled.

service porch n

A utility room.

1968 *DARE* (Qu. D16, . . *Parts added on to the main part of a house*) Inf **UT6,** Service porch. **1978** *DARE* File **cwCA** (as of 1948), In our house the service porch was between the kitchen and the garage. It was an enclosed room (part of the original structure) where laundry machines and equipment were housed, and not a porch per se. *Ibid,* My grandmother (b. 1880s) who lived successively in Missouri, southwest Kansas, Wyoming and California, used this term to refer to a utility room off the kitchen in which the backdoor was located. (This backdoor opened onto a much abbreviated back porch.) The service porch held a "linen closet" for mops and brooms etc., space for a washing machine, a laundry sink, hot water heater.

service tree n

1 See **serviceberry.**

2 =**mountain ash 1,** usu *Sorbus americana.* [*OED2* 1545 → for *Sorbus aucuparia* or its wood]

1737 (1911) Brickell *Nat. Hist. NC* 71, The *Service* Tree groweth to be very large, and beareth long Leaves like those of the *Ash* Tree. **1785** Marshall *Arbustrum* 144, *Sorbus*. The *Service Tree*, . . or *Mountain Ash*. *Ibid* 145, *Sorbus americana*. *American Service Tree*. This grows naturally upon the mountains towards Canada. . . The flowers . . are succeeded by roundish berries of a red colour when ripe. **1843** Torrey *Flora NY* 1.225, The *Mountain Ash* of this country [=*Sorbus americana*], or *American Service-tree* as it is sometimes called, is nearly allied to the *S[orbus] aucuparia* of Europe. **1910** Graves *Flowering Plants* 223 **CT**, *Sorbus americana*. . . Service Tree. . . The very astringent bark and berries are employed medicinally. **1952** Blackburn *Trees* 269, *Sorbus* . . Mountain-ashes, service-trees. **1979** Erichsen-Brown *Med. N. Amer. Plants* 88, *Sorbus decora*. . . *Common names.* Dogberry, service tree.

service winter n [*service* (at **serviceberry**)] Cf **blackberry winter**

> **1983** *MJLF* 9.1.54 ceKY, Sarvis Winter . . a period of cold weather when the sarvis is in bloom.

servigrous adj |sə(r)ˈvaɪg(ə)rəs, -gəs| Also *savig(e)rous, servigous, sevigrous, survig(e)rous, survigorous, suvigrus, suvigrous, suvvigus;* by metath *sergiverous* [Etym uncert; cf **savagerous, vigrous**] **chiefly Sth, S Midl**
Fierce, violent, powerful, ill-tempered; hence adv *servigerously* vigorously.

1835 Longstreet *GA Scenes* 227, Pretty *sevigrous,* but nothing killing yet. [*DARE* Ed: In ref to the performance of a competitor in a shooting match.] **1839** *Spirit of Times* 19 Oct 396 **NY**, If I thought he had been shot and creesed in that savigerous sorta fashion, I'd give him jessy with my butcher knife. **1883** (1971) Harris *Nights with Remus* 288 **GA** [Black], He wrinkly ole hawn en de shaggy ha'r on he neck make 'im look mighty servigous. [Footnote:] Wild; fierce; dangerous; courageous. The accent is on the second syllable, ser-*vi*-gous; or, ser-*vi*-gus, and the *g* is hard. Aunt Tempy would have said "vigrous." **1887** *Amer. Philol. Assoc. Trans. for 1886* 17.35 **sOH**, A gentleman from Ohio . . has attempted to indicate for me the words that were imported during or after the war from the South into Southern Ohio. . . He mentions as recently imported . . *savigrous* (savage). **1891** Johnston *Primes & Neighbors* 147 **GA** [Black], I found out dem ve'y time what de hick'ry was made fer; but I ain' gwine be too servigous wid 'em. **1893** Shands *MS Speech* 61, *Suvigrous* [səvaɪgrəs]. A negro word meaning *fierce, savage;* sometimes shortened to *vigrous* [vaɪgrəs], or *vigous* [vaɪgəs]. **1909** *DN* 3.367 **eAL, wGA**, *Servigrous* [sə˞ˈvaɪgrəs]. . . Headstrong, strongwilled, obstinate, pugnacious. "He's the most servigrous white man in the land." A negroism used frequently by whites. **1910** *DN* 3.458 **FL, GA**, *Servigrous*. . . A term of opprobrium, as "He is a low-down sergiverous cuss." **1913** Kephart *Highlanders* 294 **sAppalachians**, Survigrous (ser-*vi*-grus) is a superlative of vigorous (here pronounced *vi*-grus, with long *i*): as "a survigrous baby," "a most survigrous cusser." **1922** *DN* 5.184 **GA**, *Suvvigus*. . . "Sur-vigus," "sur-vigorous," of unusual vigor. Here, *angry,* applied to men or animals. . . "Brer Wolf, he say he de mos' suvvigus." Cf. *vigrus* in Ky. and Va., and *survigrus* in Ky. **1938** Matschat *Suwannee R.* 81 **GA**, Ary fowkses knows as how onion juice, rubbed in servigerously, sprouts hair like weeds after a rain. **1947** Ballowe *The Lawd* 6 **LA**, Unc' Brutus' Duppy got so savigerous, jumpin' up an' down, that Unc' Brutus had to slap him to make him behave. **1952** Brown *NC Folkl.* 1.596, *Survig(e)rous* [səˈvaɪg(ə)rəs, sɚ-]. . . Fierce.—West. **1974** Fink *Mountain Speech* 25 **wNC, eTN**, *Survigorous* . . vicious, exceedingly strong. "Hit was a powerful survigorous bear."

sesame grass n
A **gama (grass)** (here: *Tripsacum dactyloides*).
1791 Muhlenberg *Index Florae* 179 (*DAE*), *Tripsacum dactyloides,* Sesame-grass. **1859** (1880) Darlington *Amer. Weeds* 407, *T. dactyloides*. . . Sesame Grass. . . This stout and remarkable Grass is not very common on the Atlantic slope of our continent; but it is said to be abundant in the valley of the Mississippi. **1910** Graves *Flowering Plants* 48 **CT**, Sesame Grass. . . A large corn-like grass, sometimes used for fodder in the South. **1942** Hylander *Plant Life* 507, Gama Grass or Sesame Grass . . is a tall grass, six to eight feet in height, . . and. . . grows in swamps and along pond margins, from Nebraska to Florida and Texas. **1968** Barkley *Plants KS* 66, Sesame Grass. Prairies, especially along streams.

set v¹
A Forms. Note: Historically some of these forms belong to

sit rather than *set;* they are included here if used where *set* would be expected. Cf **sit** v¹

1 Infin and pres: usu *set;* also:
a *sot.*
c1937 in 1976 *Weevils in the Wheat* 233 **VA** [Black], Ole Marse let us stay up all night, an' didn't seem to mind it at all. Saw de sun sot an' befo' we know it, it was a-risin' again.
b *sit.*
1683 in 1852 *PA Prov. Council Minutes* 1.82, For sitting up of Bouyes in the River & Bay. **1843** (1916) Hall *New Purchase* 323, I fotch'd my copy-book and a bottle of red-ink to sit down siferin in—and daddy wants me to larn bookkeepin. **1851** (1976) Melville *Moby-Dick* 431, My boat's crew could only trim dish, by sitting all their sterns on the outer gunwale. **1967** *DARE* Tape **MI**42, Charlie used to sit it on top of the back of a chair. **1969** *DARE* (Qu. A4, *The time of day when the sun goes out of sight*) Inf **KY**55, When the sun sits; sitting of the sun. **1975** Gould *ME Lingo* 255, Siddout—To set out, in the sense of plan to and intend to.

2 Past: usu *set:* also;
a *sot(t).* [Cf *EDD* set v. 2.(4)]
1770 in 1915 *New Engl. Hist. & Geneal. Reg.* 69.10 **MA**, Got 15 appel trees & Sot out in my Rye field. **1776** (1886) Hutchinson *Diary* 2.67 **MA**, I sot out from Falmouth this morning in a Postchaise. **1785** (1930) Hazard *Jrl.* 76 **RI**, I made and Sott atrap [sic] with a figger 4 for quails. **1795** Dearborn *Columbian Grammar* 138, *List of Improprieties,* commonly called *Vulgarisms,* which should never be used in *Speaking, Reading, or Writing*. . . Sot for Sat or Set. **1843** (1916) Hall *New Purchase* 280, I unsot the triggurs and went right in. **1859** (1968) Bartlett *Americanisms* 429, Sot. 1. A corrupt pronunciation of the past tense or past participle of *to set.* **1871** Eggleston *Hoosier Schoolmaster* 100 **sIN**, Your mother's cryin' sot me a cryin' too. **1899** Chesnutt *Conjure Woman* 13 **csNC** [Black], I 'member well w'en he sot out all dis yer [= here] part er de plantation in scuppernon's. **1905** *DN* 3.20 **cCT**, *Sot*. . . Pret. tense of *set.* **1907** *DN* 3.218 **nwAR, cCT**, *Sot, pret.* of set. **1923** *DN* 5.221 **swMO**, *Sot*. . . Past tense of *set.* **1929** *Sale Tree Named John* 108 **MS**, Dat night dey sot de rat-trap in de crib. **c1938** in 1970 Hyatt *Hoodoo* 1.73 **Waycross GA**, He sot dat stuff afire an' it wus a long blacksnake come runnin' up. *Ibid* 123 **St. Petersburg FL**, They went then an' sot little tumblers of whiskey around. **1939** Aurand *Quaint Idioms* 27 [PaGer], She sure sot (set, or put) him down in his place (i.e. shamed him). **1975** Gould *ME Lingo* 267, Sot—Correct Maine preterit of *set:* "I sot out my tomato plants this morning."
b *sat.* **esp NEng**
1716 (1865) Church *King Philip's War* 1.119 **MA**, The fore-most sat down his load and halted. **1781** *PA Jrl. & Weekly Advt.* (Philadelphia) 16 May 1/3, I *sat* out yesterday morning, for I *set* out. **1801** in 1889 *MA Hist. Soc. Proc.* 2d ser 4.123 **MA**, I sat out from Boston on an excursion to the South Eastern parts of New England. **1817** (1930) Sewall *Diary* 10 **ME**, Father sat out for Wiscasset District Court to set there this week. **1836** *Ibid* 173 **ME**, It sat in to rain. **1909** *DN* 3.419 **Cape Cod MA** (as of a1857), I *sat* one hen, she brought out eleven chickens.

3 Past pple: usu *set;* also *sot.* [Cf *EDD* set v. 3.(9)] **chiefly Sth, S Midl**
1858 Hammett *Piney Woods Tavern* 37, The police was sot to work, and sure enough they found old Broadhorn. **1859** [see A2a above]. **1888** Johnston *Mr. Absalom Billingslea* 130 **GA**, You've all sot out yourn, I s'pose. **1899** (1912) Green *VA Folk-Speech* 403, *Sot*. . . Perfect tense and past participle of *set.* **1914** Furman *Sight* 46 **KY**, I am sot here bound hand and foot, . . a living monument to the hate and revenge and onjestice of God! **1929** *Sale Tree Named John* 34 **MS** [Black], Dat Mist' Man had a trop sot at de onliest hole whut 'uz in de gyarden fence. **1932** Randolph *Ozark Mt. Folks* 127 **nwAR, swMO**, It is not considered the proper thing for a woman to raise her voice in a crowd, and a man would be "turrible sot back" and embarrassed if his wife were to do so. **c1938** in 1970 Hyatt *Hoodoo* 2.1480 **seGA**, Now, yo' kin take red ones an' set dem in a circle. When yo' get dem sot in a circle, . . why den yo' get de Bible an' get de 23rd Psalm. **1940** Richter *Trees* 183 **OH** (as of early 19th cent), What day have you sot to git married? **1945** FWP *Lay My Burden Down* 72 **GA** (as of c1865) [Black], Rev. Dickey, he preached freedom for the niggers and say that they all should be sot free and gived a home and a mule.

4 ppl adj: usu *set;* also *sot, esp in phr sot in one's ways.*
1848 Lowell *Biglow* 146 'Upcountry' **MA**, Sot, set, obstinate, resolute. **1890** Holley *Samantha among Brethren* 6 **NY**, I see [=saw] that the hull [=whole] community was so sot on havin' them five deacons.

1908 Lincoln *Cy Whittaker* 13 **MA,** Whit was a good-hearted boy, too, but full of the Old Scratch and as sot in his ways as his dad, and if Cap'n Cy wan't sot, then there ain't no sotness. **1909** *DN* 3.373 **eAL, wGA,** *Sot.* . . Set: often in the expression "Sot in one's way." **1912** Green *VA Folk-Speech* 403, *Sot.* . . Fixed or settled, a person is said to be "*sot* in his ways." **1914** *DN* 4.80 **ME, nNH,** *Sot.* . . Obstinate (var. of *set*). **1931** Hannum *Thursday April* 50 **wNC,** Joe had often made the remark that she was uncommon sot in her ways. **1932** *DN* 6.284 **swCT,** *Set* or *sot.* Firmly fixed in an attitude or opinion or decision. "You can be *set* and you're fairly reasonable; but if you're *sot,* you won't move." **1942** McAtee *Dial. Grant Co. IN* 60 (as of 1890s), *Sot.* . . past, part. of set; "_____ in his ways". **1959** *VT Hist.* 27.156, *Set* [sŏt]. . . Stubborn. *Sot* in one's ways. Common. **1966–69** *DARE* (Qu. GG18, . . 'Obstinate': "Why does he have to be so _____.") Infs **GA30, MA5, NY202,** Sot; **LA17, TX29,** Sot in his ways; (Qu. GG19a, *When you can see from the way a person acts that he's feeling important or independent:* "He surely is _____ these days.") Inf **MA5,** Feeling his oats; set up; sot up. **1972** Cooper *NC Mt. Folkl.* 91, *Feet sot to run*—ready to hurry away. **1976** Garber *Mountain-ese* 85 **sAppalachians,** There's no use to try to change that ole man, he's already sot in his ways. **1982** Slone *How We Talked* 24 **eKY** (as of c1950), "Sot in his way."—Stubborn.

B Senses.

1 in phrr *set a good deal* (or *a lot,* etc) *by:* To think much (or a lot, etc) of; to have much (or a lot of, etc) respect for. [*OED2* set v. 91.a a1300 →; "*Obs.* exc. *arch.* or *dial.*"] **esp NEng** *old-fash* Cf **great B1**

1785 in 1853 Sparks *Corresp. Amer. Revol.* 4.118, A visit, which I shall set more by than the interest I possess in Massachusetts. **1845** Judd *Margaret* 208 **NEng** (as of 18th cent), God knows how hard it is to help setting a good deal by one's children. **1871** (1882) Stowe *Fireside Stories* 124 **MA,** Not that she sets so very gret by me neither. **1884** Baldwin *Yankee School-Teacher* 190 **VA** [Black], I don't set no gre't by her. **1887** (1967) Harris *Free Joe* 82 **GA** [Black], My mistiss sot lots by her. **1914** *Harper's Mth. Mag.* 129.362 **NEng,** You know you mustn't give goldfish too much to eat. I will own I set a lot by that bowl of goldfish.

2 with *by:* To regard highly, respect. [*OED2* set v. 91.c 1393 →; "*Obs.* exc. *arch.* or *dial.*"] **esp NEng**

1848 Bartlett *Americanisms* 291, *To set by, to set much by.* To regard; to esteem.—Johnson. . . These are very old expressions, and were once in good use in England. **1848** Lowell *Biglow* 135 'Upcountry' **MA,** He said / He'd give a fifty spot right out, to git ye, 'live or dead;/ Wite folks ain't sot by half as much. **1865** (1889) Whitney *Gayworthys* 295 **NEng,** She sets by you as she does by her life. **1868** *Atlantic Mth.* 21.15 **NEng,** "'T would kill mother, . . she sets so by him." **1871** (1882) Stowe *Fireside Stories* 208 **MA,** There wa'n't a better minister, nor no one more set by in all the State, than Parson Morrel. **1899** Brown *Tiverton Tales* 262 **NEng,** He always set by blue, didn't he, puss? **1899** (1912) Green *VA Folk-Speech* 376, *Set-by.* . . To value or hold in estimation; *to set store by.* **1922** Brown *Old Crow* 490 **NEng** [Black], Folks set by me a spell. Then they stop.

3 To court. Cf **set up** v phr **2, to**

[**1895** *DN* 1.374 **seKY, eTN, wNC,** *Set to:* to court. "Jim is going to set to his girl."] **1896** *DN* 1.424 **cTX,** *Set.* . : to court. "He's settin' her." **1923** *DN* 5.220 **swMO,** *Set.* . . To court. "Bill's a-settin' Mary."

4 with *in:* To begin (to work); to apply oneself (to a task), esp with deliberation; to start a job. [*OED2* set in (at set v.¹ 146.d. "*Obs.* exc. *dial.*")] **esp Sth, S Midl**

1800 (1907) Columbia Hist. Soc. *Records* 10.225 **PA,** The new manager went up to the farm to see it, to set in on Monday. **1834** Crockett *Narrative* 40 **TN,** I set in to work for a man by the name of James Caldwell. **1868** *Harper's New Mth. Mag.* 36.799 **NC,** It would be God's good riddance if two-thirds of them could be starved to death. The rest might set in to work. **1926** *DN* 5.403 **Ozarks,** *Set in.* . . Begins. . . A farmer sometimes sets in to pulling weeds, or cutting wood, or clearing land, and so on. **1939** *Hall Coll.* **wNC, eTN,** *Set in to.* . . I just set in to shootin' him [=a bear] as fast as I could shoot the little gun. **1951** Porter *Ragged Roads* 45 **OK,** Again in pioneer days I set in to work for a Mr. John McDergan, that is, "set in" as much as possible. **1966** *PADS* 46.29 **cnAR,** *Set in.* . . To start a process. . . "They set in and pressure cooked a lot of that beef." **1986** Pederson *LAGS Concordance* 1 inf, **cnMS,** He just set in to beat me. **1995** in 2000 *Montgomery Coll.* **wNC,** Bill set in to build a barn. **2000** in 2002 *DARE* File—Internet **cAL,** Beau would set in to crying around 4:30p. **2002** *Ibid* **csWI,**

[From a junior high school student paper:] We set in to do what we could.

5 To sew—often in phr *set a stitch.* [*OED2* set v.¹ 61 →1862]

1857 *Harper's New Mth. Mag.* 15.666 **NY,** She had not set a stitch. **1899** (1912) Green *VA Folk-Speech* 376, *Set a stitch.* . . To sew. "They never think that I set a stitch." . . *Set on.* . . To sew on, as buttons. "I must set the buttons on his jacket." **1939** in *Lib. of Congress Amer. Memory: WPA Life Hist.* (Internet) **SC,** She swiftly set tiny stitches in a sheer crepe blouse. **1958** *PADS* 29.3 **TN** (as of 1954–56), *Set a quilt together:* To piece a quilt.

6 with *off:* To clear (a table). Cf **redd 3b,** *DS* **G10**

1950 *WELS Suppl.* **seWI,** *Set off.* . . "Set off the table" = clear. Common.

7 in phr *set one's bed:* To make one's bed.

2000 *NADS Letters* **sePA,** A friend who married a woman from suburban Philadelphia used to tease her about her wanting to 'set the bed' rather than make the bed.

8 of a larval **oyster B1** or rarely a clam: To become permanently attached to some solid object; to cause to become attached; hence vbl n *setting.* Cf **set n¹ 1, strike**

1887 Goode *Fisheries U.S.* 2.540, The first thing found out was that the floating spawn would not attach itself to, or 'set' (in the vernacular of the shore) upon, anything which had not a clean surface. **1950** *AmSp* 25.151 **Puget Sound WA,** The Washington State Shellfish Laboratory biologists in their *Bulletin* issued weekly during the spawning and setting season spell the word *cultch.* **1951** Taylor *Surv. Marine Fisheries NC* 148, Oysters which had set on shells planted in Bay River . . were found to be three or four inches long after 18 months. *Ibid* 162, A byssal gland . . secretes a substance which hardens on contact with water . . , by means of which the larval clam [=*Mercenaria mercenaria*] attaches to or "sets" upon such objects as seaweed, stones, and shells. **1951** *Sun* (Baltimore MD) 12 Oct 25/3 (Hench Coll.), The larva [was] moving upstream in order to "set" on the seed beds. **1953** MD Dept. Educ. *Our Underwater Farm* 32, From the time of attachment or "setting" the oysters grow very rapidly. Within the first week they reach pinhead size. **1996** MD Sea Grant College *MD Marine Notes Online* Sept–Oct (Internet), For more than a month . . an oyster hatchery assistant had worked . . to set oyster larvae.

9 with *in:* Of a tract of land: to extend from (a specified place), begin.

1926 *DN* 5.403 **Ozarks,** *Set in.* . . Begins. This phrase is used in a peculiar sense with reference to spatial measurements. "Jim's farm sets in right hyar an' runs plum t' the creek." **1958** *PADS* 29.4 **TN** (as of 1954–56), *Set in:* Of a boundary, . . to begin. "'At track [tract] sets in at 'at big old oak."

set v² See **sit** v¹ **1a, 2a, 3a**

set n¹

1 The attachment of larval oysters to solid objects; the crop of oysters that have thus attached themselves; an oyster that has recently attached itself. Cf **blister 4, set v B8, strike**

1881 Ingersoll *Oyster-Industry* 248, *Set.*—I. A young oyster. Occasionally "Set" is used improperly for *spawn.* . . II. The appearance of young oysters in a district, as a whole, thus: "The *Set* is good in Somerset this year"; *i.e.,* there is an abundance of infant oysters. **1887** Goode *Fisheries U.S.* 5.2.515 **RI,** At only a few places does a breed of oysters, or a "set," as it is termed, occur with any regularity, or of any consequence. **1931–33** *LANE Worksheets* **CT,** Sets—six-week-old oysters. **1939** *Sun* (Baltimore MD) 19 Oct 19/4 (Hench Coll.), Old Rock and Kent Shore, where shells were planted in the spring of 1939, are showing a fine set, as many as 400 per bushel by actual count. **1948** *Ibid* 19 May 20/1 (Hench Coll.), An outstanding difficulty in the management of Maryland oyster crops is the failure to realize 'setting,' that is, an abundance of small oysters every year. Actually the sets are highly infrequent. **1951** *Ibid* 12 Oct 25/3 (Hench Coll.), Certain areas seem more suitable for oyster "set" than others. **1951** Taylor *Surv. Marine Fisheries NC* 148, After the set or "spat" (as the young oysters after attachment are called) have been secured, the oystermen may transplant them to more favorable locations or allow development . . where attachment occurred. Through microscopical examinations of water samples for the presence of larval oysters the period of setting can be accurately predicted. This information is of value when heavy sets are desired in order to have the shells or other collectors function most efficiently. *Ibid* 154, The production of seed requires preparations to secure a set of oysters. . . The theoretical yield from a heavy set would probably exceed 50 bushels of market oysters.

2 The operation of setting out and hauling in a trawl line or net—often in phr *make a set.*

1887 Goode *Fisheries U.S.* 5.1.176 **nwMA,** In addition to the night set, the fishermen . . often make a set during the day-time, or some times, too, by a process called underrunning. . . scarcity of fish prevented day sets. **1930** *AmSp* 5.391 [Language of N Atl fishermen], *Make a set.* . . To set, tow, and haul-back the trawl. **1957** *ME Coast Fisherman* July 21, When the skipper locates fish . . all hands turn to to make a set.

set n[2]

1 In logging: a crew of workers; a team of two workers.

1950 *Western Folkl.* 9.119 **nwOR** [Logger speech], *Set.* A functioning side; a team or crew of workers, "a set of fallers." **1958** McCulloch *Woods Words* 160 **Pacific NW,** *Set.* . . A pair of fallers or buckers. **1959** *AmSp* 34.79 **nwCA** [Logger lingo], *Set.* . . A pair of fallers. . . 'How many set are you going to have?'

2 A sofa, couch. [Perh from its inclusion in a *parlor set* or *living room set*]

1957 in 1974 *DARE* File **NEng,** Set—a sofa, couch, divan; any piece of furniture designed to seat three people. Used by two women of Irish background, in their thirties, one from Providence, Rhode Island, one from New Bedford, Massachusetts. **1967** *DARE* (Qu. E9, *A piece of upholstered furniture that seats three people*) Inf **NE5,** Over-stuff set.

3 A party; a social event.   *among Black speakers*

1959 *Esquire* Nov 70 [sic *OED2*—quot not found], *Set,* a party. **1968** *Current Slang* 3.2.41 [Watts slang; Black], *Set.* . . An informal party or dance. **1969** Keiser *Vice Lords* 40 **NYC** [Black], A set had been planned. . . Throughout the prior week, the set was a constant topic of conversation. The clothes that were going to be worn and the girls that were going to be present were repeatedly discussed. **1970** *DARE* (Qu. FF4, *Names and joking names for different kinds of dancing parties*) Infs **DC11, SC67,** Set. [Both Infs Black] **1970** *Current Slang* 5.2.12 [Black Univ student slang], *Set.* . . A party. **1971** Roberts *Third Ear* np [Black], *Make the set* . . to attend a social affair. **1972** (1973) Bullins *Theme is Blackness* 178 **NYC,** What's happenin'? What'cha doin' tonight, baby? Why don't we make the set? **1980** Folb *Runnin' Down* 253 **cwCA** [Black], *Set.* . . Party, social event. **1986** Pederson *LAGS Concordance (Parties)* 1 inf, **cTX,** A set. [Inf Black]

set n[3] [Prob var of *seat* or *site*]

1923 *DN* 5.220 **swMO,** *Set.* . . A site, as for a mill. **1959** Roberts *Up Cutshin* 11 **eKY,** They're several jobs around a mill set.

set a good deal by See **set** v **B1**

set-along adj, also used absol **chiefly Appalachians** Cf **floor baby**

Of a child: old enough to sit up unaided.

1917 *DN* 4.417 **wNC,** *Set-along.* . . "When my oldest was a little set-along child (settin' along the flo')." **1923** in 1952 Mathes *Tall Tales* 8 **sAppalachians,** He'd take the little setalongs on his knee and talk to 'em when they hadn't never seed no strangers afore, an' they wasn't afeard of him nary bit. **1927** *AmSp* 2.363 **cwWV,** *Set along* . . a small child that is able to sit on the floor alone. "Mrs. Smith had her little set along with her." **1930** *VA Qrly. Rev.* 6.246 **S Midl,** Adjectives arise from verbs, a set-along child. **1974** Fink *Mountain Speech* 23 **wNC, eTN,** *Set-along child* . . child big enough to sit on the floor but not walk. **1975** Chalmers *Better* 34 **Smoky Mts,** Hit's jest a lil ol' set-along chile—caint walk yet. **1996** *NY Times* (NY) 28 June sec A 14/2 **Appalachians,** A baby small enough to stay put on a blanket is . . "a set-along child."

set a lot by See **set** v[1] **B1**

set a stitch See **set** v[1] **B5**

setback n

1 Water that flows backward or overflows from a stream; a backwater. Cf **backset** n **2a**

1877 Bartlett *Americanisms* 572, *Set-back,* The reflux of water made by a counter-current, by the tide from the sea meeting the flow of a river, by a dam, &c. **1895** Remington *Pony Tracks* 139, The crane takes off from his grassy "set back" in a deliberate manner. **1968–69** *DARE* (Qu. C9, *Water from a river that comes up and covers low land when the river is high*) Inf **NY75,** Setback—a narrow place in streams that forces

water back over the land when the river rises; (Qu. C14, *A stretch of still water going off to the side from a river or lake*) Infs **NY200, 233, VT2,** Setback; (Qu. P19) Inf **MA32,** Setback—inlet in river. **1998** *DARE* File **nwMA** (as of 1920s-30s), Dad used to talk about the setback beside the road in the spring when it flooded Davis's pasture by the Connecticut River.

2 also attrib: Any of var card games in which players may lose as well as gain points, esp auction **pitch** n[2] **1.** **chiefly SE, Mid Atl, Appalachians, CT** See Map Cf **pedro**

1843 (1973) Porter *Big Bear AR* 176 **MS,** It may be crack-loo, poker, brag, or set-back-euchre. **1899** Champlin–Bostwick *Young Folks' Games* 299, *Set-back Euchre.* . . At the opening of the game each player's score is credited with five points. When he makes a point it is subtracted from the score, and when he is euchred he is set back two points. . . He whose score is first reduced to nothing, wins. **1963** Edwards *Gravel* 113 **eTN** (as of 1920s), We'll make coffee and have an all-night feed. We'll play Set-Back. **1965–70** *DARE* (Qu. DD35, . . *Card games*) 74 Infs, **chiefly SE, Mid Atl, Appalachians, CT,** Setback; **CT29,** Setback—same as pitch; **TN37,** Setback, pitch same game [Of all Infs responding to this question, 70% were comm types 4, 5, 29% gs educ or less, 63% male; of those giving this response, 84% were comm types 4, 5, 46% gs educ or less, 80% male.]; (Qu. EE40) Inf **FL6,** Set-back. **1968** Haun *Hawk's Done Gone* 134 **TN,** Him and Carlous were going to play set-back. **1969** *DARE* Tape **GA**81, We used to play . . setback. . . Four people usually play partners, and you have eleven cards, and they play with regular playing cards, and you can go set, you bid a certain amount and if you don't get all of them count cards in the game, why you're set—you know, that's what they called setback, and then you bid again and try to recover your score. **1974** Gibson *Hoyle* 214, *Pitch.* . . Its most popular form is *Auction Pitch* (also called *Setback*). *Ibid* 215, *Points* are scored at the end of play; and if the bidder fails to gain the number that he specified, he is "set back" (hence the name "set-back") that many points. [*Ibid* 216, In the earlier or standard form of pitch, there is no auction and therefore no setback.] **1976** Ryland *Richmond Co. VA* 376, Setback—a favorite game. **1986** Pederson *LAGS Concordance,* 1 inf, **nwMS,** Can't play setback. [*LAGS* Ed: a card game?]

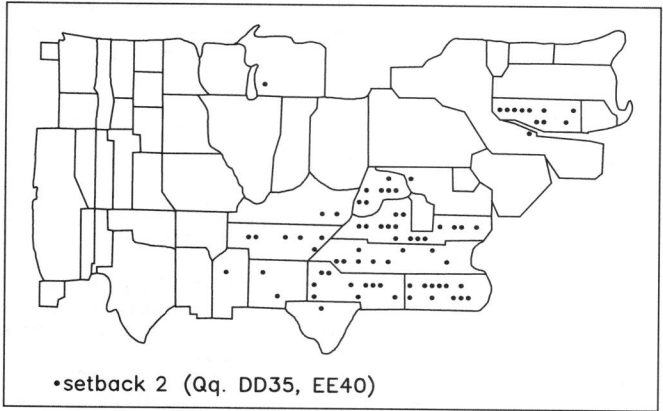

•setback 2 (Qq. DD35, EE40)

3 See quot.

1958 *PADS* 29.3 **TN** (as of 1954–56), *Set-back:* A party where no games are played.

set-back food n

1958 *PADS* 29.3 **TN** (as of 1954–56), *Set back food:* Food that has cooled for a time and then has been placed on the table. "I don't lak [like] no old set back food."

set by v phr[1] Also *sit by* Cf **set up** v phr **1**

To take one's place (at the table)—often used as an invitation to dine.

1902 *DN* 2.244 **sIL,** *Set by.* . . Form of invitation to dine. **1903** *DN* 2.329 **seMO,** *Sit by.* . . An invitation to take a seat at table. 'Sit by and have some dinner.' **1910** *DN* 3.448 **wNY,** *Set by.* . . To come out to dinner. "Well, will you set by?" Older generation. **1941** *LANE* Map 318 (*Sit down; dinner is ready*) 3 infs, **CT,** Set by; 2 infs, **CT,** Set by an' have sump'n t'eat (*or* have some dinner); 1 inf, **swMA,** Set by.

set by v phr[2] See **set** v[1] **B2**

set by ppl adj phr See **set** v¹ **B1**

set down v phr [*OED2* 1753 →]

To humble, rebuke, defeat; hence nouns *set-down, setting down* a rebuff or rebuke.

1899 (1912) Green *VA Folk-Speech* 376, *Set down.* . . A depressing or humiliating rebuke or reprehension; a rebuff; an unexpected and over- whelming answer or reply. . . *Setting-down.* . . A rebuke. "I like to see that upstart get a setting-down." **1934** Hurston *Jonah's Gourd Vine* 241 **AL** [Black], Some uh dem niggers don't b'lieve nobody kin preach but John Pearson. Let 'em see. Den maybe dey'll set 'im down. **1939** Aurand *Quaint Idioms* 29 [PaGer], She was *set down plenty hard* (hu- miliated). **1954** *Harder Coll.* **cwTN**, *Set down.* . . "We set 'em down playin' forty-two." "I sure got set down 'at time." **1965–68** *DARE* (Qu. AA11, *If a man asks a girl to marry him and she refuses,* . . *she* _____) Inf **OK**1, Set him down; (Qu. GG9, *To suddenly embarrass somebody and throw him off balance*) Inf **NH**15, Set him down.

set-down n See **sit-down** n

setfast n [*OED2* 1709 →] Cf **nigger brand**

A hard swelling or sore on a horse's back caused by an ill- fitting saddle or by over-riding.

1892 *DN* 1.231 **KY**, *Setfast* . . the knot on the horse's back made by the saddle. **1899** (1912) Green *VA Folk-Speech* 376, *Set-fast.* . . A hard swelling. **1905** *DN* 3.93 **nwAR**, *Setfast.* . . Sore on a horse's back. 'That setfast ought to be cured up.' **1916** (1918) Lomax *Cowboy Songs* 137, They saddled me up an old gray hack / With two set-fasts on his back. **1933** *AmSp* 8.1.30 **nwTX** [Ranch diction], *Set-fast.* A saddle sore on a horse's backbone. **1936** Adams *Cowboy Lingo* 87 **West**, To ride a horse until his back became sore was to 'beefsteak' or 'gimlet' him, and such sores were called 'nigger brands' or 'set fasts.'

set fire v phr Cf **all-fired, hell-fired, shit fire**

To damn, blast; hence adv *set-fired*.

1882 *Harper's Mth. Mag.* 66.129 **eMA**, I'm afeared I hev ben a set- fired bigoted old man. **1929** *AmSp* 5.124 **ME**, "Godfrey Dorman," "I swan to man," "God All-Sufficient," "Set fire you!", "Dod rot it," "By the holy smut" were emphatic and impatient exclamations. **1975** Gould *ME Lingo* 249, *Set fire you*—An admonitory exhortation of obscure ori- gin: "Now, set fire you; pay attention to what you're doin'!"

set-headed adj phr

1914 *DN* 4.113 **cKS**, *Set-headed.* . . Headstrong.

set hook n esp **SE** Cf **bank line**

A hook on a **setline**.

1963 *South Alabamian* 21 Mar 4-B/3 (*Mathews Coll.*), The party ad- journed and put out some set hooks down the river. **1967–69** *DARE* (Qu. P13, . . *Ways of fishing* . . *besides the ordinary hook and line*) Inf **LA**2, With set hooks—lines set out along the bank; **SC**45, Set hooks— fishing with set hooks—5' pole—line 2' long—let bait stay on top or deep; **GA**89, Set hook—stick in bank and leave it (hook and line); (Qu. P17, . . *When* . . *people fish by lowering a line and sinker close to the bottom of the water*) Infs **AL**28, **NC**49, Set hook fishing. **1972** Hilliard *Hog Meat* 86 **Sth**, Set hooks, trot lines, nets, seines, and baskets all were used to catch catfish.

set horses v phr Also *set horse (together), sit horses* [Varr of *set their horses together* (*OED2* at *set* v. 153.a(c) 1685); cf *gee horses* (at *gee* v² **b**), *hitch horses* (at *hitch* v **3**)] **chiefly Sth, esp S Atl** See Map *esp freq among Black speakers*

To agree, to get on well—usu used in neg constrs.

1899 (1912) Green *VA Folk-Speech* 376, *Set horses.* . . To agree. "They set horses very well." **1935** Hurston *Mules & Men* 196 **FL** [Black], Me and him ain't never gointer set hawses. [Footnote: Never going to get along. As two horses pull together.] **1946** *PADS* 6.18 **eNC**, *Horses, not to set.* . . Not to agree; to be incompatible. . . Occasional. **1965–70** *DARE* (Qu. II11a, *If two people don't get along well together* . . *"They don't* _____") Infs **FL**48, 52, **GA**3, 7, 30, 61, **SC**19, **TX**26, **VA**74, 69, Set horses; **SC**69, Set horses together; **GA**67, Sit horses; (Qu. II29a, *An unexplainable dislike that you feel from the first moment you meet a person: "I don't know why, but I just can't* _____ *him."*) Infs **FL**48, **GA**7, Set horses (with); **MS**37, Sit horses with; (Qu. II29b, . . *To explain the unpleasant effect that person has on you: "He just* _____.") Inf **TN**53, Don't set horses; (Qu. KK68, *When people don't think alike about something: "We agree on most things, but on politics we're*

_____.") Inf **TX**26, Don't set horses. [7 of 14 total Infs Black] **2000** *DARE* File **SC** (as of c1950), **GA** (as of 1999) [Black], "They don't set horse" means that they disagree.

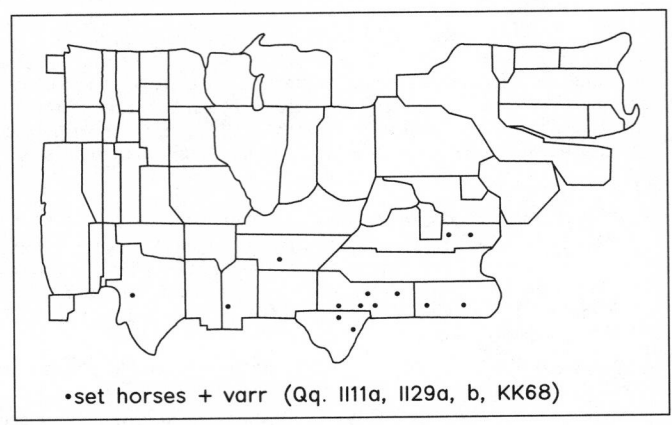

•set horses + varr (Qq. II11a, II29a, b, KK68)

set in See **set** v¹ **B4, 9**

setline n **chiefly Inland Nth, S Atl** See Map Cf **outline, trotline**

A fixed or anchored fishing line that may be left unattended; see quot 1911.

1884 U.S. Natl. Museum *Bulletin* 27.961, Set-line sinkers. **1903** *DN* 2.329 **seMO**, *Set-line.* . . A trot-line. **1907** *DN* 3.237 **nwAR**, *Set- line.* . . A long fish-line to which short lines are attached, and which is usually set over night. **1909** *DN* 3.368 **eAL, wGA**, *Set-line.* . . A fishing-line set out for fish: especially a trot-line. **1911** *Century Dict. Suppl.*, *Set-line.* . . A fish-line with a baited hook which is set or an- chored: often a long line stretched horizontally, from which several shorter lines with baited hooks hang. **1942** McAtee *Dial. Grant Co. IN* 55 (as of 1890s), *Set-line* . . a fishing line fastened to the bank and left unattended often overnight. . . [I]n our neighborhood a trotline was one with both ends fast and numerous hooks on short leaders scattered along the middle of its course, while a set-line usually had only one hook and that at the free end. **1965–70** *DARE* (Qu. P13, . . *Ways of fishing* . . *besides the ordinary hook and line*) 24 Infs, **chiefly Inland Nth, S Atl**, Setline(s); **IN**69, Setline fishing; **CA**36, Setline—a long line with many attached hooks—a buoy at both ends—also called *trot line*; **FL**48, Setlines—long lines, 50 to 60 feet for private fishing, 300 feet for commercial fishing; held above water—short lines with bait suspended at intervals; **MI**65, Setlines—spool is set with a line on, with a minnow, maybe a foot or so below the ice; flag on the line; when flag signals, walk over and take that line; five lines is the limit; **MI**84, Setlines on the ice; **ND**1, Setline—line with baited hook left over night; **NJ**1, Setline— tethered to poles; shells from a long line stretched out; **NY**207, Setline—tie it up and go away. [27 of 32 Infs male] **1982** Sternberg *Fishing* 46, *Trotlines* and *limblines* . . are commonly used on large rivers and reservoirs. A trotline, or *setline*, consists of a dozen or more hooks. . . Both types of lines are set one day and picked up the next. **2000** Chamberlain *River Stories* 38 **swWI**, I'd look out and see him qui- etly moving his boat along his set line that ran from the bank out to the middle of the river. As he worked his way along the finger-size line, he

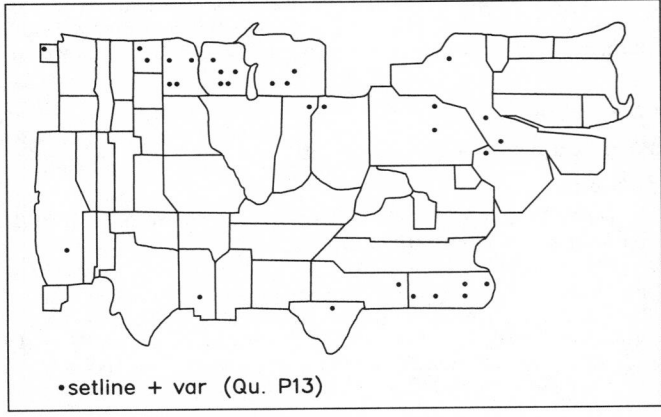

•setline + var (Qu. P13)

checked the #3 catfish hooks which hung from smaller lines attached to the main line. . . The line stretched halfway across the channel and was anchored on the far end with a hundred-pound sandbag.

set off See set v¹ B6

set-off house n
See quot.
1991 Weals *Last Train* 56 **eTN** (as of c1910), The shanties were what Mary called "set-off houses," because they were brought to the site on railroad flatcars and "set off" with a log crane. *Ibid* 98 (as of c1920), Most of the families lived in what were called "cars" or "set-off houses." . . Several units could be joined end-to-end to accommodate more people, and they amounted to a primitive version of today's mobile home.

set one's bed See set v¹ B7

set one's budget down See set the bucket down

set-out n
1 A display (of food or dinnerware).
1899 (1912) Green *VA Folk-Speech* 377, *Set out. . .* A display, as of plate, dishes, etc., at table. "There was a grand set out at the wedding." **1921** *Harper's Mth. Mag.* May 803 **MD**, There was a big supper afterward, a regular set-out, handsome vittles and plenty of them. **1940** White *Wild Geese* 339 **AK** (as of 1890s), He surveyed humorously the modest set-out of foodstuffs to be cooked.
2 A tongue-lashing; a scolding.
1970 *DARE* (Qu. II27, *If somebody gives you a very sharp scolding . . "I certainly got a _____ for that."*) Inf **MS88**, Bawling out, set-out, chewing out; **TN50**, Cussed out; bawling out, set-out.

set out v phr Cf set up v phr 2, 4
To seek a marriage partner.
1952 Brown *NC Folkl.* 1.588, *Set out. . .* To go courting.—West. **1953** Randolph–Wilson *Down in Holler* 282 **Ozarks**, *Set out. . .* To seek a husband, to show a desire for matrimony. "Old Miz Thomas is a-settin' out." I believe it refers chiefly to widows seeking to remarry. **c1960** *Wilson Coll.* **csKY**, *Set out. . .* To go courting, esp as a very young person or a widower.

set rain n
A steady rain or drizzle.
1966 *DARE* (Qu. B25, . . *Joking names . . for a very heavy rain. . . "It's a regular _____."*) Inf **FL24**, Set rain. **1986** Pederson *LAGS Concordance* (A steady drizzle) 1 inf, **seGA**, A set rain—steady and light.

setter See sitter

setters adv Cf belly-flop 1, scoocher
In coasting on a sled: in a sitting position.
1892 *DN* 1.211 **seMA**, Setters, steerers, belly-bumpers: three ways of "coasting." Salem.

set the bucket down v phr Also set one's budget down Cf budget n 1
To come to a decision; to take a stand.
1933 *AmSp* 8.1.52 **Ozarks**, *Set a budget down. . .* To take a firm or positive position on any subject. *Hit ain't no use argyfyin' 'bout it no more, 'cause I have done sot my budget down.* **1966** *DARE* File **neTX** (as of 1920s–30s), *"Set the bucket down"* means to set down anything you might be holding—face your adversary—and settle this matter— *right here and now.*

set the floor v phr among Black speakers
To dance, esp in a style involving vigorous stamping.
1937 in 1976 *Weevils in the Wheat* 106 **VA** [Black], Ole overseer was name Barnes, an' he would yell an' cuss an' lash de slaves near him wid his cowhide, but he couldn't stop all dem slaves from feelin' good, 'cause dey gonna "set de flo" dat night. **1940** Writers' Program *Negro in VA* 93 (as of c1936) [Black], Set de flo'? Dat was—well de couples would do dat in turn. Dey come up an' bend over toward each other at de waist, an' de woman put her hands on her hips an' de man roll his eyes all roun' an' dey pat de flo' wid dey feet jus' like dey was puttin' it in place. Used to do dat bes' on dirt flo' so de feet could slap down hard against it. Sometimes dey would set de flo' alone—either a

man or a woman. Den dey would set a glass of water on dey haid an' see how many kinds of steps dey could make widout spillin' de water.

set the hair See hair n C11

setting n¹ [Cf *EDD* setting sb. 3]   esp Sth
A clutch (of eggs) to be hatched by a fowl; transf: a similar number (of eggs) not intended for hatching.
1899 (1912) Green *VA Folk-Speech* 377, *Setting-of-eggs. . .* A setting of eggs must always be an odd number. For a hen, twelve chickens and a bad one. **1938** Rawlings *Yearling* 140 **nFL,** The setting was hatched. The young quail . . scattered like small windblown leaves. **1967** *Atlanta Constitution* (GA) 6 Mar 5, It has been a long time since I had even thought of the task of marking a setting of eggs. Of course it had to be done to distinguish the eggs designed for hatching from the fresh ones. **1985** Wilkinson *Moonshine* 126 **neNC,** When he was a young man on a farm, his breakfast ordinarily consisted of "a setting of eggs and a dose of ham." A setting is fifteen eggs. **1984** Wilder *You All Spoken Here* 135 **Sth,** *Settin' of eggs:* A clutch of 12 to 15 eggs, depending on heft of the broody hen. **1986** Pederson *LAGS Concordance,* 1 inf, **ceFL,** A setting of egg [sic]—enough for hen to hatch; (*A setting hen*) 1 inf, **csAL,** A setting of eggs—to be put under hen; 1 inf, **nwFL,** A setting of eggs; 1 inf, **cTX,** A setting of eggs (=15).

setting n² Also setting bee
A visit characterized by sitting and talking.
1929 Ellis *Ordinary Woman* 220 **CO** (as of early 20th cent), Every Saturday night there is a 'settin' bee' in both the front room and the kitchen. All this time I visit with Mrs. Chipman as much as possible. **1991** *DARE* File **seNY,** Parlor = the front, or more formal, living room, where you and your guests might have a settin'. Settin' = a visit. Visit = conversation.

setting vbl n See set v¹ B8

setting chair n Also sitting chair   esp Sth, S Midl
A plain, straight chair (as contrasted with a rocking chair).
1768 in 1898 Pelletreau *Early Wills* 233 **seNY,** Leaves to grandson Martines son of *Martines Van Wart* "my Dutch stove and my setting chair with two arms." **1937** Thornburgh *Gt. Smoky Mts.* 96, "Settin' chairs have curved backs, and. . . I bend 'em in this form while they're wet, to give them the right shape," she continued. . . "I can make a settin' chair in a day, but I can't a rockin' chair. It takes longer." **1937** (1977) Hurston *Their Eyes* 16 **FL** [Black], "Mah husband git so sick of 'em sometime he makes 'em all git for home." "Sam is right too. They just wearin' out yo' sittin' chairs." **1972** Cooper *NC Mt. Folkl.* 95, *Setting chair*—chair. **1974** Fink *Mountain Speech* 23 **wNC, eTN,** *Settin' cheer* . . sitting chair, no rockers. **1977** Jones *OR Folkl.* 50 (as of mid 1800s), The predominant chair-type found in the [Aurora] Colony furniture was the mule-eared slat-back chair. . . This chair-type, known in the southern mountains as a *settin' chair* can be found on the East Coast and is very common in the Midwest and in the South; it also turns up in pioneer museums throughout the Northwest. **1986** Pederson *LAGS Concordance* (Chair) 4 infs, 2 **TX,** 1 **nwLA,** 1 **cMS,** Setting chair(s); 1 inf, **ceAL,** Setting chair—straight chairs; black usage. [3 of 5 infs Black]

setting down See set down

setting hen n widespread, but somewhat less freq NEast
See Map on p. 858   Cf broody, cluck n 1
A hen that is incubating eggs.
1820 *N. Amer. Rev.* 10.195, One of our inland tavern keepers . . established himself upon the capital of a setting hen and her venerable consort. **1857** *Ladies' Repository* 17.676, Many women think it necessary to luck that an odd number of eggs should be put under a setting hen. **1937** *AmSp* 12.104 **eNE** [Farm terms], A setting hen may be a *cluck,* . . a *clucking hen,* a *settin' hen,* a *sour hen* (Scandinavian from *sur hona*) or a *skrock hen* (German). **1949** Kurath *Word Geog.* 49, The following expressions . . are current in all three of the major areas, or large parts of them, but are still paralleled by regional or local terms in certain areas: . . *setting hen.* *Ibid* 63, *Clook* (less commonly *cluck*) is an expression of Pennsylvania German origin that is extensively used for the setting hen in Pennsylvania from the Delaware to the Ohio. It is rare beyond the boundaries of the state. **1965–70** *DARE* (Qu. K72, *When the hen stops laying and begins to sit on the eggs to hatch them, she's a _____*) 509 Infs, **widespread, but somewhat less freq NEast,** Setting hen. **1973** Allen *LAUM* 1.254 **Upper MW** (as of c1950), By far the most common term is *setting hen,* with an overall average of

85%. Only Minnesota, with an overlapping frequency of 40% for *cluck (hen)* has an appreciably lower occurrence of *setting hen* (68%). **1976** Garber *Mountain-ese* 80 **sAppalachians,** We put two goose eggs under the settin' hen to hatch. **1989** Pederson *LAGS Tech. Index* 137 *(A setting hen)* 475 infs, **Gulf Region,** Setting hen.

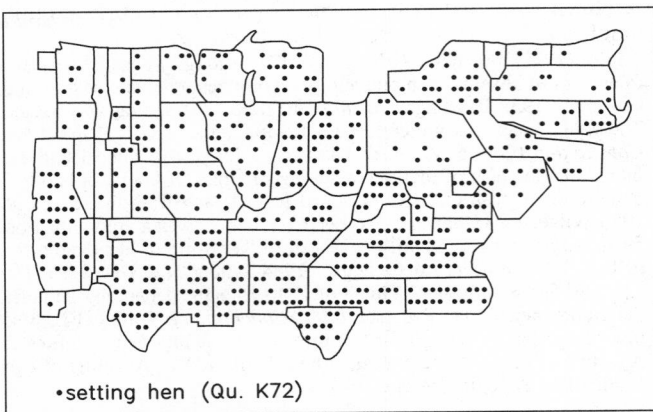

•setting hen (Qu. K72)

setting-lonely adj
=**set-along.**

1959 Lomax *Rainbow Sign* 27 **AL** [Black], He just lived to be a settin-lonely baby. . . When he got to sittin lonely on the floor, his head would just tumble him right over.

setting out n chiefly NEast old-fash
A dowry; a trousseau; the equipment necessary for establishing a household, usu in the form of a gift to a bride or newly married couple.

1833 Greene *Life Dr. Dodimus* 2.35 **NEng,** She would be likely to receive a pretty penny by way of marriage dowry; or, as the people expressed it, a good setting out. **1848** *Ladies' Repository* 8.337 **NEng,** Why don't you give Henry the old three-legged gridiron? . . I think you can afford to give that to Hen and Kate as a part of their "setting out." **1884** Baldwin *Yankee School-Teacher* 138 **VA** [Black], An' whar's her sett'n out t come fr'm now? **1893** Holley *Samantha at World's Fair* 632, A silver bedstead the Sultan is a-goin' to give to his daughter as a part of her settin' out when she marries. **1947** Bowles–Towle *New Engl. Cooking* 46, Every New England girl who lived within sound of the sea, four or five generations ago, counted a chowder kettle as an essential part of her "setting out." **1952** *NY Folkl. Qrly.* 8.187 **cwNY,** A bride's "setting out" always included a bread "peel" or board on which to cut bread. **1959** *VT Hist.* 27.156, Settin' out. . . The start of house furnishings. Obsolescent. **1967** *DARE* FW Addit **MA5,** Setting out—trousseau; included clothes and household linens.

setting room n [sit v¹ A1a] chiefly Atlantic, esp NEast old-fash
A sitting room.

1741 in 1915 NH *Prov. & State Papers* 33.30, I give to my Beloved Wife. . . ye furniture of ye Chamber over our Setting room. **1832** Williamson *Hist. ME* 2.703, Our indigenous cherry, black-birch, and curl maple . . were shoved from the parlour and setting-room, to admit articles of foreign mahogany. **1890** Holley *Samantha among Brethren* vii **NY,** The corner of the settin' room table devoted by me to literary pursuits. **1907** *DN* 3.199 **seNH,** Sett'n'-room. . . Living room. "This rag carpet I'm making is for my sett'n'-room." **1916** *DN* 4.265 **Cape Cod MA,** She tells her son not to "craunch" his toast and to take his great "clompers" off before he walks on the new "settin'-room mattin'." **1916** Lincoln *Mary-'Gusta* 18 **MA,** Mrs. Hobbs led her into the little room off the parlor, the "back settin-room." **1949** Kurath *Word Geog.* 51, *Living room* . . In all the Eastern states *living room* and *sitting room* (*settin' room* among the common folk) are the usual names for the room in which the family gathers evenings, and receives and entertains friends. **1966–69** *DARE* (Qu. D13, *The room where you entertain company*) Infs **IN54, MT4, NH14, NJ55, NY75,** Setting room. [4 of 5 Infs old] **1970** *DARE* FW Addit **seMA,** Setting room—Room between parlor and kitchen; wasn't for best company; more like living room today. Old-fashioned. **1974** *AmSp* 49.63 **sME coast,** Setting room . . Living room. **1976** Garber *Mountain-ese* 80 **sAppalachians,** Settin'-room . .

parlor, livingroom—Maudie axed her beau to come set in her ma's settin' room. **1986** Pederson *LAGS Concordance* **Gulf Region** *(Sitting room / where guests are entertained)* [Of the 15 primary infs who responded with *setting room,* 14 of 15 were 65 years of age or older.]

setting up n See set up v phr 3

setting-up adj Cf setting-lonely
=**set-along.**

1954 *Harder Coll.* **cwTN,** Settin' up kid: . . a baby old enough to sit alone.

setting up vbl n See set up v phr 3

settle v
1 Of a cow: to become pregnant.

1962 *Daily Progress* (Charlottesville VA) 19 April 19/5 *(Hench Coll.),* The inseminator will make additional trips to the farm if the cow doesn't settle on the first service. **1967–69** *DARE* Tape **ID**8, That's what dairy farmers say, is a cow won't settle. That's when she won't become pregnant and have a calf again; **MA**32, We had a little trouble in gettin' the cows to settle, if you understand farm language. **2002** *DARE* File—Internet **TX,** If a cow doesn't settle on the second artificial insemination breeding, I recommend putting her with a bull for natural service.

2 To impregnate (a cow); hence ppl adj *settled* of a cow: pregnant; n *(cow) settler* a bull of proven fertility, regardless of other traits.

1968 *DARE* (Qu. K10, *Words used about a cow that is going to have a calf*) Inf **NY**102, She's settled with calf. **1984** *MJLF* 10.155 **WI,** Settle. To get a cow with calf. *Ibid* 152 **ME,** A young bull of no particular heritage pastured with heifers to get them with calf for the first time. Maine: Settler or dunghill bull. **1999** *Cattle Today* May (Internet), He should know each breeding season how long it took to get each cow bred and settled. **1999** in 2002 *DARE* File—Internet **MO,** [Auction terms and conditions:] Any bull which settles at least one-third of the healthy cows he breeds will be considered a breeder. **2002** *DARE* File—Internet **NE,** We strongly feel that any bull you buy should be an industry improver, not just a cow settler.

settle-aged adj
1974 (1975) Shaw *All God's Dangers* 41 **AL** [Black], Old man Frank Milliken—he weren't no old man, he was settle-aged, but he could get up and work, . . and he was a good cook, too.

settled See settle 2

settle down v phr
To decide, conclude; hence ppl adj *settled down* established.

1851 Hooper *Widow Rugby's Husband* 69 **AL,** Well, arter a little while, the jury settled down that they'd wait twell the s'lic'tor should come, and they'd take *his* opinion. **1866** in 1893 *Century Illustr. Mag.* 45.892 **OH,** After much pro and con we have settled down that I shall go with Campbell. **1965** *DARE* Tape **KY**1, If they strip [=engage in strip-mining], everybody in this place is gonna have to leave here. That's a settled down proposition.

settlement n Usu |ˈsɛt̬lˌmənt|; also chiefly Sth, S Midl |ˌsɛt̬lˈmɛnt, -ˈmɪnt|; for addit varr see quots Pronc-spp *settlemaynt, settlemint*
Std senses, var forms.

1843 (1916) Hall *New Purchase* 79 **IN,** All round the settlemints. **1851** Burke *Polly Peablossom* 30 **GA,** The celebrities of which his settle*ment* (neighbourhood) boasted. **1895** *DN* 1.374 **seKY, eTN, wNC,** Settlemént. **1902** *DN* 2.245 **sIL,** Settlement [-ment]. . . settlemaynt. **1903** *DN* 2.329 **seMO,** Settlement. **1907** *DN* 3.226 **nwAR,** Settlement [setlment]. *Ibid* 237 **nwAR,** Settlemint. **1913** Kephart *Highlanders* 224 **sAppalachians,** I became a sort of "doctor to the settle*ment*." [Footnote:] In mountain dialect such words as settlement . . are accented on the last syllable, or drawled with equal stress throughout. **1923** in 1952 Mathes *Tall Tales* 1 **sAppalachians,** Indeed, old man Jake Howell, who used to be the schoolmaster in the "settle*ment*," declared once that even the name of the place had been "tore out o' the joggafy." **c1960** Wilson *Coll.* **csKY,** Settlement is often /ˈsɛtl̩mɪnt/ later /ˈsɛtlmənt/. **1967** *Mt. Life* 43.1.14 **sAppalachians,** Oncet they 'uz a fox 'at 'uz a-goin daown to the settle-mints one mornin to the store. **1968** *DARE* FW Addit **GA**40, "Settlement" pronounced [ˈsɛləˌmɪnt]. **1981** Pederson *LAGS Basic Materials,* 1 inf, nwGA, [ˈsɛʔt̬lˈmɛnt].

settlement road n Sth, S Midl Cf neighborhood road

A local rural road.

1843 (1916) Hall *New Purchase* 77 **IN**, A neighborhood road does not imply necessarily much proximity of neighbors. I have travelled all day long upon a neighborhood or settlement road and seen neither neighbors nor neighbors' cabins. **1866** Smith *Bill Arp* 127 **nwGA**, Across the country by a settlement road they called the 'cut-off.' **1968** *DARE* (Qu. N29, . . *Names . . for a less important road running back from a main road*) Inf **GA40**, Settlement road. **1986** Pederson *LAGS Concordance* **Gulf Region** *(Byway, outside of town)* 5 infs, Settlement road(s); 1 inf, Settlement road—local dirt road; 1 inf, Settlement road—out in country, usually dirt road; 1 inf, Settlement road—red rock or red gravel now; *(Lane, from public road to house)* 1 inf, Settlement road; 1 inf, Settlement road—to house; 1 inf, Settlement road—leads to a person's house; 1 inf, Settlement road—country road.

settlemint See settlement

settler See settle 2

set tub n

A permanently installed laundry tub.

1873 *Appletons' Jrl.* 10.219, Who can fail to recognize that such a phase of life, thrown back into the foggy distance of the past, will be lighted and shaded by our memories . . , after the type-kitchens of the country are all abandoned to Biddy, with the range, hot and cold water pipes and boiler, refrigerators, and "set tubs." **1885** Howells *Rise Lapham* 50 **VT**, I'll do the wash. . . I presume you'll let me have set tubs. **1925** *AmSp* 1.152, Western speech is full of differences from Eastern speech. . . What is the difference between a "set tub" and a "laundry tray?" **1961** Hall *String Too Short* 19 **sNH**, She could look at them [=flowers in the yard] while she cooked, or washed workclothes at the set-tubs. **1966** *DARE* File, *Set tubs*—Laundry tubs (stationary tubs). **c1978** *DARE* File **cnMA** (as of c1915), I knew *set tubs* as a child, built-in tubs, usually in basements, with hot and cold running water. **1980** *Ibid* **csWI**, A friend from Portland [OR] used the term "laundry tray" for what I would call a set tub. **2001** *Ibid* **cwCA** (as of c1950), A set tub was the one on the service porch that couldn't be moved.

set up v phr

1 also *sit up;* also in phr *set up to (the) table:* To pull one's chair up to the table, take one's seat for a meal; hence n *set-up* (or *sit-up*) the taking of one's place (at the table).

1843 (1916) Hall *New Purchase* 54 **IN**, "Well! come, sit up." This sit-up we instantly performed. *Ibid* 153, When the "set up" is ordered, the gentlemen seat themselves alongside, and partly under the table. **1886** *S. Bivouac* 4.350 **sAppalachians**, Set up (as "set up to table, men; supper's ready, sich as it is"). **1889** *Overland Mth.* 13.266 **IN**, He was sociable enough to "set up" to supper. **1899** (1912) Green *VA Folk-Speech* 377, *Set up.* . . A person was told to *"set up"* and *"catch hold"*: that is, to sit up to the table and help himself to the food. "Set up and take holt." **1906** *DN* 3.155 **nwAR**, Set up and have some dinner. . . Won't you take dinner with us? **1941** *LANE* Map 318 *(Sit down; dinner is ready)* **NEng**, [Both *sit up* and *set up* occur throughout the region with the latter form being far more frequent; the longer form *set up to the table* also occurs several times.] **1982** Brooks *Quicksand* 327 **swUT** (as of 1932), "We're just ready to sit up. Come and join us." . . Mary's food was delicious.

2 also *sit up;* with *to:* To pay court to (a woman); broadly, to curry favor with. [Despite the superficial similarity, prob unrelated to *set up with* (at **4** below); cf *make up to* (*OED2* at *make* v. 96.n.(b)) and *set up for* (*OED2* at *set* v. 154.mm.(c)).] **chiefly Sth, S Midl** Cf **set v B3**

1845 in 1956 Eliason *Tarheel Talk* 293 **cnNC**, Mr Bogle. . . was setting up to Miss Charinten. **1846** *Ibid* 293 **ceNC**, [He] is setting up to Fanny Hawks hard. **1873** *Overland Mth.* 10.54 **AR**, You didn't know I once set up to her myself, eh? But Nat got in ahead of me. **1874** Aldrich *Prudence Palfrey* 86 **NEng**, I'd wager a cookey, now, young Dent has ben settin' up to that Palfrey gal, an' there's ben trouble. **1901** Harben *Westerfelt* 6 **nGA**, Westerfelt certainly is settin' square up to Ab's daughter. **1905** *DN* 3.93 **nwAR**, Set up to. . . To woo, to court. 'He's settin' up to 'er.' Not uncommon. **1909** *DN* 3.369 **eAL, wGA**, *Set up to.* . . To court, woo. **1912** *DN* 3.589 **wIN**, *Set up to.* . . To court; to "spoon." **1918** *DN* 5.21 **NC**, *Set up to,* to court. **1926** *DN* 5.403

Ozarks, Jake he's a-settin' up t' a gal over on Hawg Mountain. **1927** *DN* 5.475 **Ozarks**, Jeff he sets up t' thet 'ar gal like a sick kitten t' a jam rock. **1930** *DN* 6.85 **cSC**, *To sit up to,* to woo. **1941** Writers' Program *Guide MO* 135, When he "sets up" to a girl, he usually intends to marry her. **1966–70** *DARE* (Qu. AA1, *When a man goes to see a girl often and seems to want to marry her, he's _____ her*) Infs **SC11, 19, 34**, Sitting up to [suggested resp]; (Qu. II20b, *A person who tries too hard to gain somebody else's favor: "He's always trying to _____ the boss."*) Infs **FL14, MS49, 84**, Set up to. **1986** Pederson *LAGS Concordance,* 1 inf, **cGA**, The men were sitting up to them—more serious; 1 inf, **cAL**, Setting up to her = courting.

3 also *sit up:* To stay up through the night with the body of a dead person; freq in phrr *set* (or *sit*) *up with* (or *for, by*) *the body* (or *corpse*, etc); hence vbl n *setting* (or *sitting*) *up*; n *setting up* an occasion on which this is done; a wake. **chiefly Sth, S Midl, TX** See Map

1838 (1852) Gilman *S. Matron* 81, As the visiters assembled, they crowded the hut of the deceased, and when that was full, stood around the entrance near the coffin. At short intervals some among the group commenced a hymn, in which all joined; refreshments were then decorously distributed. [Footnote:] This solemnity is usually styled by the negroes "a setting up." **1884** *Anglia* 7.271 **Sth, S Midl** [Black], *To set up wid* = to keep a lych-wake. **1892** (1893) Botume *First Days* 222 [Black], He . . died a little after dark. His friends immediately assembled and held a watch-meeting, which they call "a setting-up." **1927** Adams *Congaree* 29 **cSC** [Black], Dere was a fellow that went to one of he fren's settin-up, and dis fren' was laid out dead on de coolinboard. **1929** *AmSp* 4.304 [Iowa locutions], "Sit up" took on a somber meaning when a death had occurred and the corpse had been "laid out." It then meant sitting in pairs or groups all night by the dead, and perhaps in volved the task of dipping a cloth at intervals in the embalming fluid, and laying it on the still face. **1937** in 1977 *Amer. Slave Suppl. 1* 1.87 **AL**, Iffen any of de slaves'd die, dey would have a big settin' up party and sing and pray and nounce benedictions, bury dem and go on. **1938** Rawlings *Yearling* 207 **nFL**, Hit'd pleasure him [=a dead man], you comin' to set up with him tonight. **1952** Brown *NC Folkl.* 1.588, *Setting-up.* . . A wake.—Central and east. **1939** *FWP Guide NC* 96, In its ordinary manifestations the religious code shows its influence throughout the State. . . A wake, with the less sophisticated, becomes something of a social occasion as neighbors gather to "set up." **1944** *PADS* 2.30 **KY, NC**, *Set up with.* . . To keep a wake for a corpse. . . Common. **1965–70** *DARE* (Qu. BB60, *When friends and relatives gather together at the place where the body is, usually the night before the funeral*) 89 Infs, **chiefly Sth, S Midl, TX**, Sitting up; 17 Infs, **chiefly Sth, S Midl, TX**, Setting up; **FL19**, Setting up—at the home; do not set up at funeral parlors; **FL49**, In setting up, the body would be in bed and someone would sit by the bed till the morning of the funeral; **GA59**, Sitting up—I sat up with so-and-so; **ME5**, Sitting up with the body—a person was usually chosen to sit up with the body, to keep away rats, put ice on the body in warm weather, etc; **OK25**, Years ago they had a sitting up—one or two would sit up with the body all night; 12 Infs, **esp Lower Missip Valley**, Sitting (*or* setting) up with (him, the corpse, the body, *etc*); **GA72**, Setting up for the dead (*or* corpse); 12 Infs, **chiefly Sth, S Midl, TX**, Set (or sit) up; **GA84**, They set up—old-fashioned; **LA12**, Sit up with the dead, when it used to be done at home; **MI10**, Set up at the laying-out—used to be; **NC77**, Sit up by him; **OK1**, They just sit up with the family—no name, but people come; **VA52**, Set up—old-fashioned;

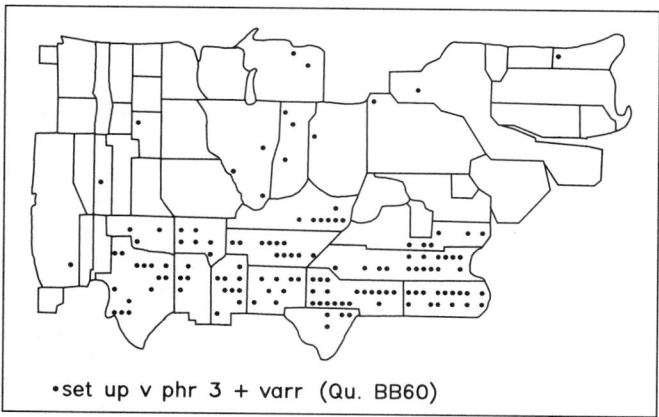

•set up v phr 3 + varr (Qu. BB60)

three nights before burial. **1966** *DARE* Tape **AL**1, When anybody died back in them days we went to sit up, people'd sit up all night with them, we'd sit up and sing and parch peanuts and pop corn. **1984** Burns *Cold Sassy* 329 **nGA** (as of 1906), "Git thet marble-top table over yonder, Will Tweedy, and set it by the head of a-thet coffin. Then see can you find a kerosene lamp to put on it." He must of thought the carbon bulb hanging from the ceiling was too raw-looking for a settin'-up. **1986** Pederson *LAGS Concordance*, 1 inf, **nwFL**, Setting up; 1 inf, **cGA**, Set up—wake a corpse; 1 inf, **cGA**, Setting up nights—with the dead, waking them; 1 inf, **neMS**, Set up many a night—with corpse; divided time; 1 inf, **nwMS**, Set up with them = wake; sit up with the corpse; 1 inf, **seMS**, Sitting up with the dead—older name for it; 1 inf, **cTN**, Sit up—wake a corpse; 1 inf, **cwTN**, Sit up with the dead—before they were buried; 1 inf, **cTN**, I've sat up with corpses = waked them.

4 also *sit up:* To stay up or stay up (with someone) in the evening for the purpose of courtship; to associate as lovers. [*EDD* at *sit* v. 1.(9)(a)] Cf *keep company* (at **keep** v **B5b**), **set up** v phr **2** above

1871 Eggleston *Hoosier Schoolmaster* 41 **sIN**, A parlor which Mirandy had made an effort to furnish a little (in hope of the blissful time when somebody should "set up" with her of evenings). **1896** *DN* 1.424 **wMA**, Sit up with: to receive courtship from. "Sarah Ann is sitting up with a young man." **1911** *DN* 3.539 **eKY**, Set up with. To call upon a woman in courtship; e.g., "He's a-setting up with Blue Joe's daughter." **1914** *DN* 4.79 **ME, nNH**, Set up with. . . To court. "Harvey's ben a-settin' up with Jane, quite a spell." **1931** *AmSp* 7.94 **eKY**, Settin'-up, having dates. "Belle 'n' Fulton'll git married soon; they've been settin'-up." **1932** Toone *Yankee Slang* 33, Sitting up: Young man paying court to girl "sits up" with her after parents have retired to bed. **1939** Aurand *Quaint Idioms* 31 [PaGer], She is now old enough to *sit up* (entertain her beau, without parental supervision, we believe). **1939** *AmSp* 14.91 **eTN**, Setting up. With reference to a girl beginning to have boy friends. 'Lida's started setting up.' **1941** LANE Map 405 *(Keeping company with her)* 2 infs, **ME, MA**, Setting up with (her); 2 infs, **ME, MA**, Setting up with her—obsolete; 1 inf, **swMA**, They are setting up together—heard as a child. **1941** Writers' Program *Guide IN* 120, Courtship was a serious business for the reason that everybody knew when a young couple began to 'set up' with each other. **1944** *PADS* 2.26 **cwNC**, Set up with. . . To court. "Where you says 'makin a call' on a gal, we says 'settin' up with.'" **1952** Brown *NC Folkl.* 1.588, Set up with. . . To court. . . General. Obsolescent. **1966** *DARE* (Qu. AA1, *When a man goes to see a girl often and seems to want to marry her, he's _____ her*) Inf **ME**5, Setting up with.

5a Of a condition, esp a disease: to become established, take hold.

1906 *DN* 3.155 **nwAR**, Set up. . . To set in, begin. "Then tuberculosis sets up and runs its course rapidly." **1967** *DARE* Tape **TX**32, When we gather our vegetables we have to work in a hurry to get them in the freezer before spoil sets up. **1986** Pederson *LAGS Concordance*, 1 inf, **nwMS**, Blood poison would set up; 1 inf, **cwTN**, Peritonitis had done set up; 1 inf, **cwTN**, Blood poisoning setting up; 1 inf, **neMS**, When gangrene would set up.

b See quot.

1932 Smiley *Gloss. New Paltz* **seNY**, Sot up or set up—to become inflamed (usually hand or foot). Has it *sot up* on you? means Has it become festered or infected.

c To come down with, develop (a disease).

1966–68 *DARE* (Qu. BB44, . . *A person just starting some sickness . . "He _____ pneumonia."*) Inf **TN**27, Set up pneumonia; **GA**8, Is setting up; is taking; took.

6 To court (a woman). [*EDD* has a single example of *sit (one) up* in this sense at *sit* v. 1.(9)(a).] Cf **set up** v phr **2** above, **set** v **B3**

1941 LANE Map 404 *(Courting her)* 2 infs, **swME**, Setting her up.

set up adj phr [Engl dial; cf *EDD* set ppl. adj. 1.(13)]
Proud; exhilarated; taken (with oneself); enlivened by drink.

1875 *Appletons' Jrl.* 14.230 **Sth**, But, if I ever take to planting, . . I don't care to do it on a large scale; I would feel quite set up with "forty acres and a mule." **1876** *Ibid* 1.336 **NEng**, But Mrs. Woodmansee was wonderfully set up with it all, and no great marvel, either. **1900** *DN* 2.58 [College slang], Set up. . . Intoxicated. . . Proud. **1929** Ellis *Ordinary Woman* 102 **CO** (as of early 20th cent), We are 'set up' over having an organ for the front room. . . no, none of us played, but—it gave such an air to the Front Room. **1931** Hannum *Thursday April* 38 **wNC**, The

wind was slushing through the thick needles of little white-pines. . . Down by the house the two balsam by the gate were heavy things that did a ponderous dance. The night, she realized suddenly, was set-up and prancy. It excited her. **1935** Porter *Flowering Judas* 82 **TX**, At the foot of the platform stairway she staggered slightly—they were both nicely set up on Thora's cocktails. **1949** Guthrie *Way West* 31, He was sad, sure enough, but set up, too. **1965–70** *DARE* (Qu. BB47, *Feeling in the best of health and spirits: "I'm feeling _____!"*) Inf **CA**97, Set up; (Qu. GG19a, *When you can see from the way a person acts that he's feeling important or independent: "He surely is _____ these days.")* Infs **CA**4, **HI**1, **IL**72, **MA**5, **NY**60, **OH**29, Set up; (Qu. II36b, *Of somebody who talks back or gives rude answers . . "She certainly is _____!"*) Inf **PA**15, Set up with herself. [7 of 8 Infs old]

set-up n See **set up** v phr **1**

set up one's ebenezer See **ebenezer 1**

set up to (the) table See **set up** v phr **1**

sevagarous, sevagerous See **savagerous**

seval See **several**

seve bean See **sieva bean**

seven n, adj Usu |'sɛvən|; also |'sɛvm̩, 'sɛbm̩|; for addit varr see quots Pronc-spp *seben, sebm, seb'n, sebun, se'm, sev'm* Similarly *sebmty, seb'nteen, seb'nty* Cf Pronc Intro 3.I.17, **eleven, heaven A**

A Forms.

1856 *S. Lit. Messenger* 23.196 [Black], 'Bout seben miles, sir. **1887** (1967) Harris *Free Joe* 119 **nGA**, You go on like a man what's done gone an' took leave of his sev'm senses. **1899** (1912) Green *VA Folk-Speech* 374, Seben. . . For seven. . . Sebm. **1922** Gonzales *Black Border* 325 **sSC, GA coasts** [Gullah glossary], Seb'n—seven. . . Sebm. . . Seb'nteen—seventeen. Seb'nty—seventy. **1930** *VA Qrly. Rev.* 6.248 **S Midl**, The hill man . . may make . . consonant changes like seben for seven. **1936** *AmSp* 11.236 **eTX**, In . . seven . . the [v] > [b] in careless or illiterate speech, the following vowel is elided, making the [n] syllabic, and then [n̩] > [m̩] by assimilation to [b] . . ['sɛbm̩]. **1936** Greene *Death Deep South* 210 [Black], Se'm o'clock. **1939** LANE Map 57, The nasal consonant in *seven, seventy*, when immediately preceded by another consonant, is usually syllabic; but in rapid utterance it may be non-syllabic. Pronunciations of the type of [sɛm, sɛmtɪ] are quick forms, used side by side with more careful pronunciations. [Proncs of the type [sɛbm, sɛvm̩, sɛbmtɪ, sɛvm̩tɪ] are found throughout the region; those of the type [sɪˑm, sæbm, sævm̩] occur infrequently.] **1953** Brewer *Word Brazos* 55 **eTX** [Black], So de fo'th Sunday comed an' 'bout sebun hunnud Town Nigguhs. **1955** Roberts *S. from Hell-fer-Sartin* 134 **seKY**, And he laid there seben days and seben nights. **1967–70** *DARE* (Qu. BB25) Infs **LA**12, **VA**52, [sɛbm̩]-year-itch. **1969** *DARE* FW Addit **ceVA**, Eighty-seven ['eɪdɪˌsɛbm̩]. **c1970** Pederson *Dial. Surv. Rural GA* **seGA** *(Seven),* [Of 64 infs, 57 gave proncs of the type ['sɛv(ə)n, -m̩, -ɛn, ʊn]; 4 infs ['sɛvm̩]; 1 inf, ['sɛbm̩]; 1 inf, ['saˀvən].] **1976** Allen *LAUM* 3.318 **Upper MW** (as of c1950), An apparent geographic pattern with a concentration of the /bm/ in eastern Nebraska is probably illusory. . . There is, however, some evidence for social differentiation, as in *seven* . . and *seventy* 62% of the speakers with the /bm/ cluster are in Type I [=old, with little educ] and only 38% in Type II [=mid-aged, with approx hs educ], with none at all in Type III [=mid-aged, with coll educ]. [21 infs have the cluster /bm/ in *seven*, and 22 in *seventy*.] **1989** Pederson *LAGS Tech. Index* 3 **Gulf Region**, [720 infs offered the pronc [sɛvn̩], 209 infs [sɛbm̩], 51 infs [sɛvm̩], 33 infs [sɛm], 9 infs [sɪvn̩], 5 infs [sɪbn̩], 2 infs [sɪvm̩].] **1994** *DARE* File **MO**, Sebmty-lebm is just a variant of forty-lebm.

B Sense.

See **seven, number.**

seven and six (or seventy six), the See **same old six and seven, the**

sevenbark n

1 A ninebark 1. *obs*

1762 Gronovius *Flora Virginica* 77, Spiræa floribus albis, foliis opuli [=*Physocarpus opulifolius*]. Sevenbark. **1806** (1905) Lewis *Orig. Jrls. Lewis & Clark Exped.* 4.49, The seven bark or nine bark as it is called in the U'States is also common [near Ft. Clatsop OR]. [**1934** Haskin *Wild Flowers Pacific Coast* 169, *Opulaster opulifolius* [here: =*Physocarpus* *capitatus*]. . . In the journals of Lewis and Clark this shrub was commonly spoken of as "seven bark," but ninebark is now its more commonly recognized name. On old mature stems the parchment-like bark will easily peel off—layer after layer—the number of them by no means confined either to seven or to nine. On very old stems twenty or more may frequently be counted.]

2 A **hydrangea 1** (here: either *Hydrangea arborescens* or *H. quercifolia*).

1876 Hobbs *Bot. Hdbk.* 105, Seven-bark, Hydrangea, Hydrangea arborescens. **1901** Mohr *Plant Life AL* 535, *Hydrangea arborescens. . . Wild Hydrangea. Sevenbark. . .* The root . . is used medicinally. *Ibid* 536, *Hydrangea quercifolia. . . Oak-leaf Hydrangea. Sevenbark. . .* The bark, "sevenbark," is used in domestic medicine. **1926** *Torreya* 26.5 **MS,** *Hydrangea quercifolia. . .* Seven-bark, Pickens, Miss. **1937** Thornburgh *Gt. Smoky Mts.* 29, Then there are . . yellow root, showy hydrangea, or seven bark, for all sorts of bodily ailments. **1986** Pederson *LAGS Concordance,* 1 inf, **ceAL,** Sevenbark = hydrangea; 1 inf, **cnAL,** Sevenbark—called as a child.

3 A birch (*Betula* spp).

1966–69 *DARE* (Qu. T15, . . *Kinds of swamp trees*) Infs **AL**33, **GA**84, Birch—also called "sevenbark"; **MS**1, Sevenbark—these are birch; **SC**32, Sevenbark. [*DARE* Ed: Some of these Infs may refer instead to other senses.]

4 A **sycamore.**

1966 *DARE* (Qu. T13, . . *Names . . for . . sycamore*) Inf **MS**16, Sycamore, sevenbark. **1986** Pederson *LAGS Concordance,* 1 inf, **nwGA,** Sevenbark = sycamore.

seven-day pickle n Cf fourteen-day pickle

A type of pickle made by a method that takes a week.

1957 Showalter *Mennonite Cookbook* 407, *Seven-Day Sweet Pickles. . .* Wash cucumbers and cover them with boiling water. Let stand 24 hours and drain. Repeat each day for 4 days. . . On the fifth day, cut cucumbers in ¼ inch rings. Combine vinegar, sugar, salt and spices. Bring liquid to a boil and pour over sliced cucmbers. Let stand 24 hours. Drain syrup and bring to a boil. Pour over cucumbers. Repeat on the sixth day. On the last day, drain off the syrup . . and bring it to a boil. Add cucumber slices and bring to the boiling point. Pack into hot jars and seal. **1965–70** *DARE* (Qu. H56, *Names for . . pickles*) Infs **GA**17, **IN**7, 19, **KY**44, **MI**96, **MO**39, **NC**68, **PA**242, Seven-day pickle(s); **AL**27, Seven-day pickle—crisp and green; takes seven days to make; **MD**27, Seven-day pickles—cucumbers kept in salt brine seven days, served with spicy syrup; **MO**20, **PA**150, Seven-day.

seven hundred dollars n

Used as a vague standard of comparison.

1923 *DN* 5.220 **swMO** *Seven hundred dollars. . .* Extraordinarily. "I'm sicker 'n seven hunderd dollars." "Hit snowed like seven hunderd dollars."

seven, number n Also seven [From the shape] Cf ell n[1] 4

1968 *DARE* (Qu. W27, . . *A three-cornered tear in a piece of clothing from catching it on something sharp*) Inf **LA**32, A number seven (named because of the shape of the tear); **NV**9, Number seven; **MD**19, Seven (due to its shape).

seven sisters n

1 The Pleiades. [*OED2* →1742]

1928 Chapman *Happy Mt.* 313 **eTN,** Seven Sisters—Pleiades. **1942** McAtee *Dial. Grant Co. IN* 55 (as of 1890s), *Seven Sisters . .* the constellation Pleiades. **2002** *DARE* File **cwCA** (as of c1955), When I was a child, my mother taught me that the Pleiades were also known as the seven sisters. They were supposed to be the seven daughters of Atlas and Pleione.

2 A **spurge** such as *Euphorbia helioscopia.*

1900 Lyons *Plant Names* 156, *E[uphorbia] Helioscopia. . .* Seven-sisters. . . *Juice* acrid, formerly used to cure warts. **c1938** in 1970 Hyatt *Hoodoo* 1.645 **csNC,** An' then yo' git a root which is called de *Seven Sisters,* an yo' take that root an' yo' wrop this hair [=the boss's] round that root an' keep that. An' when yo' go to 'em, dey says he won't deny yo' [your request].

3 A **multiplying onion;** see quot.

1968 *DARE* (Qu. I6, *The kind of onions that come up fresh early in the year, and you eat them raw*) Inf **SC**57, Seven sisters = a multiplying onion—plant one set and a cluster of 6–12 will form around it.

seventeen-year locust n Also seventeen-years locust; for addit varr see quot 1965–70

A **cicada** of the genus *Magicicada,* esp *M. septemdecim.*

1817 *Columbian Centinel. MA Federalist* (Boston MA) 14 May 1/4, The southern papers have announced that the present is the year for the appearance of what is called, in rural language, the *Seventeen Years Locust. . .* The insect lives above ground about two months, and 17 years in it. **1843** *Farmers' Cabinet* 7.368, Some discussion in regard to the exact year in which the seventeen year locusts make their appearance, is now going on in the various newspapers. [**1861** in 1865 IL Dept. Ag. *Trans.* 5.458, *Cicada septemdecim* [sic]. . . The "Seventeen-year Cicada." . . is the insect to which the name "Locust" has been so improperly applied in this country.] **1869** MO State Entomol. *Annual Rept.* 18, The year 1868 will long be remembered in the annals of insect life, as one of peculiar interest, from the fact that this singular Cicada (*Cicada septemdecim,* Linn.) popularly known as the "17-year locust," made its appearance very generally over the United States. **1884** (1885) McCook *Tenants* 313 **PA,** Then we have . . that remarkable and famous insect the so-called seventeen-year locust (*Cicada septemdecim*), and its close ally, the thirteen-year Cicada (*Cicada tredecim*). **1922** U.S. Dept. Ag. *Farmers' Bulletin* 1270.68, The periodical cicada [is] more popularly known as the "17-year locust." **1965–70** *DARE* (Qu. R7, *Insects that sit in trees or bushes in hot weather and make a sharp, buzzing sound*) Infs **KY**65, **MD**3, 32, **MI**63, **NC**8, **PA**104, **WI**20, 43, 48, **WV**2, Seventeen-year locust(s); **NY**73, 93, Seventeen-year-old locust; **PA**6, Seventeen locust; (Qu. R6, . . *Names . . for grasshoppers*) Inf **NY**53, Seventeen-year locust. **1999** in 2000 *DARE* File—Internet **neOH,** This is the summer of the return of the insect called variously as the seventeen year locust or cicada. It lies dormant in the soil for 17 years then emerges to mate and lay eggs for the next generation.

seventh day See first day 1

seventh heaven n

=**peanut gallery.**

1967–69 *DARE* (Qu. D40, *Names and nicknames . . for the upper balcony in a theater*) Infs **IL**9, 31, **MI**69, Seventh heaven.

seventh month See first month

seven-top(ped) turnip n Also seven-top

A turnip (*Brassica rapa* Rapifera Group) grown for greens.

1949 Arnow *Hunter's Horn* 339 **KY,** For seven long years . . I've planted me a late patch a seven-top turnips fer greens, an ever fall, . . fer seven falls you've been patient to wait till them turnips got big enough for winter greens, an then you've et the whole patch, pulled it up turnip by turnip, so the tops couldn't grow agin—an me a starven all winter fer turnip greens. **1966–69** *DARE* (Qu. I3, . . *The large yellowish root vegetable, similar to a turnip, with a strong taste*) Inf **MS**16, Seven-top; (Qu. I28a, . . *Kinds of things . . you call 'greens' . . [Those that are eaten raw]*) Inf **KY**28, Seven-tops; (Qu. I28b, *Kinds of greens that are cooked*) Inf **KY**28, Seven-top; **NJ**17, Seven-topped turnip. **1990** *Seed Savers Yearbook* 255, Seven Top. . . Produces heavy crop, of tender greens over a long season, old commercial var., seven crops of tops. **2000** *DARE* File—Internet, *Seven Top.* Ready in 45 days. A foliage turnip grown for the greens. Root is inedible. Young plants provide the best greens. The variety is noted for its winter hardiness.

seventy-eleven adj Cf forty-eleven

Indefinitely numerous.

1970 *DARE* FW Addit **MI**122, *Seventy-eleven*—meaning many, used by Inf's mother. "I've told you seventy-eleven times _____." **1988** Lincoln *Avenue* 144 **wNC** (as of c1940) [Black], I been here seventy-leb'n years an' I done made seventy-leb'n crops, I reckon. **1994** *DARE* File, I've got seventy-'leven things to do this morning, so I can't have lunch with you, sorry. *Ibid* **MO,** Sebmty-lebm is just a variant of forty-lebm. **2001** *Ibid* **cwCA** (as of c1950), My grandfather was a great storyteller, and I remember that "sebmty-lebm" was one of the traditional terms to indicate a large number.

seven-up n

1 A var of the card game all fours. *old-fash; chiefly among rural speakers and those with little formal educ* Cf **high-low-jack, pitch** n[2] **1, setback 2**

1830 *NY Constellation* (NY) 11 Sept 2/5, Some tugged at the bottle . . and some played seven-up. **1853** Simms *Sword & Distaff* 271 **SC,** The ordinary game with the "little dogs," was one still known and still reasonably practised among this class under the several names of Old Sledge, Seven Up, All Fours, &c. **1864** in 1996 Owen *Letters to Laura* 138 **TN**, After supper had several tables with cards some poker, some Euchre, Seven-up, Whist. **1899** (1912) Green *VA Folk-Speech* 377, *Seven-up*. . . A game with cards, the same as all-fours. **1923** (1946) Greer-Petrie *Angeline Doin' Society* 24 **csKY**, [He] 'lowd if anybody present wanted to play a game of 'Seven Up' he'd set 'em up a hot deesh [=dish], fur he was the champeen player of Merry Oaks. **1939** FWP *Guide NC* 91, A favorite game was all-fours, which was similar to seven-up and muggins. **1965–70** DARE (Qu. DD35, . . *Card games*) 83 Infs, **scattered**, Seven-up. [Of all Infs responding to the question, 70% were comm type 4 or 5, 65% old, 29% gs educ or less; of those giving this response, 84% were comm type 4 or 5, 88% old, 45% gs educ or less.]

2 A guessing game; see quots.

1966–67 DARE Tape **AL3**, They call it seven-up. . . seven people, standing up, in front, then they say "heads down." Everybody puts his head down on his desk, and . . these seven people go along the players and touch the end of their hair or tap 'em on the head lightly . . then they get back to their places real quickly. Then they say "heads up" and . . then they call on . . certain person in the room that . . has been touched, and . . he's supposed to guess the person that touched him. And if he guesses that person he sits . . down, and this person takes his place; **CA68**, [Inf:] Have you ever heard of seven-up? . . It was a classroom game. . . The people in the class pick seven people . . and then there's a whole bunch of others sitting in their desks. . . Then all the people . . put down their heads. Then the people that are up, they go around. . . The people . . on the desks put their thumb up. . . And the person touches it, and they put it down, like that. Then the people . . who are up at the front of the room, they go back up there. Then the people that were on the desks . . they say, "He did it." But sometimes they're wrong. . . [If you guess right] you get to be up. **1968–70** DARE (Qu. EE2, *Games that have one extra player*) Inf **NY98**, Seven-up—you have eight people. Seven line up, the other says "seven-up" and touches those with their heads down; they guess who it was; (Qu. EE4, *Games in which one player's eyes are bandaged and he has to catch the others and guess who they are*) Inf [**MA128**, Seven-up—a kind of tag game;] **NJ13**, Seven-up—must guess who tapped you; (Qu. EE33) Inf **CA87**, Seven-up—a rainy day game, players put heads down and the seven up tap them—then they guess who tapped them. **1976** Knapp-Knapp *One Potato* 262, Seven-up. . . Seven students stand. The rest put their heads down on their desks and shut their eyes. The seven go through the aisles, tapping students on their backs. At a signal, everyone sits up and tries to guess who touched him.

3 A marble game; see quots.

1967 DARE Tape **TX40**, Played seven-up, that is one. . . Little game, has little marbles. **1967–68** DARE (Qu. EE7, . . *Kinds of marble games*) Inf **TN24**, Seven-up—5 marbles, great big ones. [DARE Ed: The drawing in the text shows the five marbles arranged at the four corners and the center of a square]; **TX40**, Seven-up.

seven-year apple n [See quot 1884]

A small tree (*Casasia clusiifolia*) native to southern Florida; also its fruit.

[**1730** Royal Soc. London *Philos. Trans.* 36.434, The seven Years Apple . . ripens in Seven or Eight Months Time.] **1884** Sargent *Forests of N. Amer.* 95, *Genista clusiæfolia*. . . *Seven-year Apple*. Semi-tropical Florida, on the southern keys. . . The large insipid fruit popularly but incorrectly supposed to require seven years in which to ripen. **1896** *Jrl. Amer. Folkl.* 9.190 **FL**, *Randia clusiæfolia* . . , seven-year apple, Florida Keys. **1938** Baker *FL Wild Flowers* 156, The handsome seven-year apple, with starry white fragrant flowers and glistening leaves . . is closely related to the gardenia. The peculiar pear-shaped fruit, slow in ripening, contains a pulp that has the flavor of dried apples. *Casasia clusiifolia*. . . Extreme S. Fla. **1971** Craighead *Trees S. FL* 94, Some of the more characteristic trees and shrubs of the beaches and coastal ridges are . . seven-year apple, sea grape, joewood [etc]. **2000** DARE File— Internet **sFL**, *Wildlife food*. . . Seven-year apple fruit: deer, iguanas, others.

seven-year itch n Also *seven-years' itch* Cf **itch B1**

1 Any of var skin conditions that cause chronic itching. **scattered, but less freq NEast, West** See Map

1854 (1969) Thoreau *Walden* 355, If we have had the seven-years' itch, we have not seen the seventeen-year locust yet in Concord. **1909** *DN* 3.369 **eAL, wGA**, *Seven-year itch*. . . An itch supposed to last for

seven years. **1936** Sandburg *People* 112, "May you have the sevenyear itch," was answered, "I hope your wife eats crackers in bed." **1940** Stuart *Trees of Heaven* 316 **neKY**, I'd ruther have the seven-year eetch as to be bothered with that family. **1955** *Sun* (Baltimore MD) 16 May 12/7, When I was a boy, we called the skin rash from poison ivy . . "the seven-year itch" and firmly believed it would reappear every year for seven years. **1956** McAtee *Some Dialect NC* 56, *Itch*. . . "Got the seven-year itch and am a year behind in my scratchin'." Saying. **1965–70** DARE (Qu. BB25, . . *Common skin diseases around here*) 67 Infs, **scattered, but less freq NEast, West**, Seven-year itch; **LA2, 28, MI2, NY34**, Seven-years' itch [Of all Infs responding to the question, 68% were comm type 4 or 5, 29% gs educ or less; of those giving these responses, 89% were comm type 4 or 5, 46% gs educ or less.]; [(Qu. S17, . . *Kinds of plants . . that . . cause itching and swelling*) Inf **CT11**, Seven-year itch;] (Qu. BB24, . . *A rash that comes out suddenly—from hives or something else: "He's got some kind of _____ all over his chest."*) Inf **AR47**, Seven-year itch; (Qu. BB49, . . *Other kinds of diseases*) Inf **NC22**, Seven-year itch. **1982** Slone *How We Talked* 103 **eKY** (as of c1950), *Seven year etch* (itch)—caused by a parasite being under the skin. Thought to last for seven years. **1986** Pederson *LAGS Concordance*, 1 inf, **cnAL**, Seven-year itch—poison ivy; 1 inf, **swTN**, Seven-year itch—disease of hand, arms, fingers. **1990** Cavender *Folk Med. Lexicon* 31 **sAppalachians**, *Seven year itch—a.* a fungus that starts between the fingers and spreads over the hands. *b.* a prolonged rash that is difficult to cure.

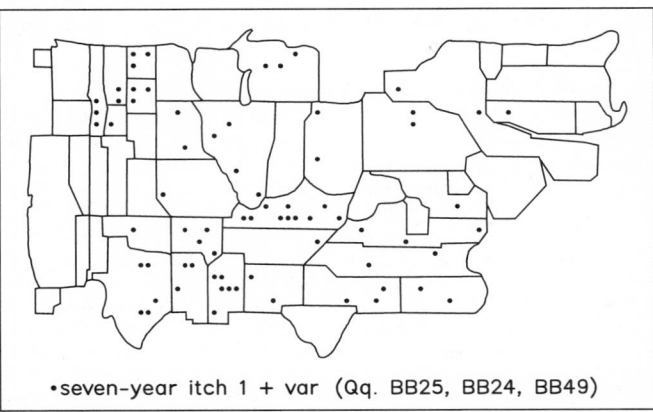

•seven-year itch 1 + var (Qq. BB25, BB24, BB49)

2 Used in var proverbial comparisons, as:

a *(as) slow as the seven-year itch* and varr: Very slow. **chiefly Midl** See Map

1899 Chesnutt *Conjure Woman* 154 **NC**, Lawsuits wuz slow ez de seben-yeah eetch. **1912** *DN* 3.590 **wIN**, *Slow as the seven year itch*. . . Very slow. **1927** *AmSp* 2.364 **cwWV**, *Slow as the seven year itch* . . very slow and sure. "That team pulls as slow as the seven year itch." **1929** *AmSp* 4.471 **NEast**, *Slow as the seven year itch*. **1942** Warnick *Garrett Co. MD* 14 **nwMD** (as of 1900–18), *"Slow as the seven-year's itch."* . . extremely slow. **1946** *PADS* 6.42 **eNC** (as of 1900–10), As *slow as the seven-year itch*. (Exasperatingly slow). . . Occasional. **1952** Brown *NC Folkl.* 430, A slow as the itch. As slow as the seven-year itch. **1965–70** DARE (Qu. A18, . . *A very slow person: "What's keeping him? He certainly is _____!"*) 22 Infs, **esp Midl**, Slow as (the) seven-year

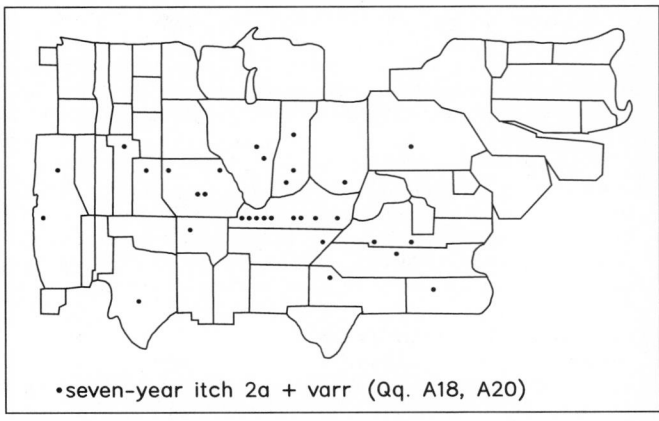

•seven-year itch 2a + varr (Qq. A18, A20)

itch; **CA**195, **GA**71, **KS**5, **MO**19, 27, **OH**49, **TN**11, Slower than the seven-year itch; **IL**113, **IN**48, Slow as (a) seven-years' itch; [**NC**41, Too slow to catch the seven-year itch; **MO**4, Slow as second ['sɛkn] year itch;] (Qu. A20, *Joking ways of telling somebody to hurry*) Inf **VA**1, Hurry up, you're as slow as seven-year itch. [27 of 33 Infs comm type 4 or 5]

b *worse* (or *meaner*) *than the seven-year itch:* Very bad (or mean).

1929 *AmSp* 5.123 **ME**, A person talked about might be "as polite as a basket of chips" or "worse than the seven-years' itch." **1942** McAtee *Dial. Grant Co. IN* 72 (as of 1890s), Worse than the seven-year eech. **1967** *DARE* (Qu. HH22b, . . *A very mean person* . . *"He's meaner than _____."*) Inf **TX**5, Seven-year itch.

seven-year locust n
?=seventeen-year locust.

1867 Mattison *Immortality* 334, The "seven year locust," as it is called, emerges from the earth at the end of its period, and crawls up upon the trees and shrubs, a rude, unsightly insect, without wings or voice, or power to eat. **1877** Leslie *California* 219, We were behind them all the way to the Geysers and back, and it was like travelling in the wake of a swarm of seven-year locusts. Not a carriage, not a house, not a bed, not a guide, not a decent dinner to be had anywhere. **1930** Ferber *Cimarron* 45, Her tone was that of one who speaks of prairie dogs, seven-year locusts, or any like Western nuisance. **1950** *Chicago Tribune* (IL) 18 Jan sec 1 12, Like the seven year locust—the interior decorating bug moves from room to room. **1967–70** *DARE* (Qu. R7, *Insects that sit in trees or bushes in hot weather and make a sharp, buzzing sound*) Infs **IA**29, **IN**31, **PA**148, **VA**26, Seven-year locust; (Qu. R8, . . *Kinds of creatures that make a clicking or shrilling or chirping kind of sound*) Infs **KY**86, **SC**46, Seven-year locust; (Qu. R30, . . *Kinds of beetles; not asked in early QRs*) Inf **IL**30, Seven-year locust; [(Qu. R5, *A big brown beetle that comes out in large numbers in spring and early summer, and flies with a buzzing sound*) Inf **GA**54, Seven-year beetle]. **1986** Pederson *LAGS Concordance,* 1 inf, ceAR, Seven-year locust.

seven-year onion n chiefly **KY** Cf **green onion 1, scallion**
An **onion** n B, probably a **multiplying onion.**

1967–70 *DARE* (Qu. I5, . . *Kind of onions that keep coming up without replanting year after year*) Infs **KY**8, 12, 34, 42, 77, **WY**3, Seven-year onions; (Qu. I6, *The kind of onions that come up fresh early in the year, and you eat them raw*) Inf **KY**12, Seven-year onion.

seven-years' itch See **seven-year itch**

seven-year weed n
A **lupine** (here: *Lupinus luteolus*).

1902 U.S. Natl. Museum *Contrib. Herbarium* 7.358 **nwCA**, *Lupinus luteolus*. . . The white people know it as "seven-year-weed" or "butterweed," the latter name referring to the color of the flowers, the former to the erroneous idea that it appears only every seventh year.

several adj, n, pron Pronc-spp *seval, severial*
A Pronc forms.

1909 *DN* 3.368 **eAL, wGA**, Seval. . . Several. **1927** *AmSp* 2.363 **cwWV**, Severial . . several. "He had severial good coon dogs."
B Gram forms.

Noun or pron pl: usu *several;* also *severals.* [Scots, Ir; cf *EDD, Concise Ulster Dict.*] Cf *others*

1767 in 1953 Woodmason *Carolina Backcountry* 244 **SC**, This has been the Case, and Ruin of severals. **1837** Sherwood *Gaz. GA* 71, *Severals,* for several. **1859** (1968) Bartlett *Americanisms* 395, *Severals,* for several, is used in Pennsylvania. "How many hats have you?" "I used to have severals, but now have got only one." **1902** *DN* 2.244 **sIL**, *Severals, n. pl.* For several used as a noun.
C Sense.

A good many; a large number. [Engl dial] esp **Appalachians, Ozarks** Cf **some several**

1911 *DN* 3.539 **eKY**, Several. . . Used only in reference to groups of about one hundred or more, even to thousands. **1913** Kephart *Highlanders* 77 **sAppalachians**, "You'll spy, to-morrow, whar several trees has been wind-throwed and busted to kindlin'." I recalled that several, in the South, means many—"a good many," as our own tongues phrase it. **1926** *DN* 5.403 **Ozarks**, Several. . . A large number. When the hillman says "they's sever'l fox in them 'ar bluffs," he does not mean three foxes, or four, or ten, but a great many. **1934** *AmSp* 9.234 **NC**, Another

peculiarity of speech here, is that the word *several* is used to mean 'a large number,' or 'a good many.' **1944** *PADS* 2.49 **wNC, VA**, *Several*. . . A great many. "There are several berries this summer." **1952** Brown *NC Folkl.* 1.588, *Several*. . . A great amount. "I have several cherries this year." **c1960** *Wilson Coll.* **csKY**, *Several*. . . An indefinite, large . . number. **1967** *DARE* (Qu. FF26, . . *A large group of people at a public gathering*) Inf **TN**6, Several. **1995** *Brophy Coll.* 66 **swMO** (as of c1960), *Several* . . many.

severaleth See **severalth**

severals See **several B**

severalth adj Also *severaleth*
Being the latest of several things in a countable series.

1902 Lewis *Wolfville Days* 238 **SW**, Re-fillin' his glass for the severaleth time. **1949** Webber *Backwoods Teacher* 23 **Ozarks**, Apologizing for the "severalth" time—to use a good word we learned at Big Piney—. . Mrs. Helms did sit down.

severe adj chiefly **sAppalachians** Cf **severely**
1 Untamed, fierce, savage.

1829 *Western Mth. Rev.* 3.120 **KY** (as of 1780s), They were in the habit of managing a wild, or, as the phrase was, a "severe" colt. **1889** *Harper's New Mth. Mag.* 78.270 **eKY**, A well-known character in the mountains . . has killed twenty-one men. . . He is called, in the language of the country, a "severe" man. **1907** White *AZ Nights* 5, The hound returned leisurely, licking from his chops the hair of his victims. Uncle Jim shook his head. "Trailer," he said sadly, "is a little severe." **1913** Kephart *Highlanders* 81 **sAppalachians**, No hound 'll raelly fight a bear—hit takes a big severe dog to do that. **1940** *Hall Coll.* **eTN**, We had two pretty severe dogs with us, Plott hounds. **1976** Garber *Mountain-ese* 80 **sAppalachians**, *Severe* . . vicious—A german shepherd makes a mighty severe watch dog. **1995** *Brophy Coll.* 66 **swMO** (as of c1960), *Severe*. [F]ierce, wild, big, terrible (S. Appalachia).
2 Vigorous, considerable, powerful.

1805 (1904) White *Jrl.* 32 **MA**, I got up this morning with the determination to have a severe nap before night. **1834** Hall *Kentucky* 2.9, Your whiskey is as good as your fire, and that is saying a great deal, for you are the *severest old beaver* to *tote* wood that I've seen for many a long day. **1913** Kephart *Highlanders* 36 **sAppalachians**, Thar, I've cl'ared me a patch and grubbed hit out—now I can raise me two or three severe craps!

severely adv Cf **severe**
Thoroughly.

1886 *S. Bivouac* 4.349 **sAppalachians**, I was thankful to hear her son speak of an Indian burying place that was "kivered severely" with stones.

severial See **several**

sevigrous See **servigrous**

sev'm See **seven**

sewage inspector n Also *sewer inspector joc*
The common carp (*Cyprinus carpio*).

1948 *WELS Suppl.* **cwWI**, And you've heard carp called sewage inspectors? That came from Colfax. **1950** *Ibid* **csWI**, Sewage inspector—joking name for carp. **1995** *Brophy Coll.* 66 **swMO** (as of c1960), *Sewer inspector.* [A] carp fish.

sew buttons on lemons v phr Also *sew buttons on ice cream,* ~ *on the ice-cream freezer*
Used as an evasive or diversionary remark to a child.

1967 *DARE* (Qu. NN12b, *Things that people say to put off a child when he asks, "What are you making?"*) Inf **OH**37, Sewing buttons on lemons. **1979** *NYT Article Letters* **cnVA**, My father has a term, origins . . unknown, for a sort of good-humored brush-off, . . as when an overly-inquisitive child wants to know what he's doing, he says, "Sewing buttons on the ice-cream freezer." **2001** *DARE* File **nwMA** (as of 1960s–70s), "Sew buttons on ice cream". . . It was a good way of stopping you kids from arguing, I remember. If I heard one of you say "sooooo" to [the] other, I'd chime in with the phrase. Then you probably got mad at me instead of each other.

sewee bean See **sieva bean**

sewer n Cf **ear cutter, ~ sewer 1, sewing needle**

A **dragonfly.**

[1949 (1972) *Funk & Wagnalls Dict. Folkl.* 324, Children are told that if they tell lies the Devil's-darning-needle will sew up their mouths; it is even likely to sew up nose and ears and go right on through the head.] **1968** *DARE* (Qu. R2, . . *The dragonfly*) Inf **WI**48, Sewer. **1973** Allen *LAUM* 1.318 **Upper MW** (as of c1950), One instance of simple *sewer* [for dragonfly] is found in Minnesota.

sewer bass n

A **white sucker** (here: *Catostomus commersoni*).

1970 *DARE* (Qu. P3, *Freshwater fish that are not good to eat*) Inf **MI**123, Grand River tuna—nickname for a sucker. [Also called] sewer bass. **1974** *DARE* File swMI (as of 1973), Sewer bass. . . A sucker fish. . . Humorous: Grand Rapids, MI.

sewer inspector See **sewage inspector**

sewer rat n [*OED2* 1851 →]

A rat that lives in a sewer; used esp of a **Norway rat.**

1851 *Harper's New Mth. Mag.* 2.203, Sewer rats, he admits, are not the very worst of the race. . . But the rats of the cellar, the warehouse, the barn, the rick-yard, the granary, and the corn-field, are the grand destroyers against whom war . . is proclaimed. **1877** Leslie *California* 107, The "braves" . . were somewhat more repulsive than the women and children, being equally dirty and more dangerous; as, for instance a sewer rat is more disagreeable than a young pig. **1890** *Century Dict.* 5534, *Sewer-rat.* . . The ordinary gray or brown Norway rat, *Mus decumanus* [=*Rattus norvegicus*]: so called as living in sewers. **1947** Cahalane *Mammals* 548, Nearly everyone knows the brown house rat by sight. Many descriptive names are given to it: gray rat, . . sewer rat, . . and Norway rat. These merely indicate its versatility. **1980** Whitaker *Audubon Field Guide Mammals* 518, *Norway Rat* . . "Sewer Rat". . . Range: entire U.S. . . Neither a native of Norway nor more common there than elsewhere. **2000** *U.S. News & World Rept.* 12 June 18 **GA,** Last October, they spotted their first sewer rat—a Norway rat the size of a small cat—when it scampered across the buffed oak floor of the breakfast room.

sewer-upper, sewing beetle (or bug) See **sewing needle**

sewing-machine bird n

=**Wilson's phalarope.**

1967 *DARE* (Qu. Q9, *The bird that looks like a small, dull-colored duck and is commonly found on ponds and lakes*) Inf **CO**7, Phalarope—the sewing-machine bird.

sewing needle n Also *sewing beetle, ~ bug, sewer-upper* **esp MI, WI, MN, MA** See Map and Map Section Cf **darning needle 1, ear sewer 1, needle 3, sewer**

A **dragonfly.**

1950 *WELS (Other names for the dragonfly)* 2 Infs, **WI,** Sewing needle. **1965–70** *DARE* (Qu. R2, . . *The dragonfly*) Infs **CT**31, **MI**37, 42, **MA**1, 8, 50, **MN**2, **WI**65, 71, Sewing needle; **MI**103, Sewing bug. **1967** *DARE* File neMA Sewing needle—dragonfly—it would sew up your eyes and mouth if you fell asleep outside. c1970 *Ibid* ceMN (as of 1940s), Sewing needle = dragonfly. **1971** Bright *Word Geog. CA & NV* 114, Sewing bug—2 [infs]—1, Contra Costa [=San Francisco Bay area] Used by mother with story of sewing lips. . . Sewing needle—2 [infs]—Los Angeles. **1971** Wood *Vocab. Change* 35 **Sth,** Darning needle,

devil's darning needle, and *sewing needle* are known in scattered instances. **1973** Allen *LAUM* 1.319 **Upper MW** (as of c1950), Sewer [1 inf, **MN**]. Sewing needle [8 infs, 7 **MN**]. **1977–78** Foster *Lexical Variation* 53 **NJ,** Numerous folk names for the dragonfly are still known in New Jersey, but they are used by only one-quarter of the informants. . . *Sewing bug,* apparently a new term representing a re-invention of the folk belief underlying *darning needle,* is most common in Mercer County, although it and its variants *sewing beetle* and *sewer-upper* (1 response each) are recorded sporadically elsewhere; seven of the eight *sewing* responses are from males. *Ibid* 120, Outside Mercer [County], responses are less accurate—one each *sewing bug, sewer-upper,* and *sewing beetle* and one "It'll sew your mouth up" . . suggesting the Mercer focus of the name and folk belief.

sexton beetle n Also *sexton* [*OED2* 1840 →]

A **burying beetle** of the genus *Nicrophorus.*

1852 *Harper's New Mth. Mag.* 5.220, These birds are for the most part too large for the sexton beetle to bury. **1854** Emmons *Agriculture NY* 5.56, The latter [=*Nicrophorus* spp] are sometimes called sexton beetles, from their habit of burying all the small dead animals which they meet with. **1869** U.S. Dept. Ag. *Rept. of Secy. for 1868* 307, The Silphidae (burying or sexton beetles, scavengers, &c) are found with dead animals, and sometimes on flowers. **1884** Kingsley *Std. Nat. Hist.* 2.385, On account of their habit of burying small dead vertebrate animals, in which they lay their eggs, these beetles [=*Nicrophorus*] are often called sextons or grave-diggers. **1949** Swain *Insect Guide* 122, Sexton Beetle (*Nicrophorus marginatus*). Widely distributed. A pair of sexton beetles will fly to a dead mouse and, by digging away the soil from below, bury it completely. **1969** *DARE* (Qu. R30, . . *Kinds of beetles;* not asked in early QRs) Inf **MI**103, Sexton beetle—they [sic] clear the woods of dead animals. **2000** *DARE* File—Internet, *Sexton Beetles: Grave-Diggers.* . . They are beautiful red and black beetles called sexton or carrion beetles. . . The sexton beetle is named after church officials whose duties once included burying the dead. . . Adult sexton beetles only feed on carrion when they are rearing young.

-sey See **-sie**

sez See **say** v **B1a, 3**

shab v Usu with *out* [Engl dial; cf *EDD shab* v. 3]

To sneak away, slink off; to go quickly; hence n *shab out* a cowardly retreat.

1902 *DN* 2.244 **sIL,** Shab out. . . To retire humiliated, or to avoid an encounter. *Ibid* 245 **sIL,** Shab out. . . A cowardly retreat. **1912** *DN* 3.589 **wIN,** Shab out. . . To sneak away; to clear out. "After he saw they were in trouble, he shabbed out." **1947** *AmSp* 22.158, The verb *shab* was commonly employed by a group of Nebraska persons who had come from Indiana. To them it meant to walk or go, especially in the sense of doing so rapidly. 'Now you shab straight home.'

‡shabbers n

See quot.

1970 *DARE* (Qu. K47, . . *Diseases . . horses or mules commonly get*) Inf **MS**87, [šæbəz]—swells under stomach. A big pone hangs under the horse. If you stop it before it get to the horse's throat, it won't kill him. [FW: Inf also pronounces this [šabəz].]

shabby adj [Scots, nEngl dial] **Sth**

Having a general feeling of unwellness; tired, "under the weather."

1926 *AmSp* 1.408 **Okefenokee GA,** A usual response to an inquiry as to his well-being was, 'I'm feelin' mighty tough this morning'—I'm feelin' mighty shabby.' **1965–68** *DARE* (Qu. BB39, *On a day when you don't feel just right, though not actually sick . . "I'll be all right tomorrow—I'm just feeling _____ today."*) Inf **MS**63, Shabby; (Qu. KK30, *Feeling slowed up or without energy: "I certainly feel —-."*) Inf **VA**15, Shabby. **1984** Wilder *You All Spoken Here* 204 **Sth,** *Shabby:* When you feel you've been sent for and cain't go. [*DARE* Ed: see **sent for and couldn't come**]. **1986** Pederson *LAGS Concordance* (Peaked) 1 inf, **cwLA,** A little shabby (=sickly, puny); (*He is worn out*) 1 inf, **cTX,** Shabby (=worn out, literally, as of clothes).

shab out See **shab**

shack n[1] [*OED2 shack* sb.[1] 1 1536 →; "Now *dial.* . . Grain fallen from the ear, and available for the feeding of pigs, poultry, etc. . . Also, fallen beech-mast or acorns."] Cf **mast** n[1]

Nuts and acorns that have fallen to the ground.

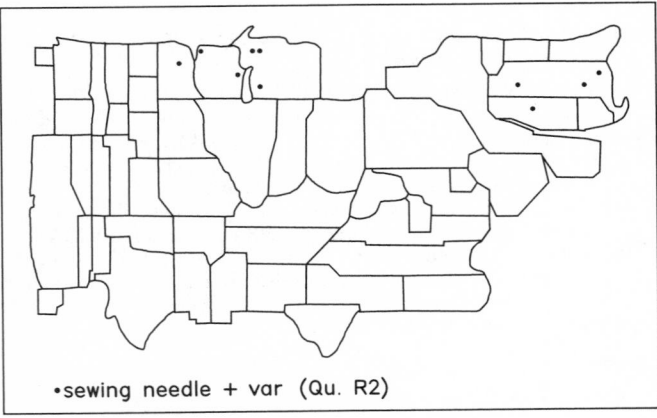

•sewing needle + var (Qu. R2)

1828 (1970) Webster *Amer. Dict., Shack.* . . In New England, *shack* is used . . for mast or the food of swine. **1849** Brown *America* 33, The pork which has been fed in the woods is called shack-fed, and is not so good as the corn-fed. **1858** Morgan *England* 57 **OH**, [Quoting a Buffalo NY newspaper:] The woods in the vicinity of Sandusky . . were frequented by vast numbers of wild hogs, which . . grew fat upon the shack which every where abounded. *Ibid*, The term shack, a provincial word for nuts, acorns and so forth, is used in America. **1911** (1913) Johnson *Highways Gt. Lakes* 128 **seMI**, Yes, there were hundreds of hogs runnin' loose, and in the autumn they got fat on the shack—that is, the acorns and the beech and hazel nuts. They lived right in the forest the whole year.

shack v[1] [Cf *EDD shake* (also *shack*) v. 5. "Of a horse: to go at a jog-trot."]

1 To amble along; to go at a slow trot; hence n *shack (gait)* a slow trot. **esp NEast**

1833 Hallett *Trial Avery* 61 **RI**, I *shacked* down some of the hills, (partly run). **1881** *Harper's New Mth. Mag.* 62.375 **NYC**, [He] walked with a peculiar shack gait. **1896** *DN* 1.424 **c,wNY**, *Shack* . . a slow trot. Also . . to go at a slow trot. "The old horse shacked along." **1900** Garland *Eagle's Heart* 144, He continued his steady onward "shack" toward the West. **1903** *DN* 2.300 **Cape Cod MA** (as of a1857), *Shack*. . . Trot listlessly. **1947** *Sat. Eve. Post* 8 Mar 53 **WI**, Each winter Steve shacked in to Barry's camp a couple of times, sat in the log office a day and shacked out.

2 See quot. [Cf *EDD shake* v. 7. "To idle away one's time; to loaf about; . . to wander about as a tramp."] Cf **shack** n[2] **2**

1969 *DARE* (Qu. Y29a, *To 'go out' a great deal, not to stay at home much: "She's always* _____.") Inf **RI**15, On the shack or shacking.

shack n[2]

1 A tramp; a bum; a good-for-nothing. [*OED2 shack* sb.[2] 1 1682 →] **esp NEast**

1828 (1970) Webster *Amer. Dict., Shack.* . . In New England . . I have heard a shiftless fellow, a vagabond, called a *shack*. **1848** Bartlett *Americanisms* 292, *Shack.* A vagabond; a low fellow. Ex. 'He's a poor *shack* of a fellow.' It is provincial in England, and applied in the same way as here. **1856** Whitcher *Bedott Papers* 34 **cNY**, All creation knows she wa'n't nobody. Why, her father was a poor drunken shack . . and her mother took in washin'. **1894** *DN* 1.342 **wCT**, *Shack*: a tramp. **1898** Westcott *Harum* 221 **cNY**, That ole shack! Who in creation could he git to take him?

2 in phr *on the shack*: On the go. [Cf *EDD to be on the shack* (at *shake* sb. 12.(4)) "to wander idly about"]

1969 [see **shack** v[1] **2**].

shack n[3] See **shack** v[1] **1**

shack n[4] Also *shacks, shag* [See quot 1940] Cf **donicker 2**
A railroad brakeman.

1897 *KS Univ. Qrly.* (ser B) 6.56 **KS**, *Shacks* . . brakeman (R.R. slang.) **1901** *Independent* 53.2886, [Caption:] Jumping a "Boxer," "Pullman Side Door."—The "Shack" Objects. **1922** *DN* 5.181 **NW**, *Shack*. . . A brakeman on a freight train. "The shack gave the wrong signal." Railroad usage. **1927** *DN* 5.448 [Underworld jargon], *Give the shacks the spiel*. . . To tell a heartwringing tale to a brakeman so that he will allow the narrator to ride on his train unmolested. **1928** in 1953 Botkin–Harlow *Treas. Railroad Folkl.* 406, I found I didn't have no air, so I whistled for brakes to beat hell. The skipper an' the shacks musta been asleep; they didn't pay me no mind. **1940** Cottrell *Railroader* 135, *Shack*—Brakeman. Probably named after the small huts which in the early days of railroading were frequently mounted on a car near the middle of a train, from which the brakeman sallied to set the hand brakes when the engineer whistled him out to "down brakes." **1956** *AmSp* 31.152 **nwCA** [Logger lingo], *Shag*. . . A brakeman on a logging railroad. **1958** McCulloch *Woods Words* 160 **Pacific NW**, *Shack*—A brakeman; head end shack is the brakeman on the engine; tail end shack is the brakeman on the last log car, or on the caboose if one is carried on the train. **1962** *AmSp* 37.135 **nwCA**, *Shack*. . . A brakeman.

shack n[5] Also *shag* [Perh related to **shack** n[1]] **NEng**

1 also *shack-bait*: See quot 1890; hence vbl nouns *shack-fishing, shag-fishing*; n *shack-fisherman*.

1890 *Century Dict.* 5539, *Shack[1]* . . n. . . . 3. In the fisheries, bait picked up at sea by any means, as the flesh of porpoises or of sea birds, refuse fish, etc., as distinguished from the regular stock of bait carried by the

vessel or otherwise depended upon. Also *shack-bait*. [*Century* Ed: New Engl.] *Ibid, Shack-fisherman*. . . A vessel which uses shack for bait. *Shack-fishing*. . . fishing with shack for bait. **1896** (1897) Kipling *Captains Courageous* 75 **NEng**, 'I mistrust shag-fishin' will pay better, ez things go.' That meant the boys would bait with selected offal of the cod as the fish were cleaned.

2 Miscellaneous fish; esp a boatload chiefly of cod, haddock, hake, and pollack, of which those caught earlier have been preserved with salt and those later with ice.

1902 *Boston Eve. Transcript* (MA) 20 Aug 13/6, A shacker, as the vessels, which bring fresh cod and haddock to the wharf are called. **1903** *DN* 2.294 **Cape Cod MA** (as of a1857), *Shack*. . . Fish which did not go into the division, either codfish or mackerel, the regular order. 'We go fishing summers and try to get enough shack to last through the winter.' **1904** *DN* 2.427 **Cape Cod MA** (as of a1857), *Shackfish*. . . The same as shack. . . It includes especially haddock and pollack. **1904** *Rep. Mass. Com. Fisheries and Game* 78 (*Century Dict.*), Such fish, tumbled together, without effort at classification, are known as shack. *Ibid* (*Century Dict. Suppl.*), While at first a shack trip referred particularly to a voyage on which cheap species of fish constituted the bulk of the catch, this system . . has now broadened . . to such a degree that it is common for vessels . . to go as far as the Grand Bank, where cod alone are taken. **1952** (1973) Thomas *Fast & Able* xii **neMA**, *Shacking*—Gloucester term for trip in which fish caught early were salted, and the rest brought in fresh, iced. *Ibid* 129 **neMA**, Most of *Arethusa*'s big producing was in shacking, both fresh and salt, and in salt bank trips. *Ibid* 156 **neMA**, In August 1918 the *Sylvania* landed a trip of shack at Gloucester. She stocked $7160 and shared $187 per man. *Ibid*, The Cape North shackers would fit out about the middle of April and would be gone on a trip from three to six weeks. . . Twenty five to 50 hogsheads of salt for salting down the first part of the trip would be taken on at Gloucester. Ice was taken at Canso or some other Nova Scotian port and bait was secured at the Magdalens, Souris, Prince Edward Island or St. Pierre.

shack v[2] [Perh var of **shag** v[2]] **esp NEast**
To retrieve stray balls (for a baseball or tennis player); to retrieve (a stray ball); broadly, to go in search of; hence nouns *shack(er)* one who retrieves stray balls.

1890 *AN&Q* 4.214, *Shack*. . . This word was formerly common in the New England States among ball players. The *shacker* stood behind the catcher to intercept, or to chase any ball that might pass the latter. To *shack* for another player meant to chase wild or fly balls for him. **1893** *KS Univ. Qrly.* 1.141 **KS**, *Shack*: to run after an errant ball. Also, the one who does this. **1895** *DN* 1.399 **cNY**, *Shag* . . of balls, to chase. . . In form *shack* common in N[ew] E[ngland] and N.Y. City. . . Also used humorously in other ways, as of hunting up a person. **1900** *DN* 2.58 **MA** [College slang], *Shack, n.* . . 2. Small boy employed to attend tennis players and retrieve stray balls. . . *Shack v. t.* 1. To gather tennis balls. . . 2. To go in search of, hunt up a person or thing. **1905** *DN* 3.18 **cCT**, *Shack*. . . To run after. 'When the bulls [sic] go over the fence we have to shack them ourselves.' **1907** *DN* 3.199 **seNH**, *Shack*. . . To search for and return a base-ball that has passed out of bounds. "Go shack the ball, will you?"

shack n[6] Cf **shack** n[1], **shuck** n[1] **2b**
A husk or shell; hence v *shack* to remove the shell (of a nut).

1903 *DN* 2.352 **neOH**, *Shack*. . . The husk or shuck of a nut. . . *Shack*. . . To remove the 'shacks,' or shucks of a nut.

shack n[7] See **shack** v[2]

shack n[8] [Var of *shock*]
1956 Ker *Vocab. W. TX* 286, *Stalks of wheat tied together*. . . *Shacks*, a variant pronunciation of *shock*, is the response of [1 inf] of Lubbock county. **1969** *DARE* (Qu. L30b, *Then these sheaves . . are set together in piles called* _____) Inf **PA**201, Shacks.

shack-bait See **shack** n[5] **1**

shackbark See **shagbark hickory**

shackelty See **shacklety**

shackely See **shackly**

shacker n[1] See **shack** v[2]

shacker n[2] See **shack** n[5] **2**

shacker n[3]

1 One whose dwelling is a shack.

1937 in Lib. of Congress *Amer. Memory: FSA/OWI* (Internet), [Captions:] The older Mr. Gavanea, a single shacker near Gibbs City, Michigan. . . Black Aleck Dickinson, single shacker. Iron County, Michigan. . . Mr. Smallwood, shacker near Alvin, Wisconsin, sawing wood. . . Shack occupied by Mr. Bastia, an unmarried shacker in Iron County, Michigan. **1969** Sorden *Lumberjack Lingo* 106 **NEng, Gt Lakes,** *Shacker*—A man who lived, generally by himself, in a small building of logs or rough lumber.

2 See quot. Cf **nester**

1958 McCulloch *Woods Words* 160 **Pacific NW,** *Shacker*—To loggers, the same as a nester to cattlemen; a small farmer moving in on the woods.

shackety See **shacklety**

shackfish See **shack** n[5] **2**

shack-fisherman (or -fishing) See **shack** n[5] **1**

shack gait See **shack** v[1] **1**

shackily See **shackly**

shacking vbl n[1] See **shack** n[5] **2**

shacking vbl n[2] Also *shagging* Cf **hooky bob, hop cars, skitching**

Holding onto a moving vehicle so as to be towed along over snow and ice.

1993 *Detroit Free Press* (MI) 30 July sec F 3/3 **Upper Peninsula MI,** *Shacking*: grabbing onto the back fender of a moving bus, truck or car and sliding along the icy or snowy road. Favorite pastime of young Yoopers. Also called skitching or shagging. **1994** *Capital Times* (Madison WI) 14 Feb sec A 10/2, It's called "hopping cars" in Philadelphia, "bumper-hitching" or "shagging" in Detroit, "skitching" along the Eastern Seaboard. In northern Indiana it's "hooky-bobbing." As long as snow is on the ground and a car is passing by, kids grab bumpers and go along for the ride. It's a dangerous thrill, and some children are learning that the hard way.

shackle v Also with *around* [Cf *EDD* shackle v.[2] 5 "To idle about; to shirk work." and *shachle* v. (also *shauchle, shackle,* etc) 2 "To walk in a shuffling, shambling, knock-kneed manner."] Cf **sanko** v, **shack** n[2] **1, shackling, shuckle**

To loaf; to saunter, mosey.

1913 Kephart *Highlanders* 203 **sAppalachians,** And "shacklin' around" pictures a shackly, loose-jointed way of walking, expressive of the idle vagabond. **1932** Randolph *Ozark Mt. Folks* 234, Come Fall I put on my store clothes an' shackled over t' Hawgleg settlement an' sot up t' teach a school myse'f.

shackledy See **shacklety**

shackle-footed adj [Cf **shackle**]

1912 *DN* 3.589 **wIN,** *Shackle-footed.* . . Awkward.

shacklety adj Also *shacke(l)ty, shackledy* [Engl dial; cf *EDD* shacklety] **Sth, S Midl** Cf **ramshacklety, shackling, shackly**

Ramshackle, rickety, shaky.

1905 *DN* 3.93 **nwAR,** *Shackelty.* . . Ram-shackle. 'It's a shackelty house.' Common. **1909** *DN* 3.368 **eAL, wGA,** *Shackelty.* . . Dilapidated, run-down. See *ramshackle.* **1915** *DN* 4.190 **swVA,** *Shackelty.* . . Loosely held together; run down. "Uncle Wesley's shackelty old mill." **1966–69** *DARE* (Qu. KK20a, *Something that looks as if it might collapse any minute: "That old shed is certainly _____."*) Inf **AL6,** Shackledy; **KY25,** Shacklety; (Qu. KK23, *Weak or unsteady: "I think the footbridge will hold but it is a bit _____."*) Infs **AL12, GA80,** Shackledy; **SC3, VA15,** Shacklety. **1967** Williams *Greenbones* 74 **GA** (as of c1910), I'll tell you about this little one-room nigger schoolhouse I come across once, a shackety cabin where someone had painted one wall for a blackboard. **1967** *DARE* FW Addit **seAR,** Oh, I'll sell you that 'un [=a table] for two and a half. It's a little shackledy ['šækldı], needs tightenin' up. **1982** Powers *Cataloochee* 381 **cwNC,** *Shackelty* (loose-jointed) . . EDP heard Weldon Williamson of Asheville, 1972, tell of a simpleton who . . saw girls bathing in Cataloochie Creek. When they took their clothes off, he said he "went all shackelty and laid down

in the corn rows so's they wouldn't see me." **1986** Pederson *LAGS Concordance,* 1 inf, **nwFL,** The building was old and shacklety.

shackley See **shackly**

shackling adj Cf **shackle, shacklety, shackly**

1 Ramshackle, rickety, run-down; gangling.

c1784 in 1966 Brown *Beverages* 34, The journey to New York took up a week. The carriages were old and shackling and much of the harness was made of ropes. **1790** (1927) Maclay *Jrl.* 266, His whole figure has a loose, shackling air. **1793** (1892) Lindley *Exped. Detroit* 17.575 **PA,** The wagon very shackling, made the tour very disagreeable. **1883** (1971) Shields *Life S. Prentiss* 62, The boat itself was a rude, shackling craft, with rickety flooring and an abundance of bilge-water beneath. **1901** *DN* 2.146 **cNY,** *Shacklin.* . . Loose-jointed, rickety. **1943** Weslager *DE Forgotten Folk* 166, One day I was feeling pretty shacklin' and I went to her with a boil. She took the boil away and also cured many of my neighbors of boils. **1955** *DE Folkl. Bulletin* 1.17, [An elderly man] may reply to an inquiry about his health . . "I feel pretty shacklin'." **1984** Wilder *You All Spoken Here* 202 **Sth,** *Shacklin':* About to fall apart.

2 See quot. [*OED2* 1788 →]

1894 *DN* 1.333 **NJ,** *Shacklin':* shiftless; lazy; going from one job to another.

shackly adj Also *shackely, shackily, shackley* **formerly widespread, now chiefly Sth, S Midl** See Map Cf **ramshackly, shacklety, shackling**

Ramshackle, rickety; gangling.

1843 in 1907 *IN Mag. Hist.* 3.191, Shackly houses, huts and hovels . . gave no great expectation of refinements. **1890** *Jrl. Amer. Folkl.* 3.311 **NEng,** *Shackly*—Tumble-down. Also *ramshackly.* **1891** (1967) Freeman *New Engl. Nun* 273, If folks want to wear them manufactured shoes, they can . . old shackly things! **1897** Twain *Following Equator* 694, A gaunt, shackly country lout six feet high. **1899** (1912) Green *VA Folk-Speech* 378, *Shackly.* . . Shaky; rickety; tottering; ramshackle. **1903** *DN* 2.300 **Cape Cod MA** (as of 1857), *Shackely.* . . Rickety. **1905** *DN* 3.18 **cCT,** *Shackely.* . . Shaky, rickety. **1907** *DN* 3.207 **nwAR,** *Shackely.* . . Rickety. **1956** McAtee *Some Dialect NC* 39, *Shackily.* . . Ramshackle. **1961** Seeman *In Arms of Mt.* 122 **eTN,** I heard a scraping sound outside. . . His old mare was dragging a shackly land sled. **1965–70** *DARE* (Qu. KK23, *Weak or unsteady: "I think the footbridge will hold but it is a bit _____."*) 26 Infs, **Sth, S Midl,** Shackly; (Qu. KK20a, *Something that looks as if it might collapse any minute: "That old shed is certainly _____."*) Infs **KY28, 33, 40, 41, 47, LA6, VA2,** Shackly; (Qu. KK20b, *Something that looks as if it might collapse any minute: "Our old washing machine is _____."*) Inf **VA15,** Shackly; (Qu. KK24, *Something that breaks easily: "She broke her arm again: Her bones must be _____."*) Inf **VA42,** Shackly; (Qu. KK70, *Something that has got out of proper shape: "That house is all _____."*) Inf **KY77,** Shackly. **1982** Powers *Cataloochee* 381 **cwNC** (as of 1972), *Shackley.* . . (loose-sounding) "That's all shackley, must be a punkin' ball loose in your gun or your gun part's loose." **1986** Pederson *LAGS Concordance,* 1 inf, **cnMS,** Wheels got shackly.

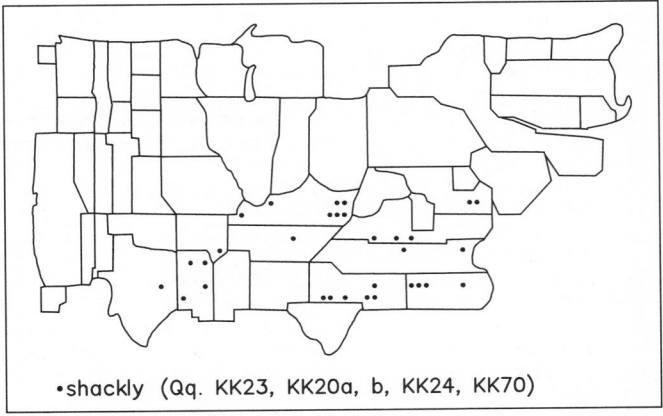

•shackly (Qq. KK23, KK20a, b, KK24, KK70)

shackpoke See **shagpoke**

shack rouster n Also *shack rouser*

One who awakens workers from sleep; also fig.

1942 (1965) Parrish *Slave Songs* 246 **GA coast,** A colored man who used to be a "shack-rouser" at a railroad camp on the Georgia Central Line sang these warning lines before he gave the rat-a-tat-tat, with a stick, on the different doors. **1943** Writers' Program NC *Bundle of Troubles* 45, The shacks was in charge of a feller they calls the shack-rouster. He keeps good order and wakes up the hands in the mornin'. **1957** *Sat. Eve. Post Letters* **neAL,** *Shack-rouser* (rouser)—nick-name for a garrulous person. Sometimes used for loud barking dogs or any loud noise.

shacks See **shack** n[4]

shack wacky adj phr Cf **cabin fever**

Nervous or irritable as a result of confinement to close quarters.

1991 *DARE* File **WI,** I wish I felt good enough to go today; I'm getting shack wacky. . . That's an old logger's and trapper's term from up north.

shacky adj

Shabby; shoddy; also fig.

1935 Davis *Honey* 71 **OR,** There was not even enough little shacky things like frugality and lechery and drunkenness for them to harden themselves around. **1937** Sandoz *Slogum* 179 **NE,** Gulla dumped the hog-ranch outfit into the road, moving the lumber of the shacky buildings to Slogum House. **1969** *DARE* FW Addit **cwNJ,** *Shacky*—shoddy, shabby.

shad n

1 also *shad fish;* pronc-spp *shard, shed:* A **herring** n[1] **1** of the genus *Alosa,* esp *A. sapidissima.* **chiefly Atl** For other names of this sp see **alewife, Connecticut River pork, jack** n[1] **24b(3), white shad** Cf **chad** n[3]

1606 in 1624 Smith *Genl. Hist. VA* 28, Of fish we were best acquainted with Sturgeon, Grampus . . Lampreys, Catfish, Shades [etc]. **1634** Wood *New Engl. Prospect* 34 **neMA,** The Shaddes be bigger than the *English* Shaddes and fatter. *Ibid* 39, The inhabitants of Watertowne . . take great store of *Shads* and *Alewives.* **1677** in 1899 Springfield MA *First Century* 2.131, And shad fish they may not sel for more then halfe pence apeice there. **1771** (1925) Washington *Diaries* 2.16 **MD,** Many Shad had been catchd on the Maryland shore. **1792** Belknap *Hist. NH* 3.61 **CT,** On the steep sides of the island rock, hang several arm chairs, fastened to ladders, and secured by a counterpoise, in which fishermen sit to catch salmon and shad with dipping nets. **1856** *Porter's Spirit of Times* 27 Dec 274 **NY,** The young shad are hauled ashore, without thought, and left to perish, high and dry, by thousands. **1902** Jordan-Evermann *Amer. Fishes* 107, Though there is but one species of shad on our Atlantic Coast it has received almost as many vernacular names as there are rivers which it enters, as Potomac shad, Susquehanna shad, Delaware shad, North River shad, and Connecticut shad; and the people on each particular stream regard their shad as the best. **1943** *Sun* (Baltimore MD) 19 Oct 16/5 *(Hench Coll.),* On The Gomicksing Up Of Shad Fish With Red Wine And Oysters With Horse Radish. **1965–70** *DARE* (Qu. P1, . . *Kinds of freshwater fish . . caught around here . . good to eat)* 32 Infs, **chiefly Atlantic,** Shad; NY58, Shed; SC40, Roe shad—a female shad; buck shad—a male shad; SC43 Shad fish; White shad—eat up with bones—very bony; (Qu. P14, . . *Commercial fishing . . what do the fishermen go out after?)* 27 Infs, 26 **Atlantic,** Shad; **CT**10, Shad fishing; NY52 Shad—old-fashioned; **RI**4, Shard; SC43, Shad fish; (Qu. P2, . . *Kinds of saltwater fish caught around here . . good to eat)* 25 Infs, 23 **Atlantic,** Shad; VA46, Shad fish; (Qu. O9, . . *Kinds of sailboats)* Inf NC81, Shad boats; (Qu. O10, . . *Kinds of boats)* Inf NC78, Shad boats—a bigger kind used in the spring; NJ21, Shad skiffs; (Qu. P3, *Freshwater fish that are not good to eat)* Inf CT9, Shad—imported from Connecticut and Hudson river—great delicacy; (Qu. P8, *Do fishermen around here use 'white bait'? If . . 'yes', what is it?;* total Infs questioned, 75) Inf MS1, Cut-up shad; (Qu. P13, . . *Ways of fishing . . besides the ordinary hook and line)* Inf GA5, Shad net or drift net—lead line on cork line strung between two boats to catch shad; GA16, SC2, 40, 43, Shad net; NC82, Shad netting—a special net for shad done in the spring; (Qu. FF16, . . *Local contests or celebrations)* Inf CT19, Rotary has its annual "shad bake." [*DARE* Ed: Some of these Infs may refer instead to **3** below.] **1975** Evanoff *Catch More Fish* 93, The shad (*Alosa sapidissima*) is also known as the common shad, white shad, American shad, Atlantic shad, and silver herring. . . Originally the shad was found on the East Coast from the St. Lawrence River in Canada to the St. John's River in Florida, but it was also intro-

duced on the Pacific Coast, and is now found there from Southern California to Alaska.

2 =**mooneye 1.**

1818 Rafinesque in *Amer. Monthly Mag. & Crit. Rev.* 3.354, [In a catalogue of newly discovered fishes of the Ohio River:] Clupea alosoides, R.—Shad. **1820** Rafinesque *Ohio R. Fishes* 42, *Amphiodon alosoides.* . . I have observed it in the lower parts of the Ohio, where it is . . often called Shad, owing to its larger size. **1956** Harlan–Speaker *IA Fish* 61, Mooneye—*Hiodon tergisus.* . . Other Names—Toothed herring, big-eyed shad.

3 also *shad salmon:* A **whitefish** (here: *Coregonus clupeaformis*).

1842 DeKay *Zool. NY* 4.248, The Common Shad Salmon. *Coregonus clupeiformis.* . . occurs in Lakes Erie and Ontario, and in the smaller lakes in the interior of the State, which still communicate with our inland seas. **1848** in 1850 Cooper *Rural Hours* 376 **NY,** It is a shad-salmon, but is commonly called the "Otsego Bass," and is considered one of the finest fresh-water fish in the world. **1886** Mather *Memoranda* 4 **NY,** A species of *Coregonus* ("whitefish" of the great lakes), is called "shad[n]" in Lake Champlain. **1949** Caine *N. Amer. Sport Fish* 165, *Coregonus clupeaformis clupeaformis.* . . This is the species of whitefish common to our Great Lakes and the smaller lakes in that region. . . It is known by numerous names, such as . . whiting and shad.

4 also *shad minnow:* A small baitfish such as the **golden shiner.**

1879 U.S. Natl. Museum *Bulletin* 9.25, Notemigonus americanus. . . This fish is rarely or never called Shiner in the Ohio Basin, and it is very often considered by the fishermen as a Shad. **1969** *DARE* (Qu. P7, *Small fish used as bait for bigger fish)* Inf AL56, Shad minnow; KY60, Shad, goldfish—types of minnows. **1986** Pederson *LAGS Concordance* **Gulf Region** *(Small fish used for bait)* 1 inf, Shad = roach, shiner; 1 inf, Shad minnows; 1 inf, Shad = minnow? 1 inf, Small shads.

5 also *chad, shag:* =**gizzard shad 1. chiefly Sth, S Midl, Missip-Ohio Valleys**

1882 U.S. Natl. Museum *Proc.* 5.248, Dorosoma cepedianum . . shad. . . Generally abundant, especially along the coast of Texas. . . This species is not used for food. **1948** in 1983 Becker *Fishes WI* 276, Fishermen along the Chippewa River are interested in the appearance of large schools of gizzard shad. . . Along with the shad come flocks of seagulls to feed on them. For a time the taking of shad was prohibited but the ban has been lifted. **1965–70** *DARE* (Qu. P3, *Freshwater fish that are not good to eat)* 79 Infs, **chiefly Sth, S Midl, Missip-Ohio Valleys,** Shad; LA44, SC57, Shads; LA26, Shad—some people eat them, but they are mainly used for crawfish bait; MA58 [FW:] Inf objects to this category for shad—good to eat, bony—must be dressed right; MO19, Shag; (Qu. P7, *Small fish used as bait for bigger fish)* 13 Infs, **chiefly Sth, S Midl,** Shad; MS81, Chad. [*DARE* Ed: Some of these Infs may refer instead to other senses.] **1967–69** *DARE* Tape LA5, [FW:] What kind of fish do you have that aren't valuable either commercially or for sport? [Inf:] Well, we have what we call shad. . . We catch 'em up to about three pounds in trammel nets. . . Some people eat 'em, mostly 'mongst colored people. . . It's a fine food, I mean for other fish. . . any kind of catfish'll eat 'em; MI109, [FW:] What's the deal with the fishing? Not enough fish anymore? [Inf:] Well, between the fishermen, the lamprey eel, and the shad, they just cleaned them up. **1986** Pederson *LAGS Concordance* **Gulf Region** *(Fish you get around here)* 24 infs, Shad; 5 infs, Shads; 1 inf, ceAL, Shad—rough fish; 1 inf, seAL, Shad—inedible; 1 inf, swGA, Shad, undesirable fish; gave to colored people; 1 inf, cMS [Black], Shad—not fit to eat, hardly; *(Small fish used for bait)* 7 infs, Shad(s); 1 inf, Crawfish—bait with shad. [*DARE* Ed: Some of these infs may refer instead to other senses.]

6 also *shad fish:* =**menhaden 1.**

1709 (1967) Lawson *New Voyage* 66 **NC, SC,** We met an Indian that had got a parcel of Shad-Fish ready barbaku'd. *Ibid* 160, Shads are a sweet Fish, but very bony; they are very plentiful at some Seasons. **1884** Goode *Fisheries U.S.* 1.576, The Gulf Menhaden has several vernacular names. . . On the Texan coast it is known as 'Herring,' 'Alewife,' 'Sardine,' and 'Shad,' each locality having its peculiar name. **1911** U.S. Bur. Census *Fisheries 1908* 9, The familiar . . name "shad" is, in North Carolina, sometimes applied to the menhaden. **1951** Taylor *Surv. Marine Fisheries NC* 93, In Maryland and Virginia it [=*Brevoortia tyrannus*] is known as *alewife,* probably a corruption of *allizes,* a colonial name used in common with *shadd,* another name for menhaden that has held through the centuries and which is still used in some places. **1986** Pederson *LAGS Concordance,* 1 inf, seMS, Shad = pogy, menhaden.

7 The white **crappie.**

1887 Goode *Amer. Fishes* 71, *Pomoxys annularis.* . . has other names of local application as "Tin Mouth" . . and "Shad." **1902** Jordan-Evermann *Amer. Fishes* 334, In other places it [=the crappie] is known as bridge perch, goggle-eye, speckled perch, shad [etc]. **1933** LA Dept. of Conserv. *Fishes* 333, The Sac-a-lait. . . This species, [sic] popularity is very well attested by the variety of names it has been given, a number matched by few other North American species. They are as follows: Crappie . . Shad [etc].

8 =**serviceberry.** [Abbr for **shadbush** or one of the other *shad-* compounds used for this plant]

1886 *Harper's New Mth. Mag.* 73.149, Kites, tops, hoops. . . all appear in due season as regularly as . . the blossoms of the "shad." **1965–69** *DARE* (Qu. I44, *What kinds of berries grow wild around here?*) Inf NY21, Shadberries or shads; (Qu. T16, . . *Kinds of trees . . 'special'*) Infs MA25, NY186, Shad.

9 See **shad fly.**

10 See **shadflower 1.**

shadback fence n Also *shadbelly fence* [Prob from the shape] Cf **backbone fence, ripgut fence**

A type of rail fence; see quot 1917.

1917 *DN* 4.399 **neOH,** *Shad-belly fence.* . . A fence made thus: two stakes are driven so as to cross each other. A rail is laid on them with one end in the notch and the other on the ground. Half way, more or less, to the lower end, two more stakes are driven astride the rail, and another rail laid in the same way, and so on. A connection suggests itself with *shad-belly coat.* **1931–33** *LANE Worksheets* seMA, *Shadback fence.* . . **1933–34** *Hanley Disks* cME, That was called rip-gut fence. [Inf says it's the same as shad-belly fence.]] **1939** *LANE* Map 117 (*Rail fence*) 1 inf, swMA, Shad back [fence].

shadbark (hickory) See **shagbark hickory**

shadbelly fence See **shadback fence**

shadberry n [See **shadbush**] =**serviceberry.**

1801 (1820) Harmon *Journal* 81 (*DCan*), The last [berries] . . exactly resemble, in shape and taste, what in the New England states are called shad berries. **1847** Wood *Class-Book* 245, *A[melanchier] Canadensis* . . Shad Berry. . . Fruit pleasant to the taste, ripening in June. **1906** Rydberg *Flora CO* 436, *Amelanchier* [spp] . . Service-berry, Juneberry, Shadberry. **1966–69** *DARE* (Qu. I44, *What kinds of berries grow wild around here?*) Infs MA6, 58, NJ16, WI58, Shadberries; MN14, Serviceberries—called shadberries out west; NY21, Shadberries or shads; NY97, Shadberries—grow on trees. **1976** Elmore *Shrubs & Trees SW* 136, Utah Serviceberry—shadberry, -bush or -blow; Juneberry. . . In the West it is called serviceberry (or sarvisberry as oldtimers were wont to say); eastern species are called shadblow because its "blows" (blossoms) appear in the spring when shad are running upstream to spawn.

shadbird n

1 =**Wilson's snipe.** [See quot 1883] Cf **shad spirit**

1883 in 1888 Trumbull *Names of Birds* 157 **DE,** Snipe are called shadbirds by many of the fishermen, and the abundance or scarcity of the one is considered highly indicative of that of the other. **1895** Elliot *N. Amer. Shore Birds* 47, Wilson's Snipe. . . It has many local appellations, and is called in different sections Jack Snipe . . Shad Bird, Shad Spirit, Gutter Snipe, etc. **1923** U.S. Dept. Ag. *Misc. Circular* 13.50 **NJ, PA, DE,** Common snipe. . . [*Names*] *in local use* . . shadbird [etc]. **1946** Hausman *Eastern Birds* 266, Wilson's Snipe. . . Other Names—Jack Snipe . . Shadbird [etc].

2 also *shad buck:* A **bittern** (here: *Botaurus lentiginosus*). [See quot]

1959 *Names* 7.118 **MD,** [In an article on the names of the American bittern:] Shad bird and shad buck . . relate to its being seen at the season of the shad fishery.

shadblossom n [See **shadbush**] =**serviceberry.**

a1817 Dwight *Travels* I.42 (*DAE*), Shad-blossom. This tree grows about fifteen feet in height. **1849** [see **shad fly**]. **1875** Holland *Sevenoaks* 288 **NEast,** The freshets of spring had passed away; the woods were filling with birds; the shad-blossoms were reaching their flat

sprays out over the river. **1896** *New Engl. Mag.* 20.346 **MA,** The pink laurel and the shad blossom sprang up from the roadside.

shadblow n [See **shadbush**] chiefly **NEast** Cf **fish blossom** =**serviceberry.**

1846 Browne *Trees* 282, *Amelanchier canadensis,* The Canadian Amelanchier. . . Wild Pear-tree, Sugar Plum, June Berry, Shad-blow, Shadflower. **1892** *Jrl. Amer. Folkl.* 5.95 **NH,** *Amelanchier Canadensis.* . . sugar plum; shad-blow. **1937** U.S. Forest Serv. *Range Plant Hdbk.* B12 **Atlantic,** On the Atlantic coast these shrubs [=*Amelanchier* spp] are often called shadblow and shadbush because they bloom when the shad are running. **1948** Stevens *KS Wild Flowers* 251, Amelanchier canadensis—Shadblow. **1967** Borland *Hill Country* 159 **nwCT,** Only a couple of weeks ago the shadblow was in bloom along the river here. . . Some call it shad bush. **1968** *DARE* (Qu. I44, *What kinds of berries grow wild around here?*) Inf NY72, Bilberries—they blow out (bloom) with white flowers in early spring; called shadblows then because they blow out about the time shad come around; berries are red, about the size of a small pea; (Qu. S26c, *Wildflowers that grow in woods*) Inf NY73, Shadblow—turns to bilberry; (Qu. T16, . . *Kinds of trees . . 'special'*) Infs CT8, NJ29, Shadblow. **1968** *DARE* Wildfl QR Pl.103 Inf NY91, *Amelanchier canadensis* . . shadblow. **1976** Bruce *How to Grow Wildflowers* 115, When shad run upstream to spawn, so runs the old legend, the Shad-blow flowers, and indeed when the plant blooms you may be sure to find shad in the rivers of the East—at least you could in the days before all our major streams were polluted. **1985** Rattray *Advent. Dimon* 244 **Long Is.** NY, Below, Napeague Beach spread dusted-white toward Montauk; the shadblow was in blossom.

shad buck See **shadbird 2**

shadbush n [Because it is said to bloom when the shad begin to run] =**serviceberry.**

1832 MA Hist. Soc. *Coll.* 2d ser 9.147 **cwVT,** Aronia botryapium . . Shad-bush. **a1862** (1865) Thoreau *Cape Cod* 152 **MA,** The Shadbush (*Amelanchier*), Beach Plums, and Blueberries . . were very dwarfish. **1872** Schele de Vere *Americanisms* 346 **NEng,** The good people of New England are prosaic enough to call the beautiful service-berry, with its beautiful sprays full of delicate white blossoms, the *shadbush,* because, forsooth, it blooms about the time when the fish ascend the rivers in early spring! **1948** Peattie *Berkshires* 68 **wMA,** The shadbush berries or Juneberries, maturing in July or August, were used a great deal by the Indians but now find favor primarily with the children, who eat them raw. **1953** Nelson *Plants Rocky Mt. Park* 96, Serviceberry or shadbush, *Amelanchier.* . . The blue or purplish berries are very good to eat, but the birds and the worms usually find them first. **1961** Douglas *My Wilderness* 192 **MD,** Early to bloom is a tree which in the Far West we call juneberry but which the people along the Potomac have dubbed the "shadbush," because its white blooms come when the shad run the river. **1968** *DARE* (Qu. I44, *What kinds of berries grow wild around here?*) Inf MN14, Serviceberries—plant called shadbush out west; (Qu. T16, . . *Kinds of trees . . 'special'*) Inf WI58, Shadbush; VA21, Sarviceberry = serviceberry = shadbush. **1968** *DARE* Wildfl QR Pl.103 Inf NY91, *Amelanchier canadensis*—shadbush. **1992** *Daily Hampshire Gaz.* (Northampton MA) 1 July 18/3, The Juneberry tree has abundant white blossoms that precede purplish berries that ripen in late June, hence the name "Juneberries." The tree is also known as shadbush.

shaddah, shadder n[1] See **shadow**

shadder n[2] See **shatter** n

shadduh See **shadow**

shade n See **shed**

shade v, hence vbl n *shading* Often with *up* chiefly **West**

To take shelter from the sun and heat; to rest.

1935 *Cattleman* May 5, Shadin', if you don't know, means in cowboy—hunting a "black spot," or shade for a few minutes rest or to eat a snack, and does not necessarily mean that the boys are "throwin' off", or soldiering, on the old man. **1959** Robertson *Ram* 205 **ID** (as of c1875), In summer they [=sheep] shade up as soon as it gets hot and won't move again until the cool of the evening. **1971** Green *Last Trail Drive* 4 **TX,** This foreman . . walked out to where I was shadin' under a tree with my horses. **1984** Wilder *You All Spoken Here* 38 **Sth** *Shade up:* Rest in the shade during the noonday sun. **1993** Doig *Heart Earth* 123

MT, The instant the sheep shaded up at midday my father was sifting his way into them on a walkthrough count of the lambs.

shade bee n

See quot.

1955 McAtee *Dial. Grant Co. IN Suppl.* 6 [2], Shade bee: . . a carpenter bee *(Xylocopa),* from their being seen buzzing about under trees in some dead part of which they doubtless had their burrows.

shade-tree n attrib Cf **jackleg** adj **1 chiefly Sth, S Midl**

Of a member of an occupational group: having little or no formal training; unprofessional; part-time—usu in phr *shade-tree mechanic.*

1946 *McDavid Coll.* **GA,** A shade tree mechanic—Country mechanic—small scale. **1966** *State* (Raleigh, N.C.) 1 Nov. 26/3 *(Mathews Coll.)* **LA,** You just drive up to his house, park under a shade-tree, and he does the best he can with such common tools as he has. This is a 'shade-tree' business, and down there people often apply it to any kind of poorly equipped business institution. **1984** *Newsweek* 16 July 63, The Rutans built the Voyager [=an experimental aircraft] with a small crew, improvising like shade-tree mechanics when they had to. **1984** Wilder *You All Spoken Here* 9 **Sth,** Sorry: Of poor quality; lazy; incompetent as a right sorry jackleg carpenter, or a ditch-bank blacksmith, or a shade-tree mechanic. **1986** Pederson *LAGS Concordance* **Gulf Region** *(Jackleg)* 22 infs, Shade-tree (mechanic(s)); 6 infs, Shade-tree (preacher(s)); 1 inf, Shade-tree—heard—associate it with mechanics; 1 inf, Shade-tree—jackleg; 1 inf, Shade-tree—tries but not good; not insulting; 1 inf, Shade-tree—heard of mechanics, painters; 1 inf, Shade-tree (mechanic—lack of skill); 1 inf, Shade-tree (mechanic—suggests not well trained); 1 inf, Shade-tree (mechanic—not insulting); 1 inf, Shade-tree (mechanic—insulting—only mechanics); 1 inf, Shade-tree (mechanic—derogatory); 1 inf, Shade-tree (mechanic—amateur); 1 inf, Shade-tree (auto mechanic—may be good); 1 inf, Shade-tree mechanic—can be lazy or amateur; 1 inf, Shade-tree mechanic—not necessarily derogatory; 1 inf, Shade-tree mechanic—works under tree, not garage; 1 inf, Shade-tree mechanic—not good; works under tree; 1 inf, Shade-tree mechanic—same as jackleg; 1 inf, Shade-tree mechanic—part-time; self-trained; hobby; 1 inf, Shade-tree mechanic—fairly-well qualified; 1 inf, Shade-tree mechanic—no shop; not very good; 1 inf, Shade-tree mechanic—not professional; insulting; 1 inf, Shade-tree mechanic—jackleg; jack-of-all-trades; 1 inf, Shade-tree mechanics—untrained; 1 inf, Shade-tree mechanics—work on side; untrained; 1 inf, Shade-tree mechanics—work on cars under trees; 1 inf, Shade-tree mechanics—kind of lazy; 1 inf, Shade-tree mechanics—work when they can; in yard; 1 inf, Shade-tree mechanics—also carpenters, preachers. **1999** *Smithsonian* Feb 95, He bought a manual and a few tools, and from then on conducted his repairs himself. He became a competent "shade-tree mechanic."

‡**shade-tree money** n Cf **rocking-chair money**

1986 Pederson *LAGS Concordance,* 1 inf, **cMS,** Shade-tree money—unemployment compensation.

shade up See **shade** v

shad fish See **shad** 1, 6

shadflower n

1 also *shad:* =**arbutus.**

1892 *Jrl. Amer. Folkl.* 5.99 **CT,** *Epigaea repens,* shad-flower. **1896** *Ibid* 10.49 **NEng, NJ,** *Epigaea repens* . . shad-flower. **1911** Henkel *Amer. Med. Leaves* 18, Gravel Plant. . . *Other common names* . . Mayflower, shad-flower [etc]. **1969** *DARE* (Qu. S4, . . *Mayapple)* Inf **MA25,** Mayflower, shad. [FW: At the next meeting, Inf's wife recalled mayflower and trailing arbutus as the same flower in this area.] **1979** Erichsen-Brown *Med. N. Amer. Plants* 307, Trailing Arbutus. . . Common names. . . ground laurel, shadflower [etc].

2 =**serviceberry.** [See **shadbush**]

1817 Eaton *Botany* 55, *Aronia . . botryapium,* (shad-flower). **1837** Darlington *Flora Cestrica* 295 **sePA,** Aronia Botryapium. . . *Vulgò* . . Snowy Medlar. Shad-flower. . . This is quite a showy little tree, when in flower;—which, happening at the fishing season, has acquired for it the name of *"Shad flower,"* or *"Shad bush."* **1843** Torrey *Flora NY* 2.1.225, Amelanchier Canadensis . . *Common June-berry.* Shad-flower. **1930** *Amer. Botanist* 30.57, Shad-flower . . may have as much significance . . as it does when associated with species of *Amelanchier.*

3 See quot.

1893 *Jrl. Amer. Folkl.* 6.137 **WV,** *Draba verna,* shad flower.

shad fly n Also *chad fly, shad, shag fly* **chiefly NEast; also Missip Valley, GA** See Map
=**mayfly 1.**

[**1825** *Canadian Mag.* 4.474 *(DCan),* Among the curious phenomena of Canada, is the ephemeral Spring fly, called . . by the English the Shad Fly, as they are supposed to indicate the approach of the fish.] **1849** (1911) Thoreau *Week on Concord* 105 **MA,** The shad make their appearance early in May, at the same time with the blossoms of the pyrus, . . which is for this reason called the shad-blossom. An insect called the shad-fly, also appears at the same time, covering the houses and fences. **1905** Kellogg *Amer. Insects* 65, May-flies, lake-flies, or shad-flies, common names for the insects of the order Ephemerida, are familiar to people who live on the shores of lakes or large rivers, but are among the unknown insects to most high-and-dry dwellers. **1950** *WELS* **WI** *(Large winged insect that hatches in summer in great numbers around lakes or rivers, crowds around lights, lives only a day or so, and is good fish bait)* 3 Infs, Shad fly; 1 Inf, Shads. **1965–70** *DARE* (Qu. R4) 34 Infs, **chiefly NEast; also Missip Valley, GA,** Shad fly; **CT**13, Shad fly—white bug one inch long—comes in June; **IA**21, Fish fly—the Illinois chad fly; **IA**22, Chad fly—hear occasionally; **IL**4, Sand fly, shad fly—alternate names; **MI**2, Shad fly—some call 'em a Canadian soldier; **VT**16, Shag fly; (Qu. R11, *A very tiny fly that you can hardly see, but that stings)* Inf **MA**6, Shad flies. **1967** *Watertown Daily Times* (NY) 14 June 8/1, The other driver . . reported a shad fly got in her eye. **1972** Swan–Papp *Insects* 166, In some localities where mayflies appear earlier than May they are (more appropriately perhaps) called shadflies.

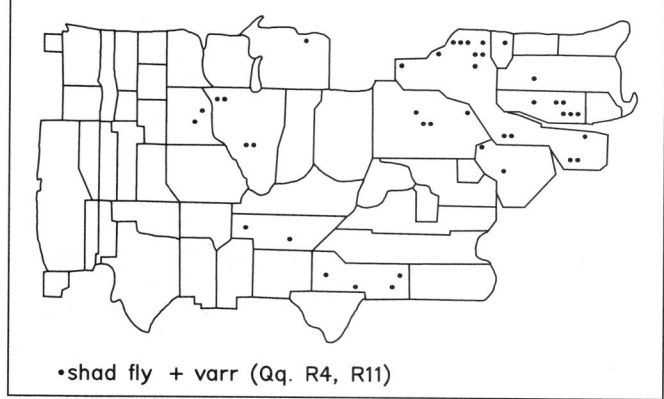

•shad fly + varr (Qq. R4, R11)

shad frog n [See quot 1791]

A **leopard frog** (here: either *Rana pipiens* or *R. sphenocephala*).

1791 Bartram *Travels* 278 **PA,** The shad frog, so called in Pennsylvania from their appearing and croaking in the spring season, at the time the people fish for shad: these are a beautiful spotted frog, of a slender form, five or six inches in length from the nose to the extremities; of a dark olive green, blotched with clouds and ringlets of a dusky colour. **1842** DeKay *Zool. NY* 3.63, The Shad Frog. Rana halecina. . . From its simultaneous appearance in the spring with our common Shad . . it is frequently called *Shad Frog.* . . The Swedish colonists named them *Sill-hoppetosser,* or *Herring-hoppers,* from their appearance at the commencement of the herring season. **1891** in 1876 *IL State Lab. Nat. Hist. Urbana Bulletin* 3.322, *Rana pipiens* . . Leopard Frog, Shad Frog. **1966–70** *DARE* (Qu. P21, *Small frogs that sing or chirp loudly in spring)* Inf **GA**3, Shad frog (small, brown); **NC**49, Shad frogs—old folks use it; **VA**46, Shad frogs—when you hear him, it's time to go catch shadfish.

shad herring n esp NY

A clupeid fish such as the **glut herring, hickory shad,** or a **thread herring** (here: *Opisthonema oglinum*).

1815 *Lit. & Philos. Soc. NY Trans.* 452, Some call this fish [=the Long-Island Herring] the *shad herring,* and some the *fall shad.* He is reckoned to be almost equal to the shad, as an article of food. He is probably the full grown fish of the *mediocris* species. **1842** DeKay *Zool. NY* 3.261, The *Autumnal* or *Fall Herring,* or *Shad Herring* [= *Alosa mattowacca*], is a common fish in our waters in the months of

September, October, and November. *Ibid* 265, It [=the thread herring] appears in our waters about the beginning of September, where it is often called the *Shad Herring.* **1872** Schele de Vere *Americanisms* 386, The *Shad-Herring* (Chatöessus signifer), sometimes called thread herring, or threadfish. **1903** NY State Museum & Sci. Serv. *Bulletin* 203, At Gravesend bay the glut herring is called shad herring. **1976** Tryckare et al. *Lore of Sportfishing* 70, Blueback herring. . . Other common names: Shad herring, glut herring.

shadine n

1 Either a **hickory shad** (here: *Alosa mediocris*) or a **menhaden 1** (here: *Brevoortia tyrannus*).

1782 Crèvecoeur *Letters* 132 **eMA,** Near Pochick Rip . . they catch their best fish, such as . . cod, smelt, perch, shadine, pike, &c. **1815** Lit. & Philos. Soc. NY *Trans.* 457, *New-York Shadine. (Clupea sadina.)* An elegant species with a small smutty spot behind the gill-cover. **1842** DeKay *Zool. NY* 4.263, The Spotted Shadine. *Alosa sadina.* . . Our species does not appear to be common. It was taken in the harbor of New-York in November, and was brought to me for a curious variety of the *menhaden,* from which it differs. **1906** NJ State Museum *Annual Rept. for 1905* 94, *Pomolobus mediocris.* . . Shadine. Herring. Fall Herring. Hickory Shad. *Ibid* 103, *Brevoortia tyrannus.* . . Menhaden. . . Shadine [etc].

2 A **menhaden 1** (here: *Brevoortia tyrannus*) when packed like a sardine as an article of food. *hist*

1878 *Amer. Naturalist* 12.736 **NJ,** Among the manufacturers in Port Monmouth, N.J., who prepare the menhaden as an article of food, a number of trade names are in use, such as "American sardine" . . "American club-fish," "shadine," and "ocean trout." **1884** U.S. Natl. Museum *Bulletin* 27.1041, An effort was made a few years ago to introduce menhaden canned in oil, under the names of "American sardines," ["]American boneless sardines," and "shadines," but as the herring has proved a much better "sardine" this industry does not appear to have prospered. **1889** *Manufacturer & Builder* 21.74, The "shadines" or American Sardines, are put up in cotton-seed oil.

shading See shade v

shad minnow See shad 4

shad-mouth n

A person whose mouth has a projecting upper lip; hence adj phr *shad-mouthed.*

1934 *AmSp* 9.288 **PA** [Black student slang], *Shad-mouth.* Applied to anyone having a projecting upper lip. **1942** Hurston *Dust Tracks* 143 **FL** [Black], It is an everyday affair to hear somebody called a . . shad-mouthed . . so-and-so.

shadow n[1], v Usu |'šædo|; also |'šædə, 'šædəˈ| Pronc-spp *shaddah, shadder, shadduh* Cf Intro "Language Changes" IV.1.c, Pronc Intro 3.1.12.d

Std sense, var forms.

1851 Hooper *Widow Rugby's Husband* 45 **AL,** I seen the shadder of my face. **1884** *Anglia* 7.270 **Sth, S Midl** [Black], *Wrassle wid yo' shadder* = to attempt the impossible. **1891** Riley *Swimmin'-Hole* 1 **IN,** My shadder smilin' up at me. **1901** *DN* 2.183 **neKY** [Black], *Shadows* . . shaddahs. **1904** Day *Kin o' Ktaadn* 6 **ME,** Then the shadders stalk an' the embers talk. **1922** Gonzales *Black Border* 325 **sSC, GA coasts** [Gullah glossary], *Shadduh*—(n. and v.) shadow, shadows, shadowed, shadowing. **1941** *Esquire* May 131 **KY,** When dinner time come we could step on the heads of shadders. **1942** Hall *Smoky Mt. Speech* 80 **wNC, eTN,** A considerable degree of education or subjection to modernizing influences is required before speakers regularly avoid [əˈ] for general American [o]. Examples: Banjo . . shadow . . yellow. **1981** Pederson *LAGS Basic Materials,* 3 infs, **GA, LA, MS,** Shadow(s) ['šædə(z)]; 1 inf, **cwAR,** Shadow ['šædoᵁ].

shadow n[2] See shatter n

‡shadow ice n

1970 *DARE* (Qu. B35, *Ice that will bend when you step on it, but not break*) Inf **VA69,** Shadow ice ['šædo aıs]; thin ice.

shadow lane n Cf *DS* N17

1968 *DARE* FW Addit **ceNM,** Shadow lane—short center lane in highway, that traffic pulls into to wait to make a left turn. [Term used on] street sign.

shadow rider n

See quots.

1936 McCarthy *Lang. Mosshorn* np **West** [Range terms], *Shadow Rider.* A cowboy who rides along gazing at his own shadow. Mirrors are sometimes scarce on the range and some fellows must admire themselves, even though only their shadow. **1949** *PADS* 11.25 **CO,** *Shadow rider.* . . A lazy cowboy who spends most of his time showing off, watching his shadow.

shadow social n Cf box social

A social or fund-raising gathering at which a person stands behind a sheet and others look at the shadow and bid for the privilege of that person's company; see quots.

1950 *WELS* (A kind of gathering called a "social" or a "sociable") 1 Inf, **cwWI,** Shadow social—girl's shadow on a sheet sold to highest bidder. **1966–68** *DARE* (Qu. FF1, . . *A kind of group meeting called a 'social' or 'sociable'. . . [What goes on?]*) Inf **DE2,** Shadow social—You have a big white cloth—one girl at a time parades across behind the cloth to cast a shadow and the men bid on the shadow—they eat ice cream or other refreshments with her—old-fashioned; **MI4,** Shadow social—With a light, throw the shadow of the person on screen, auction off shadow; **NJ8,** Shadow social—girl waits behind sheet lit by candle—men bid on her and eat her dinner; **SD3,** Shadow social—stand behind sheet—audience bids on shadow. **1967** Stegner *Little Live Things* 238 **IA,** Or that box supper in Maquoketa, the shadow social where girls brought boxed meals and walked in turn between a light and a hung sheet so that men recognizing a shadow shape would bid five, ten, fifteen dollars for the cooking and the company and the Ladies' Aid would raise a round sum.

shadow tag n

A game of tag in which the person who is "it" attempts to step on the shadow of a player who then becomes "it."

1909 (1923) Bancroft *Games* 173, *Shadow Tag.* . . This is a very pretty form of tag, suitable for little children, and they delight in playing it. It hardly need be said that it requires a sunny day. The player who is It tries to step or jump on to the shadow of some other player, and if successful, announces the fact by calling the name of the player. That player then becomes It. **1959** *DARE* File **ceMA** (as of 1920s), Around Boston we used to play shadow tag, statues, and forfeits. **1966** *DARE* (QR, near Qu. EE1) Inf **WA1,** Shadow tag. **1966** *DARE* File **swIN,** *Shadow tag*—a type of children's game. [**1969** Opie–Opie *Children's Games* 86 **Gt Britain,** *Shadow touch.* . . The game is also played in Canada and the United States ('Shadow Tag').] **1975** Ferretti *Gt. Amer. Book Sidewalk Games* 167, *Shadow Tag,* a sunny-day test in which "It" has to run after the other players and, instead of tagging them, touch their shadows with his foot. A fast, exciting game that has more than its share of arguments.

shadpoke See shagpoke

shad porgy n

A **porgy** n[1] **1b(4)** (here: *Calamus arctifrons*).

1887 Goode *Amer. Fishes* 100, There are other species, known by the name "Porgy," which are found in this region [=the Gulf of Mexico and Florida reefs], such as . . *C[alamus] arctifrons,* the "Shad Porgy." **1902** Jordan–Evermann *Amer. Fishes* 440 **FL,** The grass or shad porgy . . is a small species, rather common in shallow water among grass-patches at Key West and as far north as Pensacola. **1946** LaMonte *N. Amer. Game Fishes* 71, Grass Porgy . . Names: Shad Porgy.

shad salmon See shad 3

shad scale n Also *shad-scale saltbush* [See quot 1931] Cf red scale

=**saltbush 1,** esp *Atriplex canescens* or *A. confertifolia.*

1898 *Jrl. Amer. Folkl.* 11.278 **WY,** *Atriplex confertifolium* . . shad scale. **1913** (1979) Barnes *Western Grazing* 57, There is another favorite forage bush known as shad scale (Atriplex canescens). . . It is eagerly eaten by all stock, especially sheep. **1931** U.S. Dept. Ag. *Misc. Pub.* 101.28, Fourwing saltbush. . . This species has in the past been fairly generally known by the name "shadscale." Historically, however, shadscale pertains to *A. confertifolia* . . and the name is also picturesquely descriptive of the flattened, concentrically ringed fruits of that species. **1940** Writers' Program *Guide NV* 246, In September the floor of the valley looks as though it were covered with a dark red carpet; shadscale, evenly spaced, produces the effect. **1962** Sweet *Plants of West*

17, Shadscale saltbush, *Atriplex canescens*. . . the leaves covered with tiny white hairs and bran-like scales. **1981** Benson–Darrow *Trees SW Deserts* 168, Shadscale is found in nearly pure stands on alkaline soils in northern Arizona and in the Great Basin, and there it is an important browse plant for range livestock.

shad spirit n chiefly NEng
A bird heard in early spring and associated with the upstream passage of the shad, variously identified with **Wilson's snipe, flicker** n[2] **1**, or rarely **nighthawk 1**.

a1828 in 1841 Brainard *Poems* 21 **CT**, There is a superstition in many places, which bears, that Shad are conducted from the gulf of Mexico into Connecticut river by a kind of *Yankee bogle*, in the shape of a bird, properly called the *Shad Spirit*. It makes its appearance, annually, about a week before the Shad, calls the fish, and gives warning to the fishermen to mend their nets. **1844** DeKay *Zool. NY* 2.35, The Night Hawk. *Chordeiles americanus*. . . Its first appearance is known by a booming sound heard high in the air, while the bird itself is unseen. When a boy at school, I remember to have heard this mysterious sound along the Connecticut river, and was told that it was the *Shad Spirit*, announcing to the scholes of shad, about to ascend the river, their impending fate. **1861** Higginson in *Atlantic Mth.* 7.392 **neMA**, There is a bird known as the Shad-spirit, which I take to be identical with the flicker or golden-winged woodpecker, whose note is still held to indicate the first day when the fish ascend the river. **1881** Nuttall Ornith. Club *Bulletin* 6.184 **NEng**, The Golden-winged Woodpecker (*Colaptes auratus*) . . is variously known as follows. . . *Flicker*, or *Yellow-shafted Flicker*. . . *Shad-spirit* (New England coast.) **1883** *Century Illustr. Mag.* 923, Along the New England coast, . . it [=the Wilson's snipe] has an appellation which is rather curious. As the bird arrives about the same time as the shad, and is found on the meadows along the rivers where the nets are hauled, the fishermen, when drawing their seines at night, often start it from its moist resting-place, and hear its sharp cry as it flies away through the darkness. They do not know the cause of the sound, and from the association they have dubbed its author the "shad spirit." **1900** *Wilson Bulletin* 31.9 **NEng**, Shad-spirit. New England Coast. "A half superstitious idea of the fishermen of former days—and it may be yet—that this bird came up from the south and ascended the rivers just ahead of the vernal migration of the shad, in order to inform them of the approach of the fish; in other words, the noting of a coincidence." **1917** (1923) *Birds Amer.* 1.227, Wilson's Snipe—*Gallinago delicata*. . . Shadbird; Alewife-bird; Shad Spirit. **1955** MA Audubon Soc. *Bulletin* 39.446, Wilson's Snipe. . . Shad Spirit. . . From its flight "song" being heard at night during the time of the shad run.

shad tree n [See shadbush]
=serviceberry.

1818 in 1826 MA Hist. Soc. *Coll.* 2d ser. 8.169, The latter part of May appear . . among the trees, the elm, ash, beech, aronia or shad tree [etc]. **1880** *Harper's New Mth. Mag.* 61.71 **NEng**, Yonder on the wooded slope the feathery shad-tree blooms, like a suspended cloud of drifting snow. **1922** *Amer. Botanist* 28.7 **MI**, Over them wave and bloom the slender shad-trees.

shad trout n
A **weakfish** (here: either *Cynoscion nebulosus* or *C. regalis*).

1882 U.S. Natl. Museum *Proc.* 5.607, Cynoscion regale. . . *Trout; Shad-Trout.* **1887** Goode *Amer. Fishes* 112 **S Atl**, In the Southern Atlantic States it [=the squeteague] is called "Grey Trout," "Sun Trout" and "Shad Trout." **1892** *Outing* 20.54 **eVA**, He did say where it be called the 'gray trout,' 'sun trout' and 'shad trout,' the 'chickwit,' 'squit,' 'succoteague' and 'squitee.' **1911** U.S. Bur. Census *Fisheries 1908* 316 **Mid and S Atl**, Squeteague (*Cynoscion regalis*). . . It is known as . . "shad trout," "sea trout," and "salt-water trout" in the Middle and South Atlantic states. **1946** LaMonte *N. Amer. Game Fishes* 75, Weakfish. . . Names: Squeteague . . Shad Trout [etc]. [*Ibid*, Spotted Weakfish. . . Names: Spotted Squeteague . . also any of the names used for the Weakfish.]

shad waiter n
Usu **=round whitefish,** but also **whitefish.**

1879 U.S. Natl. Museum *Bulletin* 14.57, *Prosopium quadrilaterale* . . "Shad-waiter."—Great Lakes and northward. **1887** Goode *Amer. Fishes* 490 **NH**, The Menomonee White-fish, *Coregonus quadrilateralis*. . . The name of "Round-fish" is given to it by Richardson, and that of "Shad Waiter" (Winnipiseogee Lake) by Prescott. **1911** U.S. Bur. Census *Fisheries 1908* 318, The Menominee whitefish . . also locally known

as . . "shadwater" [sic]. **1976** Tryckare et al. *Lore of Sportfishing* 77, Round Whitefish. . . Other common names: Menominee whitefish . . shadwaiter [etc].

shaf(f) See shaft 1

shaf(f)s See shaft 2

shaft n
Std senses, var forms.

1 sg: usu |šæft|; also, by assim, |šæf|; by back-formation from pl *shavs* (see **2** below), |šæv|; also **NEng** |šaf, šav, šɑf, šɑv|. Pronc-spp *shaf(f), shav*

1917 [see **2** below]. **1939** *LANE* Map 171 **NEng** (*Shafts*), Although the singular . . is entered on the map . . [it] is rarely used. [Pronunciations of the types [šaf, šav] and occasionally [šɑf, šɑv] are found scattered throughout the region.] **1946** *PADS* 6.26 **eNC**, Shav [šæv]. . . The shaft of a cart or buggy. . . Common. **1965–70** *DARE* (Qu. L44, *On a buggy, two long pieces of wood stick out in front and the horse goes between them. You call them the _____*) 20 Infs, **scattered,** Shaft [šæft]; 9 Infs, **scattered,** Shaf [šæf]; **HI3, OH45,** Shaf [šæf]; **IA26, SC19,** 26, Shav [šæv]; **GA7,** 16, Shav; (Qu. L45, *The long piece of wood that sticks out in front of a wagon, and you put a horse on each side*) Inf **LA39,** Shaf; **MD9,** Shaf [šæf]; (Qu. L53b, *The band that goes under a horse's middle—if it's a part of a work harness*) Inf **ME5,** Shav [šɑv] girt; (Qu. JJ10b, *Parts of an ink pen*) Inf **RI4,** Shaf [šæf]. **1969** *DARE* FW Addit **cwNJ**, Shaf chimes—bells to put along shaffs of horse pulling sleigh.

2 pl: usu |šæfts|; also |šæfs, šævz|; **chiefly Sth, S Midl** |ševz|; **chiefly NEng** |šavz, šɑvz|. Pronc-spp *shaf(f)s, shalves, sharves, shav(e)s;* for addit pronc and sp varr see quots

1891 *DN* 1.120 **cNY**, [šævz] . . 'shafts'. **1892** *DN* 1.241 **swMO**, Shafts. Often . . an exact rhyme for calves. **1899** (1912) Green *VA Folk-Speech* 379, Shalves. . . Plural of shaft. *Ibid*, Sharves. . . Plural of shaft. . . Shavs. **1917** *DN* 4.399 **neOH**, Shaff, shavs. . . Shaft(s) of a one-horse vehicle. "One shaff was broken clear off." "The colt had never been in the shavs before." Also Ill., Ia., N. Eng., S. Car., N.Y. **1930** *AmSp* 5.455 **seNE**, The pronunciation "shavs" (riming with "halves"), for the bars (shafts) between which a horse is hitched to a buggy, seems to be the only one heard in Southeast Nebraska. **1939** *LANE* Map 171 (*Shafts*), [The dominant pronunciation variant throughout **NEng** is of the type [šævz]; proncs of the type [šæfs] are also found throughout, and while the same is true for proncs of the types [šavz, šɑvz, šafs, šɑfs] these appear to be more concentrated in the eastern, esp coastal, areas, of the region.] **1942** McAtee *Dial. Grant Co. IN* 56 (as of 1890s), Shavs (rhyming with calves) . . shafts of a vehicle. . . (Iowa, Md., Mo, New England, N.Y., Ohio, S.C., Va.) **1942** Warnick *Garrett Co. MD* 1 **nwMD** (as of 1900–18), Shavs (shafts). **1949** Kurath *Word Geog.* 17, From New England to Lake Erie *fills* or *thills* . . is a common name in rural areas for the shafts of a buggy. . . The Hudson Valley, the Midland, and the South have only *shafts* (pronounced *shavs* or *shaffs,* rarely *shafts*), and this term is also current throughout the *fills* area. **1963** Watkins–Watkins *Yesterday Hills* 183 **cnGA**, The shaves [of a buggy] came loose, and the lines wrapped around Henry's ankle. **1965–70** *DARE* (Qu. L44, *On a buggy, two long pieces of wood stick out in front and the horse goes between them. You call them the _____*) 429 Infs, **widespread,** Shavs [šævz]; **AL20, GA11,** 12, **HI10, IL73, MS81, PA1, WV7,** Shavs; **ME5,** 19, **MA37,** 66, 74, 75, **RI2,** [šavz]; **ME12, MA72, NH12, NJ17, WI30,** [šavz]; **CT32** [šarvz]; **IL24, SC3,** 32, 34 **TN66,** [šæivz]; **FL50, GA87, NC85,** 87, [še(i)vz] [Of all Infs responding to the question, 79% were comm types 4, 5, 76% were old, 40% gs educ or less; of those giving these responses, 83% were comm types 4, 5, 81% were old, 47% gs educ or less]; 137 Infs, **widespread,** Shafs [šæfs]; 9 Infs, **scattered,** Shafs; **MA40,** [šafs]; **NJ19,** [šaɪfs]; **NY79,** [šeæfs]; **TN53,** [šɚfs]; **VA70,** [šɛɪfs]; 113 Infs, **widespread, but less freq Sth, Gt Lakes,** Shafts; **NY36,** 48, 62, [šeæfts]; **NY45,** [šafts]; **MA51,** [šafts] [Of all Infs responding to the question, 61% were hs or coll educ; of those giving these responses, 71% were hs or coll educ]; **GA14, KY9, NE8, OK3, SC69, VA68, WV14,** [ševz]; **IN2, SC7, VA10,** [šeɪvz]; **TN30,** 58, [šæe(ɪ)vz]; **TX16,** [šeɑvz] [12 of 13 Infs comm types 4, 5]. **1965** *DARE* FW Addit **OK7,** *Jack shaft*—a long-wheelbase truck might have one or two "Jack [šævz]." **1969** *DARE* Tape **CA**128, But . . both shavs that I worked in [in a mine] are forty six hundred . . feet deep. **1981** *PADS* 67.25 **Mesabi Iron Range MN,** *Shafts*. . . The 16 Iron Range informants responding use either *shafts* or *shavs,* the usual terms with other Minnesota informants. **1983** *MJLF* 9.1.55 **ceKY** (as of 1956), *Shavs* . . shafts.

shag n[1] [*OED2* 1566 →]

Usu =**double-crested cormorant**, but also other **cormorants**.

1737 (1911) Brickell *Nat. Hist. NC* 212, The *Shag* is somewhat like the *Cormorant*, but much less [=smaller]. . . The Flesh is black, ill-tasted, and hard of digestion, being much of the same Nature with the *Cormorant*. **1796** Morse *Amer. Universal Geog.* 1.214, Shag—Pelicanus graculus. Cutler. **1872** Coues *Key to N. Amer. Birds* 302, Genus Graculus. . . *Common Cormorant. Shag.* . . Atlantic Coast of Europe and North America. **1917** (1923) *Birds Amer.* 1.97, The Cormorants have many local names, such as "Shag," "Lawyer," and "Nigger Goose." **1955** MA Audubon Soc. *Bulletin* 39.311 **ME, MA,** European Cormorant. . . Shag (Maine, Mass. In reference to the shaggy crest). . . Winter Shag (Maine). *Ibid* 312, Double-crested Cormorant. . . Shag (General). **1966** *DARE* (Qu. Q7, *Names and nicknames for . . game birds*) Inf **ME22,** Shag. **1975** Gould *ME Lingo* 249, Shag—Not a Maine exclusive, but because of the ubiquitous cormorant or *shag* that infests the Maine coast a very common word, in numerous allusions. It is inedible because of its exclusive diet of fish. Its worst offense is to clean out a pocket of herring awaiting transport. **1986** Rustad *I Married a Fisherman* 80 **AK,** The black cormorants . . are the most commonly seen of the sea birds. They're also called shags, or Norwegian turkeys.

shag v[1] [*OED2 shag* v.[4] 1 1851 →] Cf **shack** v[1]

To stroll, rove about; also with *out,* also in phrr *shag ass, it:* to make off, get going; hence n *shag* a stroll.

1928 *AmSp* 3.435, To "shag" means to amble along, saunter, or proceed: "I must shag down town and buy a drink," writes a Central Western correspondent. **1932** Farrell *Young Lonigan* 192 **Chicago IL,** He watched a familiar looking airedale dog shag about, snapping at the heels of the park sheep. **1950** Bissell *Stretch on River* 110 **Missip Valley,** After he loses his flock [of chickens] from mold or something . . he will shag ass for the river like a turtle flopping off a log. **1954** *WELS Suppl.,* Or a student may say to another, "Want to take a shag?" He is asking him to take a stroll. **1960** *AmSp* 38.270, Some of the student slang at Haskell corresponds quite closely to standard American school usage . . *shag* or *shag A[ss]* means 'to remove oneself from or leave a place.' **1964** *AmSp* 39.235 **KS,** Shag. . . To leave. **1966–69** *DARE* (Qu. Y18, *To leave in a hurry: "Before they find this out, we'd better _____!"*) Infs **GA77, TX37,** Shag out; (Qu. Y19, *To begin to go away from a place: "It's about time for me to _____."*) Inf **MI32,** Shag it; **OK28,** Shag out; (Qu. Y24, . . *To walk, to go on foot: "I can't get a ride, so I'll just have to _____."*) Inf **OR6,** Shag; (Qu. JJ26, *If somebody has been doing poor work or not enough, the boss might say, "If he wants to keep his job he'd better _____."*) Inf **MI32,** Shag it.

shag v[2] Cf **shack** v[2]

To chase, fetch; esp, to retrieve (stray balls); intr: to retrieve balls; to run an errand; hence nouns *shag(ger)* one who retrieves or fetches.

1910 *DN* 3.448 **wNY,** Shag. . . In boys' ball-games, to play in the outfield and return the ball. "You go and shag." *Shag.* . . In ball-games the boy who *shags* the ball. "I'll be shag." **1911** (1912) Claudy *Battle Base-ball* 318 **PA,** I was allowed to stand behind the catcher when the Factoryville team was playing, and "shag" foul balls. **1932** *AmSp* 7.403 [Orphanage argot], *Shag.* . . To chase. "All the guys'll be shagging rabbits." **1932** Farrell *Young Lonigan* 66 **Chicago IL,** He would have nightmares, and strange boys, like demons . . would come and lean over his bed . . until his old man came and shagged them away. **1938** Farrell *No Star* 15 **IL,** We had fun. Gettin' shagged by the guy for throwin' papers in front of the theater. **1940** (1942) Clark *Ox-Bow* 216 **NV,** Tetley sent two riders to help the Bartlett boys shag in the cattle they'd been holding. **1954** *WELS Suppl.,* A mail-shagger in our college slang is a mail-carrier. A senior might also say to a . . freshman . . , "Hey, kid, will you shag to town for me?" He is asking him to do an errand. **1989** Mosher *Stranger* 141 **nVT** (as of 1952), We went for crawdads and Frenchy LaMott came along and shagged us out on the trestle with rocks.

shag n[2] See **shag** v[2]

shag n[3] See **shag** v[1]

shag n[4] See **shack** n[4]

shag n[5] See **shack** n[5]

shag n[6] See **shad** 5

shag ass See **shag** v[1]

shagbark hickory n Also *shackbark, shadbark (hickory), shagbark, shag(gy)-barked hickory, shag* ~; also chiefly **NEng** *shagbark walnut* chiefly **NEng, N Cent, sAppalachians** See Map Cf **walnut**

Any of several **hickories B1,** but usu *Carya ovata;* also the fruit or wood of such a tree. For other names of *C. ovata* see **flying-barked hickory, kingnut, kiskitomas, redheart hickory, scaly bark, shellbark hickory, sweet walnut, upland hickory, white** ~, **walnut, white** ~

1743 (1751) Bartram *Observations* 67 **NY,** A great hill, cloathed with large *Magnolia* . . shagbark-hickory, chesnut and chesnut oak. **1777** in 1886 MA Hist. Soc. *Proc.* 2d ser 2.236 **RI,** [Buy me] a bushel or two of shagbarks. **1792** Belknap *Hist. NH* 3.100, *Walnut.* The American species of this genus, have been confounded by botanical writers. There are at least three in New-Hampshire. . . 2. *Shag-bark (juglans cineria?)* The wood of this tree is not so valuable as the white; but the fruit is preferable, being larger, and having a softer shell. **1802** *Thomas' MA Spy or Worcester Gaz.* (MA) 10 Mar, The growth of the shagbark walnuts has been remarkably slow. **1810** Michaux *Histoire des Arbres* 1.20 **NEng,** *Shell bark hickery* . . , nom le plus en usage dans tous les Etats-Unis. *Shag bark hickery,* dénomination secondaire au nord de la rivière de Connecticut. [=*Shell bark hickery* . . , the name most used throughout the United States. *Shag bark hickery,* a name of less importance, used north of the Connecticut River.] **1824** Elliott *Sketch* 2.625 **SC, GA,** One of the largest and most valuable trees of this genus [=*Carya*], remarkable for the exfoliation of the epidermis in old trees, whence it has acquired the name of shag or shaggy-barked Hickory. **1864** (1868) Trowbridge *3 Scouts* 134 **VT,** "Nuts, boys, nuts!" at length cried Jake. "We sha'n't starve now. Yonder's hickories. . . " "Shagbarks—that's what we call 'em in Vermont!" **1892** Torrey *Foot-Path Way* 225 **NEng,** Our annual wild crop—blueberries, huckleberries, blackberries, cherries, grapes, pig-nuts (a bad name for a good thing), shagbarks, acorns, and so forth. **1897** Sudworth *Arborescent Flora* 113 **VT,** *Hicoria ovata.* . . Common names. . . Shagbark Walnut. **1941** *LANE* Map 277 *(Walnut shell)* **NEng,** 14 infs, Shagbark(s); 1 inf, Shagbarks, homemade walnuts; 1 inf, Shagbarks, large: you have to pound the hide off'n 'em; 1 inf, Shagbarks, 'a little mite different' from walnuts (can be opened without a hammer); 1 inf, Shackbarks . . shagbarks, 'The kind you buy'; 1 inf, Shagbarks ('proper' pron.)—Shackbarks (usual pron.); 8 infs, Shagbark walnut; 1 inf, Shadbark walnut, wood used to make wheel spokes; 1 inf, Shagbark walnut = hickory nut; 1 inf, Shagbark hickory. **1950** *WELS,* 1 Inf, **csWI,** Hickory nut (shagbark). **1965–70** *DARE* (Qu. T16, . . *Kinds of trees . . 'special'*) 17 Infs, 11 **N Cent,** Shagbark hickory; **AL11, CT40, IL26, MD29, TN37,** Shagbark; **CT9,** Shadbark or shagbark hickory different from shadblow hickory; [**IN49,** Shadybark hickory;] **MA25,** Shadbark—called shad; **MA42,** Shagbark—the regular walnut tree = the shagbark; **SC4,** Shag hickory; (Qu. I43, *What kinds of nuts grow wild around here?*) Infs **MA5, 37, 42, 74, ME5,** Shagbark walnut(s); **CT12,** Shagbark nuts (type of walnut); **CT17,** Hickory nuts: Shagbark—best; **MD30,** Shellbark or shagbark—like hickory tree, but rougher bark—grows only in creek bottoms; **MA68,** Shagbark—also called hickory; **NH5,** Shagbark (a hickory nut).

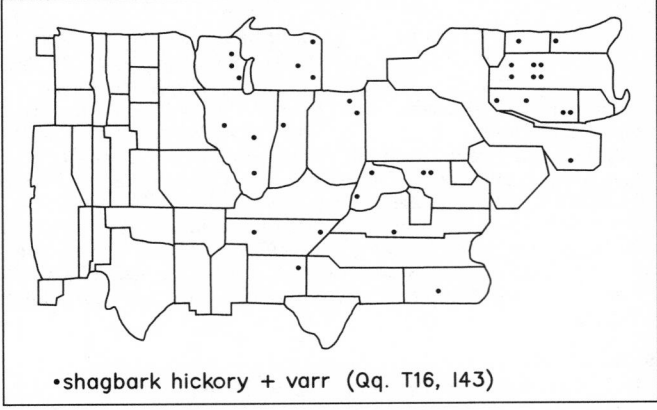

•shagbark hickory + varr (Qq. T16, I43)

shag-fishing See **shack** n[5] 1

shag fly See **shad fly**

shagger See **shag** v[2]

shagging See **shacking**

shaggy-barked hickory See **shagbark hickory**

shaggy bear n
A **milky cap** (here: *Lactarius representaneus*).
   1987 McKnight–McKnight *Mushrooms* 334, Shaggy bear—*Lactarius representaneus*. . . Large, *sticky, yellow cap;* surface *scaly,* with a *hairy margin.*

shaggymane n Also *shaggy-mane(d) mushroom*
A **mushroom B1** (here: *Coprinus comatus*).   Also called **inky cap, ~ egg, horsetail agaric**
   1885 Palmer *Mushrooms Amer.* Pl.2, [Caption:] Shaggy-Maned Mushroom. **1911** *Century Dict. Suppl.,* Shaggy-mane. . . A common edible fungus, *Coprinus comatus,* having a white pileus covered with shaggy appressed scales and black deliquescent gills. **1925** *Book of Rural Life* 6.3722, The *shaggy-mane or ink-cap, mushroom,* a common inhabitant of lawns, that is edible when young and may be recognized by the shaggy top. **1942** Hylander *Plant Life* 56, The black-spored mushrooms belong to the genus *Coprinus.* . . The Shaggy Mane is a species with yellowish scales on its cap. **1964** Kingsbury *Poisonous Plants U.S.* 96, Fisher . . records symptoms of intoxication following ingestion of *Coprinus comatus* . . the shaggy mane . . generally considered one of the better edible species. **1966–70** *DARE* (Qu. I37, *Small plants shaped like an umbrella that grow in woods and fields—which are safe to eat*) Inf MN36, Shaggymane; (Qu. S18) Inf CA155, Shaggymane; MI120, Shaggymanes—tall, white, umbrella-like; (Qu. S26e) Inf WA15, Shaggymane—grows where there's been forest fire. **1980** Marteka *Mushrooms* 172, The shaggy-mane mushroom *(Coprinus comatus)* has a cap that would arouse the envy of the shako-crowned honor guard at Buckingham Palace. The cap is barrel-shaped when young, is white to pewter in color, and has shaggy "hairs," which is why the mushroom is called shaggy-mane.

shag hickory See **shagbark hickory**

shag it See **shag** v[1]

shagpoke n Also *shackpoke, shadpoke* [Varr of **shitepoke B1**]
Any of var herons; also a **bittern;** see quots.
   1931–33 *LANE Worksheets* CT, 1 inf, Shag poke—shite poke; 1 inf, Shad poke . . a big bird. **1942** in 1945 McAtee *Nomina Abitera* 26 **CA,** Great Blue Heron . . shadpoke, shagpoke, Cedarville, California . . letter, Feb 16, 1942. **1945** *Ibid* 26 **GA,** Louisiana Heron. . . Little Blue Heron. . . Shagpoke, Savannah, Ga. *Ibid* 27 **FL, MS,** Green Heron. . . Shackpoke, Okechobee, Florida . . shagpoke, North Central Mississippi. *Ibid* 29 **OR,** American Bittern. . . shagpoke, Burns, Oregon . . [shag, probably a shortening of this term is sent from Big River, Saskatchewan.]

shagpoke gut See **shitepoke B6**

shagpoll n
=**hooded merganser.**
   1824 Latham *Genl. Hist. Birds* 10.208 **GA,** [Hooded Merganser]. . . called at Hudson's Bay, Omiska sheep; in Georgia, Shag Pole, Cotton Head, or Hairy Head; comes there in the winter. . . is a great diver. **1955** *Oriole* 8.5, Hooded Merganser. . . [also called] *Shag-poll* (in reference to the ample crest).

shagtail n
See quot.
   1899 (1912) Green *VA Folk-Speech* 378, Shagtail. . . A snapping turkle.

shake v
Std senses, var forms.
1 past: usu |šuk|; also:
a |šʌk|; pronc-spp *shu(c)k.* **chiefly Sth, S Midl**
   1838 *S. Lit. Messenger* 4.405 **GA,** So I went round the tree and shuk a vush [sic for *bush*] and fetch'd a squall. **1844** Thompson *Major Jones's Courtship* 12 **GA,** Miss Mary looked mighty sort o' redish when I shuck her hand. **1893** Shands *MS Speech* 56, Shuk [šək]. Negro for *shook.* **1899** Chesnutt *Conjure Woman* 26 **csNC** [Black], Henry's marster shuck his head. **1899** (1912) Green *VA Folk-Speech* 385, Shuck. . . Perfect tense of the verb to *shake.* "He shuck down the apples." For *shook:* "I shuck hands with him." **1903** *DN* 2.329 **seMO,** *Shuck,* pret. and *pp.* of

shake. 'We shuck hands all round.' **1907** *DN* 3.236 **nwAR,** *Shuck,* pret. and *pp.* of shake. Shook, shaken. **1908** Fox *Lonesome Pine* 61 **KY,** Yes, Rufe's going away agin and they shuk hands. **1909** *DN* 3.369 **eAL, wGA,** *Shuck,* pret. and *pp.* of *shake.* **1913** Johnson *Highways St. Lawrence to VA* 192 **nNJ,** Apples are so plenty. . . We shuck ours right off. **1923** *DN* 5.220 **swMO,** *Shuk.* . . Shook. **1927** Kennedy *Gritny* 136 **sLA** [Black], It kep' up de whole time . . till I got hyuh an' shuck you' wake. **1931** *PMLA* 46.1319 **sAppalachians,** The strong preterite with change of vowel is common: . . "shuck" (shook). **1932** Randolph *Ozark Mt. Folks* 61, Then ever'body shuck hands. **1940** (1941) Bell *Swamp Water* 153 **Okefenokee GA,** After [a] while we shuck the sand offn the quilt. **1941** *AmSp* 16.6 **eTX** [Black], *Shook* . . [šʌk]. **1942** Hall *Smoky Mt. Speech* 37 **wNC, eTN,** Often . . one hears a distinct [ʌ] in . . *shook.* **1967** *DARE* FW Addit **GA**19, "Shook" is consistently "shuck" [šʌk]

b *shaked, shaken(ed).* **esp Sth, S Midl**
   1884 *Anglia* 7.253 [Black], To the regular forms of the Irregular verbs as used by the whites, the Negro adds the following forms of his own. . . *Pres.* shake—*Past.* shuck, . . shaked, shaken-ed (I shaken de tree). **1928** in 1944 *ADD* **WV,** Shaked. . . Shook. **1940** Faulkner *Hamlet* 38 **MS,** The mule had taken the weight of it when Ab shaken out the whip. *Ibid* 49 **MS,** So I just drove under the first roof I come to and shaken Ab awake. **1965** *DARE* (Qu. Y17, *When two people agree to stop fighting and not be enemies any more . . "I hear they _____."*) Inf **OK**50, Shaked hands and made up. **1986** Pederson *LAGS Concordance* (Oats is *thrashed*) 1 inf, seAL, Shaked them.

c *shooken.*
   1898 *Century Illustr. Mag.* 56.319 [Black], It done shooken up de las' nerve I got. **1901** in 2002 (acc) De Forest *Downing Legends* 180 (Internet), An' right among the raree-shows,/ . . / The Flyin' Dutchman's near relations,/ Who shooken hands an' offered cheers. *Ibid* viii, *Shooken hands.* Surviving in country usage fifty or sixty years ago.

2 past pple, ppl adj: usu *shaken, shook;* also:
a *shooken.*
   1868 (1869) Ward *Gates Ajar* 138 **MA,** She's all shooken up, somehow. **1891** *Overland Mth.* (2d ser) 17.135, So after she'd spoke to us all . . an' shooken hands with us . . , she sot right down. **1986** Pederson *LAGS Concordance* ([They are in] *mourning*) 1 inf, ceGA, All shooken up. [Inf is Black] **1994** Bolton *Gal* 119 **seSC** [Black], Sylvie was shooken up, knowing that we was going to run away and leave her behind.

b *shuck(ed), shuk.* **chiefly Sth, S Midl**
   1858 Hammett *Piney Woods Tavern* 133, When it's been shuk up on a York cart. **1871** Eggleston *Hoosier Schoolmaster* 130 **sIN,** He felt "consid'able shuck up like." **1903** [see **1a** above]. **1906** Johnson *Highways Missip. Valley* 93 **TN** [Black], She tol' him she ain't shuck hands wid nobody. **1907** [see **1a** above]. **1909** [see **1a** above]. **1913** Kephart *Highlanders* 80 **sAppalachians,** You'll get some o' that meanness shuck outen you if you tackle an old she-bear. **1966–68** *DARE* (Qu. DD14, *When a person is partly drunk, "He's _____."*) Inf **SC**10, All shucked up; (Qu. GG7, . . *Annoyed or upset: "Though we were only ten minutes late, she was all _____."*) Inf **SC**10, Shucked up; **GA**19, 30, Shuck up; (Qu. GG11, *To be quite anxious about something . . "The letter hasn't come and he's _____."*) Inf **GA**19 Shuck up; (Qu. GG23c, . . *Expressions [to tell someone to be patient]*) Inf **GA**19, Don't get all shuck up; (Qu. GG28, *To be very pleased or happy about something: "She managed to come home for Christmas, and everybody was _____ to see her."*) Inf **SC**10, All shucked up; (Qu. GG35b, *[To sulk or pout:] "Because she couldn't go, she's been _____ all day."*) Inf **SC**10, Shucked up. **1967** *DARE* FW Addit **GA**19, I got all shuck up. **1982** Slone *How We Talked* 53 **eKY** (as of c1950), No man would ever break a promise after he had "shuck hands on it."

shake n[1]
1 also *shakes:* An earthquake; an earth tremor.
   1705 *Boston News–Letter* (MA) 25 June–2 July 2/2, There was felt in this Town a small shake of an Earthquake. [**1847** Cumings *Western Pilot* 142 (*DA*), The neighborhood of that once little lake is now called 'The Shakes.' The earthquake put a mark on that place which time only will eradicate.] **1903** *DN* 2.329 **seMO,** Shake. . . Earthquake. 'The sand-blows came up during the New Madrid shakes.' **1907** *DN* 3.236 **nwAR,** Shake. . . Earthquake. **1907** *Westminster Gaz.* 13 Apr 3/2, That earthquake at San Francisco—the 'shake,' as the local papers lightheartedly called it within a fortnight. **1931** *AmSp* 6.335 [Circus and carnival slang], An earthquake. . . "I hear they had a little shakes over in Los An-

geles yesterday." **1937** in 1972 *Amer. Slave* 2.212 **SC,** It wuz de year of de 'shake'. . . It wuz dark and we wuz eatin' supper, when sumpin started to makin' de dishes fall out'n de cupboard. . . She tole us dat it wuz er earthquake and it wasn't no day o' Judgement. **1949** *Los Angeles Times* (CA) 14 May sec 1 1/4, Newspaper and police switchboards were flooded immediately with requests for information on the shake. **c1960** *Wilson Coll.* **csKY,** Shake. . . Earthquake. **1994** NC *Lang. & Life Project Dial. Dict. Lumbee Engl.* 11 **seNC,** Since the shake. . . In a long time. This expression originated shortly after the 19th century earthquake in Charleston, South Carolina, which was felt in Robeson County. *I haven't seen you since the shake.*

2 A party, esp a **house-rent party.** Cf **shakedown 2**

1932 in 1975 Albertson *Bessie Smith* 54 [Black], [In song "Safety Mama":] Give your house rent shake on Saturday night. **1946** Blesh *Shining Trumpets* 303 **Chicago IL,** The great South Side institution of "rent party" (locally known as "skiffle," "shake," or "percolator"). **1968** *DARE* (Qu. FF4, *Names and joking names for different kinds of dancing parties*) Inf **GA**36, Shake (teenagers). **1975** *AmSp* 50.65 **AR** (as of c1970), Shake. . . Party—"There's a shake at Jim's house."

shake n[2] See **salt shake**

shake a foot v phr Also *shake a hoof, ~ leg*
To dance.

1805 (1904) Lewis *Orig. Jrls. Lewis & Clark Exped.* 2.187, Such as were able to shake a foot amused themselves in dancing on the green. **1848** in 1965 *AmSp* 40.132, I ax'd her would she hab a dance. . . I taught dat I might get a chance, To shake a foot wid her. **1872** *Harper's New Mth. Mag.* 45.516 **sAppalachians,** That young lady signified her willingness to shake a foot to any tune that could be started. **1924** (1946) Greer-Petrie *Angeline Gits an Eyeful* 15 **csKY,** When the music started, she wuz the fust one on the floor to *shake a foot.* **1927** Lewis *Elmer Gantry* 373, Come on, Reverend. I bet you can shake a hoof as good as anybody! The wife says she's going dance with you! **1942** McAtee *Dial. Grant Co. IN* 55 (as of 1890s), Shake a leg . . . hurry; also dance. Slang. *Shake one's feet* . . same meaning as the last; in the sense of "to dance", both are recorded from Va. **1944** Adams *Western Words* 141, *Shakin' a hoof*—Dancing. **1950** *WELS (Names and joking names for different kinds of dancing parties)* 1 Inf, **cwWI,** Shake a leg.

shake a lonesome See **lonesome B3**

shaked See **shake** v **1b**

shakedown n
1 A makeshift bed, usu one made up on the floor; also transf. [*OED2* c1730 →] **chiefly Nth** See Map *old-fash* Cf **pallet**

1837 *S. Lit. Messenger* 3.477 **NEast,** Come to see me when I get my cottage built, and you shall have . . a shake-down of straw. **1887** in 1950 *AmSp* 25.37, Shakedown. A lodging for a night. . . 'Couldn't give me a shakedown in some institution . . ?' **1926** *DN* 5.389 **ME,** Shakedown. . . Temporary or improvised bed; a slighting reference to any form of bed. "Can you give me a shake-down for the night?" Common. **1929** Bell *Some Contrib. KS Vocab.* 92, Shake-down. . . A temporary bed made on the floor. **1930** Shoemaker *1300 Words* 59 **cPA Mts** (as of c1900), Shake-down—Bed clothes laid on straw on the floor. **1936** Adams *Cowboy Lingo* 37, The cowboy's bed was made of blankets and . . heavy comforts. . . carried rolled in a 'tarpaulin,' . . [and] called by the various names of 'lay,' . . 'shake-down,' . . or 'flea trap.' **1949** *PADS* 11.26 **CO,** Shake-down. . . A bed made on the floor with pillows and covers. **1950** *WELS (A temporary or emergency bed made up on the floor)* 8 Infs, **WI,** Shakedown. **1953** Randolph–Wilson *Down in Holler* 282 **Ozarks,** Shake-down. . . A makeshift bed, a pallet laid on the floor. **1965–70** *DARE* (Qu. E18, *A temporary or emergency bed made up on the floor*) 10 Infs, **scattered Nth,** Shakedown; **MI**115, **NY**9, 128, 205, 215, Shakedown [FW sugg]; **IA**9, Shakedown—way back; **IL**3, Shakedown—heard but not used; **MI**51, Shakedown—never heard, only read about them; **MI**68, Shakedown—I think that's what I've heard; **NY**65, Shakedown—has heard in reference to camping—an old blanket, under the sleeping bag. [16 of 20 Infs old] **1971** Wood *Vocab. Change* 49 **Sth,** When there are more overnight guests than beds, a host and hostess may improvise beds on the floor. The only name of major importance for these beds is *pallet.* . . *shakedown* [is] reported only [three times] in Tennessee and Oklahoma. **1973** Allen *LAUM* 1.230 **Upper MW** (as of c1950), *Pallet* (bed on the floor). . . Although most infs. have no name for a temporary bed on the floor, the 35 infs. using *pallet* exhibit a clear South Midland distribution. . . Competing *shakedown,* though with only 20 occurrences [8 **ND,** 5 **IA,** 4 **SD,** 3 **MN,** 0 **NE**], has a suggestively

Northern distribution. [The term is] usually considered old-fashioned if known at all. **1995** Brophy *Coll.* 66 **swMO** (as of c1960), Shakedown. [A] pallet, a bed on the floor. "[T]wo bundles of straw are shaken down for his accommodation" (Scott).

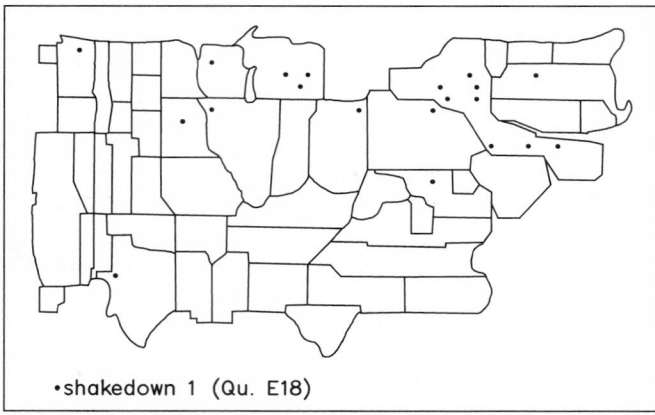

•shakedown 1 (Qu. E18)

2 also *shakedown dance:* A boisterous dance or dancing party. Cf **breakdown, kitchen dance, shake** n[1] **2**

1845 *Xenia Torchlight* 31 July 1/7 *(DAE),* The organ struck up, from which he concluded that some sort of 'shake down' was about to commence. **1908** Sinclair *Metropolis* 207, When he felt like dancing a shakedown, he could take a run out to God's country. **1941** *LANE* Map 410 *(A dance)* 3 infs, **MA, NH,** Shake-down. **1945** Saxon *Gumbo Ya-Ya* 489 **LA,** Ever since that day he's been drinkin' whiskey and makin' women do shake-down dances. Them is dances where you slide back and pull up your dress; show your linen, you know. **1954** *Harder Coll.* **cwTN,** Shake-down. . . A play or dance. **1986** Pederson *LAGS Concordance (A dance)* 1 inf, **cwGA,** Shakedowns.

shake hands with v phr Cf **howdy 2**
To greet, pay respects to; to be formally introduced to.

1906 *DN* 3.155 **nwAR,** Shake hands with. . . To be introduced to. "Mr. James, (I want you to) shake hands with my friend, Col. Caldwell." **1912** Green *VA Folk-Speech* 378, Shake hands. . . As when people speak to each other: "Shake-hands with cousin May." **1957** Battaglia *Resp. to PADS 20* **eMD,** Shake hands with—Someone introduces you: "Shake hands with John Smith." **c1960** *Wilson Coll.* **csKY,** Shake hands with. . . Meet, get acquainted with. **1960** Criswell *Resp. to PADS 20* **Ozarks,** Shake hands with. . . Get acquainted with, get an introduction to. . . "John Smith, this is _____; shake hands with _____." **1966** *DARE* (Qu. II4, *When people . . ask to be introduced to someone—for example: "I'd like to _____ John Smith."*) Inf **MT**1, Shake hands with.

shaken(ed) See **shake** v **1b**

shaker n
1 also *flour shaker:* A flour sieve. *old-fash*

1939 *LANE* Map 134 *(Flour sieve)* 1 inf, **seNH,** Shaker, older term; 1 inf, **ceMA,** Shaker. **1966–68** *DARE* (Qu. F8, *The kitchen utensil that you pass flour through*) Infs **NY**36, 43, **OH**36, Flour shaker; **WA**11, Shaker. [All Infs old]
2 See **Shaker bonnet.**

Shaker v [In allusion to the frugal habits of the *Shakers*]
1936 Carmer *Listen Drum* 124 **eNY, NEng,** And to this day in portions of York State and New England children are urged to "Shaker" their plates (eat them clean).

Shaker bonnet n Also *Shaker (straw bonnet)* [*Shaker* a member of the celibate, communal "Society of Believers in Christ's Second Appearing," brought to the US in 1774] *old-fash*
A plain bonnet or sunbonnet, esp one made from straw and having a cloth cape attached to drape over the shoulders.

1849 Howitt *Our Cousins in OH* 140, The girls wore . . a very peculiar straw bonnet, called a Shaker-bonnet, with a buff cotton curtain behind, and no ribbon excepting for strings. **1858** in 1862 Colt *Went to KS* 238 **NYC** (as of 1835), I did not wear the green silk calash, but a shaker, made of brown muslin smoothed over a pasteboard frame; it was very fashionable; besides it kept the sun out of my face, and was very genteel for a school-ma'am. **1909** *DN* 3.415 **nME,** *Shaker.* . . A palm leaf sun-bonnet. **c1916** in 1932 *AmSp* 7.170 **NE** (as of c1860), Shakers, a kind of straw bonnet having a cape of light cloth material surounding [sic] it like the lower part of a cloth sunbonnet. **1931–33** *LANE Worksheets* **RI,** *Shaker.* . . Kind of sunbonnet made of straw, had a cape attached. **1932–34** *Hanley Disks* **CT,** [Speaking of bonnets women made for themselves:] They used to call em Shaker bonnets. **1950** *WELS (A cloth bonnet worn by women for protection from the sun)* 1 Inf, **seWI,** Shakers—made of cloth. Were made of gingham or calico. Made like one-half of stovepipe cut in half lengthwise. Stretched very stiff or stiff-ened with cardboard which was put on beak to extend several inches over back of head as well [as] over face. Then some buttons put on and the buttons at back to which ruffle was buttoned that would drape over shoulders. To wash[,] cardboard would be removed[,] replaced into slots or heavily starched ridge. **1968–69** *DARE* (Qu. W2, . . *A cloth bonnet worn by women for protection from the sun*) Inf **MA57,** Shaker bon-net—no longer in use; **NY73A,** Shaker bonnet—old-fashioned; **NY214,** Shaker bonnet [FW sugg]. **1977** Neal *KY Shakers* [foll p46] (as of 19th cent), [Caption:] Kentucky Shaker straw bonnet. [*DARE* Ed: Photo shows a deeply hooded headpiece of straw, with a fabric cap attached to the bottom edge to cover the shoulders.]

shaker fork See **shaking fork**

Shaker straw bonnet See **Shaker bonnet**

shakes See **shake** n 1

shake the dew off one's lily v phr
Of a man: to urinate.
1966–67 *DARE* FW Addit **AL,** "I've got to shake the dew off my lily"—to urinate (male); **sIL,** *Shake the dew off one's lily* = urinate. . . Used among men; probably "on the way out"—men over forty. **2000** *DARE* File **IA,** My grandfather used to say he was going to shake the dew off his lily.

shake-up n Also *shake-up bed*
A makeshift bed; a **shakedown 1.**
1924 Raine *Land of Saddle-Bags* 74 **sAppalachians,** They divide up the bedding and make shake-up beds upon the floor every night. **1969** *DARE* (Qu. E18, *A temporary or emergency bed made up on the floor*) Inf **IL53,** Shake-up.

shaking ague n Also *shaking ague-fit* [*DA(E)* "Obs."] **esp Sth, S Midl** Cf **ague, dumb ague**
A high fever accompanied by convulsive chills; a fit of trem-bling.
1720 (1882) *MA Hist. Soc. Coll.* 5th ser 7.238 **MA,** My wife had a very bad night. . . had such a shaking Ague-Fit. **1835** Longstreet *GA Scenes* 210, Nancy was cured sound and well . . of a hard shakin' ager. **1856** Cartwright *Autobiog.* 433 **KY,** On my way . . I was suddenly taken ill with a real shaking ague in a large . . prairie . . and shook so severely that I could not sit in my sulky. **1899** (1912) Green *VA Folk-Speech* 379, *Shakin-ague.* . . A very violent ague. "Joe had a sheking ager yistiddy." **1903** *DN* 2.329 **seMO,** *Shaking-ague.* . . Ague accompanied by shivering. It is 'dumb ague' when no shivering occurs. **1967–69** *DARE* (Qu. BB13, . . *Chills and fever*) Infs **DE3, NC77,** Shaking agers; [**OH15,** Shaking of ague;] (Qu. DD22, . . *Delirium tremens*) Inf **NC61,** Shaking agers.

shaking disease See **shaking palsy**

shaking fork n Also *shaker fork* [Cf *OED2* shakefork "A wooden fork with two tines or prongs used by threshers to shake and remove the straw from the grain. . . Now *dial.*"] **esp PA**
See quots.
1854 *PA State Ag. Soc. Report* 1.81, Joseph Bruederly exhibited two shaking forks. **1889** *AN&Q* 4.60 **PA** (as of 1820s), It [=grass cut for hay] was then scattered with a hay fork, or *shaking fork,* and left to dry. **1968** *DARE* (Qu. L32a, *In early days, how was the grain separated from the straw?*) Inf **PA141,** Shaker fork.

shaking palsy n Also *shaking disease*
Parkinson's disease or a similar condition characterized by tremors.
1852 Beardsley *Reminiscences* 192 **NY,** I hunted with him after he was eighty years old; and though very much afflicted with . . shaking palsy, he managed to shoot a fox. **1888** *Century Illustr. Mag.* 35.571

sIL, Lazar Brown had shaking-palsy . . and, being good for nothing else, could devote his entire time to . . gossip. **1942** (1971) Campbell *Cloud-Walking* 137 **seKY,** He was up in years and had the shaking disease. **1943** *LANE* Map 505, 1 inf, **csVT,** Shaking palsy; 1 inf, **nwVT,** Shaking palsy—a nervous disease. **1968** *DARE* (Qu. BB13, . . *Chills and fever*) Inf **MN38,** Shaking palsy—the old people get. **1990** Cavender *Folk Med. Lexicon* 31 **csAppalachians,** *Shaking palsy*—Parkinson's disease.

shale ice n Also *shale* [Engl dial *shale* flake, scale] Cf **shell n[1] 3**
The first thin ice that forms on the surface of a pond or pool.
1971 Wood *Vocab. Change* 33, A large part of the Interior South does experience freezing weather. When a thin covering of ice forms on ponds, the common term is *skim;* its next nearest competitor is *shale ice.* Scattered instances of . . *shale* . . are recorded. **1973** Gawthrop *Dial. Calumet* 77 **nwIN,** *First thin layer of ice on lake or pond* . . shale ice 3 [of 125 infs].

shaller See **shallow**

Shall-I-go-naked n [Cf *EDD* shalligonaked sb. 2 "A thin, flimsy garment; cloth of an inferior kind."] Cf **Naked City**
1970 *DARE* (Qu. C34, *Nicknames for nearby settlements, villages, or districts*) Inf **MA100,** Shall-I-go-naked—a neighborhood—hardscrabble kind of place.

shallon n [Of Chinook origin; cf **salal**] **chiefly Pacific NW** =**salal.**
[**1806** (1905) Lewis *Orig. Jrls. Lewis & Clark Exped.* 4.12 **OR,** The native fruits and buries in uce among the Indians of this neighbourhood [=the Clatsops] are a deep purple burry about the size of a small cherry called by them Shal-lun [etc].] [**1814** Pursh *Flora Americae* 1.284 **OR, WA,** This elegant evergreen shrub is in high esteem among the natives, on account of its berries, which they call *Shallon.*] **1866** Lindley-Moore *Treas. Botany* 522, The Shallon or Salal of the north-west coast of America. **1946** Peattie *Pacific Coast* 71, Everywhere in these lower woods you see shallon or salal, a fine shrub whose berries are a chief vegetable in the diet of many of the Indian tribes, and are made by white settlers into pies. **1959** Carleton *Index Herb. Plants* 105, *Shallon:* Gaultheria procumbens.

shallot n Usu |ʃə'lɑt|, |'ʃælət|; also |'ʃɛlət, 'ʃɛlot, 'sælot| for addit varr see **A** below Pronc-spp *shalot, shellot, shelloat*
A Forms.
1909 *DN* 3.368 **eAL, wGA,** *Shellot.* . . Shallot. Universal. **1941** *LANE* Map 258 *(Scallion, spring onion)* 2 infs, **MA, NY,** [ʃaɫaˑt]; 1 inf, **ceMA,** [ʃɔlaˑt]; 1 inf, **ceMA,** [ʃælət]; 1 inf, **seMA,** [ʃaˑɫt]. **1965–70** *DARE* (Qu. I6) 23 Infs, **chiefly Sth, S Midl,** ['ʃælət(s), -ɪt(s)]; 21 Infs, **Sth, S Midl,** ['ʃɛlət(s), -ɑt(s)]; **LA15, 40, MI34, 68, OH38, TX12, 37,** [ʃɛˈlɑt, ʃə'lɑt]; **LA3, 20, 23, 43,** ['ʃɑlɪt(s), -ət(s)]; **MS35, TX4, VA13,** ['ʃælɑt]; **AR3, FL36, MS72,** [ʃɛˈlot]; **MS63, TN13,** ['ʃɪlɑt(s)]; **AL14,** ['ʃɛl,lɑk]; **GA72,** ['ʃɛl,auts]; **GA81,** ['ʃɪ'lɪts]; **IL77,** ['ʃə'lʌts]; **MS13,** ['ʃɑulɑts]; **MS73,** [ʃə'ruts]; **NY66,** [sæ'lʌts] [sic]; **NC10,** ['ʃæɫouts]; **TX13,** ['ʃæləps]; (Qu. I5) 13 Infs, **Sth, S Midl,** ['ʃælɛt(s), -ɪt(s)]; **AL27, 43, 58, AR52, 55, LA2, 15,** ['ʃɛlət(s), -ɑt(s)]; **AL60, NC8, 12, 81, 84,** ['ʃælo(ʊ)ts]; **AL6, MI34, 53,** [ʃɛˈlɑt, ʃə-]; **AL14, TN52, TX26,** ['ʃɛlɑk(s)]; **FL6,** [ʃɛˈlot]; **LA11,** ['ʃɛlouts]; **NC18,** [ʃə'louts]; **RI5,** ['ʃɑlɪt]; **TX4,** ['ʃælɑts]; **TX54,** ['ʃɑlɑt]; **TX89,** ['ʃælɑts]. **1966** *DARE* [see **B** below]. **1989** Pederson *LAGS Tech. Index* 189 **Gulf Region,** 39 infs, [ʃæl(l)ət(s)]; 28 infs, [ʃɛlət(s)]; 24 infs, [ʃɛlot(s)]; 22 infs, [ʃɛləts]; 17 infs, [ʃælɪt(s)]; 11 infs, [ʃælɪt(s)]; 7 infs, [ʃɛlot(s)]; 5 infs, [ʃɑlɪts]; 4 infs, [ʃælɑt(s)]; 4 infs, [ʃɑlɑts]; 2 infs, [ʃɛlʌt(s)]; 2 infs, [ʃæloz]; 2 infs, [ʃʌlat, ʃʌlot]; 2 infs, [ʃɑlat, ʃɑlot].
B Sense.
Also *shallot onion:* An **onion** n B: either *Allium ascalonicum* or a **scallion.** [*OED2* 1664 →] **chiefly Sth, S Midl, TX** See Map on p. 876 and Map Section Cf **bunch onion, green ~ 1, multiplying ~**
1709 (1967) Lawson *New Voyage* 97 **NC, SC,** The Garden-Roots that thrive well in Carolina are Carrots . . Onions, Shallot, Garlick [etc]. **1821** Cobbett *Amer. Gardener* 262, *Shalot.*—A little sort of Onion, which is taken up in the fall and kept for winter use. Each plant multi-plies itself in the summer by adding offsets all round it. **1847** (1852) Crowen *Amer. Cookery* 189, Shalots, or Green Onions. **1863** Burr *Field & Garden* 143, The Shallot (sometimes written Eschalot). . . The root of the plant is composed of numerous small bulbs, united at their base; the whole being enclosed in a thin skin. **1886** Ebbutt *Emigrant Life* 72 **KS,**

Wild onions, or shallots, were very plentiful. **1912** Green *VA Folk-Speech* 379, *Shallot. . . A small onion.* **1941** *LANE* Map 258 (*Scallion, spring onion*) 1 inf, **seMA**, Shallot. **1946** *PADS* 6.26 **eNC**, Shelloats ['ʃɛl'ots]:. . . *Shallots.* Pamlico. Formerly common among gardeners. **1950** *WELS* (*The kind of onions that last from year to year*) 1 Inf, **WI**, Shallots; [1 Inf, **KY**, Shellots;] (*The kind of onions that are served raw early in the year*) 2 Infs, **WI**, Shallots. **1965–70** *DARE* (Qu. 16, *The kind of onions that come up fresh early in the year, and you eat them raw*) 76 Infs, **chiefly Sth, S Midl, TX**, Shallots; **AR**51, Shallot onions; **KY**34, Tall shallots; **LA**2, Shallots—also called multiplying onions; **LA**28, Shallots—same as multiplying onions; (Qu. I5, *. . Kind of onions that keep coming up without replanting year after year*) 43 Infs, **chiefly Sth, S Midl, TX**, Shallot(s); **LA**15, Shallots—same as multiplying onions; **KY**85, Winter shallots; **NC**81, Shallots—a lot of people use as flavoring; **NC**84, Shallots—very little, really; have button on them which is really an onion seed which they grow back from; **TX**89, Shallots—multiplying onions; **TX**105, Shallot onions; (Qu. I7, *The small plants like onions with hollow green leaves that are cut up in a salad*) 10 Infs, **chiefly Sth, S Midl**, Shallot(s); (Qu. I35, *. . Kitchen herbs . . grown and used in cooking around here*) Infs **LA**11, 43, Shallots; (Qu. L34, *. . Most important crops grown around here*) Inf **LA**44, Shallots. **1966** Dakin *Dial. Vocab. Ohio R. Valley* 2.367, The other "spring onions" are perennial or grow from sets planted in the fall. Numerous bulbils develop, each of which grows a new blade in the very early spring. These therefore grow in clusters. . . *Shallot (onion)* and the rare *scallion* seem most often to be names for the new blade which appears in the spring. **1966** *DARE* Tape **AL**4, [FW:] You got a different name for that early onion? Is there a special name for that? [Inf:] Well, there's onions were referred to as nest onions sometimes, or shallots ['ʃɛl,ats]. . . In those days it usually, it was ['ʃɛlɨts] or nest onions. Actually, the old shallot ['ʃɛl,at], we called it, was one of the first type that I remember, because it was a hardy plant; it would live the year round pretty well. **1976** Bailey-Bailey *Hortus Third* 787, Most shallots are used as green onions since the mature bulbs are small, and, in fact, in some areas any green bunching onion is called a shallot, regardless of species. **1986** Pederson *LAGS Concordance* **Gulf Region,** 250 infs, Shallot(s); 10 infs, Shallot onion(s); 1 inf, Shallot—a little onion in bunches; 1 inf, Shallot = green onion; 1 inf, Shallot—pull up, fry green, grow in clusters; 1 inf, Shallots—too strong to use; 1 inf, Shallots = little multipliers; 1 inf, Shallots—live all winter; 1 inf, Shallots—larger than nest onions; 1 inf, Shallots = nest onions; 1 inf, Shallots—they have buttons—not winter onions; 1 inf, Shallots—not green onions, not onions or garlic; 1 inf, Shallots—cross between onion and garlic; 1 inf, Shallot onion—green onion, but grows in bunch; 1 inf, Shallot onion—has buttons that are replanted.

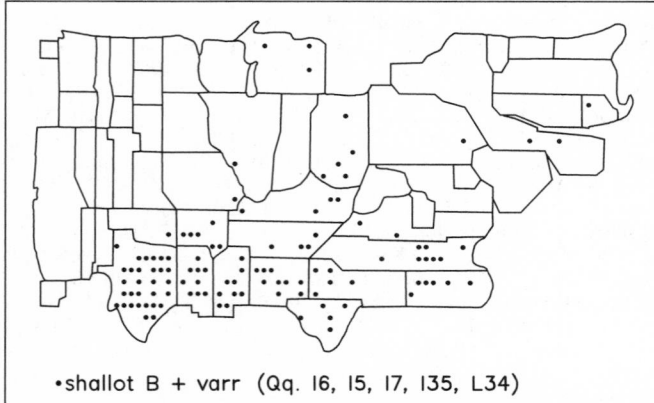

•shallot B + varr (Qq. I6, I5, I7, I35, L34)

shallow n, v, adj Usu |'ʃælo|; also **chiefly S Midl** |'ʃælə(r)|; for addit varr see quots Pronc-spp *shaller, shally* Cf Intro "Language Changes" IV.1.c, Pronc Intro 3.1.12.d

A Forms.

1867 *Atlantic Mth.* 20.551 **NEng**, I took to hevin' my porridge in a shaller plate. **1891** *DN* 1.164 **cNY**, [ʃælr] < shallow. **1895** [see **B** below]. **1902** *DN* 2.245 **sIL**, *Shaller.* . . Not full. Scant measure. **1906** *DN* 3.123 **sIN**, *Shaller.* . . Usual pronunciation of shallow. **1933** [see **C** below]. **1936** *AmSp* 11.159 **eTX**, The vowel in the final syllable of all the words listed below is usually [ə]. . . *-o, -ow:* banjo . . shallow . . yellow. *Ibid* 161, In addition to the usual sound of [ə] in the final syllable, some of the words listed above . . have [ɚ] in less literate speech. . .

mosquito . . shallow . . yellow. **1942** Hall *Smoky Mt. Speech* 80 **wNC, eTN,** The sound [ɚ], representing retroflexion of historical [ə], is the prevailing one in most words spelled with *-o, -ow.* It may be, and frequently is, modified to [ə]. . . A considerable degree of education or subjection to modernizing influences is required before speakers regularly avoid [ɚ] for general American [o]. Examples: Banjo . . shallow . . yellow. **1954** *Harder Coll.* **cwTN,** Shallow [ʃɑulɚ] . . a place in a swift stream where the surface is broken. **c1960** *Wilson Coll.* **csKY,** Shallow ['ʃælə]. **1968–70** *DARE* (Qu. C3) Inf **TN**60, [ʃæələ]; (Qu. C14) **GA**28, [ʃælɚ]; (Qu. BB38) Inf **KY**77, [ʃælə]. **1968** *DARE* Tape **GA**35, Usually the mother alligator'll take the young around the shallow ['ʃælɚ] sections. **1981** Pederson *LAGS Basic Materials* **Gulf Region,** [8 infs offered proncs of the type ['ʃæ(ɛ)lə]; 1 inf, ['ʃælo]; 1 inf, ['ʃælɚ].]

B As adj, adv.
Of musical pitch: high; at a high pitch. [Prob by analogy with *deep* low-pitched]

1895 *DN* 1.374 **seKY, eTN, wNC,** *Shaller:* shallow. "She's started it too shaller"—of a tune pitched too high. **1924** Raine *Land of Saddle-Bags* 105 **sAppalachians,** When a girl pitched a tune too high, an observer . . remarked, "She started it *too shallow.*" **1927** *DN* 5.469 **Appalachians,** *Shallow.* . . High in pitch;—of musical tones.

C As verb.
With *off:* To become shallow.

1933 *AmSp* 8.1.52 **Ozarks,** *Shally.* . . To become shallow. *Th' branch kinder shallies off just below th' spring-house.* **1954** *Harder Coll.* **cwTN,** *Shaller off.* . . To become shallow.

shallowwater cisco n Cf **deepwater cisco**
A **cisco** (here: *Coregonus artedi*).

1983 Becker *Fishes WI* 341, Cisco or Lake Herring. . . Other common names: shallowwater cisco [etc].

shally See **shallow**

shalot See **shallot**

shalves See **shaft 2**

sham adv Also *shamly*
Shoddily; dishonestly.

1883 (1885) Jewett *Mate of Daylight* 203 **ME,** [He] bought a mis'able sham-built little house down close by the mills. **c1938** in 1970 Hyatt *Hoodoo* 2.1126 **swTN** [Black], An' when he got de house shamly built . . she says he came on to de house. . . Says, "Now hit's yore house. Yo've built it an' if yo' shamly built it, den yo' gotta live in it."

shamble-sticker n [*shamble* or *shambles* a slaughterhouse + *sticker,* from the bird's habit of impaling its prey]
=**northern shrike.**

1953 Jewett *Birds WA* 543, Alaskan Great Gray Shrike. *Lanius excubitor invictus* . . Other Names: Great Northern Shrike; Butcher Bird; Shamble-sticker [etc].

shame adj *chiefly among Black speakers*
Ashamed; embarrassed.

1883 (1971) Harris *Nights with Remus* 337 **GA** [Black], Mr. Lion, he hol' he head one side en try ter look 'shame', but all de same he aint feel 'shame'. **c1885** in 1981 Woodward *Mary Chesnut's Civil War* 742 **NC** (as of 1865) [Black], Missis, ain't you 'shame—crying for joy like a beggar 'oman. **1899** (1912) Green *VA Folk-Speech* 379, Shame. . . Tendency to feel distressed at any breach of decorum: as, he is *shame* to do it. **1927** Kennedy *Gritny* 35 **sLA** [Black], Unc' Nat, ain't you shame? **1931** (1991) Hughes-Hurston *Mule Bone* 81 **cFL** [Black], You-all ought to be shame, carrying on over a brazen heifer like Daisy Taylor. **1939** Griswold *Sea Is. Lady* 515 **csSC** (as of c1893) [Gullah], Miss Em'ly, I been too shame. **1942** *AmSp* 17.18 **HI** [English of Hawaiian children], Shame. . . Includes meanings of *embarrassed* and *shy.* **1967** *DARE* (Qu. GG9, *To suddenly embarrass somebody and throw him off balance:* "When they told him what she had said about him, it certainly did _____ him.") Inf **HI**13, Make him shame—in pidgin.

shame brier n Also *shame Billy, ~ face, ~-faced brier, ~ Jim, ~ plant, ~ vine, ~ weed, shamin' Judy* [From its habit of closing its leaves when touched] Cf **be-shame' bush, hilahila 2, sensitive plant,** *DJE shamer*
A **mimosa 1;** see quots.

1896 *Jrl. Amer. Folkl.* 9.186 **swMO,** *Schrankia uncinata* . . sensitive brier, shame-faced brier. **1904** (1913) Johnson *Highways South* 41 **seGA, nFL** [Black], The boys picked . . some "shame-brier." **1917** *DN* 4.417 **wNC,** Shame-briar. . . Sensitive plant. **1922** *Amer. Botanist* 28.30, A well known member of this group [=sensitive plants] is the "sensitive rose", "sensitive brier" and "shamevine" whose scientific title is *Schrankia uncinata.* **c1938** in 1970 Hyatt *Hoodoo* 1.533 **Sumter SC** [Black], Yo' git a piece of shame brier root an' put in between dem straws. *Ibid* 646 **St. Petersburg FL** [Black], A little vine called de *shame face.* . . (Hyatt: If you touch it what will happen?) Oh! It will close. *Ibid* **Mobile AL** [Black], Yo' git cha some dis heah *Shame Jim* [Hyatt: shame brier] 'at's a root dat grows in de woods. *Ibid* **Sumter SC** [Black], Yo' kin go out on railroad track an' it's a lil vine dat grow out dere dey call de *Shamin' Judy—*yes, *Shamin'.* Some calls it *Ashamin',* but it's a *Shamin' Judy.* See, if yo' touch it, an' it close up—when yo' touch de bush de leaves close up. **1940** Writers' Program *Guide TX* 375 **neTX,** The wild rose, shame vine, Virginia creeper, and swamp pink are among the plants that ornament the roadside. **1944** AL Geol. Surv. *Bulletin* 53.124, A few other plants of this family [= Mimosaceae], such as the "shame-brier", (*Morongia uncinata* or *Leptoglottis Nuttallii*) . . are sometimes found in weedy places. **1966** *DARE* (Qu. S26d, *Wildflowers that grow in meadows;* not asked in early QRs) Inf **SC27,** Shame Billy—*Schrankia microphylla.* **1972** Brown *Wildflowers LA* 83, Mimosa, Sensitive-plant, Shame-plant. . . Abundant in Mississippi and Red river floodplains, prairie, and second growth pineland. Also Texas, Arkansas, and Mississippi. **1988** Naylor *Mama Day* 40 **sSC, GA coasts** [Black], All she needs is to get herself a little shame weed and bake it up in something sweet. The bowls come out, the flour, the butter—she'd sleep tonight, sure enough.

shameface n[1]

A **cranesbill 1** (here: *Geranium maculatum*).

1900 Lyons *Plant Names* 172, [*Geranium*] *maculatum.* . . Shame-face. **1930** Sievers *Amer. Med. Plants* 62, Wild Geranium. . . old-maid's-nightcap, shameface. **1974** (1977) Coon *Useful Plants* 144, *Geranium maculatum*—Cranesbill . . shameface [etc].

shame face n[2], **shame-faced brier, shame Jim (or plant, vine, weed)** See **shame brier**

shamey flower n

A **huisache** (here: *Acacia farnesiana*).

1950 *PADS* 14.59 **SC,** Shamey flower. . . The opopanax, so called because sensitive.

shamin' Judy See **shame brier**

shamly See **sham**

shammock v Also *shammick, shammuck, shummick* [Engl dial] **chiefly sAppalachians**

To walk in a shambling or idle way; to saunter, mosey.

1913 Kephart *Highlanders* 203 **sAppalachians,** To "shummick" (also "shammick") is to shuffle about, idly nosing into things, as a bear does when there is nothing serious in view. **1925** Dargan *Highland Annals* 76 **cwNC,** I knowed that fox 'ud take him to Katter Knob, so I let him go on by hissef an' I shammocked along toward home. *Ibid* 148, Whoever shot her is in the woods now, an' he better not come shammuckin' where I can see him. **1927** *AmSp* 2.364 **cwWV,** Shammick . . to move slowly. The man shammicked off down the road. **1944** *PADS* 2.49 **wNC,** Shammock. . . To walk in a slouchy, unsteady manner. **1972** Cooper *NC Mt. Folkl.* 96, Shammuck—to walk.

shamp v [Etym unknown]

To trim (hair).

1913 Kephart *Highlanders* 294 **sAppalachians,** To shamp means to shingle or trim one's hair.

shampoo bean n

=**jojoba.**

1993 Kingsolver *Pigs in Heaven* 112, "In the store we sell these shampoos they make with ho-hoba. . . A fellow come in today and says he's all set up down in Arizona to grow ho-hoba beans on his farm. . . They don't need nothing but a poor patch of ground and some sunshine. I'll bet you can buy you a piece of that land for nothing. . . "Why would somebody sell it for nothing if they could get rich growing shampoo beans on it?"

shampoon n, v Cf Intro "Language Changes" I.8

Shampoo; to shampoo.

1903 *DN* 2.352 **neOH,** Shampoon, n. Shampoo (rare). **1909** *DN* 3.403 **nwAR,** Shampoon, v. Shampoo. "I got him to shampoon my head."

shang See **sang** n

Shanghai n

1 A long **oyster B1.** [In allusion to the imported *Shanghai* rooster, noted for its height]

1881 Ingersoll *Oyster-Industry* 248, Shanghai.—A long, slender oyster.

2 See **Shanghai fence.**

3 See **Shanghai parade.**

Shanghai fence n Also *Shanghai*

A type of rail or board fence; see quots.

1865 IL State Ag. Soc. *Trans. for 1861–64* 5.692, Many men . . are compelled to make "Shanghai" or "Bloomer" fences (two-boarded fences). **1871** in 1951 *S. Folkl. Qrly.* 15.136, The 'Shanghai' fence is made of rail, three to five to the panel, laid on the crotches of forked stakes driven into the ground, staked and surmounted with riders. **1872** U.S. Dept. Ag. *Rept. of Secy. for 1871* 504 **WI,** Post and pole, log, brush, stone, ditch, "Shanghai," and various fancy styles, are made. *Ibid* 505, The Shanghai fence is also found in Kansas. **1937** (1943) Dick *Sod-House Frontier* 81, One type of rail fence was called the Shanghai fence. If the farmer did not desire a fence clear to the ground, a stake was driven for the rails to set on, thus allowing a space below the bottom rail like the common barbed wire fence.

Shanghai parade n Also *Shanghai* Cf **belsnickeling**

A holiday procession of people in costume; hence n *Shanghai group* a group of people engaged in such a procession; vbl n *shanghaiing* the practice of holding such a procession.

1934 in 1936 *AmSp* 11.104 **WV,** Hundreds of people from this and adjoining states attended the *Shanghai parade* here this afternoon. Shanghai is an old Lewisburg custom that was conceived by the pioneers of Greenbrier County in celebration of the New Year. . . The grand prize went to Tom Reynolds, who drove an ox team attached to a pioneer wagon. Other entries winning prizes represented periods of local history. **1964** Smith *PA Germans* 122, In the past, there was a practice in several areas of the Valley called shanghai-ing, which was similar to belsnickeling. Although this custom is remembered by older residents in many towns and villages, it was actually engaged in by relatively few, but some can be found in Augusta and Highland Counties in Virginia and in Pendleton County, West Virginia, who actually took part in this activity. Shanghai-ing took place in the daylight hours during the same season when people went belsnickeling. Grown-up males dressed in clown-like disguises, with blackened or masked faces, and rode on horses or mules. Some rode in wagons in a group. They rode in single file, eight or more horses in a shanghai group. . . The merrymakers seldom visited at homes, instead they rode by as a parade, making noise by blowing on a horn or shouting in order to attract attention. . . Some Scotch-Irish residents of Augusta and Rockbridge Counties use the term shanghai to describe belsnickeling, whereas the residents of dialect-speaking neighborhoods separate the terms as distinctly unique customs, with belsnickeling a custom practiced at night and on foot while shanghai-ing was a daytime activity on horseback. One included visiting the homes of friends, while others did not.

shank grass n

=**barnyard grass.**

1916 *Torreya* 16.236 **SC,** *Echinochloa Crus-galli* . . Shank grass, rice cousin, Oakley, S.C.

shankings n pl [Var of **chankings**]

1966 *DARE* FW Addit **MA6A,** Shankings ['šæŋkɪnz]—skins and core of apple.

shank it v phr [Scots, nEngl dial] Cf **shank's mare**

To go on foot; to walk.

1967 *DARE* (Qu. Y24, . . *To walk, to go on foot: "I can't get a ride, so I'll just have to* _____.") Inf **AR52,** Shank it. **1991** Still *Wolfpen Notebooks* 90 **sAppalachians,** And I had to shank it eight miles with the weather bumping zero.

shank of the evening n Also *shank of the afternoon, ~ day*
chiefly **Sth, S Midl, occas NEast**

The latter part of the afternoon or the **evening B.** Note: For
some quots it is not possible to ascertain the precise sense of
evening; some speakers for whom *evening* refers to the period
from suppertime onward seem to have reinterpreted *shank* to
mean the early part of their *evening* rather than the latter part
of **evening B.**

1829 *VA Lit. Museum* 1.418, "Won't you spend the *balance* of the evening with me?" In some places, *shank* is quaintly used with the same
signification. **1890** Johnston *Widow Guthrie* 219 **GA** (as of 1830s),
'Tweren't I made up my mind before I left home to stay to dinner, and
may be toward the shank of the evenin' like, I'd a not let him come.
1892 *DN* 1.231 **KY,** *Shank.* "To'ds de shank o' de evenin'" . . late in the
afternoon. A negro phrase. **1893** Shands *MS Speech* 55, *Shank of the
evening.* Used principally by negroes, meaning near the end of the evening. **1899** (1912) Green *VA Folk-Speech* 379, *Shank.* . . The latter end
or part of anything: as, the *shank* of the evening. **1905** *DN* 3.93 **nwAR,**
Shank. . . End. 'It was towards the shank of the evening.' . . Not common. **1909** *DN* 3.368 **eAL, wGA,** *Shank.* . . The latter part. "The shank
of the evening (the afternoon)." **1911** *DN* 3.539 **eKY,** *Shank o' the evening.* Latter part of the afternoon. **1939** *LANE* Map 76, *Evening.* . .
Most of our informants define the evening as beginning at or after supper time, or . . at sunset or dusk, and extending till bed time. . . Some
however claim to use evening only of the early part of this period, which
others call *the shank of the evening.* [7 infs, **CT, MA, VT,** Shank of the
evening.] **1944** *PADS* 2.49 **NC, VA,** *Shank of the evening.* . . Latter part
of the afternoon. **1947** Steed *KY Tobacco Patch* 38, In the shank of the
afternoon we take the hogs from the tier rail. **1952** Brown *NC Folkl.*
1.588, *Shank of the evening, (day).* . . The late afternoon, the early evening.—General. **1955** *Courier–Jrl.* (Louisville KY) 31 Jan sec 2, I
mused upon these grave matters till the shank of the evening, for I was
trying to solve a serious question. **c1960** *Wilson Coll.* **csKY,** *Shank of
the evening.* . . Late afternoon. **1968–69** *DARE* (Qu. A3, *The time between the middle of the day and supper time*) Inf **NY41,** Shank of the
day—old-fashioned; **NY49,** Shank of the day [FW sugg]; **NC62,** Shank
of the evening [FW sugg]; **NY76,** Shank of the evening [FW: Inf uses it
for early evening]. **1975** *DARE* File **cnMA** (as of c1920), If I complained that I didn't want to do something, that it was too late, my
grandmother said, "Why it's just the shank of the day!" **1986** Pederson
LAGS Concordance, 1 inf, **cAL,** Shank of the evening—late in the evening.

shank's horse n Also *shank's horses* **esp Inland Nth** See
Map
=**shank's mare.**

1917 *DN* 4.400 **neOH,** *Shank's horses.* . . Legs. To ride Shank's horses
= "to go afoot." Also Ill., Ia., Kan., Ky. **1927** *AmSp* 2.364 **cwWV,**
Shank's horse, to ride . . to walk. "How are you going?" "Oh, I will ride
shank's horse." **1928** *Ruppenthal Coll.* **KS,** *Shank's horses* . . on foot;
not riding. **1946** McAtee *Dial. Grant Co. IN Suppl. 3* 9 (as of 1890s),
[*Ride*] *shank's horses* . . walk. **1949** *McDavid Coll.* **cn,cwNY,** *Shanks
horses* = shanks mare. **1965–70** *DARE* (Qu. Y24, . . *To walk, to go on
foot: "I can't get a ride, so I'll just have to _____."*) 12 Infs, **esp
Inland Nth,** Ride (*or* go on, pull on, take, use) shank's horses; **WA11,**
Take shank's horse. [12 of 13 Infs old]

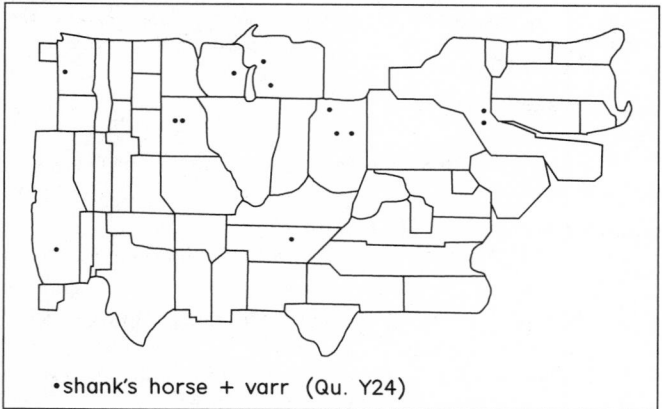

•shank's horse + varr (Qu. Y24)

shank's mare n Also *mare's shanks, shank's mares, shanks's
mare* [*OED2* (at *shank* sb. 1.b) c1774 →] Cf **shank's horse,
~ pony**

One's own legs (as a means of transportation)—usu in phr *ride
shank's mare* and varr: to go on foot.

1831 (1940) Motte *Charleston to Harvard* 30 **SC,** It appeared more
convenient to ride out, notwithstanding my general preference to *shanks-
mare.* **1896** Harris *Sister Jane* 304 **GA,** He rode 'shank's mare,' as the
saying is. **1899** (1912) Green *VA Folk-Speech* 379, *Shanks's mare.* . .
On foot is to ride *shanks's mare.* **1909** *DN* 3.363 **eAL, wGA,** *Ride
Shanks's mare.* . . To walk, go on one's own shanks. **1910** *DN* 3.455
seVT, *Shank's mare.* To "ride shank's mare" means to travel on foot or
on one's own legs. **1910** Hart *Vigilante Girl* 141 **nCA,** When tired of
riding, he would vault from the saddle without stopping his lumbering,
creaking wagon-train; then, on Shanks's mare, he would trudge by the
side of his animals until he wearied of walking. **1919** *DN* 5.76 **wMA,**
Shank's horses: the form is *shank's mare* in Western Massachusetts.
1963 Owens *Look to River* 6 **TX,** He sees me afoot and makes out like
I'm on horseback. "I cain't light," Jed said. "I'm on shanks' mare."
1965–70 *DARE* (Qu. Y24, . . *To walk, to go on foot: "I can't get a ride,
so I'll just have to _____."*) 102 Infs, **widespread,** Ride (*or* go, go
by, go on, take, use) shank's mare; **MD34, NJ36, NY199, WY5,** Ride
(*or* go on, use) shank's mares; **CA181, MA123, TX51,** Shank's mare;
NY232, PA234, Go on mare's shanks; **CT23,** Take shank's old mare.
1968 *DARE* FW Addit **seNY,** "Lost the use of *shank's mare*" (means
lost the use of one's legs). **1982** *Greenfield Recorder* (MA) 28 Aug 4/2,
They thought a five-mile-walk was no hardship. "Shanks' mare" was
kept well exercised and in good condition. **1991** Still *Wolfpen Notebooks* 59 **sAppalachians,** Them days, if you wanted to go somewhere
and you had no horse, you went shank's-mare.

shank's pony n Also *shank's ponies* **chiefly N Cent, Pacific**
See Map
=**shank's mare.**

1931 *AmSp* 7.53 **Sth, SW** [Lumberjack lingo], "Ridin' shanks ponies"
is an old phrase meaning to walk. **1944** *PADS* 2.60 **MO,** *Shank's ponies, to ride.* . . To walk instead of ride. Livingston Co. Rural. **1965**
Julian Apple Day [24] **csCA,** The boys who had cars very generously
donated them . . while the others went on horse-back or 'Shank's
Ponies.' **1965–70** *DARE* (Qu. Y24, . . *To walk, to go on foot: "I can't
get a ride, so I'll just have to _____."*) 12 Infs, **esp N Cent, Pacific,**
Ride (*or* go on, take) shank's ponies; **AL6, CA134, 165, IL39, IN19,
39, MI9, MT4, VA31,** Ride (*or* go on, use) shank's pony; **IL143,**
Shank's ponies; **MO4,** Shank's pony. [18 of 23 Infs female] **1966**
Barnes–Jensen *Dict. UT Slang* 37, *Shank's pony, on* . . on foot. "We had
no horse so I went there on shank's pony."

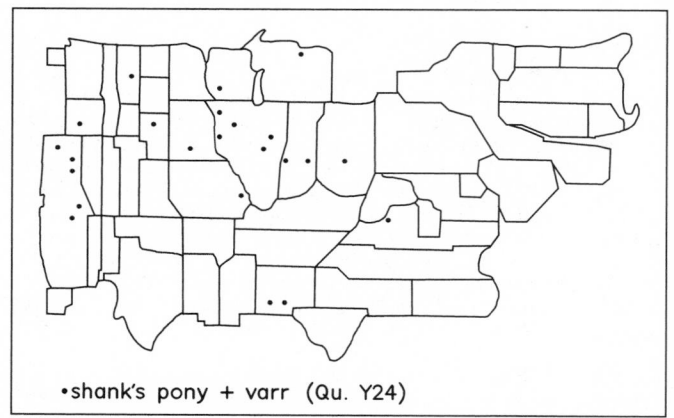

•shank's pony + varr (Qu. Y24)

shanks's mare See **shank's mare**

shanty n

1 In logging: any of the var buildings making up a logging
camp, esp the bunkhouse; hence nouns *shanty boy, ~ man* a
logger; *shanty team* a logging crew.

[**1829** Mactaggart *3 Yrs. in Canada* 1.241, The *Shantymen* live in
hordes of from thirty to forty together; throughout the day they cut down
the pine trees.] **c1847** in 1924 Gray *Songs ME Lumberjacks* xvii **MI,**

'T was in Jim Lockwell's shanty this song was sung with glee,/ And that's the end of "The Shanty Boy," and it was composed by three. **1878** *Lumberman's Gaz.* 6 Apr 310, The last of the shanty-teams of the season have about gone through here. **1926** Rickaby *Ballads Shanty-Boy* 237 **MI, MN, WI** (as of a1920), *Shanty.* Any of the several buildings comprising a logging camp. In the plural, means a camp. *Ibid, Shanty-boy.* A member of a logging crew. A lumber-jack. In the golden days of logging the woodsman evidently preferred the name "shanty-boy." At least it is the word he uses most generally in referring to himself. **1931** *AmSp* 7.49 **Sth, SW** [Lumberjack lingo], Their most common diversion during the long winter evenings is their "free-for-all" when the "shanty men" join the "bull pen boys" around the box stove. **1942** Beck *Songs MI Lumberjacks* 26, [Song title:] A Shantyman's Life. [Lyrics:] We are lying in the shanty; it's bleak and it's cold. **1958** McCulloch *Woods Words* 161 **Pacific NW**, *Shanty*—Any small camp building. Usually means built with boards, where cabin originally meant built with logs. **1961** Holbrook *Yankee Loggers* 122 **NEng,** [Glossary:] *Shantyboy*—In the United States, a now all but obsolete term for a logger. Its use is confined largely to Canada. **1964** Hargreaves–Foehl *Story of Logging* 61 **MI,** [Glossary:] *Shanty boys*—Loggers, woodsmen. **1969** Sorden *Lumberjack Lingo* 107 **NEng, Gt Lakes,** *Shanty.* . . Men's camp, men's sleeping quarters, bunkhouse. . . *Shanty man*—A lumberjack.

2 In railroading: a caboose.

1931 *Writer's Digest* 11.64 [Railroad terms], *Shanty*—A caboose. **1938** Beebe *High Iron* 224 [Railroad terms], *Shanty:* Caboose. **1945** in 1953 Botkin–Harlow *Treas. Railroad Folkl.* 345, It is a caboose, crummy, way car, . . shanty. **1948** *Sat. Eve. Post* 25 Dec 69, To understand what the shanty means to its crew, picture the 512 on its run on a blustery sleeting night. **1950** *WELS (The last car on a freight train, usually used as headquarters for the crew)* 1 Inf, **cWI,** Shanty.

3 also *shanty house:* An outdoor toilet building, privy. **esp Missip-Ohio Valleys** See Map

1965–70 *DARE* (Qu. M21a, *An outside toilet building*) Infs **MO**18, **OH**88, **WA**27, **WY**4, Shanty; (Qu. M21b, *Joking names for an outside toilet building*) Infs **IL**80, 114, **MI**116, **MO**11, **VT**2, Shanty; **KY**86, Shanty house. **1973** Allen *LAUM* 1.181 **Upper MW** (as of c1950), *Privy.* . . shanty [2 infs, **IA, MN**]. **1986** Pederson *LAGS Concordance (Outhouse)* 1 inf, **cwMS,** Shanty house.

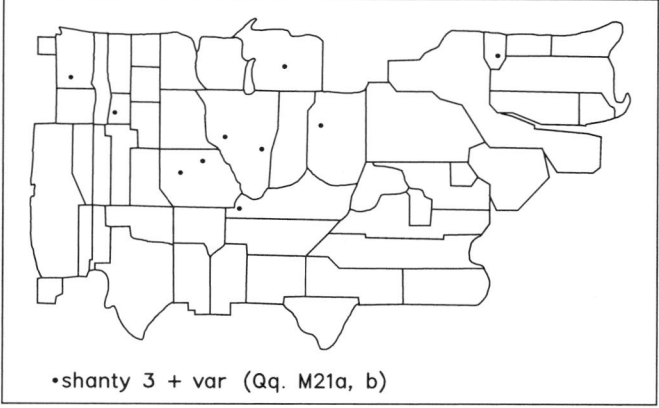

•shanty 3 + var (Qq. M21a, b)

4 A shed or lean-to attached to the main structure of a building.

1950 *WELS (Parts built on outside the main part of the house)* 1 Inf, **seWI,** Shanty. **1967–68** *DARE* (Qu. D16, . . *Parts added on to the main part of a house*) Inf **IL**9, Lean-to; shanty—old-fashioned; **NE**7, Lean-to; shanty; **MN**16, Shanty part—if [it] has a sloping roof. **1973** Allen *LAUM* 1.179 (as of c1950), *Shed* (for wood, tools, etc.) . . Attached . . shanty [2 infs, **MN, SD**]. [Unspecified as to whether an attached or unattached structure, 2 infs, **IA, MN,** Shanty.]

5 also *fish shanty, ice ~, smelt ~:* A small, portable shelter used for ice fishing.

1964 Gould *Parables of Peter* 146 **ME,** I think a smelt shanty is a special thing. The art of angling from the private isolation of a fish shanty draws a man to such an extent that he is temporarily separated from the silliness and foibles of society, including laws. **1969–70** *DARE* Tape **MI**106, [FW:] Do they ice fish and all that? . . [Inf:] Ice shanty. It's like

Shantytown out there at Black Lake. You have to make your fun here; **MI**120, [Aux Inf:] Do you remember when our dad used to go ice fishing? We had a shanty on Otsego Lake; **WI**75, Last winter they fished through the ice here in the harbor; . . they cut a hole in the ice and fish perch. . . And they used to fish 'em in these shanties. . . Now you can't catch any in the shanties—they won't bite in the shanty, you've got to fish 'em in an open hole. **1977** *Sawyer Co. Rec.* (Hayward WI) 5 Jan 1/ 3 **nWI,** The offenses are minor and range from not having a name or address on a fish shanty to possession of an untagged deer. **1989** *Yankee* Feb 130 **VT,** Kenneth Bryant . . offered to pull the girls over their collapsible shanty, which folded into a stout wooden sled. **1999** *WI State Jrl.* (Madison) 23 Feb sec B 5/6 **csWI,** No matter what the weather conditions are . . ice shanties . . must be removed from lakes by March 5.

6 A black eye—also in phrr *build* (or *hang*) *a shanty* to bruise the area around the eye by hitting a person. [Joc transf of *shanty* a crudely built shack associated with poor Irish immigrants (cf **shanty Irish**); see quot 1859]

1859 in 1983 *PADS* 70.50 **ce,sePA,** I suppose Mother told you about my building a Shanty over that Irishmans eye. **1926** Anderson–Stallings *3 Amer. Plays* 76, I hung a shanty on the bimbo's eye. **1950** *WELS (Names . . for a black eye)* 3 Infs, **WI,** Shanty. **1950** *WELS Suppl.* **cwWI,** He was in a fight, last night, and got a shanty. **1965–70** *DARE* (Qu. X20, . . *A black eye*) Infs **NJ**21, **OH**29, **PA**142, 148, **UT**3, **VA**69, **WI**27, Shanty.

7 See **shantyboat 1.**

shantyboat n

1 also *shanty:* A houseboat, esp a crudely built one; also transf; hence nouns *shanty-boater, shanty-boatman.* **chiefly Missip-Ohio Valleys**

1879 Bishop *4 Months* 59 **Missip-Ohio Valleys,** The shanty-boatman looks to the river . . for his life. *Ibid* 59, The sweeps, or oars . . govern the motions of the shanty-boat. **1906** Johnson *Highways Missip. Valley* 252, The river people themselves commonly call these floating homes "shanty-boats," and that indicates their general character. They are mostly rudely built in the first place, get little care, and in a few years go to pieces. **1935** *Lit. Digest* 17 Aug 20 **Missip-Ohio Valleys,** The latter usually is a solid citizen who resents being called a "shanty-boater." **1938** *Sat. Eve. Post* 15 Oct 58 **Missip-Ohio Valleys,** We moved on to a shanty moored to the one where we had been chatting. **1940** Writers' Program *Guide OH* 437, The shantyboat was an oddity. Its owner was the gypsy of the river, who rarely stayed more than a season in any one place. His dwelling was a low, ramshackle houseboat; his home, the river. **1953** (1977) Hubbard *Shantyboat* 2 **Missip-Ohio Valleys,** The tradition of drifting is carried into our day by an amphibious race usually called shantyboaters. A shantyboat is a scow with a small house on it. Nearly always a homemade job, it is put together of odd scraps of material and pieces of driftwood and wreckage. The shantyboat may be embellished by any of the appurtenances of living. Yet it is more than a floating homestead: it is an ark which the river bears toward a warmer climate, better fishing grounds, and more plentiful and easier work on shore. **1962** Faulkner *Reivers* 102 **swTN,** Not looking like a shantyboat swamp rat. **1970** *DARE* (Qu. O2, *Nicknames . . for an old, clumsy boat*) Inf **PA**235, Shantyboat; (Qu. O10, . . *Kinds of boats*) Inf **VA**47, Shanty—houseboat; floating shanty. **1986** Pederson *LAGS Concordance,* 2 infs, **seAR, cwMS,** Shantyboat.

2 Spec; in logging: a houseboat used as a bunkhouse or kitchen. Cf **ark 3, wanigan**

1905 U.S. Forest Serv. *Bulletin* 61.46 [Logging terms], *Shanty boat.* See Wanigan. [*Ibid* 52, *Wanigan.* . . A houseboat used as sleeping quarters or as kitchen and dining room by river drivers.] **1969** Sorden *Lumberjack Lingo* 107 **NEng, Gt Lakes,** *Shanty boat*—The cook's raft which followed the log drive down the river. Same as wanigan.

shanty-boater (or -boatman) See **shantyboat 1**

shanty boss n Cf **bull cook n, chore boy**

One who does odd jobs in a logging camp.

1905 U.S. Forest Serv. *Bulletin* 61.46 [Logging terms], *Shanty boss.* See Chore boy. [*Ibid* 33, *Chore boy.* One who cleans up the sleeping quarters and stable in a logging camp, cuts firewood, builds fires, and carries water.] **1969** Sorden *Lumberjack Lingo* 107 **NEng, Gt Lakes,** *Shanty boss*—A camp worker who got the wood and water and did chores. Same as chore boy.

shanty boy See **shanty 1**

shanty coffee n
Strong coffee.

1968 *DARE* (Qu. H74a, . . *Coffee . . very strong*) Inf **NY**43, Shanty coffee—from coffee made by fishermen who lived in shanty in area. **1968** *DARE* Tape **NY**44, Shanty coffee was usually made in a shanty; now, what is a shanty? These islands . . in the middle of the bay, where the clamdiggers and fishermen, baitmen had houses. . . And they called them shanties. . . Some of them were just shells of houses, they didn't have walls inside. . . It was just a shack to live in in the summer. . . Some of them . . were furnished nicely, had walls. . . but every time you went out there, there was always a coffee pot on; that was always very strong coffee, and everybody who makes strong coffee now, you call it shanty coffee.

shanty duck n
=**ruddy duck.**

1923 U.S. Dept. Ag. *Misc. Circular* 13.31 **TN**, Ruddy Duck. . . Vernacular Names. . . *In local use.* . . shanty duck.

shanty fever n
=**cabin fever.**

1950 *WELS Suppl.* **nWI** (as of 1945), *Shanty-fever.* . . The slight derangement of mind that comes from living too much alone in a shanty in the remote north areas. Heard. *Ibid* **nwWI**, *Shanty fever.* . . Also *cabin fever.* "He's got shanty fever." = Living in isolation or being all alone for a long time has made him a little odd. Not heard in Dane Co., though 'shanty fever' is common around Hayward. Its victims are frequently old lumberjacks or retired bootleggers. **1983** *Greenfield Recorder* (MA) 26 Feb 9, "Shanty fever" . . referred to the condition of one person who had lived alone for so long he was a little queer in some ways, a bit "tetched" in the head on some subjects, but was quite able to still live alone in spite of a few delusions. Long ago, some of the old trappers, hunters and prospectors got into that condition.

shanty fried potatoes n pl Also *shanty fries*
=**cottage fried potatoes.**

1968–69 *DARE* (Qu. H47, *Kinds of fried potatoes*) Inf **OH**38, Shanty fried—lots of water, not brown; **PA**196, Shanty fries—raw, sliced potato—fried.

shanty house See **shanty 3**

shanty Irish n pl Also *shantytown Irish* **chiefly NEast, N Cent** Cf **flannelmouth 2,** *lace curtain Irish* (at **lace curtain 2**)
Irish people or people of Irish descent, esp those belonging to the lower classes or retaining lower-class traits; hence n *shanty Irishman* such a person; adj *shanty Irish* characterized by such traits.

1928 Tully *Shanty Irish* 117 **OH**, I'm jist plain Shanty Irish an' I'll go to hell when I die. **1931–33** *LANE Worksheets* **RI**, *Shanty Irish* . . nickname for Irish. **1934** Farrell *Young Manhood* 334 **Chicago IL**, The Irish made a shanty Irishman out of Christ. **1947** *AmSp* 22.18, In America, we have . . the phrase *shanty-Irish,* meaning those Irish who have not made enough money to live in anything but a *shanty,* or in *shanty-town,* as opposed to those who have done rather better and become lace-curtain Irish. **1950** *WELS* (*Nicknames for people living in nearby settlements or places*) 1 Inf, **seWI**, Shanty Irish; (*Names and nicknames for people of foreign background: Irish*) 3 Infs, **WI**, Shanty Irish. **1964** *PADS* 42.35 **Chicago IL**, The tendency to mark social levels within a nationality group with nicknames is best seen here among the Irish. The most commonplace of these is the distinction between *shanty-* and *lace-curtain Irish,* i.e., those who remain in the lower-class communities near the center of the city (or, irrespective of residency, preserve the social traits of the shanty Irish) and those who move into lowermiddle-class communities and work hard to approximate the ideals of vulgar respectability. **1965–70** *DARE* (Qu. HH28, *Names and nicknames . . for people of foreign background: Irish*) 19 Infs, **esp NEast, N Cent,** Shanty Irish; **MA**68, Shanty Irish—used to call the poor Irish shanty Irish; **MI**72, Shantytown Irish; (Qu. HH18, *Very insignificant or low-grade people*) Inf **PA**227, Shanty Irish; (Qu. II25, . . *Poorer people*) Inf **NY**131, Shantytown Irish. **1967** *DARE* Tape **MA**71, They used to live down there on Summit Street, brick-yarders. They were Irish, and they were all country Irish. They didn't have much rubbed off of 'em. The old Yankees used to call 'em shanty Irish. . . [T]he Yankees were anything but generous when referring to the recently arrived Irish. **1985**

WI Alumnus Letters, To Protestant Irish families such as my mother came from, the term [=*Black Irish*] was used to indicate Irish of lower social orders, usually Catholic. It often was used in conjunction with "shanty," such as "that shanty Black Irishman," which was about the worst thing Mom could have called anyone. **1995** *DARE* File **csWI** (as of 1930s), My grandmother was "shanty Irish" by her own declaration, as opposed to cousin Grover's wife Stella, who "put on airs" and acted like "lace-curtain Irish."

shanty man See **shanty 1**

shanty shanty over n Cf *DS* EE22
Prob =**Antony-over** n.

1957 *Sat. Eve. Post Letters* **Chicago IL**, We played "heely, heely over⁽ⁿ⁾" or ⁽ᶜ⁾shanty, shanty over."

shanty team See **shanty 1**

shantytown Irish See **shanty Irish**

shape note n, freq attrib Also *shaped note* **chiefly Sth, S Midl** Cf **buckwheat note, fasola, patent note, round ~, sacred harp**
A musical note whose head has a distinctive shape to indicate its position in the musical scale.

1931 Goodrich *Mt. Homespun* 52 **sAppalachians,** The singers had challenged the neighboring districts to bring along their shaped-note songbooks and sing them down if they could. **1932** Randolph *Ozark Mt. Folks* 248, Round notes is all alike, an' you got t' sing by line-an'-space. Shape notes is all different, an' you sing 'em by shape an' by line-an'-space too. T' my mind th' shape-notes is best. L'arn shape-notes an' you'll be singin' in a week, but if you stick t' round-notes it'll take a right smart longer. **1941** Writers' Program *Guide AR* 332 **cAR,** Each summer the Grant County Singing Convention is held in Sheridan. Hymns are almost the only songs, but the square and triangular "shaped notes" of former times are giving way to the conventional round notes of the city-printed hymnbooks. **1942** (1960) Robertson *Red Hills* 291 **SC,** We still sing from music books printed with shaped notes instead of round notes—with shaped diamonds, circles, squares, and triangles as William & Smith devised them at Philadelphia in 1798. **1953** *Hall Coll.* **ceTN,** They was religious songs. We sung out of shaped-note books. **1972** in 1982 Powers *Cataloochee* 360 **cwNC** (as of a1940), We used shape-note songbooks altogether. **1989** Flynt *Poor But Proud* 229 **ceAL** (as of 1910–30), [The occasion was] variously called a Sacred Harp sing . . , a Fasola sing . . , or a Shaped Note sing (because a different shaped note placed on the staff represented each of the four or seven notes). **1995** Williams *Gt. Smoky Mts. Folklife* 43 **wNC, eTN,** Shape-note singing, particularly as practiced by the traditional singers, can produce a strong response. . . There is no musical accompaniment for shape-note singing.

shaps See **chaps**

shard See **shad 1**

share n, v Usu |šɛə(r), šæə(r)|; also **chiefly Sth, S Midl, occas NEast** |šir|; infreq |šʌr| Pronc-spp *shayre, shear, sheer, shur* Cf Pronc Intro 3.I.1.b, **chair**
Std senses, var forms.

1795 Dearborn *Columbian Grammar* 138, *List of Improprieties.* . . Shear for Share. **1848** Lowell *Biglow* 146 'Upcountry' **MA**, Sheer, share. **1858** Hammett *Piney Woods Tavern* 120, Some's got more'n their sheer. **1867** Allen *Slave Songs* xxxiii, "Charles, why did n't you come to school earlier?" "A-could n't come *soon* to-day, sir; de boss he sheer out [=distributes] clo' dis mornin'." **1894** Riley *Armazindy* 8 **IN**, As fer Jule and Sol, they had / Their sheer!—less o' good than bad! **1902** *DN* 2.245 **sIL**, Share. . . [šir]. **1903** *DN* 2.290 **Cape Cod MA** (as of a1857), Fishermen went on *shears* (=shares). **1903** *DN* 2.329 **seMO**, Share. . . Pronounced sheer. **1907** *DN* 3.226 **nwAR**, Share. . . [šir]. **1909** *DN* 3.368 **eAL, wGA**, Sheer. . . Common pronunciation of *share.* **1922** Gonzales *Black Border* 325 **sSC, GA coasts** [Gullah glossary], *Shayre*—share, shares, shared, sharing. **1923** *DN* 5.220 **swMO**, *Sheer.* . . Share. **1928** *AmSp* 3.401 **Ozarks** (as of 1916–27), The vowel in *care, share* and *scarce* is pronounced almost exactly as though the words were spelled *keer, sheer* and *skeerce.* **1942** Faulkner *Go Down* 223 **MS**, I reckon that aint no lie. I done fed him enough cawn to have a sheer in him. **1942** Warnick *Garrett Co. MD* 1 **nwMD** (as of 1900–18), *Shear* (share). **1944** *PADS* 2.30 **eKY, wNC**, *Shur* [šʌr]. . . Share; to share. **1954** *Harder Coll.* **cwTN,** *Share* /šər/. **1991** *Macoupin Co. Enquirer* (Carlinville IL) **cwIL** 6, [From a 1961 issue quoting "oldsters":] Most younguns were well brung up and not afeared to do their sheer of work.

share-cash tenant n Also *share-cash cropper* Cf **sharecropper, share hand, ~-tenant**

A tenant farmer who pays both money and a share of the crop as rent.

1925 Amer. Acad. Political & Social Sci. *Annals* Jan 61, Number of farms operated by tenants of various kinds (cash, share and share-cash "croppers", standing tenants, etc.) increased about 100,000. **1989** Flynt *Poor But Proud* 60 **ceAL** (as of 1880–1930), Share-cash tenants paid part of their rent in cash and part in shares of crops or livestock.

sharecrop n

1 See **sharecropper.**

2 A crop grown on shares—also in phr *make a sharecrop* = **sharecrop** v.

1928 Peterkin *Scarlet Sister Mary* 235 **SC,** The ugly . . thing would cost as much as his whole share-crop of cotton would make in five years. **1986** Pederson *LAGS Concordance,* 1 inf, **cwTN,** I made a one-horse sharecrop; 1 inf, **nwMS,** They made a sharecrop just like a colored fellow did; 1 inf, **cMS,** Made a sharecrop.

sharecrop v [Back-formation from **sharecropper**] chiefly Sth

Also with *it:* To work as a **sharecropper;** to rent out (land) on shares.

1930 DN 6.83 **cSC,** Share-crop, v. To farm "on shares." . . The word, like the practice, is very common. **1937** *Amer. Mag.* July 167, And how will you classify the case of Mr. Floyd Sprouse . . who share-crops in southern Arkansas? **1938** in Lib. of Congress *Amer. Memory: WPA Life Hist.* (Internet) **SC,** The newcomers till small farms of their own or work for the large truck planters, and some of them share crop. **1957** Faulkner *Town* 246 **MS,** For the same reason I would hunt up the best carpenter if I wanted to build a house, or the best farmer if I wanted to share-crop some land. **1968–70** DARE (Qu. L5, *When a farmer gets help on a job from his neighbors in return for his help on theirs farm years later on*) Infs **MO**20, **VA**7, 111, Sharecropping. **1986** Pederson *LAGS Concordance* **Gulf Region,** 9 infs, Sharecropping; 7 infs, Sharecropped (it).

sharecropper n Rarely *sharecrop* widespread, but esp Sth, S Midl, SW See Map Cf **cropper, furnish, share hand**

A tenant farmer who pays a share of the crop as rent, esp one who is supplied by the landowner with equipment and working stock and supplies only labor.

1923 DN 5.220 **swMO,** *Sheer crapper.* . . A tenant farmer who pays rent with a certain share of his products. **1929** Gottschalk *Era Fr. Revol.* 33, Most of them had become *métayers,* who, like our sharecroppers, farmed a piece of land for a stipulated portion . . of the harvest. **1929** *AmSp* 4.204 **Ozarks,** He aint nothin' on'y a tie-whackin' sheer-crapper noways. **1938** FWP *Guide MS* 104, The share-tenants, supplying much of their equipment, pay the landowner one-fourth or one-third of the crop. The sharecroppers, supplying almost nothing but their labor, usually pay one-half of the crop. Both groups, however, must pay out of their own share all that is supplied to them in the way of seed, fertilizer, and food. **1938** in Lib. of Congress *Amer. Memory: WPA Life Hist.* (Internet) **MS,** We was share-croppers; I guess you have heard they work. The owner stakes you to grub and seed and takes a percentage of your crop in payments. The system is only good for the party that stakes you. [**1941** Percy *Lanterns* 280 **nwMS,** Those hundred and twenty-four families . . worked "on the shares" and called themselves "croppers," but I wasn't familiar with the term "share-croppers."] **1965–70** DARE (Qu. L3, *A man who lives on the farm and does the work, but divides the expenses and profits with the owner*) 483 Infs, **widespread, but esp Sth, S Midl, SW,** Sharecropper; **AL**62, Sharecropper man; **CA**63, A sharecrop—usually gets a fourth of profit; **GA**16, Sharecrop; (Qu. L2, *The extra house on a large farm where a hired man and his family live*) Inf **AL**2, 38, **OK**43, **SC**23, Sharecropper('s) house; **MN**2, Sharecropper shack. **1986** Pederson *LAGS Concordance* **Gulf Region,** 25 infs, Sharecropper(s); 1 inf, I was a sharecrop for one year. **1989** Flynt *Poor But Proud* 60 **ceAL** (as of 1880–1930), At the bottom of the tenancy system and most pervasive in Alabama was the sharecropper. Under this arrangement, the landowner normally furnished land, housing, fuel, working-stock, livestock feed, farm implements, and seed. The cropper provided the labor and fed and clothed his family.

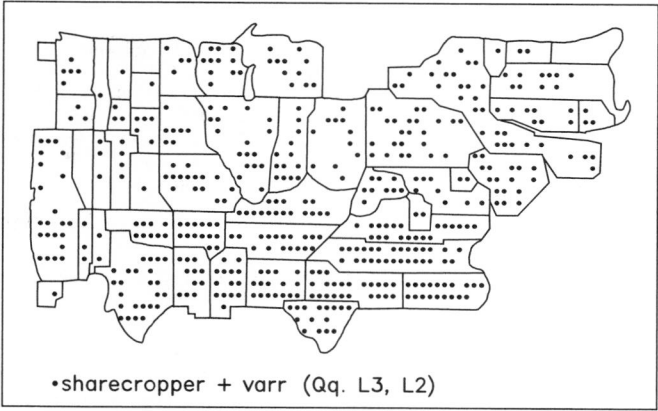

•sharecropper + varr (Qq. L3, L2)

share farmer n esp PA, N Cent See Map Cf **sharecropper**

A tenant farmer who pays a share of the crop as rent.

1933 in 1993 Major *Calling the Wind* 50 [Black], Old Jeff Patton, the black share farmer, fumbled with his bow tie. *Ibid* 51, Pine woods stretched away to the left like a black sea. Among them were scattered scores of log houses like Jeff's, houses of black share farmers. **1961** Folk *Word Atlas N. LA* map 1701, Farmer who works on shares . . [Among other responses] share farmer. **1965–70** DARE (Qu. L3, *A man who lives on the farm and does the work, but divides the expenses and profits with the owner*) 14 Infs, **esp PA, N Cent,** Share farmer [12 of 14 Infs old, 11 male]; [**PA**166, Share farming].

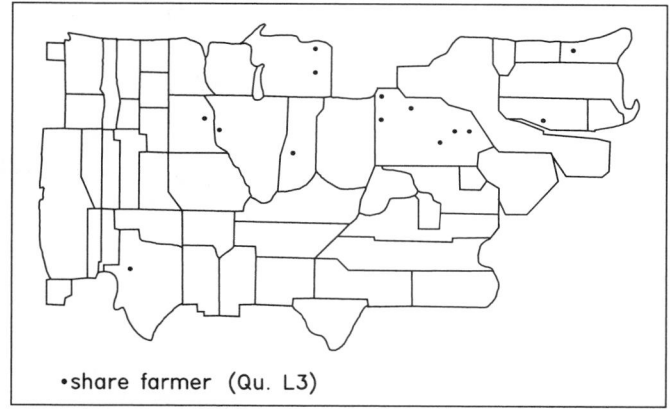

•share farmer (Qu. L3)

share hand n esp LA, MS Cf **sharecropper, shareman**

A tenant farmer who pays a share of the crop as rent, esp one who provides his own equipment and working stock.

1911 (1912) Jenks–Lauck *Immigration Problem* 83 **seLA,** Italian cotton tenants are showing the cotton growers of how much value careful cultivation, kitchen gardens and small store accounts may be to the cotton "share hand" and tenant. **1951** Faulkner *Requiem* 245 **MS,** The serried identical ranks of two-room shotgun shacks in which lived in droves with his family the Negro tenant- or share- or furnish-hand. **1965–68** DARE (Qu. L1, *A man who is employed to help with work on a farm*) Inf **MS**63, Share hand, wage hand—depending on arrangement; (Qu. L3, *A man who lives on the farm and does the work, but divides the expenses and profits with the owner*) Inf **NY**87, Share hand; **LA**10, Share hand—might be a half hand (he puts up the labor) or a fourth hand (he furnishes everything). **1976** Brown *Gloss. Faulkner* 174, The "share-hand" provides his own equipment and pays one third of his corn and one fourth of his cotton as rent. **1986** Pederson *LAGS Concordance,* 2 infs, **MS,** Share hand(s); 1 inf, **cwMS,** Share hands (=sharecroppers); 1 inf, **neLA,** Share hands—worked on halves.

share house n

A house on a farm for the **hired man** or a **shareman** and his family.

1950 WELS Suppl., Share house. . . Tenant house. "We were living in the share house on her father's place then." **1960** Criswell *Resp. to PADS 20* **Ozarks,** *Share house*—refers to extra house on farm for hired man's family. **1970** DARE (Qu. L2, *The extra house on a large farm where a hired man and his family live*) Infs **OK**53, **WV**14, Share house.

shareman n Cf sharecropper, share hand

A tenant farmer who pays a share of the crop as rent.

1950 *WELS* (*A man who lives on a farm and does the work, sharing expenses and profits with the owner*) 2 Infs, **csWI**, Shareman. **1965–70** *DARE* (Qu. L3) Infs **IN**19, **NY**220, **ND**5, **OH**22, 56, **SD**5, **TN**34, **VA**49, Shareman; **VA**40, Half-shareman; (Qu. L2, *The extra house on a large farm where a hired man and his family live*) Infs **IL**50, **TN**34, **WV**16, Shareman's house. [All Infs old, all comm type 4 or 5]

share-tenant n Also *share-renter* Cf share-cash tenant, share hand

A tenant farmer who pays a share of the crop as rent, esp one who supplies his own equipment and working stock.

1889 *N. Amer. Rev.* 148.370, The increase by subdivision is largest in the cotton-growing States, where the share-tenant system prevails. **1903** (1977) Kelsey *Negro Farmer* 29, Negroes on the farms may be divided into four classes: Owners, cash tenants, share tenants, laborers. Share tenants differ from the same class in the North in that work animals and tools are usually provided by the landlord. **1937** *Amer. Mag.* July 164 **sAL**, The share-tenant . . is a little bit better off than the share-cropper. **1938** [see **sharecropper**]. **1944** Fast *Freedom Road* 120 **SC**, All of them living on the old acreage, all of them going to get off or be share tenants when the land is sold. **1950** *WELS* **WI** (*A man who lives on a farm and does the work, sharing expenses and profits with the owner*) 3 Infs, Share-renter; 1 Inf, Share-tenant. **1966–68** *DARE* (Qu. L3, *A man who lives on the farm and does the work, but divides the expenses and profits with the owner*) Infs **MI**83, **WI**17, 44, Share-renter; **MI**23, Share-tenant. **1989** Flynt *Poor But Proud* 60 **ceAL** (as of 1880–1930), Share tenants furnished their own equipment and work animals; as a consequence they usually paid one-third of their grain and one-fourth of their cotton for rent (hence the term "farming on thirds and fourths").

shark n

1 also *job shark:* Esp in logging: An employment agent.

1927 *AmSp* 2.391 [Vagabond argot], A *shark* is an employment agent. **1930** Williams *Logger-Talk* 28 **Pacific NW**, Shark: The proprietor of an employment office. **1938** (1939) Holbrook *Holy Mackinaw* 262 [Loggers' Dictionary], Job shark. An employment agent. **1958** McCulloch *Woods Words* 99 **Pacific NW**, Job shark. *Ibid* 161, Shark. **1969** Sorden *Lumberjack Lingo* 64 **NEng, Gt Lakes**, Job shark.

2 also *shark and fish, sharks (and minnows):* A game of water tag.

1967–70 *DARE* (Qu. EE28, *Games played in the water*) Inf **GA**54, Shark—like tag, except in the water; **MI**118, Shark and fish—like tag; **TX**54, Sharks—One man tries to touch others on the head above water before he gets to the other side; when touched, he has to help catch the next; **TX**37, Sharks and minnows—One man in the middle and the rest try to get back and forth without getting caught.

shark pilot n

1 also *shark's pilot:* =**rudderfish b.**

1896 U.S. Natl. Museum *Bulletin* 47.902, *Seriola zonata.* . . Rudderfish; Shark's Pilot. **1903** NY State Museum & Sci. Serv. *Bulletin* 60.416 **NJ**, The name, shark's pilot, is in use at Somers Point N.J. **1911** U.S. Bur. Census *Fisheries 1908* 307, Amber-fish (*Seriola*).—A food fish found from Cape Cod to Cape Hatteras. It is known as "jack-fish" on the Carolina coast, and "amber-fish," "shark's pilot," and "rudderfish" elsewhere. **2000** *DARE* File—Internet **NJ**, [In a list of fish caught in Ocean County:] Banded Rudderfish (Shark Pilot, Slender Amberjack).

2 =**pilot fish 1.** [See quot]

1933 John G. Shedd Aquarium *Guide* 83, Many a tale has been told of the services rendered by the Shark-pilot to its big companion in the way of leading it to food and warning it of danger. Unfortunately for romance, however, cold scientific observations tend to show that this well known companionship is largely one of expediency on the part of the smaller fish. It feeds on the remnants of the shark's meals and will follow a ship for days for the same reason.

sharks (and minnows) See **shark 2**

shark's pilot See **shark pilot 1**

sharp adj [Cf *EDD sharp* adj. 1.4 "Of a dog: snappish, savage."]

1899 (1912) Green *VA Folk-Speech* 379, Sharp. . . Fierce: as, a *sharp* dog.

sharp v

1 To sharpen (a tool); also fig. Cf **flat v 2**

1834 *Life Andrew Jackson* 153, Your pen has touch'd this glory bisness as if it bin sharp'd on one of Packard's or Morgan's razor straps. **1888** *Overland Mth.* (2d ser) 12.507 **sAppalachians**, He will . . "sharp and pint" plows. **1902** *DN* 2.245 **sIL**, Sharp. . . To sharpen. **1907** *DN* 3.226 **nwAR**, Sharp. . . To sharpen. **1934** *AmSp* 9.124 [Engl dial of HI], The function of the suffix *-en* is not comprehended. *Sharp the knife* is typical of a large group of examples. **1940–41** Cassidy *WI Atlas*, 1 inf, **swWI**, Sharp . . sharpen. A blacksmith sharping picks and drills.

2 See quot. Cf **sharp n**

1944 Adams *Western Words* 141, Sharp—When you see a man grubbin' and sharpin' the ears of his cows, you can bet he's a thief.

sharp n Cf *DS* K18, **sharp v 2**

A type of **earmark** n; see quot.

1936 Adams *Cowboy Lingo* 131, An 'over-slope' was made by cutting the ear about two thirds of the way back from the tip straight to the center of the ear at its upper side; the 'under-slope' was the same cut on the lower side. The 'sharp' was made by cutting an under- and over-slope upon the same ear, giving it a sharp or pointed appearance and sometimes called a 'point.'

sharp-chin hawk See **sharp-shinned hawk**

sharped up adj phr

Elegantly dressed.

1967–68 *DARE* (Qu. W37, *When a woman puts on her good clothes and tries to look her best . . she's _____*) Inf **TX**37, All sharped up; (Qu. W38, *When a man dresses himself up in his best clothes . . he's _____*) Inf **PA**94, Sharped up. **1986** Pederson *LAGS Concordance*, 2 infs, **GA, TN**, Sharped up.

sharpen v [*EDD sharpen* "To rough a horse to prevent slipping in frosty weather."] Cf **sharp shoe**

1907 *DN* 3.249 **eME**, Sharpen (a horse). . . To provide (a horse) with sharp shoes. "It was long into the night before some of the horses were sharpened."

sharpen one's hoe v phr Cf **clean one's plow**

See quots.

1919 *DN* 5.35 **seKY**, Sharpen one's hoe, to. . . To whip, "thrash." The figure has its origin in the cornfield, where a boy sometimes lags behind as he hoes corn, saying that he has a dull hoe. His father "sharpens the hoe" for him. . . In Oklahoma, "to clean one's plow." **1968** Adams *Western Words* 274, Sharpen his hoe—A cowboy's expression meaning *to thrash someone*.

sharpie n

1 also sp *sharpy:* A small, flat-bottomed sailing boat with a sharp prow and broad, square stern.

1860 in 1913 *Outing* 61.688 **seNY**, I took some of the skiffs and sharpies behind the Emma S . . and we went down to Whig inlet. **1864** (1873) Webster *Amer. Dict.* 1215, Sharpie. . . A long, sharp, flat-bottomed sail-boat. [Webster: *Local U.S.*] **1882** H. Hall *Ref. Ship-build. Industry U.S.* (1884) 22 *(OED2)*, A large fleet of small flat-bottomed fishing boats are employed, called 'sharpies', which have a family resemblance to the dory. **1884** U.S. Natl. Museum *Bulletin* 27.657, The sharpy, used in the oyster and other fisheries, is a very serviceable form of boat in localities where the waters are generally shallow. Provided with center-board and sails, they are frequently swift sailers in smooth water, and on certain parts of the Atlantic coast boats of this type are in high favor as small yachts. *Ibid* 700, *Connecticut Sharpy.* . . Open; flat bottom; center-board; sharp bow; wide, square stern; single mast; leg-of-mutton sail; 2 oars. . . Length, 14½ feet. **1955** Adams *Grandfather* 138 **NY** (as of 1880s), The pride of the Hopkins family was an eighteen-foot Sandusky sharpie. She was a lovely, lively little craft, two-masted, high-prowed, drawing less than a foot of water amidships, and stabilized by a deep centerboard. **1965** Will *Okeechobee Boats* 22 **FL**, This boat had been a sailing sharpie, but Cal Buckles had got her, put in a kerosene burning engine and a propeller, and named her *Irene*. **1966–68** *DARE* (Qu. O9, . . *Kinds of sailboats*) Inf **NC**12, Sharpie—old-fashioned; **NC**81, Sharpie—flat bottom—big. **1985** Rattray *Advent. Dimon* 187 **Long Is. NY**, The buggy was at the north bank of the Creek by the time we'd anchored, and we took the sharpie and ferried the two of them across, leaving the buggy and swimming the mare. **1988** Nickerson *Days to Remember* 134 **Cape Cod MA** (as of c1915), Sharpie—There were many "sharpies" along the shore. They were flat-bottomed skiffs, rarely over 16 feet long, decked in forward with a centerboard and cockpit. They were propelled either by oars or a leg o'mutton sail permanently attached to a mast, which was stepped through a hole in the deck, and was unstepped and stowed with the sail rolled around the mast when not in use. When under sail it was steered by an oar held against the lee gunnel. It was also sometimes propelled by sculling with an oar over the stern. It had no rudder.

2 also *sharpshooter:* A type of coasting sled with a pointed front; see quots.

1931–33 *LANE Worksheets* **Marblehead MA,** Sharp shooters . . "Those sleds that runs away out to sharp points." **1943** *LANE* Map 573–574, A low sled with solid sides coming to a point in front, often home-made. . . 2 infs, **CT,** Sharpie.

3 See **sharp-shinned hawk.**

sharpridge turbot See **sharpside turbot**

sharp-set adj phr Pronc-sp *sharp-sot* [*OED2* 1540 →]
Very hungry.

1808 in 1892 *S. Hist. Mag.* 1.56 **VA,** We inquired of Dennis if we could get breakfast, being pretty sharp set with a ride of fourteen good, honest, long miles. **1867** Lowell *Biglow* 13 'Upcountry' **MA,** I hed to cross bayous an' criks . . / Upon a kin' o' corderoy, fust log, then alligator:/ Luck'ly the critters warn't sharp-sot; I guess 't was overruled / They'd done their mornin's marketin' an' gut their hunger cooled. **1891** Cooke *Huckleberries* 258 **CT,** But I am kinder sharp-set, I allow. I've driv all day to git here, and had only jest a bite to a tavern. **1899** (1912) Green *VA Folk-Speech* 379, Sharp-set. . . Hungry and ready for one's food.

sharp-shinned hawk n Also *sharp-chin hawk, sharpie, sharp-shin (hawk)* [See quot 1812]
A small, widely distributed hawk (*Accipiter striatus*). Also called **bird hawk 2, blue darter 2, bluetail hawk, brown ~, bullet ~, chicken ~ 1, fowl ~, harvest ~, partridge ~, pigeon ~ 2, privateer, quail hawk, sparrow ~**

1812 Wilson *Amer. Ornith.* 5.116, Sharp-shinned Hawk. *Falco Velox.* . . edges of the inside of the shins, below the knee, projecting like the edge of a knife, hard and sharp, as if intended to enable the bird to hold its prey with more security between them. **1858** Baird *Birds* 18, Sharp-shinned Hawk. . . Apparently, this handsome little hawk inhabits the whole of North America, from Mexico to the confines of the frigid zone. **1923** Dawson *Birds CA* 4.1659, The flight of the Sharp-shin is at times as swift as an arrow and as direct, but it is skilled in doubling and twisting; and no bird, save a swift or a swallow, can escape it in the open. **1950** *WELS (Kinds of hawks in your neighborhood),* 4 Infs, **WI,** Sharp-shinned hawk. **1965–70** *DARE* (Qu. Q4, . . *Kinds of hawks*) 19 Infs, **scattered,** Sharp-shinned (hawk); 15 Infs, **scattered,** Sharp-shin (hawk); **IL**119, Sharp-chin hawk. **1968** *PA Game News* Oct 49 **PA,** The swift, long-legged "sharpie" hunts in much the same manner as the Cooper's. . . The sharp-shinned hawk takes many small birds. . . Sharp-shins are hard to find. **1979** *UpCountry* Sept 22 **cwVT,** I could look down [through the picture-window pane] upon the inert form of a sharp-shinned hawk, its wings spread as though in death. **2000** *NADS Letters,* The New Jersey nickname for the Sharp-Shinned Hawk—'Sharpie'— . . . has spread through the birding community . . and is still in current use.

sharp shoe n Cf **sharpen**
A horseshoe provided with tapering calks to prevent slipping; hence adj *sharpshod* provided with such shoes.

1847 *Scientific Amer.* 2.122, They have had some fine sleighing at Albany, and the streets became quite slippery before the farmers had got their horses sharp-shod. [**c1855** Dana *U.S. Illustr.* 131 **NH,** The animals are also sharply shod, to make them foot-sure.] **1866** *Scientific Amer.* 14.244, You could not invent a more perfect ice breaker than a horse's sharp shoe. [**1875** in 1983 *PADS* 70.50 **ce,sePA,** Everything is frozen up so that it is almost impossible to travel with horses unless they are right sharply shod.] **1890** *Century Dict.* 5554, Sharp-shod. . . Having shoes with calks or sharp spikes for safety in moving over ice. **1907** *DN* 3.249 **eME,** Sharpen (a horse). . . To provide a horse with sharp shoes. **1925** *Book of Rural Life* 6.3714, Both work mules and fattening mules, unless sharp-shod, can advantageously be run in a lot having access to an open shed, and fed together. **1935** Davis *Honey* 289 **OR,** A man run down by a bunch of sharp-shod horses has a tendency to scatter

around badly. **1956** Almirall *From College* 191 **CO,** When deep snow . . hid the roads, bobsleds with their wide runners and horses "sharp-shod," that is, with what were known as calks, sharpened and set in their shoes, did the work. **1970** *DARE* Tape **MI**125, [FW:] How about the horses, didn't they slip on that ice? [Inf:]. . . But they had sharp shoes, they was sharp! If one of 'em stepped on your foot, you had a hole. **1984** *MJLF* 10.155 **nME, cnWI,** Sharp shod. When the calks on a horse's shoes have been drawn out to points to prevent slipping on the ice.

sharpshooter n
1 A leafhopper; see quots.

1902 U.S. Dept. Ag. *Yearbook for 1901* 377, Early cotton . . avoids to a great extent damage to the plant by the boll-worm, cotton worm, and sharp-shooter. **1906** Johnson *Highways Missip. Valley* 112 **AR,** Last year we had a bug what we call the sharpshooter. It comes when the bolls was just formin' an' blasted 'em so they dried up an' stuck thar hard an' fast. **1942** McAtee *Notes Thornton's Gloss.* [3], Sharpshooter. . . The appellation was inspired by the swift flushing (jumping or "shooting") of these insects when disturbed. Colloquially, various kinds of leafhoppers may have been included by the expression but those most frequently sent in for identification were the larger sorts (Cicadellinae, genera *Homalodisca* and *Oncometopia*). These do not have sharply conical heads as called for in *[WNID]*. **1959** *Washington Post & Times Herald* (DC) 23 July sec A 20/2 **swCA,** Priesendorfer identified them as leafhoppers, commonly called sharpshooters. **1999** (acc) CA Univ. *Xylella Fastidiosa Web Site* (Internet), Important vectors in California—*Blue-green Sharpshooter . . Green Sharpshooter . . Red-headed Sharpshooter . . Glassy-winged Sharpshooter.*

2 A spade with a long narrow blade. **esp LA, TX**

1929 Bell *Some Contrib. KS Vocab.* 253, Sharpshooter. . . A spade. . . Included on the questionnaire with the result that twenty-two marked it as their use, while ten indicated they had heard it in various Kansas and Missouri communities. **1942** *AmSp* 17.281 [TX oil pipe line terms], Sharpshooter. A tilling spade. **1967–68** *DARE* (Qu. L35, *Hand tools used for cutting underbrush and digging out roots*) Inf **LA**15, Sharpshooter—a narrow eighteen-inch shovel [*DARE* Ed: drawing in text]; **TX**8, Sharpshooter—small, pointed shovel—long narrow blade (20″ blade). **1980** *DARE* File **cMO,** Joe Wollard uses the term "sharp shooter" to describe a ditching spade. **1986** Pederson *LAGS Concordance,* 1 inf, **nwLA,** Sharpshooter—little skinny shovel; 1 inf, **neTX,** Sharpshooter—narrow, round-pointed shovel. **2000** *DARE* File—Internet **ceTX,** I had just bought me a second hand sharpshooter [for digging graves].

3 =**shotgun 1.**

1942 Perry *Texas* 137, A Negro or poor white shanty is a "shotgun shack" or a "sharpshooter." **1986** Pederson *LAGS Concordance,* 1 inf, **ceTX,** A sharpshooter; Three-room sharpshooter—straight house, shotgun.

4 also *sharpshooter casket:* A coffin with tapering ends.

1986 Pederson *LAGS Concordance (Casket)* 1 inf, **cLA,** Sharpshooter casket—broad middle, sharp ends; 1 inf, **nwMS,** Sharpshooters—plain, homemade boxes; 1 inf, **swMS,** Sharpshooters—narrow at feet, old, not used now. [All infs Black]

5 A **navy bean.**

1970 *DARE* (Qu. I18, *The smaller beans that are white when they are dry*) Inf **AR**56, Sharpshooters.

6 See **sharpie 2.**

sharpshooter casket See **sharpshooter 4**

sharpside turbot n Also *sharpridge turbot*
=**hornyhead turbot.**

1960 Amer. Fisheries Soc. *List Fishes* 75, Turbot, . . sharpridge—see turbot, hornyhead. **1973** Knight *Cook's Fish Guide* 393, Turbot . . sharpside—Hornyhead.

sharp-sot See **sharp-set**

sharptail n
1 See **sharp-tailed grouse.**
2 See **sharp-tailed sparrow.**
3 =**pintail 1.**

1874 Long *Amer. Wild-Fowl* 195, Pintail Duck (*Anas Acuta*). Local names: "Sprigtails," "Sharptails," and "Water-Pheasants." **1877** Hallock *Sportsman's Gaz.* 205, *Dafila acuta.* . . Pin-tail. Sprig-tail. Sharp-tail.

1946 Goodrich *Birds in KS* 318, Sharp-tail—pintail, American. **1982** Elman *Hunter's Field Guide* 156, Pintail . . Common & regional names: pinnie, . . sharptail [etc].

sharp-tailed finch n

=**sharp-tailed sparrow.**

1811 Wilson *Amer. Ornith.* 4.70 **GA,** The Sharp-tailed Finch is five inches and a quarter long. **1834** Audubon *Ornith. Biog.* 2.281, *The Sharp-tailed Finch.* . . spend the winter among the salt marshes of South Carolina. **1898** (1900) Davie *Nests N. Amer. Birds* 373, The Sharp-tailed Finch breeds abundantly in the salt marshes of the Atlantic coast from North Carolina northward. **1909** Field Museum Nat. Hist. *Zool. Ser.* 9.588 **IL,** Nelson's Sharp-tailed Sparrow, or Sharp-tailed Finch as it is often called, is abundant at times in Illinois during the migrations, but apparently much less common in spring than in the fall.

sharp-tailed grouse n Also *sharptail (grouse)*

A western grouse (*Pedioecetes phasianellus*) distinguished by a pointed tail edged with white. Also called **chicken B1, piketail 2, pin-tailed grouse, prairie chicken 2, ~ hen 2, specklebelly, spiketail, whitebelly, white grouse, willow ~**

1785 Pennant *Arctic Zool.* 2.306, Sharp-tailed Grous. **a1806** (1905) Clark *Orig. Jrls. Lewis & Clark Exped.* 6.121, The Prarie Fowl common to the Illinois are found as high up as the River Jacque above which the Sharpe tailed Grows [grouse] commence. **1877** Hallock *Sportsman's Gaz.* 118, The present indiscriminate netting and slaughter will soon finish the Pinnated Grouse, but the Sharp-tails have as yet escaped the pot-hunter. **1918** Grinnell *Game Birds CA* 558, The history of the Columbian Sharp-tailed Grouse, as far as it concerns California, is like that of a considerable number of North American game and non-game birds, which were once extremely abundant and are now almost or entirely extirpated. **1951** Kumlien–Hollister *Birds WI* 47, The sharp-tails seem to be rapidly giving way to the prairie hen, a species better adapted to life in a settled country. **1966–67** *DARE* (Qu. Q7, *Names and nicknames for . . game birds*) Infs **MI**10, 27, **MN**2, Sharptail grouse; **MI**2, 53, Sharptail; **MI**14, Sharptail grouse—something like the prairie chicken; **MI**42, Sharp-tailed grouse is called prairie chicken here. **1982** Elman *Hunter's Field Guide* 26, Sharptail gunning is superb on the prairies of eastern Alberta and western Saskatchewan. The birds are now hunted in all or parts of eleven states, from eastern Washington to the upper Michigan Peninsula and as far south as upper-central Colorado.

sharp-tailed snake n

A small snake of the Pacific states (*Contia tenuis*) noted for the spine in its tail. Also called **ground snake e**

1937 Pope *Snakes Alive* 218, Sharp-tailed snake (*[Contia] tenuis*). Pacific states but absent from extreme southern California. **1947** Pickwell *Amphibians* 49, The name "sharp-tailed" arises from the horny, truly sharp tip at the end of the tail. . . The Sharp-tailed Snake occurs in the Pacific states from south-central California north, possibly to Puget Sound. **1979** Behler–King *Audubon Field Guide Reptiles* 599, Sharp-tailed Snake. . . The short spine-tipped tail and *alternating black and whitish crossbars on belly* quickly identify it.

sharp-tailed sparrow n Also *sharptail (sparrow)*

A salt-marsh sparrow (*Ammospiza caudacuta*). Also called **quailhead, sharp-tailed finch**

1898 (1900) Davie *Nests N. Amer. Birds* 373, Sharp-tailed sparrow. . . Salt marshes of the Atlantic coast from Prince Edward Island and Nova Scotia to North Carolina. **1917** (1923) *Birds Amer.* 3.29, The Sharp-tailed Sparrow is a bird of the saltwater marshes along the coast of New England and New York. . . A distinguishing peculiarity is the form of its tail, which is rather long, and tapers to a point, instead of being square at the end. **1940** Weygandt *Down Jersey* 32 **sNJ,** We saw very few beach sparrows, either seaside or sharp tails. **1969–70** *DARE* (Qu. Q21, . . *Kinds of sparrows*) Infs **RI**17, Sharptail sparrow; **VA**47, Sharp-tailed sparrow. **1977** Bull–Farrand *Audubon Field Guide Birds* 440, There are few birds more unprepossessing than a threadbare Sharp-tail in August.

sharptail grouse See **sharp-tailed grouse**

sharptail sparrow See **sharp-tailed sparrow**

sharp time adv phr

Punctually.

1885 *Atlantic Mth.* 55.602 **sAppalachians,** I waited fur Sol an' the

corn right sharp time Wednesday morning. **1905** *DN* 3.93 **nwAR,** *Sharp time.* . . Sharp, punctually. 'The society will meet at eight o'clock, sharp time.' Rare.

sharpy n

1 See **sharpie 1.**

2 =**hooded merganser.**

1982 Elman *Hunter's Field Guide* 228, *Hooded Merganser* . . Common & Regional Names . . spikebill . . pickaxe, sharpy [etc].

sharves See **shaft 2**

shasha See **sashay** v

Shasta lily n

A **lily 1** (here: either *Lilium washingtonianum* subsp *purpurascens* or *L. pardalinum* subsp *shastense*).

1885 *Overland Mth.* (2d ser) 6.638 **ncCA,** [Title:] Shasta Lilies. **1900** *Sunset* Mar 197, *L. Washingtonianum,* the Shasta lily, is found in the mountains of the Shasta region and in the Sierras, where it attains its full perfection in July and August. **1915** (1926) Armstrong–Thornber *Western Wild Flowers* 34, Shasta Lily is a variety with a small bulb. **1920** Rice–Rice *Pop. Studies CA Wild Flowers* 116, The Shasta Lily, which is more plentiful than the Washington, is really a variety of *L[ilium] washingtonianum,* but it has a smaller bulb. **1959** Munz–Keck *CA Flora* 1342, Shasta Lily. . . Chaparral; base of Mt. Shasta. **1999** (acc) CA Univ. Digital Lib. Project *CalFlora* (Internet), *Lilium pardalium ssp. shastense*—Shasta lily. *Ibid,* *Lilium washingtonianum ssp. purpurascens*—purple-flowered Shasta lily.

shat n Rarely *chat* [Prob < **shatter** n, but cf *OED2 chat* sb.³] **Delmarva** Cf *chat* n², ~ n³, **longshat pine, shatter** n, **shortshat pine**

A dried **needle 1** from a pine tree.

1895 *DN* 8.393 **seMD,** Shats: dry pine leaves or needles. Worcester Co. **1898** *Amer. Forests* 4.81 **ceVA,** The Pine "chats," "needles" or "browse" are valuable for a fertilizer and are spread on the neighboring fields. **1913** Johnson *Highways St. Lawrence to VA* 239 **DE,** Cattle sheds, for instance, were roofed with brush on which pine shats were thrown. The shats would shed rain if there was enough of 'em, but they'd rot in two or three years, and then we had to take the oxen and haul more. **1938** FWP *Guide DE* 508 **seDE,** The fire was protected by "harbors" of brush made windproof and fire-proof by a covering of pine "shats" and clay. **1949** in 1986 *DARE* File **eMD,** Pick up the pine shats from under the trees. **1968–70** *DARE* (Qu. T6, *The pointed leaves that fall from pine trees*) Inf **DE**1, Pine shats; **VA**51, Shats—colored usage. **1976** Bruce *How to Grow Wildflowers* 24, Pine forests mean the South—red sand roads, shrilling cicadas, clouds of biting flies, and the pungency of sun-baked pine needles (or pine "shats" as they are called in lower Delmarva). **1976** [see **shatter** n].

shatawba n

=**catalpa B2.**

1966 *DARE* (Qu. P6) Inf **MS**11, Shatawba [šə'tɔbə].

shatter v Also with *off, out* [*OED2* shatter v. 3 1577 →]

Of grain or seed: to fall from the ear, seed pod, etc—freq in phr *shattered corn*.

1790 Deane *New Engl. Farmer* 122, [Hay] should not stand too late, or till the seed be ripe. It is not only harder to cut, but the ripeness of the seed will cause it to shatter out while drying, which will be a considerable loss. **1902** *DN* 2.245 **sIL,** Shatter. . . To shell out, by dehiscence, as over-ripe grain. **1905** *DN* 3.93 **nwAR,** Shattered corn. . . Scattered corn; corn loosened from the ear. Common. **1907** *DN* 3.226 **nwAR,** Shatter. . . To shell out by dehiscence, as over-ripe grain. **1909** *DN* 3.368 **eAL, wGA,** Shattered corn. . . Scattered corn, loose grains of corn. **1912** Green *VA Folk-Speech* 380, Shattered-corn. . . The grains of corn shattered from the husks in handling, and fed to hogs or fowls. **1966–70** *DARE* Tape **IA**10, They's some of them butterprint, too. There's little seeds in 'em, they're round and . . they get dry, they shatter out; **OK**18, Ordinarily, the oats would fall out, when they got ripe. You had to cut 'em pretty green to keep 'em from shattering off.

shatter n Pronc-sp *shadder, shadow* [Prob < **shatter** v] **chiefly VA**

=**shat.**

1831 *Genesee Farmer* 1.50/3 **VA,** I once asked a Virginia skipper . .

how they managed to keep them [=sweet potatoes] over the winter. "Why," said he "I *reckon* it is the easiest thing in *natur*,—you must first dig a big hole in a sand bank, then *tote* your *taturs* in a cart and *dump* them in, cover 'em with *pine shadows*, and so heap up the sand on the top, and I *reckon* you will have no trouble." **1860** *Harper's New Mth. Mag.* 21.641 **VA**, "Some of the negroes, I suppose, after 'shatters'." . . "No such thing," she said; "it is some one on horseback." And next moment we heard for ourselves the regular tramp of a horse's feet . . , though the sound was deadened by the thick carpet of pine-shatters that lined the woodland road. **1899** (1912) Green *VA Folk-Speech* 380, *Shatters*. . . The leaves of the pine after they have fallen. *Pine-shatters.* **1937** Hench Coll., Eastern Shore of Virginia expressions. . . He is hauling shadows (=pine needles) in to the pound (=barn yard). **c1938** in 1970 Hyatt *Hoodoo* 1.240 **seMD**, I was in the woods rakin' up, heapin' up *shadders*—you know, baiddin' [Hyatt: bedding]. *Ibid*, [Hyatt:] *Shadders* = shatters, a plural of shatter, meaning in Southern U.S.A., fallen pine leaves or needles. **1970** *DARE* (Qu. T6, *The pointed leaves that fall from pine trees*) Inf **VA**51, Shatters [ʃædɚz]—colored usage; **VA**79, Pine shatters. **1970** *DARE* FW Addit **NJ**, Pine tags or shadows—pine straw, branches of pine needles to cover vegetable beds in winter. [FW: Speaker built such beds in Virginia.] **1976** Ryland *Richmond Co. VA* 375, *Pine shadows*—pine needles (cf. Eastern Shore "pine shats") i.e. "shatters."

shattered corn, shatter off (or out) See **shatter** v

shatter worm n

A **corn earworm** or sugarcane borer; see quots.

1903 U.S. Dept. Ag. *Yearbook for 1902* 729 **VA**, *Corn stalk-borer* . . (Diatræa saccharalis). . . reported in 1902 as occasioning considerable injury in Virginia, in some portions of which it is known as the "shatter worm." **1999** (acc) Natl. Integrated Pest Management Network—NC Component *Pest Identification* (Internet), During May and June, first-generation larvae feed in the tightly coiled blades of corn. As a result, numerous ragged holes appear when the blades unfurl. . . This condition is often referred to as "shatter worm" injury.

shav See **shaft** 1

shave brush n Cf **shave grass**

A **horsetail** 1 (here: *Equisetum arvense*).

1974 (1977) Coon *Useful Plants* 131, *Equisetum arvense*—Scouring rush, joint weed, bull pipes, shave brush [etc.].

shaved-tail See **shave-tail** adj 2

shave grass n [*OED2* c1450 →] Cf **shave brush**

A **horsetail** 1 (here: *Equisetum hyemale*).

1857 Gray *First Lessons* 587, *E[quisetum] hyemale* . . Scouring Rush. Shave-Grass. . . Wet banks; common, especially northward. **1892** IN Dept. Geol. & Nat. Resources *Rept. for 1891* 158, *Equisetum hyemale* . . Scouring Rush. Shave-Grass. **1900** Lyons *Plant Names* 147, *E[quisetum] hyemale*. . . The following names apply to this and other rough species: Dutch Rush, Gun-bright . . Shave-grass [etc.].

shave ice n **chiefly HI, but now more widely recognized** Cf **snowball**

A confection of finely shaved ice with fruit syrup or other topping.

1953 *Honolulu Advertiser* 26 Apr 10/5 *(Popik Coll.)* **HI**, Long ago, as way far back as when I was one small kid in Honolulu, it was smart to find out right away quick where the nearest "Shave Ice" sign was in the neighborhood, for on those warm summer days there was nothing quite like it for bringing down the body temperature. **1972** Carr *Da Kine Talk* 147 **HI**, *Shave ice* is a fistful of joy to children—a paper cone of crushed (shaved) ice and generously doused with sweetened and colored water. **1974** *DARE* File **HI**, Shave ice. . . Shaved ice with fruit flavoring similar to a snow cone. **1975** *Sunset HI Guide* 9, Everywhere in the Islands you'll see children licking fruit-flavored "shave ice" (snow cones). **2000** in 2002 *DARE* File—Internet **HI**, My husband . . would be *ashamed* of me if I forgot to mention shave ice! It is *not* a snow cone, but shaved ice—a much finer texture. **2002** *Ibid* **UT**, Tropical Sno was founded in April of 1984 . . in Provo, Utah. Since that time it is estimated that more than 200,000,000 Tropical Sno shave ice have been sold throughout the United States and several foreign countries.

shaves See **shaft** 2

shave-tail adj

1 Of a horse or mule: having the tail shaved, freq as a sign that it is newly broken or otherwise unreliable.

1865 in 1963 Barrett *Civil War NC* 294 **NC**, He had rode upon that knock-kneed, shave tail, rail fence mule over 30 miles. **1914** Dixon *Life* 50 **KS** (as of 1867), By this time our "shave-tail" mules were under fairly good control.

2 also *shaved-tail;* Transf; of a person: inexperienced, "green"; contemptible.

1891 Bourke *On Border* 204 **AZ**, There were sarcastic references to the lack of "horse sense" shown by certain unnamed "shave-tail leftenants." **1899** Hall *Tales* 8 **AZ**, Not once . . has the boy asked his advice even about a camping place, which is quite customary and proper with 'shavetail' officers. **1908** Beach *Barrier* 283 **AR**, The first shave-tail desperado that meets him will spit in his eye. [sic] just to make a name for himself. **1949** Arnow *Hunter's Horn* 319 **eKY**, As fer me, you'll marry me off to some little shaved-tail son of a bitch when th rest gets big enough to work.

shavetail n [Absol use of **shave-tail** adj]

1 Used as a nickname for:

a A horse or mule.

1832 Paulding *Westward Ho* 111 **KY**, But somehow you don't appear to mind what's said to you any more than my old horse Shavetail, who lost his hearing at the last general training, they fired at such a rate. **1846** *N.O. Delta* 31 Aug. 366/2 *(DA)*, [This mule] was followed by Shavetail Kicky, Esq., who, in a few pertinent remarks, expressed his ass-ent to the proceedings.

b A person. Note: The implications of this nickname are not clear; the speaker in quot 1832, who applies it to himself, perh means to suggest that he is a "dangerous creature."

1832 Paulding *Westward Ho* 123 **KY**, "No, no," says I, "that won't do, there's no mistake in Shavetail, you may swear." **c1960** *Mathews Coll.* **AL** (as of c1900), It was customary for us schoolboys to nickname each other, and among the popular nicknames we applied jocosely to each other was "Shavetail." . . Where we got it I do not know, but I believe it was none other than a brother of mine that came forward at the opportune moment with this designation.

2 A mule (less freq, a horse) with its tail shaved, freq as a sign that it is newly broken or otherwise unreliable; a mule, esp a refractory one.

1870 Keim *Sheridan's Troopers* 89 **KS**, [He] gave vent to a soliloquy in denunciation of "shavetails," declaring that they [=intractable mules] were only "sulky and playing off." **1891** Bourke *On Border* 153 **MO, NE**, To contravene his [=a young mule's] maliciousness, it is necessary to mark him in such a manner that every packer will see at a glance that he is a new arrival, and thereupon set to work to drive him back to his proper place in his own herd. . . To effect this, is by neatly roaching his mane and shaving his tail so that nothing is left but a pencil or tassel of hair at the extreme end. He is now known as a 'shave-tail,' and everybody can recognize him at first sight. **1897** Lewis *Wolfville* 168 **AZ**, My off-wheel mule—a reg'lar shave-tail—is bad med'cine. Which he's not only eager to kick towerists an' others he takes a notion ag'inst; but he's likewise what you-alls calls a kleptomaniac. **1914** Dixon *Life* 47 **KS** (as of 1867), We put in ten days breaking the "shave-tails." *Ibid* 46, The mules were known as "shave-tails," which meant wild, unbroken. **1930** Cowan *Range Rider* 224 **WY**, All range horses in that country that are unbroken are called broom-tails. All broken saddle horses are called shave-tails. I just needed to say in range language that I was making shave-tails out of broom-tails, and people would know I was breaking horses. **1931** *AmSp* 7.52 **Sth, SW** [Lumberjack lingo], The "mule skinner" is frequently known as a "skinner" and the mules as "shave tails." **c1960** *Wilson Coll.* **csKY**, *Shavetail*. . . Mule, because of the custom of cutting the hair off most of its tail. **1966–70** *DARE* (Qu. K50, *Joking nicknames for mules*) Infs **IL**142, **OH**95, **WA**3, **WV**3, Shavetail; **CA**135, Shavetail—always had their tails roached; **TX**78, Shavetail—a mule who kicks a lot has tail shaved to identify. **1969** Sorden *Lumberjack Lingo* 107 **NEng, Gt Lakes**, *Shavetail*—A mule. **1980** Blair & Ketchum's *Country Jrl.* Oct 43 **SW**, That last practice started in the mines, where a "shavetail" was a snaky mule, not to be trusted.

3 A new recruit; a newly commissioned officer; now esp, a second lieutenant.

1891 Bourke *On Border* 153, Officers . . in the parlance of the packers, are known as "bell-sharps" and "shave-tails" respectively; . . the latter, [being] the youngster fresh from his studies on the Hudson, who fondly imagines he knows it all. **1902** Whitlock *13th District* 426, He was a shavetail [=a new recruit] then, and didn't know a Piegan Indian from a Sioux. **1926** *AmSp* 1.243, *"Shave-tail"*—a second lieutenant. **1936** *AmSp* 11.60 [Soldier speech], There is a part of soldier speech, however, which is not fixed by regulation. . . A young lieutenant is a *shavetail* like a newly purchased mule. **1970** *Current Slang* 5.3.18, *Shave-tail*. . . A new second Lieutenant.

shavings n Cf old man's beard 2
=fringe tree.

1900 Lyons *Plant Names* 96, [*Chionanthus*] *virginica* . . Delaware to Florida and Texas. Fringe-tree . . Shavings [etc]. **1960** Vines *Trees SW* 850, Vernacular names [of *Chionanthus virginicus*] are Flowering Ash, Old Man's Beard, Grandfather-graybeard . . Shavings, and Graybeard-tree. **1971** Krochmal *Appalachia Med. Plants* 92, Fringe tree . . old man's beard, poison ash, shavings [etc].

shavs See shaft 2

shaw n [Engl, Scots, Ir dial; cf *OED2 shaw* sb.[1] 1.a, b, *EDD shaw* sb.[1] 1] *arch*

1930 Shoemaker *1300 Words* cPA Mts (as of c1900), *Shaw*—A small grove of trees.

Shawnee n Also sp *Shawanee, Shawny, shonny* Also *Shawnee salad, ~ lettuce* esp KY Cf Indian salad

A **waterleaf** (here: *Hydrophyllum virginianum*).

1780 in 1964 *3 Pioneer TN Documents* 9, Gathered some herbs in the bottoms of Cumberland, which some of the Company called Shawanee Sallad. **1784** (1929) Filson *Kentucke* 24, The Shawanese [sic] sallad, wild lettuce, and pepper-grass, and many more . . have excellent virtues. **1793** in 1948 Toulmin *Western Country* 73, The sorts of grass are white clover . . a vegetable called . . Shawnee lettuce. **1822** *London Hort. Soc. Trans.* I Ser. IV. 445 *(DA)*, The *Hydrophyllum Virginicum* is called by the Americans of the Western States, *Indian Sallad*, or *Shawanee Sallad*, because these Indians eat it as such, when tender. Some of the first settlers do the same. **1911** *DN* 3.540 eKY, *Shawny*. . . An (unidentified) plant cooked as "greens." **1937** (1963) Hyatt *Kiverlid* 79 KY, We picked wild mustard an' Shawnee an' Injun collards, polk, blue-thistle . . an' I don't know what all. **1953** (1977) Hubbard *Shantyboat* 59 **Missip-Ohio Valleys,** One of the best greens was shawny, or milk-weed, a slender plant with tender leaves and stem and a delicate flavor. This grew in the woods and we sought our dinner among the yellow violets and trillium. **1965–70** *DARE* (Qu. I28a, *. . . Kinds of things . . you call 'greens'* . . *[Those that are eaten raw]*) Infs **KY**42, **MO**37, Shawnee; **NC**55, Shawnee lettuce; (Qu. I28b, *Kinds of greens that are cooked*) Infs **KY**28, 44, Shawnee; **KY**34, Shawnee—leaves like a nickel—big bunches; **KY**40, Shawnee—little round leaf, one inch diameter . . wild green. **1967–68** *DARE* Tape **IN**32, I get mountain sprouts, sourdock, wild beet, shawnee. . . I don't eat any of them raw; **KY**34, [FW:] What other things do people pick for salad greens? [Inf:] Mustard and turnip tops and shawnee. . . [FW:] What does shawnee taste like? [Inf:] Hit's sweet. It don't taste bitter much. . . sort of like lettuce. **1983** *MJLF* 9.1.55 ceKY (as of 1956), *Shonny* . . a wild green. **1991** Still *Wolfpen Notebooks* 77 **sAppalachians,** What I look forward to in the spring hain't garden sass. Hit's wild greens. They grow where God planted them. What you want to look for is plaintain [sic], bird's toe . . shawnee [etc]. . . And don't spare the seasoning.

Shawnee berry n Cf Shawnee haw

A **black haw 1** (here: *Viburnum prunifolium*).

1941 Writers' Program *Guide WV* 140, Teas made from herbs and roots are regarded in high favor . . Shawnee berry tea for kidney trouble . . Jerusalem oak tea for worms.

Shawnee haw n Also *shoneehaw, shonny (haw)* chiefly NC

A **viburnum** (here: usu *Viburnum nudum*).

1860 Curtis *Cat. Plants NC* 90, Possum haw. . . The fruit is a deep blue. In the Mountains I have heard this called *Shawnee Haw.* **1883** Zeigler–Grosscup *Heart of Alleghanies* 58 **wNC,** Here also spring the service tree, . . the Shawnee haw [etc]. **1911** *Century Dict. Suppl.*, *Shawnee-haw* . . The larger withe-rod, *Viburnum nudum*. **1930** Youngken *Text Book Pharmacognosy* (3d ed) 687, *Substitutes and Adulter-ants.*—The barks of other species of *Viburnum* notably *V. nudum* . . commonly known as Shonny Haw or Shawnee Haw [etc]. **1956** McAtee *Some Dialect NC* 58, *Shonny haw.* . . that is Shawnee haw, one of the black haws (*Viburnum carolinianum*). Macon County. **1968** *DARE* (Qu. I44, *What kinds of berries grow wild around here?*) Inf **VA**13, Shawnee

haws. **1971** Krochmal *Appalachia Med. Plants* 272, *Viburnum pruni-folium.* . . Common names: Black haw . . shonny [etc]. **1982** Ginns *Snowbird Gravy* 57 nwNC, When students misbehaved back then they whipped 'em. Whipped 'em with what they called a "shonny haw." That was just a long switch with no limbs off of it or anything—just a long switch. **1985** *NC Folkl. Jrl.* 33.44 wNC (as of c1912), He [=a school-teacher] walked up Clear Creek and across Little Buck Hill, stopping to select and cut a half dozen hickory and shawnee haw switches about six feet in length on the way.

Shawnee lettuce (or salad) See Shawnee

Shawnee wood n
=catalpa B1.

1818 Barton *Compendium Florae Philadelphicae* 1.9, Catalpa-tree. Catawba-tree. Schawnes-wood. **1852** *De Bow's Rev.* 12.272 **LA,** *Shaw-nee wood,* or *big-leaved cucumber* (magnolia glauca.) **1907** Hodge *Hdbk. Amer. Indians* 1.213, The western catalpa, larger Indian bean, or Shawnee wood *(C. speciosa).* **1995** Alden *Hardwoods N. Amer.* 37, *Catalpa speciosa* . . shawnee-wood.

Shawny See Shawnee

shawt-pashunt See short-patient

shay n

A type of fishing boat; see quot 1957.

1905 *Churchman* 18 Nov. 804 *(DAE)*, A 'shay'. . . is a kind of fishing boat. **1905** Wasson *Green Shay* 59 NEng, "I've seen them two Spurlings out there on their gear this fall in that big green sprits'l shay of theirn when the whole Shoal Ground was nothin' only a clear streamin' torch of breakers!" . . "I call it a fool way to resk life, myself. Some of them big shays are dretful able boats though, and no mistake." **1957** Beck *Folkl. ME* 128, At Cape Porpoise the boat used was the shay, a form of dory that differed in minor respects from the typical dory in that it was beamier and had less freeboard and a few other things.

shayre See share

she pron Cf he pron

1 Used redundantly with a noun subject. [*OED2* a1440 →; cf *EDD she* II.1] Cf **he** pron **1**, **it** pron **C2**, **they**

1850 in 1999 *AmSp* 74.274 ceSC, Me fren Mres. Maklin that be a nebr whwer i liv wit me great nefu tom McCormick en wife emily she sed she wud hep me. **1882** *Century Illustr. Mag.* 23.529 NC, Esmeraldy, she's down-stairs. **1893** Shands *MS Speech* 35, The almost universal use of the third person pronoun after names by illiterate whites of Mississippi should be noted. They very rarely say that John or Susan did it, but nearly always "John he" or "Susan she" did it. **1913** Kephart *High-landers* 112 sAppalachians, I don't know; maw, she knows. *Ibid* 122, The woman she bakes us a pone o' bread to eat. *Ibid* 224, John's Lize Ann she ain't much. **1916** Howells *Leatherwood God* 85 **OH** [sic *ADD*—quot not found], Sally she got it putty straight. **1926** Roberts *Time of Man* 138 KY, Miss Casse, she bought her a mare today. *Ibid* 326, He's done all the things Nannie she ever thought to do. **1931** Jacobson *Milwaukee Dial.* 17 seWI, Our car, she is running fine. . . Our Anna, she is pretty. **1933** *AmSp* 8.1.49 Ozarks, Th' ol' woman she scrubbed th' hull dang shanty. . . Maw she done went a-greenin' this mornin'. **1934** Carmer *Stars Fell on AL* 182, Miss B'ar she run out de cabin. **1999** *DARE* File **ME** (as of 1970s), "The phone she rings," was a common manner of speaking among those of French Canadian extraction. I don't recall ever hearing anyone use "he" in that sort of phrase.

2 Her. *esp freq among Gullah speakers* Note: The common use of *she* for *her* in compound objects (as in *I saw she and her sister*) is not treated here. Cf **he** pron **2, 3**

1922 Gonzales *Black Border* 326 sSC, GA coasts [Gullah glossary], *She'own*—her own. **1927** Adams *Congaree* 14 cSC [Black], She tongue forked just like a snake. *Ibid* 19, You know . . Ole Sister take so much interest in she friends. **1971** Cunningham *Syntactic Analysis Gullah* 40, She name is Bertha. **1987** Jones-Jackson *When Roots Die* 126 sSC coast [Gullah], The man tell she, say "Go in onion patch and try for pull up onion." **1989** Gurganus *Oldest Confederate Widow* 393 **Sth** (as of 1860s) [Black], Queen down in she parlor eating bread and money.

3 He; his. *Gullah* Cf **he** pron **4**

1926 Smith *Gullah* 26 sSC, GA coasts, A visitor to the office of a masculine attorney who had stepped out for a moment was told by the Georgetown darkey office boy: "She is out; 'e yent come back, not yit; him soon will." **1939** Griswold *Sea Is. Lady* 6 csSC (as of 1861) [Gullah], Alec whispered: "Reb'ren' say come please Maussa. She vaitin' on you at de westry in she robe an' t'ing."

she n

1a A female.   **scattered, but esp S Midl**   Cf **he** n **1**

1828 Webster *Amer. Dict., She. . . She* is sometimes used as a noun for *woman* or *female . .* but in contempt or in ludicrous language. . . *She* is also used in composition for female, representing sex; as a *she*-bear; a *she*-cat. 1889 *MLN* 4.206 **TN,** *He* and *she* are used as nouns. . . This is very common among uneducated people, especially children, who say, "It is a *he*," etc. 1899 (1912) Green *VA Folk-Speech* 381, *She's. . .* Females. "The goat has three kids, two *she's* and one *he*." 1931 Randolph *Ozarks* 79, The names of male animals must not be mentioned when women are present. . . The hillman sometimes refers to animals as the *he* or the *she*. 1939 *Hall Coll.* **wNC, eTN,** *She . .* a female bear. "They was two old *she's* and three yearlin's." 1967–69 *DARE* (Qu. K62, *. . A female sheep*) Infs **GA**74, **NC**49, She; (Qu. AA7b, *. . A woman who is very fond of men and is always trying to know more—if she's not respectable about it*) Inf **IL**5, She—she's just a she; (Qu. HH34, *General words . . for a woman, not necessarily uncomplimentary*) Infs **MI**104, **TN**15, She.

b attrib, occas used redundantly: See quots.   **scattered, but esp S Midl**   Cf **he** n **1**

1825 Neal *Brother Jonathan* 1.54 **CT,** Whenever a young she-yankee is "laying out" for a husband, she gives what is there called a *"quilting frolic."* 1828 [see **1a** above]. 1847 Howe *Hist. Coll. OH* 565, He once shot a she bear and 2 cubs in less than three minutes. 1858 Hammett *Piney Woods Tavern* 40 **TX,** Some . . it hangs to like a chinkapin bur to a she-nigger's wool. 1899 (1912) Green *VA Folk-Speech* 380, *She. . .* A female animal; a bird, beast, or fish of the female sex: as, a *she*-goat; a *she*-crab. 1927 Adams *Congaree* 19 **cSC** [Black], I ain't axed de ole she rat to pray for me. c1937 in 1972 *Amer. Slave* 2.1.16 **SC,** Every he thing from a he king down to a bunty [sic] rooster gits 'cited 'bout she things. 1939 *LANE* Map 210 *(Ewe)* 2 infs, **ME, MA,** She sheep. 1940 *AmSp* 15.46 **swVA,** Whereas in the Smokies, Cumberlands and Ozarks the usual variant for cow is *cow-brute*, in the Blue Ridge it is commonly a she-cow. 1954 *Harder Coll.* **cwTN,** *She. . .* But we found out that it was a she o'possum. 1956 *Hall Coll.* **wNC, eTN,** Then he heerd a cub bear go to bawlin'. Then he saw the old bear come runnin' out of the laurel. 1958 McCulloch *Woods Words* 161 **Pacific NW,** *She-bitch. . .* A double damned female of some kind. 1961 Seeman *In Arms of Mt.* 57 **eTN,** That young'un was only fifteen, but she was as mean as a striped snake. Law, there's a lot of she-nethin's and he-nethin's around this country. 1965–70 *DARE* (Qu. AA7b, *. . A woman who is very fond of men and is always trying to know more—if she's not respectable about it*) Infs **IL**14, **OK**55, **WA**11, She-wolf; **SC**58, Regular she-devil; (Qu. HH12, *A person who is always finding fault about unimportant things*) Inf **OH**33, A she-biddy; (Qu. HH34, *General words . . for a woman, not necessarily uncomplimentary*) Inf **FL**7, She-heifer. 1986 Pederson *LAGS Concordance* **Gulf Region** *(Cow)* 6 infs, She cow; 3 infs, She moo(s); *(Calf)* 3 infs, She calf; 1 inf, She dog and boy dog; 1 inf, He's a she dog; *(Horses)* 4 infs, She horse; *(Hogs)* 9 infs, She hog; 1 inf, She pig; 1 inf, She donkeys; 2 infs, She mule; 1 inf, She rabbit. 1996 Horton *Island Out of Time* 20 **Chesapeake Bay MD,** Among the first to arise are those immature females, "she crabs" or "maiden crabs," that did not quite make it to their final "shed" or molt before cold weather arrested them last December.

c attrib; Transf: having qualities traditionally assoc with women; see quots.   Cf **he** n **2**

1916 Macy–Hussey *Nantucket Scrap Basket* 143, *"She rig"*—A contemptuous term, reflecting on the weaker sex, applied to anything which is not properly made, set up or put together—in direct opposition to "ship shape"—implying masculine skill and efficiency. 1917 *DN* 4.420 **New Orleans LA, Baltimore MD,** *She-brick. . .* Same as *dandy-trap* [= a loose paving-brick that squirts muddy water when stepped on]. 1940 Mencken *Happy Days* 281 **Baltimore MD,** He would bring out a kitchen chair shortly after noon, plant it carefully on the narrow and squidgy sidewalk, with its treacherous "she" bricks, and proceed solemnly to business. 1945 Mencken *Amer. Lang. Suppl. 1* 658 **MD,** In my boyhood in Baltimore a loose paving brick was called a *she-brick*. On wet days it discharged a stream of dirty water on anyone who stepped on it. 1950 *WELS Suppl.* **MA, NH,** *He-dishes*—Pots and pans, utensils, Usually used in the context of washing them. Familiar to several generations of Yankees, in contrast with *she-dishes* (glass, china, silverware). 1986 *Hand Coll.* **OH** (as of 1955), Never carry a she-note (two-dollar bill), for it is bad luck.

2 A women's toilet.   Cf **he** n **4**

1969 *DARE* (Qu. F37, *Names for an indoor toilet*) Inf **NY**213, A he and a she.

sheaf n Usu |šif|; pl |šifs, šivz|; also |šiθs, šiðz| Pronc-spp *sheat(h);* by back-formation *sheave*   **widespread, but esp PA, MD, WV, OH**   See Map   **bundle** n **B1**

A quantity of cereal plants bound together after reaping.

1765 in 1904 Thwaites *Early W. Travels* 1.140 **swIN,** Reeds . . make the best pasture in the world, the young reeds being preferable to sheaf oats. 1845 (1930) Sewall *Diary* 273 **ME,** Hauled load of sheaf oats to the stable (100 bundles). 1946 *PADS* 5.36 **VA,** *Sheaf* (see *bundle*). Fairly common west of the Blue Ridge and on the Middle Neck. 1949 Kurath *Word Geog.* 67, *Sheaf . .* In the Southern area and in the South Midland *bundle* is the regular word for a sheaf of wheat. Elsewhere in the Eastern States *bundle* and *sheaf* occur side by side, the former predominating in the entire New England settlement area, the latter in Pennsylvania and adjoining parts of West Virginia. In Philadelphia and its immediate vicinity *sheaf* is used to the exclusion of *bundle*, and in the adjoining Pennsylvania German section to the west *sheaf* is much more common than *bundle*. . . *Sheaf* predominates in all the larger cities of the North and Midland, partly because it is the literary term. In the South *sheaf* is almost entirely restricted to cultured speakers. 1965–70 *DARE* (Qu. L30a, *When grain is cut it is . . tied up in ⸺*) 169 Infs, **widespread, but esp PA, MD, WV, OH,** Sheaves; 29 Infs, **scattered,** Sheafs; 20 Infs, **scattered,** Sheaths [šiθs]; 15 Infs, **scattered,** Sheaths [šiðz]; **MO**5, Sheaf; **MS**53, Sheats; **DC**2, Corn sheaves; (Qu. L31, *. . The top bundle of a shock*) 19 Infs, **scattered, but esp OH,** Cap sheaf; **IL**142, **MI**64, **MO**15, **OH**10, 88, Sheaf; **IN**77, **MO**5, **OH**72, **PA**158, Top *(or deck)* sheaf; **IL**114, Cap sheaf bundle; **MI**56, Sheave. 1968 *PADS* 49.13 **Upper MW** (as of c1950), The literary term *sheaf (of wheat* was offered by the minority of informants in each group, but the student responses suggest that this variant is becoming more widespread while *bundle* is declining in usage. 1972 *PADS* 58.19 **cwAL,** *Sheaf. Bundle* (21 [of 27 infs]) predominates over *sheaf* (3, 2 of whom are cultured informants) and *hands* (1). 1973 Flach *Yankee German-America* 23 **csTX,** When combines came they were hard to use in the small fields. Finally they made sheaf-oats and baled it. 1989 Pederson *LAGS Tech. Index* 149 **Gulf Region,** Sheaf [Of 914 infs, 494 responded with *bundle*, 87 with *sheaf*].

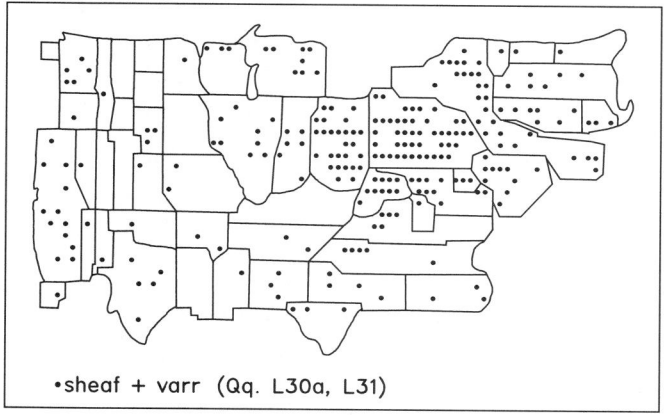

•sheaf + varr (Qq. L30a, L31)

sheafish See **sheefish**

sheal n Also, perh by folk-etym, *shield* [Cf *EDD sheal* sb.[2] 9 "A thin layer or skin, a scale"; but cf also *OED2 shield* sb. 14 "?A sheet of ice. *Obs.*"]

1966 *DARE* (Qu. B33a, *The first thin ice that forms over the surface of a pond or pool: "There's just a ⸺ of ice."*) Inf **FL**9, Shield; **IL**93, Sheal [šil]; **MS**2, Thin sheal [šiəl].

shear n[1], v See **share**

shear n[2] [Pronc-sp for *share;* cf *EDD shear* sb.[2] 11 "A plough-share."]   Cf **barshare plow**

1917 *DN* 4.400 **neOH,** Shear [šiɚ]. . . Plowshare. I have heard this word, as if it were *shear*, used by those who customarily say [plauˇšæɚ]. . . Also Ill., Kan. 1967–68 *DARE* (Qu. L18, *Kinds of* *plows*) Infs **MD26, 29, VA33,** Barshear plow; **WA20,** Shear plow. **1982** *Barrick Coll.* **csPA,** *Plowshare*—pron. plów-shear.

shear crab n Cf crab n 1
See quots.

1967 *PA Game News* Aug 4 **PA,** My two companions collected a few soft-shelled crayfish for bait. . . Everywhere we looked in the slower water the outgrown empty exoskeletons rocked gently on the bottom like pallid crayfish ghosts. Turning over the nearest rock invariably revealed the newly moulted "shear-crab," hiding out while waiting for his soft, pink shell to harden. **1968** *DARE* (Qu. P19, . . *Small, freshwater crayfish*) Inf **PA155,** Shear crab.

shearings n Cf chopping 1, slash, slashing
1984 *MJLF* 10.155 **cnWI,** Shearings. Timberland that has been clean-cut, with everything cut. Maine: A chopping.

shearwater n Also sp sheerwater [From its flying low over the waves]
1 A bird of the genus *Puffinus.* [*OED2* c1671 →] For other names of var spp see **hagdon, moaning bird, sooty shearwater, whalebird**

1834 Nuttall *Manual Ornith.* 2.335, The Cinereous Puffin or Wandering Sheerwater, visits every part of the great Atlantic Ocean, from the banks of Newfoundland to Senegal and the Cape of Good Hope. **1844** DeKay *Zool. NY* 2.287, The Large Shearwater. *Puffinus cinereus. Ibid* 288, The Little Shearwater. *Puffinus obscurus.* **1858** Baird *Birds* 833, Puffinus Major . . The Greater Shearwater. **1872** Coues *Key to N. Amer. Birds* 331, Manks *Shearwater.* . . N. Atlantic Coast, common. **1898** (1900) Davie *Nests N. Amer. Birds* 51, Audubon's Dusky Shearwater is found on the Atlantic coast of the United States from New Jersey to Florida. **1977** Udvardy *Audubon Field Guide Birds* 343, Shearwaters occur from spring to fall, but are seen most commonly in fall, when thousands congregate at favored places, such as Monterey Bay or outside San Francisco's Golden Gate. **1986** Rustad *I Married a Fisherman* 60 **AK,** Often the shearwaters were the only birds keeping us company.

2 The black **skimmer 1** (*Rynchops nigra*). Cf **cutwater 1** [*DARE* Ed: Some of these quots may refer instead to **1** above.]

1709 (1967) Lawson *New Voyage* 154 **NC, SC,** Shear-Waters are a longer Fowl than a Duck; some of them lie on the Coast, whilst others range the Seas all over. Sometimes they are met five hundred Leagues from Land. **1748** in 1970 Kalm *Resejournal* 124 **Philadelphia PA,** Strax efter middagen sågo vi en stor myckenhet af nyssomtalta foglar, som sades likna änder; styrman, som var hemma i Philadelphia, kallade dem *shearwaters.* [=Shortly after noon we saw a great multitude of the aforementioned birds, which are said to resemble ducks; the mate, who was from Philadelphia, called them shearwaters.] **1791** Bartram *Travels* 295, Rynchops niger, the shearwater or razor bill. **1844** DeKay *Zool. NY* 2.297, *Rhynchops* [sic] *nigra.* . . The *Shearwater, Razor-bill, Cutwater, Skimmer, Flood Gull,* and *Skippang,* for it is known under all these names, reaches our coast from tropical America in May. **1946** Kopman *Wild Acres* 27 **LA,** The purpose of the shape and structure of the bill . . is to allow the bird to submerge the lower mandible at a shallow and fixed angle to the water . . ; thus, . . it shears . . almost horizontally. It is from this unique adaptation that the bird gets the popular names of "shearwater" and "scissors-bill." **1949** Sprunt–Chamberlain *SC Bird Life* 61, The name "shearwater" is frequently given to the abundant Black Skimmer locally. The mistake results in much confusion, for many observers are sure they know shearwaters when actually they have never seen one. **1950** Writers' Round Table *Padre Is.* 119 **csTX,** Black skimmers are locally called shearwaters. . . They are most graceful as they skim the surface of the water with open bills to catch plankton or surface sea life. **1969** *DARE* (Qu. Q10, . . *Water birds and marsh birds*) Inf **NC78,** Shearwater.

sheat(h), sheave See sheaf

she-balsam n Also she-balsam fir [Cf OED2 she pers. pron. 5.10.e] esp NC Cf he-balsam
=Fraser fir.

1851 in 1956 Eliason *Tarheel Talk* 259 **NC,** The Balsam is of two kinds, the He and She (or Blister). The latter has blisters in the bark, which alone contain the balsam. . . It has been selling at $1.00 pr. gill. **1897** Sudworth *Arborescent Flora* 50 **NC,** She Balsam. . . She Balsam Fir. **1917** *DN* 4.407 **wNC,** She-balsam . . Frazer's balsam. **1943** Peattie *Great Smokies* 161, In the trunks of the fir under the bark, there are often big rosin blisters filled with a clear liquid (the balsam of com-

merce) which the mountain folk have whimsically compared to milk. So they named this the "she-balsam." Thinking perhaps that it needed a mate, and finding the spruce tree, which is devoid of "milk," commonly accompanying it, they named it the "he-balsam"! **1979** *S. Living* May 105 **NC,** Two trees give the forest its name, red spruce (*Picea rubens;* locally known as he balsam) and Fraser fir (*Abies fraseri;* called she balsam).

shebang n [Prob var of Ir dial shebeen unlicensed drinking place, still-cabin] old-fash
A hut, shanty, rude shelter; a disreputable tavern or other place of resort; broadly, any building or establishment. Note: The expression *the whole shebang* is widespread and is not treated here.

1862 in 1882–83 Whitman *Specimen Days* 27, I . . go occasionally on long tours through the camps, talking with the men. . . Sometimes at night among the groups around the fires, in their shebang enclosures of bushes. **1865** in 1866 U.S. Congress *Congressional Globe* 31 Jan 552 **AL,** In a visit to Spanish Fort . . we stopped at the "shebang" of one of [the poor whites]. **1868** Goss *Soldier's Story* 153, By common consent, if any one [at Andersonville Prison] had complaints to make, he carried them to the "shebang" of Big Peter. **1877** Wright *Big Bonanza* 364 **NV,** Their attention was attracted to a "shebang" near at hand, by a terrible uproar within its doors. There was a smashing of glass, a crashing of chairs, bottles, and tumblers; fierce yells, bitter curses, and, in short, a fearful commotion. **1907** Lincoln *Cape Cod* 263 **MA,** "It'll give tone to the shebang," says he, referring to the hotel. **1913** Johnson *Highways St. Lawrence to VA* 103 **PA,** A man come along and looked at the shebang and says, 'What'll you take for this shebang?' **1931–33** LANE Worksheets **CT,** Shebang. . . Building. **1947** Jones *Evergreen Land* 191 **seWA,** There was a time when it was a hell-roaring town, when Ferd Plummer, the outlaw, ran a shebang just outside the limits and was about all the law there was. **1963** Edwards *Gravel* 171 **eTN** (as of 1920s), Uncle Lat came by Charlie Harr's store, which was the neighborhood loafing place, with his hoe on his shoulder. . . laughed Charlie, . . "Lat, lemme know. I'll close up this shebang and sharpen up my hoe and jine ye." **1966** Barnes–Jensen *Dict. UT Slang* 38, Shebang . . a poor, usually temporary habitation. "Some hunters put up this log shebang for the deer season." **1973** Allen *LAUM* 1.377 **Upper MW** (as of c1950), Shebang. . . An old house [1 inf, **MN**].

sheboodle n [Blend of shebang + caboodle]
1966 *DARE* (Qu. LL8b, . . *A large number* . . "*She has a whole _____ of cousins.*") Inf **MS49,** Sheboodle; (Qu. LL25, . . *Entirely, completely:* "*He sold out the whole . . _____.*") Inf **MS73,** Sheboodle.

she-burr n [Var of sheep burr]
A **cockleburr 1.**

1970 *DARE* (Qu. S15, . . *Weed seeds that cling to clothing*) Inf **VA69,** She-burr—round, big as a shelled peanut, covered with tiny prongs, turns brown in fall.

sheckel See shickle

she-crab soup n coastal SC Cf crab soup
A bisque of the meat and roe of the female crab.

1966–67 *DARE* (Qu. H36, *Kinds of soup*) Inf **SC21,** She-crab soup; (Qu. H45, *Dishes made with meat, fish, or poultry that everybody around here would know, but that people in other places might not*) Infs **SC4, 21,** She-crab soup; **SC62,** She-crab soup—milk, sherry. **1975** *Ford Times* Oct 49 **coastal SC,** She-crab soup. The key to this Low-Country delight is the roe of the female crab. . It is only in the coastal area of South Carolina where this special dish is prepared to any extent. . . There are thousands of people all over the country who consider Charleston and she-crab soup synonymous. . . butter . . flour . . milk . . white crab meat and crab eggs . . mace . . pepper . . Worcestershire sauce . . salt . . sherry . . cream. **1976** *Star* (Kansas City MO) 7 Apr sec B 4 **coastal SC,** Without the female there can be no true she-crab soup. To be authentic, the bisque must contain the meat of the blue she-crab and, of course, the crab roe.

shed adj See shut adj c

shed v See shut v A

shed n[1] Also shade [OED2 shed sb.[3] 1648 →; "rare."] esp Mid Atl

The molted skin or shell of a snake or arthropod—freq in comb *snake shed.*

1898 (1899) Earle *Home Life* 250 **NC,** Coverlet patterns. . . "Snake Shed," "Flowers in the Mountains." **1899** (1912) Green *VA Folk-Speech* 398, *Snake-shed.* . . *Snake-shade.* The shed left by a snake when he casts his skin. Looked on as a remedy, and a charm. **1934** Carmer *Stars Fell on AL* 219, Take a snake shed (discarded skin), mix it with pepper and bury it where he will have to walk over it and it will bring him the kind of bad luck you want him to have. **c1938** in 1970 Hyatt *Hoodoo* 1.236 **ceVA,** The shed from a snake, a woman . . taken that snake shed . . an' powders it, ground it. *Ibid* 2.1104 **cSC,** Very often yo' go tuh a tree an' see where de grubworm has left his shed dere and de grubworm gone. . . Den de same thing turns to a big flopping buttahfly. **1963** *DE Folkl. Bulletin* 1.40/2, A snake-shed (snakeskin). **1968** *DARE* FW Addit **eMD,** *Shed*—The cast-off shell of a crab that has peeled; heard all over Eastern Shore of MD plus Smith Island. **1970** *DARE* Tape **VA**112, He [=a male crab]'ll hold her until she comes out of the shed; then she becomes completely soft. . . That's when they start matin'.

shed n[2] See **shad 1**

shed chamber n **NEng** Cf **chamber B1**
An attic beneath the roof of a shed.

1889 Cooke *Steadfast* 74 **CT,** Hiram Perkins, the hired man . . slept in the "shed chamber." **1895** Brown *Meadow-Grass* 13 **NH,** Mis' Jeremiah took her to the shed-chamber and trounced her soundly. **1922** Brown *Old Crow* 483 **NH,** The bed . . was the old four-poster he had packed away in the shed chamber. **1926** *AmSp* 2.79 **ME,** All upstairs rooms are known as "chambers," another good old English term. A room over the shed is a "shed-chamber," and is very likely unfinished, like an attic, while the unfinished room at the top of the main part of the house is a "garrit [sic]." The barn loft is likewise the "barn-chamber." **1929** *AmSp* 5.124 **ME,** The "shed" chamber was over the "wood house" and in it "cultch" would collect and remain for years. **1941** *LANE* Map 345 *(Attic)* 1 inf, **VT,** Shed chamber = garret. **1959** *VT Hist.* 27.129, Chamber. . . Bedroom or other room. . . Usually, in phrases, such as in the front *chamber* or in the shed *chamber.* Common. Older people. **1967** *DARE* Tape **VT**1A, [FW:] What was the shed chamber? [Inf:] Well, the shed chamber was over the wood shed and the, well, we called it, garage in the later days; wagon house was the older . . name for it. . . And the chamber, shed chamber, ran over both of those rooms. It was . . very large room . . And it was a nice place to store things and an awful place to pick up. [FW:] You didn't use it as a sleeping room them? [Inf:] No, except one summer. **1968** *DARE* (Qu. D4, *The space up under the roof, usually used for storing things*) Inf **VT**3, Shed chamber—over shed and kitchen.

shedder n, also attrib **chiefly N and Mid Atl** Cf **buckler, buckram, buster 5, comer 2, crack-buster, fat crab, leatherback 8, papershell 1, peeler crab, pink sign, poor crab, rank adj 4, red sign (crab), second, soft crab, soft-shell ~**
Usu a saltwater crab but also a **lobster B1** or **crawfish n B1** at the time of shedding its shell.

1843 DeKay *Zool. NY* 6.11, The process of sloughing or casting their shell occurs annually, and is of short duration, scarcely ever exceeding the period of forty-eight hours from the time of casting its old shell until the new one is firmly consolidated. During this interval, they [=*Lupa dicantha*] are known under the name of *Soft-shell Crabs,* or *Shedders,* and are sought after with great avidity. **1848** *S. Lit. Messenger* 14.684, We will purchase a few shedder crabs in the market. **1875** Scott *Fishing Amer. Waters* 59, Shedder or soft-shell crab is preferred as bait; but, if it can not be procured, use shedder lobster. **1905** U.S. Bur. Fisheries *Rept. for 1904* 412, Then, on the under surface of the carapace . . there appears a narrow fracture, so that the whole upper surface of the shell can be raised up from the back like a lid, to expose the soft body underneath. Such a crab is termed a "shedder" or a "buster." **1916** Kephart *Camping & Woodcraft* 2.411, Crayfish . . are found under flat stones in shallow water. They shed their hard armor periodically, and are at their best as bait when in the "shedder" stage. **1953** *Sun* (Baltimore MD) 27 Aug 13/1, **seMD,** Littleton T. Dryden, of the Dryden Bros. Seafood Co., Inc., explained that the many "shedders" now being caught are not fat. **1966–68** *DARE* Tape **DE**3, We don't have much trouble getting bait. Now, they used to use peeler crab . . they call them shedder crabs. We used to use quite a lot, but they've become scarce and they're quite expensive and . . they're very small; **ME**24, Sometimes in shedder season when the soft shedders—when the lobsters are soft—they put 'em in a different bin than they do the hard ones. **1975** Gould *ME*

Lingo 250, *Shedder*—A lobster just after the biological shedding of the old shell. . . During the shedding season, lobstermen find both hardshell and softshell lobsters in their traps. The *shedders* are softshell, as the new covering hasn't yet calcified. **1980** *DARE* File **eNJ,** "Shedder" is also pretty much of a New Jersey or Mid-Atlantic usage. When I was a kid spending summers on the Jersey shore, the locals always spoke of shedders, meaning soft crabs. In the Chesapeake they simply say *soft crabs.*

shed kitchen n Cf **summer kitchen**
A **shed room** used as a kitchen.

1865 *Ladies' Repository* 25.115, An old-fashioned house with its gable-end and shed-kitchen. **1872** Eggleston *End of the World* 62 **IN,** Got a mustache onto the top story of his mouth, somethin' like a tuft of grass on the roof of a old shed kitchen. **1885** (1886) Stapleton *Major's Christmas* 267 **eMA,** They followed her . . to a shed kitchen, where there was a cook stove and a sink. **1968–70** *DARE* (Qu. D8, *The small room next to the kitchen [in older houses] where dishes and sometimes foods are kept*) Infs **PA**66, 239, Shed kitchen; (Qu. D16, . . *Parts added on to the main part of a house*) Inf **MD**17, Shed kitchen—one story, sloping roof.

shed room n **chiefly S Atl, Gulf States, TX** See Map
A room added to the main structure of a house (or rarely barn) and covered by a pent roof.

1835 Longstreet *GA Scenes* 205, Ned . . asked the landlady where we should sleep. She pointed to an open shed-room adjoining the room in which we were sitting, and separated from it by a log partition. **1839** (1840) Simms *Border Beagles* 1.74 **MS,** But there were shed-rooms to his dwelling, and upper chambers, which were asserted to be very well fitted up, in which no limited profits were made out of the ignorant and the unwary. **1891** Johnston *Primes & Neighbors* 10 **GA,** They lived in an unpretending one-story house, with the usual shed-rooms. *Ibid* 40, He had a small back-shed room wherein he usually slept at night. **1904** (1905) Watson *Bethany* 8 **GA,** Springing off from the main roof, other rafters reached downward to rest upon outer plates—forming a shed roof; the half of this, being closed in with planks, made a shed room. **1928** Peterkin *Scarlet Sister Mary* 238 **SC,** When she ran into the shed room he paid no heed to her. **1950** *PADS* 14.59 **SC,** Shed room. . . A shed, a lean-to. A shed room is usually built on the side of the barn, but may also be built against the dwelling. **1956** McAtee *Some Dialect NC* 39, *Shed room* . . a shed or lean-to attached to another building. **c1960** Wilson *Coll.* **csKY,** *Shed* for stock, often an actual shedroom attached to the regular barn. . . *Shedroom.* . . A room built on to another, a lean-to. **1965–70** *DARE* (Qu. D16, . . *Parts added on to the main part of a house*) 32 Infs, **chiefly S Atl, Gulf States, TX,** Shed room. **1986** Pederson *LAGS Concordance,* 48 infs, **chiefly GA, TX, AL,** Shed room(s); 1 inf, **cGA,** Shed room—attached to house; 1 inf, **cwGA,** Shed room—with beds, also for storage; 1 inf, **csAR,** Shed rooms—added later, same as side rooms; 1 inf, **ceTX,** Shed rooms—for storage, use similar to pantry's.

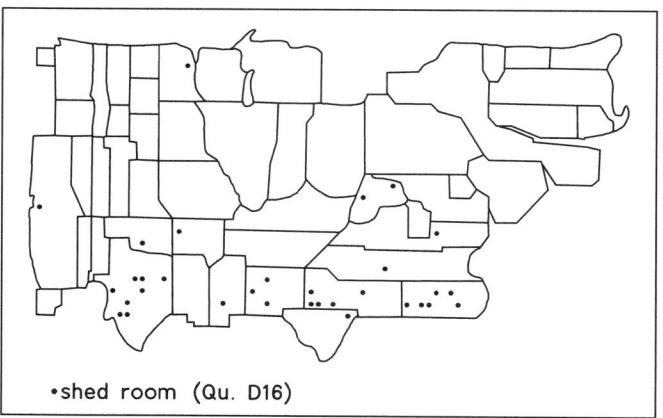

•shed room (Qu. D16)

sheefish n Also *chee, sheafish, shee, skee fish* [See quot 1991] **AK**
=inconnu.

1913 Underwood *Alaska* 197, In Lake Selawik, north of Kotzebue Sound, a fish called "Chee," very much resembling a white fish in shape and taste, but weighing from thirty to fifty pounds, can be caught in abundance during the winter months. **1935** *AK Sportsman* Jan 9 (Tabbert *Dict. Alaskan Engl.*), We had been told by Eskimos at Kotzebue that this was a favorite bend in the river for "sheefish." **1955** U.S. Arctic Info. Center *Gloss.* 43, *Inconnu.* . . A large fresh water food fish, *Stenodus leucichthys,* of the whitefish family, found in streams in Siberia, Alaska and northern Canada. Also called 'sheefish,' 'skee fish,' 'shign,' 'Yukon char.' **1958** Carrighar *Moonlight* 328 **AK,** There is one fish . . that surpasses the kings in esteem. It is the shee, a Siberian "white salmon," found as well in northwest Alaska. It has been described as tasting not like fish but like fresh, sweet cream. Eskimos seine shee in arctic rivers during the summer and take them in winter by "jigging" through holes in the five-foot-thick ice on the sea. **1964** *AK Sportsman* May 11 (Tabbert *Dict. Alaskan Engl.*), A committee established to standardize the common names of fishes has recommended that the common name of this fish be inconnu, the name originally given it by French explorers in the Mackenzie River and which means "unknown fish." However, in Alaska it is commonly known as sheefish, although shee, cony, inconnu and shovelnose whitefish are sometimes used. **1965** Bowen *Alaskan Dict.* 29, *Sheefish* or *Sheafish*—The Inconnu or unknown fish. **1991** Tabbert *Dict. Alaskan Engl.* 140, The usual Alaskan name for this fish is *shee,* or, in more recent times, *sheefish. Shee* is originally an Athabaskan word. . . The word is first recorded in an English context from the Great Slave Lake area of Canada in a 1772 journal entry of Samuel Hearne: "The Northern Indians call this fish Shees."

sheeny n[1] Also sp *sheeney* [*OED2* 1816 →; perh from Gael *sionnaí* fox-like, clever]

1 also attrib: A Jewish person. **chiefly Nth, N Midl** See Map *derog*

1857 *Sacramento Phoenix* 17 Nov. 3/2 *(Mathews Coll.),* This put some of the faithful down on him and the Sheeneys no longer deal on the cross with him. **1900** *DN* 2.59 **New Orleans LA** [College slang], *Sheeny.* . . A member of a Hebrew-letter society. **1929** *AmSp* 4.344 [Vagabond lingo], *Sheeny*—A Jew. **1932** Farrell *Young Lonigan* 15 **Chicago IL** (as of 1916), His long nose was too large for his other features; almost a sheeny's nose. **1941** *LANE* Map 455 *(Nicknames for a Jew)* **NEng,** [*Sheeny* is common and found throughout the region.] **1965–70** *DARE* (Qu. HH28, *Names and nicknames . . for people of foreign background: Jewish*) 27 Infs, **chiefly Nth, N Midl,** Sheeny; **MI26,** Sheeny—that's passé now; **MI51,** Sheeny—one that they used to use a lot; (Qu. CC4, *. . Nicknames . . for various religions or religious groups*) Inf **MO26,** Sheenies; (Qu. HH18, *Very insignificant or low-grade people*) Inf **WA1,** Sheeny—among Jews; (Qu. II25, *Names or nicknames for the part of a town where . . special groups, or foreign groups live*) Inf **IA25,** Sheenyville—the Jewish part. [24 of 30 total Infs old] **1967** *DARE* FW Addit **LA14,** *Sheeny* [ʃɪnɪ]—adj. meaning Jewish (pejorative). "That's a sheeny trick." **1982** [see **2** below]. **1986** Pederson *LAGS Concordance,* 1 inf, **neTX,** Sheeny; 1 inf, **seFL,** The goddamn kikes or sheenies—not said at home; 1 inf, **cnTN,** Sheenies. **2001** *DARE* File **wNY,** Sheeny . . a Jew (disparaging).

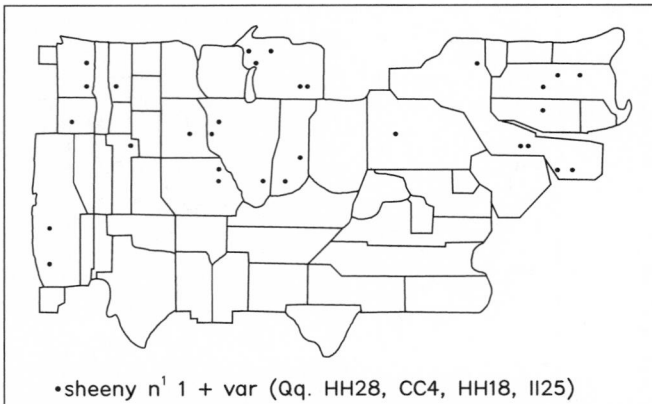

•sheeny n[1] 1 + var (Qq. HH28, CC4, HH18, II25)

2 Transf: see quots.

1982 *Barrick Coll.* **csPA,** *Sheeny*—any foreigner, esp. a Jew. **1999** *DARE* File **NYC** (as of 1950s–60s), I can't say that I remember ever having heard the word *sheeny,* even though being Jewish and living in a predominantly Irish Catholic neighborhood where other choice epithets were hurled at me on occasion, but I did know the word as an adolescent and for some reason thought that it meant an Irishman. Recently I had an occasion to ask a colleague who grew up in Milwaukee (German-Irish

background) if he had ever heard the word, and while he said that he couldn't recall ever actually having heard it, he knew what it meant, and when I asked him, he said, "An Irishman."

3 A contemptible person; see quots.

1900 *DN* 2.59 **CT** [College slang], *Sheeny.* . . A second rate person. **1942** Berrey–Van den Bark *Amer. Slang* 450.8, *Sheeny,* a stingy person. **1967** *DARE* (Qu. HH16, *Uncomplimentary words with no definite meaning—just used when you want to show that you don't think much of a person: "Don't invite him. He's a _____."*) Inf **LA8,** Sheeny.

4 also *sheeny man:* One who follows a trade traditionally associated with Jews; see quots; hence *sheeny wagon* a peddler's wagon.

1910 *DN* 4.151 [Navy slang], *Ship's sheeny.* . . A tailor aboard ship. **1941** *LANE* Map 455, 1 inf, **csCT,** A sheeny is a rag picker; 1 inf, **neMA,** Sheeny, a rag picker, not necessarily a Jew. **1956** Algren *Walk on the Wild Side* 205 **New Orleans LA,** You've been hiding them pants to keep him from loading up a sheeny wagon of green bananas and making hisself a nice profit by the time he got to Chicago. **1984** *MJLF* 10.156 **cnWI,** *Sheeny man.* Horse and cow dealer. Rag buyer. . . "A pretty sharp dealer."

sheeny n[2] [Cf *chainy, cheny, chin(e)y, chinny* (at **china**)] Cf **china B1**

A playing marble.

1967 *DARE* (Qu. EE6c, *Cheap marbles*) Inf **AR51,** Sheenies—pretty cheap. **c1970** Wiersma *Marbles Terms* **swMI** (as of 1963), Sheenies—one w[ith] swirled color, or blotched ugly marble.

sheeny man (or wagon) See **sheeny** n[1] **4**

sheep n

A Gram form.

Pl: usu *sheep;* also *sheeps.* Cf Intro "Language Changes" II.3

1860 Hundley *Social Relations S. States* 296, But let us come back to our "sheeps." **1915** in 1944 *ADD* **wTX,** Plurals. . . Double. . . Sheeps = sheep. **1939** *AmSp* 14.30 [Citadel argot], *Sheeps.* . . Cadets, especially in the classroom of a particular instructor (introduced by former Lieutenant M.S. Shockley, from the 'Popeye' cartoons). **1955** Roberts *S. from Hell-fer-Sartin* 111 **seKY,** About an hour or two atter dark they come in cattle in that house and all around, and sheeps and cats. **1967** *DARE* (Qu. E20, *Soft rolls of dust that collect on the floor under beds or other furniture*) Inf **PA52,** Sheeps. **1968** *PADS* 50.34 **swTN** [Black], *Sheep.* . . Four [of 24 infs] . . have the plural /šɪp/. One . . has /sɪps/. **1986** Pederson *LAGS Concordance* **Gulf Region** *(Ewe)* 10 infs, Sheeps; 1 inf, Female sheeps; *(Ram)* 3 infs, Sheeps; *(Wool)* 2 infs, Sheeps; 1 inf, Shear the sheeps; *(Heads* [of children]) 2 infs, Sheeps; 1 inf, Heads of goats and sheeps; [*DARE* Ed: Not in resp to a spec qu:] 23 infs, Sheeps; 1 inf, She got sheeps; 1 inf, Goats and sheeps; 1 inf, I ain't never had no dealings with no sheeps.

B Senses.

1 See **sheepshead 1, 2.**

2 Also *sheepwool:* a roll of dust under furniture.

1967–69 *DARE* (Qu. E20, *Soft rolls of dust that collect on the floor under beds or other furniture*) Infs **IL31, 36,** Sheep(wool); **PA52,** Sheeps.

sheepball tea n

=**sheep tea.**

1968 Haun *Hawk's Done Gone* 310 **TN,** I give Jamie sheepball tea to make the measles break out when he was two year old.

sheepberry n [Because the fruits are said to resemble sheep droppings]

1 A **black haw 1** (here: *Viburnum prunifolium*). Cf **nannyberry 1**

1814 Pursh *Flora Americae* 2.709, Sheep-berry. *Viburnum prunifolium.* **1897** Sudworth *Arborescent Flora* 339 **NJ,** Black Haw. . . Sheepberry. . . Nannyberry. **1950** Peattie *Nat. Hist. Trees* 513, Black Haw. . . Other Names: Stagbush. Sheepberry. Nannyberry. Sweet Haw. **1971** Krochmal *Appalachia Med. Plants* 272, Common Names: Black haw . . Sheepberry, shonny, sloe [etc].

2 also *sheepsberry:* A **nannyberry 1** (here: *Viburnum lentago*).

1822 Eaton *Botany* 510, *[Viburnum] lentago* . . sheepberry. . . Berries black, oval, and sweetish, pleasant-tasted: somewhat mucilaginous. **1832** *MA Hist. Soc. Coll.* 2d ser 9.157 **cwVT,** *[Viburnum] lentago* . .

Sheepberry. **1908** Rogers *Tree Book* 449, The sheepberry, with its shining leaves set opposite, is likely to be mistaken for a dogwood. **1938** Brown *Trees NE U.S.* 390, Nannyberry, Sheepsberry—*Viburnum lentago*. **1954** McAtee *Suppl. to Nomina Abitera* [4], Nannyberry, Nanny-Plum, Sheepberry (*Viburnum lentago* primarily, but applied also to *V. prunifolium*)—These names refer to a resemblance of the fruits (or blackhaws) to sheep turds. **1979** Little *Checklist U.S. Trees* 293, Nannyberry. . . Other common names—blackhaw, sheepberry, sweet viburnum.

sheepbine n Also *sheep-bind*

A **bindweed 1** (here: *Convolvulus arvensis*).

1911 *Century Dict. Suppl.*, Sheep-bine. . . The small bindweed, *Convolvulus arvensis.* **1949** Moldenke *Amer. Wild Flowers* 270, The field bindweed, *Strophocaulos arvensis.* . . possesses scores of common names including such picturesque ones as hedgebells, cornlily . . laplove and sheepbine. **1959** Carleton *Index Herb. Plants* 106, *Sheep-bind:* Convolvulus arvensis.

sheep buck n [Calque of Ger *Schafbock*] **Ger settlement areas** Cf **buck** n[1] **1a**

A ram.

1949 Kurath *Word Geog.* 62, Ram. . . In the Pennsylvania German settlement area one can also hear *sheep buck,* which is modeled on the German *Schafbock.* **1966** Dakin *Dial. Vocab. Ohio R. Valley* 2.239, Ram. . . The Pennsylvania German *sheep buck* appears once in Tuscawaras County, Ohio, and once in the American Bottom of Illinois. **1967** Faries *Word Geog. MO* 90, Ram. . . *Sheep buck* . . characteristic of the Pennsylvania German settlement . . appears on forty checklists, occurring especially in the German settlement areas of Missouri. **1967–69** *DARE* (Qu. K63, . . *A male sheep*) Infs **OH**27, 88, **PA**153, Sheep buck. **1973** Allen *LAUM* 1.249 **MN** (as of c1950), The one example of *sheep buck,* from a retired Winona, Mn., farmer whose father was born in Austria, surely is influenced by the German *Schafbock.* **1985** *AmSp* 60.234 se**PA**, *Sheep buck* is used by only three [of 60] informants, all of whom have a background in farming.

sheep burr n **scattered, but chiefly C and Mid Atl** See Map

Usu a **cockleburr 1,** but also any of var other plants with prickly seeds; the seed vessels or flowerheads of such a plant.

1895 *U.S. Dept. Ag. Farmers' Bulletin* 28.27, Sheep bur . . Acanthospermum xanthoides . . North Carolina to Florida. **1898** *Jrl. Amer. Folkl.* 11.275 **KS**, Echinospermum Virginicum . . sheep-burr. **1922** Gonzales *Black Border* 326 s**SC**, **GA coasts** [Gullah glossary], *Sheepbuhr* [sic]. **1954** Harder *Coll.* cw**TN**, Sheep-burr. **1965–70** *DARE* (Qu. S13, . . *A common wild bush with bunches of round, prickly seeds; when they get dry they stick to your clothing*) 16 Infs, 14 **C and Mid Atl**, Sheep burr; **NC**87, Sheep burr, cuckleburrs—same thing; (Qu. S6) Inf **AR**41, Sheep burr; (Qu. S14) Infs **MO**16, **NC**83, Sheep burr(s); (Qu. S15, . . *Weed seeds that cling to clothing*) Infs **IN**30, 32, **SC**63, **TX**32, Sheep burr(s); **KY**28, Sheep burr—flat, triangular; **NJ**56, Sheep burr—it gots pricklies all over it, size of your thumb; (Qu. S21, . . *Weeds . . that are a trouble in gardens and fields*) Inf **NC**49, Sheep burr—some call cuckleburr. [18 of 27 Infs male]

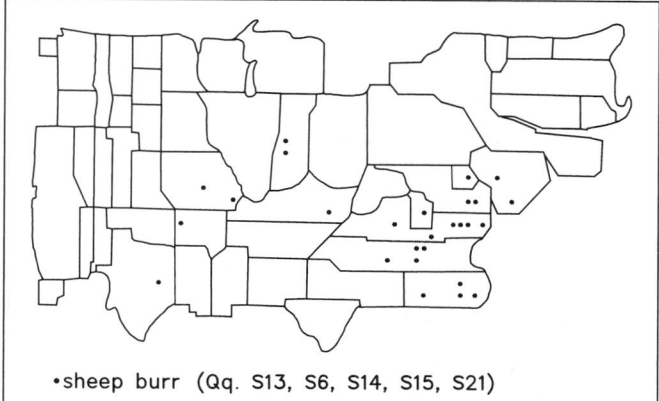

•sheep burr (Qq. S13, S6, S14, S15, S21)

sheep camp See **sheep wagon**

sheep cloud n Cf **black-sheep cloud, sheepshead 6**
See quots.

1947 (1962) Henry *Misty* 155 e**VA,** Toward evening a light wind came up, whisking sheep clouds before it. **1969–70** *DARE* (Qu. B10, . . *Long trailing clouds high in the sky*) Inf **MI**100, Sheep clouds; (Qu. B11, . . *Other kinds of clouds that come often*) Infs **PA**216, 242, Sheep clouds; **TX**102, Sheep clouds—sign of rain.

sheep dip n *joc* or *derog*

Any of var beverages with a strong or foul taste; see quots.

1939 FWP *ID Lore* 244, The following is reported as the talk of a southwest Idaho cowboy: . . the cowboys fall in line to grab their shoe soles (pancakes) and snowballs (biscuits) and sheepdip (coffee). **1942** Berrey–Van den Bark *Amer. Slang* 99.3, *Inferior liquor.* . . sheep dip. **1949** *PADS* 11.26 **CO**, Sheep dip. . . Bad whiskey. **1979** McPhee *Giving Good Weight* 168 **ME**, Breakfast at six. Strong tea. "Sheep dip" was what the lumberjacks called their tea. **1986** Pederson *LAGS Concordance,* 1 inf, nw**TN**, Sheep-dip—bad tasting whiskey.

sheep-dumpling n Cf **dumpling B, nanny** n[2] **2, sheep saffron**

A pellet of sheep dung—also in comb *sheep-dumpling tea:* =**sheep tea.**

1947 (1964) Randolph *Ozark Superstitions* 109, An infusion of sheep manure, called nanny tea or sheep-dumplin' tea, is also much in favor as a remedy for earache. **1953** Randolph–Wilson *Down in Holler* 283 **Ozarks,** Sheep dumplings. . . Sheep manure. *Sheep dumplings* are used in the home treatment of measles and certain other ailments. **1954** Harder *Coll.* cw**TN**, Sheep dumplings. . . Sheep manure. Sheep dumplings are used in the treatment of measles.

sheep fat n [See quot 1976]

A **saltbush 1** (here: *Atriplex confertifolia*).

1923 in 1925 Jepson *Manual Plants CA* 327, [*Atriplex*] confertifolia . . Sheep-fat. Spiny Saltbush. . . Common on desert mesas and hills. **1933** Harrington *Gypsum Cave NV* 196, *Atriplex confertifolia* . . Sheep fat, Spiny salt-bush. **1976** Elmore *Shrubs & Trees SW* 37, Shadscale—spiny or round-leaf saltbush; sheep-fat. . . Where it occurs in nearly pure stands on alkaline soils, it is an important browse plant for cattle, sheep and goats.

sheepfish See **sheepshead 1**

sheep fly n esp **MD, DE** See Map

A fly of the family Œstridae or Calliphoridae; see quots.

1859 Goodrich *Illustr. Nat. Hist.* 582, The *Sheep-Fly, Œstrus ovis,* is less than half an inch long; it deposits its egg in the nostrils of the sheep; the larvæ ascend to the cavity of the forehead, where they remain for the season, often producing vertigo in their victims. **1965–70** *DARE* (Qu. R12, . . *Other kinds of flies*) Infs **CA**97, **DE**4, **MD**13, 32, Sheep fly; **DE**3, Sheep fly or thin-wing fly—found around the woods; **GA**1, Sheep fly—bites; smaller than a housefly; **MD**15, Sheep fly—brown, larger than housefly, bites; **MD**34, Sheep fly—common in branches—larger than housefly, greenish head—bite leaves swelling; **MD**36, Sheep fly—small, wide wingspread; flies in faces of humans or animals; **MD**42, Sheep fly—bites any animal—greenish wings, about one-third the size of a horsefly; **MD**45, Sheep fly—same as dogfly and brown fly. **1998** Braun *Cat Stars* 11 **Upper MW**, Tourists were excited at the prospect of seeing aliens. Friendly locals referred to them as Visitors; others blamed them for every quirk of weather or outbreak of sheep-fly.

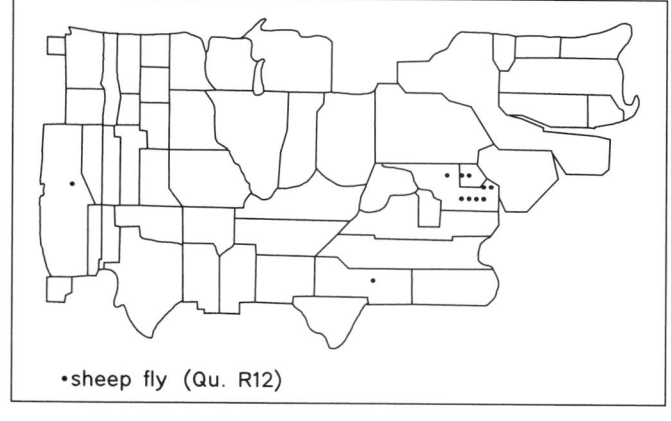

•sheep fly (Qu. R12)

sheep grass n
=**sheep sorrel.**

1967 *DARE* (Qu. S26e, *Other wildflowers not yet mentioned*; not asked in early QRs) Inf **LA**12, Sheep grass, occasionally, or sheep shower—same as sheep sorrel.

sheephead See **sheepshead**

sheepherder n **chiefly Rocky Mts, Pacific**

1 Used as an epithet, see quots. *usu derog*

[**1872** Schele de Vere *Americanisms* 210, California . . forms its vast flocks of sheep into *bands* . . and employs *herders* to tend its valuable cattle. The former is hence called *sheep-herder,* and not shepherd, because the keeping of sheep is considered unfit for man, and no one will own to it! Formerly the work was done by Indians; then by such immigrants as were utterly unable by any exertion of their own to earn a living; and finally the task has come down to the despised *greasers* or "vagrant miners" . . or runaway sailors . . or vagabond soldiers.] **1930** Williams *Logger-Talk* 28 **Pacific NW,** *Sheep-herder:* An epithet inferring laziness, stupidity, insanity, and sexual aberrations. **1932** *AmSp* 7.270 [Oil field language], *Sheep herder.* . . A Wyoming driller. **1949** *PADS* 11.26 **CO,** *Sheepherder.* . . A Mexican. **1958** McCulloch *Woods Words* 161 **Pacific NW,** *Sheepherder*—a. A logger wearing a farmer's bib overalls. b. A logger's idea of a useless man. **1963** *AmSp* 38.271 **KS** [Amer. Indian student slang], Indians from Montana or Wyoming are *sheep herders.* **1969** *AmSp* 44.208 [Trucker jargon], *Sheep herder*—Driver whose ability is questioned.

2 attrib; also *sheepherder's;* Of food and drink: characteristic of the simple but hearty dishes prepared by sheepherders.

1940 Brown *Amer. Cooks* 531 **NV,** *Sheepherder salad*—Dictated by a sheepherder I ran into. . . "Well, you take some cold beans and some cold potatoes and cut the potatoes up and throw them in with the beans, and some cold meat if you got it, and cut up an onion or anything that's around, and put the oil off some sardines on it and some vinegar and salt and pepper, and if you got some cold pancakes left, why, just cut them up, too, and shake the whole works together and you got something." **1967–70** *DARE* (Qu. H18, . . *Special kinds of bread*) Infs **CA**182, 205, **UT**8, Sheepherder('s) bread; **CA**210, Sheepherder bread—from old Basque recipe; **CA**59, Sheepherder's bread—a coarser grade of sourdough bread; **NV**1, Sheepherder's bread—made in round loaves in a Dutch oven—probably usually a starter; (Qu. H49, *Dishes made by boiling potatoes with other foods*) Inf **UT**8, Sheepherder's dinner—raw potatoes sliced, fried with ham and onions; (Qu. H65, *Foreign foods favored by people around here*) Inf **CA**210, Sheepherder's bread; (Qu. H74a, . . *Coffee . . very strong*) Inf **MT**3, Sheepherder's coffee. **1967** *DARE* FW Addit **cOR,** *Sheepherder*—a form of French bread, *round.* **1968** *DARE* File **seID,** *Sheepherder coffee*—boiled coffee. **1984** Lesley *Winterkill* 66 **neOR,** Danny had played with Judy, the marble-eyed sheepdog that Sammy claimed was part Australian, and Sammy had given Danny wedges of sheepherder's bread he'd baked in coffee cans. *Ibid* 168, They built a fire from juniper and locust. Danny chopped carrots, potatoes, and onions, then mixed them with ground beef and wrapped equal portions in tinfoil packets. When the coals were glowing, he tucked the packets in along the edge. "Sheepherder's stew," he said. **1998** *DARE* File **AZ, UT,** Ranch fried potatoes. My grandparents were sheepranchers in Utah and Arizona and this dish was eaten often by the sheepherders when they were out on the range with the sheep. We called them sheepherder potatoes. They were sliced potatoes fried with bacon and onions then a little water was added and a lid put on the pan to steam them until done. *Ibid,* The sheepherder potatoes were prepared by my Mormon grandmother. The family were originally sheepherders in Scotland but migrated to the midwest so I don't know if the term was one they used in Scotland or learned after their arrival in the midwest.

sheepherder's bread See **sheepherder 2**

sheepie exclam, often repeated Also sp *sheepy* **scattered, but chiefly Midl** See Map Cf **co-sheep(ie)** v phr
Used as a call to sheep.

1948 Davis *Word Atlas Gt. Lakes* app qu. 71, 83 (of 233) infs, **IN, IL, MI, OH,** Sheepy! **1949** Kurath *Word Geog.* 65, Calls to Sheep . . the Midland has *sheep!, sheepie!* **1965–70** *DARE* (Qu. K85, *The call to sheep to come in from the pasture*) 72 Infs, **chiefly Midl,** Sheepie; **FL**36, **KS**17, **NM**3, **OH**41, 72, **TN**26, **TX**36, Sheepie sheepie (sheepie); **PA**198, Sheepie sheep sheep. **1966** Dakin *Dial. Vocab. Ohio R. Valley* 285, *Calls to sheep.* . . Throughout Ohio and Indiana only scattered individuals use any call other than the Midland *sheep!, sheepie!*.

The latter is by far the common form. **1972** *PADS* 58.18 **cwAL,** Calls to sheep. Most informants were not familiar with a call to sheep because the animal is not commonly raised in the area. However, two informants gave Midland *sheepie.* **1973** Allen *LAUM* 1.266 **Upper MW** (as of c1950), *Calls to sheep from the pasture.* . . Midland *sheep* and *sheepy* are the most common, exclusively dominating southern Iowa and extending into southern Minnesota. **1986** Pederson *LAGS Concordance* (*Calls to sheep*) 4 infs, **TN, LA, MS,** Sheepy (x2)—falsetto; 3 infs, **TN, AR,** Sheepy (x3)—falsetto; 2 infs, **TN,** Sheepy; 2 infs, **AL, TN,** Sheepy (x2).

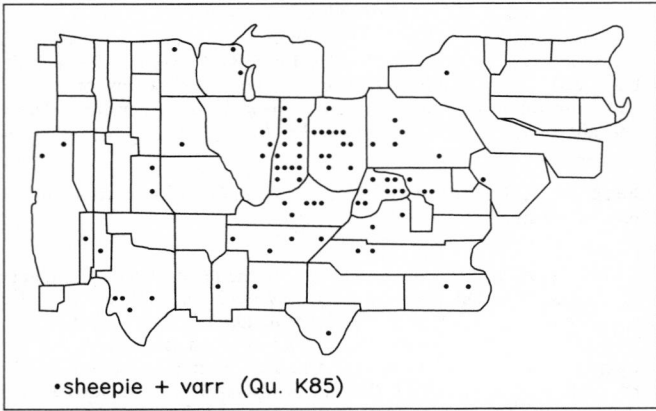

•sheepie + varr (Qu. K85)

sheepie in the bush See **sheep in the bush**

sheep in my pen n Also *sheep in the pen* Cf **beckon**
A children's outdoor hiding game; see quots.

1945 Boyd *Hdbk. Games* 69, Beckon, or *Sheep in My Pen.* **1953** Brewster *Amer. Nonsinging Games* 42 **OK,** *Sheep in My Pen.* . . There should be ten or more players for this game. One of them is chosen to be "It," and the rest hide within a certain area previously decided upon. In the middle of this area is a square space, the "pen." The player who is "It" starts out in search of the others. As soon as he has sighted a player, "It" calls out "Sheep in my pen!" The discovered player must then go to the "pen." From the "pen" he keeps on shouting "Beckon!" until another player waves to him. When this occurs he can leave the "pen" and hide again if he can escape the eye of the player who is "It." He can then wave to another player who has been caught and thus enable him to escape. The game continues until all have been captured. **1957** *Sat. Eve. Post Letters* **WI,** Games we played in my girlhood right here in Red Mound over 60 yrs. ago. . . Tintin . Sheep in the pen . . Mother mother the teakettle is boiling over.

sheep in the bush n Also *sheepie in the bush* Cf **sheep in my pen**
A hiding game; see quots.

1966 *DARE* (Qu. EE13a, *Games in which every player hides except one, and that one must try to find the others*) Inf **SC**26, Sheep in the bush—old. **1966** *DARE* Tape **SC**26, Sheepie in the bush . . one person be out . . everybody be hide. . . One person be hunting. . . Everytime this one person find, then that hunt the others . . until all of them be find. . . And there be five, ten, or fifteen we be hide and there be one person out looking for them and if I find you, you help me find the others. That's in the bush . . sheepie in the bush. . . Hide and go seek, that's the same thing. . . as sheepie in the bush. You can hide and go seek . . but sheepie in the bush, that's the old play.

sheep in the pen See **sheep in my pen**

sheepkill n [See quot 1850]
A **sheep laurel** (here: *Kalmia angustifolia*).

1850 Emerson *Rept. Trees & Shrubs* 394, The Narrow-leaved Kalmia. . . From its supposed poisonous effect upon lambs, this plant is often called *lamb-kill* or *sheep-kill.* It is found from Hudson's Bay to Georgia. **1964** Kingsbury *Poisonous Plants U.S.* 251, *Kalmia angustifolia.* . . Lambkill, sheepkill, calfkill. **1968** Radford et al. *Manual Flora Carolinas* 803, K[almia] angustifolia var *caroliniana* . . Lamb-kill or Sheep-kill.

sheep laurel n Also *sheep's laurel* [See quot 1860]
A **mountain laurel 1:** usu *Kalmia angustifolia,* but also **calico**

bush 1. For other names of the former see **bush laurel 1, dwarf ~ 1, ivory n², ivy 4, kill-calf, ~-kid, lambkill, laurel 2, low laurel, pig ~, sheepkill, sheep poison 1, spoonwood ivy, wicky**

1810 Michaux *Histoire des Arbres* 1.38, *Mountain laurel . .* dénomination la plus générale sur la chaîne des monts Alléghanys. *Sheep laurel . .* nom secondaire dans les mêmes endroits. [=*Mountain laurel . .* the name most common in the Alleghany mountain chain. *Sheep laurel . .* a secondary name in the same area.] **1860** Curtis *Cat. Plants NC* 99, Wicky. . . This is a beautiful undershrub and is greatly improved by cultivation. It is a poisonous plant, especially to sheep, and is in some places called *Sheep Laurel.* **1924** *Amer. Botanist* 30.58, *Kalmia angustifolia,* second only to *latifolia* in beauty, is disparaged by such names as "lambkill," "sheep poision," "calf kill," "kill kid" and "sheep laurel." All these allude to the poisonous foliage. **1941** *LANE* 249 (*Mountain laurel*) 21 infs, **chiefly CT, RI, MA,** Sheep laurel; 3 infs, Sheep's laurel. **1967–70** *DARE* (Qu. S26a, . . *Wildflowers. . . Roadside flowers*) Inf **MA5,** Sheep laurel; (Qu. S26c, *Wildflowers that grow in woods*) Inf **RI**15, Sheep laurel; (Qu. S26e, *Other wildflowers not yet mentioned; not asked in early QRs*) Inf **MA58,** Sheep laurel—lower, smaller leaves, smaller flowers than mountain laurel; **VA101,** Sheep laurel; (Qu. T5, . . *Kinds of evergreens, other than pine*) Inf **MA**15 Sheep laurel; (Qu. T16, . . *Kinds of trees . . 'special'*) Infs **MA5,** 100 Sheep laurel. **1967–68** *DARE* Wildfl QR Pl.160A, Infs **NH4, OH**41, Sheep laurel; **NY**91, Sheep laurel—poisonous to livestock—occurs along Massachusetts coast; Plates 156A, B, [=*Kalmia latifolia, K. polifolia*] Inf **SC**41, Sheep laurel, mountain laurel, dog laurel, mountain ivy. **1976** Bruce *How to Grow Wildflowers* 128, Sheep-laurel grows in great abundance in the New Jersey Pine Barrens, usually in drier, sunnier sections away from the pines where Mountain-laurel occurs.

sheep leg n Also *sheep's leg* [From the shape] Cf **hog leg**
A handgun.
1936 *AmSp* 11.276 eTN, *Sheep leg.* An old pistol. 'He gave away his sheep leg.' **1951** Porter *Ragged Roads* 1 **OK,** I had heard, too, that the western folks were tough and quick on the trigger, and I was beset with grave expectancy. I had a big sheep's leg on my hip at the time.

sheep lice n

1 A **hound's-tongue 1** (here: *Cynoglossum officinale*).
1892 *Jrl. Amer. Folkl.* 5.101 **nOH,** *Cynoglossum officinale,* sheep lice.
2 also *sheep needles, ~ ticks, sheep's bane:* The seed of **beggar ticks 1.**
1950 *WELS* (*Other weed seeds that cling to clothing*) 1 Inf, **cWI,** Sheep lice. **1950** *WELS Suppl. Sheep lice*—Weed seeds that are flat and have two prongs at one end. **1968–70** *DARE* (Qu. S14, . . *Prickly seeds, small and flat, with two prongs at one end, that cling to clothing*) Infs **MO**17, **TN**26, Sheep needles; **IL**37, Sheep's bane; **MA**78, Sheep lice, sheep ticks; **MO**16, Sheep burr—maybe sheep lice; (Qu. S15, . . *Weed seeds that cling to clothing*) Inf **KY**83, Sheep needles.

sheep loco n Cf **sheep pod**
A **milk vetch** (here: *Astragalus hornii* or *A. nothoxys*).
1925 Jepson *Manual Plants CA* 567, [*Astragalus*] *hornii . .* Sheep Loco. . . It is reported as poisonous to sheep. **1964** Kingsbury *Poisonous Plants U.S.* 307 **AZ, NM,** The following species of *Astragalus* and *Oxytropis* are true locoweeds—that is, they produce the symptoms characteristic of loco poisoning. . . *A. nothoxys* Gray (sheep loco). Southeast Arizona and New Mexico into Mexico. **1968** Schmutz et al. *Livestock-Poisoning Plants AZ* 26, Sheep loco, locoweed, crazyweed (*A[stragalus] nothoxys*).

sheep loon n
An immature **loon 1** (here: *Gavia immer*).
1852 in 1876 *Forest & Stream* 7.212 **eMA,** *List of Gunner's Names for Birds and Wild Fowl obtained in Plymouth Bay, Mass. . . Columbus torquatus.* Adult, Pond loon; young, sheep loon. **1955** MA Audubon Soc. *Bulletin* 39.309 **MA,** Common Loon. . . Sheep Loon . . the young.

sheep marble n Cf **sheep-dumpling, sheepball tea**
1983 *MJLF* 9.1.55 **ceKY** (as of 1956), *Sheep marbles . .* sheep manure.

sheep meat n
Lamb; mutton.
1859 (1968) Bartlett *Americanisms* 398, *Sheep-Meat.* Mutton is often so called in the West. **1860** *S. Lit. Messenger* 30.65 **VA,** Anh-a! anh a-

a! Sheep meat too good for niggers! **1884** *Gringo & Greaser* 1 Jan. 2/3 (*DAE*), [We] munch our tortiers and sheepmeat on the wing. **1986** Pederson *LAGS Concordance,* 1 inf, **cwAL,** I don't like sheep meat.

sheep mint n esp sAppalachians
A calamint; see quots.
1935 Glasgow *Vein of Iron* 76 wVA, The sheepmint in the grass gave out an aromatic scent when it was crushed. **1968** *DARE* (Qu. S21, . . *Weeds . . that are a trouble in gardens and fields*) Inf VA24, Sheep mint. **1970** *NC Folkl.* 18.27, Jimson weed and sheep mint, cooked with wax, was used as remedy for hemorrhoids.

sheep mullein n Also *sheep's mullein* Cf **lamb's tongue 3, ~ wool, sheep's ear, sheep weed 6**
A **mullein** (here: *Verbascum thapsus*).
1949 *WELS Suppl.* csWI, Burdock was correctly identified—also mullein. However, I heard "sheep mullein" or "sheep's mullein" used a few times. **1965–70** *DARE* (Qu. S20, *A common weed that grows on open hillsides: It has velvety green leaves close to the ground, and a tall stalk with small yellow flowers on a spike at the top*) 11 Infs, **scattered,** Sheep mullein; NJ67, Sheep mullein—For swollen feet . . soak feet . . in hot water and mullein; VA69, Sheep mullein—good for swelling and snakebite.

sheep mustard n esp KY
See quots.
1969 *DARE* (Qu. I28b, *Kinds of greens that are cooked*) Inf **KY**42, Sheep mustard. **1983** *MJLF* 9.1.55 ceKY (as of 1956), *Sheep mustard . .* a wild green. **2000** *NADS Letters* GA, Sheep mustard. . . Yes, it is a type of grass. I can't exactly remember what the grass is actually called. I want to say . . Sheep Sorrell, or something that sounds like that. But it is a type of grass that is edible, but very, very sour!! *Ibid* KY, Sheep Mustard: common wild mustard, used as cooked greens by older Kentuckians. Usually just referred to as wild mustard locally, but I have heard a few folks from farther east call it sheep mustard.

sheep-nanny tea See **nanny** n² **2**

sheep needles See **sheep lice 2**

sheepnose n

1 A **freshwater clam** (here: *Plethobasus cyphus*).
1941 *AmSp* 16.156, Common names as applied by the cutter and fisher of shells. . . Sheep-nose [etc]. **1982** U.S. Fish & Wildlife Serv. *Fresh-Water Mussels* 2.12, Bullhead. Sheepnose. Historically widespread, uncommon. . . Nearly extirpated. **1992** Cummings–Mayer *Field Guide Freshwater Mussels MW* 50, Sheepnose—*Plethobasus cyphus . .* Other common name—Bullhead.
2 =**black-eyed Susan 2.**
1968 *DARE* (Qu. S7, *A kind of daisy, bright yellow with a dark center, that grows along roadsides in late summer*) Inf **IN**35, Sheepnose.

sheepnut n
=**jojoba.**
1920 Saunders *Useful Wild Plants* 78, Little known to Americans but possessing a fascination all its own, is the so-called Wild Hazel, Goatnut or Sheep-nut, the fruit of a non-deciduous, grayish-green shrub, *Simmondsia Californica . .* locally abundant along the mountain borders of the desert in Southern California and extending into Arizona and northern Mexico. **1938** Van Dersal *Native Woody Plants* 353, Sheepnut (*Simmondsia chinensis*).

sheep parsnip n
A **biscuit root 1** (here: *Lomatium macrocarpum*).
1961 Thomas *Flora Santa Cruz* 261 cwCA, *L[omatium] macrocarpum . .* Sheep Parsnip. Commonly growing on open serpentine outcroppings.

sheep pen n Also *sheep yard* Cf **barsdown, sheep in my pen**
=**sic-a-nine-ten.**
1895 *DN* 1.399, *Sheep pen, sheep yard:* same as sic-a-nine-ten. **1906** *DN* 3.155 nwAR, *Sheep-pen. . .* A boys' game.

sheep pod n Cf **sheep loco**
A **ground plum 1** (here: *Astragalus crassicarpus*).
1915 (1926) Armstrong–Thornber *Western Wild Flowers* 258, Pink Lady-fingers, Sheep-pod—*Astragalus Utahensis. . .* The pod is short,

leathery, woolly, and stemless. **1959** Carleton *Index Herb. Plants* 106, *Sheep-pod:* Astragalus mexicanus.

sheep poison n

1 A **sheep laurel** (here: *Kalmia angustifolia*).

1790 Castiglioni *Viaggio* 2.272, *K[almia] Angustifolia* . . Sheep poison, Ivy, Dwarf-Laurell, Lamb-kill. **1814** Bigelow *Florula Bostoniensis* 103, *Kalmia angustifolia*. . . A low shrub with rose coloured flowers, very common in low grounds, and known by the names *sheep poison, lambkill, low laurel, &c.* **1832** MA Hist. Soc. *Coll.* 2d ser 9.151 **cwVT**, Kalmia angustifolia, Sheep poison. **1892** *Jrl. Amer. Folkl.* 5.100 **NEng**, *Kalmia angustifolia*, sheep-poison. **1924** [see **sheep laurel**]. **1935** (1943) Muenscher *Weeds* 355, *Kalmia angustifolia* . . Sheep poison.

2 A **lupine** (here: *Lupinus densiflorus*).

1884 Miller *Dict. Engl. Names of Plants* 124 **CA**, "Sheep-poison," Californian. *Lupinus densiflorus.*

sheep pole down n Cf **guard the sheep, sheep pen**

1901 *DN* 2.147, *Sheep pole down.* . . Name of an out-door game similar to *sic-a-nine-ten.*

sheep puncher n [By analogy with **cowpuncher 1**] Cf **mutton puncher, puncher 2**

1936 McCarthy *Lang. Mosshorn* np **West** [Range terms], Sheep-puncher. . . A cowboy's term for sheepherder.

sheep rain n

See quot 1995.

1954 Taylor *Widows of Thornton* 40 **TN** [Black], She liked to talk, and she talked about Aunt Munsie not in any ugly, resentful way but as she would about when the sheep-rains would begin or where the fire was last night. **1955** *Sun* (Baltimore MD) 28 Apr 38/2, The Weather Bureau delved into some ancient lore . . and announced that the period of rainy, cloudy weather from which Baltimore should emerge today was the period of "sheep rains" or "snowball rains." . . The reason for the former name is that shearing sheep was delayed until after the cold, rainy periods because it was thought that warmer weather would persist after these periods. **1995** Heatwole *Shenandoah Voices* 43 **VA**, In the Shenandoah Valley, the first sheep shearing of the year usually takes place soon after the first of May. The old timers say that a cold rain will follow within a few days of the shearing—a sheep rain. People used to use the sheep rain as a date to plan other events around. Someone might say, "Let's register that deed at the courthouse before the sheep rain," or "We'll be married after the sheep rain."

sheeps See **sheep A**

sheep saffron n Also *sheep-saffron tea* Cf **sheep-dumpling**

Sheep droppings or a medicinal infusion made from them.

1834 in 1956 Eliason *Tarheel Talk* 293 **NC**, I gave a good deal of *Sheep Saffron* to my little children hear, both white and black and they done well. **1835** Longstreet *GA Scenes* 210, *Mrs. R.* Well, I reckon sheep-saffron the onliest thing in nater for the ager. *Mrs. B.* I've always hearn it was wonderful in hives, and measly ailments. **1843** (1969) Lewis *Odd Leaves* 151, How we debated "whether the 'hives' were catchin' or not?" and were perfectly unanimous in the conclusion that "sheep safern" were wonderful "truck!" **1856** Cartwright *Autobiog.* 135 **KY, TN**, The next time these monkey-catchers come they bring sheep-saffron, that very much resembles black haws. **1983** *Barrick Coll.* **csPA**, *Sheep saffron*—sheep droppings soaked in water to produce a yellow fluid used as a folk remedy for measles, *et al.* **1986** Pederson *LAGS Concordance*, 1 inf, **cLA**, Sheep manure—boiled to make sheep-saffron tea.

sheep's bane See **sheep lice 2**

sheepsberry See **sheepberry 2**

sheep's ear n

The leaf of **mullein** (here: *Verbascum thapsus*).

1970 *DARE* (Qu. S20, *A common weed that grows on open hillsides: It has velvety green leaves close to the ground, and a tall stalk with small yellow flowers on a spike at the top*) Inf **NY**232, Leaves called sheep's ears.

sheep's eyes n Also *sheep eyes* [*OED2* 1529 →] Cf **calf-eyes**

An amorous glance; a glance of longing—usu in phrr *cast* (or *make*) *sheep's eyes* to look amorously or lovingly (upon).

1854 *Harper's New Mth. Mag.* 8.855, Never 'cast sheep's-eyes' at the fair sex during sermon-time, unless by previous arrangement. **1871** Eggleston *Hoosier Schoolmaster* 26 **sIN**, She cast at him what are commonly called sheep's-eyes. Ralph thought them more like calf's-eyes. **1955** Roberts *S. from Hell-fer-Sartin* 141 **seKY**, There was a young man . . couldn't think of anything to say when he went to see the girls. . . His daddy told him to cast sheep's eyes at the girls. **1968** Kellner *Aunt Serena* 65 **cIN** (as of c1920), Ella May was a large rawboned girl with red hair and freckles and all sorts of virtues. . . she never cast sheep's eyes at *anybody.* **1984** Wilder *You All Spoken Here* 93 **Sth**, Make sheep eyes, make time with, take a shine for.

sheep shadney n

=**sheep tea.**

1934 Hurston *Jonah's Gourd Vine* 151 **AL** [Black], Ahm gwine find some sheep pills [droppings] so de baby kin have some sheep shadney. *Ibid* 314, *Sheep shadney*, tea made from sheep droppings. It is sweetened and fed to very young babies.

sheepshank tea n

=**sheep tea.**

1970 *Clarke Co. Democrat* (Grove Hill AL) 26 Feb 4/2 *(Mathews Coll.)*, Sheep-shank tea taken hot would make measles pop out.

sheepshead n Also *sheephead*

1 also *head, sheep(fish):* A sparid fish *(Archosargus probatocephalus)* of the Atlantic and Gulf coasts. [See quot 1884] **chiefly Sth** Also called **Charleston brim, convict, gaspergou 2**

1670 (1937) Denton *Brief Descr.* 5 **Long Is. NY**, These Rivers are very well furnished with Fish, as Bosse, Sheepsheads, Place [etc]. **1687** Blome *Present State* 119 **PA**, The *Sheepshead,* so called, from the resemblance of its Mouth and Nose to a Sheep, is a Fish much preferred by some; but they keep in Salt Water. **1724** (1865) Jones *Present State VA* 41, There is Variety of excellent *Fish* . . especially *Oysters, Sheepsheads, Rocks, large Trouts, Crabs, Drums.* **1789** Morse *Amer. Geog.* 205 **RI**, In the rivers and bays are plenty of sheeps-head, black-fish, herring. **1814** in 1815 Lit. & Philos. Soc. NY *Trans.* 1.392 **NY**, Nothing, in the opinion of a New-Yorker, can exceed boiled sheep's head served up at a sumptuous dinner. . . The form of the mouth, and a certain smuttiness of the face, have a distant resemblance to the physiognomy of the sheep. **1838** [see **3** below]. **1864** in 1903 Norton *Army Letters* 212 **FL**, Sheephead, shaped like a pumpkin seed with teeth exactly like a sheep's. **1875** Scott *Fishing Amer. Waters* 91 **NYC**, The clam-rakers and crab-catchers, whose small sail and row boats dot the shores and shoals of Jamaica Bay . . advised me to use a hand-line for "head." **1884** Goode *Fisheries U.S.* 1.381, The Sheepshead is one of the choicest fishes of our coast. It derives its name from the resemblance of its profile and teeth to those of a sheep, and also from its browsing habits. . . It has only this one name by which it is known from Cape Cod to the Mexican border. The negroes of the South, however frequently drop the "s" out of the middle of the word and call it "Sheephead." **1946** Kopman *Wild Acres* 56 **LA**, The fishermen . . spend their time matching strategy . . with wily, nimble spadefish and sheephead feeding . . about the pilings. **1965–70** *DARE* (Qu. P2, . . *Kinds of saltwater fish caught around here . . good to eat*) 14 Infs, **Sth**, Sheephead(s); **AL**22, Sheephead—also called a drum; **LA**40, Sheephead or gaspergou; **MD**36, **NJ**22, **NC**82, **TN**65, Sheepshead; **TX**14, Sheepfish; (Qu. P4, *Saltwater fish that are not good to eat*) Inf **NY**132, Sheeps; (Qu. P14, . . *Commercial fishing . . what do the fishermen go out after?*) Infs **LA**37, 44, **SC**63, Sheephead; **LA**34, Sheepsheads—not striped, caught in lakes. . . caspergou; **SC**66, Sheepshead. **1966–67** *DARE* Tape **FL**46, There's plenty good fish to be caught. . . You can get . . snoop, snapper, sheephead. . . red and . . mullet; **TX**18, Sheepshead. . . That's . . a very delicious fish, very hard to clean, and we catch 'em around pilings. **1986** Pederson *LAGS Concordance*, 33 infs, **Gulf Region**, Sheepshead(s).

2 also *freshwater sheepshead, sheep:* =**freshwater drum. chiefly Gt Lakes** Cf **lake sheepshead**

1815 Lit. & Philos. Soc. NY *Trans.* 1.494, A very ill-tasted fish in Erie, is called the *sheep's head,* on account of a supposed resemblance to its salt water namesake. **1908** Forbes–Richardson *Fishes of IL* 324, In the Great Lake region it is more commonly called the sheepshead, and this is perhaps the name by which it is best known in Illinois. **1933** LA Dept. of Conserv. *Fishes* 363, The Gaspergou or Fresh-water

Sheepshead . . is an important and valuable member of the Louisiana fresh water fish fauna. **1950** *WELS (Kinds of fish not commonly eaten)* 6 Infs, **WI**, Sheephead. **1965–70** *DARE* (Qu. P3, *Freshwater fish that are not good to eat*) 12 Infs, 9 **Gt Lakes**, Sheephead; **MN38**, Carp or sheephead—Iowa people eat—all right smoked; **NY132**, Sheeps; **WI48**, Sheephead; (Qu. P1, . . *Kinds of freshwater fish . . caught around here . . good to eat*) Infs **IA14**, **MN21**, **OH16**, 29, 67, **TX19**, **WI6**, Sheephead(s); **MN42**, Sheephead—smoked; **WI22**, 32, Sheephead; (Qu. P14, . . *Commercial fishing . . what do the fishermen go out after?*) Inf **MN42**, Sheephead; **MI71**, Sheephead—shipped to the outfits that make catfood. **1985** Madson *Up River* 134 **Upper Missip Valley**, Freshwater drum (known variously as "sheepshead" or "white perch," depending on where you are) can also be fine eating.

3 A **butterfish 1** (here: *Peprilus triacanthus*).
1838 MA Zool. & Bot. Surv. *Repts. Zool.* 36, The *Sargus ovis*, a very excellent, and in many markets a highly valued fish . . and the *Peprilus cryptosus* . . used in this State only as manure, are each called "Sheep's-head." **1902** Jordan-Evermann *Amer. Fishes* 330 **MA**, *Poronotus triacanthus*—This is the butterfish of the coast of Massachusetts and New York, the harvestfish of New Jersey, the dollarfish of Maine, the sheepshead of Cape Cod, the pumpkinseed of Connecticut, and the starfish of Norfork [sic].

4 A California wrasse *(Pimelometopon pulchrum)*. Also called **fathead 2, humpy 1, redfish d**
1884 Goode *Fisheries U.S.* 1.275, The Red-fish, of California. . . is very rarely called 'Sheepshead.' **1946** LaMonte *N. Amer. Game Fishes* 92, California sheepshead—*Pimelometopon pulcher*. **1968–70** *DARE* (Qu. P2, . . *Kinds of saltwater fish caught around here . . good to eat*) Inf **CA191**, Sheephead; **CA65**, Sheephead—by the islands; (Qu. P4, *Saltwater fish that are not good to eat*) Inf **CA36**, Sheepheads—a scavenger fish. **1975** Evanoff *Catch More Fish* 108, Other fish caught by Pacific bottom anglers include the queenfish, . . sheepshead [etc].

5 A card game played with 32 cards ranked in an unusual order in which players take tricks that are scored according to the point values assigned to particular cards. [Calque of **schafskopf**] **chiefly WI** See Map
1886 E.E. Lemcke *Skat* 4 (*OED2*), Skat is of quite recent origin. . . It bears a great resemblance to the Wendish game of '*Schafskopf*' (Sheepshead). **1913** *Official Rules of Card Games* 205, Schafkopf [sic] . . *Sheephead*. . . Object of the game. . . To win in tricks certain cards of counting value. **1965–70** *DARE* (Qu. DD35, . . *Card games*) 13 Infs, 10 **WI**, Sheephead; **IN35**, **WI60**, 63, 71, 77, Sheephead. **1983** in 1998 Leary *WI Folkl.* 383, Many bartenders keep decks of cards on hand. Dirty Clubs, a variant of Euchre, is the most popular tavern game in Barron County. But old-timers also enjoy *Schafskopf*, or Sheephead. **1997** *DARE* File—Internet **WI** [Speak 'Scansin], Two card games, probably of German origin. You can watch these games and have them explained for years, and you still won't know the rules. Actual names being smear and sheephead. You can also schmear in sheephead. **1999** *Ibid* **WI** [Central Florida Green Bay Packer Backers], Sheephead: a popular Wisconsin card game.

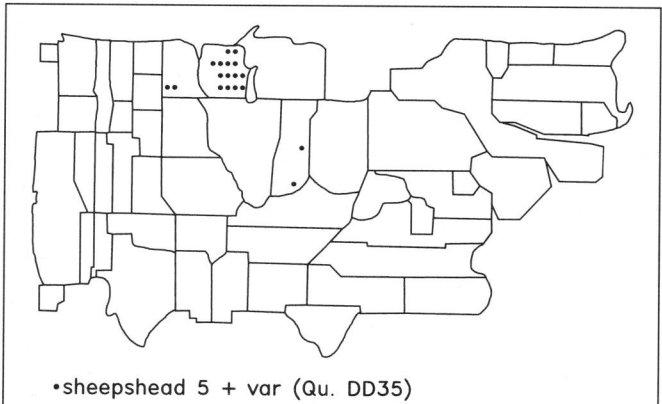

•sheepshead 5 + var (Qu. DD35)

6 A white cumulus cloud, esp a small one occurring in a group of similar clouds. **esp Nth, N Midl** Cf **black-sheep cloud, sheep ~**
1965–70 *DARE* (Qu. B11, . . *Other kinds of clouds that come often*) Infs **CT7**, **IL93**, **IN19**, **MI30**, **NJ17**, **NY116**, Sheepsheads; **OH4**,

TN52, Sheepsheads [FW sugg]; **AZ15**, Sheepsheads—small, round, in flocks; **OH99**, Sheepsheads—puffed around, billowy—farmers use this term; **TX37**, Sheepsheads—real white with patches of blue; **VT16**, Sheepsheads—little fluffly clouds; they look like a sheep's head; **WI5**, Sheepsheads—tiny, little, fluffy one—have rain in them; **WI60**, Sheepsheads—big white clouds; **WV16**, Sheepsheads—white, puffy clouds; **WV17**, Sheepsheads—large, white puffs of fog; come when weather is good; **WA18**, Sheepsheads. [14 of 17 Infs old] **1995** Brophy Coll. 66 **swMO** (as of c1960), *Sheephead*. [A] summer cumulus cloud containing no rain.

sheepshead killifish n Also *sheepshead minnow*
A **killifish 1** (here: *Cyprinodon variegatus*).
1814 in 1815 Lit. & Philos. Soc. NY *Trans.* 441, *Sheep's-Head Killifish*. . . Length about an inch and a half; and remarkably large in the girth. **1884** U.S. Natl. Museum *Bulletin* 27.470, Mummichog; Sheepshead Killifish. **1903** NY State Museum & Sci. Serv. *Bulletin* 60.315, *Cyprinodon variegatus* . . Sheepshead minnow. *Ibid* 317, The Sheepshead killifish ranges from Cape Cod to Florida. **1955** Carr–Goin *Guide Reptiles* 75, Southern Sheepshead Killifish. . . Atlantic Coast of the United States from Cape Cod southward.

sheepshead of the lake See **lake sheepshead**

sheep shear (or shire, shower) See **sheep sour**

sheepskin n
1 A sheet formed by pouring hot maple syrup on snow. Cf **air foam, leather apron, maple wax**
1939 Wolcott *Yankee Cook Book* 346, Some call the syrup [=hot maple syrup poured on snow] "sheepskins"; others refer to it as "leather aprons" or "maple wax." **1940** Brown *Amer. Cooks* 819 **VT**, Maple snow has a number of descriptive names—maple wax, sugar-on-snow, sheepskins, and leather aprons.
2 See quot.
1966 *DARE* (Qu. H77, *When you are making jam, . . the stuff that has to be skimmed off the top?*; total Infs questioned, 75) Inf **MS2**, Sheepskin—drained off syrup.
3 A type of marble; see quot.
c1970 Wiersma *Marbles Terms*, *Sheep skin*—marbles with coloring on the outside. *Ibid*, *Sheepskin(s):*. . . Marble that is brown, white, and red, and not blurred up or mixed.

sheep's laurel See **sheep laurel**

sheep's leg See **sheep leg**

sheep's mullein See **sheep mullein**

sheep sorrel n [*OED2* 1578 →]
A **dock n[1]** (here: usu *Rumex acetosella*) or a **wood sorrel** (here: *Oxalis* spp). Also called **sheep grass, ~ sour** For other names of the former see **gentleman's sorrel, horse ~ 1, house ~, rabbit's ear, red sorrel, redtop 2, redweed 2, sour dock, ~ grass, sourweed**
1806 (1807) Gass *Jrl.* 188, A great quantity of sheep-sorrel growing in the woods. **1830** Rafinesque *Med. Flora* 2.259, R[umex] acetosella or sheep sorrel . . subastringent. **1837** Darlington *Flora Cestrica* 236 **sePA**, *R. acetosella*. . . Sheep Sorrel. Field Sorrel. **1893** *Jrl. Amer. Folkl.* 6.139, *Oxalis acetosella*, sheep sorrel. Jones and Del. Co., Ia. *Ibid*, *Oxalis violacea*, sheep sorrel. Peoria, Ill. *Ibid*, *Oxalis corniculata*, var. *stricta*, sheep sorrel. Peoria, Ill.; Ferrisburgh, Vt.; Anderson, Ind. **1940** Steyermark *Flora MO* 314, Sheep Sorrel (*Oxalis pilosa* . .). *Ibid*, Sheep Sorrel (*Oxalis corniculata* . .). **1941** Cleaveland *No Life* 163 **NM** (as of a1890), In early spring we often had lamb's-quarter greens and occasionally sheep-sorrel pie if a patch of sheep sorrel could be found. The acid-sweet of sheep sorrel makes delectable pie, but it takes so much of the short-stemmed clover-leaf-shaped plant that only when all hands gathered sheep sorrel could we hope for the luxury of a pie. **1951** *PADS* 15.35 **TX**, *Oxalis* spp.—Wood sorrel; sorrel grass; sour grass; sheep sorrel. Except as pink, purple, white, or yellow, there is no differentiation between the forms, to which the above names are indiscriminately applied. **1953** Randolph–Wilson *Down in Holler* 205 **Ozarks**, The old-timers often speak extravagantly of the poverty and hardships of their youth. . . "Us boys was *drinkin' branch-water an' eatin' sheep-sorrel* in them days," another told me solemnly. **1965–70** *DARE* (Qu. I28a, . . *Kinds of things . . you call 'greens' . . [Those that are eaten raw]*) Infs **MI113**, **WV3**, 17, Sheep sorrel; (Qu. I28b, *Kinds of*

greens that are cooked) Inf **IN39**, Sheep sorrel; (Qu. S21, . . *Weeds . . that are a trouble in gardens and fields*) Infs **TN1**, **VA15**, **WV17**, Sheep sorrel; **IN54**, Sheep sorrel—fine pale-green leaves; (Qu. S2, . . *The flower that comes up in the woods early in spring, with three white petals that turn pink as the flower grows older*) Inf **MS23**, Sheep sorrel; (Qu. S11) Inf **AR35**, Wood sorrel; sheep sorrel—same; (Qu. S26d, *Wildflowers that grow in meadows; not asked in early QRs*) Infs **PA192**, **TN6**, Sheep sorrel; (Qu. S26e, *Other wildflowers; not asked in early QRs*) Inf **IL135**, Sheep sorrel or sheep sour—sour-tasting leaves, tender and small; **LA12**, Sheepgrass, occasionally, or sheep shower—same as sheep sorrel; **OR5**, Sheep sorrel. **1966–67** *DARE* Wildfl QR **WA10**, *Rumex acetosella*—Sheep Sorrel, Sour Weed; Pl.121A **AR44**, **WA15**, *Ionoxalis violacea*—Sheep-sorrel. **1976** Brown *Gloss. Faulkner* 174, *Sheep sorrel . .* not the 1′–2′ high red sorrel (*Rumex hastatulus*) commonly known by this name, but the much smaller violet wood sorrel (*Oxalis violacea*). It grows 1″–3″ high, with three greenish-bronze leaflets on each stem, and is eaten by children in the spring for its pungent sour taste. The pink flowers, growing two or three to a stem, are particularly delectable. **1985** Clark *From Mailbox* 109 **ME**, Some parts of my gardens have sheep sorrel creeping in.

sheep sour n Also *sheep shear, ~ shire, ~ shower;* for addit varr see quots [*Sheep sour* is prob by folk-etym from **sheep sorrel,** though it may instead (or also) derive from Scots *sheep sourock. Sheep shower* is prob by assim; the other varr appar represent further folk-etym alterations.] **chiefly S Midl**
=**sheep sorrel.**

1893 Shands *MS Speech* 55, Sheep-sorrel. This plant has many names in Mississippi, all of which are very common. It is called *sheep-shaw* [šip šɔ], *sheep-shire* [šip šaɪə], *sheep-sheer* [šip šiə], *sheep-shy* [šip šaɪ]; but the correct name, *sheep-sorrel,* is rarely heard. **1915** *DN* 4.228 **wTX**, Sheep-sour. . . Sheep-sorrel. **1932** *AmSp* 7.168 **NE**, Among the table delicacies of the pioneers were "sheep-shower pie," made of an herb common in Nebraska, and "plum-soup." **c1960** *Wilson Coll.* **csKY**, Sheep shower: . . Wood sorrel, sheep sorrel. **1964** Wallace *Frontier Life* 60 **OK** (as of 1893–1906), Burning the ricks of cornstocks, planting gardens, gathering the first "sheep shower," coloring Easter eggs, wearing a new Easter dress. **1965–70** *DARE* (Qu. I28b, . . *Greens . . cooked*) Inf **KY85**, Sheep sour—cooked, wild green; **MO6**, Sheep shower; (Qu. S2, . . *The flower that comes up in the woods early in spring, with three white petals that turn pink as the flower grows older*) Inf **OK3** Sheep shalos ['šaloz]; **MO10**, Sheep shower flower; (Qu. S3, *A flower like a large violet with a yellow center and small ragged leaves—it comes up early in spring on open, stony hilltops*) Inf **OK9**, Sheep shower; (Qu. S9, . . *Kinds of grass that are hard to get rid of*) Inf **VA96**, Sheep's arrow; (Qu. S22, . . *The bright yellow flowers that bloom in clusters in marshes in early springtime*) Inf **AR24**, Sheep shar; (Qu. S26e, *Other wildflowers*) Inf **IL135**, Sheep sorrel or sheep sour—sour-tasting leaves, tender and small; **LA12**, Sheep grass, occasionally, or sheep shower—same as sheep sorrel. **1967** *DARE* FW Addit **swWA**, *Sheep shower*—same as sheep sorrel. **1968** Haun *Hawk's Done Gone* 227 **eTN**, George sometimes jested Cathey about eating the grass and bushes. But she did eat them—sweetgum and sassafras and sheep sours and things I didn't know. **1970** *DARE* FW Addit **KY88**, *Sheep shears*—An edible wild green, three leaves, pink underneath; book word sheep sorrel. **1982** Slone *How We Talked* 47 **eKY** (as of c1950), Sheep's sour. **2001** *NADS Letters* **MO**, I grew up in rural Missouri near Bagnell Dam on Lake of the Ozarks. When we were kids we'd sometimes nibble on "sheep shears" which were edible "weeds" with a pleasantly sour taste. *Ibid* **neNE** (as of 1940s), We always referred to it [= sheep sorrel] as 'sheepshower' or 'sheepsour.'

sheep's quarters n
=**lamb's quarter(s) 1.**
1968–69 *DARE* (Qu. I28b, *Kinds of greens that are cooked*) Inf **IL31**, Sheep's-quarters—a weed; (Qu. S21, . . *Weeds . . that are a trouble in gardens and fields*) Inf **WI64**, Sheep's quarters.

sheep's-teats (black)berry n See **sheeptit (berry)**

sheep's tongue n
Perh a **plantain;** see quots.
1961 *Mt. Life* Spring 57 **Appalachians**, In almost any old field can be found wild lettuce, pepper grass, sheep's tongue, poke, hanner-on-the-rock, creasies, crow's foot, and a hundred others. **1973** Kluger *Wild Flavor* 72 **sIN**, I learned to know plantain as "sheep's tongue." **1982** Slone *How We Talked* 47 **eKY** (as of c1950), [In a list of "salet" plants:] Sheeps tongue.

sheepswool n Also *sheepswool sponge, sheepwool* [See quot 1981]
A Florida **sponge** (here: *Hyrtios lachne*).
1879 Hyatt *Commercial Sponges* 11, A bath sponge . . large enough to show the crater-like openings on the upper surface. The best is one of the American sponges of the coarser Sheep's Wool variety. **1881** Ingersoll *Oyster-Industry* 248, Sheepswool.—The highest grade of Florida commercial sponges, *Spongia gossypina.* **1898** (1910) Willoughby *Across Everglades* 93 **sFL**, I have a sheep's-wool in my possession that is larger than my head, but so soft that I can put it in my closed hand and it cannot be seen. **1949** Palmer *Nat. Hist.* 345, Florida and Bahamas produce sheep's-wool sponge, *H. gossypina.* **1981** Meinkoth *Audubon Field Guide Seashore* 331, Sheep's Wool Sponge. . . This is the most important commercial sponge in the New World. Its unusual softness after cleaning suggests its common name.

sheep tea n Also called **sheepball tea,** *sheep-dumpling tea* (at **sheep-dumpling**), (*sheep-*)*nanny tea* (at **nanny** n[2] 2), **sheep saffron, ~ shadney, sheepshank tea**
An infusion of sheep dung used as a remedy.
[**1872** *Appletons' Jrl.* 8.245 **England,** In cases of the measles . . a decoction, commonly known as "sheep-tea," is of modern use.] **1970** *NC Folkl.* 8.23, For breaking out hives, use sheep tea. *Ibid* 25, Sheep tea was used for breaking out measles. **1983** *MJLF* 9.1.55 **ceKY** (as of 1956), *Sheep tea . .* a medicine made by boiling sheep manure in water. Said by informant one to make measles break out when they otherwise won't. Same use reported in SC.

sheep ticks See **sheep lice 2**

sheeptit (berry) n Also *sheep's-teats (black)berry* Cf **sow-tit**
A **dewberry 1** (here: *Rubus canadensis*) or a **strawberry** (here: *Fragaria vesca*).
1942 Weygandt *Plenty* 296 **cPA**, We ran on *Rubus canadensis,* there called sheep's teats blackberry. . . These sheep's teats berries were a delicious fruit, coreless, melting, with a piquant individual flavor. **1945** McAtee *Nomina Abitera* 13 **NH**, Strawberry (*Fragaria vesca*)—Sheeptits (New Hampshire, Philip F. Allan). **1969** *DARE* (Qu. I44, *What kinds of berries grow wild around here?*) Inf **MA42**, Sheeptit berries.

sheep tobacco n [Because the leaves are densely woolly and are smoked as a treatment for asthma]
A **mullein** (here: *Verbascum thapsus*).
1974 Morton *Folk Remedies* 155 **SC**, Woolly Mullein . . Sheep Tobacco. . . *Verbascum thapsus.* . . Old fields, newly disturbed ground and roadsides.

sheep wagon n Also *sheep camp* **chiefly Rocky Mts**
An enclosed covered wagon equipped to serve as a dwelling for a sheepherder.
1909 in 1914 Stewart *Letters* 8 **WY**, About noon the first day out we came near a sheep-wagon. **1931** *AmSp* 7.120 **eID**, A *sheep camp,* or the migratory home of a pair of sheepherders, consists of a canvas-topped wagon with a stove in it and a *bunk* or bed at the back. **1936** in Lib. of Congress *Amer. Memory: FSA/OWI* (Internet), [Caption:] Sheep wagon. Natrona County, Wyoming. *Ibid,* [Caption:] Central Utah fry [sic] land adjustment project . . Tooele, Utah. Sheep wagons in which some workers on project lived. **1939** Towne *Her Majesty Montana* 84 *(Hench Coll.),* The herder is still a nomad. This necessitates a high degree of mobility for the herder and his belongings. Hence the sheep wagon. We have all seen a sheep wagon, with its short length of stove pipe sticking through a rounded canvas top covering a wagon-box on four wheels. **1954** *Middle Border Bulletin* Spring np **SD**, A recent addition to the Friends of the Middle Border Museum is the sheep wagon in which Archie Gilfillan wrote his book, Sheep. [Illustr in text] **1985** Ehrlich *Solace* 18 **WY**, Lambing, which started in late February and ended in April, was one of the times of year when everyone on the ranch worked closely together. Sheep wagons, pulled in from their lonely sentinels on the range, were lined up behind the sun sheds. **1999** *DARE* File—Internet **WY** [Steadman's Old West Miniatures], The Sheep Camp. . . Perhaps the Sheep Camp could be considered the forerunner of the modern day R.V. It was a home on wheels for those who stayed in the hills in the summer or on the desert in the winter to watch over the large herds of sheep. It contained a bed, cook stove, table, eating and cooking utensils, cupboards for storage, and a kerosene lantern for light. It was pulled from camp to camp site by a team of horses, usually behind a chuck wagon which carried the supplies. **2000** *Ibid,* Montana Abolition Coalition . . Anti-Death Penalty Sheep Wagon Trek. . . These

retired teachers pulled a sheep wagon around the entire state of Montana. . . They ate and slept in the sheep wagon.

sheepweed n

1 A **velvetleaf 1** (here: *Abutilon theophrasti*).

1892 *Jrl. Amer. Folkl.* 5.93 **cwIL,** *Abutilon Avicennae.* . . sheepweed; Mormon-weed; velvet-weed. Quincy, Ill. **1940** Clute *Amer. Plant Names* 44, Velvet-leaf. . . cotton-weed, sheep-weed.

2 =**bouncing Bet 1.**

1900 Lyons *Plant Names* 334, *S[aponaria] officinalis.* . . Sheepweed, Sweet-Betty [etc]. **1958** Jacobs–Burlage *Index Plants NC* 35, *Saponaria officinalis.* . . common soapwort; soaproot; . . sheepweed; sweet-betty.

3 A croton (here: *Croton capitatus*).

1913 *Torreya* 13.231, *Croton engelmannii.* . . Goat-weed, sheep-weed, Marksville, La.

4 A **snakeweed** (here: *Gutierrezia sarothrae*).

1943 Elmore *Ethnobotany Navajo* 86, *Solidago sarothrae.* . . Sheepweed, Dodgeweed [etc]. . . When a sheep is bitten by a snake, this plant is ground and boiled and placed on the wound as a poultice. The swelling is said to go down immediately and the sheep cured. **1960** Vines *Trees SW* 994, Broom Snakeweed. . . Other names in common use are Broom-weed, Sheep-weed [etc]. . . In times of stress it is eaten in limited amounts by sheep and horses. **1989** Mayes–Lacy *Nanise* 115, Snakeweed . . sheepweed, yellowweed.

5 An **indigo bush 2** (here: *Dalea frutescens*).

1951 *PADS* 15.35 **TX,** *Dalea frutescens* . . sheep or goat weed. The way sheep or goats devour every morsel of this perfect bouquet of pansy purple, the plant, [sic] will not last very long outside of tightly fenced areas with no "woolies" around.

6 A **mullein** (here: *Verbascum thapsus*).

1966 *DARE* (Qu. S20, *A common weed that grows on open hillsides: It has velvety green leaves close to the ground, and a tall stalk with small yellow flowers on a spike at the top*) Inf **NC27,** Mullein or sheepweed. **1966** *DARE* Tape **NC25,** And now I don't hardly ever see any of that mullein growin'. They used to call it sheepweed. . . 'cause it was furry, like.

sheepwool n

1 See **sheepswool.**

2 See **sheep B2.**

sheepy See **sheepie**

sheep yard See **sheep pen**

sheer See **share**

sheerwater See **shearwater**

sheet cotton See **cotton balls**

sheeting n [Folk-etym for *sheathing*]

See quots.

1965–70 *DARE* (Qu. D27, *Strips of wood used to cover the outside of a frame house*) 21 Infs, **scattered,** Sheeting. **1976** Wells *Barns U.S.A.* np **cnIN,** Sheeting is 1″ x 4″ hemlock with red cedar shingles. **1984** *MJLF* 10.156 **cnWI,** Sheeting. The boards or plywood covering the outside walls of a building. Perhaps from "sheathing," as in "Sheathing paper."

sheewee n Cf **shoo-shoo** n

1968 *DARE* (Qu. FF15, *When a firecracker doesn't go off, and you break it in the middle and light the powder, you call it a _____*) Inf **LA25,** Sheewee [ˌšiˈwi, ˈšiˌwi]; **LA40,** Sheewee.

sheffi n [Joc pronc of *chef*]

A cook on a ranch or trail drive.

1920 Hunter *Trail Drivers TX* 299, The chief man about the camp is the cook. . . Naturally, the cook has many names applied to him. He is called a "sheffi," . . and "biscuit shooter."

she-heifer See **heifer 1a**

sheik of Araby n Cf **Arab** n **B2**

1969 *DARE* (Qu. II21, *When somebody behaves unpleasantly or without manners: "The way he behaves, you'd think he was _____."*) Inf **CA136,** Sheik of Araby.

sheive See **chive**

sheldrake n

1 also *shell, shilldrake:* =**merganser.** Cf **shelduck 1**

1616 Smith *Descr. New Engl.* 29 **neMA,** Sheldrakes, Teale, Meawes, Guls, . . and many other sorts, whose names I knowe not. **1842** DeKay *Zool. NY* 2.318, This large species [=*Mergus merganser*] is known on our coast under the names of *Sheldrake, Sawbill,* and *Dun Diver. Ibid* 319, The Red-Breasted Sheldrake. Mergus serrator. *Ibid* 320, The Hooded Sheldrake. Mergus cucullatus. **1852** in 1876 *Forest & Stream* 7.212 **eMA,** *Mergus serrator.* Sheldrake. **1896** Robinson *In New Engl. Fields* 211, Dark and sullen the river sulks its cheerless way, enlivened but by the sheldrake that still courses his prey in the icy water. **1966–69** *DARE* (Qu. Q5, . . *Kinds of wild ducks*) Inf **CT2,** Sheldrakes—not good to eat; **MA57, NJ55,** Sheldrake; **GA11,** Shell; (Qu. Q7, *Names and nicknames for . . game birds*) Inf **ME22,** Shilldrake. **1975** Gould *ME Lingo* 251, One time a federal biologist came to Maine to lecture at a game-warden school, and when he held up what he called an American merganser the game wardens from northern Maine all hooted at him. He might have a degree and hold down a cozy government job, but he didn't know a *sheldrake* when he saw one.

2 =**canvasback duck.** *prob obs*

a1782 (1788) Jefferson *Notes VA* 77, We have. . . Sheldrach [sic], or Canvas back. **1813** (1824) Wilson *Amer. Ornith.* 8.109 **VA,** At the Susquehannah they are called *Canvass-backs,* on the Potomac *White-backs,* and on James' river *Sheldrakes.* **1925** (1986) Phillips *Nat. Hist. Ducks* 3.121, Vernacular Names—Canvas-back, White-back, Sheldrake [etc].

sheldrake loon n Cf **loon 2**

=**red-necked grebe.**

1917 *Wilson Bulletin* 29.2.74 **Long Is. NY,** *Columbus holboelli.* . . sheldrake loon, Patchogue, L.I.

shelduck n Also sp *shell duck*

1 A **merganser,** esp the female. Cf **sheldrake 1**

1888 Trumbull *Names of Birds* 68 **CT,** At Stonington, Conn., though the name Sheldrake [for red-breasted merganser] is more or less used for both sexes, many gunners distinguish the female as *shelduck.* **1917** (1923) *Birds Amer.* 1.111, Red-breasted Merganser. . . Other Names.— Shelduck; Shell-bird [etc]. **1923** U.S. Dept. Ag. *Misc. Circular* 13.5 **VA,** American Merganser. . . Vernacular Names. . . *In local use* . . shelduck [etc]. **1955** MA Audubon Soc. *Bulletin* 39.378 **RI,** Hooded Merganser. . . Shell Duck. *Ibid* 379 **CT,** Red-breasted Merganser. . . Shelduck (Conn. Pied duck.) **1970** *DARE* (Qu. Q5, . . *Kinds of wild ducks*) Inf **VA47,** Shelduck—red-breasted merganser.

2 =**shoveler.**

1927 *DN* 5.477 **Ozarks,** Shell duck. . . The shoveller, or spoonbill duck.

shelf n

A balcony in a theater.

[**1942** Berrey–Van den Bark *Amer. Slang* 587.10, Top gallery. . . top shelf.] **1966** *DARE* (Qu. D40, *Names and nicknames . . for the upper balcony in a theater*) Inf **MS1,** Buzzard roost; shelf. **2002** *DARE* File **eVA** (as of c1955), "Quiet on the *shelf,*" yells a cheeky White boy at the Blacks laughing on the balcony of the segregated movie theater.

shelf mushroom n Also *shelf (toadstool)* Cf **frogstool**

A polypore or other shelflike **mushroom B1.**

1907 *St. Nicholas* July 846, "Shelves," often called "devil's bread," . . grow on woodland stumps and trees and logs. **1965–70** *DARE* (Qu. S19, *Mushrooms that grow out like brackets from the sides of trees*) 61 Infs, **widespread exc West,** Shelf mushroom(s); **CT40, IA8,** Shelf(s); **RI15, VT16,** Shelf toadstool(s); **OH48, SC32,** Shelves; [**CT15,** Shell mushrooms].

shelf-worn adj phr

Shopworn; showing wear from having been kept too long on a store shelf or in a store display.

1833 *New Engl. Mag.* 5.100, Shelf-worn spelling-books and primers. **1887** Tourgée *Button's Inn* 188, It[=a paper of pins]'s out of season . . creased and shelf-worn. **1905** *DN* 3.93 **nwAR,** *Shelf-worn.* . . Shopworn. 'We have no old shelf-worn goods.' Common. **1909** *DN* 3.369 **eAL, wGA,** *Shelf-worn.* . . Shopworn: the only term used. **1944** Clark *Pills* 214 **Sth** (as of c1870), Ready-made clothes were poor in quality. They were notoriously shelf-worn and motheaten. **1967** *DARE* (Qu. KK6, *Something low-grade or of poor quality—for example, a piece of* *merchandise: "I wouldn't buy that, it's _____."*) Inf **TX**18, Shelf-worn.

shell n¹

1 A standard eight-ounce beer glass; a drink of beer.

[**1903** Farmer–Henley *Slang* 6.172, *Shell. . .* (old). A drinking glass.] **1919** Mencken *Amer. Lang.* 85, In the department of conviviality. . . characteristic Americanisms . . are *red-eye, corn-juice . . schooner, shell . . pony* and *chaser*. **1945** *AmSp* 20.237, At the few taverns in Austin, Texas, where draught beer is sold, a large sixteen-ounce glass, regardless of shape, is quite generally calld a *tub*. The small eight-ounce glass is called a *shell*. These uses of *tub* and *shell* are not found in the dictionaries. **1949** in 1986 *DARE* File, Shell equals spec. a kind of glass of beer—also any glass of beer. Male, about 40, midwest. "Give me a shell of beer." **1950** *WELS (A beer glass)* 8 Infs, **WI**, Shell. **1950** in 1960 Wentworth–Flexner *Slang* 465, *Shell.* . . He decanted two thirds of a beer shell of bourbon and to this he added about a teaspoon of water. **c1970** *DARE* File **seMI**, There [=Detroit]. . . a shell and a shot is a beer and a shot of whiskey as a chaser.

2 An old or weak cow or horse; hence adj *shelly.* Cf **hull n B2b(2)**

1935 *AmSp* 10.272 [Stockyard language], *Shells.* Old, thin cows, *nellies. Shelly.* The adjective applied to *shells.* **1937** *AmSp* 12.103 **eNE** [Farm terms], An old cow is designated by such terms as *nellie, hatrack, skin, shell,* or *canner.* **1953** Randolph–Wilson *Down in Holler* 283 **Ozarks**, *Shelly.* . . Inferior, of low grade, in poor condition. "An old shelly cow" is one that isn't worth much. I have heard it applied only to cattle, but believe that it sometimes refers to bony old horses as well. **1966–70** *DARE* (Qu. K15, *A thin, bony, or poor-looking cow*) Infs **LA**18, **MN**23, **TX**11, Shell; **CA**136, **ID**3, **KS**5, 17, **MD**22, **VA**89, Shelly.

3 also *shell ice*: The first thin coating of ice on a body of water; hence adj *shelly* thin. Cf **scale** n, **shale ice**

1896 *DN* 1.424 **cNY**, Shelly ice: same as *scaly ice.* **1960** Bailey *Resp. to PADS 20* **KS**, (*The first thin ice formed on a pond in the winter*) Shell. **1965–70** *DARE* (Qu. B33a, *The first thin ice that forms over the surface of a pond or pool: "There's just a _____ of ice."*) 12 Infs, **scattered**, Shell; **DE**4, Shell ice; **OK**13, Thin shell. [13 of 15 Infs old; 12 of 15 Infs comm types 4 and 5]; [[(Qu. B33b, *Talking about the first thin ice that forms over the surface of a pond or pool: "The pond is just _____ over."*) Inf **NY**19, Lightly shelled]. **1968** O'Hare *E. MT Engl. Vocab.* 62, The first thin ice. . . shell ice [1 of 10 infs]. **1973** Allen *LAUM* 1.157 **Upper MW** (as of c1950), *Scum* (first thin coating of ice). . . Shell ice [2 infs, **MN, IA**].

4 The skin or rind of a fruit. [PaGer *Schaal*] **PaGer area** Cf **hull n B2a(6)**

1935 *AmSp* 10.171 **PA** [Engl of PA Germans], *Shell.* Any peeling or skin or outer covering is called a shell. 'Banana shell' or 'orange shell.' **1968** *Helen Adolf Festschrift* 38 **cePA**, *Shell* (Pennsylvania German *Schaal*) for any 'skin,' 'peeling,' or 'outer covering'; for example, "apple shells," "orange shells," or "banana shells." **1987** *Jrl. Engl. Ling.* 20.2.175 **ePA**, *Shell* 'a peel, a skin'. . . This Germanism is now extinct.

5 The green leaves at the top of a strawberry. Cf **hull n B1**

1969 *DARE* (Qu. I47, *When you pull the stem out of a strawberry, what do you call the green part that comes off with the stem?*) Inf **MO**19, Shell.

shell v

1 with *out*: =**sell out 2.**

1909 *DN* 3.368 **eAL, wGA**, Shell out. . . To run away precipitously, leave hastily. "We had to shell out from that place."

2 in phrr *shell the brush*, *~ woods*: See quot. [Perh metaphor from threshing dried beans; cf *beat the bushes*]

1953 Randolph–Wilson *Down in Holler* 283 **Ozarks**, Shell the brush: *phr.* Used in connection with political campaigns. "Bob's been a-shellin' the brush over in Barry county" means that he has done a lot of speech-making and hand-shaking over there. *Shellin' the woods* is often used with the same meaning.

3 In var phrr with *corn*, as:

a *shell out the corn*, *~ down the corn*: To pay up. [Appar an expansion of *shell out* to pay up]

1841 *Daily Picayune* (New Orleans LA) 30 Apr 1/6, He is induced to be thus particular, (being like ten thousand of his neighbors,) not exactly prepared to "shell out the corn," and wipe out old scores. **1905** *DN* 3.93 **nwAR**, Shell down the corn. . . To produce and pay the money. 'He just had to shell down the corn, and he didn't have much money,

either.' **1909** *DN* 3.368 **eAL, wGA**, Shell out (the corn). . . To pay (the money).

b *shell down the corn*: To acknowledge one's error. Cf **acknowledge the corn**

1869 in 1981 *AmSp* 56.110 **AL**, The *Mountain Home* shells down the corn to N.S. McAfee, Esq.

c *shell corn*, *~ the corn down*: To speak bluntly or harshly.

1952 Brown *NC Folkl.* 1.589, *Shell corn to (one)*: *phr.* To talk angrily to one.—Guilford county. Rare. **1992** *Houston Chron.* (TX) 5 Apr sec G, *Tell it like it is*: Shell the corn down.

shell n² See **sheldrake 1**

shellback sturgeon n

=**lake sturgeon.**

1983 Becker *Fishes WI* 221, Lake Sturgeon. . . Other common names . . shell back sturgeon, bony sturgeon, smoothback [etc].

shell-bark n

1 See **shellbark hickory.**

2 A rough, rugged person.

1941 Ward *Holding Hills* 79 **IA** (as of early 20th cent), Then one day I told this shell-bark what his friend had said of him. For a moment he said nothing, he sat there sharp and stiff on the chair.

shellbark hickory n Also *shell-bark, shell-barked hickory, shellbark walnut* esp **NJ, PA, WV, N Cent** See Map Cf **walnut**

A hickory **B1**: either a **shagbark hickory** (here: *Carya ovata*) or *Carya laciniosa;* also the fruit or wood of such a tree. For other names of *C. laciniosa* see **kingnut, shagbark hickory**

1769 (1906) Smith *Tour Great Rivers* 21 **NY**, The Timber in these Parts . . consists of . . red Oak Hazel Bushes, Ash and Gum together with Butternut and Shellbark, Hiccory in plenty. **1785** Marshall *Arbustrum* 69, *Juglans alba ovata.* Shell-barked Hickory. . . The bark is rough and shelly or scaly. **1799** *Columbian Mirror* (Alexandria VA) 15 Feb 3/4, *Thomas Simms* Has just received, and has for sale at his Grocery Store . . a quantity of Excellent . . Shellba k [sic] Nuts, by the barrel or smaller quantity. **1810** [see **shagbark hickory**]. **1813** Muhlenberg *Catalogus Plantarum* 88, [Juglans] compressa (squamosa)—shell-bark [walnut], shag-bark [walnut]. **1843** (1844) Johnson *Farmer's Encycl.* 621, The singular disposition of the bark in this species has given rise to the descriptive names of Shellbark, Shagbark, and Scalybark hickory, the first of which is in most general use in the Middle and Southern States. **1890** (1895) Riley *Rhymes of Childhood* 31 **IN**, There, the almost pathless wood / Where the shellbark hickory tree / Rained its wealth on you and me. **1941** *LANE* Map 277 (*Walnut shell*) 6 infs, **CT, MA**, Shellbarks; 1 inf, **ceMA**, Shellbark, not a walnut, but of the same size and with a similar shell; 1 inf, **seMA**, Shellbarks, better than walnuts; 1 inf **csCT**, Shellbark walnut. **1965–70** *DARE* (Qu. I43, *What kinds of nuts grow wild around here?*) Infs **MA**83, **NJ**55, 56, **PA**9, 13, 26, 150, Shellbark; **NJ**50, Shellbark, we used to call 'em; **MO**6, Shellbark hickory nuts; **MD**30, **NY**206, **OH**42, **PA**22, 31, 126, 203, 206, Shellbarks; **PA**242, Shellbarks—variety of hickory; **MD**28, Shellbarks—another name for hickory; (Qu. T16, . . *Kinds of trees* . . '*special*') 14 Infs, **chiefly NCent, WV**, Shellbark hickory; **MA**62, **OH**61, **PA**6, 35, Shellbark. **1969** *DARE* Tape **KY**50, The one's called a shellbark. I think it's sort of medium-sized nut. **1982** *Barrick Coll.* **csPA**, Shellbark—hickory nut.

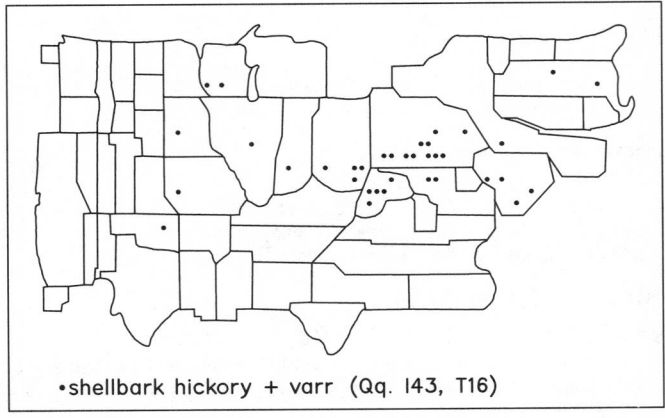

•shellbark hickory + varr (Qq. I43, T16)

shell bean n scattered, but esp NEng See Map Also called **shell-out, shelly bean** Cf **shuck bean**

A bean that is allowed to ripen and is removed from the pod before being cooked and eaten; a plant or variety of plant that produces such beans.

1818 (1920) Clark *Diary* 2324 **CT**, Boiled shell beans (first we had) made pyecrust. . **1842** in 1874 Hawthorne *Passages Amer. Note-Books* 2.88 **MA**, [We will have] shell-beans, green corn, and cucumbers from our garden. **1896** (c1973) Farmer *Orig. Cook Book* 255 **Boston MA**, *Shell Beans,* including horticultural and sieva, are sold in the pod or shelled, five quarts in pod making one quart shelled. . . Common lima and improved lima shell beans are in season in August and September. **c1938** in Lib. of Congress *Amer. Memory: WPA Life Hist.* (Internet) **VT**, They attacked the meat, potatoes, gravy; the vegetables, "succotash" (corn and shell beans canned together, then heated up in milk with a hunk of butter added), stewed tomatoes and little chunks of sweet pickle. **1942** Hale *Prodigal Women* 508 **MA**, A great pot full of shell beans and lamb. **1947** Paul *Linden* 60 **neOH**, On the other side of the house was a tomato patch . . shell beans climbing on poles that were never exactly straight or plumb, some squash and pumpkin vines. **1965–70** DARE (Qu. I20, . . *Kinds of beans*) Infs **NY1, VT2**, Shell beans; **CT4**, Pole shell beans—the horticultural bean; [there are] hundreds of varieties of shell beans here in northeast; **CT11**, Shell beans—put them in succotash; they come in pretty colors; **KY81**, Shell beans—shelled out of the pod; **MA42**, Pole beans = cranberry beans = shell beans; **MA55**, Shell beans—used to make succotash; **MA66**, Shell beans—speckled red and white or red and light brown; **NJ46**, Shell beans—more of a New England type of bean; **PA150**, Shell beans—a pole bean; (Qu. I14, *Kinds of beans that you eat in the pod before they're dry*) Inf **MA5**, Shell beans—turn bright striped red, used to make succotash; **NJ39**, Shell beans—older type of bean; **NC8**, When mature and shelled they're shell beans; **RI16**, Shell beans, yellow and green; (Qu. I15, *Some of the beans that you eat in the pod have yellow pods; you call these _____*) Inf **IN79** Shell beans = yellow beans; **MA37**, Shell beans—a kind of pole bean; **OH47**, Shell beans; (Qu. I16, *The large flat beans that are not eaten in the pod*) Infs **MO25, 36, MA16, VT16, WI29**, Shell bean(s); **MD17**, Shell beans—any beans removed from shell; (Qu. I17, *Beans . . that are dark red when they are dry*) Infs **MA13, 83, 98, VT13, WI29**, Shell beans; (Qu. I18, *The smaller beans that are white when they are dry*) Infs **NY28, 69**, Shell beans. **1986** Pederson *LAGS Concordance* 5 infs, **AL, AR, GA, MS**, Shell beans; 1 inf, **neTN**, Shell beans—generic; 1 inf, **cnGA**, Shell beans—include lima and butter beans; 1 inf, **csTN**, Shell bean—removed from hull; 1 inf, **seGA**, Shell beans—older snap beans; must be shelled; 1 inf, **csMS**, Shell beans—beans you have to shell; 1 inf, **ceLA**, Shell bean—with no string; 1 inf, **cnGA**, Shell beans—beans that are ready to be shelled; 1 inf, **csLA**, Shell beans—if you let them grow more; 1 inf, **ceTX**, Snap beans as opposed to shell beans. **1999** DARE File **nwMA**, Horticultural genetics being what they are, each stage has a strain bred particularly for it: we used . . something called French's Horticultural for shell beans. Their pods, which are green when they're growing, turn scarlet-striped when they're ripe, and the bean is a speckled cranberry-and-white when it's dead ripe. . . I think a lot of other beans could be classified as shell beans: pinto beans and such like, but they were not grown here. A shell bean, here, is a French's Horticultural bean, or one like it, . . grown to be picked when the seed is just short of hardening.

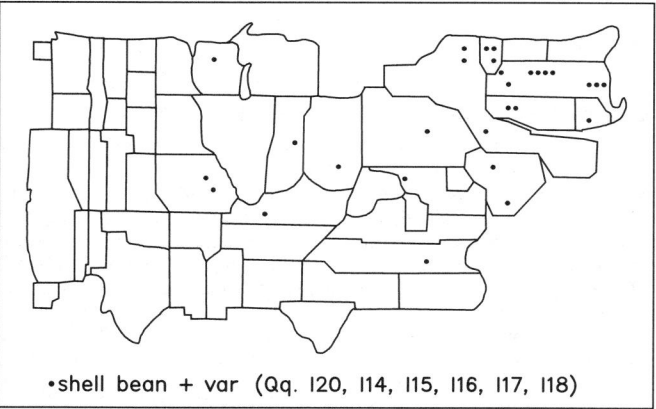

•shell bean + var (Qq. I20, I14, I15, I16, I17, I18)

shell-bird n
=**red-breasted merganser.**

1917 *Wilson Bulletin* 29.2.76 **MA**, *Mergus serrator.*—Shell-bird, Muskeget I[slan]d. **1955** Forbush–May *Birds* 93, Red-breasted Merganser. . . Other names: Shell-bird; Shelduck; Sheldrake [etc.].

shell corn See **shell** v 3c

shell-cracker n Also *shell-crackle* [See quot 1949] esp **FL**
Usu the **red-eared sunfish 1**, but also the **bluegill 1** or a **warmouth** (here: *Chaenobryttus gulosus*).

1890 *Century Dict.* 5565 **FL**, Shell-cracker. . . A kind of sunfish, *Eupomotus speciosus.* **1902** Jordan–Evermann *Amer. Fishes* 352, Shell Cracker—*Eupomotis holbrooki.* . . In Florida it is the sunfish which is most frequently taken on the hook. **1935** Caine *Game Fish* 33, Warmouth. . . *Synonyms* . . Shell-cracker [etc.]. **1949** Caine *N. Amer. Sport Fish* 46, Shellcracker—*Lepomis microlophus.* . . Name stems from the fact that it cracks snail shells to obtain part of its diet. **1965–70** DARE (Qu. P1, . . *Kinds of freshwater fish . . caught around here . . good to eat*) Infs **AL32, FL17, 35, GA41, MS73**, Shell-cracker(s); **GA7, 76**, Shell-cracker—same as brim; **FL17**, Shell-crackers or bluegills; **GA18**, Shell-crackle. **1966** *Lake Co. Citizen* (Tavares FL) 1 Apr 5/4, Jim Davis brought in a nice string of shellcrackers. . . Shellcrackers are beginning to come in to bed among the grasses and lily pads. **1968** DARE FW Addit **LA15**, [The Inf] identified the *chinquapin bream* or *chinquapin* as being the same fish as the one called *shell-cracker* in Florida. **1975** Evanoff *Catch More Fish* 70, You can locate shellcrackers . . by smelling them, according to southern anglers. They claim that they smell these beds when in the area and fish there. Most sunfish scoop out tiny depressions alongshore, and these depressions can be spotted by their lighter color. **1975** Newell *If Nothin' Don't Happen* 230 **nwFL**, That's a pretty place and it ain't far to where a feller can really catch a mess of big old shell-crackers—if he cared about fishin'. **1995** White *Sleeping* 107 **FL**, Under a scratched-up pane of glass . . are photographs of filthy, happy people . . holding the fish they have caught—warmouth perch, bluegills and shellcrackers. **2001** DARE File **FL, MS**, In Louisiana the red-ear is a chickapin; in Florida or Mississippi they call it a stump-bumper, a stump-knocker, or a shell-cracker.

shell down the corn See **shell** v 3a, b

shell duck See **shelduck**

shellfish n [Because the head and body are encased in a carapace of bony plates]
A boxfish (*Lactophrys* spp).

1896 U.S. Natl. Museum *Bulletin* 47.1722, *Lactophrys triqueter.* . . Trunk-fish; Rock Shellfish. . . West Indies, north to the Bermudas, Key West and Pensacola. *Ibid* 1723, *Lactophrys trigonus.* . . Shell-fish. . . West Indies; very common as far north as Bermuda and Key West, occasionally northward in the Gulf Stream (Holmes Hole, Mass. . . Woods Hole; Chesapeake Bay.) **1966–70** DARE (Qu. P2, . . *Kinds of saltwater fish caught around here . . good to eat*) Inf **FL24**, Shellfish—boxfish in books.

shellflower n

1 A **turtlehead** (here: *Chelone glabra*).
1837 Darlington *Flora Cestrica* 369 **sePA**, Glabrous Chelone. *Vulgò*—Shell-flower. Snake-head. **1876** Hobbs *Bot. Hdbk.* 105, Shell-flower, Balmony, Chelone glabra. **1901** Lounsberry *S. Wild Flowers* 461, *C[helone] glabra,* turtle-head, shell-flower, or balmony. **1971** Krochmal *Appalachia Med. Plants* 84, *Chelone glabra,* . . Common Names: White turtlehead . . shellflower [etc.].

2 See **shell ginger.**

3 A **false dragonhead 1** (here: *Physostegia virginiana*).
1959 Carleton *Index Herb. Plants* 93, *Pink shellflower:* Physostegia virginiana.

shell ginger n Also *shellflower* [See quot 2000] **HI**
A wild ginger (*Alpinia zerumbet*).
1929 Neal *Honolulu Gardens* 84, Shell ginger, shell flower. . . The highly ornamental shell ginger has long clusters of waxy-white, bell-like flowers touched with red, inside red and yellow. . . The roots resemble those of ginger. **1967** DARE (Qu. S11) Infs **HI6, 8**, Shell ginger [in a list of mountain plants]. **2000** DARE File **HI**, It is my impression the name "shell ginger" is in wide use in Hawaii. It applies to *Alpinia zerumbet* for the resemblance of the shape and luster of the waxy-white bracts and floral parts (in bud) to a polished sea shell.

shell ice See **shell** n¹ 3

shellie bean See **shelly bean**

shelloat, shellot See **shallot**

shell out v See **shell** v 1

shell-out n
=**shell bean.**
   1969 *DARE* (Qu. I15, *Some of the beans that you eat in the pod have yellow pods; you call these _____*) Inf **KY**40, Shell-outs—because they shell 'em out; **KY**62, Shell-outs.   **1982** *NADS Letters* **KY,** I was familiar with "shellouts" from childhood in the Blue Grass region and saw them so designated in a supermarket in Lexington just this past summer. In fact, I never heard them called cranberry beans.   **1999** *DARE* File **cnIN,** Now about shell beans—all we can think of is when green beans mature we sometimes shell them out and cook them. We always called them shell-outs.

shell out the corn See **shell** v 3a

shellpot See **skillpot**

shell road n **chiefly C and S Atl, LA, seTX** See Map
A road having a surface of marine shells.
   1801 in 1965 *AmSp* 40.200 **Long Is. NY,** Working on the shell road John P. Lott and myself Waymasters.   **1835** (1836) Power *Impressions* 2.108 **swAL,** We soon gained the shell road however, and found it as good as the streets of Mobile.   **1903** *DN* 2.329 **seMO,** *Shell-road. . .* Road made or covered with shells. Common in Florida and Louisiana.   **1909** *DN* 3.368 **eAL, wGA,** *Shell-road. . .* A road of shells, often found along the gulf-coast. A common expression for making fast time is 'to go like 2:40 on a shell-road.'   **1911** U.S. Bur. Census *Fisheries 1908* 309, *Cuneata clam. . .* This clam is found in large quantities in the Gulf of Mexico. . . The shell is used for road making. The famous shell roads of the South are constructed of these shells, taken from Lakes Pontchartrain and Salvador.   **1965–70** *DARE* (Qu. N27a, *Names . . for different kinds of unpaved roads*) 23 Infs, **chiefly C and S Atl, LA, seTX,** Shell road; [**MD**34, **WA**19, Oyster-shell road;] (Qu. N23, *Other kinds of paved roads*) Infs **MD**40, **SC**69, **TX**9, Shell; **GA**12, 15, **NJ**56, Shell road; [**NJ**20, 54, Oyster-shell].   **1990** Pederson *LAGS Regional Matrix* 84, [Regarding Qu. 31.6 concerning different types of roads, of the 49 infs who responded with *shell road,* 36 lie in the coastal region, especially the western Gulf Coast.]

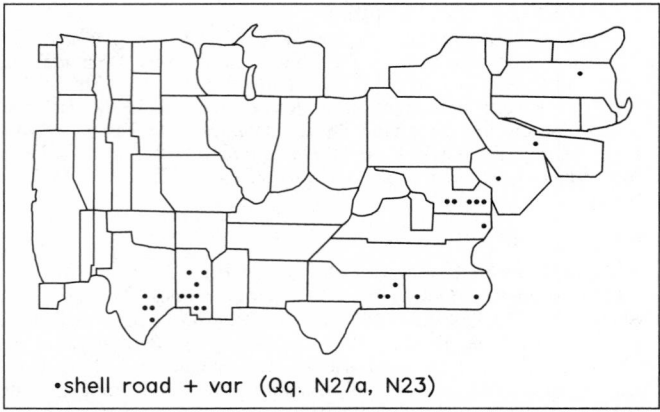

•shell road + var (Qq. N27a, N23)

shell the brush See **shell** v 2

shell the corn down See **shell** v 3c

shell the woods See **shell** v 2

shelly adj See **shell** n¹ **2, 3**

shelly n See **shelly bean**

shelly bean n Also *shelly*   Also sp *shellie bean*   **chiefly S Midl** See Map
Usu =**shell bean;** see quots.
   1939 *AmSp* 14.92 **eTN,** *Shelly beans.* Dried beans. 'We eat shelly beans of a winter.'   **1953** *PADS* 19.12 **sAppalachians,** *Leather britches. . .* Beans dried and cooked in the shell, also called *shelly beans* and, in Kentucky, *shucky beans.*   **1954** *PADS* 21.36 **SC,** *Shelly beans,*

shellies: . . Beans gathered late in the season, too mature and tough to be cooked in the pod as string beans. They are shelled out and cooked with other string beans that are not too tough.   **1958** *PADS* 29.15 **TN,** *Shelly beans:* A legume. "A kind of green bean that has the tendency to shell themselves during cooking." Rep. from Hamilton, Perry.   **1959** Roberts *Up Cutshin* 23 **seKY,** We boys would get them [=beans] right real dry, and take and put them in sacks, get us some big sticks, and go to work. I've beat 'em out a many a time that way, going atter 'em just like killing snakes, bust them hulls up, take them out on a sheet or something, and sort the beans out of the hulls. We called these shelly beans.   **1965–70** *DARE* (Qu. I14, *Kinds of beans that you eat in the pod before they're dry*) Inf **TN**11, Shelly beans—part in pod, part shelled out; (Qu. I15, *Some of the beans that you eat in the pod have yellow pods; you call these _____*) Inf **AL**52, Shelly beans; **IL**76, **NC**38, Shellies; **NC**52, Shelly beans—after they get too old, you have to shell them; (Qu. I16, *The large flat beans that are not eaten in the pod*) Inf **AL**27, Shellies; (Qu. I17, *Beans . . that are dark red when they are dry*) Inf **TN**13, Shellies; (Qu. I20, . . *Kinds of beans*) Inf **MI**88, Shelly bean; **VA**42, Shelly beans—beans eaten out of the hull.   **1969** *DARE* FW Addit **csKY,** *Shelly beans*—beans left to mature then shelled, cooked, and eaten.   **1973** *Hardin Co. Independent* (Elizabethtown IL) 26 Apr 5/4, [Canned goods:] Shelly Beans—5 for $1.00.   **1975** *Appalachian Jrl.* 2.155 **wNC,** Green beans were called *snap beans,* and *shellies* was the designation for very full beans, some of which had to be shelled.   **1986** Pederson *LAGS Concordance,* 24 infs, 19 **TN,** Shelly bean(s); 4 infs, **TN,** Shellies; 1 inf, **neTN,** Shellies—speckled, yellow beans.   **1993** Mason *Feather Crowns* 229 **KY,** On the table were two apple pies . . a white cake, a yellow cake, a coconut cake, green beans simmered with hog jaws, shelly beans, cold slaw, cornbread, green onions, and preserves. [**1999** *DARE* File—Internet **IN,** Aunt Maude's beans are excellent for canning (and of course fresh from the garden) and are always popular at pitch-in dinners. They tend to be a "shelly" type of bean when left on the plant. . Plant as you would any bush bean. . . Aunt Maude was born December 7, 1901 in Wolfe county Kentucky.]   **1999** *DARE* File **csIN,** I thought I would bring your inquiry to the experts at the local general store. Bev said shelly beans are green beans that have gotten too big so they are shelled and mixed with the regular green beans. She pulled a can of Stokley 'Shellie' Beans off the shelf and said it was green beans and pinto beans but they were out of Oconomowoc, WI so what do they know. . . My mother . . remembered a doctor from Kentucky (residing in Evansville) who used to love to come and pick the green beans that had dried on the vine. He called these shelly beans.

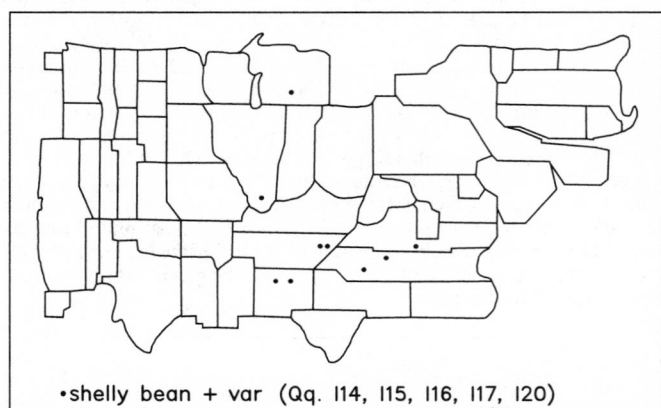

•shelly bean + var (Qq. I14, I15, I16, I17, I20)

shelter belt n **chiefly Plains States, Upper MW**
A strip of trees planted to prevent soil erosion or to protect from wind or snow.
   1869 U.S. Dept. Ag. *Rept. of Secy. for 1868* 197, For a shelter belt . . [maple] will be found suitable.   **1905** U.S. Forest Serv. *Bulletin* 61.21, *Shelterbelt. . .* Natural or artificial forest maintained as a protection from wind or snow.   **1945** *Boulder (Colo.) D. Camera* 30 Nov. 2/1 *(DA),* The Great Plains shelterbelt project has been pronounced an outstanding success.   **1966** *Wichita Eagle* (KS) 9 Apr sec B 8/4, Farm shelterbelts have proved their worth over a wide area of the Great Plains. Close plantings of trees in successive rows for a half mile or more in length, shelter belts protect the soil from blowing, control snow distribution, protect cattle and provide other valuable services.   **1966–68** *DARE* (Qu. T2a, . . *A piece of land covered with trees . . only a few acres*) Infs **MN**38, **SD**8, Shelter belt.   **1967** *DARE* FW Addit **CO**3, *Shelter belt*—row of trees

planted to protect the house.   **1973** Allen *LAUM* 1.333 **Upper MW** (as of c1950), *Clump* (of trees). . . *Shelter belt* developed during the dust bowl period of the 1930's, when drouth following excessive cultivation of arid prairie land led to such annual dust storms that federal funds were appropriated to enable farmers to plant trees as a preventive against erosion. . . [2 infs, **SD**].   **1986** Erdrich *Beet Queen* 179 **ND**, During three hard winters . . the snow packed so deep that starved deer drifted from the fields to my stock pens. . . In the shelterbelts, I came across more of the deer's frail hulks.   **1989** Frazier *Gt. Plains* 198, Farmers could plant shelterbelts around their fields and houses. . . The rows of wind-bent cottonwood, hackberry, elm, honey locust, and pine that you often see to the windward of abandoned or long-gone farmhouses are the mark [Franklin] Roosevelt left on the Great Plains.

shelter house n
A roofed structure built over a grave.
  1992 Covington *Night Ride Home* 234 **AL** (as of c1940), Constructing the burial canopy was the perfect task. . . Charles had asked Bolivia to describe the canopy. She'd called it a shelter house and said it looked like an old-fashioned latticework spring house, painted white or white-washed, either square or in an arc. "Some people make them with cinder and they got a tin roof, but that's sinful," she told him. . . "God meant graves to be simple." She told him the shelters were important, and that a Melungeon would paint his family's burial shelter before he'd paint his own house because the dead were more important than the living.

shelving n [Scots, nEngl dial; *OED2* shelving vbl. sb.[1] 1641→1871] esp NJ, NY old-fash
Also pl: A removable framework fixed to a cart or wagon in order to increase its carrying capacity; hence *shelving (wagon)* a wagon to which such a frame has been added.
  1847 *Scientific Amer.* 3.70, The following kind of wagon shelvins I have used for 28 years, and believe them to be better then [sic] any others I ever saw and they are not a few.   **1876** Knight *Amer. Mech. Dict.* 3.2149, *Shelving. . . (Husbandry.)* Additional top rails to a cart or wagon for enabling it to hold a larger load of bulky material, such as straw, sheaves, or hay.   **1889** *AN&Q* 4.71, In New Jersey a hay wagon or market wagon with shelves or removable frame of boards is called a *shelving.*   **1930** Shoemaker *1300 Words* 60 **cPA Mts** (as of c1900), *Shelvings*—Additional sides to a wagon.   **1967-68** *DARE* (Qu. L13, *The kind of wagon used for carrying hay: [. . special wagon, or frame put on ordinary wagon]*) Inf **NJ22**, Hay shelvin' [šɛlvɪn]; **NJ53**, Hay shelvin'; **NY52**, We put hay shelvings on an ordinary wagon; **NJ17**, Shelvin' wagon—the wagon with the shelvin' put on it [FW illustr]; (Qu. N41b, *Horse-drawn vehicles to carry heavy loads*) Inf **NJ18**, Shelvin'—hauling produce; (Qu. N41c, *Horse-drawn vehicles to carry light loads*) Inf **NY22**, Two-horse shelvin' wagon. [All Infs old]   **1991** *DARE* File **seNY**, Shelvins = the high racks (stakes with horizontal boards) put on the front and rear of a wagon to make it a haywagon; also collectively, the wagon with racks.

she-male n
A woman; a female.
  a1856 in 1944 Botkin *Treas. Amer. Folkl.* 8, Davy Crockett's hand would be sure to shake if his iron war pointed within a hundred mile of a shemale.   **c1863** in Lib. of Congress *Amer. Memory: America Singing* (Internet), The Rebs now get hot buttered beans,/ In *Fort Warren's* Solitude, Sir,/ The *Shemales* should have a sweet *Fort* / Made out of Sugar Candy.   **1875** *Overland Mth.* 15.563 **CA**, He also declared most emphatically that "that 'ere gal could jest knock the spots off uv any shemale in the mountings!"   **1913** Johnson *Highways St. Lawrence to VA* 218 **NJ**, Our cows were always milked by she-males. The generality of men did n't milk then, but they have to now.   **1917** Lewis *Job* 194 **NYC**, You know yourself, bein' a shemale, that there's an awful lot of cats among the ladies. *Ibid* 246, Course you high-strung virgin kind of shemales take some time . . to get over your choosey, finicky ways.   **1941** O'Donnell *Great Big Doorstep* 51 **sLA**, A bull-red [=a fish] gunna give you plenty fun to land. The bull is the she-male, and that's a funny thing. *Ibid* 125, How can that one inside be cruel to dogs like that? If they were she-males always dropping pups, I wouldn't say.   **1960** Wentworth–Flexner *Slang* 465, *Shemale.* . . A female, esp. a disliked, distrusted woman; a bitch.

she-maple n Cf she-balsam
An unidentified **maple.**
  1967 *DARE* (Qu. T14, . . *Kinds of maples*) Inf **PA35**, She-maple.

shepherd's needle n
A **beggar ticks 1** (here: *Bidens pilosa*); the seed of this plant.
  1933 Small *Manual SE Flora* 1451, *B[idens] pilosa.* . . Shepherd's-needle . . Coastal Plain, Fla. and sporadically in S Ga. and Ala.   **1934** *Torreya* 34.132 **FL**, One finds his clothing covered with spindle-shaped brown objects about one quarter of an inch long with two to four barbed prickles at the broader end. We call similar fruits in the north, Beggar ticks, but these are named Spanish or Shepherd's needles, *Bidens pilosa.*   **1979** Niering–Olmstead *Audubon Guide N. Amer. Wildflowers E. Region* 369, Shepherd's Needle. . . Southeastern North Carolina south to Florida; west to Texas.

shepherd spider n [*OED2* 1665 →]
=**daddy longlegs 1.**
  1858 Redfield *Zool. Sci.* 638, *Shepherd Spiders,* or *Harvest-men, Phalangidæ,* genus *Phalangium.* . . Their legs are long and slender, the tarsi consisting of more than fifty joints.   **1913** Comstock *Spider Book* 53, The name harvestmen was probably suggested by the fact that they are most often seen at harvest time. . . Other English names are harvest-spiders and shepherd-spiders.   **1926** Essig *Insects N. Amer.* 11, These long-legged creatures with small bodies are variously known as harvesters, harvestmen, harvest spiders, shepherd spiders, grand-daddy-long-legs, grandfather-gray beards, and so forth.

shepherd's pie n [*OED2* 1877 →]   chiefly NEast, Gt Lakes, esp PA   See Map   Cf hunter's stew
A dish whose main ingredients are meat and vegetables, usu baked in a shell of or with a topping of mashed potatoes.
  1932 (1946) Hibben *Amer. Regional Cookery* 163 **NJ**, *Shepherd's Pie* . . butter . . onion . . flour . . broth and lamb gravy mixed . . salt and pepper . . parsley . . mashed potatoes . . cold roast lamb. . . Saute the onion in the butter, add flour. . . Pour in broth mixed with . . gravy . . from the roast lamb. . . Turn in the meat. . . Line a buttered baking dish with mashed potatoes, pour in meat and gravy and cover with mashed potatoes. Bake.   **1950** *WELS (Dishes made with lamb or mutton)* 1 Inf, **cwWI**, Shepherd's pie.   **1957** Showalter *Mennonite Cookbook* 66 **PA, VA**, *Shepherd's Pie.* . . This is a good way to use leftovers from a holiday meal. Line a greased casserole with mashed potatoes. Fill with leftover vegetables and cubes of meat. Add bread crumbs and gravy and seasoning. Cover with mashed potatoes and bake.   **1965-70** *DARE* (Qu. H45, *Dishes made with meat, fish, or poultry that everybody around here would know, but that people in other places might not*) 14 Infs, 8 **PA**, Shepherd's pie; **CT11**, **PA102**, Shepherd's pie—casserole; **MI68**, Shepherd's pie—also called 'poor man's pie'; leftover meats, a kind of stew, put a pie crust or biscuit crust on top and bake it; **PA40**, Shepherd's pie—a lot of sausage, beef, and pork together; **PA159**, Shepherd's pie—mashed potato and hamburger; pie in oven; (Qu. H43, *Foods made from parts of the head and inner organs of an animal*) Inf **MA72**, Shepherd's pie; (Qu. H48, *Baked dishes made of potatoes cut up with meat or cheese*) Infs **IL99**, **MI100**, **NY48**, Shepherd's pie; **CT8**, Shepherd's pie—beef or lamb and potatoes; **GA70**, Shepherd's pie—potatoes and meat; (Qu. H49, *Dishes made by boiling potatoes with other foods*) Inf **PA196**, Shepherd's pie; (Qu. H50, *Dishes made with beans, peas, or corn that everybody around here knows, but people in other places might not*) Inf **GA75**, Shepherd's pie—peas and potatoes; **MD17**, Shepherd's pie—peas, corn, tomatoes, beans, baked in deep-dish pie. [25 of 28 Infs female]   **1967** *DARE* Tape **PA27**, Have you ever eaten . . shepherd's pie? . . It's made with meat and dumplings, and it's, uh, a deep-

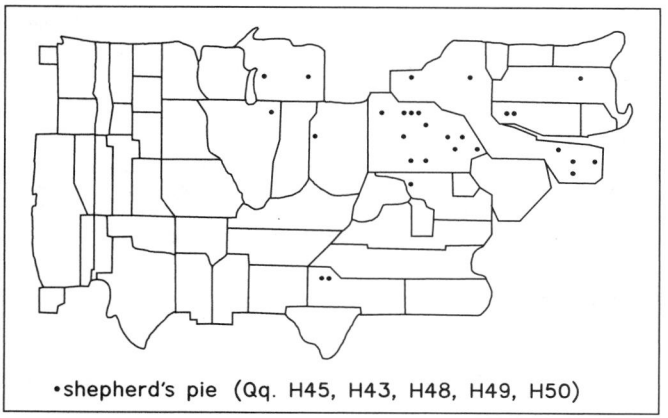

•shepherd's pie (Qq. H45, H43, H48, H49, H50)

dish pie . . mostly made in a casserole dish. . . The top is covered with mashed potatoes and browned. . . We never have anything inside the pie . . except meat and carrots, maybe peas. . . Has a gravy, white.

shepherd's purse n

Std: an introduced weed *(Capsella bursa-pastoris)*. Also called **fat hen 3, hen pepper, mother's heart, peppergrass 2, pepperweed 2, poor man's pepper 2, shepherd's sprout**

shepherd's sprout n Cf **mountain sprout**

=**shepherd's purse.**

1910 Graves *Flowering Plants* 201 **CT,** Shepherd's Purse or Sprouts. . . Valued as a pot-herb because of its earliness. **1951** *PADS* 15.12 **WV,** *Bursa bursa–pastoris* . . Shepherd's sprout, Keyser, W.Va.

she-pine n Also *she pitch pine* Cf **she-balsam**

A **slash pine** (here: *Pinus elliottii*).

1896 Mohr–Roth *Timber Pines* 74 **GA, FL,** The Cuban Pine. . . Common or local names. . . She Pitch Pine (Ga.). She Pine (Ga. and Fla.) **1911** *Century Dict. Suppl., Pine.* . . *She-pine.* . . Same as *slash-pine.*

sheriff n Usu |ˈʃɛrɪf|; also esp **Sth, S Midl** |ˈʃɝɪf|; for addit varr see quots Pronc-spp *shurf(f)*

Std sense, var forms.

1899 (1967) Chesnutt *Wife of Youth* 67 **NC** [Black], "Is de shurff in," inquired the negro. "Yas, Brer Sam, he's eatin' his dinner," was the answer. **1942** Hall *Smoky Mt. Speech* 21 **wNC, eTN,** Before *r,* [ɛ] is often retracted to [ɜ], as in . . sheriff. **1942** Faulkner *Go Down* 67 **MS** [Black], Ifn we took and fotch that kettle from whar you and Mister Roth told them shurfs it was. **1953** Brewer *Word Brazos* 16 **eTX** [Black], Dey hab passenger coaches an' de Marlin shurf allus sen' 'long a dep'ty shurf to keep down fights on de train. **1967–70** *DARE* (Qu. V9, . . *Nicknames . . for a policeman*) Inf **TN5,** [ˈʃɝɪf]; (Qu. V10a, . . *Sheriff*) Inf **FL48,** [ʃef]; **MD22,** [ˈʃɝɪf]; **NY70,** [ʃeɜ˞f]. **1972** *Atlanta Letters* ceGA, Shurf—the shurf put me in jail.

sheriff v

1 To serve as a sheriff; hence vbl n *sheriffing.* [*OED2 sheriffing* vbl. sb. 1682 →]

1896 *Harper's New Mth. Mag.* 92 **MO,** "You may think this here sheriffing is mighty funny," he confided one day to a friend, "but you ought to try it once, and see the dishonest whelps you have to deal with." **1917** *DN* 4.417 **wNC,** Sheriff. . . To serve as sheriff. **1986** Pederson *LAGS Concordance,* 1 inf, **cwAR,** The way I done most of my sheriffing.

2 To repossess (a property) as part of foreclosure proceedings; with *out:* to evict (a person) as part of foreclosure proceedings.

1959 Schiddel *Devil Bucks Co.* 131 **PA,** Even when a man's sheriffed-out in Pennsylvania, the State gives him a year or two to reclaim his property before selling it up. **1963** Teller *Area Code 215* 20 **cePA,** By this time Coryell had failed; in fact his Ferry Inn had been sheriffed.

sheriffing See **sheriff** v 1

sheriff out See **sheriff** v 2

sheriff pink n Also *sheriff weed*

=**oxeye daisy 1.**

1894 *Jrl. Amer. Folkl.* 7.91 **WV,** *Chrysanthemum leucanthemum.* . . sheriff pink. **1900** Lyons *Plant Names* 99, Pismire, Poverty-weed, Sheriff-weed. **1940** Clute *Amer. Plant Names* 79, Ox-eye Daisy. . . Dutch morgan, sheriff-pink [obsolete]. **1959** Carleton *Index Herb. Plants* 106, *Sheriff-pink:* Chrysanthemum leucanthemum.

she-root n [See quot]

=**bloodroot 1.**

1968 *Foxfire* 2.2.50 **sAppalachians,** Bloodroot. . . This is the "redcoonroot" of the mountains, and juice on a lump of sugar was a cough drop. Known as "[te]tterwort" or "sweet slumber" or "she-roots", the dried rootstocks were ground and used in an infusion. . . As "she-roots", bloodroot was a remedy for female complaints.

sherrie-varrie See **shivaree** n A

she's a honey but the bees don't know it See **honey** n 6

sheself pron Pronc-sp *shese'f* **SC** *among Gullah speakers* Cf **heself**

Herself.

1853 Simms *Sword & Distaff* 131 **SC,** He hab catch Missis Ebleigh, shese'f, and him son, Mass Art'ur, and de obe'shar. **1927** Adams *Congaree* 26 **cSC** [Black], The first thing she do been to try and make sheself satisfied. **c1937** in 1972 *Amer. Slave* 2.223 **SC,** De Missus larnt he how to read en write she self.

she-she talk n **sSC, GA coasts** *Gullah*

Woman's talk.

1922 Gonzales *Black Border* 326 **sSC, GA coasts** [Gullah glossary], *She-she talk—*woman's talk, gabble. **1926** Smith *Gullah* 34.35 **sSC, GA coasts,** *She-she talk,* used of feminine loquacity. This phrase looks, by the way, like a correct use of the feminine gender, but Mr. Gonzales sees in it an onomatopoetic origin, deriving it from the whispering froufrou of silken petticoats. **1930** Stoney-Shelby *Black Genesis* 28 **seSC,** Spite o' all de she-she talk she gi' him, what wid all de work she done for help him, an' de good bittle she cook him, Adam git jus' as fat an' sassy as a barrow-shoat.

she-stuff n Also *she-stock* **West**

Females, esp female cattle; rarely, a single female animal.

1920 Hunter *Trail Drivers TX* 378 (as of 1874), These cattle were in good shape and as fine beeves as you ever saw, no she stuff. **1923** Evarts *Tumbleweeds* 87 **SW,** The herd would have been worked on the spot . . the she-stuff . . being allowed to scatter. **1935** Sandoz *Jules* 84 **wNE** (as of 1880–1930), Big herds of longhorns still trailed in . . but their place was gradually being taken by trainloads of smooth young she stuff, with Hereford bulls to improve the strain. **1935** *AmSp* 10.272 [Stockyard language], *She stuff.* Cows and heifers. **1937** *AmSp* 12.104 **eNE** [Farm terms], On ranches, the heifers and cows are the *she stock* or *she stuff.* **1942** *AmSp* 17.75 **NE,** The word *cows* may include cattle of both sexes. *She-stuff* means only females and is not always limited to cattle. I was standing on a street corner in Arthur, Nebraska . . when a couple of girls passed. A waddie standing nearby remarked, 'Some pretty fancy she-stuff, hey?' **1949** *PADS* 11.26 **CO,** *She stuff.* . . Female cattle. **1958** McCulloch *Woods Words* 161 **Pacific NW,** *She stuff—*Women. **1958** Blasingame *Dakota Cowboy* 300 **SD,** The Matador had decided to spay this young she-stock. **1961** *Wranglin' Notes* (Eaton's Ranch, Wyoming) Nov. *(OED2),* Our hay crop was cut, baled and stacked early this year. It is fed to the 200 'she stuff' and calves that winter on the lower ranch.

shet v See **shut** v A

shet adj See **shut** adj b

sheth n [Var of *sheath;* cf *EDD sheath* sb. 1]

1899 (1912) Green *VA Folk-Speech* 252, *Knittin-sheth.* . . Sheath. A quill sewed in a piece of calico or cloth and pinned to the front of the dress to rest the end of one needle in while knitting. **1903** *DN* 2.329 **seMO,** Sheth. . . Sheath. **1912** Green *VA Folk-Speech* 381, *Sheth.* . . For *sheath.*

shetty See **shut** v A

shevaree See **shivaree** n

sheve See **shove** 1

shew intj |ʃu, ʃju| Also *pshew, shoo;* for addit varr see quots **chiefly S Midl** See Map

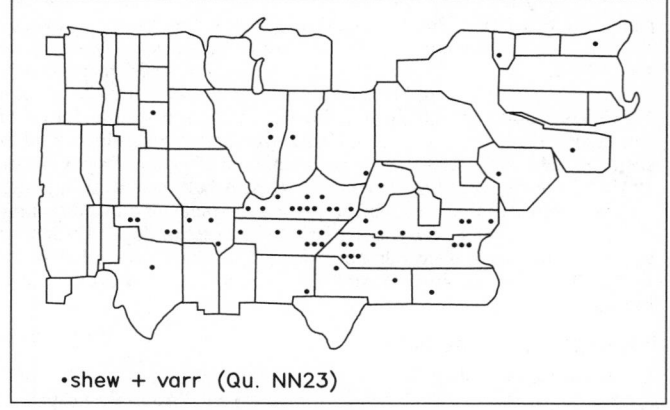

•shew + varr (Qu. NN23)

Used as an expression of disdain or disgust.

1883 (1971) Harris *Nights with Remus* 117 **GA** [Black], 'Shoo!' sezee, 'Brer B'ar foot too big en he tail too long fer ter slide down dat rock,' sezee. **1943** Chase *Jack Tales* 167 **wNC** (as of 1880s), A woman came out a-holdin' her nose, says, "Shee-ee-ew! Take them stinkin' horse hides away from here!" **1946** McCullers *Member* 17 **AL**, 'Shoo!' John Henry argued. 'She was, too.' **1965–70** *DARE* (Qu. NN23, *Exclamations when people smell a very bad odor*) 20 Infs, **chiefly S Midl**, Shew; 15 Infs, **chiefly S Midl**, [šju(:), šru, ši:ju, šiu]; **NC55, 76, 79, 82, TN44, 58, TX76, VT7,** [šu(:)]; **TN23,** Shew, that stinks; **OK42,** Shew, that would stink a dog off a gut wagon; shew, that's got odor to it; **OK18,** Pshew; **KY11, OH40, VA15, 75,** [pšju(:)]; **AR52,** [pšuw]; **KY49,** Pee-shew; **IL135, NE10,** [pi šu]; **IL17, WV12,** Pa-shew [pəšu]; **NJ70,** Fshew [fšu]. [34 of 57 Infs young or mid-aged]

shickle n Also *sheckel* [Pronc varr of *shuttle;* cf Engl dial *shittle,* Intro "Language Changes" IV.4]

1888 Johnston *Mr. Absalom Billingslea* 168 **GA,** Miss Mattox had left the shickle in the loom and was promised to return. **1917** *DN* 4.417 **wNC,** Shickle. . . Shuttle (of a loom). **c1937** in 1972 *Amer. Slave* 3.3.218 **SC coast** [Black], My mother was a weaver. Old timey loom. Cotton and wool. Sheckel (Shuttle?).

shidepoke See **shitepoke**

shield See **sheal**

shifferobe See **chifforobe**

shift v

1 To change (one's own or another's clothes); in phr *shift oneself:* change one's clothes. [Cf *OED2 shift* v. 9.a →1848, *shift* v. 9.c →1839]

1852 in 1904 *DN* 2.401, The judge shifted himself from top to toe, and put on a complete suit of the miller's clothes. **1858** *Harper's New Mth. Mag.* 17.14, Some families lost everything their houses contained; many have now neither food nor clothes to shift. **1870** *Ibid* 40.551, Let us see whether . . we have done any thing more than to shift our colonial swaddling-clothes for the beggarly rags of a scarecrow. **1899** (1912) Green *VA Folk-Speech* 381, Shift. . . To change the clothes. **1904** *DN* 2.401, Shift . . to shift one's self = to change one's clothes. **1914** *DN* 4.79 **ME, nNH,** Shift. . . To swap, exchange; as, *to shift clothes,* to change them. **1934** McDavid Coll. **GA,** To shift your clothes = change. **c1980** *DARE* File **cVT** (as of c1880), Shift his shirt and shave him.

2 To change (one's mind).

1979 *AmSp* 54.99 **sME** (as of 1899–1910), Shift. . . "He shifted his mind."

3 See quot.

1914 *DN* 4.154 **NH,** Shift. . . To trade, as horse or cattle.

shift n

1 A division of farmland. [*EDD shift* n. 11 "Obs. . . The division of land arranged with a view to the rotation of crops; any division of land."]

1838 (1930) Sewall *Diary* 197 **IL,** Shucked out 5 rows of the 14 acre shift. **1899** (1912) Green *VA Folk-Speech* 381, Shift. . . A division of land; each *shift* is planted in a different crop, or lies fallow according to the system.

2 See quots. [*OED2* →1886; "Obs. exc. dial."]

1930 *AmSp* 5.393 [Language of N Atl fishermen], Shift. . . A change of clothes. **1953** Randolph–Wilson *Down in Holler* 88 **Ozarks,** A *shift of clothes* means a change of clothes.

shifting clothes n [Scots dial]

A change of clothes.

1938 (1964) Korson *Minstrels Mine Patch* 318 **nePA,** Shifting clothes: Street clothes into which the miner changes on emerging from the mine. **1953** Randolph–Wilson *Down in Holler* 88 **Ozarks,** "He ain't got shiftin' clothes" means that he has only the garments he is wearing. [**1997** *DARE* File—Internet **cePA** [CoalSpeak], *Shiftin' clothes:* Work clothes, overalls.]

shift oneself See **shift** v 1

‡shift-robe n [Var, perh by folk-etym, of **chifforobe**]

1969 *DARE* FW Addit **KY,** *Shift-robe*—a movable closet for hanging clothes.

shifty adj

1 Resourceful, enterprising, astute. [*OED2* 1570 →] **chiefly Sth, S Midl**

1783 *MD Jrl. & Baltimore Advt.* (MD) 18 Feb 3/3, Ran away . . a Negro Man named Pompey . . very artful and shifty. **1876** Emerson *Letters & Social Aims* 124 **MA,** What a plastic little creature he [=man] is! so shifty, so adaptive. **1898** Lloyd *Country Life* 104 **AL,** I can point you out two of the thriftiest and shiftiest men in the Rocky Creek settlement—men that are clever and honest and good citizens in a general way. **1912** *DN* 3.589 **wIN,** Shifty. . . Alert; busy. "He'll get along all right; he's mighty shifty." **1915** *DN* 4.190 **swVA,** Shifty. . . Industrious and successful. **1958** *PADS* 29.15 **TN,** Shifty: Alert. "They use *shifty* in a complimentary sense. It doesn't mean *sly* but more as *provident*—the opposite of *shiftless.*" Rep[orted] from Warren. **c1960** Wilson Coll. **csKY,** Shifty. . . Alert, able to take care of oneself. **1967** *DARE* (Qu. U35, . . *Thrifty but not in a complimentary way:* "She's not a bad housekeeper, but very _____.") Inf **AL32, TN15,** Shifty; (Qu. HH27a, *A very able and energetic person who gets things done*) Inf **TX26,** Shifty. **1981** High Coll. **ceKY** (as of c1930), Shifty . . handy, resourceful, said of a person who is a hard worker and can "make something out of nothing."

2 Undependable, untrustworthy, dishonest, evasive. **chiefly Nth, N Midl** See Map

1884 *American* 7.213 **Philadelphia PA,** His political methods have been "shifty" and not straightforward. **1899** (1912) Green *VA Folk-Speech* 381, Shifty. . . Given to or characterized by shifts, tricks, or artifices; fertile in dodges or evasions; tricky. **1965–70** *DARE* (Qu. KK37, *Words to describe a very sly person:* "He's _____.") 16 Infs, **chiefly Nth, N Midl,** Shifty; **OH21,** Shifty one; **CA66,** Shifty person; (Qu. V2a, . . *A deceiving person, or somebody that you can't trust*) Infs **AL41, 42, CT34, IL22, 97, NY232, OH61, PA49, WI57,** Shifty; **NY123,** Shifty character; (Qu. V7, *A person who sets out to cheat others while pretending to be honest*) Inf **CT34,** Shifty; (Qu. II7, *Somebody who doesn't seem to 'fit in' or to get along very well . .* "He's kind of a _____.") Inf **OK1,** Shifty guy; (Qu. II33, *To get an advantage over somebody by tricky means:* "I don't trust him, he's always trying to _____.") Inf **CA66,** He's shifty; (Qu. JJ45, *When someone avoids giving a definite answer:* "We tried to pin him down, but he just kept _____.") Inf **CA66,** Being shifty. [25 of 28 total Infs coll or hs educ; 17 young or mid-aged]

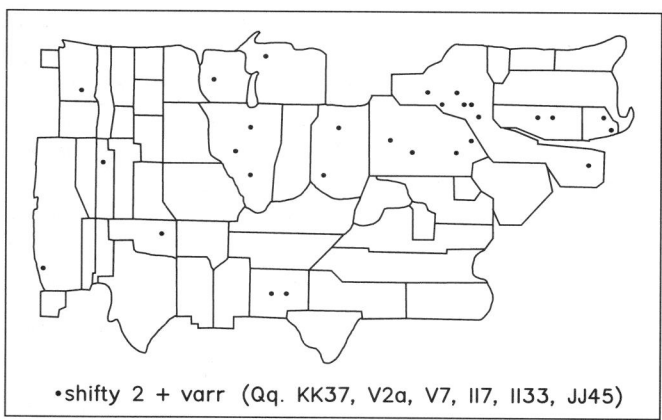

•shifty 2 + varr (Qq. KK37, V2a, V7, II7, II33, JJ45)

shikepoke See **shitepoke**

shilldrake See **sheldrake 1**

shilling n **chiefly NEast, N Cent** See Map on p. 904 *old-fash* Cf **levy** n[1], **picayune**

Any of var small sums of money, freq a "bit" or 12½ cents; rarely, a dime.

1789 in 1834 U.S. Congress *Debates & Proc.* 1.227 **MA,** The price of molasses is about twenty-ninetieths of a dollar, the duty is about five, and the expense of the distillation may be six more, in all thirty-one ninetieths, or two shillings and seven pence. **1828** Webster *Amer. Dict., Shilling.* . . Our ancestors introduced the name with the coin into this country, but by depreciation the value of the shilling sunk in New England and Virginia one fourth, or to a fraction less than 17 cents, in New York to 12½ cents, in Pennsylvania, New Jersey and Maryland to about 11 cents. This denomination of money still subsists in the United States, although there is no coin of that value current, except the Spanish coin of 12½ cents, which is a shilling in the money of the state of New York. **1831** Peck *Guide for Emigrants* 151 **Missip Valley**, One shilling per bushel, New England currency, is a common price [for wheat]. **1846** Farnham *Life in Prairie Land* 299, "I reckon you may get three," said the prudent husband, depositing a shilling in his palm. **1848** Bartlett *Americanisms* 135, The old system of reckoning by shillings and pence is continued by retail dealers generally. *Ibid* 136, In consequence of the abovenamed diversity in the colonial currencies, in New England the Spanish real of ⅛ of a dollar or 12½ cents is called *ninepence;* in New York, one *shilling.* **1891** *Century Dict.* 5572, *Shilling. . .* Reckoning by the shilling is still not uncommon in some parts of the United States, especially in rural New England. **1894** *DN* 1.342 **wCT**, *Shillin:* a "long" or "Yankee shillin" = 16⅔ cents; a "York shillin" = 12½ cents. **1909** *DN* 3.403 **nwAR**, *Shilling. . .* Sixteen and two-thirds cents. **1910** *DN* 3.448 **wNY**, *Shilling. . .* Twelve and a half cents. Especially in such expressions as "six shilling," "twelve shilling," "twenty shilling," instead of 75 cents, $1.50, $2.50. "That cost me six shilling." "He gets twelve shilling a day." "He asked twenty shilling for it." **1912** *DN* 3.569 **cNY**, *Shilling. . .* Twelve and one-half cents. Used generally by old-fashioned people in "two shillings," "five shillings," "eight shillings," etc. In Mississippi, *shilling* is used for twenty-four cents English money. **1951** *Chr. Sci. Monitor* (Boston MA) 20 Oct 8/2 **wCT**, Her shilling, in which she [=the writer's grandmother] often reckoned her purchases though the coin itself was obsolete, had the New York value of twelve and one-half cents instead of the sixteen and two-thirds cents of the rest of New England. "This goods cost me two shillings a yard," she would say. **1952** Brown *NC Folkl.* 1.589, *Shilling. . .* A dime. **1965–70** *DARE* (Qu. U23, . . *A 25-cent piece*) Infs **NJ**3, **PA**100, 234, **WI**49, Shilling; **MA**5, Shilling—cloth would be a shilling a yard; **MI**50, Shilling—I've heard my father say "shilling"; **IL**48, **MT**4, **NJ**56, **NY**68, **SC**3, 19, Two shilling; **MI**93, Two shilling—older term; **MI**97, Two shilling—very seldom anymore; **NY**163, Two shilling [FW: Inf's parents used]; **NY**232, Two shilling—old-fashioned; **MI**108, Two shillings—grandfather said this; (Qu. U24, . . *A 50-cent piece*) Infs **IL**48, **NJ**56, **NY**233, **SC**3, Four shilling; **MI**93, Four shilling—older term; **MI**97, Four shilling—older term; **NY**232, Four shilling—old-fashioned. [17 of 18 total Infs old] **1976** *DARE* File **nwPA**, *Shilling*—Two sisters nearly eighty say that in their youth, i.e. early 1900's, prices were still given in shillings sometimes. . . and a shilling was reckoned as 12½ cents. **1985** *Ibid* **eNC**, I was reared on a farm in eastern North Carolina and had a grandfather born in 1844. . . Grandmother . . called a dime (10¢) a *shilling.*

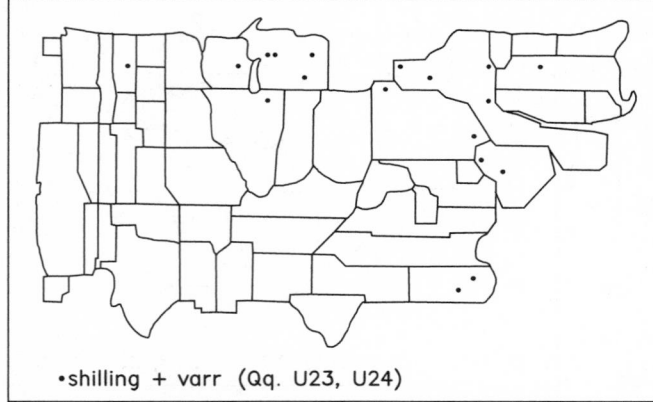

•shilling + varr (Qq. U23, U24)

shim See **shimmy** v

shimmel See **schimmel**

shimmering owl n Cf **shivering owl**

A **screech owl 1** (here: *Otus asio*).

1966 *DARE* (Qu. Q1, . . *Kind of owl that makes a shrill, trembling cry*) Inf **MS**16, Shimmering owl.

shimming See **shimmy** v

shimmy n[1] Also *shimmy-shirt,* ~*-tail* **widespread, but slightly more freq Sth, S Midl** *somewhat old-fash*

A chemise.

1858 in 1956 Eliason *Tarheel Talk* 293 **c,csNC**, These wee man [women] neds cloth for shimneys. **1903** *DN* 2.300 **Cape Cod MA** (as of a1857), *Shimmy. . .* Chemise. **1905** *DN* 3.18 **cCT**, *Shimmy. . .* A

woman's under garment. **1907** *DN* 3.207 **nwAR**, *Shimmy.* **1909** *DN* 3.368 **eAL, wGA**, *Shimmy.* . . Chemise. Also sometimes *shimmy-tail.* **1910** *DN* 3.448 **wNY**, *Shimmy.* **1912** *DN* 3.589 **wIN**, *Shimmy.* **1926** *DN* 5.389 **ME**, *Shimmy, or shimmy-shirt. . .* Common. **1938** Farrell *No Star* 13 **IL**, Now she had the corset off and he got a side shot of her. Her breasts stood up. She only had on what Aunt Peg called a shimmy. **1942** (1971) Campbell *Cloud-Walking* 112 **seKY**, Hetty could make Sabriny some under drawers and a shimmy and a petticoat. **c1950** *Halpert Coll.* 56 **wKY, nwTN**, I'm in my shimmy-tail (He's in his . .) = state of undress. **1965–70** *DARE* (Qu. W15, *A shirt-length undergarment worn by women*) 160 Infs, **widespread, but slightly more freq Sth, S Midl**, Shimmy; **CA**50, **NC**11, Shimmy-shirt [Of all Infs responding to the question, 68% were old; of those giving these responses, 79% were old.]; (Qu. W16a, *The full-length garment that a woman wears under her dress*) 9 Infs, **scattered, but esp Sth, S Midl**, Shimmy [8 of 9 Infs old]; (Qu. W14, . . *Underwear . . women's*) Infs **MS**1, **TX**42, Shimmy; (Qu. W24a, . . *Expressions . . to warn a woman slyly that her slip is showing*) Inf **AL**36, Your shimmy's showing. **1993** White *Mama* 116 **sGA**, You're no better than you ought to be, you young hussy. . . wearing that shimmy-tail dress. You had your chance to do right, but you sure went wrong with your bad ways.

shimmy v Also *shim* [Prob by folk-etym < **shinny** v, infl by *shimmy* to shake, wriggle] *esp freq among younger speakers* Cf **shinny** v

=**shinny** v; hence vbl nouns *shimming, shimmying.*

1950 *WELS Suppl.* (*To climb the trunk of a tree by holding on with your legs while you pull yourself up with your hands*) 1 Inf, **cwWI**, Shimmy up. **1965–70** *DARE* (Qu. EE36) 102 Infs, **widespread,** Shimmy up; 11 Infs, **scattered,** Shimmy; **MI**34, **NY**68, Shim up; **MI**49, **MO**26, **NY**81, Shimmying; **TN**66, Shimmying up [Of all Infs responding to the question, 64% were old; of those giving these responses, 42% were old.]; (Qu. OO10b, *Talking about climbing trees: "Some trees were dangerous—we shouldn't have _____ [those]."*) Inf **MA**128, Shimmed up. **1967** *DARE* FW Addit **CO**, *Shimmy*—"shimmy up a tree." **1983** *MJLF* 9.1.55 **ceKY** (as of 1956), *Shimmy . .* to shinny, climb by using the shins to grip. **1986** Pederson *LAGS Concordance,* 1 inf, **cAL**, Shimmy.

shimmy n[2] Cf **shinny** n[1] 1, *DS* EE10

=**cat** n 3a.

1965 *DARE* Tape **NY**245, We used to play what they called shimmy. It was a piece of a tapered-end . . broom handle about so long that when you . . tipped it with a . . stick, it would pop up and you would strike it like you would a baseball and play the 1, 2, 3, 4 bases the same as you do in baseball.

shimmying See **shimmy** v

shimmy lizard [**shimmy** n[1]]

=**shirt rabbit.**

1933 *AmSp* 8.3.31 [Prison terms], *Shimmy lizard.* Louse. [A shimmy, you may remember, was a woman's chemise. Hobos appropriated the word in behalf of their shirts.]

shimmy shirt (or tail) See **shimmy** n[1]

shin v, hence vbl n *shinning* Also with *up*

=**shinny** v.

1840 (1841) Dana *2 Yrs.* 379, We had to . . shin up and down single ropes caked with ice. **1892** *KS Univ. Qrly.* 1.98 **KS**, *Shin:* to climb, as, to shin up a tree. **1899** (1912) Green *VA Folk-Speech* 381, *Shin. . .* To use the shins in climbing; climb by hugging with arms and legs. **1905** *DN* 3.18 **cCT**, *Shin up. . .* To climb a tree by aid of hands and legs only. **1907** *DN* 3.217 **nwAR**, *Shin up. . .* To climb a tree by aid of hands and legs only. **1912** *DN* 3.589 **wIN**, Why don't you shin up that tree and get them? **1965–70** *DARE* (Qu. EE36, *To climb the trunk of a tree by holding on with your legs while you pull yourself up with your hands*) 27 Infs, **scattered,** Shin (up); **CA**24, **DE**2, 3, **FL**28, **NC**16, 37, 88, **SC**69, Shinning (up); (Qu. OO10a, *Talking about climbing trees: "When we were children we often _____ [trees]."*) Infs **MA**82, **LA**17, Shinned (up). **1995** Brophy *Coll.* 67 **swMO** (as of c1960), *Shin, shinny.* [T]o climb, scale.

shin cutter n

=**shin hoe.**

1956 Sorden–Ebert *Logger's Words* 31 **Gt Lakes**, *Shin-cutter,* An adze tool used in hewing logs to form the floors of stables and shanties. It had a handle long enough to enable a worker to use it while he was standing. The lumber-jacks called it a shin-cutter because if it slipped, a man could cut his leg. Same as adze. **1969** Sorden *Lumberjack Lingo* 108 **NEng, Gt Lakes,** *Shin cutter.*

shindy n[1]

1 A party or gathering, esp a noisy one with dancing; a spree, shindig. [*OED2* 1821 →]

1844 (1856) Neal *Peter Ploddy* 18, "Well, bang my kerkus for a drum," panted Dogberry, "if this 'ere isn't that 'ere singing chap agin. I knows him by his mulberry nose. He's on a shindy somewhere or other every night, and gets knock'd down and tuck'd up three times a week, rig'ler." **1911** *DN* 3.540 **eKY,** *Shindy. . .* A dance; a caper. **1914** *DN* 4.113 **cKS,** *Shindy . . = shindig.* **1927** *AmSp* 2.364 **cwWV,** *Shindy . .* a frolic. "The boys had a regular shindy Saturday afternoon." **1930** Shoemaker *1300 Words* 60 **cPA Mts** (as of c1900), *Shindy*—A noisy gathering. **1941** *LANE* Map 410 (*A dance*) 1 inf, **swCT,** Shindy; 1 inf, **cwCT,** Shindy, when a dancer exhibits his steps; 1 inf, **neMA,** Shindy, informal.

2 A commotion; a ruckus; a **fuss** n **B2.**

1828 (1829) Hall *Travels* 3.325 **New Orleans LA,** I never saw a more complete row, or as a fellow near me called it, 'a more regular shindy.' **1866** (1867) Locke *Swingin Round* 244, This occasioned another shindy. **1899** (1912) Green *VA Folk-Speech* 381, *Shindy. . .* A row, disturbance, or rumpus; as to kick up a *shindy.* **1903** Dawson *Birds OH* 1.243, It was just like those Titmice, anyway—inquisitive, irascible, hysterical, always kicking up a shindy among the birds. **1909** *DN* 3.368 **eAL, wGA,** *Shindy. . .* A fuss, a fracas. **1913** Beach *Iron Trail* 221 **AK,** One of his eyes was black and nearly closed, his lips were cut and swollen, but he grinned cheerfully. . . He tried to smile his appreciation, but the effort resulted in a leer so repulsive that the girl looked dismayed. "You ought to have seen the shindy." **1927** *AmSp* 3.139 **eME,** A rough perhaps not respectable party was a "shindig," a fight a "shindy." **1932** Stribling *Store* 434 **AL,** The idyah, a book on character kicking up all this shindy! **1968** *DARE* Tape CA100, They were all scared of him [=a game warden]. He . . tended to business. He thought they were trying to beat him. Said, "You'd better throw 'em [=undersized abalone] back." I said, "Take a hoe and hit 'em, can't he?" . . I thought he'd only give me a shindy, so I threw the little ones back in.

shindy n[2] See **shinny** n[1] **1**

shine v **scattered, but chiefly MI, WI, MN** See Map Cf **fire-hunt, jacklight** v

To cause (the eyes of a game animal) to glow by use of a bright light at night; to attract or locate and temporarily immobilize (fish or game) with a bright light at night; to hunt in such a way; hence vbl nouns *(night-)shining* hunting in this way; n *shiner* an animal shot in this way.

1833 Flint *Biog. Memoir D. Boone* 26, He had *shined the eyes* of a deer. *Ibid* 26, The animal is betrayed to its doom by the gleaming of its fixed and innocent eye. This cruel mode of securing a fatal shot, is called in hunter's phrase, *shining the eyes.* **1845** Thompson *Pineville* 170 **GA,** Sam was eager to show me how to shine the eyes of a buck. **1885** *S. Fla. Sentinel* (Orlando) 10 June 2/2 *(DA),* They took the smallest boat and pulled to the nearest key to shine deer. **1900** *Outing* 36.33 **NC,** Adroitly holding the light behind him and low down, he "shines" the 'possum's eyes. **1903** *DN* 2.329 **seMO,** *Shine (the eyes). . .* To throw light in the eyes of animals when hunting at night. **1909** *DN* 3.368 **eAL, wGA,** *Shine. . .* To throw or cast light in (an animal's eyes): a method of finding the quarry when hunting 'possums, coons, etc., at night. **1916** *DN* 4.346 **LA,** *Shining. . .* Hunting at night with a light that dazzles fish, alligators or bull-frogs. **1927** *AmSp* 2.364 **cwWV,** We shined the bullfrogs last night, and got a good mess. **1965–70** *DARE* (Qu. P35b, *Illegal methods of shooting deer;* not asked in early QRs) 50 Infs, **chiefly MI, WI, MN,** Shining (deer); MI76, Shining the deer; MI71, Shining them; OH20, Shining with a spotlight; MI115, WI26, Night-shining; MI13, MO13, Shine them; MI99, Shine 'em; GA84, Shine their eyes at night; (Qu. P13, *. . Ways of fishing . . besides the ordinary hook and line*) Inf GA72, Shining; (Qu. P35a, *Names or nicknames for any deer shot illegally*) Inf MN35, Shiner. **1977** Sawyer Co. *Rec.* (Hayward WI) 5 Jan 1/3, Dennis Miller and Melvin White were each fined $159 for possession of an untagged deer and shining in an area inhabited by wild animals. **1990** *WI State Jrl.* (Madison) 18 Nov sec C 1/1, A 42-year-old fugitive . . was nabbed by game wardens for shining deer. . . Hergan and another man were found shining deer with a car's headlights. **1997** *Ibid* 23 Nov sec C 4/1, Two teen-agers have been charged . . with hunting deer out of season and shining. With An-

derson driving . . , they chased deer down a road, shined the animals with light to transfix them, then struck them. . . Caldwell also was charged with . . shining deer.

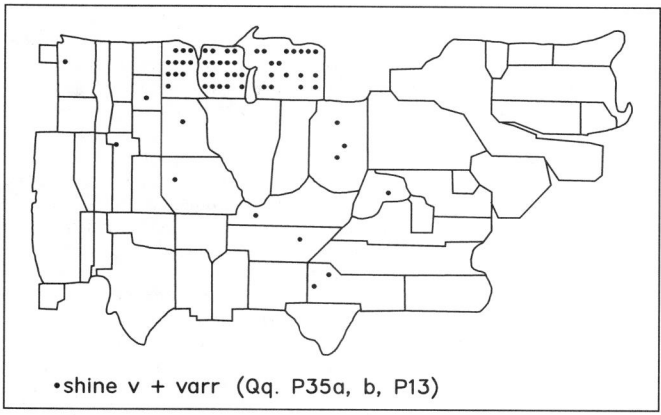

•shine v + varr (Qq. P35a, b, P13)

shine n

1 A caper; a prank—freq in phrr *cut a shine, cut shines,* and varr: to behave in a comic, boisterous, or unruly manner; to play tricks on (someone); to make a conspicuous display of oneself. **now chiefly Sth, S Midl**

1830 Ames *Mariner's Sketches* 34 **NEng,** This practice [=of harassing sailors] is so notorious and so well understood, that it is quite a question of course, to ask the crew of a *full* ship, "well, has your skipper begun to cut any *shines* yet?" **1836** (1838) Haliburton *Clockmaker* (1st ser) 143, I met a man this mornin . . all shines and didos. **1848** in 1935 *AmSp* 10.42 **Nantucket MA,** *Shines. . . Cut shines.* Cut capers. **1858** Hammett *Piney Woods Tavern* 290, You never ketch Sam tellin' the old Judge any of them dreadful shines he used to cut, when he was growin' up. **1884** *Anglia* 7.264 **Sth, S Midl** [Black], *To kick up shines* = to be proud, to put on airs. **1892** (1969) Christensen *Afro-Amer. Folk Lore* 45 **seSC,** Don't you cut up none o' you shine now. **1899** (1912) Green *VA Folk-Speech* 381, *Shine. . .* A trick, a prank; to cut up *shines.* **1905** *DN* 3.18 **cCT,** *Shine. . .* A great display, as, to cut or make a shine. **1906** Casey *Parson's Boys* 191 **sIL** (as of c1860), Ye'd better remember likewise that if I hear of any more of yer shines, the way I'll warm yer back'll be some! **1915** *DN* 4.182 **swVA,** *Cut a shine . . =* cut a dash. **1931** *AmSp* 7.121 **eID,** *To cut a shine* is to perform some antic thought clever. **1946** in 1958 Brewer *Dog Ghosts* 103 **TX** [Black], Dis boy Simon was young an' worl'y an' cut quite a shine in Dallas. **1953** *PADS* 19.13 **sAppalachians,** *Shine, cut a. . .* To behave in an unseemly manner; to display anger. "When I git mad I sure cut a shine." **1955** Ritchie *Singing Family* 202 **seKY,** I raced through the woods like a deer, swinging on grapevines and tree limbs, and laughing and making speeches on top of high rocks, and cutting such a shine that I was ashamed of myself. **1966** *DARE* Tape OK40, So I looked across and I seen she was cutting all kind of shines; she was really putting on dancing. **1968** *DARE* (Qu. KK11, *To make great objections or a big fuss about something:* "When we asked him to do that, he _____.") Inf VA29, He cut a shine. **1986** Pederson *LAGS Concordance* **neTN,** 1 inf, Cut all kinds of shines at [a] shivaree; 1 inf, He cut the awfullest shines on me that you ever seen.

2 Illegally made whiskey; also transf; hence nouns *shiner* a moonshiner, *shine house* a speakeasy. [Abbr for *moonshine*] **scattered, but chiefly S Atl** See Map on p. 906 Cf **moon** n[1] **1, shinny** n[2]

1923 (1951) Toomer *Cane* 37 **GA** [Black], Soda bottles, five fingers full of shine, are passed to those who want them. **1929** *AmSp* 4.385 **KS** [Wet words], Some of the common names for whiskey—*moonshine, moon, mooney, shine, blockade, brush whiskey, swamproot, squirrel,* and *mountain dew*—seem to refer to its alleged origin, suggesting that it is manufactured by moonlight in the wilderness. *Ibid* 440 **GA,** Some names for intoxicants of various grades and potencies are: moonshine, moon, or more commonly, 'shine. **1930** *DN* 6.89 **cWV,** *Shine,* moonshine whiskey, or other intoxicating liquor. **1930** *AmSp* 5.393 [Language of N Atl fishermen], *Shine. . .* A mixture of alky splits and water which is used as an intoxicating drink. **1931** *AmSp* 7.86 [Prohibition terms], Terms for those who deal in liquor. . . *Shiner.* **1938** Rawlings *Yearling* 12 **nFL,** "Goin' to Grahamsville allus do make me hongry." "You git a snort o' 'shine there, is the reason." **1963** Edwards *Gravel* 118 **eTN** (as of

1920s), Zeke had hung around with the 'shiners at their stills drinking and telling yarns until it was dark. **1965** Will *Okeechobee Boats* 33 **FL**, Sometimes they would git guavas from the Seminoles in exchange for *wyomee* or shine. **1965–70** *DARE* (Qu. DD21c, *Nicknames for whiskey, especially illegally made whiskey*) 27 Infs, 19 **S Atl**, Shine; (Qu. DD21a, *General words . . for any kind of liquor*) Infs **FL**1, 6, 10, **GA**19, **SC**68, Shine; (Qu. DD21b, *General words . . for bad liquor*) Infs **FL**30, 48, **GA**3, **WV**2, Shine; **GA**59, Georgia shine; (Qu. DD28b, . . *Fermented drinks . . made at home*) Infs **FL**6, 30, **GA**17, **MA**35, Shine; (Qu. DD30, *Joking names for a place where liquor is [or was] sold and consumed illegally*) Infs **FL**1, 48, **GA**30, **SC**68, Shine house; (Qu. DD31, *Joking names for homemade hard liquor;* total Infs questioned, 75) Infs **FL**6, 10, 13, 22, 30, **GA**1, **NM**11, Shine. [29 of 36 total Infs male] **1968** *DARE* Tape **GA**30, Why, I'd take a little boat and come out and get groceries and things, take 'em back in to 'em. . . Little shine, take 'em shine in. Course we'd pick up shine most anywhere we come out. **1986** Pederson *LAGS Concordance*, 1 inf, **seFL**, Shiner = moonshiner. **1989** Flynt *Poor But Proud* 167 **ceAL**, Using such a rig a shiner could make two gallons of excellent whiskey per bushel of corn. **1990** Pederson *LAGS Regional Matrix* 134, [Of the 15 infs who gave the response *shine* to the question "Terms for cheap whiskey and for home-brewed beer or whiskey," 13 were from **FL** and **GA**.] **1991** Greene *Praying for Sheetrock* 83 **seGA** [Black], I give him a pint or a half-pint. Ain't nothing to that. 'Shine houses be all over the county.

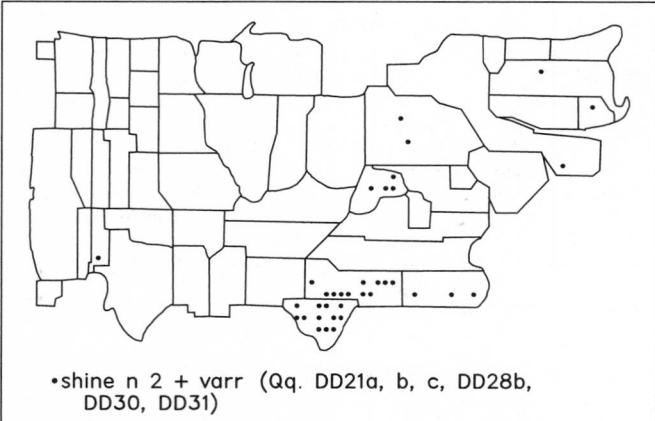

•shine n 2 + varr (Qq. DD21a, b, c, DD28b, DD30, DD31)

3 A state of intoxication—in phrr *have* (or *get*) *a shine on* to be intoxicated; similarly adj (phr) *shined (up)* intoxicated. [From the florid coloration characteristic of excessive alcohol consumption] **esp MI, WI**
1942 Berrey–Van den Bark *Amer. Slang* 106.7, *Drunk. . .* shined. **1950** *WELS* (*A person who is partly drunk:* "He's _____.") 1 Inf, **cWI**, Getting a shine on; 1 Inf, **swWI**, Shined up. **1966–69** *DARE* (Qu. DD14) Inf **MI**49, Has a shine on; **MI**10, **WI**77, Shined up; (Qu. DD13, *When a drinker is just beginning to show the effects of the liquor . . he's* _____) Inf **MN**12, Shined up. **1984** *MJLF* 10.156 **cnWI**, *Shined up.* Somewhat intoxicated.

4 also *shiner:* A Black person. **scattered, but esp Atlantic, Sth, S Midl** See Map *usu derog*
1893 in 1901 *Independent* 53.2760, Early in May, 1893, . . I saw two men coming toward me whom I took to be tramps. One of them was white, the other black. . . And it was not long before a white "hobo" and a youthful "shine" were added to my . . [photograph] gallery. **1907** in 1953 Botkin–Harlow *Treas. Railroad Folkl.* 239, A "shine" is always a Negro, so called, possibly, from the high lights on his countenance. Texas Shine or Toledo Shine convey both race and nativity. **1915** Hall *Claib Jones* 12 **KY**, Hall's girl's name was Shine Polly and shine she was. **1919** *DN* 5.42 [Hobo cant], *Shine. . .* A negro. **1926** Van Vechten *Nigger Heaven* 286 [Black], *Shine:* Negro. **1932** Farrell *Young Lonigan* 114 **Chicago IL** (as of 1916), There were more trees on Indiana [Avenue] too, and no shines, and only a few kikes. **1965–70** *DARE* (Qu. HH28, *Names and nicknames . . for people of foreign background: Negro*) 44 Infs, **scattered, but esp Atlantic, Sth, S Midl**, Shine; **MO**5, **PA**167, Shiner; (Qu. HH29b, . . *People of mixed blood—part Negro*) Inf **FL**48, Shine. [34 of 46 total Infs male] **1973** Allen *LAUM* 1.347 **Upper MW** (as of c1950), Equally demeaning are *coon, jig, jigaboo, shine* [3 infs], *skunk,* and *smoke.* **1986** Pederson *LAGS Concordance (Negro)*

1 inf, **neGA**, Shine—derogatory; 1 inf, **eTN**, Shine—very black Negro; 1 inf, **swMS**, Shine—very dark-skinned Negro; 1 inf, **cTX**, Heard a young person say shine.

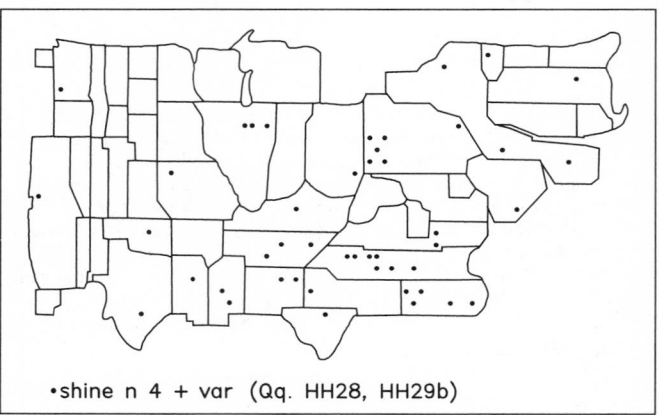

•shine n 4 + var (Qq. HH28, HH29b)

shine bone n [Perh folk-etym var of *chine bone*]
1 A cut of pork used to flavor boiled vegetables; see quots.
1981 Pederson *LAGS Basic Materials,* 1 inf, **ceGA**, Shine bone—a hog bone; 1 inf, **csGA**, A shine bone, not sure what it is, but it's a pork bone boiled with greens. **2000** *NADS Letters* **MS**, A large piece of pork cooked with greens, green beans, peas, etc. I remember joking with my grandmother about the shine bone being a hunk of (very fat) pork, and not having any bone at all. She was from east central Mississippi (born in 1914) but was raised in the Delta. *Ibid* **KY**, Shine Bone: (=Shin bone) transverse sections of pork front legs (cut off cured pork shoulders), used, as are ham hocks, as flavoring boiled with green or pinto beans.

2 also *shine ball:* **=funny bone 1.**
1966–70 *DARE* (Qu. X33, *The place in the elbow that gives you a strange feeling if you hit it against something*) Inf **MS**45, Shine ball; **TX**86, Shine bone.

shined (up) See **shine** n 3

shine house See **shine** n 2

shiner n

1 also *shiner fish,* ~ *minnow, shiny:* A small, usu silvery fish of the family Cyprinidae, esp one of the genus *Notropis*. **scattered, but esp NEast, Gt Lakes, Gulf States** See Map Cf **minnow B1** For other names of these fishes see **dace, ghost shiner, gold chub, golden shiner, hornyhead c, d, lake shiner 1, Milwaukee ~, minnow B1, mud dace 2, pugnosed shiner 2, red dace, ~ fallfish, redfin 1, redhorse shiner, red minnow, ~ shiner, redside dace, ~ shiner, river shiner, sand ~, satinfin ~, silverfin, silverfish 3, silver shiner, silversides 2, silvery minnow 2, smelt, ~ shiner, spawneater, taillight shiner, war-paint ~, weed ~**
1792 MA *Hist. Soc. Coll.* 1st ser 1.113 **cMA**, The pond. . . is supplied with pickerel, large perch, eels, shiners. **1792** Belknap *Hist. NH* 3.178, Shiner, *Perca nobilis?* **1820** Rafinesque *Ohio R. Fishes* 46, There are in the United States more than fifty species of small fresh water fishes. [sic] (and in the Ohio waters more than sixteen species) commonly called Minnies, Minnews, Bait-fish, Chubs, and Shiners. **1842** DeKay *Zool. NY* 3.211, This beautiful species [=*Leuciscus chrysopterus*] is caught in the harbor of New-York, and is popularly called *Bay Shiner,* or simply *Shiner.* **1882** U.S. Natl. Museum *Bulletin* 16.215, C[eratichthys] dissimilis . . *Spotted Shiner.* . . Ohio Valley and tributaries of the Great Lakes. **1906** NJ State Museum *Annual Rept. for 1905* 142, *Notropis analostanus* . . Silver Fin. Shiner. *Ibid* 143, *Notropis cornutus* . . Red Fin. Shiner. Minny. **1909** *DN* 3.403 **nwAR**, *Shiny. . .* A shiner; a common silvery fish used for bait. "I've got some shinies; le's go fishin'." **1939** *LANE* Map 234 (*Minnow*) 148 infs, 1 inf, **NEng**, Shiner; 1 inf, **CT**, Shiners, the young of the wind fish; 1 inf, **CT**, Shiner = minnow; 1 inf, **cnCT**, Shiner—not used locally. "If a fellow from Hartford or New Haven asked for shiners, I should know what he meant"; 1 inf, **CT**, Shiner = mummichog; 1 inf, **CT**, Shiners, in fresh water; mummichogs, in salt water; 1 inf, **VT**, Minnows, general term; shiners, specific term; 1 inf, **VT**, Shiners, a species of dace; 1 inf, **VT**, Shiners and chubs are differ-

ent kinds of minnow; 1 inf, **ME**, Shiner, a freshwater minnow. **1950** WELS **WI** (*Small fish used as bait*) 10 Infs, Shiner; (*Fish not commonly eaten*) 2 Infs, Shiner; (*Fish that are good to eat*) 1 Inf, Shiner. **1963** Sigler–Miller *Fishes* **UT** 76, Common Names: Redside shiner . . silverside minnow, red-sided bream, shiner. **1965–70** *DARE* (Qu. P7, *Small fish used as bait for bigger fish*) 168 Infs, **scattered, but esp NEast, Gt Lakes, Gulf States,** Shiner(s); **LA**15, 22, Shiners—bigger than minnows; **MD**36, **WI**32, Shiner minnow; **AL**22, Mississippi shiners; **CA**95, Shiners—a small carp; **CT**9, Shiners—sunfish; **FL**24, Shiner or percher—a little bigger than minnows; **FL**48, Shiners—silverfish and roaches are other names; **LA**34, Shiner—he's like a little goldfish; **MN**42, Crick shiner; **NY**233, Prick shiners—for size; **MI**99, Shiner minnows; **MA**45, Shiners—larger than a minnow; **NV**8, Shiners—larger minnows; **OH**67, Shiners and chubs are minnows; **OK**11, River minner doesn't glisten; shiner does; **RI**4, Proper name is minnows, but they call 'em shiners; **TX**54, Shiners, minnows—same; (Qu. P3, *Freshwater fish that are not good to eat*) 16 Infs, 13 **NEast**, Shiner(s); **IA**22, Three-toothed herring—gets to be 1 foot—or shiner; **WY**1, Shiner minnow; (Qu. P1, . . *Kinds of freshwater fish . . caught around here . . good to eat*) Infs **GA**19, **ND**1, Shiner(s); **GA**34, Shiner—he's a perch. **1971** Bright *Word Geog. CA & NV* 187, *Minnows . . shiners* 7% [of 300 infs]. **1973** Allen *LAUM* 1.331 **Upper MW** (as of c1950), *Shiners* is used as a second word by some infs., who thus refer to minnows having silvery light-reflecting scales. It seems to have a Northern speech orientation. **1986** Pederson *LAGS Concordance* **Gulf Region** (*Minnows*) 155 infs, Shiner(s); 1 inf, Shiner = minnow; 1 inf, Shiner—not a minnow; 1 inf, Shiner—small perch/big minnow; 1 inf, Shiner fish; 1 inf, Shiner minnows.

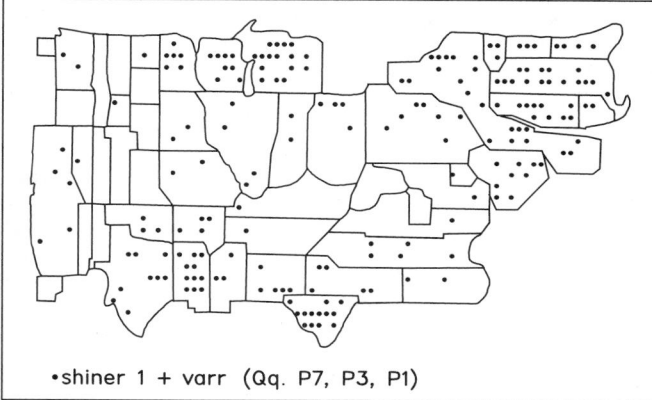

•shiner 1 + varr (Qq. P7, P3, P1)

2 Any of var other silvery fishes, as:

a A **harvest fish** (here: *Peprilus triacanthus*). **esp NY**

1815 *Lit. & Philos. Soc. NY Trans.* 1.365, *Cryptous broad shiner*. . . A curious and beautiful fish, eight inches long, and five deep. **1915** *Copeia* 23.41 **Long Is. NY**, *Poronotus triacanthus* . . "Butterfish"; "Shiner." **1917** *Ibid* 41.21 **Long Is. NY**, *Rhombus triacanthus*. Butterfish. . . It is an abundant species and better known as "Shiner." **1939** *Natl. Geogr. Soc. Fishes* 68, Other local names [for *Peprilus triacanthus*] are harvestfish . . shiner, and skipjack.

b A **mooneye 1** (here: *Hiodon tergisus*).

1842 DeKay *Zool. NY* 4.267, The lake moon-eye. . . This species is common in Lake Erie. At Buffalo and Barcelona, it is called *Moon-eye, Shiner,* and *Lake Herring.* **1971** *WI State Jrl.* (Madison) 29 Aug sec 4 5/3 **swWI**, The next strike was mine and I'll admit to being a little disappointed when it turned out to be a lowly mooneye, also, I think, known as a shiner or a gizzard shad.

c A **menhaden 1** (here: *Brevoortia tyrannus*).

1878 *Amer. Naturalist* 12.375 **FL**, The menhaden, *Brevoortia tyrannus* . . has at least thirty distinct popular names. . . [I]n the Indian river, Florida, the fish is occasionally called the "shiner" and the "herring." **1939** *LANE* Map 234 (*Minnow*) 1 inf, **ME**, Shiner, of the herring family. **1951** Taylor *Surv. Marine Fisheries* **NC** 93, Other names for the menhaden are . . shiner, herring [etc.].

d =**pinfish 1a.**

1884 Goode *Fisheries U.S.* 1.393 **nwFL**, The "Sailor's Choice" . . bears several other names, being known . . at Cedar Keys as the "Porgy" and "Shiner." **1903** *NY State Museum & Sci. Serv. Bulletin* 60.562, This [=*Lagodon rhomboides*] is called the salt water bream. . . It is also called pinfish, squirrel fish, porgee, yellowtail and shiner. **1935** Caine

Game Fish 55, Salt-water Bream or Sailor's Choice. . . *Synonyms* . . Shiner[,] Shiny Scup [etc.].

e also *shiner perch*: A **surfperch** (here: usu *Cymatogaster aggregata*, but also *Micrometrus minimus*).

1884 Goode *Fisheries U.S.* 1.278, *Sparada*. . . This fish is usually known as the "Shiner." It is found from Vancouver's Island to the Mexican line. *Ibid, Abeona minima*. . . This little fish is known as the "Shiner." . . It ranges from Tomales Bay to San Diego. **1917** *Copeia* 47.73, I observed, with much satisfaction, the breeding habits of *Cymatogaster aggregatus*. . . about twenty feet offshore . . two "Shiners" were swimming with their backs just out of the water. **1953** Roedel *Common Fishes CA* 112, Shiner Perch—*Cymatogaster aggregata*. . . Port Wrangel, Alaska, to Pt. Banda, northern Baja California. **1991** *Amer. Fisheries Soc. Common Names Fishes* 56, *Cymatogaster aggregata* . . shiner perch. *Ibid* 168, Seaperch, shiner—see shiner perch.

f =**little roncador.**

1946 LaMonte *N. Amer. Game Fishes* 82, Kingfish. . . Names: White croaker, Chenfish, Tomcod, Shiner [etc.].

g =**queenfish 1.**

1953 Roedel *Common Fishes CA* 94, Queenfish—*Seriphus politus*. . . Unauthorized Names: Herring, tomcod, shiner, sea trout.

3 A **goldfinch 1** (here: *Carduelis tristis*).

1917 (1923) *Birds Amer.* 3.13, Goldfinch. . . Other Names. . . Catnip Bird; Lettuce-bird; Shiner [etc.]. **1946** Hausman *Eastern Birds* 584, Eastern goldfinch. . . Other Names—Wild Canary, Yellowbird, Thistlebird, Catnip Bird, Shiner.

4 See **shine** v.

5 See **shine** n 2.

6 See **shine** n 4.

7 A silver dollar. [*DAE shiner* n. 1 "A silver or gold coin"; →a1861]

1921 *DN* 5.110 **CA**, *Shiner*. . . A dollar. **1942** Berrey–Van den Bark *Amer. Slang* 559.16, *Silver dollar*. . . shiner. **1968** *DARE* (Qu. U20, . . *Dollars . . "It cost a hundred _____."*) Inf **NY**109, Shiners; (Qu. U27, . . *A silver dollar*) Inf **CT**1, Shiner.

8 A clear marble. Cf **clearie, glassie, purie**

1968 *DARE* (Qu. EE6d, *Special marbles*) Inf **WI**29, Shiners. **c1970** Wiersma *Marbles Terms* **MI**, Shiner—like a pearlie or a purie, it is a clear marble of any size; it is always clear, never white. *Ibid* **MI**, Shiner—a glassy. *Ibid* **MI**, Shiner—a clear glass marble, like clearie.

shiner fish (or minnow) See **shiner** n 1

shiner perch See **shiner** n 2e

‡**shin froe** n Cf **shin hoe**

1966 *DARE* (Qu. L37, *A hand tool used for cutting weeds and grass*) Inf **NC**30, Shin froe.

shingle n

In var phrr referring to noisy activity, esp snoring: See quots.

1956 Moody *Home Ranch* 28 **CO** (as of 1911), You sure ripped off a heap of shingles last night! Hope you don't snore that-a-way 'ceptin' when you're plumb beat out. **1966–69** *DARE* (Qu. X45, . . *Joking expressions . . about snoring*) Inf **NC**61, Knocking the shingles; **SC**40, Rattling the shingles; **KS**12, See shingles fly; (Qu. FF18, *Joking words . . about a noisy or boisterous celebration or party: "They certainly _____ last night."*) Inf **NC**23, Tore off the shingles.

‡**shingle-butted** adj

See quot.

1942 Rawlings *Cross Creek* 22 **nFL**, She was shingle-butted, but what there was of butt stuck out sharply. . . I have never been able to identify any possible appeal she might have for the colored men, unless it be that little square boxlike rear.

shingle-nail bird n [Echoic]

A **wood thrush;** see quot.

1969 *DARE* (Qu. Q14, . . *Names . . for . . thrush*) Inf **MA**68, Wood thrush—shingle-nail bird—because that's what their song sounds like.

shingle oak n

Std: an **oak** (here: *Quercus imbricaria*) native chiefly to the Mississippi and Ohio Valleys. Also called **jack oak a, laurel ~ 1, peach ~ 3, pin ~ 1d, water ~**

‡shingle rave n
1968 *DARE* FW Addit **neNY,** Shingle rave—tool for splitting shingles, a froe.

shingle weaver n [Prob from the resemblance of one sitting on a shaving horse dressing shingles with a drawknife to one sitting at a loom and weaving] *joc* Cf **weave**
One who dresses wooden shingles; a shingle maker, worker in a shingle mill; also n *shingle weaving* the practice of making or dressing shingles.
1859 (1968) Bartlett *Americanisms* 401, *Shingle-Weaver.* A workman who dresses shingles. **1860** Street *Woods & Waters* 161 **NY,** At last we reached the foot of the Rapids, with the shingle-weaver's camp just above. A single light like a star told where the woodman was weaving his shingles by his pine-knot torch. **1909** *DN* 3.415 **nME,** *Shingle weaver. . .* One who shaves shingles. **1918** *DN* 5.29 **NW,** *Shingle weaver. . .* 1. A worker in a shingle mill. 2. One who shaves shingles. **1953** Van Wagenen *Golden Age* 141 **NY,** One craft . . had a very important place in our architectural economy. I refer to shingle shaving, or as it was sometimes dubbed, a bit facetiously, "shingle weaving." **1958** McCulloch *Woods Words* 162 **Pacific NW,** *Shingle weaver*—Actually a mill term, meaning a man who works in a shingle mill. **1966** *DARE* Tape **MI**14, The shingle weavers, you could tell 'em. They were quite a distinct class. They nearly all had fingers gone. . . They were . . quite a rough type of fellow; they moved around a lot from one mill to another. **1969** Sorden *Lumberjack Lingo* 108 **NEng, Gt Lakes,** *Shingle weaver*—A worker in a shingle mill. **1976** *DARE* File **IL** (as of 1928), *Shingle weaver*—One who practised the skilled trade of packing shingles at a shingle mill.

shin hoe n [See quot 1917] Cf **shin cutter, ~ froe**
An adz.
1896 Riley *Child-World* 74 **IN,** From one / Knee down, a leg was bandaged.—"Jason done / That-air with one o' these-'ere tools *we* call / A *'shin-hoe'*—but a *foot-adz* mostly all / *Hardware*-store-keepers calls 'em." **1917** *DN* 4.400 **neOH,** *Shin-hoe. . .* Adz; from the frequent experience of cutting the shins with it.

shinhopple n
Prob =**hobblebush;** see quot.
1968 *DARE* (Qu. S26e, *Other wildflowers not yet mentioned;* not asked in early QRs) Inf **NY**69, Shinhopple—has a roundish leaf and grows up about two feet high. White flowers.

shining See **shine** v

shining grass n [See quot 1892 at **1** below]
1 A **meadow rue** (here: either *Thalictrum dioicum* or *T. pubescens*).
1892 *Jrl. Amer. Folkl.* 5.91 **VT,** *Thalictrum dioicum,* shining grass. Weathersfield, Vt. [Footnote to *shining grass:*] See, also, *Impatiens.* The name is given because of the silvery appearance of the leaves when immersed in water.
2 A **jewelweed 1** (here: *Impatiens capensis*).
1892 *Jrl. Amer. Folkl.* 5.93 **VT,** *Impatiens fulva.* . . shining grass. Weathersfield, Vt.

shinleaf n Also *shinleaf lily* [See quot 1931]
A **wintergreen** (here: usu *Pyrola elliptica* or *P. rotundifolia*).
1822 Eaton *Botany* 416, *Pyrola . . rotundifolia* (shin-leaf). *Ibid,* [*Pyrola*] *secunda* (one-sided shin-leaf). **1837** Darlington *Flora Cestrica* 265 **sePA,** *P[yrola] elliptica . .* Vulgò—Shin leaf. **1899** MacMillan *MN Plant Life* 351, The shinleaf . . has papery rather than leathery leaves. **1931** Harned *Wild Flowers Alleghanies* 358, The name Shin-leaf originated from its supposed virtue as a panacea for bruises, bee-stings, etc., and the bruised leaves were applied in the form of a poultice for all such conditions. **1944** Nute *Lake Superior* 322 **nwMI,** The forest floor is dotted with flowers of many kinds, pyrola or shinleaf [etc]. **1966–68** *DARE* Wildfl QR Pl.151A Inf **MN**14, Shinleaf or bog wintergreen; **MI**31, Shinleaf lily; Pl.151B Infs **NY**91, **NH**4, Shinleaf; **MN**14, Bog wintergreen or shinleaf. **1967–68** *DARE* (Qu. S26c, *Wildflowers that grow in woods*) Inf **PA**99, Shinleaf; (Qu. S26e, *Other wildflowers not yet mentioned;* not asked in early QRs) Inf **MA**5, Shinleaf.

shinnery n Also *shinry* [Pronc-spp for *chênière;* cf **chenier**] **chiefly TX**

A dense growth of dwarf **oak** or other scrubby trees; an area covered with such growth.
1901 *Amer. Mth. Rev.* 24.310, It [="creeps"] is due mainly to an insufficiency of nourishment in the grass, particularly in pastures where "shinnery," or dwarf oak trees, abound. **1907** Cook *Border & Buffalo* 179 **wTX,** West of the pecan and oak shinnery ("cross-timber") belt . . were thousands of beautiful cottonwood groves. **1913** (1979) Barnes *Western Grazing* 268, Scrub Oak. . . Known also as "shin oak." This is the scrub oak of the western ranges, especially in the Southwest, where it forms as on the Texas staked plains great areas called "shinneries." **1916** Benedict–Lomax *Book of TX* 91, Much of the timber is stunted, and when it occurs in thick patches is called chaparral or shinnery. **1929** Dobie *Vaquero* 260 **TX,** As we rode into the shinnery a big buck deer jumped up and Ike wanted to rope it, as they are said to be easy to catch in low brush. **1937** *Natl. Geogr. Mag.* 71.709 **wOK,** The Davison Ranch itself, however, is largely covered with tiny oaks which the natives call "shinnery." Here in the dust-covered shinnery we were to study the lesser prairie chickens. **1949** *PADS* 11.10 **wTX,** *Shinnery, shinry* ['ʃɪnə,ɹɪ, 'ʃɪnrɪ]. . . Derogatory name for those areas whose principal tree is the shin oak. **1954** Tolbert *Bigamy Jones* 159 **wTX** (as of 1870s), "You better borrow a pair of chaps, too, Mister Sprain," said Grandma Renfro. "The shinnery will chew up those dress pants you're wearing." **1956** Ker *Vocab. W. TX* 81, *Land where scrubby oak grows.* . . shinnery. [48 of 67 infs] **1962** Atwood *Vocab. TX* 41, *Land where scrubby oak grows.* The thick growth of small oaks . . that covers parts of North Central and West Texas is known as the *shinnery* (95 [of approx 270 infs]). **1967** *DARE* (Qu. C28, *A place where underbrush, weeds, vines and small trees grow together so that it's nearly impossible to get through*) Infs **TX**39, 40, Shinnery; **TX**2, Shinnery—this is oak; **TX**43, Shinnery—refers to a special variety of oak; (Qu. T2a, . . *A piece of land covered with trees . . only a few acres*) Inf **TX**42, Shinnery—if it's full of shin oak. **1989** *New Yorker* 27 Feb 56 **nwTX,** Now there's houses empty with the yards all gone back to shinnery—shinnery, that's sandpiles, weeds, bushes, land not good for nothing.

shinnery oak n Also *shinnery, shinry* [**shinnery**]
A dwarf **oak:** usu *Quercus havardii,* but also a **shin oak a** (here: *Quercus mohriana*) native chiefly to the Southwest. For other names of the former, see **sand scrub 2, sand oak, shin ~**
1913 Wooton *Trees NM* 57, The Shin-Oak or Shinry (*Quercus havardii*) is a low deciduous-leaved shrub, rarely over 3 feet high . . that covers relatively large areas of sand hills in the southeastern corner of the State. **1961** Ligon *NM Birds* 90, The principal range [of the lesser prairie chicken] south of the main line of the Santa Fe Railway, west from Texico, is characterized by a dwarf oak, known as shinnery oak (*Quercus havardii*). **1975** Lamb *Woody Plants SW* 11, Shinnery probably has the largest acorns, yet is the smallest plant. **2000** (acc) Seyffert *Birds Shinnery Oak–Grasslands* (Internet) **cwOK,** The Shinnery Oak-Grasslands is a vegetation association largely unique to western Oklahoma and occurs most extensively in Beckham, Roger Mills and Ellis counties.

shinnery plum n Cf **hog plum 2**
Prob a **wild plum.**
[**1844** (1954) Gregg *Commerce* 241 **OK,** An immense sand-plain was now opening before us . . in some places . . completely covered with an extraordinarily diminutive growth which has been called *shin-oak,* and a curious plum-bush of equally dwarfish stature.] **1967** *DARE* (Qu. I46, . . *Kinds of fruits that grow wild around here*) Inf **TX**40, Hog plums, shinnery plums—old-fashioned.

shinney See **shinny** n[1]

shinnied up See **shinny** n[2]

shinning See **shin**

shinny n[1] Also sp *shinney*
1 rarely *shindy;* also *shinny on your own side* and varr: An improvised game of hockey played on the ground or on ice; see quots. [*OED2* 1672 →] **scattered exc Sth** See Map *somewhat old-fash*
1785 in 1971 Denny *Military Jrl.* 60 **Ohio Valley,** [The Indians were] exceedingly active at the game our boys call shinny. **1859** (1860) Creecy *Scenes South* 160, At bandy or shindy, one day, I was on the side opposed to a large boy . . and in a hard race for a ball, I was just in the

act of striking it, when, to prevent me, he struck my foot rather severely. **1863** in 1983 *PADS* 70.51 **ce,sePA**, After clearing our baskets of pie and apples we hie away for a game of shinny. **1891** *Jrl. Amer. Folkl.* 4.232 **Brooklyn NYC**, *Shinney*. Sides are chosen, and goals, one for each side, are agreed upon. The latter consist of two lines about three hundred feet apart, which are drawn across the street. The implements of the game consist of sticks with a crook at one end, with which each of the players are provided, and a wooden ball or a block of wood about two or three inches in length, which is placed in the middle of the street, midway between the goals. The sides form two lines facing each other, up and down the street, with a distance of about two feet between them. The two boys on opposite sides of the ball, which occupies the centre of this alley, will strike it at the cry of "Ready;" and each side then endeavors to drive it to its own goal, which constitutes the game. It is not permitted to touch the ball with the hands; and if a player crosses to the side opposite to the one to which he belongs, he is greeted with the cry of "Shinney on your own side!" and liable to a blow on the shins. **1899** (1912) Green *VA Folk-Speech* 381, *Shinny. . .* The game of bandy-ball. **1932** Farrell *Young Lonigan* 22 **Chicago IL** (as of 1916), He had shown her where they played shinny with tin cans. **1942** McAtee *Dial. Grant Co. IN* 56 (as of 1890s), *Shinny . .* a version of the game described in the dictionary as hockey. The penalty for being off-side was a rap on the shin by any opponent who could do it at the time. This feature seems sufficient to account for the name. Our shinny sticks were cut from natural growths most readily found in swampy places; they resembled in shape an "iron" among golf clubs. **1949** Hedgecock *Gone Are the Days* 70 **swMO**, When it came time for shinny, we boys all tried to see who could bring the best shinny club to school. . . If I couldn't find a limb that curved just right, I could nearly always find one that branched off from another limb at just the right angle, and, using about six inches of the larger limb for the head, and the smaller branch for a handle, I could cut myself a shinny club that suited me to a tee. **1957** *Sat. Eve. Post Letters* **neNE** (as of 1900), There was a game called shinny or shinny-on-your-own-side. It was played with broom sticks or if one had top-drawer equipment, a stick bent at the lower end like a hockey stick. The puck was a piece of wooden curtain rod about two inches long, or if the game was on ice, often a tin can was used. . . The players were divided into two teams and the captains faced each other in the middle of the field with the puck on the ground between them. Each captain hit the ground and then the adversary's stick three times synchronously and then tried to knock the puck into enemy territory. On a dirt or turf field it was permissible to pick up the puck and run across the other goal line, but one was liable to become the bottom of a pile of squirming boys trying to wrest the puck from one's grasp. *Ibid* **PA**, We played "Shinny in your own Hole", which was something like hockey. **1965–70** *DARE* (Qu. EE27, *Games played on the ice*) 86 Infs, **scattered exc Sth**, Shinny; **IA**3, **MN**38, **NV**7, **NY**44, **OR**15, Shinny on (the) ice; **VA**5, Ice shinny [Of all Infs responding to the question, 65% were old; of those giving these responses, 79% were old.]; (Qu. EE18, *Games in which the players set up a stone, a tin can, or something similar, and then try to knock it down*) 17 Infs, **scattered**, Shinny; **IA**3, Shinny—a game like hockey played with a stick and a can or rock in the street; **MO**3, Shinny—a kind of hockey played on the ground; **NM**4, Shinny—when a tin can was hit with a stick—you tried to hit the other player's [sic] shins; **OK**18, Shinny—hit tin can toward hole with sticks—two sides; **OK**28, Shinny—take turns hitting a tin can out of a ring; **WA**18, Shinny—two teams using sticks—shinny clubs—knock puck or tin can over each other's can; on ice or street or grass; **PA**71, Shinny on your own side; **PA**203, Tin shinny; (Qu. EE33, *. . Outdoor games . . that children play*) 13 Infs, **esp Midl**, Shinny; (Qu. EE2) Inf **IA**11, Shinny—kicking a can through a line of kids, played both on ice and on [the] ground; (Qu. EE10, *A game in which a short stick lying on the ground is flipped into the air and then hit with a longer stick*) Infs **MD**49, **MI**67, **MA**21, **NJ**6, **PA**49, Shinny; **IL**63, Shinny—could use stick . . if you didn't have a tin can; **NY**209, Shinny—very much like hockey; **WI**24, Shinny—with a tin can; (Qu. EE11, *Bat-and-ball games for just a few players [when there aren't enough for a regular game]*) Inf **CA**105, Shinny—hit the ball with a shinny stick over the other player's goal; (Qu. EE28) Inf **WV**7, Shinny on your own side: each player has a stick; the object knocked with the stick is [a] tin can; you have to hold your stick a particular way; if you move it, e.g., right-handed, and you're supposed to be left-handed, the opposing player says, "Shinny on your own side" and hits you across the legs with his stick; object of the game is same as ice hockey. **1967** Borland *Hill Country* 45 **NE**, The boys played shinny with a home-made wooden puck and clubs cut from the osage orange trees that lined the roadsides. **1986** Pederson *LAGS Concordance*, 1 inf, **ceTX**, Shinny—like hockey—knock tin can with stick; 1 inf, **seTX**,

Shinny—ball and stick game; 2 infs, **cwTN, cLA**, Shinny—childhood game. **2001** *DARE* File, Hockey as played very informally, such as on a frozen rural pond and without adherence to particulars of the rule book such as how many players a side, is known as "shinny."

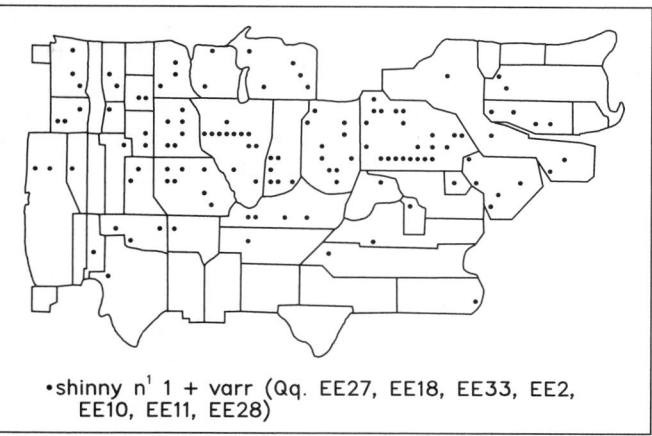

• shinny n¹ 1 + varr (Qq. EE27, EE18, EE33, EE2, EE10, EE11, EE28)

2 A marble; a marble game; see quots.　Cf **china B1**

1966–67 *DARE* (Qu. EE6b, *Small marbles or marbles in general*) Inf **OH**31, Shinnies; (Qu. EE6c, *Cheap marbles*) Inf **AR**3, Shinnies. **1968** *DARE* Tape **MD**51, Now with shinny, we're taking two players. . . You had a small hole, about four inches in diameter. You'd stand back maybe ten feet, behind a line, and throw toward a hole. Now, if a man got a . . hole-in-one on the first throw, he won the other man's marble. Now, if neither one went into the hole, the man closest to the hole would shoot at his opponent's marble. Upon hitting it—and then he would shoot toward the hole. Now, if he got his marble in the hole, then he would win the opponent's marble.

shinny v, hence vbl n *shinnying*　**widespread, but less freq Sth, S Midl**　See Map　Cf **shimmy** v, **shin**, **skin** v **3**, **skinny** v
To climb by alternately grasping with the arms and legs.

1889 Daly *Lottery of Love* 18, The way you shinnied up the side of the ship . . converted me on the spot to the Blooming costume. **1896** *DN* 1.424 **NYC**, *Shinny over:* to climb over. **1946** *AmSp* 21.98 **sIL**, *Skin down, slide down.* (Also *shinny up.*) **1965–70** *DARE* (Qu. EE36, *To climb the trunk of a tree by holding on with your legs while you pull yourself up with your hands*) 532 Infs, **widespread, but less freq Sth, S Midl**, Shinny (up); **WA**1, Shinny it up; **CO**42, **IN**58, **MO**19, 20, **NY**145, 228, Shinnying (up); (Qu. OO10a, *Talking about climbing trees: "When we were children we often _____ [trees]."*) Infs **CA**197, **CO**14, **CT**35, **IL**37, **MD**2, **MA**58, Shinned; **NY**1, **OH**44, **VA**5, Shinnied up; **IL**113, Shinny; (Qu. OO10b, *Talking about climbing trees: "Some trees were dangerous—we shouldn't have _____ [those]."*) Inf **CA**197, Shinnied. **1976** Garber *Mountain-ese* 80 **sAppalachians**, *Shinny-up* . . climb by grip—Little Albert can shinny-up that tree like a monkey. **1986** Pederson *LAGS Concordance (Climb)* 1 inf, **seLA**, Shinnied; 1 inf, **seGA**, Shinnied up the tree; 1 inf, **cwFL**, Shinny up it.

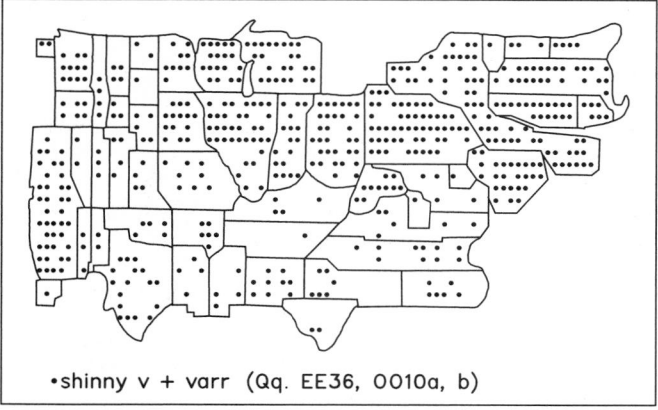

• shinny v + varr (Qq. EE36, OO10a, b)

shinny n² Also rarely *shinny whiskey*　Cf **shine** n **2**　**chiefly Gulf States**

Whiskey, esp when illegally made or of poor quality; also transf, the place where such whiskey is sold; hence adj *shinnied up* drunk.

1927 *AmSp* 3.25 eTX [Sawmill talk], The liquor on tap at these dances is called "pine-top," "Shinny," "white mule," or "corn." **c1940** Eliason *Word Lists FL* 11 wFL, *Shinny.* . . Bad liquor made from cane-skimmings. **1960** Lee *Mockingbird* 121 sAL, Miss Maudie Atkinson baked a Lane cake so loaded with shinny it made me tight. *Ibid* 135, "—besides," Atticus was saying, "you're not scared of that crowd, are you?" " . . know how they do when they get shinnied up." "They don't usually drink on Sunday, they go to church most of the day." **1966–67** *DARE* (Qu. DD21a, *General words . . for any kind of liquor*) Inf TX37, Shinny—old-timers; (Qu. DD21b, *General words . . for bad liquor*) Infs AL6, MS73, Shinny; (Qu. DD21c, *Nicknames for whiskey, especially illegally made whiskey*) Infs AL31, MS73, TX32, 37, Shinny; (Qu. DD30, *Joking names for a place where liquor is [or was] sold and consumed illegally*) Inf TX30, Shinny. **1986** Pederson *LAGS Concordance* (Cheap whiskey, home-brewed beer or whiskey) 32 infs, coastal Gulf Region, esp nwFL, Shinny; 1 inf, seMS, Shinny whiskey; (A rustic) 1 inf, swAL, Shinny makers.

shinnying See **shinny** v

shinny on a pole n [**shinny** n[1] **1**]
1966 *DARE* (Qu. EE18, *Games in which the players set up a stone, a tin can, or something similar, and then try to knock it down*) Inf OK52, Shinny on a pole—can tied on long string to upright pole and hit back and forth.

shinny on one's own side v phr [**shinny on your own side** exclam]
To mind one's own business.
1866 Smith *Bill Arp* 144 GA, Let 'em shinny on their own side, and git over among folks who don't want us reconstructed. **1887** *Courier-Jrl.* (Louisville KY) 11 Jan 1/1, If his Royal Highness does not like United States justice, he can "shinny on his own side" of the water hereafter. **1892** Johnston *Mr. Billy Downs* 36 GA, I know Jones can be made to—to shinny on his own side. **1942** McAtee *Dial. Grant Co. IN* 56 (as of 1890s), *Shinny on your own side* . . mind your own business. **1951** *MW Folkl.* (IN Univ.) 1.246 IN, The cry was, "shinny on your own side," which was part of the dialect and in ordinary use meant, "mind your own business."

shinny on your own side n See **shinny** n[1] **1**

shinny on your own side exclam Also sp *shinney on your own side* [Cf *EDD* *shin your side*, *shin you* (at *shin* int.) "A term in the game of 'shinny'. . . The call to a player who has trespassed too far into the line of his opponents."]
Used as a call in the game of **shinny** n[1] **1**; see quots.
1891 [see **shinny** n[1] **1**]. **1899** Champlin–Bostwick *Young Folks' Games* 412, Each player [in hockey or shinney] must strike the ball from right to left. If he do so in any other way, he may be told by his opponent to "shinney on his own side," and at the third offense he shall be disqualified by the umpire. **1968** *DARE* (Qu. EE28) Inf WV7, You have to hold your stick a particular way; if you move it, e.g., right-handed, and you're supposed to be left-handed, the opposing player says, "Shinny on your own side" and hits you across the legs with his stick.

shinny pea n
Prob a **black-eyed pea**; see quot.
1970 *DARE* (Qu. L9b, *Hay from other kinds of plants [not grass]*; not asked in early QRs) Inf VA77, Pea hay—use gray pea or shinny pea or cow pea.

shinny, tear up v phr Also *cut up shinny* [Perh var of **shindy** n[1] **2**] Cf **jack** n[1] **14**, **molly** n[1] **3**, **Sam** n[3] **1**
To make a fuss or disturbance.
1952 Hench *Coll.* cVA, Heard. . . "[He] . . came in here tearing up shinny about his not getting his change-of-status notice. So I tore up shinny back and told him I couldn't do everything at once." **1952** Brown *NC Folkl.* 1.589, *Shinny, cut up.* . . To create a disturbance.

shinny whiskey See **shinny** n[2]

shin oak n [Prob < **shinnery oak**] esp TX Cf **scrub oak**, **shinnery**

Any of var low-growing **oaks** native chiefly to the Southwest, esp *Quercus mohriana* and *Q. undulata*; see quots.
1844 [see **shinnery plum**]. **1882** *Bot. Gaz.* 7.48 cTX, The sides . . of this great bluff are covered with a thick growth of . . shin oak (*Q[uercus] sinuata*). **1884** *Encycl. Brit.* (9th ed) 17.693 KS, MO, *Q[uercus] Chinquapin* or *prinoides*, a dwarf variety . . forms dense miniature thickets . . ; the tree is called by the hunters of the plains the "shin-oak". **1897** Sudworth *Arborescent Flora* 159 TX, Durand Oak. . . Common names. . . Shin Oak. *Ibid* 152, *Quercus breweri*. . . Shin Oak. *Ibid* 153, *Quercus gambelii*. . . Shin Oak. *Ibid* 160, *Quercus undulata*. . . Shin Oak. *Ibid* 176 TX, *Quercus brevifolia*. . . Shin Oak. **1913** [see **shinnery oak**]. **1922** Sargent *Manual Trees* 285, Quercus Mohriana . . Shin Oak. **1960** Vines *Trees SW* 168, Gray Oak. . . Vernacular names are Shin Oak, Scrub Oak [etc]. **1967** *DARE* (Qu. T10, . . *Kinds of oak trees*) Infs TX1, 3, 4, 11, 42, 45, 68, Shin oak; TX43, Shin oak—looks like a damn little scrubby live oak; never gets more than waist-high. **1967** *DARE* Tape TX25, [FW:] What kind of things make up the brush around here? [Inf:] Mesquite, shin oak, live oak, all kinds of trees. **1979** Little *Checklist U.S. Trees* 231, *Quercus garryana*. . . shin oak. *Ibid* 232, *Quercus havardii*. . . shin oak, shinnery oak, Havard shin oak. *Ibid* 233, Bluejack oak. . . Other common names . . shin oak. *Ibid* 240, *Quercus pungens* var. *vaseyana*. . . shin oak. **1980** Little *Audubon Guide N. Amer. Trees E. Region* 399, Mohr Oak. . . The names Shin Oak and "shinnery" refer to the dense thickets, scarcely knee-high, of dwarf evergreen oaks of this and related species on uplands of western Texas and borders of adjacent states. **1980** Little *Audubon Guide N. Amer. Trees W. Region* 402, Gray Oak . . "Shin Oak." **1986** Pederson *LAGS Concordance*, 1 inf, ceTX, Shin oak—short tree—hits your shins.

shin-plasters n
A **fringed orchid** (here: *Platanthera orbiculata*).
1959 Carleton *Index Herb. Plants* 106, *Shin plasters:* Habenaria orbiculata.

shinry n
1 See **shinnery**.
2 See **shinnery oak**.

shin up See **shin**

shinwood n
A **yew** (here: *Taxus canadensis*).
1778 Carver *Travels N. Amer.* 505, *Shin Wood.* This extraordinary shrub . . runs near the ground for six or eight feet, and then takes root again; . . this proves very troublesome to the hasty traveller, by striking against his shins, and entangling his legs. **1813** Muhlenberg *Catalogus Plantarum* 93, Taxus . . Canadensis . . shin-wood. **1822** Eaton *Botany* 483, [*Taxus*] *canadensis* . . dwarf yew, shin-wood. **1900** Lyons *Plant Names* 365, [*Taxus*] *minor*. . . Canada, south to Virginia and Iowa. . . Chinwood, Shinwood.

shiny See **shiner** n **1**

‡shiny-pants Methodist n
1966 *DARE* (Qu. CC4, . . *Nicknames . . for various religions or religious groups*) Inf AL10, Shiny-pants Methodists—slide in, slide out.

ship, captain, (and) crew n Also *ship ahoy*
A dice game: see quots.
1966–68 *DARE* (Qu. EE40, . . *Table games . . using dice*) Inf MN42, Ship ahoy—three tosses of five dice for a 6, 5, 4. 6 = ship, 5 = captain, 4 = crew. Extra two are thrown for number of men; WA2, Ship, captain, and crew—4-5-6-3; CA32, Ship, captain, crew—a bar game—five dice in a box, three shakes, have to get at least two of the three [=1, 2, 3 or 6, 5, 4] in each set to hold what you've got; once you get ship you are captain; so 1, 2, 3 + two 5's, [you] would stand with ship and crew of ten. **1966** *DARE* FW Addit nwWA, Dice games played across bar counter— 1. ship, captain, and crew; 2. horses. **2001** *DARE* File seMN (as of c1980), Some college friends from Rochester, Minnesota, used to talk about playing ship, captain, and crew (a dice game sometimes played as a drinking game).

ship feed See **ship stuff**

shipmast locust n [See quots 1938, 1950]
A **black locust** (here: *Robinia pseudoacacia* var *rectissima*).
1938 Van Dersal *Native Woody Plants* 240, Var. *rectissima* . . , the shipmast locust, is a tree to 100 feet, occurring on the richer soils of the

northern and western parts of Long Island, and locally in New York and Massachusetts. The trunk is columnar, very straight and yields a wood which is harder and more durable than that of the species. **1950** Peattie *Nat. Hist. Trees* 419, Not until 1936 did botanists get around to describing, as a distinct variety . . a form of the Black Locust known as Shipmast Locust. . . The Shipmast Locust takes its name from the fact that the main stem grows straight up through the branches, without forking till near the top, like the mast of a ship. **1979** Little *Checklist U.S. Trees* 254, A clone of unknown origin, *Robinia pseudoacacia* var. *rectissima . . ,* shipmast locust, has become established from cultivation in Mass., N.Y., and N.J., and perhaps elsewhere.

shipoke See **shitepoke**

shipped stuff See **ship stuff**

shippy n [PaGer *shipli,* prob infl by *sheepy*] Cf **sheepie**
A lamb.
　1908 *German Amer. Annals* 10.42 **sePA,** *Shippy.* Lamb. "You can see the ewe and her shippy."

ship stuff n Also *ship feed, shipped stuff* [Prob because it was orig sold for provisioning ships]
A low grade of wheat flour containing considerable bran; wheat middlings, sometimes mixed with other grains and used as animal feed.
　1771 (1925) Washington *Diaries* 2.23, Sold all the Flour I have left . . ship stuff at 8/4 pr. Cwt. **1779** (1909) U.S. Continental Congress *Jrls.* 14.875, *Resolved,* That . . the said commissioners shall take effectual care that every barrel of flour shall be plainly branded on one head, so as to shew the miller's name, the quality of the flour, whether superfine, common or ship stuff [etc]. **1869** Roosevelt *Five Acres* 22 **NYC,** He went into the habits of cows in general; that he thought ship-stuff was an excellent change of diet; that they liked hay [etc]. **1909** *DN* 3.369 **eAL, wGA,** *Ship-stuff, ship-feed.* . . Wheat bran: so called because it is always *shipped* from a distance. **1912** *DN* 3.589 **wIN,** *Ship(ped) stuff.* . . Cheap feed, usually wheat bran mixed with oats and ground corn. "I must get some ship stuff for my cow." **1949** Arnow *Hunter's Horn* 146 **KY,** Maybe the molasses money would had to have gone for something ugly like ship stuff for the ewes. **1955** Bradshaw *Hist. Prince Edward Co. VA* 304 (as of a1820), In addition to manufacturing flour and meal, the mills also made feed for livestock. This was called shipstuff. **1981** Mebane *Mary* 16 **cnNC,** Slopping the hogs was Jesse's job. . . and we'd carry slops—discarded vegetables cooked with "ship stuff," a coarse thickening substance about the consistency of sawdust. We'd pour it . . into the trough and watch them eat. **1984** Wilder *You All Spoken Here* 136 **Sth,** *Ship stuff.* . . By-products in the milling of wheat. Once relegated to chicken and hog feed, they now are favored for human consumption.

shire town n [*OED2* (at *shire* sb. 8.b) 1459 →] **chiefly NEng**
A county seat.
　1648 in 1867 NH *Prov. & State Papers* 1.189, The Court doth think fitt that the shire town of Norfolke be referred to further consideration. **1717** in 1882 MA *Hist. Soc. Coll.* 5th ser 7.132, Cambridge is the Shire-Town for Middlesex. **1801** in 1889 MA *Hist. Soc. Proc.* 2d ser 4.125 **MA,** Bristol . . is the shire-town of a county of its name. **1829** in 1910 Buffalo *Hist. Soc. Pub.* 14.227 **NY,** It [=Lyons] is the shire town of Wayne county. **1851** *Hist. Gaz. Tioga Co. NY* 317 (McDavid Coll.), Owego, the shire town of Tioga county. **1881** *Century Illustr. Mag.* 23.251 **MA,** It was the central town in the county, and yet not the shire-town. **1946** Attwood *Length ME* 16 [Geographical terms], *Shire town*—The town designated by statute, or by referendum provided by statute, as the place where the business of a county is conducted. Other places may be established by statute for conduct of part of the county's business but they do not thereby become shire towns, of which there may be only one to a county. **1949** Kurath *Word Geog.* 20, Although the term *county seat* is current in all parts of New England at the present time, the older *shire town* . . is still in common use in the northern New England states and not unknown in Massachusetts. **1967** *DARE* Tape **MA34,** My mother came from Machias, Maine. . . That's the shire town . . where the courthouse is. **1999** *DARE* File **wMA,** The county seat was called the shire town, pronounced to rhyme with wire. I haven't heard anyone use the term for many years. It seems old-fashioned to me.

shirkshire n [Appar rel to the place name or nickname *Shirkshire;* this is now the official name of a small community in Franklin Co, MA]

See quot 1959.
　1956 *VT Hist.* 24.158 **Shaftsbury VT** (as of 1888), It snowed for two days and two nights. . . When the snow stopped, . . they took shovels to dig the way out. When the road was plowed out, the drifts were clear above their heads. There was a shirkshire with the snowstorm. **1959** *Ibid* 27.156 **swVT,** *Shirkshire.* . . A certain type of wind that seems to blow from every direction. Heard in and near Bennington, Bennington Co.

shirt-button n [From the shape; cf **cheese B1**] Cf **button-weed 4**
The fruit of a **mallow B** (here: *Malva rotundifolia*).
　1899 (1912) Green *VA Folk-Speech* 382, *Shirt-buttons.* . . The fruit of the mallow. **1914** Georgia *Manual Weeds* 280, Common Mallow . . Round Dock, Cheeses, Shirt-button Plant, Maul.

shirt rabbit n Also *shirt hound, ~ rat, ~ squirrel* **joc** Cf **pants rabbit**
=**louse B1.**
　1918 *Stars & Stripes* (Paris France) 22 Mar 8/2, Yes, the louse! The humble, inoffending shirt-hound, the cootie. **1918** (1919) Rowse *Doughboy Dope* 53, For the scientifically inclined, it is noted that, according to the location of the phenomenon it is described either as "leaping dandruff" or "shirt rats." **1918** Kauffman *Navy at Work* 5, They were covered with what our boys call shirt-squirrels. **1919** *Hist. 307th Field Artillery* 31, Many of us would while away the time by "reading our shirts", or "hunting shirt rabbits." **1925** Mullin *Advent. Tramp* 125, I shipped gandy-dancer with a railroad construction outfit. . . The bunkcar stunk. Oh, *boy!* And shirt-rabbits in the blankets. **1950** *WELS (Body and head lice)* 1 Inf, **ceWI,** Shirt squirrels, pants rabbits, cooties. **1968** *DARE* (Qu. R25, *Joking names for a head louse, or body louse*) Inf **NY52,** Shirt rat, seam squirrel. **1976** Gould *Blackie's RR Hdbk.* 13, *Shirt rabbits:* Body Lice.

shirt rat See **shirt rabbit**

shirttail n

1 also *shirttailful, shirttail load:* A small load or amount. **chiefly S Midl**
　1909 *DN* 3.403 **nwAR,** Shirt tail full. . . A smaller quantity than a jag. [c1920 in 1993 Farwell–Nicholas *Smoky Mt. Voices* 145 **sAppalachians,** When Matt Crisp (now preacher) was goin' to see his gal, . . [he said,] ' 'Lisbeth, I'll bet you cain't tell what I got tied up fer you in my shirt tail.'/ 'Well, what is it?'/ 'Sugar.'] **1940** Faulkner *Hamlet* 391 **MS,** There aint a piece of land . . that's been worked as much and as often as this here little shirt-tail of garden. **1940** *AmSp* 15.453 **KS,** 'Is there a load of hay out in the field?' 'No, just a jag.' A *jag,* however, was considerably more than a *shirt-tail,* which had its origin in the contemptuous remark sometimes addressed to a hay-maker who drove up to the barn with an unduly small load. 'You call that a load? Why you could have brought it up in your shirt-tail!' **1941** Writers' Program *Guide MO* 436, Miners' language . . was varied by such novel expressions as . . "an Alex Watson load" of ore, one so small as to be only a "shirt tail load." **1965–70** *DARE* (Qu. L55, *If the wagon was only partly full . . he had a _____*) Infs **AR56, CA36, IL114, MS1, OK20, VA95,** Shirttailful; **OH45, OK3,** Shirttail load; **KS12,** Shirttail; (Qu. L56, *The amount of wood a person can carry in both arms: "We're out of firewood—I'll just get in a _____."*) Inf **VA38,** Shirttail. **1986** Pederson *LAGS Concordance,* 1 inf, **cAL,** Shirttail of wood—a piece of a load.

2 also *shirttail(ed) bird, shirttail woodpecker, shirttailer:* = **red-headed woodpecker 1.** [See quot 1950] **SE** Cf **half-a-shirt**
　1913 *Auk* 30.497 **seGA,** Red-headed woodpecker; 'White Shirt'; 'Jerry Coat'; 'Shirt-tail.' **1934** Vines *Green Thicket* 60 **cnAL,** He had enough feathers from wild things to make a feather bed. . . He had a little old trunk nearly full of feathers and down from . . shirttails, sapsuckers, peckerwoods [etc]. **1943** Caldwell *GA Boy* 87, The shirt-tail woodpeckers had been bothering us for a long time. [*Ibid* 96, One of the older woodpeckers, a big cock with a long white shirt-tail, got up enough nerve to come down.] **1949** Sprunt–Chamberlain *SC Bird Life* 334, Red-headed Woodpecker. . . Local Names: Half-a-shirt; Shirt-tail Bird. **1950** *PADS* 14.60 **SC,** *Shirttail.* . . The red-headed woodpecker. So called because of white feathers on wings and under parts. *Shirttail bird.* . . The red-headed woodpecker. **1955** *Oriole* 20.1.10, Red-headed Woodpecker. . . *Shake-tail, Shirt-tailed Bird; Shirt-tail Woodpecker.* **1956** *AmSp* 31.184, The redheaded woodpecker . . is called *shirttail* throughout the Southeast, as well as *shirttailer* (Del.), *half shirt* (S.C.).

and *white shirt* (S.C., Ga.) **1966–68** *DARE* (Qu. Q17, . . *Kinds of woodpeckers*) Inf **GA**1, Shirttail—black at shoulders and tail white; (Qu. Q18, *Joking names and nicknames for woodpeckers*) Inf **SC**46, Shirttail—same as red-headed; **SC**57, Shirttail. **1986** Pederson *LAGS Concordance (Woodpecker)* 2 infs, **swGA**, Shirttail(s); 1 inf, **cAL**, Shirttail—peckerwood bird—larger than sapsucker.

shirttail adj

1 also *shirttail-size:* Very young—usu in phr *shirttail boy.* **chiefly Sth, S Midl**

1845 (1969) Hooper *Advent. Simon Suggs* 13 **GA**, From the time he was a "shirt-tail boy" [his wits] were always too sharp for his father's. **1897** (1952) McGill *Narrative* 14, About the eighth year of our lives a new era in early boyhood is opening, and he is known no more as a shirt tail boy, but assumes a place among his people. **1922** (1926) Kephart *Highlanders* 312 **sAppalachians**, It still is common in many districts of the mountain country for small boys to go about through the summer in a single abbreviated garment and that they are called "shirt-tail boys." **1937** in 1977 *Amer. Slave Suppl. 1* 1.86 **AL**, Us was called shirt-tale fellows and dey was made at home and hung below our knees, outer orsanburg. **1938** Rawlings *Yearling* 421 **nFL**, Nobody but your folks'll bother with a little ol' shirt-tail boy like you. **1952** Brown *NC Folkl.* 1.589, *Shirt-tail boy.* . . A small boy. Perhaps from the fact that some small boys in pre-Civil War days wore only a long shirt in warm weather. **1962** Dykeman *Tall Woman* 206 **NC** (as of 1860), I declare, how the years fly! Seems to me like he's still just a shirttail boy. **1966** *DARE* (Qu. HH1, *Names and nicknames for a rustic or countrified person*) Inf **FL**7, Shirttail plowboys—for youngsters. **1968** *Tuscaloosa News* (AL) 1 Aug 1/1, A shirttail-size boy in the crowd hankered to find a restroom. **1972** *Atlanta Letters* **nwGA**, A "little shirt-tail boy" is a very young male child. Long ago it was customary for *little* boys to wear only shirts until they were several years old—hence, the above expression. **1975** Newell *If Nothin' Don't Happen* 6 **nwFL**, Even when he were just a shirttail boy he were a scrappy little scaper. **1991** Still *Wolfpen Notebooks* 78 **sAppalachians**, When I was a shirttail boy my Pap used to kill us a mess of snowbirds for supper in the winter time.

2 Distantly related; loosely connected. **esp Nth** *often derog* Cf **buttonhole cousin, shoestring relation, woodpile ~**

1927 *Ruppenthal Coll.* **KS**, Shirt tail relation . . derisive. . . distant relatives. **1941** *AmSp* 16.24 **sIN**, Shirt-tail kin. A remote relationship. **1945** *WELS Suppl.* **seWI**, Shirt-tail relative. . . A not-close relative with whom one does not keep touch particularly (though one is conscious of the relation). Sometimes with the implication that these are not the relatives of whom one is proudest. **1959** *VT Hist.* 27.156, Shirt tail cousin. . . Distant cousin, not highly esteemed. Occasional. **1967–69** *DARE* (Qu. Z7, *Nicknames and affectionate words for any other relatives*) Inf **NY**165, Shirttail relation—same as buttonhole cousin; (Qu. Z9, *General word for others related to you by blood*) Inf **MN**19, Shirttail relations—if far removed; **WA**20, Shirttail relations—just distant relations—not blood; **IA**22, Shirttail relative; (Qu. CC7, . . *A person who goes to church very seldom or not at all*) Inf **IL**54, Shirttail Baptist. **1967** *DARE* Tape **WA**30, One of my illustrious relatives . . he's a shirt-tail relation somewhere. I think he was a half-brother or something [to] my grandfather. **1973** Allen *LAUM* 1.346 **Upper MW** (as of c1950), *Relatives*. . . shirt-tail relations [1 inf, **MN**]. **1985** *DARE* File **nNJ**, A . . woman . . told of a letter that came years ago from an English lawyer about a possible inheritance. . . She said she didn't follow it up because . . she would be spending a lot of money and then having "every shirt-tail relation back here" wanting part of whatever she got. **2001** *DARE* File **csWI** (as of c1970), When I asked my mother how I was related to "Aunt" Shirley and "Uncle" John, she replied, "They're not really related to us; I guess you'd say they're shirttail relatives." She also referred to distant blood relatives (such as second or third cousins) as "shirttail relatives."

3 Small; insignificant.

1929 (1954) Faulkner *Sound & Fury* 256 **MS**, My people owned slaves here when you all were running little shirt tail country stores. **1935** Sandoz *Jules* 198 **wNE** (as of 1880–1930), His shirt-tail patch of pop corn and cabbage. **1944** Adams *Western Words* 142, *Shirttail outfit*—A small ranch which employs only one or two men. **1960** Carpenter *Tales Manchaca* 1 **cTX**, How a young Tennessean migrated to frontier Texas while it was still a shirttail republic. *Ibid* 79 **cTX** (as of 1893), The Manchaca and Buda schools had a Baseball game in the Martin flat. . . I never heard such yelling and excitement over a little shirtail [sic] game in my life. **1967** *DARE* (Qu. MM24, . . *'A short distance': "The river is just a _____ from the house."*) Inf **GA**77, Shirttail distance.

4 Of a worker or member of an occupational group: inexperienced, inept, untrained. Cf **jackleg** adj **1**

1966 *DARE* (Qu. HH15, *A very inexperienced person, one who is just learning how to do a new thing*) Inf **SC**19, Shirttail fellow. **1968** *DARE* FW Addit **SC**, *Shirttail*—of a worker—not so good—working his way, gaining experience—not just a raw beginner, though. **1983** *DARE* File **cOK** (as of 1962), Shirttail mechanic—Jackleg. **1986** Pederson *LAGS Concordance*, 1 inf, **cAL**, Shirttail preacher—facetious, derogatory.

shirttail bird See **shirttail** n **2**

shirttail boy See **shirttail** adj **1**

shirttailed bird, shirttailer See **shirttail** n **2**

shirttailful, shirttail load See **shirttail** n **1**

shirttail relation (or relative) See **shirttail** adj **2**

shirttail-size See **shirttail** adj **1**

shirttail woodpecker See **shirttail** n **2**

shirt wetter n Cf *DS* B23

A very light rain.

1971 *WI Statist. Reporting Serv. Report* 6 July 2, Our rains have only been shirt wetters.

shishi n, v |ˈšiši| [Japanese *shishi* a child's word for urine] **HI**

Urine; to urinate—also in phr *make shishi* to urinate.

1967 *DARE* (Qu. BB20, *Joking names or expressions for overactive kidneys*) Inf **HI**4, Shishi all the time. **1969** *DARE* File **Honolulu HI**, *Shishi:* to make [ˈšiši]—the cat made [ˈšiši] on my dress, meaning—to make water, to pee. **1981** *Pidgin To Da Max* np **HI**, Shishi (SHEE shee)—What you do eenside da lua.

shit See **shut** v **A**

shit-across-the-creek n

A **bittern** (here: *Botaurus lentiginosus*).

1954 McAtee *Suppl. to Nomina Abitera* [7] **sNJ**, American Bittern. . . shit-across-the-creek. . . It was said if the bird ate a frog on one side of a creek and flew, it would shit it out before reaching the other side; again this term might refer to the apparent length of heron excrements—enough in this case to span a creek.

shit and caboodle See **caboodle**

shit-a-quart n Also *shit-a-rod*

=**great blue heron.**

1945 McAtee *Nomina Abitera* 26 **AK**, Great Blue Heron. . . shit-a-quart, Petersburg, Alaska. *Ibid* **CA**, Shit-a-rod.

shitass n

1 A **gull.**

1945 McAtee *Nomina Abitera* 38 **nwNV**, **neCA**, Gulls . . not further identified. . . shitass.

2 =**killdeer 1.**

1945 McAtee *Nomina Abitera* 34 **nwNV**, **neCA**, Killdeer . . Cracker-ass, shit-ass.

shitbird n

1 =**English sparrow.** [See quot] Cf **shit-eater 2**

1954 McAtee *Suppl. to Nomina Abitera* [9] **MA**, House Sparrow . . shit-bird, New Bedford, Massachusetts . . from its feeding among horse dung.

2 =**rufous-sided towhee.** [See quot]

1954 McAtee *Suppl. to Nomina Abitera* [9] **sNJ**, Red-eyed Towhee . . Shit-bird from resemblance to those words of the first two notes of the bird's song.

shit-brindle adj phr Also *turd-brindle*

Muddy brown.

1942 Whipple *Joshua* 265 **UT** (as of c1860), Blue-dyed yarn could be colored green by scalding in yellow dye . . olive green from the creosote leaves, and 'shit-brindle' from wild sage. **1950** *WELS* (*A dark, unattractive brownish color: "They painted the house a _____ color."*) 4 Infs, **WI**, Shit-brindle. **1954** *Harder Coll.* **cwTN**, Shit brindle—same as muddy. **1960** Bailey *Resp. to PADS 20* **KS**, Shit brindle . . dun.

1960 Criswell *Resp. to PADS* 20 **Ozarks,** *Shit brindle. . .* Muckle dun. **1966–69** *DARE* (Qu. K38, *A horse of a dirty white color*) Infs **ME**19, **MI**47, **NY**23, Shit-brindle; **GA**47, Turd-brindle; (Qu. K39, *. . Names . . for horses according to their colors*) Inf **NY**1, Shit-brindle (brownish). **1999** in 2002 *DARE* File—Internet **MT,** [He] wears those aviator sunglasses that turn shit-brindle brown indoors.

shit-bug See **shit-roller**

shit-digger n **LA**
=**shoveler.**

    [**1918** LA Dept. of Conserv. *Bulletin* 5.23, Bechleur [sic] de merde.] **1945** McAtee *Nomina Abitera* 31 **LA,** Shoveller (Spatula clypeata) . . shit-digger, Cameron, La. . . Mississippi Delta, La.

shit-eater n *derog*
1 A dog.

    1967–69 *DARE* (Qu. J2, *. . Joking or uncomplimentary words . . for dogs*) Infs **AR**55, **KY**27, **TN**26, Shit-eater. **1972** Shafer *Dict. Prison Slang* [34] **TX,** *Shit eaters*—dogs that chase escapees. **1986** Pederson *LAGS Concordance (Mongrel)* 1 inf, **cwFL,** A worthless shit eater.

2 also *horse-shit-eater:* =**English sparrow;** see quot.

    1967–69 *DARE* (Qu. Q21, *. . Kinds of sparrows*) Inf **SC**43, Horse-shit-eater—a kind that stayed around stables—not often seen now; (Qu. Q22, *Joking names or nicknames for the common sparrow*) Inf **MA**15, Shit-eater—heard in city (Brooklyn)—when horses were common in cities.

3 A mullet n[1] **1.**

    1968 *DARE* (Qu. P2, *. . Kinds of saltwater fish caught around here . . good to eat*) Inf **LA**44, Mullet—also called shit-eaters—eaten by Negroes; White people don't eat them.

shitepoke n Also *shidepoke, shikepoke, shitpoke, shrikepoke, shypoke, skikepoke;* for addit varr see quots at **A** below [*shite* arch var of *shit* + *poke* bag; see quot 1945 at **B1** below] Cf **pokeshite, shagpoke**
A Forms.

    1844 [see **B1** below]. **1899** in 1900 LA Soc. Naturalists *Proc.* 92, *Ardetta exilis . . Least Bittern; Shyte Poke.* An abundant resident in all marshy sections of the state. **1905** *Amer. Naturalist* 39.402, "Shikepoke" or "Quawk" = *Nycticorax nycticorax nævius.* . . Perhaps the former name refers to *Butorides virescens.* **1909** *DN* 3.368 **eAL, wGA,** *Shide-poke. Ibid* 415 **nME,** *Shitpoke.* **1911** [see **B2** below]. **1938** FWP *Guide DE* 511, Occasionally a rowboat passes through the semidarkness of overhanging pine trees and trailing vines, startling "shikepokes" (little green herons) that flap slowly ahead of the intruder. **1938** Rawlings *Yearling* 303 **nFL,** A shipoke flew. **1940** WI Conserv. Bulletin 5.8.57, *American bittern:* shypoke or shikepoke or shitepoke or shied poke. . . *Least bittern:* shypoke or shitepoke or shiedpoke or shipoke, little shikepoke. **1945** McAtee *Nomina Abitera* 25, To date I have found the following variants of shitepoke—34 in all: pokeshike[,] scheidpoke[,] scheytepoke[,] schitepoke[,] schytepoke[,] shackpoke[,] shadpoke[,] shagpoke[,] sheidpok[,] sheidpoke[,] sheilpoke[,] sheitpoke[,] shidpoke[,] shide-poke[,] shiedpoke[,] shightpoke[,] shikecoat[,] shikepoe[,] shikepoke[,] shikepolk[,] shikpoke[,] shipepoke[,] shipoke[,] shitepoke[,] shitepolk[,] shitepout[,] shitpoke[,] shypoke[,] shypook[,] shypork[,] shytepoke[,] skikepoke[,] skitepoke[,] skypoke. **1953** *AmSp* 28.253 **csPA,** *Shitepote. . .* A variant of *shitepoke,* the heron known as a 'fly-up-the-creek.' **1954** McAtee *Suppl. to Nomina Abitera* [6] **NC,** Great Blue Heron . . Shypoke, Matamuskeet Wildlife Refuge, North Carolina. *Ibid* [7], Herons. Shitepoke. Variant. . . Shite-pook, Percy Taverner (The Museum, Albion, N.Y. 1896 2.109). **1965–70** [see **B1** below]. **1984** *MJLF* 10.1.156 **cnWI,** *Shypoke.* The bittern. Maine: Shitpoke. **1997** [see **B4** below]. **2001** *NADS Letters* **Ozarks,** I've heard this bird name only as "shypoke"—from the Ozarks, where the birds are numerous along the White River in Arkansas.

B Senses.

1 A bird of the family Ardeidae, usu the **green heron** or a bittern (here: *Botaurus lentiginosus*). [See quot 1945] **chiefly Nth, Midl** Cf **flying shit-house, mudpoke, poke** n[4], **red shitepoke**

    1775 *First Book Amer. Chron.* 2.19 **eMA,** They drummed with their drums . . running to and fro like shitepokes on the muddy shore. **1799** Barton *Fragments Nat. Hist.* PA 18, *Ardea virescens.* Commonly called S——e-Poke. **1832** Williamson *Hist. ME* 1.145, The *Skouk . .* is vulgarly called a "shite-poke." **1844** DeKay *Zool. NY* 2.224, The *Poke, Chalk-line, Fly-up-the-creek,* or *Schyte Poke* as he was called by our

Dutch progenitors, is a southern species. **1899** Howe–Sturtevant *Birds RI* 44, Black-crowned Night Heron. *Night Heron. Shitepoke.* **1905** *DN* 3.18 **cCT,** *Shitepoke. . .* A species of heron. **1909** *DN* 3.368 **eAL, wGA,** *Shide-poke. . .* The small blue heron. Also called *shite-poke* and *Indian hen. Ibid* 415 **nME,** *Shitpoke. . .* The immature, black-crowned night heron. **1911** Porter *Harvester* 170 **IN,** A shitepoke, skulking along the river bank, stopped and cried, "Cowk, cowk!" **1939** FWP *Guide TN* 17, Numerous along all the State's water courses is the green heron, known variously as "shikepoke" and "fly-up-the-creek." **1945** McAtee *Nomina Abitera* 25, The name shite-poke for American herons is one of considerable interest. . . As a whole, the term seems to imply that a bird so named is a mere shitbag, capable of producing the commodity at will. As other names of herons indicate, the birds are able when flushed to lay a "chalk-line," "shit a rod," or "shit a quart," it is evident that the popular mind has been impressed with both linear and volumetric aspects of heron shitting. *Ibid* 30, Shitepoke . . application of this term to the bittern rivals its usage for the green heron. I have records from 27 States and provinces for the latter species and from 24 for the former; the distribution of "shitepoke" for the green heron is almost entirely in the eastern half of the United States, while this name for the bittern is more frequent in the Midwest and in the territory along both sides of the U.S.-Canadian boundary. **1965–70** *DARE* (Qu. Q8, *A water bird that makes a booming sound before rain and often stands with its beak pointed almost straight up*) 72 Infs, **chiefly Nth, N Midl,** Shypoke; 52 Infs, **chiefly Nth, Midl,** Shitepoke; 21 Infs, **esp KY, TN,** Shikepoke; 9 Infs, **esp Nth, N Midl,** Shidepoke; **DC**8, **MA**26, **OK**52, **PA**235, Shitpoke; **KY**9, 11, 84, Skikepoke; **CA**97, Shrikepoke—sort of small heron; **IA**22, Shikepoke—a scavenger bird, a wader—they pass bowels so much, hence the name; **ME**8, Shitpoke—American bittern or meadow hen (any heron is called a shitepoke); **MI**23, Shidepoke—belongs to the crane family; **MN**15, Shypoke or water pump or slough pump; **MN**18, Shikepoke—old-fashioned; **ND**1, Shitepoke—name from "straight gut" which releases excrement when they fly; **NH**14, Shitpoke—not same bird as stake-driver; **NJ**39, Shitepoke—pile-driver; **NY**103, Shitepoke—a little green heron; **PA**104, Shypoke—old term for heron—great heron and blue heron; **PA**147, Shitepoke—fish crane; **SD**3, Shitepoke—blue heron; **WI**78, Shypoke—quite tall—24 inches, dark, some sparkling; (Qu. Q10, *. . Water birds and marsh birds*) Infs **IN**45, **MO**11, 15, 19, **OH**74, Shitepoke; **IL**46, **NY**191, **PA**58, Shypoke; **CA**97, Shrikepoke—sort of small heron; **DE**3, Shitepokes or bitterns; **MI**76, Mud hen, shypoke—same; **MA**78, Black-crowned night heron—also called shypoke; **PA**235, Shitpoke; **WA**30, Blue heron or shitepokes or shitties; **CT**29, Shitepoke = type of heron = mud hen. **c1970** *DARE* File, In Delaware this [=*shitepoke*] is the name for the Little Blue Heron. . . In Iowa it is the name for the American Bittern. **1975** Gould *ME Lingo* 252, *Shitepoke*—Maine people make two errors with this word—they pronounce it wrong and they apply it to the wrong bird. They ignore the middle "e," and they use the word for the blue heron. The green heron is the *shitepoke.* **1991** *DARE* File **seNY,** Shite-poke = great blue heron. Shite is a delicate way to say shit.

2 Any of var other birds found near water.

    [**1844** Giraud *Birds Long Is.* 283 **Long Is. NY,** Snowy Heron. . . On Long Island it is not abundant, though by no means uncommon, and is known to the gunners by the name of "White Poke."] **1909** *DN* 3.415 **nME,** *Shitepoke. . .* The loon. **1911** (1913) Johnson *Highways Gt. Lakes* 31, Once or twice we saw a long-legged crane, or "shikepoke," flopping soberly on its way high up in the air. **1917** *Wilson Bulletin* 29.2.74 **ME,** *Columbus holboelli.*—Bobtail, Shitepoke . . Matinicus [Island], Me.; sheldrake loon, Patchogue [Long Island]. **1927** *AmSp* 2.364 **cwWV,** *Shitepoke . .* a wild duck. "He shot at a shitepoke, but missed it." **1945** McAtee *Nomina Abitera* 26 **WI,** American Egret . . White shypoke. **1954** McAtee *Suppl. to Nomina Abitera* [7] **WY, IL,** Shitepoke. . . Certain examples, somewhat suspect because not applied to herons, include . . shitepoke, the sandhill crane . . Wyoming . . [and] shitepoke, the belted kingfisher . . Illinois. **1967–69** *DARE* (Qu. Q8, *A water bird that makes a booming sound before rain and often stands with its beak pointed almost straight up*) Inf **IA**29, Shypoke or egret; **NY**84, Shypoke—egret; (Qu. Q9, *The bird that looks like a small, dull-colored duck and is commonly found on ponds and lakes*) Infs **PA**75, **TN**22, Shitepoke; **IN**42, **TN**1, Shypoke; (Qu. Q10, *. . Water birds and marsh birds*) Inf **GA**3, Cranes—also called shitepoke; **PA**168, Shypoke—also shitpoke = loon.

3 Used in proverbial comparison *crazy as a shitepoke.*

    1935 Sandoz *Jules* 28 **wNE,** He remembered . . "crazy as a shitepoke," which seemed to be a queer bird that rose heavily from the rushes along the Niobrara and made the peculiar pumping noise in the evening. Thunder-pumper, Sol Pitcher called him. **1937** Sandoz *Slogum* 200 **NE,**

Crazy as a shitepoke he was, but he did n't look crazy enough to confess to the Bullard business just because some sky pilot yelled hell-fire. **1943** Wood *Walter Reed* 133, Sometimes, after a more severe ordeal . . a man would come out crazy as—they had a word for it here—as a shitepoke, the big awkward heron that seemed to have no sense at all. **1947** *PADS* 8.20 **ceIA** (as of 1915–40), *Shite poke:* In phrase—*crazy as a shite poke.*

4 also attrib: A mean, contemptible, or uncouth person.

[**1836** (1838) Haliburton *Clockmaker* (1st ser) 130, Let them great hungry, ill-favoured, long-legged bitterns, says he, (only he called them by another name that don't sound quite pretty) from the outlandish states to Congress, *talk about* Independence.] **1925** *IL State Hist. Soc. Jrl.* 18.243 (as of 1844), Buggy riding was not common those days, such vehicles were very scarce and there was some prejudice against those who rode in them. Uncle Billie called them "Shite Pokes" and would not allow them an inch of the highway if he could help it. **1930** Shoemaker *1300 Words* 57 **cPA Mts**, *Shite-poke* . . a characterless person. **1932** Stribling *Store* 90 **AL**, I wish you'd take this to Alex Bivins at the Florence Hotel and tell him I cancel it. . . damn red-headed shike-poke! **1936** Lutes *Country Kitchen* 19 **sMI**, Of course I'll return it—when he's returned all the molasses and sugar and eggs and everything else they've borrowed in the last year—the ole shitepoke! **1941** *LANE* Map 464 *(Awkward person, lummox)* 1 inf, **cwCT**, Shigepoke. **1951** West *Witch Diggers* 60 **IN**, "Who's Ferris P. Thompson?" "An old saucer peach. . . That's what I say instead of shite-poke." **1956** Algren *Walk on the Wild Side* 56 **wTX**, Certainly didn't take long for word to get around this shite-poke town. **1958** McCulloch *Woods Words* 162 **Pacific NW**, *Shikspoke*—A man who pokes around his grub like a heron. **1967** Stegner *Little Live Things* 65 **cwCA**, Young Catlin yawns and stretches, squints at the view of Weld's shitepoke pigeon house and Tobacco-Road dog run across the gully, sips his drink, looks at me with a pleasant opaque expression. **1997** Frazier *Cold Mountain* 131 **NC** (as of c1860), It could be any time now, for my daddy's old. He could already be dead for all I know, the old shitpike. **2001** *DARE* File **KY**, When I was in high school in Louisville KY (1960–65) a classmate of mine used the word "shitepoke" (my recollection is that he pronounced it "shikepoke") to refer to people, and since nobody ever figured out what a shitepoke was, the targets of his, uh, description never could figure out whether they were being insulted or not.

5 A small child—used affectionately.

1942 Whipple *Joshua* 242 **UT** (as of c1860), Willie touched a finger to the soft down above the baby's ears. 'Little shite-poke' she cried fondly. 'See her stretch!' **2001** *NADS Letters*, Doing an undergraduate paper on "shitepoke" 30 years ago, I was surprised to discover that the term was long-established for the blue heron. (I knew only my family's use in affectionate disparagement of a child).

6 attrib, in combs *shitepoke gut, shagpoke gut*: A great capacity for food; a voracious person.

1954 *DE Folkl. Bulletin* 1.16, Shitepoke (heron-like—as in "Mom says I have a shitepoke gut": a comment on how much he could eat and never get fat.) **1958** McCulloch *Woods Words* 160 **Pacific NW**, *Shagpoke-gut*—A tremendous eater; from shagpoke, a bird which doesn't care what it eats, just so it eats all the time.

7 attrib: Long-legged.

1976 Garber *Mountain-ese* 80 **sAppalachians**, That shitepoke kid would make a good basketball player.

shitepoke gut See **shitepoke B6**

shit fire exclam Also *shit fire and flames*, euphem *shoot fire* Cf **set fire**

Used as an oath; see quots.

1949 Arnow *Hunter's Horn* 276 **KY**, Shit-fire Suse . . you're a droppen kernels in th hulls. **1986** Pederson *LAGS Concordance (Damn [it])* 1 inf, **csAL**, Shit fire—expression of disgust; *(Shucks)* 1 inf, **csTN**, Shit fire; 1 inf, **seAL**, Shit fire and flames; 1 inf, **cnAL**, Shoot fire.

shit-holer See **-holer**

shithouse n

In phr *in a shithouse with a muzzle on* and varr: See quot.

1967–69 *DARE* (Qu. V2b, *About a deceiving person, or somebody that you can't trust . . "I wouldn't trust him _____."*; not asked in early QRs) Infs **SC32, TX54, GA72**, In a shithouse with a muzzle (on); **LA2**, To the shithouse with a muzzle on.

shit-house trout n

A **sucker** (here: *Catostomus macrocheilus*).

1945 McAtee *Nomina Abitera* 20 **nOR, sWA**, Columbia River Sucker . . Shit-house trout, lower Columbia River.

shit-kicker n Also *shit-stomper*

1 A man's boot, esp one with a sharp toe; see quots. Cf **kicker** n[1] **2**

1966–69 *DARE* (Qu. W11, *Men's low, rough work shoes*) Infs **IN75, MI19, PA167**, Shit-kickers. **1975** *AmSp* 50.66 **AR** (as of c1970), *Shit stompers* . . 1: Cowboy boots. 2: Cowboys. **1986** Pederson *LAGS Concordance*, 1 inf, **csTN**, Shit kickers—boots. **1991** *DARE* File **wNE, Dallas TX**, There are two kinds of boots, both of which have pointed toes: kickers and shit-kickers. Men wore kickers for dancing. . . Shit-kickers are your everyday work boots, and that's what they're called, "shit-kickers." They're made out of horse hide or ordinary leather. People wore shit-kickers in western Nebraska too but out there nobody had kickers. **1992** *Ibid* **csWI**, I bought a pair of men's used lace-up black boots, they laced up above my ankle bones. When I showed my beautiful new boots to a friend, he said, "Shit-kickers, how post modern." I said, "Why call them that?" He said, "Because that's what they are, they're shit-kickers, work boots." I said, "Would you call them 'kickers?'" He said, "They're not kickers, they're shit-kickers." **1994** *Ibid* **nwKS** (as of 1960s), He had on a pair of shit-stompers (=cowboy boots). **1998** *Ibid* **eKS** (as of 1980s), *Shit-kicker*—Growing up in the northeast (Topeka), I heard this word used to refer to sharp-toed boots, esp. cowboy boots, the implication being that they could be used to kick the _____ out of someone. "He better watch out, 'cause I'm gonna be wearin' my shit-kickers." In any case, they were never work boots, and were usually stylish enough for school, parties, dancing, etc.

2 A **red-neck** n **2**; a cowboy or would-be cowboy. Cf **kicker** n[1] **4**

1964 *PADS* 42.29 **Chicago IL**, Any rustic . . *shit kicker.* **1968** *DARE* (Qu. HH1, *Names and nicknames for a rustic or countrified person*) Infs **NY93, PA161, WI57**, Shit-kicker. **1969** *Rolling Stone* 28 June 14 **CA**, [Country music] has also been called shitkicker music and white man's blues. **1975** [see **1** above]. **1986** Pederson *LAGS Concordance (Poor whites—black man's terms)* 1 inf, **ceTX**, Shit kicker—wants to be [a] cowboy, doesn't know how; 1 inf, **ceTX**, Shit kicker—insult; *(Poor whites—white man's terms)* 1 inf, **csTX**, Shit kicker—works around a ranch; *(A rustic)* 1 inf, **csTX**, Children call [a] cowboy shit kicker—new word; 1 inf, **csTX**, Shit kicker—wears cowboy hat, has pickup truck.

shit, meaner than adj phr Also *meaner than cat shit*; for addit varr see quot **chiefly NJ, PA, NY** See Map *esp freq among men*

Contemptible, despicable.

1965–70 *DARE* (Qu. HH22b, *. . A very mean person . . "He's meaner than _____."*) 23 Infs, **chiefly NJ, PA, NY**, Cat shit; **NJ53**, Cat shit and a damn sight nastier; **NJ20, NY59, PA29, 108, 202, VT12**, Cow (or hen, hog, owl's, skunk, snake, whale) shit; **PA245**, Lower than whale shit; **NY249, PA236**, Shit. [29 of 31 total Infs male] **2001** *DARE* File **csWI**, She's meaner than cat shit—wouldn't do a favor for anybody if her life depended on it.

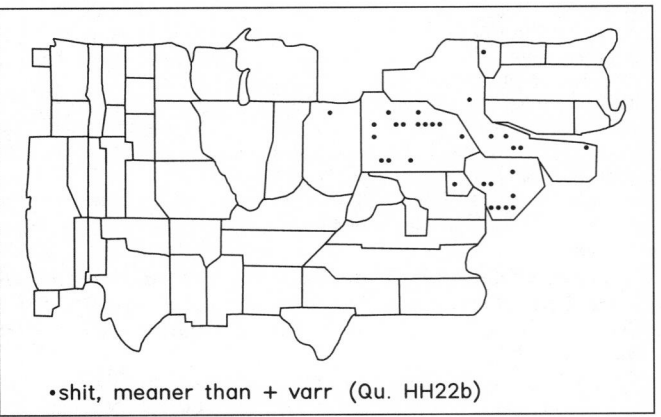

•shit, meaner than + varr (Qu. HH22b)

shit on a stick n Also *hot shit on a stick, shit on the ~* [Cf *OED2 shit-sticks* (at *shit* v. 4)] Cf **something on a stick**

An important or consequential person or thing; a big deal.

1965–70 *DARE* (Qu. GG19b, *When you can see from the way a person acts that he's feeling important or independent: "He seems to think he's _____."*) Infs **CO**22, **GA**1, 13, **IL**45, **IN**45, **KY**10, **LA**2, **MO**27, **TX**28, Shit on a stick; **LA**46, Shit on a stick but he ain't fart on a splinter; (Qu. HH8, *A person who likes to brag*) Inf **NY**241, Thinks he's hot shit on a stick; (Qu. II23, *Joking names for the people who are, or think they are, the best society of a community: The _____*) Inf **TN**53, Shit on the stick; (Qu. NN12b, *Things that people say to put off a child when he asks, "What are you making?"*) Inf **MI**33, Shit on a stick.

shitpoke See **shitepoke**

shitquick n
=**great blue heron.**
1945 McAtee *Nomina Abitera* 26 **FL**, Great Blue Heron . . shitquick, Lake Okechobee, Florida. . . As the badge worn by wardens of the National Audubon Society bore the figure of a heron, local citizens dubbed the organization the Shitquick Society.

shit-roller n Also *shit-bug* [See quot]
A **dung beetle.**
1967–68 *DARE* (Qu. R30, . . *Kinds of beetles; not asked in early QRs*) Inf **CO**7, Tumblebug—gets into a cow pie and gets out a hunk to roll [FW: Inf calls them shit-rollers.]; **IA**27, Shit-rollers—roll manure; **IA**29, Shit-roller—same as tumblebug; **OH**22, Shit-roller; **TN**22, Shit-bug—same as tumblebug.

shit-stomper See **shit-kicker**

shittim bark See **chittamwood 4**

shittimwood See **chittamwood**

shitty n
=**great blue heron.**
1967 *DARE* (Qu. Q10, . . *Water birds and marsh birds*) Inf **WA**30, Blue heron or shitepokes or shitties.

shitweed n
A **coneflower 1.**
1960 [see **piss-a-bed 2**].

shitworm n Cf **manure worm**
An **earthworm** such as a **red worm 1.**
1966 *DARE* (Qu. P5, . . *The common worm used as bait*) Inf **MI**32, Shitworm—come out of manure piles, look like an angleworm, but striped like a zebra, yellow and red.

shiv n¹ See **chive**

shiv n² See **shive** n¹

shivaree n Usu |ˌʃɪvəˈri|; also |ˈʃɪvəˌri|; for addit varr see **B1** below Also sp *chivaree, chiveree, chiverie, chivoree, shevaree, shiver(r)ee;* by folk-etym, *chivalree, shivering* For *charivari* and similar forms see **A** below [By dissim from Fr *charivari* [ʃarivaˈri]]

A Forms. Pronc-spp *cari-vari, charivari, chiravari, chivirari, sherrie-varrie* **scattered, but esp LA** *now esp freq among LaFr speakers* Note: It is often not clear to what degree spp that follow or approximate the std Fr *charivari* are meant to represent the actual pronc.

1805 [see **B2** below]. **1843** *Knickerbocker* 21.45, There is a pleasant custom . . that is nowhere more duly observed than at Idleberg. I refer to the *charavari.* **1857** (1930) DeLong *Jrls.* 9.165 **NY**, Had a grand Charivari of Gray and his bride formerly Miss Spencer. **1859** [see **B2** below]. **1883** [see **B2** below]. **1886** Amer. Philol. Assoc. *Trans.* 17.45 **Sth**, Chiravari (pron. chivaree, sort of horn-serenade). **1890** [see **B1** below]. **1891** *DN* 1.158 **cNY**, Chivirari. **1965–70** [see **B1** below]. **1966–68** [see **B2** below]. **1967** [see **B2** below]. **1984** [see **B1** below]. **1986** Pederson *LAGS Concordance (Shivaree)* 12 infs, **LA**, Charivari; 1 inf, **wLA**, Charivari wedding. [All infs LaFr speakers who offered proncs of the type [ʃaˈrɪvaˌri, ʃaˈrɪvaˌri]].

B Senses.
1 A noisy celebration or mock serenade for newlyweds; hence v *shivaree* to hold such a celebration for (a couple); to cele-

brate in such a way; vbl n *shivareeing.* **widespread, but less freq Atlantic, Gulf States exc FL** See Map and Map Section Cf **belling** vbl n², **bull band, callithumpian, horning** n 1, **serenade, skimmelton**

1843 (1916) Hall *New Purchase* 445 **IN**, In those days, was prevalent a custom derived from the Canadians, called *Chevrarai;* or, as pronounced by us . . *Shiver-ree.* . . The Shiver-reeing was done by a collection of all physical bodies capable of emitting sounds from a sugar kettle to a horse-shoe . . and all, at a signal, let off at once under the windows . . of the marriage house. *Ibid* 446, But the Shíver-ree was used, also, to annoy any unpopular person or family. . . The moment always chosen to begin the concert, was when the parties stood before the parson. **1848** Bartlett *Americanisms* 74, Charivari. (Commonly pronounced *shevaree.*) **1856** (1930) DeLong *Jrls.* 9.52 **NY**, George and Mrs. Stafford married got gloriously drunk and had a grand chiverie. **1890** *Daily Register* (Mobile AL) 3 Oct 4/5 (*AmSp* 21.176), The four came to town last night in company with about twenty others, for the purpose of charivaring a friend recently married. **1902** *DN* 2.231 **sIL**, [ʃivəˈri]. . . A boisterous serenade at a wedding. **1905** *DN* 3.65 **eNE**, Shivaree. . . Charivari. "They were given a shivaree." *Ibid* 74 **nwAR**, [ʃivəˈri]. . . To give a burlesque serenade to a newly married couple. 'They [ʃɪvərɪd] 'em.' The noun has recessive accent—[ˈʃɪvəri]. **1909** *DN* 3.415 **nME**, Shivaree. . . To serenade a newly-married couple with horns, bells, drums, etc. *Ibid*, Shiveree. . . A mock serenade to a newly-wedded couple. **1923** *DN* 5.244 **LA**, Shiveree. . . A noisy night procession around the house of a couple just married. **1944** *PADS* 2.60 **MO**, Shivaree [ˈʃɪvəˌi]. . . A boisterous party for newly-weds at which guns are fired into the air, bells are rung, etc., and at which the newly-weds are supposed to serve candy, cigars, and the like to the crowd. **1946** *Chicago Tribune* (IL) 11 Sept 31/2, *Do You Remember 'Way Back When.* . . We kids would "shivaree" at the neighborhood weddings until the bridegroom tossed us coins with which to buy treats? **1949** Kurath *Word Geog.* 78, Serenade. . . Regional and local terms . . *chivaree* . . in northern Vermont, New Hampshire and Maine . . the westernmost part of Virginia and the adjoining part of Kentucky. **1962** Atwood *Vocab.* TX 67, Burlesque serenade. . . is invariably designated in this area as a *shivaree.* . . There is no indication in Texas that the *shivaree* implies dislike of the wedded couple or that it is restricted to any particular type of wedding. **1965–70** *DARE* (Qu. AA18, . . *A noisy neighborhood celebration after a wedding, where the married couple is expected to give a treat*) 453 Infs, **widespread, but less freq Atlantic, Gulf States exc FL**, Shivaree; **AK**1, **OK**7, **RI**17, **WI**12, 27, 76, [ˌʃɪvəˈri]; **IL**118, **OK**50, **SD**3, **TN**2, [ˈʃɪvəˌi]; **FL**18, 19, [ˈʃɪvəri]; **FL**17, [ˈʃɪvəˈri]; **IL**57, [ˌʃevəˈri]; **MA**72, [ˈʃɪvəre]; **MI**64, [ʃɪˈvavəi]—most people mispronounce that word; **NE**6, [ˈʃɪvəˌi]; **OH**57, [ʃɪˈvɑri]; **PA**126, [ˈʃɪvere]; **IL**60, Shiveree dance; **IL**51, 118, **IN**82, Charivari [ʃəˈrɪvəi]; **IL**131, **KY**25, Charivari; **WI**21, Charivari [ʃərɪvəˈri]; (Qu. AA17, . . *Other people beside the bride and groom . . in a wedding party*) Inf **PA**104, Shivaree. **1967** *DARE* File **cLA**, Chiverees—When a couple married we'd wait up on the wedding night (then no one went on the honeymoon—too pore [sic]) we'd silently, about 11 p.m. begin to blow whistles, ring bells bang windows, and get them out of bed for cake and coffee. **1970** Tarpley *Blinky* 229 **neTX**, *Noisy burlesque serenade after a wedding* . . chivaree [111 of 200 infs] . . chivalree [rare] . . shivering [rare]. **1982** Slone *How We Talked* 11 **eKY** (as of c1950), To "chivoree" someone—on the night of a wedding. **1984** Head *Brogans* 116 **eKY, eTN**, A wedding which took place

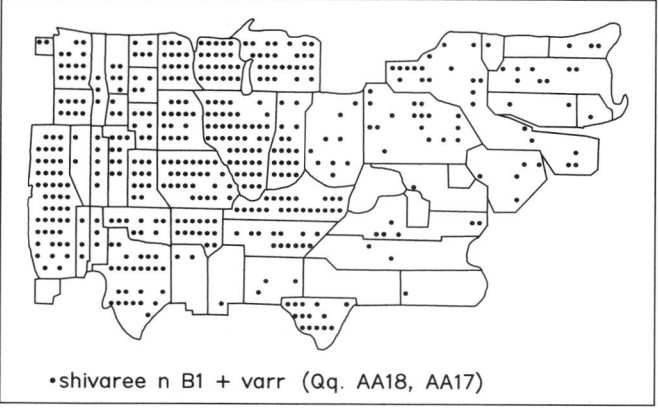

•shivaree n B1 + varr (Qq. AA18, AA17)

when I was a child . . was celebrated with due ceremony by the friends of the young couple. They were "cari-vari-ed" (chivareed) or serenaded with tin can music and the groom was ridden on a rail until he begged to be let off. **1990** Pederson *LAGS Regional Matrix* 208, [*Shivaree* occurs both as a noun (181 infs) and verb (72 infs) chiefly in **AR, LA, ceTX,** and **sMS.**] [*DARE* Ed: Some of these infs are also included in quot 1986 at **B2** below.]

2 Spec: such an event staged to call attention to a remarriage or to an unusual or unpopular marriage; hence v *shivaree* to inflict such a spectacle on (a couple); vbl n *shivareeing.* **chiefly Lower Missip Valley, esp LA** See Map

1805 in 1843 *Amer. Pioneer* 229 **New Orleans LA,** *Sherri-varries.* . . consist in mobbing the house of a *widow* when she marries. . . The house is mobbed by thousands . . ; hundreds are seen on horseback; many in disguise-dresses and masks; and all have some kind of discordant and noisy music. . . It [=a three-day *sherri-varrie*] was made extreme because the second husband was an unpopular man, of humble name, and she was supposed to have done unworthily. . . [*Amer. Pioneer* Ed: At a later period, Edward Livingston, esq., was *sherri-varried* here.] **1843** [see **B1** above]. **1859** (1860) Creecy *Scenes South* 47, The *charivari* is another extraordinary custom, in some respects peculiar to New Orleans, which is indulged in, generally, when an odd, unequal, or *uneven* pair is *married*—as a very young man to an elderly woman, or . . a very rich man marries a very poor girl, or . . when a fine-looking man marries a hard-featured woman . . or when a man or woman of doubtful or questionable blood marries one whose blood is thought to be pure and unmixed, or when old bachelors and maidens . . unexpectedly become Hymen's victims. **1883** (1919) Cable *Old Creole Days* 201 **LA,** "What is it you call this thing where an old man marries a young girl, and you come out with horns and"— "*Charivari?*" asked the Creoles. "Yes, that's it. Why don't you shivaree him?" **1961** *PADS* 36.11 **sLA,** *Shivaree.* . . In southern Louisiana the custom is usually confined to weddings in which one of the parties has been married before. **1966–68** *DARE* (Qu. AA18, . . *A noisy neighborhood celebration after a wedding, where the married couple is expected to give a treat*) Inf **LA20,** Charivari [ˌšɑrɪvɑˈri]—that's when a single boy marries a widow; **LA33,** Charivari [šɑˈrɪvɑri]—for when one has been married before; **AL30,** Shivaree—if one is a widow or widower; **LA6,** Shivaree—when somebody is married the second time, they shivaree; **LA14,** Shivaree—it was usually for a remarriage of a woman; **LA16,** Shivaree—for a second marriage; **LA25,** Shivaree—for a marriage in which one has been married before; **LA28,** Shivaree—when one of the couple has been married before; **LA31,** Shivaree—only where one of 'em is a widow; **LA40,** Shivaree—usually for a second marriage or for people who get married after they are older than usual marriageable age; **MN3,** Shivaree—used to have them more long ago, for older couples; **MS6,** Shivaree—older couples who have been married before; **MS72,** Shivaree—this is done when older couples whose mates have died marry; **MO10,** Shivaree—now it's done only on second marriage; **MO16,** Shivaree—this is done only for the widows; **TX9,** Shivaree—only when one mate was married before and is now divorced; **TX12,** Shivaree—only when an older couple get married; **TX31,** Shivaree—only if one had been previously married. **1967** LeCompte *Word Atlas* 276 **seLA,** *Noisy burlesque serenade after a wedding.* . . charivari [18 of 21 infs]. . . The *charivari* is particularly associated with hazing of a person marrying for a second time. **1986** Pederson *LAGS Concordance (Shivaree)* 22 infs, 16 **LA,** Shivaree; 13 infs, **LA,** Charivari. [*DARE* Ed: All infs describe *shivaree* as a hazing (or the carrying out of such a hazing) following a marriage regarded as

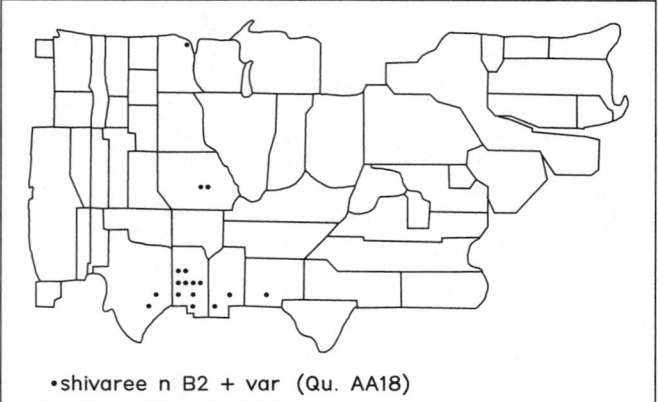

•shivaree n B2 + var (Qu. AA18)

diverging from the community norm, such as that of widows, widowers, or the divorced, or when the ages or races are incommensurate, etc.]

shivaree v, **shivareeing** See **shivaree** n **B1, 2**

shive n¹ Also *shiv(v)*

1 =**needle 1,** esp of the **juniper 1.** **ME**

1851 (1856) Springer *Forest Life* 80 **ME,** My . . clothes were considerably torn and thoroughly wet, and the shives of the old bough bed were sticking into them nearly as thickly as a fleece of porcupine quills. **1860** *Harper's New Mth. Mag.* 20.447 **ME,** Naught disturbs their [= lumbermen's] heavy slumbers . . unless, perchance, a startling cry of "Fire!" and insidious flames darting through the dry hemlock shives . . wake them with sudden alarm. **1913** *DN* 4.5 **ME,** Shives. . . The needles of the juniper tree. Northport. **1941** *Nature Mag.* 34.139 **ME,** In northern Maine, spills is the indigenous term for the leaves of pine, those of juniper being known as shives.

2 A broken fragment or splinter of wood; also fig. [*OED2 shive* sb.² 1 "*Obs. exc. dial.*"] Cf **shiver** n **1**

1958 McCulloch *Woods Words* 162 **Pacific NW,** Shiv (or *shivv*)—A splinter which comes out of the chipper too long to be pulped; hence something no good. The term has worked its way back to the woods in this sense.

3 See quot. Cf **shiver** n **2**

1967 *DARE* (Qu. B33a, *The first thin ice that forms over the surface of a pond or pool: "There's just a _____ of ice."*) Inf **AR52,** Shiv.

shive n² See **chive**

shiveling owl n Also *shivel owl* Cf **shivering owl**

A **screech owl 1** (here: *Otus asio*).

1934 Vines *Green Thicket* 85 **cnAL,** "Oh, listen, there's an old scrootch owl," she said. "The little old shivelin owl," Clay replied. **c1940** *LAMSAS Materials,* 4 infs, **NC, SC,** Shivel owl; 1 inf, **NC,** Shiveling owl. [3 of 5 infs Black]

shiver v

1 To split, splinter (wood); also transf; hence ppl adj *shivered.* [*OED2* c1200 →]

1688 (1892) Hammond *Diary* 148 **MA,** I find ye post I was by shivered on 3 sides [by lightning]. **1901** *DN* 2.147 **NY,** Shiver. . . A child's word for *grate, v.* "Let me shiver the potatoes for you." Gouverneur, N.Y. **1902** *DN* 2.245 **sIL,** Shivered, adj. Splintered; wind-racked, as a tree. **1903** *DN* 2.329 **seMO,** Shiver. . . To split. 'The tree was shivered by lightning.' **1907** *DN* 3.226 **nwAR,** Shivered, adj. Splintered. *Ibid* 236 **nwAR,** Shiver, v. tr. To split. **[1924** *DN* 5.277 [Exclams], Shiver my timbers. [*DARE* Ed: now formulaic and unlikely to be understood in its literal sense]] **1986** Klinkenborg *Making Hay* 27 **wMT,** We walked past a homemade logsplitter where Russ and the boys shiver kindling for Russ's mom's woodstove.

2 See quot.

1927 *DN* 5.477 **Ozarks,** Shiver. . . To propel, to throw, to fire. "They done shivered four bullets inter Jim Yancey 'fore he c'd git t' whar his weepon was at."

shiver n Cf **shive** n¹

1 A fragment, splinter. [*OED2* c1205 →; "Now *rare* exc. in phrases"]

1832 (1919) Irving *Jrls.* 3.141 **NY,** By and by down comes the tree with great crash and breaks to shivers. **1899** (1912) Green *VA Folk-Speech* 382, Shivers. . . Pieces; atoms; the cup fell on the floor and broke to shivers. **c1920** in 1993 Farwell–Nicholas *Smoky Mt. Voices* 146 **sAppalachians,** A little shiver of bone come out.

2 See quot.

1968 *DARE* (Qu. B33a, *The first thin ice that forms over the surface of a pond or pool: "There's just a _____ of ice."*) Inf **CT14,** Shivers [ˈšɪvɚz] of ice.

shivered See **shiver** v **1**

shiveree, shivering See **shivaree** n

shivering owl n Cf **cold owl, freeze ~, quivering ~**

1 also *shiver owl, shivery ~:* A **screech owl 1** (here: *Otus asio*). [See quot 1931] **chiefly S Atl, Gulf States** See Map *esp freq among Black speakers*

1911 *Forest & Stream* 77.174 **NC,** *Otus asio.*—Shivering Owl,

Church's Island, N.C. **1923** WV State Ornith. *Birds WV* 22, The screech owl is sometimes called . . shivering owl. **1931** LA Dept. of Conserv. *Bulletin* 20.351, "Shivering owl" is in recognition of the "shivering" quality of its tremulous, wailing whistle, a doleful ditty that gives superstitious folk the "shivers" as well, for to some it means a death in the family! **c1940** LAMSAS Materials, [*Shivering owl* was the resp of 71 infs, most of them in coastal **NC** and **SC**. One **SC** inf gave *shivery owl*.] **1952** Brown *NC Folkl.* 1.589, *Shivering owl*. . . The screech owl.—Central and east. **1965–70** *DARE* (Qu. Q1, . . *Kind of owl that makes a shrill, trembling cry*) Infs **LA**7, **MS**81, **NC**3, 24, 85, 87, **OK**13, **SC**7, Shivering owl; **SC**24, Shivering owl [FW sugg]; if he takes up near your house, that forecasts a death in the family; if you turn your pockets inside out, they'll quit shivering; **SC**43, Shivering owl—used by some people; **NC**49, Shiver owl ['ʃɪvə aʊl]; (Qu. Q2, . . *Kinds of owls*) Infs **NC**13, 21, Shivering owl; **GA**3, Shivering owl—makes an awful shivering noise; small. [5 of 14 Infs Black] **1967** *DARE* FW Addit **SC**, Note the Santee River as a boundary of *shivering owl/screech owl.* . . My mother and father are from opposite sides of the river, and neither knew of the other's name for the bird, though both knew of its supposed forecast of death and of turning the pockets inside out to make him leave. **1969** Kantor *MO Bittersweet* 218, Another name [for the screech owl] is the Shivering Owl. **1972** [see **scrooch owl**]. **1986** Pederson *LAGS Concordance* (Screech owl) 9 infs, **Gulf Region,** Shivering owl; 2 infs, **MS,** Shivering owl = screech owl; 1 inf, **neAR,** Shivering owl—hollers when someone dies; 1 inf, **swAL,** Shivering owl—cry is a sign of impending death; 1 inf, **csGA,** Shivering owl—small one, brings bad luck; 1 inf, **seGA,** Shivering owl—small, noise gives you the creeps; 1 inf, **cMS,** Shivering owl—hollers like he's shivering; 1 inf, **ceMS,** Shivering owl—small, sits on ground at night; 1 inf, **cwMS,** Shivering owl = death owl/squinch owl; 1 inf, **nwMS,** Shivering owl—smaller; 1 inf, **seMS,** Shivering owl—small, makes strange noise; 1 inf, **ceTX,** Shivering owl—small, in graveyard, scary call; 2 infs, **nwGA, cwFL,** Shiver owl. [17 of 22 total Infs Black]

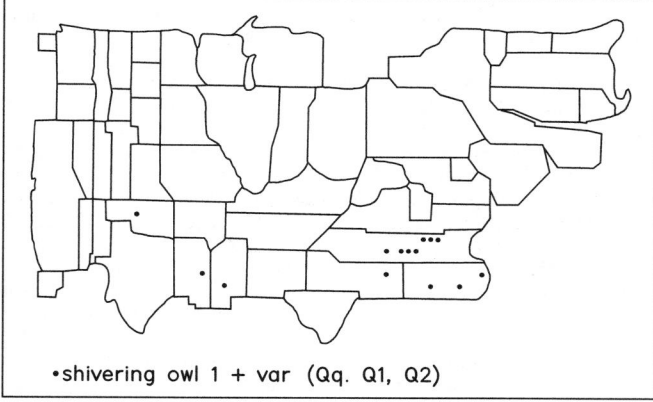

•shivering owl 1 + var (Qq. Q1, Q2)

2 See quot. Cf **screech owl 2, scrooch owl**

1986 Pederson *LAGS Concordance,* 1 inf, **nwFL,** Shivering owl—large, death omen, not screech owl.

shiver owl See **shivering owl 1**

shiverree See **shivaree n**

shivery owl See **shivering owl 1**

shives n pl [Pronc-sp for *chives.* This pronc of *chives* is given by Sheridan (*A General Dictionary of the English Language,* 1780) and a few of the later English orthoepists, and appears also in Engl dial.] *old-fash*

1948 WELS Suppl. **cnWI,** In my unabridged dictionary I do not find "shives," a plant which has a top which looks like that of an onion. **1950** WELS **WI** (*The small plants like onions with hollow green leaves that are cut up in salad*) 1 Inf, Chives, sometimes spelled shives; 1 Inf, Chives [ʃaɪvz]; 1 Inf, Chives—have heard pronunciation [ʃaɪvz], but it is not common. **1965–70** *DARE* (Qu. I7, *The small plants like onions with hollow green leaves that are cut up in a salad*) 39 Infs, **scattered,** Shives; **CA**151, **HI**11, **WI**25, Chives, shives; **MO**1, [FW: Inf acknowledged "shives"; repeated "chives."]; (Qu. I35, . . *Kitchen herbs . . grown and used in cooking around here*) Infs **CA**151, **NY**206, Shives; **AK**3, Some say "shives." [40 of 43 total Infs old; 15 gs educ or less]

shivv See **shive n**[1]

shlep See **schlepper**

shlepp v See **schlepp v**

shlepp n
1 See **schlepper.**
2 See **schlepp n 2.**

shlepper See **schlepper**

shlook v, n Pronc-sp *schlut;* cf "Pronc Intro" 3.I.14 [Ger *schlucken* to swallow, *Schluck* a swallow] **Ger settlement areas**

To swallow; a swallow.

1939 Aurand *Quaint Idioms* 19 [PaGer], I was so scared I nearly shlook'd (swallowed) my Adam's apple. **1964** *Ferhoodled Engl.* [5] [PaGer], Dunk your fastnacht (doughnut) but don't shlook (swallow) so fast. **1967–68** *DARE* (Qu. DD18, *A drink of liquor, or the amount of liquor taken in one swallow:* "He took a good _____.") Inf **MO**36, Shlook [ʃlʊk]; **SC**21, Schlut—"Let's take a schlut [ʃlʌt]"—the Charleston Germans, 25 years ago. **2000** *DARE* File **Milwaukee WI** (as of c1960), I remember my German-Bohemian mother using this word for a drink or gulp of liquid—usually medicine or liquor: "He took a big shlook of it and almost gagged."

shnibbel See **schnibble**

shnovvel See **schnabel**

shnozz See **schnozzle**

sho See **sure**

shoal v[1]

Of fish: to gather in shallow water, esp for breeding or spawning.

1933 *AmSp* 8.1.52 **Ozarks,** Shoal. . . To spawn. This is used particularly with reference to fish of the sucker family, which lay their eggs in shallow water. **1954** *Harder Coll.* **cwTN,** Shoal. . . To assemble for breeding or spawning.

shoal v[2] See **shool**

shoal duck n
=**eider duck.**

1807 in 1846 MA Hist. Soc. Coll. 2d ser 3.54 **seMA,** The birds, which frequent this and the adjacent islands, are . . the wild goose; the brant; the shoal duck [etc]. **1844** DeKay *Zool. NY* 2.333 **Long Is. NY,** The *Eider Duck* . . is known on Long island [sic] under the names of *Black* and *White Coot, Big Sea Duck,* and *Shoal Duck.* **1888** Trumbull *Names of Birds* 94, At Barnstable, Mass., *Shoal Duck* and *Isle of Shoals Duck;* the latter name being likewise heard at New Bedford, same state, and in Connecticut at Stonington and Stony Creek. **1925** (1928) Forbush *Birds MA* 1.264, *Eider. Other names:* American Eider; Shoal Duck [etc]. **1982** Elman *Hunter's Field Guide* 214, *American Eider* . . common & regional names . . sea duck, shoal duck [etc].

shoaling n [Cf *OED2 shoaling* vbl. sb.[1] 3 "Sc[ots dial]. Spearing fish in shallow water."]
The taking of fish stranded in shallow water.

1941 Writers' Program *Guide OK* 408, Red horse, a delicious, hard-fighting fish, varying in size from three to eight pounds, is seldom taken except during "shoalings." The floater fortunate enough to be on the river just after a period of high water and just before it has subsided to the normal stage may see a shoaling, a local term used to describe the taking of red horse. The flood carries them downstream over shoals to the deep pools, and as the water subsides they (like salmon) fight back upstream. In that period, a stretch of shoal water will sometimes seem to be choked with them. Then local shoaling parties rush to the scene with long heavy lines to which large hooks are attached at intervals of about six inches. The lines are thrown into the water in big loops and, though the hooks are not baited, the red horse take them or are caught by the gills as the lines are pulled in.

shoalwater trout n
=**lake trout 1.**

1884 Goode *Fisheries U.S.* 1.488 **swMI,** At Grand Haven there are two forms of Mackinaw Trout, known as the 'Shoal-water Trout' and the 'Deep-water Trout.'

shoat n Also sp *shote* [Transf from *shoat* a young hog; cf *EDD shoot* sb. 6 "A pig between a 'sucker' and a 'porker'; a term of contempt for a young person."] **esp NEast**
Used as a derog term for a person—esp in phr *poor shoat.*

1809 Weems *Life George Washington* 38, The poorest shoat, if wearing the proud epaulette of a Briton, might command a Wolfe, if so unlucky as to be an American. **1844** Stephens *High Life in NY* 2.155 **CT,** I'm afeard he's a gone shote. *Ibid* 205, I'll settle your hash for you, you mean old shote! **1867** Lowell *Biglow* 107 **'Upcountry' MA,** Long'z you elect for Congressmen poor shotes thet want to go. **1869** Stowe *Oldtown Folks* 134 **MA,** Where a plague is that lazy shote of a boy. **1899** (1912) Green *VA Folk-Speech* 384, *Shote. . .* A trifling worthless fellow: as, "a poor shote." *Shote.* **1903** *DN* 2.300 **Cape Cod MA** (as of a1857), *Shote. . .* In expression 'a poor shote,' a shiftless person. **1953** *AmSp* 28.254 **csPA,** *Shoat, shote. . .* A worthless fellow. 'He's a pretty poor shoat.' Popular speech. **1979** *AmSp* 54.99 **sME** (as of 1899–1910), *Shoat. . .* "He's a poor shoat."

shock n[1] [Transf from *shock* a conical pile of sheaves of grain or stalks of corn] Cf **shook** n, v[2]

1 also *hayshock*, rarely *chock*: A small, round pile of hay in a field; hence v *shock*, rarely *chock* to gather (hay) into small piles; vbl n *shocking*. **chiefly Midl, Sth, West** See Map Cf **cock** n[2]

1891 *PMLA* 6.174 **TN,** *Shock* is the usual word for a conical pile of hay. **1902** *DN* 2.245 **sIL,** *Shock. . .* A cock, as 'A shock of hay.' **1906** *DN* 3.123 **sIN,** *Shock. . .* Cock, as of hay. **1909** *DN* 3.403 **nwAR,** *Shock. . .* Cock, as of hay. "The field was full of little shocks of hay." **1937** *AmSp* 12.107 **eNE** [Farm terms], *Cocking* is done by hand with a pitchfork by laying three or four forkfuls on top of each other. Also called *shocking*. **1946** *PADS* 5.37 **VA,** *Shock. . .* A pile of hay in the field at haying time; common everywhere. **1949** Kurath *Word Geog.* 54, *Hay cock. . .* For the temporary small heaps of hay in the meadow two regional terms are widely current, *cock* in the New England area and the North Midland, *shock* in the Southern area and in the South Midland. **1958** *AmSp* 33.272 **eWA** [Ranching terms], *Shock. . .* A small pile of hay, forked from the windrow for drying and for ease in loading. **c1960** Wilson Coll. **csKY,** *Hayshock* is rarely used to mean haystack; usually a shock is a small pile out in the field, not a stack. **1965–70** *DARE* (Qu. L12, . . *The small piles of hay standing in the field*) 251 Infs, **chiefly Midl, Sth, West,** Shocks; 73 Infs, **Midl, Sth, West,** Hayshocks; **MS58, OK52,** Shocks of hay; **LA3,** Chock of hay; (Qu. L14, *A large pile of hay stored outdoors*) 12 Infs, **scattered Sth, S Midl,** Shock; **LA8, MS87,** Hayshock; **NC49,** Big shocks; (Qu. L11, *What do you do to hay in the field after it's cut?*) 23 Infs, **Sth, S Midl, West,** Shock it; **MS81,** Chock it; **AR18, CO12,** Rake (it) and shock it; **CO33,** Mow and shock it; **MS58,** Shock it up; **UT3,** Put it in shock [sic] and later stack it; **MO35,** Put it up in shocks; **OK18,** Rake it and put it in small shocks. **1968** *PADS* 49.13 **Upper MW** (as of c1950), There are a few examples of regional farm terms increasing in usage. *Hay) shock,* the Southern and Midland term for the small pile of hay in a field, is increasing while the Northern term, *hay) cock,* is decreasing. **1971** *AmSp* 46.182, Words with Midland and Southern designations brought to Chicago by recent migrants, especially blacks: . . hay shock. **1983** *MJLF* 9.1.55 **ceKY,** *Shock . .* a small pile of hay.

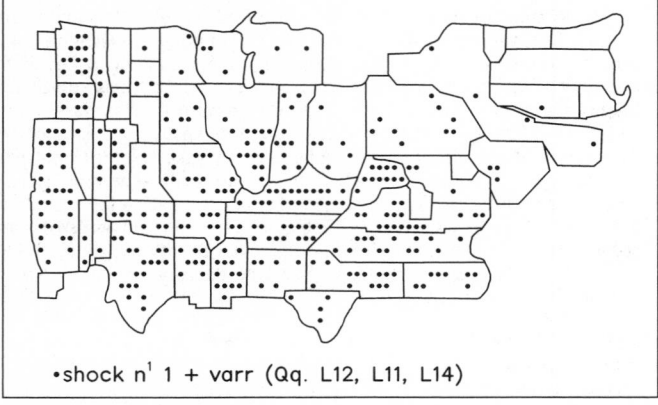
•shock n[1] 1 + varr (Qq. L12, L11, L14)

2 pl: Great numbers, lots. [*OED2* c1430 →]
1938 Matschat *Suwannee R.* 159 **neFL, seGA,** The little-un will need shocks of things from home.

shock v[1], hence vbl n *shocking* [Var of **shuck** v[1]] **chiefly NEng**
To remove an outer covering from; to remove from an outer covering; also fig; see quots.

1856 Reynolds *Peter Gott* 266 **neMA,** They are employed in shocking them, as it is called, that is, in opening the shells and taking out the clam, which is done with a small, stout knife. **1881** Ingersoll *Oyster-Industry* 248 **NEng,** Shock. . . To open or "shuck" clams or oysters. **1894** *DN* 1.333 **NJ,** *Shuck, shock:* to open oysters. To husk corn. **1941** *LANE* Map 260 *(To shell beans)* 1 inf, **seME,** [ʃɒˑk bijnz]. **1975** Gould *ME Lingo* 252, *Shock*—Shuck; to remove the shells or husks from about anything. Also, to *shock* off a jacket or boots. One exception seems to be crabmeat; clams are *shocked* but crabmeat is picked. An attentive ear will observe that Mainers sometimes *shock* one thing and shuck another. Clams almost always get *shocked*, but green peas may get shucked. **1977** *Yankee* Jan 112 **Isleboro ME,** What you do to a clam when you open it with a knife is called shocking.

shock n[2] [Scots dial] **chiefly NEast**
A paralytic stroke.

1818 *N. Amer. Rev.* 7.255, A paralytic shock compelled him to retire in December, 1779. **1860** *New Englander & Yale Rev.* 18.346, He had a shock of paralysis, which took away his power of speech. Another shock . . closed his life. **1903** Wiggin *Rebecca* 279, We had three o' the worst shocks in our family that there ever was . . and I know every symptom of 'em better 'n the doctors. **1908** Wasson *Home from Sea* 60 **sME coast,** He up and died all of a sudden, and quick's ever Ezry learnt the news, he took a shock like. **1910** *DN* 3.448 **cwNY,** *Shock. . .* Stroke of apoplexy. **1915** (1916) Johnson *Highways New Engl.* 131 **VT,** He'd only taken a few mouthfuls when he gave a kind of groan, and his right hand dropped by his side. He'd had a shock, and when I spoke to him he really didn't act as if he knew much. **1916** Lincoln *Mary-'Gusta* 28 **MA,** Cal'late my head must have stopped goin'; maybe the shock I had a spell ago broke the mainspring. **1926** *DN* 5.389 **ME,** *Shock. . .* A paralytic stroke. "He has had a shock." Universal. **1959** *VT Hist.* 27.156, *Shock. . .* A paralytic stroke. Common. **1966–69** *DARE* (Qu. BB6, *A sudden feeling of weakness, when sometimes the person loses consciousness*) Inf **CT6,** Shock; **NH11,** She had a shock; **MA73,** Might be a shock; (Qu. BB7, *A feeling that lasts for a short while, with difficult breathing and heart beating fast*) Inf **NH11,** Shock; **NY86,** Shock; (Qu. BB14, *To suddenly become unconscious and fall: "Just as she came to the door she _____."*) Inf **NH11,** Had a shock [FW: apparently used for *stroke*]; (Qu. BB49, . . *Other kinds of diseases*) Inf **MA5,** Apoplexy—some form of a shock, i.e., a stroke; **MA6,** Shocks—strokes. **1968** *DARE* FW Addit **cwNY,** *Shock*—"a stroke of apoplexy." **1980** *DARE* File **cnMA** (as of 1920s), I never heard any word for a paralytic stroke but *shock* when I was growing up.

shock n[3] See **shuck** n[1] **1b(1)**

shock v[2] See **shock** n[1] **1**

shock fodder n Cf **blade fodder, fodder 1**
Fodder consisting of stalks and blades of corn cut and arranged in shocks in the field.

1845 (1930) Sewall *Diary* 280 **IL,** Shucked out a little shock fodder. **1949** Hornsby *Lonesome Valley* 12 **eKY,** Chester was up in the cornfield, getting a sledload of shockfodder. **1963** Allen *Legends & Lore S. IL* 269, Farmers . . thus would have a few weeks of rest before time to strip cane, cut shock fodder, sow wheat, gather in the fall crops, and arrange a wood supply for the winter.

shocking vbl n[1] See **shock** n[1] **1**

shocking vbl n[2] See **shock** v[1]

shod See **shoe 1**

shodded, shodden See **shoe 3b**

shoe v
Std sense, var forms.
1 infin: usu *shoe;* also *shod.*
1937 in 1976 *Weevils in the Wheat* 216 **VA** [Black], Presently slaves

begin to cut timber, an' marser had us wid oxen drawin' timber to build de vessels wid. Haulin' was so hawd, dey had to shod de oxen's feet.

2 past: usu *shod;* also *shoed.*

    1906 *DN* 3.156 **nwAR,** *Shoed,* v. pret., pp. Shod. "The blacksmith shoed my horse." **1946** *PADS* 6.29 **eNC** (as of 1900–10), *Shoed.* . . Past tense and past participle of *shoe.* . . Common. **1947** *PADS* 9.18 **seIA** (as of 1915–40), *Shoed* [*DARE* Ed: as in quot 1946]. **1986** Pederson *LAGS Concordance,* 1 inf, **neMS,** Shoed the horse.

3 past pple, ppl adj: usu *shod;* also:

a *shoed.*

    1906 [see **2** above]. **1946** [see **2** above]. **1947** [see **2** above]. **c1960** *Wilson Coll.* **csKY,** *Shod* (sometimes *shoed*). . . With shoes nailed on, as a horse. **1965–70** *DARE* (Qu. K49, *You take a horse to the blacksmith to have it* _____) 193 Infs, **widespread,** Shoed. [Of all Infs responding to the question, 73% were old; of those giving this response, 58% were old.] **1965** *DARE* Tape **MS61,** I have been the blacksmith for about forty years, and I have shoed a many, a many of horses and mules. **1970** GA Dept. Ag. *Farmers Market Bulletin* 5 Aug np, Beautiful 3 yr. old paint mare. exc. conf., perf. halter mare, over 15 hands, just reshoed. **1986** Pederson *LAGS Concordance,* 1 inf, **ceAL,** Had my horse shoed; 1 inf, **seAL,** Have them shoed.

b *shodded, shodden.*

    1899 (1912) Green *VA Folk-Speech* 383, *Shodden.* . . Past participle of *shoe.* **1967** *DARE* (Qu. K49, *You take a horse to the blacksmith to have it* _____) Inf **MO21,** Shodded. **1986** Pederson *LAGS Concordance (Horseshoes)* 1 inf, **cwMS,** Shodded (p[ast] p[article]).

c *shone.*

    1970 *DARE* (Qu. K49, *You take a horse to the blacksmith to have it* _____) Inf **OK56,** Shone [šon].

shoe-around See **shoo-round**

shoebe(e), shoebie See **shoobie**

shoe-black plant n Also *shoe-black, shoe plant* [See quots] =**China rose.**

    [**1837** J. Macfadyen *Flora Jamaica* 1.66 *(OED2),* The flowers, from the mucilaginous juice they contain, are employed to give a polish to the leather of shoes; and hence the plant has received the name of the shoe-black.] **1900** Lyons *Plant Names* 190, *[Hibiscus] Rosa Sinensis* . . Shoe-black plant. . . *Flowers* yield a black dye. **1965** Neal *Gardens HI* 557, Red hibiscus, Chinese hibiscus. . . When crushed, the red flowers turn black, yielding dark purplish dye; they are used in India for blacking shoes (hence "shoe-black plant") and in China by women to dye hair and eyebrows. **1982** Perry–Hay *Field Guide Plants* 60, *Hibiscus rosa-sinensis* . . China rose; rose of China; shoe plant.

shoed See **shoe 2, 3a**

shoehead cat n
Perh a **channel catfish** or a **flathead catfish 1.**

    1967 *DARE* (Qu. P1, . . *Kinds of freshwater fish* . . *caught around here* . . *good to eat*) Inf **AL17,** Shoehead cat; **SC40,** Shoehead cat—all head.

shoelace See **shoestring 3**

shoe-leather express n Cf **shank's mare**
One's own feet (as a means of transportation).

    1934 (1940) Weseen *Dict. Amer. Slang* 64 [Hoboes and tramps], *Shoe leather express*—Walking; traveling afoot. **1969** *Capital Times* (Madison WI) 13 May 9 **ceFL,** When I was . . using the old "shoe leather express." **1970** *DARE* (Qu. Y24, . . *To walk, to go on foot: "I can't get a ride, so I'll just have to* _____.") Inf **PA243,** Go by shoe leather express. **1984** Wilder *You All Spoken Here* 148 **Sth,** *Shoe leather express:* Pick 'em up an' lay 'em down. **2000** *NY Times* (NY) 27 June sec D 3/3, San Diego to New York on the Shoe Leather Express. . . Mittleman . . ran and walked an average of 52 miles a day.

shoemake See **sumac**

shoemaker n[1]

1 =**hog sucker.**

    1836 Richardson *Fauna Boreali-Amer.* 3.120, *Cyprinus (Catastomus* [sic] *) nigricans.* . . This species is . . an inhabitant of Lake Erie, where it is known to the fishermen by the names of 'Shoemaker,' and 'Black Sucker.' **1903** NY State Museum & Sci. Serv. *Bulletin* 60.104, *Catos-*

tomus nigricans. . . *Hog Sucker; Stone Roller.* . . The name, shoemaker, was formerly applied to this species in Lake Erie, perhaps on account of the resemblance of its color to that of shoemaker's pitch.

2 also *shoemaker-fish:* A **threadfish** (here: *Alectis crinitus*).

    1862 Acad. Nat. Sci. Philadelphia *Proc. for 1861* 36, *Blepharichthys crinitus* . . "Shoemaker." **1884** Goode *Fisheries U.S.* 1.326, The Thread-fish—*Blepharis crinitus.* This fish, also known as the "Shoemaker-fish," is found along our coast from Cape Cod to the Caribbean Sea, as also on the Pacific coast of tropical America. **1906** NJ State Museum *Annual Rept. for 1905* 259, *Alectis crinitus* . . Shoe Maker.

3 =**rainbow runner.**

    1884 Goode *Fisheries U.S.* 1.332 **FL,** *Elagatis pinnulatus.* This West Indian fish, known at Key West as "Skipjack" or "Runner," and at Pensacola as "Yellow-tail" or "Shoemaker," is, according to Stearns, "abundant on the western and southern coasts of Florida." **1946** LaMonte *N. Amer. Game Fishes* 37, Rainbow Runner . . Names . . Skipjack, Shoemaker. **1976** Tryckare et al. *Lore of Sportfishing* 108, Rainbow Runner. . . Other common names . . skipjack, shoemaker.

4 An inept worker or professional; see quots.

    1936 *Hench Coll.,* [Prison language:] *Shoemaker*—a poor lawyer. **1958** McCulloch *Woods Words* 163 **Pacific NW,** *Shoemaker*—A doggone poor logger. **1988** *Spinner* 4.135 **seMA** (as of c1938) [Rubber industry jargon], *Shoemaker:* A crude, inefficient, unskilled workman in the rubber fabrics and hard rubber plants. (Not in the footwear factories.)

shoemaker n[2] See **sumac**

shoemaker berry n Also *shoemaker's berry, shumaker* [Folk-etyms for *shoemake,* var of **sumac**]
A **sumac;** see quots.

    1926 *Torreya* 26.5 **GA,** *Rhus copallina* . . Shoemaker berry, Sapelo I[slan]d, Ga. **1940** Clute *Amer. Plant Names* 269, *Rhus copallina.* Shoe-maker's berry [etc]. **1943** Weslager *DE Forgotten Folk* 163, The following record . . applies only to the Cheswold Moors. . . Shoemaker Berry (Shoemaker—Smooth Sumac)[,] *Rhus glabra* . . Syrup for coughs and colds. **1974** Morton *Folk Remedies* 127 **SC,** Sumac; "shumaker" . . *Rhus copallina.*

shoemaker-fish See **shoemaker** n[1] **2**

shoemaker's berry See **shoemaker berry**

shoemaker's black team n [Cf *EDD shoemaker's black galloway* (at *shoemaker* 1) "one's feet, 'Shanks' pony'"] Cf *DS* Y24
One's own legs (as a means of transportation).

    1897 *KS Univ. Qrly.* (ser B) 6.91 **neKS,** *Shoemaker's black team:* on foot.

shoemaker's heels n
A **goosefoot** (here: *Chenopodium bonus-henricus*).

    1900 Lyons *Plant Names* 95, *[Chenopodium] Bonus*–Henricus. . . Shoemaker's-heels [etc]. [*DARE* Ed: This may have been based on a British source.]

shoe mold See **mold** n[1]

shoe-mouth n chiefly **S Midl**
The opening on the top of a shoe that accommodates the tongue—usu in phr *shoe-mouth deep* to the height of the top of a shoe; ankle deep.

    1890 *Scribner's Mag.* 7.56 **AR,** Mud ain't more'n shoe-mouth deep. **1903** *DN* 2.329 **seMO,** *Shoe-mouth deep.* . . Ankle deep. **1914** *DN* 4.112 **cKS,** *Shoe-mouth.* . . The opening where the shoe is laced. **1917** *DN* 4.417 **wNC,** *Shoe-mouth.* . . "The fog is friz shoe-mouth deep on the mountains." **1920** *DN* 5.86 **NC,** *Shoe-mouth,* the opening down the front of a laced shoe. **1923** *DN* 5.220 **swMO,** *Shoe mouth deep.* . . To a depth equal to the height of an ordinary shoe, as in mud or snow. **1927** *AmSp* 2.364 **cwWV,** *Shoe-mouth* . . deep as the mouth of a shoe. "The snow was shoe-mouth deep this morning." **1938** Stuart *Dark Hills* 230 **KY,** When the farmers dug them out of the mine, they had to wade in a puddle of blood shoe-mouth deep to get to Ennis. **1939** *Hall Coll.* **wNC, eTN,** They said he was a-steppin' on the ground so hard he went in shoe-mouth deep. **1942** *AmSp* 17.130 **IN,** *Shoe-mouth deep* (said of mud, water, snow). 'The water was shoe-mouth deep on our front walk this morning.' **1946** *Harder Coll.* **cwTN,** [Letter:] It come a snow snowed all night and all day to day it is shoe mouth deep and Elsie made some snow cream. **1951** Porter *Ragged Roads* 21 **OK,** I "browsed" around through the wagon yards, wandered up and down Main Street, which in places was shoe-mouth deep in worn-out hay and sand. **1967** *DARE* FW Addit **TN12,** "The apples are shoe-mouth deep" meaning "the ground is covered with apples." **2001** *NADS Letters* **AR,** An old friend used to say, "It rained to my shoemouth."

shoenaher n [Perh *shoe* or Ger *Schuh* + Ger *Näher* one who sews] Cf **shoemaker** n[1] **1**
=Missouri sucker.
   1887 Goode *Amer. Fishes* 436, The Black Horse, *Cycleptus elongatus,* also called "Missouri Sucker," "Gourd-seed Sucker," "Suckerel" and "Shoenaher" is found in the river channels of the Ohio and Mississippi.

shoepack n Also *shoepac* [Folk-etym < Delaware trade jargon *seppock, sippack* shoes] Cf **bootpack, larrigan, pac**
Orig a moccasin; later a usu high-topped waterproof rubber-soled shoe or boot, esp with a leather upper.
   1755 in 1898 Hamilton *Letters to Washington* 1.99, It would be a good thing to have Shoe-packs or Moccosons for the Scouts. **1824** Doddridge *Notes Indian Wars* 144 **sAppalachians,** Those who could not make shoes, could make shoepacks. These like moccassons were made of a single piece of leather with the exception of a tongue piece on the top of the foot. . . To this the main piece of leather was sewed. . . To the shoepack a soal was sometimes added. **1916** [see **pac**]. **1920** Lewis *Main Street* 82 **MN,** All over town small boys were squealing . . "Look at my shoe-packs!" **1923** *DN* 5.237 **swWI,** *Shoepack.* . . boot-pack. **1949** Guthrie *Way West* 1, Seeing the path lead down to the muddy barnyard and the tracks of his shoepacks splashed in it, Lije Evans was just as well satisfied that things were wet. **1965** Bowen *Alaskan Dict.* 29, *Shoe pac.* A boot with a flexible, waterproof moccasin lower. Most shoe pacs have laced, leather legs or uppers and rubber bottoms or lowers. Shoe pacs are worn with felt inner soles and thick socks and are normal gear for winter and swamp travel. **1966** *DARE* Tape **ME1,** [FW:] What kind of boots did they use? . . [Inf:] They used to use just all leather—what they called a shoepack. . . It was just like a shoe, only a top of about 6 inches high. It was just—just leather. **1969** Sorden *Lumberjack Lingo* 108 **NEng, Gt Lakes,** *Shoe packs*—Rubber bottoms with leather tops worn in cold weather. Worn with several pairs of socks. Same as packs. **1991** [see **pac**].

shoe-peg n[1]
1 See **shoe-peg corn.**
2 Either of two games; see quot. Cf **mumblety-peg**
   1967–70 *DARE* (Qu. EE5, *Games where you try to make a jackknife stick in the ground*) Inf **VA46,** Shoe-peg; (Qu. EE18, *Games in which the players set up a stone, a tin can, or something similar, and then try to knock it down*) Inf **LA11,** Shoe-peg—if you use your feet, it would be shoe-peg.

shoe-peg n[2] See **choupique**

shoe-peg corn n Also *shoe-peg* [From the resemblance of the kernels to the wooden pegs once used in shoemaking]
A variety of **Indian corn 1** with long, roughly cylindrical kernels.
   1856 Davis *Farm Book* 27 *(DA),* I planted the shoe peg corn on the lower part of the T ditch. **1942** Weygandt *Plenty* 96 **sePA,** There were no varieties of sweet yellow corn in those days . . that have never [sic] rivaled, in my estimation, the shoepeg or evergreen for juiciness and sweetness. **1969** *DARE* (Qu. I33, . . *Ears of corn that are just right for eating*) Inf **NJ56,** Sweet corn, sugar corn, shoe-peg, evergreen. **1979** McPhee *Giving Good Weight* 15, He doesn't even know what shoe-peg corn is. **1992** Rule *Everything* 180 **cwGA,** And she *always* took a hot dish to the house when somebody died. . . Once . . she stood there and gave the whole recipe for the escalloped corn she brought—it had to be shoepeg corn and all—to these people who were *grieving.* **1993** *DARE* File **nKY,** Shoepeg corn—my husband says it is corn which has tall thin kernels. His grandfather . . was native to the hill country of . . northern Kentucky. *Ibid* **TX,** Shoepeg corn I've seen in the stores—canned . . It's little white pieces of corn. **1999** *DARE* File, [Package label:] Green Giant Shoepeg White Corn.

shoe-pick See **choupique**

shoe plant See **shoe-black plant**

shoe-round See **shoo-round**

shoe sole n Also *sole* [From the resemblance]
Any of var comestibles; see quots.
   1930 *DN* 6.88 **sWV,** *Shoe soles,* a cook-shack term for fried beef. **1939** FWP *ID Lore* 244, The following is reported as the talk of a southwest Idaho cowboy: . . the coolie yells beans, and the cowboys fall in line to grab their shoe soles (pancakes) and snowballs (biscuits) and sheepdip (coffee). **1955** *Western Folkl.* 14.136 **CA** [San Quentin prison slang], *Shoesole.* Roast beef. **1968** *DARE* (Qu. H32, . . *Fancy rolls and pastries*) Inf **LA23,** Sole or shoe sole is a large, flat, sweet, sugar-coated pastry embedded with nutmeats. **1968** *DARE* File **neOH,** Shoe Soles— a crisp Danish Pastry, known variously as *Pecan Crisps, Elephant Ears, Danish.*

shoespoon n [Calque of Ger *Schuhlöffel*]
A shoehorn.
   1930 Shoemaker *1300 Words* 59 **cPA Mts** (as of c1900), *Shoe-spoon*—A lady's shoe horn. **1968** *DARE* FW Addit **csOK,** Shoe-spoon—shoehorn; old-fashioned. **1970** *DARE* File **nePA,** *Shoespoon*— a shoehorn. **1986** *Ibid* **csWI,** [Speaker from **NYC:**] Do you have a shoehorn? [Speaker from **WI:**] You mean a slipper-spoon, a shoe-spoon.

shoes, throw up one's v phr Also *heave up one's shoelaces;* for addit varr see quots **chiefly Nth, West** Cf **boots, throw up one's; socks, throw up one's**
To vomit profusely.
   1914 *DN* 4.81 **ME, nNH,** *Throw up Jonah,* also, *throw up yer shoe-taps.* . . To be extremely nauseated. **1950** *WELS* (To vomit a great deal) 3 Infs, **WI,** Throw up his (*or* your) shoes; 1 Inf, **swWI,** Almost threw up their shoestrings; 1 Inf, **cwWI,** Throw up the soles of your shoes. **1965–70** *DARE* (Qu. BB18) Inf **OH74,** Throw up his shoes; **NY219,** Throw up everything but his shoestrings; **NY150,** Throwed up all but your shoes; **WI44,** Throwed up his shoes; **CA202,** Gonna lose your shoes; **CA199, CO14, NY105, SC19,** Heave up your shoelaces (*or* shoe soles, shoe-tops); **MN42,** Heaved up his shoelaces; **TX65,** Lost his shoes; **NC33,** Puke up the soles of your shoes; **OH78,** Turn up your shoe-tops; **TX36,** Vomit up your shoes; [**NY209,** Bottom of his shoes was coming up]. [13 of 15 Infs old] **1973** Allen *LAUM* 1.369 **Upper MW** (as of c1950), *Vomit.* . . Throw up one's shoe soles. [1 inf, **SD**].

shoestring n, usu pl
1 Any of several plants with long, flexible stems or roots, as:
a also *prairie shoestring:* A **false indigo 1** (here: usu *Amorpha canescens*). Cf **devil's shoestring 5**
   1892 *Jrl. Amer. Folkl.* 5.94 **IL,** *Amorpha canescens,* shoestrings. **1896** *Ibid* 9.185 **MN, SD,** *Amorpha canescens* . . Shoe-strings, Minn.; Burnside, S. Dak. [Footnote to *shoe-strings:* From the long, tough roots]. . . *Amorpha microphylla* . . shoe-string, Burnside, S. Dak. **1929** Bell *Some Contrib.* **KS** Vocab. 190, A bit of legend connected with the *shoestring* plant is that the Indians used the fibrous stem of the plant as moccasin ties. *Ibid* **IA,** In Iowa, years ago, old settlers counted that it would be good farming land where the *shoestring* grew. **1937** Stemen-Myers *OK Flora* 236, *Amorpha canescens* . . Lead-plant or Shoe-strings. . . Prairies. Common. **1991** Heat Moon *PrairyErth* 242 **ceKS,** White settlers heard the long and slender lateral roots snap on the blade of their breaking plows, pop sharply like old bootlaces drawn too tight, and they named the plant prairie shoestring.
b =**trumpet creeper.** Cf **devil's shoestring 3**
   1924 Deam *Shrubs IN* 289, This vine [=*Campsis radicans*] in the Wabash bottoms where it is a menace to the farmers, is known as "hell-vine" and "shoe-strings."
c A **goat's rue** (here: *Tephrosia virginiana*). Cf **devil's shoestring 1**
   1953 Greene-Blomquist *Flowers South* 58, Shoe-Strings, Cat-Gut, Dolly-Varden *(Tephrosia virginiana).*
2 See **shoestring potato.**
3 also *shoelace, shoestring licorice:* A thin strand of licorice candy. **chiefly NYC, C Atl** See Map *old-fash*
   1965–70 *DARE* (Qu. H82b, *Kinds of cheap candy that used to be sold years ago*) Infs **NY27, 48, 90,** (Licorice) shoelaces; **NJ59, NY35, 65, PA52,** Shoestring licorice (*or* lickrish); **NY49, PA40, 49,** Shoestrings; **NJ29, PA26, 31,** Licorice (*or* lickrish) shoestrings; (Qu. H82a, *Cheap candies sold especially for schoolchildren*) Inf **DE3,** Shoelaces; **NY36,** Shoestrings. [13 of 15 Infs old]

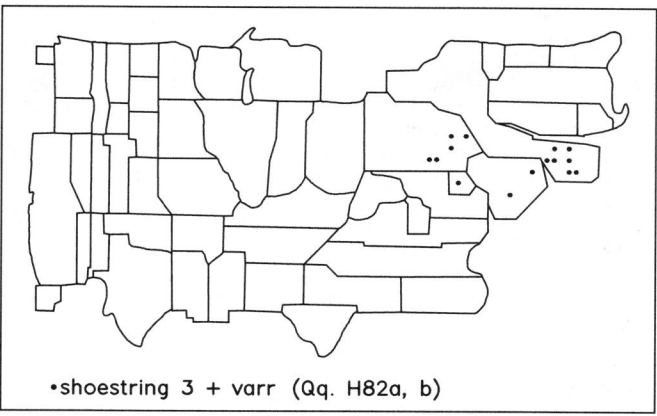

•shoestring 3 + varr (Qq. H82a, b)

shoestring fern n [See quot 1942]
A fern of the genus *Vittaria.*

   1942 Hylander *Plant Life* 112 **FL**, The narrow, grass-like fronds of the Shoestring or Grass Fern *(Vittaria)* form bunches of pendant dark-green along the trunks of the Cabbage Palms. **1969** Lyons *My Florida* 20, My Florida is . . shoestring ferns in the hammock's shade. **2000** (acc) U.S. Dept. Ag. *Plants Database* (Internet), *Vittaria lineata* . . shoestring fern.

shoestring fungus n
=**honey mushroom.**

   1938 Boyce *Forest Pathology* 110, *Armillaria mellea.* . . has also been referred to as honey agaric, oak fungus, and shoestring fungus. *Ibid,* The disease has also been called shoestring fungus rot [etc].

shoestring licorice See **shoestring 3**

shoestring potato n Also *shoestring* **scattered, but esp West, Lower Missip Valley** See Map
A thin strip of potato that is usu fried or deep-fried.

   1906 Hobart *Skiddoo* 30 **NYC**, The next course was French fried potatoes with some shoe-string potatoes on the side. **1931** B. Starke *Touch & Go* x.156 *(DA)*, I. . found that the word 'shoe-strings' on the menu really meant Julienne potatoes. I ate every last shoe-string. **1940** *Amer. Mercury* 51.42 **SW**, Old Fred Harvey . . [turned] a shoestring potato into a 2500-mile string of railroad eating-places. **1965–70** *DARE* (Qu. H47, *Kinds of fried potatoes*) 19 Infs, **esp West, Lower Missip Valley,** Shoestring(s); 9 Infs, **esp Lower Missip Valley,** Shoestring potatoes; **MS2, ND2, TX5, 9, 10, 69,** Shoestring—[same as] french fried; **KS8, OK51, TX1,** Shoestring—[same as] french fried, [only] smaller; **CO35,** Shoestring—[same as] french fried; sometimes made at home; **MI18,** French fried—we call them shoestrings here [FW: This term very prevalent here; verified with another Inf and noted in one restaurant.]; **TX15,** French fried—shoestring—thinner strips; **MD37,** Shoestrings—long strips of potato fried with onions; **NV7,** Shoestrings—narrow. **1978** *Sat. Review* 22 July 51 **NYC**, Me, it's the shoestring potatoes and the sirloin and a spinach salad on the side. **2002** *DARE* File—Internet, *Hot Shoestring Potato Salad.* . . 1 lb Medium Russet Potatoes, Cut Into Julienne Strips. . . Arrange Potatoes in A Single Layer in A Large Shallow Pan Coated With Cooking Spray. Bake at 450 F. For 30 Min.

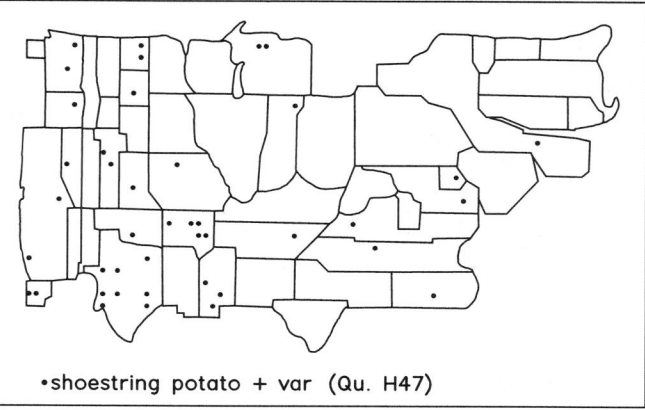

•shoestring potato + var (Qu. H47)

shoestring relation n Cf **shirttail** adj **2**
A distant relative.
   2001 *DARE* File **MO**, I think we're shoestring relations of some sort.

shoestring weed n [In ref to the stringlike vines or branches of these plants]
1 also *(wild) shoestring:* Either **poison ivy 1** or a **sumac.**
   1920 *Torreya* 20.22 **NC**, *Toxicodendron radicans* . . shoestring weed, Church's I[slan]d, N.C. **1968** *DARE* (Qu. S17, . . *Kinds of plants* . . *that* . . *cause itching and swelling*) Inf **MO9,** Wild shoestring. **1986** Pederson *LAGS Concordance (Sumac)* 1 inf, **cnLA,** Shoestring—has heard of—a bush.
2 =**coralberry 1.**
   1951 *PADS* 15.19 **VA**, *Symphoricarpos orbiculatus* . . shoestring weed, Rockbridge County, Va.

shoe, throw a v phr [Cf *throw a shoe* of a horse: to lose a shoe]
To lose one's temper.
   1967–69 *DARE* (Qu. GG15, . . *A person who became over-excited and lost control, "At that point he really _____."*) Inf **CO21,** Threw a shoe; [**KY65,** Blew his shoes;] (Qu. KK11, *To make great objections or a big fuss about something: "When we asked him to do that, he _____."*) Inf **TX43,** Threw a shoe; **TX37,** Throwed a shoe. **1995** *Signal Mag.* Dec np **cwTX**, *Throw a shoe*—"He th'oed a shoe." To get mad and express it.

shoetop cotton n
See quots.
   1941 Writers' Program *Guide AR* 59, After the destructive years of the War between the States, cotton again began to spread along the narrowest creek valleys and over the ridges, sometimes in patches so small there was barely room to turn a mule. It was here the "shoetop cotton" grew, and here it got its name from pickers who had to stoop nearly to the ground to gather the lint from scrubby plants. **1975** McDonough *Garden Sass* 245 **AR**, People of the Ozarks. . . call . . the short cotton of the mountains "shoetop cotton."

shonacker See **shonicker**

shone See **shoe 3c**

shoneehaw See **Shawnee haw**

shonicker n Also *schonocker, shonacker, shonnicker, shon(n)iker* [Etym unknown] *derog* Cf *DS* HH28
A Jew.
   [**1914** Jackson *Criminal Slang* 75, *Shoniker.* . . Current amongst cosmopolitan thieves, especially Jews. A neophyte or inexperienced hand at the game.] [**1927** *DN* 5.462 [Underworld jargon], *Shonniker.* . . A Jewish pawnbroker.] **1932** Farrell *Young Lonigan* 269 **Chicago IL** (as of 1916), Andy and Johnny O'Brien, the two youngest in the gang, stopped the shonickers. Sock one of 'em Andy, Studs said. Sa-ay, Christ Killer! Johnny said to his man. *Ibid* 271, Hit 'im again, he's ony a shonicker, said Davey. **1942** Berrey–Van den Bark *Amer. Slang* 385.12, *Jew.* . . shonacker, shonniker. **1964** *PADS* 42.33 **Chicago IL**, Jew . . shonicker. *Ibid* 45, My colleague . . suggests a derivation from Hanukkah /xánǝkǝ̀/ with the palatalization in American English of the unfamiliar velar fricative (/x/ > /š/) and with either a derivational (agentive) suffix /ər/ or simply excrescent /r/. [**1970** Feinsilver *Yiddish* 338, *Shon, shonk, shonky, shoncker, shonnicker*—These opprobrious terms for a Jew in England are supposed to have come from Yiddish *shoniker* (petty trader or peddler).] **1983** Allen *Lang. Ethnic Conflict* 61, Jews. . . *schonocker.*

shonny n
1 See **Shawnee.**
2 See **Shawnee haw.**

shonny haw See **Shawnee haw**

shoo intj[1] Cf **scat** intj
Used as a response when someone sneezes.
   1909 *DN* 3.403 **nwAR**, *Shoo, interj.* Sometimes said when one sneezes. **1968** *DARE* (Qu. NN18, *When somebody sneezes, what do people say to him?*) Inf **LA32,** Shoo.

shoo intj[2] See **shew**

shoo-ants oil n [Folk-etym for **insurance oil**]　Cf **insurance, showancy**

    1983 Reinecke Coll. **LA,** Insurance oil. . . Black folk etym. "shoo-ants oil." **1986** Pederson LAGS Concordance, 1 inf, **seLA,** Shoo-ants [=insurance] oil—scared away ants.

shoobie n　Also shoebe(e), shoebie, shub(i)e　[See quots]　**sNJ**　Cf **benny 3**

A person who visits the seashore for the day.

    1968 Sun. Bulletin (Philadelphia PA) 9 June mag sec 6/1 **sNJ,** "Well, there goes another Shoobie," he remarked with casual contempt. . . "A Shoobie? What's that?" "A Shoobie," he declared with satisfaction, "is a guy who comes down [to Atlantic City] for the day with his lunch in a shoe box." **1977–78** Foster Lexical Variation 28 **NJ,** Bennie, referring to tourists from New York City and North Jersey, is universal in Monmouth County. . . Shubie is the only form recorded in southern Ocean . . and Atlantic . . Counties. . . Shubie is probably related to shoe; a reference to Philadelphians who formerly came to the Shore on one-day excursions carrying their lunch in shoe boxes bears more weight than the explanation that only tourists wear shoes on the beach. **1986** DARE File **sNJ,** "Shoebe" ("shoebee"? "shube"?) . . has been used for at least forty years to refer to tourists, chiefly from the Philadelphia and New York areas, who visit the New Jersey shore. Apparently, the term alludes to their habit, at one time, of bringing lunch in a shoe box while visiting resorts like Atlantic City. **1997** Beach Haven Times (NJ) 27 Aug 19/1, That distinctively South Jersey expression "shoobie"—a person who visits the seashore for a single day, primarily to use the beach. . . [T]he origins of "shoobie" are back in the mid 1940s. . . We used to see strangers get out of their cars in their bathing suits . . but they were wearing street shoes to walk the graveled side streets up to the beach. "Here come the 'shoobies'," we would say. Their feet were too tender for the gravel. **2000** NADS Letters **NJ,** I heard the word from residents of Atlantic City. Shoebie or bee. Referring to day visitors to Atlantic City, years ago who came on day trip[s] from Philadelphia and carried their food in shoe boxes.

shoofly n

1 Any of var devices intended to ward off flies; see quots.

    1879 Glendale (Mont.) Atlantis 28 Dec. 4/4 (DA), A Dutchman drove rapidly along Main Street, with a new shoo-fly attached to his wagon, making forty flips a second. **1949** AmSp 24.113 **neSC,** Shoo-fly. . . A type of overhead fan, like the Indian punkah for dining room or living room, worked by ropes pulled by a servant stationed in another part of the house. **1967** DARE FW Addit **seLA,** Punkah—large fan suspended over table to shoo flies, operated by servant boy pulling a rope. Servants called it the "shoofly" ['ʃu,flaɪ]; **cnNY,** A shoofly—a paper flour sack shredded at one end & nailed to a stick at the other end—used to shoo flies.

2 A local train.　**scattered, but esp S Atl**

    1907 DN 3.249 **eME,** Shoo-fly. . . Suburban railway train. **1922** Gonzales Black Border 75 **sSC, GA coasts,** At 9 o'clock Sam arrived from Charleston on "de shoofly strain [sic]," as the negroes call the local which stops at all way stations. **1929** Macon (Ga.) Telegraph 2 July (News of Twenty Years Ago) (DA), There comes into Macon every morning on the Eatonton Shoo Fly a very old white woman. **1938** (1964) Korson Minstrels Mine Patch 318 **nePA,** Shoofly: Miners' work train. **1956** McAtee Some Dialect NC 39, Shoo-fly . . a railway train on a small branch line. **1967–69** DARE (Qu. N37, Joking names for a branch railroad that is not very important or gives poor service) Inf **GA89,** The shoofly—a train from Savannah, Georgia, to Montgomery, Alabama, around 1930; **TX5,** Shoofly. **1986** Pederson LAGS Concordance, 1 inf, **cnGA,** The Shoofly—a train from Atlanta to Lithonia; 1 inf, **ceGA,** The Shoofly—commuter train from Miller to Macon.

3 also shoofly ribbon, shu-fly: A necktie or ribbon bow worn around the neck.　**esp S Midl**

    1933 AmSp 8.1.52 **Ozarks,** Shoofly. . . The big bow of ribbon which some elderly mountain women wear as a necktie. **1940** AmSp 15.447 **eTN,** Shu-fly. Necktie. 'I like to wear my red shu-fly.' **1946** Richter Fields 278 **OH,** Huldah had gone with Amy MacMahon, a red shoofly ribbon low on both their necks. **1954** Harder Coll. **cwTN,** Shoo-fly. . . The big bow of ribbon which some elderly women wear as a necktie. **1983** MJLF 9.1.55 **ceKY** (as of 1956), Shoo fly . . a big bow or ribbon which elderly women wear as a necktie.

4 See **shoofly pie.**

5 A **wild indigo** (here: Baptisia tinctoria). [See quots]

    1893 Jrl. Amer. Folkl. 6.140 **WV,** Baptisia tinctoria, shoo fly. **1911**

Century Dict. Suppl., Shoo-fly. . . The wild indigo, Baptisia tinctoria: so called in allusion to the widespread belief that the mere presence of the plant attached to the harness will keep away horseflies. **1922** Amer. Botanist 28.31, "Horse-fly weed" "horse-flea weed" and "shoofly" alludes [sic] to the belief that sprays of this plant fastened to the harness will protect the horses from flies. **1951** Teale North with Spring 218 **NC,** The harvest of an American plant hunter may include badman's oatmeal, truelove, tread-softly, simpler's joy, lords-and-ladies, shoofly, nature's mistake [etc].

6 also shoofly plant: =**flower-of-an-hour.**

    1898 Jrl. Amer. Folkl. 11.224 **IA,** Hibiscus trionum . . shoo-fly. **1935** (1943) Muenscher Weeds 336, Hibiscus Trionum . . Modesty, Shoo-fly. **1949** Palmer Nat. Hist. 264, Bladder Ketmia. . . Known as modesty, shoofly . . devil's-head-in-a-bush [etc].

shoofly adj

Slipshod, shoddy, frivolous.

    1927 Kennedy Gritny 39 **sLA** [Black], "De Sperret goin' stop his shoo-fly ways one dese days; an' den dey ain' goin' be nobody kin tetch him raisin' his voice to give Gawd de praise he done helt back for so long;" the old church members would comment, after having listened to some of the "shoo-fly ballets." **1947** Ballowe The Lawd 220 **LA,** A tin-peddler, who made rounds from time to time, selling pots, pans, and shoofly jewelry to the hands on the plantation. **1956** Sorden–Ebert Logger's Words 31 **Gt Lakes,** Shoo-fly-sacking, Not sacking thoroughly. Not getting all of the logs thrown up on the river bank back into the river during a river-drive or following a log-jam.

shoofly pie n　Also shoofly (cake)　**chiefly PA**　See Map

A molasses pie or cake; see quots.

    1908 Lee–Hansey Std. Domestic Sci. Cook Book 286 (Popik Coll.), Shoo Fly Pie. Into a pie tin lined with crust pour mixture of 1 cup of New Orleans molasses and 1 cup of hot water in which 1 teaspoonful of soda has been dissolved. Sprinkle into the liquor mixture of 1 cup of brown sugar, butter the size of 1 egg, 2 cups of flour and cinnamon or nutmeg to taste. When soaked in, bake. **1932** Hench Coll., Mother told me that in Western Penna. the pie she always called Shoofly pie is called 'granger pie'. **1940** Sat. Eve. Post 30 Mar 42, No account of the Amish is complete without a mention of shoo-fly pie and schnitz pie. The former is a molasses crumb cake. **1949** Life 14 Nov 12, What are the ingredients of a shoo-fly pie, a regional dish of Pennsylvania? . . Molasses, baking soda, brown sugar, flour, shortening, salt and boiling water. According to some folklore experts, the term 'shoo-fly' comes from the sweet, syrupy substance of the pie, which attracts flies that have to be shooed away. **1950** Klees PA Dutch 425, The Shoofly is not a pie but a wonderful molasses cake with a rich pie crust below and a top covered with crumbs. . . Although counted as a breakfast cake, it is good at any hour of the day or night. . . Some prefer their shooflies gummy at the bottom and some do not. **1951** Reading Times (PA) 24 Sept. 20/1 (Mathews Coll.), Shoofly [sic] cake, speck and sauer-kraut, snitz and nepp and many other tasty dishes common to the inhabitants of the region were served. **1965–70** DARE (Qu. H63, Kinds of desserts) 11 Infs, **PA,** Shoofly pie; **PA9, 49,** Shoofly; **PA203,** Wet-bottom shoofly pie; (Qu. H45) Inf **OH80,** Shoofly pie; (Qu. H65, Foreign foods favored by people around here) Infs **NJ2, PA146,** Shoofly pie. [14 of 17 Infs old] **1977** Anderson Grass Roots Cookbook 52 **sePA,** "I don't often anymore make Shoo-Fly pies," admits Mrs. Rohrer, "because I have to have helpers to eat." **1998** Millersville Univ. Center for PA Ger. Studies Jrl. Au-

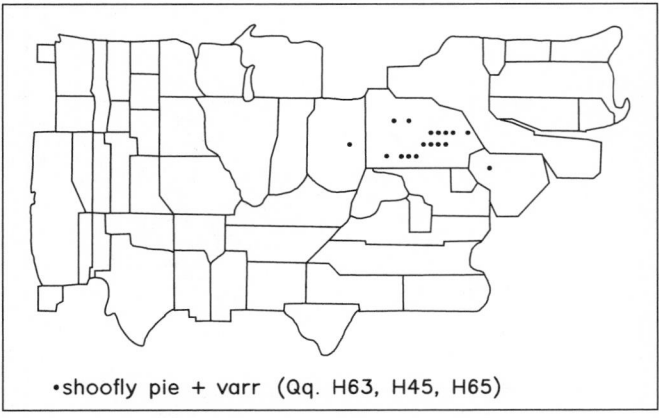

•shoofly pie + varr (Qq. H63, H45, H65)

tumn 11, Before leaving for the coal mine, she would hand him his water flask and lunch pail that she had prepared earlier. Inside the pail you might find several Lebanon bologna sandwiches, hard boiled eggs, and a large piece of shoofly pie.

shoofly plant See **shoofly** n 6

shoofly ribbon See **shoofly** n 3

shook v[1] See **shake** v 2

shook n, v[2] [Var of *shock;* this form is occas attested in Engl dial (see *OED2 shock* sb.[1].β, *EDD shock* sb.[1]), but may represent an independent formation infl by **stook** or *shook* a bundle of barrel or box parts]
A shock of grain; to gather into a shock.
   1939 *LANE* Map 126 (*Sheaf; shock*) 23 infs, **chiefly nNEng,** Shook [proncs of the type [šʊk]]; 1 inf, **neMA,** Shooking the wheat into bundles. **1965–70** *DARE* (Qu. L30b, *Then these sheaves . . are set together in piles called _____*) Infs **ME**12, **MO**11, **OK**53, Shooks; **IN**35, **MA**66, [šʊks]; **CA**97, **NH**12, **NY**198, **OR**10, **TX**31, Shook [FW sugg].

shooken See **shake** v 2a

shool v, hence vbl n *shooling,* n *shooler* Also *shoal, shul(e);* also with *around* [Cf *EDD shool* v.[1] 9 "To saunter, idle about;" 10 "To go about begging;" *shooler* (at *shool* v.[1] 9(1)) "An idle, lazy fellow."] **chiefly Atl, esp NEng**
To roam or idle about; to loaf; with *after:* to follow, go in search of.
   a1874 in 1949 *PADS* 11.36 **eME,** He knew I was not shuling around. **1887** (1895) Robinson *Uncle Lisha* 88 **wVT,** I wish 't the' wa'n't a haoun' dawg ner a fox in this wide-livin' world for men t' go shoolin' an' runnin' an' traipsin' arter. **1896** *DN* 1.424 **Nantucket MA,** *Shool:* to saunter. **1916** Macy-Hussey *Nantucket Scrap Basket* 144, "*Shooler*"—The old English verb "shool" is rarely heard, but its derivative, "Shooler" is still used occasionally, and is applied to any one who likes to roam about the shores or over the commons in search of a "mess" or a "voyage" of fish, clams, berries or game, or for any other object. **1946** *PADS* 6.26 **eNC** (as of 1900–10), *Shool* [ʃul]. . To waste time doing a task. . . Occasional. **1950** *PADS* 14.60 **SC,** *Shool.* . . To drag the feet in walking; to walk with a shuffle. **1953** Randolph-Wilson *Down in Holler* 283 **Ozarks,** A village preacher once told me that serenades are sinful, "just an excuse for young folks to go a-shoalin' round of a night." **1956** *AmSp* 31.137 **CT,** *Shool (shule)* 'to saunter.' This word . . has so far, I believe, been reported in America only from Nantucket Island. . . I should like to add to the record that *shool* passes current in Waterford, Connecticut. **1966** *DARE* (Qu. A9, . . *Wasting time by not working on the job*) Inf **AL**1, Shooling.

shoo-round n Also *shoe-(a)round* [Cf *EDD shoo* v.[2], *SND shue* v. 1 "To swing, rock or sway backwards and forwards"] Cf **play-party**
A party with games and dancing; a party game or dance.
   1918 *DN* 5.19 **NC,** *Shoe-round,* a common dance. **1935** Hurston *Mules & Men* 179 **FL,** The children played "Shoo-round," and "Chickmah-Chick." **1952** Brown *NC Folkl.* 1.589, *Shoe-around.* . . A country dance, a frolic, a party.—West. **1981** Pederson *LAGS Basic Materials* (*A dance*) 1 inf, **cLA,** [ˈʃuˑuˑˌraˑʔən] dance.

shoo-shoo n Also *shoo-shoo baby* [Prob echoic] **chiefly LA**
A failed firecracker that is later broken open and lit.
   1917 *DN* 4.420 **LA,** *Shoo-shoo* [šušu]. . . A fire-cracker that has failed to go off. The 'shoo-shoo' is broken and lighted for the flare of the loose powder. **1967–68** *DARE* (Qu. FF15, *When a firecracker doesn't go off, and you break it in the middle and light the powder, you call it a _____*) Infs **LA**23, 35, 37, Shoo-shoo [ˈšuˌšu]; **LA**20, Shoo-shoo [ˌšuˈšu]; **LA**46, Shoo-shoo; **HI**6, 9, Shoo-shoo baby.

shoo-shoo v [Cf *DJE susu* "To whisper (behind one's back); to gossip; to speak ill."]
   1935 Hurston *Mules & Men* 191 **FL,** Lucy and Ella were alternately shoo-shooing [Footnote: Whispering] to each other and guffawing.

shoot n
1 The discharge of a firearm; a shot. [*OED2 shoot* sb.[1] 1.a "Arch."] **esp S Midl**
   1775 *PA Eve. Post* (Philadelphia) 30 Nov 551/1 **VA,** The riflemen . .

declare that they can hit a man every shoot if within two hundred and fifty yards. **1891** *PMLA* 6.167 **WV,** *Shoot* is very common for *shot;* as, "he made a good shoot." **1899** (1912) Green *VA Folk-Speech* 383, *Shoot.* . . The act of shooting; the discharge as of a gun: as, "Let me have a shoot." **1908** Fox *Lonesome Pine* 84 **KY,** Eight fellers with bead on one another and not a shoot shot. **1913** Kephart *Highlanders* 91 **sAppalachians,** I fired a shoot as she riz in the air. **1926** *DN* 5.403 **Ozarks,** *Shoot.* . . substitutes for the noun *shot,* as in the sentence: "I heerd th' shoot, but I never seen nobody a-runnin'." **1939** Hall Coll. **wNC, eTN,** *Shoot.* . . Shot. He shot 'im—broke his neck the first shoot. . . I shot him nine shoots. **c1960** Wilson Coll. **csKY,** *Shoot.* . . A shot. "We heard two shoots down in the holler last night."
2 See quot. [Prob by analogy with *catch* a quantity caught at one time]
   1940 *AmSp* 15.52 **sAppalachians, Ozarks,** 'Josh came a-packin' his shoot' (animals killed in a hunt, a kill).
3 The quantity of an explosive used in a single discharge. [*OED2 shoot* sb.[1] 1.d "*Obs.*"]
   1974 Fink *Mountain Speech* 23 **wNC, eTN,** *Shoot* . . charges or loads, as *"two shoots of powder."* **1976** Garber *Mountain-ese* 81 **sAppalachians,** *Shoot* . . charge or load—They set off three shoots of dannymite in the rocks.

shoot an anvil See **shoot the anvil**

shoot and caboodle (or capoodle) See **caboodle**

shoot anvils See **shoot the anvil**

shoot dozens at one See **dozen** n B1

shooter n
1 A usu large marble, esp one propelled from the hand at other marbles. **widespread, but less freq NEng, Inland Sth, Lower Missip Valley** See Map Cf **taw**
   1927 *88 Successful Play Activities* 29, "*Shooter*"—Taw—Large marble (½ to ⅞ inch) shot from the hand. **1957** *Sat. Eve. Post Letters* **neIL** (as of 1910–20), Our "mibs" included "glassies, steelies, snotties, chickadees, bulls eyes, clays and shooters." **1965–70** *DARE* (Qu. EE6a, . . *Different kinds of marbles—the big one that's used to knock others out of the ring*) 310 Infs, **widespread, but less freq NEng, Inland Sth, Lower Missip Valley,** Shooter; **MI**49, **OK**58, Big shooter; **NC**36, **OH**88, Shooter marble; (Qu. EE7, . . *Kinds of marble games*) Inf **MI**19, Marbles were shot out of a circle with a shooter; (Qu. EE6b, *Small marbles or marbles in general*) Infs **MS**30, **NC**35, **ND**9, **PA**165, Shooters; (Qu. EE6d, *Special marbles*) Infs **CA**137, **PA**71, Shooters; **WI**40, Glass shooters. **c1970** Wiersma *Marbles Terms, Shooter.* . . Not quite so large as a boulder, but usually considered the second-largest marble. It is also used for shooting at the opponent's group of marbles. *Ibid* **swMI** (as of 1960), *Shooters.* . . A large marble. Like [a] Boulder. **1984** *WI State Jrl.* (Madison) 8 Apr sec 9 1/4, The better shooters are made of agate, usually chalcedony, a kind of quartz that has the luster of wax and contains a variety of colors sometimes referred to as cat's eyes, carnelian or neelies. **1986** Pederson *LAGS Concordance,* 1 inf, **csGA,** Shooter—special marble; 1 inf, **neFL,** Shooter—type of marble; 1 inf, **neFL,** Shooter—big marble.

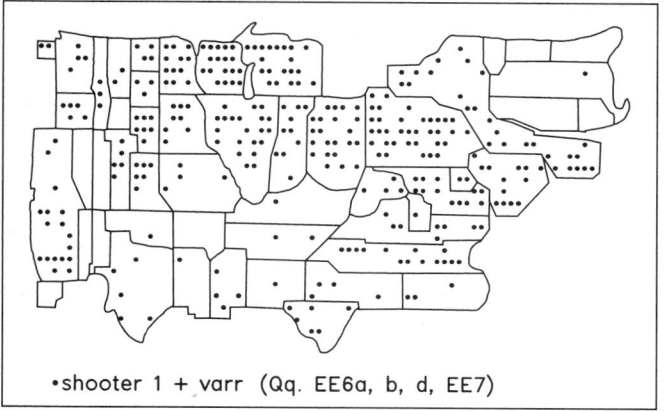

•shooter 1 + varr (Qq. EE6a, b, d, EE7)

2 pl: A marbles game; see quot 1976.
   1957 *Sat. Eve. Post Letters* **neNJ** (as of 1920–25), We played the fol-

lowing games. . . Alleys, shooters. . . shooters I believe originated possibly from the fact that one of our favorite marbles or alleys were used as a shooter. **1976** *WI Acad. Rev.* Mar 9/2 (as of 1920s), Another game similar to Mibs was called *Shooters,* in which only glass marbles were used. One or more players shot from talls [=taws] after properly calling the order of play backwards: there was an advantage in shooting last with opponent's shooters on the field. No ring was used, and only one shooter per player entered the game. The object of this game was to hit another player's shooter with yours. If successful, you kept the hit shooter and received another turn. The loser returned to talls to enter the game again with a new shooter. As many as five or six players made this game not only exciting but challenging as considerable skill was required. It was usually a game for older boys.

3 A drink or measure of liquor. **esp Sth**

1967–70 *DARE* (Qu. BB50a, . . *Favorite remedies . . for a cough*) Inf **NC69,** Shooter—a drink of liquor; (Qu. BB50b, *Remedies for chest colds*) Inf **NC69,** Shooter—a drink of liquor; (Qu. DD18, *A drink of liquor, or the amount of liquor taken in one swallow:* "He took a good _____.") Infs **SC40, VA35,** Shooter; (Qu. DD21a, *General words . . for any kind of liquor*) Inf **TX81,** Shooter—as in "have a shooter." **1971** *Car & Driver* Jan. 75/1 *(OED2),* He made his famous call for 'shooters.' Now in case you haven't heard, a 'shooter' is a Turner variation of the word 'shot', as in a 'shot of likker', and . . refers to a shot of Canadian Club mixed into a few fingers of 'Co-cola'. **1981** *NYT Mag.* (NY) 3 May 16/5, The word coming up fast for a *straight shot* is a *shooter.* "A shooter is a shot of liquor swallowed in one quick gulp," says Jeff Dee in Sarasota, Fla.

shoot fire See **shit fire**

shooting capoodle See **caboodle**

shooting cracker n Also *shooting popper* **PA, OH, MD, KY**
A firecracker.

1849 Howitt *Our Cousins in OH* 123, Some of the company brought Willie a large packet of shooting-crackers; not the little feeble things which he had hitherto been accustomed to, but seventy-five large red rolls, each of which would make a tremendous report—pop!pop!-bang!!—and not only help to keep all the dogs barking, but furnish him with the means of making a terrific noise on his own account, greatly to the joy of himself and his sisters. **1867** *Amer. Philos. Soc. Proc.* 10.344 **PA,** There was also a loud report, described as resembling the noise of a large shooting-cracker. **1890** Howells *Boy's Town* 110 **sOH,** The boys began to celebrate [Christmas] . . with shooting-crackers and torpedoes. **1957** Battaglia *Resp. to PADS 20* **eMD,** Other names for firecrackers: *Shootin cracker.* **1968–69** *DARE* (Qu. FF14, . . *Kinds of firecrackers*) Infs **KY54, MD25, 31,** Shooting crackers. **1983** *MJLF* 9.1.55 **ceKY** (as of 1956), *Shooting cracker* . . a fire cracker. . . *Shooting popper* . . a fire cracker.

shooting in the New Year vbl n
Celebrating the arrival of a new year by firing guns.

1950 Klees *PA Dutch* 354, "Shooting in the New Year" is one of the most firmly entrenched of New Year customs in the Dutch country. **1964** Smith *PA Germans* 101, In the past, many Pennsylvania Germans of the Shenandoah Valley were reminded of a New Year by being awakened during the wee hours by the loud voice of the captain of the New Year Shooters, who would call out, "Hello, Ben _____!" When a response was given, the captain recited a greeting which consisted of a series of verses, and the "Shooters" fired their guns and made other loud noises. Although the custom of "shooting in the New Year" is only a memory, some elderly residents still remember the shooters and others can describe their experiences as members of shooting parties.

shooting popper See **shooting cracker**

shooting star n
Std: a plant of the genus *Dodecatheon.* Also called **bird bill 1, cowslip 2, mosquito bill, pink n² 2, pinky-winky;** for other names of the common *D. meadia* see **compass plant 5, gentlemen-and-ladies, Indian chief 1, johnny-jump, lady's slipper 7, mad violet, prairie pointers;** for other names of var spp see **jack-in-the-pulpit 2h, rooster head 2, sailor's caps**

shooting taw See **taw**

shooting toy See **toy**

shoot, Luke, or give up the gun phr For varr see quots **esp S Midl**
You must act or give up the attempt—also used as a quasinoun.

1903 (1965) Adams *Log Cowboy* 294 **West,** It's either swim or say he's afraid to,—it's "Shoot, Luke, or give up the gun" with him. **1909** *DN* 3.369 **eAL, wGA,** *Shoot Luke, or give up the gun.* Imperative sentence, begin or give place to another. **1912** *DN* 3.589 **wTN,** *Shoot, Luke, or give up the gun.* . . Do something, or give somebody else the opportunity. **1919** *DN* 5.35 **KY,** *Shoot, or give up your gun.* An expression often heard when some one keeps threatening to do something, and doesn't. Knott Co. **1941** *AmSp* 16.24 **sIN, MO,** *Shoot or give up the gun.* **c1950** Halpert *Coll.* 39 **wKY, nwTN,** Shoot, Luke, or give up your gun (. . or give me the fowling piece) = hurry up and act or let someone else do it.

shoot one's face See **face n 1**

shoot out v phr
To throw away, discard.

2000 *DARE* File **cNY,** Some folks from the rural areas around Syracuse say "shoot out" in place of "throw out" or "throw away." A secretary I know says "Just shoot it out when you're done with it."

shoot the anvil v phr Also *shoot an anvil, shoot anvils* Cf **anvil** n
To explode black powder in a hole in a blacksmith's anvil as a celebratory noisemaker.

1946 McAtee *Dial. Grant Co. IN Suppl. 3* 9 (as of 1890s), *Shoot an anvil* . . use an anvil in Fourth of July celebration to put pressure on a charge of powder so that it would make a louder report upon exploding. **1956** *KY Folkl. Rec.* 2.96, "Shooting the anvil". . . This feat was accomplished by filling the large hole in the base of the anvil with black powder, . . and driving a wooden peg in the hole. The fuse would be lighted and the powder would explode with an earth-shaking roar. [*DARE* Ed: Hopkins and Webster Counties. 4th of July and Christmas noisemaker] **1967** Borland *Hill Country* 212 **NE,** A dozen of the town's young men got up at dawn and "shot the anvil". . . It was the Fourth of July. . . They took a blacksmith's anvil, set it in the middle of Main Street, and poured gunpowder into the hole that took the colter. . . The load was fused and wadded. The fuse was lit and everybody ran. When the blast went off it sometimes hoisted the anvil ten feet into the air. . . It was like a cannon blast. **1970** *DARE* (Qu. FF15, *When a firecracker doesn't go off, and you break it in the middle and light the powder, you call it a _____*) Inf **TX91,** Shooting an anvil—powder was exploded in a hole in an anvil. Done at Christmas. **1975** McDonough *Garden Sass* 198 **AR,** He also recalled that "depending if anybody had any money, they'd get a keg of powder and they'd get a couple of anvils and shoot the anvils. . . They'd shoot anvils then till they used up that keg of powder." **1984** Wilder *You All Spoken Here* 192 **Sth,** *Shoot the anvil:* Wake up the neighborhood for miles around by exploding black powder in the blacksmith's anvil. To properly shoot an anvil you remove it from the blacksmith's shop to the open, turn it upside-down and fill the hole in the bottom with black gun powder—a teacup is enough—and place another anvil or a heavy flat rock on top of the hole. Somewhere along here you lay a fuse or a trail of powder. . . Shooting the anvils used to be customary on special occasions such as Christmas Eve, New Year's Eve, and election nights. Or whenever the blacksmith took a mind to celebrate. **1986** Pederson *LAGS Concordance,* 1 inf, **seAR,** Shooting the anvil—on holidays; fuse; black powder.

shoot the hook See **hook, shoot a**

shord'n bread See **shortening bread**

shore berry n
=**chokeberry 1.**

1916 *Torreya* 16.238 **ME,** *Pyrus arbutifolia* (L.) var. *atropurpurea* . . Shore berry, Matinicus I[slan]d, Me.

shore day n
1957 Rose *Block Is.* 24 **RI,** A local term. When a fisherman has a 'shore day' he catches up on the tag ends, odd jobs he has to neglect when out. So it is with the man ashore. When major work is accom-

plished, the planting is done and the hoeing caught up, and naught but routine chores for a very brief interval, he catches up on his tag ends.

shore dinner n

1 A meal consisting largely of seafood served by the seashore; a set restaurant meal featuring a similar menu. **esp NEng**

1872 *Scribner's Mth.* 3.333 **RI,** It was announced in the bills as "a first-class shore dinner." . . The bill of fare on these occasions is inexorable, and consists of three courses and a dessert. First course: baked clams, with green corn and melted butter. Second course: clam chowder. Third course: baked fish, with raw tomatoes and cucumbers. . . Dessert: clamcakes, which are fritters made of clams chopped very small and fried in butter. **1885** *Bay State Mth.* 3.197 **Nantucket MA,** After a shore dinner at the Wauwinet House, and another stroll on the beaches, they started for the town on the yacht "Lilian." **1895** *Outing* 26.408 **NEng,** Happy-Go-Lucky Beach is proud of their achievements . . in the ordering of and presiding at a good shore-dinner. **1920** *DN* 5.83 **nwWA,** Shore dinner. Mrs. _____ gave a shore dinner at Sunlight Beach. **1939** Wolcott *Yankee Cook Book* 58, *New Hampshire Shore Dinner*—Clam or Fish Chowder . . Steamed Hampton River Clams with Clam Bouillon and Drawn Butter . . Broiled Rock Cod—Fried Clams . . Broiled Lobster—Potato Chips . . Corn on the Cob—Tomato and Cucumber Salad . . Rolls . . Apple Pie—Cheese—or Ice Cream . . Coffee. **1947** Paul *Linden* 267 **ceMA,** It was arranged for the party to eat at the Massasoit a shore dinner cooked by Jeff. **1966** *York Co. Coast Star* (Kennebunk ME) 28 Apr 6/5, Now Open / For the Season / Serving Everyday from 11:30 A.M. / Shore Dinners / Prime Steaks / Chicken / Luncheons / A La Carte Menu. **1975** Gould *ME Lingo* 253, *Shore dinner.* . . The *shore dinner* originated before the turn of the century at New Meadows Inn at West Bath, where it was a seafood meal prepared on a range and served at a table in the dining room. . . The meal began with fried and steamed clams, followed by a lobster stew or bisque. Then came a boiled lobster. Dessert was traditionally a thin sugar cookie . . with vanilla ice cream. **1978** *DARE* File **ME,** [Picture post card:] Down East Gourmet's Delight "Shore Dinner" Famed throughout the world as New England's greatest contribution in delightful food. **1994** Mariani *Dict. Amer. Food & Drink* 285, *Shore Dinner.* A large meal based mostly on fresh, locally caught seafood. The term is most readily associated with the eastern coastline cities from New York to Maine, where restaurants feature lavish spreads of steamed clams in clam broth, mussels, lobsters, and corn on the cob. In New York the offerings might include shrimp or crabmeat cocktail and broiled fish as well.

2 also *shore lunch:* A meal consisting primarily of the fish one has just caught.

1999 *DARE* File—Internet **Upstate NY,** To top a perfect day of fishing is the shore dinner. . . The guides of this section are famous for their ability to cook over an open fireplace. The guide will take you ashore at noon . . and prepare some of the morning's catch for your dinner. *Ibid* **MI,** Top notch guides, rod & reel, flies, leaders and—on full-day guided outings—a delicious shore lunch. **2001** *Ibid* **csWI,** When my husband goes on a fishing trip to the lakes and rivers of Ontario, the goal is always to catch enough fish early in the day for a shore lunch, or later for a shore dinner. *Ibid* **nWI,** On the Wisconsin Public Television program "Outdoor Wisconsin," the host told of a guide who would "serve up a cisco shore lunch" after a fishing trip on a lake.

shore lark n
=horned lark.

[**1731** Catesby *Nat. Hist. Carolina* 32, *The Lark.* In size and shape this resembles our Sky-Lark. . . They frequent the Sand-Hills upon the Seashore of *Carolina.*] **1771** Forster *Catalogue Animals N. Amer.* 12, Lark Shore—Alauda alpestris. **1808** Wilson *Amer. Ornith.* 1.85, [The] *Shore Lark.* . . is one of our winter birds of passage. **1903** Dawson *Birds OH* 1.198, Shore Lark. (This name is perpetuated solely through an accident of discovery, the type specimen having been described by Catesby from "the Seashore of Carolina.") **1927** Forbush *Birds MA* 2.364, The old term, Shore Lark, is a most appropriate name for this bird, as it is generally seen near the shore. Here it is equally at home on the beach, among the dunes, and in the salt marshes. **1928** Beston *Outermost House* 112 **Cape Cod MA,** The birds keep well up on the beach and never seem to venture close to ocean. This same shore lark, *Otocoris alpestris,* is perhaps the bird I encounter most frequently during the winter months. **1956** *MA Audubon Soc. Bulletin* 40.84 **MA,** Horned Lark. Shore Lark (Mass. Also in British folk usage. From being often observed along the seashore.)

shoreline n Cf *DS* N44

1984 *DARE* File **cwGA,** Strip of grass between the sidewalk and the curb. . . Fred Rutledge, a blind Black student, said he and his family and the folks around them call the strip *the shoreline.* Rutledge says they got it from their grandmother who grew up in La Grange, Georgia.

shore lunch See **shore dinner 2**

shore pine n

1 **=jack pine 1.**

1894 *Jrl. Amer. Folkl.* 7.100 **cME,** Pinus Banksiana. . . shore-pine, rock-pine, Grand Lake section of Penobscot River.

2 **=lodgepole pine.**

1908 Britton *N. Amer. Trees* 27, The Shore pine occurs chiefly along the coast from Alaska to Mendocino county, California. **1939** Medsger *Edible Wild Plants* 93 **CA,** When hard pressed for food, they [=Indians] also make use of the inner bark of two or three species of pines. The Shore or Scrub Pine . . is one of these. **1966** *DARE* (Qu. T17, . . *Kinds of pine trees;* not asked in early QRs) Inf **WA33,** Shore pine. **1980** Little *Audubon Guide N. Amer. Trees W. Region* 274, Shore Pine (var. *contorta*), the Pacific Coast variety [of lodgepole pine] is a small tree with spreading crown.

short adj

1 also *short-aged:* In comb with a noun specifying an animal's age: barely that age—used in comb *short yearling.* Cf **long** adj B4

1907 Love *Deadwood Dick* 52, Short yearlings were those over one year old and short of two years, long yearlings those two years and short of three years, tail end and scabs mean nearly the same thing, and comprise all the very young stock of all classes not yet reached the dignity of yearlings. [*DARE* Ed: This definition appears to be erroneous.] **1923** *DN* 5.225 **swMO,** A . . 'short' yearlin' is one . . less than a year old. **1935** *AmSp* 10.272 [Stockyard language], *Short yearlings.* Cattle too old to be called calves but less than a year old. **1937** *AmSp* 12.104 **eNE** [Farm terms], A *short yearling* or *short-aged* yearling lacks a little of being a year old. **1992** Atteberry *Sheep* 37 **swID, eOR,** They may be segregated by age (the short yearlings—that is, the ewe lambs about ten months old—two-year-olds, and so on).

2 Cheap; niggardly. **esp Gulf States** Cf **narrow** B1, **short John, ~ skate**

1967–68 *DARE* (Qu. U33, *Names or nicknames for a stingy person*) Infs **AR48, LA28,** Short; (Qu. U36b, . . *A person who saves in a mean way or is greedy in money matters:* "She certainly is _____.") Inf **LA15,** Short. **1986** Pederson *LAGS Concordance* (He is a [tightwad]) 2 infs, **cwLA, neTX,** Short.

short n Also *short lobster* Pronc-sp *shot* **esp ME**
An illegal, undersized lobster.

1966 *DARE* Tape **ME17,** Well they haul up the trap an' when they haul up the trap . . there may be one or two counters in it and maybe seven or eight lobsters in it but the rest of 'em are small, short lobsters, so they have to heave 'em overboard. **1969** *DARE* FW Addit **seCT,** Shorts—undersize lobsters. **1978** Merriam *Illustr. Lobstering* 79 **ME,** *Short*—A lobster under the legal size. **1983** *DARE* File **eME,** The word *shot* is Mainiac for short or illegal, undersized lobsters. There is a lobsterman's chanty about them which contains the lines "He put three shots in my lobster pots,/ But that don't frighten me." The chanty is about an enemy who put three short lobsters in the pots of another lobsterman on the wharf. This would make him subject to a $50 fine for each short.

short-aged See **short** adj 1

short-billed gar n Also *shortbill (gar)*
=shortnose gar.

1908 Forbes–Richardson *Fishes of IL* 35, The short-nosed gar. . . is locally known by Illinois River fishermen as the "duck-bill gar," though the name "short-billed gar" is commoner. **1933** LA Dept. of Conserv. *Fishes* 406, Short-Nosed Gar. . . Known also under the names of Duck-billed and Short-billed Gar. **1951** Harlan–Speaker *IA Fish* 49, Short-nose Gar. . . Other Names—Short bill, stub-nose gar, billy gar. **1983** Becker *Fishes WI* 241, Shortnose Gar. . . broadnosed gar, stubnose gar, shortbill gar [etc].

short bit n [*bit* a unit of value equal to 12 ½ cents] **esp West** Cf **long bit**

A dime; the sum of 10 cents.

1854 Paige *Dow's Patent Sermons* 4.219 (1912 Thornton *Amer. Gloss.*), The will, that cuts off an expectant heir with a 'short bit.' **1877** Wright *Big Bonanza* 268 **West**, The smallest coin in use is the bit, or ten-cent piece—sometimes spoken of as a "short bit," as not being twelve and one half cents, the "long bit." **1879** in 1944 *ADD* 59 **Pacific**, Short bit . . long bit. **1915** *DN* 4.245 **MT**, Short bit. . . Ten cents. "Gave two short bits for that." **1944** (1967) McNichols *Crazy Weather* 113 **SW**, "Buy yourself a short-bit's worth of toothache the next time you go to the Fort," he said, in way of reward. **1957** *Seattle Daily Times* (WA) 25 July 11, When dimes finally came in, they were called short bits, and eight of them passed for a dollar. When one bought something for a bit and tendered a 25-cent piece, he received a dime in change, and paid a long bit.

shortbread See **shortcake**

short bred n

A cow recently bred.

1994 *WI State Jrl.* (Madison) 4 Oct sec D 2, [Advt:] 120 short breds, 1000 lbs., bred 3–4 months. 150 short breds, 1100 lbs., bred 5–7 months. 80 Springers, 1250 lbs.

shortcake n Also *shortbread* =**shortening bread.**

1899 (1912) Green *VA Folk-Speech* 383, Short-cake. . . Corn bread made "short" by putting grease in it. **1940** Richter *Trees* 107 **OH** (as of early 19th cent), She used the kettle a third time to fry the shortcake in. **1967** *DARE* (Qu. H14, *Bread that's made with cornmeal*) Inf **MI68**, Cornbread—I've heard it called shortcake too. **1986** Pederson *LAGS Concordance* (Corn bread) 1 inf, **seLA**, Shortbread; shortcake—in skillet, but it rises a little.

short-circuit beetle n

A **powder-post beetle** (here: *Scobicia declivis*).

1949 Swain *Insect Guide* 141 **CA**, In California, a small bostrichid is called the "lead cable borer" and "short-circuit beetle" because of the frequency with which it penetrates telephone cables. **1954** Borror–DeLong *Intro. Insects* 381, One species in the family bostrichidae which occurs in the West, *Scobicia declivis* . . is rather unusual in that the adults often bore into the lead sheathing of telephone cables. . . This insect is commonly known as the lead-cable borer or "short-circuit" beetle.

short-coupled adj [By ext from *short-coupled* of a horse: having a relatively short back] Cf **long-coupled**

1958 McCulloch *Woods Words* 163 **Pacific NW**, Short coupled. . . A runty man.

short dog n esp **sAppalachians**

1 A dance step—used in phr *cut the short dog;* also fig.

1888 *Harper's New Mth. Mag.* July 294 **GA**, Unc' Tom . . uz er-jumpin' roun' cuttin' de short dog good es de bes'. **1946** *PADS* 6.11 **swVA, eNC**, Cut the short dog. . . To caper and frisk around when tipsy. . . Occasional among *bons vivants.*

2 A local train or bus.

1955 Ritchie *Singing Family* 266 **seKY**, Wouldn't a day pass . . but what five or six big long trainloads of coal would rumble by. Then no time passed before they went to hauling out limber and livestock and such on the freight trains. Then they sent the short dog on the tracks, too, for people to travel on. **1963** Edwards *Gravel* 151 **eTN** (as of 1920s), This little short-dog doesn't go any farther than Knoxville. Here you change to the Memphis Special. . . But I had learned something too: that was only a short-dog train. There were much better and faster trains. I would ride those some day. **1991** Still *Wolfpen Notebooks* 163 **sAppalachians**, Short dog bus: connecting line between Hindman and Vicco, Kentucky.

short-eared owl n

Std: a widely distributed owl (*Asio flammeus*) distinguished by short ear tufts. Also called **cat owl, cob ~, day ~ 2, field ~, hawk ~ 2, prairie ~ 2, pueo, swamp owl** See also **hunting owl, marsh ~, meadow ~** Cf **long-eared owl**

shortened bread See **shortening bread**

shortened dodger n

A **corn dodger 1** made with shortening.

1890 *DN* 1.64 **KY**, Dodger. . . "shortened dodger," in which the meal is made up with lard, or grease of some kind. **1909** *DN* 3.403 **nwAR**, Shortened dodger. . . Corn-bread, the meal of which is made up with lard or grease of some kind.

shortening bread n Also *shortened bread, shortening corn bread* Pronc-spp *shord'n bread, shortning ~* **Sth, S Midl** Cf **fatty-bread 1, shortcake**

Corn bread made with cooking fat, esp lard; often =**crackling bread.**

1898 *Century Mag.* 55.600 **KY**, "My Baby Loves Shortenin'-Bread." **1915** *Jrl. Amer. Folk.* 28.142 **eTN**, Run hyeur, mammy, run hyeur quick!/ Shord'n bread made baby sick. **c1920** in 1993 Farwell–Nicholas *Smoky Mt. Voices* 146 **sAppalachians**, Shortened bread. . . bread made with cooking fats. . . "My baby's sick; I believe it's [from] eatin' that shortened bread." **1946** *Ag. Hist.* Apr 97 **wNC, eTN** (as of 1870s), What gave to lard rendering its glow and its glamor was its byproduct, cracklings, the precious ingredient of "shortnin' bread," so celebrated in song and story. **1966** Dakin *Dial. Vocab. Ohio R. Valley* 2.318, Shortening bread (most often) = *fatty bread* (sometimes). These are names for corn bread baked with "lots of lard" shortening. **1967–69** *DARE* Tape **GA**81, That's what makes . . shortning bread. . . It's made with corn meal just like a corn bread, and then the cracklings . . where the lard has been rended out, they're real brown and crispy, an' that's crumbled up in the cornmeal . . and that's used instead of . . the other fat; **SC**46, Crackling bread was made with corn bread like making a corn pone. Put your cracklings in it and thoroughly mix it and bake it. Some call it shortening bread; some crackling bread. Same thing. **1969–70** *DARE* (Qu. H14, *Bread that's made with cornmeal*) Inf **NC**72, Shortening bread—cornbread made with ground cracklings left after rendering lard; (Qu. H18, . . *Special kinds of bread*) Inf **KY**74, Shortening bread = crackling bread. **1972** *PADS* 58.20 **cwAL**, Cracklin bread. Southern and South Midland *cracklin bread . .* is most frequent, with *shortening bread . .* as an apparent synonym. **1981** Howell *Surv. Folklife* 104 **neTN, seKY**, White corn meal was used for bread. . . The addition of cracklings, the crispy residue left from rendering lard or frying meat, made cracklin' bread or shortenin' bread. **1986** Pederson *LAGS Concordance* (Cornbread) 1 inf, **nwGA**, Shortening bread; 1 inf, **csTN**, Shortening bread—crackling bread; (*Other kinds of bread . . made from cornmeal*) 2 infs, **cnGA, cwMS**, Shortening bread—crackling bread; 1 inf, **cnAL**, Shortening bread; 1 inf, **cnGA**, Shortening corn bread—has cracklings in it; [*DARE* Ed: Addit resps] 1 inf, **nwAL**, Shortening bread—made with lard, in pones; 1 inf, **cAL**, Shortening bread—made from cracklings; 1 inf, **nwAR**, Shortening bread—made with cracklings in it; 1 inf, **ceTN**, Shortening bread—has grease in it; 1 inf, **csMS**, Shortening bread; 1 inf, **neGA**, Shortening bread—with cracklings.

short grass n, freq attrib **esp KS**

Any of var low, drought-resistant grasses, esp **grama grass 1** or **buffalo grass a,** characteristic of the high plains of the Central US; hence n *short-grass country* an area dominated by such grasses.

1844 Gregg *Commerce* 2.139, We succeeded in reaching a spot of short-grass prairie. **1897** *KS Univ. Qrly.* (ser B) 6.91 **neKS**, Short grass country: the western third of Kansas. **1900** *Congressional Record* 26 Jan 1222 **KS**, It is a part of the public domain, away out in what is called the short-grass country. **1929** Bell *Some Contrib. KS Vocab.* 254, Short grass country. . . Western Kansas; so-called because, on account of the arid climate, grass does not grow tall and rank, and short grass, especially *buffalo grass,* is that most found. **1944** Wellman *Bowl* 11 **KS**, The farmers of the Short Grass Country—as it was commonly called—labored against unrelenting handicaps. *Ibid* 82, It certainly had been powerful hot and dry, even for the Short Grass. Here it was, June yet, and the buffalo sod already curing and crumbling as in August. **1945** Wodehouse *Hayfever Plants* 53, Blue grama. . . Along with buffalo grass it constitutes most of what is known in the Middle West as "Short Grass". **1966–68** *DARE* Tape **KS**20, This is short-grass country; **SD**8, They take these cattle off the short-grass country here and go any place with them, they'd match the corn-fed beef. **1995** *Brophy Coll.* 67 **swMO** (as of c1960), Short-Grass Country. [W]estern Kansas, the Plains Proper.

short growth n

Failure of a child to grow as expected.

1965 *Good Old Days* 2.8.11 ceIL, "Short Growth" was if a child was poorly or skinny. The parent would measure him or her with a string of certain length to see just how tall they would grow to be. If the string came up short the child was given special cures and foods to correct their height. **1970** *DARE* File **PA,** *Short-growth.* . . Undergrowth, failure of growth in a child. "The child was pow-wowed for short-growth."

short handles n pl Cf **long handles**
Men's short underwear.

1968–69 *DARE* (Qu. W14, *Names for underwear, including joking names.* . . *Men's—short*) Infs **MO15, UT4,** Short handles; **VA2,** Short handles—heard. **1986** Pederson *LAGS Concordance,* 1 inf, **seMS,** Short handles—underwear.

shorthead mullet n Cf **muley carp**
A **redhorse 1** (here: *Moxostoma macrolepidotum*).

1983 Becker *Fishes WI* 665, *Moxostoma macrolepidotum.* . . Other common names . . redhorse mullet, common mullet, shorthead mullet, mullet.

shorthorn n

1 Someone not from Texas or the Southwest; an outsider; a neophyte, greenhorn.   **chiefly SW**   Cf **longhorn 2**

1885 Siringo *TX Cowboy* 75, Mr. Black was a Kansas "short horn" and he had brought his outfit of "short horn" men and horses, to drive the herd "up the trail." **1888** *Outing* 13.129 **SW,** Besides a few snipe killed at a swamp called by Shorthorns "cinky," from the Spanish *sieneca,* we still depended upon Uncle Sam's subsistence stores for our daily bread. **1896** in 1980 Turner *Earps Talk* 133 (as of 1877), In the vernacular of the feud the . . [Texans] were "longhorns," and the Northerners "shorthorns." **1897** Lewis *Wolfville* 115 **AZ,** 'Shall we take this he-shorthorn along?' An' he p'ints where them four tenderfoots is mixed up together in the back of the stage. **1907** White *AZ Nights* 321, "Say, boys, did you get into the *pisano*-looking shorthorn at Willets last week?" "Nope." "He sifted in wearin' one of these hard-boiled hats, and carryin' a brogue thick enough to skate on. Says he wants a job drivin' team—that he drives a truck plenty back to St. Louis, where he comes from." **1920** Hunter *Trail Drivers TX* 29 (as of 1884), This trip [on the Chisholm Trail] was made while working for Cul Juvanel, who was from Indiana and had a lot of Indiana boys with him, whom we called "Short Horns." *Ibid* 476 (as of 1883), We had some trouble in the Indian Territory. . . My boss, Zack Stucker, being a fighting man of some reputation, said that a "bunch of shorthorns could not turn him back," and we went straight ahead, ignoring the signboard instructions. **1925** Hunter *Trail Drivers TX* 550 (as of 1872), Before I got to the river, there came about twenty "short horns" armed with double-barreled shot guns. . . All at once there came a "short horn" on a big horse to where I was. **1933** *AmSp* 8.1.30 nwTX [Ranch diction], *Short-horn.* A man from the East come to learn cow work.

2 See quot.
1899 (1912) Green *VA Folk-Speech* 384, *Short-horn.* . . An ordinary person, one of indifferent quality and not belonging to the best sort.

3 See quot.
1930 Williams *Logger-Talk* 18 **Pacific NW,** *Short-horn:* A young lad.

short in one's mind See **short-minded 2**

shortjaw cisco n Also *shortjaw chub*   **Gt Lakes**   Cf **longjaw**
A **cisco** (here: *Coregonus artedi* or *C. zenithicus*).

1947 Hubbs–Lagler *Fishes Gt. Lakes* 42, Shortjaw chub—*Leucichthys zenithicus.* . . Lakes Michigan, Huron, Superior and Nipigon. **1972** Sparano *Outdoors Encycl.* 359, Lake Erie cisco . . shortjaw chub [etc]. . . *Coregonus artedii* (and others). **1983** Becker *Fishes WI* 350, Shortjaw Cisco. . . Other common names: shortjaw chub, longjaw . . Lake Superior longjaw.

short John n [**short** adj 2]   Cf **cheap John 1**
1909 *DN* 3.369 eAL, wGA, *Short John.* . . Same as *cheap John. Ibid* 298, *Cheap John.* . . A niggardly or stingy person, one who does things in a cheap style: often used attributively.

short joint See **short thigh**

shortleaf pine n [From the relatively short needles; cf **leaf** n[1] **B1, longleaf pine**]
1 also *short-leafed pine, short-leaved ~:* A short-needled **pine 1** (*Pinus echinata*) native to the southeastern US.   Also

called **armored pine, bastard ~ 1a, bull ~ 1c, forest ~, fox-tail ~ 3, hard ~ 3, longtag ~, old-field ~, pitch ~ b(3), poor ~, rosemary ~, scrub ~, shortshat ~, shortstraw ~, slash ~, spruce ~, swamp ~, yellow ~**

1743 Catesby *Nat. Hist. Carolina* 2 app xxii, The *Short-leav'd Pine* is usually a small Tree, with short Leaves and small Cones. It delights in middling Land, and usually grow [sic] mixed with Oaks. **1796** in 1916 Hawkins *Letters* 24 **GA,** [I] came . . to oak and short leaf pine. **1810** Michaux *Histoire des Arbres* 1.52, *Pinus mitis.* . . est connu sous le nom de *Yellow pine* . . ; dans les Carolines et la Géorgie, sous celui de *Spruce pine* . . , mais plus communément sous celui de *Short leaved pine.* [= *Pinus mitis.* . . is known as *Yellow pine* . . ; in the Carolinas and Georgia as *Spruce pine* . . , but most commonly as *Short leaved pine.*] **1860** Curtis *Cat. Plants NC* 19, Yellow pine. . . This, with us, is called *Short-leaved Pine* and *Spruce Pine.* The first is objectionable, because we have at least two species with shorter leaves. **1890** *Century Dict.* 4496, Yellow Pine . *Pinus mitis.* . . the most valuable of the yellow pines except the long-leafed, in contrast with which it is called *short-leafed pine.* **1942** Perry *Texas* 163, The noble forests of short leaf, long leaf, and loblolly pine. **1965–70** *DARE* (Qu. T17, . . *Kinds of pine trees;* not asked in early QRs) 101 Infs, **chiefly Sth, S Midl,** Shortleaf pine; [**WV16,** Shortleaf needle;] (Qu. T5, . . *Kinds of evergreens, other than pine*) Inf **DC8,** Shortleaf pine; (Qu. T15, . . *Kinds of swamp trees*) Inf **FL6,** Shortleaf pines; (Qu. T16, . . *Kinds of trees . . 'special'*) Infs **FL18, NC24, OK20,** Shortleaf pine. [*DARE* Ed: Some of these Infs may refer instead to other senses.] **2000** (acc) MO Dept. Conserv. *Forestry Page* (Internet), The shortleaf pine forests of southeast Missouri lured eastern lumbermen to our state at the turn of the century. It grows very well on the dry, upland sites in the Ozark region.

2 also *short pine, short-leaved pine:* =**Jersey pine.**
1860 Curtis *Cat. Plants NC* 20, Jersey Pine. . . This tree is generally confounded in this State with the preceding [=yellow pine], and also called *Short-leaved Pine* and *Spruce Pine.* **1901** Lounsberry *S. Wild Flowers* 4, Jersey pine . . is very often mistaken, through the south, for *Pinus echinata,* and bears without distinction the common name of short-leaved pine. **1908** Britton *N. Amer. Trees* 47, Jersey Pine. . . It is also called by many other names, as Scrub pine, Short pine, Short-leaved pine [etc]. **1910** Shreve *MD Plant Life* 391, *Pinus virginiana* . . Scrub Pine, Shortleaf Pine.

3 =**loblolly pine 1.**
1896 Mohr–Roth *Timber Pines* 106 **LA, VA, NC, SC,** Loblolly Pine. . . Common or Local Names. . . Shortleaf Pine. **1960** Vines *Trees SW* 23, Loblolly Pine. . . Other vernacular names are Frankincense Pine, Black Pine, Lowland Shortleaf Pine . . Shortleaf Pine [etc]. **1979** Little *Checklist U.S. Trees* 199, *Pinus taeda* . . Other common names—oldfield pine, shortleaf pine, North Carolina pine.

4 A **slash pine** (here: *Pinus elliottii*).
1922 U.S. Dept. Ag. *Farmers' Bulletin* 1256.2, Slash or "yellow slash" pine was formerly referred to in forestry literature as Cuban pine. . . In its younger stages on abandoned fields it is somewhat widely known as "oldfield," and even as "shortleaf" pine.

short-leaved pine See **shortleaf pine 1, 2**

short leg See **short thigh**

short lobster See **short** n

short log n, often attrib **Pacific NW**
The marketable trunk of a tree (esp a pine), which is significantly shorter than the bole of a tree such as a fir or spruce.

1947 Jones *Evergreen Land* 254 **WA,** The tree business, the wood products business, is still the leading basic industry of the State, whether you are thinking of the fir and spruce and hemlock and cedar of the western slope, or the "short log" trees east of the Cascades, the white pine and the Ponderosa, the cottonwood and the aspen. **1958** McCulloch *Woods Words* 163 **Pacific NW,** *Short log*—The 16 or 20 foot log frequently cut in the pine country, as opposed to the 32, 40, or longer log cut in the fir belt. . . *Short-log country*—The pine country. . . *Short-log logger.* . . A logger in the pine country. . . *Short-log show.* . . A pine operation.

short meter n Formerly also sp *short metre* [Perh transf < *short meter* a form of stanza used in hymn writing]
1 also *short-meter time:* A short time; hence adv phr *short meter* in a short time; quickly.   **chiefly Nth**

1833 in 1834 Smith *Life Jack Downing* x **ME,** I guess I can work it out in short metre. **1842** Kirkland *Forest Life* 2.215 **MI,** He would bear it no longer, but take the law into his own hands, and "settle up with the Ardens, short metre." **1848** Lowell *Biglow* 26 'Upcountry' **MA,** An' ef it worn't fer wakin' snakes, I'd home agin short meter. **1850** *Quincy Whig* (IL) 19 Nov 2/2 **NEng,** He put through all the money she had, in short meeter [sic], and left her without a cent. **1859** Taliaferro *Fisher's R.* 129 **nwNC** (as of 1820s), Everything were so nasty, I determined to shift my boardin' and lodgin' in short-metre time. **1863** in 1986 Messer *Civil War Letters* 21 **VT,** Would to God that all the officers in the army thought as he does, and all the citizens of the north to [sic], and then rebellion would be put down in short metre.

2 in phr *make short meter of:* To dispose of quickly. [Prob infl by *make short work of*]

1916 *DN* 4.343 **KS,** Make short meter of. . To get rid of quickly.

short meter adv phr, **short-meter time** See **short meter** n **1**

short metre See **short meter** n

short-minded adj phr

1 Slow-witted.

1862 in 1889 U.S. War Dept. *War of Rebellion* (3d ser) 2.59 **seSC** [Gullah], This conscription . . has created a suspicion that the Government has not the interest in the negroes that it has professed, and many of them sighed yesterday for the "old fetters" as being better than the new liberty. My own heart well-nigh failed me, and but for the desire to still sympathize with this, as they call themselves, "short-minded" but peculiar people, I should desire to commit my charge to some person with a stronger mind and sterner heart than my own. **1972** *Atlanta Letters* **GA,** We took her son to help with some yard work and she called out, "Tell him zactly what you-all wants him to do, he's a little 'short-minded' ye know.["]

2 also *short in one's mind:* Forgetful.

1908 *German Amer. Annals* 10.42 **sePA,** Short in one's mind. Forgetful. "He'll never remember, he's so short in his mind." . . The form *short-minded* also occurs. **1966** *DARE* (Qu. JJ30a, *Other words or expressions for forgetting something: "I _____."*) Inf **MA6,** Am short-minded.

3 Quick-tempered.

1986 Pederson *LAGS Concordance* (Touchy) 1 inf, **cwAR,** Short-minded.

short name n [*EDD short name* (at *short* adj. 8.(21)) "a nickname."]

1986 Pederson *LAGS Concordance* 2 infs, **csAL, ceMS,** Short name—(a) nickname. [Both infs Black]

shortneck n

=**pectoral sandpiper.**

1844 Giraud *Birds Long Is.* 235, To some of the residents of the Island, it is known by the name of "Meadow Snipe," and I have heard the baymen term it "Short-neck." **1880** *Forest & Stream* 15.4/3 **NJ,** On account of its creaking, shrill cry, it [=the pectoral sandpiper] is called the krieker on the Northern New Jersey coast, but further south it changes its name to short-neck and fat bird. **1956** MA Audubon Soc. *Bulletin* 40.19 **CT,** Pectoral Sandpiper. . . Short-neck, Squat Snipe.

short-necked goose n Cf **long-necked goose**

=**Hutchins's goose.**

1917 (1923) *Birds Amer.* 1.161, Hutchins's Goose. . . is variously known also as Goose-brant . . Short-necked Goose, or Mud Goose. **1955** MA Audubon Soc. *Bulletin* 39.313 **MA,** Canada Goose. . . Long-necked Goose (Mass. For the larger Canada subspecies.); Short-necked Goose (Mass. For the smaller Hutchins subspecies.)

shortning bread See **shortening bread**

shortnose gar n Also *shortnose, short-nosed gar(-pike)* Cf **longnose gar**

A **gar** n **1** (here: *Lepisosteus platostomus*). Also called **duck-bill gar, flat-nosed bony pike, short-billed gar**

1879 U.S. Natl. Museum *Bulletin* 14.64, *Lepidosteus platystomus* . . Short-nosed Gar Pike.—Great Lakes and streams south and west to the Rocky Mountains. **1882** U.S. Natl. Museum *Bulletin* 16.91, Short-nosed Gar. . . Great Lakes and southern and western rivers. **1933** [see

short-billed gar]. **1966** WI Acad. *Trans.* 55.94, In southern Wisconsin the shortnose gar is found in the same habitat as the longnose gar. . . A shortnose . . with a total length of 22⅛ inches weighed 23.7 ounces. **1991** Amer. Fisheries Soc. *Common Names Fishes* 15, *Lepisosteus platostomus* . . shortnose gar.

short-patience adj phr See **short-patient**

short-patience v phr

1933 *N. Amer. Rev.* 236.541 **seSC,** "Doan' short-patience me" means "Don't lose your temper with me" or, conversely, "Don't make me lose my temper."

short-patient adj phr Also *short-patience(d),* ~-patiented Pronc-sp *shawt-pashunt* **chiefly S Atl** See Map *esp freq among Black speakers*

Quick-tempered; excitable; touchy.

1922 Gonzales *Black Border* 325 **sSC, GA coasts** [Gullah glossary], *Shawt*—short—"shawt-pashunt," short patience or irritable, irritability. **1930** Stoney-Shelby *Black Genesis* 20 **seSC,** An' he aint 'tend to what you tell him. An' he aint 'tend to what I tell him. He git short-patience! **c1940** *LAMSAS Materials* **GA NC, SC, VA,** 27 infs, Short patient; 6 infs, Short patient [FW sugg]; 2 infs, Short patient—heard; 1 inf, Short patient—heard—Negro; 3 infs, Short patience; 2 infs, Short patienced; 1 inf, Short patiented—heard; 1 inf, Short patient—doesn't like to be crossed; 1 inf, He's so short patient; 1 inf, Very short patient; 1 inf, This [=short patient] is universal on the [Sea] islands in the sense of easily offended. [15 of 46 infs Black] **1965–70** *DARE* (Qu. GG41, *To lose patience easily: "You never did see such a _____ person."*) Infs **GA3, 11, 61, 77, MO23, NC49, PA66, SC19,** Short-patient; **DC8, TN53, TX71,** Short-patient [FW: sugg]; **GA67,** Short-patiented; **GA15,** Short-patience; [**SC5,** He certainly has short patience]; (Qu. GG8, *When a person is very easily offended: "Be careful what you say to him, he's _____."*) Inf **SC10,** Short-patient; (Qu. GG22a, *When you have come to the end of your patience . . "Well that's the _____."*) Inf **GA67,** I'm very short-patiented. [5 of 14 Infs Black] **1986** Pederson *LAGS Concordance* (Touchy) **AL, GA,** 5 infs, Short patient; 1 inf, Short patience. [4 of 6 infs Black]

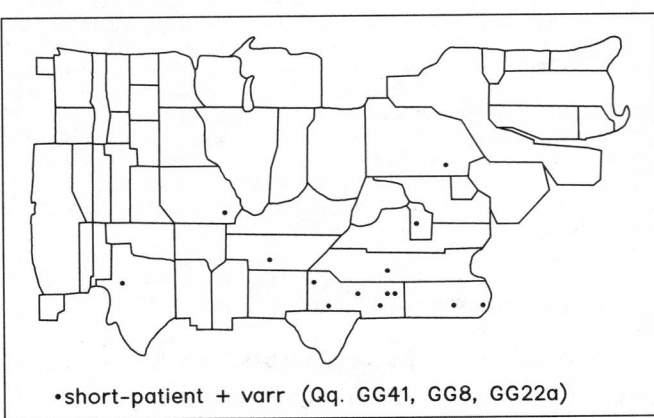

•short-patient + varr (Qq. GG41, GG8, GG22a)

short pine See **shortleaf pine 2**

short pot v phr [Transf from gambling usage] **esp TX, OK** To cheat or deceive (someone); to give less than the expected amount.

1940 *AmSp* 15.222 **cwTX,** The gay *vaquero* is usually faithful to one sweetheart, it not being 'in the cards' to 'roach,' 'short pot,' or 'cabbage' on her. **1966–69** *DARE* (Qu. LL22, *Less than you should get: "They'll try to give you _____ every time."*) Infs **OK**25, 45, **TX**18, 43, 70, Short pot you.

short road n

In logging: =**go-back road** (at **go-back** adj **2**).

1905 U.S. Forest Serv. *Bulletin* 61.46 [Logging terms], *Short road. See* Go-back road. [=A road upon which logging sleds can return to the skidways for reloading, without meeting the loaded sleds en route to the landing.] **1958** McCulloch *Woods Words* 163 **Pacific NW,** *Short road*—Same as go-back road. **1969** Sorden *Lumberjack Lingo* 109

NEng, Gt Lakes, *Short road*—A road upon which unloaded logging sleighs can return for reloading without meeting a loaded sleigh.

short rows n pl

1 in phrr *be in* (or *be getting into*) *the short rows:* To be near the end or the climax of something.

1894 *DN* 1.342 **wCT**, *Short rows:* in a field not quite rectangular, planted in rows, there will be a few rapidly shortening rows at the end which hoe off with surprising rapidity after the rest are done. Hence the proverbial expression "gittin' into the short rows" = nearly finished. **1909** *DN* 3.369 **eAL, wGA**, *Short rows.* . . In the sense reported, D.N. i, p. 342. **1938** [see **2** below]. [**1954** *Harder Coll.* **cwTN**, *Short rows.* . . The state of a person when he has almost reached the limit of his ability. . . The state of a person about to achieve the orgasm in sexual intercourse.] **1984** Wilder *You All Spoken Here* 97 **Sth**, In the short rows: The moments just preceding orgasm.

2 in phr *have one in the short rows:* See quot. [Appar by confusion with *have one by the short hairs*]

1938 *AmSp* 13.4 **seAR**, 'I have him in the short rows now,' that is, where I can control him. [Footnote:] The short rows of cotton are usually found at the end of a field. Thus, 'we're in the short rows now' may mean that we are near the end of our task.

short sauce n esp NEng obs Cf long sauce, sauce B1

See quot 1859.

1809 Ritson *Poetical Picture* 76, Their [=New England vessels'] long sauce [Footnote: Carrots, parsnips, &c], and their short sauce too [Footnote: Turnips, potatoes, &c.],/ About their boats are laid in view. **1815** Humphreys *Yankey in England* 41, Long sairse and short sairse; consisting of a variety of leetle notions too tedious to mention. **1825** Neal *Brother Jonathan* 1.76 **CT**, A quantity of long, short, and round sauce, or "sarse," *i.e.* carrots, turnips, and potatoes. **1859** (1968) Bartlett *Americanisms* 255, *Long sauce.* Beets, carrots, and parsnips are *long sauce.* Potatoes, turnips, onions, pumpkins, etc. are *short sauce.* **1947** Bowles–Towle *New Engl. Cooking* 104, At one time some of the vegetables were classified as short sauce, others as long sauce, but these finer distinctions have been lost, and in northern New Hampshire and Maine, even today, garden sass is the accepted phrase for all green vegetables.

shortshat pine n Also sp shortschat pine Cf longshat pine, shat

Either the **Jersey pine** or **shortleaf pine 1.**

1897 Sudworth *Arborescent Flora* 27 **DE**, *Pinus virginiana* . . Shortschat Pine. *Ibid* 29 **DE**, *Pinus echinata.* . . Shortschat Pine. **1908** Britton *N. Amer. Trees* 33, [Shortleaf pine] is known under many common names, most of which have also been applied to other species of pine, as Yellow pine . . Shortschat pine [etc]. *Ibid* 47, [Jersey pine] is also called by many other names, as Scrub pine . . Shortschat pine, and Shortshucks. **2001** (acc) Forest Products Lab. Center for Wood Anatomy Research *Tech. Transf. Fact Sheet* (Internet), *Virginia Pine.* . . Other Common Names: . . Jersey pine, . . shortleaf pine, shortleaved, shortschat pine, shortshat pine, shortshucks.

shortshucks n Cf longshucks

=**Jersey pine.**

1897 Sudworth *Arborescent Flora* 27 **MD, VA**, *Pinus virginiana.* . . Short Shucks. **1908** [see **shortshat pine**]. **2001** [see **shortshat pine**].

short skate n [short adj 2 + skate n² 1]

A cheapskate; hence v phr *short skate* to act like a cheapskate.

1909 Engeln *At Cornell* 57 **cNY**, Don't shortskate; buy a season ticket, good for all the games. **1953** in 1960 Wentworth–Flexner *Slang* 472, *Short skate.* . . He must be a . . short skate. A short skate like you've been speakin' of here. **1967** *DARE* (Qu. U17, *Names or nicknames for a person who doesn't pay his bills*) Inf **OH11**, Short skate.

short staker n Also short stake hobo Cf boomer n²

An itinerant worker; see quots.

1925 *AmSp* 1.138 **Pacific NW** [Logger talk], The first gang of logger delegates to go to an I.W.W. convention called itself "the overall brigade." The brigade horrified the gentle idealists who controlled the Eastern end of the movement; they called it "the bummery" and deserted it. The trouble was that the men in this brigade were real workers; they returned to their jobs with a new name, "pink-pretties," for gentle Socialists; and they made "scissor bill," "boss-simple," "job-simple," "home guard," "fink," "slave-puncher," "job hog," "garbage-kisser," "short-

staker," and "bull-killer" common terms in the woods. **1927** *DN* 5.462 [Underworld jargon], *Short staker.* . . A restless hobo who works only long enough to get a few dollars together before he is off again. **1935** Davis *Honey* 82 **OR**, Any set of short-stake hoboes would be apt to steal his horse and maybe his shoes while he slept. **1938** (1939) Holbrook *Holy Mackinaw* 263, *Short staker.* A very migratory worker. **1941** *AmSp* 16.233 [Lumberjack jargon], *Short staker.* A *boomer* who quits after earning a day's pay or so. **1950** *Western Folkl.* 9.381 **neCA** [Lumberjack language], *Short staker.* A man who works just long enough to get a few dollars in order to travel on. **1958** McCulloch *Woods Words* 163 **Pacific NW**, *Short staker*—A man who works in any one place only long enough to make a small stake. **1969** Sorden *Lumberjack Lingo* 109 **NEng, Gt Lakes**, *Short staker*—A very migratory worker. One who stayed only a short time at any one camp.

shortstraw pine n Cf longstraw pine, straw

=**shortleaf pine 1.**

1859 Perry *Turpentine Farming* 26, Among the various qualities of pines, we may distinguish . . common short-straw pine. **1946** *Clarke County Democrat* (Grove Hill AL) 26 Dec 1/1 *(DA)*, The following native pines are listed in the order of . . susceptibility . . slash (short straw for gum production). **1980** Little *Audubon Guide N. Amer. Trees E. Region* 287, "Shortstraw Pine". . . The most widely distributed of the southern yellow pines.

short sweetening n Also short sweetning [OED2 short a. 20 "Of edible substances: Friable, easily crumbled"] chiefly Sth, S Midl Cf long sweetening

Sugar in crystalline form.

1856 Lanman *Advent. Wilds U.S.* 192 **seMS**, The mother added the sugar or "short sweetning" to the coffee with her fingers, and tasted each cup before sending it round to ascertain if it was right. **1885** *Harper's New Mth. Mag.* Aug 399 **GA**, He set out the glass with its little quota of "short sweetening." **1887** Amer. Philol. Assoc. *Trans. for 1886* 46 **Sth**, *Short sweetening* (sugar). **1899** (1912) Green *VA Folk-Speech* 432, *Short sweetening*, sugar. **1909** *DN* 3.378 **eAL, wGA**, *Short sweetnin'* . . sugar. **1911** *DN* 3.540 **eKY**, *Short-sweetening.* . . Sugar. **1923** (1946) Greer-Petrie *Angeline Doin' Society* 11 **csKY**, If thar wan't no short sweetnin' (sugar) handy, long sweetnin' (molasses) would do. **1931** Randolph *Ozarks* 34, Granulated sugar is called "short sweetnin'," and is still regarded as a luxury in some isolated sections. **1933** Rawlings *South Moon* 102 **nFL**, Will you have long or short sweetnin'? **1936** *AmSp* 11.317 **Ozarks**, *Pour short sweetening into long.* . . Literally, to pour sugar into molasses. It means to paint the lily, to gild the rose, etc. **1938** Matschat *Suwannee R.* 107 **neFL, seGA**, There were raw rations in plenty—white flour and coffee and short sweetnin' (sugar). **1959** Roberts *Up Cutshin* 8 **seKY**, Made our molasses into long sweetening and tapped the sugartrees for short sweetening. **1966–67** *DARE* (Qu. H21, . . *The sweet stuff that's poured over these [pan]cakes*) Inf **NC34**, Short sweetening—sugar; **SC46**, Short sweetening—a solid-crystal sugar. **1969** Sorden *Lumberjack Lingo* 109 **NEng, Gt Lakes**, *Short sweet'nin'*—A lump of sugar to sweeten coffee. **1978** *NADS Letters* **MS**, In my youth, sorghum molasses was referred to as "long sweetenin'"; granulated sugar was "short sweetenin'." **1986** Pederson *LAGS Concordance*, 3 infs, **FL, GA, MS**, Short sweetening—sugar; [1 inf, **neFL**, Short sweetening—syrup;] 1 inf, **cTX**, Short sweetening—less heavy; 1 inf, **neTN**, Short sweetening is sugar; 1 inf, **seMS**, Long and short sweetening—syrup [and] sugar respective[ly].

shorttag pine n Cf longtag pine, tag

Prob = **Jersey pine.**

1970 *DARE* (Qu. T17, . . *Kinds of pine trees;* not asked in early QRs) Inf **VA105**, Shorttag pine.

short-tailed house wren See short-tailed wren

short-tailed tern n prob obs

=**black tern.**

1813 Wilson *Amer. Ornith.* 7.84 *(DAE)*, The short-tailed tern measures eight inches and a half from the point of the bill to the tip of the tail. **1874** NY Acad. Sci. *Annals Lyceum Nat. Hist.* 10.13 **UT**, *Hydrochelidon fissipes.* . . Short-tailed Tern. . . "Breeds in marshes of Salt Lake." **1890** Warren *Birds PA* 23, The Black or Short-tailed Tern is a rather irregular, though an uncommon visitor during the spring and fall in different sections of Pennsylvania. **1936** Roberts *MN Birds* 1.566, The Black Tern . . once upon a time called the short-tailed tern.

short-tailed wren n Also *short-tailed house wren*
=house wren 1.

1917 (1923) *Birds Amer.* 3.192, House Wren. . . Other Names. . . Short-tailed House Wren [etc]. **1923** *WV State Ornith. Birds WV* 74, House Wren. . . Common Names—Brown Wren . . Short-tailed Wren.

short talk n
Quarrelsome talk; hence v phr *short talk* to speak rudely, curtly, or in a quarrelsome manner to (someone).

1931 *VA Qrly. Rev.* Jan 111, Ooman! . . Dat ain't no way to short-tawk yo' husband. **1934** Carmer *Stars Fell on AL* 213, But on some short talk Wade pulled out his gun and shot him. **1952** Brown *NC Folkl.* 1.589, Short-talk. . . To talk crossly. "It would shame Lige powerfully if you'd short-talk him in company."—West. **1972** Cooper *NC Mt. Folkl.* 96, Short talk—quarrelsome talk.

short thigh n Also *short joint, ~ leg* **chiefly Sth** Cf **second joint**
The thigh of a chicken.

1960 *DE Folkl. Bulletin* 1.36, Short joints (chicken thighs). **1986** Pederson *LAGS Concordance (Poultry)* 1 inf, **cTX**, Short thigh; 1 inf, **ceTX**, Short thigh—near ankle, not same as drumstick; [*(Leg)* 1 inf, **neFL**, Short thigh—thigh, of [a] human]. [All infs Black] **2000** *NADS Letters* **TN**, I grew up with the term "short leg" to refer to the thigh of a chicken (as opposed to the drumstick). *Ibid* **NC, VA**, Short thigh is a term used in my family to refer to the thigh of a chicken. It is also known as a short leg and is, I believe just a mashing together of two more commonly used terms for the same portion of a chicken, the "thigh" and the "short leg" to form "short thigh". Both my mother and grandmother were fine Southern cooks and both cooked a lot of chicken. All three of us use(d) the term short thigh. My mother and grandmother were born in rural North Carolina and I was born in Virginia. When I saw your inquiry I was surprised as I thought the term quite common. *Ibid* **AL, GA**, I was born in 1950 and grew up in southwest Georgia where the term "short thigh" was the accepted way to refer to the upper portion of the chicken leg. Both of my grandmothers . . always used only the term "short thigh" to refer to that piece of chicken. The term is still in common use in that area. I have friends of a similar age from southeast Alabama who also use the term in the same way as my family. My mother still calls it the "short thigh." I have never heard anyone use "long thigh." *Ibid* **cGA**, Growing up in middle Georgia (born 1955) we referred to the thigh of the chicken as the "short" thigh. Everyone I know there uses this term, particularly my grandparents. Only in adult life, away from Georgia, have I wondered if there was such a thing as a "long" thigh, or why the use of "short" at all. *Ibid* **SC**, Short-thigh. . . I've occasionally heard my ex-husband use this term. He is black, 42 years old, and lives in SC, Piedmont/Sandhill area. *Ibid* **sFL**, My brother was a manager and regional director of fried chicken franchise stores for over twenty-five years, approximately 15 of which he spent in South Florida. According to him, the term "short thigh" is used by Florida blacks (but not whites) to specify just the thigh portion of a chicken leg, i.e., the leg minus the "drumstick."

shortwoods n Also *shortwoodard*
A rustic.

1931–33 *LANE Worksheets* **swCT**, Shortwoods. . . A rustic. Short-woodards. . . Rustics. **1932** *DN* 6.284 **swCT**, Shortwoods. A country bumpkin.

short yearling See **short** adj **1**

shot v See **shut** v **A**

shot adj See **shut** adj **d**

shot n See **short** n

shot-borer beetle See **shot-hole borer**

shotbush n [From the masses of small, round, black berries]
A **spikenard**, usu **Hercules'-club 1** or **wild sarsaparilla**.

1784 in 1785 *Amer. Acad. Arts & Sci. Memoirs* 1.431 **PA**, *Aralia.* . . Berry-Bearing Angelica. Shot Bush. . . Common in new plantations. **1876** Hobbs *Bot. Hdbk.* 106, Shot bush, Prickly elder, Aralia spinosa. **1930** Sievers *Amer. Med. Plants* 62, Wild-sarsaparilla. . . Other common names.—False sarsaparilla . . shotbush, wild licorice. **1950** Peattie *Nat. Hist. Trees* 493, Hercules'-club . . Other Names . . Toothache-tree. Shotbush. Pigeontree. **1968** *Foxfire* 2.2.49, Aralia racemosa, called

spignet . . shotbush, or indian-root, is a very tall, dramatic plant with huge divided leaves and a very showy panicle of fragrant flowers.

shote See **shoat**

shotgun n

1 attrib, also used absol; Of a dwelling: consisting of a row of interconnecting rooms—usu in comb *shotgun house.* **chiefly Sth, S Midl** Cf **gun-barrel house, gunshot ~, sharpshooter 3**

1936 in 1953 Botkin–Harlow *Treas. Railroad Folkl.* 48, Sim Webb sits in the warm sunshine on the porch of his little shotgun house. **c1939** in 1984 Lambert–Franks *Voices* 165 **OK**, Ma's still livin'. She's in the house next door there. . . [a] two-room shotgun house. **1940** Writers' Program *Guide TX* 388 **neTX**, Five-sixths of the population of this vicinity live on farms, and rural habitations are largely "shotgun" houses one room wide, extending back one or two rooms to a lean-to. **1941** Writers' Program *Guide AL* 166, Between the various residential sections are the homes of Negroes, ranging from the tumbledown, poorly constructed "shotgun" type to the well-kept, comfortable house occupied by business and professional men. **1941** Writers' Program *Guide LA* 158, The "shotgun" house, in which the rooms are one behind the other and the doors separating each are in line, so that a shot fired in the front entrance would go out the rear, and the "camel-back" house . . are all of frequent occurrence in New Orleans. **1942** *AmSp* 17.171 **sIL**, Shot-gun house. Used to describe a house whose rooms are all in a line. **1945** FWP *Lay My Burden Down* 98 **TX** (as of c1865) [Black], And then they had to go out and live in sod houses and little old boxed shotguns and turn their Negroes loose. **1952** Brown *NC Folkl.* 1.590, Shot-gun house. . . A house having all its rooms in one row. **1960** (1966) Percy *Moviegoer* 21 **New Orleans LA**, The two of them are forever buying shotgun cottages in rundown neighborhoods and fixing them up. **1965–70** *DARE* (Qu. D21, *A small, poorly-built house, or one in rundown condition*) Infs **SC66, TX11, 51**, Shotgun house; **AR56, TX33**, Shotgun (shack); **FL15**, Shotgun shanty; (Qu. D23, *A house that is divided in two through the middle so that two families can live in it*) Inf **CA34**, Double shotgun house; shotgun house; **KS8, LA23**, Shotgun (double); (Qu. M22, . . *Kinds of buildings . . on farms*) Inf **LA3**, Shotgun house. **1984** Stall *Proud New Orleans* 167, Shotgun double: The same as [shotgun house] . . except two narrow, long houses were put together for larger Irish families. **1989** Pederson *LAGS Tech. Index* 388 **Gulf Region** (Shotgun house) 53 infs, Shotgun house; 23 infs, Shotgun; 1 inf, Shotgun shack; 1 inf, Shotgun doubles; 1 inf, Straight shotgun; 1 inf, Three room shotgun house. **1997** *NY Times* (NY) 15 Mar 8/1 **New Orleans LA**, Down here . . eating poorly is a mortal sin and good food simmers in both $100-a-plate restaurants and in the most humble shotgun houses.

2 also attrib; also abbr *shotty:* The privilege of riding in the front passenger seat of a car—also used as a call claiming this privilege; also *shotgun(ner):* the person occupying this seat. [From the phr *ride shotgun* (at **ride** v[1] **B12**)]

1979 Jordan *Yesterday in TX Hill Country* 75, This going to church meant a caravan of horses and vehicles, led by the two-span hack, with my father in the driver's seat on the right, my mother in the shotgun seat to the left. **1995** Karr *Liars' Club* 211 **eTX**, He slouched behind the wheel. . . Mother stretched out on the shotgun side of the car, her cowboy boots propped on the front dash. **1998** *Post–Reg.* (Idaho Falls ID) 17 Nov (Internet), Here, culled from Web pages, are some common rules: . . The caller must pronounce the word "shotgun" in a clear voice and the call must be acknowledged by the driver. . . If one of the occupants is too wide or too tall to fit comfortably in the backseat, then the driver may . . award shotgun to the genetic misfit. . . Responsibilities of the Shotgun [include] Controlling the radio. . . If the car is forced to stop due to a serious infraction of the shotgunner, the seat must be relinquished. . . The Rotating Shotgun Rule from a Philadelphia suburb. . . explains how each passenger on a trip may sit in the coveted front seat. . . The Five Minute Rule, originating in Massachusetts. In the event that the passenger riding shotgun leaves the car, he/she is allowed five minutes to return and retain the prized front seat. **1999** *DARE* File **cMS** (as of 1950s), When gaggles of teenagers in Jackson, Mississippi, in the mid-to-late '50s started heading toward a car, there was always a contest for who could holler out "I want shotgun!" first. *Ibid*, Ride shotgun. . . Today, it's referred to as "shotty" by many. "I got shotty." *Ibid* **csWI**, "Shotgun!" my son said as we walked into the garage. He wanted to sit in front, in the passenger seat of the car.

shotgun bunk n
=muzzle loader.

1956 Sorden–Ebert *Logger's Words* 31 **Gt Lakes,** *Shot-gun-bunks.* **1969** Sorden *Lumberjack Lingo* 109 **NEng, Gt Lakes,** *Shot gun bunks*— Old-fashioned bunks into which the lumberjack crawled from the foot of the bed. Same as muzzle loaders.

shotgun chaps n pl   Cf **batwing 2, chaps**

Leather leggings that totally encompass each leg in the manner of trousers.

1937 Sandoz *Slogum* 21 **NE,** The newcomers with the Wyoming herd, still in their shotgun chaps, looking bashfully in at the door. *Ibid* 207, He wore the same bowlegged shotgun chaps that he had on when he came up the Texas trail in the seventies. **1980** *AZ Highways* Feb 7, In the Southwest, the cowboys adopted the Mexican "shotgun" chaps, which fit snugly around the legs and were more like a second pair of pants. **1981** *KS Qrly.* 13.2.70, *Shotgun chaps* . . leather chaps of straight, narrow shape that completely cover a rider's legs.

shotgun house See **shotgun 1**

shotgunner See **shotgun 2**

shotgunning vbl n

1942 Henry *High Border* 309 **nRocky Mts,** Some wheat you'll drill into the stubble. Shotgunning, that is called.

shot-hole borer n   Also *shot-borer beetle*   [See quot 1997]

A bark beetle (here: usu *Scolytus rugulosus*).

1890 Ormerod *Manual Injurious Insects* 331, I found that the cause of the injury was the "Shot-borer" Beetle (as it is called in America). **1916** U.S. Dept. Ag. *Farmers' Bulletin* 763.2, The shot-hole borers or barkbeetles burrow into the bark. **1938** Brimley *Insects NC* 245, *S[colytus] rugulosus*. . . Shot-Hole Borer. State-wide; the larvae bore in the bark of sick or weakly fruit trees. [**1954** Borror–DeLong *Intro. Insects* 424, When the larvae [of bark beetles] complete their growth they pupate at the ends of their tunnels, and emerge through a round hole eaten through the bark. These numerous emergence holes resemble the holes which would be made by a charge of small lead shot.] **2000** (acc) VT Univ. Ext. *Insects in Firewood* (Internet), *Bark Beetles* (Scolytidae). . . The adults emerge en masse through small, circular holes, giving them the common name "shot-hole" borers.

shot house n

A place where liquor is sold by the drink.

1974 Dabney *Mountain Spirits* 140 **sFL,** The "bumper joints" in Miami's Negro sections dispensed moonshine by the drink, for thirty-five to fifty cents a shot, a common practice of the "shot houses" and "crack joints" in such areas. **1996** McDowell *Leaving Pipe Shop* 154 **AL** (as of 1960s), [Black], The story goes that Grandma tracked Daddy Frank to Georgia's shot house, where he was passed out on the floor.

shot-pouch n   [See quot 1888]

=**ruddy duck.**

1888 Trumbull *Names of Birds* 111 **MI,** Others at Detroit, and the "punters" of St. Clair Flats, refer to the species [=the ruddy duck] still as Fool-Duck, Deaf-Duck, and Shot-Pouch (the latter—considering the bird's ability to carry away shot—being not far from inappropriate). **1926** (1986) Phillips *Nat. Hist. Ducks* 4.159, Ruddy Duck. . . Vernacular Names. . . Shot-pouch [etc].

shots n pl   Cf **jimmies** n pl[2]

Bits of candy used as a topping for ice cream or cakes.

1973 *DARE* File **CT,** Shots. . . The small bits of chocolate on an ice cream cone—so in Conn.; called jimmies in Boston, sprinkles in NY. **1982** *NY Times* (NY) 25 Nov sec A 22, What do you call the tiny multi-colored flecks of candy that are . . scattered on . . cakes, or into which ice cream cones are dipped? . . To one friend from the West they are "shots"; to another, "cake decorators." **1982** Chaika *Speaking RI* [7], *Jimmies* . . outsidas [sic] may know them as shots. **1997** *DARE* File **CT,** When I was a child . . I used the word "shots" for the little things you put on ice cream. "I'd like a vanilla cone with chocolate shots, please." . . Mostly everyone uses the expression in my home town of Shelton, Connecticut.

shot-sling n   [By metath from *slingshot;* cf Intro "Language Changes" I.1]

c1937 in 1977 *Amer. Slave Suppl. 1* 1.319, Every boy, white and black, would have a shot-sling or air gun.

shotten ppl adj   [Var of *shot*]   Cf **bloodshotten,** *hipshotten* (at **hipshot**)

1906 *DN* 3.156 **nwAR,** *Shotten.* . . Shot. "It was all shotten up."

shotten herring n   Also *shotten shad*   esp NEng   Cf **last run of shad 1**

A herring (or shad) that has released its roe—in similes *lean* (or *thin*) *as a shotten herring* and varr: very thin; emaciated.

1885 *Catholic World* 40.654, Imagine a man about forty years of age, of medium height, as lean, as the saying is, as a shotten herring. **1903** *DN* 2.300 **Cape Cod MA** (as of a1857), *Shotten.* . . Cast its spawn. 'You look as lean as a shotten herring.' **1918** *DN* 5.16 **Martha's Vineyard MA,** *Shotten.* . . Thin because the roe has been ejected. "The oxen are looking fat now. Before grass came they were as thin as shotten herring." **1942** ME Univ. *Studies* 56.65, A person or animal might be thin as a *shotten* (i.e., spawned or spent) shad or herring.

shotty See **shotgun 2**

should v

Used with perf infin in place of the past or perf to mark that a statement (direct or indirect) is based on hearsay.   [The exx in quot 1953 correspond exactly to the idiom described in *OED2* at *shall* v. 15.a (c888 →; "*Obs.* exc. *dial.*") and *EDD* at *shall* v.[1] 4; most of the other exx can be explained as natural extensions of this idiom, but there has perh been (as appar in quot 1930) some infl from the use of the cognate verbs in Ger and Scan langs to mean "is said to."]

1863 IN House of Repr. *Rept. Arbitrary Arrests* 71 **seIN,** Colonel Landrum read a paper to me which asserted that I had said that I intended to sell my potatoes to the South, and some thing else I should have said about the soldiers being d—d rogues. **1892** *KS Univ. Qrly.* 1.98 **KS,** *Should have said:* said, as, He should have said yes, i.e., indeed he said yes. [*DARE* Ed: This prob reflects an imperfect understanding of the idiom.] **1914** Ruppenthal in *DN* 4.112 **cKS,** *Should.* . . "He should have said that I was lazy"; that is, he is reported to have said so. **1923** *DN* 5.220 **swMO,** *Should.* . . In indirect discourse, supposedly. "'Cordin' to Bill, Sam sh'd 'a' [sic] said I was a liar." **1927** Ruppenthal *Coll.* **KS,** *Should have said.* . . Miller told me what Renker should have said—testimony in court at Wakeeney, Kansas, 1926. **1930** *AmSp* 6.217 **IL, MN, WI** [Idioms illustrating infl of Sw], [Sw Engl:] *He should be a good man.* [Std Engl:] He is said to be a good man. [Sw:] *Han skulle vara en god man.* **1953** Randolph–Wilson *Down in Holler* 42 **Ozarks,** "They do say Jim Burwell should have set his barn afire, to git the insurance money" means that Jim probably *did* set the barn afire. In the sentence "I hear that Mabel should have been a-runnin' after Lucy's man," the *should* stands between the speaker and a direct accusation of misconduct.

shoulda See **have** v[2]

shoulder-buster See **buster 6**

should ought See **ought** v C1b, 2d

shout v, hence vbl n *shouting* (also attrib), n *shouter*

1 To evidence religious enthusiasm by loud cries or vigorous bodily motions; hence phr *shout oneself happy* to bring oneself to a state of exaltation in this way.   [Cf *OED2 shouter* sb.[2] "A name given to some Methodist congregations in the north of Ireland who used to leap and shout in their ecstasies." 1820]   **chiefly Sth, S Midl**   See also **shouting Methodist**   Cf **holler B6**

c1806 in 1927 IN *Mag. Hist.* 23.22, He says, they had shouting times, but he could not form a class. **1807** McNemar *KY Revival* 73 **KY, NC, OH, wPA, TN, VA,** There were regular societies of these people. . . Praying, shouting, jerking, barking, or rolling. **1839** *Knickerbocker* 14.213 **MD,** He was sternly opposed to what are called 'shouting meetings.' **1844** *Ladies' Repository* 4.179, I . . inquired of a friend as to her religious "whereabouts," when he told me, with a smile, that after having "*confessed*" with the Catholics—shouted with the Methodists—stood awhile with the Presbyterians, and been baptized with the Baptists, she had finally 'gone to sleep' with the Quakers." *Ibid,* She called herself a Quaker; yet when she got warmed with religious enjoyment, she *would shout,* and sometimes sing her favorite Methodist hymn. **1859** Taliaferro *Fisher's R.* 33 **nwNC** (as of 1820s), I've hearn uv this feller Beller's shoutin' night meetin's, and I'm a-gwine to one on 'um. **1884**

Baldwin *Yankee School-Teacher* 111 **VA** [Black], When de Lawd gets hold o' us we're boun' f'r ter shout an' praise Him.   **1913** (1980) Hardy *OH Schoolmistress* 91 (as of c1850), One of these [forms of religious expression] very common in the Methodist churches . . was what was called "Shouting." Not only at revivals, but at the ordinary Sunday meetings, some old-fashioned people when they got, as they said, very "happy," would walk up and down the aisles of the church waving their arms and shouting in a half-breathless voice "Glory!" (or "Praise the Lord!" or "Hallelujah!").   **1939** in Lib. of Congress *Amer. Memory: WPA Life Hist.* (Internet) **GA** [Black], Everybody 'gin to git happy, and when that old song, *Amazing Grace How Sweet the Sound,* was sung the shouting could be heard for a mighty long ways off 'cause didn't nobody stay home 'cause they didn't have no clothes to wear. Everybody was there shouting.   **1942** (1960) Robertson *Red Hills* 204 **SC,** Aunt Coot told us one morning that she tried to be graceful when she shouted—took two steps to the left, then two steps to the right. And Margit was famous for her shouting. Margit was the biggest shouter in our county.   **1953** Randolph–Wilson *Down in Holler* 167 **Ozarks,** When backwoods Christians get to shoutin', they dance or jump or roll in a religious frenzy. Usually this is accompanied by loud yells, but it is quite possible for a worshipper to *shout* without opening his mouth, or making any sound at all. Sometimes hillfolk *shout* at funerals, too. [A woman] tells of a little boy going with his elders to a buryin' ground. "Granny'll shout," he said. "Granny's nigh ninety, but she'll shout."   *c1960* Wilson *Coll.* **csKY,** Shout. . . Manifest religious exaltation.   **1975** McDonough *Garden Sass* 153 **AR,** You could tell who was gonna shout because it was the same people did it all the time. For instance, Savannah Agar at Highland—the girls used to follow and pick up her hairpins, and I've known her even to fall over to the floor with her hair flying and she was shouting—and sometimes the men did too. **1982** *Foxfire 7* 187 **nwAL,** I've seen my own mother shout up and down that aisle when I was a young child. You don't see it any more.   **1986** Pederson *LAGS Concordance,* 1 inf, **swAL,** Shouting—in Holiness church; drums, pianos, guitars; 1 inf, **seAL,** Go to shouting; 1 inf, **nwAR,** Go to shouting—at a revival; 1 inf, **ceMS,** Got to shouting; 1 inf, **nwAR,** Shouting revival.   **1996** Horton *Island Out of Time* 186 **Chesapeake Bay MD,** But no man ever had more fun in the pulpit than Joshua Thomas. He was a mover and a shaker, literally, a fine dancer and an exhorter who is said to have often "shouted himself happy."

2 Spec: to perform a **shout** n **1.** **chiefly sSC, GA coasts** *chiefly among Black speakers*

1863 in 1865 Post *Soldiers' Letters* 225 **SC** [Black], After the meeting, there was a "shout," which is a most extraordinary performance. They all walk and shuffle round in a ring, singing and chanting, while three or four stand in a corner and clap their hands to mark the time. At certain parts of the chorus, they all give a duck, the effect of which is very peculiar. This shuffling is what they call "shouting."   **1867** Allen *Slave Songs* xiv **SC,** All stand up in the middle of the floor, and when the 'sperichil' is struck up, begin first walking and by-and-by shuffling round, one after the other, in a ring. The foot is hardly taken from the floor, and the progression is mainly due to a jerking, hitching motion, which agitates the entire shouter, and soon brings out streams of perspiration.   *Ibid,* In the form here described, the "shout" is probably confined to South Carolina and the States south of it. It appears to be found in Florida, but not in North Carolina or Virginia. It is, however, an interesting fact that the term "shouting" is used in Virginia in reference to a peculiar motion of the body not wholly unlike the Carolina shouting.   *Ibid* xv **SC,** The shouting may be to any tune. . . In practice, however, a distinction is generally observed. . . The shouting step varied with the tune. . . So far as I can learn, the shouting is confined to the Baptists.   **1880** *Amer. Missionary* 34.109 **GA,** At these feasts they have the colored people come into the big house . . and shout for them, as it is called here, but I call it dancing. They are given ginger snaps, rum and wine. This kind of a party, or feast, or shout, was given last Sunday (they are called by all these names).   **1930** Woofter *Black Yeomanry* 220 **seSC,** There is . . a sharp line between shouting and dancing. . . To shuffle without crossing the feet is legitimate shouting; to "cross-um-foot" is a sin.   **1936** Smith–Sass *Carolina Rice* 75 **SC coast** (as of 1850s), But it must not be supposed that John the leader could induce our negroes entirely to accept "shoutings" as a substitute for dances. I have attended both many times, and am competent to describe them. Shouting was a religious dance, the music of which was supplied by the lookers-on singing in a high-key a religious song.   **1938** in Lib. of Congress *Amer. Memory: WPA Life Hist.* (Internet) **NYC** [Black], 'Dat's owah faith' / 'Owah faith' / 'Some uh us stan' still' / 'Yeah' / 'Some uh us shouts' / 'Yeah' / 'Ah don' condemn neither' / 'Amen, amen' / 'We got diffunt ways uh showin' we's sanctified' / 'Amen. Dat's de trufe!'   **1942** (1965)

Parrish *Slave Songs* 35 **GA coast,** In the House of Prayer in Savannah (where the pillars are thickly padded, and the sawdust is inches deep on the floor) I saw a "lone shouter" fall into a trance that lasted half an hour.   **1972** Jones–Hawes *Step it Down* 143 **GA,** No, the ring plays are not exactly like the ring shouts, because you are *playing*—you see, the children are playing and they *mean* to play. . . Some ring plays seem just like a shout in some ways but they are plays. . . You see, if you're going to play, you *play,* and if you're going to shout, you *shout.*   **1987** Jones-Jackson *When Roots Die* 31 **sSC coast** [Gullah], Though many of the men act as responders to the minsters, few shout or become "happy" as many of the women do. However, those who do join in the movements of the shout do so with considerable zeal.

shout n

1 A chiefly religious dance, usu involving a shuffling step and accompanied by strongly rhythmic singing; a religious meeting devoted to dancing of this sort; hence combs *ring shout* such a dance in which the performers move in a circle, *shout step* a step used in this dance.   [**shout** v 2] Sth, esp sSC, GA **coasts** *esp freq among Black speakers* Cf **holy dance, shout song**

1862 in 1906 Pearson *Letters from Port Royal* 27 **csSC,** We asked Cuffy if they considered the "shout" as part of their religious worship. *Ibid* 34, They had had a "Shout" which I had heard distinctly at three o'clock in the morning.   **1867** *Nation* 30 May 432 **sSC, GA coasts,** This is a ceremony which the white clergymen are inclined to discountenance, and even of the colored elders some of the more discreet try . . to put on a face of discouragement; and although, if pressed for Biblical warrant for the shout, they generally seem to believe "he in de Book," . . still, it is not considered blasphemous or improper if "de chillen" and "dem young gal" carry it on in the evening for amusement's sake, and with no well-defined intention of "praise." But the true "shout" takes place on Sundays or on "praise" nights through the week.   **1867** Allen *Slave Songs* ii **csSC,** When visitors from the North were on the islands, there was nothing that seemed better worth their while than to see a "shout" or hear the "people" sing their "sperichils." . . All of them were sung, and then the glorious shout, "I can't stay behind, my Lord," was struck up, and sung by the entire multitude with a zest and spirit, a swaying of the bodies and nodding of the heads and lighting of the countenances and rhythmical movement of the hands, which I think no one present will ever forget.   **1880** [see **shout** v 2].   **1925** Scarborough *On Trail Negro Folk-Songs* 269 **nwAL,** The church would hold "shouts," when the benches would be pushed back and a lively tune played.   **1926** Ferber *Show Boat* 155, In the Louisiana bayou country she saw the Negroes perform that weird religious rite known as a ring shout, semi-savage, hysterical, mesmerizing.   **1931** *VA Qrly. Rev.* Jan 98, Even in his sermon which preceded the sing [sic]-shout he urged the unmarried men and women to leave the church. "Old Satan hangs mighty close to de shoutin' line."   **1938** FWP *Guide MS* 24 [Black], Soon a woman leaps out into the aisle. She is "moved by the spirit" she cries, and slowly, rigidly, she begins "the shout" or if it is a Holiness meeting, the "Holy Dance." It is shuffling, intricate; her heels thud on the floor. . . The ring . . moves faster and faster, yet the feet keep the step; the rhythm is not broken.   **1942** (1965) Parrish *Slave Songs* 13 **sSC, GA coasts,** In the coastal section of South Carolina and Georgia, the ring-shout, a semi-religious survival of African dancing—not a vocal performance as the name implies—is accompanied by a melodious chant which generally concerns itself with the simplest of Biblical narratives and admonitions.   **1942** *Sat. Eve. Post* 3 Oct 17 **GA coast,** "Shout"—which isn't a sound made with the mouth, but a kind of ecstatic sacred dance.   **1972** Jones–Hawes *Step it Down* 45 **GA,** The nonreligious shout step appears in several traditional children's plays.   *Ibid* [see **shout** v 2].

2 See **shout song.**

shouter, shouting See **shout** v

shouting Methodist n [**shout** v 1] scattered, but esp C Atl, **PA, OH, WV** See Map Cf **howling Methodist**

A Methodist who exhibits religious enthusiasm with loud cries or vigorous bodily motions; the denomination whose adherents express themselves in such a manner.

1851 Burke *Polly Peablossom* 87 **GA,** Forgeron was from that time "a shouting Methodist."   **1855** (1856) Manship *13 Yrs.* 122 **MD,** She had long been a shouting Methodist, and on this occasion, she was powerfully blessed. . . And while she leaped and praised God, we heard her exclaim: "Glory to God, the Roman Catholics shall never have that church." **1884** Baldwin *Yankee School-Teacher* 39 **VA,** They're all pious (real shouting Methodists), and they never do nothin' else that's foolish. **1893** Frederic *Copperhead* 66 **nNY,** People used to say, though, that he behaved like a shouting Methodist. This was another way of saying that he made a nuisance of himself in church. **1923** Cook *50 Yrs.* 231, A great revivalist of the shouting Methodist school, who could soon have great numbers of blind followers under the influence of . . "the power." **1942** Handy *Father of Blues* 158 **nwAL,** My mother was a "shouting Methodist". **1965–70** *DARE* (Qu. CC4, . . *Nicknames . . for various religions or religious groups*) 67 Infs, **scattered, but esp C Atl, PA, OH, WV,** Shouting Methodists; [**LA**11, **NC**36, **SC**46, Shouting Baptists;] (Qu. CC2, . . *Predominant religious denominations*) Inf **IA**3, Shouting Methodist; (Qu. CC3, . . *Religions that have come in recently . . or are a bit different from the common ones*) Inf **NY**73, Shouting Methodists. **1986** Pederson *LAGS Concordance,* 1 inf, **nwAR,** Shouting Methodist.

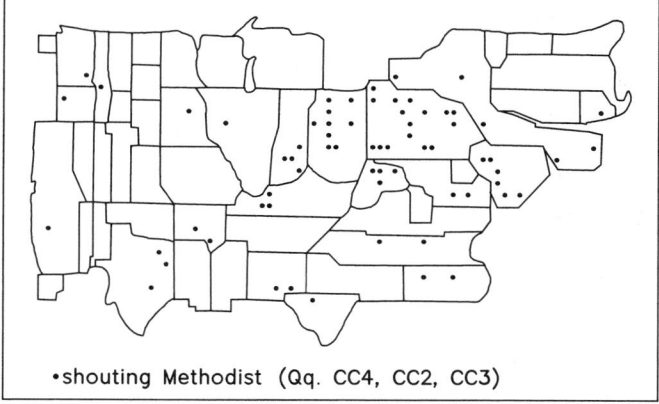

•shouting Methodist (Qq. CC4, CC2, CC3)

shout oneself happy See **shout** v 1

shout song n Also *(ring) shout* *esp freq among Black speakers*

A song used to accompany a **shout** n 1; hence n *shout singer.*

1867 Allen *Slave Songs* 44 **csSC,** *Early in the Morning.* . . This shout is accompanied by the peculiar shuffling dance except in the chorus, where they walk around in slow time, keeping step to their song. **1920** (1921) Moton *Finding a Way* 18 [Black], He must have inherited his ability to sing from his father, "Uncle Jim," who was a noted "shout singer" in the neighborhood. Sam was not a "Christian" and so sang everything. **1925** Scarborough *On Trail Negro Folk-Songs* 269 **nwAL,** The "shout" songs were lively religious songs introduced to give the Negroes something of the emotional thrill that they might have had from dancing, if that amusement had not been sternly forbidden in many sections. **1926** Van Vechten *Nigger Heaven* 84 **NYC,** When she got through dancing, she'd sit down to the piano and sing a shout or a lively Spiritual. **1929** Gordon *Born to Be* 106 [Black], It was at these religious gatherings that I saw how mother got the fear of God ground into her soul: it was by dominating characters singing, barking and stomping their belief into susceptible minds, made so by suffering. . . Probably if mother had been dead at the time, I might have had a different feeling about the affair. Maybe I would not have gotten the amusement out of joining in on the ring shouts, as I did. **1934** Couch *Culture South* 554 **SC, GA** [Gullah], The "shout songs" are fascinating but little known. They are now sung only in the sea-island and tidewater section of South Carolina and Georgia. They are characterized by simple and monotonous music, insistent rhythms, and a shuffling movement by the singers. *Ibid* 555, Typical "shout song" lines are: Leaders: I'm a soldier./ All: In de army of de Lawd!/ Leaders: I'm a soldier./ All: In de army of de Lawd! **1970** Major *Dict. Afro-Amer. Slang* 103, Shout: (1920's) . . a slow blues or spiritual done like a chant.

shout step See **shout** n 1

shove v

1 pronc-sp *sheve:* To move (down, over, etc), esp in crowded circumstances, to make room for another person. **scattered, but chiefly Nth, N Midl, esp NEast** See Map Cf **scoot** v 2

1923 (1946) Greer-Petrie *Angeline Doin' Society* 21 **csKY,** He could sheve up and make room fur Tomkins. **1950** *WELS (To move over [for* example on a long bench] without getting up: "Can you _____ and make room for one more?") 8 Infs, **WI,** Shove over. **1960** Criswell *Resp. to PADS 20* **Ozarks,** Shove over. . . Move over; when in close quarters or a crowd, one moves over to make room. **1965–70** *DARE* (Qu. Y52, *To move over—for example on a long bench: "We have to make room for one more. Can you _____ [a little]?"*) 142 Infs, **scattered, but chiefly Nth, N Midl, esp NEast,** Shove over; **CT**8, **IA**17, **MA**76, **NJ**36, **NY**92, 136, **OH**11, Shove along; **MA**123, **SC**21, **WI**8, Shove down; **CO**15, **MS**6, Shove up.

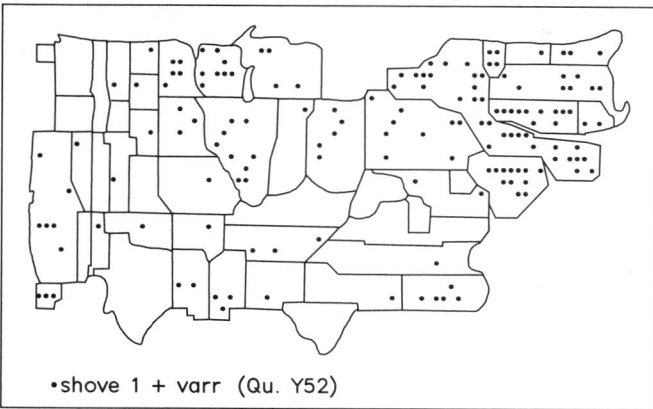

•shove 1 + varr (Qu. Y52)

2 also with *down, up:* To drive (cattle), esp rapidly. **West** Cf **shove-down** n, **shove-up** n

1922 Rollins *Cowboy* 253 **West,** For the first week, the herd was "shoved" to the reasonable limit of its speed, that the beasts might tire into submissiveness, and thereafter willingly keep to the course which their owners had planned. **1926** Bennet *Boss Diamond A* 34 **WY,** To shove cows up on the high range too soon meant scant grass and poisoning from larkspur and loco weed. *Ibid* 195, You might drift all the herd along, and shove bunches ahead to load 'em as fast as they get here. **1929** *AmSp* 5.72 **NE** [Cattle country talk], "Cattle-drives" . . are not the difficult tasks they once were. . . The men "shove" the cattle or "push" them to the limit of speed the first day in order to tire the cattle and make them submissive. **1944** Adams *Western Words* 143, Shove down—This term is used in certain mountain ranges when, during the fall months, cattle are rounded up from the higher country and shoved down into the valleys or lower country to winter. **1961** [see **shove-down** n].

shoved ppl adj

Hard-pressed (by circumstances).

1859 Taliaferro *Fisher's R.* 196 **nwNC** (as of 1820s), I'd . . git out'n the scrap ef possible, fur I were shoved fur the rent. **1952** Brown *NC Folkl.* 1.590, Shoved to death: . . Very busy. "I'm shoved to death trying to finish my plowing."—Central and east.

shove down v See **shove** 2

shove-down n Cf **shove** 2

The driving of cattle into lower ranges for the winter; hence comb *shove-down crew.*

1926 Bennet *Boss Diamond A* 153 **WY,** I should not leave until the shove-down. **1961** Adams *Old-Time Cowhand* 252, Sometimes in the fall months in the mountain ranges cattle would be rounded up from the higher country and drove into the valley or lower country to winter, and this was called "shovin' down." The men doin' this work were called the "shove-down crew."

shovelbill n

1 also *shovel duck, shovelmouth, shovelnose:* =**shoveler.** [*OED2* 1864 →]

1888 Trumbull *Names of Birds* 42 **MD, NJ,** Shoveller. . . At Tuckerton, N.J., and Crisfield, Md., it is the shovel-bill. **1917** *Wilson Bulletin* 29.2.77 **SC,** *Spatula clypeata.*—Shovel-mouth, Oakley, S.C. **1940** *WI Conserv. Bulletin* 5.8.55, Shoveler: spoonbill, shovelbill . . shovel nose, shovel duck [etc]. **1965–70** *DARE* (Qu. Q5, . . *Kinds of wild ducks*) Infs **SC**24, **VA**47, Shovelbill; **DE**4, Butterball or shovelbill.

2 also *shovelbill cat, shovel-billed cat(fish):* Usu the **paddlefish,** but also **flathead catfish 1.**

1878 U.S. Natl. Museum *Bulletin* 12.72 **TN,** *List of Fishes of Nashville* . . Shovel-bill Cat. **1890** TX Geol. Surv. *Report* 487, Of the catfish there are four kinds, channel cats, yellow cats, mud cats, and shovel-billed cats. **1906** *DN* 3.156 **nwAR,** Shovel-bill cat. . . A kind of catfish. **1944** *Chicago Daily News* (IL) 17 July 21/1 **Ozarks,** If you are a born hillbilly, . . you jab at . . red-horse, shovel-bills, and other strangely named creatures of the river. **1965–70** *DARE* (Qu. P1, . . *Kinds of freshwater fish* . . *caught around here* . . *good to eat*) Inf **KY**16, Shovel cat or shovelbill; **OK**52, Shovelbill; **OK**23, Shovelbill cat—bill four inches wide, twelve inches long; **KY**86, Shovelbill cat—same as spoonbill cat; **TN**26, Shovelbill cat; **OK**11, Shovel-billed catfish, spoonbill catfish. **1969** *DARE* FW Addit **KY,** Shovelbill cat—book name: spoonbill—a fish. **1986** Pederson *LAGS Concordance,* 1 inf, **neTX,** Shovelbill cats—freshwater. **2000** *DARE* File—Internet **swVA,** The Clinch boasts the largest variety of fish to be found in any Virginia stream. Small and largemouth bass, red-eye, blue-gill, channel, blue, and shovel-bill cat fish . . are abundant.

shovel cat n
=**paddlefish.**

1908 Forbes–Richardson *Fishes of IL* 18, Various names . . have been applied to this fish [=the paddlefish], the commonest of which are spoonbill, shovel-fish or shovel-cat, duck-bill cat, and spade-fish. **1969** *DARE* (Qu. P1, . . *Kinds of freshwater fish* . . *caught around here* . . *good to eat*) Inf **KY**16, Shovel cat or shovelbill. **2000** *DARE* File—Internet **nKY,** *Shovel Cats*—are being caught on goldfish, shiners and bluegills.

shovel duck See **shovelbill 1**

shoveler n Also *shoveler duck, shuffler* Also sp *shoveller* [*OED2* 1674 →]

A duck (*Anas clypeata*) noted for its spatulate bill. Also called **broadbill 2, cow frog 2, dredge boat, feather bed 3, Irish mallard, jew duck 3, mud ~ 2, mud lark 3, ~ shoveler, mule duck 1, pile it, pipebill, scooper, shelduck 2, shit-digger, shovelbill 1, spoonbill, swaddle-bill, turd-rassler**

1709 (1967) Lawson *New Voyage* 149 **NC, SC,** Shovellers (a sort of Duck) are gray, with a black Head. **1731** Catesby *Nat. Hist. Carolina* 1.96, *Anas Americanus lato rostro. The Blue-wing Shoveler.* . . It's [sic] Bill is three inches long, coal black . . much broader toward the tip than at the base. **1838** Geol. Surv. OH *Second Annual Rept.* 186, The shoveler duck receives its name from the form of its bill. **1842** DeKay *Zool. NY* 2.342, The *Shoveller,* or *Spoonbill* . . is more frequently obtained along the rivers and lakes than on the coast. **1890** Warren *Birds PA* 39, The Shoveller is a rare and rather irregular spring and fall migrant in all sections of the state. **1951** *AmSp* 26.92 **MD, NC,** The standard name *shoveler,* for the spoonbill duck, has been rendered as *shuffler* (Indian Head, Md.; Roanoke Island, N.C.) **1965–70** *DARE* (Qu. Q5, . . *Kinds of wild ducks*) 10 Infs, **scattered,** Shoveler. **1982** Elman *Hunter's Field Guide* 127, Dippers or puddle ducks . . include the black duck, gadwall, mallard, pintail, shoveler [etc].

shovelfish n

1 also *shovelfish sturgeon:* =**shovelnose sturgeon.** *obs*

1816 (1819) Thomas *Travels W. Country* 211 **IN, IL,** The *shovel fish* or *flat nose* is another species of sturgeon. It ways [sic] about twenty pounds. **1820** Rafinesque *Ohio R. Fishes* 80, Shovelfish Sturgeon. . . It is very good to eat and bears many names, such as Spade-fish, Shovelfish, Shovel-head, Flat-head, Flat-nose, &c. having reference to the shape of its head, which is flattened somewhat like a spade. **1837** (1924) Higbee *Diary* 23 **NJ,** Saw for the first time a shovel fish they had caught weighing 12 lbs. and very good eating they seemed to think it was. **1852** Fisher *Indiana* 21, The varieties of fish . . in the tributaries of the Ohio are the pike, perch, sucker, shovel fish [etc].

2 =**paddlefish.** Cf **spadefish**

1818 *Amer. Monthly Mag. & Crit. Rev.* 3.354, Polyodon folium . . [Vulgar name:] Shovel-fish. **1847** *Knickerbocker* 29.332, The shovel or spoon-bill fish is only found in the Alabama and its tributaries. **1911** U.S. Bur. Census *Fisheries 1908* 313, Paddle-fish. . . Local names are "spoonbill," "duckbill cat," and "shovelfish." **1933** LA Dept. of Conserv. *Fishes* 374, Spoonbill, Duckbill Cat, Shovelfish and Spadefish, all these popular names refer to the Paddlefish's most striking characteristic, the long, thin, expanded, blade-like snout which, extending far beyond its mouth, appears to be a sensitive organ of touch. **2001** *DARE* File **LA,** A shovelfish is a spoonbill catfish.

shovelfish sturgeon See **shovelfish 1**

shovelhead cat n Also *shovelhead (catfish)*
=**flathead catfish 1.**

1943 Eddy–Surber *N. Fishes* 160, Farther south the shovelhead catfish is sometimes found in submerged hollow logs, from which it is often taken by hand. **1957** Trautman *Fishes* 430, Since 1900 this species, usually called Shovelhead Cat in southern Ohio, was common and much sought after in the Ohio River. **1968** *DARE* (Qu. P3, *Freshwater fish that are not good to eat*) Inf **NC**53, Shovelhead catfish. **2000** *DARE* File—Internet **nKY,** [Fishing report:] Shovelheads—pace picking up . . on shiners, and goldfish! *Ibid,* Shovelhead Cats very slow. Blue Cats doing well on shiners. *Ibid,* Shovelhead Catfish—being caught in paylakes with suckers, and bluegills.

shovelhead shark n

A hammerhead shark (here: usu *Sphyrna tiburo*).

1873 in 1878 Smithsonian Inst. *Misc. Coll.* 14.2.35, *Reniceps tiburo.* . . Shovel-head shark. Cape Cod to Florida. **1933** LA Dept. of Conserv. *Fishes* 220, The Bonnethead or Shovelhead Shark, *Reniceps tiburo* . . is a common species along our Gulf Coast and exhibits a curious broad, flattened expansion of the head.

shoveller See **shoveler**

shovelmouth See **shovelbill 1**

shovelnose n

1 See **shovelnose cat.**
2 See **shovel-nosed shark 1.**
3 See **shovelnose pike.**
4 See **shovelnose sturgeon.**
5 See **shovelbill 1.**

shovelnose cat n Also *shovelnose*
=**paddlefish.**

1951 Harlan–Speaker *IA Fish* 34, Paddlefish. . . Other Names—Spoonbill cat, boneless cat, shovel-nose cat, flatbill, and incorrectly, spoonbill sturgeon. **1969** *DARE* (Qu. P14, . . *Commercial fishing* . . *what do the fishermen go out after?*) Inf **IL**81, Catfish is what they're after; shovelnose and flatheads—varieties of cat.

shovel-nosed shark n

1 also *shovelnose (shark):* Any of several sharks such as a hammerhead shark, a **man-eater 1,** or a sand tiger; see quots. Cf **shovelhead shark**

[**1707** Funnell *Voyage* 5.120 (*OED2*), The Shovel-nos'd Shark.] **1709** (1967) Lawson *New Voyage* 158, *Sharks.* . . Of these there are two sorts; one call'd *Paracooda* [Barracuda]-Noses; the other Shovel-Noses. [**1805** in 1815 *Lit. & Philos. Soc. NY Trans.* 1.282, Three sharks of the shovel-nosed species were taken in a net by Mr. Joshua Terry, of Riverhead. The largest was eleven feet in length. On opening him many detached parts of a man were found in his belly.] **1832** Williamson *Hist. ME* 1.161, The *Shark,* among fishermen, is called the "maneater," the "shovel-nose," and the "swingle-tail;" these being varieties of the species. **1842** DeKay *Zool. NY* 4.362, The Hammer-head Shark . . is popularly termed *Shovel-nose* and *Hammer-head,* by our fishermen, and is much dreaded for its boldness and ferocity. **1865** *Ladies' Repository* July 442, The sunfish, sawfish, white shark, blue or shovel-nose shark, were often seen. **1884** Goode *Fisheries U.S.* 1.671 **ME,** The Sand Shark—Odontaspis littoralis. This species, known also on the coast of Maine as the "Shovel-nosed Shark" . . is found on our coast from New England southward to Charleston. *Ibid* 672, Bonnet-headed Shark—Sphyrna tiburo. This species is found in our waters in company with [Sphyrna zygaena], and when both are known to fishermen, the names "Hammer-head" and "Shovel-nosed" are used indiscriminately for both. *Ibid* 676 **Pacific,** Heptranchias maculatus. This species is usually known as the "Shovel-nosed Shark". . . It ranges from Monterey Bay northward, being most abundant in Northern California. **1906** NJ State Museum *Annual Rept. for 1905* 52, Carcharias littoralis. . . Possibly the shovel nose shark of the fishermen is this species. *Ibid* 65, Bonnet-Headed Shark. . . Possibly reports of the "shovel nose shark" from Cape May may in part refer to this species. **2000** *DARE* File—Internet **seFL,** The shallow waters of Florida Bay also make it possible to land pretty fair-sized sharks on light tackle. Lemons, duskies, bulls, shovelnose and occasional hammerheads can all be caught this way.

2 also *shovelnose shark*, ~ *guitarfish:* A guitarfish (here: *Rhinobatos productus*). **CA**

1933 John G. Shedd Aquarium *Guide* 22 **CA,** *Rhinobatos productus*. . . The California Guitar Fish is abundant in the vicinity of Los Angeles, where it is incorrectly called Shovel-nosed Shark. **1936** Barnhart *Marine Fishes S. CA* 11, *Rhinobatos productus*. . . Commonly though inaccurately known as "shovel-nose shark." **1953** Roedel *Common Fishes CA* 24, Shovelnose Guitarfish. . . It is often caught by sport fishermen who usually call it "shovelnose shark." **2001** (acc) U.S. Dept. Ag. *Integrated Taxonomic Info. System* (Internet), *Rhinobatos productus*—Vernacular Name: shovelnose guitarfish.

shovel-nosed snake n [See quot 1974]

A western snake of the genus *Chionactis*.

1947 Pickwell *Amphibians* 50, *Chionactis occipitalis*, the Spade-nosed, or Shovel-nosed, Snake . . has an upper jaw longer than the lower, with the snout long, rounded, and depressed or flattened, apparently for burrowing. **1974** Shaw–Campbell *Snakes West* 156, The beautiful western shovel-nosed snake is highly adapted to a life of sand swimming. Its head is indeed shaped somewhat like a shovel; from the top of its head to the snout there is a continuous slope.

shovel-nosed sturgeon See shovelnose sturgeon

shovelnose guitarfish See shovel-nosed shark 2

shovelnose pike n Also *shovelnose*

=**northern pike 1.**

1894 *Outing* 24.59, The big "pike" was slow in its movements, and Jack had plenty of warning before the shovel-nose showed in the rapid right at his feet. **1927** Weed *Pike* 44 **nMI,** *Esox lucius*. . . Shovelnose Pike; northern Michigan and western Ontario. **1967** *DARE* (Qu. P1, . . *Kinds of freshwater fish . . caught around here . . good to eat*) Inf **MI**47, Shovelnose pike.

shovelnose shark See shovel-nosed shark 1, 2

shovelnose sturgeon n Also *shovelnose*, *shovel-nosed sturgeon*

A **sturgeon** of the genus *Scaphirhynchus* (here: usu *S. platorhynchus*). Also called **hackleback 1.** For other names of *S. platorhynchus* see **flathead sturgeon, sand ~, shovelfish 1, switchtail**

1849 U.S. Congress *Serial Set* 570 Doc 5.1025, *Ho-tan-ke* . . is applied . . by the Sioux to the shovel-nosed sturgeon of the Mississippi. **1911** U.S. Bur. Census *Fisheries 1908* 317, *Sturgeon*. . . The various species are known as "lake sturgeon," "white sturgeon," "shovelnose," etc. **1945** *AmSp* 20.278, The 'esturgeon' is the shovelnose (also called *switchtail, hackleback,* or *sand sturgeon*). **1968** *WI Conserv. Bulletin* May–June 14, The gar are sometimes mistaken for the hackleback or shovelnose sturgeon. **2000** (acc) N. Prairie Wildlife Research Center *Biol. Resources* (Internet) **ND,** The only other fish that may be confused with the pallid is the shovelnose sturgeon. Both these fish inhabit the Missouri and Yellowstone Rivers of North Dakota.

shovel plow n scattered, but chiefly W Midl See Map

A cultivator with one or more broad, approximately triangular shares—often in var combs indicating the number or style of the shares, as *single-shovel plow, double-shovel (plow).*

1793 (1948) Toulmin *Western Country* 57 **VA,** A man runs with a shovel plow (which is in fact a shovel fixed in a plow-frame) drawn by a poor horse through the rows of Indian corn, by which means they tumble the stones over and just scrape the surface of the soil. **1805** Parkinson *Tour* 492, What they [=Americans] call a shovel-plough, [is] something like a paring-spade. **1838** in 1952 Green *Samuel Maverick* 82 **TX,** He had better not go until he goes out and gets timber sufficient, and makes 3 common ploughs & two shovel ploughs and one with stout beams for a coulter to go before a "bull-tongue." **1853** PA State Ag. Soc. *Report* 1.180 **sePA,** There [is] . . the *Double Shovel Plow,* for dressing corn. **1897** (1968) Sears *Catalogue* 158, Steel Beam Double Shovel Plow for $2.50. . . Shovels are 6 inches wide and 11 inches long, of hardened steel. **1899** Garland *Boy Life* 124 **nwIA** (as of c1870s), They had to ride horse to the single-shovel plough or to pull weeds with their brown and warty hands. **1924** Raine *Land of Saddle-Bags* 228 **sAppalachians,** There is a very large acreage where even the turning plow cannot be used. A makeshift, called a "hillside turner," is widely used, and the simple "bull-tongue" or shovel plow (occasionally the "double-

shovel") does what plowing is possible. **1965–70** *DARE* (Qu. L18, *Kinds of plows*) 37 Infs, **chiefly S Midl,** Double-shovel plow; 23 Infs, **scattered,** Shovel plow; **IN**3, **KY**14, **MO**37, **OH**58, **TN**26, **WV**2, Single-shovel plow; **IN**45, **OH**95, Five-shovel plow; **OH**95, Multiple-shovel plow; **GA**74, Half-shovel plow; **IN**27, One-shovel plow; **MD**29, Triple-shovel plow; **TX**32, Twist-and-shovel plow; **LA**8, Walking double-shovel plow; (Qu. L25, *The implement used to clean out weeds and loosen the earth between rows of corn*) 9 Infs, **esp KY,** Double-shovel plow; **KY**68, **OH**72, **PA**191, Shovel plow; [**OH**50, Double-shoveled plow]. **1966** *Cynthiana Democrat* (KY) 28 Apr 6/7, *Public Auction* . . 2–3 shovel plows; rastas. **1986** Pederson *LAGS Concordance* **Gulf Region,** 16 infs, Shovel plow(s); 3 infs, Double shovel plow; 2 infs, Half shovel plow(s); 1 inf, Single shovel plow.

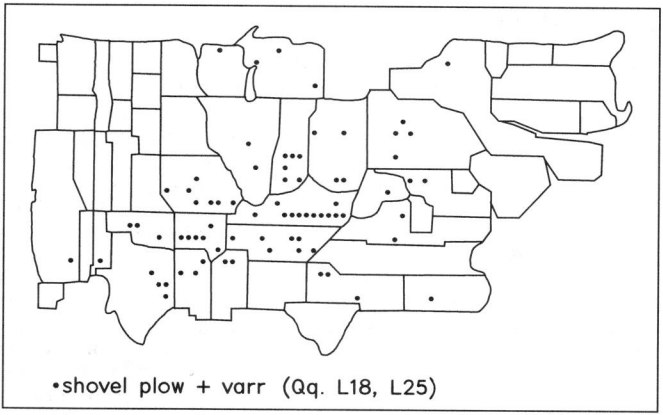

•shovel plow + varr (Qq. L18, L25)

shove up v See shove 2

shove-up n Cf shove 2

The driving of cattle into higher ranges for the summer.

1926 Bennet *Boss Diamond A* 31 **WY,** Dolan . . goes with the chuck wagon when we pull out for the shove-up.

show n

1 also rarely *showing:* A prospect, chance, promise; an opportunity, opening.

1856 (1930) Buck *Yankee Trader* 162, I do not suppose Fillmore has that much show. **1860** (1937) Lewis *Diary Pike's Peak* 14.214 **PA,** Walked over to Graves' ranch this morn. Good show for mules. **1864** in 1926 Twain *Sketches* 141, Give him another show. **1878** Hart *Sazerac Lying Club* 51 **NV,** I thought if I could only reach that thar gun I'd have something like an even show with the bar [=a grizzly bear]. **1884** *Anglia* 7.277 **Sth, S Midl** [Black], *To give er ne'er (another) showin'* = to give another opportunity. **1899** (1912) Green *VA Folk-Speech* 385, *Show.* . . Chance; opportunity; appearance. "There is some show for rain this afternoon." **1899** (1977) Norris *McTeague* 215 **nCA,** The old invariable formula came back to McTeague on the instant. "What's the show for a job?" **1907** Wright *Shepherd* 34 **Ozarks,** The worst of it is, there ain't much show to get a man; unless that one over on Bear Creek will come. **1912** (1914) Sinclair *Flying U Ranch* 188, Our only show is to stop with our toes on the right side of the dead line. **1926** Roberts *Time of Man* 207 **KY,** There's a pretty gal that's got bright glossy hair all done up high and a blue ribbon around her neck. She'll beat your time. . . You got no show, Sallie Brown. **1951** Hench *Coll.* **csWV,** He [=a resident of Marlinton WV] was telling me about his chances of going home soon [from the hospital]: There's no show for me to go home before the middle of next week. . . I . . don't think there's any show that I'll be going for some days yet. **c1960** Wilson *Coll.* **csKY,** *Show.* . . Chance, prospect, promise. "We've got a good show of taters."

2 A logging operation; the operating conditions that affect a logging operation. Cf **chance B5**

1938 (1939) Holbrook *Holy Mackinaw* 263, *Show.* A logging chance. Spoken of as a *good show* or a *poor show.* **1941** *AmSp* 16.233 [Lumberjack jargon], *Show.* A word with many general uses applied to almost everything. Thus, the *logger* speaks of the *whole show,* a *poor* or *bum show,* a *haywire show.* **1942** *AmSp* 17.223 [Loggers' talk], *Nosebag show.* A camp where the midday meal is carried to the woods in dinner pails. Badly thought of by modern loggers. **1950** *Western Folk.* 9.119 **nwOR** [Logger speech], *Show.* Site of logging operations. **1956** *Ibid* 15.202 [Logger talk], *Hemlock show,* an old-time term for logging in a poor, scrubby kind of timber. Hemlock was once a weed tree, unwanted by the mills, hence its term. Pulp mills have made it an aristocrat of the forests, so the term, "hemlock show," is no longer a slur. **1958** McCulloch *Woods Words* 163 **Pacific NW,** *Show*—a. A logging operation (cat show, high lead show, winter show, summer show, etc.). b. The operating conditions which affect logging, as a poor show, a good show. **1961** Labbe–Goe *Railroads* 259 **Pacific NW,** [Glossary:] *Show:* Used to indicate the immediate area of operation. Also the type of logging, such as donkey show, caterpillar show, etc. **1969** Sorden *Lumberjack Lingo* 109 **NEng, Gt Lakes,** *Show*—A logging operation or a logging chance.

showancy n Cf **pushency**
   1952 Brown *NC Folkl.* 1.590, *Showancy. . .* Aggressiveness, "pushiness." A variant of *assurancy* (?).—Granville county. Illiterate.

show daylight See **daylight 3**

shower of rain n Also *shower rain* [*OED2 shower of rain* (at *shower* sb.¹ 1.b) a1300 →]   **esp SE**   See Map
A rain shower.
   1756 in 1931 Washington *Writings* 1.355 **VA,** A hard shower of rain prevented their making a farther search. **1835** *N. Amer. Rev.* 40.404, They suffered from the burning heat, and were completely drenched by an unexpected shower of rain. **1869** in 1980 *Ho for CA* 224 **TX,** Had nice shower of rain last night. *c***1938** in Lib. of Congress *Amer. Memory: WPA Life Hist.* (Internet) **GA,** I've been interviewed by social workers that haven't had sense enough to get out of a shower of rain. **1941** *Hall Coll.* **wNC, eTN,** Shower of rain. A passing shower. Common. **1965–70** *DARE* (Qu. JJ15a, *Sayings about a person who seems to you very stupid: "He hasn't sense enough to _____."*) Infs **AL**8, 46, **AR**22, **FL**6, 22, 39, **GA**86, **SC**54, Get out (*or* come (in) out) of a shower of rain; **SC**40, Get out a shower of rain; **GA**12, Get out of a hard shower rain; **NC**51, Get out of a shower rain. **1986** Pederson *LAGS Concordance (Heavy rain)* 3 infs, **TN, ceGA,** A shower of rain; *(A steady drizzle)* 3 infs, **cnLA, seMS, cTX,** A shower of rain.

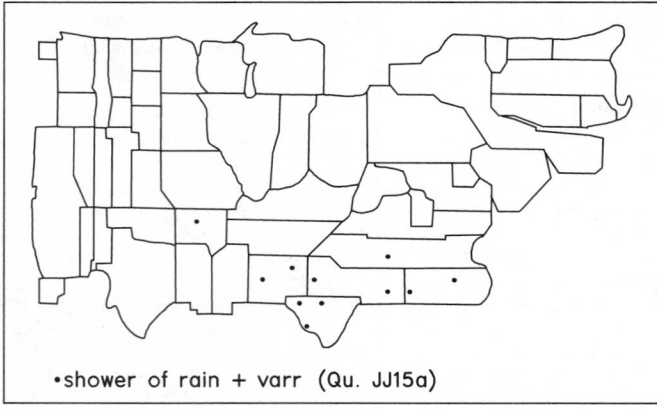

•shower of rain + varr (Qu. JJ15a)

show for v phr [Engl dial]
Of weather: to promise, portend.
   1969 *DARE* (Qu. B5, *When the weather looks as if it will become bad, you say . . _____*) Inf **OH**88, It shows for storm.

show house n Also *show hall*   **scattered, but esp West, WI**
See Map
A movie theater.
   *c***1938** in Lib. of Congress *Amer. Memory: WPA Life Hist.* (Internet) **NE,** [It is] the same equipment in the . . most modern equipped show house in the world, the Radio City Music Hall. **1950** *WELS (The place where you go to see a motion picture)* 12 Infs, **WI,** Show house. **1954** *Harder Coll.* **cwTN,** Show house. . . Motion picture house. **1960** Bailey *Resp. to PADS 20* **KS,** Show house. *c***1960** *Wilson Coll.* **csKY,** Show house. . . A moving-picture showhouse. **1965** *Rockport Democrat* (IN) 13 Aug 11/2, And those good times enjoyed down at the old Show House on Main Street where even some had held jobs as ticket-taker and piano player at the picture shows. **1965–70** *DARE* (Qu. FF24) 18 Infs, **scattered, but esp West, WI,** Show house; **KY**54, Show hall; **WA**18, Moving-picture show house; **NC**33, Picture show house. **1971** Bright *Word Geog. CA & NV* 200, *Theater . . show house* 7% [of 300 infs]. **1973** *Fairbanks Daily News–Miner* (AK) July 9 *(Tabbert Coll.),* There was a free movie at the Agimak's show hall that evening. **1977** Miles

Ozark Dict. 9, *Show house*—Movie Theatre. "The show house is across the street from the church house and just down the hill from the school house." **1983** *MJLF* 9.1.55 **ceKY,** *Show house . .* a movie theater. **1986** Pederson *LAGS Concordance (Theater)* 1 inf, **cnAR,** A show-house.

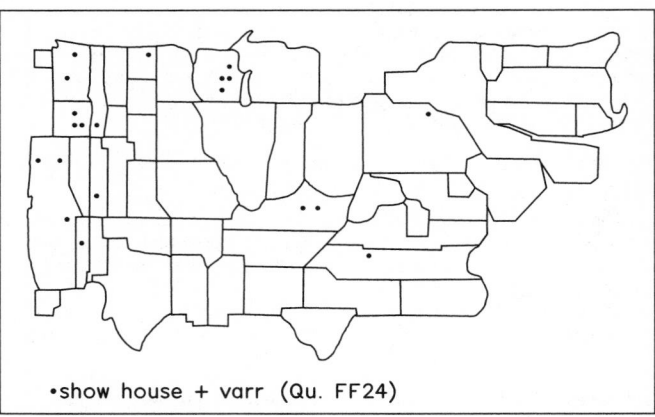

•show house + varr (Qu. FF24)

showing See **show 1**

show out v phr, hence vbl n *showing out*   **chiefly Sth, S Midl**
See Map
To make a display of oneself, behave extravagantly, esp in order to draw attention to oneself; to brag, show off; hence n *show-out* one who does this.
   1841 *Ladies' Repository* 1.368, T_____ came forward before this assembled multitude with almost an *audacious* air, deliberately made his best bow, and so far from being abashed, became quite graceful, in the gratified opportunity, as it seemed, of *showing out.* **1859** Taliaferro *Fisher's R.* 176 **nwNC,** He . . buckled up to the 'squire, like a little dog does to a big one when he wants to show out. **1891** Freeman *Far-Away Melody* 258 **NEng,** See that old lady trailing her best black silk by. . . Ain't it ridiculous how she keeps on showing out? **1932** Stribling *Store* 125 **AL,** The little idiot says he doesn't believe in God. . . I think . . he does it to show-out. **1940** *AmSp* 15.220 **cwTX,** If a Westerner is vexed with someone who is 'showing out' (bragging), he is capable of saying quite a few things. **1944** *PADS* 2.49 **NC, VA,** Show out. . . To show off. "They was great folks for showing out." **1945** *AmSp* 20.306 **SW** [Cowboy slang], He's showing out. (He's bragging.) **1954** *Harder Coll.* **cwTN,** Show out. . . To move around in such a way that people will take notice. . . A loud, self-assertive person. *c***1960** *Wilson Coll.* **csKY,** Show out. . . To show off, often with the added idea of letting the cat out of the bag, revealing too much. **1965–70** *DARE* (Qu. Y22, *To move around in a way to make people take notice of you: "Look at him _____."*) 11 Infs, **Sth, S Midl,** Show out; **MO**23, **NC**55, **VA**2, Showing out; (Qu. AA8, *When people make too much of a show of affection in a public place . . "There they were at the church supper _____ [with each other]."*) Infs **AL**4, **KY**11, 44, **LA**2, **TX**36, Showing out; **AR**24, Trying to show out; (Qu. DD13, *When a drinker is just beginning to show the effects of the liquor . . he's _____*) Inf **GA**26, A-showin' out; (Qu. FF18, *Joking words . . about a noisy or boisterous celebration or party: "They certainly _____ last night."*) Infs **AL**62, **MS**56, **OK**55, **TN**46, Showed out; (Qu. GG15, *. . A person who became over-excited and lost control, "At that point he really _____."*) Inf **NC**55, Showed out; (Qu. GG19a, *When you can see from the way a person acts that he's feeling important or independent: "He surely is _____ these days."*) Infs **NC**36, **SC**34, Showing out; (Qu. GG42, *A reckless person, one who takes foolish chances*) Inf **KY**85, Show-out; (Qu. HH16, *Uncomplimentary words with no definite meaning—just used when you want to show that you don't think much of a person: "Don't invite him. He's a _____."*) Infs **TX**40, **VA**2, Show-out; (Qu. JJ22, *To express your opinion . . "I went to the meeting, and _____."*) Inf **GA**19, Showed out. **1986** Pederson *LAGS Concordance,* 1 inf, **csAL,** He's showing out = acting foolishly; 1 inf, **swAR,** Show out = show off; 1 inf, **cwTN,** Showing out—of the revellers, who are cutting up; 1 inf, **ceTX,** Fool is always showing out = showing off. **1988** Naylor *Mama Day* 237 **sSC, GA coasts** [Black], You in this house by my good graces, 'cause I don't feel like showing out in front of real company. But I got a reckoning with you. **1996** *Atlanta Jrl.–Constitution* (GA) 11 Feb sec M 3/1, Y'all just showed out, didn't you? (when children misbehaved in public).

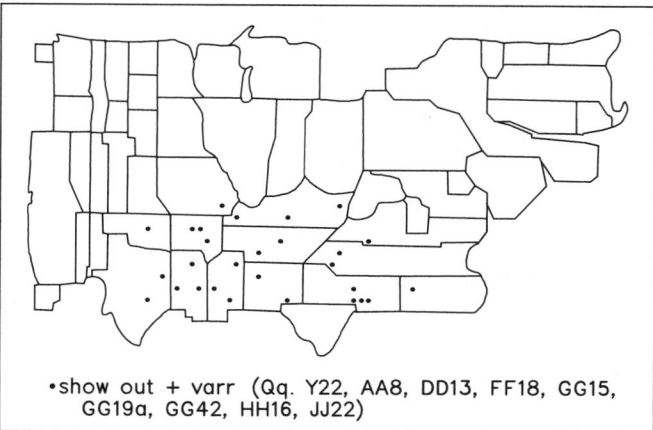

•show out + varr (Qq. Y22, AA8, DD13, FF18, GG15, GG19a, GG42, HH16, JJ22)

show someone where to head in See **head in 3**

shrank See **shrink B2, 4**

shranked See **shrink B2**

shrew n
Std: a small insectivorous mammal of the family Soricidae. For other names of var spp see **ground-mole rat, meadow mole 2, mole** n[1] **3, mole mouse 2, ~ shrew 1, water shrew**

shrew mole n [*OED2* 1614 →]
A **mole** n[1] **1:** either *Scalopus aquaticus* of the eastern US or *Neurotrichus gibbsii* of the Pacific coast.   Cf **mole shrew 2**
    1826 Godman *Amer. Nat. Hist.* 1.84, The shrew-mole is found abundantly in North America, from Canada to Virginia.   **1842** DeKay *Zool. NY* 1.16, The Shrew-mole, for its size, is remarkably strong, and is capable of domestication.   **1917** Anthony *Mammals Amer.* 306, The tunnels of the Shrew Mole resemble those of the Star-nosed Mole more than those of others.   **1952** Burt *Field Guide Mammals* 4, Shrew-mole. *Neurotrichus gibbsi.* . . Smallest of the North American moles, this miniature edition is found along the humid northwest coast.   **1961** Jackson *Mammals WI* 61, *Scalopus aquaticus machrinus.* . . Prairie Mole. . . Other names include common mole, common shrew-mole [etc].   **1980** Whitaker *Audubon Field Guide Mammals* 296, Shrew-mole *(Neurotrichus gibbsii).* . . This creature is aptly named, for it is characterized by the size and forefeet of a shrew and the large head and dental structure of a mole.

shriek n, v Usu |šrik|; also |srik| Pronc-sp *sriek*   Cf **shrimp, shrink**
Std senses, var form.
    1856 [see **shrimp**].   **1907** *DN* 3.250 eME, *Sriek, v.i.* Shriek.   **1940** *AmSp* 15.50 **sAppalachians, Ozarks,** [ʃ] before [r] becomes [s] . . sriek (shriek).   **1941** *AmSp* [see **shrimp**].   **1943** *AmSp* 18.271 **VA,** The [ʃ] before [r] is almost impossible for many Virginians to make; it frequently becomes [s] . . *shrieked* [srikt].

shriek owl n [*OED2* 1567 →; "*Obs.*"]
A **screech owl 1** (here: *Otus asio*).
    1824 *Old Colony Mem.* (Plymouth MA) 6 Mar 180/1 **NEng,** Out squealed cousin Betty Diggins, as loud as a shriek-owl.   **1966–68** *DARE* (Qu. Q1, . . *Kind of owl that makes a shrill, trembling cry*) Infs **IA7, PA26, WA3, WI41,** Shriek owl; (Qu. Q2, . . *Kinds of owls*) Inf **NJ22,** Shriek owl.   **1986** Pederson *LAGS Concordance (Screech owl)* 1 inf, **cTX,** Shriek owl.

shrikepoke See **shitepoke**

shrimp n, v Usu |šrimp|; also **chiefly Sth, S Midl** |šrɛmp, srimp, swimp, swɛmp| Pronc-spp *srimp, swimp*   Similarly adj *srimpy* [Spp of the type *srimp* are also found in Engl dial; cf *EDG* §338]   Cf **shriek, shrink, shrivel** v[1]
Std senses, var forms.
    1804 (1904) Clark *Orig. Jrls. Lewis & Clark Exped.* 1.110, I cought a Srimp.   **1856** in 1941 *AmSp* 16.253, Sometimes the words *shrink, shriek, shrine,* &c., are pronounced as if written *srink, sriek, srine,* the letter *h* being entirely suppressed. This is the affected pronunciation of

over-refined school girls, who cannot bring themselves to utter the homely English sound of *sh* when combined with an *r,* for fear apparently of distorting their faces. The utterance of this combination of sounds certainly does require a projection of the lips beyond what is beautiful; but still all good authority requires that these and similar words should have the full sound of the *sh.* . . The following are the words thus mispronounced: *shred* . . *shrimp* . . *shrivel* . . *shrub.*   **1883** (1971) Harris *Nights with Remus* 143 **GA** [Black], I ketch-a dem swimp, I ketch-a dem crahb.   **1899** (1912) Green *VA Folk-Speech* 413, *Srimps.* . . Shrimps.   **1922** Gonzales *Black Border* 331 **sSC, GA coasts** [Gullah glossary], *Swimp*—shrimp.   **1941** Writers' Program SC *Folk Tales* 101, He lib where dere's ister [oyster] en swimps en crabs.   **1941** O'Donnell *Great Big Doorstep* 19 **sLA,** This meal costed two dollar and eighty cents without the swimps.   **1941** *AmSp* 16.119 **VA,** In words like *shrimp, shriek,* and *shrink,* half of the speakers from all sections said [sr] for [ʃr].   Ibid 251, From childhood I have been familiar with the pruncation in Virginia of *srimp* for "shrimp". . . I have heard it used by people from widely separated parts of Virginia and by people from other southern states, particularly Maryland, the Carolinas, and Georgia.   **1942** *Sat. Eve. Post* 12 Dec 91 **Sth** [Black], I had to wait for my b'iled swimps to cool.   **1943** in 1944 *ADD* **WV,** Shrimp. . . [swɪmps].   **1947** Ballowe *The Lawd* 127 **LA,** To git fust to a rabbit gum, er to a swimp box.   **1956** Algren *Walk on the Wild Side* 148 **New Orleans LA,** Because there *aint* no srimps because we 'et em all.   **1966** *DARE* Tape **FL14,** Srimp and stone crabs and blue crabs, we got plenty of them.   **1967** *DARE* FW Addit **cLA,** Swimp [swɪmp]—Negro pronunciation of shrimp.   **1968** *DARE* (Qu. LL3b, *Shrunk, dried up:* "*He's a little _____ old man.*") Inf **WV3,** Srimpy [srɪmpɪ].   **1989** Pederson *LAGS Tech. Index* 212 **Gulf Region,** [*Shrimp:* 237 infs offered proncs of the type [srɪmp], 46 infs [swɪmp], 31 infs [šrɛmp], 1 inf [swɛmp].]

shrimp bug See **shrimp moth**

shrimp mammy n
See quot.
    1954 *PADS* 21.37 **SC,** *Shrimp mammy.* . . A squid, often caught in the net with shrimp. Coastal area.

shrimp moth n Also *shrimp bug*   **LA**   Cf **fish fly 2**
Perh =**mayfly 1.**
    1981 Pederson *LAGS Basic Materials,* 1 inf **cLA,** River shrimp—live in fresh water; produce "shrimp moth," which fly 2 days & return to water to become shrimp.   **2000** *NADS Letters* **LA,** Shrimp moth/Shrimp bug. . . My husband, who is from St. Francisville, Louisiana, says that these are very common bugs that fly around lights at night. These bugs are mainly seen around the [Mississippi] River. He says they look like shrimp, are white, but have wings like a moth. He has heard this term all his life.

shrimp snapper n
A **mantis shrimp 1** (here: *Squilla empusa*).
    1981 Meinkoth *Audubon Field Guide Seashore* 599, Common Mantis Shrimp. . . This is the "shrimp snapper" well known and respected by shrimp trawlers. A quick slash of one of its large appendages can cut a shrimp in two—or lacerate a finger.

shrink v Usu |šrɪŋk|; also **chiefly Sth, S Midl** |srɪŋk, swɪŋk| Pronc-spp *shwink, srink, swink, swrink* (and similarly with other gram forms); for addit pronc and sp varr see quots   Cf **shrimp, shriek, shrivel** v[1]
A Proncs.
    1808 in 1956 Eliason *Tarheel Talk* 317 **NC,** *Srinking.*   **1825** *Ibid, Swrink.*   **1837** *Ibid, Surink.*   **1847** *Ibid, Serinking.*   **1853** *Ibid, Swrunk.*   **1883** (1971) Harris *Nights with Remus* 159 **GA** [Black], Skin, 'e do swink, 'e do swivel.   **1890** *DN* 1.69 **KY, NEng,** *Srink:* for *shrink.*   **1891** *PMLA* 172 **TN,** *S'rink* is used for shrink.   **1892** *DN* 1.218 **PA,** *Srink.* . . It is common in New England. . . *Srink* is "heard among Philadelphians of fair education."   **1893** *DN* 1.278 **nwCT,** [Pres:] *Srink* . . [preterit and past participle:] *srunk.*   **1898** Lloyd *Country Life* 145 **AL,** If he keeps on swinkin, I reckon he will dry up and blow away some of these days.   **1899** (1912) Green *VA Folk-Speech* 413, *Srink.* . . For *Shrink.*   Ibid 434, *Swink.* . . A form of shrink.   **1905** *DN* 3.97 **nwAR,** *Swunk up.* . . Exhausted. 'The cook's kinder swunk up.' Originally a negroism from "shrunk up." Rare.   **1906** *DN* 3.158 **nwAR,** *Srinked.* . . Shrank, did shrink.   **1907** *DN* 3.250 **eME,** *Srink.* . . Shrink.   **1909** *DN* 3.378 **eAL, wGA,** *Swink.* . . To shrink. Pret. *swunk.*   **1930** Stoney-Shelby *Black Genesis* 31 **seSC,** De cooter swink down in de mud.   **1952**

Brown *NC Folkl.* 1.597, *Swink*. . . To shrink.—Granville county. . . *Swunk*. . . Past tense and past participle of *swink* . . —Granville county. **1953** [see B2 below]. **c1960** *Wilson Coll.* **csKY,** *Shrunk* is rarely, still /swʌŋk/. **1965–70** *DARE* (Qu. OO37b, . . *"I can't get them on because they've _____ [too much]."*; not asked in early QRs) 18 Infs, **esp Sth, S Midl,** Srunk; **KY**60, 71, **NY**237, **SC**40, Srank; **KY**81, Sranked; **FL**51, **SC**10, Swank; **TX**106, Swunk; **LA**8, **VA**73, Shwank; **DC**13, Swrank; **MO**8, Shtrunk; [**AL**50, Shrunk—[FW: [Inf] has difficulty with this; probably says [srʌŋk]];] (Qu. OO37a, . . *"The first time my wool socks were washed they _____."*; not asked in early QRs) Infs **FL**51, **KY**33, 77, 85, **NC**40, 41, **NJ**67, **TX**86, **VA**42, **WV**7, Srunk; **KY**60, 71, **TX**82, **VA**35, 102, Srank; **GA**59, **TX**106, Swunk; **SC**10, Swank; **VA**73, Shwink; **LA**8, Shwank; (Qu. X51, . . *"He was sick all winter and _____ [quite a bit]."*) Inf **TX**16, Srunk; (Qu. Y32, . . *"If you're going to fit in there you'll have to _____."*) Inf **NC**35, Srink; (Qu. LL3a, . . *"These apples are all _____."*) Inf **AR**47, Swunk up; (Qu. LL3b, . . *"He's a little _____ old man."*) Inf **VA**37, Srunk-up. **1989** Pederson *LAGS Tech. Index* 101, [Of the 1727 instances of *shrink* and its forms collected, 1211 had initial [ʃr-], 416 [sr-], 82 [sw-], 10 [str-], 4 [ʃw-], 2 [skr-], 1 [tsr-], and 1 [č-].]

B Gram forms.

1 pres: usu *shrink;* for varr see quots.

1965 *DARE* Tape **FL**22, It destroyed it, destroyed by the tidal wave and yellow fever. . . It started to shrunk. **1989** Pederson *LAGS Tech. Index* 101, [Of 702 instances of the present tense of *shrink* collected, 542 had the vowel [ɪ], 81 [ɛ], 66 [i], 6 [æ], 6 [e], and 1 [ʌ].]

2 past: usu *shrank* or *shrunk;* also rarely *shrinked, shranked;* for addit varr see quots. Note: Although both *shrank* and *shrunk* are widespread, they are illustr here with the other varr. *Shrunk* was widely used in std Brit and Amer writing throughout the 18th and into the 19th century. Std Brit writing appar settled on *shrank* in the 19th cent, which explains its dominance in the written lang of both countries, with *shrunk* remaining more common in spoken usage in the US.

a1651 (1912) Bradford *Hist. Plymouth* 1.35, Some few shrunk . . at these . . conflicts. **1828** Webster *Amer. Dict., Shrink* . . pret. and pp. *Shrunk*. The old pret *shrank* and p.p. *shrunken* are nearly obsolete. **1829** Kirkham *Engl. Grammar* 146, Shrink—shrunk—shrunk. **1837** *S. Lit. Messenger* 13.107, I always shrank from verbal communication on the subject. **1843** *Ladies' Repository* 3.351, We involuntarily shrunk from the anticipation of the labor which was before him. **1893** [see A above]. **1906** [see A above]. **1909** [see A above]. **1952** [see A above]. **1953** Atwood *Survey of Verb Forms* 21, *Shrink*. . . The preterite *shrunk* /ʃrʌŋk/ or often /srʌŋk/ strongly predominates among all types in all areas. . . though a good many [cultured informants] . . use *shrunk* and *shrank* interchangeably. *Shrank* /ʃræŋk/ or /sræŋk/ is scattered throughout the East, though it is almost unknown in the South. . . *Shrinked* /ʃrɪŋkt/ is extremely rare and scattered, showing nothing like concentration except in the Susquehanna Valley. . . *Swunk* /swʌŋk/ occurs twice in N. Eng. [out of 413 infs], twice in the M[iddle] A[tlantic] S[tates] [out of 475 infs], and 11 times in the S[outhern] A[tlantic] S[tates] [out of 550 infs]. *Swinked* /swɪŋkt/ is used by five Southern informants (three Negro), *swink* /swɪŋk/ by one (Negro), *shrink* /ʃrɪŋk/ by six (three Negro), *shranked* /ʃræŋkt/ by one (N.J.), and *strinked* /strɪŋkt/ by one (N.J.) **1956** *Newsweek* 3 Dec 71, The Suez shutdown shrunk U.S. Middle East oil imports by one-third. **1965–70** *DARE* (Qu. OO37a, . . *"The first time my wool socks were washed they _____."*; not asked in early QRs) 586 Infs, **widespread,** Shrunk (up) [also in phrr]; 10 Infs, 9 **Sth, S Midl,** Srunk; **GA**59, **TX**106, Swunk; 392 Infs, **widespread,** Shrank (up); **KY**60, 71, **TX**82, **VA**35, 102, Srank; **LA**8, Shwank, **SC**10, Swank; **AR**47, **KY**44, **MS**57, 83, **MO**26, **NY**73, **SC**68, **TN**50, **VA**2, 9, Shrinked (up); **KY**81, **MO**8, **NC**50, Shranked (up); **CA**202, **GA**28, **SC**26, Shrink; **VA**73, Shwink; **NJ**55, Shrunken. **1968** *PADS* 50.35 **swTN** [Black], For the past tense of *shrink* three of the seven type I [= infs with little formal educ] . . , and three of the six type II [=those with approx hs educ] informants, . . have /ʃrɪŋkt/. Five, two type I . . and three type II . . have /ʃrʌŋk/. Two type I informants . . have /ʃrɪŋk/. **1973** *PADS* 60.69 **seNC,** Although four of our [12] informants said *shrunk*, all the rest said *shrank*. **1981** *PADS* 67.45 **Mesabi Iron Range MN,** *Shrink* (pret.). . . *Shrunk* is usual . . and *shrank* infrequent . . for both Iron Range and other Minnesota informants. **1989** Pederson *LAGS Tech. Index* 101, [Of the 571 instances of the past tense of *shrink* collected, 522 were strong and 48 weak (with suffixed [-t]). Of the strong forms, 344 had the vowel [ʌ], 125 [æ], 22 [ɛ], 20 [ɪ], 10 [e], and 1 [ɔ]. Of the weak forms, 34 had the vowel [ɪ], 7 [i], 5 [ɛ], and 2 [ʌ]. There was one doubly inflected form: [swɛntɨd].] **1989** *Webster's Dict.*

Engl. Usage 848, The past tense *shrunk* is undoubtedly standard, but we have relatively little evidence of its use in writing.

3 past pple: usu *shrunk;* also *shrank, shrunken;* for addit varr see quots.

1838 *S. Lit. Messenger* 4.541, I have shrank from their intercourse for years, and now I wish again to mingle with them. **1854** *Ladies' Repository* 14.257, The young mother . . has shrunken mournfully into the forlorn, and wrinkled, and unlovely old woman. **1893** *Overland Mth.* 22.622, And yet you have shrank from wooing women. **1953** Atwood *Survey of Verb Forms* 21, *Shrink*. . . A sizeable minority in N. Eng. (64/413) use *shrunken* . . as a past participle. . . *Shrinked* is used as the past participle by two informants, and *swunk* by two. **1965–70** *DARE* (Qu. OO37b, . . *"I can't get them on because they've _____ [too much]."*; not asked in early QRs) [790 Infs, **widespread,** Shrunk (up) [also in phrr]; 18 Infs, **esp Sth, S Midl,** Srunk; **TX**106, Swunk; **MO**8, Shtrunk]; 125 Infs, **widespread,** Shrank (up); **KY**60, 71, **NY**237, **SC**40, Srank; **FL**51, **SC**10, Swank; **LA**8, **VA**73, Shwank; **DC**13, Swrank; 51 Infs, **scattered,** Shrunken; [**MD**17, **MA**73, They [a]re shrunken;] **IL**117, **KS**5, **KY**44, **MS**30, 57, 63, 83, **NY**73, **SC**68, Shrinked; **NC**72, **VA**28, Shranked; **KY**81, Sranked; **GA**77, **TX**76, Shranken; **SC**26, **TN**50, Shrink; **VA**69, Shrinken. [Of all Infs responding to the question, 27% were gs educ or less, 32% coll educ, 60% female; of those giving the response *shrank,* 32% were gs educ or less, 22% coll educ, 52% female; of those giving the response *shrunken,* 12% were gs educ or less, 35% coll educ, 78% female.] **1989** Pederson *LAGS Tech. Index* 101, [Of the 467 instances of the past participle of *shrink* collected, 399 ended with [-ŋk], 35 had suffixed [-ŋ], and 31 suffixed [-t]. Of the forms ending with [-ŋk], 348 had the vowel [ʌ], 24 [æ]; 15 [ɛ], 6 [ɪ], 3 [e], 2 [ɔ], and 1 [i]. Of the forms ending in [-ŋ], 28 had the vowel [ʌ], 5 [ɪ], 1 [i], and 1 [ɛ]. Of the forms ending in [-t], 17 had the vowel [ɪ], 7 [ɛ], 5 [i], 2 [æ]. One doubly inflected form, [swɪŋktɨd], was recorded, as well as one entirely anomalous form, [swænčt].]

4 ppl adj: usu *shrunken* or *shrunk;* also rarely *shrank, shrunkened.*

1965–70 *DARE* (Qu. LL3a, *Shrunk, dried up: "These apples are all _____."*) [21 Infs, **scattered,** Shrunk [alone and in longer phrr]; 15 Infs, **scattered,** Shrunken; 21 Infs, **scattered,** Shrunk up; **LA**11, **NE**4, **SC**26, Shrunken up; **AR**47, Swunk up;] **CA**105, Shrank; **IL**30, Shrunkened; [(Qu. LL3b, *Shrunk, dried up: "He's a little _____ old man."*) 65 Infs, **scattered,** Shrunk-up; 32 Infs, **scattered,** Shrunken; 9 Infs, **scattered,** Shrunk; **CA**107, **ID**5, **MN**33, **NY**2, **SC**2, Shrunken-up; **VA**37, Srunk-up.]

shrinked See **shrink** B2

shrink of the moon n Also *shrinking moon* [Cf *EDD shrink*. . . "Of the moon: to wane."] Cf **dark of the moon**
The period of the waning moon.

1970 *NC Folkl.* 18.62, Kill hogs on shrinking moon, and your meat will shrink when you cook it. **1984** Wilder *You All Spoken Here* 61 **Sth,** Dark of the moon, waste of the moon, downside of the moon, shrink of the moon: when the moon is waning, or decreasing.

shrivel v[1], hence ppl adj *shrivel(l)ed* Usu |ˈʃrɪvəl(d)|; also **chiefly Sth, S Midl** (See Map) |ˈswɪvəl(d)|; also |ˈsrɪvəl(d)|; for addit varr see quots Pronc-spp *scriveled, skrivvel, swivel(ed), swivveled, swivelled* Similarly adj *swivelly* Cf **swizzle**
Std senses, var forms.

1856 [see **shrimp**]. **1883** (1971) Harris *Nights with Remus* 145 **nGA** [Black], 'E . . tail swivel wit' da' fier. **1898** Lloyd *Country Life* 53 **AL,** I . . filled my pockets full of scalybarks and peanuts and some swivelled up apples of my own raisin. **1899** (1912) Green *VA Folk-Speech* 434, *Swivel*. . . To shrivel; to *swivel* up. **1899** Chesnutt *Conjure Woman* 13 **csNC** [Black], De grapes begin ter swivel up des a little wid de wrinkles er old age. **1923** *DN* 5.222 **swMO,** *Swivel*. . . To shrivel. **1924** *DN* 5.295 **csNH,** *Skrivvel, v.i.* To shrink up (or dry corn). Compare shrivel. **1938** Rawlings *Yearling* 204 **nFL,** And him a swivveled, no-account thing, too. **1939** FWP *ID Lore* 242, *Swivel*—shrivel. **1939** FWP *Guide TN* 503, Kill hogs in the dark of the moon and the meat will "swivel" away and make more lard. **1946** *PADS* 6.29 **ceNC,** *Swivel*. . . *Shrivel*. Pamlico. Common. **1956** McAtee *Some Dialect NC* 45, *Swivelled:* pronunc., shrivelled. **1965–70** *DARE* (Qu. LL3a, *Shrunk, dried up: "These apples are all _____."*) [577 Infs, **widespread,** Shriveled (up); **MO**21, **SC**65, Shrivel (up); **GA**23, Shriveled away;] 90 Infs, **chiefly Sth, S Midl, TX, esp KY,** Swiveled (up); **VA**2, Swivelly; **ME**22, Scriveled up; (Qu. LL3b, *Shrunk, dried up: "He's a little*

_____ *old man.")* [239 Infs, **widespread,** Shriveled (up); **SC**9, 65, Shrivel up; **MA**1 Shrively;] 15 Infs, **chiefly Sth, S Midl,** Swiveled (up); **GA**89, Swivelly; **NY**123, [ˈsrɪvld] up; **ME**22, **PA**82, Scriveled up; (Qu. I8, *When root vegetables get old and tough)* [16 Infs, **chiefly Nth, N Midl,** Shriveled (up);] **KY**28, 56, 90, Swiveled; **OH**41, Swivel up; (Qu. Y32, *To squeeze yourself into a small space)* [6 Infs, **scattered,** Shrivel up;] **MS**16, Swivel up; (Qu. DD24, . . *Diseases that come from continual drinking)* Inf **AR**47, Swivels up your brain. **1968** *DARE* FW Addit **GA**22, "He's a swiveled [ˈswɪvəld] up feller"—describing a little old man he knows. **1970** *Foxfire* 4.93 **nGA,** Dig yer sweet 'taters an' sun 'em 'till they gets just th' least bit swiveled, I call it. **1989** Pederson *LAGS Tech. Index* 190, [Among the proncs recorded for *shriveled* and other forms of the verb *shrivel* there are 248 instances of initial [šr-], 130 of [sw-], 59 of [sr-], and 4 of [šw-].] **1993** Mason *Feather Crowns* 139 **KY,** We ain't hardly got any taters left, and they're all swiveled up like little old men.

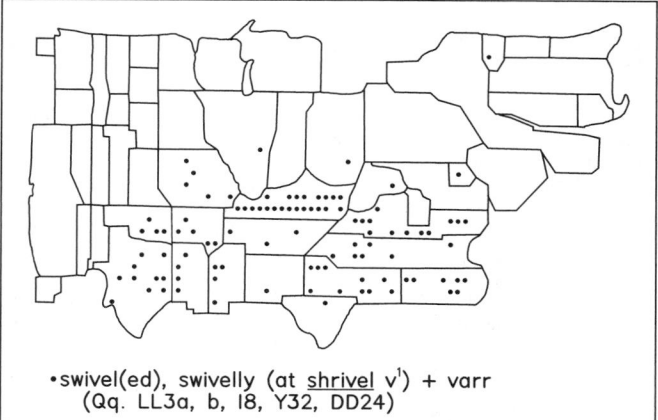

•swivel(ed), swively (at <u>shrivel</u> v¹) + varr
(Qq. LL3a, b, I8, Y32, DD24)

shrivel v² [By hypercorrection for *swivel;* cf **shrivel** v¹]
   1966 *DARE* FW Addit **OK**18, Shrivel [ˈšrɪvəl]—Used for "swivel."

shrivel(l)ed See **shrivel** v¹

shrub n¹ Usu |šrʌb|; also |srʌb| Pronc-spp *srub, swub* Cf **shriek, shrimp, shrink**
   A Proncs.
   1804 (1904) Clark *Orig. Jrls. Lewis & Clark Exped.* 1.96 **swIA,** Two Kind of honeysuckle one which grows to a kind of a Srub. **1856** [see **shrimp**]. **1899** (1912) Green *VA Folk-Speech* 432, *Sweet-shrub. . .* Sweet-*swub.* **1941** *AmSp* 16.251 **VA,** From childhood I have been familiar with the pronunciation . . of . . *srub* for 'shrub.' **1953** *AmSp* 28.254 **csPA,** Shrub. . . Frequently pronounced in popular speech as [srʌb].
   B Sense.
   =Carolina allspice.
   1896 *Jrl. Amer. Folkl.* 9.180 **swOH,** *Calycanthus floridus* . . shrub, sweet-scented shrub, Sulphur Grove, Ohio. **1933** Small *Manual SE Flora* 631, *C[alycanthus] floridus. . .* Shrub. Strawberry-shrub.

shrub v, hence vbl n *shrubbing* Also with *off, out* [*OED2* *shrub* v. 4 "*Obs.*"; →1611] **chiefly S Midl**
To clear the underbrush from (a piece of land); to clear land of brush.
   1851 *U.S. Democratic Rev.* 29.152 **KY,** "Hyah, hyah!" laughed a big, goggle-eyed negro, leaning on his shrubbing hoe, and gazing at the fleeing Yankee. **1855** *De Bow's Rev.* 19.6 **SC,** A church-yard is generally selected as the depository of the remains of the deceased. It is enclosed and shrubbed out until the plat is covered with graves. **1902** *DN* 2.245 **sIL,** Shrub, v. tr. To clear the land of small growth by cutting it off at the ground. **1903** *DN* 2.329 **seMO,** Shrub off. . . To clear land superficially. To cut only the smallest trees. **1907** *DN* 3.226 **nwAR,** *Shrub, v. tr.* To clear land of small growth by cutting it off at the ground. *Ibid* 236, Shrub off. . . To clear land superficially. **1940** Harris *Folk Plays* 33 **NC,** First thing you know he'll be . . a-shrubbin' land. *Ibid* 293, Shrub land, to cut away the undergrowth. **1970** *DARE* (Qu. L36, . . *When you dig out roots and underbrush to make a new field)* Inf **KY**90, Shrubbing—cutting underbrush. **1986** Pederson *LAGS Concordance* (We cleared [the land]) 2 infs, **cAL, neTN,** Shrubbed it (out); 1

inf, **ceTN,** Shrubbing—like "grubbing"; getting everything out; 1 inf, **cAL,** Some say shrubbing; 1 inf, **cwAL,** Shrubbing—if small stuff; 1 inf, **neTN,** Shrubbing off—clearing off. **2002** *DARE* File—Internet **csNC,** Shrubbing tools are intended to cut weeds, vines, briars, wood and other similarly soft materials.

shrub n² Pronc-sp *srub*   **scattered, but esp freq NEng**
A sweetened fruit syrup; a drink made by diluting such a syrup with water (or sometimes with alcohol)—freq in comb *raspberry shrub.*
   1787 in 1915 MA Hist. Soc. *Coll.* 7th ser. 10.310, When our People begin to drink Punch, we will try what can be done with the Arrack and Schrub [sic]. **1831** Child *Frugal Housewife* 82 **MA,** Raspberry shrub mixed with water is a pure, delicious drink for summer. **1861** Holmes *Venner* 1.126 **wMA,** "Is this to be a Temperance Celebration, Mrs. Sprowle?" asked Mr. Silas Peckham. Mrs. Sprowle replied, "that there would be lemonade and srub for those that preferred such drinks . . and that those that didn't like srub . . would find somethin' that would suit them better." *Ibid* 1.143, Silas Peckham . . took from the table a small glass cup, containing a fluid reddish in hue and subacid in taste. This was *srub,* a beverage in local repute, of questionable nature, but suspected of owing its color and sharpness to some kind of syrup derived from the maroon-colored fruit of the sumac. [*Century* Ed: U.S.] **1890** James *Mother James' Cooking* 343, *Currant shrub. . .* To each pint of juice add three-quarters of a pound of white sugar. . . This is a delicious drink when used with equal quantity of ice water. [*Century* Ed: U.S.] **1891** *Century Dict.* 5602, *Shrub. . .* A cordial or syrup consisting of the acid juice of some fruit, as the raspberry, cooked with sugar and vinegar, and diluted with water when used. [*Century* Ed: U.S.] **1900** *Hyde Park Cuisine* 95 **neIL,** *Grape shrub.* **1930** Shoemaker *1300 Words* 52 **cPA Mts** (as of c1900), *Shrub*—A drink made of fruit juices, with a strong alcoholic basis. **1932** (1946) Hibben *Amer. Regional Cookery* 335 **NH,** Raspberry Shrub. **1938** Rawlings *Yearling* 117 **FL,** Jody wished it [=a glass of wine] was something sweeter, blackberry shrub, perhaps. **1939** Wolcott *Yankee Cook Book* 320 **ME,** My grandmother was a Quaker and very, very temperate. . . However, she got thirsty now and then even as you or I, and so she made rasberry shrub. **1950** *WELS* (Home-made . . *drinks)* 1 Inf, **cWI,** Shrub is made of most any kind of berry & sugar. **1953** Piercy *Shaker Cook Book* 33, *Shaker fruit shrub. . .* Crush berries [=red raspberries] and pour hot syrup over fruit. Let stand until cool, and strain. Add lemon juice and a little ice. . . Strawberries, blackberries, or black raspberries can be used in the same way. **1967–69** *DARE* (Qu. DD28b, . . *Fermented drinks . . made at home)* Inf **KY**11, Shrub—grape juice partially fermented; **NY**24, Shrub—raspberry or fruit wine slightly fermented. **1975** Gould *ME Lingo* 254, *Shrub*—A temperance drink much esteemed in early Maine, and still made by many housewives, usually from raspberries. Laid down with sugar and vinegar, the liquid was strong in the bottle and was diluted with cold spring water when served. Absolutely non-alcoholic. A genteel refreshment during an afternoon chat, with cookies. *Shrub* seldom stood by itself as a word; usually in full: *rawzbreeshrub.* **1980** *DARE* File **MA** (as of 1915–20), Raspberry shrub was a cooling summer drink (more elegant than switchel) served before the days when ice was plentiful. It is bottled in a concentrated form (like grapejuice) and combined with cold water when served. It is made of raspberries, sugar, and some vinegar. . . cooked and strained.

shrubbing See **shrub** v

shrubby horsetail n
=Mormon tea 1.
   1889 *Century Dict.* 2893, *Shrubby horsetail,* a popular name for plants of the genus *Ephedra.* **1931** U.S. Dept. Ag. *Misc. Pub.* 101.12, Jointfirs (Ephedra spp.) . . All the species are known also as Mormon-tea, canatillo, Brigham tea, teamsters' tea, shrubby horsetail, and by other local names. **1966** Barnes–Jensen *Dict. UT Slang* 31, Mormon tea. . . Besides Mormon tea and Brigham's tea there were other names including: canatillo, teamsters' tea, shrubby horse tail.

shrubby trefoil n Also *shrub trefoil* [*OED2* 1597]
=hop tree.
   1785 Marshall *Arbustrum* 115, Ptelea trifoliata. *Carolinian Shrub-Trefoil.* **1847** Wood *Class-Book* 202, P[telea] trifoliata. *Shrubby Trefoil. . .* An ornamental shrub, 6–8f high. . . Rare in Western N.Y. **1890** *Century Dict.* 4824, *Ptelea. . . P. trifoliata* is the hop-tree, known also as *wingseed . . wafer-ash,* and *shrubby trefoil.* **1960** Vines *Trees SW* 591, Vernacular names are Three-leaf Hop-tree, Shrubby-trefoil [etc.].

shrub oak n Cf scrub oak

1 A **bear oak** (here: *Quercus ilicifolia*).

1778 Carver *Travels N. Amer.* 508, The *Shrub Oak* is exactly similar to the oak tree. **1792** Belknap *Hist. NH* 3.100, *Shrub* oak. (*quercus pumila* [=*Q. ilicifolia*].) It is found on barren hills and plains. It produces a gall, which is evidently the *nidus* of an insect, and has been used [as] an ingredient in writing ink. **1824** Bigelow *Florula Bostoniensis* 352, The shrub oak grows on dry hills and barren plains, and is commonly considered an indication of a sterile soil. **1847** Wood *Class-Book* 495, Shrub or Scrub Oak. Bear Oak. **a1862** (1865) Thoreau *Cape Cod* 93 **MA**, [Bayberry bush], next to the Shrub-oak, was perhaps the most common shrub thereabouts. Location: sand & sand-banks of Cape Cod. The beach. **1907** *St. Nicholas* May 620, He wore . . stout shoes, strong gray trousers to brave shrub-oaks and smilax.

2 =**chinquapin oak 1.**

1897 Sudworth *Arborescent Flora* 157 **NE**, *Quercus acuminata*. . . Shrub Oak. **1940** Clute *Amer. Plant Names* 163, *Q[uercus] Muhlenbergii* . . shrub oak, scrub oak [etc.]. **1968–70** *DARE* (Qu. T10, . . *Kinds of oak trees*) Infs **IN9, NJ69**, [šrʌb].

shrub off (or out) See shrub v

shrub trefoil See shrubby trefoil

shrunk See shrink B2

shrunken See shrink B3

shrunkened See shrink B4

shub(i)e See shoobie

shuck n[1] Cf hull n, husk n

1a also *cornshuck:* One of the leaves surrounding an ear of corn; the leaves considered as a unit. **chiefly Sth, S Midl** Cf **corn shucking, shuck v[1] 1a**

1782 in 1891 Washington *Writings* 109 **VA**, My countrymen are too much used to corn blades and corn shucks; and have too little knowledge of the profit of grass lands. **1805** in 1924 Steele *Papers* 2.864 **NC**, Anderson . . cribbed 40 waggon Loads of corn in shucks. **1816** in 1824 Knight *Letters* 82 **VA**, What in New England is called the husk of corn, in Virginia is called the *shuck.* **1838** (1930) Sewall *Diary* 197 **ME**, My wagon . . holds 19 bushels [of corn] in the shuck. **1856** in 1956 Eliason *Tarheel Talk* 294 **csNC**, 41 loads [of corn] in the uper crib and 20 in the shuck in the other. **1892** Eggleston *Hoosier Schoolmaster* 55 **IN**, [Footnote:] On the northern belt, shucks are the outer covering of nuts; in the middle and southern regions the word is applied to what in New England is called the husks of the corn. *Shuck*, however, is much more widely used than *husk* in colloquial speech—the farmers in more than half of the United States are hardly acquainted with the word *husk* as applied to the envelope of the ear. **1899** (1912) Green *VA Folk-Speech* 385, *Shuck.* . . The covering of ears of corn. **1902** *DN* 2.245 **sIL**, *Shuck, n.* Husk, which is not used. **1904** *DN* 2.421 **nwAR**, *Shuck.* . . A husk. "I bought seven bushels of corn in the shuck." **1906** *DN* 3.123 **sIN**, *Shuck, n.* Husk, as of corn. **1909** *DN* 3.369 **eAL, wGA**, *Shuck.* . . The husk of an ear of Indian corn: usually in the plural. **1946** *PADS* 6.27 **ceNC** (as of 1900–10), *Shuck.* . . The husk of corn; to husk corn. *Husk* means the cover of a grain of corn, wheat, etc. **1949** Kurath *Word Geog.* 47, The North and the Midland have . . *corn husks* . . against Southern *corn shucks. Ibid* 73, *Corn husks* . . The cover leaves of an ear of corn are called *husks* in the North and the North Midland, *shucks* in the South and the South Midland. **1966** *DARE* (Qu. I32, *How do you know when corn is ready to eat?;* total Infs questioned, 75) Inf **MS45**, Feel corn through shuck for size of ear; **FL27**, Pull down shuck and look to see if grains are filled out; **OK32**, Open shuck, pinch kernels. **1983** *MJLF* 9.1.55 **ceKY** (as of 1956), *Shuck* . . a corn husk. **1989** Pederson *LAGS Tech. Index* 192 **Gulf Region** (*Shuck*) 671 [of 914] infs, Shuck; 23 infs, Corn shuck.

b Used attrib, as:

(1) rarely sp *shock; shuck bed,* ~ *mattress,* ~ *tick:* A mattress stuffed with such leaves; hence *shuck bed* a bed having such a mattress. **chiefly Sth, S Midl**

1835 Kennedy *Horse Shoe Robinson* 2.126 **SC**, A shock-bed was spread for the lady. **1860** *Knickerbocker* June 613, We . . enjoyed in common our shuck-mattress and scanty quilts. **1885** Twain in *Century Illustr. Mag.* 24.547 **MO**, There's always cobs around about in a shuck tick, and they poke into you. **1891** Johnston *Primes & Neighbors* 27

GA, She got out some of the most worn of the bedclothes, and, along with a shuck mattress, she and the cook took them to the cotton-house. **1906** *DN* 3.156 **nwAR**, *Shuck-bed, shuck-mattress*. . . A bed or mattress filled with corn-husks. **1942** Faulkner *Go Down* 62 **MS**, He lay beneath the quilt on the shuck mattress. **1949** Arnow *Hunter's Horn* 199 **KY**, She had known . . innerspring mattresses instead of shuck ticks. **1951** *DE Folk. Bulletin* 1.8 (as of c1870–1900), Enough [corn shuck] was torn to fill a large ticking and was known as a shuck bed. **1956** Algren *Walk on the Wild Side* 10 **wTX**, "It were Ma's stid 'n all the makin's was Ma's too"—"makin's" being the shuck-mattress, quilt coverlet, and two square pillows of the kind still called "shams." **c1960** Wilson *Coll.* **csKY**, Shuck bed. . . A tick or mattress made of shucks. **1969** *DARE* FW Addit **KY5**, Mattresses stuffed with corn shucks; old-fashioned. **1983** *MJLF* 9.1.55 **ceKY** (as of 1956), *Shuck bed* . . a bed with a mattress stuffed with corn husks. **1986** Pederson *LAGS Concordance* **Gulf Region**, 5 infs, Shuck bed; 2 infs, Shuck mattress; 1 inf, Shuck tick.

(2) *shuck broom,* ~ *brush,* ~ *mop,* ~ *scrub (broom):* An implement for sweeping, brushing, or cleaning made from such leaves affixed to a handle. **Sth, S Midl**

1841 [see **1b(3)** below]. **1904** (1913) Johnson *Highways South* 308 **NC**, Another broom was a shuck broom made of corn husks fastened to the end of a stick. **1966–68** *DARE* Tape [**MD24**, My grandfather used to make a broom out of a hickory stick that he called a shuck broom. He would have a sharp knife and would whittle up one end of the stick until he got it all whittled up as fine as he could and then he'd take a piece of wire and up next to the top he'd wrap around it. And that's what we always used to sweep off rough boards in the barn or in the porches or even out in the yard;] **SC12**, They'd get coarse white sand. . . and they'd sprinkle it all over the floor, and they had a shuck scrub broom that had a frame made of about three inches of thick board. . . they bored holes in that frame. . . About four holes crosswise and about six longwise, and they'd go to the cornhouse and get shucks and strip them shucks to about an inch width. . . you could push it through them holes. . . and you'd have a big bushy brush. . . That floor would be white when you scrubbed it with that sand and that shuck broom. **1968** *DARE* (Qu. F36, . . *Kinds of brooms*) Infs **LA28, 33, MD24**, Shuck broom. **1968** *DARE* FW Addit **csLA**, *Shuck broom* = broom made by sticking corn shucks through holes in a board, then affixing a handle. **1983** *MJLF* 9.1.55 **ceKY** (as of 1956), *Shuck broom* . . a broom with the sweeping end made of corn husks. **1986** Pederson *LAGS Concordance* **Gulf Region, exc FL**, 15 infs, Shuck mop(s); 7 infs, Shuck broom(s); 2 infs, Shuck brush; 2 infs, Shuck scrub.

(3) *shuck (horse) collar:* A collar for horses (or mules) made from such leaves plaited into strips and sewn together. **Sth, S Midl**

1781 in 1875 VA *Calendar State Papers* 1.589, Many of these [horses] are sent with "shuck-collars" which are of little use. **1841** *S. Lit. Messenger* 7.775, The more provident part of the slaves . . manufacture . . shuck-bottomed chairs, mats, shuck collars, brooms, and the like. **1896** Read *Jucklins* 128 **nAL**, I saw . . a red-looking negro, with a string of shuck horse collars. **1901** Harben *Westerfelt* 35 **nGA**, Slogan was astride of his bony horse, which was already clad in shuck collar and clanking harness. **1944** Clark *Pills* 278 **Sth**, A fifty-cent shuck collar was good enough for an ordinary plow mule. **1986** Pederson *LAGS Concordance,* 1 inf, **cwMS**, Shuck collars of corn shucks for mules.

(4) *shuck bottom:* A seat, as of a chair, made of such leaves woven together; hence adj phr *shuck-bottomed.*

1841 [see **1b(3)** above]. **1872** Eggleston *End of the World* 282 **CA**, Jonas . . was sitting on a "shuck-bottom" chair. **1899** (1912) Green *VA Folk-Speech* 385, *Shuck-bottom.* . . Having a seat made of the shucks of corn: as, a chair. **1907** Obenchain *Aunt Jane* 4 **KY**, The chairs were ancient Shaker rockers, some with homely "shuck" bottoms. **1938** *AmSp* 13.22 **NE** [Cornhusking terms], Cornhusks helped furnish the pioneer's home. *Shuck bottom* or *Shaker* chairs had seats woven of cornhusks. **1976** Ryland *Richmond Co. VA* 376, *Shuck-bottom*—in a chair, a bottom woven of corn-shucks.

(5) *shuck house:* A farm building in which fodder is stored.

1856 in 1927 Jones *FL Plantation Rec.* 487, 1 [hand], Renty, gitten sills to go under shucke house. **1969** *DARE* (Qu. M22, . . *Kinds of buildings . . on farms*) Inf **GA74**, Shuck house—with shucks from grain.

(6) *shuck pen:* See **pen** n[1] **B3.**

(7) *(corn) shuck tea:* An infusion of such leaves used as a remedy.

1888 *Whitewater Reg.* (WI) 23 Feb 3/5, Oftentimes the simplest remedies, such as pine-water or shuck-tea, were made to serve a timely and efficient turn. **1945** Saxon *Gumbo Ya-Ya* 531 **LA,** Medicine [for Measles]: Shuck tea and sheep pills (dung). **1966** *DARE* Tape **AL1,** Chills and fever . . we had shuck tea for that. . . Go out in the crib and get an ear of corn and pull that shuck off, and boil them shucks, and make a tea out of those shucks. **1970** Anderson *TX Folk Med.* xvii, Field corn supplied shucks . . for the shuck tea that appears in so many cures. *Ibid* 34, *Fever.* . . drink corn shuck tea. **1986** Pederson *LAGS Concordance* 1 inf, **swGA,** Shuck tea—for measles; from boiled corn shucks, served with sugar and whiskey; 1 inf, **cAL,** Shuck tea.

(8) *shuck sausage:* See quot. Cf **slip shuck**

1931 Randolph *Ozarks* 32, Sausage was usually put up in cornshucks. It is easy to pull an ear of corn out of the shuck without damaging the latter, put the sausage inside, and tie the ends of the husk together. These "shuck-sassages" were hung up in the smokehouse and smoked with the other meat, and were usually left hanging there until needed. [**1986** Pederson *LAGS Concordance,* 1 inf, **cwTN,** Shucks—sausage was "put up" in these; 1 inf, **neMS,** [Corn] shucks—used to stuff sausage into; 1 inf, **cwAR,** Shucks—mother used them to stuff sausage; 1 inf, **cnGA,** Corn shucks—to put sausage in.]

c in phr *not to hold shucks;* Fig:

(1) Of a person's skin: to be riddled with holes—used in hyperbolic threats; see quots.

1838 *New-Yorker* (NY NY) 30 June 229/1, If he slopes off in this way again when I want him, his hide won't hold shucks in two minutes arter. **1851** Burke *Polly Peablossom* 176 **OH,** Buckeyes . . will fight the enemies of their country, until their hides cannot hold shucks for the bullet holes. **1871** Eggleston *Hoosier Schoolmaster* 119 **sIN,** I'd lick you till yer hide wouldn' hold shucks. **1953** Randolph–Wilson *Down in Holler* 216 **Ozarks,** I once heard an Arkansas storekeeper roaring threats against a competitor. . . When I git through, *his hide won't hold shucks in a tan-yard!* **1968** Kellner *Aunt Serena* 157 **IN,** Get your stingy old threads and get out of here, or I'll fill your hide so full of buckshot that it won't hold shucks! **1984** Wilder *You All Spoken Here* 48 **Sth,** Tan: Thrash, as "I'll tan yore hide till it won't hold shucks."

(2) To be incapable of withstanding scrutiny; not to "hold water."

1960 Criswell *Resp. to PADS 20* **Ozarks,** Hold water, hang together, hold shucks. **1967–69** *DARE* (Qu. KK58, *An excuse that looks as if it would not stand up under questioning: "His story won't _____."*) Infs **SC34, 40, TX72,** Hold shucks.

d also *corn shuck;* usu pl; Fig: the smallest amount, anything at all—usu used in neg constrs, esp in phrr *not to amount to* (or *be worth*) *shucks.* **formerly more widespread, now esp Nth** See Map

1847 (1962) Robb *Squatter Life* 135 **MO,** He aint wuth *shucks,* and ef you don't lick him fur his onmannerly note, you aint wuth shucks, nuther. **1859** (1965) Marcy *Prairie Traveler* 211, But the Injun he don't care shucks for you. **1887** (1967) Harris *Free Joe* 107 **GA,** This yer one what I'm already got don't amount to shucks. **1893** Shands *MS Speech* 56, *Shucks.* . . As the husks of corn are the most worthless part, the saying arose, "That is not worth shucks"; i.e. not worth anything. **1904** *DN* 2.421 **nwAR,** The old man ain't worth shucks. **1905** *DN* 3.19 **cCT,** *Shucks.* . . 'Not worth shucks' means good for nothing. **1906** *DN* 3.123 **sIN,** *Shucks, ain't worth.* . . Worthless, shiftless. Utter comtempt. **1910** *DN* 3.448 **wNY,** *Shucks.* . . "That aint worth shucks," that is, is worth nothing. **1914** Dickinson *WI Plays* 28, But barrin' Christmas

week I don't believe that amounts to shucks. **1919** Kyne *Capt. Scraggs* 3 **CA,** I never did see a ferry-boat skipper that knew shucks about sailorizing. **1965–70** *DARE* (Qu. HH20b, *Of an idle, worthless person* . . *"He doesn't amount to _____."*) 18 Infs, **Nth,** Shucks; **CT23, NY232,** Row of shucks; **MA58,** A shuck; (Qu. HH20c, *Of an idle, worthless person* . . *"He isn't worth _____."*) Infs **CA161, IL92, MA47, NY12, PA126,** Shucks; **IL96,** A corn shuck. [24 of 26 total Infs old] **1972** *Atlanta Letters* **GA,** What cher doin'? Nothing worth a shuck.

e in phr *to shucks:* Into pieces; also fig.

1901 *DN* 2.147 **NY,** Shuck, n. In phr. 'all pulled to shucks' = pulled to pieces. Oneida, Orleans Co., N.Y. In phr. 'gone to shucks' = gone to pieces financially, failed, petered out. Washington Co., N.Y.

f in phr *if I can't be corn I won't be shucks;* Fig: if I can't be in charge I won't be a subordinate. Cf **dishrag 2**

1968 *DARE* (Qu. II19, *When you think somebody has been put ahead of you or has been given something you deserved*) Inf **VA31,** If I can't be corn, I won't be shucks.

g See **hit the shucks.**

h See **light a shuck.**

2 The covering of a nut, spec:

a The hard shell of a nut, esp of a walnut or hickory nut.

1837 *Yale Lit. Mag.* 2.220 **NC,** He thumped round the deck like a cat shod with walnut shucks. **1941** *LANE* Map 277 *(Walnut shell)* 21 infs, **wNEng,** (Walnut) shuck. **1950** *WELS (The hard part [of a walnut] that comes next [after the thick outside covering])* 1 Inf, **cWI,** Shuck. **1966** Dakin *Dial. Vocab. Ohio R. Valley* 2.363, The hard inner cover surrounding the kernel of a walnut. . . A Franklin County, Ohio, speaker says *shuck* for the hard inner cover of the nut itself in contrast to *shell* for the soft cover. . . It is the only such instance and the only use of *shuck* attested in any sense when speaking of a walnut. **1967–69** *DARE* (Qu. I40, *The hard part inside the husk* . . *of a walnut that you have to break*) Infs **NY12, 159,** Shuck. **1971** Wood *Vocab. Change* 42 **Sth,** The hard inner cover of a walnut is a *shell* in over one-third of the choices. In descending order are *hull, husk,* and *shuck* [with 13 of c1000 infs], the last being unreported from Louisiana.

b The fleshy, outer layer surrounding the shell, esp of a walnut or hickory nut. **chiefly NEast, Gt Lakes** See Map

1853 *Knickerbocker* 42.369, He [=a squirrel] sat bolt upright in a hickory, eating nuts, and throwing the shucks on the ground. [*DARE* Ed: This quot may refer instead to **2a** above.] **1880** *Harper's New Mth. Mag.* 61.865 **NEng,** There was a splendid tall shagbark close by, with branches fairly loaded with the white nuts in their open shucks. **1894** Eggleston in *Century Illustr. Mag.* 47.850 **NY,** About Lake George, . . I find "shuck" used . . for the outer covering of the hickory nut. **1941** *LANE* Map 277 **chiefly wNEng,** Terms for the green outer covering of the walnut . . were incidentally offered. . . [by 28 infs, 23 **CT,** 2 **wMA,** 3 **NH**] shuck. **1950** *WELS (The thick outside covering of a walnut)* 9 Infs, **WI,** Shuck. **1965–70** *DARE* (Qu. I39, . . *The thick outside covering of a walnut*) 67 Infs, **chiefly NEast, Gt Lakes,** Shuck. [Of all Infs responding to the question, 64% were female; of those giving this response, 49% were female.] **1971** Wood *Vocab. Change* 302 **Sth,** [The green outer cover of a walnut:] 31 [infs of c1000] shuck. **1973** Allen *LAUM* 1.307 (as of c1950), *Hull* (the green outer covering of a walnut or hickory nut). . . Southwestern New England *shuck* survives in the older Northern settlement areas of Minnesota, Iowa, and South Dakota.

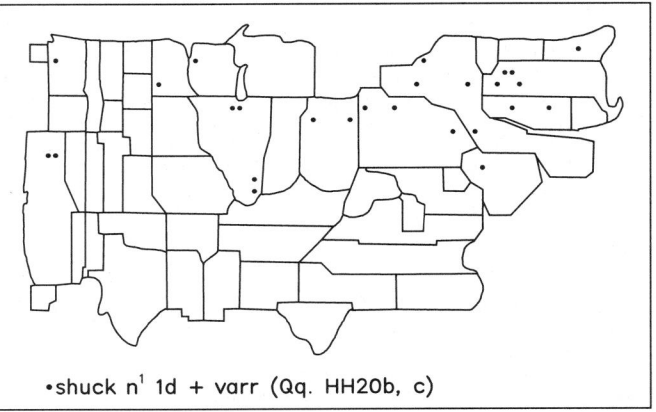

•shuck n¹ 1d + varr (Qq. HH20b, c)

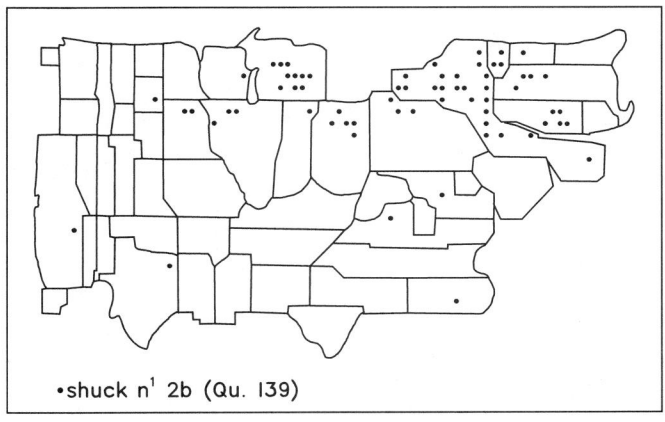

•shuck n¹ 2b (Qu. I39)

3 The shell of an oyster.

1859 (1968) Bartlett *Americanisms* 404, *Shucks*. . . At the South the term is also applied to the shells of oysters. **1881** Ingersoll *Oyster-Industry* 248 **Sth**, *Shuck*. . . An oyster shell.

4 The pod of a bean or pea. [*OED2* 1674 →] **scattered, but chiefly Nth** See Map Cf **shuck v¹ 1c, shuck bean**

c1960 *Wilson Coll.* **csKY** *Shuck*. . . Outside covering of beans. **1965–70** *DARE* (Qu. I12, *The outside covering of dry beans*) 32 Infs, **scattered, but chiefly Nth,** *Shuck*; (Qu. I10, *The outside covering of green peas that you break open to get the peas out*) 16 Infs, **chiefly Nth,** *Shuck*.

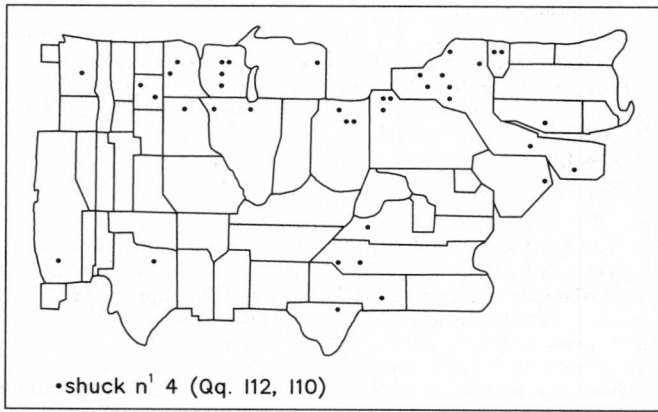

•shuck n¹ 4 (Qq. I12, I10)

5 in combs *longshucks, shortshucks:* =**needle 1.**

1896 Mohr–Roth *Timber Pines* 106 **MD, VA,** *Pinus taeda*. . . *Local or common names*. . Long Shucks. **1897** [see **shortshucks**]. **1908** [see **shortshat pine**]. **1960** Vines *Trees SW* 23, Vernacular names [for *Pinus taeda*] are . . Long-shucks Pine [etc]. **2001** [see **shortshat pine**].

6 The calyx of a fruit, esp a berry.

1941 *LANE* Map 275 (*Hull—of a strawberry*) 1 inf, **csCT**, *Shuck*, the hull of a raspberry; 1 inf, **neCT**, The shuck is what holds the berry onto the stalk. **1965–70** *DARE* (Qu. I47, *When you pull the stem out of a strawberry, what do you call the green part that comes off with the stem?*) Infs **AR27, LA2, MS59, NY28,** *Shuck*. **1968** *DARE* Tape **GA69,** Then after it begins to grow a little bit the petals fall and the shuck sheds, or the husk, around the little peach.

7 See quot.

1968 *DARE* FW Addit **LA15,** *Flag, shucks*—leaves on sugar cane.

shuck v¹, hence vbl n *shucking* [**shuck n¹**]

1 To remove the outer covering of (var plants), spec: see below. Cf **hull v, husk v**

a To strip the leaves from (an ear of corn); rarely, to break (an ear of corn) from the stalk. **scattered, but chiefly Sth, S Midl** Cf **shock v¹, shucking n**

1772 in 1906 *William & Mary Qrly.* 14.39, Just so these Ears; when shucked the husk and grain seem really more than the shuck could contain. **1818** in 1824 Knight *Letters* 100 **KY**, In "shucking" seasons, the slaves split the welkin with their boisterous glee. **1834** Nott *Novellettes* 2.144 **NC**, The farmers occasionally employed the mountaineers to . . shuck corn. **1894** *DN* 1.333 **NJ**, *Shuck, shock*. . . To husk corn. **1899** (1912) Green *VA Folk-Speech* 385, *Shuck*. . . To remove the shucks of corn from the ears. **1899** Garland *Boy Life* 219 (as of c1870s), Already in Sun Prairie husking the corn or "shucking" it, as people from the South called it, was a considerable part of the fall work. **1903** *DN* 2.329 **seMO** *Shuck, v. tr.* Husk. **1904** *DN* 2.421 **nwAR**, *Shuck*. . . "Can you help me shuck this corn?" **1905** *DN* 3.18 **cCT**, *Shuck*. . . To strip off the husks. **1907** *DN* 3.226 **nwAR**, *Shuck*. . . To husk. (The latter word not used.) **1909** *DN* 3.369 **eAL, wGA**, *Shuck*. . . To remove the husk from an ear of corn. **1938** *AmSp* 13.19 [Cornhusking terms], Pulling the ripe ear from its covering of dried shucks on the stalk, in western Nebraska and South Dakota is sometimes called *snapping* or *picking* as well as husking. Boys from Missouri farms have told me that they also call it *peeling* and *shucking*. . . 'Snapping' to some farmers in western Nebraska means breaking the ear from the stalk but not husking or stripping the sheath from the ear. 'Shucking' may also refer to either of these operations. **1942** *Sun* (Baltimore MD) 25 Sept 16/1, The farmers in the North and West say "husk," and those in the South say

"shuck," and one word is quite as good as the other. **1942** Perry *Texas* 138, We don't husk corn; we "shuck" it. **1965–70** *DARE* Tape **IN30**, They would shuck this corn or husk it by hand and break it off; **MI**120 A whole bunch of us kids'd get together and get in the barn and we'd husk corn, shuck it; **OK**48, They call them a husking bee. The men would go and shuck corn. **1984** *Grandfather Tell Me a Story* 17 **OK**, All the farmers would gather their corn and they would shuck it and they would put it in sacks and they would bring it to the corn mill where they would grind their meal.

b as vbl n: Removing the soft outer covering from a nut.

1845 Kirkland *Western Clearings* 101, We were soon well pelted with [hickory] nuts, and busily engaged in freeing them from their aromatic wrappers—an operation which we of the West call "shucking."

c To remove the shells of (peas and beans). **chiefly NEast, N Cent, Upper MW** See Map

1941 *LANE* Map 260 (*To shell beans*) 7 infs, **CT, NH, VT**, *Shuck*. **1948** Davis *Word Atlas Gt. Lakes* app qu 44, 5 [of 233] infs, **MI, IL, OH**, To shuck. **1955** Potter *Dial. NW OH* 77, To shell (beans) . . The Northern and Midland verb *to shell* is the common term for the removal of beans from their pods. . . There were also six instances of *to shuck* [out of a total of 60 infs]. **1960** Bailey *Resp. to PADS 20* **KS**, [Referring to taking beans out of their covers:] I believe a housewife would call it "shucking." **1965–70** *DARE* (Qu. I11, *When somebody takes peas out of the covering* . . "She's _____ peas.") 45 Infs, **chiefly NEast, N Cent, Upper MW**, *Shucking*; (Qu. I13, *When you take dry beans out of the cover you are _____ them*) 29 Infs, **NEast, N Cent, Upper MW**, *Shucking*. **1971** Wood *Vocab. Change* 301 **Sth**, [Activities: of beans] 16 [infs of c1000], To shuck. **1973** Gawthrop *Dial. Calumet* 73 **nwIN**, *Of beans* . . to shuck 13 [of a total of 125 checklist infs]. **1983** *MJLF* 9.1.55 **ceKY** (as of 1956), *Shuck* . . to remove dried beans from the pods. **1986** Pederson *LAGS Concordance*, 1 inf, **seMS**, Shucking some beans.

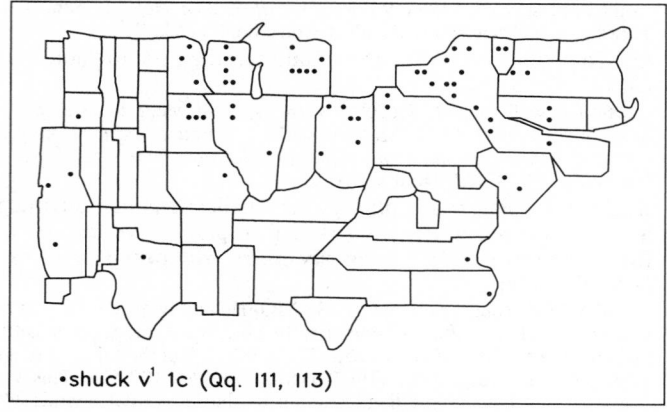

•shuck v¹ 1c (Qq. I11, I13)

d To remove the calyx and stem from (a berry).

1941 *LANE* Map 275 **NEng**, Verbs to denote the process of removing the hulls from a dish of strawberries were recorded incidentally . . *shuck*. **1950** *WELS Suppl.*, *Shuck* (of strawberries)—take out stems in preparation for preserving. In some places it's "hull."

2 To remove the shell from (a shellfish, esp an oyster); hence n *shucker*.

1864 *Scientific Amer.* 10.28 **MD**, I claim the combined steam chamber and shucking box, B, constructed, arranged and operating substantially as hereinbefore described. **1867** *De Bow's Rev.* 3.44 **MD**, From 1,500 to 2,000 persons chiefly negroes of both sexes, were employed in "shucking" or opening the oysters. **1879** *Harper's New Mth. Mag.* 59.64 **eMD**, The oysters are generally shucked early in the morning. . . At the first glance into a shucking house it looks terribly dirty, . . but in the shining pans in front of the shuckers are quarts of clean, fat, succulent oysters. **1939** Berolzheimer *U.S. Cookbook* 62 **NEng**, Buy quahogs shucked or have the fishman shuck them. **1965** *PADS* 43.19 **seMA**, Process of removing scallops from shell: shucking [9 of 9 infs]. **1965** *DARE* Tape **FL21**, The business people buy 'em [=oysters] an' have 'em shucked, have 'em opened and prepared for shipping. **1977** Anderson *Grass Roots Cookbook* 6 **cME**, If the fish man simply dips into a vat of shucked oysters, your pint of oysters may consist largely of juice. **2000** *NADS Letters* **neMA**, When the clams are dug they then have to be "shucked"; **FL, GA**, Shuck oysters (open them); **LA**, I want you to shuck me a half dozen oysters; **neMA,** Shuck a clam; **NH,** One can shuck a clam, a mussel, a quahog, a scallop etc., but one would never shuck a shrimp. (That would have to be shelled.)

3 To strip (oneself); to disrobe; also with *off:* to take off (clothing or harness); with *out of:* to remove (something) from (what contains it); fig: to shed, abandon; hence n *shucker.* **chiefly Sth, S Midl**

1843 (1973) Porter *Big Bear AR* 55, Young men in *my* time'd just get in a spree, sorter open thar shirt collars, and shuck themselves with a growl. **1870** (1935) Duval *Advent. Big Foot* 150 **TX,** "See here, my friend," said our little author, stepping boldly forward, and beginning to shuck off his coat. **1887** (1967) Harris *Free Joe* 42 **GA,** Will you shuck them duds? **1897** *KS Univ. Qrly.* (ser B) 6.91 **MO,** *Shuck:* to undress. **1909** *DN* 3.369 **eAL, wGA,** *Shuck.* . . [T]o remove. "Shuck them duds." **1940** *AmSp* 15.205 [Entertainment world words], *Shucker.* A burlesque performer who specializes in disrobing. **1942** McAtee *Dial. Grant Co. IN* 56 (as of 1890s), *Shuck* . . to remove clothing. **1960** (1962) Eichenlaub *Minnesota Dr.* 227, They can also help you shuck off the cares and worries of daily life. **1963** Burroughs *Head-First* 140 **wCO,** I might add that boys who lived on ranches were inducted into the mysteries of handling livestock as well as performing the thousand-and-one other chores that go to make a ranchman's life almost as soon as they shucked their diapers. **1966–70** *DARE* (Qu. II5b, *When you don't want to have anything to do with a certain person because you don't like him . . "I'd certainly like to give him the _____.")* Inf **TX**81, Shuck him; (Qu. II32, *To manage some way to shift the responsibility: "He said it wasn't his fault and tried to _____.")* Inf **MS**6, Shuck his responsibility. **1967** Green *Horse Tradin'* 271 **TX,** I helped him unhitch and shuck the rigging off his team. **1992** McCarthy *All Pretty Horses* 89 **TX** (as of c1950), Rawlins shucked the rifle backward out of the bootleg scabbard. *Ibid* 276, [He] told the captain to shuck his foot out of the stirrup. **1995** Brophy *Coll.* 67 **swMO** (as of c1960), *Shuck oneself.* [T]o undress. **2000** *NADS Letters* **wNC,** Let's shuck school and go fishing; **VA,** *[Shuck]* is used as someone needing to "shuck" that image if he wants to improve his reputation or shucking a jacket if it gets hot; **wNC,** My grandmother . . would shuck the baby's dress; **KY,** Shuck your coat and come sit a spell. **2001** *Ibid* **Upstate NY,** Shuck off your clothes; **eTN,** I shucked off and jumped into the water.

4 with *out:* To leave in a hurry; to set out. **Cf light a shuck**

1932 Randolph *Ozark Mt. Folks* 35, Right then an' thar th' ol' man seen how things was, an' he come a-runnin' up t' th' house. . . Wal, sir, Tom he shucked right out an' dug up th' corner post whar th' money was vaulted, an' they melted up three half-dollars. **1939** in 1944 *ADD* **Sth,** *Shuck out.* To depart. . . He shucked out. **1942** *Sat. Eve. Post* 17 Jan 56 **NC,** Uncle Bob shucked out for Laurel Springs.

5a To cheat, deceive, mislead (someone).

[**1926** in 1983 Taft *Blues Lyric Poetry* 126, [Title:] Shuckin' Sugar.] **1959** Lipton *Holy Barbarians* 25 **CA,** I didn't shuck the customers enough to please the crook who was running the car lot. **1975** *AmSp* 50.66 **AR** (as of c1970), *Shuck* vt—Trick, deceive, fool. **1977** Morrison *Song of Solomon* 181 [Black], You come running after me with a dynamite proposition, and for three days we talk about it, . . but when we get down to business, you come up with some shit about how it can't be done. You shucking me or what? **1982** Slone *How We Talked* 9 **eKY** (as of c1950), "Shucking someone in a trade"—getting the best of them or the best end of the deal. "Shucking someone"—getting them to believe a ridiculous story.

b esp in phr *shuck and jive:*

(1) To be deceptive or evasive; to tell tall tales or lies; to fool around. *esp freq among Black speakers*

1968 *Current Slang* 3.2.42 [Watts slang; Black], *Shuck.* . . To kid; to tease.—He didn't mean anything, he was just shucking. **1970** *Ibid* 5.2.12 [Black Univ student slang], *Shuck-and-jive.* . . To act irresponsibly; to "fool around." **1970** *DARE* (Qu. JJ6, *To stay away from school without an excuse)* Inf **TN**46, Shuck and jive. [Inf Black] **1971** Roberts *Third Ear* np [Black], *Shuckin(g)* . . fooling; not for real; e.g. And I'm not just shuckin' and jivin'. **1974** Foster *Ribbin'* 195 [Black], For many blacks, shuckin' and jivin' is a survival technique to avoid and stay out of trouble. **1986** Pederson *LAGS Concordance,* 1 inf, **cwFL,** Shuck and jive with them—play around with them. [Inf Black] **2000** *NADS Letters* **AR,** We have used *shuck,* as in . . setting around telling stories, lies, or tall tales; **cwIN,** Shuck and jive . . means to tell a tall tale; **wOR,** Shuck and jive . . [meant] stalling or obfuscating, especially to avoid having to admit that you did not know something or were trying to di

vert someone's attention; **TX** (as of 1963), I heard Black men say a person was "shuckin' and jivin'" when . . dissembling and trying to extricate oneself from a difficult situation. **2001** *Ibid* **GA,** When asked to explain, Jim started shucking and jiving.

(2) To dance.

1972 Claerbaut *Black Jargon* 79, *Shucking and jiving* . . dancing. **2000** *NADS Letters* **MA** (as of c1970), I remember . . "shuck and jive" referring to dancing to jazz type music or rock and roll; **wOR** (as of c1965), I remember . . "shuck and jive" . . to describe dancing, generally not slow dancing, often with fancy footwork; **MS,** "Shuck" was used with "jive" by my mother to describe dancing, mainly the way Black people dance. They "shuck and jive."

shuck v[2] [*EDD shuck* v.[1] 1. "To shake"; 2. "To slip; to move about; to move from a certain position; to wriggle."] **chiefly NEast, esp NEng**

1 also with *around;* Of something loose or unsteady; to shift, slide; hence vbl n *shucking.*

1859 Storke *Family Farm* 2.172 **NY,** Shake the barrel frequently, and when full arrange the apples so that the head will rest upon them smoothly, and in order to secure them from shucking in the barrel. **1959** *VT Hist.* 27.157 **nwVT,** *Shuck around.* . . To fit loosely. Rare. Chittenden. **1999** *DARE* File **nwMA,** Yes, I can remember using "shuck", though I can't recall hearing it used lately. It's used in reference to unwanted movement from things that don't fit right or aren't secured properly. After a while the leather on your snowshoe bindings stretches, and your feet will shuck; if your hiking boots don't fit right, your feet might shuck around in them; if you don't put enough newspaper in the packing box, the vase will shuck around and break when you're moving. I suppose you could say that when the Starship Enterprise encounters an alien gravitational field, the crew gets shucked around in there. Why don't they ever use seatbelts? I seem to be able to construct the verb-adverb combination: "shuck around", more naturally. I have no idea why. **2000** *NADS Letters* **NEng,** *[Shuck]* meaning "to shift about" or to slide about, especially in an enclosed space—is one I have heard all my life. My mother was born in Hyde Park, MA in 1878 and she used it. I recall her using it to describe a loose page in a three-ring notebook. When I came to Vermont I heard my mother-in-law use it also. **2001** *DARE* File—Internet **CT,** It should be able to "shuck" around slightly side-to-side if pushed. *Ibid* **MI,** Deep sheepskin pile is also in the bottom [of the quiver] so broadheads will not shuck around and get dull. **2002** *DARE* File **cNY,** It could shuck back and forth and work itself loose if we don't tie it good.

2 To shift or shake (something that is loose or unsteady); to attempt to do this; hence vbl n *shucking.*

1982 Watson *Hand Tools* 20 **VT,** The bench should be completely solid with the floor. . . Test it by shucking it end-to-end and front-to-back. *Ibid* 178, Make a pencil mark on the wall. . . Stand the bookcase against the wall, then shuck it one way or another until it touches the mark. **1999** [see **1** above]. **2002** *DARE* File **csMI,** [He said he] could shuck it [=a door] wherever he wanted it. To me he clearly meant "to move it around and position it."

3 with *together:* See quot.

1959 *VT Hist.* 27.157 **neVT,** *Shucked together.* . . Mixed; shuffled. Common. Essex.

shuck n[2] [**shuck** v[2] 1]
Unsteadiness.

1982 Watson *Hand Tools* 17 **VT,** A bench should be as solid as a butcher's chopping block—no vibration when you pound on it, no shuck, and no creeping along the floor when you plane on it.

shuck v[3] See **shake** v **1a, 2b**

shuck and jive See **shuck** v[1] **5b**

shuck around See **shuck** v[2] **1**

shuck bean n Also *shucky bean* **chiefly sAppalachians** Cf **fodder bean, leather breeches 1, shell bean, shelly ~**
A bean that is dried in the pod for storage; esp such a bean that is later shelled before being eaten.

1913 Kephart *Highlanders* 292 **sAppalachians,** Green beans in the pod are called snaps; when shelled they are shuck-beans. [*DARE* Ed: Cf following quot] **1917** Kephart in *DN* 4.417 **wNC,** *Shuck-beans.* . .

Beans in the pod. **1917** in 1944 *ADD* **sWV,** *Shuck-beans. . .* Shelled string-beans. **1924** Raine *Land of Saddle-Bags* 11 **sAppalachians,** She dries apples and corn and shucky beans. The latter she strings with a needle and thread and hangs overhead. **1939** *Hall Coll.* **wNC, eTN,** *Shuck(y) beans. . .* Beans strung on strings and dried in their shells. **1940** in 1944 *ADD* **WV,** *Shucky beans.* Fodder beans; dried beans in the pod. . . Reported. **1940** (1978) *Still River of Earth* 3 **KY,** The strings of shucky beans dried in the fall would not last until a new garden could be raised. **1946** *AmSp* 21.191 **seKY,** *Shucky beans,* green beans dried in the pod. . . In eastern Kentucky, the green beans are threaded and hung to dry in long strings, usually from porch rafters in the sun. To prepare them for cooking, the housewife washes the pods and cuts them up as she would cut green string beans. **1950** Stuart *Hie Hunters* 22 **eKY,** Hanging to nails driven in the walls, were strings of bright red pepper pods, shuck beans, leather britches, dried apples, drying peaches, and drying ears of white and yellow corn. **1965–70** *DARE* (Qu. H50, *Dishes made with beans, peas, or corn that everybody around here knows, but people in other places might not*) Inf **KY63,** Shuck beans—whole beans dried and cooked later—includes bean and pod; **VA13,** Dry beans = shuck beans = leather britches—green beans dried, later soaked and cooked; **KY34,** Shucky beans—they are made by stringing green beans together and letting them dry like peppers; (Qu. I20, . . *Kinds of beans*) Inf **KY37,** Shuck beans—hulled green beans. **1975** McDonough *Garden Sass* 74 **AR,** Green Beans were usually "nipped" and strung on a thread to make what most people call shuck beans. **1982** Slone *How We Talked* 56 **eKY** (as of c1950), Served with soup beans, shucky beans, or as a side dish. **1986** Pederson *LAGS Concordance* (Butter beans) 1 inf, **nwFL,** Shucky bean. **1995** Williams *Gt. Smoky Mts. Folklife* 99, Many older women fondly remember "bean stringings." Dried beans took two forms: "leather britches"—dried green beans—and "shucky beans"—dried beans that would later be shucked.

shuck bed See **shuck** n[1] **1b(1)**

shuck-bottom(ed) See **shuck** n[1] **1(b)4**

shuck broom (or brush) See **shuck** n[1] **1b(2)**

shuck collar See **shuck** n[1] **1b(3)**

shucked See **shake** v **2b**

shuckens See **shuckins** intj

shucker See **shuck** v[1] **2, 3**

shuck horse collar See **shuck** n[1] **1b(3)**

shuck house See **shuck** n[1] **1b(5)**

shucking n Also *shucking bee* **chiefly S Midl** Cf **bee** n[2], **corn shucking, husking** vbl n **2, shuck** v[1] **1a**
A social gathering at which the surrounding leaves are stripped from ears of corn, the event often including music and dancing.
1817 in 1830 Royall *Letters AL* 31, I only got a little lively at brother I's shucking. **1849** in 1956 Eliason *Tarheel Talk* 294 **cn,cNC,** There is a great many shuckings about now, the negroes enjoy themselves at them singing and frolicking. **1852** *Knickerbocker* 40.45 **wIL,** At a 'shucking-bee,' as they have to work, the feasting is gratis, for those who would feast. [**1871** Eggleston *Hoosier Schoolmaster* 25 **sIN,** Spelling and "shucking" are the only public competitions.] **1884** Baldwin *Yankee School-Teacher* 21 **VA,** Percy Darnell was t' have a shuckin t'night; wants t' git his corn out the way 'fore Christmas. **1903** *DN* 2.329 **seMO,** *Shucking. . .* A husking bee. 'There will be a shucking and a dance at the Widow Smith's to-night.' **1907** *DN* 3.236 **nwAR,** *Shucking. . .* A husking party.

shucking vbl n[1] See **shuck** v[1]

shucking vbl n[2] See **shuck** v[2] **1, 2**

shucking bee See **shucking** n

shucking peg n Cf **husking pin**
A tool for removing the leaves that surround an ear of corn.
1886 Ebbutt *Emigrant Life* 180 **KS,** The hand is armed with a "shucking-peg,"—either of wood or iron fastened on with a thong,—which tears open the shucks on the ears of corn. **1946** Adams *Album Amer. Hist.* 3.376, [Caption:] *Above* is a shucking (or husking) peg that was used every fall during the 1880's. **1950** Stuart *Hie Hunters* 153 **eKY,**

They didn't have fancy store-bought shucking pegs. Each man had made his peg from a piece of seasoned hickory wood.

shuckins intj Also sp *shuckens* **esp Sth, S Midl**
Used as an expression of annoyance, irritation, contempt, or disbelief.
1893 Shands *MS Speech* 56, *Shucks. . .* An exclamation indicative of . . contempt. . . *Shuckins . .* is a form of this word frequently met with. **1906** *DN* 3.156 **nwAR,** *Shuckins. . .* Pshaw. "O shuckins! what's the use?" **1935** Davis *Honey* 255 **OR,** Well, shuckins, mister, ef you'd stood up ary longer you'd had me broke plumb in two! **1956** Ker *Vocab. W. TX* 386, *Expressions of mild disgust. . .* shuckens. [1 of 67 infs] **1966–69** *DARE* (Qu. NN8a, *Exclamations of annoyance or disgust:* "Oh _____. I've lost my glasses again.") Inf **GA84,** Shuckins; [(Qu. NN29b, *Exclamations beginning with 'land':* "Land _____!") Inf **MS69,** Oh, shuckin]. **1971** *Today Show Letters* **cnAL** (as of a1940), Just as we sometimes [say] "Pshaw" or "Shucks" the Southerners say "Shuckin's.["]

shuckins n
In phr *some shuckins:* =*some pumpkins* (at **pumpkin** n[1] **B2**)
c1939 in 1984 Lambert–Franks *Voices* 75 **OK,** The day tour is *the* tour to work on, and most contractors won't put a man on that shift unless he's had plenty of experience and unless he's their best man. . . This company I was with must have thought I was some shuckins to put me on day tour.

shuckle v Cf **shuck** v[1] **4**
To run fast; to hurry.
1933 *AmSp* 8.1.52 **Ozarks,** *Shuckle. . .* To hurry, to bustle about, to make haste. *I jest let on like th' shanty was afire, an' you orter of saw them fellers shuckle out o' thar!* **1954** Harder *Coll.* **cwTN,** *Shuckle. . .* To hurry, to bustle about.

shuck mattress See **shuck** n[1] **1b(1)**

shuck mop See **shuck** n[1] **1b(2)**

shuck off See **shuck** v[1] **3**

shuck out See **shuck** v[1] **4**

shuck out of See **shuck** v[1] **3**

shuck pen See **pen** n[1] **B3**

shuck-pulling n
=**shucking** n.
1975 Gainer *Witches* 16 **sAppalachians,** *Shuck-pullin'* (n.), corn-husking party. "There's goin' to be a shuck-pullin' at Hart's barn tonight."

shuck sausage See **shuck** n[1] **1b(8)**

shuck scrub(broom) See **shuck** n[1] **1b(2)**

shucks, go v phr [Perh var of *EDD shag* sb.[3] "A share; esp in phr *to go shags*"; cf also **chuckers, snooks**]
To agree to share equally.
1897 *KS Univ. Qrly.* (ser B) 6.57 **KS,** *Shucks:* 'havers', as 'to go shucks with one.' **1968** *DARE* (Qu. II9, *If several people have to contribute in order to pay for something . .* "Let's all _____.") Inf **PA118,** Go shucks on that.

shuck tea See **shuck** n[1] **1b(7)**

shuck-tearing party n Cf **shuck** n[1] **1b(1)**
1951 *DE Folkl. Bulletin* 1.8 (as of c1850), Shuck-tearing parties provided good times in the middle of the century. Corn shucks were gathered during the day. . . At night neighbors . . tore or shredded the corn shuck into narrow strips. Enough was torn to fill a large ticking and was known as a shuck bed.

shuck tick See **shuck** n[1] **1b(1)**

shuck together See **shuck** v[2] **3**

shucky bean See **shuck bean**

shud See **shut** adj a

shuffler n[1]
1 Either the **greater scaup** or the **lesser scaup.**

1845 Hooper *Advent. Simon Suggs* 111 **AL,** Sol . . went under the water in the "Buck Hole," "like a shuffler duck with his wing broke." [*DARE* Ed: This quot may refer instead to **2** below.] **1858** Baird *Birds* 791, *Fulix marila*. . *Broad-bill; Blue-bill; Shuffler;* Vulgo. **1872** Coues *Key to N. Amer. Birds* 289, Greater Scaup Duck. . . Shuffler. *Ibid,* Lesser Scaup Duck. . . with other names of the foregoing. **1898** (1900) Davie *Nests N. Amer. Birds* 87, American Scaup Duck. . . This and the next species [=the lesser scaup duck] are closely allied, and are variously known as Bluebills, Raft Duck, Floating Fowl and Shufflers. **1923** U.S. Dept. Ag. *Misc. Circular* 13.19 **Mid Atl,** *Scaup Ducks. . . shufflers* (Md. to N.C.) *Ibid* 20 **MD, VA,** *Greater Scaup Duck. . .* bay shuffler. *Ibid, Lesser Scaup Duck. . .* river shuffler (Potomac River). **1951** *AmSp* 26.92 **Mid Atl,** In Atlantic states (Maryland to the Carolinas), ever since colonial days, the name *shufflers,* in allusion to their noisy take-off, has been given primarily to the scaups.

2 A coot n[1] **1** (here: *Fulica americana*).

1889 *Century Dict.* 1252, The common or bald coot of Europe is *F[ulica] atra;* that of America is *F. americana,* sometimes called *shuffler.* **1917** (1923) *Birds Amer.* 1.214, *Coot. . . Other Names. . .* Splatter; Shuffler [etc.].

shuffler n[2] See **shoveler**

shuffy n [Var of **chufa**]
1959 McAtee *Oddments* 6 **cNC,** *Shuffies* . . chufas or grass nuts; really tubers of a sedge (*Cyperus esculentus*).

shu-fly See **shoofly** n **3**

shuk See **shake** v **1a, 2b**

shul(e) See **shool**

shum See **see** v **A**

shumaker See **shoemaker berry**

Shumard oak n
Std: an *oak* (*Quercus shumardii*) of the southern and eastern US. Also called **leopard oak, scarlet ~ 2, Spanish ~,** spotted **~,** swamp red **~**

shummick See **shammock**

shun v [*EDD* shun v.[1] 4 "To cover, hide, screen, shelter."]
To protect; to shield.
1936 Hench *Coll., Shun*—Told to me by one of my students . . of Warm Springs, Va., who says that it is used thus in the neighborhood of his house: I was in trouble and my sister . . shunned . . me (=protected me). **1936** *AmSp* 11.372 **VA,** A woman, speaking of her older sister, who had always tried to make things easy for her, said '_____ always did *shun* me.' The idea was rather that of shielding from hardship or work. The idea of protecting from danger did not enter into this, but the people who use the word may not make the distinction.

shunning n [Calque of Ger *Meidung*] Cf **finger-pointing**
The Mennonite practice of ostracism of one who has been excommunicated from the church; also vbl n *shunning* carrying out that practice; n *shun* the judgment of ostracism.
1947 *Sun* (Baltimore MD) 6 Nov (*Hench Coll.*), Ex-Mennonite Sues Church for 'Shunning'. . . Bishop John W. Helmuth . . said the Scriptures were responsible for the "shunning" of [the] former Amish Mennonite church member. . . "The Scriptures put the shun on him . . I didn't." **1963** Hostetler *Amish Soc.* 14, Major offenses are punishable by excommunication, which requires avoidance [by members of the church district]—the latter is called shunning, or the ban. . . No member may knowingly eat at the table with an expelled member or have normal work or domestic relations with him. *Ibid* 28, The controversy [between Amish or Mennonite sects in the seventeenth century] centered around three specific norms of practice: the *Meidung* or shunning (also called avoidance) of excommunicated members [etc.]. *Ibid* 63, The strict interpretation requires shunning of all (1) members who leave the Amish church to join another and (2) members who marry outside the brotherhood. *Ibid* 210, The *streng* [=strict] *Meidung* groups lose fewer members than those who practice the mild form of shunning. **1966** *DARE* Tape **PA**30, He is not what they call on the shun side. I guess this is not a strange term to you, *shunning. . .* Because . . he has never taken up the obligations of the church, they cannot hold him responsible to them, so he will not be shunned. **1980** Mead *Hdbk. Denominations*

U.S. 168, The Amish movement within the ranks of the Mennonites . . insisted upon strict conformation to the confession of faith, especially in the matter of "shunning" excommunicated members.

shunpike n Also *shunpike road* **esp NEast**
A road used to avoid the payment of tolls on a toll road; by ext, a back road; hence v *shunpike* to use an alternate route in order to avoid the payment of tolls; to drive back roads for pleasure; vbl n *shunpiking;* n *shunpiker* one who drives free roads; a tourist who drives back roads.
1853 in 1919 *DN* 5.53 **NY,** Some of this very loan is to be applied to the Oswego Canal, which has been called a 'shun-pike.' **1867** Lowell *Biglow* 52 '**Upcountry**' **MA,** Ef your soul / Don't sneak thru shun-pikes so 's to save the toll. **1881** Pierson *In the Brush* 27 **KY,** At various points along the "pike," as it was universally called, I saw tracks leading off into the woods, and was told that they were known as "shunpikes," and that some people in traveling would take these and go through the woods around the toll-gates, in order to avoid paying toll. **1931–33** *LANE Worksheets* **VT,** *Shunpike*—A side road. **1951** *New Yorker* 8 Dec 88, This was a third-rate troupe of dust-eaters, shun-pikers, and swing-kettles. **1952** *Lamp* June 10 (*Mathews Coll.*), Don't shunpike unless prepared to drive more skillfully than turnpiking demands. **1953** in 1968 *DARE* File **AR,** [Newspaper clipping:] Many there were who saved toll by taking the Shun Pike Road into and out of Magnolia. **1964** *Collier's Encycl. Yearbk.* 70 (*OED2*), Besides making long trips at high speeds, motorists could take part in sports car rallies, chug about in antiques, 'shunpike' on quiet back roads. **1968** *Yankee* Dec 141 **NEng,** [Advt:] Every time Fred goes "shun piking" he stops at the Colonial Inn. **1968** *DARE* FW Addit **NJ,** *Shunpike*—a road taken to avoid driving on a turnpike. **1989** *DARE* File **nwMA,** We'll take route 80 through Pennsylvania; we're shunpikers. **1990** *Ibid* **nwMA,** [Historical marker:] *Shunpike*—To the Thrifty Travelers of the Mohawk Trail who in 1797 here forded the Deerfield River rather than pay toll at the Turnpike Bridge and who in 1810 won the battle for free travel on all Massachusetts Roads.

shunt See **shut** adj **a**

shur See **share**

shurf(f) See **sheriff** n

shurn v [Perh blend of *shun* + *spurn;* but cf *OED2 shurn* v. "*Obs. rare. . .* Altered form of *scurn* v."; →1546. Alternatively, perh simply a pronc var; cf Intro "Language Changes" I.8 and quot 1961 at **shut** v **A**]
To avoid, shun.
1970 *DARE* (Qu. Y51, *. . . Ways of saying 'to avoid' things or people . . "He's not your kind—you'd better _____ him."*) Inf **FL**51, Shurn [šɝ·n]; **VA**69, Shurn [šɜn]; (Qu. II32, *To manage some way to shift the responsibility: "He said it wasn't his fault and tried to _____."*) Inf **FL**52, Shurn the responsibility; (Qu. II6, *If you meet somebody who used to be a friend, and he pretends not to know you: "When I met him on the street he _____."*) Inf **FL**52, Shurned [šɜ·nd]. [All Infs Black]

shut v
A Pronc and gram forms.
Pronc-spp **chiefly Sth, S Midl, NEng** *shed, shet;* also **esp Sth, S Midl** *shit, shot;* rarely *Gullah, shetty* [Cf *EDD*] Note: A few quots suggest grammatical differentiation among these forms, with *shet* used for the present tense and *shot* for the past, past pple, and ppl adj; the evidence is insufficient to determine how common this is. For the ppl adj in the phr *get shut of* see **shut** adj.
1795 Dearborn *Columbian Grammar* 138, *List of Improprieties. . . Shot* or *Shet* for *Shut.* **1843** (1916) Hall *New Purchase* 144 **IN,** My ole womin she always shot the door at night. **1851** Hooper *Widow Rugby's Husband* 39 **AL,** He's got hardly any skin to shet his eyes with. **1883** (1971) Harris *Nights with Remus* 80 **GA** [Black], Brer Fox, he come up little nigher en play, but Brer Tarrypin, he keep he eyes shot en he stay still. *Ibid* 144, 'E is shed 'e y-eye, un opun 'e mout', un tek e' nap. *Ibid* 155, I shetty me y-eye, I shekkey me head. **1888** Jones *Negro Myths* 3 **GA coast,** Eh shet eh yeye. **1893** Shands *MS Speech* 56, *Shet. . .* Negro for *shut.* **1893** *DN* 1.278 **nwCT,** [Pres:] *shet* [pret and past pple:] *shet.* **1899** (1912) Green *VA Folk-Speech* 381, *Shet,* v. A form of *shut.* Closed. **1903** *DN* 2.329 **seMO,** *Shut. . .* Pronounced shet. 'Shet the door.' . . Pret. pronounced shot, as 'he shot the door in my

face.' **1909** *DN* 3.368 **eAL, wGA,** *Shet. . . To shut. Ibid* 369, *Shot,* *pret.* of *shut.* **1912** Green *VA Folk-Speech* 384, *Shot. . . To shut.* "He shot the door." **1926** *AmSp* 2.80 **ME,** Old people and others who have grown up in smaller communities still say "shet" for *shut.* **1930** *AmSp* 5.205 [Ozark dialect], *Shut* is usually pronounced *shet* by the Ozarkers. **1934** Hurston *Jonah's Gourd Vine* 11 **AL** [Black], Come out dat do' way and shet it tight. **1952** Brown *NC Folkl.* 1.589, *Shet. . . To shut. . . All* tenses. *Ibid, Shot. . . Past tense and past participle of* shut. **1953** *AmSp* 28.254 **csPA,** *Shut. . . Often pronounced* [ʃɛt] *in popular speech.* **1961** Kurath–McDavid *Pronc. Engl.* 146, *Shut. . . The verb in the phrase* shut the door! *usually rimes with* bet *in the folk speech (1) of the South and the South Midland and (2) of northeastern New England, rarely elsewhere. In large parts of the South, this pronunciation is used also by some middle-class speakers, but not by the better educated. In the Low Country of South Carolina and in Georgia . . the vowel in* shut *is rather frequently pronounced as a mid-central* [ɜ] *. . so that* shut *would seem to rime with* shirt /šɜrt/. **1965–70** DARE (Qu. X10b, *To tell a person to stop talking—not very politely*) Infs **GA**43, **MS**45, **MO**29, Shet up; **FL**2, Shet your mouth; (Qu. NN19, *When you want people to stop talking for a moment so that you can listen for something*) Inf **MS**84, Sheddup; **MO**23, Shet up. [5 of 6 Infs Black] **1975** *Appalachian Jrl.* 2.151 **wNC,** Over the years the letter *u* also suffered a certain instability, becoming *. . o, e,* or *i* in *shot, shet* or *shit* the door. **1986** Pederson *LAGS Concordance (Shut)* 1 inf, **cTX,** You didn't shut the door, you shot it. **1989** Pederson *LAGS Tech. Index* 43 **Gulf Region,** *Shut:* [Of 914 primary infs, 531 gave the pronc [šʌt], 77 infs [šɛt], 7 infs [šʊt], 3 infs [šɪt], and 1 inf [šat]].

B Sense.

To turn off (a light).   Cf **close** v, **open** C3

1966–69 *DARE* (Qu. Y42, *Expressions for putting out a lamp or light*) Infs **MA**2, **NJ**21, 56, **NY**50, 201, **TX**53, Shut (the light). **1968** *DARE* FW Addit **NYC,** "Shut the light" (NYC—Jewish). **1999** *DARE* File— Internet, [Song lyrics:] I shut the light and then let go of my brain. *Ibid,* You shut the light, and closed the door. **2000** *Ibid* [Lois & Clark Message Board], Topic: . . and shut the light on your way out. **2000** *NADS Letters,* My girlfriend and her friends from middle Wisconsin would say "shut the light" where I would say "turn off the light." **2001** *DARE* File—Internet **HI** [Hanabuddah Days], And it was usually the last person's job that came in to shut the light.

shut adj For varr see below   [*OED2* (at *shut* v. 11) 1575–6 →; "*dial.* and *colloq.*"; *EDD* (at *shut* v. 3.(2)).   Orig ppl adj of **shut** v in the obs sense "to set (one) free from (something)." The form *shed* is derived from *shet* partly by the typical Amer voicing of intervocalic *t* in the comb *shet of* and partly by folk-etym infl from *shed* get rid of. *OED2* regards *shot* as of separate origin (at *shoot* v. 37.b 1802 →), but as *shot* is attested as a form of *shut* in both Brit and US dial, this seems unlikely.]

In phrr *get* (or *be*) *shut of* (rarely *on*): To get (or be) rid, free, or clear of, as:

a pronc-spp *shut, shud;* rarely *shunt.* **formerly chiefly Sth, S Midl, NEast; now more widespread**

1827 (1939) Sherwood *Gaz. GA* 139, *Get shut of,* for get rid of. **1858** Hammett *Piney Woods Tavern* 230, When you get shut of the timber and strike into the perara, there's a house. **1865** in 1983 *PADS* 70.35 **ce,sePA,** There was heavy fighting going on in the advance but we got shut of participation in it. **1902** *DN* 2.235 **sIL,** *Get shut of. . . To get rid* of; dispose of. **1905** *DN* 3.94 **nwAR,** I couldn't get shut of him. **1907** *German Amer. Annals* 9.376 **sePA,** I have more apples than I'll get shut of. **1913** Johnson *Highways St. Lawrence to VA* 307 **VA,** He would use it [=a sinkhole] to get shut of a lot of stumps and stones. **1929** (1951) Faulkner *Sartoris* 293 **MS,** Well, I've had 'em around so long I don't know how to get shut of 'em, 'less I drown 'em. **1940** (1941) Bell *Swamp Water* 24 **Okefenokee GA,** Being shut of him for good was the next best thing. **1943** *LANE* Map 569 *(Get rid of him)* 4 infs, **CT, MA,** Get shut of. **1946** *PADS* 5.37 **VA,** *(Get) shut of (someone):* (Get) rid of (someone); common everywhere. **1952** Brown *NC Folkl.* 1.590, *Shut, get (be) _____ of: . . To get rid of. . . General. Illiterate.* **1959** *VT Hist.* 27.157 **swVT,** *Get shut of. . . To get rid of. Rare.* **1965–70** *DARE* (Qu. II5a, *When you don't want to have anything to do with a certain person because you don't like him . . "I'd certainly like to get _____ of him."*) 66 Infs, **scattered,** Shut; **AL**6, **GA**67, Shut—Negroes; **AL**43, **MA**5, Shut—heard; **MO**11, Shut—they used to say; **NJ**69, Shut—old-fashioned; **WI**73, Shut—in the South; **MT**4, Shud; **GA**72, [šʊt]; (Qu. II18, *Someone who joins himself on to you and your group without being asked and won't leave*) Inf **VA**25, We couldn't get shut of him. **1966–70** *DARE* Tape **FL**37, That man stayed with us for I don't know how

long. We couldn't get shut of him. He just stayed; **KY**13, Your . . big furrows brought it out or shoved it out the side and got shut of it; **KY**85, They all fell off, and she [=the queen bee] went in and they all follered, so I got shut of 'em. **1982** Heat Moon *Blue Highways* 33 **cTN,** Hangin' on the drop edge of yonder. I said to Thurmond, "Thurmond, unless you want shut of me, call the doctor." **1984** Wilder *You All Spoken Here* 167 **Sth,** They got shud of their preacher. **1989** Pederson *LAGS Tech. Index* 355 **Gulf Region,** *Get rid of . . get shut of* (5 [of 914 primary infs]) get shut of (134). **2000** *NADS Letters,* Have you run into the phrase "git shunt of", meaning to get rid of? I last heard it used in north east Maryland in 1970, but when growing up in east Tennessee in the 1930s and '40s it was used often. In some of the area it was "get shut of", but usually "shunt".

b *shet.* **scattered, but more freq Sth, S Midl, TX** See Map

1837 Sherwood *Gaz. GA* 70, *Get shet of,* for get rid of. **1853** Simms *Sword & Distaff* 317 **SC,** Why, Lord bless you, Cappin, ef once they git here, you'll never git shet of them. **1859** Taliaferro *Fisher's R.* 54 **nwNC** (as of 1820s), I got shet uv my inimy. **1891** *PMLA* 6.169 **WV,** *Let on* is common in nearly the whole country; and so is *to get shet (shut) of.* **1895** *DN* 1.374 **eTN, seKY, wNC,** *Get shet on:* get rid of. "I can't get shet on that dog." **1903** *DN* 2.329 **seMO,** *Shut. . . Get shet of,* get rid of. 'I haven't got shet of my cold.' **1912** *DN* 3.576 **wIN,** *Get shet of. . . To get rid of.* **1915** (1916) Johnson *Highways New Engl.* 202 **Nantucket MA,** The people have backslid from the old habits of thrifty industry. Lots of 'em will do anything to get shet of hard work. **1916** *DN* 4.275 **NE,** *Get shet of. . . To get rid of.* "I'd like to get shet of those Missourians for neighbors." **1923** *DN* 5.220 **swMO,** *To git shet of* = to be rid of. **1924** Raine *Land of Saddle-Bags* 135 **sAppalachians,** I wish to the Lord we could get shet of the whiskey. **1927** *AmSp* 2.355 **cwWV,** We were glad to get shet of that family in the next house. **1942** Faulkner *Go Down* 68 **MS,** We offered to help us git shet of it. **1943** *LANE* Map 569 *(Get rid of him)* 6 infs, **scattered NEng,** Get shet of. **1963** Owens *Look to River* 118 **TX,** Ain't nothing else that'll get shet o' the scent. **1965–70** *DARE* (Qu. II5a, *When you don't want to have anything to do with a certain person because you don't like him . . "I'd certainly like to get _____ of him."*) 48 Infs, **scattered, but more freq Sth, S Midl, TX,** Shet; **FL**52, Shet—what the old folks say; **IL**76, They do say "shut of him"; they used to say "shet of him"; **LA**32, Shet—colored people say this; **SC**2, Shet—[I] hear it frequently, never used it; **SC**54, Shet—joking; a countrified expression; [**NM**6, Shet him out of my hair]; (Qu. Y51, *. . Ways of saying 'to avoid' things or people . . "He's not your kind—you'd better _____ him."*) Infs **TN**23, **WI**33, Get shet of. **1994** NC Lang. & Life Project *Dial. Dict. Lumbee Engl.* 11 **seNC,** If she could just get shet of that man, she'd be a lot better off.

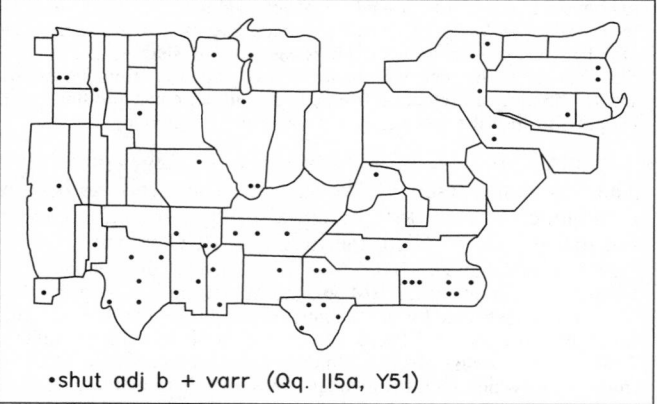

•shut adj b + varr (Qq. II5a, Y51)

c *shed.* **chiefly Sth, S Midl**

1868 *Radical Rule GA* 64, I then put whip to my horses to get shed of him. *Ibid* 129, He was very sick, and asked me if I could take him to his father's so he could get shed of the chills. **1871** Eggleston *Hoosier Schoolmaster* 218 **sIN,** I'm glad to be shed of you! **1892** *KS Univ. Qrly.* 1.98 **KS,** *Shet, shut, shed:* rid, as, to get shut of anything. **1909** *DN* 3.368 **eAL, wGA,** "I couldn't get shed of him." Also *shet.* **1910** *DN* 3.457 **seKY,** I was glad to get shed of that fellow. **1916** *DN* 4.342 **seOH,** *Get shed of.* To be rid of. In the south and Kan., *get shed of.* **1932** (1974) Caldwell *Tobacco Road* 51 **GA,** It will help you get shed of your sins, like Jeeter did. **1948** Hurston *Seraph* 115 **FL,** If she wanted to get shed of him, he would grant it. **1950** Faulkner *Stories* 72 **MS,** But hit ain't no law making you go up there and get shed of them. **1953** Brewer *Word Brazos* 33 **eTX** [Black], De Lawd was gonna lay a heavy han' on 'em if'n dey didn' git shed of dey sinful ways. **1954** *Harder Coll.* **cwTN**, Get shet of . . also get shed of. **1963** *Watkins–Watkins Yesterday Hills* 49 **cnGA**, Some people just got used to the bugs and let them bite and never tried to get shed of them. **1965–70** *DARE* (Qu. II5a, *When you don't want to have anything to do with a certain person because you don't like him . . "I'd certainly like to get _____ of him."*) 19 Infs, **scattered, but somewhat more freq Sth, S Midl**, Shed; **CA**115, Shed—I've heard people say; **LA**14, Shed—very occasionally; **NC**88, Shed—what poor Whites say; I've never heard a Negro use it; **TN**43, Shed—old folks say; [**MI**108, Like to shed him]. [13 of 23 total Infs coll educ] **1966** *PADS* 46.26 **AR**, Wait till I get shed of these things. **1970** *DARE* Tape **VA**114, That was after we'd got shed of our sheep and people had quit raising 'em nearly around here. **1989** [see **a** above]. **2001** *DARE* File **swNM**, An informant from here in Silver City uses . . *to get shed of.*

d *shot.*
1912 Green *VA Folk-Speech* 384, To get *shot* of, is to get rid of. **1943** *LANE* Map 569 *(Get rid of him)* 1 inf, **ceMA**, Git shot of him. **1952** Brown *NC Folkl.* 1.590, *Shot, get _____:* See *shut.*

shut-in n **sAppalachians, Ozarks**
A gorge, canyon.
1913 Kephart *Highlanders* 283 **sAppalachians**, That Natahala is a master shut-in, jest a plumb gorge. *Ibid* 300, The Shut-In is a gorge. **1931** *PMLA* 46.1319 **sAppalachians**, That'ere big cove is a plum' shut-in. **1933** *AmSp* 8.1.52 **Ozarks**, *Shut-in.* . . The canyon formed by a stream with high, steep banks. Perhaps the most famous are the Black River *shut-ins* in Reynolds County, Mo., but there are many others in various parts of the Ozark country. **1972** Cooper *NC Mt. Folkl.* 95, *Shut-in*—gorge. **1996** *DARE* File, I have been to Johnson Shut-ins State Park in Missouri. The sides of the banks are formed by great slabs of rock, haphazardly thrown together. At the bottom, the Black River is a shallow playground, with small waterfalls and waist high (to an adult) pools to splash in.

shut-knife n [Engl dial]
1967 *DARE* (Qu. F39, *A large pocket knife with blades that fold in and out*) Inf **WY**4, Shut-knife.

shut-mouth n **chiefly Sth, S Midl** See Map
A person who says little—also in phr *play shut-mouth* and varr, to keep silent; hence adj *shut-mouth(ed)* silent, secretive, reserved.
1891 Henry *Narrative* 32 **NC** (as of 1781), Instantly after Ferguson's defeat, McGirt, Cunningham and Brown quit their robbing, murdering, burning and destroying and played the game of "the least in sight" and "shut-mouth" into the bargain. **1909** *S. Atl. Qrly.* 8.47 **seSC**, *Shut-mout'*; i. e., *shut-mouthed,* meaning *ill-naturedly secretive and reserved:* "*Buh Wolf too shut-mout'.*" **1932** (1970) Natl. Comm. Defense Political Prisoners *Harlan Miners* 32 **KY**, There wa'n't nothing else for us to do. There wa'n't nothing to eat. No man could play shut mouth here and lie by himself, alone and quiet. **1937** Thornburgh *Gt. Smoky Mts.* 94, Thar wuz lawin' about it, but my folks kept outen it by keeping shet mouth. And thar'd be a sight less trouble in the world, ef folks would mind their own business and keep shet mouth. **1944** *PADS* 2.12 **AL**, *Shut-mouth.* . . One who says little about his own or others' personal affairs. . . Common in South. . . Popular. **1954** *Harder Coll.* **cwTN**, *Shut-mouth.* . . One who says little; *To play shut mouth.* . . To avoid saying anything. "He shore played shut-mouth 'bout 'at killin' at Kelley's Land-

ing." **1960** Criswell *Resp. to PADS* 20 **Ozarks**, *Shut-mouth.* . . A person who says little, reveals little; close-mouthed, tight-lipped. **1965–70** *DARE* (Qu. HH24, *Somebody who doesn't talk very much, who keeps his thoughts to himself*) 18 Infs, **chiefly Sth, S Midl**, Shut-mouth; **SC**34, **TN**15, Plays shut-mouth; (Qu. HH25, *One who never has anything to say: "What's the matter with him? _____?"*) Inf **TX**35, Shut-mouthed; (Qu. JJ44, *Expressions about someone who can be trusted to keep a secret: "Don't worry about him, he'll _____."*) Inf **OK**9, Be a shut-mouth; **TX**99, Be shut-mouthed; **IL**76, He's a shut-mouth; **KY**40, **SC**34, Play (it) shut-mouth. [19 of 24 total Infs old, 18 female] **1996** *Atlanta Jrl.–Constitution* (GA) 26 Feb sec D 1, In many North Georgia counties, wild ginseng . . can still be found. But the people who know about it are pretty shut-mouthed.

shut one's face See **face** n 1

shut one's head See **head** n B2

shutter n Also *door-shutter* old-fash
A door (as distinguished from the opening to which it is fitted).
1863 *Ladies' Repository* 23.91, The cabin was ten by twelve feet on the ground; no floor, no shutter to the door, and no fireplace. **1865** Byrn *Advent. Fudge Fumble* 123 **TN**, At the very moment that I went to lay down, what should I hear but the door-shutter, which flew open & struck against the wall with considerable force. **1875** *Appletons' Jrl.* 13.252, I once observed . . one of these spiders at work in the upper corner of an open outside door-shutter. **1900** Harris *Reminiscences* 4.108 **TX** (as of 1834), The floor was made of heavy hewed logs, called puncheons, and there were no windows nor any shutter to the door. **1903** *DN* 2.312 **seMO**, The door-shutter is offen its hinges. **1986** Pederson *LAGS Concordance,* 1 inf, **neFL**, Shutter—his word for "door." [Inf old]

shuttle n [Folk-etym for *scuttle*]
1947 *McDavid Coll.* **neFL**, Coal shuttle = scuttle. **1965–70** *DARE* (Qu. F44, . . *A container for coal to use in a stove*) Infs **CA**134, **CO**8, **MD**39, **NY**144, **OH**21, **PA**176, **WI**60, (Coal) shuttle; **CA**139, Shuttle-bucket; **AR**47, Stove shuttle. **1986** Pederson *LAGS Concordance* **Gulf Region**, 22 infs, (Coal) shuttle [=scuttle].

shuttlecock n
=gadwall.
1911 *Forest & Stream* 77.172 **FL**, Gadwall. . . Shuttlecock, Apalachicola and St. Vincent Island, Fla.

shut up one's head See **head** n B2

shwink See **shrink**

shy(te)poke See **shitepoke**

s'l See **say** v B1b

si-antigodlin adv, adj Cf **antisigodlin, si-godlin, si-gogglin**
1913 Kephart *Highlanders* 295 **sAppalachians**, Slaunchways denotes slanting, and si-godlin or si-antigodlin is out of plumb or out of square (factitious words, of course—mere nonsense terms, like catawampus).

sib adj, n [*OED2 sib* a. and sb.[2]]
Akin, similar (to); a relative, companion.
1930 Shoemaker *1300 Words* 57 **cPA Mts** (as of c1900), *Sib*—A sister or relative. **1944** *PADS* 2.49 **NC, VA**, *Sib.* . . A companion. . . Reported. *Sib.* . . Akin to, having similar tastes, like. "That city fellow is sib to us country folks; he likes our mountain ways." . . Common. **1952** Brown *NC Folkl.* 1.590, *Sib.* . . A companion, a relative.—East.

sibby bean See **sieva bean**

Siberian elm n
A naturalized elm (*Ulmus pumila*). Also called **cork elm 4**
1904 *Outing* 84, The English elm and the cork-back [sic] and Siberian elms are also desirable. **1931** Otis *MI Trees* 154, The Siberian, Chinese or Dwarf Elm, *Ulmus pumila . . ,* is a small, rapidly-growing tree of dense habit. **1966–68** *DARE* (Qu. T11, . . *Kinds of elm trees*) Infs **OR**13, **UT**7, Chinese elm, Siberian elm; **OR**16, Siberian elm; **WA**8, Siberian elm, cork elm.

sibitron n
A **bittern** (here: *Botaurus lentiginosus*).
1917 *Wilson Bulletin* 29.2.78 **NJ**, *Botaurus lentiginosus.* . . sibitron,

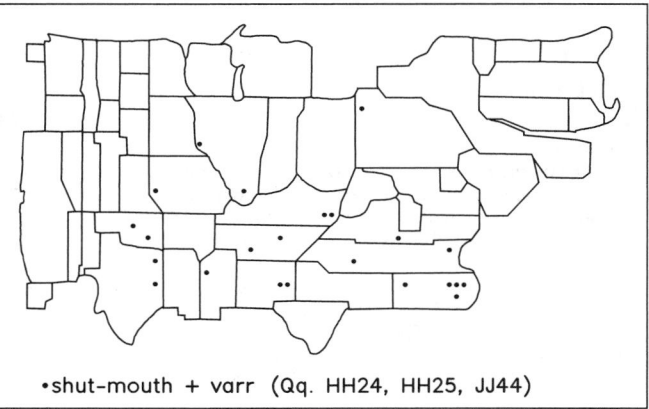

•shut-mouth + varr (Qq. HH24, HH25, JJ44)

Newark and Flemington, N.J. . . probably residuum of the phase [sic] "it's a bittern."

sic v Also by metanalysis (from *sic-calf*) *si* [Cf *EDD* sic int. "A call to pigs. . . A sheep-call"] Cf **sook**

Come!—used as a call to animals; freq in combs *si(c)-calf* and varr.

1965–70 *DARE* (Qu. K83, *To call a calf to you at feeding time*) Infs **IA**36, **PA**178, Si-calf; **IN**72, Si-calf ['sɪ kɑf]; **MO**3, **OK**1, Si-calf [sɪ kæːf] si-calf; **OK**33, Si-calf [si 'kæ·f] si-calf; **IN**63, **PA**198, Si-calfy [sɪ kæfi] (si-calfy); **PA**207, Si-calfy si-calf; **CO**11, 44, **KS**9, Si-calf; (Qu. K80, *The call that's used . . to get the cows in from the pasture*) Inf **MO**17, Sic—we used to say [sɪk] or [zɪk] or something like that; **CO**11, **IN**63, Sic-boss. **1973** Allen *LAUM* 1.261 **Upper MW** (as of c1950), *Calls to calves. . .* sic calf [3 infs, **IA, NE, SD**].

sic-a See **senkah**

si-calf See **sic**

sic-a-nine-ten n Cf **barsdown, guard the sheep**

1895 *DN* 1.399 **cNY**, *Sic-a-nine-ten:* an outdoor game very similar to hi-spy, but somewhat more complicated. A stick is used as a "gool"; if a player not previously "caught" throws the stick, all who have been "caught" are said to be "home free" and may hide again. The one who is "it" then returns the stick to its place and proceeds again to "catch" those hiding. The game is also known as *sheep pen, sheep yard,* and *bars down.*

sicarum adj, n Also sp *sukkuhr'um* Cf **senkah**

See quots.

1908 *S. Atl. Qrly.* 7.341 [Gullah], Me yent no sicarum; me holleh one patty-augah. [Footnote:] No sicarum: no such a thing—*sic'a* is probably not *sich a . .* but a variant of *sakes-a* or *senka . .* with euphonic *r,* and that general-purpose substantive " 'um:" translation in full, "I did nothing like that." **1922** Gonzales *Black Border* 330 **sSC, GA coasts** [Gullah glossary], *Sukkuhr'um*—same like, or like him, her, it, them.

sic-calf See **sic**

sic 'em, not to know v phr Also sp *siccum, sickem, sickom, sickum;* also in phr *not to know sic 'em from come here* and varr **chiefly Inland Nth, esp Pacific NW, Rocky Mts, Upper MW** See Map

To be very ignorant or stupid; hence adj phr *not worth sic 'em* worthless.

1907 White *AZ Nights* 27, You see, for all their plumb nerve in comin' so far, the most of them didn't know sic 'em. *Ibid* 134, I didn't know sic em' [sic] about minin'; and before long I *knew* that I didn't know sic 'em. **1942** Whipple *Joshua* 494 **UT**, I don't know sickom about this business, myself. **1950** *WELS* (*Saying about somebody who seems to you to be very stupid . . "He doesn't know _____."*) 4 Infs, **WI**, Sic 'em; (*The most basic thing, the simplest things: "He doesn't know _____ about plumbing."*) 1 Inf, **cWI**, Come here from sic 'em. **1958** Hench Coll., [A person from] Worcester Mass, said about somebody, "He doesn't know sickum about that." When I asked him about it he said he had used it all his life. **1961** *AmSp* 36.233 **sCA**, He doesn't know sick 'em from com'ere (come here). **1965–70** *DARE* (Qu. JJ15b, *Sayings about a person who seems to you very stupid: "He doesn't know*

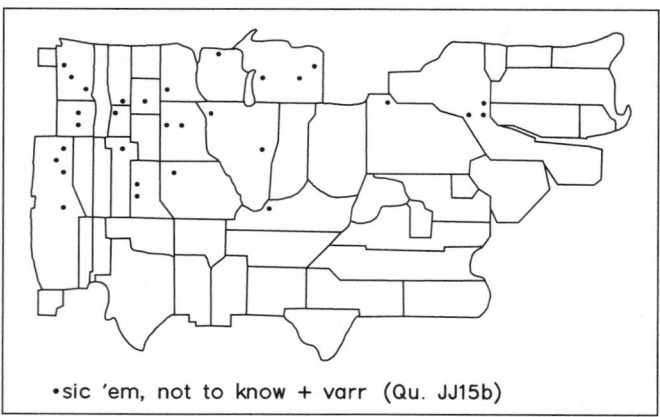

•sic 'em, not to know + varr (Qu. JJ15b)

_____.")* 27 Infs, **chiefly Inland Nth, esp Pacific NW, Rocky Mts, Upper MW**, Sic 'em; **NY**113, Here from sic 'em; **KY**78, Sic 'em from come here; **IL**4, Sic 'em from go get 'em. [23 of 30 Infs old] **1965** *DARE* File **csWI**, Doesn't know sic 'em from come 'ere (indication of stupidity). **1988** *Ibid* **swWI**, "He don't know sic 'em!" means that he's ignorant or stupid. *Ibid* **Upstate NY, nePA**, We used to say that a person "don't know sic 'em." This meant that the person was pretty stupid. **1989** *Ibid* **sWI**, *Not worth sic 'em*—Not worth beans; worthless. Common. **1995** Lesley *Sky Fisherman* 126 **OR**, Some of those girls didn't know sickem. **1998** Daheim *Wed & Buried* 154 **WA**, "The bean pole." Judith exuded patience. "The woman who left with Mr. Tenino." . . "What bean pole?" Gertrude scowled at her daughter. "I don't know siccum about any bean poles." **2001** *DARE* File **OR** (as of c1930), He doesn't know sic 'em from come back.

sick adj

1 In labor; confined to childbed. [*OED2* sick a. A.1.e "*north. dial.*"]

[**1798** in 1956 Eliason *Tarheel Talk* 294 **se,cwNC**, I do not think yr sick time will be before the last of Decbr.] **1805** (1905) Lewis *Orig. Jrls. Lewis & Clark Exped.* 7.142, One of our Indian women was taken Sick a little back of this and halted a fiew minutes on the road and had hir child and went on without Detaining us. **1941** *LANE* Map 392 (*Pregnant*) 2 infs, **MA, NH**, (About to be) sick. **1959** *VT Hist.* 27.157, *Be sick. . .* A euphemism for the phrase, to have a baby. Old fashioned. Rare. **1969–70** *DARE* (Qu. AA28, . . *Joking or sly expressions . . women use to say that another is going to have a baby . . "She['s] _____.")* Infs **PA**216, **VA**80, Going to (or gonna) be sick.

2 Menstruating. Cf **come sick, sickness**

1948 *Word* 4.185 [Vernacular of menstruation], I am sick. **1960** Criswell *Resp. to PADS 20* **Ozarks**, Sick meant menstruating. **1965–70** *DARE* (Qu. AA27, . . *A woman's menstruation*) Infs **LA**14, **MD**21, **MO**12, **OH**65, **VA**2, 31, Sick; **IL**75, 88, **KY**28, **MA**55, Being sick; **GA**81, **MS**51, **MT**4, **UT**9, She's (or she is) sick; [**NJ**59, Her monkey's sick].

sick abed in the woodbox adj phr Also *sick abed on two chairs;* for addit varr see quots **chiefly NEast**

Quite well—used as a facetious response to queries about one's health or to imply that someone is pretending to be ill; slightly unwell.

1914 *DN* 4.79 **ME, nNH**, Sick abed in the wood-box. . . In good health. A common answer to any inquiry after one's condition. **1939** (1962) Thompson *Body & Britches* 498 **NY**, He's sick abed on two chairs with his feet in the woodbox: (not seriously ill; sometimes means shamming illness). **1957** Eaton Coll. **Upper MW**, How are you?—I'm sick in bed with one foot in the wood box—smart answer: the person is not really sick. **1959** *VT Hist.* 27.157, Sick-abed in the woodbox. . . Quite well. A frequent reply to the question of how one feels, when the person wishes to be facetious. **1968** *DARE* (Qu. BB41, *Not seriously ill, but sick enough to be in bed: "He's been _____ for a week."*) Inf **NH**14, Sick abed in the woodbox; **NY**94, **PA**115, Sick abed (or in bed) on two chairs.

sick as a dog See **dog** n[1] B16f

sick-bird winter n

A late spring storm.

1991 Still *Wolfpen Notebooks* 91 **sAppalachians**, There are several winters: blackberry, redbud, and dogwood. After they're past, sometimes we have Sick Bird winter. Birds get wet and chilled, look pretty droopy.

sickem, not to know See **sic 'em, not to know**

sicklebill n

1 also *sickle-bill(ed) curlew, sicklebill plover:* =**long-billed curlew.**

1844 Giraud *Birds Long Is.* 272, The Long-billed Curlew, or "Sickle-bill," as many term it, frequents the muddy shores of beaches and marshes, where it collects minute shell-fish. **1876** *Forest & Stream* 7.149 **Long Is. NY**, The biggest of all the snipes is the sickle billed curlew, which is almost as large as a hen, and has a bill about six inches long, curved just about the same as a jack curlew. **1916** *Times–Picayune* (New Orleans LA) 2 Apr mag sec 8/4, Long-billed curlew. . . Corbigeau; Sickle bill. The extremely long, curved bill of this most curious of all shore birds at once identifies it. **1955** MA Audubon Soc. *Bulletin* 39.446, Long-billed Curlew. . . Old Sicklebill (From its long curved bill). . . Sicklebill, Sicklebill Curlew (General) . . Sicklebill Plover (Maine).

2 also *sickle-billed thrush:* The California **thrasher** *(Toxostoma redivivum).*

1872 Coues *Key to N. Amer. Birds* 75, Sickle-billed Thrush. Californian Mockingbird. . . Coast region of California. . . *[Harporhynchus] redivivus.* **1881** *Amer. Naturalist* 15.210 **CA,** The California sickle-bill *(Harporhynchus redivivus),* a thrush . . is a resident . . in Southern California.

3 =**bluestocking 2.**

1917 *Wilson Bulletin* 29.2.79 **WA,** *Recurvirostra americana.* . . sicklebill, Willapa Harbor, Wash.

4 =**Hudsonian curlew.**

1955 MA Audubon Soc. *Bulletin* 39.446 **MA,** Hudsonian Curlew. . . Sicklebill.

5 A **mosquito** n[1] **B1** (here: *Toxorhynchites rutilus*).   [From its strongly curved proboscis]

1938 Brimley *Insects NC* 322, *M[egarhinus] septentrionalis.* . . Sicklebill. State-wide, July–September. One of our largest mosquitoes but does not bite.

sickle-bill(ed) curlew See **sicklebill 1**

sickle-billed thrush See **sicklebill 2**

sicklebill plover See **sicklebill 1**

sicklepod n

1 A rock cress *(Arabis canadensis).*

1824 Bigelow *Florula Bostoniensis* 251, Arabis falcata. . . *Sickle Pod.* . . Pods long and curved, resembling a crooked sword blade. **1843** Torrey *Flora NY* 1.55, Sickle-pod. Turkey-pod. . . Rocky woods and hill sides. **1910** Shreve *MD Plant Life* 439, *Arabis canadensis.* . . Sicklepod. Midland and Mountain Zones. **1950** Gray–Fernald *Manual of Botany* 727, *[Arabis] canadensis* . . Sicklepod. . . Rich woods, thickets, and rocky banks.

2 also *sickle senna:* A **senna** n[1] **1** (here: *Senna obtusifolia*). Also called **coffeeweed 1b**

1876 Hobbs *Bot. Hdbk.* 156, Cassia Tora, Sickle senna. **1922** *Amer. Botanist* 28.30, *Cassia tora* of the Southern States is known as "sicklepod" and "coffee-weed," these names referring to the shape of the pods and the hard dark seeds. **1970** Correll *Plants TX* 791, Sickle-pod. Erect malodorous herb. **2000** *DARE* File—Internet **MS,** [Title:] Why is sicklepod such a problem weed?

sickletop n Also *sickletop lousewort*

A western **lousewort 1** (here: *Pedicularis racemosa*) that has flowers with the upper lip of the corolla extended into a slender beak and curved like a sickle.

1937 U.S. Forest Serv. *Range Plant Hdbk.* W142, Sickletop . . , one of the most widespread of the western species, occurs chiefly on open mountain sides. **1973** Hitchcock–Cronquist *Flora Pacific NW* 430, Sickletop l[ousewort] . . *P. racemosa.*

sickness n Also with *the*   Also *monthly sickness*   **scattered, but esp C and Mid Atl**   See Map   *euphem*   Cf **sick time**
Menstruation.

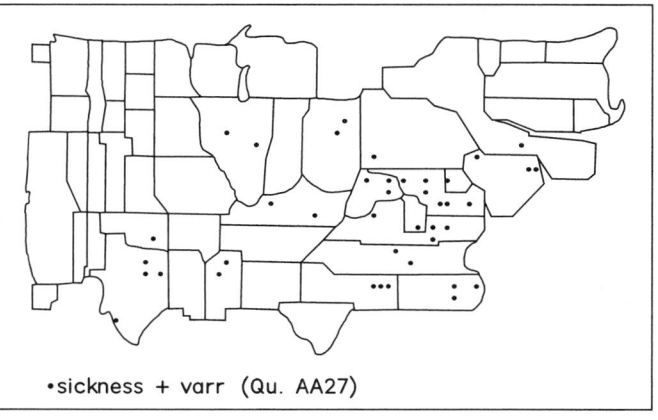

•sickness + varr (Qu. AA27)

1948 *Word* 4.185 [Vernacular of menstruation], To be suffering from the monthly sickness. [Used by women.] **c1960** *Wilson Coll.* **csKY,** *The sickness.* . . The menstrual period. **1965–70** *DARE* (Qu. AA27, . . *A woman's menstruation*) 34 Infs, **scattered, but esp C and Mid Atl,** Sickness; **MD17, NY66,** Her sickness; **MD19, NJ41,** (Got) my sickness; **KY19,** Monthly sickness; **MD15,** She has her sickness; **MD9,** She's having her sickness.

sick of one's stomach See **of** prep **C10**

sickom, not to know See **sic 'em, not to know**

sick on one's stomach See **on** prep **B9**

sick period See **sick time**

sick shrimp n

The black-tailed shrimp *(Crangon nigricauda).*

1968 *DARE* (Qu. P14, . . *Commercial fishing . . what do the fishermen go out after?*) Inf **LA44,** Black shrimp are often called sick shrimp.

sick time n Also *sick period*   [**sick** adj 2]   **chiefly Inland Nth, N Midl, West**   See Map   Cf **sickness**
A menstrual period.

1965–70 *DARE* (Qu. AA27, . . *A woman's menstruation*) 16 Infs, **chiefly Inland Nth, N Midl, West,** Sick time; **CA144, OH64,** Her sick time; **IL45,** My sick time; **MO37, SC58,** Her sick period(s); **KS12, MO21, OH23,** Sick period. **2001** *DARE* File **csWI** (as of late 1970s), My grandmother invariably referred to a woman's menstrual period as her "sick time."

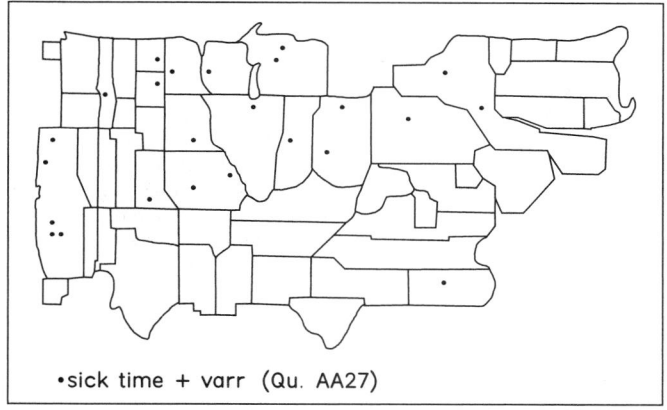

•sick time + varr (Qu. AA27)

sickum, not to know See **sic 'em, not to know**

siddity See **siditty**

side n[1] See **scythe**

side n[2]

1 A self-contained crew within a logging operation; hence combs *side push,* ~ *rod* the foreman of such a unit. **chiefly Nth, esp Pacific NW**   Cf **pusher 1, ramrod** n

1938 (1939) Holbrook *Holy Mackinaw* 263, Side. One complete yarding and loading crew, with spar tree and donkey engines. A *two-side camp* has two spars and crews. *Side push.* A minor foreman. **1942** *AmSp* 17.224 **Nth** [Loggers' talk], Side. One complete yarding and loading crew in high-line operation, usually consisting of 22 men equipped with spar tree and donkey engine. A two-side camp has two sets of equipment and crews. Inevitably one *side* is the *haywire* and the other side the *candy* side. **1950** *Western Folkl.* 9.119 **nwOR** [Logger speech], *Side rod.* Woods foreman. *Ibid* 381 **neCA** [Lumberjack language], *Side rod.* A boss; usually second in command in the woods. **1956** *AmSp* 31.152 **nwCA** [Logger lingo], *Siderod.* . . The boss of a yarding crew in the woods. **1958** McCulloch *Woods Words* 164 **Pacific NW,** *Side*—A logging unit: the men and equipment needed to fall, buck, yard, and load any one unit of an operation. Known as cat side, high lead side, skidder side, etc. *Ibid,* *Side push*—The foreman of a crew on one side. *Side rod*—The man in charge of a side, or one unit of a logging operation. *Ibid* 84, *Hemlock side*—The poorest side in any logging operation. **1959** *AmSp* 34.79 **nwCA** [Logger lingo], *Side.* . . The crew of men, including fallers, buckers, rigging men, loaders, and all others working with the yarding donkey. **1961** Labbe–Goe *Railroads* 259 **Pacific NW,** [Glossary:] *Side:* The operation revolving around one landing. An operation could be made up of several sides. **1969** Sorden *Lumberjack Lingo* 109 **NEng, Gt Lakes,** *Side*—The crew and equipment in yarding and loading logs at one landing.

2 See **side meat.**

side v

1 To fillet (a fish). [*OED2 side* v.¹ 1 "*Obs.*"]

1985 Madson *Up River* 213 **Upper Missip Valley,** He swiftly "sided" the fish with a thin-bladed, very sharp knife and cubed the fillets into chunks.

2 To accompany; to support or stand by (someone). [*OED2* 1591 →]

1923 *DN* 5.220 **swMO,** *Side.* . . To accompany. "If he wants a pardner I'll side 'im." **1945** Thorp *Pardner* 32 **SW,** I sided these boys all morning. They were studying some about me, I judged. Had I just talked big to show off? Or could I ride? **1956** Almirall *From College* 97 **CO,** I was more than glad of my brother's suggestion to have this old-timer side me for a while. **1960** Criswell *Resp. to PADS 20* **Ozarks,** *Side.* . . To support, stand by (one). "Bill wouldn't side me or I would a' tackled them fellers."

3 To cultivate close to a row of (a crop); hence vbl n *siding.* **esp SE** Cf **bar off, side harrow**

1847 in 1927 Jones *FL Plantation Rec.* 245 **nwFL,** 1, [named] winey, sewing for negroes, 9 sideing cotton [in] hous field. **1851** *Ibid* 383, 14 [hands] Ploughing Cotton at Cars, sideling [sic] it. **1886** *Century Illustr. Mag.* 32.200 **eVA,** I tell Hannah I ain' done sidin' meh corn. **1909** *DN* 3.369 **eAL, wGA,** *Side.* . . To plow close to young cotton so as to throw the soil from it. This enables the choppers to work more rapidly. **1918** *DN* 5.19 **NC,** *Side,* to plow on the side of the row. **1947** McDavid *Coll.* **cSC,** Siding cotton—working between the rows. **1986** Pederson *LAGS Concordance,* 1 inf, **ceAL,** Sided the cotton—with a scrape or sweep; 1 inf, **csAL,** Siding—procedure after chopping/before hoeing; 1 inf, **swGA,** Siding it [=cotton]—using a plow that throws dirt to it.

4 also with *up:* To clean up; to put in order. [Engl dial; cf *EDD side* v.¹ 8] **esp NEast** Cf **aside** adj, **siden,** *DS* E21

1895 *DN* 1.383 **NJ,** *Side up:* to clean up, put in order (a room). **1941** *LANE* Map 336 (*She cleans up every morning*) 1 inf, **sME,** Sides up, reported as a Lancashire term heard from mill workers. **1950** *WELS Suppl.,* 1 Inf, **csWI,** Side the table—for clear the table. **2000** *NADS Letters* **seMA,** I . . got these words from my mother, who was born and bred in New Bedford, MA. She's 50. . . *Blueberry grunt* is still in use . . , but she only uses *side the table* to tease us and out-of-state visitors. **2001** *DARE File* **seMA,** [She] sided the table and washed the few breakfast dishes.

side prep Also *side of* Cf **of** prep **Bh**

1 On the side of—usu in phrr *take one side (of) the head* and varr.

1880 (1881) Harris *Uncle Remus Songs* 24 **GA** [Black], Brer Rabbit draw back wid his fis', he did, en blip he tuck 'er side er de head. **1887** (1967) Harris *Free Joe* 172 **GA** [Black], Dat nigger man tuck'n lam me side the head. **1905** *DN* 3.10 **cCT,** He gin me a crack side of the head. **1909** *DN* 3.369 **eAL, wGA,** *Side the head.* . . Equivalent to 'on the side of the head.' **1927** *DN* 5.473 **Ozarks,** An' then I jes' clewd him side o' th' head.

2 Beside, alongside. **chiefly S Atl, Gulf States**

1922 Gonzales *Black Border* 326 **sSC, GA coasts** [Gullah glossary], *Side'uh*—on the side of, alongside. **1927** Adams *Congaree* 8 **cSC** [Black], White folks an' niggers, all both of them, an' all lined up 'side of the road. **1934** *AmSp* 9.127 [Engl dial of HI], Prepositions may be combined to form entirely new compound prepositions. . . Among new compound prepositions are . . *side of,* 'beside.' . . *The deer would eat side of them.* **1937** in 1958 Brewer *Dog Ghosts* 89 **TX** [Black], So he . . picks up a Coca Cola bottle what layin' on de groun' side de wagon he been settin' in. **1965–69** *DARE* (Qu. MM1, . . '*Opposite to*' . . "The shed is _____ the barn.") Inf **NY9,** Side of it; (Qu. MM6, . . '*Very close*' or '*only a short distance away*': "The house is _____ the park.") Infs **FL26, MS61,** Right side; **GA7, MA73,** (Right) side of. **1968** *DARE* Tape **GA25,** And my grandfather, he cut out a road ran right side the swamp. **1971** in 1993 Major *Calling the Wind* 312 **LA** [Black], Lucy's playing side the house. . . I go side the house and play with Lucy. *Ibid* 316, Daddy lays there side me a long time. **1986** Pederson *LAGS Concordance,* 1 inf, **csAR,** Hang clothes

here side the wall; 1 inf, **swGA,** Lit right down side of me; 1 inf, **nwLA,** Sat down side of me; 1 inf, **cMS,** Side the highway.

side and side adv phr Cf **side by each,** *neck and neck* **chiefly NEast; also Sth, S Midl** See Map *old-fash*

Side by side; abreast; close together.

1834 *S. Lit. Messenger* 1.104, Day after day . . you would find . . these two young innocents sitting side and side, cheek and joke [sic], feasting on each others' eyes. **1883** *Overland Mth.* 2.266, We were riding side and side when he fell. **1913** *DN* 4.5 **ME,** *Side and side.* . . Side by side. "They lived side 'n side." **1914** *DN* 4.112 **cKS,** *Side and side* . . side by side. **1923** *DN* 5.220 **swMO,** *Side an' side.* . . Side by side. **1945** *FWP Lay My Burden Down* 40 **Sth** (as of c1865) [Black], Us three, me and Green and Isham, was riding along side and side. **1950** *WELS* (*One next to the other:* "He put the two boxes _____ on the table.") 1 Inf, **seWI,** Side and side. **1951** Johnson *Resp. to PADS 20* **DE,** One next to the other. . . Old-fashioned . . side and side. **c1960** *Wilson Coll.* **csKY,** *Side and side.* . . Next to one another; usually side by side. **1965–70** *DARE* (Qu. MM17, *If two things are next to each other* . . "He put the two boxes on the table . . _____.") 27 Infs, **chiefly NEast; also Sth, S Midl,** Side and side; (Qu. KK54, *Just about equal, very close:* "They were both fast runners and it was _____ all the way.") Inf **MO8,** Side and side. [22 of 27 total Infs old] **1966** *DARE* Tape **SC9,** Put two side and side and roll one on the top. **1986** Pederson *LAGS Concordance,* 1 inf, **nwLA,** Side and side—side by side.

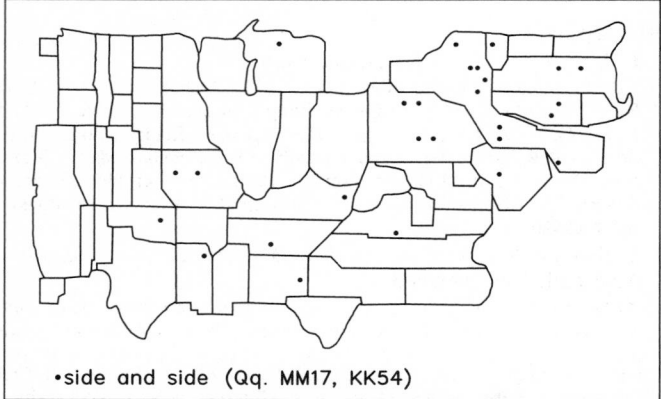

•side and side (Qq. MM17, KK54)

side bacon n
=**side meat.**

1850 (1926) Sawyer *Way Sketches* 108 **MO,** Each man . . fifty pounds of smoked side bacon. **1909** Porter *Roads of Destiny* 140 **TX,** Frijoles and side bacon would do me about as well. **1962** Atwood *Vocab. TX* 62, *Salt pork* . . Other terms in occasional use . . bacon, side bacon . . sowbosom. **1965–70** *DARE* (Qu. H38, . . *Words for bacon [including joking ones]*) Infs **IL103, NY70, OH89, OK32, SC11, 43, 46,** Side bacon; **IN76,** Jowl bacon, side bacon; **KY84,** Fresh side bacon. **1966** Dakin *Dial. Vocab. Ohio R. Valley* 336, *Side bacon = salt pork* is fairly common in the Mountains, but is only scattered elsewhere in Kentucky (chiefly the Bluegrass) and is rare in all the states above the Ohio. . . The most common practice generally throughout the Ohio Valley is simply to refer to smoked (and possibly sugar-cured) side pork as *bacon.* In Illinois . . the terms *side* (sometimes *slab*) bacon . . are usual. *Side bacon* . . [is] also scattered throughout eastern Kentucky. **c1970** Pederson *Dial. Surv. Rural GA* **seGA** (*Meat from the side of a hog, salted but not smoked*) 2 [of 64] infs, Side bacon. **1986** Pederson *LAGS Concordance* (*Salt pork*) 4 infs, **AL, GA, TN, TX,** Side bacon; (*Side [of bacon]*) 4 infs, **AR, GA, TN,** Side bacon; (*Smoked meat*) 3 infs, **AL, GA, TX,** Side bacon; (*Bacon*) 1 inf, **TX,** Side bacon.

side beard n
A side-whisker, sideburn.

1869 *Galaxy* 7.210, Tall and light-made . . pale face, black silky side-beard. **a1876** in 2002 (acc) Brigham Young Univ. *Book of Abraham Project* (Internet) **OH,** Having shaved himself in his usual style, leaving side beards, [he] started on his return to the mill. **1927** Kennedy *Gritny* 8 **sLA** [Black], I ain' trus' *no* ooman w'at got side-b'yeards growin' 'long-side her jaws like Bell got.

side-box kitchen n
A kitchen forming an addition to a house.

1971 *Foxfire* Spring–Summer 40 **nGA,** There was a side-box kitchen we called it, on th' far side.

side by each adv phr **scattered, but less freq Sth, S Midl**
See Map   *often joc*
Side by side.
　1923 *DN* 5.220 **swMO,** *Side and side.* . . Side by side. Also, *side by each.* 1927 *Ruppenthal Coll.* **KS,** *Side by each.* . . Two or more objects that are close together. . . Jocularly "side by each" is used. 1950 *WELS* (One next to the other: "He put the two boxes ＿＿＿ on the table.") 2 infs, **WI,** Side by each; 1 Inf, **csWI,** Side by each—heard in jocular use—common; 1 Inf, **cwWI,** Side by each—humorous and in Germanic communities; 1 Inf, **cWI,** Side by each. . . German. 1950 *Western Folkl.* 9.119 **nwOR** [Logger speech], *Side by each.* Side by side. 1951 Johnson *Resp. to PADS 20* **DE,** One next to the other. . . Old-fashioned—side by each. 1960 Bailey *Resp. to PADS 20* **KS,** *Side by side.* . . side by each: facetiously. 1960 Criswell *Resp. to PADS 20* **Ozarks,** Together, side by side, side by each (humorous). Perhaps this last was at one time a serious expression though I do not remember so far back. 1965–70 *DARE* (Qu. MM17, *If two things are next to each other* . . "*He put the two boxes on the table* . . ＿＿＿.") 74 Infs, **scattered, but less freq Sth, S Midl,** Side by each. 1967 *DARE* FW Addit **CO4,** Side by each—a three-team is arranged "side by each." 1968 *DARE* Tape **WI27,** We went along side by each with the train. 1999 *DARE* File—Internet **WI** [Central Florida Green Bay Packer Backers], *Side-by-each:* used instead of, "next to each other."

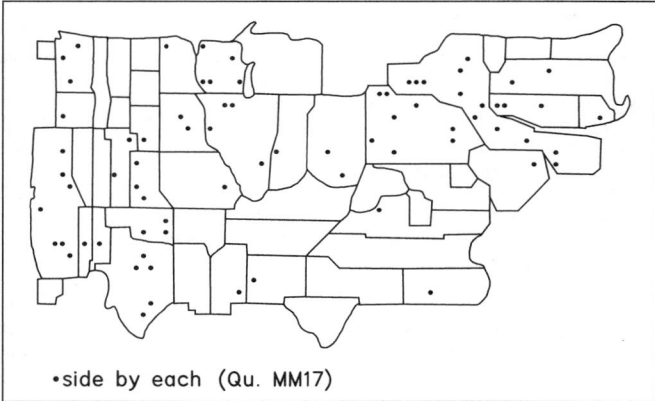

•side by each (Qu. MM17)

side delivery bunk See **side loader**

side ditch n Also *side drain, ～ gutter* **chiefly Midl, esp Mid Atl** See Map   Cf **drain** n[1] **C1**
　1965–70 *DARE* (Qu. N24, *A ditch along the side of a graded road*) 17 Infs, **chiefly Midl, esp Mid Atl,** Side ditch; **MD20, VA59,** Side drain; **MD29, PA204,** Side gutter.

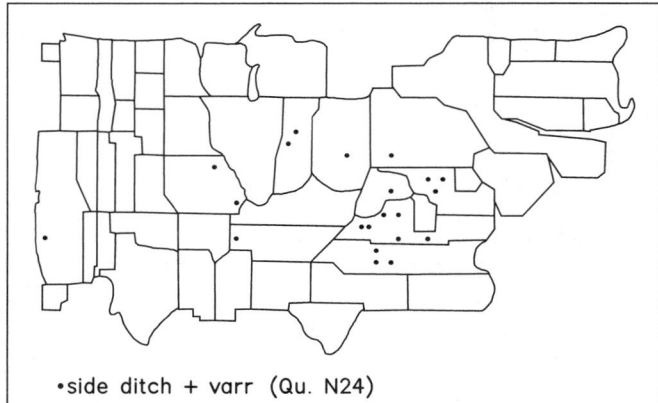

•side ditch + varr (Qu. N24)

side entry n Cf **back entry**
In coal mining: a passageway; see quot.
　1973 *PADS* 59.52 **wKY** [Bituminous coal mining vocab], *Side entry.* . . = *entry* [=any passageway opened for the removal, haulage, access to, or temporary storage of the coal or for the movement of men,

vehicles, or machinery] . . *slant* [=an *entry cut* off a *main entry* at more than a ninety degree angle].

sidegadling See **si-godlin**

side gal See **side girl**

sidegartlin' See **si-godlin**

side girl n Also *side gal*
A woman with whom a man has an illicit or secret relationship.
　1928 Peterkin *Scarlet Sister Mary* 122 **SC,** I want a charm for July, Daddy Cudjoe. July's got a side-gal. 1934 Hurston *Jonah's Gourd Vine* 250 **AL** [Black], Harris knew that he must find some other weapon to move the man who had taken his best side-girl from him. 1984 Wilder *You All Spoken Here* 95 **Sth,** *Side gal:* One courted on the sly, or side, unbeknownst to one's steady.

sidegodlin See **si-godlin**

sidegoglin See **si-gogglin**

side gutter See **side ditch**

side harrow n **esp Lower Missip Valley** See Map   Cf **gee whiz** n, **side** v 3
A type of harrow used with row crops, esp cotton.
　1844 in 1969 Turner *Cotton Planter's Manual* 174 **seGA,** I have been using, for some time, the plough in the cultivation of the Sea Island cotton . . and I intend . . to facilitate my work by the side-harrow and the cultivator. 1925 *Book of Rural Life* 3.1368, The first cultivation of cotton must be of such a nature as to stir the soil close to the plants without covering them. Either double cultivators with fenders attached or single cultivators made similar to a side harrow may be satisfactorily used. 1944 Clark *Pills* 283 **Sth,** Crowded along the aisles . . were the assembled implements such as middle busters . . side harrows, spring tooth cultivators. 1965–70 *DARE* (Qu. L18, *Kinds of plows*) Infs **AR15, LA7, MS63, 87,** Side harrow; (Qu. L20, *The implement used in a field after it's been plowed to break up the lumps*) Infs **AR55, LA10,** Side harrow(s); **LA2,** Side harrow—also called "gee whiz"—used for cultivating when corn is young; **LA3,** Side harrow—for cultivating cotton, etc.; (Qu. L25, *The implement used to clean out weeds and loosen the earth between rows of corn*) Inf **LA7,** Side harrow. 1986 Pederson *LAGS Concordance* (Harrow) 32 infs, 30 **LA, MS,** Side harrow(s).

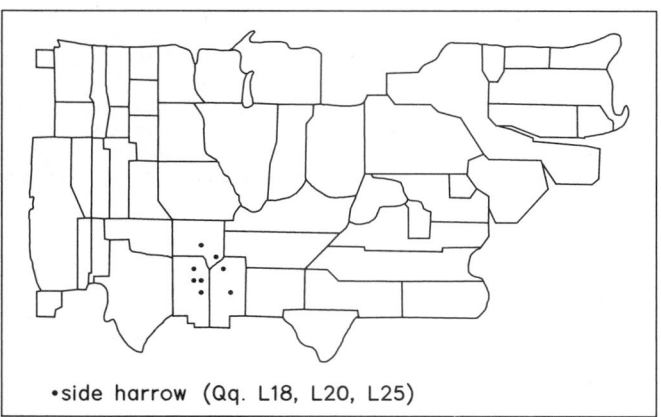

•side harrow (Qq. L18, L20, L25)

sidehead n With *the*
A condition, caused by an inflammation of the external ear, in which a dog holds its head on one side or shakes it persistently.
　1949 Arnow *Hunter's Horn* 65 **KY,** Mark was struggling to his knees, shaking his bloody head like a hound with the sidehead.

sidehill n [*OED2* "Now U.S."]
1 A hillside, slope. **chiefly Nth, esp NEast**
　1674 *Groton Rec.* 178 (*DAE*) **MA,** His houselot . . [is] bounded on the north with the sidhill. 1711 in 1892 MA Hist. Soc. *Coll.* 6th ser 5.242 **CT,** You must all get out at the Barbers Bason, being a bad side hill. 1843 *Ladies' Repository* 3.49 **NEng,** And I now recall the whole scene before me, . . the many boats filled with spectators, and the silent, sol-

emn, gazing multitutde on the side hill and the shore. **1847** Hurd *Grammatical Corrector* 67, *Side-hill,* for *hill-side;* as, "He lives on the side-hill." **1851** in 1940 *AmSp* 15.391 **VA,** Thence . . to a white oak on E Side hill. **1898** *Overland Mth.* (2d ser) 32.32 **CA,** Here I was, more'n a hundred feet from the gulch, up on the side hill. **1911** in 1914 Stewart *Letters* 137, My house faces east and is built up against a side-hill, or should I say hillside? **1938** in Lib. of Congress *Amer. Memory: WPA Life Hist.* (Internet) **NE,** They would . . gather berries on the side hills. *Ibid* **cwCT,** The side hills was dotted with his sheep and cattle. **1939** *Ibid* **nwMA,** Then they's this side hill where the snakes are. **1968** *DARE* Tape **NH**14, They was just a dirt, a dirt road and you'd strike a place where it'd be say a sidehill like; sometime they'd dig that edge off, you know, and level it down. **1968** *DARE* FW Addit **NY**93, *On the sidehill* = on the side of the hill, on the hillside. **1978** Doig *This House* 73 **MT** (as of c1950), Hold on, I'm gonna give her [=pickup truck] snoose to get up this sidehill. **2000** *NADS Letters* **wPA,** Have you recorded "side-hill" as a variant of hillside? My brother used this term once and his wife, who grew up in our same area, made fun of it. It didn't sound at all odd to me, but I don't know which term I would use.

2 Attrib:

a Built or established on sloping ground.

1848 *De Bow's Rev.* 5.84, The latter—the guard-drain or side-hill ditch—is as yet a thing unheard-of by ninety-nine in a hundred of the hill-planters of the South. **1859** Jacques *House* 140 **NY,** The advantages of a side-hill barn are, the warmth of its stables in winter and their coolness in summer; storage for roots, if required; [etc]. **1862** U.S. Patent Office *Annual Rept. for 1861: Ag.* 415 **NY,** During one season a side-hill lot on his farm . . yielded no less than *twelve tons* of hay. **1890** *Century Dict.* 5615, *Side-hill.* . . A hillside; an acclivity; especially, any rise or slope of ground not too steep for cultivation or other use: as, a house built on a *side-hill; a side-hill* farm. . . [*Century* Ed: U.S.] **1891** *Harper's New Mth. Mag.* 83.192 **Boston MA,** In the humbler side-hill streets . . they have their homes. **1969** *DARE* (Qu. M1, . . *Kinds of barns*) Inf **MA**58, Sidehill barn.

b in comb *sidehill plow:* A plow that can be set to throw the furrow to either side. **chiefly NEast** See Map *old-fash* Cf **flatland plow, hillside ~**

1830 *N.C. Spectator* (Rutherfordton) 13 Aug. 1/3 *(DA),* The *patent revolving side hill plough* has . . the following advantages. **1848** *De Bow's Rev.* 6.131, We noticed the Side Hill or Swivel Plows, . . so constructed that the mould-board can be instantly changed from one side to the other, which enables the operator to perform the work horizontally upon side hills, going back and forth on the same side, and turning all the furrow slices with great accuracy, downward. **1876** Knight *Amer. Mech. Dict.* 2173, *Side-hill Plow.* A plow whose cutting apparatus is reversible, so as to throw its furrow-slice to the right or left, as may be desired. **1965–70** *DARE* (Qu. L18, *Kinds of plows*) 34 Infs, **chiefly NEast,** Sidehill plow. [30 Infs old, 29 male] **1992** Phelps *Famous Last Words* 22 **NEng,** I learned to plow with a side hill plow or swivell plow as it was called, as at the end of a furrow a latch was released and the mold board could be rolled over and it would turn the other way going back.

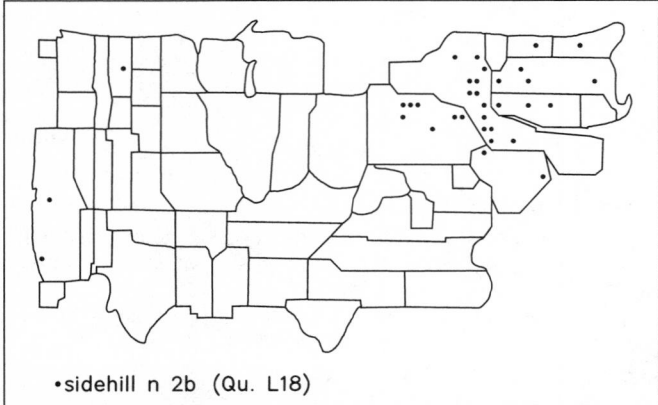

•sidehill n 2b (Qu. L18)

c in combs *sidehill badger, ~ clincher, ~ critter, ~ gopher, ~ gouger, ~ hoofer, ~ lounger, ~ mootie, ~ ranger, ~ slicker, ~ walloper, ~ winder, ~ wowser:* An imaginary creature alleged to frequent hillsides, usu described as having the legs on one side shorter than those on the other. **chiefly Nth** See Map

1849 Willis *Rural Letters* 93 **csNY,** "It's a *side-hill* critter! Two off legs so lame, she can't stand even." It was certainly a new idea, that a horse with two spavins on a side, might be used with advantage on a hill farm. **1904** Day *Kin o' Ktaadn* 132 **ME,** I have heard some of you woodsmen talk about the ha'nts and the swogons and the witherlicks and the side-hill loungers—says The Stranger.—I know these are jokes, my friends. **1907** *DN* 3.249 **eME,** Side hill badger. . . A fabulous creature which belongs to woodsmen's lore. Its legs on one side are longer than those on the other. Hence it can travel unimpeded only on a sidehill and in one direction. Formerly called *side-winder.* **1914** *DN* 4.79 **ME, nNH** Side-hill ranger. . . Mythical animal in lumber-woods. **1922** *DN* 5.188 **NEng,** Side hill winder. A badger with the right foreleg abnormally short. **1939** (1962) Thompson *Body & Britches* 299 **NY,** The Side-Hill Gouger, or Walloper, . . has legs on one side so that he can manage the steepest hill. **1939** Tryon *Fearsome Critters* 39, The Side-Hill Gouger. . . there are some vigorous proponents of [the name] . . "Side-Hill Wowser." . . [H]is nigh legs are shorter than the off pair. . . Gougers must obviously travel counter-clockwise around the hillside, and in making their daily rounds for food they wear the characteristic, partly gouged-out paths so familiar to woodsmen. **1950** *WELS* **WI** (Imaginary wild animals that people tell stories about) 2 Infs, Sidehill gouger; 1 Inf, Sidehill badger; 1 Inf, Sidehill gopher. **1953** Randolph–Wilson *Down in Holler* 284 **Ozarks,** Side-hill hoofer. . . A mythical beast which runs around mountain tops, always in the same direction because the legs on one side of its body are longer than those on the other side. The *side-hill slicker* and the *side-hill walloper* are variants. These imaginary creatures play an important part in Ozark folklore. **1958** McCulloch *Woods Words* 164 **Pacific NW,** Side hill gouger—Most famous of the imaginary critters found in loggers' yarns. Has two long legs on the downhill side and two short legs on the uphill side so it can stand upright. **1959** *VT Hist.* 27.157, Side hill gouger. **1965–70** *DARE* (Qu. CC17, *Imaginary animals or monsters that people . . tell tales about—especially to tease greenhorns*) Infs **IL**37, **MI**24, **MN**3, **NY**23, 34, **WA**30, **WI**19, 30, Sidehill gouger; **MA**100, Sidehill badger; **NY**219, Sidehill-clincher; **CO**14, Sidehill gopher; [(Qu. BB1) Inf **CO**14, A sidehill gopher—facetious remark made about one who limps;] (Qu. NN12b, *Things that people say to put off a child when he asks, "What are you making?"*) Inf **NY**219, Sidehill clincher. **1975** Gould *ME Lingo* 255, Sidehill winder. Or, sidehill gouger. A native Maine animal living on mountain slopes and having shorter legs on one side than on the other (except on Mt. Blue, where it's the other way around). **1979** *Oregonian Article Letters,* Side hill gouger. **1983** Glimm *Flatlanders* 34 **cnPA,** The sidehill mootie is an animal peculiar to the hills of northern Pennsylvania. These hills are so steep that in order to survive, the sidehill mootie developed one set of downhill and one set of uphill legs.

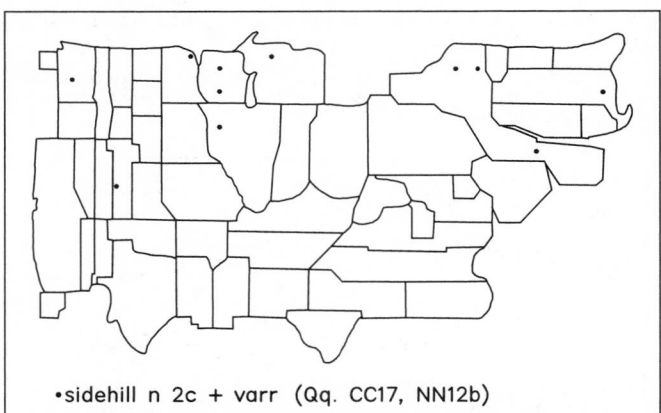

•sidehill n 2c + varr (Qq. CC17, NN12b)

d in var joc combs referring to bacon or to illegally killed venison; see quots. **Pacific NW** Cf **mountain trout 4**

1958 McCulloch *Woods Words* 164 **Pacific NW,** Side hill salmon—Bacon. **1967–69** *DARE* (Qu. H38, . . *Words for bacon [including joking ones]*) Inf **CA**136, Sidehill salmon; (Qu. P35a, *Names or nicknames for any deer shot illegally*) Inf **AK**1, Sidehill halibut; **CA**145, Sidehill salmon; **OR**1, Sidehill jerky.

e in var other combs: See quots. Cf **hillside**

1948 *WELS Suppl.* **cwWI,** Home cured tobacco we call dynamite fuse or side hill navy. **1958** McCulloch *Woods Words* 164 **Pacific NW,** *Side hill mechanic*—A skinner on an early day steam or gas log hauling tractor. **1962** Atwood *Vocab. TX* 66, *Illegitimate child.* . . Uncommon and perhaps sometimes improvised terms, occurring from one to six times each, include . . *sidehill baby.*

f Sloping.

1958 McCulloch *Woods Words* 164 **Pacific NW,** *Side hill load*—Big logs on one side of the truck, small logs on the other.

3 in phr *on a sidehill:* Askew.

1960 *VT Hist.* 28.119, Button. To be buttoned on a side hill. (To be buttoned crookedly)

sidehill v, hence vbl n, ppl adj *sidehilling*

To cross a steep slope obliquely.

2000 in 2002 *DARE* File—Internet **NV,** The trail sidehilled to the west of this point, crossed a sketchy scree slope, and achieved another saddle just below the main summit. *Ibid* **CA,** A narrow, sidehilling trail, with three big, fallen logs across it, leads 1.2 miles to the lookout. **2001** *DARE* File **AK,** When planning hiking trips, it is good to plan routes that won't involve too much sidehilling. Hiking across scree or loose gravel or even tundra slopes is exhausting and dangerous. **2002** *DARE* File—Internet, Crossing a Slope (Sidehilling)—Sidehilling can be very dangerous and is not recommended for inexperienced snowmobilers.

sidehill badger (or clincher, critter, gopher, gouger, hoofer) See **sidehill** n 2c

sidehill halibut See **sidehill** n 2d

sidehilling See **sidehill** v

sidehill lounger (or mootie) See **sidehill** n 2c

sidehill plow See **sidehill** n 2b

sidehill ranger See **sidehill** n 2c

sidehill salmon See **sidehill** n 2d

sidehill slicker (or walloper, winder, wowser) See **sidehill** n 2c

side line n Cf **forehopple** esp **TX, KS**

A cord used to hobble an animal by tying together a foreleg and hind leg of the same side; hence v phr *side line* to secure (an animal) in such a way.

1837 Irving *Rocky Mts.* 1.36 **KS,** The horses were "side-lined," as it is termed: that is to say, the fore and hind foot on the same side of the animal were tied together so as to be within eighteen inches of each other. **1844** (1954) Gregg *Commerce* 44 **KS,** [With] the 'side line' (a hopple connecting a fore and a hind leg) . . an animal can hardly increase his pace beyond a hobbling walk. **1869** *Overland Mth.* 3.128 **TX,** In addition to the usual methods of hoppling a horse, the Texans often "side line" him, by tying a fore to a hind leg. **1887** *Outing* 10.11 **ND,** "Side-lines" is the army substitute for hobbles. They connect a fore and hind foot, and consist . . of two leather leglets joined by an iron chain. **1903** (1965) Adams *Log Cowboy* 151 **TX,** We hobbled every horse and side-lined certain leaders. **1920** Hunter *Trail Drivers TX* 298, To "fair ground" is to rope an animal by the head, throw the rope over the back while still running and then throw the animal violently to the ground where it will usually lay until . . "sidelined," tying two feet together on the same side. **1949** *PADS* 11.10 **wTX** (as of 1911–29), *Side-line.* . . A hobble joining a front and a back foot; to hobble in such a fashion. **1954** *True* June 65 **TX,** The wild-cattle catcher has a standing offer in print in the cattlemen's magazines to pay $100 for any wild steer, bull, or cow that he can't find and pen or sideline.

side line v phr

1 See quot; hence n *side-liner.* [By metath from **linesides**]

1953 Randolph–Wilson *Down in Holler* 284 **Ozarks,** *Side-line.* . . To catch bass, usually bigmouth bass which are called linesides, by forcing them to leap into a boat. Same as *jumping, bumping,* and *goosing.* A man who makes a business of this kind of fishing is called a *side-liner.*

2 See **side line** n.

sideliner n¹ See **sidewinder** 1

side-liner n² See **side line** v phr **1**

sideling adj Also sp *sidling* [*OED2 sideling* v. 3 1611 →]

1 also rarely *sidely;* Of a topographical feature: sloping, esp to one side; steep.

1789 in 1940 *AmSp* 15.391 **VA,** To a white oak, pine and reed oak Saplin on sidling ground. **1805** (1905) Lewis *Orig. Jrls. Lewis & Clark*

Exped. 158 **KY,** We Suped on a little portable Soup and lay down on this Sideling mountn. **1834** (1925) Evans *Jrl.* 3.187 **IN,** Encamped on a sidling eminence. **1841** *S. Lit. Messenger* 7.525 **VA,** I mounted my horse, and cantered up the sidling road which led over the mountain of stone-coal, immediately back of the fort. **1851** *De Bow's Rev.* 11.64, It is not the weight usually put on them [=wagon wheels] that racks them to pieces, but the strain to which they are subjected from running on steep sideling declivities. **1859** (1864) Browning *Hunter* 15 **wMD,** By and by we arrived at a very sideling place, with a considerable precipice on our left. **1874** Chappell *Misc. GA* 2.29, This new road struck the mountain some few miles north-west from Hamilton, and by a gentle sidling ascent, rose gradually above the continually expanding campaign below. **1887** *Overland Mth.* (2d ser) 10.398 **CA,** Down this declivity by a sidling pathway I went in safety till I reached the bed of the cañon. **1935** Sandoz *Jules* 385 **NE,** On a sidling place the long tugs let the tongue fall from the neck yoke. It plunged into the ground, broke, pitching her forward, across the doubletrees. **1940–41** Cassidy *WI Atlas* 1 inf, **swWI,** The land was a little [sɑɪdlɪŋ]. **1968** *DARE* Tape **NH**14, In the winter, when they hauled the wood out, they used to put brush in, in what we always called a sidelin place. . . It would be where it was downhill—build that side in with brush and put snow on top. Level the road up. **1981** Pederson *LAGS Basic Materials,* 1 inf, **neTN,** Hillside plow used where the land was hilly or sidely ['saɛdlɪ̣]. **1982** Slone *How We Talked* 30 **eKY** (as of c1950), *Sidelin'*—slanting; "Sidelin' ground"—steep; at an angle.

2 Of a structure: leaning, lopsided.

1874 *Appletons' Jrl.* 11.489 **Gt Lakes,** Beyond, the long log dock, sidling and dilapidated, stretched out into the bay. **1953** Randolph–Wilson *Down in Holler* 284 **Ozarks,** Sidelin'. . . Leaning, inclined, not horizontal. A woman complained that her house, built on a steep hillside, was not level. "That shanty is so sidelin'," she said, "I cain't git a toehold nowheres." **1954** *Harder Coll.* **cwTN,** Sideling. . . Leaning, inclined, not horizontal. **1995** Brophy *Coll.* 67 **swMO** (as of c1960), *Sideling, sidlin.* [L]eaning to one side, tilted, aside.

side loader n Also *side delivery bunk* Cf **muzzle loader, shotgun bunk**

Among loggers: see quot 1969.

1969 Sorden *Lumberjack Lingo* 109 **NEng, Gt Lakes,** *Side delivery bunk*—Bunks, built parallel to the deacon seat, into which the lumberjack crawled from the side, in contrast to muzzle-loaders which he entered from the end. **1972** *Yesterday* 1.2.22 **WI** (as of c1890), Bunks which were built parallel to the center aisle of the building were called "side loaders."

sidely See **sideling** 1

side meat n Also *side* widespread, but more freq Midl, Sth See Map on p. 954 Cf **middling** n, **meat** n 2, **plate meat, side pork**

Meat from the side of a hog, usu salted or smoked.

1868 *Overland Mth.* 1.468, But they do not thrive after transplanting any better than do the corn pone of Virginia . . and the "side-meat" of Missouri. **1903** *DN* 2.329 **seMO,** *Side-meat.* . . Bacon. **1905** *DN* 3.93 **nwAR,** *Salt side-meat.* . . Salt pork. **1907** *DN* 3.237 **nwAR,** *Side-meat.* . . Bacon. **1909** *DN* 3.369 **eAL, wGA,** *Side-meat.* . . Bacon. Universal. **1938** Rawlings *Yearling* 274 **nFL,** The meat itself was dressed out into hams and shoulders, side-meat and belly-bacon. **1942** Faulkner *Go Down* 139 **MS,** They would eat once without haste or hurry after five days—the sidemeat, the greens, the cornbread, the buttermilk from the well-house. **1945** FWP *Lay My Burden Down* 71 **GA** (as of c1865) [Black], The biggest what they would give the field hands to eat would be the truck what us had on the place, like greens, turnips, peas, side meat, and they sure would cut the side meat awful thin too, boss. **1949** Kurath *Word Geog.* 39, *Middlin(s)* and *middlin meat* . . are the regular designations for salt pork throughout the South and South Midland . . but in western Maryland, the Valley of Virginia, and northern West Virginia the Midland term *side meat* is also still used. **1958** Humphrey *Home from the Hill* 193 **neTX,** Grabbing a bite to eat on the run—collard greens and poke salad and underdone salty sidemeat. **1965–70** *DARE* (Qu. H38, . . Words for bacon [including joking ones]) 176 Infs, **widespread, but more freq Midl, Sth,** Side meat; **CA**32, Side meat—not cured; **CA**54, Side meat—more the salt pork idea than bacon; **CA**202, Side meat—before it's smoked; **TN**24, Side meat—it can be smoked for bacon; **WA**31, Side meat—from the side that isn't cured; **MD**39, **OH**80, Smoked side meat; **MO**20, Salt side meat; **IN**60, **MD**50, **OH**44, Side. **1966** Dakin *Dial. Vocab. Ohio R. Valley* 2.333, It is . . evident that *side meat . . middlin meat,* and *middlin(s)* are more truly names for the piece of meat than for the type (fresh, salted, smoked) and as such are quite commonly used to refer to the pork side in any condition. . . It is clear that many speakers who say *middlin meat* or *middlins* also use *side* . . and that *side* is in fact the usual name for the piece of meat . . throughout the Valley. **c1970** Pederson *Dial. Surv. Rural GA* **seGA** *(Meat from the side of a hog, salted but not smoked)* 2 [of 64] infs, Side. [Both infs Black] **1978** Massey *Bittersweet Country* 20 **Ozarks,** Bacon was called side meat and it was quite fat. **1988** Lincoln *Avenue* 96 **wNC** (as of c1940) [Black], But on Saturdays the store stayed open late to fill the orders of the country croppers who came to buy cornmeal, . . side meat, lard, and suchlike necessities. **1989** Pederson *LAGS Tech. Index* 158 **Gulf Region,** *Salt pork* . . side meat (85 [infs]). *Ibid* 159, *Side (of bacon)* . . side meat (104 [infs]); *Smoked meat* . . side meat (17 [infs]). *Ibid* 160, *Bacon* . . side meat (8 [infs]). *Ibid* 392, *Cuts of pork* . . side meat (1 [inf]).

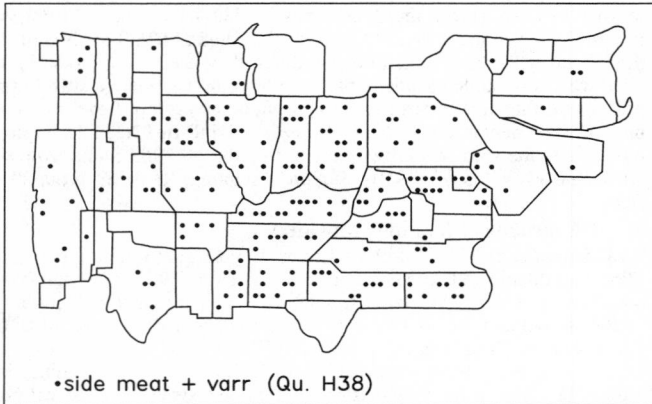

•side meat + varr (Qu. H38)

siden v [*EDD* siden "To put in order; to clear away"] Cf **side** v **4**

1936 *AmSp* 11.191 **seWY,** To *siden*. To straighten up or tidy a table or room, not a thorough cleaning. 'You need only to siden the house a bit.'

side'n prep Also sp *siding* Cf **-en** suff[3], **of** prep **Bh, outsiden** Alongside; besides.

1899 Chesnutt *Conjure Woman* 13 **csNC** [Black], Dey [=there] ain' nuffin dat kin stan' up side'n de scuppernon' fer sweetness. **1946** *McDavid Coll.* **ceGA,** Siding = 'besides'.

side-oats grama n Also *side-oat grama, side-oats* A **grama grass 1** (here: *Bouteloua curtipendula*).

1911 *Century Dict. Suppl.,* *Side-oats.* . . A grama-grass, *Atheropogon curtipendulus,* ranging from New Jersey to the Rocky Mountains and southward into Mexico. **1912** Wooton–Standley *Grasses NM* 106, Tall Grama. Side-oats Grama. *(Atheropogon curtipendulus).* **1923** in 1925 Jepson *Manual Plants CA* 133, Side-oat Grama. Tall Grama. . Plains and rocky hills . . Mont. to Mex. **1945** Wodehouse *Hayfever Plants* 53, Side-oats grama *(B[outeloua] curtipendula)* . . the tallest species sometimes reaching 3 ft. **1967** *DARE* FW Addit **CO,** Side oat grama—Native Colorado grass. Common. Found in museum in Sterling.

side of See **side** prep

side of a barn n
In phr *not to know one from the side of a barn* and varr: Not to know one at all.

1965–70 *DARE* (Qu. II26, *Joking ways of saying that you would not know who somebody is: "I wouldn't know him from _____."*) Infs **KY**85, **OK**48, **PA**185, [The] side of a (*or* the) barn; **VA**38, [The] side of a house; [**NC**35, [A] side of bacon].

side of sole leather n Also *sole leather*
In phr *not to know one from a side of sole leather:* Not to know one at all.

1855 *Harper's New Mth. Mag.* 11.779, She doesn't know me from a side of sole-leather, probably never heard of me. **1893** *Scribner's Mag.* 14.253, If you mean Commodore Ketcham . . I don't know him from a side of sole leather. **1941** *AmSp* 16.23 **sIN,** I don't know him from a side of sole leather. **1965–70** *DARE* (Qu. II26, *Joking ways of saying that you would not know who somebody is: "I wouldn't know him from _____."*) Infs **GA**9, **KY**30, **MA**71, **NC**52, **SC**39, **VA**11, 74, A side of sole-leather; **VA**38, Sole leather.

side-plate meat See **plate meat**

side pleurisy n **Sth, S Midl** Cf Intro "Language Changes" I.4 Pleurisy; also used vaguely for other sharp internal pains.

1939 in Lib. of Congress *Amer. Memory: WPA Life Hist.* (Internet), Mother got T.B. from having the flu and side pleurisy and only lived three months. **1940** Jesse Stuart in *Esquire* Sept 132 **KY,** Then the side-pleurisy got im . . He had to sit up straight in a chear. He couldn't bend over to unlace his shoes. **1966–70** *DARE* (Qu. BB3c, *A sudden pain that comes in the side*) Inf **VA**1, Side pleurisy; **SC**27, The side pleurisy—Negro; (Qu. BB8, *When a person's joints and muscles ache and sometimes swell up, especially in damp weather, he may have _____*) Inf **NC**50, Side pleurisy [sɑɪd plʊɹɪs]—that's what the doctor calls it; (Qu. BB49, . . *Other kinds of diseases*) Infs **GA**82, **VA**52, Side pleurisy. **1973** Van Noppen–Van Noppen *Western NC* 105 (as of 1880s), Other well-known diseases of the area, in the vernacular, were "pneumony fever," "side pleurisy," [etc]. **1986** Pederson *LAGS Concordance* 1 inf, **cnGA,** Appendicitis—formerly called side pleurisy; 1 inf, **neGA,** Butterfly root is good for side pleurisy; [1 inf, **seGA,** Pneumonia from your side, pleurisy of the side]. **1990** Cavender *Folk Med. Lexicon* 31 **sAppalachians,** *Side pleurisy*—a. inflammation of the pleura accompanied by pain when breathing. *b.* appendicitis.

side pork n **chiefly Inland Nth, IA** See Map Cf **side meat** Meat from the side of a hog, whether salted, smoked, or fresh; see quots.

1949 Kurath *Word Geog.* 14, *Salt pork* . . is a Northern expression which we find in New England and the greater part of New York State. In northern Pennsylvania and seemingly in the Buffalo sector *side pork,* a blend of Northern *salt pork* and the Pennsylvania term *side meat,* has become established, and this expression is not unknown in the Hudson Valley and in parts of New Jersey. **c1955** Reed–Person *Ling. Atlas Pacific NW,* 3 infs, Side pork [= salt pork]. **1956** Ker *Vocab. W. TX* 268, *Salt pork; home cured bacon* . . side pork [1 of 67 infs]. **1964** O'Hare *Ling. Geog. E. MT* 121, *Salted side of pork.* . . side pork [4 of 10 infs; according to 1 inf, "'side pork' = fresh"]. **1965–70** *DARE* (Qu. H38, . . *Words for bacon*) Infs **IA**22, **MO**10, **NE**8, **NJ**21, **OH**70, **PA**165, **WA**7, **WI**24, 66, Side pork; **IA**2, 12, **MI**100, Side pork—not smoked; **IA**13, Side pork—unsmoked; **MI**119, Side pork—uncured bacon; **NY**9, 12, Side pork—not (actually) bacon; **NY**75, Side pork—just salted down, not smoked; **NY**92, Side pork is fresh—not smoked or salted; **NY**94, Side pork—before it's cured; **NY**230, Side pork—thick bacon, no lean; **OH**15, Side pork is fresh; **PA**234, Side pork—before it's smoked; **WA**31, Fresh side pork; **WI**20, Side pork—may not be smoked; **WI**29, Side pork—not salted. **1966** Dakin *Dial. Vocab. Ohio R. Valley* 2.333, *Salt pork; bacon.* . . The majority of the terms . . recorded all seem to be used in some instances for salted, smoked, and fresh side meat. At times this multiple meaning is the usage of the same individual. . . the following are all used . . for side meat in all three conditions . . bacon . . side meat . . side pork . . boiling meat. **1967** Faries *Word Geog. MO* 240, *Side pork* (salt pork) . . 41 [of 700 infs]. **1971** *PADS* 56.16 **AL,** Terms of the North and Midland in Alabama . . side pork . . rare. **1971** Bright *Word Geog. CA & NV* 178, *Salt pork.* . . *side pork,* 10 [of 300 infs]. **1973** Gawthrop *Dial. Calumet* 72 **nwIN,** *Meat from sides of hog, salted but not smoked:* . . side pork 11 [of 125 checklist infs]. **1986** Pederson *LAGS Concordance (Salt pork)* 3 infs, **AL, GA,** Side pork; *(A side)* 3 infs, **AL, GA, TN,** Side pork.

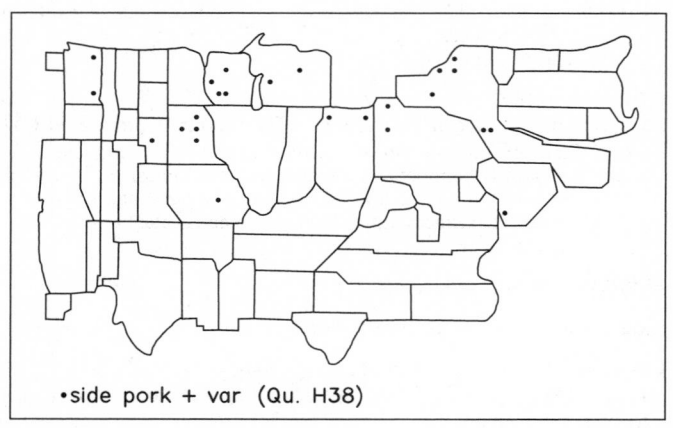

•side pork + var (Qu. H38)

side push (or rod) See **side** n[2] **1**

side room n **Sth, S Midl** See Map
A secondary room in a house or other structure, often one that has been added on and is used as a kitchen, storeroom, or bedroom.

1923 *DN* 5.221 **swMO,** *Side room.* . . An additional room built against a cabin. **1956** Ker *Vocab. W. TX* 107, *Room for storing disused articles* . . side room [3 of 67 infs]. **1961** Folk *Word Atlas N. LA* map 404, Small room off the kitchen to store food, pans, etc. . . Pantry . . kitchen closet . . side room [lowest frequency]. **1965–70** DARE (Qu. D16, . . *Parts added on to the main part of a house*) 10 Infs, **scattered Sth, S Midl,** Side room; (Qu. D7, *A small space anywhere in a house where you can hide things or get them out of the way*) Inf **MS1,** Side room; (Qu. D8, *The small room next to the kitchen [in older houses] where dishes and sometimes foods are kept*) Inf **GA8,** Side room; (Qu. D15a, *Other rooms; total Infs questioned, 75*) Inf **MS3,** Side room. **1967** Faries *Word Geog. MO* 73, *Store room.* . . Write-in terms are: *plunder hole* . . *side room* . . *storage room.* . . other responses . . side room. **1970** Tarpley *Blinky* 82 **neTX,** *Room for storing unused articles* . . other responses . . side room. **1983** *MJLF* 9.1.56 **ceKY** (as of 1956), *Side room* . . an ell. **1986** Pederson *LAGS Concordance* **Gulf Region,** 85 infs, Side room(s) *or* a side room [*DARE* Ed: These resps represent the name given to a room in a floor plan of their house which they were asked to draw and in most cases no further information is given; where there are descriptions, the *side room* is said to be a kitchen, dining room, pantry, storeroom, or bedroom; only a small number of infs describe the *side room* specifically as an extension to an existing structure.]; *(Junk room)* 11 infs, Side room; *(Bedroom)* 4 infs, Side room; *(Pantry)* 2 infs, Side room; 1 inf, **nwAR,** Side room—lean-to off house; *(Clothes closet)* 1 inf, **nwTN,** Side room—built to the side of the house; *(Corn crib)* 1 inf, **nwFL,** Side room—on side of crib for storing seed.

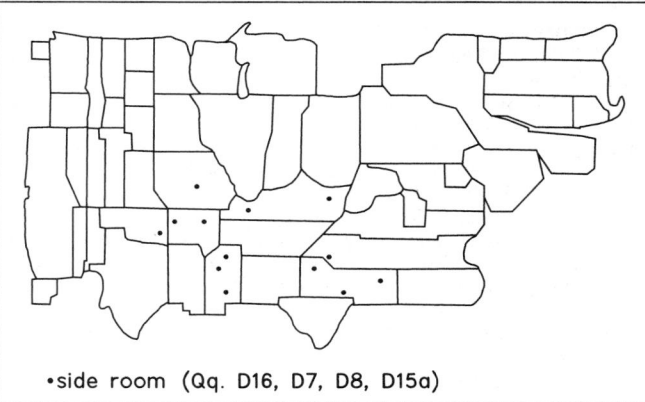

•side room (Qq. D16, D7, D8, D15a)

sides adv, prep [Aphet form of *besides; OED2* "Now *dial.* and *colloq.*"] **chiefly Sth; formerly also NEast** *esp freq among Black speakers*

1860 *Harper's New Mth. Mag.* 20.244 **NEng** [Black], I allers knowed yer was one; and 'sides dat, I heered yer Onkle John tell Sar yer was. **1887** Jackson *Between Whiles* 290 **neNY,** If thar war n't jest a hull lifetime o' misery in 't, 'sides the joy o' findin' him, I ain't no jedge. **1892** *Century Illustr. Mag.* 43.458 **GA,** Ma don't know how, an' 'sides she's dead. **1899** Chesnutt *Conjure Woman* 15 **csNC** [Black], She wuz a witch 'sides bein' a conjuh 'oman. **1931** (1991) Hughes–Hurston *Mule Bone* 92 **cFL** [Black], Oh, nigger, I'm tired of seein' you cut the fool. 'Sides that, I been playin' all afternoon for the white folks. **1945** FWP *Lay My Burden Down* 84 **AL** [Black], 'Sides the crops of cotton and corn and rice and ribbon cane we raised . . , we had vegetables and sheep and beef. **1947** Ballowe *The Lawd* 6 **LA** [Black], "You saw the Duppy?" "Nossuh, A warn't bawn with no double caul, an' 'sides, when you looks at a Duppy, hit fades." **1968** in 1972 King *Black Anthol.* 37, No, he didn't bother me, sides looking mean.

sidesaddle flower n Also *saddle flower, ~ plant, sidesaddle (plant)*
=pitcher plant 1. Cf **California sidesaddle flower**

1738 Royal Soc. London *Philos. Trans.* 40.347 **VA,** From the Shape of the Flower, they are in *Virginia* called the Side-saddle-flower. **1822** Eaton *Botany* 447, *Sarracenia* . . *purpurea* (side-saddle). **1840** MA Zool. & Bot. Surv. *Herb. Plants & Quadrupeds* 82, Side-saddle Flower. . . has its name from the resemblance in shape and position of its curved and hollow leaf, to the horn of a *side-saddle*. **1863** Porcher *Re-*

sources 53 **SC,** *Sarracenia flava* . . and *variolaris* . . Fly-catchers; side-saddle flowers. Diffused; grow in bogs; Charleston; Newbern. **1876** Hobbs *Bot. Hdbk.* 39, Forefathers' cup, Side saddle plant. **Ibid** 100, Saddle flower, Saddle plant, Side saddle plant. **1938** FWP *Guide MN* 438, In the tamarack swamps near Detroit Lakes grows the pitcher plant or side-saddle flower whose leaves hold a gill of water. **1941** Writers' Program *Guide SC* 326, Masses of golden growth catch the attention; but on closer inspection the gold turns to a sickly green as the apparent lily is found to be a flycatcher, pitcher plant, side-saddle flower, or jack-in-the-pulpit—all local names for the *Sarracenia flava*. **1966** *DARE* Wildfl. QR. Pl.83 Inf **NC28,** Sidesaddles.

side up See **side** v 4

sidewalk plot n **esp Sth, S Midl**
The strip of grass between the sidewalk and the curb.

1966–70 DARE (Qu. N44, *In a town, the strip of grass and trees between the sidewalk and the curb*) Infs **IN19, MD34, NC40, SC11, TN37, VA70, 73,** Sidewalk plot [8 of 25 total infs]. **1971** Wood *Vocab. Change* 53, A grass strip . . between the sidewalk and street. It is regularly called a *sidewalk plot* in Tennessee, Georgia, and Mississippi. **2000** Launspach *ID Dial. Project* 3 **seID,** *(Grassy strip between a sidewalk and the street)* 3 infs, Sidewalk plot. **2001** DARE File—Internet **NJ,** Of the sidewalk plot, at least four (4) feet . . shall be reserved for the ornamental planting of trees, grass and the like.

sidewalk weed n
A **knotgrass 1** (here: *Polygonum aviculare*).

1953 Nelson *Plants Rocky Mt. Park* 60, Sidewalk weed or dooryard knotweed, *Polygonum aviculare.* . . A common weed introduced from Europe; found around dwellings.

sideways adv
To an extreme degree.

1988 Kingsolver *Bean Trees* 111 **KY,** If Mama ever got married again I'd dance a jig at her wedding. I'd be thrilled sideways.

sideways n **chiefly Sth, S Midl, West** See Map
Suicide.

1942 Berrey–Van den Bark *Amer. Slang* 117.14, *Commit suicide.* . . commit sideways. **1960** Bailey *Resp. to PADS 20* **KS** (as of c1918), *Commit sideways* was heard often, usually, I think by young people and used facetiously. **1965–70** DARE (Qu. BB57, *If someone committed suicide . . he _____*) 31 Infs, **chiefly Sth, S Midl, West,** Committed sideways; [**TX12,** Went sideways; (Qu. OO8b, *If a man committed suicide by hanging, you'd say he _____ [himself]*; not asked in early QRs) Inf **IL81,** Went sideways].

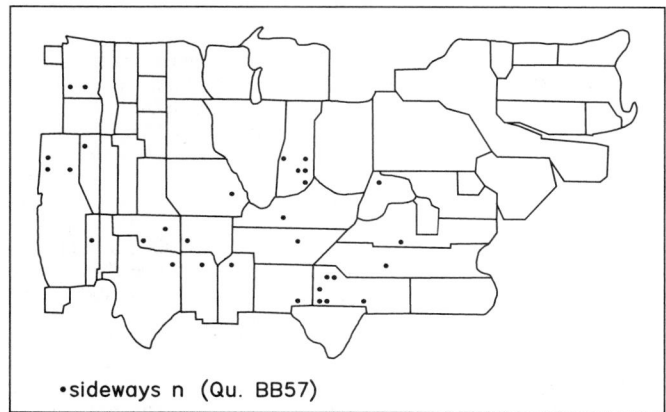

•sideways n (Qu. BB57)

sidewinder n

1 also *sideliner, sidewiper:* A **rattlesnake 1** of the Desert Southwest (here: *Crotalus cerastes*). [See quot 1947] Also called **horned rattlesnake** Cf **mountain sidewinder**

1875 Yarrow in *100th Meridian Rep.* V.535 (DA), They were also seen in Arizona, and are called 'side-winders' by the settlers, owing to their peculiar lateral progressive motion. **1877** Hodge *Arizona* 226, Another kind [of rattlesnake], called the side wiper, from its peculiar habit of locomotion sideways, instead of ahead, is found through most of the valleys and plains. **1885** Kingsley *Std. Nat. Hist.* 3.402 **NM** The New Mexicans have named this animal the 'side-winder,' because of the slightly lateral motion which they have in passing forwards. **1890** *Century Dict.* 5615, *Sideliner.* . . A sidewinder, sidewiper, or massasauga. **1918** *Copeia* 54.35 **CA,** Sidewinder—I have taken three individuals in La Puerta Valley. . . in San Diego County. **1947** Pickwell *Amphibians* 58, The name "Sidewinder" refers to the peculiar method of locomotion—a sidewise looping movement quite unlike the locomotion of other North American Snakes—which enables this species to move rapidly over loose sand. **c1955** Reed–Person *Ling. Atlas Pacific NW,* 3 infs, Sidewinder. **1965–70** *DARE* (Qu. P25, . . *Kinds of snakes*) 14 Infs, **sCA, AZ, NM,** Sidewinder. **2000** *DARE* File—Internet, Care of the Sidewinder—*Enclosure:* First and most important the cage should be secure and escape proof.

2 In logging: a tree that does not fall in the direction anticipated; a tree or limb unexpectedly knocked down by a falling tree.

1905 U.S. Forest Serv. *Bulletin* 61.46 [Logging terms], *Side winder.* A tree knocked down unexpectedly by the falling of another. (Gen[eral]). **1942** *AmSp* 17.224 [Loggers' talk], *Side-winder.* A falling tree which strikes another tree and is deflected from the line of fall selected by the fallers. Such a tree is extremely dangerous to men near by. It may even bounce back and kill the fallers. **1950** *Western Folkl.* 9.119 **nwOR** [Logger speech], *Side winder.* A falling tree that twists and slides backward off its stump. **1958** McCulloch *Woods Words* 165 **Pacific NW,** *Sidewinder.* . . A tree unexpectedly knocking down another in falling or in yarding. **1959** *AmSp* 34.79 **nwCA** [Logger lingo], *Sidewinder.* . . A falling limb or snag that may fall from above. **1963** *Western Folkl.* 22.265 **CA,** *Sidewinder* and *widow maker* are widely used expressions for anything that may fall from above, causing injury to a person. . . In the Redwood Country the term refers to a falling limb or snag that may fall from above in falling trees or in yarding. . . *Sidewinders* and *widow makers* have been the cause of many deaths and injuries in logging. **1969** Sorden *Lumberjack Lingo* 110 **NEng, Gt Lakes,** *Sidewinder.* . . A falling tree, which, hitting another, rolls on its axis. . . A tree knocked down by the fall of another tree. **1982** *Smithsonian Letters* **Pacific NW,** I was raised in the lower Columbia River logging country . . (Early 1900). . . When a tree was about to fall the faller yelled "timber" and probably "look out for widow makers" or "Sidewinders." If the falling tree fell close to another tree the other tree would bend over and then snap back and if there was any loose limbs on it they were thrown back. My uncle was killed this way.

sidewiper See **sidewinder 1**

siding v See **side** v **3**

siding prep See **side'n**

siditty adj, also used absol Also *saddity, sadiddy, saditty, seditty, siddity* [Etym unknown] *among Black speakers; derog*
Exhibiting an unwarranted air of superiority; conceited, pretentious.

1967 *Jet* 20 July 43 (OED2), Eartha . . is considered 'seditty' by many Negroes. **1968–70** *DARE* (Qu. GG19a, *When you can see from the way a person acts that he's feeling important or independent: "He surely is _____ these days."*) Inf **OH**103, ['sɪdɪti]; (Qu. GG19b, *When you can see from the way a person acts that he's feeling important or independent: "He seems to think he's _____."*) Inf **FL**52, [sə'dɪdi]—old word; (Qu. HH35, *A woman who puts on a lot of airs: "She's too _____ for me."*) Inf **CA**81, ['sʌdɪti]; Inf **OH**103, ['sɪdɪti]; **TX**86, [sə'dɪdi] [FW: Inf doesn't know derivation; she says she's heard it all her life]; (Qu. II23, *Joking names for the people who are, or think they are, the best society of a community: The _____*) Inf **GA**90, ['sɪdɪti]; **MO**23, ['sʌdɪdi]; **OH**103, ['haɪ 'sɪdɪti]; **PA**239, ['sɪd,ɪdɪs]. [All Infs Black] **1969** (1970) Angelou *Caged Bird* 62 **AR** (as of 1935) [Black], St. Louis teachers, on the other hand, tended to act very siditty, and talked down to their students from the lofty heights of education and whitefolks' enunciation. *Ibid* 232, I would stop the car when we reached the kiosk and put on my siddity [sic] air. I would speak to him like the peasant he was. I would order him to start the car and then tip him a quarter or even a dollar from Dad's pocket before driving on. **1972** Kochman *Rappin'* 318, That's all I hear lately—soul food, soul food. If you say you don't eat it you get accused of being saditty [affected, considering oneself superior]. **1973** *Black World* Aug 61, Them big man-eatin' dogs them saddity niggers had roun' the house. **1980** Folb *Runnin' Down* 33 **Los Angeles CA** [Black], Get some yella brother think he so bad, real siditty, . . [and] rank d' dude in front a young lady. **1992** *DARE* File **ceAL** [Black], Sadiddy—stuck up, conceited. **1992** in 1993 Adero *Up South* 178 **GA** [Black], Richardson

siddity, just like Susie'd said, kept her nose in the air like she was always smelling something. **1992** Morrison *Jazz* 40 **E. St. Louis IL** (as of c1926) [Black], If you don't want to dance, we can just sit there at the table, looking siditty by the lamplight and listen to the music. **1996** McDowell *Leaving Pipe Shop* 183 **AL** (as of 1960s) [Black], Mama thought the ball was just a bunch of saddity folks putting on airs, not to mention a waste of money.

sidling See **sideling**

-sie suff Also sp -*s(e)y*, -*zee*, -*zey* [*SND* -*sie* suff. 2] **chiefly Nth, N Midl** Cf **-ie** suff[3]
Used to form diminutives or hypocoristic nouns.

1894 *DN* 1.328 **NJ,** Boyzee: boy; as, "when I was a boyzee." **1906** *DN* 3.128 **neAR,** Boysie. . . Dear boy. *Ibid* 147, Momsey, momzey. **1917** *Los Angeles Examiner* (CA) 16 Mar sec 2 6 (Zwilling Coll.), [Cartoon caption:] Bulling a skating instructor out of lessons by telling him a bunch of guff about your rich "popsie." **1941** *LANE* Map 372 (*Mother, ma*) 4 infs, **NEng,** Mumsy. **1950** *WELS* (*Affectionate words meaning brother*) 1 Inf, **WI,** Boysie. **1968–70** *DARE* (Qu. W21, *Soft shoes that people wear only inside the house*) Inf **PA**167, Footsies; (Qu. Z1, . . '*Father*') Inf **KY**60, Popsy; (Qu. Z2, . . '*Mother*') Infs **CA**80, 107, **CT**16, **NY**167, **OH**72, Mumsy; **MN**33, Momsy; (Qu. AA3, *Nicknames or affectionate names for a sweetheart*) Inf **OH**23, Boopsie; (Qu. AA23, *Joking names that a woman may use to refer to her husband*) Inf **PA**234, Boopsie. **1971** *Today Show Letters* **MA,** Hoodsie—a small paper cup of ice cream; it is the trade name of H.P. Hood and Sons, Boston.

siebegodlin See **si-godlin**

siehst du interrog exclam Also *siehst;* pronc-sp *seesta* [Ger *siehst du* Do you see?] **chiefly N Cent, Upper MW** See Map Cf **capish, compree, fersteh**
1950 *WELS* (*Other ways of saying "Do you understand?": "You take hold of it this way, _____?"*) 1 Inf, **ceWI,** Seest [sic] du? (German); 1 Inf, **cwWI,** Siehes [sic] du? **1965–70** *DARE* (Qu. NN5) 12 Infs, **N Cent, Upper MW,** Siehst du; **WI**12, Siehst du—by more German types; **WI**13, Siehst du—German, still used some; **MI**18, Siehst—used to say that a lot when we were in high school, but I haven't heard that for years; **IN**5, **KS**8, **PA**148, 163, Seesta. [14 of 20 Infs female] **1985** *Lutz Coll.* "Seesta?"—When my mother was explaining something or showing how to do somthing, when we were children, she would pause to ask, "Seesta?" When I began to study German in college, I realized that she might have been using a variant of "Siest [sic] du?" Her parents were both from England, but they lived in the Germantown section of Philadelphia, Pa. We guess that "Seesta?" may have been picked up from neighbors and children with whom she played. To us, when we were youngsters, it was just Mother's word that meant, "Do you understand?"

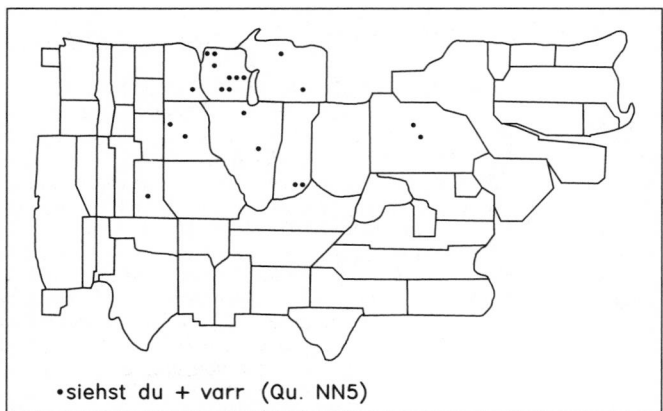

•siehst du + varr (Qu. NN5)

siene bean n Also *seenie bean, senna, siene (weed)* **esp SW**
A **rattlebox 1h:** usu *Sesbania drummondii,* but also **Colorado River hemp.**
1920 *Torreya* 20.22 **LA,** *Daubentonia longifolia* . . Seenie bean, Indigo, Cameron Parish, La. **1929** Dobie *Vaquero* 9 **swTX,** We cut siene (rattle pod) switches. **1960** Vines *Trees SW* 545, Other common names for the Drummond Rattlebox are Siene Bean, Rattle-bush, Rattle Bean, Coffee Bean, and Senna. *Ibid* 546, *Sesbania punicea.* . . Other names

are Sesban, Locust, and Red Siene Bean. *Ibid* 547, Hemp Sesbania. . . Other vernacular names are . . Siene Weed [etc]. **2000** *DARE* File—Internet **TX**, Question: . . My father . . is including in his writings a certain plant found around lakes and ponds (in Texas . .) which have bean-like pods hanging on them. He knows these plants by the name seen-a-bean. That's how it's pronounced—now how is it really spelled and what plant is it? [Answer:] One of the common names for Rattlebox is Siene Bean.

sierra n Also *searer, serin, sier, siering, sierra mackerel* [Span *sierra*, literally "saw"]
=**Spanish mackerel.**

1882 U.S. Natl. Museum *Bulletin* 16.427, [Scomberomorus] caballa. . . Sierra. . . Warm parts of the Atlantic; occasional on our coast. **1906** NJ State Museum *Annual Rept. for 1905* 246, *Scomberomorus regalis*. . . Cero. Sier. Siering. Searer. . . It is an excellent food-fish, more abundant in tropical waters, and to be considered rather scarce on our coast. **1919** *Copeia* 71.59, *Scomberomorus cavalla*. Sierra; (Serin). . . two fine specimens. **1946** LaMonte *N. Amer. Game Fishes* 28, Sierra Mackerel—*Scomberomorus sierra*. . . Names . . Cero, Sierra [etc].

Sierra laurel n
A **fetterbush 3** (here: *Leucothoe davisiae*).

1959 Munz–Keck *CA Flora* 414, *L[eucothoe] Davisiae*. . . Sierra-Laurel. . . Sierra Nevada from Fresno Co. to Lassen Peak. **2000** *DARE* File—Internet, *Leucothoe davisiae*—Vernacular Name: *Sierra Laurel*.

sierra mackerel See **sierra**

Sierra maple n
=**dwarf maple.**

1910 Jepson *Silva CA* 268, The Sierra Maple, also called Dwarf Maple, grows on the rocky sides of cañons at 6000 to 8000 feet in the Sierra Nevada Mountains. **1979** Little *Checklist U.S. Trees* 40, Rocky Mountain maple. . . Other common names—dwarf maple, mountain maple, Sierra maple [etc].

sieva bean n Also *seewee bean, seve ~, sewee ~, sibby ~, sieva lima, sivvy bean* [Sewee an Amer Ind tribe that formerly lived along the Santee River in South Carolina] **esp SC**
A **lima bean** (here: *Phaseolus lunatus*).

1737 in 1909 Wesley *Jrl.* 1.402 **eGA**, Sewee-beans, about the size of our scarlet, but to be shelled and eaten like Windsor beans. **1841** MA Ag. Surv. *Rept. for 1840* 405, Another profitable crop was saba, or as they are sometimes called seve beans. There were 1248 hills, which, on the first picking yielded 38 dollars. **1866** Copeland *Country Life* (5th ed) 554, By the third week in May it is safe to plant Lima and Sieva Beans. The seed of the former is sometimes out of the market. . . The Sieva is next to it in quality. **1930** *DN* 6.83 **cSC**, Sivvy beans. . . Butter beans, or Lima beans. Used interchangeably with *butter beans*. *Lima beans* is never heard. **1931–33** *LANE Worksheets*, 1 inf, **CT**, Sieva lima—a variety of bean. **c1940** *LAMSAS Materials* (Lima bean) 30 infs, 19 **SC**, 8 **GA**, 3 **NC**, Sivvy (beans). **1950** *PADS* 14.61 **SC**, *Sivvy bean*. . . Sieva bean. Originating in Charleston, this form has come into use in other parts of the state. "From the *Seewee* Indians. Many Charlestonians pronounce it *seewee* bean". . . *Sewee* bay, whence the seed came is also suggested as the origin. **1950** Jr. League Charleston *Receipts* 148 **seSC**, Boil sieva beans in salted water until almost done, add tender raw corn, cut from cob, and cook until both are tender. Drain, add butter, seasoning and serve. **1955** *PADS* 23.45 **e,cSC**, **eNC**, **seGA**, *Sivvy-beans, sewee beans* 'lima beans'. **1966** *DARE* (Qu. I16, *The large flat beans that are not eaten in the pod*) Inf **SC4**, Sivvy beans—more common in an earlier day [FW: He spells it "siva"—reports Negroes as using [sɪvɨ]]; **SC9**, [sɪbɨ] beans; **SC19**, [sɪvɨ]; **SC21**, Sivvy beans—the colored bean; **SC22**, ['siwɪ]—always heard this—old name, not freq now; **SC26**, ['sɪbɨ]—all I ever know; **SC43**, Sewee beans [Inf's spelling]—[sɪbɨ, sɪvɪ]; **SC66**, Sivvy beans—a small butter bean. **1966** *DARE* Tape **SC14**, [Inf:] We call 'em sibby bean, them run on some high sticks. [FW:] Same thing most people call butter beans. [Inf:] Sure right; **SC15**, We plant beans, butter beans. . . [FW:] Them old people used to call butter beans "sibby beans." [Inf:] That's right, sibby bean. **1986** Pederson *LAGS Concordance*, 1 inf, **ceGA**, Sieva bean—like a velvet bean—large.

sieve n Usu |sɪv|; also |siv| Pronc-sp *seeve*
Std sense, var form.

1909 *DN* 3.369 **eAL**, **wGA**, *Sieve,n*. Pronounced [siv]. Not in com-

mon use, *sifter* being the usual word. **1972** *Atlanta Letters* **csGA**, I was born in & lived most of my life in Georgia & am now seventy one & I assure you I have heard & still do hear lots of [Georgia colloquialisms] . . yet! . . "Seeve" (sieve).

si-fodlin adv [Var of **si-godlin**]
1986 *DARE* File **swIN**, In 1980 my mother, then 80, living in my hometown of Sullivan, Indiana used a term I had never heard before to describe her cousin's new dentures. Mother said: "Edna's new teeth don't fit—they are si-fodlin." She said that meant they were out of line, from side to side. I am struck by your remark that you can't see any reason for the change of g to f (in *si-fodlin*). My instinctive (amateur) theory is that some of those devout farm families of the Midwest and South were loath to appear to be taking the Lord's name lightly.

si-fog v |'saɪˌfag, -ˌfɔg| **esp AR** Cf **fag** v[2], **fog** v[2] 1, **si-fugle around**
Often with *around*: To roam or loaf about.

1968 *DARE* FW Addit **cAR**, *Si-fogging* ['saɪˌfagɪn]—rambling about aimlessly. . . "You boys don't need the car tonight. All you want to do is go si-fogging around anyway." **1970** *DARE* (Qu. Y27, *To go about aimlessly, with nothing to do:* "He's always _____ around the drugstore.") Inf **AR56**, Si-foggin [saɪfɔgɪn]. **1993** *DARE* File **cwAR**, He was just si-foggin' ['saɪˌfɔgɪn] around.

sift v
1 also with *around, in*: To walk casually; to drift. **West**

1904 White *Mountains* 237 **CA**, A cowboy once told me of the arrival of a tramp by saying, "He *sifted* into camp." Could any verb be more expressive? Does not it convey exactly the lazy, careless, out-at-heels shuffling gait of the hobo? **1921** Thorp *Songs Cowboys* 108 **West**, Oh, say, little dogies, when are you goin' to lay down / And quit this forever siftin' around? **1929** Ellis *Ordinary Woman* 210 **CO**, I manage to keep high and dry until one day John has a horse in the corner of the stable, and in a drunken rage is beating it dreadfully. I grit my teeth, trying to stand it, but it gets unbearable, and I sift in on him, when he lets up on the mare only to grab a hatchet and start for me.

2 also *sift dirt;* To go very fast.

1941 *Sat. Eve. Post* 11 Oct 50 **NC**, Mighty fine-lookin' car. . . Dog-gone it, I'll bet she can sift. **1984** Wilder *You All Spoken Here* 68 **Sth**, Sift dirt: Move into high gear; high-tail it.

sift around See **sift 1**

sift dirt See **sift 2**

sift in See **sift 1**

si-fugle around v phr Cf *DS* Y27
=**si-fog.**

1912 *DN* 3.589 **wIN**, *Sifugle*. . . To loaf about, possibly for the purpose of picking up desired information. "I've seen him sifuglin' around for a week or two."

sigging See **signify 1**

sigh See **scythe**

sight n

1 rarely pl: A multitude; a large amount or number; a lot. [*OED2* 1390 →; "Now *colloq.* or *slang*"] **chiefly Sth, S Midl, NEng**

1809 (1814) Weems *F. Marion* 126 **SC**, Besides them plaguy guns, they have got a *tarnal nation sight* of pistols. **1810** (1912) Bell *Journey to OH* 39 **MA**, I don't know exactly how many a heap is, or a *sight* either, which is another way of measuring people. **1862** in 1962 Truxall *Respects To All* 31 **PA**, It was a terrible battle and we lost an awful sight of men. **1876** in 1969 *PADS* 52.55 **seIL**, I learned a sight too. **1876** in 1983 *PADS* 70.51 **ce,sePA**, Wagons were overturned, fences Blown down and an immense sight of damage done to property of different kinds. **1887** (1967) Harris *Free Joe* 131 **GA**, Some un's a-losin' a mighty sight of fencin'; an' timber's timber these days, lemme tell you. **1894** *Century Illustr. Mag.* 48.872 **sIN**, "Sight" is also used for a great quantity, or a great number. . . Sight is intensified by becoming plural, as "There 's goin' to be sights and sights of people at the barbecue." **1902** (1904) Rowe *Maid of Bar Harbor* 249 **ME**, It makes a mighty sight o' difference where the land is. **1905** *DN* 3.19 **cCT**, Sight. . . A great many. 'A sight of people.' **1907** *DN* 3.217 **nwAR**, Sight. . . A great many. **1908** Fox *Lonesome Pine* 37 **KY**, It makes a mighty sight o' difference to some folks. **1909** *DN* 3.369 **eAL, wGA,** *Sight.* . . A crowd, a number. "There was a sight of folks at meetin' to-day." **1916** *DN* 4.341 **seOH,** *Sights.* . . Heaps. "We have great sights of corn." General. **1926** *AmSp* 1.416 **Okefenokee GA,** I seed a sight er them things one evenin', jest like a bunch er sheep. **1929** *AmSp* 5.127 **ME,** There might be a "sight of berries." **1941** Writers' Program *Guide WV* 416 **cwWV,** Young folks wander off in couples, for, as everybody knows and expects, 'they's a sight o' courtin' been did at 'lasses lickin's.' **1968** *DARE* (Qu. LL8b, . . *A large number* . . "She has a whole _____ of cousins.") Inf **VA24,** Sight. **1970** *DARE* FW Addit **KY75,** I don't do a big sight of business. **1986** Pederson *LAGS Concordance,* 1 inf, **neTN,** A sight of rails—a large number of rails; 1 inf, **seGA,** A sight of sweet potatoes; 1 inf, **ceTN,** Gatlinburg turned out a sight of teachers and preachers; 1 inf, **cTN,** There's a sight of them; 1 inf, **seGA,** Not a great sight—not a whole lot of material; 1 inf, **neGA,** A sight of niggers—a lot; 1 inf, **neGA,** There's a sight of seed comes out of them. **1998** *Atlanta Jrl.-Constitution* (GA) 4 Oct sec M 1/1 **Sth,** We think "sight" a good word for "much," as in, "We've had a sight of stormy weather."

2 in adv phr *a sight:* Much; a lot. **chiefly Sth, S Midl** See also *heap sight* (at **heap** n 3b)

1854 in 1893 Bridge *Personal Recoll. N. Hawthorne* 144, It is a devilish sight harder to write to the President . . than to a private man. **1876** in 1969 *PADS* 52.51 **seIL,** It rained a fearful sight last night. **1909** *DN* 3.369 **eAL, wGA,** *Sight.* . . A great deal. "I'd a sight rather not do it." *Ibid* 404 **nwAR,** *Sight.* . . Amount, great deal. "He thinks a sight of his new barn." **1911** Porter *Harvester* 515 **IN,** "Is your chest any better?" "A sight better." **1923** (1946) Greer-Petrie *Angeline Steppin'* 41 **csKY,** Maybe I oughten to criticise that thar Shakespeare feller who writ the play, but I could give him a few p'ints which would a-hope [=have helped] hit a sight. **1939** *Hall Coll.* **wNC, eTN,** *Sight.* . . We 'ud play marbles a sight. **1952** Brown *NC Folkl.* 1.590, *Sight, a.* . . "I've studied about it a sight." . . General. *Ibid* 591, I'd a sight rather see her dead than married to that skunk. **1953** Brewer *Word Brazos* 61 **eTX** [Black], De white folks in de Bottoms sho' a long sight better'n dey was reckly attuh 'mansuhpation. **1954** *Harder Coll.* **cwTN,** *A sight.* . . Aunt Marthy's shore fell off a sight. **1961** Hall *String Too Short* 76 **NH,** The old dog was gone, and Ben figured he'd gone off into the woods to die. A week or so later and Ben figured he'd died a sight closer, but he couldn't find him. **1968–69** *DARE* (Qu. BB18, *To vomit a great deal at once*) Inf **NC72,** Spewed up a sight; (Qu. JJ32, *If you have to make up your mind between two things—for example, a dog and a cat* . . "I'd _____ [have a dog].") Inf **PA138,** [A] darn sight sooner. **1986** Pederson *LAGS Concordance,* 1 inf, **nwMS,** [A] damn sight better; 1 inf, **seGA,** [A] darn sight better; 1 inf, **seMS,** A damn sight better than we get now; 1 inf, **seFL,** They get a hell of a sight bigger than that; 1 inf, **ceGA,** A darn sight more; 1 inf, **cnGA,** A darn sight tougher. **1988** Kingsolver *Bean Trees* 54 **KY,** "Oh, honey, we seen plenty from the bus," Ivy said. . . "I expect we'll see a good sight more on the way home."

3 in adv phrr *by a damn* (or *long,* etc) *sight:* By a large margin—usu in neg constrs.

1834 Davis *Letters Downing* 41, 'Gineral, do you want another report?' 'Not by a darn'd sight.' **1844** *Republican Sentinel* (Richmond, Va.) 22 June 1/2 *(OED2),* These animals begin to venture out a little of nights, since the Baltimore Convention, but are slyer by a long sight than foxes. **1885** Twain *Huck. Finn* 20 **MO,** I asked her if she reckoned Tom Sawyer would go there, and, she said, not by a considerable sight. **1893** Shands *MS Speech* 73, *Long sight.* This expression always occurs in the phrase "by a long sight," which means "by a great deal"; as, "He is not a good man by a long sight." **1896** Harris *Sister Jane* 63 **GA,** That ain't all by a long sight. **1915** *DN* 4.185 **swVA,** *Long shot or sight, not by a.* . . Decidedly not. **1942** McAtee *Dial. Grant Co. IN* 41 (as of 1890s), *Long sight,* . . *not by a* . . not by a good deal, far from it. **1956** McAtee *Some Dialect NC* 28, *Long sight, not by a.* . . not by a good deal, far from it. **1959** *VT Hist.* 27.132, *Not by a damsite.* . . Occasional. **1965–70** *DARE* (Qu. KK55a, *To deny something very firmly:* "No, not by a _____.") 250 Infs, **widespread, but more freq Nth, N Midl, West,** Damn (or *dang, darn, durn, long*) sight; **CT25,** God damn sight; **NE1,** Hell of a sight; (Qu. KK55c, . . *Expressions of strong denial*) 12 Infs, **scattered,** Not by a damn (or darn) sight; (Qu. NN4, . . *Ways of answering 'no':* "Would you lend him ten dollars?" "_____.") Infs **CA127, MA37, MI10, 28, MT4, NY105, VT12, WI48,** Not by a damn (or darn) sight; **PA227,** Not on a damn sight; (Qu. JJ24, *To refuse firmly:* "He wanted to get some more money, but this time I _____.") Inf **MA79,** Said not by a darn sight; (Qu. KK55b, *To deny something very firmly:* "Would you work for him?") Inf **TX16,** Not by a damn sight. **1966** Barnes–Jensen *Dict. UT Slang* 29, *Long sight,*

not by a . . far from it. **1976** M. Machlin *Pipeline* xxii.272 *(OED2),* The excitement ain't through here by a damn sight.

4 The distance one can see, esp along a road; an indefinite short distance. Cf **look** n

1848 Bartlett *Americanisms* 303 **NC,** *Sight.* In North Carolina the distance that can be seen on a road is called a sight. **1891** *Century Dict., Sight.* . . a line uninterrupted by a bend or an elevation: as, go on three sights, and stop at the first house. **1931** *PMLA* 46.1310 **sAppalachians,** Thus "sight" means not only a "great deal," as in "I love you a sight," or "It's one sight to know!" etc.; it also means a "short distance," as in "It's just a sight up to where the road forks." **1952** Brown *NC Folkl.* 1.590, *Sight, a.* . . The distance one can see. **1967** *DARE* FW Addit **MA,** A sight and a half—as far as you can see and half that distance again. For example, "How far is it to town?" "Oh, about a sight and a half."

5 An opportunity, chance, prospect.

1849 (1914) Kingsley *Diary* 74 **CT,** I began on some wheels for wheelbarrows but had a hard sight to get the lumber suitable for them. **1891** *Century Dict., Sight.* . . an opportunity for doing something; an opening; a chance . . as, he has no sight against his opponent. (Colloq.) **1936** Smiley *Gloss. New Paltz* **seNY,** "Will there be any 'site' [sic] for a job up there this spring". Means chance.

6 The pupil of the eye. [*OED2* c1400 →; "Now *dial.*"]

a1877 in 1950 *AmSp* 25.182 **NEng,** *Sight.* The pupil or interior of the eye, as distinguished from the white of the eye; as, 'He was hurt in the sight of his eye.' **1917** *DN* 4.417 **wNC, IL, KS,** *Sight of the eye.* Pupil. **1927** *AmSp* 2.364 **cwWV,** *Sight of the eye* . . the pupil. "The stick hit him in the sight of the eye." **1946** *PADS* 6.27 **ceNC** (as of 1900–10), *Sight of the eye.* . . The pupil of the eye. . . Common. **1952** Brown *NC Folkl.* 1.590, *Sight.* . . The pupil of the eye. "Henry's gal's got danged funny eyes. The sight o' one's bigger'n the other'n."

sight v

1 To look at (something). [Cf *OED2* sight v.[1] 1 "*Obs.*"]

1991 Still *Wolfpen Notebooks* 103 **sAppalachians,** Old Son, just you sight that corn patch. I'd bet my thumb it would 'still [=distill] up to a hundred gallons to the acre.

2 See quot.

1952 Brown *NC Folkl.* 1.591, *Sight.* . . To point or show the way. "I'll sight you to his house."—Central and east.

sign n[1]

Used as a mass noun: The tracks or other traces of an animal or person; hence v phrr *cut sign, cut off the sign* to intercept the track of an animal or person. See also **bear sign 1**

1692 in 1875 VA *Calendar State Papers* 1.44, We Ranged about to see if we could find ye tract of any Indians, but we could not see any fresh signe. **1803** (1904) Clark *Orig. Jrls. Lewis & Clark Exped.* 1.29, Great Deel of Deer Sign on the Bank. **1822** (1898) Fowler *Jrl.* 97, The men are all feerfull of meeting With the Indeans as We . . Have maid So much Sign in the Snow that the[y] Will track us up. **1848** Ruxton *Advent. Rocky Mts.* 173 **TX,** I saw some fresh beaver "sign." . . we saw Indian sign on the banks of the river. **1853** Hammett *Stray Yankee in TX* 117, Nothing leaves a *mark* to him, he sees only *sign,* whether of bird or beast, friend or enemy. You hear of *turkey sign, bear sign, hog sign, cow sign, Indian sign.* **1886** *S. Bivouac* 4.350 **sAppalachians,** Sign (track of wild beast). **1923** *DN* 5.237 **swWI,** *Sign.* . . Dung. "That wolf's been round again; he left some sign over there by the bush." **1929** Dobie *Vaquero* 163 **SW,** Every cowman represented would if necessary take his entire outfit and do his best to hang any cow thief who made sign north of the Canadian [River]. **1938** Rawlings *Yearling* 302 **nFL,** They hitched Cæsar to a magnolia and skirted the spring for 'gator sign. **1968** Abbey *Desert Solitaire* 211 **seUT,** There is no discernible trail on the slickrock but by walking around his final resting place in a big half-circle we cut sign—intersect his tracks—in a ravine a hundred yards away. **1970** *DARE* Tape **AR56,** He had some sows that he hadn't seen. They'd gotten wild. . . We was goin' along, found some fresh sign where they'd been rootin'. **1974** Dabney *Mountain Spirits* xxiv **sAppalachians,** *Sign:* The physical evidence leading to a distillery: tracks, broken undergrowth, spilled sugar, a trail. A favorite moonshiner expression was "put out the sign," i.e., sweep away the tracks. Revenue agents sought to "find the sign" or "cut off the sign."

sign n[2] See **scion**

sign v

To recognize the presence of something by its characteristic mark or marks.

1936 *Hench Coll.* **seVA,** On a guided fishing trip in Lynnhaven Bay, we heard a guide speak about how "to sign clams." He meant to spot them. You sign them by looking for holes in the sand beneath which they are. **1984** Wilder *You All Spoken Here* 169 **Sth,** *Sign clams:* Discover clams by walking in clear, shallow water and watching for their signs: keyhole-shaped depressions made as they ingest and expel water.

signify v

1 To use language in a cunning, indirect, and often malicious way; to make a sly verbal attack (on someone); broadly, to engage in deceptive, manipulative, or mocking behavior; hence vbl n *signifying,* abbr *sigging.* *among Black speakers*

1929 Gordon *Born to Be* 162 [Black], The crew was too hot, thats all, too tight. No signifying with that gang, they laid it. **1929** in 1983 Taft *Blues Lyric Poetry* 207, Now sister fooled brother man : and brother moved down / The broad catch you signifying : you breaking her down. **1934** *AmSp* 9.24 [Black], One of the most interesting of these Negro words is *signify,* a verb which is used to indicate the act of a poorly informed person talking on a subject with the confidence of a recognized authority. At times some of the more ignorant Negro prisoners will gather in a group and with the use of long, high-sounding words (meaningless to the user) will begin a discussion on a subject almost as far above their heads as the words they use. The more intelligent Negroes label this verbal display as *signifying.* **1935** Hurston *Mules & Men* 161 **FL,** "Aw, woman, quit tryin' to signify." [Footnote: To show off] "Ah kin signify all Ah please . . , so long as Ah know what Ah'm talkin' about." **1968** *Down Beat* 7 Mar 38 **Harlem NYC,** One night Billie [Holiday] brought the personal element into focus by "signifying," which in Harlemese means making a series of pointed but oblique remarks apparently addressed to no one in particular, but unmistakable in intention in such a close-knit circle. **1969–70** *DARE* (Qu. Y3, *To say uncomplimentary things about somebody*) Inf **NC68,** Signifying is Negro term for "gossip"; (Qu. Y5, *. . To urge somebody to do something he shouldn't:* "*Johnny wouldn't have tried that if the other boys hadn't _____ .*") Inf **NY249,** Signifying; (Qu. HH26, *A person who is always ready to stir up trouble*) Inf **SC69,** Signifying. **1970** Bullins *Electronic* 11 **sCA** [Black], He started agitatin' and signifyin' 'bout who the Muslims think they was. **1970** Abrahams *Deep Down* 54 **Philadelphia PA** [Black], The term "signifying" seems to be characteristically Negro in use if not in origin. It can mean any number of things; in the case of the toast, it certainly refers to the monkey's ability to talk with great innuendo, to carp, cajole, needle and lie. It can mean in other instances the propensity to talk around a subject, never quite coming to the point. It can mean "making fun" of a person or situation. . . Thus it is "signifying" to stir up a fight between neighbors by telling stories; it is signifying to make fun of the police by parodying his motions behind his back; it is signifying to ask for a piece of cake by saying, "My brother needs a piece of that cake." It is, in other words, many facets of the smart-alecky attitude. **1971** Roberts *Third Ear* np [Black], *Siggin(g) . .* language behavior that makes direct or indirect implications of baiting or boasting, the essence of which is making fun of another's appearance, relatives, or situation. Variations include joning, playing the dozens, screaming on, sounding. **1973** *AmSp* 47.153 (as of 1970) [Black], Quit signifying on me! **1980** Folb *Runnin' Down* 98 **cwCA** [Black], You signifyin' and say, 'Looky here brother, I don' sell wolf tickets and I sho' ain' buyin' none.' So you lettin' him know you sho' ain' goin' for what he sayin'. **1986** Pederson *LAGS Concordance* (Initiation rites) 1 inf, **cTX** When she was very young heard signifying; (Playing the dozens) 1 inf, **csTX,** Get down in signifying a case. [Both infs Black] **1996** McDowell *Leaving Pipe Shop* 54 **AL** (as of 1950s) [Black], "Be sure you pee before you go to get your hair cut," people would joke, signifying on his wife, who was suspicious and afraid of everybody and everything entering her house, especially anybody who might need to pee.

2 To inform (on someone); to "squeal."

1985 Wilkinson *Moonshine* 59 **neNC,** "It's been a long time ago, but I always did wonder who signified on me." "No one signified." "Well, then, how did you find me?" "I followed Jim, the man you had working for you."

signifying See signify 1

sigo See sego lily

si-godlin adj, adv Also *sidegadling, sidegartlin', sidegodlin, siebegodlin, si-godling* esp **Appalachians** Cf **anti-godlin, si-antigodlin, si-gogglin, si-waddlin**

Askew, lopsided, uneven; cater-cornered, diagonal(ly).

1896 *DN* 1.424 **swNC,** *Siebegodlin:* deformed, crooked, one-sided.

1917 *DN* 4.417 **wNC,** *Si-godlin'. . .* = *slantindicular.* "You sawed that log off a little si-godlin'." **1942** Hall *Smoky Mt. Speech* 28 **wNC, eTN,** *Si-godling* ['saɪgɒdlɪn] ('catter-cornered'?) was reported [among old men]; younger speakers always say [gɑd]. **1950** *PADS* 14.60 **SC,** *Sidegadling* ['saɪd̩gædlɪŋ] . . Awry, askew, off the main track. Applied to a path which wanders aimlessly from the main track. . . *Sidegodlin* ['saɪd̩gɑdlɪn] . . Same as *sidegadling.* **1954** *PADS* 21.37 **SC,** Sigodlin. . . Same as *squawed* [out of plumb]. **c1960** Wilson Coll. **csKY,** *Sidegodlin.* . . Awry, out of balance. **1966** *DARE* (Qu. KK70, *Something that has got out of proper shape:* "*That house is all _____ .*") Inf **AR41,** Sidegodlin; (Qu. MM13, *The table was nice and straight until he came along and knocked it _____*) Inf **NC33,** Si-godlin [ˌsɑːˈgɒdlɪn]. **1975** *Appalachian Jrl.* 2.159 **wNC,** Four terms suggest something out of line or out of plumb: *catty-cornered, cattywampus, slaunchways,* or *sigodlin* (also pronounced *si-goglin*). **1984** Wilder *You All Spoken Here* 163 **Sth,** *Slaunchways, sidegartlin':* Slanchwise; antigodlin; slanting; on a diagonal; awry; askew; off the main track; out of square; out of plumb; cattercornered; cattywampused; hipsheltered; crook-sided; slanchindicular. **1986** Pederson *LAGS Concordance* (Kitty-cornered) 1 inf, **ceTN,** Sigodlin.

si-gogglin adj, adv Also *sidegoglin, si-goglin, si-goggling* esp **sAppalachians** Cf **antigoglin** =**si-godlin.**

1930 *Herald–Advt.* (Huntington WV) 30 Nov sec 3 6/7 **KY, WV,** If one looks askance at another, one is then said to be looking "si-gogglin'." **1939** *AmSp* 14.266 **swIN,** Objects 'out of plumb' (i.e. off-center) are 'si-gogglin'. **1941** *AmSp* 16.24 **sIN,** *Si-gogglin. . .* [Footnote:] See *anti-si-gogglin, catawampus, etc.* **1968–69** *DARE* (Qu. KK70, *Something that has got out of proper shape:* "*That house is all _____ .*") Inf **KY70,** Si-gogglin; (Qu. MM13, *The table was nice and straight until he came along and knocked it _____*) Inf **KY36,** Si-gogglin [ˌsaɪ ˈgaglɪn]; (Qu. MM14, *If a drugstore is on one corner of a square and a gas station is on the far corner . .* "*The drugstore is _____ the gas station.*") Inf **VA15,** Si-gogglin ['saɪ ˌgaglɪn]; (Qu. MM15, *If a carpenter nails a board crossing another board at an angle . .* "*He nailed the board on _____ .*") Inf **VA15,** Si-gogglin. **1973** Allen *LAUM* 1.402 **Upper MW** (as of c1950), *Askew or diagonal. . .* sidegoglin [1 inf, **NE**]. **1975** [see **si-godlin**]. **1998** Kingsolver *Poisonwood Bible* 25 **GA,** I have such a small mouth, my wisdom teeth are coming in all sigoggling.

si'l See say v B1b

silencer n Cf husher

A pad or cover for the lid of a chamber pot; see quots.

1928 *Ruppenthal Coll.* **KS,** *Silencer. . .* A woven circular web placed around the top of a metal or china night vessel to prevent the sharp ringing noise otherwise caused by removing and replacing the top of the vessel. **1989** *DARE* File **csWI** (as of c1940), A padded or cloth cover for a chamber pot lid was called a silencer.

silent v

To silence.

1862 *De Bow's Rev.* 32.191, The older boys are immediately silenced by exclaiming; "Bonaparte is coming!" [*DARE* Ed: Perh a typographical error.] **1940** *AmSp* 15.52 **sAppalachians,** Parts of speech are promiscuously interchanged. Adjectives may serve as verbs: . . 'That silented him.' . . 'She littled her eyes at me.' **1982** Slone *How We Talked* 74 **eKY** (as of c1950), *To silent someone*—To not allow them to preach.

silent city n Also *silent village*

A cemetery.

1965–70 *DARE* (Qu. BB61b, *. . Joking names for a cemetery*) 10 Infs, **scattered,** Silent city; **WI12,** Silent village; (Qu. BB61a, *Other words . . for a cemetery*) Inf **MI96,** Silent city.

silent love n

=**evening primrose a.**

1959 Carleton *Index Herb. Plants* 107, Silent Love—Oenothera [spp].

silent policeman n

Any of var constructions or devices used to direct the flow or speed of traffic; see quots.

1920 in 2001 (acc) Lexis–Nexis. Legal Research *State Case Law: CT* (Internet), A so-called silent policeman consisting of a heavy circular base and an unpright post, surmounted by a sign and a suitable light . . toppled over and lay in the travelled part of the highway. **1923** in 2001 (acc) Lexis–Nexis. Legal Research *State Case Law: IL* (Internet), The post also served as a "silent policeman" . . separating the traffic. **1948** in 2001 (acc) Lexis–Nexis. Legal Research *State Case Law: CT* (Internet), The city maintained a stanchion, known as a silent policeman, at a street intersection. **1967–69** *DARE* (Qu. N20, . . *A circular arrangement on one level at a big intersection, where cars can go around till they come to the road they want*) Inf **NY23**, Silent policeman—cement block and post with light in center of intersection; (Qu. N30, . . *A sudden short dip in a road*) Inf **IL73**, Silent policeman. **1967** *DARE* FW Addit **neNY**, *Silent policeman*—The cement and metal structure in the middle of an intersection, often topped by a traffic light. **1985** *WI Alumnus Letters* **seWI**, Those built-in bumps on the road to slow one down are now called "silent policeman." **1999** *DARE* File—Internet [Cokato MN Hist. Soc.], *The Silent Policeman*. . . To keep drivers honest and make streets safer, the city council (in the 1920's) . . approved the construction of two traffic guides, later called "Silent Policemen". . . Made of solid concrete . . the guides featured a glass globe for lighting and flower beds. . . Drivers of both cars and horse teams were to keep fully to the right of the guides.

silent village See **silent city**

silf See **self**

silk aloe n

A **yucca** (here: *Yucca filamentosa*).

    1830 Rafinesque *Med. Flora* 2.276, *Y[ucca] filamentosa* called *Adam's needle, Silk Aloes, Beargrass*. . . Leaves . . furnishing a silky thread, fine strong flax, twisted ropes, traces, and even cables.

silk crab n **Chesapeake Bay MD** Cf **peeler crab, sook**

A mature female blue crab (*Callinectes sapidus*); hence comb *silk run* the annual migration of these crabs.

    1942 Chesapeake Biol. Lab. *Pub.* 52.9 **Chesapeake Bay,** It is at this final molt that the female acquires the broad semi-circular apron and becomes a "sook," "silk" or "sow" crab. **1953** *Sun* (Baltimore MD) 27 Aug 13/1 **Chesapeake Bay,** The annual "silk run," as the migration of female crabs up Chesapeake Bay is called, is now in full swing.

silk flower See **silk tree**

silk grass n

1 A **milkweed 1.** *obs* Cf **silkweed 1**

    1633 Gerarde *Herball* 899, There groweth in that part of Virginia . . a kinde of *Asclepias*, or Swallow-woort, which the Savages call *Wisanck*. . . This Plant . . is kept in some gardens by the name of Virginia Silke Grasse. **1664** in 1916 MA (Colony) Probate Court (Essex Co.) *Records* 1.457, 2 beds mad of silkgras with bolster and blankits. **1792** Belknap *Hist. NH* 3.126, The *silk grass,* another species of the *asclepias,* bears a pod, containing a down, which may be carded and spun into candle wicks. **1832** Williamson *Hist. ME* 1.127, *Milkweed,* sometimes called *Silk-grass* . . bears pods four inches in length enfolding a downy substance, soft like silk and good for bedding. **1885** *Century Illustr. Mag.* 29.878 (as of 17th cent), The cotton from the milkweed, then called "silk-grass," was used for pillows and cushions.

2 A **yucca** (here: *Yucca filamentosa*). [*DARE* Ed: Some of these quots may apply instead to other senses.]

    1610 in 1844 Force *Tracts* 22 **VA,** A kinde of hempe or flax, and silke grasse doe grow there naturally. [**1696** (1977) Dickinson *God's Providence* 28, In a little time some raw *Deare*-Skins were brought in and given to my Wife and *Negroe-Women,* and to us Men such as the *Indian-Men* wear, being a piece of Platt work of Straws wrought of diverse colours and of a Triangular Figure . . fastened behind with a *Horsetail* or a Bunch of Silk-grass exactly resembling it, of a flaxen coulour.] **1709** (1967) Lawson *New Voyage* 196 **NC,** The Baskets our Neighbouring *Indians* make, are all made of a very fine sort of Bulrushes, and sometimes of Silk-grass, which they work with Figures of Beasts, Birds, Fishes, &c. **1743** (1946) Gronovius *Flora Virginica* 152, Yucca flore albo, foliorum marginibus filamentosis. *Silkgrass.* In littoribus arenosis fluminum crescit. [=White flowered Yucca with the edges of the leaves filamentous. *Silkgrass.* It grows on sandy river-banks.] **1775** (1962) Romans *Nat. Hist. FL* 156, *Silk Grass* grows on the most barren sand hills of *Florida* (called black Jack ridges) . . the root having been found by experience to wash woollen the cleanest and whitest of any thing yet known. **1829** Eaton *Botany* 449, *Y[ucca] filamentosa* (silk-grass, beargrass). **1836** (1840) Phelps *Lectures on Botany* 151, *Yucca*. . . *filamentosa* (silk-grass). **1859** (1968) Bartlett *Americanisms* 26, Bear-Grass. (*Yucca filamentosa*) Sometimes called Silk Grass, from the fibres which appear on the edges of the leaves. It is not a grass. **1900** Lyons *Plant*

Names 401, Adam's-needle, Adam's-needle-and-thread . . Bear-grass, Silk-grass. **1952** Blackburn *Trees* 308, *Y[ucca] filamentosa* (Georgia to New Jersey)—silkgrass. **1970** *DARE* (Qu. S26e) Inf **VA77**, Adam-and-Eve thread, a soap-plant. [FW:] Silkgrass, a yucca, probably *Yucca filamentosa*.

3 A western **mountain rice** (here: *Achnatherum hymenoides*).

    1890 *Century Dict.* 5630, *Silk-grass*. . . A grass, *Oryzopsis cuspidata,* of the western United States, whose flowering glumes are densely covered with long silky hairs; also, the similar *Stipa comata* of the same region.

4 A **golden aster 2** (here: usu *Heterotheca graminifolia*).

    1900 Lyons *Plant Names* 100, *C[hrysopsis] graminifolia*. . . Silver-grass, Silk-grass, Scurvy-grass. **1940** Clute *Amer. Plant Names* 79, Silver-grass. Silk-grass [etc]. **1979** Ajilvsgi *Wild Flowers* 291, Silk-grass—*Heterotheca graminifolia*. . . soft, silvery white pubescence throughout.

5 A **bentgrass 1** (here: *Agrostis hyemalis*).

    1910 Graves *Flowering Plants* 64 **CT,** Agrostis hyemalis. . . Hair or Rough Hair Grass. Rough Bent. Fly-away or Silk Grass. **1912** Baker *Book of Grasses* 119, Before the panicles expand they are sometimes gathered and sold as "Silk-grass." **1930** OK Univ. Biol. Surv. *Pub.* 49, *Agrostis hyemalis*. . . Rough Hair-grass. Silk-grass.

6 A chiefly western **needlegrass 1** (here: *Hesperostipa comata* subsp *comata*).

    1937 U.S. Forest Serv. *Range Plant Hdbk.* G116, Needle-and-thread. . . is also called long-awned porcupinegrass, common or western needlegrass, sandgrass, and silkgrass.

silkroot n Cf **silkweed 2**

A **dogbane a.**

    c1938 in 1970 Hyatt *Hoodoo* 1.484 **seNC,** You see, the first time you take de *silkroot*—and you cut it a inch long and you steep dat in *overnight water* and put a cover over it. Well, it bitter, and it'll swell. You'll throw up ev'rything in you.

silk run See **silk crab**

silk-stocking n attrib Also rarely *silk-stockings* [*OED2* silk stocking a member of the wealthy or upper class; attrib use 1798 →] **scattered, but esp Gulf States, TX, Cent, Upper Missip Valley** See Map

Exclusive; upper-class—used to designate a place where people of wealth and high social standing live.

    1893 *World's Fair Puck* 18 Sept. 231/2 (*OED2*), Mr. Astorbilt (of the silk-stocking district). **1903** *N.Y. Even. Post* 30 Oct. 2 (*OED2*), Political conditions change even in the 'silk-stocking' quarter—the middle reaches of Manhattan, between 14th Street and 96th Street. **1949** Dean *Diamond Bess* 38 **TX,** Jefferson was truly a frontier town to a certain extent with its "silk stocking" row and Southern aristocracy forming its backbone of society. **1965–70** *DARE* (Qu. II24, *Names or nicknames for the part of a town where the well-off people live*) 56 Infs, **scattered, but esp Gulf States, TX, Cent, Upper Missip Valley,** Silk-stocking row (*or* area, avenue, district, hill, neighborhood, road, section, street, ward); (Qu. C35, *Nicknames for the different parts of your town or city*) Infs **FL15, KY60, MN6, MO14, OK25, 31, TX37,** Silk-stocking avenue (*or* area, district, road, row, street, ward); **TX80,** Silk-stockings avenue. **1976** Lynn–Vecsey *Loretta Lynn* 3 **eKY,** The foremen had nice

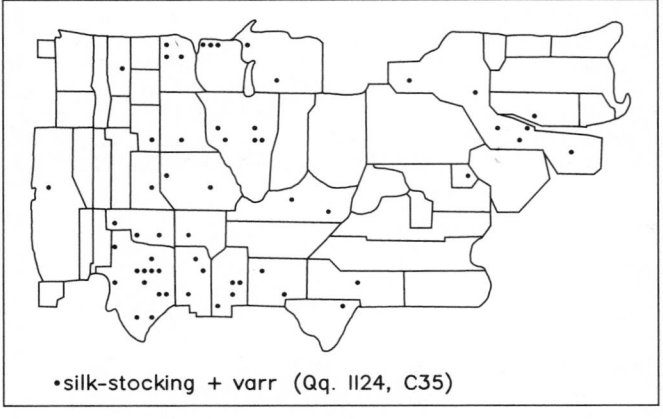

•silk-stocking + varr (Qq. II24, C35)

homes up on Silk Stocking row, and the bosses had real beautiful homes. Off to one side was a row of houses called Nigger Holler where the black miners lived.

silk tassel n Also *silk-tassel bush, silk tassels silk-tassel tree* [From the silky, pendent catkins]

A western plant of the genus *Garrya*. For other names of var spp see **bearberry 9, bear brush, coffeeberry 2c, fever bush 3, quinine ~ 1, skunkbush 2, tassel tree**

1897 Parsons *Wild Flowers CA* 370, Silk-tassel tree. Quinine-bush. *Garrya elliptica.* **1898** *Jrl. Amer. Folkl.* 11.228 **CA,** *Garrya* (sp.), silk-tassel tree, fringe bush, quinine bush. **1920** Saunders *Useful Wild Plants* 206 **CA,** *Garrya elliptica* . . is a common shrub of the California chaparral, that has been considered ornamental enough to be introduced into gardens both in this country and abroad under the name "Silk-tassel bush." **1938** Van Dersal *Native Woody Plants* 133, *Garrya flavescens.* . . Silktassel. *Ibid, Garrya fremontii.* . . Fremont silktassel. **1961** Douglas *My Wilderness* 87 **AZ,** Here also are numerous stands of the bush known as silk tassels, growing six feet or so high. Its evergreen leaves—thick and leathery—have a sharp quinine taste. **2000** *DARE* File—Internet **CA,** The more common *Coast Silk-tassel* (Garrya elliptica) is easily found between Curry Point and Sycamore Canyon in February and March.

silk-top palmetto n **FL**

A thatch palm: usu *Thrinax radiata*, but also *T. floridana*.

1884 Sargent *Forests of N. Amer.* 217, Silk-top Palmetto. Semi-tropical Florida, southern keys from Bahia Honda to Long's Key. **1890** *Century Dict.* 4249 **FL,** *Silk-top palmetto,* the name in Florida of *Thrinax parviflora,* found there and in the West Indies. **1908** Rogers *Tree Book* 120, The Thatch, or Silk-top Palmetto (*Thrinax Floridana,* Sarg.) has a silver lining in its glossy green fan leaves, making it a beautiful and showy tree. **1979** Little *Checklist U.S. Trees* 285, *Thrinax radiata.* . . Other common names . . silktop thatchpalm, silktop palmetto, silktop thatch.

silk tree n Also *silk flower* [*OED2* 1852 →]

A small tree of the genus *Albizia* (here: usu *A. julibrissin*). For other names of the latter see **mimosa tree, powder-puff ~**

1868 (1870) Gray *Field Botany* 114, *A[lbizzia] Julibrissin,* Silk-Flower or Silk-Tree . . with panicled heads of rather large pale rose-purple flowers, the long and lustrous filaments, like silky threads in tufts (giving the popular name). **1901** Mohr *Plant Life AL* 553, *Albizzia julibrissin.* . . Silk Tree. . . Florida to Louisiana. **1953** Greene–Blomquist *Flowers South* 128, Mimosa or Silk-tree. . . Ethereal brushes of clusters of numerous slender stamens cover the tree in a soft haze of pink from late spring throughout most of the summer. **1980** Little *Audubon Guide N. Amer. Trees W. Region* 486, Silktree—"Mimosa-tree" [etc]. **2000** *DARE* File—Internet, Albizia are called silk trees because of the exotic pink flowers which have delicate silky filaments.

silkweed n

1 A **milkweed 1,** esp *Asclepias syriaca.* [See quot 1784]

1784 in 1785 *Amer. Acad. Arts & Sci. Memoirs* 1.424 **PA,** The seeds are contained in large pods, and are crowned with white down . . resembling silk, which has occasioned the name of Silkweed. **1828** Rafinesque *Med. Flora* 1.78, *A. syriaca* or common Silkweed, grows all over the United States near streams. **1895** U.S. Dept. Ag. *Farmers' Bulletin* 28.26, Milkweed, cottonweed, silkweed. Asclepias syriaca. **1936** Whitehouse *TX Flowers* 100, Green-Flowered Milkweed. Silkweed. (*Asclepiodora decumbens*). **1963** Craighead *Rocky Mt. Wildflowers* 148, Pink Milkweed—*Asclepias speciosa.* . . Other names: Silkweed, Butterflyweed [etc]. **1967** *DARE* Wildfl QR Pl.173 Inf **NC28,** Silkweed. **1974** *WI Acad. Rev.* Summer 18, Common Milkweed (*Asclepias syriaca*) Silkweed.

2 An **Indian hemp 1** (here: *Apocynum cannabinum*). Cf **silkroot**

1876 Hobbs *Bot. Hdbk.* 106, Silkweed, Rose colored, White Indian hemp, Asclepias incarnata. **1940** Writers' Program *Guide VA* 30, The [Indian] women wore skirts of fringed deerskin or woven silkgrass (silk weed or Indian hemp). **1971** Krochmal *Appalachia Med. Plants* 52, *Apocynum cannabinum.* . . Common names: Hemp dogbane . . silkweed, wild cotton. **1974** (1977) Coon *Useful Plants* 61, The Dogbane Family. . . The long central stems are full of fibers (cf. the name "silkweed") and in California, Indians used the dried fibers to make twine, nets, and even clothing.

sill cock n **chiefly NEng, N Cent** See Map

A water faucet placed on the outside of a building.

1927 (1970) Sears *Catalogue* 566, Sill Cocks. **1939** *LANE* Map 143 (*Faucet*) 1 inf, **csCT,** Sill cock; 1 inf, **csCT,** Sill cock, a faucet on the sill of the house, for the water hose. **1965–70** *DARE* (Qu. F27b, *What you turn on and off outside the house to get running water*) 26 Infs, **chiefly NEng, N Cent,** Sill cock. [23 of 26 Infs old] **1971** *AmSp* 46.171 [Chicago words], 'Outdoor water outlet at the side of the house' . . (*hose, sill, square,* or *water*) *cock* 5 [of 37 infs]. **1986** Pederson *LAGS Concordance* (*Faucet*) 1 inf, **swAL,** Sill cock; 1 inf, **csGA,** Sill cock—in [the] yard, "if you want to be technical."

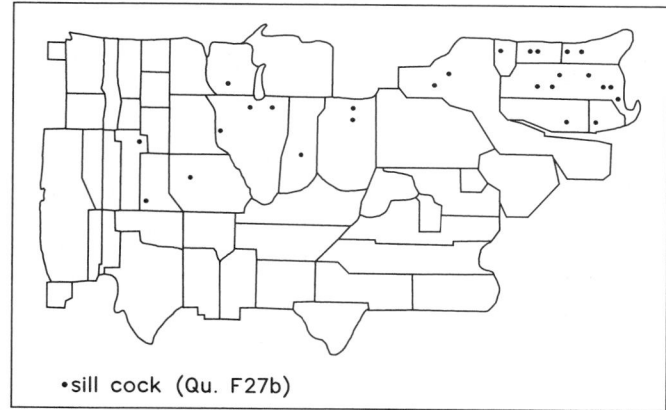

•sill cock (Qu. F27b)

sill salad n [Norw *sildesalat* herring salad]

A salad with sliced herring as the principal ingredient.

[**1951** Tufford *Scandinavian Recipes* 18 **MN,** Sildesalat (Herring Salad) . . salt herring . . potatoes . . beets . . apples . . cooked veal . . onion . . celery . . cucumber pickle.] **1967** *DARE* (Qu. H65, *Foreign foods favored by people around here*) Inf **MN6,** Sill salad—a Norwegian herring salad, potatoes, pickled beets, apple, onion, vinegar, water, sugar, hard-cooked eggs. **1981** Hachten *Flavor WI* 263, Sillsalad (Norwegian) . . salt herring . . roast meat . . cooked beets . . boiled potatoes . . dill pickle . . apples . . vinegar . . sugar . . white pepper . . heavy cream . . Hard-boiled eggs.

silver n

1 See **silver salmon.**

2 See **silver crappie.**

silver-and-gold n [See quot 1948] Cf **silverleaf 10, silverweed 1**

A **cinquefoil** (here: *Potentilla anserina*).

1948 Wherry *Wild Flower Guide* 78, Silver-and-gold. . . Flowers . . golden yellow. . . Leaves . . dark green above and silvery-hairy beneath. **1961** Smith *MI Wildflowers* 183, Silverweed, Silver-and-Gold—*Potentilla anserina.* . . Very common on lake shores in Michigan. **1966** *DARE* Wildfl QR Pl.92b Inf **MI31,** Silver-and-gold.

silver aster n Cf **silver grass**

A **golden aster 2** (here: *Pityopsis graminifolia*).

1900 Lyons *Plant Names* 100, *C[hrysopsis] graminifolia.* . . Silver Aster, Silver-grass. **1940** Clute *Amer. Plant Names* 220, *Chrysopsis graminifolia.* Golden star, silver aster.

silverback n Cf **silver plover**

=**knot** n[2].

1888 Trumbull *Names of Birds* 179 **MA,** At Ipswich, Mass., [the knot is called] Buff-breast, Blue plover, and Silver-back. **1925** (1928) Forbush *Birds MA* 1.402, *Calidris canutus* . . Other names: Red-breasted sandpiper; Gray-back; Silver-back [etc]. **1956** MA Audubon Soc. *Bulletin* 40.18 **MA,** Silver-back (Mass. See note on Blue Plover.) [Note to Blue plover:] In winter plumage the wings and back are brownish gray, the feathers edged with white.

silverback fern n Also *silver fern*

A **goldenback fern** (here: *Pityrogramma triangularis* var *viscosa*).

1937 St. John *Flora SE WA & ID* 3, Pityrogramma triangularis. . . Silver Fern. **1959** Munz–Keck *CA Flora* 38, [*Pityrogramma triangularis*]

Var. *viscosa*. . . Silverback Fern. Stipes red-brown; blades viscid above, with white powder beneath.

silver bass n

1 =**mooneye 1.**

1884 Goode *Fisheries U.S.* 1.612, "Silver Bass," *Hyodon selenops*. . . confined to the rivers of the Southern States. **1903** *NY State Museum & Sci. Serv. Bulletin* 60.185, This species [=*Hiodon tergisus*] is called mooneye, toothed herring and silver bass. It is found in Canada, the Great lakes region and the upper part of the Mississippi valley. **1935** Pratt *Manual Invertebrate Animals* 35, *H[iodon] tergisus*. . . Mooneye; silver bass.

2 The black **crappie** (*Pomoxis nigromaculatus*).

1887 Goode *Amer. Fishes* 69, In Lake Erie, and in Ohio generally, it [=*Pomoxys sparoides*] is the "Strawberry Bass". . . It is also called "Bar Fish," "Razor Back," "Chinquapin Perch," "Silver Bass" [etc]. **1938** Schrenkeisen *Field Book Fishes* 260, The calico bass is also known as Grass Bass, . . Silver Bass . . and Black Crappie.

3 Either of two closely related fishes: a **white perch** (here: *Morone americana*) or a **white bass** (here: *Morone chrysops*).

1897 *Outing* 30.437, Most prized of the lot were the black bass, especially the small-mouth. His big-mouthed cousin ranked second, calico and silver were equally esteemed, while the rock-bass was by no means to be despised. **1906** *NJ State Museum Annual Rept. for 1905* 440, *Roccus chrysops*. . . White Bass. Silver Bass. . . Introduced from the Great Lake and Mississippi valley regions. **1951** Harlan–Speaker *IA Fish* 101, Only two of the sea bass family are native to Iowa waters. They are the white, or silver, and the yellow bass. **1966–69** *DARE* (Qu. P1, . . *Kinds of freshwater fish . . caught around here . . good to eat*) Inf **NY**151, Silver bass; **OK**52, Silver bass—also called white perch. **1975** Evanoff *Catch More Fish* 91, The white bass (*Roccus chrysops*) is also called the silver bass, barfish, gray bass, sand bass, silversides [etc].

4 =**freshwater drum.**

1951 Harlan–Speaker *IA Fish* 138, The freshwater drum. . . is called sheepshead, white perch, croaker, grunter, grinder and, incorrectly, silver bass. **1968** *DARE* (Qu. P3, *Freshwater fish that are not good to eat*) Inf **NY**74, Silver bass—get up to two or three pounds. **2000** *DARE* File—Internet **IL**, I have seen Drum at the Jewel stores being sold as "silver bass."

silver bell n

1 also *Carolina silver bell, silver-bell tree:* A tree of the genus *Halesia*, esp *H. carolina* which is also called **belltree, calico wood, chittamwood 3, opossum wood, peawood, possum wood 2, rattlebox 1c, tisswood, wild olive.** For other names of var spp see **cowlicks, snowdrop tree.**

1785 Marshall *Arbustrum* 57, Halesia, or silver-bell tree. [*Ibid*, Halesia tetraptera. . . The flowers . . are bell-shaped and pendulous, of a white colour.] **1857** Gray *Manual of Botany* 266, Halesia. . . Snowdrop or Silver-bell-Tree. **1897** Sudworth *Arborescent Flora* 322, Mohrodendron carolinum. . . Silverbell-tree (R.I. (cult.), Ala., Fla., Miss.) **1937** Thornburgh *Gt. Smoky Mts.* 20, There is the rose tint of redbud, or Judas tree; the white of . . silver bell. **1961** Douglas *My Wilderness* 160 **wNC**, The silver-bells had reclaimed it. This tree, which the mountain people call "peawood," often sends a shaft seventy-five feet into the sky. **1980** Little *Audubon Guide N. Amer. Trees E. Region* 638, Carolina Silverbell. . . Common and of largest size in the southern Appalachians, where it is known as "Mountain Silverbell."

2 also *silver top:* A chocolate drop wrapped in silver-colored foil. [Cf *silver paper* tinfoil] **esp Sth**

1966–70 *DARE* (Qu. H82a, *Cheap candies sold especially for schoolchildren*) Inf **GA**11, Silver bells, **GA**88, Silver bells—chocolate drops; **MS**2, Silver bells, kisses—same; (Qu. H82b, *Kinds of cheap candy that used to be sold years ago*) Inf **SC**51, Silver bells; **LA**3, Silver bells—chocolate wrapped in foil [FW: What are now called Hershey's Kisses]; **VA**39, Silver tops.

silver-bell tree See silver bell 1

silverberry n

A **buffalo berry** (here: *Shepherdia argentea*).

1857 Gray *Manual of Botany* 381, *Eleagnus argentea*, . . the Silver-Berry, may perhaps be found within our northwestern limits. **1898** *Jrl. Amer. Folkl.* 11.278 **WY**, *Elaeagnus argentea*, Pursh, silver berry. **1900** Lyons *Plant Names* 143, *Elaeagnus* [spp]. . . Silver-berry. *Ibid*, *E. argentea*. . . Silver-berry. **2000** *DARE* File—Internet, Silverberry is na-

tive to North America and is grown for its silver foliage. . . Silvery fruit follow [sic] the flowers.

silver birch n [Because the bark is a silvery white]

Either a **paper birch** (here: *Betula papyrifera*) or the **yellow birch.**

1839 *S. Lit. Messenger* June 398, And see the silver birch; with every pointed leaf dancing gaily on its silver stem. **1848** Thoreau in *Union Mag.* (NY NY) 3.220 **ME**, It is a country full of evergreen trees, of mossy silver birches and watery maples. **1897** Sudworth *Arborescent Flora* 140 **MN**, *Betula papyrifera*. . . Common Names. . . Silver Birch. *Ibid* 142 **NH**, *Betula lutea*. . . Silver Birch. **1950** Peattie *Nat. Hist. Trees* 165, Paper Birch. . . Other Names: Canoe, White or Silver Birch. *Ibid* 170, Yellow Birch. . . Other Names: Bitter, Silver, or Gray Birch. **1966–70** *DARE* (Qu. T15, . . *Kinds of swamp trees*) Inf **WA**1, Silver birch; (Qu. T16, . . *Kinds of trees . . 'special'*) Infs **MA**78, **NY**213, Silver birch. **2001** *DARE* File **nwMA**, The silver birch is the yellow birch. *Ibid* **ME** (as of 1970s), Young yellow birch was commonly called silver birch because the bark is silvery.

silver boa n Also *silver snake* [From the grayish color of the skin]

=**rubber boa.**

1952 Ditmars *N. Amer. Snakes* 153, Rubber Boa, Silver Boa, "Two-headed" Snake. *Charina bottae*. . . Washington to California; eastward to Idaho, Montana, Wyoming, Nevada and Utah.N *Ibid* 173, Rubber Boa . . Silver Snake.

silver brant n

=**blue goose n 1.**

[**1911** *Forest & Stream* 77.173 **Canada**, Blue Goose. . . Silver Brant, Manitoba.] **1982** Elman *Hunter's Field Guide* 292, Blue Goose. . . Common & Regional Names: . . *blue brant, gray brant, silver brant* [etc].

silver button n

=**pearly everlasting 1.**

1900 Lyons *Plant Names* 32, [*Anaphalis*] *margaritacea* . . Silver-button, Silver-leaf. **1935** (1943) Muenscher *Weeds* 450, Pearly everlasting, Silver leaf, . . Silver button.

silver buttonwood See buttonwood 3

silver cactus See silver cholla

silver carp n

Either a carpsucker (*Carpiodes* spp) or the common carp (*Cyprinus carpio*).

1908 Forbes–Richardson *Fishes of IL* 78, *Carpiodes velifer*. . . Quillback; silver carp. **1951** Harlan–Speaker *IA Fish* 61, Quillback. . . Other Names—White carp, carpsucker, silver carp and white sucker. *Ibid* 62, Northern River Carpsucker. . . Other Names—Carpsucker, white carp, quillback and silver carp. **1975** Evanoff *Catch More Fish* 96, The carp (*Cyprinus carpio*) is also called the German carp, European carp, golden carp, silver carp [etc].

silver cat See silver catfish 2

silver catfish n

1 also *silver cat, silvery catfish:* Usu a **channel catfish** (here: *Ictalurus punctatus*); rarely, the **blue catfish 1.**

1819 Rafinesque in 1820 *Qrly. Jrl. Sci. Lit. Arts* 9.50, *Silurus argentinus*. Silvery cat-fish. Body compressed, entirely of a silvery white. . . A small species, rather scarce, seen only once in the lower parts of the Ohio. Length six inches. **1877** U.S. Natl. Museum *Bulletin* 10.76, *Ichthælurus punctatus*. . . Blue Cat—White Cat—Silver Cat—Channel Cat. **1903** *NY State Museum & Sci. Serv. Bulletin* 60.80, *Ictalurus punctatus*. . . This species is variously styled the channel cat, white cat, silver cat, blue cat and spotted cat. It is found over a vast extent of country comprising the Mississippi and Ohio valleys and the Great lakes region. **1946** LaMonte *N. Amer. Game Fishes* 161, Channel Catfish. . . Names: Speckled Catfish, Fiddler, White Cat, Silver Cat. . . Averages 5 pounds; runs to 25 or more. **1957** Trautman *Fishes* 415 **OH**, Channel Catfish. . . Young less than 14.0″ long . . colloquially called squealers, ladycats, spotted and silver cats. . . Adults . . colloquially called silver, channel, and blue cats. **1965** Teale *Wandering Through Winter* 173 **OK**, Silver cats may even go as high as a hundred [pounds]. **1975** Evanoff *Catch More Fish* 94, The channel catfish (*Ictalurus punctatus*) is one of the gamest and is also called the speckled catfish, fiddler, and silver catfish.

2 as *silver (sea) cat*: A **sea catfish** (here: *Arius felis*).

1933 LA Dept. of Conserv. *Fishes* 251, The Silver Sea Cat or Six-whiskered Cat is much more numerous than the Gaff Topsail. . . The Silver Cat is found around Grande Isle in depths from two to ninety feet.

silver chain n Cf **silver locust**

A **black locust** (here: *Robinia pseudoacacia*).

1900 Lyons *Plant Names* 323, R[obinia] *pseudoacacia*. . . Bastard or False Acacia, Silver-chain. **1922** *Amer. Botanist* 28.27, "Silver chain," sometimes heard is clearly patterned after "golden chain", a name given to laburnum . . whose golden flower-clusters much resemble those of the locust in size and shape. **1960** Vines *Trees SW* 566, Other vernacular names [of *Robinia pseudo-acacia*] are White Locust . . Silver-chain [etc].

silver cholla n Also *silver cactus* Cf **golden cholla**

Either of two **prickly pears 1**: *Opuntia bigelovii* or *O. echino-carpa*.

1939 Pickwell *Deserts* 65, So notorius is Cholla that in the desert it is known by many different names: "Silver Cactus" (the new stems at the top are silvery in color, older stems nearly black) [etc]. **1940** Benson *Cacti AZ* 4.42, *Opuntia echinocarpa*. . . Two chief forms occur among the plants growing north of the Bill Williams River as follows: (1) "silver cholla," distinguished as an erect plant not more than 3 feet high with a compact head of short branches densely armed with silvery spines; (2) "golden cholla," distinguished by . . its bright golden spines. **1971** Dodge *100 Desert Wildflowers* 57, Teddy bear cholla—Also known as "silver cholla". . . Joints broken off by the wind fall to the ground and take root in the sandy soil, gradually developing forests of this striking cactus, easily recognized by the silvery sheen of the spines.

silver chub n

A chub: usu *Macrhybopsis storeriana*, but also *Notropis amblops* or *Semotilis corporalis*.

1882 U.S. Natl. Museum *Bulletin* 16.222, S[emotilus] *bullaris* . . Fall-fish; Silver Chub. . . Abundant from Massachusetts to Virginia, east of the Alleghanies. **1902** Jordan–Evermann *Amer. Fishes* 74, The common names which this fish [=the fallfish] has received are numerous. . . It has been variously called chub, roach, silver chub, or wind-fish. **1908** Forbes–Richardson *Fishes of IL* 165, Hybopsis amblops. . . Big-eyed chub; Silver chub. **1930** OK Univ. Biol. Surv. *Pub.* 1.65, *Hybopsis storerianus*. . . Silver chub. **1967** Cross *Hdbk. Fishes KS* 93, The silver chub inhabits large, sandy rivers; it seems common only in the Kansas and Missouri rivers. **2000** (acc) IA Dept. Nat. Resources *IA Fish & Fishing: IA Fishes* (Internet), Silver chub populations are scattered throughout Iowa streams, but this species is most frequently found in the Mississippi, Des Moines, Skunk, and Nishnabotna rivers.

silver cloud n esp eTN, wNC Cf **gray cloud**

In moonshining: liquor produced in a still of galvanized steel which, in corroding, imparts a cloudy color to the liquor; a galvanized metal still pot.

1955 Dykeman *French Broad* 244 eTN, These galvanized drums are called "silver clouds." **1956** Hall Coll. wNC, eTN, Silver cloud. . . "Silver cloud is liquor made in a galvanized still. When the whiskey boiled off, it would be cloudy looking." (The metals used in galvanizing would be corroded by the acid of the mash.) **1959** Ibid, Silver cloud still. . . A moonshine liquor still made of galvanized steel in which the "galvanize" corrodes, making the liquor cloudy in color. **1966** DARE (Qu. DD21b, *General words . . for bad liquor*) Inf NC36, Silver cloud—because made in galvanized containers. **1974** Dabney *Mountain Spirits* xxiii eTN, A localized version of the metal pot still is the "silver cloud," common in East Tennessee, particularly around Cosby. They are cylindrical pots made of galvanized steel, with heat being applied by burners through single or twin flues through the lower third of the pot.

silver crappie n Also *silver* Cf **silver perch 2**

The white **crappie** (*Pomoxys annularis*).

1951 Harlan–Speaker *IA Fish* 122, White Crappie. . . Other Names—Crappie, silver crappie, bachelor. . . The color of the fish is silvery-olive, shading to green or brown on the back. **1970** DARE (Qu. P1, . . *Kinds of freshwater fish . . caught around here . . good to eat*) Inf VA79, Silver—same as crappie. **2000** DARE File—Internet IL, White Crappie—*Common Names*: Crappie, silver crappie, bachelor, newlight.

silver dollar n Also *silver-dollar plant* Cf **silverleaf 7, silver shilling(s)**

An **honesty** (here: *Lunaria annua*).

1940 Clute *Amer. Plant Names* 263, *Lunaria annua*. . . Silver platter, silver-bloom, . . silver dollar. **1950** *WELS Suppl.* csWI, Silver dollar (plant) . . has seed-leaves about the size of a silver dollar. Outer husk dries, is carefully peeled off from both sides, leaving a thin silvery membrane. Used for winter bouquets. **1976** Bailey–Bailey *Hortus Third* 685, [*Lunaria*] *annua*. . . Honesty, bolbonac, silver-dollar.

silver-dollar bird n

A **flicker** n[2] **1** (here: *Colaptes auratus*).

1900 *Wilson Bulletin* 7.2.9 PA, Silver Dollar Bird. Pennsyvlania. "From its white rump mark which it shows so conspicuously when rising from the ground."

silver-dollar plant See **silver dollar**

silver ear n

A **jelly fungus** (here: *Tremella fuciformis*).

1985 Weber–Smith *Field Guide S. Mushrooms* 42, *Tremella fuciformis*. . . Silver ear. . . This ghostly white fungus is jellylike and translucent when fresh but thin, pale tan, rigid, and almost lacy when dry. The fruiting bodies are distinctly and complexly lobed.

silver eel See **eel** n **3**

silver fern See **silverback fern**

silverfin n Also *silverfin minnow*

A **shiner 1** (here: usu *Notropis whipplei*).

1883 U.S. Natl. Museum *Bulletin* 16.179, Silver-fin. . . Pennsylvania and Central New York to Mississippi Valley. **1903** NY State Museum & Sci. Serv. *Bulletin* 145, The silverfin ranges from western New York to Virginia and west to Minnesota and Arkansas. **1935** Pratt *Manual Vertebrate Animals* 76, [*Cyprinella*] *whipplii*. . . Silver-fin. **2000** DARE File—Internet, Spotfin Shiner—*Notropis spilopterus*. . . Other names—satin-finned minnow, blue minnow, silverfin minnow, lemonfin minnow [etc].

silver fir n [From the silvery color of the bark or underside of the leaf]

1 A fir of the eastern US, as:

a A **balsam fir** (here: *Abies balsamea*). *obs*

1791 in 1982 Jefferson *Papers* 20.463 ceNY, Lake George is without comparison the most beautiful water I ever saw . . its waters limpid as chrystal and the mountain sides covered with rich groves of Thuja, silver fir, white pine, Aspen and paper birch down to the water edge. **a1817** (1821) Dwight *Travels* 2.210 ME, I first took a particular notice of a silver light, diffused over the leaves. . . This, I presume, is the silver fir. **1832** *N. Amer. Rev.* 35.427, That elegant tree, the *Abies Balsamifera*, is not only known by its most proper and expressive name, the Silver Fir, but also by that of Fir Balsam and Balm of Gilead. **1844** Lapham *Geogr. Descr. WI* 82, [*Pinus*] *balsamea* . . silver fir. **1869** Porcher *Resources* 585, *American silver fir, or balm of Gilead tree*. . . Grows on the summits of the mountains of Va. and the Carolinas. **1900** Lyons *Plant Names* 7, [*Abies*] *balsamea*. . . American Silver Fir.

b =**Fraser fir**.

1901 Lounsberry *S. Wild Flowers* 11, She Balsam, Silver Fir. Fraser's Balsam Fir. . . This most beautiful of firs inhabits only the higher mountains of the Alleghanies. **1908** Britton *N. Amer. Trees* 76, Fraser's Balsam Fir. . . also called She Balsam, Balsam fir, Silver fir . . occurs in the higher mountains of Virginia and West Virginia to North Carolina and Tennessee. **1933** Small *Manual SE Flora* 8, A[bies] *Fraseri*. . . Silver-fir. . . Acid swamps, slopes, and summits, Blue Ridge to Appalachian Plateau, N.C. and Tenn. to W. Va.

2 Any of several firs native to the western US, as:

a A Pacific fir (*Abies amabilis*). Also called **red fir d, white fir**

1857 U.S. War Dept. *Rept. Explor. Railroad* 6.3.48 **Pacific NW**, As will be seen from the figures now published, . . there is an entire correspondence between Douglas' *P. amabilis* and the "silver fir" of the Cascade mountains. **1873** *Overland Mth.* 10.357 cCA, Here the cañon is all broadly open again—a dead lake, luxuriantly forested with pine, and spruce, and silver fir, and brown-trunked *Librocedrus*. **1908** Sudworth *Forest Trees Pacific* 125, Amabilis fir is known by woodsmen as "white" fir or "silver" fir, from the white, smooth bark. **1953** Peattie *Nat. Hist. W. Trees* 198, Silver Fir [=*Abies amabilis*] . . The shining silvery undersides of the needles give this tree its name. **1967** *DARE* (Qu. T5, . . *Kinds of evergreens, other than pine*) Inf **WA**24, Silver fir. [*DARE* Ed: This quot may refer instead to **2c** below.] **1972** Viereck–Little *AK Trees* 61, Pacific Silver Fir. . . Other names: silver fir, white fir.

b =**grand fir.**
1880 Bessey *Botany* 412, The genus *Abies* contains . . the Giant Silver Fir, *A. grandis*, of Oregon and California. **1881** Muir in *Scribner's Mth.* 22.921, *Grand silver-fir. White-fir. (Picea grandis.)* **1897** Sudworth *Arborescent Flora* 53, Abies grandis. . . Great Silver Fir. *Ibid* 54 **MT, ID,** Silver Fir. **1938** Van Dersal *Native Woody Plants* 335, Fir . . Silver . . *Abies grandis.* **1973** Hitchcock–Cronquist *Flora Pacific NW* 60, Lovely, red, or silver f[ir]. (*A. grandis* var. *densifolia*).

c Any of several others, such as a **white fir** (here: *Abies concolor*) or the bristlecone fir of California (*Abies bracteata*).
1869 *Atlantic Mth.* 23.502 **CO,** A silver-fir or spruce is the one charm among the trees. **1874** *Overland Mth.* 12.467 **nCA,** As the small cones of the silver-fir [=*Abies procera*] grow at the very top of the tree, he has to climb 150 feet to get the choicest. **1897** Sudworth *Arborescent Flora* 55 **CA,** *Abies concolor*. . . Common Names. . . Silver Fir. **1900** Muir in *Atlantic Mth.* 86.179, And I pointed to a blossom-laden *Abies magnifica* . . in front of the house, used as a hitching post. And seeing its beauty for the first time, their wonder could hardly have been greater or more sincere had their silver fir hitching post blossomed for them at that moment as suddenly as Aaron's rod. *Ibid,* Our two silver firs [extend] to Mount Shasta, thence the fir belt is continued through Oregon, Washington, and British Columbia by four other species, *Abies nobilis, grandis, amabilis*, and *lasiocarpa*. **1908** Britton *N. Amer. Trees* 85, Bristle cone fir. . . This, the most peculiar, as well as the rarest of the North American Fir trees, is also called Santa Lucia fir, Silver fir, and Fringed spruce. **1979** Little *Checklist U.S. Trees* 34, Bristlecone fir. . . Other common names—Santa Lucia fir, silver fir. *Ibid,* Abies concolor. . . Other common names . . silver fir, white balsam [etc]. **2000** (acc) U.S. Dept. Ag. *Integrated Taxonomic Info. System* (Internet), *Abies bracteata*. . . Vernacular Name: silver fir.

silverfish n
1 =**tarpon.**
1775 (1962) Romans *Nat. Hist. FL* app lii, The fish caught here are . . *silver-fish, jew-fish, rock fish* [etc]. **1884** Goode *Fisheries U.S.* 1.610 **FL,** The sailors' name for this fish . . is "Tarpum" or "Tarpon". . . It is the "Silver-fish" of Pensacola. *Ibid* 611, The Silver-fish, or Grande Écaille, is common everywhere on the Gulf coast. . . During September of 1879, I saw large numbers of Silver-fish eight or ten miles up the Apalachicola River, and am told this is not an unusual occurrence. They go up the Homosassa River in Florida, and several of the Texas rivers. **1946** LaMonte *N. Amer. Game Fishes* 11, Tarpon. . . Names: Tarpum, Silverfish. . . The body is densely silver with iridescent reflections. **1975** Evanoff *Catch More Fish* 217, The tarpon . . is also called the tarpum, silver fish, grande ecaille, sabalo, and silver king.

2 A freshwater fish such as a **white bass** (here: *Morone chrysops*); see quots.
1804 (1904) Clark *Orig. Jrls. Lewis & Clark Exped.* 1.110, Cought . . a kind of perch Called Silver fish, on the Ohio. **1951** Harlan–Speaker *IA Fish* 119, White Bass . . Other Names . . silver fish, streaker. **1983** Becker *Fishes WI* 789, *Morone chrysops*. . . Other common names: silver bass, . . silver fish.

3 also *silver:* A **shiner 1. esp S Atl**
1875 (1876) Hallock *Camp Life* 162 **FL,** In deeper spots clustered bass, a spotted fish I could not learn the name of, and fish called silver fish. **1966–70** *DARE* (Qu. P7, *Small fish used as bait for bigger fish*) Infs **GA**3, **NY**54, **SC**9, 19, 63, Silverfish; **FL**48, Shiners—silverfish and roaches are other names. **1986** Pederson *LAGS Concordance (Minnows, shiners)* 2 infs, neGA, cLA, Silverfish; 1 inf, cnFL, Silvers.

4 A **moonfish 2** (here: either *Selene setipinnis* or *S. vomer*).
1879 U.S. Natl. Museum *Bulletin* 14.41, *Vomer setipinnis*. . . Silverfish.—Maine to Florida. *Ibid, Argyreiosus vomer*. . . Silver-fish.—Cape Cod to Florida. **1906** NJ State Museum *Annual Rept. for 1905* 260, *Selene vomer*. . . Hair Finned Silver Fish. Dollar Fish.

5 Either of two **weakfish:** *Cynoscion nebulosus* or *C. regalis*.
1892 *Outing* Apr 54 **MA,** The squetauge or weak-fish [is] . . known about Cape Cod as the 'drummer,' 'silver fish,' and 'spotted boy.'

6 The Atlantic cutlass fish (*Trichiurus lepturus*).

1896 U.S. Natl. Museum *Bulletin* 47.889, *Trichiurus lepturus*. . . Cutlass Fish, Scabbard Fish; Silverfish. . . Warm seas, chiefly of the western Atlantic, north to Virginia. **1933** LA Dept. of Conserv. *Fishes* 165, [Caption:] Among the many popular names applied to the Cutlass Fish are Silverfish, Hairtail, Savola, Scabbardfish.

silver fox n
A color phase of the **red fox 1** in which the black pelt has white-tipped guard hairs.
[**1792** Cartwright *Jrl. Labrador* 3.ix, Silver-fox. A black-fox, with white king-hairs dispersed on the back of it.] **1806** (1905) Clark *Orig. Jrls. Lewis & Clark Exped.* 4.88 **OR,** The *Silver Fox*. . . is very rare even in the countrey where it exists. **1826** Godman *Amer. Nat. Hist.* 1.274, *The Black or Silver Fox*. . . resembles the kindred species in the unpleasant odour it diffuses. **1880** (1884) U.S. Census Office *Rept. Population Industries Resources AK* 58, The king among the various tribes of the *vulpes* family is the black or silver fox. **1965–70** *DARE* (Qu. P32, . . *Other kinds of wild animals*) 9 Infs, **scattered,** Silver fox. **1968** *DARE* Tape **AK**11, The natives from . . the Canadian side. . . would come down the river into Juneau and bring the furs. . . They had very beautiful furs: white fox, silver fox, blue fox [etc]. **2000** (acc) AK Dept. Fish & Game *Notebook* (Internet), Red foxes displaying a distinct color pattern are referred [sic] by the name of that phase (i.e., red, cross, silver, black). . . The silver and black phases are similar. However, the black does not have the silver-tipped guard hairs characteristic of the silver fox.

silver gar n Also *silver garfish, silvery gar*
A **needlefish 1** (here: *Strongylura marina*).
1855 Smithsonian Inst. *Annual Rept. for 1854* 346, *Belone truncata*. . . The Bill-Fish—Sea-Pike—Silver Gar-Fish. . . They have been seen at Columbia, Pennsylvania, in the Susquehanna. **1859** (1968) Bartlett *Americanisms* 32, Bill-fish. (*Belone truncata.*) A small sea-fish fond of running up into fresh water during the summer. . . Also called Seapike, Silver Gar-fish, etc. **1873** in 1878 Smithsonian Inst. *Misc. Coll.* 14.2.30, *Belone longirostris*. . . Silver-gar; bill-fish. Cape Cod to Florida. **1906** NJ State Museum *Annual Rept. for 1905* 204, *Tylosurus marinus*. . . Silvery Gar. . . Silver Gar Fish. . . Silver Gar. **1933** John G. Shedd Aquarium *Guide* 63, The Silver Gar is the common needlefish of the Atlantic coast. It is found from Cape Cod to Texas.

silver grass n Cf **silver aster**
A **golden aster 2** (here: *Heterotheca graminifolia*).
1900 Lyons *Plant Names* 100, [*Chrysopsis*] *graminifolia*. . . Southeastern U.S. . . Silver Aster, Silver-grass. **1901** Lounsberry *S. Wild Flowers* 505, Silver grass. . . Its tall and leafy stem is considerably marked, as is its grass-like foliage, with white, silky and lustrous hairs, giving the plant an intense and silvery sheen.

silver-gray squirrel n
A **gray squirrel 1:** in the eastern US, *Sciurus carolinensis;* on the West Coast, *S. griseus*.
1857 U.S. Patent Office *Annual Rept. for 1856: Ag.* 66, [The southern grey or Carolina squirrel, *Sciurus carolinensis*] is known among hunters as the "Silver-grey Squirrel." **1928** Anthony *N. Amer. Mammals* 255, The Gray Squirrels of the *griseus* group are found in forested areas. . . Where they occur together with the large, grayish Ground Squirrels of the *Otospermophilus grammurus* group, the hunters sometimes apply the name Silver-gray Squirrel to these tree-climbing Squirrels.

silver hake n
1 =**hake 1a.**
1873 in 1878 Smithsonian Inst. *Misc. Coll.* 14.2.18 **ME,** *Merlucius bilinearis*. . . American hake; silver hake. **1902** Jordan–Evermann *Amer. Fishes* 507, The silver hake, New England hake, or whiting, is common from Newfoundland to Cape Cod, and south to the Bahamas in deep water. **1942** Hale *Prodigal Women* 494 **MA,** He squatted beside her and put down a string of silver haik [sic] where she could see it. **1975** Evanoff *Catch More Fish* 106, Another popular winter fish is the silver hake or whiting, caught also in North Atlantic waters. **2000** *DARE* File—Internet **NY,** The two most abundant local species are red hake and silver hake. *Silver hake is also known as 'whiting'.*

2 =**walleye pollack.**
1884 U.S. Natl. Museum *Bulletin* 27.407 **AK,** *Pollachius chalcogrammus*. . . Silver Hake. . . Very abundant around the Shumagin Islands. **1968** *DARE* (Qu. P2, . . *Kinds of saltwater fish caught around here . . good to eat*) Inf **AK**1, Silver hake.

silverjaw minnow n Also *silverjaw, silver-mouthed dace,* ~
minnow

A **minnow B1** (here: *Notropis buccatus*).

1884 U.S. Natl. Museum *Bulletin* 27.484, *Ericymba buccata* . . Silver-mouthed Dace. Western Pennsylvania; Ohio Valley; Mississippi Valley. **1908** Forbes–Richardson *Fishes of IL* 156, *Ericymba buccata* . . Silver-mouthed minnow. **1957** Trautman *Fishes* 393, Silverjaw minnow. *Ibid* 395, The Silverjaw is a sand-inhabiting species. **1983** *Audubon Field Guide N. Amer. Fishes* 414, Silverjaw Minnows run in schools near the bottom.

silver jenny n Cf **silver perch 3**

A **mojarra 1** (here: *Eucinostomus gula*).

1898 U.S. Natl. Museum *Bulletin* 47.1370, Silver Jenny. . . Color silvery, greenish, darker above. **1902** Jordan–Evermann *Amer. Fishes* 446, *E[ucinostomus] gula,* known . . as silver jenny . . is excessively common everywhere in shallow water and on sandy shores from the Carolinas to Brazil. **1991** Amer. Fisheries Soc. *Common Names Fishes* 53, *Eucinostomus gula* . . silver jenny.

silver king n Cf **silverfish 1**
=tarpon.

1889 *Scribner s Mag.* 6.155 **FL,** The body [of the tarpon] is covered with brilliant argentine scales, which give the fish the effect of having been laved in silver, and which have won for it the title of the "Silver King." **1902** Jordan–Evermann *Amer. Fishes* 85, Every lover of the rod has heard of the silver king and has hoped that he might some day have an opportunity to test the great fish's strength and skill. **1931** *Field & Stream* Oct 24 **FL,** Lightning speed, silver sides, spectacular leaps, untiring endurance—this is the tarpon. *Grande écaille* of the Louisiana cajun and Silver King of the Florida guides. **1972** Sparano *Outdoors Encycl.* 379, Common Names: Tarpon, silver king, sabalo. **2000** DARE File—Internet **sFL,** *Tarpon.* . . The "Silver King" of the Keys!

silver lace vine n
=climbing false buckwheat.

1967 DARE Wildfl QR Pl.15B Inf **OH**14, Silver lace vine? A buckwheat; **TX**34, Silver lace vine—grows in swampy places.

silver lamprey n Also *silvery lamprey*

A **lamprey** (here: *Ichthyomyzon unicuspis*).

1838 Geol. Surv. OH *Second Annual Rept.* 170, Petromyzon argenteus . . *Silvery Lamprey.* **1882** U.S. Natl. Museum *Bulletin* 16.10, *Silvery Lamprey.* . . Great Lakes and Mississippi Valley. **1905** U.S. Bur. Fisheries *Rept. for 1904* 579 **OH,** The fishermen told me that "lamper eels" were "common" up the Portage River, and I often found them among the fish brought to the wholesale house from both the river and the lake. This was the so-called silvery lamprey, *Ichthyomyzon concolor.* **1947** Hubbs–Lagler *Fishes Gt. Lakes* 27, Silver lamprey. . . Generally in larger lakes and rivers. **1983** Becker *Fishes WI* 201, Silver Lamprey—*Ichthyomyzon unicuspis.* . . lamprey eel, lamper eel.

silverleaf n

1 also *silver-leaf magnolia,* ~ *umbrella tree, silver-leaved magnolia:* A **magnolia 1** (here: *Magnolia macrophylla*).

1813 Muhlenberg *Catalogus Plantarum* 53, [Magnolia] discolor . . Silver-leaved [magnolia]. **1830** Rafinesque *Med. Flora* 2.31, Bigleaf Magnolia. . . *Vulgar.* Laurel, Elk Wood, Itomico, Silverleaf. . . Leaves at the end of the branches very large . . white beneath, and bright green above. **1876** [see **2** below]. **1900** Lyons *Plant Names* 236, *M[agnolia] macrophylla.* . . Silver-leaf, Silver-leaf Umbrella-tree. **1933** Small *Manual SE Flora* 536, Great-leaf magnolia. . . Silver-leaf. **1960** Vines *Trees SW* 282, Vernacular names are Large-leaf Magnolia . . Silver-leaf, and Elk-bark. **1979** Little *Checklist U.S. Trees* 167, Large-leaf magnolia . . silverleaf magnolia [etc].

2 =pearly everlasting 1.

1830 Rafinesque *Med. Flora* 2.224, The *Gn[aphalium] margaritaceum* also called *Silver leaf, None so pretty,* is anodyne and pectoral, used in colds and coughs, pains in the breast. **1876** Hobbs *Bot. Hdbk.* 106, Silver leaf . . Stillingia sylvatica. . . Gnaphalium margaritaceum. . . Magnolia macrophylla. **1931** Harned *Wild Flowers Alleghanies* 565, A number of household names cling to it [=*Anaphalis margaritacea*], among them are Silver-leaf . . and Ladies'-tobacco.

3 A **queen's delight** (here: *Stillingia sylvatica*).

1854 King *Amer. Eclectic Dispensatory* 910, *Stillingia sylvatica.* Queen's Root. . . This plant is also known by the name of *Queen's De-*

light, *Yaw-root,* and *Silver-leaf.* . . This plant is found growing in pine-barrens and sandy soils from Virginia to Florida, and in Mississippi and Louisiana. **1876** [see **2** above]. **1901** Lounsberry *S. Wild Flowers* 303, Queen's delight. Silver-leaf. *Stillingia sylvatica.* **1974** Morton *Folk Remedies* 149 **SC,** Queen's delight; Queen's root; Yaw-root; Silver-leaf. . . The local people used to gather the roots and sell them to pharmacists for making "bitters."

4 A **buffalo berry** (here: *Shepherdia argentea*).

1890 *Century Dict.* 5634, *Silver-leaf.* . . A name of the buffalo-berry (*Shepherdia argentea*). **1976** Elmore *Shrubs & Trees SW* 32, Silver Buffaloberry . . silverleaf. . . Its leaves give the name "silver" to it, as they look as if they have been sprayed with silver on both sides. The twigs, too, are silvery gray and often spiny.

5 A **jewelweed 1** (here: *Impatiens capensis*).

1899 (1909) Earle *Child Life* 398 **NEast,** When the leaves were hung with dew it deserved its title of jewelweed, and when they were immersed in water its other pretty descriptive folk name of silver-leaf. **1903** Porter *Flora PA* 206, *Impatiens biflora.* . . Spotted Touch-me-not. Silver-leaf. **1936** Winter *Plants NE* 92, Spotted or Wild Touch-me-not. Silver-leaf. . . In moist places, open woods and along streams over most of the state.

6 also *silverleaf hydrangea:* **=hydrangea 1.**

1901 Lounsberry *S. Wild Flowers* 221, Silver Leaf. . . The early autumn breeze waved upward its still beautiful leaves and thus showed their silver-grey linings as soft and sheeny as velvet. **1942** Tehon *Fieldbook IL Shrubs* 88, The Silverleaf Hydrangea, *H. radiata* . . has been reported from two counties in the state.

7 An **honesty** (here: *Lunaria annua*). Cf **silver dollar,** ~
shilling(s)

1940 Clute *Amer. Plant Names* 226, *Lunaria biennis.* Silver-leaf.

8 A shrub of the genus *Leucophyllum,* esp *L. frutescens,* native chiefly to Texas. Also called **barometer bush, cenizo 2, whiteleaf;** for other names of *L. frutescens* see **purple sage 2**

1960 Vines *Trees SW* 920, Texas Silverleaf—*Leucophyllum frutescens.* . . Texas Silverleaf is distributed in central, western, and southwestern Texas, New Mexico, and in Mexico. *Ibid,* Lesser Texas Silverleaf—*Leucophyllum minus.* **1970** Correll *Plants TX* 1420, *Leucophyllum frutescens.* . . Cenizo, purple sage, Texas silver-leaf. *Ibid, Leucophyllum minus.* . . Big Bend silver-leaf. **1985** Dodge *Flowers SW Deserts* 111, Silverleaf. . . In southern Texas, thick patches of this shrub are sometimes found. . . Since the leaves are a light gray-green, plants appear to be ashy in color.

9 See **silverleaf maple.**

10 A **cinquefoil** (here: *Potentilla anserina*). Cf **silver-and-gold, silverweed 1**

1967 DARE Wildfl QR Pl.92B Inf **OR**12, Silverleaf.

11 =lamb's quarter(s) 1.

1968 DARE Tape **WI**30, [FW:] You remember that weed you showed me today? What were some of the names for that? [Inf:] Well, lamb's quarter, silverleaf, and pigweed, as it was called.

silver-leafed maple See **silverleaf maple**

silverleaf hydrangea See **silverleaf 6**

silver-leaf magnolia See **silverleaf 1**

silverleaf maple n Also *silverleaf, silver-leafed* (or *-leaved*)
maple
=silver maple.

1773 in 1943 Amer. Philos. Soc. *Trans.* 33.2.137 **eGA,** The Timber of this land is of an emence bulk; Chiefly Hicory[,] Ash, White & black Oak[,] Silver leaf't Maple[,] Hornbeam[,] Papaw, or Wahoo, Linden & Cane thickets. **1785** Marshall *Arbustrum* 2, Acer glaucum. *The Silver-leaved Maple.* . . The leaves . . are of a lucid green on the upper side and a bright silver colour on their under. **1837** Darlington *Flora Cestrica* 245 **sePA,** [Acer] eriocarpum. . . Silver-leaved Maple. White Maple. **1846** Browne *Trees* 95 **NY,** *Acer eriocarpum.* . . Silver Maple, Silver-leaved Maple. **1897** Sudworth *Arborescent Flora* 287 **DE, NJ,** *Acer saccharinum.* . . Silver-leaved Maple. **1950** Moore *Trees AR* 94, Silver Maple. . . Local Names: Soft, River, White, Water, and Silver-Leaved Maple. **1965–70** DARE (Qu. T14, . . *Kinds of maples*) 54 Infs, **scattered,** Silverleaf; **AR**5, 16, 32, **CA**99, **OK**7, Silverleaf maple; **WI**61, Silver-leafed maple; (Qu. T13) Inf **OR**1, Silverleaf maple; (Qu. T16, . . *Kinds of trees* . . '*special*') Infs **IA**8, **KS**16, **VA**2, Silverleaf maple.

1979 Little *Checklist U.S. Trees* 42, Silver maple. . . Other common names—soft maple, river maple, silverleaf maple. **1986** Pederson *LAGS Concordance* **Gulf Region,** 12 infs, Silverleaf maple(s).

silverleaf nightshade n Also *silver nightshade, silver-leaved nightshade*
=**trompillo.**
   1901 Mohr *Plant Life AL* 714, *Solanum elaeagnifolium.* . . Silver-leaf Nightshade. **1914** Georgia *Manual Weeds* 367, White Horse Nettle. . . *Other English names:* Prickly Nightshade, Silver-leaved Nightshade [etc]. **1936** Whitehouse *TX Flowers* 128, Purple Nightshade *(Solanum eleagnifolium)* is sometimes called silver-leaved nightshade or "trompillo." **1967** *DARE* (Qu. S21, . . *Weeds . . that are a trouble in gardens and fields)* Inf **TX1,** Silver nightshed [FW: sic]. **1979** Ajilvsgi *Wild Flowers* 259, Silver-leaf nightshade. . . plant with conspicuous, silvery pubescence mostly throughout.

silverleaf oak n Also *silver-leaved oak, silver oak*
=**whiteleaf oak.**
   1913 Wooton *Trees NM* 53, For decorative purposes perhaps the most important oak is Silver-Leaved Oak *(Quercus hypoleuca)* of the southwestern corner of the State. **1938** Van Dersal *Native Woody Plants* 347, Oak, Silver *(Quercus hypoleuca).* **1961** Douglas *My Wilderness* 86 **AZ,** The Arizona white oak is there, mixed with the silverleaf oak. **1976** Elmore *Shrubs & Trees SW* 23, Silverleaf Oak. . . This is the only one of our oaks to have silver-felt undersides on its lustrous, dark green leaves.

silverleaf poplar n Also *silverleaf popple, silver-leaved poplar*
Cf **silver poplar**
A **white poplar** (here: *Populus alba*).
   1847 Wood *Class-Book* 507, Abele or Silver-leaf Poplar. **1903** Porter *Flora PA* 98, *Populus alba.* . . White or Silver-leaf Poplar. . . In yards and along roadsides. **1917** (1923) Rogers *Trees Worth Knowing* 76, The white poplar is sometimes called the silver-leaved poplar because its dark, glossy leaves are lined with cottony nap. **1953** Strausbaugh–Core *Flora WV* 284, Silverleaf poplar. . . Frequently cultivated in West Virginia in yards and along roadsides. **1965–70** *DARE* (Qu. T12, *The kind of poplar tree that has sticky, sweet-smelling buds)* Infs **IN67, MO39, SD1, WI8,** Silverleaf poplar; **WI22,** Silverleaf popple; (Qu. T13, . . *Poplar)* Infs **KY75, MI79, MO39, TX51, 52,** Silverleaf poplar; **NM6,** Silverleaf or silver poplar.

silver-leaf umbrella tree See **silverleaf 1**

silverleaf willow n Also *silver-leaved willow* Cf **silver willow**
A **willow** of the western US (here: either *Salix exigua* or *S. sessilifolia*).
   1908 Rogers *Tree Book* 158, The Silver-leaved Willow *(Salix sessilifolia,* Nutt.), with scarcely any stem for its narrow silky-lined leaves, is a little tree that follows stream borders from Puget Sound south to the western slopes of the Sierra Nevada. **1937** U.S. Forest Serv. *Range Plant Hdbk.* B141, Most members of the genus that occur in the mountains, including silverleaf willow *(S. argophylla)* . . are distinctly shrubby in character. **1960** Vines *Trees SW* 97, Silver-leaf Willow— *Salix argophylla.* . . Also known under the vernacular name of Coyote Willow.

silver-leaved magnolia See **silverleaf 1**

silver-leaved maple See **silverleaf maple**

silver-leaved nightshade See **silverleaf nightshade**

silver-leaved oak See **silverleaf oak**

silver-leaved poplar See **silverleaf poplar**

silver-leaved willow See **silverleaf willow**

silverling n Cf **silver sage**
A **groundsel tree** (here: *Baccharis halimifolia*).
   1933 Small *Manual SE Flora* 1398, *[Baccharis] halimifolia.* . . Groundsel-tree. Silverling. **1969** *DARE* FW Addit **ceNC,** Silverling— plant common on Hatteras Island. (Genus *Baccharis).* **1974** Morton *Folk Remedies* 35 **SC,** Silverling. . . Seeds minute, bearing tufts of ¼-in.-long silvery-white hairs. The great mass of pappus is highly conspicuous, giving the tops of the plants a snowy, billowing aspect. **1977** Kibler *Simms as Naturalist* 2 **SC,** *Baccharis halimifolia,* called locally "saltwater-myrtle," "silverling," or "groundsel."

silver locust n Cf **silver chain**
=**black locust.**
   1960 Vines *Trees SW* 566, Black Locust. . . Other vernacular names are White Locust . . Silver Locust [etc].

silver lupine n
A **lupine** (here: usu *Lupinus albifrons,* but also *L. argenteus* or *L. caudatus*).
   1911 Jepson *Flora CA* 217, *[Lupinus] albifrons.* . . Silver Lupine. . . leaflets . . silvery-silky on both sides. **1937** U.S. Forest Serv. *Range Plant Hdbk.* W114, Tailcup lupine, sometimes called silver lupine, is a perennial herb. **1961** Thomas *Flora Santa Cruz* 205 **cwCA,** *[Lupinus] albifrons.* . . White-foliaged, Silver, or Bentham's Bush Lupine. Chaparral, brush-covered canyon slopes, and road embankments. **1982** *Plants SW* (Catalog) 21, Silver Lupine—*L. argenteus.* . . Silvery gray perennial.

silver maple n
Std: a **maple** *(Acer saccharinum)* whose leaves are silvery white beneath. Also called **creek maple, gray ~, hard ~, red ~, Red River ~, river ~, silverleaf ~, soft ~, sugar ~, swamp ~, water ~, white ~** Cf **branch maple**

silver minnow See **silvery minnow 1**

silver-mouthed dace (or minnow) See **silverjaw minnow**

silver muskellunge See **silver pike 2**

silver nightshade See **silverleaf nightshade**

silver oak n
1 A **flannel bush** (here: *Fremontodendron californicum*).
   1897 Sudworth *Arborescent Flora* 272 **CA,** *Fremontia.* . . Common Names. . . Silver Oak. **1908** Sudworth *Forest Trees Pacific* 382, The commonest name of *Fremontodendron californicum* is "slippery elm". . . It is also called "silver oak," because of the white undersurface of its leaves.
2 See **silverleaf oak.**

silver palm n Also *silver thatch palm* [Because the leaves are silvery white beneath]
A **fan palm** *(Coccothrinax argentata).* Also called **Biscayne-palm, bay-top palmetto, silvertop ~**
   1908 Britton *N. Amer. Trees* 134, Silver Thatch Palm. . . The leaves . . are yellow-green and shining on the upper side, silvery-white beneath, at least when young. **1929** Neal *Honolulu Gardens* 38 **HI,** Silver thatch palm, silver-leaved palmetto. . . Several silver-backed, round leaves, with folds like a fan, cluster at the end of the trunk on slender stems. **1960** McGeachy *Hdbk. FL Palms* 41, When the wind tosses their leaves it is easy to see how they came by the name of "Silver Palm". **1979** Little *Checklist U.S. Trees* 93, *Coccothrinax argentata.* . . Florida silverpalm.

silver perch n
1 also *silvery perch:* =**mademoiselle.**
   1814 in 1815 Lit. & Philos. Soc. NY *Trans.* 1.417, *Silvery Perch. (Bodianus argyro-leucos.)* With white and silvery scales. **1842** DeKay *Zool. NY* 4.74, *The Silvery Corvina.* . . This fish has so much of the port and habit of a perch, that it is frequently called *Silvery Perch* by the fishermen. **1884** Goode *Fisheries U.S.* 1.375 **NJ,** The Yellow-tail, known as "Silver Perch" on the coast of New Jersey, is quite an important food-fish in the Southern States. **1933** John G. Shedd Aquarium *Guide* 116, The Silver Perch is a small fish, abundant on the sandy shores from Long Island to Texas. **1973** Knight *Cook's Fish Guide* 384, Mademoiselle—Perch, Silver.
2 =**white crappie.** Cf **silver crappie**
   1820 *Western Rev.* 2.53, *Pomoxis annularis.* . . Vulgar names Goldring and Silver-perch. Found in August at the falls [of the Ohio River]. **1897** Johnston *Old Times GA* 144 (as of 1830s), If it was fish, all the invalid had to do, was to specify the kind, say sucker, cat-fish, eel, or perch, and if the latter, whether bream, silver, or red-belly. **1933** LA Dept. of Conserv. *Fishes* 333, More northern anglers know this fish better under the name of White Crappie. . . names it has been given [include]. . . Silver Perch [etc]. **1970** *DARE* (Qu. P1, . . *Kinds of freshwater fish . . caught around here . . good to eat)* Infs **VA75, 110,** Silver perch. [*DARE* Ed: These Infs may refer instead to **4** below.]
3 =**mojarra 1.** Cf **silver jenny**

1929 Pan-Pacific Research Inst. *Jrl.* 4.8, Gerridae. The Mojarras; Silver Perch.

4 A **white perch** (here: *Morone americana*).

1938 Schrenkeisen *Field Book Fishes* 265, White Perch. . . Common names.—Silver Perch; Sea Perch. **1976** Tryckare et al. *Lore of Sportfishing* 98, White Perch. . . Other common names: Silver perch [etc].

silver pike n

1 A **smelt** (here: *Osmerus mordax*).

1870 (1871) *Amer. Naturalist* 4.109 **NJ,** The frost-fish are occasionally seen with a few herring in the small ditches, and are known then by juvenile anglers as the "silver pike." Hearing frequent mention of silver pike, I found this to be the fish referred to. **1906** NJ State Museum *Annual Rept. for 1905* 115, *Osmerus mordax.* . . Silver Pike.

2 also *silver muskellunge:* A mutation of the **northern pike 1.** [*OED2* 1804 →]

1927 Weed *Pike* 42, Esox [spp] . . Silver Pike; Northern Michigan eastward to Georgian Bay. **1943** Eddy–Surber *N. Fishes* 169, In recent years a distinct variation . . of the northern pike has appeared in several places in northern Minnesota. This variant has the morphological characters of *E[sox] lucius* but lacks spots or other markings. . . It was named "silver muskellunge" by the fishermen, though it is undoubtedly related to *E. lucius* rather than to *E. masquinongy.* **1949** Caine *N. Amer. Sport Fish* 109, In some parts of the country, during recent years, there has appeared a pike lacking the spots and other usual markings of a true pike. . . This interloper is called Silver Pike and Silver Muskellunge but apparently it is related closer to the pike than the muskellunge. **1983** Becker *Fishes WI* 398, The silver pike is a mutation or "sport" of the northern pike. It is a solid silver or gray color, sometimes flecked with gold, and not marked like the typical northern pike.

silver pine n

Usu a **white pine** (here: *Pinus monticola*), but also **digger pine** or **ponderosa pine 1.**

1869 (1911) Muir *First Summer* 69 **eCA,** Well may this shining species be called the silver pine. **1890** *Century Dict.* 4496, Yellow pine. . . *Pinus ponderosa.* . . Also called *bull-pine, silver-pine.* **1908** Britton *N. Amer. Trees* 9, Western White Pine. . . It is also known as Silver pine, Finger-cone pine [etc]. **1923** Davidson–Moxley *Flora S. CA* 29, [*Pinus*] *sabiana.* . . Digger pine, or Silver pine. **1949** *Pacific Discovery* Jan–Feb 29, Thus we find . . "hickory pine" for bristlecone pine, and "silver pine" for western white pine. **1968–69** DARE (Qu. T17, . . *Kinds of pine trees;* not asked in early QRs) Infs **MO**20, **NY**37, 209, Silver pine.

silver plover n Cf **silverback**

=**knot** n^2.

1917 (1923) *Birds Amer.* 1.231, Knot. . . Other Names. . . Silver Plover. **1956** MA Audubon Soc. *Bulletin* 40.18 **MA,** American Knot. . . Silver Plover (Mass. Also in British provincial use).

silver poplar n Also *silver popple* Cf **silverleaf poplar**

A **white poplar** (here: *Populus alba*).

1859 (1880) Darlington *Amer. Weeds* 332, White Populus. Silver Poplar. . . Some of the grass-plats in the public squares of New York have been quite overrun by the wide-spreading suckers of this tree. **1897** Sudworth *Arborescent Flora* 137, Populus alba canescens . . *Silver Poplar.* **1940** Steyermark *Flora MO* 112, Although a very ornamental tree, the Silver Poplar has a bad name because of its habit of sending up shoots around its base. **1959** Munz–Keck *CA Flora* 910, Silver Poplar. Tree with mostly grayish-white smooth bark. **1965–70** DARE (Qu. T13, . . *Names . . for . . poplar*) 11 Infs, **scattered,** Silver poplar; **MN**38, **NY**24, **WI**37, Silver popple; (Qu. T12, *The kind of poplar tree that has sticky, sweet-smelling buds*) 10 Infs, **scattered,** Silver poplar; **ND**1, Silver popple. **1986** Pederson *LAGS Concordance,* 1 inf, **nwLA,** Silver poplar.

silverrod n

A **goldenrod 1** (here: *Solidago bicolor*). Cf **silverweed 3**

1896 *Jrl. Amer. Folkl.* 9.193 **ME,** Solidago bicolor, L., silver rod, belly-ache weed, Paris, Me. **1898** *Ibid* 11.230 **ME,** Solidago bicolor, L., white goldenrod, silver rod, South Berwick, Me. **1901** Lounsberry *S. Wild Flowers* 509, Early in the season the silver-rod first blooms and until the late autumn is a familiar figure. **1932** *Sun* (Baltimore MD) 13 Sept 6/7 (*Hench Coll.*), The golden rod and silver rod both waving a princely salute. **1941** Walker *Lookout* 53 **seTN,** In late summer a per-

son going on foot meets the silver-rod, the only known white species of goldenrod. **1953** Greene–Blomquist *Flowers South* 134, White-Goldenrod, Silver-Rod. . . The only goldenrod in our area with whitish or cream-colored flowers. **1972** Courtenay–Zimmerman *Wild Flowers* 124, Silver Rod, *Solidago bicolor.* . . Dry woods, sunny places, often rocky.

silver sage n Cf **silverling**

A **groundsel tree** (here: *Baccharis halimifolia*).

1974 Morton *Folk Remedies* 35 **SC,** Lowbush merkle . . Silverling . . Silver Sage.

silver salmon n Also *silver*

Usu =**coho salmon,** but also **chum salmon** or **sockeye salmon.**

1878 in 1880 Jackson *Alaska* 209, A silver salmon, weighing thirty-eight to forty pounds, is sold for fifteen or twenty cents. **1896** Scidmore *Appletons' Guide-Book AK* 56 **AK,** Oncorhynchus kisutch, the silver salmon, is the most beautiful of its kind and the most spirited. **1946** LaMonte *N. Amer. Game Fishes* 106, Kokanee. . . Names: Kikanniny . . Silver Salmon. This fish is found from Idaho and Oregon to Alaska. . . It is bright silver-bluish except in the breeding season. **1966** *Flathead Courier Vacation Guide* (Polson MT) Summer sec B 3/2, Silver Salmon—Silvers or kokanee tend to average around 12–14 inches with the top being in the 3¼ pound bracket. **1966–68** DARE (Qu. P1, . . *Kinds of freshwater fish . . caught around here . . good to eat*) Infs **CA**105, **WA**24, Silver salmon; **ID**4, Kokanee—this is a landlocked salmon—called silvers around Spokane; (Qu. P2, . . *Kinds of saltwater fish caught around here . . good to eat*) Infs **AK**9, **WA**22, 24, Silver salmon; **CA**105, Silvers. **1983** *NY Times* (NY) 17 Apr Travel sec 12/2 [Canadian author], Although there is only one species of Atlantic salmon, there are five Pacific salmon species. They are: sockeye (which Americans usually call red), coho (which Americans sometimes call silver), pink (both agree on this one), chum (sometimes called Keta on both sides of the border) and spring (which Americans call chinook or king). **1991** Tabbert *Dict. Alaskan Engl.* 137, Silver salmon[,] silver. . . Names used in the upper Yukon River for fall-run chum salmon. From the bright, shiny appearance of this fish, people locally call it *silver* (*salmon*), leading to potential confusion with the more general use of *silver salmon* to name the coho. **1994** Guterson *Snow Falling* 295 **nwWA,** The silvers were running in immense schools, . . mostly on the flood tide. There were fish on the ebb tide, too, though. . . it would be possible to take two hundred or more working the flood alone. *Ibid* 299, He was happy to find there were salmon coming up as well, big silvers mostly over ten and eleven pounds.

silver sea cat See **silver catfish 2**

silver seatrout See **silver trout 4**

silver shilling(s) n

An **honesty** (here: *Lunaria annua*). Cf **silver dollar, silverleaf 7**

1898 *Jrl. Amer. Folkl.* 11.222 **eMA,** Lunaria biennis. . . silver shillings. **1911** *Century Dict. Suppl.,* Silver-shilling. . . The honesty, *Lunaria annua,* so called from the large, nearly circular, shining septum of the fruit, which remains after the valves fall away. **1968** Coatsworth *ME Memories* 155, The honesty by the door is still called "silver shillings," as the bright scarlet flower is called "redcoats."

silver shiner n

A **shiner 1** (here: usu *Notropis photogenis*).

1947 Hubbs–Lagler *Fishes Gt. Lakes* 65, Silver shiner—*Notropis photogenis.* **1967** DARE (Qu. P3, *Freshwater fish that are not good to eat*) Inf **NY**6, Silver shiner. **1983** Becker *Fishes WI* 518, Common Shiner. . . Other common names: eastern shiner, redfin shiner, silver shiner. **1991** Amer. Fisheries Soc. *Common Names Fishes* 23, *Notropis photogenis.* . . silver shiner.

silverside See **silversides**

silverside fallfish See **silversides 2**

silverside mullet See **silversides 6**

silversides n Also *silverside*

1 A fish of the family Atherinidae, esp one of the genus *Menidia.* **chiefly Atlantic** For other names of *Menidia* spp see **capelin 2, friar, glass minnow, green smelt, merit-fish,**

spearing; for other names of var fish in this family see **ghost minnow, grunion, horse smelt, jack ~, minnow B2f, skipjack 1e, smelt, top smelt**

1814 in 1815 *Lit. & Philos. Soc. NY Trans.* 1.446, *Large Silverside. (Atherina mordax.)* . . A white satin-coloured riband from head to tail, along the broad side. Below that stripe, the belly silvery bright. . . *Small Silverside. (Atherina notata.)* **1839** MA Zool. & Bot. Surv. *Fishes Reptiles* 62, Atherina. . . *Boscii.* . . *The small Silver Side.* . . The several species of foreign Atherinæ, are known by the names *"Atherine," "Sand Smelts,"* and *"Anchovies,"* and are much valued as articles of food. **1862** Acad. Nat. Sci. Philadelphia *Proc. for 1861* 40 **NY**, Argyrea notata. . . "Silver-side." *Ibid*, Atherina carolina. . . "Silver-side," "Sand Smelt." **1873** in 1878 Smithsonian Inst. *Misc. Coll.* 14.2.30 **NEng**, Chirostoma notata. . . Silver-sides; friar. **1902** Jordan–Evermann *Amer. Fishes* 249, The true silversides (*Menidia*) are numerous as to species, there being about a dozen or more in our waters. **1968–70** DARE (Qu. P7, *Small fish used as bait for bigger fish*) Inf **NJ39**, Spearing—silversides; **VA47**, Silversides, cut menhaden, cut spot. **1991** Amer. Fisheries Soc. *Common Names Fishes* 35, Atherinomorus stipes . . hardhead silverside. . . Hypoatherina harringtonensis. . . reef silverside. *Ibid* 36, Membras martinica . . rough silverside.

2 also *silverside fallfish:* A **shiner 1**; see quots.

1820 Rafinesque *Ohio R. Fishes* 50, Silverside Fallfish. *Rutilus plargyrus.* . . Length from four to six inches: vulgar names, Silverside, Shiner, white Chub, &c. Common in the streams of Kentucky. **1851** (1874) Glisan *Jrl. Army Life* 88, The purer streams from the hills abound in freshwater bass, sunfish, perch, and silversides. **1902** Jordan–Evermann *Amer. Fishes* xli, For bass fishing the following . . species are superior live-bait: . . redfin or common silverside (*Notropis cornutus*) [etc]. **1906** Casey *Parson's Boys* 63 **sIL** (as of c1860), The river was soon in view, and the boys caught sight of the broad lake-like ford, where silversides were jumping out of the water after flies. **1909** DN 3.369 **eAL, wGA**, Silver-side. . . A small minnow with bright silverlike side scales. **1966–69** DARE (Qu. P3, *Freshwater fish that are not good to eat*) Inf **AL7**, Silverside—never eat—for bait; (Qu. P7, *Small fish used as bait for bigger fish*) Infs **NC1, VA33**, Silversides; **TN7**, Silversides—a kind of minnow; **MD36**, Shiner minnow, silversides—same; **GA72**, Silverside. [DARE Ed: Some of these Infs may refer instead to **1** above.] **1986** Pederson *LAGS Concordance,* 1 inf, **ceTX**, Silverside minnows; 1 inf, **seAL**, Silversides.

3 also *silverside salmon:* A fish of the family Salmonidae: usu **coho salmon,** but also **Dolly Varden 1** or **sockeye salmon. chiefly Pacific** Cf **silver salmon**

1892 *Courier-Jrl.* (Louisville KY) 2 Oct 17/8, Capt. Olsen . . while still fishing for groupers four miles off shore, hooked and landed a silverside salmon. **1920** DN 5.83 **WA**, *Silverside.* A sort of salmon. "Silverside eggs are a little smaller and are bright red." **1935** *AK Sportsman* Jan 29 (Tabbert *Dict. Alaskan Engl.*), The ubiquitous Dolly Varden is chiefly responsible for the many bizarre forms which often parade as separate species. Their tendency to change, chameleon-like in sympathy with their surroundings, has given rise to such confusing names as silver sides, silver trout [etc]. **1967** DARE (Qu. P1, . . *Kinds of freshwater fish . . caught around here . . good to eat*) Inf **WA30**, Salmon—jack salmon, silverside. **1968** DARE Tape **CA100**, You could catch trout or steelhead, silverside—they were salmon; **CA104**, Silversides—they have the same thing in Oregon. [Aux Inf:] There's a good many different breed of salmon here. **1972** Sparano *Outdoors Encycl.* 354, Kokanee Salmon—Common names: Kokanee, silver trout, . . silversides. **1978** *AK Fishing Guide* 52, Silver Salmon. . . Also called coho or silversides.

4 =**tarpon.** Cf **silverfish 1**

1935 Caine *Game Fish* 134, Tarpon. *Synonyms:* Silverfish[,] Silver King[,] Silversides.

5 A **white bass** (here: *Morone chrysops*).

1949 Caine *N. Amer. Sport Fish* 124, White Bass. . . *Colloquial Names.* . . Silver Bass[,] Silversides. **1975** Evanoff *Catch More Fish* 91, The white bass (*Roccus chrysops*) is also called the silver bass, . . silversides [etc].

6 as *silverside (mullet):* =**white mullet.**

1951 Taylor *Surv. Marine Fisheries NC* 114, Two species of mullet are caught and marketed . . in North Carolina, namely, the striped or jumping mullet . . and the white or silverside mullet (*M[ugil] curema*). . . The jumping mullet is more abundant than the silverside in North Carolina.

silverside salmon See **silversides 3**

silverskin onion n Also *silverskin, silver-skinned onion*

A cultivated **onion** n B (here: *Allium cepa* var *cepa*).

1843 (1844) Johnson *Farmer's Encycl.* 859, There are 14 distinct varieties of this vegetable. . . Silver-skinned onion . . early silver-skinned [etc]. **1863** Burr *Field & Garden* 138, The Silver-skin Onion is much esteemed in the middle and southern sections of the United States, and is cultivated to a considerable extent in New England. . . The application of the term "Silver-skin" to the common Yellow Onion, as very extensively practised by seedsmen and marketmen in the Eastern States, is neither pertinent nor authorized. **1967–70** DARE (Qu. I5, . . *Kind of onions that keep coming up without replanting year after year*) Inf **LA6**, Silver-skinned onions die down and you have to take them out; they have to be replanted; (Qu. I6, *The kind of onions that come up fresh early in the year, and you eat them raw*) Infs **CA90, VA46**, Silverskin(s); **LA6**, Silverskin—you just pull them up early; **VA40**, Silverskin—a white onion. **1990** *Seed Savers Yearbook* 136, White Portugal. . . a.k.a. Portugese [sic] Silverskin, large, thick flat onion, clear silver-white skin for pickling, bunching.

silver slipper n Cf **golden slipper 1**

A **lady's slipper 1** (here: either *Cypripedium candidum* or *C. reginae*).

1933 Small *Manual SE Flora* 367, *C[ypripedium] reginae.* . . Silverslipper. **1949** Moldenke *Amer. Wild Flowers* 384, Best known of this group is *C[ypripedium] hirsutum,* the showy ladyslipper. . . It is sometimes called the whippoorwills-shoe, silverslipper, or queens-slipper, and blooms from June to September. **1950** Correll *Native Orchids* 29, *Cypripedium candidum.* . . Common names . . Silver Slipper [etc]. *Ibid* 39, *Cypripedium reginae.* . . Common names . . Silver-slipper.

silver snake See **silver boa**

silver spruce n

Usu =**blue spruce,** but also Engelmann **spruce** or Sitka **spruce.**

1869 Bowles *New West* 106, The silver spruce is the one gem of the trees; a sort of first cousin of the evergreen we call the balsam fir in our New England yards. **1892** Apgar *Trees Nth. U.S.* 181, *Picea pungens.* . . (Silver Spruce). . . From the Rocky Mountains. **1908** Britton *N. Amer. Trees* 60, Blue Spruce—*Picea pungens.* . . Also called Colorado blue spruce, . . silver spruce [etc]. **1966–68** DARE (Qu. T5, . . *Kinds of evergreens, other than pine*) Infs **AK9, CA53, CO39, OH78, PA162**, Silver spruce; **IL50**, Silver spruce—a fancy name for spruce. **1972** Viereck–Little *AK Trees* 54, Sitka Spruce. . . Other names: tideland spruce, . . silver spruce [etc]. **1979** Little *Checklist U.S. Trees* 185, Engelmann spruce. . . Other common names—Columbian spruce, mountain spruce, silver spruce [etc].

silver tea n

A social event held as a fund-raiser; see quots.

1894 *Banner of Gold* 28 Apr 264/2 (*Mathews Coll.*), The last thing we had was a Keeley Silver Tea, and it was given just like a complimentary entertainment. . . At the door each guest was met by a young lady with a silver basket, and they could drop in any amount they wished in silver coins. **1942** *Sun* (Baltimore MD) 18 May 12/7 (*Hench Coll.*), "Silver tea" means merely that everyone on arriving pays an admission of silver by putting 10 cents, 25 cents, 50 cents or a silver dollar . . into a collection plate or box or basket. The proceeds are afterward given to whatever the tea was for. The tea service—or services—are likely to be of silver, but they may equally well be . . of anything else. **1968–69** DARE (Qu. W32, . . *A group of women that meet to sew together*) Inf **NY219**, Silver tea—a church affair; (Qu. FF1, . . *A kind of group meeting called a 'social' or 'sociable'. . . [What goes on?]*) Inf **NY48**, Silver tea—tea party to raise money; (Qu. FF2, . . *Kinds of parties*) Inf **DE2**, Silver teas—silver serving dishes and you contribute silver to help the church; **GA81**, Silver teas—to raise money; (Qu. FF3, . . *'Showers' or 'gift parties'*) Inf **GA75**, Silver tea—to raise money. **1975** DARE File (as of c1917), *Silver tea*—I knew these in Massachusetts, WWI period. Church groups had them to raise money. Everyone contributed silver coins. (And I expect any one who had a silver tea set used it!)

silver thatch palm See **silver palm**

silver thaw n [DCan 1770 →] esp **OR, WA**

A freezing rain; see quots.

1936 Adams *Cowboy Lingo* 203 **West**, A 'silver thaw' was rain that froze as it hit. **1956** in 1965 *Perrin Coll.* **OR, WA**, *Silver thaw*—In western Oregon and Washington the usual term for a freezing rain, a storm in which ice forms on branches and wires. **1967** *DARE* FW Addit **WA29,** *Silver thaw*—ice formed on trees from freezing rain. A killing frost; **OR,** *Silver thaw*—rain followed by heavy freeze (followed by chinook—warm wind that thaws). Gets heavy on branches and might break them off. **1979** *NYT Article Letters* **cwWA,** "Silver thaw," called in the East "ice storm," when water freezes on trees and bushes. "Silver thaw" is a term used in both Oregon and Washington. **1980** *DARE* File **Portland OR,** During the silver thaw we could hear the trees cracking during the night. We lost all the tops out of our fir trees. **1982** *Smithsonian Letters,* Some N.W. regionalisms—silver thaw = Freezing rain that coats everything with clear (silver) Ice.

silvertip n

1 also *silvertip grizzly, silver-tipped bear:* A **grizzly bear** (here: usu *Ursus arctos horribilis,* but also *U. a. middendorffi*), usu one with white-tipped hairs.

1880 *Rept. Supt. Yellowstone Natl. Pk.* 40 *(DA),* Silver-tipped bear.— This animal is nearly destitute of a mane, and is somewhat smaller, less powerful and ferocious than the true grizzly. **1886** *Turf Field & Farm* 26 Mar 238 **seOR,** A silver tip is bad enough when he's wounded, and about as active a bear as there is. **1889** *Harper's New Mth. Mag.* 78.876, In western America there are two bears that claim the sportsman's attention—the grizzly and the black. The former, hunters have endowed with many aliases, such as "silver-tip," "brown," "cinnamon," "bald-face," and "range" bear. These names do not mean anything, for the grizzly, like the dog, is of many colors. **1907** White *AZ Nights* 47, It seemed that he was out for big game, and intended to go after silvertips somewhere in these very mountains. **1917** Anthony *Mammals Amer.* 91, With regard to color, Grizzlies show considerable variety. . . The standard color (in winter) is brown next to the skin, the extremities of the hair being tipped with silvery gray, from which has come the common name of "Silver-tip." *Ibid* 96 **AK,** Suddenly he came face to face with a 'Silver-tip' (the local name for the Kodiak). **1935** Davis *Honey* 138 **OR,** The next likeliest possibility was a bear, though it would have to be a big one to make all that racket and a mean one not to be more cautious. An old silver-tip, maybe. **1939** *AK Sportsman* Apr 25 (Tabbert *Dict. Alaskan Engl.*), He looked in that direction, too, and saw a big silvertip grizzly coming down the mountainside. *Ibid* 26, Early next morning the three of us took up the trail of the silvertip and followed him a mile or so down the river. **1984** Davis *Be Tough* 184, They had called him a "real silver tip" but I knew there is no separate species of silver tip grizzlies. They're simply a bear in one of his seasonal color phases, when his fur is prime and the silver guard hair is predominant.

2 =**red fir b.**

1949 Peattie *Cascades* 203 **Pacific NW,** The red firs are highly prized for Christmas trees under the name of silver-tips, and they fetch fantastic prices. **1958** McCulloch *Woods Words* 165 **Pacific NW,** *Silver tip.* . . A young Shasta red fir. **1969** *DARE* (Qu. T17, . . *Kinds of pine trees;* not asked in early QRs) Inf **CA113,** Silvertip. **1980** Little *Audubon Guide N. Amer. Trees W. Region* 254, California Red Fir. . . "Silvertip."

silvertip grizzly See silvertip 1

silver-tipped bear See silvertip 1

silver top See silver bell 2

silvertop palmetto n

A thatch palm (here: *Thrinax morrisii*) or **silver palm.**

1884 Sargent *Forests of N. Amer.* 218 **FL,** *Thrinax argentea.* . . Silvertop Palmetto. Brickley Thatch. Brittle Thatch. Semi-tropical Florida. **1901** Lounsberry *S. Wild Flowers* 31 **FL,** *T[hrinax] microcarpa,* silvertop palmetto, or brittle thatch . . is more frequently seen than any other palm on the keys of south Florida. **1908** Britton *N. Amer. Trees* 121 **FL,** The Silver-top Palmetto (*T[hrinax] microcarpa,* Sarg.) has its leaves coated when they unfold with dense white down. . . It inhabits No Name and Bahio Hondo Keys, south of Florida. **1979** Little *Checklist U.S. Trees* 285, *Thrinax morrisii.* . . Other common names—silvertop palmetto [etc].

silver trout n

1 =**cutthroat trout.**

1871 (1872) Kneeland *Wonders Yosemite* 64 **neCA,** Both these lakes are noted for their silver trout, which attain the weight of 20 pounds, and test the skill of the angler to the utmost. **1873** Hallock *Fishing Tourist* 30, To the above should be added the . . brook-trout, the silver-trout, and

the . . salmon-trout—these varieties peculiar to California. **1876** (1877) Williams *Pacific Tourist* 218 **neCA,** The silver trout are most highly esteemed, are always taken in deep water, and attain a size of thirty-two pounds. The silver trout of Donner Lake grow from eight to ten pounds, and those in the river are not so large. **1884** Goode *Fisheries U.S.* 1.475, *The Black spotted Trout.* . . This fish is known as the "Trout," . . "Silver Trout," etc., in the mountains, but when in the ocean, full grown, as "Salmon Trout" or "Steel-head." **1946** LaMonte *N. Amer. Game Fishes* 115, Lake Tahoe Cut-throat. . . Names: Lake Tahoe Trout, Silver Trout of Lake Tahoe [etc]. **1968** *DARE* (Qu. P1, . . *Kinds of freshwater fish . . caught around here . . good to eat*) Inf **NV8,** Silver trout.

2 =**rainbow trout.**

1976 *DARE* File **Isle Royale MI,** A silver trout is the same as a salmon trout. **1983** Becker *Fishes WI* 298, Rainbow Trout. . . Other common names . . silver trout [etc].

3 The arctic char (*Salvelinus alpinus*).

1850 *Amer. Whig Rev.* 11.43, The *silver trout,* a common trout, is found in almost all of our swift running northern streams, and weighs from one to fifteen pounds. **1903** NY State Museum & Sci. Serv. *Bulletin* 278, Salvelinus alpinus aureolus. . . *Sunapee Trout; Golden Trout; Silver Trout.* **1905** U.S. Bur. Fisheries *Rept. for 1904* 104 **ME,** Attempts were made to secure specimens of the Floods Pond saibling, locally known as silver trout, supposed to be *Salvelinus aureolus.*

4 also *silver seatrout:* A **weakfish** (here: usu *Cynoscion nothus*).

1935 Caine *Game Fish* 145, Spotted Weakfish—*Cynoscion nebulosus.* . . *Synonyms:* Salmon . . Silver Trout [etc]. **1939** Natl. Geogr. Soc. *Fishes* 82, The bastard, or silver, trout (*Cynoscion nothus*) . . found from Chesapeake Bay to Texas. **1966** WI Acad. *Trans.* 55.127 **LA,** *C[ynoscion] nothus* . . silver seatrout. **1991** Amer. Fisheries Soc. *Common Names Fishes* 54, *Cynoscion nothus* . . silver seatrout.

5 =**Dolly Varden 1.**

1935 [see **silversides 3**].

6 =**sockeye salmon.**

1939 Natl. Geogr. Soc. *Fishes* 287 **cwWA,** These landlocked red salmon, or redfish, may be caught in Lake Washington, at Seattle. . . While in the lake they pass under the name of "silver trout" but by the time of the first autumn rain or even before, the "silver trout" find their way to the mouths of streams that flow into this lake. **1949** Peattie *Cascades* 325 **cWA,** There are cutthroat, rainbow, and silver trout (landlocked blueback salmon) in its depths.

silverweed n

1 also *silverweed cinquefoil:* A **cinquefoil** (here: *Potentilla anserina*). [*OED2* 1578 →] Also called **cramp weed, goose grass 1c** Cf **silver-and-gold, silverleaf 10**

1824 Bigelow *Florula Bostoniensis* 203 **MA,** Potentilla anserina. . . *Silver Weed.* . . A handsome plant common on the marshes at South Boston and Cambridge. **1876** Hobbs *Bot. Hdbk.* 45, Grass, Goose, Silverweed, Potentilla anserina. **1934** Haskin *Wild Flowers Pacific Coast* 184, Silver-Weed. . . This is the "cinquefoil" that holds so prominent a place in the tales and myths of the Coast Indians from Oregon to British Columbia. **1961** Douglas *My Wilderness* 251 **ME,** A new friend known as silverweed cinquefoil . . has yellow flowers reminiscent of its western cousins. But the leaves are sharply toothed, silver-colored underneath, and covered with soft, silky hairs. **1969** *DARE* (Qu. I28b, *Kinds of greens that are cooked*) Inf **MA15,** Silverweed.

2 A **jewelweed 1** (here: either *Impatiens capensis* or *I. pallida*).

1893 *Jrl. Amer. Folkl.* 6.139 **NY,** *Impatiens pallida,* silver weed. *Ibid, Impatiens fulva.* . . silver weed. **1910** Graves *Flowering Plants* 274 **CT,** Spotted Touch-me-not. Snap-weed. Silver Weed.

3 A **goldenrod 1** (here: *Solidago bicolor*). Cf **silverrod**

1894 *Jrl. Amer. Folkl.* 7.92 **NY,** *Solidago bicolor* . . silver-weed.

4 A **meadow rue** (here: *Thalictrum pubescens*). Cf **quicksilver weed**

1896 *Jrl. Amer. Folkl.* 9.180 **cME,** *Thalictrum polygamum.* . . silver weed, musquash weed, celandine, Oxford County.

silverweed cinquefoil See silverweed 1

silver willow n

Any of several **willows,** but esp **pussy willow** n[1]. Cf **silver-leaf willow**

1897 Sudworth *Arborescent Flora* 122 **CA,** *Salix sessilifolia*. . . Silver Willow. *Ibid* 124 **KS,** *Salix discolor*. . . Silver Willow. **1910** Jepson *Silva CA* 181, *Salix macrocarpa* Nutt. var. *argentea* Bebb. Silver Willow. **1938** Van Dersal *Native Woody Plants* 361, Willow, . . Silver *(Salix argyrocarpa, Salix discolor, Salix geyeriana)*. **1968** *DARE* (Qu. T15, . . *Kinds of swamp trees*) Inf NY109, Silver willow. **1972** Viereck–Little *AK Trees* 115, Silver Willow *(Salix candida)*. *Ibid* 116, Silver willow is a rare shrub in Alaska, having been collected only a few times in bogs and other wet sites along the Tanana and Yukon Rivers. The silvery appearance of leaves, twigs, and catkins, and the narrow leaf shape give it a characteristic appearance. **1979** Little *Checklist U.S. Trees* 262, Geyer willow. . . Other common name—silver willow.

silvery catfish See **silver catfish 1**

silvery gar See **silver gar**

silvery lamprey See **silver lamprey**

silvery minnow n

1 also *silver minnow:* A **minnow B1,** esp *Hybognathus nuchalis*.

1882 U.S. Natl. Museum *Bulletin* 16.156, H[ybognathus] nuchalis. . . Silvery Minnow. . . A graceful minnow, abundant in most streams from New Jersey to the Upper Missouri and southward. **1906** NJ State Museum *Annual Rept. for 1905* 127, *Hybognathus nuchalis regius*. . . Gudgeon. Silvery Minnow. **1929** OK Univ. Biol. Surv. *Pub.* 91, *Hybognathus nuchalis*. . . Silver minnow. **1957** Trautman *Fishes* 396, Western Silvery Minnow—*Hybognathus nuchalis nuchalis*. **1983** *Audubon Field Guide N. Amer. Fishes* 419, Mississippi Silvery Minnow *(Hybognathus nuchalis)*. . . Western Silvery Minnow *(H. argyritis)*. . . Eastern Silvery Minnow *(H. regius)*.

2 A **shiner 1** (here: *Notropis hudsonius*).

1906 NJ State Museum *Annual Rept. for 1905* 141, *Notropis hudsonius amarus*. . . Gudgeon. . . Silvery Minnow. **1973** Allen *LAUM* 1.331 (as of c1950) 1 inf, **MN,** Silvery minnows.

silvery perch See **silver perch 1**

simarron See **cimarron**

simball See **cymbal**

simblin See **cymling**

simblin-head See **cymling-head**

similar adj Usu |ˈsɪmələ(r)|; also, perh infl by such words as *regular, singular* |ˈsɪmjulər, ˈsɪmjələr|; also, prob infl by such words as *familar, peculiar* |sɪˈmɪlɪjər| Pronc-spp *similiar, simular;* hence *similiarity* [Cf *OED2* (at *simular*) "Some examples (in the 17th and 18th cents.) of *simular, simularity, simularly,* in the sense of *similar,* etc., are app. mere misprints or individual errors."]

Std sense, var forms.

1777 in 1933 Washington *Writings* 8.53 **VA,** Their appearance has convinced me fully of the danger which I always apprehended from the Similiarity of their Uniform to that of the British Horse. **1782** in 1938 *Ibid* 24.487 **VA,** Non commissioned officers and soldiers who have served with equal reputation more than six years are to be distinguished by two pieces of cloth set in parallel to each other in a simular form. **1838** *S. Lit. Messenger* 4.633, The products of the industry of those States, are, in general, similiar to those of the rest of the civilized world. **1869** *Stranger's Guide Boston* 68 **MA,** You . . can have an opportunity to see . . the Pratt estate, and numerous others of simular beauty and costliness. **1876** Gray *Darwiniana* 175, We also advise against a similar credulity on the other side. **1912** *DN* 3.589 **wIN,** Simular. . . Similar. **1922** *DN* 5.135 **NE** [Intentional mispronunciations], There is consonant insertion as well as vowel change in *vilyan* for *villain*, *simular*, . . etc. **1939** in Lib. of Congress *Amer. Memory: WPA Life Hist.* (Internet) **IL,** But in Robbins the top functionary is never alluded to as "The President of the Board," as is customary in towns of similiar size. **1940** in 1944 *ADD* **NY,** Similar. . . [ˈsɪmjələr]. **1968–70** *DARE* (Qu. KK65, . . *'The same sort'*: "If you like Bob, I'm sure you'll like his brother—they're _____.") Inf **KS**18, Similar [sɪmjələ]; **KY**92, Similiar; **NY**205, Very similar [ˈsɪmjuˈlɚ]. **1968** *DARE* FW Addit **GA**25, *"Similar"* consistently pronounced [sɪˈmɪlɪjɚ].

simlin(g) See **cymling**

simlin-head See **cymling-head**

simmer down on v phr

See quot 1933.

1933 *AmSp* 8.1.52 **Ozarks,** Simmer down on. . . To concentrate upon, to specialize in, to devote one's entire attention to. A famous *gigger* of fish once told me: *I'm a-goin' t' simmer down on suckers from now on, an' let them dang linesides go!* **1954** Harder *Coll.* **cwTN,** Simmer down on. . . To concentrate upon, to specialize in.

'simmern See **persimmon**

simmetery See **cemetery**

'simmon See **persimmon**

'simmon bull n

The larva of the **royal walnut moth.**

1938 Brimley *Insects NC* 266, The larva is known as the "hickory devil" or "simmon bull" and feeds on cotton, hickory, sweet gum, walnut, pecan, persimmon, sourwood, Paulownia.

simmy n [Cf *SND simmy* v. "To mope about, wander around in an aimless indolent manner."]

1968 *DARE* FW Addit **LA**15, Simmy [ˈsɪmɪ]—a weakling, one lacking in spirit or vigor. (Comparing the sporting qualities of black crappie, which fights hard, and white crappie, which gives up easily.) "That white one, he's a simmy."

simon See **salmon**

‡**Simon's off-ox** n Cf **Adam's off-ox 2**

1958 *VT Hist.* 26.286, Older than Simon's off ox.

simple adj [*OED2 simple* a. A.1 c1220 →]

Sincere, unassuming.

1949 Webber *Backwoods Teacher* 158 **Ozarks,** "I don't know how smart you are, but Pa taken to you—an' in this trouble we're in now, I feel like yo're right simple." It was obviously a compliment. It was some time before I learned that in a general way it meant "good-hearted" and the opposite of "uppity."

Simpson honey plant n

A **figwort 1** (here: *Scrophularia marylandica*).

1948 Stevens *KS Wild Flowers* 193, Plants of this species yield enough nectar in some seasons and localities to add appreciably to the honey crop, and among apiarists the common name for the species is Simpson honey plant.

simular See **similar**

sin n

Illicit sexual relations—usu in v phr *have sin* to engage in illicit sexual relations.

1928 Peterkin *Scarlet Sister Mary* 35 **SC** [Gullah], May-e, you an' July is been a-havin sin, enty? **1939** Griswold *Sea Is. Lady* 176 **sSC** [Gullah], I sho ain' gwine allow no gal [=unmarried daughter] of mine fuh hab sin. *Ibid* 788, Planty gal hab sin an' chile at breas' befo' milk dry 'pon dey own mout'.

since adv, prep, conj Pronc-spp *sence, sense*

A Forms.

1795 Dearborn *Columbian Grammar* 138, *List of Improprieties*. . . Sense for Since. **1871** Eggleston *Hoosier Schoolmaster* 83 **sIN,** Felt that way ever sence they put my father into the graveyard. **1890** Holley *Samantha among Brethren* 187 **NY,** That wuz some 10 years prior and before this, and she had gone round sewin' ever sense. **1899** (1912) Green *VA Folk-Speech* 375, Sence. . . Since. **1905** *DN* 3.18 **cCT,** Sence. . . Since. **1906** *DN* 3.155 **nwAR,** Sence [sɛnts]. . . Since. "It happened sence then." **1907** *DN* 3.217 **nwAR,** Sence, adv., prep., conj. Since. **1909** *DN* 3.367 **eAL, wGA,** Sence, adv., prep., conj. Since. **1912** *DN* 3.589 **wIN,** Sence, adv., conj., and prep. Since. Very common. **1922** Gonzales *Black Border* 325 **sSC, GA coasts** [Gullah glossary], Sence—since. **1923** *DN* 5.220 **swMO,** Sence, adv. Since. **1927** *AmSp* 3.140 **eME,** "Sence" (since) "narves" and "narvous," "duberous" (dubious) were often heard. **1943** *AmSp* 18.264 **VA,** The lowering of [ɪ] to [ɛ] is fairly common throughout the state in words like *since*. **1989** Pederson *LAGS Tech. Index* 365 **Gulf Region,** [Of 914 primary infs, 708 offered proncs of the type [sıns, sınts]; 86 offered proncs of the type [sens, sents].]

B As conj.

Provided that.

1965 Brewer *Worser Days* 57 **NC** [Black], De woman say, "I don't care who it be, Lord, just since it's a man."

since God was a little boy See **God was a little boy, since**

since Hector was a pup See **Hector 1**

since the hog et grandma See **hogs ate my brother up, since the**

sinch n See **cinch** n¹ **1, 3**

sinch v See **cinch** v **5**

sinche See **cinch** n¹ **1**

sind See **send 1**

sing v

A Gram forms.

1 pres: usu *sing;* rarely *sang.*   Cf Pronc Intro 3.1.6.d

1993 Mason *Feather Crowns* 355 **KY,** "I reckon that's how we got all our songs," said the middle one. "Big, did Mama sang that last song we sanged?"

2 past: usu *sang, sung;* rarely *sanged, sing(ed), singt, sunged.*

1884 *Anglia* 7.253 [Black], To the regular forms of the Irregular verbs as used by the whites, the Negro adds the following forms of his own. . . *Pres.* sing—*Past.* sing, singed, sunged, singt—*Pass. Part.* sing. **1910** *DN* 3.448 **cwNY,** Sing, pret. of *sing.* "I set there and *sing* for an hour." **1940** in Lib. of Congress *Amer. Memory: WPA Life Hist.* (Internet) **FL** [Black], She say you want to know bout mah life an do [sic] songs whut us sanged in de Slavery time.   **1993** [see **A1** above].

3 past pple: usu *sung;* rarely *sing.*

1884 [see **A2** above].

B Sense.

Of a rattlesnake: to rattle; hence vbl n *singing.*

1937 *Hall Coll.* **wNC, eTN,** Sing. . . Rattle (of a rattlesnake). "Hit was intentioned to bite me. I never heerd a snake sing so vigorous." **1966** *DARE* Tape **FL16,** They sing with their rattlers and they coil and they'll strike.   **1967** Fetterman *Stinking Creek* 119 **seKY,** Snakes is the worst at berrypicking time. They'll sit in the bushes, and sometimes you can't even hear a rattlesnake singing.   **1995** *Brophy Coll.* 67 **swMO** (as of c1960), Singing. [T]he buzzing or rattling of a rattlesnake.

sing n *among Black speakers; arch*

A song.

1867 Allen *Slave Songs* **seSC** xvii, 'Den I made a sing, just puttin' a word, and den anudder word.' . . Then he began singing, and the men, after listening a moment, joined in the chorus as if it were an old acquaintance. . . I saw how easily a new 'sing' took root among them. **1883** (1971) Harris *Nights with Remus* 256 **GA** [Black], 'E mek up one sing in 'e head, un 'e l'arn da lilly gal fer answer da sing. [Footnote:] "'E mek up one sing." She composed a song and taught the child the refrain.   **c1937** in 1972 *Amer. Slave* 2.1.116 **SC,** That wus a sing we used to have on the plantation.

singe cat See **singed cat**

singed See **sing** v **A2**

singed cat n Also *singe cat, singed colt, swinge(d) cat* [From the proverbial simile *like a singed cat, better than it looks* and varr]   Cf **ash-cat 1, swinge**

Someone or something having a shabby or unprepossessing appearance, esp when such an appearance is misleading.

1836 *Spirit of Times* 9 Apr. 61/1 *(OED2),* Without our Jersey friends bring on a 'singed cat,' or some nag, now outside the fence, turns up a trump, the above comprise the entries for the 4 mile day.   **1842** *Spirit of Times* 2 Apr 54 *(AmSp* 40.180), There is a rumor current that this two-mile horse has gone to Canada. . He will turn out 'a singed colt' to any one who picks him up for 'a sucker.'   **1857** *S. Lit. Messenger* 25.305 **cVA,** A superficial view of him would lead you to believe that Delaware had little or no more gumption than the law allows. But don't be too certain about this. Physically and intellectually, he is a Singe Cat.   **1875**

(1876) Twain *Tom Sawyer* 20 **MO,** I reckon you're a kind of a singed cat, as the saying is—better'n you look.   **1892** *KS Univ. Qrly.* 1.98 **KS,** Singed cat: a shrewd 'rustler,' of unpretentious appearance.   **1899** (1912) Green *VA Folk-Speech* 388, Singed-cat. . . A cat disfigured with burnt fur; hence, a person of unprepossessing appearance—different from what he looks.   **1909** *S. Atl. Qrly.* 8.47 **seSC,** The description of an humorously wretched object, or person of ill and unprepossessing appearance, as *a swinge-cat, i.e., a singed cat,* is graphic.   **1914** *DN* 4.113 **cKS,** Swinged. . . Singed; as, a swinged cat.

singer See **swinger**

singing vbl n See **sing** v **B**

singing n

1 also *singing bee;* pronc-sp *sanging:* A social gathering devoted to singing, esp of hymns.   **chiefly Sth, S Midl**   Cf **all-day singing**

1859 (1922) Jackson *Col.'s Diary* 17 **PA,** I was at a singing at the Woodward church.   **1887** (1967) Harris *Free Joe* 117 **GA,** Mr. Peevy simply asked me to tell Miss Babe that there would be a singing at Philadelphia campground Sunday.   **1906** Johnson *Highways Missip. Valley* 130 **Ozarks,** It was customary in the neighborhood to have frequent "singings." The young people assemble at one home or another for the purpose nearly every Saturday night. . . The house [this night] was packed, and for two hours I heard the participants singing Gospel Hymns with loud, uncultured, unabashed voices.   **1915** *DN* 4.228 **wTX,** Singing. . . A musicale. "Going to the singing to-night?"   **1923** *DN* 5.221 **swMO,** Singin,' . . A social gathering where the chief form of entertainment is the singing of hymns.   **1934** Carmer *Stars Fell on AL* 49, Ain't seen him since the singin' down at Samanthy.   **1963** Hostetler *Amish Soc.* 255, The accepted occasion for association among Amish young people is the "singing" held on Sunday evening in the same home where preaching was held in the forenoon. The traditional singing takes the form of sitting around a long table with boys on one side and girls on the other.   **1966–70** *DARE* (Qu. FF1, . . *A kind of group meeting called a 'social' or 'sociable'.* . . *[What goes on?]*) Inf **TX33,** All-day singings and eating on the ground; **AL5,** Singing—on the fourth Sunday in May, people boarded a local train to go about 30 miles . . to a 'singing'; **WV1,** Singings—one person leads, then another; (Qu. FF2, . . *Kinds of parties*) Inf **VA42,** Singing bees—old-fashioned—church event, though not necessarily.   **1968** *Budget* (Sugarcreek OH) 25 July 10/2, A singing last night.   **1971** *Foxfire* 5.102 **nGA,** When you'd have a singin', you'd usually have a group of people get together and sing and have refreshments.   **1986** Pederson *LAGS Concordance,* 1 inf, **cnGA,** We'd have singings at somebody's house; *(A dance)* 1 inf, **nwFL,** A singing on Saturday night; 1 inf, **csMS,** A singing—singing sacred songs in house.   **2000** *DARE* File **seKY** (as of c1950), Sanging—(Singing) "Are you going to the Sanging tonight?"

2 See **singing convention.**

3 See **singing school.**

singing-all-day See **all-day singing**

singing bee See **singing 1**

singing bird n

=**mockingbird 1.**

1966–70 *DARE* (Qu. Q14, . . *Names* . . *for* . . *mockingbird*) Infs **KY11, MS11, 81, VA7, 38,** Singing bird.

singing convention n Also *singing (match)*   **chiefly Sth, S Midl**

A meeting or festival devoted to singing, often involving a competition.

1906 *DN* 3.156 **nwAR,** Singing convention. . . A festival at which there is singing and the discussion of subjects pertaining to vocal music. "One of the most enjoyable occasions we ever witnessed was at Shady Grove last Sunday in the way of a singing convention and dinner on the ground."   **1909** *DN* 3.370 **eAL, wGA,** Singing convention. . . A singing festival.   **1927** *DN* 5.477 **Ozarks,** Singing convention. . . A competitive meeting of the local singers. These gatherings were formerly called singing matches, but the term *convention* is regarded as more dignified.   **1940** in Lib. of Congress *Amer. Memory: FSA/OWI* (Internet) **NM,** [Caption:] President of the singing convention. He is also a homesteader, on the right presenting the banner to Mr. Whinnery as representative of one group of the contesting singers. Pie Town, New Mexico.   *Ibid,* [Caption:] A group of singers from Quemado who are competing for the

Catron County championship at the Pie Town, New Mexico, singing convention. **1967** *Asheville Citizen* (NC) 20 May sec 2 16/8, An Old Time Singing Convention Saturday . . will benefit the Buncombe County unit, American Cancer Society. **1967** *DARE* FW Addit **LA,** A singing or singing convention—usually on the last Sunday of each month. People from the parish get together for gospel singing. Occasionally there is a Tri-Parish singing convention. **1968** *DARE* (Qu. FF1, . . *A kind of group meeting called a 'social' or 'sociable'. . . [What goes on?]*) Inf **MO34,** Singing convention. **c1970** *DARE* File **neTX,** "Sunday we had a fine singing." An event, well advertised and attended by hundreds of people. The singers, almost all untrained, sit together in a bandstand and entertain the crowd for hours. Usually it is a capella; sometimes leaders use harmonicas; sometimes tuning fork used to set the pitch. **2000** *DARE* File—Internet **MS,** Pearl River South Singing Convention—This event brings together singers from four African-American churches in southern Mississippi's rural Marion and Walthall Counties. **2001** *Ibid* **NC,** Welcome to the 81 th [sic] State Annual Singing Convention and Talent Search . . Benson NC. *Ibid* **PA,** Pennsylvania State Singing Convention . . Elysburg, PA.

singing duck n [Because of its varied notes]
=old-squaw.

1923 U.S. Dept. Ag. *Misc. Circular* 13.24 **AK,** Old-squaw. . . Vernacular Names. . . *In local use.* . . singing duck. **1982** Elman *Hunter's Field Guide* 232, Oldsquaw. . . Common & Regional Names: longtail . . singing duck [etc.].

singing fish n [Because the male makes a humming sound]
A **midshipman** (here: *Porichthys notatus*).

1884 Goode *Fisheries U.S.* 1.253, The *Batrachidae* are represented on the Pacific coast by the "Singing-fish" or "Toad-fish," *Porichthys porosissimus*. **1939** Natl. Geogr. Soc. *Fishes* 220, The name "singing fish" is appropriate, . . for the creatures produce a peculiar humming sound during the breeding season. **1998** Cornell Univ. *News Serv.* 25 June (Internet), Called midshipman fish because some varieties of *Porichthys notatus* have bioluminescent spots that resemble rows of uniform buttons, they are also known as California singing fish and canary bird fish.

singing match See **singing convention**

singing school n Also *singing*
A class or meeting in which singing and the rudiments of music are taught, esp the reading of musical notation.

1723 *New-Engl. Courant* (Boston MA) 1 Apr 2/2, The Singing-School in that Place is broken up by Order of the Select Men. **1835** *New Engl. Mag.* 9.121, The 'ear-piercing' harmonies of a choir of fifty-three singing-school children. **1857** (1930) DeLong *Jrls.* 9.131 **NY,** Got home about 9 oclock at night; then went to singing school but did not stay long. **1877** Bartlett *Americanisms* 595, *Singing.* In Pennsylvania, a singing-school. **1900** *Amer. Missionary* 54.69 **AL,** The teachers visit the people in their cabin homes, hold mothers' meetings . . a literary society and singing-school. **1903** *DN* 2.329 **seMO,** *Singing.* . . Singing school. 'There will be a singin to-night.' **1907** *DN* 3.236 **nwAR,** *Singin'.* . . Singing-school. **1939** in Lib. of Congress *Amer. Memory: WPA Life Hist.* (Internet) **NE** (as of 1880s), We had a fine choir . . and they all had attended singing schools. It cost a dollar apiece to attend a term of singing school. A capable person would conduct it. . . He would use the black board for teaching us to read the notes and time. We really became quite good sight readers and learned the rudiments of music. **1956** Hall *Coll.* **wNC, eTN,** *Singin' schools.* . . In churches we had singin' schools. **1968–69** *DARE* (Qu. FF1, . . *A kind of group meeting called a 'social' or 'sociable'. . . [What goes on?]*) Inf **PA135,** Singing school; (Qu. FF22a, . . *Clubs and societies . . for women*) Inf **MA73,** Singing schools—years past; (Qu. FF22b, . . *Clubs and societies . . for men*) Inf **MA73,** Singing schools—years past. **1969** *DARE* Tape **IL55,** When my father was a boy, he had an older brother-in-law who taught singing school at night in schoolhouses. . . Those who wanted to learn to read music paid a fee. **1986** Pederson *LAGS Concordance,* 1 inf, **cnAL,** His father taught singing school. **2000** *DARE* File—Internet **VA,** The Potomac River Sacred Harp Singers Present All-Day Singing School. . . [The singing master] has taught three 4-shape Singing Schools and one 7-shape Singing School.

sing jawbone See **jawbone** n 2

single balsam n Cf **double balsam fir**
See quot.

1986 *DARE* File **cnWI,** People always say that they want a double

balsam for a Christmas tree. The double balsam refers to balsams that grow in optimal conditions; in full sun. The needles grow all the way around the branch. You can have double and single balsam all on the same tree. If it's a tall, mature tree, the top will be double because it gets the sun and the lower branches will have needles growing on two sides of the twig, giving it a flat look.

single-barreled See **single-fire**

single-bitting n Cf **double-bitting, single jack**
1967 *DARE* FW Addit **neOR,** Single-bitting—one man working both hammer and spike.

single dory n
A **dory** n[2] intended to be handled by one person.

1884 U.S. Natl. Museum *Bulletin* 27.680, This schooner carries twenty "single" dories, each of these being 13 feet long on the bottom. **1890** *Century Dict.* 5646, A *single* dory (a boat manned by one person). **1952** (1973) Thomas *Fast & Able* 13 **neMA,** They set their trawls from single dories (one man to a dory) and fished from the nearby banks from Georges to Brown's off the southern tip of Nova Scotia.

single-fire adj, also used absol Also *single-barreled* **West** Cf **double-barrel(ed), double-fire, single-rigged**
=center fire.

1942 Berrey–Van den Bark *Amer. Slang* 915.4, *Saddle.* . . Single-barreled saddle *or* rig, single-fire saddle *or* rig . . *a saddle with but one cinch.* **1944** Adams *Western Words* 145, Single-fire—Another name for the one-cinch saddle.

single-foot plow See **foot** n C3

single jack n **West** Cf **double jack** n
In mining: a drilling hammer designed to be wielded with one hand; hence n *single-jacker* a miner who uses such a hammer.

1923 Sinclair *Parowan Bonanza* 12 **NV,** You bet! Solid ledge of gold, Jim. Knock it off in chunks with a single-jack and gadget. **1929** *AmSp* 5.147 **CO** [Mining expressions], One who wields with both hands a large hammer and strikes the jack or wedge used to separate rocks broken by blasting is called a *double-jacker;* if he uses a smaller hammer—a *single jack*—in one hand, he is a *single-jacker.* **1949** Emrich *Wild West Custom* 251 **West,** The hardrock men, who worked with steel and drill, singlejack and doublejack—the heavy hammers . . were the recognized lords of the shift. **1966** *DARE* Tape **NM15,** [Inf:] The old hand drillers, they used to drill the rock . . by hand steel—a single jack. [FW:] What's a single jack? [Inf:] It's a hammer that you handle with one hand. **1968** Thrush *Dict. of Mining* 1016, Single jack. . . A lightweight hammer (usually 4 pounds or less). When used in hand drilling holes in rock, the hammer is held in one hand and the drill is held in the other.

single-rigged adj, also used absol Also *single-rig* **West** Cf **double-rigged, rim-fire, single-fire**
=center fire.

1887 *Scribner's Mag.* 2.509 **West,** Rig, single-rig, double-rig (in very general use throughout the Western States). **1927** (1944) Russell *Trails Plowed Under* 203, You know Texas men ain't got much love for a single rig. **1944** Adams *Western Words* 145, Single fire—Another name for the one-cinch saddle. *Single-rigged*—Still another title for the saddle mentioned above. **1956** Almirall *From College* 30 **CO,** Stock saddles with one cinch or girth, which held the saddle firmly on the horse's back, were mostly called center-fire or single-rigged. **1966** *DARE* (Qu. L42, *Do you use the word 'rig' around here? What kind of thing do you call a 'rig'?*) Inf **NM13,** Single-rig saddle.

single-shovel (plow) See **shovel plow**

single spruce n

1 Usu a **white spruce** (here: *Picea glauca*), but also **red spruce.** Cf **double spruce 1**
1810 Michaux *Histoire des Arbres* 1.133 **ME,** *Abies alba.* The White (Single) Spruce. . . Cette espèce de sapin . . est nommée en Canada Epinette blanche; à la Nouvelle-Ecosse *White spruce,* Sapin blanc; et *Single spruce,* Sapin simple, à la Nouvelle Brunswick et dans le District de Maine. [=This species of fir . . is named Epinette blanche in Canada; *White spruce* . . in Nova Scotia; and *Single spruce* . . in New Brunswick and the District of Maine.] **1832** MA Hist. Soc. *Coll.* 2d ser 9.153 **cwVT,** [Pinus] alba, Single spruce. **1850** Emerson *Rept. Trees & Shrubs* 81, The two species of spruce, the black and the white, or, as

they are more commonly called, the double and the single. **1916** *Torreya* 16.236 **ME,** *Picea rubra.* . . Common, white or yellow spruce, Matinicus I[sland], Me. At this locality I found the names single and double spruce, sometimes said to be specific designations, applied respectively to the less and the more luxuriantly leaved individuals of either this species or the last [=*P. canadensis*]. **1950** Peattie *Nat. Hist. Trees* 45, White Spruce. . . Other Names: Skunk, Cat, or Single Spruce. **1967** *DARE* (Qu. T17, . . *Kinds of pine trees;* not asked in early QRs) Inf **PA**44, White or single spruce.

2 =balsam fir. Cf **double spruce 2**

1900 Lyons *Plant Names* 7, *A[bies] balsamea.* . . Single Spruce. **1908** Britton *N. Amer. Trees* 75, The Balsam fir, also called Balm of Gilead fir, . . Single spruce, . . occurs from Labrador, west to Alberta and southward to the mountains of Virginia and to Minnesota.

singletree n [Folk-etym for **swingletree.** Perh of nIr origin, although first noted there in a collection begun in the last decades of the 19th cent] **widespread exc NEast, MI** See Map Cf **whiffletree**

A bar attached at the ends to the traces of a horse harness and having a flexible coupling in the center by which the draft is transmitted to a vehicle or other load.

1833 in 1956 Eliason *Tarheel Talk* 298 **NC,** Single-[tree]. **1860** (1937) Lewis *Diary Pike's Peak* 14.213 **PA,** White broke singletree. **1876** Knight *Amer. Mech. Dict.* 2769, *Whiffle-tree.* . . A *whippletree.* The terms *single, double,* and *treble tree* are more convenient, and expressive of their capacity. **1895** (1969) Montgomery Ward *Catalogue* 597, Singletrees and Neck Yokes. . . Strap End Singletrees. . . Davis Safety Singletrees. **1899** (1912) Green *VA Folk-Speech* 388, *Single-tree.* . . A bar of wood with a hook in the middle, and a cuff at each end to which traces may be fastened for hauling. **1902** *DN* 2.245 **sIL,** *Singl* [sic] *tree.* . . Whippletree. **1905** *DN* 3.94 **nwAR,** *Singletree.* . . Whiffletree. **1909** *DN* 3.371 **eAL, wGA,** *Singletree.* . . A swingletree, whiffletree. Neither of the latter terms is used. **1915** *DN* 4.190 **swVA,** *Singletree.* . . Used exclusively for *whiffle-tree.* **1949** Kurath *Word Geog.* 58, The bar to which the traces of a horse are fastened is called a *singletree* . . in all of the South and Midland. . . In the North Midland *singletree* is now almost universal. **1958** McCulloch *Woods Words* 166 **Pacific NW,** *Singletree*—The bar to which the traces were fastened when skidding with one horse. **1965–70** *DARE* (Qu. L46, *Behind each horse there's a movable bar* [*the leathers or ropes from the collar are fastened to it*]) 627 Infs, **widespread exc NEast, MI,** Singletree; **NJ**6, Two small singletrees; (Qu. L47, *The two movable bars behind a team of horses are fastened to a longer piece; this is a* _____) Infs **NE**7, **WA**8, **WI**6, Singletree; **MO**19, Singletree [This Inf responded "doubletree, eveners" to Qu. L46.]; **CA**101, Singletree, [corr to] doubletree; **CA**193, Pair of singletrees; **IA**6, Singletree—an evener behind one horse; **NC**81, Another singletree; **ND**2, Singletree [FW sugg]; **UT**2, Singletree—one horse; doubletree—two horses; (Qu. L44, *On a buggy, two long pieces of wood stick out in front and the horse goes between them*) Inf **IL**59, Singletree [Inf doubtful]; **MD**3, Singletree, [corr to] shafs; **MO**7, Singletree, braces; (Qu. L45, *The long piece of wood that sticks out in front of a wagon, and you put a horse on each side*) Inf **GA**60, Singletree, whiffletree; (Qu. L49, *Leathers or ropes, fastened to the collar, that a horse or mule pulls by*) Inf **OR**1, Singletree. [*DARE* Ed: The apparent confusion at Qq. L44, 45, 47, and 49 prob reflects lack of familiarity with the implements; cf **doubletree.**] **1972** *PADS* 58.16 **cwAL,** *Singletree.* Only *singletree* (20 [of 27 infs]) occurs. In addition,

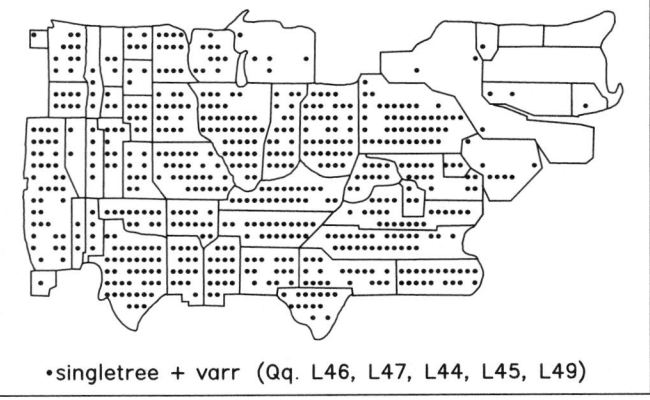

•singletree + varr (Qq. L46, L47, L44, L45, L49)

double-tree (12) and *double singletree* (1) are used for the two-horse rig. **1982** *Barrick Coll.* **csPA,** *Singletree*—whiffletree. **1989** Pederson *LAGS Tech. Index* 80, *Singletree* (549 [of 914 primary infs]).

singlings n Rarely *singling* [*SND* 1796 →] **chiefly sAppalachians** Cf **backings, doublings, first shot**

In moonshining: the crude, low-proof liquor produced from the first distillation.

1808 in 1956 Eliason *Tarheel Talk* 294 **nwNC,** Beaten Allum put in the singling will make the whiskey good & clear. **1867** U.S. Congress *Congressional Globe* 39th Cong 2d Sess 21 Jan app 60/1 **KY,** The singling tub is placed aside and the doubling tub put to the outlet of the worm. **1884** Knight *New Mech. Dict.* 816, *Singlings.* The first to come over, the crude spirit of distillation. **1911** *DN* 3.540 **eKY,** *Singlings.* . . The first weak run of whiskey from the still. **1917** *DN* 4.417 **wNC,** *Singlings.* . . The liquor of first distillation ("low wines" of the trade) which moonshiners redistill at a lower temperature to make whiskey. **1924** Raine *Land of Saddle-Bags* 131 **sAppalachians,** "Beer" is poured into the still, the fire lighted, and the vapors start through the copper spiral pipe. Cooled by the running water surrounding the "worm," the vapors condense into a liquid called "singlings" which drips or runs into a receptacle. **1968** *Foxfire* 2.3.55 **nGA,** All the beer was run through, a stillful at a time; and the results of each run ("singlins") saved at the other end. When all the beer had been run through once, the still was thoroughly cleaned, and then all the "singlins" placed into the still at one time. Then the stillful of "singlins" was run through. The result was the "doublins," or good whiskey. **1969** *DARE* Tape **GA**72, If you're making pure corn whiskey, you run what you call the singlings first. . . You run stillful after stillful of. . . singlings, which is the equivalent to backings. **1976** Garber *Mountain-ese* 82 **sAppalachians,** Sam's singlings ain't as good as his last batch uv doublings.

sing small v phr [Cf *EDD sing small* (at *sing* v. 1.(6))]

To restrain or humble oneself.

1845 Thompson *Pineville* 139 **GA,** If he don't sing small, the fust thing he'll know he'll git the worst lickin' he ever had in his life. **1852** *U.S. Democratic Rev.* 31.335, These Spaniards . . appreciate rightly those with whom they deal, and advance or hold back, frown or smile, talk big or sing small, according to the character . . of their adversary. **1875** *Atlantic Mth.* 36.23 **PA,** He feels mighty big after catching and caging me. I sing small enough in here just now, but among horsethieves and their good friends . . I am a man of mark. **1975** Gould *ME Lingo* 256, *Sing small*—To change your tune; one who has been boasting and runs into a comeuppance will *sing small* after that. Usually the term suggests the aftermath of an embarrassment.

singt See **sing** v A2

sinita See **senita**

sink n obs

=sinkboat.

1793 (1930) Hazard *Jrl.* 148 **RI,** John Congdon workt on Skif. I went to the old mill after aboard for Sink. . . I went to the meeting house for Board to make asink. **1857** E.J. Lewis *Amer. Sportsman* 284 (*OED2*), It is better . . to have two or more double-barrelled guns in the Sink. **1874** Long *Amer. Wild-Fowl* 252, The usual method of taking canvas-back in the West is by the aid of decoys, shooting . . from a sink box. . . [T]he brush may be thrown off, and the labor of towing about the "sink" avoided.

sink bedroom n Cf **sinkroom**

=bedsink.

1949 *McDavid Coll.* **nNY,** Sink bedroom = 'bedsink'—windowless alcove off kitchen. [Inf:] Male; 81; village clerk; 2 yr HS.

sinkboat n esp **MD** old-fash Also called **battery 1**

A small, narrow boat or raft, usu with floating outriggers, that can be ballasted to float nearly level with the surface of the water and that serves to conceal a waterfowl hunter.

1853 *Md. Laws* 220 (*DAE*), If any person or persons shall use any sink boats . . while engaged in shooting at . . wild fowl, he or they shall be subject to a fine. **1873** *Appletons' Jrl.* 10.467 **Chesapeake Bay,** Perhaps a description of the sink-boat may be novel and interesting to many who are unfamiliar with its construction. The shell, or boat proper, is just large enough to hold the gunner and his armament, the weight sinking it below the surface of the water, which is kept out by a light combing around the gunwale. Broad canvas frames, like outriggers, surround the boat, slightly submerged. Upon these are placed the decoys... The days of sink-boats are over, and only two modes of shooting are now regarded as legitimate—on "points" and over decoys. **1877** Hallock *Sportsman's Gaz.* 215 **Chesapeake Bay,** Although they are but little used at present, a brief description of the sink-boat may interest the reader. The sink-boat or battery was a long, narrow boat... It was loaded with old iron, so that it could be sunk nearly flush with the water's edge. From stem, stern and sides floating wings projected. **1877** Bartlett *Americanisms* 33, A friend in Maryland informs me that the usual term there is *Sink-boat,*—so called, because the whole body of the boat is below the surface. **1940** Writers' Program *Guide MD* 119 **cn,neMD,** The name of Susquehanna Flats is synonymous with good duck hunting. To old-timers it brings to mind sink boats, sneakboxes, swivel guns, 'long tom' and pump guns.

sinkbox n

1 An open, waterproof box buried in a beach or marsh so that its top is level with the surface, serving to conceal a waterfowl hunter.

1877 Hallock *Sportsman's Gaz.* 199 **neNC,** By far the most successful mode employed for the capture of the Wild Goose is that generally in vogue along the South Shore and at Currituck.., viz.: over live decoys from sink boxes... These boxes sunk in the sand until the tops are just flush with the surface of the ground, constitute the sportsman's blind. **1969** *DARE* Tape NC76, Nowadays we use stilt blinds, sinkboxes. The sinkboxes are usually made out of concrete and they have a curtain... When you're not using the box, you drop the curtain down and let it fill up with water. When you get ready to go hunting, you raise your curtain. It's made out of canvas or nylon; .. you have to waterproof it. You raise that and bail it out. **1988** Nickerson *Days to Remember* 167 **Cape Cod MA** (as of c1925), The shooting was done from "sink boxes" off on the outer edges of the marsh, and hence were usually under water at the top of the tide.

2 also *sinkbox boat:* =**sinkboat. esp MD** *old-fash*

1874 [see **sink**]. **1887** *Amer. Field* 27.3 **wCO,** In order to get any ordinary shooting [of wild ducks] one has to have a battery or sink-box in the middle of the ponds. **1900** *Outing* 37.148 **eMD,** On the Chesapeake .. the "sink-box," or "battery," is much used... It consists of a box big enough for a man to lie at full length, with flaps of wood and canvas extending on all sides, forming a platform about nine by thirteen feet. **1935** *Sun* (Baltimore MD) 8 Nov 14/1 *(Hench Coll.),* If I was asking you to allow sinkboxes it would be another matter... We can't do gunning from a blind 100 feet from shore. **1948** Camp *Hunter's Encycl.* 912, The sink-box, so-called, was designed for use in open water where diving ducks were feeding a considerable distance out of range from the shore. The first of these boats were built with water compartments .. which could be filled by pulling a plug or opening a small valve, thus sinking the hull down nearly level with the water. They were designed to circumvent the law which eliminated the use of batteries by providing that it was unlawful to shoot ducks from any boat propelled otherwise than by oars. **1989** (1990) Baden *Maryland's E. Shore* 69, The punt gun, used on the sink box boat, weighed one hundred and fifty pounds or more... The sink box boat was preferable to the blind. This raft had a sunken box in the middle where the hunter sat, covered all over with decoys, and floated along the shore looking to the birds like part of the landscape. **1996** Horton *Island Out of Time* 135 **Chesapeake Bay MD** (as of c1975), The fellow was a'huntin' out of a sink box, which is a rig where you are hidden in the middle part, which is below the water with just a little rail sticking up around the sides, and your decoys are spread out all around.

3 Perh a **fish basket.**

1967 *DARE* (Qu. P13, .. *Ways of fishing .. besides the ordinary hook and line*) Inf **PA35,** Sinkboxes [FW illustr].

sinkbox boat See sinkbox 2

sinker n

1 A silver dollar. [*OED2 sinker* sb.[1] 5.c "A base coin; also U.S. a dollar." 1839 →]

1894 *Century Illustr. Mag.* 47.713 **IN,** When I left the parson give me the sinker. **1900** *DN* 2.59 [College slang], *Sinker.* . . A silver dollar. **1900** Willard *Tramping* 397, *Sinker:* a dollar. **1967** *DARE* (Qu. U27, .. *A silver dollar*) Inf **IA3,** Sinker.

2 Any of var breadlike foods, as:

a A biscuit, dumpling, roll, or pancake.

1870 Beadle *Life in UT* 223, Our favorite dinner, when we could get

the meat, was of fried ham and "sinkers," the latter peculiar to the plains. Here is the recipe: Flour, *ad libitum;* water, *quant. suff.;* soda, a spoonful, if you have it, if not a pinch of ashes. Make in thin cakes, and fry rapidly in hot grease, with long handled frying pans. **1900** *DN* 2.59 [College slang], *Sinker.* . . A wheat or buckwheat cake... A hot roll... A doughnut. **1905** *DN* 3.94 **nwAR,** *Sinker.* . . Cream of tartar biscuit. 'The biscuits at the dorm are called "sinkers." **1917** J.A. Moss *Officer's Manual* 485 *(DA),* Sinkers, dumplings. **1919** *DN* 5.68 **NM** [Among hs students], *Sinker,* a biscuit. "We had some sinkers for breakfast and I can feel them yet." **1929** Ruppenthal *Coll.* **KS,** *Sinkers* . . dumplings. **1933** *AmSp* 8.1.27 **nwTX** [Ranch diction], *Sinker.* Biscuit. **1948** Hanna–Hanna *Lake Okeechobee* 116, Fat, white bacon warmed through will be as delicate to his taste as turkey's breast, and 'sinkers' will set as lightly on his stomach as the lightest white bread. **1952** Brown *NC Folkl.* 1.591, *Sinkers.* . . Dumplings cooked with chicken or some other meat. **1966–68** *DARE* (Qu. H19, *What do you mean by a biscuit? How are they made?*) Inf **CO5,** Sinkers—some biscuits are called sinkers (heavy ones); (Qu. H20b, .. *Names .. for pancakes*) Inf **ID4,** Sinkers; **MN14,** Sinkers—if they're not good. **1969** Sorden *Lumberjack Lingo* 110 **NEng, Gt Lakes,** *Sinkers.* . . Biscuits.

b also *belly-sinker;* Spec: a doughnut. **chiefly Nth, N Midl, West** See Map

1900 [see **2a** above]. **1903** Smith *How Paris* 48, The New York Dairy Lunch, with .. its elevating Bible texts and depressing "sinkers," .. would never make a success with Parisians. **1926** Ferber *Show Boat* 268, That famous refuge for the temporarily insolvent was so named because of the optical peculiarity of the lady who owned it and who dispensed its coffee and sinkers. **1929** *AmSp* 4.344 [Vagabond lingo], *Sinkers*—Doughnuts. **1936** *AmSp* 11.45 [Soda jerker jargon], *Sinkers and suds.* Doughnuts and coffee. **1940** *AmSp* 15.450 [Argot of the sea], *Coffee an, Coffee and.* Coffee and *sinkers* (doughnuts) or coffee and *snails* (cinnamon rolls). **1941** *LANE* Map 284 *(Doughnut)* 4 infs, **NEng,** Sinker. **1942** Beck *Songs MI Lumberjacks* 250, Say what you will, if the pie and sinkers choppers eat / That gets results. **1955** Taber *Stillmeadow Daybook* 120 **swCT,** The sinkers were very large and very heavy, very dark and extremely greasy. If you bit in with valor, you came on a lump of red stuff, supposed to be real jelly. **1965–70** *DARE* (Qu. H27, .. *Joking names for doughnuts*) 296 Infs, **chiefly Nth, N Midl, West,** Sinker; **MD8,** Belly-sinker; (Qu. H28, *Different shapes or types of doughnuts*) Inf **OK51,** Sinker—some are long and rectangular. **1986** Pederson *LAGS Concordance (Doughnut)* 1 inf, **seTX,** Sinkers; 1 inf, **csAL,** Sinkers—because heavy, like fishing sinkers; 1 inf, **ceTX,** Sinkers—called in restaurant.

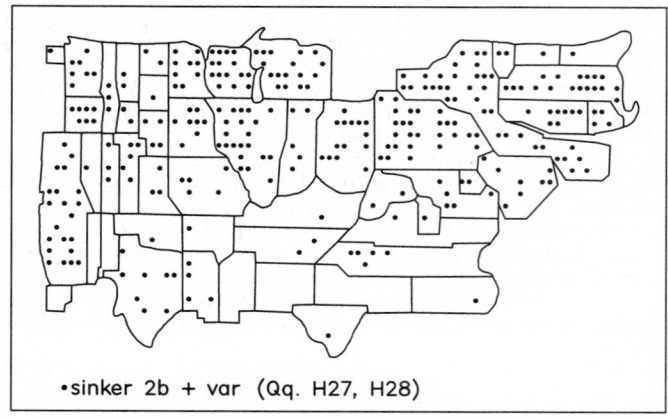

•sinker 2b + var (Qq. H27, H28)

3 In logging: a log that is too dense to float; hence comb *sinker boat* a boat for recovering sunken logs. **chiefly Pacific NW** Cf **deadhead n 4**

1884 *Redwood & Lumbering in Calif. Forests* (Edgar Cherry & Co.) 95 *(OED2),* The well matured heartwood of the base of these trees is so solid as to sink in water—hence designated as 'sinkers.' **1905** U.S. Forest Serv. *Bulletin* 61.46 [Logging terms], *Sinker.* . . See Deadhead. [*Ibid* 34, *Deadhead.* . . A sunken or partly sunken log.] *Ibid* 46, *Sinker boat.* See Catamaran. [*Ibid* 33, *Catamaran.* . . A small raft carrying a windlass and grapple, used to recover sunken logs.] **1950** *Western Folkl.* 9.381 **neCA** [Lumberjack language], *Sinker.* An extremely heavy log; usually sinks when dumped into the pond. **1953** *Mountain Messenger* (Downieville CA) 15 Jan 4/5 *(Mathews Coll.),* About 15 men were scheduled to return to work Monday.., weather permitting, to saw up sinkers and other logs left in the pond when bad weather caused a shutdown a few weeks ago.   **1956** *AmSp* 31.152 **nwCA** [Logger lingo], *Sinker.* . . A saw-log too heavy to float in a pond.   **1958** McCulloch *Woods Words* 166 **Pacific NW,** *Sinker*—A heavy log, usually a butt log, which will sink.   **1968** *DARE* Tape **CA**103, [**CA**104:] The first log that's cut off is the . . butt log. [**CA**103:] Is the butt log, and that's the sinker. [**CA**104:] Yeah. [FW:] What's the sinker? [**CA**103:] A sinker's full of water. [**CA**104:] Well, it's the heaviest part of the tree.

4 =**ruddy duck.**

1917 *Wilson Bulletin* 29.2.77 **WA,** *Erismatura jamaicensis.* . . sleepy jay, sinker, Willapa Harbor.   **1982** Elman *Hunter's Field Guide* 192, Ruddy Duck. . . Common & Regional Names: booby . . sinker.

5 =**red-necked grebe.**

1917 *Wilson Bulletin* 29.2.74 **WA,** *Colymbus holboelli.* . . red-eyed devil, sinker, Willapa Harbor.

sinker boat See **sinker 3**

sinkfield n

1 also *sinkfiel:* See **cinquefoil.**

2 =**man-of-the-earth 1.**

1974 Morton *Folk Remedies* 83 **SC,** Sinkfield; Man-root; Man-of-the-earth; Wild potato vine; Bigroot morning glory—*Ipomoea pandurata.*

sinking Peter n Cf **blue Peter, sinker 4**

A wild duck or similar bird; see quots.

1966–68 *DARE* (Qu. Q5, . . *Kinds of wild ducks*) Inf **NC**80, Sinking Peter; (Qu. Q9, *The bird that looks like a small, dull-colored duck and is commonly found on ponds and lakes*) Inf **NC**27, Dipper or sinking Peter.

sinking spell n

An episode of weakness, shortness of breath, palpitations, or the like.

1874 *Overland Mth.* 13.406 **CA,** "Will she die, Mrs. Brown?" said Billy, during one of these (literal) sinking spells.   **1888** *Ibid* (2d ser) 11.315, He revived a little towards evening, but this rally was followed by a sinking spell so profound that for a time we thought him dead.   **1954** *Harder Coll.* **cwTN,** *Sinking spell.* . . A feeling that lasts for a short while, with difficult breathing and heart beating fast.   **c1960** *Wilson Coll.* **csKY,** *Sinking spell* . . a spell of difficult breathing.   **1960** Bailey *Resp. to PADS 20* **KS,** Sinking spell; indisposition.   **1965–70** *DARE* (Qu. BB7, *A feeling that lasts for a short while, with difficult breathing and heart beating fast*) 37 Infs, **scattered,** Sinking spell; (Qu. BB6, *A sudden feeling of weakness, when sometimes the person loses consciousness*) Infs **MA**5, **MI**115, **NC**33, Sinking spell. [30 of 38 total Infs old]   **1983** *MJLF* 9.1.56 **ceKY,** *Sinking spell* . . a condition in which it is hard to breathe and the heart beats fast.   **1990** Cavender *Folk Med. Lexicon* 31 **sAppalachians,** *Sinking spell*—*a.* fainting. *b.* loss of energy or feeling tired.

sinkroom n **NEng**

A small room adjoining the kitchen equipped with a sink and often used as a pantry.

1833 *Trial E.K. Avery* 55 *(DAE),* [I] found him in the sink room.   **1865** *Ladies' Repository* 25.110, The house had formerly been the rebel General Lee's head-quarters. . . A thrifty Yankee would have made it conveniently accommodate two or three families. But it had only four rooms in it—no pantry, or closet, or sink-room.   **1869** Stowe *Oldtown Folks* 66 **NEng,** The conversation was interrupted by a commotion in the back sink-room. . . My grandmother . . [was] startled by a peculiar hissing sound in the sink-room. "Well, now, you have been and done it! You've gone and fidgeted the tap out of my beer-barrel, and here's the beer all over the floor."   **1887** Freeman *Humble Romance* 331 **NEng,** I hadn't any more'n shut the sink-room door.   **1941** *LANE* Map 344 *(Pantry)* 6 infs, **CT, MA, NH, RI,** Sink room; 1 inf, **csCT,** Sink room—for washing pots and kettles; 1 inf, **seCT,** Sink room—a pantry with a sink; 1 inf, **seMA,** Sink room—a back kitchen.   **1968–69** *DARE* (Qu. D8, *The small room next to the kitchen [in older houses] where dishes and sometimes foods are kept*) Infs **CT**18, **RI**1, Sinkroom.   **1970** *DARE* Tape **MA**98, In the house that we live in . . we tore off the rear of the house, which was a big, old-fashioned, almost a two-story, with all the beams showing, which was called the old sinkroom. But . . there was not only a sink there, there was a stove, and—it was the regular kitchen. And there was an ell to that which had been added apparently afterward, which was the dining room. . . The roof level was different from either . . the main part of the house or the sinkroom.

sink spout n **NEng**

The drain of a kitchen sink, orig one that discharged water out the side of the house; also fig.

1859 Nash *Progr. Farmer* 180 **MA,** As the spring opens, he will find a great quantity of manure in his yard, under his barn, in his pig-pen, under the necessary and at the sink-spout, already composted and ready for use.   **1859** (1860) Benedict *50 Yrs.* 43 **RI,** Illiterate as Elder Cornell was, yet many of the students in college . . were pleased to visit him to hear his sage advice and profit by his apt and shrewd remarks. One of these students was a good deal troubled with the blues, and had much to say against himself, of the badness of his feelings, etc. "You are wrong, my brother," said the elder to the complaining young man; "you have got your sink spout in front of your house; put it at the back side, my brother, where it will be out of sight."   **1926** *DN* 5.386 **ME,** *Drain* (dreen). . . Sink spout.   **1930** in 1931 McCorrison *Letters Fraternity* 248 **NEng,** One cold night in winter, . . some jovial young men were going by when one—a noted wag—seeing the light in the kitchen window, said: "There's Uncle Daniel reading history. I'm going to talk to him, up the sink spout."   **1975** Gould *ME Lingo* 256, *Sink spout weather*—The first indoor plumbing was the gooseneck to drain kitchen sinks. Suspended in midair outside the house wall, the pipe made a kind of flute on which the wind would play. The whoooo-whooo could be heard in the house, and, since weather changes with the wind, the tone of the sink spout could be a portent. *Sink spout weather* wasn't any particular kind of weather, because not all homes faced the same way, but each householder got his own kind of tootle-tootle and made what he wanted to of it.   **1979** *DARE* File **cnMA** (as of c1915), In the kitchen we poured liquids down the sink spout, not the drain. I'm not sure that we would have used *sink spout* of the bathroom bowl and tub, but I think so.

sinner n Pronc-sp *sinnuh* **esp Sth, S Midl** *esp freq among Black speakers* Cf Intro "Language Changes" I.4

Used attrib of a person, esp in comb *sinner man;* see quots.

1899 Chesnutt *Conjure Woman* 122 **csNC** [Black], I's be'n a monst'us sinner man.   **1917** in 1932 Sharp *Engl. Folk Songs* 2.289 **KY,** O sin-ner-man, where are you going to run to?   **c1938** in 1970 Hyatt *Hoodoo* 1.450 **seVA** [Black], I've heard some people say you go to the graveyard and get some dirt from a sinner-man's grave.   **1945** Saxon *Gumbo Ya-Ya* 137 **LA** [Black], Then I joined the Baptist Church. Went straight from sinner-man to board member to deacon to head deacon.   **1953** Brewer *Word Brazos* 105 **eTX** [Black], He de son of Jim Perkins, a sinnuh man.   **1967** Fetterman *Stinking Creek* 146 **seKY,** Sinner people don't understand prayin'. I tell you, I never did want to be a sinner person.   **1977** Dillard *Lexicon* 50 [Black], The person who has not yet begun to seek [religion] can be described in many ways: a *sinner man,* a *sinner boy,* or a *sinner girl.*

sinus n

A Gram form.

Sg. used as pl.

1970 *Thompson Coll.* **seMI** (as of 1950s), My sinus are all chugged up to where I cayn't hardly breathe.

B Sense.

Sinusitis; an inflammation of a sinus; a cold.

1967–70 *DARE* (Qu. BB9, *A sickness in which you have a severe cough and difficult breathing—it often starts with a cold, and lasts a week or two*) Infs **LA**37, **OH**45, Sinus; (Qu. BB13, . . *Chills and fever*) Inf **LA**37, Sinus; (Qu. BB49, . . *Other kinds of diseases*) Infs **CA**21, **CT**39, **IN**32, **MD**39, **MO**29, Sinus.   **1970** *Thompson Coll.* **seMI** (as of 1950s), I got sinus real bad again jus like I always get it in this kinda weather.   **1986** Pederson *LAGS Concordance (Caught a cold)* 1 inf, **cGA,** Sinus.

sipe v See **seep** v 1

sipe n

1 See quot.   [*EDD sipe* sb. 6]

1993 Doig *Heart Earth* 83 **MT,** I negotiate for a sip—a sipe, Grandma's way of saying it—just to confirm that coffee in this diluted fashion is as awful as it figures to be.

2 See **seep** n.

siphon-neck n

A bird of the family Ardeidae; see quot.

1970 *DARE* (Qu. Q10, . . *Water birds and marsh birds*) Inf **TN**65, Siphon-neck.

sircy See **sirsee**

sire n

1 also *herd* (or *breed, head, range*) *sire*: A male animal kept for breeding purposes. **widespread, but somewhat more freq Nth, N Midl** See Map *sometimes euphem* Cf **male** adj

1939 *LANE* Map 190 *(Bull)* 26 infs, **scattered**, Sire; 1 inf, **swCT**, The word *sire* is a little nicer; 1 inf, **nwCT**, Sire, 'high-toned'; 1 inf, **cCT**, Nowadays you can say *bull* in the presence of women, but not when I was a boy. You used *sire* then; 1 inf, **cnCT**, Sire, daughter-in-law's term; 1 inf, **csMA**, Sire, used 'in print'; 1 inf, **cwVT**, Sire, the bull regarded as the head of a herd. *Ibid* Map 197 *(Stallion)* 4 infs, **CT**, Sire [used euphemistically]; 2 infs, **MA**, Sire [used synonymously]. *Ibid* Map 200 *(Ram)* 2 infs, **CT**, Sire [used euphemistically]. *Ibid* Map 206 *(Boar)* 1 inf, **neCT**, Sire [used euphemistically]; 1 inf, **nwMA**, Sire [used synonymously]. **1950** *WELS* **WI** *(A bull)* 33 Infs, Sire; 5 Infs, Herd sire; *(Words used by women or in mixed company for a bull)* 16 Infs, Sire; 3 Infs, Herd sire; *(Words used by women or in mixed company for a male breeding pig)* 6 Infs, Sire. **1965–70** *DARE* (Qu. K22, *Words used for a bull)* 205 Infs, **widespread, but somewhat more freq Nth, N Midl**, Sire; **AL26, CA152, IL44, NY155, RI2**, Herd sire; **HI12**, Range sire [Of all Infs responding to the question, 67% were male; of those giving these responses, 79% were male.]; (Qu. K23, *Words used by women or in mixed company for a bull)* 26 Infs, **chiefly Nth, Midl**, Sire; 14 Infs, **scattered**, Herd sire; **NY99**, Breed sire; **NE3**, Head sire; **NY163**, Sire of the herd; (Qu. K52, *A male pig kept for breeding)* Infs **IN63, ND3, RI3, WI52**, Sire. **1973** Allen *LAUM* 1.244 *Upper MW* (as of c1950), *Bull. . . herd sire* [1 inf] *. . . sire* [29 infs]. *Ibid* 247, *Stallion. . . Big horse*, appearing once, and *sire* [3 infs] are apparently euphemistic. *Ibid* 250, *Boar. . . sire* [1 inf]. **1983** *DARE* File **CA, ID**, *(Words used for a bull)* Sire; *(Words used by women or in mixed company for a bull)* Sire. **1986** Pederson *LAGS Concordance* **Gulf Region** *(Bull)* 8 infs, Sire; 1 inf, **seAL**, Sire—euphemism; 1 inf, **nwAR**, Sire—in mixed company; 1 inf, **neTX**, Sire—guessing—euphemism; 1 inf, **ceTN**, Herd sire—mother used phrase as euphemism; *(Stallion)* 3 infs, Sire.

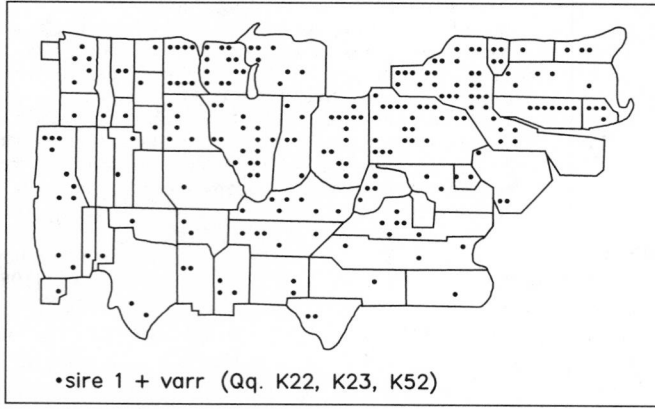

•sire 1 + varr (Qq. K22, K23, K52)

2 A father. [*OED2* c1250 →]

1931–33 *LANE Worksheets* **VT**, Sire. . . Father. How's your sire. People used to say this when asking for your father's health. **1966** Dakin *Dial. Vocab. Ohio R. Valley* 2.419, *Father. . . miscellaneous terms the old man* (fairly common), *sire, (the) gov'ner*, and *pater* (only single instances of the last three) are all attested by informants as their actual usage. **1966** *DARE* (Qu. Z1, . . *'Father')* Inf **ME13**, Sire.

siree bob See **sirree bob**

siren n Usu |ˈsaɪrən|; also |ˌsaɪˈrin|; for addit varr see quots Pronc-spp *si-reen, sirene, sy-reen*

A Forms.

1925 Lardner *What of It* 170 **WY**, He . . staid home . . with the windows open so as he would . . hear what is known in the town as the sireen. Well, the sireen did not blow. **1927** in 1944 *ADD* **sCA**, Siren. . . Sirene [ˈsaɪˈriːn]. Heard only from clerks & orchardists. **c1930** *Ibid* **eWV**, Siren. . . [ˈsaɪˈrin]. **1942** *Ibid* **NC**, [ˈsaɪrin]. **1965** Wolfe *Kandy-Kolored Baby* 129 **NC**, There he goes again, it was him, Junior Johnson! with a gawdam agent's si-reen and a red light in his grille! **1966** *DARE* (Qu. HH34, *General words . . for a woman, not necessarily uncompli-*

mentary) Inf **SC24**, Siren [saɪˈriən]. **1967** *DARE* FW Addit **nwLA**, Siren [ˌsaɪˈrin]. **1979** *DARE* File **csMA** (as of c1915), I don't remember that adults pronounced it so, but children used to talk about a [ˌsaɪˈrin]. **1981** Pederson *LAGS Basic Materials*, 1 inf, **cnAL**, [ˈsaˀˌriˀn] (=siren); 1 inf, **neTX**, [ˌsaˀˀriˀ·n]—has heard for siren. **1984** Burns *Cold Sassy* 216 **nGA** (as of 1906), And all of a sudden those empty pages were like the si-rene call I'd heard when I looked up at Blind Tillie Trestle. **1990** Smith *Understanding Speaking S. Lang.* 8, *Sy reen*—The noisy thing on top of an ambulance.

B Sense.

Std: a two-limbed salamander of the genus *Siren* or *Pseudobranchus striatus*. For other names of *Siren* spp see **congo eel 2, ditch ~ 2, eel** n **4, lamper eel 3**; for other names of *S. lacertina* see **alligator** n[1] **B1, lamprey eel 2, mud ~ 1, mudpuppy d, two-legged eel, water lizard**; for other names of *Pseudobranchus striatus* see **mud siren**

sirree bob n Also *siree bob, sirree bobcat, ~ bobtail* (cat); for addit varr see quots [*sirree* var of *sir* + *Bob* masculine name] **scattered, but esp Sth, wTX, N Midl, NYC** See Map Used for emphasis following *yes* or *no*.

1857 *Sun* (Baltimore MD) 30 Mar (1859 Bartlett *Americanisms* 408), "Sir, are you drunk?" The juror . . replied, *"No, sirree, bob!"* "Well," said the judge, "I fine you five dollars for the *'ree'* and ten for the *'bob.'"* [*DARE* Ed: According to a note that appeared in **1955** *Sun* (Baltimore MD) 3 Nov (B ed.) 18/7 *(Hench Coll.)*, the quot is not found in the issue cited by Bartlett.] **1859** (1968) Bartlett *Americanisms* 408, *Sirree*. "Yes, *sirree*," and, "No, *sirree*" for "Yes sir," and "No sir." This vulgar slang, which originated in New York, is now heard throughout the Union. Sometimes, as if not already puerile enough, the word *"bob"* is added, as *"Yes, sirree, bob."* [**1861** Burton *City Saints* 335 **UT**, The orderlies say "Sir," not Sirree nor Sirree-bob.] **1909** *DN* 3.362 **eAL, wGA**, *Rebob(tail)*. . . "No (yes), sir, rebobtail!" Probably originally "No, siree, Bob!" **1911** *DN* 3.546 **NE**, *No-sirree-bob, no-sirree-bob-tailed-rooster*. . . Used in emphatic denial. "Will you go with me?" "No-sirree-bob-tailed-rooster!" **1915** *DN* 4.186 **swVA**, *No sir-ee Bob*. . . Emphatic for *no*,—sometimes with the addition of *tail*. **1938** *AmSp* 13.74 **OH**, No siree, Bob. **1940** *AmSp* 15.219 **wVT**, 'No sirree Bub' (not 'Bob'; no comma heard; the double r was usual in writing, and the two r's were separately sounded when the emphasis was heightened by slow speech). **1942** Warnick *Garrett Co. MD* 11 **nwMD** (as of 1900–18), *No sir-ree*, or *no sir-ree bob* . . emphatic negatives. **1942** Whipple *Joshua* 469 **UT** (as of c1860), "So you believe in baptism by immersion?" . . "Yessiree-bob," says I. **1956** (1973) Holiday–Dufty *Lady Sings* 203, Yes siree bob, life is just a bowl of cherries. **1965–70** *DARE* (Qu. KK55c, . . *Expressions of strong denial)* 65 Infs, **scattered, but esp Sth, wTX, N Midl, NYC**, No sirree bob; **MS14, SC40, 44, 54, 59**, No sirree bobtail; **MS73**, No sirree bobcat; (Qu. NN1, . . *Words like 'yes'*: *"Are you coming along too?")* Inf **MT1**, Yes sirree bob; (Qu. NN2, *Exclamations of very strong agreement: Somebody says, "I think Smith is absolutely right," and you reply, "_____.")* Inf **LA17**, Yes sirree bob; yes sirree bobtail cat. **1976** Garber *Mountain-ese* 61 **sAppalachians**, *No-siree-bobtail* . . absolutely not—No-siree-bobtail, they's nobody gonna borry my coondog. *Ibid* 104, *Yes-siree-bobtail* . . yes. . . Yessiree bobtail that's a fine piece uv horseflesh. **1981** Harper–Presley *Okefinokee* 43 (as of 1912) **seGA**, No sirree-man-bob, you cain't make me believe that. **1986** Pederson *LAGS Concordance*, 1 inf, **swLA**, Yes sirree bob.

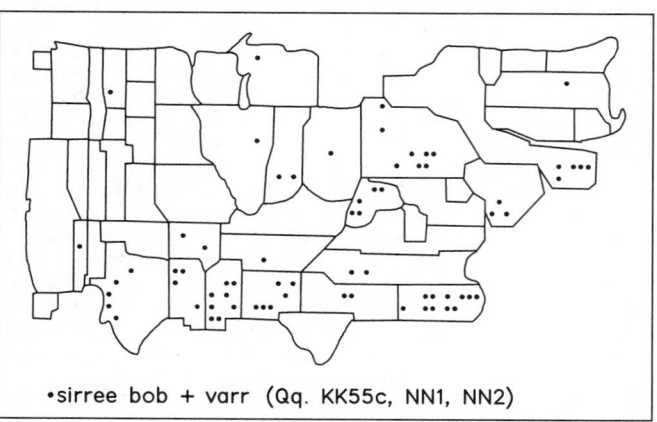

•sirree bob + varr (Qq. KK55c, NN1, NN2)

sirsee n Also sp *circe, searcy, sircy, surcy, sursie, sussie;* for addit varr see quots [Etym unknown] **scattered, but chiefly S Atl**

A small gift, esp one given impromptu.

1968 *DARE* File **GA,** *Searcy* ['sɜ·si]—noun—Surprise, small gift. Reported . . by a girl from Thomson, Ga., and another from Augusta, Ga. Also known in various locations in South Carolina. **1969** *Ibid* **Philadelphia PA,** My office mate and colleague in folklore . . has what strikes me as a rather unusual word in her family vocabulary—"circe" . . pronounced "sir-see," like the name of the Greek goddess. In her family and her mother's family (from the Philadelphia area), the word has been long used to mean a small gift, given for no special reason. . . My office mate's mother has known it for as long as she can recall. She now lives in Raleigh, North Carolina, and has discovered that the family next door, who originally came from the Midwest, also uses it. **1981** *Ibid* **GA,** Fourteen years ago I found myself set down in the middle of the deep South, due to my husband's career demands. . . I keep coming up with regionalisms. One of these is surcy (sircy? searcy?), meaning a surprise, a small treat, as in "Bring me a surcy when you come back." **1982** *Smithsonian Letters* **NC,** A friend came up to me and said "I have a *Sir'see* [that is my own phonetic spelling] for you." It was a photograph of her son and mine together. *Sir'see* she explained when I asked is a little surprise gift. . . The friend who used the word is from Scotland Neck, N.C. and says it is used there and also was used at St. Mary's College in Raleigh, N.C. **1992** *DARE* File **SC,** This [=*sirsee*] is widely known in Columbia, S.C., particularly at a women's college there, where it is almost a trademark of the school (i.e. people associate the word with the students). It is usually a small gift given in appreciation, as for help, hospitality, etc. **1997** *Ibid* **GA, SC,** I'm trying to determine both the spelling and origin of a word that I have only heard used by two different friends. The first friend was born and lived her life in Columbia, SC. . . The word means "a little gift," not necessarily a surprise but special. It sounds like cersi . . cercy . . sursy . . sirsy. *Ibid* **KY, NC,** I have heard this all my life, but more in NC than in KY; assume it is from surprise (I had a mental picture of its being spelled 'sursie'). . . One wheedles in order to obtain one, or promises one as if placating a young, fond, foolish recipient—or intimate, in a teasing manner. **1999** *Ibid* **TX,** We have a patron looking for the correct spelling of the term "Sussie," which she states means a small gift. **2001** *Ibid* **SC,** We heard it [=*searcy*] from a 57-year-old South Carolina native—a woman. In asking around, we have found native South Carolinians who've heard it, and a couple nonnatives who've lived here awhile and heard it from a South Carolinian.

sisco See **cisco**

siscowet n Also *ciscowet, siscowet salmon, siskawit(z), siskiwit, siskowit(z);* for addit varr see quots [Ojibway *pemitewiskawet;* see quot 1910]

A fatty, stout-bodied, deepwater **lake trout 1** (usu *Salvelinus namaycush siscowet*) of Lake Superior.   For other names see **fat lake trout, half-breed, humper** n[1], **potbelly 1**

1847 Lanman *Summer in Wilderness* 159 **nMI,** A fish called ciscovet [sic; cf **1856** below]. **1851** Herbert *Frank Forester's Fish & Fishing* 112, The Siskawitz in its coloring and general appearance, as regarded by an uninstructed eye, bears a very considerable resemblance to the Mackinaw Salmon, or Namaycush. **1852** MI State Ag. Soc. *Trans. for 1851* 3.230, *Siskowit.* These are mostly found in Lake Superior, and are thought by some to be the best fish in the lake. They are of the trout family, and are probably the fatest [sic] fish known. **1853** U.S. Congress *Serial Set* 622 Doc 112 241, Of all the fish caught up on the lake [=Superior] the siskawit is most prized by the natives on account of its fatness. **1856** Lanman *Advent. Wilds U.S.* 125, A fish called ciscowet, is unquestionably of the trout genus, but much more delicious, and seldom found to weigh more than a dozen pounds. **1861** *Atlantic Mth.* 7.235, In Lake Superior is likewise found that remarkable salmon, the Siscowet,—which is so fat and luscious as to be uneatable in a fresh state. **1882** U.S. Natl. Museum *Bulletin* 16.318, *Siscowet salmon.* **1904** *Salmon & Trout* 287, This charr is. . . the "siscowet" or "siskowitz" in some parts of Lake Superior. **1910** Hodge *Hdbk. Amer. Indians* 2.580, *Siskawet.* A name, with many variants, such as *siskowet, siskiwit, siskowit, siskwoet, ciscovet,* etc., for *Salvelinus namaycush,* var. *siscowet,* a large, thick-bodied salmon of the deep waters of L. Superior. . . The name is a Canadian French contraction and corruption of the cumbersome Chippewa name *pemitewiskawet,* 'that which has oily flesh.' **1976** *DARE* File **Isle Royale MI,** Siscowets are deep-water lake

trout, down to 800 feet. Weigh 50 to 60 pounds, are shorter and thicker than lake trout. Can't be broiled or baked, too oily—up to 85 percent—and fat, but very good smoked. **1983** Becker *Fishes WI* 331, The so-called half-breed is considered by fishermen to be the result of a cross between the lean lake trout and the fat siscowet.

siskin See **pine siskin**

siskiwit, siskowit(z) See **siscowet**

sisper shame exclam Also *sisper shame on you* **Philadelphia PA** Cf **abasicky**

Among children: see quots.

[**1980** *NADS* 12.3.16, A word that children say while making a gesture meaning "shame on you": the "shamer" points at the "shamed" with one index finger while moving the other index finger across it with a whittling motion.] **1980** *NADS Letters* **Philadelphia PA,** *Sispershame*—used with the whittling motion of the fingers described in *NADS* 12.3 with the meaning "shame on you." **1992** *DARE* File **Philadelphia PA** (as of 1950s), Word used when we were young—sisper—sisper shame on you.

siss v [*OED2* 13 . . →; "Now dial. and *U.S.*"] **esp NEast** old-fash Cf **sizz, sizzer** n[1]

To hiss.

1828 Webster *Amer. Dict., Siss.* . . To hiss; *a legitimate word in universal popular use in New England.* **1854** *Ladies' Repository* 14.431 **OH,** Verily, if frying be a process by which ideas may be generated, ideas hot and sissing ought to have been radiating from us. **1859** (1968) Bartlett *Americanisms* 409, *To Siss.* To hiss. A colloquialism also used in England. **1871** (1882) Stowe *Fireside Stories* 87 **MA,** There wa'n't nothin' a goin' on but jest . . the geese a sissin' and a pickin' at the grass. **1899** (1912) Green *VA Folk-Speech* 388, *Siss.* . . To hiss. **1932** *DN* 6.284 **swCT,** *Sissing hot.* Very hot. **1985** Rattray *Advent. Dimon* 201 **Long Is. NY** (as of c1890), He understood one no more than the other, but he had the words just right, save for his sissing on the S's and C's.

siss n, **sisser** See **sizzer** n[1]

sissler See **sizzler 3**

sissy-britches n pl but sg in constr Also *sissy-breeches, sissy-pants*

A sissy; an effeminate boy or man.

1946 *PADS* 6.27 **swVA** (as of 1940), *Sissy-britches.* . . An effeminate man. . . Rare. **1947** *PADS* 8.20 **ceIA** (as of 1930s), *Sissy-pants. Ibid* 8.23 **KY,** *Sissy-britches:* more often, I believe, *sissy-pants. Ibid* 8.25 **wNY,** *Sissy-britches.* **1950** *WELS* (A womanish man) 1 Inf, **cWI,** Sissy-pants. **1960** Wentworth–Flexner *Slang* 479, *Sissy-pants.* . . a sissy. **c1960** Wilson *Coll.* **csKY,** *Sissy-breeches.* . . A sissy man or boy. **1966–67** *DARE* (Qu. HH38) Infs **NC**36, 38, Sissy-britches. [**1986** Pederson *LAGS Concordance,* 1 inf, **seAL,** Sissy-breeches—common dance, at local gatherings.]

sistern n pl Also *sisterin(g), sistren, sistrin, sisturn* [Cf *OED2* sister sb. 1.b "In general literary use these [=plurals with -*n*] were finally discarded about 1550 in favour of the pl. in -*s*."]

Sisters—used esp in religious contexts.

1843 (1916) Hall *New Purchase* 172 **IN,** Brethurn and sisturn. **1871** Eggleston *Hoosier Schoolmaster* 106 **sIN,** My brethering—ah and sistering—ah. **1888** *Harper's New Mth. Mag.* 76.868 **Lower Missip Valley** [Black], An' I tell yer, my sistren an' bredren, . . my sperit was cramped dat day. **1890** *DN* 1.67 **KY,** *Bretheren.* . . I tell you, breetherin and sisterin. **1893** Shands *MS Speech* 56, *Sistern* [sɪstən]. Negro for *sisters* (in a church), formed upon analogy with *brethren.* **1894** *DN* 1.333 **NJ,** *Sistern:* pl. of *sister.* Used in Baptist and Methodist churches. **1899** (1912) Green *VA Folk-Speech* 388, *Sistren.* . . Sisters of a society or guild. Sisters. **1906** Casey *Parson's Boys* 31 **sIL** (as of c1860), "Brethren and sistern," he said with a deep sigh, "it is now goin' on forty years since I give my heart to the Lord and felt his savin' grace." **1909** *DN* 3.370 **eAL, wGA,** *Sist(e)rin.* . . Sisters. **1911** *DN* 3.540 **eKY,** *Sistren.* . . Sisters, chiefly heard in the phrase, "brethren and sistren." **1942** McAtee *Dial. Grant Co. IN* 57 (as of 1890s), *Sistern* . . sisters. **1942** Whipple *Joshua* 484 **UT** (as of c1860), His few words might be of value to the brethren and sistern. **1952** Brown *NC Folkl.* 1.591, *Sistren.* . . Sisters. **1956** *AmSp* 31.160 **cnIN** (as of 1890s), *Sistern.* . . Sisters, that is, women collectively. 'The sistern seem to think the new minister is the proper article.' **1968** *DARE* FW Addit **PA**78, *Sistern* [sɪstɚn]. Plural of sister. Very old, rare term.

sister, since the hogs ate little See **hogs ate my brother up, since the**

sistren, sistrin, sisturn See **sistern**

sit v¹ Cf **set** v¹

Std senses, var forms.

1 infin and pres: usu *sit;* also:

a *set.*

   1650 (1923) Bland *New Brittaine* 3 **VA,** Downe he sets, and looks about him. **1810** (1912) Bell *Journey to OH* 18 **MA,** Nothing vexes me more than to see them set & look at us. **1817** [see **set** v **A2b**]. **1837** Sherwood *Gaz. GA* 71, *Set,* sit. **1884** *Anglia* 7.253 [Black], To the regular forms of the Irregular verbs as used by the whites, the Negro adds the following forms of his own. . . *Pres.* set (for sit). **1893** *DN* 1.278 **wCT,** Set [Pret. forms:] set, sot (the verb *sit* is not used: *set* when transitive has pret. *set,* when intr. *set* or *sot*). [*DARE* Ed: Author states that pret and past participle are in all cases alike.] **1899** Garland *Boy Life* 16 **nwIA** (as of c1870s), Say, s'pose we set together at school. **1899** (1912) Green *VA Folk-Speech* 375, Set. . . To sit: as, "I was setting in my chair." **1909** *DN* 3.368 **eAL, wGA,** Set. . . Almost universal for *sit.* **1910** *DN* 3.448 **cwNY,** I hadn't ought to set out here, I'll take cold. **1915** *DN* 4.189 **swVA,** Set. Variant of *sit.* **1935** Hurston *Mules & Men* 190 **FL,** Everybody done fell but you. You must be setting on roots. **1942** Faulkner *Go Down* 13 **MS,** Then all you needs to do is set down and wait. **1945** Thorp *Pardner* 123 **SW,** "If you don't think Coaly is fast," she went on, "you don't know the feel of cactus when you're settin' in the middle of it." **1953** Atwood *Survey of Verb Forms* 21, *Sit.* . . Two present forms (or separate verbs) are current, *sit* /sɪt/ and *set* /sɛt/. *Sit* predominates . . in New York City, n. N.J., the lower Hudson Valley, and Pa. east of the Susquehanna. Elsewhere in Pa. and N.Y. the forms are about equally distributed. In the entire area to the south of Pa., outside of the larger cities, *sit* is rather uncommon except in cultured speech. **1965–70** *DARE* (Qu. II15, *When somebody is passing by and you want him or her to stop and talk a while*) 29 Infs, **scattered,** Come in and set a spell (var phrr: see *DS*]; (Qu. Y29b, . . *About a man [who doesn't stay home much]*) Inf **DC**13, Can't set still; (Qu. Z13, *If a mother has to leave her baby for a little while, she might ask a neighbor, "While I'm gone, will you _____ the baby for me?"*) Infs **NY**10, **OH**89, Set with; [**MI**102, Set;] (Qu. CC11, *When somebody has had a lot of good luck . . he _____*) Inf **AR**18, Is setting in easy street; **MD**20, Is setting pretty; (Qu. GG11, *To be quite anxious about something . . "The letter hasn't come and he's _____."*) Inf **AR**39, Setting on pins; **PA**234, Setting on tenterhooks; (Qu. GG23c, . . *Expressions [to tell someone to be patient]*) Inf **DC**12, Set on it; (Qu. KK4, *When things turn out just right . . "Everything is _____ now."*) Inf **IN**61, Setting pretty; (Qu. KK42b, *Expressions about a person who does something very easily: "He could do that _____."*) Inf **AZ**9, Setting down; (Qu. KK60, *Having nothing in particular to do: "I'd just as soon go with you this afternoon—I'm _____ anyway."*) Inf **MO**2, Just setting around; (Qu. NN11, *Informal ways of saying 'good-bye' to people you know quite well*) Inf **WI**26, See you in church, if you set by the window. **1968–69** *DARE* Tape **CA**87, Did your father set under that tree and wait? **FL**36A, We always made benches to put around the . . table for the children to set on; **CA**136, They'd get in there and set til they'd get a big sweat; **KY**16A, He says, "I'm a-huntin' me a woman." She says, "Well, get right down 'n' come in. I'm a-huntin' me a man, too." And he thought he was settin' good; **VA**9, He had the chairs for us all to set in. **1973** *PADS* 60.70 **seNC,** All of our Carteret County informants said *sit : sat* except one who said *set : set.* **1989** Pederson *LAGS Tech. Index* 167 **Gulf Region** *(Sit),* [Of the 773 infs who answered the question, 193 infs responded with *set* for the infinitive and 9 infs responded with *sets* for the present 3rd singular.] *Ibid (Sit down),* [Of the 616 infs who answered the question, 81 infs responded with *set (right) down, set here, take a chair and set down,* etc.] **1991** Pederson *LAGS Social Matrix* 130 **Gulf Region,** [Of all those who responded to the question to elicit the principal parts of *sit,* 635 infs offered *sit* for the infinitive, of whom 280 had a 10th-grade educ or less and 364 belonged to the lower or lower middle class; of the 190 infs who offered *set* for the infinitive, 145 had a 10th-grade educ or less and 155 belonged to the lower or lower middle class.]

b *sot.*

   1917 in 1944 *ADD* **cwWV,** *Sot.* . . To sit. . . 'Sot' = Sit down. **1967**

DARE FW Addit **AR**55, Just sottin' ['sɑtn̩] here—joking pronunciation for *setting* (common) or *sitting* (formal).

2 past: usu *sat;* also:

a *set.* *chiefly rural; esp freq among speakers with little formal educ*

   1800 (1907) Columbia Hist. Soc. *Records* 10.132 **PA,** We went first to Mrs Knapp's—We set there a little. **1810** (1912) Bell *Journey to OH* 16 **MA,** We set down to tea. **1820** in 1956 Eliason *Tarheel Talk* 317 **cs,seNC,** Set. **1837** Sherwood *Gaz. GA* 71, *Set,* sat. **1884** *Anglia* 7.253 [Black], *Past.* [of *sit*] set, sot. **1893** Shands *MS Speech* 56, *Set* is also used for *sat.* **1893** [see **1a** above]. **1910** *DN* 3.448 **cwNY,** Set. . . Also as *pret.* . . "They set there in the house, talking and talking." **1932** Stribling *Store* 295 **AL,** Yes, suh, Miss Gracie set down on my mammy. **1953** Atwood *Survey of Verb Forms* 21, Of the informants who use the present *sit,* those in the coastal areas strongly prefer the preterite *sat* /sæt/. Farther inland, particularly in c. and w. Pa. and in W. Va., there is a tendency to use the leveled forms *sit : sit.* More than a few use the combination *sit : set,* chiefly in c. and w. Pa. and W. Va., and three or four in N.Y. and n.e. Pa. use *sit : sot* /sɑt/. Among informants who use the present *set,* by far the most common preterite throughout the M[iddle] A[tlantic] S[tates] is the leveled form *set.* This is also true in the S[outh] A[tlantic] S[tates] except in the areas where *sot* predominates. . . A combination that is far from uncommon in the S.A.S. is *set : sot.* Almost all the informants in the East who gave *sot* as the preterite . . use *set* as the present. . . *Sot* . . is distinctly an archaism, and . . is most common in the more conservative areas—n.e. N. Eng., the South, and parts of the South Midland. **1959** *VT Hist.* 27.155, [set]. . . Past tense of *to sit.* . . Common. Rural areas. **1965–70** *DARE* (Qu. OO44a, *About somebody in a chair: "He did nothing at all—he just _____ [there]."*) 189 Infs, **widespread,** Set; **NH**14, Set up; **AL**3, Set like a mummy; **TN**23, Set there like a stump. [Of all Infs responding to the question, 68% were comm type 4 or 5, 28% gs educ or less; of those giving these responses, 82% were comm type 4 or 5, 47% gs educ or less.] **1967–68** *DARE* FW Addit **CA**99, Our old house set way back there, so we didn't have far to move our furniture; **MI**72, And I set here for awhile. **1973** [see **1a** above]. **1991** Pederson *LAGS Social Matrix* 130 **Gulf Region,** [Of all those who responded to the question to elicit the principal parts of *sit,* 309 infs offered *sat* for the preterite, of whom 93 had a 10th-grade educ or less and 126 belonged to the lower or lower middle class; of the 164 infs who offered *set* for the preterite, 118 had a 10th-grade educ or less and 129 belonged to the lower or lower middle class; of the 81 infs who offered *sit* for the preterite, 54 had a 10th-grade educ or less and 71 belonged to the lower or lower middle class.]

b *sit.* **scattered, but more freq Sth, S Midl** See Map *chiefly rural; esp freq among speakers with little formal educ*

   1800 (1907) Columbia Hist. Soc. *Records* 10.89 **PA,** Mr. T- Peter called and sit awhile. **1832** *Political Examiner* (Shelbyville KY) 8 Dec 4/1, Well feeling pretty kind tired, I sit down. **1843** (1916) Hall *New Purchase* 280, And so I sit down just here . . where I always before tried our guns. **1893** Shands *MS Speech* 56, *Sit* is also very frequently used for *sat* by all classes. **1912** *DN* 3.589 **wIN,** After he left, I sit there and read for two hours. **1953** [see **2a** above]. **1965–70** *DARE* (Qu. OO44a, *About somebody in a chair: "He did nothing at all—he just _____ [there]."*) 100 Infs, **scattered, but more freq Sth, S Midl,** Sit; **CO**4, **MO**37, **TX**26, Sit around. [Of all Infs responding to the question, 68% were comm type 4 or 5, 28% gs educ or less; of those giving these responses, 85% were comm type 4 or 5, 51% gs educ or less.] **1991** Pederson [see **2a** above].

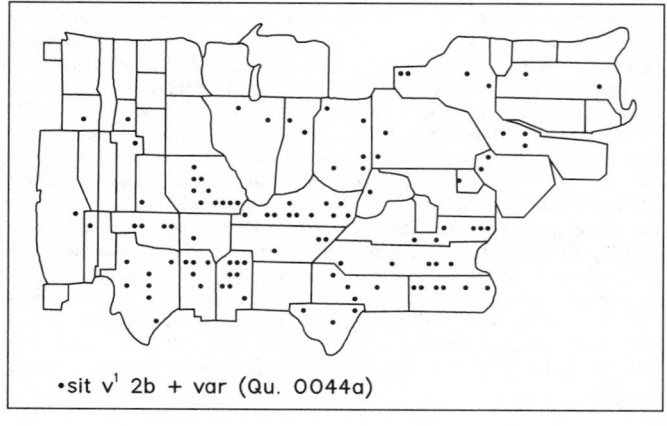

•sit v¹ 2b + var (Qu. OO44a)

c *sot.*

1795 Dearborn *Columbian Grammar* 138, *List of Improprieties. . .* Sot for Sat. **1851** Hooper *Widow Rugby's Husband* 50 **AL,** So I gits under a big red-oak, and thar I sot 'twell the lightnin' struck it! **1867** Harris *Sut Lovingood Yarns* 22 **TN,** Mam an' me made geers fur dad, while he sot on the fence a-lookin at us. **1871** (1882) Stowe *Fireside Stories* 13 **MA,** There, to be sure, sot old Cack beside a great blazin' fire. **1884** [see **2a** above]. **1893** [see **1a** above]. **1899** Chesnutt *Conjure Woman* 14 **csNC,** He en de oberseah sot up nights. **1909** *DN* 3.373 **eAL, wGA,** *Sot, pret.* and *pp.* of *sit.* **1915** *DN* 4.190 **swVA,** Variant of *sat.* **1923** *DN* 5.221 **swMO,** *Sot. . .* Past tense of sit. **c1940** Eliason *Word Lists FL* 11 **wFL,** *Sot* [sɑt]: *past tense* of *sit* and *set.* Once *common,* now *rare.* **1953** [see **2a** above]. **1955** Ritchie *Singing Family* 63 **seKY,** I sot on the porch awhile until I heard them coming out of the kitchen. **1968–70** *DARE* (Qu. OO44a, *About somebody in a chair: "He did nothing at all—he just _____ [there]."*) Infs **IN**32, **NY**69, **NY**232, Sot. **1968** *DARE* FW Addit **GA**30, "*Sot*" [sɑt]—past tense of "sit." **1989** Pederson *LAGS Tech. Index* 167 **Gulf Region,** [Principal parts of *sit:*] 9 infs, Sot—preterite; 1 inf, Sot—past participle.

3 past pple: usu *sat;* also:

a *set.* *chiefly rural; esp freq among speakers with little formal educ*

1884 *Anglia* 7.253 [Black], Pass. Part. [of *sit*] set, sot. **1893** [see **1a** above]. **1965–70** *DARE* (Qu. OO44a, *About somebody in a chair: "All day long he has just _____ [in that chair]."*) 239 Infs, **widespread,** Set. [Of all Infs responding to the question, 68% were comm type 4 or 5, 28% gs educ or less; of those giving these responses, 81% were comm type 4 or 5, 44% gs educ or less.] **1991** Pederson *LAGS Social Matrix* 130 **Gulf Region,** [Of all those who responded to the question to elicit the principal parts of *sit,* 186 infs offered *sat* for the past participle, of whom 30 had a 10th-grade educ or less and 61 belonged to the lower or lower middle class; of the 95 infs who offered *set* for the past participle, 48 had a 10th-grade educ or less and 69 belonged to the lower or lower middle class; of the 73 infs who offered *sit* for the past participle, 54 had a 10th-grade educ or less and 60 belonged to the lower or lower middle class.]

b *sit.* **scattered, but chiefly Sth, S Midl** See Map *chiefly rural; among speakers with little formal educ*

1837 (1940) Arnold *Diaries* 131 **VT,** Mrs. Nutting has sit there more than a year. **1965–70** *DARE* (Qu. OO44b, *About somebody in a chair: "All day long he has just _____ [in that chair]."*) 67 Infs, **scattered, but chiefly Sth, S Midl,** Sit; **MO**18, Sit there. [Of all Infs responding to the question, 68% were comm type 4 or 5, 28% gs educ or less; of those giving these responses, 87% were comm type 4 or 5, 65% gs educ or less.] **1973** in 1993 Major *Calling the Wind* 357 **NYC** [Black], You are not one of the riffraff or else you would of sit with them good-timers and bullshitters 'cross the room. **1991** [see **3a** above].

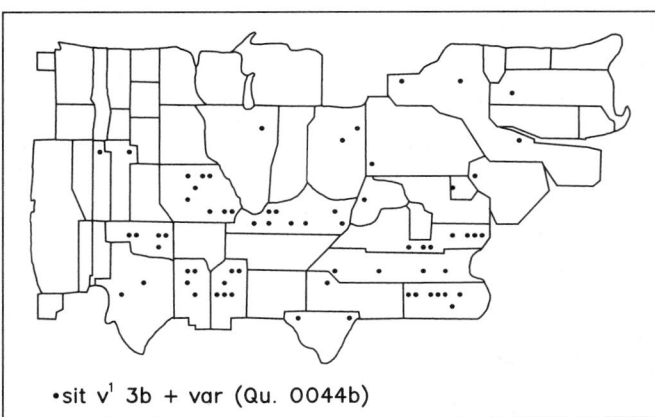

•sit v¹ 3b + var (Qu. OO44b)

c *sot.*

1858 in 1968 Bartlett *Americanisms* 430, Yes, sir-ee! for I have *sot,* and *sot,* and *sot,* till I have about tuk root! **1884** [see **2a** above]. **1893** [see **1a** above]. **1909** [see **2c** above]. **1968** *DARE* (Qu. OO44b, *About somebody in a chair: "All day long he has just _____ [in that chair]."*) Infs **IN**32, **NY**69, Sot. **1989** [see **2c** above]. **1991** Still *Wolfpen Notebooks* 19 **sAppalachians,** One said to me, "He's quit a good job and come over in here and sot down."

d *sitten.*

1781 *PA Jrl. & Weekly Advt.* (Philadelphia) 16 May, Sit has three terminations, sit, sat, sitten. **1967–69** *DARE* (Qu. OO44b, *About somebody in a chair: "All day long he has just _____ [in that chair]."*) Infs **GA**82, **NJ**3, Sitten. **1989** Pederson *LAGS Tech. Index* 167 **Gulf Region,** [Principal parts of *sit:*] 5 infs, Sitten—past participle.

sit v² See **set** v¹ **A1b**

sit-alone baby n [Perh folk-etym for *set-along child* (at **set-along**)]

1959 Roberts *Up Cutshin* 41 **seKY,** Its family broke up and scattered when it was just a sit-alone baby.

sit by See **set by** v phr¹

sit down v phr *euphem*
To go to the toilet.

1968 Kellner *Aunt Serena* 95 **sIN** (as of c1920), [At school] girls might whisper primly, "I would like to sit down."

sit-down n Also *set-down, sit-down piece, sitdownski, sit(ting)-down place* Cf **sitter, sit-upon**
The posterior, the buttocks; a buttock.

1915 (1916) Johnson *Highways New Engl.* 218, If we did get caught the watchman would take the wooden end of his hook, slap our set-downs, then give us a kick and say, 'Get out!' **1942** Berrey–Van den Bark *Amer. Slang* 121.71, *Posteriors. . .* set-down. . . sit-down. **1947** Ballowe *The Lawd* 11 **LA,** Unc' Brutus' [Duppies] had plenty [heat]. He swinged the set-downs o' the mullader women. **1965–70** *DARE* (Qu. X35, *Joking words for the part of the body that you sit on . . "He slipped and came down hard on his _____."*) 14 Infs, **scattered,** Sit-down; **NC**49, Set-down; **IL**5, Sit-down piece; **GA**9, 82, **LA**11, **NC**86, **NJ**1, Sit(ting)-down place; **IA**17, Sitdownski. [17 of 22 Infs old] **1986** Pederson *LAGS Concordance,* 1 inf, swGA, [A licking] on your sit-downs.

sithe n, v, hence vbl n *sithing* Also sp *scythe, sythe* [*OED2 sithe* v.² c1275 →; "Now *dial.*"; *sithe* sb.² 1609 →]
A sigh; to sigh.

1795 Dearborn *Columbian Grammar* 138, *List of Improprieties. . .* Scythe for Sigh. **1858** Stearns *Practical Guide Pronc.* liii, The following words have no connection . . yet those of the first list are perpetually confounded with those of the second. . . sigh (sy)—scythe. **1914** *DN* 4.81 **ME, nNH,** Sythe. . . To sigh. **1929** *AmSp* 5.122 **ME,** "Sithe" (Prov. Eng.) for sigh was not infrequent. **1968** *DARE* (Qu. X46, *When a person's getting sleepy and opens his mouth wide and takes a deep breath, that's a _____*) Inf **NY**75, Sithing ['saɪθɪn].

sit horses See **set horses**

Sitka spruce n Also *Sitka pine*
Std: a **spruce** (here: *Picea sitchensis*) of the Pacific coast from California to Alaska. Also called **Columbia River spruce, Oregon ~, silver ~, tideland ~, yellow ~**

sitten See **sit** v¹ **3d**

sitter n Also *seater, setter, sitters* **scattered exc NEast, West** See Map
The buttocks.

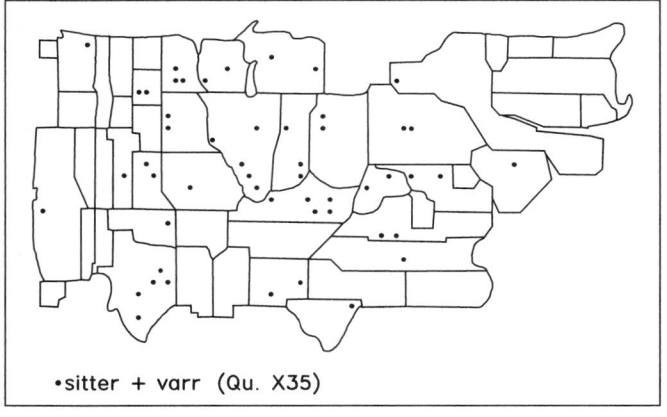

•sitter + varr (Qu. X35)

1942 Berrey–Van den Bark *Amer. Slang* 121.71, *Posteriors. . .* sitter(s). **1950** *WELS* WI *(Joking words for the part of the body that you sit on)* 11 Infs, Sitter; 2 Infs, Seater; 1 Inf, Setter. **1965–70** *DARE* (Qu. X35) 29 Infs, **scattered exc NEast, West,** Sitter; 16 Infs, **scattered exc NEast, West,** Setter; 9 Infs, **esp N Cent,** Seater. [43 of 52 total Infs old] **1984** Wilder *You All Spoken Here* 38 **Sth,** Setter: Buttocks. **1986** Pederson *LAGS Concordance (The haunches)* 1 inf, **cAR,** Setter.

sitting chair See **setting chair**

sitting-down place See **sit-down** n

sitting up See **set up** v phr 3

sit up v phr See **set up** v phr **1, 4**

sit up n See **set up** v phr **1**

sit-upon n Also *sit-upons* Cf **sit-down** n, **sitter**
The buttocks; the posterior.
1942 Berrey–Van den Bark *Amer. Slang* 121.71, *Posteriors. . .* sit-upon(s). **1969** *DARE* (Qu. X35, *Joking words for the part of the body that you sit on . . "He slipped and came down hard on his _____."*) Inf MO20, Sit-upon.

sive See **scythe**

sivvy bean See **sieva bean**

si-waddlin adv, adj Cf **si-godlin, si-gogglin**
See quots.
1941 *AmSp* 16.24 **sIN,** Si-waddlin. . . [Footnote:] Same meaning as *si-gogglin.* **1969** *DARE* (Qu. MM14, *If a drugstore is on one corner of a square and a gas station is on the far corner . . "The drugstore is _____ the gas station."*) Inf KY24, [ˌsaɪˈwɔdlɪn]—diagonally or straight across from.

si-wankert adj Also *si-wichered, siwickerin*
Lopsided; crooked.
1967 *DARE* (Qu. KK70, *Something that has got out of proper shape: "That house is all _____."*) Inf OH31, Si-wankert. **1976** *Harper's Weekly* 26 Jan 19 **OH, WV,** "Siwickerin" is my favorite expression here in our Appalachian area of West Virginia and southeastern Ohio. It means twisted, wrong, out of joint. **1982** *NYT Article Letters,* "Si wichered". . . It means out of balance, lopsided. I think I got the phrase from my mother who was western Pennsylvania Dutch.

Siwash n |ˈsaɪˌwɑš| [Chinook Jargon < CanFr *sauvage* an American Indian]
1 rarely *Siwasher:* An American Indian, esp of the Pacific Northwest coast and Alaska; a person of mixed ancestry. **chiefly NW, AK** *often derog*
[**1847** Palmer *Jrl.* 150, [Chinook Jargon:] *Si-wash* Indians.] **1869** *Overland Mth.* 3.170 **csWA,** The banks of the [Columbia] river were enlivened by busy *siwashes* of both sexes, catching and curing salmon. **1890** *Puyallup* (Wash.) *Commercial* 17 Oct. 7/4 *(DA),* A stolid Siwash and his wife were seated on a box in front of a Puyallup store from noon till 8 p.m. **1918** *DN* 5.28 **eWA,** Siwash. . . 1. An Indian. 2. A slovenly, lazy, drunken Indian. . . General. . . *Siwasher.* . . A siwash man. Rare. **1930** Williams *Logger-Talk* 16 **Pacific NW,** Siwash: A canoe Indian. **1936** Adams *Cowboy Lingo* 205 **NW,** 'Siwash' . . an Indian and used in the sense of not being up to the white man's standard. **1943** *Sun* (Baltimore MD) 11 Oct 2/7 *(Hench Coll.)* **Seattle WA,** When a wife is trying to raise five children and at the same time hold down a full-time war job her husband ought not to take the Siwash's view that housework is entirely the wife's business. . . "That's the Siwash way, you know, for the buck to lie around and let the squaw do all the work," [the Justice of the Peace] told the husband. **1944** Williamson *Far North* 48 **AK,** They paused long enough to tell Henderson that there was a big strike at Bonanza Creek. White man and a couple of siwashes started it off. **1951** in 1981 Tabbert *Dict. Alaskan Engl.* 55, *Siwash.* . . All Indians in the North are spoken of as "natives" respectfully, and "siwashes" disrespectfully. **1958** McCulloch *Woods Words* 166 **Pacific NW,** Siwash. . . An Indian. **1966–68** *DARE* (Qu. HH28, *Names and nicknames . . for people of foreign background: Indian*) Infs AK5, MI55, WA1, 3, Siwash; AK8, Siwash [ˈsaɪwɑš]—derogatory term—used by Indians of Whites or vice versa; (Qu. HH29a, *. . People of mixed blood—part Indian*) Inf MN18, Siwash—heard, unsure of exact meaning. **c1971** Hall *Snake River Valley* **swID,** *(Terms for Indians)* 1 inf, Siwash. **1979** *Oregonian Article*

Letters **OR,** Regarding the word *siwash* most of the people in Ore & Wash think it is a tribe or low class Indian. I asked an Indian about this and he said it was what the Indians called all of them. **1987** *Fairbanks Daily News–Miner* 3 May sec H 14 (Tabbert *Dict. Alaskan Engl.*), Fred and I just preferred to stay away from each other because of his family and the people here. . . He was half-Eskimo, a 'siwash' to most of the people.
2 Transf: a White person. **esp NW, AR** *derog*
1918 *DN* 5.28 **eWA,** Siwash. . . An uncouth ruffian (white). General. **1924** C.E. Mulford *Rustler's Valley* xiii.158 *(OED2),* So-long, you Siwash! **c1929** Bowen *Sea Slang* 124, Siwash. In Nova Scotian and American ships, the meanest type of seaman, just as the Siwash is described as the meanest kind of Red Indian. **1965** Bowen *Alaskan Dict.* 29, Siwash. . . a derogatory term for a Caucasian who has gone native. **1968** *DARE* (Qu. HH28) Inf AK8, Siwash [ˈsaɪwɑš]—derogatory term—used by Indians of Whites or vice versa.
3 See **Siwash dog.**
4 A small, second-rate college. [From *Siwash* the fictional college created by George Fitch (1887–1915)] *joc* or *derog* Cf **jerkwater** adj **2**
[**1911** Fitch *At Good Old Siwash* [title].] **1932** *AmSp* 7.336 [Johns Hopkins jargon], *Siwash*—term facetiously used to designate any college. **1940** *Topeka Daily Capital* (KS) 9 May 4 *(AmSp* 16.309), From fresh water Siwashes to the greatest universities. **1984** *Washington Post* (DC) 9 Oct sec C 6 (Internet), Podunk has been playing Siwash for 75 years now. **1991** *Ibid* 27 Aug sec F 1 (Internet), Siwash State collides with Opalousa Tech tonight in a game between traditional rivals that will decide the conference championship, as well as establish bragging rights around the state for the winner.

siwash v, hence vbl n *siwashing*
1 also with *it:* To camp out or travel with little or no equipment or provisions. **AK** Cf **Siwash camp**
1904 *Churchman* 21 May 626 **AK,** I have a lame shoulder . . , the result of continuous 'siwashing' and sleeping in the snow. **1913** Beach *Iron Trail* 78 **AK,** Help Tom load the lightest boat with rations for five days. If we run short we'll 'Siwash' it. **1939** FWP *Guide AK* xli, Siwash. . . (C[hinook]) to sleep out without shelter. **1940** White *Wild Geese* 156 **AK,** Unless you want to siwash it, it's hard work. **1950** *AK Sportsman* Dec 12, We had all given up and were preparing to siwash, or camp in the open, that night. **1976** Hobbs–Specht *Tisha* 204 **AK,** "These people just don't appreciate me," he said, "so I'm gonna siwash it back to my own people."
2 To bar (a person) from obtaining alcoholic drink. **esp NW**
1929 Willoughby *Trail Eater* 183 **AK,** I'm going to have you siwashed! By the Holy Mackinaw, I'm going to the judge tonight and fix it so you'll never get another drink in this town. **1958** *AmSp* 33.272 **eWA** [Ranching terms], *Siwashed, to be.* . . To be blackballed. Liquor stores keep (or did keep) lists of Indians who attempted to buy liquor, as well as the names of liquor offenders. This was known as the 'Indian list' and seems to be the origin of the expression. **1967** *DARE* FW Addit **cOR,** Siwash—[ˈsaɪwɑš]—When you can't handle any more beer they siwash you, *cut you off,* say you can't have any more. **1979** *Oregonian Article Letters* **neOR,** "To siwash" is to refuse to serve liquor to someone, whether Indian or white, because the person cannot tolerate it, or is already too drunk to be safe to either himself or others. *Ibid* **OR,** Siwash. . . means taking their [=Indians'] whisky away by the U.S. Gov't. They were "siwashed."
3 In logging: see quots. Cf **Siwash logger, ~ outfit, ~ tree**
1950 *Western Folkl.* 9.119 **nwOR** [Logger speech], *Siwash, To.* In cat or horse logging, to place a line around a stump to secure the desired lead instead of rigging a block. **1956** Sorden–Ebert *Logger's Words* 31 **Gt Lakes** (as of a1920), Siwash. . . To drag logs up to the main hauling cable. *Siwashing,* Tangling of a line on a stump or other obstruction. **1958** McCulloch *Woods Words* 101 **Pacific NW,** Kick—To siwash, or change the direction of lead by using a rub tree. **1967** *DARE* FW Addit **cwOR,** Siwash [ˈsaɪwɑš]—to throw a line around log and pull it at an angle.

Siwash camp n **AK** Cf **siwash** v **1** Addit exx in Tabbert *Dict. Alaskan Engl.*
An improvised overnight shelter.
1924 Mason *Arctic Forests* 28 **AK** (Tabbert *Dict. Alaskan Engl.*), All Indians, and many white men, build what is known as a 'siwash' camp. The snow is scraped away with a snowshoe to leave a rectangular patch

of bare ground. Round this the camper builds a windbreak two or three feet high of young spruce-trees at the back and sides. **1978** in 1981 Tabbert *Alaskan Engl.* 229, *Siwash camp.* . . A variety of "siwash" camps are known and used . . depending upon the circumstances of the situation. Snow caves, lean-tos, tarp "half-tents", and many other techniques are utilized.

Siwash dog n Also *Siwash* **AK**   Addit exx in Tabbert *Dict. Alaskan Engl.*

A dog of an indigenous breed.

1898 Henderson *Rainbow's End* AK 191, I can well believe that, but with my knowledge of "Siwash" dogs, I can scarcely credit that they actually spurned food of any kind. **1923** *Anchorage Daily Times* 13 Mar 4 (Tabbert *Dict. Alaskan Engl.*), A man who spent much time in Alaska and the Klondike. . . say[s] that he fed his animals, malamutes, huskies, siwashes—all Indian breeds—with an occasional white man's dog thrown in, on an almost purely vegetarian diet. **1946** *AK Sportsman* Mar 28, Ah, little did I dream, then, in after years I would yearn for the sight of every man, woman, dirty-faced child, and "siwash" dog that made up the community.

Siwasher See **Siwash** n 1

Siwash harness n **AK**   Addit exx in Tabbert *Dict. Alaskan Engl.*

A type of sled-dog harness; see quot 1914.

1914 (1915) Stuck *10000 Miles* 397 **AK,** The "Siwash harness" is simply a band that goes round the shoulders and over the breast. **1959** *AK Sportsman* Apr 40, Martingale or "Siwash" harness. This is by far the most commonly used sled dog harness.

siwashing See **siwash** v

siwash it See **siwash** v 1

Siwash logger n

1958 McCulloch *Woods Words* 166 **Pacific NW,** *Siwash logger*—Along the coast, a man who got his logs by beach combing, not by logging.

Siwash outfit n

An enterprise, as a logging operation or ranch, that operates in a makeshift way.

1930 Williams *Logger-Talk* 28 **Pacific NW,** *Siwash* . . a slack and unenterprizing outfit is a *Siwash outfit.* **1944** Adams *Western Words* 145, *Siwash outfit*—Contemptuous name for an unenterprising ranch. **1965** Bowen *Alaskan Dict.* 29, A *Siwash outfit* is a rough outfit or an outfit in bad repair.

Siwash side n Cf **Indian side**

1958 *AmSp* 33.272 **eWA** [Ranching terms], *Siwash side; Indian side.* The right side of a horse, or the left side of a milch cow; said, therefore, of anything done backward or ineptly. I have not found any record of the word as applied to a cow.

Siwash tree n Cf **siwash** v 3

See quots.

1956 *AmSp* 31.152 **nwCA** [Logger lingo], *Siwash tree.* . . A tree used in place of a block to deflect a cable. **1958** McCulloch *Woods Words* 166 **Pacific NW,** *Siwash tree*—A tree left standing to change the direction of a line in yarding.

si-wichered, siwickerin See **si-wankert**

six n Cf **eight**

One of the pair of draft animals before the **pointers** n 1 in a team.

1967 *DARE* Tape **NV2,** The next horse [to the wheeler] is the pointer. . . Then the next is the six and the eights.

sixes and sevens, the same old See **same old six and seven, the**

six months' cake n

See quot 1902.

1902 in 1959 *AmSp* 34.31 **cME,** *Six months' cake.* . . A nice loaf of cake which can be kept six months or longer. **1906** *Pocumtuc Housewife* 30 **nwMA,** *Six months cake.* . . Sugar . . butter, four eggs . . molas-

ses . . milk, spices . . raisins, citron, currants . . saleratus, four and a half cups flour.

six o'clock, it's See **one o'clock, it's**

six-shooter coffee n Also *six-shooter* **West** Cf *DS* H74a

Strong coffee.

1968 Adams *Western Words* 282, *Six-shooter coffee*—A cowboy's term for the strong coffee of the cow camp—said to be strong enough to float a six-shooter. **1984** Lesley *Winterkill* 137 **neOR,** "Give him some coffee," Red Shirt said. "You want to bust his innards? It's six-shooter." . . When he drank some, the liquid burned bittersweet all the way down. "That's got a stiff punch," he said. . . "Why do you call it six-shooter?" "Either because it's thick enough to float a pistol or because there's six tablespoons for a four-cup pot. I can't remember which." **2000** in 2001 *DARE* File—Internet [Museum of New Mexico—Cowboy Dict.], *Six-shooter coffee*—good, strong coffee. **2001** *Ibid* **NV** [Camp Woofer], Campers will wash down their own hardtack with six-shooter coffee.

sixth day See **first day 1**

sixth month See **first month**

sixty n esp **sAppalachians**

The game of **hide-and-seek A;** also used as a call in the game.

1916 *DN* 4.346 **TN,** *Sixty.* . . The game of hide and seek: so called from counting sixty while the players hide. **c1960** *Wilson Coll.* **csKY,** *Sixty.* . . A child's game; I spy. **1968** *DARE* (Qu. EE13a, *Games in which every player hides except one, and that one must try to find the others*) Inf **VA9,** Hide-and-go-seek = sixty; **VA13,** Sixty. **c1970** *DARE* File **swVA,** *Sixty*—hide and seek. 1. *it* counted to sixty while the rest hid; 2. *it* looked for them and called *sixty* when he found them; 3. they raced back to **base. 2001** *DARE* File **Chicago IL** (as of 1940s), Games of tag were: 60 or Kick the Can. For some unknown or forgotten reason we used to yell "Oly, Oly Ocean Free" to avoid being caught.

sixty-six n esp in Ger settlement areas

A type of **pinochle.**

1857 Frère *Hoyle's Games* 4, The German game of "Sechs und Sechszig," or Sixty-six, has never before, that we are aware of, been dressed in an English garb. *Ibid* 95, *Sixty-Six.* . . This is a German game, played almost universally among the Germans in the United States. **1875** [see **pinochle**]. **1944** *Sat. Eve. Post* 25 Nov 26, The card games America plays today . . Rummy . . sixty-six . . calabrasella. **1950** *WELS* (Card games played a good deal in your neighborhood) 1 Inf, **seWI,** Sixty-six. **1968–69** *DARE* (Qu. DD35 . . *Card games*) Inf **NY226,** Sixty-six—years ago they played this; **PA93,** Sixty-six—this is an abbreviated form of pinochle, with only the face cards doubled; played by the old Germans in the area. **1974** Gibson *Hoyle* 311, *Sixty-six:* An abbreviated, fast moving game similar to two-handed pinochle.

sixty-three n [From the highest possible bid]   esp **nNEng**

A var of the card game **cinch** n[1] **3.**

1913 *Official Rules of Card Games* 157, *Sixty-Three.* The game is a modification of Cinch. . . Sixty-three is the highest bid possible to make. **1966–69** *DARE* (Qu. DD35, . . *Card games*) Infs **ME19, 22, VT16,** Sixty-three; **ME6,** Sixty-three—used to play; **VT12,** Sixty-three—old-fashioned.

six-up n Also *six-up team* Cf **eight-up**

A team of six draft animals.

[**1963** Burroughs *Head-First* 14 **wCO,** When, at the top of the hill, the driver suddenly snatched the whip out of its socket and lashed the horses (there were "six up") into a run, the passengers were very nearly scared out of their wits.] **1967–70** *DARE* Tape **CA205,** My dad drove a six-up team and a freight wagon; **TX26,** We call 'em a six-up or eight-up, or whatever, how many of 'em you got.

six ways for Sunday See **Sunday, forty ways till**

six-week pea See **six-weeks pea**

six-weeks grama n [See quot 1912]

A **grama grass 1,** usu *Bouteloua barbata.*

1894 Coulter *Botany W. TX* 532, *B[outeloua] polystachys.* . . Six-weeks grama. . . River valleys, western Texas to southern California. **1912** Wooton–Standley *Grasses NM* 96, Of the annual species three are referred to as Six-weeks Gramas because they reach maturity in the short rainy season of late summer and early fall. Of these three, one *(B. prostrata)* occurs in the timbered parts of the mountains. . . The other two species *(B. aristidoides* and *B. polystachia)* usually occur on the over-stocked mesas at the lower levels where and when there is little else in the way of food for stock. **1945** Wodehouse *Hayfever Plants* 53, Sixweeks grama . . really includes at least two species, *B. barbata* . . , a low tufted annual, and *B. Parryi* . . , both of the Southwest. **1969** *DARE* (Qu. S9, . . *Kinds of grass that are hard to get rid of*) Inf **TX**68, Six-weeks grama.

six-weeks grass n

1 A **needlegrass 2** (here: *Aristida adscensionis* or *A. dichotoma*).

1912 Wooton–Standley *Grasses NM* 56, *Aristida Bromoides*. . . A common "six weeks" grass on the mesas and to some extent in the fields after the summer rains, in the southern part of the State, in the Lower Sonoran Zone. **1923** Abrams *Flora Pacific States* 1.126, *Aristida adscensionis*. . . Six-weeks Grass. . . Open ground, southern California . . to New Mexico and south to South America.

2 also *six-week grass:* A **bluegrass 1** (here: *Poa annua*).

1877 Hodge *Arizona* 54, The wild grasses of the country are very nutritious, embracing varieties of the wild clover, wild barley and oats, black, white, and curly gramma grass, sacatone, six week grass, many varieties of bunch grass, etc. **1901** Mohr *Plant Life AL* 384, *Poa annua*. . . Spear Grass. Six-weeks Grass. . . Naturalized throughout the continent. **1933** Small *Manual SE Flora* 130, *P[oa] annua*. . . Six week's grass. . . Open grounds, throughout N[orth] A[merica]. **1976** Bailey–Bailey *Hortus Third* 889, *[Poa] annua*. . . six-weeks g[rass].

six-weeks pea n Also *six-week pea*

=black-eyed pea.

1883 *Bot. Gaz.* 8.357 **FL,** Mr. Allen says, speaking of the Whip-poor-will pea, that, "It is generally known among farmers here as six-weeks pea, and is used both as a snap and shell. They are quite palatable. Farmers here make great use of them. In picking we pick partly full-grown pods, and partly mature peas that have not yet become dry. These are boiled together, and are a popular dish." **1966** *DARE* (Qu. I20, . . *Kinds of beans*) Infs **NC**12, Six-week peas; **NC**5, Six-weeks peas.

size See scythe

sizz v Also sp *scizz* [*OED2* a1700 →; "Chiefly *dial.* or *U.S.*"] Cf **siss** v, **sizzer** n[1]

To hiss, sizzle, buzz.

1845 Kirkland *Western Clearings* 70 **MI,** I've worked many an afternoon after my fit [of ague] was over, when my head felt as big as a half-bushel, and my hands would ha' sizzed if I'd put 'em in water. **1858** *S. Lit. Messenger* 26.123 **VA,** I went to bed rite erly, for my eyes wus akin and my hed a sizzing. **1867** Harris *Sut Lovingood Yarns* 81 **TN,** An' I felt sumthin cumin up my swaller, monstrus like a hi pressur steamboat. I cud hear hit a-snortin, and scizzin. **c1885** in 1981 Woodward *Mary Chesnut's Civil War* 79 **SC, GA,** (as of 1861), Keitt quoted a funny Georgia man who says we try our soldiers if they are hot enough before we enlist them. If when water is thrown on them, they do not sizz—they won't do—their patriotism is too cool. **1899** (1912) Green *VA Folk-Speech* 389, *Sizz*. . To hiss; sizzle. **1903** Brady *Bishop* 158 **SW,** He kin watch the thing [=a fuse] sizzin' along the floor better in the dark. **1936** in Lib. of Congress *Amer. Memory: WPA Life Hist.* (Internet) **TX,** While seated around the campfire, with the branding iron sizzing in the fire, they were served the famous dish of son-of-a-gun and black coffee. **1948** Manfred *Chokecherry* 62 **nwIA,** The bumblebee sizzed right up under his straw hat.

sizzer n[1] Also *siss(er)* Also sp *scissor, scizzor* [**sizz, siss** v] chiefly **NEast,** esp **NY** See Map Cf **fizzle** n 3

=sizzler 3.

1897 *Chicago Daily Tribune* (IL) 5 July 6/4, The last cracker will have cracked, the last torpedo will have popped, the last "sizzer" will have hissed. **1907** *DN* 3.183 **NYC,** Two fire-crackers . . are broken on one side in the middle, bent back in a V-shape, and placed apex to apex. The powder overflowing between the two apexes is then ignited. . . Called by New York City children, *scissors* (sizzers). **1947** Weitenkampf *Manhattan Kaleidoscope* 83 **NYC** (as of 1870s), "Scizzors" were firecrackers that had not exploded, bent double so as to crack open, and lighted. **1965–70** *DARE* (Qu. FF15, *When a firecracker doesn't go off, and you break it in the middle and light the powder, you call it a* _____) 13 Infs, 10 **NY, NJ,** Sizzer; **CT**6, **PA**223, Sisser; **CT**10, Siss. [12 of 16 Infs old]

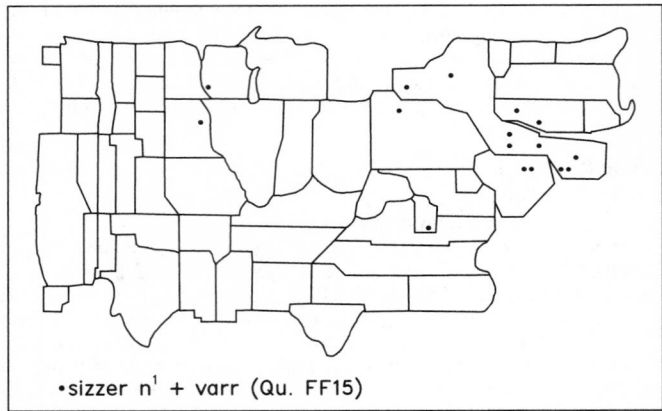

•sizzer n[1] + varr (Qu. FF15)

sizzer n[2] See scissorbill 2a

sizzerbill See scissorbill

sizzery bug n Cf sizz

=cicada.

1910 Johnson *Highways Rocky Mts.* 34 **KS,** He . . held up for my inspection the dry discarded shell of a big beetle which he had in his hand. "It's a sizzery bug," said he, poking it meditatively. *Ibid* 35, Just then the boy's father happened along and remarked: "That's a dry weather fly. They make a kind of a funny noise buzzing with their wings. So the kids call 'em sizzery bugs. We see 'em around most all summer, but they don't do any harm that I've ever heard anybody say."

sizzle n

1 See **sizzler 3.**

2 See **sizzle-sozzle.**

sizzle-britches n

A **goldeneye 1** (here: *Bucephala clangula*).

1956 MA Audubon Soc. *Bulletin* 316 **MA,** American Golden-eye. . . Sizzle-britches. . . In allusion to its speed or to the whistling sound made by the wings in flight.

sizzler n

1 The cook of a logging or construction camp. Cf **boiler** n[1] 3

1925 *AmSp* 1.137 **Pacific NW,** A camp cook is simply a cook until the loggers have graded him; and for each grade of cook they have a name full of meaning. "Gut-burglar," "stomach-robber," "stewbum," "sizzler," "dough-roller," and "star chief." **1927** *DN* 5.462 [Underworld jargon], *Sizzler*. . . The cook at a construction camp. **1938** (1939) Holbrook *Holy Mackinaw* 263, *Sizzler*. See *boiler*. **1942** *AmSp* 17.224 [Loggers' talk], *Sizzler*. A better cook than a *boiler*. **1969** Sorden *Lumberjack Lingo* 110 **NEng, Gt Lakes,** *Sizzler*—A cook who generally fried food. **1975** Gould *ME Lingo* 256, *Sizzler*—Another term for a woods cook. . . As the *boiler* knew how to boil food, the *sizzler* knew how to fry it. (Neither term should be spoken directly to a cook at any time.)

2 A turnover fried in deep fat.

1939 Wolcott *Yankee Cook Book* 364, "Sizzlers." A New England dessert similar to a fried pie. **1952** Tracy *Coast Cookery* 108 **MA,** *Sizzlers* . . flour . . sugar . . baking powder . . salt . . butter . . egg . . milk . . blueberries . . Fat for deep-frying. . . Combine egg and milk and stir into dry ingredients. Roll thin . . and cut about the size of a saucer. Place . . blueberries on each round of pastry and seal the edges with water. Fry in deep hot fat.

3 also *sissler, sizzle:* A firecracker that is broken open and lit to make a hissing noise. **scattered, but chiefly NEast, N Cent, West** See Map Cf **sizzer** n[1]

1965–70 *DARE* (Qu. FF15, *When a firecracker doesn't go off, and you break it in the middle and light the powder, you call it a* _____) 90 Infs, **scattered, but chiefly NEast, N Cent, West,** Sizzler; **MD**28, **MO**19, **NY**70, Sizzle; **NJ**55, Sissler. [Of all Infs responding to the question, 66% were old; of those giving these responses, 76% were old.] **1984** *DARE* File **csWI** (as of 1930s), Cat-and-dog fight—[These were] sizzlers in Cottage Grove, Wisconsin.

sizzle-sozzle n Also *sizzle(-sazzle), sizzle-sozzle rain, sizzly-sozzly* Cf **drizzle-drazzle**

A gentle rain, drizzle.

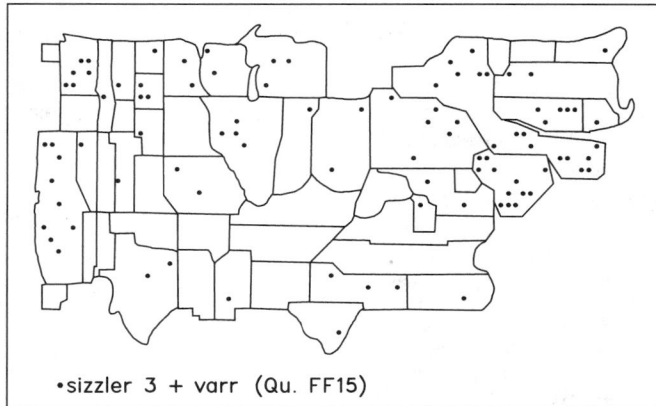

•sizzler 3 + varr (Qu. FF15)

1931 *AmSp* 7.49 **Sth, SW** [Lumberjack lingo], Perhaps one fellow will tell about a "sizzle-sozzle," another a "gully washer" rain, and then some other will tell about a rain "over in Arkansas that was so long and hard that it made Noah's flood look like a spring shower." **1946** *PADS* 6.27 **ceNC,** *Sizzly-sozzly.* . . Very light garden-variety rain. Jocular. . . Occasional. **1949** *Richmond Times–Dispatch* (VA) 26 Dec 6/5 *(Hench Coll.)* **eTN, wNC,** A light rain; a "sizzle-sozzle." **1968** Haun *Hawk's Done Gone* 78 **TN,** One cloudy night, after the thunder and lightning had quit and the rain had slacked to a mere sizzle-sozzle, I went out on the porch. **1968** *DARE* (Qu. B21, *When fine drops of moisture are falling . . it's doing what?*) Inf **NJ20,** Sizzle-sozzle. **1971** WI Statist. Reporting Serv. *Report* 23 Aug 2, A welcome gentle "sizzle-sozzle" rain falling. **1979** *NYT Article Letters,* The aforesaid fable also used "sizzle-sazzle" for a light rain. **1984** Wilder *You All Spoken Here* 140 **Sth,** *Sizzle sozzle, sizzly sozzly . . :* A good season. From a prayer by Uncle Billy Duke, of the Duke University generation of Dukes: "O Lord, send us some rain. We need it. But don't let it be a gully washer. Just give us a sizzle sozzle." **1986** Pederson *LAGS Concordance (A steady drizzle)* 1 inf, **cTN,** Sizzle—lighter than a sprinkle.

sizzletail n Also *sizzletail swallow*
=scissortail 1.
   1965–68 *DARE* (Qu. Q20, . . *Kinds of swallows and birds like them)* Inf **OK13,** Sizzletail; **KS12,** Sizzletail swallow.

sizzly sod-soaker n Cf **sizzle-sozzle,** *DS* B25
A steady rain.
   1991 Still *Wolfpen Notebooks* 91 **sAppalachians,** When the old folks wanted a rain they'd look up at the sky and say, 'I wish hit would come a sizzly sod-soaker.' *Ibid* 92, *Rain making*—For a sizzly sod-soaker: Three snakes.

sizzly-sozzly See **sizzle-sozzle**

skace See **scarce**

skadoodles See **scadoodles**

skaffle See **scaffold** n

skag n Also sp *scag* [Var of *skeg,* perh by analogy with *kag,* var of **keg**]
   1875 in 1876 Hallock *Camp Life* 270, Length of Spray, twenty-one feet; beam, seven feet; cat rigged; centre-board; form of bottom, midway between bateau and yacht; deep scag forward. **1927** *AmSp* 2.364 **cwWV,** *Skag* . . a rudder fastened to the bottom of a boat. "The skag became loose the last rise in the river." **1953** (1977) Hubbard *Shantyboat* 49 **Missip-Ohio Valleys,** A skag was placed on the stern rake. This is a sort of permanent rudder or fin. **1969** *DARE* Tape **NC76,** [FW:] What are the parts of a [surf]board? [Inf:] Just the board and the skag. [FW:] Skag. [Inf:] Skag . . it does the same job a rudder would do.

skag v [*EDD skog* v. 3 "To tear obliquely; to split; to wound slightly"]
?To split.
   1929 *AmSp* 4.356 **ME,** Skag every stick of it once or twice with your axe, to let in the air, and put it under cover, or you will find it doted in the spring. White birch always gets doted if it ain't clifted.

skal(l)awag See **scalawag**

skallyhoot See **scallyhoot** v

Skandihoovian See **Scandihoovian**

skapaug See **scuppaug**

skase See **scarce**

skat n |skat| [*OED2* 1864 →] **chiefly in Ger settlement areas** Cf **five hundred 1**
A card game similar to **sheepshead 5,** with the added feature that players bid to determine which of several variations to play.
   1913 *Official Rules of Card Games* 172, *Skat.* . . 32-card pack, Ace (high) to 7 (low). . . For three players. If more than three play, . . the players not receiving cards share the fortunes of the two who play against the successful bidder. [*Ibid* 174, *Objects of the Game.*—There are two general classes of games—those in which the player's object is to take no trick, and those in which the player's object is to win enough counting cards in tricks to make 61.] **1950** *WELS (Card games played a good deal in your neighborhood)* 12 Infs, **WI,** Skat. **1967–69** *DARE* (Qu. DD35, . . *Card games)* Infs **IL98, NE6,** Skat; **IA18,** Skat—old Germans here played—a very difficult game; **MN36,** Skat [skɑt]; **TX64,** Skat—German game; **WI12,** Skat [skɑt]. **1973** Flach *Yankee German-America* 24 **csTX,** Singing was heard in the cafes where the men gathered to drink beer and play pinochle and skat.

skate n[1]
Std: a fish of the family Rajidae. For other names of var of these see **hedgehog ray, sea possum, stingaree, tobacco box;** for names of the egg case of these fishes see **mermaid's pouch, sailor's purse**

skate n[2] [Sense **1** is of Scots origin. It is unclear if the other senses are related or not; see the individual senses below.]
1 A low, mean, contemptible person. Note: The comb *cheapskate* is std and is not illustrated here. [*SND skate* n.[1] 3 "a term of contempt for a stupid or despicable person"; regarded by *SND* as a fig use of *skate,* the fish, but perh a (euphem?) var of *skite* n.[2] 2 (cf **skite** n).]
   1896 *Typographical Jrl.* 9.6 **IN,** The voracious and rapacious "skate," . . roars himself hoarse in advocacy of reform, gaining position and prominence, only to sell himself in the end to the best advantage. **1898** Dunne *Mr. Dooley Peace & War* 198, If th' skate fr'm Okalahoma is allowed f'r to belch anny in this here assimblage, th' diligates fr'm th' imperyal Territ'ry iv New Mexico'll lave th' hall. **1900** *DN* 2.59 [College slang], *Skate.* . . 1. A reckless fellow. 2. A contemptuous epithet applied to a mean fellow, especially to one who does not pay his debts. 3. A cad, in the phrase 'a cheap *skate.*' 4. An intoxicated person. **1905** *DN* 3.95 **nwAR,** *Skate.* . . Reprobate. 'He's a tough old skate.' Common. **1929** [see **2** below]. **1967** *DARE* (Qu. U17, *Names or nicknames for a person who doesn't pay his bills)* Inf **MA34,** Poor skate—that's a slangy word; **OH11,** Short skate [FW queries]; (Qu. HH40, *Uncomplimentary words for an old man)* Infs **NM6,** Old skate, old stiff; **NY24,** Just an old skate; **TX101,** Old grampa, old skate. **1993** *DARE* File **PA,** How about *skate* for the person who always has to leave when it's their turn to buy a round?
2 A bony, decrepit horse or cow. [This sense is attested only in the US and is perh unrelated to **1** above.] **chiefly Nth, N Midl** See Map on p. 984
   1890 *DN* 1.75 **MA, NH,** *Skate* [skeɪt]: a worn-out horse. Plymouth, Mass. . . Cape Cod and New Hampshire. **1894** Kipling in *Century Illustr. Mag.* 49.493 **VT,** You intoed, shufflin', sway-backed, wind-suckin' skate, you! **1905** *DN* 3.89 **nwAR,** *Old skate.* . . An old, broken-down horse. 'He doesn't give the old skate anything to eat.' Common. **1912** *DN* 3.585 **wIN,** *Old skate.* . . A worn-out horse. **1929** *AmSp* 5.122 **ME,** A poor or worn-out horse was an "old plug" or an old "skate." These were also opprobrious epithets for the intoxicated. **1931** *AmSp* 7.121 **eID,** *Skate* or *nag* means a horse of poor quality. **1935** Davis *Honey* 57 **OR,** Everybody knew that Joel Hardcastle's horses were underfed, badly shod, and skates to start with. **1937** *AmSp* 12.103 **eNE** [Farm terms], Old, worn-out horses are known by a variety of terms, such as *crow bait, skates, skinflints, plugs, nags.* **1958** *AmSp* 33.271 **eWA** [Ranching terms], *Scate* [sic] *See horse.* *Ibid* 270, Here I bring together all the current terms. The most common are: *pony, cayuse, shitter,* and *scate.* **1965–70** *DARE* (Qu. K44, *A bony or poor-looking horse)* 14 Infs, **esp Nth, N Midl, West,** (Old) skate; (Qu. K15, *A thin, bony, or poor-looking cow)* Infs **CT17, KS18, PA21, TX16, VT2,** (Old) skate. [15 of 17 total Infs old]

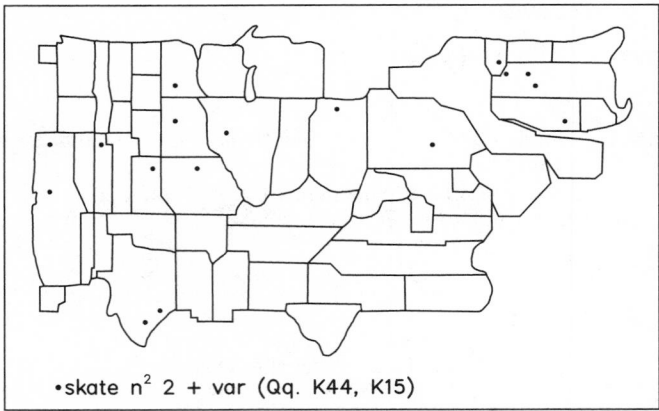

•skate n² 2 + var (Qq. K44, K15)

3 A state of drunkenness—usu in phr *have a skate on* to be drunk. [Cf **skate** v **4** and *SND skite* n.¹ 3 "A jollification, spree . . , esp. in phr *on the skite*"]

1900 *DN* 2.59 [College slang], *Skate. . .* The condition of being intoxicated. **1931** *AmSp* 7.87 [Prohibition terms], Terms referring to the state of intoxication. . . Have a skate on. **1968** *DARE* (Qu. DD14, *When a person is partly drunk, "He's _____."*) Inf **MI**76, Feels pretty high, got a skate on [laughter].

skate v, hence vbl n *skating*

1 To leave, go; to move rapidly. Cf **skeet** v **1, skite** v

1900 *DN* 2.59 [College slang], *Skate. . .* 1. To go, in general. 2. To hurry. **1915** Johnson *Battleground Advent.* 418 **nVA,** Holt met the ol' man comin' from the barn as hard as he could run. Oh! he was comin' from thar skatin'. **1970** *Current Slang* 4.3–4.23 [NM State Univ slang], *Skate. . .* To leave. **1970** *DARE* (Qu. N7, *If you had made a trip by car to a city . . "We _____ to X last week."*) Inf **MI**118, Skated. **1990** Burke *Morning for Flamingos* 120 **seLA,** "I heard you were in 'Nam. . . Those scars on your thigh, you got hit?" "A bouncing Betty on a trail. . ." "Then you got to go back to the States?" "Sure. . ." "In the corps, unless you get the big one, you got to earn two Hearts before you skate."

2 To cause (a stone) to skip; to skip a stone. **esp Sth, S Midl** See Map [Cf **skeet** v **3** and *SND skite* v.¹ "to cause (a stone) to skip over the surface of water"]

a1861 (1880) Eastman *Poems* 186 **VT,** For there [at a swamp] were the boys of the village seen / When the ice was strong, or the leaves were green,/ From morn till the night at play,/ Skating stones, or rolling the snow. **1965–70** *DARE* (Qu. EE30, *Throwing a flat stone over the surface of water so that it jumps several times*) 10 Infs, **esp Sth, S Midl,** Skating (rocks *or* stones); **TN**16, Skating them on the water; **TX**101, Rock skating. [11 of 12 Infs male, 10 old] **1983** *MJLF* 9.1.56 **ceKY** (as of 1956), *Skate rocks. . .* to skip rocks across water.

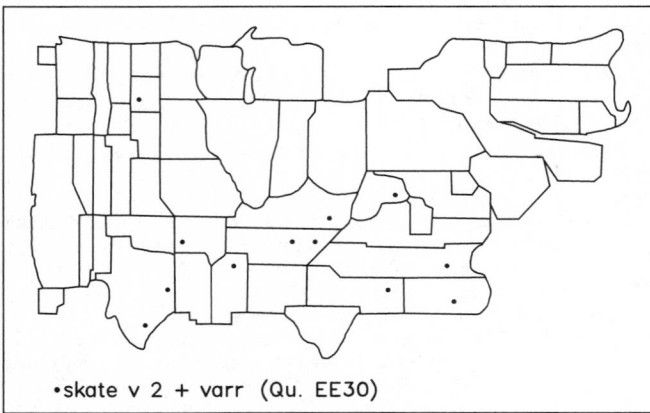

•skate v 2 + varr (Qu. EE30)

3 To shirk one's duties; to get away with something. [Perh by ext from **1** above]

1945 L. Shelly *Jive Talk Dict.* 17 (OED2), *Skate,* to get away with something. **1969** *DARE* (Qu. A9, *. . Wasting time by not working on the job*) Inf **IN**58, Skating. **1970** Major *Dict. Afro-Amer. Slang* 104,

Skate: (1940's) to escape paying a debt. **1975** *AmSp* 50.66 **AR** (as of c1970), *Skate. . .* Shirk duties—"The new pledges are really skating this week." (fraternity and sorority use)

4 To become intoxicated. [Cf *SND skite* v.¹ 5(2) "To conduct oneself in a wild, boisterous or madcap manner, to spree; to carouse"] Cf **skate** n² **3**

1900 *DN* 2.59 [College slang], *Skate, v.i. . .* To get intoxicated.

skater n Also *pond skater*

A **water strider** (family Gerridae).

1905 Kellogg *Amer. Insects* 196, On the surface are the familiar water-striders, or skaters. . . They are members of the family Hydrobatidae. **1911** *Century Dict. Suppl., Pond-skater. . .* Any one of the aquatic bugs of the family *Hydrobatidae.* **1964** Wigglesworth *Insects* 47, Perhaps the most familiar of the insects of water surfaces are the pond skaters, *Gerris* and its allies. **1967** *DARE* (Qu. R28, *. . Kinds of spiders*) Inf **MI**42, Water spider—some call them skaters; **PA**49, Skaters = water spiders; **WY**5, Water spider or skater. **1980** Milne–Milne *Audubon Field Guide Insects* 468, Common Water Strider—"Skater"—(*Gerris remigis*).

skawcoo n

A **nightshade 1** (here: *Solanum dulcamara*).

1900 Lyons *Plant Names* 349, Bittersweet, Nightshade . . Skawcoo, Snake-berry [etc]. **1930** Sievers *Amer. Med. Plants* 11, Bitter Nightshade. . . Other common names. . . skawcoo.

skay'd See **scare B**

skean See **skein**

skear See **scare A**

skearce See **scarce**

skeared, skeart See **scare B**

skeary See **scary**

skeat See **skeet** v

sked See **scare B**

skedunk See **squeedunk**

skee n [Abbr]

Whiskey.

1929 *AmSp* 4.385 **KS** [Wet words], The term *skee* is used indiscriminately for either white or colored whiskey. **1930** *Amer. Mercury* 21.456 [Racketeer argot], We hist the mutt's plant for fifty cases of skee. **1942** Berrey–Van den Bark *Amer. Slang* 100.12, Whiskey. . . Skee. **1967** *DARE* (Qu. DD21a, *General words . . for any kind of liquor*) Inf **NE**9, Skee—for whiskey; (Qu. DD21c, *Nicknames for whiskey, especially illegally made whiskey*) Inf **CA**15, Skee.

skee- pref See **skew-**

skeebald See **skewbald**

skee-daddlin See **skew- f**

skee fish See **sheefish**

skee-gee(d) See **skew- a**

skee-haw(ed) See **skew- b**

skee-jawed See **skew- c**

skeel n Cf **keeler**

See quot.

1939 Wolcott *Yankee Cook Book* 367, *Skeel:* a shallow wooden vessel used to "set" milk until the cream gathers.

skeelings n [Cf *SND keel* v.³ "To skim the floating fat from soup, etc."] Cf **air foam**

Froth that forms on the top of boiling food, esp jam.

1950 *WELS Suppl., Skeelings*—skimmings from top of a boiling pot; if unpleasant, [it's called] scum. ([Of] jam, etc.)

skeen See **skein**

skeer See **scare A**

skeerce See **scarce**

skeered See **scare B**

skeersely See **scarcely**

skeert See **scare B**

skeery See **scary**

skeesick(s), skeesix See **skeezicks**

skeester n Also *skeeter*   esp S Atl   Cf **kewster, scutter** n[1], **skeezicks**

A rascal, rogue—often used as an affectionate term for a child.

1966–69 *DARE* (Qu. Z12, *Nicknames and joking words meaning 'a small child': "He's a healthy little _____."*) Infs **NC**37, **SC**40, Skeester; **GA**73, Skeeter.   **1975** Newell *If Nothin' Don't Happen* 23 **nwFL**, I remember when I were just a little bit of a skeester.   **1997** *DARE* File—Internet **GA**, A Big, ugly skeester open hand slapped me for 'lookin' at his fat, ugly wife.   **2001** *NADS Letters* **cGA**, My mother uses the term "skeester" fairly often, and she uses it to describe a rascal or impish person—often a child. She is 86 years old and was born and grew up in Crawford Co., GA (middle of the state just west of Macon).

skeesucks See **skeezicks**

skeet n[1] Also sp *skete*   [*SND skeet* n.[1] "The variant forms *ske(a)te, skeet(e)*, are found in 17–18th c. Eng., but the phonology is difficult to explain."]   Cf **skeet** v 2

An ice skate.

1800 (1898) Hunt *Diary* 2 **PA**, The Squire and myself took each of us a pair of skeets and went up the creek to look for rock fern.   **1818** in 1824 Knight *Letters* 107 **KY**, Some words are used, even by genteel people, from their imperfect educations, in a new sense; and others, by the lower classes in society, pronounced very uncouthly, as . . sketes.   **1894** [see **skeet** v 2].

skeet v   [Cf *EDD skeet* v., *SND* v.[1], v.[2]]   Also sp *skeat, skeete*

1 also *skeeter:* To scoot, move quickly; to move (something) quickly.   [*EDD skeet* v. 4]   **chiefly Sth, S Midl**   Cf **skate** v 1

1838 Neal *Charcoal Sketches* 97 **sePA**, You'd better emigrate—the old man's coming. . . You must skeete, even if you have to cut high-dutchers with your irons loose.   **1861** in 1867 Baker *Hist. U.S. Secret Serv.* 101 **Sth**, Burn the letter unless you can safely carry, and then get in your hole and skeet for Dixie.   **1870** Twain in *Galaxy* 10.731, I hain't got time to be palavering along here . . ; and if you'll just give me a lift we'll skeet him into the hearse and meander along.   **1883** (1971) Harris *Nights with Remus* 86 **GA** [Black], Little ole Jack Sparrer en all er his fambly conneckshun wuz skeetin' 'roun' dar dippin' in dar bills.   **1886** *Atlantic Mth.* 57.13 **wNC**, I want ter see what Tad does when he skeets off an' hides that-a-way.   **1893** Shands *MS Speech* 57, Skeet [skit]. Illiterate whites use this word to mean *to move swiftly, to flee, to run,* and also *to skate.*   **1925** Greer-Petrie *Angeline of the Hill Country* 18 **eKY**, Here comes a mighty impudent lookin' darky a-skeetin' towards us.   **1954** Tolbert *Bigamy Jones* 78 **wTX** (as of 1870s), Pretty soon Bigamy came creeping into the stable. He said, "Put a halter on Joe. And let's skeeter out of here."

2 To skate or slide on ice; hence vbl n *skeeting.*   [*EDD skeet* v. 5]   **chiefly Sth, S Midl**

1872 Schele de Vere *Americanisms* 539, In the South the boys and all the negroes say *skeating* instead of *skating.*   **1892** *DN* 1.231 **KY**, Skeet [skit]: skate.   **1893** [see **1** above].   **1894** *Century Illustr. Mag.* 48.870, When I was a little boy my playmates at a country school in southeastern Indiana wore "skeets" and went "skeeting," though the village boys said *skates.* . . A New York journal of 1784 complains of the time wasted in "skeating" on Collect Pond.   **1899** (1912) Green *VA Folk-Speech* 389, Skeet. . . To skate.   **1916** *DN* 4.346 **TN**, Skeet. . . To skate or slide on ice. Gen'l South.   **1927** Mason *Lure Great Smokies* 26 **wNC, eTN**, You young uns quit skeetin' [=sliding on bare feet] on thet ice!

3 =**skate** v 2.   [*SND skeet* v.[1] 1 "To (make to) skim over the surface of water"]   **Sth, S Midl**   See Map

1965–70 *DARE* (Qu. EE30, *Throwing a flat stone over the surface of water so that it jumps several times*) 17 Infs, **chiefly Sth, S Midl**, Skeeting (rocks *or* stones); **SC**32, **GA**1, (Making it) skeet; [**KY**23, Skeet the water].   **1967** Marshall *Christy* 204 **eTN** (as of 1912), They would select smooth pebbles and skip them across the water, what they called "skeeting the rocks."

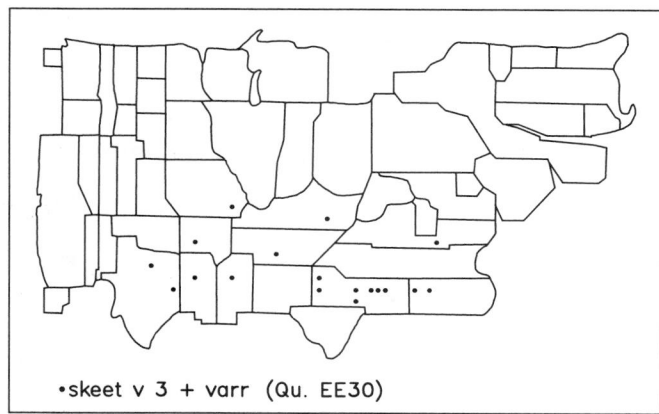

•skeet v 3 + varr (Qu. EE30)

4 To squirt (fluid or rarely gas); to spray a liquid.   [*EDD skeet* v. 1]   **chiefly Sth, S Midl**

1898 *Century Illustr. Mag.* 57.159 **SC**, Go git de gyahden-hose, an' skeet on it quick as ebah you can!   **1909** *DN* 3.370 **eAL, wGA**, *Skeet.* . . To scoot (water), spew out of the mouth, especially between the teeth.   **1935** Hurston *Mules & Men* 64 **neFL**, Julius spat out into the yard, trying to give the impression that he was skeeting tobacco juice like a man.   **1946** McCullers *Member* 33 **AL**, Mrs. Marlowe's atomizer which skeeted perfume.   **1954** *PADS* 21.37 **SC**, *Skeet:* . . To spurt water or saliva between the teeth. "To skeet ambeer," to squirt tobacco spittle between the teeth.   **1963** Wright *Lawd Today* 30 **Chicago IL** [Black], They say them German guys got some kind of a poison gas over there that's so strong and powerful that all they got to do is just skeet some of it in the air and when you smell it you'll curl up and die like a chinch!   **1967** *DARE* FW Addit **LA**, *Skeet*—to squirt. "Negro usage passed over to Whites"—explanation of origin given by a White. (I have heard *skeet* in this sense from a White man from Georgia.)

skeet n[2]   [Echoic]

A **junco** n[1] (here: *Junco hyemalis*).

1955 *Oriole* 20.1.14, Slate-colored Junco. . . skeet (sonic).

skeet n[3] See **mosquito** n[1]

skeet n[4] See **mesquite**

skeetch v   Cf **skeet** v 2, **skitching**

=**hooky bob.**

1979 *DARE* File **csWI**, *Skeetch.* . . To hang onto the back of a vehicle in order to be pulled when one is on skates, a sled, skis, etc. Common among young people in the area.   **1989** *Ibid* **cWI**, *Skeetch*—grabbing on to the back of a car and being pulled behind it, with snow on the ground, of course.

skeete See **skeet** v

skeeter n[1] See **mosquito** n[1]

skeeter v See **skeet** v 1

skeeter n[2] See **skeester**

skeeter hawk See **mosquito hawk 2b**

skeeter kite n   Cf **skeet** v 1

1993 *DARE* File **Montgomery AL**, A skeeter kite is a homemade kite. It is made out of a sheet of plastic attached to crossed stakes.

skeeter leg n

A very thin leg; a person with thin legs.

1889 *Harper's New Mth. Mag.* 79.126 **S Midl**, It's lucky you come upon me 'fo' you run them skeeter legs o' yourn plum' off.   **1966** *DARE* (Qu. X49, *Expressions . . about a person who is very thin*) Inf **AR**40, Skeeter legs.

skeeting See **skeet** v 2

skeets n pl   Often with *the*   Also *skids, skits, skites*   [**skeet** v 4; Engl dial < ON *skitr* excrement]

=**squirts.**

1966 *DARE* (Qu. BB19, *Joking names for looseness of the bowels*) Inf **GA**13, Squirts, skeets [skɪts]; **MN**38, The skites [skaɪts]; **OH**23, The skits; **PA**147, Skids.

skeeve v Also with *out* [Ital *schifare* to disgust, *schifarsi* to be disgusted] **NEast, esp NY** Cf **skeevers**

To be disgusted by; to disgust; hence adjs *skeevie, skeevy, skievy* disgusting, sleazy, disreputable.

1976 *Philadelphia Mag.* Mar 125 **sePA,** The word "skeevie" used by South Philadelphians to indicate something disgusting is from Italian "schifare," to loathe. **1996** Salvucci *Philadelphia Dial.* 58 **sePA,** *Skeeve* v. *Italians.* disgust: *Dat skeeves me. . . skeeve (someone) aout,* thoroughly disgust: *He skeeved me aout. Ibid, Skeevie . .* something disgusting. **1997** *DARE* File **eMA,** Skeeve . . means, as nearly as I can describe it, "to be made squeamish by." For example, "she skeeves spiders." **1998** *Sheidlower Coll.* **NYC,** I heard *skeevy,* meaning disgusting, in Bensonhurst [Brooklyn] in the early 1960s. I'm absolutely sure I heard it by 1965 because a girl I knew in junior high used it all the time, and I went to high school in 1965. **1999** *DARE* File—Internet **ceMA** [Boston Online *Wicked Good Guide to Boston English*], Skeeve—To be grossed out by something. Actual overheard conversation: "Ah youse gonna gowout wit Mahkie again?" "Ah youse plugged in? He skeeves me!" **2000** *NADS Letters* **cNY,** When entering a filthy home, one says, "I skeeve this place." If a man is creepy, a woman might say, "I skeeve him." I have heard people say they skeeve the retained sludge in sink drain traps; a house which has not been cleaned in a long time; and a person who looks or smells like he has not bathed in a long time. . . The actual sources in Italian: schifare, schifo, scifezza, and schifoso, all having to do with disgust, loathing and avoidance. . . I don't know . . if this word has gotten out to the greater Syracuse community, or if it is confined to Italian-Americans. . . "I skeeve that man" is the preferred construction on the "North Side" of Syracuse. "That man skeeves me," or "That man skeeves me out" is the preferred construction in Solvay, a western suburb of Syracuse where people from Tyrol live. . . The adjective "skeevy" for disgusting, slimy, or creepy is used everywhere in the area. *Ibid* **sNJ,** Skeevy is very much a part of the South Jersey vocab. My cousins (all from Gloucester County) have been using it for years to describe something that's gross or disgusting. . . Actual quote from cousin Joe for example's sake, "That skeevy cat snotted on my last beer." I never said I was proud of my relatives. *Ibid* **CT,** My teenage kids use "skeevy" in the 'gross' or 'questionable' sense, esp. my 18-year old Connecticut-raised daughter. *Ibid* **NY,** I distinctly remember hearing "skeevy" 15+ years ago in New York from a young woman, probably late-20s/early 30s, of Jewish background. *Ibid* **seNY,** I heard it [= *skeevy*] a couple of years ago from a fortyish female who has lived all her life on Staten Island, NY. She used it in conveying her sense of the sleazy ways in which males sometimes come on to females they believe are unattached. *Ibid* **NJ,** I teach at Rutgers. . . This year I heard my students using an adjective pronounced /skiːviː/, which they asserted meant "annoying" and came from Italian, where there is a word "schivi." They claim that the word had been around for about 10 years (which is about the range of their historical memory). *Ibid* **NYC,** My thirtyish-year-old daughter was using the term as early as twenty years ago, as well as related verby locutions like "That skeeves me out!" I still hear it/them. Maybe that generation is easily skeeved. *Ibid* **NY,** From Herkimer NY a female medical student, only part Italian, who believes that it [= *skeeve*] is such a nasty word that it should not be uttered in polite company. . . From Long Island a non-Italian who knows only the adjective "skeevy." *Ibid* **NYC,** I have heard Italian-Americans in the New York metropolitan area call a dishonest, slimy individual skeevy. *Ibid* **Long Is. NY,** Skeeve: we used this in an adjectival form, "skeevy." It meant nasty, gross, slimy, filthy, icky and could be applied to people as well as things. *Ibid,* I grew up in Yonkers, New York in the 1950s and 60s . . and we used "skeevy" as an adjective for anything disgusting. **2001** *Ibid* **wNY,** Skeevy—adj., underhanded, dishonest, hypocritical. **2001** *Wall St. Jrl.* (NY NY) 29 May sec A 22/4, No one should have been surprised. Everyone should have been calculating that he would do this [= switch political parties]. . . But what a skievy choice.

skeevers n Also *skeevies*
=**heebie-jeebies 1.**

1930 Shoemaker *1300 Words* 54 **cPA Mts** (as of c1900), *Skeevers*—Fright, uneasiness. **1994** *NYT Mag.* 20 Nov 124/2 **NYC,** I like how dirty New York is. Put me in nature and I get the skeevies.

skeevie See **skeeve**

skeevies See **skeevers**

skeevy See **skeeve**

skee-wampus, skee-wampy See **skew- d**

skee-wee adj
Tiny.

1930 Stoney–Shelby *Black Genesis* 106 **seSC,** Den he squeal out in a li'l skee-wee voice, like Br' Anch' own: "Git 'way from here."

skee-whiffed See **skew- e**

skee-whonked, skee-winkle See **skew- g**

skeezicks n Also sp *skeesick(s), -six, -sucks, -zacks, -zecks, -zix, -zucks* [Cf 1863 Gibbs *Chinook Jargon* 23, "*skasiks*. . . A friend. Used only toward men."] **chiefly Nth, N Midl**
A rascal, good-for-nothing—now usu used affectionately of a child.

1850 *Frontier Guardian* (Kanesville IA) 2 Oct 2/5, Though Kister that skeezecks with Hall at his back,/ Should come again thieving. **1858** *Harper's New Mth. Mag.* 18.138 **CA,** He's the same little skeesick that told me to call for *Jones!* **1875** Holland *Sevenoaks* 40 **NEng,** If there's anything awful bad . . in Skeezacks—I should say that Tom Buffum was an old Skeezacks. **1885** *Atlantic Mth.* 55.332, The old skeesix was still so mad that he would n't give me back the place. **1890** *DN* 1.62 **sePA,** *Skeezix.* In use in and around Philadelphia, to designate a man not altogether to be trusted, *ein pfiffiger Patron,* but somewhat uncouth also. [*DN* Ed: Used by Bret Harte in the sense of a shiftless, good-for-nothing fellow, as the title of a story.] **1890** *Jrl. Amer. Folkl.* 3.311 **NEng, OH,** *Skeezicks*—A worthless fellow, "scallawag." **1891** Garland *Main-Travelled Roads* 50 **West,** The doggoned old skeesucks! **1892** *DN* 1.218 **seNY,** *Skeezix.* . . "Slang about New York City, where, I should say, it has the force of a slightly contemptuous but good-natured appellative; as who should say 'old stick-in-the-mud.'" **1901** *DN* 2.147 **cNY, neNY, swOH,** *Skeezix.* . . In Otsego, Steuben Co., N.Y., used only of a person dishonest in business; in Washington Co., N.Y., Dayton, O., of mischievous persons; in Seneca Co., N.Y., only of children. **1905** *DN* 3.64 **eNE,** *Skeezicks.* . . Mischievous child. **1906** *DN* 3.156 **nwAR,** *Skeezicks.* . . A term of endearment. **1906** Casey *Parson's Boys* 260 **sIL** (as of c1860), I'd take the old skeezix out and drownd him in the river, or I'd smother him in bed some night. **1914** *DN* 4.79 **ME, nNH,** *Skeezucks, little.* . . A mischievous child (endearing, in many cases). **1915** *DN* 4.203 **sePA,** *Skeezicks,* a mean, contemptible fellow. **1939** Rollins *Gone Haywire* 117 *(DA),* Eb Hawkins, that ol' skeesicks you met on th' railway train an' liked, is th' feller that's acted as th' owners' agent in sellin' rights to your uncle. **1969** *DARE* (Qu. Z12, *Nicknames and joking words meaning 'a small child': "He's a healthy little _____."*) Inf **KY**25, Skeezicks.

skehaw See **skew- b**

skein n Usu |sken|; also |skin| Pronc-spp *skean, skeen, skene* [This sense of *skein* is from Du *scheen* and is unrelated to *skein* coil of yarn or thread; the origin of the variant pronc is not clear.]
Std sense, var forms.

1850 U.S. Army Ordnance Dept. *Ordnance Manual* 48, Gun Carriage. . . Iron. . . 8 axle skeans; 16 nails. **1899** (1912) Green *VA Folk-Speech* 389, Skene. . . A thin iron strip on the lower side of the arm of a wooden axletree to save wear. **1920** Hunter *Trail Drivers TX* 303 (as of c1865), In those days wagons had wooden axles with an iron skean, and lynch-pins to hold the wheels on the axle. **1942** Hall *Smoky Mt. Speech* 18 **wNC, eTN,** *Skeins,* the metal covering of the axle, is apparently always [skinz]. **1967** *DARE* FW Addit **SC,** *Skeen*—the part that a wagon wheel turned on.

skel See **skelly 2**

skeleton n Pronc-spp *skeletum, skellikin, skileton, skilleten, skilligan*
A Forms.

1858 Hammett *Piney Woods Tavern* 121, Pretty nigh the same as if the bony old skilleten . . had got his grip fastened onto their coat-tails and petticoats. **1895** *N. Amer. Rev.* 160.756, They do not dare . . to go to bed without a light for fear of ghosts, "skilligans" they call them. **1915** *DN* 4.190 **swVA,** *Skileton.* Variant of *skeleton.* **1943** *Sun* (Baltimore MD) 11 June 12/7, I had gotten used to the classic corruption [of the pronunciation of *skeleton*] "skellikin." **1944** *PADS* 2.49 **NC, VA,** *Skeletum*. . . Skeleton. Mainly illiterates. Occasional.

‡**B** Sense.
   1936 *AmSp* 11.317 **Ozarks,** *Skeleton*. . . A skull. On digging into some Indian burials, a Missouri hillman said: 'Thar was plenty o' leg-bones, an' back-bones, an' ribs, but nary sign of a skeleton.'

skeleton orchard n Also *skeleton park*, ~ *yard* Cf **marble orchard**
A cemetery.
   1936 *AmSp* 11.201 [Euphemisms for the cemetery], Skeleton park. **1942** Berrey–Van den Bark *Amer. Slang* 117.7, Cemetery. . . Skeleton Park. **1966–69** *DARE* (Qu. BB61b, . . *Joking names for a cemetery*) Infs **IN**13, **MS**1, **WV**8, Skeleton orchard; **IL**98, **NY**115, 211, Skeleton park; **IN**13, Skeleton yard.

skeleton plant See **skeletonweed 3**

skeleton shrimp n Also *skeleton screw* [*OED2* 1882 →]
A slender crustacean of the family Caprellidae. Also called **mantis shrimp 2**
   1890 *Century Dict.* 5667, *Skeleton-shrimp*. . . A small, slender crustacean of the family *Caprellidae*, as *Caprella linearis*; a specter-shrimp; a mantis-shrimp. Also called *skeleton-screw*. **1981** Meinkoth *Audubon Field Guide Seashore* 607, Linear Skeleton Shrimp (*Caprella linearis*). *Ibid* 608, Smooth Skeleton Shrimp (*Caprella laeviuscula*). . . The California Skeleton Shrimp (*C. californica*) is larger. *Ibid*, Long-horn Skeleton Shrimp (*Aeginella longicornis*).

skeletonweed n
1 =**gum succory.**
   1894 *Jrl. Amer. Folkl.* 7.91 **WV,** *Chondrilla juncea* . . skeleton weed, naked weed [etc]. **1925** *Book of Rural Life* 9.5087, The Eastern Skeleton Weed (*Chondrilla juncea*), also known as *naked weed, devil's greens,* and *condrille,* is a weed of wheat fields, corn, meadows and pastures in Delaware, Maryland, Pennsylvania and the Virginias. **1946** Tatnall *Flora DE* 281, Skeleton-weed. . . Rather frequent and abundant where it occurs, in dry, sandy fields. **1968** *DARE* (Qu. S26e, *Other wildflowers not yet mentioned;* not asked in early QRs) Inf **VA**24, Skeleton weed.
2 A **wild buckwheat** of the southwestern US, usu *Eriogonum deflexum.*
   1923 in 1925 Jepson *Manual Plants CA* 309, E[*riogonum*] *deflexum*. . . Skeleton Weed. . . Desert washes and flats, Colorado and Mohave deserts . . e[ast] to Nev. and Ariz. **1941** Jaeger *Wildflowers* 31 **Desert SW,** Skeleton Weed. . . Very common in late summer . . along the highways where the soil has been disturbed. **1968** Abbey *Desert Solitaire* 28 **seUT,** I can see . . skeleton weed . . so delicately formed as to be almost invisible. **2001** (acc) AZ Univ. Herbarium *Flora & Vegetation* (Internet) **AZ,** *Eriogonum deflexum*. . . Skeleton weed. Widespread annual; common on roadsides, disturbed soils and along washes.
3 also *skeleton plant:* A plant of the genus *Lygodesmia*, esp *L. juncea.* For other names of *L. juncea* see **devil's shoestring 13, gumweed 3, milk pink;** for other names of var spp see **buckwheat 2, flowering straw 2, prairie pink 2, rush ~, wild asparagus**
   1925 *Book of Rural Life* 9.5087, The Western Skeleton Weed (*Lygodesmia juncea*) is troublesome in the plains region of the Northwest. **1941** Jaeger *Wildflowers* 311, Thorny Skeleton-plant. *Lygodesmia spinosa.* **1963** Craighead *Rocky Mt. Wildflowers* 223, Rushpink— *Lygodesmia grandiflora.* . . Other names: Skeleton plant. **1968** *DARE* FW Addit **CO**7A, Skeleton weed . . milk pink—*Lygodesmia juncea.* **1975** Zwinger *Run River* 218 **UT,** Clusters of white mustards, wild four o'clock, skeleton plant and purple scorpionweed are a startling green against the pallid ground. **2000** (acc) N. Prairie Wildlife Research Center *Biol. Resources* (Internet) **ND,** Nearly every county in North Dakota is home to the skeleton-weed. . . The plant looks like a slender bare branch about six inches to a foot tall, but close inspection will reveal a few tiny needle-like leaves on the upper branches.
4 A **wire lettuce.**
   1973 Hitchcock–Cronquist *Flora Pacific NW* 552, *Stephanomeria* [spp]. . . Skeletonweed; Wirelettuce [etc].

skeleton yard See **skeleton orchard**

skeletum See **skeleton**

skeller-eyed adj [Scots, Ir, nEngl dial; *EDD skelly-eyed* (at *skelly* adj. 7.(2)) "having a squint, cross-eyed"]
Cross-eyed.
   1927 in 1944 *ADD* **WV,** *Skelter-eyed,* or *skeller-eyed*. . . Cross-eyed. **1930** Shoemaker *1300 Words* 59 **cPA Mts** (as of c1900), *Skeller-eyed*— Cross-eyed. [**1967** *DARE* (Qu. X26b, *If a person's eyes look in different directions, looking outward, he's* _____) Inf **WA**28, Scally [skæli]-eyed.]

skellikin See **skeleton**

skellion See **scallion**

skelly n [Origin unknown] **NYC**
1 also *skelsy, scully pit, skellzies, skully:* A children's street game; see quots.
   1953 Brewster *Amer. Nonsinging Games* 115, Skelly [New York]— This game is usually played in the street. Each player is equipped with one "checker," a small block of wood or a flat stone. He pitches first at square 1. If his "checker" stops inside that square, he is entitled to another shot, and so on. . . The space separating the boxes in the inner group is called "skelly," and no player whose "checker" lands here may shoot again until some kind-hearted player knocks it out. **1967** *DARE* FW Addit **NYC,** Skully—game board chalked on sidewalk, yard square; bottle caps filled with wax must be shot to different points within the square. **1975** Ferretti *Gt. Amer. Book Sidewalk Games* 230, Skelly, surely the quintessential New York City street game, uses checkers— bottle caps filled with wax for weight, glass bottle tops worn smooth, brick chips, and the caps from half-gallon wine jugs as shooters. . . Also known as *Skelsy, Scully Pit, Tops,* and *Caps*. . . The object of the game is to go from box 1 to box 13 (in . . progression . .), then return the same way from 13 to 1. **1977** *NY Times* (NY) 6 July 29/3 **NYC,** As everyone knows, skelsy—or skelly—is a form of street pool played with bottle caps in which players go through, croquet-style, a series of boxes numbered 1 to 13. **1980** *DARE* File **NYC,** One friend tells me it [= *skelly*] is also called *scully;* another that it was known as *skelsy.* **1994** *NY Times* (Natl. ed.) (NY) 18 Aug sec B 8/1 **NYC,** All it takes to play skellzies (also known as skelly or skully) is chalk, a sidewalk and a bottle cap for each player. The game's name comes from the skull and crossbones that surround the No. 9 box. [*Ibid,* The game . . has lasted a long time; about as long as the crown-rimmed bottle cap (circa 1910).] **2001** *DARE* File **Bronx NYC** (as of 1955), The essence of skelly was to fillip a weighted "checker"—usually a bottle-cap into which a washer had been placed and hot wax poured in—through a course of numbered boxes painted on the ground. The weight allowed one to strike the checkers of one's opponents out of the course with added force increasing your chance of completing the course and winning the game before they did. Skelly was a fixture of playground life and the Parks Department and Housing Authority would paint skelly courses on playground surfaces.
2 also *skel;* See quots.
   1953 [see **1** above]. **1975** Ferretti *Gt. Amer. Book Sidewalk Games* 232 **NYC,** Getting to the 13 box carries with it much danger. In some versions, the four areas around the 13 box (called "skels") have number values. If you land in any of them, you are forced to stay there for as long as the other players want you to.

skelp See **scalp**

skelsy See **skelly 1**

skemelton See **skimmelton**

skene See **skein**

skeow See **scow** n[2]

skep n[1] Also *scape, skip* [*skep* a large basket; a straw beehive; the var *skip* is widespread in Engl dial, while *scape* is an older Scots var] **esp NEast**
A beehive; a bee house. Note: *Skep* in hist refs to the obsolete straw beehive is not illustrated here.
   1901 *DN* 2.147 **cNY,** *Skip*. . . A bee-hive; still heard occasionally in N.Y. c., where, according to report, it was formerly the universal name. **1930** Shoemaker *1300 Words* 54 **cPA Mts** (as of c1900), *Scape*—A beehive. **1950** *WELS* (The place where bees live and store their honey: . . *Wild bees*) 1 Inf, **cnWI,** Nest, skep. **1953** Van Wagenen *Golden Age* 179 **NY,** Within my memory a half-dozen or more hives (often called

"skips") in some sheltered spot not too far from the kitchen door were a common feature of the countryside. **1968** *DARE* (Qu. R19a, *The place where bees live and store their honey—tame bees*) Inf **NY**73, Skip [FW: used in conv]; **NY**93, Skep; (Qu. R19b, . . *The place where wild bees live and store their honey*) Inf **NJ**8, Skip—a skip of bees is the bees in the hive, like a flock.

skep n[2], v   See **scalp**

skere   See **scare A**

skered   See **scare B**

skerse   See **scarce**

skery   See **scary**

sketch n   [*SND sketch* n.[2] "a brief period of time, a short spell"] A short period; a thin layer.

  1968–70 *DARE* (Qu. A14, . . *A very short period of time: "I'll be ready in _____." or "It won't take any longer than _____."*) Inf **NH**14, Sketch of time; (Qu. B33a, *The first thin ice that forms over the surface of a pond or pool: "There's just a _____ of ice."*) Inf **MO**4, Sketch of ice.

sketch over v phr

To skim (a piece of reading matter).

  1893 Shands *MS Speech* 57, *Sketch over.* . . Illiterate white for *glance over.* They sketch over a newspaper before reading it closely. **1906** *DN* 3.156 **nwAR**, *Sketch over.* . . To read superficially. "I didn't read that book really; I just sketched over it to see what it was like."

skete   See **skeet** n[1]

skevish   See **scabish 2**

skew- pref   Also *screw-, skee-, squee-*; for addit varr see below [*skew* adj; the form *skee* may come from an emphatic pronc ['ski,ju]. *Screw-* has clearly been infl by *screw* to twist (cf **ascrew, screwy**), and *squee-* perh by *squeeze* or, in the comb *squeegee*, by the folk var *squeege*. For Engl dial antecedents see senses **d, e, g** below]   Cf **sky west and crooked, sky-winding, squawed**

In var adj or adv combs (see below): Slantwise, diagonal(ly), out of square; distorted, damaged, rickety; also fig, usu of a person: peculiar, confused, awkward.

a *skew-gee(d)*; also *screw-gee(d), ~-gied, skee-gee(d), skwee-geed, skru-gee, squee-gee(d).*   **chiefly Nth, CA**   See Map   Cf **gee-hawed**

  1896 (1897) Brodhead *Bound in Shallows* 165 **csKY**, When folks gets all skew-gee brooding on things, why, it seems only right to straighten 'em out. **1896** *DN* 1.424 **cwNY**, *Skew-gee.* . . In Ontario Co., N.Y., equivalent to *askew. Ibid* **NYC**, *Skew-geed* [skju'ʒid], *skwee-geed* [skwi'ʒid], for *askew.* **1905** *DN* 3.64 **eNE**, *Skewgee, skewjaw.* . . Twisted, askew. "Your tie is on all skewgee." *Ibid* 65, *Skrugee.* . . Awry, twisted, cf. *skewgee.* . . *Squeegee.* . . (2) same meaning as *skewgee,* perhaps by confusion with the latter. **1913** *DN* 4.5 **ME**, *Skewgee.* . . Askew. **1916** *DN* 4.280 **NE**, *Skeegee.* . . On the bias. "Those clothes should be cut skeegee." **1931** Hannum *Thursday April* 127 **wNC**, The wagon . . ascended the other side with a suddenness which knocked Thursday April's hat squeegee over her eyes. **1943** *LANE* Map 547, 1 inf, **swVT**, Skew-gee = out of square. **1950** *WELS* **WI** (*When a collar or other clothing works itself up out of place, you say it's _____*) 3 Infs, Skew-gee; (*A necktie that is out of place*) 1 Inf, Skew-gee; 1 Inf, Screw-geed; (*Out of shape: "Now you've knocked it all _____."*) 4 Infs, Skee-gee; 1 Inf, Squee-gee; (*Diagonally. . . "He nailed the boards on _____."*) 1 Inf, Skew-gee; (*Uneven, not square or at straight angles: "That house is all _____."*) 3 Infs, Skew-gee; 2 Infs, Skee-geed; 4 Infs, Squee-gee; 1 Inf, Squee-geed; 1 Inf, Screw-geed. **1954** Forbes *Rainbow* 335 **NEng**, My guess is he always had been a little skee-gee. That doesn't mean he wasn't smart and tricky, for he was, but good sense and he weren't acquainted. **1959** *VT Hist.* 27.160 **nwVT**, *Squeegee.* . . Rickety: Rare. Chittenden. **1965–70** *DARE* (Qu. KK70, *Something that has got out of proper shape: "That house is all _____."*) 33 Infs, **chiefly Nth, esp NEast,** Skew-gee; **AZ**10, **CA**99, **CT**6, **NY**52, 211, **VT**16, Screw-gee; **WI**34, **WY**3, Screw-geed; **CA**101, **CT**19, **HI**1, **MA**6, **NY**70, Squee-gee; **CO**29, **NJ**53, Squee-geed; (Qu. MM13, *The table was nice and straight until he came along*

and knocked it _____) 24 Infs, **chiefly Nth,** Skew-gee; **NY**68, Skee-geed; **NY**199, 211, 226, **VT**16, **WI**21, **WY**5, Screw-gee; **HI**1, **PA**234, Squee-geed; (Qu. MM15, *If a carpenter nails a board crossing another board at an angle* . . "*He nailed the board on _____.*") Infs **NY**68, 163, Skew-gee; **VT**10, Screw-gee. [60 of 70 total Infs old] **1966** *Julian Apple Day* [2] **csCA**, We probably have some of the facts skewgeed and there are some more than likely downright errors. **1973** Allen *LAUM* 1.402 **Upper MW** (as of c1950), Askew or diagonal. . . screwgied [1 inf, **IA**]. **1995** *Brophy Coll.* 71 **swMO** (as of c1960), Squeegee. [C]rooked, aslant, out of plumb.

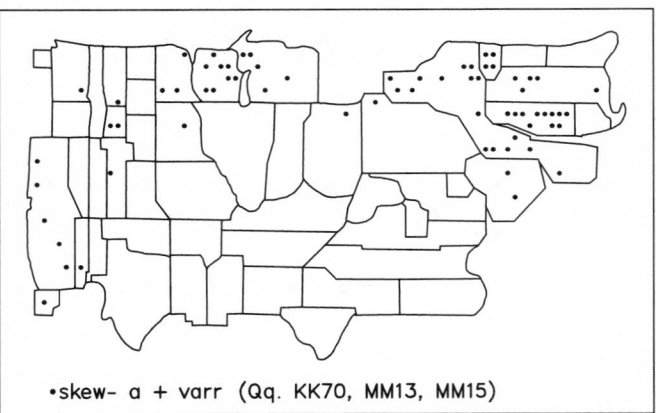

  •skew- a + varr (Qq. KK70, MM13, MM15)

b *skew-haw(ed)*; also *screw-awed, ~-haw(ed), skee-haw(ed), skehaw, skew-raw, squee-haw(ed).*   **chiefly Nth, esp NY, MI, WI**   See Map   Cf **gee-hawed**

  1896 *DN* 1.424 **nOH**, *Skew-raw:* for *askew.* **1903** *DN* 2.301 **Cape Cod MA**, *Screw-awed.* . . Askew. **1916** *DN* 4.281 **NE**, *Skeehaw.* . . Crooked, out of place. "Her collar was on skeehaw." **1923** *DN* 5.237 **swWI**, *Skew-haw.* . . Askew, out of order. "This harvestin' machine's all skew-haw." **1950** *WELS* (*Uneven, not square or at straight angles: "That house is all _____."*) 1 Inf, **cwWI**, Skew-haw—old-fashioned. **1950** *Western Folkl.* 9.120 **nwOR** [Logger speech], *Squeehawed.* Crooked, or out of line. **1965–70** *DARE* (Qu. KK70, *Something that has got out of proper shape: "That house is all _____."*) Infs **MI**9, 114, **NY**73, Squee-hawed; **WI**77, Skew-hawed; **MI**51, Screw-hawed; (Qu. MM13, *The table was nice and straight until he came along and knocked it _____*) Infs **NY**73, 94, Squee-hawed; **NY**220, Squee-haw; **MI**51, Screw-haw; **AZ**10, Screw-hawed. **1969** *DARE* FW Addit **Washington Is. WI**, Skee-hawed [offered by a member of **WI**77's family as a var of his *skew-hawed*]. **1978** *AP Letters* **MI**, Don't overlook "skehaw"—Michigan rural for askew or wrenched out of shape. Usually as "all skehaw." **2000** *NADS Letters* **cNY**, I encountered the word "squee-hawed" in my former husband's family. The most recent two generations were born in Ithaca.

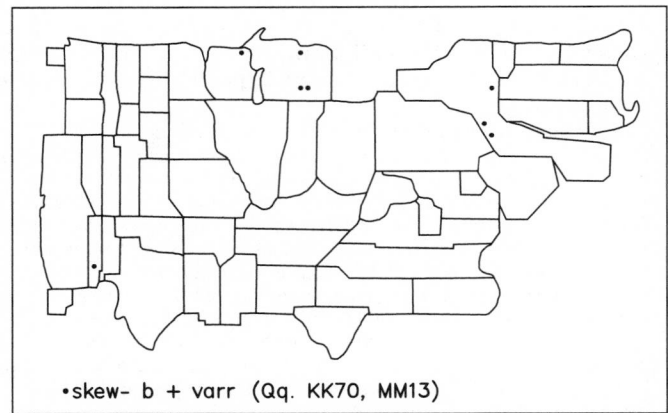

  •skew- b + varr (Qq. KK70, MM13)

c *skew-jaw(ed)*; also *screw-jawed, skee-jawed, skew-gawed, ski-jawed, squee-jaw(ed).*   **esp Gt Lakes, CA**   See Map   Cf **whomper-jawed**

  1905 [see **a** above]. **1927** *DN* 5.477 **Ozarks**, *Squee-jawed.* . . Crooked, irregular. "Thet 'ar smokehouse is plum squee-jawed." [**1942** *AmSp* 17.29 **IA**, Another word which I have never heard outside

Dubuque (or, more exactly, Dubuque County) is *screw jay,* used derisively by boys while playing marbles. *To shoot screw jay* is to dribble the marble or taw ineffectively instead of propelling it with speed and accuracy.] **1950** *WELS* **WI** *(When a collar or other clothing works itself up out of place, you say it's _____)* 1 Inf, Skew-gawed; *(Out of shape: "Now you've knocked it all _____.")* 1 Inf, Skew-gawed; 1 Inf, Ski-jawed; *(Uneven, not square or at straight angles: "That house is all _____.")* 1 Inf, Skew-jawed; 1 Inf, Skew-gawed; 1 Inf, Skee-jawed; 1 Inf, Ski-jawed; 1 Inf, Squee-jawed. **1953** Randolph–Wilson *Down in Holler* 288 **Ozarks,** Squee-jawed. . . Distorted, misshapen, lopsided. **1965–70** *DARE* (Qu. KK70, *Something that has got out of proper shape: "That house is all _____.")* Infs **CA**2, 87, **MI**104, **NY**92, **WA**3, Squee-jawed; **MI**100, **PA**220, Skew-jawed; **MI**61, Skew-jaw; **CA**39, Skew-gawed; (Qu. MM13, *The table was nice and straight until he came along and knocked it _____)* Infs **CA**22, **NY**92, 109, Squee-jaw; **CA**87, Squee-jawed; **NY**219, **PA**220, Skew-jawed; **CA**2, **MI**110, Screw-jawed; (Qu. MM15, *If a carpenter nails a board crossing another board at an angle . . "He nailed the board on _____.")* Inf **NY**109, Squee-jaw. **2000** *NADS Letters,* My late mother (born 1910, eastern Nebraska, Portland OR 1920–1930, SF Calif 1930–1980) used the term "skee-jawed" to mean out of whack, out of plumb. If something was manufactured out of square, it was skee-jawed. Sort of a superior term for "crooked."

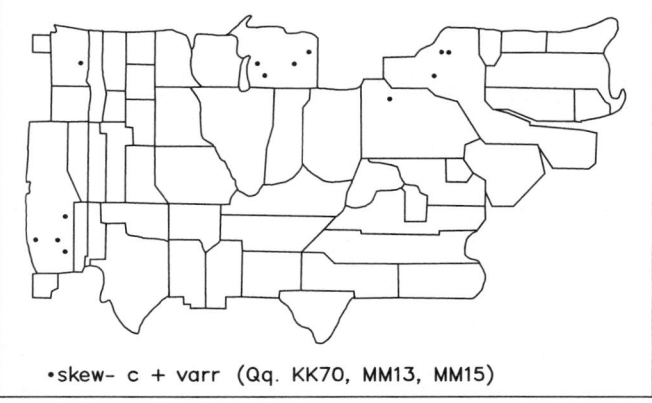

• skew- c + varr (Qq. KK70, MM13, MM15)

d *skew-wampus;* also *skee-wampus, ~-wampy, ski-wampus, sky-wampus, squee-wampus.* [Cf *EDD* skew-wamp "Awry, crooked" and **catawampus, whomper-jawed**] **scattered, but esp freq West** See Map

1905 *DN* 3.95 **nwAR,** Skiwampus [skaɪˈwɛmpəs]. . . Catty-cornered. Common. **1942** McAtee *Dial. Grant Co. IN* 57 (as of 1890s), Skeewampus, skew-wampus . . oblique, kattywampus (*q.v.;* under katty-cornered). **1953** Randolph–Wilson *Down in Holler* 284 **Ozarks,** I believe that . . *sky waddlin'*, and *sky-wampus* are very close to *sky-gogglin*. **1967–69** *DARE* (Qu. KK70, *Something that has got out of proper shape: "That house is all _____.")* Inf **CA**127, Skee-wampus; **UT**3, Skew-wampus [skjuwampəs]; **UT**6, Skew-wampy [ˈskiwampɪ]; **UT**8, Squee-wampus [ˌskwiˈwampɪs]; (Qu. MM13, *The table was nice and straight until he came along and knocked it _____)* Inf **NC**14, Skew-wampus [skjuˈwɔmpəs]; **UT**8, Skew-wampus; **WA**18, Skee-wampus [ˌskiˈwampəs].

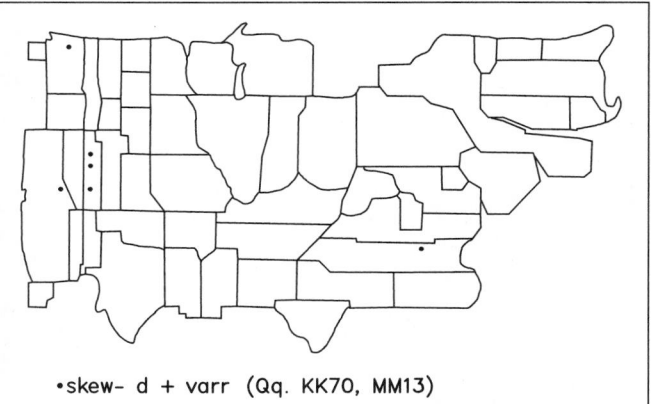

• skew- d + varr (Qq. KK70, MM13)

e *skew-wiff, skee-whiffed.* [*EDD* skew-whiff (also *skee-wiff, skew-w(h)ift,* among other varr) "Askew, crooked, awry; zigzag; cornerwise; also *fig.* out of temper, cross."]

1966–69 *DARE* (Qu. MM13, *The table was nice and straight until he came along and knocked it _____)* Infs **ME**16, **MA**61, Skew-wiff. **1993** *Coast Watch* Sept/Oct 14 **Outer Banks NC,** [Caption:] Skee-whiffed—broken; damaged.

f *skew-godlin, skee-daddlin.* Cf **antigodlin, sky-gogglin**

1967–69 *DARE* (Qu. KK70, *Something that has got out of proper shape: "That house is all _____.")* Inf **TX**11, Skee-daddlin; (Qu. MM13, *The table was nice and straight until he came along and knocked it _____)* Inf **IL**96, Skew-godlin.

g *skee-whonked, ~-winkle, skewaggy, skew-woggly, ~-wottemus, ~-yank, skwee-wab, squee-wobbled, squiogling, squiwinikie.* [Cf *EDD* skew-wabble "Unsteady, out of line" and **wopsided**]

1885 *World* (NY NY) 13 Sept 18/3 **Nantucket MA,** "Squiwinikie," blundering, awkward. **1896** *DN* 1.425 **Nantucket MA,** *Squiogling:* askew, oblique. **1905** *DN* 3.64 **eNE,** *Skew-woggly.* . . Same as *skewgee.* "That skirt hangs skew-woggly." *Ibid,* Skew-wottemus. . . Same as *skewgee,* or *skew-woggly.* **1916** *DN* 4.280 **NE,** *Skeewinkle.* . . Twisted. "Her tie's all skeewinkle." *Ibid,* Skwee-wab. . . Same meaning as *skeehaw* or *skeewinkle.* "That picture hangs all skwee-wab." **1950** *WELS (Out of shape: "Now you've knocked it all _____.")* 1 Inf, ceWI, Skewaggy. **1967** *DARE* (Qu. KK70, *Something that has got out of proper shape: "That house is all _____.")* Inf **OR**6, Squee-wobbled. **1967** *DARE* File **cwAL,** Antigodlin—out-of-plumb, skeewhonked, cut on the bias, whampus-jawed. **2001** *DARE* File **ME,** *Skew-yank.* I used it to describe a picture hanging on a wall that was out of line as in "That painting is all skew-yank!" Something that is "out-of-whack."

h *skew-balled, screw-eyed, skew-shy, screw-~.*

1966–69 *DARE* (Qu. KK70, *Something that has got out of proper shape: "That house is all _____.")* Inf **NC**33, Skew-balled; **MA**48, Skew-shy; **OH**5, Screw-shy; (Qu. MM13, *The table was nice and straight until he came along and knocked it _____)* Inf **MA**56, Screw-eyed.

skewaggy See **skew- g**

skewbald adj Pronc-spp *skeebald, skewball, sque-ball* [*OED2* 1654 →] **chiefly Sth, S Midl**
Usu of an animal, esp a horse: marked with irregular areas of white and other colors; of an ear of corn: variegated; hence n *skewbald* a horse or an ear of corn marked in this manner—also used as a nickname for a horse.

1845 *Amer. Whig Rev.* 2.504 **sKY,** The steed himself was a regular vicious-looking, pied, skewball of a mustang. **1855** Bowen *Rambles* 228, But seldom do you hear his morning song, as he rides the skew-ball horse to the plough. **1883** Amer. Philol. Assoc. *Trans.* 14.52 **Sth,** *Skewbald,* same as 'piebald,' given as obsolete in Webster, is still sometimes used of a horse in the South. **1886** *Century Illustr. Mag.* 32.608 **VA,** Well, Skewball, you are all the Yankees left me, but we'll tickle our good Amelia ground and make bread for Kitty and the children. **1906** *DN* 3.156 **nwAR,** *Skeebald, adj.* Piebald. **1920** Thomas–Thomas *KY Superstitions* 221, In corn-husking, a blue-spotted red ear brings the best luck. It is called in the Kentucky mountains a "skew ball." **1934** (1970) Wilson *Backwoods Amer.* 104 **AR, MO,** Lean, rangy skewbald hounds that leaped and yapped with impatience. **1966–69** *DARE* (Qu. K37, *. . A horse of mixed colors)* Inf **DC**8, Skewball—big spots, three colors; **VA**24, Piebald [ˈpaɪbɔld], skewbald [ˈskjubɑld]. **1976** Garber *Mountain-ese* 83 **sAppalachians,** *Skewball* (n) pibald [sic] pony or corn—At the corn-shuckin' whoever gits a skewball ear gits a free drink. **1982** Slone *How We Talked* 91 **eKY** (as of c1950), Finding a white ear [of corn] did not count anything. A red ear was twenty points, a blue fifty, and a speckled one fifteen. A "sque-ball" (one of many colors) was one hundred points. **1991** Still *Wolfpen Notebooks* 73 **sAppalachians,** *Rule for Corn-Shucking Contest*—(Stillhouse Branch)—White ear: 0 points—Speckled ear: 5 points—Skewbald ear: 15 points.

skew-balled See **skew- h**

skew-gawed See **skew- c**

skewgee adj[1] Also *skewvee, skrugee, squeegee, squeachy*
Fine, correct, as it should be.

1892 *Atlantic Mth.* 69.343 **NEast,** Say! . . I don't see no hotel register around here, but I guess that's all skewvee. My name 's Pettingill, and it would be the same if it was wrote down in a book. *Ibid* 345, " 'E spik only French, . . but dat make no diffrance. 'E can show you de 'ouse." "All skewvee. . . If he can walk in English, that's enough for me." **1896** *DN* 1.424 **NYC,** *Skewgee:* correct. "Not quite skew-gee," not quite right. **1905** *DN* 3.65 **eNE,** *Skrugee* . . as it should be, just right (perhaps by confusion with *squeegee*). *Ibid, Squeegee.* . . All right, as it should be. **1909** *DN* 3.370 **eAL, wGA,** *Skew vee,* see *all skew vee* [*DARE* Ed: =all right]. **1916** *DN* 4.281 **NE,** *Squeachy.* . . Term of eulogy. "This is a squeachy book."

skew-gee adj², adv See **skew- a**

skewgee v See **squeegee**

skew-geed See **skew- a**

skew-godlin See **skew- f**

skew-haw(ed) See **skew- b**

skewiness See **skewy**

skewing See **skewy**

skew-jaw(ed) See **skew- c**

skew, out of adj phr [Appar blend of *askew* + *out of kilter* and similar phrr]
Askew.
  1905 *DN* 3.89 **nwAR,** *Out of skew.* . . Not straight. Common. **1942** McAtee *Dial. Grant Co. IN* 47 (as of 1890s), *Out of skew* . . oblique, not at right angles. **1943** *LANE* Map 547, 1 inf, **swRI,** Catty-corner = out of skew, ~ of plumb. **1966–70** *DARE* (Qu. MM13, *The table was nice and straight until he came along and knocked it* _____) Infs **ME**19, **MA**81, Out of skew.

skew-raw See **skew- b**

skew-shy See **skew- h**

skewvee See **skewgee**

skew-wampus See **skew- d**

skew-wiff See **skew- e**

skew-woggly (or -wottemus) See **skew- g**

skewy adv, adj Also *skewing* Cf **screwy**
Askew, awry; hence n *skewiness* the quality of being skewy.
  1862 Dodge *Country Living* 62 **NEast,** Though freedom from foreign growth discovered an intention of straightness, the most casual observer could not but see that skewiness had usurped its place. **1896** *DN* 1.424 **cNY,** *Skewing:* for *askew.* **1940** *AmSp* 15.131, The occasional *out-a-kelter* and *woppersided* seem not to have been recorded in lists of colloquialisms. They have the same meaning as awry or 'skewy.' **1942** Berrey–Van den Bark *Amer. Slang* 42.3, Crooked; askew. . . Skewy. **1950** *WELS* (Uneven, not square or at straight angles: "That house is all _____.") 1 Inf, **seWI,** Skewy; (When a collar or other clothing works itself up out of place, you say it's _____) 1 Inf, **seWI,** Askew, skewy. **1968** *DARE* (Qu. KK10, . . *Words for something failing* . . "He didn't work it out carefully enough, and his plan _____.") Inf **WI**70, Went skewy.

skew-yank See **skew- g**

ski n Cf **snowshoe**
A large foot or shoe.
  1935 *AmSp* 10.9, The American imagination is fertile in creating humorous names, usually metaphorical, for human feet and the shoes that protect them. . . Exaggeration of size appears in *baggage-carriers, fiddle cases,* and *skis.* **1942** Berrey–Van den Bark *Amer. Slang* 87.34, *Large shoes.* . . Skis. **1967–70** *DARE* (Qu. W42a, . . *Nicknames . . for men's sharp-pointed shoes*) Inf **MN**2, Used to call them skis; **NY**30, Skis; (Qu. X38, *Joking names for unusually big or clumsy feet*) Infs **AL**8, **MI**70, **MN**2, **NY**10, **OK**57, **WI**47, Skis. **1972** Claerbaut *Black Jargon* 79, *Skis* . . very large shoes; large-size footwear.

ski v Cf **skate** v 2
To skip (a stone).

1967 *DARE* (Qu. EE30, *Throwing a flat stone over the surface of water so that it jumps several times*) Inf **SC**34, Skiing [ski-ɪn] rocks; **AL**32, Skiing [ski-ɪn] a rock.

-ski suff See **-sky** suff

skibby n [Perh Japanese *sukebei* lewdness (see 1946 *AmSp* 21.308)] **chiefly CA, Pacific NW** *derog*
A person of Japanese ancestry.
  1920 *DN* 5.84 **NW,** *Skibby.* A rough name for a Japanese. Common nowadays for Japanese without distinction. Is said to have been used ten years ago only for Japanese women of ill repute. **1927** *AmSp* 2.278 **CA** [Stanford expressions], *Skibby*—Japanese and Chinese (2) [=used on the Pacific Coast]. **1942** *Daily Mirror* (NY NY) 11 Feb 30/1 **swCA,** "Skibby" is what the Jap is called to this day by most Californians even in polite circles. **1967–68** *DARE* (Qu. HH28, *Names and nicknames . . for people of foreign background: Japanese*) Inf **CA**15, Skibby; **CA**74, ['skɪbiz]—old-fashioned.

skid v

1 also with *up;* In logging: to provide (a road) with skids; hence vbl n *skidding;* ppl adj *skidded.* Cf **skidder 1, skid road 1**
  1870 *Overland Mth.* 5.57 **WA,** Sometimes ten or a dozen logs are coupled together by short chains. Their appearance, when worming down the well-skidded, meandering trail, is not unlike an immense, jointed serpent. **1905** U.S. Forest Serv. *Bulletin* 61.46 [Logging terms], *Skid.* . . As applied to a road, to reenforce by placing logs or poles across it. (Gen.) *Ibid* 47, *Skid up, to.* . . To level or reenforce a logging road by the use of skids. (Gen.) **1942** ME Univ. *Studies* 57.38, It may be necessary to grub out stumps or knolls which are too high, and conversely it may be necessary to fill in depressions between knolls with material removed. Skidding of depressions and side slopes is necessary but can be minimized by proper location.

2a also with *out, up;* In logging: to bring (a log) from the stump to a **skidway a;** to stack (logs) on skids for loading; to drag (a log) to some central point; hence vbl n *skidding;* ppl adj *skidded.* Cf **deck** v, **skidder 2a, b, c, snake** v, **twitch** v, **yard**
  [**1872** see **skidway 1.**] **1873** *Appletons' Jrl.* 9.101 **MI,** I was left to go on with the skidding. **1877** *Scribner's Mth.* 15.147, "Skidding" is hauling them [=logs] together . . and placing them on skids, convenient for loading. It is an easier and quicker method than "loading from the stump." **1878** *Lumberman's Gaz.* 6 Apr 314/2 **WI,** The absence of snow during the past winter, and the consequent almost universal shortage in the log crop, has led lumbermen to cast about for some means to get their skidded logs to the streams. **1893** *Amer. Missionary* 47.127 **wVA,** There was not a day too cold for Mr. S_____ to be found "skidding out saw logs" at twenty cents per day. **1899** *Century Illustr. Mag.* 57.636 **WI,** For the benefit of the unsophisticated it may be well to add that the "skidway" is a sort of heavy bench or platform from which the logs are loaded upon the sleighs, and that "skidding" by the "skidder" is the process of placing the logs upon this platform. **1905** U.S. Forest Serv. *Bulletin* 61.46 [Logging terms], *Skid.* . . To draw logs from the stump to the skidway, landing, or mill. (Gen.) Syn.: snake, twitch. *Ibid* 47, *Skid up, to.* . . To collect logs and pile them on a skidway. (Gen.) **1931** *AmSp* 7.49 **Sth, SW** [Lumberjack lingo], The timber is sometimes "skidded" on the ground; sometimes it is loaded, one end on a forked sapling, and "lizzarded" to the "stack ground." **c1950** *WELS Suppl.* **cwWI,** My father tells of a more primitive form of go-devil used in the woods to snake out logs, called the crotch. It was a Y-shaped somewhat curved log, to which was fastened the timber, with chains, and could be drawn with one horse or two as necessary, in skidding up logs. **1958** McCulloch *Woods Words* 166 **Pacific NW,** *Skid.* . . To haul logs from the woods to a landing. **1959** *AmSp* 34.79 **nwCA** [Logger lingo], *Skid.* . . To haul logs by 'snaking' them over the surface of the ground. **1967–69** *DARE* Tape **MN**4, The old style was . . cutting it and piling it by hand out in the woods, and then they'd dray it in or they'd skid it in; **NY**219, [Inf:] I always drove those skidding horse, skidding the logs. And sometimes I cut. [FW:] The skidding horse pulled the logs? [Inf:] Pulled the logs to the skidway. **1981** *Blair & Ketchum's Country Jrl.* June 7 **ceVT,** I discovered that in Orange County they didn't "snake" logs [as in Cheshire County NH]. They "skidded" them. **1986** Pederson *LAGS Concordance Gulf Region,* 1 inf, Skid it = drag it; 2 infs, Skid it (out); 2 infs, Skid them (out); 1 inf, Skid them up—of logs, drag them up with chains; 2 infs, Skidded = dragged; 2 infs, Skidded it in (*or* out); 2 infs, Skidding.

b as vbl n *skidding;* used attrib in var combs: See quots.

1877 *Lumberman's Gaz.* 8 Dec 371 **MI,** *Pevys, Skidding Tongs,* always on hand. **1893** *Scribner's Mag.* 13.707 **MI,** The skidding-team is brought in and the log is . . hauled away. . . [I]n the case of small logs, it is grappled with "skidding-tongs," which seize the log like a pair of pinchers. **1905** U.S. Forest Serv. *Bulletin* 61.47 [Logging terms], *Skidding chain.* A heavy chain used in skidding logs. (Gen.) *Skidding hooks.* See Skidding tongs. *Skidding sled.* See Dray. *Skidding tongs.* A pair of hooks attached by links to a ring and used for skidding logs. (Gen.) . . *Skidding trail.* See Gutter road. **1942** *AmSp* 17.224 [Loggers' talk], *Skidding leverman.* The man whose job it is to wind and unwind cables on the drums of the donkey engine which operates as *skidding machine* in high-lead logging assembly. . . *Skidding line.* The line which runs from the donkey engine to the sky-line carriage in a high-lead assembly rig. **1970** *DARE* Tape **MI125,** You'd hook onto it after you had your log cut off. . . With the horses maybe you'd use a skidding tongs or just a chain. **1984** *MJLF* 10.156 **WI,** Skidding tongs. Heavy tongs used for skidding, instead of a chain.

3 =**skate** v **2.** Cf **skift** v[1]

1965–70 *DARE* (Qu. EE30, *Throwing a flat stone over the surface of water so that it jumps several times*) Infs **HI9, MO30, NM9,** Skidding; **GA23, IL97,** Skidding rocks; **MI34,** 118, Skidding stones; [**LA43,** Skidding along the water; **MO1,** Skids; **MI49,** Skids over the water].

skid n[1] See **skid grease**

skid n[2]
=**skift** n[2] **1.**

1977 Jones *OR Folkl.* 63 (as of 1910), There was a skid of snow on the ground between the river and the lake, a third lake, and they tracked him into Albany.

skidded See **skid** v **1, 2a**

skidder n

1 In logging: one who installs skids in a road; one who builds or maintains a **skid road 1.** [**skid** v **1**]

1870 *Overland Mth.* 5.56 **WA,** Two men called "swampers" make the roads, under the direction of the "boss." Another, called the "skidder," skids the road. **1905** U.S. Forest Serv. *Bulletin* 61.47 [Logging terms], *Skidder. . . 1.* One who skids logs. (Gen.) *2.* A steam engine, usually operating from a railroad track, which skids logs by means of a cable. (Gen.) Syn.: steam skidder. *3.* The foreman of a crew which constructs skid roads. (P[acific] C[oast] F[orest]). **1958** McCulloch *Woods Words* 166 **Pacific NW,** *Skidder. . .* A logger who kept the skid road in shape; forerunner of today's road monkey.

2 In logging: one that skids logs, as: see below. [**skid** v **2a**]

a A person engaged in skidding logs.

1899 *Century Illustr. Mag.* 57.636 **WI,** *The Skidder's Chorus.* When the logs go down in the spring,/ Sow-meat and dough-god, good-by! **1905** [see **1** above]. **1942** Beck *Songs MI Lumberjacks* 37, The skidders and the swampers,/ They haul it [=timber] to and fro. **1956** Sorden–Ebert *Logger's Words* 31 **Gt Lakes,** *Skidder,* A teamster skidding logs out of the woods.

b A two-wheeled vehicle used to support the front end of a log in skidding.

1905 U.S. Forest Serv. *Bulletin* 61.32, *Bummer. . .* A small truck with two low wheels and a long pole, used in skidding logs (N[orthern] F[orest], S[outhern] F[orest]) Syn.: drag cart, skidder. **1913** Bryant *Logging* 178, A low truck called a bummer or self-loading skidder has come into extensive use in the flat and rolling hardwood and yellow pine forests of the South, especially in Arkansas and Louisiana. **1967** *DARE* (Qu. N41b, *Horse-drawn vehicles to carry heavy loads*) Inf **MI40,** Two-wheel skidder—for hauling logs out of the woods, wheels 8 to 10 feet in diameter.

c Any of var powered machines used for skidding, and sometimes also loading, logs; see quots.

1885 *Manufacturer & Builder* 17.105 **Pacific NW,** The way we log here at Tallman is to give the steam skidder all the pot holes and swampy places and the hardest places to log. **1905** [see **1** above]. **1931** *AmSp* 7.49 **Sth, SW** [Lumberjack lingo], The "skidder" is a $50,000 machine operated on the railroad spurs to pull logs from places where teams or even oxen can not go. **1941** Writers' Program *Guide SC* 407 **neSC,** To the top of a tall straight 'rig' tree, stripped of its branches, are attached guy wires and a cable, like streamers from a Maypole; the puffing steam engine, or 'skidder,' furnishes power for the ca-

ble, which hauls great logs from the depth of the swamp to the loading yard. **1958** McCulloch *Woods Words* 166 **Pacific NW,** *Skidder*—a. A big donkey powering a skidder system. *Ibid* 167, *Skidder car*—A heavily built railroad car used as a permanent base for a skidder. **1961** Labbe–Goe *Railroads* 260 **Pacific NW,** *Skidder:* A logging machine combining yarder and loader, and mounted on railroad trucks. There were two types: tree rigged, which made use of a regular spar tree; and tower skidders, which carried a steel tower in lieu of a spar tree. **1967–68** *DARE* Tape **AR50,** They got these great big skidders, regular log skidders. . . They're similar to a Caterpillar. . . They're on rubber wheels and both ends of 'em will guide around . . and they'll pull. They're built specially for just skidding timber in the woods; **GA30,** [FW:] What's a skidder? [Inf:] That's these overhead riggings that they pull logs with— set up a head tree to the skidder and reach out about six hundred feet to the side, you know, and pull all the logs in; **MN4,** Now they're going into what they call skidders. Some of those are factory-built machines capable of, oh, I don't know just how big a load some of them are willing to haul. **1979** McPhee *Giving Good Weight* 151 **NEng,** The skidder, which vaguely resembles a pair of tractors coupled together and is flexible in its motions through the forest, replaced the horse not long ago. **1994** *Jrl.–Patriot* (N. Wilkesboro NC) 25 Aug sec D 5/4 [Logging terms], The grabs were driven into one or both ends of a log. On the other end was a chain that was attached to the animal or tractor. The skidder and cable replaced this.

skidding vbl n

1 See **skid** v **1.**

2 See **skid** v **2a.**

3 See **skid** v **2b.**

4 also *skid-hopping:* =**skitching.**

1985 *DARE* File **neIL,** In the 60's and 70's in Chicago/Oak Park, we kids called such an activity [=holding on to the bumper of a car as it drives on snow or ice] "skidding" or "to hitch a skid." *Ibid* **ceMA,** Back in Boston we used to call it "skid-hopping" when I was in high school, six or seven years ago. I myself was among those who called it crazy.

skiddle See **skittle** n[1]

skid grease n Also abbr *skid* [From its resemblance to the grease used on the skids of a **skid road 1**]
Chiefly among loggers: butter.

1921 *DN* 5.110 **CA,** *Skid. . .* Butter. In hot weather, butter looks like grease used on skidways. Lumbercamp in Sierra County. **1925** *AmSp* 1.137 **Pacific NW,** Each man has a certain place. His plate, cup and saucer are his "set-up." Knife, fork and spoon are "tools." "Chase is the password. . . " "Chase down the punk and the skidgrease (bread and butter)." **1936** *AmSp* 11.45 [Soda jerker jargon], *Skid grease.* Butter. **1950** *Western Folkl.* 9.381 **neCA** [Lumberjack language], *Skid grease.* Butter.

skid-hopping See **skidding 4**

skid out See **skid** v **2a**

skid road n chiefly Pacific NW

1 A roadway along which logs are dragged, esp one provided with skids consisting of logs laid transversely at regular intervals and notched to form a guide for the logs. Cf **saddle** n **1**

1880 *N.Y. Adirondack Survey 7th Rep.* 176 *(DA),* Advised that lumbermen had cut 'skid-roads' on which logs were drawn . . , I changed the route. **1892** *Overland Mth.* 20.266 **nCA,** When the logs are brought to the landing or "dump," the oxen are turned back up the skid road. **1893** *Atlantic Mth.* 71.194 **WA,** It was an ordinary roadway, across which, corduroy fashion, half embedded logs, "skids," lay at intervals of several feet. . . As we climbed upward, the clanking of chains . . prepared us for the procession that the lift of the hill showed advancing toward us down the skid road. **1905** U.S. Forest Serv. *Bulletin* 61.47 **Pacific coast** [Logging terms], *Skid road. . .* A road over which logs are dragged, having heavy transverse skids partially sunk in the ground, usually at intervals of about 5 feet. **1913** Bryant *Logging* 219, The roads are constructed in two different ways, one of which is known as the skid road, and the other as the fore-and-aft or pole road. **1939** *Hall Coll.* **wNC,** On a steep place on a skid-road, you'd have a jay hole for your team to run into so as not to be injured by the logs. **1947** Jones *Evergreen Land* 248 **WA,** You can still see some of the old skid-roads in the woods if you look for them—logs imbedded partially in the soft earth, parallel like the ties of a railroad, over which the beasts pulled the fallen trees. **1950** *Western Folkl.* 9.123 **nwOR** [Team-logging terms], *Skid road.* A graded road having small logs about eight feet long embedded crosswise at four-foot intervals. The logs were embedded to about half of their diameter, and a semicircular notch, or "saddle," cut out of the upper half at the center; the logs slid through these "saddles." Considerable skill was required to construct a skid road so that the several logs comprising a "turn" would follow one another around a curve. **1956** *AmSp* 31.152 **nwCA** [Logger lingo], *Skid road.* . . A tractor road used to bring in logs. **1967–68** *DARE* Tape **CA**103, They used bull teams, they built skid roads. . . like a railroad. And instead of putting ties down, they would cut a small tree. . . and embed half of it in the ground; **WA**20, Timber was felled and bucked or sawed into logs in the woods. . . and they were drug on the ground into a skid road or pole road or something and finally pushed down in the water. . . The skid road is . . short logs, usually ten, twelve inches through, laying crossways of the direction you're going with to pull your logs. The skids were notched and they were greased with tallow. **1994** Guterson *Snow Falling* 119 **nwWA**, In his thoughts were vestiges of old skid roads and forgotten farm paths that bled into vales of ghost fern and hollows filled with skunk cabbage.

2 An area of town frequented by loggers after working hours; a red-light district. [See quot 1958] Note: This is appar the origin of the widespread *skid row.*

    1906 *Log of 'Columbia'* I.8/1 *(OED2)*, "We'll likely see him in town." . . "He'll be in the Skid road somewhere." **1925** *AmSp* 1.135 **Pacific NW** [Logger talk], Some of the old terms remained in use, but with a changed significance. When the logger of to-day speaks of the "skid-road" he means the place where loggers gather when they are in town. **1938** in Lib. of Congress *Amer. Memory: WPA Life Hist.* (Internet) **WA**, Stevens has been a tattoo artist nearly all his life and has worked on the edge of Seattle's "skidroad" district 22 years. **1941** *AmSp* 233 **MT** [Lumberjack jargon], *Skidroad.* The path made by the logs in skidding over the ground. More often applied to that section of a city frequented by destitutes and bums. **1947** Jones *Evergreen Land* 248 **WA**, Today in Northwest towns the area below the tracks, where the bums sleep off their canned heat or their gasoline-and-milk, and where in the old days the loggers used to spend their money and raise hell, is always called "The Skid-Road." **1958** McCulloch *Woods Words* 167 **Pacific NW**, *Skidroad.* . . A street in the tougher parts of West Coast towns where loggers hang out. Careless reporters with dirt in their ears have written skidrow or skid row so often that this miserable, phoney term is accepted by the ignorant. There's no such damn thing as skidrow and there never was. The street of saloons, card rooms, flop houses, sporting houses, etc., is *the skidroad.* The present day use came from the famous skidroad built by Henry Yesler to skid logs from the woods to his mill on the Seattle waterfront in 1852. After it was no longer used for skidding this became just a road, and stores, saloons, and other establishments grew up alongside. Much of the old road remains today but is known by the more genteel name of Yesler Way.

skids See **skeets**

skid up See **skid** v 1, 2a

skidway n
In logging:
a A ramp or platform on which logs are stacked and from which they can be loaded onto a vehicle; broadly, an area where logs are collected prior to loading; the logs piled there. **chiefly Gt Lakes, NY** Cf **deck** n 1, **landing** 1, **yard**

    [**1872** *Appletons' Jrl.* 8.573 **Canada**, By skidding is meant the placing of the logs on two parallel skids raised from the ground to facilitate the loading and drawing of the same. A skidway contains from ten to three hundred logs, depending on the thickness of the timber and the make of the ground.] **1878** *Lumberman's Gaz.* 6 Apr 302/4 **MI**, These pole roads can be laid in the "branch roads" direct to the skidways. **1888** *Scribner's Mag.* 4.655 **NY**, The logs are then "skidded" by horses or oxen into skidways, which hold from one to two hundred. **1893** *Ibid* 13.707 **MI**, The skidway consists of two logs or timbers about ten feet apart, laid perpendicular to the log-road and well blocked up, upon which a tier of logs is placed ready to be loaded. **1913** Bryant *Logging* 140, Where sleds are used the skidway consists of a skeleton log structure built crib-fashion, and so placed that the logs can be stored parallel with the road. *Ibid* 144, Where power loaders are used, skidways are often merely areas along the track from which the brush and débris have been removed so that the teams can deliver the logs. . . It is unnecessary to have logs arranged parallel to the track or placed on skids since the

loader can pick them up readily at distances not to exceed 100 feet. **1926** Rickaby *Ballads Shanty-Boy* 237 **MI, MN, WI** (as of a1920), *Skidway.* The point to which the logs were skidded, and where they were piled convenient for loading on sleighs for hauling to the landings. The skidways were at points along the prepared roads from the river back into the timber. **1966–69** *DARE* Tape **MA**5C, That's just a skidway. That['s] where they dump the logs onto those logs, then roll 'em from there onto a truck to take 'em to the mill; **MI**56, I used to like to cut the logs, watch the trees fall, and we'd drag 'em out to the skidways. . . It was nothing to have, oh, I'd say seventy-five- to ninety-feet skidways. High, I mean. A man . . up there on the skidway between six and seven, well—five foot; he looked awful small way up on top of the skidway; **NY**26, You see, what I mean by skidding is, you bring 'em in with . . horses or tractors along your skidway. Your skidway runs this way; well, you'd be bringing your logs in this way, and you roll 'em up on your skidway, see. You can roll two, three high, whatever you want; **NY**219, [FW:] The skidding horse pulled the logs? [Inf:] Pulled the logs to the skidway. [FW:] What was the skidway? [Inf:] The skidway's where they piled 'em. **1968** *Daily Republican Eagle* (Red Wing MN) 1 May 17/2, *Wanted*—Standing timber or logs on skidway.

b A path provided with skids along which a log can be rolled or slid; a **rollway** 1; a **skid road** 1. Cf *DCan skidway* 1a, b

    1906 *Outing* Feb 539 **WA**, Once in a while open lanes run from the water's edge up to the hilltop. Down these "skidways" slid the great logs, cleaving the blue waters with a splash that sent the spray flying high into the air. **1958** McCulloch *Woods Words* 167 **Pacific NW**, *Skidway.* . . A skidroad. **1968** *DARE* Tape **WV**4, Well, your mill has a carriage. . . A sawyer stands right here, the man that works the levers . . pulls the lever that brings the carriage back. When it comes back, there's a skidway comes right up to it.

skievy See **skeeve**

skiff n See **skift** n[2] 1

skiff v See **skift** v[2]

skiffing See **skift** n[2] 1

skiffle n [Prob < *skiffle* a style of music combining jazz, blues, and other varieties, but cf *OED2 scuffle* v.[1] 2.b "To obtain, collect, raise (money).")] *among Black speakers* Cf **percolator, shake** n[1] 2
=**house-rent party.**

    1946 Blesh *Shining Trumpets* 303 **Chicago IL**, These piano blues players . . , making the rounds of the innumerable "skiffles," subsisted on the free food and drink. **1956** Longstreet *Real Jazz* 126, You could always . . get together . . and charge a few coins and have a skiffle. . . The money paid the rent. **1974** Foster *Ribbin'* 141, In Chicago, these parties were called a . . "percolator," "too terrible party," or the "skiffle."

skiffling See **skift** n[2] 1

skift n[1] [Var of *skiff; SND skift* n.[2] 1889 →, but prob much older in Brit use; cf **clift** (at **cliff;** *OED2* c1385 →) and *graft* (1483 → for earlier *graff*).] Cf Intro "Language Changes" I.8
1 Used in std senses of *skiff.* **scattered, but chiefly Midl** See Map

    1656 *Suffolk Co.* (Mass.) *Deeds* (1880) I.2 [sic *OED2*—quot not found], [We are] desired by Jno. Blackman to App[rize] a smale skifte taken up adrift. **1807** (1919) Bedford *Tour to New Orleans* 118 **VA**, They would . . board us in their skift without the inconvenience to us of going to shore. **1823** (1928) Kennerly *Diary* 51 **VA**, Sold the red boat . . but reserved my skift for my own use. **1873** in 1955 Lee *Mormon Chron.* 2.228 **UT**, We brought what the skift would carry conveniently. **1885** *Century Illustr. Mag.* Aug 505 **cnNY**, Visitors call it a skiff, natives a skift. **1894** *DN* 1.333 **eNJ**, *Skift:* for *skiff.* A yawl used in E[astern] [New] J[ersey]. **1903** *DN* 2.329 **seMO**, *Skift.* . . Skiff. A small boat. **1906** Johnson *Highways Missip. Valley* 181 **MO**, Most of us used to like to get in a skiff after school and go off fishin'. **1906** *DN* 3.156 **nwAR**, *Skift.* . . Any kind of boat or canoe. **1909** *DN* 3.370 **eAL, wGA**, *Skift.* . . Skiff. **1915** *DN* 4.190 **swVA**, *Skift.* Variant of *skiff.* **1917** *DN* 4.417 **wNC**, *Skift.* . . Variant of *skiff.* **1923** *DN* 5.221 **swMO**, *Skift.* . . A long, narrow, flat-bottomed boat. **1933** Williamson *Woods Colt* 222 **Ozarks**, Them fellers down there has got a flat-bottomed skift prob'ly, one man a-standin' up in each end of it. **1965–70** *DARE* (Qu. O1, . . *A small rowboat, not big enough to hold more than two people*) 30 Infs, **scattered, but chiefly Midl,** Skift; (Qu. O2, *Nicknames . . for* *an old, clumsy boat)* Inf **MO**9, Skift; (Qu. O9, . . *Kinds of sailboats)* Inf **IN**18, Skifts; (Qu. O10, . . *Kinds of boats)* Inf **DE**4, Skifts. [25 of 31 total Infs male, 25 old] **1966** Dakin *Dial. Vocab. Ohio R. Valley* 184, The *batteau* was essentially a large *skiff,* and in a smaller version which can be handled by a single person it survives by that name—frequently pronounced *skift*—throughout the valley.

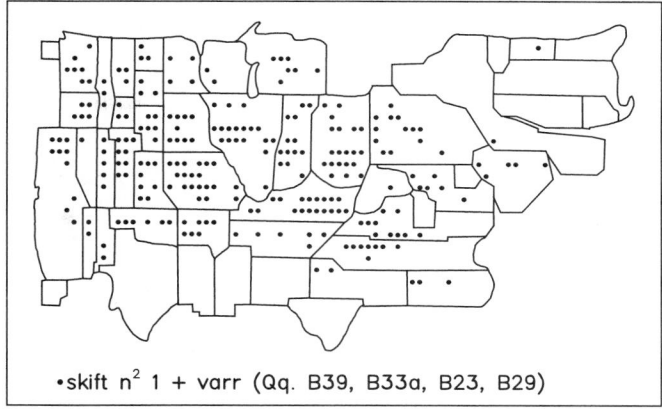

•skift n² 1 + varr (Qq. B39, B33a, B23, B29)

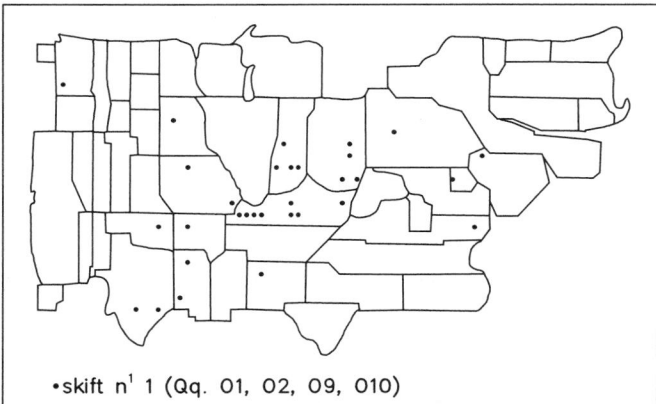

•skift n¹ 1 (Qq. O1, O2, O9, O10)

2 =**stoneboat.**
    1936 *AmSp* 11.317 **Ozarks,** *Skift.* . . The sled or sledge used for hauling stone.

skift n² [*SND skift* n.¹ 2, *skiff* n.¹ 2 "A slight or flying shower of rain or snow", *skiftin* "A light fall or sprinkling of snow"]
1 also often *skiff,* rarely *skiffing, skiffling:* A light fall of snow (or, rarely, rain); a thin layer of snow or frost on the ground, or of ice on water. **widespread exc NEast, Sth, SW** See Map
    1808 (1898) Hunt *Diary* 17 **PA,** May be call'd a green Christmass: a small skift of Snow. **1834** in 1956 Eliason *Tarheel Talk* 294 **NC,** Last night we had a little skift of snow. **1857** *Harper's New Mth. Mag.* 15.726 **nwNC,** Well, there was a little skift of snow on the ground, . . but nothing could I see of the sow, nor yet of her tracks. **1897** *KS Univ. Qrly.* (ser B) 6.57 **KS,** Skift: a small quantity; as, a small skift of snow; i.e., a light snow. Used only in this connection. **1903** *DN* 2.329 **seMO,** There was a skift of snow on the ground in the morning. **1907** *DN* 3.236 **nwAR,** Skift (of snow). **1914** *DN* 4.112 **cKS,** Skift. . . A thin coat or layer, as of snow. Also, *skiff.* **1915** *DN* 4.190 **swVA,** Skift. . . A thin layer of snow. **1917** *DN* 4.417 **wNC,** A thin skift of snow. **1923** *DN* 5.221 **swMO,** Skift. . . a light fall of snow. *Ibid* 236 **swWI,** Skift. **1930** *DN* 6.88 **cWV,** Skiff or skift, as applied to snow, as it seems to be in particular, means a thin coating. **1939** *Hall Coll.* **wNC, eTN,** We just got out on the top and there was a little skift of snow a-fallin'. **1940** *Hench Coll.* **wVA,** Some months ago I made a note of Tom Alphin's use of the word "skiff of snow" or "skift." . . It is a form that snow takes on cold windy days. . . Little stretches of snow will form on the streets, which will blow along as the wind blows across them. These . . are skiffs. **1949** *AmSp* 24.113 **nwGA,** Skift. . . A thin coating. 'A skift of ice.' **1953** *AmSp* 28.254 **csPA,** Skift, skiff. . . A slight flurry of snow, especially as it swirls and eddies over the ground. 'There was a skift of snow on the highway, but it wasn't enough to make it slippery.' **1954** *WELS Suppl.* **nwMO,** In referring to a thin coating of ice my parents said a skiff of ice. I have therefore always used that expression. And I am sure a very old man at a motel in Vicksburg Miss. used the same expression in referring to a small amount of ice on water in a tub. **1965–70** *DARE* (Qu. B39, *A very light fall of snow)* 122 Infs, **widespread exc NEast, Sth, SW,** Skift (of snow); 119 Infs, **widespread exc NEast, Sth, SW,** Skiff (of snow); **VA**1, Light skiff of snow; **SC**32, Skiffing of snow; **SC**34, Thin skiffing; (Qu. B33a, *The first thin ice that forms over the surface of a pond or pool: "There's just a _____ of ice."*) 37 Infs, **chiefly Inland Nth, Midl,** Skiff; 24 Infs, **chiefly Midl, West,** Skift; **VA**1, Thin skift; **SC**32, 34, Skiffing; (Qu. B23, . . *A light rain that doesn't last . . it's just a _____*) Inf **NM**11, Light skiff; (Qu. B29, *A frost that does not kill plants)* Inf **TN**30, Skiff of a frost. **1973** Allen *LAUM* 1.157 **Upper MW** (as of c1950), First thin coating of ice. . . skiff of ice [8 infs]. . . skiffling of ice [1 inf]. **1986** Pederson *LAGS Concordance,* 4 infs **eTN, cwAR,** Skift of ice; 1 inf, **neAR,** Ice skift; 1 inf, **cTN,** Frozen skift of ice. **2000** Launspach *ID Dial. Project* 1 **seID,** *(The first thin coat of ice on a pond or lake)* 2 infs, Skift of ice; 1 inf, Skift.

2 A wisp of clouds.
    1891 Riley *Swimmin'-Hole* 76 **IN,** Some little skift o' clouds'll shet / the sun off now and then. **c1920** in 1993 Farwell–Nicholas *Smoky Mt. Voices* 149 **sAppalachians,** "A skift o' clouds." "A thin skift o' clouds." **1967** *DARE* (Qu. B10, . . *Long trailing clouds high in the sky)* Inf **OR**14, Skift of clouds; **OH**87, Skifts, scuts.

skift v¹ [Cf *SND skiff* v. 5 "to make a flat stone skip over water", *skift* v. 2(1) "To . . skim, scud, skip. . . Deriv. *skifters,* the game of ducks and drakes"]
To skip (stones).
    1968 *DARE* (Qu. EE30, *Throwing a flat stone over the surface of water so that it jumps several times)* Inf **NJ**9, Skifting the stone; [**OH**63, Skimming stones, skiffs [Inf queries]].

skift v² Also *skiff* [**skift** n² 1]
To freeze over in a thin coat.
    1943 *LANE* Map 648 *(Froze)* 1 inf, **cwNH,** Skiffed over. **1967** *DARE* (Qu. B33b, *Talking about the first thin ice that forms over the surface of a pond or pool: "The pond is just _____ over."*) Inf **SC**32, Skiffed; **SC**29, Skifted.

ski-goglin See **sky-gogglin**

ski-jawed See **skew- c**

skijoring n Also sp *skijouring* [From Norw *skikjøring,* literally "ski-driving"] **Nth, esp AK, NEast** Cf **hooky bob**
A sport in which a person on skis is pulled over snow or ice by a dog, horse, or vehicle; hence v *skijor* to be pulled on skis over ice or snow; vbl n *skijoring.*
    [**1910** *Country Life* Dec 205 **Switzerland,** In January . . there are skee-jumping, . . skee-joring and horse racing.] **1942** Peattie *Friendly Mts.* 293 **cnNY,** Horses have recently found themselves put to another winter use as well: skijoring. . . At Saranac Lake they skijor by automobile. **1958** Carrighar *Moonlight* 371 **AK,** There are skijoring contests, dog-sled rides for spectators, an Eskimo skin-toss, and food and coffee. **1976** Hobbs–Specht *Tisha* 145 **AK,** The one thing I would have liked to learn was ski-joring—holding onto a string of dogs and letting them pull you—but I wasn't any good at it. *Ibid* 150, Instead of the two of us ski-joring out, he slung the skis over his shoulder and held the dogs on the lead. **1985** *DARE* File **CT,** I learned the word "skijoring" years ago; we skijor every winter in Connecticut, behind a horse, not a car! *Ibid* **MA,** With a rope and skiis, it [=holding onto the bumper of a car as it drives on snow or ice] is called, in Massachusetts, ski-jouring. **1989** *Ibid* **nwMA,** Skijoring is getting to be quite a popular sport now. People on skis get towed behind a vehicle of some kind; a truck or snowmobile. I think it is an old word. **1992** *Silent Sports* Jan 42, Unlike Alaskan mushing, Nordic mushing, or Skijouring, requires the minimum of equipment. All one needs is skis, a dog who is willing to pull, a belt, and a line to connect the two. Snow, of course, is helpful; however, a line tied to a bicycle can be enjoyable for both dog and musher, too. **1994** *WI Nat. Resources* Feb 11 **nWI,** Skijoring—wherein a cross-country skier and harnessed dog are tethered by straps hooked to a carabiner and a quick release. The dog can comfortably pull the skier 20 miles or more. **2000** *Anchorage Daily News* (AK) 31 May (Internet), The idea of a rental car park . . generated strong opposition from people who like to walk, skijor or watch birds in the bog.

skikepoke See **shitepoke**

skil See **skilfish**

skileton See **skeleton**

skilfish n Also *skil* [See quot 1910]
Either of two related fishes: a **sablefish** (here: *Anoploma fimbria*) or *Erilepis zonifer*. For other names of the latter see **giant sea bass 3**

   1910 Hodge *Hdbk. Amer. Indians* 2.591, *Skil.* A local name of the black candlefish (*Anoplopoma fimbria*), an excellent food fish of the waters of the n. Pacific coast. . . The word is derived from *sqil*, the name of this fish in the Haida language. **1911** U.S. Bur. Census *Fisheries 1908* 309, The skilfish (*Anoplopoma fimbria*) is known as the "black cod." **1918** *Copeia* 54.29, The flavor is rich and delicate. . . It is in fact very much like that of the Skil-fish, (*Anoplopoma fimbria*), which is now being largely pushed under the name of "Sablefish." **1983** *Audubon Field Guide N. Amer. Fishes* 724, Skilfish (*Erilepis zonifer*) has light blotches on head and anterior part of body.

skiligollee, skillagalee See **skillygoelle**

skillet n
1 A metal cooking vessel with a handle, formerly often having legs and a lid but now usu a shallow pan, esp one of cast iron, used for frying. [*OED2* a1403 →] **widespread, but somewhat more freq Midl, Gulf States, TX** See Map Cf **frying pan 1, skillet-and-lid**

   1630 in 1869 Winthrop *Life & Letters* 2.38, Be sure to have ready at sea 2 : or 3 : skilletts. **1723** *New-Engl. Courant* (Boston MA) 18–25 Nov 2/1, She does not know . . how to boil a Skillet of Beaslings without letting it turn. **1740** in 1914 NH (Colony) Probate Court *Records* 2.809, I Give & Bequeath to my . . wife . . my Brass Skellet. **1794** in 1956 Eliason *Tarheel Talk* 294 **ce,seNC,** 1 iron skillet with legs, 1 Frying pan, 1 Franklin skillet without legs. **1895** *DN* 1.374 **seKY, eTN, wNC,** A skillet is a fry-pan with legs. **1899** (1912) Green *VA Folk-Speech* 390, *Skillet.* . . Of brass; cast not beaten, a semi-globe in form, having three short, straight legs of about three inches in length cast on its bottom. The handle is tapering, but flat and quite straight, longer than that of common saucepans. . . The *skillet* is only suitable to be used with a wood fire on the hearth. For boiling water; or stewing. **1903** *DN* 2.330 **seMO,** *Skillet.* . . A shallow iron vessel with iron cover used for cooking or baking at a fireplace. In baking the skillet lid is covered with hot embers. **1909** *DN* 3.370 **eAL, wGA,** *Skillet.* . . An iron cooking vessel, having (usually) three pot-like legs, a long handle, and a cover,—commonly used for baking in an open fireplace. **1942** McAtee *Dial. Grant Co. IN* 58 (as of 1890s), *Skillet* . . the skillet of the pioneers was a heavy iron cooking utensil with legs and fitted lid, suited for cooking among the coals in fireplaces; with the adoption of stove cooking, the term was applied to a similar vessel without legs and with loose-fitting lid; its heavy construction, good for holding heat, however, still characterized the skillet; lighter sheet-metal fryers were called frying-pans. Apparently this distinction still widely applies. **1946** *PADS* 5.37 **VA,** *Skillet.* . . Now a cast iron frying pan, formerly a three legged, long handled pan for use in the fireplace; common in the western Piedmont and westward, scattered elsewhere. **1949** Kurath *Word Geog.* 56, *Frying pan* (of cast iron). . . *Skillet* is current in all of the Midland from New Jersey to western South Carolina and westward. It is also the old term in the Virginia Piedmont, but it has here been largely supplanted by *frying pan.* **1958** *PADS* 29.16 **TN,** *Skillet.* . . A cooking utensil. "A cast iron pan as distinguished from a light steel frying pan." **1965–70** *DARE* (Qu. F1, . . *A heavy metal pan that's used to fry foods*) 705 Infs, **widespread, but somewhat more freq Midl, Gulf States, TX,** (Iron) skillet; **MS55,** Black iron skillet; **DC12,** Frying skillet; **FL19,** Electric skillet. **1967** *DARE* Tape **AL14,** We had a iron skillet that had four legs to it, and it set on a . . open fireplace. And then it had a iron cover. **1972** *PADS* 58.15 **cwAL,** *Skillet* (15 [of 27 infs]) is most frequent, but *frying pan* (9), *frier* (2), and *fry pan* also occur. Nine of the informants using these general terms gave *skillet* as an alternate. Northern and Southern *spider* does not occur. **1983** *MJLF* 9.1.56 **ceKY** (as of 1954), *Skillet.* . . a frying pan made of cast iron. **1991** Pederson *LAGS Regional Pattern* 9, [Data show that *skillet* is relatively frequent in **TN, nAL, MS, LA, e,sAR,** and eastern and coastal **TX** and relatively infrequent in **GA** and **FL.**]

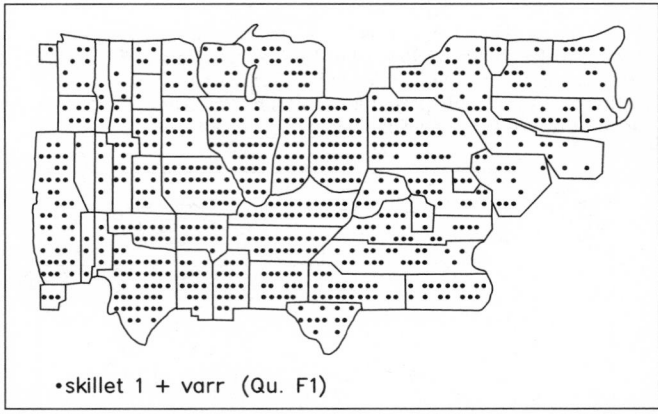

•skillet 1 + varr (Qu. F1)

2 A Black person; hence n *skillet blonde* a Black woman. Cf **coal-scuttle blond**
   1935 Hurston *Mules & Men* 125 **FL,** Dat skillet blonde [Footnote: Very black person] was too lazy to work. **1942** *Amer. Mercury* 55.92 **Harlem NYC** [Black], You skillets is trying to promote a meal on me. **1970** Major *Dict. Afro-Amer. Slang* 104, *Skillet:* a black person.

skillet-and-lid n **chiefly S Midl** Cf *oven-and-lid* (at **oven 1**)
A Dutch oven.
   1904 *DN* 2.421 **nwAR,** *Skillet and lid.* . . A circular oven resting on legs and having a removable cover. This contrivance, also called *"oven and lid"* (led), is set on the hearth of a fire-place and heated with live coals for the purpose of baking. "They cooked by the fire-place with a skillet and lid." **1932** Randolph *Ozark Mt. Folks* 153, They jest went into that 'ar cave-hole an' started in a-diggin', an' purty soon they struck somethin' hard, an' hit was a ol'-fashion skillet-an'-led. **c1960** *Wilson Coll.* **csKY,** *Skillet and lid.* . . An oven with legs and a lid on which coals can be placed. **1966** Dakin *Dial. Vocab. Ohio R. Valley* 2.121, Older informants in north-central Kentucky (and several in southern Kentucky) also speak of a *skillet and lid* [skɪlət n̩ lɛd]—cast-iron, usually described as having legs—and used for baking rather than frying. **1966** *DARE* Tape **NM14,** The way we cooked this food [=sourdough bread] is what we called skillet-and-lid. That's Dutch ovens. . . Anywhere from sixteen to twenty-four inches in diameter, eight to ten inches high. We put the skillet on the fire and get it good and hot and the lid red-hot. When . . whatever we're cooking . . is ready, . . we lift the lid from the fire with . . a pothook. . . Rake a little fire on the shovel, then take it over and put it on top of the lid. . . There's no way in the world that you can cook better food than you can cook in that old black skillet-and-lid. **1970** Tarpley *Blinky* 94 **neTX,** Heavy iron pan used for frying . . skillet and lid [rare]. **1975** McDonough *Garden Sass* 77 **AR,** My mama was the mother of four children before she ever cooked on a stove. It was a skillet and lid, in the winter by a fireplace. And in summer when it was too hot, it was under a tree. **1983** *MJLF* 9.1.56 **ceKY** (as of 1954), *Skillet and lid* . . a skillet for baking at a fireplace. The lid is constructed so that hot coals can be put on top.

skillet blonde See **skillet 2**

skillet bread n Also *skillet cake*
1 also *skillet corn bread:* Corn bread cooked in a **skillet 1.**
   c1960 *Wilson Coll.* **csKY,** *Skillet bread.* . . Bread cooked in a skillet and lid. **c1965** Randle *Cookbooks* (Ask Neighbor) 3.29, *Skillet Corn Bread*—First heat oven to 400. Then . . in 9 inch iron skillet (with metal handle or wrap handle in foil) . . pour [the ingredients]. . . This is cornbread with a custard layer. **1966–69** *DARE* (Qu. H14, *Bread that's made with cornmeal*) Inf **CA87,** Skillet bread—baked on the stove top; **KY15,** Skillet corn bread; [(Qu. H15, *Bread made with wheat flour*) Inf **TX1,** Light bread, skillet bread;] (Qu. H18, . . *Special kinds of bread*) Inf **TX4,** Skillet bread; (Qu. H25, . . *Names or nicknames . . for fried cornmeal*) Inf **FL15,** Skillet bread, hoecake, johnnycake. **1986** Pederson *LAGS Concordance,* 1 inf, **ceTX,** Skillet corn bread—cooked in skillet; 1 inf, **cnTN,** Skillet bread—corn bread, baked in oven/skillet; 1 inf, **nwMS,** Skillet bread—poured into a skillet.
2 Pancakes; a pancake. Cf *DS* H20a, b
   1947 McDavid *Coll.* **cnSC,** Skillet bread = pancakes. **1986** Pederson *LAGS Concordance (Pancakes)* 1 inf, **neTX,** Skillet cakes.

skillet corn bread See **skillet bread 1**

skilleten See **skeleton**

skillet greasy, keep one's See **keep** v **B5d**

skillethead n esp **LA**
=**blue goose** n **1.**
   1916 *Times–Picayune* (New Orleans LA) 26 Mar mag sec 2/7, Blue goose. . . Oie Bleu; Blue Brant; Gray Brant; Oie Aigle; Skillet Head. . . The head and neck is white, sometimes tinged "rusty," while the general color is a slaty blue. **1923** *U.S. Dept. Ag. Misc. Circular* 13.33 **LA,** Blue Goose. . . skillet-head. **1931** Read *LA French* 52, Oie Aigle . . "Eagle Goose"; the Blue Goose . . in English called also *Blue Brant, Skillet Head,* and *Eagle-headed Brant.* **1982** Elman *Hunter's Field Guide* 292, Blue Goose. . . Common & Regional Names. . . skillet-head.

skilligalee n Also sp *skillygalee;* abbr *skill(e)y* [*OED2* 1819 →] Cf **lobscouse 1**
A gruel or stew usu thickened with bread or meal.
   1834 *New Engl. Mag.* 7.368, Presently the delightful sound of "Skilly, ho!" warns me to thrust out my pan and receive half a gallon of that delicious mixture. It is a kind of gruel, made by mixing a few handsful of Indian meal in the liquor in which the above-mentioned offal has been boiled. **1835** *Ibid* 8.30, But to be dogged by a d—d constable, and clapped within four stone walls, and fed on skilly soup is enough to frighten the devil. **1916** Kephart *Camping & Woodcraft* 1.376, *Skilligalee.*—The best thing in a fixed camp is the stock-pot. . . Into it go all the clean fag-ends of game—heads, tails, wings, feet, giblets, large bones—also the leftovers of fish, flesh, and fowl, of any and all sorts of vegetables, rice or other cereals, macaroni, stale bread, everything edible except fat. This pot is always kept hot. Its flavors are forever changing. . . It is always ready, day or night. . . No cook who values his peace of mind will fail to have skilly simmering at all hours. [**1925** *DN* 5.342 **Nfld,** *Skilly* = lob scouse. *Ibid* 335, Lob scouse. Soup of turnips, salt meat, and potatoes.] **1927** *AmSp* 2.281 [Prison lingo], *Skilley*—Gravy. **1951** Catton *Mr. Lincoln's Army* 186, Now and then a whole hardtack was soaked in water, drained, and fried in pork fat, when it went under the name of "skillygalee" and was, said a veteran, "certainly indigestible enough to satisfy the cravings of the most ambitious dyspeptic."

skilligan See **skeleton**

skilligolee See **skillygoelle**

skillion See **scallion**

skillpot n Also *shellpot, skillipot, skilliput, skillpot turtle, skilly-pot, skilpot* [Folk-etyms for Du *schildpad,* literally "shield-toad," or perh one of the cognate Scan forms (Dan *skildpadde,* Norw *skilpadde,* Sw *sköldpadda*)] esp **DC, MD, VA, WV** See **Map** Cf **kettlepot, killpot, steelpot, stinkpot, tillpot**
Usu a **red-bellied turtle** (here: *Chrysemys picta*), but also a **mud turtle 2b(1)** or **musk turtle 1.**
   1790 *Thomas' MA Spy or Worcester Gaz.* (MA) 24 June 4/1 **VA,** A negro man . . saw, and caught, a small turtle (*or what is more generally known by the name of shellpot*). **1807** Irving *Salmagundi* 61, Famous place for *skilly-pots;* Philadelphians call 'em tarapins. **1851** *De Bow's Rev.* 11.53 **LA,** *Skillpot Turtle, Testudo Picta,* or *Emys Guttata,* the most common kind here, seen by dozens in spring and summer. . . These are esculent, as also are their eggs. **1853** Cozzens *Prismatics* 110, Here he was . . royally feasted upon skillipots and snappers, . . and other delicacies. **1868** Pinckney et al. *Reminiscences Catskill* 64, It was a bright idea of his . . to found a Turtle Club. The Delaware Indians believe that this world is supported by an enormous skilliput. **1899** (1912) Green *VA Folk-Speech* 390, *Skillpot.* . . A red-bellied tarrapin. **1930s** in 1944 *ADD* **eWV,** *Skillpot.* . . Common. **1948** in 1951 *DE Folkl. Bulletin* 1.6, A yellow-belly skilpot is the small kind, the red-belly skilpot the kind that gets as big as a small snapping turtle—maybe four pounds. . . [H]ere in Delaware it is commonly called a skilpot from Indian River clear up to Shellpot Creek. **1965–70** *DARE* (Qu. P24, . . *Kinds of turtles*) Infs **DC8, MD13,** 20, **VA64,** 105, 110, **WV10,** Skillpot; **DC2,** Skillpot = mud turtle; **WV8,** Skillpot—dry land; **VA47,** Skillpot—a highland turtle; **VA79,** Skillpot—small water turtle. **1986** Pederson *LAGS Concordance (Turtle)* 1 inf, **cwMS,** Skillpot—not edible, small, like turtle; 1 inf, **swMS,** Skillpot—scalloped shell, not edible.

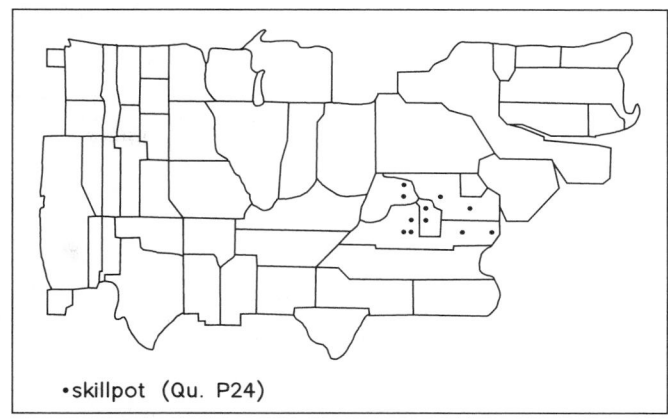

•skillpot (Qu. P24)

skilly(galee) See **skilligalee**

skillygoelle n Also sp *skiligollee, skillagalee, skilligolee*
A spearfish (here: *Tetrapterus albidus*).
   1932 *AmSp* 7.234, *The New York Times* of June 21, 1931, analyzing a catch of fish, identifies the "skillagalee" as the billfish. **1941** *Old Farmer's Almanac* 38 **NEng** (Hench Coll.), One of the most frequent visitors to the waters of southern New England is that excellent game fish the white marlin, called by exasperated commercial fishermen the "skilligolee." **1947** Caine *Salt Water* 24, The white marlin. . . is also known as billfish, skillygoelle, spikefish and spearfish. **1976** Tryckare et al. *Lore of Sportfishing* 125, White Marlin. . . Other common names: skiligollee (U.S.A.)

skilly-pot, skilpot See **skillpot**

skim v
A Gram forms.
Past, past pple, ppl adj: usu *skimmed;* also *scum, skum;* rarely *scoom.* Cf **skin** v, **scum** v[1]
   1887 (1895) Robinson *Uncle Lisha* 93 **wVT,** You've skum the milk, I s'pose, an' got the pans washed an' scalded? **1895** *DN* 1.393 **seMA,** *Scoom:* pret. of *skim.* **1899** (1912) Green *VA Folk-Speech* 373, *Scum-milk.* . . Milk with the cream taken off. **1903** *DN* 2.330 **seMO,** *Skum.* . . Skimmed. 'They sold skum milk.' **1909** *DN* 3.367 **eAL, wGA,** *Scum,* pret. and pp. of *skim.* **1937** (1963) Hyatt *Riverlid* 110 **KY,** Milk that ever drap o' cream has been scum off'n. **1943** *LANE* Map 648, [The field workers were instructed to record the preterite of the verb *freeze* in the sentence *The pond froze over last night.* . . About half our informants offered also terms referring to the formation of a thinner coating of ice. [124 infs offered *skimmed over,* 56 infs, *skum over,* 5 infs, *scummed over,* and 3 infs, *skum.*] 1 inf, I wisht I had as many dollars as I've scum (i.e. skimmed) cans of milk! **1966–69** *DARE* (Qu. B33b, *Talking about the first thin ice that forms over the surface of a pond or pool:* "The pond is just _____ over.") Infs **ME1, MA47,** Scum; **VT16,** Glazed, iced, scum. **1979** Lewis *How to Talk Yankee* [14] **nNEng,** I ice-fished Moosehead opening day, and *Gorry, wan't it cold! Holes skum over fast as you cut 'em.*
B Sense.
Freq with *over:* To freeze in a thin layer—hence ppl adjs *skimmed, scum.* Cf **scum** v[1] **2**
   1860 Hawthorne *Marble Faun* 2.181, The fountain of Trevi skimmed almost across with a glassy surface. **1943** [see **A** above]. **1950** *WELS* (*The pond is just _____ with ice*) 9 Infs, **WI,** Skimmed (over); 1 Inf, **ceWI,** Skimming over. **1965–70** *DARE* (Qu. B33b, *Talking about the first thin ice that forms over the surface of a pond or pool:* "The pond is just _____ over.") 208 Infs, **widespread, but more common Atlantic,** Skimmed; **NY144, WA18,** Skimming; **ME1, MA47, VT16,** Scum; (Qu. B33a, *The first thin ice that forms over the surface of a pond or pool*) Infs **GA11, NH5,** 10, Skimmed (over); **CT14, MA6, NY31,** 127, **RI15, SC9,** Skimming; **ME5, MA82,** Skimming over. **1970** *DARE* Tape VA112, They [=crabs] don't bury in shallow water because the ice, when the ice skims, it pulls them up out of the mud, see. In other words, the ice'll draw, will draw anything up. **1973** Allen *LAUM* 1.157 **Upper MW** (as of c1950), The lake *froze over* last night. . . skimmed over [4 infs, **IA, seSD, cNE**]. **1986** Pederson *LAGS Concordance,* 12 infs, **Gulf Region,** Skimmed over.

skim n

1 The impurities that collect on the surface of a boiling liquid; scum. [*OED2* "Obs." 1539–1764]

1909 *DN* 3.370 **eAL, wGA,** *Skim, n.* Scum. **1945** Saxon *Gumbo Ya-Ya* 563 **LA,** *Skim:* the trash and silt from boiling juice. **1966** *Record* (Columbia SC) 7 Dec sec b 1, Any skim that is still left on the syrup in the tub is ladled off and . . [she] uses it in gingerbread. **1983** *MJLF* 9.1.56 **ceKY** (as of 1954), *Skim . .* the foam that appears when making jam.

2 A thin layer, as:

a Of ice; hence adj *skimmy* thin. Cf **scum** n

1807 (1919) Bedford *Tour to New Orleans* 50 **VA,** Nothing worth noting . . but the intense severity of the cold . . occasioning a very thin skim of ice on the river. **1860** (1938) Lewis *Diary Pike's Peak* 15.30 **PA,** There was a sharp frost this morning, and skims of ice on the pools. **1869** Twain *Innocents* 206, [Lake Tahoe] never has even a skim of ice upon its surface. **1899** (1912) Green *VA Folk-Speech* 390, *Skim. . .* Thin layer. "There is a skim of ice on the pond." **1942** Warnick *Garrett Co. MD* 13 **nwMD** (as of 1900–18), *Skim . .* a thin layer; "a skim of ice." **1942** McAtee *Dial. Grant Co. IN* 58 (as of 1890s), *Skim . .* thin layer; "a skim of ice". **1950** *WELS* (*The first thin ice that forms on a pond or pool*) 7 Infs, **WI,** A skim of ice. **1965–70** *DARE* (Qu. B33a, *The first thin ice that forms over the surface of a pond or pool: "There's just a _____ of ice."*) 381 Infs, **widespread,** Skim; **AR**17, **MO**21, **NC**1, 13, Thin (*or* light) skim; **IL**75, Skimmy ice; (Qu. B33b, *Talking about the first thin ice that forms over the surface of a pond or pool: "The pond is just _____ over."*) Inf **SC**51, Covered over with a skim of ice; **MD**14, **MO**11, Skim of ice; **MD**19, It got a skim of ice; **AR**25, Coat, skim, skimmed; **SC**9, Skim. **1973** Allen *LAUM* 1.157 **Upper MW** (as of c1950), *Scum* (first thin coating of ice). . . skim of ice [30 infs]. **1986** Pederson *LAGS Concordance,* 39 infs, **Gulf Region,** (A) skim (of ice). **2000** Launspach *ID Dial. Project* 1 **seID,** (*The first thin coat of ice on a pond or lake*) 3 infs, Skim.

b also *skimming:* Of snow.

1908 Day *King Spruce* 250 **ME,** 'Beautiful snow'! He sure got a load of supplies started on that first skim o' snow, and they're due here tonight. **1965–70** *DARE* (Qu. B39, *A very light fall of snow*) 23 Infs, **chiefly Inland Nth, Midl,** Skim (of snow); **MI**110, **NY**75, Skimming (of snow).

skimback n Also *skimfish* [See quot 1820] **chiefly Missip-Ohio Valleys**

A carpsucker (here: *Carpiodes velifer*).

1820 Rafinesque *Ohio R. Fishes* 57, It [=*Catostomus velifer*] has received the vulgar names of Sailor fish, Flying fish, and Skimback, because, when it swims, its large dorsal fin appears like a sail, and it often jumps or flies over the water for a short distance. **1887** Goode *Amer. Fishes* 437, *Carpiodes velifer,* the "Spear-fish," "Sail-fish," "Quill-back" or "Skim-back" of the Ohio River, is a fish often seen in the markets. **1983** Becker *Fishes WI* 638, Highfin Carpsucker. . . Other common names: highfin, . . skimback, skimfish.

skimbling, skimelton, skimerton See **skimmelton**

skimfish See **skimback**

skimhog n [By analogy with **quahog**]

A **skimmer 2.**

1931–33 *LANE Worksheets* **CT,** Skimhog—a yellow pleated clam. A skimhog grows on quicksand—used for codfish bait.

skim hole See **skimmings hole**

skim ice n Cf **skift** n² 1, **skim** n 2a, *DS* BB33a, b

A thin layer or covering of ice.

1938 Faulkner *Unvanquished* 196 **MS,** Its head fixed in the skim ice like it was set into a mirror. **1942** *Sun* (Baltimore MD) 27 Feb 1/5 (*Hench Coll.*), Four schoolboys were drowned late yesterday afternoon when they fell through skim ice on a pond. **1950** *WELS* (*The first thin ice that forms on a pond or pool*) 2 Infs, **WI,** Skim ice. **1968** *DARE* Tape **NY**43, So that never, they said, never froze over—not completely. I mean it might have just had skim ice. **1971** Bright *Word Geog. CA & NV* 142, First thin coating of ice. . . *Skim ice* 2% [of 300 infs]. **1986** Pederson *LAGS Concordance,* 2 infs, **seTX, nwTN,** Skim ice; 1 inf, **ceMS,** Skim ice—barely frozen over. **2000** Launspach *ID Dial. Project* 1 **seID,** (*The first thin coat of ice on a pond or lake*) 9 infs, Skim ice.

skimilton See **skimmelton**

skimmed See **skim** v B

skimmelton n Also *skemelton, skimbling, skimelton, skimilton, skim(m)erton, skimmington, skimmiton* [*OED2 skimmington* sb. 2 1634 →; "A ludicrous procession . . usually intended to bring ridicule or odium upon a woman or her husband in cases where the one was unfaithful to, or ill-treated, the other." Var forms recorded in the *EDD* include *skimitin* and *skimmerton.*] **chiefly Hudson Valley, nNJ, nePA** See Map

=**shivaree** n B1, 2.

1868 *Putnam's Mag.* 11.225 **NYC,** [We tax] puns, poke-juice, thimbleriggers'-peas, essence of fudge and all other essences, skimmerton-pans, corncobs when used as corks, shades of trees when more than forty feet high [etc]. **1886** Roe *He Fell In Love* 230 **seNY,** Let's give old Holcroft and his poorhouse bride a skimelton that will let 'em know what folks think of 'em. **1904** *DN* 2.401 **NY,** *Skimelton. . .* A variant of skimmington, in the sense of charivari. **1913** *DN* 4.55 **cNY,** *Skimmelton. . .* A tin horn serenade given to newly married couples upon their return from a wedding journey or shortly after the marriage ceremony, "Didn't they give you a skimmelton when you came to town?" **1932** Smiley *Gloss. New Paltz* **seNY,** I have heard Tony Brooks use the expression "skimmelton" or "skimmerton". **1941** *LANE* Map 409 **seCT,** The map shows the terms . . denoting a noisy burlesque serenade given to a newly married couple, or a similar celebration. . . [4 infs] *skimmiton. . .* [1 inf, **seCT**] [skɪmblən], thought to be a New Hampshire word. **1943** *AmSp* 18.236, [He] inquires concerning the term *skemelton,* used in the sense of 'charivari,' which he heard in his New York region. **1949** Kurath *Word Geog.* 24, *Skimerton* or *skimilton* for the mock serenade is current in a well-defined area extending from the Housatonic in Connecticut to the upper Delaware in northeastern Pennsylvania, including the lower Hudson Valley and the Catskills. **1965–70** *DARE* (Qu. AA18, . . *A noisy neighborhood celebration after a wedding, where the married couple is expected to give a treat*) 15 Infs, **NY, NJ, PA,** Skimmelton; **NY**69, Skimmington; **NY**83, Skimbling. [16 of 17 Infs old] **1968** *DARE* Tape **PA**84, [FW:] Do you know what a skimmelton is? [Inf:] Yes, it's actually "skimmington." . . In Skimmington, England, the way they serenaded a young couple . . was by making all manner of noises on horns and a saw they'd beat and bring out the dishpans. . . The word was corrupted to skimmelton. The Westerners have called it a chivaree, but it was a little different because a chivaree really was good music.

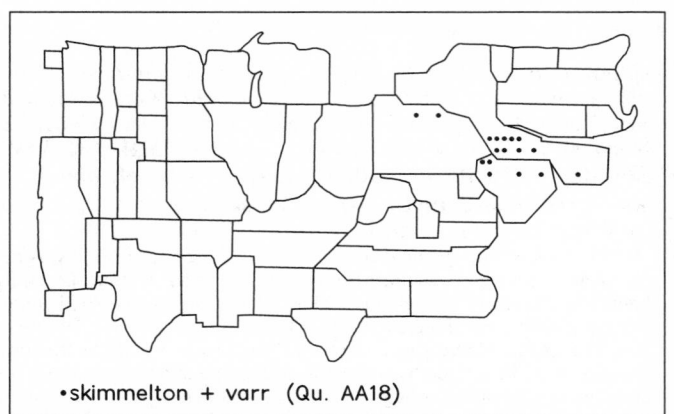

•skimmelton + varr (Qu. AA18)

skimmer n

1 freq in comb *black skimmer (gull):* A sea bird (*Rynchops nigra*) that skims the water with its lower jaw. Also called **cutwater 1, flood gull 2, razorbill, scissorbill 1, sea crow b, ~ dog, shearwater 2, storm gull** Cf **foam-eater**

1813 (1824) Wilson *Amer. Ornith.* 7.89 **NJ,** Black Skimmer, or Shearwater. *Rhynchops nigra. . .* [is a] truly singular fowl. **1844** DeKay *Zool. NY* 2.297, The Black Skimmer—*Rhynchops nigra. . .* The Shearwater, Razor-bill, Cutwater, Skimmer, Flood Gull, and *Skippang,* for it is known under all these names, reaches our coast from tropical America in May. **1907** *Auk* 24.315 **LA,** Black Skimmer (*Rhynchops nigra*). A common resident along the coast, breeding on most of the islands. **1919** Pearson et al. *Birds NC* 40, Skimmers are largely crepuscular in their feeding habits. . . [F]ar into the night, especially when the moon is bright, their weird, harsh bark may be heard as they fly slowly over the water, the under mandible slanting downward and cutting the surface like a knife-blade. **1938** Matschat *Suwannee R.* 97 **neFL, seGA,** A flock of skimmers flew low over the reeds, uttering their trumpetlike yaup-yaups. **1946** Kopman *Wild Acres* 26 **LA,** Just how the skimmer can pick up small shrimp . . on the thin edge of its lower mandible has had no satisfactory explanation. . . The bill is black. **1969** Longstreet *Birds FL* 70, Black Skimmer—*Other names:* Razorbill; Black Skimmer Gull [etc].

2 also *skimmer clam:* Usu a **surf clam** (here: *Spisula solidissima*), but occas a **quahog 2. N and Mid Atl** Cf **skimhog**

[**1864** *Atlantic Mth.* 14.473 **Cape Cod MA,** He stated that peddlers came round there, and sometimes tried to sell the women-folks a skimmer, but he told them that their women had got a better skimmer than they could make, in the shell of their clams.] **1878** *Appletons' Jrl.* 5.455, The majority of the bait, however, consists of the animals removed from the shell, salted and packed in barrels, and much of it is not the edible species, but an inferior one, known to the fishermen as the "skimmer." **1881** Ingersoll *Oyster-Industry* 248 **Long Is. NY,** Skimmer.—The *Cyprina islandica,* or big beach clam. (South shore of Long Island.) **1951** Taylor *Surv. Marine Fisheries NC* 183, The surf clams or skimmers (*Spisula solidissima*) have long been known to grow in abundance along the beaches of the northern states. **1958** *Washington Post & Times Herald* (DC) 1 Aug sec D 5/3 **NJ,** The captain encouraged us to catch more sea-robins. . . "Best bait for fluke you ever saw and much cheaper than squid or skimmer clam." **1966** *Fishing World* 13.6.39 **RI,** Favored bait when fishing the clam beds is a piece of skimmer clam. **1968** DARE (Qu. P7, *Small fish used as bait for bigger fish*) Inf **NY47,** Skimmer clam. **1975** Evanoff *Catch More Fish* 161 **NJ, NY,** For stripers in New Jersey and New York waters . . they use the larger sea or surf clams called "skimmers." **1981** Rehder *Audubon Field Guide Seashells* 753 **Mid Atl,** Atlantic Surf Clam. . . In the Middle Atlantic states this shell is called the Beach Clam or Skimmer Clam.

3 A **dragonfly** of the family Corduliidae or Libellulidae. Cf **globe-skimmer, saddlebag** n 3

1905 Kellogg *Amer. Insects* 92, The members of the family Libellulidae are called "skimmers." They may be seen continually hovering over the surface of still water, or swiftly foraging over fields. **1954** Borror–DeLong *Intro. Insects* 115, Family Libellulidae—Skimmers. *Ibid,* The tenspot skimmer, *L. pulchella. Ibid,* The white-tailed skimmer, *L.* (*Plathemis*) *lydia.* **1967** DARE (Qu. R2, . . *The dragonfly*) Inf **CA26,** Skimmer—looks like a dragonfly, but the wings are different; **MI67,** Skimmer. **1980** Milne–Milne *Audubon Field Guide Insects* 368, Green-eyed Skimmers (Family Corduliidae). *Ibid* 369, Common Skimmers (Family Libellulidae). **1986** Pederson *LAGS Concordance* (*Dragonfly*) 1 inf, **cAL,** Skimmers. **1994** Stone–Pratt *Hawai'i's Plants* 225, The common skimmers (Libellulidae) . . are dragonflies.

4 =**barn swallow 1.**

1911 *Forest & Stream* 77.174 **seLA,** *Hirundo erythrogastra.*—Skimmer, Red-Breasted Swallow, Chef Menteur, La. **1916** *Times–Picayune* (New Orleans LA) 23 Apr mag sec 5/7, Barn Swallow . . Martinet a ventre bronze; Skimmer; Red-breasted Swallow.

5 also *skimmer hawk:* See quot.

1968–70 DARE (Qu. Q4, . . *Kinds of hawks*) Inf **MD15,** Skimmer hawk—small, hunts mice; **VA40,** Skimmer—big hawk.

6 in phr *let one's skimmer leak* and var: To be foolish, unaware, or improvident.

1927 *AmSp* 2.359 **cwWV,** Leak in her skimmer . . a happy-go-lucky person. "She has always had a leak in her skimmer." **1953** Randolph–Wilson *Down in Holler* 195 **Ozarks,** In Conway, Arkansas, I heard a man say: "Nancy sure let her skimmer leak when she married that feller from Little Rock." **1968** DARE (Qu. HH13, *Expressions meaning that a person is not very alert or not aware of things: "He's certainly _____."*) Inf **IN39,** Lets his skimmer leak. **1995** Brophy *Coll.* 43 **swMO** (as of c1960), *Let one's skimmer leak.* [T]o miss an opportunity.

7 also *skimmering:* =**skim** n 2a, b.

1965–70 DARE (Qu. B33a, *The first thin ice that forms over the surface of a pond or pool: "There's just a _____ of ice."*) 12 Infs, **chiefly NEast, N Cent,** Skimmer; **WI13,** Skimmer—heard, but don't use; **UT3,** Skimmer of ice; **LA40,** Skimmering; (Qu. B39, *A very light fall of snow*) Inf **IL17,** Skimmer.

skimmer clam See **skimmer 2**

‡skimmer handle, go up the v phr Cf DS GG22a, b

1986 DARE File **sIA** (as of 1920s), When my mother (who was from north central Missouri) was extremely annoyed with us kids, and had

just about reached her limit, she would say, "I'm going up the skimmer handle!" and we would know we had to behave. I think she was referring to a molasses skimmer, but we didn't have one on the place, so she didn't mean she was going to get one to paddle us with. It was just her expression.

skimmer hawk See **skimmer 5**

skimmering See **skimmer 7**

skimmerton See **skimmelton**

skimming See **skim** n **2b**

skimmings hole n Also *skim(ming) hole* **KY**
A hole dug in the earth into which the frothy residue of boiled cane or sorghum is discarded.

1949 (1958) Stuart *Thread* 78 **KY,** We went to the sorghum mill, shoved each other in the skimmings-hole. **1955** Ritchie *Singing Family* 207 **seKY,** Help yourselves to some good juicy cane stalks to suck on, then you can help dig the skimming hole. *Ibid* 208, He dipped off as much as he could of the green jellyish skim which lay on the top, and the boys emptied it . . into the skimming hole. **c1960** *Wilson Coll.* **csKY,** Skimhole. . . The hole dug in the ground near the sorghum mills to receive the skimmings from the cooking molasses. Greenhorns were often lured into this hole, esp. when a group of young people would visit the sorghum-making.

skimmington, skimmiton See **skimmelton**

skimmy n Cf **pail feed** n
An orphan calf raised on skim milk.

1911 DN 3.550 **WY,** Skimmies, same meaning as "pail feeds." **1916** DN 4.280 **NE,** Skimmies. . . Calves raised on skim milk.

skimmy adj See **skim** n **2a**

skimp n, v Cf **skift** n² 1, **skim** n 2a, b, **skim** v B
A thin coat of snow or ice; to freeze in a thin layer.

1967–69 DARE (Qu. B33a, *The first thin ice that forms over the surface of a pond or pool: "There's just a _____ of ice."*) Inf **IA4,** Skimp; (Qu. B39, *A very light fall of snow*) Inf **KY28,** Skimp; [**IN48,** Skimp coat of snow;] **KY5,** Skimp of snow. **1986** Pederson *LAGS Concordance* (The lake froze over last night) 1 inf, **cnAR,** It's skimping over.

skimpies n pl [Cf *skivvies* underclothes]
1965–70 DARE (Qu. W14, *Names for underwear, including joking names. . . Women's—short*) Infs **IA8, IL113, OK1, TX68, WA11, WV16,** Skimpies.

skimption n Also *skimpton* Also sp *scimption* **chiefly S Midl**
A **scrimption**; a trivial matter.

1919 DN 5.40 **VA,** Scimption. . . A small thing. "That's a small scimption," equivalent to "I should worry." **1942** Hurston *Dust Tracks* 52 **FL** [Black], A fist fight was a small skimption. **1952** *Courier–Jrl.* (Louisville KY) 9 Dec sec 2, When we want to indicate a small amount of something, we say it is just a skimption. **1952** Brown *NC Folkl.* 1.591, Skimption. . . A small amount; not enough to be concerned over. **1956** McAtee *Some Dialect NC* 40, Skimption. . . A small amount. **c1960** *Wilson Coll.* **csKY,** Skimpton (or *scrimption* or *skimption*). . . A very small quantity; usually humorous. **1965** Davis *Summer Land* 14 **cnNC,** Not quiiiiiiite enough. Just a skimption more. Just a think-you-do. **1966–70** DARE (Qu. L56, *The amount of wood a person can carry in both arms: "We're out of firewood—I'll just get in a _____."*) Inf **KY16,** Small skimption ['skɪmpčən]; (Qu. KK42a, *Expressions about a person who does something very easily: "For him that would be _____."*) Inf **NC84,** Small skimption ['skɪmpšɪn]—an old, old expression; (Qu. LL6a, *A small, indefinite amount . . "I'll take just a _____ of cream in my coffee."*) Inf **DC3,** Skimption ['skɪmpšən]. **1975** *Appalachian Jrl.* 2.156 **wNC,** A small portion was a *taddle,* or *tad,* or *sup,* a *dab,* a *skimption,* or a *grain.*

skimptum See **scrimptom**

skim up v phr
1912 DN 3.589 **wIN,** Skim up. . . To get along; to prosper. Used chiefly in the expression, "Well, how are you skimmin' up these days?"

skin n

1 also *skin game, skinning:* A card game that usu includes betting. **chiefly Sth** *esp freq among Black speakers* Cf **Georgia skin (game)**

1925 *Messenger* Dec. 386/1 *(OED2),* Playing 'skin' for matches. **1935** Hurston *Mules & Men* 72 **FL** [Black], Ah played skin wid de Devil for mah life. **c1938** in 1970 Hyatt *Hoodoo* 1.556 **St. Petersburg FL** [Black], Jis' have a deck of cards an' split [Hyatt: cut] 'em off an' ah turn yo' seven spot an' I got a ten, I'll bet chew a dollar dat mah ten falls, yo' win; if de seven fall, ah win. Dey call dat *skin game*. . . So Saturday night come an' we'd check up an' maybe . . ah'd have 'bout two-three dollahs fer de *skinning,* an' ah jes' losin' mah money. **1939** FWP *Guide FL* 119, Negro churches sponsor concerts, picnics, and fish fries; social clubs provide opportunities for dancing and sometimes for games of chance such as skin (a card game), bolita, and dice. **1965–70** *DARE* (Qu. DD35, . . *Card games*) Infs **MS**88, **NY**249, **VA**73, Skin; **SC**69, Skin, Georgia skin; **TN**53, Skin [FW: Inf does not know how it's played.]; **FL**7, Skinning; **GA**89, Skinning—old niggers play; **AL**4, Coon skin—nigger game [FW: doesn't know how played]; (Qu. DD37, . . *Table games played a lot by adults*) Inf **GA**30, Skin game—nigger game, niggers call it "skinnin'" instead of "gamblin'." [5 of 9 Infs Black] **1986** Pederson *LAGS Concordance,* 1 inf, **ceGA**, A skin game—a popular card game. [Inf Black]

2 The palm of the hand, offered in a gesture of greeting or solidarity—usu in imper phr *give me some skin;* see quots. *chiefly among Black speakers*

1942 *Amer. Mercury* 55.86 **Harlem NYC** [Black], "Hi there, Sweet Back!" he exploded cheerfully. "Gimme some skin!" "Lay de skin on me, pal!" Sweet Back grabbed Jelly's outstretched hand and shook hard. *Ibid* 223.90, Lay de skin on me! **1965** Little *Autobiog. Malcolm X* 217 [Black], Gim'me some skin, man! A drink here, bartender. **1971** Roberts *Third Ear* np [Black], *Give me some skin*—a greeting requesting a handshake in which the palm is held flat while the greeter slides his hand along the open palm to the end of the fingers. **1972** Kochman *Rappin'* 33, The gestural expressions of "giving skin" and "getting skin" are very common in the black community. **1974** Foster *Ribbin'* 119, The viewer of TV sporting events will often observe black athletes, and whites too now, giving skin after a home run, a touchdown, or at the start of a basketball game. **1986** Pederson *LAGS Concordance,* 1 inf, **cnAL**, Give me some skin—with friends—informal. [Inf Black] **1994** Smitherman *Black Talk* 125, *Give somebody five*—To slap someone's hand in greeting, to show strong agreement, etc. Also *give somebody skin/some skin.*

3 See **skinner 2, 3.**

skin v

A Gram forms.

Past, past pple, ppl adj: usu *skinned;* also *skint, scun, skun(ned), skunt.*

1837 (1955) *Crockett Almanacks* 92 **TN**, I was so wrothy I should have scun him alive. **1840** *S. Lit. Messenger* 6.509, 'My conscience!' says the Major, looking at his cretur's head all skun and bloody. **1871** [see **B**3 below]. **1883** (1971) Harris *Nights with Remus* 282 **GA** [Black], Dey tuck'n kilt a cow . . . en atter dey done skunt'er Brer Rabbit, he up'n 'low, he did, dat Brer Fox . . better run home. **1884** *Anglia* 7.253 [Black], To the regular forms of the Irregular verbs as used by the whites, the Negro adds the following forms of his own. . . *Pres.* skin—*Past.* skint, skunt—*Pass. Part.* —. **1892** *DN* 1.234 **KY**, Skint or skunt: skinned. "He skunt [*DN* Ed: pronounced [skʌnt]?] his hand." **1897** *KS Univ. Qrly.* (ser B) 6.57 **KS**, Skun, pret. and p.p. of skin: 'skinned,' especially in the game of 'keeps'. **1899** Chesnutt *Conjure Woman* 49 **csNC** [Black], He had a big skyar on his lef' leg, des lack it be'n skunt. **1903** *DN* 2.330 **seMO**, Skint, pret. and *pp.* Skinned. 'I fell down and skint my shin.' **1903** *DN* 2.353 **neOH**, Skin. . . To hasten; get away quickly. Pret. sometimes skun. **1906** *DN* 3.156 **nwAR**, Skun, pret. v. Cheated. "He skun me." *Skunt, pp.* Cheated, "skinned." "I got skunt." **1907** *DN* 3.236 **nwAR**, Skint, pret. and *pp.* of skin. Skinned. **1909** *DN* 3.367 **eAL, wGA**, Scun(t), pret. and *pp.* of *skin.* *Ibid* 370, Skint, pret. and *pp.* of *skin.* See also *skunt.* *Ibid,* Skun(t), pret. and *pp.* of *skin.* **1912** *DN* 3.589 **wIN**, Skunt, pret. and *pp.* of *skin.* Sometimes *skint* is heard. "Have you skunt the rabbits yet?" **1913** *DN* 4.1 **ME**, Skun, pret. and *pp.* of skin. "He skun the fish." "We bait with a skun perch." **1915** *DN* 4.228 **wTX**, Skunt, *pp.* Analogical participle of *skin,* often heard. **1923** *DN* 5.221 **swMO**, Skun. . . Skinned. **1942** Perry *Texas* 23, We'll make out. . . Heap o' times befo' . . we been whettin' on the point, but we al-

ways skunt through somehow. **1945** FWP *Lay My Burden Down* 88 **AL** (as of c1865) [Black], The bureau come by that year looking at niggers' contracts, to see they didn't git skunt out their rightful wages. **1957** TN Folk Lore Soc. *Bulletin* 23.75 **TN**, We . . all went into skinnin' that bear, skun it all out. **1959** *VT Hist.* 27.157, *Skun* . . p.p. of *to skin.* I *skun* a beef. Rare. **1966** *DARE* (Qu. LL23, . . *"These apples are wormy, I think you got _____."*) Inf **MA**11, Skun. **1966** *DARE* FW Addit **wNC**, Skinned—[skɪnt]; [skʌnd]. **1982** *Barrick Coll.* **csPA**, *Skint—skinned,* p.t. and p.p. of skin. **1984** Wilder *You All Spoken Here* 186 **Sth**, Skunned. **1990** Smith *Understanding Speaking S. Lang.* 7, *Skint up*—Having lost a lot of hide in a beating or accident. **1991** Still *Wolfpen Notebooks* 80 **sAppalachians**, We had that old cat and was she mean! . . [W]e killed her, skint her and made a banjo head out of her hide. **1993** *DARE* File **WI**, You know what we did with that varmint after we trapped 'm? We skun 'm.

B Senses.

1 To deprive of money or property unfairly or fraudulently; to fleece, swindle; hence n *skinning* a loss inflicted by cheating. **scattered, but somewhat more freq S Midl, West** See Map

1819 *Thomas' MA Spy or Worcester Gaz.* (MA) 24 Mar 3/1, They will not be able to *skin* the people as deep as they did during their former reign. **1856** *Harper's New Mth. Mag.* 13.307 **VA** [Black], Fact is, Massa, I larnt day way to thumb a Jack, . . and so I skun dem nigger waiters at Lynchburg and Charlottesville outen dat money honestly. **1899** (1912) Green *VA Folk-Speech* 390, Skin. . . To strip of valuable properties or possession; fleece; plunder; rob; cheat; swindle. **1907** *DN* 3.249 **eME**, Skin out of one's eye-teeth. . . To cheat. "Why, he'd skin you out of your eye-teeth." **1930** Shoemaker *1300 Words* 54 **cPA Mts** (as of c1900), Skin—To cheat, to defraud. **1942** McAtee *Dial. Grant Co. IN* 58 (as of 1890s), *Skin one out of his eye teeth* . . cheat, swindle. **1942** Faulkner *Go Down* 23 **MS**, You run a hard race and you run a good one, but you skun the hen-house one time too many. **1945** [see **A** above]. **1954** Tolbert *Bigamy Jones* 46 **wTX** (as of 1870s), One fellow I talked with, a very sharp Tascosa steer trader, said no place would be paradise unless he could skin him a sucker in a cow deal now and then. **1965–70** *DARE* (Qu. LL23, *Cheated, treated dishonestly: "These apples are wormy, I think you got _____."*) 40 Infs, **chiefly S Midl, West**, Skinned; **MA**11, Skun; (Qu. LL22, *Less than you should get: "They'll try to give you _____ every time."*) 12 Infs, **scattered**, Skin you (out of it); **MO**3, Try and skin you; **IN**28, **MO**19, **OH**1, 59, (A) skinning; (Qu. II33, *To get an advantage over somebody by tricky means: "I don't trust him, he's always trying to _____."*) Infs **CA**161, **CO**7, **LA**40, **KY**60, 74, **MN**42, **MO**19, **UT**8, Skin me (or somebody, you); (Qu. V1, *When you suspect that somebody is trying to deceive you, or that something is going on behind your back . . "There's _____."*) Inf **IL**72, They'll try to skin you; (Qu. V7, *A person who sets out to cheat others while pretending to be honest*) Inf **NM**9, He'll skin you alive. **1967** *DARE* FW Addit **CO**7, To skin him—to cheat him, to best him in a deal, etc. **1968** Moody *Horse* 69 **nwKS** (as of c1920), I skun them gazabos out of close onto ten bucks.

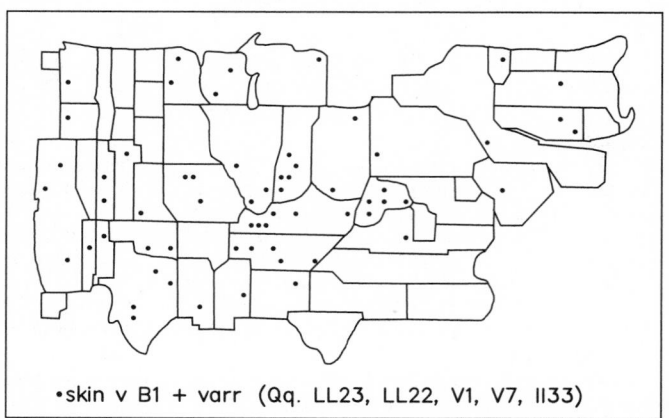

•skin v B1 + varr (Qq. LL23, LL22, V1, V7, II33)

2 in phr *skin one's eye(s), keep one's eyes skinned:* To be vigilant, on the lookout. **chiefly Sth, S Midl**

1833 *Political Examiner* (Shelbyville KY) 22 June 4/1, You had better keep your eyes skinned so that you can look powerful sharp, lest we get rowed up the river this heat. **1860** *S. Lit. Messenger* 31.458 **VA**, "S-s-s s-s-s-h" resounds through the tree "Hold your jaw and skin your eyes."

1872 Schele de Vere *Americanisms* 199, But of all these tracks, the often almost imperceptible *Indian sign* is most anxiously looked for. . . To perceive them the backwoodsman says, in his high-flown language, you must *keep your eyes skinned*. **1898** Frederic *Deserter* 69 **Upstate NY**, That German fellow . . kept them big eyes of his skinned for me all day long. **1940** (1978) Still *River of Earth* 25 **KY**, Skin your eyes and see the fishes. **1945** Hubbard *Railroad Ave.* 360, *Skin your eye*—Engineer's warning to man on left side of cab when approaching curve. **1953** Randolph–Wilson *Down in Holler* 284 **Ozarks**, *Skin your eyes: phr.* To be alert, to keep a sharp lookout. "You got to keep your eyes skinned, if you figure on gettin' a deer in this country." **c1960** *Wilson Coll.* **csKY**, *Skin your eyes.* . . Watch out, peel your eyes.

3 To climb (up or down), esp by gripping with one's arms and legs; to climb (something) in this way; hence v phr *skin the bark* to climb a tree. **chiefly Sth, S Midl, TX** See Map Cf **shinny** v, **skinny** v

1871 *Galaxy* Jan 156, The beaver skun up a tree. **1881** *Scribner's Mth.* 22.452 **GA** [Black], Brer Rabbit, he skint down outer de tree. **1909** *DN* 3.370 **eAL, wGA**, *Skin, v. tr.* To climb: usually with *up*. "You ought to 'a seen him skin up that tree." Sometimes *shin up* is heard. **1909** *DN* 3.404 **nwAR**, *Skin up*. . . To shin up. "Skin up that tree and rustle us some apples." **1916** Wilson *Somewhere* 312, I guess you can see plain enough now he ain't no rabbit, the way he skinned up that tree. **1946** *AmSp* 21.98 **sIL**, *Skin down*, slide down. (Also *shinny up*.) . . Such words as *reckon*, . . *skun down* . . are still heard from time to time. **1965–70** *DARE* (Qu. EE36, *To climb the trunk of a tree by holding on with your legs while you pull yourself up with your hands*) 84 Infs, **chiefly Sth, S Midl, TX**, Skin(ning) up; 19 Infs, Skin(ning) the tree(s) (*or* a tree, it); 17 Infs, Skin(ning); **KY**11, Skinning the bark; **NM**12, Barking? Skinning the bark? (Qu. OO10a, . . *"When we were children we often _____ [trees]."*) Infs **OH**74, **TN**59, Skinned (up). **1986** Pederson *LAGS Concordance*, 1 inf, **cnAR**, Skin up—climb; 1 inf, **seGA**, She'd skin up that pecan tree clean as a darn squirrel.

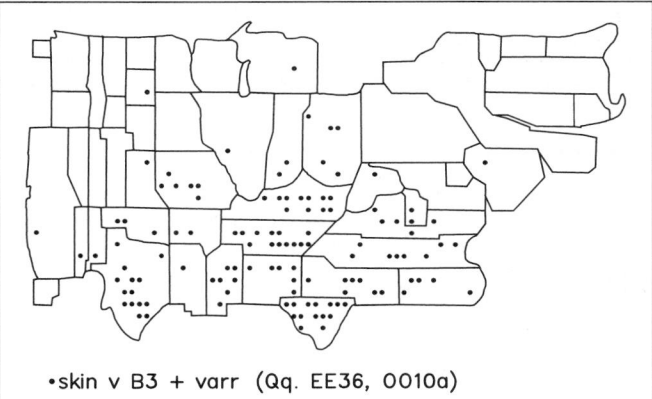

•skin v B3 + varr (Qq. EE36, OO10a)

4 freq with *out*: To leave quickly, run away.

1881 *NY Times* (NY) 18 Dec 4/3 **MT**, *Skin out.*—To leave secretly and hastily, as when pursued by an enemy. Sitting Bull "skinned out" from the Yellowstone Valley and sought refuge in Canada. **1892** *KS Univ. Qrly.* 1.98 **KS**, *Skin:* to run, as, Skin out, i.e., run away. **1894** *Outing* 24.442, The hero . . would never have been one could he have skinned for cover in time. **1903** *DN* 2.353 **neOH**, *Skin*. . . To hasten; get away quickly. Pret. sometimes skun. **1909** *DN* 3.370 **eAL, wGA**, *Skin out*. . . To leave suddenly, run away. **1915** *DN* 4.235 **neOH** [College slang], *Skin*. . . To hurry. **1931–33** *LANE Worksheets* **RI**, *Skin out*. . . Sneak away from school. "The boys'll skin out and go a fishin'." **1933** Williamson *Woods Colt* 246 **Ozarks**, This is as good a place to hide as any they'll find. An' they'll be skinnin' out the first thing in the mornin'. **1937** Sandoz *Slogum* 62 **NE**, How could she be sure that Hab and Cash had n't departed, skinned out, as the cowboys called it, gone to set up for themselves somewhere. **1950** *WELS* (*To run very fast, especially running away from something*) 1 Inf, **csWI**, Scram, skin out, dig out. **1968** *DARE* (Qu. Y18, *To leave in a hurry: "Before they find this out, we'd better _____!"*) Inf **CA**36, Skin out. **1986** *DARE* File **csWI** (as of 1940s), *Skin out* is also used in similar context [to **dig** v¹ 6]—somewhat old-fashioned now.

5 To squeeze one's way; to move in a constricted space; also fig.

1920 Camp *Football without a Coach* 57 (*DAE*), The best a runner can hope for is a chance to skin through that opening before it ceases to exist. **1958** McCulloch *Woods Words* 167 **Pacific NW**, *Skin around a tree*—To move a yarder from one side of the setting to the other in order to log the other half of the setting. **1970** *DARE* (Qu. II33, *To get an advantage over somebody by tricky means: "I don't trust him, he's always trying to _____."*) Inf **KY**72, Skin around you.

6 with *by* or *through*: To succeed by a small margin.

1902 (1903) Lorimer *Letters* 141 **Chicago IL**, I would feel a good deal happier . . if you would make a downright failure or a clean-cut success once in a while, instead of always just skinning through this way. **1942** [see **A** above]. **1950** *PADS* 14.61 **SC**, *Skin by*. . . To qualify on the narrowest margin, with the minimum performance. **1954** *Harder Coll.* **cwTN**, *Skin by*. . . Barely succeed.

7 with *back*: See quot.

1914 *DN* 4.112 **cKS**, *Skin back, v. phr.* To retract, as a false charge.

8 To haul or drag (something), esp a log or logging equipment. Cf **snake** v

1931 *AmSp* 7.119 **eID**, There is a growth of stunted and twisted red cedars, highly valued in this desert land, for posts and fuel. It is *snaked* or *skinned* into camp or settlement, piled high on the wagons, the load fastened with chains. **1958** McCulloch *Woods Words* 167 **Pacific NW**, *Skin 'er back*—Go ahead on the haulback, take the butt rigging back to the woods. **1967** *DARE* (Qu. OO46a, *Talking about dragging something heavy: "We hitched the log on and _____ it out [of the woods]."*) Inf **HI**14, Dragged, skinned; (Qu. OO46b, *Talking about dragging something heavy: "Half a mile or so we must have _____ [it]!"*) Inf **HI**14, Dragged, skinned.

9 in phr *skin the cat* (or *water*), *skin stones* (or *rocks*): To skip or skim stones on the surface of water.

1966–68 *DARE* (Qu. EE30, *Throwing a flat stone over the surface of water so that it jumps several times*) Infs **NC**82, **NH**11, Skinning the water; **OK**25, Skinning stones or rocks; **LA**14, Skin the cat.

10 To play the game of **skin** n 1; hence vbl n *skinning*.

1935 Hurston *Mules & Men* 70 **FL** [Black], Jack took his money and went on down de road skinnin' and winnin'. . . Den he met a man says, "Come on, le's skin some." De man says "Money on de wood" and he laid down a hundred dollars. *Ibid* 71, Dey went to skinnin'. **1952** Himes *Cast the First Stone* 238, They were skinning; a group of varicolored faces ringed about the table, cards spinning face-upward from the box. **1965–70** [see **skin** n].

skin a cat See **skin the cat** v phr 1

skin a flea for its hide (and tallow) v phr Also esp **NJ** *skin a louse;* for addit varr see quots

Fig: to go to great lengths to save money; to be avaricious or mean.

1803 Davis *Travels* 374, You *New Jersey Men* are close shavers; I believe you would skin a louse. **1819** in 1823 Faux *Memorable Days* 10, Being one of those Yankees . . who, in the Southern States, are said to skin a flea for . . its hide and tallow. **1856** Kelly *Humors of Falconbridge* 213 (Taylor–Whiting *Dict. Amer. Proverbs*), The old school gentlemen who split a knife that cost a fourpence, in skinning a flea for his hide and tallow. **1945** *AmSp* 20.306 **SW** [Cowboy slang], He would skin a flea for the hide and tallow and covet the use of the bones. (He was very miserly.) **1952** Brown *NC Folkl.* 1.409, He would skin a flea for its hide and tallow. He'd skin a flea fur hits hide and taller. Skin a flea fur its hide. **1957** *Sat. Eve. Post Letters* **cnKY**, Skin a flea for its hide and tallow. **1965–70** *DARE* (Qu. HH22c, . . *A very mean person . . "He's mean enough to _____."*) Inf **NJ**57, Skin a louse; **NJ**2, Skin a louse for a cent; **NJ**39, 53, Skin a louse for his hide; (Qu. U33, *Names or nicknames for a stingy person*) Inf **NY**163, Skin a flea for the hide and tallow; **OR**5, Skin a gnat for a penny; **NJ**39, Would skin a louse for his hide and tallow; (Qu. U36a, . . *A person who saves in a mean way or is greedy in money matters: "He's an awful _____."*) Inf **WI**64, Skin a flea for the hide; **MD**36, **MA**58, Skin a louse for (his hide and) tallow.

skin a goat v phr Cf *DS* BB17, 18

1901 *DN* 2.147 **cNY** [College words], *Skin a goat*. . . To vomit. Ithaca.

skin a louse See **skin a flea for its hide (and tallow)**

skinamelink, skinamulink See **skinny malink**

skin back See **skin** v B7

skin by See **skin** v B6

skin cap n Cf **curtain B2, onion skin, veil**

A caul.

1960 in 1966 Goldstein–Byington *Two Penny Ballads* 140 **PA,** Some babies are born with a skin cap, and if the mother keeps it and puts it away safely the child will have good luck. If someone else gains possession of it the child is jinxed. "There was a child born like that, and when he grew up he won a big prize in a raffle and bought his own business."

skinch v [*OED2* "*north* and *Midland dial.*"] **esp NEng**

To scrimp, economize; also with *out:* to short, cheat.

1848 in 1935 *AmSp* 10.41 **Nantucket MA,** *Skinch.* To cut short. **1861** *Vanity Fair* 4.59 **ME,** When the man knocked on the top of my curtain and sed, mam, I shal hev ter put some young women in the berths above you, I dident raze no objection; I see they was skinched fur room. **1903** *DN* 2.300 **Cape Cod MA** (as of a1857), *Skinch, v. tr.* To skimp. **1904** Day *Kin o' Ktaadn* 197 **ME,** Figgerin' up what hired men have skinched us out on time. **1941** *LANE* Map 484 **seMA,** Skinching = 'skimping, scrimping': She skinches on butter in a recipe. **1968** *DARE* (Qu. LL22, *Less than you should get: "They'll try to . . every time."*) Inf **NY105,** Short-weight, skinch.

skinching See **skinchy**

skinch out See **skinch**

skinchy adj Also *skinching, skincy* [**skinch** v; cf *EDD* skingy "Stingy"] Cf **chinchy** adj

Stingy, frugal; meager.

1866 *Atlantic Mth.* 18.524 **NEng,** She was determined to do her part, she said: she would be mighty glad to help get that skinchy-skrimpy look out of Miss Lucretia's face, just like a sour raisin. **1931–33** *LANE Worksheets* **seMA,** *Skinchin'. . .* Stingy. "I might have saved one thousand dollars more, if I had been a little more skinchin'." **1942** Berrey–Van den Bark *Amer. Slang* 376.7, *Niggardly; stingy. . .* Skinchy. **1969** *DARE* (Qu. U35, . . *Thrifty but not in a complimentary way: "She's not a bad housekeeper, but very _____."*) Inf **PA199,** Skincy [skɪnsi].

skin ex exclam [Cf *EDD* skinch int. 5 "A cry of truce used by boys at play"]

=**king's ex.**

1968 *DARE* (Qu. EE17, *In a game of tag, if a player wants to rest, what does he call out so that he can't be tagged?*) Inf **GA18,** Skin ex [skɪn'ɛks].

skinflint n Cf **skate** n² **1, snag**

An old, worn-out, or scrawny creature.

1937 *AmSp* 12.103 **eNE** [Farm terms], Old, worn-out horses are known by a variety of terms, such as . . skinflints, plugs, nags. **1967–69** *DARE* (Qu. K44, *A bony or poor-looking horse*) Infs **MN31, MO19,** Skinflint; (Qu. X49, *Expressions . . about a person who is very thin*) Infs **CO47, MN33, PA134,** (Old) skinflint.

skin game See **skin** n 1

skink n

Std: a **lizard 1** of the family Scincidae. For other names of var spp see **blue-tailed skink, glassy lizard, ground ~ 2, jackswift, mole skink, redhead 2, red-headed scorpion, redtailed skink, scorpion B2, slick lizard** Cf **blue scorpion**

skinned corn n Cf **sofkee**

1992 *DARE* File **OK,** A Cherokee Indian . . who has lived all his life around Tahlequah Okla. . . said "this kind of hominy that you buy in cans in the store now—the old-timers called it 'skinned corn.'" . . "Skinned corn" seems to be identical with what is called "sofkee" among Creek Indians in Oklahoma—identical also with modern canned hominy.

skinner n

1 A teamster, driver of draft animals—freq in comb *mule skinner;* by ext, a driver of a motorized vehicle or operator of a machine. **chiefly West**

1850 McCallum *ME Letters* [2], He put [=harnessed] four of his mules into his grain waggon, put two skinner chairs in and mounted one of the mules. **1870** Beadle *Life in UT* 224, I took to the plains . . in the

capacity of a "mule-skinner" . . seated on the back of my "near wheeler," and wielding a whip nearly half as large as myself over the backs of three spans of mules. **1918** *DN* 5.28 **NW,** *Skinner. . .* A good driver (on a combine or other vehicle) of many horses. **1920** *DN* 5.83 **NW,** *Mule skinner.* A mule driver. **1929** *AmSp* 5.58 **NE** [Cattle country talk], The "hand" who formerly drove wagons from the "ranch" to the "cow town" for supplies, etc., was a "bull whacker," "mule skinner," or "freighter." *Ibid* 147 **CO** [Mining expressions], Since the driver of the old time orecar was called a *mule-skinner* or *mule-whacker,* the driver of the modern motor-propelled car is a *motor-skinner.* **1931** *AmSp* 7.52 **Sth, SW** [Lumberjack lingo], The "mule skinner" is frequently known as a "skinner." **1950** *Western Folkl.* 9.123 **nwOR,** *Skinner.* One who drives logging horses. **1958** McCulloch *Woods Words* 168 **Pacific NW,** *Skinner*—a. In early camps, a mule driver or a freighter, or a horse teamster. b. A machine operator, usually a tractor driver. **1967–70** *DARE* Tape **CA160,** I used to have to . . hook up the mules and help the mule skinners; **CA208,** He was an old mule skinner. . . He used to . . haul all the produce from Bishop . . clean to Los Angeles; **IA8,** It was all horse and mule work . . so he had to have mule skinners. **1969** *DARE* (Qu. L1, *A man who is employed to help with work on a farm*) Inf **CA161,** Mule skinner.

2 also *skin(ny):* An old or worthless farm animal. Cf **skinflint**

1935 *AmSp* 10.272 [Stockyard language], *Skins.* Thin, common hogs. Also thin, shelly cows. **1937** *AmSp* 12.103 **eNE** [Farm terms], An old cow is designated by such terms as *nellie, hatrack, skin, shell,* or *canner.* **1952** FWP *Guide SD* 85, *Skinny:* an old ewe. **1968–69** *DARE* (Qu. K15, *A thin, bony, or poor-looking cow*) Inf **CT2,** Skinner; (Qu. K44, *A bony or poor-looking horse*) Inf **IL104,** Skinner.

3 also *skin:* A cheater, swindler. [**skin** v B1]

1887 (1892) Hinman *Corporal Si Klegg* 222, He went to the sutler—or "skinner," as he was better known—and paid ten cents for a sheet of paper and an envelope. **1942** Berrey–Van den Bark *Amer. Slang* 436.2, *Dishonest person. . . Cheat. . .* Skinner. **1950** WELS (*Names and nicknames for a person who doesn't pay his bills*) 1 Inf, **swWI,** A skinner. **1967–70** *DARE* (Qu. U17, *Names or nicknames for a person who doesn't pay his bills*) Inf **NC82,** Skinner; (Qu. U33, *Names or nicknames for a stingy person*) Inf **NJ17,** Skinner; (Qu. U36a, . . *A person who saves in a mean way or is greedy in money matters: "He's an awful _____."*) Inf **KY77,** Skinner; (Qu. V2a, . . *A deceiving person, or somebody that you can't trust*) Inf **TX33,** Skinner; (Qu. V6, . . *Words . . for a thief*) Inf **NC62,** Robber, deadbeat, skin—general term for thief; (Qu. V7, *A person who sets out to cheat others while pretending to be honest*) Inf **TX42,** Skinner; (Qu. HH44, *Joking or uncomplimentary names for lawyers*) Inf **NC61,** Skinner.

skinning vbl n See **skin** v B10

skinning n¹ See **skin** n 1

skinning n² See **skin** v B1

skinnings n

Frothy residue skimmed from a boiling liquid; skimmings.

1986 Pederson *LAGS Concordance,* 1 inf, **ceAL,** Skinnings . . scum on cooking syrup; (Hominy) 1 inf, **nwFL,** Skinnings . . drunk while product ages.

skinning the cat See **skin the cat** v phr 1

skinny n

1 See **skinner 2.**

2 A haircut in which all of the hair is cut off or shaved. *esp freq among Black speakers*

1970 *DARE* (Qu. X5, . . *Different kinds of men's haircuts*) Inf **KY94,** Skinny—all the hair is cut off; **NC88,** Skinny—Negro, looks nearly shaved all over; **VA39,** Skinny—Afro, shingle, skinny; **WV20,** Afro, skinny. [All Infs Black, female] **1986** Pederson *LAGS Concordance* (Hairstyles) 1 inf, **seFL,** Skinny—male. [Inf Black, male]

skinny v [Blend of **shinny** v + **skin** v B3] **esp S Midl** See Map

=**shinny** v.

1965–70 *DARE* (Qu. EE36, *To climb the trunk of a tree by holding on with your legs while you pull yourself up with your hands*) 10 Infs, **esp S Midl,** Skinny up; **KY17,** Skinnying up.

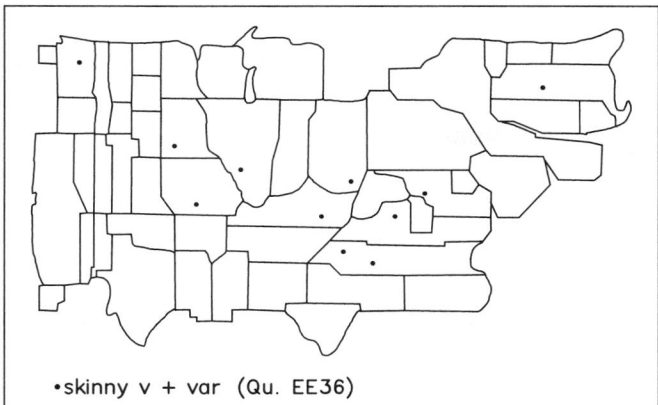

•skinny v + var (Qu. EE36)

skinny malink n Also *skinamelink, skinamulink, skinny marink, ~ merink, skittamalink* [*OED2* (at *skinny* a. 6) 1892 →; "chiefly *Sc.*" *SND* (at *skinny* adj. 2) "*skinnymalink(ie), skinamalink(ie),* . . *skinnylinky,* a thin skinny person or animal"] **esp NY**
A thin or emaciated person; also used as a derog term for a person.

1870 *Punchinello* 2.27 **Upstate NY,** I had sent too many of such skinamelinks to the clay banks when I was Gustise of the Peece to allow 'em to fool me much. **1898** Westcott *Harum* 221 **nNY,** "I think the squire 'd ortter be 'shamed of himself," she reiterated. "S'pose them two old skinamulinks was to go an' have children?" **1916** *DN* 4.280 **NE,** *Skinnymalink.* . . A very thin person. "O, she's a regular skinnymalink." Usage jocular. **1954** Collans–Sterling *House Detective* 98 **NYC,** The elevator man was a tall skinnymarink with very little meat on him. **1966** *DARE* FW Addit **cMA,** *Skittamalink* ['skɪtəmə,lɪŋk]—rascal, bad-acting woman. **1968** *DARE* (Qu. X49, *Expressions . . about a person who is very thin*) Infs **NY**67, **OH**76, Skinny merink [məˈrɪŋk]. **1989** *MetroWest Jewish News* (East Orange NJ) 27 July 19 **NYC,** My sister Pearl was beautiful; round and plump with apple red cheeks. I was a skinny *malink* and each summer Mama tried unsuccessfully to put a few pounds on me. **1993** Isaacs *After All* 94 **Long Is. NY,** "Rose!" my mother shouted, even though I was right beside her. "Who's that skinny marink over there, bawling her head off?" . . She resembled Veronica, the rich girl in the Archie comic books, grown to bulimic middle age. **1996** *DARE* File **NYC,** Skinny marink. . . For me, it's a childhood term from the 1950's in New York. *Ibid* **NYC,** My mother used to say skinny malink. Stress was *ski*nny ma*link.* I haven't thought about that or heard it in years—or from anyone else ever. I was raised in NY in 1950's. **2001** *Ibid* **wNY,** Skinny-marink . . a thin usu. awkward youth.

skin one's eye(s) See **skin** v **B2**

skin out See **skin** v **B4**

skin rocks (or stones) See **skin** v **B9**

skint See **skin** v **A**

skin the bark See **skin** v **B3**

skin the cat v phr

1 also rarely *skin a cat, skin the monkey, ~ tiger:* To perform a gymnastic feat involving hanging from a bar and passing the body through the opening formed by the arms; occas applied to other activities involving climbing or hanging; hence vbl n *skinning the cat;* n *skin the cat* and varr, such a feat.

1843 Thompson *Major Jones' Courtship* 19 **GA,** Thinks I to myself, how it would 'stonish 'em all now to see me skin the cat. . . So up I pulls my feet and twisted 'em round through my arms over backwards, and was lettin my body down tother side foremost, when they all hollered out, "Oh, look at Majer Jones!" **1845** Judd *Margaret* 199 **NEng,** Their several diversions, snapping-the-whip, skinning-the-cat, racing round the Meeting-house, or what not. **1861** *Atlantic Mth.* 7.291, Now hang to the bar by the knees . . ; then seize the bar with your hands and thrust the legs still farther and farther forward, pulling with your arms at the same time, till you find yourself unaccountably on the bar itself. This our boys cheerfully denominate "skinning the cat," because the sensations it suggests . . are supposed to resemble those of pussy with her skin drawn

over her head. **1893** *Jrl. Amer. Folkl.* 6.143 **NYC,** A boy hangs by the hands from a trapeze, and passes his legs through the circle formed by the wooden rod and the upper part of his body. Boys commonly 'skin the cat' both forwards and backwards. **1896** *DN* 1.424 **c,wNY, nOH,** *Skin the cat:* a feat performed on the horizontal bar. **1907** Mulford *Bar-20* 112 **West,** Don't yu remember how I used to shinny up this here wall an' skin th' cat gettin' through that hole up there what yu said was a window? **1910** *DN* 3.448 **cwNY,** *Skin the cat.* . . To perform, on the limb of a tree or on a horizontal bar, the feat of turning the body thru the suspended arms and back again. **1942** McAtee *Dial. Grant Co. IN* 58 (as of 1890s), *Skin the cat,* v. phr. a mostly youthful exercise in which, suspended by his hands, a person passed his feet, legs and body in a turn between his arms, and back again. **1965–70** *DARE* (Qu. EE9a, *The children's trick of turning over rapidly straight forward close to the ground*) Inf **GA**77, Skinning the cat—hands held on to horizontal pole, legs and body go through arms; (Qu. EE9b, *If children jump forward, land on the hands, and turn over*) Inf **VA**9, Skinning the cat—holding on to a bar with your hands, turning over it, and coming down through your arms; (Qu. EE33, . . *Outdoor games . . that children play*) Infs **MI**67, **NY**144, **PA**138, 203, Skin the cat; **OH**68, Skin the monkey—you hang on a tree limb and do a half-somersault; **LA**28, Skinning the cat; **MS**46, Skin the cat—hang by your feet; **LA**40, Skinning the cat—hang from a limb, flip your feet up between your arms, and flip over; (Qu. EE36, *To climb the trunk of a tree by holding on with your legs while you pull yourself up with your hands*) Inf **ME**4, Skinning the cat; **CA**202, Skinning the cat—on a ladder; **FL**48, Skinning the monkey (*or* cat); **AL**32, Skin the tiger—climb it (a tree) that way, slide back down; **NJ**4, Skin the cat; (Qu. OO10b, *Talking about climbing trees:* "*Some trees were dangerous—we shouldn't have _____ [those]."*) Inf **ME**4, Climbed—called skin the cat. **1966** Barnes–Jensen *Dict. UT Slang* 38, *Skin the cat, to:* . . to hang by the hands from a trapeze and pass the legs through the circle thus formed. **1976** Garber *Mountain-ese* 83 **sAppalachians,** Come watch little Eli skin a cat on the tree branch. **1986** Pederson *LAGS Concordance,* 1 inf, **ceMS,** Skinned a cat—sliding down a tree.

2 To take off a garment in such a way as to leave it inside out.

1983 *Lutz Coll.* **NJ** (as of c1915), Mother would sometimes say, "Skin the cat," as she took off a small child's shirt or sweater over his head, turning it wrong side out.

3 See **skin** v **B9**.

skin the cat n

1 See **skin the cat** v phr **1**.

2 Any of var games; see quot. Cf **cat and mouse 1, flies and skinners**

1966–68 *DARE* (Qu. EE11, *Bat-and-ball games for just a few players [when there aren't enough for a regular game]*) Inf **TX**54, Skin the cat, flies and skinners; (Qu. EE27, *Games played on the ice*) Inf **NY**69, Skin the cat—all take ahold of hands, one would be the leader and stop, and the one who was on the end, boy, they really had to hang on; (Qu. EE38a, *A game played with pencil and paper where the players try to get three X's or three O's in a row*) Inf **SD**2, Skin the cat.

skin the monkey (or tiger) See **skin the cat** v phr **1**

skin the water See **skin** v **B9**

skin through See **skin** v **B6**

skin timber n Also *skin wood*
Among loggers: see quots.

1950 *Western Folkl.* 9.119 **nwOR** [Logger speech], *Skin timber* or *trading timber.* Wood impregnated with pitch. **1958** McCulloch *Woods Words* 168 **Pacific NW,** *Skin timber*—Pitchy wood, useful for starting fires. In the old days of wood-fired stoves it was greatly prized, especially by women cooks. *Skin wood*—Same as skin timber.

skip v

1 To stay away from (school) without permission; also with *out:* to absent oneself from school. [*OED2 skip* v.¹ 6.b c1810 →] **widespread, but esp freq Nth** See Map on p. 1002

1900 *DN* 2.60 [College slang], *Skip.* . . To absent one's self from a recitation. **1901** *DN* 2.147 **cNY,** Skip, v. tr. To cut a class. Wells College. **1951** Salinger *Catcher* 270 **NYC,** If I let you skip school this afternoon and go for a little walk, will you cut out the crazy stuff? **1965–70**

DARE (Qu. JJ6, *To stay away from school without an excuse*) 161 Infs, **widespread, but esp freq Nth,** Skip school (*or* class, etc); 41 Infs, **chiefly Nth, Midl,** Skip; **AK**8, **MS**37, **PA**165, Skip out. **1965–69** *DARE* Tape **CA**162, High school down here, there's . . sometimes as many as a fourth that skip school in a day. . . They're just not interested in it for some reason; **MA**92, Half the time during school I skipped, you might say, to go over and help on something. **1989** Pederson *LAGS Tech. Index* 304 **Gulf Region** (*A boy left home to go to school and didn't show; he* _____) 60 infs, Skip (ed/ing) school; 56 infs, Skip (ed/ing) (his) class(es); 47 infs, Skip (ed/ing).

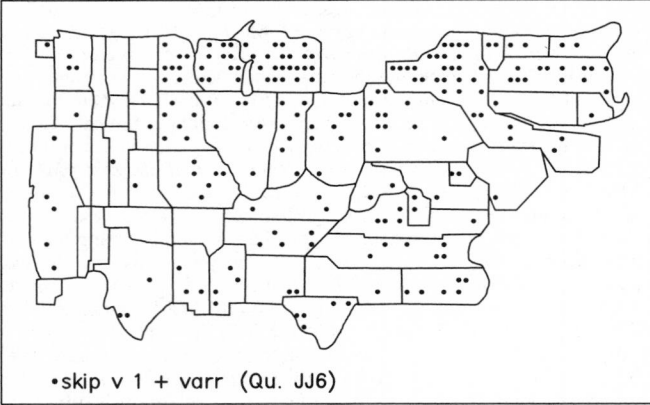

•skip v 1 + varr (Qu. JJ6)

2 See quot.
1937 *Hall Coll.* **wNC, eTN,** Skip. . . To graze (of a bullet). "I shot but just skipped him."
3 See quot. Cf *DS* P13
1907 *DN* 3.199 **seNH,** Skip. . . To fish by causing a baited hook to bound on the surface of the water. "I always use a frog's leg when I skip for pickerel."

skip n[1] *joc*
Nothing to eat—sometimes used in an evasive reply to an inquiry about a coming meal.
1939 (1962) Thompson *Body & Britches* 504 **NY,** If the evening meal is to be omitted on Sunday, the mother says, "We'll have *skip* for supper." **1968** *DARE* FW Addit **cPA,** What are we having for dinner? Skip and molasses—i.e., none of your business. **1976** *Yankee* Oct 56 **RI,** Whenever he asked his mother what they were having for dinner, she always answered, "bread and skip." **1981** *NADS Letters* **Sth,** Bread and skip: "bread and molasses, and skip the molasses," or whatever the sweet stuff mout be.

skip n[2] [Engl dial var of *skep* a large basket]
1 See **skep** n[1].
2 Among miners: an open car or bucket on a vertical shaft for carrying workers and equipment and for raising coal or ore out of the mine.
1941 Writers' Program *Guide LA* 440, An elevator, or "skip," takes sightseers down the mine to a world composed entirely of salt. **1944** Nute *Lake Superior* 251 **MI, WI, MN,** Besides such common mining terms as "adit," "skip" (an elevator in a mine), "whim," and many others, they [=Cornish miners] gave the Copper Country their delicious pasties or meat turnovers. **1947** Natl. Coal Assoc. *Gloss.* 21, Skip—A bin-like cage, open at the top, used for hoisting coal in place of the cage-and-car method. The skip is either partially automatically inverted to empty coal into the tipple or automatically discharges from a hinged bottom. **1952** Peattie *Black Hills* 298, The ore buckets, or skips, have a capacity of nine tons. . . The skips operate in pairs, like old oaken buckets in two-bucket pulley wells. **1966–69** *DARE* Tape **CA**120, Maybe they can dump a hundred fifty cars in, and a skip from the main shaft comes down to that underneath the chute; **CA**128, You run the hoist; that pulls what they call the skips, the buckets on the end of the rope, that go down underground; **NM**15, These incline shafts, they have rails and wheels on the skips. . . A skip is . . the same as a cage on a vertical shaft. It's . . got wheels on it and it runs on tracks on an incline shaft. . . They fill . . the skip up with ore. . . pull it out with the hoist; **SD**4, And the engineer had made a mistake on his . . markings on his cables . . where his skips were, and he had dropped a skip three hundred feet farther down in the [gold] mine . . than he was supposed to, and I had a man, had three men work-

ing, and one of 'em got caught in the skip and was killed. **1970** Wilhelm *Last Rig* 308 **West,** We liked it around the mines, where we could hear the blasts and watch the muckers coming out of the tunnels, or watch the skips coming out of the shafts, where the people talked our language and lived like people should.

skip n[3] Also *skipt* [Cf **skift** n[2] 1]
1967–69 *DARE* (Qu. B39, *A very light fall of snow*) Inf **KY**44, Skip [skɪp] of snow; **NJ**1, Skipt.

skip(-and)-hop See **skip-scotch**

skip ice n
1969 *DARE* (Qu. B33a, *The first thin ice that forms over the surface of a pond or pool: "There's just a _____ of ice."*) Inf **MI**91, Skip ice—a stone will skip on it.

skipjack n
1 Any of var fishes that leap above the water, as:
a =**bluefish 1. esp S Atl**
1734 Royal Soc. London *Philos. Trans.* 38.317 **NC, SC,** *Saltatrix.* The *Skip-Jack.* It hath obtained its Name from its frequent Skipping out of the Water. It is tolerable good Meat. **1787** Gesellschaft Naturforschender Freunde *Schriften* 168, *Gasterosteus Sallatrix* [sic]. . . Skipjach [sic]. **1842** DeKay *Zool. NY* 4.131 **NC, SC,** The *Blue-fish,* or, as it is sometimes called, the *Horse Mackerel, Green-fish* in Virginia, and *Skip-jack* in Carolina, is a common inhabitant of our waters from May until late in the autumn. **1874** *Harper's New Mth. Mag.* July 223 **SC,** In New Jersey and at Newport he [=the bluefish] is the horse-mackerel, in Maryland the tailor, in Virginia the green-fish, in South Carolina the skip-jack. **1882** Eggleston *Wreck Red Bird* 18 **S Atl,** They call them blue fish up North, I believe, but we call them skip-jacks or jack mackerel. **1973** Knight *Cook's Fish Guide* 391, Skipjack. . . see Bluefish.
b also *skipjack herring*: A **herring** n[1] **1** (here: *Alosa chrysochloris*). Also called **blueback herring, golden shad a, inland alewife, Ohio shad, river herring, shad 1**
1791 Bartram *Travels* 67 **GA,** The coasts . . abound with a variety of excellent fish, particularly Rock, Bass, . . Skate, Skipjack [etc]. [*DARE* Ed: This quot may refer instead to another sense.] **1838** Geol. Surv. OH *Second Annual Rept.* 195, The gold shad or skip-jack is a very rare fish that has a slight resemblance to a mackerel. **1882** U.S. Natl. Museum *Bulletin* 16.266, C[lupea] chrysochloris . . *Ohio Shad; Skipjack.* . . Gulf of Mexico and Mississippi Valley; abundant, and resident in all the larger streams, and . . Lake Erie and Lake Michigan. **1957** Trautman *Fishes* 177, Skipjack Herring—*Pomolobus chrysochloris. Ibid* 179, The species was universally known as the "Skipjack" because of its frequent leapings into the air to capture the jumping minnows. **1991** Amer. Fisheries Soc. *Common Names Fishes* 18, *Alosa chrysochloris.* . . skipjack herring.
c A **bonito 1:** usu the Atlantic *Sarda sarda* or the Pacific *S. chiliensis.*
1839 MA Zool. & Bot. Surv. *Fishes Reptiles* 49, Pelamys. . . P. sarda. . . *The Skip Jack.* . . This species is by our fishermen incorrectly called *"Bonito."* **1846** in 1884 Goode *Fisheries U.S.* 1.317 **Boston MA,** This species, called by the fishermen in Boston Market the 'Skip-jack,' and by those at the extremity of Cape Cod the 'Bonito,' is very rarely met with in Massachusetts Bay. **1882** U.S. Natl. Museum *Bulletin* 16.427, S[arda] mediterranea. . . Bonito; Skip-jack. *Ibid* 428, S. chilensis [sic]. . . Skip-jack. **1933** Bryan *Hawaiian Nature* 226, The skipjack, Sarda chilensis [sic] . . is rather slender, with a head which is longer than the depth of the body. **1947** Caine *Salt Water* 16, The bonito . . is often referred to as "the torpedo of the sea". It is also known as . . skipjack.
d The Atlantic saury (*Scomberesox saurus*).
1873 in 1878 Smithsonian Inst. *Misc. Coll.* 14.2.31, *Scomberesox scutellatus.* . . Skipper; saury; skip jack. Nova Scotia to Florida. **1884** Goode *Fisheries U.S.* 1.460, The Skipjack, although in general appearance very dissimilar to the Flying-fish, is a member of the same family.
e A **silversides 1** (here: *Labidesthes sicculus*).
1882 U.S. Natl. Museum *Bulletin* 16.406, L[abidesthes] sicculus. . . Skipjack. **1902** Jordan–Evermann *Amer. Fishes* 249, L[abidesthes] sicculus, a small transparent fish, known as the lake silverside or skipjack . . abundant in most of the Great Lakes and the small lakes of the upper Mississippi Valley. **1943** Eddy–Surber *N. Fishes* 223, Northern Brook Silverside (Skipjack). **1983** Becker *Fishes WI* 769, Brook Silverside. . . skipjack.

f =rainbow runner.

1884 Goode *Fisheries U.S.* 1.332 **seFL,** The Runner—Elagatis pinnulatus. This West Indian fish [is] known at Key West as "Skipjack" or "Runner." **1946** LaMonte *N. Amer. Game Fishes* 37, Rainbow Runner. . . Names: Runner, Yellowtail, Skipjack, Shoemaker.

g A **butterfish 1** (here: *Peprilus triacanthus*).

1884 Goode *Fisheries U.S.* 1.333 **Cape Cod MA,** The "Butter-fish" of Massachusetts and New York, sometimes known in New Jersey as the "Harvest-fish," in Maine as the "Dollar-fish," about Cape Cod as the "Sheepshead" and "Skipjack." **1939** *Natl. Geogr. Soc. Fishes* 68, Other local names [for *Peprilus triacanthus*] are harvestfish . . and skipjack.

h =leatherjacket 2.

1884 Goode *Fisheries U.S.* 1.332, The Leather-Jacket—Oligoplites saurus. . . It is known to fishermen as the "Skipjack," sharing this name with a number of other scombroid fishes which leap from the water as they pursue their prey.

i A **crevalle:** usu **hardtail 1,** but also *Caranx hippos* or *C. georgianus.*

1884 Goode *Fisheries U.S.* 1.324 **FL,** The Jurel—Caranx pisquetus. . . known about Pensacola as the "Jurel," "Cojinua," and "Hard-tail"; along the Florida coast as "Jack-fish" and "Skipjack." **1935** Caine *Game Fish* 48, Blue Runner—*Caranx chrysos.* . . *Synonyms:* Cojinua . . Skipjack. **1973** Knight *Cook's Fish Guide* 391, Skipjack . . see Jack, Crevalle. **2000** (acc) U.S. Food & Drug Admin. *Seafood List* (Internet), Caranx ruber. . . Little Skipjack. . . Skipjack. *Ibid,* Caranx georgianus. . . Skipjack.

j A **ten-pounder** (here: *Elops saurus*).

1931 *Copeia* 2.46 **TX,** *Elops saurus.* . . One "skipjack" . . from Corpus Christi. **1935** Caine *Game Fish* 98, Ladyfish. . . Skipjack. [*Ibid* 99, It is a savage striker and will break water and leap more than any other game fish.]

k also *skipjack tuna:* A **tuna:** usu *Katsuwonus pelamis,* but also *Euthynnus lineatus* or **kawakawa. esp CA, HI**

1933 Bryan *Hawaiian Nature* 228 **HI,** The oceanic bonito, *Euthynnus pelamis.* . . is sometimes called a "skipjack" by fishermen, although that name is more properly applied to *Sarda chilensis* [sic]. **1953** Roedel *Common Fishes CA* 86, Black Skipjack—*Euthynnus lineatus.* **1960** Gosline–Brock *Hawaiian Fishes* 258, *Euthynnus yaito* (Kawakawa, Little tuna, Black skipjack, Bonito). **1967–70** DARE (Qu. P2, . . *Kinds of saltwater fish caught around here . . good to eat)* Inf **HI4,** Aku—same as tuna, skipjack; **CA191,** Skipjack. **2000** (acc) U.S. Dept. Ag. *Integrated Taxonomic Info. System* (Internet), Katsuwonus pelamis. . . skipjack tuna. *Ibid,* Euthynnus affinis. . . Black Skipjack. *Ibid,* Euthynnus lineatus. . . Black Skipjack.

l A **bonefish 1** (here: *Albula vulpes*).

1935 Caine *Game Fish* 50, Bonefish. *Synonyms:* Bananafish . . Skipjack. **1946** Stilwell *Hunting in TX* 93, You will also catch skipjacks, a fish that in some parts of the world is called a ladyfish, although I never heard of a sillier name for a first-rate scrapper. The skipjack is a miniature tarpon hopped up on a supercharger. It's impossible to keep a tight line on one, for he'll leap horizontally and he may cover eight or ten feet in a leap. **1968** DARE (Qu. P4, *Saltwater fish that are not good to eat)* Inf **LA37,** Bananafish—this is the same fish called skipjack in south Texas, horse mackerel farther north and east in Texas. (May be same as ladyfish in Florida.)

m A **gizzard shad 1** (here: *Dorosoma cepedianum*).

1943 Eddy–Surber *N. Fishes* 73, Gizzard shad frequently travel in schools close to the surface and when surprised will skip over the surface of the water. This habit has caused local fishermen to apply the name skipjack to this species. **1951** Harlan–Speaker *IA Fish* 60, Gizzard Shad. . . Other Names—Shad, skipjack, and flatfish. **2000** (acc) U.S. Dept. Ag. *Integrated Taxonomic Info. System* (Internet), Dorosoma cepedianum. . . skipjack.

n An **alewife** (here: *Alosa pseudoharengus*).

1946 LaMonte *N. Amer. Game Fishes* 150, Alewife. . . Names: Branch Herring, . . Skipjack. **1967–70** DARE (Qu. P1, . . *Kinds of freshwater fish . . caught around here . . good to eat)* Inf **WI32,** Skipjacks—feed on top, at night; (Qu. P3, *Freshwater fish that are not good to eat)* Infs **IL119, IN42,** 45, Skipjack; **OH58,** Skipjacks; (Qu. P7, *Small fish used as bait for bigger fish)* Inf **IN45,** Skipjack. [*DARE* Ed: Some of these quots may refer instead to **1b** above.] **1968** *DARE* Tape **IN45,** If you can get skipjack bait [for catfish], it's the best. That's a real oily fish; **OH58,** Nobody I know of that eats skipjacks. . . They're more like a herring; they're real thin . . and . . bony as they can be. **1976** Tryckare et

al. *Lore of Sportfishing* 70, Alewife. . . Other common names: Ellwife . . skipjack.

2 A **click beetle** of the family Elateridae. [*OED2* 1817 →] Cf **jumping jack 1**

1853 *Scientific Amer.* 11 June 312, The skip-jack, the glow-worm, the death-watch. **1905** Kellogg *Amer. Insects* 267, When a click-beetle—snapping-bugs and skipjacks are other common names for them—is disturbed it falls to the ground, lying there for a little while as if dead. Then if it has alighted, as it usually does, on its back, it suddenly gives a spasmodic jerk which throws it several inches high and brings it down right side up. **1933** Bryan *Hawaiian Nature* 188, The click beetles . . are sometimes called "skipjacks" because of their ability to flip around and click out of one's hand by violently snapping their bodies, which are hinged between the front and the middle parts of the thorax.

3 A shallow, V-bottomed, centerboard, usu sloop-rigged sailboat. **esp Chesapeake Bay** Cf **sharpie 1**

1882 *Century Illustr. Mag.* 24.359, The skip-jack is another curious and by no means ungainly craft, evolved out of the sharpie by adding to the latter a rising floor. . . She can be constructed at much less expense, her frame being composed of straight timbers. **1893** *Ibid* 46.163 **ceFL,** The *Minnehaha* was of a type common on Indian River, locally known as a "skipjack." She was flat-sided, with a rise of floor of about fifteen inches. . . Over all she was 28 feet 7 inches; extreme beam, 12 feet 9 inches. **1940** Writers' Program *Guide MD* 430 **csMD,** The skipjacks are one-mast, sloop-rigged vessels of several lengths between 60 and 30 feet; the small ones are used in winter also to scrape hard crabs out of the mud. Big and little, there are (1940) about 150 skipjacks here. **1942** Footner *MD Main* 206, Single-masted vessels, larger than the canoes, are called "batteaus" in Crisfield, "skip-jacks" in other parts of the Bay. **1965** Will *Okeechobee Boats* 97 **FL,** In the year of 1916 his boat was a 34 foot skipjack with a hiked up bow and stern, a sharp V bottom and a windowless cabin. **1968–70** DARE (Qu. O9, . . *Kinds of sailboats)* Inf **DE4,** Skipjack—one-mast boat with a sharp sail; **MD11,** *Skipjack*—has jib and mainsail, about 50–60 feet, common in Chesapeake Bay area, where it originated; **MD36,** Skipjack—one mast, two sails; **MD40,** Skipjack—one or two masts, square at one end; **VA47,** Skipjack—old-fashioned, a work boat used in the Bay; (Qu. O10, *What other kinds of boats are used around here?)* Inf **MD15,** Skipjacks—for dredging; like workboat, but has sails. **1982** Heat Moon *Blue Highways* 403 **Chesapeake Bay,** One other thing made for the survival of that single-masted, double-sailed boat of low and majestic lines. People here, now that the bugeye are gone, consider the skipjack the very symbol of the Eastern Shore. It is to them what the beanpot is to a Bostonian. **1996** Horton *Island Out of Time* 44 **Chesapeake Bay MD,** They have been adopted as the Maryland state boat, and are called "skipjacks." But that was a city word, islanders say. They always called them, simply, "drudge boats."

4 =jumper 7c. Upstate NY Cf *jack jump(er)* (at **jumper 7c**), **skipper 4**

1948 *McDavid Coll.* **cNY,** Skip jack—improvised sled; seat on barrel stave. **1967** *Good Old Days* 4.1.31 **cnNY,** We lived on a farm and used to make skip jacks. A barrel stave became a runner, a block of wood was fastened to the runner with a board on top for seat. . . Old sealing wax from preserves was used to rub on the runner to make it go faster. These have been replaced today by the new "skippers." **1997** in 2001 *DARE* File—Internet **cnNY** (as of 1920s), Homemade skip-jacks—a barrel stave with an upright post and a small board seat, provided a thrilling ride for the venturesome. **2001** *Ibid* **ceNY** [Museum exhibit], Skipjack. . . A single-runner sled with a seat. **2001** *DARE* File **cNY,** My next-door neighbors . . made a skipjack for us kids to use in the late 1950's, early 1960's. Its runner was about 4″ wide and 36″ long and curved up sort of like a barrel stave (which it might have been). It was attached to a piece of wood, probably a 2″ by 4″ perhaps 18″ tall, and braced in front and back with shorter pieces of wood. The seat was a flat board about 4″ by 12″ set on top of the 2″ by 4″, perpendicular to the runner. To ride it, you would sit on it at the top of a hill with the runners [sic] between your feet, then push off with your feet.

skipjack herring (or tuna) See **skipjack 1b**

skip mackerel n esp NY
=bluefish 1.

1874 *Harper's New Mth. Mag.* July 223 **NY,** Even in New York he [= the bluefish] is not sure of his name; the young go by the name of skip-mackerel in the city. **1884** Goode *Fisheries U.S.* 1.433 **NY,** The Bluefish. . . This fish . . is also known in Rhode Island as the "Horse Mackerel"; south of Cape Hatteras as the "Skipjack." . . About New

York they are called "Skip Mackerel." **1903** NY State Museum & Sci. Serv. *Bulletin* 446 **NY,** Some of the many names applied to this widely distributed fish are the following: mackerel (New Jersey), . . skip mackerel (New York) [etc]. **1935** Caine *Game Fish* 46, Bluefish. . . Skip Mackerel. **1973** Knight *Cook's Fish Guide* 384, Mackerel[,] . . skip see Bluefish.

skip out See **skip** v 1

skippaug n [Appar var of **scuppaug**] **NY**
=**menhaden 1.**

1842 DeKay *Zool. NY* 4.260 **Long Is. NY,** At the east end of the island, they [=mossbonkers] are called *Skippangs* [sic] or *Bunkers*. **1848** Bartlett *Americanisms* 222 **NY,** In Massachusetts and Rhode Island, they are called Menhaden; in New York, Mossbonkers and Skippaugs. **1902** *Jrl. Amer. Folk.* 15.248, In Massachusetts, Rhode Island, etc., the name *menhaden* is the more common one; in New York, mossbunker and *skippaug;* in other regions *pauhagen, paughaden, poghaden,* sometimes cut down to *poggie, poggy,* or *pog*.

skipper n

1 also *skipper fly:* A maggot that infests meat or cheese; hence adj *skippery* infested with such maggots. **chiefly Sth, S Midl**

1805 Parkinson *Tour* 221, The reason why many [Americans] . . smoke their bacon and fish, is, that there are many sorts of reptiles that would absolutely destroy it, were it not for the smoke, particularly what is called the skippers, or salt-worm. **1819** *Amer. Farmer* 1.126 **MD,** We lost at least one third of our ham meat, by the skippers. **1861** IL State Ag. Soc. *Trans. for 1859–60* 4.100, The skipper fly . . has been a pest to all cheese makers of Illinois. **1879** (1965) Tyree *Housekeeping in Old VA* 126, This may be remedied by keeping it [=bacon] in ashes . . for a few weeks before using. Must then be hung up, with ashes adhering, until needed. This also prevents skippers. **1899** (1912) Green *VA Folk-Speech* 390, Skipper. . . Certain larvae in bacon and cheese. *Skippery, adj.* Abounding in skippers. **1904** *DN* 2.428 **Cape Cod MA** (as of a1857), *Skipper.* . . The maggot in cheese, meat, etc. **1905** *DN* 3.19 **cCT,** *Skipper.* . . The cheese mite. **1907** *DN* 3.217 **nwAR,** *Skipper.* . . The cheese mite. Also used of mites appearing in cured meat. **1909** *DN* 3.347 **eAL, wGA,** *Maget.* . . Maggot, skipper. "The meat has magets in it." *Skipper* is used quite as frequently. **1938** *Hench Coll.* **VA,** Skipper. . . This is the word I've heard ever since I've come to Virginia used to describe the destructive worm that eats cured hams. Folk-lore says that the little silver-white streaks in excellent country hams . . are skippers after being cooked. **1967–70** *DARE* (Qu. R13, *Flies that come to meat or fruit*) Infs **TX35, VA57,** Skipper fly; **VA43,** Skipper fly—the worm that never dies; **TN30,** Skippers. **1969** *DARE* FW Addit **KY5, 6,** *Skippers*—small white worms that get in cheese or cured meat, particularly ham. Old-fashioned. **1970** *DARE* Tape **KY90,** [Inf:] They got to buying a skipper compound at the stores. They'd sprinkle it on to keep the skippers from eating that meat. [FW:] Are those little worms? [Inf:] Yeah. I guess they have them everywhere where they have meat; **VA38,** The old people used to put black pepper, red pepper, sprinkle lead on there [=the curing ham]. They always have put borax on it. That's to help to keep the skipper flies away. **1986** Pederson *LAGS Concordance Gulf Region,* 5 infs, Skipper(s); 1 inf, Skippers—maggots—they got into the meat; 1 inf, Skippers—in cured meat; 1 inf, Skipper fly—smaller than maggot; 1 inf, Skippers—white worms—get in poorly stored meat; 1 inf, Skippers—green flies that get around raw meat.

2 also *water skipper:* A **water strider** (family Gerridae). **esp PA**

1854 Emmons *Agriculture NY* 5.167, *Hydrometridae.* . . Individuals of this family, . . from their mode of progression over the surface of the water, have been called *skippers*. **1890** in 1896 IL State Lab. Nat. Hist. Urbana *Bulletin* 3.173 **IL,** *Limnotrechus marginatus.* . . The eggs of this "skipper" are attached to aquatic plants. **1930** Shoemaker *1300 Words* 59 **cPA Mts** (as of c1900), *Skipper*—A water spider. **1967–68** *DARE* (Qu. R28, . . *Kinds of spiders*) Inf **PA6,** Water spider, skipper; **PA104,** Skipper insects; **PA155,** Water skipper.

3 also *water skipper:* The larva of a **mosquito** n[1] **B1.**

1968–70 *DARE* (Qu. R14, *Small worm-like things [seen in rain barrels or standing water] that hatch into mosquitoes*) Inf **VA73,** Skipper; **PA231,** Skippers; **KY88,** Skippers, wiggle-tails; **VA2,** Water skippers, water lice, wiggle-tails.

4 =**jumper 7c.** Cf **skipjack 4**

1943 *LANE* Map 573–74, A crude small sled with a barrel-stave run-

ner. . . *skipper* [1 inf, **neMA**]. **1969** *DARE* FW Addit **ceNY,** Jumper or skipper—barrel stave and a post and a seat on top, bear grease on bottom. [Inf born 1909]

5 A kind of playing marble: see quot. Cf **jumper 13**

c1970 Wiersma *Marbles Terms* **MI,** Skippers. . . A light marble, like [a] jumper.

skipper fly See **skipper 1**

skippick n Also *snippick*
A **needlefish 1** (here: *Strongylura marina*).

1906 NJ State Museum *Annual Rept. for 1905* 204, *Tylosurus marinus.* . . Snippick. . . Abundant on our coast, and in the Delaware as far as Trenton at least, also in the Raritan. **1946** LaMonte *N. Amer. Game Fishes* 18, The Needlefishes. . . Names: Gar, . . Skippick [etc].

skipping Jenny n Cf **hopping John 1, limping Kate**

1952 Brown *NC Folkl.* 1.591, Skipping-jenny. . . Rice and peas cooked together.—East.

skip-scotch n Also *skip(-and)-hop*
The children's game of **hopscotch.**

1965–70 *DARE* (Qu. EE19, *The game in which children mark a 'court' on the ground or sidewalk, throw a flat stone in one section, then go on one foot and try to kick it or carry it out*) Inf **MO2,** Skip-and-hop; **MO34,** Skip-hop; **OH50,** Skip-scotch.

skipt See **skip** n[3]

skip tag n
Prob a game of tag in which the players must skip (instead of run or walk).

1957 *Sat. Eve. Post Letters* **ceMN,** When I was a child . . , we called the games we played by these names . . Tag: squat-tag, skip-tag. . . This was in Elk River, Minnesota . . about 1890–1897.

skip the gutter v phr
To hurry—used as imper.

1957 *Sat. Eve. Post Letters* **swOH,** Expressions Used By My Grandfather. . . Skip the gutter (hurry up, get going). **1979** *DARE* File **MA,** When we children were making a nuisance of ourselves or getting in her way, she would say: *"Come now, skip the gutter,"* which meant that she wanted us to get going, preferably out of doors.

skirmish n, v, hence vbl n *skirmishing* Also *scrimitch, scrim(m)age, scrummish, scrum(m)age, skrim(m)age, skurmage* [All the varr represent old types; see *OED2 scrimish, scrimmage,* and *skirmish,* and cf **rubbage.**]

A Forms. Note: *Skirmish* and *scrimmage* are now often regarded as separate words, with the former used in reference to armed conflicts and the latter more common in extended senses, as esp in ref to football; nevertheless, as the evidence assembled here shows, the semantic split is still not complete.

1758 in 1988 Washington *Papers—Colonial Ser.* 5.423, He left us with Six more from the Dunkers just before the Scrumage at the Great meadoes. **1776** in 1903 Lincoln *Papers* 3 **MA,** They have Scrimageing from there every Day. **1781** *PA Jrl. & Weekly Advt.* (Philadelphia) 23 May, A gentleman writes to his friend that on such a day they had a smart *scrimitch,* for *skirmish.* **1834** *Life Andrew Jackson* 157, At this time the war becom'd bloody, the scrimmages frequent, the deths many. **1844** (1846) Kendall *Santa Fé Exped.* 1.66, We felt confident that we should meet with large bands of Indians . . with whom we should have an occasional "skrimmage." **1851** Burke *Polly Peablossom* 59 **IN,** He'd walked away before the skurmage commenced. **1874** *Appletons' Jrl.* 12.494, The queer, urn-shaped sign-board . . still constitutes an item of the rubbish stored away in the garret, whose floor was laid eleven years before the little scrimmage at Lexington. **1874** *Galaxy* 17.149 **CA,** One good thing, it's goin' to cum as nigh killin' uv 'em to start 'em out this time uv year as ef we had an out scrummage with 'em. **1899** (1912) Green *VA Folk-Speech* 372, Scrimmage. . . A confused row or contest; a tussle. **1902** *DN* 2.245 **sIL,** Scrimmage. . . 1. Skirmish. 2. Scramble. 3. Altercation. 4. Fight. **1907** *DN* 3.227 **nwAR,** Scrimmage. **1925** [see C below]. **c1937** in 1976 *Weevils in the Wheat* 138 **VA** [Black], We had a number of little scrummages wid ole Confederates upon Black Water near Windsor, Virginia, an' several men was killed. **c1938** in Lib. of Congress *Amer. Memory: WPA Life Hist.* (Internet) **TX,**

A fellow named Chub Mullins . . with one other waddy and me, had a nice little scrimmage with a party of rustlers. **1946** *AmSp* 21.146 [Army mispronunciations], Every time he wanted his squad to defile right (or left)—'Skirmishes Right' is the command—he shouted 'Skirmages Right! Skrimages Left!' **1966** [see **B1** below]. **1967–68** [see **B3** below]. **1968** *DARE* (Qu. Y13, *A fist fight with several people in it*) Inf **IN**39, Scrimmage; [**MD**41, Skirmish; (Qu. Y12b, *A real fight in which blows are struck*) Inf **CA**177, Skirmish]. **1968–70** [see **B2** below]. **2001** *NADS Letters* csGA, "Scrimmage" . . etc., a small or low violence fight.

B As noun.

1 =**skift** n² **1.**
1966 *DARE* (Qu. B39, *A very light fall of snow*) Inf **ID**1, Skurmage ['skɜ·məʃ] of snow. **1984** Wilder *You All Spoken Here* 141 **Sth**, *Skift of snow; skirmish of snow:* A light snowfall; a flurry.

2 An informal game of baseball or hockey. [Transf from football use]
1968–70 *DARE* (Qu. EE11, *Bat-and-ball games for just a few players*) Infs **MI**75, **PA**134, 221, Scrimmage; **NY**234, Skirmish. **2001** *DARE* File cwNY, [J.K. Chambers' "Dialect Topography of the Golden Horseshoe" collected 1 ex of *scrimmage* for an informal baseball game and 3 exx for an informal hockey game from 80 Buffalo-area infs surveyed in 1991–92. (The same responses were collected from 9 and 41 infs respectively of 935 nearby Canadians.)]

3 in comb *skirmish line:* A nonexistent item used as the basis of a practical joke. [In allusion to *skirmish line* a group of soldiers deployed ahead of a line of battle]
1918 *DN* 5.29 **NW**, To get a fire closer. . . Test of intelligence, as in "He would get a fire closer." Jocose use among college students. [*T]o get a skirmish line with(out) handles,* vb. phr. See above. **1967–68** *DARE* (Qu. HH14, *Ways of teasing a beginner or inexperienced person—for example, by sending him for a 'left-handed monkey wrench':* "Go get me _____.") Inf **AZ**10, Some skirmish line; **NY**66, A skirmish line—Navy; **GA**84, Yard of skirmish line; **TX**5, In Army sent for yards of skirmish line; **NJ**18, **NY**73, (A yard of) scrimmage line.

C As verb.

Also with *about, around, up:* To search, scout, rummage; to hunt up, search out; hence n *skirmisher.*
[**1855** *Harper's New Mth. Mag.* 11.571, He had started in the morning without any breakfast; and when E_____ hove in sight, he gathered himself up for a general skirmish for any and all kinds of provisions.] **1864** in 1926 Twain *Sketches* 129, His first cousin . . is a skirmisher and is with the parson—he goes through the camp-meetings and skirmishes for raw converts. **1878** *Appletons' Jrl.* 5.133, Well, let us see. . . Suppose we skirmish about in a general way. Shall we begin with geography? **1907** White *AZ Nights* 17, We skirmished around and found a condemned army pack saddle with aparejos. **1925** Dargan *Highland Annals* 99 **cwNC**, I told him we'd scrummish around the mountain toward the sun, an' maybe I could shake off my chill. **1935** Davis *Honey* 51 **OR**, They went out all in a pack to skirmish up a fresh team. **1946** McAtee *Dial. Grant Co. IN Suppl. 3* 9 (as of 1890s), Skirmish around . . hunt for; "Let me _____ a while and see if I can find it."

skirmish line See **skirmish B3**

skirmish up See **skirmish C**

skirrup n, v Also with *around*
1896 *DN* 1.424 **NY**, Skirrup [skɪrəp]: a good time. Also as v. *skirrup, skirrup around,* to frisk, frolic. N.Y.c., n. Also [skjurəp], N.Y.w.

skirs See **scarce**

skirt n [Cf *SND* skirp n. 1 "A small drop, . . *specif.* of a slight shower of rain"] Cf **scutch** n, **skit** n
=**skift** n² **1.**
1968 *DARE* (Qu. B39, *A very light fall of snow*) Inf **DE**3, Light skirt of snow—old-fashioned; **MD**35, Skirt of snow [Inf queries].

skit n Also *skitter* [*OED2* skit sb.² 3 "A slight shower (*of rain or snow*)."]
=**skift** n² **1.**
1968–69 *DARE* (Qu. B33a, *The first thin ice that forms over the surface of a pond or pool:* "There's just a _____ of ice.") Inf **IN**79, Skit; **MO**39, Skitter; (Qu. B39, *A very light fall of snow*) Infs **IN**54, 79, **MD**21, **OH**72, Skit [skɪt] (of snow).

skit v [Perh var of *scat,* but cf **skite** v]
To leave in a hurry, to rush away—usu used in imper.
1912 *DN* 3.589 **wIN**, Skit, v.i. To go. Used only in the imperative "Skit," or "You skit, now." **1945** FWP *Lay My Burden Down* 5 **Sth** (as of c1865) [Black], He skitted to the hog pen with a heavy mallet in his hand. **1966–70** *DARE* (Qu. NN22b, *Expressions used to drive away children*) Infs **KS**13, **KY**72, Skit [skɪt]; (Qu. NN22c, *Expressions used to drive away a dog*) Inf **NC**14, Skit [skɪt]; (Qu. NN22d, . . *Expressions used to drive away people or animals*) Infs **LA**45, **NC**14, Skit; **CA**66, Skit—a cat.

skitching vbl n esp NEast, Gt Lakes Cf **hooky bob, shacking** vbl n², **skeetch, skidding 4**
Holding on to the back of a vehicle so as to be pulled over snow or ice; transf: holding on to a vehicle while on a bicycle.
1983 *NY Times* (NY) 21 Aug sec 11 L[ong] I[sland] 14/1 (Internet) seNY, Then there was the game of trying to hang onto the back bumper of a truck and riding the bumper like a ski—"skitching," according to Van Patten. **1990** *DARE* File seCT, neIL, seNY, csPA, seVA (as of 1974–81), [Response given by University of Virginia students and faculty when asked, "What words do you have for the act of hanging onto the back bumper of a moving vehicle as it drives on snow or ice?":] Skitching. **1993** *Detroit Free Press* (MI) 30 July sec F 3/3 **Upper Peninsula MI**, *Shacking:* grabbing onto the back fender of a moving bus, truck or car and sliding along the icy or snowy road. Favorite pastime of young Yoopers. Also called skitching or shagging. **1994** *Capital Times* (Madison WI) 14 Feb sec A 10/2, It's called "hopping cars" in Philadelphia, "bumper-hitching" or "shagging" in Detroit, "skitching" along the Eastern Seaboard. In northern Indiana it's "hooky-bobbing." As long as snow is on the ground and a car is passing by, kids grab bumpers and go along for the ride. It's a dangerous thrill, and some children are learning that the hard way. **1995** *DARE* File, My friend from Chicago . . knows this by the terms *flippin' cars* or *skitchin'.* **2001** *Ibid* **Long Is. NY**, One of my sons-in-law, now 30, grew up on Long Island—in Babylon, New York, specifically—and when a boy there, the activity was known as "skitching." *Ibid,* In a National Public Radio interview, a bike messenger told of hitching rides by holding onto cars. He called it *skitching.*

skite v Also sp *skyt* Often with adv [Engl dial; *EDD* skite "To move in leaps and bounds; to run swiftly and lightly; to fly off hastily"; *OED2* 1721 →] esp Nth, N Midl
To go or leave quickly; to hurry; to run about—freq used in imper.
1859 (1968) Bartlett *Americanisms* 410, *To Skite.* To *skite about* is to go running about. **1890** *DN* 1.75 sePA, Skite . . [skaɪt]: skedaddle. Philadelphia. **1894** Riley *Armazindy* 144 **IN**, The next thing they did sight / Was a great big bulldog chasing them,/ And a farmer, hollerin' "Skite!" **1896** *DN* 1.424 cNY, Skite: "Skite out!" get out, run away quickly. **1903** *DN* 2.300 **Cape Cod MA** (as of a1857), Skite. . . To dodge about. *Ibid* 353 **eIA, neOH**, Skite out. . . To run hastily. *Skite up* might be used for running up stairs, or up the hill. **1912** *DN* 3.589 **wIN**, Skite. . . To hurry. "You skite, now." Sometimes *skite out* and *skite off* are heard. **1930** Shoemaker *1300 Words* 52 **cPA Mts** (as of c1900), Skyt—Be off, "go". **1942** Warnick *Garrett Co. MD* 13 **nwMD** (as of 1900–18), Skite . . to go hurriedly (Dial.) **1950** *WELS Suppl.* cwWI, Skite for hurry as "Now skite along to school and don't be late." **1975** Gould *ME Lingo* 257, Skite . . to sail fast or move right along: "Well, I'll skite along now, I've got things to do."

skite n [*OED2* 1790 →; "Sc. and north. dial."; *SND* skite n.² 2 "A nasty or objectionable person"] Cf **skate** n² **1**
See quots.
1790 in 1988 Maclay *Diary* 306 **PA**, Hamilton has a very boyish giddy Manner. our Scotch Irish People would call him a Skite. **1911** *DN* 3.547 **NE**, Skite . . (1) A cross or unlikeable man, somewhat miserly, or inclined to be dishonest in money matters. "Old man Smith is a regular skite." Reported from Saline and Lancaster counties. (2) A small cute or mischievous person. "That little skite has hidden my book." Reported from south central Nebraska. **1995** *Brophy Coll.* 68 swMO (as of c1960), Skite. [A]n unreliable or extravagant person (Scotch-Irish usage).

skit(e)s See **skeets**

skittamalink See **skinny malink**

skitter n¹ See **mosquito** n¹

skitter n[2] See **skit** n

skitters n Often with *the* [Engl dial; *OED2* a1585 →] **chiefly PA, MD, WV, OH** See Map Cf **skeets**
Diarrhea.

   1899 (1912) Green *VA Folk-Speech* 390, Skitters. . . Diarrhoea. **1930** Shoemaker *1300 Words* 56 **cPA Mts** (as of c1900), Skitters—Diarrhea. **1935** *AmSp* 10.172 **PA** [Engl of PA Germans], Other terms more rarely used include the following: . . *Skitters* for diarrhea. **1939** Steinbeck *Grapes* 431, They et green grapes. They all five got the howlin' skitters. Run out ever' ten minutes. **1965–70** *DARE* (Qu. BB19, *Joking names for looseness of the bowels*) 25 Infs, **chiefly PA, MD, WV, OH,** (The) skitters. [16 of 25 Infs male, 12 young or mid-aged]

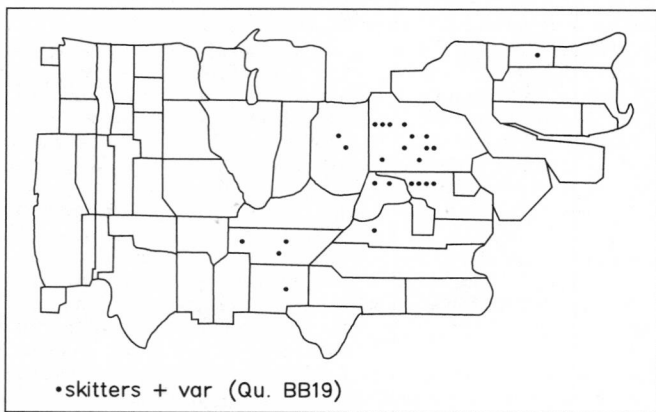

•skitters + var (Qu. BB19)

skitter-skatter adv [Redup] Cf *hither-scather* (at **hither and thither**)
Helter-skelter.

   1967–68 *DARE* (Qu. MM12a, . . *'In all directions'* . . "He shot into a flock of birds and they went _____.") Infs **PA**167, **TX**10, Skitterskatter.

skittle n[1] Also *skiddle* [Perh by metath, but perh blend of *skillet* + *kittle*] Cf *DS* F1
=**skillet** n **1.**

   1900 *Overland Mth.* (2d ser) 36.473 **CA**, With my hat fairly lifting with the bristling secrets which were now crowded under it, so that it felt ready to pop off like a hot skittle-lid, I took to the woods. **1950** *WELS Suppl.* **csWI**, Skittle—for skillet. Her mother always said "skittle" and she says it too. **1973** Allen *LAUM* 1.200 **ceMN, nwND** (as of c1950), *Frying pan.* . . Skittle. **2000** *NADS Letters* **MI**, Oh! how my grandmother could fry chicken! It wasn't just because we were young & hungry, it was because of her special touch with the hot skiddle on a wood fire.

skittle n[2] [Var of *scuttle*]
A coal scuttle.

   1973 Allen *LAUM* 1.224 **ND, WI** (as of c1950), *Coal hod.* . . Two North Dakota infs. use the variant *skittle,* also reported once in Wisconsin.

skittle-dog n [*OED2* 1862 →]
A **dogfish 1** (here: *Squalus acanthias*).

   1873 in 1878 Smithsonian Inst. *Misc. Coll.* 14.2.36, *Squalus americanus.* . . Picked dog-fish, dog-fish; bone-dog; skittle-dog [etc]. **1896** U.S. Natl. Museum *Bulletin* 47.54, *Squalus acanthias.* . . Dogfish; Picked Dogfish; Bonedog; Skittle-dog. **1935** Caine *Game Fish* 156, Sand Shark—*Squalus acanthias.* . . Known variously as the dogfish, dogshark, bone-dog, and skittle-dog, this species of shark is probably the most numerous of the entire shark family.

skittling adj [Cf *EDD skiddley* "Small, diminutive", *skiddick* sb. 1 "An atom, particle."]
   1959 *VT Hist.* 27.157, Skittling. . . Poor; inadequate. Rare.

skitty-wampus adv Cf **kitty-wampus, sky west and crooked**
Helter-skelter.

   1968 *DARE* (Qu. MM12b, . . *'In all directions'* . . "When she was out

on the dance floor, she broke her beads and they went _____.") Inf **WI**27, Skitty-wampus.

skive v[1] Also with *around* [*OED2* "dial."; 1854 →] Cf **skiver** v
To run, dart; to tumble.

   1855 Hammond–Mansfield *Country Margins* 263 **NY**, Our progress is stayed here, unless we choose to climb where a false step . . would send us skiving in the gulf below. **1857** Holland *Bay-path* 334 **CT**, Don't you want a little tot . . to be skiving round the cabin here, and making a fuss, and learning to do things, and full of fun? **1906** Casey *Parson's Boys* 61 **sIL** (as of c1860), Ye'd both better git into the wagon, and not go skivin' about like a couple of Injins. **1914** *DN* 4.71 **ME, nNH**, He come a-skivin', suthin desprit! *Ibid* 79, Skive. . . To go, run, hurry.

skive v[2] [By ext from *skive* to shave, pare (esp leather)]
With *up*: To tear up (earth or turf).

   1940 Stuart *Trees of Heaven* 202 **eKY**, That bluff is skived up where the mules dug in with their hoofs to pull this load. **1946** Stuart *Tales Plum Grove* 191 **eKY**, The sheriff took Willard to the scaffold. Willard scooted and skived-up the grass, cussed, hollered and prayed.

skive around See **skive** v[1]

skiver v Also with *around* Also *skivver* [Cf **skive** v[1]]
To scatter, scurry.

   1881 Hapgood–Roosevelt *Shore Birds* 33 **Long Is. NY**, At the report [of a gun] the frightened flock will dart about in terror, "skiver," as it is technically called, making the second shot as difficult as the first is easy. **1942** *Amer. Mercury* 55.85 **Harlem NYC** [Black], So Jelly . . got out to skivver around and do himself some good. **1977** *Yankee* Jan 73 **ME**, You can at least tell the chickens to skiver! and disperse them with a wave of your hand.

skiver n Pronc-sp *skivver* [Brit dial *skiver* skewer, splinter]
1 =**husking pin.**
   1976 *PA Folklife* Spring 30, *Corn skiver* (pron. *skivver*), a husking peg.
2 A small amount; a trace; also fig.
   1925 Dargan *Highland Annals* 196 **cwNC**, Len sowed an acre of rye for green winter picking; also a "skiver of wheat" which was to be all Serena's, as a basis for "feed," but I suspected that the hens would anticipate that harvest—and they did. **1944** Holton *Yankees Were Like This* 102 **Cape Cod MA** (as of c1890), Poor Miriam, they say, had got to be all of twenty-eight without as much as a skiver of a beau. **1996–97** in 2000 *Montgomery Coll.* **eTN**, [Skiver] = a small amount, as "We thought we were going to have one big storm, but we only got a skiver."

skiver around See **skiver** v

skive up See **skive** v[2]

skivver v See **skiver** v

skivver n See **skiver** n

ski-wampus See **skew-** d

skluff v [Cf *EDD sklouff* v. 1 "To strike with a dull, heavy blow; . . to trail the feet on the ground."]
   1911 *DN* 3.550 **WY**, Skluff, scuff. "Dont skluff your feet."

skoggin See **scoggin** 2

skoke See **scoke**

skoodle v [Cf **scoot** v 3, *EDD scroodle* "To crouch, cower, stoop down"]
   1916 Macy–Hussey *Nantucket Scrap Basket* 144 **MA**, "Skoodle"—To squat or crouch down; rarely heard now, though in common use fifty years ago.

skookum n **chiefly NW** Cf *DCan*
A ghost, demon, spirit.

   [**1838** Parker *Jrl. Rocky Mts.* 336, Evil spirit, skookoom / Hell, skookoom.] [**1844** Lee–Frost *10 Yrs. OR* 180, He [=a medicine man] approaches his patient, and . . with his mouth applied as a cupping-glass, he transfers the "sko-kum," or "tam-an-a-was," or disease, wholly or in part from himself to himself!] **1900** *OR Hist. Soc. Hist. Qrly.* 1.185, The benefits of his fishery had gone, not to the people, but to the wicked skookum. **1982** Heat Moon *Blue Highways* 223 **cwOR**, Coast was full of skookums. That's what the Chinooks called ghosts. **1995** Lesley *Sky Fisherman* 111 **OR,** We hit the whitewater, and I . . realized the current was sweeping us too far right. . . After bumping twice we cleared the shelf. . . He climbed out of the boat. "Come on. Let's pull Old Skookum out and take a look downstream." According to Jake, "Skookum" was an Indian word that meant something like "powerful spirit." On this river, I was happy for any extra help I could get.

skookum adj [Chinook Jargon]   **chiefly NW, AK**   Cf *DCan*
Strong, powerful; good.
    [**1847** Palmer *Jrl.* 151 **OR** [Chinook Jargon], *Sko-kum*—Strong, stout.] **1894** *Harper's New Mth. Mag.* 88.790 **nwWA,** Quarts to the horses and quarts to the Siwashes and a skookum-peck of trouble all round. **1913** *DN* 4.28 **NW,** *Skookum.* . . A Chinook Indian word meaning all right, *strong,* big. Used also in Alaska and Canada. "He feels quite skookum to-day." **1918** *DN* 5.28 **NW,** *Skookum,* adj. Good, fine, etc. Indian word of approval, also. General. **1935** *AK Sportsman* Jan 19 (Tabbert *Dict. Alaskan Engl.*), You go up the "crick" . . till you come to a "skookum" lake, chock full of rainbows, cutthroats and dollies. **1949** Sierra Club *Bulletin* June 105 **AK** (as of 1910), Billy and Pete were skookum, and I was pretty good myself in those days. **1956** *AmSp* 31.152 **nwCA** [Logger lingo], *Skookum.* . . Strong, good, powerful. A Chinook word. Examples: 'A skookum job well done'; 'a skookum drink.' **1964** Jackman-Long *OR Desert* 180, In Oregon one hears "skookum," "cultus," "potlatch," but you don't hear those words in Pennsylvania. **1966–67** *DARE* FW Addit **swWA,** ['skukəm]—strong; **cnWA,** ['skukəm]—good, "He's a pretty skookum old guy." **1976** Hobbs–Specht *Tisha* 76 **AK,** He cuts it a little thin sometimes and he's tough on horses, but he's skookum— he's got guts. **1988** *Fairbanks Daily News–Miner* (AK) 7 July 8 (Tabbert *Dict. Alaskan Engl.*), You've got a skookum road up for the first 50 miles.

skookum chuck n [Chinook Jargon < **skookum** adj + **chuck** n[4]]   **chiefly NW, AK**   Cf **saltchuck,** *DCan*
A turbulent channel of water, as a rapids in a river or a tidal channel—often used in place names.
    1854 in 1855 U.S. War Dept. *Rept. Explor. Railroad* 1.468, After receiving the Nawaukum and the Skookum Chuck, two bold streams rising in the Cascade mountains, it [=the Chihalis] bends to the westward, and empties finally into Gray's harbor. **1871** *Overland Mth.* 7.284 **wWA,** We continue . . southward, till we come to the large open bay of Port Madison, on the south bank of which branches the Skookum Chuck into Bainbridge Island. **1899** U.S. Fish & Wildlife Serv. *Fishery Bulletin* 1870, At the end of this arm is a narrow passage, or "skookum chuck," as it is called in this country, leading into a bay. **1899** U.S. Fish Comm. *Bulletin for 1898* 73 **AK,** The passage is a 'skookum chuck', through which the water runs in whirls and rapids almost constantly and with great velocity. **1915** Muir *Travels AK* 220, We were startled by Captain Tyeen shouting, "Skookum chuck! Skookum chuck!" (strong water, strong water), and found our canoe was being swept sideways by a powerful current. **1958** McCulloch *Woods Words* 168 **Pacific NW,** *Skookumchuck*—Fast, dangerous, or tricky waters, as falls, narrows, or tide rips.

skookum house n [**skookum** adj]   **chiefly NW, AK**   Cf *DCan*
A jail.
    1885 *Century Illustr. Mag.* 29.842 **WA,** [An Indian] had recently been arrested by the agent, put in the "skookum-house" (jail), and fined sixty dollars for having two wives. **1894** *Harper's New Mth. Mag.* 89.514 **swID,** Maybe he catch E-egante, maybe put him in skookum-house [prison]? **1910** Porter *Whirligigs* 232 **NYC,** The skookum house for yours! **1914** *DN* 4.164 **NW,** *Skookum-house.* . . A strong house or jail on an Indian reservation. **1934** *Anchorage Daily Times* (AK) 2 Oct np, And dusky maiden also is in the local skookum house for having imbibed too freely. **1939** FWP *Guide AK* xli, *Skookum-house.* . . (C[hinook]) jail. **1966–68** *DARE* (Qu. V11, . . *Joking names . . for a county or city jail*) Inf **AK**1, Skookum house ['skukəm] house; **WA**13, Skookum ['skukəm] house—Indian word.

skootch See **scooch**

skootched up See **scooch 5**

skoplotch See **scobolotch**

skouk See **scouck**

skow See **scow** n[2]

skowitz n [Nisqualli; see quot 1884]   **esp WA**
=**coho salmon.**
    1856 U.S. Army Corps Topog. Engineers *Rept. RR* 12.3.320 **WA,** The Nisqually Indians say that the majority of the *Tl'hwhai* salmon return to salt water after spawning; that many of the skowitz return, but that *more* die in fresh water. **1884** Goode *Fisheries U.S.* 1.477 **WA,** The Silver Salmon. . . On Frazer River it is known by the Musquam name of "Coho"; at Seattle, by the Nisqually name of "Skowitz." **1949** Caine *N. Amer. Sport Fish* 53, Silver Salmon. . . This salmon is also known as the Coho Salmon, . . Skowitz, Silversides [etc].

skowk See **scouck**

skrag See **scrag**

Skratch See **Scratch** n[2]

skreak See **screak** v

skreaky See **screaky**

skreek See **screak** v

skreeky See **screaky**

skrid See **scrid**

skriek See **screak** n

skrieky See **screaky**

skrim(m)age See **skirmish**

skrinch owl See **scrinch owl**

skrivvel See **shrivel** v[1]

skrook n Also *skrock hen*   [Dan *skrukhøne* brooding hen]   Cf **cluck** n 1
A setting hen.
    1937 *AmSp* 12.104 **eNE** [Farm terms], A setting hen may be a *cluck,* . . a *clucking hen,* a *settin' hen,* a *sour hen* (Scandinavian from *sur hona*) or a *skrock hen* (German). **1983** *DARE* File **cUT,** In Danish settlements in Sanpete County, a setting hen is a "skrook." **1984** *Ibid* **sID,** Skrook—a setting hen.

skrootch See **scrooch**

skroud See **scrowd**

skrouge See **scrouge** v

skrugee adj See **skewgee**

skru-gee pref See **skew- a**

skrutch See **scrooch**

skulch See **sculch**

skulheeg n Cf **killhag**
    1914 *DN* 4.79 **ME, nNH,** *Skulheeg.* . . A deadfall trap.

skull buster n Also *skull (bust),* ~ *cracker,* ~ *varnish*   **esp Sth, S Midl**   Cf **busthead 1**
=**popskull.**
    1952 Peattie *Black Hills* 167 **SD,** Not even the skull varnish sold in the Deadwood saloons could cause double vision with the two images a hundred miles or more apart. **1963** Carson *Social Hist. Bourbon* 139 **West** (as of 19th cent), Most of the potions available deserved the names bestowed upon them—skull varnish [etc]. **1965–70** *DARE* (Qu. DD21b, *General words . . for bad liquor*) Infs **IL**128, **MD**4, **MS**1, **SC**10, 68, 69, Skull buster; **FL**52, Skull. **c1970** Pederson *Dial. Surv. Rural GA* **seGA** (*What do you call cheap whiskey?*) 1 inf, Skull bust. **1985** Wilkinson *Moonshine* 28 **neNC,** "After that they'd serve you North Carolina Corn." It is called . . skull cracker. **1986** Pederson *LAGS Concordance* (Cheap whiskey) 1 inf, **swTN,** Skull bust; 1 inf, **cAR,** Skull buster.

skullcap n
    1 Std: a plant of the genus *Scutellaria.*   Also called **helmetflower.**   For other names of var spp see **hoodwort, hyssop skullcap, mad-dog** ~   Cf **mad-tail weed**

2 also *skullcap speedwell;* also sp *scullcap:* A **speedwell** (here: *Veronica scutellata*).

1822 Eaton *Botany* 508, [*Veronica*] *scutellata* (scull-cap speedwell). **1832** MA Hist. Soc. *Coll.* 2d ser 9.157 **cwVT**, Veronica scutellata, Scull-cap, speedwell. **1847** Wood *Class-Book* 406, V[eronica] *scutellata*. *Skull-cap or Marsh Speedwell*. . . in swamps and marshes, N. Eng. and Western States, and Brit. Am[erica], common. **1938** Madison *Wild Flowers OH* 108, Skullcap; Marsh Speedwell. **1959** Anderson *Flora AK* 464, Veronica scutellata. . . *Skullcap Speedwell*. . . Moist places, bogs, swamps, and lake shores.

skull cracker See **skull buster**

skulljoe n Also *scully-joe, skully-jo* Also sp *sculjo, sculljoe*
seMA

Salted and dried haddock or codfish.

1884 Goode *Fisheries U.S.* 1.228 **seMA**, At Provincetown a Haddock salted and dried after being split is called by the name of "Skulljoe," or "Scoodled Skulljoe." **1890** *Century Dict.* 5430, *Sculjo, sculljoe*. . . A haddock not split, but with the belly cut off, slack-salted, and dried hard. [*Century* Ed: Provincetown, Massachusetts.] *Ibid* 5679, *Skulljoe*. . . A variant of *sculjo*. **1933** *Sun* (Baltimore MD) 30 Mar 10/6 (Hench Coll.) **MA**, *Cape Cod Faces Skully-Jo Lack*. . . Provincetown faces a real problem. What's to be done about skully-jo? . . Skully-jo is petrified fish—haddock, to be exact, although some say a small cod will do as well. It is eaten raw. . . The fact is, it can't be "eaten," exactly. It's too solid. Perhaps "gnaw" would be the word. . . Two appellations are in general use: "skulljoe"—probably the original—and "skully-jo," a derivation. **1937** FWP *Guide MA* 331 **seMA**, *Skully-jo*, once popular, is no longer made by any but a few Portuguese families. This is codfish or haddock cured in the sun, 'till it's hard enough to bend lead pipe around.' When fish was plentiful the Portuguese made barrels of it and the children carried it about in their pockets and chewed it instead of candy. It was said that 'the longer you chewed on a junk of skully-jo, the more you had.' **1988** Nickerson *Days to Remember* 135 **Cape Cod MA** (as of c1915), *Scully-Joe*—Small cod or flatfish (flounder), dry salted (corned), then cured by drying in the sun. Often eaten without cooking by cutting strips of it for a snack.

skull orchard n **chiefly Appalachians, SE** See Map   Cf **marble orchard**

A cemetery.

c1960 Wilson Coll. **csKY**, *Skull orchard*. . . Jocose name for graveyard. **1965–70** *DARE* (Qu. BB61b, . . *Joking names for a cemetery*) 12 Infs, **chiefly Appalachians, SE**, Skull orchard; TN43, Skull orchard—has heard; VA69, Skull orchard—Inf says she uses quite a bit; (Qu. BB61a, *Other words . . for a cemetery*) Inf GA72, Skull orchard—not joking. [11 of 15 Infs male] **1971** Mitchell *Blow My Blues Away* 183 **nwMS** [Black], Let me tell you something about the stamps. . . If it wasn't for them stamps, one-half of us would be over yonder in the skull orchard. Be dead somewhere. **1986** Pederson *LAGS Concordance* (Cemetery) 2 infs, **seAL, seMS**, Skull orchard.

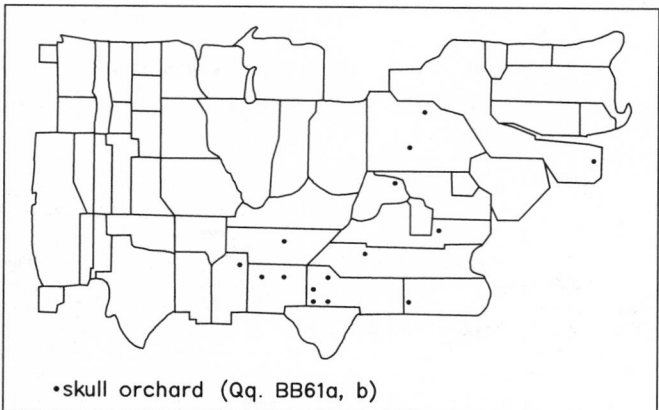

•skull orchard (Qq. BB61a, b)

skull varnish See **skull buster**

skully n[1] [Choctaw *iskąli* a dime, a ninepence, a bit < **escalin**]
1966 *DARE* (Qu. U19a, . . *Money in general: "He's certainly got the _____."*) Inf OK20, Skully—Choctaw for money, used among Indians.

skully n[2] See **skelly 1**

skully-jo See **skulljoe**

skulp See **scalp**

skum See **scum** v[1]

skummed See **scum** v[1] 1

skun See **skin** v A

skunk n

1 Std: a usu striped or spotted American mammal of the genus *Mephitis, Conepatus,* or *Spilogale* known for its repellent scent. For other names of var of these see **bet-piyan, civet cat 2, civic ~, civvy ~, essence peddler, fitch** n, **four-lined skunk, freeze-cat 2, gander skunk, hognose ~, honeycat, house kitty, hump puss, hydrophobia skunk, kitty** n 1, **musk cat 1, perfume(d) pussy, petunia, piss cat, P.K., polecat 1, polekitty, pussy** n 2, **rooter skunk, spotted ~, striped ~, two-lined ~, white-backed ~, wood pussy, woods kitty**
2 in phrr *meaner than a skunk* (or *skunk meat, ~ shit*): Very mean or unkind. Cf **dirt** n 2, **cat shit, dog** n B17d

[**1859** *Harper's New Mth. Mag.* June 106, It was he was afraid—the mean skunk!] **1966–68** *DARE* (Qu. HH22b, . . *A very mean person . . "He's meaner than _____."*) Infs AZ3, MA5, MN15, 36, NH10, (A) skunk; WI9, Skunk meat; PA108, Skunk shit; [(Qu. HH22c, . . *A very mean person . . "He's mean enough to _____."*) Inf MA3, Kill a skunk].

skunk v

1 To outdo decisively; to vanquish completely.

1843 *Quincy* (Ill.) *Herald* 24 Nov. 2/1 *(DA)*, The Legislature will be Democratic by an overwhelming majority; and it is more than probable that the Whigs have been 'skunked.' **1850** Stacy *Memoirs* 109 **NEng**, But I was so unfortunate as not to get a king, before she had taken every "man" from me. . . But again I had no better success—she "skunked" me a second time [in a game of checkers]. **1859** (1968) Bartlett *Americanisms* 410, *To skunk*. . . To utterly defeat. In games of chance, if one of the players fails to make a point, he is said to be *skunked*. **1892** *DN* 1.231 **KY**, *Skunked:* beaten in a game without having made a single point, "whitewashed." . . [*DN* Ed: Also in New England.] **1905** *DN* 3.19 **cCT**, *Skunk*. . . To defeat utterly. **1907** *DN* 3.217 **nwAR**, *Skunk*. . . To defeat utterly. To whitewash in a card game. **c1970** Wiersma *Marbles Terms* **swMI** (as of 1924), When you play with someone and end up winning all of his marbles you have "skunked" him. **1975** Gould *ME Lingo* 257, In the popular Maine game of cribbage, to defeat an opponent by thirty-one holes or more is to *skunk* him. . . This cribbage *skunk* is adapted to other situations where one has come off badly; an angler who catches nothing is *skunked*. **1976** Garber *Mountain-ese* 83 **sAppalachians**, Old Si got skunked in his checker match with Roger. **1982** *Barrick Coll.* **csPA**, *Skunk*—hold scoreless in a game; shut out.

2 in phrr *be* (or *get*) *skunked:* To be totally unsuccessful in an endeavor.

1942 McAtee *Dial. Grant Co. IN* 58 (as of 1890s), *Skunk* . . besides the dictionary meaning of utter defeat in a game, the word was applied to failure in hunting, fishing, etc. "We were skunked, we didn't get a thing." **1950** *WELS (What do you say when you are having bad luck in fishing?)* 2 Infs, **WI**, (Get) skunked. **1965–70** *DARE* (Qu. P9, *When you're fishing but not catching any*) 38 Infs, **scattered, but esp Nth, West**, (Been *or* got, was, etc) skunked (today). **1975** [see **1** above]. **1986** Pederson *LAGS Concordance*, 4 infs, **AL, FL, TX**, Got skunked (didn't catch any fish); 1 inf, **ceAL**, I was skunked (unsuccessful). **1986** *DARE* File **WI**, I went fishing last weekend, but I got skunked.
3 To cheat, deceive.

1890 Haskins *Argonauts CA* 250, I got skunked once out of a good claim. **1950** *WELS* **WI** *(When you think someone has charged you too high a price for something, you might say: . . "I _____." [Include humorous expressions])* 1 Inf, Got skunked; *(To cheat somebody: "He _____ me out of $10.")* 1 Inf, Skunked; *("These apples are wormy; I think you got _____.")* 1 Inf, Skunked. **1968–69** *DARE* (Qu. LL23, *Cheated, treated dishonestly: "These apples are wormy, I think you got _____."*) Infs CA39, IN31, PA167, VA31, VT12, WI30, Skunked.

skunk ape n **FL** Cf **sasquatch**, *DS* CC17
See quots.

1978 *Time* 29 May 101 **FL,** In Florida, the legislature recently indulged in boisterous repartee over a measure that would have made it a crime to molest the "skunk ape," a mythical critter occasionally sighted around the state that is said to stand 7 ft. tall, weigh 700 lbs. and smell like swamp gas. **1982** *Smithsonian Letters* **FL,** Regional names for the two-footed, hairy, human-like "monster" known as . . *skunk ape* (Florida).

‡skunk barn n

1968 *DARE* (Qu. M1, . . *Kinds of barns . . according to their use or the way they are built*) Inf **PA**127, Skunk barn—on the level, no stable underneath.

skunk bear n [See quot 1946]
=wolverine.

1876 U.S. Army Corps Engineers *Rept. Reconnaissance Yellowstone* 1.65 **swMT,** *Gulo luscus.* . . In this region they were spoken of as the "Skunk-bear;" farther south they are called "Carcajou." **1916** Kephart *Camping & Woodcraft* 1.262 **NC,** The wolverine, also called glutton, carcajou, skunk bear, and Indian devil, is the champion thief of the wilderness. **1946** Dufresne *AK's Animals* 93, The term "skunk-bear" is roughly descriptive of this burly marauder. Its 25 to 35 pound bear-like body is low slung on powerful legs terminating in large feet capably armed with long, curved claws. The glossy dark brown fur is marked with two pale lateral stripes converging at the base of a skunk-like bushy tail. Moreover, the wolverine is capable of emitting a disagreeable musky odor from specialized anal glands. **1980** Whitaker *Audubon Field Guide Mammals* 579, Wolverine—"Glutton"—"Skunk Bear."

skunkberry n

1 **=bearberry honeysuckle.**

1931 U.S. Dept. Ag. *Misc. Pub.* 101.146, *Bearberry honeysuckle* . . known also as bearberry, fly honeysuckle, . . and skunkberry, . . is probably the commonest and best known of the western honeysuckles. **1937** U.S. Forest Serv. *Range Plant Hdbk.* B95, Bearberry honeysuckle . . The glossy, dark, almost black fruits, with their unpleasant taste, give rise to the common names of inkberry and skunkberry.

2 Either of two **sumacs:** *Rhus trilobata* or **fragrant sumac.**

1933 *Torreya* 33.84 **cnNE,** *Rhus trilobata.* . . Skunk-berry. **1957** Barnes *Nat. Hist. Wasatch Summer* 85, A bush somewhat resembling an oak but with dark red berry clusters arrests our attention. It is a sumac (*Rhus trilobata),* locally known as squawbush, sunkberry [sic], or aromatic sumac.

3 See **skunk currant.**

skunkbill (coot) See **skunk coot**

skunk bird n

1 See **skunk blackbird.**

2 See **skunk coot.**

skunk-bit adj Cf *DS* DD15
=skunk-drunk.

1958 McCulloch *Woods Words* 168 **Pacific NW,** *Skunk-bit*—Stinking drunk.

skunk blackbird n Also *skunk bird* **chiefly Nth**
The male **bobolink B.**

[**1836** *Penny Cyclop.* 5.30, [The male bobolink's] variegated dress, . . from a resemblance in its colours to that of the quadruped, obtained for it the name of 'skunk-bird' among the Cree Indians.] **1841** *Daily Picayune* (New Orleans LA) 19 Mar 2/4, The intarpriter he sot tu and talked to him agin, as fast as a skunk blackbird. **1871** (1882) Stowe *Fireside Stories* 130 **MA,** He no more sung tenor than a skunk-blackbird, but he made b'lieve he did. **1890** *Century Dict.* 5679, *Skunk-bird.* . . Same as *skunk-blackbird.* *Ibid,* Skunk blackbird. . . The male bobolink in full plumage. **1894** *DN* 1.342 **wCT,** *Skunk blackbird:* the bobolink. **1896** Robinson *In New Engl. Fields* 57, Our New England fathers . . gave him [=the bobolink] the uncouth and malodorous name of skunk blackbird. **1950** *WELS* (Bobolink) 1 Inf, **csWI,** Skunk blackbird. **1957** Barnes *Nat. Hist. Wasatch Spring* 84 **Sth,** It surprises one to know that this bird of rapturous roulade unexcelled in the variety and beauty of its melodic outbursts by any other American feathered lyrist, is treated with enmity by the rice-growers of the south, where it is sometimes called "skunk blackbird" in reference to its colors. **1966–69** *DARE* (Qu. Q14, . . *Names . . for . . bobolink*) Infs **CT**23, **MA**68, **NY**148, Skunk blackbird; **IA**3, **MI**2, Skunk bird.

skunkbrush n Cf **skunkbush 1, 4**

1 A **sumac** (here: *Rhus trilobata*).

1926 *Torreya* 26.5 **seAZ,** *Rhus trilobata.* . . Skunk-brush, Graham Mts. **1937** [see **skunkbush 1**]. **1951** Porter *Ragged Roads* 80 **OK,** Over the sage and skunk brush hummocks we went.

2 **=fool's huckleberry.**

1972 Viereck–Little *AK Trees* 212, Rusty Menziesia. . . Other names: skunkbrush, fools-huckleberry.

skunkbush n

1 also *skunkbush sumac:* A **sumac:** usu *Rhus trilobata,* but also **fragrant sumac.** Cf **skunkbrush 1**

1903 Small *Flora SE U.S.* 728, *Schmaltzia trilobata.* . . An offensive-scented shrub 0.5–1 m. or rarely 2 m. tall, the branches often gnarled. . . *Skunk Bush. Ill-scented sumac.* **1924** Hawkins *Trees & Shrubs* 80, Skunk-bush is a spreading, stiff, angular shrub from two to six feet high with small, yellow blossoms and oval, lens-shaped, rank-smelling seeds. **1937** U.S. Forest Serv. *Range Plant Hdbk.* B129, Skunkbush. . . is often known as squawberry, squawbush, and skunkbrush. **1960** Vines *Trees SW* 630, Skunk-bush Sumac—*Rhus aromatica.* . . An offensive-scented shrub. **1967** *DARE* (Qu. S26e, *Other wildflowers not yet mentioned;* not asked in early QRs) Inf **CO**22, Skunkbush—looks like a currant bush but stinks. **1974** (1977) Coon *Useful Plants* 57, *Rhus aromatica*—Fragrant or sweet-scented sumac, stink bush, skunk bush.

2 A **silk tassel** (here: *Garrya fremonti*).

1911 *Century Dict. Suppl.,* Skunk-bush. . . The bear-brush, *Garrya Fremontii.* **1942** Amer. Joint Comm. Horticult. Nomenclature *Std. Plant Names* 270, [Garrya] fremonti. . . *Skunkbush; Squawbush.*

3 A **hop tree** (here: *Ptelea trifoliata*). Cf **polecat tree 3**

1913 Wooton *Trees NM* 107, The Rue Family . . is represented in New Mexico by 2 species of the Hop Tree or what is sometimes called Skunk Bush (*Ptelea*). . . The leaves have a peculiar spicy odor, which is rather offensive when too intense. **1946** *Nat. Hist.* 55.143, Some give it the epithet of Skunk Bush, or Polecat Tree, because of the unpleasant odor of its crushed leaves. **1960** Vines *Trees SW* 593, Vernacular names [of *Ptelea trifoliata*] are Three-leaf Hop-tree, . . Skunk-bush [etc].

4 **=fool's huckleberry.** Cf **skunkbrush 2**

1931 U.S. Dept. Ag. *Misc. Pub.* 101.131, *Menziesias.* . . They are sometimes called fools' huckleberry . . and skunkbush (because of the mephitic odor of the freshly bruised foliage).

5 **=osoberry.**

1934 Haskin *Wild Flowers Pacific Coast* 159, The flowers [of the osoberry], like many early blossoms that depend on flies, rather than bees for fertilization, are strongly rank-scented. From this they receive their common name of skunk-bush.

skunkbush sumac See **skunkbush 1**

skunk cabbage n

1 Either of two related plants of the family Araceae:

a also *skunk's cabbage, skunk cabbage weed:* A malodorous perennial plant (*Symplocarpus foetidus*) of the eastern US. Also called **devil's tobacco 2, Irish cabbage 1, meadow ~, parson-in-a-pillory, poke** n³ **2, pokeweed 2, polecat weed, skunkweed 1, stinkweed, swamp cabbage** Cf **Indian collard**

1778 Carver *Travels N. Amer.* 518, *Skunk Cabbage* or *Poke* is an herb that grows in moist and swampy places. . . There issues a strong musky smell from this herb. **1832** Williamson *Hist. ME* 1.128, *Skunk-cabbage* or *Skunk-weed* possesses an odour too distinctive ever to be mistaken. **1849** (1914) Kingsley *Diary* 15, The fruit [of the banana] grows on the extreme top with a blow or flower resembling our Skunks Cabbage. **1878** (1977) Stowe *Poganuc People* 182 **CT,** The honest, great green leaves of the old skunk cabbage, most refreshing to the eye in its hardy, succulent greenness, though an abomination to the nose. **1905** *DN* 3.19 **cCT,** Skunk cabbage. . . A strong scented plant, the *symplocarpus foetidus.* **1950** *Chicago Tribune* (IL) 28 Mar 14/3, Some watch for skunk cabbages poking mottled brown snouts thru the swamp muck. **1965–70** *DARE* (Qu. S26b, *Wildflowers that grow in water or wet places*) 25 Infs, **chiefly NEast, Gt Lakes,** Skunk cabbage; (Qu. S21, . . *Weeds . . that are a trouble in gardens and fields*) Infs **DE**4, **MA**50, **NY**73, **OH**88, Skunk cabbage; (Qu. S26c, *Wildflowers that grow in woods*) Infs **MI**65, 116, **NY**30, **OH**98, **VA**26, Skunk cabbage; (Qu. S26d, *Wildflowers that grow in meadows;* not asked in early QRs) Infs **OH**37, **RI**15, **VA**21, Skunk cabbage; **MI**114, Skunk cabbage weed;

(Qu. S26e, *Other wildflowers not yet mentioned;* not asked in early QRs) Infs **IL**30, 135, **PA**35, 49, **WI**78, Skunk cabbage. [*DARE* Ed: Some of these Infs may refer instead to other senses below.] **1965–70** *DARE* Wildfl QR Pl.5 20 Infs, **chiefly Atlantic, N Cent,** Skunk cabbage. **1976** Bruce *How to Grow Wildflowers* 191, Leave it to an unlettered farmer to call the plant Skunk-cabbage because it has big leaves, which smell precisely like skunk when they are bruised.

b also *yellow skunk cabbage:* A similar plant *(Lysichiton americanus)* of the Pacific coast. Also called **pisser's flower, swamp lily**

1897 Parsons *Wild Flowers CA* 166, *Lysichiton Camtschatcensis.* . . In our northwestern counties, before the frost is entirely out of the ground, the leaves of the skunk-cabbage may be seen pushing their way up through the standing water of marshy localities. **1934** Haskin *Wild Flowers Pacific Coast* 5, There is nothing more typical of this humid western coast in early spring than the big swamps of yellow skunk cabbage. **1949** Peattie *Cascades* 225, The scientist calls it Lysichitum americanum, a few people call it swamp lily, but to everyone else it is skunk cabbage and our noses say this is right. **1956** St. John *Flora SE WA* 77, *Lysichitum americanum.* . . *Yellow Skunk Cabbage.* . . The brilliant malodorous flowers appear before the leaves. **1965–70** *DARE* (Qu. S11) Inf **CA**87, Skunk cabbage; (Qu. S22, . . *The bright yellow flowers that bloom in clusters in marshes in early springtime)* Infs **WA**6, 20, Skunk cabbage; **WA**1, Skunk cabbages; (Qu. S26a, . . *Wildflowers. . . Roadside flowers)* Inf **WA**33, Skunk cabbage; (Qu. S26b, *Wildflowers that grow in water or wet places)* Infs **OR**4, **WA**28, Skunk cabbage; (Qu. S26c, *Wildflowers that grow in woods)* Inf **CO**39, Skunk cabbage; (Qu. S26d, *Wildflowers that grow in meadows;* not asked in early QRs) Infs **CA**126, **CO**39, Skunk cabbage; (Qu. S26e, *Other wildflowers not yet mentioned;* not asked in early QRs) Infs **AK**1, **CA**140, Skunk cabbage; (Qu. BB50c, *Remedies for infections)* Inf **WA**19, Boil down skunk cabbage roots (or salal berries), use as poultice. [*DARE* Ed: Some of these Infs may refer instead to other senses.] **1967** *DARE* Wildfl QR Pl.5 Infs **CO**29, **OR**9, 12, **WA**10, 12, 15, Skunk cabbage. *Ibid* (Craighead) Pl.1.5 Inf **CO**29, Skunk cabbage. **1977** Churchill *Don't Call* 166 **nwOR** (as of c1918), Skunk cabbage grows in low, moist places and has big greenish yellow leaves with a bright yellow hooded sheath enclosing the yellow flower stalk.

2 A **false hellebore 1** (here: either *Veratrum californicum* or **Indian poke 1**).

1751 in 1934 Eliot *Field Husbandry* 3.70, *Take the Roots of Swamp Hellebore,* sometimes called *Skunk Cabbage, Tickle Weed, Bear Root.* This Root is known by these several Names in different Places. **1897** Parsons *Wild Flowers CA* 108, Californian False Hellebore. . . The mountaineers commonly call this plant "skunk cabbage," a deplorable misnomer. **1937** U.S. Forest Serv. *Range Plant Hdbk.* W201, The name skunkcabbage, no doubt, alludes to the general resemblance of the young plants of western false-hellebore to the true skunkcabbage. **1963** Craighead *Rocky Mt. Wildflowers* 31, False Hellebore. . . sometimes erroneously called Skunkcabbage. **1969** *DARE* (Qu. S26e, *Other wildflowers not yet mentioned;* not asked in early QRs) Inf **CA**140, Indian toilet paper—another name for skunk cabbage; it's very pliable, has small hairs on, and that's what the Indians used them for. There's smooth-leaved skunk cabbage and this kind with hairy leaves. **1971** *Today Show Letters* **seNY,** Local residents refer to American white hellebore *(Veratrum viride)* as skunk cabbage.

3 A **pitcher plant 1** (here: *Sarracenia purpurea).*

1896 *Jrl. Amer. Folkl.* 9.181 **MN,** *Sarracenia purpurea,* . . skunk-cabbage, St. Paul, Minn.

4 =**galax.**

1915 *Torreya* 15.16 **nwGA,** There is nothing sharp or pungent about the galax, like the knock-down odor of the polecat, and the misnomer, "skunk cabbage," sometimes applied to it in the Georgia mountains, was no doubt suggested by the malodorous reputation of the true skunk cabbage *(Symplocarpus foetidus)* and intended to emphasize the abominableness of the smell rather than to describe its quality.

5 A **trillium** (here: *Trillium erectum).* Cf **skunk flower 3**

1968 *DARE* (Qu. S2, . . *The flower that comes up in the woods early in spring, with three white petals that turn pink as the flower grows older)* Inf **OH**80, Skunk cabbage.

skunk cabbage weed See **skunk cabbage 1a**

skunk coot n Also *skunkbill (coot), skunk bird* [See quot 1928] **NEng**
The male **surf scoter.**

1888 Trumbull *Names of Birds* 103 **eME,** Surf scoter. . . at Machiasport and Jonesport, Skunk-bill. **1928** Beston *Outermost House* 102 **Cape Cod MA,** A "raft" of skunk coots is spending the winter. Patches of white on the forehead and the hind neck of the glossy black head of the male are responsible for this local name. **1955** MA Audubon Soc. *Bulletin* 39.377 **NEng,** Surf scoter. . . Skunk-bill (Maine, N.H.); Skunkbill Coot (Maine. From the partly black and white coloration of the bill of the adult male.); Skunk-bird, Skunk Coot (Mass.)

skunk currant n Also *skunkberry* esp **NEng**
Usu a **currant B1** (here: *Ribes glandulosum),* but also a **gooseberry 1** (here: *Ribes hirtellum).* For other names of the former see **fetid currant, mountain ~**

a1817 (1821) Dwight *Travels* 2.312 **NEng,** Three sorts of currants are found in the forest: the red, the black, and a peculiar kind, called Skunk currants. **1847** Wood *Class-Book* 273, *[Ribes] prostratum.* . . ill-scented, and with ill-flavored berries—sometimes called *Skunk Currant.* **1892** *Jrl. Amer. Folkl.* 5.96 **ME,** *Ribes prostratum,* skunk currant. [Footnote:] From the offensive musky smell of the fruit. **1896** *Ibid* 9.187 **ME,** *Ribes prostratum* . . skunk currant, Oxford and Washington counties. **1916** *Torreya* 16.238 **ME,** *Ribes hirtellum.* . . Skunk currant, Matinicus I[slan]d. **1943** Fernald–Kinsey *Edible Wild Plants E. N. Amer.* 227, The bristly fruit of *R[ibes] glandulosum* . . is known as *Skunk-Currant,* but, although the bruised shrub and berries have the pole-cat-odor, the berries are juicy and palatable. **1961** Douglas *My Wilderness* 214 **NH,** Deeper in shade are skunk currants and blueberry bushes. **1966** *DARE* (Qu. I44, *What kinds of berries grow wild around here?)* Inf **MI**23, Skunkberries or skunk currant.

skunk-drunk adj [Cf *drunk as a skunk*] esp **Sth, S Midl**
Very intoxicated.

1939 Hench *Coll.* **cVA,** [Heard from a student:] Skunk drunk—very drunk. **1966–70** *DARE* (Qu. DD15, *A person who is thoroughly drunk)* Infs **AL**6, 8, **IL**11, **MS**43, **TN**53, **TX**5, Skunk-drunk. **1967** *DARE* Tape **TX**19, And another term they give a guy that's drunk as Cooter Brown, they say he was skunk-drunk.

skunk duck n [See quot 1955]
The male **surf scoter.**

1940 Gabrielson *Birds OR* 170, The Surf Scoter, or Skunk Duck, is a very common species on the Oregon coast, where it is a familiar inhabitant of the bays and lakes. **1955** *AmSp* 30.179, Those [names] incorporating the word *skunk* relate to boldly contrasted black-and-white markings. . . The surf scoter has had several such cognomens: *skunkbill* (Maine, N.H.), *skunkbill coot* (Maine), *skunk coot* (Mass.), *skunk·duck* (Oreg.), *skunktop* (Conn.), *skunkhead* (Quebec to Long Island, N.Y.), *skunk-head coot* (Maine, N.H., Mass., Conn., Nova Scotia), *skunkhead diver* (Wis.), and *skunktop* (Conn.)

skunked See **skunky**

skunk flower n

1 =**devil's bouquet.**

1936 Whitehouse *TX Flowers* 20, Devil's Bouquet . . is also called skunk flower because of its heavy disagreeable odor.

2 =**scarlet gilia.** Cf **skunkweed 2**

1967 Dodge *Roadside Wildflowers* 37, The crushed leaves of skyrocket have a skunky odor, hence the name polecat plant or skunkflower. **1979** Spellenberg *Audubon Guide N. Amer. Wildflowers W. Region* 664, Skyrocket. . . Its beauty compensates for the faint skunky smell of its glandular foliage, responsible for the less complimentary name Skunk Flower.

3 A **trillium** (here: *Trillium erectum).* Cf **skunk cabbage 5**

1968 *DARE* (Qu. S2, . . *The flower that comes up in the woods early in spring, with three white petals that turn pink as the flower grows older)* Inf **CT**6, Skunk flower—same as trillium.

skunk grape n
=**fox grape 1.**

1913 (1919) *WNID* 1970, Skunk grape. The fox grape. **1940** Clute *Amer. Plant Names* 275, *Vitis labrusca.* Skunk-grape.

skunk grass n

1 =**love grass.**

1906 Rydberg *Flora CO* 38, *Eragrostis* [spp]. . . Skunk-grass, Stink-grass. **1933** Small *Manual SE Flora* 122, *Eragrostis* [spp]. . . Love-grasses. Skunk-grasses. **1950** Gray–Fernald *Manual of Botany* 124,

[Eragrostis] megastachya. . . Stink-, Snake- or Skunk-Grass. . . Strong-scented (when fresh) annual.

2 A **musk grass** (here: *Chara* spp).

1913 *Torreya* 13.225 **seMA,** *Chara* sp. . . skunk grass, Squibnocket, Marthas Vineyard, Mass.

skunkhead n Note: The headword was also applied to the now extinct pied duck, *Camptorhynchus labradorius*.

1 also *skunkhead coot, ~ diver, skunk-headed coot, skunktop:* The male **surf scoter.**

1898 Elliot *Wild Fowl* 203, The Surf Scoter has many trivial names, and is known as the Hollow-billed Coot, Skunk Head Coot [etc]. **1902** *Jrl. Amer. Folkl.* 15.258, Skunk-head or skunk-top . . the surf-scoter. **1949** Kitchin *Birds Olympic Peninsula* 54, The surf scoter. . . has a white patch on the crown of [sic] head and another on the nape of the neck, hence the eastern name of "skunk-headed coot." **1955** [see **skunk duck**].

2 =**bufflehead 2.**

1955 MA Audubon Soc. *Bulletin* 39.316 **MA,** Buffle-head. . . Skunk-head (Mass. from the very dark green (called black) and white coloration of the head of the male.)

skunkhead coot (or diver), skunk-headed coot See **skunkhead 1**

Skunk Hollow See **Skunk's Misery**

skunk meadow-rue n

A **meadow rue** (here: *Thalictrum revolutum*).

1933 Small *Manual SE Flora* 525, *[Thalictrum] revolutum*. . . Skunk meadow-rue. **1950** Gray–Fernald *Manual of Botany* 659, *T[halictrum] revolutum*. . . Purple, Skunk- or Wax-leaved M[eadow-rue].

skunk owl n

=**great horned owl.**

1956 MA Audubon Soc. *Bulletin* 40.81 **MA,** Great Horned Owl. . . Skunk Owl. . . It more or less regularly preys upon skunks and sometimes gets well scented while so doing.

skunk's cabbage See **skunk cabbage 1a**

Skunk's Misery n Also *Skunk Hollow, ~ Town;* for addit varr see quot 1965–70

Used as a name or nickname for an unimportant or out-of-the-way place.

1847 *Yankee Doodle* 12 June 92 **NYC,** Irving has immortalized Dutch-street, (Skunk's Misery,) Mulberry-street and the Bowery, by merely incidentally mentioning them. **1869** Meader *Merrimack R.* 148 **ceNH,** In several towns in this section of the State terms are used to designate many localities, which, though they may not be euphonious, are considered peculiarly appropriate and descriptive; for instance, a certain locality is known as . . "Skunk's Misery." **1875** in 1876 Berkey *Money Question* 152, The fellow from Frogtown would get away out into Skunktown, another almost inaccessible place, and he would effect an exchange of ten, twenty, or thirty thousand dollars of Frogtown bank notes for a like amount of Skunktown bank notes. **1880** Howells *Undiscovered Country* 197 **MA,** "What place is this?" he asked. "Well," said the woman, with sober apolog, while her man grinned, "I d' know 's you may say it *has* any name. Skunk's Misery, they *call* it." **1965–70** *DARE* (Qu. C33, . . *Joking names . . for an out-of-the-way place, or a very small or unimportant place*) Inf **IA**11, Skunk Valley; (Qu. C34, *Nicknames for nearby settlements, villages, or districts*) Infs **MS**1, **NY**170, **PA**72, Skunk Hollow; **MA**42, **NJ**15, **NY**75, 84, Skunk's Misery; **NY**123, Skunk Town; (Qu. C35, *Nicknames for the different parts of your town or city*) Infs **CA**129, **MA**50, **MS**1, **VT**16, Skunk Hollow; **NY**170, Skunk City; **MA**55, Skunk's Neck; (Qu. N29, . . *Names . . for a less important road running back from a main road*) Inf **NY**198, Side road, skunk roads; (Qu. II25, *Names or nicknames for the part of a town where the poorer people, special groups, or foreign groups live*) Inf **MI**4, Skunk Road—"Skunk" is the proper name of this road. **1983** in Lib. of Congress *Amer. Memory: Omaha Indian Music* (Internet) **NE,** [Caption:] Looking up Skunk Hollow Road from Pow-Wow to North.

skunk spruce n Cf **cat spruce**

A **white spruce** (here: *Picea glauca*).

1894 *Jrl. Amer. Folkl.* 7.99 **ME,** *Picea alba*. . . skunk-spruce, Mt. Desert, Me., Washington Co., Me., Islands of Penobscot Bay, Me. [Foot-

note to *skunk-spruce:*] From supposed unpleasant smell of foliage. **1937** FWP *Guide ME* 13, Trees common throughout the State are . . white spruce, called 'skunk spruce' by lumbermen because of the odor of its foliage. **1948** *Sun* (Baltimore MD) 21 Dec 14/2, Last week, some New York city Christmas-tree dealers, with a notable lack of seasonal good will, burst out in protest against the Roosevelt Christmas trees. They are not, it seems, "real"[?] Christmas trees: only "skunk spruce." **1979** Little *Checklist U.S. Trees* 185, *Picea glauca*. . . Other common names—Canadian spruce, skunk spruce, cat spruce [etc].

skunk the line n

c**1970** Wiersma *Marbles Terms* **swMI** (as of 1930s), *Skunk the Line* . . game where all players throw their marbles, trying to get the closest to a line drawn on the ground.

skunktop See **skunkhead 1**

Skunk Town See **Skunk's Misery**

skunk tree n

A deciduous tropical tree (*Sterculia foetida*).

1948 Neal *In Gardens HI* 507, Java olives, kelumpang. . . Flowers are larger, red and yellow, or purple, and have an extremely unpleasant odor, giving rise to the name "skunk tree."

skunk turtle n

Prob =**musk turtle 1.**

1970 *DARE* (Qu. P24, . . *Kinds of turtles*) Inf **MA**80, Skunk turtle.

skunkweed n

1 =**skunk cabbage 1a.**

1742 (1849) Darlington *Mem. John Bartram* 156, The Skunk-weed thrives well. **1743** Catesby *Nat. Hist. Carolina* 2.71, *Arum Americanum, Betae folio*—The Scunk Weed. This Plant before the Leaves appeared, arrived at its full Size . . consisting of three succulent, monopetalous, hollow Flowers, with short stems. **1784** in 1785 Amer. Acad. Arts & Sci. *Memoirs* 1.407 **PA,** Scunk Cabbage. Scunkweed. **1837** Darlington *Flora Cestrica* 112 **sePA,** Fetid Symplocarpus. *Vulgò*—Swamp cabbage. Skunk weed. **1958** Jacobs–Burlage *Index Plants NC* 17, *Symplocarpus foetidus*. . . Rockweed; skunk cabbage; . . skunk weed [etc].

2 A **gilia** (here: *Navarretia squarrosa*). Also called **pepperweed 1, stinkweed** Cf **skunk flower 2**

1898 *Jrl. Amer. Folkl.* 11.275 **CA,** *Gilia squarrosa* . . skunk weed. **1914** Georgia *Manual Weeds* 329, Skunkweed. . . A troublesome and most disagreeable weed, viscidly glandular and unpleasant to touch, very bitter to the taste, and emitting a strong, fetid odor. **1961** Thomas *Flora Santa Cruz* 280 **cwCA,** *N[avarretia] squarrosa*. . . Skunkweed. The most common species of *Navarretia* locally, growing in dry, hard-packed soils, vernal pools, and as a weed in disturbed areas. San Francisco southward.

3 =**Rocky Mountain bee plant.**

1898 *Jrl. Amer. Folkl.* 11.223 **CO,** *Cleome integrifolia*. . . skunkweed, bee-plant. **1915** (1926) Armstrong–Thornber *Western Wild Flowers* 188 **AZ,** The foliage when it is crushed gives off a rank, unpleasant smell, which is responsible for the local name of Skunk-weed. **1920** *Torreya* 20.21 **West,** *Cleome serrulata*. . . Skunk-weed.

4 =**false hellebore 1.** Cf **skunk cabbage 2**

1926 *Torreya* 26.4 **AZ,** *Veratrum speciosum*. . . Skunk-weed, Graham Mts.

5 =**Jacob's ladder 1.**

1932 Rydberg *Flora Prairies* 654, *Polemonium* [spp]. . . Jacob's Ladder, Skunk-weed. **1937** U.S. Forest Serv. *Range Plant Hdbk.* W152, The plant [=*Polemonium albiflorum*] is occasionally called white skunk-leaf or skunkweed, but the skunklike odor, strong in many species of *Polemonium*, is faint in this species. **1961** Smith *MI Wildflowers* 305, Some of the numerous western species of this genus [=*Polemonium*] have a very disagreeable odor and are known as "skunkweed."

6 A **croton** (here: *Croton texensis*).

1933 Small *Manual SE Flora* 783, *[Croton] texensis*. . . Skunkweed. . . Dry soil, low hills and plains.

skunky adj Also *skunked*

=**skunk-drunk.**

1965–70 *DARE* (Qu. DD15, *A person who is thoroughly drunk*) Inf **MN**28, Skunked; **CA**114, Skunky.

skunned, skunt See **skin** v A

skurce See **scarce**

skurmage See **skirmish**

skurry See **scary**

skurse See **scarce**

skuse v See **excuse** v

skuse n See **excuse** n

skusin See **excusing** prep

skutch v[1] See **scooch**

skutch v[2] See **scutch** v[1]

skuze See **excuse** v

skwee-geed See **skew-** a

skweejee See **squeegee**

skwee-wab See **skew-** g

skwy adv Also *skwywise* Cf **skew-**
  1892 *DN* 1.211 seMA, *Skwy* [skwaɪ]: askew. "Put the book on the table skwy." "This picture hangs skwy." Salem. *Skwywise* [skwaɪwaɪz]: the same as *skwy.* Salem.

sky v See **skyhoot**

-sky suff Also sp *-ski* [Appar in imitation of Russ (or other Slavic) names or other words ending with this element; cf **Polski, Russki**] See also **buttinsky**
  Used as a joc word-forming suff.
  1902 Ade *Girl Proposition* 70 (*OED2*), The Friend belonged to the Buttinsky Family and refused to stay on the Far Side of the Room. **1916** *DN* 4.304, The suffix *-ski,* or *-sky,* seems to be gaining foothold, judging from the following examples, all but the first of which have come to my notice recently. All are in jocular or facetious usage only. *Buttinsky[i]* . . *darnfoolski[i]* . . *dumbski[i]* . . *smartski.* . . A well-dressed uppish-looking woman who passed a group of young people brought from one of them the comment, "There goes Madame Uppsky!" To a youth who announced that he was going to Burma, the remark was made, "You'll be a regular Burmese-ski, when you get back." *Ibid* 354, *Allrightsky.* "Pearl, bring me that new brush." "Allrightsky, Mrs. Bell." [Louisiana]. . . *Bumsky.* "What a bumsky shot." Exclamation of woman who missed her approach in a golf match. [Louisiana]. . . *Hurryupsky. Youbetsky.* "Will you do that for me?" "Youbetsky."! The vogue of the suffix *-sky* followed the Russo-Japanese war, as the vogue of *-fest* has accompanied the present war. **1942** Berrey–Van den Bark *Amer. Slang* 396, *Terms of disparagement.* . . nimski. **1953** *AmSp* 28.118 [Carnie talk], *Sawbuck, sawski.* . . A ten-dollar bill. 'A double sawski,' a twenty-dollar bill. **1965–70** *DARE* (Qu. II18, *Someone who joins himself on to you and your group without being asked and won't leave*) 111 Infs, **widespread,** Buttinsky; (Qu. GG36a, *The kind of person who is always poking into other people's affairs: "She's an awful _____."*) 21 Infs, **scattered,** Buttinsky; (Qu. U28b, . . *A ten-dollar bill*) Infs **NY**119, **OH**76, Tenski; **MA**3, Sawski; (Qu. X35, *Joking words for the part of the body that you sit on*) Inf **IA**17, Sitdownsky; (Qu. Y9) Inf **MO**17, Buttinsky; (Qu. BB19, *Joking names for looseness of the bowels*) Inf **CA**49, Trotsky; (Qu. GG39) Inf **NY**70, Buttinsky; (Qu. HH26) Inf **NE**1, Buttinsky; (Qu. II22) Inf **NM**6, He's a buttinsky. **1978** *NBC's Saturday Night* (NBC-TV) (Lighter *Random House Dict. Slang*), Here you go. A couple of brewskis. **2001** *WI State Jrl.* (Madison) 30 Aug sec E 4/1, [Comic strip *Bizarro:*] [Seeker:] "I'm looking for faith and hope." [Wise man:] "They're inside making potato salad. Did you bring the *brewskis?*"

skyarpin See **scorpion**

sky-ball n
  See quots.
  1966–69 *DARE* (Qu. EE10, *A game in which a short stick lying on the ground is flipped into the air and then hit with a longer stick*) Inf **FL**6, Sky-ball; (Qu. EE33, . . *Outdoor games . . that children play*) Inf **TN**1, Sky-ball—drove stake in ground, laid ball on it, hit straight up with

larger stick; see who can hit the highest. **1986** Pederson *LAGS Concordance,* 1 inf, swGA, Sky ball—childhood game.

skybloom See **skyflower 1**

sky blue n chiefly Chicago IL
  =**hopscotch;** also the area at the top of a hopscotch diagram.
  1957 *Sat. Eve. Post Letters* **Detroit MI,** Children now never heard of "Sky Blue," a variation of Hop Scotch played with a stone. *Ibid* **Chicago IL,** "Sky blue" was a hop scotch game played on the sidewalk. **1975** Ferretti *Gt. Amer. Book Sidewalk Games* 31, The most widely known and remembered sidewalk game is Pottsie. Oh, people from such places as Boston and Nottingham call it *Hopscotch;* and in Chicago, it is *Sky Blue.* **2001** *NADS Letters* **Chicago IL** (as of c1972), I was engaged in some fieldwork . . on children's folklore. . . In all cases, 'sky blue' referred not to the game of hopscotch itself, but to the zone at the top of a hopscotch diagram. . . My father (born 1927 and a native of Chicago) reported this term from his childhood. A Chicago-born contemporary of mine (born ca. 1952) also reported the term, and I saw it very much in use in Chicago in 1972. . . [A girl of about 16 in East Peoria, IL reported the term 'blue sky' . . as her term for the same space.] *Ibid* **neIL,** When I was growing up in Maywood, IL—suburb of Chicago—in the late 60's, all the hopscotch was called sky blue—it referred to the top area of the hopscotch game. On several of the permanent games, the "sky blue" area was painted blue with clouds on it. **2001** *DARE* File **Chicago IL** (as of c1910), My grandmother (b. 1901) described playing "sky blue" as a girl. It was a variety of hopscotch; the square at one end of the figure was home and that at the other end was "sky blue."

sky-bottlin adj, adv Also *sky-waddlin*
  =**sky-gogglin.**
  1953 Randolph–Wilson *Down in Holler* 284 **Ozarks,** I believe that . . *sky-waddlin* . . [is] very close to *sky-gogglin.* **1995** Brophy *Coll.* 68 **swMO** (as of c1960), Skybottlin . . also in the sense of *skygogglin.*

skybound adj
  Of a tree or of logging equipment: see quots. Note: It seems probable that the quots intend adjectival rather than nominal use.
  1939 FWP *ID Lore* 244, Lumberjack jargon in the St. Maries area and elsewhere: . . *Skybound*—a tree hard to fell. **1958** McCulloch *Woods Words* 168 **Pacific NW,** *Skybound*—a. A doggone ornery tree that won't fall down after it has been cut off. b. A falling tree hung up in another. c. Butt rigging fouled in the high lead block at the top of a spar tree. d. Rigging motionless in the air. **1969** Sorden *Lumberjack Lingo* 111 **NEng Gt Lakes,** *Skybound*—A tree that refuses to fall even when wedged.

skybugging vbl n
  1982 Powers *Cataloochee* 382 **cwNC** (as of a1940), "Skybugging" has a certain charm. It means scanning the sky aimlessly as one's trusted old horse walks along a Cataloochee trail. Or, it can simply mean "not paying attention".

sky bugler n
  A **whooping crane** (here: *Grus americana*).
  1965 Teale *Wandering Through Winter* 168, A lone whooping crane lifted into the air. . . Because early frontiersmen thought the call suggested the war whoop of an Indian, the bird received its common name. Another . . name—sky bugler—is also derived from the call.

skybust v
  To shoot at game birds that are out of effective range; to expend (ammunition), shoot at (a bird) ineffectually; hence ppl adj, vbl n *skybusting,* n *skybuster.*
  1967 *WI Conserv. Bulletin* 32.2.23 **WI,** There's nothing economical about leaving the gun on the rack all summer, then in fall getting ineffective "practice" by sky-busting box after box of shells in the general direction of game. **1997** *MO Conservationist Online* Aug (Internet) **seMO,** One of the common problems I face is skybusting, or shooting at ducks and geese that are beyond the effective range of shotguns. **2000** in 2001 *DARE* File—Internet **nIL,** The bad weather finally drove down ducks & geese to me on a day when I was out. It seems that it drove away the skybusting weekend warriors. **2001** *Ibid* **ID,** "Skybusting" or shooting at birds over 50 yards from you results in excessive crippling losses of waterfowl and reduced opportunity for good shots by you and other hunters. *Ibid* **DE,** Shell limit: There is no limit—but do not

skybust. *Ibid* **AL**, Learn from ducks instead of teaching them. . . Don't skybust 'em. They're bright enough already. *Ibid* **AR**, If you decide to go it alone, make sure to get a good map . . and have lots of patience for the skybusters. . . Although it is "duck hunter's etiquette" not to skybust another guy's ducks, they have as much right to be there as anybody else. **2001** *DARE* File **WI, Upstate NY, NEng,** Those goose hunters were just skybusting. The geese were way out of range.

sky cone n
A church steeple.

1969 *DARE* (Qu. CC1, *On a church building . . the part that sticks up high*) Inf **GA72,** Sky cone [laughter].

skyduster palm n
A **fan palm** (here: *Washingtonia robusta*).

1965 Neal *Gardens HI* 99, The southern, or Mexican, washingtonia, or skyduster palm.

sk'yeard See scare B

skyflower n
1 also *skybloom:* =**bluet 2.**

1898 *Jrl. Amer. Folkl.* 11.228 **CT,** *Houstonia caerulea. . .* Sky flower. **1902** *New Engl. Mag.* 26.260, In open, moist, grassy places you will find the Houstonia that delicate little flower with so many pretty local names, bluets, innocence, Quaker-ladies, and sky-bloom.

2 =**golden dewdrop.**

1946 West–Arnold *Native Trees FL* 192, The skyflower or golden dewdrop, *Duranta repens* L., usually seen as a shrub and widely grown as an ornamental, is native only in the Everglade Keys and the Florida Keys. It is characterized by long, drooping spikes of pale-purple flowers and yellow fruits. **1960** Vines *Trees SW* 894, Creeping Skyflower—*Duranta repens.*

skygazer n
=**bittern.**

1955 *Oriole* 20.1.2, American Bittern. . . *Sky-gazer, Star-gazer* (in its "freezing" pose, while the bird's bill points toward the sky, the eyes do not, being directed forward.)

sky-gogglin adj, adv Also *sky-godlin, sky-gog* Also sp *ski-goglin, sky-goglin* [Cf *EDD* sky-wannocking "awry, crooked, warped, . . unsteady," *sky-wannock, sky-whiffy*] Cf **antigoglin, si-godlin, si-gogglin, skew-, sky west and crooked, sky-winding**
Crooked, lopsided, irregular; obliquely, askew.

1869 *Overland Mth.* 3.128 **TX,** He will run "skygodlin" (obliquely). **1916** *DN* 4.280 **NE,** Skygog, adj. Same as skwee-wab. Out of true, or crooked. "She always gets her hats on skygog." **1953** Randolph–Wilson *Down in Holler* 284 **Ozarks,** Sky-gogglin: *adj.* Crooked, irregular, lopsided, askew, aslant, awry. A *sky-gogglin* field is one with irregular borders, limited on one side by a meandering stream or by a road which winds around a bluff. Sometimes the word has particular reference to unusual or unexpected angles. Mrs. Bess Allman, of Galena, Mo., once told me that "the streets in Boston are all sky-gogglin." **1956** McAtee *Some Dialect NC* 40, Skygodlin, skygoglin. . . Leaning, oblique, crooked. **1981** Pederson *LAGS Basic Materials,* 1 inf, **ceTN,** That field is laid out so that it's absolutely skigoglin ['skaᵊᵋgɑglɪn] (going every which way, of planting, sewing without a pattern, or whatever).

skyhook n Also rarely *skyjack, skyrod, skywrench* [*OED2* 1915 →]
An imaginary object used as the basis of a practical joke.

1939 in Lib. of Congress *Amer. Memory: WPA Life Hist.* (Internet) **ceNE,** Small unsophisticated boys and gullible adults were often sent on "round robin" tours or "Wild goose chases" for "meat augurs," "sky hooks," and . . "round squares." *Ibid* **Chicago IL,** "What about falls[?] I[=a sign writer]'ll need 200 footers on that wall if I remember right!⁽ˣ⁾ and here with hidden wink at Happy he said "What about sky hooks₍₉₎ you still got that pair I brought you the last time I came through here?" **1950** *Western Folkl.* 9.159 **nCA** [Mountaineering vocab], Skyhook. A mythical hook used to clutch at overhanging rocks that must be climbed. **1959** *VT Hist.* 27.157, Sky-hook. . . An imaginary tool with which to accomplish the impossible. Occasional. **1965–70** *DARE* (Qu. HH14, *Ways of teasing a beginner or inexperienced person—for example, by sending him for a 'left-handed monkey wrench': "Go get me _____."*) 152 Infs, **widespread,** Skyhook(s); **FL**28, **KY**11, **LA**11,

SC40, Set of skyhooks; **NY**232, **OK**45, Skyjack; **GA**9, Skyrod; **PA**167, Skywrench; (Qu. NN12b, *Things that people say to put off a child when he asks, "What are you making?"*) Inf **NE**3, Go and look for skyhooks; **CA**105, Skyhook; **NJ**28, Skyhook to hang you up. **1969** Sorden *Lumberjack Lingo* 111 **NEng, Gt Lakes,** *Sky hook*—Mythical, all-powerful hook. One end of a line fastened to the sky, which hook tenders cried for when they had to fight against bad hang ups.

skyhoot v Rarely *sky*
To go quickly, scoot; to skyrocket.

1900 Day *Up in ME* 56, That air pessle, sir, it come / Sky-hootin' like a ten-inch bumb. **1922** Wilson *Merton of Movies* 5 **IL,** Skyhootin' around in here, leavin' the front of the store unpertected for an hour or two, like your time was your own. **1928** Ritchie *Forty-Niners* 8 **CA,** There were not supplies enough in camp to last the winter . . , to say nothing of sky-hooting over wilder country. **1942** Berrey–Van den Bark *Amer. Slang* 53.9, *Go fast. . .* Skyhoot. *Ibid* 58.6, *Depart hurriedly; "cut and run." . .* Sky-hoot. **1943** in 1944 *ADD* 565, Prices have gone skyhooting way up out of proportion to what the farmer gets . . Attrib. to a S. Carolinian, Assoc. Press, Apr. 3. **1970** *DARE* (Qu. A19, *Other ways of saying "I'll have to hurry": "I'm late, I'll have to _____."*) Inf **FL**51, Sky, fly, run.

sky-inning n
1967 *DARE* (Qu. EE11, *Bat-and-ball games for just a few players [when there aren't enough for a regular game]*) Inf **HI**6, Sky-inning—throw ball in air, bat it out to players in field, whoever catches it goes to bat; if they don't catch it, one who gets it rolls it toward bat lying on ground; if he hits bat, he goes to bat; **HI**9, Sky-inning.

skyjack See skyhook

sky juice n Cf Adam's ale
Water.

1941 *AmSp* 16.24 **sIN,** Sky juice. Water. **1942** Berrey–Van den Bark *Amer. Slang* 71.8, *Rain. . .* Sky-juice. *Ibid* 72.2, *Water. . .* Sky juice. **1943** *AmSp* 18.67 [**IN** sayings used elsewhere], *Sky juice* (water). S.C., N.C., Tenn.

skylark n Cf lark n¹
1 =**horned lark.**

a1782 (1788) Jefferson *Notes VA* 74, Alavda alpestris—Alavda guttere flavo. . . Lark. Sky lark. **1792** Belknap *Hist. NH* 3.172, Sky Lark, *Alauda alpestris.* **1858** Baird *Birds* 403, *Eremophila cornuta. . .* Sky Lark; Shore Lark. **1956** MA Audubon Soc. *Bulletin* 40.84 **MA,** Horned Lark. . . Skylark. . . It resembles the European Skylark in singing on the wing. **1965–70** *DARE* (Qu. Q15, *. . Kinds of larks*) Infs **CA**80, **IL**32, 81, **NC**27, 41, 44, **NY**87, 100, **TN**22, **UT**5, Skylark. [*DARE* Ed: Some of these Infs may refer instead to other senses.]

2 Either of two **pipits:** *Anthus spinoletta* or *A. spragueii.*

1874 Coues *Birds NW* 43, It is not a little singular that the Skylark should have so long continued to be rare in collections, since it is very abundant in the extensive region which it inhabits. **1883** Nuttall Ornith. Club *Bulletin* 8.78, As for *Pipit* or *Pipit Lark. . .* In my long list of local American names for this species occur the following: *Titlark, Prairie Titlark, Lark, Skylark* [etc.]. **1936** Roberts *MN Birds* 2.147, American Pipit. . . *Other names:* American Titlark, American Skylark. **1956** MA Audubon Soc. *Bulletin* 129 **MA,** American Pipit. Skylark. . . It has some resemblance to the European Skylark and, like that species, sings on the wing.

sky parlor n [*OED2* 1785 →] Cf DS D4
A room, esp a habitable one, on the top floor of a house directly beneath the roof.

1832 *New Engl. Mag.* 3.391 **ceMA,** I've a snug sky-parlor in Ward No. 5. **1863** *Atlantic Mth.* 12.174 **MA,** He climbed the four flights that led to his "sky-parlor." **1899** (1912) Green *VA Folk-Speech* 391, *Sky-parlour. . .* A room next the sky, or at the top of the building; hence, an attic. **1914** *DN* 4.155 **Cape Cod MA,** Sky-parlor. . . The long, low (usually unplastered) rooms under the eaves, one at the front and one at the back. These are sometimes called 'front-parlor' and 'back-parlor.' The best room in the house is invariably the 'front room.' These 'parlors' have usually at each end a small window. I have seen one carpeted, wall-papered, and carefully painted, though it was used only for storage. **1930** Shoemaker *1300 Words* 55 **cPA Mts** (as of c1900), Sky-parlor—The attic, or garret. **1941** *LANE* Map 345 *(Attic)* 1 inf, **cwCT,** Some term it as a sky parlor; 1 inf, **ceMA,** Sky parlor; [1 inf, **swNH,** Sky parlor, a glassed-in room]. **1971** Wood *Vocab. Change* 95 **GA, FL,** *Unfinished room at the top of the house. . . Sky parlor.* **1986** Pederson *LAGS Concordance (Room at the top of the house just under the roof)* 1 inf, **cGA,** Sky parlor; 1 inf, **cnFL,** Sky parlor—when you'd have a dormer window.

sky piece n

A hat, cap, or bonnet; a hairpiece.

1898 *Century Illustr. Mag.* 56.147 **NM,** But there was "nuthin' wrong with that there sky-piece," as Rod Marks, the boss rider of Williams Ranch, . . very sagely remarked. **1913** *DN* 4.28 **NW,** *Sky piece. . . A* hat. **1916** *DN* 4.329 **NE,** *Skypiece. . .* Hat. Slang. **1956** Sorden–Ebert *Logger's Words* 32 **Gt Lakes,** *Sky-piece,* A hat. **1967** *DARE* (Qu. X1a, *Names . . for false hair, worn by men*) Infs **IA5, IL12,** Sky piece. **1968** *Current Slang* 2.4.9, *Sky piece. . .* A hat.—College males, New York— Where did you get that sharp sky piece? **1971** Roberts *Third Ear* np [Black], *Sky piece . .* hat; beret. **1972** Claerbaut *Black Jargon* 79, *Sky piece . .* a hat; headwear: *Here's your sky piece.*

sky pilot n

1 also *sky writer:* A clergyman.

1882 *Living Age* 155.305 **SW,** Wall, happened once when the bishop was prospecting round, to see that the sky pilots on his claim was all at work. **1883** Peck *Mirth for Million* 414, Look-a-here you sky-pilot, this thing has gone far enough. **1904** (1913) Johnson *Highways South* 62 **nFL, seGA,** I ain't no infidale [sic], but I don't take any stock in sky pilots. **1919** *DN* 5.65 **NM** [Among hs students], *Sky-pilot,* a preacher. "We have a new sky-pilot over in the camp." **1929** *AmSp* 5.76 **NE** [Cattle country talk], On a Sunday, a cowhand might take his "girl friend" to church and listen to the "tear squeezing" appeals of a "sky pilot," an itinerant minister, perhaps not ordained, whose ignorance may be so obvious that the cowhand will say, "He knows as much as a pig does about religion." **1930** Shoemaker *1300 Words* 58 **cPA Mts** (as of c1900), *Sky-pilot*—A country preacher. **1941** Writers' Program *Guide WY* 465, *Sky pilot*—Preacher. **1965–70** *DARE* (Qu. CC10, *. . . An unprofessional, part-time lay preacher*) Infs **IL11, NY7, 219, VT12, WA3, 20, WV2,** Sky pilot; **WA3,** Sky writer; **NY7,** Lumberjack sky pilot. **1986** Pederson *LAGS Concordance,* 1 inf, **neAR,** Sky pilot—not abusive, nickname for clerics. **1997** Hassler *Dean's List* 388 **nMN,** "The rev-runt's dead, I s'pose you heard." "I'm sorry, Johnny, it's going to be lonely at the men's end of the dining table, isn't it." "Naw, I never had no time for sky pilots anyhow."

2 =**Jacob's ladder 1.** West

1949 Moldenke *Amer. Wild Flowers* 246 **CA,** At altitudes of 11,000 to 13,000 feet in the Sierra Nevada of California, grows a lovely plant bearing the singularly appropriate name of skypilot, *Polemonium eximium.* **1953** Nelson *Plants Rocky Mt. Park* 128, Alpine polemonium, sky pilot, or sticky polemonium. . . It is well named "sky pilot," for it has been found above 13,000 feet. **1961** Douglas *My Wilderness* 19 **CO,** Sky pilot *(Polemonium viscosum)* marches with the alpine forget-me-not to the rocky pinnacles. Its flowers are blue, each has five petals, and they grow in clusters a few inches wide. **1968** Abbey *Desert Solitaire* 224 **seUT,** *Polemonium viscosum,* alias Sky Pilot, for it often lives at 13,000 feet or more. **1973** Hitchcock–Cronquist *Flora Pacific NW* 376, *Polemonium* [spp]. . . Sky-pilot (dwarf alp[ine] spp).

sky pond n

1950 *AmSp* 25.164 **CO,** In the dry-farming area of Colorado, the word *lagoon. . .* means a small, shallow, usually dry lake. . . not fed by streams. Some term was needed to distinguish between such a dry lake and a lake fed by streams. Sometimes the term is *dry lake* or *sky pond.*

skyrocket n Also *scarlet skyrocket, skyrocket gilia*
=**scarlet gilia.**

1925 Jepson *Manual Plants CA* 794, *[Gilia] aggregata. . .* Skyrocket. **1953** Nelson *Plants Rocky Mt. Park* 128, Skyrocket gilia or fairy trumpet, *Gilia aggregata.* **1967** *DARE* FW Addit **OR**12, Skyrocket . . locally: stinkweed. **1987** Bowers *100 Roadside Wildflowers* 63, Skyrocket has evolved with hummingbirds over thousands of years so that each is perfectly suited to the other. **2000** (acc) U.S. Dept. Ag. *Inte-*

grated *Taxonomic Info. System* (Internet), *Ipomopsis aggregata* ssp. *formosissima. . .* Vernacular Name: scarlet skyrocket.

skyrod See **skyhook**

skyt See **skite** v

skyuse See **cayuse**

sky-waddlin See **sky-bottlin**

sky-wampus See **skew-** d

sky west and crooked adv phr, adj phr Also *sky-ways and crooked, sky west, ~ end crooked, sky western crooked, sky-wise and crooked* **chiefly Sth, S Midl, West** Cf **galley-west, sky-winding**

Into confusion, flying in all directions; cockeyed, askew; also fig—often hyperbolically in phr *knock one sky west and crooked* to deal one a severe blow.

1905 *DN* 3.94 **nwAR,** Sky west end crooked. . . Helpless, senseless. 'He knocked him sky west end crooked.' Common. **1909** *DN* 3.371 **eAL, wGA,** Sky western crooked. . . Helpless, senseless, winding. **1915** *DN* 4.228 **wTX,** Sky-wise and crooked. . . Dumbfounded, extremely startling. "It knocked me _____." **1931** *AmSp* 7.51 **Sth, SW** [Lumberjack lingo], A spokesman for the "bunch" would say, "Let's walk her boys" and some boot-clad, hairy-chested fellows would mount the table at either end and walking down to the center would kick every dish and glass "sky, west, and crooked." **1942** Berrey–Van den Bark *Amer. Slang* 42.3, *Crooked; askew. .* Skygog, sky-west, sky-west and crooked, sky-western crooked. *Ibid* 221.5, *Violently. .* Skywest, skywest and crooked. **1953** Randolph–Wilson *Down in Holler* 285 **Ozarks,** Skyways: *adv.* This word must be somehow akin to *sky-gogglin.* I have not heard it often. But in a fist fight at Reeds Springs, Mo., it was said that somebody attacked the sheriff and "knocked him *sky-ways* an' crooked." **c1960** Wilson Coll. **csKY,** *Sky west and crooked*—said of something out of order; often part of a threat to knock something or somebody in this way. **1965–70** *DARE* (Qu. KK70, *Something that has got out of proper shape: "That house is all _____."*) Inf **TX1,** Sky west and crooked; (Qu. MM3, *When someone does something the wrong way round . . "This is the front, you've got the whole thing turned _____."*) Inf **IL96,** Sky west and crooked; (Qu. MM12a, *. . 'In all directions' . . "He shot into a flock of birds and they went _____."*) Inf **CA105, IL96, IN32, TX70,** Sky west and crooked; (Qu. MM12b, *. . 'In all directions' . . "When she was out on the dance floor, she broke her beads and they went _____."*) Infs **IL96, TX1,** Sky west and crooked; (Qu. MM13, *The table was nice and straight until he came along and knocked it _____*) Inf **TX67,** Sky western crooked; **AR39,** Sky west and ['wæstn] crooked; **AR3, TX11,** Sky west and crooked; **AR52,** Sky western crooked. **1996** *Verbatim* Autumn 1 **Sth,** If plans went haywire, they went *skywest* and *crooked.*

sky-winding adv **chiefly Sth, S Midl** Cf **sky-gogglin, sky west and crooked, winding**

Into turbulent motion; cockeyed, askew—often hyperbolically in phr *knock one sky-winding* to deal one a severe blow.

c1910 in **1944** *ADD* **cAR,** I knocked him sky-winding. **1930** *DN* 6.83 **cSC,** *Sky-windin'.* In the phrase, "to knock one sky-windin'." To hit one a terrific blow. Common. **1944** *PADS* 2.60 **nwMO, sVA, nNC, cnSC,** *Sky-windin'. .* "The mule kicked the dog sky-windin'." **1950** *PADS* 13.19 **cTX,** *Sky-windin'. . .* To a great height, usually over and over in the air. "He knocked me sky-windin'." **1950** *PADS* 14.77 **FL,** *Sky-winding, knock something* or *someone: . .* To knock toward the sky. **c1960** Wilson Coll. **csKY,** *Sky-winding. . .* Going in no certain way, awkwardly. **1967–68** *DARE* (Qu. MM13, *The table was nice and straight until he came along and knocked it _____*) Infs **AZ1, VA5,** Sky-winding.

sky-wise and crooked See **sky west and crooked**

skywrench See **skyhook**

sky writer See **sky pilot 1**